CHAMBERS

CONCISE DICTIONARY & THESAURUS

CHAMBERS

CONCISE DICTIONARY & THESAURUS

Edited by

Mary O'Neill

CHAMBERS

CHAMBERS

An imprint of Chambers Harrap Publishers Ltd
7 Hopetoun Crescent, Edinburgh EH7 4AY

First published by Chambers Harrap Publishers Ltd 2001

Reprinted 2003
Previously published as *Chambers Combined Dictionary and Thesaurus* 1995
© Chambers Harrap Publishers Ltd 2001

A CIP catalogue record for this book is available from the British Library.

We have made every effort to mark as such all words
which we believe to be trademarks.
We should also like to make it clear that the presence of a
word in the dictionary, whether marked or unmarked, in
no way affects its legal status as a trademark.

ISBN 0550 15016 1

Designed and typeset by Chambers Harrap Publishers Ltd
Printed and bound in Finland by WS Bookwell

CONTENTS

CONTRIBUTORS

Publishing Manager	Patrick White
Project Editor	Mary O'Neill
External Readers	Alice Grandison
	Michael Munro
Prepress	Clair Cameron

The publishers would like to thank the following for their work on the previous edition:

Martin Manser
Megan Thomson

PREFACE

This book represents an innovation in dictionary publishing. There are dictionaries, and there are thesauruses, and there are dictionaries with thesauruses printed as parallel texts. But no other reference book combines all the features you will find here: a comprehensive dictionary with fully integrated information on alternative and opposite words (synonyms and antonyms), plus additional information on word families (hyponyms). A synonym answers the question "what is another word for...?". An antonym answers the question "what is the opposite of...?". A hyponym answers the question "what kinds of... are there?".

Take the word *lock*. It has synonyms such as *fastening*, *bolt*, and *clasp*; hyponyms (kinds of lock) such as *mortise* and *deadlock*; and (as a verb) an antonym, *unlock*. There are not many words having all three relationships, and some are even more deficient; for example, many concrete nouns such as *window* and *water* have few genuine synonyms and no antonyms; and the same is true of classifying adjectives such as *oval* and *German*. There is no opposite of *dance* or *party*. Other words, however, because of the type of meaning they have, are highly productive of synonyms and antonyms, especially descriptive adjectives such as *large* and *pure*, verbs denoting general or basic actions such as *see* and *take*, and names denoting qualities and attributes, for example *deceit* and *pleasure*.

The correct choice of alternative words is influenced by what is called *register*, or the appropriacy of particular words to particular occasions. The synonyms of *lavatory* illustrate this point well: *toilet* and *washroom* are neutral or 'unmarked' alternatives that would do as well as the headword in many contexts; *loo* is only used in informal contexts (especially in conversation), and is therefore marked as 'colloquial'; *bog* is restricted in use to the most informal contexts or to particular social groups (in this case, often schoolchildren), and is therefore marked as 'slang'. The importance of register is shown by the bizarre and often hilarious effects produced when it is confused or mixed, as in *do you require the bog?*, where *require* belongs to a much higher register than *bog*.

At the other extreme, there are words that are marked as 'formal', for example *nuptials* as an alternative for *marriage*, which would not normally be used in general conversation or writing, but would be appropriate in a formal speech or a serious or technical piece of writing.

Many words have more than one meaning, and the alternative words that are valid for one meaning are not necessarily valid for others. To clarify this aspect, we have distinguished the meanings of words by relating the synonyms to the sense numbers of the dictionary section of each entry to which they apply. A good example of this treatment will be found at the entry for *dry*, where three principal meanings give rise to three sets of synonyms headed by *arid*, *boring*, and *ironic* respectively.

In this dictionary, there is a wealth of information of this kind, and it is supported and amplified by a clear and accessible dictionary text that explains the meaning and function of words, as well as other aspects usual in a dictionary, including pronunciation (where this might cause difficulty), inflection, and word origins. Information on routine derivatives of words, for example nouns ending in *-ization* formed from verbs ending in *-ize*, has been confined to those that have some currency and usefulness in English. To avoid wasting space, we have not entered nouns ending in *-ness* and adverbs ending in *-ly* when they are routine and predictable, since practically every descriptive adjective is capable of forming a noun and many adjectives form adverbs of manner ending in *-ly*. They are given, however, when there is a special point of meaning or spelling, as with *happiness* and *equally*.

This edition has been enriched by the inclusion of hundreds of extra entries, senses, and synonyms, giving even more comprehensive and up-to-date coverage of the language.

This is an ideal resource for those who want to use English effectively and productively, as well as to understand the language they hear and read. No other reference book provides such a ready means of finding the right word for every occasion.

The Editors

Notes on verb transitivity

1. In English, verbs commonly take a subject and an object and are called *transitive* (as in *people watch television,* in which *people* is the subject, *watch* is the verb, and *television* is the object of the verb). Transitivity is regarded as the normal function of verbs, and is only indicated (*trans.*) when it is noteworthy in particular cases. The typical object of transitive verbs is identified by being put in round brackets.

2. Some verbs describe an action in which no object is involved, such as verbs of motion including *go* and *arrive,* and verbs of state including *be* and *exist.* These are called intransitive and are labelled *intrans.* in the dictionary.

3. Other verbs are both transitive and intransitive in different uses (eg *move* is transitive in *we moved the car* and intransitive in *the car has moved*). In these cases the less usual uses are noted, normally intransitive (as at *break*) but sometimes transitive.

PRONUNCIATION GUIDE

Pronunciations are given for words that might cause difficulty in general use. The following phonetic symbols are used:

CONSONANTS

p	/piː/	pea
t	/tiː/	tea
k	/kiː/	key
b	/biː/	bee
d	/daɪ/	die
g	/gaɪ/	guy
m	/miː/	me
n	/njuː/	new
ŋ	/sɒŋ/	song
θ	/θɪn/	thin
ð	/ðɛn/	then
f	/fan/	fan
v	/van/	van
s	/siː/	sea
z	/zuːm/	zoom
ʃ	/ʃiː/	she
ʒ	/beɪʒ/	beige
tʃ	/iːtʃ/	each
dʒ	/ɛdʒ/	edge
h	/hat/	hat
l	/leɪ/	lay
r	/reɪ/	ray
j	/jɛs/	yes
w	/weɪ/	way
x	/lɒx/	loch

VOWELS

Short vowels

ɪ	/bɪd/	bid
ɛ	/bɛd/	bed
a	/bad/	bad
ʌ	/bʌd/	bud
ɒ	/pɒt/	pot
ʊ	/pʊt/	put
ə	/ə'baʊt/	about

Long vowels

iː	/biːd/	bead
ɑː	/hɑːm/	harm
ɔː	/ɔːl/	all
uː	/buːt/	boot
ɜː	/bɜːd/	bird

Diphthongs

eɪ	/beɪ/	bay
aɪ	/baɪ/	buy
ɔɪ	/bɔɪ/	boy
aʊ	/haʊ/	how
oʊ	/goʊ/	go
ɪə	/bɪə(r)/	beer
ɛə	/bɛə(r)/	bare
ʊə	/pʊə(r)/	poor

Notes

1. The stress mark (') is placed before the stressed syllable (*eg* **belong** /bɪ'lɒŋ/).

2. The symbol '(r)' is used to represent *r* when it comes at the end of a word, to indicate that it is pronounced when followed by a vowel.

ABBREVIATIONS USED IN THE BOOK

abbrev. = abbreviation
adj. = adjective
adv. = adverb
Aeron. = Aeronautics
Afr. = Africa, African
Agric. = Agriculture
Amer. = America, American
Anat. = Anatomy
Anthropol. = Anthropology
Antiq. = Antiquity
Archaeol. = Archaeology
Archit. = Architecture
Astrol. = Astrology
Astron. = Astronomy
Austral. = Australian
aux. = auxiliary

Biochem. = Biochemistry
Biol. = Biology
Bot. = Botany
Brit. = British

c = century (5c, 11c, etc)
c. = circa (about, around, especially before a date)
Chem. = Chemistry
Church of E. = Church of England
colloq. = colloquial

Comput. = Computing
conj. = conjunction
contr. = contraction

derog. = derogatory

Econ. = Economics
Electr. = Electricity
Electron. = Electronics
esp. = especially (only in labels)

fl. = flourished

Geog. = Geography
Geol. = Geology
Geom. = Geometry

Hist. = History

interj. = interjection
intrans. = intransitive

m = metre(s), million
Maths. = Mathematics
Mech. = Mechanics
Meteorol. = Meteorology
mi = miles
Microbiol. = Microbiology
Mil. = Military

Mus. = Music
Mythol. = Mythology

Naut. = Nautical

Pathol. = Pathology
Philos. = Philosophy
Photog. = Photography
Physiol. = Physiology
pl. = plural
prep. = preposition
pron. = pronoun
Psychol. = Psychology

RC = Roman Catholic
rel. = relative
Relig. = Religion

Scot. = Scottish
sing. = singular
Sociol. = Sociology

Telecomm. = Telecommunications
Theatr. = Theatre
trans. = transitive

Zool. = Zoology

GUIDE TO USING THIS BOOK

build — *verb* (PAST TENSE AND PAST PARTICIPLE **built**) **1** to make or construct from parts. **2** to develop gradually. **3** to make in a particular way or for a particular purpose. — *noun* physical form, especially of the human body: *a slim build*. — **build one thing into** or **on to another** to make a construction such that it is a permanent part of or addition to a larger one: *built a garage on to the side of the house*. **build on something 1** to add on by building. **2** to use (a previous success, etc) as a basis from which to develop: *build on previous experience*. **3** to base hopes, achieve success, etc on something: *success built on a popular product*. **4** to depend on something. **build up** to increase gradually in size, strength, amount, etc. **build something up 1** to build it in stages. **2** to make it bigger, stronger, or healthier. **3** to speak with great enthusiasm about it. See also BUILD-UP. [from Anglo-Saxon *byldan*]

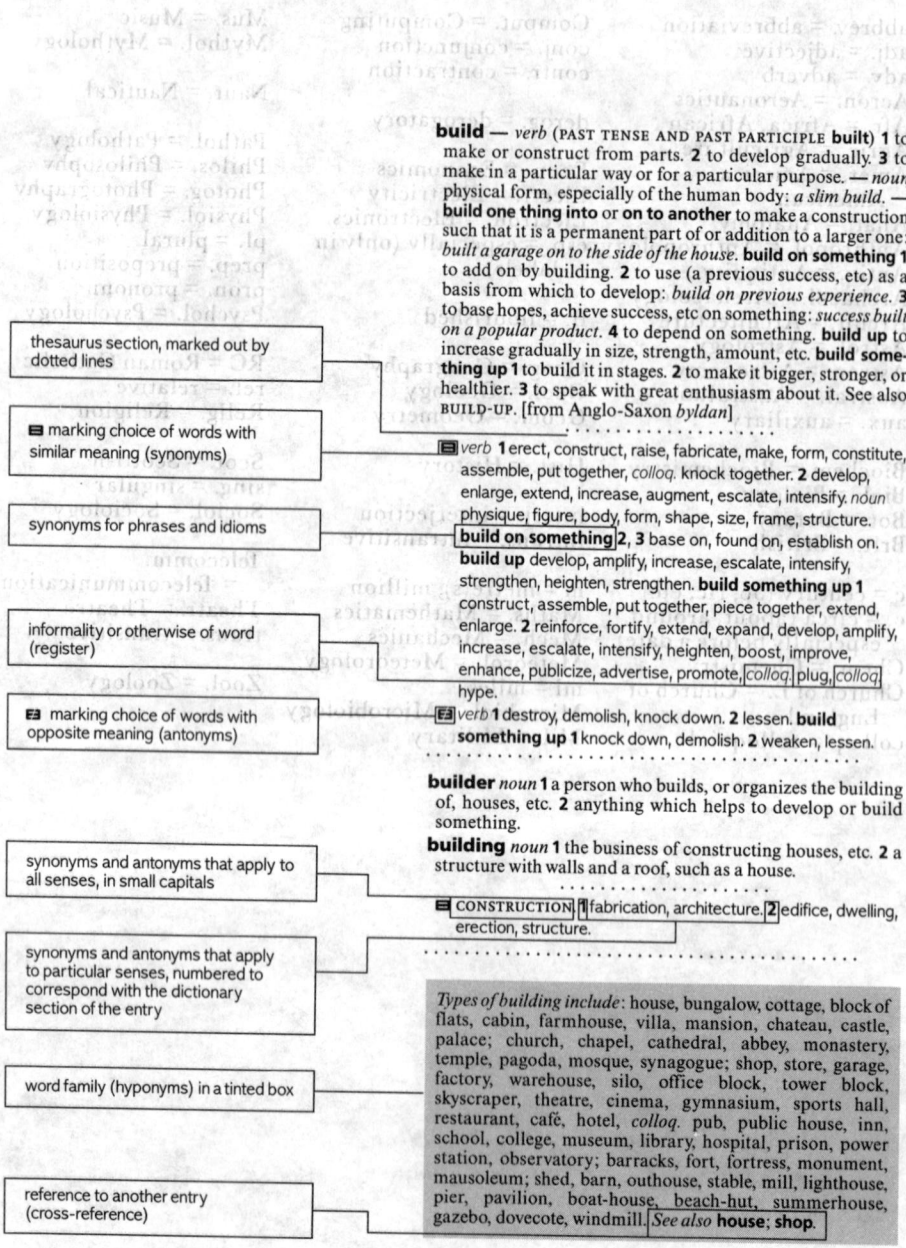

verb **1** erect, construct, raise, fabricate, make, form, constitute, assemble, put together, *colloq.* knock together. **2** develop, enlarge, extend, increase, augment, escalate, intensify. *noun* physique, figure, body, form, shape, size, frame, structure. **build on something 2, 3** base on, found on, establish on. **build up** develop, amplify, increase, escalate, intensify, strengthen, heighten, strengthen. **build something up 1** construct, assemble, put together, piece together, extend, enlarge. **2** reinforce, fortify, extend, expand, develop, amplify, increase, escalate, intensify, heighten, boost, improve, enhance, publicize, advertise, promote, *colloq.* plug, *colloq.* hype.

verb **1** destroy, demolish, knock down. **2** lessen. **build something up 1** knock down, demolish. **2** weaken, lessen.

builder *noun* **1** a person who builds, or organizes the building of, houses, etc. **2** anything which helps to develop or build something.

building *noun* **1** the business of constructing houses, etc. **2** a structure with walls and a roof, such as a house.

CONSTRUCTION. **1** fabrication, architecture. **2** edifice, dwelling, erection, structure.

Types of building include: house, bungalow, cottage, block of flats, cabin, farmhouse, villa, mansion, chateau, castle, palace; church, chapel, cathedral, abbey, monastery, temple, pagoda, mosque, synagogue; shop, store, garage, factory, warehouse, silo, office block, tower block, skyscraper, theatre, cinema, gymnasium, sports hall, restaurant, café, hotel, *colloq.* pub, public house, inn, school, college, museum, library, hospital, prison, power station, observatory; barracks, fort, fortress, monument, mausoleum; shed, barn, outhouse, stable, mill, lighthouse, pier, pavilion, boat-house, beach-hut, summerhouse, gazebo, dovecote, windmill. *See also* **house**; **shop**.

Annotation labels (left margin):

- thesaurus section, marked out by dotted lines
- marking choice of words with similar meaning (synonyms)
- synonyms for phrases and idioms
- informality or otherwise of word (register)
- marking choice of words with opposite meaning (antonyms)
- synonyms and antonyms that apply to all senses, in small capitals
- synonyms and antonyms that apply to particular senses, numbered to correspond with the dictionary section of the entry
- word family (hyponyms) in a tinted box
- reference to another entry (cross-reference)

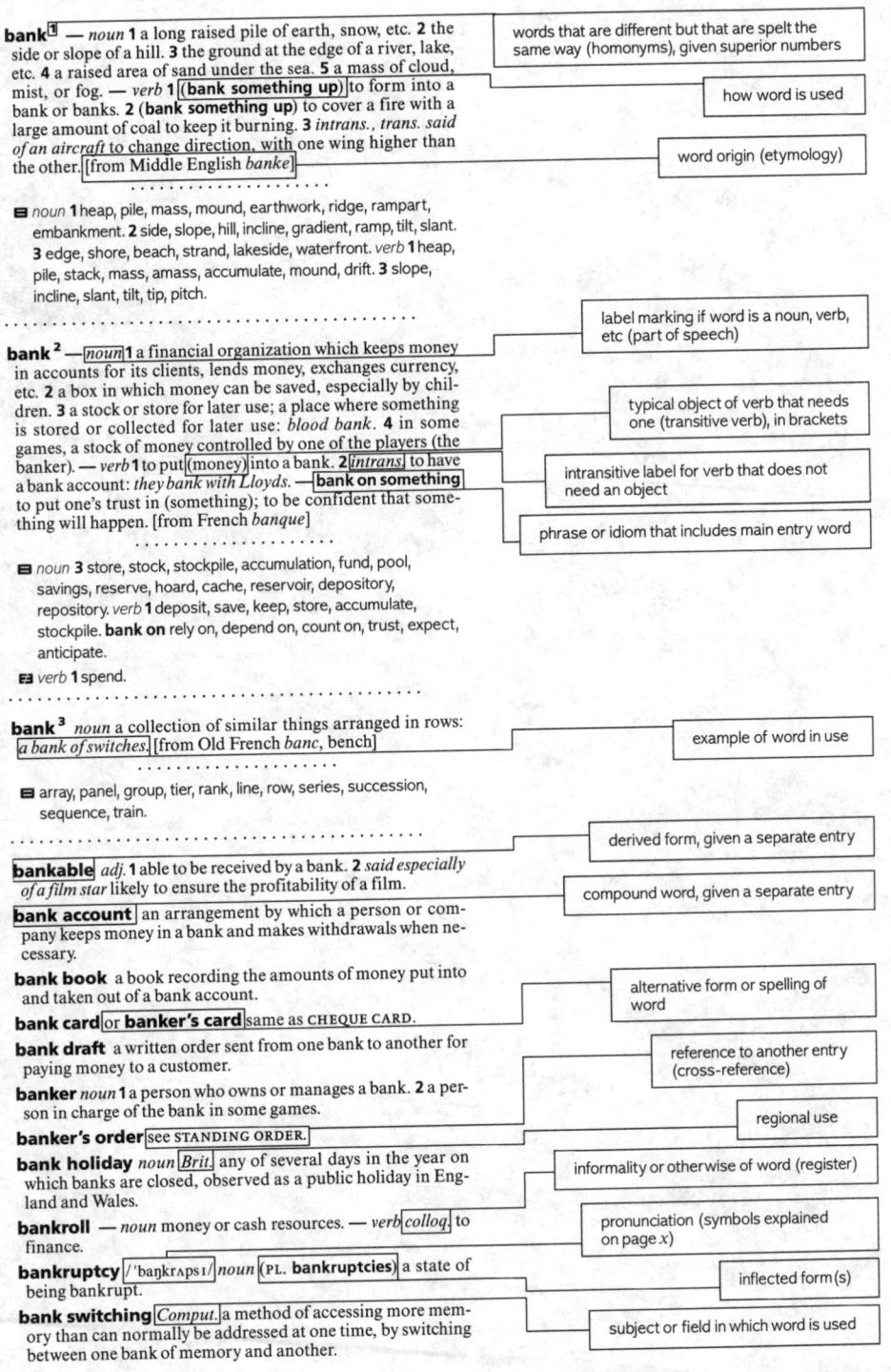

bank[1] — *noun* **1** a long raised pile of earth, snow, etc. **2** the side or slope of a hill. **3** the ground at the edge of a river, lake, etc. **4** a raised area of sand under the sea. **5** a mass of cloud, mist, or fog. — *verb* **1** (**bank something up**) to form into a bank or banks. **2** (**bank something up**) to cover a fire with a large amount of coal to keep it burning. **3** *intrans., trans. said of an aircraft* to change direction, with one wing higher than the other. [from Middle English *banke*]

> words that are different but that are spelt the same way (homonyms), given superior numbers

> how word is used

> word origin (etymology)

⊟ *noun* **1** heap, pile, mass, mound, earthwork, ridge, rampart, embankment. **2** side, slope, hill, incline, gradient, ramp, tilt, slant. **3** edge, shore, beach, strand, lakeside, waterfront. *verb* **1** heap, pile, stack, mass, amass, accumulate, mound, drift. **3** slope, incline, slant, tilt, tip, pitch.

bank[2] — *noun* **1** a financial organization which keeps money in accounts for its clients, lends money, exchanges currency, etc. **2** a box in which money can be saved, especially by children. **3** a stock or store for later use; a place where something is stored or collected for later use: *blood bank*. **4** in some games, a stock of money controlled by one of the players (the banker). — *verb* **1** to put (money) into a bank. **2** *intrans.* to have a bank account: *they bank with Lloyds*. — **bank on something** to put one's trust in (something); to be confident that something will happen. [from French *banque*]

> label marking if word is a noun, verb, etc (part of speech)

> typical object of verb that needs one (transitive verb), in brackets

> intransitive label for verb that does not need an object

> phrase or idiom that includes main entry word

⊟ *noun* **3** store, stock, stockpile, accumulation, fund, pool, savings, reserve, hoard, cache, reservoir, depository, repository. *verb* **1** deposit, save, keep, store, accumulate, stockpile. **bank on** rely on, depend on, count on, trust, expect, anticipate.

⊟ *verb* **1** spend.

bank[3] *noun* a collection of similar things arranged in rows: *a bank of switches*. [from Old French *banc*, bench]

> example of word in use

⊟ array, panel, group, tier, rank, line, row, series, succession, sequence, train.

bankable *adj.* **1** able to be received by a bank. **2** *said especially of a film star* likely to ensure the profitability of a film.

> derived form, given a separate entry

> compound word, given a separate entry

bank account an arrangement by which a person or company keeps money in a bank and makes withdrawals when necessary.

bank book a book recording the amounts of money put into and taken out of a bank account.

bank card or **banker's card** same as CHEQUE CARD.

bank draft a written order sent from one bank to another for paying money to a customer.

banker *noun* **1** a person who owns or manages a bank. **2** a person in charge of the bank in some games.

banker's order see STANDING ORDER.

> alternative form or spelling of word

> reference to another entry (cross-reference)

> regional use

bank holiday *noun* *Brit.* any of several days in the year on which banks are closed, observed as a public holiday in England and Wales.

bankroll — *noun* money or cash resources. — *verb* *colloq.* to finance.

bankruptcy /'baŋkrʌpsɪ/ *noun* (PL. **bankruptcies**) a state of being bankrupt.

> informality or otherwise of word (register)

> pronunciation (symbols explained on page *x*)

> inflected form(s)

bank switching *Comput.* a method of accessing more memory than can normally be addressed at one time, by switching between one bank of memory and another.

> subject or field in which word is used

A

A¹ or **a** *noun* (PL. **As, A's, a's**) **1** the first letter of the English alphabet. **2** (*usually* **A**) the highest grade or quality, or a mark indicating this. **3** (**A**) *Mus.* **a** the sixth note in the scale of C major. **b** a musical key with the note A as its base. — **from A to B** from one unspecified place to another. **from A to Z** from beginning to end; completely.

A² *abbrev.* **1** advanced. **2** alto. **3** America. **4** ampere. **5** answer. **6** Associate (of a society, etc). **7** atomic: *A-bomb.* **8** Australia. **9** *as an international vehicle mark* Austria.

Å *abbrev.* angstrom.50

a¹ or **an** *indefinite article: a* is used before words beginning with a consonant or consonant sound (eg *one, united, historical*), and *an* before words beginning with a vowel or vowel sound (eg *apple, only, heir, honour*) **1** one: *here is a book.* **2** used before a word describing quantity: *a dozen eggs / a lot of trouble.* **3** any; every: *a fire is hot.* **4** each or every; per: *once a day / 60p a pound.* **5** one of a stated type: *a real Romeo.* [from Anglo-Saxon *an*, one]

a² *abbrev.* **1** *ante* (Latin), before. **2** acre.

a³ *prefix* **1** to or towards: *ashore.* **2** in the process of: *abuzz.* **3** on: *afire.* **4** in: *nowadays.* [from Anglo-Saxon *an*, on]

a-¹ *prefix* (*also* **an-** before a vowel) not; without; opposite to: *amoral / asymmetrical / agnostic.* [from Greek]

a-² *prefix* of: *akin / afresh.* [from Anglo-Saxon *of*]

AA *abbrev.* **1** Automobile Association, a UK organization which helps drivers with breakdowns or technical problems, gives travel information, etc. **2** Alcoholics Anonymous, an association for alcoholics who are trying to give up alcohol completely.

AAA *abbrev.* **1** *Brit.* Amateur Athletic Association. **2** *North Amer.* American Automobile Association.

AAC *abbrev.* Amateur Athletics Club.

AAM *abbrev.* air-to-air missile.

aardvark /ˈɑːdvɑːk/ *noun* a nocturnal African burrowing mammal which feeds on termites. It has a large snout, donkey-like ears, and a tough grey skin sparsely covered with coarse hair. [from Dutch *aarde*, earth + *vark*, pig]

AB *abbrev.* **1** *Brit.* able seaman. **2** *North Amer., esp. US artium baccalaureus* (Latin), Bachelor of Arts.

aback — **taken aback** surprised or shocked, especially by something unpleasant or unexpected. [from Anglo-Saxon *on bæc*, on back]

abacus /ˈabəkəs/ (PL. **abaci**) *noun* **1** an arithmetical calculating device, known to the Greeks and Romans and to other ancient peoples, consisting of several rows of beads strung on horizontal wires or rods mounted in a frame. **2** *Archit.* the flat upper part of a column or capital. [from Latin *abacus*, from Greek *abax*, drawing-board]

abaft — *adv.* in or towards the stern of a ship. — *prep.* behind. [from A³ + Anglo-Saxon *beæftan*, after]

abalone /abəˈloʊnɪ/ *noun* a marine gastropod mollusc of the genus *Haliotis*, related to the limpet, found mainly in warm shallow coastal waters. It has a single flattened oval shell lined with bluish mother-of-pearl, with a series of holes around the edge which provide an exit for water currents. [from Spanish *abulón*]

abandon — *verb* (**abandoned, abandoning**) **1** to give up completely: *abandon hope.* **2** to leave (a person, animal, vehicle, etc) usually intending not to return. **3** to leave (a place of danger or difficulty, etc) intending either not to return at all or not until the danger or difficulty is past. **4** to give up to another person's control. **5** (**abandon oneself to something**) to let oneself be overcome by strong emotion, passion, etc. — *noun* uncontrolled, uninhibited, reckless feelings. — **abandon ship** *said of the crew and passengers* to leave a ship at sea when it is in danger of sinking. [from Old French *abandoner*, to put under someone's control]

⊟ *verb* **1** renounce, resign, give up, forego, relinquish, surrender, yield, waive, drop. **2** desert, leave, forsake, jilt, *slang* ditch, *colloq.* leave in the lurch, maroon, strand, leave behind, scrap. **3** vacate, evacuate, withdraw from, quit.
⊟ *verb* **1** continue. **2** support, maintain, keep.

abandoned *adj.* **1** having been abandoned: *an abandoned car.* **2** having, or behaving as if one has, no sense of shame or morality.

⊟ **1** deserted, unoccupied, derelict, neglected, forsaken, forlorn, desolate. **2** dissolute, wild, uninhibited, wanton, wicked.
⊟ **1** kept, occupied. **2** restrained.

abandonment *noun* **1** the act of giving up (an aim, a task, etc). **2** the act of abandoning (a person, animal, vehicle, etc) or the condition of being abandoned. **3** *Legal* the act of relinquishing a legal right; eg a tenant may abandon a tenanted property. However, it is often difficult to establish in law that abandonment has taken place, and it cannot be used by people to extricate themselves from a continuing liability.

⊟ **1** renunciation, resignation, giving up, sacrifice. **2** desertion, leaving, forsaking, jilting, neglect, scrapping. **3** relinquishment, surrender, waiver, discontinuation.

abase *verb* to humiliate or degrade (a person or oneself). [from Old French *abaissier*, from Latin *bassus*, low]

abasement *noun* **1** being humbled or degraded. **2** humiliation.

abashed *adj.* **1** embarrassed and ashamed, especially because of shyness. **2** in a state of discomposure or confusion. [from Old French *esbahir*, to astound]

⊟ **1** ashamed, shamefaced, embarrassed, mortified, humiliated, humbled. **2** confused, bewildered, nonplussed, confounded, discomposed, disconcerted, taken aback, dumbfounded, *colloq.* floored, dismayed.
⊟ **2** composed, at ease.

abate *verb* **1** *intrans.* to become less strong or severe: *the storm abated.* **2** to make (a problem, etc) less strong or severe. [from Old French *abatre*, to bring down]

⊟ DECREASE, REDUCE, LESSEN, DIMINISH, WEAKEN, MODERATE, EASE. **1** decline, dwindle, subside, *colloq.* let up, sink, wane, fade. **2** relieve, alleviate, mitigate, pacify, quell.
⊟ INCREASE, STRENGTHEN.

abatement noun **1** the act of abating. **2** the sum or quantity abated.

abattoir /'abɒtwɑ:(r)/ noun a slaughterhouse. [from Old French abatre, to bring down]

abbacy /'abəsɪ/ noun (PL. **abbacies**) the office or authority of an abbot or abbess. [from Latin abbatia, abbey]

Abbasids (8c–13c) a dynasty of caliphs that replaced the Ummayyad dynasty in 749, reached the peak of its power under Harun al-Rashid (786–809), and remained in Baghdad until its sack by the Mongols (1258).

abbess noun a woman in charge of a group of nuns living in an abbey. [from Old French abbesse]

abbey noun (PL. **abbeys**) **1** a group of nuns or monks living as a community under an abbot or abbess. **2** the buildings occupied by such a community. **3** a church associated with such a community. [from Old French abeie]

■ **2** monastery, priory, friary, seminary, convent, nunnery, cloister.

abbot noun the man in charge of a group of monks living in an abbey. [from Latin abbas, from Aramaic abba, father]

abbrev. or **abbr.** abbrev. **1** abbreviated. **2** abbreviation.

abbreviate /ə'bri:vɪeɪt/ verb to shorten, especially to represent (a long word) by a shortened form. [from Latin abbreviare, to shorten]

■ shorten, cut, trim, clip, truncate, curtail, abridge, summarize, précis, abstract, digest, condense, compress, reduce, lessen, contract.

🗲 extend, lengthen, expand, amplify.

abbreviation noun **1** the act of shortening. **2** a part of a word used to stand for the whole.

■ **1** shortening, clipping, curtailment, abridgement, summarization, compression, reduction, contraction.
🗲 **1** extension, expansion, amplification.

ABC¹ /eɪbi:'si:/ noun (PL. **ABCs**, **ABC's**) **1** the alphabet. **2** the basic facts about a subject, especially when arranged alphabetically in a book. **3** an alphabetical guide.

ABC² /eɪbi:'si:/ abbrev. **1** American Broadcasting Company. **2** Australian Broadcasting Corporation.

abdicate /'abdɪkeɪt/ verb **1** intrans., trans. to give up one's right to (the throne). **2** to refuse or fail to carry out (one's responsibilities). [from Latin ab-, away, from + dicare, to proclaim]

■ **1** renounce, give up, relinquish, surrender, cede, yield, forego, abandon, quit, vacate, retire, resign, colloq. step down.

abdication noun the act of giving up an office, especially the throne.

abdomen /'abdəmən/ noun **1** in vertebrates, the lower part of the main body cavity, containing the digestive, excretory, and reproductive organs, and in mammals separated from the thorax (chest) by the diaphragm. **2** Zool. in arthropods (eg insects), the rear part of the body, behind the head and thorax. [from Latin abdomen]

■ **1** belly, guts, stomach, colloq. tummy, paunch, midriff.

abdominal /ab'dɒmɪnəl/ adj. relating to or concerning the abdomen.

■ ventral, intestinal, visceral, gastric.

abduct verb to take (someone) away illegally by force or deception. [from Latin abducere, to lead away]

■ carry off, run away with, colloq. run off with, make off with, spirit away, seduce, kidnap, snatch, seize, appropriate.

abduction noun kidnapping.

abductor noun a person who abducts.

abeam adv. in a line at right angles to the length of a ship or aircraft. [from A³ + BEAM]

Aberdeen Angus /'abədi:n 'aŋgəs/ an early maturing breed of hornless beef cattle having short black hair, so called because it was developed from a mixture of breeds in Aberdeen and Angus in Scotland.

aberrance /a'berəns/ or **aberrancy** /a'berənsɪ/ noun (PL. **aberrancies**) a departure from what is normal or accepted.

aberrant /a'berənt/ adj. changing or departing from what is normal or accepted as standard. [from Latin aberrare, to wander away]

aberration /abə'reɪʃən/ noun **1** a temporary, usually brief and often surprising change from what is normal or accepted as standard. **2** a sudden and usually temporary drop in standards of behaviour, thought, etc. **3** Optics the failure of a lens in an optical system to form a perfect image.

■ **1** deviation, straying, wandering, divergence, irregularity, nonconformity, anomaly, oddity, peculiarity, eccentricity, quirk, freak. **2** lapse, fall, error, defect.
🗲 **1** conformity.

abet verb (**abetted**, **abetting**) especially Legal to help or encourage (someone) to commit an offence. [from Old French abeter, to entice]

abetter Legal **abettor** noun a person who abets.

abeyance /a'beɪəns/ noun **1** said of laws, customs, etc the condition, usually temporary, of not being used or followed: fall into abeyance. **2** said of a position, eg a peerage the state, usually temporary, of not being filled or occupied. [from Old French abeance, from a, to + baer, to gape]

abhor /ab'hɔ:(r)/ verb (**abhorred**, **abhorring**) to hate or dislike very much (usually something one considers morally wrong). [from Latin ab- from, away + horrere, to shudder]

■ hate, detest, loathe, abominate, shudder at, recoil from, shrink from, spurn, despise.
🗲 love, adore.

abhorrence noun **1** hatred or extreme dislike; disgust. **2** something that is abhorred.

■ **1** hate, hatred, aversion, loathing, abomination, horror, repugnance, revulsion, disgust, distaste.
🗲 **1** love, adoration.

abhorrent adj. **1** utterly detestable; causing disgust or revulsion. **2** (**abhorrent to someone**) hated or disliked by them.

■ **1** detestable, loathsome, abominable, execrable, heinous, obnoxious, odious, hateful, horrible, horrid, offensive, repugnant, repellent, repulsive, revolting, nauseating, disgusting, distasteful. **2** detestable to, loathsome to, hateful to, repugnant to, repellent to.
🗲 **1** delightful, attractive.

abide verb (PAST TENSE AND PAST PARTICIPLE **abode**, **abided**) **1** (**usually cannot** or **could not abide** or as a question) to put up with or tolerate: we cannot abide dishonesty / how could you abide him? **2** intrans. (**abide by something**) to follow, stay faithful to or obey (a decision, rule, etc). **3** intrans. old use to live. [from Anglo-Saxon abidan]

■ **1** bear, stand, endure, tolerate, put up with, *colloq.* stomach, accept. **2** obey, observe, follow, comply with, adhere to, hold to, stand by, keep to, conform to, submit to, agree to, go along with, fulfil, discharge, carry out.

abiding *adj.* permanent; lasting or continuing for a long time.

■ permanent, lasting, enduring, continuing, persisting, remaining.

ability *noun* (PL. **abilities**) **1** the power, skill, or knowledge to do something. **2** great skill or intelligence. [from Old French *ablete*, from Latin *habilitas*, suitability]

■ **1** capability, capacity, faculty, facility, potentiality, power. **2** skill, dexterity, deftness, adeptness, competence, p1roficiency, qualification, aptitude, talent, gift, endowment, knack, flair, touch, expertise, *colloq.* know-how, genius, forte, strength.
■ **1** inability. **2** incompetence, weakness.

-ability *suffix* forming nouns corresponding to adjectives in *-able*: *capability*.

ab initio /abɪˈnɪʃɪoʊ/ from the beginning; afresh. [Latin, = from the beginning]

abject /ˈabdʒɛkt/ *adj.* **1** *said of conditions, etc* extremely sad, miserable or poor; wretched. **2** *said of people* showing lack of courage or pride, etc; shameful. [from Latin *abjicere*, to throw away]

■ **1** miserable, wretched, forlorn, hopeless, pitiable, pathetic, low, mean. **2** shameful, ignoble, dishonourable, deplorable, despicable, contemptible, worthless, low, mean, vile, sordid, debased, degenerate, submissive, servile, grovelling, slavish.
■ **2** proud, exalted.

abjection /abˈdʒɛkʃən/ *noun* a state of degradation or misery.

abjuration /abdʒʊˈreɪʃən/ *noun* the act of abjuring.

abjure *verb* to promise solemnly, especially under oath, to stop believing, doing, etc (something). [from Latin *ab*, away, from + *jurare*, to swear]

ablative /ˈablətɪv/ — *noun* Grammar the case which, especially in Latin, expresses the place, means, manner or instrument of an action. — *adj.* of or in the ablative case. [from Latin *ablativus*, from *ablatus*, carried off, removed]

ablaut /ˈablaʊt/ *noun* Grammar a variation of a root vowel in the forms of a word, as in *sing*, *sang*, *song*, and *sung*. [from German *ab*, off + *Laut*, sound]

ablaze *adj.* **1** burning, especially strongly. **2** brightly lit. **3** (**ablaze with something**) feeling an emotion with great passion.

■ **1** blazing, flaming, burning, on fire, ignited, lighted, alight. **2** illuminated, luminous, glowing, aglow, radiant, flashing, gleaming, sparkling, brilliant.

able *adj.* **1** having the necessary knowledge, power, time, opportunity, etc to do something. **2** clever, skilful. [from Latin *habilis*, handy]

■ **1** capable, fit, fitted, strong, powerful, effective, adequate, efficient, competent, proficient, qualified, practised, experienced, skilled, accomplished. **2** clever, expert, masterly, adept, dexterous, adroit, deft, skilful, ingenious, talented, gifted.
■ **1** unable, incapable, ineffective, incompetent.

-able *suffix* forming adjectives meaning: **1** that may or must be: *eatable* / *payable*. **2** that may be the subject of: *objectionable*. **3** that is suitable for: *seasonable*/*fashionable*. See also -IBLE. [from Latin *abilis*]

able-bodied — *adj.* fit and healthy. — *pl. noun* fit and healthy people.

■ *adj.* fit, healthy, sound, strong, robust, hardy, tough, vigorous, powerful, hale, hearty, lusty, sturdy, strapping, stout, stalwart, staunch.
■ *adj.* infirm, delicate.

abled *adj.* having a range of abilities or a specified type of ability: *holidays for the abled older person.*

able seaman or **able-bodied seaman** a sailor able to perform all duties, with more training and a higher rating than an ordinary seaman.

ablution /əˈbluːʃən/ *noun* (*usually in pl.*) **1** the washing of parts of the body as part of a religious ceremony. **2** *colloq.* the ordinary washing of oneself. **3** a place for washing oneself in a camp, on board ship, etc. [from Latin *abluere*, to wash away]

-ably *suffix* forming adverbs corresponding to adjectives in *-able*: *capably* / *understandably*.

ABM *abbrev.* anti-ballistic missile.

abnegation /abnəˈɡeɪʃən/ *noun* **1** the act of giving up something one has or would like to have. **2** the act of renouncing a doctrine, etc. [from Latin *abnegare*, to deny]

abnormal *adj.* not normal; different from what is expected or usual. [from French *anormal*, from Greek *anomalos*]

■ odd, strange, peculiar, curious, queer, eccentric, unnatural, extraordinary, exceptional, unusual, uncommon, irregular, anomalous, aberrant, deviant, divergent, different.
■ normal, regular, typical.

abnormality /abnɔːˈmalɪtɪ/ *noun* (PL. **abnormalities**) **1** something which is abnormal. **2** the condition of being abnormal.

■ ODDITY, PECULIARITY, ECCENTRICITY, IRREGULARITY, ABERRATION. **1** anomaly, deformity, flaw, exception, difference. **2** singularity, strangeness, bizarreness, unnaturalness, unusualness, deviation, divergence.
■ REGULARITY. **2** normality.

Abo /ˈabəʊ/ or **abo** — *noun* (PL. **Abos**) *offensive slang* an Australian aborigine. — *adj.* aboriginal.

ABO blood group system *Medicine* a classification of human blood into four types (A, B, AB, and O), based on the presence or absence of antigens A and B.

aboard *adv., prep.* **1** on, on to, in or into (a ship, train, aircraft, etc). **2** *Naut.* alongside. [from Middle English *aborde*]

abode[1] *noun formal* the house or place where one lives; a dwelling. — **of no fixed abode** *Brit. Legal* having no regular home or address. [from ABIDE]

abode[2] see ABIDE.

abolish *verb* to stop or put an end to (customs, laws, etc). [from French *abolir*]

■ do away with, annul, nullify, invalidate, quash, repeal, rescind, revoke, cancel, obliterate, blot out, suppress, destroy, eliminate, eradicate, get rid of, stamp out, stop, end, put an end to, terminate, subvert, overthrow, overturn.
■ create, retain, continue, authorize.

abolition *noun* **1** the act of abolishing something; the state of being abolished. **2** *Hist.* the abolishing of slavery.

■ **1** annulment, nullification, invalidation, quashing,

repeal, abrogation, cancellation, obliteration, suppression, eradication, extinction, end, ending, termination, subversion, overturning, dissolution. 🔁 1 creation, retention, continuance.

abolitionism *noun* a 19c movement to end slavery in the southern states of the USA.

abolitionist *noun* a person who seeks to abolish a custom or practice, especially capital punishment or (formerly) slavery.

A-bomb see ATOM BOMB.

abominable *adj.* **1** greatly disliked, usually because morally bad. **2** *colloq.* very bad. [from Latin *abominari*, to hate]

🔁 **1** loathsome, detestable, hateful, horrible, abhorrent, execrable, odious, repugnant, repulsive, obnoxious, foul, vile, heinous, atrocious, appalling, terrible, contemptible, despicable. **2** awful, terrible, foul, vile, appalling. 🔁 **1** delightful, desirable.

abominable snowman a yeti. [a loose translation of Tibetan *metohkangmi*, literally 'snowfield man-bear']

abominate *verb* to dislike or hate greatly. [from Latin *abominari*]

🔁 hate, loathe, detest, abhor, *formal* execrate, despise, condemn. 🔁 love, adore.

abomination *noun* **1** anything one hates or dislikes greatly. **2** great dislike or hatred.

🔁 **1** anathema, bête noire, curse, plague, torment, outrage, disgrace. **2** hate, hatred, aversion, loathing, abhorrence, repugnance, revulsion, disgust, distaste, horror, outrage. 🔁 **2** adoration, delight.

aboriginal *or* **Aboriginal** /abəˈrɪdʒɪnəl/ — *noun* **1** a member of a people forming the original inhabitants of a place. **2** an Australian Aboriginal language. — *adj.* earliest, primitive, or indigenous.

aborigine /abəˈrɪdʒɪnɪ/ *noun* **1** (*also* **Aborigine**) a member of a people forming the original inhabitants of Australia. **2** a member of any people who were the first to live in a country or region, especially as compared to later arrivals. [from Latin *aborigines*, pre-Roman inhabitants of Italy, from *ab origine*, from the beginning]

abort *verb* **1** *intrans.* to expel (an embryo or fetus) spontaneously from the uterus (womb) before it is capable of surviving independently; to miscarry. **2** *intrans. said of a baby* to be lost in this way. **3** to induce termination of pregnancy, by surgical procedures or the use of drugs, before the embryo or fetus is capable of surviving independently. **4** *trans., intrans.* to stop (a plan, space flight, etc), or to be stopped, earlier than expected and before reaching a successful conclusion, usually because of technical problems or danger. **5** *Comput.* to stop the execution of (a program) before it has been completed, either because it is unsuitable or because it cannot continue owing to an error or system failure. [from Latin *abortus*, miscarried]

🔁 **1** miscarry. **3** terminate, end. **4, 5** stop, terminate, end, halt. 🔁 **4, 5** continue.

abortion *noun* **1** the removal of an embryo or fetus from the uterus (womb) before it is sufficiently developed to survive independently, deliberately induced by the use of drugs such as prostaglandins, or by surgical procedures, for medical or social reasons. Also called TERMINATION. **2** the spontaneous expulsion of an embryo or fetus from the uterus (womb) before it is sufficiently developed to survive independently. Also called MISCARRIAGE. **3** the failure of a plan, project, etc. **4** anything which has failed to grow properly or enough.

🔁 **3** failure, frustration, misadventure, termination, ending. 🔁 **3** success, continuation.

abortionist *noun* **1** a person who performs abortions, especially illegally. **2** a person who is in favour of abortion.

abortion pill *Medicine* a pill containing prostaglandins or other drugs that is taken by mouth in order to induce labour and bring about termination of pregnancy.

abortive *adj.* ending in failure.

🔁 failed, unsuccessful, fruitless, unproductive, barren, sterile, vain, idle, futile, useless, ineffective, unavailing. 🔁 successful, fruitful.

abound *verb intrans.* **1** to exist in large numbers. **2** (**abound in** *or* **with something**) to be rich in it or filled with it. [from Latin *abundare*, to overflow]

🔁 **1** be plentiful, proliferate, flourish, thrive, superabound, run riot. **2** swarm with, teem with.

abounding *adj.* plentifully supplied.

about — *prep.* **1** concerning; relating to; on the subject of. **2** near to. **3** around; centring on. **4** here and there in; at points throughout. **5** all around; surrounding. **6** occupied or busy with: *What are you about?* **7** on the person of. — *adv.* **1** nearly or just over; approximately. **2** nearby; close: *is there anyone about?* **3** scattered here and there. **4** all around; in all directions. **5** in or to the opposite direction: *turn about.* **6** on the move; in action: *be up and about again after an illness.* — **about to do something** on the point of doing it. **not about to do something** determined not to do it. **that's about it** *or* **about all** *colloq.* almost everything that needs to be said or done has been. [from Anglo-Saxon *onbutan*]

🔁 *prep.* **1** regarding, concerning, relating to, referring to, connected with, concerned with, as regards, with regard to, with respect to, with reference to. **2** close to, near, beside, adjacent to. **3** round, around, encircling. **4** throughout, all over. **5** round, around, surrounding, encircling, encompassing. *adv.* **1** around, approximately, roughly, in the region of, more or less, almost, nearly, approaching, nearing. **3** here and there, throughout, all over. **4** to and fro, here and there, from place to place. **about to** on the point of, on the verge of, ready to, intending to, preparing to.

about turn *or* **about face 1** a turn made so that one is facing in the opposite direction. **2** a complete change of direction.

about-turn *or* **about-face** *verb intrans.* to turn round so as to be facing in the opposite direction.

above — *prep.* **1** higher than; over. **2** more or greater than in quantity or degree. **3** higher or superior to in rank, importance, ability, etc. **4** too good or great for: *above petty quarrels.* **5** too good, respected, etc to be affected by or subject to. **6** too difficult to be understood by; beyond the abilities of. — *adv.* **1** at, in or to a higher position, place, rank, etc. **2** in addition: *over and above.* **3** in an earlier passage of written or printed text. **4** *literary* in heaven. — *adj.* appearing or mentioned in an earlier or preceding passage of written or printed text. — *noun* something already mentioned. — **above all** most of all; more than anything else. **above and beyond** more than is required by. **above oneself** having an inflated opinion of one's importance; conceited, arrogant. [from Anglo-Saxon *abufan*]

🔁 *prep.* **1** over, higher than, on top of. **2** over, in excess of, exceeding, surpassing, beyond. *adv.* **1** overhead, aloft, on high. **3** earlier, before. *adj.* above-mentioned, above-stated,

foregoing, preceding, previous, earlier, prior.
■ *prep.* **1, 2** below, under. *adv.* **1, 3** below, underneath.

· ·

above-board *adj.* honest; open; not secret.

· ·

■ honest, legitimate, straight, *slang* on the level, fair, fair and
square, square, true, open, frank, candid, guileless,
straightforward, forthright, truthful, veracious, trustworthy,
honourable, reputable, upright.
■ dishonest, *colloq.* shady, underhand.

· ·

abracadabra /abrəkə'dabrə/ *interj.* a word which supposedly has magic power, often used by people when
doing magic tricks.
abrade *verb* to scrape or wear away, especially by rubbing.
[from Latin *abradere*, to scrape away]
abrasion *noun* **1** a damaged area of skin, rock, etc, which
has been worn away by scraping or rubbing. **2** the act of
scraping or rubbing away.

· ·

■ **1** graze, scratch, scrape. **2** scratching, scraping, scouring,
grating, grinding, abrading, chafing, friction, rubbing,
erosion, wearing away, wearing down.

· ·

abrasive /ə'breɪsɪv, ə'breɪzɪv/ — *adj.* **1** denoting a material
that is capable of wearing away the surface of skin, wood,
etc, by rubbing and scraping. **2** denoting a material
that is used to smooth or polish a softer surface by rubbing. **3** relating to the process of abrasion. **4** *said of people
or their actions* likely to offend others by being harsh and
rude. — *noun* any hard material, such as sandpaper,
pumice, or emery, that is used to wear away the surface of
softer materials, usually in order to shape or smooth
them.

· ·

■ *adj.* **3** scratching, scraping, grating, rough, harsh,
chafing, rubbing, frictional. **4** sharp, biting, caustic,
harsh, hurtful, nasty, unpleasant, rude, galling,
irritating, annoying.
■ *adj.* **3** smooth. **4** pleasant.

· ·

abreast — *adv.* side by side and facing in the same direction. — *adj.* (**abreast of something**) up to date concerning it; having the most recent information: *keep abreast
of events.* [from A³ + BREAST]

· ·

■ *adj.* acquainted with, informed about, knowledgeable
about, au courant with, up to date with, in touch with,
au fait with, conversant with, familiar with.
■ *adj.* unaware of, out of touch with.

· ·

abridge *verb* to make (a book, etc) shorter. [from Old
French *abregier*, from Latin *abbreviare*, to abbreviate]

· ·

■ shorten, cut (down), prune, curtail, abbreviate, contract,
reduce, summarize, précis, abstract, digest, condense,
compress, concentrate.
■ expand, amplify, pad out.

· ·

abridgement or **abridgment** *noun* **1** a shortening or
curtailment. **2** a shorter form of a work, especially a book.

· ·

■ **1** shortening, cutting, reduction, concentration, contraction,
curtailment, restriction, limitation. **2** summary, synopsis,
résumé, outline, précis, abstract, digest.
■ **1** expansion, padding.

· ·

abroad *adv.* **1** in or to a foreign country or countries. **2** in
circulation; at large. **3** over a wide area; in different directions. **4** *old use* out of or away from one's home. [from Middle English *abrod*]

· ·

■ **1** overseas, in foreign parts, out of the country. **2** at large,

around, about, circulating, current. **3** far and wide, widely,
extensively.
■ **1** at home.

· ·

abrogate /'abrəgeɪt/ *verb* to cancel (a law, agreement, etc)
formally or officially. [from Latin *abrogare*]
abrogation /abrə'geɪʃən/ *noun* the act of abrogating.
abrupt *adj.* **1** sudden and unexpected; very quick. **2** *said
especially of speech, etc* rather sharp and rude. **3** sloping
or descending sharply or suddenly. [from Latin *abrum-
pere*, to break off]

· ·

■ **1** sudden, unexpected, unforeseen, surprising, quick, rapid,
swift, hasty, hurried, precipitate. **2** brusque, curt, terse,
short, brisk, snappy, gruff, rude, uncivil, impolite, blunt,
direct. **3** sheer, precipitous, steep, sharp.
■ **1** gradual, slow, leisurely. **2** expansive, ceremonious, polite.
3 gradual.

· ·

abscess /'abses/ *noun* a localized collection of pus in a
cavity surrounded by inflamed tissue, usually caused by
bacterial infection. [from Latin *abscessus*, going away]
abscisic acid /ab'sɪsɪk/ *Bot.* a plant growth substance that
plays an important role in plant development by inhibiting
growth, and promoting leaf ageing and the shedding of
leaves, fruit, etc from the plant.
abscissa /ab'sɪsə/ *noun* (PL. **abscissas, abscissae**) *Maths.*
in coordinate geometry, the first of a pair of numbers (x,
y), known as the x coordinate. It specifies the distance of
a point from the vertical or y-axis. See also ORDINATE.
[from Latin *abscissus*, cut off]
abscission /ab'sɪʃən/ *noun* **1** an act of cutting off, or the
state of being cut off. **2** *Bot.* the shedding of leaves, fruit,
and other parts from a plant by the formation of a layer of
thin-walled cells, which subsequently breaks down, at the
base of the part which is to be shed. [from Latin *abscindere
abscissum*, to cut off]
abscond /ab'skɒnd/ *verb intrans.* to depart or leave quickly
and usually secretly, especially because one has done
something wrong and wants to avoid punishment or arrest. [from Latin *abscondere*, to hide]

· ·

■ run away, run off, make off, decamp, flee, fly, escape, bolt,
quit, *colloq.* clear out, disappear, take French leave.

· ·

absconder *noun* a person who has absconded.
abseil /'abseɪl/ — *verb intrans.* to make a descent down a
rock face, etc using a double rope wound round the body
and fixed to a point higher up. — *noun* an act of abseiling.
[from German *abseilen*, from *ab*, down + *Seil*, rope]
abseiling *noun* the sport of making a descent of a rock
face etc by means of a doubled rope fixed to a point higher
up.
absence *noun* **1** the state of being away or not present. **2**
the time when a person is away from work, etc. **3** the state
of not existing or being lacking. — **absence of mind** a lack
of attention or concentration. [from Latin *absentia*, from
abesse, to be away]

· ·

■ **1** non-attendance, non-appearance, truancy, absenteeism.
3 non-existence, lack, need, want, deficiency, dearth,
scarcity, unavailability, default, omission.
■ **1** presence, attendance, appearance. **3** existence.

· ·

absent /'absənt, ab'sent/ — *adj.* (with stress on *ab-*) **1** not in
its or one's expected place; not present. **2** not existing,
especially where normally to be expected. **3** showing that
one is not paying attention or concentrating. — *verb* (with
stress on -*sent*) (**absent oneself**) to stay away from a meeting, gathering, etc.

· ·

■ *adj.* **1** missing, not present, away, out, unavailable, gone,
truant, lacking. **3** inattentive, daydreaming, dreamy, faraway,

elsewhere, absent-minded, vacant, vague, distracted, preoccupied, unaware, oblivious, unheeding.
⊟ adj. **1** present. **3** alert, aware.

absentee /absən'ti:/ noun a person who is not present at a particular or required time.

absenteeism noun frequent and continued absence from work, school, etc.

absentee landlord a landlord who does not live in the property he lets out.

absentia see IN ABSENTIA.

absent-minded adj. **1** having a tendency to forget. **2** not noticing what one is doing or what is going on around one, especially because one is thinking about something else; preoccupied.

⊟ **1** forgetful, scatterbrained. **2** absent, abstracted, withdrawn, faraway, distracted, preoccupied, absorbed, engrossed, pensive, musing, dreaming, dreamy, inattentive, unaware, oblivious, unconscious, heedless, unheeding, unthinking.
⊟ **2** attentive, alert.

absinthe or **absinth** /'absɪnθ/ noun a strong green alcoholic drink flavoured with substances from certain plants, such as aniseed and wormwood. [from French absinthe, from Latin absinthium, wormwood]

absolute — adj. **1** complete; total; perfect. **2** without limits; not controlled by anything or anyone else. **3** certain; undoubted. **4** not measured in comparison with other things; not relative: an absolute standard. **5** pure; not mixed with anything else. **6** Grammar, said of a part of a sentence, etc not dependent on the rest of the sentence, but able to stand alone. See also RELATIVE 6. — noun **1** a rule, standard, etc which is thought to be true or right in all situations. **2 (the absolute)** Philos. that which can exist without being related to anything else.

⊟ adj. **1** utter, total, complete, entire, full, thorough, exhaustive, perfect, supreme, consummate, definitive, decisive, conclusive, final, sheer, unqualified, out-and-out, outright. **2** unlimited, unrestricted, omnipotent, totalitarian, autocratic, tyrannical, despotic, dictatorial, sovereign. **3** sure, certain, undoubted, positive, definite, categorical, unequivocal, unquestionable, unqualified, decided. **5** pure, unmixed, genuine.
⊟ adj. **3** uncertain, questionable, qualified. **5** impure, mixed.

absolute alcohol Chem. ethanol containing not more than one per cent water.

absolutely adv. **1** completely. **2** independently of anything else. **3** colloq. in actual fact; really; very much. **4** (with negatives) at all: absolutely nothing / absolutely no use. **5** yes; certainly.

⊟ **1** utterly, totally, completely, entirely, fully, wholly, thoroughly, exhaustively, perfectly, supremely, purely, unconditionally. **3** really, genuinely, actually, very, extremely. **5** certainly, positively, definitely, categorically, unequivocally, unambiguously, unquestionably, decidedly, decisively, conclusively, finally, exactly, precisely.

absolute majority noun a number of votes for a candidate in an election which is greater than the number of votes received by all the other candidates put together.

absolute pitch see PERFECT PITCH.

absolute zero the lowest temperature theoretically possible, 0 K on the kelvin scale, equivalent to $-273.15°$C or $-459.67°$F. It is the temperature at which atoms and molecules have minimal kinetic energy (energy of motion).

absolution /absə'lu:ʃən/ noun the formal forgiving of a person's sins, especially by a priest. [from Latin absolutio, acquittal]

absolutism noun the theory or practice of government by a person who has total power.

absolutist — noun a person who supports absolute government. — adj. practising or supporting absolute government; despotic.

absolve /əb'zɒlv/ verb **1** (**absolve someone from** or **of something**) to release them or pronounce them free from a promise, duty, blame, etc. **2** said of a priest to forgive (someone) formally for the sins they have committed. [from Latin absolvere, to loosen]

absorb verb **1** to take in or suck up (liquid, knowledge, etc). **2** to take up or receive matter or energy, eg water or radiation. **3** Physics to take up (energy) without reflecting or emitting it. **4** to receive or take in as part of oneself or itself. **5** to have all of the attention or interest of. **6** to reduce or lessen (the shock, force, impact, etc of something). [from Latin ab, away, from + sorbere, to suck in]

⊟ **1** take in, ingest, drink in, imbibe, suck up, soak up, consume, devour, engulf, digest, assimilate, understand. **2** take up, receive, hold, retain. **5** engross, involve, fascinate, enthral, monopolize, preoccupy, occupy, fill (up).
⊟ **1** exude.

absorbed adj. **1** soaked up, swallowed up; taken in, incorporated. **2** engrossed.

absorbency noun (PL. **absorbencies**) **1** the ability to absorb liquids, etc. **2** the degree to which something is able to absorb liquids, etc.

absorbent — adj. able to absorb liquid, etc. — noun an absorbent material.

absorbing adj. **1** soaking up; incorporating. **2** occupying or engrossing the mind.

⊟ **2** interesting, amusing, entertaining, diverting, engrossing, preoccupying, intriguing, fascinating, captivating, enthralling, spellbinding, gripping, riveting, compulsive, colloq. unputdownable.
⊟ **2** boring, colloq. off-putting.

absorptance noun Physics (SYMBOL α) a measure of the ability of a body to absorb radiation, measured as the ratio of energy absorbed by that body to the energy that is incident (falling) on it, and formerly known as absorptivity.

absorption noun **1** the act of taking in, sucking up or absorbing, or the process of being taken in, absorbed, etc. **2** the state of having all one's interest or attention occupied by something. [from Latin absorptio]

absorptive adj. **1** capable of absorbing. **2** engrossing.

abstain verb intrans. (**abstain from something** or **from doing something**) **1** to choose not to take or have it, or to do or undertake it: abstain from alcohol / abstain from having fun. **2** to formally record one's intention not to vote in an election. See also ABSTENTION, ABSTINENCE. [from Latin ab, away, from + tenere, to hold]

⊟ **1** refrain from, decline, refuse, reject, resist, shun, avoid, forbear from, keep from, stop, cease, desist, give up, renounce, forego, go without, deny oneself.
⊟ **1** indulge in.

abstainer noun a person who abstains, especially from alcohol.

abstemious /ab'sti:mɪəs/ adj., said of people, habits, etc taking food, alcohol, etc in very limited amounts; moderate or restrained in what one eats or drinks. [from Latin abstemius, from abs, away, from + temetum, strong drink]

⊟ abstinent, self-denying, self-disciplined, disciplined, sober, temperate, moderate, restrained, sparing, frugal, austere, ascetic.
⊟ intemperate, gluttonous, luxurious.

abstention *noun* **1** the act of choosing not to do something, especially not to take food or alcohol. **2** a refusal to vote; a person who has abstained from voting. [from Latin *abstinere*, to abstain]

abstinence /ˈabstɪnəns/ *noun* the practice or state of choosing not to do or take something, especially alcohol. [from Latin *abstinere*, to abstain]

· ·

🔳 abstaining, abstention, abstemiousness, self-denial, non-indulgence, avoidance, forbearance, refusal, restraint, self-restraint, self-control, self-discipline, sobriety, teetotalism, temperance, moderation, frugality, asceticism.
🔳 indulgence, self-indulgence.

· ·

abstinent *adj.* keeping oneself from indulgence, especially in alcohol.

abstract /ˈabstrakt, abˈstrakt/ — *adj.* (with stress on *ab-*) **1** referring to something which exists only as an idea or quality. **2** concerned with ideas and theory rather than with things which really exist or could exist. **3** *said of art forms, especially painting* representing the subject by shapes and patterns, etc rather than in the shape or form it actually has. — *noun* (with stress on *ab-*) **1** a brief statement of the main points (of a book, speech, etc). **2** an abstract idea, theory, etc. **3** an example of abstract painting, etc. — *verb* (with stress on *-stract*) **1** to take out or remove. **2** to summarize (a book, speech, etc). — **in the abstract** in theory rather than in reality. [from Latin *abs*, away, from + *trahere*, to draw]

· · · · · · · · · · · · · · · · · · · ·

🔳 *adj.* **1** non-concrete, conceptual, hypothetical, theoretical, general, generalized, indefinite. **2** unpractical, theoretical, metaphysical, philosophical, complex, abstruse, deep, profound, subtle. *noun* **1** synopsis, outline, summary, recapitulation, résumé, précis, epitome, digest, abridgement, compression. *verb* **1** extract, remove, withdraw, isolate, detach, dissociate, separate. **2** summarize, outline, précis, digest, condense, compress, abridge, abbreviate, shorten.
🔳 *adj.* **1** concrete, real, actual. *verb* **1** insert. **2** expand.

· ·

abstract art a general term for the many forms of non-figurative art which have developed since the beginning of the 20c. Abstract art is defined by its rejection of any attempt to represent the exterior world, and instead makes use of arrangements of lines, shapes, and colours to establish an independent 'reality' and aesthetic appeal.

abstracted *adj.* thinking about something so much that one does not notice what is happening around one.

abstraction *noun* **1** the act, or an example of, abstracting. **2** something which exists as a general idea rather than as an actual example. **3** the state of thinking about something so much that one does not notice what is happening around one.

· · · · · · · · · · · · · · · · · · · ·

🔳 **1** extraction, withdrawal, isolation, separation. **2** idea, notion, concept, thought, conception, theory, hypothesis, theorem, formula, generalization, generality. **3** inattention, dreaminess, absent-mindedness, distraction, pensiveness, preoccupation, absorption.

· ·

abstruse /abˈstruːs/ *adj.* hard to understand. [from Latin *abstrusus*, pushed away]

· · · · · · · · · · · · · · · · · · · ·

🔳 complex, puzzling, recondite, deep, profound, unclear, cryptic, enigmatic, mysterious.

· ·

absurd *adj.* not at all suitable; ridiculous. [from Latin *absurdus*, out of tune]

· · · · · · · · · · · · · · · · · · · ·

🔳 ridiculous, ludicrous, preposterous, fantastic, incongruous, illogical, paradoxical, implausible, untenable, unreasonable, irrational, nonsensical, meaningless, senseless, foolish, silly, stupid, idiotic, crazy, *colloq.* daft, farcical, comical, funny, humorous, laughable, risible.
🔳 logical, rational, sensible.

· ·

absurdism *noun* the expression in art of a vision of mankind as being essentially absurd and without purpose.

absurdity *noun* (PL. **absurdities**) **1** being absurd. **2** something that is absurd.

ABTA *abbrev.* Association of British Travel Agents.

abulia or **aboulia** /əˈbuːlɪə/ *noun Psychol.* a reduction in or absence of willpower, a common symptom of schizophrenia. [from A-¹ + Greek *boule*, will]

abundance *noun* **1** a large amount, sometimes more than is needed. **2** wealth. [from Old French *abundance*, from Latin *abundare*, to overflow]

abundant *adj.* **1** existing in large amounts. **2** (**abundant in something**) having or providing a large amount or variety of something.

· · · · · · · · · · · · · · · · · · · ·

🔳 **1** plentiful, in plenty, ample, generous, bountiful, copious, profuse, lavish, exuberant. **2** full of, filled with, well-supplied with, rich in, teeming with, overflowing with.
🔳 **1** scarce, sparse.

· ·

abundantly *adv.* **1** very; completely. **2** in large amounts.

abuse /əˈbjuːz, əˈbjuːs/ — *verb* (pronounced *-yuze*) **1** to use (one's position, power, etc) wrongly. **2** to treat (someone or something) cruelly or wrongly. **3** to speak rudely or insultingly to or about (someone). — *noun* (pronounced *-yuse*) **1** wrong use of one's position, power, etc. **2** bad or cruel treatment of someone or something. **3** (*in full* **child abuse**) the physical, mental, or emotional maltreatment of a child by one of its parents or another adult. **4** (*in full* **drug abuse**) the excessive use of alcohol, drugs, or other harmful substances, especially as distinguished from the more severe form of dependence known as *addiction*. **5** offensive or insulting words said to or about someone. [from Latin *abusus*, using up, wasting]

· · · · · · · · · · · · · · · · · · · ·

🔳 *verb* **1** misuse, misapply, exploit, take advantage of. **2** illtreat, maltreat, oppress, wrong, hurt, injure, molest, damage, spoil, harm. **3** insult, swear at, defame, libel, slander, smear, disparage, malign, revile, scold, upbraid. *noun* **1** misuse, misapplication, exploitation. **2** illtreatment, maltreatment, imposition, oppression, wrong, hurt, injury, molestation, damage, spoiling, harm. **5** insults, swearing, cursing, offence, defamation, libel, slander, disparagement, reproach, scolding, upbraiding, tirade.
🔳 *verb* **2** cherish, care for. **3** compliment, praise. *noun* **2** care, attention. **5** compliment, praise.

· ·

abusive /əˈbjuːsɪv/ *adj.* insulting or rude; using insulting or rude language.

· · · · · · · · · · · · · · · · · · · ·

🔳 insulting, offensive, rude, scathing, hurtful, injurious, cruel, destructive, defamatory, libellous, slanderous, derogatory, disparaging, pejorative, vilifying, maligning, reviling, censorious, reproachful, scolding, upbraiding.
🔳 complimentary, polite.

· ·

abut *verb* (**abutted**, **abutting**) **1** *intrans.* (**abut against** or **on something**) *said of countries, areas of land, buildings, etc* to join, touch, or lean against another. **2** to lean on or touch (something): *a wall abutting the house*. [from Old French *abouter*, to touch with an end]

abutment *noun* the support at the end of an arch, eg in a bridge or similar structure.

abuzz *adj.* in a state of noisy activity or excitement.

abysmal /əˈbɪzml/ *adj.* **1** *colloq.* extremely bad. **2** very deep; very great: *abysmal ignorance*. [from Old French *abisme*, abyss]

abyss /əˈbɪs/ *noun* **1** a very large and deep hole. **2** hell. **3** a deep part of the ocean, generally more than 2000m below the surface. [from Latin *abyssus*, from Greek *abyssos*, bottomless]

. . . .

■ **1** gulf, chasm, crevasse, fissure, gorge, canyon, crater, pit, depth, void.

. . . .

abyssal /ə'bɪsəl/ *adj. Biol.* deep or bottomless, especially of ocean depths. [from Greek *abyssos* bottomless]

abyssal hills *Geol.* low hills which occur on the deep sea floor, often as a series of parallel ridges 1 to 10km across.

abyssal plains *Geol.* extremely flat areas of the deep ocean floor which may extend for more than 1000km.

Ac *symbol Chem.* actinium.

a/c *abbrev.* account.

a.c. *abbrev.* alternating current.

acacia /ə'keɪʃə/ *noun* any of various trees and shrubs belonging to the genus *Acacia*, found mainly in warm dry regions of Australia, Africa, and S America. Most species bear large spines and clusters of small yellow flowers, and many produce branches suitable for making interwoven (wattle) roofs and fencing. [from Greek *akakia*]

academe /'akədi:m/ *noun formal* the world of scholars or academic life. [see ACADEMY]

academic /akə'dɛmɪk/ — *adj.* **1** to do with learning, study, education or teaching. **2** to do with a university, college or academy. **3** theoretical rather than practical. **4** of no practical importance, eg because impossible or unreal: *what we would do with a car is quite academic, since we can't afford one.* **5** *said of a person* fond of intellectual pursuits. — *noun* a member of the teaching or research staff at a university or college.

. . . .

■ *adj.* **1** scholastic, pedagogical, educational, instructional, scholarly, erudite. **3** theoretical, hypothetical, conjectural, speculative, notional, abstract, impractical. **5** studious, bookish, learned, well-read, scholarly, erudite, intellectual, highbrow. *noun* professor, don, master, fellow, lecturer, tutor.

3 *adj.* **3** practical.

. . . .

academically *adv.* as regards academic matters.

academician /əkadə'mɪʃən/ *noun* a member of an academy (sense 2), especially the Royal Academy of Arts, the French Académie Française, or the Russian Academy of Sciences.

academy /ə'kadəmɪ/ *noun* (PL. **academies**) **1** a school or college giving training in a particular subject or skill. **2** a society which encourages the study of science, literature, art, or music. **3** (*usually* **Academy**) a society of distinguished scholars, scientists, painters, etc. **4** in Scotland, a school for children between the ages of 11 and 18. [from Greek *Akademeia*, the garden outside Athens where the philosopher Plato taught, named after the hero *Akademos*]

Academy Award or **Oscar** *noun* any of the various prizes given each year by the American Academy of Motion Picture Arts and Sciences to the best film, actor, actress, etc.

acanthus /ə'kanθəs/ *noun* **1** any of various herbaceous perennial plants of the genus *Acanthus*, native to the Mediterranean region, and having spiny leaves and bracts. **2** *Archit.* a stone carving of an acanthus leaf used for decorations on columns. [from Greek *akanthos*]

ACAS *abbrev.* in the UK, the Advisory, Conciliation, and Arbitration Service, a body set up under the Employment Protection Act (1975). Its function is to provide facilities for conciliation, arbitration, and mediation in industrial disputes.

acc. *abbrev.* **1** (*also* **acc**) account. **2** accusative.

accede /ək'si:d/ *verb intrans.* (*often* **accede to something**) **1** to take office, especially to become king or queen. **2** to agree: *accede to the proposal.* **3** to join with others in a formal agreement. [from Latin *accedere*, to go near]

accelerate /ək'sɛləreɪt/ *verb* **1** *intrans., trans.* to increase or cause to increase speed. **2** *intrans.* to be completed more quickly. **3** to make (something) happen sooner. [from Latin *accelare*]

. . . .

■ **1** quicken, speed, speed up. **3** expedite, hurry, hasten, step up, precipitate, stimulate, facilitate, advance, further, promote, forward.

3 **1** decelerate, slow down. **2** delay.

. . . .

acceleration /əksɛlə'reɪʃən/ *noun* **1** *Physics* (SYMBOL **a**) the rate of change of velocity with time, equal to force divided by mass. It is a vector quantity, and is expressed in metres per second per second (m s^{-2}). **2** any increase of speed, eg of a vehicle.

acceleration due to gravity *Physics* (SYMBOL **g**) the downward acceleration of an object falling freely due to the Earth's gravitational attraction alone. Close to the Earth's surface, it has an international standard value of 9.81m s^{-2}, which is the same for all objects regardless of their mass. It decreases with increasing height above sea level.

accelerator /ək'sɛləreɪtə(r)/ *noun* **1** *Engineering* a pedal or lever designed to control the speed of an electric motor or engine by varying the amount of electric current or fuel supplied. **2** a piece of apparatus designed to increase the velocity of charged atomic particles, eg a cyclotron, used to accelerate protons, etc. **3** any substance that increases the rate at which a process occurs, eg a catalyst.

accent /'aksənt, ək'sɛnt/ — *noun* (with stress on *ac-*) **1** the particular way in which words are pronounced by speakers who live in a particular place, belong to a particular social group, etc. **2** emphasis or stress put on a particular syllable in speaking. **3** a mark put over or under a letter or syllable to show how it is pronounced. **4** a feature, mark, or characteristic which makes something distinct or special. **5** emphasis or stress placed on certain notes or chords in a piece of music. — *verb* (with stress on -*cent*) **1** to pronounce with an accent. **2** to write accents on. **3** to emphasize or stress. [from Latin *accentus*]

. . . .

■ *noun* **1** pronunciation, enunciation, articulation, tone, pitch, intonation, inflection, brogue, *colloq.* twang. **2** accentuation, stress, emphasis, intensity, force. **5** cadence, rhythm, beat, pulse, pulsation.

. . . .

accentor /ək'sɛntə(r)/ *noun* a sparrow-like bird native to N Africa, Europe, and Asia, brownish-grey to chestnut above, often streaked, and grey beneath. [from Latin *accentor*, one who sings with another, from *cantor*, singer]

accentuate /ək'sɛntjʊeɪt/ *verb* to emphasize or make more evident or prominent. [from Latin *accentuare*]

. . . .

■ accent, stress, emphasize, underline, highlight, intensify, strengthen, deepen.

3 play down, weaken.

. . . .

accentuation /əksɛntjʊ'eɪʃən/ *noun* emphasis; stress.

accept *verb* **1** to agree to take or receive (something offered). **2** *trans., intrans.* to agree to (a suggestion, proposal, etc). **3** to agree to do (a job, etc) or take on (a responsibility, etc). **4** to believe to be true or correct. **5** to be willing to listen to and follow (advice, etc). **6** to be willing to suffer or take (blame, etc). **7** to take as suitable or appropriate: *won't accept cheques.* **8** to allow into a group, treat as a colleague, etc. **9** to tolerate calmly. [from Latin *acceptare*, to receive]

. . . .

■ **1** take, receive, obtain, acquire, gain, secure. **2** agree to, consent to, approve. **3** take on, undertake, adopt. **4** acknowledge, recognize, admit, allow. **9** tolerate, put up with, stand, bear, abide.

3 **1** refuse, turn down. **2** reject.

. . . .

acceptability *noun* being acceptable.

acceptable *adj.* **1** worth accepting. **2** welcome or pleasing; suitable. **3** good enough, but usually only just; tolerable.

. . . .

⊟ **2** suitable, conventional, correct, desirable, pleasant, gratifying, welcome. **3** satisfactory, unexceptionable, tolerable, moderate, passable, admissible, adequate, all right, *colloq.* OK, *colloq.* so-so.
⊞ **2** unsuitable, unwelcome. **3** unacceptable, unsatisfactory.

. . . .

acceptance *noun* **1** the act or state of accepting something offered. **2** the act of agreeing to something; favourable or positive reception of something. **3** the act of believing something.

. . . .

⊟ **1** taking, accepting, receipt, obtaining, acquiring, gaining, securing. **2** agreement, concurrence, assent, consent, permission, ratification, approval, stamp of approval, *colloq.* OK. **3** acknowledgement, recognition, admission, concession, affirmation, belief, credence.
⊞ **1** refusal. **2** rejection, dissent.

. . . .

accepted *adj.* customary or conventional; generally recognized as correct, suitable, etc.

. . . .

⊟ authorized, approved, ratified, sanctioned, agreed, acknowledged, recognized, admitted, confirmed, acceptable, correct, conventional, orthodox, traditional, customary, time-honoured, established, received, universal, regular, standard, normal, usual, common.
⊞ unconventional, unorthodox, controversial.

. . . .

accepting house *Commerce* a merchant bank which 'accepts', ie buys three-month bills of exchange issued by companies.

acceptor *noun* **1** someone who accepts something, especially a bill of exchange. **2** a substance which is added as an impurity to a semiconductor material in order to increase the conductivity of the material by attracting electrons.

access /'akses/ — *noun* **1** a means of approaching or entering a place. **2** the right, opportunity, or ability to use, approach, meet with, or enter. **3** a sudden and usually brief period of strong emotion. **4** *Comput.* the right and opportunity to log on to a computer system, and to read and edit files that are held within it. **5** *Comput.* the possibility of transferring data to and from a memory device. — *verb* to locate or retrieve (information stored in the memory of a computer). [from Latin *accessus*, from *ad*, to + *cedere*, to go]

. . . .

⊟ *noun* **1** entrance, gateway, door, key, approach, passage, road, path, course. **2** admission, admittance, entry, entering.
⊞ *noun* **1** exit, outlet.

. . . .

accessary see ACCESSORY.

accessibility *noun* being accessible.

accessible *adj.* **1** able to be reached easily. **2** willing to talk to or have friendly discussions with other people. **3** easy to understand and enjoy or get some benefit from.

. . . .

⊟ **1** reachable, *colloq.* get-at-able, attainable, achievable, possible, obtainable, available, on hand, ready, handy, convenient, near, nearby. **2** friendly, affable, approachable, sociable, informal.
⊞ **1** inaccessible, remote. **2** unapproachable.

. . . .

accession /ək'seʃən/ *noun* **1** the act or process of taking up a new office or responsibility, or becoming a king or queen. **2** a person or thing added, eg a new book to a library. **3** the formal act of agreeing to, and coming under the rules of, an international agreement or treaty. [from Latin *accedere*, to accede]

accessory — *noun* (PL. **accessories**) **1** something additional to, but less important than, something else. **2** an item of dress, such as a bag, hat, etc which goes with a dress, coat, etc. **3** (*also* **accessary**) a *Legal* a person who helps a criminal do something wrong. **b** a person who helps somone to do something. — *adj.* adding to something but only in a minor way. — **accessory before** or **after the fact** *Legal* a person who helps a criminal before or after the crime. [from Latin *accessorius*]

. . . .

⊟ *noun* **1** extra, supplement, addition, appendage, attachment, extension, component, fitting. **2** accompaniment, decoration, adornment, frill, trimming. **3** accomplice, partner, associate, colleague, confederate, assistant, helper, help, aid.

. . . .

access road a minor road built specially to give access to a house, etc.

access time *Comput.* the time interval between the issue of a command requesting the retrieval of data from memory, and the stage at which data is finally obtained.

accident /'aksɪdənt/ *noun* **1** an unexpected event which causes damage or harm. **2** a collision involving vehicles, pedestrians, or other road users. **3** something which happens without planning or intention; chance: *managed it by accident*. [from Latin *accidere*, to happen]

. . . .

⊟ **1** misfortune, mischance, misadventure, mishap, casualty, blow, calamity, disaster. **2** collision, crash, *colloq.* shunt, *colloq.* prang, pile-up. **3** chance, hazard, fortuity, luck, fortune, fate, serendipity, contingency, fluke.

. . . .

accidental /aksɪ'dentəl/ — *adj.* happening or done by accident; not planned. — *noun* **1** a sign, such as a sharp or flat, put in front of a note in written music to show that it is to be played higher or lower. **2** something which is not a necessary feature of something.

. . . .

⊟ *adj.* unintentional, unintended, inadvertent, unplanned, uncalculated, unexpected, unforeseen, unlooked-for, chance, fortuitous, fluky, uncertain, haphazard, random, casual, incidental.
⊞ *adj.* intentional, deliberate, calculated, premeditated.

. . . .

accidentally *adv.* by chance.

accident-prone *adj.*, *said of a person* frequently causing or involved in accidents, usually minor ones.

acclaim — *verb* **1** to declare (someone) to be (something) with noisy enthusiasm. **2** to receive or welcome with noisy enthusiasm. — *noun* **1** a shout of praise or welcome; applause. **2** strong approval. [from Latin *acclamare*]

. . . .

⊟ *verb* **1** praise, commend, extol, exalt, honour. **2** hail, salute, welcome, applaud, clap, cheer. *noun* **1** applause, ovation, clapping, cheers, cheering, shouting, welcome, celebration. **2** acclamation, approval, approbation, praise, commendation, homage, tribute, eulogy, exaltation, honour.
⊞ *noun* **2** criticism, disapproval.

. . . .

acclamation /aklə'meɪʃən/ *noun* a loud showing of approval, agreement, applause, etc.

acclimatization or **acclimatisation** /ə'klaɪmətaɪ-'zeɪʃən/ *noun* becoming accustomed to a new climate or environment.

acclimatize or **acclimatise** /ə'klaɪmətaɪz/ *verb trans., intrans.* to make or become accustomed to a new place, situation, climate, etc. [from French *acclimater*, from *climat*, climate]

acclivity /ə'klɪvɪtɪ/ *noun* (PL. **acclivities**) *formal* an upward slope. See also DECLIVITY. [from Latin *acclivitas*]

accolade /'akəleɪd/ *noun* **1** a sign or expression of great praise or approval. **2** a touch on the shoulder with a sword when giving a person a knighthood. [from Old French *accoler*, to embrace]

accommodate /ə'kɒmədeɪt/ *verb* **1** to provide (someone) with a place in which to stay. **2** to be large enough for; to be able to hold. **3** to do what (someone) wants; to do (someone) a favour. **4** (**accommodate oneself to something**) to adapt one's habits or plans in order to be more like, more acceptable to, or more helpful to someone or something. [from Latin *accommodare*, to adapt]

■ **1** lodge, board, put up, house, shelter. **2** contain, hold. **3** oblige, help, assist, aid, serve, provide with, supply with, comply with. **4** adapt to, adjust to, fit in with, harmonize with, get accustomed to, reconcile oneself to.

accommodating *adj.* helpful; willing to do what another person wants.

■ obliging, indulgent, helpful, co-operative, willing, kind, considerate, unselfish, sympathetic, friendly, hospitable.
🔄 disobliging, selfish.

accommodation /əkɒmə'deɪʃən/ *noun* **1** (*also North Amer.* **accommodations**) a room or rooms in a house or hotel in which to live. **2** willingness to accept other people's wishes, etc. **3** (**accommodations**) *North Amer.* a reserved place on a bus, train, ship, or aircraft. **4** in vertebrates, adjustment of the shape of the lens of the eye by ciliary muscles, which contract to make the lens thinner in order to focus on distant objects, or relax to make it thicker in order to focus on nearby objects.

Types of accommodation include: flat, apartment, bedsit, bedsitter, *colloq.* digs, lodgings, hostel, halls of residence, rooms, residence, dwelling, shelter, *colloq.* pad, *colloq.* squat; bed and breakfast, board, guest house, hotel, youth hostel, villa, timeshare, motel, inn, pension, boarding-house; barracks, billet, married quarters. *See also* **house**; **room**.

accommodation address an address used on letters to a person who cannot give, or does not want to give, his or her permanent address.

accommodation ladder a small ladder on the side of a large ship by means of which one can get to or from a smaller boat.

accompaniment /ə'kʌmpənɪmənt/ *noun* **1** something that happens or exists at the same time as something else, or which comes with something else. **2** music played to accompany or support a singer or another instrument.

accompanist *noun* a person who plays a musical instrument to accompany or support a singer or another player.

accompany *verb* (**accompanies, accompanied**) **1** to come or go with. **2** to be done or found with. **3** to play a musical instrument to support (someone who is playing another instrument or singing). [from Old French *accompagnier*, from *a*, to + *compaignon*, companion]

■ **1** escort, attend, convoy, chaperon, usher, conduct, follow. **2** coexist with, coincide with, belong to, go with, complement, supplement.

accomplice /ə'kʌmplɪs/ *noun* a person who helps another commit a crime. [from Middle English *complice*, from Latin *complex*, joined]

■ accessory, abettor, helper, assistant, mate, henchman, conspirator, collaborator, ally, confederate, partner.

accomplish *verb* to manage to do; complete. [from Old French *acomplir*]

■ achieve, attain, do, perform, carry out, execute, fulfil,

discharge, finish, complete, conclude, consummate, realize, effect, bring about, engineer, produce, obtain.

accomplishable *adj.* capable of being achieved or done.
accomplished *adj.* **1** clever or skilled. **2** completed or finished.

■ **1** clever, skilled, practised, proficient, professional, gifted, talented, skilful, adroit, adept, expert, masterly, consummate, polished, cultivated. **2** finished, complete, done, achieved.
🔄 **1** unskilled, inexpert, incapable. **2** incomplete, undone.

accomplishment *noun* **1** a social or other skill developed through practice. **2** something special or remarkable which has been done; an achievement. **3** the finishing or completing of something.

■ **1** skill, art, aptitude, faculty, ability, capability, proficiency, gift, talent, forte. **2** achievement, exploit, feat, deed, stroke, triumph. **3** achievement, attainment, doing, performance, carrying out, execution, fulfilment, discharge, finishing, completion, conclusion, consummation, perfection, realization, fruition, production.

accord — *verb* **1** *intrans.* (**accord with someone** or **something**) to agree or be in harmony with them. **2** to give (a welcome, etc) or grant (permission, a request, etc). — *noun* agreement or consent; harmony. — **of one's own accord** willingly; without being told to or forced to. **with one accord** with everyone in agreement and acting at the same time. [from Old French *acorder*, from Latin *ad*, to + *cor*, heart]

■ **1** agree with, concur with, harmonize with, match, conform with, correspond with, suit. **2** give, tender, grant, bestow, endow, confer. *noun* accordance, agreement, consent, assent, harmony, unanimity, concert, unity, correspondence, conformity, sympathy.
🔄 *verb* **1** disagree with. **2** deny. *noun* conflict, discord, disharmony.

accordance *noun* agreement or harmony: *in accordance with the law.*

according *adv.* **1** (**according to someone**) as said or told by: *according to my doctor.* **2** (**according to something**) in agreement with: *live according to one's principles.* **3** (**according as ...**) *formal* in proportion as ... ; depending on whether: *pay according as one is able.*

■ **2** in accordance with, in agreement with, in keeping with, obedient to, in conformity with, in line with, consistent with, commensurate with, in proportion to, in relation to.

accordingly *adv.* **1** in an appropriate way: *act accordingly.* **2** therefore; for that reason.

■ **1** in accordance, correspondingly, appropriately, properly, suitably. **2** therefore, thus, so, hence, as a result, consequently, in consequence.

accordion /ə'kɔːdɪən/ *noun* a musical instrument consisting of two box-like parts joined by a folding middle section, played by pushing the box-like parts together and pulling them apart again to create a sound which is changed into different notes by pressing a series of buttons and piano-like keys with the fingers. [from German *Akkordion*, from French *accorder* or Italian *accordare*, to harmonize]

accordionist *noun* a person who plays the accordion.
accost *verb* **1** to approach and speak to (someone), especially boldly or in a threatening way. **2** *said of a prostitute*

to offer to have sexual intercourse with (a person) in return for money. [from Latin *accostare*]

. . . .

▣ **1** approach, confront, buttonhole, waylay, stop, halt, detain, importune.

. . . .

account — *noun* **1** a description or report. **2** an explanation, especially of one's behaviour. **3** an arrangement by which a bank or building society allows a person to have banking or credit facilities; a deposit of money in a bank or building society. **4** a statement of the money owed to someone for goods or services. **5** (*usually* **accounts**) a record of money received and spent. **6** an arrangement by which a shop allows a person to buy goods on credit and pay for them later. **7** importance or value. **8** behalf or sake. — *verb formal* to consider (someone or something) to be as specified: *accounted them all fools.* — **account for something 1** to give a reason or explanation for it. **2** to make or give a reckoning of money spent, etc. **account for something** or **someone** to succeed in destroying or disposing of them. **bring someone to account** to punish them for something wrong that has been done. **by all accounts** according to general opinion. **call someone to account** to demand an explanation from them for their action or behaviour. **give a good** or **poor account of oneself** to give a good or bad performance; to make a good or bad impression. **hold someone to account** to consider them responsible. **leave something out of account** not to consider (a problem, factor, etc) when making a decision, calculation, etc. **on account 1** to be paid for at a later date. **2** as partial payment. **on account of something** because of it. **on no account** not for any reason. **on one's own account 1** on one's own responsibility. **2** for one's own benefit. **put something to good account** to use a situation, ability, etc to one's advantage. **take something into account** or **take account of something** to consider (a problem, opinion, or other factor) when making a decision or assessment. **turn something to good account** to use it to one's advantage. [from Old French *aconter*]

. . . .

▣ *noun* **1** description, narrative, story, tale, record, chronicle, history, memoir, report, statement, communiqué, write-up, version, portrayal, sketch, presentation. **4** statement, invoice, bill, *North Amer.* tab, charge, reckoning, computation, tally, score, balance. **5** ledger, book, books, records. *verb* consider, regard, think, deem, judge, rate, count. **account for** *something* explain, elucidate, illuminate, clear up, rationalize, justify, vindicate, answer for. *something or someone* destroy, put paid to, dispose of, kill.

. . . .

accountability *noun* responsibility.
accountable *adj.* **1** responsible; having to explain or defend one's actions or conduct. **2** explicable.

. . . .

▣ **1** answerable, responsible, liable, amenable, obliged, bound.

. . . .

accountancy *noun* the profession of preparing and keeping the financial records of a business or organization.
accountant *noun* a person who is trained to keep accounts.
accounting *noun* the skill or practice of preparing or keeping the financial records of a company, etc.
accoutrements /əˈkuːtrəmənts/ *pl. noun* **1** equipment. **2** a soldier's equipment apart from clothing and weapons. [from Old French *acoustrer*, to equip]
accredit *verb* (**accredited, accrediting**) **1** (**accredit something to someone** or **someone with something**) to attribute a saying, action, etc to someone: *accredited the idea to us* / *should accredit them with devising the scheme.* **2** (**accredit someone to** or **at a place**) to send an ambassador or diplomat to a foreign country with official authority. **3** to state officially that (something) is of a satisfactory standard. [from Old French *acrediter*]

accreditation /əkredɪˈteɪʃən/ *noun* the action of accrediting or being accredited.
accredited *adj.* **1** officially recognized. **2** *said of a belief, etc* generally accepted.
accretion /əˈkriːʃən/ *noun* **1** *Geol.* a gradual increase in land area resulting from offshore deposition of sediment carried by river or stream currents, tides, or wave action. **2** the process of separate things growing into one. **3** an increase in size of a particle, eg a hailstone, as a result of the formation of additional outer layers. [from Latin *accretio*, growing together]
accrual /əˈkruːəl/ *noun* **1** the act of accruing. **2** something which has been accrued.
accrue /əˈkruː/ *verb* **1** *intrans.* (*usually* **accrue to someone** or **something**) to come in addition, as a product, result, or development. **2** *intrans.* to fall to naturally. **3** to collect: *accrued a collection of antique vases.* [from Old French *acrue*, from Latin *accrescere*, to grow together]
acct. *abbrev.* (*also* **acct**) account.
acculturation /əkʌltʃəˈreɪʃən/ *noun* the process of one group of people becoming more like another group of people in behaviour, customs, etc, usually because of living near them for a long time. [from Latin *ad*, to + CULTURE]
accumulate /əˈkjuːmjʊleɪt/ *verb* **1** to collect or gather (something) in an increasing quantity. **2** *intrans.* to grow greater in number or quantity. [from Latin *accumulare*, from *cumulus*, heap]

. . . .

▣ **1** gather, assemble, collect, amass, accrue, aggregate, cumulate, hoard, stockpile, *slang* stash, store. **2** grow, increase, multiply, build up.
▣ **1** disseminate. **2** decrease.

. . . .

accumulation /əkjuːmjʊˈleɪʃən/ *noun* **1** the act of accumulating. **2** a mass or pile.

. . . .

▣ **1** gathering, assembly, collection, aggregation, conglomeration, increase, build-up. **2** mass, heap, pile, stack, stock, store, reserve, hoard, stockpile.

. . . .

accumulative /əˈkjuːmjʊlətɪv/ *adj.* **1** becoming greater over a period of time. **2** tending to gather, buy, etc many things.
accumulator /əˈkjuːmjʊleɪtə(r)/ *noun* **1** *Electr.* a storage battery that can be recharged by passing a current through it from an external DC (direct current) supply. **2** *Brit.* (*also* **accumulator bet**) a bet on four or more races, where the original money bet and any money won are bet on the next race, so that the better either wins a lot of money or loses it all. **3** *Comput.* a part of the memory of a computer that is used as a temporary store for the results of an arithmetical calculation or logic operation.
accuracy *noun* exactness; the state of being absolutely correct and making no mistakes, especially through careful effort.

. . . .

▣ exactness, precision, correctness, authenticity, truth, veracity, closeness, faithfulness, fidelity, carefulness.
▣ inaccuracy.

. . . .

accurate *adj.* **1** exact; absolutely correct; making no mistakes. **2** agreeing exactly with the truth or a standard. [from Latin *accuratus*, performed with care]

. . . .

▣ **1** exact, precise, correct, right, unerring, well-directed, *colloq.* spot-on, faultless, perfect, word-perfect. **2** true, truthful, veracious, factual, authentic, proper, close, faithful, well-judged, careful, rigorous, scrupulous, meticulous, minute, nice.
▣ INACCURATE. **1** inexact, imprecise, wrong. **2** untrue, false.

. . . .

accursed /əˈkɜːsɪd, əˈkɜːst/ *adj.* **1** *colloq.* disliked or hated. **2** having been cursed. [from Anglo-Saxon *acursod*]

accusation *noun* **1** the act of accusing someone of having done something wrong. **2** *Legal* a statement charging a person with having committed a crime.

    ▣ **1** imputation, denunciation, impeachment, incrimination, recrimination, complaint. **2** charge, allegation, indictment, complaint.

accusative /əˈkjuːzətɪv/ *Grammar* — *noun* in certain languages, eg Latin, Greek and German, the grammatical case of a noun, etc when it is the object of an action or the point towards which something is moving. — *adj.* of or in the accusative. [from Latin *accusativus*]

accuse *verb* (**accuse someone of something**) to charge them with an offence. — **the accused** the person or people accused of an offence. **stand accused** *Legal* to appear in court charged with an offence. [from Latin *accusare*]

    ▣ charge with, indict with, reproach with, arraign with, impeach for, incriminate for, blame for, censure for.

accuser *noun* a person who accuses or blames.

accusing *adj.* blaming, condemning; reproachful.

accustom *verb* (**accustomed, accustoming**) (**accustom someone** or **oneself to something**) to make them become familiar with it. [from Old French *acostumer*]

accustomed *adj.* **1** (**accustomed to someone** or **something**) familiar with them; experienced in something. **2** usual; customary: *the accustomed practice*.

    ▣ **1** used to, in the habit of, given to, acquainted with, familiar with, experienced in, trained in, adapted to, acclimatized to, hardened to, inured to. **2** usual, habitual, wonted, routine, regular, customary, conventional, traditional, established, fixed, general, normal, ordinary, everyday.
    ▨ **1** unaccustomed to, unused to, unfamiliar with. **2** unaccustomed, unusual.

AC/DC or **ac/dc** /eɪsiːˈdiːsiː/ *abbrev.* alternating current/direct current. — *adj. slang* sexually attracted to both men and women; bisexual.

ACE *abbrev.* Advisory Centre for Education.

ace — *noun* **1** *Cards* the card in each of the four suits with a single symbol on it, having either the highest value or the value one. **2** a person who is extremely good at something. **3** a fighter pilot who has shot down many enemy aircraft. **4** *Tennis* a serve that is so fast and cleverly placed that the opposing player cannot hit the ball. — *adj. colloq.* excellent. — **an ace up one's sleeve** a hidden or secret advantage, argument, etc that will help one to beat an opponent. **hold all the aces** to be in a powerful or winning position. **play one's ace** to put into action a plan for the final defeat of one's opponent. **within an ace of something** or **of doing something** very close to it: *came within an ace of winning*. [from Old French *as*, from Latin *as*, unit]

acellular /eɪˈsɛljʊlə(r)/ *adj. Biol.* not containing cells; not made up of cells.

acerbic /əˈsɜːbɪk/ *adj.* **1** bitter and sour in taste. **2** bitter and harsh in manner, speech, etc. [from Latin *acerbus*, sour]

acerbity *noun* **1** bitterness, sourness. **2** harshness.

acesulfame K /asɪˈsʌlfeɪm/ *Chem.* an artificial sweetener, 130 times sweeter than sugar. [from *K* for *potassium*, + *sulfamic acid*]

acetal /ˈasɪtəl/ *noun Chem.* a substance formed by the reaction of an alcohol with an aldehyde. [from Latin *acetum*, vinegar]

acetaldehyde /asɪtˈaldəhaɪd/ *noun Chem.* (FORMULA CH_3CHO) a colourless volatile pungent-smelling liquid used as a solvent and reducing agent, and in the manufacture of acetic acid and polymers such as paraldehyde (a sleep-inducing drug) and metaldehyde (a slug poison and fuel for portable stoves).

acetate /ˈasɪteɪt/ *noun* **1** a salt or ester of acetic acid. Also called ETHANOATE. **2** any of various synthetic fibres that are made from cellulose acetate. **3** a piece of transparent film on which information, diagrams, etc, may be written or drawn for display by an overhead projector.

acetic /əˈsiːtɪk, əˈsetɪk/ *adj.* of or like vinegar. [from Latin *acetum*, vinegar]

acetic acid *Chem.* (FORMULA CH_3COOH) a clear colourless viscous liquid with acidic properties and a characteristic pungent odour. It is present in vinegar, and is formed by the fermentation of alcohol. Acetic acid is used in the production of plastics, dyes, and food additives. Also called ETHANOIC ACID.

acetone /ˈasɪtoʊn/ *noun Chem.* (FORMULA CH_3COCH_3) a colourless flammable volatile liquid with a characteristic pungent odour, widely used as a solvent for paints, varnishes, nail-varnish remover, etc, and as a raw material in the manufacture of plastics. Also called PROPANONE. [from acetic]

acetylcholine /asiːtaɪlˈkoʊliːn/ *noun Biochem.* a neurotransmitter found in the brain, spinal cord, and ganglia of the autonomic nervous system in mammals.

acetylene /əˈsetɪliːn/ *noun Chem.* (FORMULA C_2H_2) a colourless highly flammable gas with a characteristic sweet odour, used for lighting, oxyacetylene welding, and in the manufacture of organic compounds. It is the simplest member of the alkyne series of hydrocarbons. Also called ETHYNE. [from ACETIC]

acetyl group /ˈasətaɪl/ *Chem.* in organic chemical compounds, the CH_3CO- group.

Achaean *noun* **1** the archaic name for a Greek, found frequently in Homer. **2** in Classical Greece, an inhabitant of Achaea, the territory to the south of the Corinthian Gulf. *adj.* relating to the Achaeans.

ache /eɪk/ — *verb intrans.* **1** to feel or be the source of a dull continuous pain. **2** (**ache for something**) to want it very much. — *noun* a dull continuous pain. [from Anglo-Saxon *acan*, to ache; *æce*, an ache]

    ▣ *verb* **1** hurt, be sore, pain, agonize, throb, pound, twinge. **2** desire, yearn for, long for, pine for, hanker after, crave, hunger for, thirst for, itch for. *noun* pain, hurt, soreness, agony, anguish, throb, throbbing, pounding, pang, twinge.

achene /əˈkiːn/ *noun Bot.* a dry one-seeded fruit that is indehiscent (ie it does not split to release its seed), formed from a single carpel, as in the buttercup. [from A-[1] + Greek *chainein*, to gape]

achievable *adj.* capable of being achieved.

achieve *verb* **1** to reach, realize, or attain (a goal, ambition, etc), especially through hard work. **2** to earn or gain (a reputation, etc). **3** *intrans.* to be successful. [from Old French *achever*]

    ▣ **1** accomplish, attain, reach, realize, finish, complete, do, perform, carry out, execute, fulfil, effect, bring about, produce. **2** earn, win, gain, get, obtain, acquire, procure. **3** succeed, prosper.
    ▨ **1** miss. **2** lose. **3** fail.

achievement *noun* **1** the gaining of something, usually after working hard for it. **2** something that has been done or gained by effort.

    ▣ ACCOMPLISHMENT, ATTAINMENT. **1** realization, completion, performance, execution, fulfilment, success, fruition. **2** acquirement, gain, feat, exploit.

achiever *noun* a person who achieves success.

Achilles' heel /əˈkɪliːz/ a person's weak or vulnerable point.

Achilles' tendon the tendon situated at the back of the ankle, that connects the muscles in the calf of the leg to the heelbone.

achondroplasia /akɒndroʊˈpleɪʒə/ *Medicine* an inherited form of dwarfism, in which the arms and legs are abnormally short, but the head and body are of normal size. [from A-¹ + Greek *chondros*, cartilage + *plassein*, to make]

achromatic /eɪkroʊˈmatɪk/ *adj.* **1** without colour. **2** *said of a lens* capable of transmitting light without separating it into its constituent colours. [from A-¹ + Greek *khroma*, colour]

achromatically *adv.* in an achromatic way; without colour.

achromatic lens *Astron.* a composite lens, consisting of two or more lenses each made of a different type of glass, that has the same focal length for two or more wavelengths of light, and greatly reduces the effects of chromatic aberration in optical systems.

achy *adj.* (**achier**, **achiest**) full of or troubled by pain.

acid /ˈasɪd/ — *noun* **1** any of a group of chemical compounds that have a sour or sharp taste, turn blue litmus paper red, and react with bases to form salts. Acids dissociate (break down) in water to form positively charged hydrogen ions and negatively charged anions. **2** any sour substance. **3** *slang* LSD. — *adj.* **1** containing acid; sour to taste. **2** *said of remarks, etc* expressing bitterness or anger. [from Latin *acidus*, sour]

▤ *adj.* SOUR, BITTER, TART, SHARP, PUNGENT, ACERBIC, CAUSTIC, STINGING, BITING. **1** acidic, vinegary, corrosive. **2** cutting, incisive, trenchant, mordant, harsh, hurtful.

acid house a type of electronically produced disco music with a repetitive hypnotic beat, often associated with the use of certain drugs, and usually played at large parties.

acidic *adj.* like, or containing, acid.

acidification *noun* the act or process of acidifying.

acidify *verb trans., intrans.* (**acidifies**, **acidified**) to make or become acid.

acidity *noun* (PL. **acidities**) **1** the quality of being acid or sour. **2** the extent to which a given solution is acid, as indicated by its pH value, which is in turn dependent on the concentration of hydrogen ions (H ions) in the solution.

acidosis /asɪˈdoʊsɪs/ *noun Medicine* a condition in which the blood and other body fluids are abnormally acidic, eg as a result of kidney failure or diabetes.

acid rain rain or other forms of precipitation (eg snow) containing dissolved sulphur dioxide and nitrogen oxides that have been released into the atmosphere as a result of the burning of fossil fuels, eg coal or oil.

acid test a decisive test to determine that something is genuine or valid. [originally a test using acid to determine whether a substance contained gold]

ack-ack *adj. old colloq. use* anti-aircraft. [formerly, British signaller's code for the letters *AA*, standing for *anti-aircraft*]

acknowledge /əkˈnɒlɪdʒ/ *verb* **1** to admit or accept the truth of (a fact or situation). **2** to accept as valid or legal; to recognize. **3** to report that one has received (what has been sent). **4** to express thanks for. **5** to show that one has noticed or recognized (someone), by greeting them, nodding one's head, etc. **6** to accept someone (as something); to accept a person's claim to be (something). [from obsolete *acknow*, to acknowledge]

▤ **1** admit, confess, own up to, declare, recognize, accept, grant, allow, concede. **2** accept, recognize. **3** answer, reply to, respond to. **5** greet, address, notice, recognize.
▣ **1** deny. **5** ignore.

acknowledged *adj.* generally recognized or accepted as valid, legal, rightful, true, etc.

▤ recognized, accepted, approved, accredited, declared, professed, attested, avowed, confirmed.

acknowledgement or **acknowledgment** *noun* **1** the act of acknowledging someone or something. **2** something done, given, or said to acknowledge something.

▤ **1** admission, confession, declaration, profession, recognition, notice, acceptance. **2** answer, reply, response, receipt, thanks, gratitude, appreciation, tribute, greeting, salutation.

acme /ˈakmɪ/ *noun* the highest point of achievement, success, excellence, etc. [from Greek *akme*]

▤ peak, pinnacle, summit, top, height, zenith, culmination, climax.

acne /ˈaknɪ/ *noun Medicine* a skin disorder, common in adolescence, caused by overactivity of the sebaceous glands, especially on the face, chest, and back. The pores become blocked by *sebum*, an oily secretion of the sebaceous glands, forming a plug which develops into a pimple or blackhead. [from Latin *acne*]

acolyte /ˈakəlaɪt/ *noun* **1** a person who assists a priest in certain religious ceremonies. **2** an assistant or attendant. [from Latin *acolytus*, from Greek *akolouthos*, follower]

aconite /ˈakənaɪt/ *noun* any of various herbaceous plants belonging to the genus *Aconitum*, native to Europe and NW Asia, especially *A.napellus* (commonly known as *monkshood*), which has deeply divided leaves and hooded bluish-purple flowers. Its roots contain the toxic alkaloid compound aconitine, formerly used to poison wolves (giving rise to the plant's other popular name, *wolfsbane*), and once used as a narcotic and analgesic drug. [from Latin *aconitum*]

acorn *noun* the nut-like fruit of the oak tree, which has a cup-shaped outer case. [from Anglo-Saxon *æcern*]

acoustic /əˈkuːstɪk/ *adj.* **1** relating to, producing, or operated by sound. **2** relating to acoustics. **3** relating to the sense of hearing. **4** *said of a musical instrument, eg a guitar or piano* amplifying the sound by means of its body, not using an electrical amplifier. **5** *said of building materials, etc* designed so as to reduce the disturbance caused by excessive noise. [from Greek *akoustikos*, from *akouein*, to hear]

acoustically *adv.* **1** relating to the hearing of sound. **2** without electronic amplification.

acoustic coupler **1** a device that is used to transmit digital data along telephone lines to and from the modem of a computer terminal, without making direct connections to the telephone system. **2** any device that is used to convert electrical signals to sound signals, or vice versa.

acoustics *noun* **1** (*sing.*) the scientific study of the production and properties of sound waves. **2** (*pl.*) the characteristics of a room, concert hall, theatre, etc, that determine the nature and quality of sounds such as music and speech heard within it.

acquaint *verb* (**acquaint someone with something**) to make them aware of or familiar with it. [from Old French *acointer*]

▤ tell about, notify of, advise of, inform of, brief on, enlighten about, familiarize with, accustom to.

acquaintance *noun* **1** slight knowledge of something or someone. **2** someone whom one knows slightly. — **make someone's acquaintance** to get to know them.

▤ **1** awareness, knowledge, understanding, experience, familiarity, intimacy, relationship, association, fellowship, companionship. **2** friend, companion, colleague, associate, contact.

acquaintanceship *noun* slight knowledge, especially of a person.

acquainted adj. 1 (**acquainted with someone**) knowing them personally but only slightly. 2 (**acquainted with something**) familiar with it: acquainted with her books.

acquiesce /akwɪˈɛs/ verb intrans. (**acquiesce in** or **to something**) to accept it or agree to it without objection. [from Latin acquiescere]

acquiescence noun quiet or tacit agreement or acceptance.

acquiescent adj. quietly accepting or agreeing.

acquire verb 1 to get, gain, or develop. 2 to achieve or reach (a reputation). [from Latin acquirere]

◼ 1 get, obtain, procure, buy, purchase, gain, secure, earn, win, receive, collect, gather, pick up, develop. 2 achieve, attain, realize.

◩ 1 relinquish, forfeit, lose.

acquired immune deficiency syndrome see AIDS.

acquired taste 1 a liking for something that develops as one has more experience of it. 2 the thing liked.

acquirement noun something learned or developed through hard work and not a natural gift.

acquisition /akwɪˈzɪʃən/ noun 1 a thing obtained or acquired. 2 the act of obtaining, developing, or acquiring something. [from Latin acquisitio]

◼ ACHIEVEMENT, ATTAINMENT. 1 gain, purchase, colloq. buy, property, possession. 2 development, gaining, procurement, securing.

acquisitive /əˈkwɪzɪtɪv/ adj. very eager to obtain and possess things. [from Latin acquisitivus]

acquit verb (**acquitted, acquitting**) 1 (**acquit someone of something**) said of a court or jury, etc to declare a person accused of a crime to be innocent. 2 (**acquit oneself**) to behave or perform in a particular way: acquitted themselves with distinction. [from Old French aquiter]

◼ 1 absolve of, clear of, exonerate of, excuse for. 2 behave, conduct oneself, act, perform.

◩ 1 convict for.

acquittal noun 1 a declaration in a court of law that someone is not guilty of the crime, etc of which they have been accused. 2 performance of a duty.

◼ DISCHARGE. 1 absolution, clearance, exoneration, exculpation, vindication, liberation, release, dismissal. 2 performance, execution, fulfilment.

◩ 1 conviction.

acre /ˈeɪkə(r)/ noun 1 a measure of land area equivalent to 4,047 sq m or 4,840 sq yd. 2 (**acres**) a large area of land. [from Anglo-Saxon æcer, field]

acreage /ˈeɪkərɪdʒ/ noun the number of acres in a piece of land.

acrid /ˈakrɪd/ adj. 1 having a very strong, bitter taste, or smell. 2 said of speech, manner, etc sharp or bitter. [from Latin acer, sharp, keen]

◼ SHARP, STINGING, CAUSTIC, ACID, ACERBIC, BITING, BITTER, HARSH. 1 pungent, burning. 2 cutting, incisive, trenchant, sarcastic, sardonic, acrimonious, virulent, vitriolic, venomous.

acridity noun being acrid, bitterness.

acrimonious /akrɪˈmoʊnɪəs/ adj., said of speech, etc bitter; accusing.

◼ bitter, rancorous, cutting, trenchant, sharp, virulent, severe, spiteful, malicious, venomous, vitriolic, nasty, ill-tempered.

◩ peaceable, kindly.

acrimony /ˈakrɪmənɪ/ noun bitterness in feeling, temper, or speech. [from Latin acrimonia]

◼ bitterness, rancour, resentment, ill-will, petulance, irascibility, sarcasm, trenchancy, astringency, acerbity, harshness, virulence.

acrobat noun an entertainer, eg in a circus, who performs skilful balancing acts and other athletic tricks. [from French acrobate, from Greek akrobatos, walking on tip-toe]

acrobatic adj. 1 able to perform gymnastic feats; agile. 2 liable to change one's opinion or allegiance frequently.

acrobatically adv. in an acrobatic way.

acrobatics noun 1 (sing.) the art or skill of an acrobat. 2 (pl.) acrobatic movements.

acromegaly /akroʊˈmɛgəlɪ/ noun Medicine a disorder characterized by abnormal enlargement of the face, hands, and feet. It is caused by overproduction of growth hormone. [from Greek akron point, megas, megalos great]

acronym /ˈakrənɪm/ noun a word made from the first letters or syllables of other words, eg NATO is an acronym of North Atlantic Treaty Organization. [from Greek akron, point, end + onyma, name]

acrophobia /akrəˈfoʊbɪə/ noun fear of heights. [from Greek akron, point, summit + phobos, fear]

acropolis /əˈkrɒpəlɪs/ noun 1 the upper fortified part or citadel of an ancient Greek city. 2 (**Acropolis**) the citadel of ancient Athens. [from Greek akron, point, summit + polis, city]

across — prep. 1 to, at, or on the other side of. 2 from one side of to the other. 3 so as to cross: arms folded across the chest. — adv. 1 to, at, or on the other side. 2 from one side to the other. — **across the board** general or generally; applying in all cases. [from A³ + CROSS]

acrostic /əˈkrɒstɪk/ noun a poem in which the first letters in each line form a word or proverb. [from Greek akron, end + stichos, line]

acrylic /əˈkrɪlɪk/ — noun any of various synthetic products derived from acrylic acid, especially acrylic fibre or acrylic resin. — adj. relating to, containing, or derived from acrylic acid. [from Latin acer, sharp + olere, to smell]

acrylic acid Chem. (FORMULA CH_2:$CHCOOH$) a highly reactive colourless liquid with a pungent odour and acidic properties, used in the manufacture of numerous acrylic polymers, including acrylic resins, acrylic fibres, adhesives, and artists' acrylic paint. Also called PROPENOIC ACID.

acrylic painting in art, the use of plastic paints, ie pigments mixed with an acrylic resin binder such as poly-methyl methacrylate in mineral spirits.

acrylic resin Chem. any of a large number of synthetic resins, eg Acrilan, Perspex, formed by the polymerization of derivatives of acrylic acid. Acrylic resins are used to make artificial fibres, lenses for optical instruments, protective coatings, waxes, paints, and adhesives.

ACT abbrev. Australian Capital Territory.

act — noun 1 a thing done; a deed. 2 the process of doing something: caught in the act. 3 behaviour that is intended to make an impression on people and is not a sincere expression of feeling. 4 a short piece of entertainment, usually one of a series in a show; the person or people performing this. 5 a major division of a play, opera, etc. See also SCENE. 6 a formal decision reached or a law passed by a law-making body. — verb 1 intrans. to function in a specified or usual way. 2 intrans. to do something: need to act fast. 3 intrans. (**act as, act for**) to perform the actions or functions (of). 4 intrans. to perform in a play or film. 5 to perform (a part) in a play or film; to perform (a play). 6 to show (feelings one does not really have). 7 intrans. (**act on, act upon**) to have an effect or influence on. — **act of God** an event beyond human control, especially a natural disaster such as an earthquake. **act on** or **upon something** to follow advice, etc; to obey instructions, etc. **act some-thing out** to express one's feelings, fears, etc in one's behaviour, usually unconsciously. **act up** *intrans. colloq.* **1** *said of a machine, etc* to fail or function erratically. **2** to behave badly. **get in on the act** *colloq.* to start taking part in some profitable activity, plan, etc in order to share in the benefits. **get one's act together** *colloq.* to become organized and able to act, especially in relation to a specific undertaking. [from Latin *actum*, thing done]

⊟ *noun* **1** deed, action, undertaking, enterprise, operation, manoeuvre, move, step, accomplishment, achievement, exploit, feat, stroke. **2** execution, accomplishment, doing. **3** pretence, make-believe, sham, fake, feigning, dissimulation, affectation, show, front. **4** turn, item, routine, sketch, performance, show, *slang* gig. **5** law, statute, ordinance, edict, decree, resolution, measure, bill. *verb* **1** behave, perform, conduct oneself, exert oneself, work, function, operate. **2** do, perform. **3** function as. **4** perform. **5** perform, enact, play, portray, represent, impersonate, imitate, mimic, mime. **6** pretend, feign, put on, assume, affect, simulate. **7** affect, influence, alter, modify, change, transform. **act on** carry out, fulfil, comply with, conform to, obey, follow, heed, take.

acting — *noun* the profession or art of performing in a play or film. — *adj.* temporarily doing someone else's job or duties.

⊟ *noun* theatre, drama, stagecraft, artistry, performing, playacting, melodrama, dramatics, theatricals, portrayal, characterization, impersonation, imitating. *adj.* temporary, provisional, interim, stopgap, supply, stand-by, substitute, reserve.

actinide /ˈaktɪnaɪd/ or **actinoid** /ˈaktɪnɔɪd/ *noun Chem.* any chemical element with an atomic number between 89 and 104, the best-known being uranium (92) and plutonium (94). All actinides are radioactive. [from Greek *aktis aktinos*, ray]

actinium /akˈtɪnɪəm/ *noun Chem.* (SYMBOL **Ac**, ATOMIC NUMBER **89**) a silvery-white radioactive metal, found in uranium ores, and formed by the decay of uranium-235, or by bombarding radium with neutrons. It is used as a source of alpha particles. [from Greek *aktis*, ray (from its being radioactive)]

actinotherapy /aktɪnoʊˈθɛrəpɪ/ *noun Medicine* the treatment of diseases and disorders by exposure to infrared or ultraviolet radiation.

action *noun* **1** the process of doing something: *put ideas into action.* **2** something done. **3** activity, force, or energy: *a woman of action.* **4** a movement or gesture. **5** the working part of a machine, instrument, etc; a mechanism. **6** a battle; fighting. **7** (**the action**) the events of a play, film, etc. **8** *colloq.* exciting activity or events going on around one: *get a piece of the action.* **9** a legal case. — **out of action** not working. [from Latin *actio*, from *agere*, to do, drive]

⊟ **1** performance, execution, operation, motion, functioning, process. **2** act, proceeding, move, step, deed, exploit, feat, accomplishment, achievement, undertaking, endeavour, enterprise. **3** activity, liveliness, spirit, energy, vigour, power, force, effort, exertion, work, exercise. **4** movement, gesture, motion. **5** mechanism, workings, *colloq.* works. **6** battle, warfare, conflict, combat, fighting, engagement, skirmish, clash. **9** litigation, lawsuit, suit, case.

actionable *adj.* giving reasonable cause for legal action.
action-packed *adj. colloq.* filled with exciting activity.
action painting a style of painting in which paint is dripped, splashed, or spilled on to the canvas; it draws attention to the significance of the act of painting in itself.
action potential *Physiol.* a brief electrical signal consisting of a change in electrical potential, produced across

the membrane of a nerve or muscle fibre in response to stimulation. It is an easily measurable indication of the passage of a nerve impulse.

action replay on television, the repeating of a piece of recorded action (eg the scoring of a goal in football), usually in slow motion or from another angle.

action stations positions taken by soldiers, etc who are ready for battle, etc.

activate /ˈaktɪveɪt/ *verb* **1** to make (something) start working or go into operation. **2** to increase the energy of (something). **3** to make (a material) radioactive. **4** to increase the speed of or cause (a chemical reaction). **5** to increase the capacity of (carbon or charcoal) to adsorb impurities, especially gases. **6** to increase the biological activity of (sewage) by treatment with air and bacteria.

⊟ **1** start, initiate, trigger, set off, fire, switch on, actuate, set in motion, launch, propel, stimulate, impel, energize, galvanize.
⊟⊟ **1** deactivate, stop.

activated charcoal or **activated carbon** *Chem.* a form of charcoal that is a very efficient absorber of gases. It is prepared by heating wood in a limited supply of air, and is used in gas masks and cooker hoods, and also for removing the colouring matter from solutions.

activation /aktɪˈveɪʃən/ *noun* the act or process of activating.

activation energy *Chem.* the amount of energy that is needed to start a chemical reaction by breaking and reforming chemical bonds.

active — *adj.* **1** moving, working, and doing things; full of energy. **2** involved or committed; not passive: *an active supporter.* **3** operating; working. **4** having an effect: *the active ingredients.* **5** radioactive. **6** *said of a volcano* liable to erupt, not extinct. **7** *said of verbs* in the form that is used when the subject of the sentence performs the action of the verb. See also PASSIVE. — *noun* **1** (*also* **active voice**) the form a verb takes when its subject performs the action or has the state that the verb denotes, eg the verbs in *the man fell, smoking kills you,* and *God exists* (see also PASSIVE). **2** a verb in the active. [from Latin *activus*]

⊟ *adj.* **1** busy, occupied, *colloq.* on the go, industrious, diligent, hard-working, forceful, spirited, animated, lively, energetic, vigorous, agile, nimble, sprightly, quick, alert. **2** involved, committed, engaged, devoted, enthusiastic, militant, activist. **3** in operation, functioning, working, running.
⊟⊟ *adj.* **1, 3** inactive, idle, inert. **2** passive, apathetic. **4** inactive. **6** dormant. **7** passive.

active service *Mil.* service by a member of the armed forces, or by a military unit, in a battle area. The term is also applied, especially in the USA, to service in the fighting forces at any time, whether in peacetime or in war.

active transport *Biochem.* the transport of a solute across a cell membrane against a concentration gradient or electrochemical potential gradient (ions), and therefore requiring the input of energy.

activist *noun* a person who is very active, especially as a member of a political group.

activity *noun* (PL. **activities**) **1** the state of being active or busy. **2** (*often* **activities**) something that a person does or people do, especially for pleasure, interest, exercise, etc. **3** *Physics* the rate at which the atoms of a radioactive substance disintegrate per unit time. [from Latin *activitas*]

⊟ **1** liveliness, activeness, action, motion, movement, commotion, bustle, hustle, industry, labour, exertion, exercise. **2** pursuit, hobby, pastime, interest, occupation, job, work, act, deed, project, scheme, task, venture, enterprise, endeavour, undertaking.
⊟⊟ **1** inactivity.

act of God *Legal* an extraordinary event, beyond human control, which could not be foreseen and guarded against.

Act of Parliament a bill which has passed five stages (first reading, second reading, committee stage, report stage, third reading) in both houses of the UK parliament (the House of Commons and the House of Lords), and received the royal assent.

actor *noun* a man or woman who performs in plays or films, especially professionally. [from Latin *actor*, doer]

⊟ actress, comedian, tragedian, ham, player, performer, artist, artiste, impersonator, mime.

actress *noun* a woman whose job is performing in plays or films.

actual /'aktʃʊəl/ *adj.* **1** existing as fact; real. **2** not imagined, estimated, or guessed. [from Latin *actualis*]

⊟ **1** real, existent, substantial, tangible, material, physical, concrete, true, genuine, legitimate, bona fide, authentic, current, present, prevailing. **2** positive, definite, absolute, certain, unquestionable, indisputable, confirmed, verified, factual.
⊠ **1** apparent, imaginary, theoretical.

actuality /aktʃʊ'alıtı/ *noun* (PL. **actualities**) **1** fact; reality. **2** (*usually* **actualities**) an existing condition.

actually *adv.* **1** really; in fact. **2** *usually said in surprise or disagreement* as a matter of fact: *actually, I think she's right.*

⊟ **1** really, truly, indeed, in fact, in truth, in reality. **2** as a matter of fact, as it happens.

actuarial /aktjʊ'ɛərɪəl/ *adj.* relating to actuaries or their work.

actuary /'aktjʊərɪ/ *noun* (PL. **actuaries**) a person who calculates insurance risks, and gives advice to insurance companies, etc on what premiums to set. [from Latin *actuarius*, clerk]

actuate /'aktjʊeɪt/ *verb* **1** to cause (a mechanism, etc) to go into action. **2** to cause (someone) to act the way he or she does. [from Latin *actuare*, from *actus*, act]

actuation /aktjʊ'eɪʃən/ *noun* putting in motion, movement.

acuity /ə'kjuːɪtɪ/ *noun* **1** sharpness or acuteness, eg of the mind or senses. **2** (*also* **visual acuity**) sharpness of vision. [from Latin *acuitas*, from *acus*, needle]

acumen /'akjʊmən/ *noun* the ability to judge quickly and well; keen insight. [from Latin *acumen*, point, from *acus*, needle]

⊟ astuteness, shrewdness, sharpness, keenness, penetration, insight, intuition, discrimination, discernment, judgement, perception, sense, wit, wisdom, intelligence.

acupressure /akjʊ'preʃə(r)/ *noun Medicine* **1** the arrest of a haemorrhage by a needle pressing across the artery. **2** in acupuncture or related treatments, pressure (as opposed to a needle) applied to specified points (acupoints). [from Latin *acus*, needle + PRESSURE]

acupuncture /'akjʊpʌŋktʃə(r)/ *noun* a traditional Chinese method of healing in which symptoms are relieved by the insertion of thin needles at specific points beneath the skin. [from Latin *acus*, needle + PUNCTURE]

acupuncturist *noun* a practitioner of acupuncture.

acute — *adj.* **1** extremely severe; very bad. **2** *said of the senses* keen or sharp; highly sensitive. **3** *said of mental powers, etc* quick and accurate. **4** *said of a disease or symptoms* arising suddenly and often severe, but of short duration: *acute bronchitis* / *acute pain*. **5** *said of a sound* high, sharp, and shrill. **6** *Geom.*, *said of an angle* of less than 90°. — *noun* (*also* **acute accent**) a mark placed over a

vowel (eg *á, é*) in some languages, showing pronunciation. [from Latin *acuere*, to sharpen]

⊟ *adj.* **1** severe, intense, extreme, violent, dangerous, serious, grave, urgent, crucial, vital, decisive. **2** keen, sharp, penetrating, sensitive. **3** sharp, keen, incisive, penetrating, astute, shrewd, judicious, discerning, observant, perceptive. **4** severe, intense, sharp, cutting, stabbing, distressing. **5** shrill, high, piercing, penetrating.
⊠ *adj.* **1** mild, slight. **2, 3** dull.

-acy *suffix* forming nouns denoting: **1** a quality: *accuracy*. **2** a state, condition, office, etc: *supremacy* / *piracy*. [from latin *-acia*]

acyl group /'eɪsɪl/ *Chem.* in an organic chemical compound, the general name for the functional group RCO−, where R is either hydrogen or a hydrocarbon group (eg CH_3).

AD or **A.D.** *abbrev.* Anno Domini: used in dates of the modern era. See also BC.

ad *noun colloq.* short form of ADVERTISEMENT.

ADA or **Ada** *noun Comput.* a programming language originally devised for military use, one of its applications being simultaneous control of diverse operations. [named after Ada Lovelace (1816–52), daughter of Byron and assistant to the computer pioneer, Charles Babbage]

adage /'adɪdʒ/ *noun* a proverb or maxim. [from French *adage*, from Latin *adagium*]

adagio /ə'dɑːdʒɪoʊ/ *Mus.* — *adv.* slowly. — *noun* (PL. **adagios**) a slow movement or piece of music. [from Italian *adagio*]

Adam the first man, according to the Biblical account in the Book of Genesis. — **not know someone from Adam** to be unable to distinguish or recognize someone. [from Hebrew *adam*, man]

adamant /'adəmənt/ *adj.* completely determined; not likely to change one's mind or opinion. [from Old French *adamaunt*, from Latin *adamas*, hard steel]

⊟ resolute, determined, set, firm, insistent, rigid, stiff, inflexible, unbending, unyielding, intransigent, stubborn, fixed, immovable, unshakable.
⊠ hesitant, flexible, yielding.

Adam's apple the projection of the thyroid cartilage lying just beneath the skin at the front of the throat. It is more prominent in men than in women, and is so called because it was formerly associated with the forbidden fruit that was thought to have stuck in Adam's throat.

adapt /ə'dapt/ *verb* **1** to change (something, oneself, etc) so as to fit new circumstances, etc; to make suitable for a new purpose. **2** *intrans.*, *said of a person, animal, etc* to adjust to a new environment, way of life, method of working, etc. **3** to alter or modify. [from Latin *ad*, to or *aptare*, to fit]

⊟ **1** adjust, convert, remodel, customize, fit, tailor, fashion, shape, familiarize, acclimatize. **2** adjust, harmonize, match, fit, conform. **3** alter, change, modify.

adaptability *noun* the capability of adapting; versatility.

adaptable *adj.* **1** *said of a person* good at fitting into new circumstances, situations, etc. **2** *said of a machine, device, etc* that can be adapted.

⊟ **1** flexible, compliant, amenable, colloq. easy-going, versatile. **2** adjustable, alterable, changeable, variable, modifiable, convertible, conformable, versatile, plastic, malleable, flexible.
⊠ INFLEXIBLE.

adaptation /adəp'teɪʃən/ *noun* **1** a thing which is adapted. **2** the process of adapting. **3** *Biol.* a particular change in the structure, function, or behaviour of a living organism that improves its chances of survival in its environment.

∎ **1** variation, version, conversion, modification. **2** alteration, change, shift, transformation, modification, adjustment, accommodation, conversion, remodelling, reshaping, reworking, revision.

adaptive radiation /ə'daptɪv/ *Biol.* a burst of evolution in which a single ancestral type gives rise to a number of different forms, each of which occupies a different ecological niche. It usually takes place over a relatively short period of time, and may occur after the colonization of a new habitat.

adaptor or **adapter** *noun* **1** an attachment or accessory enabling a piece of apparatus to be used for a purpose or in conditions other than those originally intended. **2** a person who adapts.

ADAS *abbrev.* Agricultural Development and Advisory Service.

ADC *abbrev.* aide-de-camp.

ADD *abbrev.* attention defect disorder.

add *verb* **1** (**add something to something else**) to put something together with something else, so that they are counted or regarded together: *we'll add our money to yours.* **2** (**add things** or **add things together**) to put together or combine (two or more things). **3** (*also* **add up**) to calculate the sum of two or more numbers in order to obtain their total value; to carry out the process of addition. **4** to say or write (something) further: *they added a remark about the bad weather.* — **add something in** to include it, especially as an extra. **add something on** to attach (something) to something else. See also ADD-ON. **add up** *colloq.* to make sense; to be coherent. **add up to something** to be the equivalent of it or amount to it: *it all adds up to a great success.* [from Latin *addere*, from *ad*, to + *dare*, to put]

∎ **2** join, combine, put together. **3** sum up, tot up, total, tally, count (up), reckon, compute. **4** append, annex. **add on** attach, affix, tack on. **add up** make sense, be coherent, be consistent, hang together, fit, be plausible, be reasonable. **add up to** amount to, come to, constitute, mean, signify, indicate.

✶ **1** take away, remove. **3** subtract, take away.

added *adj.* **1** attached. **2** extra, additional.

addendum /ə'dɛndəm/ *noun* (PL. **addenda**) **1** an addition. **2** (*usually* **addenda**) an extra piece of text added to the end of a book. [from Latin *addere*, to add]

adder *noun* a brown, olive, grey, or cream-coloured snake with a dark zigzag line running down its back, belonging to the viper family and found in most of Europe and across Asia. [from Anglo-Saxon *nædre*; in Middle English *a nadder* became understood to be *an adder*]

addict /'adɪkt/ *noun* **1** a person who is physically or psychologically dependent on the habitual intake of a drug such as alcohol, nicotine, caffeine, barbiturates, heroin, etc. **2** *colloq.* a person who is extremely fond of a hobby, etc: *a chess addict.* [from Latin *addicere*, to surrender]

∎ **1** drug addict, *colloq.* user, *colloq.* dope-fiend, *slang* junkie, *slang* tripper, *slang* mainliner. **2** enthusiast, fan, *colloq.* buff, fiend, freak, devotee, follower, adherent.

addicted /ə'dɪktəd/ *adj.* **1** (**addicted to something**) dependent on something, especially a drug. **2** unable to give something up, eg a habit.

∎ **1** dependent on, *colloq.* hooked on. **2** obsessed, *colloq.* hooked, absorbed, devoted, dedicated, inclined, disposed, accustomed.

addiction *noun* a habit that has become impossible to break, especially one involving physical and psychological dependence on the intake of harmful substances such as alcohol or narcotic drugs; the state of being addicted.

∎ dependence, craving, habit, obsession.

addictive *adj.* relating to or tending to cause addiction; habit-forming.

addition *noun* **1** the act or operation of adding. **2** a person or thing that is added. **3** the combining of two or more numbers in such a way as to obtain their sum. **4** *Chem.* a chemical reaction in which one molecule combines with another to form a third more complex molecule, without the formation of a by-product such as water. — **in addition** as well; besides. [from Latin *additio*, from *addere*, to add]

∎ **1** adding, combination, inclusion, extension, enlargement, increasing, increase. **2** adjunct, supplement, additive, addendum, appendix, appendage, accessory, attachment, extra, increment. **3** summing-up, totting-up, totalling, counting, reckoning. **in addition** additionally, too, also, as well, besides, moreover, further, furthermore, over and above.

✶ **1** removal. **3** subtraction.

additional *adj.* extra; more than usual.

∎ added, extra, supplementary, spare, more, further, increased, other, new, fresh.

additionally *adv.* also, besides.

additive /'adɪtɪv/ — *noun* any chemical substance that is deliberately added to another substance, usually in small quantities, for a specific purpose, eg food flavouring or colouring, or antiknock compounds added to petrol to improve engine performance. — *adj. Maths.* relating to addition. [from Latin *additivus*]

addle *verb* **1** to confuse or muddle. **2** *intrans.*, *said of an egg* to go bad. [from Anglo-Saxon *adela*, mud]

addle-brained *adj.* confused; crazy.

addled *adj.* **1** rotten. **2** confused.

add-on *noun* **1** anything added to supplement something else. **2** *Comput.* any device that can be added to a basic computer system in order to increase its capabilities, eg an extra program, circuit, or piece of hardware: *add-on memory.* **3** an extra charge added to the basic charge of something.

address /ə'drɛs/ — *noun* **1** the number or name of the house or building, and the name of the street and town, where a person lives or works. **2** a speech or lecture. **3** *Comput.* a name, label, or number that identifies the location of a stored item of data in the memory of a computer. **4** *Comput.* a specific location, usually capable of storing one byte of information, within the memory of a computer. — *verb* **1** to put the name and address on (an envelope, etc). **2** to make a speech, give a lecture, etc to. **3** to speak to. **4** to give one's attention to (a problem, etc). **5** *Comput.* to identify (a specific location) within the memory of a computer and either obtain data from it or store data within it. — **address oneself to someone** or **something 1** to speak or write to them. **2** to deal with a problem, matter, etc. [from Old French *adresser*]

∎ *noun* **1** residence, dwelling, abode, house, home, lodging, direction, whereabouts, location, situation, place. **2** speech, talk, lecture, discourse, sermon, dissertation. *verb* **2** lecture, speak to. **3** speak to, talk to, greet, salute, accost, approach, buttonhole.

address bus *Comput.* a set of wires connecting the processor to the memory, used to inform the memory of the address which the processor wishes to read or write to.

addressee /ədrɛ'si:/ *noun* the person to whom a letter, etc is addressed.

adduce /ə'dju:s/ *verb* to mention (a fact) as a supporting reason, piece of evidence, etc. [from Latin *ad*, to + *ducere*, to lead]

adducible /ə'dju:sɪbl/ *adj.* capable of being adduced.

adenine /'adəni:n/ *noun Biochem.* a base derived from purine, and one of the four bases found in nucleic acids (RNA and DNA). [from Greek *aden*, gland]

adenoidal /adə'nɔɪdəl/ *adj.* 1 relating to the adenoids. 2 *said of a person* having swollen adenoids. 3 *said of the voice* having the blocked nasal tone normally associated with swollen adenoids.

adenoids /'adənɔɪdz/ *pl. noun Anat.* a pair of lymph glands found in the upper part of the throat, at the back of the nasal cavity, in children. [from Greek *adenoiedes*, from *aden*, gland]

adenosine diphosphate /ə'dɛnoʊsi:n daɪ'fɒsfeɪt/ (ABBREV. **ADP**) *Biochem.* an organic compound, composed of adenine, ribose, and two phosphate groups, involved in processes requiring the transfer of energy in living cells. It is formed by the breakdown of adenosine triphosphate (ATP), during which process energy is released. See also ADENOSINE TRIPHOSPHATE.

adenosine triphosphate /ə'dɛnoʊsi:n traɪ'fɒsfeɪt/ (ABBREV. **ATP**) *Biochem.* an organic compound, composed of adenine, ribose, and three phosphate groups, the main form in which energy is stored in the cells of living organisms. Energy is released, and so made available for muscle contraction, synthesis of complex molecules, etc, when ATP loses one or two of its phosphate groups.

adept /ə'dɛpt, 'adɛpt/ — *adj.* (with stress on -*dept*; *often* **adept at something**) skilful at doing it; proficient. — *noun* (with stress on *ad-*) an expert at something. [from Latin *adeptus*, having attained an art]

⊟ *adj.* skilful, skilled, accomplished, expert, masterly, experienced, versed, practised, polished, proficient, able, adroit, deft, nimble.

adequacy /'adəkwəsi/ *noun* being adequate; sufficiency.

adequate /'adəkwət/ *adj.* 1 enough; sufficient. 2 (**adequate to something**) competent to do a particular job, task, etc. 3 only just satisfactory. [from Latin *ad*, to + *aequus*, equal]

⊟ 1 enough, sufficient, commensurate, requisite. 2 competent to, capable of, able to, fit for, suitable for. 3 acceptable, satisfactory, passable, tolerable, fair.
⊟ 1 inadequate, insufficient. 2 incompetent, incapable.

à deux /a 'dɜ:/ for two people; involving two people. [French, = for two]

adhere /ad'hɪə(r)/ *verb intrans.* (*often* **adhere to something**) 1 to stick or remain fixed to it. 2 to remain loyal to a religion, etc. 3 to follow a plan, rule, etc exactly. [from Latin *ad*, to + *haerere*, to stick]

⊟ 1 stick to, fasten to, attach to, join, combine with, coalesce with, cohere with. 2 cling to, cleave to, hold to. 3 follow, observe, abide by, comply with, fulfil, obey, keep, heed, respect, stand by.

adherence /ad'hɪərəns/ *noun* 1 the act of adhering. 2 steady loyalty.

adherent /ad'hɪərənt/ — *noun* a follower; a supporter. — *adj.* sticking or adhering to.

⊟ *noun* supporter, upholder, advocate, partisan, follower, disciple, satellite, henchman, hanger-on, votary, devotee, admirer, fan, enthusiast.

adhesion /ad'hi:ʒən/ *noun* 1 the process of sticking or adhering. 2 the sticking together of two surfaces, especially by means of an adhesive. 3 *Physics* the attraction between atoms or molecules of different substances, eg water and glass, that produces surface tension effects such as the formation of a meniscus. See also COHESION. 4 (*often* **adhesions**) *Medicine* a mass or band of fibrous connective tissue that develops between membranes or other structures which are normally separate, such as the stomach and intestines. [from Latin *adhaesio*]

⊟ 1 adherence, adhesiveness, bond, grip, cohesion.

adhesive /ad'hi:zɪv/ — *adj.* sticky; able to make things stick together. — *noun* a substance that is used to bond two surfaces together. Adhesives can be made from natural materials, eg gelatine or vegetable gums, or manufactured synthetically, eg epoxy resins which set when mixed with a separate hardener. [from French *adhésif*, from Latin *adhaerere*, to adhere]

⊟ *adj.* sticky, tacky, self-adhesive, gummed, gummy, gluey, adherent, adhering, sticking. *noun* glue, gum, paste, cement.

ad hoc /ad hɒk, ad hɔk/ *adj.*, *adv.* for one particular purpose, situation, etc only. [from Latin *ad hoc*, to this]

ad hominem /ad 'hɒmɪnəm/ *adj.* relating to an individual person. [Latin, = to the man]

adiabatic process /adɪə'batɪk/ *Physics* any process that occurs without the exchange of heat between a system and its surroundings. [from A-[1] + Greek *dia*, through + *batos*, passable]

adieu /ə'dʒu:/ — *noun* (PL. **adieus**, **adieux**) a goodbye. — *interj.* goodbye. [from French *adieu*, from *à*, to + *dieu*, God]

ad infinitum /ad ɪnfɪ'naɪtəm/ *adv.* for ever; without limit. [from Latin *ad infinitum*, to infinity]

adipose /'adɪpoʊs/ *adj.* relating to, containing, or consisting of fat; fatty. [from Latin *adiposus*, from *adeps*, soft fat]

adipose tissue body tissue consisting of large spherical cells specialized for the storage of fat and oil, found mainly beneath the skin, in the buttocks, and around the heart and kidneys. It provides insulation and serves as an energy reserve.

adiposity /adɪ'pɒsɪtɪ/ *noun* 1 fatness. 2 tendency to fatness.

adj. *abbrev.* adjective.

adjacent /ə'dʒeɪsənt/ *adj.* (*often* **adjacent to something**) lying beside or next to it: *adjacent houses / a house adjacent to the church*. [from Latin *adjacere*, to lie by the side of]

⊟ adjoining, abutting, touching, contiguous, bordering, juxtaposed, next-door, neighbouring, next, closest, nearest, close, near.
⊟ remote, distant.

adjectival /adʒək'taɪvəl/ *adj. Grammar* 1 having the role of an adjective. 2 using many adjectives.

adjectivally *adv.* as an adjective.

adjective /'adʒəktɪv/ *noun* a word that describes or modifies a noun or pronoun, as *dark* describes *hair* in *she has dark hair*, and *sad* describes *him* in *the story made him sad*. [from Latin *adjicere*, to throw to, to apply]

adjoin *verb* to be next to and joined to (something). [from Old French *ajoindre*, from Latin *ad*, to + *jungere*, to join]

⊟ abut, touch, meet, border, interconnect, link, connect, join, unite.

adjoining *adj.* 1 lying next to; neighbouring. 2 in contact, connected.

adjourn /ə'dʒɜːn/ *verb* **1** to put off (a meeting, etc) to another time. **2** to finish (a meeting, etc), intending to continue it at another time or place. **3** *intrans.* to move to another place, usually for refreshment or rest. **4** *intrans.* to finish a meeting and separate. [from Old French *ajorner*]

⊟ **1** defer, postpone, put off, delay, stay. **2** interrupt, suspend, discontinue, break off. **3** retire. **4** recess.
⊟ **2** continue. **4** assemble, convene.

adjournment *noun* an act of adjourning; postponement.

⊟ interruption, suspension, discontinuation, break, pause, recess, dissolution, deferment, deferral, postponement, putting off, delay, stay.

adjudge *verb* to declare or judge officially. [from Old French *ajuger*, from Latin *adjudicare*, to adjudicate]
adjudgement or **adjudgment** *noun* an official judgement or declaration.
adjudicate /ə'dʒuːdɪkeɪt/ *verb* **1** *intrans.* to act as judge in a court, competition, etc. **2** to give a decision on (a disagreement between two parties, etc). [from Latin *adjudicare*, from *judex*, judge]

⊟ **1** judge, arbitrate, umpire, referee. **2** settle, determine, decide.

adjudication /ədʒuːdɪ'keɪʃən/ *noun* **1** the act or process of adjudicating. **2** a judgement. **3** a decision.
adjudicator /ə'dʒuːdɪkeɪtə(r)/ *noun* a person who adjudicates.
adjunct /'adʒʌŋkt/ *noun* **1** something attached or added to something else but not an essential part of it. **2** a person who is below someone else in rank. **3** *Grammar* a word or clause that adds information about the subject, etc of a sentence. [from Latin *adjungere*, to join to]
adjuration /adʒʊə'reɪʃən/ *noun* the act of adjuring.
adjure /ə'dʒʊə(r)/ *verb formal* to request, beg, or command formally or solemnly. [from Latin *adjurare*, to swear to]
adjust *verb* **1** to change slightly so as to be more suitable for a situation, etc. **2** to change or alter, especially only slightly, to make more correct or accurate. **3** to calculate or assess the amount of money payable in an insurance claim, etc). **4** (**adjust to something**) to change so that one fits in with it or becomes suited to it. [from Old French *ajuster*, to make conform to]

⊟ **1** modify, change, alter, adapt, convert, reshape, remodel, fit, accommodate, arrange, compose. **2** change, alter, *colloq.* tweak, rectify, regulate, balance, temper, tune, fine-tune, fix, set. **3** calculate, assess. **4** adapt to, accustom oneself to, acclimatize oneself to, reconcile oneself with, harmonize with, conform to.

adjustable *adj.* capable of adjustment.
adjustment *noun* the act or process of adjusting; the state of being adjusted.

⊟ modification, change, alteration, adaptation, conversion, remodelling, reshaping, fitting, accommodation, arrangement, rectification, regulation, tuning, setting, orientation, acclimatization, habituation, naturalization, harmonization, reconciliation.

adjutant /'adʒʊtənt/ *noun* an army officer who does administrative work. [from Latin *adjutare*, to assist]
ad-lib — *verb intrans., trans.* (**ad-libbed, ad-libbing**) to say (something) without preparation, especially as a departure from a prepared text or to fill time; to improvise

(music, etc). — *adj.*, *said of speeches, etc* made up as the speaker speaks; improvised. — *adv.* (**ad lib**) **1** without preparation. **2** *colloq.* without limit; freely. [short for Latin *ad libitum*, at pleasure]

⊟ *verb* improvise, extemporize. *adj.* impromptu, improvised, extempore, extemporaneous, off-the-cuff, unprepared, unpremeditated, unrehearsed, spontaneous, made up. *adv.* **1** impromptu, extempore, extemporaneously, off the cuff, off the top of one's head, spontaneously, impulsively.
⊟ *adj.* prepared.

ad litem /ad 'laɪtəm/ *said of a guardian* appointed to act in court. [Latin, = for the lawsuit]
Adm. *abbrev.* Admiral.
adman *noun colloq.* a person whose job is to produce or write advertisements for commercial organizations, etc.
admin *noun colloq.* short form of ADMINISTRATION.
administer /əd'mɪnɪstə(r)/ *verb* (**administered, administering**) **1** to manage, govern, or direct (one's affairs, an organization, etc). **2** to give out formally: *administer a rebuke.* **3** to supervise a person taking (an oath). **4** to apply or provide (medicine). **5** to give: *administer justice.* **6** *intrans.* to act as an administrator. [from Latin *administrare*]

⊟ **1** govern, rule, administrate, manage, run, organize, direct, conduct, lead, head, preside over, officiate, control, regulate, superintend, supervise, oversee. **2** give, provide, supply, distribute, dole out, dispense, measure out, mete out, execute, impose, apply. **4** apply, provide, supply, give.

administrate *verb* **1** to administer (a company, organization, etc). **2** *intrans.* to act as an administrator.
administration /ədmɪnɪ'streɪʃən/ *noun* **1** the directing, managing or governing of a company's affairs, etc. **2** a period of government by a particular party, etc. **3** *North Amer., esp. US* a period of government by a particular president. **4** the group of people who manage a company's affairs or run the business of government.

⊟ **1** administering, governing, ruling, leadership, management, execution, running, organization, direction, control, superintendence, supervision, overseeing. **2, 3** government, term of office. **4** directorship, board, management, executive, regime, government, ministry, leadership.

administrative /əd'mɪnɪstreɪtɪv/ *adj.* of or concerned with administration.

⊟ governmental, legislative, authoritative, directorial, managerial, management, executive, organizational, regulatory, supervisory.

administrative law the body of law relating to powers exercised by central and local government. The exercise of these administrative powers may be subject to scrutiny by the courts on legal, but not policy, grounds.
administrator /əd'mɪnɪstreɪtə(r)/ *noun* a person who manages, governs, directs, etc the affairs of an organization, estate, etc.
admirable /'admɪrəbl/ *adj.* **1** worthy of being admired. **2** very good; excellent.

⊟ **1** praiseworthy, commendable, laudable, creditable, deserving, worthy, respected. **2** excellent, superior, wonderful, fine, exquisite, choice, rare, valuable.
⊟ **1** contemptible, despicable, deplorable.

admiral /'admɪrəl/ *noun* **1** a high-ranking naval officer commanding a fleet of ships. **2** a name applied to several species of butterfly. [from Old French *amiral*, from Arabic *amir-al-bahr*, lord of the sea]

admiral of the fleet *noun* the highest-ranking admiral in the Royal Navy.

Admiralty *noun* (**the Admiralty**) *Brit. Hist.* the government department that managed the Royal Navy until the responsibility passed to the Ministry of Defence in 1964.

admiration /admɪ'reɪʃən/ *noun* 1 an act of admiring. 2 wonder, approval. 3 an object of wonder or approval.

▤ 1 esteem, regard, respect, reverence, veneration, worship, praise, adoration. 2 approval, appreciation, pleasure, delight, wonder, astonishment, amazement, surprise.
▣ 1 contempt.

admire *verb* to regard with respect or approval. [from Latin *admirari*]

▤ esteem, respect, revere, venerate, worship, idolize, adore, approve, praise, applaud, appreciate, value.
▣ despise, censure.

admirer *noun* 1 someone who admires a particular person or thing. 2 a man who is attracted to a particular woman.

▤ 1 follower, disciple, adherent, supporter, fan, enthusiast, devotee, worshipper, idolizer. 2 suitor, boyfriend, sweetheart, lover.
▣ 1 critic, opponent.

admiring *adj.* full of admiration.

admissibility *noun* fitness or ability to be admitted.

admissible *adj.* that can be allowed or accepted, especially as proof in a court of law. [from Latin *admissibilis*, from *admittere*, to admit]

▤ acceptable, tolerable, tolerated, passable, allowable, permissible, allowed, permitted, lawful, legitimate, justifiable.
▣ inadmissible, illegitimate.

admission *noun* 1 the act of allowing in or being allowed in. 2 the cost of entry. 3 an act of admitting the truth of something. [from Latin *admissio*]

▤ 1 admittance, admitting, letting in, access, entrance, entry. 3 confession, acknowledgement, recognition, acceptance, concession, affirmation, declaration, profession, disclosure, divulgence, revelation.
▣ 3 denial.

admit *verb* (**admitted**, **admitting**) 1 to agree to the truth of (something), especially unwillingly. 2 *trans., intrans.* (**admit something** or **admit to something**) to agree that one is responsible for a deed or action, especially an offence or wrongdoing. 3 to allow to enter. 4 to allow to take part in; to accept as a member or patient. 5 *formal* to have the capacity for: *a room admitting forty people.* — **admit of something** to agree that it is possible or valid. [from Latin *admittere*]

▤ 1 grant, acknowledge, recognize, accept, allow, concede, agree. 2 confess, own (up). 3 let in, give access, accept, receive, take in. 4 accept, receive, take in.
▣ 1 deny. 2 shut out, keep out, exclude.

admittance *noun* 1 the right to enter; permission to enter. 2 the act of entering; entry.

▤ 1 admitting, admission, letting in, access, entrance, entry, acceptance. 2 entrance, entry, reception, introduction, initiation.
▣ 1 exclusion.

admittedly *adv.* as is known to be true; as one must admit.

admixture *noun* 1 anything that is added to the main ingredient of a mixture. 2 the mixture itself. 3 any material other than cement, aggregate, or water that is added to wet concrete in order to improve its properties. [from Latin *ad*, to + *miscere*, to mix]

admonish /əd'mɒnɪʃ/ *verb* 1 to warn. 2 to scold or tell off firmly but mildly. 3 to advise or urge. [from Old French *amonester*]

▤ 2 scold, rebuke, reprimand.

admonishingly *adv.* so as to admonish.

admonition /admə'nɪʃən/ *noun* a scolding or warning. [from Latin *admonitio*, from *admonere*, to admonish]

admonitory /əd'mɒnɪtərɪ/ *adj.* containing a scolding or warning.

ADN *abbrev., as an international vehicle mark* Republic of Yemen (capital Aden).

ad nauseam /ad 'nɔːzɪam/ to the point of producing disgust; excessively. [Latin, = to sickness]

ado /ə'duː/ *noun* (PL. **ados**) difficulty or trouble; fuss or bustle. — **without more** or **further ado** without any more delay; immediately; promptly. [from Middle English *at do*, to do]

adobe /ə'dəʊbɪ/ *noun* 1 a kind of building material made of clay and straw, which is dried in the sun. 2 a sun-dried brick made from such material. 3 a building made from such bricks. [from Spanish *adobe*, from Arabic *at tub*, the brick]

adolescence /adə'lesəns/ *noun* the period of human development between the onset of puberty and adulthood, during which physical and emotional changes take place as a result of hormonal activity.

▤ teens, puberty, youth, minority, boyhood, girlhood, development, immaturity, youthfulness, boyishness, girlishness.

adolescent /adə'lesənt/ — *adj.* 1 *said of a young person* at the stage of development between childhood and adulthood, or between puberty and adulthood. 2 relating to or typical of this state. 3 *colloq., said of behaviour* of the kind often associated with adolescence; silly and immature. — *noun* a young person between childhood and adulthood, or between puberty and adulthood. [from Latin *adolescere*, to grow up]

▤ *adj.* 1 teenage, young, youthful, growing, developing. 3 juvenile, puerile, boyish, girlish, immature. *noun* teenager, youth, juvenile, minor.

adopt *verb* 1 *trans., intrans.* to take (a child of other parents) into one's own family, becoming its legal parent. 2 to take up (a habit, position, policy, etc). 3 to take (an idea, etc) over from someone else. 4 to choose formally (especially a candidate for an election). [from Old French *adopter*, from Latin *ad*, to + *optare*, to choose]

▤ 2 take up, embrace, follow. 3 take on, assume, appropriate, accept. 4 choose, select, support, maintain, back, endorse.
▣ 2 repudiate, disown.

adopted *adj.* 1 taken as one's own. 2 taken up. 3 chosen. 4 approved.

adoption *noun* the act of adopting; the state of being adopted.

adoptive *adj.* that adopts or is adopted.

adorable /ə'dɔːrəbl/ *adj.* 1 worthy of being adored. 2 *colloq.* very charming and attractive. [from Latin *adorare*, from *ad*, to + *orare*, to pray]

▤ 1 lovable, dear, darling, precious. 2 appealing, sweet,

winsome, charming, enchanting, captivating, winning, delightful, pleasing, attractive, fetching.
☒ 1 hateful, abominable.

. . . .

adoration /ədəˈreɪʃən/ *noun* **1** great love. **2** worship.
adore /əˈdɔː(r)/ *verb* **1** to love deeply. **2** *colloq.* to like very much. **3** to worship (a god).

. . . .

☐ 1 love, cherish, dote on. **3** worship, revere, venerate, idolize, exalt, glorify.
☒ 1 hate, abhor.

. . . .

adorer *noun* a worshipper, a lover.
adoring *adj.* **1** loving, doting. **2** worshipful.
adorn /əˈdɔːn/ *verb* **1** to decorate. **2** to add beauty to. [from Latin *adornare*]

. . . .

☐ 1 decorate, deck, bedeck, ornament, trim, garnish. **2** enhance, embellish, enrich, grace, crown, gild.

. . . .

adornment *noun* decoration, ornament.
ADP *abbrev.* **1** automatic data processing. **2** adenosine diphosphate.
adrenal /əˈdriːnəl/ *adj.* **1** on or near the kidneys. **2** relating to the adrenal glands. [from Latin *ad*, to + RENAL]
adrenal gland *Anat.* in mammals, either of a pair of flattened endocrine glands situated one above each kidney, and consisting of a central region or *medulla* that secretes the hormones adrenaline and noradrenaline, and an outer region or *cortex* that secretes small amounts of sex hormones (androgens and oestrogens) and various corticosteroids, such as as cortisol and cortisone.
adrenaline or **adrenalin** /əˈdrenəlɪn/ *noun* **1** *Biochem.* a hormone secreted by the *medulla* (inner part) of the adrenal glands in response to fear, excitement, or anger. It causes an increase in heartbeat, blood pressure, blood sugar levels, muscle power, and the rate and depth of breathing, and it constricts certain blood vessels, diverting blood away from the intestines and towards the muscles. **2** this hormone produced synthetically, used to reduce blood loss during surgery (by constricting blood vessels), and to treat asthma.
adrenocorticotrophic hormone /ədriːnoʊ kɔːtɪkoʊˈtrɒfɪk ˈhɔːmoʊn/ (ABBREV. **ACTH**) *Physiol.* a hormone that is produced by the front lobe of the pituitary gland. It controls the release of corticosteroid hormones from the adrenal glands, and is released in response to physical or emotional stress. It is also used to treat rheumatic diseases and asthma.
adrift *adj., adv.* **1** *said of a boat* not tied up; floating about without being steered. **2** without help or guidance. **3** *colloq.* off course.
adroit /əˈdrɔɪt/ *adj.* quick and clever in action or thought. [from French *à droit*, according to the right, rightly]
ADSL *abbrev.* Asymmetric Digital Subscriber Line.
adsorb /ədˈsɔːb/ *verb Chem.*, *said of a solid or liquid* to hold a thin layer of atoms or molecules of a solid, liquid, or gas on its surface. [from Latin *ad*, to + *sorbere*, to suck in]
adsorbent *adj.* denoting a substance on whose surface adsorption takes place.
adsorption *noun Chem.* the accumulation of a thin layer of atoms or molecules of a solid, liquid, or gas on the surface of a solid (eg charcoal, silica) or, more rarely, a liquid. This process is utilized in certain types of chromatography.
adulate /ˈadjʊleɪt/ *verb* to praise or flatter far too much. [from Latin *adulari*, to fawn upon]
adulation /adjʊˈleɪʃən/ *noun* excessive praise; flattery.
adulatory /ˈadjʊleɪtərɪ/ *adj.* flattering, fawning.
adult /ˈadʌlt, əˈdʌlt/ — *adj.* **1** fully grown; mature. **2** typical of, or suitable for, a fully grown person. **3** *said especially of films* containing sexually explicit or indecent scenes, and therefore regarded as unsuitable for children. — *noun* a fully grown person, animal, or plant. [from Latin *adultus*, grown-up]

. . . .

☐ *adj.* **1** grown-up, of age, fully grown, developed, mature, ripe, ripened.
☒ *adj.* **1** immature.

. . . .

adult education the provision of further or continuing educational opportunities for people over the minimum school-leaving age.
adulterate /əˈdʌltəreɪt/ *verb* to debase or render impure, by mixing with something inferior or harmful. [from Latin *adulterare*]

. . . .

☐ debase, contaminate, pollute, taint, corrupt, defile, dilute, water down, weaken, devalue, deteriorate.
☒ purify.

. . . .

adulteration /ədʌltəˈreɪʃən/ *noun* **1** the act of adulterating or making less pure. **2** the state of being adulterated.
adulterer /əˈdʌltərə(r)/ *noun* a man or woman who commits adultery.
adulteress *noun* a woman who commits adultery.
adulterous *adj.* **1** relating to or in the nature of adultery. **2** *said of a person* who has committed adultery.
adultery /əˈdʌltərɪ/ *noun* sexual relations willingly undertaken between a married person and a person who is not his or her spouse. [from Latin *adulterare*, to defile]
adulthood *noun* maturity.
adumbrate /ˈadʌmbreɪt/ *verb* **1** to indicate or describe in a general way. **2** to suggest or indicate (something likely to happen in the future); to foreshadow. **3** to throw a shadow over. [from Latin *adumbrare*, to shade in, sketch]
adumbration /adʌmˈbreɪʃən/ *noun* act or process of adumbrating.
adv. *abbrev.* adverb.
advance — *verb* **1** *intrans.* to move or go forward, sometimes in a threatening way. **2** to put or send forward, sometimes in a threatening way. **3** *intrans.* to make progress. **4** to help the progress of; to improve or promote. **5** to propose or suggest (an idea, etc). **6** to put at an earlier time or date than that previously planned. **7** (**advance someone something**) to lend them money, or pay them money before payment is due. **8** *trans., intrans.* to increase (a price) or be increased. — *noun* **1** progress; a move forward. **2** a payment made before it is due. **3** money lent to someone. **4** an increase, especially in price. **5** (**advances**) friendly or sexual approaches to a person. — *adj.* done, made or given beforehand. — **in advance** ahead in time, place, or development. [from Old French *avancer*, from Latin *abante*, in front]

. . . .

☐ *verb* **1** proceed, go forward, move on, go ahead. **3** progress, prosper, flourish, thrive, improve, increase, grow. **4** accelerate, speed, hasten, further, promote, upgrade, foster, support, assist, benefit, facilitate. **5** present, submit, suggest, put forward, offer. **6** bring forward. **7** lend, loan, pay, give. *noun* **1** progress, forward movement, onward movement, headway, step, advancement, furtherance, breakthrough, development, growth, increase, improvement, amelioration. **2** deposit, down payment, prepayment. **3** credit, loan. **in advance** beforehand, previously, earlier, sooner, ahead.
☒ *verb* **1** retreat. **4** retard, impede. **5** withdraw. *noun* **1** retreat, recession. **in advance** later, behind.

. . . .

advanced *adj.* **1** having progressed or developed well or far. **2** modern; new; revolutionary.

. . . .

☐ 1 leading, foremost, ahead, forward, precocious, sophisticated, complex, higher. **2** progressive, forward-

looking, modern, ultra-modern, avant-garde, revolutionary, new, innovative.
⊟ **1** backward, retarded, elementary.

advanced gas-cooled reactor (ABBREV. **AGR**) a type of nuclear reactor that operates at high temperatures, using graphite as a moderator and carbon dioxide as a coolant.

Advanced-level see A-LEVEL.

advancement *noun* **1** progress and development. **2** promotion in rank or improvement in status. **3** payment in advance.

⊟ **1** advance, progress, headway, development, growth, rise, gain. **2** promotion, preferment, furtherance, betterment, improvement.
⊟ **1** retardation. **2** demotion.

advantage /əd'vɑːntɪdʒ/ *noun* **1** a favourable circumstance; benefit or usefulness. **2** a circumstance that may help one to succeed, win, etc. **3** superiority over another. **4** *Tennis* the point scored after deuce. — **have the advantage of someone** to know something that is not known to them; to be in a better position than them. **take advantage of someone** or **something 1** to make use of a situation, a person's good nature, etc in such a way as to benefit oneself. **2** *old use* to seduce someone. **to advantage** in such a way as to emphasize the good qualities. **to one's advantage** of benefit or importance to one. **turn something to advantage** to use a circumstance, situation, etc in such a way as to get some benefit from it. [from Old French *avantage*, from *avant*, before; see also ADVANCE]

⊟ **1** asset, blessing, benefit, good, service, help, aid, assistance, use, avail, convenience, usefulness, utility, profit, gain. **2** start, lead, edge. **3** superiority, precedence, pre-eminence, sway, upper hand.
⊟ **1** disadvantage, drawback, hindrance.

advantaged *adj.* having a good social or financial situation.

advantageous /ədvən'teɪdʒəs/ *adj.* giving help or benefit in some way.

⊟ beneficial, favourable, opportune, convenient, helpful, useful, worthwhile, valuable, profitable, gainful, remunerative, rewarding.
⊟ disadvantageous, adverse, damaging.

advantageously *adv.* **1** in an advantageous manner. **2** so as to produce an advantage.

advent /'advent/ *noun* **1** coming or arrival; first appearance. **2** (**Advent**) the period including the four Sundays before Christmas. **3** (**Advent**) the first or second coming of Christ. [from Latin *adventus*, arrival]

Adventist *noun* a member of a Christian group which believes the second coming of Christ will happen very soon.

adventitious /ədvən'tɪʃəs/ *adj.* **1** happening by chance; accidental. **2** denoting tissues or organs that grow in an unusual position, eg a root arising from a stem. [from Latin *adventicius*, coming from the outside]

adventure /əd'ventʃə(r)/ *noun* **1** an exciting and often dangerous experience. **2** the excitement of risk or danger: *a sense of adventure.* [from Latin *adventurus*, about to happen]

⊟ **1** exploit, venture, undertaking, enterprise, experience, incident, occurrence. **2** excitement, risk, hazard, chance, speculation.

adventure playground a playground with things for children to climb on and equipment for them to build with.

adventurer *noun* **1** a person who is eager for personal adventure. **2** a person who enjoys taking risks in business.

adventuress *noun* a woman who is eager for personal adventure.

adventurous *adj.* **1** ready to act boldly and take risks; enjoying adventure; daring. **2** full of excitement, danger, daring activities, etc.

⊟ **1** venturesome, enterprising, daring, intrepid, bold, audacious, headstrong, impetuous, reckless, rash. **2** risky, dangerous, exciting, thrilling.
⊟ **1** cautious, prudent.

adverb *noun* a word or group of words which describes or adds to the meaning of a verb, adjective, or another adverb, such as *very* and *quietly* in *they were talking very quietly.* [from Latin *adverbium*, a word added after]

adverbial /əd'vɜːbɪəl/ *adj.* having the role of an adverb.

adverbially *adv.* like or as an adverb.

adversarial /ædvə'seərɪəl/ *adj.* **1** involving opposition. **2** hostile.

adversary /'ædvəsərɪ/ *noun* (PL. **adversaries**) **1** an opponent in a competition, etc. **2** an enemy. [from Latin *adversarius*]

adverse /'ædvɜːs, ad'vɜːs/ *adj.* **1** unfavourable to one's interests. **2** *said of criticism, etc* expressing disapproval. **3** *said of comments, etc* causing offence or injury. **4** *said of a wind* coming from in front of one and not from behind. [from Latin *adversus*, hostile]

⊟ **1** disadvantageous, unfavourable, inauspicious, unfortunate, unlucky, inopportune, hostile, antagonistic, opposing, counter, contrary, counterproductive, negative, detrimental, harmful. **2** disapproving, negative, unfavourable, hostile. **3** hurtful, injurious, unfriendly, uncongenial.
⊟ **1** advantageous, favourable.

adversity /ad'vɜːsətɪ/ *noun* (PL. **adversities**) **1** circumstances that cause trouble or sorrow. **2** an event or circumstance that causes trouble or sorrow; a misfortune.

⊟ **1** misfortune, ill fortune, bad luck, ill luck, hardship, hard times, misery, wretchedness, affliction, suffering, distress, sorrow, woe, trouble. **2** misfortune, reverse, affliction, woe, trouble, trial, tribulation, calamity, disaster, catastrophe.
⊟ **1** prosperity.

advert[1] /'ædvɜːt/ *noun colloq.* short form of ADVERTISE-MENT.

advert[2] /ad'vɜːt/ *verb intrans. formal* (**advert to something**) to refer to it or mention it in speaking or writing. [from Old French *avertir*, from Latin *advertere*, to direct one's attention to]

advertise /'ædvətaɪz/ *verb* **1** to draw attention to or describe (goods for sale, services offered, etc) in newspapers, on television, etc, to encourage people to buy or use them. **2** to make known publicly or generally. **3** *intrans.* to ask for or seek (something or someone) by putting a notice in a newspaper, shop window, etc. [from Old French *avertir*, from Latin *advertere*, to direct one's attention to]

⊟ **1** publicize, promote, push, *colloq.* plug, praise, *colloq.* hype, trumpet, blazon, herald. **2** announce, declare, proclaim, broadcast, publish, display, make known, inform, notify.

advertisement /əd'vɜːtɪsmənt/ *noun* a public notice, announcement, picture, etc in a newspaper, on a wall in the street, etc, which advertises something; a short television film advertising something.

⊟ *colloq.* advert, *colloq.* ad, commercial, publicity, promotion, *colloq.* plug, *colloq.* hype, display, blurb, announcement, notice, poster, leaflet, handout.

advertiser /'advətaɪzə(r)/ *noun* a person who advertises.

advertising /'advətaɪzɪŋ/ *noun* the business of producing advertisements for goods.

advice /əd'vaɪs/ *noun* **1** suggestions or opinions given to someone about what he or she should do in a particular situation. **2** in business, etc, an official note about a transaction, etc. — **take advice 1** to ask someone for an opinion about what one should do. **2** to act on advice given. [from Old French *avis*]

⊟ **1** counsel, help, guidance, direction, instruction, suggestion, recommendation, opinion, view, warning, caution. **2** notification, notice, memorandum, communication.

advisability /ədvaɪzə'bɪlɪtɪ/ *noun* being recommended, sensible, or wise.

advisable /əd'vaɪzəbl/ *adj.* said of action to be taken, etc, to be recommended; wise or sensible.

⊟ suggested, recommended, sensible, wise, prudent, judicious, sound, profitable, beneficial, desirable, suitable, appropriate, fitting, proper, correct.
⊞ inadvisable, foolish.

advise /əd'vaɪz/ *verb* **1** to give advice to. **2** to recommend. **3** (**advise someone of something**) to inform them about it. **4** *trans., intrans.* to act as an adviser to someone. [from Old French *aviser*]

⊟ **1** counsel, guide, warn, forewarn, caution, instruct, teach. **2** recommend, suggest, commend, urge. **3** notify of, inform of, tell about, acquaint with.

advised /əd'vaɪzd/ *adj.* (*especially in compounds*) considered; judged: *well-advised / ill-advised.*

advisedly /əd'vaɪzədlɪ/ *adv.* after careful thought; on purpose.

adviser or **advisor** *noun* a person who advises, especially professionally.

⊟ counsellor, consultant, authority, guide, teacher, tutor, instructor, coach, aide, right-hand man, mentor, confidant(e), counsel, lawyer.

advisory /əd'vaɪzərɪ/ — *adj.* giving advice. — *noun* an official statement giving advice on a particular subject or a warning about something.

advocaat /'advəkɑːt/ *noun* a liqueur made from raw eggs, sugar, and brandy. [from Dutch *advocaatenborrel*, a lawyer's drink, originally to clear the throat]

advocacy /'advəkəsɪ/ *noun* **1** recommendation or active support of an idea, etc. **2** the function or job of an advocate, eg in a particular trial. [from Latin *advocatia*, from *advocatus*, legal counsellor]

advocate /'advəkət, 'advəkeɪt/ — *noun* (pronounced -kət) **1** especially in Scotland, a lawyer who speaks for the defence or prosecution in a trial. See also BARRISTER, SOLICITOR. **2** a person who supports or recommends an idea, proposal, etc. — *verb* (pronounced -keɪt) to recommend or support (an idea, proposal, etc), especially in public. [from Old French *avocat*, from Latin *advocatus*, legal adviser]

⊟ *noun* **2** supporter, upholder, defender, champion, campaigner, proponent, promoter. *verb* defend, champion, campaign for, press for, argue for, plead for, urge, encourage, advise, recommend, suggest, propose, promote, endorse, support, uphold, subscribe to, favour.
⊞ *noun* **2** opponent, critic. *verb* impugn, disparage, deprecate.

adze *noun* a tool with an arched blade set at right angles to its handle, used for cutting and shaping wood. [from Anglo-Saxon *adesa*]

AEA *abbrev.* (in the UK) Atomic Energy Authority.

AEB *abbrev.* Associated Examining Board.

Aegean civilization the Bronze Age cultures which flourished in the third and second millennia BC on the islands of the Aegean Sea and around its coasts.

aegis /'iːdʒɪs/ — **under the aegis of someone** or **something** under the supervision and with the support of an official organization, etc. [from Greek *aigis*, the shield of Zeus in Greek mythology]

aeolian harp /eɪ'oʊlɪən/ a box-like musical instrument which has strings stretched across a hole, and which makes musical sounds when the wind passes through it. [from Latin *Aeolus*, god of the winds]

aeon /'iːən/ *noun* same as EON.

aerate /'ɛəreɪt/ *verb* **1** to expose to or mix with air or oxygen, eg to aerate the blood by mixing it with oxygen. **2** to charge a liquid with carbon dioxide or some other gas, eg when making fizzy drinks. [from Latin *aer*, air]

aeration /ɛə'reɪʃən/ *noun* **1** mixing or saturating with air or other gas. **2** oxygenation of the blood by breathing. **3** exposure to the air.

aerenchyma /ɛə'reŋkɪmə/ *noun Bot.* a type of tissue most commonly found in aquatic plants, in which there are large air spaces between the cells. [from Greek *aer*, air + *en*, in + *chyma*, that which is poured]

aerial /'ɛərɪəl/ — *noun* a wire, rod, or other device, especially on a radio or television receiver, used to receive or transmit electromagnetic waves, especially radio waves. Dish-shaped aerials are used to receive and transmit microwaves. Also called ANTENNA. — *adj.* **1** relating to or found in the air. **2** like air; ethereal. **3** relating to or using aircraft. [from Latin *aerius*, from *aer*, air]

aerially *adv.* in or through the air.

aerial photography photography of the Earth's surface from an aerial viewpoint such as a balloon, aircraft, spacecraft, or satellite.

aerie /'ɛərɪ/ *noun* same as EYRIE.

aero- *combining form* **1** relating to air: *aerodynamics.* **2** relating to aircraft: *aerodrome.* [from Greek *aer*, air]

aerobatic *adj.* relating to aerobatics.

aerobatics *noun* **1** (*pl.*) spectacular or dangerous manoeuvres, such as flying upside down or looping the loop, in an aircraft or glider. **2** (*sing.*) the art of performing such manoeuvres in the air. [from AERO- + ACROBATICS]

aerobe /'ɛəroʊb/ *Biol.* any organism that requires oxygen in order to obtain energy from the breakdown of carbohydrates or other foodstuffs by the process of respiration. With the exception of certain bacteria and yeasts, most living organisms are aerobes. [from AERO- + Greek *bios*, life]

aerobic /ɛə'roʊbɪk/ *adj.* **1** *Biol.* denoting an organism that requires oxygen in order to obtain energy from the breakdown of carbohydrates or other foodstuffs by the process of respiration. **2** relating to any form of physical exercise that produces an increase in the use of oxygen by the body, eg walking, jogging, swimming, cycling. **3** *Biochem.* denoting a form of respiration in living organisms in which oxygen is required for the complete oxidation (breakdown) of foodstuffs, especially carbohydrates, to carbon dioxide and water. [from AERO- + Greek *bios*, life]

aerobics *noun* **1** (*sing.*) a system of physical exercise consisting of rapidly repeated, energetic movements, which increases the supply of oxygen in the blood and strengthens the heart and lungs. **2** (*sing., pl.*) energetic exercises.

aerodrome *noun Brit.* an area of land and its associated buildings, smaller than an airport, used for the take-off and landing of private and military aircraft. [from AERO- + Greek *dromos*, course]

aerodynamic /ɛəroʊdaɪ'namɪk/ *adj.* **1** relating to aerodynamics. **2** making effective use of aerodynamics so as to minimize air resistance and drag.

aerodynamically *adv.* so as to be aerodynamic; as regards aerodynamics.

aerodynamics *noun* **1** (*sing.*) *Aeron.* the scientific study of the movement of air or other gases relative to solid bodies immersed in them. **2** (*pl.*) the qualities required for fast and efficient movement through the air.

aerofoil *noun* any body or part shaped so as to provide a desirable aerodynamic reaction, such as lift or thrust, when it is moving through the air, eg the wings, tail fins, and propeller blades of aeroplanes, and the rotor blades of helicopters. [from AERO- + FOIL²]

aerogramme or **aerogram** *noun* a thin piece of paper on which to write letters for sending by air, designed so that it can be folded and sealed without being put into an envelope. [from AERO- + GRAM]

aerometry /ɛəˈrɒmətrɪ/ *noun Phonetics* the measurement of airflow through the nose and mouth during speech. Variations in oral and nasal airflow are plotted on instruments such as an *aerometer.*

aeronautic /ɛərəʊˈnɔːtɪk/ or **aeronautical** /ɛərəʊˈnɔːtɪkl/ *adj.* relating to aeronautics.

aeronautics *sing. noun* the scientific study of travel through the Earth's atmosphere.

aerophone *noun* any musical instrument in which sound is produced using air as the main vibrating agent. These include the so-called 'free' aerophones, eg the mouth organ and harmonium, in which a reed is vibrated by air passing across it; and wind instruments of all types. [from Greek *aer*, air + *phone*, sound]

aeroplane *noun* a powered machine used for travelling in the air that is heavier than air and supported in its flight by fixed wings. [from AERO- + PLANE¹]

aerosol /ˈɛərəʊsɒl/ *noun* **1** a cloud of fine particles of a solid or liquid suspended in a gas. **2** a can containing a product that can be sprayed to produce such a suspension, eg paint, polish, insecticide. [from AERO- + SOL²]

aerospace *noun* **1** the Earth's atmosphere and the space beyond it, considered as a zone available for the flight of aircraft and spacecraft. **2** (*attributive*) denoting the branches of technology or industry concerned with the design, development, manufacture, and sale of aircraft and spacecraft: *the aerospace industry.*

aesthete /ˈiːsθiːt/ *noun* a person who has or claims to have a special appreciation of art and beauty. [from Greek *aisthetes*, one who perceives]

aesthetic /ɪsˈθɛtɪk/ *adj.* **1** able to appreciate beauty. **2** artistic; tasteful. [from Greek *aisthetikos*, from *aisthanesthai*, to perceive]

aesthetically *adv.* in an aesthetic way.

aesthetics *sing. noun* **1** the branch of philosophy concerned with the study of the principles of beauty, especially in art. **2** the principles of good taste and the appreciation of beauty.

aestivation /iːstɪˈveɪʃən/ *noun Bot.* **1** in certain animals, eg tropical amphibians, a state of inactivity that enables them to survive prolonged periods of heat or drought. **2** the arrangement of the petals and sepals in a flower bud. [from Latin *aestivus*, relating to summer]

aether /ˈiːθə(r)/ same as ETHER 2, 3.

aetiological *adj.* **1** relating to aetiology. **2** giving a cause or reason.

aetiology or **etiology** /iːtɪˈɒlədʒɪ/ *noun* **1** the science or philosophy of causes. **2** the scientific study of the causes or origins of diseases. **3** the cause of a specific disease. [from Latin *aetiologia*, from Greek *aitia*, cause + *logos*, discourse]

AEU *abbrev.* Amalgamated Engineering Union.

AF *abbrev.* audio frequency.

AFA *abbrev.* Amateur Football Association.

Afar a Cushitic-speaking people of the Horn of Africa, also known as Danakil.

afar *adv.* at a distance; far away. — **from afar** from a great distance.

AFC *abbrev.* **1** Air Force Cross. **2** Association Football Club.

affability *noun* being affable.

affable /ˈafəbl/ *adj.* pleasant and friendly in manner; easy to talk to. [from Latin *affabilis*, from *affari*, to speak to]

■ friendly, amiable, sociable, approachable, open, expansive, genial, good-humoured, good-natured, pleasant, agreeable, benevolent, kindly, gracious, obliging, amicable, congenial, cordial.

◼ unfriendly, reserved, reticent, cool.

affair *noun* **1** a concern, matter, or thing to be done. **2** an event or connected series of events. **3** a sexual relationship between two people, usually when at least one of them is married to someone else. **4** (**affairs**) matters of importance and public interest: *current affairs.* **5** (**affairs**) private or public business matters. [from Old French *afaire*, from *a*, to + *faire*, to do]

■ **1** concern, matter, question, issue, subject, topic, responsibility, interest. **2** event, occurrence, incident, episode, happening, circumstance. **3** relationship, liaison, intrigue, affaire, love affair, romance, amour. **5** business, transactions, operations, proceedings, undertakings, activities.

affaire /afɛ(r)/ *noun* **1** a liaison or intrigue. **2** an incident arousing speculation and scandal. [French, = affair]

affect¹ *verb* **1** to have an effect on. **2** to cause (someone) to feel strong emotions, especially sadness or pity. **3** *said of diseases* to attack or infect. [from Latin *afficere*]

■ **1** act on, change, transform, alter, modify, influence, sway, bear upon, impinge upon, concern, regard, involve, relate to, apply to. **2** move, touch, upset, disturb, perturb, trouble, stir, impress, interest. **3** attack, strike.

affect² *verb* **1** to pretend to feel or have. **2** to use, wear, etc (something) in a way that is intended to attract attention. **3** to have an obvious liking for: *affect fast cars.* [from Old French *affecter*, from Latin *afficere*, to affect = have an effect on]

■ **1** adopt, assume, put on, feign, simulate, imitate, fake, counterfeit, sham, pretend.

affectation /afɪkˈteɪʃən/ *noun* **1** unnatural behaviour or pretence which is intended to impress people. **2** the act of pretending.

■ **1** airs, pretentiousness, mannerism, pose, act, show, appearance, façade. **2** pretence, sham, simulation, imitation, artificiality, insincerity.

◼ **1** artlessness, ingenuousness.

affected *adj.* **1** not genuine; false; pretended. **2** *said of a manner of speaking or behaving* put on to impress people.

■ **1** assumed, pretended, feigned, simulated, artificial, fake, false, counterfeit, sham, *colloq.* phoney, contrived, studied. **2** unnatural, put-on, precious, mannered, pretentious, pompous, stiff, insincere.

◼ **1** genuine. **2** natural.

affecting *adj.* causing people to feel strong emotion, especially sadness, pity, sympathy, joy, etc.

affection *noun* **1** a feeling of love or strong liking. **2** (**affections**) feelings: *play on his affections.* **3** a disease. [from Latin *affectio*, from *afficere*, to affect = have an effect on]

■ **1** liking, fondness, attachment, devotion, love, passion,

tenderness, care, warmth, kindness, friendliness, goodwill, favour, partiality, inclination, penchant.
■ 1 dislike, antipathy.

affectionate /ə'fɛkʃənɪt/ adj. showing love or fondness.

■ fond, attached, devoted, doting, loving, passionate, tender, caring, warm, kind, friendly, amiable, cordial.
■ cold, undemonstrative.

affective disorder Psychol. any of various disorders whose primary characteristic is a disturbance of mood or emotion, eg depression, mania.

afferent /'afərənt/ adj. 1 Anat. denoting an anatomical structure, especially a nerve or blood vessel, that leads inwards or towards a central part. 2 denoting a nerve or neurone that carries nerve impulses from the sense organs and other sensory receptors to the central nervous system (the brain and spinal cord). See also EFFERENT. [from Latin afferre, from ad, to + ferre, to carry]

affianced /ə'faɪənst/ adj. old use engaged to be married. [from Old French afiancer, to pledge in marriage]

affidavit /afə'deɪvɪt/ noun a written statement, sworn to be true by the person who makes it, for use as evidence in a court of law. [from Latin affidavit, he or she swears on oath]

affiliate /ə'fɪlɪeɪt, ə'fɪlɪət/ — verb trans., intrans. (pronounced -eit) (usually be affiliated with or to something) to connect or associate a person or organization to a group or a larger organization. — noun (pronounced -ət) a person or organization, etc having an association with a group or larger body. [from Latin affiliatus, adopted]

affiliation noun the act or process of affiliating; the state of being affiliated.

affiliation order Legal a court order instructing a man to pay money towards the support of his illegitimate child.

affinity /ə'fɪnɪtɪ/ noun (PL. **affinities**) 1 a strong natural liking for or feeling of attraction or closeness towards someone or something. 2 (**affinity with someone**) relationship to them, especially by marriage. 3 similarity in appearance, structure, etc, especially one suggesting relatedness. 4 (**affinity for something**) chemical attraction between substances; readiness to combine chemically with another substance and remain in combination. [from Latin affinitas, from affinis, neighbouring]

affirm /ə'fɜːm/ verb 1 to state positively and firmly; to state as a fact. 2 to uphold or confirm (an idea, belief, etc). 3 intrans. in a court of law, to promise solemnly to tell the truth, without swearing a religious oath. [from Old French afermer, from Latin ad, to + firmare, to make firm]

■ 1 state, assert, declare, pronounce, maintain, swear, testify. 2 confirm, corroborate, verify, endorse, ratify, uphold, support.
■ 1 deny. 2 refute.

affirmation /afə'meɪʃən/ noun 1 assertion. 2 something which is affirmed. 3 a positive judgement or proposition. 4 a solemn declaration.

affirmative /ə'fɜːmətɪv/ — adj. expressing agreement; giving the answer 'yes'. — noun an affirmative word or phrase.

■ adj. agreeing, concurring, assenting, approving, confirming, corroborative, positive, emphatic.
■ adj. negative, dissenting.

affix /ə'fɪks, 'afɪks/ — verb (with stress on -fix) to attach or fasten. — noun (with stress on a-) a word or syllable added to the beginning or end of a word to form another, related, word, eg un- to happy to make unhappy, and -ness to sad to make sadness; a prefix or suffix. [from Latin affixus, fastened to]

afflict verb to cause (someone) physical or mental suffering. [from Latin affligere, to cast down]

■ strike, trouble, burden, oppress, distress, grieve, pain, hurt, harm, beset, plague, torment, torture.
■ comfort, solace.

affliction noun distress or suffering, or a cause of this.

■ distress, grief, sorrow, misery, suffering, pain, torment, disease, illness, plague, curse, ordeal, trial, tribulation, trouble, hardship, adversity, misfortune, calamity, disaster.
■ comfort, consolation, solace, blessing.

affluence /'afluəns/ noun wealth, abundance.

■ wealth, riches, fortune, substance, property, wealthiness, prosperity, opulence, abundance, profusion, plenty.
■ poverty.

affluent /'afluənt/ adj. having more than enough money; rich. [from Latin affluere, to flow freely]

■ wealthy, rich, moneyed, colloq. loaded, colloq. flush, well-off, prosperous, well-to-do, opulent, luxurious.
■ poor, impoverished.

affluent society a society in which ordinary people benefit materially from general prosperity, especially in being able to afford things that were once regarded as luxuries.

afford /ə'fɔːd/ verb 1 (used with can, could, be able to) to have enough money, time, etc to spend on (something). 2 (used with can, could, be able to) to be able to do (something), or allow (something) to happen, without risk: cannot afford to take chances. 3 to give; to provide: a room affording a view of the sea. [from Anglo-Saxon geforthian, to further, promote]

■ 1 have enough for, spare, allow, manage. 3 provide, supply, give, grant, offer, produce, yield, generate.

affordable adj. that can be afforded.

afforest /ə'fɒrɪst/ verb to carry out the process of afforestation on (a piece of land). [from Latin afforestare]

afforestation /afɒrɪ'steɪʃən/ noun the process whereby a forest is established for the first time on bare or cultivated land, either by planting seeds, or by transplanting seedlings or young trees.

affray /ə'freɪ/ noun a fight in a public place; a breach of the peace by fighting. [from Old French esfrei]

affront /ə'frʌnt/ — noun an insult, especially one delivered in public. — verb 1 to insult, especially in public. 2 to offend the pride of; to embarrass. [from Old French afronter, to slap in the face]

■ noun insult, slur, rudeness, discourtesy, snub, slight, offence, wrong, injury, provocation, vexation, outrage. verb 1 insult, abuse, snub, slight, provoke, irritate, annoy, anger, vex, incense, outrage. 2 offend, embarrass.
■ noun compliment. verb 1 compliment, appease.

AFG abbrev., as an international vehicle mark Afghanistan.

Afghan /'afgan/ — adj. of Afghanistan or its inhabitants. — noun 1 (also **Afghani**) a citizen of, or person born in, Afghanistan. 2 the official language of Afghanistan. 3 (also **Afghan hound**) a type of tall thin dog with long silky hair, originally used for hunting. [from Pashto]

aficionado /əfɪʃɪə'nɑːdoʊ/ noun (PL. **aficionados**) a person who takes an enthusiastic interest in a particular sport or pastime. [Spanish, = amateur]

afield adv. to or at a distance; away from home: far afield. [from Anglo-Saxon, from A[3] + FIELD]

afire adj., adv. on fire; burning.

aflame adj. 1 in flames; burning. 2 very excited.

aflatoxin /afləˈtɒksɪn/ noun Biol. a toxic substance produced by the fungus Aspergillus flavus, which contaminates stored corn, soya beans, peanuts, etc, in warm humid regions. [from Aspergillus flavus, from Latin aspergere, to sprinkle + flavus, yellow]

AFL/CIO abbrev. American Federation of Labor-Congress of Industrial Organizations.

afloat adj., adv. 1 floating. 2 at sea; aboard ship. 3 out of debt; financially secure. [from Anglo-Saxon, from A³ + FLOAT]

AFM abbrev. 1 Air Force medal. 2 audio frequency modulation.

afoot adj., adv. being prepared or already in progress.

afore adj., prep. old use, dialect before. [from Anglo-Saxon onforan]

afore- combining form before; previously: aforementioned.

aforementioned — adj. already mentioned. — sing. or pl. noun a person or group of people already mentioned.

aforesaid /əˈfɔːsɛd/ adj. said or mentioned already.

aforethought — with malice aforethought Legal, said of a criminal act done deliberately; planned beforehand.

a fortiori /eɪ fɔtɪˈɔːriː/ for an even better or stronger reason. [from Latin a fortiori, from the stronger]

AFP abbrev. Agence France Press.

afraid adj. 1 (often afraid of someone or something) feeling fear; frightened. 2 (afraid to do something) reluctant to do something out of fear or concern for the consequences: they are afraid to go out at night. 3 as a formula of regret, politely sorry: I'm afraid we're going to be late. [past tense of the obsolete verb affray, to disturb or frighten]

. . . .
■ 1 frightened, scared, alarmed, terrified, fearful, daunted, intimidated, faint-hearted, cowardly, timorous, timid, distrustful, suspicious. 2 reluctant to, apprehensive about, anxious about, nervous about.
■ 1 unafraid, brave, bold, confident.
. . . .

AFRC abbrev. in the UK, the Agricultural and Food Research Council, now superseded by the Biotechnology and Biological Sciences Research Council (BBSRC).

afresh adv. again, especially from the beginning; with a fresh start.

African — adj. belonging to the continent of Africa, its inhabitants or languages. — noun a person, especially a dark-skinned person, who is native to Africa or of African descent. [from Latin Africanus]

African-American — noun a person of African descent living in America. — adj. of African-Americans.

African elephant the larger of the two living species of elephant (Loxodonta africana), also differing from the other species in that it has larger ears, and a triangular lip on the top and bottom of the trunk (not just on the top as in the other species).

African lily see AGAPANTHUS.

African violet noun any of various herbaceous perennial plants of the genus Saintpaulia, native to tropical E Africa, having rounded hairy leaves and violet, bluish-purple, pink, or white flowers.

Afrikaans /afrɪˈkɑːnz/ noun one of the official languages of South Africa, developed from Dutch. [from Dutch Afrikaans, African]

Afrikaner /afrɪˈkɑːnə(r)/ noun a white inhabitant of S Africa whose native language is Afrikaans and who is usually of Dutch descent. [from Dutch Afrikaans, African]

Afro noun (PL. Afros) a hairstyle consisting of thick bushy curls standing out from the head.

Afro- combining form forming words meaning 'African, African and ...': Afro-Caribbean. [from Latin Afer, African]

Afro-American — noun an American whose ancestors came from Africa. — adj. of Afro-Americans, their music, culture, etc.

Afro-Asiatic /afroʊeɪzɪˈatɪk/ — adj. denoting a major family of African languages used in Africa and SW Asia. It contains over 200 languages and is usually divided into six groups (thought to be derived from a common language of the 7th millennium BC), Semitic, Berber, Chadic, Cushitic, Egyptian (now extinct), and Omotic. — noun the languages forming this family.

Afro-Caribbean /afroʊkærɪˈbɪən/ — noun a person living in the Caribbean whose ancestors came originally from Africa. — adj. of Afro-Caribbeans, their music, culture, etc.

aft adv., adj. at or towards the stern, rear, or tail. [from Anglo-Saxon æftan, behind]

after — prep. 1 coming later in time than. 2 following in position; behind. 3 next to and following in importance, order, arrangement, etc. 4 because of; considering: you can't expect to be promoted after that mistake. 5 in spite of: he's still no better after all that medicine. 6 about: ask after her. 7 in pursuit of: run after him. 8 said of a painting or other work of art in the style or manner of (someone else). 9 given the same name as; in imitation of: called her Mary after her aunt. 10 North Amer., esp. US past (an hour): it's twenty after six. — adv. later in time, behind in place. — conj. after the time when. — adj. 1 later; following: in after years. 2 further towards the stern of a ship: after cabins. See also AFT. — after all 1 in spite of all that has happened or has been said. 2 contrary to what is or was expected: the shop was closed after all. after one's own heart of exactly the kind one likes. after you please go before me. be after someone or something to be pursuing or chasing a person or animal. [from Anglo-Saxon æfter]

. . . .
■ prep. 1 following, subsequent to. 2 following, behind. 3 following, below. 4 because of, in consequence of, as a result of, in view of.
■ prep. 1, 2, 3 before.
. . . .

afterbirth noun Medicine the placenta, blood, and ruptured membranes expelled from the uterus after the birth of a mammal.

afterburning noun Aeron. a system whereby the thrust of a jet engine is increased by injecting fuel into the hot exhaust gases leaving the engine. The fuel is ignited by the hot gases, providing additional thrust.

aftercare noun care and support given to someone after a period of treatment, a surgical operation, a prison sentence, etc.

after-effect noun a circumstance or event, usually an unpleasant one, that follows as the result of something.

afterglow noun 1 a glow remaining in the sky after the sun has set. 2 an impression or feeling, usually a pleasant one, that remains when the experience, etc that caused it is over.

afterlife noun the continued existence of one's spirit or soul after one's death.

aftermath noun circumstances that follow and are a result of something, especially a great and terrible event. [from Anglo-Saxon mæth, mowing]

afternoon noun the period of the day between noon and the evening.

afters pl. noun Brit. colloq. dessert; pudding.

aftershave noun a scented lotion for putting on the face after shaving.

aftertaste noun the taste that remains in the mouth after one has eaten or drunk something.

afterthought noun an idea thought of after the main plan, etc has been formed.

afterwards or **afterward** adv. later; following (an earlier event of time).

Ag symbol Chem. silver. [from Latin argentum, silver]

again adv. 1 once more; another time. 2 back to a previous condition, situation, etc: *get well again.* **3** in addition: *twice as much again.* **4** however; on the other hand: *He might come, but then again he might not.* **5** further; besides. — **again and again** very often; repeatedly. [from Anglo-Saxon *ongean*]

▣ **1** once more, once again, another time, over again, afresh, anew, encore.

against *prep.* **1** close to or leaning on; in contact with. **2** into collision with. **3** in opposition to: *against the law.* **4** in contrast to: *against a dark background.* **5** with a bad or unfavourable effect on: *His youth is against him.* **6** as a protection from; in anticipation of or preparation for. **7** in return for: *exchange rate against the franc.* — **as against something** in comparison with it. **have something against someone** or **something** to have a reason for disliking or disapproving of them. [from Middle English *ageynes*]

▣ **1** close to, adjacent to, abutting, touching, in contact with, on. **3** opposing, confronting, facing, versus, opposed to, in opposition to, hostile to, resisting, in defiance of.

▣ **3** for, pro.

agamid /ˈagəmɪd/ *noun* a lizard native to Africa (except Madagascar), S and SE Asia, and Australia. Its body is usually broad, and it has a large head, scales with ridges and spines, and a thick fleshy tongue. [from a Carib name]

agapanthus /agəˈpanθəs/ *noun* an evergreen perennial plant (*Agapanthus africanus*), native to S Africa, up to 1m tall, with strap-shaped leathery leaves, and bell-shaped blue (or rarely white) flowers. Also called AFRICAN LILY. [from Greek *agape*, love + *anthos*, flower]

agape[1] /əˈɡeɪp/ *adj.* **1** *said of the mouth* gaping; open wide. **2** *said of a person* very surprised.

agape[2] /ˈaɡəpeɪ, əˈɡɑːpɪ/ *noun* Christian brotherly love, as distinct from erotic love. [from Greek *agape*, love]

agar /ˈeɪɡə(r)/ *noun* a gelatinous substance extracted from the dried stems of certain species of red seaweed. It is the main ingredient of media used for growing cultures of bacteria and other micro-organisms, and is also used as a stabilizer for emulsions and as a thickening agent in foods and cosmetics. [from Malay]

agaric /ˈaɡərɪk, əˈɡarɪk/ *noun* any of various fungi belonging to the order Agaricales, which produce an umbrella-shaped spore-bearing structure with a central vertical stem supporting a circular cap, eg cultivated mushroom, field mushroom, fly agaric, death cap. [from Latin *agaricum*]

agate /ˈaɡət/ *noun Geol.* a fine-grained variety of chalcedony (a form of quartz), which usually forms within rock cavities, and consists of concentrically arranged bands of two or more colours, eg black and white, as in onyx. It is used as a semi-precious stone in jewellery and ornaments. [from Old French *agathes*]

agave /əˈɡɑːvɪ/ *noun* any of various evergreen perennial plants of the genus *Agave*, native to Central and S America, and having fleshy sword-shaped often spiny leaves arranged in a rosette, and tall flower stalks. [from Latin, from the Greek name *Agave*]

age — *noun* **1** the period of time during which a person, animal, plant, or phenomenon has lived or existed. **2** a particular stage in life. **3** the fact of being old. **4** any great division of world, human, or individual history. **5** in the earth's history, an interval of time during which specific life forms, physical conditions, geological events, etc, were dominant, eg Ice Age. **6** (*usually* **ages**) *colloq.* a very long time. — *verb* (**ageing, aging**) **1** *intrans.* to show signs of growing old. **2** *intrans.* to grow old. **3** *intrans.* to mature. **4** to cause to seem older or look old. — **act** or **be one's age** to behave sensibly. **come of age** to become legally old enough to have an adult's rights and duties. **of an age** of the same, or a similar, age. **over age** too old. **under age** too young to be legally allowed to do something, eg buy alcoholic drink. [from Old French *aage*, from Latin *aetas*]

▣ *noun* **3** old age, maturity, elderliness, seniority, dotage, senility, decline. **4** era, epoch, time, period, date, generation, day, days, years, aeon. *verb* **2** grow old, decline. **3** mature, ripen, mellow, season.

▣ *noun* **3** youth.

-age *suffix* forming nouns meaning: **1** a collection or set: *baggage.* **2** an action: *breakage.* **3** the result of an action or event: *wreckage.* **4** a condition: *bondage.* **5** the home, house, or place of: *orphanage / anchorage.* **6** cost: *postage.* [from Old French]

aged /ˈeɪdʒd, ˈeɪdʒɪd/ — *adj.* **1** (pronounced ˈeɪdʒd) having a particular age. **2** (pronounced ˈeɪdʒɪd) very old. — *noun* (pronounced ˈeɪdʒɪd) old people as a group.

age group or **age bracket** the people between two particular ages, considered as a group.

ageing or **aging** *noun* the period during which the physical condition of a living organism deteriorates, leading to death; in biological terms this corresponds to the entire life process.

ageism or **agism** /ˈeɪdʒɪzəm/ *noun* the practice of treating people differently, usually unfairly, on the grounds of age only, especially because they are too old.

ageist or **agist** — *noun* a person who discriminates against people on the grounds of age. — *adj.* discriminating on the grounds of age.

ageless *adj.* never growing old or fading; never looking older.

age limit the age under or over which one may not do something.

Agence France Presse (ABBREV. **AFP**) an international news agency, with headquarters in Paris.

agency /ˈeɪdʒənsɪ/ *noun* (PL. **agencies**) **1** an office or business providing a particular service. **2** an active part played by someone in bringing something about. **3** *North Amer., esp. US* a government department providing a particular service. **4** the business of an agent. [from Latin *agere*, to do]

▣ **1** office, bureau, department, organization, business, work. **2** intervention, means, medium, instrumentality, power, force, influence, effect, action, activity, operation.

agenda /əˈdʒɛndə/ *noun* a list of things to be done or discussed; a written list of subjects to be dealt with at a meeting, etc. [from Latin *agenda*, things to be done]

agent /ˈeɪdʒənt/ *noun* **1** a person who represents an organization and acts on its behalf; a person who deals with someone else's business matters, etc. **2** (*also* **secret agent**) a spy. **3** a substance that is used for producing a particular result. **4** a person who is the cause of something. [from Latin *agens*, from *agere*, to do]

▣ **1** substitute, deputy, delegate, envoy, emissary, representative, *colloq.* rep, broker, middleman, go-between, intermediary, negotiator. **4** instrument, vehicle, channel, means, agency, cause, force.

agent provocateur /aʒɒn prəvɒkəˈtɜː(r)/ *noun* (PL. **agents provocateurs**) a person employed to incite others by pretended sympathy to perform illegal acts. [French, = provocative agent]

age of consent the age at which consent to sexual intercourse is permitted by law.

age-old *adj.* done, known, etc for a very long time.

aggiornamento /adʒɔːnaˈmɛntoʊ/ *noun* **1** political or religious reform. **2** *Christianity* the process of modernizing the belief, structure, and discipline of the Roman Catholic Church and making it more effective in the modern world. It was one of the aims of the Second Vatican Council (1962–5) called by Pope John XXIII. [from Italian *aggiornamento*, modernization]

agglomerate /ə'glɒməreɪt, ə'glɒmərət/ — *verb trans., intrans.* (pronounced -reɪt) to make into or become an untidy mass. — *noun* (pronounced -rət) **1** an untidy mass or collection of things. **2** a type of volcanic rock consisting of a mass of coarse angular fragments of solidified lava embedded in a matrix of ashy material. — *adj.* (pronounced -rət) formed into a mass. [from Latin *agglomerare*, to wind on to a ball]

agglomeration /əglɒmə'reɪʃən/ *noun* **1** the act of collecting in a mass; heaping together. **2** a mass or cluster.

agglutinate /ə'glu:tɪneɪt/ *verb* **1** to stick or glue together. **2** *trans., intrans.* Grammar, *said of a language* to create (words) by joining together simpler words or word elements, each of which corresponds to a particular element of meaning. **3** *Biol., said of red blood cells, bacteria, etc* to clump together forming a visible precipitate as a result of mixing blood cells from two incompatible blood groups, or of the reaction of an antigen (foreign particle) to its specific antibody. [from Latin *agglutinare*, to glue together]

agglutinating language or **agglutinative language** *Linguistics* a language type in which words are typically made up of elements, with each element expressing a particular grammatical meaning, as in the English word *de-human-ize*. Japanese, Turkish, and Finnish are examples of agglutinating languages. See also ANALYTIC LANGUAGE.

agglutination /əglu:tɪ'neɪʃən/ *noun* **1** act of agglutinating. **2** an agglutinated mass. **3** a process of word-formation in which words are inflected by the addition of one or more meaningful elements to the stem. **4** *Biol.* the process of agglutinating. Agglutination tests are used to determine blood groups, and to establish the identity of bacteria.

agglutinative /ə'glu:tɪnətɪv/ *adj.* tending to or able to agglutinate.

aggrandize or **aggrandise** /ə'grandaɪz/ *verb* **1** to increase the power, wealth, etc of (a person, country, etc). **2** to make (someone or something) seem greater than they really are. [from Old French *aggrandir*]

aggrandizement or **aggrandisement** /ə'grandɪzmənt/ *noun* making someone or something seem greater than they really are.

aggravate /'agrəveɪt/ *verb* **1** to make (a bad situation, an illness, etc) worse. **2** to make (someone) angry; to annoy. [from Latin *aggravare*, to make heavier or worse]

⊟ **1** exacerbate, worsen, inflame, increase, intensify, heighten, magnify, exaggerate. **2** annoy, irritate, vex, irk, anger, exasperate, incense, provoke, tease, pester, harass.
⊟ **1** improve, alleviate. **2** appease, mollify.

aggravating *adj.* **1** worsening. **2** annoying.

aggravatingly *adv.* so as to aggravate or annoy.

aggravation /agrə'veɪʃən/ *noun* **1** something that increases the gravity of an illness or crime etc. **2** irritation, annoyance.

aggregate /'agrəgət, 'agrəgeɪt/ — *noun* (pronounced -gət) **1** a collection of separate units brought together; a total. **2** any material, especially sand, gravel, or crushed stone, that is mixed with cement to form concrete. **3** a mass of soil grains or rock particles, or a mixture of both. — *adj.* (pronounced -gət) *said of separate units* combined together. — *verb* (pronounced -geɪt) **1** *trans., intrans.* to combine or be combined into a single unit or whole. **2** *colloq.* to amount to. **3** *formal* to add as a member to a society, group, etc. — **in the aggregate** taken all together. **on aggregate** in total. [from Latin *aggregare*, to herd or bring together]

⊟ *noun* **1** total, sum, amount, whole, totality, entirety, combination, collection, accumulation. *adj.* accumulated, collective, combined, united, added, total, complete, composite, mixed. *verb* **1** combine, unite, collect, accumulate.
⊟ *adj.* individual, particular.

aggregation /agrə'geɪʃən/ *noun* the act or process of aggregating.

aggression *noun* **1** the act of attacking another person or country without being provoked; an instance of hostile behaviour towards someone. **2** the tendency to make unprovoked attacks. **3** hostile feelings or behaviour. [from Latin *aggredi*, to attack]

⊟ HOSTILITY. **1** attack, offensive, assault, onslaught, raid, incursion, invasion, provocation, offence. **2** aggressiveness, militancy, belligerence, combativeness. **3** antagonism.
⊟ **1** peace, resistance. **2** passivity, gentleness.

aggressive *adj.* **1** *said of a person* always ready to attack; hostile. **2** *said of a person* strong and determined; self-assertive. **3** *said of an action* hostile.

⊟ **1** argumentative, quarrelsome, contentious, belligerent, hostile. **2** bold, assertive, self-assertive, *slang* in-your-face, pushy, *colloq.* go-ahead, forceful, vigorous, zealous, ruthless. **3** hostile, offensive, provocative, intrusive, invasive.
⊟ **1** friendly. **2** submissive, timid. **3** peaceable.

aggressor *noun* in a fight, war, etc, the person, group or country that attacks first, especially if the attack is unprovoked.

aggrieved *adj.* **1** angry, hurt, or upset because one feels that one has been badly or unfairly treated. **2** *Legal* having suffered because of someone else's illegal behaviour. [from Old French *agrever*, to press heavily upon]

⊟ **1** offended, hurt, injured, insulted, wronged, maltreated, ill-used, resentful, distressed, upset, annoyed, angry.
⊟ **1** pleased.

aggro /'agrəʊ/ *noun Brit. slang* **1** fighting; violent or threatening behaviour. **2** problems or difficulties. [abbreviation of AGGRAVATION or AGGRESSION]

aghast /ə'gɑːst/ *adj.* filled with fear or horror. [from Anglo-Saxon *gæstan*, to frighten]

⊟ shocked, appalled, horrified, horror-stricken, thunderstruck, stunned, stupefied, astonished, astounded, dismayed, terrified.

agile /'adʒaɪl/ *adj.* able to move, change direction, etc quickly and easily; nimble; active. [from Latin *agilis*, from *agere*, to do]

⊟ active, lively, nimble, spry, sprightly, mobile, flexible, lithe, quick, swift, brisk, prompt, sharp, acute.
⊟ clumsy, stiff.

agilely *adv.* in an agile way.

agility /ə'dʒɪlɪtɪ/ *noun* being agile; the ability to move quickly and easily.

agin /ə'gɪn/ *prep. Scot. colloq.* against. [from Anglo-Saxon *ongean*, opposite to]

agitate /'adʒɪteɪt/ *verb* **1** to excite or trouble (a person, their feelings, nerves, etc). **2** *intrans.* to stir up public opinion for or against an issue. **3** to stir or shake (a liquid) vigorously, usually in order to mix it with another liquid or to dissolve a solid in it. [from Latin *agitare*]

⊟ **1** excite, stimulate, rouse, arouse, stir up, incite, inflame, work up, worry, trouble, upset, alarm, disturb, unsettle, discompose, fluster, ruffle, unnerve, confuse, disconcert. **3** shake, stir, beat, churn, toss.
⊟ **1** calm, tranquillize.

agitated *adj.* distressed, excited, and worried.

agitation /adʒɪ'teɪʃən/ noun **1** public discussion for or against something. **2** a disturbed or nervous state of mind; anxiety.

agitator /'adʒɪteɪtə(r)/ noun **1** a person who tries continually to stir up public feeling, especially over serious political or social issues. **2** a tool or machine for stirring or shaking a liquid.

■ **1** troublemaker, rabble-rouser, revolutionary, colloq. stirrer, inciter, instigator.

agitprop /'adʒɪtprop/ noun the spreading of political propaganda, especially by communists. [from Russian agitatsiya, agitation + propaganda, propaganda]

aglow adj., adv. shining with colour or warmth; glowing.

AGM abbrev. annual general meeting.

agnosia /əg'nəʊzɪə/ noun Medicine a brain disorder characterized by inability to interpret information from the sense organs correctly, eg an affected person may have unimpaired hearing, but be unable to interpret sounds. [from A-¹ + Greek gnosis, knowledge, recognition]

agnostic /əg'nɒstɪk/ — noun a person who believes that one can know only about material things and so believes that nothing can be known about the existence of God. — adj. relating to this view. [from Greek agnostos, not known]

agnosticism /əg'nɒstɪsɪzəm/ noun the belief that nothing can be known about the existence of God.

ago adv. in the past; earlier. [from Anglo-Saxon agan, to pass by]

agog /ə'gɒg/ — adj. very interested and excited; eager to know more. — adv. eagerly; expectantly. [from Old French en gogues, in fun]

agonist /'agənɪst/ noun **1** someone engaged in a struggle, whether physical or spiritual. **2** Biol. a muscle whose contraction results in movement of a body part. **3** a drug whose action is complementary to that of another drug.

agonize /'agənaɪz/ or **agonise** verb **1** intrans. (**agonize about** or **over something**) to worry intensely or suffer great anxiety about it. **2** trans. to cause great anxiety or worry to. [from Greek agonizesthai, to struggle]

agonized or **agonised** adj. suffering or showing great anxiety, worry or agony.

agonizing or **agonising** adj. causing great bodily or mental suffering.

agonizingly or **agonisingly** adv. **1** so as to cause agony; painfully. **2** acutely, severely: an agonizingly difficult decision.

agony /'agənɪ/ noun (PL. **agonies**) severe bodily or mental pain. [from Latin agonia, from Greek agon, struggle]

■ anguish, torment, torture, pain, throes, suffering, affliction, tribulation, distress, woe, misery, wretchedness.

agony aunt colloq. a person who answers letters sent in to an agony column.

agony column part of a newspaper or magazine where advice is offered to readers who write in with their problems.

agoraphobia /agərə'fəʊbɪə/ noun an irrational fear of open spaces or public places. [from Greek agora, marketplace + phobos, fear]

agoraphobic /agərə'fəʊbɪk/ — noun a person who is suffering from agoraphobia. — adj. suffering from agoraphobia.

agouti /ə'guːtiː/ noun a rodent like a cavy, native to Central and S America and the Caribbean Islands, about 500mm in length, resembling a rat in appearance, and having long legs and a minute black tail. [from Guarani acuti]

AGR abbrev. advanced gas-cooled reactor.

agranulocytosis /ə'granʊləʊsaɪ'təʊsɪs/ noun Medicine a disorder in which there is a marked decrease in the number of granulocytes (a particular type of white blood cell) in the blood as a result of damage to the bone marrow, eg by toxic drugs. It results in greatly increased vulnerability to infection. [from A-¹ + GRANULE]

agraphia /eɪ'grafɪə, ə'grafɪə/ noun Psychol. loss of the ability to write, although hand co-ordination remains unaffected, caused by brain disorder. [from A-¹ + Greek graphein, to write]

agrarian /ə'grɛərɪən/ adj. **1** relating to land or its management. **2** relating to the uses of land, especially agriculture or the cultivation of plants. [from Latin agrarius, from ager, field]

agree verb, usually intrans. **1** (**agree with someone** or **something**) to be of the same opinion as someone else about something. **2** (**agree to something**) to say yes to a suggestion, request, or instruction. **3** (**agree on** or **upon something**) to reach a joint decision about something after discussion. **4** trans. to reach agreement about (something). **5** (**agree with someone**) usually said of food to be suitable or good for them: milk doesn't agree with me. **6** (**agree with something**) to be consistent with it. **7** Grammar to have the same number, person, gender, or case. — **agree to differ** said of two or more people to agree to accept each other's different opinions. **be agreed** to have reached the same conclusion. [from Old French agreer]

■ **1** concur with, see eye to eye with. **2** consent to, assent to, accede to, grant, yield to, comply with. **3, 4** settle, decide on. **5** suit. **6** accord with, match, fit, tally with, correspond with, conform with.

E3 1 disagree with, differ from. **2** refuse. **5** disagree with. **6** conflict with.

agreeable adj. **1** said of things pleasant. **2** said of people friendly. **3** (**agreeable to something**) said of people willing to accept a suggestion, etc.

■ **1** pleasant, congenial, nice, attractive, delightful, enjoyable, gratifying, satisfying, palatable, acceptable. **2** pleasant, likable, friendly, affable.

E3 1, 2 disagreeable, nasty.

agreement noun **1** a contract or promise. **2** a joint decision made after discussion. **3** the state of holding the same opinion. **4** Grammar the state of having the same number, person, gender, or case.

■ **1** contract, deal, bargain, arrangement, understanding, promise, compact, covenant, treaty, pact. **2** settlement. **3** concurrence, accord, unanimity, concord, harmony, sympathy, affinity, similarity, compatibility, correspondence, consistency.

E3 3 disagreement.

agricultural /'agrɪkʌltʃərəl/ adj. relating to agriculture.

■ agronomic, agrarian, farming, farmed, cultivated, rural, pastoral, bucolic.

agricultural controls a term commonly applied to UK government controls over agricultural production and pricing during World War II, continuing up to 1953. Agricultural controls are now mainly concerned with the restriction of surplus production through quotas, and with disease prevention and control.

agriculturalist or **agriculturist** noun **1** an expert on agriculture. **2** a farmer.

Agricultural Revolution a series of changes in farming practice that started in England and then spread throughout W Europe between 1700 and 1850. The main changes included greater intensity of productive land use, a reduction in the area of fallow land and wasteland, the introduction of crop rotation, the development of artificially bred grasses, and scientific animal breeding.

agriculture /ˈaɡrɪkʌltʃə(r)/ *noun* the cultivation of the land in order to grow crops or raise animal livestock as a source of food or other useful products, eg wool, cotton. [from Latin *ager*, field + *cultura*, cultivation]

⊟ farming, husbandry, cultivation, agronomy, culture, tillage.

agrimony /ˈaɡrɪmənɪ/ *noun* an erect perennial plant (*Agrimonia eupatoria*), native to Europe, W Asia, and N Africa. It has hairy leaves with pairs of small leaflets alternating with large ones, and small yellow flowers borne in long terminal spikes. [from Greek *argemone*, a long prickly-headed poppy]

agro- *combining form* agricultural: *agrochemical*. [from Latin *ager*, field]

agrochemical or **agrichemical** — *noun Agric.* any chemical compound that is used to improve the quality of farm products, eg inorganic fertilizers, insecticides, and herbicides. — *adj.* relating to the use of such chemical compounds.

agro-industry *noun* an industry embracing all aspects of agricultural production and distribution, including the supply of equipment and chemicals, finance, marketing, processing, and transportation of commodities.

agronomy /əˈɡrɒnəmɪ/ *noun Agric.* the scientific study of the cultivation of field crops and soil management. It includes plant breeding and other methods of improving crop production, and soil conservation. [from AGRO- + Greek *nomos*, law]

aground *adj. adv.*, *said of ships* stuck on the bottom of the sea or rocks, usually in shallow water.

ague /ˈeɪɡjuː/ *noun* **1** *old use* a burning fever. **2** malaria. **3** a fit of shivering. [from Old French *fièvre ague*, acute fever]

AH *abbrev. anno Hegirae* (Latin), in the year of the Hegira.

ah *interj.* used to express surprise, sympathy, admiration, pleasure, etc, according to the intonation of the speaker's voice.

aha *interj.* used to express pleasure, satisfaction, triumph or surprise, according to the intonation of the speaker's voice.

ahead *adv.* **1** at or in the front; forward. **2** earlier in time; before. **3** in the lead; further advanced: *ahead on points*. — **ahead of someone** or **something** in advance of them. **get ahead** to make progress, especially socially.

⊟ **1** forward, onward, at the head, in front. **2** in advance, before, earlier on. **3** in the lead, winning, at an advantage, superior, to the fore, in the forefront.
⊠ BEHIND.

ahem /əˈhɛm/ *interj.* a sound made in the back of the throat, used to gain people's attention or express doubt or disapproval.

-aholic or **-oholic** *colloq.* an element forming words meaning 'addicted to': *workaholic*. [modelled on ALCOHOLIC]

ahoy *interj. Naut.* a shout to greet or attract the attention of another ship. [from AH + HOY]

AI *abbrev.* **1** artificial insemination. **2** artificial intelligence.

AID *abbrev.* artificial insemination by donor.

aid — *noun* **1** help. **2** help or support in the form of money, supplies or services given to people who need it. **3** a person or thing that helps do something: *a hearing aid*. — *verb* **1** to help or support (someone). **2** to help (something) happen; to promote. — **aid and abet** *Legal* to help and encourage (someone) to do something wrong, especially disobey the law. **in aid of someone** or **something** in support of them. **what's this in aid of?** *colloq.* what is the reason for, or purpose of, this? [from Old French *aidier*]

⊟ *noun* **1** help, assistance, service, prop, support. **2** relief, benefit, subsidy, donation, contribution, funding, grant, sponsorship, patronage. *verb* **1** help, assist, succour, rally

round, relieve, support, subsidize, sustain, second, favour. **2** promote, boost, encourage, expedite, facilitate, ease.
⊠ *noun* **1** hindrance, impediment, obstruction. *verb* HINDER, IMPEDE, OBSTRUCT.

aide /eɪd/ *noun* an assistant or adviser, especially to the head of a government. [from French *aide*]

aide-de-camp /ˈeɪd də ˈkɒŋ/ *noun* (PL. **aides-de-camp**) an officer in the armed forces who acts as assistant to a senior officer.

aide-mémoire /ˈeɪd mɛmˈwɑː/ *noun* (PL. **aides-mémoire**) something that helps one to remember something, especially a note listing the main points mentioned in a paper, speech, etc. [from French *aide-mémoire*, help-memory]

AIDS or **Aids** *noun* acquired immunodeficiency syndrome: caused by infection with the human immunodeficiency virus (HIV).

AIDS-related complex a condition related to AIDS and characterized by infection with the HIV virus. It is less severe than AIDS, although it sometimes develops into AIDS. The main symptoms are swollen lymph nodes, fever, weight loss, and diarrhoea.

AIF *abbrev.* Australian Imperial Force.

aikido /aɪˈkiːdəʊ/ *noun* a Japanese form of self-defence, based on a system of locks and holds and the movements of the attacker or opponent. [from Japanese *ai*, to harmonise + *ki*, breath + *do*, way]

ail *verb* **1** *intrans.* to be ill and weak. **2** *trans. old use* to cause pain or trouble to. [from Anglo-Saxon *eglan*, to trouble]

aileron /ˈeɪlərɒn/ *noun* one of a pair of hinged flaps situated at the rear edge of each wing of an aircraft. Ailerons can be moved differentially on either side of the aircraft in order to control roll about its longitudinal axis. [a French diminutive of *aile*, wing]

ailing *adj.* unwell; in poor health.

⊟ unwell, ill, sick, poorly, indisposed, *colloq.* out of sorts, *colloq.* under the weather, off-colour, suffering, sickly, invalid, infirm, unsound, frail, weak, feeble, failing.
⊠ healthy, thriving, flourishing.

ailment *noun* an illness, especially a minor one.

⊟ illness, sickness, complaint, malady, disease, infection, disorder, affliction, infirmity, disability, weakness.

aim — *verb* **1** *trans., intrans.* (**aim at** or **for something**) to point or direct a weapon, attack, remark, etc at someone or something. **2** *intrans.* to plan, intend, or try. — *noun* **1** what a person, etc intends to do; the achievement aimed at. **2** the ability to hit what is aimed at: *good aim*. — **take aim** to point a weapon at a target so as to be ready to fire. [from Old French *esmer*, from Latin *aestimare*, to estimate]

⊟ *verb* **1** point at, direct at, take aim at, level on, train on, *colloq.* zero in on, target. **2** plan, intend, propose, mean, resolve, purpose, aspire, want, wish, seek, strive, try, attempt, endeavour. *noun* **1** plan, design, scheme, purpose, motive, end, intention, object, objective, target, mark, goal, aspiration, ambition, hope, dream, desire, wish.

aimless *adj.* without any purpose.

⊟ pointless, purposeless, unmotivated, directionless, rambling, undirected, unguided, chance, random, haphazard, erratic.
⊠ purposeful, positive.

ain't *contr. colloq.* **1** am not; is not; are not. **2** has not; have not.

air — *noun* 1 the invisible odourless tasteless mixture of gases that forms the atmosphere surrounding the Earth. 2 the space above and around the earth, where birds and aircraft fly. 3 an appearance, look, or manner. 4 (**airs**) behaviour intended to impress others, to show off, etc: *put on airs/airs and graces*. 5 a tune. 6 a breeze. — *verb* 1 *trans., intrans.* **a** to hang (laundry) in a warm dry place to make it completely dry or to remove unpleasant smells. **b** *said of laundry* to be hung in a warm dry place for this purpose. 2 *trans., intrans.* **a** to let fresh air into (a room, etc). **b** *said of a room, etc* to become cooler or fresher in this way. 3 to make warm (the sheets and blankets of a bed, especially one that has not been used recently). 4 to make (one's thoughts, opinions, etc) known publicly. 5 *old use* to make a show or of parade. 6 *trans., intrans. North Amer., esp. US* to broadcast or be broadcast on radio or television. — **by air** in an aircraft. **a change of air** a beneficial change from one's usual routine. **clear the air** to remove or reduce misunderstanding or disagreement by speaking openly and honestly. **in the air** 1 *said of projects, etc* uncertain or undecided. 2 *said of opinions, news, etc* being generally considered, thought, or talked about. **into thin air** mysteriously and leaving no trace. **off the air** no longer or not yet broadcasting on radio or television. **on the air** broadcasting on radio or television. **take the air** *old use* to go for a walk. **walk on air** to be elated. [from Old French, from Greek *aer*]

. . . .

▤ *noun* 1 atmosphere. 2 sky, heavens. 3 appearance, look, aspect, aura, bearing, demeanour, manner, effect, impression. 6 breeze, wind, draught, blast, breath, puff, waft. *verb* 2 ventilate, aerate, freshen. 4 utter, voice, express, give vent to, make known, communicate, tell, declare, reveal, disclose, divulge, make public, publicize, broadcast, publish, disseminate. 5 exhibit, display, parade.

. . . .

airbag *noun* a safety device installed in some motor vehicles, consisting of a bag which inflates automatically if the vehicle is involved in a collision, preventing the driver and front-seat passenger from coming into immediate contact with the steering-wheel and dashboard.

air base a centre from which military aircraft operate.

air bed an inflated mattress.

airborne *adj.* 1 *said of aircraft* flying in the air, having just taken off. 2 transported by air.

Airborne Warning and Control System (ABBREV. **AWACS**) a radar system mounted on an aircraft and able to detect and track hostile intruders at long range, and direct friendly fighters to intercept them.

air brake a mechanism in which the pressure of compressed air acting on a piston is used to stop or slow down a moving part. Air brakes are commonly used on lorries and railway rolling stock.

air brick a brick with small holes, put into the side of a building to allow ventilation.

airbrush — *noun* an instrument for painting which uses compressed air to form a spray. — *verb* 1 to paint using an air brush. 2 to cover up the undesirable aspects of something.

air chief marshal *Brit.* an air force officer equal in rank to a general and admiral.

air commodore *Brit.* a senior officer in the air force.

air-conditioned *adj., said of a building, etc* equipped with air-conditioning.

air-conditioner *noun* an apparatus for providing air-conditioning.

air conditioning *noun* 1 any system that is used to control the temperature, relative humidity, or purity of air, and to circulate it mechanically, in an enclosed space such as a room, building, or motor vehicle. 2 the control of room temperature, etc, using such a system.

air cover the use of aircraft to protect against enemy attack.

aircraft *noun* (PL. **aircraft**) any structure, machine, or vehicle, such as an aeroplane or helicopter, that is designed for travelling through air, and is supported either by its own buoyancy or by the action of air on its surfaces.

Types of aircraft include: aeroplane, plane, jet, jumbo, Concorde, airbus, helicopter, monoplane, two-seater, air ambulance, freighter, seaplane, glider, hang-glider, microlight, hot air balloon; fighter, spitfire, bomber, *colloq.* kite, jump jet, dive-bomber, *slang* chopper, spy plane, delta-wing, swing-wing, troop-carrier, airship, turbojet, VTOL (vertical take-off and landing), warplane, zeppelin.

aircraft carrier a large naval warship with a flat deck, serving as a base for military aircraft.

aircraftman or **aircraftwoman** *noun Brit.* a man or woman of the lowest rank in the air force.

aircrew *noun* the people in an aircraft who are responsible for flying it and looking after the passengers.

air cushion 1 a cushion that can be filled with air. 2 a pocket of air used for supporting a hovercraft, etc.

air-drop — *noun* a delivery of military equipment, troops, supplies, etc by air. — *verb* to deliver by aircraft.

airfield *noun* an open expanse that is used by aircraft for landing and take-off.

air force that part of a country's defence forces which uses aircraft for fighting.

airgun *noun* a gun that uses air under pressure to fire small pellets.

airhead *noun slang* a stupid or dull person.

air hostess *Brit.* a woman member of an airliner's crew, responsible for the comfort of passengers.

airily *adv.* in an airy manner; jauntily.

airiness *noun* an airy or jaunty manner or state.

airing *noun* 1 the act of airing (laundry, a room, the sheets, etc on a bed, etc) or fact of being aired. 2 the stating and discussing of opinions, etc publicly. 3 a short walk, etc taken in order to get some fresh air.

airing cupboard a heated cupboard in which laundry is put to become completely dry and warm.

air lane a route through the air regularly used by aircraft.

airless *adj.* 1 *said of the weather* unpleasantly warm, with no wind. 2 *said of a room* lacking fresh air; stuffy.

. . . .

▤ 1 suffocating, stifling, sultry, muggy, close, heavy, oppressive. 2 unventilated, stuffy, musty, stale.

▤ 1 fresh. 2 airy.

. . . .

air letter same as AEROGRAMME.

airlift — *noun* the transporting of large numbers of people or large amounts of goods in aircraft when other routes are blocked. — *verb* to transport in this way.

airline *noun* a company or organization which provides a regular transport service for passengers or cargo by aircraft.

airliner *noun* a large passenger aeroplane.

airlock *noun* 1 a bubble of air or gas that obstructs or blocks the flow of liquid through a pipe. 2 an airtight chamber with controllable air pressure and two entrances, which enables a person to move between two areas on either side of it with different air pressures (eg between a space vehicle and outer space) without air escaping, or between air and water (eg between a submarine and the sea) without water entering.

airmail *noun* 1 the system of carrying mail by air. 2 mail carried by air.

airman or **airwoman** *noun* a pilot or member of the crew of an aeroplane, especially in an air force.

air mile (*usually* **air miles**) a point gained by a purchaser of air tickets or other products, which are accumulated and exchanged for free air travel to a certain distance.

air miss a situation in which two aircraft on different routes come dangerously close together.

airplane *noun North Amer.* an aeroplane.

air plant *Bot.* a plant that grows on another plant and uses it for support, but is not a parasite. Also called EPIPHYTE.

air pocket an area of reduced pressure in the air or a downward current which can cause an aircraft to suddenly lose height.

air pollution *Environ.* the presence of gases, smoke, dust, fumes, and other contaminants in the atmosphere at levels considered to be detrimental to living organisms.

airport *noun* a place where civil aircraft arrive and depart, with facilities for passengers and cargo, etc.

air pressure the pressure exerted by the air as a result of the movements of air molecules.

air pump an instrument for pumping air out or in.

air raid an attack by aircraft.

air resistance *Aeron.* the drag experienced by a body passing through air.

air rifle a rifle that is fired by air under pressure.

air sac *Zool.* 1 in birds, any of nine thin-walled extensions of the lung, which increase the efficiency of breathing. 2 in insects, an extension of the trachea (one of various tubes through which air moves into the body tissues).

air-sea rescue the use of both aircraft and boats to rescue people from the sea.

airship *noun* a power-driven steerable aircraft, developed from the air balloon, that is lighter than air, and consists of a streamlined envelope or hull containing helium gas, which provides buoyancy, with engines and gondolas (cabins) suspended from it. Formerly used for military purposes, airships are now used mainly for aerial photography and advertising. Also called DIRIGIBLE.

airsick *adj.* sick due to the motion of an aircraft.

airsickness *noun* nausea affecting travellers by air.

airspace *noun* the part of the sky directly above a country, considered as part of the country.

airstrip *noun* a strip of ground where aircraft can land and take off but which has no facilities.

air terminal an office or other place in a town from where passengers are taken, usually by bus, to an airport nearby.

airtight *adj.* 1 *said of a container, etc* which air cannot get into, out of, or through. 2 *said of an opinion, argument, etc* having no weak points.

airtime *noun* the length of time given to a particular item or programme on television or radio.

air-to-air *adj., said of a weapon* fired from one aircraft to another in flight.

air traffic control a system or organization which manages the passage of aircraft and sends instructions to aircraft by radio communication.

air vice-marshal a senior rank in the air force.

airwaves *pl. noun* 1 an informal term for the radio waves used for radio and television broadcasting. 2 the particular frequencies used for such broadcasting.

airway *noun* 1 a route regularly followed by aircraft. 2 (**airways**) an airline.

airwoman see AIRMAN.

airworthiness *noun* the condition of being airworthy.

airworthy *adj., said of aircraft* in a condition to fly safely.

airy *adj.* (**airier, airiest**) 1 with plenty of fresh, cool air. 2 not thinking about or dealing with something as seriously as one should; flippant. 3 lively; light-hearted.

■ 1 well-ventilated, open, roomy, spacious, draughty, breezy, windy. 2 flippant, casual, nonchalant, offhand. 3 lively, high-spirited, cheerful, happy, light-hearted.
■ 1 airless, stuffy, close, heavy, oppressive.

airy-fairy *adj. colloq.* showing or suggesting a lack of sense or good planning; not based on facts or on awareness of real situations.

aisle /aɪl/ *noun* 1 a passage between rows of seats, eg in a church or theatre. 2 the side part of the inside of a church.

[from Latin *ala*, wing; spelling influenced by ISLE]

■ gangway, corridor, passage, passageway.

aitch /eɪtʃ/ *noun* the letter H or h. — **drop one's aitches** to fail to pronounce the sound of the letter *h* when it comes at the beginning of words. [from Old French *ache*]

aitchbone *noun* 1 the rump bone in cattle. 2 a cut of beef from this. [from Old French *nache*, from Latin *natis*, buttocks]

ajar *adj., adv.* partly open. [from Anglo-Saxon *on*, on + *cierr*, turn]

AK *abbrev.* Alaska.

AK-47 a type of Kalashnikov submachine gun.

AKA or **aka** *abbrev.* also known as.

akimbo /əˈkɪmboʊ/ *adj., adv.* with hand on hip and elbow bent outward. [from Middle English *in kenebowe*, in a sharp bend]

akin *adj.* 1 similar; of the same kind. 2 related by blood. [from A-² + KIN]

AL *abbrev.* 1 Alabama. 2 *as an international vehicle mark* Albania.

Al *symbol Chem.* aluminium.

-al *suffix* 1 forming adjectives from nouns: *parental.* 2 forming nouns denoting an action or occurrence: *arrival.*

Ala. *abbrev.* Alabama.

alabaster /ˈaləbɑːstə(r)/ — *noun* a type of white stone used for ornaments, etc. — *adj.* of or like alabaster. [from Old French *alabastre*]

à la carte /a la ˈkɑːt/ *said of a meal in a restaurant* with each dish priced and ordered separately. [French, = from the menu]

alacrity /əˈlakrɪtɪ/ *noun* quick and cheerful enthusiasm. [from Latin *alacritas*]

à la mode /a la ˈmɒd/ in fashion; according to current fashion. [French, = in fashion]

alanine /ˈaləniːn/ *noun Biochem.* an amino acid that is found in proteins. [from German *Alanin*]

alarm — *noun* 1 sudden fear produced by awareness of danger. 2 a noise warning of danger. 3 a bell, etc which sounds to warn of danger or, eg on a clock, to waken a person from sleep. 4 an alarm clock. — *verb* 1 to frighten. 2 to warn of danger. 3 to fit an alarm on (a house, car, etc). — **give** or **raise** or **sound the alarm** to give warning of danger by shouting, ringing a bell, etc. [from Old French *alarme*, from Italian *all'arme*, to arms]

■ *noun* 1 fright, fear, terror, panic, horror, shock, consternation, dismay, distress, anxiety, nervousness, apprehension, trepidation, uneasiness. 2 danger signal, alert, warning, distress signal, siren, bell. *verb* 1 frighten, scare, startle, *colloq.* put the wind up, terrify, panic, unnerve, daunt, dismay, distress, agitate.
■ *noun* 1 calmness, composure. *verb* 1 reassure, calm, soothe.

alarm clock a clock that can be set to make a noise at a particular time to wake someone up.

alarming *adj.* causing alarm or concern; disturbing or frightening.

■ frightening, startling, terrifying, unnerving, daunting, ominous, threatening, disturbing, distressing, shocking, dreadful.
■ reassuring.

alarmism *noun* the spreading of unnecessary alarm.

alarmist — *noun* a person who feels or spreads unnecessary alarm. — *adj.* causing unnecessary alarm.

Alas. *abbrev.* Alaska.

alas *interj. old use, literary* used to express grief or misfortune. [from Old French *ha*, ah + *las*, wretched, from Latin *lassus* weary]

alb /alb/ noun a long white garment reaching to the feet, worn by some Christian priests. [from Latin albus, white]

Albanian /al'beɪnɪən/ — noun 1 a person born in, or a citizen of, Albania. 2 the language spoken in Albania. — adj. of Albania, its inhabitants, or its language.

albatross /'albətrɒs/ noun a large seabird of the genus Diomedea with remarkable powers of flight. It is found mainly in the oceans of the southern hemisphere, and has a powerful hooked beak and long narrow wings with a span of up to 3m. [from Portugese alcatraz, pelican]

albeit /ɔːl'biːɪt/ conj. even if; although. [from Middle English al be it, although it be]

Albigenses or **Albigensians** the followers of a form of Christianity especially strong in the 11c and 12c in the town of Albi, SW France.

albinism /'albɪnɪzm/ noun the inherited lack of pigmentation in a living organism, eg the congenital absence of pigment from the skin, hair, and eyes of a human being.

albino /al'biːnoʊ/ noun (PL. **albinos**) in an animal or human being, an abnormal lack of pigmentation in the hair, skin, and eyes; in a plant, a total or partial lack of chlorophyll or other pigments. [from Portuguese, from Latin albus, white]

album /'albəm/ noun 1 a book with blank pages for holding photographs, stamps, etc. 2 a long-playing record. [from Latin album, blank tablet, from albus, white]

albumen /'albjʊmən, al'bjuːmən/ noun the white of an egg, the nutritive material surrounding the yolk in the eggs of birds and some reptiles. It consists mainly of the protein albumin. [from Latin albumen, white of egg, from albus, white]

albumin /al'bjuːmɪn, 'albjʊmɪn/ noun Biochem. any of various water-soluble globular proteins that coagulate when heated, found in egg white, milk, blood serum, and many other plant and animal tissues.

albuminuria /albjʊmɪ'njʊərɪə/ noun Medicine the presence of albumin (a soluble protein) in the urine, sometimes but not always associated with kidney or heart disease. [from Latin albumen, from albus white]

alchemist /'alkəmɪst/ noun a person who practises or studies alchemy.

alchemy /'alkəmɪ/ noun the forerunner of modern chemistry, which centred around attempts to convert ordinary metals such as lead into gold, and to discover a universal remedy for illness, known as the elixir of life. [from Latin alchymia, from Arabic al, the + kimiya, from Greek kemeia, transmutation]

alcohol /'alkəhɒl/ noun 1 any of a large group of organic chemical compounds that contain one or more hydroxyl ($-OH$) groups and react with acids to form esters, eg ethanol (C_2H_5OH), methanol (CH_3OH). Alcohols are used as solvents for dyes, resins, varnishes, perfume oils, etc, and as fuels and antiseptic medical products, eg surgical spirit. 2 ethanol (C_2H_5OH), a colourless volatile flammable liquid that is produced by fermentation of the sugar in fruit or cereals, and is used as an intoxicant in alcoholic beverages. 3 any beverage containing this substance, eg wine, beer, spirits. [from Arabic al, the + kohl, kohl]

▣ **3** drink, slang booze, liquor, spirits, slang hard stuff, intoxicant.

alcohol abuse excessive drinking of alcoholic liquor, to the point where it becomes harmful.

alcoholic /alkə'hɒlɪk/ — adj. 1 relating to, containing, or having the properties of alcohol. 2 relating to alcoholism. — noun a person who is suffering from alcoholism.

▣ adj. 1 intoxicating, brewed, fermented, distilled, strong, hard. noun drunk, drunkard, inebriate, hard drinker, dipsomaniac, slang wino, slang alkie.

Alcoholics Anonymous a self-help group for alcoholics trying to stop drinking.

alcoholism /'alkəhɒlɪzəm/ noun 1 a severe and potentially fatal condition caused by physical dependence on alcohol, habitual consumption of which occurs to such an extent that it interferes with normal everyday activities and impairs physical and mental health. 2 used loosely to refer to heavy drinking habits.

alcopop noun colloq. a drink containing alcohol but packaged and tasting like a soft drink. [from ALCOHOL and POP¹ 2]

alcove /'alkoʊv/ noun a recess in the wall of a room or garden. [from Spanish alcoba, from Arabic al, the + qubbah, vault]

▣ niche, nook, recess, bay, corner, cubbyhole, compartment, cubicle, booth, carrel.

aldehyde /'aldəhaɪd/ noun Chem. any member of a class of organic chemical compounds that are formed by the oxidation of alcohols and contain the $-CHO$ group, eg formaldehyde (methanal), acetaldehyde (ethanal). See also ACETALDEHYDE, FORMALDEHYDE. [a shortening of Latin alcohol dehydrogenatum, alcohol derived from hydrogen]

al dente /al 'dente/ adj., said of pasta and vegetables cooked so as to remain firm when bitten. [from Italian al dente, to the tooth]

alder /'ɔːldə(r)/ noun 1 any of various deciduous trees and shrubs of the genus Alnus, usually found growing by water or on wet soils in northern temperate regions, and having male and female flowers borne on separate plants. 2 the timber of this tree, which is resistant to underwater rot and is used to make bridges and piles. [from Anglo-Saxon alor]

alderman /'ɔːldəmən/ noun 1 in England and Wales until 1974 a member of a town, county or borough council elected by fellow councillors, below the rank of mayor. 2 in the US and Canada a member of the governing body of a city. [from Anglo-Saxon ealdormann, nobleman of the highest rank]

aldosterone /al'dɒsteroʊn/ noun Physiol. a steroid hormone that is secreted into the bloodstream by the adrenal cortex of the adrenal glands. It stimulates the reabsorption of sodium ions and the excretion of potassium ions by the kidneys, in order to help maintain the balance of salts and water in the body.

ale noun 1 a light-coloured beer, higher in alcohol content than lager and with a fuller body, flavoured with hops. 2 beer. [from Anglo-Saxon ealu]

aleatory /'eɪlɪətərɪ, eɪlɪ'eɪtərɪ/ adj. depending on chance. [from Latin aleator, dice-player]

aleatory music music in which the choice of notes in the composition or performance is determined to a greater or lesser extent by chance or whim. [from Latin aleatorius, from aleator, a dicer, from alea, a die]

alehouse noun old use an inn or public house.

alert — adj. 1 watchful; paying attention. 2 thinking and acting quickly. 3 (alert to something) aware of a danger, etc. — noun 1 a warning of danger. 2 the period of time covered by such a warning. — verb (alert someone to something) to warn them of a danger; to make them aware of a fact or circumstance. — on the alert watchful. [from French alerte, from Italian all 'erta, to the watchtower]

▣ adj. 1 attentive, wide-awake, watchful, vigilant, on the lookout, sharp-eyed, observant, perceptive. 2 sharp-witted, colloq. on the ball, active, lively, spirited, quick, brisk, agile, nimble. 3 ready for, prepared for, aware of, heedful of, wary of. verb warn of, forewarn of, notify of, inform of, tip off about.

◪ adj. 2 slow, listless. 3 unprepared for, unaware of.

Aleut /'aljʊt/ — noun (PL. **Aleut**, **Aleuts**) 1 a member of a people, related to the Inuit, inhabiting the Aleutian Islands and part of Alaska. 2 the language of this people.

— *adj.* (*also* **Aleutian** /al'juːʃən/) relating to this people or their language. [from Russian]

A-level or **Advanced-level** in England, Wales, and Northern Ireland, an examination taken by school and college students which qualifies them for entrance to higher education and the professions. It is a single-subject examination at a level representing two further years of study beyond the GCSE.

Alexander technique *Medicine* a system of exercises, etc, designed to improve posture and breathing habits, and by reducing muscular tension and promoting relaxation to bring about a general improvement in health. [named after the Australian therapist F M Alexander]

alexandrine /alag'zaːndraɪn/ — *noun* a verse of six iambic feet (in English) or twelve syllables (in French). — *adj.*, *said of verse* written in alexandrines. [from French *Alexandre*; Alexander the Great was the subject of an Old French romance written in this metre]

alexia /a'lɛksɪə/ *noun Psychol.* loss of the ability to read, caused by brain disease. [from A-¹ + Greek *legein*, to speak, confused with Latin *legere*, to read]

ALF *abbrev.* Animal Liberation Front.

alfalfa /al'falfə/ *noun* **1** a perennial plant (*Medicago sativa*) of the pea family (Leguminosae) with purple flowers, small divided leaves, and spirally twisted pods. **2** the young leaves of this plant used as a salad vegetable. [from Spanish, from Arabic *al-fasfasah*]

alfresco /al'freskəʊ/ *adj., adv.* in the open air. [from Italian *al fresco* in the fresh air]

alga /'algə/ *noun* (PL. **algae**) (*usually* **algae**) *Bot.* any of a large and very diverse group of mainly aquatic organisms, ranging from single-celled members of the plant plankton, eg diatoms, to large multicellular algae, including nearly all brown, green, and red seaweeds. [from Latin *alga*, seaweed]

algebra /'aldʒəbrə/ *noun* the branch of mathematics that uses letters and symbols to represent variable quantities and numbers, and to express generalizations about them. [from Italian and Spanish, from Arabic *al-jebr*, from *al*, the or *jebr*, reunion of broken parts]

algebraic /aldʒə'breɪɪk/ *adj.* relating to or occurring in algebra.

algebraically *adv.* by the use of algebra.

-algia *combining form* pain in the part of the body stated: *neuralgia*. [from Greek *algos*, pain]

alginate /'aldʒɪneɪt/ *noun Biochem.* a salt of alginic acid, found in seaweeds and forming viscous solutions which hold large amounts of water. Alginates are used in food manufacturing as thickening agents. [from Latin *alga*, seaweed]

ALGOL /'algɒl/ *noun Comput.* an acronym for the first high-level computer programming language to be used as much for scientific problem solving as for manipulating mathematical data. It is no longer widely used, but many subsequent computer languages have been influenced by it. [from *algorithmic language*]

Algonkian or **Algonquian** /al'gɒŋkɪən/ — *adj.* denoting a family of over 30 Amerindian languages used in central and E Canada and parts of the USA. — *noun* the languages forming this family.

Algonkin or **Algonquin** any of the scattered small groups of Native Americans speaking Algonkian languages, living in forest regions around the Ottawa River in Canada.

algorithm /'algərɪðəm/ *noun* **1** any procedure involving a series of steps that is used to find the solution to a specific problem, eg to solve a mathematical equation. **2** *Comput.* the sequence of operations, often represented visually by means of a flow chart, that are to be performed by and form the basis of a computer program. [from Latin *algorismus*, from *Al-Khwarizmi*, 9c Arab mathematician]

algorithmic /algə'rɪðmɪk/ *adj.* relating to algorithms; involving the use of an algorithm.

alias /'eɪlɪəs/ — *noun* a false or assumed name. — *adv.* also known as: *John Smith, alias Mr X*. [from Latin *alias*, at another time, otherwise]

☐ *noun* pseudonym, false name, assumed name, nom de plume, pen name, stage name, nickname, sobriquet. *adv.* also known as, also called, otherwise, formerly.

alibi /'alɪbaɪ/ *noun* **1** a plea of being somewhere else when a crime was committed. **2** *colloq.* an excuse. [from Latin *alibi*, elsewhere]

☐ **1** defence, justification, story, explanation. **2** excuse, pretext, reason.

alien /'eɪlɪən/ — *noun* **1** a foreign-born resident of a country who has not adopted that country's nationality. **2** an inhabitant of another planet, especially in science fiction stories. **3** a plant introduced to an area by people rather than by nature. — *adj.* **1** of or from a different country, planet, etc. **2** (**alien to someone** or **something**) not in keeping with them; unfamiliar to them. [from Latin *alienus*, foreign]

☐ *noun* **1** foreigner, immigrant, newcomer, stranger, outsider. **2** extraterrestrial. *adj.* **1** foreign, exotic, outlandish, extraterrestrial, extraneous, remote. **2** strange to, unfamiliar to, estranged from, opposed to, contrary to, conflicting with, incompatible with, incongruous with.
Ⓕ₃ *noun* **1** native. *adj.* **1** native. **2** akin to.

alienable *adj. Legal, said of property* able to be transferred to another owner.

alienate *verb* **1** to make (someone) feel unfriendly or strange. **2** to make (someone) feel unwelcome or isolated. **3** *Legal* to transfer ownership of (property) to another person.

alienation /eɪlɪə'neɪʃən/ *noun* **1** estrangement. **2** mental or emotional detachment; the state of not being involved. **3** *Legal* the transfer of ownership of property to another person.

alienation effect *Theatr.* a device or series of devices used to create a sense of detachment from the subject-matter of a play and intended to remind the audience of the strangeness of familiar things which hitherto they had taken for granted. These include interruption of the action, deliberate lowering of dramatic tension, and the introduction of placards, strip cartoons, and film. [a translation of German *Verfremdungseffekt*]

alight¹ *adj.* **1** on fire. **2** lighted up; excited: *a face alight with wonder*.

☐ **1** lighted, lit, ignited, on fire, burning, blazing, ablaze, flaming, fiery. **2** lighted up, lit up, illuminated, bright, radiant, shining.
Ⓕ₃ **2** dark.

alight² *verb intrans.* **1** *old use* to get down from or out of a vehicle. **2** (**alight on something**) to settle or land on it. [from Anglo-Saxon *alihtan*]

☐ **1** descend, get down, dismount, get off, disembark, land. **2** land on, settle on, light on, perch on.
Ⓕ₃ **1** ascend, board.

align /ə'laɪn/ *verb* **1** to put in a straight line or bring into line. **2** *trans., intrans.* to bring (someone, a country, etc) into agreement with others, or with a political belief, cause, etc. [from French *à ligne*, into line]

☐ **1** straighten, range, line up, make parallel, even (up), adjust, regulate, order. **2** ally, associate, affiliate, join.

alignment *noun* **1** setting in a line or lines. **2** a row arranged in this way. **3** the taking of a side, or the side taken with others in a debate, dispute, etc.

alike — *adj.* like one another; similar. — *adv.* in a similar manner. [from Anglo-Saxon *gelic*]

■ *adj.* similar, resembling, comparable, akin, analogous, corresponding, equivalent, equal, the same, identical, duplicate, even, uniform. *adv.* similarly, correspondingly, equally, in common.
✏ *adj.* dissimilar, unlike, different.

alimentary /alɪˈmɛntərɪ/ *adj.* **1** relating to digestion. **2** relating to food, diet, or nutrition. [from Latin *alimentarius*, from *alere*, to nourish]

alimentary canal *Anat.* in vertebrate animals, a tubular organ along which food passes, and in which it is digested. It extends from the mouth, where food is ingested (taken in) to the anus, where waste material is eliminated.

alimony /ˈalɪmənɪ/ *noun Legal* money for support paid by a man to his wife or by a woman to her husband, when they are legally separated or divorced. See also MAINTENANCE. [from Latin *alimonia*, nourishment]

aliphatic /alɪˈfatɪk/ *adj. Chem.*, *said of an organic compound* having carbon atoms arranged in chains rather than in rings. See also AROMATIC. [from Greek *aleiphar*, oil]

aliphatic compound *Chem.* any of a major class of organic chemical compounds having carbon atoms arranged in straight or branched chains, rather than in rings. Aliphatic compounds include alkanes, alkenes, and alkynes.

aliquot /ˈalɪkwɒt/ *noun* **1** *Maths.* a number or quantity into which a given number or quantity can be exactly divided without any remainder. **2** *Chem.* a sample of a material or chemical substance that is analysed in order to determine its properties. [Latin, = some, several]

alive *adj.* **1** living; having life; in existence. **2** lively; active. **3** (**alive to something**) aware of it; responsive to it. **4** (**alive with something**) full of it; abounding in it. — **alive and kicking** *colloq.* living and active. [from Anglo-Saxon *on life*, in life]

■ **1** living, having life, live, animate, breathing, existent, in existence, real. **2** lively, animated, spirited, awake, alert, active, energetic, vigorous, vivacious, vital. **3** aware of, heedful of, alert to, sensitive to. **4** full of, crawling with, teeming with, swarming with, abounding in.
✏ **1** dead, extinct. **2** lifeless, apathetic. **3** unaware of, blind to, deaf to.

alkali /ˈalkəlaɪ/ *noun* a hydroxide of any of the alkali metals, eg sodium hydroxide, that dissolves in water to produce a solution with a pH greater than 7, known as a *basic solution*. Alkalis turn red litmus paper blue, and neutralize acids to form salts and water. [from Arabic *al-qaly*, calcinated ashes]

alkali metal *Chem.* any of the metals belonging to group IA of the periodic table of chemical elements, namely lithium, sodium, potassium, rubidium, caesium, and francium.

alkaline /ˈalkəlaɪn, ˈalkəlɪn/ *adj.* **1** relating to or having the properties of an alkali. **2** denoting a solution that has a pH greater than 7, owing to the presence of an excess of hydroxide (OH⁻) ions.

alkaline earth *Chem.* any of the metals belonging to group IIA of the periodic table of chemical elements, namely beryllium, magnesium, calcium, strontium, barium, and radium.

alkalinity /alkəˈlɪnɪtɪ/ *noun* **1** the quality of being alkaline. **2** the extent to which a substance is alkaline.

alkaloid /ˈalkəlɔɪd/ *noun Biochem.* any of a group of nitrogen-containing organic compounds occurring naturally in certain plants, with toxic or medicinal properties, eg caffeine, morphine, nicotine, codeine. More than 1,000 alkaloids have been identified to date.

alkalosis /alkəˈloʊsɪs/ *noun Medicine* a condition in which the blood and other body fluids are abnormally alkaline,

eg as a result of excessive vomiting, or overconsumption of antacids.

alkane /ˈalkeɪn/ *noun Chem.* the general name for any of a series of hydrocarbons having the general formula C_nH_{2n+2}, eg methane (CH_4), ethane (C_2H_6). Alkanes are saturated, ie they contain only single bonds. Also called PARAFFIN.

alkene /ˈalkiːn/ *noun Chem.* the general name for any of a series of hydrocarbons having the general formula C_nH_{2n}, eg ethene (ethylene) (C_2H_4). Alkenes contain one or more double bonds, and are therefore said to be unsaturated. Also called OLEFIN.

alkyl group /ˈalkaɪl/ *Chem.* in an organic chemical compound, the general name for the hydrocarbon group that is formed by the removal of one hydrogen atom from an alkane, eg the methyl group (CH_3), which is derived from methane (CH_4), and the ethyl group (C_2H_5), which is derived from ethane (C_2H_6).

alkyne /ˈalkaɪn/ *noun Chem.* the general name for any of a series of hydrocarbons having the general formula C_nH_{2n-2}, eg ethyne (acetylene) (C_2H_2). Alkynes contain one or more triple bonds, and are therefore said to be unsaturated. Also called ACETYLENE. [*alky*d and ethy*ne*]

all — *adj.* **1** the whole amount, number, or extent of; every. **2** the greatest possible: *run with all speed*. **3** any whatever: *beyond all doubt*. — *noun* **1** every one of the people or things concerned; the whole of (something). **2** one's whole strength, resources, etc: *give one's all*. **3** *in scores in games* on each side. — *adv.* **1** entirely, quite. **2** *colloq.* very: *go all shy*. — **after all** in spite of what has been said, been done or happened. **all along** the whole time. **all and sundry** everyone. **all but ...** very nearly: *he all but drowned*. **all in 1** *colloq.* exhausted. **2** with all expenses included. **all in all** considering everything. **all over 1** finished. **2** everywhere in or on: *all over the world*. **3** *colloq.* exactly what one would expect from someone: *that's her all over*. **all right** see as separate entry. **all there** *colloq.* completely sane; mentally alert. **all told** including everyone or everything. **be all for something** be enthusiastic about it. **for all that** in spite of it. **in all** all together. [from Anglo-Saxon *eall*]

■ *adj.* **1** each, every, each and every, every single, every one of, the whole of, every bit of. **2** full, total, utter, complete, entire, outright, perfect, greatest. *noun* **1** everything, sum, total, aggregate, whole, entirety. **2** utmost. *adv.* **1** completely, entirely, wholly, fully, totally, utterly, quite, altogether.
✏ *noun* **1** nothing, none.

alla breve /ˈalə ˈbreɪvɪ/ *adj.*, *adv. Mus.* played quickly with two beats to the bar instead of four. [from Italian *alla breve*, at the breve, there originally being one breve to the bar]

Allah *Islam* the principal Muslim name for God.

all-American *adj.* typically American in quality, appearance, etc.

allantois /əˈlantoʊɪs/ *noun Anat.* a membranous sac-like appendage for effecting oxygenation in the embryos of mammals, birds, and reptiles. [from Greek *allas, -antos*, sausage + *eidos*, form]

allay *verb* to make (pain, fear, suspicion, etc) less intense. [from Anglo-Saxon *alecgan*]

■ alleviate, relieve, soothe, ease, calm, tranquillize, quell, pacify, mollify, soften, blunt, lessen, reduce, diminish, moderate.
✏ exacerbate, intensify.

all clear a signal or statement that the threat of danger is over.

allegation /alɪˈɡeɪʃən/ *noun* an unsupported claim, statement, or assertion, especially when unfavourable or depreciatory. [from Latin *allegatio*, from *allegare*, to allege]

■ accusation, charge, claim, assertion, affirmation, declaration, statement, testimony.

allege /əˈlɛdʒ/ *verb* to claim or declare to be the case, usually without proof. [from Old French *aleguer*, from Latin *allegare*, to allege, mixed with Old French *alegier*, from Latin *alleviare*, to justify, lighten]

▣ claim, profess, assert, affirm, declare, state, attest, maintain, insist, hold, contend.

alleged /əˈlɛdʒd/ *adj.* presumed or claimed to be so, but not proved.

▣ supposed, reputed, putative, inferred, so-called, professed, declared, stated, claimed, doubtful, dubious, suspect, suspicious.

allegedly /əˈlɛdʒɪdlɪ/ *adv.* seemingly, supposedly.

allegiance /əˈliːdʒəns/ *noun* commitment and duty to obey and be loyal to a government, sovereign, etc. [from Middle English *aliegiaunce*, from Old French *liege*, liege]

▣ loyalty, fidelity, faithfulness, constancy, duty, obligation, commitment, obedience, devotion, support, adherence, friendship.
▣ disloyalty, enmity.

allegorical /aləˈgɒrɪkəl/ *adj.* 1 relating to or in the nature of an allegory. 2 being or containing an allegory.

allegorize /ˈaləgəraɪz/ or **allegorise** *verb* to put in the form of an allegory.

allegory /ˈaləgərɪ/ *noun* (PL. **allegories**) a story, play, poem, picture, etc in which the characters represent moral or spiritual ideas or messages. [from Old French *allegorie*, from Greek *allos*, other + *agoreuein*, to speak]

allegro /əˈlɛɡroʊ/ *Mus.* — *adj.*, *adv.* in a quick, lively manner. — *noun* (PL. **allegros**) a piece of music to be played like this. [from Italian *allegro*]

allele /əˈliːl/ *Genetics* one of the alternative forms of a gene which can occur at a given point on a chromosome. There is usually a pair of alleles for any one gene, one having been received from each parent. [from German *Allel*, a shortening of *allelomorph*, from Greek *allelos*, one another]

alleluia /alɪˈluːjɑː, aleɪˈluːjɑː/ or **hallelujah** *interj.* praise the Lord. [from Greek *allelouia*, from Hebrew *halleluyah*, praise Jehovah]

allemande /ˈaləmand/ *noun* 1 a dance originating in Germany in the 16c and adopted by the French and English; also, the music for it. 2 a quick dance in triple time, popular in Swabia and Switzerland in the late 18c and early 19c. [from French *allemande*, (feminine) German]

all-embracing *adj.* including everything; missing nothing out.

allergen /ˈalədʒən/ *noun Medicine* any foreign substance, usually a protein, that induces an allergic reaction in the body of a person who is hypersensitive to it, eg pollen. See also ALLERGY.

allergic /əˈlɜːdʒɪk/ *adj.* 1 (**allergic to something**) having an allergy caused by abnormal sensitivity to it: *is allergic to shellfish.* 2 relating to or caused by an allergy: *an allergic reaction.*

▣ 1 sensitive to, hypersensitive to, susceptible to, affected by, incompatible with.

allergy /ˈalədʒɪ/ *noun* (PL. **allergies**) 1 a hypersensitive reaction of the body to certain foreign substances, called allergens. These react with antibodies produced within the body by the immune system, resulting in the release of histamine and other substances that cause cell damage, inflammation, and the symptoms of the particular allergy. 2 *colloq.* a dislike. [from Greek *allos*, other + *ergia*, activity]

alleviate /əˈliːvɪeɪt/ *verb* to make (pain, a problem, suffering, etc) less severe. [from Latin *alleviare*, to lighten]

▣ relieve, soothe, ease, palliate, mitigate, soften, cushion, dull, deaden, allay, abate, lessen, reduce, diminish, moderate, temper, subdue.
▣ aggravate.

alleviation *noun* making (pain, a problem, suffering, etc) less severe; relief.

alley /ˈalɪ/ *noun* (PL. **alleys**) 1 (*also* **alleyway**) a narrow passage behind or between buildings. 2 a long narrow channel used for bowling or skittles. 3 a path through a garden or park. [from Old French *alee*, passage, from *aler*, to go]

alliance /əˈlaɪəns/ *noun* 1 the state of being allied; a group of allied countries, organizations, people, etc. 2 an agreement or treaty by which people, countries, etc ally themselves with one another.

▣ 1 confederation, federation, association, affiliation, coalition, league, bloc, cartel, conglomerate, consortium, syndicate, guild, union, partnership, marriage. 2 agreement, treaty, pact, compact, bond.
▣ 1 separation, divorce, estrangement.

allied /ˈalaɪd/ *adj.* 1 joined by political agreement or treaty. 2 (**Allied**) of Britain and its allies in World Wars I and II. 3 similar; related.

alligator /ˈalɪɡeɪtə(r)/ *noun* a large reptile similar to a crocodile but with a broader head and blunter snout. The fourth tooth from the front on each side of the lower jaw is hidden when the mouth is closed, whereas in the crocodile it is visible. There are two species, the American alligator, found in the SE USA, and the rare Chinese alligator, found only in the Yangtze River Basin. [from Spanish *el lagarto*, the lizard]

all-in wrestling a style of wrestling with few rules or restrictions.

alliterate /əˈlɪtəreɪt/ *verb intrans.* to use or show alliteration.

alliteration /əlɪtəˈreɪʃən/ *noun* the repetition of the same sound at the beginning of each word or each stressed word in a phrase, as in *sing a song of sixpence.* [from Latin *allitteratio*, from *ad*, to + *littera*, letter]

alliterative /əˈlɪtərətɪv/ *adj.* in the nature of or using alliteration.

allocate /ˈaləkeɪt/ *verb* to give, set apart, or assign (something) to someone or for some particular purpose. [from Latin *ad*, to + *locus*, place]

▣ assign, designate, budget, allow, earmark, set aside, allot, apportion, share out, distribute, dispense, mete.

allocation *noun* 1 allocating. 2 a share or part allocated.

▣ 1 allotment, apportionment. 2 lot, allotment, measure, share, portion, stint, ration, quota, budget, allowance, grant.

allophone /ˈaləfoʊn/ *noun Linguistics* a phonetic variant of a phoneme. A phoneme may be produced using two (or more) different 'shapes', without altering the basic sound: for example, the English phoneme /t/ is pronounced with the lips spread in the word *tan*, but with the lips rounded in the word *too*. [from Greek *allos*, other + *phone*, sound, voice]

allot /əˈlɒt/ *verb* (**allotted**, **allotting**) to give to (each of a group) a share of or place in (something). [from Old French *aloter*]

▣ share out, apportion, divide, ration, distribute, dispense, mete, dole out, allocate, assign, allow, grant, give.

allotment *noun* **1** a small part of a larger piece of public ground rented to a person to grow vegetables, etc. **2** the act of allotting. **3** a share or portion allotted.

- **2** division, partition, allocation, apportionment. **3** lot, portion, share, percentage, ration, quota, allowance, grant.

allotrope /ˈalətrəʊp/ *noun Chem.* one of the forms of a chemical element that shows allotropy.

allotropic /aləˈtrɒpɪk/ *adj.* **1** relating to allotropy. **2** having the property of allotropy.

allotropy /əˈlɒtrəpɪ/ *noun Chem.* the existence of an element in two or more structural forms (allotropes), often due to differences in crystal structure, eg graphite and diamond (allotropes of carbon), red and white phosphorus. [from Greek *allos*, other + *tropos*, manner]

all-out *adj.* using all one's strength, powers, etc.

- complete, full, total, comprehensive, exhaustive, thorough, intensive, thoroughgoing, wholesale, full-scale, no-holds-barred, vigorous, powerful, maximum, utmost, unlimited, unrestrained.
- perfunctory, half-hearted.

allow /əˈlaʊ/ *verb* **1** to permit (someone to do something, something to happen, etc). **2** *intrans.* (**allow for something**) to take it into consideration when judging or deciding something. **3** to give, provide, or set aside, usually for a specific purpose: *allow £10 for food.* **4** to admit or agree to (a point, claim, etc). **5** to permit (oneself to do something). [from Old French *aloer*]

- **1** permit, let, enable, authorize, sanction, approve, tolerate. **2** take into account, make provision for, make allowances for, provide for, foresee, plan for, bear in mind, keep in mind, consider, include. **3** allot, allocate, assign, apportion, afford, give, provide. **4** admit, confess, own, acknowledge, agree, concede, grant.
- **1** forbid, prevent. **2** discount. **4** deny.

allowable *adj.* able to be admitted or accepted.

allowance *noun* **1** a fixed sum of money, amount of something, etc given regularly. **2** something allowed. — **make allowances for something** to take it into consideration in one's plans. **make allowances for someone** to judge them less severely, or expect less of them, because of particular circumstances applying to them.

- **1** allotment, lot, amount, allocation, portion, share, ration, quota, grant, pocket money, maintenance, stipend, pension, annuity, subsidy, weighting, discount, concession.

allowedly *adv.* as is generally admitted or believed.

alloy /ˈalɔɪ/ — *noun* a material consisting of a mixture of two or more metals, or a metal and a non-metal, eg bronze, brass, steel. — *verb* to add one metal or alloy to another. [from Old French *alei*, from Latin *alligare*, to bind]

- *noun* blend, compound, composite, amalgam, combination, mixture.

all-purpose *adj.* useful for many different purposes.

all right 1 unhurt; safe: *are you all right?* **2** adequate; satisfactory. **3** satisfactorily; properly: *it worked out all right.* **4** *colloq.* used as an intensive, with little real meaning: *it's broken all right.* **5** used to express agreement or approval: *all right, you can go.*

- **1** unhurt, uninjured, unharmed, unimpaired, whole, sound, well, healthy, safe, secure. **2** adequate, satisfactory,

passable, unobjectionable, acceptable, fair, average, *colloq.* OK. **3** adequately, satisfactorily, well enough, properly, passably, acceptably, suitably, appropriately, reasonably, *colloq.* OK.

- **1** hurt, injured. **2** inadequate, unacceptable. **3** unsatisfactorily, unacceptably.

all-round *adj.* **1** having many different skills. **2** including everyone or everything: *an all-round education.*

all-rounder *noun* a person with a lot of different skills.

All Saints' Day a Christian festival commemorating all Church saints collectively. Formerly known as All Hallows' Day, it is held on 1 Nov in the Catholic and Anglican churches (the preceding evening being Hallowe'en), and on the first Sunday after Pentecost in the Eastern Churches.

all-singing all-dancing *colloq.* **1** performing superlatively. **2** having many special features: *an all-singing all-dancing computer.*

All Souls' Day the day (2 Nov) set apart in the Roman Catholic Church as a day of prayer for souls in purgatory; also celebrated by some Anglicans. In the Eastern Orthodox Church, it is celebrated about two months before Easter.

allspice /ˈɔːlspaɪs/ *noun* **1** an aromatic spice prepared from the dried unripe berries of a small tropical evergreen tree, so called because it has an aroma and flavour similar to a mixture of cinnamon, cloves, and nutmeg. It is used to flavour foods, especially meat. **2** the pimento or Jamaican pepper tree (*Pimenta officinalis*), cultivated mainly in Jamaica, that yields this spice.

all-time *adj. colloq.* **1** *said eg of a sporting record* best to date; unsurpassed. **2** of great and permanent importance: *one of the all-time greats of jazz.*

allude /əˈluːd, əˈljuːd/ *verb intrans.* (**allude to something**) to speak of it indirectly or mention it in passing. [from Latin *alludere*]

allure /əˈlʊə(r), əˈljʊə(r)/ — *noun* attractiveness, appeal or charm. — *verb* to attract, charm or fascinate. [from Old French *alurer*, from *a*, to + *lurer*, to lure]

- *noun* appeal, attraction, magnetism, fascination, glamour, attractiveness, charm, enchantment, lure, enticement, seduction, temptation. *verb* attract, lure, entice, seduce, tempt, cajole, win over, disarm, charm, enchant, fascinate, captivate, entrance, beguile.
- *verb* repel.

allurement *noun* **1** the act of alluring. **2** fascination, attraction. **3** someone or something that allures.

alluring *adj.* enticing, seductive, attractive.

allusion /əˈluːʒən, əˈljuːʒən/ *noun* an indirect reference. [from Latin *allusio*, from *alure*, to allure]

- mention, reference, citation, quotation, remark, observation, suggestion, hint, intimation, implication, insinuation.

allusive /əˈluːsɪv, əˈljuːsɪv/ *adj.* referring indirectly.

alluvial /əˈluːvɪəl, əˈljuːvɪəl/ *adj.* relating to or consisting of alluvium.

alluvium /əˈluːvɪəm, əˈljuːvɪəm/ *noun* (PL. **alluvia**) fine particles of silt, clay, mud, and sand that are carried and deposited by rivers. [from Latin *alluvius*, washed up]

ally /ˈalaɪ, əˈlaɪ/ — *noun* (with stress on *al-*) (PL. **allies**) **1** a country or person, etc that has formally agreed to help and support another. **2** (**Allies**) the term generally applied to the nations that fought the 'Axis' powers during World War II. — *verb* (with stress on *-ly*) (*usually* **ally oneself** or **be allied with** or **to someone**) to align oneself politically or militarily with another person or country, especially by a formal agreement. [from Old French *aleier*, from Latin *alligare*, to bind]

◨ *noun* confederate, associate, consort, partner, colleague, co-worker, collaborator, helper, accomplice, accessory, friend. *verb* confederate, affiliate, league, associate, collaborate, join forces, band together, team up, fraternize, side, join, combine, marry, unite, amalgamate.

◪ *noun* antagonist, enemy. *verb* estrange, separate.

alma mater /ˈalmə ˈmɑːtə(r)/ the school, college, or university that one attended, and from which one graduated. [from Latin *alma mater*, bountiful mother]

almanac /ˈɔːlmənak, ˈalmənak/ *noun* a book, published yearly, with a calendar, information about the moon and stars, religious festivals, public holidays, etc. [from Latin *almanach*, from Arabic *al*, = + *manakh*, calendar]

almighty — *adj.* 1 having complete power. 2 *colloq.* very great. 3 (**the Almighty**) God. — *adv. colloq.* extremely. [from Anglo-Saxon *ælmihtig*]

◨ *adj.* 1 omnipotent, all-powerful, supreme, absolute, great, invincible. 2 enormous, severe, intense, overwhelming, overpowering, *colloq.* terrible, *colloq.* awful. *adv.* very.

◪ extremely, *colloq.* terribly, *colloq.* awfully. *adj.* 1 impotent, weak.

almond /ˈɑːmənd/ *noun* 1 a small deciduous tree (*Prunus amygdalus*) of the rose family, native to the Near East, and widely grown in temperate regions for its ornamental pink blossom and oval edible nut. 2 the nut-like kernel of the fruit of this tree. [from Old French *almende*]

almond-eyed *adj.* with long, almond-shaped eyes.

almoner /ˈɑːmənə(r), ˈalmənə(r)/ *noun* 1 *old use* a distributor or giver of alms. 2 *old use* a medical social worker attached to a hospital. [from Old French *aumonier*]

almost *adv.* nearly but not quite. [from Anglo-Saxon *ælmæst*]

◨ nearly, well-nigh, practically, virtually, just about, as good as, all but, not quite, close to, approaching, nearing.

alms /ɑːmz/ *pl. noun Hist.* donations of money, food, etc to the poor. [from Anglo-Saxon *ælmesse*, from Greek *eleemosyne*]

alms-house *noun Hist.* a house for the poor, paid for by charity.

Alnico *noun trademark* an alloy containing iron, nickel, aluminium, cobalt, and copper, used to make permanent magnets.

aloe /ˈaloʊ/ *noun* 1 any of various succulent plants of the genus *Aloe*, native to Africa, and having tall trunk-like stems, long sword-shaped fleshy leaves with spiny edges, and bell-shaped or tubular yellow to red flowers borne on long stalks. 2 (*usually* **aloes**) the dried juice of the leaves of this plant, formerly used as a purgative drug known as bitter aloes. [from Anglo-Saxon *alewe*]

aloe vera /ˈaloʊ ˈvɛrə, ˈvɪərə/ *noun* 1 a species of aloe plant, the leaves of which contain a juice that is said to have healing properties. 2 the juice of the leaves of this plant, used in skin lotions, ointment, etc.

aloft *adv.* 1 in the air; overhead. 2 *Naut.* in a ship's rigging. [from Norse *a lopti*, in the sky]

alone *adj., adv.* without anyone else; by oneself; apart from other people. — **go it alone** *colloq.* to act on one's own and without help. **leave someone** or **something alone** to avoid bothering or interfering with them. [from Middle English *al one*, all one]

◨ apart, by oneself, by itself, on one's own, on its own, unaccompanied, unescorted, unattended, solo, single-handed, unaided.

◪ together.

along — *adv.* 1 in some direction: *saw him walking along*. 2 in company with others: *go along for the ride*. 3 into a more advanced state: *coming along nicely*. — *prep.* beside or over all or part of the length of. — **along with something** or **someone** in addition to them; as well as them. [from Anglo-Saxon *andlang*]

alongside — *prep.* close to the side of. — *adv.* to or at the side.

aloof — *adj.* unfriendly and distant. — *adv.* away; apart; distant: *stand aloof from the group*. [from A³ + Middle English *loof* = LUFF]

◨ *adj.* unfriendly, unsociable, distant, remote, stand-offish, haughty, supercilious, unapproachable, detached, formal, cool, cold, unsympathetic. indifferent, reserved, unforthcoming.

◪ *adj.* sociable, friendly, warm.

alopecia /aləˈpiːʃə/ *noun Medicine* hair loss resulting from failure of the hair follicles to form hairs. It may be hereditary (eg the usual gradual loss of head hair in men), or it may be a result of disease or old age. [from Greek *alopekia*, fox-mange]

aloud *adv.* 1 loud enough to be able to be heard; not silently. 2 in a loud voice; not quietly.

◨ 1 out loud, audibly, intelligibly, clearly, plainly, distinctly. 2 loudly, resoundingly, sonorously, noisily, vociferously.

◪ 1 silently. 2 quietly.

ALP *abbrev.* Australian Labor Party.

alp /alp/ *noun* 1 a high mountain. 2 in Switzerland, pasture land on a mountainside. [from Latin *Alpes*, the Alps, a mountain range running through Switzerland, France, and Italy]

alpaca /alˈpakə/ *noun* 1 a herbivorous hoofed mammal (*Lama pacos*), closely related to the lama, that lives at high altitudes in the mountains of Peru, Bolivia, and Chile, and is reared mainly for its long straight fleece, which yields a fine silky wool. 2 the wool of this animal, or cloth made from it. [from Spanish *alpaca*, from Aymara (a S American Indian language) *allpaqa*]

alpha /ˈalfə/ *noun* 1 the first letter of the Greek alphabet (A, α). 2 a mark indicating the best or top grade. — **alpha and omega** 1 the beginning and the end. 2 the most important part. [from Greek *alpha*]

alphabet /ˈalfəbɛt/ *noun* the set of letters, usually in a fixed order, used in writing and printing a language. [from Greek *alphabetos*, from *alpha* + *beta*, the first two letters of the Greek alphabet]

Alphabets and writing systems include: Byzantine, Chalcidian alphabet, cuneiform, Cyrillic, devanagari, estrangelo, finger-alphabet, futhark, Glagol, Glossic, Greek, Gurmukhi, hieroglyphs, hiragana, ideograph, initial teaching alphabet (i.t.a.), International Phonetic Alphabet (IPA), kana, kanji, katakana, Kufic, linear A, linear B, logograph, nagari, naskhi, ogam, pictograph, romaji, Roman, runic, syllabary.

alphabetical /alfəˈbɛtɪkəl/ or **alphabetic** *adj.* in the form of an alphabet; in the order of the letters of an alphabet.

alphabetically *adv.* in terms of or in relation to the alphabet or alphabetical order: *listed alphabetically*.

alphabetize or **alphabetise** /ˈalfəbɛˈtaɪz/ *verb* to arrange or list alphabetically.

alpha decay *Physics* a form of radioactive decay in which a radioactive nucleus spontaneously emits an alpha particle that is identical to a helium nucleus.

alphanumeric /alfənjuˈmɛrɪk/ or **alphanumerical** *adj.* 1 *Comput.* denoting characters, codes, or data that consist of letters of the alphabet and numerals (digits between 0 and 9), and do not include punctuation marks or special characters. 2 *said of a machine* using letters of the alphabet and numerals. [from ALPHABET + NUMERICAL]

alphanumerically *adv.* in an alphanumeric way; so as to be alphanumeric.

alpha particle a positively charged particle produced by radioactive decay and consisting of two protons and two neutrons bound together, identical to the nucleus of a helium atom. Alpha particles have a low energy content and are stopped by a sheet of paper or a few centimetres of air.

alpha ray *Physics* a stream of alpha particles.

alpha test *Comput.* an initial test of new software by the manufacturer.

alphorn /'alphɔ:n/ or **alpenhorn** /'alpənhɔ:n/ *noun* a long straight or slightly curved horn with an upturned bell, used by Alpine cowherds.

alpine /'alpaɪn/ — *adj.* **1** of alps or high mountains. **2 (Alpine)** of or in the region of the Alps. — *noun* a plant growing in high mountain areas.

already *adv.* **1** before the present time or the time in question: *we've already paid.* **2** so soon or so early: *was already reading at the age of four.* [from Middle English *al redy*, completely ready]

alright a less acceptable spelling of *all right*.

Alsatian /al'seɪʃən/ *noun* **1** a large breed of dog resembling a wolf, and having a thick coat, a long pointed muzzle, and pointed ears, widely used by police and security officers because of its high intelligence and strength, and its aggressive nature. Also called GERMAN SHEPHERD. **2** a person born or living in Alsace, a region in NE France. [from Latin *Alsatia*, Alsace]

also *adv.* in addition; too; besides. [from Anglo-Saxon *ealswa*, all so, wholly]

▣ too, as well, and, plus, additionally, in addition, besides, further, furthermore, moreover.

also-ran *noun* **1** a horse, dog, person, etc not finishing in one of the top three places in a race. **2** an unimportant, undistinguished person.

altar /'ɔ:ltə(r)/ *noun* **1** a special table at the front of a Christian church, near which the priest stands. **2** a table on which sacrifices are made to a god. — **lead a woman to the altar** to marry her. [from Anglo-Saxon *alter*, from Latin *altaria*]

altar boy a young man or boy who assists a priest during a service.

altarpiece *noun* a religious picture or carving placed above and behind an altar, usually a carved or painted screen made up of a single panel, or a series of panels, often elaborately decorated.

alter /'ɔ:ltə(r)/ *verb* (**altered, altering**) **1** to make different. **2** *intrans.* to become different. [from Old French *alterer*, from Latin *alter*, other]

▣ CHANGE, VARY, ADAPT, ADJUST, TURN, CONVERT. **1** modify, transform, reshape, remodel, reform, revise, amend, *colloq.* tweak.

alterable /'ɔ:ltərəbl/ *adj.* capable of being altered.

alteration /ɔ:ltə'reɪʃən/ *noun* **1** altering or being altered. **2** a change made.

▣ CHANGE, VARIATION, MODIFICATION, ADJUSTMENT, TRANSFORMATION, METAMORPHOSIS, REVISION, AMENDMENT. **1** variance, diversification, adaptation, conversion, reshaping, remodelling.

altercation /ɔ:ltə'keɪʃən/ *noun* a heated argument. [from Latin *altercari*, to quarrel]

alter ego /'ɔ:ltər 'i:goʊ/ *noun* (PL. **alter egos**) **1** a person's second or alternative character. **2** a close and trusted friend. [from Latin *alter ego*, other self]

alternate /ɒl'tɜ:nət, 'ɔ:ltəneɪt/ — *adj.* (pronounced -nət) **1** arranged or coming one after the other by turns: *alternate periods of misery and joy.* **2** (*with plural nouns*) every other; one out of two: *alternate Mondays.* — *verb* (pronounced -neɪt) **1** *intrans.* *said of two things* to succeed each other by turns. **2** to cause two things to succeed each other by turns. **3** *intrans.* (**alternate between two things**) to change from one thing to another by turns. [from Latin *alternare*, to do things by turns]

▣ *adj.* **1** alternating, interchanging, reciprocal, rotating. **2** every other, every second. *verb* **1** interchange, reciprocate, rotate, take turns. **2** replace, substitute, intersperse. **3** change between, oscillate between, fluctuate between.

alternate angles *pl. noun Geom.* each of a pair of angles that lie on opposite sides and at opposite ends of a line, known as a *transversal*, that cuts two other lines. If the other two lines are parallel, the alternate angles are equal.

alternately *adv.* in an alternating position or sequence: *houses that were alternately grey and black*.

alternating current (ABBREV. **a.c.**) an electric current that reverses its direction of flow with a constant frequency, and is therefore continuously varying. Almost all electric power is distributed as alternating current. See also DIRECT CURRENT.

alternation /ɔ:ltə'neɪʃən/ *noun* a pattern or sequence of repeated change from one action, state, etc, to another and back again.

alternation of generations *Biol.* the occurrence within the life cycle of certain living organisms (such as ferns, mosses, and coelenterates, eg corals) of a sexually reproducing generation that alternates with an asexually reproducing generation.

alternative /ɔ:l'tɜ:nətɪv/ — *adj.* **1** available as a choice between two or more possibilities. **2** *said of a lifestyle, culture, etc* different from what is usually done, especially in being less conventional or materialistic, and more natural. — *noun* **1** the possibility of choice between two or more things. **2** any one of two or more choices or possibilities. [from Latin *alternare*, to do things by turns]

▣ *adj.* **1** substitute, second, another, other. **2** different, unorthodox, unconventional, fringe. *noun* **1** option, choice, selection. **2** option, choice, selection, preference, recourse, substitute, back-up.

alternative energy *Environ.* energy derived from sources other than nuclear power or the burning of fossil fuels such as coal, oil, and natural gas. The main sources of alternative energy are tidal power, wind power, wave power, hydroelectricity, solar radiation, and geothermal energy.

alternatively *adv.* as an alternative.

alternative medicine the treatment of disease using procedures other than those practised in orthodox medicine.

alternative technology intermediate technology.

alternator /'ɔ:ltəneɪtə(r)/ *noun* an electricity generator that produces alternating current by means of one or more coils rotating in a magnetic field, eg a bicycle dynamo. Large alternators are used in power stations.

although *conj.* in spite of the fact that; apart from the fact that; though. [from Middle English *al thogh*, all though]

altimeter /al'tɪmətə(r), 'ɔ:ltɪmi:tə(r)/ *noun Aeron.* an instrument used in aircraft for measuring height (altitude) above sea or ground level, and usually based on the change in air pressure with height, or the time taken for radio waves to be reflected back to a recording device on the aircraft. [from Latin *altus*, high + -METER]

altitude /'altɪtju:d/ *noun* **1** height, especially above sea level. **2** *Astron.* the angular distance between a celestial body and the horizon. See also AZIMUTH. **3** *Geom.* in a plane or solid figure, eg a triangle or pyramid, the perpendicular distance from an angle or *vertex* to the side opposite the angle (the *base*). [from Latin *altitudo*, from *altus*, high]

. . . .

◨ **1** height, elevation, loftiness, tallness, stature.
◧ **1** depth.

. . . .

alto /ˈɔːltəʊ/ — *noun* (PL. **altos**) **1** the lowest female singing voice. **2** the highest adult male singing voice. **3** a singer with an alto voice. **4** a part or piece of music written for a voice or instrument at this pitch. — *adj.*, *said of a musical instrument, etc* having this pitch. [from Italian *alto*, from Latin *altus*, high]

altocumulus /ˌæltəʊˈkjuːmjʊləs/ *adj. Meteorol.* denoting middle-level clouds of the cumulus family that occur at altitudes of about 2,000m to 7,000m. They are white and/or grey in colour, and usually indicate fine weather. [from Latin *altus*, high + CUMULUS]

altogether *adv.* **1** completely. **2** on the whole. **3** taking everything into consideration. — **in the altogether** *colloq.* naked. [from Middle English *altogeder*, all together]

. . . .

◨ **1** totally, completely, entirely, wholly, fully, utterly, absolutely, quite, perfectly, thoroughly. **2** on the whole, generally, in general. **3** in all, all told, in toto, all in all, as a whole.

. . . .

altostratus /ˌæltəʊˈstreɪtəs/ *adj. Meteorol.* denoting middle-level clouds of the stratus family, similar to stratus clouds but less dense and occurring at higher altitudes, typically about 2,000m to 7,000m. They are greyish in colour with a sheet-like appearance, and give a warning of warm rainy weather associated with the passage of a warm front. [from Latin *altus*, high + STRATUS]

altruism /ˈæltrʊɪzm/ *noun* an unselfish concern for the welfare of others. [from French *altruisme*, from Italian *altrui*, someone else]

altruist *noun* an altruistic person.

altruistic /ˌæltrʊˈɪstɪk/ *adj.* having or involving an unselfish concern for the welfare of others.

. . . .

◨ unselfish, self-sacrificing, disinterested, public-spirited, philanthropic, charitable, humanitarian, benevolent, generous, considerate, humane.
◧ selfish.

. . . .

altruistically *adv.* in an altruistic way.

alum /ˈæləm/ *noun* **1** *Chem.* aluminium potassium sulphate, a white crystalline compound that occurs naturally as the mineral kalinite, used in dyeing and tanning, and as a medical astringent to stop bleeding. **2** any of various double-sulphate salts with a similar composition to this compound. [from Latin *alumen*]

alumina /əˈluːmɪnə, əˈljuːmɪnə/ *Chem.* (FORMULA Al_2O_3) aluminium(III) oxide, a white crystalline compound that is the main ingredient of bauxite (the chief ore of aluminium), and also occurs in the form of the mineral corundum, which is used as an abrasive.

aluminium /ˌæljʊˈmɪnɪəm, əˈljuːmɪnɪəm/ *noun* (SYMBOL **Al**, ATOMIC NUMBER **13**) a silvery-white metal that is strong when alloyed, light, a good electrical conductor, and protected against corrosion by the formation of a thin surface layer of its oxide. Aluminium alloys are used in the construction of aircraft and vehicles, and in door and window frames, household utensils, drink cans, etc. [from ALUM]

aluminosilicate /əˌluːmɪnəʊˈsɪlɪkət/ *Chem.* a chemical compound, consisting mainly of alumina and silica, that is found in many rocks and minerals (eg clays and mica) and is also a constituent of glass and some ceramics.

alumnus /əˈlʌmnəs/ *noun* (PL. **alumni**) a former pupil or student of a school, college or university. [from Latin *alumnus*, pupil]

alveolar /ˈælvɪələ(r)/ *adj.*, *said of a speech sound* produced by putting the tip of the tongue against the ridge behind the upper front teeth, eg *t* and *n*. [from Latin *alveolus*, small cavity]

alveolitis /ˌælvɪəˈlaɪtɪs/ *noun Medicine* inflammation of the alveoli in the lungs.

alveolus /ælˈvɪələs/ *noun* (PL. **alveoli**) **1** *Anat.* each of the millions of thin-walled air sacs in the lungs, in which oxygen from inhaled air is exchanged for carbon dioxide in the blood. **2** a tooth socket in the jaw bone. **3** *Zool.* any small depression in the surface of an organ. [from Latin *alveolus*, a diminutive of *alveus*, a hollow]

always *adv.* **1** at all times. **2** continually. **3** in any case; if necessary: *you can always stay if you want to.* [from Middle English *alwayes*]

. . . .

◨ **1** every time, consistently, invariably, without exception, unfailingly. **2** continually, constantly, regularly, repeatedly, perpetually, unceasingly, eternally, endlessly, evermore, forever, ever.
◧ **1, 2** never.

. . . .

alyssum /ˈælɪsəm, əˈlɪsəm/ *noun* **1** any of various low-growing bushy plants of the genus *Alyssum*, native to the Mediterranean region, but widely cultivated as an ornamental plant, especially in rock gardens. **2** (**sweet alyssum**) a related plant (*Lobularia maritima*) of the mustard family, widely cultivated as an ornamental plant. [from Greek *alysson*]

Alzheimer's disease /ˈæltshaɪməz/ a disease in which degeneration of the brain cells results in gradual loss of memory, confusion, and impairment of other mental functions, eventually leading to total disintegration of the personality.

AM *abbrev.* amplitude modulation.

Am *symbol Chem.* americium.

am see BE.

a.m. or **am** *abbrev.* ante meridiem (Latin), before midday; in the morning.

amalgam /əˈmælɡəm/ *noun* **1** a mixture or blend. **2** *Chem.* an alloy of mercury with one or more other metals, eg silver or tin, which forms a soft paste on mixing, and later hardens, used in dentistry to fill holes in drilled teeth. [from Latin *amalgama*]

amalgamate /əˈmælɡəmeɪt/ *verb* **1** *trans., intrans.* to join together or unite to form a single unit, organization, etc. **2** *intrans. said of metals* to form an alloy with mercury. [from AMALGAM]

. . . .

◨ **1** merge, blend, mingle, alloy, integrate, compound, fuse, synthesize, combine, unite.
◧ **1** separate.

. . . .

amalgamation /əˌmælɡəˈmeɪʃən/ *noun* blending; merging; joining together.

amanuensis /əˌmænjʊˈɛnsɪs/ *noun* (PL. **amanuenses**) a literary assistant or secretary, especially one who writes from dictation or copies from manuscripts. [from Latin *amanuensis*, from *manu*, by hand]

amaranth /ˈæmərænθ/ *noun* **1** any of various plants of the genus *Amaranthus*, native to tropical and temperate regions, that produce spikes of small brightly coloured flowers. **2** a dark red dye obtained from the flowers of this plant, or manufactured artificially, used as a food colouring. **3** *poetic* a fabled flower that never fades, and is regarded as a symbol of immortality. [from Greek *amarantos*, everlasting]

amaryllis /ˌæməˈrɪlɪs/ *noun* **1** any of various plants of the genus *Amaryllis*, especially *A. belladonna* (the belladonna lily), native to S Africa. It is widely grown as an ornamental plant. **2** used loosely to refer to any of various plants of the genus *Hippeastrum*, native to tropical America, hybrids of which are popular house plants. [from the name of a shepherdess in Virgil's *Eclogues*]

amass *verb* to gather or collect (money, possessions, knowledge, etc) in great quantity. [from French *amasser*]

amateur /ˈæmətə(r), æməˈtɜː(r)/ — *noun* **1** a person who takes part in a sport, pastime, etc as a hobby and without being paid for it. **2** a person who is not very skilled in an activity, etc. — *adj.* of amateurs; not professional. [from French *amateur*, from Latin *amator*, lover]

▤ *noun* **1** non-professional, layman, ham, dilettante, dabbler, enthusiast, *colloq.* buff. *adj.* non-professional, lay, unpaid, unqualified, untrained, amateurish, inexpert, unprofessional.
▣ *noun* PROFESSIONAL. *adj.* professional.

amateurish *adj.*, *said of a person or a person's work, etc* characteristic of an amateur; not particularly skilful; inexperienced.

amateurism *noun* attitudes or behaviour associated with amateurs.

amatory /'amətərɪ/ *adj.* of or showing sexual love. [from Latin *amatorius*, loving]

amaze *verb* to surprise greatly; to astonish. [from Anglo-Saxon *amasian*]

▤ surprise, startle, astonish, astound, stun, stupefy, daze, stagger, *colloq.* floor, dumbfound, *colloq.* flabbergast.

amazed *adj.* astonished.

amazedly *adv.* so as to astonish.

amazement *noun* astonishment; incredulity.

▤ surprise, astonishment, incredulity, disbelief, shock, bewilderment, admiration, wonderment, wonder.

amazing *adj.* astonishing; wonderful.

amazingly *adv.* so as to cause amazement or surprise: *an amazingly quiet child / amazingly, he said nothing.*

Amazon /'aməzən/ *noun* **1** *Greek Mythol.* a member of a nation of women warriors from Scythia. **2** (**amazon**) an immensely strong woman, usually one who is good at sport. [from Greek; the Greeks understood it to mean 'lacking a breast', from *mazos*, breast, but it was more probably a foreign word]

Amazonian /amə'zəʊnɪən/ *adj.* **1** relating to or like an Amazon. **2** relating to or in the region of the River Amazon.

ambassador /am'basədə(r)/ *noun* **1** a diplomat of the highest rank appointed by a government to act for or represent it abroad. **2** a representative, messenger, or agent. [from Old French *ambassateur*, from Latin *ambactus*, servant]

▤ **1** diplomat, consul, plenipotentiary, emissary, envoy, legate. **2** representative, agent, deputy, delegate, messenger.

ambassadorial /ambasə'dɔːrɪəl/ *adj.* relating to or having the status of an ambassador.

ambassadorship *noun* the office or function of an ambassador.

ambassadress *noun* **1** a woman ambassador. **2** the wife of an ambassador.

amber — *noun Geol.* a transparent yellow or reddish fossilized resin that was exuded by coniferous trees, and is found in rock strata worldwide. It can be carved and polished, and is used to make jewellery and ornaments. — *adj.* relating to this substance or to its colour. [from Old French *ambre*, from Arabic *anbar*, ambergris]

ambergris /'ambəgriːs/ *noun* a pale grey waxy substance with a strong smell produced in the intestines of sperm whales, found in lumps floating on the water or washed ashore. Until the recent decline in whaling it was widely used in the perfume industry. [from Old French *ambre gris*, grey amber]

ambidextrous /ambɪ'dekstrəs/ *adj.* able to use both hands equally well. [from Latin *ambi*, both + *dexter*, right]

ambience or **ambiance** /'ambɪəns/ *noun* the surroundings or atmosphere of a place. [from Latin *ambiens*, surrounding, from *ambi*, about + *ire*, to go]

ambient *adj.* **1** *said of air, temperature, etc* surrounding. **2** *said of music* intended to be relaxing, and played at a low volume to provide atmosphere. **3** describing processed foods that can be preserved for a long time at room temperature.

ambiguity /ambɪ'gjuːɪtɪ/ *noun* (PL. **ambiguities**) **1** uncertainty of meaning. **2** an ambiguous word or statement.

▤ **1** double meaning, equivocality, equivocation, obscurity, unclearness, vagueness, woolliness, doubt, uncertainty. **2** double entendre, enigma, puzzle.
▣ **1** clarity.

ambiguous /am'bɪgjʊəs/ *adj.* having more than one possible meaning; not clear. [from Latin *ambiguus*, from *ambi*, both ways + *agere*, to drive]

▤ equivocal, multivocal, double-edged, backhanded, cryptic, enigmatic, puzzling, confusing, obscure, unclear, vague, indefinite, woolly, dubious, doubtful, uncertain, inconclusive, indeterminate.
▣ clear, definite.

ambit *noun* range, extent, or bounds. [from Latin *ambitus*, from *ambi*, about + *ire*, to go]

ambition *noun* **1** a strong desire for success, fame, or power. **2** a thing one desires to do or achieve. [from Latin *ambitio*, going round, canvassing, from *ambi*, about + *ire*, to go]

▤ **1** desire, yearning, longing, striving, eagerness, push, thrust, drive, enterprise, commitment, zeal. **2** aspiration, aim, goal, target, objective, purpose, design, object, ideal, dream, hope, wish.
▣ **1** apathy.

ambitious *adj.* **1** having a strong desire for success, etc. **2** requiring hard work and skill.

▤ **1** aspiring, hopeful, desirous, intent, purposeful, pushy, assertive, *colloq.* go-ahead, enterprising, enthusiastic, eager, keen, zealous. **2** formidable, hard, difficult, arduous, strenuous, demanding, challenging, exacting, impressive, grandiose, elaborate.
▣ **1** apathetic. **2** undemanding, modest, uninspiring.

ambivalence /am'bɪvələns/ *noun* the state of holding two opposite views or feelings about a person or subject at the same time. [from Latin *ambi*, both + *valere*, to be worth]

ambivalent *adj.* relating to or involving ambivalence.

▤ contradictory, conflicting, clashing, opposed, inconsistent, mixed, confused, vacillating, wavering, hesitant, irresolute, undecided, unresolved, uncertain, unsure, doubtful.

amble — *verb intrans.* to walk without hurrying; to stroll. — *noun* a leisurely walk. [from Old French *ambler*, from Latin *ambulare*, to walk about]

▤ *verb* walk, saunter, stroll, ramble, wander.
▣ *verb* march.

amblygonite /am'blɪgənaɪt/ *noun Geol.* a mineral that occurs as white or greenish masses in pegmatites in Europe and the USA. It is an important ore of lithium. [from Greek *amblus*, dull + *gonia* angle]

ambrosia /am'brəʊzɪə/ *noun* **1** *Greek Mythol.* the food of the gods, which gave them eternal youth and beauty. **2** something with a delicious taste or smell. [from Greek *ambrosia*, from *ambrotos*, immortal]

ambulance /'ambjʊləns/ *noun* a specially equipped vehicle for carrying sick or injured people to hospital. [from Latin *ambulare*, to walk about]

ambush — *noun* **1** the act of lying in wait to attack someone by surprise. **2** an attack made in this way.

3 the person or people making such an attack. **4** the place of concealment from which the attack is made. — *verb* to lie in wait for or attack (someone) in this way. [from Old French *embuschier*, to place men in the woods]

....

◨ *noun* **1** waylaying. **2** surprise attack, trap, snare. **4** cover, hiding-place. *verb* lie in wait, waylay, surprise, trap, ensnare.

....

ameliorate /ə'miːlɪəreɪt/ *verb trans., intrans.* to make or become better. [from Old French *ameillorer*, from Latin *melior*, better]

amelioration /əmiːlɪə'reɪʃən/ *noun* making better; improvement.

amen /ɑː'mɛn, eɪ'mɛn/ *interj., usually said at the end of a prayer* so be it. [from Hebrew *amen*, certainly]

amenable /ə'miːnəbl/ *adj.* **1** ready to accept advice or guidance. **2** legally responsible. [from Old French *amener*, to lead to]

....

◨ **1** accommodating, flexible, open, persuadable, agreeable, compliant, tractable, submissive, responsive. **2** responsible, liable, susceptible.
◧ **1** intractable.

....

amend *verb* to correct, improve, or make minor changes to (a book, document, etc). — **make amends for something** to make up for or compensate for some injury, insult, etc. See also EMEND. [from Old French *amender*, from Latin *emendare*]

....

◨ revise, correct, rectify, emend, change, alter, modify, adjust, enhance, improve, ameliorate, better. **make amends for** make up for, compensate for, indemnify, recompense, make reparations for, make redress for, requite, expiate, atone for.
◧ impair, worsen.

....

amendment *noun* correction, improvement, alteration.

....

◨ revision, correction, corrigendum, rectification, emendation, change, alteration, modification, adjustment, addendum, addition, adjunct, improvement.
◧ impairment, deterioration.

....

amenity /ə'miːnɪtɪ, ə'mɛnɪtɪ/ *noun* (PL. **amenities**) **1** anything that makes life more comfortable and pleasant. **2** pleasantness of situation. **3** a public facility. [from Latin *amoenus*, pleasant]

amenorrhoea or **amenorrhea** /amɛnə'rɪə/ *noun Medicine* the absence or stopping of normal menstruation. [from A-¹ without + Greek *men*, month + *rhoia*, a flowing]

American — *adj.* of the United States of America or the American continent, the people who live or were born there, and the languages they speak. — *noun* a person born or living in the United States of America, or the American continent. [from *America*, named after *Amerigo* Vespucci (1454–1512), Italian navigator]

American Indian a member of any of the original peoples of N America.

Americanism *noun* a word, phrase, custom, etc that is characteristic of Americans.

americium /aməˈrɪʃɪəm/ *noun* (SYMBOL **Am**, ATOMIC NUMBER **95**) a silvery-white radioactive metallic element that occurs naturally in trace amounts in uranium ores such as pitchblende. It is produced artificially in nuclear reactors by bombarding plutonium with neutrons, and is used as a source of alpha particles. [from *America*, where it was first produced]

Amerindian — *adj.* **1** Native American. **2** denoting a family of over 1000 languages used by Native Americans in N, Central, and S America. It is divided into North American (including the group Eskimo-Aleut, Na-Dené, Algonkian, and Macro-Siouan), Mesoamerican, and South American. — *noun* **1** a Native American. **2** the languages forming the Amerindian family.

amethyst /'aməθɪst/ — *noun* a pale to deep purple transparent or translucent variety of the mineral quartz that is used as a gemstone. Its colour is due to the presence of impurities, especially iron oxide. — *adj.* of or coloured like this material. [from Greek *amethystos*, not drunken; the stone was supposed to prevent drunkenness]

Amharic /am'harɪk/ — *noun* the official language of Ethiopia, related to Hebrew and Arabic. — *adj.* of or in this language.

amiability /eɪmɪə'bɪlɪtɪ/ *noun* being amiable.

amiable /'eɪmɪəbl/ *adj.* likeable; friendly, pleasant and good-tempered. [from Latin *amicabilis*, amicable, confused with Old French *amable*, lovable]

....

◨ likeable, pleasant, agreeable, congenial, companionable, sociable, friendly, affable, approachable, genial, cheerful, good-tempered, good-natured, kind, obliging.
◧ unfriendly, curt, hostile.

....

amicability /amɪkə'bɪlɪtɪ/ *noun* **1** being amicable. **2** friendly feelings; a friendly relationship.

amicable /'amɪkəbl/ *adj.* friendly. [from Latin *amicabilis*, from *amicus*, friend]

amid or **amidst** *prep.* in the middle of; among. [from Anglo-Saxon *onmiddan*, in the centre]

....

◨ in the midst of, in the thick of, in the middle of, surrounded by, among.

....

amide /'eɪmaɪd, 'amaɪd/ *noun Chem.* **1** any member of a class of organic chemical compounds that contain the $-CONH_2$ group (known as the amide group), formed when one or more of the hydrogen atoms of ammonia is replaced by an acyl group. **2** any member of a class of inorganic chemical compounds that contain the NH_2^- ion, formed when one of the hydrogen atoms of ammonia is replaced by a metal, eg sodium amide ($NaNH_2$). [from AMMONIA]

amidships or **midships** *adv.* in, into, or near the middle of a ship.

amine /'eɪmaɪn, 'amaɪn/ *noun Chem.* any member of a class of organic chemical compounds in which one or more of the hydrogen atoms of ammonia has been replaced by an organic group, eg a methyl (CH_3) group. Amines are produced by decomposing organic matter. [from AMMONIA]

amino acid /ə'miːnoʊ/ any of a group of water-soluble organic compounds that contain an amino ($-NH_2$) group and a carboxyl ($-COOH$) group, and form the individual subunits of proteins.

amino group /ə'miːnoʊ/ *Chem.* the $-NH_2$ group in amino acids and other nitrogen-containing organic compounds.

amir /ə'mɪə(r)/ same as EMIR.

Amish a US pietistic sect, founded (c.1693) in Berne, Switzerland, by Jacob Amman, a conservative Mennonite preacher.

amiss — *adj.* wrong; out of order. — *adv.* wrongly. — **take something amiss** to be upset or offended by it. [from MISS¹]

amity /'amɪtɪ/ *noun formal* friendship. [from Old French *amitie*, from Latin *amicus*, friend]

ammeter /'amiːtə(r)/ *noun* an instrument used for measuring electric current in a circuit, usually in amperes. [from AMPERE + METER]

ammo *noun colloq.* short form of AMMUNITION.

ammonia /ə'moʊnɪə/ *noun* **1** (FORMULA NH_3) a colourless pungent gas that is very soluble in water, formed naturally by the bacterial decomposition of proteins, urea, etc, and manufactured industrially from nitrogen and hydrogen in the Haber process. **2** an alkaline solution of ammonia in water (ammonium hydroxide), used as a bleach and household cleaning agent. [from Latin *sal ammoniacus*, salt of Ammon, ammonia in salt form first found near a temple to the god Ammon in Libya]

ammonite /'æmənaɪt/ *noun Geol.* an extinct marine cephalopod mollusc, with a flat tightly coiled shell, widespread during the Mesozoic era; the fossilized remains, especially the shell, of this animal. [from Latin *ammonites*, horn of Ammon]

ammonium /ə'moʊnɪəm/ *Chem.* (FORMULA NH$_4^+$) a cation (a positively charged ion), formed by the reaction of ammonia with acid. It behaves like a metal ion, and is found in many salts, particularly ammonium chloride (sal ammoniac) and ammonium carbonate (sal volatile).

ammunition /æmjʊ'nɪʃən/ *noun* **1** bullets, shells, bombs, etc made to be fired from a weapon. **2** facts, etc which can be used against someone in an argument. [from French *amunitions*, military supplies]

amnesia /æm'niːzɪə/ *noun* the loss or impairment of memory, caused by physical injury, disease, drugs, or emotional trauma. [from Greek *amnesia*, forgetfulness]

amnesiac *noun* a person who suffers from amnesia.

amnesic /æm'niːzɪk/ *adj.* **1** relating to amnesia. **2** suffering loss of memory.

amnesty /'æmnəstɪ/ *noun* (PL. **amnesties**) **1** a general pardon, especially for people convicted or accused of political crimes. **2** a period of time during which criminals may admit to crimes, hand in weapons, etc, with the promise of a pardon. [from Greek *amnestia*, oblivion]

> ▣ **1** pardon, forgiveness, absolution, mercy, indulgence, reprieve, remission.

amnio *noun colloq.* amniocentesis.

amniocentesis /æmnɪoʊsen'tiːsɪs/ *noun Medicine* the insertion of a hollow needle through the abdominal wall into the uterus (womb) of a pregnant woman in order to withdraw a sample of the amniotic fluid surrounding the embryo. The sample is analysed in order to detect fetal abnormalities such as Down's syndrome or spina bifida. [from *amnion*, the membrane enclosing the foetus + *centesis*, puncture]

amnion /'æmnɪən/ *noun* (PL. **amnia**) *Anat.* the innermost membrane that surrounds the embryo of mammals, birds, and reptiles.

amniotic fluid /æmnɪ'ɒtɪk/ *Zool.* the clear fluid that surrounds and protects the embryo in the amniotic cavity of mammals, birds, and reptiles. [from *amnion*, the membrane enclosing the foetus]

amoeba /ə'miːbə/ *noun* (PL. **amoebae**, **amoebas**) a microscopic animal belonging to the phylum Protozoa, which has no fixed shape and moves by continually pushing out 'arms' or *pseudopodia* in different directions. [from Greek *amoibe*, change]

amoebic /ə'miːbɪk/ *adj.* relating to or characteristic of amoebae.

amok /ə'mɒk, ə'mʌk/ or **amuck** — **run amok** or **amuck** to rush about violently and out of control. [from Malay *amoq*, frenzied]

among or **amongst** *prep.*, *used of more than two things, people, etc* **1** in the middle of: *among friends*. **2** between: *divide it among them*. **3** in the group or number of: *among his best plays*. **4** with one another: *decide among yourselves*. [from Anglo-Saxon *ongemang*]

> ▣ **1** in the middle of, surrounded by, amid, in the midst of, in the thick of, with.

amoral /eɪ'mɒrəl, a'mɒrəl/ *adj.* having no moral standards or principles.

amorality *noun* being amoral.

amorous /'æmərəs/ *adj.* showing, feeling, or relating to love, especially sexual love. [from Latin *amorosus*, from *amor*, love]

amorphous /ə'mɔːfəs, eɪ'mɔːfəs/ *adj.* with no definite shape or structure. [from Greek *amorphos*, shapeless]

amortization /əmɔːtaɪ'zeɪʃən/ or **amortisation** *noun* **1** the process of amortizing a debt. **2** the money used for this.

amortize /ə'mɔːtaɪz/ or **amortise** *verb* **1** to gradually pay off (a debt) by regular payments of money. **2** to gradually write off the initial cost of (an asset) over a period. [from Old French *amortir*, to kill]

amount — *noun* a quantity; a total or extent: *a large amount of money*. — *verb intrans.* (**amount to something**) to be equal to it or add up to it in size, number, etc: *their assets amounted to several millions*. [from Old French *amonter*, to climb up]

> ▣ *noun* quantity, number, sum, total, whole, entirety, aggregate, lot, quota, supply, volume, mass, measure, magnitude, extent. *verb* add up to, total, come to, make, equal, mean, be tantamount to, be equivalent to, approximate to.

amour /a'mʊə(r)/ *noun old use* a love affair, especially one that is kept secret. [from French *amour*, love]

amour-propre /'amʊə prɒprə/ *noun* self-esteem. [from French *amour-propre*]

amp *noun* **1** an ampere. **2** *colloq.* an amplifier.

amperage /'æmpərɪdʒ/ *noun* the magnitude or strength of an electric current expressed in amperes.

ampere /'æmpeə(r)/ *noun* (SYMBOL **A**) the SI unit of electric current, equivalent to one coulomb per second. One ampere is the current that would produce a force of 2 x 10^{-7}Nm^{-1} between two parallel conductors of infinite length placed 1m apart in a vacuum. [named after the French physicist André Marie Ampère]

ampersand /'æmpəsand/ *noun* the sign &, meaning 'and'. [short form of *and per se and*, ie 'and' by itself means 'and']

amphetamine /æm'fɛtəmiːn/ *noun Medicine* any of a group of potentially addictive drugs that stimulate the central nervous system and produce a sense of well-being and mental alertness. [from the chemical name *alpha-methylphenethylamine*]

amphibian /æm'fɪbɪən/ *noun* **1** *Zool.* any cold-blooded vertebrate animal belonging to the class Amphibia, which includes frogs, toads, newts, and salamanders. **2** a vehicle that can operate both on land and in water, eg an aircraft that can land and take off on either land or water. [from Greek *amphi*, both + *bios*, life]

> *Amphibians include:* frog, bullfrog, tree frog, toad, horned toad, midwife toad, natterjack, newt, eft, salamander, congo eel, axolotl.

amphibious /æm'fɪbɪəs/ *adj.* **1** *said of a living organism* capable of living both on land and in water. **2** *said of vehicles, equipment, etc* designed to be operated or used on land, or on or in water, usually for military or rescue purposes. **3** *said of a military operation* using troops that have been conveyed across the sea or other water before landing on enemy-held territory.

amphibole /'æmfɪboʊl/ *noun Geol.* any of a group of complex silicate minerals that are widely distributed in igneous and metamorphic rocks. Common varieties include hornblende, and fibrous forms belong to the asbestos group of minerals. [from Greek *amphibolos*, ambiguous, on account of the resemblance between hornblende and tourmaline]

amphipod /'æmfɪpɒd/ *noun* any of more than 4600 species of crustacean belonging to the order Amphipoda, eg sandhoppers, freshwater shrimps, with different pairs of legs specialized for swimming, walking, and jumping. [from Greek *amphi*, both + *pous podos*, foot]

amphitheatre /'æmfɪθɪətə(r)/ *noun Hist.* a round building without a roof, with tiers of seats round a central open area, used as a theatre. [from Greek *amphi*, around + *theatron*, theatre]

amphora /'æmfərə/ *noun* (PL. **amphoras**, **amphorae**) *Hist.* a Greek or Roman narrow-necked jar with a handle on each side and a pointed bottom, used to hold wine. [from

Latin and Greek *amphora*, from Greek *amphi*, on both sides + *phoreus*, bearer]

amphoteric /amfoʊ'terɪk/ *adj. Chem.*, *said of a chemical compound* having two different properties, usually that of being an acid and a base, eg aluminium hydroxide is amphoteric, because it forms salts both with acids (by behaving as a base) and with alkalis (by behaving as an acid). [from Greek *amphoteros*, both]

ample *adj.* **1** more than enough; plenty. **2** extensive, abundant. **3** *said especially of people* very large. [from Latin *amplus*]

. . . .

▣ **1** plenty, profuse, copious, lavish, liberal, generous, bountiful, munificent, handsome. **2** large, big, extensive, expansive, broad, wide, full, voluminous, roomy, spacious, commodious, great, considerable, substantial, plentiful, abundant.
▣ **1** insufficient, inadequate, meagre.
. . . .

amplification /amplɪfɪ'keɪʃən/ *noun* **1** the act, process, or result of amplifying. **2** material added to a report, story, etc to expand or explain it. **3** a story or account with details added.

amplifier /'amplɪfaɪə(r)/ *noun* an electronic device that increases the strength of an electrical or radio signal without appreciably altering its characteristics, by transferring power from an external source to the signal.

amplify /'amplɪfaɪ/ *verb* (**amplifies, amplified**) **1** to increase the strength of an electrical or radio signal by transferring power from an external energy source so that the intensity of the output signal is greater than that of the input signal. **2** *trans., intrans.* (**amplify on** or **upon something**) to add details or further explanation to an account, story, etc. [from Latin *amplificare*, from *amplus*, ample]

. . . .

▣ **1** boost, enhance, intensify, strengthen, increase, raise. **2** enlarge on, expand on, dilate, fill out, add to, supplement, augment, extend, lengthen, widen, broaden, develop, elaborate on.
▣ **1** reduce, decrease. **2** abridge.
. . . .

amplitude *noun* **1** spaciousness, wide range or extent. **2** *Physics* for any quantity that varies in periodic cycles, eg a wave or vibration, the maximum displacement from its mean position, eg the angle between the vertical and the peak position during the swing of a pendulum. [from Latin *amplitudo*, from *amplus*, ample]

amplitude modulation *Radio* (ABBREV. **AM**) in radio transmission, the process whereby the amplitude of the carrier wave (signal-carrying wave) is made to increase or decrease instantaneously in response to variations in the characteristics of the signal being transmitted.

amply /'amplɪ/ *adv.* well; more than is necessary.

ampoule /am'puːl/ *noun Medicine* a small sealed container, usually of glass or plastic, containing one sterile dose of a drug for injecting. [from French, from Latin *ampulla*, bottle]

ampulla /am'pʊlə/ *noun* (PL. **ampullae**) **1** *Hist.* a small round glass bottle with two handles, used by ancient Romans for holding oil, perfume, or wine. **2** a container for oil, water, or wine used in religious ceremonies. [from Latin *ampulla*]

amputate /'ampjʊteɪt/ *verb Medicine* to remove surgically all or part of (a limb), usually in cases of severe injury or following death and decay of the tissue caused by gangrene or frostbite. [from Latin *amputare*, to cut off]

. . . .

▣ cut off, remove, sever, separate, dock, lop, curtail, truncate.
. . . .

amputation *noun* **1** the surgical removal of all or part of a limb, or any other part of the body (eg a breast), usually in cases where there is severe injury or infection, or an inop-

erable tumour is present. **2** the loss of a limb or other body part as a result of an accident.

amputee *noun* someone who has had a limb amputated.

amt. *abbrev.* amount.

amuck /ə'mʌk/ see AMOK.

amulet /'amjʊlət/ *noun* a small object or jewel worn to protect the wearer from evil or disease. [from Latin *amuletum*]

amuse *verb* **1** to make (someone) laugh. **2** to keep (someone) entertained and interested. [from Old French *amuser*, to cause to muse]

. . . .

▣ ENTERTAIN, DIVERT. **1** make laugh, regale, *colloq.* tickle, *colloq.* crease, *colloq.* slay, cheer (up), gladden. **2** occupy, interest, absorb, engross, enthral, charm, delight, please.
▣ **2** bore, displease.

amused *adj.* **1** made to laugh. **2** entertained; happily occupied.

amusement *noun* **1** the state of being amused. **2** something that amuses. **3** a machine for riding on or playing games of chance.

. . . .

▣ **1** entertainment, diversion, distraction, recreation, fun, enjoyment, pleasure, delight, merriment, mirth, hilarity, laughter. **2** entertainment, diversion, distraction, recreation, sport, game, hobby, pastime, interest, joke, prank.
▣ **1** boredom.
. . . .

amusement arcade a public building with machines for gambling, video games, etc.

amusement park *North Amer.* a funfair.

amusing *adj.* mildly funny, diverting, entertaining.

. . . .

▣ funny, humorous, comical, laughable, ludicrous, droll, witty, facetious, jocular, jolly, enjoyable, pleasant, entertaining, diverting, interesting.
▣ dull, boring.
. . . .

amylase /'amɪleɪs/ *noun Biochem.* any of various enzymes present in digestive juices, which play a part in the breakdown of starch and glycogen. [from Greek *amylon*, starch]

an see A[1].

an- see A-[1].

Anabaptism /anə'baptɪsm/ *noun* belief in adult baptism. [from Greek *ana*, again + *baptizein*, to dip]

Anabaptist *noun* a member of various groups of believers who adopted the more radical elements of the 16c Reformation and advocated the baptism of believing adults only, refusing to recognize infant baptism. Also called REBAPTIZERS.

anabatic /anə'batɪk/ *adj. Geol.* denoting a local upward-moving wind, which most commonly develops in a valley, and reaches speeds of 10 to 15 metres per second. [from Greek *anabasis* going up]

anabolic steroid /anə'bɒlɪk/ *Biochem.* a synthetic male sex hormone (androgen) that promotes tissue growth by increasing protein synthesis. [from ANABOLISM]

anabolism /ə'nabəlɪzm/ *noun Biochem.* in the cells of living organisms, the process whereby complex molecules such as proteins, fats, and carbohydrates are manufactured from smaller molecules. This process requires energy in the form of the chemical compound adenosine triphosphate (ATP). [from Greek *ana*, up + *bole*, throw]

anachronism /ə'nakrənɪzm/ *noun* **1** the attribution of something to a historical period in which it did not exist. **2** a person, thing, or attitude that is out of date and old-fashioned. [from Greek *ana*, backwards + *chronos*, time]

anachronistic /ənakrə'nɪstɪk/ *adj.* involving an anachronism.

anachronistically *adv.* in an anachronistic way.

anaconda /anə'kɒndə/ *noun* a non-venomous constrictor

snake (*Eunectes murinus*), belonging to the boa family, found in or near water in tropical S America, and having an olive green body covered with large round black spots. [from Sinhalese *henakandaya*, the name of a Sri Lankan snake]

anaemia /ən'iːmɪə/ or **anemia** *noun Medicine* a condition characterized by a reduction in the amount of the oxygen-carrying pigment haemoglobin in the red blood cells. [from Greek *an-*, without + *haima*, blood]

anaemic or **anemic** *adj.* **1** suffering from anaemia. **2** pale or weak; lacking in energy.
. . . .
◨ **2** bloodless, ashen, chalky, livid, pasty, pallid, sallow, whey-faced, pale, wan, colourless, insipid, weak, feeble, enervated, sickly.
◨ **2** ruddy, sanguine, full-blooded.
. . . .

anaemically *adv.* in an anaemic way; without energy.

anaerobe /'anərəʊb/ *Biol.* any organism that does not require oxygen in order to obtain energy from the breakdown of carbohydrates or other foodstuffs by the process of respiration, or that cannot survive in the presence of oxygen, eg certain bacteria and yeasts.

anaerobic /anə'rəʊbɪk/ *Biol.* **1** denoting an organism, especially a bacterium, that does not require oxygen in order to obtain energy from the breakdown of carbohydrates or other foodstuffs, or that cannot survive in the presence of oxygen. **2** *Biochem.* denoting a form of respiration in which oxygen is not required for the oxidation (breakdown) of foodstuffs, especially of carbohydrates. It occurs in certain bacteria and yeasts, and in muscle tissue when all the available oxygen has been used up.

anaesthesia /anəs'θiːzɪə/ *noun* **1** a reversible loss of sensation in all or part of the body, usually induced by drugs which may be inhaled or injected intravenously, although in suitable cases it is sometimes induced by acupuncture or hypnosis. **2** loss of sensation that may be a symptom of disease. [from Greek *an-*, without + *aisthesis*, feeling]

anaesthetic /anəs'θɛtɪk/ — *noun* any agent, especially a drug, that is capable of producing anaesthesia either by causing complete loss of consciousness (*general anaesthetic*) or by producing loss of sensation in a specific part of the body (*local anaesthetic*). — *adj.* denoting an agent or procedure (eg acupuncture) that is capable of producing anaesthesia in this way.

anaesthetist /ə'niːsθətɪst/ *noun* a medically qualified doctor who is trained to administer anaesthetics.

anaesthetize or **anaesthetise** /ə'niːsθətaɪz/ *verb* to administer an anaesthetic to (someone).
. . . .
◨ desensitize, numb, deaden, dull, drug, dope, stupefy.
. . . .

anaglyph /'anəglɪf/ *noun* **1** an ornament in low relief. **2** a picture made up of two prints in complementary colours, seen stereoscopically through spectacles of these colours. [from Greek *anaplyphos*, in low relief]

anaglypta /anə'glɪptə/ *noun* plain white wallpaper with a raised pattern on it, usually for painting over. [from Greek *anaglyptos*, in low relief]

anagram /'anəgram/ *noun* a word, phrase, or sentence formed from a changed arrangement of the letters of another. [from Greek *ana*, back + *gramma*, letter]

anal /'eɪnəl/ *adj.* **1** relating to or in the region of the anus. **2** *Psychol.* the stage of development where a child's interest is concentrated on excretion. **3** *Psychol. said of an adult* having personality traits such as obsessiveness and obstinacy, thought to result from fixation at the anal stage.

analgesia /anal'dʒiːzɪə/ *noun Physiol.* a reduction in or loss of the ability to feel pain, without loss of consciousness or deadening of sensation. It may be deliberately induced by pain-killing drugs such as aspirin or paracetamol, or it may be a symptom of diseased or damaged nerves. [from Greek *an*, not + *algeein*, to feel pain]

analgesic /anal'dʒiːzɪk/ — *noun* any drug or other agent that relieves pain. — *adj.* having the effect of relieving pain.

analogical /anə'lɒdʒɪkl/ *adj.* relating to or expressing an analogy.

analogous /ə'naləgəs/ *adj.* **1** similar or alike in some way. **2** *Biol.* denoting plant or animal structures that are similar in function, but that have evolved completely independently of each other in different plant or animal groups, eg the wings of insects and birds. See also HOMOLOGOUS. [from Greek *analogos*, proportionate]

analogue /'anəlɒg/ — *noun* **1** a thing regarded in terms of its similarity or parallelism to something else. **2** *Chem.* a chemical compound, especially a drug, that differs slightly in molecular structure and chemical properties from the parent compound from which it is derived. Analogues of drugs are often used because they have fewer side-effects, or are more potent, etc. **3** *Biol.* any organ or part of an animal or plant that is similar in function, though not in origin, to an organ or part in a different organism. — *adj.*, *said of a device or physical quantity* changing continuously rather than in a series of discrete steps, and therefore capable of being represented by a dial or an electrical voltage, eg analogue watch, analogue computer. See also DIGITAL. [from Greek *analogos*, analogous]

analogue computer or **analog computer** *Comput.* a computer in which data is stored and processed in the form of continuously varying signals representing the changing size of a physical quantity such as voltage or current, rather than in the form of individual numerical values as in a digital computer. See also DIGITAL COMPUTER.

analogy /ə'naledʒɪ/ *noun* (PL. **analogies**) **1** a likeness or similarity in some ways. **2** a way of reasoning which makes it possible to explain one thing or event by comparing it with something else. [from Greek *analogia*, from *analogos*, analogous]
. . . .
◨ **1** likeness, resemblance, similarity, correspondence, equivalence, parallel, relation, correlation, agreement. **2** comparison, simile, metaphor.
. . . .

anal retentive *Psychol.* an adult with anal personality traits.

anal-retentive *adj. Psychol.* displaying anal personality traits.

analysable /anə'laɪzəbl/ *adj.* capable of being analysed.

analyse /'anəlaɪz/ *verb* **1** to examine the structure or content of (something) in detail, eg to examine data in order to discover the general principles underlying a particular phenomenon. **2** to resolve or separate a thing into its component parts. **3** to detect and identify the different chemical components present in a mixture, or to determine the relative proportions of the different components in a mixture. **4** to psychoanalyse (someone). [from Greek *analyein*, to undo, set free]
. . . .
◨ **1** examine, scrutinize, sift, investigate, study, review, interpret, judge, evaluate, consider. **2** break down, separate, divide, take apart, dissect, resolve, reduce.
. . . .

analysis /ə'nalɪsɪs/ *noun* (PL. **analyses**) **1** a detailed examination of the structure and content of something. **2** a statement of the results of such an examination. **3** *North Amer.* psychoanalysis. — **in the final analysis** after everything has been considered.
. . . .
◨ **1** examination, test, scrutiny, sifting, investigation, study, review, separation, division, dissection, resolution, reduction. **2** breakdown, exposition, explanation, interpretation, opinion, evaluation, reasoning.
◨ **1** synthesis.
. . . .

analyst /'anəlɪst/ *noun* **1** someone who is skilled in analysis, especially chemical, political, or economic. **2** *North Amer.* a psychoanalyst.

analytic /anə'lɪtɪk/ or **analytical** *adj.* **1** concerning or involving analysis. **2** examining or able to examine things in detail to learn or make judgements about them.

■ **1** systematic, methodical, logical, rational, interpretative, explanatory, expository. **2** detailed, in-depth, searching, questioning, inquiring, investigative, diagnostic.

analytically *adv.* by an analytic method.

analytic language *Linguistics* a language type in which words do not vary in their internal structure, and their grammatical function is determined solely by their position in the sentence. Also called ISOLATING ROOT LANGUAGE. See also AGGLUTINATING LANGUAGE.

analytic philosophy a movement, associated particularly with Bertrand Russell and the early work of Ludwig Wittenstein, which sees the primary task of philosophy as one of analysing language (usually by means of formal logic) in order to resolve philosophical issues. The analytic approach has been the dominant tradition in Anglo-American academic philosophy for most of the 20c.

anamorphosis /anəˈmɔːfəsɪs, anəmɔːˈfəʊsɪs/ *noun* (PL. **anamorphoses**) in drawing and painting, an image executed in trick perspective so that it is distorted when seen from a normal viewpoint but appears in normal proportion when seen from a particular angle, or reflected in a curved mirror. [from Greek *anamorphosis*, transformation]

anapaest /ˈanəpiːst, ˈanəpest/ *noun Prosody* a foot consisting of two short or unstressed beats followed by one long or stressed beat, as in *with a leap* and *and a bound*. [from Greek *anapaistos*, reversed, because it is the reverse of a dactyl]

anapaestic *adj.*, *said of verse* composed using anapaests.

anaphase /ˈanəfeɪz/ *noun Genetics* the stage of mitosis during which the chromosomes move to opposite poles (ends) of the cell by means of a structure composed of protein fibres, known as the *spindle*, that is formed in the cytoplasm. [from Greek *ana* up, back + PHASE]

anaphylaxis /anafɪˈlaksɪs/ or **anaphylaxy** *noun Medicine* a sudden severe hypersensitive reaction to the injection of a particular foreign substance or antigen (eg certain drugs) into the body of a person who has already been exposed to that substance and is abnormally sensitive to it. [from Greek *ana* back, *phylaxis* protection]

anarchic /aˈnɑːkɪk/ *adj.* involving anarchy; lawless.

■ lawless, ungoverned, anarchistic, libertarian, nihilist, revolutionary, rebellious, mutinous, riotous, chaotic, disordered, confused, disorganized.
E3 submissive, orderly.

anarchically *adv.* in an anarchic way; lawlessly.

anarchism /ˈanəkɪzm/ *noun* a political belief that governments and laws are unnecessary and should be abolished.

anarchist *noun* **1** a person who believes in anarchism. **2** a person who tries to overthrow the government by violence. **3** a person who tries to cause disorder of any kind.

■ **1** libertarian, nihilist. **2** revolutionary, rebel, insurgent, terrorist.

anarchistic /anəˈkɪstɪk/ *adj.* characterized by anarchism; believing in anarchy.

anarchy /ˈanəkɪ/ *noun* **1** confusion and lack of order, especially political; the failure of law and government. **2** the absence of law and government. [from Greek *an*, without + *arche*, government]

■ **1** lawlessness, misrule, revolution, rebellion, insurrection, mutiny, riot, pandemonium, chaos, disorder, confusion. **2** lawlessness, anarchism, nihilism.
E3 CONTROL, ORDER.

anathema /əˈnaθəmə/ *noun* **1** a person or thing one detests. **2** *Christianity* a person or doctrine that has been cursed or denounced. [from Greek *anathema*, thing devoted to evil]

■ **1** abomination, object of loathing, bête noire, bugbear, bane, curse.

anathematize or **anathematise** /əˈnaθəmətaɪz/ *verb trans., intrans.* to curse or denounce.

Anatolian /anəˈtoʊlɪən/ — *noun* a group of extinct languages, mainly of the Indo-European family, and spoken c.2000BC in Anatolia, in the area of present-day Turkey and Syria. The main Anatolian language is Hittite. — *adj.* relating to this group of languages.

anatomical /anəˈtɒmɪkəl/ *adj.* **1** relating to anatomy. **2** relating to the human body.

Anatomical terms include: aural, biceps, bone, cardiac, cartilage, cerebral, dental, diaphragm, dorsal, duodenal, elbow, epidermis, epiglottis, Fallopian tubes, foreskin, funny bone, gastric, genitalia, gingival, gristle, groin, gullet, hamstring, helix, hepatic, hock, intercostal, jugular, lachrymal, ligament, lumbar, mammary, membral, muscle, nasal, neural, ocular, oesophagus, optical, pectoral, pedal, pulmonary, renal, spine, tendon, triceps, umbilicus, uterus, uvula, voice-box, vulva, windpipe, wisdom tooth, womb. *See also* **bones**.

anatomically *adv.* as regards anatomy or the body.

anatomist /əˈnatəmɪst/ *noun* a scientist who specializes in anatomy.

anatomy /əˈnatəmɪ/ *noun* (PL. **anatomies**) **1** the scientific study of the structure of living organisms, including humans, especially as determined by dissection and microscopic examination. **2** the art of dissection. **3** *colloq.* a person's body. [from Greek *anatome*, dissection]

ANC *abbrev.* African National Congress.

-ance *suffix* forming nouns denoting a state, quality, or action: *abundance / performance*. [from French *-ance*, from Latin *-antia*]

ancestor /ˈansəstə(r)/ *noun* **1** a person who was a member of one's family a long time ago, and from whom one is descended. **2** an earlier example or version. [from Latin *antecessor*, from *ante*, before + *cedere*, to go]

■ **1** forebear, forefather, progenitor, predecessor. **2** forerunner, precursor, antecedent.
E3 DESCENDANT.

ancestor worship deification or veneration of dead members of a family, group, or society, found in many primitive societies and religious cults.

ancestral /anˈsɛstrəl/ *adj.* of or inherited from one's ancestors.

■ familial, parental, genealogical, lineal, hereditary, genetic.

ancestry /ˈansəstrɪ/ *noun* (PL. **ancestries**) one's family descent.

■ ancestors, forebears, forefathers, progenitors, parentage, family, lineage, line, descent, blood, race, stock, roots, pedigree, genealogy, extraction, derivation, origin, heritage, heredity.

anchor /ˈaŋkə(r)/ — *noun* **1** a heavy piece of metal with hooks which dig into the seabed, attached by a cable to a ship and used to restrict its movement. **2** a weight used to hold a balloon to the ground. **3** anything that gives security or stability. See also ANCHORMAN. — *verb* **1** to fasten (a ship or balloon) using an anchor. **2** to fasten

anchorage securely. **3** *intrans.* to drop an anchor and become moored by it; to be moored by an anchor. [from Anglo-Saxon *ancor*]

⊟ *verb* **1** moor, tie up, make fast. **2** fasten, attach, fix.

anchorage *noun* **1** a place where a ship may anchor. **2** a safe place in which to rest. **3** the act of anchoring.

anchorite /'aŋkəraɪt/ *noun* a man or woman who, for religious reasons, lives alone and separate from other people. [from Greek *anachoretes*, from *ana*, apart + *choreein*, to withdraw]

anchorman or **anchorwoman** *noun* **1** a man or woman who presents a television programme and is responsible for keeping the discussion running smoothly, linking up with reporters outside, etc. **2** (*also* **anchor**) a man or woman running last in a relay team.

anchovy /'antʃəvɪ, an'tʃoʊvɪ/ *noun* (PL. **anchovies**) any of about 100 species of small fish (*Engraulis encrasicholus*), related to the herring, up to about 20cm in length, found in large shoals in surface waters around the coasts of Europe. It has a pungent flavour and is sometimes eaten as a food fish, but is most widely used as a garnish, and as a flavouring for fish pastes and other foods. [from Spanish and Portuguese *anchova*]

ancient /'eɪnʃənt/ — *adj.* **1** dating from very long ago. **2** very old. **3** dating from before the end of the Western Roman Empire in AD 476. — *noun* (*usually* **ancients**) people who lived in ancient times, especially the Greeks and Romans. [from Old French *ancien*, from Latin *antianus*, former, old]

⊟ *adj.* **1** archaic, antediluvian, prehistoric, primeval, immemorial, bygone, early, original. **2** old, aged, time-worn, age-old, antique.

⊟ *adj.* **1** modern, contemporary. **2** new, young.

ancient history 1 the history of the countries surrounding the Mediterranean Sea, especially Greece, Asia Minor, Italy, and Egypt, before the end of the Western Roman Empire in AD 476. **2** *colloq.* information, news, etc one has known for a long time.

ancillary /an'sɪlərɪ/ *adj.* **1** helping or giving support, especially to medical services. **2** being used as an extra. [from Latin *ancillaris*, from *ancilla*, maid-servant]

-ancy *suffix* forming nouns denoting a state or quality, or something which shows this: *expectancy / vacancy.* [from Latin *-antia*]

AND *abbrev., as an international vehicle mark* Andorra.

and *conj.*, *used to join two or more statements, words, or clauses* **1** used to show addition: *two and two.* **2** used to show a result or reason: *fall and bang one's head.* **3** used to show repetition or duration: *It rained and rained.* **4** used to show progression: *bigger and bigger.* **5** used to show variety or contrast: *There are good cars and bad cars.* **6** *colloq.* used instead of *to* after some verbs: *come and try.* — **and/ or** either or both of two possibilities stated: *cakes and/or biscuits.* [from Anglo-Saxon *and*]

andalusite /andə'luːsaɪt/ *noun Geol.* one of the three varieties of mineral aluminium silicate found in metamorphic rocks. It is an important indicator of the pressure and temperature of metamorphism in rocks. [from *Andalusia* in Spain, where it was first found]

andante /an'dantɪ/ — *adj., adv. Mus.* played at a slow steady tempo. — *noun* a piece of music to be played like this. [from Italian *andante*, from *andare*, to go]

andesite /'andəsaɪt/ *noun Geol.* a dark-coloured igneous rock, containing large amounts of feldspar minerals, produced during the eruption of volcanoes.

andiron /'andaɪən/ *noun* an iron bar, usually one of a pair, supporting logs and coal in a fireplace. [from Old French *andier*]

androecium /an'driːsɪəm/ *noun Bot.* the male reproductive parts of a flower, consisting of the stamens. [from Greek *oikion*, house]

androgen /'andrədʒən/ *noun* **1** *Physiol.* any of a group of steroid hormones, produced mainly by the testes, that control the growth and functioning of the male sex organs and the appearance of male secondary sexual characteristics, eg beard growth, deepening of the voice. **2** a synthetic form of any of these hormones that has a similar effect. [from Greek *aner andros*, man, male]

androgynous /an'drɒdʒɪnəs/ *adj.* **1** *Biol.* denoting an animal or plant that shows both male and female characteristics, especially one that possesses both male and female sex organs; hermaphrodite. **2** *Psychol.* showing both male and female traits, eg a woman who resembles a man in outward appearance. [from Greek *androgynos*, from *aner*, man + *gyne*, woman]

android — *noun* a robot that resembles a human being in form or features. — *adj.* relating to or resembling a human being. [from Greek *aner*, man]

Andromeda galaxy or **Andromeda nebula** /an'drɒmədə/ *Astron.* a bright spiral galaxy in the constellation Andromeda, about 2.2m light years away from Earth. It is the largest of the nearby galaxies, and the most distant object visible to the naked eye.

anecdotal /anək'doʊtəl/ *adj.* **1** consisting of or in the nature of anecdotes. **2** *said of information, etc* based on chance accounts of incidents rather than systematic explanation; unsystematic.

anecdote /'anəkdoʊt/ *noun* a short and entertaining account of an incident. [from Greek *anekdota*, unpublished things, from *an*, not + *ekdotos*, published]

⊟ story, tale, yarn, sketch, reminiscence.

anechoic /anə'koʊɪk/ *adj.* **1** *Physics* denoting a room, chamber, etc, in which there is little or no reflection of sound, and hence no echoes. **2** denoting wall tiles that absorb sound and so prevent reflection of sound waves by the wall.

anemia *North Amer., esp. US* same as ANAEMIA.

anemometer /anə'mɒmɪtə(r)/ *noun Meteorol.* an instrument for measuring and recording wind speed. [from Greek *anemos*, wind + -METER]

anemone /ə'nɛmənɪ/ *noun* any plant of the genus *Anemone* of the buttercup family (Ranunculaceae), including the cultivated anemone, which bears red, purple, blue, or white cup-shaped flowers on a tall slender stem, and wild species such as the wood anemone. [from Greek, = flower of the wind]

aneroid /'anərɔɪd/ *noun* (*also* **aneroid barometer**) *Meteorol.* a type of barometer used to measure atmospheric pressure and to estimate altitude. It consists of a sealed metal box from which most of the air has been removed, that expands or contracts like a bellows as the atmospheric pressure rises or falls, respectively. [from Greek *a*, without + *neros*, water]

anesthesia, anesthetic *North Amer., esp. US* same as ANAESTHESIA, ANAESTHETIC.

aneurysm or **aneurism** /'anjʊərɪzm/ *noun Medicine* a balloon-like swelling in the wall of an artery, caused by a congenital defect in the muscular wall, or a disorder such as arteriosclerosis (formation of fatty deposits on the inner walls of arteries). Aneurysms most commonly occur in the aorta. [from Greek *aneurysma*, from *ana*, up + *eurys*, wide]

anew *adv.* **1** again. **2** in a different way. [from NEW]

angel *noun* **1** a messenger or attendant of God. **2** a representation of this in human form, with a halo and wings. **3** *colloq.* a good, helpful, pure, or beautiful person. **4** *colloq.* a person who puts money into an enterprise, in particular in the theatre. — **angels on horseback** oysters wrapped in slices of bacon, grilled until crisp. [from Greek *angelos*, messenger]

⊟ **1** divine messenger, archangel, cherub, seraph. **3** darling, treasure, saint, paragon, ideal.

1 devil, fiend.

....

angel cake a light sponge cake.

angel dust *Medicine* the street name of the drug phencyclidine piperidine (PCP), a hallucinogen, abuse of which can lead to serious psychological disturbances. [from Greek *angelos* a messenger]

angelfish *noun* **1** any of various unrelated fishes, so called because their pectoral fins resemble wings. **2** any of various freshwater fishes of this type belonging to the genus *Pterophyllum*, native to S America, having a very deep body, flattened from side to side and covered with dark vertical stripes, and elongated winglike or flaplike pectoral fins. **3** any of various small brightly coloured marine fishes of this type, especially of the genus *Pomacanthus*, found in shallow tropical waters, especially around coral reefs, and having a deep body and a sharp backwardly pointing spine on the gill cover. **4** an alternative name for the monkfish.

angelic /anˈdʒɛlɪk/ *adj.* of or like an angel, especially in being pure and innocent.

....

cherubic, seraphic, celestial, heavenly, divine, holy, pious, saintly, pure, innocent, unworldly, virtuous.

devilish, fiendish.

....

angelica /anˈdʒɛlɪkə/ *noun* **1** any of various tall perennial plants of the genus *Angelica*, found mainly in Europe and Asia. The young stem and leaf stalks of *A. archangelica* are used as a food flavouring and cake decoration, and the roots produce an aromatic oil that is used in perfumes and as an ingredient of herbal liqueurs such as vermouth and Chartreuse. **2** pieces of the young stem and leaf stalks of this plant, crystallized in sugar and used as a food flavouring and cake decoration. [from Latin *herba angelica*, angelic herb]

angel shark monkfish.

angelus /ˈandʒələs/ *noun* **1** a Roman Catholic prayer said in the morning, at noon, and at sunset, in honour of the Incarnation. **2** a bell rung to announce these prayers. [from Latin *Angelus domini*, the angel of the Lord, the opening words of the prayer]

anger — *noun* a feeling of great or violent displeasure. — *verb* (**angered**, **angering**) to make angry; to displease. [from Norse *angr*, grief]

....

noun annoyance, irritation, antagonism, displeasure, irritability, temper, pique, vexation, ire, rage, *colloq.* red mist, fury, wrath, exasperation, outrage, indignation. *verb* annoy, irritate, *colloq.* aggravate, *colloq.* wind up, vex, irk, rile, *colloq.* miff, *colloq.* needle, nettle, provoke, antagonize, madden, enrage, incense, infuriate, exasperate, outrage.

noun forgiveness, forbearance. *verb* please, appease, calm.

....

Angevins three ruling families of the medieval county (and later duchy) of Anjou in W France.

angina /anˈdʒaɪnə/ *noun* (*in full* **angina pectoris**) *Medicine* severe pain behind the chest-bone, which often spreads to the left shoulder and arm, and is induced by exertion, eg physical exercise, and usually relieved within a few minutes by rest. [from Latin *angina*, a throat disease + *pectus*, breast]

angiosperm /ˈandʒɪoʊspɜːm/ *Bot.* any plant belonging to the subdivision Angiospermae (often referred to as flowering plants), which characteristically produce flowers, and bear ovules that subsequently develop into seeds, enclosed within an ovary, the wall of which subsequently develops into a fruit. [from Greek *angeion*, vessel + *sperma*, seed]

Angle /ˈaŋgl/ *noun* (*usually* **Angles**) a member of a N German tribe which settled in N and E England and southern Scotland in the 5c. [from Anglo-Saxon *Angel*]

angle[1] — *noun* **1** *Maths.* a measure of the rotation of a line about a point, usually measured in degrees, radians, or revolutions. A complete revolution or circle corresponds to 360° or 2π radians. Angles are formed at the point where two lines or planes intersect. An acute angle is less than 90°, a right angle is exactly 90°, an obtuse angle is greater than 90° but less than 180°, and a reflex angle is greater than 180° but less than 360°. **2** the amount by which one line slopes away from another. **3** a corner. **4** a point of view; an aspect; a way of considering or being involved in something. — *verb* **1** *intrans.* to move in or place at an angle. **2** *trans.* to present (a news story, information, etc) from a particular point of view. [Latin *angulus*]

....

noun **3** corner, nook, bend, flexure, hook, crook, elbow, knee, point. **4** point of view, viewpoint, standpoint, position, aspect, outlook, facet, side, approach, slant, perspective.

....

angle[2] *verb intrans.* **1** to use a rod and line for catching fish. **2** (**angle for something**) to try to get it in a devious or indirect way. [from Anglo-Saxon *angul*, hook]

angle of incidence *Physics* the angle between a ray (eg a light ray) that strikes a surface (eg glass) and the normal (a line drawn perpendicular to that surface) at the point where the ray strikes the surface.

angle of reflection *Physics* the angle between a ray (eg a light ray) leaving a reflecting surface (eg glass) and the normal (a line drawn perpendicular to that surface) at the point where the ray leaves the surface. It is equal to the angle of incidence.

angle of refraction *Physics* the angle between a ray (eg a light ray) that is refracted (bent) at an interface between two different media (eg water and glass) and the normal (a line drawn perpendicular to that interface) at the point where the ray is refracted.

angler *noun* a person who fishes with a rod and line.

anglerfish *noun* any of about 13 families of bizarre shallow to deep-sea fishes which have a dorsal fin spine modified to form a lure to attract prey. Also called GOOSEFISH.

Anglican /ˈaŋglɪkən/ — *adj.* relating to the Church of England or another Church in communion with it. — *noun* a member of an Anglican Church. [from Latin *Anglicanus*, from *Anglus*, Angle]

Anglicanism *noun* the principles of the Church of England and other Anglican churches.

anglicism /ˈaŋglɪsɪzm/ *noun* a word or custom that is peculiar to the English.

anglicization or **anglicisation** *noun* making or becoming English.

anglicize or **anglicise** /ˈaŋglɪsaɪz/ *verb* to make English in form or character. [from Latin *Anglus*, Angle]

angling *noun* the sport of catching fish with rod, line, and hook; one of the world's most popular pastimes. There are many forms, including freshwater fishing, fly fishing, game fishing, coarse fishing, and deep sea fishing.

Anglo- *combining form* forming words meaning 'English, British' or 'English or British and ...': *Anglo-American*. [from Latin *Anglus*, English]

Anglo-Catholic — *noun* a member of an Anglican Church which emphasizes the Church's Catholic traditions. — *adj.* relating to Anglo-Catholics.

Anglo-Catholicism *noun* the beliefs and practices of Anglo-Catholics.

Anglo-Indian — *noun* **1** a person of British descent who has lived in India for a long time. **2** a person of mixed English and Indian descent. — *adj.* of Anglo-Indians.

Anglo-Norman — *noun* **1** the Old French dialect introduced into England by the Norman invaders in 1066, and spoken in England by the aristocracy for about 200 years. **2** a Norman inhabitant of England after 1066. — *adj.* of the Anglo-Norman language or people.

anglophile /ˈaŋgloʊfaɪl/ *noun* a person who admires England and the English. [from ANGLO- + Greek *philos*, friend]

anglophobe /'aŋgloʊfoʊb/ noun a person who hates or fears England and the English. [from ANGLO- + Greek *phobos*, fear]

anglophone /'aŋgloʊfoʊn/ noun an English-speaking person, especially in states where other languages are also spoken. [from ANGLO- + Greek *phone*, voice]

Anglo-Saxon — noun 1 a member of any of the Germanic tribes which settled in England and parts of Scotland in the 5c. 2 Old English, the English language before about 1150. — adj. of the Anglo-Saxons or the Old English language.

angora or **Angora** /aŋ'gɔːrə/ — noun the wool or cloth made from the soft silky wool of the Angora goat. — adj. 1 denoting a garment made from this material. 2 denoting a breed of domestic goat that originated in Turkey, but is now bred mainly in N America, S Africa, and Australasia for its soft silky wool, known as mohair. 3 denoting a breed of rabbit, native to the island of Madeira, that produces fine white silky wool. 4 denoting a breed of domestic cat that originated in Turkey, and resembles the Persian cat in having a long smooth white coat, but has a more pointed head, longer body and fuller tail. [from *Angora*, old name for Ankara, capital of Turkey]

angostura /aŋgə'stjʊərə/ noun an essential oil distilled from the bitter aromatic bark of a S American tree (*Galipea cusparia*), formerly used in medicines. It is blended with herbs to make *angostura bitters*, which are used as a flavouring in cocktails and other alcoholic drinks, and some fruit juices. [from *Angostura*, now called Ciudad Bolfívar, a town in Venezuela]

Angostura bitters *trademark* a bitter liquid for flavouring drinks, made from angostura bark.

angrily adv. with an angry manner.

angry adj. (**angrier, angriest**) 1 feeling or showing anger. 2 *said of a wound* red and sore. 3 dark and stormy: *an angry sky*.
· · · · · · · · · · · · · · · · · · · ·

▣ 1 annoyed, cross, irritated, *colloq.* aggravated, displeased, *colloq.* uptight, irate, *colloq.* mad, enraged, incensed, infuriated, furious, raging, passionate, heated, hot, exasperated, outraged, indignant. 2 red, inflamed, sore, painful. 3 dark, louring, threatening, stormy.
▣ 1 content, happy, calm. 3 clear, bright.
· ·

angst /aːŋst/ noun a feeling of anxiety or foreboding. [from German *Angst*, fear]

angstrom or **ångstrom** /'aŋstrəm/ noun (SYMBOL Å) a unit of length equal to 10^{-10}m, sometimes used to measure wavelengths of electromagnetic radiation (eg visible light, X-rays) and the sizes of molecules and atoms. In the SI system it has been replaced by the nanometre (10^{-9}m). [named after the Swedish physicist Anders Ångström]

anguish /'aŋgwɪʃ/ noun great pain or suffering, especially mental. [from Latin *angustia*, tightness]
· · · · · · · · · · · · · · · · · · · ·

▣ pain, agony, suffering, distress, misery, sorrow, grief.
· ·

anguished adj. feeling, showing, or suggesting great pain.

angular /'aŋgjʊlə(r)/ adj. 1 *said of a person, etc* thin and bony; sharp or awkward in manner. 2 having an angle or angles. 3 measured by an angle: *angular distance*. [from Latin *angularis*, from *angulus*, angle]

angularity /aŋgjʊ'larɪtɪ/ noun 1 being angular. 2 an angular shape or form.

angular momentum *Physics* for a particle moving about an axis, the product of its angular velocity and its moment of inertia about the axis of rotation.

anhydride /an'haɪdraɪd/ noun *Chem.* any chemical compound formed by the removal of water from another compound, especially an acid. [from A-¹ + Greek *hydor, hydr-*, water]

anhydrous adj. denoting a chemical compound that contains no water, especially one that lacks water of crystallization. [from Greek *an*, without + *hydor*, water]

aniline /'anɪliːn/ noun (FORMULA $C_6H_5NH_2$) a colourless oily liquid organic compound that is highly toxic and turns brown on exposure to air or sunlight. It is widely used in the manufacture of rubber, plastics, drugs, dyes, and photographic chemicals. [from Arabic *an-nil*, indigo, from which it was first obtained]

animadversion /anɪmad'vɜːʃən/ noun criticism or censure. [from Latin *animus*, mind + *ad*, to + *vertere*, to turn]

animal — noun 1 any member of the kingdom of organisms that are capable of voluntary movement, possess specialized sense organs that enable them to respond rapidly to stimuli, can only grow to a limited size, lack the pigment chlorophyll, and are unable to manufacture complex organic compounds from simple molecules obtained from the environment. Animal cells differ from plant cells in that they are surrounded by a cell membrane instead of a cell wall. 2 a person who behaves in a rough, uncivilized way. 3 *colloq.* a person or thing. — adj. 1 of, from, or like an animal. 2 of the physical desires of animals; brutal; sensual. [from Latin *animalis*, having breath]
· · · · · · · · · · · · · · · · · · · ·

▣ noun 1 creature, beast, mammal. 2 brute, beast, barbarian, savage, monster, cur, pig, swine. adj. 2 bestial, brutish, inhuman, savage, wild, instinctive, bodily, physical, sensual, carnal, fleshly.
· ·

Animals include: cat, dog, hamster, gerbil, mouse, rat, rabbit, hare, fox, badger, beaver, mole, otter, weasel, ferret, ermine, mink, hedgehog, squirrel, horse, pig, cow, bull, goat, sheep; monkey, lemur, gibbon, ape, chimpanzee, orang-utan, baboon, gorilla; seal, sea lion, dolphin, walrus, whale; lion, tiger, cheetah, puma, panther, cougar, jaguar, ocelot, leopard; aardvark, armadillo, wolf, wolverine, hyena, mongoose, skunk, racoon, wombat, platypus, koala, polecat; deer, antelope, gazelle, eland, impala, reindeer, elk, caribou, moose; wallaby, kangaroo, bison, buffalo, gnu, camel, zebra, llama, panda, giant panda, grizzly bear, polar bear, giraffe, hippopotamus, rhinoceros, elephant. *See also* **amphibian**; **bird**; **cattle**; **dog**; **fish**; **insect**; **reptile**.

animalcule /anɪ'malkjuːl/ noun (PL. **animalcules, animalcula**) formerly used to refer to any microscopic animal, ie one that cannot be seen by the naked eye. [from Latin *animalculum*]

animal experimentation any type of experiment performed on living animals, especially in order to test the effects of chemical compounds, such as new drugs, cosmetics, food additives, and pesticides, on the body functions and behaviour of animals (eg guinea pigs, rabbits, hamsters, rats, mice, dogs, cats, monkeys) as an alternative to using human subjects.

animal husbandry the branch of agriculture concerned with the breeding, care, and feeding of domesticated animals.

animalism noun 1 the state of having the physical desires of an animal. 2 the belief that man is no better than other animals.

animality /anɪ'malɪtɪ/ noun 1 animal nature or behaviour. 2 the state of being an animal, especially a lower animal.

animalize or **animalise** /'anɪmələɪz/ verb to make (a person) brutal or sensual.

animal rights the rights of animals to exist without being exploited by humans.

animate /'anɪmeɪt, 'anɪmət/ — verb (pronounced -meɪt) 1 to give life to. 2 to make lively. 3 to record (still drawings telling a story) on film in such a way as to make the images seem to move: *animated cartoon*. — adj. (pronounced -mət) alive. [from Latin *animare*, from *anima*, breath, life or soul]
· · · · · · · · · · · · · · · · · · · ·

▣ adj. alive, living, live, breathing, conscious.
▣ adj. inanimate.
· ·

animated adj. 1 lively, spirited. 2 living. 3 moving as if alive.

▣ **1** lively, spirited, buoyant, ebullient, vivacious, quick, brisk, vigorous, energetic, active, passionate, impassioned, vehement, ardent, fervent, excited, enthusiastic.

▣ **1** lethargic, sluggish, inert.

animation /anɪˈmeɪʃən/ *noun* **1** liveliness, vivacity. **2** the techniques used to record still drawings on film in such a way as to make the images seem to move.

animator /ˈanɪmeɪtə(r)/ *noun* a person who makes the drawings used to develop animated films and cartoons.

animatronics /anɪməˈtrɒnɪks/ *noun* in film-making, the art of animating a life-like figure of a person, animal, etc, by means of computer technology. [from ANIMAL + ELECTRONICS]

animism /ˈanɪmɪzm/ *noun* the belief that plants and natural phenomena (eg rivers, mountains, etc) have souls. [from Latin *anima*, soul]

animist *noun* a believer in animism.

animistic *adj.* relating to or characterized by animism.

animosity /anɪˈmɒsɪtɪ/ *noun* (PL. **animosities**) a strong dislike or hatred. [from Latin *animositas*]

▣ hate, hatred, loathing, antagonism, hostility, enmity, ill-feeling, ill-will, acrimony, bitterness, rancour, resentment, spite, malice.

▣ goodwill.

animus /ˈanɪmʊs/ *noun* a feeling of strong dislike or hatred. [from Latin *animus*, spirit, soul]

anion /ˈanaɪən/ *noun Physics* any negatively charged ion, which moves towards the anode during electrolysis. See also CATION. [from Greek *ana*, up + *ienai*, to go]

anise /ˈanɪs/ *noun* an umbelliferous plant (*Pimpinella anisum*), native to China but widely cultivated elsewhere, that produces clusters of small yellowish-white flowers, and small greyish-brown fruits that yield an oil used in cough medicines and lozenges, and aromatic seeds (known as aniseed) used as a food flavouring. [from Greek *anison*]

aniseed *noun* the liquorice-flavoured seeds of the anise plant (*Pimpinella anisum*), used as a food flavouring in cakes and other baked products, sweets, liqueurs, and other beverages.

ankh /aŋk/ *noun* a T-shaped cross with a loop above the horizontal bar. It was a symbol of life in ancient Egypt. [from Egyptian *ankh*, life]

ankle *noun* **1** the hinge joint between the bones of the leg (the tibia and fibula) and the ankle bone (the talus). **2** the region of this joint, ie the part of the leg just above the foot. [from Anglo-Saxon *ancleow*]

anklet *noun* a chain or ring worn around the ankle.

ankylosaur /ˈaŋkɪlɒsɔː(r)/ *noun* a small plant-eating dinosaur, known from the Cretaceous period, with a small head, a flattened body covered with rectangular bony plates, and short legs. [from Greek *ankylos*, crooked + *sauros*, lizard]

ankylosis /aŋkɪˈloʊsɪs/ *noun* a disorder characterized by immobility or stiffening of a joint, the bones of which often become fixed in an abnormal position, as a result of injury, disease (eg rheumatoid arthritis), surgery, or prolonged inflammation of the joint as as a result of infection. [from Greek *ankylosis*]

annalist *noun* a person who compiles annals.

annals /ˈanəls/ *pl. noun* **1** a yearly historical record of events. **2** regular reports of the work of an organization. [from Latin *annales libri*, yearly books]

anneal /əˈniːl/ *verb Engineering* to heat a material such as metal or glass and then slowly cool it in order to make it softer, less brittle, and easier to work. [from Anglo-Saxon *onælan*, to burn]

annealing *noun Engineering* the process whereby metal or glass is heated to a predetermined temperature for a specified length of time, and then allowed to cool slowly, in order to bring about a desirable change in its properties, eg in order to make it softer or less brittle, or to relieve internal stresses.

annelid /ˈanəlɪd/ *noun Zool.* any invertebrate animal belonging to the phylum Annelida, consisting of segmented or true worms, which characteristically have long, soft, cylindrical bodies consisting of many similar ring-shaped body segments. [from Latin *annellus*, little ring]

annex /əˈnɛks/ *verb* **1** to take possession of (land, territory), especially by conquest or occupation. **2** to add or attach (something) to something larger. **3** *colloq.* to take without permission. [from Latin *annectere*, to tie to]

▣ **1** occupy, conquer, seize, usurp, take over. **2** add, append, affix, attach, fasten, adjoin, join, connect, unite, incorporate. **3** appropriate, acquire.

annexation /anəkˈseɪʃən/ *noun* **1** annexing or being annexed. **2** something annexed.

annexe or **annex** /ˈanɛks/ *noun* a building added on to, or used as an addition to, another.

▣ wing, extension, attachment, addition.

annihilate /əˈnaɪəleɪt/ *verb* **1** to destroy completely. **2** to defeat or crush, especially in an argument. [from Latin *annihilare*, from *ad*, to + *nihil*, nothing]

▣ **1** eliminate, eradicate, obliterate, erase, wipe out, exterminate, *slang* liquidate, murder, assassinate, extinguish, raze.

annihilation /ənaɪəˈleɪʃən/ *noun* **1** destruction; reduction to nothing. **2** an act of annihilating.

anniversary /anɪˈvɜːsərɪ/ *noun* (PL. **anniversaries**) **1** the date on which some event took place in a previous year. **2** the celebration of this event on the same date each year. [from Latin *anniversarius*, from *annus*, year + *vertere*, to turn]

Anno Domini /ˈanoʊ ˈdɒmɪnaɪ/ **1** 'in the year of our Lord', used in giving dates since the birth of Christ. **2** *colloq.* old age. [from Latin *anno domini*]

annotate /ˈanoʊteɪt/ *verb* to add notes and explanations to (a book, etc). [from Latin *annotare*]

▣ note, comment on, explain, interpret, elucidate, gloss.

annotation *noun* **1** the making of notes. **2** an explanatory note or comment.

▣ **2** note, footnote, gloss, comment, commentary, exegesis, explanation, elucidation.

annotator /ˈanoʊteɪtə(r)/ *noun* a person who annotates a book.

announce *verb* **1** to make known publicly. **2** to make known (someone's) arrival. **3** to be a sign of: *dark clouds announcing a storm*. [from Latin *annuntiare*]

▣ **1** declare, proclaim, report, state, reveal, disclose, divulge, make known, publish, broadcast, promulgate, propound, advertise, publicize, blazon.

▣ **1** suppress.

announcement *noun* **1** a public or official statement, notice, or advertisement. **2** the act of announcing.

▣ DECLARATION, PROCLAMATION, REVELATION, DISCLOSURE, DIVULGENCE, PUBLICATION, BROADCAST, ADVERTISEMENT. **1** report, statement, communiqué, dispatch, bulletin, notification, notice.

announcer *noun* a person who introduces programmes on radio or television.
. . . .
◨ broadcaster, compère, master of ceremonies, MC, commentator, newscaster, newsreader.
. . . .

annoy *verb* **1** to anger or distress. **2** to harass or pester, especially sexually. [from Latin *inodiare*, to cause aversion]
. . . .
◨ **1** irritate, rile, *colloq.* aggravate, displease, anger, vex, irk, madden, exasperate, tease, provoke, ruffle, upset, distress. **2** trouble, disturb, bother, pester, plague, harass, molest.
◪ **1** please, gratify, comfort.
. . . .

annoyance *noun* **1** something that annoys. **2** the act of annoying. **3** the state of being annoyed.
. . . .
◨ **1** nuisance, pest, bother, trouble, bore, *colloq.* bind, *colloq.* pain, *colloq.* headache, tease. **2** irritation, *colloq.* aggravation, provocation, disturbance, harassment. **3** irritation, *colloq.* aggravation, displeasure, anger, vexation, exasperation.
◪ **3** pleasure.
. . . .

annoyed *adj.* displeased, irritated.
. . . .
◨ irritated, cross, displeased, angry, vexed, piqued, exasperated, provoked, harassed.
◪ pleased.
. . . .

annoying *adj.* irritating, troublesome.
. . . .
◨ irritating, *colloq.* aggravating, vexatious, irksome, troublesome, bothersome, tiresome, trying, maddening, exasperating, galling, teasing, provoking, harassing.
◪ pleasing, welcome.
. . . .

annual /'anjʊəl/ — *adj.* **1** happening every year. **2** lasting for a year. — *noun* **1** *Bot.* a plant that germinates, flowers, produces seed, and dies within a period of one year, eg marigold. See also BIENNIAL, PERENNIAL. **2** a book published every year, especially an illustrated gift-book for children. [from Latin *annualis*, from *annus*, year]

annual general meeting (ABBREV. **AGM**) a yearly meeting of a public company, society, etc to report on the year's activity and to hold elections, etc.

annualize or **annualise** *verb* to calculate (rates of interest, inflation, etc) for a year based on the figures for only part of it.

annually *adv.* yearly.

annual ring *Bot.* each of the concentric rings visible in a cross-section of the stem of a woody plant, eg certain trees. It generally represents the amount of new wood produced in one year, and can thus be used to estimate the age of the plant.

annuity /ə'nju:ɪtɪ/ *noun* (PL. **annuities**) **1** a yearly grant or allowance. **2** money invested providing a fixed amount of interest every year. [from Latin *annuitas*, from *annus*, year]

annul /ə'nʌl/ *verb* (**annulled**, **annulling**) to declare publicly that (a marriage, legal contract, etc) is no longer valid. [from Latin *annullare*, from *ad*, to + *nullus*, none]
. . . .
◨ nullify, invalidate, void, cancel, abolish, terminate, end, quash, repeal, revoke, rescind, countermand, negate, retract.
◪ enact, restore.
. . . .

annular /'anjʊlə(r)/ *adj.* ring-shaped. [from Latin *annularis*, from *anulus*, ring]

annular eclipse *Astron.* an eclipse in which a thin ring of light can be seen around the edge of the obscuring body, eg a solar eclipse during which a ring of sunlight remains visible around the Moon's shadow.

annulate /'anjʊlət/ *adj.* formed from or marked with rings.

annulment *noun* **1** the act of annulling. **2** the formal ending of a marriage, legal contract, etc.

annulus /'anjʊləs/ *noun* **1** *Geom.* the figure formed by two concentric circles on a plane surface, ie a disc with a central hole. **2** *Biol.* any ring-shaped structure, eg the ring of cells that surrounds the spore-bearing structure in ferns, and by constriction causes the structure to rupture, releasing its spores. [from Latin *annularis*, little ring]

Annunciation /ənʌnsɪ'ɛɪʃən/ *noun* **1** (**the Annunciation**) *Christianity* the announcement by the Angel Gabriel to Mary that she would be the mother of Christ. **2** the festival celebrating this, on 25 March; Lady Day. [from Latin *annuntiare*]

annus horribilis /'anʊs hɒ'ri:bɪlɪs/ a particularly unpleasant year. [Latin, by analogy with ANNUS MIRABILIS]

annus mirabilis /'anʊs mi:'rɑ:bɪlɪs/ a remarkably successful or auspicious year. [Latin, = year of wonders]

anode /'anoʊd/ *noun* **1** the positive electrode in an electrolytic cell, towards which negatively charged ions, usually in solution, are attracted. **2** the negative terminal in a battery. See also CATHODE. [from Greek *anodos*, way up, from *ana*, up + *hodos*, way]

anodize or **anodise** /'anədaɪz/ *verb* to coat an object made of metal, especially aluminium) with a thin protective oxide film by making that object the anode in a cell to which an electric current is applied. Such an oxide coating can also be made to absorb coloured dyes, so producing a decorative finish. [from ANODE]

anodyne /'anədaɪn/ — *adj.* **1** able to relieve physical pain or mental distress. **2** able to prevent argument or criticism. — *noun* an anodyne medicine or drug. [from Greek *an*, without + *odyne*, pain]

anoint *verb* to put oil or ointment on (especially a person's head) as part of a religious ceremony, eg baptism. [from Latin *inungere*, from *in*, on + *ungere*, to smear with oil]
. . . .
◨ oil, embrocate, rub, smear, daub, bless, consecrate, sanctify, dedicate.
. . . .

anointment *noun* **1** the action of anointing. **2** ointment, material to use in anointing.

anomalous /ə'nɒmələs/ *adj.* different from the usual; irregular.
. . . .
◨ abnormal, atypical, exceptional, irregular, inconsistent, incongruous, aberrant, deviant, freakish, eccentric, peculiar, singular, odd, unusual, rare.
◪ normal, regular, ordinary.
. . . .

anomaly /ə'nɒməlɪ/ *noun* (PL. **anomalies**) something which is unusual or different from what is normal. [from Greek *an*, without + *homalos*, even]
. . . .
◨ abnormality, exception, irregularity, inconsistency, incongruity, aberration, deviation, divergence, freak, eccentricity, peculiarity, oddity, rarity.
. . . .

anomia /a'noʊmɪə/ *noun Psychol.* a disorder characterized by an inability to name familiar objects, although their uses are understood, and the affected person's speech is not impaired in any other way. [from Greek *anomia*, lawlessness]

anomie or **anomy** /'anoʊmɪ/ *noun* a lack of moral standards in a person or social group. [from Greek *an*, without + *nomos*, law]

anon *adv.* old use soon. [from Anglo-Saxon *on an*, into one]

anon. *abbrev.* anonymous.

anonymity /anɒˈnɪmətɪ/ *noun* the state of being a-nonymous; lack of identity.

anonymous /əˈnɒnɪməs/ *adj.* 1 having no name. 2 *said of an act, piece of writing, etc* by a person whose name is not known or not given. 3 without character. [from Greek *an*, without + *onoma*, name]

⊟ 1 nameless, unnamed, unidentified, unknown, incognito. 2 unsigned, unacknowledged, unspecified, unidentified, unknown. 3 unexceptional, nondescript, faceless, impersonal.
⊟ 1 named. 2 signed, identifiable. 3 distinctive.

anonymously *adv.* without giving a name or revealing one's identity: *an obituary written anonymously.*

anorak /ˈanərak/ *noun* 1 a hooded waterproof jacket. 2 *colloq.* a person who is obsessively interested in a hobby. [from Inuit]

anorexia /anəˈrɛksɪə/ *noun* 1 loss of appetite. 2 a common name for anorexia nervosa. [from Greek *an*, without + *orexis*, longing]

anorexia nervosa /anəˈrɛksɪə nɜːˈvəʊsə/ a psychological illness, mainly affecting adolescent girls and young women, and characterized by a significant decrease in body weight, deliberately induced by refusal to eat because of an obsessive desire to lose weight, usually associated with a distorted perception of actual body shape.

anorexic — *noun* a person suffering from anorexia or anorexia nervosa. — *adj.* 1 relating to or suffering from anorexia or anorexia nervosa. 2 relating to loss of appetite for food.

another *adj., pron.* 1 one more. 2 a person comparable to one already known: *another Mozart.* 3 one of a different kind: *another country.* [Middle English, from *an other*]

anserine /ˈansəraɪn/ *adj. formal* 1 of or like a goose. 2 stupid. [from Latin *anser*, goose]

answer /ˈɑːnsə(r)/ — *noun* 1 something said or done in reply or response to a question, request, letter, etc. 2 the solution to a mathematical problem. — *verb* (**answered, answering**) 1 *trans., intrans.* to make a reply or answer to someone. 2 to react or respond to (a doorbell, the telephone, etc). 3 *intrans.* (**answer to someone for something**) to have to account to them for it. 4 *trans., intrans.* to be suitable (for something). 5 to fulfil or satisfy (a need, etc). 6 to match or be the same as, especially a description. 7 *intrans.* (**answer for something**) to be punished for it. — **answer back** to reply rudely. [from Anglo-Saxon *andswaru*]

⊟ *noun* 1 reply, acknowledgement, response, reaction, rejoinder, retort, riposte, comeback, retaliation. 2 solution, explanation. *verb* 1 reply, acknowledge, respond, retort, riposte, retaliate. 2 react, respond. 4 suit, fit, serve. 5 fulfil, fill, meet, satisfy. 6 match, fit, correspond with, conform with, agree with. **answer back** talk back, retort, riposte, retaliate, contradict, disagree, dispute, rebut.

answerability *noun* the state or obligation of being answerable.

answerable *adj.* (**answerable to someone for something**) accountable for it to them.

⊟ accountable to, responsible for, liable for, to blame for.

answering machine a tape-recording device attached to a telephone, which automatically answers incoming calls by playing a pre-recorded message to the caller and recording the caller's message for subsequent playback.

answering service an organization which takes messages and answers telephone calls for its customers.

ant /ant/ *noun* any of a vast family of insects belonging to the same order (Hymenoptera) as the bees and wasps, and characteristically having elbowed antennae and narrow waists. [from Anglo-Saxon *æmette*]

-ant *suffix* used to form words denoting: 1 a quality or function: *pleasant / expectant.* 2 a person who performs an action: *assistant.* [from Latin *-ant-*, the stem of verb participles]

antacid /antˈasɪd/ — *noun Medicine* an alkaline substance that neutralizes excess acidity in the digestive juices of the stomach, and is used to relieve pain and discomfort in disorders of the digestive system. — *adj.* denoting a substance, especially a medicine, that neutralizes the acidity of the stomach.

antagonism /anˈtagənɪzm/ *noun* openly expressed dislike or opposition.

⊟ opposition, hostility, rivalry, dislike, antipathy, ill-feeling, ill-will, animosity, friction, discord, dissension, conflict.
⊟ rapport, sympathy, agreement.

antagonist /anˈtagənɪst/ *noun* 1 an opponent or enemy. 2 a muscle whose contraction opposes the action of another muscle. 3 *Physiol.* a drug, hormone, or other chemical substance which has the opposite effect to that of another drug, hormone, or chemical substance in the body, and therefore inhibits it. [from Greek *anti*, against + *agon*, contest]

⊟ 1 opponent, adversary, enemy, foe, rival, competitor, contestant, contender.
⊟ 1 ally, supporter.

antagonistic /antagəˈnɪstɪk/ *adj.* hostile; actively opposing.

⊟ opposed, conflicting, hostile, adverse, at variance, incompatible, belligerent, contentious, ill-disposed, unsympathetic.
⊟ sympathetic.

antagonistically *adv.* in an antagonistic or hostile way.

antagonize or **antagonise** /anˈtagənaɪz/ *verb* to make (someone) feel anger or hostility.

⊟ alienate, estrange, disaffect, repel, embitter, offend, insult, provoke, annoy, irritate, anger, incense.
⊟ disarm.

Antarctic /anˈtɑːktɪk/ — *noun* (**the Antarctic**) the area round the South Pole. — *adj.* relating to this area. [from Greek *anti*, against + *arktikos*, the Arctic]

antbird *noun Zool.* a forest-dwelling bird, native to the New World tropics, that feeds on insects, spiders, lizards, and frogs, so called because it follows army ants, feeding on the animals they disturb.

ante /ˈantɪ/ — *noun* 1 a stake put up by a player in poker before receiving any cards. 2 an advance payment. — *verb* 1 to put up as a stake. 2 (**ante up**) to pay. — **up** or **raise the ante** *colloq.* to increase the risks involved in, or the demands to be met before, some action. [from Latin *ante*, before]

ante- *combining form* before in place or time: *anteroom / antenatal.* [from Latin *ante*, before]

anteater *noun* any of various mammals found in swamps, grasslands, and open forests of Central and S America and belonging to the same order (Edentata) as armadillos and sloths.

antecedence /antɪˈsiːdəns/ *noun* the act or state of going before.

antecedent — *noun* 1 an event or circumstance which precedes another. 2 *Grammar* a word or phrase to which another word, especially a relative pronoun, refers. 3 (*usually* **antecedents**) a person's past history. — *adj.* going before in time. [from Latin *ante*, before + *cedere*, to go]

antechamber /ˈantɪtʃeɪmbə(r)/ *noun* an anteroom.

antedate /antɪˈdeɪt/ *verb* 1 to belong to an earlier period than. **2** to put a date (on a document, letter, etc) that is earlier than the actual date.

antediluvian /antɪdɪˈluːvɪən/ adj. **1** belonging to the time before the Flood. **2** facetious very old or old-fashioned. [from ANTE- + Latin diluvium, flood]

antelope /ˈantəloʊp/ noun (PL. **antelope**, **antelopes**) any of various species of hoofed mammal with a smooth brown or grey coat, belonging to the same family (Bovidae) as cattle, goats, and sheep, and found mainly in Africa, although a few species live in Asia. [from Greek antholops]

ante meridiem /antɪ məˈrɪdɪəm/ see A.M.

antenatal /antɪˈneɪtəl/ adj. **1** formed or occurring before birth. **2** relating to the health and care of women during pregnancy. [from ANTE- + Latin natalis, of one's birth]

antenna /anˈtɛnə/ noun **1** (PL. **antennae**) one of a pair of long slender jointed structures on the head of certain invertebrate animals, especially insects and crustaceans (eg crabs), which act as feelers but are also concerned with the sense of smell, and are sometimes modified for other functions (eg swimming). **2** (PL. **antennas**) an aerial. [from Latin antenna, yard of a mast]

antepenultimate /antɪpəˈnʌltəmət/ noun, adj. third from last.

anterior /anˈtɪərɪə(r)/ adj. **1** earlier in time. **2** at or nearer the front. [from Latin anterior, from ante, before]

anteroom noun a small room which opens into another, more important, room.

anthem noun **1** a usually complicated piece of music sung by a church choir, usually with words from the Bible. **2** a song of praise or celebration, especially of a nation: national anthem. [from Anglo-Saxon antefn, from Latin antiphona, antiphon]

🔲 HYMN, SONG. **1** chorale, psalm, canticle, chant.

anther noun in flowering plants, the two-lobed structure at the tip of the stamen which contains the pollen sacs within which the pollen grains are produced. The anther is usually borne on a long slender stalk or filament. [from Greek anthos, flower]

anthesis /anˈθiːsɪs/ noun Bot. **1** the opening of a flower-bud. **2** the period of time during which a flower is in full bloom. [from Greek anthesis, flowering]

ant hill a mound of earth deposited around the entrance to the underground nest of ants or termites.

anthocyanin /anθoʊˈsaɪənɪn/ noun Bot. any of a group of pigments that are found in certain cells in plants, and are responsible for many of the red, purple, and blue colours of flowers, fruits, and leaves. [from Greek anthos, flower + kyanos, blue]

anthologist noun a person who compiles an anthology.

anthology /anˈθɒlədʒɪ/ noun (PL. **anthologies**) a collection of pieces of poetry or other writing. [from Greek anthos, flower + logia, gathering]

🔲 selection, collection, compilation, compendium, treasury, miscellany.

anthracite /ˈanθrəsaɪt/ noun Geol. a hard shiny black coal with a very high carbon content, that burns with a short blue flame and generates much heat but little or no smoke. [from Greek anthrax, coal]

anthrax /ˈanθraks/ noun Medicine an acute infectious disease, now rare in the UK, that is most common in sheep and cattle, but can be transmitted to humans by contact with infected meat, hides, excrement, etc. [from Greek anthrax, = coal, carbuncle]

anthropo- combining form of or like human beings. [from Greek anthropos, man]

anthropocentric /anθrəpoʊˈsɛntrɪk/ adj. believing that mankind is the central element of existence.

anthropocentrically adv. in an anthropocentric way.

anthropoid /ˈanθrəpɔɪd/ — adj. like a human being in form. — noun an ape that is like a human being in form, eg the gorilla. [from Greek anthropoeides, man-like]

anthropoidal adj. like an anthropoid.

anthropological /anθrəpəˈlɒdʒɪkəl/ adj. relating to anthropology; relating to the nature and natural history of human beings.

anthropologist noun a person who studies anthropology.

anthropology /anθrəˈpɒlədʒɪ/ noun the study of human beings, especially their society, customs, and beliefs.

anthropomorphic /anθroʊpəˈmɔːfɪk/ adj. **1** characterized by anthropomorphism. **2** human in form.

anthropomorphism noun the attribution of human behaviour, feelings, and beliefs to animals, gods, objects, etc. [from ANTHROPO- + Greek morphe, form]

anthropomorphous adj. human in form.

anti /ˈantɪ, ˈantaɪ/ — adj. opposed to something. — noun a person who is opposed to something. [from Greek anti, against]

anti- combining form **1** opposed to; against: anti-aircraft. **2** opposite to: anticlockwise / anticlimax. [from Greek anti, against]

anti-aircraft adj., said of a gun or missile used to attack enemy aircraft.

anti-ballistic missile /antɪbəˈlɪstɪk/ a missile that is used to intercept and destroy a ballistic missile.

antibiotic /antɪbaɪˈɒtɪk/ — noun a substance, produced by or derived from a micro-organism, that can selectively destroy or inhibit other bacteria and fungi without damaging the host. — adj. of or relating to antibiotics. [from ANTI- + Greek bios, life]

antibody /ˈantɪbɒdɪ/ noun (PL. **antibodies**) a protein that is produced by certain white blood cells in response to the presence in the body of an antigen (a foreign substance, usually a protein). The antibody combines with the antigen that caused its production, and renders it harmless. The production of antibodies is an important part of the body's immune response.

Antichrist noun **1** an enemy of Christ. **2** Christianity the great enemy of Christ who is expected to appear before the end of the world. [from Greek anti, against + Christos, Christ]

anticipate /anˈtɪsɪpeɪt/ verb **1** to see what will be needed or wanted in the future and do what is necessary in advance. **2** to expect. **3** to look forward to. **4** to mention (part of a story, what a person thinks, etc) before the proper time. **5** to spend (eg one's salary) before receiving it. [from Latin anticipare, from ante, before + capere, to take]

🔲 **1** forestall, pre-empt, prepare for, intercept, prevent. **2** expect, foresee, predict, forecast. **3** look forward to, await, look for, hope for, bank on, count on. **4** forestall, pre-empt.

anticipation noun anticipating, expectation.

anticipatory /anˈtɪsɪpeɪtərɪ/ adj. anticipating.

anticlerical adj. opposed to public and political power being held by members of the clergy.

anticlericalism noun opposition to the clergy, especially to their having power in politics.

anticlimactic /antɪklaɪˈmaktɪk/ adj. relating to or in the nature of an anticlimax.

anticlimax /antɪˈklaɪmaks/ noun a dull or disappointing end to a series of events which seemed to be leading to a climax.

🔲 comedown, let-down, disappointment, bathos.

anticline /ˈantɪklaɪn/ noun Geol. a geological fold in the form of an arch, formed as a result of compressional forces acting in a horizontal plane on rock strata. [from ANTI- + Greek klinein, to lean]

anticlockwise adv., adj. in the opposite direction to that in which the hands of a clock move.

anticoagulant /ˌantɪkoʊˈagjʊlənt/ *noun Medicine* a drug or other substance that prevents or slows the clotting of blood.

anticonvulsant /ˌantɪkənˈvʌlsənt/ *noun Medicine* a drug that is used to prevent or reduce convulsions, especially in epilepsy.

antics *pl. noun* odd or foolish behaviour. [from Italian *antico*, grotesque]

············

☰ foolery, tomfoolery, silliness, buffoonery, clowning, frolics, capers, skylarking, playfulness, mischief, tricks, monkey-tricks, pranks, stunts.

············

anticyclone /ˌantɪˈsaɪkloʊn/ *noun Meteorol.* an area of relatively high atmospheric pressure from which light winds spiral outward in the opposite direction to that of the Earth's rotation. Anticyclones are generally associated with calm settled weather, and are shown on weather charts as a series of widely spaced concentric isobars.

antidepressant /ˌantɪdɪˈpresənt/ — *noun* any drug that prevents or relieves the symptoms of depression. — *adj.* denoting a drug or any other agent that has this effect.

antidote /ˈantɪdoʊt/ *noun* **1** any agent (eg a drug) that counteracts or prevents the action of a poison. **2** anything that counteracts or prevents something bad. [from Greek *anti*, against + *didonai*, to give]

············

☰ REMEDY. **1** cure, counter-agent, antitoxin, neutralizer. **2** countermeasure, corrective.

············

antifreeze *noun* any substance that is added to water or some other liquid in order to lower its freezing point, especially a mixture of ethylene glycol and water which is widely used to protect cooling systems that rely on circulating water, eg the radiators of motor vehicles.

antigen /ˈantɪdʒən/ *noun Biol.* any foreign substance, usually a protein, that stimulates the body's immune system to produce antibodies. Common antigens include bacteria, viruses, allergens, and the proteins of incompatible blood groups or tissues. [from ANTI- + Greek *genes*, born, produced]

antihero /ˈantɪhɪəroʊ/ *noun* (PL. **antiheroes**) a principal character in a book, play, film, etc who has no noble qualities but is just like an ordinary person.

antihistamine /ˌantɪˈhɪstəmiːn/ *noun Medicine* any of a group of drugs that counteract the effects of histamines in allergic reactions, such as hay fever. Antihistamines are also used to treat disorders that cause nausea and vomiting, such as travel sickness.

anti-inflammatory *adj. Medicine* denoting a drug that reduces inflammation.

antiknock *noun* (*attributive*) any substance that is added to petrol in order to reduce knocking, especially in the engines of motor vehicles. The most widely used antiknock compound, tetraethyl lead, causes environmental pollution and is being increasingly replaced by non-metallic compounds in unleaded petrols.

anti-lock *adj., said of a braking system* designed to prevent the wheels of a vehicle locking when the brakes are applied.

antilog *abbrev.* antilogarithm.

antilogarithm *noun* (ABBREV. **antilog**) *Maths.* the number *x* whose logarithm to a specified base is a given number *y*.

antimacassar /ˌantɪməˈkasə(r)/ *noun* a covering for the back of a chair to stop it getting dirty. [from ANTI- + *macassar*, an oil once used on hair]

antimatter *noun* a substance that is composed entirely of antiparticles, ie subatomic particles with the opposite electric charge, magnetic moment, and spin to other subatomic particles of the same mass.

antimony /ˈantɪmənɪ/ *noun Chem.* (SYMBOL **Sb**, ATOMIC NUMBER **51**) a brittle bluish-white metal that is a poor conductor of heat and electricity, and is added to lead alloys to increase their hardness. It is used in storage batteries, semiconductors, flameproofing, paints, ceramics, and enamels, and its compounds are used in paint pigments. [from Latin *antimonium*]

antinode *noun Physics* a point that is halfway between the nodes in a stationary wave (a standing wave, produced when a travelling wave is reflected back along its own path). It indicates a position of maximum displacement or intensity.

antinomian /ˌantɪˈnoʊmɪən/ — *adj.* denoting the view that Christians do not have to observe moral law. — *noun* a person holding this view. [from Latin *Antinomi*, the name of a sect believing this, from ANTI- + Greek *nomos*, law]

antinomy /anˈtɪnəmɪ/ *noun* (PL. **antinomies**) a contradiction between two laws or beliefs that are reasonable in themselves. [from Greek *anti*, against + *nomos*, law]

antinovel *noun* a novel in which the accepted elements of novel-writing are ignored or avoided.

antinuclear *adj.* opposed to the use of nuclear power or nuclear weapons.

antioxidant *noun Chem.* a substance that slows down the oxidation of other substances, often by being oxidized itself. The term is usually applied to additives in foods and plastics.

antiparticle *noun Physics* an elementary particle that has the same mass and spin as another elementary particle, but opposite electrical and magnetic properties, eg the positron is the antiparticle of the electron, because it has a positive charge of the same magnitude as the negative charge of an electron. When an elementary particle is brought together with its antiparticle, mutual destruction results.

antipasto /antɪˈpasto/ *noun* (PL. **antipasti**, **antipastos**) food served at the beginning of a meal to sharpen the appetite. [from Italian *antipasto*]

antipathetic /ˌantɪpəˈθetɪk/ *adj.* arousing or having an antipathy.

antipathetically *adv.* in an antipathetic way.

antipathy /anˈtɪpəθɪ/ *noun* (PL. **antipathies**) strong dislike or hostility.

············

☰ aversion, dislike, hate, hatred, loathing, abhorrence, distaste, repulsion, hostility, opposition, enmity, antagonism, animosity, ill-will.
☲ liking, affection, sympathy, rapport.

············

anti-personnel *adj., said of weapons and bombs* designed to attack and kill people rather than destroy buildings and other weapons.

antiperspirant /ˌantɪˈpɜːspərənt/ *noun* a substance applied to the skin to help stop perspiration.

antiphon /ˈantɪfən/ *noun* a hymn or psalm sung alternately by two groups of singers. [from Latin *antiphona*, from Greek *anti*, in return + *phone*, voice]

antipodean /antɪpəˈdɪən/ *adj.* relating to the antipodes.

antipodes /anˈtɪpədiːz/ *pl. noun* (also **Antipodes**) two points on the Earth's surface that are diametrically opposite each other, especially Australia and New Zealand as being opposite Europe. [from Greek *antipodes*, from *anti-pous*, having the feet opposite]

antipope /ˈantɪpoʊp/ *noun* a pope elected in opposition to one already elected.

antipyretic /ˌantɪpaɪəˈretɪk/ — *adj.* denoting any drug that reduces or prevents fever, eg aspirin, paracetamol. — *noun* any drug that has this effect. [from ANTI- + Greek *pyretos*, fever]

antiquarian /ˌantɪˈkweərɪən/ — *adj.* of or dealing in antiques and rare books. — *noun* an antiquary.

antiquary /ˈantɪkwərɪ/ *noun* (PL. **antiquaries**) a person who collects, studies, or deals in antiques and antiquities. [from Latin *antiquarius*, from *antiquus*, ancient]

antiquated *adj.* old and out of date; old-fashioned. [from Latin *antiquare*, to make old]

antique /anˈtiːk/ — *noun* **1** a piece of furniture, china, etc which is old and often valuable, and is sought after by collectors. **2** (**the Antique**) art from the time of Classical antiquity, especially sculpture. It has been regarded by artists since the Renaissance both as a source of motifs, and as a model for style. — *adj.* **1** old and often valuable. **2** *colloq.* old-fashioned. [from Latin *antiquus*, ancient]

▤ *noun* **1** antiquity, relic, bygone, period piece, heirloom, curio, museum piece, curiosity, rarity. *adj.* **1** old, ancient, antiquarian, veteran, vintage. **2** antiquated, old-fashioned, outdated, archaic, obsolete.

antiquity /anˈtɪkwətɪ/ *noun* (PL. **antiquities**) **1** ancient times, especially before the end of the Roman Empire in AD 476. **2** great age. **3** (**antiquities**) works of art or buildings surviving from ancient times. [from Latin *antiquitas*, from *antiquus*, ancient]

▤ **1** ancient times, time immemorial, distant past, olden days. **2** age, old age, oldness, agedness.
▣ **2** modernity, novelty.

antiracism *noun* support for policies that promote equality among, and tolerance between, groups of different racial origins, and opposition to prejudice or persecution on grounds of race.

antiracist *adj.* supporting or characterized by antiracism.

antirrhinum /antɪˈraɪnəm/ *noun* any of various bushy perennial plants of the genus *Antirrhinum*, native to Europe and N America, and having large brightly coloured two-lipped flowers. Many varieties are cultivated as ornamental garden plants. Also called SNAPDRAGON. [from Greek *antirrinon*, from *anti*, mimicking + *rhis*, nose]

antiscorbutic /antɪskɔːˈbjuːtɪk/ — *adj.* preventing or curing scurvy. — *noun* an antiscorbutic drug.

anti-semite /antɪˈsemaɪt/ *noun* a person who is hostile to or prejudiced against Jews.

anti-semitic /antɪsəˈmɪtɪk/ *adj.* disliking or prejudiced against Jews.

anti-semitism /antɪˈsemətɪzm/ *noun* hostility to or prejudice against Jews.

antiseptic /antɪˈseptɪk/ — *adj.* denoting any substance that kills or inhibits the growth of bacteria and other micro-organisms, but is not toxic to the skin or mucous membranes, and so can be used to clean wounds and prevent infections. — *noun* denoting any substance that has this effect, eg ethanol (alcohol), iodine.

▤ *adj.* disinfectant, medicated, germicidal, cleansing, purifying, aseptic, germ-free, sterile, sanitary, hygienic. *noun* disinfectant, germicide, bactericide, purifier, cleanser.

antiserum /ˈantɪsɪərəm/ *noun* (PL. **antisera**) a blood serum containing antibodies that are specific for and neutralize the effects of a particular antigen. Antisera are used in vaccines to provide immunity to specific diseases. [from ANTIBODY + SERUM]

antisocial *adj.* **1** unwilling to mix socially with other people. **2** *said of behaviour* causing harm or annoyance to other people.

▤ ASOCIAL. **1** unfriendly, unsociable, uncommunicative, reserved, retiring, withdrawn, alienated, unapproachable. **2** harmful, annoying, unacceptable, disruptive, disorderly, hostile, antagonistic.
▣ **1** sociable, gregarious.

antistatic *adj.* denoting any substance that prevents the accumulation of static electric charges on a surface (eg clothing, vinyl records) as a result of friction during operation or wear.

antitank *adj.*, *said of weapons* designed to destroy military tanks.

antithesis /anˈtɪθəsɪs/ *noun* (PL. **antitheses**) **1** a direct opposite. **2** the placing together of contrasting ideas, words, or themes in any oral or written argument, especially to produce an effect. [from Greek *antitithenai*, to set against]

antithetic or **antithetical** *adj.* **1** of the nature of antithesis. **2** directly opposite; contrasted.

antithetically *adv.* in direct opposition.

antitoxin *noun* Medicine a type of antibody produced by the body in order to neutralize a toxin released by invading bacteria, viruses, etc. Some antitoxins are deliberately introduced into the body by vaccination.

antitrades *pl. noun* winds blowing above, and in the opposite direction to, trade winds.

anti-trust *adj.* North Amer., esp. US, *said of a law* protecting small companies and trade from domination by monopolies.

antiviral *adj.* Medicine denoting a drug that destroys viruses or prevents their multiplication.

anti-vivisection *noun* opposition to scientific experiments on living animals.

anti-vivisectionist *noun* a person who opposes scientific experiments being made on living animals.

antler *noun* either of a pair of solid bony outgrowths, which may or may not be branched, on the head of an animal belonging to the deer family. Antlers are usually present only in the male and are shed annually. [from French *antoillier*]

antonym /ˈantənɪm/ *noun* a word opposite in meaning to another word. [from Greek *anti*, opposite + *onyma* or *onoma*, name]

antonymous /anˈtɒnəməs/ *adj.*, *said of a word* opposite in meaning to another word.

antonymy /anˈtɒnəmɪ/ *noun* oppositeness of meaning.

antrum /ˈantrəm/ *noun* (PL. **antra**) **1** Anat. a cavity or sinus, especially in a bone. **2** Anat. the part of the stomach next to the opening that leads into the duodenum. [from Greek *antron*, cave]

ANU *abbrev.* Australian National University.

anus /ˈeɪnəs/ *noun* the opening at the end of the alimentary canal between the buttocks, through which faeces leave the bowels. [from Latin *anus*, ring]

anvil *noun* a heavy iron block on which metal objects can be hammered into shape. [from Anglo-Saxon *anfilt*]

anxiety /aŋˈzaɪətɪ/ (PL. **anxieties**) *noun* a strong feeling of fear or distress either as a normal response to a dangerous or stressful situation, or as a form of neurosis in which there is excessive and lasting fear, often for no apparent reason. Symptoms of anxiety may include trembling, sweating, breathlessness, rapid pulse rate, dry mouth, and nausea.

▤ worry, concern, care, distress, nervousness, apprehension, dread, foreboding, misgiving, uneasiness, restlessness, fretfulness, impatience, suspense, tension, stress.
▣ calm, composure, serenity.

anxious /ˈaŋkʃəs/ *adj.* **1** worried, nervous, or fearful about what will or may happen. **2** causing worry, fear, or uncertainty. **3** very eager: *anxious to do well.* [from Latin *anxius*, from *angere*, to press tightly]

▤ **1** worried, concerned, nervous, apprehensive, afraid, fearful, uneasy, restless, fretful, impatient, in suspense, on tenterhooks, tense, distressed, disturbed, troubled, stressed. **2** worrying, alarming, frightening, disturbing, stressful.
▣ **1** calm, composed.

anxiously *adv.* in an anxious state; nervously.

anxiousness *noun* a state of anxiety.

any — *adj.* **1** one, no matter which: *can't find any answer.* **2** some, no matter which: *have you any apples?* **3** a very small amount of: *won't tolerate any nonsense.* **4** large or indefinite: *have any number of dresses.* **5** whichever or whatever: *any child could tell you.* — *pron.* any one or any amount. — *adv.* (*in questions and negative sentences*) in any way whatever: *it isn't any better.* [from Anglo-Saxon *ænig*]

anybody *pron.* **1** any person, no matter which. **2** *in questions and negative sentences* an important person.

anyhow *adv.* **1** in spite of what has been said, done, etc; anyway. **2** carelessly; in an untidy state.

anyone same as ANYBODY.

anyplace *North Amer., esp. US* same as ANYWHERE.

anything — *pron.* a thing of any kind; a thing, no matter which. — *adv.* in any way; to any extent: *she isn't anything like her sister.* — **anything but ...** not ... at all: *was anything but straightforward.* **like anything** *colloq.* with great speed or enthusiasm.

anyway *adv.* **1** nevertheless; in spite of what has been said, done, etc. **2** in any way or manner.

anywhere — *adv.* in, at, or to any place. — *pron.* any place.

Anzac /ˈanzak/ *noun* **1** (*also* **ANZAC**) the Australia and New Zealand Army Corps, a unit in which troops from both countries fought during World War I in the Middle East and on the Western Front. **2** a soldier serving in this unit.

Anzac Day 25 Apr, a public holiday in Australia and New Zealand in memory of the Anzac landing in Gallipoli in 1915.

AOB or **AOCB** *abbrev.* any other business or competent business: the last item on the agenda for a meeting, when any matter not already dealt with may be raised.

AOC *abbrev.* appellation d'origine contrôlée.

A1 or **A-1** *adj. colloq.* first-class; of the highest quality.

aorist /ˈɛərɪst/ *noun Grammar* a tense of a verb in some inflecting languages, especially Greek, expressing action in simple past time with no implications of completion, duration, or repetition. [from Greek *aoristos*, indefinite]

aorta /eɪˈɔːtə/ *noun Anat.* in mammals, the main artery in the body, that carries oxygenated blood from the heart to the smaller arteries that in turn supply the rest of the body. [from Greek *aorte*]

AP *abbrev.* Associated Press.

apace *adv. literary* quickly. [from A[3] + PACE[1]]

Apache a Native American people who dominated much of the SW during the 19c. The surviving Apache population (c.11,000) live on reservations (eg in Arizona and New Mexico).

apart *adv.* **1** in or into pieces: *come apart.* **2** separated by a certain distance or time. **3** to or on one side. **4** (*after a noun*) leaving aside: *joking apart.* — **apart from something** or **someone** except for them; leaving them out of consideration. [from Old French *a part*, to one side]

≡ **1** to pieces, to bits, into parts, in pieces, in bits, piecemeal. **2** away, afar, distant, separated, divorced, cut off, isolated. **3** aside, to one side, aloof, separately, independently, individually, alone, on one's own, by oneself.

≠ **1, 2** together.

apartheid /əˈpɑːtheɪt, əˈpɑːthaɪt/ *noun* an official policy of separate development for different races in a state, especially formerly in South Africa. [from Afrikaans *apart*, apart + *heid*, -hood]

apartment *noun* **1** a large room. **2** *North Amer.* a set of rooms for living in on one floor; a flat. **3** (**apartments**) a set of rooms used for accommodation, usually in a large building. [from French *appartement*, from Italian *appartare*, to separate]

apathetic *adj.* feeling or showing little or no emotion; indifferent.

≡ uninterested, unenthusiastic, uninvolved, indifferent, unemotional, emotionless, impassive, unmoved, unconcerned, cold, unresponsive, passive, listless, unambitious.

≠ enthusiastic, involved, concerned, responsive.

apathetically *adv.* with an apathetic manner; without caring.

apathy /ˈapθəɪ/ *noun* lack of interest or enthusiasm. [from Greek *a*, without + *pathos*, feeling]

≡ uninterestedness, indifference, impassivity, unconcern, coldness, insensibility, passivity, listlessness, lethargy, sluggishness, torpor, inertia.

≠ enthusiasm, interest, concern.

apatite /ˈapətaɪt/ *noun Geol.* a common phosphate mineral widely distributed in small amounts in many igneous and metamorphic rocks. [from Greek *apate* deceit, from its having been confused with other minerals]

apatosaurus /əpatəˈsɔːrəs/ *noun* (*also called* **brontosaurus**) a huge semi-aquatic dinosaur of the Jurassic period, up to 20m in length and weighing about 30 tonnes, with massive limbs, a small head and tiny teeth, a long neck, and a whip-like tail. [from Greek *apate*, deceit + *sauros*, lizard]

ape — *noun* **1** any of 11 species of primate that differ from most monkeys, and resemble humans, in having no tail and in walking upright some of the time. Their brains are much more highly developed than those of other primates. **2** an ugly, stupid, or clumsy person. — *verb* to imitate (someone's behaviour, speech, etc). — **go ape** *North Amer. slang* to go crazy. [from Anglo-Saxon *apa*]

≡ *verb* copy, imitate, echo, mirror, parrot, mimic, take off, caricature, parody, counterfeit, affect.

apeman *noun* any of various extinct primates thought to have been intermediate in development between humans and the higher apes.

aperient /əˈpɪərɪənt/ — *adj.* having a mild laxative effect. — *noun* an aperient substance or drug. [from Latin *aperire*, to open]

aperitif /əˈperɪtiːf/ *noun* an alcoholic drink taken before a meal to stimulate the appetite. [from French *apéritif*, from Latin *aperire*, to open]

aperture /ˈapətʃə(r)/ *noun* **1** a small hole or opening. **2** the opening through which light enters an optical instrument such as a camera or telescope. **3** the effective diameter of the lens in such an instrument. [from Latin *apertura*, from *aperire*, to open]

APEX /ˈeɪpeks/ *abbrev.* advance purchase excursion: a reduced fare for journeys booked a certain period in advance.

apex /ˈeɪpeks/ *noun* (PL. **apexes**, **apices**) the highest point or tip. [from Latin *apex*, peak]

aphasia /əˈfeɪzɪə/ *noun Psychol.* loss or impairment of the ability to speak or write, or to understand the meaning of written or spoken language. In right-handed people it is caused by damage to the left side of the brain. It is treated by similar methods to those used for teaching deaf people. [from A-[1] not + Greek *phanai*, to speak]

aphelion /aˈfiːlɪən, apˈhiːlɪən/ *noun* (PL. **aphelia**) the point in a planet's orbit when it is furthest from the sun. See also PERIHELION. [from Greek *apo*, from + *helios*, sun]

aphid /ˈeɪfɪd/ or **aphis** /ˈeɪfɪs/ *noun* (PL. **aphids**, **aphides**) any of about 4,000 species of small bug belonging to the family Aphididae, found mainly in north temperate regions, and having a soft pear-shaped body, with or without wings, and a small head with slender beaklike mouthparts that are used to pierce plant tissues and suck the sap on which the animal feeds. Some aphid species (eg greenfly, blackfly) are serious plant pests.

aphonia /eɪˈfoʊnɪə/ *noun Psychol.* inability to speak, which may be caused by hysteria, laryngitis or some other disorder of the larynx or brain damage. [from A-[1] + Greek *phone*, voice]

aphorism /ˈafərɪzm/ *noun* a short, often clever or humorous saying expressing some well-known truth. [from Greek *aphorizein*, to define]

aphoristic *adj.* characteristic of an aphorism; short and pithy.

aphrodisiac /afrə'dızıak/ — *noun* a food, drink, or drug that is said to stimulate sexual desire, eg oysters, ginseng. — *adj.* sexually exciting. [from Greek *aphrodisiakos*, from *Aphrodite*, the goddess of love]

apiarist /'eɪpɪərɪst/ *noun* a bee-keeper.

apiary /'eɪpɪərɪ/ *noun* (PL. **apiaries**) a place where honey bees are kept, usually for the purpose of breeding and honey production, but sometimes to aid the pollination of seed and fruit crops. [from Latin *apiarum*, from *apis*, bee]

apical /'apɪkəl, 'eɪpɪkəl/ *adj.* of, at, or forming an apex.

apiculture /'eɪpɪkʌltʃə(r)/ *noun* the rearing and breeding of honey bees, especially on a commercial scale, to obtain honey, beeswax, or royal jelly. [from Latin *apis*, bee]

apiece *adv.* to, for, by, or from each one.

apish *adj.* 1 like an ape. 2 imitative. 3 affected; silly.

aplomb /ə'plɒm/ *noun* calm self-assurance and poise. [from French *à plomb*, straight up and down]

   ▣ calmness, coolness, confidence, assurance, self-assurance, poise, balance, composure, equanimity.
   ▣ discomposure.

apnoea or **apnea** /ap'nɪə/ *noun Medicine* a temporary cessation of breathing, as occurs in some adults during sleep (*sleep apnoea*) and in some newborn babies. [from Greek *apnoia*]

apocalypse /ə'pɒkəlɪps/ *noun* 1 (**Apocalypse**) the last book of the New Testament, also called the Revelation of St John, which describes the end of the world. 2 any revelation of the future, especially future destruction or violence. [from Greek *apocalypsis*, uncovering]

apocalyptic *adj.* 1 like an apocalypse. 2 *said of an event* signalling or foretelling an upheaval, disaster, etc.

Apocrypha /ə'pɒkrɪfə/ *pl. noun* those books of the Bible included in the ancient Greek and Latin versions of the Old Testament, but not in the Hebrew version. They are excluded from modern Protestant Bibles but included in Roman Catholic and Orthodox Bibles. [from Greek *apocryphos*, hidden]

apocryphal /ə'pɒkrɪfəl/ *adj.*, *said of a story, etc* unlikely to be true.

   ▣ unauthenticated, unverified, unconfirmed, unsubstantiated, questionable, doubtful, dubious, spurious, fabricated, concocted, fictitious, imaginary, legendary, mythical.
   ▣ true, authentic.

apogee /'apoʊdʒiː/ *noun* 1 *Astron.* the point in the orbit of the Moon or an artifical satellite around the Earth when it is at its greatest distance from the Earth. See also PERIGEE. 2 *Physics* the greatest height reached by a missile whose velocity is not high enough for it to escape from a gravitational field. [from Greek *apo*, away + *gaia*, Earth]

apolitical /eɪpə'lɪtɪkəl/ *adj.* not interested or active in politics.

apolitically *adv.* without concern for politics.

apologetic /əpɒlə'dʒɛtɪk/ *adj.* showing or expressing regret for a mistake or offence.

   ▣ sorry, repentant, penitent, contrite, remorseful, conscience-stricken, regretful, rueful.
   ▣ unrepentant, impenitent, defiant.

apologetically *adv.* in an apologetic way.

apologia /apə'loʊdʒɪə/ *noun* a formal statement in defence of a belief or cause.

apologist /ə'pɒlədʒɪst/ *noun* a person who formally defends a belief or cause.

apologize or **apologise** /ə'pɒlədʒaɪz/ *verb intrans.* to acknowledge or express regret for a mistake or offence.

apology /ə'pɒlədʒɪ/ *noun* (PL. **apologies**) 1 an expression of regret for a mistake or offence. 2 a formal defence of a belief or cause. — **apology for something** a poor example of it: *what's that apology for a pudding?* [from Greek *apologia*, from *apologeisthai*, to speak in defence]

   ▣ 1 acknowledgement, confession, excuse, explanation. 2 defence, apologia, justification, vindication, plea.

apophthegm /'apəθɛm/ *noun* a short saying expressing some general truth. [from Greek *apophthegma*, from *apo*, forth + *phthengesthai*, to speak]

apoplectic /apə'plɛktɪk/ *adj.* 1 of or relating to apoplexy. 2 *colloq.* red-faced and very angry.

apoplectically *adv.* with, or as if with, symptoms of apoplexy.

apoplexy /'apəplɛksɪ/ *noun* a former name for a stroke caused by a cerebral haemorrhage. [from Greek *apoplexia*, being struck down]

apostasy /ə'pɒstəsɪ/ *noun* (PL. **apostasies**) the giving up of one's religion, principles, or political party. [from Greek *apo*, away + *stasis*, standing]

apostate /ə'pɒsteɪt/ — *noun* a person who renounces a former religion or belief. — *adj.* relating to or involved in this renunciation.

a posteriori /eɪ pɒstɪərɪ'ɔːraɪ, ɑː pɒstɛrɪ'ɔːriː/ *said of an argument or reasoning* working from effect to cause or from particular cases to general principles; based on observation or experience. See also A PRIORI. [from Latin *a posteriori*, from what comes after]

apostle /ə'pɒsl/ *noun* 1 (*often* **Apostle**) a person sent out to preach about Christ in the early Christian church, especially one of his twelve original disciples. 2 an enthusiastic champion or supporter of a cause, belief, etc. [from Greek *apostolos*, from *apo*, away + *stellein*, to send]

Apostles' Creed *Christianity* the most ancient creed of the Christian faith, widely used in Roman Catholic and Protestant churches, and recognized by Orthodox Churches. It is a statement which stresses the threefold nature of God (as Father, Son, and Holy Spirit) and the work of Christ as God's representative on Earth. In its present form, it dates back to the 8c, though its origins go back at least as far as the 3c.

apostolic /apə'stɒlɪk/ *adj.* 1 relating to the apostles in the early Christian Church, or to their teaching. 2 relating to the Pope: *the Apostolic See*.

apostolically *adv.* as regards the apostles or the Pope.

apostolic succession *Christianity* the theory in the Christian Church (notably the Roman Catholic Church), that certain spiritual powers conferred on the first Apostles by Christ have been handed down from one generation of bishops to the next in an unbroken chain of transmission. It is disputed by many New Testament scholars, and rejected by many Churches.

apostrophe /ə'pɒstrəfɪ/ *noun* 1 a punctuation mark ('), used to show the omission of a letter or letters, eg *I'm* for *I am*, and possession, eg *Ann's book*. 2 a passage in a speech, poem, etc which turns away from its course to address a person (especially dead or absent) or thing. [from Greek *apostrephein*, to turn away]

apostrophize or **apostrophise** /ə'pɒstrəfaɪz/ *verb* to speak an apostrophe to.

apothecary /ə'pɒθəkərɪ/ *noun* (PL. **apothecaries**) *old use* a chemist licensed to dispense drugs. [from Greek *apotheke*, storehouse]

apotheosis /əpɒθɪ'oʊsɪs/ *noun* (PL. **apotheoses**) 1 a raising to the rank of god. 2 a perfect example. [from Greek *apo*, completely + *theos*, god]

appal *verb* (**appalled**, **appalling**) to shock or horrify. [from French *appallir*, to grow pale]

▣ horrify, shock, outrage, disgust, dismay, daunt, intimidate, unnerve, alarm, scare, frighten, terrify.
▣ reassure, encourage.

appalling *adj.* **1** causing feelings of shock or horror. **2** *colloq.* extremely bad.

▣ **1** horrifying, horrific, shocking, outrageous, atrocious, disgusting, hideous, ghastly, horrible, daunting, alarming, frightening, terrifying. **2** *colloq.* awful, *colloq.* frightful, *colloq.* terrible, dreadful, dire.
▣ **1** reassuring, encouraging.

apparatchik /ɑːpəˈrɑːtʃɪk/ *noun* **1** a member of a communist bureaucracy or party machine. **2** a bureaucratic hack. [from Russian *apparat*, apparatus, machine]

apparatus /apəˈreɪtəs, apəˈrɑːtəs/ *noun* (PL. **apparatuses, apparatus**) **1** the equipment needed for a particular purpose; a piece of equipment; a machine or appliance. **2** an organization or system made up of many different parts. [from Latin *apparatus*, from *apparare*, to prepare for]

▣ **1** equipment, gear, tackle, tools, implements, utensils, materials, machinery, machine, appliance, gadget, device, contraption. **2** system, machinery, mechanism, means.

apparel /əˈparəl/ *noun old use, formal* clothing. [from French *apareillier*, to make fit]

apparent /əˈparənt, əˈpeərənt/ *adj.* **1** easy to see or understand. **2** seeming to be real but perhaps not actually so. See also HEIR. [from Latin *apparere*, to appear]

▣ **1** visible, evident, noticeable, perceptible, plain, clear, distinct, marked, unmistakable, obvious, manifest, patent. **2** seeming, outward, superficial.
▣ **1** hidden, obscure.

apparently *adv.* **1** as it seems. **2** evidently, clearly.

▣ **1** seemingly, ostensibly, outwardly, superficially. **2** evidently, plainly, clearly, obviously, manifestly, patently.

apparition /apəˈrɪʃən/ *noun* **1** a sudden, unexpected appearance, especially of a ghost. **2** a ghost. [from Latin *apparitio*]

▣ **1** appearance, manifestation, materialization. **2** ghost, spectre, phantom, spirit, vision.

appeal — *verb intrans.* **1** to make an urgent or formal request. **2** (**appeal to someone**) to be pleasing, interesting, or attractive. **3** *Legal* to request a higher authority or law court to review or change a decision given by a lower one. **4** (**appeal to someone**) to call on them for support: *tried to appeal to her better nature.* **5** *Cricket* to ask the umpire whether a batsman is out or not. — *noun* **1** an urgent or formal request for help, money, etc. **2** *Legal* a request to a higher authority or law court for a review or change of a decision taken by a lower one. **3** the quality of attracting, interesting, or pleasing. [from Latin *appellare*, to address by name]

▣ *verb* **1** ask, request, call, apply, petition, sue, plead, beg, pray. **2** attract, allure, lure, tempt, entice, interest, engage, fascinate, charm, please. **4** address, beseech, implore, entreat, supplicate, invoke, call upon. *noun* **1** request, application, petition, suit, plea, entreaty, supplication, prayer, invocation. **3** attraction, allure, interest, fascination, enchantment, charm, attractiveness, winsomeness, beauty, charisma, magnetism.

appealing *adj.* **1** pleasing, attractive, or interesting. **2** arousing sympathy.

appear *verb intrans.* **1** to become visible or come into sight. **2** to seem. **3** to present oneself formally or in public, eg on stage. **4** to be present in a law court as either accused or counsel. **5** to be published. [from Latin *apparere*]

▣ **1** show (up), materialize, come into sight, come into view, loom, rise, surface, come to light, come out, emerge, arrive, turn up. **2** seem, look. **3** enter, make one's début, act, perform, play, take part. **4** attend. **5** be published, come out.
▣ **1** disappear, vanish.

appearance *noun* **1** an act or instance of appearing. **2** how a person or thing looks, whether or not this reflects reality. — **keep up appearances** to keep up an outward show of happiness, wealth, etc when this is really lacking. **put in an appearance** to attend a meeting, party, etc only briefly. **to all appearances** so far as it can be seen.

▣ **1** appearing, arrival, advent, coming, rise, emergence, début, introduction. **2** look, expression, face, aspect, air, bearing, demeanour, manner, looks, figure, semblance, show, front, guise, illusion, impression, image.
▣ **1** disappearance.

appease *verb* **1** to calm or pacify, especially by agreeing to demands made on one. **2** to satisfy (an appetite or doubt). [from French *apeser*, from *a*, to + *pes*, peace]

appeasement *noun* **1** the act or process of appeasing; conciliation. **2** the state of being appeased or conciliated.

appellant /əˈpɛlənt/ — *noun* a person who makes an appeal to a higher court to review or change the decision of a lower one. — *adj.* of an appeal or appellant. [from Latin *appellare*, to address by name]

appellate /əˈpɛlət/ *adj. Legal, said especially of a court* concerned with appeals. [from Latin *appellare*, to address by name]

appellation /apəˈleɪʃən/ *noun formal* a name or title. [from Latin *appellare*, to address by name]

append *verb* to add or attach, especially as a supplement to a document. [from Latin *appendere*, to hang]

appendage *noun* anything added or attached to a larger or more important part.

appendectomy /apɛnˈdɛktəmɪ/ or **appendicectomy** /əpɛndɪˈsɛktəmɪ/ *noun* (PL. **appendectomies, appendicectomies**) *Medicine* an operation for the surgical removal of the appendix. [from APPENDIX + Greek *ektome*, a cutting out]

appendicitis /əpɛndɪˈsaɪtɪs/ *noun Medicine* inflammation of the appendix, causing abdominal pain and vomiting. Usually the appendix is surgically removed to prevent it bursting and leading to the development of peritonitis.

appendix /əˈpɛndɪks/ *noun* (PL. **appendixes, appendices**) **1** a section containing extra information, notes, etc at the end of a book or document. **2** *Anat.* a short tube-like sac attached to the lower end of the caecum at the junction of the small and large intestines. [from Latin *appendere*, to hang]

▣ **1** addendum, supplement, epilogue, codicil, postscript, rider, addition, adjunct.

appertain /apəˈteɪn/ *verb intrans.* to belong or relate. [from Latin *ad*, to + *pertinere*, to belong]

appetite *noun* **1** a natural physical desire, especially for food. **2** (**have an appetite for something**) to favour or enjoy it. [from Latin *appetitus*, from *appetere*, to seek after]

▣ **1** hunger, stomach, relish, desire, longing, yearning, craving. **2** taste for, propensity for, inclination for,

liking for, passion for, zest for.
▣ 2 distaste for.
. . . .

appetizer or **appetiser** /ˈapətaɪzə(r)/ *noun* a small amount of food or drink eaten before a meal to increase the appetite.

appetizing or **appetising** *adj.* increasing the appetite, especially by looking or smelling delicious.
. . . .
▣ mouthwatering, tempting, inviting, appealing, palatable, tasty, delicious, *colloq.* scrumptious, succulent, piquant, savoury.
▣ disgusting, *colloq.* off-putting.

applaud /əˈplɔːd/ *verb* **1** *trans., intrans.* to praise or show approval by clapping. **2** to express approval of. [from Latin *applaudere*, to clap]
. . . .
▣ **1** clap, cheer. **2** acclaim, compliment, congratulate, approve, commend, praise, extol.
▣ **1** boo, hiss. **2** criticize, censure.
. . . .

applause /əˈplɔːz/ *noun* praise or approval shown by clapping.
. . . .
▣ ovation, clapping, cheering, cheers, acclaim, acclamation, accolade, congratulation, approval, commendation, praise.
▣ criticism, censure.
. . . .

apple *noun* **1** any small deciduous tree of the genus *Malus* of the rose family (Rosaceae), with pink or white flowers and edible fruit. There are thousands of varieties of cooking, dessert, and cider apples. **2** the firm round edible fruit of this tree, with a green, red, or yellow skin and white flesh. It is consumed fresh or cooked, or used to make fruit juice, cider, etc. — **the apple of one's eye** a person or thing one is proud or fond of. **in apple-pie order** neat and tidy. **upset the apple cart** to disrupt carefully made plans. [from Anglo-Saxon *æppel*]

apple-pie bed a bed made with the sheets doubled up so that one cannot stretch out one's legs, usually as a joke.

applet *noun Comput.* a program that carries out a single task in a set. [from APPLICATION 7 + -LET]

appliance /əˈplaɪəns/ *noun* any electrical device, usually a tool or machine, that is used to perform a specific task, usually of a domestic nature, eg washing machine, food processor, electric heater. [from APPLY]
. . . .
▣ machine, device, contrivance, contraption, gadget, tool, implement, instrument, apparatus, mechanism.
. . . .

applicable /əˈplɪkəbl, ˈaplɪkəbl/ *adj.* that may be applied; suitable; appropriate. [from Latin *applicare*, to apply]
. . . .
▣ suitable, appropriate, relevant, pertinent, apposite, apt, fitting, suited, fit, proper, valid, legitimate.
▣ inapplicable, inappropriate.
. . . .

applicant /ˈaplɪkənt/ *noun* a person applying for a job, a university place, a grant, etc. [from Latin *applicare*, to apply]
. . . .
▣ candidate, interviewee, contestant, competitor, aspirant.
. . . .

application /aplɪˈkeɪʃən/ *noun* **1** a formal request, eg for a job. **2** the act of putting something on to a surface; the thing put on to a surface. **3** the act of using something for a particular purpose. **4** hard work and effort. **5** relevance. **6** *Comput.* the specific task or function that a computer system or program is designed to perform (eg payroll processing, stock control). **7** *Comput. colloq.* an applications package. [from Latin *applicare*, to apply]
. . . .
▣ **1** request, appeal, petition, suit, claim, inquiry. **2** applying, spreading, painting, smearing. **3** function, purpose, use. **4** industry, diligence, assiduity, effort, commitment, dedication, perseverance, keenness, attentiveness. **5** relevance, pertinence, value.
. . . .

applications package *Comput.* a set of integrated programs designed for a particular purpose, usually to perform a specific task (eg payroll processing, stock control). Examples of applications packages include word processors, spreadsheets, and databases.

applicator /ˈaplɪkeɪtə(r)/ *noun* a device for putting something on to a surface, especially the skin. [from Latin *applicare*, to apply]

applied /əˈplaɪd/ *adj.*, *said of a skill, theory, etc* put to practical use: *applied science.*

applied linguistics the application of linguistic theory, methods, and practice to situations which present language-related problems and tasks.

applied mathematics *Maths.* the branch of mathematics concerned with the formation and solution of equations whose variables relate to real physical systems, such as experimental data.

appliqué /aˈpliːkeɪ/ *noun* decoration for clothes, fabric, etc, in which material is cut into shapes which are sewn on to the clothes, etc to make patterns and designs. [from French *appliqué*, applied]

apply *verb* (**applies**, **applied**) **1** *intrans.* (**apply for something**) to make a formal request, eg for a job. **2** to put or spread on a surface: *applied three coats of paint to each wall.* **3** *intrans.* to be relevant or suitable. **4** to put (a skill, rule, theory, etc) to practical use. — **apply oneself to something** to give one's full attention or energy to a task, etc. [from Latin *applicare*, to attach]
. . . .
▣ **1** request, ask for, requisition, put in for, appeal for, petition for, solicit, sue for, claim, inquire about. **2** put, spread, lay, paint, smear, rub. **3** refer, relate, be relevant, pertain, fit, suit. **4** use, utilize, exercise, employ, engage, harness, ply, wield, administer, execute, implement, direct, bring to bear. **apply oneself to** address oneself to, buckle down to, settle down to, commit oneself to, devote oneself to, dedicate oneself to, concentrate on, study, persevere with.
. . . .

appoint *verb* **1** to give (a person) a job or position: *appointed him to the chairmanship / was appointed chairman.* **2** to fix or agree on (a date, time, or place). **3** to equip or furnish: *well-appointed rooms.* [from French *apointer*, from *à*, to + *point*, point]
. . . .
▣ **1** name, nominate, elect, install, choose, select, engage, employ, take on, commission, delegate, assign, designate, command, direct, charge, detail. **2** fix, set, decide, determine, agree on, arrange, settle, establish, ordain, decree.
▣ **1** reject, dismiss, discharge.
. . . .

appointee *noun* a person appointed.

appointment *noun* **1** an arrangement to meet someone. **2** the act of giving someone a job or position. **3** the job or position a person is given. **4** the person given a job or position: *you were a surprise appointment.* **5** (**appointments**) *formal* equipment and furnishings.
. . . .
▣ **1** arrangement, engagement, date, meeting, rendezvous, interview, consultation. **2** nomination, election, choosing, selection, commissioning, delegation. **3** job, position, situation, post, office, place.
. . . .

apportion /əˈpɔːʃən/ *verb* to share out fairly. [from Latin *apportionare*]

apposite /'apəzɪt/ *adj.* suitable; well chosen. [from Latin *appositus*, from *apponere*, to put to]

appositeness *noun* relevance, applicability.

apposition /apə'zɪʃən/ *noun* a grammatical construction in which two or more nouns or noun phrases are put together without being linked by *and*, *but*, *or*, etc, eg *his wife the doctor*. [from Latin *appositio*, from *apponere*, to put to]

appraisal *noun* evaluation; estimation of quality.

■ evaluation, assessment, estimate, estimation, judgement, reckoning, valuation, rating, survey, inspection, review, examination.

appraise /ə'preɪz/ *verb* 1 to decide the value or quality of (a person's skills, ability, etc). 2 to put a price on, especially officially. [from Old French *aprisier*, from *a*, to + *prisier*, to price or prize]

appraiser *noun* 1 a person who values property. 2 a person who estimates quality.

appreciable /ə'priːʃəbl/ *adj.* noticeable; significant. [from Latin *appretiare*, to appreciate]

appreciably *adv.* so as to be appreciable; significantly.

appreciate /ə'priːʃieɪt/ *verb* 1 to be grateful or thankful for. 2 to be aware of the value, quality, etc of. 3 to understand or be aware of. 4 *intrans.* to increase in value. [from Latin *appretiare*, from *ad*, to + *pretium*, price]

■ 1 welcome, take kindly to. 2 prize, treasure, value, cherish, admire, respect, regard, esteem, enjoy, relish, savour. 3 understand, comprehend, perceive, realize, recognize, acknowledge, sympathize with, know. 4 grow, increase, rise, mount, gain, improve.

🗲 2 despise. 3 overlook. 4 depreciate.

appreciation /əpriːʃi'eɪʃən/ *noun* 1 gratitude or thanks. 2 sensitive understanding and enjoyment of the value or quality of something: *an appreciation of good music*. 3 the state of knowing or being aware of. 4 an increase in value.

■ 1 gratitude, gratefulness, thanks, thankfulness, indebtedness, obligation. 2 liking, sensitivity, responsiveness, enjoyment, relish, admiration, respect, regard, esteem. 3 knowledge, understanding, comprehension, perception, awareness, realization, recognition, acknowledgement, sympathy. 4 growth, increase, rise, inflation, gain, improvement, enhancement.

🗲 1 ingratitude. 4 depreciation.

appreciative /ə'priːʃiətɪv/ *adj.* feeling or expressing appreciation.

■ grateful, thankful, obliged, indebted, pleased, admiring, encouraging, enthusiastic, sensitive, responsive.

🗲 ungrateful.

apprehend /aprə'hend/ *verb* 1 to arrest. 2 to understand. [from Latin *apprehendere*, to seize]

apprehension *noun* 1 uneasy concern about the imminent future; fear or anxiety. 2 the act of arresting. 3 understanding. [from Latin *apprehendere*, to seize]

■ 1 dread, foreboding, misgiving, qualm, uneasiness, anxiety, worry, concern, disquiet, alarm, fear, doubt, suspicion, mistrust.

apprehensive *adj.* anxious or worried; uneasily concerned about the imminent future.

■ nervous, anxious, worried, concerned, uneasy, doubtful, suspicious, mistrustful, distrustful, alarmed, afraid.

🗲 assured, confident.

apprentice /ə'prentɪs/ *noun* a young person who works for an agreed period of time in order to learn a craft or trade. — *verb* to assign as an apprentice. [from French *apprentiz*, from Latin *apprehendere*, to lay hold of]

■ *noun* trainee, probationer, student, pupil, learner, novice, beginner, starter, recruit.

🗲 *noun* expert.

apprenticeship *noun* 1 the status of an apprentice. 2 a time of training for a trade, etc.

apprize or **apprise** *verb* (**apprize someone of something**) to give them information about it. [from French *appris*, learnt]

appro /'aproʊ/ *noun* — **on appro** *colloq.* on approval.

approach — *verb* 1 *trans., intrans.* to come near or nearer in space or time. 2 to ask (someone) for help, support, etc; to suggest or propose something to (someone). 3 to begin to deal with (a problem, subject, etc). 4 to be like or similar to: *nothing approaches this for quality.* — *noun* 1 the act of coming near. 2 a way to, or means of reaching, a place. 3 a request for help, support, etc; a suggestion or proposal. 4 a way of considering or dealing with, eg a problem: *a new approach.* 5 the course that an aircraft follows as it comes in to land. 6 an approximation. [from Latin *appropriare*, from *ad*, to + *prope*, near]

■ *verb* 1 draw near, near. 2 apply to, appeal to, sound out, suggest to, propose to. 3 begin, commence, set about, undertake. 4 resemble, be like, compare with, approximate to, come close to. *noun* 1 advance, coming, advent, arrival. 2 access, road, avenue, way, passage, entrance, doorway, threshold. 3 application, appeal, overture, proposition, suggestion, proposal. 4 attitude, manner, style, technique, procedure, method, means.

approachable *adj.* 1 friendly and ready to listen and help. 2 that can be reached.

approbation /aproʊ'beɪʃən/ *noun* approval; consent. [from Latin *approbatio*, from *approbare*, to approve of]

appropriate /ə'proʊprɪət, ə'proʊprɪeɪt/ — *adj.* (pronounced -ət) suitable or proper. — *verb* (pronounced -eɪt) 1 to take (something) as one's own, especially without permission. 2 to put (money) aside for a particular purpose. [from Latin *appropriare*, from *ad*, to + *proprius*, one's own]

■ *adj.* suitable, fit, befitting, becoming, proper, right, correct, *colloq.* spot-on, applicable, relevant, pertinent, to the point, apt, fitting, well-chosen, well-timed, timely, seasonable, opportune. *verb* 1 seize, take, expropriate, commandeer, requisition, confiscate, impound, assume, usurp, steal, embezzle, misappropriate.

🗲 *adj.* inappropriate, unsuitable, irrelevant.

appropriation /əproʊprɪ'eɪʃən/ *noun* the act of appropriating.

approval /ə'pruːvəl/ *noun* 1 a favourable opinion. 2 official permission. — **on approval** *said of goods for sale* that may be returned if not satisfactory.

■ 1 good opinion, favour, approbation, admiration, esteem, regard, respect, liking, appreciation, recommendation, praise, commendation, acclaim, acclamation. 2 permission, consent, assent, agreement, leave, sanction, authorization, licence, mandate, *colloq.* go-ahead, *colloq.* green light, *colloq.* OK, blessing, certification, ratification, validation, confirmation.

🗲 1 disapproval, condemnation.

approve /ə'pru:v/ *verb* **1** to agree to or permit. **2** *intrans.* (**approve of someone** or **something**) to be pleased with or think well of them. [from Latin *approbare*, to approve of]

....

▣ **1** agree to, assent to, consent to, accede to, allow, permit, pass, sanction, authorize, mandate, *colloq.* OK, ratify, rubber-stamp, validate, endorse, support, uphold. **2** admire, esteem, regard, like, favour, recommend, praise, commend, acclaim.
🔄 **2** disapprove, condemn.

....

approving *adj.* favourable.
approvingly *adv.* with approval.
approx. *abbrev.* approximate.
approximate /ə'prɒksɪmət, ə'prɒksɪmeɪt/ — *adj.* (pronounced -mət) almost exact or accurate. — *verb trans., intrans.* (pronounced -meɪt) (**approximate to something**) to come close to it in value, quality, accuracy, etc. [from Latin *approximare*, from *ad*, to + *proximus*, nearest]

....

▣ *adj.* estimated, guessed, rough, inexact, loose, close, near, like, similar. *verb* approach, border on, verge on, be tantamount to, resemble.
🔄 *adj.* exact.

....

approximately *adv.*, *said of a number, estimate, etc* nearly; roughly.

....

▣ roughly, around, about, circa, more or less, nearly, approaching, close to, just about.

....

approximation /əprɒksɪ'meɪʃən/ *noun* **1** a figure, answer, etc which is almost exact. **2** the process of estimating a figure, etc.
appurtenance /ə'pɜ:tənəns/ *noun* (*usually* **appurtenances**) an accessory to, or minor detail of, something larger, such as duties or rights connected with owning property. [from French *apertenance*, from Latin *appertinere*, to belong]
APR *abbrev.* annual percentage rate.
Apr or **Apr.** *abbrev.* April.
apraxia /eɪ'praksɪə/ *noun Psychol.* an inability to make deliberate movements with accuracy, usually as a result of brain disease. [from Greek *apraxia*, inaction]
après-ski /apreɪ'ski:/ — *noun* evening social activities after a day's skiing. — *adj.*, *said of clothes, etc* suitable for such activities. [French, = after-skiing]
apricot /'eɪprɪkɒt/ — *noun* **1** a small deciduous tree (*Prunus armeniaca*), native to the Far East, and widely cultivated in warm regions of Europe and the USA, and in N Africa, for its edible fruit. **2** the small edible fruit of this plant, which has yellow flesh surrounded by a soft furry yellowish-orange skin, eaten fresh, and also used to make jams, preserves, etc. — *adj.* apricot-coloured or apricot-flavoured. [from Portuguese *albricoque*, from Latin *praecox*, early-ripening]
April /'eɪprɪl/ *noun* the fourth month of the year, following March. [from Latin *aperire*, to open]
April fool a person tricked or made a fool of on 1 Apr (All Fools' Day or April Fools' Day); also, the trick made.
a priori /eɪ praɪ'ɔ:raɪ/ *said of an argument or reasoning* working from cause to effect or from general principles to particular cases. See also A POSTERIORI. [from Latin *a priori*, from what is before]
apron /'eɪprən/ *noun* **1** a piece of cloth, plastic, etc worn over the front of clothes to protect them. **2** a hard-surface area at an airport where aircraft are loaded. **3** the part of a theatre stage in front of the curtain. — **tied to his mother's** or **wife's apron strings** *said of a boy or man* completely dominated by and dependent on his mother or wife. [from Middle English *napron*, from Old French *naperon*; *a napron* came to be understood as *an apron*]

apropos /aprə'pou, 'aprəpou/ — *adj.*, *said of remarks* suitable or to the point. — *prep.* (**apropos of something**) with reference to it. — *adv.* by the way; appropriately. [from French *à propos*, to the purpose]
apse *noun* the arched, domed east end of a church. [from Greek *hapsis*, arch]
apsis /'apsɪs/ *noun* (PL. **apsides**) either of the two points in the orbit of a planet, satellite, etc, that lie furthest from or closest to the centre of gravitational attraction (the body about which it is orbiting). [from Greek *hapsis*, arch]
APT *abbrev.* Advanced Passenger Train.
apt *adj.* **1** *said of a remark, etc* particularly appropriate or suitable for the situation, circumstances, etc. **2** (**apt to do something**) inclined or likely to do it. **3** (**apt at something**) clever or quick to learn it. [from Latin *aptus*, fit]

....

▣ **1** appropriate, apposite, relevant, applicable, suitable, fit, fitting, seemly, proper, correct, accurate, *colloq.* spot-on. **2** inclined to, prone to, given to, disposed to, likely to, liable to. **3** clever at, gifted with, talented with, skilful at, expert at, quick at.
🔄 **1** inapt.

....

apteryx /'aptərɪks/ *noun* any flightless bird belonging to the kiwi family, found in New Zealand. See also KIWI. [from Greek *a*, without + *pteryx*, wing]
aptitude /'aptɪtju:d/ *noun* **1** (**aptitude for something**) a natural skill or talent. **2** ability or fitness. [from Latin *aptitudo*]

....

▣ **1** inclination for, gift for, talent for, flair for. **2** ability, capability, capacity, faculty, fitness, suitability.
🔄 **2** inaptitude.

....

aptly *adv.* in an apt way; suitably.
aptness *noun* suitability, being apt.
aqua- *combining form* denoting water: *aqualung*.
aquaculture or **aquiculture** /'akwəkʌltʃə(r)/ *noun Agric.* the practice of using the sea, lakes, and rivers for cultivating aquatic animals (eg fish, shellfish) and plants (eg seaweed), mainly for consumption as food. [from Latin *aqua* water + CULTURE]
aquafit *noun* a system of aerobic exercises performed in chest-high water.
aqua fortis /'akwə fɔ:tɪs/ *old use* nitric acid. [from Latin *aqua fortis*, strong water]
aqualung *noun* a device that enables a diver to breathe under water, consisting of a mouth tube connected to one or more cylinders of compressed air strapped to the diver's back, and regulated by a valve system.
aquamarine /akwəmə'ri:n/ — *noun* **1** *Geol.* a transparent bluish-green gemstone that is a variety of the mineral beryl. **2** the colour of this gemstone. — *adj.* relating to this stone or its colour. [from Latin *aqua marina*, sea water]
aquaplane — *noun* a thin board which a person stands on to be towed very fast by a motor boat. — *verb intrans.* **1** to ride on an aquaplane. **2** *said of a vehicle* to slide along out of control on a thin film of water.
aqua regia /'akwə 'ri:dʒə/ a highly corrosive mixture of one part concentrated nitric acid to three parts concentrated hydrochloric acid, so called because it dissolves the noble metals, such as gold and platinum. It is a powerful oxidizing agent and dissolves all metals except silver. [from Latin *aqua regia*, royal water]
Aquarian /ə'kweərɪən/ — *noun* a person born under the sign of Aquarius. — *adj.* born under or characteristic of the sign of Aquarius.
aquarium /ə'kweərɪəm/ *noun* (PL. **aquariums, aquaria**) a glass tank, or a building containing several such tanks (eg in a zoo), for keeping fish and other water animals. [from Latin *aquarius*, of water]
Aquarius /ə'kweərɪəs/ *noun* **1** *Astron.* the Water Bearer, a large but dim southern constellation of the zodiac, lying between Pisces and Capricornus. **2** a person born be-

tween 21 January and 19 February, under this sign. [from Latin *aquarius*, water-carrier]

aquatic /ə'kwatɪk/ — *adj.* **1** denoting any organism that lives or grows in, on, or near water. **2** *said of sports* taking place in water. — *noun* **1** an aquatic animal or plant. **2** (**aquatics**) water sports. [from Latin *aquaticus*, from *aqua*, water]

aquatint /'akwətɪnt/ *noun* a picture produced by printing with a copper plate that has been etched using acid and wax. [from Italian *aqua tinta*, dyed water]

aquatube *noun* an extended water chute with twists and bends, down which users slide on a stream of water into a swimming pool.

aqua vitae /'akwə vaɪti:/ a strong alcoholic drink, especially brandy. [from Latin *aqua vitae*, water of life]

aqueduct /'akwɪdʌkt/ *noun* a channel or canal carrying water, especially in the form of a tall bridge across a valley. [from Latin *aqua*, water + *ducere*, to lead]

aqueous /'eɪkwɪəs, 'akwɪəs/ *adj.* **1** relating to water. **2** denoting a solution that contains water, or in which water is the solvent. [from Latin *aqua*, water]

aqueous humour *Anat.* the clear liquid between the lens and the cornea of the eye.

aqueous solution *Chem.* any solution in which the solvent is water.

aquifer /'akwɪfɛ(r)/ *noun Geol.* water-bearing rock strata, commonly sandstones or chalk, that are highly porous and permeable to water. They provide much of the world's water supply, which may be tapped directly by sinking wells or pumping the water into a reservoir. [from Latin *aqua*, water, + *ferre*, to carry]

aquilegia /akwɪ'li:dʒɪə/ *noun* any of various garden hybrids of a perennial plant (*Aquilegia vulgaris*, or columbine), native to Europe, N Africa, and Asia, and having pink, crimson, violet, yellow, orange, or white flowers. [probably from Latin *aquila*, eagle]

aquiline /'akwɪlaɪn/ *adj.* **1** of or like an eagle. **2** *said of a nose* curved like an eagle's beak. [from Latin *aquila*, eagle]

AR *abbrev.* Arkansas.

Ar *symbol Chem.* argon.

Arab — *noun* **1** a member of a Semitic people living in the Middle East and N Africa. **2** a breed of horse famous for its grace and speed. — *adj.* relating to Arabs or Arabia. [from Greek *Araps*]

arabesque /arə'besk/ *noun* **1** *Ballet* a position in which the dancer stands with one leg stretched out backwards and the body bent forwards from the hips. **2** a complex design of leaves, flowers, etc woven together. **3** a short ornate piece of music. [from Italian *arabesco*, in the Arabian style]

Arabian /ə'reɪbɪən/ — *adj.* of Arabia or the Arabs. — *noun old use* an Arab.

Arabic /'arəbɪk/ — *noun* the Semitic language of the Arabs. — *adj.* of the Arabs, their language or culture.

Arabic numeral any of the numbers 0, 1, 2, 3, 4, 5, 6, 7, 8, and 9, based on Arabic characters.

Arabist *noun* an expert in or student of Arabic culture, history, and language.

arable /'arəbl/ *adj. Agric.* **1** *said of land* suitable or used for ploughing and growing crops. **2** *said of a crop* that has to be sown on ploughed land, eg cereals, potatoes, root crops. [from Latin *arare*, to plough]

arachnid /ə'raknɪd/ *noun* **1** any invertebrate animal belonging to the class Arachnida, which contains about 65,000 species, including spiders, scorpions, mites, ticks, and harvestmen. **2** relating to such an animal. [from Greek *arachne*, spider]

arachnoid /ə'raknɔɪd/ — *adj.* **1** relating to or resembling an arachnid. **2** resembling a cobweb. — *noun Anat.* (*also* **arachnoid membrane**) the middle of the three membranes (known as the *meninges*) that cover the brain and spinal cord, so called because it resembles a cobweb in texture.

aragonite /ə'ragənaɪt, 'arəgənaɪt/ *noun Geol.* a mineral form of calcium carbonate that occurs in some alpine metamorphic rocks, sedimentary rocks, and the shells of certain molluscs, of which it forms the lining (mother-of-pearl). [from *Aragon*, in Spain]

arak same as ARRACK.

Aramaic /arə'meɪɪk/ — *noun* any of a group of Semitic languages, including the language spoken by Christ and modern forms spoken in parts of Syria. — *adj.* of or in Aramaic. [from Greek *Aramaios*]

arbiter /'ɑ:bɪtə(r)/ *noun* **1** a person with the authority or influence to settle arguments between other people. **2** a person with great influence in matters of style, taste, etc. [from Latin *arbiter*]

arbitrarily /'ɑ:bɪtrərɪlɪ/ *adv.* in an arbitrary or random way; capriciously, despotically.

arbitrariness *noun* **1** being arbitrary; capriciousness. **2** tyranny.

arbitrary /'ɑ:bɪtrərɪ/ *adj.* **1** based on subjective factors or random choice, and not on objective principles. **2** *said of a person* unpredictably dictatorial or authoritarian. [from Latin *arbitrarius*]

⊟ **1** random, chance, capricious, inconsistent, discretionary, subjective, instinctive, unreasoned, illogical, irrational. **2** dictatorial, despotic, tyrannical, autocratic, absolute, imperious, magisterial, authoritarian, domineering, overbearing, high-handed, dogmatic.

⊞ **1** reasoned, rational, circumspect.

arbitrate /'ɑ:bɪtreɪt/ *verb trans., intrans.* to act as a judge in a quarrel or disagreement. [from Latin *arbitrari*, to judge]

⊟ judge, adjudicate, referee, umpire, mediate, settle, decide, determine.

arbitration /ɑ:bɪ'treɪʃən/ *noun* the settling of a quarrel or disagreement between two or more groups by a neutral person.

⊟ judgement, adjudication, intervention, mediation, negotiation, settlement, decision, determination.

arbitrator /'ɑ:bɪtreɪtə(r)/ *noun* a person who arbitrates; an arbiter.

⊟ judge, adjudicator, arbiter, referee, umpire, moderator, mediator, negotiator, intermediary, go-between.

arbor *noun* **1** a tree-like structure. **2** the axle or spindle on which a revolving cutting tool (eg a reamer) is mounted. **3** the axle of a wheel in a clock or watch. [from Latin *arbor*, tree]

Arbor Day in the USA, New Zealand, and parts of Canada and Australia, a day (which varies from place to place) set apart each year for planting trees and increasing public awareness of the value of trees. It was first observed in the state of Nebraska, USA in 1872 and became an official holiday there in 1885.

arboreal /ɑ:'bɔ:rɪəl/ *adj.* **1** relating to or resembling a tree. **2** denoting an animal that lives mainly in trees. [from Latin *arboreus*, from *arbor*, tree]

arboretum /ɑ:bə'ri:təm/ *noun* (PL. **arboreta**) *Bot.* a botanical garden used for the display of trees and shrubs for scientific, educational, and recreational purposes. [from Latin *arbor*, tree]

arboriculture /ɑ:'bɔrɪkʌltʃə(r)/ *noun* the cultivation of trees and shrubs, especially for ornamental or scientific purposes, rather than for profit. [from Latin *arbor*, tree]

arborio rice /ɑ:'bɔrɪoʊ/ a starchy short-grain rice from Italy, used for making risotto.

arbour /'ɑ:bə(r)/ *noun* a shady area in a garden formed by trees or climbing plants, usually with a seat. [from Latin *herba*, grass, influenced by Latin *arbor*, tree]

ARC *abbrev.* **1** Aeronautical Research Council. **2** the Agriculture Research Council, superseded first by the Agricultural and Food Research Council, and then by the Biotechnology and Biological Sciences Research Council. **3** AIDS-related complex.

arc — *noun* **1** *Geom.* a continuous section of a circle or other curve. A *minor arc* is less than a semicircle and a *major arc* is greater than a semicircle. **2** the graduated scale of an instrument or device that is used to measure angles. **3** a continuous electric discharge (of low voltage and high current), giving out heat and light, that is maintained across the space between two electrodes. Electric arcs are used in welding. Also called ELECTRIC ARC. **4** an island arc. — *verb intrans.* (**arced, arcing**) to form an arc. [from Latin *arcus*, bow]

arcade /ɑ:ˈkeɪd/ *noun* **1** a covered walk or passage, usually lined with shops. **2** a row of arches supporting a roof, wall, etc. [from Italian *arcata*]

Arcadian /ɑ:ˈkeɪdɪən/ *adj.* relating to or like Arcadia; characterized by simple rural pleasures.

arcane /ɑ:ˈkeɪn/ *adj.* mysterious, secret; understood only by a few. [from Latin *arcanus*, shut]

arch¹ — *noun* **1** a curved structure forming an opening, and consisting of wedge-shaped stones or other pieces supporting each other by mutual pressure, used to sustain an overlying weight such as a roof or bridge, or for ornament. **2** anything shaped like an arch, especially a monument. **3** the bony structure of the foot between the heel and the toes, normally having an upward curve. — *verb* **1** *intrans.* to form an arch. **2** *trans.* to span as an arch or like an arch. [from Latin *arcus*, bow]

⊟ *noun* **1** archway, bridge, span, dome, vault. **2** bend, curve, curvature, bow, arc, semicircle. *verb* **1** bend, curve, bow, arc, vault, camber.

arch² *adj.* self-consciously playful or coy. [from ARCH-, originally in *arch rogue*, etc]

arch- or **archi-** *combining form* chief; most important: *archangel / archduke.* [from Anglo-Saxon *arce*, from Greek *archos*, chief]

Archaean or **Archean** /ɑ:ˈkɪən/ *adj. Geol.* the earlier of the two geological eons into which the Precambrian period is divided, corresponding to the period of time from the formation of the Earth (about 4600 million years ago) to about 2500 million years ago. [from Greek *archaios*, ancient]

archaeological /ɑ:kɪəˈlɒdʒɪkl/ *adj.* relating to archaeology; discovered or known from archaeology.

archaeologist *noun* a person who studies or practises archaeology.

archaeology /ɑ:kɪˈɒlədʒɪ/ *noun* the excavation and study of the physical remains of earlier civilizations, especially buildings and artefacts. [from Greek *archaiologia*, ancient history]

archaeopteryx /ɑ:kɪˈɒptərɪks/ *noun* the oldest fossil bird, known from the Jurassic period in Europe, and having feathers and a wishbone, but distinguished from modern birds by reptilian features such as a long bony tail supported by vertebrae, three clawed fingers on the wings, and sharp teeth on both jaws. [from Greek *archaios*, ancient + *pteryx*, wing]

archaic /ɑ:ˈkeɪk/ *adj.* **1** ancient; of or from a much earlier period. **2** out of date; old-fashioned. **3** *said of a word, phrase, etc* no longer in general use, but sometimes used for special effect. [from Greek *archaikos*, from *archaios*, ancient]

⊟ **1** old, ancient, antique, primitive. **2** out of date, outdated, antiquated, obsolete, old-fashioned, outmoded, *colloq.* old-hat, passé.

⊟ **1** recent. **2** modern.

archaically *adv.* in an archaic way.

archaism /ˈɑ:keɪɪzm/ *noun* **1** an archaic word or expression. **2** the deliberate use of archaic words or expressions.

archangel /ˈɑ:keɪndʒəl/ *noun* an angel of the highest order. [from Greek *archos*, chief + *angelos*, messenger]

archbishop /ɑ:tʃˈbɪʃəp, ˈɑ:tʃbɪʃəp/ *noun* a chief bishop, in charge of all the other bishops, clergy, and churches in a particular area. [from Anglo-Saxon *arcebiscop*]

archbishopric *noun* the office or diocese of an archbishop.

archdeacon /ɑ:tʃˈdi:kən/ *noun* in the Church of England, a member of the clergy ranking just below a bishop. See also ARCHIDIACONAL. [from Anglo-Saxon *arcediacon*]

archdeaconry *noun* (PL. **archdeaconries**) the office or residence of an archdeacon.

archdiocese /ɑ:tʃˈdaɪəsɪs/ *noun* in the Church of England, an area under the control of an archbishop.

archduchess *noun* **1** *Hist.* a princess in the Austrian royal family. **2** the wife of an archduke.

archduchy *noun* (PL. **archduchies**) the area ruled by an archduke.

archduke *noun* the title of some princes, especially formerly the son of the Emperor of Austria.

arched *adj.* **1** having an arch or arches. **2** shaped like an arch.

archenemy *noun* (PL. **archenemies**) **1** a chief enemy. **2** the Devil.

archeology *North Amer., esp. US* same as ARCHAEOLOGY.

archer *noun* **1** a person who shoots with a bow and arrows. **2** (**the Archer**) the constellation and sign of the zodiac Sagittarius. [from Latin *arcus*, bow]

archery *noun* the art or sport of shooting with a bow.

archetypal /ɑ:kɪˈtaɪpəl/ *adj.* serving as an archetype or an original or typical model of something.

archetype /ˈɑ:kɪtaɪp/ *noun* **1** an original model; a prototype. **2** a perfect example. [from Greek *arche*, beginning + *typos*, model]

⊟ MODEL. **1** original, prototype, pattern, standard, form, type. **2** classic, paradigm, ideal.

archfiend *noun* the Devil.

archidiaconal /ɑ:kɪdaɪˈakənəl/ *adj.* of an archdeacon or archdeaconry. [from Greek *archidiakonos*]

archiepiscopal /ɑ:kɪeˈpɪskəpəl/ *adj.* of an archbishop or an archbishopric. [from Greek *archiepiskopos*]

archimandrite /ɑ:kɪˈmandraɪt/ *noun Christianity* in the Greek Church, a priest in charge of a group of monks. [from Greek *archos*, chief + *mandra*, monastery]

Archimedes' principle /ɑ:kɪˈmi:di:z/ *Physics* the principle that, when a body is wholly or partly immersed in a liquid, the weight of the fluid displaced by the body is equal to the weight of the body.

Archimedes screw or **Archimedean screw** /ɑ:kɪˈmi:di:z, ɑ:kɪˈmi:dɪən/ a device for raising water against gravity, especially for irrigation, consisting of a spiral screw that rotates inside an inclined close-fitting cylinder, so called because it is thought to have been invented by the Greek mathematician Archimedes (c.287–c.212BC).

archipelago /ɑ:kɪˈpɛləgoʊ/ *noun* (PL. **archipelagos**) **1** *Geog.* a group or chain of islands separated from each other by narrow bodies of water. **2** formerly used to refer to an area of sea containing many small islands, eg the Aegean. [from Italian *arcipelago*, from Greek *archi*, chief + *pelagos*, sea]

architect /ˈɑ:kɪtekt/ *noun* **1** a person qualified to design buildings and other large structures. **2** a person responsible for creating something: *the architect of the European Union.* [from Greek *archi*, chief + *tekton*, builder]

⊟ **1** designer, planner, master builder. **2** creator, originator, founder, instigator, prime mover, author, inventor, engineer, maker, constructor.

....

architectural /ɑːkɪˈtɛktʃərəl/ *adj.* relating to or belonging to the realm of architecture.

Architectural and building terms include: alcove, annexe, architrave, baluster, barge-board, baroque, bas-relief, capstone, casement window, classical, coping stone, Corinthian, corner-stone, cornice, coving, dado, decorated, dogtooth, dome, Doric, dormer, double-glazing, drawbridge, dry-stone, duplex, Early English, eaves, Edwardian, elevation, Elizabethan, façade, fanlight, fascia, festoon, fillet, finial, flamboyant, Flemish bond, fletton, fluting, French window, frieze, frontispiece, gable, gargoyle, gatehouse, Georgian, Gothic, groin, groundplan, half-timbered, Ionic, jamb, lintel, mullion, Norman, pagoda, pantile, parapet, pinnacle, plinth, Queen-Anne, rafters, Regency, reveal, ridge, rococo, Romanesque, roof, rotunda, roughcast, sacristy, scroll, soffit, stucco, terrazzo, Tudor, Tuscan, wainscot, weathering.

architecture *noun* 1 the art of designing and constructing buildings. 2 a particular historical, regional, etc style of building design: *Victorian architecture*. 3 the buildings built in any particular style.

architrave /ˈɑːkɪtreɪv/ *noun* 1 a beam that rests on top of a row of columns. 2 a moulded frame around a door or window. [from French, from Greek *archi*, chief + *trabs*, beam]

archive /ˈɑːkaɪv/ *noun* (*usually* **archives**) 1 a collection of old public documents, records, etc. 2 a place where such documents are kept. 3 *Comput.* infrequently used data stored on disk or tape. — *verb* to store (records, data, etc) in an archive. [from Greek *archeion*, public office]

■ 1 records, annals, chronicles, papers, documents, deeds, ledgers, registers.

....

archivist /ˈɑːkɪvɪst/ *noun* a person in charge of archives.
archly *adv.* with an arch or self-consciously playful manner.
arch stone see VOUSSOIR.
archway *noun* a passage or entrance under an arch or arches.
arc lamp *Engineering* a type of electric lamp, no longer in general use, in which the source of light is an arc produced when an electric current flows through ionized gas between two electrodes.
Arctic /ˈɑːktɪk/ — *noun* (**the Arctic**) the area round the North Pole. — *adj.* 1 relating to this area. 2 (**arctic**) *colloq.* extremely cold. [from Greek *arktikos*, from *arktos*, (the constellation of) bear]
Arctic fox a fox (*Alopex lagopus*) widespread on Arctic land masses, having hairy feet and small ears. There are two forms, one of which is white in winter and brown in the summer, and the other is pale blue-grey in winter and darker blue-grey in the summer.
Arctic tern a small tern, found worldwide, that migrates further than any other bird (approximately 36,000km per year), spending the northern summer in the Arctic, and the northern winter in the Antarctic.
arc welding *Engineering* a form of welding in which two pieces of metal are joined by raising the temperature at the joint by means of a continuous electric arc. The high temperature melts the material on either side of the join, forming a welded joint.
ardent *adj.* 1 enthusiastic; eager. 2 burning; passionate. [from Latin *ardere*, to burn]

■ 1 enthusiastic, eager, keen, dedicated, devoted, zealous. 2 fervent, fiery, burning, warm, passionate, impassioned, fierce, vehement, intense, spirited.
✢ 1 apathetic, unenthusiastic.

....

ardour /ˈɑːdə(r)/ *noun* a great enthusiasm or passion. [from Latin *ardor*, from *ardere*, to burn]
arduous /ˈɑːdjʊəs/ *adj.* 1 difficult; needing much work or energy. 2 steep. [from Latin *arduus*, steep]

....

■ 1 hard, difficult, tough, rigorous, severe, harsh, formidable, strenuous, tiring, taxing, exhausting, backbreaking, punishing, gruelling, uphill, laborious, onerous.
✢ 1 easy.

....

arduously *adv.* with difficulty; laboriously.
arduousness *noun* lasting difficulty.
are[1] see BE.
are[2] /ɑː(r)/ (PL. **ares**) *noun* a metric unit of land area, used mainly in agriculture, and equal to 100 square metres. There are 100 ares in a hectare. [from French *are*, from Latin *area*, open space]
area /ˈɛərɪə/ *noun* 1 a measure of the size of a flat surface, measured in square units, eg m^2. 2 a region or part, especially of a town, country, etc. 3 any space set aside for a particular purpose. 4 the range of a subject, activity, or topic. 5 *North Amer., esp. US* a sunken space in front of a building's basement. [from Latin *area*, open space]

....

■ 2 region, zone, sector, part, portion, section, district, locality, neighbourhood, environment, patch, territory, department, province. 4 range, scope, compass, size, extent, expanse, width, breadth, field, sphere, realm, domain.

....

arena /əˈriːnə/ *noun* 1 an area surrounded by seats, for public shows, sports contests, etc. 2 a place of great activity, especially conflict: *the political arena*. 3 the open area in the middle of an amphitheatre. [from Latin *arena*, sanded area for combats]
arena stage *North Amer.* same as THEATRE-IN-THE-ROUND.
aren't *contr.* 1 are not: *they aren't coming.* 2 (*in questions*) am not: *aren't I lucky?*
areola /əˈrɪələ/ *noun* (PL. **areolae**, **areolas**) 1 *Anat.* the ring of brownish or pink pigmented tissue surrounding a nipple. 2 *Anat.* the part of the iris that surrounds the pupil of the eye. [a Latin diminutive of *area*, open space]
arginine /ˈɑːdʒɪniːn, ˈɑːdʒɪnaɪn/ *noun Biochem.* one of the essential amino acids, and a constituent of many proteins.
argon /ˈɑːgɒn/ *noun Chem.* (SYMBOL **Ar**, ATOMIC NUMBER 18) a colourless odourless inert gas, representing 0.93% of the air by volume. It is one of the rare or noble gases, does not form any compounds, and is used to provide inert atmospheres in light bulbs, discharge tubes, and in arc welding. [from Greek, = inactive, from *a*, without + *ergon*, work]
Argonauts in Greek mythology, the 50 heroes who sailed with Jason in the ship the *Argo* to find the Golden Fleece.
argot /ˈɑːgoʊ/ *noun* slang used and understood only by a particular group of people. [from French *argot*]
arguable /ˈɑːgjʊəbl/ *adj.* 1 capable of being argued or disputed. 2 *said of a proposition, statement, etc* capable of being maintained.
arguably *adv.* as can be defended by argument; possibly: *arguably the finest singer in Italy.*
argue *verb* 1 *intrans.* (**argue with someone**) to exchange views with them, especially heatedly or angrily. 2 *trans., intrans.* to suggest reasons for or against (something), especially clearly and in a proper order: *declined to argue the point / argued against capital punishment.* 3 (**argue someone into** or **out of something**) to persuade them to do or not to do something: *persuaded us to stay.* 4 to show or be evidence for: *it argues a degree of enthusiasm on their part.* [from Latin *arguere*, to show, accuse]

....

■ 1 quarrel with, squabble with, bicker with, row with, wrangle with, haggle with, remonstrate with, fight with, feud with, fall out with, disagree with, debate with, discuss with. 2 reason, contend, plead. **4** show, exhibit, display, manifest, demonstrate, indicate, denote, prove, evidence, suggest, imply.

· · · · · · · · · · · · · · · · · · · ·

argument /'ɑːgjʊmənt/ *noun* **1** a quarrel or unfriendly discussion. **2** a reason for or against an idea, etc. **3** the use of reason in making decisions. **4** a summary of the theme or subject of a book, etc. [from Latin *argumentum*, from *arguere*, to show, accuse]

· · · · · · · · · · · · · · · · · · · ·

◨ **1** quarrel, squabble, row, wrangle, controversy, debate, discussion, dispute, disagreement, clash, conflict, fight, feud. **2** reason, assertion, contention, claim, defence, case. **3** reasoning, logic. **4** synopsis, summary, theme.

· · · · · · · · · · · · · · · · · · · ·

argumentation /ɑːgjʊmən'teɪʃən/ *noun* sensible and methodical reasoning.
argumentative /ɑːgjʊ'mentətɪv/ *adj.* fond of arguing; always ready to quarrel.

· · · · · · · · · · · · · · · · · · · ·

◨ quarrelsome, contentious, polemical, opinionated, belligerent, perverse, contrary.
◨ obliging, complaisant, peaceable.

· · · · · · · · · · · · · · · · · · · ·

aria /'ɑːrɪə/ *noun Mus.* a long accompanied song for one voice, especially in an opera or oratorio. [from Italian *aria*]
Arian[1] /'ɛərɪən/ — *noun* a person who believes in the doctrine of Arianism. — *adj.* relating to or following Arius or Arianism.
Arian[2] /'ɛərɪən/ — *noun* a person born under the sign of Aries. — *adj.* born under or characteristic of the sign of Aries.
Arianism *noun* the doctrine of Arius of Alexandria, who denied that Christ was God.
arid /'arɪd/ *adj.* **1** denoting a region or climate characterized by very low rainfall (usually less than 250mm a year). Arid regions are extremely dry and often support only desert vegetation. **2** lacking interest; dull. [from Latin *aridus*]

· · · · · · · · · · · · · · · · · · · ·

◨ DRY. **1** parched, waterless, desiccated, torrid, barren, infertile, unproductive, desert, waste. **2** dull, uninteresting, boring, monotonous, tedious, dreary, colourless, lifeless, spiritless, uninspired.
◨ **1** fertile. **2** lively.

· · · · · · · · · · · · · · · · · · · ·

aridity *noun* an arid or dry state.
Aries /'ɛəriːz/ *noun* **1** *Astron.* the Ram, a small zodiacal constellation, most clearly seen in the autumn, situated between Pisces and Taurus. Its brightest star is *Hamal*. **2** the first sign of the zodiac, falling between 21 Mar and 20 Apr, represented by the Ram. **3** a person born under this sign. [from Latin *aries*, ram]
aright *adv. old use* correctly. [from Anglo-Saxon *ariht*]
arise *verb intrans.* (PAST TENSE **arose**; PAST PARTICIPLE **arisen**) **1** to come into being. **2** (**arise from** or **out of something**) to result from it or be caused by it. **3** to get up or stand up. **4** to come to one's notice. [from Anglo-Saxon *arisan*]

· · · · · · · · · · · · · · · · · · · ·

◨ **1** originate, begin, start, commence, emerge, appear, come to light, occur, happen. **2** originate from, derive from, stem from, spring from, proceed from, flow from, result from, ensue from, follow. **3** rise, get up, stand up, go up, ascend, climb, mount, lift, soar, tower.

· · · · · · · · · · · · · · · · · · · ·

aristocracy /arɪ'stɒkrəsɪ/ *noun* (PL. **aristocracies**) **1** the highest social class, usually owning land and having titles. **2** government by this class. **3** people considered to be the best representatives of something. [from Greek *aristos*, best + *kratos*, power]

· · · · · · · · · · · · · · · · · · · ·

◨ **1** upper class, gentry, nobility, peerage, ruling class, gentility, élite.
◨ **1** common people.

· · · · · · · · · · · · · · · · · · · ·

aristocrat /'arɪstəkrat, ə'rɪstəkrat/ *noun* a member of the aristocracy.

· · · · · · · · · · · · · · · · · · · ·

◨ noble, patrician, nobleman, noblewoman, peer, peeress, lord, lady.
◨ commoner.

· · · · · · · · · · · · · · · · · · · ·

aristocratic *adj.* **1** of the aristocracy. **2** proud and noble-looking.

· · · · · · · · · · · · · · · · · · · ·

◨ **1** upper-class, high-born, well-born, noble, patrician, blue-blooded, titled, thoroughbred, élite.
◨ plebeian, vulgar.

· · · · · · · · · · · · · · · · · · · ·

aristocratically *adv.* with an aristocratic manner.
Aristotelian /arɪstɒ'tiːlɪən/ — *adj.* relating to the Greek philosopher Aristotle (384–322 BC) or his ideas. — *noun* a student or follower of Aristotle.
arithmetic /ə'rɪθmətɪk/ — *noun* (with stress on *-rith-*) **1** the branch of mathematics that uses numbers to solve theoretical or practical problems, mainly by the processes of addition, subtraction, multiplication, and division. **2** ability or skill at this: *my arithmetic is poor.* — *adj.* (with stress on *-met-*) (*also* **arithmetical**) relating to arithmetic. [from Greek *arithmetike*, of numbers, from *arithmos*, number]
arithmetically *adv.* in terms of or by means of arithmetic.
arithmetician /ərɪθmə'tɪʃən/ *noun* a person skilled in arithmetic.
arithmetic mean *Maths.* the average of a set of n numbers, equal to the sum of the numbers divided by n.
arithmetic progression a sequence of numbers such that each number differs from the preceding and following ones by a constant amount, eg 4, 10, 16, 22,...
Ariz. *abbrev.* Arizona.
ark *noun* **1** *Biblical* the vessel built by Noah in which his family and animals survived the Flood. **2** (**Ark**) *Judaism* a chest or cupboard in a synagogue in which the law scrolls are kept. [from Anglo-Saxon *arc*, from Latin *arca*, chest]
ark. *abbrev.* Arkansas.
arm[1] *noun* **1** in humans and other two-footed animals, that part of the upper limb that extends from the shoulder to the hand. **2** a similar structure in any other animal, eg a tentacle. **3** anything that resembles the human arm: *an arm of the sea*. **4** the sleeve of a garment. **5** the part of a chair, etc that supports an arm. **6** a section or division of a larger group, eg of the army, etc. **7** power and influence: *the long arm of the law.* — **arm in arm** with arms linked together. **at arm's length** at a distance, especially to avoid becoming too friendly. **with open arms** with a friendly welcome. [from Anglo-Saxon *earm*]

· · · · · · · · · · · · · · · · · · · ·

◨ **1** limb, upper limb. **3** branch, bough, projection, extension, offshoot, appendage. **6** section, division, detachment, department.

· · · · · · · · · · · · · · · · · · · ·

arm[2] — *noun* **1** (*usually* **arms** or in compounds such as *firearm, sidearm*) a weapon. **2** a branch of a military force. **3** (**arms**) fighting; soldiering. **4** (**arms**) the heraldic design which is the symbol of a family, school, country, etc. — *verb* **1** to equip with weapons. **2** *intrans.* to equip oneself with weapons. **3** (**arm someone with something**) to supply them with whatever is needed. **4** to prepare (a bomb) for use. — **bear arms** to serve as a soldier. **lay down one's arms** to stop fighting. **take up arms** to begin fighting. **under arms** armed and ready to fight. **up in arms** openly angry and protesting. [from Latin *arma*]

· · · · · · · · · · · · · · · · · · · ·

◨ *noun* **1** weapon, armament, instrument of war, firearm, gun, weaponry, artillery, ordnance, munitions, ammunition. **4** coat of arms, armorial bearings, insignia, heraldic device, escutcheon, shield, crest. *verb* **1** equip, fortify, protect. **3** provide with, supply with, furnish with, equip with, forearm with. **4** prepare, prime.

....

armada /ɑːˈmɑːdə/ *noun* **1** a fleet of ships. **2** (**Armada**) *Hist.* the fleet of Spanish ships sent to attack England in 1588. [from Spanish *armada*, from Latin *armata*, armed forces]

armadillo /ɑːməˈdɪloʊ/ *noun* (PL. **armadillos**) a small nocturnal burrowing mammal of N and S America, belonging to the same order (Edentata) as anteaters and sloths. Its head and body are covered with horny plates, and it uses its large sickle-like claws to forage for ants, termites, small reptiles, leaves, and shoots. [from Spanish, from *armado*, armed]

Armageddon /ɑːməˈgɛdn/ *noun* a large-scale and bloody battle, especially the final battle between good and evil before the Day of Judgement, as described in the New Testament (Revelation 16.16). [from Hebrew *Megiddo*, a place in northern Palestine]

armament /ˈɑːməmənt/ *noun* **1** (*usually* **armaments**) arms, weapons, and military equipment. **2** preparation for war. [from Latin *armamenta*]

armature /ˈɑːmətjʊ(r)/ *noun* **1** *Engineering* the moving part of an electromagnetic device in which an electromotive force (voltage) is induced by a magnetic field, eg the rotating wire-wound coil of an electric motor or generator. **2** a piece of soft iron placed across the two poles of a permanent magnet that is not in use, in order to preserve its magnetic properties. Also called KEEPER. **3** a wire framework around which a sculpture is modelled. [from Latin *armatura*, armour]

armband *noun* **1** a strip of cloth worn round the arm, usually to indicate an official position or as a sign of mourning. **2** an inflatable plastic band worn round the arm by beginners in swimming.

armchair — *noun* a comfortable chair with arms at each side. — *adj.* taking no active part.

armed *adj.* **1** supplied with arms. **2** provided with means of defence. **3** *said of a weapon or bomb* ready for use.

armed forces or **armed services** the military forces of a country, such as the army and navy.

Units in the armed services include: task-force, militia, garrison; *air force*: wing, squadron, flight; *army*: patrol, troop, corps, platoon, squad, battery, company, brigade, battalion, regiment; *marines*: Royal Marines, commandos; *navy*: fleet, flotilla, squadron, convoy. *See also* **rank**.

Armenian /ɑːˈmiːnɪən/ — *noun* **1** a member of the people of Armenia. **2** an Indo-European language spoken by some 56 million people in the Republic of Armenia, parts of Turkey, and the Middle East. — *adj.* relating to Armenia, or its people or language.

armful *noun* (PL. **armfuls**) an amount that can be held in one's arms.

armhole *noun* the opening at the shoulder of a garment through which the arm is put.

armistice /ˈɑːmɪstɪs/ *noun* a stopping of hostilities; a truce. [from Latin *armistitium*, from *arma*, arms + *sistere*, to stop]

Armistice Day the anniversary of the day (11 Nov 1918) when fighting ended in World War I; replaced after World War II by Remembrance Day.

armlet *noun* a band or bracelet worn round the arm.

armorial /ɑːˈmɔːrɪəl/ *adj.* relating to heraldry or coats of arms. [from Latin *arma*, arms]

armour /ˈɑːmə(r)/ *noun* **1** *Hist.* a metal suit or covering worn by men or horses as a protection against injury in battle. **2** metal covering to protect ships, tanks, etc against damage from weapons. **3** armoured fighting vehicles as a group. **4** a protective covering on some animals and plants.

5 heraldic designs and symbols. [from French *armure*, from Latin *armatura*, armour]

armoured *adj.* **1** protected by armour. **2** *Mil.* made up of armoured vehicles.

▣ **1** armour-plated, steel-plated, ironclad, reinforced, protected, bullet-proof, bomb-proof.

....

armoured car a light-armoured fighting vehicle, usually with four-wheel drive and armed with a machine gun or small calibre cannon on a rotating turret.

armoured fighting vehicle (**AFV**) any military vehicle, whether on tracks or on wheels, that is protected by metal armour.

armourer *noun* **1** a person who makes or repairs arms and armour. **2** a person in charge of a regiment's arms.

armour-plate *noun* strong metal or steel for protecting ships, tanks, etc.

armour-plated *adj.* fitted with armour-plate.

armoury *noun* (PL. **armouries**) **1** a place where arms are kept. **2** a collection of arms and weapons.

....

▣ ARSENAL. **1** ordnance depot, ammunition dump, magazine, repository. **2** stock, stockpile.

....

armpit *noun* the hollow under the arm at the shoulder.

arms race a contest between countries for superiority in weapons.

army *noun* (PL. **armies**) **1** a large number of people armed and organized for fighting on land. **2** the military profession. **3** a large number. **4** a group of people organized for a particular cause: *Salvation Army*. [from French *armee*, from Latin *armare*, to arm]

▣ **1** armed force, land force, soldiers, troops, legions, cohorts. **2** military, militia. **3** multitude, throng, host, horde.

....

A-road *noun Brit.* a main or principal road.

aroma /əˈroʊmə/ *noun* **1** a distinctive, usually pleasant smell that a substance has or gives off. **2** a subtle quality or charm. [from Greek *aroma*, spice]

....

▣ **1** smell, odour, scent, perfume, fragrance, bouquet, savour.

....

aromatherapist *noun* a person skilled in aromatherapy.

aromatherapy /əroʊməˈθɛrəpɪ/ *noun* a form of therapy involving the use of essential plant oils (which are usually diluted in a 'carrier' oil), generally in combination with massage. It is used to treat physical ailments, and many of the oils are also reputed to have calming or mood-elevating properties.

aromatic /arəˈmatɪk/ *adj.* **1** having a spicy or distinctive fragrance. **2** *Chem.*, *said of an organic compound* having carbon atoms arranged in one or more rings rather than in chains. See also ALIPHATIC.

....

▣ perfumed, fragrant, sweet-smelling, spicy, pungent, redolent, savoury.

....

aromatically *adv.* in an aromatic way; fragrantly.

aromatic compound any of a major class of organic chemical compounds that contain one or more *benzene rings* (five or six carbon atoms joined in a very stable ring structure), or that resemble benzene in their chemical properties. Aromatic compounds are unsaturated hydrocarbons, and usually have a strong odour, eg benzene, naphthalene.

arose see ARISE.

around — *adv.* **1** on every side. **2** here and there; in different directions or to different places. **3** in existence. **4** near at hand. — *prep.* **1** on all sides of. **2** at or to different points in. **3** somewhere in or near. **4** approximately in or at;

about. **5** *North Amer., esp. US* round. — **have been around** *colloq.* to have a great deal of experience of life.

■ **1** everywhere, all over, on all sides, in all directions. **2** here and there, to and fro, about. **4** near, nearby, close, close by, at hand. *prep.* **1** surrounding, round, about, encircling, encompassing, enclosing. **4** approximately, roughly, about, circa, more or less.

arousal *noun* being aroused; an aroused state.

arouse *verb* **1** to cause or produce (an emotion, reaction, sexual desire, etc). **2** to cause to become awake or active.

■ ROUSE. **1** stimulate, cause, produce, instigate, prompt, provoke, excite, spark, kindle, inflame, whet, sharpen. **2** wake (up), waken, awaken, animate, galvanize, goad, spur, incite, agitate, stir up.
◸ **1** calm. **2** lull.

arpeggio /ɑːˈpedʒɪoʊ/ *noun* (PL. **arpeggios**) a chord whose notes are played one at a time in rapid succession. [from Italian *arpeggiare*, to play the harp]

arquebus /ˈɑːkwəbʌs/ *noun Hist.* an early type of portable gun. [from Dutch *hakebusse*, from *hake*, hook + *busse*, gun]

arr. *abbrev.* **1** *Mus.* arranged by. **2** arrival; arrives.

arrack /ˈarək/ *noun* an alcoholic drink made from grain or rice. [from Arabic *'araq*, sweat]

arraign /əˈreɪn/ *verb* **1** to bring into a court of law, usually to face serious charges. **2** to find fault with. [from French *aresnier*]

arraignment *noun* arraigning or being arraigned.

arrange *verb* **1** to put into the proper order. **2** *trans., intrans.* (**arrange something** or **for something**) to plan it in advance. **3** *intrans.* (**arrange with someone**) to come to an agreement about something: *arrange with him to take time off.* **4** to make (a piece of music) suitable for particular voices or instruments. [from Old French *arangier*, from *a*, to + *rangier*, to put in a row]

■ **1** order, tidy, range, array, marshal, dispose, position, set out, lay out, align, group, classify, categorize, file, systematize, organize. **2** plan (for), prepare (for), organize, co-ordinate. **4** adapt, set, score, orchestrate, instrument, harmonize.
◸ **1** disorganize, muddle.

arrangement *noun* **1** (*usually* **arrangements**) a plan or preparation for some future event. **2** the act of putting things into a proper order or pattern. **3** the order, pattern, etc which results from things being arranged. **4** an agreement. **5** a piece of music which has been made suitable for particular voices or instruments.

■ **1** plan, scheme, design, schedule, preparation, organization. **3** order, array, display, pattern, disposition, layout, line-up, grouping, classification, structure, system, method. **4** agreement, settlement, contract, terms, compromise. **5** adaptation, version, interpretation, setting, score, orchestration, instrumentation.

arrant /ˈarənt/ *adj.* out-and-out; notorious: *an arrant liar.* [a Middle English variant of *errant*]

arras /ˈarəs/ *noun* a tapestry for hanging on a wall or concealing an alcove. [from Arras, the capital of Pas-de-Calais department, N France]

array — *noun* **1** a large and impressive number or collection. **2** a well-ordered arrangement: *troops in battle array.* **3** *Maths.* an arrangement of numbers or other items of data in rows and columns, eg a matrix. **4** *Comput.* an arrangement of individual elements of data in such a way that any element can be located and retrieved. In most arrays each item of data is identified by a subscript. **5** *poetic* fine clothes. — *verb* **1** to put in order, eg for battle. **2** to

dress (someone or oneself) in fine clothes. [from Old French *areer*, to arrange]

■ *noun* **1** assortment, collection, assemblage, muster. **2** arrangement, order, formation, line-up, parade, display, show, exhibition, exposition. *verb* **1** arrange, order, range, dispose, group, line up, align, marshal, assemble, muster, parade, display, show, exhibit. **2** clothe, dress, robe, deck, adorn, decorate.

arrears *pl. noun* an amount or quantity which still needs to be done or paid back. — **in arrears** late in paying money owed or doing the required work. [from Old French *arere*, from Latin *ad*, to + *retro*, back, behind]

arrest — *verb* **1** to take (a person) into custody, especially by legal authority. **2** to stop or slow the development of (a disease, etc). **3** to catch or attract (a person's attention). — *noun* **1** the act of taking, or being taken, into custody, especially by the police. **2** a stopping: *cardiac arrest.* — **under arrest** having been arrested by the police. [from Old French *arester*, from Latin *ad*, to + *restare*, to stand still]

■ *verb* **1** capture, apprehend, catch, seize, *colloq.* nick, run in, detain. **2** stop, stem, check, restrain, inhibit, halt, interrupt, delay, slow, retard, block, obstruct, impede, hinder.

arresting *adj.* strikingly individual or attractive.

arris /ˈarɪs/ *noun Archit.* a sharp edge on stone, metal, or wood where two surfaces meet. An arris rail is a wood or metal rail of triangular section; and an arris tile is an angular roofing tile used where hips and ridges intersect. [from French *arête*, a sharp ridge]

arrival *noun* **1** the act of arriving. **2** a person or thing that has arrived, especially a newborn baby.

■ **1** appearance, entrance, advent, coming, approach, occurrence.
◸ **1** departure.

arrive *verb intrans.* **1** to reach a place or destination. **2** (**arrive at something**) to come to a conclusion, decision, etc. **3** *colloq.* to be successful. **4** *said of a child* to be born. **5** *said of a thing* to be brought. **6** *said of a time* to occur. [from Old French *ariver*, from Latin *ad*, to + *ripa*, shore]

■ **1** turn up, *colloq.* show up, *colloq.* roll up, appear, *colloq.* materialize, enter, come. **2** reach, come to. **6** occur, happen.
◸ **1** depart, leave.

arrogance /ˈarəgəns/ *noun* arrogant behaviour; an arrogant manner.

arrogant *adj.*, *said of a person or behaviour* aggressively and offensively self-assertive; having or showing too high an opinion of one's own abilities or importance. [from Latin *arrogare*, to arrogate]

■ self-important, presumptuous, overbearing, high-handed, imperious, self-assertive, assuming, proud, conceited, boastful, high and mighty, lordly, haughty, supercilious, disdainful, scornful, contemptuous, superior, condescending, patronizing.
◸ humble, unassuming, bashful.

arrogate /ˈarəgeɪt/ *verb* (**arrogate something to oneself**) to claim a responsibility, power, etc without having any legal right to it. [from Latin *ad*, to + *rogare*, to ask]

arrogation /arəˈgeɪʃən/ *noun* an act of arrogating; an undue claim or attribution.

arrow *noun* **1** a thin, straight stick with a point at one end and feathers at the other, fired from a bow. **2** an arrow-shaped sign, eg one showing the way to go or the position of something. [from Anglo-Saxon *arwe*]

arrowhead *noun* the pointed tip of an arrow.

arrow-poison frog a slender frog, native to Central and S America, and often brightly coloured. Its skin is highly poisonous, and local American Indians rub arrow-heads on live frogs to poison the tips for hunting. Also called POISON-ARROW FROG.

arrowroot *noun* 1 a tropical perennial plant (*Maranta arundinacea*), native to S America, and cultivated in the West Indies for its swollen underground tubers, which produce a highly digestible form of starch. 2 the fine-grained starch obtained from the tubers of this plant, used as a food thickener and in bland low-salt diets, and so called because it was formerly used by the S American Indians to treat wounds made by poisoned arrows.

arse *noun coarse slang* the buttocks. [from Anglo-Saxon *ears*]

arsehole *noun coarse slang* 1 the anus. 2 a term of contempt for a person.

arsenal /'ɑːsənəl/ *noun* 1 a factory or store for weapons, explosives, etc. 2 the weapons, etc available to a country or group. [from Arabic *dar sina'ah*, workshop]

arsenic /'ɑːsənɪk/ — *noun* 1 (SYMBOL **As,** ATOMIC NUMBER 33) a metalloid chemical element that occurs in three different forms, the commonest and most stable of which is a highly toxic grey shiny solid. 2 a powerful poison, an oxide of arsenic, usually found in the form of a white powder, used in insecticides. — *adj.* of, containing or using arsenic. [from Greek *arsenikon*, yellow arsenic]

arson *noun* the crime of deliberately setting fire to a building, etc. [from Latin *arsio*, from *ardere*, to burn]

arsonist *noun* a person who commits arson.

art[1] *noun* 1 the creation of works of beauty. 2 (**arts**) the different branches of creative activity, eg music, painting, and literature, as a group. 3 one of these branches. 4 (**arts**) the branches of learning linked to creative skills, eg languages, literature and history: *Faculty of Arts*. 5 human skill and work as opposed to nature. 6 a skill, especially gained through practice. 7 (**arts**) *colloq.* cunning schemes. [from Latin *ars*]

▣ 1 fine art, painting, sculpture, drawing, artwork, craft, artistry, draughtsmanship, craftsmanship. 5 skill, aptitude, facility, dexterity, finesse, mastery, expertise. 6 skill, knack, technique, method.

Arts and crafts include: painting, oil painting, watercolour, fresco, portraiture; architecture, drawing, sketching, caricature, illustration; graphics, film, video; sculpture, modelling, woodcarving, woodcraft, marquetry, metalwork, enamelling, cloisonné, engraving, etching, pottery, ceramics, mosaic, jewellery, stained glass, photography, lithography, calligraphy, collage, origami, spinning, weaving, batik, silk-screen printing, needlework, tapestry, embroidery, patchwork, crochet, knitting.

art[2] *verb old use* the form of the present tense of the verb *be* used with *thou*.

artefact /'ɑːtəfakt/ *noun* an object made by human effort, eg a tool, especially one having historical or archaeological interest. [from Latin *arte*, by art + *factum*, made]

artemisia /ɑːtə'miːzɪə/ *noun Bot.* any plant of the genus *Artemisia* of composites, including wormwood, southernwood, etc. [from Greek *artemisia*]

arterial /ɑː'tɪərɪəl/ *adj.* 1 of or like an artery. 2 *said of a road, etc* connecting large towns or cities; main.

arteriole /ɑː'tɪərɪoʊl/ *noun Anat.* a small artery.

arteriosclerosis /ɑːtɪərɪoʊsklə'roʊsɪs/ *noun* (PL. **arterioscleroses**) *Medicine* a general term for any of various disorders of the arteries, especially atherosclerosis (atheroma or hardening of the arteries), in which fatty deposits and scar tissue develop on the inner walls of arteries, making them narrower and eventually obstructing the flow of blood. [from ARTERY + SCLEROSIS]

artery /'ɑːtərɪ/ *noun* (PL. **arteries**) 1 *Anat.* a blood vessel that carries oxygenated blood from the heart to the body tissues, the only exception being the pulmonary artery, which conveys deoxygenated blood from the heart to the lungs. Artery walls are thicker than those of veins, and contain a layer of muscle. 2 a main road, railway or shipping lane. [from Greek *arteria*, windpipe]

artesian basin /ɑː'tiːzɪən/ *Geol.* a shallow basin-shaped aquifer surrounded above and below by rocks that are impermeable to water, so that the groundwater in the aquifer is confined under pressure. Consequently, if a well is sunk into the aquifer, water will rise to the surface without the need for pumping. [from *Artesian*, of Artois (Latin *Artesium*) in N France]

artesian well *Geol.* a deep well that is drilled into an aquifer in an artesian basin, so that water trapped under pressure in the aquifer is forced to flow upward in the well. Artesian wells are often used as a source of drinking water.[from *Artesian*, of Artois (Latin *Artesium*) in N France, where such wells were common]

art form a recognized form for music or literature, eg the novel or the sonnet.

artful *adj.* 1 cunning; able to achieve what one wants, often by illicit or underhand means. 2 skilful.

▣ 1 cunning, crafty, sly, foxy, wily, tricky, scheming, designing, deceitful, devious, subtle, sharp, astute, shrewd. 2 skilful, dexterous, clever, masterly, ingenious, resourceful.
▣ 1 artless, naïve, ingenuous.

artfulness *noun* being artful; craftiness.

▣ cunning, craftiness, slyness, guile, deceit, trickery, astuteness, shrewdness.

art house a cinema that shows films regarded as artistic rather than popular.

arthritic /ɑː'θrɪtɪk/ — *noun* a person suffering from arthritis. — *adj.* relating to or typical of arthritis.

arthritis /ɑː'θraɪtɪs/ *noun* inflammation of one or more joints, associated with swelling, pain, redness, local heat, nd often restricted movement of the affected part. [from Greek *arthron*, joint or -ITIS]

arthropod /'ɑːθrəpɒd/ *noun Zool.* any invertebrate animal belonging to the phylum Arthropoda, the largest phylum in the animal kingdom, which contains over a million species, including insects, crustaceans (eg crabs, shrimps), arachnids (eg spiders, scorpions), and myriapods (eg centipedes, millipedes). [from Greek *arthron*, joint + *pous*, foot]

artichoke /'ɑːtɪtʃoʊk/ *noun* 1 (*in full* **globe artichoke**) a tall perennial plant (*Cynara scolymus*) native to the Mediterranean region, and widely cultivated in temperate regions for the edible fleshy oval bracts that form the base of the unopened flower-heads. It is also grown as an ornamental plant. 2 the fleshy base of the immature flower-head of this plant, eaten as a vegetable. 3 (*in full* **Jerusalem artichoke**) a tall perennial plant (*Helianthus tuberosus*) native to N America, and widely cultivated elsewhere for its edible underground tubers. 4 the underground tubers of this plant, with white flesh and knobbly brownish or reddish skin, eaten as a vegetable. [from Arabic *al-kharshuf*]

article *noun* 1 a thing or object. 2 a usually short written composition in a newspaper or magazine. 3 a clause or paragraph in a document, legal agreement, etc. 4 *Grammar* the definite article *the* or the indefinite article *a* or *an*, or an equivalent word in another language. [from Latin *articulus*, little joint]

▣ 1 item, thing, object, commodity, unit, part, piece. 2 feature, report, story, account, piece, item, review, commentary, composition, essay, paper. 3 clause, paragraph, section, subsection.

articled *adj., said of a lawyer, accountant, etc* bound by a legal contract while working in an office to learn the job.

articular /ɑːˈtɪkjʊlə(r)/ *adj.* relating to or associated with a joint of the body. [from Latin *articularis*, from *articulus*, little joint]

articulate /ɑːˈtɪkjʊleɪt, ɑːˈtɪkjʊlət/ — *verb* (pronounced -leɪt) **1** *trans., intrans.* to pronounce (words) or speak clearly and distinctly. **2** to express (one's thoughts, feelings, ideas, etc) clearly. — *adj.* (pronounced -lət) **1** able to express one's thoughts clearly. **2** *said of speech* pronounced clearly and distinctly so that each sound can be heard. **3** having joints. [from Latin *articulare*, to divide into distinct parts]

⊞ *verb* **1** speak, talk, vocalize, verbalize, enunciate. **2** express, voice, state, utter, pronounce. *adj.* **1** coherent, fluent, vocal, lucid. **2** distinct, clear, well-spoken, intelligible, comprehensible, understandable, meaningful.
⊟ *adj.* **1** inarticulate, incoherent. **2** inarticulate, indistinct.

articulated /ɑːˈtɪkjʊleɪtɪd/ *adj.* having joints.

articulated lorry a lorry constructed in two main sections, of which the front section can turn at an angle to the rear section, making it easier to deviate from a straight course.

articulation /ɑːˌtɪkjʊˈleɪʃən/ *noun* **1** the act of speaking or expressing an idea in words. **2** the word, idea, etc expressed. **3** the state of being jointed together. **4** a joint.

⊞ **1** speaking, speech, talking, utterance, expression, vocalization, verbalization, pronunciation, enunciation, diction, delivery.

artifact /ˈɑːtɪfakt/ same as ARTEFACT.

artifice /ˈɑːtɪfɪs/ *noun* **1** a clever trick. **2** clever skill and tricks; cunning. [from Latin *artificium*, from *ars*, arts + *facere*, to make]

artificer /ɑːˈtɪfɪsə(r)/ *noun* a skilled craftsman, especially a mechanic in the army or navy.

artificial /ɑːtɪˈfɪʃəl/ *adj.* **1** made by human effort; not occurring naturally. **2** made in imitation of a natural product. **3** *said of a person, behaviour, etc* not genuine or sincere. [from Latin *artificialis*, from *ars*, art + *facere*, to make]

⊞ **1** synthetic, plastic, man-made, manufactured. **2** imitation, simulated, mock, false, fake, faux, bogus, counterfeit, *colloq.* phoney, pseudo, sham. **3** insincere, false, assumed, affected, mannered, forced, contrived, feigned, pretended.
⊟ **1** natural. **2** real, genuine. **3** genuine, sincere.

artificial insemination (ABBREV. AI) the introduction of semen into the vagina using some form of instrument in order to facilitate conception. The semen may be that of the husband or partner, in which case the procedure is known as AIH (artificial insemination by husband), or in cases where the partner is infertile it may be that of an anonymous donor, in which case the procedure is known as AID (artificial insemination by donor).

artificial intelligence *noun Comput.* (ABBREV. AI) the development and use of computer systems that can perform some of the functions normally associated with human intelligence, such as learning, problem-solving, decision-making, and pattern recognition.

artificiality /ɑːtɪfɪʃɪˈalɪtɪ/ *noun* being artificial.

artificial language 1 an invented language, created to overcome difficulties of understanding caused by the diversity of the world's languages. Many such languages have been devised over the centuries, with Esperanto achieving the widest international success. See also AUXILIARY LANGUAGE. **2** an invented language used in computer programming. See also COMPUTER LANGUAGE.

artificial radioactivity *Physics* a form of radioactivity that results from the absorption of ionizing radiation, eg

alpha particles, neutrons, by a stable substance that is not normally radioactive.

artificial respiration respiration that is stimulated and maintained manually (eg by the 'kiss of life') or mechanically (eg using a respirator) by forcing air in and out of the lungs when normal spontaneous breathing has stopped.

artificial satellite *Astron.* a man-made spacecraft that is placed in orbit around the Earth or a celestial object such as a planet.

artillery /ɑːˈtɪlərɪ/ *noun* (PL. **artilleries**) **1** large guns for use on land. **2** the part of an army equipped with such guns. [from French *artillier*, to arm]

artiness *noun* affected or ostentatious artistry.

artisan /ɑːtɪˈzan, ˈɑːtɪzan/ *noun* a person who does skilled work with his or her hands. [from French *artisan*, from Latin *artitus*, trained in arts and crafts]

⊞ craftsman, craftswoman, artificer, expert, skilled worker, mechanic, technician, artist.

artist *noun* **1** a person who produces works of art, especially paintings. **2** a person who is skilled at some particular thing. **3** an artiste. [from Latin *ars*, art]

Types of artist include: architect, graphic designer, designer, draughtsman, draughtswoman, illustrator, cartoonist, photographer, printer, engraver, goldsmith, silversmith, blacksmith, carpenter, potter, weaver, sculptor, painter; craftsman, craftswoman, master.

artiste /ɑːˈtiːst/ *noun* a professional performer, especially a singer or dancer, in a theatre, circus, etc. [from French *artiste*]

⊞ performer, entertainer, artist, variety artist, comic, comedian, comedienne, singer, dancer, player, actor, actress.

artistic *adj.* **1** liking or skilled in painting, music, etc. **2** made or done with skill and good taste.

⊞ **1** creative, imaginative, cultured, skilled, talented. **2** tasteful, refined, sensitive, aesthetic, ornamental, decorative, beautiful, exquisite, elegant, stylish, graceful, harmonious.
⊟ **2** tasteless, inelegant.

artistically *adv.* in an artistic way.

artistry *noun* artistic skill and imagination.

⊞ craftsmanship, workmanship, skill, craft, talent, flair, finesse, style, mastery, expertise, proficiency, touch, sensitivity, creativity, imagination.
⊟ ineptitude.

artless *adj.* **1** simple and natural in manner. **2** honest, not deceitful.

⊞ **1** simple, natural, unpretentious. **2** honest, open, frank, ingenuous.
⊟ **2** artful, deceitful, dishonest.

art therapy *Psychol.* art used as a means of communication, or as a creative activity, to gain insight into psychological and emotional disorders, and to aid recovery.

artwork *noun* any original material in the form of illustrations, drawings, design, etc, produced by an artist, illustrator, or designer for reproduction in a book, magazine, or other printed medium.

arty *adj.* (**artier, artiest**) *colloq.* affectedly or ostentatiously artistic.

arum /ˈeərəm/ *noun* any of various perennial plants of the genus *Arum* and related genera of the family Araceae, having a characteristic flower-head consisting of numerous tiny flowers borne around the base of a club-shaped structure. [from Greek *aron*]

arum lily a perennial plant (*Zantedeschia aethiopica*) of the family Araceae, with large leaves shaped like arrow-heads, native to South Africa, and widely cultivated elsewhere for its ornamental flower.

-ary *suffix* forming adjectives or nouns meaning 'of or connected with': *budgetary / dignitary*. [from Latin *arius*]

Aryan /ˈɛərɪən, ˈɑːrɪən/ — *noun* 1 a member of the peoples speaking any of the Indo-European languages, now especially the Indo-Iranian languages. 2 *Hist.*, *in Nazi Germany* a Caucasian, especially of northern European type. — *adj.* of the Aryans or Aryan languages. [from Sanskrit *arya*, noble]

As *symbol Chem.* arsenic.

as[1] — *conj.* 1 when; while; during. 2 because; since. 3 in the manner which: *behave as one likes.* 4 that which; what: *do as one's told.* 5 although: *Try as he might, he still couldn't reach.* 6 for instance: *large books, as this one for example.* — *prep.* in the role of: *speaking as her friend.* — *adv.* to whatever extent or amount. — *pron.* 1 that, who, or which also: *She is a singer, as is her husband.* 2 (after **so**) for the reason that: *Come early so as to avoid the rush.* 3 a fact that: *he'll be late, as you know.* — **as for** or **to** ... with regard to ...; concerning ... **as from** or **as of**... starting at (a particular time). **as if** or **as though** ... as it would be if ... **as it were** in a way; to some extent. **as well** also. **as yet** until now. [from Anglo-Saxon *eallswa*, just as]

⊟ *conj.* 1 when, while, during. 2 because, since, seeing that, considering that. 4 what, whatever. 6 such as, for example, for instance. **as for** as to, as regards, with regard to, with reference to, on the subject of, in connection with, in relation to, with respect to. **as well** also, too, in addition.

as[2] /əz, az/ *noun* (PL. **asses**) an ancient Roman copper coin. [from Latin *as*, unit]

ASA *abbrev.* American Standards Association, used eg in labelling photographic film speeds.

asafoetida or **asafetida** /asəˈfɛtɪdə, asəˈfiːtɪdə/ *noun* a gum resin with an unpleasant smell of onions, obtained from the roots of plants of the genus *Ferula*, and formerly used medicinally. [from Persian *aza*, gum + Latin *foetida*, fetid]

ASAP or **asap** *abbrev.* as soon as possible.

asbestos /azˈbɛstɒs, asˈbɛstɒs/ *noun Geol.* any of a group of fibrous silicate minerals that are resistant to heat and chemically inert.

asbestosis /azbɛˈstoʊsɪs, asbɛˈstoʊsɪs/ *noun* a chronic inflammatory disease of the lungs, caused by inhalation of asbestos dust over a long time period. It is associated with a high incidence of lung cancer.

ascend /əˈsɛnd/ *verb* 1 to climb or go up. 2 *intrans.* to rise or move upwards. — **ascend the throne** to become king or queen. [from Latin *ascendere*]

⊟ CLIMB, MOUNT, GO UP. 1 scale, move up. 2 rise, move upwards, take off, lift off, float up, fly up, soar, slope upwards.
⊟ DESCEND, GO DOWN.

ascendancy or **ascendency** *noun* controlling or dominating power.

ascendant or **ascendent** *adj.* 1 having more influence or power. 2 *Astrol.* rising over the eastern horizon. — *noun* 1 increasing influence or power. 2 *Astrol.* the sign of the zodiac rising over the eastern horizon at the time of an event, especially birth.

ascending *adj.* from the lowest to the highest, the least to the greatest, or the worst to the best.

ascension /əˈsɛnʃən/ *noun* 1 an ascent. 2 (**Ascension**) *Christianity* Christ's ascent to heaven on the fortieth day after the Resurrection. [from Latin *ascensio*, from *ascendere*, to ascend]

Ascension Day *Christianity* the Thursday ten days before Whit Sunday, on which Christ's Ascension is commemorated.

ascent /əˈsɛnt/ *noun* 1 the act of climbing, ascending, or rising. 2 an upward slope.

⊟ 1 ascending, ascension, climb, climbing, scaling, escalation, rise, rising. 2 slope, gradient, incline, ramp, hill, elevation.
⊟ DESCENT.

ascertain /asəˈteɪn/ *verb* to find out; to discover (the truth, etc). [from Old French *acertener*]

⊟ find out, learn, discover, determine, establish, settle, detect, identify, verify, confirm, make certain.

ascertainable *adj.* capable of being ascertained; verifiable.

ascetic /əˈsɛtɪk/ — *noun* a person who avoids all physical comfort and pleasure, especially as a way of achieving holiness. — *adj.* avoiding physical pleasure and comfort; self-denying. [from Greek *asketikos*, from *askein*, to practise, train]

ascetically *adv.* in an ascetic way.

asceticism /əˈsɛtɪsɪzm/ *noun* the philosophy or practice of an ascetic.

ASCII /ˈaskɪ/ *abbrev. Comput.* acronym for American Standard Code for Information Interchange, the most common way of representing text characters by binary code in digital computing systems.

ascorbic acid /əˈskɔːbɪk/ *noun* vitamin C. [from A-[1] + SCORBUTIC]

ascribable /əˈskraɪbəbl/ *adj.* capable of being ascribed; attributable.

ascribe *verb* to think of (something) as done, made, or caused by someone or something: *ascribe their success to hard work.* [from Latin *ascribere*]

⊟ attribute, credit, assign, charge, put down.

ascus /ˈaskəs/ *noun Bot.* in fungi belonging to the subdivision Ascomycetes, a small elongated reproductive structure that usually contains eight spores known as *ascospores*. [from Greek *askos*, bag]

asdic *noun* the name for the system of submarine detection using ultrasonic waves which was used on warships of the Royal Navy up to 1963, and which afterwards was known as sonar (see also SONAR). [an acronym for *Allied Submarine Detection Investigation Committee*, the body set up in 1917 to develop the system]

ASE *abbrev.* Association for Science Education.

aseptic /eɪˈsɛptɪk/ *adj.*, *said of a procedure, environment, etc* free from disease-causing bacteria or other micro-organisms; sterile. [from A-[1] + Greek *sepein*, to cause to decay]

asexual /eɪˈsɛkʃʊəl/ *adj.* 1 denoting reproduction that does not involve sexual processes, and in which genetically identical offspring are produced from a single parent, eg budding of yeasts, asexual spore formation in fungi, vegetative propagation in plants. 2 without functional sexual organs. 3 not sexually attracted to others.

asexuality /eɪsɛkʃʊˈalɪtɪ/ *noun* being asexual.

ASH *abbrev.* Action on Smoking and Health.

ash[1] *noun* 1 the dust that remains after something is burnt. 2 (**ashes**) the remains of a human body after cremation. [from Anglo-Saxon *asce*]

ash[2] *noun* 1 any deciduous tree or shrub of the genus *Fraxinus* of the olive family, with compound leaves, small clusters of greenish flowers, and winged fruits. 2 the strong pale timber obtained from this tree, used to make hockey sticks, tool handles, furniture, etc. [from Anglo-Saxon *æsc*]

ashamed *adj.* 1 (*often* **ashamed of someone** or **something**) feeling shame or embarrassment about them. 2

(**ashamed to do something**) hesitant or reluctant to do it through shame or a fear of disapproval. [from Anglo-Saxon *ascamian*, to feel shame]

. . . .

⊟ **1** shamefaced, sheepish, abashed, embarrassed, red-faced, mortified, sorry, apologetic, remorseful, contrite, guilty, conscience-stricken. **2** hesitant, reluctant, shy, self-conscious, bashful, modest, prudish.

⊞ **1** proud, shameless.

. . . .

ashamedly /əˈʃeɪmɪdlɪ/ *adv.* in an ashamed or shameful way.

ashcan *noun North Amer., esp. US* a dustbin.

ashen *adj.*, *said of a face* grey or very pale, usually from shock.

Ashes *pl. noun* (**the Ashes**) a trophy which goes to the team winning the regular series of cricket matches played by England and Australia. [thought to be so called from a newspaper announcement after Australia's defeat of England in 1882, that the ashes of English cricket were to be taken to Australia]

Ashkenazim Jews of Central and E European descent, as distinguished from Sephardim Jews, who are of Spanish or Portuguese descent.

ashlar or **ashler** /ˈaʃlə(r)/ *noun* **1** a large stone cut square, used for building or facing walls. **2** masonry made of ashlars. [from Old French *aiseler*, from Latin *axilla*, small plank]

ashore *adv.* on or on to the shore or land (from water).

ashram /ˈɑːʃrəm, ˈaʃrəm/ *noun Relig.* especially in India, a hermitage for a holy man, or a place of retreat for a religious community where members lead lives of austere self-discipline and dedicated service according to the teachings and practice of their particular school. The ashram of Mahatma Gandhi is a well known example. [from Sanskrit]

ashtray *noun* a dish or other container for the ash from cigarettes.

Ashura /ˈaʃərə/ *noun* a Muslim fast day observed on the 10th of Muharram, the first month of the Muslim calendar. It is of special significance to Shiite Muslims, being a day of mourning for Husain, grandson of Muhammed, who was killed in 680 by soldiers of Caliph Yazid. It is an official holiday in predominantly Shiite Muslim countries such as Iran. [from Arabic *'Ashūrā*]

Ash Wednesday the first day of Lent.

ashy *adj.* (**ashier, ashiest**) **1** covered in ash. **2** grey; ashen.

Asian /ˈeɪʃən, ˈeɪʒən/ — *noun* **1** a person born and living in Asia. **2** a person of Asian descent. — *adj.* of Asia, its people, languages, and culture. [from Greek *Asianos*]

Asiatic /eɪʃɪˈatɪk, eɪzɪˈatɪk/ *adj.* Asian. [from Greek *Asiatikos*]

A-side *noun* the side of a two-sided gramophone record that is more actively promoted. See also B-SIDE.

aside — *adv.* **1** on or to one side. **2** (**aside from something**) apart from it. — *noun* **1** words said by a character in a play which the audience hears, but the other characters do not. **2** a remark unrelated to the main subject of a conversation.

. . . .

⊟ *adv.* **1** apart, on one side, in reserve, away, out of the way, separately, in isolation, alone, privately, secretly. *noun* **1** stage whisper, whisper. **2** digression, parenthesis, departure.

. . . .

asinine /ˈasɪnaɪn/ *adj.* of or like an ass, especially in being stupid and stubborn. [from Latin *asininus*, from *asinus*, ass]

ask *verb* **1** *trans., intrans.* to put a question to (someone) or call for an answer to (a question). **2** to inquire about: *ask the way.* **3** *trans., intrans.* (*often* **ask for something**) to make a request for it; to seek it. **4** to invite. **5** *intrans.* (**ask something of someone**) to expect it of them: *don't ask too much of him.* — **ask after someone** to ask for news of them. **ask for it** or **ask for trouble** *colloq.* to behave in a

way that is likely to bring trouble on oneself. [from Anglo-Saxon *ascian*]

. . . .

⊟ **1** question, interrogate. **2** inquire about, query. **3** request, appeal for, petition for, plead (for), beg (for), entreat, crave, demand, require, seek, solicit. **4** invite, summon.

. . . .

askance /əˈskans/ *adv.* sideways. — **look askance at something** or **someone** to consider them with suspicion or disapproval.

askew /əˈskjuː/ *adv., adj.* not properly straight or level; awry. [from A³ + SKEW]

asking price the price of an object proposed by the seller.

ASL *abbrev.* American Sign Language.

asleep — *adj.* **1** sleeping; not awake. **2** *colloq.* not paying attention. **3** *said of limbs* numb. — *adv.* into a sleeping state: *fall asleep.* [from Anglo-Saxon *on slæpe*]

. . . .

⊟ *adj.* **1** sleeping, napping, snoozing, dozing, resting, dormant, inactive, inert, unconscious. **2** dreaming, daydreaming, inattentive, absent, absent-minded, oblivious. **3** numb, dead.

⊞ **1** awake. **2** awake, alert, attentive.

. . . .

ASLEF *abbrev.* Associated Society of Locomotive Engineers and Firemen.

ASM *abbrev.* air-to-surface missile.

asocial /eɪˈsoʊʃəl/ *adj.* **1** not social, antisocial; not gregarious. **2** hostile to, or against the interests of, society.

asp /asp/ *noun* **1** any of various small venomous snakes, including *Vipera aspis*, related to the adder. **2** the Egyptian cobra, a venomous snake (*Naja haje*), native to Africa, which is said to have caused the death of the Egyptian queen Cleopatra. [from Greek *aspis*]

asparagine /əˈsparədʒiːn/ *noun Biochem.* an amino acid, first discovered in asparagus, derived from aspartic acid. It is an important nitrogen reserve in many plants, and a requirement of the human diet.

asparagus /əˈsparəgəs/ *noun* **1** any plant of the genus *Asparagus* of the lily family (Liliaceae), especially *A. officinalis*, which is cultivated as a garden vegetable and has cylindrical green shoots or 'spears' that function as leaves. The true leaves are reduced to scales. **2** the harvested shoots of this plant, which can be cooked and eaten. [from Greek *asparagos*]

aspartame /əˈspɑːteɪm/ *noun Food Science* an artificial sweetener, 200 times sweeter than sugar, but without the bitter aftertaste of saccharin. It is widely used in the food industry, and by diabetics and dieters. [from *asparagine*]

aspartic acid /əˈspɑːtɪk/ *Biochem.* an amino acid formed by the hydrolysis of asparagine. [from ASPARAGINE + ACID]

aspect /ˈaspɛkt/ *noun* **1** a particular or distinct part or element of a problem, subject, etc. **2** a particular way of considering a matter. **3** look or appearance. **4** the direction in which a building faces. **5** *Astron.* the position of a planet in relation to the Sun as viewed from the Earth. [from Latin *aspectus*, from *ad*, to + *specere*, to look]

. . . .

⊟ **1** part, element, angle, side, facet, feature. **2** attitude, position, standpoint, point of view, view, outlook. **3** look, appearance, face, expression, air, manner, bearing. **4** direction, elevation, situation, position, view, outlook, prospect.

. . . .

aspen /ˈaspən/ *noun* a deciduous tree (*Populus tremula*), also called quaking aspen, belonging to the poplar family and widespread in Europe, having smooth greyish-brown bark and oval greyish-green leaves that are borne on long flattened leaf stalks and tremble in the slightest breeze. [from Anglo-Saxon *æspe*]

aspergillosis /aspədʒɪˈləʊsɪs/ *noun Medicine* a rare disease in which spores of the fungus *Aspergillus*, normally harmless when inhaled, settle and multiply in parts of the lung that have previously been damaged, eg by tuberculosis. [from Latin *aspergere*, from *ad* to, *spargere* to sprinkle]

asperity /ə'sperɪtɪ/ *noun* (PL. **asperities**) roughness, bitterness, or harshness, especially of temper. [from Latin *asper*, rough]

aspersion — **cast aspersions on someone** or **something** to make damaging or spiteful remarks about them. [from Latin *aspersio*, sprinkling, slander]

asphalt /'asfalt/ — *noun* a brown or black semi-solid bituminous material consisting mainly of hydrocarbons, occurring in natural deposits and also prepared synthetically by distillation from petroleum. It is used in the construction industry for roofing, and is mixed with rock chips or gravel to make paving and road-surfacing materials. — *adj.* relating to or containing this material. — *verb* to cover with asphalt. [from Greek *asphaltos*]

asphyxia /as'fɪksɪə/ *noun* 1 the absence of pulse. 2 suffocation caused by any factor that interferes with respiration and prevents oxygen from reaching the body tissues, such as choking, drowning, inhaling poisonous gases, and some diseases, eg diphtheria. Unless emergency treatment is given asphyxia causes death within minutes. [from A-¹, without + Greek *sphyxis*, pulse]

asphyxiate /as'fɪksɪeɪt/ *verb trans., intrans.* to stop or cause to stop breathing.

asphyxiation *noun* 1 producing asphyxia. 2 being asphyxiated; suffocation.

aspic /'aspɪk/ *noun* a savoury jelly, made from meat or fish, used as a glaze, or to make a mould for fish, eggs, etc. [from French *aspic*, possibly connected with ASP]

aspidistra /aspɪ'dɪstrə/ *noun* an evergreen perennial plant (*Aspidistra elatior*) of the lily family, native to E Asia, and having long-lasting broad leathery leaves borne on long stalks, and dull purple bell-shaped flowers. It is a popular house plant. [from Greek *aspis*, shield]

aspirant /'aspɪrənt, ə'spaɪərənt/ *noun* a person who aspires to something.

aspirate /'aspɪrət, 'aspɪreɪt/ — *noun* (pronounced -rət) the sound represented in English and several other languages by the letter *h*. — *verb* (pronounced -reɪt) 1 *trans., intrans.* to pronounce (a word, etc) with a breath at the beginning. 2 to remove (liquid or gas) from a cavity by suction. [from Latin *aspirare*, from *ad*, to + *spirare*, to breathe]

aspiration /aspɪ'reɪʃən/ *noun* 1 eager desire, ambition. 2 *Medicine* the removal of fluid from a cavity in the body such as a cyst or an inflamed joint, or from the mouth during dental treatment, by suction using an instrument known as an aspirator.

⊟ 1 ambition, hope, dream, ideal, wish, desire, yearning, longing, aim, intent, purpose, endeavour, object, objective, goal.

aspirator /'aspɪreɪtə(r)/ *noun* 1 an instrument that is used to withdraw liquid, gas, or solid debris from a cavity of the body, eg during dental treatment. See also ASPIRATION. 2 an apparatus that is used to draw air or other gases through bottles or other vessels.

aspire *verb intrans.* (**aspire to** or **after something**) to have a strong desire to achieve or reach an objective or ambition. [from Latin *aspirare*, from *ad*, to + *spirare*, to breathe]

⊟ hope for, dream of, wish for, desire, yearn for, long for, crave, aim for, seek, pursue.

aspirin /'aspɪrɪn, 'aspɪrɪn/ *noun* acetylsalicylic acid, an analgesic drug that is widely used to relieve mild to moderate pain, eg headache, toothache, rheumatic pain, or neuralgia, and to reduce inflammation and fever caused by influenza and the common cold. [from German (originally a trademark), from *acetyl* + *spiraeic* (= salicylic) acid]

aspiring *adj.* ambitious, hopeful.

⊟ ambitious, enterprising, keen, eager, would-be, hopeful, optimistic, wishful, longing, striving.

ass¹ *noun* 1 any of various species of hoofed mammal with a grey or brownish coat, related to and resembling the horse, but having a smaller body, longer ears, a short erect mane, and a characteristic bray. 2 *colloq.* a stupid person. [from Anglo-Saxon *assa*]

ass² *North Amer., esp. US* same as ARSE.

assagai same as ASSEGAI.

assail *verb* 1 to make a strong physical or verbal attack on. 2 to make a determined start on (a task). [from Latin *ad*, to + *salire*, to leap]

assailant *noun* an attacker.

Assamese /asə'miːz/ — *noun* a language spoken in the eastern parts of N and Central India. — *adj.* relating to or spoken or written in Assamese.

assassin /ə'sasɪn/ *noun* a killer, especially for political or religious reasons. [from Arabic *hashshashin*, hashisheaters: originally applied to Muslim fanatics sent on murder missions at the time of the Crusades]

⊟ murderer, killer, cut-throat, executioner, *colloq.* hatchet man, gunman, *colloq.* hit-man, *colloq.* liquidator.

assassinate *verb* 1 to murder, especially for political or religious reasons. 2 to destroy the good reputation of (someone).

⊟ 1 murder, kill, dispatch, *slang* hit, *slang* eliminate, *slang* liquidate.

assassination *noun* 1 murder by an assassin. 2 the malicious ruining of a person's reputation.

assassin bug a small bug that feeds mainly on the body fluids of small arthropods. Some species suck the blood of vertebrates and are carriers of disease.

assault /ə'sɔːlt/ — *noun* 1 a violent physical or verbal attack. 2 *euphemistic* rape. — *verb* to make an assault on. [from French *asaut*, from Latin *ad*, to + *saltus*, leap]

⊟ *noun* 1 attack, offensive, onslaught, strike, raid, invasion, incursion, charge, battery, grievous bodily harm, *colloq.* GBH, *slang* mugging, abuse. *verb* attack, raid, invade, strike, hit, fall on, *colloq.* beat up, *slang* mug, molest, abuse.

assault and battery *Legal* the crime of threatening to attack a person, followed by an actual attack.

assault course an obstacle course with walls, pools, nets, etc, used for training soldiers.

assay /ə'seɪ, a'seɪ/ — *noun Metall.* the analysis and assessment of the composition and purity of a metal in an ore or mineral, or of a chemical compound in a mixture of compounds. — *verb* to perform such an analysis, or to determine the commercial value of an ore or mineral on the basis of such an analysis. [from Old French *assaier*]

assegai /'asəgaɪ/ *noun* a thin light iron-tipped wooden spear used in southern Africa. [from Arabic *az-zagayah*, the spear]

assemblage /ə'semblɪdʒ/ *noun* 1 a collection of people or things. 2 a gathering together.

assemble *verb* 1 *trans., intrans.* to gather or collect together. 2 *trans.* to put together the parts of (a machine, etc). [from Old French *asembler*, from Latin *ad*, to + *simul*, together]

⊟ 1 gather, muster, rally, collect, accumulate, amass, group. 2 construct, build, put together, piece together, compose, make, fabricate, manufacture.

⊟ 1 scatter, disperse. **2** dismantle, take apart.

. . . .

assembler *noun Comput.* a computer program designed to convert a program written in assembly language into one written in machine code.

assembly *noun* (PL. **assemblies**) **1** a group of people gathered together, especially for a meeting. **2** the act of assembling.

. . . .

⊟ GATHERING, COLLECTION. **1** meeting, rally, convention, conference, convocation, congress, council, group, body, company, congregation, crowd, multitude, throng. **2** construction, building, fabrication, manufacture.

. . . .

assembly language *Comput.* a low-level programming language that uses mnemonic codes consisting of short sequences of letters to represent machine code programs in a form that can be easily understood by the user.

assembly line a continuous series of machines and workers along which an article, product, etc passes in the stages of its manufacture.

assent — *noun* consent or approval, especially official. See also ROYAL ASSENT. — *verb intrans.* (**assent to something**) to agree to it. [from Latin *assentari*]

assert *verb* **1** to state firmly. **2** to insist on or defend (one's rights, opinions, etc). — **assert oneself** to state one's wishes, defend one's opinions, etc confidently and vigorously. [from Latin *asserere*]

. . . .

⊟ 1 declare, profess, state, lay down, affirm, attest, contend, maintain, claim, allege. **2** insist on, stress, protest, defend, vindicate, uphold, promote.

⊟ 1 deny.

. . . .

assertion *noun* a positive or strong statement or claim.

. . . .

⊟ declaration, profession, statement, affirmation, attestation, word, contention, claim, allegation, insistence.

⊟ denial.

. . . .

assertive *adj.* expressing one's wishes and opinions in a firm and confident manner.

. . . .

⊟ confident, self-assured, bold, forward, *slang* in-your-face, pushy, insistent, emphatic, forceful, firm, decided, strong willed, dogmatic, opinionated, presumptuous, assuming, overbearing, domineering, aggressive.

⊟ timid, diffident.

. . . .

assess *verb* **1** to judge the quality or importance of. **2** to estimate the cost, value, etc of. **3** to fine or tax by an amount stated: *were assessed at £500.* [from Latin *assidere*, to sit as a judge]

. . . .

⊟ 1 judge, consider, weigh, size up, evaluate, appraise, review. **2** gauge, estimate, value, cost, compute, determine.

. . . .

assessment *noun* **1** the act of assessing. **2** evaluation, estimation. **3** a valuation or estimate. **4** an amount to be paid.

. . . .

⊟ 1 gauging, estimation, calculation, determination. **2** evaluation, appraisal, review, estimation, opinion, judgement, consideration. **3** valuation, rating, estimate, quotation. **4** tax, duty, levy, fine.

. . . .

assessor *noun* **1** a person who assesses the value of property, etc for taxation. **2** a person who advises a judge, etc on technical matters. **3** a person who assesses the importance or quality of eg a job.

asset /ˈaset/ *noun* **1** a valuable skill, quality, or person. **2** (**assets**) the total value of the property and possessions of a person or company, especially as able to cover debts. [from Old French *asez*, enough]

. . . .

⊟ 1 strength, resource, virtue, *colloq.* plus, benefit, advantage, blessing, boon, help, aid. **2** estate, property, possessions, goods, holdings, securities, money, wealth, capital, funds, reserves, resources, means.

⊟ 1 weakness, disadvantage. **2** liabilities.

. . . .

asset-stripping *noun* the practice of buying an unsuccessful company at a low price and selling off its assets separately for a profit.

asseverate /əˈsevəreit/ *verb* to state solemnly. [from Latin *asseverare*]

assiduity /asɪˈdjuːɪtɪ/ *noun* (PL. **assiduities**) constant care and attention to a person, or to what one is doing.

assiduous /əˈsɪdjʊəs/ *adj.* **1** hard-working. **2** done carefully and exactly. [from Latin *assiduus*, persistent]

assign /əˈsaɪn/ *verb* **1** to give (a task, etc) to someone or appoint (someone) to a position or task. **2** to fix (a time, place, etc) for a purpose. **3** *Legal* assign something to someone) to give one's title, property, interest, etc to someone else by contract. [from Latin *assignare*, to mark out]

. . . .

⊟ 1 give, allocate, apportion, allot, distribute, delegate, name, nominate, designate, appoint, choose, select. **2** fix, set, determine, specify, stipulate.

. . . .

assignation /asɪgˈneɪʃən/ *noun* a secret appointment to meet, especially between lovers.

assignee /asaɪˈniː/ *noun Legal* a person to whom property, interest, etc is given by contract.

assignment /əˈsaɪnmənt/ *noun* **1** a task or duty assigned to someone. **2** the act of assigning. **3** *Legal* a transfer of property, interest, etc to someone else.

. . . .

⊟ 1 task, job, project, commission, errand, duty, responsibility, charge, appointment, position, post. **2** allocation, distribution, delegation, designation, nomination, selection, appointment.

. . . .

assignor /asɪˈnɔː(r)/ *noun Legal* a person who gives property, interest, etc by contract.

assimilable /əˈsɪmɪləbl/ *adj.* capable of being assimilated.

assimilate /əˈsɪmɪleɪt/ — *noun Biol.* any of the complex organic compounds initially produced by green plants and certain bacteria that manufacture complex molecules from simple molecules obtained from the environment, such as carbon dioxide, nitrogen, or water. — *verb* **1** to become familiar with and understand (facts, information, etc) completely. **2** *trans., intrans.* to become part of, or make (people) part of, a larger group, especially of a different race or culture. **3** *Biol., said of a plant or animal* to manufacture complex organic compounds. **4** to cause to resemble, especially to make (a sound) like another. [from Latin *ad*, to + *similis*, like]

assimilation /əsɪmɪˈleɪʃən/ *noun Biol.* in autotrophic organisms (green plants and certain bacteria), the manufacture of complex organic compounds from simple molecules obtained from the environment, such as carbon dioxide, nitrogen, or water; in animals, the manufacture of complex organic compounds, such as proteins and fats, from simple molecules derived from digested food material.

assist *verb* **1** *trans., intrans.* (often **assist in** or **with something**) to help (someone) with it. **2** *intrans.* to take part in a ceremony, etc. [from Latin *assistere*, to take a stand beside]

. . . .

⊟ 1 help, aid, co-operate, collaborate, benefit, serve, enable, facilitate, expedite, advance.

⊟ 1 hinder, thwart.

. . . .

assistance *noun* the act of helping someone with something; the help given in this way.

■ help, aid, co-operation, collaboration, support, relief, benefit, service.
🔁 hindrance.

assistant *noun* 1 a person employed to help someone of higher rank, position, etc. 2 a person who serves customers in a shop.

■ 1 helper, aide, right-hand man, auxiliary, ancillary, subordinate, accomplice, accessory, abettor, collaborator, colleague, partner. 2 shop assistant, salesperson, salesman, saleswoman.

assistant referee in soccer, an official whose job it is to indicate when the ball has gone out of play and to assist the referee in his decisions.

assizes /əˈsaɪzɪz/ *pl. noun Hist.* a court sitting at regular intervals in each county in England and Wales. [from Latin *assidere*, to sit as a judge]

assoc. *abbrev.* 1 associated. 2 association.

associate /əˈsəʊʃɪeɪt, əˈsəʊʃɪət/ — *verb* (pronounced -eɪt) 1 to connect in the mind: *associate lambs with spring.* 2 *intrans.* to mix socially: *don't associate with him.* 3 to involve (oneself) in a group because of shared views or aims. 4 *intrans.* to join with people for a common purpose. — *noun* (pronounced -ət) 1 a business partner. 2 a colleague or friend. 3 a person admitted to a society without full membership. — *adj.* (pronounced -ət) 1 joined with another, especially in a business: *an associate director.* 2 not having full membership of a society. [from Latin *associare*, from *ad*, to + *socius*, companion]

■ *verb* 1 connect, link, correlate, relate, couple, pair, yoke. 2 mix, mingle, socialize, fraternize, consort, *colloq.* hang around. 4 join, combine, unite, ally, league, affiliate, confederate. *noun* 1 partner, ally, confederate, affiliate. 2 colleague, co-worker, peer, fellow, mate, comrade, companion, friend, *colloq.* sidekick.

associated *adj.* (*usually* **Associated**) used in the name of a company to show that it has been formed from several smaller companies.

association /əsəʊʃɪˈeɪʃən, əsəʊsɪˈeɪʃən/ *noun* 1 an organization or club. 2 a friendship or partnership. 3 a connection in the mind. 4 the act of associating.

■ 1 organization, corporation, company, partnership, league, alliance, confederation, consortium, cartel, syndicate, union, society, club, fraternity, fellowship, clique, group, band. 2 friendship, companionship, fellowship, partnership, relationship, bond, tie. 3 connection, link, correlation, relation.

associative /əˈsəʊʃɪətɪv, əˈsəʊsɪətɪv/ *adj. Maths.* denoting any mathematical operation whose result does not depend on the order in which the operation is carried out, eg multiplication, because 2 x (3 x 4) gives the same result as (2 x 3) x 4. Addition is also an associative operation.

assonance /ˈasənəns/ *noun Poetry* 1 the rhyming of vowel sounds but not consonants, as in *load* and *cold.* 2 the use of a consonant or consonants with different vowel sounds, as in *milled* and *mulled.* [from Latin *assonare*, to sound]

assorted *adj.* 1 mixed; of or containing various different kinds. 2 arranged in sorts; classified. [from Latin *ad*, to + *sors*, lot]

■ 1 miscellaneous, mixed, varied, different, heterogeneous, diverse, sundry, various, several, manifold.

assortment *noun* a mixed collection.

■ miscellany, medley, potpourri, jumble, mixture, variety, diversity, collection, selection, choice.

assuage /əˈsweɪdʒ/ *verb* to make (a pain, sorrow, hunger, etc) less severe. [from Latin *ad*, to + *suavis*, mild, sweet]

assume /əˈsjuːm, əˈsuːm/ *verb* 1 to accept (something), though without proof; to take for granted. 2 to take upon oneself (a responsibility, duty, etc). 3 to take on or adopt (an appearance, quality, etc): *an issue assuming immense importance.* 4 to pretend to have or feel. [from Latin *assumere*, to take to oneself]

■ 1 presume, surmise, accept, take for granted, expect, understand, deduce, infer, guess, postulate, suppose, think, believe, imagine, fancy. 2 undertake, adopt, embrace, seize, arrogate, commandeer, appropriate, usurp, take over. 3 take on, adopt. 4 pretend, affect, feign, fake, counterfeit, simulate, put on.

assumed *adj.* 1 false; not genuine. 2 accepted as true before proof is available.

■ 1 false, bogus, counterfeit, fake, *colloq.* phoney, sham, affected, feigned, simulated, pretended, made-up, fictitious. 2 hypothetical, imagined, presumed, supposed, putative.
🔁 1 real, actual, true, genuine. 2 proven.

assuming *adj., said of a person* arrogant; presumptuous.

assumption /əˈsʌmʃən, əˈsʌmpʃən/ *noun* 1 something accepted as true without proof. 2 the act of accepting something as true without proof. 3 the act of assuming. 4 (**Assumption**) *Christianity* see separate entry. [from Latin *assumptio*, from *assumere*, to take to oneself]

■ 1 presumption, surmise, inference, supposition, guess, conjecture, theory, hypothesis, premise, postulate, idea, notion, belief, fancy. 2 presumption, surmise, inference, supposition, conjecture. 3 adoption, undertaking, feigning, simulation.

assurance *noun* 1 a promise, guarantee, or statement that a thing is true. 2 confidence. 3 *Brit.* insurance, especially of one's life.

■ 1 guarantee, pledge, promise, vow, word, assertion, declaration, affirmation. 2 confidence, self-confidence, self-assurance, aplomb, boldness, audacity, courage, nerve, conviction, sureness, certainty.
🔁 2 shyness, doubt, uncertainty.

assure *verb* 1 to state positively and confidently. 2 (**assure someone of something**) to convince them or make them sure about it: *can assure you of my innocence.* 3 to make (an event, etc) certain: *assure her success.* 4 *Brit.* to insure, especially one's life. [from Latin *ad*, to + *securus*, safe]

■ 1 declare, affirm, guarantee, warrant, pledge, promise, vow, swear. 2 convince, persuade, reassure, tell. 3 ensure, secure, confirm.

assured *adj.* 1 *said of a person* confident. 2 certain to happen.

■ 1 confident, self-confident, self-assured, self-possessed, bold, audacious, assertive. 2 sure, certain, indisputable, positive, definite, settled, fixed, guaranteed, secure.
🔁 1 shy. 2 uncertain.

assuredly *adv.* certainly.

Assyrian /ə'sɪrɪən/ *Hist.* — *noun* **1** an inhabitant of Assyria. **2** the Semitic language of Assyria. — *adj.* of Assyria, its people, language and culture. [from Greek *Assyrios*]

astatine /'astəti:n/ *noun Chem.* (SYMBOL **At**, ATOMIC NUMBER **85**) a radioactive element, the heaviest of the halogens, that has several isotopes, all of which are radioactive but have very short half-lives, ranging from fractions of a second to eight hours. Astatine is prepared by bombarding bismuth with alpha particles. [from Greek *astatos*, unstable]

aster *noun* any of a large group of mainly perennial plants of the genus *Aster*, native to Europe, Asia, America, and Africa, and having daisy-like flower-heads. Many species are popular ornamental plants, including the Michaelmas daisy (*A.nova-belgii*). [from Greek *aster*, star]

asterisk /'astərɪsk/ — *noun* a star-shaped mark (*) used in printing and writing to mark especially a reference to a note or an omission. — *verb* to mark with an asterisk. [from Greek *asteriskos*, small star]

astern *adv.*, *adj.* **1** in or towards the stern. **2** backwards. **3** behind. [from A³ + STERN]

asteroid *noun* any of thousands of small rocky objects, 1km to 1,000km in diameter, that revolve around the Sun, mainly between the orbits of Mars and Jupiter. Asteroids are thought to be fragments of the material from which the Solar System was formed. Also called MINOR PLANET. [from Greek *asteroeides*, star-like]

asthenosphere /as'θenəsfɪə(r)/ *noun Geol.* the upper layer of the mantle that lies immediately below the Earth's crust. [from Greek *astheneia*, weakness]

asthma /'asmə/ *noun* a respiratory disorder in which breathlessness and wheezing occur as a result of narrowing and obstruction of the bronchi and bronchioles (the air passages). [from Greek *asthma*, from *aazein*, to breathe hard]

asthmatic /as'matɪk/ — *adj.* relating to or suffering from asthma. — *noun* a person who suffers from asthma.

asthmatically *adv.* with symptoms of asthma.

astigmatic /astɪg'matɪk/ *adj.* relating to, affected by, or correcting astigmatism: *astigmatic lens.*

astigmatism /ə'stɪgmətɪzm/ *noun Physics* a defect in a lens, especially abnormal curvature of the lens or cornea of the eye. Astigmatism causes distortion of the image of an object because not all light rays from it are brought to the same focus on the retina. It is corrected by wearing spectacles or contact lenses that produce exactly the opposite degree of distortion. [from A-¹ without + Greek *stigma*, point]

astir *adj.*, *adv.* **1** awake and out of bed. **2** in a state of motion or excitement. [from A³ + STIR]

astonish *verb* to surprise greatly. [from Old French *estoner*, from Latin *ex*, out + *tonare*, to thunder]

....
⊟ surprise, startle, amaze, astound, stun, stupefy, daze, stagger, *colloq.* floor, dumbfound, *colloq.* flabbergast, shock, confound, bewilder.
....

astonished *adj.* extremely surprised.

astonishing *adj.* wonderful or surprising; extraordinary.

astonishingly *adv.* in an astonishing way; to an astonishing extent: *they were astonishingly brave.*

astonishment *noun* wonder; complete surprise.

....
⊟ surprise, amazement, wonder, shock, confusion, bewilderment.
....

astound *verb* to amaze or shock. [from obsolete *astone*, to astonish]

astounded *adj.* amazed, shocked, bewildered.

astounding *adj.* amazing, shocking.

....
⊟ amazing, astonishing, surprising, startling, shocking,

bewildering, stunning, breathtaking, stupefying, overwhelming, staggering.
....

astoundingly *adv.* in a surprising and shocking way.

astrakhan /astrə'ka:n/ *noun* dark tightly curled wool from lambs, used to make cloth. [from Astrakhan in SE Russia]

astral *adj.* of or like the stars. [from Latin *astralis*, from *astrum*, star]

astray *adj.*, *adv.* out of the right or expected way. — **go astray** to become lost.

....
⊟ adrift, lost, amiss, wrong, awry.
....

astride — *adv.* **1** with a leg on each side. **2** with legs apart. — *prep.* **1** with a leg on each side of. **2** stretching across.

astringency /ə'strɪndʒənsɪ/ *noun* being astringent; severity, harshness.

astringent /ə'strɪndʒənt/ — *adj.* **1** severe and harsh. **2** *said of a substance* causing cells to shrink. — *noun* a substance that causes cells to shrink, used in medical preparations to stop bleeding from minor cuts, etc, and in cosmetic lotions to harden and protect the skin. Astringents are also used in throat lozenges and antiperspirants. [from Latin *astringere*, to draw tight]

astringently *adv.* with an astringent or harsh manner.

astro- *combining form* relating to stars or space. [from Greek *astron*, star]

astrodome *noun* an open space or building covered by a large translucent plastic dome, usually a sports centre or arena.

astrolabe /'astrəuleɪb/ *noun Astron.* a former navigational instrument used to observe the positions of the Sun and bright stars, and to estimate the local time by estimating the altitude of the Sun or specific stars above the horizon. [from ASTRO- + *lab-*, root of Greek *lambanein* to take]

astrologer /ə'strɒlədʒə(r)/ *noun* a person who studies or practises astrology.

astrological *adj.* relating to astrology.

astrology /ə'strɒlədʒɪ/ *noun* the study of the movements of the stars and planets and their influence on people's lives. [from Greek *astron*, star + *logos*, discourse]

astrometry *noun Astron.* the branch of astronomy concerned with the precise measurement of the positions of stars, planets, and other celestial bodies on the celestial sphere.

astronaut /'astrənɔ:t/ *noun* a person trained to travel in a space vehicle. [from ASTRO- + Latin *nautes*, sailor]

astronautics *sing. noun* the science of travel in space.

astronomer /ə'strɒnəmə(r)/ *noun* a person who studies or practises astronomy.

Astronomer Royal formerly the title of the Director of the Royal Greenwich Observatory, but since 1972 an honorary title awarded to a distinguished British astronomer.

astronomical or **astronomic** *adj.* **1** *said of numbers, amounts, etc* large; extreme. **2** relating to astronomy.

astronomically *adv.* **1** *colloq.* extremely; enormously: *an astronomically large bill.* **2** as regards or in terms of astronomy.

astronomical unit (ABBREV. **AU**) *Astron.* the mean distance between the Earth and the Sun, about 149.6m km (93m mi), used to measure distances within the Solar System. There are 63,240 astronomical units in a light year.

astronomy /ə'strɒnəmɪ/ *noun* the scientific study of celestial bodies, including the planets, stars, and galaxies, as well as interstellar and intergalactic space, and the universe as a whole. [from Greek *astron*, star + *nomos*, law]

astrophysical *adj.* relating to astrophysics.

astrophysicist *noun* a person who studies astrophysics.

astrophysics *sing. noun Astron.* the application of physical laws and theories to astronomical objects and phenomena, especially stars and galaxies, with the aim of deriving theoretical models to explain their behaviour.

astute *adj.* able to judge and act intelligently and decisively; mentally perceptive. [from Latin *astutus*, from *astus*, craft]

．．．．．．．．．．．．．．．．．．

🔁 shrewd, prudent, sagacious, wise, canny, knowing, intelligent, sharp, penetrating, keen, perceptive, discerning, subtle, clever, crafty, cunning, sly, wily.

🔁 stupid, slow.

．．．．．．．．．．．．．．．．．．

asunder *adv.* apart or into pieces. [from Anglo-Saxon *on-sundran*]

asylum /ə'saɪləm/ *noun* (PL. **asylums**) 1 a place of safety or protection. 2 the granting of protection. See also POLITICAL ASYLUM. 3 *Hist.* a mental hospital. [from Greek *asylon*, from A-[1], not + Greek *sylon*, right of seizure]

．．．．．．．．．．．．．．．．．．

🔁 1 haven, sanctuary, refuge, shelter, retreat. 2 protection, safety.

．．．．．．．．．．．．．．．．．．

asymmetric /eɪsɪ'mɛtrɪk, asɪ'mɛtrɪk/ or **asymmetrical** *adj.* lacking symmetry.

．．．．．．．．．．．．．．．．．．

🔁 unbalanced, uneven, crooked, awry, unequal, disproportionate, irregular.

🔁 symmetrical.

．．．．．．．．．．．．．．．．．．

asymmetrically *adv.* without symmetry; in an asymmetrical way.

asymmetry /eɪ'sɪmətrɪ, a'sɪmətrɪ/ *noun* a lack of symmetry. [from A-[1] not + Greek *symmetria*, symmetry]

asymptote /'asɪmtəʊt/ *noun Geom.* a line (usually straight) which is continually approached by a curve that never actually meets the line. [from Greek *asymptotos*, apt to fall together]

At *symbol Chem.* astatine.

at *prep.* expressing: 1 position or location. 2 direction: *look at the book*. 3 position in time. 4 state or occupation: *children at play*. 5 time during which: *work at night*. 6 rate or level: *work at speed*. 7 cost: *sell at £5 each*. 8 cause: *shocked at his behaviour*. — **at that** 1 at that point. 2 as well. [from Anglo-Saxon *æt*]

atavism /'atəvɪzm/ *noun* 1 a resemblance to ancestors rather than immediate parents. 2 reversion to an earlier, especially more primitive, type. [from Latin *atavus*, great-great-grandfather]

atavistic *adj.* 1 relating to or resembling ancestors. 2 involving reversion to an earlier type.

ataxia /ə'taksɪə/ *noun Medicine* inability of the brain to coordinate voluntary movements of the limbs, resulting in jerky movements and a staggering gait. It is caused by a disorder of the sensory nerves or by disease of the cerebellum. [from Greek *ataxia*, disorder]

ATC *abbrev.* Air Training Corps.

ate /ɛt, eɪt/ see EAT.

-ate *suffix* 1 forming verbs meaning 'cause to be': *hyphenate*. 2 forming nouns denoting rank, profession, or group: *doctorate* / *magistrate* / *electorate*. 3 forming nouns denoting a salt: *carbonate*. See also -IDE, -ITE. 4 forming adjectives meaning 'having, showing features of, like or related to': *passionate* / *fortunate*. [from the Latin ending *-atus*, sometimes via Old French]

atelier /ə'tɛlɪeɪ/ *noun* 1 a workshop or artist's studio. 2 an abbreviated form of *atelier libre*, free studio (free in the sense that anyone may attend, on payment of a fee). Found throughout Europe, these studios provide a nude model for artists to work from, but offer no instruction. [from French *atelier*]

atheism /'eɪθiːɪzm/ *noun* the belief that there is no God. [from A-[1] without + Greek *theos*, god]

🔁 unbelief, non-belief, disbelief, scepticism, irreligion, ungodliness, godlessness, impiety, infidelity, paganism, heathenism, freethinking, rationalism.

．．．．．．．．．．．．．．．．．．

atheist *noun* a person who believes that there is no God.

．．．．．．．．．．．．．．．．．．

🔁 unbeliever, non-believer, disbeliever, sceptic, infidel, pagan, heathen, freethinker.

．．．．．．．．．．．．．．．．．．

atheistic or **atheistical** *adj.* 1 characteristic or typical of an atheist. 2 relating to or involving atheism.

atheistically *adv.* in an atheistic way.

atherosclerosis /'aθərəʊsklə'rəʊsɪs/ *noun* (PL. **atheroscleroses**) *Medicine* a form of arteriosclerosis (thickening and hardening of the arteries) in which cholesterol and other fatty substances are deposited on the inner walls of arteries, making them narrow and eventually obstructing the flow of blood. [from Greek *athere*, gruel + SCLEROSIS]

atherosclerotic /aθərəʊsklə'rɒtɪk/ *adj.* relating to or typical of atherosclerosis.

athlete *noun* 1 a person who is good at sport, especially track and field events such as running. 2 a healthy person with athletic ability. [from Greek *athlos*, contest]

．．．．．．．．．．．．．．．．．．

🔁 1 sportsman, sportswoman, runner, gymnast, competitor, contestant, contender.

．．．．．．．．．．．．．．．．．．

athlete's foot a fungal infection of the skin of the feet, caused by a type of ringworm, and usually characterized by itching lesions on the skin between the toes.

athletic *adj.* 1 *said of people* physically fit and strong. 2 relating to athletics.

．．．．．．．．．．．．．．．．．．

🔁 1 fit, energetic, active, sporty, strong, powerful, muscular, sinewy, brawny, strapping, robust, sturdy.

🔁 1 unfit, weak, puny.

．．．．．．．．．．．．．．．．．．

athletics *sing. noun* competitive track and field sports for athletes, including running, jumping, throwing, and walking.

．．．．．．．．．．．．．．．．．．

🔁 sports, games, races, track events, field events, exercises, gymnastics.

．．．．．．．．．．．．．．．．．．

athwart /ə'θwɔːt/ *adv.*, *prep.* across, from side to side (of). [from A-[3] + THWART]

-ation *suffix* forming nouns meaning 'the process or result of'; sometimes corresponding to verbs in *-ize*: *expectation* / *mechanization* / *representation*.

-ative *suffix* forming adjectives denoting a particular attribute or tendency: *authoritative* / *talkative*.

Atlantic — *noun* (**the Atlantic**) an ocean between the Americas to the W and Europe and Africa to the E. — *adj.* in or relating to the Atlantic. [from Greek *Atlantikos*, from *Atlas*, so called because it lay beyond the Atlas mountains]

atlas *noun* (PL. **atlases**) 1 a book of maps and geographical charts. 2 *Anat.* the topmost vertebra of the neck. [from *Atlas* in Greek mythology, a Titan who was made to hold up the heavens with his hands, as a punishment for taking part in the revolt against the Olympians. In early atlases, he was often portrayed as the frontispiece]

atlas vertebra *Anat.* the topmost bone of the spine, which joins the skull to the spine and pivots on the axis vertebra, enabling nodding movements of the head to be made.

ATM *abbrev.* automatic teller machine.

atman /'ɑːtmən/ *noun Hinduism* the human soul or essential self. In the teachings of the Upanishads (Sanskrit texts that form the basis of much Hindu philosophy), it is seen as being one with the Absolute, and is identified with Brahman. [from Sanskrit *atman*, self, soul]

atmosphere /'atmosfɪə(r)/ *noun* 1 the layer of gas surrounding a planet, and held to it by gravity. 2 the air in a particular place. 3 the mood of a place, book, etc or the general impression one has of it. 4 a unit of atmospheric pressure, equal to normal air pressure at sea level. [from Greek *atmos*, vapour + *sphaira*, ball]

....

◫ **1** air, sky, aerospace, heavens, ether. **3** ambience, aura, feel, feeling, impression, mood, spirit, tone, tenor, character, quality.

....

atmospheric /atmos'ferɪk/ *adj.* **1** relating to or occurring within the Earth's atmosphere. **2** *said of a place* strongly suggestive of a particular mood or feeling.

atmospherically *adv.* as regards the atmosphere.

atmospheric interference same as ATMOSPHERICS.

atmospheric pollution *Environ.* air pollution.

atmospheric pressure *Physics* the pressure exerted by the atmosphere at any point on the Earth's surface, due to the weight of the air above it. Atmospheric pressure decreases with increasing altitude.

atmospherics *pl. noun* radio-frequency electromagnetic radiation, produced by lightning discharges and other natural electrical disturbances in the Earth's atmosphere, that interferes with radio communications. Also called ATMOSPHERIC INTERFERENCE.

atoll /'atɒl/ *noun* a continuous or broken circle of coral reef that surrounds a lagoon, and is itself surrounded by open sea. [from *Atolu*, a name in the Maldive Islands]

atom *noun* **1** the smallest unit of a chemical element that can display the properties of that element. Atoms are composed of subatomic particles, and combine to form molecules. **2** formerly used to refer to the smallest particle of matter that can exist. **3** a very small amount or piece: *not an atom of use*. [from Greek *atomos*, undivided]

....

◫ **3** bit, particle, morsel, crumb, grain, spot, speck, shred, scrap, hint, trace, jot, iota.

....

atom bomb or **atomic bomb** *Mil.* a powerful explosive device that derives its force from the sudden release of enormous amounts of nuclear (atomic) energy during nuclear fission. Also called NUCLEAR BOMB.

atomic *adj.* **1** relating to atoms. **2** obtained by atomic phenomena, especially nuclear fission: *atomic energy / atomic weapons.*

atomically *adv.* as regards atoms or atomic energy.

atomic clock *Physics* a precise clock that measures time by using the regular oscillations of individual atoms or molecules to regulate its movement.

atomic energy nuclear energy.

atomicity /atə'mɪsɪtɪ/ *noun Chem.* the number of atoms in a molecule of a chemical element.

atomic mass unit *Chem.* an arbitrary unit that is used to denote the masses of individual atoms or molecules. It is equal to one twelfth of the mass of an atom of the carbon-12 isotope of carbon. Also called DALTON.

atomic number *Chem.* (SYMBOL Z) the number of protons in the nucleus of an atom of a particular element. In the periodic table, the chemical elements are arranged in order of increasing atomic number.

atomic orbital *Chem.* a wave function that represents the region in space occupied by an electron that is orbiting round the nucleus of an atom.

atomic weight relative atomic mass.

atomism *noun* (*also* **atomic theory**) a philosophical tradition dating back to the 5c BC and particularly associated with the Greek philosophers Leucippus, Democritus, and Epicurus. It maintains that all that exists is made up of minute indivisible particles, and that all phenomena must be explained in terms of these 'fundamental particles' and their interactions in space (the *void*).

atomize or **atomise** *verb* **1** to reduce to atoms or small particles. **2** to reduce (a liquid) to a spray or mist of fine droplets by passage through a nozzle or jet under pressure. **3** to destroy by means of atomic weapons.

atomizer or **atomiser** *noun* a container from which liquid can be released as a fine spray.

atonal /eɪ'tɒʊnl, a'tɒʊnl/ *adj. Mus.* lacking tonality; not written in a particular key. [from Greek *atonos*, toneless]

atonality /eɪtɒʊ'nalɪtɪ, atɒʊ'nalɪtɪ/ *noun* being atonal; lack of tonality.

atone *verb intrans.* (**atone for something**) to make amends for a wrongdoing. [from Middle English; originally to 'make at one', to reconcile]

atonement *noun* **1** an act of atoning. **2** (**Atonement**) *Christianity* the reconciliation of God and man through the death of Christ.

ATP *abbrev. Biochem.* adenosine triphosphate.

atrial /'eɪtrɪəl/ *adj.* relating to or in the style of an atrium.

atrium /'eɪtrɪəm/ *noun* (PL. **atria**, **atriums**) **1** a central court or entrance hall in an ancient Roman house. **2** *Anat.* either of the two upper chambers of the heart that receive blood from the veins. Also called AURICLE. **3** *Anat.* any of various other chambers or cavities in the body. [from Latin *atrium*]

atrocious /ə'trɒʊʃəs/ *adj.* **1** *colloq.* very bad. **2** extremely cruel or wicked. [from Latin *atrox*, cruel]

....

◫ **1** dreadful, shocking, appalling, terrible, awful, abominable. **2** shocking, appalling, wicked, heinous, cruel, savage, vicious, monstrous, ruthless.

◪ **1** excellent. **2** admirable, fine.

....

atrociousness *noun* being atrocious; extreme wickedness.

atrocity /ə'trɒsɪtɪ/ *noun* (PL. **atrocities**) **1** wicked or cruel behaviour. **2** (*usually* **atrocities**) an act of wickedness or cruelty.

....

◫ **1** wickedness, heinousness, evil, villainy, savagery, barbarity, brutality, cruelty, viciousness. **2** outrage, abomination, evil, barbarism.

....

atrophy /'atrəfɪ/ — *verb trans., intrans.* (**atrophies**, **atrophied**) to make or become weak and thin through lack of use or nourishment. — *noun* the process of atrophying. [from Greek *a*, not + *trophe*, nourishment]

atropine or **atropin** /'atrəpiːn, 'atrəpɪn/ *noun Medicine* a poisonous alkaloid drug, obtained from deadly nightshade, that relaxes smooth muscle and reduces secretions of the salivary glands, stomach, and intestines. Also called BELLADONNA. [from Greek *Atropos*, the Fate that cut the thread of life]

attach *verb* **1** to fasten or join. **2** to associate (oneself) with or join. **3** to attribute or assign: *attach great importance to detail*. **4** *intrans.* (**attach to something**) to be connected with or form part of it: *certain conditions attach to the offer.* **5** *Legal* to arrest (a person) or seize (property) by legal authority. — **be attached to someone** or **something** be fond of them. [from French *atachier*]

....

◫ **1** fasten, fix, secure, tie, bind, affix, stick, adhere, join, unite, connect, link, couple, add, annex. **3** ascribe, attribute, assign, impute.

◪ **1** detach, unfasten.

....

attaché /ə'taʃeɪ/ *noun* a junior official in an embassy. [from French *attaché*, attached]

attaché-case *noun* a small rigid leather case for documents, etc.

attached *adj.* joined, connected.

attachment *noun* **1** an act or means of fastening. **2** liking or affection. **3** an extra part that can be fitted to a machine to change its function slightly. **4** a legal seizure of a person or property. **5** a temporary period of working with a different group.

....

◫ **1** fastening, connection, link. **2** fondness, affection, tenderness, love, liking, partiality, loyalty, devotion, friendship, affinity, attraction, bond, tie. **3** accessory, fitting, fixture, extension, appendage, extra, supplement, addition, adjunct.

attack — *verb* **1** to make a sudden, violent attempt to hurt, damage, or capture. **2** to criticize strongly in speech or writing. **3** *intrans.* to make an attack. **4** to begin to do (something) with enthusiasm or determination. **5** to begin to damage. **6** *intrans.* to take the initiative in a game, contest, etc to attempt to score points. — *noun* **1** an act or the action of attacking. **2** a sudden spell of illness. [from Italian *attaccare*]

■ *verb* **1** invade, raid, strike, storm, charge, assault, assail, set about, set upon, fall on, lay into, *slang* do over. **2** criticize, censure, blame, denounce, revile, malign, abuse. *noun* **1** offensive, blitz, bombardment, invasion, incursion, raid, strike, charge, rush, onslaught, assault, aggression, criticism, censure, abuse. **2** bout, fit, seizure, convulsion, paroxysm, spasm, stroke.
F3 *verb* **1** defend, protect. *noun* **1** defence, protection.

attacker *noun* a person who makes an attack.

■ assailant, *slang* mugger, aggressor, invader, raider, critic, detractor, persecutor,
F3 defender, supporter.

attack helicopter a military helicopter designed or adapted for attacking or engaging an enemy, whether on land or at sea.

attain *verb* **1** to complete successfully; to accomplish. **2** to reach or arrive at; to gain. [from Latin *ad*, to + *tangere*, to touch]

■ **1** accomplish, achieve, complete, fulfil, effect, realize. **2** reach, get to, arrive at, touch, grasp, gain, win, get, acquire, obtain, procure, secure.

attainable *adj.* capable of being attained; achievable.
attainment *noun* **1** attaining; achieving by effort. **2** something that is attained.

■ ACCOMPLISHMENT, ACHIEVEMENT. **1** completion, fulfilment, realization. **2** feat, skill, art, proficiency, mastery.

attar / 'atɑː(r)/ *noun* a fragrant oil made from rose petals. [from Persian]
attempt — *verb* **1** to try (to do something); to make an effort to achieve (something). **2** to try to climb or master (a mountain, problem, etc). — *noun* (*often* **attempt at something**) an endeavour to achieve something. — **an attempt on someone's life** an attempt to kill them. [from Latin *attemptare*, to test]

■ *verb* **1** try, endeavour, seek, strive, venture. **2** tackle, undertake. *noun* try, endeavour, *colloq.* shot, *colloq.* go, *colloq.* stab, *colloq.* bash, effort, struggle, bid, undertaking, venture, trial, experiment.

attend *verb* **1** *trans., intrans.* to be present (at). **2** to go regularly to (eg a school). **3** *intrans.* (**attend to something** or **someone**) to devote oneself to them or take action about them. **4** *formal* to accompany or escort. **5** *trans. formal* (**attend on** or **upon something**) to follow as a result of it. **6** *trans.* to serve or wait on. [from Latin *attendere*, to direct one's attention to]

■ **1** be present (at), go (to), visit. **2** frequent. **3** deal with, see to, take care of, look after, manage, direct, control,

supervise. **4** escort, chaperone, accompany, usher, guard. **6** serve, help, wait on, minister to.

attendance *noun* **1** the act of attending. **2** the number of people attending. **3** regularity of attending.

■ **1** presence, appearance. **2** turn-out, audience, house, crowd, gate.

attendance allowance *Brit.* money paid by the government to severely disabled people to pay for a nurse, etc to help them.
attendant — *noun* a person employed to help, especially the public. — *adj.* **1** giving attendance. **2** accompanying.

■ *noun* helper, assistant, auxiliary, steward, waiter, servant, page, retainer, guide, marshal, usher, escort, companion, follower, guard, custodian. *adj.* **2** accompanying, attached, associated, related, incidental, resultant, consequent, subsequent.

attention *noun* **1** the act of concentrating or directing the mind. **2** special care and consideration. **3** (**attentions**) an act of politeness or courtship. **4** *Mil.* a position in which one stands rigidly erect with heels together and hands by one's sides. [from Latin *attentio*]

■ **1** concentration, attentiveness, alertness, vigilance, heed, notice, observation, regard, awareness, recognition, thought, contemplation. **2** care, concern, consideration, treatment, service.
F3 **1** inattention. **2** disregard, carelessness.

attention deficit disorder (ABBREV. **ADD**) a disorder, especially in children, characterized by hyperactivity and the inability to concentrate.
attentive *adj.* **1** concentrating; paying attention. **2** polite, helpful, and caring.

■ **1** concentrating, alert, awake, vigilant, watchful, observant, heedful, mindful, careful, conscientious. **2** polite, courteous, caring, considerate, thoughtful, kind, helpful, obliging, accommodating, devoted.
F3 **1** inattentive, heedless. **2** inconsiderate.

attenuate / ə'tɛnjʊeɪt/ *verb* **1** *trans., intrans.* to make or become thin and weak. **2** to reduce the strength or value of. **3** *Physics, said of sound, radiation, electric current, etc* to decrease in intensity as a result of absorption or scattering on passing through a medium. **4** *Medicine* to treat bacteria or viruses in such a way as to diminish greatly their capacity to cause disease, while retaining their ability to evoke an immune response. This procedure is used to produce certain vaccines. [from Latin *attenuare*]
attenuated *adj.* **1** thin. **2** thinned, diluted. **3** tapering.
attenuation / ətenjʊ'eɪʃən/ *noun* **1** the process of making slender. **2** reduction in strength, virulence, etc. **3** *Physics* a reduction in amplitude or intensity of sound, electromagnetic radiation, etc, caused by absorption, scattering, or friction as it passes through a medium.
attest *verb* **1** to affirm or be proof of the truth or validity of. **2** *trans., intrans.* (**attest to something**) to certify that it is so. [from Latin *attestari*, from *ad*, to + *testare*, to witness]
attestation / ate'steɪʃən/ *noun* **1** an act of attesting. **2** the administration of an oath.
attested *adj.* **1** *said of a fact, statement, etc* supported by evidence or proof. **2** *Brit., said of cattle* officially certified free from disease, especially tuberculosis.
Attic — *adj.* **1** relating to ancient Athens or Attica, or the form of Greek spoken there. **2** elegant. — *noun* the form of Greek spoken in ancient Athens. [from Greek *attikos*]
attic *noun* a space or room at the top of a house under the

roof. [from ATTIC; such a structure is supposedly in the Athenian style]

attire *noun* clothing, especially formal or elegant. [from French *atirier*, to put in order]

attired *adj.* dressed, especially formally or elegantly.

attitude / 'atıtju:d/ *noun* **1** a way of thinking or behaving. **2** a position of the body. **3** a pose, especially adopted for dramatic effect: *strike an attitude*. **4** the angle made by the axes of an aircraft or space vehicle in relation to some plane, especially the relative airflow or the Earth's surface. [from French *attitude*, from Latin *aptitudo*, suitability]

   1 feeling, disposition, mood, point of view, opinion, view, outlook, perspective, approach. **2** position, posture, stance, pose, manner, bearing.

attitudinize or **attitudinise** / atı'tju:dənaız/ *verb intrans.* to adopt an opinion or position for effect.

atto- *combining form* a million million millionth, 10⁻¹⁸. [from Danish or Norwegian *atten*, eighteen]

attorney / ə'tɜ:nɪ/ *noun* (PL. **attorneys**) **1** a person able to act for another in legal or business matters. **2** *North Amer., esp. US* a lawyer. — **power of attorney** the right to act for another person in legal and business matters. [from French *atourner*, to turn over to]

Attorney General *noun* (PL. **Attorneys General, Attorney Generals**) the principal law officer in England, the USA, and several other countries. In England and Wales, he is a member of the House of Commons and of the government.

attract *verb* **1** to cause to come close or stay close. **2** to arouse or draw to oneself: *attract attention*. **3** to arouse liking or admiration; to be attractive to. [from Latin *ad*, to + *trahere*, to draw]

   1 pull, draw, lure, allure, entice, tempt, invite. **2** draw, arouse, excite. **3** appeal to, interest, engage, fascinate, enchant, charm, bewitch, captivate.

   REPEL.

attraction *noun* **1** the act or power of attracting. **2** a person or thing that attracts. **3** *Physics* a force that tends to pull two objects closer together, such as that between opposite electric charges or opposite magnetic poles. See also RE-PULSION.

   1 pull, draw, magnetism, lure, allure, appeal, interest, fascination, enchantment, charm, captivation. **2** bait, enticement, inducement, temptation, invitation. **3** magnetism.

   1, 3 repulsion.

attractive *adj.* **1** capable of attracting attention; appealing. **2** good-looking.

   1 pleasant, pleasing, agreeable, appealing, winsome, seductive, tempting, inviting, interesting, fascinating, charming, captivating, magnetic. **2** pretty, fetching, good-looking, handsome, beautiful, gorgeous, stunning, glamorous, lovely.

   UNATTRACTIVE. **1** repellent. **2** repulsive.

attributable / ə'trɪbjutəbl/ *adj.* capable of being attributed.

attribute / ə'trɪbju:t, 'atrɪbju:t/ — *verb* (with stress on *-trib-*) (**attribute something to someone** or **something**) to think of it as being written, made, said, or caused by them. — *noun* (with stress on *at-*) a quality, characteristic, or feature. [from Latin *attribuere*, to assign to]

   verb ascribe to, credit to, assign to, put down to. *noun* quality, property, virtue, point, aspect, facet, feature, trait, characteristic, peculiarity, mark, sign.

attribution / atrı'bju:ʃən/ *noun* **1** the act of attributing. **2** something that is attributed.

attributive / ə'trɪbjutɪv/ *adj. Grammar, said of an adjective or noun* placed before the noun which it modifies, eg in *young girl* and *buffet car*. See also PREDICATIVE.

attributively *adv. Grammar* with an attributive function.

attrition / ə'trɪʃən/ *noun* **1** a rubbing together; friction. **2** a wearing away or making weaker, especially by continual friction or attacks: *a war of attrition*. **3** *Geol.* the process whereby rock fragments become worn, smooth and smaller in size as they scrape against each other while being transported by water, wind, or gravity. [from Latin *attritio*, from *atterere*, to rub]

attune *verb* **1** to adjust to or prepare for (a situation, etc). **2** to put (a musical instrument, an orchestra, etc) into tune.

atypical / eɪ'tɪpɪkəl/ *adj.* not typical.

Au *symbol Chem.* gold. [from Latin *aurum*]

aubergine / 'oʊbəʒi:n/ *noun* **1** a bushy perennial plant (*Solanum melongena*) native to SE Asia, and widely cultivated as an annual in temperate regions for its edible fruit. **2** the egg-shaped edible fruit of this plant, about 30cm long, with a smooth skin that is usually deep purple in colour, but sometimes white, yellow, or striped, eaten as a vegetable, especially in moussaka and ratatouille. [from Sanskrit *vatinganah*]

aubrietia / ɔ:'bri:ʃə/ or **aubretia** *noun* a dwarf perennial plant of the genus *Aubrieta*, native to SE Europe, especially *A.deltoidea*, varieties of which are widely cultivated as ornamental plants in rock gardens. [named after Claude Aubriet (1665–1742), French botanist]

auburn / 'ɔ:bə:n/ *adj., said especially of hair* reddish-brown. [from Latin *alburnus*, whitish, from *albus*, white]

   red, chestnut, tawny, russet, copper, Titian.

auction / 'ɔ:kʃən/ — *noun* a public sale in which each item is sold to the person who offers the most money. — *verb* (*also* **auction something off**) to sell it by auction. [from Latin *auctio*, an increase]

auctioneer *noun* a person who conducts an auction, especially professionally.

audacious / ɔ:'deɪʃəs/ *adj.* **1** bold and daring. **2** disrespectful; impudent. [from Latin *audax*, bold]

audacity / ɔ:'dasɪtɪ/ *noun* boldness.

audibility / ɔ:dɪ'bɪlətɪ/ *noun* capacity to be heard.

audible / 'ɔ:dɪbl/ *adj.* loud enough to be heard. [from Latin *audire*, to hear]

   clear, distinct, perceptible, discernible, detectable, appreciable.

   inaudible, silent, unclear.

audibly *adv.* so as to audible.

audience / 'ɔ:dɪəns/ *noun* **1** a group of people watching a performance. **2** the people reached by a film, radio broadcast, book, magazine, etc. **3** a formal interview with an important person. [from Latin *audientia*, from *audire*, to hear]

   1 house, auditorium, spectators, onlookers, crowd, turn-out. **2** viewers, listeners, readers, fans, devotees, following, public. **3** interview, consultation, talk, dialogue, meeting, conference.

audio *adj., combining form* relating to hearing, sound, or the recording and broadcasting of sound. [from Latin *audire*, to hear]

audio frequency any frequency that can be detected by the human ear, in the range 20 to 20,000Hz for normal hearing.

audiogram / 'ɔ:dɪoʊgram/ *noun Medicine* a record of a person's hearing ability, in the form of a graph, as measured by an audiometer. It usually indicates hearing ability for a range of sounds of different frequency.

audiometer /ɔːdɪˈɒmɪtə(r)/ *noun* **1** *Medicine* an instrument used to measure a person's hearing ability at different sound frequencies. It is used in the diagnosis of deafness. **2** an instrument that is used to measure the intensity of sounds.

audio-typing *noun* the typing of material recorded on a dictating machine.

audio-typist *noun* a person who types letters, etc which have been recorded on a dictation machine.

audiovisual *adj.* **1** concerned simultaneously with seeing and hearing. **2** *said of a device or teaching method* using both sound and vision, especially in the form of film strips, video recordings, television programmes or computer programs, as a teaching or training aid.

audit /ˈɔːdɪt/ — *noun* an official inspection of an organization's accounts by an accountant. — *verb* (**audited, auditing**) to examine accounts officially. [from Latin *audire*, to hear]

. . . .

🔳 *noun* inspection, examination, check, verification, investigation, scrutiny, analysis, review. *verb* inspect, examine, check, verify, investigate, scrutinize.

. . . .

audition /ɔːˈdɪʃən/ — *noun* a short performance as a test of the suitability of an actor, singer, musician, etc for a particular part or role. — *verb trans., intrans.* (**auditioned, auditioning**) to test or be tested by means of an audition. [from Latin *auditio*, from *audire*, to hear]

auditor *noun* a person who audits accounts, especially professionally.

auditorium /ɔːdɪˈtɔːrɪəm/ *noun* (PL. **auditoriums, auditoria**) the part of a theatre, hall, etc where the audience sits. [from Latin *auditorium*, a lecture-room, court, etc.]

auditory /ˈɔːdɪtərɪ/ *adj.* relating to hearing. [from Latin *audire*, to hear]

auditory nerve *Anat.* the eighth cranial nerve, which carries nerve impulses concerned with hearing and balance from the inner ear to the brain.

AUEW *abbrev.* Amalgamated Union of Engineering Workers.

au fait /oʊ feɪ/ well informed or familiar. [French, = to the point]

Aug or **Aug.** *abbrev.* August.

Augean /ɔːˈdʒiːən/ *adj. literary* filthy. [from the name *Augeas*, a king in Greek mythology whose stables were cleaned by Heracles]

auger /ˈɔːgə(r)/ *noun* a hand-tool with a corkscrew-like point for boring holes in wood. [from Anglo-Saxon *nafogar*; in Middle English, *a nauger* was understood as *an auger*]

aught /ɔːt/ *pron. old use* anything. [from Anglo-Saxon *awiht*]

augment /ɔːgˈment/ *verb trans., intrans.* to make or become greater in size, number, strength, amount, etc. [from Latin *augere*, to increase]

augmentation /ɔːgmənˈteɪʃən/ *noun* increase, addition.

augmentative *adj.* tending to augment or increase.

augmented *adj.* **1** having become or been made greater in size, etc. **2** *Mus.* increased by a semitone.

au gratin /oʊ ˈgratan/ *adj., said of food* covered and cooked with breadcrumbs and often with grated cheese. [from French *au gratin*]

augur /ˈɔːgə(r), ˈɔːgjə(r)/ *verb intrans.* (*usually* **augur well** or **ill**) to be a good or bad sign for the future. [from Latin *augur*, soothsayer]

. . . .

🔳 bode, forebode, promise, herald, prophesy.

. . . .

augury /ˈɔːgjʊrɪ/ *noun* (PL. **auguries**) **1** a sign or omen. **2** the practice of predicting the future.

August /ˈɔːgəst/ *noun* the eighth month of the year. [from Latin *Augustus*, the first Roman emperor]

august /ɔːˈgʌst/ *adj.* noble; imposing. [from Latin *augustus*, grand]

Augustinian — *noun* a member of a religious order united in 1255 which follows the monastic teaching and 'rule' of St Augustine (of Hippo). There are also Augustinian nuns of second or third orders ('tertiaries'). — *adj.* relating to the Augustinians.

auk /ɔːk/ *noun* any of various species of small diving seabirds belonging to the same family (Alcidae) as razorbills, puffins, and guillemots, and having a heavy body, black and white plumage, and short wings, found in cool seas in the northern hemisphere. [from Norse *alka*]

auld lang syne /ɔːld laŋ saɪn/ *Scot.* days of long ago.

aunt /ɑːnt/ *noun* **1** the sister of one's father or mother, or the wife of one's uncle. **2** a close female friend of a child's parents. [from Latin *amita*, father's sister]

auntie or **aunty** *noun* (PL. **aunties**) *colloq.* an aunt.

Aunt Sally *noun* (PL. **Aunt Sallies**) **1** a game in which sticks or balls are thrown at a dummy. **2** a target of abuse.

au pair /oʊ peə(r)/ *noun* a young person from abroad, usually a woman, who lives with a family and helps with housework, looking after children, etc in return for board and lodging. [from French *au pair*]

aura /ˈɔːrə/ *noun* (PL. **auras, aurae**) **1** a distinctive character or quality around a person or in a place. **2** a fine substance coming out of something, especially that supposedly coming from and surrounding the body, which many mystics claim is visible as a faint light. **3** an unusual sensation that precedes the onset of an attack, especially such a sensation occurring before a migraine attack or epileptic seizure. [from Greek *aura*, breeze]

aural /ˈɔːrəl/ *adj.* relating to the sense of hearing or the ears. [from Latin *auris*, ear]

aurally *adv.* by hearing; by ear.

aureate /ˈɔːrɪət, ˈɔːrɪeɪt/ *adj.* **1** golden. **2** elaborately ornamental. [from Latin *aurum*, gold]

aureole /ˈɔːrɪoʊl/ or **aureola** /ɔːˈrɪələ/ *noun* **1** *said of painting* a bright light surrounding the head or body of a holy figure. **2** *Astron.* a hazy bluish-white halo surrounding the sun or moon. **3** *Astron.* a corona. **4** *Geol.* a ring-shaped area of metamorphosed rock surrounding an igneous intrusion. [from Latin *aureolus*, golden]

au revoir /oʊ rəv'wa/ *interj.* goodbye; until we meet again. [from French *au revoir*]

auricle /ˈɔːrɪkəl/ *noun Anat.* **1** the outer part of the ear. **2** the ear-shaped tip of the atrium of the heart. **3** any ear-shaped appendage. [from Latin *auricula*, little ear]

auricular /ɔːˈrɪkjʊlə(r)/ *adj.* **1** belonging or relating to the ear or sense of hearing. **2** known by hearing or report. **3** shaped like an ear. **4** relating to an auricle.

auriferous /ɔːˈrɪfərəs/ *adj., said of a substance, mineral deposit, etc* containing or yielding gold. [from Latin *aurum*, gold]

aurochs /ˈɔːrɒks, ˈaʊərɒks/ *noun* (PL. **aurochs**) an extinct wild ox, formerly widespread in Europe, SW Asia, and N Africa, considered to be the ancestor of domestic cattle, and depicted in numerous Stone Age cave paintings. Also called URUS. [from German *urohso*]

aurora /ɔːˈrɔːrə/ *noun* (PL. **auroras, aurorae**) **1** *Astron.* the appearance of diffuse bands or curtains of red, green or yellow coloured lights in the night sky, most often observed from the Arctic and Antarctic regions. It is known as the *aurora borealis* (northern lights) in the northern hemisphere, and the *aurora australis* (southern lights) in the southern hemisphere. **2** *poetic* the dawn. [from Latin *aurora*, dawn]

AUS *abbrev., as an international vehicle mark* Australia.

auscultation /ɔːskəlˈteɪʃən/ *noun Medicine* the practice of listening, usually with the aid of a stethoscope, to the sounds produced by the movement of blood, air, or gas within the internal organs of the body, especially the heart and lungs, in order to ascertain their physical state and diagnose any abnormalities. [from Latin *ascultare*, to listen]

auspices /ˈɔːspɪsɪz/ *pl. noun* protection; patronage. — **un-**

der the auspices of someone or something *said of an activity or undertaking* arranged or supported by a person, society, etc. [from Latin *auspicium*, foretelling the future by watching birds]

▣ patronage, sponsorship, backing, support, protection, charge, care, supervision, control, authority. **under the auspices of** under the aegis of.

auspicious /ɔːˈspɪʃəs/ *adj.* promising future success; favourable. [see AUSPICES]

▣ favourable, propitious, encouraging, cheerful, bright, rosy, promising, hopeful, optimistic, fortunate, lucky, opportune, happy, prosperous.
▣ inauspicious, ominous.

Aussie /ˈɒzɪ/ *noun, adj. colloq.* Australian.
austere /ɔːˈstɪə(r)/ *adj.* **1** severely simple and plain. **2** serious; severe; stern. **3** severe in self-discipline. [from Greek *austeros*, strict, rigorous]

▣ SEVERE, SOBER. **1** plain, simple, unadorned, stark, bleak, grim, forbidding. **2** serious, grave, solemn, stern, strict, cold, formal, rigid, rigorous, exacting, hard, harsh, spartan. **3** self-disciplined, ascetic, puritanical, chaste, abstinent, abstemious, self-denying, restrained, economical, frugal.
▣ **1** ornate, elaborate. **2** genial. **3** self-indulgent.

austerity /ɔːˈstɛrɪtɪ/ *noun* (PL. **austerities**) **1** the state of being austere; strictness or harshness. **2** severity and extreme simplicity of dress, etc. **3** a period of economic depression. [from Latin *Auster*, the south wind]

▣ **1** severity, sternness, strictness, coldness, formality, harshness, seriousness, solemnity, asceticism, abstinence, abstemiousness, economy. **2** plainness, simplicity, severity.
▣ **2** elaborateness.

austral *adj.* southern.
Australasian *adj.* of or relating to Australia, New Zealand, and the nearby Pacific islands.
Australia Day /ɔːˈstreɪlɪə/ a public holiday in Australia, 26 January or the first Monday after that, celebrating the landing of the British in 1788.
Australian — *adj.* relating to Australia. — *noun* a person born or living in Australia. [from Latin *australis*, southern]
Australian Rules Football an Australian version of football, developed in Melbourne, Victoria c.1858. It is a handling and kicking game which is a cross between association football, rugby and Gaelic football.
Austro-Asiatic — *adj.* denoting a family of over 100 languages used in SE Asia. It includes three main branches, Mon-Khmer, Munda, and Nicobarese. — *noun* the languages forming this family.
Austronesian — *adj.* denoting the most numerous and (after Indo-European) the most widely dispersed of the world's great language families. It includes some 700 languages in two main groups: the western group of c.400 languages spoken in Madagascar, Malaysia, Indonesia, the Philippines, Taiwan, and W New Guinea; and the smaller eastern group, also known as Oceanic, spoken in Melanesia, Micronesia, and Polynesia. — *noun* the languages forming this group.
AUT *abbrev.* Association of University Teachers.
autarchy /ˈɔːtɑːkɪ/ *noun* (PL. **autarchies**) government of a country by a ruler who has absolute power. [from Greek *autos*, self + *archein*, to rule]
autarky /ˈɔːtɑːkɪ/ *noun* (PL. **autarkies**) economic self-sufficiency: the condition of a country that is a closed economy conducting no international trade. [from Greek *autarkeia*, from *autos*, self + *arkeein*, to suffice]

authentic /ɔːˈθɛntɪk/ *adj.* **1** genuine; not false or fake. **2** reliable; trustworthy. [from Greek *authentikos*]

▣ **1** genuine, true, real, actual, certain, bona fide, legitimate, honest, valid, original, pure, factual, accurate, true-to-life, faithful. **2** reliable, dependable, trustworthy.
▣ **1** false, fake, counterfeit, spurious. **2** unreliable.

authentically *adv.* in an authentic way; so as to be authentic.
authenticate *verb* to prove to be true or genuine.

▣ validate, certify, endorse, confirm, verify, corroborate, attest, guarantee, warrant, vouch for, authorize, accredit.

authentication *noun* **1** proof of being genuine or valid. **2** the state of having validity.
authenticity /ɔːθənˈtɪsɪtɪ/ *noun* **1** the quality of being authentic; genuineness. **2** being true.

▣ **1** genuineness, accuracy, faithfulness, fidelity, reliability, dependability, trustworthiness, certainty, authoritativeness. **2** validity, truth, veracity, truthfulness, honesty.
▣ **1** spuriousness. **2** invalidity.

author /ˈɔːθə(r)/ *noun* **1** the writer of a book, article, play, etc. **2** the creator or originator of an idea, event, etc. [from Latin *auctor*]

▣ **1** writer, novelist, dramatist, playwright, pen. **2** creator, originator, initiator, instigator, parent, prime mover, inventor, designer, architect, planner, maker, producer.

authoring *noun* the process of creating multimedia documents.
authoritarian /ɔːˌθɒrɪˈtɛərɪən/ — *adj.* in favour of, or insisting on, strict authority. — *noun* an authoritarian person.

▣ *adj.* strict, severe, harsh, rigid, inflexible, unyielding, doctrinaire, absolute, autocratic, dictatorial, despotic, tyrannical, oppressive, domineering, imperious. *noun* disciplinarian, autocrat, despot, tyrant.
▣ *adj.* LIBERAL.

authoritarianism *noun* being authoritarian; authoritarian behaviour.
authoritative /ɔːˈθɒrɪtətɪv/ *adj.* **1** accepted as a reliable source of knowledge. **2** having authority; official.

▣ **1** scholarly, learned, sound, reliable, dependable, trustworthy, accepted, definitive, authentic, factual, true, truthful, accurate, faithful, convincing. **2** official, authorized, legitimate, valid, approved, sanctioned.
▣ **1** unreliable. **2** unofficial.

authority /ɔːˈθɒrɪtɪ/ *noun* (PL. **authorities**) **1** the power or right to control or judge others. **2** (*often* **authorities**) the person or people who have power, especially political or administrative. **3** a position which has such a power or right: *be in authority.* **4** authorization; official permission. **5** the ability to influence others, usually as a result of knowledge or expertise. **6** an expert: *an authority on birds.* **7** a passage in a book used to support a statement. [from Latin *auctoritas*, from *auctor*, author]

▣ **1** sovereignty, supremacy, rule, sway, control, dominion, influence, power, force. **2** government, administration, officialdom. **4** authorization, permission, sanction, permit, warrant, licence, credentials, right, prerogative. **6** expert, pundit, specialist, connoisseur, professional, *colloq.* guru, master, scholar.

authorization or **authorisation** *noun* 1 the act of authorizing; permission. 2 legality, right.

authorize or **authorise** /'ɔːθəraɪz/ *verb* 1 to give (someone) the power or right to do something. 2 to give official permission for. [from Latin *auctorizare*, from *auctor*, author]

⊟ 1 empower, enable, commission, warrant, license, entitle, accredit. 2 permit, allow, consent to, approve, sanction, legalize, validate, ratify, confirm.

authorship *noun* 1 the origin, or attribution to an author, of a particular piece of writing. 2 the profession of writing.

autism /'ɔːtɪzm/ *noun Psychol.* a rare and severe mental disorder that develops in early childhood, characterized by learning difficulties, extreme self-absorption, inability to relate to other people and the outside world, repetitive body movements, and strong resistance to changes in familiar surroundings. [from Greek *autos*, self]

autistic *adj.* relating to, affected by, or characteristic of autism.

autistically *adv.* in a way suggestive of or characterized by autism.

auto /'ɔːtoʊ/ *noun* (PL. **autos**) *North Amer. colloq.* a motor car. [abbreviation of AUTOMOBILE]

auto- *combining form* of or by oneself or itself: *autograph / automatic.* [from Greek *autos*, self]

autobahn /'ɔːtoʊbɑːn, 'aʊtɔːbɑːn/ *noun* a motorway in Austria, Switzerland, or Germany. [from German *Auto*, car + *Bahn*, road]

autobiographer *noun* a person who writes an autobiography.

autobiographical /ɔːtoʊbaɪə'ɡrafɪkl/ *adj.* relating to or in the nature of autobiography.

autobiography /ɔːtoʊbaɪ'ɒɡrəfɪ/ *noun* (PL. **autobiographies**) 1 the story of a person's life written by that person. 2 this as a literary form.

autocatalysis /ɔːtoʊkə'talɪsɪs/ *noun Chem.* a catalytic reaction initiated by the products of another catalytic reaction.

autoclave /'ɔːtoʊkleɪv/ *noun* a strong steel vessel that can be made airtight and filled with pressurized steam, used to carry out chemical reactions at high temperature and pressure, and to sterilize equipment, eg surgical instruments. [from Greek *autos*, self + Latin *clavis*, key or *clavus*, nail]

autocracy /ɔː'tɒkrəsɪ/ *noun* (PL. **autocracies**) absolute government by one person; dictatorship. [from Greek *autos*, self + *kratos*, power]

⊟ absolutism, totalitarianism, dictatorship, despotism, tyranny, fascism, authoritarianism.
⊟ democracy.

autocrat /'ɔːtəkrat/ *noun* 1 a ruler with absolute power. 2 an authoritarian person.

⊟ 1 absolutist, totalitarian, dictator, despot, tyrant, fascist. 2 authoritarian, *colloq.* (little) Hitler.

autocratic *adj.* typical of an autocrat; authoritarian.

⊟ absolute, all-powerful, totalitarian, despotic, tyrannical, authoritarian, dictatorial, domineering, overbearing, imperious.
⊟ democratic, liberal.

autocratically *adv.* with an autocratic manner.

autocross /'ɔːtoʊkrɒs/ *noun* motor-racing on a rough grass track.

Autocue /'ɔːtoʊkjuː/ *noun trademark Broadcasting* a screen, unseen by an audience, which displays a speaker's script.

auto-da-fé /ɔːtoʊdə'feɪ/ *noun* (PL. **autos-da-fé**) 1 *Hist.* the ceremonial passing of sentence on heretics by the Spanish Inquisition. 2 the public burning of a heretic. [from Portuguese *auto da fé*, act of the faith]

autogenics /ɔːtoʊ'ɡɛnɪks/ *sing. noun Medicine* a system of relaxation, also used in the treatment of psychosomatic disorders, designed to facilitate voluntary control of bodily tension. [from Greek *autogenes*, self-generated]

autograph /'ɔːtəɡrɑːf/ — *noun* 1 a person's signature, especially a famous person's, kept as a souvenir. 2 a manuscript in the author's handwriting. — *verb* to sign (a photograph, etc). [from Greek *autos*, self + *graphein*, to write]

autoimmunity *noun* the production by the body of antibodies that attack constituents of its own tissues, treating them as foreign material.

autolysis /ɔː'tɒlɪsɪs/ *noun Biol.* the breaking down of dead tissue by enzymes produced in the organism's own cells. [from Greek *autos*, self + *lysis*, loosening]

automat /'ɔːtəmat/ *noun North Amer., esp. US* an automatic vending machine.

automate /'ɔːtəmeɪt/ *verb* to apply automation to (a technical process).

automated *adj.* mechanized and automatic.

automatic /ɔːtə'matɪk/ — *adj.* 1 *said of a machine or instrument* capable of operating on its own by means of a self-regulating mechanism, and requiring little human control once it has been activated, eg a vehicle assembly plant. 2 *said of an action* done without thinking; unconscious; spontaneous. 3 happening as a necessary and inevitable result. 4 *said of a firearm* able to reload itself and so able to fire continuously. 5 *said of a motor vehicle* having automatic transmission. — *noun* 1 an automatic firearm. 2 a vehicle with automatic transmission. [from Greek *automatos*, self-moving]

⊟ *adj.* 1 automated, self-regulating, mechanical, mechanized, programmed, computerized, push-button, robotic, self-propelled, unmanned. 2 spontaneous, reflex, involuntary, unwilled, unconscious, unthinking, natural, instinctive, routine. 3 necessary, certain, inevitable, unavoidable, inescapable.
⊟ *adj.* 1 manual.

automatically *adv.* 1 with automatic action; in an automatic way. 2 as a necessary consequence: *unattended bags are automatically impounded.*

automatic data processing (ABBREV. **ADP**) *Comput.* the use of computer systems to process information, especially business data, with little or no human assistance.

automatic pilot or **autopilot** 1 an electronic control device that automatically steers a vehicle, especially an aircraft, space vehicle, or ship, and enables it to maintain a preset course at a specific speed without the need for human intervention. 2 automatic or involuntary actions or behaviour occurring as a result of fatigue, boredom, or abstraction: *he was working on automatic pilot.*

automatic teller machine (ABBREV. **ATM**) an electronic panel set into the exterior wall of a bank, etc from which (on insertion of one's cash card and the keying of one's personal identification or 'PIN' number) cash or account information can be obtained.

automatic transmission in a motor vehicle, a system that allows the gears to be selected and engaged automatically in response to variations in speed, gradient, etc, as opposed to a manually controlled gearbox.

automation /ɔːtə'meɪʃən/ *noun* the use of automatic machinery in manufacturing and data-processing, so that entire procedures can be automatically controlled with minimal or no human intervention.

automaton /ɔː'tɒmətən/ *noun* (PL. **automatons**, **automata**) 1 a machine or robot that has been programmed to perform specific actions in a manner imitative of a human or animal, especially such a device used as a toy, amusement, or decoration. **2** a person who acts like a machine, according to routine and without thinking.

automobile /ˈɔːtəməbiːl, ɔːtəməˈbiːl/ *noun North Amer., esp. US* a motor car. [from French *automobile*, from Greek *autos*, self + Latin *mobilis*, mobile]

automotive /ɔːtəˈmoʊtɪv/ *adj.* relating to motor vehicles. [from Greek *autos*, self + Latin *motivus*, causing to move]

autonomic nervous system *Physiol.* (ABBREV. **ANS**) that part of the nervous system which supplies the glands (eg the salivary and sweat glands), heart muscle, and smooth muscle (eg the walls of blood vessels and the bladder). It consists of the sympathetic nervous system and the parasympathetic nervous system. See also SYMPATHETIC NERVOUS SYSTEM, PARASYMPATHETIC NERVOUS SYSTEM.

autonomous /ɔːˈtɒnəməs/ *adj.* **1** self-governing. **2** independent of others.

autonomy /ɔːˈtɒnəmɪ/ *noun* (PL. **autonomies**) **1** the power or right of self-government. **2** personal freedom. [from Greek *autos*, self + *nomos*, law]

. . . .

⊟ INDEPENDENCE, SELF-DETERMINATION. **1** self-government, self-rule, home rule, sovereignty. **2** freedom, free will.
⊡ **1** subjection.
. . . .

auto-oxidation *noun Chem.* oxidation brought about by oxygen in the atmosphere.

autopilot same as AUTOMATIC PILOT.

autopsy /ˈɔːtɒpsɪ, ɔːˈtɒpsɪ/ *noun* (PL. **autopsies**) the dissection and examination of the internal organs of the body after death, in order to determine the cause of death. Also called POST MORTEM. [from Greek *autos*, self + *opsis*, sight]

autoradiography *noun Physics, Biol.* a technique for showing the positions of radioactively labelled molecules within the cells or tissues of a specimen, by placing the specimen over a photographic emulsion. The emulsion is then developed, and the image formed represents the distribution of the radioactive content of the specimen.

auto-reverse *noun* a feature on a cassette recorder, etc causing automatic playing of the reverse side after completion of the first.

autoroute /ˈɔːtuːruːt/ *noun* a motorway in France. [French, from *auto*, car + *route*, road]

autosome /ˈɔːtousoum/ *noun Genetics* a chromosome other than a sex-chromosome. [from Greek *autos*, self + *soma*, body]

autostrada /ˈaʊtoustrɑːdə/ *noun* a motorway in Italy. [Italian, from *auto*, car + *strada*, road]

auto-suggestion *noun Psychol.* a form of psychotherapy that involves repeating ideas to oneself in order to change attitudes or habits, eg to reduce anxiety.

auto-suggestive *adj.* relating to or typical of auto-suggestion.

autotrophism /ɔːˈtoʊˈtrɒfɪzm/ *Biol.* the capability of building up food materials from inorganic matter. [from Greek *autos*, self + *trophe*, food]

autumn /ˈɔːtəm/ *noun* **1** the season of the year, between summer and winter, when leaves change colour and fall. **2** a period of maturity before decay. [from Latin *autumnus*]

autumnal /ɔːˈtʌmnəl/ *adj.* **1** associated with or typical of autumn. **2** characteristic of the later part of a person's life.

autumnal equinox *Astron.* the equinox that occurs annually around 23 Sep, when the Sun's path crosses the celestial equator from north to south, so that day and night are of equal length.

autumnally *adv.* in an autumnal way; so as to suggest autumn.

autumn crocus a plant (*Colchicum autumnale*) that produces corms and has lance-shaped glossy leaves, so called because the lilac goblet-shaped flowers appear during the autumn. Also called MEADOW SAFFRON.

auxiliary /ɔːɡˈzɪlɪərɪ/ — *adj.* **1** helping or supporting. **2** additional or extra. — *noun* (PL. **auxiliaries**) **1** a helper. **2** (**auxiliaries**) foreign troops helping another nation at war. **3** *Grammar* an auxiliary verb. [from Latin *auxiliarius*, from *auxilium*, help]

. . . .

⊟ *adj.* **1** helping, assisting, aiding, ancillary, supporting, supportive. **2** subsidiary, secondary, accessory, additional, extra, supplementary, spare, reserve, back-up, emergency, substitute. *noun* **1** helper, assistant, ancillary worker.
. . . .

auxiliary language a natural language adopted by people of different speech communities to aid communication. English and French are often used in this way, for example, in many parts of Africa, and particularly in the spheres of trade and education. The term is also used for certain artificial languages, especially Esperanto.

auxiliary verb *noun* a verb which shows the tense, voice, or mood of the main verb in a phrase, eg *should, will, can.*

auxin /ˈɔːksɪn/ *noun Bot.* any of a large group of plant hormones that promote growth of plant tissues by an increase in the size of existing cells, rather than an increase in cell number. Low levels of auxin promote growth and high levels inhibit it. Auxins are used commercially as 'rooting powders' and weedkillers. [from Greek *auxein*, to increase]

AV *abbrev.* Authorized Version (of the Bible).

avail — *verb trans., intrans.* to help or be of use. — *noun* use; advantage: *of no avail.* — **avail oneself of something** to make use of it or take advantage of it. [from Latin *valere*, to be worth]

availability *noun* the state or degree of being available: *special offers are subject to availability.*

available *adj.* able or ready to be obtained or used.

. . . .

⊟ free, vacant, to hand, within reach, at hand, accessible, handy, convenient, on hand, ready, on tap, obtainable.
⊡ unavailable.
. . . .

availably *adv.* so as to be available.

avalanche /ˈavəlɑːnʃ/ *noun* **1** the rapid movement of a large mass of snow or ice down a mountain slope under the force of gravity. **2** a sudden appearance of a large number of people or things. [from French *avalanche*]

. . . .

⊟ **1** landslide, landslip. **2** cascade, torrent, deluge, flood, inundation, barrage.
. . . .

avant-garde /avɔːnˈɡɑːd/ — *noun* those writers, painters, musicians, etc whose ideas and techniques are the most modern or advanced. — *adj.*, *said of a work of art, idea, etc* using or supporting the most modern and advanced ideas in literature, art, music, etc. [from French *avant-garde*, vanguard]

. . . .

⊟ *adj.* innovative, innovatory, pioneering, experimental, unconventional, *slang* way-out, progressive, advanced, forward-looking, enterprising, inventive.
⊡ *adj.* conservative.
. . . .

avarice /ˈavərɪs/ *noun* a great desire for money, possessions, etc. [from Latin *avaritia*, from *avere*, to crave]

. . . .

⊟ covetousness, rapacity, acquisitiveness, greed, greediness.
⊡ generosity.
. . . .

avaricious /avəˈrɪʃəs/ *adj.* greedy for money, possessions, etc.

. . . .

⊟ covetous, grasping, rapacious, acquisitive, greedy, mercenary.
⊡ generous.
. . . .

avatar /ˈavətɑː(r), avəˈtɑː(r)/ *noun* the appearance of a Hindu god in human or animal form. [from Sanskrit *ava*, down + *tar*, pass over]

Ave or **Ave Maria** /ˈɑːveɪ məˈrɪə/ a prayer to the Virgin Mary. See also HAIL MARY. [from Latin *ave*, from *avere*, to be well; the opening words of the angel's greeting to Mary in Luke 1.28]

Ave. *abbrev.* avenue.

avenge *verb* to punish (someone) in return for (harm they have done to someone). [from Old French *avengier*, from Latin *vindicare*, to claim]

⊟ take revenge for, take vengeance for, requite, repay.

avenger *noun* a person who takes avenging action.

avenging *adj.* wanting to be avenged; in or for revenge.

avenue /ˈavənjuː/ *noun* **1** a broad road or street, often with trees along the sides. **2** a tree-lined approach to a house. **3** a means or way: *explored several avenues before deciding on a plan.* [from Latin *advenire*, to come to]

aver /əˈvɜː(r)/ *verb* (**averred, averring**) to state firmly. [from Latin *ad*, to + *verus*, true]

average /ˈavərɪdʒ/ — *noun* **1** the usual or typical amount or number. **2** any number that is representative of a group of numbers or other data, especially the *arithmetic mean*, which is equal to the sum of a set of *n* numbers, divided by *n*. — *adj.* **1** usual or ordinary. **2** estimated by taking an average. **3** mediocre. — *verb* **1** to obtain the numerical average of. **2** to amount to on average. — **average out** to result in an average or balance: *it averaged out at 3 each.* **on average** usually; normally. [from Arabic *awariya*, damaged goods]

⊟ *noun* **1** norm, standard, rule, par, medium. **2** mean, median, midpoint. *adj.* **1** usual, normal, regular, standard, ordinary, everyday, common, typical, unexceptional, undistinguished, run-of-the-mill. **2** mean, medial, median, middle, intermediate. **3** mediocre, middling, indifferent, *colloq.* so-so, passable, tolerable, satisfactory, fair, medium, moderate.
⊟ *noun* **1** extreme, exception. *adj.* **1, 3** exceptional, remarkable.

averse *adj.* (**averse to something**) reluctant about it or opposed to it: *not averse to helping.* [from Latin *aversus*]

⊟ reluctant to, unwilling to, loath to, disinclined to, ill-disposed to, hostile to, opposed to.
⊟ willing to, keen to.

aversion *noun* **1** a strong dislike. **2** an object of strong dislike. [from Latin *aversio*, from *aversus*, averse]

⊟ **1** dislike, hatred, loathing, detestation, abhorrence, horror, phobia, reluctance, unwillingness, disinclination, distaste, disgust, repugnance, hostility, opposition, antagonism.
⊟ **1** liking, sympathy, desire.

aversion therapy a form of behaviour therapy that aims to eliminate an undesirable habit or a compulsive form of behaviour (eg drug addiction or alcoholism) by repeatedly linking the undesirable response with an unpleasant stimulus (eg by linking the taste of alcohol with feelings of nausea).

avert *verb* **1** to turn away: *avert one's eyes.* **2** to prevent (especially danger). [from Latin *ab*, from + *vertere*, to turn]

⊟ TURN AWAY, TURN ASIDE. **2** prevent, obviate, avoid, evade, forestall, frustrate, fend off, ward off, stave off, deflect, parry.

Aves /ˈeɪviːz, ɑːˈweɪs/ *pl. noun Zool.* in the animal kingdom, the class of vertebrates that comprises the birds. [from Latin *avis*, bird]

Avesta the scriptures of Zoroastrianism, written in Avestan (a language of the eastern branch of the Indo-European family) and assembled in the 3c–7c AD. Traditionally believed to have been revealed to Zoroaster, only the *Gathas*, a set of 17 hymns, may be attributed to him, and only a few parts of the original survive.

aviary /ˈeɪvɪərɪ/ *noun* (PL. **aviaries**) a large enclosed area in which birds are kept. [from Latin *aviarium*, from *avis*, bird]

aviation /eɪvɪˈeɪʃən/ *noun* **1** the science or practice of mechanical flight through the air, especially by powered aircraft. **2** the production, design, and operation of aircraft. **3** the aircraft industry. [from Latin *avis*, bird]

⊟ **1** aeronautics, flying, flight.

aviator /ˈeɪvɪeɪtə(r)/ *noun old use* an aircraft pilot.

avid /ˈavɪd/ *adj.* **1** enthusiastic. **2** (**avid for something**) eagerly wanting it. [from Latin *avidus*, from *avere*, to crave]

⊟ **1** eager, earnest, keen, enthusiastic, fanatical, devoted, dedicated, zealous, ardent, fervent, intense, passionate, insatiable. **2** greedy for, ravenous for, hungry for, thirsty for.
⊟ **1** indifferent.

avidity *noun* greediness, eagerness.

avionics /eɪvɪˈɒnɪks/ *Aeron.* the scientific study of the development and use of electronic and electrical devices for aircraft and spacecraft. [from AVIATION + ELECTRONICS]

avocado /avəˈkɑːdoʊ/ *noun* (PL. **avocados**) **1** a tropical evergreen tree of the genus *Persea* of the laurel family (Lauraceae), with large oval leaves, small yellowish flowers, and a pear-shaped fruit. **2** (*also* **avocado pear**) the edible pear-shaped fruit of this tree, which has a large hard seed enclosed by creamy flesh and a rough thick greenish-brown skin. It is eaten fresh, eg as a starter or in salads. [from Aztec *ahuacatl*]

avocado oil an edible oil used in salad dressings, hair and skin conditioners, and as a base for cosmetics.

avocation /avəˈkeɪʃən/ *noun old use* **1** a diversion or distraction from one's main occupation; a hobby. **2** *colloq.* a vocation. [from Latin *avocatio*, from *ab*, from + *vocare*, to call]

avocet or **avoset** /ˈavəset/ *noun* any of various large wading birds of the genus *Recurvirostra*, found in fresh and saline waters worldwide, and having black and white plumage, long legs, and a long slender upward curving bill. [from French *avocette*]

Avogadro's constant or **Avogadro's number** /avəˈgɑːdroʊz/ *Chem.* the number of atoms, molecules, or ions that are present in a mole of any substance. It has a value of 6.02×10^{23}.

Avogadro's law or **Avogadro's rule** *Chem.* the law which states that under the same conditions of temperature and pressure equal volumes of gases contain the same number of molecules.

avoid *verb* **1** to keep away from (a place, person, action, etc). **2** to stop, prevent, manage not to, or escape. [from French *avoidier*]

⊟ EVADE, DODGE. **1** steer clear of, shun, abstain from, refrain from, bypass, circumvent, elude, sidestep. **2** escape, get out of, shirk, *colloq.* duck, stop, balk, prevent, avert.

avoidable *adj.* capable of being avoided; unnecessary.

⊟ escapable, preventable, unnecessary.
⊟ inevitable.

avoidably *adv.* so as to be avoidable; unnecessarily.

avoidance *noun* the act of avoiding or shunning, especially a duty or responsibility.

avoirdupois /avwɑːdjuːˈpwɑː, avədəˈpɔɪz/ — *noun* a system of units of mass based on a *pound* (0.45kg) consisting of 16 *ounces*, formerly widely used in English-speaking countries, but now increasingly replaced by SI units. — *adj.* of or relating to this system of units. [from Old French *aveir de pes*, to have weight]

avow *verb* to state openly; to declare; to admit. [from Latin *advocare*]

avowal *noun* a declaration, acknowledgement, or confession.

avowed *adj.* declared; admitted: *their avowed intention.*

☐ sworn, declared, professed, confessed, admitted, acknowledged, open, overt.

avowedly *adv.* as is avowed; admittedly.

avuncular /əˈvʌŋkjʊlə(r)/ *adj.* of or like an uncle, especially in being kind and caring. [from Latin *avunculus*, maternal uncle]

AWACS *abbrev.* Airborne Warning and Control System, an aircraft-mounted radar system able to detect and track hostile intruders at long range and direct friendly fighters to intercept them.

await *verb* **1** to wait for. **2** to be certain to happen (to someone) in the future. [from French *awaitier*]

awake — *verb intrans., trans.* (PAST TENSE **awoke**; PAST PARTICIPLE **awoken**) **1** to stop sleeping or cause to stop sleeping. **2** to become active or cause to become active. — *adj.* **1** not sleeping. **2** alert or aware. [from Anglo-Saxon *awæcnian* & *awacian*]

☐ *verb* **1** awaken, waken, wake, wake up. *adj.* **1** wakeful, wide-awake, aroused, conscious. **2** alert, attentive, aware, conscious, vigilant, watchful, observant.
☒ *adj.* **1** asleep. **2** unaware.

awaken *verb trans., intrans.* (**awakened, awakening**) **1** to awake. **2** to start feeling or be aware of.

awakening *noun* **1** becoming awake; emerging from sleep. **2** wakening; rousing from sleep. **3** reanimating.

☐ **1** awaking, waking. **2** awaking, wakening, waking, rousing. **3** reawakening, revival, rebirth, arousal, stimulation.

award — *verb* to give (someone something) especially as a payment or prize. — *noun* **1** a payment, prize, etc awarded. **2** a legal judgement. [from French *awarder*]

☐ *verb* give, present, distribute, dispense, bestow, confer, endow, gift, grant, allot, assign, allow. *noun* **1** prize, trophy, decoration, medal, endowment, gift, grant, allowance. **2** judgement, adjudication, decision, order.

aware *adj.* **1** (*often* **aware of something** or **someone**) knowing about them or conscious of them. **2** well-informed. [from Anglo-Saxon *gewær*]

☐ **1** conscious, cognizant, mindful, heedful, attentive, observant. **2** knowledgeable, familiar, conversant, well-acquainted, well-informed, enlightened, au courant, sharp, alert, *colloq.* on the ball, shrewd, sensible.
☒ UNAWARE. **1** oblivious. **2** ignorant.

awareness *noun* being aware, consciousness.

awash *adj.* **1** covered or flooded by water. **2** (**awash with something**) covered by a large amount of it.

away — *adv.* **1** (*often* **away from something**) showing distance or movement from a particular place, position, person, or time. **2** in or to another, usual, or proper place: *put the books away.* **3** gradually into nothing: *fade away.* **4** continuously: *work away.* **5** as one wishes: *ask away.* **6** *said of a sporting event* on the opponent's ground. — *adj.* **1** not present. **2** distant: *not far away.* **3** *said of a sporting event* played on the opponent's ground. — *noun* a match won by a team playing on their opponent's ground. [from Anglo-Saxon *aweg, onweg*]

awe — *noun* admiration, fear, and wonder. — *verb* to fill with awe. [from Norse *agi*]

☐ *noun* wonder, admiration, respect, reverence, amazement, astonishment, fear, terror, dread, apprehension.

aweigh *adv., said of an anchor* in the process of being raised from the bottom of the sea. [from A³ + WEIGH]

awe-inspiring *adj.* causing awe.

☐ wonderful, sublime, magnificent, overwhelming, breathtaking, stunning, astonishing, amazing, impressive, imposing, majestic, solemn, moving, awesome, formidable, daunting, intimidating, fearsome.
☒ contemptible.

awesome *adj.* causing awe; dreaded.

awestricken or **awestruck** *adj.* filled with awe.

awful — *adj.* **1** *colloq.* very bad. **2** *colloq.* very great: *an awful shame.* **3** awe-inspiring, terrible or shocking. — *adv. colloq.* very.

☐ *adj.* **1** terrible, frightful, dreadful, dire, abysmal, atrocious, ghastly, unpleasant, nasty, horrible. **2** terrible, dreadful, frightful, fearful. **3** dreadful, terrible, frightful, horrific, shocking, appalling, spine-chilling.
☒ *adj.* **1** wonderful, excellent.

awfully *adv.* **1** very badly. **2** *colloq.* very; extremely: *awfully expensive.*

awfulness *noun* being bad or awful; horror.

awhile *adv.* for a short time. [from Anglo-Saxon *æne hwil*, a while]

awkward /ˈɔːkwəd/ *adj.* **1** clumsy and ungraceful. **2** embarrassed or embarrassing. **3** difficult, dangerous or inconvenient to deal with: *an awkward customer / make things awkward for him.* [from Norse *ofugr*, turned the wrong way + -WARD]

☐ **1** clumsy, gauche, inept, inexpert, unskilful, bungling, ham-fisted, unco-ordinated, ungainly, graceless, ungraceful, inelegant, cumbersome, unwieldy. **2** embarrassed, uncomfortable, ill at ease. **3** difficult, inconvenient, fiddly, troublesome, obstinate, stubborn, unco-operative, irritable, touchy, rude, unpleasant.
☒ **1** graceful, elegant. **2** comfortable, relaxed. **3** convenient, handy, amenable, pleasant.

awkwardly *adv.* with an awkward or clumsy manner; so as to cause embarrassment.

awkwardness *noun* **1** being awkward. **2** clumsiness. **3** an embarrassing situation or circumstance.

awl *noun* a pointed tool used for boring small holes, especially in leather. [from Anglo-Saxon *æl*]

awn *noun Bot.* in some grasses, eg barley, a small stiff bristle projecting from the lemma (one of the bracts enclosing a floret) or glumes (bracts at the base of the spikelet); a similar structure projecting from a fruit or leaf tip. [from Norse *ogn*]

awning *noun* a soft plastic or canvas covering above the entrance to a shop, hotel, etc which can be extended to give shelter from the sun or rain.

awoke, awoken see AWAKE.

AWOL *abbrev.* absent without leave: absent from one's place of duty without official permission.

awry /əˈraɪ/ *adj., adv.* **1** twisted to one side; crooked(ly). **2** wrong; amiss. [from A³ + WRY]

AWU *abbrev.* Australian Workers' Union, the largest Australian trade union from the early 1900s to 1970, and still one of the largest, with 120,000 members in 1985.

axe — *noun* **1** a tool with a long handle and a heavy metal blade, for cutting down trees, chopping wood, etc. **2** a severe cut in spending or staff. — *verb* **1** to get rid of or dismiss. **2** to reduce (costs, services, etc). — **have an axe to grind** to have a personal, often selfish, reason for being involved in something. [from Anglo-Saxon *æcs*]

⊟ *noun* **1** hatchet, chopper, cleaver, tomahawk, battle-axe. *verb* **1** get rid of, throw out, dismiss, discharge, *colloq.* sack, *colloq.* fire, remove, withdraw. **2** cut (down), *colloq.* slash, reduce, curtail, cancel, terminate, discontinue.

axial /'aksɪəl/ *adj.* of, forming, or placed along an axis.

axiality *noun* an axial state or quality.

axil /'aksl/ *noun Bot.* the angle between the upper surface of a leaf or stem and the stem or branch from which it grows. [from Latin *axilla*, armpit]

axillary /ak'sɪlərɪ/ *adj. Bot.* relating to the axil. [from Latin *axilla*, armpit]

axiom /'aksɪəm/ *noun* **1** a fact or principle which is generally accepted as true. **2** a self-evident statement. [from Greek *axios*, worthy]

⊟ **1** principle, fact, truth. **2** truism, precept, dictum, byword, maxim, adage, aphorism.

axiomatic *adj.* **1** obvious; self-evident. **2** containing or based on axioms.

axiomatically *adv.* so as to be axiomatic; self-evidently.

axis *noun* (PL. **axes**) **1** an imaginary straight line around which an object, eg a planet, rotates. **2** an imaginary straight line about which a body is symmetrical. **3** *Geom.* one of the lines of reference used to specify the position of points on a graph, eg the horizontal x-axis and vertical y-axis in Cartesian co-ordinates. **4** *Anat.* in vertebrates, the second cervical vertebra, which articulates with the atlas vertebra and enables the head to be moved from side to side. [from Latin *axis*, axle, pivot]

⊟ **1** centre-line, vertical, horizontal, pivot, hinge. **2** centre-line, vertical. **3** horizontal, vertical.

axle *noun* a fixed or rotating rod that is designed to carry a wheel or one or more pairs of wheels which may be attached to it, driven by it, or rotate freely on it. [from Norse *öxull*]

⊟ shaft, spindle, rod, pin, pivot.

axolotl /'aksəlɒtl/ *noun* a rare salamander (*Ambystoma mexicanum*), found in certain lakes at high altitude in Mexico, that has a newt-like body, usually black or dark brown in colour (although albino forms are fairly common), small weak limbs, three pairs of feathery gills (used for breathing), and a long deep tail (used for swimming). [an Aztec word, from *atl*, water + *xolotl*, servant]

axonometric /'aksənɒ'metrɪk/ *noun* an architectural drawing showing a building in three dimensions. It is produced by placing the plan at an angle and projecting the verticals upwards; all lines are drawn to scale, with parallel lines remaining parallel, so that the drawing appears distorted due to lack of perspective. [from Greek *axon*, axis + *metron*, measure]

ayah /'aɪə/ *noun* a native maid, especially formerly in India and some other parts of the British Empire. [from Hindi *aya*, from Latin *avia*, grandmother]

ayatollah /aɪə'tɒlə/ *noun* a Shiite religious leader in Iran. [from Arabic *ayatollah*, sign of God]

aye¹ or **ay** /aɪ/ — *interj. dialect* yes. — *noun* a vote in favour. [equivalent to *I*, expressing agreement]

aye² /eɪ/ *adv. old use, poetic* always. [from Norse *ei*, ever]

aye-aye /'aɪaɪ/ *noun* a nocturnal primitive primate from Madagascar, having a shaggy coat, a long bushy tail, large ears, and extremely long slender fingers, especially the third finger, which is used to probe for wood-boring insects. It lives in trees. [from Malagasy *aiay*]

ayurveda or **Ayurveda** /ɑːjʊə'veɪdə/ *noun* an ancient system of Hindu medicine, still widely practised in India, and based on principles derived from the *Vedas* (ancient Hindu scriptures). The different forms of treatment for disease include herbal remedies, fasting, bathing, special diets, enemas, massage, prayers, and yoga. [Sanskrit, from *ayur*, life, and *veda*, knowledge]

AZ *abbrev.* Arizona.

azalea /ə'zeɪlɪə/ *noun* **1** any of various deciduous shrubs of the genus *Rhododendron*, closely related to the evergreen rhododendron, native to Asia and N America, although many hybrid varieties are widely cultivated for their large clusters of flowers. **2** the flower of this plant. [from Greek *azaleos*, dry]

azimuth /'azɪməθ/ *noun Astron.* in astronomy and surveying, the bearing (direction) of an object, eg a planet or star, measured in degrees as the angle around the observer's horizon clockwise from north, which is the zero point. See also ALTITUDE. [from Arabic *al*, the + *sumut*, directions]

Aztec /'aztɛk/ — *noun* **1** a member of a Mexican Indian people whose great empire was overthrown by the Spanish in the 16c. **2** the language spoken by this people, also called *Nahuatl*. — *adj.* of the Aztec people, their language and culture. [from Aztec *aztecatl*, men of the north]

azure /'aʒə(r), 'eɪʒʊə(r)/ — *adj.* of a deep sky-blue colour. — *noun* a deep sky-blue colour. [from Persian *lajward*, lapis lazuli]

B

B¹ or **b** noun (PL. **Bs, B's, b's**) **1** the second letter of the English alphabet. **2** (usually **B**) the second highest grade or quality, or a mark indicating this. **3** (**B**) Mus. **a** the seventh note in the scale of C major. **b** a musical key with the note B as its base.

B² abbrev. **1** Bachelor. **2** bass. **3** as an international vehicle mark Belgium. **4** Chess bishop. **5** on pencils black.

B³ symbol Chem. boron.

b. abbrev. **1** born. **2** Cricket bowled.

BA abbrev. **1** Bachelor of Arts. **2** British Airways.

BAA abbrev. British Airports Authority.

baa /bɑː/ — noun the cry of a sheep or lamb. — verb intrans. (**baaed, baaing**) to make this cry.

baba or **rum baba** noun a type of small sponge cake soaked in a rum-flavoured syrup. [from French baba, from Polish]

babble — verb **1** trans., intrans. to talk or say quickly, especially in a way that is hard to understand. **2** intrans. colloq. to talk foolishly. **3** intrans. formal literary, used of water, especially a stream to make a low murmuring sound. **4** trans. to give away (a secret) carelessly. — noun speech that is too quick or too unclear to be easily understood. [probably imitative]

. . . .
▣ verb **1** chatter, gabble, jabber, cackle, prate, mutter, mumble, murmur. **2** burble, blather, jabber. **3** burble, gurgle. noun chatter, gabble, clamour, hubbub, gibberish, burble, murmur.
. . . .

babbler noun a songbird native to warmer regions of the Old World, and having soft, usually brown, fluffy plumage and short wings.

babbling adj. **1** making a murmuring sound, as of gently flowing water. **2** said of a person making incomprehensible sounds.

babe noun **1** colloq. North Amer., esp. US, often used as a term of affection a girl or young woman. **2** old use, literary a baby. **3** colloq. an attractive girl or young woman. [probably imitative of the sound made by a baby]

babel noun **1** a confused sound of voices. **2** a scene of noise and confusion. [from Hebrew Babel]

Babinski reflex or **Babinski effect** Psychol. a reflex curling upwards of the big toe when the outer side of the foot is stroked, normal in children up to two years of age. [named after the French neurologist Joseph Babinski (1857–1932)]

baboon /bəˈbuːn/ noun **1** any of various large ground-dwelling monkeys, most of which are native to Africa, having long dog-like muzzles with large teeth, and long tails. **2** derog. a clumsy or stupid person. [from Old French babuin]

baby — noun (PL. **babies**) **1** a newborn or very young child or animal. **2** an unborn child. **3** the youngest member of a group. **4** derog. a childish person. **5** colloq. a person's own particular project, responsibility, etc. **6** colloq. North Amer., esp. US a term of affection. — verb (**babies, babied**) to treat as a baby. — adj. **1** newborn or very young. **2** smaller than usual; miniature. — **be left holding the baby** colloq. to be left with the responsibility for something. **throw out the baby with the bathwater** colloq. to give up or throw away the important part of something when getting rid of an unwanted part. [probably imitative of the sound a baby makes]

. . . .
▣ noun **1** babe, infant, suckling, child, tiny, toddler. adj. **2** miniature, small-scale, colloq. mini, midget, small, little, tiny, minute, diminutive.
. . . .

babyhood noun the time of life when one is a baby.

babyish adj. derog. childish; immature.

. . . .
▣ childish, juvenile, puerile, infantile, silly, foolish, colloq. soft, colloq. sissy, baby, young, immature, naïve.
▣ mature, precocious.
. . . .

baby-sit verb trans., intrans. to look after a child (usually in its own home) while the parents are out.

baby-sitter noun a person who looks after a child while the parents are out.

baby-sitting noun looking after a child while the parents are out.

baby talk the way in which adults talk to very young children, mimicking the immature speech forms perceived as the main features of infant language. See also CARETAKER SPEECH, MOTHERESE.

baby-walker noun a frame with a seat and wheels in which a baby can sit while learning to walk.

BAC abbrev. British Aircraft Corporation.

baccalaureate /bakəˈlɔːrɪət/ noun **1** formal a Bachelor's degree. **2** a diploma of a lower status than a degree. [from French baccalauréat, from Latin baccalaureus, bachelor]

baccarat /ˈbakərɑː/ noun a card game in which players bet money against the banker. [from French baccarat]

bacchanal /ˈbakənəl/ noun **1** literary a noisy and drunken party. **2** a follower of Bacchus (Dionysus), the god of wine and pleasure in ancient Greece and Rome. [from Latin bacchanalis]

bacchanalia /bakəˈneɪlɪə/ pl. noun orgiastic feasts in honour of Bacchus (Dionysus).

bacchanalian /bakəˈneɪlɪən/ adj. literary characteristic of a bacchanal; riotous.

baccy noun (PL. **baccies**) colloq. tobacco.

bachelor /ˈbatʃələ(r)/ noun **1** an unmarried man. **2** (**Bachelor**) a first university degree, or a person who has taken a degree: Bachelor of Arts. See also MASTER. [from Old French bacheler]

bachelorhood noun the time of life when one is a bachelor.

Bach flower healing Medicine a form of homeopathic therapy in which the healing properties of flowers are used to treat disease by relieving mental and emotional symptoms which are thought to be its cause. [named after the UK physician Edward Bach]

bacillus /bəˈsɪləs/ noun (PL. **bacilli**) **1** Biol. any of a large group of rod-shaped Gram-positive bacteria of the genus Bacillus that are widely distributed in soil and air, mainly as spores. Most bacilli are harmless to humans, but many species cause food spoilage, and some are responsible for serious diseases, eg anthrax, tuberculosis, diphtheria, and tetanus. **2** any rod-shaped bacterium. [from Latin bacillus, little stick]

back — *noun* 1 the rear part of the human body from the neck to the base of the spine. 2 the upper part of an animal's body. 3 the part of an object that is opposite to or furthest from the front. 4 the side of an object that is not normally seen or used. 5 the upright part of a chair. 6 *Football, Hockey* a player whose role is to defend. — *adj.* 1 located or situated behind or at the back. 2 of or from an earlier date: *back pay.* 3 away from or behind (especially something more important): *back roads.* — *adv.* 1 to or towards the rear; away from the front. 2 in or into an original position or condition. 3 in return or in response: *hit back.* 4 in or into the past: *look back to happier days.* — *verb* 1 to help or support, usually with money. 2 a *intrans.* (*often* **back away** or **out** or **out of**) to move backwards. b *trans.* to cause to move backwards. 3 to bet on the success of (a horse, etc). 4 to provide a back or support for. 5 to accompany (a singer) with music. 6 to lie at the back of. 7 *intrans. Naut., said of the wind* to change direction anticlockwise. — **back down** to concede an argument or claim, especially under pressure or opposition. **back off** 1 to move backwards or retreat. 2 to back down. **back on to something** *said of a building, etc* to have its back next to or facing something. **back out of something** to withdraw from a promise or agreement, etc. **back to front** 1 with the back where the front should be. 2 in the wrong order. **back someone up** to support or assist them. **back something up** 1 to confirm that something is true or accurate. 2 to copy computer data on to a disk or tape. **get off someone's back** *colloq.* to stop annoying or troubling them. **have one's back to the wall** *colloq.* to be in a very difficult or desperate situation. **put one's back into something** *colloq.* to do a task with all one's energy. **put someone's back up** *colloq.* to make them annoyed or resentful. **see the back of someone** or **something** *colloq.* to be rid of or finished with someone or something unpleasant or tiresome. [from Anglo-Saxon *bæc*]

▣ *noun* 1 posterior, backside. 2 tail, hindquarters. 3 rear, stern, end, tail, tail end, hind part. 4 reverse, underside. *adj.* 1 rear, end, tail, posterior, hind, hindmost, reverse. *verb* 1 support, sustain, assist, side with, champion, advocate, encourage, promote, boost, favour, sanction, countenance, endorse, second, countersign, sponsor, finance, subsidize, underwrite. 2 move backwards, reverse, withdraw, back away. **back down** concede, yield, give in, surrender, submit, retreat, withdraw, back-pedal. **back out of something** abandon, give up, *colloq.* chicken out of, withdraw from, *colloq.* pull out of, resign from, recant, go back on, cancel. **back someone up** support, reinforce, bolster, assist, aid, second, champion. **back something up** 1 confirm, corroborate, substantiate, endorse, second.

▣ *noun* 3 front, face. *adj.* 1 front. *verb* 1 discourage, weaken. 2 advance, approach. **back someone up** let down.

backache *noun* a pain in the back.

backbench *adj.* relating to the back benches in parliament.

backbencher *noun* in the UK, Australia, etc, a Member of Parliament who sits on the back benches, ie does not hold an official position in either the government or the opposition. See also FRONTBENCHER.

backbite *verb intrans. colloq.* to speak unkindly about someone who is absent.

backbiting *noun* unkind remarks about someone who is absent.

backbone *noun* 1 the spine. 2 the main support of something (in physical and abstract senses): *the chairman is often the backbone of a company.* 3 firmness and strength of character.

▣ 1 spine, spinal column, vertebrae, vertebral column. 2 mainstay, support, core, foundation, basis, character. 3 courage, mettle, pluck, nerve, grit, determination, resolve, tenacity, steadfastness, toughness, stamina, strength, power.

▣ 3 spinelessness, weakness.

backbreaking *adj.*, *said of a task, etc* extremely hard or tiring.

▣ hard, difficult, arduous, laborious, tiring, exhausting.

backchat *noun Brit.* impertinent or rude replies, especially to a superior.

backcloth or **backdrop** *noun* the painted cloth at the back of a stage, forming part of the scenery.

backcomb *verb* to comb (the hair) towards the roots to make it look thicker.

back-cross *Genetics* a cross between a hybrid and a parent.

backdate *verb* 1 to put a date on (a document, etc) that is earlier than the actual date. 2 to make effective from a date in the past.

back door 1 the rear door to a building. 2 a clandestine or illicit means of achieving an objective: *by the back door.* 3 (*attributive*) (*often* **back-door**) denoting an activity done secretly, and often dishonestly.

backdrop SEE BACKCLOTH.

backer *noun* a person who gives financial support to a project, etc.

backfire /bak'faɪə(r)/ *verb intrans.* 1 *said of an engine or vehicle* to produce a loud bang caused by the explosion of accumulated unburned or partially burned gases in the exhaust or inlet system. 2 *said of a plan, etc* to go wrong and have a bad effect on the originator.

▣ 2 recoil, rebound, boomerang, miscarry, fail, flop.

back-formation *noun Grammar* 1 the making of a new word as if it were the root or simpler form of an existing word. 2 a word made in this way, eg *laze* from *lazy.*

backgammon *noun* a board game for two people, with pieces moved according to the throws of a dice. [from BACK + Middle English *gamen*, game]

background *noun* 1 the space behind the main figures of a picture or scene. 2 a less noticeable or less public position: *stay in the background.* 3 the events or circumstances that precede and help to explain an event, etc. 4 a person's social origins, education, etc.

▣ 1 setting, surroundings, scenery, environment. 3 context, circumstances, conditions, environment, milieu, perspective, setting. 4 history, record, credentials, experience, grounding, preparation, education, upbringing, breeding, culture, tradition.

background radiation *Physics* naturally occurring radiation which can be detected at any place on Earth, and results from cosmic rays reaching the Earth from outer space, and from natural radioactive sources on Earth, eg certain rocks.

backhand *noun* 1 *Tennis* a stroke made with the back of the hand turned towards the ball (see also FOREHAND). 2 handwriting with the letters sloping backwards.

backhanded *adj.* 1 made with or as a backhand. 2 *said of a compliment* ambiguous or doubtful in effect.

backhander *noun* 1 a backhand stroke of a ball. 2 *colloq.* a bribe.

backing *noun* 1 support, especially financial. 2 material, etc that supports the back of something. 3 music accompanying a singer.

▣ 1 support, aid, assistance, encouragement, promotion, endorsement, seconding, patronage, sponsorship, finance, funds, grant, subsidy.

backing store *Comput.* a large-capacity computer data store supplementary to a computer's main memory.

backlash *noun* 1 a sudden violent reaction to an action, situation, etc. 2 a jarring or recoil between parts of a machine that do not fit together properly.

▤ **1** reaction, response, repercussion, reprisal, retaliation. **2** recoil, kickback.

backless *adj.* lacking or not requiring a back.

backlog *noun* a pile or amount of uncompleted work.

▤ accumulation, stock, supply, resources, reserve, reserves, excess.

backmarker *noun* a competitor at the back of the field in a race.

back number 1 a copy or issue of a newspaper or magazine that is earlier than the current one. **2** *colloq.* a person or thing that is out of date or no longer useful.

backpack — *noun North Amer., esp. US* a rucksack. — *verb intrans.* to go hiking with a pack on the back.

backpacker *noun* a person who travels with a backpack.

backpacking *noun* the activity of travelling with a backpack.

back passage *colloq.* the rectum.

back-pedal *verb intrans.* **1** to turn the pedals on a bicycle backwards. **2** to withdraw rapidly or suddenly from one's previous opinion or course of action.

backroom *attributive noun* denoting important work done secretly behind the scenes.

back seat an inferior or unimportant position: *take a back seat.*

back-seat driver a person, especially a passenger in a car, who gives unwanted advice.

back shift 1 a group of workers whose working period comes between the night shift and day shift. **2** this period.

backside *noun colloq.* the buttocks.

back slang a type of informal language in which words are spelt backwards and pronounced according to the new spelling, as in English *neetrith*, 'thirteen', and *yob*, 'boy'.

backslide *verb intrans.* to relapse into former bad behaviour, habits, etc.

backslider *noun* a person who declines into bad habits.

backsliding *noun* a decline into former bad habits.

▤ lapse, relapse, apostasy, defection, desertion, defaulting.

backspace — *verb intrans.* to move the carriage of a typewriter or a computer cursor back one or more spaces. — *noun* the key on a typewriter or computer keyboard used for backspacing.

backspin *noun Sport* the spinning of a ball in the opposite direction to the way it is travelling, reducing its speed on hitting a surface. See also SIDESPIN, TOPSPIN.

backstage *adj., adv.* **1** behind a theatre stage. **2** not seen by the public.

backstreet *noun* **1** a street away from a town's main streets. **2** (*attributive*) secret or illicit: *a backstreet abortion.*

backstroke *noun* a swimming stroke performed on the back, with the arms raised alternately in a backward circular motion, and the legs kicked in a paddling action.

backtrack *verb intrans.* **1** to return the way one came. **2** to reverse one's previous opinion or course of action.

backup *noun* **1** support, assistance. **2** *Comput.* a copy made of a program or of data, stored separately in case the main copy is lost as a result of damage or system failure.

backward — *adj.* **1** directed behind or towards the back. **2** less advanced than normal in mental, physical, or intellectual development. **3** reluctant or shy. — *adv.* same as BACKWARDS.

▤ *adj.* **2** immature, underdeveloped, primitive, retarded, subnormal, stupid, slow, behind, behindhand, late. **3** shy,

bashful, reluctant, unwilling, hesitant, hesitating, wavering.
▤ *adj.* **1** forward. **2** precocious.

backwardness *noun* **1** being backward, especially mentally or intellectually. **2** sluggishness; slowness.

backwards *adv.* **1** towards the back or rear. **2** with one's back facing the direction of movement. **3** in reverse order. **4** in or into a worse state. — **backwards and forwards** first in one direction, and then in the opposite direction. **bend** or **fall** or **lean over backwards** *colloq.* to try extremely hard to please or accommodate someone. **know something backwards** *colloq.* to know it thoroughly.

backwash *noun* **1** waves washed backwards by the movement of a ship, oars, etc through the water. **2** a repercussion.

backwater *noun* **1** a pool of stagnant water connected to a river. **2** *derog.* an isolated place, not affected by what is happening elsewhere.

backwoods *pl. noun* **1** remote uncleared forest. **2** a remote region.

backwoodsman *noun* **1** an inhabitant of backwoods. **2** a coarse person.

bacon *noun* meat from the back and sides of a pig, usually salted or smoked. [from Old French *bacon*]

bacteraemia or **bacteremia** *noun Medicine* the presence of bacteria in the blood.

bacteria SEE BACTERIUM.

bacterial /bak'tɪərɪəl/ *adj.* relating to or caused by bacteria.

bactericide /bak'tɪərɪsaɪd/ *noun Chem.* a substance that destroys bacteria.

bacteriological /baktɪərɪə'lɒdʒɪkəl/ *adj.* relating to bacteriology.

bacteriologist /baktɪərɪ'ɒlədʒɪst/ *noun* a person who studies bacteriology, especially professionally.

bacteriology /baktɪərɪ'ɒlədʒɪ/ *noun* the scientific study of bacteria and their effects.

bacteriolysis /baktɪərɪ'ɒlɪsɪs/ *noun Biol.* the breakdown of bacterial cells.

bacteriolytic /baktɪərɪoʊ'lɪtɪk/ *adj. Biol.* relating to or involving bacteriolysis.

bacteriophage /bak'tɪərɪəfɑːʒ/ *noun Biol.* a virus that infects bacteria. Bacteriophages are widely used in genetic research. [from BACTERIUM + Greek *phagein*, to eat]

bacteriostatic /baktɪərɪoʊ'statɪk/ *adj. Chem.* denoting a substance that inhibits the growth of bacteria but does not kill them.

bacterium /bak'tɪərɪəm/ *noun* (PL. **bacteria**) *Biol.* any of an extremely diverse group of microscopic and usually single-celled organisms that are prokaryotes, ie their genetic material consists of a large loop of DNA in the cytoplasm, and there is not a distinct nucleus containing chromosomes. [from Greek *bakterion*, little stick]

bad — *adj.* (**worse, worst**) **1** not good; of poor quality; inferior. **2** wicked; immoral. **3** naughty; misbehaving or disobedient. **4** (**bad at something**) not skilled or clever at some activity. **5** (**bad for someone**) harmful to them. **6** causing distress or misfortune. **7** rotten; decayed. **8** of a serious nature; severe. **9** unwell; injured; causing physical pain or discomfort. **10** sorry, upset, or ashamed. **11** not valid; worthless. **12** *slang* very good. — *noun* **1** unpleasant events. **2** evil; badness: *take the good with the bad.* — **go to the bad** to become morally bad. **in a bad way** very ill or in serious trouble. **not bad** *colloq.* quite good. **too bad** *colloq.* unfortunate. [from Middle English *badde*]

▤ *adj.* **1** poor, inferior, substandard, imperfect, faulty, defective, deficient, unsatisfactory, worthless. **2** evil, immoral, wicked, sinful, criminal, corrupt, vile. **3** naughty, mischievous, ill-behaved, disobedient. **4** incompetent at, incapable of, inexpert at, unskilful at, stupid at, useless at. **5** harmful to, damaging to, injurious to, detrimental to. **6** unpleasant, disagreeable, nasty, undesirable, unfortunate, distressing. **7** rotten, mouldy, decayed, spoilt, putrid, rancid, sour, off, tainted, contaminated. **8** serious, grave, severe, harsh. **9** unhealthy, unwell, unfit, ill, sick, poorly, injured, painful, sore, aching. **10** sorry, upset, ashamed, regretful, remorseful, guilty, contrite, embarrassed.

▣ *adj.* **1** good. **2** virtuous. **3** well-behaved. **4** competent at, skilled at, capable of. **5** harmless to. **6** pleasant. **7** fresh. **8** mild, slight. **9** well, healthy. **10** happy, cheerful.

bad blood or **bad feeling** angry or bitter feelings.

bad debt a debt which will never be repaid.

baddy *noun* (PL. **baddies**) *colloq.* a criminal or villain, especially in films, etc.

bade see BID.

bad faith dishonesty; treachery.

bad feeling see BAD BLOOD.

badge *noun* **1** a small emblem or mark worn to show rank, membership of a society, etc. **2** any distinguishing feature or mark. [from Middle English *bage*]

▣ **1** identification, emblem, device, insignia. **2** sign, mark, token, stamp, trademark.

badger — *noun* a small burrowing mammal belonging to the same family (Mustelidae) as stoats and weasels, and having a stocky body about 1m long, a short tail, and short powerful legs, with strong claws on the front feet. — *verb* (**badgered**, **badgering**) to pester or worry. [probably from BADGE, from the white mark on its forehead]

bad hair day *colloq.* a day that does not go well.

bad language coarse words and swearing.

badly *adv.* (**worse**, **worst**) **1** in an incorrect, unsatisfactory, or inefficient manner. **2** to someone's disadvantage. **3** extremely; severely: *they are badly in arrears with the rent.* **4** in a wicked or cruel manner. — **badly off** poor.

▣ **1** wrong, wrongly, incorrectly, improperly, defectively, faultily, imperfectly, inadequately, unsatisfactorily, poorly, incompetently, negligently, carelessly. **2** unfavourably, adversely, unfortunately, unsuccessfully. **3** greatly, extremely, exceedingly, intensely, deeply, acutely, bitterly, painfully, seriously, desperately, severely, critically, crucially. **4** wickedly, criminally, immorally, shamefully, unfairly. **badly off** poor, hard-up, *colloq.* broke, needy.

▣ **1** well.

badminton /ˈbadmɪntən/ *noun* a game for two or four players played with rackets and a shuttlecock which is hit across a high net. [from *Badminton* in southern England]

badmouth *verb colloq.* to criticize or malign.

badness *noun* being bad; poor or evil quality.

bad-tempered *adj.* easily annoyed or made angry.

▣ irritable, cross, crotchety, crabbed, crabby, snappy, grumpy, querulous, petulant, fractious, *colloq.* stroppy.

▣ good-tempered, genial, equable.

BAF *abbrev.* British Athletics Federation.

baffle — *verb* **1** to confuse or puzzle. **2** to hinder. — *noun* a device for controlling the flow of gas, liquid, or sound through an opening. [perhaps related to Old French *befe*, mockery]

▣ *verb* **1** puzzle, perplex, mystify, bemuse, bewilder, confuse, confound, *colloq.* bamboozle, *colloq.* flummox, daze, upset, disconcert. **2** foil, thwart, frustrate, hinder, check, defeat, stump.

▣ **1** enlighten, help.

bafflement *noun* mental confusion; bewilderment.

baffling *adj.* causing mental confusion; mystifying.

bafflingly *adv.* so as to confuse or mystify: *a bafflingly strange story.*

BAFTA /ˈbaftə/ *abbrev.* in the UK, the British Academy of Film and Television Arts.

bag — *noun* **1** a container made of a soft material with an opening at the top, for carrying things. **2** (**bags of something**) *colloq.* a large amount of it. **3** the amount a bag will hold. **4** an amount of fish or game caught. **5** *offensive colloq.* a woman, especially an unpleasant or ugly one. **6** (**bags**) loose wide-legged trousers. — *verb* (**bagged, bagging**) **1** *trans., intrans.* (also **bag up**) to put (something) into a bag. **2** to kill or catch (game). **3** *colloq.* to obtain or reserve (a seat, etc). **4** *intrans.* said especially of clothes to hang loosely or bulge. — **bag and baggage** completely: *clear out bag and baggage.* **in the bag** *colloq.* as good as secured or done. [from Middle English *bagge*]

▣ *noun* **1** container, sack, case, suitcase, grip, carrier, holdall, handbag, shoulder-bag, satchel, rucksack, haversack, pack. *verb* **2** kill, shoot, catch, capture, trap, land. **3** obtain, acquire, get, gain, reserve, corner, appropriate, commandeer, take, grab.

bagatelle /bagəˈtel/ *noun* **1** a game played on a board with holes into which balls are rolled. **2** an unimportant thing. **3** a short piece of music. [from French *bagatelle*, from Italian *bagatella*, trick, trifle]

bagel or **beigel** /ˈbeɪgl/ *noun* a hard ring-shaped bread roll. [from Yiddish *beygel*]

baggage *noun* **1** a traveller's luggage. **2** the portable equipment of an army. **3** the outlook and experiences a person has, especially when brought inappropriately from one situation into another: *emotional baggage from his last relationship.* [from Old French *bagage*]

▣ **1** luggage, suitcases, bags, belongings, things, equipment, gear, paraphernalia.

baggily *adv.* in a loose or baggy manner.

bagginess *noun* a loose or baggy state or quality.

baggy *adj.* (**baggier, baggiest**) hanging loose or bulging.

▣ loose, slack, roomy, ill-fitting, billowing, bulging, floppy, sagging, droopy.

▣ tight, firm.

bag lady a homeless woman who carries her belongings around with her in bags.

bagpiper *noun* a person who plays the bagpipes; a piper.

bagpipes *pl. noun* a musical instrument consisting of a bag into which air is blown through a pipe and from which air flows through other pipes to form notes. Drone pipes make single sustained notes, and a 'chanter' or fingered pipe makes the melody.

baguette /baˈget/ *noun* a long narrow French loaf. [from French *baguette*]

bah *interj.* expressing displeasure or disgust.

Baha'i or **Bahai** /bəˈhɑːɪ/ *noun Relig.* **1** (also **Baha'ism**) a religious movement that arose out of the Persian Islamic sect Babi in the 1860s, teaching the oneness of God and the unity of all faiths, the inevitable unification of humankind, the harmony of all people, universal education, and obedience to government. **2** an adherent of Baha'ism. [from Persian *baha*, splendour]

Bahasa Indonesian /bəˈhɑːsə/ the Malay dialect of the S Malay Peninsula, and the official language of Indonesia since 1949. [from Malay *bahasa*, language]

bail¹ — *noun* money required as security for a person's temporary release while awaiting trial. — *verb* (also **bail out**) to provide bail for. — **bail someone out** *colloq.* to help or rescue them. **forfeit** or **jump bail** to fail to return for trial after being released on bail. **on bail** released once bail money has been given to the court. **put up** or **stand or**

go bail to provide bail for a prisoner. [from Old French *bail*, custody]

⊟ *noun* security, surety, pledge, bond, guarantee, warranty. **bail out** help, aid, assist, relieve, rescue, finance.

bail² or **bale** *verb trans., intrans.* (*usually* **bail** or **bale out**) **1** to remove (water) from a boat with a bucket. **2** to escape from an aeroplane by jumping out. **3** *colloq.* to escape from a difficult situation. [from French *baille*, bucket]

⊟ **3** escape, withdraw, retreat, quit, back out, *colloq.* cop out.

bail³ *noun* (*usually* **bails**) one of the cross-pieces laid on top of the stumps in cricket.

bailey *noun* (PL. **baileys**) the outer wall of a castle, or a courtyard within the wall. [from Old French *baille*, enclosure]

Bailey bridge a temporary lattice bridge that can be assembled rapidly from prefabricated pieces of welded steel, widely used as a military bridge during World War II. [named after the UK engineer Sir Donald Bailey (1901–85)]

bailiff /ˈbeɪlɪf/ *noun* **1** an officer of a lawcourt, especially one with the power to seize the property of a person who has not paid money owed to the court. **2** a person who looks after property for its owner. [from Old French *baillier*, to control, hand over]

bain-marie /banmaˈriː/ *noun* a pan filled with hot water in which a container of food can be cooked gently or kept warm. [from French *bain-marie*, bath of Mary, from medieval Latin *balneum Mariae*, 'Maria' being the name of an alleged alchemist]

bairn /beərn/ *noun dialect* a child. [from Anglo-Saxon *bearn*, to bear]

bait — *noun* **1** food put on a hook or in a trap to attract fish or animals. **2** anything intended to attract or tempt. — *verb* **1** to put food on or in (a hook or trap). **2** to harass or tease wilfully. **3** to set dogs on (another animal). [from Norse *beita*, to cause to bite]

⊟ *noun* **2** lure, incentive, inducement, bribe, temptation, enticement, allurement, attraction. *verb* **2** tease, provoke, goad, irritate, annoy, irk, *colloq.* needle, harass, persecute, torment.
⊞ *noun* **2** disincentive.

baize *noun* a woollen cloth, usually green and used as a covering on snooker and card tables. [from Old French *baies*, chestnut-coloured]

bake *verb* **1** *trans., intrans.* to cook (cakes, bread, vegetables, etc) using dry heat in an oven. **2** *trans., intrans.* to dry or harden by heat from the sun or a fire. **3** *intrans. colloq.* to be extremely hot. [from Anglo-Saxon *bacan*]

baked beans haricot beans baked in tomato sauce and usually tinned.

bakehouse *noun old use* a bakery.

Bakelite /ˈbeɪkəlaɪt/ *noun trademark* a type of hard plastic formerly used to make dishes, buttons, etc. [named after L H Baekeland (1863–1944), its inventor]

baker *noun* a person who bakes and sells bread, cakes, etc.

baker's dozen thirteen.

bakery *noun* (PL. **bakeries**) a place where bread, cakes, etc are made or sold.

baking *adj.* extremely hot, especially from the sun.

baking powder a powder containing sodium bicarbonate, used to make cakes, etc rise.

baking soda sodium bicarbonate, used to make baking powder.

baklava or **baclava** /ˈbakləvə/ *noun* a rich cake of Middle Eastern origin made of layers of flaky pastry with a filling of honey, nuts, and spices. [from Turkish]

baksheesh /ˈbakʃiːʃ/ *noun* in some eastern countries, money given as a tip or present. [from Persian *bakshish*]

balaclava /baləˈklɑːvə/ *noun* a knitted hat that covers the head and neck, with an opening for the face. [from *Balaclava* in the Crimea]

balalaika /baləˈlaɪkə/ *noun* a Russian stringed musical instrument with a triangular body, a neck like a guitar and normally three strings. [from Russian *balalaika*]

balance — *noun* **1** an instrument for weighing, usually with two dishes hanging from a bar supported in the middle. **2** a state of physical stability in which the weight of a body is evenly distributed. **3** a state of mental or emotional stability. **4** a state existing when two opposite forces are equal. **5** something that is needed to create such equality. **6** the amount by which the two sides of an account (money spent and money received) differ. **7** an amount left over. **8** a device which regulates the speed of a clock or watch. — *verb* **1** *trans., intrans.* to be or put into a state of physical balance. **2** to compare two or more things in one's mind. **3** to find the difference between money put into an account and money taken out of it, and to make them equal: *balance the books.* **4** *intrans.* (*also* **balance out**) to be or become equal in amount. — **in the balance** not yet decided. **on balance** having taken all the advantages and disadvantages into consideration. [from Latin *bilanx*, having two scales]

⊟ *noun* **2** equilibrium, steadiness, stability. **3** composure, self-possession, poise, equanimity. **4** evenness, symmetry, equality, parity, equity, equivalence, correspondence. **5** remainder, rest, residue, surplus, difference. *verb* **1** steady, poise, stabilize, level, square, equalize, equate, match, counterbalance, counteract, neutralize, offset. **2** compare, consider, weigh, estimate.
⊞ *noun* **2** imbalance, instability. *verb* **1** unbalance, overbalance.

balanced *adj.* **1** in a state of balance. **2** fair; considering all sides of an argument, etc. **3** *said of a person* calm and sensible.

⊟ **1** stable, steady. **2** fair, impartial, objective, unbiased, unprejudiced. **3** calm, sensible, level-headed, sane, rational, reasonable, realistic.

balance of payments the difference in value between the amount of money coming into a country and the amount going out of it, over a period of time.

balance of power the equal distribution of political or military power, with no one nation or group having supremacy. — **hold the balance of power** to be in a position where either of two equal and opposed groups, etc can be made more powerful than the other through one's support.

balance of trade the difference in value of a country's imports and exports.

balance sheet a summary and balance of financial accounts.

balcony /ˈbalkənɪ/ *noun* (PL. **balconies**) **1** a platform surrounded by a wall or railing, projecting from the wall of a building. **2** an upper tier in a theatre or cinema. [from Italian *balcone*]

⊟ **1** terrace, veranda. **2** gallery, upper circle, the gods.

bald /bɔːld/ *adj.* **1** *said of a person* having little or no hair on the head. **2** *said of birds or animals* not having any feathers or fur. **3** bare or plain. **4** making no attempt to disguise, soften, or elaborate the facts. [perhaps from Middle English *balled*, rounded]

⊟ **1** bald-headed, hairless, smooth, uncovered. **3** unadorned, bare, plain, simple, severe, stark, barren, naked. **4** blunt, forthright, direct, straight, outright, downright, straightforward

⊞ **1** hairy, hirsute. **3** adorned.

baldacchino /bɔːldəˈkiːnoʊ/ or **baldachin** or **balda-quin** /ˈbɔːldəkɪn/ *noun* **1** a canopy, especially the canopy supported at each corner by a pole and carried over a sacred object in a religious procession, or placed over a throne, altar, or pulpit. **2** *Archit.* a fixed structure with a canopy supported at each corner by a column, found over the high altar in many Baroque churches. [from Italian *Baldacco*, Baghdad, originally the source of the silk used for the canopy]

bald eagle a large eagle, native to N America, but now found only in Florida and Alaska, so called because its head and neck are covered with distinctive white feathers, whereas the rest of its plumage is black. It is the national emblem of the USA.

balderdash /ˈbɔːldədaʃ/ *noun old use* nonsense.

balding *adj.* becoming bald.

baldly *adv.* in a plain and often hurtful way: *told them baldly they were not wanted.*

⊞ plainly, bluntly, outright, frankly, candidly, curtly.

baldness *noun* the partial or total loss of hair from parts of the body where it normally grows, especially the head. See also ALOPECIA.

baldric or **baldrick** /ˈbɔːldrɪk/ *noun Hist.* a broad leather belt or silk sash (often highly ornate), worn around the waist or over the right shoulder to support a sword. [from Old French *baudrei*; related to Middle High German *balderick*, girdle]

bale¹ — *noun* a large tied bundle of a commodity such as cloth or hay. — *verb* to make into bales. [from Old French *bale*]

⊞ *noun* bundle, truss, pack, package, parcel. **bale out** see **bail out.**

bale² see BAIL².

baleen /bəˈliːn/ *noun* whalebone. [from Latin *balaena*, whale]

baleful *adj.* **1** evil; harmful. **2** threatening; gloomy. [from Anglo-Saxon *bealu*, evil]

balefully *adv.* with menace; threateningly.

balefulness *noun* a harmful or threatening state.

Balinese /bɑːlɪˈniːz/ — *noun* **1** (PL. **Balinese**) a native of Bali. **2** the Austronesian language of Bali, spoken by c.2–3 million people. — *adj.* relating to Bali or its language or Hindu culture, especially its distinctive dance, music, and drama.

balk or **baulk** /bɔːlk/ *verb* **1** *intrans.* (*usually* **balk at something**) to hesitate or refuse to go on because of some obstacle. **2** *trans.* to check or block. [from Anglo-Saxon *balca*, ridge]

⊞ **1** flinch, recoil, shrink, jib, boggle, hesitate, refuse, resist, dodge, evade, shirk. **2** thwart, frustrate, foil, forestall, disconcert, baffle, hinder, obstruct, check, stall, bar, prevent, defeat, counteract.

Balkan /ˈbɔːlkən/ — *adj.* **1** relating to the peninsula in SE Europe surrounded by the Adriatic, Aegean, and Black seas. **2** of its peoples or countries. — *noun* (**Balkans**) the Balkan countries.

ball¹ — *noun* **1** a round or roundish object used in some sports. **2** anything round or nearly round in shape: *a snow-ball.* **3** the act of throwing a ball, or the way a ball is thrown. **4** a rounded fleshy part of the body: *the ball of the foot.* **5** (*usually* **balls**) *coarse slang* a testicle (see also BALLS). — *verb trans., intrans.* to form or gather into a ball. — **have the ball at one's feet** to have the opportunity to do something. **on the ball** *colloq.* well-informed; alert. **play ball** *colloq.* to co-operate. **start** or **set** or **keep the ball roll-** ing to begin, or continue, an activity, conversation, etc. [from Middle English *bal*]

⊞ *noun* **1** sphere, globe, orb. **2** globule, pellet, pill, shot, bullet, *colloq.* slug.

ball² *noun* **1** a formal social meeting for dancing. **2** *colloq.* an enjoyable time: *have a ball.* [from French *bal*]

⊞ **1** dance, dinner-dance, party, soirée, masquerade, carnival, assembly.

ballad *noun* **1** a slow, usually romantic song. **2** a poem or song with short verses, which tells a popular story. [from Provençal *balada*, dance]

⊞ POEM, SONG, FOLKSONG, SHANTY, CAROL, DITTY.

ballade /bəˈlɑːd/ *noun* **1** a poem consisting of verses grouped in threes, with a repeated refrain, and a final short concluding verse (an envoy). **2** *Mus.* a short lyrical piece for piano. [an earlier form of BALLAD]

ball-and-socket a joint consisting of the ball-shaped head of one bone partially enclosed by the cup-shaped cavity of another bone, allowing considerable freedom of movement, eg the hip joint between the pelvis and the femur.

ballast *noun* **1** heavy material used to keep a balloon or a ship without cargo steady. **2** broken rocks or stones used as a base for roads and railway lines. [probably from Old Swedish *bar*, bare + *last*, load]

ball-bearing *noun* **1** a device consisting of a ring of steel balls whose rolling action in the spherical grooves between a fixed housing and a rotating shaft serves to minimize friction. **2** one of these balls.

ballcock *noun* in a lavatory cistern or similar tank, a floating ball that rises and falls as the water level changes, opening or closing a valve to which it is attached, and so regulating the supply of water to the cistern.

ballerina /baləˈriːnə/ *noun* a female ballet-dancer, especially one taking leading roles. [from Italian *ballerina*, feminine of *ballerino*, dancing-master]

ballet /ˈbaleɪ/ *noun* a classical style of dancing and mime, using set steps and body movements; a performance of this. [from French *ballet*, diminutive of *bal*, dance]

ballet-dancer *noun* a dancer of ballet.

balletic /baˈlɛtɪk/ *adj.* of or like ballet or a ballet; dance-like.

balletically *adv.* with dance-like movement; gracefully.

ball game *noun* **1** *North Amer.* a baseball game. **2** *colloq.* a situation: *a whole new ball game.*

ballistic /bəˈlɪstɪk/ *adj.* **1** relating to projectiles. **2** operating under the force of gravity. — **go ballistic** *colloq.* **1** to become hugely successful. **2** to become extremely angry.

ballistic missile a type of missile which is initially guided but drops on its target under gravity.

ballistics *sing. noun* the scientific study of the movement, behaviour and effects of projectiles, such as bullets, rockets, and guided missiles. [from Latin *ballista*, a military machine for throwing large rocks at buildings, etc]

balloon /bəˈluːn/ — *noun* **1** a small rubber pouch with a neck, filled with air or other gas and used as a toy or decoration. **2** an aircraft that is lighter than air and has no propulsive power, usually consisting of a large non-porous bag filled with hot air or a gas such as helium that is lighter than air, and having a basket or gondola for carrying passengers, weather-recording instruments, etc, suspended beneath it. **3** an inflatable plastic cylinder that is used to dilate blood vessels or parts of the alimentary canal in areas where they have become narrowed as a result of obstruction. **4** an outline containing the words or thoughts of characters in a cartoon. — *verb intrans.* **1** to swell out like a balloon. **2** to increase dramatically: *the costs started bal-*

looning alarmingly. **3** to travel by balloon. — **go down like a lead balloon** *colloq.*, *said of an action or statement* to be received with hostility or disapproval. **when the balloon goes up** when the trouble starts. [from Italian *ballone*]

ballooning *noun* the activity of travelling in a balloon, especially for recreation.

balloonist *noun* a person who travels in a balloon, especially for recreation.

ballot — *noun* **1** a method or act of voting, usually in secret, by putting a marked paper into a box or other container. **2** the total number of votes recorded in an election. **3** a piece of paper, etc used in voting. — *verb* (**balloted, balloting**) **1** *intrans.* to vote by ballot. **2** *trans.* to take a ballot of. [from Italian *ballotta*, little ball]

....

◗ *noun* **1** poll, polling, vote, voting, election, referendum, plebiscite.

....

ballot-box *noun* **1** the box into which voters put marked ballot-papers. **2** the system of voting in secret by ballot, especially as a sign of political freedom.

ballot-paper *noun* a piece of paper used for voting in a ballot.

ballpark *North Amer., esp. US* — *noun* a baseball field. — *adj.* approximate, rough: *a ballpark figure.* — **in the right ballpark** approximately correct or relevant.

ballpoint or **ballpoint pen** *noun* a pen having a tiny ball as the writing point.

ballroom *noun* a large hall where balls are held.

ballroom dancing a formal kind of dancing, in which couples dance to music with a strict rhythm.

balls *sing. noun coarse slang* **1** *North Amer., esp. US* courage or bravery. **2** *also interj.* rubbish or nonsense. — **balls something up** *Brit. coarse slang* to make a complete mess of it; to bungle it. See also BALL¹ 5.

bally *adj. Brit. old colloq. use* a mild form of BLOODY.

ballyhoo /balɪ'huː/ *noun colloq.* **1** a noisy confused situation. **2** noisy or sensational publicity or advertising.

balm /baːm/ *noun* **1** an oil obtained from certain types of trees, having a pleasant smell, and used in healing or reducing pain. **2** something comforting to either the body or the spirit. [from Old French *basme*]

balmily *adv., said of the air* warmly and softly.

balminess *noun, said of the air* a warm and soft quality.

balmy¹ /baːmɪ/ *adj.* balmier, balmiest *said of the air* warm and soft. [from Old French *basme*, balm]

balmy² same as BARMY.

baloney or **boloney** /bə'ləʊnɪ/ *noun slang* nonsense. [perhaps from *Bologna*, a type of sausage]

balsa /'bɔːlsə, 'bɒlsə/ *noun* **1** a large fast-growing tree, native to lowland areas of tropical America, having broadly oval to circular leaves, and yellowish or brownish flowers. **2** (*also* **balsa-wood**) the very light soft timber of this tree, used for insulation and panelling, and in the construction of models. [from Spanish *balsa*, raft]

balsam /'bɒlsəm/ *noun* **1** any of various plants of the genus *Impatiens*, most of which are native to tropical regions, having irregular flowers with five petals forming a broad lip, a hood, and a curved nectar-filled spur. **2** a resinous oily substance obtained from trees of the genus *Commiphora*, and used in various medicines and as a base for perfumes. [from Latin *balsamum*]

balsamic vinegar /bɔːl'samɪk/ a vinegar from Italy that is matured in wooden casks, giving it a sweet flavour and a dark colour.

balti /'baltɪ/ *noun* **1** a style of Indian cooking originating in Britain, in which food is both cooked and served in a pan resembling a wok. **2** the pan in which this is cooked. [from Hindi, = bucket]

Baltic /'bɒltɪk/ — *adj.* **1** denoting the sea separating Scandinavia from Germany and Russia, or the countries in this area. **2** denoting a group of Indo-European languages, of which the main surviving examples are Latvian and

Lithuanian. Both of these have written records dating from the 14c, and each has a standard form and many dialects. See also SLAVIC. — *noun* the Baltic languages.

baluster /'baləstə(r)/ *noun* each of a series of posts or pillars supporting a rail. [from French *balustre*]

balustrade /balə'streɪd/ *noun* a row of posts or pillars, joined by a rail, on the edge of a balcony, staircase, bridge, etc. [from French *balustrade*, from *balustre*, baluster]

bamboo /bam'buː/ *noun* **1** a tall grass that very rarely flowers, found mainly in tropical regions, with jointed hollow woody stems and deciduous leaves. Bamboo shoots are a popular food. **2** the stem of this grass, used in furniture making, basketry, building, etc, and as a garden cane. [probably from Malay *bambu*]

bamboo curtain *Politics* a term used in the West for the political and military barrier to communications around the People's Republic of China, especially in the 1950s and 1960s.

bamboozle /bam'buːzl/ *verb colloq.* **1** to trick or cheat. **2** to confuse.

bamboozlement *noun* cheating, trickery.

ban — *noun* an official order that something may not be done: *a ban on advertising.* — *verb* (**banned, banning**) to forbid or prevent, especially officially or formally. [from Anglo-Saxon *bannan*, to summon]

....

◗ *noun* prohibition, embargo, veto, boycott, stoppage, restriction, suppression, censorship, outlawry, proscription, condemnation, denunciation, curse, taboo. *verb* forbid, prohibit, disallow, proscribe, bar, exclude, ostracize, outlaw, banish, suppress, restrict.

◗ *noun* permission, dispensation. *verb* allow, permit, authorize.

....

banal /bə'nɑːl/ *adj.* not original or interesting; tedious. [earlier meanings 'compulsory, common to all': from French *banal*]

....

◗ trite, commonplace, ordinary, everyday, humdrum, boring, unimaginative, hackneyed, clichéd, stock, stereotyped, *colloq.* corny, stale, threadbare, tired, empty.

◗ original, fresh, imaginative.

....

banality /bə'nalɪtɪ/ *noun* (PL. **banalities**) something tedious or commonplace.

banana /bə'nɑːnə/ *noun* **1** a large perennial plant of the genus *Musa*, superficially resembling a tree, native to SE Asia, and cultivated throughout the tropics as a staple food crop. **2** the long curved fruit of this plant, which despite its appearance is a berry. It is often sold as an unblemished yellow fruit, but is not fully ripe until it is flecked with brown spots. The seeds within the fruit are sterile. [from a native name in Guinea]

banana republic *derog.* a poor country whose economy is dependent on foreign capital.

bancassurance /baŋkə'ʃʊərəns/ *noun* the selling of insurance policies by a bank or building society through a wholly-owned subsidiary company.

band¹ — *noun* **1** a flat narrow strip of cloth, metal, paper, etc used to hold things together or as a decoration. **2** a stripe of colour or strip of material differing from its background or surroundings. **3** a belt for driving machinery. **4** a group or range of radio frequencies between two limits: *waveband.* **5** a range of values between two limits. — *verb* to fasten or mark with a band. [from Old French *bande*]

....

◗ *noun* **1** strip, belt, ribbon, tape, bandage, binding, tie, ligature, bond, strap, cord, chain. **2** strip, stripe, line, bar, streak.

....

band² — *noun* **1** a group of people with a common purpose or interest. **2** a group of musicians who play music other than classical music: *a rock band.* — *verb intrans., trans.* (**band together**) to unite to work for a common purpose. [from Old French *bande*]

■ *noun* **1** troop, gang, crew, group, herd, flock, party, body, association, company, society, club, clique. **2** group, orchestra, ensemble. *verb* group, gather, join, unite, ally, amalgamate, merge, affiliate, federate.

🔁 *verb* disband, disperse.

bandage — *noun* a pad or strip of gauze or other material, applied to a cut or other injury in order to protect it, or wrapped around an injured part of the body, eg a broken limb. — *verb* to wrap (a wound or a broken limb) in a bandage. [from French *bandage*]

■ *noun* dressing, plaster, compress, ligature, tourniquet, swathe, swaddle. *verb* bind, dress, cover, swathe, swaddle.

bandana or **bandanna** /banˈdanə/ *noun* a large brightly coloured cotton or silk square, folded and worn around the neck or head. [from Hindi *ba(n)dhnu*, a type of dyeing]

B and B or **B & B** or **b & b** *abbrev.* bed and breakfast.

bandbox *noun* a light round box for holding hats.

bandeau /ˈbandoʊ/ *noun* (PL. **bandeaux**) a narrow band of soft material worn around the head. [from French *bandeau*]

banded *adj.* marked with a stripe or stripes of a different colour.

banderole /ˈbandəroʊl/ *noun* **1** a long narrow flag, usually with a forked end. **2** a flat, ribbon-like band carved into a stone wall, etc with writing on it. [from French *banderole*]

bandicoot /ˈbandɪkuːt/ *noun* a nocturnal marsupial resembling a rat, but similar in size to a rabbit, found in Australia, Tasmania, and Papua New Guinea, and having elongated hind legs and a long flexible snout. [from Telugu (Indian language) *pandikokku*]

bandicoot rat a giant rat found in India and Sri Lanka, where it is an agricultural pest. It is unrelated to the marsupial bandicoot.

bandit *noun* an armed robber, especially a member of a gang which attacks travellers. [from Italian *bandito*, outlaw]

■ robber, thief, brigand, marauder, outlaw, highwayman, pirate, buccaneer, hijacker, cowboy, gunman, desperado, gangster.

bandmaster *noun* the conductor of a musical, especially brass, band.

bandog *noun* **1** an aggressive dog kept chained or tied up. **2** a dog that is a cross between an American pit bull terrier and a mastiff, rottweiler, or Rhodesian ridgeback, bred for exceptional ferocity. [from Middle English *band-dogge*, from *bande*, a tie or bond + DOG]

bandoleer or **bandolier** /bandəˈlɪə(r)/ *noun* a leather shoulder belt, especially for carrying bullets. [from Old French *bandouillere*]

band-saw *noun* a saw consisting of a blade with teeth attached to a metal band which moves very fast around two wheels.

bandsman *noun* a member of a musical, especially brass, band.

bandstand *noun* a platform with a roof, often in a park, where bands play music.

bandwagon — **jump** or **climb on the bandwagon** to join or show interest in an activity that is fashionable and likely to succeed.

bandwidth *noun Telecomm.* **1** the width or spread of the range of frequencies used for the transmission of radio or television signals. **2** the space in the frequency-domain occupied by signals of a specified nature, eg television, radar, telephone-quality speech, etc.

bandy[1] *verb* (**bandies, bandied**) (**bandy something about** or **around**) **1** to pass (a story, information, etc) from one person to another. **2** to mention (someone's name) in rumour: *her name is being bandied about.* — **bandy words with someone** to exchange (cross words, etc) with someone: *don't bandy words with me!* [origin unknown]

■ **1** exchange, swap, trade, barter, interchange, reciprocate, pass, toss, throw. **2** pass, circulate, spread, toss.

bandy[2] *adj.* (**bandier, bandiest**) *said of a person's or animal's legs* curved or bending wide apart at the knee.

■ bandy-legged, bow-legged, curved, bowed, bent, crooked.

bandy-legged *adj.* having bandy legs.

bane *noun* the cause of trouble or evil: *the bane of my life.* [from Anglo-Saxon *bana*, murderer]

baneful *adj.* evil; causing harm.

bang[1] — *noun* **1** a sudden loud explosive noise. **2** a heavy blow. **3** *coarse slang* an act of sexual intercourse. **4** *slang* an injection of an illegal drug. — *verb trans., intrans.* **1** to make a loud noise by hitting, dropping, closing violently, etc. **2** to hit sharply, especially by accident: *banged her elbow on the table.* **3** to make or cause to make the sound of an explosion. **4** *coarse slang* to have sexual intercourse with (someone). — *adv. colloq.* **1** exactly: *bang on time.* **2** suddenly. — **bang away** *colloq.* **1** to make a continuous noise. **2** **go off with a bang** to be a great success. [from Norse *banga*, to hammer]

■ *noun* **1** explosion, detonation, pop, boom, clap, peal, clang, clash, thud, thump, slam, noise, report, shot. **2** blow, hit, knock, bump, crash, collision, smack, punch, thump, *colloq.* wallop, stroke, whack. *verb* **1** explode, burst, detonate, boom, echo, resound, crash, slam, clatter, clang, peal, thunder. **2** strike, hit, bash, knock, bump, rap, drum, hammer, pound, thump, stamp. *adv.* **1** exactly, straight, directly, right, precisely. **2** suddenly, abruptly, *colloq.* slap, *colloq.* smack, hard.

bang[2] *noun North Amer., esp. US* (*usually* **bangs**) hair cut in a straight line across the forehead.

banger *noun* **1** *colloq.* a sausage. **2** *colloq.* an old car, usually noisy and in poor condition. **3** a loud firework.

bangle *noun* a piece of jewellery in the form of a solid band, worn round the arm or leg. [from Hindi *bangri*, glass ring]

banian see BANYAN.

banish *verb* **1** to send (someone) away from a place, usually the country of origin. **2** to put (thoughts, etc) out of one's mind. [from Old French *bannir*]

■ **1** expel, eject, evict, deport, transport, exile, outlaw, ban, bar, debar, exclude, shut out, ostracize, excommunicate, dismiss, oust, dislodge, remove, get rid of, discard. **2** dismiss, eliminate, eradicate, reject, repudiate, dispel.

🔁 RECALL. **1** welcome.

banishment *noun* the act or an instance of banishing.

■ expulsion, eviction, deportation, expatriation, transportation, exile, outlawry, ostracism, excommunication.

🔁 return, recall, welcome.

banister or **bannister** *noun* (*usually* **banisters**) a row of posts and the hand-rail they support, running up the side of a staircase. [from BALUSTER]

banjo *noun* (PL. **banjos, banjoes**) a stringed musical instrument with a long neck and a round body, played like a guitar. [probably of African origin]

banjoist /ˈbandʒoʊɪst/ *noun* a person who plays a banjo.

bank[1] — *noun* **1** a long raised pile of earth, snow, etc. **2** the side or slope of a hill. **3** the ground at the edge of a river, lake, etc. **4** a raised area of sand under the sea. **5** a mass of cloud, mist, or fog. — *verb* **1** (**bank something up**) to form into a bank or banks. **2** (**bank something up**) to cover a fire with a large amount of coal to keep it burning. **3** *intrans., trans. said of an aircraft* to change direction, with one wing higher than the other. [from Middle English *banke*]

▣ *noun* **1** heap, pile, mass, mound, earthwork, ridge, rampart, embankment. **2** side, slope, hill, incline, gradient, ramp, tilt, slant. **3** edge, shore, beach, strand, lakeside, waterfront. *verb* **1** heap, pile, stack, mass, amass, accumulate, mound, drift. **3** slope, incline, slant, tilt, tip, pitch.

---

bank² — *noun* **1** a financial organization which keeps money in accounts for its clients, lends money, exchanges currency, etc. **2** a box in which money can be saved, especially by children. **3** a stock or store for later use; a place where something is stored or collected for later use: *blood bank*. **4** in some games, a stock of money controlled by one of the players (the banker). — *verb* **1** to put (money) into a bank. **2** *intrans.* to have a bank account: *they bank with Lloyds*. — **bank on something** to put one's trust in (something); to be confident that something will happen. [from French *banque*]

▣ *noun* **3** store, stock, stockpile, accumulation, fund, pool, savings, reserve, hoard, cache, reservoir, depository, repository. *verb* **1** deposit, save, keep, store, accumulate, stockpile. **bank on** rely on, depend on, count on, trust, expect, anticipate.
▣ *verb* **1** spend.

---

bank³ *noun* a collection of similar things arranged in rows: *a bank of switches*. [from Old French *banc*, bench]

▣ array, panel, group, tier, rank, line, row, series, succession, sequence, train.

---

bankable *adj.* **1** able to be received by a bank. **2** *said especially of a film star* likely to ensure the profitability of a film.

bank account an arrangement by which a person or company keeps money in a bank and makes withdrawals when necessary.

bank book a book recording the amounts of money put into and taken out of a bank account.

bank card or **banker's card** same as CHEQUE CARD.

bank draft a written order sent from one bank to another for paying money to a customer.

banker *noun* **1** a person who owns or manages a bank. **2** a person in charge of the bank in some games.

banker's order see STANDING ORDER.

bank holiday *noun Brit.* any of several days in the year on which banks are closed, observed as a public holiday in England and Wales.

banking *noun* the business done by a bank.

banknote *noun* a piece of paper money issued by a bank.

bankroll — *noun* money or cash resources. — *verb colloq.* to finance.

bankrupt — *noun* a person who is legally recognized as not being able to pay debts. — *adj.* **1** not having money to pay one's debts. **2** (**bankrupt of something**) exhausted of or lacking some quality, etc: *bankrupt of ideas*. — *verb* to make bankrupt. [from French *banqueroute*, altered under the influence of Latin *banca rupta*, bank broken]

▣ *noun* insolvent, debtor, pauper. *adj.* **1** insolvent, in liquidation, ruined, failed, beggared, destitute, impoverished, *colloq.* broke. **2** exhausted of, depleted in, lacking in. *verb* impoverish, ruin.
▣ *adj.* **1** solvent, wealthy.

---

bankruptcy /'baŋkrʌpsɪ/ *noun* (PL. **bankruptcies**) a state of being bankrupt.

banksia *noun* a low shrub or small tree of the genus *Banksia*, native to Australia, and having small sharply-toothed leathery leaves, and cream, orange, red, or purplish flowers with four petals and a protruding style. [named after the UK botanist Sir Joseph Banks]

bank switching *Comput.* a method of accessing more memory than can normally be addressed at one time, by switching between one bank of memory and another.

banner /'banə(r)/ *noun* **1** a large piece of cloth or cardboard, with a design, slogan, etc carried at public meetings and parades. **2** a military flag. [from Old French *baniere*]

▣ **1** placard, notice, sign. **2** flag, standard, colours, ensign, pennant, streamer.

---

banner headline a newspaper headline written in large letters across the width of the page.

bannock *noun dialect* a small flat round cake, usually made from oatmeal. [from Anglo-Saxon *bannuc*]

banns *pl. noun* a public announcement in church of two people's intention to marry. [from Anglo-Saxon *bannan*, to summon]

banoffee pie a dessert of a pastry case with a filling of toffee, bananas, and cream. [BANANA + TOFFEE]

banquet /'baŋkwɪt/ — *noun* **1** a sumptuous formal dinner. **2** *loosely* an elaborate meal. — *verb trans., intrans.* (**banqueted**, **banqueting**) to entertain with or take part in a banquet. [from French *banquet*]

▣ *noun* FEAST, DINNER, REPAST, *colloq.* TREAT.

---

banshee /'banʃiː/ *noun, especially in Irish and Scottish folklore* a female spirit whose sad cries outside a house warn that a member of the family will die. [from Irish Gaelic *bean sidhe*, woman of the fairies]

bantam /'bantəm/ *noun* **1** a small variety of the common domestic fowl. **2** a small but forceful person. [probably from *Bantam* in Java, from where such chickens may have been first imported]

bantamweight *noun* **1** a class for boxers, wrestlers, and weightlifters of not more than a specified weight (54kg in professional boxing, slightly more in the other sports). **2** a boxer, etc of this weight.

banter — *noun* light-hearted friendly talk. — *verb intrans.* (**bantered**, **bantering**) to make teasing or joking remarks.

▣ *noun* joking, pleasantry, badinage, repartee, word play, chaff, chaffing, *colloq.* kidding, *colloq.* ribbing, *old use* jesting, derision, mockery, ridicule. *verb* tease, joke, chaff, *old use* jest, mock.

---

bantering — *adj.* light-heartedly teasing. — *noun* light-hearted teasing.

Bantu /'bantuː/ — *noun* **1** a group of languages spoken in southern and central Africa. **2** (*pl.*) the group of peoples who speak these languages. **3** *offensive* a black speaker of one of these languages. — *adj.* denoting these languages or the Bantu-speaking people. [from Bantu *people*]

Bantustan /bantu:'stɑːn/ *noun, often offensive* any of the partially self-governing regions reserved for black South Africans. [from BANTU + *-stan* as in Hindustan]

banyan or **banian** /'banjan/ *noun* a large evergreen species of fig (*Ficus benghalensis*), native to tropical Asia, and regarded as a sacred tree in India. [from Portuguese *banian*, from Gujarati *vaniyo*, man of the trading caste]

baobab /'beɪoʊbab/ *noun* a large deciduous African tree of the genus *Adansonia*, with a massive soft trunk which serves as a water store, and a relatively small crown. It produces an edible fruit (monkeybread) resembling a gourd, and the trunk is sometimes hollowed out for use as a human dwelling. [probably from an African language]

BAOR *abbrev.* British Army of the Rhine.

baptism /'baptızm/ *noun* the religious ceremony of baptizing a person.

■ christening, dedication, beginning, initiation, introduction, début, launch, launching, immersion, sprinkling, purification.

baptismal *adj.* relating to or for baptism.

baptist *noun* 1 a person who baptizes, especially John the Baptist. 2 **(Baptist)** a member of a Christian group which believes that only people who are able to profess their religious beliefs should be baptized, and that they should be completely immersed in water.

baptistery or **baptistry** /'baptistri/ *noun* (PL. **baptisteries**) 1 the part of a church where baptisms are carried out. 2 a tank of water for baptisms in a Baptist church.

baptize or **baptise** /bap'taız/ *verb* 1 to sprinkle with or dip in water as a sign of having become a member of the Christian Church. In the case of babies, this is usually accompanied by name-giving. 2 to give a name to. [from Greek *baptizein*, to immerse]

■ 1 christen, name, introduce, initiate, enrol, recruit, immerse, sprinkle, purify, cleanse. 2 name, call, term, style, title, nickname.

bar¹ — *noun* 1 a block of some solid substance: *bar of soap.* 2 a rod or long piece of a strong rigid material used as a fastening, weapon, obstruction, etc. 3 anything that prevents or hinders: *a bar to progress.* 4 a line or band of colour, light, etc, especially a stripe on a shield. 5 a room or counter in a restaurant, hotel, etc, or a separate establishment, where alcoholic drinks are sold and drunk. 6 a small café where drinks and snacks are served: *a coffee bar.* 7 a counter where some special service is available: *a heel bar.* 8 a vertical line marked on music, dividing it into sections of equal value; one of these sections. 9 the rail in a law court where the accused person stands. 10 **(the Bar)** the profession of barristers and advocates. 11 a raised area of sand, mud, stones, etc at the mouth of a river or harbour. 12 an addition to a medal, usually to show that it has been won more than once: *DSO and bar.* — *verb* **(barred, barring)** 1 to fasten with a bar. 2 **(bar someone from a place)** to forbid them to enter it. 3 to prevent (progress). 4 to mark with a stripe or bar. — *prep.* except. — **be called to the Bar** to be made a barrister. **behind bars** in prison. [from Old French *barre*]

■ *noun* 1 slab, block, lump, chunk, wedge, ingot, nugget. 2 rod, stick, shaft, pole, stake, stanchion, batten, cross-piece, rail, railing, paling, barricade. 3 obstacle, impediment, hindrance, obstruction, barrier, stop, check, deterrent. 4 stripe, band, chevron, streak. 5 public house, *colloq.* pub, inn, tavern, saloon, lounge, counter. *verb* 1 barricade, lock, bolt, latch, fasten, secure. 2 exclude, debar, ban, forbid, prohibit. 3 prevent, preclude, hinder, hamper, impede, obstruct, restrain. 4 stripe, streak, band.

bar² *noun* a unit of (especially atmospheric) pressure, 10^5 newtons per square metre. See also MILLIBAR. [from Greek *baros*, weight]

barb — *noun* 1 a point on a hook facing in the opposite direction to the main point, which makes it difficult to pull the hook out. 2 a humorous but hurtful remark. — *verb* to fit with barbs. [from Latin *barba*, beard]

barbarian /ba:'beərıən/ — *noun* 1 a person who is cruel and wild in behaviour. 2 a person who is uncivilized and uncultured. — *adj.* typical of a barbarian. [from Greek *barbaros*, foreign]

■ *noun* 1 savage, brute, ruffian, hooligan, vandal, lout, oaf. 2 boor, philistine, ignoramus, illiterate. *adj.* cruel, wild, brutal,

savage, primitive, boorish, uncivilized, uncultured, uneducated, ignorant, illiterate, philistine.

barbaric /ba:'barık/ *adj.* 1 cruel and brutal. 2 coarse and rude.

■ BARBAROUS. 1 cruel, inhuman, brutal, brutish, wild, savage, fierce, ferocious. 2 coarse, crude, rude, uncivilized, uncouth, loutish, oafish, vulgar.
F3 1 humane. 2 civilized, gracious.

barbarically *adv.* in a barbaric or cruel manner; brutally.

barbarism /'ba:bərizm/ *noun* 1 the state of being uncivilized, coarse, etc. 2 a coarse or ignorant act. 3 an utterance which is considered coarse or ungrammatical.

barbarity /ba:'barıtı/ *noun* (PL. **barbarities**) 1 the state of being cruel, coarse, uncivilized, etc. 2 a cruel, coarse, or uncivilized act.

■ 1 cruelty, inhumanity, brutality, wildness, savagery, ferocity, viciousness, barbarousness, brutishness, coarseness, rudeness.
F3 1 civilization, humanity, civility.

barbarous /'ba:bərəs/ *adj.* 1 uncultured and uncivilized. 2 extremely cruel or brutal. 3 coarse or rude.

■ 1 uncivilized, primitive, savage, wild, uncultured, unenlightened, unsophisticated, barbarian. 2 cruel, inhuman, brutal, brutish, savage, fierce, ferocious. 3 coarse, crude, rude, uncouth, loutish, oafish, vulgar.
F3 1 humane. 2 civilized, gracious.

barbarously *adv.* in an uncivilized or brutal manner.

barbarousness *noun* the state of being uncivilized or brutal.

barbecue /'ba:bıkju:/ — *noun* 1 a frame on which food is grilled over an open fire. 2 food cooked in this way. 3 a party held out of doors at which food is cooked on a barbecue. — *verb* to cook on a barbecue. [from S American Arawak *barbacòa*, framework of sticks]

barbed *adj.* 1 having a barb or barbs. 2 *said of a remark* intended to hurt someone.

■ 1 prickly, spiny, thorny, spiked, pronged, hooked, jagged, toothed, pointed. 2 cutting, hurtful, unkind, nasty, spiteful, vindictive, snide, hostile, critical, caustic, acid.

barbed wire wire with short sharp points twisted on at intervals, used for making fences, etc.

barbel *noun* 1 a large freshwater fish (*Barbus barbus*) of the carp family, widespread in European rivers, and having a slender body and four long sensory feelers or *barbels* around the mouth, used for detecting prey. 2 a fleshy whisker-like outgrowth, covered with taste buds, on the mouth or nostril of some fishes, especially catfish or barbels. [from Latin *barba*, beard]

barbell *noun* a bar with heavy metal weights at each end, used for weightlifting exercises.

barber *noun* a person who cuts and styles men's hair, and shaves their beards. [from Old French *barbeor*, from Latin *barba*, beard]

barberry /'ba:bərı/ *noun* (PL. **barberries**) a deciduous or evergreen shrub of the genus *Berberis*, native to north temperate regions and S America, and having long spiny shoots and elongated clusters of small yellow or orange flowers, which are followed by red, yellow, black, or blue fleshy berries. [from Latin *berberis*]

barbershop *noun* a type of singing in which four men sing in close harmony without musical accompaniment.

barbet /'ba:bıt/ *noun* a plump brightly coloured bird that inhabits the tropics worldwide, especially Africa, and is usually a forest-dweller, named after its 'beard' of feathers at the base of its large bill. It feeds on fruit, flowers, and insects. [from Latin *barba*, beard]

barbican /'bɑːbɪkən/ *noun* a tower over the outer gate of a castle or town, allowing the gate to be defended. [from Old French *barbacane*]

barbiturate /bɑːˈbɪtjʊərət/ *noun Medicine* a salt or ester of barbituric acid, used as a source of sedative and hypnotic drugs, eg sleeping pills, and anaesthetics.

barcarole or **barcarolle** /bɑːkəˈrɒl/ *noun* a gondolier's song, or a piece of music with a similar rhythm. [from Italian *barcarola*, boat-song]

bar chart or **bar graph** a graph in which horizontal or vertical rectangular blocks, known as *bars*, are used to represent data, the height or length of the bars being proportional to the quantities they represent. See also PIE CHART.

bar code a series of numbers and black parallel lines of varying thickness, commonly used on product labels such as food packaging and book jackets, and corresponding to binary numbers representing information about the product, such as price, source, and stock level. Bar codes are scanned and 'read' by optical devices known as barcode readers.

bard *noun* 1 *literary* a poet. 2 a poet who has won a prize at the Eisteddfod in Wales. [from Scots Gaelic *bàrd* and Irish Gaelic *bard*, poet]

bardic *adj.* relating to bards or to heroic poetry.

bare — *adj.* 1 not covered by clothes; naked. 2 without the usual or natural covering: *bare trees*. 3 empty: *the cupboard was bare*. 4 simple; plain: *the bare facts*. 5 basic; essential: *the bare necessities*. — *verb* to uncover. — **bare one's heart** or **soul** to make known one's private thoughts and feelings. **lay something bare** to make known a secret, etc. **with one's bare hands** without weapons or tools. [from Anglo-Saxon *bær*]

◨ *adj.* 1 naked, nude, unclothed, undressed, stripped, uncovered. 2 exposed, denuded, barren, leafless, treeless, desolate. 3 empty, unfurnished, unfilled, hollow. 4 plain, simple, unadorned, bald, stark, basic, essential. *verb* uncover, strip, unclothe, expose, denude, divest.

◪ *adj.* 1 clothed. 4 decorated, detailed.

bareback *adv.*, *adj.* riding on a horse without a saddle.

bare bones the essential facts.

barefaced *adj.* having no shame or regret.

barefacedly /bɛəˈfeɪsɪdlɪ/ *adv.* without shame; openly.

barefoot or **barefooted** *adj.*, *adv.* not wearing shoes or socks.

bareheaded *adj.*, *adv.* not wearing a hat.

barelegged *adj.*, *adv.* with the legs uncovered.

barely *adv.* 1 scarcely or only just: *barely enough*. 2 plainly, simply: *barely furnished*.

◨ 1 hardly, scarcely, only just, just, almost.

bareness *noun* being bare or naked.

bargain /'bɑːgɪn/ — *noun* 1 an agreement made between people buying and selling things, offering and accepting services, etc: *strike a bargain*. 2 something offered for sale, or bought, at a low price. — *verb intrans.* to discuss the terms for buying or selling, etc. — **bargain for something** (*often in the negative*) to expect; to be prepared for. **bargain on something** to rely on it or expect it to happen. **drive a hard bargain** to enter into an agreement only after bargaining hard for the best terms. **into the bargain** in addition; besides. [from Old French *bargaine*]

◨ *noun* 1 deal, transaction, contract, treaty, pact, pledge, promise, agreement, understanding, arrangement, negotiation. 2 discount, reduction, *colloq.* snip, give-away, special offer. *verb* negotiate, haggle, deal, trade, traffic,

barter. **bargain for something** expect, anticipate, plan for, reckon on, look for, imagine, contemplate, consider. **bargain on something** rely on, bank on, count on.

bargainer *noun* a person who bargains, especially of a specified kind: *a hard bargainer*.

barge — *noun* 1 a long flat-bottomed boat used on rivers and canals. 2 a large boat, often decorated, used in ceremonies, celebrations, etc. — *verb* 1 (**barge about** or **around**) to move in a clumsy ungraceful way. 2 (**barge in** or **into something**) to hit or knock it clumsily. 3 (**barge past** or **through**) to make one's way rudely or roughly. 4 (**barge in**) to interrupt a conversation, especially rudely or abruptly. [from Old French *barge*, from Latin *barga*]

◨ *noun* 1 canal boat, flatboat, narrow boat, houseboat, lighter. *verb* 2 bump (into), hit, knock (into), collide with. 3 shove, elbow, jostle, push (in), interrupt, butt in, muscle in, intrude, interfere, gatecrash.

bargee /bɑːˈdʒiː/ *noun* a person in charge of a barge.

bargepole *noun* a long pole used to move or guide a barge. — **not touch someone** or **something with a bargepole** *colloq.* to refuse to have anything to do with them.

barite /'bɛəraɪt/ *noun Geol.* barytes.

baritone /'barɪtəʊn/ *noun* 1 the second lowest male singing voice, between bass and tenor. 2 a singer with such a voice. 3 in music, a part that is written for such a voice. [from Greek *barytonos*, deep-sounding]

barium /'bɛərɪəm/ *noun Chem.* symbol Ba, ATOMIC NUMBER 56) a soft silvery-white metal mainly obtained from the mineral barytes. [from Greek *barys*, heavy]

barium meal *Medicine* a preparation of barium sulphate and water drunk by a patient prior to X-ray of the digestive system. It cannot be penetrated by X-rays, and so forms an opaque shadow which shows the outline of the stomach and intestines.

bark¹ — *noun* the short sharp cry of a dog, fox, etc. — *verb* 1 *intrans.* to make this sound. 2 (**bark out** or **bark something out**) to speak loudly and sharply: *barked out a series of commands*. — **bark up the wrong tree** *colloq.* to have the wrong idea. [from Anglo-Saxon *beorcan*]

◨ *noun* yap, woof, yelp, snap, snarl, growl, bay, howl. *verb* 1 yap, woof, yelp, snap, snarl, growl, bay, howl.

bark² — *noun Bot.* the tough protective outer layer, consisting mainly of dead cells, that covers the stems and roots of woody plants, eg trees. It includes all the tissue lying external to the cambium. — *verb* 1 to scrape or rub off the skin from (one's leg). 2 to strip or remove the bark from (a tree, etc). [from Norse *börkr*]

bark³ see BARQUE.

barker *noun* a person outside a circus, show, etc who shouts to attract customers.

barley *noun* 1 a cereal (*Hordeum vulgare*) of the grass family (Gramineae), which bears a dense head of grains with long slender bristles (awns). 2 the grain of this plant, which when partially germinated is used in the brewing of beer and the production of whisky. It is also used as feed for animal livestock. [from Anglo-Saxon *bærlic*, of barley]

barleycorn *noun* same as BARLEY 2.

barley sugar a kind of hard orange-coloured sweet, made by melting and cooling sugar.

barley water a drink made from water in which barley has been boiled, usually with orange or lemon juice added.

barmaid *noun* a woman who serves drinks in a bar.

barman *noun* (PL. **barmen**) a man who serves drinks in a bar.

bar mitzvah /bɑː ˈmɪtsvə/ 1 a Jewish ceremony in which a boy usually aged 13 formally accepts full religious responsibilities. 2 a boy for whom this ceremony is conducted. [from Hebrew *bar mitzvah*, son of the law]

barmy *adj.* (**barmier, barmiest**) *colloq.* crazy. [originally 'bubbling or fermenting', from Anglo-Saxon *beorma*, froth on fermenting liquor]

barn *noun* 1 a building in which grain, hay, etc is stored, or for cattle, etc. 2 a large, bare building. [from Anglo-Saxon *bere*, barley + *ærn*, house]

barnacle /'baːnəkəl/ *noun* a marine crustacean that cements itself firmly by means of its head to rocks, hulls of boats, and other underwater objects. [from Old French *bernaque*]

barnacle goose a goose with a white face and black neck and breast, native to the N Atlantic Ocean, so called because in the Middle Ages it was thought that these geese hatched from goose-necked barnacles.

barn dance 1 a kind of party at which there is music and country dancing, originally held in a barn. 2 a particular kind of country dance.

barney *noun* (PL. **barneys**) *colloq.* a rough noisy quarrel.

barn owl an owl of worldwide distribution, which inhabits forests and open country, has a pale heart-shaped face, and feathered legs.

barnstorm *verb intrans.* 1 to tour a country, stopping briefly in each town to give theatrical performances, formerly often in barns. 2 *North Amer.* to travel about the country making political speeches just before an election.

barnstormer *noun* a person who barnstorms, especially a politician.

barnyard *noun* the area around a barn.

barograph /'barougraːf/ *noun Meteorol.* a type of barometer that produces a continous printed chart recording fluctuations in atmospheric pressure over a period of time. [from Greek *baros*, weight + *graphein*, to write]

barometer /bə'rɒmɪtə(r)/ *noun* 1 *Meteorol.* an instrument for measuring atmospheric pressure, especially in order to predict changes in the weather, or to estimate height above sea level 2 anything that indicates a change: *a barometer of public opinion*. [from Greek *baros*, weight + *metron*, measure]

barometric /barou'metrɪk/ *adj.* relating to the barometer or to atmospheric pressure.

barometrically *adv.* as shown by a barometer.

baron /'barən/ *noun* 1 a man holding the lowest rank of nobility. 2 a powerful businessman: *an oil baron*. [from Latin *baro*, man]

baroness *noun* 1 a baron's wife. 2 a woman holding the title of baron in her own right.

baronet /'barənet/ *noun* (ABBREV. **Bart**) in the UK, a title below that of baron. [diminutive of BARON]

baronetcy *noun* (PL. **baronetcies**) the rank or title of a baronet.

baronial /bə'rouniəl/ *adj.* relating to or suitable for barons.

barony *noun* (PL. **baronies**) 1 the rank of baron. 2 land belonging to a baron.

baroque /bə'rɒk/ — *noun* 1 (*also* **Baroque**) a bold complex decorative style of architecture, art, decoration, and music, popular in Europe from the late 16c to the early 18c. 2 (*also* **the Baroque**) this period in European cultural history. — *adj.* (*also* **Baroque**) 1 written or executed in such a style. 2 excessively complicated or ornate. [from French *baroque*, from Portuguese *barroco*, irregularly shaped pearl]

▣ *adj.* 1 elaborate, ornate, rococo, florid, flamboyant, exuberant, vigorous, bold. 2 convoluted, overdecorated, overwrought, extravagant, fanciful, fantastic, grotesque.

▣ *adj.* PLAIN, SIMPLE.

barperson *noun* a person who serves drinks in a bar.

barque or **bark** /baːk/ *noun* 1 a small sailing ship with three masts. 2 *literary* any boat or small ship. [from French *barque*, from Latin *barca*, small boat]

barrack[1] /'barək/ — *noun* see BARRACKS. — *verb* to house (soldiers) in barracks. [from French *baraque*]

barrack[2] /'barək/ *verb trans., intrans.* to shout and laugh rudely at (a speaker, sports team, etc).

barracking *noun* shouting and jeering at a public meeting, sports event, etc.

barracks *sing. or pl. noun* a building or group of buildings for housing soldiers.

▣ garrison, camp, encampment, guardhouse, quarters, billet, lodging, accommodation.

barracuda /barə'kuːdə/ *noun* (PL. **barracuda, barracudas**) a large predatory marine fish, widespread in tropical and warm temperate waters, and having a long slender body, a pointed head with a jutting lower jaw, and many sharp fang-like teeth. [from Spanish *barracuda*]

barrage /'baraːdʒ/ *noun* 1 a long burst of gunfire which keeps an enemy back while soldiers move forward. 2 a large number of questions, criticisms, etc coming in quickly one after the other. 3 a man-made barrier across a river. [from French *barrage*, from *barrer*, to block]

▣ 1 bombardment, shelling, gunfire, cannonade, broadside, volley, salvo, burst, assault, attack, onset, onslaught. 2 deluge, torrent, stream, storm, hail, rain, shower, mass, profusion.

barrage balloon a large balloon attached to the ground by a cable and often with a net hanging from it, used to prevent attack by low-flying aircraft.

barre /bar/ *noun* a rail fixed to a wall at waist level, which ballet dancers use to balance themselves while exercising. [from French *barre*]

barred *adj.* 1 having bars. 2 closed off; blocked.

barrel /'barəl/ — *noun* 1 a large round container with a flat top and bottom and curving out in the middle, usually made of planks of wood held together with metal bands. 2 the amount a barrel will hold. 3 a measure of capacity, especially of industrial oil. 4 the long hollow tube-shaped part of a gun, pen, etc. — *verb* (**barrelled, barrelling**) to put in barrels. — **have someone over a barrel** to be in a position to get whatever one wants from them. [from Old French *baril*]

▣ *noun* 1 cask, keg, tun, butt, water-butt.

barrel-chested *adj.*, *said of a person* having a large round chest.

barrel organ a large instrument which plays music when a handle is turned.

barrel vault *Archit.* a vault which has a semi-cylindrical roof.

barren *adj.* 1 *said of a living organism* incapable of bearing offspring or producing seed. 2 *said of land* incapable of producing crops, vegetation, etc. 3 not producing results. 4 dull. [from Old French *brahaigne*]

▣ 1 infertile, sterile, childless, unprolific, unbearing. 2 infertile, arid, dry, desert, desolate, waste, empty, unfruitful. 3 unrewarding, unproductive, profitless, fruitless, pointless, useless. 4 dull, uninteresting, uninspiring, boring, flat, uninformative, uninstructive.

▣ 1, 2 fertile. 2, 3 productive, fruitful, useful.

barrenness *noun* 1 a barren or unproductive state. 2 inability to produce children.

barricade /'barɪkeɪd/ — *noun* a barrier made of anything which can be piled up quickly, eg to block a street. — *verb* 1 to block or defend with a barricade. 2 (**barricade someone** or **oneself in**) to shut them away behind a barrier. [from French *barricade*, from *barrique*, barrel: barricades were often made from barrels]

▣ *noun* blockade, obstruction, barrier, fence, stockade, bulwark, rampart, protection. *verb* **1** block, obstruct, bar, fortify, defend, protect.

barrier *noun* **1** a fence, gate, bar, etc put up to defend, block, protect, separate, etc. **2** any thing, circumstance, etc that separates things, people, etc: *a language barrier*. [from Old French *barriere*]

▣ **1** wall, fence, railing, barricade, blockade, boom, rampart, fortification, ditch, frontier, boundary, bar, check. **2** obstacle, hurdle, stumbling-block, impediment, obstruction, hindrance, handicap, limitation, restriction, drawback, difficulty.

barrier cream cream used to protect the skin, especially of the hands, against dirt, oil, and solvents.

barrier island *Geol.* a long straight narrow island or peninsula which generally lies parallel to the coast and is separated from the mainland by a lagoon or salt marsh.

barrier reef a long narrow actively growing coral reef that lies parallel to the coast of a continent or encircles a volcanic island, but is separated from the land by a wide deep lagoon.

barring *prep.* except for; leaving out of consideration: *barring accidents.*

barrister /ˈbarɪstə(r)/ *noun* in England and Wales, a lawyer qualified to act for someone in the higher law courts. [from Latin *barra*, bar]

barrow[1] *noun* **1** a small one-wheeled cart used to carry tools, earth, etc. **2** a larger cart, with two or four wheels, from which goods are often sold in the street. [from Anglo-Saxon *bearwe*, bier]

barrow[2] *noun Archaeol.* a large pile of earth over an ancient grave. [from Anglo-Saxon *beorg*, hill]

barrow boy a boy or man who sells goods from a barrow.

Bart *abbrev.* (*also* **Bart.**) Baronet.

bartender *noun North Amer.* a person who serves drinks in a bar.

▣ barman, barmaid, barkeeper, publican.

barter — *verb trans., intrans.* to trade or exchange (goods or services) without using money. — *noun* trade by exchanging goods rather than selling them for money. [from Old French *barater*, to trick or cheat]

▣ *verb* exchange, swap, trade, traffic, negotiate, bargain.

barterer *noun* a person who barters or exchanges goods.

baryon /ˈbarɪɒn/ *noun Physics* a heavy subatomic particle involved in strong interactions with other subatomic particles and composed of three quarks bound together by gluons. [from Greek *barys*, heavy]

barytes /bəˈraɪtiːz/ *noun Geol.* the mineral form of barium sulphate, the chief ore of barium. Also called BARITE.

baryton or **barytone** /ˈbarɪtɒn/ *noun* an obsolete stringed musical instrument of the violin family, popular during the 17c and 18c. [from Greek *barytonos*, deep-sounded, not accented]

BAS *abbrev.* **1** Bachelor of Agricultural Science. **2** British Antarctic Survey.

basal /ˈbeɪsl/ *adj.* at or forming a base.

basalt /ˈbasɔːlt/ *noun Geol.* a fine-grained dark igneous (volcanic) rock formed by the solidification of thin layers of molten lava that spread out following a volcanic eruption. It is the commonest volcanic rock in the Earth's crust, and is quarried for use in the construction of buildings and roads. [from Greek *basanites*]

basaltic *adj.* consisting of basalt.

base[1] — *noun* **1** the lowest part or bottom; the part which supports something or on which something stands. **2** the origin, root, or foundation of something. **3** a headquarters; a centre of activity or operations. **4** a starting point. **5** the main part of a mixture: *rice is the base of this dish.* **6** *Chem.* any of a group of chemical compounds, eg metal oxides and hydroxides, that can neutralize an acid to form a salt and water. An aqueous solution of a base contains OH^- ions and will turn litmus blue. **7** *Baseball* one of several fixed points which players run between. **8** *Maths.* in a numerical system, the number of different symbols used, eg in the binary number system the base is two, because only the symbols 0 and 1 are used. In the decimal system the base is 10. **9** *Maths.* in logarithms, the number that when raised to a certain power has a logarithm equal in value to that power. In common logarithms the base is 10; in natural logarithms the base is *e*. **10** *Geom.* the usually horizontal line or surface on which a geometric figure rests. — *verb* **1** to found or establish (an argument, etc): *reasoning based on self-interest.* **2** to give as a headquarters or centre of operations: *troops based in France.* [from Latin *basis*, pedestal]

▣ *noun* **1** bottom, foot, pedestal, plinth, stand, rest, support, foundation, bed, groundwork. **2** root, origin, source, basis, foundation, fundamental, essential, key, heart, core, essence. **3** headquarters, centre, post, station, camp, settlement. *verb* **1** establish, found, ground, build, construct, derive. **2** locate, station, install, establish, post, garrison.

base[2] *adj.* **1** lacking morals; wicked. **2** not pure. **3** low in value. [from Latin *bassus*, low, short]

▣ **1** immoral, wicked, ignoble, dishonourable, disreputable, unprincipled, degenerate, treacherous.

baseball *noun* **1** a team game played with a bat and ball on a diamond-shaped pitch by two teams each with nine players. **2** the ball used in this game.

baseless *adj.* having no cause or foundation: *baseless fears.*

▣ groundless, unfounded, unsupported, unsubstantiated, unauthenticated, unconfirmed, unjustified, uncalled-for, gratuitous.
▣ justifiable.

baseline *noun* **1** one of the two lines which mark the ends of a tennis court. **2** an amount or value taken as a basis for comparison.

basely *adv.* impurely, immorally.

basement *noun* the lowest floor of a building, usually below ground level.

base metal any metal that readily corrodes, tarnishes, or oxidizes on exposure to air, moisture, or heat, eg zinc, copper, and lead, as opposed to a precious metal such as gold or silver.

baseness *noun* immorality; wickedness.

base rate the rate used by a bank to fix its charges for lending money to customers.

bases pl. of BASE[1], BASE[2], BASIS.

BASF *abbrev. Badische Anilin und Soda-Fabrik* (a German chemical company).

bash — *verb colloq.* **1** to strike or smash bluntly. **2** (**bash someone up**) to attack someone violently. **3** (**bash something down** or **in**) to damage or break by striking very hard. **4** (**bash into something**) to collide violently with it. — *noun* **1** a heavy blow or knock. **2** a mark caused by a heavy blow. **3** *slang* a noisy party. — **have a bash at something** *colloq.* to attempt it.

bashful *adj.* lacking confidence; shy. [from Old French *abaissier*, to bring low]

▣ shy, retiring, backward, reticent, reserved, unforthcoming, hesitant, shrinking, nervous, timid, coy, diffident, modest,

inhibited, self-conscious, embarrassed, blushing, abashed, shamefaced, sheepish.
- ✤ bold, confident, aggressive.

bashfully *adv.* with a shy or bashful manner.

bashfulness *noun* being shy or bashful.

-bashing *combining form colloq.* forming words meaning:
1 making strong and often unjustified physical or verbal attacks on a person or group of people that one dislikes or is opposed to: *union-bashing*. **2** any of various other activities associated with the word *bash*: *Bible-bashing* (enthusiastic evangelical Christian preaching).

BASIC /'beɪsɪk/ *noun Comput.* a high-level computer programming language. [from *Beginner's All-purpose Symbolic Instruction Code*]

basic — *adj.* **1** of or forming the base or basis. **2** of or at a very simple or low level. **3** without additions: *basic pay.* — *noun* (*usually* **basics**) the essential parts or facts; the simplest principles. [from Latin *basis*, pedestal]

- ✤ *adj.* **1** fundamental, root, underlying, bottom, key, central, inherent, intrinsic, essential, indispensable, vital, necessary, important. **2** elementary, rudimentary, primary, introductory. *noun* fundamentals, rudiments, principles, essentials, necessaries, practicalities, *colloq.* brass tacks, grass roots, bedrock, rock bottom, core, facts.
- ✤ *adj.* **1** inessential, minor, peripheral. **2** complicated.

basically /'beɪsɪklɪ/ *adv.* mostly, essentially; described in simple or general terms: *the argument is basically sound.*

- ✤ essentially, fundamentally, at bottom, at heart, inherently, intrinsically, principally, primarily.

Basic English a simplified version of English with a vocabulary of 850 words supplemented by international words (eg names of countries), and scientific words.

basic-oxygen process or **basic process** *Engineering* the most widely used method of producing steel, in which oxygen is blown at high pressure through molten pig iron.

basil /'bazɪl/ *noun* a bushy aromatic annual plant (*Ocimum basilicum*), native to the tropics, and having square stems, purplish-green oval leaves, and white or purplish two-lipped flowers, borne in whorls. It is widely cultivated in Europe, Africa, tropical Asia, and N America as a culinary herb. [from Old French *basile*, from Greek *basilikon*, royal]

basilica /bə'zɪlɪkə/ *noun* **1** an ancient Roman public hall, with a rounded wall at one end and a row of stone pillars along each side, used as a lawcourt. **2** a church shaped like this. [from Greek *basilike*, hall]

basilisk /'bazɪlɪsk/ *noun* **1** a mythical serpent which could kill with a glance or breath. It was so named, according to Pliny, from its crown-like crest. **2** any of various species of lizard, related to the iguanas, native to tropical forests of Central and S America. [from Greek *basiliskos*, prince]

basin *noun* **1** a wide shallow circular container or dish, used to hold water and other liquids. **2** a bowl or sink in a bathroom, etc for washing oneself in. **3** the amount a basin will hold. **4** the area drained by a river and its tributaries: *Mississippi basin.* **5** *Geol.* a low-lying area of land, surrounded wholly or in part by higher land, or any area in which rock beds dip downward from all sides toward a central point. **6** the deep part of a harbour. [from Latin *bacinum*, water vessel]

basis *noun* (PL. **bases**) **1** a principle on which an idea, theory, etc is based. **2** a starting point: *a basis for discussion.* **3** the main part of a mixture. [from Latin *basis*, pedestal]

- ✤ **1** principle, premise, base, foundation, fundamental. **2** foundation, groundwork, support. **3** heart, core, essence.

bask /bɑːsk/ *verb intrans.* to lie in comfort, especially in warmth or sunshine. — **bask in something** to enjoy and take great pleasure in something: *basking in her approval.* [from Norse *bathask*, to bathe]

- ✤ sunbathe, lie, lounge, relax, laze, wallow. **bask in something** revel in, delight in, enjoy, relish, savour.

basket *noun* **1** a container made of strips of wood or cane, woven together. **2** the amount a basket will hold. **3** one of two nets into which the ball is thrown in basketball. **4** a goal scored in basketball.

- ✤ **1** hamper, creel, pannier, punnet, bassinet.

basketball *noun* **1** a game in which two teams of five players score by throwing a ball into a net on a high post at each end of the court. **2** the ball used in this game.

basket case 1 a person who is agitated and seems unable to cope. **2** a country with a struggling economy.

basket chair a chair made from strips of wood or cane woven together.

basketful *noun* (PL. **basketfuls**) the amount a basket will hold.

basketry *noun* the art or business of making baskets.

basketwork *noun* **1** articles made of strips of wood or cane woven together. **2** the art of making these.

basking shark a large but harmless shark, the second-largest living fish, up to 10m in length, and weighing about 6000kg.

Basque /bɑːsk/ — *noun* **1** a member of a people living in the western Pyrenees, in Spain and France. **2** the language spoken by these people. — *adj.* relating to the Basque people or their language. [from French *Basque*, from Latin *Vasco*]

basque *noun* a tight-fitting garment for women, covering the body between the shoulders and the hips.

bas-relief /basrɪ'liːf/ *noun* a technique of cutting and shaping stone or wood so that the figures on it are only slightly raised from the background. [a French word, from Italian *basso rilievo*, low relief]

bass[1] /beɪs/ — *noun* **1** the lowest male singing voice. **2** a singer with such a voice. **3** in music, a part written for such a voice or for an instrument of the lowest range. **4** *colloq.* a bass guitar or double bass. — *adj.* sounding, singing, or playing at a low musical pitch. [from Latin *bassus*, low]

- ✤ *adj.* deep, low, low-toned, grave, resonant.

bass[2] /bas/ *noun* (PL. **bass, basses**) **1** (*in full* **common bass**) a marine fish (*Perca fluviatilis*), resembling but unrelated to the salmon, found in European coastal waters, especially near rocks and reefs, and having a greenish-grey body with silvery sides, and spiny fins. **2** any of various freshwater and marine fishes, especially N American species, having spiny fins similar to those of the common bass. [from Anglo-Saxon *bærs*, perch]

bass clef a sign at the beginning of a piece of written music which places the note F below middle C on the fourth line of the staff.

bass drum a large drum that produces a very low sound.

basset *noun* **1** (*in full* **basset hound**) a breed of dog having a long body with a short black, tan, and white coat, short legs, a long broad muzzle, and long pendulous ears, formerly used in France and Belgium for hunting. **2** *Geol.* an outcrop, representing the edge of a geological structure exposed at the Earth's surface. [from French *bas*, low]

basset horn a musical instrument of the clarinet family, with a lower range of pitch than that of a standard clarinet. [a partial translation of French *cor de bassette* and Italian *corno di bassetto*]

bass guitar or **bass** in popular music, an electric guitar which plays the bass part.

bassinet /'basɪnet/ *noun* a baby's basket-like bed or pram, usually covered at one end. [diminutive of French *bassin*, basin]

bassist /'beɪsɪst/ *noun* a person who plays a bass guitar or double bass.

bassoon /bə'suːn/ *noun* a woodwind instrument with a double reed, producing a deep plangent sound. [from Italian *basso*, low]

bassoonist *noun* a person who plays a bassoon.

bast /bast/ *noun* threads of the soft inner bark of some trees, woven together and used to make ropes, mats, etc. [from Anglo-Saxon *bæst*]

bastard /'bɑːstəd/ — *noun* 1 often *offensive* a child born of parents not married to each other. 2 *coarse slang* a term of abuse or sympathy for a man: *rotten bastard / poor bastard*. 3 *coarse slang* something annoying or difficult. — *adj.* 1 born to parents not married to each other. 2 not genuine, standard, original or pure. [from Latin *bastardus*]

bastardization or **bastardisation** *noun* the process of making something less genuine or pure.

bastardize or **bastardise** *verb* to make less genuine or pure.

bastardized or **bastardised** *adj.* impure; no longer genuine.

bastardy /'bɑːstədɪ/ *noun* the state of being a bastard.

baste[1] *verb* to pour hot fat or butter over (especially roasting meat).

baste[2] /beɪst/ *verb* to sew with temporary loose stitches. [from German *basten*, to sew]

baste[3] *verb* to beat or thrash. [probably from Norse *beysta*]

bastinado /bastɪ'neɪdoʊ/ — *noun* (PL. **bastinadoes**) beating of the soles of the feet with a stick as torture or punishment. — *verb* (**bastinadoes, bastinadoed**) to beat on the soles of the feet with a stick. [from Spanish *bastonada*, from *bastón*, stick]

bastion /'bastɪən/ *noun* 1 a kind of tower which sticks out at an angle from a castle wall. 2 a person, place, or thing regarded as a defender of a principle, etc. [from Italian *bastire*, to build]

⊟ 1 stronghold, citadel, fortress, defence. 2 bulwark, mainstay, support, prop, pillar, rock.

BASW *abbrev.* British Association of Social Workers.

BAT *abbrev.* British-American Tobacco Company.

bat[1] — *noun* 1 a shaped piece of wood, with a flat or curved surface, for hitting the ball in cricket, baseball, table tennis, etc. See also RACKET. 2 a batsman, especially in cricket. — *verb* (**batted, batting**) 1 *intrans.* to take a turn at hitting a ball with a bat in cricket, baseball, etc. 2 to hit with, or as if with, a bat. — **off one's own bat** 1 without help. 2 without being prompted by anyone else. [from Anglo-Saxon *batt*]

bat[2] *noun* any of more than 1000 species of nocturnal mammal, the only mammal capable of sustained flight, found mainly in the tropics, and also widely distributed in warm and temperate regions. — **have bats in the belfry** *colloq.* to be crazy or slightly mad. See also BATS, BATTY. **like a bat out of hell** *colloq.* very fast. [from Middle English *bakke*]

bat[3] *verb* (**batted, batting**) to open and close (one's eyelids) very quickly, usually to attract sympathy or admiration. — **not bat an eye** or **eyelid** *colloq.* to show no surprise or emotion. [from Middle English *baten*, to flap]

batch — *noun* a number of things or people prepared, delivered, dealt with, etc at the same time. — *verb* to arrange in batches. [from Middle English *bache*, from Anglo-Saxon *bacan*, to bake]

⊟ *noun* lot, consignment, parcel, pack, bunch, set, assortment, collection, assemblage, group, contingent, amount, quantity.

batch file *Comput.* a text file containing a series of commands which are executed in order when the name of the file is called.

batch processing *Comput.* a procedure whereby a number of batches of data are prepared in advance and then processed periodically in a single program run, eg overnight. It is widely used for frequently repeated tasks, such as the processing of a company payroll.

bated — **with bated breath** feeling anxiety, excitement, or fear. [from ABATE]

bath — *noun* 1 a large open container for water, in which to wash the whole body. 2 an act of washing the body in a bath. 3 the water filling a bath: *run a bath*. 4 (**baths**) a public swimming pool. 5 a liquid, or its container, in which something is washed, etc, usually as part of a technical process such as developing photographs. 6 (**Order of the Bath**) a British order of chivalry. — *verb trans., intrans.* to wash in a bath. [from Anglo-Saxon *bæth*]

⊟ *noun* 1 tub, trademark Jacuzzi. 2 wash, scrub, soak, shower, douche. *verb* bathe, wash, clean, soak, shower.

Bath bun a small sweet cake.

Bath chair *formerly* a kind of chair with three wheels in which an invalid can be pushed.

bathcube *noun* a small block of bath salts.

bathe /beɪð/ — *verb* 1 *intrans.* to swim in the sea, etc for pleasure. 2 *intrans. chiefly North Amer.* to have a bath. 3 to wash or treat (part of the body) with water, a liquid, etc to clean it or to lessen pain. 4 to cover and surround (eg in light). — *noun* an act of swimming in the sea, etc. [from Anglo-Saxon *bathian*, to wash]

⊟ *verb* 1 swim. 3 wash, cleanse, rinse, wet, moisten, immerse, soak, steep. 4 cover, suffuse, flood, drench. *noun* swim, dip, paddle.

bather *noun* a person who bathes or is bathing.

bathetic /bə'θetɪk/ *adj.* characterized by bathos.

bathing cap a tight rubber cap worn to keep the hair dry when swimming.

bathing costume a swimming costume or swimsuit.

batholith /'baθɒlɪθ/ *noun Geol.* a large igneous rock mass, typically granite, that has intruded while molten into the surrounding rock. [from Greek *bathos*, depth, or *bathys*, deep + *lithos*, stone]

bathos /'beɪθɒs/ *noun literary* in speech or writing, a sudden change from very important, serious, or beautiful ideas to very ordinary or trivial ones. [from Greek *bathos*, depth]

bathrobe *noun* a loose towelling coat used before and after taking a bath.

bathroom *noun* 1 a room containing a bath and often other washing facilities. 2 a room with a lavatory.

bath salts a sweet-smelling substance in the form of large grains, which perfumes and softens the water in a bath.

bathtub *noun* a movable or fixed receptacle for a bath.

bathymetry /bə'θɪmətrɪ/ *noun Geol.* the measurement of the depths of sea bottom features in large bodies of water, especially by echo-sounding. [from Greek *bathys*, deep]

bathyscaphe or **bathyscaph** /'baθɪskaf/ *noun* an electrically powered crewed vessel with a spherical observation cabin on its underside, used for exploring the ocean depths. [from Greek *bathys*, deep + *skaphos*, ship]

bathysphere /'baθɪsfɪə(r)/ *noun* a deep-sea observation chamber, consisting of a spherical watertight steel sphere that is lowered and raised from a surface vessel such as a ship by means of cables. It has now been largely superseded by the bathyscaphe. [from Greek *bathys*, deep + SPHERE]

batik /ba'ti:k/ *noun* **1** a technique of printing coloured patterns on cloth, in which those parts not to be coloured or dyed are covered with wax. **2** cloth coloured in this way. [from Malay]

batman *noun* (PL. **batmen**) an officer's personal servant in the armed forces. [from French *bat*, pack-saddle]

baton /'batɒn/ *noun* **1** a light thin stick used by the conductor of an orchestra. **2** a short heavy stick carried by a policeman as a weapon. **3** a short stick passed from one runner to another in a relay race. **4** a stick carried by a person at the head of a marching band. [from French *bâton*, stick]

bats *adj. colloq.* crazy. [from the phrase *have bats in the belfry*]

batsman or **batswoman** *noun* a person who bats or is batting in cricket.

battalion /bə'talɪən/ *noun* an army unit made up of several smaller units (companies), and forming part of a larger unit (a brigade). [from French *bataillon*, from Italian *battaglione*, squadron of soldiers]

▣ unit, force, brigade, regiment, squadron, company, platoon, division, contingent, army, legion, horde, multitude, throng, host.

battels *pl. noun Brit.* accounts for provisions received from college kitchens and butteries, especially at Oxford University. [perhaps connected with dialect *battle*, to feed]

batten — *noun* **1** a long flat piece of wood used for keeping other pieces in place. **2** a strip of wood used to fasten the covers over the hatches in a ship's deck, etc. — *verb* to fasten or shut with battens. — **batten down the hatches** to prepare for a danger or crisis. [from Old French *batre*, to beat]

batter¹ *verb* (**battered**, **battering**) **1** *trans., intrans.* to strike or hit hard and often, or continuously. **2** (**batter something down** or **in**) to break down or to destroy by battering. **3** to damage or wear through continual use. **4** to subject (someone) to repeated physical violence. [from Old French *batre*, to beat]

▣ **1** beat, pound, pummel. **2** break down, smash, demolish, destroy, ruin, wreck. **3** damage, wear down, wear out, erode, mangle, distress. **4** abuse, maltreat, ill-treat, assault, hurt, injure, bruise, disfigure.

batter² *noun* a mixture of eggs, flour, and either milk or water, beaten together and used in cooking. [from Old French *bateure*, beating]

batter³ *noun* a person who bats or is batting, especially in baseball. See also BATSMAN.

battered *adj.* coated and cooked in batter.

battering *noun* a beating.

battering-ram *noun* a large wooden beam with a metal head, formerly used in war for breaking down walls or gates.

battery *noun* (PL. **batteries**) **1** a device that converts chemical energy into electrical energy in the form of direct current, eg a car battery. Dry batteries, in which the electrolyte is in the form of a paste instead of a liquid, are used as portable energy sources in torches, etc. See also ELECTROLYTIC CELL. **2** a number of similar things: *a battery of questions*. **3** a long line of small cages in which eg hens are kept. **4** *Legal* a physical attack on a person. See also ASSAULT AND BATTERY. **5** a group of heavy guns and the place where they are mounted. [from French *batterie*, from *battre*, to strike]

battle — *noun* **1** a fight between opposing armies or people. **2** fighting; warfare. **3** a competition between opposing groups or people: *a battle of wits*. **4** a long or difficult struggle: *a battle for equality*. — *verb intrans.* **1** to fight. **2** to struggle; to campaign vigorously or defiantly. — **do battle** to fight. **fight a losing battle** to try to do something

which is sure to fail. **half the battle** something that takes one well on the way to success. **join battle** to begin to fight. [from French *bataille*]

▣ *noun* **1** fight, engagement, encounter, combat, attack, fray, skirmish, row, disagreement, dispute, debate. **2** warfare, war, combat, hostilities, action, conflict, strife. **3** competition, contest, bout, clash, encounter, tournament, rivalry. **4** struggle, campaign, crusade, movement. *verb* **1** fight, combat, war, feud, contend, contest, argue, dispute. **2** struggle, strive, campaign, crusade, agitate, clamour.

battle-axe *noun* **1** a type of axe formerly used in warfare. **2** *colloq.* a fierce and domineering older woman.

battle-cruiser *noun* a large warship, the same size as a battleship but faster and with fewer guns.

battle-cry *noun* **1** a shout given by soldiers charging into battle. **2** a slogan.

▣ **1** war cry, war song. **2** slogan, motto, watchword, catchword.

battledress *noun* a soldier's ordinary uniform.

battle fatigue or **combat fatigue** a usually temporary mental disorder caused by the anxiety of fighting for a long time.

battlement *noun* a low wall around the top of a castle, etc with gaps for shooting through. [from Old French *bataillier*, to provide with ramparts]

battleship *noun* the largest type of warship.

batty *adj.* (**battier**, **battiest**) *colloq.* crazy; eccentric. [from BAT²]

bauble /'bɔːbl/ *noun* a small cheap ornament or piece of jewellery. [from Old French *babel*, a child's toy]

baud rate /bɔːd/ *Comput.* the speed at which information is passed between computers, eg along a telephone line, given in bits per second. [named after the French inventor Emil Baudot]

baulk see BALK.

bauxite /'bɔːksaɪt/ *noun Geol.* the main ore of aluminium, consisting of a white, yellow, red, or brown claylike substance that is formed by the weathering of igneous rocks in tropical regions. [from the name *Les Baux* in S France, where it was first found]

bawdily *adv.* with bawdy or coarse humour.

bawdiness *noun* being bawdy; coarse humour.

bawdy *adj.* (**bawdier**, **bawdiest**) *said of language, writing, etc* containing coarsely humorous references to sex. [from Old French *baude*, dissolute]

▣ coarse, lewd, ribald, smutty, earthy.

bawl *verb intrans., trans.* (*also* **bawl out**) to cry or shout loudly. — **bawl someone out** *colloq.* to scold them angrily. [from Latin *baulare*, to bark]

▣ shout, scream, shriek, yell, *colloq.* holler, bellow, roar.

bay¹ *noun* a body of water that forms a wide-mouthed indentation in the coastline. It is larger than a cove, and differs from a gulf in that it is usually broader at its seaward end than it is long. [from Old French *baie*]

▣ gulf, bight, arm, inlet, cove.

bay² *noun* **1** a small area of a room set back into a wall. **2** an area for parking vehicles, or for loading and unloading. **3** a compartment for storing or carrying. **4** an enclosed or partly enclosed area within a building for storage or some other purpose. [from Old French *baer*, to gape]

1 recess, alcove, niche, nook, opening. **4** compartment, cubicle, booth, stall, carrel.

bay³ — adj., said of a horse reddish-brown in colour. — noun a bay-coloured horse. [from Old French bai, chestnut-coloured]

bay⁴ noun **1** any of various evergreen trees of the laurel family, having shiny dark green leaves, especially the Mediterranean laurel (Laurus nobilis), the dried leaves of which are often used as a flavouring agent during the cooking of soups and stews. **2** (usually **bays**) a wreath of bay leaves, usually worn on the head by champions in some competitions, etc. [from Old French baie]

bay⁵ — verb intrans., said of a dog to make a deep howling bark or cry, especially when hunting. — noun the baying sound of a dog. — **at bay 1** not able to escape, forced to face an attacker. **2** at a distance: keep poverty at bay. **bring to bay** to trap. [from Old French abai, barking]

▤ verb howl, roar, bellow, bell, bawl, cry, colloq. holler, bark.

bayonet /'beɪənɛt/ — noun a steel knife fixed to the end of a soldier's rifle. — verb (**bayoneted, bayoneting**) to stab with a bayonet. [from French baïnnette, from Bayonne in SW France, where bayonets were first made]

bayou /'baɪuː/ noun in the US, a marshy offshoot of a lake or river. [from Louisiana French]

bay window a three-sided or rounded window that juts out from the wall of a building.

bazaar /bə'zɑː(r)/ noun **1** in Eastern countries a market place. **2** a sale of goods, etc, usually in order to raise money for a particular organization or purpose. [from Persian bazar, market]

▤ **1** market, market-place, mart, exchange, souk. **2** sale, fair, fête, bring-and-buy.

bazooka /bə'zuːkə/ noun a gun which fires small rockets, especially at tanks. [from the name of a toy wind-instrument]

bazouki same as BOUZOUKI.

BB abbrev. **1** Boys' Brigade. **2** on pencils very black.

BBB abbrev., on pencils blacker than BB.

BBBC abbrev. British Boxing Board of Control.

BBC abbrev. British Broadcasting Corporation.

BBFC abbrev. **1** British Board of Film Censors. **2** British Board of Film Classification.

BBSRC abbrev. Biotechnology and Biological Sciences Research Council.

BC or **B.C.** abbrev. **1** before (the birth of) Christ: used in dates. See also AD. **2** British Columbia.

BCC abbrev. British Council of Churches.

BCE or **B.C.E.** abbrev. before the common era: used instead of BC in dates.

BCG or **bcg** abbrev. bacillus Calmette-Guérin, a vaccine given to a person to prevent tuberculosis.

BCL abbrev. Bachelor of Civil Law.

BCom. or **BComm.** abbrev. Bachelor of Commerce.

BD abbrev. **1** Bachelor of Divinity. **2** as an international vehicle mark Bangladesh.

BDA abbrev. British Dental Association.

BDI abbrev. Bundesverband der Deutschen Industrie (German) Federation of German Industry.

BDS abbrev., as an international vehicle mark Barbados.

BE abbrev. Bachelor of Engineering.

Be symbol Chem. beryllium.

be /biː/ — verb (PRESENT TENSE **am, are, is, are**; PAST TENSE **was, were**; PAST PARTICIPLE **been**) intrans. **1** to exist or live: I think, therefore I am. **2** to occur or take place: lunch is in an hour. **3** to occupy a position in space: she is at

home. **4** (in past tense) to go: he's never been to Italy. **5** to remain or continue without change: let it be. **6** used to link a subject and what is said about it: she is a doctor/he is ill. **7** intrans. used with the infinitive form of a verb to express a possibility, command, intention, outcome, etc: if it were to rain/we are to come tomorrow/it was not to be. — verb, aux. **1** used with the past participle of a verb to form a passive: the film was shown last night. **2** used with a present participle to form the continuous tenses: he was running. — **the be-all and end-all** the only thing of importance. **be that as it may** although that may be true. [present tense from Anglo-Saxon beon, to live or exist; past tense from Anglo-Saxon weran, to be]

▤ verb **1** exist, breathe, live, inhabit, reside, dwell. **2** happen, occur, arise, come about, take place, come to pass, befall, develop. **4** go, travel, journey. **5** stay, remain, abide, last, endure, persist, continue, survive, stand, prevail.

be- an element forming words meaning: **1** all over or all around; thoroughly or completely: beset/bedazzle. **2** considering as or causing to be: befriend/benumb. **3** having or covered with; affected by: bejewelled. **4** affecting someone or something by an action: bereave. [from Anglo-Saxon]

BEAB abbrev. British Electrical Approvals Board.

beach — noun the sandy or stony shore of a sea or lake. — verb to push or pull (a boat) on to a beach.

▤ noun sand, sands, shingle, shore, strand, seashore, seaside, coast, seaboard, bank, riverside, lakeside, water's edge.

beachcomber noun a person who searches beaches for things of interest or value.

beachcombing noun the activity of searching beaches for things of interest or value.

beachhead noun an area of shore captured from the enemy, on which an army can land men and equipment.

beacon noun **1** a fire on a hill or mountain, lit as a signal. **2** Brit. (chiefly in place names) a hill, etc on which a beacon could be lit. **3** a warning or guiding device for aircraft or ships, eg a lighthouse. **4** (in full **radio beacon**) a radio transmitter that broadcasts signals. [from Anglo-Saxon beacen]

▤ **1** signal, fire, watch fire, bonfire. **3** light, beam, lighthouse, flare, rocket, sign.

bead — noun **1** a small and usually round ball of glass, stone, etc strung with others, eg in a necklace. **2** (**beads**) a string of beads worn as jewellery, or one used when praying; a rosary. **3** a small drop of liquid: beads of sweat. — verb to decorate with beads. — **draw a bead on something** colloq. to aim a gun at it. [from Anglo-Saxon biddan, to pray]

▤ noun **1** pearl, jewel. **3** drop, droplet, drip, globule, colloq. glob, blob, dot, bubble.

beaded adj. consisting of or in the form of beads.

beading noun thin strips of patterned wood used to decorate the edges of furniture, walls, etc.

beadle noun **1** a person who leads formal processions in church or some old British universities. **2** in Scotland, a church officer. **3** formerly in England, a minor parish official who had the power to punish minor offences. [from Anglo-Saxon bydel, from beodan, to proclaim]

beady adj. (**beadier, beadiest**) usually derog., said of a person's eyes small, round, and bright.

beagle — noun a medium-sized breed of hunting dog with a sturdy body, broad pendulous ears, a deep muzzle, and usually a short white, tan, and black coat. — verb intrans. to hunt with beagles. [from Old French baer, to gape + goule, throat, mouth]

beak noun **1** the horny projecting jaws of a bird. Also called BILL. **2** any pointed projection that resembles this, eg the projecting jaws of certain fishes (eg sawfish) and other animals. **3** colloq. a nose, especially if big and pointed. **4** Brit. old slang use a headmaster, judge, or magistrate. [from Old French bec]

beaked adj. having a beak.

beaker noun **1** a large drinking-glass, or a large (often plastic) cup without a handle. **2** a deep glass container with a lip, used in chemistry. **3** the amount a beaker will hold. [from Norse bikarr]

▣ **1, 3** glass, tumbler, jar, cup, mug, tankard.

beakerful noun (PL. **beakerfuls**) the amount a beaker will hold.

beam — noun **1** a long straight thick piece of wood, used eg in a building. **2** the widest part of a ship or boat. **3** a ray of light. **4** the part of a set of scales from which the weighing-pans hang. **5** a narrow wooden bar on which gymnasts perform balancing exercises. — verb **1** intrans. to smile broadly with pleasure. **2** intrans. to shine. **3** trans. to send out (rays of light, radio waves, etc). — **broad in the beam** colloq. having wide hips. **off beam** colloq. wrong; misguided. **on the beam** colloq. on the right track. **on one's beam ends** Brit. colloq. with only a very small amount of money left. **on the port** or **starboard beam** Naut. on the left, or right, side of a ship. [from Anglo-Saxon, = tree]

▣ noun **1** plank, board, timber, rafter, joist, girder, spar, boom, bar, support. **3** ray, shaft, gleam, glint, glimmer, glow. verb **1** smile, grin. **2** shine, glare, glitter, glow, glimmer. **3** emit, broadcast, transmit, radiate.

bean noun **1** the edible kidney-shaped seed of plants belonging to the pea family (Leguminosae), especially those of the genus Phaseolus, eg runner bean. **2** any plant belonging to the pea family that bears such seeds. **3** any other seed that superficially resembles those of the pea family, eg coffee bean. — **full of beans** colloq. full of energy; lively and cheerful. [from Anglo-Saxon]

bean bag 1 a small cloth bag filled with dried beans, or something similar, thrown like a ball in children's games. **2** a very large floor cushion.

bean curd a soft paste made with soya beans, used in Chinese and vegetarian cookery.

beanfeast noun Brit. colloq. a party or celebration.

beansprout or **beanshoot** noun the young shoot of the mung bean or certain other beans, used as a vegetable, especially in Chinese cookery.

beanstalk noun the stem of a bean plant.

bear[1] /beə(r)/ verb (PAST TENSE **bore**; PAST PARTICIPLE **borne**, **born** in sense 4 also) **1** to carry, bring, or take: bear gifts. **2** to support (a weight). **3** to produce: bear fruit. **4** past participle in the passive is **born**, or **borne** when followed by by and a name) to give birth to: has she borne children?/a child borne by Mary/he was born in 1960. **5** to take or accept: bear the blame. **6** to put up with or like. **7** to show or be marked by: bear the traces of tears. **8** to carry in thought or memory: bear a grudge. **9** intrans. to turn slightly in a given direction: bear left. **10** to have: bear no resemblance to. **11** to behave: bear oneself well. — **bear down on someone** to move towards them threateningly. **bear on something** to affect or concern it. **bear something** or **someone out** to support or confirm them: the evidence bears him out. **bear up** said of a person to remain strong, brave, etc under strain. **bear with someone** to be patient with them. **bring something to bear** to apply pressure or influence. [from Anglo-Saxon beran]

▣ **1** carry, take, bring, convey, transport, move, remove. **2** hold, support, shoulder, uphold, sustain, maintain. **3** produce, generate, develop, yield, bring forth. **4** give birth to, breed, propagate, engender, beget, old use bring forth. **5**

accept, carry, admit, acknowledge. **6** tolerate, stand, put up with, endure, abide, suffer, permit, allow, admit. **7** show, exhibit, manifest, present, reveal. **8** harbour, cherish, entertain, foster, nourish, nurture. **9** turn, veer, bend, curve, swerve. **bear on** affect, concern, refer to, relate to, involve. **bear out** confirm, endorse, support, uphold, prove, demonstrate, corroborate, substantiate, vindicate, justify. **bear up** persevere, soldier on, carry on, suffer, endure, survive, withstand. **bear with someone** tolerate, put up with, endure, suffer, forbear, be patient with, make allowances for.

bear[2] /beə(r)/ noun **1** any of various large carnivorous animals belonging to the family Ursidae, and having heavily built bodies covered with thick fur, short powerful limbs, small eyes and ears, strong claws, and short tails. **2** a rough ill-mannered person. **3** Stock Exchange a person who sells shares, hoping to buy them back later at a much lower price. [from Anglo-Saxon bera]

bearable adj. able to be suffered or tolerated.

▣ tolerable, endurable, sufferable, supportable, sustainable, acceptable, manageable.
▣ unbearable, intolerable.

bearably adv. in a bearable or tolerable way; to a tolerable degree: bearably cold.

beard /bɪəd/ — noun **1** the hair that grows on a man's chin and cheeks. **2** a beard-like growth on certain animals, especially the hairy tuft on the lower jaw of a goat. **3** the awns or hair-like spikes on the head of barley and certain other grasses. — verb to face or oppose openly or boldly. [from Anglo-Saxon]

bearded adj. having a beard, or a growth resembling a beard.

▣ unshaven, bristly, stubbly, whiskered, tufted, hairy, hirsute, shaggy, bushy.
▣ beardless, clean-shaven, smooth.

beardless adj. lacking a beard.

bearer noun **1** a person or thing that bears or carries. **2** a person who helps carry equipment on an expedition. **3** a person who holds a banknote, cheque, or other money order which can be exchanged for money.

▣ **1** carrier, conveyor, porter, courier, messenger, runner. **2** porter, Sherpa. **3** holder, possessor, payee.

bear-garden noun a noisy or rowdy gathering or scene.
bear hug colloq. a rough tight squeeze with the arms.
bearing noun **1** the way a person stands, walks, etc. **2** a relation or effect: that has no bearing on the situation. **3** the horizontal direction of a fixed point, or the path of a moving object, measured from a reference point on the Earth's surface, and normally expressed as an angle measured in degrees clockwise from the north. **4** (usually **bearings**) position, or a calculation of position: a ship's bearings. **5** (**bearings**) colloq. a sense or awareness of one's own position or surroundings: lose one's bearings. **6** any part of a machine or device that supports another part and allows free movement between the two parts, eg a ball bearing which allows a shaft to rotate freely within a housing.

▣ **1** demeanour, manner, mien, air, aspect, attitude, behaviour, comportment, poise, deportment, carriage, posture. **2** relation, reference, relevance, significance, connection. **5** position, location, situation, whereabouts, orientation, direction, course, track, way, aim.

bearish adj. **1** said of a person bad-tempered. **2** Stock Exchange causing or linked with a fall in prices.

bearskin *noun* **1** the skin of a bear. **2** a tall fur cap worn as part of some military uniforms.

beast *noun* **1** any large wild animal, especially a four-footed one. **2** *colloq.* a cruel brutal person. **3** *colloq.* a difficult or unpleasant person or thing. [from Old French *beste*]

⊟ **1** animal, creature. **2** brute, monster, savage, barbarian, devil, fiend. **3** pig, swine, devil.

beastliness *noun* fierceness; unpleasantness.

beastly — *adj.* (**beastlier, beastliest**) **1** like a beast in actions or behaviour; fierce, brutal. **2** *colloq.* unpleasant; horrid. — *adv.* extremely and unpleasantly: *beastly hot.*

⊟ *adj.* **1** animal, bestial, fierce, brutal, ferocious, savage, wild, inhuman. **2** unpleasant, horrible, horrid, nasty, unkind, awful.

beat — *verb* (PAST TENSE **beat**; PAST PARTICIPLE **beaten**) **1** to hit violently and repeatedly, especially to harm or punish. **2** to strike repeatedly, eg to remove dust or make a sound. **3** *intrans.* to knock or strike repeatedly: *rain beating against the door.* **4** to defeat; to do something better, sooner, or quicker than (someone else). **5** to be too difficult to be solved or understood by: *the last puzzle had me beaten.* **6** to mix or stir thoroughly: *beat eggs.* **7** (**beat something** or **beat something out**) to make or shape it by striking the raw material. **8** *intrans.* to move in a regular pattern of strokes, etc: *a beating heart.* **9** (**beat out time**) to mark or show musical time. **10** *trans., intrans.* to move rhythmically up and down. **11** (**beat someone** or **something back** or **down** or **off**) to push, drive, or force them away. **12** *trans., intrans.* to strike (bushes, trees, etc) to force birds or animals into the open for shooting. — *noun* **1** a regular stroke, or its sound: *the beat of a heart.* **2** the main accent in music. **3** a regular or usual course or journey, especially one made by a policeman or policewoman. — **beat about the bush** to talk tediously about a subject without coming to the main point. **beat down** *said of the sun* to give out great heat. **beat someone down** to force (a person) to reduce (the price of something) by bargaining. **beat a hasty retreat** to go away in a hurry. **beat it** *slang* to go away immediately and quickly. **beat someone off** to check them, or succeed in overcoming them. **beat someone up** to punch, kick, or hit them severely and repeatedly. **dead beat** *colloq.* very tired. **off the beaten track** away from main roads and towns; isolated. [from Anglo-Saxon *beatan*]

⊟ *verb* **1** hit, whip, flog, lash, *colloq.* tan, cane, strap, thrash, *colloq.* whack, lay into, punch, strike, bash, *colloq.* wallop. **2** strike, knock, bang, *colloq.* wallop, whack, wham. **3** knock, pound, hammer, batter. **4** defeat, trounce, best, worst, *slang* hammer, *colloq.* slaughter, conquer, overcome, overwhelm, vanquish, subdue, surpass, excel, outdo, outstrip, outrun. **5** baffle, perplex, puzzle, confound, confuse, *colloq.* bamboozle, *colloq.* flummox, stump. **6** mix, blend, stir, whisk, whip. **7** shape, mould, form, fashion, hammer out, forge. **8** pulsate, pulse, throb, thump, race, palpitate, flutter, vibrate, quiver, tremble, shake, quake. *noun* **1** pulsation, pulse, stroke, throb, thump, palpitation, flutter. **2** rhythm, time, tempo, metre, measure, rhyme, stress, accent. **3** round, rounds, territory, circuit, course, journey, way, path, route. **beat off** drive off, drive back, repel, repulse, check, ward off. **beat up** attack, assault, knock about, knock around, batter, *slang* do over.

beater *noun* **1** a person who forces animals into the open for shooting. **2** an instrument used for beating: *an egg-beater.*

beat generation a group of US writers and poets whose work was popular in the 1950s.

beatific /biə'tɪfɪk/ *adj.* **1** showing great happiness: *a beatific smile.* **2** making blessed. [from Latin *beatus*, blessed + *facere*, to make]

beatification /bɪatɪfɪ'keɪʃən/ *noun RC Church* the act of declaring a dead person 'blessed', as a step towards full canonization.

beatify /bɪ'atɪfaɪ/ *verb* (**beatifies, beatified**) **1** *RC Church* to declare the blessed status of (someone who has died), usually as the first step towards canonization. **2** to make extremely happy. [from Latin *beatus*, blessed + *facere*, to make]

beating *noun* **1** physical assault or punishment. **2** a severe defeat.

⊟ **1** corporal punishment, chastisement, whipping, flogging, caning, thrashing. **2** defeat, rout, thrashing.

beatitude /bɪ'atɪtjuːd/ *noun* **1** a state of extreme happiness and peace. **2** Beatitudes) the blessings from Christ's Sermon on the Mount, recorded in Matthew 5.3–11. [from Latin *beatitudo*, from *beatus*, blessed]

beatnik *noun* a young person, especially in the 1950s, who rejected conventional social and political ideas and wore unusual clothes, long hair, etc.

beat-up *adj. colloq.* old and worn; in very bad condition.

beau /bəʊ/ *noun* (PL. **beaux**) *old use* **1** a boyfriend or male lover. **2** a man who thinks a lot about his clothes and appearance. [from French *beau*, beautiful]

Beaufort scale /'bəʊfət/ *Meteorol.* a system for estimating wind speeds without using instruments, based on a scale ranging from 0 (calm) to 12 (hurricane). [named after the British admiral Sir Francis Beaufort]

beauteous /'bjuːtɪəs/ *adj. poetic* beautiful.

beauteously *adv. poetic* beautifully.

beautician /bjuː'tɪʃən/ *noun* a person who styles women's hair, treats their skin, applies their make-up, etc, especially in a beauty parlour.

beautification /bjuːtɪfɪ'keɪʃən/ *noun* making beautiful, especially by decoration.

beautiful /'bjuːtɪfʊl/ *adj.* **1** having an appearance or qualities which please the senses. **2** pleasing or enjoyable.

⊟ **1** attractive, fair, pretty, lovely, good-looking, handsome, gorgeous, exquisite, radiant, ravishing, *colloq.* stunning, appealing, alluring, charming. **2** pleasing, enjoyable, delightful, lovely, charming, fine.
⊞ **1** ugly, plain, hideous.

beautifully *adv.* in a manner that pleases the senses: *the stories are beautifully written.*

beautify /'bjuːtɪfaɪ/ *verb* (**beautifies, beautified**) to make beautiful, often by decorating.

⊟ embellish, enhance, improve, grace, gild, garnish, decorate, ornament, deck, bedeck, adorn, array, glamorize, titivate, *slang* tart up.
⊞ disfigure, spoil.

beauty /'bjuːtɪ/ *noun* (PL. **beauties**) **1** a quality pleasing to the senses, especially the eye or ear. **2** a beautiful woman or girl. **3** *colloq.* an excellent example of something. **4** a benefit: *the beauty of the plan.* [from Old French *biaute*]

⊟ **1** attractiveness, fairness, prettiness, loveliness, (good) looks, handsomeness, glamour, appeal, allure, charm, grace, elegance, symmetry, excellence.
⊞ **1** ugliness, repulsiveness.

beauty contest a competition in which young women are judged by the beauty of their faces and bodies.

beauty parlour or **beauty salon** a place which offers hairdressing, make-up, massage, etc to women.

beauty queen the winner in a beauty contest.

beauty spot 1 a place of great natural beauty. **2** a small dark natural or artificial mark on the face, considered to enhance beauty.

beaver *noun* **1** either of two species of large semi-aquatic squirrel-like rodent, the European beaver and the N American beaver, renowned for their industry and their ability to construct dams. **2** its fur. **3** a hat made of beaver fur. — **beaver away at something** *colloq.* to work very hard at it. [from Anglo-Saxon *befer*]

bebop /'biːbɒp/ *noun* a jazz style which evolved in the 1940s, characterized by fast tempos, complex agitated rhythms, and a continuous, improvised melodic line.

becalmed *adj.*, *said of a sailing ship* unable to move because of lack of wind.

became see BECOME.

because /bɪ'kɒz/ *conj.* for the reason that. — **because of something** or **someone** on account of them; by reason of them. [from *by cause of*]

▣ as, for, since. **because of** owing to, on account of, by reason of, thanks to.

beck[1] — **at someone's beck and call** having to be always ready to carry out their orders or wishes. [from Anglo-Saxon *biecnan*, to beckon]

beck[2] *noun* a stream. [from Norse *bekkr*]

beckon *verb trans., intrans.* (**beckoned, beckoning**) **1** to call (someone) towards oneself, especially by making a sign with the hand. **2** to exert an attraction (over); to draw the attention (of). [from Anglo-Saxon *biecnan*]

▣ CALL. **1** gesture (to), signal, nod (to), wave, gesticulate (to). **2** attract, allure, entice, tempt.

become /bɪ'kʌm/ *verb usually intrans.* (PAST TENSE **became**; PAST PARTICIPLE **become**) **1** to come or grow to be. **2** (**become of someone** or **something**) to happen to: *whatever became of Donald?* **3** *trans. formal*, *said especially of dress* to suit, or look good on: *that hat becomes you.* [from Anglo-Saxon *becuman*, to come, approach]

▣ **1** turn, grow, get, change into, develop into. **3** suit, befit, flatter, enhance, grace, embellish, ornament.

becoming *adj.* **1** attractive. **2** *said of behaviour, etc* suitable or proper.

becomingly *adv.* in a proper or attractive way: *he is becomingly modest.*

becquerel /'bekərel/ *noun* (SYMBOL **Bq**) the SI unit of radioactivity, equivalent to one disintegration of a radioactive source per second.

BEd. *abbrev.* Bachelor of Education.

bed — *noun* **1** a piece of furniture for sleeping on. **2** the bottom of a river, lake, or sea. **3** an area of ground in a garden, for growing plants: *flower-bed.* **4** a structure or surface which underlies or supports something. **5** a layer, especially of rock. — *verb* (**bedded, bedding**) **1** (**bed down** or **bed someone down**) to go to bed, or put them in bed or a place to sleep: *bedded down on the sofa.* **2** *colloq.* to have sexual intercourse with. **3** (**bed something out**) to plant it in a garden. **4** to place or fix firmly. **5** *trans., intrans.* to arrange in, or form, layers. — **bed and board** lodgings and food. **a bed of roses** an easy or comfortable place or situation. **go to bed with someone** *colloq.* to have sexual intercourse with someone. **make the bed** to make the bedclothes tidy after the bed has been slept in. [from Anglo-Saxon *bedd*]

▣ *noun* **1** divan, couch, bunk, berth, cot, mattress, pallet, sack. **2** bottom, floor, watercourse, channel. **3** border, patch, plot, garden. **4** support, foundation, groundwork, base. **5** layer, stratum, substratum.

bedazzle /bɪ'dazəl/ *verb* **1** to impress greatly. **2** to confuse.

bedazzled *adj.* impressed; confused.

bedazzlement *noun* a state of dazzlement or confusion.

bedbath *noun* a complete wash of the body of a person who is unable get out of bed.

bedbug *noun* the common name for any of various species of household pest that infest bedding, and feed on human blood.

bedclothes *pl. noun* the sheets, blankets, etc used to cover a bed.

▣ bedding, bed linen, sheets, pillowcases, pillowslips, covers, blankets, bedspreads, coverlets, quilts, eiderdowns, pillows.

bedcover *noun* a top cover for a bed.

bedding *noun* **1** mattresses, blankets, etc. **2** straw, etc for animals to sleep on.

bedeck /bɪ'dek/ *verb* to cover with decorations; to adorn.

bedevil /bɪ'devɪl/ *verb* (**bedevilled, bedevilling**) **1** to cause continual difficulties or trouble to. **2** to confuse.

bedevilment *noun* continual difficulty or trouble.

bedfellow *noun* **1** a person with whom one shares a bed. **2** a partner or associate.

bedlam /'bedləm/ *noun colloq.* a noisy confused place or situation. [from *Bedlam* Royal Hospital in London]

bed linen the sheets and pillowcases used on a bed.

Bedlington terrier a UK breed of dog with a tapering muzzle and a pale curly coat. [from Bedlington in NE England, where it was first bred]

Bedouin /'beduɪn/ *noun* (PL. **Bedouin, Bedouins**) a member of a wandering Arab tribe that lives in the deserts of the Middle East. [from Arabic *badawi*, desert-dweller]

bedpan *noun* a wide shallow pan used as a receptacle for urine and faeces by a patient confined to bed.

bedraggled /bɪ'dragld/ *adj.*, *said of a person or animal* very wet and untidy.

▣ untidy, unkempt, dishevelled, disordered, scruffy, slovenly, wet, soaked, sodden, drenched, messy, dirty, muddy, muddied, soiled.
▣ neat, tidy, clean.

bedridden *adj.* not able to get out of bed, especially because of old age or sickness.

bedrock *noun* **1** the solid rock forming the lowest layer under soil and rock fragments. **2** the basic principle, idea, etc on which something rests.

bedroom *noun* **1** a room for sleeping in. **2** (*attributive*) denoting sexual relations: *bedroom comedy.*

Beds. *abbrev.* Bedfordshire.

bedside *noun* the place or position next to a bed, especially of a sick person.

bedsit or **bedsitter** *noun Brit. colloq.* a bedsitting room.

bedsitting room *noun Brit.* a single room for both eating and sleeping in.

bedsore *noun* an ulcer on a person's skin, caused by lying in bed for long periods.

bedspread *noun* a top cover for a bed.

bedstead *noun* the frame of a bed.

bedstraw *noun* a small annual or perennial plant of the genus *Gallium*, found almost everywhere, and having a fragile stem, narrow leaves arranged in whorls, and tiny white, yellow, or greenish flowers borne in open clusters.

bed-wetting *noun* accidental urination in bed at night.

bee *noun* **1** any of various insects of the family Apidae, having four membranous wings, and living in communities for which it collects pollen and makes honey and wax. **2** *North Amer.* a meeting of friends or neighbours to work or for enjoyment. **3** *old use* a friendly competition. — **a bee in one's bonnet** *colloq.* a notion or wish with which one is preoccupied. **the bee's knees** *Brit. colloq.* a person or thing that is extremely good. [from Anglo-Saxon *beo*]

beech — *noun* **1** a deciduous tree or shrub of the genus *Fagus* which has smooth grey bark, pale green glossy leaves, and produces triangular edible nuts. **2** the hard straight-grained wood of this tree, widely used for furniture making. — *adj*. made from the wood of the beech tree. [from Anglo-Saxon *bece*]

beech mast the nuts of the beech tree.

bee-eater *noun* a brilliantly coloured bird, usually bright green with red, blue, or yellow patches, native to the Old World, especially Africa and S Asia, and having a slender pointed bill. It feeds on ants, bees, and wasps caught in flight.

beef — *noun* **1** the flesh of a bull, cow, or ox, used as food. **2** *colloq*. muscle, strength. **3** *colloq*. a complaint. — *verb intrans. colloq*. to complain. — **beef something up** *colloq*. **1** to make something stronger or heavier. **2** to make something more interesting or exciting. [from Old French *boef*, ox]

beefburger *noun* a piece of finely chopped beef, made into a flat round shape, grilled or fried.

beefcake *noun colloq., derog*. very muscular men displayed in photographs. See also CHEESECAKE.

Beefeater *noun* a guard at the Tower of London.

beefiness *noun* a beefy or fat condition.

beefsteak *noun* a thick slice of beef for grilling or frying.

beef tea the juice of chopped beef, sometimes taken by people who are ill.

beefy *adj*. (**beefier, beefiest**) **1** of or like beef. **2** *colloq*. having a lot of fat or muscle.

beehive *noun* **1** a box or hut in which bees are kept, and where they store their honey. **2** a place where a lot of people are working hard. **3** shaped like a traditional round-topped beehive: *a beehive hairstyle*.

beekeeper *noun* a person who keeps bees for their honey.

beekeeping *noun* the keeping of bees for their honey.

beeline *noun* a straight line between two places. — **make a beeline for something** to go to it directly or purposefully: *made a beeline for the cake-stall*.

been see BE.

beep — *noun* a short high-pitched sound, eg made by a car horn. — *verb intrans., trans*. to produce a beep (on or for something): *do stop beeping the horn*. [imitative of the sound]

beeper *noun* an instrument that makes a beep, eg to attract someone's attention.

beer *noun* **1** an alcoholic beverage prepared by the slow fermentation of malted cereal grains, usually barley, flavoured with hops, eg ale, lager, stout. **2** a glass, can, or bottle of this beverage. **3** any other fermented liquor, eg ginger beer. — **beer and skittles** *Brit*. fun; pleasure. [from Anglo-Saxon *beor*]

beer garden a garden, usually attached to a pub, where beer and other refreshments can be drunk.

beery *adj*. (**beerier, beeriest**) **1** of or like beer. **2** *colloq*. affected by drinking beer.

beeswax *noun* a solid yellowish substance produced by bees for making the cells in which they live, used as a polish.

beeswing *noun* a filmy crust of tartar formed in port and some other wines after long keeping.

beet *noun* any of several types of plant with large round or carrot-shaped roots, used as food or for making sugar. [from Anglo-Saxon *bete*]

beetle[1] — *noun* any of over 350,000 species of winged insect belonging to the order Coleoptera, with thickened forewings that are not used for flight but modified to form rigid horny wing-cases. — *verb intrans*. (**beetle about, around**, etc) *Brit*. to move quickly or as if in a hurry. [from Anglo-Saxon *bitela*]

beetle[2] *noun* a tool with a heavy head for crushing, beating, etc. [from Anglo-Saxon *bietle*]

beetle[3] *verb intrans*. to project; to overhang.

beetle-browed *adj*. having bushy eyebrows.

beetling *adj*. projecting; overhanging.

beetroot *noun* a type of plant with a round red root which is cooked and used as a vegetable. [from Anglo-Saxon *bete*, beet]

BEF *abbrev*. British Expeditionary Force.

befall /bɪˈfɔːl/ *verb intrans., trans*. (PAST TENSE **befell**; PAST PARTICIPLE **befallen**) *old use, literary* to happen; to happen to (someone). [from Anglo-Saxon *befeallan*]

befit /bɪˈfɪt/ *verb* (**befitted, befitting**) *formal* to be suitable or right for.

befitting *adj. formal* suitable for.

befittingly *adv. formal* in a way that is suitable.

before /bɪˈfɔː(r)/ — *prep*. **1** earlier than: *before noon*. **2** ahead of; in front of: *stand before the table*. **3** in the presence of; for the attention of: *the question before us*. **4** *formal, literary* in the face of: *draw back before the blast*. **5** rather than; in preference to: *put money before friendship*. — *conj*. **1** earlier than the time when: *do it before you forget*. **2** rather than; in preference to: *I'd die before I'd surrender*. — *adv*. **1** *formal* in front; ahead: *go before*. **2** previously; in the past: *haven't we met before?* [from Anglo-Saxon *beforan*]

▣ *adv*. **1** ahead, in front, in advance. **2** previously, sooner, earlier, formerly, beforehand.
▣ *adv*. **1, 2** after. **2** later.

beforehand *adv*. before the arranged or due time; in preparation.

▣ in advance, preliminarily, already, before, previously, earlier, sooner.

befriend /bɪˈfrend/ *verb* to become the friend of; to help or support.

▣ make friends with, get to know, take under one's wing, *colloq*. chum up with, team up with, welcome, help, aid, assist, back, support, stand by, comfort, encourage.
▣ neglect, oppose.

befuddle /bɪˈfʌdl/ *verb* to confuse, especially with the effects of alcohol.

befuddled *adj*. confused, especially by the effects of alcohol.

beg *verb intrans., trans*. (**begged, begging**) (*usually* **beg for something**) **1** to ask for (money, food, etc). **2** to ask earnestly or humbly. — **beg the question** to assume in an argument the truth of something which is part of what is to be proved. **beg to differ** to disagree. **go begging** to be unused or unwanted. [from Anglo-Saxon *bedecian*]

▣ REQUEST. **1** ask for, cadge, scrounge, sponge, solicit. **2** ask, plead, entreat, implore, beseech, pray, desire, crave, supplicate, petition, solicit.

began see BEGIN.

beget /bɪˈget/ *verb* (**begetting**; PAST TENSE **begot, begat**; PAST PARTICIPLE **begotten**) **1** *old use* to be the father of. **2** to cause. [from Anglo-Saxon *begietan*]

beggar — *noun* **1** a person who lives by begging. **2** *colloq*. an affectionate term for a person: *cheeky beggar*. — **beggar description** or **belief** to be impossible to describe or believe.

▣ **1** mendicant, supplicant, pauper, down-and-out, tramp, vagrant, cadger, scrounger, sponger. **2** rascal, rogue, devil.

beggarly *adj*. extremely small or poor.

begin /bɪˈgɪn/ *verb* (**beginning**; PAST TENSE **began**; PAST PARTICIPLE **begun**) **1** *trans., intrans*. to start. **2** *trans*. to bring into being. **3** *intrans*. to come into being. **4** *intrans*.

to start speaking. **5** *intrans.* to be the first, or take the first step. **6** (**begin with someone** or **something**) to deal with them first. **7** *intrans. colloq.* to have the ability or possibility: *I can't even begin to understand.* — **to begin with** at first; firstly. [from Anglo-Saxon *beginnan*]

■ **1** start, commence. **2** originate, initiate, introduce, found, set in motion, activate, institute, instigate. **3** arise, spring, emerge, appear.
F3 **1, 2, 3** end, finish, cease.

beginner *noun* someone who is still learning how to do something.

■ novice, tiro, starter, learner, trainee, apprentice, student, freshman, fresher, recruit, cub, tenderfoot, fledgling.
F3 veteran, old hand, expert.

beginning *noun* **1** the point or occasion at which something begins. **2** the origin of something.

■ **1** start, commencement, onset, outset, appearance, emergence, opening, preface, prelude, introduction, initiation, establishment, inauguration, inception, starting point, birth, dawn. **2** origin, source, fountainhead, root, seed, rise.
F3 **1** end, finish.

begone /bɪˈgɒn/ *interj. old use, poetic* go away.

begonia /bəˈgoʊnɪə/ *noun* a kind of tropical plant with brightly coloured waxy flowers and unevenly shaped leaves. [named after Michel Bégon (1638-1710), French patron of botany]

begot /bɪˈgɒt/ see BEGET.

begrudge /bɪˈgrʌdʒ/ *verb* **1** to do, give, or allow unwillingly or with regret. **2** (**begrudge someone something**) to envy or resent them for it.

■ **1** regret, resent, grudge, deplore, object to, stint.
F3 **1** allow.

beguile /bɪˈgaɪl/ *verb* **1** to charm. **2** to cheat, trick, or deceive. [from BE- + *guile*, to deceive]

■ **1** charm, enchant, bewitch, captivate, amuse, entertain, divert, distract, occupy, engross. **2** deceive, fool, hoodwink, dupe, trick, cheat, delude, mislead.

beguilement *noun* charm; deception.
beguiling *adj.* deceptively charming or amusing.
beguilingly *adv.* with deceptive charm: *a beguilingly friendly person.*
begun see BEGIN.
behalf /bɪˈhɑːf/ — **on behalf of 1** of, for, or in the interests of. **2** as a representative of. [from Anglo-Saxon *be*, by + *healfe*, side]

■ **on behalf of 1** for the sake of, for the good of, in the interest(s) of, for the benefit of, to the advantage of. **2** in the name of, on the authority of.

behave /bɪˈheɪv/ *verb* **1** *intrans.* to act in a specified way: *behave well.* **2** *intrans., trans.* to act or conduct (oneself) in a suitable, polite or orderly way: *mind you behave yourself at the party.* [from BE- + HAVE]

■ **1** act, react, respond, conduct oneself, acquit oneself, comport oneself.

behaviour /bɪˈheɪvɪə(r)/ *noun* **1** way of behaving; manners: *good behaviour.* **2** *Psychol.* a response to a stimulus. — **be on one's best behaviour** to behave as well as one can.

■ **1** conduct, comportment, manner, manners, actions, doings, dealings, ways, habits. **2** action, reaction, response.

behavioural *adj.* relating to or concerned with behaviour.
behaviourally *adv.* in terms of behaviour.
behaviourism *noun Psychol.* a school of psychology that interprets behaviour solely in terms of events that can be physically observed or measured, such as the activity of nerves and glands, and does not take account of mental experiences such as thoughts and emotions.
behaviourist or **behaviorist** — *noun* a person who studies or advocates behaviourism. — *adj.* relating to behaviourism.
behaviour therapy *Psychol.* a form of psychotherapy which aims to modify undesirable behaviour patterns. It is often used in the treatment of neuroses.
behead /bɪˈhed/ *verb* to cut off the head of (someone), usually as a form of capital punishment. [from Anglo-Saxon *beheafdian*]

■ decapitate, execute, guillotine.

beheld see BEHOLD.
behest /bɪˈhest/ *noun old use, formal* a command or request: *at his behest.* [from Anglo-Saxon *behæs*, vow]
behind /bɪˈhaɪnd/ — *prep.* **1** at or towards the back of or the far side of. **2** later or slower than; after in time: *behind schedule.* **3** supporting: *we're all behind you.* **4** in the past with respect to: *those problems are all behind me now.* **5** not as far advanced as. **6** being the cause of: *reasons behind the decision.* — *adv.* **1** in or to the back or far side of. **2** remaining: *leave something behind.* **3** following: *run behind.* — *adj.* (**behind with**) **1** not up to date; late: *behind with the payments.* **2** not having progressed enough: *get behind with one's work.* — *noun* the part of the body a person sits on. — **behind someone's back** without their knowledge or permission. **put something behind one** to try to forget something unpleasant. [from Anglo-Saxon *behindan*]

■ *prep.* **2** following, after, later than. **3** supporting, backing, for. **6** causing, responsible for, instigating, initiating. *adv.* **3** after, following, next, subsequently. *adj.* **1** behindhand, late, overdue, in arrears, in debt. **2** behindhand, late, overdue. *noun* rump, rear, posterior, buttocks, seat, bottom, *colloq.* backside, *colloq.* bum, *North Amer. colloq.* butt, *colloq.* tail.

behindhand *adj.* **1** late. **2** (**behindhand with something**) not up to date with regard to it; in arrears.
behold /bɪˈhoʊld/ *old use, literary* — *verb* (PAST TENSE AND PAST PARTICIPLE **beheld**) to see; to look at. — *interj.* look. [from Anglo-Saxon *behealdan*, to hold, observe]
beholden *adj.* (**beholden to someone**) *formal* owing them a debt or favour; grateful to them. [from Anglo-Saxon *behealdan*, to hold, observe]
beholder *noun literary* an observer or onlooker.
behove /bɪˈhoʊv/ *verb old use* to be necessary or fitting on the part of: *it behoves me to tell you the truth.* [from Anglo-Saxon *behofian*, to have need of]
beige /beɪʒ/ *noun* a pale pinkish-yellow colour. — *adj.* of this colour. [from French *beige*]

■ BUFF, MUSHROOM, CAMEL, SANDY, KHAKI, COFFEE.

beigel see BAGEL.
being *noun* **1** existence; life. **2** any living person or thing.

■ **1** existence, actuality, reality, life, animation, essence, substance, nature, soul, spirit. **2** creature, animal, beast, human being, mortal, person, individual, thing, entity.

bejewelled *adj.* wearing or decorated with jewels.

bel *noun* (SYMBOL **B**) a quantity used to represent the ratio of two different power levels, eg of sound, equal to 10 decibels. [named after the US inventor Alexander Graham Bell]

belabour /bɪˈleɪbə(r)/ *verb old use* **1** to beat thoroughly. **2** to argue about or discuss at excessive length.

belated /bɪˈleɪtɪd/ *adj.* happening or coming late or too late.

🔲 late, tardy, overdue, delayed, behindhand, unpunctual.
🔁 punctual, timely.

belatedly *adv.* tardily; too late.

belay /bɪˈleɪ/ — *verb* **1** *Mountaineering* to make (a climber) safe by tying his or her rope to a rock or pin. **2** *Naut.* to make (a rope) secure by winding it round a hook, peg, etc. — *noun* **1** an act of belaying. **2** a piece of rock used for belaying. [from Anglo-Saxon *belecgan*]

bel canto *Mus.* a term applied to operatic singing in the Italian manner with the emphasis on beauty of tone and phrasing. [Italian, = beautiful singing]

belch — *verb* **1** *intrans.* to give out air noisily from the stomach through the mouth. **2** *trans.* (*also* **belch something out**) *said of a chimney, volcano, etc* to send out smoke, etc. — *noun* an act of belching. [from Anglo-Saxon *bealcan*]

🔲 *verb* **1** *colloq.* burp, hiccup. **2** emit, discharge, disgorge, spew. *noun colloq.* burp, hiccup.

beleaguer /bɪˈliːgə(r)/ *verb* (**beleaguered**, **beleaguering**) **1** to surround with an army and lay siege to. **2** to cause (someone) bother or worry. [from Dutch *belegeren*, to besiege]

beleaguered *adj.* besieged, overwhelmed with criticism, difficulty, etc.

🔲 harassed, pestered, badgered, bothered, worried, vexed, plagued, persecuted, embattled, surrounded, beset, besieged.

belemnite /ˈbelemnaɪt/ *noun Geol.* an extinct mollusc, resembling a squid, found extensively as fossil shells from the Carboniferous period to the Eocene epoch. [from Greek *belemnon*, dart]

belfry /ˈbelfrɪ/ *noun* (PL. **belfries**) **1** a tower for bells, usually attached to a church. **2** the upper part of it, containing the bells. — **have bats in the belfry**. See BAT². [from French *berfroi*, watch tower]

belie /bɪˈlaɪ/ *verb* (**belied**, **belying**) **1** to show to be untrue or false. **2** to give a false idea or impression of. **3** to fail to fulfil or justify (a hope, etc). [from Anglo-Saxon *beleogan*, to deceive by lying]

belief /bɪˈliːf/ *noun* **1** a principle, idea, etc accepted as true, especially without proof: *belief in the afterlife.* **2** acceptance of an idea, principle *etc* as true. **3** trust or confidence: *has no belief in people.* **4** a person's religious faith. **5** a firm opinion. — **beyond belief** difficult to believe; incredible. **to the best of one's belief** as far as one knows. [from Anglo-Saxon *geleafa*]

🔲 **1** principle, doctrine, dogma, tenet, article of faith. **2** acceptance, conviction, acknowledgement, recognition, credit. **3** trust, reliance, confidence, assurance, certainty, sureness. **4** religion, faith, creed, persuasion, theology, ideology. **5** conviction, presumption, expectation, opinion, judgement, theory, view, notion, feeling, intuition, impression.
🔁 **2** disbelief, doubt, scepticism.

believable *adj.* capable of being believed; credible.

🔲 credible, imaginable, conceivable, acceptable, plausible, possible, likely, probable, authoritative, reliable, trustworthy.
🔁 unbelievable, incredible, unconvincing.

believe /bɪˈliːv/ *verb* **1** to accept (something said or proposed) as true. **2** to accept what is said by (a person) as true. **3** to think, assume, or suppose. **4** (**believe in something**) **a** to have religious faith or other forms of conviction about it. **b** to consider it right or good: *believe in telling the truth.* **5** (**believe in someone** or **something**) to be convinced of the existence of a God or another supreme being. **6** (**believe in someone**) to have trust or confidence in them. — **not be able to believe one's ears** or **eyes** *colloq.* to find it hard to believe in what one is hearing or seeing. [from Anglo-Saxon *belyfan*]

🔲 **1**, **2** accept, *colloq.* wear, *colloq.* swallow, credit. **3** think, consider, hold, maintain, deem, judge, reckon, suppose, assume, presume, postulate, gather, speculate, conjecture, guess, imagine. **6** trust, count on, depend on, rely on, swear by.
🔁 **1**, **2** disbelieve, doubt.

believer *noun* a person who believes, especially in God.

🔲 convert, proselyte, disciple, follower, adherent, devotee, zealot, supporter, upholder.
🔁 unbeliever, sceptic.

Belisha beacon /bəˈliːʃə/ in the UK, a tall black and white post with a flashing orange light on top, marking a pedestrian crossing on a road. [named after L Hore-Belisha, the Minister of Transport who introduced them in 1934]

belittle /bɪˈlɪtl/ *verb* to treat as unimportant, especially disparagingly.

🔲 minimize, play down, dismiss, underrate, undervalue, underestimate, lessen, diminish, detract from, deprecate, decry, disparage, run down, deride, scorn, ridicule.
🔁 exaggerate, praise.

belittlement *noun* treating as unimportant; disparagement.

belittling *adj.* treating as unimportant; disparaging.

bell *noun* **1** a deep hollow object, usually of metal, rounded at one end and wide and open at the other, with a small hammer or clapper inside, which gives a ringing sound when struck. **2** the sound made by such an object. **3** any other device which makes a ringing sound. **4** anything shaped like a bell. **5** the ringing of a bell on board ship to tell the time. **6** *Brit. colloq.* a telephone call: *give me a bell.* — **bell the cat** to do something daring and dangerous. **ring a bell** *Brit. colloq.* to sound familiar; to remind one of something. **sound as a bell** *Brit. colloq.* in very good condition or health. [from Anglo-Saxon *belle*]

belladonna /beləˈdɒnə/ *noun* **1** a poisonous plant, deadly nightshade. **2** a drug obtained from this plant, used in medicine. [from Italian *bella donna*, beautiful lady, so called because the drug was formerly used as a cosmetic]

bell-bottomed *adj.* having bell-bottoms.

bell-bottoms *pl. noun* trousers with legs which are much wider at the bottom than at the top.

bell-boy or *North Amer.* **bell-hop** *noun* a man or boy who works in a hotel, carrying guests' bags, delivering messages, etc.

belle /bel/ *noun old use* a beautiful woman, especially the most beautiful woman at a dance: *belle of the ball.* [from French *belle*, beautiful, fine]

belles-lettres /belˈletrə/ *pl. noun* works of literature, especially poetry and essays, valued for their style rather than their content. [from French *belles-lettres*, beautiful letters]

bell-hop *noun North Amer.* same as BELL-BOY.

bellicose /'bɛlɪkoʊs/ *adj. literary* likely or wanting to cause an argument or war. [from Latin *bellicosus*]

belligerence or **belligerency** *noun* aggressiveness; hostility.

belligerent /bə'lɪdʒərənt/ — *adj.* **1** aggressive and unfriendly. **2** fighting a war. — *noun* a person or country fighting a war. [from Latin *belligerare*, to wage war]

⊟ *adj.* **1** aggressive, militant, argumentative, quarrelsome, contentious, combative, pugnacious, violent, bullying, antagonistic, warlike, bellicose. **2** combatant, warring.
🗷 peaceable.

belligerently *adv.* in a belligerent or warlike way.

bell jar a bell-shaped glass cover put over instruments, experiments, etc in a laboratory, to stop gases escaping.

bellow — *verb* **1** *intrans.* to make a loud deep cry like that of a bull. **2** *trans.* to shout loudly or angrily. — *noun* **1** the loud roar of a bull. **2** a deep loud sound or cry. [from Anglo-Saxon *bylgan*]

⊟ *verb* **2** roar, yell, shout, bawl, cry, scream, shriek, howl, clamour. *noun* **2** roar, yell, shout, cry, scream, shriek.

bellows *sing. or pl. noun* **1** a device consisting of or containing a bag-like or box-like part with folds in it which is squeezed to create a current of air. **2** on some cameras, a sleeve with bellows-like folds connecting the body of the camera to the lens. [from Anglo-Saxon *belg*, bag]

bell-pull *noun* a handle or cord which operates a bell.

bell-push *noun* a button which, when pressed, operates an electric bell.

bell-ringer *noun* a person who rings a bell in a church, or who plays tunes with hand-held bells.

bell-ringing *noun* the art or practice of ringing bells.

bells and whistles *colloq.* additional, largely decorative rather than functional features.

Bell's palsy *Medicine* a sudden paralysis of the muscles of one side of the face, caused by damage to the facial nerve. [named after the UK surgeon Sir Charles Bell]

bellwether *noun* the leading sheep in a flock, with a bell on its neck.

belly — *noun* (PL. **bellies**) **1** the part of the body below the chest containing the organs used for digesting food. **2** the stomach. **3** the lower or under part of an animal's body, which contains the stomach and other organs. **4** a part of a structure shaped like a belly. — *verb intrans.* (**bellies, bellied**) (*usually* **belly out**) to swell out. [from Anglo-Saxon *belg*, bag]

bellyache — *noun* a pain in the belly. — *verb intrans. slang* to complain noisily or repeatedly.

belly button *colloq.* the navel.

belly dance — *noun* an erotic eastern dance performed by women, in which the belly and hips are moved around, often very fast. — *verb intrans.* to perform a belly dance.

belly dancer a woman who performs belly dances.

belly-flop *noun* a dive into water in which the body hits the surface flat, instead of at an angle.

bellyful *noun* (PL. **bellyfuls**) enough to eat. — **have had a bellyful of something** *colloq.* to have had more of it than one can bear.

belly-landing *noun, said of an aircraft* a landing without using the landing wheels, usually because of a fault.

belly laugh a loud deep laugh.

belong /bɪ'lɒŋ/ *verb intrans.* **1** (**belong to**) to be the property or right of. **2** (**belong to**) to be a native of, member of a group, etc. **3** (**belong with** or **in something**) to have a proper place; to go together; to have the right qualities to fit in. [from Middle English *belongen*]

⊟ **3** fit in (with), go with, be part of, attach to, link up with, tie up with, be connected with, relate to.

belongings *pl. noun* personal possessions.

⊟ possessions, property, chattels, goods, effects, things, *colloq.* stuff, *colloq.* gear, paraphernalia.

beloved /bɪ'lʌvd, bɪ'lʌvɪd/ — *adj.* much loved. — *noun* a much loved person. [from an obsolete verb *belove*, to love]

⊟ *adj.* loved, adored, cherished, treasured, prized, precious, pet, favourite, dearest, dear, darling, admired, revered. *noun* darling, pet, favourite, dearest, dear.

below /bɪ'loʊ/ — *prep.* **1** in a lower position than. **2** lower in status, rank, amount, etc than. **3** not worthy of. — *adv.* **1** at, to, or in a lower place, point, or level. **2** further on in a book, etc: *see page 23 below.* [from Middle English *bilooghe*]

⊟ *prep.* **1** under, underneath, beneath. **2** inferior to, lesser than, subordinate to, subject to. *adv.* beneath, under, underneath, down, lower, lower down.
🗷 *prep.* **1, 2** above. *adv.* above.

belt — *noun* **1** a long narrow piece of leather or cloth worn around the waist to keep clothing in place or for decoration. **2** a strap passed across the body, to secure a person in a seat: *a seat-belt.* **3** an area, usually relatively long and narrow: *a belt of rain.* **4** a band of rubber, etc moving the wheels, or round the wheels, of a machine: *a conveyor belt.* **5** *slang* a hard blow. — *verb* **1** to put a belt round. **2** (**belt something on**) to fasten it with a belt. **3** to beat with a belt. **4** *trans., intrans. colloq.* (**belt into someone**) to hit them repeatedly. **5** *intrans. colloq.* (**belt along, home,** etc) to move very fast in the direction stated. — **below the belt** *colloq.* unfair; unfairly. **belt something out** *colloq.* to sing or say it very loudly. **belt up 1** to attach a seat-belt. **2** *colloq.* to stop talking. **tighten one's belt** *colloq.* to reduce one's spending, and live more economically. **under one's belt** *colloq.* as part of one's experience: *have a good education under one's belt.* [from Anglo-Saxon, from Latin *balteus*]

⊟ *noun* **1** sash, girdle, waistband, girth, strap. **3** strip, band, swathe, stretch, tract, area, region, district, zone, layer.

Beltane /'bɛlteɪn/ *noun* an ancient Celtic festival formerly held at the beginning of May, with bonfires on hills. [from Gaelic *bealtainn*, apparently 'bright fire']

belted *adj.* **1** having or wearing a belt. **2** *said especially of an animal* marked with a band of different colour.

beluga /bə'luːgə/ *noun* **1** a small toothed whale, native to shallow Arctic seas and rivers, having a white body when adult, and no dorsal fin. **2** a large sturgeon found in the Black Sea and Caspian Sea, one of the largest freshwater fish known, up to 5m in length, and having rows of large bony plates along its back and sides. It is a source of caviar. [a Russian word, from *beliy*, white]

belvedere /'bɛlvədɪə(r)/ *noun Archit.* a pavilion, or a raised turret or lantern on the top of a house, built to provide a view (or admit light and air). The term is also applied to a summer-house built on high ground. [from Italian, from *bel*, beautiful + *vedere*, to see]

BEM *abbrev.* British Empire Medal.

bemoan /bɪ'moʊn/ *verb* to express great sadness or regret about (something).

⊟ bewail, deplore, lament, regret.

bemuse /bɪˈmjuːz/ *verb* to make unable to understand or think clearly.

⊟ confuse, muddle, bewilder, puzzle, perplex, daze, befuddle, stupefy.

bemused *adj.* unable to understand or think clearly.

⊟ confused, muddled, bewildered, puzzled, perplexed, dazed, befuddled, stupefied.
⊟ clear-headed, clear, lucid.

ben *noun Scot.*, *in place names* a mountain. [from Gaelic *beann*]

bench *noun* **1** a long wooden or stone seat. **2** a work-table for a carpenter, scientist, etc. **3** (**the bench**) a judge's seat in court. **4** (**the bench**) judges and magistrates as a group. See also QUEEN'S BENCH. **5** a seat in the House of Commons. See also BACKBENCH, FRONTBENCH. — **raise someone to the bench** to make someone a judge or a bishop. [from Anglo-Saxon *benc*]

⊟ **1** seat, form, settle, pew, ledge, counter, table, stall. **2** workbench, work-table. **4** the courts, tribunal, the judiciary, judges, magistrates.

benchmark *noun* **1** a mark on a post, etc giving the height above sea level of the land at that exact spot, used when measuring land and making maps. **2** anything used as a standard or point of reference.

bend — *verb* (PAST TENSE AND PAST PARTICIPLE **bent**) **1** *trans.*, *intrans.* to make or become angled or curved. **2** *intrans.* to move or stretch in a curve: *a road bending to the left.* **3** *intrans.* (**bend down** or **over**) to move the top part of the body forward and down to reach the ground. **4** *trans.*, *intrans.* to submit or force to submit: *bent them to his will.* — *noun* **1** a curve or bent part. **2** the act of curving or bending. — **bend over backwards** *Brit.* to try very hard to be helpful. **bend the rules** interpret the rules in one's favour, without actually breaking them. **round the bend** *colloq.* mad; crazy. [from Anglo-Saxon *bendan*]

⊟ *verb* **1** curve, turn, deflect, twist, contort, flex, shape, mould, buckle. **2** turn, curve, swerve, veer. **3** bow, incline, lean, stoop, crouch. *noun* **1** curvature, curve, arc, bow, loop, hook, crook, elbow, angle, corner, turn, twist, zigzag.
⊟ *verb* **1, 2, 3** straighten.

bends *sing. or pl. noun* (**the bends**) decompression sickness: severe pains affecting divers who come to the surface too quickly from deep in the sea.

bendy *adj.* (**bendier, bendiest**) **1** having many bends or curves. **2** able to bend easily.

beneath /bɪˈniːθ/ — *prep.* **1** in a lower position than. **2** not worthy of. — *adv.* at a lower place, point, or level. [from Anglo-Saxon *beneothan*]

⊟ *prep.* **1** under, underneath, below, lower than. **2** unworthy of, unbefitting, unbecoming. *adv.* below, under, underneath, lower, lower down.

Benedictine /benɪˈdɪktɪn/ — *noun* **1** a member of a scholarly Christian religious order that follows the teachings of St Benedict of Nursia. **2** a strong greenish-yellow alcoholic drink first made by Benedictine monks in France in the 16c. — *adj.* relating to the Benedictines or to St Benedict.

benediction /benɪˈdɪkʃən/ *noun* **1** a prayer giving blessing, especially at the end of a religious service. **2** in the Roman Catholic church, a short service in which the congregation is blessed. [from Latin *benedictio*]

benedictory *adj.* in the nature of or serving as a blessing.

benefaction /benɪˈfakʃən/ *noun* a gift or donation from a benefactor.

benefactor /ˈbenɪfaktə(r)/ *noun* a person who gives financial help to an institution or cause. [from Latin *bene*, good + *facere*, to do]

⊟ philanthropist, patron, sponsor, *colloq.* angel, backer, supporter, promoter, donor, contributor, subscriber, provider, helper, friend, well-wisher.
⊟ opponent, persecutor.

benefactory *adj.* serving as a gift or donation.

benefice /ˈbenɪfɪs/ *noun* a position as priest or a church office, and the income (from land, buildings, etc) which is attached to it. [from Latin *beneficium*, favour]

beneficed *adj.*, *said of a person* holding a benefice or church office.

beneficence /bɪˈnefɪsəns/ *noun formal* generosity.

beneficent *adj.* actively kind and generous. [from Latin *beneficium*, favour]

beneficently *adv.* with kindness and generosity.

beneficial /benɪˈfɪʃəl/ *adj.* having good results or benefits. [from Latin *beneficialis*, generous]

⊟ advantageous, favourable, useful, helpful, profitable, rewarding, valuable, improving, edifying, wholesome.
⊟ harmful, detrimental, useless.

beneficially *adv.* with good results or benefits.

beneficiary /benɪˈfɪʃərɪ/ *noun* (PL. **beneficiaries**) **1** a person who benefits from something. **2** *Legal* a person who receives land, money, etc, in a will. [from Latin *beneficiarius*]

⊟ **1** payee, receiver, recipient. **2** inheritor, legatee, heir, heiress, successor.

benefit /ˈbenɪfɪt/ — *noun* **1** something good gained or received. **2** advantage or sake: *for your benefit.* **3** (*often* **benefits**) a payment made by a government or company insurance scheme, usually to someone who is ill or out of work: *social security benefit.* **4** a game, performance at a theatre, etc from which the profits are given to a person or people in need. — *verb* (**benefited, benefiting**) **1** (**benefit from** or **by something**) to gain an advantage or receive something good. **2** to do good to. — **give someone the benefit of the doubt** to believe them although there may be doubts. [from Old French *benfet*, from Latin *benefactum*, good deed]

⊟ *noun* **1** good, favour, help, aid, assistance, service, use, avail, gain, profit, asset, blessing. **2** advantage, good, welfare, interest, favour. *verb* **1** gain, profit, improve. **2** help, aid, assist, serve, avail, advantage, improve, enhance, better, further, advance, promote.
⊟ *noun* **1** disadvantage, harm, damage. *verb* **2** hinder, harm, undermine.

benefit society a society to which people pay money, as an investment against illness or old age.

benevolence /bəˈnevələns/ *noun* **1** the desire to do good; kindness; generosity. **2** an act of kindness or generosity. [from French *benivolence*, from Latin *bene*, good + *volens*, wishing]

⊟ **1** kindness, philanthropy, charity, generosity, liberality, munificence, altruism, benignity, humanity, compassion.

benevolent *adj.* showing or involving kindness and generosity.

⊟ philanthropic, humanitarian, charitable, generous, liberal, munificent, altruistic, benign, humane, kind, kindly, well-

disposed, compassionate, caring, considerate.
⊟ mean, selfish, malevolent.

benevolently *adv.* with kindness and generosity.

Bengali /bɛŋ'gɔːlɪ/ — *noun* 1 a member of a people living in Bangladesh and the state of West Bengal in India. 2 the language of this people. — *adj.* relating to this people or language.

benighted /bɪ'naɪtɪd/ *adj.* lacking intelligence or a sense of morality. [from obsolete *benight*, to overcome with darkness]

benign /bɪ'naɪn/ *adj.* 1 kind; gentle. 2 favourable. 3 *Medicine, said of a disorder* not having harmful effects, especially a non-cancerous tumour, ie one that does not invade and destroy the surrounding tissue or spread to more distant parts of the body. See also MALIGNANT. [from Latin *benignus*, gentle]

⊟ 1 good, gentle, kind, benevolent, obliging, friendly, gracious, amiable, genial, sympathetic. 2 favourable, propitious, beneficial, temperate, mild, warm, refreshing, restorative, wholesome. 3 curable, harmless.
⊟ 1 hostile. 2 harmful, unpleasant. 3 malignant.

benignant /bɪ'nɪgnənt/ *adj.* 1 kind. 2 favourable. 3 *said of a disease, growth, etc* not fatal.

benignity /bɪ'nɪgnɪtɪ/ *noun* (PL. **benignities**) kindness, or an act of kindness.

benignly /bɪ'naɪnlɪ/ *adv.* in a benign or gentle way.

bent — *adj.* 1 not straight. 2 (**bent on something**) with one's attention or energy directed on it: *bent on revenge.* 3 *Brit. slang* dishonest. 4 *Brit. derog. slang* homosexual. — *noun* a natural liking or aptitude.

⊟ *adj.* 1 angled, curved, bowed, arched, folded, doubled, twisted, hunched, stooped. 2 intent on, determined on *or* to, set on, resolved on, fixed on, out to, committed to. 3 dishonest, crooked, *colloq.* illegal, criminal, corrupt, untrustworthy. *noun* tendency, inclination, leaning, preference, aptitude, ability, capacity, faculty, facility, gift, talent, knack, flair, forte.
⊟ *adj.* 1 straight, upright. 3 honest.

benthic *adj. Biol.* denoting or relating to benthos.

benthos *noun Biol.* the living organisms that are found at the bottom of a sea or lake. [from Greek *benthos*, depth]

bentonite *noun Geol.* a type of clay formed by the decomposition of volcanic ash, used in paper-making. [from Fort Benton, Montana, USA, where it was found]

benumb /bɪ'nʌm/ *verb* to make numb.

benzene *noun* a colourless flammable liquid hydrocarbon that has an aromatic odour. [see BENZOIN]

benzene ring *Chem.* a ring consisting of six linked carbon atoms, as in a molecule of benzene.

benzine *noun* a motor fuel obtained from petroleum.

benzodiazepine /benzəʊdaɪ'azəpiːn/ *noun Psychol.* any of various minor tranquillizers and hypnotic drugs, eg diazepam (Valium).

benzoic acid /ben'zoʊɪk/ *Chem.* (FORMULA C_6H_5COOH) a white crystalline compound obtained by the oxidation of toluene. Its sodium salt, sodium benzoate, is used as a preservative.

benzoin /'benzoʊɪn/ *noun* a thick liquid obtained from a tree native to Java and Sumatra, used to make perfumes. [from Arabic *luban jawa*, incense of Java]

bequeath /bɪ'kwiːð/ *verb* to leave (personal belongings) in a will. [from Anglo-Saxon *becwethan*]

⊟ will, leave, bestow, gift, endow, grant, settle, hand down, pass on, impart, transmit, assign, entrust, commit.

bequest /bɪ'kwest/ *noun* 1 an act of leaving (personal belongings) in a will. 2 anything left or bequeathed in someone's will. [from Anglo-Saxon *becwethan*, to bequeath]

⊟ 1 bestowal, endowment, settlement. 2 legacy, inheritance, heritage, trust, endowment, gift, donation, estate, settlement.

berate /bɪ'reɪt/ *verb* to scold severely. [from *rate*, to scold]

Berber — *noun* 1 a person belonging to a Muslim race of North Africa. 2 the language spoken by these people. — *adj.* of the Berber people or language. [from Arabic *barbar*]

bereaved /bɪ'riːvd/ *adj.* having recently suffered the death of a close friend or relative. [from Anglo-Saxon *bereafian*]

bereavement *noun* the death of a close friend or relative.

⊟ death, loss, deprivation.

bereft /bɪ'reft/ *adj.* (**bereft of something**) deprived of it; having had it taken away. [from the past tense of *bereave*: see BEREAVED]

⊟ deprived of, robbed of, stripped of, destitute of, devoid of, lacking, wanting.

beret /'bɛreɪ/ *noun* a round flat cap made of soft material. [from French *béret*, cap]

bergamot /'bɜːgəmɒt/ *noun* a fruit related to the orange and lemon, from which an oil is obtained which is used in perfumes and for flavouring food. [from Bergamo in N Italy]

beribboned /bɪ'rɪbənd/ *adj.* decorated with ribbons.

beriberi /'berɪberɪ/ *noun Medicine* a tropical deficiency disease caused by lack of vitamin B1 (thiamine), which results in inflammation of the nerves, paralysis of the limbs, oedema, and heart failure. [from Sinhalese *beri*, weakness]

berk or **burk** /bɜːk/ *noun Brit. slang* a fool. [short for *Berkeley Hunt*, rhyming slang for CUNT]

berkelium /bɜː'kiːlɪəm/ *noun* (SYMBOL **Bk**, ATOMIC NUMBER **97**) a radioactive metallic element manufactured artificially by bombarding americium-241 with alpha particles. [from Berkeley, California, where it was first made]

Berks. *abbrev.* Berkshire.

Bermuda shorts or **Bermudas** close-fitting shorts reaching almost to the knee. [from *Bermuda*, in the west Atlantic]

Bermuda Triangle a name for the area of sea between Florida, Bermuda, and Puerto Rico, where there is an unusually high number of unexplained disappearances of ships and aircraft.

berry *noun* (PL. **berries**) 1 *Bot.* a fleshy fruit containing seeds which are not surrounded by a stony protective layer, eg grape, cucumber, tomato, citrus fruits. 2 *Zool.* a dark structure resembling a knob on the bill of a swan. [from Anglo-Saxon *berie*]

berserk /bə'zɜːk/ *adj.* violently angry; wild and destructive. [from Norse *berserkr*, probably from *bern*, bear + *serkr*, coat]

⊟ mad, crazy, demented, insane, deranged, frantic, frenzied, wild, raging, furious, violent, rabid, raving.
⊟ sane, calm.

berth — *noun* 1 a sleeping-place in a ship, train, etc. 2 a place in a port where a ship or boat can be tied up. 3 enough room for a ship to be able to turn round in. — *verb* 1 to tie up (a ship) in its berth. 2 *intrans. said of a ship* to arrive at its berth. 3 to provide a sleeping-place for. — **give a wide berth to someone** or **something** to stay well away from them.

⊟ *noun* **1** bed, bunk, hammock, billet. **2** mooring, anchorage, quay, wharf, dock, harbour, port.

beryl *noun Geol.* beryllium aluminium silicate, a mineral that occurs in the form of green, blue, yellow, or white crystals, and is often used as a gemstone, the most valuable varieties being emerald and aquamarine. It is also the main source of the element beryllium. [from Greek *beryllos*]

beryllium /bəˈrɪlɪəm/ *noun Chem.* (SYMBOL **Be**, ATOMIC NUMBER **4**) a silvery-grey metal, obtained from the mineral beryl, which is used for windows in X-ray tubes, and together with copper is used to make very strong alloys. [from BERYL]

beseech /bɪˈsiːtʃ/ *verb* (PAST TENSE AND PAST PARTICIPLE **beseeched, besought**) *formal, literary* to ask earnestly; to beg. [from obsolete *secan*, to seek]

⊟ beg, implore, entreat, plead with, pray, supplicate.

beseeching *adj.* imploring; earnestly seeking something: *a beseeching smile.*

beset /bɪˈset/ *verb* (**besetting**; PAST TENSE AND PAST PARTICIPLE **beset**) *literary* to attack on all sides; to worry: *beset by problems.* [from Anglo-Saxon *besettan*]

beside /bɪˈsaɪd/ *prep.* **1** next to, by the side of or near. **2** compared with. **3** not relevant to: *beside the point.* — **beside oneself** in a state of uncontrollable anger, excitement, or other emotion: *beside oneself with worry.* [from Anglo-Saxon *be*, by + *sidan*, side]

⊟ **1** alongside, abreast of, next to, adjacent, abutting, bordering, neighbouring, next door to, close to, near, overlooking.

besides — *prep.* in addition to; as well as. — *adv.* in addition to something previously mentioned.

⊟ *prep.* **1** in addition to, as well as, over and above. **2** apart from, other than. *adv.* also, as well, too, in addition, additionally, further, furthermore, moreover.

besiege /bɪˈsiːdʒ/ *verb* **1** to surround (a town or stronghold) with an army in order to force it to surrender. **2** to gather round in a crowd. **3** to bother; to annoy constantly: *were besieged with questions.*

⊟ **1** lay siege to, blockade, surround, encircle, confine. **2** surround, crowd (around), mob, hem in. **3** trouble, bother, importune, assail, beset, beleaguer, harass, pester, badger, nag, hound, plague.

besmirch /bɪˈsmɜːtʃ/ *verb formal* **1** to make dirty. **2** to spoil the reputation of.

besom /ˈbiːzəm/ *noun* a large brush made from sticks tied to a long wooden handle. [from Anglo-Saxon *besma*]

besotted /bɪˈsɒtɪd/ *adj.* **1** foolishly infatuated. **2** confused, especially through having drunk too much alcohol.

⊟ **1** infatuated, doting, obsessed, smitten, hypnotized, spellbound, intoxicated. **2** confused, befuddled, tipsy, drunk.
⊟ **1** indifferent, disenchanted.

besought see BESEECH.

bespangle /bɪˈspaŋgl/ *verb* to decorate with objects which shine or sparkle.

bespatter /bɪˈspatə(r)/ *verb* (**bespattered, bespattering**) to cover with spots, splashes, large drops, etc.

bespeak /bɪˈspiːk/ *verb* (PAST TENSE **bespoke**; PAST PARTICIPLE **bespoken**) *formal* **1** to claim in advance. **2** to show or be evidence of.

bespoke /bɪˈspəʊk/ *adj.* **1** *said of clothes* made to fit a particular person. **2** *said of a tailor* making clothes to fit individual customers.

Bessemer process /ˈbesɪmə/ *Chem.* a process for converting pig iron (which has a high carbon content) into steel (an iron alloy with a low carbon content). Air is blown through the molten iron, and oxygen in the air converts the carbon in the iron to carbon dioxide, which escapes. This reaction produces heat which keeps the iron molten.

best — *adj.* **1** most excellent, suitable, or desirable. **2** most successful, clever, etc: *is the best at swimming.* **3** the greatest or most: *the best part of an hour.* — *adv.* **1** most successfully, etc: *who did best in the exam?* **2** more than all others: *I like her best.* — *noun* **1** the most excellent or suitable person or thing, most desirable quality, etc: *the best of the bunch/bring out the best in them.* **2** the greatest effort: *do one's best.* **3** a person's finest clothes: *Sunday best.* **4** victory or success: *get the best of an argument.* — *verb* to beat or defeat. — **as best one can** as well as one can. **at best** considered in the most favourable way; in the best circumstances. **at the best of times** in the most favourable circumstances. **the best bet** *colloq.* the most appropriate course of action. **for the best** likely or intended to have the best results possible. **had best** would find it wisest to. **make the best of something** to do as well as possible in unfavourable circumstances. **put one's best foot forward** to make the best attempt possible. **to the best of one's knowledge** or **belief** or **ability** as far as one knows, or believes, or is able. [from Anglo-Saxon *betst*]

⊟ *adj.* **1** optimum, optimal, first, foremost, leading, greatest, highest, largest, finest, excellent, outstanding, superlative, first-rate, first-class, unequalled, unsurpassed, matchless, incomparable, supreme, perfect. **2** first, foremost, leading, excellent, outstanding, superlative, first-rate, first-class, greatest, finest, unequalled, unsurpassed, matchless, incomparable, supreme. *adv.* **2** greatly, extremely, exceptionally, excellently, superlatively. *noun* **1** finest, cream, prime, élite, top, first, pick, choice, favourite.
⊟ *adj.* **1, 2** worst. *adv.* **1, 2** worst. *noun* **1** worst.

best-before date a date stamped on a perishable product (especially food) to indicate the day or month by which the product should be used.

best boy the charge-hand electrician in a film or television production crew, working directly under the gaffer.

bestial *adj.* **1** of or like an animal. **2** *derog.* cruel. [from Latin *bestia*, animal]

bestiality /bestɪˈalɪtɪ/ *noun* **1** disgusting or cruel behaviour. **2** sexual intercourse between a human and an animal.

bestially *adv.* with great cruelty.

bestiary /ˈbestɪərɪ/ *noun* (PL. **bestiaries**) a kind of book popular in Europe in the Middle Ages, containing pictures and descriptions of animals, often used for moral instruction. [from Latin *bestia*, animal]

bestir /bɪˈstɜː(r)/ *verb* (**bestirred, bestirring**) (**bestir oneself**) to make an effort to become active, start moving, etc.

best man a bridegroom's main male attendant at a wedding.

bestow /bɪˈstəʊ/ *verb formal* (**bestow something on** or **upon someone**) to give them a title, award, quality, etc. [from Anglo-Saxon *stow*, spot or position]

⊟ award, present, give, donate, grant, confer, endow, bequeath, commit, entrust, impart, transmit, allot, apportion, accord, lavish.
⊟ withhold, deprive.

bestowal *noun* an act or instance of bestowing.

bestrewn /bɪˈstruːn/ *adj. formal, literary* covered loosely, usually with things which have been thrown or scattered: *a beach bestrewn with shells.* [from Anglo-Saxon *bestreowian*, to strew]

bestride /bɪˈstraɪd/ *verb* (PAST TENSE **bestrode**; PAST PARTICIPLE **bestridden**) *formal*, *literary* to sit or stand across (something) with one leg on each side. [from Anglo-Saxon *bestridan*]

best seller 1 a book or other item which sells in large numbers. **2** the author of a best-selling book.

best-selling *adj.* that sells in large numbers.

bet — *verb* (**betting**; PAST TENSE AND PAST PARTICIPLE **betted, bet**) **1** *intrans.*, *trans.* to risk (an asset, usually money) on predicting the outcome or result of a future event, especially a race or other sporting event. The better wins money if the outcome is as predicted, and loses the money betted if it is not. **2** *trans. colloq.* to feel sure or confident: *I bet they'll be late.* — *noun* **1** an act of betting. **2** a sum of money betted. **3** *colloq.* an opinion. — **an even bet** an equal chance that something will happen or not. **you bet** *North Amer.*, *esp. US slang* certainly; definitely; of course. [origin uncertain]

▣ *verb* **1** wager, gamble, punt, speculate. *noun* **1** wager, *colloq.* flutter, gamble, speculation, risk, venture. **2** stake, ante, bid, pledge.

beta /ˈbiːtə/ *noun* **1** the second letter of the Greek alphabet (Β, β). **2** a mark indicating the second highest grade or quality.

beta-blocker *noun Medicine* a drug that slows the heartbeat by blocking certain receptors of the sympathetic nervous system.

beta decay *Physics* a form of radioactive decay in which a neutron in an atomic nucleus spontaneously breaks up into a proton, which remains within the nucleus, and an electron, which is emitted.

betake /bɪˈteɪk/ *verb* (PAST TENSE **betook**; PAST PARTICIPLE **betaken**) *literary* (**betake oneself**) to go somewhere specified.

beta particle an electron or positron produced when a neutron inside an unstable radioactive nucleus turns into a proton, or a proton turns into a neutron.

beta test *Comput.* a second round of tests run on new software before it is marketed, designed to recreate normal working conditions.

betel /ˈbiːtl/ *noun* **1** (*in full* **betel pepper**) an Asian climbing plant (*Piper betle*), the leaves of which are chewed in the East, together with the betel nut and lime, as a mild stimulant. **2** (*also* **betel nut**) a preparation consisting of the dried seed of the betel palm (*Areca catechu*), mixed with lime and wrapped in the leaf of the betel pepper (*Piper betle*), chewed by the Malays and southern Indians for its mild stimulatory properties. [from Malayalam (S Indian language) *vettila*]

bête noire /bet nwaː(r)/ *noun* (PL. **bêtes noires**) a person or thing that especially bothers, annoys or frightens one. [French, = black beast]

betide — **woe betide** see WOE. [from Anglo-Saxon *tidan*, to befall]

betoken *verb* (**betokened, betokening**) *formal* to be evidence or a sign of. [from Anglo-Saxon *betacnian*]

betook see BETAKE.

betray *verb* **1** to hand over (a friend, one's country, etc) to an enemy. **2** to give away (a secret, etc). **3** to break (a promise, confidence, etc) or be unfaithful to (someone): *betray a trust.* **4** to be evidence of: *her face betrayed her unhappiness.* [from Latin *tradere*, to hand over]

▣ **1** inform on, *slang* grass (on), *colloq.* rat on, *slang* shop, sell (out), double-cross. **2** disclose, give away, tell, divulge, expose, reveal. **3** break, go back on, neglect, disregard, break faith with, let down, fail, desert, abandon, forsake. **4** show, manifest, reveal, expose, disclose, express.

▣ **1** defend, protect. **2, 4** conceal, hide.

betrayal *noun* an act or instance of betraying.

▣ treachery, treason, sell-out, disloyalty, unfaithfulness, double-dealing, duplicity, deception, trickery, falseness.
▣ loyalty, protection.

betrayer *noun* a person who betrays or breaks a confidence.

▣ traitor, Judas, informer, *slang* grass, *slang* supergrass, *colloq.* double-crosser, deceiver, conspirator, renegade, apostate.
▣ protector, supporter.

betrothal *noun formal* engagement to be married.

betrothed *noun, adj. formal* engaged to marry someone. [from Middle English *betrouth*, from *treuth*, truth]

better¹ — *adj.* **1** good to a greater extent; more excellent, suitable, desirable, etc. **2** (**better at something**) more successful, etc in doing it. **3** partly or fully recovered from illness. **4** greater: *the better part of a day.* — *adv.* **1** more excellently, successfully, etc. **2** in or to a greater degree. — *noun* (*often* **betters**) a person superior in quality, rank, etc: *one's elders and betters.* — *verb* (**bettered, bettering**) **1** to beat; to improve on. **2** *trans.* to make better. **3** *intrans.* to become better. **4** (**better oneself**) to improve one's position or social standing. — **all the better for something** very much better as a result of it. **better off** more affluent or fortunate. **a change for the better** an improvement. **for better or for worse** no matter what happens. **get the better of someone** to gain the advantage over them. **go one better than someone** to do, offer, etc something better or more than them. **had better** ought to: *we'd better hurry or we'll be late.* **so much the better** that is, or would be, preferable. [from Anglo-Saxon *betera*]

▣ *adj.* **1** superior, bigger, larger, longer, greater, worthier, finer, surpassing, preferable. **3** improving, progressing, on the mend, recovering, fitter, healthier, stronger, recovered, restored. *verb* **1** surpass, top, beat, outdo, outstrip, overtake. **2** enhance, raise, further, promote, forward, reform, mend, correct. **3** improve, ameliorate.
▣ *adj.* **1** inferior. **1, 3** worse. *verb* **2, 3** worsen. **3** deteriorate.

better² or **bettor** *noun* a person who bets.

betterment *noun* improvement; advancement.

betting *noun* gambling by predicting the outcome of a race etc.

betting-shop *noun Brit.* a licensed establishment where the public can place bets; a bookmaker.

between — *prep.* **1** in, to, through, or across the space dividing (two people, places, times, etc). **2** to and from: *a regular bus service between Leeds and Bradford.* **3** in combination; acting together: *they bought a car between them.* **4** shared out among: *divide the money between them.* **5** involving choice: *choose between right and wrong.* **6** including; involving: *a fight between rivals.* — *adv.* (**in between**) in, into the middle (of two points in space, time) etc: *time for a quick lunch (in) between.* — **between you and me** or **between ourselves** as a matter of confidence. [from Anglo-Saxon *betweonum*]

▣ *prep.* **1** mid, amid, amidst, among, amongst.

betweentimes *adv.* (*also* **in betweentimes**) at intervals between other events.

betwixt /bɪˈtwɪkst/ *prep.*, *adv. old use* between. [from Anglo-Saxon *betweox*]

betwixt and between undecided; in a middle position.

bevel — *noun* **1** a sloping edge. **2** a tool which makes a sloping edge on a piece of wood or stone. — *verb* (**bevelled, bevelling**) **1** to give a bevel or slant to. **2** *intrans.* to slope at an angle. [from Old French *baif*, from *baer*, to gape]

bevelled *adj.* having a bevel or slant.

beverage /ˈbɛvərɪdʒ/ *noun formal* a prepared drink, especially a hot or alcoholic drink. [from Old French *beuvrage*, from Latin *bibere*, to drink]

....
☐ drink, draught, liquor, liquid, refreshment.
....

bevy /ˈbɛvɪ/ *noun* (PL. **bevies**) **1** a group, originally of women or girls. **2** a flock of larks, quails, or swans.

....
☐ **1** group, gathering, band, company, troupe, pack, bunch, crowd, throng. **2** flock, gaggle.
....

bewail *verb literary* to express great sorrow or be very sad about.

....
☐ lament, grieve over, mourn, bemoan.
....

beware *verb* **1** *intrans.* (**beware of something**) to be careful of it; to be on one's guard. **2** *trans. old use, literary* to be on one's guard against. [from Anglo-Saxon *bewarenian*, to be on one's guard]

....
☐ **1** watch out, look out, mind out, take heed. **2** steer clear of, avoid, shun, guard against.
....

bewilder *verb* (**bewildered, bewildering**) to confuse or puzzle. [from obsolete *wilder*, to lose one's way]

....
☐ confuse, muddle, disconcert, confound, *colloq.* bamboozle, baffle, puzzle, perplex, mystify, daze, stupefy, disorient.
....

bewildered *adj.* utterly confused.

....
☐ confused, muddled, uncertain, disoriented, nonplussed, *colloq.* bamboozled, baffled, puzzled, perplexed, mystified, bemused, surprised, stunned.
☒ unperturbed, collected.
....

bewildering *adj.* confusing; puzzling.

bewilderment *noun* being confused or puzzled.

bewitch *verb* **1** to cast a spell on. **2** to charm. [from Anglo-Saxon *wiccian*, to use witchcraft]

....
☐ CHARM, ENCHANT, ENTRANCE. **1** hypnotize. **2** allure, beguile, spellbind, possess, captivate, enrapture, obsess, fascinate.
....

bewitching *adj.* alluring; charming.

bewitchingly *adv.* in a bewitching way; alluringly.

bey /beɪ/ *noun Hist.* a title given to a Turkish governor in the Ottoman Empire. [from Turkish *bey*]

beyond — *prep.* **1** on the far side of: *beyond the hills.* **2** farther on than (something) in time or place. **3** out of the range, reach, power, understanding, possibility, etc of: *it's quite beyond me/beyond recognition.* **4** greater or better than in amount, size, or level. **5** other than; apart from: *unable to help beyond giving money.* — *adv.* farther away; to or on the far side of. — **the back of beyond** a lonely isolated place. **the beyond** the unknown, especially life after death. **beyond a joke** more than one can reasonably tolerate. [from Anglo-Saxon *begeondan*]

....
☐ *prep.* **1, 2** past, further than, after, apart from. **3** out of range of, out of reach of, above, remote from. **4** above, over, superior to. **5** apart from, besides, except for, other than, further than.
....

bezique /bɪˈziːk/ *noun* a card game for two, three, or four players. It is played with two packs of cards from which all cards of a value below seven have been removed. [from French *bésigue*]

b.f. *abbrev., in accounts, etc* brought forward.

B-film or **B-movie** *noun* a supporting film in a cinema programme, usually less ambitious than the main film.

BFPO *abbrev.* British Forces Post Office (written on mail sent to British forces abroad, with the number or name of the military unit).

BG *abbrev., as an international vehicle mark* Bulgaria.

BH *abbrev., as an international vehicle mark* Belize (formerly British Honduras).

bhaji /ˈbɑːdʒɪ/ *noun Cookery* an Indian appetizer of vegetables, chickpea flour, and spices, formed into a ball and deep-fried. [Hindi]

bhakti /ˈbʌktɪ/ *noun Hinduism* loving devotion and surrender to God, recommended as the most effective path to salvation in most popular Hindu texts. [from Sanskrit *bhakti*, portion]

bhangra /ˈbaŋgrə/ *noun* a style of music combining traditional Punjabi and Western pop rhythms. [Punjabi, the name of a traditional harvest dance]

bhp *abbrev.* brake horsepower.

Bi *symbol Chem.* bismuth.

bi- *prefix* forming words meaning: **1** having, involving, etc two: *bicycle.* **2** happening twice: *biennial.* **3** on or from two sides or directions: *bilateral.* **4** *Chem.* a non-technical term for an acid salt: *bicarbonate* (technically known as *hydrogen carbonate*). [from Latin *bis*, twice]

biannual *adj.* occurring twice a year.

biannually *adv.* twice a year.

bias /ˈbaɪəs/ — *noun* **1** a disposition to favour or disfavour one side against another in a dispute or rival claim. **2** a tendency or principal quality of a person's character. **3** a weight on or in an object, such as a bowl in the game of bowls, which makes it move in a particular direction. **4** *Statistics* a lack of balance in a result. **5** a line cut across the grain of a fabric. — *verb* (**biased, biasing** or **biassed, biassing**) **1** to influence in favour of or against somebody or something, especially unfairly. **2** to give a bias to. [from French *biais*]

....
☐ *noun* **1** prejudice, partiality, one-sidedness, unfairness, favouritism, bigotry, intolerance. **2** bent, tendency, leaning, inclination, propensity, partiality. **4** slant, angle, distortion. *verb* **1** prejudice, influence, sway, slant, colour, condition, distort.
☒ *noun* **1** impartiality, fairness.
....

bias binding a long narrow strip of cloth sewn on or into the edges or corners of garments to make them strong.

biased or **biassed** *adj.* **1** predisposed to favour one side rather than another. **2** not balanced; weighted more towards one side, aspect *etc* than another.

....
☐ **1** prejudiced, partial, predisposed, one-sided, unfair, bigoted, blinkered, jaundiced, warped, twisted. **2** weighted, loaded, slanted, angled, one-sided, distorted.
☒ **1** impartial, fair.
....

biathlon /baɪˈæθlən/ *noun* an outdoor sporting event in which competitors cross a 20km course on skis, stopping at intervals to shoot at targets with rifles. [from BI- + Greek *athlon*, contest]

bib *noun* **1** a piece of cloth or plastic fastened under a child's chin to protect its clothes while eating. **2** the top part of an apron or overalls, covering the chest.

Bible *noun* **1** the sacred writings of the Christian Church, consisting of the Old and New Testaments. **2** (**bible**) a copy of these. **3** (**bible**) an authoritative and comprehensive book on a subject, regarded as definitive. [from Latin *biblia*, from Greek *biblos*, papyrus]

Bible belt those areas of the Southern USA where the population is predominantly Christian fundamentalist.

biblical or **Biblical** *adj.* relating to or in accordance with the Bible.

bibliographer /bɪblɪ'ɒɡrəfə(r)/ *noun* a person who compiles a bibliography.

bibliographic /ˌbɪblɪə'ɡrafɪk/ or **bibliographical** *adj.* relating to or in the nature of bibliography.

bibliography /ˌbɪblɪ'ɒɡrəfɪ/ *noun* (PL. **bibliographies**) **1** a list of books by one author or on one subject. **2** a list of books used as the sources of a book and usually given in a list at the back of it. [from Greek *biblion*, book + *graphein*, to write]

bibliophile /'bɪblɪəfaɪl/ *noun* an admirer or collector of books. [from Greek *biblion*, book + *philos*, friend]

bibulous /'bɪbjʊləs/ *adj. humorous* liking alcohol too much, or drinking too much of it. [from Latin *bibulus*, drinking freely]

bicameral /baɪ'kamərəl/ *adj.*, *said of a legislative body* made up of two parts, such as the House of Commons and the House of Lords in the British parliament. [from BI- + Latin *camera*, a chamber]

bicarb short form of BICARBONATE OF SODA.

bicarbonate /baɪ'kɑ:bənət/ *noun Chem.* a common name for hydrogen carbonate.

bicarbonate of soda *colloq.* sodium bicarbonate, a white powder used in baking, as a cure for indigestion, and in some types of fire extinguisher. See also BAKING SODA.

BICC *abbrev.* British Insulated Callender's Cables.

bicentenary /baɪsɛn'tiːnərɪ/ — *noun* (PL. **bicentenaries**) a two-hundredth anniversary of an event, especially as a cause for celebration. — *adj.* of or concerning a bicentenary.

bicentennial /baɪsɛn'tɛnɪəl/ *noun North Amer., esp. US* a bicentenary.

biceps /'baɪsɛps/ *noun* (PL. **biceps**) *Anat.* any muscle that has two heads or points of origin, especially the *biceps brachii*, at the front of the upper arm, which is used to flex the forearm. [from BI- + Latin *caput*, head]

bicker *verb intrans.* (**bickered**, **bickering**) *colloq.* to argue or quarrel, especially about trivial matters. [from Middle English *biker*]

· · · · · · · · · · · · · · · · · · ·

▣ squabble, row, quarrel, wrangle, argue, scrap, spar, fight, clash, disagree, dispute.

▨ agree.

· ·

bickering *noun* tedious and usually trivial quarrelling.

biconcave /baɪ'kɒnkeɪv/ *noun Physics* denoting a structure, especially a lens, that is concave on both surfaces.

biconvex /baɪ'kɒnvɛks/ *noun Physics* denoting a structure, especially a lens, that is convex on both surfaces.

bicuspid /baɪ'kʌspɪd/ — *adj.* having two points or cusps. — *noun North Amer.* a premolar tooth.

bicycle /'baɪsɪkəl/ — *noun* a vehicle driven by pedals, consisting of a metal frame with two wheels, one behind the other, and a saddle. — *verb intrans.* to ride a bicycle. [from BI- + Greek *kyklos*, circle, wheel]

· · · · · · · · · · · · · · · · · · ·

▣ *noun* cycle, *colloq.* bike, two-wheeler, pushbike, racer, mountain bike, tandem, penny-farthing. *verb* ride, cycle, pedal.

· ·

bicycle chain a metal chain connecting the pedals to the back wheel of a bicycle, making it move when the pedals are turned.

bicycle clip a metal clip worn around the bottoms of a cyclist's trousers, keeping them close to the leg and free of the chain.

bicyclist *noun formal* a rider of a bicycle; a cyclist.

bid¹ — *verb* (**bidding**; PAST TENSE AND PAST PARTICIPLE **bid**) **1** *trans.*, *intrans.* to offer (an amount of money) when trying to buy something, especially at an auction. **2** *intrans.*, *trans. Cards* to state in advance (the number of tricks one will try to win). **3** *intrans.* to state a price one will charge for work to be done. — *noun* **1** an offer of a

price, especially at an auction. **2** *Cards* a statement of how many tricks one hopes to win. **3** an attempt to obtain something: *make a bid for freedom.* — **bid fair** *formal* to seem likely. [from Anglo-Saxon *beodan*, to command, summon]

· · · · · · · · · · · · · · · · · · ·

▣ *verb* **1** offer, tender, submit, propose. *noun* **1** offer, tender, sum, amount, price, advance, submission, proposal. **3** attempt, effort, try, *colloq.* go, endeavour, venture.

· ·

bid² *verb* (**bidding**; PAST TENSE **bade**; PAST PARTICIPLE **bidden**) *formal* **1** to command. **2** to invite: *bid her to start.* **3** to express a wish, greeting, etc: *bid him welcome.* [from Anglo-Saxon *biddan*, to beg, pray]

· · · · · · · · · · · · · · · · · · ·

▣ **1** instruct, command, direct, enjoin, require, charge, call, summon. **2** ask, invite, request, desire, solicit.

· ·

biddable *adj.* compliant; obedient.

bidder *noun* a person who bids, especially at an auction.

bidding *noun* **1** a command, request, or invitation. **2** the offers at an auction. **3** *Cards* the act of making bids. — **be at** or **do someone's bidding** to be ready to carry out someone's orders or commands.

bide *verb intrans.* (PAST TENSE **bided**, **bode**; PAST PARTICIPLE **bided**) *old use* to wait or stay. — **bide one's time** to wait patiently for a good opportunity. [from Anglo-Saxon *bidan*]

bidet /'biːdeɪ/ *noun* a small low basin with taps, on which one sits to wash the genital area. [from French *bidet*, pony]

biennial /baɪ'ɛnɪəl/ — *adj.* **1** occurring once in every two years. **2** lasting two years. — *noun Bot.* a plant that takes two years to complete its life cycle, eg carrot. Biennials germinate and accumulate food reserves in the first year, and flower, produce seed, and die during the second year. See also ANNUAL, PERENNIAL. [from BI- + Latin *annus*, year]

biennially *adv.* every two years.

bier /bɪə(r)/ *noun* a movable stand on which a coffin rests or is transported. [from Anglo-Saxon *bær*]

biff — *verb slang* to hit very hard. — *noun* a blow.

bifocal /baɪ'fəʊkəl/ *adj. Optics* **1** having two different focal lengths. **2** denoting spectacles or contact lenses having two separate sections with different focal lengths, one for near vision (eg reading) and one for viewing distant objects.

bifocals *pl. noun* a pair of glasses with bifocal lenses, which allow the wearer to look at distant objects through the upper part of the lens, and to read through the lower part.

bifurcate /'baɪfəkeɪt/ *verb intrans. formal*, *said of roads, etc* to divide into two parts; to fork. [from Latin *bifurcus*, two-forked]

bifurcated *adj.* divided into two parts.

bifurcation /baɪfə'keɪʃən/ *noun* division into two parts or branches.

big — *adj.* (**bigger, biggest**) **1** large or largest in size, weight, or number: *the big toe.* **2** significant or important to someone: *his big day.* **3** important, powerful, successful: *the big four.* **4** older or adult: *my big sister.* **5** *often ironic* generous: *that was big of him.* **6** boastful; extravagant; ambitious: *big ideas.* **7** *old use* in an advanced state of pregnancy: *big with child.* — *adv. colloq.* boastfully; extravagantly: *talk big/think big.* — **big deal!** *slang* an expression of indifference. **make it big** *colloq.* to become successful and famous. **too big for one's boots** *colloq.* having an inflated view of one's importance; conceited. [from Middle English, of uncertain origin]

· · · · · · · · · · · · · · · · · · ·

▣ *adj.* **1** large, great, sizeable, considerable, substantial, huge, enormous, immense, massive, colossal, gigantic, mammoth, burly, bulky, extensive, spacious, vast, voluminous. **2** important, significant, momentous, serious. **3** main, principal, leading, eminent, prominent, influential.

5 generous, magnanimous, gracious, unselfish.
adj. **1** small, little. **3** insignificant, unknown.

. . . .

bigamist noun a person who commits bigamy.

bigamous adj. married to two wives or husbands at the same time.

bigamously adv. with two wives or husbands.

bigamy /ˈbɪgəmɪ/ noun (PL. **bigamies**) the crime of being married to two wives or husbands at the same time. [from BI- + Greek gamos, marriage]

Big Bang 1 a hypothetical model of the origin of the universe, now generally accepted, which postulates that all matter and energy were once concentrated into an unimaginably dense state, which underwent a gigantic explosion (the Big Bang) between 13 and 20 billion years ago. **2** Brit. colloq. the change, in 1986, of the regulations controlling the British Stock Exchange.

big business powerful commercial and industrial organizations or activities.

big cat a large member of the cat family, such as a lion, tiger, or leopard.

big dipper 1 a rollercoaster. **2** (**Big Dipper**) North Amer. the N American name for the Plough, a prominent group of seven bright stars in the constellation Ursa Major.

big end Brit. in an internal combustion engine, the larger end of the main connecting rod.

big game large animals, such as lions, tigers, etc that are hunted for sport.

biggish adj. fairly big.

big guns colloq. the most important or powerful people in an organization.

bighead noun colloq., derog. a conceited or arrogant person.

big-headed adj. conceited; arrogant.

big-headedness noun conceit; arrogance.

big-hearted adj. thoughtful and generous.

bighorn noun either of two species of a wild sheep that inhabit mountains, especially cliffs: the American bighorn sheep from N America, and the Siberan bighorn or snow sheep from NE Siberia. The male has large curling horns.

bight /baɪt/ noun **1** a stretch of gently curving coastline. **2** a loose curve or loop in a length of rope. [from Anglo-Saxon byht]

big mouth colloq. a boastful talkative person.

bigot /ˈbɪgət/ noun a person who is persistently prejudiced, especially about religion and politics, and refuses to tolerate the opinions of others. [from Old French bigot]

. . . .

☰ chauvinist, sectarian, racist, sexist, dogmatist, fanatic, zealot.
☲ liberal, humanitarian.

. . . .

bigoted adj. persistently prejudiced, especially about religion and politics, and refusing to tolerate the opinions of others.

. . . .

☰ prejudiced, biased, intolerant, illiberal, narrow-minded, narrow, blinkered, closed, dogmatic, opinionated, obstinate.
☲ tolerant, liberal, broad-minded, enlightened.

. . . .

bigotry noun persistent prejudice and intolerance.

. . . .

☰ prejudice, discrimination, bias, injustice, unfairness, intolerance, narrow-mindedness, chauvinism, jingoism, sectarianism, racism, racialism, sexism, dogmatism, fanaticism.
☲ tolerance.

. . . .

big time colloq. success in an activity or profession, especially in show business: hit the big time.

big top a large round tent in which a circus gives its performances.

bigwig noun colloq. an important person.

bijou /ˈbiːʒuː/ — noun a small delicate jewel or object. — adj. small and elegant. [from French bijou]

bike noun colloq. a bicycle or motorcycle.

biker noun colloq. a person who rides a motorcycle.

biker jacket or **biker's jacket** a blouson-style leather jacket, often having a number of zips, studs, etc.

bikeway noun chiefly North Amer. a lane, road, etc, specially designed or set aside for the use of pedal cycles.

biking noun the sport or pastime of cycling or riding a motorcycle.

bikini /bɪˈkiːnɪ/ noun a two-piece swimming costume for women. [from Bikini, an atoll in the west Pacific, and a former site of nuclear tests. The allusion is to the costume's supposed 'explosive' effect]

bilabial /baɪˈleɪbɪəl/ — adj., said of a consonant made with both lips touching, or almost touching, each other, as with the letter b. — noun a bilabial consonant. [from BI- + Latin labium, lip]

bilateral /baɪˈlatərəl/ adj. **1** of or on two sides. **2** affecting, or signed or agreed by, two countries, groups, etc: a bilateral agreement. [from BI- + Latin latus, side]

bilateralism noun equality, especially in the value of trade between two countries.

bilaterally adv. **1** on two sides. **2** concerning two countries or parties.

bilateral symmetry Biol. the condition in which an organism is divisible into similar halves by one plane only.

bilberry /ˈbɪlbərɪ/ noun (PL. **bilberries**) **1** a small deciduous shrub (Vaccinium myrtilis), native to heaths and moorland of Europe and N Asia, and having bright green oval leaves with a toothed margin, and pink globular flowers borne singly or in pairs in the axils of leaves. The fruit is a round edible black berry with a bluish-white bloom. **2** a berry from this plant.

Bildungsroman /ˈbɪldʊŋsrəʊmaːn/ noun a novel which deals with the formative stages of the life of the hero or heroine. [German, = education novel]

bile noun **1** a thick yellowish-green alkaline fluid produced by the liver, stored by the gall bladder, and periodically secreted into the duodenum, where it plays an important role in the breakdown and absorption of fats during digestion. **2** literary anger or bad temper (see also BILIOUS). [from Latin bilis]

bilge noun **1** the broadest part of a ship's bottom. **2** (also **bilge-water**) the dirty water that collects in a ship's bilge. **3** colloq. rubbish or nonsense. [probably a variant of BULGE]

bilingual adj. **1** written or spoken in two languages. **2** speaking two languages very well. [from BI- + Latin lingua, tongue]

bilingualism /baɪˈlɪŋgwəlɪzm/ noun the ability to speak two languages fluently.

bilinguist /baɪˈlɪŋgwɪst/ noun a person who speaks two languages.

bilious /ˈbɪlɪəs/ adj. **1** sick. **2** derog., said of a colour unpleasant, nauseous. **3** peevish; bad-tempered. See BILE. [from Latin biliosus, from bilis, bile]

. . . .

☰ **1** sick, queasy, nauseated, sickly, colloq. out of sorts. **2** nauseous, sickly, ghastly, revolting. **3** irritable, choleric, cross, grumpy, crotchety, testy, grouchy, peevish.

. . . .

biliously adv. with a bilious or bad-tempered manner.

bilirubin /bɪlɪˈruːbɪn/ noun Biochem. a yellowish-orange pigment that is found in the bile, and is formed from another bile pigment, biliverdin. [from Latin bilis, bile + ruber, red]

biliverdin /bɪlɪˈvɜːdɪn/ noun Biochem. a green pigment that is found in the bile, and is formed as a result of the breakdown of the pigment haem during the disintegration of old red blood cells. [from Latin bilis, bile + verd as in VERDURE]

bilk *verb* **1** to avoid paying (someone) money one owes. **2** (**bilk someone out of something**) to cheat or trick someone. [perhaps from *balk*, a term in cribbage]

bill[1] — *noun* **1** a printed or written statement of the amount of money owed for goods or services received. **2** a written plan for a proposed law. **3** *North Amer., esp. US* a banknote. **4** an advertising poster or leaflet. **5** a list of items, events, performers, etc. — *verb* **1** to send a bill to (someone), requesting payment for goods, etc. **2** to advertise or announce (a person or event) in a poster, etc. — **fit** or **fill the bill** *colloq.* to be suitable, or what is required. [from Latin *bulla*, seal, document bearing a seal]

◼ *noun* **1** invoice, statement, account, charges, reckoning, tally, score. **2** proposal, measure, legislation. **4** advertisement, notice, poster, placard, circular, leaflet, handout, bulletin, handbill, broadsheet. **5** playbill, programme, line-up, listing. *verb* **1** invoice, charge, debit. **2** advertise, announce, publicize, hype, proclaim, trumpet.

bill[2] *noun* **1** the beak of a bird. **2** any structure which resembles this in appearance or function. **3** a long thin piece of land that extends into the sea, eg Portland Bill. — **bill and coo** *colloq.* to kiss and whisper affectionately. [from Anglo-Saxon *bile*]

bill[3] *noun Hist.* a weapon with a long handle and a hook-shaped blade. [from Anglo-Saxon *bil*]

billabong /ˈbɪləbɒŋ/ *noun Austral.* **1** a cut-off loop of a river, forming a long stagnant pool or lagoon that is replenished seasonally only by flooding. **2** a branch of a river that comes to a dead end in a dry stream bed. [from Australian Aboriginal *billa*, river + *bung*, dead]

billboard *noun* a large board on which advertising posters are displayed.

billet[1] /ˈbɪlɪt/ — *noun* **1** a formal order to provide lodgings for a soldier. **2** a house, often a private home, where soldiers are given food and lodging temporarily. **3** *colloq.* a job. — *verb* (**billeted, billeting**) to give lodging to (soldiers, etc). [from Old French *billette*]

◼ *noun* **2** accommodation, quarters, barracks, lodging, housing, berth. **3** job, employment, post, occupation.

billet[2] /ˈbɪlɪt/ *noun* **1** a small log of wood. **2** a bar of metal. [from Old French *billette*]

billet-doux /bɪlɪˈduː/ *noun* (PL. **billets-doux**) *old use* a love-letter. [from French *billet*, letter + *doux*, sweet]

billiards /ˈbɪlɪədz/ *sing. noun* an indoor table game played on a cloth-covered table with pockets at the sides and corners, into which coloured balls are struck with a cue. See also SNOOKER, POOL. [from French *billard*, from *bille*, narrow stick]

billing *noun* the importance of a performer in a play or concert, especially as shown by the position of the name on the poster advertising the performance: *top billing*.

billion — *noun* (PL. **billions**, **billion** after a number) **1** a thousand million; in the UK formerly also a million million. **2** *colloq.* a billion pounds or dollars. **3** (*often* **billions**) *colloq.* a great number: *billions of books*. — *adj.* a thousand million in number. [from BI- + MILLION]

billionaire /bɪljəˈneə(r)/ *noun* a person owning money and property worth a billion pounds, dollars, etc.

billionairess *noun* a female billionaire.

billionth *noun, adj.* a thousand millionth.

bill of exchange a written order to a person to pay a specified sum of money to some other person on a certain date or when payment is asked for.

bill of fare a menu.

bill of lading a receipt for goods transported by ship.

Bill of Rights a written declaration of the rights of the citizens of a country.

bill of sale in English law, a formal legal paper stating that something has been sold by one person to another.

billow — *noun* **1** a large wave. **2** an upward-moving mass of smoke, mist, etc. — *verb intrans.* **1** to move in large waves or clouds. **2** (**billow out**) to swell or bulge like a sail in the wind. [from Norse *bylgja*]

◼ *noun* **1** wave, roller, breaker, comber, white horse. **2** cloud, pillar, column, wreath. *verb* **1** heave, surge, roll, undulate, rise, belch, pour. **2** swell, expand, bulge, puff out, fill out, balloon.

billowing or **billowy** *noun* moving in large waves; swelling.

billowy *adj.* same as BILLOWING.

billposter or **billsticker** *noun* a person who puts up advertising posters.

billy or **billycan** *noun* (PL. **billies**) *Brit., Austral.* a metal container used for cooking in or for eating and drinking from, especially when camping.

billy goat a male goat. See also NANNY GOAT. [from the name *Billy*]

billy-o or **billy-oh** — **like billy-o** or **-oh** *Brit. old slang use* quickly, powerfully, or forcefully: *raining like billy-oh*.

BIM *abbrev.* British Institute of Management.

bimbo *noun* (PL. **bimbos**) *slang* a young woman who is physically attractive but empty-headed. [from Italian *bimbo*, baby, small child]

bimetallic /baɪməˈtalɪk/ *adj.* **1** composed of or using two metals. **2** denoting a monetary system in which gold and silver are used in fixed relative values.

bimetallic strip *Physics* a strip consisting of two lengths of different metals welded or riveted together face to face, which expand to different extents on heating, forming a curved shape. Bimetallic strips are used in thermostats.

bimonthly — *adj.* **1** occurring once every two months. **2** occurring twice a month. — *adv.* **1** every two months. **2** twice a month.

bin — *noun* **1** a large container for storing or depositing rubbish. **2** a container for storing some kinds of food: *a bread bin*. **3** a large industrial container for storing goods in large quantities. **4** a stand or case with sections in, for storing bottles of wine. — *verb* to dispose of or store in a bin. [from Anglo-Saxon *binn*]

◼ *noun* **1** container, receptacle, litter bin, *Brit.* dustbin, *North Amer.* garbage can, *North Amer.* trash can, waste bin, waste-paper basket. *verb* throw away, dump, dispose of, *colloq.* chuck (out).

binary /ˈbaɪnərɪ/ — *adj.* **1** consisting of or containing two parts or elements. **2** denoting a system that consists of two components, especially a number system which uses the digits 0 and 1. See also BINARY SYSTEM. — *noun* (PL. **binaries**) **1** a thing made up of two parts. **2** a binary star. [from Latin *binarius*]

binary code *Comput.* a code of numbers that involves only two digits, 0 and 1. See also BINARY SYSTEM.

binary fission *Biol.* the division of an organism or cell into two parts.

binary star *Astron.* a system of two stars that share and orbit around the same centre of mass, and are held together by gravitational attraction.

binary system *Maths.* a number system to the base 2 that uses only the binary digits (*bits*) 0 and 1. It forms the basis of the internal coding of information in electronics and computers, where 1 and 0 represent high and low voltages in circuits, or on and off states of switches.

binary weapon a type of chemical weapon, usually an artillery shell, packed with two chemicals which are individually harmless but which combine on detonation to form a deadly toxic agent.

bind /baɪnd/ — *verb* (PAST TENSE AND PAST PARTICIPLE **bound**) **1** to tie or fasten tightly. **2** (**bind something up**) to tie or pass strips of cloth, bandage, etc around it. **3** to control or prevent from moving. See also BOUND[1]. **4** to make (someone) promise (to do something). **5** to require or oblige (to do something): *legally bound to reply*. **6** to fasten together and put a cover on (the separate pages of a book). **7** to put a strip of cloth on the edge of (something) to strengthen it. **8** to cause dry ingredients to stick together. **9** *intrans.* to stick together. — *noun colloq.* a difficult or boring situation. — **bind someone over** to make them legally obliged to do a particular thing, eg to keep the peace and not cause a disturbance. [from Anglo-Saxon *bindan*]

. . . .

▤ *verb* **1** tie, attach, fasten, secure, clamp, stick, lash, truss. **2** bandage, cover, dress, wrap, strap. **5** oblige, force, compel, constrain, necessitate, restrict, confine, restrain.

. . . .

binder *noun* **1** a person who binds books. **2** a hard book-like cover in which loose pieces of paper can be kept in order. **3 a** an attachment to a reaping machine, used for tying cut grain into bundles. **b** a reaping machine provided with such an attachment. **4** a cementing agent that causes loose particles of a mixture to adhere.

bindery *noun* (PL. **binderies**) a place where books are bound.

binding — *noun* **1** the part of a book cover on to which the pages are stuck. **2** cloth, etc used to bind something. — *adj.* formally or legally obliging (someone) to do (something).

. . . .

▤ *noun* **2** border, edging, trimming, tape, bandage, covering, wrapping. *adj.* obligatory, compulsory, mandatory, necessary, requisite, permanent, irrevocable, unalterable, indissoluble, strict.

. . . .

bindweed *noun* **1** any plant belonging to the Convolvulaceae, a large family of perennial plants, native to temperate regions, many species of which are climbers that twine around the stems of other plants. See also CONVOLVULUS. **2** (*in full* **common bindweed**) a perennial plant, widespread in Europe, with long slender twining stems, arrowhead-shaped leaves, and funnel-shaped white or pink flowers.

binge — *noun colloq.* a bout of extravagant eating and drinking. — *verb intrans.* to indulge in a binge. [perhaps originally a dialect word meaning 'soak']

bingo — *noun* a game of chance in which each player has a card with a set of numbers on it. Numbers are called out at random, and the winner is the first player with a card on which all the numbers have been called out. — *interj.* **1** the word shouted by the winner of a game of bingo. **2** an expression of success or sudden pleasure.

bin-liner *noun* a disposable plastic bag used as a lining in a rubbish bin.

binnacle *noun* a case for a ship's compass. [earlier *bittacle*, from Latin *habitaculum*, habitation]

binocular /baɪˈnɒkjʊlə(r)/ *adj.* **1** relating to the use of both eyes simultaneously. **2** denoting an optical instrument that requires the use of both eyes simultaneously, producing a stereoscopic effect: *binocular microscope*.

binoculars /bɪˈnɒkjʊləz/ *pl. noun* an optical instrument designed for viewing distant objects, and consisting of two small telescopes arranged side by side so that the observer is able to use both eyes at once. [from Latin *bini*, two by two + *oculus*, eye]

binocular vision the ability of animals with forward-facing eyes to focus both eyes on an object at the same time, producing a three-dimensional image.

binomial /baɪˈnəʊmɪəl/ — *noun Maths.* an algebraic expression that contains two variables (terms consisting of numbers or letters), eg $6x-3y$. — *adj.* containing two variables. [from BI- + Latin *nomen*, name]

binomial nomenclature *Biol.* the system (introduced by Linnaeus) of denoting a plant or animal by two Latin words, the first (with an initial capital letter) being the name of the genus, and the second (with an initial small letter) that of the species. Both names are conventionally written in italics.

binomial theorem a general mathematical formula for calculating any power of a *binomial quantity* (an algebraic expression consisting of the sum of two variables raised to a given power), without the need for progressive multiplications.

bio- *combining form* forming words denoting life or living things: *biology*. [from Greek *bios*, life]

bioassay /baɪəʊˈaseɪ/ *noun Biol.* the assessment of the concentration of a chemical substance by testing its effect on a living organism, eg its effect on plant or bacterial growth.

biochemical *adj.* relating to biochemistry.

biochemist *noun* a scientist who specializes in biochemistry.

biochemistry *noun* the scientific study of the chemical compounds and chemical reactions that occur within the cells of living organisms.

biocontrol *noun* biological control.

biodegradable /baɪəʊdɪˈɡreɪdəbl/ *adj.* denoting a substance that is capable of being broken down by living organisms (mainly bacteria and fungi), so that its constituents are released and can then be recycled.

biodegradation /baɪəʊdɛɡrəˈdeɪʃən/ *noun Biol.* the breakdown of substances by living organisms, especially bacteria and fungi.

biodiesel *noun* a biofuel that is used instead of diesel.

biodiversity *noun Biol.* a measure of the number of different species of living organism that are present within a given area. [a shortening of *biological diversity*]

bioenergetics *sing. noun Biol.* the scientific study of the use of energy by living organisms, including its conversion from one form to another.

bioengineering *noun Medicine* the application of engineering methods and technology to biology and medicine, eg in the production of artificial limbs.

biofeedback *noun Psychol.* the technique of controlling certain body functions by monitoring and displaying them to the patient using electronic instruments, so that the patient becomes aware of them and can learn to control the underlying process.

biofuel *noun* a fuel that is made immediately from living matter that can be replenished, as opposed to fossil fuel.

biogeography *noun Biol.* the scientific study of the distributions of plants and animals.

biographer /baɪˈɒɡrəfə(r)/ *noun* a writer of biography or of a particular biography: *one of Shaw's biographers*.

biographical or **biographic** /baɪəˈɡrafɪkəl/ *adj.* relating to or in the nature of biography.

biographically *adv.* in the nature of or as regards biography.

biography /baɪˈɒɡrəfɪ/ *noun* (PL. **biographies**) **1** an account of a person's life, usually written by someone else and published or intended for publication. **2** the art of writing biographies. [from BIO- + Greek *graphein*, to write]

. . . .

▤ **1** life story, life, history, autobiography, memoirs, recollections, curriculum vitae, account, record.

. . . .

biological /baɪəˈlɒdʒɪkəl/ *adj.* **1** relating to biology. **2** physiological. **3** *said of a detergent* containing enzymes which are said to remove dirt of organic origin, eg blood, grass, and egg stains.

biological clock a supposed natural mechanism inside the body which controls the rhythm of the body's functions.

biological control *Biol.* the control of plant or animal pests by the introduction of natural predators, parasites, etc.

biological engineering SEE BIOENGINEERING.

biologically *adv.* as regards biology.

biological rhythm SEE BIORHYTHM.

biological warfare the use of toxins and micro-organisms as weapons in war.

biologist /baɪˈɒlədʒɪst/ *noun* a scientist who specializes in biology.

biology *noun* the scientific study of living organisms.

bioluminescence *noun Biol.* the emission of light by living organisms, such as certain insects, deep-sea fishes, bacteria, and fungi.

biomass *noun Biol.* the total mass of living organisms in an ecosystem, population, or designated area at a given time. It is usually expressed as dry weight per unit area.

biome *noun Biol.* a major ecological community of living organisms, usually defined by the plant habitat with which they are associated, eg grassland, rainforest.

biomechanics *noun* the mechanics of movement in living things.

bionic *adj.* **1** relating to or using bionics. **2** *colloq.* especially in science fiction, denoting an electronic or mechanical device that is used to replace a part of the human body, usually in order to provide an increase in strength, eg bionic arm. **3** *colloq.* having extraordinary powers of speed, strength, etc.

bionics *sing. noun* **1** the scientific study of the functions and characteristics of living systems, and the application of this knowledge to the design and development of electronic and mechanical devices that function in a similar way, eg artificial limbs. **2** the replacement of damaged parts of the human body, such as limbs and heart valves, by electronic or mechanical devices. [from BIO- + ELECTRONICS]

biophysicist *noun* a person who studies or practises biophysics.

biophysics *sing. noun* the application of the ideas and methods of physics to the study of biological processes.

biopsy *noun* (PL. **biopsies**) *Pathol.* the removal of a small piece of living tissue from an organ or part of the body in order to determine the nature of any suspected disease. It is an important means of diagnosing cancer. [from BIO- + Greek *opsis*, sight or appearance]

biorhythm *noun* **1** *Biol.* a periodic change in the behaviour or physiology of many animals and plants (eg winter hibernation or migration, spring flowering), mediated by hormones which are in turn influenced by changes in day-length. **2** a circadian (24-hour) rhythm associated, for example, with sleep, and independent of daylength. **3** any of three cyclical patterns which have been suggested as influencing physical, intellectual, and emotional aspects of human behaviour.

biosphere *noun* that part of the Earth's surface and its atmosphere in which living organisms are known to exist. Also called ECOSPHERE.

biosynthesis *noun* the manufacture by living organisms of complex organic compounds, such as proteins, fats, and other major components of cells from simpler molecules.

biota /baɪˈoʊtə/ *noun Biol.* the living organisms present in a particular area. [from Greek *bios*, life]

biotechnology *noun Biol.* the use of living organisms, eg bacteria, or the enzymes produced by them, in the industrial manufacture of useful products, or the development of useful processes.

biotin /ˈbaɪoʊtɪn/ *noun Biochem.* a member of the vitamin B complex that functions as a *coenzyme* for various enzymes involved in the chemical reactions in living cells. Also called VITAMIN H. [from Greek *bios*, life]

bipartisan /baɪˈpɑːtɪzən/ *adj.* of or involving two groups or political parties. [from BI- + PARTISAN]

bipartite /baɪˈpɑːtaɪt/ *adj.* **1** consisting of two parts. **2** involving, or agreed by, two parties: *a bipartite agreement*. [from BI- + Latin *partire*, to divide]

biped /ˈbaɪped/ — *noun* any animal that has two feet or uses two feet for walking, eg a human or bird. — *adj.* (also **bipedal**) having two feet. [from BI- + Latin *pes*, foot]

biplane /ˈbaɪpleɪn/ *noun* an aeroplane or glider with two sets of wings, one above the other.

bipolar /baɪˈpoʊlə(r)/ *adj.* have two poles or extremes.

birch — *noun* **1** a slender deciduous tree or shrub of the genus *Betula*, found in north temperate and Arctic regions, with smooth silvery-white bark. **2** the strong fine-textured wood of this tree, used to make furniture, plywood, charcoal, etc. **3** a bundle of birch branches, formerly used as a punishment. — *adj.* made of birch wood. — *verb* to beat with a birch, as a punishment. [from Anglo-Saxon *beorc*]

bird *noun* **1** any warm-blooded vertebrate animal belonging to the class Aves, which consists of about 8,600 species, distinguished from all other animals by the possession of feathers. **2** *Brit. slang* a girl or woman. **3** *old colloq. use* a person, especially a strange or unusual one. **4** (**the bird**) harsh criticism: *gave them the bird*. — **the birds and the bees** *colloq.* sex and reproduction. **birds of a feather** *Brit. colloq.* people who are like each other, share the same ideas, the same way of life, etc. **do bird** *Brit. slang* to serve a prison sentence. **kill two birds with one stone** *colloq.* to achieve two things with a single action. **strictly for the birds** *colloq.* worthless; unimportant. [from Anglo-Saxon *bridd*, young bird]

Birds include: sparrow, thrush, starling, blackbird, bluetit, chaffinch, greenfinch, bullfinch, dunnock, robin, wagtail, swallow, tit, wren, martin, swift, crow, magpie, dove, pigeon, skylark, nightingale, linnet, warbler, jay, jackdaw, rook, raven, cuckoo, woodpecker, yellowhammer; duck, mallard, eider, teal, swan, goose, heron, stork, flamingo, pelican, kingfisher, moorhen, coot, lapwing, peewit, plover, curlew, snipe, avocet, seagull, guillemot, tern, petrel, crane, bittern, petrel, albatross, gannet, cormorant, auk, puffin, dipper; eagle, owl, hawk, sparrowhawk, falcon, kestrel, osprey, buzzard, vulture, condor; emu, ostrich, kiwi, peacock, penguin; chicken, grouse, partridge, pheasant, quail, turkey; canary, budgerigar, *colloq.* budgie, cockatiel, cockatoo, lovebird, parakeet, parrot, macaw, toucan, myna bird, mockingbird, kookaburra, bird of paradise.

birder *noun colloq.* a bird-watcher.

birdie — *noun* **1** a child's word for a little bird. **2** *Golf* a score of one stroke less than the fixed standard number of strokes (par) for a particular hole on a course. — *verb* (**birdying**) *Golf* to complete a hole with a birdie score.

bird-lime *noun* a sticky substance put on the branches of trees to catch small birds.

bird of paradise 1 any of about 40 species of bird, native to the forests of New Guinea and neighbouring islands, of which the males have brightly coloured plumage. **2** (*also* **bird-of-paradise flower**) an evergreen perennial plant (*Strelitzia reginae*), native to South Africa, growing up to 1m high, with brightly-coloured flowers.

bird of passage 1 a bird that flies to different parts of the world as the seasons change. **2** a person who constantly moves around and never settles in one place.

bird of prey any of several types of bird, eg eagle, vulture, hawk, that hunt other birds and small mammals for food.

bird's-eye view 1 a general view from above. **2** a general impression.

birdsfoot trefoil a small perennial plant (*Lotus corniculatus*), native to Europe, Asia, and Africa, and having leaves composed of five oval leaflets.

bird's nest fern a perennial fern (*Asplenium nidus*), native to Old World tropical forests, with leaves consisting of bright green undivided fronds that form a nest-like rosette in which humus accumulates.

bird strike a collision of a bird or birds with the engine of a flying aircraft.

bird-watcher *noun* a person who studies birds by observing them closely, especially as a hobby.

bird-watching *noun* the scientific observation of birds.

bireme /ˈbaɪriːm/ *noun* a type of ancient galley with two banks of oars on either side, and a square sail. [from Latin *biremis*, from *bi-*, two + *remus*, an oar

biretta /bɪˈrɛtə/ *noun* a stiff square cap with upright projections on top, worn by Roman Catholic clergy. [from Italian *berretta*]

biriani or **biryani** /bɪrɪˈɑːnɪ/ *noun* a type of highly seasoned Indian dish consisting mainly of rice, with meat or fish. [from Urdu]

Biro *noun* (PL. **Biros**) *Brit. trademark* a type of pen with a writing tip consisting of a small ball. [named after L Biró (1899–1985), the inventor]

birth *noun* 1 the act or process of being born or of bearing children. 2 family history or origin: *of humble birth.* 3 beginning; origins: *the birth of socialism.* — **give birth to someone** *said of a mother* to bear or produce a baby. **give birth to something** to produce or be the cause of something: *give birth to a new idea.* [from Norse *byrthr*]

⊞ 1 childbirth, *Medicine* parturition, confinement, delivery, nativity. 2 ancestry, family, parentage, descent, line, lineage, genealogy, pedigree, blood, stock, race, extraction, background, breeding. 3 beginning, rise, emergence, origin, source, derivation.

birth certificate an official record of a person's birth, stating the time and place, the parents, etc.

birth control the use of contraception or sterilization to prevent pregnancy.

birthday *noun* 1 the anniversary of the day on which a person was born. 2 (*also* **birth day**) the day on which a person was born.

birthday honours in the UK, titles or medals awarded to people on the official birthday of the king or queen.

birthday suit — **in one's birthday suit** *humorous colloq.* naked.

birthing pool a portable pool in which a woman can sit partially immersed in water during labour and childbirth.

birthmark *noun* a blemish or mark that is present on the skin at birth.

birth mother the mother who gives birth to a child, as contrasted with the adoptive or genetic mother.

birthplace *noun* 1 the place where a person was born. 2 the place where something important or well known began: *the birthplace of medicine.*

⊞ 1 place of origin, native town, native country, fatherland, mother country, roots.

birth rate the ratio of the number of live births occurring over a period of a year in a given area per thousand inhabitants, or per thousand women of childbearing age.

birthright *noun* the rights a person may claim by being born into a particular family, social class, etc.

biscuit /ˈbɪskɪt/ — *noun* 1 a crisp flat cake. 2 (*also* **biscuitware**) objects made from baked clay that have not been glazed. 3 a pale brown colour. — *adj.* pale brown in colour. — **take the biscuit** *colloq.* to be worse than everything else that has happened. [from Old French *bescoit*, from Latin *bis*, twice + *coquere*, to cook]

bisect /baɪˈsɛkt/ *verb* to divide into two equal parts. [from BI- + Latin *secare*, to cut]

⊞ halve, divide, separate, split, intersect, cross.

bisection *noun* division into two equal parts.

bisexual /baɪˈsɛkʃʊəl/ — *adj.* 1 sexually attracted to both males and females. 2 having the sexual organs of both male and female. — *noun* a bisexual person. See also UNISEXUAL.

bisexuality /baɪsɛkʃʊˈalɪtɪ/ *noun* the state of being bisexual.

bishop *noun* 1 a senior Christian priest or minister in the Roman Catholic, Anglican, and Orthodox Churches, in charge of a group of churches in an area, or of a diocese. 2 *Chess* a piece shaped like a bishop's mitre at the top. It may

only be moved diagonally across the board. [from Anglo-Saxon *bisceop*, from Greek *episkopos*, overseer]

bishopric *noun* 1 the post or position of bishop. 2 the area under the charge of a bishop.

bismuth /ˈbɪzməθ/ *noun* (SYMBOL **Bi**, ATOMIC NUMBER 83) a hard silvery-white metal with a pinkish tinge, used to make lead alloys. [from German *Wismut*]

bison *noun* (PL. **bison**) either of two species of a large hoofed mammal with a dark brown coat, broad humped shoulders, and short upward curving horns: the American bison (*Bison bison*) or buffalo, and the European bison or wisent (*Bison bonasus*) which is larger than the American bison and has a shorter coat and longer horns. [from Latin *bison*, probably of Germanic origin]

bisque[1] /bɪsk/ *noun* a thick rich soup, usually made from shellfish, cream, and wine. [from French *bisque*]

bisque[2] /bɪsk/ *noun* a type of baked clay or china, which has not been glazed. [see BISCUIT 2]

bistort /ˈbɪstɔːt/ *noun* any of various plants belonging to the genus *Polygonum*, found mainly in north temperate regions, and including some aquatic species [from Latin *bis torta*, twice twisted]

bistro /ˈbiːstroʊ/ *noun* (PL. **bistros**) a small bar or informal restaurant. [from French *bistro*]

bisulphate /baɪˈsʌlfeɪt/ *noun Chem.* hydrogen sulphate.

bit[1] *noun* a small piece. — **a bit** *colloq.* 1 a short time or distance: *wait a bit.* 2 a little; slightly; rather: *a bit of a fool.* 3 a lot: *takes a bit of doing.* **a bit much** or **thick** or **rich** *colloq.* behaviour that is unacceptable, unreasonable, or unfair. **a bit off** *Brit. colloq.* bad manners, taste, or behaviour. **bit by bit** gradually. **do one's bit** to do one's fair share. [from Anglo-Saxon *bita*]

⊞ 1 piece, fragment, part, segment, slice, crumb, morsel, scrap, atom, mite, whit, jot, iota, grain, speck. **bit by bit** gradually, little by little, step by step, piecemeal.

⊟ wholesale.

bit[2] see BITE.

bit[3] *noun* 1 a small metal bar which a horse holds in its mouth as part of the bridle with which it is controlled. 2 a tool with a cutting edge, which can be fitted into a drill and turned at high speed. 3 the part of a key which connects with the lever in a lock. — **take the bit between one's teeth** to act decisively and with determination. [from BITE]

bit[4] *noun Comput.* a binary digit with a value of either 0 or 1, representing the smallest piece of information that can be dealt with by a computer. [a contraction of *binary digit*]

bitch — *noun* 1 a female animal of the dog family. 2 *offensive slang* a bad-tempered, unpleasant, spiteful woman. 3 *slang* a difficult or unpleasant thing. — *verb intrans.* 1 to speak scathingly or spitefully. 2 to complain. [from Anglo-Saxon *bicce*]

bitchily *adv.* with a bitchy or spiteful manner.

bitchiness *noun* being bitchy or spiteful.

bitchy *adj.* (**bitchier, bitchiest**) *colloq.* 1 spiteful. 2 petulantly bad-tempered.

⊞ 1 spiteful, catty, snide, nasty, mean, malicious, vindictive, backbiting, venomous. 2 petulant, snappy, irritable, bad-tempered, grouchy.

⊟ 1 kind.

bite — *verb* (**biting**; PAST TENSE **bit**; PAST PARTICIPLE **bitten**) 1 to grasp or cut with the teeth. 2 (**bite something away** or **off** or **out**) to remove or tear it with the teeth. 3 *trans., intrans., said of animals and humans* to attack or wound with the teeth. 4 *trans., intrans., said of insects and snakes* to penetrate a victim's skin and suck blood. 5 *intrans., said of fish* to be caught on the hook on a fishing line. 6 *intrans.* to start to have an effect (usually adverse): *the spending cuts are beginning to bite.* 7 *intrans., said of a wheel, screw, etc* to grip firmly. 8 *intrans.* to cause a stinging sensation. **9** *colloq.* to annoy or worry: *what's biting him?* — *noun* **1** an act of biting. **2** a wound caused by biting. **3** a small amount of food: *a bite to eat.* **4** strength, sharpness, or bitterness of taste. — **bite something back** *colloq.* to restrain oneself from saying something as if by biting the lips. **bite someone's head off** *colloq.* to reply with unexpected fierceness or anger. **bite one's tongue** to restrain oneself from saying something one wants to say. [from Anglo-Saxon *bitan*]

⊟ *verb* **1** chew, masticate, munch, gnaw, nibble, champ, crunch, crush. **3** nip, wound, pierce, tear, rend. **6** take effect, become effective, pinch, work. **7** grip, hold, seize. **8** smart, sting, tingle. *noun* **2** nip, wound, sting, pinch. **3** snack, refreshment, mouthful, morsel, taste. **4** pungency, piquancy, *colloq.* kick, punch.

biting *adj.* **1** bitterly and painfully cold: *a biting wind.* **2** *said of a remark* sharp and hurtful.

⊟ **1** cold, freezing, bitter, harsh, severe. **2** cutting, incisive, piercing, penetrating, raw, stinging, sharp, tart, caustic, scathing, cynical, hurtful.
⊠ **1** mild. **2** bland.

bitmap *noun Comput.* an image created by bit-mapping.
bit-mapping *noun Comput.* a graphics display technique in which the brightness and colour of each point or *pixel* of the image displayed on the screen is controlled by one or more bits stored in the memory of the computer.
bit-part *noun* a small acting part in a play or film.
bits and pieces or **bits and bobs** *Brit. colloq.* small objects or possessions.
bitter — *adj.* **1** having a sharp, acid, and often unpleasant taste. **2** feeling or causing sadness or pain: *bitter memories.* **3** difficult to accept: *a bitter disappointment.* **4** showing an intense dislike, hatred, or opposition: *bitter criticism.* **5** *said of the weather, etc* extremely and painfully cold. — *noun Brit.* a type of beer with a slightly bitter taste, strongly flavoured with hops. — **a bitter pill to swallow** something difficult to accept. **to the bitter end** up to the very end, however unpleasant, and in spite of difficulties. [from Anglo-Saxon *biter*]

⊟ *adj.* **1** sour, tart, sharp, acid, vinegary, unsweetened. **2** resentful, embittered, jaundiced, cynical, rancorous, acrimonious, acerbic, hostile. **3** intense, acute, painful, deep, profound. **4** severe, harsh, fierce, cruel, savage, merciless, painful, stinging. **5** freezing, raw, biting.
⊠ *adj.* **1** sweet. **2** contented. **3** slight. **4, 5** mild.

bitter lemon a carbonated lemon-flavoured drink.
bitterly *adv.* **1** in a bitter manner, especially with fierce resentment: *he looked bitterly back at them.* **2** extremely, painfully: *bitterly cold.*
bittern /ˈbɪtən/ *noun* any of various species of bird of the heron family, found in reed-beds of Europe and Asia, having a long pointed bill. [from Old French *butor*]
bitterness *noun* a bitter state or quality, especially a feeling of fierce resentment: *I felt no bitterness towards them.*

⊟ resentment, rancour, animosity, malice, vindictiveness, hurt, injury.

bitters *pl. noun* a liquid made from bitter herbs or roots, used to help digestion or to flavour certain alcoholic drinks.
bittersweet *adj.* pleasant and unpleasant, or bitter and sweet, at the same time.
bittiness *noun* being bitty or scrappy.
bitty *adj.* (**bittier, bittiest**) *colloq.* consisting of small unrelated pieces or parts, especially awkwardly or untidily.

⊟ fragmentary, disjointed, disconnected, scrappy, sketchy, episodic.

bitumen /ˈbɪtjʊmɪn/ *noun* any of various black solid or tarry flammable substances composed of an impure mixture of hydrocarbons, such as petroleum or asphalt, either occurring naturally (eg in tar pits) or obtained by the distillation of petroleum. [from Latin *bitumen*]
bituminous /bɪˈtjuːmɪnəs/ *adj.* **1** containing bitumen. **2** denoting a dark brown or black coal containing more than 80% carbon, which burns with a smoky yellowish flame.
bivalent /baɪˈveɪlənt/ *adj.* same as DIVALENT.
bivalve /ˈbaɪvalv/ — *noun* any of about 20,000 species of mollusc having a shell composed of two parts, known as *valves*, hinged together by a tough horny ligament. They include clams, cockles, mussels, scallops, oysters, and razor shells. — *adj.* having a shell composed of two parts.
bivariate /baɪˈvɛərɪət/ *adj. Maths.* involving two variables.
bivouac /ˈbɪvʊak/ — *noun* a temporary camp without tents, especially used by soldiers and mountaineers. — *verb intrans.* (**bivouacked, bivouacking**) to camp out temporarily at night without a tent. [from French *bivouac*, from Swiss German *Beiwacht*, an additional guard at night]
bizarre /bɪˈzɑː(r)/ *adj.* weirdly odd or strange. [from Spanish *bizarro*, gallant or brave]

⊟ strange, odd, queer, curious, weird, peculiar, eccentric, *colloq.* left-field, *slang* way-out, outlandish, ludicrous, ridiculous, fantastic, extravagant, grotesque, freakish, abnormal, deviant, unusual, extraordinary.
⊠ normal, ordinary.

bizarrely *adv.* in a weird or bizarre way.
Bk *symbol Chem.* berkelium.
BL *abbrev.* **1** Bachelor of Law. **2** British Library.
blab *verb* (**blabbed, blabbing**) **1** *intrans., trans.* (usually **blab out** or **blab something out**) to tell a secret, etc. **2** *intrans.* to chatter foolishly. [from Middle English *blabbe*]

⊟ **1** tell, *slang* split (on), *slang* grass (on). **2** chatter, babble, jabber, cackle.

blabber *verb intrans.* (**blabbered, blabbering**) to talk nonsense, especially without stopping.
blabbermouth *noun* a person who talks foolishly and indiscreetly.
black — *adj.* **1** of the colour of coal, the night sky, etc. **2** without light. **3** (*also* **Black**) *used of people* dark-skinned, especially of African, West Indian, or Australian Aboriginal origin. **4** (*also* **Black**) belonging or relating to black people: *black rights.* **5** *used of drinks* without added milk: *black coffee.* **6** angry; threatening: *black looks.* **7** dirty: *they came in from the garden with their hands black.* **8** sad, gloomy: *a black mood.* **9** promising trouble; likely to be bad in some way: *the future looks black.* **10** wicked or sinister: *black-hearted/black comedy.* **11** *said of goods, etc* not allowed by a trade union to be handled, especially during a strike. — *noun* **1** the colour of coal, the night sky, etc. **2** anything which is black in colour. **3** (*also* **Black**) a person of African, West Indian, or Australian Aboriginal origin. **4** black clothes worn when in mourning. — *verb* **1** to make black. **2** to clean with black polish. **3** to forbid work to be done on or with (certain goods). — **black and blue** *colloq.* covered in bruises. **black and white 1** *used of photographs or television images* having no colours except black, white, and shades of grey. **2** either good or bad, right or wrong, etc, with no compromise. **black out** to lose consciousness. **black something** or **someone out 1** to deprive them of light. **2** to prevent information from being broadcast or published. **in the black** with assets on the credit side of an account. **in black and white** in writing or print. [from Anglo-Saxon *blæc*]

. . . .

■ *adj.* **1** jet-black, coal-black, jet, ebony, sable, inky, sooty. **2** dark, unlit, moonless, starless, overcast, dingy, gloomy, sombre, funereal. **3** dark, dark-skinned, dark-complexioned, dusky, swarthy. **6** angry, threatening, menacing, hostile. **7** filthy, dirty, soiled, grimy, grubby. **8** sad, depressed, gloomy, despondent, downcast, dejected, morose, sombre. **9** gloomy, depressing, bleak, ominous, dismal, cheerless. *verb* **3** boycott, blacklist, ban, bar, taboo. **black out** faint, pass out, collapse, *colloq.* flake out. **black something** or **someone out 1** darken, eclipse. **2** cover up, conceal, suppress, withhold, censor, gag.

■ *adj.* **1** white. **2** bright. **7** clean.

. . . .

Black Africa the part of Africa south of the Sahara desert, where the population is mainly black.

blackamoor *noun old use,* usually *derog.* a dark-skinned or black person.

black art same as BLACK MAGIC.

blackball *verb* **1** to vote against (a candidate for membership), originally by putting a black ball in the ballot-box. **2** to refuse to see or speak to (someone).

black belt 1 a belt indicating that the wearer has reached the highest level of skill in judo and karate. **2** a person who is entitled to wear a black belt.

blackberry *noun* **1** a very variable perennial plant (*Rubus fruticosus*), native to the Mediterranean region and introduced elsewhere, having long prickly woody stems and white or pale pink flowers. Also called BRAMBLE. **2** the edible fruit of this plant.

blackbird *noun* **1** a bird belonging to the thrush family, native to Europe, N Africa, and Asia, and found mainly in hedgerows, woodland, and scrub, but also in gardens in urban areas. The male has a glossy black plumage and a yellow bill. **2** any of various unrelated birds of the oriole family, found in most parts of N America, and so called because the male has dark plumage.

blackboard *noun* a dark-coloured board for writing on with chalk, especially used in schools.

black body *Physics* a hypothetical body that absorbs all the radiation that falls on it, reflecting none.

black box a flight recorder in an aircraft.

blackcap *noun* a slender-billed bird belonging to the warbler family, found in mature deciduous woodland from Europe to Siberia, and so called because the top of the head is black in the male (in the female it is reddish-brown).

blackcock *noun* the male of the black grouse.

black comedy a kind of comedy (in narrative or dramatic form) which derives its humour from exposing the absurd accidents and misfortunes of life.

blackcurrant *noun* **1** a bushy shrub (*Ribes nigrum*), native to Europe and temperate Asia, but widely cultivated for its small edible purplish-black fruit. **2** the fruit of this shrub, which is used to make jam and tarts.

black economy unofficial business, trade, etc, undertaken clandestinely to evade payment of tax.

blacken *verb* (**blackened, blackening**) **1** *trans., intrans.* to make or become black or very dark in colour. **2** *trans.* to speak evil or badly of: *tried to blacken their name.*

. . . .

■ **1** darken, dirty, soil, smudge, cloud. **2** defame, malign, slander, libel, vilify, revile, denigrate, detract, smear, besmirch, sully, stain, tarnish, taint, defile, discredit, dishonour.

■ **2** praise, enhance.

. . . .

black eye an eye with darkened swollen skin around it, usually caused by a blow.

black fly *noun* a small biting fly found near running water. The females of some species are bloodsuckers and serious cattle pests.

Black Friar *Relig.* a monk of the Dominican Order: from their black mantles worn over white habits.

blackguard / ˈblagaːd, ˈblagəd/ *noun old use* a rogue or villain.

blackguardly *adj. old use* villainous; unscrupulous.

blackhead *noun* a small black spot on the skin caused by sweat blocking one of the skin's tiny pores.

black hole *Astron.* a region in space believed to be formed when a star has collapsed in on itself in a huge implosion at the end of its life, when it has exhausted all its nuclear fuel. It is seen as a 'hole' because the force of gravity is so strong that not even light waves can escape from the star.

black ice a type of ice that is thin and transparent. It forms on road surfaces, where the blackness of the road makes it barely visible and therefore highly dangerous.

blacking *noun old use* black polish, especially for shining shoes.

blackjack *noun* **1** pontoon or a similar card-game. **2** *North Amer.* a length of hard flexible leather, especially used for hitting people.

black lead same as GRAPHITE.

blackleg — *noun derog.* a person who refuses to take part in a strike. — *verb intrans.* (**blacklegged, blacklegging**) to refuse to take part in a strike.

blacklist — *noun* a list of people convicted or suspected of something, or not approved of. — *verb* to put (a person, etc) on such a list.

. . . .

■ *verb* ban, bar, boycott, black, outlaw, ostracize.

. . . .

blackly *adv.* in an angry or threatening way.

black magic magic which supposedly invokes the power of the devil to perform evil.

blackmail — *verb* **1** to extort money illegally from (a person) by threatening to reveal harmful information about them. **2** to try to influence (a person) using unfair pressure. — *noun* an act of blackmailing someone.

. . . .

■ *verb* **1** extort, *colloq.* bleed, *colloq.* milk, squeeze, hold to ransom. **2** threaten, *colloq.* lean on, force, compel, coerce. *noun* extortion, chantage, *colloq.* hush money, intimidation, protection, *colloq.* pay-off, ransom.

. . . .

blackmailer *noun* a person who commits blackmail.

Black Maria *colloq.* a police van for transporting prisoners.

black mark an indication of disapproval or criticism.

black market the illegal buying and selling, at high prices, of goods which are scarce or in great demand.

black-marketeer *noun* a person who trades in a black market.

black mass a ceremony parodying the Christian mass, conducted in worship of Satan.

Black Muslim a member of a US black religious movement known as the Nation of Islam.

blackness *noun* a black or very dark state or quality.

blackout 1 a loss of memory or consciousness. **2** a loss of sight or vision. **3** a suppression of information. **4** a sudden interruption in the supply of electrical power or in radio, television *etc* reception. **5** an enforced period during which lights are turned out over an area as a precaution during an air raid at night.

. . . .

■ **1** faint, coma, unconsciousness, oblivion. **3** suppression, censorship, cover-up, concealment, secrecy. **4** power failure, power cut.

. . . .

black pepper pepper produced by grinding the dried fruits of the pepper plant without removing their dark outer covering.

black pudding a dark sausage made from pig's blood and fat.

Black Rod in the UK, a ceremonial official of the House of

Lords, who summons the Commons at the opening of Parliament.

black sheep a member of a family or group who is disapproved of in some way.

Blackshirt *noun* a member of the Italian Fascist Party before and during World War II.

blacksmith *noun* a person who makes and repairs by hand things made of iron, such as horseshoes.

black spot *Brit.* **1** a dangerous stretch of road where accidents often occur. **2** an area where an adverse social condition is prevalent: *an unemployment black spot.*

Black Studies educational courses centred on the history, culture, and development of black people, especially those of African origin or descent in N America, the Caribbean, and Europe.

black swan a swan native to Australia and Tasmania, and now introduced to New Zealand, so called because of its dark plumage. It nests in reed beds.

blackthorn *noun* a thorny deciduous shrub (*Prunus spinosa*), or occasionally a small tree, native to Europe, often forming dense thickets in woodland, and so called because it has conspicuous black twigs on which the small white flowers appear in early spring before the oval toothed leaves have emerged. The rounded fruits, known as *sloes*, are bluish-black with a waxy bloom.

black-tie — *noun* a black bow-tie. — *adj.*, *said of a celebration or function* very formal, with guests expected to wear evening dress.

black widow any of various species of venomous spider found in warm regions worldwide, especially the N American species (*Latrodectus mactans*), the female of which has a black shiny body with a red hourglass-shaped mark on the underside of its almost spherical abdomen.

bladder *noun* **1** in some fishes, amphibians, and reptiles, and all mammals, a hollow sac-shaped organ with a thin muscular wall, in which urine produced by the kidneys is stored before it is discharged from the body. **2** any of various similar hollow organs in which liquid or gas is stored. **3** a hollow bag made of leather, etc stretched by filling with air or liquid. **4** a hollow sac-like structure in certain plants. [from Anglo-Saxon *blædre*, blister, pimple]

bladder wrack a tough brown seaweed (*Fucus vesiculosus*) whose fronds are supported in water by its air-filled bladders.

blade *noun* **1** the cutting part of a knife, sword, etc. **2** the flat, usually long and narrow part of a leaf or petal. **3** the wide flat part of an oar, bat, etc. **4** a flat bone, especially in the shoulder. [from Anglo-Saxon *blæd*]

▣ **1** edge, knife, dagger, sword, scalpel, razor.

blag *verb trans.*, *intrans. slang* **1** to rob or steal. **2** to scrounge or wheedle.

BLAISE *abbrev.* British Library Automated Information Service.

blame — *verb* (**blame someone for something** or **blame something on someone**) **1** to consider a person or thing as responsible for something bad or undesirable. **2** to find fault with a person. — *noun* **1** responsibility for something bad or undesirable. **2** criticism; censure. — **be to blame for something** to be responsible for something bad or undesirable. [from Old French *blasmer*, from Latin *blasphemare*, to blaspheme]

▣ *verb* **1** accuse, charge, indict, denounce, condemn, incriminate. **2** find fault with, reproach, censure, criticize, reprimand, chide, reprove, upbraid, reprehend, admonish, rebuke, disapprove, condemn. *noun* **1** guilt, culpability, fault, responsibility, accountability, liability, onus. **2** censure, criticism, *colloq.* stick, reprimand, reproof, reproach, recrimination, condemnation, accusation, charge, *slang* rap, incrimination.
▣ *verb* **1** exonerate, vindicate. **2** praise. *noun* **1** credit. **2** praise.

blameless *adj.* free from blame; innocent.

▣ innocent, guiltless, clear, faultless, perfect, unblemished, stainless, virtuous, sinless, upright, above reproach, irreproachable, unimpeachable.
▣ guilty, blameworthy.

blamelessly *adv.* without incurring or involving blame: *they were judged to have acted blamelessly.*

blamelessness *noun* lack of blame; innocence.

blameworthy *adj.* deserving blame.

blanch /blɑːntʃ/ *verb* **1** to make white by removing the colour. **2** *intrans.*, *trans.* to make or become white, especially through fear. **3** to prepare (vegetables or meat) for cooking or freezing by boiling in water for a few seconds. **4** to remove the skins (from almonds, etc) by soaking them in boiling water. [from Old French *blanchir*]

▣ **1** whiten, fade, bleach. **2** blench, turn pale.
▣ **1, 2** colour. **2** blush, redden.

blancmange /bləˈmɒndʒ/ *noun* a cold sweet jelly-like pudding made with milk. [from Old French *blanc*, white + *manger*, food]

bland *adj. derog.* **1** *said of food* having a very mild taste. **2** *said of people or their actions* mild or gentle; showing no strong emotions. **3** insipid; lacking interest: *a bland appearance.* [from Latin *blandus*, soft, smooth]

▣ **1** mild, tasteless, weak, smooth. **2** mild, gentle, soft, calm, detached, unemotional. **3** boring, monotonous, humdrum, tedious, dull, uninspiring, uninteresting, unexciting, nondescript, characterless, flat, insipid.
▣ **1** sharp, tasty. **2** emotional, excitable. **3** lively, stimulating.

blandish *verb* to persuade by gentle flattery; to cajole. [from Old French *blandir*]

blandishments *pl. noun* flattery intended to persuade.

blandly *adv.* in a bland or insipid manner; without interest.

blandness *noun* a bland or insipid state or quality.

blank — *adj.* **1** *said of paper* not written or printed on. **2** *said of magnetic tape, etc* with no sound or pictures yet recorded on it. **3** with spaces left for details, information, a signature, etc: *a blank form.* **4** not filled in; empty. **5** showing no expression or interest: *a blank look.* **6** having no thoughts or ideas: *my mind suddenly went blank.* **7** without a break or relieving feature: *a blank wall.* — *noun* **1** an empty space. **2** an empty space left on forms, etc to be filled in with particular information. **3** a printed form with blank spaces. **4** a state of having no thoughts or ideas: *my mind went a complete blank.* **5** a dash written in place of a word. **6** a blank cartridge. — *verb* (**blank something off** or **out**) to hide it or form a screen in front it: *clouds blanking out the sun.* — **draw a blank** to get no results; to fail. [from French *blanc*, white]

▣ *adj.* **1, 3, 4** empty, unfilled, void, clear, bare, unmarked, plain, clean, white. **5** expressionless, deadpan, poker-faced, impassive, apathetic, glazed, vacant, uncomprehending. *noun* **1** space, gap, break, void. **4** emptiness, vacancy, vacuity, nothingness, vacuum.

blank cartridge a cartridge containing an explosive but no bullet.

blank cheque **1** a cheque which has been signed but on which the amount to be paid has been left blank. **2** complete freedom or authority.

blanket /ˈblaŋkɪt/ — *noun* **1** a thick covering of wool or other material, used to cover beds or for wrapping a person in for warmth. **2** a thick layer or mass which covers something: *a blanket of fog.* **3** (*attributive*) general; applying to or covering all cases, etc: *a blanket rule.* — *verb* (**blanketed, blanketing**) **1** to cover with, or as if with, a blanket. **2** to keep quiet or suppress. [from Old French *blankete*, from *blanc*, white]

. . . .

◫ *noun* **1** covering, cover, sheet, carpet, rug, coat, cloak, mantle, wrapper, wrapping. **2** layer, coating, coat, film, carpet, mantle. *verb* **1** cover, cloak, surround, envelop, carpet, enwrap, shroud, swathe, conceal, mask, obscure, cloud. **2** suppress, muffle, deaden, dampen, quieten.

. . . .

blanket bath the washing of a sick person in bed.

blankly *adv.* in a blank or inexpressive manner: *stared at us blankly.*

blankness *noun* lack of interest or expression.

blank verse poetry which does not rhyme, especially iambic pentameters.

blanquette /blɒŋˈkɛt/ *noun* a dish made with white meat such as chicken or veal, cooked in a white sauce. [from French *blanquette*, related to BLANKET]

blare — *verb* **1** *intrans.* to make a sound like a trumpet. **2** *intrans., trans.* to sound or say loudly and harshly. — *noun* a loud, harsh sound. [from Middle English *blaren*]

. . . .

◫ *verb* TRUMPET, ROAR, BOOM, RESOUND. **1** blast, ring, peal, clang, hoot, toot. **2** bellow, bawl, clamour. *noun* roar, bray, blast, boom, clang, bellow, bawl, clamour.

. . . .

blarney — *noun* flattering words used to persuade or deceive. — *verb* (PAST TENSE AND PAST PARTICIPLE **blarneyed**) to persuade using flattery. [from *Blarney* Castle in the Irish Republic; kissing the Blarney Stone traditionally bestows the power of eloquence]

blasé /ˈblɑːzeɪ/ *adj.* lacking enthusiasm or interest, unconcerned, especially through over-familiarity. [from French *blasé*]

. . . .

◫ nonchalant, offhand, unconcerned, unimpressed, unmoved, unexcited, unmoved, jaded, weary, bored, uninterested, apathetic, indifferent, cool.

◫ excited, enthusiastic.

. . . .

blaspheme /blasˈfiːm/ *verb* **1** *intrans., trans.* to speak disrespectfully or rudely about God or sacred matters. **2** *intrans.* to swear or curse using the name of God. [from Latin *blasphemare*]

. . . .

◫ **2** swear, curse, imprecate, damn.

. . . .

blasphemer *noun* a person who blasphemes.

blasphemous /ˈblasfəməs/ *adj.* involving blasphemy; using divine names profanely.

. . . .

◫ profane, impious, sacrilegious, godless, ungodly, irreligious, irreverent.

. . . .

blasphemously *adv.* with blasphemy; profanely.

blasphemy /ˈblasfəmɪ/ *noun* (PL. **blasphemies**) speaking about God or sacred matters in a disrespectful or profane way.

. . . .

◫ impiety, irreverence, sacrilege, desecration, violation, outrage, profanity, curse, expletive, imprecation, cursing, swearing, *formal* execration.

. . . .

blast /blɑːst/ — *noun* **1** an explosion, or the strong shockwaves spreading out from it. **2** a strong sudden stream or gust (of air, wind, etc). **3** a sudden loud sound of a trumpet, car horn, etc. **4** a sudden and violent outburst of anger or criticism. — *verb* **1** to blow up (a tunnel, rock, etc) with explosives. **2** to destroy: *blast one's hopes.* **3** to wither or cause to shrivel up. **4** to criticize severely. **5** (*often* **blast out**) to make a sudden loud noise; to say or produce very loudly: *music was blasting out from the radio.* — *interj.* col-

loq. an expression of annoyance, etc. — **at full blast** at full power, speed, etc. **blast off** *said of a spacecraft* to take off from its launching pad. [from Anglo-Saxon *blæst*]

. . . .

◫ *noun* **1** explosion, detonation, bang, crash, clap, crack, burst, discharge. **2** draught, gust, gale, squall, storm, tempest. **3** sound, blow, blare, roar, boom, peal, hoot, wail, scream, shriek. **4** outburst, broadside, volley, eruption, storm. *verb* **1** explode, blow up, burst, bomb, quarry. **2** shatter, destroy, demolish, ruin, blight. **3** wither, shrivel, blight, canker, mildew, rot, decay. **4** criticize, attack, condemn, *slang* slam, *colloq.* slate. **5** sound, blare, roar, boom, peal, hoot, wail, scream, shriek. **blast off** lift off, take off, launch.

. . . .

blasted — *adj. colloq.* annoying. — *adv. colloq.* extremely: *blasted cold.*

blast furnace a tall furnace that is used to extract iron from iron ores such as haematite and magnetite.

blasting *noun* **1** blowing up with explosives. **2** swearing; cursing.

blastula /ˈblastjʊlə/ *noun Zool.* an early embryonic stage in the development of multicellular animals. It typically consists of a hollow ball of cells. [from Greek *blastos*, bud]

blatant /ˈbleɪtənt/ *adj.* **1** very obvious and without shame: *a blatant lie.* **2** very noticeable and obtrusive. [probably invented by Edmund Spenser (1596)]

. . . .

◫ OBVIOUS. **1** flagrant, brazen, barefaced, shameless, arrant, sheer, outright, gross, unmitigated, undisguised, open, overt, ostentatious. **2** glaring, conspicuous, obtrusive, prominent, pronounced, manifest.

. . . .

blatantly *adv.* in a blatant or flagrant manner.

blather see BLETHER.

blaze[1] — *noun* **1** a bright strong fire or flame. **2** a sudden and sharp bursting out of feeling or emotion. **3** a brilliant display. — *verb intrans.* **1** to burn or shine brightly. **2** to show great emotion, especially anger. — **blaze away 1** to fire a gun rapidly and without stopping. **2** *colloq.* to work very hard. **blaze up 1** to suddenly burn much more brightly. **2** to become very angry. **like blazes** *colloq.* with great energy, speed, or enthusiasm. [from Anglo-Saxon *blse*, torch]

blaze[2] — *noun* **1** a white mark on an animal's face. **2** a mark made on the bark of a tree, especially to show a route or path. — *verb* to mark (a tree, path, etc) with blazes. — **blaze a trail** to be the first to do, study, discover, etc something. [perhaps related to Norse *blesi*]

blaze[3] *verb* (*usually* **blaze something abroad**) to make news or information widely known. [related to Norse *blasa*, to blow]

blazer *noun* a light jacket, often in the colours of a school or club and sometimes worn as part of a uniform. [from BLAZE[1]]

blazing *adj.* **1** burning brightly. **2** *colloq.* extremely angry.

blazon /ˈbleɪzn/ — *verb* (**blazoned, blazoning**) **1** to make public. **2** to describe (a coat of arms) in technical terms. **3** to paint names, designs, etc on (a coat of arms). — *noun* a shield or coat of arms. [from Old French *blason*, shield]

bleach — *verb trans., intrans.* to whiten or remove colour from a substance by exposure to sunlight or certain chemicals. — *noun* any liquid chemical, eg hydrogen peroxide, sodium hypochlorite, used to whiten or remove colour from cloth, paper, hair, etc. All bleaches are oxidizing agents. [from Anglo-Saxon *blæcan*]

. . . .

◫ *verb* whiten, blanch, decolorize, fade, pale, lighten.

. . . .

bleaching powder a white powder used in bleaching, a compound of calcium, chlorine, and oxygen.

bleak *adj.* **1** exposed and desolate. **2** cold and not welcoming. **3** offering little or no hope. [from Anglo-Saxon *blac*, pale]
. . . .

▣ **1** exposed, open, barren, bare, empty, desolate, unsheltered, windy, windswept, gaunt, weatherbeaten. **2** cold, unwelcoming, chilly, raw, freezing, bitter, uninviting, dismal, cheerless. **3** gloomy, sombre, leaden, grim, dreary, dismal, depressing, joyless, cheerless, comfortless, hopeless, discouraging, disheartening.
▣ **1** sheltered. **2** cosy, inviting. **3** bright, cheerful.
. . . .

bleakly *adj.* drearily; without promise.
bleakness *noun* a bleak or desolate state or quality.
blearily *adv.* dimly; indistinctly.
bleary *adj.* **(blearier, bleariest) 1** *said of a person's eyes* red and dim, usually from tiredness or through crying. **2** blurred, indistinct, and unclear.
bleat *verb* **1** *intrans.* to cry like a sheep, goat or calf. **2** *intrans., trans.* **(bleat something out)** to speak or say something foolishly and in a weak, high voice. [from Anglo-Saxon *blætan*]
bleed *verb* (PAST TENSE AND PAST PARTICIPLE **bled**) **1** *intrans.* to lose or let out blood. **2** to remove or take blood from. **3** *intrans. said of plants, etc* to lose juice or sap. **4** to empty liquid or air from (a machine, radiator, etc). **5** *colloq.* to obtain money from (someone), usually illegally. **6** *intrans. said of dye* to come out of the material when wet. **— one's heart bleeds** *ironic* one is sad or pitying. [from Anglo-Saxon *bledan*]
. . . .

▣ **1** haemorrhage, gush, spurt, flow, run, exude, ooze, seep, trickle. **4** drain, empty, tap, siphon. **5** drain, suck dry, squeeze, *colloq.* milk, sap, reduce, deplete.
. . . .

bleeding *adj., adv. slang* expressing anger or disgust: *a bleeding fool/he's bleeding lying.*
bleep **—** *noun* **1** a short high burst of sound, usually made by an electronic machine. **2** same as BLEEPER. **—** *verb* **1** *intrans.* to give out a short, high sound. **2** *trans.* to call (someone) using a bleeper. [probably imitative]
bleeper *noun* a portable radio receiver that emits a single short bleeping sound when it picks up a signal, used especially to call a doctor or police officer carrying such a device.
blemish /'blemɪʃ/ **—** *noun* a stain, mark, or fault. **—** *verb* to stain or spoil the beauty of. [from Old French *blesmir*]
. . . .

▣ *noun* flaw, imperfection, defect, fault, deformity, disfigurement, birthmark, naevus, spot, mark, speck, smudge, blotch, blot, stain, taint, disgrace, dishonour. *verb* flaw, deface, disfigure, spoil, mar, damage, impair, spot, mark, blot, blotch, stain, sully, taint, tarnish.
. . . .

blench *verb intrans.* to start back or move away, especially in fear. [from Anglo-Saxon *blencan*]
blend *verb* **1** to mix (different sorts or varieties) into one. **2** *intrans.* **(blend in** or **with something)** to form a mixture or harmonious combination; to go well together. **3** to mix together. **4** *intrans. said especially of colours* to shade gradually into another: *the blue of the sea blending into the sky.* **—** *noun* a mixture or combination. [from Middle English *blenden*]
. . . .

▣ *verb* **1, 3** mix, mingle, merge, combine, amalgamate, coalesce, compound, synthesize, fuse, unite. **2** harmonize, complement, fit, match. *noun* mixture, mix, combination, union, compound, composite, alloy, amalgam, amalgamation, synthesis, fusion, concoction.
▣ *verb* **1, 3** separate.
. . . .

blende /blɛnd/ *noun* **1** any naturally occurring metal sulphide, eg zinc blende (zinc sulphide). **2** sphalerite, a

mineral consisting mainly of zinc sulphide. [from German *blenden*, to deceive]
blender *noun* a machine for mixing food or making it into a liquid.
blenny *noun* (PL. **blennies**) the common name for any of various small fishes found worldwide, mainly in shallow temperate and tropical seas, and having a long tapering slimy body, no scales, long pelvic fins, and jaws bearing many small teeth. [from Greek *blennos*, mucus]
bless *verb* (PAST TENSE **blessed**; PAST PARTICIPLE **blessed**, **blest**) **1** to ask for divine favour or protection for. **2** to make or pronounce holy; to consecrate. **3** to praise; to give honour or glory to. **4** to thank or be thankful for: *I bless the day I met him.* **5** to make happy, prosperous, or successful. **6** to give consent and approval to. **— be blessed with something** to have the benefit or advantage of a natural quality or attribute: *to be blessed with good health.* **bless me** or **bless my soul** an expression of surprise, pleasure, dismay, etc. **bless you!** said to a person who has just sneezed. [from Anglo-Saxon *bletsian*]
. . . .

▣ **2** anoint, sanctify, consecrate, hallow, dedicate, ordain. **3** praise, extol, magnify, glorify, exalt. **6** approve, countenance, favour, grace.
▣ **2** curse. **3** condemn.
. . . .

blessed /'blesɪd, blest/ *adj.* **1** holy. **2** that brings happiness or benefits; happy, joyful. **3** *RC Church, said of a dead person* pronounced holy by the Pope, usually as the first stage of becoming a saint. **4** *euphemistic colloq.* damned.
. . . .

▣ **1** holy, sacred, hallowed, sanctified, revered, adored, divine. **2** fortunate, prosperous, auspicious, beneficial, happy, contented, glad, joyful, joyous.
▣ **1** cursed.
. . . .

blessedly /'blesɪdlɪ/ *adv.* fortunately; happily.
blessing *noun* **1** a wish or prayer for happiness or success. **2** a cause of happiness; a benefit or advantage. **3** approval or good wishes. **4** a short prayer said before or after a meal. **— a blessing in disguise** something that has proved to be fortunate after seeming unfortunate. **count one's blessings** to be grateful for one's advantages.
. . . .

▣ **1** benediction, prayer, consecration, dedication, invocation. **2** benefit, advantage, favour, godsend, windfall, gift, gain, profit, help, service. **3** approval, concurrence, backing, support, authority, sanction, consent, permission, leave. **4** grace, benediction, thanksgiving.
▣ **2** curse, blight. **3** condemnation.
. . . .

blether or **blather** *verb intrans.* **(blethered, blethering)** *chiefly Scot.* to talk foolishly. [from Norse *blathra*]
blew see BLOW[1].
blight /blaɪt/ **—** *noun* **1** *Agric.* a fungal disease of plants that usually attacks an entire crop, or one specific crop throughout a particular region, eg potato blight. **2** a person or thing that causes decay or destruction, or spoils things. **—** *verb* **1** to affect with blight. **2** to harm or destroy. **3** to disappoint or frustrate: *blighted hopes.* [origin unknown]
. . . .

▣ *noun* **1** fungus, mildew, canker, rot, disease. **2** curse, bane, evil, scourge, affliction, disease, cancer, pollution, contamination, corruption, infestation. *verb* **1** wither, shrivel, mildew, rot. **2** harm, destroy, spoil, mar, injure, ruin, wreck, crush, shatter. **3** frustrate, disappoint, dash, thwart, undermine.
▣ *noun* **2** blessing, boon. *verb* **2** bless.
. . . .

blighter *noun old colloq. use* **1** a person one dislikes. **2** a person one feels some sympathy for or envy of: *poor old blighter.* [from BLIGHT]

blimey /'blaɪmɪ/ *interj. Brit. slang* used to express surprise or annoyance. [from *gorblimey*, God blind me]

Blimp or **blimp** *noun* a very conservative, old-fashioned, reactionary person. [from the fat pompous cartoon character Colonel *Blimp*, used in anti-German and antigovernment cartoons during World War II]

blimp *noun* **1** a type of large balloon or airship, used for publicity, observation, or defence. **2** a soundproof cover for a camera used to shoot films.

blimpish *adj.* characteristic of (Colonel) Blimp; reactionary.

blind /blaɪnd/ — *adj.* **1** not able to see. **2** (**blind to something**) unable or unwilling to understand or appreciate something unwelcome: *blind to one's faults.* **3** without preparation or previous knowledge. **4** unthinking; without reason or purpose: *blind hatred.* **5** hidden from sight: *a blind entrance.* **6** not allowing sight of what is beyond: *a blind summit.* **7** *said of flying* using instruments only, without visual contact. **8** having no openings: *a blind wall.* **9** closed at one end. **10** *said of a pastry case* cooked without a filling. **11** *said of plants* failing to produce flowers. **12** *colloq.* for the use of people who are blind: *a blind crossing.* — *adv.* blindly: *flying blind.* — *noun* **1** a screen to stop light coming through a window. **2** a person, action, or thing which hides the truth or deceives. **3** anything which prevents sight or blocks out light. **4** (**the blind**) people who cannot see. — *verb* **1** to make (someone) blind. **2** to cause (someone) to become unreasonable, foolish, etc, especially uncharacteristically: *blinded by anger.* **3** (**blind someone with something**) to confuse or dazzle them: *tried to blind me with science.* — **blind drunk** *colloq.* completely drunk. **swear blind** *colloq.* to state with certainty. **turn a blind eye to something** to pretend not to notice it. [an Anglo-Saxon word]

▣ *adj.* **1** sightless, unsighted, unseeing, eyeless, purblind, partially sighted. **2** ignorant of, oblivious of or to, unaware of, unconscious of, inattentive to, neglectful of, indifferent to, insensitive to. **3** unprepared, unready, cold, unrehearsed. **4** impetuous, impulsive, hasty, rash, reckless, wild, mad, indiscriminate, careless, heedless, mindless, unthinking, unreasoning, irrational. **5** hidden, concealed, obscured, closed, obstructed. *noun* **1** shade, screen, curtain. **2** cover, cloak, mask, camouflage, masquerade, front, façade, distraction, smokescreen, *colloq.* cover-up.
▣ *adj.* **1** sighted. **2** aware of, sensitive to. **4** careful, cautious.

blind alley 1 a narrow road with an opening at one end only. **2** a situation or course of action which is leading nowhere.

blind date 1 a date with a person one has not met before, often arranged by a third person. **2** the person met on such a date.

blindfold — *noun* a piece of cloth used to cover the eyes to prevent a person from seeing. — *adj., adv.* with one's eyes covered. — *verb* to cover the eyes of (someone) to prevent them from seeing.

blinding *noun* **1** making someone blind, especially violently. **2** the process of filling the cracks of a newly made road with grit. — *adj., said of a light, etc* intensely strong and bright, causing temporary lack of vision. — **clear and intense**: *the answer came in a blinding flash.*

blindly *adv.* without being able to see: *groped blindly for the switch.*

▣ **2** without preparation, thought, or plan. **2** impulsively, rashly, recklessly, indiscriminately, carelessly, heedlessly, impetuously.

blindman's-buff *noun* a children's game in which one child wears a blindfold and tries to catch the other children.

blindness *noun* serious or total loss of vision in one or both eyes.

blind-side — *noun* a person's weak spot, or an area where they fail to see danger. — *verb* to cause a problem for or injury to (someone) by exploiting their blind-side.

blind spot 1 *Anat.* a small area on the retina of the eye where nerve fibres from the light-sensitive rods and cones lead into the optic nerve. There are no rods and cones in this area, and so no visual images can be transmitted from it. **2** an area of poor reception within the normal range of radio transmission, caused by tall buildings or other obstructions. **3** an area of poor or no visibility, especially in the window area of a motor vehicle. **4** a subject in which a particular person lacks understanding or interest: *communication was his blind spot.*

blindworm *noun* same as SLOW-WORM.

blink — *verb usually intrans.* **1** to open and shut the eyes quickly. **2** *trans.* to open and shut (an eyelid or an eye) very quickly. **3** *said of a light* to flash on and off or shine unsteadily. **4** (**blink at something**) to refuse to recognize or accept something unwelcome. — *noun* **1** an act of blinking. **2** a brief period of sunshine, etc. — **in the blink of an eye** quickly; suddenly. **on the blink** *colloq.* not working properly. [from Middle English *blinken*]

blinker — *noun* (*usually* **blinkers**) one of two small flat pieces of leather attached to a horse's bridle to prevent it from seeing sideways. — *verb* (**blinkered, blinkering**) **1** to provide (a horse) with blinkers. **2** to limit or obscure sight or awareness. [from BLINK]

blinkered *adj.* **1** *said of a horse* wearing blinkers. **2** *derog., said of a person* narrow in outlook; unwilling to consider the opinions of others.

▣ **2** narrow-minded, small-minded, prejudiced, bigoted, insular, parochial.

blinking *colloq.* — *adj.* used to express mild annoyance or disapproval: *broke the blinking thing.* — *adv.* very. [from BLINK]

blip — *noun* **1** a sudden sharp sound produced by a machine. **2** a spot of light on a screen showing the position of an object. **3** a sudden and fleeting deviation from what is normal or correct. — *verb intrans.* (**blipped, blipping**) to make a blip. [imitative]

bliss *noun* **1** very great happiness. **2** the special happiness of heaven. [from Anglo-Saxon *bliths*]

▣ **1** happiness, blissfulness, ecstasy, euphoria, rapture, joy, gladness, paradise, heaven. **2** blessedness, beatitude.
▣ HELL. **1** misery. **2** damnation.

blissful *adj.* completely happy; utterly joyful.

▣ ecstatic, euphoric, elated, enraptured, rapturous, delighted, enchanted, joyful, joyous, happy.
▣ miserable, wretched.

blissfully *adv.* happily; joyfully.

blister — *noun* **1** a small swelling on or just beneath the surface of the skin, containing watery fluid (serum) and occasionally blood or pus, usually caused by friction or a burn, but sometimes occurring as an allergic reaction. **2** a bubble in a thin surface coating of paint, varnish, etc, or on the surface of previously molten metal or plastic that has solidified. — *verb* **1** to cause a blister on (skin, a surface, etc). **2** *intrans.* to erupt in blisters. **3** to criticize or attack sharply. [from Norse *blastr*]

▣ *noun* **1** sore, swelling, cyst, boil, abscess, ulcer, pustule, pimple, carbuncle.

blistered *adj.* having many blisters.

blistering *adj.* **1** very hot. **2** angry and aggressive: *blistering criticism.*

blister pack same as BUBBLE PACK.

blithe /blaɪð/ *adj.* **1** happy, without worries or cares. **2** *derog.* done without serious thought; casual. [an Anglo-Saxon word]

blithely *adv.* without concern; casually.

blithering *adj. colloq.* stupid. [from *blither*, a form of BLETHER]

BLitt *abbrev. Baccalaureus Litterarum*, Bachelor of Letters.

blitz — *noun* 1 (*also* **blitzkrieg**) a sudden strong attack, or period of such attacks, especially from the air. 2 (**the Blitz**) the German air raids on Britain in 1940. 3 a period of hard work, etc to get something finished. — *verb* 1 to attack, damage, or destroy as if by a blitz or air raid. 2 to work hard at for a short period. [from German *Blitzkrieg*, lightning war, a sudden and intensive attack to win a quick victory in war]

blizzard /'blɪzəd/ *noun* a severe snowstorm characterized by low temperatures and strong winds that blow large drifts of dry powdery snow upward from the ground, resulting in much reduced visibility.

⊟ snowstorm, squall, storm.

bloat *verb* 1 *trans., intrans.* to swell or cause to swell or puff out with air, pride, etc. 2 *trans.* to prepare (fish, especially herring) by salting and half drying in smoke. [from Norse *blautr*, wet, soft]

⊟ 1 swell, puff up, blow up, inflate, distend, dilate, expand, enlarge.

bloated *adj.* inflated; swollen; puffed out.

⊟ swollen, puffy, blown up, inflated, distended, dilated, expanded, enlarged.
⊞ thin, shrunken, shrivelled.

bloater *noun* a herring that has been salted in brine and partially smoked.

blob *noun* 1 a small soft round mass of something: *a blob of jam.* 2 a small drop of liquid. [imitative of the sound of dripping]

⊟ 1 dab, spot, *colloq.* gob, lump, mass, ball, pellet, pill. 2 drop, droplet, globule, *colloq.* glob, bead, pearl, bubble.

bloc *noun* a group of countries, people, etc who have a common interest, purpose or policy. [from French *bloc*, block, group]

block — *noun* 1 a mass of solid wood, stone, ice, or other hard material, usually with flat sides. 2 a piece of wood, stone, etc used for chopping and cutting on. 3 (*usually* **blocks**) a wooden or plastic cube, used as a child's toy. 4 a large building containing offices, flats, etc. 5 a group of buildings with roads on all four sides. 6 a group of seats, tickets, etc thought of as a single unit: *a block booking.* 7 something which causes or acts as a stopping of movement, thought, etc: *a road block.* 8 a piece of wood or metal which has been cut to be used in printing. 9 *Athletics.* same as STARTING-BLOCK. 10 a series of ropes and wheels for lifting things, or pulleys, mounted in a case. See also BLOCK AND TACKLE. 11 *slang* a person's head. — *verb* 1 to obstruct or impede; to put an obstacle in the way of. 2 to print (a design, title, etc) on (the cover of a book, piece of material, etc). 3 *Cricket* to stop (a ball) with one's bat resting upright on the ground. — **block someone** or **something in** 1 to prevent them from moving or from getting out; to confine them. 2 to draw or sketch them roughly. 3 (**block something off**) to restrict or limit the use of an area: *the police have blocked off several streets.* **block something out** 1 to shut out light, an idea, etc. 2 to draw or sketch something roughly. **block something up** 1 to block it completely. 2 to fill a window, doorway, etc with bricks, etc. [from French *bloc*]

⊟ *noun* 1 mass, piece, lump, chunk, hunk, square, cube, brick, bar. 7 obstacle, barrier, bar, jam, blockage, stoppage, resistance, obstruction, impediment, hindrance. *verb* 1 obstruct, impede, hinder, choke, clog, plug, stop up, dam

up, close, bar, stop, check, arrest, halt, thwart, scotch, deter. 3 stonewall.

blockade — *noun* the closing off of a port, region, etc by military means in order to stop people, goods, etc from passing in and out. — *verb* to put a blockade round (a port, etc).

⊟ *noun* barrier, barricade, siege, obstruction, restriction, stoppage, closure.

blockage /'blɒkɪdʒ/ *noun* 1 anything that causes a pipe, etc to be blocked. 2 the state of being blocked.

⊟ OBSTRUCTION. 1 block, clot, jam, log jam, hindrance, impediment. 2 stoppage, congestion.

block and tackle a series of ropes and wheels used for lifting heavy objects. See also BLOCK 10.

blockbuster *noun colloq.* 1 a highly popular and successful film, book, etc. 2 an extremely powerful bomb.

block capital or **block letter** a capital letter written in imitation of printed type.

blocked *adj.* affected by an obstruction or blockage.

⊟ obstructed, clogged, choked, jammed, barred, barricaded, impassable.

blockhead *noun colloq.* a stupid person.

⊟ fool, idiot, imbecile, *colloq.* ass, *colloq.* dimwit, dolt, dunce.

blockhouse *noun* 1 a small shelter made from very strong concrete, used for watching battles, spacecraft take off, etc. 2 a small, temporary fort.

block letter same as BLOCK CAPITAL.

block vote a vote by a delegate, eg at a conference, that is proportional in power to the number of people the delegate represents.

bloke *noun Brit. colloq.* a man.

⊟ man, *colloq.* guy, *Brit. colloq* chap, fellow.

blond *adj.* 1 *said of a person* having pale yellow hair and light-coloured or pale skin. 2 *said of a person's hair* pale yellow. [from Latin *blondus*, yellow]

⊟ *adj.* 2 fair, flaxen, golden, fair-haired, golden-haired, light-coloured, bleached.

blonde /blɒnd/ — *noun* a woman with pale yellow hair. — *adj., said of a woman* having pale yellow hair.

blood /blʌd/ — *noun* 1 a fluid tissue that circulates in the arteries, veins, and capillaries of the body as a result of muscular contractions of the heart. It conveys nutrients and oxygen to the organs and tissues, and removes carbon dioxide and other waste products. 2 the taking of life; murder. 3 relationship through belonging to the same family, race, etc.; descent: *of royal blood.* 4 near family: *my own flesh and blood.* 5 temper, passion. 6 a group of people seen as adding new strength to an existing group: *new blood in the teaching profession.* 7 a man who is interested in fashion, etc and takes a strong interest in his appearance. — *verb* 1 to give a (young hunting dog) its first taste of a freshly killed animal. 2 to give (a person, etc) the first experience of (war, battle, etc). — **be after** or **out for someone's blood** to be extremely angry with a person and to want revenge, to fight him or her, etc. **in cold blood** deliberately and cruelly, showing no concern or passion. **make one's blood boil** to make one extremely angry. **make one's blood run cold** to frighten or horrify one. **sweat**

blood to work very hard. [from Anglo-Saxon *blod*]
················

▤ *noun* **3** extraction, birth, descent, lineage, ancestry, descendants, kinship, relationship. **4** family, kin, kindred, kith and kin, relations.
·····························

blood-and-thunder *adj.*, *said of a film, etc* including much violent action and excitement.

blood bank a department in a hospital or blood transfusion centre where blood collected from donors is stored, categorized according to blood group, and tested (for the presence of the HIV virus), prior to transfusion into patients.

bloodbath *noun* a massacre.

blood brother a man or boy who has promised to treat another as his brother, usually in a ceremony in which some of their blood has mixed.

blood count a numerical calculation to determine the number of red or white blood cells in a known volume of blood.

bloodcurdling *adj.* causing great fear.
··················

▤ horrifying, chilling, spine-chilling, hair-raising, terrifying, frightening, scary, dreadful, fearful, horrible, horrid, horrendous.
·····························

blood donor a person who donates blood under medical supervision for storage in a blood bank until it is required for transfusion into a patient with a compatible blood group.

blood group or **blood type** any one of the four types into which human blood may be classified, A, B, AB and O.

blood heat the normal temperature of human blood (37°C or 984°F).

bloodhound *noun* a large breed of dog, known for its keen sense of smell, having a powerful body with loose-fitting skin, a short tan or black and tan coat, long pendulous ears, and a long deep muzzle.

bloodily *adv.* in a bloody or cruel manner.

bloodiness *noun* **1** being bloody or covered in blood. **2** cruelty; much killing.

bloodless *adj.* **1** without violence or anybody being killed. **2** pale and lifeless. **3** having little vitality or interest.

▤ **1** peaceful, non-violent, amicable. **2** anaemic, pale, wan, sallow, ashen, colourless, lifeless, weak, frail. **3** dull, tedious, boring, insipid, bland, anaemic, lifeless, colourless.
·····························

bloodlessly *adv.* without violence or killing.

bloodletting *noun* **1** killing. **2** the removal of blood by opening a vein, formerly used to treat numerous diseases and disorders.

blood-money *noun* **1** money paid for committing murder. **2** money paid in compensation to the relatives of a murdered person.

blood orange a variety of orange having deep red pulp, or orange pulp streaked with red, when ripe.

blood poisoning a serious condition caused by the presence of either bacterial toxins or large numbers of bacteria in the bloodstream.

blood pressure the pressure of the blood within the blood vessels. It usually refers to the pressure within the arteries, the pressure within capillaries and veins being much lower.

blood relation a person related to another by birth rather than by marriage.

bloodshed *noun* the shedding of blood or killing of people.
··················

▤ killing, murder, slaughter, massacre, bloodbath, butchery, carnage, gore, bloodletting.
·····························

bloodshot *adj.*, *said of the eyes* sore and red with blood.

blood sports sports that involve the killing of animals.

bloodstained *adj.* stained with blood.

bloodstock *noun* horses that have been bred specially for racing.

bloodstone *noun Geol.* a type of chalcedony, a fine-grained variety of the mineral quartz. It is dark green with red flecks.

bloodstream *noun* the flow of blood through the arteries, veins, and capillaries of an animal's body.

bloodsucker *noun* **1** an animal that sucks blood, eg the leech. **2** *colloq.* a person who extorts money from another.

bloodsucking *adj.* extortionate.

blood test a test in which a small amount of blood is analysed in order to determine its blood group, or to detect the presence of alcohol, drugs, bacteria, or viruses.

bloodthirstily *adv.* with eagerness or fondness for killing.

bloodthirstiness *noun* eagerness or fondness for killing.

bloodthirsty *adj.* **1** eager for or fond of killing or violence. **2** *said of a film, etc* including much violence and killing.
··················

▤ **1** murderous, homicidal, warlike, savage, barbaric, barbarous, brutal, ferocious, vicious, cruel, inhuman, ruthless. **2** violent, bloody, gory.
·····························

blood transfusion the introduction of whole blood directly into a person's bloodstream in order to replace blood that has been lost as a result of injury, severe burns, surgery, etc, or that is of defective quality as a result of disease. See also TRANSFUSION.

blood type same as BLOOD GROUP.

blood vessel in the body of an animal, any tubular structure through which blood flows, ie an artery, vein, or capillary.

bloody — *adj.* (**bloodier**, **bloodiest**) **1** stained or covered with blood. **2** involving or including much killing. **3** cruel. **4** *slang* used to express annoyance, etc: *a bloody fool.* — *adv. slang* extremely. — *verb* (**bloodies**, **bloodied**) to stain or cover with blood.
··················

▤ *adj.* **1** bleeding, bloodstained, gory. **2** gory, bloodthirsty, sanguinary. **3** cruel, murderous, savage, brutal, ferocious, fierce, sanguinary.
·····························

bloody Mary a drink made from vodka and tomato juice.

bloody-minded *adj. derog.* deliberately unco-operative and inclined to cause difficulties for others.

bloody-mindedness *noun* being deliberately unco-operative and causing difficulties.
··················

▤ unco-operative, unhelpful, contrary, perverse, obstinate, stubborn, intransigent, refractory, troublesome.
·····························

bloom — *noun* **1** a flower, especially on a plant valued for its flowers. **2** the state of flowering: *in bloom.* **3** a state of perfection or great beauty: *in full bloom.* **4** a glow or flush on the skin. **5** a powdery or waxy coating on the surface of certain fruits (eg grapes) or leaves. **6** a rapid seasonal increase in the rate of growth of certain algae in lakes, ponds, etc, often as a result of pollution of the water by nitrate fertilizers applied to the surrounding land, but sometimes occurring naturally. — *verb intrans.* **1** to be in flower. **2** to be in or achieve a state of great beauty or perfection. **3** to be healthy; to be growing well; to flourish. [from Norse *blom*]
··················

▤ *noun* **1** blossom, flower, bud. **3** prime, heyday, perfection, beauty, radiance, lustre. **4** blush, flush, glow, rosiness, health, vigour, freshness. *verb* **1** blossom, flower, blow, open, bud, sprout. **3** grow, wax, develop, mature, flourish, thrive, prosper.

▣ *verb* FADE, WITHER.
·····························

bloomer *noun colloq.* a silly mistake. [from BLOOMING]

⊟ mistake, blunder, *colloq.* clanger, *colloq.* boob, *colloq.* booboo, gaffe.

bloomers *pl. noun* **1** *formerly* short loose trousers gathered at the knee, worn by women. **2** *old colloq. use* women's underpants or knickers. [named after Amelia *Bloomer* (1818–94), an American social reformer who believed women should dress in short full skirts and bloomers]

blooming — *adj.* **1** flowering. **2** bright; beautiful. **3** healthy and flourishing. **4** *slang* used as an expression of annoyance, etc: *a blooming idiot.* — *adv. slang* very.

blossom — *noun* **1** a flower or mass of flowers, especially on a fruit tree. **2** the state of flowering: *in blossom.* — *verb intrans.* blossomed, **blossoming**) **1** to develop flowers. **2** to grow well or develop: *she has blossomed into an accomplished dancer.* [from Anglo-Saxon *blostm*]

⊟ *noun* BLOOM, FLOWER, BUD. *verb* **1** bloom, flower, blow. **2** develop, mature, flourish, thrive, prosper, succeed.
⊟ *verb* FADE, WITHER.

blossoming *adj.* flowering; maturing, thriving.

blot — *noun* **1** a spot or stain, especially of ink. **2** a spot or blemish which spoils the beauty of something. **3** a stain on a person's good reputation or character. — *verb* (**blotted, blotting**) **1** to make a spot or stain on, especially with ink. **2** to dry with blotting-paper. — **blot one's copybook** to spoil one's good reputation, etc, especially through a small mistake. **blot something out 1** to hide it from sight. **2** to refuse to think about or remember a painful memory. [from Middle English *blotte*]

⊟ *noun* SPOT, STAIN, BLEMISH. **1**, **2** smudge, blotch, smear, mark, speck. **2** flaw, fault, defect. **3** taint. *verb* **1** spot, mark, stain, smudge, blur, sully, taint, tarnish, spoil, mar, disfigure, disgrace. **blot out 1** hide, conceal, cloak, eclipse, obscure, darken, shadow. **2** obliterate, cancel, erase, eradicate, expunge, delete.

blotch — *noun* **1** a large coloured or sore spot or mark on the skin. **2** a large discoloured patch or stain. — *verb* to cover or mark with blotches. [perhaps from **blot**]

⊟ *noun* PATCH, MARK, BLEMISH. **2** splodge, splotch, splash, smudge, blot, spot, stain. *verb* mark, blemish, smudge, blot, spot, stain.

blotchy *adj.* (**blotchier, blotchiest**) covered in blotches; discoloured in patches.

⊟ spotty, spotted, patchy, uneven, smeary, blemished, reddened, inflamed.

blotter *noun* a large sheet or pad of blotting-paper with a hard backing.

blotting-paper *noun* soft, thick paper used for drying wet ink when writing.

blouse /blaʊz/ — *noun* **1** a woman's shirt-like garment. **2** a loose jacket gathered in at the waist, part of a soldier's uniform. — *verb* to arrange in loose folds. [from French *blouse*]

blouson /'bluːzɒn/ *noun* a loose jacket fitting tightly at the waist. [from French *blouson*]

blow[1] — *verb* (PAST TENSE **blew**; PAST PARTICIPLE **blown**) **1** *intrans* said of a current of air, wind, *etc* to be moving, especially rapidly. **2** *intrans., trans.* (often **blow along** or **down**) to move or be moved by a current of air, wind, etc. **3** to send (air) from the mouth. **4** to form or shape by blowing air from the mouth: *blow bubbles/blow glass.* **5** to shatter or destroy by the strength of its blast: *the explosion blew*

the chimney off the roof. **6** to produce (a sound) by blowing: *blow a whistle.* **7** *intrans.* to breathe heavily. **8** to clear by blowing through: *blow one's nose.* **9 a** to cause (a fuse) to break. **b** *said of a fuse* to break, causing an interruption in the flow of current. **10** to break into (a safe, etc) using explosives. **11** *colloq.* to spoil or bungle (an opportunity, etc): *he had his chance, and he blew it.* **12** *colloq.* to spend a large amount of money: *blew £10 on a round of drinks.* **13** *intrans., trans. slang* to leave (a place) quickly and suddenly. **14** *intrans. said of a whale* to send out air and water through a hole in the top of its head. — *noun* **1** an act or example of blowing. **2** a spell of exposure to fresh air: *let's go for a blow on the cliffs.* — *interj.* an expression of annoyance. — **blow someone away** *North Amer. slang* to murder them with a gun. **blow something away** or **off** to remove it by blowing. **blow hot and cold** *colloq.* to keep changing one's mind. **blow something out 1** to put a flame, etc out by blowing. **2** to send something forcibly outwards through an explosion. See also BLOW-OUT. **blow over** *said of an incident, threat, etc* to come to an end, especially without having any harmful effect. **blow one's own trumpet** *colloq.* to praise oneself and one's abilities, etc. **blow something sky-high** to destroy it completely. **blow one's top** *colloq.* to lose one's temper. **blow up 1** to explode. **2** to fill up or swell up with air or gas. **3** *colloq.* to lose one's temper. **blow someone up** *colloq.* to lose one's temper with them. **blow something up 1** to explode something; to destroy something by an explosion. **2** to inflate something. **3** to produce a larger version of (a photograph, etc). **4** *colloq.* to make something seem more serious or important than it really is. **blow the whistle on someone** *colloq.* to inform on them. **blow the whistle on something** *colloq.* to bring it to an abrupt end. [from Anglo-Saxon *blawan*]

⊟ *verb* **1** gust. **1**, **2** rush, flow, waft, whirl, whisk, swirl, sweep. **2** flutter, flap, ripple, ruffle, toss, sway, bend. **3** breathe, exhale, puff, waft. **6** play, sound, pipe, toot. **7** pant, puff, gasp. **12** spend, squander, waste, lavish. *noun* **1** puff, draught, flurry, gust, blast, wind, gale, squall, tempest. **blow over** die down, subside, end, finish, cease, pass, vanish, disappear, dissipate, fizzle out, peter out. **blow up 1** explode, go off, detonate, burst, blast, bomb. **2** inflate, swell, fill (out), distend, dilate, expand. **3** lose one's temper, *colloq.* blow one's top, erupt, *colloq.* hit the roof, *colloq.* go mad. **blow someone up** tell off, reprimand, *colloq.* haul over the coals, *colloq.* tear a strip off, give a dressing-down to. **blow something up 1** explode, set off, detonate, blast, shatter, destroy, mine, bomb. **2** inflate, pump up, fill, bloat, distend. **3** enlarge, magnify. **4** exaggerate, overstate, amplify, embellish, embroider.

blow[2] *noun* **1** a stroke or knock with the hand or a weapon. **2** a sudden shock or misfortune. — **come to blows** to end up fighting.

⊟ **1** knock, stroke, thump, punch, rap, box, cuff, clip, clout, swipe, *slang* biff, bash, slap, smack, *colloq.* whack, *colloq.* wallop, *slang* belt, buffet, bang. **2** misfortune, affliction, reverse, setback, shock, upset, *colloq.* whammy, jolt, bombshell, disappointment, comedown, calamity, catastrophe, disaster.

blow-by-blow *adj., said of a description, account, etc* giving all the details in the right order.

blow-dry — *verb* to dry (hair) in a particular style with a hair-drier. — *noun* an act of blow-drying.

blower *noun* **1** a device for blowing out a current of air. **2** (**the blower**) *colloq.* the telephone.

blowfly *noun* any of various species of fly whose eggs are laid in rotting flesh or excrement on which the hatched larvae (maggots) subsequently feed, eg the bluebottle.

blowhole *noun* **1** a nostril high on the head of a whale, which can be closed by means of valves during diving, and through which a compressed stream of water droplets and air is released, forming a 'spout', as the animal surfaces. **2** *Geol.* an aperture near a clifftop through which air or water compressed in a sea cave by breaking waves and rising tides is forcibly expelled. **3** *Geol.* a small vent on the surface of a thick lava flow.

blowlamp or **blowtorch** *noun* a small portable burner, usually fuelled with liquid gas, that produces an intense hot flame, used for paint-stripping, melting soft metal, etc.

blown see BLOW[1].

blow-out *noun colloq.* **1** the bursting of a car tyre. **2** a violent escape of gas, etc, especially on an oil rig. **3** a large meal.

blowpipe *noun* **1** in glass-blowing, a long narrow iron tube on which a mass of molten glass is gathered. Air is then forced down the tube, forming a bubble of air within the glass, which can then be shaped as it cools. **2** a small often curved tube that carries a stream of air into a flame in order to concentrate and direct it, eg for brazing and soldering.

blowtorch same as BLOWLAMP.

blow-up **1** an enlargement of a photograph. **2** an explosion.

blowy *adj.* (**blowier, blowiest**) blustery; windy.

. . . .

   🖃 breezy, windy, fresh, blustery, gusty, squally, stormy.

. . . .

blowzy or **blowsy** *adj.* (**blowzier, blowziest**) *derog. colloq., said of a woman* **1** fat and red-faced. **2** dirty and untidy. [from *blowze*, beggar's woman]

blubber — *noun* a thick insulating layer of fat beneath the skin of whales, seals, etc. — *verb* **1** *intrans.* to weep convulsively. **2** to try to say (words, etc) while weeping. [imitative]

bludgeon /ˈblʌdʒən/ — *noun* a stick or club with a heavy end. — *verb* (**bludgeoned, bludgeoning**) **1** to hit with, or as if with, a bludgeon. **2** to force or bully into doing something.

. . . .

   🖃 *noun* club, cudgel, cosh. *verb* **1** beat, strike, club, batter, *colloq.* cosh, cudgel. **2** force, coerce, bully, bulldoze, badger, hector, harass, browbeat, terrorize, intimidate.

. . . .

blue — *adj.* **1** of the colour of a clear, cloudless sky. **2** sad or depressed. See also BLUES. **3** *said of a film, etc* pornographic or indecent. **4** politically conservative. **5** with a skin which is pale blue or purple because of the cold. — *noun* **1** the colour of a clear, cloudless sky. **2** blue paint or dye. **3** blue material or clothes: *dressed in blue.* **4** a person who has been chosen to represent a college or university at sport, especially at Oxford or Cambridge. **5** *Brit. colloq.* a supporter of the Conservative Party. — *verb* (**bluing, blueing**) **1** to make blue. **2** *colloq.* to waste. — **do something till one is blue in the face** to do it repeatedly but without any effect. **once in a blue moon** hardly ever. **out of the blue** without warning; unexpectedly. [from Old French *bleu*]

. . . .

   🖃 *adj.* **1** azure, sapphire, cobalt, ultramarine, navy, indigo, aquamarine, turquoise, cyan. **2** sad, depressed, low, *colloq.* down in the dumps, dejected, downcast, dispirited, downhearted, despondent, gloomy, glum, dismal, unhappy, miserable, melancholy, morose, fed up. **3** pornographic, obscene, offensive, indecent, improper, coarse, vulgar, lewd, dirty, bawdy, smutty, near the bone, near the knuckle, risqué. **4** Conservative, Tory, right-wing. *noun* **1** azure, sapphire, cobalt, ultramarine, navy, indigo, aquamarine, turquoise, cyan.

   🖃 *adj.* **2** cheerful, happy. **3** decent, clean.

. . . .

blue baby *Medicine* a newborn baby suffering from congenital heart disease that results in some or all of the deoxygenated (blue) blood being pumped around the body (giving the skin and lips a bluish tinge) instead of passing through the lungs. It is treated by cardiac surgery early in life.

bluebell *noun* **1** a bulbous perennial plant (*Hyacinthoides*

non-scriptus), native to W Europe, that produces clumps of narrow strap-shaped shiny leaves in spring. **2** the Scottish name for harebell (*Campanula rotundifolia*). **3** any of various other plants having blue bell-shaped flowers.

blueberry *noun* (PL. **blueberries**) **1** any of various species of deciduous shrub of the genus *Vaccinium*, native to N America, having white or pinkish bell-shaped flowers and bluish-black edible berries with a waxy bloom, containing numerous tiny seeds. Also called HUCKLEBERRY. **2** the fruit of this plant.

bluebird *noun* **1** any of various species of bird belonging to the thrush family, native to N and Central America, and so called because the male has bright blue plumage on its back (the female is dull grey in colour). **2** any of various other birds having blue plumage.

blue blood royal or noble blood or descent.

bluebottle *noun* a large buzzing fly, so called because its abdomen has a metallic blue sheen.

blue cheese cheese with thin lines of blue mould running through it.

blue-chip *adj. Stock Exchange* used to describe shares that are secure, although less secure than gilt-edged.

blue-collar *adj., said of workers* doing manual or unskilled work. See also WHITE-COLLAR.

blue-eyed boy *derog. colloq.* a favourite.

bluegrass or **bluefunk** *noun* a simple style of country music popular in southern states of America.

blue-green alga *Biol.* common name for any of a group of single-celled prokaryotic organisms capable of photosynthesis. Also called CYANOBACTERIA.

blue movie or **blue film** a titillating or pornographic film.

blueness *noun* a blue state or quality.

blue note *Mus.* a flattened note, usually the minor third and seventh of the scale, characteristic of the blues.

blue-pencil *verb* (**blue-pencilled, blue-pencilling**) to correct, edit, or cut parts out of (a piece of writing).

Blue Peter a blue flag with a white square, flown on a ship which is about to sail.

blueprint *noun* **1** a photographic print of plans, designs, etc consisting of white lines on a blue background. **2** a detailed plan of work to be done.

. . . .

   🖃 **2** plan, scheme, pattern, design, outline, draft, sketch, project, model, archetype, prototype, pilot, guide.

. . . .

blues *noun* **1** (*usually* **the blues**) a feeling of sadness or depression. **2** slow melancholy jazz music of Black American origin.

bluestocking *noun* often *derog.* a highly educated woman who is interested in serious academic subjects.

blue tit a small bird belonging to the tit family, native to Europe, N Africa, and SW Asia, and having a bright blue crown, wings, and tail, yellow underparts, and a narrow black line running down the centre of its breast.

blue whale a rare baleen whale of the rorqual family, the largest living animal. It grows to a length of up to 30m, and is blue with pale spots.

bluff[1] — *verb* **1** *intrans.* to try to deceive someone by pretending to be stronger, cleverer, etc than one really is. **2** *trans.* (**bluff someone into something**) to trick them by bluffing: *let's bluff him into doing all the work.* — *noun* an act of bluffing. — **call someone's bluff** to challenge another person's bluff. [from Dutch *bluffen*, to play a trick at cards]

. . . .

   🖃 *verb* **1** lie, pretend, feign, sham, fake. **2** trick, deceive, delude, mislead, hoodwink, blind, *colloq.* bamboozle, fool. *noun* lie, idle boast, bravado, humbug, pretence, show, sham, fake, fraud, trick, subterfuge, deceit, deception.

. . . .

bluff[2] — *noun* a steep cliff or bank of ground. — *adj.* **1** *usually said of a cliff or the bow of a ship* steep and upright. **2** rough, cheerful, and honest in manner.

■ *noun* cliff, bank, face, scarp, escarpment. *adj.* **3** hearty, frank, blunt, honest, straightforward, forthright, cheerful, jovial, genial.

bluffly *adv.* **1** steeply. **2** in a straightforwardly cheerful manner.

bluffness *noun* a bluff or rough manner; abruptness.

bluish *adj.* somewhat blue; close to blue.

blunder — *verb intrans.* (**blundered, blundering**) **1** to make a foolish and usually serious mistake. **2** to move about awkwardly and clumsily: *her brother blundered in while we were kissing.* — *noun* a foolish and usually serious mistake. [from Middle English *blunderen*, from Norse *blunda*, to shut one's eyes]

■ *verb* **1** make a mistake, err, *colloq.* slip up, miscalculate, misjudge, bungle, botch, *colloq.* fluff, mismanage, *slang* cock up. **2** barge, stumble, flounder, stagger, bumble. *noun* mistake, error, *colloq.* bloomer, *colloq.* clanger, *colloq.* howler, inaccuracy, slip, solecism, *colloq.* boob, indiscretion, gaffe, faux pas, *colloq.* slip-up, oversight, fault, *slang* cock-up.

blunderbuss *noun Hist.* a type of shotgun with a short wide barrel. [from Dutch *donderbus*, from *donder*, thunder + *bus*, gun]

blunderer *noun* a person who blunders; a clumsy person.

blundering *adj.* making or involving many clumsy mistakes.

blunt — *adj.* **1** having no point or sharp edge. **2** not sharp. **3** honest and direct in a rough way. — *verb* to make blunt or less sharp.

■ *adj.* **1, 2** unsharpened, dull, worn, pointless, rounded, stubbed. **3** honest, frank, candid, direct, forthright, unceremonious, explicit, plain-spoken, downright, outspoken, tactless, insensitive, rude, impolite, uncivil, brusque, curt, abrupt. *verb* dull, take the edge off, dampen, soften, deaden, numb, anaesthetize, alleviate, allay, abate, weaken.
🔁 *adj.* **1, 2** sharp, pointed. **3** subtle, tactful. *verb* sharpen, intensify.

bluntly *adv.* in a blunt direct manner: *replied bluntly that she was staying.*

■ frankly, candidly, directly, forthrightly, unceremoniously, explicitly, insensitively, rudely, impolitely, brusquely, curtly, abruptly.

bluntness *noun* directness of manner: *the bluntness of his reply took them by surprise.*

blur — *noun* **1** a thing not clearly seen or heard. **2** a smear or smudge. — *verb* (**blurred, blurring**) **1** *trans., intrans.* to make or become less clear or distinct. **2** to rub over and smudge. **3** to make (one's memory, judgement, etc) less clear.

■ *noun* **1** shape, shadow, haze, mist, fog, muddle, confusion, babble, hubbub. **2** smear, smudge, blotch, splotch, splodge. *verb* **1** obscure, darken, mask, conceal, mist, fog, befog, cloud, becloud. **2** smear, smudge.

blurb *noun* a brief description of a book, usually printed on the jacket in order to promote it. [invented by Gelett Burgess, an American author (died 1951)]

blurred or **blurry** *adj.* (**blurrier, blurriest**) **1** indistinct. **2** smudged.

■ **1** indistinct, vague, unclear, out of focus, fuzzy, ill-defined,

faint, hazy, misty, foggy, cloudy, bleary, dim, obscure, confused. **2** smudged, smeared, blotted.
🔁 **1, 2** clear, distinct.

blurt *verb* (*usually* **blurt something out**) to say or reveal suddenly or without thinking of the effect or result.

■ exclaim, cry, shout (out), utter, tell, reveal, disclose, divulge, *colloq.* blab, let out, let slip.

blush — *noun* **1** a red or glow on the skin of the face, caused by shame, embarrassment, etc. **2** a pink, rosy glow. — *verb intrans.* **1** to become red or pink in the face because of shame, embarrassment, etc. **2** to feel ashamed or embarrassed: *blush when one thinks of past mistakes.* [from Anglo-Saxon *blyscan*]

■ *noun* FLUSH. **1** reddening, ruddiness, colour. **2** rosiness, glow. *verb* **1** flush, redden, colour, glow.
🔁 *verb* **1** blanch.

blusher *noun* a pink or pale orange cream or powder used to give colour to the cheeks.

blushing *adj.* red or pink in the face from embarrassment.

■ flushed, red, rosy, glowing, confused, embarrassed, ashamed, modest.
🔁 pale, white, composed.

blush wine a white wine with a pink tint, made from red grape varieties.

bluster — *verb intrans.* (**blustered, blustering**) **1** to speak in a boasting, angry, or threatening way, often to hide fear. **2** *said of the wind, waves, etc* to blow or move roughly. — *noun* **1** speech that is ostentatiously boasting, angry, or threatening. **2** the roaring noise of the wind or sea on a rough day. [probably from German dialect *blustern*, to blow violently]

■ *verb* **1** boast, brag, crow, *colloq.* talk big, swagger, strut, vaunt, show off, rant, roar, storm, bully, hector. *noun* **1** boasting, crowing, bravado, bluff, swagger.

blusterer *noun* **1** a person who blusters or speaks loudly and boastfully. **2** a rough windy day.

blustery *adj.*, *said of the weather* rough and windy.

■ windy, gusty, squally, stormy, tempestuous, violent, wild, boisterous.
🔁 calm.

blvd *abbrev.* boulevard.

BM *abbrev.* **1** Bachelor of Medicine. **2** British Museum.

BMA *abbrev.* British Medical Association.

BMEWS *abbrev.* ballistic missile early warning system.

BMJ *abbrev.* British Medical Journal.

BMus *abbrev.* Bachelor of Music.

BMW *abbrev. Bayerische Motoren Werke*, Bavarian motor works.

BMX *noun* **1** bicycle riding and racing over a rough track with obstacles. **2** a bicycle designed for this. [abbreviation of bicycle moto-*cross*]

BNEC *abbrev.* British National Export Council.

BNFL *abbrev.* British Nuclear Fuels Ltd.

BO *abbrev. colloq.* body odour.

boa /ˈbəʊə/ *noun* **1** any constricting snake belonging to the family Boidae, which also includes the pythons and anaconda. **2** (*also* **boa constrictor**) a tropical American ground-dwelling snake, 3m to 4m in length, that coils around and kills its prey by suffocation rather than crushing. **3** a woman's long thin scarf, usually made of feathers or fur. [from Latin *boa*, a kind of snake]

boar *noun* **1** (*in full* **wild boar**) a wild ancestor of the domestic pig, native to Europe, NW Africa, and S Asia, and having thick dark hair. The male has tusks. **2** a mature uncastrated male pig. **3** the flesh of this animal. [from Anglo-Saxon *bar*]

board — *noun* **1** a long flat strip of wood. **2** a piece of material resembling this, made from fibres compressed together: *chipboard*. **3** a flat piece of wood, etc for a stated purpose: *notice board/chessboard*. **4** thick stiff card used eg for binding books. **5** a person's meals, provided in return for money: *bed and board*. **6** an official group of people controlling or managing an organization, etc, or examining or interviewing candidates: *a board of examiners*. **7** (**boards**) a theatre stage: *tread the boards*. **8** *Naut.* the side of a ship. — *verb* **1** to enter or get on to (a ship, aeroplane, bus, etc). **2** *intrans.* to receive accommodation and meals in someone else's house, in return for payment. **3** to provide (someone) with accommodation and meals in return for payment. **4** (*also* **board someone out**) to arrange for someone to receive accommodation and meals away from home. **5** (*also* **board something up**) to cover a gap or entrance with boards. — **across the board**. See ACROSS. **go by the board** *colloq.* to be given up or ignored. **on board** on or into a ship, aeroplane, etc. **sweep the board** to win everything. **take something on board** to understand or accept new ideas, responsibilities, etc. [from Anglo-Saxon *bord*]

■ *noun* **1** strip, sheet, panel, slab, plank, beam, timber, slat. **5** meals, food, provisions, rations. **6** committee, council, panel, jury, commission, directorate, directors, trustees, advisers. *verb* **1** get on, embark on, mount, enter, catch. **2** lodge. **3** put up.

boarder *noun* **1** a person who receives accommodation and meals in someone else's house, in return for payment. **2** a pupil who lives at school during term time.

board game a game played with pieces to be moved on a board, eg chess.

boarding *noun* **1** a collection of wooden boards laid next to each other. **2** the act of boarding a ship, aeroplane, etc.

boarding house a house where people live and take meals as paying guests.

boarding pass or **boarding card** a card or piece of paper which allows a person to board an aeroplane, etc.

boarding school a school where pupils may live during term time.

boardroom *noun* **1** a room in which the directors of a company meet. **2** the highest level of management of a company.

boast — *verb* **1** *intrans.* to talk with excessive pride (about one's own abilities, achievements, etc). **2** *trans.* to own or have (something it is right to be proud of): *the hotel boasts magnificent views across the valley*. — *noun* **1** an act of boasting. **2** a thing one is proud of. [from Middle English *bost*]

■ *verb* **1** brag, crow, *colloq.* swank, exaggerate, *colloq.* talk big, bluster, swagger, show off. **2** possess, have, enjoy. *noun* **1** brag, claim, vaunt. **2** pride, joy, jewel, treasure.

boastful *adj. derog.* **1** given to boasting about oneself. **2** showing or characterized by boasting.

■ **1** proud, conceited, vain, swollen-headed, *colloq.* big-headed, puffed up, bragging, crowing, *colloq.* swanky, cocky, swaggering.
⬛ modest, self-deprecating, self-effacing, humble.

boastfully *adv.* in a boastful manner; with excessive pride.

boastfulness *noun* tending to boast often.

boasting *noun* talking with excessive pride about oneself.

boat — *noun* **1** a small vessel for travelling over water. **2** *colloq., loosely* a larger vessel; a ship. **3** a boat-shaped dish for serving sauce, etc. — *verb intrans.* to sail in a boat for pleasure. — **in the same boat** in the same difficult circumstances. **miss the boat** to lose an opportunity. **rock the boat** to disturb the balance or calmness of a situation. [from Anglo-Saxon *bat*]

■ *noun* **2** ship, vessel, craft. *verb* row, sail, punt, cruise.

Types of boat or ship include: canoe, dinghy, lifeboat, rowing boat, kayak, coracle, skiff, punt, sampan, dhow, gondola, pedalo, catamaran, trimaran, yacht; cabin cruiser, motor boat, motor launch, speedboat, trawler, barge, narrow boat, houseboat, dredger, junk, smack, lugger; hovercraft, hydrofoil; clipper, cutter, ketch, packet, brig, schooner, square rigger, galleon; ferry, paddle steamer, tug, freighter, liner, container ship, tanker; warship, battleship, destroyer, submarine, U-boat, frigate, aircraft carrier, cruiser, dreadnought, corvette, minesweeper, man-of-war.

boater *noun* **1** a person who sails in a boat, especially for pleasure. **2** a straw hat with a flat top and a brim.

boathook *noun* a metal hook fixed to a pole, for pulling or pushing a boat.

boathouse *noun* a building where boats are stored, especially by a lake or river.

boating *noun* the sailing of boats for pleasure.

boatman *noun* a man in charge of a small boat which carries passengers.

boat people refugees who have fled their country by boat.

boatswain or **bosun** /ˈbəʊtswein, ˈbəʊsn/ *noun* a ship's officer in charge of the lifeboats, ropes, sails, etc and crew. [from Anglo-Saxon *batswegen*, boatman]

boat train a train which takes passengers to or from a ship.

bob[1] — *verb* (**bobbed**, **bobbing**) **1** *intrans.* to move up and down quickly. **2** *intrans.* to curtsy. **3** *trans.* to move (the head) up and down, usually as a greeting. — *noun* **1** an up-and-down bouncing movement. **2** a curtsy. — **bob up** to appear or reappear suddenly. [from Middle English *bobben*]

■ *verb* **1** bounce, hop, skip, spring, jump, leap, twitch, jerk, jolt, shake, quiver, wobble, oscillate. **2** curtsy, bow. **bob up** appear, reappear, emerge, surface, rise, pop up, arrive, *colloq.* show up, materialize, spring up, arise.

bob[2] — *noun* **1** a short hairstyle for women and children, with the hair cut square across the face and evenly all round the head. **2** a hanging weight on a clock's pendulum. **3** a bobsleigh. — *verb* (**bobbed**, **bobbing**) **1** to cut (hair) in a bob. **2** *intrans.* to ride on a bobsleigh. [from Middle English *bobbe*, spray, cluster]

bob[3] *noun* (PL. **bob**) *old colloq. use* a shilling.

bob[4] — **bob's your uncle** *Brit. colloq.* an expression used to show that something should follow as a matter of course: *just turn the knob and bob's your uncle!* [from *Bob*, a pet form of the name *Robert*]

bobbin *noun* a small cylindrical object on which thread is wound, used in sewing and weaving machines. [from French *bobine*]

bobble *noun* a small ball, often made of wool, used to decorate clothes. [from BOB[1]]

bobby *noun* (PL. **bobbies**) *Brit. colloq.* a policeman. [from the name *Bob*, after Sir Robert Peel who founded the Metropolitan Police in 1828]

bobsleigh or **bobsled** *noun* a sleigh with metal runners used in crossing, and sometimes racing on, snow and ice.

bobtail *noun* a short or cut tail, or an animal having this.

bobtailed *adj., said of an animal* having a bobtail.

Boche /bɒʃ/ *noun derog. slang* **1** a German, especially a German soldier. **2** (**the Boche**) the Germans, especially

German soldiers. [from French *boche*, rascal, applied to Germans in World War I]

bod *noun colloq.* a person. [from BODY]

bodacious /bɒˈdeɪʃəs/ *adj. slang* extraordinary; outstanding. [perhaps a mixture of BOLD and AUDACIOUS]

bode¹ *verb* to be a sign of. — **bode ill** or **well** to be a bad or good sign for the future. [from Anglo-Saxon *bodian*, to announce]

bode² see BIDE.

bodge *verb intrans., trans. colloq.* to make a mess of something; to do something badly or carelessly. [from BOTCH]

Bodhisattva /bɒdɪˈsatvə/ *noun (also* **bodhisattva)** *Relig.* in Mahayana Buddhism, one who has attained enlightenment but who has chosen not to pass into nirvana, voluntarily remaining in the world to help lesser beings attain enlightenment; a personal saviour. [from Sanskrit *bodhi*, enlightenment + *sattva*, existence]

bodice /ˈbɒdɪs/ *noun* **1** the part of a dress covering the upper part of the body. **2** a woman's close-fitting outer garment, worn over a blouse. **3** *formerly* a similar close-fitting undergarment. [from *bodies*, plural of BODY]

-bodied a word-forming element meaning 'having a body of the type specified': *able-bodied/wide-bodied.*

bodily — *adj.* of or concerning the body. — *adv.* **1** as a whole. **2** in person.

. . . .

▣ *adj.* physical, corporeal, carnal, fleshly, real, actual, tangible, substantial, concrete, material. *adv.* **1** altogether, en masse, collectively, as a whole, completely, fully, wholly, entirely, totally, in toto.
▣ *adj.* spiritual. *adv.* **1** piecemeal.

. . . .

bodkin *noun* a large blunt needle. [from Middle English *badeken*]

body — *noun* (PL. **bodies**) **1** the whole physical structure of a person or animal. **2** the physical structure of a person or animal excluding the head and limbs. **3** a corpse. **4** the main or central part of anything. **5** a person's physical needs and desires as opposed to spiritual concerns. **6** a substantial section or group: *a body of opinion.* **7** a group of people thought of as a single unit. **8** a quantity: *a body of water.* **9** a piece of matter: *a heavenly body.* **10** *said of wine, music, etc* a full or strong quality or tone. **11** *colloq.* a person. **12** thickness; substantial quality. **13** a body stocking. — *verb* (**bodies, bodied**) to give body or form to. — **keep body and soul together** to barely manage to survive. **over my dead body** *colloq.* not if I can prevent it. [from Anglo-Saxon *bodig*]

. . . .

▣ *noun* **1** anatomy, physique, build, figure. **2** trunk, torso. **3** corpse, cadaver, carcase, *slang* stiff. **7** company, association, society, corporation, confederation, bloc, cartel, syndicate, congress, collection, group, band, crowd, throng, multitude, mob, mass. **12** consistency, density, solidity, firmness, bulk, mass, substance, essence, fullness, richness.

. . . .

body bag a bag made of heavy material used to transport a dead body, especially that of a war casualty or accident victim.

body builder a person who undertakes body-building exercises.

body building physical exercise designed to develop the muscles and strengthen the body.

body double a person who takes the place of a film actor in scenes which focus on the body, such as nude scenes.

bodyguard *noun* a person or group of people guarding an important person, etc.

. . . .

▣ guard, protector, *colloq.* minder.

. . . .

body language *Psychol.* the communication of information by means of conscious or unconscious gestures, attitudes, facial expressions, etc.

body piercing the practice of inserting metal studs or rings through parts of the body for decoration.

body politic all the people of a nation in their political capacity.

body-snatcher *noun Hist.* a person who robs graves of their dead bodies.

body stocking a garment worn next to the skin, covering all of the body and often the arms and legs.

bodysuit *noun* a close-fitting one-piece garment for women, worn especially during exercise and sporting activities.

bodywork *noun* **1** the outer painted structure of a motor vehicle. **2** any form of alternative therapy which concentrates on releasing tension or balancing energies in the body.

Boer /bɔː(r)/ — *noun* a descendant of the early Dutch settlers in South Africa. — *adj.* of or relating to the Boers. [a Dutch word]

boffin *noun Brit. colloq.* a scientist engaged in research, especially in military concerns.

bog — *noun* **1** a flat or domed area of wet spongy poorly drained ground, composed of acid peat and slowly decaying plant material, and dominated by *Sphagnum* moss, sedges, rushes, etc. **2** *Brit. slang* a lavatory. — *verb* (**bogged, bogging**) (*usually* **be bogged down**) to be prevented from progressing: *got bogged down in difficulties.* [from Gaelic *bogach*, from *bog*, soft]

. . . .

▣ *noun* **1** marsh, swamp, fen, mire, quagmire, quag, slough, morass, quicksands, marshland, swampland, wetlands. *verb* encumber, hinder, impede, overwhelm, deluge, sink, stick, slow down, slow up, delay, retard, halt, stall.

. . . .

bog asphodel a perennial plant (*Narthecium ossifragum*), native to boggy regions of NW Europe, and having yellow flowers that turn deep orange after fertilization, and woolly stamens.

bog burial *Archaeol.* a burial of prehistoric human remains found in peat bogs in N Europe.

bogey¹ or **bogy** *noun* (PL. **bogeys, bogies**) **1** an evil or mischievous spirit. **2** something specially feared.

bogey² *noun* (PL. **bogeys**) *Golf* a standard score for a hole or a course, formerly par but now usually a score of one stroke more than par for each hole. [perhaps from the name of an imaginary player]

bogeyman or **bogyman** *noun* a cruel or frightening person, existing or imaginary, used to deter or frighten children.

boggle *verb intrans. colloq.* **1** to be amazed at something, or unable to understand or imagine it: *the mind boggles.* **2** (**boggle at something**) to hesitate over it.

boggy *adj.* (**boggier, boggiest**) *said of an area of ground* wet and spongy like bog.

bogie *noun* a frame with four or six wheels which supports part of a long vehicle, such as a railway carriage.

bog-standard *adj.* ordinary and unexceptional.

bogus *adj.* false; not genuine.

. . . .

▣ false, fake, counterfeit, forged, fraudulent, *colloq.* phoney, spurious, sham, pseudo, artificial, imitation, dummy.
▣ genuine, true, real, valid.

. . . .

bogy same as BOGEY¹.

bohemian /bəʊˈhiːmɪən/ — *noun* **1** (**Bohemian**) a person from Bohemia, formerly a kingdom, later a part of the Czech Republic. **2** a person, especially a writer or an artist, who lives in a way which ignores standard customs and rules of social behaviour. — *adj.* **1** (**Bohemian**) of or from Bohemia. **2** ignoring standard customs and rules of social behaviour. [from French *bohémien*, Bohemian, gypsy]

. . . .

▣ *noun* **2** beatnik, hippie, dropout, nonconformist.
adj. **2** artistic, *colloq.* arty, unconventional, unorthodox,

nonconformist, alternative, eccentric, offbeat, *slang* way-out, bizarre, exotic.

◼ *noun* bourgeois, conformist. *adj.* bourgeois, conventional, orthodox.

. . . .

boho *adj. colloq.* unconventional and artistic. [from BOHE-MIAN2]

boil[1] — *verb* **1** *intrans. said of a liquid* to change rapidly from a liquid to a vapour on reaching a temperature known as the *boiling point*. Boiling is accompanied by the (often violent) formation of copious bubbles of vapour within the liquid. See also BOILING POINT. **2** *said of a container, eg a kettle* to reach a temperature corresponding to the boiling point of its contents. **3** to cause (a liquid or its container) to reach its boiling point rapidly. **4** *trans., intrans. said of food* to cook or be cooked by heating in boiling liquid. **5** *said of a person* to be extremely angry or agitated. **6 (be boiling)** *colloq.* to be very hot. **7** to treat with boiling water, especially to clean. **8** *intrans. said of the sea, etc* to move and bubble as if boiling. — *noun* the act or point of boiling. — **boil away** or **down** *said of a liquid* to be reduced by boiling. **boil something away** or **down** to reduce a liquid by boiling. **boil something down** to reduce something to its essentials. **boil down to something** *colloq.* to mean; to have as the most important part or factor: *it all boils down to a question of cost.* **boil over 1** *said of a liquid* to boil and flow over the edge of its container. **2** to speak out angrily. **boil up 1** *said of a liquid* to become heated to boiling point. **2** to come to a dangerous level. **boil something up** to heat a liquid until it boils. [from Old French *boillir*, from Latin *bullire*, to bubble]

. . . .

◼ *verb* **1** simmer, seethe, bubble, steam. **4** stew, steam. **5** erupt, explode, rage, rave, storm, fulminate, fume. **6** bake, roast, swelter, sizzle. **8** froth, foam, seethe, bubble. **boil something down** reduce, concentrate, distil, condense, digest, abstract, summarize, abridge.

. . . .

boil[2] *noun* a reddened and often painful swelling in the skin, containing pus, and usually caused by infection of a hair follicle with the bacterium *Staphylococcus aureus*. [from Anglo-Saxon *byl*]

. . . .

◼ pustule, abscess, gumboil, ulcer, tumour, pimple, carbuncle, blister, inflammation.

. . . .

boiler *noun* **1** any closed vessel that is used to convert water into steam, especially by burning coal, oil, or other fuel, used to drive steam turbines (eg in power stations), steamships, steam locomotives, etc. **2** an apparatus for heating a building's hot water supply. **3** a metal vessel, tub, etc for boiling and washing clothes in.

boiler suit a one-piece suit worn over normal clothes to protect them while doing manual or heavy work.

boiling point 1 (ABBREV. **bp, b.p.**) the temperature at which a particular substance changes from a liquid to a vapour. The boiling point can be lowered by decreasing the air pressure, eg water boils at a lower temperature at high altitudes. **2** a point of great anger, high excitement, etc at which emotions can no longer be controlled.

boisterous *adj.* **1** very lively, noisy, and cheerful. **2** *said of the sea, etc* rough and stormy. [from Middle English *boistous*]

. . . .

◼ **1** exuberant, *Brit. colloq.* rumbustious, rollicking, bouncy, tumultuous, loud, noisy, clamorous, rowdy, rough, disorderly, riotous, wild, unrestrained, unruly, obstreperous. **2** rough, choppy, stormy, turbulent, tempestuous.

◼ QUIET, CALM, RESTRAINED.

. . . .

boisterously *adv.* with a lively, noisy manner.

bold *adj.* **1** daring or brave. **2** not showing respect; impudent. **3** striking and clearly marked. **4** *Printing* printed in boldface. [from Anglo-Saxon *beald*]

. . . .

◼ **1** fearless, dauntless, daring, audacious, brave, courageous, valiant, heroic, gallant, intrepid, adventurous, venturesome, enterprising, plucky, spirited, confident, outgoing. **2** impudent, brazen, brash, forward, shameless, unabashed, *colloq.* cheeky, insolent. **3** eye-catching, striking, conspicuous, prominent, strong, pronounced, bright, vivid, colourful, loud, flashy, showy, flamboyant.

◼ **1** cautious, timid, shy. **2** modest, unassuming, shy. **3** faint, restrained.

. . . .

boldface *noun Printing* thicker stronger letters, as used in the word **boldface**.

boldly *adv.* in a daring or striking manner; so as to attract the attention.

boldness *noun* daring; forwardness of manner; impertinence.

bole *noun* **1** the trunk of a tree. **2** *Geol.* a fine earthy clay, usually red, but sometimes yellow or brown in colour, consisting mainly of aluminium silicates. [from Norse *bolr*]

bolero /bəˈlɛərəʊ/ *noun* (PL. **boleros**) **1** a traditional Spanish dance, or the music for it. **2** a short open jacket reaching not quite to the waist. [from Spanish *bolero*]

boll /bəʊl/ *noun Bot.* a rounded capsule containing seeds, especially of a cotton or flax plant. [from Anglo-Saxon *bolla*, bowl]

bollard *noun* **1** *Brit.* a small post used to mark a traffic island or to keep traffic away from a certain area. **2** a short but strong post on a ship, quay, etc round which ropes are fastened. [probably from BOLE]

bollocks *noun coarse slang* **1** (*pl.*) the testicles. **2** (*sing.*) rubbish, nonsense. [from Anglo-Saxon *beallucas*, testicles]

boll-weevil *noun* a small weevil, found in Mexico and the southern USA, whose larvae infest and destroy young cotton bolls.

boloney same as BALONEY.

Bolshevik /ˈbɒlʃəvɪk/ — *noun* **1** *Hist.* a member of the radical faction of the Russian socialist party, which became the Communist Party in 1918. **2** a Russian communist. **3** *derog. colloq.* (often **bolshevik**) any radical socialist. — *adj.* **1** of the Bolsheviks. **2** communist. [from Russian, from *bolshe*, greater, because they were in the majority at the 1903 party congress or because they favoured more extreme measures]

Bolshevism *noun* the political principles and philosophy of the Bolsheviks.

Bolshevist *noun* an adherent of Bolshevism; a Bolshevik. — *adj.* relating to Bolshevism.

bolshie or **bolshy** *derog. slang* — *adj.* (**bolshier, bolshiest**) **1** bad-tempered and unco-operative. **2** left-wing. — *noun* (PL. **bolshies**) a Bolshevik.

bolster /ˈbəʊlstə(r)/ — *noun* **1** a long narrow pillow. **2** any pad or support. — *verb* (**bolstered, bolstering**) (*usually* **bolster something up**) to support it, make it stronger, or hold it up. [an Anglo-Saxon word]

. . . .

◼ *verb* support, boost, reinforce, strengthen, buttress, shore up, sustain.

. . . .

bolt[1] — *noun* **1** a bar to fasten a door, gate, etc. **2** a small thick round bar of metal with a screw thread, used with a nut to fasten things together. **3** a flash of lightning. **4** a sudden movement or dash away, especially to escape: *make a bolt for it.* **5** a roll of cloth. **6** a short arrow fired from a crossbow. — *verb* **1** to fasten (a door, window, etc) with a bolt. **2** to eat very quickly. **3** *intrans.* to run or dash away suddenly and quickly. **4** *intrans. said of a horse* to run away out of control. **5** to fasten together with bolts. **6** *intrans. Bot.* to flower and produce seed too early, usually in response to low temperatures; (of a biennial) to behave like an annual. — **a bolt from the blue** a sudden, unexpected, and usually unwelcome event. **bolt upright** very straight and stiff. **have shot one's bolt** to have failed in one's final or only available attempt. [from Anglo-Saxon]

. . . .

🔳 *noun* **1** bar, rod, shaft, fastener, latch, catch, lock. **2** screw, pin, peg, rivet. *verb* **1** fasten, secure, bar, latch, lock. **2** gulp, *colloq.* wolf, gobble, gorge, devour, cram, stuff. **3** escape, flee, fly, run, sprint, rush, dash, hurtle.

. . . .

bolt² or **boult** *verb* **1** to pass (flour, etc) through a sieve. **2** to examine or investigate. [from Old French *bulter*]

bolthole *noun* a refuge from danger; a means of escape.

bomb — *noun* **1** a hollow case or other device containing substances capable of causing explosions, fires, etc. **2** (**the bomb**) the atomic bomb, especially regarded as the most powerful destructive weapon. **3** (**a bomb**) *Brit. colloq.* a lot of money: *it cost a bomb.* **4** *North Amer. colloq.* a failure: *the film was a bomb.* — *verb* **1** to attack, damage, etc with a bomb or bombs. **2** *intrans. colloq.* to move or drive quickly: *bombing along the road.* **3** *intrans. colloq. North Amer.* to fail badly. — **go like a bomb** *colloq.* **1** to move very quickly. **2** to sell extremely well; to be very successful. [from French *bombe*, from Greek *bombos*, humming sound]

. . . .

🔳 *noun* **1** shell, bombshell, explosive, charge, grenade, mine, torpedo, rocket, missile, projectile, petrol bomb. **2** atom bomb, atomic bomb, hydrogen bomb, nuclear bomb. *verb* **1** bombard, shell, torpedo, attack, blow up, destroy.

. . . .

bombard *verb* **1** to attack with large heavy guns or bombs. **2** to direct questions or abuse at (someone) very quickly and without stopping. **3** *Physics* to subject (a target, especially an atom) to a stream of high-energy particles. [from French *bombarder*, from *bombarde*, machine for throwing stones]

. . . .

🔳 **1** attack, assault, assail, pound, strafe, blast, bomb, shell, blitz, besiege. **2** overwhelm, inundate, hound, harass, pester.

. . . .

bombardier /bɒmbə'dɪə(r)/ *noun* **1** *Brit.* a noncommissioned officer in the Royal Artillery. **2** *North Amer., esp. US* the member of an aircraft's crew who releases the bombs. [from BOMBARD]

bombardment *noun* **1** a fierce attack with heavy weapons. **2** a fierce onslaught of questions or criticism.

. . . .

🔳 BARRAGE. **1** attack, assault, air raid, bombing, shelling, blitz, cannonade, fusillade, salvo, fire, flak. **2** onslaught, broadside.

. . . .

bombast /'bɒmbast/ *noun* pretentious, boastful, or insincere words having little real force or meaning. [from Middle English *bombace*, cotton padding]

bombastic *adj.*, *said of language* sounding impressive but insincere or meaningless.

. . . .

🔳 grandiloquent, magniloquent, grandiose, pompous, high-flown, inflated, *colloq.* windy, wordy, verbose.

. . . .

bombastically *adv.* with an impressive but insincere manner.

Bombay duck a slender-bodied fish with large jaws and barb-like teeth, common in the tropical Indian Ocean, especially the Bay of Bengal.

bomb disposal the science or process of incapacitating unexploded bombs.

bomber *noun* **1** an aeroplane built for bombing. **2** a person who bombs something.

bomber jacket a short jacket gathered tightly at the waist.

bombing *noun* a period of dropping bombs; an attack with bombs.

bombshell *noun* **1** a piece of surprising and usually disappointing news. **2** *colloq.* a stunningly attractive woman.

bombsite *noun* an area where buildings have been destroyed by a bomb.

bona fide /'bəʊnə 'faɪdɪ/ — *adj.* genuine or sincere. — *adv.* genuinely or sincerely. [from Latin *bona fide*]

. . . .

🔳 *adj.* genuine, honest, true, real, legitimate, veritable, sincere. 🔳 *adj.* bogus, counterfeit.

. . . .

bona fides /'bəʊnə 'faɪdɪz/ **1** (*sing.*) genuineness; honesty. **2** (*sing. or pl.*) proof or evidence of trustworthiness.

bonanza *noun* **1** an unexpected and sudden source of good luck or wealth. **2** a large amount, especially of gold from a mine. [from Spanish *bonanza*, good weather at sea]

Bonapartism *noun* advocacy or support of the policies of the French emperor Napoleon Bonaparte, and his dynasty.

bonbon /'bɒnbɒn/ *noun* a sweet. [from French *bon-bon*]

bond — *noun* **1** something used for tying, binding, or holding. **2** (*usually* **bonds**) something which restrains or imprisons (a person): *break one's bonds.* **3** something that unites or joins people together: *a bond of friendship.* **4** a binding agreement or promise. **5** a certificate issued by a government or a company, which promises to pay back money borrowed at a fixed rate of interest at a stated time. **6** *Legal* a written agreement to pay money or carry out the terms of a contract. **7** *Chem.* the strong force of attraction that holds together two atoms in a molecule or a crystalline salt; a chemical bond. — *verb* **1** to join or tie together. **2** *intrans.* to hold or stick together. **3** to put (goods) into a bonded warehouse. — **in** or **out of bond** *said of goods* in or out of a bonded warehouse. [from Norse *band*]

. . . .

🔳 *noun* **1** cord, band, binding, tie, string, rope. **2** fetter, shackle, manacle, chain, cord. **3** connection, relation, link, tie, union, affiliation, attachment, affinity. **4** contract, agreement, covenant, pledge, promise, word, obligation. *verb* **1** connect, fasten, bind, unite, fuse, glue, gum, paste, stick, seal.

. . . .

bondage *noun* **1** slavery. **2** the state of being confined, imprisoned, etc. **3** a sado-masochistic sexual practice in which one partner is physically restrained. [from Latin *bondagium*]

. . . .

🔳 **1** slavery, enslavement, serfdom, servitude, subservience, subjection, subjugation, yoke. **2** imprisonment, incarceration, captivity, confinement, restraint. 🔳 FREEDOM, INDEPENDENCE.

. . . .

bonded warehouse a building in which goods are kept until customs or other duty on them is paid.

bond energy *Chem.* the energy released or absorbed during the formation of a chemical bond.

bonding *noun* **1** an act or process of making a bond. **2** *Psychol.* the forming of a close emotional attachment, especially between a mother and her newborn child.

bond paper a type of very good quality paper.

bone — *noun* **1** the hard dense tissue that forms the skeleton of vertebrates. It provides structural support for the body, and serves as an attachment for muscles, as well as being the site of red blood cell production, and a store for mineral salts. **2** any of the components of the skeleton, made of this material. **3** (**bones**) the skeleton. **4** (**bones**) the body as the place where feelings come from: *feel it in one's bones.* **5** a substance similar to human bone, such as ivory, whalebone, etc. **6** (**bones**) the basic or essential part: *the bare bones.* — *verb* **1** to take bone out of (meat, etc). **2** to make (a piece of clothing) stiff by adding pieces of bone or some other hard substance. — **a bone of contention** something which causes arguments or disagreement. **bone up on something** *colloq.* to learn or study a subject. **have a bone to pick with someone** to have a reason to argue with them about something. **make no bones about something 1** to admit or allow it without fuss or bother. **2**

to be quite willing to say or do it openly. **near** or **close to the bone** *colloq.* **1** lewd or mildly indecent. **2** *said of criticism, etc* personal; almost offensive. **to the bone 1** thoroughly and completely. **2** to the minimum. **work one's fingers to the bone** to work long and hard, especially in physical work. [from Anglo-Saxon *ban*]

Human bones include: clavicle, coccyx, collar-bone, femur, fibula, hip-bone, humerus, ilium, ischium, mandible, maxilla, metacarpal, metatarsal, patella, pelvic girdle, pelvis, pubis, radius, rib, scapula, shoulder-blade, skull, sternum, stirrup-bone, temporal, thigh-bone, tibia, ulna, vertebra.

bone china a type of fine china made from clay mixed with ash from burnt bones.

bone-dry *adj.* completely dry.

bonehead *noun slang* a stupid person.

bone-headed *adj.* stupid; dense.

bone idle *colloq.* utterly lazy.

boneless *adj.* lacking bones; having the bones removed.

bone meal dried and ground bones, used as a plant fertilizer and as a supplement to animal feed.

bone of contention a point over which there is much disagreement.

boneshaker *noun colloq.* an old uncomfortable and unsteady vehicle, especially a bicycle.

bonfire *noun* a large outdoor fire, often burned as a celebration or signal. [from Middle English *bonefire*: bones were formerly used as fuel]

Bonfire Night in the UK, the evening of 5 November, Guy Fawkes Day, when bonfires are lit, accompanied by fireworks displays.

bong[1] *noun* a long, deep sound such as is made by a large bell. — *verb intrans.* to make this sound. [imitative]

bong[2] *noun* a water pipe used for smoking marijuana, etc.

bongo *noun* (PL. **bongos**, **bongoes**) (*also* **bongo drum**) each of a pair of small drums held between the knees and played with the hands. [from Spanish *bongó*]

bonhomie /ˈbɒnɒmiː/ *noun* an easy, friendly nature. [from French, from *bonhomme*, good fellow]

bonk — *verb trans., intrans.* **1** to bang or hit. **2** *coarse slang* to have sexual intercourse with (someone). — *noun* **1** the act of banging. **2** *coarse slang* an act of sexual intercourse. [imitative]

bonkers *adj. slang* mad, crazy.

■ mad, crazy, *colloq.* cracked, *colloq.* crackers, *colloq.* off one's head, out of one's mind, *colloq.* barmy.

bon mot /bɒn moʊ/ *noun* (PL. **bons mots**) a short and clever remark. [from French *bon mot*]

bonne-bouche /bɒnˈbuːʃ/ *noun* a delicious morsel. [from French *bonne bouche*, good mouth]

bonnet *noun* **1** a type of hat fastened under the chin with ribbon, formerly worn by women but now worn especially by babies. **2** *Brit.* the hinged cover over a motor vehicle's engine. **3** a soft Scottish cap. [from Old French *bonet*]

bonny *adj.* (**bonnier**, **bonniest**) **1** *chiefly Scot.* attractive; pretty. **2** looking very healthy and attractive.

bonsai /ˈbɒnsaɪ/ *noun* (PL. **bonsai**) **1** the ancient Japanese art of cultivating artificially miniaturized trees in small containers. **2** a miniature tree cultivated in this way. [from Japanese, from *bon*, tray, bowl + *sai*, cultivation]

bonus *noun* (PL. **bonuses**) **1** an extra sum of money given on top of what is due as interest or wages. **2** an unexpected extra benefit. [from Latin *bonus*, good]

■ **1** commission, dividend, premium, honorarium, tip, gratuity, gift, handout. **2** advantage, benefit, *colloq.* plus, extra, *colloq.* perk, perquisite, prize, reward.

■ **2** disadvantage, disincentive.

bon vivant or **bon viveur** /bɒn viˈvɒn, viˈvɜː(r)/ (PL. **bons vivants** or **bons viveurs**) a person who enjoys good food and wine. [French, = good liver]

bon voyage /bɒn vwaɪˈaʒ/ *interj.* an expression of good wishes said to a person about to travel. [from French *bon voyage*]

bony *adj.* (**bonier**, **boniest**) **1** of or like bone. **2** full of bones. **3** thin.

■ **3** thin, lean, angular, lanky, *colloq., derog.* gawky, gangling, skinny, scrawny, emaciated, rawboned, gaunt, drawn.
■ **3** fat, plump.

bonzer *adj. Austral. slang* good, excellent. [perhaps from French *bon*, good, influenced by BONANZA]

boo — *interj.*, *noun* a sound expressing disapproval or made when trying to frighten or surprise someone. — *verb intrans., trans.* to shout boo to express disapproval (of). — **one could not** or **would not say boo to a goose** one is very shy or easily frightened. [imitative]

boob[1] — *noun colloq.* **1** (*also* **booboo**) a stupid or foolish mistake. **2** a stupid or foolish person. — *verb intrans. colloq.* to make a stupid or foolish mistake. [from BOOBY]

■ *noun* **1** mistake, blunder, lapse, *colloq.* clanger, *colloq.* bloomer, gaffe, *slang* cock-up. *verb* blunder, slip up, *colloq.* fluff, *slang* cock up, miscalculate.

boob[2] *noun slang* a woman's breast.

booby *noun* (PL. **boobies**) **1** *old colloq. use* a stupid or foolish person. **2** any of various species of large seabird belonging to the gannet family, native to tropical waters, and having white plumage with dark markings, long powerful wings, a large head, and a colourful conical bill.

booby prize a prize for the lowest score, the person coming last, etc in a competition.

booby trap 1 a bomb or mine which is disguised so that it is set off by the victim. **2** something placed as a trap, eg a bucket of water put above a door so as to fall on the person who opens the door.

booby-trap *verb* to put a booby trap in or on (a place).

■ sabotage, mine, tamper with.

boodle *noun old use, slang* money, especially when gained dishonestly or as a bribe. [from Dutch *boedel*, possessions]

boogie *colloq.* — *verb intrans.* (**boogieing**, **boogying**) to dance to pop or jazz music. — *noun* a dance to pop or jazz music.

book — *noun* **1** a number of printed pages bound together along one edge and protected by covers. **2** a piece of written work intended for publication. **3** a number of sheets of blank paper bound together: *a notebook*. **4** (*usually* **books**) a record of the business done by a company, a society, etc. **5** a major division of a long literary work. **6** a number of stamps, matches, cheques, etc bound together. **7** the words of an opera or musical; a libretto. **8** a record of bets. **9** (**the book**) the current telephone directory: *they're not in the book.* — *verb* **1** *trans., intrans.* to reserve a ticket, seat, etc, or engage a person's services in advance. **2** to enter (a person's name, etc) in a book or list. **3** to record the details of (a person who is being charged with an offence). — **be in someone's good** or **bad books** to be in, or out of, favour with them. **book in 1** to sign one's name on the list of guests at a hotel, etc. **2 book someone in** to reserve a place for them in a hotel, etc. **book something up** to complete arrangements for (a holiday, etc). **be booked up** have no more places or tickets available. **bring someone to book** to punish them or make them account for their behaviour. **by the book** strictly according to the rules. **in my book** in my opinion. **suit one's book** to be what one wants or likes. **take a leaf out of someone's book** to profit or benefit from their example or experience. **throw the book at someone** *colloq.* to deal with them as severely as possible. [from Anglo-Saxon *boc*]

....

◨ *noun* **1, 2** volume, tome, publication, work, booklet, tract. *verb* **1** reserve, *slang* bag, engage, charter, procure, order, arrange, organize, schedule, programme.
◪ *verb* **1** cancel.

....

Types of book include: hardback, paperback, best seller; fiction, novel, story, thriller, romantic novel; children's book, primer, picture-book, annual; reference book, encyclopedia, dictionary, lexicon, thesaurus, concordance, anthology, compendium, omnibus, atlas, guidebook, gazetteer, directory, anthology, pocket companion, handbook, manual, cookbook, yearbook, almanac, catalogue; notebook, exercise book, textbook, scrapbook, album, sketchbook, diary, jotter, pad, ledger; libretto, manuscript, hymn-book, hymnal, prayer-book, psalter, missal, lectionary. *See also* **literature**.

bookable *adj.* **1** able to be booked or reserved in advance. **2** *said of an offence* that makes the offender liable to be charged.

bookbinder *noun* a person whose job is to bind books.

bookbinding *noun* the art or business of binding books.

bookcase *noun* a cabinet of shelves for books.

book club a club which sells books to its members at reduced prices.

book end each of a pair of supports used to keep a row of books standing upright.

book fair a trade fair of publishers and booksellers.

bookie *noun colloq.* a bookmaker.

booking *noun* **1** a reservation of a seat, hotel room, etc. **2** *especially in sport* the recording of an offence with details of the offender.

bookish *adj.* **1** devoted to reading. **2** *often derog.* learned and serious; with knowledge or opinions based on books rather than practical experience.

bookishness *noun* devotion to reading; learned seriousness.

bookkeeper *noun* a person who keeps official accounts.

bookkeeping *noun* the keeping of financial accounts.

booklet *noun* a small book or pamphlet with a paper cover.

bookmaker *noun* a person who takes bets on horseraces, etc and pays out winnings.

bookmark — *noun* **1** a strip of leather, card, etc put in a book to mark a particular page, especially the reader's place. **2** *Comput.* a tag added by a user to a website, allowing them to access it easily in subsequent searches. — *verb* to add a bookmark to website.

bookplate *noun* a piece of decorated paper stuck into the front of a book and bearing the owner's name.

bookseller *noun* an individual or business that sells books, either direct to the public, to bookshops and book clubs, or to institutional buyers such as libraries and schools.

bookshelf *noun* (PL. **bookshelves**) a shelf for storing books in an upright position.

bookshop *noun* a shop that sells books to the public.

bookstall *noun* a small shop in a station, etc where books, newspapers, magazines, etc are sold.

book token a card containing a token worth a specified amount of money which can be used to buy books.

bookworm *noun* **1** *colloq.* a person devoted to reading. **2** a type of small insect which feeds on the paper and glue used in books.

Boolean algebra /ˈbuːlɪən/ *Maths.* a form of algebra that is closely related to logic, and uses algebraic symbols and set theory, instead of arithmetical quantities, to represent logic operations. It is used in computer programming. [named after the UK mathematician George Boole]

boom[1] — *noun* a deep resounding sound, like that made by a large drum or gun. — *verb intrans.* to make a deep resounding sound. — **boom something out** to say something with a booming sound. [probably imitative]

....

◨ *noun* bang, clap, crash, roar, thunder, rumble, reverberation, blast, explosion, burst. *verb* bang, crash, roar, thunder, roll, rumble, resound, reverberate, blast, explode.

boom[2] — *noun* a sudden increase or growth in business, prosperity, etc. — *verb intrans.* to prosper rapidly. [perhaps from BOOM[1]]

....

◨ *noun* increase, growth, expansion, gain, upsurge, jump, spurt, boost, upturn, improvement, advance, escalation, explosion. *verb* flourish, thrive, prosper, succeed, develop, grow, increase, gain, expand, swell, escalate, intensify, strengthen, explode.
◪ *noun* failure, collapse, slump, recession, depression. *verb* fail, collapse, slump.

....

boom[3] *noun* **1** a pole to which the bottom of a ship's sail is attached, keeping the sail stretched tight. **2** a heavy pole or chain, etc across the entrance to a harbour. **3** a long pole with a microphone attached to one end, allowing the microphone to be held above the heads of people being filmed. [from Dutch *boom*, beam]

boomerang /ˈbuːməraŋ/ — *noun* **1** a piece of flat, curved wood used by Australian Aborigines for hunting, often so balanced that, when thrown to a distance, it returns to the thrower. **2** a malicious act or statement which harms the perpetrator rather than the intended victim. — *verb intrans.*, *said of an act, statement, etc* to go wrong and harm the perpetrator rather than the intended victim. [from Dharuk (Australian Aboriginal language) *bumariny*]

....

◨ *verb* backfire, rebound.

boon[1] *noun* **1** an advantage, benefit, or blessing. **2** *old use* a gift or favour. [from Norse *bon*, prayer]

....

◨ **1** blessing, advantage, benefit, godsend, windfall, favour, kindness, gift, present, grant, gratuity.
◪ **1** disadvantage, blight.

....

boon[2] *adj.* close, intimate, or favourite: *a boon companion.* [from Old French *bon*, good]

boor /buː(r)/ *noun derog.* a coarse person with bad manners. [from Dutch *boer*, farmer, peasant]

....

◨ lout, oaf, barbarian, savage, philistine.

....

boorish *adj.*, *said of a person, or a person's manner* coarse and unfriendly.

....

◨ uncouth, oafish, loutish, ill-mannered, rude, coarse, crude, vulgar, unrefined, uncivilized, uneducated, ignorant.
◪ polite, refined, cultured.

....

boorishly *adv.* with a coarse and unfriendly manner.

boorishness *noun* a coarse and unfriendly manner.

boost — *verb* **1** to improve or encourage: *boost the spirits.* **2** to make greater or increase: *boost profits.* **3** to promote by advertising. — *noun* **1** a piece of help or encouragement, etc. **2** a push upwards. **3** a rise or increase.

....

◨ *verb* **1** improve, lift, encourage, foster, support, sustain, bolster, advance, further. **2** increase, augment, supplement, enhance, develop, enlarge, expand, amplify, heighten. **3** promote, advertise, *colloq.* plug, *colloq.* hype, praise. *noun* **1** help, advancement, promotion, encouragement, fillip, lift. **2** lift, hoist, heave, push, thrust. **3** increase, improvement, enhancement, expansion, rise, jump, increment, addition, supplement, booster. ▣ *verb* **1** hinder, undermine. *noun* **1, 3** setback, blow.

booster *noun* **1** a person or thing that boosts. **2** *Medicine* a dose of vaccine that is given in order to renew or increase the immune response to a previous dose of the same vaccine. **3** *Engineering* an engine in a rocket that provides additional thrust at some stage of the vehicle's flight. **4** (*also* **booster rocket**) a rocket that is used to launch a space vehicle, before another engine takes over. **5** *Electron.* a radio-frequency amplifier that is used to amplify a weak television or radio signal, and to rebroadcast such a signal so that it can be received by the general public.

boot [1] — *noun* **1** an outer covering, usually of leather, for the foot and lower part of the leg. **2** *Brit.* a compartment for luggage in a car, usually at the back. **3** *colloq.* a hard kick. **4** (**the boot**) *colloq.* dismissal from a job: *get the boot.* — *verb* to kick. — **boot something** or **someone out** to throw them out or remove them with force. **boot someone out** to dismiss them from employment, etc. **boot up** *Comput.* to start (a computer) by loading the programs which control its basic functions. **the boot is on the other foot** or **leg** *colloq.* the situation is now the reverse of what it was before, especially as regards advantage, responsibility, etc. **lick someone's boots** *derog. colloq.* to try to win a person's favour by flattery, excessive obedience, etc. [from Old French *bote*]

▣ *noun* **1** gumboot, wellington, *colloq.* welly, galosh, overshoe, walking-boot, riding-boot, top boot.

boot [2] — **to boot** as well; in addition. [from Anglo-Saxon *bot*, help, advantage]

boot camp *colloq.* **1** a training centre for young US naval recruits. **2** a place for punishing and reforming young offenders.

bootee /buːˈtiː/ *noun* a soft knitted boot for a baby.

booth *noun* **1** a small temporary roofed structure, or a tent, especially at a fair. **2** a small compartment, structure, or building for a stated purpose: *a polling booth.* [from Norse *buth*]

▣ **1** sideshow, stall, kiosk, stand, hut. **2** box, compartment, cubicle, carrel.

bootlace *noun* a piece of string, ribbon, etc used to fasten boots.

bootleg — *verb* (**bootlegged, bootlegging**) to make or transport alcoholic drinks illegally, especially in a time of prohibition. — *adj.*, *said of alcoholic drinks* illegally produced or transported.

bootlegger *noun* a person who produces or sells alcoholic drinks illegally, especially in a time of prohibition.

bootlegging *noun* the practice of producing or selling alcoholic drinks illegally.

bootlicker *noun colloq.* a person who tries to gain the favour of someone in authority by flattery, excessive obedience, etc.

boots *noun old use* a person in a hotel who carries guests' bags and cleans their shoes.

bootstrap *Comput.* — *noun* a short program used to boot up a computer by transferring the disk-operating system program from storage on disk into a computer's working memory. — *verb trans., intrans.* to boot up (a computer) by activating the bootstrap program.

booty *noun* (PL. **booties**) **1** valuable goods taken in wartime or by force. **2** *humorous* anything gained, earned, or won. [from Middle English *botye*]

▣ **1** loot, plunder, pillage, spoils, *colloq.* swag, haul. **2** pickings, gains, takings, winnings, profits.

booze — *noun slang* **1** alcoholic drink. **2** the drinking of alcohol: *on the booze.* — *verb intrans. slang* to drink a lot of, or too much, alcohol. [from Old Dutch *busen*, to drink in excess]

boozer *noun slang* **1** a person who drinks much alcohol. **2** a public house.

booze-up *noun slang* an occasion when much alcohol is drunk.

boozy *adj.* (**boozier, booziest**) *slang* **1** given to drinking a lot of alcohol. **2** drunken.

bop [1] — *verb intrans.* (**bopped, bopping**) *colloq.* to dance to popular music. — *noun colloq.* a dance. [from *bebop*, a type of 1940s jazz music]

bop [2] *verb* (**bopped, bopping**) *colloq.* to hit lightly. [imitative]

bopper *noun colloq.* a person who dances to popular music.

boracic *adj.* same as BORIC.

boracic acid same as BORIC ACID.

borage /ˈbɒrɪdʒ/ *noun* an annual plant (*Borago officinalis*), native to Central and S Europe, having oval hairy leaves and small bright blue star-shaped flowers. It is used medicinally. [from Old French *bourache*]

borax /ˈbɔːraks/ *noun Chem.* (FORMULA $Na_2B_4O_7.10H_2O$) a colourless crystalline salt or white greasy powder found in saline lake deposits and used in the manufacture of enamels, ceramics, and heat-resistant glass, eg Pyrex, and as a cleaning agent, mild antiseptic, astringent, and source of boric acid. Also called SODIUM BORATE. [from Latin *borax*, from Arabic *buraq*]

border — *noun* **1** the edge or boundary of something; a band or margin along the edge of something. **2** the boundary of a country, state *etc.* **3** the land on either side of a country's border. See also BORDERS. **4** a narrow strip of ground planted with flowers, surrounding a small area of grass. **5** any decorated or ornamental edge. — *verb* **1** to provide with a border. **2** to be a border to or on the border of. **3** (**border on something**) to be nearly the same as some specified quality or condition: *actions bordering on stupidity.* [from Middle English *bordure*]

▣ *noun* **1** boundary, bound, bounds, confine, confines, limit, demarcation line, edge, rim, brim, verge, brink, margin, fringe, periphery, surround, perimeter, circumference. **2** frontier, borderline, boundary, line, state line. **3** borderland, march. **4** bed, flowerbed, plot. **5** trimming, frill, valance, skirt, hem, frieze. *verb* **1** edge, hem. **2** adjoin, abut, touch, impinge, join, connect, communicate with. **border on** resemble, approach, verge on.

bordered *adj.* having a border.

borderer *noun* a person who lives on the border of a country.

borderland *noun* **1** land at or near the country's border. **2** a condition between two states, eg between sleeping and waking.

borderline — *noun* **1** the border between one thing, country, etc and another. **2** a line dividing two opposing or extreme conditions: *the borderline between passing and failing.* — *adj.* on the border between one thing, state, etc and another.

▣ *noun* **1** frontier, border, boundary, line, demarcation line, margin. *adj.* marginal, doubtful, dubious, debatable, moot.

Borders *pl. noun* the area adjoining a border between two countries, especially Scotland and England.

bore [1] — *verb* **1** (*also* **bore a hole in something**) to make a hole in (something) by drilling. **2** to produce (a tunnel, mine, etc) by drilling. — *noun* **1** the hollow barrel of a gun. **2** the diameter of the hollow barrel of a gun, especially to show which size of bullets the gun requires. **3** same as BOREHOLE. [from Anglo-Saxon *borian*]

◳ *verb* DRILL. **1** pierce, perforate, penetrate. **2** sink, burrow, tunnel, mine, undermine, sap.

bore[2] — *verb* to make (someone) feel tired and uninterested, by being dull, uninteresting, unimaginative, etc. — *noun* a dull, uninteresting, tedious person or thing.

◳ *verb* tire, weary, fatigue, jade, trouble, bother, worry. *noun* nuisance, bother, *colloq.* bind, *colloq.* drag, *colloq.* pain, headache.
◪ *verb* interest, excite. *noun* pleasure, delight.

bore[3] *noun* a solitary high wave of water that moves rapidly upstream and is caused by constriction of the spring tide as it enters a narrow shallow estuary.[from Norse *bara*, wave]

bore[4] see BEAR[1].

boreal forest *Bot.* the vast area of dense coniferous forest that extends from the arctic tundra to the N temperate forests in N America, Europe, and Asia.

bored *adj.* tired and without interest from being unoccupied or under-occupied.

◳ uninterested, *colloq.* fed up, weary, tired, worn out, listless, jaded.

boredom *noun* the state of being bored.

◳ tedium, tediousness, monotony, dullness, apathy, listlessness, weariness, worldweariness.
◪ interest, excitement.

borehole *noun* a deep narrow hole made by boring, especially one made in the earth to find oil, water, etc.

borer *noun* a machine or tool for boring holes.

boric *adj.* relating to or containing boron. Also called BORACIC.

boric acid *Chem.* (FORMULA H_3BO_3) a white or colourless crystalline solid, obtained from borax, that is soluble in water and has antiseptic properties. It is used in pharmaceutical products and as a food preservative.

boring *adj.* tedious and uninteresting.

◳ tedious, monotonous, routine, repetitious, uninteresting, unexciting, uneventful, dull, dreary, humdrum, commonplace, trite, unimaginative, uninspired, stale, flat, insipid.
◪ interesting, exciting, stimulating, original.

born *adj.* **1** brought into being by birth. **2** having a natural quality or ability: *a born leader.* **3** destined to do something stated: *born to lead men.* **4** having a stated given status by birth: *Scots-born.* — **in all one's born days** *colloq.* in all one's lifetime or experience. **not born yesterday** alert; shrewd. [from BEAR[1]]

◳ **2** natural, instinctive.

born-again *adj.* **1** converted to a fundamentalist Christian faith. **2** *colloq.* showing a new and strong enthusiasm for something: *a born-again vegetarian.*

borne see BEAR[1].

boron /'bɔːrɒn/ *noun Chem.* (SYMBOL **B**, ATOMIC NUMBER **5**) a non-metallic element consisting of a dark brown powder or black crystals, that is found only in the form of its compounds, eg borax, boric acid. It is used in semiconductors and as a component of control rods and shields in nuclear reactors. See also BORAX, BORIC ACID.

borough /'bʌrə/ *noun* **1** in Britain, a town or urban area which sends a member to Parliament. **2** *Hist.* in Britain, a town with special rights granted by royal charter. **3** a divi-

sion of a large town, especially of London or New York. [from Anglo-Saxon *burg*]

borrow *verb* **1** to take (something) temporarily, usually with permission and with the intention of returning it. **2** *intrans.* to get money in this way. **3** to take, adopt, or copy (words, ideas, etc) from another language, person, etc. — **live on borrowed time** to live longer than expected. [from Anglo-Saxon *borgian*, from *borg*, pledge]

◳ **1** take, take out, draw, derive, obtain, acquire, use, appropriate, usurp, *colloq.* scrounge, *derog.* cadge. **2** *colloq.* scrounge, *derog.* cadge, sponge. **3** adopt, lift, plagiarize, crib, copy, imitate, mimic, echo.
◪ **1, 2** lend.

borrower *noun* a person who borrows, especially from a bank or building society.

borrowing *noun* a thing borrowed, especially a word taken from one language into another.

borstal *noun Brit. Hist.* an penal institution to which young criminals were formerly sent; now replaced by *detention centre* and *young offender institution*. [from *Borstal* in Kent, where the first of these was established]

borzoi /'bɔːzɔɪ/ *noun* a large originally Russian breed of dog with a tall slender body, a long thin muzzle, a long tail, and a long soft coat which may be straight or curly. [from Russian *borzii*, swift]

Bosch process /bɒʃ/ *Chem.* an industrial process whereby hydrogen is obtained by reducing (removing oxygen from) steam using carbon monoxide. [named after the German chemist Carl Bosch]

bosh /bɒʃ/ *noun, interj. colloq.* nonsense. [from Turkish *bo*, worthless, empty]

bosom /'bʊzəm/ *noun* **1** a person's, especially a woman's, chest or breast. **2** *colloq.* (*also* **bosoms**) a woman's breasts. **3** the part of a dress covering the breasts and chest. **4** a loving or protective centre: *the bosom of one's family.* **5** the seat of emotions and feelings. [from Anglo-Saxon *bosm*]

◳ **1** bust, chest, breast. **2** breasts, bust, *colloq.* boobs, *coarse slang* tits. **4** heart, core, centre, midst, protection, shelter, sanctuary. **5** breast, heart, soul.

bosom friend a close friend.

boson /'bəʊsɒn/ *noun Physics* one of two categories of subatomic particle (the other being *fermion*). [named after the Indian physicist Satyendra Nath Bose]

boss[1] — *noun colloq.* a person who employs or who is in charge of others. — *verb* (*also* **boss someone about** or **around**) *colloq.* to give them orders in a domineering way. [from Dutch *baas*, master]

◳ *noun* employer, governor, master, owner, captain, head, chief, leader, supremo, administrator, executive, director, manager, foreman, *colloq.* gaffer, superintendent, overseer, supervisor. *verb* order around, order about, domineer, tyrannize, bully, bulldoze, browbeat, push around, dominate.

boss[2] *noun* **1** a round raised knob for decoration on a shield etc. **2** a round raised decorative knob, found where the ribs meet in a vaulted ceiling. [from Old French *boce*]

bossa nova /'bɒsə 'nəʊvə/ **1** a dance like the samba, which originated in Brazil. **2** music for this dance. [from Portuguese *bossa*, trend + *nova*, new]

boss-eyed *adj. Brit. colloq.* **1** having only one good eye. **2** cross-eyed. **3** crooked, squint.

bossily *adv.* in a bossy or domineering manner.

bossiness *noun* a bossy or domineering manner.

bossy *adj.* bossier, **bossiest**) *colloq.* prone to give orders; disagreeably domineering.

◳ authoritarian, autocratic, tyrannical, despotic, dictatorial, domineering, overbearing, oppressive, lordly, high-handed, imperious, insistent, assertive, demanding, exacting. ⊟ unassertive.

. . . .

bossy-boots noun colloq. a bossy domineering person.

bosun same as BOATSWAIN.

botanic or **botanical** adj. relating to botany or plants.

botanic garden or **botanical garden** a garden in which a diverse collection of plants is developed and maintained for educational, scientific, and conservation purposes. Many botanic gardens also include a herbarium and research laboratories.

botanist noun a person who specializes in or has a detailed knowledge of botany.

botany noun the branch of biology concerned with the scientific study of plants, including their structure, function, ecology, evolution, and classification. [from Greek botane, plant]

botch colloq. — verb (also **botch something up**) 1 to do something badly and without skill. 2 to repair something carelessly or badly. — noun (also **botch-up**) a badly or carelessly done piece of work, repair, etc.

. . . .

⊟ verb 1 bungle, mismanage, colloq. mess up, colloq. foul up, slang cock up, slang screw up.

. . . .

botched adj. bungled; done badly or clumsily.

botcher noun a person who does things carelessly or clumsily.

both — adj., pron. the two. — adv. as well: she both works and runs a family. [from Norse bathir]

bother — verb (**bothered, bothering**) 1 to annoy, worry, or trouble. 2 intrans. (**bother about** or **with something**) to take the time or trouble to consider it. 3 intrans. (**bother about something**) to worry about it. — noun 1 a minor trouble or worry. 2 a person or thing that causes bother. 3 trouble, worry and inconvenience. — interj. an exclamation of slight annoyance or impatience. [perhaps from Irish bodhair, to annoy]

. . . .

⊟ verb 1 annoy, irritate, irk, trouble, worry, concern, disturb, alarm, dismay, distress, upset, inconvenience, harass, colloq. hassle, pester, molest, plague, nag, vex. noun TROUBLE. 1 inconvenience, problem, difficulty. 2 nuisance, pest, annoyance, irritation. 3 inconvenience, colloq. hassle, colloq. aggravation, vexation, worry, strain, bustle.

. . . .

botheration noun, interj. colloq. a minor trouble or worry.

bothersome adj. causing bother or annoyance.

bottle — noun 1 a hollow glass or plastic container with a narrow neck, for holding liquids. 2 the amount a bottle will hold. 3 a baby's feeding bottle, or the liquid in it. 4 slang courage, nerve, or confidence. 5 (usually **the bottle**) slang drinking of alcohol, especially to excess. — verb to put into or store in bottles. — **bottle out** slang to lose one's courage and decide not to do something. **bottle something up** to restrain or suppress one's feelings. [from Old French botele, from Latin buttis, cask]

. . . .

⊟ noun 1 phial, flask, carafe, decanter, flagon, demijohn. **bottle out** colloq. chicken out, colloq. cop out. **bottle something up** hide, conceal, restrain, curb, hold back, suppress, inhibit, restrict, enclose, contain.

. . . .

bottle bank a large container, usually in the street or a public place, where people can put empty bottles so that the glass can be used again.

bottle-feed verb to feed (a baby) with milk from a bottle.

bottle-feeding noun the practice of feeding a baby from a bottle.

bottle-green noun a dark green colour. adj. of this colour.

bottleneck noun 1 a place or thing which impedes the movement of traffic, especially a narrow part of a road. 2 an obstacle to progress.

. . . .

⊟ 1 hold-up, traffic jam, colloq. snarl-up, congestion. 2 clogging, blockage, obstruction, block, obstacle.

. . . .

bottlenose whale a toothed whale with a narrow projecting beak.

bottom — noun 1 the lowest position or part. 2 the point farthest away from the front, top, most important or most successful part: the bottom of the garden/bottom of the class. 3 the part of the body on which a person sits. 4 the base on which something stands. 5 the seat of a chair. 6 the ground underneath a sea, river, or lake. 7 the part of a ship which is under the water. — adj. lowest or last. — verb (**bottomed, bottoming**) 1 to put a bottom on. 2 intrans. said of a ship to reach or touch the bottom. — **at bottom** in reality. **be at the bottom of something** to be the basic cause of it. **bet one's bottom dollar** colloq. to be quite certain. **bottom out** said of prices, etc to reach the lowest level and begin to rise again. **get to the bottom of something** to discover the real cause of a mystery, etc. [from Anglo-Saxon botm]

. . . .

⊟ noun 1 underside, underneath, sole, base, foot. 2 foot, back, rear, end, far end, tail end, rock bottom, depths, nadir. 3 rump, rear, behind, facetious posterior, buttocks, seat, colloq. backside, Brit. colloq. bum, North Amer. colloq. butt. 4 base, plinth, pedestal, support, foundation, substructure, ground, floor, bed. 6 floor, bed, channel. ⊟ noun 1 top.

. . . .

bottom drawer Brit. the sheets, cups and saucers, plates, etc that a woman traditionally collects ready for when she gets married and has her own home.

bottomless adj. extremely deep or plentiful.

. . . .

⊟ deep, profound, fathomless, unfathomed, unplumbed, immeasurable, measureless, infinite, boundless, limitless, unlimited, inexhaustible. ⊟ shallow, limited.

. . . .

bottom line 1 the last line of a financial statement showing profit or loss. 2 colloq. the essential or most important part of a situation.

botulism /ˈbɒtjʊlɪzm/ noun Medicine a severe form of food poisoning, caused by swallowing a toxin produced by the bacterium Clostridium botulinum, which is most commonly found in canned raw meat. The toxin, which is destroyed by cooking, damages the central nervous system and can cause death by heart and lung failure. [from Latin botulus, sausage, from the shape of the bacteria]

bouclé /ˈbuːkleɪ/ noun 1 a type of wool with curled or looped threads. 2 a material made from this. [from French bouclé, curled, looped]

boudoir /ˈbuːdwɑː(r)/ noun old use a woman's private sitting-room or bedroom. [from French boudoir, from bouder, to sulk]

bouffant /ˈbuːfɒn/ adj., said of a hairstyle or dress, etc very full and puffed out. [from French bouffant]

bougainvillaea or **bougainvillea** /buːgənˈvɪlɪə/ noun any of various species of climbing shrub of the genus Bougainvillea, native to S America and having oval leaves and conspicuous flower-heads. [named after the 18c French navigator Louis Bougainville]

bough /baʊ/ noun a branch of a tree. [from Anglo-Saxon bog, arm, shoulder]

bought see BUY.

bouillabaisse /buːjɑːˈbes/ noun a thick spicy fish soup from Provence. [a French word]

bouillon /ˈbuːjɒn/ noun a thin clear soup made by boiling meat and vegetables in water, often used as a basis for thicker soups. [from French bouillon, from bouillir, to boil]

boulder /'bəʊldə(r)/ *noun* a large piece of rock with a diameter greater than 25.6cm, that has been rounded and worn smooth by weathering and abrasion. [from Middle English *bulderston*]

boules /buːl/ *sing. noun* a ball-game popular in France, played on rough ground. The players try to hit a small metal ball, the jack, with larger balls rolled along the ground. [from French *boule*, bowl²]

boulevard /'buːləvɑːd/ *noun* a broad tree-lined street. [from French *boulevard*, from German *Bollwerk*, bulwark: originally used of roads built on a town's demolished fortifications]

bounce — *verb* **1** *intrans. said of a ball, etc* to spring or jump back from a solid surface. **2** to make (a ball, etc) spring or jump back from a solid surface. **3** *intrans.* (**bounce about** or **up**) to move or spring suddenly: *bounce about the room.* **4** (**bounce in** or **out**) to rush noisily, angrily, with a lot of energy, etc: *bounced out in a temper.* **5** *colloq., said of a cheque* to be returned without being paid, because of lack of funds in a bank account. — *noun* **1** the act of springing back from a solid surface. **2** the ability to spring back or bounce well. **3** a jump or leap. **4** *colloq.* energy and liveliness. — **bounce back** *intrans.* to rapidly recover one's health or good fortune after a difficult or adverse period. [from Dutch *bonzen*, to thump]

⊟ *verb* **1** spring, jump, leap, bound, bob, ricochet, rebound, recoil. *noun* **1** rebound, recoil. **2** spring, springiness, elasticity, give, resilience. **3** jump, leap, spring, bound. **4** energy, liveliness, vitality, vivacity, ebullience, exuberance, vigour, *colloq.* go, *colloq.* zip, animation.

bouncer *noun colloq.* a strong person employed by clubs and restaurants, etc to stop unwanted guests entering and to throw out people who cause trouble.

bouncily *adv.* in a bouncy or lively manner.

bounciness *noun* liveliness, energy.

bouncing *adj., said especially of a baby* strong and lively.

bouncy *adj.* (**bouncier, bounciest**) **1** able to bounce well. **2** *said of a person* noticeably lively and energetic.

⊟ **2** lively, animated, spirited, vivacious, energetic, vigorous, jaunty, sprightly.

bound¹ *adj.* **1** tied with, or as if with, a rope, etc. **2** (*in compounds*) restricted to or by the thing specified: *housebound/snowbound.* **3** obliged: *duty bound.* **4** *said of a book* fastened with a permanent cover. — **bound up with something** closely linked with it. See also BIND. **bound to do something** certain or obliged to do it: *it is bound to happen/we are bound to comply.* [past participle of BIND]

⊟ **1** fastened, secured, fixed, tied (up), chained, held, restricted, bandaged. **3** obliged, required, forced, compelled, constrained, liable, committed. **bound to do something** sure, certain, destined, fated, doomed.

bound² *adj.* **1** (**bound for a place**) going to or towards it. **2** (*in combination*) going in a specified direction: *southbound.* [from Norse *bua*, to get ready]

bound³ — *noun* (*often* **bounds**) **1** a limit or boundary. **2** a limitation or restriction. — *verb* **1** to form a boundary of. **2** to set limits to; to restrict. — **out of bounds** outside the permitted area or limits. [from Old French *bonde*]

⊟ *noun* LIMIT. **1** border, line, borderline, demarcation, confine, margin, verge, brink, edge, perimeter, circumference, extremity, termination. **2** limitation, restriction, check, curb, restraint. *verb* LIMIT, CIRCUMSCRIBE. **1** border, outline, enclose. **2** restrict, regulate, contain.

bound⁴ — *noun* **1** a jump or leap upwards. **2** a bounce back from a solid surface. — *verb intrans.* **1** to move energetically; to spring or leap: *bound down the stairs.* **2** to move with leaps. **3** *said of a ball* to bounce back from a solid surface. [from French *bondir*, to spring]

⊟ *noun* **1** jump, leap, vault, spring, hop, skip, gambol, frolic, caper. **2** bounce, rebound. *verb* **1** jump, leap, spring, vault, hurdle. **2** bounce, bob, hop, skip, frisk, gambol, caper, prance.

boundary *noun* (PL. **boundaries**) **1** a line marking the farthest limit of an area, etc. **2** the marked limits of a cricket field. **3** *Cricket* a stroke that hits the ball across the boundary line, scoring four or six runs. [from BOUND³]

⊟ border, frontier, barrier, line, borderline, demarcation, bounds, confines, limits, margin, fringe, verge, brink, edge, perimeter, extremity, termination.

bounden *adj. old use* which must be done; obligatory. [old past participle of BIND]

bounder *noun old colloq. use* a badly behaved person; a cad.

boundless *adj.* having no limit; extensive: *boundless energy.*

⊟ unbounded, limitless, unlimited, countless, untold, incalculable, vast, immense, measureless, immeasurable, infinite, endless, unending, inexhaustible, unflagging, indefatigable.

⊟⊟ limited, restricted.

boundlessly *adv.* without limit.

bounteous /'baʊntɪəs/ *adj.* **1** generous. **2** freely given. [from BOUNTY]

bounteously *adv.* generously or freely; plentifully.

bountiful *adj.* **1** generous. **2** in plenty. [from BOUNTY]

bountifully *adv.* generously; plentifully.

bounty *noun* (PL. **bounties**) **1** the giving of things generously; generosity. **2** a generous gift. **3** a reward given, especially by a government, as encouragement eg to kill or capture dangerous animals, criminals, etc. [from Old French *bonte*, goodness, from Latin *bonus*, good]

⊟ **1** generosity, liberality, munificence, largesse, almsgiving, charity, philanthropy, beneficence, kindness. **2** gift, present, offering. **3** reward, recompense, premium, bonus, gratuity, grant, allowance.

bouquet /'buːkeɪ/ *noun* **1** a bunch of flowers arranged in an artistic way, given as a gift, carried by a bride, etc. **2** the delicate smell of wine. [from French *bouquet*, from *bois*, a wood]

⊟ **1** bunch, posy, nosegay, spray, corsage, buttonhole, wreath, garland. **2** aroma, smell, odour, scent, perfume, fragrance.

bouquet garni /buːkeɪ gɑːˈniː/ a bunch or small packet of mixed herbs used to add flavour to food, usually removed before serving. [from French *bouquet* + *garnir*, to garnish]

bourbon /'bɜːbən/ *noun* a type of whisky made from maize and rye, popular in the USA. [from *Bourbon* county, Kentucky, where it was first made]

bourgeois /'bʊəʒwɑː/ — *noun* (PL. **bourgeois**) *usually derog.* a member of the middle class, especially regarded as politically conservative and socially self-interested. — *adj.* of or like the middle class or bourgeois people. [from French *bourgeois*]

⊟ *adj.* middle-class, materialistic, conservative, traditional, traditionalist, conformist, conventional, hidebound, unadventurous, dull, humdrum, banal, commonplace, trite, unoriginal, unimaginative.

■ *adj.* bohemian, unconventional, original.
. . . .

bourgeoisie /ˈbʊəʒwaːziː/ *noun* (**the bourgeoisie**) *derog.* the middle classes, especially regarded as politically conservative and socially self-interested.

bourn¹ *noun* a small stream. [from BURN²]

bourn² *noun old use* a boundary or limit. [from Old French *bodne*, boundary]

boustrophedon /buːstrəˈfiːdn/ an ancient method of writing, particularly in early Greek, in which lines go alternately from left to right and right to left. [from Greek *boustrophe*, turning like ploughing oxen, from *bous*, ox + *strophe*, a turning]

bout *noun* **1** a period or turn of some activity: *a drinking bout.* **2** a period of illness: *a bout of flu.* **3** a boxing or wrestling match. [from obsolete *bought*, bend, turn]
. . . .

■ **1** period, spell, time, stint, turn, go, term, stretch, session, spree. **2** attack, spell. **3** fight, battle, engagement, encounter, struggle, set-to, match, contest, competition, round, heat.
. . . .

boutique /buːˈtiːk/ *noun* a small shop, especially one selling fashionable clothes. [from French *boutique*]

bouzouki or **bazouki** /buːˈzuːkiː/ *noun* a plucked metal-stringed musical instrument, used especially in Greece. It has a long neck, a fretted fingerboard, and three or four courses of strings played with a plectrum. [from modern Greek]

bovine *adj.* **1** of or like cattle. **2** *derog.*, *said of people* dull or stupid. [from Latin *bos*, ox]

bovine spongiform encephalopathy (ABBREV. BSE) a highly infectious brain disease of cattle, characterized by spongy degeneration of the brain, nervousness, a clumsy gait, and eventual collapse and death. Also called MAD COW DISEASE.

bow¹ /baʊ/ — *verb* **1** *intrans.* to bend the head or the upper part of the body forwards and downwards, usually as a sign of greeting, respect, shame, etc or to acknowledge applause. **2** to bend (the head or the upper part of the body) forwards and downwards: *bow one's head.* **3** (**bow to something**) to accept or submit to it, especially unwillingly: *must bow to the inevitable.* — *noun* an act of bowing or bending the body forwards and down. — **bow and scrape** *derog.* to behave with excessive politeness or deference. **bow down to someone** to submit to them or agree to obey them: *bow down to one's enemies.* **bow out** to stop taking part; withdraw: *bow out of the contest.* **take a bow** to acknowledge applause. [from Anglo-Saxon *bugan*]
. . . .

■ *verb* **1** nod, bob, curtsy, genuflect, kowtow, salaam, stoop. **2** bend, incline. **3** accept, submit to, give in to, consent to, surrender to, acquiesce in, concede, comply with, defer to. *noun* inclination, bending, nod, bob, curtsy, genuflexion, kowtow, salaam, obeisance, salutation, acknowledgement. **bow down to** surrender to, yield to, give way to, capitulate to, *colloq.* knuckle under to, *colloq.* cave in to. **bow out** withdraw, pull out, desert, defect, back out, *colloq.* chicken out, retire, resign, quit, stand down, step down, give up.
. . . .

bow² /boʊ/ — *noun* **1** a knot with a double loop. **2** a weapon made of a piece of curved wood, bent by a string attached to each end, for shooting arrows. **3** a long thin piece of wood with horsehair stretched along its length, for playing the violin, cello, etc. **4** anything which is curved or bent in shape. — *verb* to use a bow on (a violin, cello, etc). [from Anglo-Saxon *boga*, arch]

bow³ /baʊ/ *noun* **1** (*often* **bows**) the front part of a ship or boat. **2** *Rowing* the rower nearest the bow. [from German dialect *boog* or Dutch *boeg*, a ship's bow]

bowdlerization or **bowdlerisation** *noun* expurgation of a book or text.

bowdlerize or **bowdlerise** /ˈbaʊdləraɪz/ *verb* to remove passages or words from (a book, play, etc), especially on moral and social rather than aesthetic grounds; to expurgate. [named after Thomas Bowdler, who produced an expurgated edition of Shakespeare in 1818]

bowel /baʊəl/ *noun* an intestine, especially the large intestine in humans. [from Old French *buel*, from Latin *botellus*, sausage]

bowels *pl. noun* **1** the intestines. **2** the depths or innermost part of something, especially when deep or mysterious: *the bowels of the earth.*
. . . .

■ **1** intestines, guts, entrails, viscera, insides, innards. **2** depths, interior, inside, middle, centre, core, heart.
. . . .

bower /baʊə(r)/ *noun* **1** a place in a garden which is shaded from the sun by plants and trees. **2** *literary* a lady's private room. [from Anglo-Saxon *bur*, chamber]

bower-bird *noun* any of 18 species of a family of birds that are native to Australia and New Guinea, so called because the males construct bowers out of twigs, usually decorated with flowers, berries, leaves, shells, etc, in order to attract the females.

bowl¹ *noun* **1** a round deep dish for mixing or serving food, for holding liquids or flowers, etc. **2** the amount a bowl will hold; the contents of a bowl. **3** the round hollow part of an object, such as a spoon or pipe. [from Anglo-Saxon *bolla*]
. . . .

■ **1** receptacle, container, vessel, dish, basin, sink.
. . . .

bowl² — *noun* a large wooden or plastic ball designed to run in a curve, used in the game of bowls; a similar metal ball used in boules. — *verb* **1** to roll (a ball, hoop, etc) smoothly along the ground. **2** *intrans.* to play bowls. **3** *intrans.*, *trans.* Cricket to throw (a ball) with a straight arm towards the person batting. **4** to throw (something), usually with an overarm movement. — **bowl along** to move smoothly and quickly: *a little car was bowling along the road.* **bowl someone out** *Cricket* to put out the person batting by hitting the wicket with the ball. **bowl someone over 1** to knock them over. **2** *colloq.* to surprise or impress them greatly. [from French *boule*]
. . . .

■ *verb* **1** roll, run, propel. **4** throw, hurl, fling, deliver, pitch, toss, lob, spin. **bowl over 1** knock down, knock over, up-end, *colloq.* flatten. **2** surprise, amaze, astound, astonish, stagger, stun, dumbfound, *colloq.* flabbergast, *colloq.* floor.
. . . .

bow-legged *adj.*, *said of a person* having legs which curve out at the knees.

bowler¹ *noun* **1** a person who bowls the ball in cricket, etc. **2** a person who plays bowls or goes bowling.

bowler² *noun* (*also* **bowler hat**) a man's hard round felt hat with a narrow brim. [named after *Bowler*, a 19c hatter]

bowlful *noun* (PL. **bowlfuls**) the amount a bowl will hold.

bowline /ˈboʊlaɪn/ *noun* **1** a rope used to keep a sail taut against the wind. **2** a knot which makes a loop that will not slip at the end of a piece of rope. [from Old German dialect *boline*]

bowling *noun* **1** the game of bowls. **2** a game played indoors, in which a ball is rolled along an alley at a group of skittles, the object being to knock over as many as possible.

bowling alley 1 a long narrow channel made of wooden boards used in bowling (sense 2). **2** a building containing several of these.

bowling green an area of smooth grass set aside for the game of bowls.

bowls *sing. noun* a game played on smooth grass with bowls, the object being to roll these as close as possible to a smaller ball called the jack.

bowshot *noun* the distance which an arrow can be shot from a bow.

bowsprit / 'bəusprıt/ *noun* a pole projecting from the front of a ship, with ropes from the sails fastened to it. [from Old German dialect *boch*, bow (of a ship) + *spret*, pole]

bowstring *noun* the string on a bow, tension in which projects the arrow.

bow tie a tie which is tied in a double loop to form a horizontal bow at the collar.

bow window a window which is curved out at the centre.

bow-wow — *noun* a child's word for a dog. — *interj.* an imitation of a dog's bark.

box [1] — *noun* 1 a usually square or rectangular container made from wood, cardboard, plastic, etc and with a lid. 2 the amount a box will hold. 3 a separate compartment for a particular purpose, eg for a group of people in a theatre, for a horse in a stable or vehicle, or a witness in a lawcourt. 4 a small enclosed area for a particular purpose: *a telephone box*. 5 a section on a piece of paper, field, road, etc marked out by straight lines: *a penalty box*. 6 a newspaper office or agency which collects mail and sends it on to the person it is intended for: *a post-office box/a box number*. 7 (**the box**) *Brit. colloq.* the television. 8 a raised seat for the driver on a carriage. 9 a small country house, used as a base for some sports: *a shooting-box*. 10 a gift of money given to tradesmen and, formerly, servants: *a Christmas box*. — *verb* 1 (**box something up**) to put it into or provide with a box or boxes. 2 (**box someone** or **something in** or **up**) to stop them moving; confine or enclose them. — **box the compass** to name all the 32 points of the compass in their correct order. [from Latin *buxis*]

⊟ *noun* 1 container, receptacle, case, crate, carton, packet, pack, package, chest, coffer, trunk, coffin. 2 case, crate, carton, packet, pack. 3, 4 booth, compartment, stall. *verb* 1 case, encase, package, pack, wrap. 2 enclose, surround, confine, restrict, circumscribe, cordon off, hem in, corner, trap, imprison, cage, coop up, contain.

box [2] — *verb* 1 *trans., intrans.* to fight with the fists and protected by thick leather gloves, especially as a sport. 2 *trans.* to hit (especially someone's ears) with the fist. — *noun* (*usually* **a box on the ears**) a punch with the fist, especially on the ears. [from Middle English *box*, blow]

⊟ *verb* 1 fight, spar. 2 punch, hit, strike, slap, buffet, cuff, *colloq.* clout, *slang* sock, *colloq.* wallop, *colloq.* whack. *noun* punch, cuff, *colloq.* clout, *slang* sock, *colloq.* wallop, *colloq.* whack.

box [3] *noun* 1 (*also* **boxtree**) an evergreen shrub or small tree (*Buxus sempervirens*), native to north temperate regions and Central America, having small leathery paired leaves, glossy green above and paler underneath, and tiny green flowers lacking petals. 2 (*also* **boxwood**) the hard durable fine-grained yellow wood of this tree, which is used for fine carving, inlay work, and for making rules and chess pieces. [from Anglo-Saxon, from Latin *buxus*]

boxed *adj.* contained in or provided with a box.

Boxer *noun* a member of a 19c nationalistic secret society in China, who led an anti-foreign uprising in 1898. [a translation of Chinese *yi he tuan*, = right harmonious fist]

boxer *noun* 1 a person who boxes, especially as a sport. 2 a large breed of dog with a muscular body, rounded compact head, and a short broad muzzle with pronounced jowls. It was developed from the bulldog in Germany in the late 19c.

⊟ 1 pugilist, fighter, prize-fighter, sparring partner, flyweight, featherweight, bantamweight, lightweight, welterweight, middleweight, heavyweight.

boxer shorts loose shorts worn by men as underpants.

boxful *noun* (PL. **boxfuls**) the amount a box will hold.

box girder *Engineering* a hollow girder made of steel,

timber, or concrete, and having thin walls, often used in bridge construction.

boxing *noun* the sport or practice of fighting with the fists, especially in padded gloves.

⊟ pugilism, prize-fighting, fisticuffs, sparring.

Boxing Day 1 26 December, the day after Christmas Day. 2 the first weekday after Christmas, a public holiday in the UK.

boxing-glove *noun* each of a pair of thick leather gloves worn by boxers.

box junction *Brit.* an area at the intersection of a road junction, marked with a grid of yellow lines painted on the ground, which vehicles may enter only if the exit is clear.

box-kite *noun* a kite in the form of a box with open ends.

box office 1 an office which sells theatre tickets. 2 theatrical entertainment regarded in terms of its commercial value: *the new show is wonderful box office*.

box pleat on a skirt or dress, a large double pleat formed by folding the material in two pleats facing in opposite directions.

boxroom *noun Brit.* a small room used to store bags, boxes, etc or as an extra bedroom.

box set *Theatr.* a system of stage scenery used to represent the interior of a room. It consists of a three-dimensional arrangement of three walls covered by a stretched canvas cloth to form the ceiling.

boy — *noun* 1 a male child. 2 a son. 3 a young man, especially regarded as still immature. 4 (**the boys**) *colloq.* a group of men with whom a man regularly socializes: *go out with the boys*. 5 *offensive* a black male servant. — *interj.* (*also* **oh boy**) an expression of excitement, surprise, or pleasure.

⊟ 1 lad, youngster, *colloq.* kid, *colloq.* nipper. 2 teenager, adolescent, youth, *colloq.* kid, fellow.

boycott — *verb* (**boycotted**, **boycotting**) 1 to refuse to have any business or social dealings with (a company, a country, etc), especially as a form of disapproval or coercion. 2 to refuse to handle or buy (goods). — *noun* an act of boycotting. [named after Charles Boycott]

⊟ *verb* BLACKLIST, BLACK, OUTLAW, BAR, EXCLUDE. 1 ostracize, cold-shoulder, ignore, spurn. 2 refuse, reject, embargo, ban, prohibit, disallow. *noun* embargo, ban, prohibition, rejection, refusal.

🔁 *verb* 1 encourage, support.

boyfriend *noun* a person's regular male companion, often with a romantic or sexual relationship.

⊟ young man, man, *colloq.* bloke, *colloq.* fellow, admirer, date, sweetheart, lover, fiancé.

boyhood *noun* the period of life when a person is a boy.

boyish *adj.* like a boy in appearance or behaviour: *boyish good looks*.

boyishly *adv.* with a boyish manner; like a boy.

boyishness *noun* a boyish manner or quality.

Boyle's law *Physics* a law which states that the volume of a given mass of gas at a constant temperature is inversely proportional to its pressure.

Boys' Brigade an organization for boys which encourages discipline, self-respect, etc.

Boy Scout see SCOUT.

BP *abbrev.* 1 blood pressure. 2 British Petroleum. 3 British Pharmacopoeia.

Bq *symbol* becquerel.

BR *abbrev.* 1 *as an international vehicle mark* Brazil. 2 British Rail.

Br¹ *abbrev.* **1** Britain. **2** British. **3** brother.

Br² *symbol Chem.* bromine.

bra or **brassière** /brɑː, 'brɑːzɪə(r)/ *noun* an undergarment worn by a woman to support the breasts. [from French *brassière*, baby's vest]

brace — *noun* **1** a device, usually made from metal, which supports, strengthens, or holds two things together. **2** **(braces)** *Brit.* straps worn over the shoulders, for holding trousers up. **3** a wire device worn on the teeth to straighten them. **4** (PL. **brace**) a pair or couple, especially of game birds: *four brace of pheasants.* **5** *Printing* either of two symbols, or , used to show that lines, figures, parts of text, etc are connected. **6** a rope attached to a ship's yard, used for adjusting the sails. — *verb* **1** to make tight or stronger, usually by supporting in some way. **2** **(brace oneself)** to prepare oneself for a blow, shock, etc. [from Old French *brace*, arm, power, from Latin *bracchium*]

. . . .

▤ *noun* **1** support, beam, bar, prop, truss, member, strut, cross-piece. **4** pair, couple. *verb* **1** strengthen, reinforce, fortify, bolster, buttress, prop, shore (up), support, steady, tighten, fasten, tie, strap, bind, bandage.

. . . .

brace and bit a hand tool for drilling holes.

bracelet /'breɪslɪt/ *noun* **1** a band or chain worn as a piece of jewellery round the arm or wrist. **2** **(bracelets)** *slang* handcuffs. [from Old French, little arm]

brachiopod /'brakɪəpɒd/ *noun* any marine invertebrate animal belonging to the phylum Brachiopoda, having an asymmetrical chalky shell consisting of two unequal valves. Also called LAMPSHELL. [from Greek *brachion*, arm + *podos*, foot]

bracing *adj.* **1** *said of the wind, air, etc* stimulatingly cold and fresh. **2** invigorating.

. . . .

▤ REFRESHING. **1** fresh, crisp, cool, cold. **2** invigorating, strengthening, fortifying, tonic, rousing, stimulating, reviving, exhilarating, enlivening, energizing, brisk, energetic, vigorous.

▨ WEAKENING, DEBILITATING.

. . . .

bracken *noun* the commonest species of fern in the UK (*Pteridium aquilinum*), which has tall fronds and spreads rapidly across hillsides and woodland by means of its underground rhizomes. [from Middle English *braken*]

bracket — *noun* **1** each of a pair of symbols, [], (), {}, or <>, used to group together or enclose words, figures, etc (see also BRACE 5, PARENTHESIS). **2** a group or category falling within a certain range: *out of my price bracket.* **3** an L-shaped piece of metal or strong plastic, used for attaching shelves, etc to walls. — *verb* (**bracketed, bracketing**) **1** to enclose or group together (words, etc) in brackets. **2** to put (people, things, etc) into a group or category.

bracket fungus the fruiting body (spore-bearing structure) of fungi belonging to the family Polyporaceae, commonly found growing on tree trunks or stumps in north temperate regions, and so called because it resembles a hemispherical shelf or bracket in shape.

brackish *adj.*, *said of water* tasting slightly salty. [from Dutch *brak*, salty]

brackishness *noun* a slightly salty taste of water.

bract *noun* a modified leaf in whose axil an inflorescence or flower develops. Bracts are usually smaller than a true leaf, and green in colour, but in some plants (eg poinsettia, bougainvillea) they are large and brightly coloured, and resemble petals. [from Latin *bractea*, thin plate of metal or gold-leaf]

brad *noun* a thin flat nail with a small head. [from Norse *broddr*, spike]

bradawl *noun* a small hand tool for making holes in wood, leather, etc.

bradycardia /bradɪ'kɑːdɪə/ *noun Medicine* a condition in which the heartbeat is slower than normal (less than 50

to 60 beats per minute). [from Greek *bradys*, slow + *kardia*, heart]

brae /breɪ/ *noun Scot.* a slope on a hill. [from Norse *bra*, brow]

brag — *verb intrans.* (**bragged, bragging**) to talk boastfully or too proudly about oneself, what one has done, etc. — *noun* **1** a boastful statement or boastful talk. **2** a card game like poker. [from Middle English *brag*, arrogance]

. . . .

▤ *verb* boast, crow, *colloq.* swank, *colloq.* talk big.

. . . .

braggart /'bragət/ *noun* a person who brags a lot. [from French *bragard*, vain, bragging]

braggingly *adv.* in a boastful or over-proud manner; as if bragging.

Brahma *noun* the first god of the Hindu triad, the creator of the Universe.

Brahman or **Brahmin** *noun* a member of the highest or priestly class of Hinduism.

Brahmanism *noun* one of the religions of India, involving the worship of Brahma.

braid — *noun* **1** a band or tape, often made from threads of gold and silver twisted together, used as a decoration on uniforms, etc. **2** a length of hair consisting of several lengths which have been twisted together. — *verb* **1** to twist (several lengths of thread, hair) together. **2** to decorate with braid. [from Anglo-Saxon *bregdan*, to weave]

. . . .

▤ *noun* **2** plait, pigtail. *verb* **1** plait, interweave, interlace, intertwine, weave, lace, twine, entwine, ravel, twist, wind.

▨ *verb* **1** undo, unravel.

. . . .

braided *adj.* decorated with braid.

braiding *noun* braid decoration.

Braille /breɪl/ *noun* a system of printing for the blind, in which raised dots are used to represent printed characters. [named after its inventor Louis Braille]

brain — *noun* **1** the highly developed mass of nervous tissue that co-ordinates and controls the activities of the central nervous system of animals. Virtually all the functions of the human body are controlled by the brain. **2** **(brains)** *colloq.* cleverness, intelligence. **3** *colloq.* a very clever person. **4** (*also* **brains**) *colloq.* the person responsible for devising a plan, undertaking, etc. — *verb colloq.* to hit hard on the head. — **have something on the brain** *colloq.* to be preoccupied with it. [from Anglo-Saxon *brægen*]

. . . .

▤ *noun* **1** cerebrum, grey matter, head, mind, intellect. **2** intelligence, cleverness, wit, nous, sense, common sense, shrewdness, understanding. **3** intellectual, highbrow, *colloq.* egghead, scholar, expert, boffin, genius, mastermind, prodigy. **4** mastermind, planner, prime mover.

▨ *noun* **3** simpleton.

. . . .

brainchild *noun* a person's particular theory, idea, or plan.

brain-dead *adj.* denoting a person in whom brain death has occurred or has been diagnosed.

brain death the functional death of the centres in the brain stem that control breathing and other vital reflexes, so that the affected person is incapable of surviving without the aid of a ventilator.

brain drain *colloq.* the loss of scientists, academics, professionals, etc to another country, usually because the prospects are better.

braininess *noun* cleverness, intelligence.

brainless *adj. colloq.* stupid, silly.

brainstem *noun Anat.* the part of the brain that is connected to the top of the spinal cord. It consists of the midbrain, medulla oblongata, and pons.

brainstorm *noun* **1** a sudden loss of the ability to think clearly and act properly. **2** *North Amer. colloq.* same as BRAINWAVE 1.

brainstorming *noun* the practice of seeking solutions to problems or developing new ideas by intensive group discussion of spontaneous suggestions.

brainteaser *noun* a difficult exercise or puzzle.

brainwash *verb* to force (someone) to change their beliefs, ideas, etc by continually applying mental pressure.

brainwashing *noun* the process of forcing someone to change their ideas by mental pressure.

brainwave *noun* **1** *Physiol.* a wave representing the pattern of electrical activity in the brain, recorded by electrodes placed on the scalp. **2** *colloq.* a sudden bright or clever idea.

brainy *adj.* (**brainier, brainiest**) *colloq.* clever, intelligent.

⊟ intellectual, intelligent, clever, smart, bright, brilliant.
🞐 dull, stupid.

braise *verb* to cook (meat, etc) slowly with a small amount of liquid in a closed dish. [from French *braiser*, from *braise*, live coals]

braised *adj.*, *said of meat* cooked by braising.

brake[1] — *noun* **1** a device that is used to slow down or stop a moving vehicle or machine, usually by applying friction to the surface of a rotating part such as a wheel, brake drum, or disc. **2** anything which makes something stop, prevents progress, etc: *a brake on public spending.* **3** an implement for crushing flax or hemp. **4** (*also* **brake harrow**) a heavy harrow used to break up large clods of earth. — *verb* **1** *intrans.* to apply or use a brake. **2** to use a brake to make (a vehicle) slow down or stop. **3** to crush (flax or hemp) by beating.

⊟ *noun* **2** check, curb, rein, restraint, control, restriction, constraint, drag. *verb* **1** slow, decelerate, halt, stop, pull up. **2** slow, retard, delay, slacken, moderate, check, halt, stop.
🞐 *verb* **1, 2** accelerate, speed up.

brake[2] *noun* **1** an area of wild rough ground covered with low bushes, etc. **2** a thicket. [probably from an Old German dialect word meaning 'thicket']

brake drum *Engineering* a revolving cylinder, attached to a rotating piece of machinery, eg the wheel of a car, against which the brake shoes press when the brake is applied.

brake horsepower (ABBREV. **bhp**) the power developed by an engine as measured either by the force that must be applied to a friction brake in order to stop it, or by a dynamometer applied to the flywheel.

brake light each of two red lights at the back of a vehicle which light up when the driver applies the brakes.

brake shoe either of two semicircular metal structures within a rotating brake drum, which press against the inner wall of the drum when the brake is applied.

braless *adj.* not wearing a bra.

bramble *noun* **1** a blackberry bush. **2** any other wild prickly shrub. **3** *Scot.* a blackberry. [from Anglo-Saxon *bremel*]

brambling *noun* a small bird belonging to the finch family, that breeds in N Europe and Asia, but overwinters in S Europe and the Middle East, and has an orange breast and shoulder patch, a white rump, and a black tail. [from BROOM + LING]

bran *noun* the outer covering of cereal grain which is removed during the preparation of white flour. It is an important source of vitamin B and dietary fibre. [from Old French]

branch — *noun* **1** an offshoot arising from the trunk of a tree or the main stem of a shrub. **2** a main division of a railway line, river, road, or mountain range. **3** a division in a family, subject, group of languages, etc. **4** a local office of a large company or organization. — *verb intrans.* (*also* **branch off**) **1** to send out branches. **2** to divide from the main part: *a road branching off to the left.* — **branch out** to develop different interests, projects, etc. [from Old French *branche*, from Latin *branca*, paw]

⊟ *noun* **1** bough, limb, sprig, shoot, offshoot. **2** division, arm, extension. **4** department, office, part, section, division, subsection, subdivision. *verb* **2** diverge, separate, divide, fork. **branch out** diversify, vary, develop, expand, enlarge, extend, broaden out, increase, multiply, proliferate.

branched *adj.* having or formed into branches.

branching *adj.* forming branches.

branchless *adj.* not having branches.

brand — *noun* **1** a maker's name or trademark. **2** a variety or type: *a special brand of humour.* **3** an identifying mark on cattle, etc, usually burned on with a hot iron. **4** (*also* **branding-iron**) an iron used for burning identifying marks on cattle, etc. **5** a sign of disgrace or shame. **6** a piece of burning or smouldering wood. **7** *literary* a torch. **8** *literary* a sword. — *verb* **1** to mark (cattle, etc) with a hot iron. **2** to make a permanent impression on (someone). **3** to give (someone) a bad name or reputation: *branded him a liar.* [from Anglo-Saxon *brand*, fire, flame]

⊟ *noun* **1** make, brand-name, tradename, trademark, logo, mark, symbol, sign, emblem, label, stamp, hallmark. **2** variety, type, class, kind, sort, line, species, grade, quality. *verb* MARK, STAMP. **1** label, tag. **2** burn, scar, sear. **3** stigmatize, denounce, censure.

brandish *verb* to wave (a weapon, etc) as a threat or display. [from Old French *brandir*]

⊟ wave, flourish, shake, raise, swing, wield, flash, flaunt, exhibit, display, parade.

brand-new *adj.* completely new.

brandy *noun* (PL. **brandies**) a strong alcoholic drink made from wine or fermented fruit juice. [from Dutch *brandewijn*, from *branden*, to burn or distil + *wijn*, wine]

brandy-snap *noun* a thin biscuit in the form of a hollow tube, flavoured with ginger and usually served filled with cream.

bran tub *Brit.* a lucky dip consisting of a tub filled with bran, paper, wood shavings, etc with prizes hidden in it.

brash *adj.* **1** very loud or showy. **2** unpleasantly self-confident and disrespectful. **3** over-hasty, rash.

⊟ **1** loud, showy, *colloq.* flashy, gaudy, jazzy, garish, ostentatious. **2** rude, brazen, forward, impertinent, impudent, insolent, cocky, assured, bold, audacious. **3** reckless, rash, impetuous, impulsive, hasty, precipitate, foolhardy, incautious, indiscreet.
🞐 **1** subdued. **2** reserved. **3** cautious.

brashly *adv.* in a brash or vulgar manner or style.

brashness *noun* a brash manner; vulgarity.

brass — *noun* **1** an alloy of copper and zinc, which is strong and ductile, resistant to corrosion, and suitable for casting. It is used to make electrical fittings, screws, and decorative items such as buttons and buckles. **2** objects, tools, etc made of brass. **3** wind instruments made of brass, such as the trumpet. **4** the people who play brass instruments in an orchestra. **5** a piece of flat brass with a figure, design, name, etc on it, usually found in a church, in memory of some dead person. **6** a small, flat, brass ornament with a design on it, for a horse's harness. **7** (**top brass**) *colloq.* people in authority or of high military rank. **8** (**the brass** or **the brass neck**) *colloq.* over-confidence or effrontery; nerve: *he had the brass to call me a wimp.* **9** *colloq.* money. — *adj.* made of brass. — **brassed off** *colloq.* fed up; annoyed. See also BRAZIER[2]. [from Anglo-Saxon *bræs*]

brass band a band consisting mainly of brass instruments.

brasserie /ˈbrasəri/ *noun* a small and usually inexpensive restaurant, especially one serving French food, and originally also beer. [from French *brasserie*, brewery]

brass hat *Brit. colloq.* a high-ranking military officer.

brassica /ˈbrasɪkə/ *noun* any plant belonging to the genus *Brassica* of the family Cruciferae, including several commercially important crop vegetables, eg cabbage, cauliflower, broccoli. [from Latin *brassica*, cabbage]

brassière see BRA.

brassily *adv.* in a brassy or pretentious manner or style.

brassiness *noun* being brassy; vulgarity.

brass rubbing 1 a copy of the design on a brass (sense 5) made by putting paper on top of it and rubbing with coloured wax or charcoal. **2** the process of making of such a copy.

brass tacks *colloq.* the essential details: *get down to brass tacks.*

brassy *adj.* (**brassier, brassiest**) **1** like brass in appearance, especially in colour. **2** like a brass musical instrument in sound. **3** *colloq.* loudly confident and rude. **4** flashy or showy.

brat *noun* a child, especially a rude or badly behaved one.

bravado /brəˈvɑːdoʊ/ *noun* a display of confidence or daring, often boastful and insincere. [from Spanish *bravada*]

. . . .
- ◫ swagger, boasting, bragging, bluster, bombast, talk, boast, vaunting, showing-off, parade, show, pretence.
- ◲ modesty, restraint.
. . . .

brave — *adj.* **1** without fear of danger, pain, etc. **2** fine, excellent. — *verb* (*usually* **brave something out**) to meet or face up to danger, pain, etc: *brave the storm.* — *noun formerly* a warrior from a Native American tribe. [from Old French, from Latin *barbarus*, barbarous]

. . . .
- ◫ *adj.* **1** courageous, plucky, unafraid, fearless, dauntless, undaunted, bold, audacious, daring, intrepid, stalwart, hardy, stoical, resolute, stouthearted, valiant, gallant, heroic, indomitable. *verb* face, confront, defy, challenge, dare, stand up to, face up to, suffer, endure, bear, withstand.
- ◲ *adj.* **1** cowardly, afraid, timid. *verb* capitulate.
. . . .

bravely *adv.* with bravery; boldly.

bravery *noun* a brave quality; being brave or courageous.

. . . .
- ◫ courage, pluck, *colloq.* guts, fearlessness, dauntlessness, boldness, audacity, daring, intrepidity, fortitude, resolution, stout-heartedness, valour, gallantry, heroism, indomitability, *colloq.* grit, mettle, spirit.
- ◲ cowardice, faint-heartedness, timidity.
. . . .

bravo[1] /brɑːˈvoʊ/ — *interj.* well done! excellent! — *noun* (PL. **bravos**) a cry of 'bravo'. [from Italian *bravo*]

bravo[2] /ˈbrɑːvoʊ/ *noun* (PL. **bravos, bravoes**) a hired killer. [from Italian *bravo*]

bravura /brəˈvjʊərə/ *noun* **1** a display of great spirit or daring. **2** a piece of music, especially for the voice, requiring considerable technical ability. [from Italian *bravura*]

brawl — *noun* a noisy quarrel or fight, especially in public. — *verb intrans.* to quarrel or fight noisily. [from Middle English *bralle*]

. . . .
- ◫ *noun* fight, *colloq.* punch-up, *colloq.* scrap, scuffle, *colloq.* dust-up, melee, free-for-all, fray, affray, fracas, rumpus, disorder, row, argument, quarrel, squabble, altercation, dispute, clash. *verb* quarrel, fight, *colloq.* scrap, scuffle, wrestle, tussle, row, argue, squabble, wrangle, dispute.
. . . .

brawler *noun* a person who brawls or is brawling.

brawling *noun* noisy fighting or quarrelling.

brawn *noun* **1** muscle or physical strength. **2** boiled, jellied meat from the head of a pig. [from Old French *braon*, meat]

brawniness *noun* having strong muscles; muscularity.

brawny *adj.* (**brawnier, brawniest**) muscular; strong.

. . . .
- ◫ muscular, strong, sinewy, well-built, burly, beefy, hefty, solid, bulky, hulking, massive, strapping, powerful, vigorous, sturdy, robust.
- ◲ slight, frail.
. . . .

bray — *noun* the loud harsh sound made by an ass or donkey. — *verb* **1** *intrans. said of an ass or donkey* to make a braying noise. **2** *intrans. said of a person* to make a loud harsh sound. **3** to say in a loud harsh voice. [from Old French *braire*]

braze *verb Engineering* to join (two pieces of metal) by melting an alloy with a lower melting point than either of the metals to be joined, and applying it to the joint. [from French *braser*, from *braise*, live coals]

brazen — *adj.* **1** (**brazen-faced**) without shame or any attempt at concealment. **2** of or like brass, especially in sound or colour. — *verb* (**brazened, brazening**) (**brazen something out**) to face an embarrassing or difficult situation boldly and without shame. [from Anglo-Saxon *bræsen*, from *bræs*, brass]

. . . .
- ◫ *adj.* **1** blatant, flagrant, brash, brassy, bold, forward, saucy, pert, barefaced, impudent, insolent, defiant, shameless, unashamed, unabashed, immodest.
- ◲ *adj.* **1** shy, shamefaced, modest.
. . . .

brazenly *adv.* in a brazen or impudent manner.

brazenness *noun* boldness; impudence.

brazier[1] /ˈbreɪzɪə(r)/ *noun* a metal frame or container for holding burning coal, especially used by people who have to work outside in cold weather. [from French *brasier*, from *braise*, live coals]

brazier[2] /ˈbreɪzɪə(r)/ *noun* a worker in brass. [from BRASS]

brazil or **Brazil** /brəˈzɪl/ *noun* **1** the hard reddish wood of any of various tropical trees. **2** (*also* **Brazil nut**) the large three-sided oily edible seed (commonly referred to as a 'nut') of an evergreen tree (*Bertholletia excelsa*), native to S American rainforests. [from *Brazil* in S America, the country itself being so named from the similarity of the red wood found there to that found in the East and known as *brasil*]

brazing *Engineering* the process of joining two pieces of metal by fusing a layer of brass (sometimes known as spelter) between the adjoining surfaces.

BRCS *abbrev.* British Red Cross Society.

breach — *noun* **1** a breaking (of a law, promise, etc) or failure to carry out (a duty). **2** a serious disagreement. **3** a breaking of a relationship. **4** a gap, break, or hole. — *verb* **1** to break (a promise, etc) or fail to carry out (a duty). **2** to make an opening or hole in. — **in breach of something** not following or agreeing with a law, etc. **step into the breach** to take responsibility, or an absent person's place, in a crisis. [from Anglo-Saxon *bryce*]

. . . .
- ◫ *noun* **1** violation, contravention, infringement, trespass, disobedience, offence, transgression, lapse, disruption. **2** quarrel, disagreement, dissension, difference, clash, row. **3** rift, rupture, split, schism, division, separation, parting, estrangement, alienation, disaffection, dissociation. **4** break, crack, gap, hole, space, chasm, rift, rupture, fissure, cleft, crevice, opening, aperture. *verb* **1** break, violate, infringe, contravene, disobey, flout. **2** hole, broach, crack, split, tear, rupture, fissure.
- ◲ *verb* **1** keep, respect, obey.
. . . .

breach of confidence a divulging of information received in confidence.

breach of contract failure to fulfil the terms of a contract.

breach of promise the breaking of a promise, especially a promise of marriage.

breach of the peace a riot or disturbance which violates the public peace.

bread — *noun* 1 a food prepared from wheat or rye flour that is mixed with water or milk, kneaded into a dough with yeast or some other leavening agent to make it rise, and baked. 2 food and other necessities of life: *earn one's bread.* 3 *slang* money. — *verb* to cover (food) with breadcrumbs. — **know which side one's bread is buttered** to know how to act for one's own best interests. [from Anglo-Saxon]

....

☐ *noun* 1 loaf, roll. 2 food, provisions, diet, fare, nourishment, nutriment, sustenance, subsistence, necessities.

....

bread and butter 1 sliced and buttered bread. 2 a means of earning a living.

bread basket 1 a basket for holding bread. 2 an area which produces large amounts of grain for export. 3 *slang* the stomach.

breadboard *noun* 1 a wooden board on which bread, etc is cut. 2 a board for making a model of an electric circuit.

breadcrumbs *pl. noun* crumbs of bread, used in cooking.

breaded *adj.*, *said of food* covered with breadcrumbs.

breadfruit *noun* 1 a tall tropical tree (*Artocarpus altilis*), native to SE Asia, and cultivated throughout the Pacific islands and parts of S America for its large edible fruit. 2 the large oval starchy fruit of this tree, so called because it has a texture similar to that of bread.

breadline — **on the breadline** having an income that is barely enough to live on.

breadth *noun* 1 the measurement from one side to the other. 2 the broad extent or scope of something. 3 openness and willingness to understand and respect other people's opinions, beliefs, etc: *breadth of vision.* [from Anglo-Saxon *brǽd*]

....

☐ 1 width, broadness, wideness, thickness, size, magnitude, measure. 2 scale, range, reach, scope, compass, span, sweep, extent, expanse, spread, comprehensiveness, extensiveness, vastness. 3 tolerance, latitude, open-mindedness, broad-mindedness, permissiveness.

....

breadthways or **breadthwise** *adv.* as measured or regarded from one side to the other.

breadwinner *noun* the person who earns money to support a family.

break — *verb* (PAST TENSE **broke**; PAST PARTICIPLE **broken**) 1 *trans.*, *intrans.* to divide or become divided into two or more parts as a result of stress or a blow. 2 *trans.*, *intrans.*, *said of a machine or tool, etc* to damage or become damaged, so as to stop working and be in need of repair: *the scissors have broken/try not to break the radio.* 3 to fracture a bone in (a limb, etc): *break one's leg.* 4 to burst or cut (the skin) or the skin of (the head). 5 to do something not allowed by (a law, agreement, promise, etc). 6 to interrupt (a journey). 7 *intrans.* to stop work, etc for a short period of time: *break for tea.* 8 to achieve better than (a sporting record, etc). 9 *trans.*, *intrans. said of news, etc* to make or become known. 10 *intrans. said of the weather* to change suddenly, especially after a fine spell. 11 *trans.*, *intrans.* to make or become weaker: *tried to break his spirit.* 12 to defeat or destroy: *break a strike.* 13 to make (the force of something) less: *the trees broke her fall.* 14 to decipher: *break a code.* 15 (**break someone of something**) to make someone give up a bad habit, etc: *tried to break him of smoking.* 16 (**break with someone**) to stop associating with them: *broke with his former friends.* 17 *intrans.* to come into being: *day breaking over the hills.* 18 *intrans. said of a storm* to begin violently. 19 *intrans.* to cut or burst through: *sun breaking through the clouds.* 20 *intrans.* (**break into song** or **laughter**) to begin singing or laughing, especially unexpectedly. 21 *intrans. said of a boy's voice* to become lower in tone on reaching puberty. 22 to disprove (an alibi, etc). 23 to interrupt the flow of electricity in (a circuit). 24 to force open with explosives: *break a safe.* 25 *intrans. said of waves, etc* to collapse into foam. 26 to lose or disrupt the order or form of: *break ranks.* 27 *in-*

trans. Snooker to take the first shot at the beginning of a game. 28 *Tennis* to win (an opponent's service game). 29 *intrans. Boxing* to come out of a clinch. 30 *intrans. Cricket, said of a ball* to change direction on hitting the ground. — *noun* 1 an act of or result of breaking. 2 a brief pause in work, lessons, etc. 3 a change: *a break in the weather.* 4 a sudden rush, especially to escape: *make a break for it.* 5 *colloq.* an unexpected or sudden opportunity. 6 *colloq.* a piece of good or bad luck: *a bad break.* 7 *Snooker* a series of successful shots played one after the other. 8 *Snooker* the opening shot of a game. 9 an interruption in the electricity flowing through a circuit. 10 *Mus.* a short improvised solo passage in jazz. — **break away** *intrans.* 1 to become detached from. 2 to escape from control. 3 to put an end to one's connection with a group, etc. **break the back of something** to complete the heaviest or most difficult part of a job, etc. **break camp** to pack up the equipment after camping. **break cover** to come out of hiding. **break down** 1 *said of a person* to fail in mental health. 2 to give way to one's emotions; to burst into tears. 3 *said of a machine, etc* to stop working properly. 4 *said of human relationships* to be unsuccessful and so come to an end. **break something down** 1 to use force to knock down a door, etc. 2 to divide something into parts and analyse it. **break even** to make neither a profit nor a loss in a transaction. **break in** 1 to enter a building by force, especially to steal things inside. 2 to interrupt a conversation, etc. **break in a horse** to train a horse to carry a saddle and a rider. **break something in** to wear new shoes, boots, etc so that they lose their stiffness. **break loose** or **free** 1 to escape from control. 2 to become detached: *the boat broke loose from its mooring.* **break new** or **fresh ground** to do something in an original way. **break off** 1 to stop talking. 2 to become detached by breaking. 3 to come to an end abruptly. **break something off** 1 to detach it by breaking. 2 to end something abruptly. **break something open** to open a box, door, etc by force. **break out** 1 to escape from a prison, etc using force. 2 to begin suddenly and usually violently: *then war broke out.* **break out in spots**, etc to become suddenly covered in spots, a rash, etc. **break step** *said of soldiers, etc* to become irregular and out of step in marching. **break through** 1 to force a way through. 2 to make a new discovery or be successful, especially after a difficult or unsuccessful period. **break up** 1 to break into pieces. 2 to come to an end; to finish. 3 *said of people* to end a relationship or marriage: *his parents have broken up.* 4 *said of a relationship, marriage, etc* to come to an end: *their marriage has broken up.* 5 *said of a school or a pupil* to end term and begin the holidays. **break someone up** *North Amer. colloq.* to make them laugh convulsively. **break something up** 1 to divide it into pieces. 2 to make it finish or come to an end. **break wind** to release gas from the bowels through the anus. [from Anglo-Saxon *brecan*]

....

☐ *verb* 1 divide, fracture, crack, snap, split, sever, separate, rend. 2 smash, splinter, shatter. 5 violate, contravene, infringe, breach, disobey, flout. 6 interrupt, suspend, stop, halt, discontinue. 7 rest, pause, stop, halt. 8 exceed, beat, better, excel, surpass. 11 weaken, lessen, erode. 12 defeat, destroy, crush, overpower, quell, subdue, demoralize. 13 soften, dampen, deaden, lessen, moderate, reduce. *noun* 1 fracture, crack, split, tear, gash, fissure, cleft, crevice, opening, gap, hole, breach, rift, rupture, schism, separation. 2 interval, intermission, interlude, interruption, pause, halt, lull, *colloq.* let-up, respite, rest, *colloq.* breather, *North Amer.* time out, holiday. 4 rush, dash, run. 5 opportunity, chance, fortune, luck. **break away** 1 separate, split off, break off, snap off. 2 run away, escape, flee, fly. 3 leave, depart, quit, part company, secede. **break down** 1 *colloq.* crack up, *colloq.* go to pieces. 3 fail, stop, *colloq.* pack up, *slang* conk out, seize up. 4 collapse, fail, fall apart, *colloq.* come to grief, come to an end. **break something down** 1 demolish, knock down, tear down, destroy. 2 analyse, dissect, separate, itemize, detail. **break in 2** interrupt, butt in, interpose, interject, intervene, intrude, encroach, impinge. **break off** 1 pause, cease, stop, fall silent, take a break. **break something off 1** detach, snap off, sever, separate, part, divide, disconnect. **2** end, finish, terminate, discontinue, halt, stop, cease, interrupt, suspend. **break out 1** escape, abscond, bolt, flee. **2** start, begin, commence, happen, occur, erupt, flare up, burst out. **break up 1** divide, split, crack. **2** stop, finish, terminate, adjourn, dissolve, disband. **3** part, separate, split up, divorce, part company. **4** break down, fail. **break something up 1** divide, dismantle, take apart, demolish, destroy, disintegrate, splinter, sever, split, part, separate. **2** adjourn, suspend, stop, finish, terminate, disband, disperse, dissolve.

◨ *verb* **1, 2** mend. **5** keep, observe, abide by. **6, 7** continue. **11** strengthen.

breakable — *adj.* able or liable to be broken. — *noun* (*usually* **breakables**) a breakable object.

◨ *adj.* brittle, fragile, delicate, flimsy, insubstantial, frail.
◨ *adj.* unbreakable, durable, sturdy.

breakage *noun* **1** the act of breaking. **2** a broken object; damage caused by breaking.

breakaway *noun* **1** an act of breaking away or escaping from control. **2** (*attributive*) that has broken away; separate: *a breakaway republic*.

breakdancing *noun* an energetic style of dancing which involves complicated jumps and twists, originally developed by young black Americans.

breakdown *noun* **1** a failure in a machine or device. **2** (*attributive*) used in connection with a breakdown, especially of a road vehicle: *a breakdown van*. **3** *used of a person* a failure in mental health. **4** a failure or collapse of a process: *a breakdown in communications*. **5** a detailed analysis.

◨ **1** failure, malfunction, interruption, stoppage. **3** failure, collapse. **4** failure, collapse, disintegration, cessation. **5** analysis, dissection, itemization, classification, categorization.

breaker *noun* **1** a person or thing that breaks something. **2** a large wave which breaks on rocks or the beach.

◨ **2** wave, surf, roller.

breakfast /'brɛkfəst/ — *noun* the first meal of the day. — *verb intrans.* to have breakfast. [from *break fast*, ie begin to eat after fasting]

break-in *noun* an illegal entry by force into a building, especially to steal things inside.

◨ burglary, house-breaking, robbery, raid, invasion, intrusion, trespass.

breaking and entering the act of breaking into a building to steal things inside.

breaking-point *noun* a point at which a person or thing can no longer stand a stress or strain.

breakneck *adj.*, *used of speed* extremely fast.

break of day *literary* dawn.

breakout *noun* an escape by force.

breakthrough *noun* **1** a decisive advance or discovery. **2** an act of breaking through something.

◨ **1** discovery, find, finding, invention, innovation, advance, progress, headway, step, leap, development, improvement.

break-up *noun* **1** the ending of a relationship or situation. **2** a dispersal or scattering.

◨ **1** divorce, separation, parting, split, rift, finish, termination,

dissolution. **2** dispersal, scattering, dissolution, disbanding, disintegration, crumbling.

breakwater *noun* a wall built on a beach to break the force of the waves.

◨ groyne, mole, jetty, pier, quay.

bream *noun* (PL. **bream**) **1** any of various freshwater fish belonging to the carp family, found in slow-moving rivers and lowland lakes throughout N and E Europe, and having a deep body covered with silvery scales, and mouthparts which can be pushed out to form a tube for feeding. **2** (*in full* **sea bream**) an unrelated deep-bodied marine fish, some species of which are important food fish. [from Old French *bresme*]

breast — *noun* **1** the front of the human body between the neck and the belly. **2** in women, each of the two mammary glands, forming soft protuberances on the chest, and each consisting of a group of milk-secreting glands embedded in fatty tissue. **3** the source or seat of emotions. **4** the part of a garment covering the breast. — *verb* **1** to face or oppose: *breast the wind*. **2** to come to the top of a hill, etc. **3** *Athletics* to touch (the tape) at the end of a race with the chest. — **make a clean breast of something** to be frank and honest about something one has done, feels, or thinks, etc. [from Anglo-Saxon *breost*]

breastbone *noun* the sternum.

breastfed *adj.*, *said of a baby* fed with milk from the breast.

breastfeed *verb trans.*, *intrans.* to feed a baby with milk from the breast.

breastfeeding *noun* feeding a baby with milk from the breast.

breastplate *noun* a piece of armour which protects the chest.

breaststroke *noun* a style of swimming in which the arms are pushed out in front and then pulled backwards together.

breastwork *noun* a temporary wall built from earth for defence, reaching up to a person's chest.

breath *noun* **1** the air drawn into and then expelled from the lungs. **2** a single inhalation of air. **3** exhaled air as odour, vapour, or heat: *bad breath*. **4** a faint breeze. **5** a slight trace of perfume, etc. **6** a slight hint, suggestion, or rumour (especially of scandal). — **catch one's breath** to stop breathing for a moment, from fear, amazement, pain, etc. **draw breath** to breathe. **get one's breath back 1** to begin breathing normally again after strenuous exercise. **2** to recover from a shock or surprise. **hold one's breath** to stop breathing, usually because of worry or to avoid being heard. **out of** or **short of breath** breathless, especially after strenuous exercise. **take one's breath away** to astound or amaze one (see also BREATHTAKING). **under one's breath** in a whisper. **waste one's breath** to speak without any effect. [from Anglo-Saxon *bræth*]

◨ **2** breathing, respiration, inhalation, exhalation. **4** breeze, puff, waft, gust. **5** aroma, smell, odour, whiff. **6** hint, suggestion, suspicion, undertone, whisper, murmur.

breathalyse *verb* to test (a driver) with a Breathalyser.

Breathalyser or **Breathalyzer** *noun trademark* an instrument used to test the amount of alcohol on a driver's breath.

breathe *verb* **1** *intrans.*, *trans.* to respire by alternately drawing air into and expelling it from the lungs. **2** *trans.* to say quietly. **3** *intrans.* to make a very quiet sound; to blow softly. **4** *trans.* to show or express: *breathe defiance*. **5** *intrans.* to take breath or pause. **6** *trans.* to communicate; to instil: *breathe some life into the proceedings*. **7** *intrans. said of wine* to be exposed to the air so as to improve in flavour. — **breathe again** or **freely** to feel at ease after a period of anxiety or fear. **breathe down**

someone's neck to watch or supervise someone so closely that they feel uncomfortable. **breathe fire** *colloq.* to speak very angrily. **breathe one's last** to die. [from BREATH]

....

⊞ **1** respire, inhale, exhale, expire, sigh, gasp, pant, puff. **2** say, utter, express, articulate, murmur, whisper, impart, tell. **3** murmur, whisper, sigh, rustle. **6** instil, imbue, infuse, inject, inspire.

....

breather *noun colloq.* a short break from work.

....

⊞ break, pause, halt, *colloq.* let-up, respite, rest, *North Amer.* time out.

....

breathily *adv.* with a sound of breathing.

breathing *noun* **1** in terrestrial animals, the process whereby air is alternately drawn into the lungs and then expelled from them, as a result of which oxygen is taken into the body and carbon dioxide is released from it. Also called RESPIRATION. **2** a sign in Greek indicating that the initial vowel is pronounced with an h- sound (aspirate).

breathing space a short time allowed for rest.

breathless *adj.* **1** having difficulty in breathing normally, either from illness or from hurrying, etc. **2** very eager or excited. **3** with no wind or fresh air.

....

⊞ **1** short-winded, out of breath, panting, puffing, puffed (out), exhausted, winded, gasping, wheezing, choking. **2** eager, excited, expectant, impatient, agog, feverish, anxious.

....

breathlessly *adv.* with difficulty in breathing normally; with a lack of breath: *replied breathlessly that she was exhausted.*

breathlessness *noun* being breathless; a lack of breath.

breathtaking *adj.* very surprising, exciting, or impressive.

....

⊞ awe-inspiring, impressive, magnificent, overwhelming, amazing, astonishing, stunning, exciting, thrilling, stirring, moving.

....

breathtakingly *adv.* astoundingly; amazingly.

breath test *Brit.* a test given to drivers to check the amount of alcohol in their blood.

breathy *adj.* (**breathier, breathiest**) *said of the voice* producing a sound of breathing when speaking.

breccia /ˈbrɛtʃɪə/ *noun Geol.* coarse sedimentary rock composed of a mixture of angular rock cemented together by finer-grained material. It is usually formed by processes such as landslides and geological faulting, in which rocks become fractured. [from Italian *breccia*]

bred see BREED.

breech *noun* **1** the back part of a gun barrel, where it is loaded. **2** *old use* the buttocks. [from Anglo-Saxon *brec*]

breech birth or **breech delivery** the birth of a baby buttocks first instead of the normal head-first position.

breeches *pl. noun* **1** short trousers fastened below the knee. **2** *humorous colloq.* trousers.

breeches buoy a pair of canvas breeches on a rope, used for rescuing people, especially from ships.

breed — *verb* (PAST TENSE AND PAST PARTICIPLE **bred**) **1** *intrans. said of animals and plants* to reproduce or cause them to reproduce sexually in order to transmit certain selected characteristics from parents to offspring. **2** to keep (animals or plants) for the purpose of producing offspring, or developing new types with selected characteristics. **3** to train or educate: *well-bred children.* **4** to cause or produce (usually something bad): *dirt breeds disease.* **5** *Physics* to produce more fissile fuel (atoms that can be split) than is consumed in a nuclear reaction. See also BREEDER REACTOR. — *noun* **1** an artificially maintained subdivision within an animal species, especially farm live-

stock or pet animals, produced by domestication and selective breeding, eg Friesian cattle, Irish wolfhound. **2** a race or lineage. **3** a kind or type. [from Anglo-Saxon *bredan*, to produce, cherish]

....

⊞ *verb* **1** reproduce, procreate, multiply, propagate, bear, bring forth. **2** farm, cultivate, plant. **3** rear, raise, bring up, educate, train, instruct. **4** produce, create, originate, arouse, cause, occasion, engender, generate, make, nourish, develop. *noun* **1** strain, variety, stock, family, species. **2** race, lineage, stock, family, line, pedigree. **3** sort, kind, type, species.

....

breeder *noun* a person who breeds animals, especially for a living.

breeder reactor a type of nuclear reactor which produces more fissile material than it consumes as fuel, used mainly to produce plutonium for the nuclear weapons industry. Also called FAST BREEDER REACTOR.

breeding *noun* **1** *Biol.* controlling the manner in which plants or animals reproduce in such a way that certain characteristics are selected for and passed on to the next generation. **2** the result of a good education and training: *show good breeding.*

....

⊞ **1** reproduction, procreation, nurture, development, rearing, raising. **2** manners, politeness, civility, gentility, urbanity, refinement, culture, polish.

⊞ **2** vulgarity.

....

breeding-ground *noun* **1** a place where animals, birds, etc produce their young. **2** a place, situation, etc which encourages the development of something usually regarded as bad: *a breeding-ground for crime.*

breeze[1] — *noun* **1** a gentle wind. **2** *colloq.* any job, etc which is easily done. — *verb intrans. colloq.* **1** to move briskly and confidently: *breezed into the room.* **2** (**breeze through something**) to do it easily and quickly: *breezed through the exam.* [probably from Old Spanish *briza*, north-east wind]

....

⊞ *noun* **1** wind, gust, flurry, waft, puff, breath, draught, air.

....

breeze[2] *noun* ashes from coal, coke or charcoal. [from French *braise*, live coals]

breezeblock *noun* a type of brick made from breeze and cement, used for building houses, etc.

breezily *adv.* in a breezy or carefree manner: *walked breezily into the room.*

breeziness *noun* a breezy or carefree manner.

breezy *adj.* (**breezier, breeziest**) **1** slightly windy. **2** *said of a person* lively, confident, and casual.

....

⊞ **1** windy, blowing, fresh, airy, gusty, blustery, squally. **2** animated, lively, confident, vivacious, jaunty, blithe, debonair, carefree, cheerful, easy-going, casual, informal, assured.

⊞ **1** still. **2** staid, serious.

....

Bren gun or **bren gun** a light, quick-firing machine-gun used during World War II. [from *Brno* in Czechoslovakia, where it was originally made + *Enfield* in England, where it was later made]

brethren see BROTHER.

Breton /ˈbrɛtən/ — *noun* **1** a person from Brittany in France. **2** the Celtic language spoken in Brittany. — *adj.* of Brittany, its people, or language. [from French *Breton*]

breve /briːv/ *noun* **1** *Mus.* a note twice as long as a semibreve. **2** a mark sometimes put over a vowel to show that it is short or unstressed. [from Latin *brevis*, short]

breviary /ˈbriːvɪərɪ/ *noun* (PL. **breviaries**) *RC Church* a book containing the hymns, prayers, and psalms which form the daily service. [from Latin *breviarum*, summary]

brevity /ˈbrɛvɪtɪ/ noun 1 using few words; conciseness. 2 shortness of time. [from Old French brievete, from Latin brevis, short]

⊟ 1 conciseness, terseness, succinctness, pithiness, crispness, incisiveness, abruptness, curtness. 2 briefness, shortness, impermanence, ephemerality, transience, transitoriness.
⊟ 1 verbosity. 2 permanence, longevity.

brew — verb 1 to make beer or other alcoholic beverage by infusion, boiling, and fermentation of malted barley. 2 (also **brew up** or **brew something up**) to make (tea, coffee, etc) by mixing the leaves, grains, etc with boiling water. 3 intrans. to be prepared by brewing: the tea is brewing. 4 (also **brew up**) to become stronger and threatening: there's a storm brewing. 5 (also **brew something up**) to plan or prepare something (usually unwelcome): brew up trouble. — noun 1 a drink produced by brewing, especially tea or beer. 2 an amount of beer, etc produced by brewing: last year's brew. 3 the quality of what is brewed: a good strong brew. [from Anglo-Saxon breowan]

⊟ verb 1 infuse, stew, boil, seethe, ferment, prepare, soak, steep. 2, 3 infuse, stew, boil. 4 build up, develop, gather, threaten. 5 plot, scheme, plan, prepare, project, devise, contrive, concoct, hatch, excite, foment. noun 1 infusion, drink, beverage, liquor, potion, mixture, blend, concoction.

brewer noun a person or company that brews and sells beer.
brewer's yeast a type of yeast (especially Saccharomyces cerevisiae) used in the brewing of beer, and as a source of vitamins of the vitamin B complex for use in dietary supplements.
brewery noun (PL. **breweries**) a place where beer and ale are brewed.
brewing noun the process by which alcoholic beverages, especially beer, are produced by the slow fermentation of malted cereal grains, usually barley, flavoured with hops.
brewpub noun a pub, often incorporating a restaurant, where beer is brewed. See also MICROBREWERY.
briar¹ or **brier** /ˈbraɪə(r)/ noun any of various prickly shrubs, especially a wild rose bush. [from Anglo-Saxon brer]
briar² or **brier** /ˈbraɪə(r)/ noun 1 a shrub or small tree (Erica arborea), native to S Europe, the woody root of which is used to make tobacco pipes. 2 a tobacco pipe made from the root of this plant. [from French bruyère, heath]
bribe — noun a gift, usually of money, offered to someone to persuade them to do something illegal or improper. — verb to offer or promise a bribe, etc to (someone). [from Old French briber]

⊟ noun incentive, inducement, allurement, enticement, colloq. backhander, kickback, payola, colloq. sweetener, colloq. hush money, protection money. verb corrupt, buy, buy off, suborn.

bribery noun the practice of offering bribes.

⊟ corruption, slang graft, colloq. palm-greasing, inducement.

bric-à-brac /ˈbrɪkəbrak/ noun small objects of little financial value kept as decorations or ornaments. [from French à bric et à brac, at random]

⊟ knick-knacks, ornaments, curios, antiques, trinkets, baubles.

brick — noun 1 a rectangular block of baked clay used for building. 2 the material used for making bricks. 3 a child's plastic or wooden rectangular or cylindrical toy for build-ing. 4 something in the shape of a brick: a brick of ice-cream. 5 Brit. colloq. (only in sing.) a trusted and helpful person. — adj. made of bricks, of the dull red colour of bricks. — verb (**brick something in** or **up**) to close or fill it in with bricks: brick up the window. — **drop a brick** Brit. colloq. to do or say something embarrassing or insulting without realizing that it is. **like banging** or **knocking one's head against a brick wall** colloq. having no effect despite much effort. **make bricks without straw** to do a job without having the proper materials for it. [from Old Dutch bricke]

brickbat noun 1 an insult or criticism. 2 a piece of brick, or anything hard, thrown at someone.
bricklayer noun a person who builds with bricks.
bricklaying noun the skill or practice of laying bricks in building.
brickwork that part of a building, eg the walls, that is made of brick.

⊟ masonry, shell, walls.

brickyard noun a place where bricks are made.
bridal adj. of a wedding or a bride. [from Anglo-Saxon brydeala, wedding feast, from bryd, bride + ealu, ale]

⊟ wedding, nuptial, marriage, matrimonial, marital, conjugal.

bride noun a woman who has just been married, or is about to be married. [from Anglo-Saxon bryd]
bridegroom noun a man who has just been married, or is about to be married.
bridesmaid noun a girl or unmarried woman attending the bride at a wedding.
bridewealth noun Anthropol. in some societies, property or money given by a bridegroom to the relatives of his bride, especially her parents, as a means of compensating them for her loss to the family, or to establish his rights over her.
bridge¹ — noun 1 a structure that spans a river, road, railway, valley, ravine, or other obstacle, providing a continuous route across it for pedestrians, motor vehicles, or trains. 2 anything joining or connecting two separate things. 3 Comput. a component which connects the parts of a communications network. 4 the narrow raised platform from which the captain of a ship directs its course. 5 the hard bony upper part of the nose. 6 a small piece of wood on a violin, guitar, etc which keeps the strings stretched tight. 7 a fixed replacement for one or more missing teeth, consisting of a partial denture that is permanently secured to one or more adjacent natural teeth. 8 same as BRIDGEWORK. — verb 1 to form or build a bridge over. 2 to make a connection, close a gap, etc. — **cross a bridge when one comes to it** to deal with a problem when it arises and not before. [from Anglo-Saxon brycg]

⊟ noun 1 arch, span, causeway. 2 link, connection, bond, tie. verb 1 span, cross, traverse. 2 fill, link, connect, couple, join, unite, bind.

Types of bridge include: suspension bridge, archbridge, cantilever bridge, flying bridge, flyover, overpass, footbridge, railway bridge, viaduct, aqueduct, humpback bridge, toll bridge, pontoon bridge, Bailey bridge, rope bridge, drawbridge, swing bridge.

bridge² noun a card game for four people playing in pairs, developed from whist. A player declares trumps, and also plays the hand of that player's partner, which is laid down face upwards.
bridge-builder noun 1 a person who builds bridges. 2 a person who tries to settle a dispute between two other people.
bridgehead noun a position well into enemy land from which an attack can be made.

bridgework *Dentistry* a plate with false teeth, which is connected to the real teeth on either side of it (see BRIDGE[1] 6).

bridging loan a loan of money, usually from a bank, to cover the period between buying one house and selling another.

bridle — *noun* 1 the leather straps on a horse's head which help the rider control the horse. 2 anything which controls or restrains. — *verb* 1 to put a bridle on (a horse). 2 to bring under control: *bridle one's anger.* 3 *intrans.* (*also* **bridle up**) to show anger or resentment by moving the head upwards proudly. [from Anglo-Saxon *bridel*]

⊟ *noun* 2 check, curb, restraint. *verb* 2 check, curb, restrain, control, govern, master, subdue, moderate, repress, contain.

bridle path or **bridle way** a path for riders and horses.
Brie /briː/ *noun* a French soft cheese. [from *Brie*, in NE France, where it is made]

brief — *adj.* 1 lasting only a short time. 2 short or small. 3 said of writing or speech using few words; concise. *noun* 1 *Legal* a summary of the facts and legal points of a case, prepared for the barrister who will be dealing with the case in court. b a case taken by a barrister. c *colloq.* a barrister: *who's your brief?* 2 instructions given for a job or task. 3 *RC Church* a letter from the Pope on a matter of discipline. — *verb* 1 to prepare a person by giving them instructions in advance: *we need to brief them in detail.* 2 *Legal* to inform a barrister about a case by brief. — **hold no brief for someone** or **something** to decline to support or be in favour of them.[from Old French *brief, from Latin brevis, short*]

⊟ *adj.* SHORT. 1 short-lived, momentary, ephemeral, transient, fleeting, passing, transitory, temporary, limited, cursory, hasty, quick, swift, fast. 2 small, *colloq.* mini, skimpy. 3 terse, succinct, concise, pithy, crisp, compressed, thumb-nail, laconic, abrupt, sharp, brusque, blunt, curt, surly. *noun* 1 dossier, case, defence, argument, outline. 2 orders, instructions, directions, remit, mandate, directive, advice, briefing, data, information. *verb* 1 instruct, direct, explain, guide, advise, prepare, prime, inform, bring up to date, *colloq.* fill in, *colloq.* gen up.
⊠ *adj.* 1, 2 long. 3 lengthy, verbose.

briefcase *noun* a light, usually flat case for carrying papers, etc.
briefing *noun* 1 a meeting at which instructions and information are given. 2 the instructions or information given at a meeting. 3 the act of giving information or instructions.

⊟ 1 meeting, conference, session, forum. 2 information, advice, guidance, directions, instructions, orders, *colloq.* gen, *colloq.* low-down. 3 preparation, priming, *colloq.* filling-in, bringing up to date.

briefly *adv.* 1 using few words: *I will try to explain it briefly.* 2 for a short time: *visited her briefly at her house.*

⊟ 1 tersely, succinctly, concisely, pithily, crisply, laconically, in brief, in short. 2 momentarily, fleetingly, temporarily, quickly.

briefness *noun* being brief, especially using few words; brevity.
brier see BRIAR[1], BRIAR[2].
Brig. *abbrev.* brigadier.
brig *noun* a type of sailing ship with two masts and square sails. [from BRIGANTINE]
brigade *noun* 1 one of the divisions in the army, usually commanded by a brigadier. 2 a group of people organized

for a particular purpose: *the fire brigade.* [a French word, from Old Italian *brigata*, company of soldiers]
brigadier /brɪgəˈdɪə(r)/ *noun* 1 an officer commanding a brigade. 2 a staff officer of similar rank, above a colonel but below a major-general.
brigadier general in the US army, an officer ranking above a colonel.
brigand *noun* a member of a band of robbers, especially one operating in quiet mountain areas. [from French *brigand*, from Old Italian *brigante*, member of an armed band]
brigantine /ˈbrɪgəntiːn/ *noun* a type of sailing ship with two masts, with square sails on the main mast, and sails set lengthwise on the second mast. [from Old Italian *brigantino*, armed escort ship.]
bright — *adj.* 1 giving out or shining with much light. 2 said of a colour strong, light, and clear. 3 lively, cheerful. 4 (**bright at something**) clever and quick to learn it. 5 full of hope or promise: *a bright future.* 6 said of a day or the weather with clear skies and sunshine: *bright periods and showers.* — *adv.* brightly: *a fire burning bright.* — **bright and early** very early in the morning. **look on the bright side** to be cheerful and optimistic in spite of problems. [from Anglo-Saxon *beorht*]

⊟ *adj.* 1 luminous, illuminated, shining, beaming, gleaming, glistening, glittering, sparkling, glowing, brilliant, resplendent, glorious, splendid, dazzling, glaring, blazing, intense. 2 clear, light, vivid, strong, intense, brilliant, glowing. 3 lively, vivacious, happy, cheerful, glad, joyful, merry, jolly. 4 clever, *colloq.* brainy, smart, intelligent, quick-witted, quick, sharp, acute, keen, astute, perceptive. 5 promising, propitious, auspicious, favourable, rosy, optimistic, hopeful, encouraging. 6 fine, sunny, cloudless, unclouded.
⊠ *adj.* 1, 2, 6 dark, dull. 3 sad. 4 stupid. 5 depressing. 6 dark.

brighten *verb trans., intrans.* (*also* **brighten up**) 1 to make or become bright or brighter. 2 to make or become happier or more cheerful.

⊟ 1 light up, illuminate, lighten, clear up, shine, colour. 2 cheer up, gladden, *colloq.* buck up, perk up, liven up.
⊠ 1 darken, dull.

bright lights a big city seen as a place of entertainment and excitement.
brightly *adv.* 1 with brightness. 2 with enthusiasm; cheerfully: *he said brightly that it would be no trouble.*
brightness *noun* being bright or shining, especially in physical senses: *the brightness of the walls took us aback.*
bright spark *often derog.* a lively and eager young person.
brill *noun* (PL. **brill, brills**) a large flatfish, found mainly on sandy bottoms in shallow waters around the coasts of Europe, and having a freckled sandy brown body, up to 60cm in length, with both eyes on the left side. It feeds mainly on sand eels and whiting, and is valued as a food fish.
brilliance or **brilliancy** *noun* 1 being bright and sparkling. 2 outstanding intelligence or skill.

⊟ 1 radiance, brightness, sparkle, dazzle, intensity, vividness, gloss, lustre, sheen, glamour, glory, magnificence, splendour. 2 intelligence, genius, talent, virtuosity, greatness, distinction, excellence, aptitude, cleverness.

brilliant — *adj.* 1 very bright and sparkling. 2 said of a colour bright and vivid. 3 of outstanding intelligence or talent. 4 making a great display or show: *a brilliant display of flowers.* 5 *colloq.* excellent. — *noun* a diamond cut to have a lot of facets so that it sparkles brightly. [from French *briller*, to shine]

⊟ *adj.* magnificent, splendid. 1 scintillating, dazzling, glaring, blazing, bright, shining, sparkling, glittering. 2 intense, vivid, bright, glossy. **3** clever, *colloq.* brainy, intelligent, quick, astute, gifted, talented, accomplished, expert, skilful, masterly, exceptional, outstanding. **4** showy, flamboyant, colourful, rich, striking, breathtaking, glorious. **5** excellent, wonderful, marvellous, great, terrific, fabulous.

▣ *adj.* **1, 2** dull. **3** stupid, undistinguished.

brilliantine /'brɪljənti:n/ *noun old use* a perfumed oil used by men to make the hair shiny. [from French *brillantine*, from *brillant*, shining]

brilliantly *adv.* with brilliance, especially with outstanding intelligence.

brim — *noun* **1** the top edge or lip of a cup, glass, bowl, etc. **2** the projecting edge of a hat. — *verb intrans.* brimmed, brimming) to be full to the brim: *eyes brimming with tears.* — **brim over** *intrans.* to become full and begin to overflow. [from Middle English *brymme*]

▣ *noun* **1** rim, perimeter, circumference, lip, edge, margin, border, brink, verge, top, limit.

brimful or **brim-full** *adj.* full to the brim.

brimless *adj.*, *said especially of a hat* not having a brim.

brimstone *noun old use* sulphur. [from Anglo-Saxon *bryne*, burning + STONE]

brimstone butterfly a wide-winged butterfly that breeds in hedgerows and the margins of deciduous woodland, and is commonly found in gardens, so called because the male has brilliant yellow wings

brindled *adj.*, *said of animals* brown or grey, and marked with stripes of a darker colour. [from Middle English *brended*, from *brend*, burnt]

brine *noun* **1** very salty water, used for preserving food. **2** *literary* the sea. [from Anglo-Saxon *bryne*]

bring *verb* (PAST TENSE AND PAST PARTICIPLE **brought**) **1** to carry or take (something or someone) to a stated or implied place or person. **2** to cause or result in: *war brings misery.* **3** to cause to be in or reach a certain state: *bring him to his senses/bring into effect.* **4** to make or force (oneself): *I can't bring myself to tell her.* **5** to be sold for; to produce as income. **6** to make (a charge) against someone: *bring a case against him.* **7** to give (evidence) to a court, etc. — **bring something about** to cause it to happen. **bring something** or **someone along 1** to bring or convey them with one. **2** to help something develop. **bring something back** to cause a thought or memory to return. **bring someone down** to make them sad, disappointed, etc. **bring something** or **someone down** to cause them to fall. **bring forth** *formal* to give birth to or produce (an offspring). **bring something forward 1** to move an arrangement to an earlier date or time. **2** to draw attention to it. **bring something home to someone** to prove or show it clearly. **bring the house down** (of an actor, performer, etc) to receive ecstatic applause; to be brilliantly successful. **bring something in 1** to introduce it, make it effective, etc. **2** to produce income or profit. **bring something off** *colloq.* to succeed in doing something difficult. **bring something on 1** to cause it to happen or appear. **2** to help it to develop or progress. **bring something out 1** to emphasize or clarify it. **2** to publish it. **bring someone out in spots, a rash**, etc to cause them to be affected with spots or a rash: *cats bring me out in spots.* **bring someone over** to convert them to one's own opinion, etc. **bring someone round 1** to cause them to recover consciousness. **2** to convince them that one's own opinions, etc are right. **bring someone to** to cause someone who is asleep or unconscious to wake up. **bring something to mind** to cause it to be remembered or thought about. **bring someone up** to care for and educate them when young. **bring something up 1** to introduce a subject for discussion. **2** to vomit or regurgitate something eaten. **bring up the rear** to come last or behind. **bring someone up short** to cause them to stop suddenly. [from Anglo-Saxon *bringan*]

▣ **1** take, carry, bear, convey, transport, fetch, deliver, escort,

accompany, usher, guide, conduct, lead. **2** cause, produce, engender, create, prompt, provoke, force. **bring something about** cause, occasion, create, produce, generate, effect, accomplish, achieve, fulfil, realize, manage. **bring something** or **someone down** knock down, shoot down, fell, topple, unseat, overthrow, oust. **bring something in 1** introduce, inaugurate, initiate, originate, pioneer, set up, usher in. **2** earn, net, gross, produce, yield, fetch, return, accrue, realize. **bring something off** succeed in, achieve, accomplish, fulfil, execute, discharge, perform, win. **bring something on 1** cause, occasion, induce, lead to, give rise to, generate, inspire, prompt, provoke, precipitate. **2** advance, expedite, accelerate, foster, nurture. **bring something out 1** emphasize, stress, highlight, enhance, draw out. **2** publish, print, issue, launch, introduce. **bring someone round 1** revive, rouse, awaken, resuscitate. **2** persuade, convince, win over, convert, coax, cajole. **bring someone up** care for, rear, raise, foster, nurture, educate, teach, train, form. **bring something up 1** introduce, broach, mention, submit, propose. **2** vomit, regurgitate, *colloq.* throw up.

▣ **bring something on** INHIBIT.

brink *noun* **1** the edge or border of a steep, dangerous place or of a river. **2** the point immediately before the start of something dangerous, unknown, exciting, etc: *on the brink of new discoveries.* [probably from Danish *brink*, declivity]

▣ VERGE, THRESHOLD. **1** edge, lip, rim, brim, bank, margin, fringe, border, boundary, limit, extremity.

brinkmanship *noun colloq.* the art of going to the very edge of a dangerous situation before moving back or withdrawing.

briny — *adj.* (brinier, briniest) *said of water* very salty. — *noun* (**the briny**) *colloq.* the sea.

brioche /bri:'ɒʃ/ *noun* a type of bread-like cake made with a yeast dough, eggs, and butter. [from French *brioche*]

briquette /brɪ'kɛt/ *noun* a brick-shaped block made from coal dust, used for fuel. [from French *briquette*, little brick]

brisk *adj.* **1** lively, active, or quick: *a brisk walk.* **2** *said of the weather* pleasantly cold and fresh.

▣ **1** energetic, vigorous, quick, snappy, lively, spirited, active, busy, bustling, agile, nimble, alert. **2** fresh, crisp, invigorating, exhilarating, stimulating, bracing, refreshing.

▣ **1** lazy, sluggish.

brisket /'brɪskɪt/ *noun* the breast of an animal, especially of a bull or cow, when eaten as food. [from Middle English *brusket*]

briskly *adv.* with a lively or keen manner: *they responded briskly to our offer.*

briskness *noun* being brisk or lively.

brisling /'brɪslɪŋ/ *noun* a small marine fish (*Sprattus sprattus*) of the herring family, fished in Norwegian fjords, that has been processed and canned in oil. [a Norwegian word]

bristle — *noun* **1** a short stiff hair on an animal or plant. **2** something like this but man-made, used eg for brushes. — *verb* **1** *intrans.*, *trans. said of hair* to stand or cause it to stand upright. **2** *intrans.* to show anger, rage, etc. **3** (**bristle with someone** or **something**) to be covered with or full of them. [from Anglo-Saxon *byrst*]

▣ *noun* **1** hair, whisker, stubble, spine, prickle, barb, thorn.

bristling *adj.*, *said of a beard, eyebrows, etc* thick and rough.

bristly *adj.* (bristlier, bristliest) **1** having bristles; rough. **2** likely to be or quickly get angry.

⊟ PRICKLY, SPIKY. **1** hairy, whiskered, bearded, unshaven, stubbly, rough, spiny, thorny. **2** irritable, touchy, grumpy, short-tempered.
⊞ **1** clean-shaven, smooth.

Brit *noun colloq.* a British person.

Brit- *combining form* forming words denoting something produced in contemporary Britain and having features regarded as typical: *Britpop / Britart.*

Brit. *abbrev.* **1** Britain. **2** British.

Britannia *noun* a female warrior wearing a helmet and carrying a shield and a trident, used as an image or personification of Britain. [from Latin *Britannia*, Britain]

Britannia metal a silvery-white alloy, similar to pewter, consisting of 80 to 90 per cent tin, together with antimony, and sometimes containing small amounts of copper, lead, and zinc. It is used to make bearings and tableware.

Britannic /brɪˈtanɪk/ *adj. formal* of Britain: *His Britannic Majesty.* [from Latin *britannicus*, from *Britannia*, Britain]

British — *adj.* of Great Britain or its people. — *noun* (**the British**) people from Great Britain. [from Anglo-Saxon *Bryttisc*, from *Bryt*, Briton]

British Summer Time the system of time used in Britain in the summer to give extra daylight in the evenings, one hour ahead of Greenwich Mean Time.

British thermal unit *Physics* (ABBREV. **Btu**) the imperial unit of heat energy, equal to the amount of heat required to raise the temperature of one pound of water by one degree Fahrenheit. It is equivalent to 1054.5 joules or 252 calories.

Briton *noun* **1** one of the Celtic people living in S Britain before the Roman conquest. **2** a British person. [from Old French *breton*, from Latin *britto*]

brittle *adj.* **1** hard but easily broken or likely to break. **2** sharp or hard in quality: *a brittle laugh.* [from Anglo-Saxon *breotan*, to break in pieces]

⊟ **1** breakable, fragile, delicate, frail, crisp, crumbly, crumbling, friable.
⊞ **1** durable, resilient.

brittle bone disease a hereditary disease characterized by abnormal fragility of the bones of the skeleton, resulting in fractures and physical deformities. Its cause is unknown, although it is associated with an abnormality of the structural protein *collagen.*

brittlely or **brittly** *adv. so as to break easily.*

brittleness *noun* being brittle or apt to break easily.

brittlestar *Zool.* a starfish-like member of the Echinodermata, with five slender mobile arms radiating from a disc-like body. Each arm bears a large number of suckers called *tube feet*, which aid movement over the sea bed. In some species the arms are branched.

BRN *abbrev., as an international vehicle mark* Bahrain.

broach — *verb* **1** to raise (a subject, especially one likely to cause arguments or problems) for discussion. **2** to open (a bottle or barrel, etc) to remove liquid. **3** to open and start using the contents of: *broach a new bottle.* — *noun* **1** a tool for making holes. **2** a roasting-spit. [from Middle English *broche*]

⊟ *verb* **1** raise, introduce, bring up, mention, put forward. **2, 3** open, tap.

B-road *noun Brit.* a road of secondary importance.

broad — *adj.* **1** large in extent from one side to the other. **2** wide and open; spacious. **3** general, not detailed: *a broad inquiry.* **4** clear: *in broad daylight.* **5** strong; obvious: *a broad hint.* **6** main: *the broad facts.* **7** tolerant, not prejudiced or narrow-minded: *take a broad view.* **8** *said of an accent or speech* strongly marked by local features: *broad Scots.* **9** *usually said of a joke, anecdote, etc* rather rude and vulgar. — *noun* **1** the broad part of anything. **2** *North*

Amer., esp. US offensive slang a woman. [from Anglo-Saxon *brad*]

⊟ *adj.* **1** wide. **2** spacious, large, vast, roomy, capacious, ample, extensive, widespread. **3** wide-ranging, far-reaching, encyclopedic, catholic, eclectic, all-embracing, inclusive, comprehensive, general, sweeping, universal, unlimited. **7** tolerant, liberal, enlightened, unprejudiced, broad-minded, latitudinarian, permissive.
⊞ *adj.* **1, 7** narrow. **2, 3** restricted.

broad-based *adj.* including a wide range of opinions, people, political groups, etc.

broad bean 1 an annual plant (*Vicia faba*) of the bean family, native to Europe and Asia, but cultivated worldwide for its large edible seeds, which are borne in pods. **2** one of the large flattened pale green edible seeds of this plant, eaten as a vegetable, and sometimes used to feed livestock.

broadcast — *verb* (PAST TENSE AND PAST PARTICIPLE **broadcast**) **1** *trans., intrans.* to transmit (a radio or television programme, speech, etc) for reception by the public. **2** to make (something) widely known. **3** to sow (seeds) by scattering (them) in all directions, especially by hand, as opposed to sowing in drills. — *noun* **1** a radio or television programme. **2** the transmission of a radio or television programme for reception by the public. — *adv.* **1** communicated or sent out by radio or television. **2** widely known or scattered. [from BROAD + CAST]

⊟ *verb* **1** air, show, transmit, beam, relay, televise, report. **2** announce, publicize, advertise, publish, circulate, promulgate, disseminate, spread. *noun* **1** transmission, programme, show.

broadcaster *noun* a person who takes part in broadcasts, especially on a regular or professional basis.

broadcasting *noun* the transmission of radio and television programmes.

broadcloth *noun* a thick cloth of good quality made from wool, cotton, or silk.

broaden *verb trans., intrans.* (**broadened, broadening**) (*also* **broaden out**) to make or become broad or broader.

⊟ widen, thicken, swell, spread, enlarge, expand, extend, stretch, develop, open up, branch out, diversify.
⊞ narrow, contract.

broad gauge a railway track wider than the standard size.

broadloom *adj., said especially of a carpet* woven on a wide loom to give broad widths.

broadly *adv.* widely; generally: *broadly speaking.*

broad-minded *adj.* **1** tolerant of others' opinions, etc. **2** not prudish.

⊟ TOLERANT, PERMISSIVE. **1** liberal, unprejudiced, latitudinarian, enlightened, sophisticated, free-thinking, open-minded, receptive, charitable, lenient. **2** unshockable.
⊞ **1** narrow-minded. **2** prudish, strait-laced.

broad-mindedly *adv.* with tolerance; liberally.

broad-mindedness *noun* being broad-minded; tolerance.

broadness *noun* being broad, especially extensive in scope, taste, etc.

broadsheet *noun* **1** a large sheet of paper usually printed on one side only, for advertisements, etc. **2** a newspaper printed on large sheets of paper. See also TABLOID.

broadside *noun* **1** the firing of all guns on one side of a warship. **2** a strong verbal attack. — **broadside on** sideways.

broadsword *noun* a heavy sword with a broad blade, used for cutting rather than stabbing.

brocade /brə'keɪd/ *noun* a heavy silk material with a raised design on it. [from Italian or Spanish *broccato*, from *brocco*, twisted thread or spike]

brocaded *adj.*, *said of material* woven with a brocade design on it.

broccoli /'brɒkəlɪ/ *noun* **1** a type of cultivated cabbage (*Brassica oleracea*) grown for its green leafy stalks and branched heads of immature flower buds, which are eaten as a vegetable. **2** the immature buds of this plant, eaten as a vegetable. [from Italian *broccoli*, sprouts]

brochure /'brəʊʃə(r)/ *noun* a short book or pamphlet giving information about holidays, products, etc. [from French *brocher*, to stitch]

🖿 leaflet, pamphlet, booklet, prospectus, broadsheet, handbill, circular, handout, folder.

broderie anglaise /'brəʊdərɪ ɒŋ'gleɪz/ a technique of decorating cotton and linen by making patterns with tiny holes and stitches. [French, = English embroidery]

brogue[1] /brəʊg/ *noun* a type of strong outdoor shoe. [from Gaelic *bròg*, shoe]

brogue[2] /brəʊg/ *noun* a strong but gentle accent, especially of the Irish speaking English.

broil /brɔɪl/ *verb chiefly North Amer.* to grill (food). [from Old French *bruiller*, to burn]

broiler *noun* **1** a small chicken suitable for broiling. **2** *North Amer.* a grill. **3** *colloq.* a very hot day.

broke *adj. colloq.* having no money. — **go for broke** to risk all one has left in a last attempt at success. [old past participle of BREAK]

🖿 insolvent, penniless, bankrupt, *colloq.* bust, ruined, impoverished, destitute.
🖽 rich, affluent, solvent.

broken *adj.* **1** smashed, fractured. **2** disturbed or interrupted: *broken sleep*. **3** not working properly. **4** *said of a promise, agreement, etc* not kept. **5** *said of language, especially speech* not perfect or fluent. **6** exhausted and despairing, as a result of illness, misfortune, *etc*. [from BREAK]

🖿 **1** fractured, burst, ruptured, smashed, shattered, destroyed, demolished, severed, separated. **2** interrupted, intermittent, spasmodic, disjointed, disconnected, fragmentary, discontinuous, erratic. **3** faulty, defective, out of order, unserviceable. **5** hesitant, stammering, halting, imperfect. **6** beaten, defeated, crushed, demoralized, down, weak, feeble, exhausted, tamed, subdued, oppressed.
🖽 **1, 3** mended. **2** unbroken, continuous. **5** fluent.

broken chord *Mus.* an arpeggio.

broken-down *adj.* **1** not in working order. **2** not in good condition or good health.

🖿 **1** faulty, defective, out of order, unserviceable. **2** dilapidated, worn out, ruined, collapsed, decayed, inoperative, out of order.

broken-hearted *adj.* overwhelmed with sadness or grief.

🖿 heartbroken, inconsolable, devastated, grief-stricken, desolate, despairing, miserable, wretched, mournful, sorrowful, sad, unhappy, dejected, despondent.
🖽 happy, ecstatic, euphoric.

broken home a home that has been disrupted by the separation or divorce of parents.

broken-in *adj.* **1** *said of an animal* made tame through training. **2** *said of shoes, etc* made comfortable by being worn.

brokenly *adv.*, *said of language* imperfectly; without fluency.

brokenness *noun* being broken; a broken state.

broken reed a weak person that can no longer be relied on.

broker *noun* **1** a person employed to buy and sell shares for others (see also STOCKBROKER). **2** a person who buys and sells secondhand goods. [from Old French *brocour*]

brokerage *noun* the profit or fee charged by a broker.

broking *noun* the trade or business of a broker.

brolly *noun* (PL. **brollies**) *Brit. colloq.* an umbrella. [a shortening of UMBRELLA]

bromeliad /brə'miːlɪad/ *noun Bot.* any plant belonging to the pineapple family (Bromeliaceae). [named in honour of the 17c Swedish botanist Olaus Bromel]

bromide *noun* **1** *Chem.* any chemical compound that is a salt of hydrobromic acid (HBr). Various bromides are used as sedatives in medicine, and silver bromide is used to coat photographic film. **2** a much-used and now meaningless statement or phrase. [from BROMINE + -IDE]

bromide paper a type of paper with a surface which has been coated with silver bromide to make it sensitive to light, used for printing photographs.

bromine *noun Chem.* (SYMBOL **Br**, ATOMIC NUMBER **35**) a non-metallic element consisting of a dark red highly corrosive liquid with a pungent smell, that gives off a reddish-brown vapour. It is used in the manufacture of plastics and organic chemicals. [from Greek *bromos*, stink]

bronchial /'brɒŋkɪəl/ *adj.* relating to the bronchi (either of the two main airways to the lungs).

bronchitic /brɒŋ'kɪtɪk/ — *adj.* relating to or suffering from bronchitis. — *noun* a person suffering from bronchitis.

bronchitis /brɒŋ'kaɪtɪs/ *noun Medicine* inflammation of the mucous membrane of the bronchi (the two main airways to the lungs), which often also affects the throat, larynx, and bronchioles (minute branches of the bronchi).

bronchodilator /brɒŋkəʊdaɪleɪtə(r)/ *noun Medicine* any drug or other agent that relaxes the smooth muscle of the bronchi, causing the air passages in the lungs to widen.

bronchus /'brɒŋkəs/ *noun* (PL. **bronchi**) *Anat.* either of the two main airways to the lungs that branch off the lower end of the trachea (windpipe). [from Greek *bronchus*, windpipe]

bronco /'brɒŋkəʊ/ *noun* (PL. **broncos**) a wild or half-tamed horse from the western USA. [from Spanish *bronco*, rough]

brontosaurus /brɒntə'sɔːrəs/ *noun* the name in general use for the dinosaur now officially termed *apatosaurus*. [from Greek *bronte*, thunder + *sauros*, lizard]

bronze — *noun* **1** a hard alloy of copper and up to 25 per cent tin, sometimes also containing small amounts of lead and zinc, and resistant to corrosion. **2** the dark red-brown colour of bronze. **3** a work of art made of bronze. — *adj.* **1** made of bronze. **2** of the colour of bronze. — *verb* **1** to give a bronze colour or surface to: *sun bronzing the skin*. **2** *intrans.* to become the colour of bronze. [from French *bronze*, from Italian *bronzo*, of uncertain origin]

Bronze Age (*usually* **the Bronze Age**) the period in the history of mankind when tools, weapons, etc were made out of bronze, between about 3000 and 1000BC.

bronzed *adj.* having a bronze colour; suntanned.

bronze medal a medal given to the person who comes third in a race, etc.

brooch /brəʊtʃ/ *noun* a decoration or piece of jewellery, fastened to clothes by a pin. [from Middle English *broche*]

🖿 badge, pin, clip, clasp.

brood — *noun* **1** a number of young animals, especially birds, that are produced or hatched at the same time, or that are being cared for by adults. **2** *often humorous* all the children in a family. — *verb intrans.* **1** *said of a bird* to sit on eggs in order to hatch them. **2** (**brood about** or **on** or **over something**) to think anxiously or resentfully about it for a period of time. **3 (brood over someone)** to be imminent or threatening. [from Anglo-Saxon *brod*]

■ *noun* **1** clutch, chicks, hatch, litter, young, offspring. **2** issue, progeny, children, family. *verb* **2** ponder, ruminate over, meditate on, muse about, agonize over, fret about.

broodily *adv.* with a broody or sullen manner.
broodiness *noun* a broody or sullen manner.
brooding *adj.* thinking anxiously or resentfully about something.
broodingly *adv.* with brooding or sullen thoughts: *sat broodingly over his coffee.*
broody *adj.* (**broodier, broodiest**) **1** *said of a bird* ready and wanting to brood. **2** deep in anxious thought. **3** *colloq.*, *said of a woman* eager to have children.
brook[1] *noun* a small stream. [from Anglo-Saxon *broc*]

■ stream, rivulet, beck, burn, watercourse, channel.

brook[2] *verb* to tolerate or accept: *brook no criticism.* [from Anglo-Saxon *brucan*, to enjoy]
broom *noun* **1** any of various deciduous shrubby plants of the pea family with yellow, white, or purple flowers, especially the common broom (*Cytisus scoparius*), native to Europe. **2** a long-handled sweeping brush, formerly made from the stems of this plant, but now usually made from straw or synthetic material. [from Anglo-Saxon *brom*]
broomrape *noun* an annual or perennial plant, belonging to the genus *Orobanche*, that is a parasite and lacks chlorophyll.
broomstick *noun* the long handle of a broom.
Bros. *abbrev.* Brothers, especially in the name of a company.
broth *noun* a thin, clear soup made by boiling meat, fish, or vegetables. [from Anglo-Saxon *broth*]
brothel /ˈbrɒθl/ *noun* a house where men pay money for sexual intercourse with women. [from Middle English *brothel*, worthless person, prostitute]
brother *noun* (PL. **brothers**) **1** a boy or man with the same parents as another person or people. **2** a man belonging to the same group, society, church, trade union, etc as another or others. **3** (PL. *also* **brethren**) a man who is a member of a religious group, especially a monk. [from Anglo-Saxon *brothor*]

■ **1** sibling, relation, relative. **2** comrade, friend, mate, partner, colleague, associate, fellow, companion. **3** monk, friar.

brotherhood *noun* **1** the state of being a brother. **2** friendliness felt towards people one has something in common with. **3** an association of men for a particular, especially religious, purpose.

■ **3** fraternity, association, society, league, confederation, confederacy, alliance, union, guild, fellowship, community, clique.

brother-in-law *noun* (PL. **brothers-in-law**) **1** the brother of one's husband or wife. **2** the husband of one's sister. **3** the husband of the sister of one's own wife or husband.
brotherly *adj.* like a brother; kind, affectionate.
brougham /ˈbruːəm/ *noun* a type of light closed carriage pulled by four horses, with a raised open seat for the driver. [named after Lord Brougham (1778–1868)]
brought SEE BRING.
brouhaha /ˈbruːhɑːhɑː/ *noun* noisy, excited, and confused activity. [from French *brouhaha*]
brow *noun* **1** (*usually* **brows**) an eyebrow. **2** the forehead. **3** the top (of a hill, road, pass, etc). **4** the edge (of a cliff, etc). [from Anglo-Saxon *bru*]
browbeat *verb* (PAST TENSE **browbeat**; PAST PARTICIPLE **browbeaten**) to frighten (someone) by speaking angrily or looking fierce; to bully.

■ bully, coerce, dragoon, bulldoze, awe, cow, intimidate, threaten, tyrannize, domineer.

browbeaten *adj.* bullied and intimidated.
brown — *adj.* **1** of the colour of dark soil or wood. **2** *of bread* made from wholemeal flour and therefore darker in colour than white bread. **3** having a dark skin or complexion. **4** having a skin tanned from being in the sun. — *noun* **1** any of various dark colours similar to bark, tanned skin, coffee, etc. **2** brown paint, dye, material or clothes. — *verb trans., intrans.* to make or become brown by cooking, burning in the sun, etc. — **browned off** *colloq.* **1** bored; fed up. **2** discouraged. [from Anglo-Saxon *brun*]

■ *adj.* **1** mahogany, chocolate, coffee, hazel, bay, chestnut, umber, sepia, tan, tawny, russet, rust, rusty, brunette, browned, toasted. **3** dark, dusky. **4** sunburnt, tanned, bronzed. *noun* **1** mahogany, chocolate, coffee, hazel, chestnut, umber, sepia, tan, russet, rust.

brown alga (PL. **algae**) *Bot.* any alga belonging to the class Phaeophyceae, characterized by the presence of a brown pigment known as *fucoxanthin*, which masks the green pigment chlorophyll. Most brown algae are marine species, eg the kelps.
brown bear a bear widespread in the N hemisphere, and having a thick brown coat and a pronounced hump on its shoulders.
brown dwarf *Astron.* a hypothetical very cool 'star' with a mass that is intermediate between that of a planet and a small star.
brownfield *noun* a potential site for building that has previously undergone agricultural development.
Brownian movement or **Brownian motion** *Physics* the ceaseless random movement of small particles suspended in a liquid or gas. It is caused by the continual bombardment of the particles by molecules of the liquid or gas, which are in a state of constant agitation. [named after Robert Brown (1773–1858), Scottish botanist]
brownie *noun* **1** *Folklore* a friendly goblin or fairy. **2** (**Brownie** or **Brownie Guide**) a young member of the Girl Guides in Britain or of the Girl Scouts in the US. **3** *North Amer., esp. US* a small square chocolate cake with nuts.
Brownie Guider a woman in charge of a group of Brownie Guides.
brownie point *colloq.* a mark of approval earned by doing something good, useful, etc.
browning *noun* *Brit.* a substance used to turn gravy brown.
brownish *adj.* somewhat brown in colour.
brownness *noun* a brown state or colour.
brown owl **1** the tawny owl. **2** (**Brown Owl**) same as BROWNIE GUIDER.
brown paper very thick brown-coloured paper used eg for wrapping up parcels sent through the post.
brown rice unpolished rice from which only the fibrous husk has been removed, leaving the yellowish-brown bran layer intact.
Brownshirt *noun* **1** a member of the German Nazi stormtroopers, formed in 1920. **2** a member of any fascist organization.
brown study **1** deep thought. **2** absent-mindedness.
brown sugar sugar that is unrefined or only partially refined.
browse — *verb* **1** *intrans., trans.* to read a book or look around casually or haphazardly. **2** *intrans., trans. said of certain animals, eg deer* to feed by continually nibbling on young buds, shoots, leaves, and stems of trees and shrubs, as opposed to grazing. **3** *Comput.* to examine stored information, especially on the Internet. — *noun* **1** an act of

browsing. **2** young shoots, twigs, leaves, etc used as food for cattle. [from Old French *brost*, new shoot]

∎ *verb* **1** leaf through, flick through, skim through, look around, look through. **2** graze, feed (on), eat, nibble.

....

browser *noun* **1** a person or thing that browses. **2** *Comput.* software that acts as an interface between the user and the content on the Internet.

BRS *abbrev.* British Road Services.

BRU *abbrev.*, *as an international vehicle mark* Brunei.

brucellosis /bruːsəˈləʊsɪs/ *noun Agric.* an infectious disease, mainly associated with cattle, in which it causes reduced milk yields, infertility, and abortion of calves. [from *Brucella*, the name of the bacterium causing the disease]

bruise /bruːz/ — *noun* an area of skin discoloration and swelling caused by the leakage of blood from damaged blood vessels following injury. — *verb* **1** to mark and discolour (the surface of the skin) in this way. **2** *intrans.* to develop bruises. **3** *trans.*, *intrans.* to hurt or be hurt emotionally or mentally, to crush (a foodstuff). [from Anglo-Saxon *brysan*, to crush, and Old French *bruiser*, to break]

....

∎ *verb* **1**, **2** discolour, blacken, mark, blemish. **3** hurt, injure, offend, grieve. **4** pound, pulverize, crush. *noun* contusion, discoloration, black eye, *colloq.* shiner, mark, blemish, injury.

....

bruised *adj.* **1** affected by bruising. **2** emotionally hurt.

bruiser *noun colloq.* a big strong person, especially one who likes fighting.

bruising *noun* dark-coloured marks which show on bruised skin.

bruit /bruːt/ *verb* (**bruit something about** or **around**) *old use* to spread or report news, rumours, etc. [from French *bruit*, noise]

brûlé /ˈbruːleɪ/ *adj.*, *said of food* having brown sugar on top and cooked so that the sugar melts. [French, = burnt]

brunch *noun colloq.* a meal eaten late in the morning combining breakfast and *lunch*. [from *breakfast* + *lunch*]

brunette /bruːˈnet/ *noun* a woman with brown or dark hair and a fair skin. [from French *brunette*, from *brun*, brown]

brunt *noun* the main force or shock of a blow, attack, etc: *his wife bore the brunt of his anger.* [Middle English, of unknown origin]

bruschetta /bruːˈʃetə/ *noun* (PL. **bruschettas** or **bruschette**) toasted bread coated in olive oil and topped with grilled tomatoes, olives, basil, etc. [from Italian *bruscare*, from *abbrustolire*, to toast]

brush — *noun* **1** a tool with lengths of stiff nylon, wire, hair, bristles, etc, for tidying the hair, cleaning, painting, etc. **2** an act of brushing. **3** a short fight or disagreement: *a brush with the law.* **4** a fox's brush-like tail. **5** *Engineering* a metal or carbon conductor that maintains sliding contact between the stationary and moving parts of an electric motor or generator. **6** brushwood. — *verb* **1** (*also* **brush something down**) to rub it with a brush or other object to remove dirt, dust, etc. **2** (**brush something on** or **away**, **off**, etc) to apply or remove it with a brush or brushing movement. **3** (**brush against something**) to touch it lightly in passing. — **brush something aside** to pay no attention to it; to dismiss it as unimportant. **brush something** or **someone off** to refuse to listen to, to ignore it or them. **brush up** to make oneself clean, tidy one's appearance, etc. **brush something up** or **brush up on something** to improve or refresh one's knowledge of a subject, language, etc. [from Old French *brosse*, brushwood]

....

∎ *noun* **1** broom, sweeper, besom. **2** clean, sweep, polish, confrontation, encounter, clash, conflict, fight, *colloq.* scrap, skirmish, set-to, tussle, *colloq.* dust-up, fracas. **6** brushwood, scrub, thicket, bushes, shrubs, undergrowth, ground cover. *verb* **1** clean, sweep, flick, polish, burnish,

shine. **3** touch, contact, graze, kiss, stroke, rub, scrape. **brush aside** dismiss, *colloq.* pooh-pooh, belittle, disregard, ignore, flout, override. **brush something** or **someone off** disregard, ignore, slight, snub, coldshoulder, rebuff, dismiss, spurn, reject, repulse, disown, repudiate. **brush up** freshen up, smarten up, wash, tidy oneself. **brush something up** revise, relearn, improve, polish up, study, read up, swot .

....

brushed *adj.*, *said of a material* treated by a brushing process so that it feels soft and warm: *brushed cotton.*

brush fire a fire of dead and dry bushes and trees, which usually spreads quickly.

brush-off *noun colloq.* an abrupt dismissal; a rebuff or rejection.

brush-up *noun* a tidying or cleaning up.

brushwood *noun* **1** dead and broken branches, etc from trees and bushes. **2** small trees and bushes on rough land. **3** rough land covered by such trees and bushes.

brushwork *noun* the particular way a painter has of putting paint on to canvas.

brusque /bruːsk/ *adj.* blunt and often impolite in manner. [from French *brusque*, from Italian *brusco*, sour]

....

∎ abrupt, sharp, short, terse, curt, gruff, surly, discourteous, impolite, uncivil, blunt, tactless, undiplomatic.
𝔼 courteous, polite, tactful.

....

brusquely *adv.* bluntly; impolitely.

brusqueness *noun* a brusque or blunt manner.

Brussels sprout or **brussels sprout** **1** a type of cultivated cabbage now widely grown in temperate regions for its swollen edible buds, resembling miniature cabbages, which develop in the leaf axils along the main stem. **2** the bud of this plant, eaten as a vegetable. [first grown near *Brussels*, capital of Belgium]

brutal *adj.* **1** savagely cruel or violent. **2** ruthlessly harsh. [from Latin *brutalis*]

....

∎ CRUEL, INHUMANE, RUTHLESS, REMORSELESS, PITILESS, MERCILESS. **1** animal, bestial, beastly, brutish, inhuman, savage, bloodthirsty, vicious, ferocious, callous, insensitive, unfeeling, heartless. **2** harsh, severe, draconian.
𝔼 **1** kindly, humane, civilized. **2** lenient.

....

brutality *noun* (PL. **brutalities**) **1** a brutal act. **2** brutal behaviour or treatment.

....

∎ CRUELTY, BARBARITY. **1** atrocity, outrage, enormity. **2** savagery, bloodthirstiness, viciousness, ferocity, inhumanity, violence, ruthlessness, callousness, barbarism.
𝔼 **2** gentleness, kindness.

....

brutalization or **brutalisation** *noun* making brutal; brutal treatment.

brutalize or **brutalise** *verb* **1** to make brutal. **2** to treat brutally.

brutally *adv.* with a brutal or cruel manner.

brute — *noun* **1** an animal other than man. **2** a cruel and violent person. — *adj.* **1** not able to use reason or intelligence. **2** coarse and animal-like. [from Latin *brutus*, heavy, irrational]

....

∎ *noun* **1** animal, beast, swine, creature. **2** monster, ogre, devil, fiend, savage, sadist, bully, lout.

....

brute force sheer physical strength, with no thought or skill.

brutish *adj.* of or like a brute.

brutishly *adv.* with cruelty or violence.

brutishness *noun* being brutish; cruelty.

bryony /ˈbraɪənɪ/ *noun* (PL. **bryonies**) **1** (*in full* **black bry-**

ony) a perennial climbing plant (*Tamus communis*), related to the yam, native to Europe, W Asia, and N Africa, and having slender twining stems up to 4m long, heart-shaped or three-lobed glossy green leaves, and sprays of tiny yellowish-green flowers. **2** (*in full* **white bryony**) a perennial climbing plant (*Bryonia cretica*), related to the pumpkin, native to Europe, W Asia, and N Africa, and having long slender stems, lobed leaves, and greenish-white flowers. [from Latin *bryonia*]

bryophyte /'braɪəʊfaɪt/ *noun Bot.* any plant belonging to the division Bryophyta of the plant kingdom, which includes mosses (Musci) and liverworts (Hepaticae).

Brythonic /brɪ'θɒnɪk/ — *noun* the early Celtic language of southern Britain and Brittany. — *adj.* relating to this language or its speakers. [from Celtic *Brython,* Britons]

BS *abbrev.* **1** Bachelor of Surgery. **2** *as an international vehicle mark* Bahamas. **3** British Standard(s): marked on manufactured goods that conform to an acceptable standard.

BSc. *abbrev.* Bachelor of Science.

BSE *abbrev.* bovine spongiform encephalopathy.

BSI *abbrev.* British Standards Institution, an organization which controls the quality and safety of manufactured goods, etc.

B-side *noun* the side of a two-sided gramophone record that is less actively promoted.

BSL *abbrev.* British Sign Language.

BSM *abbrev.* British School of Motoring.

BST *abbrev.* British Summer Time.

BT *abbrev.* British Telecom.

Bt. *abbrev.* Baronet.

BTA *abbrev.* British Tourist Authority.

BTEC *abbrev.* Business and Technician Education Council.

BTW *abbrev.* by the way.

bubble — *noun* **1** a thin film of liquid forming a hollow sphere filled with air or gas, especially one which floats in liquid. **2** a ball of air or gas which has formed in a solid or liquid: *an air bubble in glass.* **3** a dome made of clear plastic or glass. **4** an unrealistic or over-ambitious plan or scheme. — *verb intrans.* **1** to form or rise in bubbles. **2** (**bubble away**) to make the sound of bubbling liquid: *water bubbling away in the pan.* — **bubble over** *intrans.* **1** to boil over. **2** to be full of happiness, excitement, enthusiasm, good ideas, etc: *they're bubbling over with excitement.* [from Middle English *bobel*]

- -
■ *noun* **1** blister, globule, ball, drop, droplet, bead. *verb* **1** effervesce, fizz, sparkle, froth, foam, seethe, boil, burble, gurgle.
- -

bubble and squeak *Brit.* cold cooked cabbage and potatoes mixed together and then fried.

bubble bath a scented liquid which is put into bath water to make bubbles.

bubble chamber *Physics* a device that enables the movements of charged subatomic particles to be observed and photographed as trails of gas bubbles within a container of superheated liquid (a pressurized liquid kept at slightly above its boiling point).

bubble gum a type of chewing gum which can be blown into bubbles.

Bubble-jet *noun trademark* a type of ink-jet printer which heats the ink in a fine tube to form a bubble, which then bursts and projects the ink on to the paper.

bubble memory a form of computer memory in which microscopic artificially produced irregularities known as *magnetic bubbles* float in a thin film of magnetic material. The presence of a bubble in a particular region of the film represents the binary digit 1, and the absence of a bubble represents the binary digit 0.

bubble pack a clear plastic bubble, usually on cardboard, in which goods for sale are packed.

bubbly — *adj.* (**bubblier, bubbliest**) **1** having or being like bubbles. **2** very lively and cheerful and full of high spirits. — *noun colloq.* champagne.

- - - - - - - - - - - - - - - - - - - -
■ *adj.* **1** effervescent, fizzy, sparkling, carbonated, frothy, foaming, sudsy. **2** lively, bouncy, cheerful, happy, merry, ebullient, elated, excited.
🗴 *adj.* **1** flat, still. **2** lethargic.
- -

bubo /'bju:bəʊ/ *noun* (PL. **buboes**) a swollen tender lymph node, especially in the armpit or groin, commonly developing as a symptom of bubonic plague, syphilis, or gonorrhoea. [from Latin *bubo,* swelling]

bubonic plague /bju:'bɒnɪk/ the commonest form of plague, an infectious epidemic disease, the main symptoms of which are fever, delirium, and swelling of the lymph nodes (*buboes*). It is caused by the bacterium *Yersinia pestis,* which is transmitted to humans via fleas carried by rats.

buccal *adj. Anat.* relating to the mouth or the inside of the cheek. [from Latin *bucca* cheek]

buccaneer /bʌkə'nɪə(r)/ *noun* a pirate, especially one who attacked Spanish ships in the Caribbean during the 17c. [from French *boucanier*]

buccaneering *noun* pirating; unscrupulous adventuring.

buck[1] — *noun* **1** a male animal, especially a male deer, goat, antelope, rabbit, hare, or kangaroo. **2** a lively young man. **3** an act of bucking. — *verb* **1** *intrans. said of a horse* to make a series of rapid jumps into the air, with the back arched and legs held stiff, especially in an attempt to throw a rider. **2** *said of a horse* to throw (a rider) from its back in this way. **3** *colloq.* to oppose or resist (an idea, etc). — **buck up** *colloq.* **1** to become more cheerful. **2** to hurry. **buck someone up** to make them more cheerful. **buck something up** to improve one's ways, ideas, etc. [from Anglo-Saxon *bucca*]

buck[2] *noun North Amer. colloq.* a dollar. — **make a fast** or **quick buck** to make money quickly and often dishonestly. [perhaps from BUCKSKIN: deer-skins were used as a unit of exchange by Native Americans and frontiersmen in the 19c in the USA]

buck[3] *noun* **1** an item placed before the person who is to deal next in poker. **2** *colloq.* the responsibility, especially to deal with a problem: *pass the buck.* [from *buckhorn knife,* an item which used to be used as a buck in poker]

bucked *adj. Brit. colloq.* pleased and encouraged.

bucket — *noun* **1** a round open-topped container for holding or carrying liquids, sand, etc. **2** the amount a bucket will hold. **3** the scoop of a dredging machine. — *verb intrans.* (**bucketed, bucketing**) *colloq.* (*also* **bucket down**) *said of rain* to pour down heavily. — **kick the bucket** *slang* to die. **rain buckets** to rain hard and continuously. **weep buckets** to weep long and bitterly. [from Anglo-Saxon *buc*]

- - - - - - - - - - - - - - - - - - - -
■ *noun* **1** pail, can, bail, scuttle, vessel. *verb* pour (down), teem (down), pelt (down).
- -

bucketful *noun* (PL. **bucketfuls**) the amount a bucket will hold.

bucket seat a small seat with a round back, for one person, eg in a car.

bucket shop **1** *Brit. colloq.* a travel agent which sells cheap airline tickets. **2** an office where one may deal in shares, gamble on the money market, etc.

buckle — *noun* a flat piece of metal attached to one end of a strap or belt, with a pin in the middle which goes through a hole in the other end of the strap or belt to fasten it. — *verb* **1** *trans., intrans.* to fasten or be fastened with a buckle. **2** *trans., intrans. said of metal* to bend or become bent out of shape, especially as a result of great heat or force. — **buckle down** or **to** to begin working seriously at something. **buckle under** *intrans.* to collapse under strain. [from Old French *boucle,* from Latin *buccula,* cheek-strap of a helmet]

- - - - - - - - - - - - - - - - - - - -
■ *noun* clasp, clip, catch, fastener. *verb* **1** fasten, catch, hook,

hitch, connect, close, secure. **2** bend, warp, twist, distort, bulge, cave in, fold, wrinkle, crumple, collapse.

· · · · · · · · · · · · · · · · · ·

buckled *adj.*, *said of metal* bent out of shape, especially from heat or force.

buckler *noun* a small round shield. [from Old French *bocler*, from *bocle*, boss (round knob)]

buckminsterfullerene /bʌkmɪnstəˈfʊləriːn/ *Chem.* (FORMULA **C₆₀**) an almost spherical molecule, thought to be an ingredient of soots. [named after Buckminster Fuller (1895–1983), US inventor and designer]

buckram /ˈbʌkrəm/ *noun* stiffened cotton or linen, used to line clothes or cover books. [from Middle English *bukeram*, perhaps from *Bukhara*, a town in central Asia once noted for its textiles]

Bucks *abbrev.* Buckinghamshire.

buckshee *adj.*, *adv. slang* free of charge. [from BAKSHEESH]

buckshot *noun* large lead shot used in hunting.

buckskin *noun* **1** the skin of a deer. **2** a soft leather made from deer-skin.

buckthorn *noun* any of various deciduous or evergreen shrubs or small trees, native to north temperate regions, especially *Rhamnus catharticus*, a thorny deciduous shrub with bright green oval toothed leaves, and small yellowish-green sweetly scented flowers borne on short shoots.

bucktooth *noun* a tooth which sticks out in front.

bucktoothed *adj.* having projecting front teeth.

buckwheat *noun* **1** an erect fast-growing annual plant (*Fagopyrum esculentum*), native to Central Asia, having leathery spear-shaped leaves and tiny pink or white flowers borne in terminal clusters. **2** the greyish-brown triangular seeds of this plant, which are highly nutritious. [from Dutch *boekweit*, beech wheat, from the shape of the seeds]

bucolic /bjʊˈkɒlɪk/ — *adj.* concerned with the countryside or people living there; pastoral. — *noun* a poem about the countryside. [from Greek *boukolos*, herdsman]

bucolically *adv.* with reference to the countryside or pastoral life.

bud — *noun* **1 a** in a plant, an immature knob-like shoot, often enclosed by protective scales, that will eventually develop into a leaf or flower. **b** a flower or leaf that is not yet fully open. **2** in yeasts and simple animals, a small outgrowth from the body of the parent that becomes detached and develops into a new individual capable of independent existence. **3** in an embryo, an outgrowth from which a limb develops. — *verb intrans.* (**budded, budding**) **1** to put out buds. **2** *Bot.* to reproduce asexually by the production of small outgrowths from the body of the parent, which become detached and develop into new individuals. — **in bud** producing buds. **nip something in the bud** to put a stop to an activity or plan at an early stage. [from Middle English *budde*]

· · · · · · · · · · · · · · · ·

◼ *noun* **1** shoot, sprout. **2** germ, embryo. *verb* **1** shoot, sprout, burgeon, develop, grow.

· ·

Buddhism /ˈbʊdɪzm/ *noun* the religion founded by the *Buddha*, Gautama, in the 6cBC, which teaches spiritual purity and freedom from human concerns. The goal is nirvana, which means 'the blowing out' of the fires of all desires, and the absorption of the self into the infinite. [from Sanskrit *budh*, to awaken, notice or understand]

Buddhist — *noun* a person who practises Buddhism. — *adj.* relating to Buddhism.

budding — *adj.* developing, beginning to show talent: *a budding pianist.* — *noun* **1** the formation of buds on a plant shoot, or the artificial propagation of a plant by grafting of a bud. **2** a method of asexual reproduction involving the production of one or more outgrowths or buds that develop into new individuals.

· · · · · · · · · · · · · · · · · ·

◼ *adj.* potential, promising, up-and-coming, gifted, embryonic, burgeoning, developing, growing.

· ·

buddleia or **buddleja** /ˈbʌdlɪə/ *noun* any of various deciduous shrubs or small trees of the genus Buddleia, native to China and naturalized in many parts of the world, and having spear-shaped leaves and long pointed purple or white flower-heads. [named after the English botanist Adam Buddle (d.1715)]

buddy — *noun* (PL. **buddies**) **1** *North Amer. colloq.* a friend or companion. **2** a volunteer who helps care for a person suffering from AIDS. — *verb* (**buddies, buddied**) **1** *intrans. colloq.* (*usually* **buddy up**) to become friendly. **2** *trans.* to help care for (someone suffering from AIDS). [perhaps from *butty*, companion]

buddy movie *colloq.* a film, usually with two central characters, exploring male or female camaraderie.

budge *verb* **1** *intrans.*, *trans.* to move or cause to move. **2** *trans.* to persuade or influence. **3** to change one's mind or opinions: *nothing you say will make me budge.* [from Old French *bouger*]

· · · · · · · · · · · · · · · · · · ·

◼ MOVE, SHIFT. **1** stir, dislodge, roll, slide. **2** sway, influence, persuade, convince. **3** bend, yield, give (way).

· ·

budgerigar /ˈbʌdʒərɪgɑː(r)/ *noun* a small parrot, native to Central Australia, the wild form of which has a yellow head with a blue patch on each cheek, bright green underparts, a greyish-green back with black and yellow barred markings, and a long tapering blue tail. Budgerigars are popular cagebirds, and readily mimic human speech and other sounds. [from Australian Aboriginal *gijirriga*]

budget /ˈbʌdʒɪt/ — *noun* **1** a plan, especially for a particular period of time, showing how money coming in will be spent. **2** (**the Budget**) *Brit.* a periodic assessment of national revenue and expenditure proposed by the government. **3** the amount of money set aside for a particular purpose. **4** (*attributive*) low in cost: *a budget holiday.* — *verb* (**budgeted, budgeting**) **1** *intrans.* to calculate how much money one is earning and spending, so that one does not spend more than one has. **2** *intrans.* (**budget for something**) to allow for it in a budget: *next year we'll budget for a new car.* **3** to provide (an amount of money) in a budget: *budget £600 for a holiday.* [from Old French *bougette*, diminutive of *bouge*, pouch]

· · · · · · · · · · · · · · · · · · ·

◼ *noun* **1** plan, estimate, allocation, cash flow. **3** finances, funds, resources, means, allowance, allotment, allocation. *verb* **1** plan, estimate, calculate. **3** allow, allot, allocate, apportion, ration.

· ·

budget account an account with a bank or shop into which regular payments are made to sustain a credit level.

budgetary *adj.* relating to or connected with a budget or finance.

budgeting *noun* the process or practice of drawing up budgets; financial planning.

budgie *noun colloq.* a budgerigar.

buff[1] — *noun* **1** a dull yellow colour. **2** a soft undyed leather. **3** a piece of soft material used for polishing. **4** *colloq.* a person who is enthusiastic about and knows much about a subject: *an opera buff.* — *adj.* dull yellow in colour. — *verb* **1** (*also* **buff something up**) to polish with a buff or piece of soft material: *buff up one's shoes.* **2** to make (leather) soft like buff. — **in the buff** *Brit. colloq.* naked. [from French *buffle*, buffalo]

· · · · · · · · · · · · · · · · · · · ·

◼ *noun* **4** expert, connoisseur, enthusiast, fan, admirer, devotee, addict, *colloq.* fiend, freak. *adj.* yellowish-brown, straw, sandy, fawn, khaki. *verb* **1** polish, burnish, shine, smooth, rub, brush.

· ·

buffalo /'bʌfələʊ/ *noun* (PL. **buffalo**, **buffaloes**) **1** (*in full* **African buffalo**) a member of the cattle family (*Syncerus caffer*) native to S and E Africa, and having a heavy black or brown body, thick horns curving upwards at their tips, and large drooping ears. **2** (*in full* **Indian buffalo**) a SE Asian member of the cattle family (*Bubalus bubalus*), that lives in swampy areas or near rivers. **3** the American bison. [from Portuguese *bufalo*]

buffer[1] *noun* **1** an apparatus, especially one using springs, on railway carriages, etc, or a cushion of rope on a ship, which takes the shock when the carriage or ship hits something. **2** a person or thing which protects from harm or shock. **3** *Comput.* a temporary storage area for data that is being transmitted from the central processing unit to an output device such as a printer. **4** *Chem.* a chemical solution that maintains its pH at a constant level when an acid or alkali is added to it, or when the solution is diluted. Buffers are used to prepare solutions that are required to have a specific pH, eg for dyeing, food technology, brewing, or for intravenous medical injections. [from Middle English *buffe*, blow]

▤ **1** shock absorber, bumper, fender, pad, cushion, pillow. **2** cushion, intermediary, screen, shield.

buffer[2] *noun Brit. colloq.* a rather foolish or dull person, especially a man: *old buffer.*

buffer[3] *noun* a person or thing that buffs or polishes.

buffered *adj.* **1** equipped with a buffer or buffers. **2** protected.

buffer state a neutral country situated between two larger countries which are potentially hostile towards each other, making war less likely.

buffer stock stock held in reserve to try and control prices.

buffet[1] /'bʊfeɪ/ *noun* **1** a place where light meals and drinks may be bought and eaten. **2** a meal set out on tables from which people help themselves. **3** a sideboard or cupboard for holding china, glasses, etc. [from Old French *buffet*]

▤ **1** snack bar, counter, café, cafeteria.

buffet[2] /'bʌfɪt/ — *noun* a blow with the hand. — *verb* (**buffeted**, **buffeting**) **1** to strike or knock with the fist. **2** to knock about: *a ship buffeted by the waves.* [from Old French *buffe*, blow]

▤ *noun* blow, knock, bang, push, shove, thump, box, cuff, *colloq.* clout, slap, smack. *verb* **1** hit, strike, knock, bang, push, shove, pummel, beat, thump, box, cuff, *colloq.* clout, slap. **2** batter, pound.

buffet car /'bʊfeɪ/ a carriage in a train, in which light meals and drinks can be bought.

buffeting /'bʌfɪtɪŋ/ *noun* repeated knocks or blows.

buffoon /bə'fuːn/ *noun often derog.* a person who does amusing or foolish things. [from French *bouffon*, from Italian *buffone*]

buffoonery *noun* comic or foolish behaviour.

bug — *noun* **1** a common name for any of thousands of species of insect belonging to the order Hemiptera, eg aphids and bedbugs. True bugs have flattened oval bodies and mouthparts modified into a beak for piercing and sucking. **2** *North Amer.* a popular name for any kind of insect. **3** *colloq.* a popular name for a bacterium or virus that causes infection or illness: *a stomach bug.* **4** *colloq.* a small microphone hidden so as to spy on conversations. **5** *colloq.* a fault in a computer program or hardware. **6** *colloq.* an obsession or craze: *get the skiing bug.* — *verb* (**bugged**, **bugging**) **1** *colloq.* to hide a microphone in (a room, etc) so as to spy on conversations. **2** *slang* to annoy or worry. [from Anglo-Saxon *budda*, beetle]

▤ *noun* **3** virus, bacterium, germ, microbe, micro-organism, infection, disease. **5** fault, defect, flaw, blemish, imperfection, failing, error, gremlin. *verb* **2** annoy, irritate, vex, irk, *colloq.* needle, bother, disturb, harass, badger.

bugaboo *noun* an imaginary thing which causes fear.

bugbear *noun* a thing which causes fear or annoyance. [originally a hobgoblin, from Middle English *bugge*, perhaps from Welsh *bwg*, hobgoblin]

bug-eyed *adj.* with eyes that stick out from the face, especially with astonishment.

bugger *coarse slang* — *noun* **1** a person or thing considered to be difficult or awkward. **2** a person one feels affection or pity for: *poor old bugger.* **3** a person who practises anal sex. — *verb* (**buggered**, **buggering**) **1** to practise anal sex with (someone). **2** to tire or exhaust. — *interj.* (*also* **bugger it**) an expression of annoyance. — **bugger about** or **around** to waste time; to do things flippantly or without due attention. **bugger someone about** to mislead them or cause them problems. **bugger all** nothing at all. **bugger off** to go away. **bugger something up** to spoil or ruin it. [from Old French *bougre*, from Latin *Bulgarus*, a heretic (literally, a Bulgarian), from the large number of heretical beliefs, including deviant sexual practices, thought in the Middle Ages to have come from the Balkans]

buggery *noun* anal sex.

buggy *noun* (PL. **buggies**) **1** a light open carriage pulled by one horse. **2** *North Amer., esp. US* a pram.

bugle — *noun* a brass instrument like a small trumpet, used mainly for military signals. — *verb* **1** *intrans.* to sound a bugle. **2** *trans.* to sound (a call) on a bugle. [an Old French word, from Latin *bos*, ox]

bugler *noun* a person who plays a bugle.

build — *verb* (PAST TENSE AND PAST PARTICIPLE **built**) **1** to make or construct from parts. **2** to develop gradually. **3** to make in a particular way or for a particular purpose. — *noun* physical form, especially of the human body: *a slim build.* — **build one thing into** or **on to another** to make a construction such that it is a permanent part of or addition to a larger one: *built a garage on to the side of the house.* **build on something 1** to add on by building. **2** to use (a previous success, etc) as a basis from which to develop: *build on previous experience.* **3** to base hopes, achieve success, etc on something: *success built on a popular product.* **4** to depend on something. **build up** to increase gradually in size, strength, amount, etc. **build something up 1** to build it in stages. **2** to make it bigger, stronger, or healthier. **3** to speak with great enthusiasm about it. See also BUILD-UP. [from Anglo-Saxon *byldan*]

▤ *verb* **1** erect, construct, raise, fabricate, make, form, constitute, assemble, put together, *colloq.* knock together. **2** develop, enlarge, extend, increase, augment, escalate, intensify. *noun* physique, figure, body, form, shape, size, frame, structure. **build on something 2, 3** base on, found on, establish on. **build up** develop, amplify, increase, escalate, intensify, strengthen, heighten, strengthen. **build something up 1** construct, assemble, put together, piece together, extend, enlarge. **2** reinforce, fortify, extend, expand, develop, amplify, increase, escalate, intensify, heighten, boost, improve, enhance, publicize, advertise, promote, *colloq.* plug, *colloq.* hype.

▩ *verb* **1** destroy, demolish, knock down. **2** lessen. **build something up 1** knock down, demolish. **2** weaken, lessen.

builder *noun* **1** a person who builds, or organizes the building of, houses, etc. **2** anything which helps to develop or build something.

building *noun* **1** the business of constructing houses, etc. **2** a structure with walls and a roof, such as a house.

■ CONSTRUCTION. **1** fabrication, architecture. **2** edifice, dwelling, erection, structure.

Types of building include: house, bungalow, cottage, block of flats, cabin, farmhouse, villa, mansion, chateau, castle, palace; church, chapel, cathedral, abbey, monastery, temple, pagoda, mosque, synagogue; shop, store, garage, factory, warehouse, silo, office block, tower block, skyscraper, theatre, cinema, gymnasium, sports hall, restaurant, café, hotel, *colloq.* pub, public house, inn, school, college, museum, library, hospital, prison, power station, observatory; barracks, fort, fortress, monument, mausoleum; shed, barn, outhouse, stable, mill, lighthouse, pier, pavilion, boat-house, beach-hut, summerhouse, gazebo, dovecote, windmill. *See also* **house**; **shop**.

building-block *noun* any of the separate parts out of which something is built.

building society *Brit.* a finance company that lends money for buying or improving houses and in which customers can invest money to earn interest.

build-up *noun* **1** a gradual increase. **2** a gradual approach to a conclusion or climax. **3** publicity or praise of something or someone given in advance of its, his, or her appearance.

■ **1** increase, enlargement, expansion, development, gain, growth, escalation, accumulation, storing, stockpiling. **2** crescendo. **3** publicity, promotion, *colloq.* plug, *colloq.* hype. ▪ **1** reduction, decrease.

built-in *adj.* **1** forming an integral part of a structure. **2** inherent.

■ STRUCTURAL. **1** fitted, integrated, incorporated. **2** inherent, intrinsic, inbuilt, essential. ▪ **1** free-standing.

built-up *adj.* **1** *said of land, etc* covered with buildings, especially houses. **2** increased in height by additions. **3** made up of separate parts.

bulb *noun* **1** *Bot.* in certain plants, eg tulip, onion, a swollen underground organ consisting of a modified shoot, with overlapping layers of fleshy leaf bases or scales, and roots growing from the lower surface. It functions as a food store. **2** a flower grown from a bulb, eg a daffodil or hyacinth. **3** *Electr.* the airtight glass envelope that encloses the electric filament of an incandescent lamp, the electrodes of a vacuum tube, etc. **4** anything which is shaped like a pear. [from Latin *bulbus*, from Greek *bolbos*, onion]

bulbous *adj.* **1** like a bulb in shape; fat or bulging. **2** having or growing from a bulb.

Bulgar *noun* a member of a Turkic-speaking people who settled in what is now Bulgaria and adopted the Slavonic language.

Bulgarian /bʌlˈɡɛərɪən/ — *noun* **1** a native or citizen of Bulgaria. **2** the language of Bulgaria, a S Slavic language of the Indo-European family, spoken by c.8 million people in Bulgaria and neighbouring countries. — *adj.* of Bulgaria or its people or language.

bulge — *noun* **1** a swelling, especially where one would expect to see something flat. **2** a sudden and usually temporary increase, eg in population. — *verb intrans.* to swell outwards. [from Old French *boulge*, from Latin *bulga*, knapsack]

■ *noun* **1** swelling, bump, lump, hump, distension, protuberance, projection. **2** rise, increase, surge, upsurge, intensification. *verb* swell, puff out, bulb, hump, dilate, expand, enlarge, distend, protrude, project.

bulghar wheat or **bulgur wheat** wheat that has been boiled, dried, lightly milled, and cracked. [from Turkish]

bulging *adj.* **1** swollen because very full. **2** swelling or increasing suddenly.

■ **1** swollen, crammed, stuffed, overflowing.

bulgy *adj.* having a bulge or bulges; swollen.

bulimia /buˈlɪmɪə/ *noun Medicine* **1** compulsive overeating, caused either by psychological factors or by damage to the hypothalamus of the brain. **2** same as BULIMIA NERVOSA. [from Greek *boulimia*, great hunger, from *bous*, ox + *limos*, hunger]

bulimia nervosa /buˈlɪmɪə nɜːˈvoʊzə/ *Medicine* a psychological disorder, most common in female adolescents and young women, in which episodes of excessive eating are followed by self-induced vomiting or laxative abuse in an attempt to avoid any increase in weight.

bulk *noun* **1** size, especially when large and awkward. **2** the greater or main part of: *the bulk of the task is routine.* **3** a large body, shape, or person. **4** a large quantity: *buy in bulk/bulk buying.* **5** roughage. — **bulk large** to be or seem important: *an issue which bulks large in his mind.* [from Norse *bulki*, cargo]

■ **1** size, magnitude, dimensions, extent, amplitude, bigness, largeness, immensity, volume, mass, weight, substance, body. **2** preponderance, majority, most.

bulk carrier a ship which carries dry goods such as grain, in bulk and unpackaged.

bulked yarn *Textiles* a yarn made of (usually synthetic) fibres modified chemically or physically to induce a high volume or loftiness to the yarn by crimping the fibres during processing.

bulkhead *noun* a wall in a ship or aircraft which separates one section from another, so that if one section is damaged, the rest is not affected. [from Middle English *bulk*, stall]

bulkily *adv.* with a large and awkward size.

bulkiness *noun* being bulky or awkward in size.

bulky *adj.* (**bulkier**, **bulkiest**) large in size and awkward to carry or move.

■ large, big, substantial, huge, enormous, immense, massive, hulking, hefty, heavy, weighty, unmanageable, unwieldy, awkward, cumbersome. ▪ insubstantial, small, handy.

bull[1] *noun* **1** the uncastrated male of animals in the cattle family. **2** the male of the elephant, whale, and various other large animals. **3** (**the Bull**) the constellation and sign of the zodiac Taurus. **4** *Stock Exchange* a person who buys shares hoping to sell them at a higher price at a later date. **5** same as BULL'S-EYE 1. — **a bull in a china shop** a person who acts in a rough and careless way and is likely to cause damage. **take the bull by the horns** to deal boldly and positively with a challenge or difficulty. [from Middle English *bole*]

bull[2] *noun* an official letter or written instruction from the Pope. [from Old French *bulle*, from Latin *bulla*, seal]

bull[3] *noun* **1** an illogical, nonsensical statement, eg 'if you don't receive this card, you must write and tell me'. **2** *slang* nonsense. **3** tedious and sometimes unnecessary routine tasks.

bull-baiting *noun* the sport of baiting bulls with dogs, popular in 16c England, forbidden by law in 1835.

bull bar a strong metal bar on the front of a vehicle to protect it from damage if struck by an animal.

bulldog *noun* a breed of dog with a heavy body, a short brown or brown and white coat, a large square head with a flat upturned muzzle, short bowed legs, and a short tail.

bulldog clip a clip with a spring, used to hold papers together or on to a board.

bulldoze *verb* **1** to use a bulldozer to move, flatten, or demolish. **2 (bulldoze someone into something)** to force them to do something they do not want to do: *bulldoze him into taking part.*

    ◫ **1** demolish, raze, flatten, level. **2** force into, coerce into, bully into, pressurize into, pressgang into.

bulldozer *noun* a large powerful tractor with a vertical blade at the front, for pushing heavy objects, clearing the ground or making it level.

bullet *noun* a small metal cylinder with a pointed end, for firing from small guns and rifles. [from French *boulette*, little ball]

    ◫ shot, pellet, ball, *colloq.* slug, missile, projectile.

bulletin /ˈbʊlɪtɪn/ *noun* **1** a short official statement of news issued as soon as the news is known. **2** a short printed newspaper or leaflet, especially one produced regularly by a group or organization. [from French *bulletin*, from Italian *bullettino*]

    ◫ **1** report, newsflash, dispatch, communiqué, statement, announcement, notification, communication, message.

bulletin board 1 a notice-board. **2** *Comput.* an electronic data system containing messages and programs accessible to a number of users.

bullet-proof *adj.*, *said of a material, etc* strong enough to prevent bullets passing through.

bullet train a high-speed passenger train, especially in Japan.

bullfight *noun* a public show, especially in Spain, in which men on horseback and on foot bait and kill a bull. See BULLFIGHTING.

bullfighter *noun* a person who takes part in a bullfight.

bullfighting *noun* the sport or practice of baiting and killing bulls as a spectacle.

bullfinch *noun* a small bird belonging to the finch family, native to Europe and Asia, and having a short black bill and a white rump.

bullfrog *noun* **1** any of various large frogs with a loud call. **2** the largest N American frog (*Rana catesbiana*), up to 20cm long, which seldom leaves water.

bullhead *noun* a small bottom-dwelling fish found in clear streams and lakes of N Europe, and having a stout body up to 10cm in length, with a broad flattened head.

bullion /ˈbʊlɪən/ *noun* gold or silver in large bars. [from Old French *bouillon*, boiling]

bullish *adj.* **1** like a bull, especially in temper. **2** *Stock Exchange* tending to cause or hoping for rising prices. **3** very confident about the future.

bullishly *adv.* with a bullish or very confident manner.

bullishness *noun* being bullish or confident.

bull mastiff a breed of dog with a thick-set body, a short brown coat, soft ears, and a powerful muzzle.

bull-necked *adj.*, *said of a person* having a short thick strong neck.

bullock *noun* **1** a young male ox. **2** a castrated bull. Also called STEER.

bullring *noun* an arena where bullfights take place.

bull's-eye *noun* **1** the small circular centre of a target used in shooting, darts, etc. **2** a shot hitting this. **3** *colloq.* anything which hits its target or achieves its aim, etc. **4** a large, hard, round peppermint sweet. **5** a thick round disc of glass forming a window, especially on a ship. **6** a thick round boss in a sheet of glass. **7** a round lens in a lantern, or a lantern with such a lens.

bullshit *coarse slang* — *noun* nonsense. — *verb intrans.* **(bullshitted, bullshitting)** to talk bullshit.

bull terrier a breed of dog with a heavy body, a short smooth coat (usually white), a broad head with small eyes, pointed erect ears, and a long tail, originally developed by crossing bulldogs and terriers.

bully¹ — *noun* (PL. **bullies**) a person who hurts or frightens weaker or smaller people. — *verb* (**bullies, bullied**) **1** to act like a bully towards. **2 (bully someone into something)** to force them to do something they do not want to do: *they bullied us into helping.* — *adj.* excellent; very good. [from Old Dutch *boele*, lover]

    ◫ *noun* persecutor, tormentor, browbeater, intimidator, *colloq.* bully-boy, *slang* heavy, ruffian, tough. *verb* **1** persecute, torment, terrorize, *colloq.* push around, intimidate, tyrannize, domineer, overbear, oppress. **2** force, coerce, browbeat, bulldoze.

bully² or **bully beef** corned beef. [from French *bouilli*, boiled beef]

bully³ *verb intrans.* (**bullies, bullied**) (*usually* **bully off**) to begin a game, especially in hockey, by hitting one's stick three times against an opponent's before going for the ball.

bully-boy *noun colloq.* a rough person employed to bully and threaten people.

bullying *noun* pressuring or coercing someone weaker by use of force.

bulrush /ˈbʊlrʌʃ/ *noun* **1** a tall waterside plant of the genus *Typha* with long narrow greyish leaves and one or two thick spikes of tightly packed dark brown flowers. **2** *Biblical* a papyrus plant. [perhaps from BULL + RUSH²]

bulwark /ˈbʊlwək/ *noun* **1** a wall built as a defence, often made of earth. **2** a thing or person that defends a cause, way of life, etc. **3** (*usually* **bulwarks**) the side of a ship projecting above the deck. [from Old Dutch *bolwerc*]

bum¹ *noun Brit. colloq.* the buttocks. [from Middle English *bom*]

bum² *colloq. esp. North Amer.* — *noun* **1** a person who lives by begging. **2** a person who is lazy and shows no sense of responsibility. — *verb* (**bummed, bumming**) to get by begging, borrowing or cadging: *bum a lift.* — **bum around** or **about** to travel around or spend one's time doing nothing in particular. [perhaps from German *Bummler*, loafer]

bumbag *noun colloq.* a small bag on a belt, worn round the waist.

bumble *verb intrans.* **1** to speak in a confused or confusing way. **2** to move or do something in an awkward or clumsy way.

bumble bee a large hairy black and yellow bee found in most temperate regions. Like the honey bee it is a social insect, but it forms smaller colonies, and only the queen bee survives the winter. [from Middle English *bomblen*, to boom or buzz]

bumbling *adj.* inept; blundering.

bumf or **bumph** *noun Brit. colloq.* miscellaneous useless leaflets, documents. [short for *bum-fodder*]

bummer *noun* **1** a lazy or idle person. **2** *colloq.* a difficult or unpleasant thing.

bump — *verb* **1** *trans., intrans.* to knock or hit something. **2** to hurt or damage by hitting. **3** *intrans.* (*usually* **bump together**) *said of two moving objects* to collide. **4** *intrans.* (*also* **bump along**) to move or travel with jerky or bumpy movements: *bump along the road.* — *noun* **1** a knock, jolt, or collision. **2** a dull sound caused by a knock, collision, etc. **3** a lump or swelling on the body, especially one caused by a blow. **4** a lump on a road surface. — **bump into someone** *colloq.* to meet them by chance. **bump someone off** *slang* to kill them. **bump something up** *colloq.* to increase it: *bump up production.* [imitative]

    ◫ *verb* **1** hit, knock, strike, bang, crash (into), collide (with). **2** damage, dent, scrape, hurt, bruise, injure. **4** jolt, jerk, jar, rattle, shake, bounce. *noun* **1** blow, hit, knock, smash, crash, collision, impact, jolt, jar, shock. **2** bang, thump, thud. **3** lump, swelling, bulge, hump, protuberance. **bump into someone** meet, encounter, run into, chance upon, come across. **bump off** kill, murder, assassinate, *slang* eliminate, *slang* liquidate, *slang* do in. **bump up** increase, raise, boost, add to, *colloq.* jack up.

bumper — *noun* **1** *Brit.* a bar on the front or back of a motor vehicle which lessens the shock or damage if it hits anything. **2** an exceptionally good or large example. **3** a large full glass. — *adj.* exceptionally good or large: *a bumper crop.*

🔲 *adj.* plentiful, abundant, large, great, enormous, massive, excellent, exceptional.

🔳 *adj.* small.

bumph same as BUMF.

bumpily *adv.* with a bumpy or uneven manner, ride, etc.

bumpiness *noun* being bumpy or uneven.

bumpkin *noun colloq.* an awkward, simple or stupid person, especially one from the country. [from Old Dutch *bommekijn,* little barrel]

bumptious /ˈbʌmpʃəs/ *adj.* offensively or irritatingly conceited. [from BUMP + FRACTIOUS]

🔲 self-important, conceited, pompous, officious, overbearing, pushy, assertive, over-confident, presumptuous, forward, impudent, arrogant, cocky, boastful, full of oneself.

🔳 humble, modest.

bumptiously *adv.* with a bumptious or conceited manner.

bumptiousness *noun* being bumptious or conceited.

bumpy *adj.* (**bumpier, bumpiest**) **1** having a lot of bumps: *a bumpy road.* **2** affected by bumps: *a bumpy ride.*

🔲 **1** uneven, irregular, lumpy, knobbly, knobby. **2** jerky, jolting, bouncy, choppy, rough.

🔳 SMOOTH, EVEN.

bun *noun* **1** a small round sweetened roll, often containing currants, etc. **2** a mass of hair fastened in a round shape on the back of the head. [from Middle English *bunne*]

BUNAC *abbrev.* British Universities North America Club.

bunch — *noun* **1** a number of things fastened or growing together: *a bunch of flowers.* **2** (**bunches**) long hair divided into two pieces and tied separately at each side or the back of the head. **3** *colloq.* a group or collection. **4** *colloq.* a group of people; gang. — *verb trans., intrans.* to group together in or form a bunch. [from Middle English *bunche*]

🔲 *noun* **1** bouquet, posy, spray, bundle, sheaf, tuft, clump, cluster. **3** group, number, quantity, collection, assortment, batch, lot, heap, pile, stack, mass. **4** gang, band, troop, crew, team, party, gathering, flock, swarm, crowd, mob, multitude. *verb* group, bundle, cluster, collect, assemble, congregate, gather, herd, crowd, mass, pack, huddle.

🔳 *verb* disperse, scatter, spread out.

bunching *noun* **1** gathering together in bunches. **2** a situation in which traffic on a motorway travels in groups with little distance between vehicles.

bunch of fives *noun Brit. slang* a fist; a blow with a fist.

bunchy *adj.* (**bunchier, bunchiest**) resembling or in the form of a bunch or bunches.

Bundesbank /ˈbʊndəzbaŋk/ *noun* the state bank of Germany. [German, from *Bund,* confederacy + *Bank,* bank]

Bundestag /ˈbʊndəztɑːg/ *noun* the lower house of parliament of Germany. [German, from *Bund,* confederacy + *tagen,* confer]

bundle — *noun* **1** a number of things loosely fastened or

tied together. **2** a loose parcel, especially one made from cloth. **3** *Bot.* (*in full* **vascular bundle**) one of many strands of conducting vessels, fibres, etc, that serve to conduct water and nutrients and to provide mechanical support in the stems and leaves of higher plants. **4** *slang* a large amount of money. — *verb* **1** to make into a bundle. **2** to sell (especially specific computer software along with hardware) as a single package. — **be a bundle of nerves** to be extremely nervous. **bundle someone** or **something away** or **off** to put them somewhere quickly and roughly or untidily: *let's bundle him into a taxi/bundled the papers into the drawer.* **go a bundle on someone** or **something** *slang* to like them. [from Middle English *bundel*]

🔲 *noun* **1** bunch, sheaf, roll, bale, truss, batch, consignment, group, collection, set, pile, stack. **2** parcel, package, packet, bag, pack, load, knapsack. *verb* pack, wrap, bale, truss, bind, tie, fasten.

bun fight *Brit. colloq.* a noisy tea party.

bung — *noun* a small round piece of wood, rubber, cork, etc, which closes a hole in the bottom of a barrel, a small boat, etc. — *verb* **1** to block (a hole) with a bung. **2** *slang* to throw or put in a careless way. — *colloq.* **bung something up** to block it. [from Old Dutch *bonge,* stopper]

bungalow /ˈbʌŋgəloʊ/ *noun* a single-storey house. [from Gujarati *bangalo,* from Hindi *bangla,* in the style of Bengal]

bungee jumping /ˈbʌndʒi/ the sport of jumping from a height with strong rubber ropes or cables attached to the ankles to ensure that the jumper bounces up before reaching the ground or other surface. [of unknown origin]

bunghole *noun* a hole by which a barrel, etc is emptied or filled.

bungle — *verb trans., intrans.* to do (something) carelessly or badly. — *noun* carelessly or badly done work; a mistake.

🔲 *verb* botch (up), *slang* cock up, *slang* screw up, *colloq.* foul up, *colloq.* mess up, fudge, blunder. *noun slang* cock-up, *slang* screw-up, *colloq.* foul-up, fudge, mistake, blunder.

bungled *adj.* done badly; mishandled.

bungler *noun* a person who does things badly.

bungling *noun, adj.* doing things badly or carelessly: *their bungling attempts to put things right.*

bunion /ˈbʌnjən/ *noun* a painful swelling on the first joint of the big toe. [perhaps from Old French *buigne,* bump on the head]

bunk[1] — *noun* a narrow bed attached to the wall in a cabin in a ship, caravan, etc. — *verb intrans. colloq.* (**bunk down**) to lie down and go to sleep, especially in an improvised place.

bunk[2] same as BUNKUM.

bunk[3] *noun Brit. slang* the act of running away: *do a bunk.* — **bunk off** *intrans.* to stay away from school or work when one ought to be there.

bunk bed each of a pair of narrow beds fixed one on top of the other.

bunker *noun* **1** a large container or cupboard for storing coal. **2** an obstacle on a golf course consisting of a hollow containing sand. **3** an underground shelter. [from Scots *bonker,* box or chest]

bunkhouse *noun* a building with many beds, usually for workers.

bunkum /ˈbʌŋkəm/ or **bunk** *noun colloq.* nonsense; foolish talk. [from *Buncombe,* a county in N Carolina, whose congressman is said to have excused a rambling speech in Congress on the grounds that he was only speaking for Buncombe]

bunny *noun* (PL. **bunnies**) (*also* **bunny rabbit**) a child's word for rabbit. [from *bun,* rabbit, from Scots Gaelic *bun,* bottom]

bunny girl a club hostess or waitress whose costume includes false rabbit's ears and tail.

bunsen burner *Chem.* a gas burner, used mainly in laboratories. Natural gas enters via a jet at the lower end of a vertical metal tube, and air is drawn through an adjustable inlet hole. By controlling the gas-air mixture, it is possible to produce a very hot flame with no smoke. [named after the 19c German chemist Robert Bunsen]

bunting[1] *noun* 1 a row of small cloth or paper flags and other decorations. 2 thin loosely woven cotton used to make flags, especially for ships.

bunting[2] *noun* any of various small finch-like birds, found in N America, Europe, Africa, and Asia, having a sturdy body and a short stout bill with a hump in the roof of the mouth for crushing seeds.

buoy /bɔɪ/ — *noun* a brightly coloured floating object fastened to the bottom of the sea by an anchor, to warn ships of rocks, etc or to mark channels, etc. — *verb* to mark with a buoy or buoys. — **buoy something** or **someone up** 1 to keep them afloat. 2 to raise or boost (someone's spirits); to make (someone) cheerful, excited, etc. [from Middle English *boye*, float]

⊟ *noun* float, marker, signal, beacon. **buoy up** SUPPORT. **2** raise, lift, boost, encourage, cheer, hearten.

⊟ **2** depress, discourage.

buoyancy /ˈbɔɪənsɪ/ *noun* the upward force exerted on an object that is immersed in or floating on the surface of a fluid (a liquid or gas). It is equal to the weight of fluid displaced (Archimedes' principle).

buoyant /ˈbɔɪənt/ *adj.* 1 *said of an object* able to float in a liquid. 2 *said of a liquid or gas* able to keep an object afloat. 3 *said of a person* cheerful. 4 *said of sales, profits, etc* increasing. 5 *said of a business, etc* having increasing trade, rising profits, etc. [from BUOY]

⊟ **1** floatable, floating, afloat, light, weightless. **3** light-hearted, carefree, bright, cheerful, happy, joyful, lively, animated, bouncy.

⊟ **1** heavy. **3** depressed, despairing.

buoyantly *adv.* with a buoyant or cheerful manner.

BUPA /ˈbuːpə/ *abbrev.* British United Provident Association, a private medical insurance scheme.

BUR *abbrev., as an international vehicle mark* Burma (Myanmar).

bur or **burr** *noun* 1 the rough prickly seed-case or flower of some plants, which sticks readily to things it touches. 2 any plant which produces burs. [from Middle English *burre*]

burble *verb* 1 *intrans.* to speak at length but with little meaning. 2 *intrans., said of a stream, etc* to make a bubbling, murmuring sound. 3 to say (something) in a way that is hard to understand. [probably imitative]

⊟ BABBLE. **2** murmur, bubble, gurgle. **3** jabber, gabble, mumble, mutter.

burbot *noun* (PL. **burbot, burbots**) a large fish, the only freshwater species in the cod family, found in lowland rivers and lakes of N Europe, Asia, and N America. [from Old French *bourbotte*]

burden[1] — *noun* 1 something to be carried; a load. 2 a duty, obligation, etc which is difficult, time-consuming, costly, etc. 3 the carrying of loads: *a beast of burden.* 4 (*also* **burthen**) the amount a ship can carry. — *verb* (**burdened, burdening**) to load with a burden, difficulty, problem, etc. — **the burden of proof** the responsibility for proving something, especially in a law court. [from Anglo-Saxon *byrthen*]

⊟ *noun* 1 cargo, load, weight, deadweight, encumbrance, millstone. 2 obligation, duty, onus, responsibility, strain, stress, worry, anxiety, care, trouble, trial, affliction, sorrow.

verb load, weigh down, encumber, handicap, bother, worry, tax, strain, overload, lie heavy on, oppress, overwhelm.

⊟ *verb* unburden, relieve.

burden[2] *noun* 1 the main theme (of a book, speech, etc). 2 a line repeated at the end of each verse of a song; a refrain. [from Old French *bourdon*, droning sound]

burdensome *adj.* difficult to carry, support, or tolerate.

⊟ heavy, onerous, hard, laborious, troublesome, demanding, taxing, exacting.

⊟ light, easy, undemanding.

burdock *noun* any of various perennial plants of the genus *Arctium*, native to Europe and Asia, having long-stalked heart-shaped lower leaves, and oval flower-heads each composed of many tiny purple flowers. [from BUR + DOCK[3]]

bureau /ˈbjʊərəʊ/ *noun* (PL. **bureaux, bureaus**) 1 *Brit.* a desk for writing at, with drawers and usually a front flap which opens downwards to provide the writing surface. 2 *North Amer., esp. US* a chest of drawers. 3 an office or department for business, especially for collecting and supplying information. 4 *North Amer., esp. US* a government or newspaper department. [from Old French *burel*, dark red cloth]

⊟ **3** office, branch, department, division, service, agency, counter, desk.

bureaucracy /bjʊˈrɒkrəsɪ/ *noun* (PL. **bureaucracies**) 1 a system of government by officials who are responsible to their department heads and are not elected. 2 these officials as a group, especially when regarded as oppressive. 3 a country governed by officials. 4 any system of administration in which matters are complicated by complex procedures amd trivial rules. [from BUREAU + Greek *kratos*, power]

⊟ **1, 2** administration, government, ministry, civil service, the authorities, officialdom. **4** officialdom, red tape, regulations.

bureaucrat /ˈbjʊərəkrat/ *noun* 1 a government official. 2 an official who follows rules rigidly, so creating delays and difficulties.

bureaucratic /bjʊərəˈkratɪk/ *adj.* involving a complex and inflexible administration or organization.

bureaucratically *adv.* with a bureaucratic or inflexible manner.

bureau de change /ˈbjʊərəʊ də ʃɒnʒ/ a place where one can change money from one currency to another.

burette /bjʊˈret/ *noun Chem.* a long vertical glass tube marked with a scale and having a tap at the bottom, used to deliver controlled volumes of liquid, eg during chemical titrations. [from French *burette*]

burgeon /ˈbɜːdʒən/ *verb intrans. literary* to grow or develop quickly; to flourish. [from Old French *burjon*, bud, shoot]

burgeoning *adj. literary* beginning to grow or flourish.

burger *noun* 1 a hamburger. 2 a hamburger covered or flavoured with something: *a cheeseburger.* 3 an item of food shaped like a hamburger but made of something different: *a nutburger.* [a shortening of HAMBURGER]

burgess /ˈbɜːdʒɪs/ *noun* 1 *Brit.* in England an inhabitant of a town or borough, especially a person who has the right to elect people to government. 2 *Brit. Hist.* a Member of Parliament for a borough, a town with a municipal corporation or a university. [from Old French *burgeis*, from Latin *burgus*, borough]

burgh /ˈbʌrə/ *noun* in Scotland until 1975, a town or borough with a certain amount of self-government under a town council. [Scots form of BOROUGH]

burgher /'bɜːgə(r)/ *noun* a citizen of a town or borough, especially on the Continent. [from Old German *burger*, from *burg*, borough]

burghul wheat /bər'guːl/ same as BULGHAR WHEAT. [from Persian]

burglar *noun* a person who enters a building, etc illegally to steal from it. [from Old French *burgler*]

▣ housebreaker, robber, thief, pilferer, trespasser.

burglar alarm an alarm fitted to a building, which is activated by an intruder.

burglary *noun* (PL. **burglaries**) the crime or an act of entering a building, etc illegally to steal.

▣ housebreaking, break-in, robbery, theft, stealing, trespass.

burgle *verb* 1 *trans.* to enter (a building, etc) illegally and steal from it; to steal from (a person). 2 *intrans.* to commit burglary.

burgomaster /'bɜːgəmɑːstə(r)/ *noun* a mayor of a town in Germany, Belgium, the Netherlands, and Austria. [from Dutch *burgemeester*, from *burg*, borough + *meester*, master]

burial *noun* 1 the burying of a dead body in a grave. 2 *Archaeol.* a grave and the remains found in it. [from Anglo-Saxon *byrgels*, tomb]

▣ burying, interment, entombment, funeral, obsequies.

burin /'bjʊərɪn/ *noun* a steel tool for engraving copper, wood, etc. [from French *burin*]

burk same as BERK.

burlesque /bɜː'lesk/ — *noun* 1 a piece of literature, acting, etc which exaggerates and mocks a serious subject or art form. 2 *North Amer., esp. US* a type of theatrical entertainment involving humorous sketches, songs, and usually strip-tease. — *adj.* of or like a burlesque. — *verb* to make fun of (something) using burlesque. [from Italian *burlesco*, from *burla*, jest]

▣ *noun* satire, take-off, *Brit. colloq.* send-up, skit, parody. *verb* satirize, take off, *Brit. colloq.* send up, parody, ridicule.

burliness *noun*, *said especially of a person* a strong heavy build.

burly *adj.* (**burlier**, **burliest**) *said of a person* strong and heavy in build. [from Middle English *borli*]

▣ big, well-built, hulking, hefty, heavy, stocky, sturdy, brawny, beefy, muscular, strapping, strong, powerful.

▣ small, puny, thin, slim.

Burmese — *noun* 1 (PL. **Burmese**) a native or citizen of Burma (Myanmar). 2 a Sino-Tibetan language spoken by c.25 million people in Burma (Myanmar), the official language of the country. — *adj.* of Burma (Myanmar) or its people or language.

burn[1] — *verb* (PAST TENSE AND PAST PARTICIPLE **burned**, **burnt**) 1 *intrans.* to be on fire. 2 to set alight; to consume or destroy by means of fire. 3 *trans., intrans.* to damage or injure, or be damaged or injured, by fire or heat. 4 to use as fuel. 5 to make (a hole, etc) by or as if by fire, heat, etc: *acid can burn holes in material.* 6 *trans., intrans.* to kill or die by fire. 7 *intrans.* to be or feel hot: *my face is burning.* 8 *intrans., trans.* to feel or cause to feel a stinging pain: *vodka burns my throat.* 9 *intrans.* to feel strong emotion: *burn with shame.* 10 *intrans. colloq.* to want to do something very much: *is burning to get his revenge.* 11 *trans., intrans.* to char or scorch or become charred or scorched: *I think the potatoes are burning.* 12 to write material onto (a compact disc) using a laser. — *noun* 1 an injury or mark caused by fire, heat, acid, etc. 2 an act of burning. 3 an act of firing the engines of a space rocket. — **burn one's boats** or **bridges** *colloq.* to destroy all chance of escape or retreat. **burn the candle at both ends** to become over-tired by working for excessively long periods, especially from early in the morning till late at night. **burn down** *said of a large structure such as a building* to be destroyed by fire. **burn something down** to destroy a building, etc by fire. **burn one's fingers** or **get one's fingers burnt** *colloq.* to become involved in something foolish, dangerous, etc and suffer as a result. **burn the midnight oil** to work late into the night. **burn out** 1 to be completely burnt and reduced to nothing. 2 *said of a rocket engine* to stop working when the fuel is used up. **burn out** or **burn something out** to stop or cause something to stop working because of too much use or heat. **burn out** or **burn oneself out** *North Amer., esp. US* to be exhausted from too much work or exercise. **burn up** 1 to be destroyed by fire, heat, acid, etc. 2 *North Amer. slang* to become very angry. **burn up fuel** *said of an engine* to use it in large quantities. **burn someone up** *North Amer., esp. US slang* to make them very angry. [from Anglo-Saxon *biernan*, to be on fire, and *bærnan*, to cause to burn]

▣ *verb* 1 flame, blaze, flare, flash, glow, flicker, smoulder, smoke, fume. 2 ignite, light, kindle, incinerate, cremate, consume. 3 scald, scorch, parch, shrivel, singe, char, sear. 4 use, run on. 8 smart, sting, bite, hurt, tingle.

burn[2] *noun Scot.* a small stream. [from Anglo-Saxon *burna*, brook]

burner *noun* the part of a gas lamp, stove, etc which produces the flame. — **put something on the back burner** *colloq.* to put it aside for future consideration.

burning *adj.* 1 on fire. 2 feeling extremely hot. 3 stinging painfully. 4 very strong or intense: *a burning desire.* 5 very important or urgent: *a burning issue.*

▣ 1 ablaze, aflame, afire, fiery, flaming, blazing, flashing, gleaming, glowing, smouldering, alight. 2 hot, scalding, scorching, searing, piercing, acute. 3 smarting, stinging, prickling, tingling, biting, caustic, pungent. 4 ardent, fervent, eager, earnest, intense, vehement, passionate, impassioned, frantic, frenzied, consuming. 5 urgent, pressing, important, significant, crucial, essential, vital.

▣ 2 cold. 4 apathetic. 5 unimportant.

burnish *verb* to make (metal) bright by polishing. [from Old French *brunir*, from *brun*, brown]

▣ polish, buff (up), shine, rub (up), brighten.

burnished *adj.* made bright by polishing.

burnishing *noun* making bright by polishing.

burnous /bɜːˈnuːs/ *noun* a long cloak with a hood, worn by Arabs. [from Arabic *burnus*]

burn-out *noun North Amer.* 1 physical or emotional exhaustion caused by overwork or stress. 2 the point at which a rocket engine stops working when the fuel is used up.

burnt see BURN.

burnt ochre or **burnt sienna** a natural reddish-brown pigment made dark by being burnt.

burnt umber umber heated to a dark reddish-brown colour.

burp *colloq.* — *verb* 1 *intrans.* to let air escape noisily from one's stomach through one's mouth. 2 *trans.* to rub or pat (a baby) on the back to help get rid of air in its stomach. — *noun* a belch. [imitative]

burr[1] same as BUR.

burr[2] — *noun* 1 in some accents of English, a rough 'r' sound pronounced at the back of the throat. 2 a continual humming sound. 3 a rough edge on metal or paper. 4 a small drill used by a dentist or surgeon. — *verb* 1 *intrans.* to make a burring sound. 2 *trans.* to pronounce with a burr.

burrito /bʊˈriːtoʊ/ *noun* (PL. **burritos**) a Mexican dish of a folded flour tortilla stuffed with meat, beans, chillis, etc. [from Spanish, a diminutive of *burro*, donkey]

burrow — *noun* a hole in the ground, especially one dug by a rabbit or other small animal for shelter or defence. — *verb* **1** *intrans.*, *trans.* (**burrow in** or **into something**) to make a hole or tunnel in or under it. **2** *intrans.* to live in a burrow. **3** *intrans.* *said of people* to hide or keep warm as if in a burrow. **4** (**burrow into something**) to search or investigate it: *burrow into one's pockets.* [from Middle English *berg*, refuge]

▣ *noun* warren, hole, earth, set, den, lair, retreat, shelter, tunnel. *verb* **1** tunnel, dig, delve, excavate, mine, undermine.

bursar *noun* **1** a treasurer in a school, college, or university. **2** a student or pupil who has a bursary. [from Latin *bursa*, bag, purse]

bursary *noun* (PL. **bursaries**) **1** an award or grant of money made to a student; a scholarship. **2** the bursar's room in a school, college, etc.

burst — *verb* (PAST TENSE AND PAST PARTICIPLE **burst**) **1** *intrans.*, *trans.* to break open or into pieces, usually suddenly and violently. **2** *intrans.* to make one's way suddenly or violently: *burst into the room.* **3** *intrans.* to appear suddenly and be immediately important or newsworthy: *burst on to the political scene.* **4** *intrans.* (**be bursting**) **a** to be quite full. **b** to break open, overflow, etc. **c** to be consumed with emotion, vitality, etc: *bursting with life/bursting with anger.* — *noun* **1** an instance of, or the place of, bursting or breaking open. **2** a sudden brief period of some activity: *a burst of speed/a burst of gunfire.* — **burst into song** to begin singing, especially suddenly or unexpectedly. **burst into tears** to begin weeping suddenly or unexpectedly. **burst open** *usually said of a door* to open suddenly and violently. **burst out laughing** to begin laughing suddenly or unexpectedly. [from Anglo-Saxon *berstan*]

▣ *verb* **1** puncture, rupture, tear, split, crack, break, fragment, shatter, shiver, disintegrate, explode, blow up. **2** rush, run, dash. *noun* **1** puncture, *colloq.* blow-out, rupture, split, crack, break, breach, explosion, blast, bang, eruption. **2** spurt, surge, rush, spate, torrent, outpouring, outburst, outbreak, fit, discharge.

bursting *adj. colloq.* **1** very eager to do something: *we're bursting to tell you the news.* **2** (**bursting with something**) having too much of it: *bursting with pride.* **3** urgently needing to urinate.

burthen SEE BURDEN.

burton — **gone for a burton** *Brit. slang* lost, broken, dead, no longer in existence, etc.

bury *verb* (**buries**, **buried**) **1** to place (a dead body) in a grave, the sea, etc. **2** to hide in the ground: *a dog burying a bone.* **3** to put out of sight; to cover: *bury one's face in one's hands.* **4** to lose (a close relative) by death: *she has already buried three husbands.* — **bury oneself in something** to occupy oneself completely with it: *bury oneself in one's work.* **bury the hatchet** to stop quarrelling and become friends again. **bury one's head in the sand** to refuse to think about or accept something unpleasant. [from Anglo-Saxon *byrgan*]

▣ **1** inter, entomb, lay to rest, shroud. **2** sink, submerge, immerse, plant, implant, embed. **3** cover, conceal, hide, enshroud, engulf, enclose. **bury oneself in something** engross oneself in, occupy oneself with, involve oneself in, absorb oneself in.

▣ **1** disinter, exhume. **2, 3** uncover.

bus — *noun* **1** a usually large road vehicle which carries passengers to and from established stopping points along a fixed route for payment. **2** *colloq.* a car or aeroplane, especially one which is old and shaky. **3** *Comput.* a set of electrical conductors that form a channel or path along which data (in the form of digital signals) or power may be transmitted to and from all the main components of a computer. — *verb* (**bused**, **busing** or **bussed**, **bussing**) **1** *intrans.*, *trans.* to go or take by bus. **2** *trans. North Amer., esp. US* to transport (children) by bus to a school in a different area, as a way of promoting racial integration. — **miss the bus** to lose an opportunity. [from OMNIBUS]

busby /ˈbʌzbɪ/ *noun* (PL. **busbies**) a tall fur hat worn as part of the uniform of some British soldiers.

bus conductor an official on a bus who collects fares from passengers and issues tickets.

bush[1] *noun* **1** a low woody perennial plant, especially one having many separate branches originating at or near ground level. **2** anything resembling this, especially in thickness or density: *a bush of hair.* **3** (*usually* **the bush**) wild uncultivated land covered with shrubs or small trees, and ranging from open countryside to forest, especially in semi-arid regions of Africa or Australia. [from Middle English *busshe*; some uses are from Dutch *bosch*]

▣ **1** shrub, hedge, thicket. **3** scrub, brush, scrubland, backwoods, wilds.

bush[2] — *noun* a sheet of thin metal lining a cylinder in which an axle revolves. — *verb* to provide with a bush. [from Old Dutch *bussche*, box]

bushbaby *noun* an agile nocturnal primate of sub-Saharan Africa with thick fur, large eyes and ears, a long tail, and long hind legs that enable it to leap easily from branch to branch.

bushed *adj. colloq.* extremely tired.

bushel /ˈbʊʃəl/ *noun* **1** a unit for measuring dry or liquid goods (especially grain, potatoes, or fruit), by volume, equal to 8 gallons or 36.4 litres in the UK, or 35.2 litres in the USA. **2** a container with a capacity of 36.4 litres in the UK or 35.2 litres in the USA. — **hide one's light under a bushel** to keep one's good qualities or abilities hidden from other people. [from Old French *boissiel*]

bushido /bʊˈfiːdoʊ/ *noun* the Japanese code of chivalry practised by the samurai until 1868. [from Japanese *bushi*, warrior + *do*, doctrine]

bushily *adv.* with a bushy style or appearance.

bushiness *noun* a bushy style or appearance.

bush jacket same as BUSH SHIRT.

bushman *noun* **1** a person who lives or travels in the bush in Australia or New Zealand. **2** (**Bushman**) a member of an aboriginal tribe in S Africa. **3** (**Bushman**) the language spoken by this tribe.

bushranger *noun Austral. Hist.* a robber or criminal living in the bush.

bush shirt or **bush jacket** a light cotton jacket with four pockets and a belt.

bush telegraph the rapid spreading of information, rumours, etc, usually by word of mouth.

bushwhack *verb intrans.* to travel through woods or bush clearing it.

bushwhacker *noun* a person who lives or travels in bush country.

bushwhacking *noun* living or travelling in bush country.

bushy *adj.* (**bushier**, **bushiest**) **1** covered in bushes. **2** *said of hair, etc* thick and spreading.

busily *adv.* with a busy or occupied manner.

business /ˈbɪznɪs/ *noun* **1** the buying and selling of goods and services. **2** a shop, firm, commercial company, etc. **3** one's regular occupation, trade, or profession. **4** the things that are one's proper or rightful concern: *mind one's own business.* **5** serious work or activity: *get down to business.* **6** an affair, matter: *a nasty business.* **7** *colloq.* a difficult or complicated problem; a bother or nuisance: *It's a real business filling in this form.* — **like nobody's business** *colloq.* very fast, very well, or very efficiently. **mean business** *colloq.* to be very serious about something. **on business** in the process of doing business or something official. **out of

business no longer able to function as a business. **send someone about their business** to dismiss them or send them away. [from Anglo-Saxon *bisig*, busy + *-nes*, -ness]

⊟ **1** trade, commerce, industry, manufacturing, dealings, transactions, bargaining, trading, buying, selling. **2** company, firm, corporation, establishment, organization, concern, enterprise, venture. **3** job, occupation, work, employment, trade, profession, line, calling, career, vocation, duty, task, responsibility. **6** affair, matter, issue, subject, topic, question, problem, point.

business card a card carried by businessmen and businesswomen showing their name and business address.

business class a class of comfort in air travel intermediate between standard class and first class.

business end *colloq.* the part of something which does the work the thing is made for.

businesslike *adj.* practical and efficient.

⊟ professional, efficient, thorough, systematic, methodical, organized, orderly, well-ordered, practical, precise, correct, formal.
⊟ inefficient, disorganized.

businessman *noun* a man who works in trade or commerce, especially at a senior level.

⊟ entrepreneur, industrialist, trader, merchant, tycoon, magnate, capitalist, financier, employer, executive.

business park an area, usually on the edge of a town, specially designed to accommodate business offices and light industry.

businesswoman *noun* a woman who works in trade or commerce, especially at a senior level.

⊟ entrepreneur, industrialist, trader, merchant, tycoon, magnate, capitalist, financier, employer, executive.

busk *verb intrans.* to sing, play music, etc in the street for money. [probably from Spanish *buscar*, to seek]

busker *noun* a person who performs in the street for money.

busking *noun* the activity of performing in the street for money.

busman's holiday leisure time spent doing what one normally does at work.

bust[1] *noun* **1** the upper front part of a woman's body. **2** a sculpture of a person's head, shoulders, and chest. [from French *buste*]

⊟ **1** bosom, breasts, chest, breast. **2** sculpture, head, torso, statue.

bust[2] — *verb* (PAST TENSE AND PAST PARTICIPLE **bust**, **busted**) **1** *trans., intrans. colloq.* to break or burst. **2** *slang* to arrest. **3** *slang* to raid or search. — *noun slang* **1** a police raid. **2** a drinking bout; a spree. — *adj. colloq.* **1** broken or burst. **2** having no money left; bankrupt. — **go bust** *colloq.* to go bankrupt. [from BURST]

bustard /ˈbʌstəd/ *noun* any of various species of large ground-dwelling bird of open plains, fields, and desert, found mainly in Africa, and also in S Europe, S Asia, and Australia, and having speckled grey or brown plumage and long powerful legs. Several species have been hunted almost to extinction. [from Old French *bistarde*, from Latin *avis tarda*, slow bird (although it is not slow)]

buster *noun North Amer. slang* a form of address used for a man or boy.

bustle[1] /ˈbʌsl/ — *verb* **1** *intrans.* (*usually* **bustle about**) to busy oneself noisily and energetically. **2** to make (someone) hurry, work hard, etc: *bustled her out of the room.* —

noun hurried, noisy, and excited activity. [from Middle English *bustelen*, to hurry along aimlessly]

⊟ *verb* **1** dash, rush, scamper, scurry, hurry, hasten, scramble, fuss. *noun* activity, stir, commotion, tumult, agitation, excitement, fuss, ado, flurry, hurry, haste.

bustle[2] /ˈbʌsl/ *noun Hist.* a frame or pad for holding a skirt out from the back of the waist.

bustler *noun* a person who bustles or works with ostentatious haste.

bustling *adj.* ostentatiously lively and busy.

bust-up *noun colloq.* **1** a quarrel; the ending of a relationship or partnership. **2** an explosion or collapse.

busty *adj.* (**bustier, bustiest**) *colloq., said of a woman* having large breasts.

busy — *adj.* (**busier, busiest**) **1** fully occupied; having much work to do. **2** full of activity: *a busy day/a busy street.* **3** *North Amer., esp. US, said of a telephone line* engaged. **4** constantly working or occupied. **5** fussy and tending to interfere in the affairs of others. — *verb* (**busies, busied**) (**busy someone with something**) to occupy them with a task, etc. [from Anglo-Saxon *bisig*]

⊟ *adj.* **1** occupied, engaged, *colloq.* tied up, employed, working. **2** active, lively, energetic, strenuous, tiring, full, hectic, eventful, crowded, swarming, teeming, bustling. **4** diligent, industrious, stirring, restless, tireless. *verb* occupy, engage, employ, engross, absorb, immerse, interest, concern, bother.
⊟ *adj.* **1, 4** idle, lazy. **2** quiet.

busybody *noun* a person who is always interfering in other people's affairs.

⊟ meddler, *colloq.* nosy parker, intruder, pry, gossip, eavesdropper, snoop, snooper, troublemaker.

busy Lizzie a fast-growing plant of the genus *Impatiens*, usually having pink, red, or white flowers, and widely grown as a house plant.

busyness /ˈbɪznəs/ *noun* a busy or occupied state.

but — *conj.* **1** contrary to expectation: *she fell down but didn't hurt herself.* **2** in contrast: *you've been to Spain but I haven't.* **3** other than: *you can't do anything but wait.* — *prep.* except: *they are all here but him.* — *adv.* only: *I can but try.* — *noun* an objection or doubt: *no buts about it.* — **but for** were it not for; without: *I couldn't have managed but for your help.* **the last but one** the one before the last. [from Anglo-Saxon *butan*, outside of, without]

butane /ˈbjuːteɪn/ *noun Chem.* (FORMULA C_4H_{10}) a colourless highly flammable gas belonging to the alkane series of hydrocarbon compounds, and obtained from petroleum. It is used in the manufacture of synthetic rubber, and liquid butane is used as a fuel. [from Latin *butyrum*, butter]

butch *adj. slang, of a person, usually a man* tough and strong-looking. [from a boy's nickname in the US]

butcher — *noun* **1** a person or shop that sells meat. **2** a person who kills animals for food. **3** a person who kills people needlessly and savagely. — *verb* **1** to kill and prepare (an animal) for sale as food. **2** to kill cruelly. **3** to ruin or spoil. [from Anglo-Saxon *bouchier*, person who kills and sells he-goats]

butcher bird *Zool.* **1** any of six species of a bird from Australia and New Guinea that impales its prey on thorns. It is similar in size to the crow, and has a large powerful hooked beak. **2** the name sometimes given to shrikes.

butchery *noun* **1** the preparing of meat for sale as food. **2** senseless or cruel killing.

butler *noun* the head male servant in a house, in charge of the wine cellar, dining table, etc. [from Old French *bouteillier*, from *botele*, bottle]

butt[1] — *verb trans., intrans.* **1** to push or hit hard or roughly with the head like a ram or goat. **2** to join or be joined end to end. — *noun* **1** a blow with the head or horns. **2** the place where two edges join. — **butt in** *colloq.* to interrupt or interfere. [from Old French *boter*, to push or strike]

▪ *verb* hit, bump, knock, push, shove, ram, thrust, jab, prod, poke. *noun* **1** blow, bump, knock, push, shove, thrust, jab, prod, poke. **butt in** interrupt, cut in, interpose, interfere, intrude, meddle.

butt² *noun* a large barrel for beer, rain, etc. [from Old French *bout*, from Latin *buttis*, cask]

butt³ *noun* **1** a person who is often a target (of jokes, ridicule, criticism, etc). **2** a mound of earth behind a target on a shooting range. [from French *but*, goal]

▪ **1** target, mark, object, subject, victim, laughing-stock, dupe.

butt⁴ *noun* **1** the thick, heavy, or bottom end of a tool or weapon. **2** the unused end of a finished cigar, cigarette, etc. **3** *North Amer. colloq.* the buttocks. [from Middle English *bott*, from Anglo-Saxon *butt*, tree stump]

▪ **1** base, foot, shaft, stock, handle, haft. **2** stub, end, tip.

butte /bjuːt/ *noun Geol.* an isolated flat-topped residual hill with steep sides, formed by erosion. [from French *butte*]

butter — *noun* **1** a creamy yellowish food that is made by pasteurizing, souring, and churning the cream from milk. **2** any of various substances that resemble this food in appearance or texture, eg peanut butter. — *verb* to put butter on or in. — **butter someone up** *colloq.* to flatter them, especially in order to gain a favour. [from Anglo-Saxon *butere*, from Greek *boutyron*, probably meaning 'ox-cheese']

butter bean 1 any of several varieties of lima bean having large edible seeds. **2** the large pale flat edible seed of this plant.

buttercup *noun* any of various perennial plants of the genus *Ranunculus*, native to north temperate and alpine regions, with bright yellow flowers.

buttered *adj.* coated in or made with butter.

butterfingers *noun colloq.* a person who often drops things, or who does not manage to catch things.

butterfly *noun* (PL. **butterflies**) **1** the common name for any of about 20,000 species of winged insect belonging to the order Lepidoptera, and having four broad wings covered with tiny overlapping scales, and a feeding tube (known as a *proboscis*) for sucking nectar from flowers. **2** a not very serious person, only interested in pleasure: *a social butterfly.* **3** (**butterflies**) a nervous feeling in the stomach. **4** same as BUTTERFLY STROKE. [from Anglo-Saxon *buter-fleoge*, butter-fly]

butterfly fish angelfish.

butterfly nut a screw or nut with two flat projections which allow it to be turned with the fingers.

butterfly stroke a swimming stroke in which both arms are brought out of the water and over the head at the same time.

butter knife a blunt knife for spreading butter.

buttermilk *noun* the slightly sharp-tasting liquid left after all the butter has been removed from milk.

butter muslin a loosely woven cloth, originally used for wrapping butter.

butterpat *noun* **1** a small lump of butter. **2** a piece of wood used for shaping butter.

butterscotch *noun* a kind of hard sweet made from butter and sugar.

butterwort *noun* a small carnivorous perennial plant of the genus *Pinguicula*, native to the northern hemisphere

and the mountains of S America. It has a rosette of oval slightly rolled leaves, and produces solitary white, lilac, or violet flowers on leafless stems.

buttery¹ *adj.* having a taste or consistency of butter.

buttery² *noun* (PL. **butteries**) a room, especially in a college or university, where food is kept and supplied to students. [from Old French *boterie*, place for storing butts]

buttock *noun* **1** (*usually* **buttocks**) each of the fleshy parts of the body between the back and the legs. **2** the similar part of some animals. [probably from BUTT⁴]

▪ **1** rump, hindquarters, rear, *humorous* posterior, seat, bottom, behind, *colloq.* backside, *coarse slang* arse.

button — *noun* **1** a small round piece of metal, plastic, etc sewn on to clothes, which fastens them by being passed through a slit or hole. **2** a small disc pressed to operate a door, bell, etc. **3** a small round object worn as decoration or a badge. **4** any small round object more or less like a button: *chocolate buttons/a button nose.* — *verb* (*usually* **button something up**) to fasten it using a button or buttons. — **button up** *slang* to stop talking. **button something up** to bring it to a successful conclusion. **on the button** *colloq.* exactly right or correct. [from Old French *bouton*]

button cell a small flat circular battery, used to power a watch, etc.

buttoned-down *adj. colloq.* conservative and restrained.

buttonhole — *noun* **1** a small slit or hole through which a button is passed to fasten a garment. **2** a flower or flowers worn in a buttonhole or pinned to a lapel. — *verb* to stop and force conversation on (a usually reluctant person).

▪ *verb* waylay, catch, grab, nab, detain, importune, accost.

button mushroom the head of an unexpanded mushroom.

buttress — *noun* **1** a support built on to the outside of a wall. **2** any support or prop. — *verb* **1** to support (a wall, etc) with buttresses. **2** to support or encourage (an argument, etc). [from Old French *bouterez*, thrusting]

▪ *noun* **2** support, prop, shore, stay, brace, pier, strut, stanchion, mainstay, reinforcement. *verb* SUPPORT, STRENGTHEN, REINFORCE. **1** prop up, shore up, hold up, brace, bolster up. **2** back up, substantiate, corroborate, sustain.

◨ *verb* UNDERMINE, WEAKEN.

butty *noun* (PL. **butties**) *Brit. colloq.* a sandwich. [from BUTTER]

buxom *adj., said of a woman* attractively plump and healthy-looking. [from Middle English *buhsum*, pliant]

buy — *verb* (PAST TENSE AND PAST PARTICIPLE **bought**) (*usually trans.*) **1** to obtain something by paying a sum of money for it. **2** to be a means of obtaining something: *there are some things money can't buy.* **3** to obtain by giving up or sacrificing something: *success bought at the expense of happiness.* **4** *colloq.* to believe or accept as true. **5** to bribe someone. — *noun* a thing bought: *a good buy.* — **buy something in** to buy a stock or supply of it. **buy into something 1** to buy shares in a company, etc. **2** to accept or agree with an idea, etc. **buy someone off** to get rid of a threatening person, etc by paying them money. **buy someone out** to buy all the shares held by someone in a company. **buy oneself out** to pay to be released from the armed forces. **buy time** *colloq.* to gain more time before a decision, action, etc is taken. **buy something up** to buy the whole stock of it. **have bought it** *slang* to have been killed. [from Anglo-Saxon *bycgan*]

▪ *verb* **1** purchase, pay for, procure, acquire, obtain, get. **3** gain, secure, get. **4** *colloq.* swallow, *colloq.* wear, *colloq.* go for, believe, accept. *noun* purchase, acquisition, bargain, deal.

◨ *verb* **1** sell.

buyer *noun* **1** a person who buys; a customer. **2** a person employed by a large shop or firm to buy goods on its behalf.

⊟ PURCHASER. **1** customer, shopper, consumer, vendee, emptor.

⊟ **1** seller, vendor.

buyer's market a situation where there are more goods for sale than people wanting to buy them, so keeping prices low.

buyout *noun Commerce* the purchase of all the shares in a company in order to gain control of it.

buzz — *verb* **1** *intrans.* to make a continuous humming or rapidly vibrating sound. **2** *intrans.* to be filled with activity or excitement: *buzzing with activity.* **3** *colloq.* to call (someone) on the telephone. **4** *colloq.* to call (someone) using a buzzer. **5** *colloq., said of an aircraft* to fly very low over or very close to (another aircraft, a building, etc.) — *noun* **1** a humming or rapidly vibrating sound, eg as made by a bee. **2** a low murmuring sound eg as made by many people talking. **3** *colloq.* a telephone call. **4** *colloq.* a sense of activity, excitement, etc. **5** *colloq.* a rumour. — **buzz about** or **around** to move quickly or excitedly. **buzz off** *colloq.* to go away. [imitative]

⊟ *verb* **1** hum, whirr, drone. **2** hum, throb, pulse. *noun* **1** hum, whirr, drone. **2** hum, murmur. **3** ring, call, *Brit. colloq.* bell, *colloq.* tinkle. **4** thrill, *colloq.* kick.

buzzard /ˈbʌzəd/ *noun* **1** one of a number of large hawks that resemble eagles in their effortless gliding flight, rising on warm air currents for long distances. Buzzards hunt by pouncing on rabbits, voles, mice, lizards, and other small animals. **2** *North Amer.* a vulture. [from Old French *busard*]

buzzer *noun* an electrical device which makes a buzzing sound.

buzz word *colloq.* a fashionable new word or expression, often in a particular subject or social group.

BV *abbrev. Beata Virgo* (Latin) Blessed Virgin.

BVM *abbrev. Beata Virgo Maria* (Latin) Blessed Virgin.

bwana /ˈbwɑːnɑː/ *noun, often used as a form of address in E Africa* master; sir. [a Swahili word]

by — *prep.* **1** next to, beside, near. **2** past: *drive by the house.* **3** through, along, or across: *enter by the window.* **4** used to show the person or thing that does, causes, produces, etc something: *bitten by a dog/a play by Shakespeare.* **5** used to show method or means: *travel by air.* **6** not later than: *be home by 10pm.* **7** during: *escape by night.* **8** used to show extent or amount: *bigger by six feet.* **9** used in stating rates of payment, etc: *paid by the hour.* **10** according to: *by my watch.* **11** used in giving measurements, compass directions, etc: *a room measuring six feet by ten/north-north-east by north.* **12** used to show the number which must perform a mathematical operation on another: *divide six by two/multiply three by four.* **13** with regard to: *do his duty by them.* — *adv.* **1** near: *live close by.* **2** past: *drive by without stopping.* **3** aside; away; in reserve: *put money by.* — *noun* (PL. **byes**) same as BYE¹. — **by and by** after a short time. **by the by** or **bye** *colloq.* while I think of it; incidentally. **by and large** generally; all things considered. **by oneself** **1** alone. **2** without anyone else's help. [from Anglo-Saxon *be*]

⊟ *prep* **1** near, next to, beside. **3** through, via, along, over. *adv.* **1** near, close, handy, at hand.

bye¹ or **by** *noun* **1** a pass to the next round of a competition given to a competitor or team that has not been given an opponent in the current round. **2** *Cricket* a run

scored from a ball which the batsman has not hit or touched. — **by the bye** see BY. [from BY]

bye² or **bye-bye** *interj. colloq.* goodbye.

bye-law same as BY-LAW.

by-election *noun* an election during the sitting of parliament to fill a seat which has become empty because the member has died or resigned.

bygone — *adj.* past, former. — *noun* (*usually* **bygones**) a past event or argument. — **let bygones be bygones** to agree to forget past disagreements.

by-law or **bye-law** *noun* a law or rule made by a local authority. [from Norse *byjar-log*, town law]

byline *noun* a line under the title of a newspaper or magazine article which has the author's name on it.

byname *noun* another name by which a person is known; a nickname.

bypass — *noun* **1** a road which avoids a busy area or town. **2** a channel, pipe, etc which carries gas, electricity, etc when the main channel is blocked. **3** an electrical circuit that carries current around one or more circuit components instead of through them. **4** the redirection of blood flow so as to avoid a blocked or diseased blood vessel, especially a coronary artery, usually by grafting a blood vessel taken from another part of the body, such as the patient's leg. — *verb* **1** to avoid (a place) by taking a road which goes around it or avoids it. **2** to leave out (a step in a process) or ignore and not discuss something with (a person). **3** to provide with a bypass.

⊟ *noun* **1** ring road, detour, diversion. *verb* **1** avoid, skirt, circumvent, dodge, sidestep. **2** ignore, neglect, omit.

by-play *noun* less important action happening at the same time as the main action.

by-product *noun* **1** a secondary product that is formed at the same time as the main product during a chemical reaction or manufacturing process. By-products of industrial processes are often commercially important. **2** an unexpected, extra result; a side effect.

⊟ **2** side effect, fallout, repercussion, after-effect, consequence, result.

byre /baɪə(r)/ *noun Scot.* a cowshed. [from Anglo-Saxon *byre*, stall, shed]

byroad or **byway** *noun* a minor road.

bystander *noun* a person who watches but does not take part in what is happening.

⊟ spectator, onlooker, looker-on, watcher, observer, witness, eyewitness, passer-by.

byte or **bite** *noun* (ABBREV. **B**) **1** *Comput.* a group of adjacent binary digits (bits) that are handled as a single unit. It usually consists of eight bits, representing one alphanumerical character or two decimal digits. **2** the amount of storage space occupied by such a group.

byway same as BYROAD.

byword *noun* a person or thing well known as an example of something: *a byword for luxury.*

Byzantine /ˈbɪzəntaɪn, bɪˈzæntaɪn/ — *adj.* **1** relating to Byzantium (now Istanbul in Turkey) or the eastern part of the Roman Empire from AD395 to 1453. **2** of the style of architecture or painting developed by the Byzantine Empire, with domes, arches, mosaics, etc. **3** secret; complex and impenetrable. — *noun* an inhabitant of Byzantium. [from Latin *byzantinus*]

C

C¹ or **c** *noun* (PL. **Cs, C's, c's**) **1** the third letter of the English alphabet. **2** (*usually* **C**) the third highest grade or quality, or a mark indicating this. **3** (**C**) *Mus.* the note on which the Western system of music is based. **4** a musical key with the note C as its base.

C² *abbrev.* **1** Celsius. **2** centigrade. **3** century: *C19.* **4** *as an international vehicle mark* Cuba.

C³ *symbol* **1** the Roman numeral for 100. **2** *Chem.* carbon.

c *abbrev.* **1** centi-. **2** cubic. **3** *Physics* the speed of light.

c. *abbrev.* **1** *Cricket* caught. **2** cent. **3** century. **4** *circa* (Latin), approximately. **5** chapter.

© *symbol* copyright.

CA *abbrev.* **1** California. **2** Chartered Accountant.

Ca *symbol Chem.* calcium.

CAA *abbrev.* Civil Aviation Authority.

CAB *abbrev.* **1** Civil Aeronautics Board (USA). **2** Citizens Advice Bureaux.

cab *noun* **1** a taxi. **2** the driver's compartment in a lorry, railway engine, etc. **3** *Hist.* a carriage for hire, pulled by a horse. [short for CABRIOLET]

cabal /kə'bal/ *noun* **1** a small group formed within a larger body, for secret, especially political, discussion, planning, etc. **2** a political plot or conspiracy. [from French *cabale*, from Hebrew *qabbalah*, tradition]

cabaret /'kabəreɪ/ *noun* **1** an entertainment with songs, dancing, etc at a restaurant or nightclub. **2** a restaurant or nightclub providing this. [from French *cabaret*, tavern]

cabbage *noun* **1** any of several varieties of a leafy biennial plant (*Brassica oleracea*), grown for its compact head of edible leaves, which are usually green, although in some varieties they are white or red. **2** the leaves of this plant, which can be cooked, eaten raw in salads, or pickled. **3** *derog.* a dull inactive person. **4** *offensive* a person so severely brain-damaged or mentally subnormal as to be completely dependent on other people for survival. [from French *caboche*, head]

cabbage-white butterfly a large butterfly, found in Europe and N Africa, and having wings that are mainly white with black markings, and yellow on the undersides of the hind wings. The caterpillars are pests of plants belonging to the cabbage family (Cruciferae).

cabby or **cabbie** *noun* (PL. **cabbies**) *colloq.* a taxi-driver. [from CAB]

caber *noun Athletics* in the contest of *tossing the caber*, a heavy wooden pole, c.3-4m in length, that must be carried upright and then tipped end over end. [from Gaelic *cabar*, pole]

cabin *noun* **1** a small house, especially made of wood. **2** a small room on a ship for living, sleeping or working in. **3** the passenger section of a plane. **4** the section at the front of a plane for pilot and crew. **5** the driving compartment of a large commercial vehicle; the cab. [from French *cabane*, cabin]

⊟ **1** hut, shack, shanty, lodge, chalet, cottage, shed, shelter. **2** berth, quarters, compartment, room.

cabin boy *Hist.* a boy who serves officers and passengers on board ship.

cabin crew the members of an aircraft crew who attend to the passengers.

cabin cruiser a large, especially luxurious, power-driven boat with living and sleeping accommodation.

cabinet *noun* **1** a piece of furniture with shelves and doors, for storing or displaying things. **2** the casing round a television set, music centre, etc. **3** (*also* **Cabinet**) the group of ministers in charge of the various departments of government who meet regularly for discussion with the prime minister. [diminutive of CABIN]

⊟ **1** cupboard, closet, dresser, locker. **2** casing, case.

cabinet-maker *noun* a skilled maker and repairer of fine furniture.

cabinet-making *noun* the occupation or skills of a cabinet-maker.

cabinet minister *Politics* in the UK, a senior government minister with responsibility for a particular government department who is also a member of the policy- and decision-making council chaired by the prime minister. Not all government ministers are members of the cabinet.

cabinet picture a small easel painting, carefully executed in minute detail, intended for close viewing and suitable for display in a small private room; a speciality of the 17c Dutch masters.

cable — *noun* **1** a strong wire cord or rope used for supporting loads, lifting, hauling, towing, etc, or for attaching a ship or boat to its mooring. **2** two or more electrical wires bound together but separated from each other by insulating material, and covered by a protective outer sheath, used to carry electricity, telephone messages, television signals, etc. **3** *Naut.* a measure of length or depth, about 600 ft (220 m). **4** a telegram sent by cable. **5** (*in full* **cable stitch**) a pattern in knitting that looks like twisted cable. — *verb intrans., trans.* to send a cable, or send (a message) to (a person) by cable. [from Latin *caplum*, halter]

⊟ *noun* **1** line, rope, cord, chain, wire. **2** flex, lead, wire, line. **4** telegram, wire, *Brit. trademark* Telemessage.

cable car a small box-shaped vehicle suspended from a continuous moving cable, for carrying passengers up or down a steep mountain, across a valley, etc.

cablegram *noun* same as CABLE *noun* 4.

cable television or **cable TV** or **cablevision** a television broadcasting system in which signals are relayed directly to individual subscribers by means of underground or overhead cables, instead of being broadcast by radio waves and received by an aerial.

caboodle /kə'bu:dl/ — **the whole caboodle** *colloq.* the whole lot; everything. [originally US; perhaps from *boodle*, collection]

caboose *noun* **1** *North Amer.* a guard's van on a railway train. **2** *Naut.* a ship's galley or kitchen. [from Dutch *cabuse*, ship's galley]

cabriole *noun* a furniture leg ornamentally curved to resemble an animal's leg. [from French *cabriole*, goat-like leap]

cabriolet /kabrıoʊ'leı/ *noun* **1** *Hist.* a light two-wheeled carriage drawn by one horse. **2** a car with a folding roof. [from French *cabriole*, goat-like leap]

cacao /kə'kɑːoʊ/ *noun* **1** a small evergreen tree (Theobroma cacao), native to S and Central America, and widely cultivated in other tropical regions. It has oblong leaves and pink flowers borne in clusters directly on trunks and older branches. The fruit is a yellow leathery grooved pod, enclosing up to 60 seeds embedded in soft pink pulp. **2** the edible seed of this tree. [from Spanish, from Aztec *cacauatl*, cacao tree]

cache /kaʃ/ — *noun* **1** a hiding-place, eg for weapons. **2** a collection of hidden things. — *verb* to put or collect in a cache. [from French *cacher*, to hide]

cache memory *Comput.* an extremely fast part of the main store of computer memory, often used to execute instructions.

cachet /'kaʃeı/ *noun* **1** something that brings one respect or admiration; a distinction. **2** a distinguishing mark. **3** an official seal. **4** a special commemorative postmark. **5** *old medical use* a small edible container for a pill, etc. [from French *cachet*, something compressed]

cachexia /ka'kɛksıə/ *noun Medicine* a condition characterized by physical weakness, abnormally low body weight, and general ill health, usually associated with a chronic disease such as cancer or tuberculosis. [from Greek *kachexia*, from *kakos* bad, *hexis* condition]

cack-handed *adj. colloq.* **1** clumsy; awkward. **2** left-handed. [from dialect *cack*, excrement]

cackle — *noun* **1** the sound that a hen or goose makes. **2** *derog.* a laugh like this. **3** shrill, silly chatter. — *verb intrans.* **1** to laugh with a hen-like sound. **2** to chatter shrilly. — **cut the cackle** *colloq.* to stop meaningless talk and come to the point. [imitative]

CACM *abbrev.* Central American Common Market.

cacophonous /kə'kɒfənəs/ *adj.* harsh, jarring.

cacophony /kə'kɒfənı/ *noun* a disagreeable combination of loud noises. [from Greek *kakos*, bad + *phone*, sound]

cactus *noun* (PL. **cacti, cactuses**) any member of a large family of mostly spiny plants (the Cactaceae), almost all of which are confined to the arid deserts of N and Central America. Miniature cacti are grown as house plants. [from Greek *kaktos*, prickly plant in Sicily]

CAD *abbrev.* computer-aided design.

cad *noun old derog. use* a man who behaves discourteously or dishonourably. [short for *caddie*, odd-job man]

cadaver /kə'dɑːvə(r)/ *noun* a dead body, especially a human one. [from Latin *cadaver*]

cadaverous /kə'davərəs/ *adj.* corpse-like in appearance; pale and gaunt.

caddie or **caddy** — *noun* (PL. **caddies**) a person whose job is to carry the golf clubs for a golf-player. — *verb intrans.* (**caddies, caddied, caddying**) (**caddie for someone**) to act as their caddy. [originally Scot., from French *cadet*, cadet]

caddis fly a small or medium-sized moth-like insect with brown or black wings covered with fine hairs. Caddis-fly larvae are found in ponds and streams, each larva building itself a protective cylindrical case consisting of sand grains, fragments of shell, small pieces of twig, and leaf fragments.

caddish *adj.* dishonourable, ungentlemanly.

caddy [1] *noun* (PL. **caddies**) a small container for tea leaves. [from Malay *kati*, a unit of weight]

caddy [2] see CADDIE.

cadence /'keɪdəns/ *noun* **1** a fall of pitch in the voice. **2** the rising and falling of the voice in speaking. **3** rhythm or beat. **4** a pattern of notes that closes a musical passage. [from French *cadence*, from Latin *cadere*, to fall]

cadenza /kə'dɛnzə/ *noun* an elaborate variation played by a solo musician at the end of a concerto movement, etc. [from Italian *cadenza*, from Latin *cadere*, to fall]

cadet /kə'dɛt/ *noun* **1** a student at a military, naval or police training school. **2** a schoolboy or schoolgirl training in a cadet corps. [from French dialect *capdet*, chief]

cadet corps in some schools, a group of pupils organized into a unit for military training.

cadge *verb trans., intrans. derog.* (**cadge something from** or **off someone**) to get it by begging or scrounging.

🔲 scrounge, sponge, beg.

cadger *noun* a scrounger or sponger.

cadi /'kɑːdı/ or **kadi** *noun* a judge in Muslim countries. [from Arabic *qadi*, judge]

cadmium *noun Chem.* (SYMBOL **Cd**, ATOMIC NUMBER **48**) a soft bluish-white metal used in alloys with low melting points, and as a corrosion-resistant plating, a component of control rods in nuclear reactors, and in nickel-cadmium batteries. Cadmium compounds, the soluble forms of which are highly toxic, are used as yellow and red pigments, and as phosphorescent coatings in television tubes. [from Greek *kadmeia*, calamine]

cadre /'kɑːdə(r)/ *noun* **1** a basic, highly trained military unit that can be expanded in emergencies. **2** an inner group of politically active people, eg within the Communist party. **3** a member of a cadre. [from French *cadre*, framework]

CAE *abbrev.* **1** College of Advanced Education. **2** *Comput.* computer-aided engineering, the use of computers to replace the manual control of machine tools by automatic control in order to increase accuracy and efficiency.

caecal /'siːkəl/ *adj.* relating to or in the region of the caecum.

caecilian /siː'sılıən/ *noun* an amphibian found in tropical regions worldwide, up to 1.5m in length, and having a worm-like body with encircling rings and no legs. Some species have fish-like scales. It burrows into forest floors or river beds, and feeds on invertebrates. [from Latin *caecus*, blind]

caecum /'siːkəm, 'kaɪkʊm/ *noun* (PL. **caeca**) *Anat.* the blind-ended pouch, to the lower end of which the appendix is attached, at the junction of the small and large intestines. [from Latin *intestinum caecum*, blind-ended intestine]

Caenozoic /siːnoʊ'zoʊɪk/ same as CENOZOIC.

caesarean /sɪ'zɛərıən/ *noun* (*in full* **caesarean section**) *Medicine* a surgical operation in which a baby is delivered through an incision in the lower abdomen. It is usually performed when normal delivery through the vagina would place the mother or baby at risk. [from the name of Julius Caesar, who was said to have been delivered by this method]

caesium /'siːzıəm/ *noun Chem.* (SYMBOL **Cs**, ATOMIC NUMBER **55**) a soft silvery-white metal formed by the fission of uranium, and used in photoelectric cells and certain optical instruments. The radioactive isotope caesium-137 is used in radiotherapy to treat cancer. [from Latin *caesius*, bluish-grey]

caesura /sɪ'zjʊərə/ *noun* a pause in a line of poetry, usually in the middle of it. [from Latin *caedere*, to cut]

café or **cafe** /'kafeı/ *noun* a usually small restaurant serving meals or snacks. [from French *café*, coffee, coffee house]

🔲 coffee shop, teashop, tearoom, coffee bar, cafeteria, snack bar, bistro, brasserie, restaurant.

cafeteria /kafə'tıərıə/ *noun* a self-service restaurant. [from Spanish *cafeteria*, coffee shop]

cafetière /kafə'tjɛə/ *noun* a coffee-pot with a plunger mechanism for separating the grounds from the liquid. [from French]

caffeine /'kafiːn/ *noun Biochem.* an alkaloid with a bitter taste, found in coffee beans, tea leaves, and kola nuts. It is a stimulant of the central nervous system and a diuretic. [from French *caféine*, from *café*, coffee]

caftan or **kaftan** /'kaftan/ *noun* **1** a long loose-fitting garment worn by men in Middle Eastern countries. **2** a similarly shaped garment worn as a dress by Western women. [from Turkish *qaftan*]

cage — *noun* **1** a container with bars, etc, in which to keep captive birds or animals. **2** a lift for taking mineworkers up and down a shaft in a mine. **3** any structure or framework something like a bird's or animal's cage: *the ribcage.* — *verb* to put in a cage. — **cage someone in 1** to imprison or confine them. **2** to limit their freedom of action; to inhibit them. [from French *cage*, from Latin *cavea*, hollow place]

. . . .
⊟ *noun* **1** aviary, coop, hutch, enclosure, pen, pound, corral.
cage in 1 encage, confine, imprison, lock up, shut up, coop up, fence in, impound, incarcerate. **2** limit, inhibit, restrict, restrain, confine, fence in.
⊟ **1** release, let out, free.
. . . .

cagebird *noun* a bird, eg a canary, suitable for keeping in a cage.

caged *adj.* kept in a cage.

cagey *adj.* (**cagier, cagiest**) *colloq.* not speaking frankly and openly; secretive and cautious. [possibly from CAGE]

cagily *adv.* with a cagey manner.

caginess *noun* secretiveness, wariness.

cagoule /kəˈguːl/ *noun* a light waterproof hooded outer garment, especially one that is made of thin nylon, is pulled over over the head, and reaches down to the knees. [from French *cagoule*, hood]

cahoots /kəˈhuːts/ — **in cahoots with someone** *colloq.*, *usually derog.* working in close partnership with them, especially in the planning of something unlawful.

caiman /ˈkeɪmən/ see CAYMAN.

Cainozoic /kaɪnoʊˈzoʊɪk/ same as CENOZOIC. [from Greek *kainos*, new + *zoe*, life]

caique /kɑːˈiːk/ *noun* **1** a light narrow boat propelled by one or two oars and used in Turkish waters, particularly on the Bosporus. **2** any small rowing boat, skiff, or lateen-rigged sailing vessel of the Levant (including modern motorized versions), used mainly for island trade. [from French, from Turkish *kaik*, a boat]

cairn[1] *noun* a heap of stones piled up to mark eg a grave or pathway. [from Gaelic *carn*]

cairn[2] *noun* (*in full* **cairn terrier**) a small breed of dog with short legs, a thick shaggy brown coat, and erect ears, developed in Scotland and formerly used for flushing foxes out of their burrows. [from Gaelic *carn*, cairn; the dogs were believed to come from rocky areas]

cairngorm *noun Geol.* a yellow or smoky brown variety of the mineral quartz, often used as a gemstone, and so called because the Cairngorms, a group of mountains in Scotland, are among the places where it occurs. [from Gaelic *carn gorm*, blue cairn]

caisson /ˈkeɪsən/ *noun* a watertight rectangular or cylindrical chamber used to protect construction workers during the building of underwater foundations, bridges, piers, etc. [from French *caisson*, large box]

caisson disease same as DECOMPRESSION SICKNESS.

cajole /kəˈdʒoʊl/ *verb* (**cajole someone into something**) to use flattery, promises, etc to persuade them to do something. [from French *cajoler*, to coax]

. . . .
⊟ coax, persuade, wheedle, flatter, *colloq.* sweet-talk, *colloq.* butter up, tempt, lure, seduce, entice, beguile, mislead, dupe.
⊟ bully, force, compel.
. . . .

cajolery *noun* coaxing, flattery, wheedling.

cake — *noun* **1** a solid food made by baking a mixture of flour, fat, eggs, sugar, etc. **2** an individually baked portion of this food. **3** a portion of some other food pressed into a particular shape. **4** a solid block of soap, etc. — *verb* **1** *intrans.* to dry as a thick hard crust. **2** *trans.* to cover in a thick crust: *skin caked with blood.* — **piece of cake** *colloq.* a very easy task. **have one's cake and eat it** *colloq.* enjoy

the advantages of two alternatives, usually as an unattainable ideal when each excludes the other. **sell** or **go like hot cakes** *said especially of a new product* to be bought enthusiastically in large numbers. [from Norse *kaka*]

. . . .
⊟ *noun* **1** gâteau. **2** bun, fancy, madeleine. **4** lump, bar, block, slab, loaf, mass. *verb* **1** dry, harden, solidify, consolidate, coagulate, congeal, thicken. **2** coat, cover, encrust.
. . . .

cakehole *noun slang* the mouth.

cakewalk *noun* **1** a prancing march with intricate improvised steps once performed by Black Americans in competition for the prize of a cake. **2** a dance developed from this. **3** *colloq.* something accomplished with extreme ease. — *verb intrans.* **1** to perform a cakewalk. **2** to accomplish something with extreme ease.

Cal *abbrev.* California.

cal. *abbrev.* calorie.

calabash *noun* **1** (**calabash tree**) an evergreen tree (*Crescentia cujete*), native to tropical S America, that grows to a height of 12m and has clusters of lance-shaped leaves, and bell-shaped flowers that are borne directly on the trunk and branches. **2** a trailing or climbing vine (*Lagenaria siceraria*), native to warm regions of the Old World, and having white flowers and woody bottle-shaped fruits. **3** the dried, hollowed-out shell of one of these fruits, used as a bowl or water container. [from French *calebasse*]

calaboose /ˈkaləbuːs/ *North Amer. noun slang* a small local prison. [from Spanish *calabozo*, dungeon]

calabrese /kaləˈbreɪzeɪ, ˈkaləbriːs/ *noun* a type of green sprouting broccoli, eaten as a vegetable. [from Italian *calabrese*, Calabrian]

calamine /ˈkaləmaɪn/ *noun* **1** a fine pink powder or a solution of this containing zinc oxide and small amounts of ferric oxide, and used in the form of a lotion or ointment to soothe insect bites and stings, and to treat sunburn, eczema, and other skin complaints. **2** *North Amer.* zinc ore consisting mainly of zinc oxide. [from Latin *calamina*]

calamitous /kəˈlamɪtəs/ *adj.* disastrous, tragic, or dreadful.

. . . .
⊟ disastrous, catastrophic, ruinous, devastating, ghastly, dreadful, tragic, woeful, grievous, dire, deadly, fatal.
⊟ good, fortunate, happy.
. . . .

calamitously *adv.* so as to be calamitous.

calamity /kəˈlamɪtɪ/ *noun* (PL. **calamities**) a catastrophe, disaster or serious misfortune, causing great loss or damage. [from Latin *calamitas*, harm]

. . . .
⊟ catastrophe, disaster, mishap, misadventure, mischance, misfortune, adversity, reverse, trial, tribulation, affliction, distress, tragedy, ruin, downfall.
⊟ blessing, godsend.
. . . .

calcareous /kalˈkɛərɪəs/ *adj.* relating to, containing, or resembling calcium carbonate; chalky. [from Latin *calcarius*, from *calx*, lime]

calceolaria /kalsɪoʊˈlɛərɪə/ *noun* any of various annual and perennial plants and shrubs belonging to the genus Calceolaria, native to Central and S America, and having wrinkled leaves and characteristic two-lipped yellow, orange, or red spotted flowers, the lower lip being inflated and pouch-like. [from Latin *calceus*, shoe]

calcicole /ˈkalsɪkoʊl/ *noun Bot.* a plant that requires soil rich in lime or chalk. [from Latin *calx calcis*, lime, limestone + *colere*, to dwell]

calciferol /kalˈsɪfərɒl/ *noun* vitamin D$_2$. [from *calciferous*, calcium-carrying, as it increases the absorption of calcium, from Latin *calx*, lime]

calciferous /kalˈsɪfərəs/ *adj. Chem.* containing lime. [from Latin *calx calcis*, lime, limestone + *ferre*, to bear]

calcification /kalsɪfɪˈkeɪʃən/ *noun* the process of calcifying or becoming calcified; a conversion into lime.

calcifuge /'kalsɪfjuːd/ *noun Bot.* a plant that requires an acid soil with a low lime or chalk content. [from Latin *calx calcis*, lime, limestone + *fugere*, to flee]

calcify /'kalsɪfaɪ/ *verb trans., intrans.* (**calcifies, calcified**) **1** to harden as a result of the deposit of calcium salts. **2** to change or be changed into lime. [from CALCIUM + *-ify*]

calcite *noun Geol.* crystalline calcium carbonate, a white or colourless mineral that is the main constituent of limestone and marble rocks. [from Latin *calx*, lime]

calcium *noun* (SYMBOL **Ca**, ATOMIC NUMBER **20**) a soft silvery-white metal (an alkaline earth) that is the fifth most abundant element in the Earth's crust, occurring mainly in the form of calcium carbonate minerals such as chalk, limestone, and marble. [from Latin *calx*, lime]

calcium carbide *Chem.* (FORMULA **CaC₂**) a solid grey compound, formerly used to produce acetylene in acetylene lamps.

calcium carbonate *Chem.* (FORMULA **CaCO₃**) a white powder or colourless crystals, only slightly soluble in water, occurring naturally as limestone, marble, chalk, and various other sedimentary rocks, and also found in the bones and shells of animals. It is used in the smelting of iron ore to make steel, and in the manufacture of glass, cement, bleaching powder, white paints, antacids, and tooth powders.

calcium chloride *Chem.* (FORMULA **CaCl₂**) a white crystalline compound that absorbs moisture from the atmosphere and is used to dry gases, and as a de-icing agent.

calcium hydroxide *Chem.* (FORMULA **Ca(OH)₂**) a white crystalline powder that dissolves sparingly in water to give an alkaline solution known as limewater. It is used as a neutralizer for acid soil, and in the manufacture of mortar, cement, bleaching powder, whitewash, and water softeners. Also called SLAKED LIME.

calcium oxide *Chem.* (FORMULA **CaO**) a white crystalline powder, formed by heating limestone, which is used in mortar and cement, and as a neutralizer for acid soils. Also called QUICKLIME.

calcium phosphate *Chem.* (FORMULA **Ca₃(PO₄)₂**) a white crystalline salt that is essential for the formation of bones and teeth in animals, and for the healthy growth of plants. It occurs in the mineral apatite.

calcium sulphate *Chem.* (FORMULA **CaSO₄**) a white crystalline solid that occurs naturally as the mineral gypsum, and is used to make plaster of Paris, paint, paper, ceramics, and blackboard chalk. It causes permanent hardness of water.

calculable /'kalkjʊləbl/ *adj.* **1** capable of being calculated. **2** predictable.

calculably *adv.* in a calculable or predictable way.

calculate *verb* **1** to work out, find out, or estimate, especially by mathematical means. **2** (**calculate on something**) to make plans that depend on or take into consideration some probability or possibility, designed to, intended to, or likely to do something: *measures calculated to increase profits.* [from Latin *calculare*, to calculate]

. . . .
■ **1** compute, work out, count, enumerate, reckon, figure, determine, weigh, rate, value, estimate, gauge, judge. **2** plan, intend, aim, consider.
. . . .

calculated *adj.* intentional; deliberate: *a calculated insult.*

calculated risk a possibility of failure that has been taken into consideration before some action is taken.

calculating *adj. derog.* inclined to see other people, or situations, in terms of how one can use them to benefit oneself.

. . . .
■ crafty, cunning, sly, devious, scheming, designing, contriving, sharp, shrewd.
🔁 artless, naïve.
. . . .

calculatingly *adv.* in a calculating or scheming manner.

calculation *noun* **1** the act or process of calculating. **2** something estimated or calculated. **3** *derog.* the cold and deliberate use of people or situations to benefit oneself.

. . . .
■ **1** reckoning, figuring, planning, deliberation. **2** sum, computation, answer, result, estimate, forecast, judgement.
. . . .

calculator *noun* a small usually hand-held electronic device that is used to perform numerical calculations, especially addition, subtraction, multiplication, and division, and is usually also capable of more complex operations, such as statistical analysis of data.

calculus /'kalkjʊləs/ *noun* (PL. **calculi**) **1** *Maths.* the branch of mathematics concerned with the differentiation and integration of functions. **2** *Medicine* a hard mass or 'stone' consisting of calcium salts and other compounds (eg cholesterol) that forms within hollow body structures such as the kidney, urinary bladder, gallbladder, or bile ducts. [from Latin *calculus*, pebble, as formerly used in counting]

caldera /kal'dɛərə/ *noun Geol.* a large crater formed when the remains of a volcano subside down into a magma chamber that has been emptied during a violent eruption. The caldera may subsequently fill with water and become a *crater lake.* [from Spanish *caldera*, cauldron]

Caledonian /kalɪ'doʊnɪən/ — *adj.* concerning or belonging to Scotland. — *noun facetious* a Scot. [from Latin *Caledonia*, Scotland]

calendar *noun* **1** a booklet or chart, or an adjustable device, that shows the months and days of the year. **2** any system by which the beginning, length, and divisions of the year are fixed: *the Julian calendar.* **3** a timetable or list of important dates, events, appointments, etc. [from Latin *calendrium*, account book]

calender — *noun* a machine consisting of a vertical arrangement of heated rollers through which paper or cloth is passed in order to give it a smooth shiny finish. — *verb* (**calendered, calendering**) to give a smooth finish to (paper or cloth) by passing it through such a machine. [from French *calandre*, from Greek *kylindros*, cylinder, roller]

calends /'kaləndz/ *pl. noun* in the Roman calendar, the first day of the month. [from Latin *calendae*]

calf¹ *noun* (PL. **calves**) **1** the young of any bovine animal, especially domestic cattle. **2** the young of certain other mammals, such as the elephant and whale. **3** a large mass of ice that has broken off a glacier or an iceberg. **4** same as CALFSKIN. — **in calf** pregnant with a calf. [from Anglo-Saxon *cælf*]

calf² *noun* (PL. **calves**) the thick fleshy part of the back of the leg, below the knee. [from Norse *kálfi*]

calf love romantic love between adolescents, or the love of an adolescent for an older person.

calfskin *noun* leather made from the skin of a calf.

calibrate *verb* **1** to measure (the diameter of a gun barrel or tube). **2** to mark (a scale on a measuring instrument) so that it can be used to take readings in suitable units. **3** to determine (a correct value) by comparison with an accurate standard. [see CALIBRE]

calibrated airspeed *Aeron.* an airspeed value obtained from an airspeed indicator and corrected for instrument error but not for altitude. See also TRUE AIRSPEED.

calibration *noun* **1** the act of calibrating a measuring instrument by checking it against fixed standards and then marking a scale on it. **2** one of the individual marks on the scale of a measuring instrument. **3** any measurement that is made against a fixed standard.

calibre /'kalɪbə(r)/ *noun* **1** the internal diameter of a gun barrel or tube. **2** the outer diameter of a bullet, shell, or other projectile. **3** quality; standard; ability. [from French *calibre*, from Arabic *qalib*, mould]

. . . .
■ **1, 2** diameter, bore, gauge, size, measure. **3** quality, standard, merit, character, ability, capacity, faculty, stature, worth, distinction, talent, gifts, strength.
. . . .

calico *noun* (PL. **calicoes**) a kind of cotton cloth, usually plain white or in its natural, unbleached state. [from Calicut in India, from where the cloth was first brought]

Calif. *abbrev.* California.

californium /ˌkalɪˈfɔːnɪəm/ *noun Chem.* (SYMBOL **Cf**, ATOMIC NUMBER 98) a synthetic radioactive metal produced by bombarding curium-242 with alpha particles. One of its isotopes, californium-252, is produced in nuclear reactors, and is a strong neutron source. [from the name California, where the element was first made]

caliph /ˈkeɪlɪf, ˈkalɪf/ or **khalif** *noun* a Muslim civil and religious leader. [from Arabic *khalifah*, successor (of Mohammed)]

caliphate *noun* the rank of, or area ruled by, a caliph.

call — *verb* **1** *trans., intrans.* (*also* **call out**) to shout or speak loudly in order to attract attention or in announcing something. **2** to ask (someone) to come, especially with a shout. **3** to ask for a professional visit from. **4** to summon or invite. **5** *trans., intrans.* to telephone. **6** to waken. **7** *intrans.* to make a visit: *call at the grocer's*. **8** *intrans.* to stop at a place during a journey: *does the train call at York?* **9** to give a name to: *called her Mary / let's call this group A*. **10** to regard or consider (something) as: *I call that strange*. **11** to say or imply that (someone) is (something unpleasant): *are you calling me a liar?* **12** to summon or assemble people for (a meeting). **13** to announce or declare: *call an election*. **14** *intrans.* (**call for something**) to make a demand or appeal for it. **15** *trans., intrans.* to make a bid, or choose (a suit for trumps), in a card game. **16** *said of an umpire, etc* to judge (a ball) to be in or out of play. **17** *intrans., said of a bird, etc* to make its typical or characteristic sound. — *noun* **1** a shout or cry. **2** the cry of a bird or animal. **3** an invitation; a summons. **4** a demand, request, or appeal. **5** (**call on something**) a claim or demand for it: *too many calls on my time*. **6** a brief visit. **7** an act of contacting someone by telephone; a telephone conversation. **8** a need or reason: *not much call for Latin teachers*. **9** an act of waking someone, usually by arrangement. **10** a signal blown on a bugle, etc. **11** a feeling that one has been chosen to do a particular job; a vocation. **12** a player's turn to bid or choose trumps in a card game. **13** the decision of a referee, etc on whether a ball is in or out of play. **14** an instrument that imitates a bird's call. — **call back** to visit or telephone again. **call someone back** to contact them again or in return by telephone. **call collect** *North Amer., esp. US* to have the telephone call one is making charged to the receiver of the call; to reverse the charges. **call something down on someone** to try to inflict it on them as if from heaven. **call for something** or **someone 1** to require them. **2** to collect or fetch them. **call something forth** to elicit or evoke it. **call someone in** to invite or request their help. **call something in** to request the return of (eg library books, a batch of faulty products, etc). **call in on** or **in at someone** to visit them, usually briefly. **call something into question** to suggest reasons for doubting it. **call it a day** to decide to finish work, etc. **call something off 1** to cancel a meeting, arrangement, etc. **2** to order (a dog) to stop attacking (someone). **3** to give orders for (something) to be stopped: *call off the search*. **call on** or **upon someone 1** to visit them. **2** to appeal to them. **3** to request or invite them: *call on the secretary to read the minutes*. **call on something** to gather or summon up one's strength, courage, etc. **call people out 1** to instruct (workers) to strike. **2** to summon (eg the fire brigade, the army, etc) to help with an emergency, etc. **call round** to make an informal visit. **call something** or **someone to mind 1** to remember them. **2** to remind you of something. **call someone up 1** to conscript them into the armed forces. **2** *colloq.* to telephone them. **call something up** to cause (memories, images, etc) to come into the mind. **have first call on something** to have the right to (someone's help, attention, etc) before anyone else. **on call** *said of a doctor* available if needed, eg to deal with an emergency. **within call** close enough to hear if called. [from Anglo-Saxon *ceallian*]

· · · · · · · · · · · · · · · · · ·

▣ *verb* **1** shout, yell, roar, bellow, cry (out), exclaim. **2, 3, 4** summon, invite, bid. **5** telephone, phone, ring (up), contact.

6 waken, wake (up), awake, rouse. **7** drop in, call in. **9** name, christen, baptize, title, entitle, dub, style, term, label, designate. **10** consider, regard, think. **12** summon, convene, assemble, rally, muster, gather, collect. **14** demand, appeal for, request, ask for, order. *noun* **1** cry, shout, exclamation, yell, roar, scream. **2** cry, chirp, song. **3** invitation, summons, notification, order, command. **4** demand, request, appeal, plea, order, command, claim. **7** phone call, ring, *Brit. colloq.* bell, *colloq.* buzz, *colloq.* tinkle. **8** demand, need, occasion, cause, excuse, justification, reason, grounds, right. **call down** inflict, invoke. **call for 1** demand, require, need, necessitate, involve, entail, occasion, suggest. **2** fetch, collect, pick up. **call forth** elicit, evoke, invoke, summon. **call off 1, 3** cancel, drop, abandon, discontinue, break off. **call on 1** visit, drop in on. **2, 3** appeal to, entreat, ask, request, invite. **call to mind 1** remember, recall, recollect. **2** remind of, put in mind of. **call someone up 1** conscript, *North Amer., esp. US* draft, enlist, recruit. **2** telephone, phone, ring (up). **within call** within earshot.

· ·

call box a public telephone box.

caller *noun* a person visiting or making a telephone call.

call girl a prostitute with whom appointments are made by telephone.

calligrapher /kəˈlɪɡrəfə(r)/ or **calligraphist** *noun* a person skilled in calligraphy.

calligraphy /kəˈlɪɡrəfɪ/ *noun* **1** handwriting as an art. **2** beautiful, decorative handwriting. [from Greek *kallos*, beauty + *graphein*, to write]

calling *noun* **1** a trade or profession. **2** an urge to follow a particular profession, especially the ministry or one involving the care of other people.

· · · · · · · · · · · · · · · · · ·

▣ **1** trade, profession, career, occupation, job, vocation, mission, business, line, work, employment, field, province, pursuit. **2** vocation, mission.

· ·

calling card 1 *North Amer.* a card bearing one's name, etc that one leaves when calling at someone's house; a visiting card. **2** an unmistakable and usually disagreeable sign, especially deliberately left, that a particular person has been present.

calliper *noun* **1** (**callipers**) a measuring instrument with two prongs, resembling a large pair of geometrical dividers attached to a scale which is used to measure the linear distance between them, eg to determine the diameters of pipes. **2** a splint for supporting an injured or paralysed leg by keeping it rigid and taking most of the weight of the body. It consists of metal rods that extend from a metal plate under the foot to a padded ring surrounding the upper thigh. [another form of CALIBRE]

callisthenic /ˌkalɪsˈθɛnɪk/ *adj.* relating to or typical of callisthenics.

callisthenics *noun* a system of physical exercises for increasing the body's strength and grace. [from Greek *kallos*, beauty + *sthenos*, strength]

callosity /kaˈlɒsɪtɪ/ *noun* (PL. **callosities**) a callus. [from Latin *callositas*]

callous[1] /ˈkaləs/ *adj.* lacking any concern for others; unfeeling; coldly and deliberately cruel. [from Latin *callosus*, thick-skinned]

· · · · · · · · · · · · · · · · · ·

▣ heartless, hard-hearted, cold, indifferent, uncaring, unsympathetic, unfeeling, insensitive, hardened, thick-skinned, cruel.

▣ kind, caring, sympathetic, sensitive.

· ·

callous[2] /ˈkaləs/ SEE CALLUS.

callousness *noun* lack of feeling, brutality.

callow /ˈkaloʊ/ *adj. derog.* young and inexperienced. [from Anglo-Saxon *calu*, bald]

call sign or **call signal** a word, letter, or number that identifies a ship, plane, etc when communicating with another by radio.

call-up *noun* an order to join the armed forces as a conscript.

callus /ˈkaləs/ or **callous** *noun* **1** a thickened hardened pad of skin which develops on parts of the body that are subjected to constant friction or pressure, such as the palms of the hands and soles of the feet. **2** a mass of tissue, consisting of large thin-walled parenchyma cells, that forms around a wound on the surface of a plant. **3** a mass of blood and connective tissue that forms around the exposed ends of a fractured bone, and represents an important part of the healing process. [from Latin *callus*, hardened skin or tissue]

calm — *adj.* **1** relaxed and in control; not anxious, upset, angry, etc. **2** *said of the weather, etc* still, quiet, peaceful; not rough or stormy. — *noun* **1** peace, quiet, tranquillity. **2** stillness of weather. **3** a lack of sufficient wind for sailing. — *verb trans., intrans.* **1** (**calm down**) to become calmer. **2** (**calm someone** or **something down**) to make them calmer. [from French *calme*, from Greek *kauma*, (a rest during) the heat of noon]

. . . .

▣ *adj.* **1** composed, self-possessed, collected, cool, dispassionate, unemotional, impassive, unmoved, relaxed, placid, sedate, imperturbable, unflappable, unexcitable, *colloq.* laid back, unexcited, unruffled, unflustered, unperturbed, undisturbed, untroubled, unapprehensive. **2** still, windless, unclouded, mild, quiet, peaceful, tranquil, serene, uneventful, restful, smooth. *noun* **1**, **2** stillness, calmness, peace, quiet, tranquillity, serenity, peacefulness, hush. *verb* **1** quieten, compose oneself, relax, hush. **2** soothe, placate, pacify, hush, sedate, tranquillize.

▣ *adj.* **1** excitable, worried, anxious, upset, angry. **2** rough, wild, stormy. *noun* **1**, **2** restlessness, storminess. *verb* **2** excite, worry.

. . . .

calmly *adv.* with a calm manner.

calmness *noun* the quality or state of being calm.

Calor gas *trademark* a mixture of liquefied butane and propane gases, stored under pressure in metal cylinders, and used as a fuel supply for portable stoves, etc. [from Latin *calor*, heat]

calorie *noun* the amount of heat required to raise the temperature of one gram of water by 1°C (1K) at one atmospheric pressure. Also called SMALL CALORIE. See also KILOCALORIE. [from French, from Latin *calor*, heat]

calorific /kaləˈrɪfɪk/ *adj.* **1** of, relating to, or generating heat. **2** of or relating to calories. [from Latin *calorificus*, warming]

calorific value *Physics* the amount of heat liberated during the complete combustion of unit mass of a fuel or food.

calorimeter /kaləˈrɪmɪtə(r)/ *noun Chem.* an instrument for measuring the thermal properties of a substance, especially its calorific value. [from Latin *calor*, heat + -METER]

calque /kalk/ *noun* a loan translation, ie a compound word or phrase that is a literal translation of the parts of a foreign expression, as in the German word for 'telephone', *Fernsprecher* (= *fern*, distant + *Sprecher*, speaker). In English, *superman* is a calque of German *Übermensch*. [from Latin *calcare*, to tread]

calumniate /kəˈlʌmnɪeɪt/ *verb* to utter a calumny against (someone).

calumniator *noun* a person who utters calumny.

calumnious /kəˈlʌmnɪəs/ *adj.* of the nature of calumny; slanderous.

calumny /ˈkaləmnɪ/ *noun* (PL. **calumnies**) an untrue and malicious spoken statement about a person, or the act of uttering this. [from Latin *calumnia*, false accusation]

calve *verb intrans.* **1** to give birth to (a calf). **2** *said of a glacier or iceberg* to release (masses of ice) on breaking up.

calves pl. of CALF[1], CALF[2].

Calvinism *noun* the teachings of John Calvin, laying emphasis on mankind's inability to repent and believe in Christ without God's help, and on predestination (God's deciding in advance who will go to heaven and who will not).

Calvinist *noun* a follower of Calvinism.

Calvinistic *adj.* **1** relating to or typical of Calvinism. **2** following the doctrines of Calvinism.

calx /kalks/ *noun* (PL. **calxes**, **calces**) **1** the powdery metal oxide that remains after an ore has been roasted in air. **2** lime (calcium oxide). [from Latin *calx*, lime]

Calypso /kəˈlɪpsoʊ/ *Astron.* the fourteenth moon of Saturn, 30km in diameter, discovered in 1980.

calypso /kəˈlɪpsoʊ/ *noun* (PL. **calypsos**) a type of popular song invented in the West Indies, usually dealing with current happenings in an amusing way, and often made up by the singer as he or she goes along.

calyx /ˈkeɪlɪks, ˈkalɪks/ *noun* (PL. **calyces**, **calyxes**) *Bot.* the outermost whorl (circle) of a flower, consisting of the sepals, which are often green and leaf-like. The calyx encloses the petals, stamens, and carpels, and protects the developing flower bud. [from Greek *calyx*, covering, husk]

calzone /kaltˈsoʊne/ *noun* a folded round of pizza dough stuffed with a savoury filling. [from Italian *calzone*, trouser leg]

CAM *Comput.* computer-aided manufacture, the use of computers to control any part of a manufacturing process.

cam *noun Engineering* an irregular projection on a wheel or rotating shaft, shaped so as to transmit regular movement to another part, eg to operate the cylinder valves of a car engine. [from Dutch *kam*, comb]

camaraderie /kaməˈrɑːdərɪ/ *noun* a feeling of friendship and cheerful support for one another within a group or team of people. [from French *camaraderie*]

camber *noun* **1** a slight convexity on the upper surface of a road, ship's deck, wing section of an aeroplane, etc, designed to promote drainage of water. **2** to form (a slight convexity) on the upper surface of a structure or to give (a slight convexity) to such a surface. [from French *cambre*]

cambium *noun Bot.* in the roots and stems of woody plants, a layer of actively dividing cells between the xylem and the phloem, which produces an increase in lateral growth or girth. [from Latin *camire*, to exchange]

Cambrian *adj.* **1** *Geol.* relating to the earliest geological period of the Palaeozoic era, lasting from about 580 million to 505 million years ago. During this period there were widespread seas, and Cambrian rocks contain a large variety of marine invertebrate fossils, including trilobites, and primitive shellfish, corals, and crustaceans. **2** relating to rocks formed during this period. [from Latin *Cambria*, from Welsh *Cymru*, Wales]

cambric /ˈkambrɪk, ˈkeɪmbrɪk/ *noun* a fine white cotton or linen cloth. [from Cambrai, in N France, where the cloth was first made]

Cambs. *abbrev.* Cambridgeshire.

camcorder *noun* a portable video camera that is used to record images and sound as electronic signals on a small cassette of video tape. The tape can then be played back through a standard television receiver using a videocassette recorder that is incorporated within the camera. [a shortening of *camera video recorder*]

came see COME.

camel *noun* **1** a herbivorous (plant-eating) mammal belonging to the family Camelidae, standing up to 1.8m high at the shoulder, and having a long neck and legs, coarse hair, a tufted tail, and one or two humps on its back, which contain fat and serve as a food reserve. **2** the pale brown colour of this animal. [from Greek *kamelos*, from a Semitic source]

camelhair *noun* **1** a soft usually pale brown cloth made from camels' hair. **2** hair from a squirrel's tail used to make paintbrushes.

camellia /kəˈmiːlɪə, kəˈmɛlɪə/ *noun* **1** an evergreen shrub of the genus Camellia, native to SE Asia, but widely cultivated for its conspicuous white, pink, or crimson flowers and glossy dark green leaves. **2** the flower of this plant. [named after the I7c plant collector Josef Kamel]

Camembert /'kaməmbeə(r)/ *noun* a kind of soft white French cheese with a strong flavour and smell. [from Camembert in N France, where originally made]

cameo /'kamɪoʊ/ *noun* (PL. **cameos**) **1** a smooth rounded gemstone with a raised design, especially a head in profile, carved on it. See also INTAGLIO. **2** a piece of jewellery containing such a gemstone. **3** the design itself. **4** (*also* **cameo role**) a small part in a play or film performed by a well-known actor. **5** a short descriptive piece of writing. [from Italian *cammeo* or *cameo*]

camera[1] *noun* **1** an optical device that focuses light from an object on to light-sensitive film, in order to record the image as a photograph. **2** a device in a television broadcasting system that converts visual images into electrical signals for transmission. — **on camera** in front of the camera; being filmed. [from Latin *camera*, vaulted chamber]

camera[2] see IN CAMERA.

camera lucida /'luːsɪdə/ a mechanical aid used in drawing and painting, whereby an image is projected through a prism onto the paper, thus providing the artist with an accurate guide from which to work. It makes use of light reflected from a scene in the same way as the camera obscura, but has no 'chamber', and is operated in full daylight. [from Latin, = light chamber]

cameraman *noun* a person who operates a camera in television or film-making.

camera obscura /ɒbs'kjʊərə/ a darkened box or room with a small hole in one wall, through which light from outside can enter, pass through a lens, and form an inverted image of the scene outside, which is projected on to the opposite wall of the chamber. [from Latin *camera obscura*, dark chamber]

camera-shy *adj.* having a dislike of being photographed.

camiknickers /'kamɪnɪkəz/ *pl. noun* **1** loose-legged knickers for women, usually of a silky material. **2** a woman's undergarment consisting of a camisole and knickers combined.

camisole *noun* a woman's loose undergarment for the top half of the body with narrow shoulder straps. [from French *camisole*]

camomile or **chamomile** /'kaməmaɪl/ *noun* **1** a strongly scented perennial plant (Anthemis nobilis), native to Europe and SW Asia, having leaves divided into narrow fine-pointed segments, and daisy-like flower-heads consisting of outer white ray florets and inner yellow disc florets. **2** the dried crushed flowers or leaves of this plant, infused to make a popular herbal tea, and also used for their soothing medicinal properties or added to some types of shampoo. [from Greek *chamaimelon*, literally 'earth apple' (from its smell)]

camouflage /'kaməflɑːʒ/ — *noun* **1** any device or means of disguising or concealing a person or animal, or of deceiving an adversary, especially by adopting the colour, texture, etc, of natural surroundings or backgrounds. **2** the use of such methods to conceal or disguise the presence of military troops (including soldiers' uniforms), equipment, vehicles, or buildings, by imitating the colours of nature. **3** objects such as tree branches, undergrowth, etc, used to disguise military equipment, etc. **4** the colour pattern or other physical features that enable an animal to blend with its environment and so avoid detection by predators. — *verb* to disguise or conceal with some kind of camouflage. [from French *camouflage*, from *camoufler*, to disguise]

....

▣ *noun* **1** disguise, guise, masquerade, mask, cloak, screen, blind, front, cover, concealment, deception. **2** disguise, concealment, deception. *verb* disguise, mask, cloak, veil, screen, cover, conceal, hide, obscure.

▣ *verb* uncover, reveal.
....

camp[1] — *noun* **1** a piece of ground on which tents have been erected. **2** a collection of buildings, huts, tents, etc used as temporary accommodation or for short stays for a particular purpose. **3** a permanent site where troops are housed or trained. **4** *Archaeol.* an ancient fortified site. **5** a party or side in a dispute, etc; a group having a particular set of opinions, beliefs, etc. — *verb intrans.* to stay in a tent or tents, cooking meals in the open, etc. — **break camp** to take down tents, etc when leaving a campsite. **camp out 1** to live and sleep in the open, with or without a tent. **2** to stay in temporary accommodation with a minimum of furniture, equipment, etc. [from Latin *campus*, field]

camp[2] *derog. colloq.* — *adj.* **1** said of a man or his behaviour using mannerisms that are typically associated with women, especially in a deliberate, exaggerated, or theatrical way. **2** said of a man homosexual. **3** theatrical and exaggerated, especially amusingly so. — *noun* camp behaviour or style. — *verb* **1** *intrans.* to behave in a camp way. **2** (**camp something up**) to make it camp. — **camp it up** to behave in an exaggerated, theatrical way; to overact.

campaign /kam'peɪn/ — *noun* **1** an organized series of actions to gain support for or build up opposition to a particular practice, group, etc. **2** the operations of an army while fighting in a particular area or to achieve a particular goal or objective. — *verb intrans.* (**campaign for** or **against something**) to organize, or take part in, a campaign in support of or against something. [from French *campagne*, countryside, campaign]

....

▣ *noun* **1** crusade, movement, promotion, operation, drive, push, offensive. **2** offensive, attack, battle, expedition, operation. *verb* crusade, push, fight, battle.
....

campaigner *noun* **1** a person actively involved in a campaign. **2** an army veteran; someone who has served in several campaigns.

campanile /kampə'niːleɪ, 'kampənaɪl/ *noun* a bell tower standing by itself, ie not attached to a church, etc, found especially in Italy. [from Italian *campanile*, from Latin *campana*, bell]

campanologist *noun* a bell-ringer.

campanology *noun* **1** the art of bell-ringing. **2** the study of bells. [from Latin *campana*, bell + -LOGY]

campanula /kam'panjʊlə/ *noun* any of about 250 species of annual and perennial plants belonging to the genus Campanula, native to north temperate regions, and having very narrow to almost circular leaves, and bell-shaped flowers, usually blue but sometimes white or pink, borne either singly or in long flower-heads. Many frost-hardy species are cultivated as ornamental garden plants. Also called BELL-FLOWER. [diminutive of Latin *campana*, bell]

camp bed a light folding bed consisting of a metal or wooden frame with canvas stretched across it.

camper *noun* **1** a person who camps. **2** a motor vehicle equipped for sleeping in, with cooking and washing facilities, etc.

camp-follower *noun* **1** *derog.* a person who supports a particular group, party, etc only because it is fashionable. **2** a person who travels about with an army or other moving group in order to earn money eg as a prostitute or by doing odd jobs for them.

camphor *noun* (FORMULA $C_{10}H_{16}O$) a white or colourless crystalline compound with a strong aromatic odour, that occurs naturally in the leaves of an Asian evergreen tree (Cinnamomum camphora), and can also be manufactured artificially. It is used as a plasticizer in the manufacture of celluloid, as a medicinal liniment and inhalant, and as an insect repellent. [from Latin *camphora*]

camphorated *adj.* containing camphor.

camping *noun* living in a tent or makeshift accommodation, especially for recreation.

campion *noun* any of various annual or perennial plants belonging to the genus Silene, native to north temperate regions, especially the *red campion* (S.dioica) and *white campion* (S.alba), which have bright pink and white flowers respectively, and a tubular calyx. In both species the male and female flowers are borne on separate plants. [an old form of CHAMPION, translating *stephanomatikos*, part of the Greek name meaning 'for making champions' wreaths']

campsite *noun* a piece of land for camping on.

campus *noun* **1** the grounds of a college or university. **2** a university, or the university as an institution. **3** the academic world. — **on campus** within university premises or grounds. [from Latin *campus*, field]

Campylobacter /kampɪloʊ'baktə(r)/ *noun Biol.* a spiral-shaped Gram-negative bacterium of the genus Campylobacter, that occurs in the reproductive and digestive tracts of humans and animals, and can cause diarrhoea and gastritis (inflammation of the stomach lining) in humans, and genital diseases in cattle and sheep. [from Greek *kampylos* bent, *bacterion* a little rod (from its shape)]

CAMRA *abbrev.* Campaign for Real Ale.

camshaft *noun Engineering* a shaft to which one or more cams are attached.

Can. *abbrev.* **1** Canada. **2** Canadian.

can[1] *verb, aux.* **1** to be able to: *Can you lift that?* **2** to know how to: *Can he swim yet?* **3** to feel able to; to feel it right to: *How can you believe that?* **4** used to express surprise: *Can it really be that late?* **5** used to express a possibility: *The weather can change so quickly in the mountains.* **6** to have permission to: *Can I take an apple?* **7** used when asking for help, etc: *Can you give me the time?* See also CANNOT, CAN'T, COULD, COULDN'T. [from Anglo-Saxon *cunnan*, to know]

can[2] — *noun* **1** a sealed container, usually of tin plate or aluminium, for preventing bacterial contamination of preserved food, or for retaining the carbon dioxide in fizzy drinks. **2** a large container made of metal or another material, for holding liquids, eg oil, paint. **3** the amount a can will hold. **4** *slang* prison. **5** *North Amer. slang* a lavatory. — *verb* (**canned, canning**) to seal (food or drink) in metal containers in order to preserve it. — **carry the can** *colloq.* to take the blame. **in the can** *colloq.* completed; finished. [from Anglo-Saxon *canne*, pot, can]

Canada Day a public holiday in Canada (1 Jul), commemorating the anniversary of the union of the provinces in 1867 which created the Dominion of Canada.

Canada goose a goose native to N America, and introduced to Europe and New Zealand. It has a black head and neck and a white chin, and feeds on grass and water plants. It migrates, the females often returning to their birthplace to breed.

Canadian /kə'neɪdɪən/ — *noun* a native or citizen of Canada. — *adj.* relating or belonging to Canada.

canal /kə'nal/ *noun* **1** an artificial channel or waterway, usually constructed to allow shipping to pass between two adjacent bodies of water, but sometimes built to improve irrigation or drainage of a particular area of land. **2** *Anat.* any tubular channel or passage that conveys air, fluids, or semi-solid material from one part of the body to another, eg the alimentary canal. **3** *Astron.* any of the indistinct channel-like markings apparent on the surface of Mars when viewed through a telescope. [from Latin *canalis*, water pipe, channel]

canal boat a barge; a narrow boat.

canalization or **canalisation** /kanəlaɪ'zeɪʃən/ *noun* **1** the act or process of canalizing. **2** direction into a fixed channel.

canalize or **canalise** /'kanəlaɪz/ *verb* **1** to make or convert into an artificial channel or system of channels, especially to deepen, widen, or straighten (a river) in order to allow the passage of shipping or prevent flooding. **2** to guide or direct into a useful, practical, or profitable course.

canapé /'kanəpeɪ/ *noun* a type of food served at parties, etc consisting of a small piece of bread or toast spread or topped with something savoury. [from French *canapé*]

canard /'kanɑːd/ *noun* an untrue report or piece of news; a rumour, hoax, etc. [from French *canard*, duck]

canary /kə'neərɪ/ *noun* (PL. **canaries**) a small bird belong-

ing to the finch family, and native to the Canary Islands, the Azores, and Madeira, which has been bred to produce varieties with bright yellow plumage, although in the wild form it is usually green or grey. It is best known for its melodic song, and is very popular as a caged bird. [named after the Canary Islands]

canasta *noun* a card game played with two packs of cards, in which the aim is to collect sets of cards of the same value. [from Spanish *canasta*, basket, into which rejected cards were thrown]

cancan *noun* a lively dance originally from Paris, usually performed in the theatre by dancing girls, who execute high kicks, raising their skirts to reveal their petticoats, etc. [from French *cancan*]

cancel *verb* (**cancelled, cancelling**) **1** to stop (something already arranged) from taking place, by an official announcement, etc. **2** to stop (something in progress) from continuing. **3** *intrans.* to withdraw from an engagement, etc. **4** to tell a supplier that one no longer wants (something). **5** to put an end to (an existing arrangement, rule, law, etc). **6** to cross out, delete. **7** to put an official stamp on (eg a cheque or postage stamp) so that it cannot be reused. **8** *Maths.* to eliminate (common numbers or terms), especially to strike out (equal quantities) from opposite sides of an equation, or (common factors) from the numerator and denominator of a fraction. **9** *Comput.* to stop (a process) before or shortly after it has started. — **cancel something out** to remove the effect of it, by having an exactly opposite effect. [from Latin *cancellare*, to cross out]

▤ **1, 2** call off, abort, abandon, drop. **5** abolish, annul, quash, rescind, revoke, repeal, countermand, nullify. **6** delete, erase, obliterate, eliminate. **cancel out** offset, compensate, redeem, neutralize, nullify.

cancellation *noun* **1** cancelling. **2** something which has been cancelled, especially a theatre ticket which can then be transferred to another person.

Cancer *noun* **1** *Astron.* the Crab, a faint uniform constellation lying on the zodiac between Gemini and Leo. At its centre is a star cluster, Praesepe, which can be seen with the naked eye. **2** the Crab, the fourth sign of the zodiac. **3** a person born between 22 June and 22 July, under the sign of Cancer. [from Latin *cancer*, crab]

cancer *noun* **1** any form of malignant tumour that develops when the cells of a tissue or organ multiply in an uncontrolled manner. In contrast to benign tumours, malignant tumours invade and destroy the surrounding tissues, and may then spread to other parts of the body via the bloodstream or the lymphatic system. **2** one of these diseased areas. **3** an evil within an organization, community, etc that is gradually destroying it. See also ONCOGENE. [from Latin *cancer*, crab, cancerous growth]

▤ **1** tumour, growth, malignancy, carcinoma. **3** evil, blight, canker, pestilence, sickness, corruption, rot.

Cancerian /kan'sɪərɪən/ — *noun* a person born under the sign Cancer. — *adj.* relating to this sign.

cancerous *adj.* relating to or affected by cancer.

candela /kan'delə, kan'diːlə/ *noun* (SYMBOL **cd**) the SI unit of luminous intensity, equal to the luminous intensity in a given direction of a source that emits monochromatic radiation of frequency 540×10^{12} Hz and has a radiant intensity in that direction of 1/683 watts per steradian. [from Latin *candela*, candle]

candelabrum /kandə'lɑːbrəm/ *noun* (PL. **candelabra** sometimes used as a singular, **candelabrums**) a decorative candle-holder with branches for several candles. [from Latin *candela*, candle]

candid *adj.* **1** saying honestly and openly what one thinks; outspoken. **2** *colloq., said of a photograph* taken of someone without their knowledge so as to catch them unawares in an informal situation. [from Latin *candidus*, shining white, pure, honest]

● ●

▣ **1** frank, open, honest, truthful, sincere, outspoken, forthright, blunt, straightforward, unequivocal, ingenuous, guileless, simple, plain, clear.

▣ **1** guarded, evasive, devious.

● ●

candidacy /'kandɪdəsɪ/ or **candidature** /'kandɪdətʃə(r), 'kandɪdeɪtʃə(r)/ noun (PL. **candidacies**) the position or status of being a candidate.

candidate /'kandɪdət, 'kandɪdeɪt/ noun **1** a person who is competing with others for a job, prize, parliamentary seat, etc. **2** a person taking an examination. **3** a person or thing considered suitable for a particular purpose or likely to suffer a particular fate: *is a candidate for promotion.* [from Latin *candidatus*; Roman candidates always wore white (Latin *candidus*)]

● ● ● ● ● ● ● ● ● ● ● ● ● ● ● ● ● ● ●

▣ **1** applicant, aspirant, contender, contestant, competitor, entrant, runner, nominee, claimant, pretender, suitor. **2** entrant. **3** contender, possibility.

● ●

candidness noun being candid; honesty, frankness.

candied adj. preserved or encrusted with sugar; crystallized.

candle noun a stick or block of wax or (especially formerly) tallow, usually long and cylindrical in shape but sometimes more ornamental, containing a wick that is burnt to provide light. — **burn the candle at both ends** to exhaust oneself with work or activity from early morning till late in the night; to try to do too many things. **not fit or able to hold a candle to something** or **someone** to be noticeably inferior to them. **not worth the candle** *said of a task, etc* not worth the trouble and effort it would take. [from Latin *candela*]

candlelight noun the light given by a candle or candles.

candlelit adj. lit by candles.

Candlemas /'kandlməs/ noun a festival of the Christian church on 2 February celebrating the purification of the Virgin Mary after childbirth, at which candles are carried in procession. [from Anglo-Saxon *Candelmasse*, candle mass]

candlestick noun a holder for a candle.

candlewick noun a cotton fabric with a tufted surface formed by cut loops of thread, used for bedcovers, etc. [from the similarity of the thread used to a candle's wick]

can-do adj. colloq. denoting a willing and positive attitude.

candour noun the quality of being candid; frankness and honesty. [from Latin *candor*, purity, sincerity]

● ● ● ● ● ● ● ● ● ● ● ● ● ● ● ● ● ● ●

▣ frankness, openness, truthfulness, honesty, plain dealing, sincerity, straightforwardness, outspokenness, bluntness, directness, unequivocalness, ingenuousness, guilelessness, naïvety, artlessness, simplicity, plainness. evasiveness, deviousness.

● ●

candy — noun (PL. **candies**) North Amer. **1** a sweet. **2** sweets or confectionery. — verb **1** to reduce (sugar) to a crystalline form by boiling and evaporating slowly. **2** to preserve (fruit, peel, etc) by boiling in sugar or syrup. **3** to coat or encrust with sugar or candied sugar. [from Old French *sucre candi*, candied sugar, from Persian *qandi*, sugar]

candyfloss noun a fluffy mass of spun sugar usually coloured and served on a stick.

candy-striped adj. having a pattern of stripes, usually pink or red on a white background.

candytuft noun an annual or perennial evergreen plant of the genus *Iberis*, native to Europe and Asia, having narrow leaves and flattened heads of small white or mauve flowers. Several large-flowered species are cultivated as ornamental garden plants. [from Candia, in Crete, from where the plant was brought + TUFT]

cane — noun **1** the long jointed hollow or pithy stem of certain plants, especially various small palms (eg rattan) and larger grasses (eg bamboo and sugar cane). **2** same as SUGAR CANE. **3** the woody stem of a raspberry, blackberry, or loganberry plant. **4** a slender stick used as a support for plants, etc. **5** thin stems or strips cut from stems, eg of rattan, for weaving into baskets, etc. **6** a walking-stick. **7** a long slim stick for beating people as a punishment, or for supporting plants. — verb **1** to beat with a cane, as a punishment. **2** to construct or mend with cane. [from Greek *kanna*, reed]

cane-sugar noun Biochem. sucrose, especially that obtained from sugar-cane.

canful noun (PL. **canfuls**) the amount a can will hold.

canine /'keɪnaɪn/ — adj. **1** relating to or resembling a dog. **2** relating to the dog family in general, including wolves and foxes as well as the domestic dog. **3** relating to a canine tooth. — noun **1** any animal belonging to the dog family, especially a domestic dog. **2** a canine tooth. [from Latin *canis*, dog]

canine tooth in most mammals, any of the long sharp pointed teeth, two in each jaw, located between the incisors and premolars, and used for catching and killing prey and tearing flesh. Canine teeth are particularly well developed in carnivorous mammals, eg dogs. Also called EYE TOOTH.

caning noun **1** a beating with a cane. **2** colloq. a severe defeat or humiliation.

canister noun **1** a metal or plastic container for tea or other dry foods. **2** Mil. a metal cylinder filled with gas or metal shot, which explodes when thrown or fired. [from Latin *canistrum*, basket]

canker noun **1** a fungal, bacterial, or viral disease of trees and woody shrubs, eg fruit trees, in which hardened tissue forms over sunken or cracked dead areas on the bark or near a wound. The affected stem eventually dies. **2** ulceration of the lips, mouth, or tongue. **3** an ulcerous disease of animals that causes several conditions, eg inflammation and decay of the hooves of horses, inflammation of the ears of cats and dogs. **4** an evil, destructive influence, etc. [from Anglo-Saxon, from Latin *cancer*, crab, ulcer]

cankerous adj. corroding like a canker.

cannabis noun **1** a narcotic drug, prepared from the leaves and flowers of the hemp plant (Cannabis sativa), that produces euphoria or hallucinations when smoked or swallowed. Also called MARIJUANA, HASHISH, POT. **2** a common name for the hemp plant from which this drug is obtained. [from Greek *kannabis*, hemp]

cannabis resin a resin obtained from the dried leaves and flowers of the cannabis plant, and used to make hashish.

canned adj. **1** contained or preserved in cans. **2** slang drunk. **3** colloq. previously recorded.

cannelloni /kanə'loʊnɪ/ noun a kind of pasta in the form of large tubes, served with a filling of meat, cheese, etc. [from Italian *cannelloni*, from *cannello*, tube]

cannery noun (PL. **canneries**) a factory where goods are canned.

cannibal noun **1** a person who eats human flesh. **2** an animal that eats others of its own kind. [from Spanish *canibal*, from Caribes, the Caribs of the W Indies, once believed to be cannibals]

cannibalism noun the practice of eating human flesh.

cannibalistic /kanɪbə'lɪstɪk/ adj. relating to or practising cannibalism.

cannibalize or **cannibalise** verb colloq. to take parts from (a machine, vehicle, etc) for use in repairing another.

cannily adv. in a canny way.

canniness noun being canny.

cannon — noun (PL. **cannon, cannons**) **1** Hist. a large gun mounted on wheels. **2** a rapid-firing gun fitted to an aircraft or ship. **3** a stroke in billiards in which the cue ball strikes the other balls one after the other; a similar stroke in other related games. — verb **1** (**cannon into something**) to hit or collide with it while moving at speed. **2** (**cannon off something**) to hit with force and bounce off it. [from Old French *canon*, from Italian *cannone*, from *canna*, tube]

cannonade /kanə'neɪd/ *noun* a continuous bombardment by heavy guns. [from French *cannonnade*, from Italian *cannonata*, cannon shot]

cannonball *noun Hist.* a ball, usually of iron, for shooting from a cannon.

cannon fodder *colloq.* soldiers regarded merely as material to be sacrificed in war.

cannot /'kanət, 'kanɒt/ *verb, aux.* can not. See also CAN'T. — **cannot but** see CAN'T.

cannula or **canula** /'kanjʊlə/ *noun Medicine* a thin hollow tube that is used to remove fluid from body cavities. [from Latin, a diminutive of *canna*, reed]

canny *adj.* (**cannier, canniest**) **1** wise, clever, and alert, especially in business matters; shrewd. **2** careful; cautious. **3** *dialect, said of a person* nice; good. [from CAN[1], in the sense of 'to know how']

canoe /kə'nuː/ — *noun* a light narrow boat propelled by one or more single or double-bladed paddles by an occupant or occupants facing the direction of travel. — *verb intrans.* (**canoes, canoed, canoeing**) to travel by canoe. — **paddle one's own canoe** *colloq.* **1** to manage without other people's help. **2** to look after one's own affairs; to mind one's own business. [from Spanish *canoa*]

canoeing *noun* the sport or activity of paddling a canoe.

canoeist *noun* a person who canoes.

canon /'kanən/ *noun* **1** a basic law, rule, or principle. **2** a member of the clergy attached to a cathedral or, in the Church of England, a member of the clergy having special rights with regard to the election of bishops. **3** an officially accepted collection of eg religious writings, or of works considered to be by a particular writer. **4** in the Christian church, a list of saints. **5** a section of the Roman Catholic mass. **6** a piece of music similar to a round, in which a particular sequence is repeated, with a regular overlapping pattern, by different voices or instruments. [from Greek *kanon*, rod, rule; sense 2 via Anglo-Saxon *canonic*, from Latin *canonicus*, person under a monastic rule]

canonical /kə'nɒnɪkəl/ *adj.* **1** of the nature of, according to, or included in a canon. **2** regular. **3** orthodox or accepted. **4** ecclesiastical.

canonical hours *RC Church* set hours for prayer. See also COMPLINE, LAUDS, MATINS, NONE[2], SEXT, TERCE, VESPERS.

canonization or **canonisation** *noun* **1** the action of canonizing a saint. **2** being canonized.

canonize or **canonise** *verb* to declare (someone) officially to be a saint.

canon law the law of the Christian church.

canoodle /kə'nuːdl/ *verb intrans. colloq.* to hug and kiss; to cuddle.

can-opener *noun* a small tool for opening cans.

canopied *adj.* covered by or provided with a canopy.

canopy *noun* (PL. **canopies**) **1** a covering hung or held up over something or someone for shelter or ornament, or ceremonially. **2** a wide overhead covering. **3** *Archit.* a roof-like structure over an altar, recess, etc. **4** a transparent cover over the cockpit of an aeroplane. **5** *Bot.* the top layer of a wood or forest, consisting of the uppermost leaves and branches of trees. **6** the fabric part of a parachute, that opens like an umbrella. [from Latin *conopeum*, mosquito net]

∷∷∷∷∷∷∷∷∷∷∷∷∷∷∷∷
⊟ **1** awning, covering, shade, shelter, sunshade.
∷∷∷∷∷∷∷∷∷∷∷∷∷∷∷∷∷∷∷∷

canst *old use* the form of the verb **can** used in the 2nd person singular with **thou**.

cant[1] — *noun* **1** *derog.* insincere talk, especially with a false display of moral or religious principles. **2** the special slang or jargon of a particular group of people, eg thieves. — *verb intrans.* to talk in a preaching way. [from Latin *cantare*, to chant]

cant[2] — *noun* **1** a slope. **2** a jerk or toss that makes something tilt. **3** a sloping or tilting position or plane. — *verb trans., intrans.* to tilt, slope or tip up. [from Middle English *cant*, border, side]

can't /kɑːnt/ *contr.* cannot. — **one can't but** ... one has to ... or is obliged to: *you can't but admire her perseverance.*

Cantab. *abbrev.* Cantabrigiensis (Latin), belonging to Cambridge.

cantabile /kan'tɑːbɪleɪ/ *adj. Mus.* in an easy, flowing, melodious style. [from Italian *cantabile*, suitable for singing]

cantaloup /'kantəluːp/ or **cantaloupe** *noun* a large melon with a thick, ridged skin and orange-coloured flesh. [from French *cantaloup*, probably from Cantaluppi in Italy, where first cultivated in Europe]

cantankerous *adj.* bad-tempered; irritable.

∷∷∷∷∷∷∷∷∷∷∷∷∷∷∷∷∷∷
⊟ bad-tempered, irritable, irascible, grumpy, grouchy, crusty, *colloq.* crotchety, *colloq.* crabby, crabbed, testy, ill-humoured, peevish, difficult, perverse, contrary, quarrelsome, cross.
⊟ good-natured, *colloq.* easy-going.
∷∷∷∷∷∷∷∷∷∷∷∷∷∷∷∷∷∷∷∷∷

cantankerousness *noun* a bad-tempered or quarrelsome nature or state.

cantata *noun* a sung musical work, especially on a religious theme, with parts for chorus and soloists. [from Italian *cantata aria*, sung air]

canteen *noun* **1** a restaurant, especially a cafeteria, attached to a factory, office, etc for the use of employees. **2** a shop selling food and drink in an army camp, etc. **3** a case containing cutlery; a full set of knives, forks, spoons, etc. **4** a flask for water, etc carried by soldiers or campers. [from French *cantine*, a shop in a barracks, etc.]

canteen culture *derog.* an alleged attitude within the police force of resistance to change or progress.

canter — *noun* a horse-riding pace between trotting and galloping. — *verb intrans., trans.* (**cantered, cantering**) to move or cause to move at this pace. [originally Canterbury gallop, the pace used by the pilgrims riding to Canterbury in the Middle Ages]

canticle *noun* a hymn or chant with a text taken from the Bible. [from Latin *canticulum*, diminutive of *canticum*, song]

cantilever /'kantɪliːvə(r)/ *noun* **1** a beam or other support projecting from a wall to support a balcony, staircase, etc. **2** *Engineering* a beam that is securely fixed at one end and hangs freely at the other, although it may be supported at some point along its length. Cantilevers are widely used in structural engineering. [perhaps from CANT[2] + LEVER]

cantilever bridge a fixed bridge consisting of two outer spans that project towards one another and support a suspended central span, eg the Forth Road Bridge in Scotland.

canting *adj.* pretending to be religious; whining.

cantingly *adv.* with a canting manner.

canto *noun* (PL. **cantos**) a section of a long poem. [from Italian *canto*, song]

canton /'kantɒn, kan'tɒn/ *noun* a division of a country, especially one of the separately governed regions of Switzerland. [from Old French *canton*]

Cantonese /kantə'niːz/ — *noun* **1** the dialect of Chinese used in the Canton area of China. **2** (*sing., pl.*) a person or the people, belonging to Canton. — *adj.* belonging to Canton.

cantonment /kan'tɒnmənt/ *noun Hist.* a permanent military station in India.

cantor *noun* **1** a man who chants the liturgy and leads the congregation in prayer in a synagogue. **2** a person who leads the choir in a Christian church service. [from Latin *cantor*, singer]

canvas *noun* **1** a thick heavy coarse cloth used for sails, tents, etc and for painting pictures on. **2** a painting done on canvas, or a piece of canvas prepared for painting. **3** the sails of a ship. — **under canvas 1** in tents. **2** *Naut.* with sails spread. [from Anglo-Saxon *canevas*, from Latin *cannabis*, hemp]

canvass *verb* **1** *trans., intrans.* to ask for votes or support from (someone) for a person or proposal. **2** to find out the opinions of, on a particular matter. **3** to discuss or examine (a question) in detail. [from CANVAS in an old sense, to toss in a sheet, or to criticize severely]

....

🔢 **1** electioneer, campaign, solicit, ask for, seek, agitate. **2** poll, question. **3** discuss, debate, examine, inspect, scrutinize, study, scan, investigate, analyse, sift.

....

canvasser *noun* a person who canvasses opinions, etc.

canyon *noun* a deep gorge or ravine with steep sides, usually cut into the bedrock of arid and semi-arid regions by the action of a stream or river. [from Spanish *cañón*, tube, hollow]

....

🔢 gorge, ravine, gully, valley.

....

canyoning *noun* an extreme sport that involves coursing down rapidly flowing water in mountain gullies.

CAP *abbrev.* Common Agricultural Policy.

cap — *noun* **1** a hat with a flat or rounded crown and a peak, of any of various types, some worn as part of a uniform or issued to members of a team. **2** a small hat of any of various shapes, many worn as an indication of occupation, rank, etc. **3** (*usually in compounds*) a close-fitting hat of various sorts. **4** a lid, cover, or top, eg for a bottle or pen. **5** (*also* **percussion cap**) a little metal or paper case containing a small amount of gunpowder, that explodes when struck, used eg to make a noise in toy guns. **6** a protective or cosmetic covering fitted over a damaged or decayed tooth. **7** a covering or top layer: *icecap*. **8** the top or top part. **9** a person chosen for a team representing a country, etc, or the fact of being chosen for such a team. **10** (*also* **Dutch cap**) a contraceptive device consisting of a rubber cover that fits tightly over the woman's cervix (opening into the womb) and prevents the male sperm entering; a diaphragm. — *verb* (**capped**, **capping**) **1** to put a cap on, or cover the top or end of, with a cap. **2** to be or form the top of. **3** to choose for a team by awarding a cap to. **4** to do better than, improve on or outdo: *cap someone's achievement*. **5** to set an upper limit to (a tax), or to the tax-gathering powers of (a local authority). — **cap in hand** humbly. **if the cap fits, wear it** *colloq.* you can take the general criticism, etc personally if you think it applies to you. **set one's cap at someone** *old colloq. use, said of a woman to* make obvious efforts to attract a particular man. **to cap it all** *colloq.* as a final blow; to make matters worse. [from Anglo-Saxon *cæppe*, from Latin *cappa*, hooded cloak]

....

🔢 *noun* **1, 2** hat, skullcap, beret, tam-o'-shanter. *verb* **1, 2** top, cover. **4** exceed, surpass, transcend, better, improve on, beat, outdo, outstrip, eclipse, crown.

....

cap. *abbrev.* capital (letter).

capability /keɪpə'bɪlɪtɪ/ *noun* (PL. **capabilities**) **1** ability or efficiency. **2** a power or ability, often one that has not yet been made full use of.

....

🔢 ABILITY, CAPACITY, EFFICIENCY, PROFICIENCY, POWER, POTENTIAL, SKILL, COMPETENCE, FACILITY, FACULTY, MEANS, QUALIFICATION.
🔢 INABILITY, INCOMPETENCE.

capable *adj.* **1** (**capable of something**) having the ability or the personality for a task, objective, etc. **2** clever; able; efficient. [from French *capable*, from Latin *capabilis*]

....

🔢 ABLE, COMPETENT, QUALIFIED, EXPERIENCED, ACCOMPLISHED, SKILFUL, PROFICIENT, EFFICIENT, GIFTED, TALENTED, MASTERLY, CLEVER, INTELLIGENT, FITTED, SUITED.

🔢 INCAPABLE, INCOMPETENT, USELESS.

capably *adv.* in a capable way; ably.

capacious /kə'peɪʃəs/ *adj. formal* having plenty of room for holding things; large; roomy. [from Latin *capax*]

capaciously *adv.* in a capacious way; with plenty of room.

capaciousness *noun* plenty of space; roominess.

capacitance /kə'pasɪtəns/ *noun Electr.* the ability of the conductors in a capacitor to store electric charge. It is equal to the ratio of the stored charge on one of the conductors to the potential difference between them. The SI unit of capacitance is the farad.

capacitor /kə'pasɪtə(r)/ *noun Electr.* a device consisting of two conducting surfaces separated by a dielectric material (insulator), eg waxed paper, that can store energy in the form of electric charge. Capacitors can smooth the flow of an electric current and are used in electrical oscillators, eg in radio.

capacity /kə'pasɪtɪ/ *noun* (PL. **capacities**) **1** the amount that something can hold. **2** the amount that a factory, etc can produce. **3** (**capacity for something**) the ability or power to achieve it. **4** function; role. [from Latin *capacitas*, from *capax*, capable, roomy]

....

🔢 **1** volume, space, room, size, dimensions, magnitude, extent, compass, range, scope. **2** output, volume. **3** capability, ability, faculty, power, potential, competence, efficiency, skill, gift, talent, genius, cleverness, intelligence, aptitude, readiness. **4** role, function, position, office, post, appointment, job.

....

caparison /kə'parɪsən/ — *noun* **1** *Hist.* a decorative covering, harness, etc for a horse. **2** *formal* a fine set of clothes. — *verb* (**caparisoned**, **caparisoning**) **1** to put a caparison on. **2** *formal facetious* to dress up. [from Spanish *caparazón*, saddle cloth]

cape [1] *noun* **1** a short cloak. **2** an extra layer of cloth attached to the shoulders of a coat, etc. [from Latin *cappa*, hooded cloak]

....

🔢 **1** cloak, shawl, wrap, robe, poncho, coat.

....

cape [2] *noun* **1** a part of the coast that projects into the sea. **2** (**the Cape**) **a** the Cape of Good Hope, the most southerly part of Africa. **b** Cape Province in South Africa. [from Middle English *cap*, from Latin *caput*, head]

....

🔢 **1** headland, head, promontory, point, peninsula, ness.

....

Cape Coloured relating to the Coloured population of Cape Province in South Africa.

caper [1] — *verb intrans.* (**capered**, **capering**) to jump or dance about playfully. — *noun* **1** a playful jump. **2** *old use* a playful trick or joke. **3** *derog.* a scheme, activity, etc, especially something dishonest or illegal. [from Latin *caper*, goat]

caper [2] *noun* **1** a small deciduous spiny shrub (*Capparis spinosa*), native to S Europe, and having oval slightly fleshy leaves and conspicuous white or lilac flowers with four petals and a large number of long purple stamens. **2** a young flower bud of this plant, pickled in vinegar and used as a condiment. [from the earlier form *capers* (mistaken as a plural), from Greek *kapparis*]

capercaillie or **capercailzie** /kapə'keɪlɪ/ *noun* either of two species of large game bird native to Europe and N Asia, the male of which is dark grey with a blue-green sheen on its neck and breast, and the female of which is smaller, with speckled brown plumage. [from Gaelic *capull coille*, horse of the wood]

capillarity /kapɪ'larɪtɪ/ *noun* the phenomenon whereby a liquid such as water rises up a narrow tube placed in the liquid, caused by surface tension effects in which water molecules at the surface of the liquid are attracted to the solid molecules of the glass tube, and the liquid rises until its weight balances the surface tension. [from Latin *capillus*, hair]

capillary /kəˈpɪləri/ — *noun* (PL. **capillaries**) **1** a tube, usually made of glass, having a very small diameter. **2** in vertebrates, the narrowest type of blood vessel, many of which form a network connecting the arteries with the veins. The walls of capillaries are extremely thin, consisting of a single layer of cells through which nutrients, dissolved gases, and waste products can readily pass into and out of the surrounding tissues. — *adj.* **1** resembling a hair. **2** *said of a tube* having a very small diameter. **3** *Physics* of or relating to capillarity.

capita see PER CAPITA.

capital[1] — *noun* **1** the chief city of a country, usually where the government is based. **2** a capital letter. **3** the total amount of money or wealth possessed by a person or business, etc, especially when used to produce more wealth. — *adj.* **1** principal; chief. **2** *said of a letter of the alphabet* in its large form, as used eg at the beginnings of names and sentences. **3** *said of a crime* punished by death. **4** *Brit. old colloq. use* excellent. — **make capital out of something** to use a situation or circumstance to one's advantage. **with a capital A** or **B** or **C** (etc) in a very real or genuine sense: *poverty with a capital P.* [from Latin *capitalis*, from *caput*, head]

▣ *noun* **3** money, funds, finance, principal, cash, savings, investment(s), wealth, means, wherewithal, resources, assets, property, stock. *adj.* **1** principal, chief, main, primary, prime, first. **2** upper-case. **4** excellent, first-rate, splendid, *colloq.* super.

capital[2] *noun Archit.* the slab of stone, etc, usually ornamentally carved, that forms the top section of a column or pillar. [from Latin *capitellum*, diminutive of *caput*, head]

capital assets the things a person or company owns that could be sold to raise capital.

capital expenditure the money that a company, etc uses to buy equipment, buildings, etc.

capital gains money obtained from selling possessions.

capital gains tax (ABBREV. **CGT**) *Commerce* a UK tax on the profit or gain obtained by selling or exchanging an asset.

capital-intensive *adj., said of an industry, etc* needing a lot of capital to keep it going. See also LABOUR-INTENSIVE.

capitalism *noun* an economic system based on private rather than state ownership of businesses, factories, transport services, etc, with free competition and profit-making.

capitalist — *noun* **1** a person who believes in capitalism. **2** *derog.* a wealthy person, especially one who is obviously making a great deal of personal profit from business, etc. — *adj.* believing in capitalism.

capitalistic *adj.* relating to or typical of capitalism or capitalists.

capitalization or **capitalisation** *noun* the action or process of capitalizing.

capitalize or **capitalise** *verb* **1** to write with a capital letter or in capital letters. **2** to sell (property, etc) in order to raise money. **3** to supply (a business, etc) with needed capital. **4** (**capitalize on something**) to exploit an asset, achievement, etc to one's advantage.

▣ **4** profit from, take advantage of, exploit, *colloq.* cash in on.

capitally *adv. Brit. old colloq. use* in a capital or excellent way.

capital punishment punishment of a crime by death.

capital sum a sum of money paid all at once, eg to someone insured.

capital transfer tax in the UK, a tax payable on gifts of money or property over a certain value.

capitation *noun* a tax of so much paid per person. [from Latin *capitatio*, poll tax, from *caput*, head]

capitulate /kəˈpɪtjʊleɪt/ *verb intrans.* **1** to surrender formally, usually on agreed conditions. **2** to give in to argument or persuasion. [from Latin *capitulare*, to set out (conditions) under headings]

▣ SURRENDER, YIELD, GIVE IN, SUBMIT, RELENT, SUCCUMB, *colloq.* THROW IN THE TOWEL.
▣ FIGHT ON.

capitulation *noun* surrender.

caplet *noun* a small, solid, usually oval medicinal pill. [from CAPSULE + TABLET]

capon /ˈkeɪpən/ *noun* a male chicken that has been castrated, usually by implantation of pellets of female sex hormone rather than by surgical methods, in order to increase the tenderness of its flesh and fatten it for eating. [from Latin *capo*]

cappuccino /kapʊˈtʃiːnoʊ/ *noun* (PL. **cappuccinos**) coffee with frothy hot milk and usually chocolate powder on top. [from Italian *cappuccino*]

capriccio /kaˈprɪtʃɪoʊ/ *noun* (PL. **capricci**, **capriccios**) **1** *Art* a picture or print depicting a scene or incident that is a product of the artist's imagination. **2** *Mus.* a free composition, not keeping to the rules of any particular form. [from Italian *capriccio*, fancy]

caprice /kəˈpriːs/ *noun* **1** a sudden and unexplained change of mood or behaviour. **2** a sudden strange wish or desire. **3** the tendency to have caprices. **4** *Mus.* a lively composition in an original style. [from French *caprice*, from Italian *capriccio*, fancy]

capricious /kəˈprɪʃəs/ *adj.* often changing one's mind for no good reason; changeable in behaviour, mood or opinion. [from Italian *capriccioso*, wayward, fanciful]

Capricorn *noun* **1** (*also* **Capricornus**) *Astron.* the Sea Goat, a large but dim zodiacal constellation lying between Sagittarius and Aquarius. **2** the Goat, the tenth sign of the zodiac. **3** a person born between 23 December and 19 January, under the sign of Capricorn. [from Latin *caper*, goat + *cornu*, horn]

Capricornian /kaprɪˈkɔːnɪən/ — *noun* a person born under the sign Capricorn. — *adj.* relating to this sign.

caps. *abbrev.* capital letters.

capsicum *noun* **1** any of various tropical shrubs of the genus Capsicum (see PEPPER). **2** the red, green, or yellow fruit of this plant, which has a hollow seedy interior. It is eaten raw in salads when green and unripe, or cooked as a vegetable. The powdered dried fruit is used to make cayenne pepper. [probably from Latin *capsa*, box, case]

capsizable /kapˈsaɪzəbl/ *adj.* capable of being capsized.

capsize *verb* **1** *intrans.*, *usually said of a boat* to tip over completely; to overturn. **2** *trans.* to cause (a boat) to capsize.

▣ OVERTURN, TURN OVER, TIP OVER, INVERT. **1** turn turtle, keel over. **2** upset.

capstan *noun* **1** an upright mechanical device consisting of a cylindrical barrel turned by levers, bars, or a motor, used for winding in heavy ropes or cables, especially such a device mounted on the deck of a ship. **2** in the magnetic tape drive of a tape recorder, computer, etc, the rotating spindle that pulls the tape past the electromagnetic recording head at a constant speed. [from Provençal *cabestan*]

capsular *adj.* in the form of or resembling a capsule.

capsule *noun* **1** a hard or soft soluble case, usually made of gelatine, containing a single dose of a powdered drug that is to be taken by mouth. **2** (*in full* **space capsule**) a small spacecraft or a compartment within a spacecraft that houses the instruments and crew for the duration of a space flight. **3** *Anat.* a membranous sheath, sac, or other structure that surrounds an organ or tissue, eg the capsule that surrounds the lens of the eye or the moving parts of a joint. **4** *Bot.* in some flowering plants, eg poppy, a dry dehiscent fruit, formed by the fusion of two or more carpels, that splits open to release its many seeds. **5** *Biol.* the gelatinous envelope of protein or polysaccharide that surrounds and protects certain bacteria. [from Latin *capsula*, diminutive of *capsa*, box]

⊟ **1** pill, tablet, lozenge. **2** module, pod. **4** pod, shell, receptacle.

capsulize or **capsulise** *verb* to present (information) in a concise form.

Capt. *abbrev.* Captain.

captain — *noun* **1** a leader, chief. **2** the commander of a ship. **3** the commander of a company of troops. **4** a naval officer below a commodore and above a commander in rank. **5** an army officer of the rank below major and above lieutenant. **6** the chief pilot of a civil aircraft. **7** the leader of a team or side, or chief member of a club. — *verb* to be captain of. [from Old French *capitain*, from Latin *capitaneus*, chief]

⊟ *noun* **1** leader, chief, boss, head, commander, master, skipper. **2** skipper, master. **7** chief, leader, boss, head, officer.

captaincy *noun* (PL. **captaincies**) the rank or office of a captain.

caption — *noun* **1** the words that accompany a photograph, cartoon, etc to explain it. **2** a heading given to a chapter, article, etc. **3** wording appearing on a television or cinema screen as part of a film or broadcast. — *verb* (**captioned**, **captioning**) to provide with a caption or heading. [from Latin *captio*, act of seizing]

captious *adj.* inclined to criticize and find fault. [from Latin *captiosus*, arguing falsely]

captivate *verb* to delight, charm, or fascinate. [from Latin *captivare*, to take captive]

⊟ delight, charm, fascinate, enthral, hypnotize, mesmerize, enchant, bewitch, beguile, lure, allure, seduce, win, attract, enamour, infatuate, enrapture, dazzle.

⊟ repel, disgust, appal.

captivating *adj.* enchanting, fascinating.

captivation *noun* being captivated or enchanted.

captive — *noun* a person or animal that has been caught or taken prisoner. — *adj.* **1** kept prisoner. **2** held so as to be unable to get away. **3** forced into a certain state or role. [from Latin *captivus*, prisoner]

⊟ *noun* prisoner, hostage, slave, detainee, internee, convict. *adj.* **1**, **2** imprisoned, caged, confined, restricted, secure, locked up, enchained, enslaved, ensnared.

⊟ *adj.* **1**, **2** free.

captivity /kap'tıvıtı/ *noun* the condition or period of being captive or imprisoned.

⊟ custody, detention, imprisonment, incarceration, internment, confinement, restraint, bondage, duress, slavery, servitude.

⊟ freedom.

captor *noun* the capturer of a person or animal. [from Latin *captor*]

capture — *verb* **1** to catch; to take prisoner. **2** to gain possession or control of. **3** to succeed in recording (a subtle quality, etc): *the camera captured her smile.* — *noun* **1** the capturing of someone or something. **2** the person or thing captured. [from Latin *captura*]

verb **1** catch, trap, snare, take, seize, arrest, apprehend, imprison. **2** take, seize, secure, win, conquer. *noun* **1** catching, trapping, taking, seizure, arrest, imprisonment.

capturer *noun* a captor.

Capuchin /'kapjʊ ın/ *noun* a member of an order of friars that originated as a branch of the Franciscan order, observing a strict rule of poverty and austerity. — *adj.* relating to the Capuchins. [from Italian *cappuccio*, a kind of cowl worn by them, from Latin *cappa*]

capuchin /'kapjʊ ın/ *noun* a New World monkey, the most numerous captive monkey in the USA and Europe. It has a prehensile tail (adapted for grasping), often carried curled at the tip, and is acrobatic and intelligent. It was formerly a popular pet for street musicians. [so called because its thick hair resembles a monk's cowl]

capybara /kapı'bɑːrə/ *noun* a cavy-like rodent, native to Central and S America, and the largest living rodent, growing to a length of over 1m. It is dog-like in appearance, with a deep square snout, partially webbed toes, and no tail. It lives in or near water, and feeds on plant material. [from Portuguese, from a S American name]

car *noun* **1** a self-propelled four-wheeled road vehicle designed to carry passengers and powered by an internal combustion engine. Also called MOTOR CAR, AUTOMOBILE. **2** a wheeled vehicle of a specified type, eg tramcar. **3** a railway carriage, especially of a specified type, eg buffet car, sleeping car. **4** *North Amer. combining form* any railway carriage, wagon, or truck. **5** the part of an airship, balloon, or cable car that carries passengers. [from Middle English *carre*, from Latin *carrum*, cart]

⊟ **1** automobile, motor car, motor, vehicle.

Types of car include: saloon, hatchback, fastback, estate, sports car, cabriolet, convertible, limousine, *colloq.* limo, *slang* wheels, *colloq.* banger, Mini, bubble-car, coupé, station wagon, shooting brake, veteran car, vintage car, *colloq.* Beetle, four-wheel drive, jeep, buggy, Land Rover, Range Rover, panda car, patrol car, taxi, cab.

carafe /kə'raf/ *noun* a wide-necked bottle or flask for wine, etc, for use on the table. [from French *carafe*, from Spanish *garrafa*]

carambola /karəm'boʊlə/ *noun* **1** a small evergreen tree (*Averrhoa carambola*), native to SE Asia, and widely cultivated in the tropics for its edible fruit. **2** the smooth-skinned yellow fruit of this plant, star-shaped in cross-section, which can be eaten raw or cooked. Its juice is used as a stain remover. Also called STAR FRUIT. [from Spanish *carambola*, word]

caramel /'karəməl/ *noun* **1** a brown substance with a characteristic flavour produced by heating sugar solution until it darkens. It is used as a food colouring, eg in beer, and as a flavouring. **2** a toffee-like sweet made from sugar, animal fat, and milk or cream. **3** a pale yellowish brown colour. [from French, from Spanish *caramelo*]

caramelization or **caramelisation** *noun* the process of turning sugar into syrup.

caramelize or **caramelise** *verb* **1** *trans.* to change (sugar) into caramel. **2** *intrans.* to turn into caramel.

carapace /'karəpeıs/ *noun* **1** *Zool.* the hard thick shell, resembling a shield, that covers the upper part of the body of some reptiles of the order Chelonia (tortoises and turtles) and crustaceans, eg crabs. **2** a layer of heat-resistant tiles covering a spacecraft. [from Spanish *carapacho*, shell]

carat *noun* **1** a unit of mass, equal to 0.2g, used to measure the mass of gemstones, especially diamonds. **2** a unit used to express the purity of gold in an alloy with another metal (usually copper). It is equal to the number of parts of gold in 24 parts of the alloy, so pure gold is described as *24-carat* gold. [from Arabic *qirat*, 4-grain weight, from Greek *keration*, carob bean, 3.3-grain weight]

caravan /'karəvan/ — noun **1** a large vehicle fitted for living in, designed for towing by a motor vehicle or, especially formerly, a horse. **2** Hist. a group of travellers, merchants, etc usually with camels, crossing the desert in company for safety. — verb intrans. (**caravanned, caravanning**) to go travelling with, or stay in, a caravan. [from Persian karwan, company of travellers]

caravanette /karəvə'nɛt/ noun a motor vehicle with a compartment equipped for living in while touring.

caravanning noun holidaying in or travelling with a caravan.

caravanserai /karə'vansəraɪ/ noun in some Eastern countries, an inn with a central courtyard, for receiving caravans crossing the desert, etc. [from Persian karwansarai, caravan inn]

caravan site a place where caravans may be parked, permanently or temporarily, usually with showers and toilets, a shop, etc.

caravel noun a light sailing vessel used for trade in the Mediterranean in the 14c–17c. [from French caravelle, from Italian caravella; compare late Latin carabus, Greek karabos, a light ship]

caraway noun **1** an annual plant (Carum carvi), native to Europe and Asia, having finely divided leaves and clusters of small white flowers with deeply notched petals. **2** (in full **caraway seed**) the dried ripe fruit of this plant, which contains an aromatic oil, and is widely used as a spice for flavouring bread, cakes, and cheese, and is also an important ingredient of Kümmel liqueur. [from Arabic karawiya]

caraway seed the small, strong-flavoured fruit of this plant, used in baking.

carbide noun Chem. any chemical compound consisting of carbon and another element (except for hydrogen), usually a metal. Carbides are extremely hard, and are widely used as abrasives.

carbine noun a short light rifle. [from French carabine]

carbohydrate /kɑːbəʊ'haɪdreɪt/ noun Biochem. any of a group of organic compounds that are present in the cells of all living organisms, and consist of carbon, hydrogen, and oxygen. Carbohydrates are formed in green plants during photosynthesis, and are an important source of energy for both plants and animals. [from CARBON + HYDRATE]

carbolic acid /kɑː'bɒlɪk/ same as PHENOL.

carbolic soap soap containing carbolic acid.

carbon noun **1** (SYMBOL **C**, ATOMIC NUMBER **6**) a non-metallic element that occurs in various pure amorphous forms, such as coal, coke, and charcoal, and as two crystalline allotropes, namely diamond and graphite. **2** a sheet of carbon paper. **3** a carbon copy. [from French carbone, from Latin carbo, charcoal]

carbonaceous /kɑːbə'neɪʃəs/ adj. containing large amounts of carbon, or resembling carbon.

carbonate — noun Chem. a salt of carbonic acid containing the carbonate (CO_3^{2-}) ion. Carbonates commonly occur as rock-forming minerals, eg chalk, limestone, dolomite, and they all react with acids to produce carbon dioxide. — adj. relating to such a compound.

carbonated adj., said of a drink made fizzy by being filled with carbon dioxide.

carbonation noun Chem. the addition of carbon dioxide gas to a liquid under pressure, eg to make fizzy drinks.

carbon black Chem. a form of finely divided carbon, produced by partial combustion of natural gas or petroleum oil, used in pigments and printer's ink.

carbon copy 1 a copy of typewritten matter, etc made using carbon paper. **2** colloq. a person or thing that looks exactly like someone or something else.

carbon cycle a series of reactions in which carbon, either as the free element or in the form of one of its many compounds, is exchanged between living organisms and their non-living environment, including the atmosphere, oceans, and soil.

carbon dating Archaeol. a scientific method of estimating the age of archaeological specimens, based on measurements of the radioactive isotope carbon-14, which is present in all living organisms, but on their death gradually decays and is not replaced.

carbon dioxide (FORMULA CO_2) a colourless odourless tasteless gas that is chemically unreactive and does not burn or support the combustion of other materials. It is denser than air, and represents about 0.03% of the atmosphere by volume.

carbon fibre a high-strength material prepared by heating textile fibres in the absence of air. Carbon fibres are more than twice as stiff as steel, and are used in fibre-reinforced plastics to make extremely strong lightweight materials which are used in components of aeroplanes and rockets, and in sports equipment such as fishing rods, rackets, and skis.

carbonic /kɑː'bɒnɪk/ adj., said of a compound containing carbon, especially carbon having a valency of four.

carbonic acid (FORMULA H_2CO_3) a weak acid formed by dissolving carbon dioxide in water. Its salts are carbonates and hydrogencarbonates.

carboniferous /kɑːbə'nɪfərəs/ adj. **1** producing carbon or coal. **2** (**Carboniferous**) Geol. relating to the fifth period of the Palaeozoic era, lasting from about 360 million to 290 million years ago, and characterized by extensive swampy forests containing clubmosses, ferns, and horsetails, which subsequently formed coal deposits. Amphibians became more numerous, and the first reptiles appeared. **3** relating to rocks formed during this period. [from CARBON + -FEROUS]

carbonization or **carbonisation** noun the action or process of carbonizing.

carbonize or **carbonise** verb **1** trans., intrans. to convert or reduce (a substance containing carbon) into carbon, either by heating or by natural methods such as fossilization. **2** to coat (a substance) with a layer of carbon.

carbon monoxide Chem. (FORMULA **CO**) a poisonous colourless odourless gas formed by the incomplete combustion of carbon, eg in car exhaust gases, and manufactured industrially by the oxidation of methane for use as a reducing agent, eg to extract metals from ores. It binds to iron in the blood pigment haemoglobin, preventing the uptake of oxygen, and levels as low as 0.1% in the air can be fatal.

carbon paper a thin sheet of paper coated on one side with a dark waxy material (usually containing carbon black), so that when it is placed with the waxy side facing downward between two sheets of paper, information typed or written on the top sheet is transferred by pressure to the bottom sheet. Carbon paper has now been largely superseded by the use of word processors and photocopiers.

carbon steel Engineering steel containing carbon, with different properties according to the quantity of carbon used.

carbon tax a tax on fossil fuels, intended to discourage their use and the consequent damaging effects of carbon monoxide emissions on the environment.

carbonyl group /'kɑːbənɪl, 'kɑːbənaɪl/ Chem. in certain organic chemical compounds (aldehydes, ketones, and carboxylic acids), the C=O group, consisting of a carbon atom joined to an oxygen atom by a double bond.

carborundum /kɑːbə'rʌndəm/ noun Chem. an extremely hard black crystalline substance, consisting of silicon carbide, that is used as an abrasive and semiconductor. [from CARBON + CORUNDUM]

carboxyl group /kɑː'bɒksɪl, kɑː'bɒksaɪl/ Chem. in certain organic chemical compounds, the –COOH group, characteristic of carboxylic acids.

carboxylic acid /kɑːbɒk'sɪlɪk/ Chem. an organic acid containing a carboxyl (–COOH) group bonded to hydrogen or a hydrocarbon, eg methanoic acid (formic acid), which has the formula HCOOH, ethanoic acid (acetic acid), which has the formula CH_3COOH.

carboy noun a large glass or plastic bottle, usually protected by a basketwork casing, used for storing or transporting corrosive liquids. [from Persian *qaraba*, glass flagon]

carbuncle *noun* **1** a cluster of boils on the skin, usually caused by infection with the bacterium Staphylococcus aureus, and characterized by the presence of several drainage ducts. **2** a rounded red gemstone, especially a garnet that has not been cut with facets. [from Latin *carbunculus*, diminutive of *carbo*, coal]

carburettor /ˈkɑːbəretə(r)/ *noun* the part of an internal combustion engine in which the liquid fuel (eg petrol) and air are mixed in the correct proportions and vaporized before being sucked into the cylinders. [from obsolete *carburet*, carbide]

carcase /ˈkɑːkəs/ or **carcass** *noun* **1** the dead body of an animal. **2** *colloq.* a living person's body. **3** the rotting remains of something, eg a ship. **4** the basic structure or framework of something. [from Old French *carcasse*]

. . . .

▣ **1** body, corpse, cadaver, remains. **3** remains, relics, skeleton, hulk. **4** structure, framework, shell, skeleton, body.

. . . .

carcinogen /kɑːˈsɪnədʒən/ *noun Medicine* any substance capable of causing cancer in a living tissue that is exposed to it, eg X-rays and other ionizing radiation, many chemical compounds (eg constituents of cigarette smoke), and some viruses. Carcinogens damage the DNA of a cell, which may then become cancerous if the cell divides before the damage has been repaired. [from Greek *karkinos*, crab, cancer + -GEN]

carcinogenic /kɑːsɪnəˈdʒɒnɪk/ *adj.* denoting any agent that is capable of causing cancer in a living tissue that is exposed to it.

carcinoma /kɑːsɪˈnoʊmə/ *noun Medicine* any cancer that occurs in epithelial tissue, ie the skin, or the tissue that lines the internal organs of the body, such as the digestive tract and lungs. It may then spread to other parts of the body via the bloodstream. [from Greek *karkinos*, crab, cancer]

card[1] *noun* **1** a thick stiff kind of paper or thin cardboard. **2** (*also* **playing card**) a rectangular piece of card bearing a design, usually one of a set of 52, for playing games with. **3** a small rectangular piece of card or plastic, showing eg one's identity, job, membership of an organization, etc. **4** a small rectangular piece of stiff plastic issued by a bank, etc to a customer, used instead of cash or a cheque when making payments, as a guarantee for a cheque, for operating a cash machine, etc. **5** *Electron.* a printed circuit board. **6** *Comput.* a piece of card on which information is stored in the form of punched holes or magnetic codes. **7** a piece of card, usually folded double, bearing a design and message, sent to someone on a special occasion. **8** a postcard. **9** *old colloq. use* an amusing person. **10** *Racing* same as RACECARD. **11** (**cards**) games played with playing cards. **12** (**cards**) an employee's personal documents held by his or her employer. — **the cards are stacked against someone** or **something** *colloq.* circumstances do not favour them. **get one's cards** *colloq.* to be dismissed from one's job. **have a card up one's sleeve** in an argument or contest, to have something to one's advantage that one's opponent is not aware of and that one can still make use of. **hold all the cards** *colloq.* to have the stronger or strongest position of opposing parties; to have all the advantages. **lay** or **put one's cards on the table** *colloq.* to announce one's intentions, reveal one's thoughts, etc openly. **on the cards** *colloq.* likely to happen. **play one's best** or **strongest** or **trump card** *colloq.* to make use of one's strongest advantage. **play one's cards close to one's chest** to be secretive about one's intentions. **play one's cards right** *colloq.* to make good use of one's opportunities and advantages. [from French *carte*]

card[2] — *noun* a comb-like device with sharp teeth for removing knots and tangles from sheep's wool, etc before spinning, or for pulling across the surface of cloth to make it fluffy. — *verb* to treat with a card. [from Middle English *carde*, teasel head]

cardamom or **cardamum** /ˈkɑːdəməm/ or **cardamon** *noun* **1** a tropical perennial shrub (Elettaria cardamomum), native to India and Sri Lanka, having two rows of large hairy leaves with stalks sheathing the stem, and clusters of small white flowers with blue and yellow markings on the petals. **2** the dried aromatic seeds of this plant, which are used as a spice, especially in curry powder or paste. [from Greek *kardamomum*]

cardboard — *noun* a stiff material manufactured from pulped waste paper, used for making boxes, card, etc. — *adj.* **1** made of cardboard. **2** *derog., said eg of characters in a play, etc* not realistic or lifelike.

cardboard city an area in which homeless people live or sleep, using cardboard boxes, etc, as shelter. These camp sites have become a feature of many large cities in Europe and the USA in the late 1980s and 1990s.

card-carrying *adj.* **1** officially registered as a member of a political party, etc and openly supporting it. **2** *colloq.* strongly supporting.

cardiac *adj.* **1** relating to or affecting the heart. **2** relating to the upper part of the stomach, in the region of the junction between the stomach and the oesophagus. [from Greek *kardia*, heart]

cardiac arrest *Medicine* the stopping of the heartbeat and therefore the pumping action of the heart, usually as a result of myocardial infarction (death of part of the heart muscle). There is an immediate loss of consciousness, breathing stops, and brain damage and death may occur within minutes unless emergency treatment is given.

cardiac massage rhythmic stimulation of the heart in order to restart or maintain blood circulation after heart failure. It is achieved either by exerting manual pressure on the chest, or by massaging the heart itself after the chest has been opened surgically.

cardiac muscle *Anat.* specialized muscle, found only in the walls of the heart, consisting of long fibres with unique physiological properties that enable them to expand and contract indefinitely.

cardigan *noun* a long-sleeved knitted jacket that fastens down the front. [named after the 7th Earl of Cardigan]

cardinal — *noun* **1** one of a group of leading clergy in the Roman Catholic Church, who elect the pope and advise him, their official dress being bright red. **2** a cardinal number. **3** either of two species of songbird, native to temperate regions of N America and introduced to Bermuda and Hawaii, so called because the plumage of the male is bright red. In Hawaii it breeds all year round and has become a serious pest of fruit trees. **4** (*also* **cardinal red**) a bright red colour. — *adj.* of the highest importance; principal or fundamental. [from Latin *cardinalis*, principal]

cardinalate *noun* **1** the rank or office of a cardinal. **2** the cardinals as a body.

cardinal number one of a series of numbers expressing quantity (eg 1, 2, 3,...), as opposed to an *ordinal number* which expresses order (eg 1st, 2nd, 3rd,...). See also ORDINAL NUMBER.

cardinal point *noun* any of the four main points of the compass: north, south, east, or west.

cardinal virtue any of the most important virtues, usually listed as justice, prudence, temperance, fortitude, faith, hope, and charity.

carding *noun Weaving* the process of blending and disentangling fibres in preparation for spinning. In mechanized carding systems, fibres are passed between a series of rollers covered with projecting steel wires and rotating at different speeds, and emerge in the form of a light fluffy web or sliver.

cardio- *combining form* belonging or relating to the heart. [from Greek *kardia*, heart]

cardiogram *noun Medicine* an electrocardiogram.

cardiograph *noun Medicine* an electrocardiograph.

cardiographer /kɑːdɪˈɒɡrəfə(r)/ *noun* a person who operates an electrocardiograph.

cardiography /kɑːdɪˈɒɡrəfɪ/ *noun* the branch of medicine concerned with the recording of the movements of the heart.

cardiologist /kɑːdɪˈɒlədʒɪst/ *noun* a doctor who specializes in cardiology.

cardiology /kɑːdɪˈɒlədʒɪ/ *noun* the branch of medicine concerned with the study of the structure, function, and diseases of the heart. [from CARDIO- + -LOGY]

cardiopulmonary *adj. Anat.* relating to the heart and lungs.

cardiovascular *adj.* relating to the heart and blood vessels. [from CARDIO- + VASCULAR]

cardphone *noun* a payphone operated with a phonecard. See also CASHPHONE.

card-sharp or **card-sharper** *noun derog.* a person who makes a business of cheating at card games played for money.

card table a small folding table, usually covered with green cloth, for playing card games on.

card vote *Brit.* a vote by representatives of bodies, each vote counting in proportion to the number of members represented.

care — *noun* **1** attention and thoroughness. **2** caution; gentleness; regard for safety. **3** the activity of looking after someone or something, or the state of being looked after. **4** worry or anxiety. **5** a cause for worry; a responsibility. — *verb intrans.* **1** to mind or be upset by something, or the possibility of something. **2** (**care about** or **for someone** or **something**) to concern oneself about them or be interested in them. **3** (**care for something** or **someone**) to have a wish or desire for: *would you care for a drink?* **4** to wish or be willing: *would you care to come?* — **as if I care** or **cared** *colloq.* it doesn't matter to me, etc. **care for someone** or **something 1** to look after them. **2** to be fond of or love them. **3** to like or approve of them: *I don't care for mushrooms.* **care of** ... (*usually* **c/o** ...) written on letters, etc addressed to a person at someone else's address. **for all I care** *colloq.* without upsetting me, etc in the least. **have a care!** *old use* to be more careful, considerate, etc. **I couldn't care less** *colloq.* it doesn't matter to me, etc in the least. **in care** being looked after by a local authority, etc, or in a hospital, etc, instead of at home. **take care** to be cautious, watchful or thorough. **take care of someone** or **something 1** to look after them. **2** to attend to or organize them. [from Anglo-Saxon *caru*, anxiety, sorrow]

⊟ *noun* **1** attention, thoroughness, carefulness, meticulousness, regard, consideration. **2** caution, vigilance, watchfulness, prudence, heed. **3** keeping, custody, guardianship, protection, charge, responsibility, control, supervision. **4** worry, anxiety, stress, strain, pressure, concern, trouble, distress, affliction, tribulation, vexation. **5** worry, problem, concern, trouble, responsibility. *verb* **1** worry, mind, bother, be concerned. **2** concern oneself, be interested, bother. **3, 4** want, like, fancy. **care for 1** look after, nurse, tend, mind, watch over, protect, minister to, attend. **2** like, be fond of, love, be keen on. **3** enjoy, be fond of, love, be keen on, delight in.

⊞ *noun* **1, 2** carelessness, thoughtlessness, inattention, neglect.

careen /kəˈriːn/ *verb* **1** to turn (a boat) over on its side for cleaning, etc. **2** *intrans. said of a ship* to lean over to one side; to heel over. **3** *intrans. North Amer., esp. US, said of a vehicle, etc* to swerve or lurch violently from side to side. [from Latin *carina*, keel]

career — *noun* **1** one's professional life; one's progress in one's job. **2** a job, occupation, or profession. **3** one's progress through life generally. **4** a swift or headlong course. — *verb intrans. colloq.* to rush in an uncontrolled or headlong way. [from French *carrière*, racecourse, career]

⊟ *noun* **1, 2** vocation, calling, occupation, pursuit, profession, trade, job, employment, livelihood. *verb* rush, dash, tear, hurtle, race, run, gallop, speed, shoot, bolt.

careerism *noun* concern with the advancement of one's career.

careerist *noun derog.* a person who is chiefly interested in his or her own advancement or promotion.

careers adviser or **careers officer** in schools, etc, a person whose job is to help young people choose a suitable career.

carefree *adj.* having few worries; cheerful.

⊟ unworried, untroubled, unconcerned, cheerful, happy, breezy, cheery, blithe, happy-go-lucky, light-hearted, *colloq.* easy-going, *colloq.* laid back.

⊞ worried, anxious, despondent.

careful *adj.* **1** giving or showing care and attention; thorough. **2** gentle; watchful or mindful; cautious. **3** taking care to avoid harm or damage. **4** (**careful of something**) protective of it.

⊟ **1** meticulous, thorough, painstaking, conscientious, scrupulous, detailed, punctilious, particular, accurate, precise, thoughtful. **2, 3** cautious, prudent, circumspect, judicious, wary, chary, vigilant, watchful, alert, attentive, mindful, thoughtful.

⊞ **1** careless. **2, 3** careless, inattentive, thoughtless, reckless.

carefully *adv.* with care; in a careful way.

carefulness *noun* being careful.

careless *adj.* **1** not careful or thorough enough; inattentive. **2** lacking, or showing a lack of, a sense of responsibility. **3** effortless: *careless charm.*

⊟ **1** unthinking, inattentive, thoughtless, inconsiderate, uncaring, unconcerned, heedless, unmindful, forgetful, remiss, negligent, irresponsible, unguarded. **2** neglectful, slipshod, slap-dash, sloppy, hasty, cursory, offhand, casual, disorderly, inaccurate, messy, untidy.

⊞ **1** careful, thorough, thoughtful, prudent. **2** careful, accurate, meticulous.

carelessly *adv.* without care; in a careless way.

carelessness *noun* **1** being careless. **2** a careless action.

carer *noun* the person who has the responsibility for looking after an ill, disabled, or otherwise helpless person.

caress /kəˈrɛs/ — *verb* to touch or stroke gently and lovingly. — *noun* a gentle, loving touch; a gentle embrace. [from Italian *carezza*]

⊟ *verb* stroke, touch, rub, pet, fondle, cuddle, hug, embrace, kiss. *noun* stroke, fondle, pat, embrace, cuddle, hug, kiss.

caret /ˈkarət/ *noun* a mark (∧) made on written or printed material to show where a missing word, letter, etc should be inserted. [from Latin *caret*, there is missing]

caretaker — *noun* a person employed to look after a public building, eg a school, or a house, eg if the owner is away. — *adj.* taking temporary responsibility.

⊟ *noun North Amer., Scot* janitor, porter, watchman, keeper, custodian, curator, warden, superintendent.

caretaker speech the speech used by adults when talking to young children. It has shorter sentences, is grammatically simple, and has clear pronunciation, often with exaggerated intonation and repetition.

careworn *adj.* worn out with, or marked by, worry and anxiety.

cargo *noun* (PL. **cargoes**) the goods carried by a ship, aircraft, or other vehicle. [from Spanish *cargo*, burden]

⊟ goods, freight, load, payload, lading, tonnage, shipment, consignment, merchandise, contents, baggage.

cargo pants same as COMBAT TROUSERS.

Carib — *noun* **1** an aboriginal inhabitant of the southern West Indies or of parts of Central and S America. **2** their language. — *adj.* relating to the Caribs or their language. [from Spanish *Caribe*, from the Arawak language of the West Indies]

Caribbean /karɪˈbɪən/ — *noun* the part of the Atlantic between the West Indies and Central and S America. — *adj.* relating to this region.

caribou /ˈkarɪbuː, karɪˈbuː/ *noun* (PL. **caribous**, **caribou**) a large deer belonging to the same species as the reindeer, and roaming wild in large herds in N America and Siberia. [from Canadian French *caribou*, from a native American language]

caricature /ˈkarɪkətʃʊə(r)/ — *noun* **1** a representation, especially a drawing, of someone, with his or her most noticeable and distinctive features exaggerated for comic effect. **2** a ridiculously poor attempt at something. — *verb* to make or give a caricature of. [from Italian *caricatura*, from *caricare*, to distort]

⊟ *noun* **1** cartoon, parody, lampoon, burlesque, satire, *Brit. colloq.* send-up, take-off, imitation, representation, distortion. **2** travesty, parody, imitation, distortion. *verb* parody, mock, ridicule, satirize, *Brit. colloq.* send up, take off, mimic, distort, exaggerate.

caricaturist /ˈkarɪkətʃʊərɪst/ *noun* a person who makes a caricature.

CARICOM *abbrev.* Caribbean Community.

caries /ˈkɛəriːz, ˈkɛərɪz/ *noun* the progressive decomposition and decay of a tooth or a bone, accompanied by softening and discoloration. [from Latin *caries*, decay]

carillon /kəˈrɪljən/ *noun* **1** a set of bells hung usually in a tower and played by means of a keyboard or mechanically. **2** a tune played on such bells. [from French *carillon*, from Latin *quaternio*, probably a set of four bells]

caring *adj.* **1** showing concern for others; sympathetic and helpful. **2** denoting a profession or activity concerned with the social or medical welfare of people.

carjacking *noun* the practice of hijacking a car with its driver and passengers.

Carmelite — *noun* a mendicant friar or nun of a monastic order that originated in the 12c from the hermits of Mt Carmel, following a strict rule. — *adj.* relating to the Carmelites.

carmine /ˈkɑːmaɪn, ˈkɑːmɪn/ *noun* **1** a deep red colour; crimson. **2** a red colouring substance obtained from the cochineal insect. [from French *carmine*]

carnage /ˈkɑːnɪdʒ/ *noun* great slaughter. [from French *carnage*, from Latin *carnaticum*, payment in meat]

⊟ slaughter, butchery, bloodshed, bloodbath, killing, murder, massacre, holocaust.

carnal *adj.* **1** belonging to the body or the flesh, as opposed to the spirit or intellect. **2** sexual. [from Latin *caro*, flesh]

carnality *noun* a carnal or bodily state.

carnally *adv.* in a carnal way.

carnassial tooth /kɑːˈnasɪəl/ *Anat.* in carnivorous animals, a molar or premolar tooth that is adapted for tearing flesh. [from French *carnassier*, flesh-eating, from Latin *caro carnis*, flesh]

carnation *noun* **1** a perennial plant (Dianthus caryophyllus), native to the Mediterranean region, having tufted leaves and pink strongly scented flowers with spreading slightly frilled petals. Many double-flowered varieties with white, pink, red, yellow, peach, or multicoloured flowers have been developed by selective breeding and are widely cultivated as ornamental garden plants and for floristry. **2** a deep pink colour. [from Latin *carnatio*, flesh colour, from *caro*, flesh]

carnelian /kɑːˈniːljən/ see CORNELIAN.

carnival *noun* **1** a period of public festivity with eg street processions, colourful costumes, and singing and dancing. **2** a circus or fair. [from Latin *carnelevarium*, probably from *caro*, flesh + *levare*, to remove, the original carnival being Shrove Tuesday, the day before the start of the Lent fast]

⊟ **1** festival, fiesta, gala, jamboree, fête, fair, holiday, jubilee, celebration, merrymaking, revelry. **2** circus, fair, fête, gala, jamboree.

carnivore *noun* **1** commonly used to refer to an animal that feeds mainly on the flesh of other vertebrate animals; a meat-eating animal. **2** any of a group of mammals belonging to the order Carnivora, whose teeth are specialized for biting and tearing flesh, eg dogs, cats, seals, although some are omnivores, eg bears, or even herbivores, eg panda. See also HERBIVORE. [from Latin *carnivorus*, flesh-eating]

carnivorous /kɑːˈnɪvərəs/ *adj.* **1** denoting an animal, especially a mammal, that feeds mainly on the flesh of other vertebrate animals. **2** denoting a plant which traps animals, usually insects and small invertebrates, and secretes enzymes which digest the prey, allowing the products of digestion to be absorbed by the plant.

carob /ˈkarəb/ *noun* **1** an evergreen tree (Ceratonia siliqua), native to the Mediterranean region, which produces large reddish-brown seedpods rich in sugars and gums. Also called LOCUST TREE. **2** the edible seedpod of this tree, ground and used as a substitute for chocolate and as a food stabilizer, or as a feed for animal livestock. [from French *carobe*]

carol — *noun* a religious song, especially one sung at Christmas in honour of Christ's birth. — *verb intrans.* (**carolled**, **carolling**) **1** to sing carols. **2** to sing joyfully. [from Old French *carole*]

Carolingian /karəˈlɪndʒɪən/ — *noun* a member of a Frankish dynasty which replaced the Merovingians in the 8c. — *adj.* relating to the Carolingians.

carom /ˈkarəm/ *noun* a form of billiards popular in Europe, played on a table without pockets with the object of making cannons. [short form of *carambole*, a cannon in billiards, from French *carombole*, from Spanish *carambola*, the red ball in billiards]

carotene or **carotin** /ˈkarətiːn/ *noun Biochem.* any of a number of reddish-yellow pigments, widely distributed in plants, that are converted to vitamin A in the body. [from Latin *carota*, carrot]

carotenoid or **carotinoid** /kəˈrɒtɪnɔɪd/ *noun Biochem.* any of a group of plant pigments that absorb light during photosynthesis.

carotid /kəˈrɒtɪd/ — *noun* (*in full* **carotid artery**) either of the two major arteries that supply blood to the head and neck. — *adj.* relating to either of these arteries. [from Greek *karotides*, from *karos*, stupor, pressure on these arteries causing unconsciousness]

carousal /kəˈraʊzəl/ *noun* a drinking bout or party; a noisy revel.

carouse /kəˈraʊz/ *verb intrans.* to take part in a noisy drinking party. [from German *gar aus*, all out, ie completely emptying the glass]

carousel /karəˈsɛl/ *noun* **1** a revolving belt in an airport, etc on to which luggage is unloaded so that passengers can collect it as it passes by. **2** a revolving case for holding photographic transparencies, for use in a projector. **3** *North Amer.* a merry-go-round. [from Italian *carusello*, kind of ball game]

carp[1] *noun* (PL. **carp**, **carps**) **1** a freshwater fish belonging to the carp family, native to the Danube basin and the northern Balkans and now introduced worldwide, found mainly in warm shallow waters of slow-flowing rivers and large lakes with abundant vegetation. **2** any of various freshwater fishes found worldwide and characterized by soft fins and a sucker-like mouth. [from Middle English *carpe*]

carp² *verb intrans.* to complain, find fault, or criticize, especially unnecessarily. [from Norse *karpa*, to boast, dispute]

carpal *Anat.* — *noun* in terrestrial vertebrates, any of the bones that form the *carpus* (the wrist or corresponding part of the forelimb). — *adj.* relating to the carpus. [from Greek *karpos*, wrist]

car park a building or piece of land where cars can be parked.

carpel *noun Bot.* the female reproductive part of a flowering plant, consisting of a stigma, style, and ovary. There may be one or many carpels in a flower, either fused together or free. [from Greek *karpos*, fruit]

carpenter *noun* a skilled workman in wood, eg in building houses, etc or in making and repairing fine furniture. [from Latin *carpentarius*, person who builds wagons]

carpentry *noun* the work or skill of a carpenter.

carper *noun* a person who carps.

carpet — *noun* 1 a covering for floors and stairs, made of heavy, usually woven and tufted, fabric. 2 something that covers a surface like a carpet does. — *verb* 1 to cover with, or as if with, a carpet. 2 *colloq.* to reprimand or scold. — **on the carpet** *colloq.* being scolded or reprimanded. [from Middle English *carpete*, from Italian *carpita*, woollen bedcovering]

carpet-bag *noun* an old-fashioned travelling-bag made of carpeting.

carpetbagger *noun derog.* a politician seeking election in a place where he or she is a stranger.

carpeting *noun* 1 fabric for making carpets. 2 carpets generally.

carpet slippers slippers, especially men's, with the upper part made of carpeting or a fabric resembling it.

carpet-sweeper *noun* a long-handled device fitted with a revolving brush, that picks up dust, etc from carpets as it is pushed along.

car phone a portable telephone for use in a car, operating by cellular radio. See CELLULAR RADIO.

carping *adj.* critical, over-critical.

carpingly *adv.* with a carping manner.

carport *noun* a roofed shelter for a car, attached to the side of a house.

carpus *noun* (PL. **carpi**) *Anat.* in terrestrial vertebrates, the set of small bones (eight in humans) that forms the wrist or corresponding part of the forelimb. [from Greek *karpos*, wrist]

carrel or **carrell** *noun* a small compartment or desk in a library, for private study. [from Middle English *carole*, enclosure for study in a cloister]

carriage / ˈkarɪdʒ / *noun* 1 a four-wheeled horse-drawn passenger vehicle. 2 a railway coach for carrying passengers. 3 the process or cost of transporting goods. 4 a moving section of a machine, eg a typewriter, that carries some part into the required position. 5 the way one holds oneself in standing or walking. [from Middle English *cariage*, from Old French *carier*, to carry]

▪ 1 coach, wagon, vehicle. 2 coach, wagon, *North Amer.* car. 3 delivery, postage, transport, transportation, carrying, conveyance. 5 bearing, posture, deportment, air, manner, mien, demeanour.

carriage clock a small ornamental clock with a handle on top, originally used by travellers.

carriageway *noun* the part of a road used by vehicles, or a part used by vehicles travelling in one direction.

carrier *noun* 1 a person or thing that carries. 2 a person or firm that transports goods; a haulier. 3 an individual who is infected by a disease-causing micro-organism (a bacterium or virus), and who may remain without symptoms but is still capable of transmitting that organism to other individuals. 4 a vector. 5 *Genetics* an individual who carries a gene for a particular disorder (eg haemophilia) without

displaying signs or symptoms of that disorder, and who may pass on the gene to his or her offspring. 6 *Radio* a carrier wave. 7 *Physics* a charge carrier, such as an electron. 8 a non-radioactive material mixed with, and chemically identical to, a radioactive compound. 9 a carrier bag.

carrier bag a plastic or paper bag with handles, supplied to shop customers for carrying purchased goods.

carrier pigeon any pigeon with homing instincts, especially one used for carrying messages.

carrier wave *Physics* in radio transmission, a continuously transmitted radio wave whose amplitude or frequency is made to increase or decrease instantaneously in response to variations in the characteristics of the signal being transmitted.

carrion — *noun* the dead and rotting body or flesh of any animal. — *adj.* relating to or feeding on dead and rotting flesh. [from Old French *charogne*, from Latin *caro*, flesh]

carrion crow a crow native to Europe and Asia, usually having black plumage, that inhabits forest, grassland, and cultivated land, and eats virtually anything.

carrot *noun* 1 a biennial plant (Daucus carota), native to Europe, temperate Asia, and N Africa, having divided leaves, leaflets with toothed oval segments, small white, pink, or yellow flowers borne in dense rather flat-topped clusters, and spiny fruits. It is widely cultivated for its edible orange root. 2 the large fleshy orange root of this plant, eaten raw in salads or cooked as a vegetable. Its orange colour is due to the presence of the pigment carotene, which is a rich source of vitamin A. 3 *colloq.* something offered as an incentive. [from Old French *carrotte*]

carroty *adj. derog., said of hair* having a strong reddish colour.

carry *verb* (**carries, carried**) 1 to hold in one's hands, have in a pocket, bag etc, or support the weight of on one's body, while moving from one place to another. 2 to bring, take, or convey. 3 to have on one's person. 4 to be the means of spreading (a disease, etc). 5 to support: *the walls carry the roof*. 6 to be pregnant with. 7 to hold (oneself or a part of one's body) in a certain way: *carry oneself well*. 8 to bear (responsibilities, etc). 9 to bear the burden or expense of: *we can't carry unprofitable enterprises*. 10 to do the work of (someone who is not doing enough) in addition to one's own. 11 to print or broadcast. 12 to stock or sell. 13 to have, involve, etc: *a crime carrying the death penalty*. 14 *intrans. said of a sound or the source of a sound* to be able to be heard a distance away. 15 to pass or agree to by majority vote. 16 to win the support of (voters, an audience, etc). 17 to bear the effects of: *he carries his age well*. 18 to take to a certain point: *carry politeness too far*. 19 *Maths.* to transfer (a figure) in a calculation from one column to the next. 20 *intrans. said of a golf ball, etc* to travel (a certain distance). 21 *Mil.* to capture (a town, etc). — **be** or **get carried away** *colloq.* to become over-excited or over-enthusiastic. **carry something forward** to transfer a number, amount, etc to the next column, page, or financial period. **carry something off** 1 to manage an awkward situation, etc well. 2 to win a prize, etc. 3 to take something away by force. **carry on** 1 to continue; to keep going. 2 *colloq.* to make a noisy or unnecessary fuss. **carry something on** to conduct or engage in business, etc. **carry on with someone** to have a love affair with someone. **carry something out** to accomplish it successfully. **carry something over** 1 to continue it on the following page, etc; to carry forward. 2 to postpone it. **carry someone through** to help them to survive a difficult period, etc. **carry something through** to complete or accomplish it. [from Old French *carier*, from Latin *carricare*, to cart]

▪ *verb* 1, 2 bear, convey, bring, take, fetch, move, transfer, relay. 4 transmit, spread. 5 support, bear, underpin, uphold, sustain, shoulder. 6 bear. 8, 9 bear, support, maintain, sustain, uphold, shoulder, stand. 11 print, broadcast, report, present, release, contain. 12 stock, sell, retail, have. **carry off** 1 manage, bring off, succeed. 2 win, gain, capture, walk off with. 3 take, capture, seize, abduct, kidnap. **carry on** 1 continue, keep going, keep on, persist, persevere, proceed, maintain, last, endure. **2** fuss, misbehave, *colloq.* go on. **carry something on** conduct, engage in, operate, run, manage, administer. **carry out** accomplish, achieve, realize, bring off, do, perform, undertake, discharge, conduct, execute, implement, fulfil. **carry someone through** help, sustain. **carry something through** complete, accomplish, achieve, realize, bring off, effect, implement, execute, fulfil.

🔁 **carry on 1** stop, finish.

carrycot *noun* a light, box-like cot for a baby, with handles for carrying it.

carrying *adj., said of a voice* easily heard at a distance.

carry-on *noun* **1** an excitement or fuss. **2** a romance or love-affair.

carry-out *noun colloq.* **1** *North Amer., esp. US, Scot.* cooked food bought at a restaurant, etc for eating elsewhere. **2** *North Amer., esp. US, Scot.* a shop or restaurant supplying such food. **3** *Scot.* an alcoholic drink bought in a shop or pub for drinking elsewhere.

car-sick *adj.* feeling sick as a result of travelling in a car.

car-sickness *noun* the tendency to be car-sick; a bout of being car-sick.

cart — *noun* **1** a two- or four-wheeled, horse-drawn vehicle for carrying goods or passengers. **2** a light vehicle pushed or pulled by hand. — *verb* **1** to carry in a cart. **2** (**cart something around** or **off**, etc) *colloq.* to carry or convey it. — **in the cart** *colloq.* in difficulties. **put the cart before the horse** to reverse the normal or logical order of doing things. [related to Norse *cartr*]

🔁 *noun* **1** wagon. **2** barrow, handcart, wheelbarrow. *verb* **1** carry, move, convey, transport, haul. **2** carry, haul, *colloq.* lug, *colloq.* hump.

carte blanche /kɑːt ˈblɑːtʃ/ *noun* complete freedom of action or discretion. [from French *carte blanche*, blank paper]

cartel /kɑːˈtɛl/ *noun* a group of firms that agree, especially illegally, on similar fixed prices for their products, so as to reduce competition and keep profits high. [from French *cartel*, from Italian *cartello*, letter of defiance]

Cartesian *adj.* relating to the 17c French philosopher and mathematician Descartes, or his works. [from Cartesius, the Latinized form of his name]

carthorse *noun* a large strong horse bred for pulling heavy loads on farms, etc, and formerly used to pull carts and carriages.

Carthusian /kɑːˈθuːzɪən/ — *noun* a member of a monastic order founded in 1084 by St Bruno in Chartreuse in France, having a strict rule of abstinence and solitary living. — *adj.* relating to the Carthusians.

cartilage *noun* a tough flexible semi-opaque material that forms the skeleton of cartilaginous fish, eg sharks, dogfish. In other vertebrates, including man, it forms the skeleton of the embryo, but is converted into bone before adulthood. In the adult, cartilage persists in structures such as the larynx, trachea, nose, and discs between the vertebrae, and also surrounds the ends of bones at joints. [from French *cartilage*, from Latin *cartilago*]

cartilaginous /kɑːtɪˈlædʒɪnəs/ *adj.* of the nature of or like cartilage.

cartographer /kɑːˈtɒɡrəfə(r)/ *noun* a person who makes charts or maps.

cartographic /kɑːtəʊˈɡræfɪk/ *adj.* relating to cartography.

cartography /kɑːˈtɒɡrəfɪ/ *noun* the art or science of making maps. [from French *carte*, chart + -GRAPHY]

carton *noun* **1** a plastic or cardboard container in which food of various types is packaged for sale. **2** a cardboard box. [from French *carton*, pasteboard, from Italian *cartone*, strong paper]

🔁 BOX, CONTAINER, PACK, CASE, PACKET, PACKAGE, PARCEL.

cartoon *noun* **1** a humorous drawing in a newspaper, etc, often ridiculing someone or something. **2** (*also* **animated cartoon**) a film made by photographing a series of drawings, each showing the subjects in a slightly altered position, giving the impression of movement when the film is run at normal speed. **3** (*also* **strip cartoon**) a strip of drawings in a newspaper, etc showing a sequence of often humorous events. **4** a preparatory drawing of a subject done by an artist before attempting a large painting of it. [from Italian *cartone*, strong paper, or a drawing on it]

🔁 **1** caricature, parody. **2** animated cartoon, animation. **3** strip cartoon, comic strip. **4** sketch, drawing.

cartoonist *noun* an artist who draws cartoons for newspapers, etc.

cartouche /kɑːˈtuːʃ/ *noun Hist.* **1** a paper case containing the explosive charge for a gun, etc; a cartridge. **2** *Archit.* a scroll-like ornament or decorative border with rolled ends. **3** in Egyptian hieroglyphics, an oval figure enclosing a royal or divine name. [from French *cartouche*, from Italian *cartoccio*, from Latin *carta*, *charta*, paper]

cartridge *noun* **1** a metal case containing the propellant charge for a gun. A *blank cartridge* contains powder alone, whereas a *ball cartridge* contains a bullet as well. **2** the part of the pick-up arm of a record-player that contains the needle or stylus. **3** a small plastic tube containing ink for loading into a fountain pen. **4** a plastic container holding a continuous loop of magnetic tape which can be easily inserted and removed from a tape deck, video recorder, etc. **5** a plastic container holding photographic film, which can be inserted into and removed from a camera without exposing the film to light. [from the earlier form *cartage*, a variant of French *cartouche*, cartridge]

🔁 **1** shell, magazine, canister, round, charge, case, container. **4, 5** cassette.

cartridge belt a wide belt with a row of loops or pockets for gun cartridges.

cartridge paper thick rough-surfaced paper for drawing on.

cartwheel — *noun* **1** the wheel of a cart. **2** an acrobatic movement in which one throws one's body sideways with the turning action of a wheel, putting one's weight on each hand and foot in turn. — *verb intrans.* to perform a cartwheel.

carve *verb* **1** to cut (wood, stone, etc) into a shape. **2** to make (something) from wood or stone by cutting into it. **3** to produce (a design, inscription, etc) in wood or stone. **4** to cut (meat) into slices; to cut (a slice) of meat. **5** *intrans.* to cut meat into slices. **6** (**carve something out**) to establish or create an opportunity, etc for oneself through personal effort: *carve out a career*. — **carve something up 1** to cut it up. **2** *colloq.* to divide territory, spoils, etc, especially in a crude or wholesale manner. **carve someone up** *slang* to attack and cut someone with a knife. [from Anglo-Saxon *ceorfan*, to cut]

🔁 **1, 2** cut, hew, chisel, chip, sculpt, sculpture, shape, form, fashion, mould. **3** etch, engrave, incise, indent. **4** slice.

carvel-built *adj., said of a boat* built with planks laid flush, not overlapping. See also CLINKER-BUILT. [from *carvel*, a type of ship]

carver *noun* **1** a person who carves. **2** a carving-knife.

carvery *noun* (PL. **carveries**) a restaurant where meat is carved from a joint for customers on request.

carve-up *noun* a wholesale division of territory or spoils.

carving *noun* a figure or pattern etc produced by carving.

carving fork a large fork with two long prongs, for holding meat steady during carving.

carving knife a long sharp knife for carving meat.

car wash a place at a petrol station, etc fitted with automatic equipment for washing cars.

caryatid /karı'atıd/ *noun* (PL. **caryatids, caryatides**) *Archit.* a carved female figure used as a support for a roof, etc, instead of a column or pillar. [from Greek *Karyatides*, priestesses of the goddess Artemis at Caryae in S Greece, or columns in the form of women]

Casanova *noun derog.* a man with a reputation for having many love affairs. [named after Giacomo Casanova]

cascade — *noun* 1 a waterfall or series of waterfalls. 2 something resembling a waterfall in appearance or manner of falling. 3 a large number of things arriving or to be dealt with suddenly: *cascades of letters.* — *verb intrans.* to fall like a waterfall. [from French *cascade*, from Italian *cascare*, to fall]

▣ *noun* 1 waterfall, falls, cataract, 2 fountain, shower. 3 rush, gush, flood, deluge, torrent, avalanche. *verb* overflow, spill, pour, tumble, fall, descend, plunge, pitch, rush, gush, surge, flood, shower.
▣ *noun* 3 trickle. *verb* trickle.

case[1] — *noun* 1 a box or container for storage, display, carrying, etc. 2 the outer covering of something, especially providing protection. 3 a suitcase or briefcase. 4 *Printing* a tray with compartments for type, the terms *lower case* for small letters and *upper case* for capital letters resulting from the traditional positioning of the trays containing those letters. — *verb* 1 to put in a case. 2 *slang* to have a good look at (a house, etc) with the intention of breaking into it and stealing (see also JOINT). [from Latin *capsa*, case for holding a scroll]

▣ *noun* 1 box, carton, casket, chest, crate, container, receptacle, holder, cabinet, showcase. 2 cover, casing, sheath, jacket, wrapper, cartridge, shell, capsule. 3 suitcase, briefcase, trunk, bag.

case[2] *noun* 1 a particular occasion, situation, or set of circumstances. 2 an example, instance, or occurrence. 3 a person receiving some sort of treatment or care. 4 a matter requiring investigation: *the police are looking into the case.* 5 a matter to be decided in a law court. 6 (**case for** or **against something**) the argument for or against something, with the relevant facts fully presented. 7 *Grammar* the relationship of a noun, pronoun or adjective to other words in a sentence, or the form the noun, etc takes which shows this relationship. 8 an odd character. — **as the case may be** according to how things turn out. **be the case** to be true. **a case in point** a good example, relevant to the present discussion. **in any case** whatever happens; no matter what happens. **in case** so as to be prepared or safe (if a certain thing should happen). **in case of something** if a certain occurrence happens. **in that case** if that happens, since that has happened, etc. [from French *cas*, from Latin *casus*, fall]

▣ 1 occasion, situation, circumstances, occurrence, event, context, state, condition, position, contingency. 2 example, instance, occurrence, event, illustration, point, specimen. 3 patient, client. 5 lawsuit, suit, trial, proceedings, action, process.

casebook *noun* a written record of cases dealt with by a doctor, etc.

case-harden *verb* 1 *Metall.* to harden the surface layer of steel by diffusing carbon into it at high temperatures so that the outer surface is tough and resistant to wear, while the inner core remains resistant to fracture. 2 *Geol.*, *said of a mineral* to form a coating on the surface of porous rock as a result of the evaporation of a solution containing that mineral. 3 to make (someone) insensitive or callous.

case history a record of relevant details from a person's past kept by a doctor, social worker, etc.

casein /'keɪsiːn, 'keɪsiːɪn/ *noun Biochem.* a milk protein that is the main constituent of cheese. [from Latin *caseus*, cheese]

case law law based on decisions made about similar cases in the past, as distinct from statute law established by the government.

case load the number of cases a doctor, etc has to deal with at any particular time.

casement or **casement window** *noun* a window that opens outwards like a door. [from Middle English, from CASE[1]]

casework *noun* social work with individuals, in which family background and environment are closely studied.

cash — *noun* 1 coins or paper money, as distinct from cheques, credit cards, etc. 2 *colloq.* money in any form. — *verb* to obtain or give cash in return for (a cheque, traveller's cheque, postal order, etc). — **cash down** *colloq.* with payment immediately on purchase. **cash something in** to exchange tokens, vouchers, etc for money. **cash in on something** *colloq.* to make money, or profit in some other way, by taking advantage of a situation, etc. **cash on delivery** (ABBREV. **c.o.d.**) with payment for goods immediately on delivery. **cash up** *Brit. colloq.*, *said of a shopkeeper, etc* to count up the money taken, usually at the end of a day. [from Old French *casse*, box]

▣ *noun* MONEY, HARD MONEY, READY MONEY, BANKNOTES, NOTES, COINS, CHANGE, LEGAL TENDER, CURRENCY. 2 funds, resources, hard currency. *verb* encash, exchange, realize, liquidate.

cash-and-carry — *noun* a large often wholesale shop where accredited customers pay for goods in cash and take them away immediately. — *adj.*, *said of a business, etc* using this system.

cashback *noun* 1 a cash discount made on a particular purchase. 2 a service offered by some retailers whereby a customer can withdraw money from their own account using a debit card.

cash book a written record of all money paid out and received by a business, etc.

cash box a box, usually metal and with a lock, for keeping cash in.

cash card a card, issued by a bank, etc, with which one can obtain money from a cash machine.

cash crop a crop that is grown for sale rather than for consumption by the farmer's household or by animal livestock.

cash desk a desk in a shop, etc at which one pays for goods.

cashew /kə'ʃuː, 'kaʃuː/ *noun* 1 a small evergreen tree (Anacardium occidentale), native to tropical regions of Central and S America, having oval leaves, and red flowers borne in terminal clusters. 2 (*in full* **cashew nut**) the curved edible seed, rich in oil and protein, produced by this tree. [from Portuguese *caj*, from Tupi (a S American Indian language)]

cash flow the amount of money coming into, and going out of, a business, etc.

cashier[1] /ka'ʃɪə(r)/ *noun* the person in a business, firm, etc who receives, pays out, and generally deals with, the cash. [from Old French *caissier*, from *caisse*, cash box]

▣ clerk, teller, treasurer, bursar, purser, banker, accountant.

cashier[2] /ka'ʃɪə(r)/ *verb* (**cashiered, cashiering**) to dismiss (an officer) from the armed forces in disgrace. [from Old Dutch *kasseren*]

cashless *adj.* using payment by credit card or electronic transfer of money, rather than by cash or cheque.

cash machine or **cash dispenser** an electronic machine, eg fitted into the outside wall of a bank, from which one can obtain cash using one's personal cash card. See also ATM.

cashmere /'kaʃmɪə(r)/ *noun* **1** very fine soft wool from a long-haired Asian goat. **2** a fabric made from this. [from Kashmir, in N India, where shawls were woven from this wool]

cashphone *noun* a coin-operated payphone, as distinct from a cardphone.

cash point 1 the place in a supermarket, etc where money is taken for goods purchased. **2** a cash machine.

cash register a machine in a shop, etc that calculates and records the amount of each sale and from which change and a receipt are usually given.

casing *noun* a protective covering, eg of plastic for electric cables.

casino /kə'si:nou/ *noun* (PL. **casinos**) a public building or room for gambling. [Italian diminutive of *casa*, house]

cask *noun* **1** a barrel for holding liquids, especially alcoholic liquids. **2** the amount contained by a cask. [back-formation from CASKET, the ending *et* having been understood as a diminutive suffix]

. . . .

▣ barrel, tun, hogshead, firkin, vat, tub, butt.

. . . .

casket *noun* **1** a small case for holding jewels, etc. **2** *North Amer.* a coffin. [from Middle English]

cassava /kə'sɑːvə/ *noun* **1** a perennial shrubby plant of the genus Manihot, belonging to the spurge family (Euphorbiaceae) and native to Brazil, but cultivated throughout the tropics for its fleshy tuberous edible roots. **2** a starchy substance that is obtained from the root of this plant, and is stored and exported in the form of tapioca. [from Spanish *cazabe*, from Taino (W Indian language)]

casserole — *noun* **1** a dish with a lid, in which meat, vegetables, etc can be cooked and served. **2** the food produced in a casserole. — *verb* to cook in a casserole. [from French *casserole*]

cassette *noun* **1** a small usually plastic case, containing a long narrow ribbon of magnetic tape, that can be inserted into a suitable audio or video tape recorder for recording or playback, during which the tape passes from one reel of the cassette to the other. **2** a small lightproof plastic cartridge containing photographic film for loading into a camera. [from French *cassette*, from Italian *cassetta*, diminutive of *cassa*, box]

cassette recorder or **cassette-player** a machine that records or plays material on cassette.

Cassini /ka'si:nɪ/ *noun* a space probe scheduled by NASA and the European Space Agency to be launched in 1997, and to go into orbit around Saturn in 2004.

cassiterite /kə'sɪtərʌɪt/ *noun Geol.* a hard black mineral, consisting mainly of tin oxide (SnO_2), that is the chief ore of tin. [from Greek *kassiteros*, tin]

cassock *noun* a long black or red garment worn in church by clergymen and male members of a church choir. [from Old French *casaque*, type of coat]

cassowary /'kasəwəri, 'kasəweəri/ *noun* (PL. **cassowaries**) a large flightless bird, native to New Guinea and N Australia, up to 1.5m in height and having a bony crest or *casque* on its head. [from Malay *kasuari*]

cast — *verb* (PAST TENSE AND PAST PARTICIPLE **cast**) **1** *usually old use* to throw. **2** to turn, direct, shed, or cause to fall or arise: *cast doubt on* / *cast a shadow* / *cast one's eye over* / *cast a spell*. **3** *trans., intrans.* to throw (a fishing-line) out into the water. **4** to let down (an anchor). **5** to release from a secured state: *cast adrift*. **6** *said of animals* to get rid of or shed (a skin, horns, etc). **7** (**cast something off** or **aside** or **out**) to throw it off or away; to get rid of it. **8** to give (an actor) a part in a play or film; to distribute the parts in (a film, play, etc). **9** to shape (molten metal, plastic, plaster, etc) by pouring it into a mould and allowing it

to set. **10** to create (an object) by this means. **11** to give or record (one's vote). **12** to work out (a horoscope). **13** to present (work, facts, etc) in a certain way. — *noun* **1** a throw; an act of throwing (dice, a fishing-line, etc). **2** an object shaped by pouring molten metal, plastic, plaster, etc, into a mould and allowing it to set. **3** (*also* **plaster cast**) a rigid casing, usually of gauze impregnated with plaster of Paris, moulded round a broken limb or other body part while the plaster is still wet, and then allowed to set in order to hold the broken bone in place while it heals. **4** the set of actors or performers in a play, opera, etc. **5** *formal* type, form, shape, or appearance: *an analytical cast of mind*. **6** a slight tinge; a faint colour. **7** the slight turning inwards of an eye; a squint. **8** a coiled heap of indigestible material (mainly earth or sand) ejected by an earthworm. — **cast about** or **around for something 1** to look about for it. **2** to try to think of it: *cast about for ideas*. **cast someone away** to cause them to be abandoned on a remote piece of land after shipwreck, etc. **cast someone down** to depress or discourage them. **cast one's mind back** to think about something in the past. **cast off** or **cast something off 1** to untie a boat ready to sail away. **2** to finish off and remove knitting from the needles. **cast on** *trans., intrans.* to form (stitches or knitting) by looping and securing the wool, etc over the needles. **cast something up 1** to mention (a person's past faults, etc) to them, as a reproach. **2** to throw (a body, etc) up on to a beach. **cast up figures** to find their total. [from Norse *kasta*, to throw]

. . . .

▣ *verb* **1** throw, hurl, lob, pitch, fling, toss, sling, launch, impel, drive. **2** turn, direct, shed, emit, project, diffuse, spread, scatter. **4** let down, drop. **6** slough. **7** throw off, throw away, get rid of, rid oneself of, shed, discard, expel, eject, oust. **9, 10** mould, shape, form, model, found. **13** present, represent, express. *noun* **1** throw, toss, pitch, fling, sling, heave, lob. **2** casting, mould, shape, form. **4** actors, characters, dramatis personae, players, performers, entertainers, company, troupe. **6** tint, trace, touch, shade, hint. **cast about** or **around for 1** look for, search for, hunt for, seek. **cast down** depress, discourage, dishearten, deject, sadden, crush, desolate.

▣ **cast down** cheer up, encourage.

. . . .

castanets /kastə'nɛts/ *pl. noun* a musical instrument consisting of two small hollow pieces of wood or plastic attached to each other by string, held in the palm and struck together rhythmically, used especially by Spanish dancers to accompany their movements. [from Spanish *castañeta*, from *castaña*, chestnut, the wood used]

castaway *noun* a person who has been shipwrecked.

caste /kɑːst/ *noun* **1** any of the four hereditary social classes into which Hindus are divided. **2** this system of division into classes, or any system of social division based on inherited rank or wealth. — **lose caste** to drop to a lower social class. [from Portuguese *casta*, breed, race]

castellated *adj., said of a building* having turrets and battlements like those of a castle. [from Latin *castellare*, to fortify]

castellation *noun* **1** building castles. **2** providing a house with battlements. **3** a castellated structure; a battlement.

caster¹ see CASTOR².

caster² or **castor** *noun* a closed container with holes in its lid, through which to sprinkle the contents, eg sugar or flour, over food. [see CAST]

caster sugar finely crushed white sugar used in baking, etc.

castigate *verb* to criticize or punish severely. [from Latin *castigare*, to whip]

castigation *noun* severe punishment or criticism.

casting *noun* **1** *Engineering* the process of forming a solid object with a fixed shape by pouring molten material, eg metal, alloy, glass, or plastic, into a mould and allowing it to cool and solidify. **2** an object formed in this way.

casting vote the deciding vote of a chairperson when the votes taken at a meeting, etc are equally divided.

cast iron any of a group of hard heavy alloys of iron, containing more carbon than steels, and cast into a specific shape when molten because it is too brittle to work when solid. It is used to make machine and engine parts, stoves, pipes, radiators, cooking utensils, etc.

cast-iron adj. **1** made of cast iron. **2** very strong. **3** said of a rule or decision firm; not to be altered. **4** said of an argument, etc with no flaws, loopholes, etc.

castle / 'kɑːsl/ — noun **1** a large fortified, especially medieval, building with battlements and towers. **2** Chess a piece that can be moved any number of squares forwards, backwards, or sideways (also called ROOK). — verb intrans. Chess to make a move allowed once to each player in a game, in which the king is moved two squares along its rank towards either castle, and the castle is placed on the square the king has passed over. [from Latin castellum]

. . . .
▣ noun **1** stronghold, fortress, citadel, keep, tower, château.
. . . .

castles in the air or **castles in Spain** grand but impossible schemes; daydreams.

cast-off — noun something, especially a garment, discarded or no longer wanted. — adj. no longer needed; discarded.

castor[1] See CASTER[2].

castor[2] or **caster** noun a small swivelling wheel fitted to the legs or underside of a piece of furniture so that it can be moved easily. [see CAST]

castor oil a yellow or brown non-drying oil obtained from the seeds of a tropical African plant (Ricinus communis), used as a lubricant and in soap manufacture, and formerly used medicinally as a laxative.

castrate verb **1** to remove the testicles of. **2** to deprive of masculinity or strength. [from Latin castrare]

castrated adj. **1** gelded. **2** made ineffective.

castration noun the action of castrating.

castrato / kaˈstrɑːtoʊ/ noun (PL. **castrati**, **castratos**) formerly, a male singer castrated before puberty in order to preserve his soprano or contralto voice.

casual adj. **1** happening by chance. **2** careless; showing no particular interest or concern. **3** without serious purpose or intention. **4** (of clothes) informal. **5** said of work, etc occasional; not permanent or regular. [from Latin casualis, accidental]

. . . .
▣ **1** chance, fortuitous, accidental, unintentional, unpremeditated, unexpected, unforeseen, irregular, random, occasional, incidental. **2** careless, superficial, cursory, nonchalant, blasé, lackadaisical, negligent, colloq. couldn't-care-less, apathetic, indifferent, unconcerned, offhand, relaxed, colloq. laid back. **3** informal, light-hearted, passing. **5** temporary, occasional.
▣ **1** deliberate, planned, intentional. **3, 4** formal. **5** permanent, regular.
. . . .

casually adv. in a casual way.

casualness noun being casual.

casualty noun (PL. **casualties**) **1** a person who is killed or hurt in an accident or war. **2** the casualty department of a hospital. **3** something that is lost, destroyed, sacrificed, etc as a result of some event. [see CASUAL]

. . . .
▣ **1** injury, victim, sufferer, injured person, wounded, loss, death, fatality, dead person.
. . . .

casualty department or **casualty ward** the part of a hospital where casualties from an accident, etc are attended to.

casuist / 'kazjʊɪst/ noun a person who uses cleverly misleading arguments, especially to make things that are really morally wrong seem acceptable. [from French casuiste, from Latin casus, case]

casuistic / kazjʊˈɪstɪk/ adj. involving clever and misleading argument or casuistry.

casuistry / 'kazjʊɪstrɪ/ noun the use of clever and misleading argument.

casus belli / 'keɪsəs 'bɛlaɪ/ circumstance or situation that causes a war. [Latin, = occasion of war]

CAT abbrev. College of Advanced Technology.

cat[1] noun **1** any of a wide range of carnivorous mammals belonging to the family Felidae, including such large cats as the lion, tiger, jaguar, leopard, cheetah, and lynx, as well as the common domestic cat. **2** a popular name for the domestic cat, Felis catus, which belongs to this family. **3** derog. colloq. a person, especially a woman, with a spiteful tongue. **4** slang a person. **5** same as CAT-O'-NINE-TAILS. — **the cat's whiskers** or **pyjamas** colloq. the best or greatest thing. **fight like cat and dog** colloq. to quarrel ferociously. **let the cat out of the bag** colloq. to give away a secret unintentionally. **like a cat on a hot tin roof** or on **hot bricks** colloq. very nervous or uneasy. **like something the cat brought in** colloq. messy, dirty, untidy, or bedraggled in appearance. **no room to swing a cat** having very little space; cramped. **not have a cat in hell's chance** colloq. to have absolutely no chance. **play cat and mouse with someone** to keep chasing and almost catching them; to tease them cruelly. **put** or **set the cat among the pigeons** to do or say something that is generally upsetting or disturbing. **rain cats and dogs** colloq. to rain long and hard. **see which way the cat jumps** colloq. to wait on events before acting. [from Latin cattus]

cat[2] noun colloq. short for CATALYTIC CONVERTER.

catabolism / kəˈtabəlɪzəm/ noun Biochem. the metabolic processes whereby complex organic compounds in living organisms are broken down into simple molecules. [from Greek katabole, throwing down]

catachumen noun a person who is being taught about the main beliefs of Christianity.

cataclysm / 'katəklɪzm/ noun **1** an event causing tremendous change or upheaval. **2** a terrible flood or other disaster. [from Greek kataklysmos, flood]

cataclysmic / katəˈklɪzmɪk/ adj. disastrous; involving great change or upheaval.

catacomb / 'katəkuːm, 'katəkoʊm/ noun (usually **catacombs**) a system of underground tunnels containing burial places. [from Latin catacumbas]

catafalque / 'katəfalk/ noun a platform on which the coffin of a king or other important person is placed for the lying-in-state or funeral. [from French catafalque, from Italian catafalco]

Catalan — noun a Romance language of the Indo-European family, spoken by c.57 million people in NE Spain and Andorra, and in neighbouring areas of France. — adj. relating to or spoken or written in Catalan.

catalepsy / 'katəlɛpsɪ/ noun **1** a trance-like state characterized by the abnormal maintenance of rigid body postures, and an apparent loss of sensation, most commonly associated with catatonia. **2** cataplexy in animals. [from Greek katalepsis, seizing]

cataleptic / katəˈlɛptɪk/ — adj. relating to or affected by catalepsy. — noun a person affected by catalepsy.

catalogue / 'katəlɒg/ — noun **1** a list of items arranged in a systematic order, especially alphabetically. **2** a brochure, booklet, etc containing a list of goods for sale. **3** a list or index of all the books in a library. **4** a series of things mentioned one by one as though in a list: the catalogue of his faults. — verb **1** to make a catalogue of (a library, books, etc). **2** to enter (an item) in a catalogue. **3** to list or mention one by one: He catalogued her virtues. [from Greek katalegein, to reckon up]

. . . .
▣ noun **1** list, inventory, roll, register, roster, schedule, record, table, index, directory, gazetteer, brochure, prospectus.
verb **1, 2** list, register, record, index, classify, alphabetize, file.
. . . .

cataloguer noun a person who compiles a catalogue.

catalyse or **catalyze** verb, said of a chemical substance, known as a 'catalyst' to alter (the rate of a chemical reaction), usually by increasing it, without itself undergoing any permanent chemical change.

catalysis /kə'taləsɪs/ noun the process whereby a catalyst alters the rate of a chemical reaction, usually by increasing it. See also CATALYST. [from Greek catalysis, breaking up]

catalyst /'katəlɪst/ noun **1** Chem. any substance that changes the rate of a chemical reaction, especially by increasing it, without itself undergoing any permanent chemical change, eg finely divided metals, metal oxides, enzymes in living cells. **2** something or someone that causes, or speeds up the pace of, change.

catalytic /katə'lɪtɪk/ adj. of the nature of or involving catalysis.

catalytic converter a device, fitted to the exhaust system of a motor vehicle with a petrol or diesel engine, that is designed to reduce toxic emissions from the engine, and thereby reduce environmental pollution.

catalytic cracking in the petrochemical industry, the process whereby long-chain hydrocarbons produced during petroleum refining, eg heavy oils, are broken down into lighter, more useful, short-chain products, eg petrol or kerosene, using a catalyst such as silica or alumina.

catamaran /'katəməran, katəmə'ran/ noun **1** a sailing-boat with two hulls lying parallel to each other, joined across the top by the deck. **2** a raft made of logs or boats lashed together. [from Tamil kattumaram, tied wood]

cataplectic /katə'plɛktɪk/ adj. relating to or affected by cataplexy.

cataplexis /katə'plɛksɪs/ noun Zool. a physical state resembling death, adopted by some animals to discourage predators. [from Greek kataplexis, astonishment]

cataplexy /'katəplɛksɪ/ noun Medicine a sudden attack of muscular weakness that affects the whole body and causes collapse without loss of consciousness. It is triggered by strong emotion such as laughter, anger, or excitement.

catapult — noun **1** a Y-shaped stick with an elastic or rubber band fitted between its prongs, used especially by children for firing stones, etc. **2** Hist. a weapon of war designed to fire boulders. **3** an apparatus on an aircraft-carrier for launching aircraft. — verb **1** to fire or send flying with, or as if with, a catapult. **2** intrans. to be sent flying as if from a catapult. [from Greek kata, against + pallein, to throw]

☰ verb **1** hurl, propel, launch, fling, throw, pitch, toss, sling, shoot, fire.

cataract noun **1** Medicine an opaque area within the lens of the eye that produces blurring of vision, and may be caused by ageing, injury, diabetes, prolonged exposure to ionizing radiation, or various hereditary disorders. It is treated by surgical replacement of the affected lens, or by its removal and the use of corrective spectacles. **2** a succession of steep waterfalls within a river. **3** an immense rush of water, eg from a large waterfall that consists of a single vertical drop. [from Greek katarraktes, waterfall]

☰ **2** waterfall(s), falls, rapids. **3** cascade, downpour, torrent, deluge, force.

catarrh /kə'tɑː(r)/ noun inflammation of the mucous membranes lining the nose and throat, causing an excessive discharge of thick mucus. [from Greek kata, down + rheein, to flow]

catarrhal adj. of the nature of or relating to catarrh.

catastrophe /kə'tastrəfɪ/ noun **1** a terrible blow or calamity. **2** a great disaster, causing destruction, loss of life, etc. **3** a disastrous ending or conclusion. **4** a violent event in the geological history of the earth. [from Greek catastrophe, overturning, conclusion]

☰ **1, 2** disaster, calamity, cataclysm, debacle, fiasco, failure, ruin, devastation, tragedy, upheaval.

catastrophic /katə'strɒfɪk/ adj. of the nature of a catastrophe; disastrous.

catastrophically adv. so as to cause a catastrophe; disastrously.

catatonia /katə'təʊnɪə/ noun Medicine an abnormal mental state characterized either by stupor, mutism, and immobility, or by excessive excitement and violent or uncoordinated activity. It may be a symptom of a form of schizophrenia, or of hysteria or encephalitis. [from Greek kata, down + tonos, tension]

catatonic /katə'tɒnɪk/ — adj. relating to catatonia. — noun a person affected by catatonia.

cat burglar a burglar who breaks into buildings by climbing walls, water pipes, etc.

catcall noun a long shrill whistle expressing disagreement or disapproval.

catch — verb (PAST TENSE AND PAST PARTICIPLE caught) **1** to stop (a moving object) and hold it. **2** to manage to get hold of or trap, especially after a hunt or chase. **3** to be in time to get, reach, see, etc: catch the last post. **4** to overtake or draw level with. **5** to discover so as to prevent, or to encourage, the development of: the disease can be cured if caught early / catch children young for athletic training. **6** to surprise (someone) doing something wrong or embarrassing. **7** to trick or trap. **8** to become infected with. **9** trans., intrans. to become or cause to become accidentally attached or held: my dress caught on a nail. **10** to hit. **11** to manage to hear, see, or understand. **12** to attract (attention, etc): catch her eye. **13** intrans. to start burning. **14** to succeed in recording (a subtle quality, etc): the artist perfectly caught her expression. **15** Cricket to put (a batsman) out by catching the ball he has struck before it touches the ground. — noun **1** an act of catching. **2** a small device for keeping a lid, door, etc closed. **3** something caught. **4** the total amount of eg fish caught. **5** a hidden problem or disadvantage; a snag; some unsuspected trick in a question, etc. **6** something or someone that it would be advantageous to get hold of, eg a certain person as a husband or wife. **7** a slight breaking sound in one's voice, caused by emotion. **8** a children's game of throwing and catching a ball. **9** Mus. a humorous round sung by two or three people. — **be caught short** see SHORT. **be** or **get caught up in something** to be or get involved in it, especially unintentionally. **catch at something** to try to catch or hold it; to hold on to it briefly. **catch fire** to start burning. **catch hold of something** to grasp or grab it. **catch it** colloq. be scolded, punished, etc. **catch on** colloq. to become popular. (**catch on to something**) to understand it. **catch someone out 1** to trick them into making a mistake. **2** to discover them or take them unawares in embarrassing circumstances. **catch sight of** or **catch a glimpse of someone** or **something** to see them only for a brief moment. **catch up** or **catch up with someone** to draw level with someone ahead. (**catch up on something**) to bring oneself up to date with one's work, the latest news, etc. **catch something up** to pick it up or grab it hastily. [from Old French cachier, from Latin captiare, to try to catch]

☰ verb **1** hold, take, grasp, seize, grab, grip, clutch. **2** capture, trap, entrap, snare, ensnare, hook, net, arrest, apprehend. **6** surprise, expose, unmask, find (out), discover, detect. **7** trick, trap, dupe, fool, hoodwink. **8** contract, get, develop, go down with. **9** hook, snag, entangle. **11** hear, see, recognize, understand, grasp, perceive, discern, colloq. get. **13** ignite, light, flare. **14** capture, portray, evoke. noun **2** fastener, clip, hook, clasp, hasp, latch, bolt. **5** problem, disadvantage, drawback, snag, hitch, obstacle. **6** prize, conquest. **catch on to** understand, grasp, colloq. cotton on to, colloq. get. **catch out** discover, expose, unmask, find out. **catch up with someone** draw level with, gain on, overtake.

🔁 *verb* **1** drop. **2** release, free. **3** miss.

catch-22 *noun* a set of circumstances by which one is permanently frustrated and from which one cannot escape, all possible courses of action either having undesirable consequences or leading inevitably to further frustration of one's aims. [from the name of a novel by Joseph Heller (1961)]

catch-all *adj.*, *said of a phrase in an agreement, etc* covering all possibilities.

catch crop *Agric.* a fast-growing crop that is either planted between the rows of a main crop, or grown in the time interval between two main crops.

catcher *noun Baseball* the fielder who stands behind the batter.

catching *adj.*, *said of a disease* that is passed from one person to another.

🔲 infectious, contagious, communicable, transmittable.

catchment *noun* **1** the area of land that is drained by a particular river system or lake. **2** the population within the catchment area of a school, hospital, etc.

catchpenny *adj. derog.* poor in quality but designed to appeal to the eye and sell quickly.

catch phrase *noun* a frequently used popular and fashionable phrase or slogan.

catchword *noun* **1** a much-repeated, well-known word or phrase. **2** each of the two words printed in the top corners of each page of a dictionary or encyclopedia, indicating the first and last entry to be found on that page. **3** the first word of a page, printed at the bottom of the previous page.

🔲 **1** catch phrase, slogan, motto, watchword, byword, password.

catchy *adj.* (**catchier**, **catchiest**) *said of a song, etc* tuneful and easily remembered.

🔲 tuneful, memorable, haunting, popular, melodic, attractive, captivating.
🔁 dull, boring.

catechism /'katəkızəm/ *noun* **1** a series of questions and answers about the Christian religion, or a book containing this, used for instruction. **2** any long series of difficult questions, eg in an interview.

catechize /'katəkaız/ or **catechise** *verb* **1** to teach by means of a catechism, or using a question-and-answer method. **2** to question (a person) very thoroughly. [from Greek *katechizein*, to instruct orally]

categorical /katə'gɒrıkəl/ or **categoric** *adj.*, *said of a statement, refusal, denial, etc* absolute or definite; making no exceptions and giving no room for doubt or argument. [from Greek *kategorikos*; see CATEGORY]

🔲 absolute, definite, total, unqualified, unreserved, unconditional, unequivocal, clear, explicit, express, direct, utter, downright, positive, emphatic.
🔁 tentative, qualified.

categorically *adv.* so as to be categorical; definitely.

categorization or **categorisation** *noun* classification.

categorize or **categorise** *verb* to put into a category or categories; to classify.

🔲 classify, class, group, sort, grade, rank, order, list.

category /'katəgərı/ *noun* (PL. **categories**) a group of things, people, or concepts classed together because of some quality or qualities that they all have. [from Greek *kategoria*, statement, affirmation]

🔲 class, classification, group, grouping, sort, type, section, division, department, head, heading, grade, rank, order, list.

catenary /kə'tiːnərı, 'katənərı/ *noun* **1** *Maths.* the curve formed by a flexible chain or cable supported at both ends and hanging freely, acted on by no force other than gravity. **2** *Engineering* a similar structure, consisting of an overhead cable, that is used to deliver electric current to an electric railway locomotive or tram. [from Latin *catena*, chain]

cater *verb intrans.* (**catered**, **catering**) **1** (**cater for someone**) to supply food, accommodation, or entertainment for. **2** (**cater for someone or something**) to make provision for them; to take them into account. **3** (**cater to something**) to indulge or pander to unworthy desires, etc. [from Middle English *acatour*, buyer, from Old French]

🔲 **1, 2** provide, supply, furnish, serve.

caterer *noun* a person whose job is to provide food, etc for social occasions.

catering *noun* the job of a caterer.

caterpillar *noun* **1** the larva of a butterfly, moth, or sawfly, with a segmented worm-like body. **2** (*usually* **Caterpillar**) *trademark* **a** a continuous band or track made up of metal plates driven by cogs, used instead of wheels on heavy vehicles for travelling over rough surfaces. **b** a vehicle fitted with such tracks. [probably from Old French *chatepelose*, hairy cat]

caterwaul /'katəwɔːl/ — *verb intrans.* **1** *said of a cat* to make a loud high wailing noise. **2** to wail or shriek in this way. — *noun* a loud high wail. [formed from CAT¹]

caterwauling *noun* howling, wailing.

catfish *noun* any of several hundred mainly freshwater species of fish, all of which have long whisker-like sensory barbels around the mouth. The European catfish or *wels* has a large flattened body, up to 3m long, and feeds on frogs and fishes, and the *banjo catfishes* of S America have flat bodies and long thin tails.

catgut *noun* a strong cord made from the dried intestines of sheep and other animals (and formerly from those of cats), used in surgery for making stitches and ligatures, and also used for stringing violins and (now rarely) tennis rackets.

Cath. *abbrev.* Catholic.

catharsis /kə'θɑːsıs/ *noun* (PL. **catharses**) **1** *Psychol.* the emotional relief that results either from allowing repressed thoughts and feelings to surface, as in psychoanalysis, or from an intensely dramatic experience, originally a stage tragedy that inspired acute fear and pity in the onlooker. **2** *Medicine* the process of clearing out or purging the bowels. [from Greek *kathairein*, to purify]

cathartic /kə'θɑːtık/ *adj.* **1** resulting in catharsis. **2** cleansing; purgative.

cathedral /kə'θiːdrəl/ *noun* the principal church of a diocese (the area presided over by a bishop), in which the bishop has his throne. [from Greek *kathedra*, seat]

Catherine wheel /'kaθərın/ a wheel-like firework which is fixed to a post, etc and which whirls round when set off. [named after St Catherine, who escaped being martyred on a spiked wheel]

catheter /'kaθıtə(r)/ *noun Medicine* a hollow slender flexible tube that can be introduced into a narrow opening or body cavity in order to drain a liquid, most commonly inserted into the urethra in order to drain urine from the urinary bladder. [from Greek *kathienai*, to send down]

cathode *noun* **1** the negative electrode in an electrolytic cell, towards which positively charged ions, usually in solution, are attracted. **2** the positive terminal of a battery. See also ANODE. [from Greek *kathodos*, descent]

cathode rays a stream of electrons emitted from the surface of a cathode (negative electrode) in a vacuum tube.

cathode-ray tube an evacuated glass tube (vacuum

tube) in which streams of electrons, known as cathode rays, are produced. Cathode-ray tubes are used to display images in television sets, the visual display units of computers, cathode-ray oscilloscopes, and radar equipment.

catholic — *adj.* **1** (**Catholic**) relating or belonging to the Roman Catholic Church. **2** (**Catholic**) relating to the whole Christian Church, or to the Church before the East – West split of 1054, or to the Western Church before the split caused by the Reformation. **3** *said especially of a person's interests and tastes* broad; wide-ranging. — *noun* (**Catholic**) a member of the Roman Catholic Church. [from Greek *katholikos*, universal]

⊟ *adj.* **3** broad, wide, wide-ranging, universal, global, general, comprehensive, inclusive, all-inclusive, all-embracing, liberal, tolerant, broad-minded.

⊟ *adj.* narrow, limited, narrow-minded.

catholicity /kaθəˈlɪsɪtɪ/ *noun* **1** universality. **2** liberality or breadth of view. **3** Catholicism.

cation /ˈkataɪən/ *noun Physics* any positively charged ion, which moves towards the cathode during electrolysis. See also ANION. [from Greek *kateinai*, to go down]

catkin *noun Bot.* in certain tree species, eg birch, hazel, a flowering shoot that bears many small unisexual flowers, adapted for wind pollination. [from Old Dutch *kateken*, kitten]

catmint or **catnip** *noun Bot.* a square-stemmed perennial plant (Nepeta cataria), native to Europe and Asia, and having oval toothed leaves and spikes of white two-lipped flowers spotted with purple, so called because its strong scent is attractive to cats.

catnap — *noun* a short sleep. — *verb intrans.* (**catnapped, catnapping**) to doze; to sleep briefly, especially without lying down.

cat-o'-nine-tails *noun Hist.* a whip with nine knotted rope lashes, used as an instrument of punishment in the navy.

CAT scanner *abbrev. Medicine* computer-assisted or computed axial tomography scanner, a machine that produces X-ray images of cross-sectional 'slices' through the brain or other soft body tissues.

cat's cradle a game with a long piece of string, which is looped over the fingers and passed from person to person in a series of changing patterns.

cat's eye 1 (**Cat's eye**) *trademark* a small glass reflecting device, one of a series set into the surface along the centre of a road to guide drivers. **2** a type of precious stone.

cat's paw a person used by someone else to perform an unpleasant job.

catsuit *noun* a woman's close-fitting garment, combining trousers and top.

cattery *noun* (PL. **catteries**) a place where cats are bred or looked after. [see CAT[1]]

cattily *adv.* in a catty way.

cattiness *noun* being catty.

cattle *pl. noun* **1** any of various large, heavily built, grass-eating mammals, including wild species, which are all horned (eg the bison, buffalo, and yak), and domestic cattle, which are descended from the auroch, a wild species that once lived in Europe but is now extinct. **2** often used to refer to domesticated forms of this animal which are farmed for their milk, meat, and hides. [from Old French *catel*, property]

⊟ COWS, BULLS, OXEN, LIVESTOCK, STOCK, BEASTS.

Breeds of cattle include: Aberdeen Angus, Africander, Alderney, Ankole, Ayrshire, Blonde d'Aquitaine, Brahman, Brown Swiss, cattabu, cattalo, Charolais, Chillingham, Devon, dexter, Durham, Friesian, Galloway, Guernsey, Hereford, Highland, Holstein, Jersey, Latvian, Limousin, Longhorn, Luing, Red Poll, Romagnola, Santa Gertrudis, Shetland, Shorthorn, Simmenthaler, Teeswater, Ukrainian, Welsh Black.

cattle cake a concentrated processed food for cattle, made from the compressed seeds of soya bean, groundnut, and various other plants.

cattle grid a grid of parallel metal bars covering a trench or depression in a road where it passes through a fence, designed to allow pedestrians and wheeled vehicles to pass unhindered, while preventing the passage of animal livestock.

cattleya /ˈkatlɪə/ *noun* one of the most popular cultivated orchids, an epiphyte, native to SE Asia and S America. It has swollen green bulb-like stems for storing water, and produces spikes of up to 47 large showy flowers. [named after the English botanist William Cattley]

catty *adj.* (**cattier, cattiest**) inclined to talk spitefully about other people. [see CAT[1]]

catwalk *noun* **1** a narrow walkway, usually at a high level, eg alongside a bridge. **2** the narrow raised stage along which models walk at a fashion show.

Caucasian /kɔːˈkeɪʒən/ — *adj.* **1** relating to the Caucasus, a mountain range between the Black Sea and the Caspian Sea, representing the boundary between Europe and Asia. **2** belonging to one of the light-skinned or white races of mankind. **3** denoting a family of 38 languages spoken in the area of the Caucasus mountains, between the Black Sea and the Caspian Sea. — *noun* **1** an inhabitant or native of the Caucasus. **2** a white-skinned person. **3** the languages forming the Caucasian family.

Caucasoid /ˈkɔːkəzɔɪd/ *adj.* belonging to the Caucasian race.

caucus *noun* (PL. **caucuses**) **1** *derog.* a small dominant group of people taking independent decisions within a larger organization. **2** *North Amer., esp. US* a group of members of a political party, or a meeting of such a group for some purpose.

caudal *adj.* **1** *Anat.* relating to, resembling, or in the position of a tail. **2** relating to the tail end of the body. [from Latin *cauda*, tail]

caudate *adj. Zool.* having a tail or a tail-like appendage. [from Latin *caudatus*, from *cauda*, tail]

caught /kɔːt/ see CATCH.

caul *noun* a membrane that sometimes surrounds an infant's head at birth, and consists of part of the amnion (the innermost membrane that surrounds the fetus). [from Old French *cale*, little cap]

cauldron *noun* a very large bowl-shaped metal pot for boiling or heating liquids. [from Old French *cauderon*]

cauliflower *noun* **1** a biennial plant that is a type of cultivated cabbage (Brassica oleracea), widely cultivated for its edible flower-head. **2** the edible immature flower-head of this plant, consisting of a mass of creamy-white flower buds, which can be cooked and eaten as a vegetable. [from the earlier *colieflorie*, with spelling influenced by Latin *caulis*, cabbage, and FLOWER]

cauliflower ear an ear permanently swollen and misshapen by injury, especially from repeated blows.

caulk /kɔːk/ *verb* to fill up (the seams or joints of a boat) with tarred rope, called oakum; to make (a boat) watertight by this means. [from Latin *calcare*, to trample]

causal *adj.* **1** relating to, or being, a cause. **2** relating to cause and effect. [from Latin *causalis*]

causality *noun* **1** the relationship between cause and effect. **2** the principle that everything has a cause. **3** the process at work in the causing of something.

causally *adv.* in a causal way.

causation *noun* **1** the relationship of cause and effect; causality. **2** the process of causing. [from Latin *causatio*]

causative — *adj.* **1** making something happen; producing an effect. **2** *Grammar* expressing the action of causing. — *noun* a causative verb. [from Latin *causativus*]

causatively *adv.* in a causative way.

cause — *noun* **1** something which produces an effect; the person or thing through which something happens. **2** a reason or justification: *there is no cause for concern*. **3** an ideal, principle, aim, etc, that people support and work for. **4** a matter that is to be settled by a lawsuit; the lawsuit itself. — *verb* to produce as an effect; to bring about. — **make common cause with someone** to co-operate with them, so as to achieve a common aim. [from Latin *causa*]

. . . .

▣ *noun* **1** source, origin, beginning, root, basis, spring, originator, creator, maker, agent, agency. **2** reason,

motive, justification, grounds, motivation, stimulus, incentive, inducement, impulse. **3** ideal, principle, aim, object, purpose, end, belief, conviction, movement, undertaking, enterprise. *verb* bring about, give rise to, lead to, result in, begin, occasion, effect, produce, generate, create, precipitate, motivate, stimulate, provoke, incite, induce.

▣ *noun* **1** effect, result, consequence. *verb* stop, prevent.

. . . .

'cause *contr. colloq.* because.

cause célèbre /'kɔːz 'səlɛbrə/ *noun* (PL. **causes célèbres**) a legal case, or some other matter, that attracts much attention and causes controversy. [French, = famous case]

causeway *noun* **1** a raised roadway crossing low-lying, marshy ground or shallow water. **2** a stone-paved pathway. [from Old French *caucie*, from Latin (*via*) *calciata*, limestone-paved (way)]

caustic /'kɔːstɪk/ — *adj.* **1** *Chem.*, *said of a chemical substance* strongly alkaline and corrosive to living tissue, eg sodium hydroxide (caustic soda). **2** *said of remarks, etc* sarcastic; cutting; bitter. — *noun* **1** caustic soda. **2** *Optics* the curve produced when parallel rays of light are reflected in a large concave mirror, or refracted by a convex lens. [from Greek *kaustikos*, capable of burning]

. . . .

▣ *adj.* **2** cutting, bitter, acrimonious, sarcastic, biting, stinging, acid, mordant, scathing, virulent, burning, trenchant, keen, pungent, severe.

▣ *adj.* **2** soothing, mild.

. . . .

caustically *adv.* with a caustic effect or manner.

causticity /kɔːˈstɪsɪtɪ/ *noun* being caustic.

caustic soda same as SODIUM HYDROXIDE.

cauterization or **cauterisation** /kɔːtəraɪˈzeɪʃən/ *noun Medicine* the intentional destruction of living tissue by the direct application of a heated instrument (a cautery), an electric current, a laser beam, or a caustic chemical, in order to remove small warts, seal blood vessels, etc.

cauterize or **cauterise** *verb* to destroy (living tissue) by the direct application of a heated instrument, an electric current, a laser beam, or a caustic chemical. See also CAUTERIZATION. [from Latin *cauterizare*, from Greek *kauter*, branding-iron]

caution *noun* **1** care in avoiding danger; prudent wariness. **2** a warning. **3** a reprimand or scolding for an offence, accompanied by a warning not to repeat it. **4** *Legal* a warning from the police to someone suspected of an offence, that anything he or she says may be used as evidence. **5** *old colloq. use* an amusing person or thing. — *verb* (**cautioned, cautioning**) **1** *trans., intrans.* to warn or admonish someone. **2** to give (someone) a legal caution. [from Latin *cautio*]

. . . .

▣ *noun* **1** care, carefulness, prudence, vigilance, watchfulness, alertness, heed, discretion, forethought, deliberation, wariness. **2** warning, caveat, injunction, admonition, advice, counsel. **3** reprimand, scolding, warning, admonition, injunction, rebuke, *colloq.* dressing-down. *verb* **1** warn, advise, urge, admonish, rebuke.

▣ *noun* **1** carelessness, recklessness.

. . . .

cautionary *adj.* giving, or acting as, a warning: *cautionary remarks.*

cautious *adj.* having or showing caution; careful; wary. [see CAUTION]

▣ careful, wary, circumspect, chary, guarded, tentative, softly-softly, *colloq.* cagey, judicious, prudent, vigilant, watchful, alert, heedful, discreet, tactful, unadventurous.

▣ incautious, imprudent, heedless, reckless, rash.

. . . .

cautiously *adv.* in a cautious way.

cautiousness *noun* being cautious.

cavalcade /kavlˈkeɪd, ˈkavlkeɪd/ *noun* a ceremonial procession of cars, horseback riders, etc. [from French *cavalcade*, from Italian *cavalcata*, raid on horseback]

. . . .

▣ procession, parade, march-past, troop, array, retinue, train.

. . . .

cavalier /kavəˈlɪə(r)/ — *noun* **1** *old use* a horseman or knight. **2** *old use* a courtly gentleman. **3** *now facetious* a man acting as escort to a lady. **4** (**Cavalier**) *Hist.* a supporter of Charles I during the 17c English Civil War. — *adj. derog.*, *said of a person's behaviour, attitude, etc* thoughtless, offhand, casual, or disrespectful. [from Italian *cavaliere*, from Latin *caballarius*, horseman]

. . . .

▣ *noun* **1** horseman, equestrian, knight. **3** gallant, escort, partner, gentleman. *adj.* offhand, thoughtless, casual, disrespectful, arrogant, supercilious, condescending, scornful, disdainful, curt, lordly, haughty, lofty, swaggering, insolent.

. . . .

cavalierly *adv.* with a cavalier manner.

cavalry *noun* (PL. **cavalries**) (*sing.*) **1** *usually Hist.* the part of an army consisting of soldiers on horseback. **2** the part of an army consisting of soldiers in armoured vehicles. [from French *cavallerie*, from Latin *caballarius*, horseman]

cavalryman *noun* a member of a cavalry troop.

cave *noun* a large natural hollow chamber either underground, usually with an opening to the surface, or in the side of a mountain, hillside, or cliff. Underground caves are often associated with limestone rocks, which are slowly dissolved by underground streams, and frequently contain stalactites and stalagmites. Sea caves are formed as a result of wave action. — **cave in 1** *said of walls, a roof, etc* to collapse inwards. **2** *colloq.*, *said of a person* to give way to persuasion. [from Latin *cavus*, hollow]

. . . .

▣ *noun* cavern, grotto, hole, pothole, hollow, cavity. **cave in 1** collapse, subside, give way, fall, slip. **2** give way, give in, yield, succumb, capitulate, concede, submit, surrender.

. . . .

caveat /'kavɪat, 'keɪvɪat/ *noun* **1** a warning. **2** *Legal* an official request that a court should not take some particular action without warning the person who is making the request. [from Latin *caveat*, let him or her beware]

cave-in *noun* **1** the sudden collapse of a roof, mine workings, etc. **2** a submission or surrender.

caveman *noun* **1** (*also* **cave-dweller**) a person of prehistoric times, living in caves. **2** *derog.* a man of crude, brutish behaviour.

caver *noun* a person whose pastime is exploring caves.

cavern /'kavən/ *noun* a large cave or an underground chamber. [from Latin *caverna*, from *cavus*, hollow]

cavernous *adj.* **1** *said of a hole or space* deep and vast. **2** *said of rocks* full of caverns.

. . . .

▣ **1** deep, vast, gaping, yawning, sunken, hollow, concave, echoing, resonant.

. . . .

cavetto /ka'vɛtəʊ/ *noun* (PL. **cavetti**) *Archit.* a hollowed moulding with a curvature of a quarter of a circle, used chiefly in cornices, eg on ancient Egyptian buildings. [an Italian diminutive of *cavo*, from Latin *cavus*, hollow]

caviare /'kavɪɑː(r)/ or **caviar** *noun* the salted hard roe of the sturgeon, used as food and considered a delicacy. [perhaps from Turkish *havyar*]

cavil /'kavıl/ — *verb intrans.* (**cavilled, cavilling**) (**cavil at** or **about something**) to object to it, or find fault with it, especially trivially or unnecessarily. — *noun* a trivial objection. [from Latin *cavillari*, to scoff]

caviller *noun* a person who cavils.

caving *noun* the sport of exploring caves.

cavitation *noun Physics* **1** the formation of cavities in a structure. **2** the formation of gas bubbles in a liquid. **3** the formation of a partial vacuum in a liquid moving at high speed.

cavity *noun* (PL. **cavities**) **1** a hollow or hole. **2** a hole in a tooth, caused by decay. [from Latin *cavitas*, hollowness]

. . . .
🔳 **1** hollow, hole, gap, dent, crater, pit, well, sinus, ventricle.
. . . .

cavity wall a wall of a building constructed in two separate layers or partitions with a space between them.

cavort /kə'vɔːt/ *verb intrans.* to jump, prance, or caper about.

. . . .
🔳 jump, prance, caper, frolic, gambol, romp, skip, dance, frisk, sport.
. . . .

cavy /'keıvı/ *noun* (PL. **cavies**) any of various rodents native to S America, including guinea pigs and a wide range of rodents. [from Cabiai, a native name in French Guiana]

caw — *noun* the loud harsh cry of a crow or rook. — *verb intrans.* to make this cry. [imitative]

cay see KEY[2].

cayenne /keɪ'en/ or **cayenne pepper** *noun* a hot spice made from the seeds of certain types of capsicum, a tropical American vegetable. [formerly *cayan*, from Tupi (S American language), changed by association with Cayenne in French Guiana]

cayman or **caiman** /'keɪmən/ *noun* (PL. **caymans**) a reptile closely related to the alligator, native to tropical regions of Central and S America, up to 2m long, and often having bony plates embedded in the skin of its belly. [from Spanish *caimán*, from Carib, a West Indian language]

CB *abbrev.* **1** Citizens' Band. **2** Companion of the Order of the Bath.

CBC *abbrev.* Canadian Broadcasting Corporation.

CBE *abbrev.* Commander of the Order of the British Empire.

CBS *abbrev.* Columbia Broadcasting System.

CBSO *abbrev.* City of Birmingham Symphony Orchestra.

cc or **c.c.** *abbrev.* **1** carbon copy or copies. **2** cubic centimetre.

CCC *abbrev.* County Cricket Club.

CCD *abbrev. Electron.* charge-coupled device.

CCTV *abbrev.* closed-circuit television.

CD *abbrev.* **1** compact disc. **2** civil defence, or Civil Defence (Corps), a voluntary organization of civilians, active especially in World War II, trained to cope with the effects of enemy attack. **3** Corps Diplomatique (French), Diplomatic Corps, the body of diplomats in the service of any country.

Cd *symbol Chem.* cadmium.

cd *abbrev.* candela.

CD-i or **CDI** or **CD-I** *abbrev. Comput.* compact disc interactive.

CDN *abbrev., as an international vehicle mark* Canada.

Cdr *abbrev.* Commander.

CD-ROM *abbrev. Comput.* compact disc read-only memory.

CDT *abbrev.* craft, design, technology.

CE or **C.E.** *abbrev.* Common Era: used instead of AD in dates.

Ce *symbol Chem.* cerium.

cease *verb trans., intrans.* to bring or come to an end. — **without cease** *formal* continuously. [from Old French *cesser*]

. . . .
🔳 end, stop, desist, refrain, halt, call a halt, break off, discontinue, finish, conclude, terminate.
🔳 begin, start, commence.
. . . .

cease-fire *noun* **1** a break in the fighting during a war, agreed to by both sides. **2** the order to stop firing.

ceaseless *adj.* continuous; going on without a pause or break.

. . . .
🔳 continuous, non-stop, incessant, interminable, constant, perpetual, continual, persistent, endless, unending, never-ending, everlasting, eternal, untiring, unremitting.
🔳 occasional, irregular.
. . . .

ceaselessly *adv.* without ceasing; endlessly.

cedar *noun* **1** any of various tall coniferous trees of the genus Cedrus of the pine family, noted for its flat crown with widely spreading branches, its needle-like foliage and reddish-brown bark. **2** the hard yellow sweet-smelling wood of this tree, used as building timber and for making furniture. [from Greek *kedros*]

cedarwood *noun* same as CEDAR 2.

cede *verb* **1** to hand over or give up formally. **2** *intrans.* to yield or give way: *cede to a higher authority.* [from Latin *cedere*, to yield]

. . . .
🔳 **1** hand over, give up, surrender, relinquish, forego, waive, resign, abdicate, renounce, abandon, convey, transfer. **2** yield, give way, surrender, concede, succumb, capitulate, submit, acquiesce, accede, grant, allow.
. . . .

cedilla /sə'dɪlə/ *noun* **1** in French and Portuguese, a mark put under *c* in some words (eg *façade*) to show that it is to be pronounced like *s*, not like *k*. **2** the same mark used under other letters in other languages to indicate various sounds. [from Spanish, a variant of *zedilla*, diminutive of *zeda*, z]

Ceefax /'siːfaks/ *noun trademark* a television information service provided by the BBC. [from the phrase *see facts*]

CEGB *abbrev.* Central Electricity Generating Board.

ceilidh /'keılı/ *noun* originally in Scotland and Ireland, an informal gathering, especially with entertainment in the form of songs, story-telling, instrumental music, and dancing. [from Gaelic *ceilidh*, visit]

ceiling *noun* **1** the inner roof of a room, etc. **2** an upper limit. **3** the maximum height that a particular aircraft can reach. **4** the height above the ground of the base of the cloud-layer. [from Middle English *celen*, to panel]

celandine *noun* (*also* **lesser celandine**) a low-growing perennial plant (Ranunculus ficaria), native to Europe and W Asia, found mainly in damp woods and meadows and along hedgerows, having heart-shaped dark green leaves, and flowers with eight to twelve glossy golden-yellow petals that gradually fade to white. [from Greek *chelidonion*, from *chelidon*, swallow, the flowering of the plant coinciding with the arrival of the swallows in spring]

celebrant *noun* a person who performs a religious ceremony.

celebrate *verb* **1** to mark (eg a success or other happy occasion, a birthday or other anniversary) with festivities. **2** *intrans.* to do something enjoyable to mark a happy occasion, anniversary, etc. **3** to give public praise or recognition to, eg in the form of a poem. **4** to conduct (a religious ceremony, eg a marriage or mass). [from Latin *celebrare*, to honour]

. . . .
🔳 **1** commemorate, mark, remember, observe, keep. **2** rejoice. **3** praise, extol, eulogize, commend, honour, exalt, glorify, toast, drink to. **4** conduct, solemnize.
. . . .

celebrated *adj.* famous; widely acclaimed.

▪ famous, acclaimed, well-known, famed, renowned, illustrious, glorious, eminent, distinguished, exalted, revered, notable, prominent, outstanding, popular.
▪ unknown, obscure, forgotten.

celebration *noun* the action or state of celebrating.

▪ merrymaking, festivity, revelry, jollification, party, *colloq.* rave-up, festival, gala, commemoration, observance, anniversary, jubilee, remembrance.

celebrator *noun* a person who celebrates.
celebratory /sɛlə'breɪtərɪ/ *adj.* of the nature of a celebration.
celebrity *noun* (PL. **celebrities**) **1** a famous person. **2** fame. [from Latin *celebritas*, fame]

▪ **1** personality, star, superstar, *colloq.* VIP, name, big name, personage, dignitary, luminary, worthy. **2** fame, renown, stardom, prominence, eminence, illustriousness, glory, honour, esteem.
▪ **1** nobody, nonentity.

celeriac /sə'lerɪak/ *noun* **1** a variety of celery (Apium graveolens var. *rapaceum*), widely cultivated for the swollen edible base of its stem. **2** the swollen base of the stem of this plant, which is eaten raw in salads or cooked as a vegetable.
celerity *noun formal* quickness. [from Latin *celeritas*]
celery *noun* **1** a biennial plant (Apium graveolens var. *dulce*), native to Europe, W Asia, and Africa, having shiny leaves divided into segments, and tiny greenish-white flowers borne in flat-topped clusters. It is widely cultivated for its edible deeply grooved swollen leaf stalks. **2** the edible leaf stalks of this plant, which can be eaten raw or cooked as a vegetable. [from French *céleri*, from Greek *selinon*, parsley]
celesta *noun* a keyboard instrument, resembling a small upright piano, from which soft bell-like sounds are produced by hammers striking steel plates suspended over wooden resonators. [from French *céleste*, heavenly]
celestial /sə'lestɪəl/ *adj.* **1** belonging to, or relating to, the sky: *celestial bodies*. **2** belonging to heaven; heavenly; divine: *celestial voices*. [from Latin *celestialis*, from *caelum*, the heavens]
celestial equator *Astron.* the great circle in which the plane of the Earth's equator meets the celestial sphere and divides it into northern and southern hemispheres. The angular distance of a star or planet north or south of the celestial equator is known as *declination*.
celestial mechanics *Astron.* the branch of astronomy concerned with the movement of celestial bodies in gravitational fields, especially the motion of planets, binary stars, artificial satellites, and other objects that are in orbit. It is based on Newton's laws of motion and gravity.
celestial sphere *Astron.* an infinitely large imaginary sphere on which the stars and other celestial bodies appear to lie when viewed by an observer at the centre of the sphere, represented by the Earth. It is used to specify the position of stars and other celestial bodies in relation to the Earth.
celiac /'siːlɪak/ *adj., noun North Amer., esp. US* same as COELIAC.
celibacy *noun* the state or habit of being celibate.

▪ singleness, chastity, virginity, purity, abstinence, continence, bachelorhood, spinsterhood.

celibate — *adj.* **1** unmarried, especially in obedience to a religious vow. **2** having no sexual relations with anyone. — *noun* a person who is unmarried, especially because of a religious vow. [from Latin *caelebs*, unmarried]

cell *noun* **1** a small room for an inmate in a prison or monastery. **2** *Biol.* the basic structural unit of all living organisms (except viruses), consisting of a mass of protein material (the protoplasm), which is composed of the cytoplasm (a watery jelly-like material) and usually a nucleus. **3** *Electr.* an electrolytic cell, consisting of two electrodes (an anode and a cathode) immersed in an electrolyte. When an electric current is passed through the electrolyte from an external source, electrolysis occurs. **4** a voltaic cell, which produces a current as a result of the conversion of chemical energy to electrical energy at the surface of two electrodes (an anode and a cathode) immersed in an electrolyte. **5** one of the cavities or compartments in a honeycomb or in a structure similarly divided. **6** *Radio* a radio transmitter serving one of the geographical areas into which a country is divided for coverage by cellular radio. **7** one of these geographical areas. **8** *Comput.* a unit or area of storage in computing, eg the smallest unit capable of storing a single bit. **9** a small group of people (especially spies or terrorists) conducting their own operation within a larger organization. **10** *Hist.* a tiny one-roomed dwelling used by a hermit. [from Latin *cella*, room, small apartment]

▪ **1** room, cubicle, prison, dungeon. **5** cavity, compartment, chamber.

cellar — *noun* **1** a room, usually underground, for storage, eg of wine. **2** a stock of wines. — *verb* (**cellared, cellaring**) to store in a cellar. [from Latin *cellarium*, storeroom, pantry]

▪ *noun* **1** room, basement, wine cellar, storeroom, vault, crypt.

cellarage *noun* **1** the volume of cellar space in a building. **2** the cost of storing goods in a cellar.
cell body *Anat.* the enlarged part of a neurone (nerve cell) that contains the nucleus and cytoplasm, and from which the long thread-like axon extends.
cellist /'tʃɛlɪst/ *noun* a person who plays the cello.
cell membrane *Biol.* the surface membrane surrounding a cell.
cello /'tʃɛləʊ/ *noun* (PL. **cellos**) a stringed musical instrument similar to a violin but much larger, played sitting, with the neck of the instrument against the player's shoulder. It has four strings tuned an octave below the viola; 17c and early 18c versions had five strings. [short for VIOLONCELLO]
Cellophane *noun trademark* a material consisting of thin transparent sheeting manufactured from regenerated cellulose, used as a wrapping material for food and other products, and in dialysis tubes. [from CELLULOSE + Greek *phainein*, to shine or appear]
cellphone *noun Radio* a portable telephone for use in a cellular radio system.
cellular *adj.* **1** composed of cells, or divided into cell-like compartments. **2** containing many cavities or holes; porous. **3** knitted with an open pattern. [from Latin *cellula*, tiny cell or room]
cellular radio a system of mobile radio communication, widely used in car phones, based on a network of roughly hexagonal geographical areas (about 5km across) known as *cells*, each of which is served by a separate transmitter. The receiving equipment automatically tunes in by switching frequencies as it passes from one cell to another.
cellule *noun Biol.* a small cell. [from Latin *cellula*, tiny cell or room]
cellulite *noun* deposits of fat cells that do not respond to a change in diet or exercise regime, and which give the skin a dimpled pitted appearance. [from French, from Latin *cellula*, little cell]
celluloid *noun trademark* **1** a transparent highly flammable plastic material made from cellulose nitrate and camphor, formerly widely used in photographic film, but

now largely superseded by cellulose acetate, which is non-flammable. **2** cinema film.

cellulose /ˈsɛljʊlouz/ *noun* a complex carbohydrate that is the main constituent of plant cell walls, and is responsible for their strength and rigidity. It is used in the manufacture of paper, rope, textiles (eg cotton, linen, viscose, and acetate), and plastics (eg cellophane and celluloid). [from French *cellule*, tiny cell]

cellulose acetate *Chem.* a tough, flexible, non-flammable, thermoplastic resin formed by treating cellulose with acetic acid, and used to make photographic film, magnetic tape, lacquers, varnishes, and acetate fibres, eg rayon.

cellulose nitrate *Chem.* a highly flammable pulpy solid prepared by treating cellulose with concentrated nitric acid. It is used as an explosive and propellant, and was formerly used in photographic film, plastics, and lacquers.

cell wall *Bot.* in plant cells, the relatively rigid outer wall that surrounds the membrane of the cell, and consists mainly of cellulose. Animal cells do not have cell walls.

Celsius or **Celsius scale** (ABBREV. **C**) a scale of temperature, formerly known as the centigrade scale, in which the freezing point of water is 0°C and its boiling point is 100°C, the temperature range between these fixed points being divided into 100 degrees. [named after Anders Celsius]

Celt /kɛlt/ *noun* a member of one of the ancient peoples that inhabited most parts of Europe in pre-Roman and Roman times, or of the peoples descended from them, eg in Scotland, Wales, and Ireland. [from Greek *Keltoi*, Celts]

Celtic — *adj.* relating to the Celts or their languages. — *noun* the group of languages spoken by the Celts, including Gaelic, Irish, Manx, Welsh, Cornish, and Breton.

cement /səˈmɛnt/ — *noun* **1** a fine powder that hardens when mixed with water, and is formed by grinding a heated mixture of clay and limestone. It is used in building as an ingredient of mortar and concrete. **2** any of various substances used as adhesives for bonding to a hard material. **3** the thin layer of hard bony tissue that anchors the roots of the teeth to the jaws. **4** *Geol.* any material, especially precipitated mineral salts, that binds loose particles of sediment together to form solid rock. — *verb* **1** to stick together with cement. **2** to apply cement. **3** to bind or make firm (eg a friendship). [from Old French *ciment*, from Latin *caementum*, quarried stone]

⋯⋯⋯⋯⋯⋯⋯⋯⋯⋯⋯

◩ *noun* **2** adhesive, glue, gum, paste. *verb* **1** stick, bond, join, unite, bind. **3** bind, bond, join, unite, seal, weld.

⋯⋯⋯⋯⋯⋯⋯⋯⋯⋯⋯⋯⋯⋯⋯⋯

cementation *noun* **1** the act of cementing. **2** the process of impregnating the surface of one substance with another by surrounding it with powder and applying heat. Cementation is used in case-hardening and the conversion of glass into porcelain, and was formerly used in steel-making. **3** the process of injecting fluid cement mixture into a hole or cavity for strengthening purposes.

cemetery /ˈsɛmɪtrɪ/ *noun* (PL. **cemeteries**) a burial ground for the dead, especially one that is not attached to a church. [from Greek *koimeterion*, sleeping-room, burial place]

⋯⋯⋯⋯⋯⋯⋯⋯⋯⋯

◩ burial ground, graveyard, churchyard.

⋯⋯⋯⋯⋯⋯⋯⋯⋯⋯⋯⋯⋯⋯⋯⋯

cenotaph *noun* a tomb-like monument in honour of a person or people buried elsewhere, especially soldiers killed in war. [from Greek *kenos*, empty + *taphos*, tomb]

Cenozoic /siːnoʊˈzoʊɪk/ or **Cainozoic** *adj. Geol.* denoting the most recent era of the Phanerozoic eon, lasting from about 65 million years ago to the present day, and subdivided into the Tertiary and Quaternary periods. [from Greek *kainos*, new + *zoe*, life]

censer *noun* a container in which incense is burnt, used eg in some churches. [from Latin *incensarium*]

censor — *noun* an official who examines books, films, newspaper articles, etc and has the power to cut out any

parts thought undesirable (eg because containing information a government wants kept secret) or offensive (eg because over-violent or sexually too explicit), and to forbid publication or showing altogether. — *verb* to alter or cut out parts of, or forbid publication, showing, or delivery of. [from Latin *censor*, a Roman official empowered to punish moral and political offences]

⋯⋯⋯⋯⋯⋯⋯⋯⋯

◩ *verb* cut, edit, blue-pencil, bowdlerize, expurgate.

⋯⋯⋯⋯⋯⋯⋯⋯⋯⋯⋯⋯⋯⋯⋯⋯

censorial *adj.* relating to a censor or the activity of a censor.

censorious *adj.* inclined to find fault; severely critical. [from Latin *censorius*, relating to a censor, hence severe]

⋯⋯⋯⋯⋯⋯⋯⋯⋯

◩ critical, hypercritical, disparaging, fault-finding, condemnatory, disapproving, carping, cavilling, severe.
◪ complimentary, approving.

⋯⋯⋯⋯⋯⋯⋯⋯⋯⋯⋯⋯⋯⋯

censoriously *adv.* in a censorious or critical manner.

censorship *noun* **1** the practice of censoring. **2** the job of a censor.

censurable *adj.* **1** deserving censure. **2** capable of being censured.

censure /ˈsɛnʃə(r)/ — *noun* severe criticism or disapproval. — *verb* to criticize severely or express strong disapproval of. [from French *censure*, from Latin *censura*, the job of a censor]

⋯⋯⋯⋯⋯⋯⋯⋯⋯

◩ *noun* criticism, disapproval, condemnation, blame, admonishment, admonition, reprehension, reproof, reproach, rebuke, reprimand, *colloq.* telling-off. *verb* criticize, condemn, denounce, blame, castigate, admonish, reprehend, reprove, upbraid, reproach, rebuke, reprimand, scold, *colloq.* tell off.
◪ *noun* praise, compliments, approval. *verb* praise, compliment, approve.

⋯⋯⋯⋯⋯⋯⋯⋯⋯⋯⋯⋯⋯⋯⋯

census *noun* **1** an official count, carried out at intervals, of a population, covering information such as sex, age, job, etc. **2** an official count made of something else, eg vehicles using a particular road. [from Latin *census*, from *censere*, to assess]

cent *noun* a currency unit of several countries, worth one-hundredth of the standard unit, eg of the US dollar. [from Latin *centum*, a hundred]

cent. *abbrev.* **1** centigrade. **2** central. **3** century.

centaur *noun* Greek *Mythol.* a creature with a man's head, arms, and trunk joined to the four-legged body of a horse. [from Greek *kentauros*]

centenarian /sɛntəˈnɛərɪən/ — *noun* a person who is 100 years old or more. — *adj.* **1** 100 years old or more. **2** relating to a centenarian. [from Latin *centenarius*, composed of 100]

centenary /sɛnˈtiːnərɪ/ — *noun* (PL. **centenaries**) the 100th anniversary of some event, or the celebration of it. — *adj.* **1** occurring every 100 years. **2** relating to a period of 100 years. [from Latin *centenarius*, composed of 100]

centennial /sɛnˈtɛnɪəl/ — *noun* North Amer. a centenary. — *adj.* **1** relating to a period of 100 years. **2** occurring every 100 years. **3** lasting 100 years. [from Latin *centum*, 100 + *-ennial* as in BIENNIAL]

centi- *combining form* denoting a hundred. [from Latin *centum*, hundred]

centigrade or **centigrade scale** (ABBREV. **C**) the former name for the Celsius scale of temperature. [from Latin *centum*, 100 + *gradus*, step]

centime /ˈsɒtiːm/ *noun* a currency unit of several countries, worth one-hundredth of the standard unit, eg of the French franc. [from Old French *centiesme*, from Latin *centesimum*, one-hundredth]

centimetre *noun* (**cm**) in the metric system, a basic unit of length equal to 0.01m (one hundredth of a metre).

centipede *noun* any of about 3,000 species of terrestrial arthropods belonging to the class Chilopoda, having long rather flat segmented bodies and usually either 15 or 23 pairs of legs, one pair for each body segment (as opposed to millipedes, which have two pairs per segment). [from CENTI- + Latin *pes*, foot]

central *adj.* **1** at, or forming, the centre of something. **2** near the centre of a city, etc; easy to reach. **3** principal or most important. [from Latin *centralis*, from *centrum*, centre]

. . . .

◉ **1** middle, mid, inner, interior. **3** principal, important, significant, main, chief, key, primary, fundamental, focal, vital, essential.
◨ **1, 2** peripheral. **3** minor, secondary, peripheral.

. . . .

central bank a national bank acting as banker to the government, issuing currency and having control over interest rates.

central government the government that has power over a whole country, as distinct from local government.

central heating a system for heating a whole building, by means of pipes, radiators, etc connected to a central source of heat.

centralism *noun* the policy of bringing the administration of a country under central control, with a decrease in local administrative power.

centralist — *noun* a person who supports centralism. — *adj.* characterized by centralism.

centrality /sen'tralıtı/ *noun* the condition or state of being central.

centralization or **centralisation** *noun* the action or process of centralizing; centralism.

centralize or **centralise** *verb trans., intrans.* to bring under central control.

central locking in a motor vehicle, a system whereby all the doors (including the boot or trunk) are locked or unlocked automatically when the key is turned in any one of the locks.

centrally *adv.* in a central way or position; in or with regard to the centre.

centrally-heated *adj.* provided with or warmed by central heating.

central nervous system (ABBREV. CNS) the part of the nervous system that is responsible for the co-ordination and control of the various body functions. In vertebrates it consists of the brain and the spinal cord.

central processing unit (ABBREV. CPU) *Comput.* the part of a digital computer that controls and co-ordinates the operation of all the other parts, and that performs arithmetical and logical operations on data loaded into it, according to the individual instructions of a program that it holds. Also called CENTRAL PROCESSOR, MICROPROCESSOR.

central processor *Comput.* a central processing unit.

central reservation *Brit.* a narrow strip of grass, concrete, etc dividing the two sides of a dual carriageway, especially a motorway.

centre — *noun* **1** a part at the middle of something: *chocolates with soft centres.* **2** a point inside a circle or sphere that is an equal distance from all points on the circumference or surface, or a point on a line at an equal distance from either end. **3** a point or axis round which a body revolves or rotates. **4** a central area. **5** a place where a particular activity is concentrated or particular facilities, information, etc are available: *a sports centre.* **6** something that acts as a focus: *the centre of attraction.* **7** a point from which activities radiate and are controlled: *the centre of operations.* **8** a position that is at neither extreme, especially in politics. **9** in some playing-field sports, a position in the middle of the field, or a player in this position. — *adj.* at the centre; central. — *verb* **1** to place in or at the centre; to position centrally or symmetrically. **2** to adjust or focus (eg one's thoughts). **3** *intrans., trans.* (**centre on** or **upon something**) to concentrate on it. [from Latin *centrum*,

from Greek *kentron*, sharp point, the point round which a circle is drawn]

. . . .

◉ *noun* **1, 4** middle, core, nucleus, heart, hub, focus, crux. **2** midpoint. **3** axis, pivot, hub. **6** focus, focal point, heart, core, nucleus, hub, crux, target. **7** hub, heart, core, nerve centre. **8** middle ground. *verb* **2** focus, adjust, concentrate. **3** converge on, revolve around, pivot on, hinge on, gravitate towards.
◨ *noun* **1, 4** edge, periphery, outskirts.

. . . .

centreboard *noun* a movable plate in a sailing boat or dinghy, which can be let down through the keel to prevent sideways drift.

centrefold *noun* the sheet that forms the two central facing pages of a magazine, etc, or a picture, etc occupying it.

centre-half *noun Sport* in some field games, the position in the centre of the half-back line, or the player in this position.

centre of gravity *Physics* a theoretical fixed point in a body about which its weight may be considered to be uniformly distributed. If the body is situated in a uniform gravitational field, the centre of gravity is the same as the centre of mass.

centre of mass or **centre of inertia** *Physics* centre of gravity.

centrepiece *noun* **1** a central or most important item. **2** an ornament or decoration for the centre of a table.

centre spread same as CENTREFOLD.

centri- *combining form* denoting a centre or middle. [from Latin *centrum*, centre]

-centric *combining form* having a stated centre, focus, basis, etc.

centrifugal /sentri'fju:gəl/ *adj.* acting or moving away from the centre of a circle along which an object is moving, or away from the axis of rotation. [from CENTRI- + Latin *fugere*, to flee]

centrifugal force an apparent force that seems to exert an outward pull on an object that is moving in a circular path. In fact such a force does not exist. See also CENTRIPETAL FORCE.

centrifuge /'sentrifju:dʒ/ — *verb* to separate substances by spinning them at high speed in a rotating device. — *noun* an instrument containing a rotating device that is used to separate solid or liquid particles of different densities, by spinning them at high speed in a tube in a horizontal circle. The heaviest particles become sedimented in the form of a pellet at the end of the tube.

centriole *noun Biol.* a cylindrical structure that plays a role in cell division in animal cells. [a diminutive of Latin *centrum*, centre]

centripetal /sen'tripitəl/ *adj.* acting or moving towards the centre of a circle along which an object is moving, or towards the axis of rotation. [from CENTRI- + Latin *petere*, to seek]

centripetal force the force that is required to keep an object moving in a circular path. It is directed inwards towards the centre of the circle, and for an object of mass m moving with a constant speed v in a circle of radius r, the centripetal force is mv^2/r. See also CENTRIFUGAL FORCE.

centrism *noun* the practice of adopting the middle ground in politics; the holding of moderate political opinions.

centrist — *adj.* having moderate, non-extreme political opinions. — *noun* a person holding such opinions. [from CENTRE + -IST]

centromere *noun Genetics* the part of a chromosome that attaches it to the spindle during cell division. [from Latin *centrum*, from Greek *kentron*, a sharp point + *meros*, part]

centurion *noun Hist.* in the army of ancient Rome, an officer in charge of a century. [from Latin *centurio*, from *centum*, a hundred]

century *noun* (PL. **centuries**) **1** any of the 100-year periods counted forwards or backwards from an important event, especially the birth of Christ. **2** a period of 100 years. **3** in the game of cricket, 100 runs made by a batsman in a single innings. **4** *Hist.* in the army of ancient Rome, a company of (originally) 100 foot soldiers. [from Latin *centuria*, unit of 100 parts]

CEO *abbrev.* Chief Executive Officer.

cephalic *adj.* relating to the head or the head region. [from Greek *kephale*, head]

cephalic index *Anthropol.* a skull's breadth as a percentage of its length. Skulls of different relative breadths are termed *brachycephalic* (broad), *mesaticephalic* (intermediate), and *dolichocephalic* (long).

cephalopod /ˈsɛfələpɒd, ˈkɛfələpɒd/ *noun* any invertebrate animal belonging to the class Cephalopoda, eg squid, octopus, cuttlefish, nautilus. Cephalopods include several large fossil groups such as the ammonites and belemnites. [from Greek *kephale*, head + *pous podos*, foot]

ceramic *adj.* **1** any of a number of hard brittle materials, eg enamels, all kinds of pottery, porcelain, tiles, and brick, produced by moulding or shaping and then baking or firing non-metallic mineral substances (clays) at high temperatures. **2** relating to or made of such a material. [from Greek *keramos*, potter's clay]

ceramics *noun* **1** (*sing.*) the art of making pottery. **2** (*pl.*) articles made of pottery.

cereal — *noun* **1** an edible member of the grass family (Gramineae) that is cultivated as a food crop for its nutritious seeds (grains). **2** the grain produced. **3** a breakfast food prepared from grain. — *adj.* relating to edible grains. [from Latin *Cerealis*, relating to Ceres, goddess of agriculture]

cerebellar /sɛrəˈbɛlə(r)/ *adj.* relating to or in the region of the cerebellum.

cerebellum /sɛrəˈbɛləm/ *noun* (PL. **cerebella**) *Anat.* the main part of the hindbrain in vertebrates, concerned primarily with the co-ordination of movement. [from Latin, diminutive of *cerebrum*, brain]

cerebral /ˈsɛrəbrəl/ *adj.* **1** relating to or in the region of the brain. **2** intellectual in nature rather than practical or emotional: *a cerebral piece of music.* [from CEREBRUM]

cerebral cortex *Anat.* the outer layer of the cerebral hemispheres of the brain. In humans it consists of highly convoluted folds of *grey matter*, about 2mm deep, and contains over 12,000 million nerve cells. It is responsible for consciousness (including perception, memory, and learning) and the initiation of voluntary movement.

cerebral hemisphere *Anat.* in higher vertebrates, either of the two halves of the cerebrum. The cerebral hemispheres form the major part of the human brain, each having a much folded outer layer of grey matter (the *cerebral cortex*) and controlling the opposite side of the body.

cerebral palsy *Medicine* a failure of the brain to develop normally in young children due to brain damage before or around the time of birth.

cerebrate *verb intrans. facetious* to think; to use one's brain. [from CEREBRUM]

cerebration *noun* action of the brain, especially unconscious.

cerebrospinal /sɛrəbrəʊˈspaɪnl/ *adj.* relating to the brain and spinal cord together: *cerebrospinal fluid.*

cerebrum /ˈsɛrəbrəm/ *noun* (PL. **cerebra**) *Anat.* in higher vertebrates, the part of the brain that consists of two cerebral hemispheres linked by a band of nerve fibres (the *corpus callosum*). It initiates and co-ordinates all voluntary activity. [from Latin *cerebrum*]

ceremonial *adj.* relating to, used for, or involving a ceremony. [from Latin *caerimonia*, rite]

▤ ritual, ritualistic, formal, official, stately, solemn.
▨ informal, casual.

ceremonially *adv.* in a ceremonial way.

ceremonious *adj.* elaborately formal. [from Latin *caeremoniosus*, full of religious rites]

▤ formal, stately, dignified, solemn, ritual, deferential, stiff, starchy, punctilious, precise, exact, grand, courtly.
▨ unceremonious, informal, relaxed.

ceremony *noun* (PL. **ceremonies**) **1** a ritual performed to mark a particular, especially public or religious, occasion. **2** formal politeness. — **stand on ceremony** to insist on behaving formally. **without ceremony** in a hasty, informal way. [from Latin *caerimonia*, rite]

▤ **1** ritual, rite, commemoration, celebration, function, service, observance. **2** formality, form, politeness, propriety, etiquette, protocol, decorum, niceties.

cerise /səˈriːz, səˈriːs/ — *noun* cherry-red. — *adj.* of this colour. [from French *cerise*, cherry]

cerium /ˈsɪərɪəm/ *noun* *Chem.* (SYMBOL **Ce**, ATOMIC NUMBER 58) a soft silvery-grey metal belonging to the lanthanide series, used in catalytic converters for car exhausts, alloys for cigarette-lighter flints, cores for carbon arc lamps, and as an agent for removing fission products from spent nuclear fuel. [named after the asteroid Ceres]

cermet *noun* *Engineering* **1** a hard strong composite material, resistant to corrosion and wear, made from a ceramic and a metal, and used to make cutting tools and brake linings. **2** a type of electronic resistor made of such material. [from CERAMIC + METAL]

CERN *abbrev.* Conseil Européen pour la Recherche Nucléaire (French), European Organization for Nuclear Research, now known as the European Laboratory for Particle Physics.

ceroc *noun* a contemporary style of jive dancing to rock-and-roll music. [from French Le Roc dancing, on which it is based]

cert *noun colloq.* a certainty.

cert. *abbrev.* **1** certificate. **2** certified.

certain — *adj.* **1** proved or known beyond doubt. **2** (**certain about** or **of something**) having no doubt about it; absolutely sure. **3** *used with reference to the future* definitely going to happen, etc. **4** able to rely on or be relied on. **5** particular, and, though known, not named or specified: *a certain friend of yours.* **6** used before a person's name to indicate either their obscurity or one's own unfamiliarity with them: *a certain Mrs Smith.* **7** *said of a quality* present without being clearly definable: *the beard gave his face a certain authority.* **8** some, though not much: *that's true to a certain extent.* — *pron.* some. — **for certain** definitely; without doubt. **make certain of something** to take action so as to ensure it or be sure about it. [from Old French, from Latin *certus*, sure]

▤ *adj.* **1** proved, proven, known, positive, undoubted, indubitable, unquestionable, incontrovertible, undeniable, conclusive, irrefutable, sure, plain, absolute, convincing, true. **2** sure, confident, convinced, definite. **3** inevitable, definite, fixed, established, settled, decided, unavoidable, bound, assured, destined, fated. **4** reliable, dependable, trustworthy, constant, steady, stable. **5** particular, specific, special, individual.
▨ *adj.* **1** uncertain, unsure, doubtful. **2** uncertain, unsure, hesitant, doubtful. **3** unlikely, doubtful. **4** unreliable.

certainly *adv.* **1** without any doubt. **2** definitely. **3** *in giving permission* of course.

▤ **1, 2** definitely, undoubtedly, doubtlessly, naturally, of course, for sure. **3** of course, yes, go ahead.

certainty *noun* (PL. **certainties**) **1** something that cannot be doubted or is bound to happen. **2** freedom from doubt; the state of being sure. **3** the state of being bound to happen: *the certainty of death.*

◨ **1** fact, reality, inevitability. **2** sureness, positiveness, confidence, conviction, assurance, faith, trust, truth. **3** inevitability, sureness, fact.
◨ UNCERTAINTY. **2** doubt, hesitation. **3** doubtfulness.

certifiable /'sɜːtɪfaɪəbl/ *adj.* **1** capable of or suitable for being certified. **2** *colloq.* mad, crazy.

certificate /sə'tɪfɪkət, sə'tɪfɪkeɪt/ — *noun* (pronounced -kət) an official document that formally acknowledges or witnesses a fact (eg *a marriage certificate*), an achievement or qualification (eg *a First-Aid certificate*), or one's condition (eg *a doctor's certificate*). — *verb* (pronounced -keɪt) to provide with a certificate. See also CERTIFY. [from Latin *certificare*, to certify]

◨ *noun* document, qualification, licence, authorization, credentials, testimonial, guarantee, endorsement, warrant, pass, voucher, award, diploma. *verb* authorize, certify, accredit, license, empower, warrant.

certificated *adj.* qualified by a particular course of training.

certificate of deposit a certificate representing a fixed-term interest-bearing deposit in large denominations, which may be bought and sold. First introduced by Citibank in New York in 1961, Sterling certificates were introduced in 1968.

certification *noun* **1** certifying or being certified. **2** a document that certifies something.

certified *adj.* **1** possessing a certificate. **2** endorsed or guaranteed. **3** *said of a person* insane.

certify *verb* (**certifies, certified**) **1** to declare or confirm officially. **2** to declare (someone) insane. **3** to declare to have reached a required standard, passed certain tests, etc. See also CERTIFICATE. [from Latin *certificare*]

◨ **1** declare, confirm, assure, guarantee, endorse, corroborate, vouch, testify, witness, verify. **3** authenticate, certify, validate, authorize, license, accredit, empower, warrant.

certitude *noun* a feeling of certainty. [from Latin *certitudo*, from *certus*, sure]

cervical /'sɜːvɪkəl, sə'vaɪkəl/ *adj.* relating to or in the region of the cervix.

cervical smear *Pathol.* the collection of a sample of cells from the cervix for staining and examination under a microscope, in order to detect any abnormal changes indicative of cancer. Also called SMEAR TEST.

cervix *noun* **1** *Anat.* the neck of the uterus (womb), consisting of a narrow passage leading to the inner end of the vagina. **2** *Anat.* the neck. [from Latin *cervix*, neck]

cesium same as CAESIUM.

cessation *noun* stopping or ceasing; a pause. [from Latin *cessare*, to cease]

cession *noun* the giving up or yielding of territories, rights, etc to someone else. [from Latin *cessio*, from *cedere*, to yield]

cesspit or **cesspool** *noun* a pool, pit, or tank for the collection and storage of sewage and waste water. [from Italian *cesso*, latrine]

cetacean /sɪ'teɪʃən/ — *noun* any animal belonging to the order Cetacea, which includes dolphins, porpoises, and whales. — *adj.* relating to this group. [from Greek *ketos*, whale]

cetane *noun* (FORMULA $C_{16}H_{34}$) a colourless liquid hydrocarbon found in petroleum, used as a solvent and in the determination of the *cetane number* of diesel fuel. Also called HEXADECANE. [from Greek *ketos*, whale, cetane also being obtainable from *cetyl* compounds found in spermaceti]

cetane number a measure of the ignition quality of diesel fuel when it is burnt in a standard diesel engine.

Cf *symbol Chem.* californium.

cf. *abbrev. confer* (Latin), compare.

CFC *abbrev.* chlorofluorocarbon.

CGI or **CLGLI** *abbrev.* City and Guilds (of London) Institute.

CFS *abbrev.* chronic fatigue syndrome.

cgs unit *Physics* centimetre-gram-second unit, a system of measurement based on the use of the centimetre, gram, and second as the fundamental units of length, mass, and time, respectively, for most purposes now superseded by SI units.

CH *abbrev.* **1** Companion of Honour, a British title awarded to people who have given particular service to the nation. **2** *as an international vehicle mark* Confederatio Helvetica (Latin), Switzerland.

ch. *abbrev.* **1** chapter. **2** *Chess* check. **3** church.

cha-cha or **cha-cha-cha** *noun* a Latin American dance, or music for it. [from American Spanish *cha-cha*]

chaconne /ʃa'kɒn/ *noun* an old Spanish dance, probably originating in Mexico; also, a piece of music for it. [from French *chaconne*, from Spanish *chacona*, from Basque *chucun*, pretty]

Chadic — *noun* a group of more than 100 languages spoken by c.25 million people in parts of Ghana and the Central African Republic. The group is assigned to the Afro-Asiatic family of languages, although its status within the family is unclear. The most important language of the group is Hausa. — *adj.* relating to this group of languages.

chador or **chadar** or **chuddar** /'tʃʌdə(r)/ *noun* a thick veil worn by Muslim women covering the head and body. [from Persian *chador*]

chafe *verb* **1** *trans., intrans.* to make or become sore or worn by rubbing. **2** to make warm by rubbing. **3** (**chafe at** or **under something**) to become angry or impatient at: *chafe at the rules*. [from Old French *chaufer*, to heat]

chafer *noun* any of various species of large nocturnal beetle, found mainly in the tropics, and including several pests, eg the cockchafer, whose fleshy C-shaped larvae burrow in soil and cause serious damage to plant roots. [from Anglo-Saxon *ceafor*]

chaff¹ /tʃɑːf/ *noun* **1** the husks that form the outer covering of cereal grain, and are separated from the seeds during threshing. **2** chopped hay or straw used as animal feed or bedding. **3** worthless material. **4** thin strips of metallic foil fired into or dropped through the atmosphere in order to deflect radar signals and so prevent detection.[from Anglo-Saxon *ceaf*]

chaff² /tʃɑːf/ — *noun* light-hearted joking or teasing. — *verb* to tease or make fun of.

chaffinch /tʃafɪntʃ/ *noun* either of two species of bird belonging to the finch family, especially the *common chaffinch*, which is native to Europe and W Asia, and has a blue crown, brown body, stout bill, conspicuous white wing bars, white outer tail feathers, and a greenish rump. [from Anglo-Saxon *ceaffinc*, chaff finch]

chagrin /'ʃagrɪn/ *noun* acute annoyance or disappointment. [from French *chagrin*]

chain — *noun* **1** a series of connected links or rings, especially of metal, used for lifting, supporting, pulling, restraining, fastening, binding, or holding objects, for transmitting motion or, eg in jewellery, for ornament. **2** a series or progression: *a chain of events*. **3** a number of shops, hotels, etc under common ownership or management. **4** (**chains**) something that restricts or frustrates. **5** *Chem.* a number of atoms of the same type that are joined in a line to form a molecule. **6** an old measure of length equal to 22 yards (about 20m). **7** a mountain range. **8** a string of islands. **9** (**chains**) circular apparatus consisting of metal links fitted to the wheels of a car to provide traction in icy conditions. — *verb* to fasten, bind, or restrict with, or as if with, chains. — **in chains** bound by chains, as a prisoner or slave. [from Old French *chaeine*, from Latin *catena*]

◨ *noun* **2** series, sequence, succession, progression, string, train, set. **4** fetters, manacles, restraints, bonds, ties. *verb* fasten, bind, tether, fetter, shackle, secure, restrain, restrict, confine, enslave, manacle.
◨ *verb* release, free.

chain gang a group of prisoners chained together for working outside the prison.

chain letter a letter copied to a large number of people, especially with a request for and promise of something (eg money), each recipient being asked to copy the letter to a stated number of acquaintances.

chainmail same as MAIL².

chain of office a heavy ornamental chain worn round the neck as a symbol of office, eg by a mayor.

chain reaction 1 *Physics* a nuclear reaction that is self-sustaining, eg nuclear fission, in which the splitting of atomic nuclei is accompanied by the release of neutrons, which themselves cause the splitting of more nuclei. Such chain reactions may be controlled, as in a nuclear reactor, or uncontrolled, as in a nuclear explosion. **2** *Chem.* a chemical reaction that is self-sustaining because a change in one molecule causes many other molecules to undergo change, eg during combustion. **3** a series of events, each causing the next.

chainsaw *noun* a portable power-driven saw with cutting teeth linked together in a continuous chain, used mainly for cutting timber.

chain-smoke *verb trans., intrans.* to smoke (cigarettes) continuously.

chain-smoker *noun* a person who smokes cigarettes continuously.

chain store one of a series of shops, especially department stores, owned by the same company and selling the same goods.

chair — *noun* **1** a seat for one person, with a back-support and usually four legs. **2** the office of chairman or chairwoman at a meeting, etc, or the person holding this office. **3** a professorship. **4** *Hist.* a sedan chair. — *verb* **1** to control or conduct (a meeting) as chairman or chairwoman. **2** to lift up and carry (a victor, etc) in triumph. **3** to place (someone) in a seat of authority. — **the chair** *colloq. North Amer., esp. US* the electric chair as a means of capital punishment. **in the chair** acting as chairman. **take the chair** to be chairman or chairwoman. [from Old French *chaiere*, from Greek *kathedra*, seat]

chairlift *noun* a series of seats suspended from a moving cable, for carrying skiers, etc up a mountain.

chairman or **chairwoman** or **chairperson** *noun* (PL. **chairmen**, **chairwomen**, **chairpersons**) **1** a person who conducts or controls a meeting or debate. **2** a person who presides over a committee, a board of directors, etc.

◨ CHAIR, CHAIRPERSON. **1** president, convenor, organizer, director, speaker, master of ceremonies, MC, toastmaster.

chaise /ʃeɪz/ *noun Hist.* a light open two-wheeled horse-drawn carriage. [from French *chaise*, chair]

chaise longue /ʃeɪz ˈlɒŋ/ (PL. **chaises longues**) a long seat with a back and one arm-rest, on which one can recline at full length. [from French *chaise longue*, long chair]

chalaza /kəˈleɪzə/ (PL. **chalazas**, **chalazae**) *noun* **1** *Zool.* in a bird's egg, one of a pair of twisted strands of albumen that hold the yolk sac in position. **2** *Bot.* the base of a plant ovule, where the nucellus (a mass of thin-walled cells in the centre of the ovule) merges with the integuments. [from Greek *chalaza*, hail, lump]

chalcedony /kalˈsedənɪ, ˈkalsədoʊnɪ/ *noun Geol.* a fine-grained variety of the mineral quartz, which occurs in various forms, including several semiprecious gemstones, eg agate, jasper, onyx. [from Greek *chalkedon*]

Chalcolithic /kalkoʊˈlɪθɪk/ *adj.* belonging to the Copper or earliest Bronze Age: the period of transition between

the Neolithic and Bronze Ages when copper was already in use. [from Greek *chalkos*, copper + *lithos*, stone]

chalcopyrite /kalkoʊˈpaɪəraɪt/ *noun Geol.* a copper iron sulphide mineral ($CuFeS_2$), found in veins associated with igneous rocks. It is golden-yellow in colour, and is the main ore of copper. Also called COPPER PYRITES. [from Greek *chalkos*, copper + PYRITE]

chalet /ˈʃaleɪ/ *noun* **1** a style of house typical of snowy Alpine regions, built of wood, with window-shutters and a heavy, sloping, wide-eaved roof. **2** a small cabin for holiday accommodation, especially one of a number at a holiday camp, etc. **3** a wooden villa. [from Swiss French *chalet*]

chalice /ˈtʃalɪs/ *noun* **1** *poetic* a wine cup; a goblet. **2** in the Christian Church, the cup used for serving the wine at Communion or Mass. [from Old French *chalice*, from Latin *calix*, cup]

chalk /tʃɔːk/ — *noun* **1** a soft fine-grained porous rock, composed of calcium carbonate, often pure white or very light in colour, and formed from the shell fragments of countless millions of minute marine organisms that were deposited on the ocean bed during the Cretaceous period. It is used in writing materials, paints, putty, cement, and fertilizers. **2** a material similar to this, usually calcium sulphate, or a stick of it, often coloured, used for writing and drawing, especially on a blackboard. — *verb* to write or mark in chalk. — **by a long chalk** *colloq.* by a considerable amount. **chalk and cheese** *colloq.* completely different things. **chalk something up** to add an item to one's list of successes or experiences. **chalk something up to someone** to add it to the account of money owed by or to them. **not by a long chalk** *colloq.* not at all. [from Anglo-Saxon *cealc*, from Latin *calx*, limestone]

chalkboard *noun North Amer., esp. US* a blackboard.

chalkiness *noun* the quality of being chalky.

chalky *adj.* (**chalkier**, **chalkiest**) **1** like, or consisting of, chalk. **2** *said eg of a face* very pale.

challenge /ˈtʃaləndʒ/ — *verb* **1** to call on (someone) to settle a matter by any sort of contest: *challenge him to a duel.* **2** to cast doubt on or call in question: *challenge her right to dismiss staff.* **3** to test, especially in a stimulating way: *a task that challenges you.* **4** (of a guard or sentry) to order (someone) to stop and show official proof of identity, etc. **5** *Legal* to object to the inclusion of (a person) on a jury. — *noun* **1** an invitation to a contest. **2** the questioning or doubting of something. **3** a problem or task that stimulates effort and interest. **4** an order from a guard or sentry to stop and prove identity. **5** *Legal* an objection to the inclusion of (someone) on a jury. [from Old French *chalenge*]

◨ *verb* **1** dare, defy, throw down the gauntlet to, invite. **2** question, contest, dispute, query, impugn. **3** test, tax, try. **5** object to, dispute, question. *noun* **1** invitation, dare, provocation, confrontation, ultimatum. **2** questioning, question, doubting. **3** problem, test, trial, hurdle, obstacle.

challenged *adj.* a supposedly neutral term in political correctness, meaning handicapped, impaired, or deficient in some specified way. It was first used in the USA when discussing physical or mental handicap, but is now applied in a wide variety of contexts: *physically challenged* (= disabled) / *financially challenged* (= poor).

challenger *noun* a person who issues a challenge.

challenging *adj.* demanding; difficult but rewarding.

challengingly *adv.* in a challenging way.

chalumeau /ʃalʊˈmoʊ/ *noun* **1** an early reed-pipe which evolved into the clarinet at the beginning of the 18c. **2** the lowest register of the clarinet. [from French *chalumeau*, from Late Latin *calamellus*, diminutive of *calamus*, a pipe, reed]

chamber /ˈtʃeɪmbə(r)/ *noun* **1** *old use* a room, especially a bedroom. **2** a hall for the meeting of an assembly, especially a legislative or judicial body. **3** one of the houses of which a parliament consists. **4** (**chambers**) a suite of rooms used by eg a judge or lawyer. **5** an enclosed space or hollow; a cavity. **6** the compartment in a gun into which the bullet or cartridge is loaded. **7** a room or compartment with a particular function: *a decompression chamber*. [from Old French *chambre*, from Latin *camera*, room]

chamberlain /ˈtʃeɪmbəlɪn/ *noun* **1** a person who manages a royal or noble household. See also LORD CHAMBERLAIN. **2** the treasurer of a corporation, etc. [from Old French *chambrelenc*, from Latin *camera*, room]

chambermaid *noun* a woman in a hotel, etc who cleans bedrooms.

chamber music music composed for a small group of players, suitable for performing in a room rather than a concert hall, with only one player to a part.

chamber of commerce an association of business people formed to promote local trade.

chamber orchestra a small orchestra that plays classical music.

chamberpot *noun* a receptacle for urine, etc for use in a bedroom.

chambré /ˈʃɒmbreɪ/ *adj., said of wine* at room temperature. [French, = put into a room]

chameleon /kəˈmiːlɪən/ *noun* **1** a slow-moving lizard, found mainly in Africa, with a sticky tongue that can be extended further than its own body length in order to trap prey. Its eyes can be swivelled independently of each other, and its granular skin changes colour rapidly in response to changes in its environment, acting as camouflage and as a means of communication with rivals. **2** someone who readily adapts to any new environment. **3** *derog.* a changeable, unreliable person. [from Greek *chamai*, on the ground + *leon*, lion]

chamfer /ˈtʃamfə(r), ˈʃamfə(r)/ — *verb* (**chamfered, chamfering**) to give a smooth rounded shape to (an edge or corner). — *noun* a rounded or bevelled edge. [from Old French *chamfrein*, from *chant*, edge + *fraindre*, to break]

chamois /ˈʃamwɑː, ˈʃamɪ/ *noun* (PL. **chamois**) **1** an agile hoofed mammal, native to S Europe, Asia Minor, and the Caucasus region, having short vertical horns with backward-pointing tips. **2** soft suede leather, formerly made from the skin of this animal, but now usually made from the hides of sheep, lambs, or goats. **3** a piece of this used to polish or dry glass and other materials. [from French *chamois*]

champ[1] — *verb trans., intrans.* to munch noisily. — *noun* the sound of munching. — **champ at the bit** to be impatient to act. [imitative]

champ[2] *noun colloq.* a champion.

champagne /ʃamˈpeɪn/ *noun* **1** a sparkling white French wine traditionally drunk at celebrations. **2** a pale pinkish-yellow colour. [from Champagne, the French district where the wine was originally made]

champers /ˈʃampəz/ *noun colloq.* champagne.

champion — *noun* **1** in games, competitions, etc, a competitor that has defeated all others. **2** the supporter or defender of a person or cause. — *adj., adv. dialect* fine. — *verb* to strongly support or defend (a person or cause). [from Old French, from Latin *campio*, from *campus*, battlefield, place for exercise]

⊞ *noun* **1** winner, victor, conqueror, hero. **2** supporter, defender, protector, guardian, upholder, patron, backer, advocate, vindicator. *verb* support, defend, stand up for, back, *formal* espouse, advocate, promote, maintain, uphold.

championship *noun* **1** a contest held to find the champion. **2** the title or position of champion. **3** the strong defending or supporting of a cause or person.

champlevé /ˈʃamplə'veɪ/ *noun* a technique of enamelling on metal, in which the surface of the metal is first engraved with the pattern or image, the engraved channels are filled with vitreous pastes or powders of different colours, and then the metal is fired. [French, = raised field]

chance — *noun* **1** the way that things happen unplanned and unforeseen; fate or luck as causing this to happen, or something that happens in this way. **2** an unforeseen, unexpected occurrence. **3** a possibility or probability. **4** a possible or probable success: *not stand a chance*. **5** an opportunity: *your big chance*. **6** risk, or a risk: *take a chance*. — *verb* **1** to risk. **2** *intrans.* to do or happen by chance: *I chanced to meet her*. — **be in with a chance** to have some hope of success. **a chance in a million** the faintest possibility. **2** (*also* **chance of a lifetime**) an opportunity not to be missed. **chance it** or **chance one's luck** or **chance one's arm** to take a risk. **chance on** or **upon someone** or **something** to meet or find them by accident. **the chances are … it is likely that … an eye to the main chance** a tendency to act from motives of personal advantage rather than consideration for others. **on the off chance** in hope rather than expectation. **an outside chance** a very faint possibility. **take a chance on something** to act in the hope of it being the case. **take one's chance** or **chances** to make the most of whatever opportunities arise. [from Old French *cheance*, from Latin *cadere*, to fall]

⊞ *noun* **1** luck, fortune, providence, fate, destiny. **2** accident, fortuity, coincidence, *colloq.* fluke. **3** possibility, probability, likelihood, risk, gamble, speculation, prospect, odds. **4** hope. **5** opportunity, opening, occasion, time. **6** risk, gamble, speculation. *verb* **1** risk, hazard, gamble, wager, stake, try, venture. **2** happen, occur. *adj.* fortuitous, casual, accidental, inadvertent, unintentional, unintended, unforeseen, unlooked-for, random, haphazard, incidental.

⊟ *noun* **3** certainty. *adj.* deliberate, intentional, foreseen, certain.

chancel *noun* the eastern part of a church, where the altar is, formerly separated from the nave by a screen. [from Latin *cancelli*, lattice, grating]

chancellery /ˈtʃɑːnsələrɪ/ *noun* (PL. **chancelleries**) **1** the rank of a chancellor. **2** a chancellor's department or staff. **3** Also called CHANCERY. **a** the offices or residence of a chancellor. **b** the office of an embassy or consulate.

chancellor *noun* **1** the head of the government in certain European countries. **2** a state or legal official of various kinds. See also LORD CHANCELLOR. **3** in the UK, the honorary head of a university. **4** in the US, the president of a university or college. [from Latin *cancellarius*, court usher]

Chancellor of the Exchequer *noun* the chief minister of finance in the British government.

chancellorship *noun* the position or office of chancellor.

chancer *noun colloq., derog.* a person inclined to take any opportunity to profit, whether honestly or dishonestly.

chancery *noun* (PL. **chanceries**) **1** (*usually* **Chancery**) a division of the High Court of Justice. **2** a record office containing public archives. **3** Also called CHANCELLERY. **a** the offices or residence of a chancellor. **b** the office of an embassy or consulate. — **in chancery 1** *said of a legal case* being heard in a court of chancery. **2** in the charge of a lord chancellor. **3** in an awkward or difficult situation. [a contracted form of CHANCELLERY]

chanciness *noun* being chancy; uncertainty.

chancre /ˈʃaŋkə(r)/ *noun Medicine* a small hard growth that develops in the primary stage of syphilis and certain other diseases. [from Old French]

chancrous *adj.* relating to or of the nature of a chancre.

chancy *adj.* (**chancier, chanciest**) risky; uncertain.

chandelier /ʃandəˈlɪə(r)/ *noun* an ornamental light-fitting hanging from the ceiling, with branching holders for candles or light-bulbs. [from Old French *chandelier*, candle-holder]

chandler *noun* **1** a dealer in ship's supplies and equipment. **2** a dealer in certain other goods: *corn chandler*. **3** *old use* a grocer. **4** *old use* a dealer in candles, oil, etc. [from Old French *chandelier*, dealer in candles]

chandlery *noun* (PL. **chandleries**) **1** a place where candles are kept. **2** goods sold by a chandler.

change — *verb* **1** *trans., intrans.* to make or become different. **2** (**change one thing for another**) to give, leave, or substitute one thing for another. **3** to exchange (usually one's position) with another person, etc: *change places.* **4** *trans., intrans.* (**change into** or **out of something**) to remove (clothes, etc) and replace them with clean or different ones. **5** to put a fresh nappy or clothes on (a baby), or clean sheets on (a bed). **6** *trans., intrans.* (**change into something**) to make into or become something different. **7** to obtain or supply another kind of money for: *change pounds into francs.* **8** *intrans., trans.* to go from one vehicle, usually a train or bus, to another to continue a journey: *change trains at Didcot / we need to change at the depot.* **9** *intrans., trans.* to put a vehicle engine into (another gear): *change into third.* — *noun* **1** the process of changing or an instance of it. **2** the replacement of one thing with another; the leaving of one thing for another. **3** a variation, especially a welcome one, from one's regular habit, etc: *eat out for a change.* **4** the leaving of (one vehicle) for another during a journey. **5** a fresh set (of clothes) for changing into. **6** (**small** or **loose change**) coins as distinct from notes. **7** coins or notes given in exchange for ones of higher value. **8** money left over or returned from the amount given in payment. **9** (*usually* **changes**) any of the various orders in which a set of church bells can be rung. **10** (**change of life**) *colloq.* the menopause. — **change down** to change to a lower gear. **change hands** to pass into different ownership. **change one's mind** to adopt a different intention or opinion. **change over 1** to change from one preference or situation to another. **2** to exchange (jobs, roles, etc): *I drove for two hours, then we changed over.* **change up** to change to a higher gear. **get no change out of someone** *colloq.* to get no help from them. [from French *changer*]

⊟ *verb* **1** alter, vary, convert, reorganize, reform, remodel, restyle, transform, mutate, shift. **2, 3** exchange, swap, trade, switch, transpose, substitute, replace, alternate, interchange. **6** make into, become, mutate, transform, transfigure, metamorphose, convert, alter, modify, remodel, revise. **9** shift. *noun* **1** alteration, modification, conversion, transformation, variation, fluctuation, shift. **2** exchange, transposition, substitution, interchange. **3** difference, diversity, novelty, innovation, variety, transition, revolution, upheaval.

changeability or **changeableness** *noun* **1** a tendency to be changeable; fickleness. **2** the power of being changed.

changeable *adj.* **1** inclined or liable to change often. **2** able to be changed.

⊟ **1** variable, mutable, fluid, kaleidoscopic, shifting, mobile, unsettled, uncertain, unpredictable, unreliable, erratic, irregular, inconstant, fickle, capricious, volatile, unstable, unsteady, wavering, vacillating. **2** variable, adaptable, alterable, modifiable, convertible, transformable.

⊞ **1** constant, reliable.

changeably *adv.* in a changeable or changing way.

changeless *adj.* never-changing.

changelessly *adv.* without change.

changeling *noun* in folklore, a child substituted by the fairies for an unbaptized human baby. [see CHANGE]

change-over *noun* a change from one preference or situation to another.

change-ringing *noun* a British form of bell-ringing devised by the 17c Cambridge printer Fabian Stedman. A set of differently tuned bells is rung in various permutations so that no sequence (or 'change') is sounded more than once. With a full diatonic scale of eight bells 40,320 changes are possible: a peal of 5,000 changes takes as much as three hours to ring.

changing-room *noun* a room in a sports centre, etc where one can change one's clothes.

channel — *noun* **1** any natural or artificially constructed water course, eg the bed of a stream, or an irrigation channel. **2** the part of a river, waterway, etc, that is deep enough for navigation by ships. **3** a wide stretch of water, especially between an island and a continent, eg the English Channel. **4** *Electron.* the frequency band that is assigned for sending or receiving a clear radio or television signal. **5** a groove, furrow, or any long narrow cut, especially one along which something moves. **6** *Comput.* the path along which electrical signals or data flow. **7** (**channels**) a means by which information, etc is communicated, obtained, or received. **8** a course, project, etc into which some resource may be directed: *a channel for one's energies.* **9** (**the Channel**) the English Channel, the stretch of sea between England and France. — *verb* (**channelled, channelling**) **1** to make a channel or channels in. **2** to convey (a liquid, information, etc) through a channel. **3** to direct (a resource, eg talent, energy, money) into a course, project, etc. [from Old French *chanel*]

⊟ *noun* **1** canal, waterway, watercourse, duct, conduit, trough, gutter, main, flume. **2, 3** strait, sound. **5** groove, furrow, duct, conduit. **7** route, means, medium, way, course, path, avenue, approach, passage. **8** outlet. *verb* **2, 3** direct, guide, conduct, convey, send, transmit.

chant — *verb trans., intrans.* **1** to recite in a singing voice. **2** to keep repeating, especially loudly and rhythmically. — *noun* **1** a type of singing used in religious services for passages in prose, with a simple melody and several words sung on one note. **2** a phrase or slogan constantly repeated, especially loudly and rhythmically. [from Old French *chant*, song, and *chanter*, to sing]

⊟ *verb* RECITE, INTONE, CHORUS. *noun* **1** plainsong, psalm. **2** chorus, refrain, slogan, war cry.

chanter *noun* **1** the pipe on which the melody is played on a set of bagpipes. **2** this pipe adapted for separate use as a practice instrument. **3** someone who chants. [from Old French *chanteor*, singer]

chanterelle /tʃantəˈrɛl/ *noun* the bright yellow funnel-shaped fruiting body of the fungus Cantharellus cibarius, native to Europe and N America, and often found in clusters on the ground in beech or oak woods. The soft apricot-scented flesh is edible, and chanterelles are highly prized as a delicacy. [from French *chanterelle*, from Latin *cantharellus*, diminutive of *cantharus*, tankard]

chanting *noun* **1** performing a chant. **2** the sound of a chant or chants.

chantry *noun* (PL. **chantries**) a chapel, or a sum of money, provided for the chanting of masses. [from Old French *chanter*, sing]

chanty see SHANTY².

Chanukkah /ˈhɑːnəkə/ same as HANUKKAH.

chaos /ˈkeɪɒs/ *noun* **1** complete confusion; utter disorder. **2** *Physics* a state of disorder and irregularity that is an intermediate stage between highly ordered motion and entirely random motion. [from Greek *khaos*]

⊟ **1** disorder, confusion, disorganization, anarchy, lawlessness, tumult, pandemonium, bedlam.

⊞ **1** order, organization.

chaotic /keɪˈɒtɪk/ *adj.* lacking any order; utterly confused.

⊟ disordered, confused, disorganized, topsy-turvy, deranged, anarchic, lawless, riotous, tumultuous, unruly, uncontrolled.

⊞ ordered, organized.

chaotically *adv.* in a chaotic way.

chap¹ *noun colloq.* a man or boy; a fellow. [formerly a customer; shortened from CHAPMAN]

□ fellow, *colloq.* bloke, *colloq.* guy, man, boy, person, individual, character, sort, type.

chap[2] — *verb trans., intrans.* (**chapped, chapping**) *said of the skin* to make or become cracked, roughened, and red as a result of rubbing or exposure to cold. — *noun* a cracked, roughened, and red patch on the skin, formed in this way. [from Middle English *chappen*]

chap[3] *noun* 1 a chop or jaw. 2 a cheek. [ultimately from Norse *kjaptr*, jaw]

chap. *abbrev.* chapter.

chaparral /ʃapəˈral/ *noun* in the southwestern USA, a dense growth of low evergreen thorny shrubs and trees, often forming tangled thickets. [from Spanish *chaparral*, from *chaparro*, evergreen oak]

chapati or **chapatti** /tʃəˈpɑːtɪ/ *noun* in Indian cooking, a thin flat portion of unleavened bread. [from Hindi *capati*]

chapel *noun* 1 a recess within a church or cathedral, with its own altar. 2 a place of worship attached to a house, school, etc. 3 *especially in England and Wales* a place of Nonconformist worship, or the services held there. 4 an association of workers in a newspaper office, or a printing- or publishing-house. [from Latin *cappella*, cloak, ie the cloak of St Martin, which was kept in a shrine, to which the word became attached]

chaperone or **chaperon** /ˈʃapərəʊn/ — *noun* 1 formerly an older woman accompanying a younger unmarried one on social occasions, for respectability's sake. 2 an older person accompanying and supervising a group of young people. — *verb* to act as chaperone to. [from Old French *chaperone*, hood]

chaplain *noun* a clergyman or -woman attached to a chapel, to a school, hospital, or other institution, or to the armed forces. [from Latin *cappellanus*, custodian of St Martin's cloak; see etymology for CHAPEL]

chaplaincy *noun* (PL. **chaplaincies**) the position or office of chaplain.

chaplet *noun* 1 a wreath of flowers or a band of gold, etc for the head. 2 a string of beads, especially one used by Roman Catholics as a short version of the rosary. [from Old French *chapel*, wreath, hat]

chapman *noun* (PL. **chapmen**) *Hist.* a travelling dealer; a pedlar. [from Anglo-Saxon *ceapman*, from *ceap*, trading]

chapped *adj.*, *said of the skin* dry and cracked.

chappie *noun colloq.* diminutive of **chap**[1].

chaps *pl. noun* a cowboy's protective leather riding leggings, worn over the trousers. [from Spanish *chaparejos*]

chapter *noun* 1 one of the numbered or titled sections into which a book is divided. 2 a period associated with certain happenings: *an unfortunate chapter in my life.* 3 a sequence or series: *a chapter of accidents.* 4 *North Amer., esp. US* a branch of a society, or its meeting. 5 the body, or a meeting, of canons of a cathedral, or of the members of a religious order. — **chapter and verse** an exact reference, description of circumstances, etc quoted in justification of a statement, etc. [from Old French *chapitre*, from Latin *caput*, head]

□ 1 part, section, division. 2 period, episode, phase, stage. 3 sequence, series, succession, set, run, chain, string, train.

chapter house the building used for the meetings of a cathedral chapter.

char[1] *verb trans., intrans.* (**charred, charring**) 1 to blacken by burning. 2 *said of wood* to turn into charcoal by partial burning. [shortened from CHARCOAL]

char[2] — *verb intrans.* (**charred, charring**) to do paid cleaning work in someone's house, an office, etc. — *noun colloq.* a charwoman. [from Anglo-Saxon *cierran*, to turn; later, as *chare*, to accomplish (a task)]

char[3] *noun old colloq. use* tea. [from Hindi *ca* and Chinese *ch'a*]

char[4] or **charr** *noun* (PL. **char, charr, chars, charrs**) a fish related to and resembling the salmon, native to cool lakes and rivers of the northern hemisphere, and otherwise living mainly at sea, especially in the Arctic Ocean, and ascending rivers in order to spawn. [probably of Celtic origin]

charabanc /ˈʃarəbaŋ/ *noun old use* a single-decker bus for tours, sightseeing, etc; a coach. [from French *char à bancs*, carriage with seats]

character /ˈkarəktə(r)/ *noun* 1 the combination of qualities that makes up a person's nature or personality. 2 the combination of qualities that typifies anything. 3 type or kind. 4 strong, admirable qualities such as determination, courage, and honesty. 5 interesting qualities that make for individuality: *a house with character.* 6 a person in a story or play. 7 an odd or amusing person. 8 *colloq.* a person. 9 reputation: *blacken someone's character.* 10 a letter, number, or other written or printed symbol. — **in** or **out of character** typical or untypical of a person's nature. [from Greek *charaktēr*, engraving tool, branding-iron, hence a distinctive mark impressed on something]

□ 1 personality, nature, disposition, temperament, temper, constitution, make-up, characteristics, features, qualities, traits. 2 nature, characteristics, features, qualities. 3 type, kind, sort, nature. 4 personality. 5 style, individuality. 6 role, part. 7 case, *colloq.* oddball, oddity, eccentric, crank, *old colloq. use* card. 8 person, individual, soul, type. 9 reputation, status, name. 10 letter, number, figure, symbol, sign, mark, type, cipher, hieroglyph, ideograph.

character actor an actor who specializes in character parts.

character assassination the destruction of a person's good name, reputation, etc, by slander, rumour, etc.

character code *Comput.* the particular binary code used to represent a character in a computer, eg ASCII.

characteristic /karəktəˈrɪstɪk/ — *adj.* 1 typical. 2 distinctive. — *noun* a typical or distinctive feature.

□ *adj.* 1 typical, representative. 2 distinctive, distinguishing, individual, idiosyncratic, peculiar, specific, special. *noun* feature, quality, trait, attribute, property, symptom, hallmark, mark, mannerism, peculiarity, idiosyncrasy.

□ *adj.* 1 uncharacteristic, unrepresentative, untypical.

characteristically *adv.* in a characteristic manner; typically.

characterization or **characterisation** /karəktəraɪˈzeɪʃən/ *noun* 1 characterizing. 2 the process by which a writer builds up the characters in a story or play so that their individual personalities emerge. 3 the art of an actor in giving a convincing performance as a particular character.

characterize or **characterise** *verb* 1 to describe or give the chief qualities of. 2 to be a distinctive and typical feature of.

□ 1 portray, represent. 2 typify, mark, stamp, brand, identify, distinguish.

characterless *adj. derog.* dull; uninteresting; lacking individuality.

character part a colourful part in a play or film, giving good opportunities for characterization.

character sketch a quick description of someone, mentioning his or her chief qualities.

charade /ʃəˈrɑːd/ *noun derog.* a ridiculous pretence; a farce. [from French *charade*, from Provençal *charrado*, entertainment]

charades *noun* a party game in which players act out each syllable of a word, or each word of a book title, etc in successive scenes, while the watching players try to guess the complete word or title.

charcoal *noun* **1** a black porous form of carbon produced by heating organic material, especially wood, in the absence of air. It is used for adsorbing gases and clarifying liquids, and charcoal derived from wood is used as a fuel and as an artist's material for making black line drawings. **2** a stick of charcoal used for drawing. **3** a line drawing made using charcoal. **4** (*also* **charcoal grey**) a dark grey colour. [from Middle English *charcole*]

Chardonnay /ˈʃɑːdɒneɪ/ *noun* **1** a grape variety, originally from the Burgundy region of France, now grown also in California, Australia, New Zealand, etc. **2** a dry white wine made from this grape. [from French *Chardon*]

charge *verb* **1** to ask for (an amount) as the price of something: *charged us £20 for mending the window.* **2** to ask (someone) to pay an amount for something: *I'll have to charge you.* **3** (**charge something to someone**) to record it as a debt against them: *charge the breakages to me.* **4** to accuse (someone) officially of a crime: *was charged with manslaughter.* **5** *trans., intrans.* to rush at in attack. **6** *intrans.* to rush. **7** *formal* to order officially: *she was charged to appear in court.* **8** (**charge someone with something**) *formal* to give them a task or responsibility: *he was charged with looking after the books.* **9** to load (a gun, furnace, etc) with explosive, fuel, etc. **10** *old use, formal* to fill up: *charge your glasses.* **11** *said of a battery, capacitor, etc* to take up or store electricity. **12** to cause (a battery, capacitor, etc) to take up or store electricity. **13** to load or saturate: *the liquid is made fizzy by charging it with carbon dioxide.* **14** to fill: *the moment was charged with emotion.* — *noun* **1** an amount charged; a price, fee, or cost. **2** control, care, responsibility; supervision or guardianship: *in charge of repairs / the police arrived and took charge.* **3** something or someone, eg a child, that is in one's care. **4** something of which one is accused: *a charge of murder / they face several charges.* **5** a rushing attack. **6** (**electrical charge**) a deficiency or excess of electrons on a particular object, giving rise to a *positive* or *negative* charge, respectively. The SI unit of electrical charge is the coulomb. **7** the total amount of electricity stored by an insulated object such as an accumulator or capacitor, a quantity of material appropriate for filling something. **8** an amount of explosive, fuel, etc, for loading into a gun, furnace, etc. **9** an order. **10** a task, duty, or burden: *undertake a difficult charge.* **11** a debt or financial liability. — **press** or **prefer charges** to charge someone officially with a crime, etc. [from Old French *chargier* or *charger*, from Latin *carricare*, to load a vehicle]

▣ *verb* **1** ask, demand, levy, exact, debit. **2** invoice, debit. **4** accuse, indict, impeach, incriminate, blame. **5** attack, assail, storm, rush. **6** rush, race, stampede, tear, career, dash, bolt, fly. **7** order, command, instruct, direct. **8** entrust, delegate, depute. *noun* **1** price, cost, fee, amount, rate, expense, expenditure, outlay, payment. **2** control, care, responsibility, custody, keeping, safekeeping, trust, supervision, guardianship. **3** ward, responsibility. **4** accusation, indictment, allegation, imputation. **5** attack, assault, onslaught, rush. **10** task, duty, job, burden, responsibility, obligation.

chargeable *adj.* **1** *said of costs, etc* that may or should be charged to someone. **2** permitted or liable to be charged: *a fee is chargeable for missed appointments.* **3** incurring tax or duty: *chargeable assets.* **4** *said of an offence* serious enough to justify a legal charge by the police.

charge card a small card entitling one to make purchases on credit, supplied to one by a shop with which one has a credit account.

charge-coupled device (ABBREV. **CCD**) **1** *Comput.* a unit of memory in which information is stored using electrically charged particles that circulate continuously through cells printed on a semiconductor. The memory storage capacity of a single computer chip can be greatly enhanced in this way. **2** *Electron.* a semiconductor device that converts an optical image into an electronic signal.

charged *adj.* filled with excitement or other strong emotion: *the charged atmosphere in the room.*

chargé d'affaires /ˈʃɑːʒeɪ daˈfɛə(r)/ (PL. **chargés d'affaires**) a deputy to, or substitute for, an ambassador. [French, = person in charge of affairs]

charge hand the deputy to a foreman in a factory, etc.

charge nurse a nurse in charge of a hospital ward, especially if a male; the equivalent of a sister.

charger *noun Hist.* a strong horse used by a knight in battle, etc.

chargrilled *adj.* grilled over burning charcoal.

charily *adv.* with a chary or guarded manner.

chariness *noun* being chary.

chariot *noun Hist.* a two-wheeled vehicle pulled by horses, used in ancient times for warfare or racing. [diminutive of Old French *char*, carriage]

charioteer /tʃærɪəˈtɪə(r)/ *noun* a chariot-driver.

charisma /kəˈrɪzmə/ *noun* (PL. **charismata**) **1** a strong ability to attract people, and inspire loyalty and admiration. **2** *Relig.* a divinely bestowed talent or power. [from Greek *charis*, grace]

charismatic /kærɪzˈmatɪk/ *adj.* relating to or having charisma; attracting loyalty and admiration.

charismatic movement a movement within Christianity that emphasizes the power of the Holy Spirit at work within individuals, manifesting itself as an ability to heal, a talent for prophecy, etc.

charitable *adj.* **1** kind and understanding in one's attitude to others. **2** generous in assisting people in need. **3** relating to, belonging to, or in the nature of, a charity: *charitable institutions.* [from Old French *charite*, charity]

▣ **1** kind, compassionate, sympathetic, understanding, considerate, generous, magnanimous, liberal, tolerant, broad-minded, lenient, forgiving, indulgent, gracious, benign. **2**, **3** philanthropic, humanitarian, benevolent. ▣ **1** uncharitable, inconsiderate, unforgiving.

charitably *adv.* in a charitable way; with generosity.

charity *noun* (PL. **charities**) **1** assistance given to those in need. **2** an organization established to provide such assistance. **3** kindness and understanding in one's attitude towards, or judgement of, other people. **4** *Biblical* compassionate love for others. [from Old French *charite*, from Latin *caritas*, love]

▣ **1** assistance, aid, relief, alms, gift, handout. **3**, **4** kindness, goodness, love, humanity, compassion, indulgence, benignness, unselfishness, altruism, benevolence, tender-heartedness, affection, generosity, bountifulness, alms-giving, beneficence, philanthropy. ▣ **3**, **4** selfishness, malice.

charlady see CHAR².

charlatan /ˈʃɑːlətən/ *noun derog.* a person posing as an expert in some profession, eg medicine. [from Old French, from Italian *ciarlare*, to chatter]

charlatanism *noun* the practices of a charlatan.

Charles's law *Physics* a law which states that, if the pressure remains constant, the volume of a given mass of gas is directly proportional to its absolute temperature. [named after the French physicist Jacques Charles]

Charleston *noun* a vigorous dance popular in the 1920s, its characteristic step being a pivot on one leg with a side-kick of the other from the knee. [from Charleston, a town in South Carolina, USA]

charlie *noun Brit. colloq.* a fool.

charlock /ˈtʃɑːlɒk/ *noun* a rough hairy annual plant (Sinapis arvensis) with toothed and lobed leaves and yellow cross-shaped flowers. It is related to mustard, and was formerly grown as a leaf vegetable, but is now a pernicious weed of arable land. [from Anglo-Saxon *cerlic*]

charm — *noun* **1** the power of delighting, attracting, or fascinating. **2 (charms)** delightful qualities possessed by a person, place, thing, etc. **3** an object believed to have magical powers. **4** a magical saying or spell. **5** a small ornament, especially of silver, worn on a bracelet. — *verb* **1** to delight, attract, or fascinate. **2 (charm someone into** or **out of something)** to influence or persuade by charm. **3** to control as if by magic: *charm snakes.* — **work like a charm** to produce the desired result as if by magic. [from Old French *charme*, from Latin *carmen*, song, spell]

. . . .

▨ *noun* **1** attraction, allure, magnetism, appeal, fascination, enchantment. **2** allure, magnetism, appeal, attractiveness, desirability. **3** amulet, talisman, fetish, idol, trinket. **4** spell, sorcery, magic. *verb* delight, attract, fascinate, enrapture, captivate, enamour, win. **2** influence, persuade, beguile, enchant, bewitch, mesmerize, cajole. **3** bewitch.

▨ *verb* **1** repel.

. . . .

charmed *adj.* seeming to be protected by magic: *lead a charmed life.*

charmer *noun* **1** *colloq.* a person with an attractive, winning manner. **2** *combining form* a person who can charm animals: *a snake-charmer.*

charming *adj.* delightful; pleasing; attractive; enchanting.

. . . .

▨ delightful, pleasing, attractive, enchanting, pleasant, appealing, lovely, captivating, fetching, sweet, winsome, seductive, winning, irresistible.

▨ ugly, unattractive, repulsive.

. . . .

charmingly *adv.* in a charming way.

charmless *adj.* lacking charm; unattractive.

charmlessly *adv.* in a charmless way.

charm offensive a method of getting what one wants from someone by overwhelming them with reasonableness, kind offers, etc.

charnel house *Hist.* a building where dead bodies or bones are stored. [from Old French *charnel*, burial place]

chart — *noun* **1** a map, especially one designed as an aid to navigation by sea or air, or one on which weather developments are shown. **2** a sheet of information presented as a table, graph, or diagram. **3 (charts)** *colloq.* weekly lists of top-selling pop records. — *verb* **1** to make a chart of (eg part of the sea). **2** to plot the course or progress of. **3** *intrans. colloq.* to appear in the record charts. [from Old French *charte*, from Latin *charta*, leaf of paper]

. . . .

▨ *noun* **1** map, plan. **2** diagram, table, graph, plan, blueprint. *verb* **1** map, map out, sketch, draw, plot, draft. **2** plot, map, map out, outline, delineate, mark, place.

. . . .

charter — *noun* **1** a document guaranteeing the rights and privileges of subjects, issued by a sovereign or government. **2** a document in which the constitution and principles of an organization are presented. **3** a document creating a borough. **4** the hire of aircraft or ships for private use, or a contract for this. — *verb* **(chartered, chartering) 1** to hire (an aircraft, etc) for private use. **2** to grant a charter to. [from Old French *chartre*, from Latin *charta*, paper]

. . . .

▨ *noun* **1** Bill of Rights, constitution. **2** constitution. **4** permit, licence, lease, franchise, concession, contract. *verb* **1** hire, rent, lease, license, commission, engage, employ. **2** authorize, sanction, license.

. . . .

chartered *adj.* **1** qualified according to the rules of a professional body that has a royal charter: *chartered accountant.* **2** having been granted a charter.

charterer *noun* **1** the holder of a charter; a freeholder. **2** a person who charters transport.

charter flight a flight in a chartered aircraft.

Chartism *noun* a radical movement for political reform active in Britain from 1837 to 1848. [from Latin *charta*, charter]

Chartist — *noun* an advocate or supporter of Chartism. — *adj.* relating to or supporting Chartism.

chartreuse /ʃɑːˈtrɜːz/ *noun* a green or yellow liqueur made from brandy and herbs. [named after the monastery of Chartreuse where it was first distilled]

charwoman or **charlady** *noun* a woman employed to clean a house, office, etc.

chary *adj.* **(charier, chariest, of) 1** cautious; wary: *chary of lending money.* **2** sparing; rather mean: *chary of praise.* [from Anglo-Saxon *cearig*, sorrowful, anxious]

Charybdis /kəˈrɪbdɪs/ see SCYLLA.

chase¹ — *verb* **1 (chase someone** or **chase after someone)** to follow or go after them in an attempt to catch them. **2 (chase someone away** or **off**, etc) to drive or force them away, off, etc. **3** *intrans.* to rush; to hurry. **4** *colloq.* to try to achieve, especially with difficulty: *too many applicants chasing too few jobs.* **5** to pursue a particular matter urgently with (someone): *chase the post office about the missing parcel.* — *noun* **1** a pursuit. **2 (the chase)** the hunting of animals, eg foxes. **3** a large area of open land, originally where wild animals were kept for hunting. — **chase something up** to inquire about (a matter) or seek out (information). **chase someone up** to speak to (the person responsible) in order to get something done. **give chase** to rush off in pursuit. [from Old French *chasser*, from Latin *captare*, to try to catch]

. . . .

▨ *verb* **1** pursue, follow, track. **2** drive, force, send, expel. **4** go after, go for. *noun* **1, 2** hunt, pursuit.

. . . .

chase² *verb* to decorate (metal) with engraved or embossed work. [short for *enchase*, to engrave or emboss]

chase³ *noun Printing* a metal frame that holds assembled type in position for printing. [from Old French *chas*, from a variant of Latin *capsa*, case]

chaser *noun* **1** *colloq.* a drink taken after one of a different kind, eg beer after spirits. **2** a person, animal, etc that chases. **3** a horse for steeplechasing.

chasing *noun* the art or technique of engraving or embossing metal; also, the patterns produced.

chasm /ˈkazəm/ *noun* **1** a deep crack or opening in the ground or in the floor of a cave. **2** a wide difference in opinion, feeling, etc. [from Greek *chasma*]

. . . .

▨ **1** gap, opening, gulf, abyss, void, hollow, cavity, crater, breach, rift, split, cleft, fissure, crevasse, canyon, gorge, ravine. **2** difference, discrepancy, divergence, rift, split, gulf.

. . . .

chassé /ˈʃaseɪ/ — *noun* a gliding step used in ballroom dancing, etc. — *verb intrans.* (PAST TENSE AND PAST PARTICIPLE **chasséd**) to perform this step. [from French *chassé*]

chassis /ˈʃasɪ/ *noun* (PL. **chassis**) **1** the structural framework of a motor vehicle, to which the body and movable working parts (eg wheels) are attached. **2** the rigid structural framework of an electronic device, such as a radio or television set, on which the circuit components, etc, are mounted. **3** the landing gear of an aeroplane. [from French *châssis*, frame]

chaste *adj.* **1** sexually virtuous or pure; refraining from sexual relations either outside marriage or altogether. **2** *said of behaviour, etc* modest; decent. **3** *said of clothes, jewellery, style, etc* simple; plain; unadorned. See also CHASTITY. [from Old French *chaste*]

. . . .

▨ **1** pure, virginal, virtuous, moral, unsullied, undefiled, celibate, innocent, abstinent, continent. **2** modest, decent, restrained, wholesome. **3** plain, simple, modest, decent, austere.

▨ **1** promiscuous, loose, immoral, licentious. **2** corrupt, lewd, vulgar, indecorous. **3** vulgar, loud, indecorous.

. . . .

chasten /'tʃeɪsn/ *verb* to produce in (someone) a feeling of guilt and a resolve to improve. [from Old French *chastier*, to punish]

∎ humble, humiliate, tame, subdue, repress, curb, discipline, punish, correct, chastise, castigate, reprove.

chasteness *noun* being chaste; chastity.

chastise /tʃa'staɪz/ *verb* 1 to punish severely, especially by beating. 2 to scold. [from Latin *castigare*, to punish]

∎ 1 punish, discipline, correct, castigate, beat, flog, whip, lash, scourge, smack, spank. 2 scold, reprove, admonish, castigate, berate, censure.

chastisement /tʃa'staɪzmənt/ *noun* 1 physical punishment. 2 a scolding.

chastity /'tʃastɪtɪ/ *noun* 1 the state of refraining entirely from sexual intercourse or from sex outside marriage; chasteness. 2 simplicity or plainness of style. [from Old French *chasteté*]

chastity belt *Hist.* a leather garment said to have been worn by the wives of absent crusaders, covering the genitals in such a way as to prevent sexual intercourse.

chasuble /'tʃazjʊbl/ *noun* a long sleeveless garment, usually elaborately embroidered, worn by a priest when celebrating Mass or Communion. [from French *chasuble*, from Latin *casubla*, variant of *casula*, hooded cloak]

chat[1] — *verb intrans.* (**chatted**, **chatting**) to talk or converse in a friendly, informal way. — *noun* informal familiar talk; a friendly conversation. — **chat someone up** *colloq.* to speak to them flirtatiously, or in the hope of gaining a favour. [shortened from CHATTER]

∎ *verb* chatter, talk, *colloq.* natter, gossip, *colloq.* rabbit (on). *noun* talk, conversation, *colloq.* natter, gossip, *colloq.* chinwag, tête-à-tête, heart-to-heart.

chat[2] *noun* any of various songbirds belonging to several different families, and noted for their harsh chattering calls, especially certain small brightly coloured members of the thrush family, and five species of small birds found in dry regions of Australia, known as Australian chats. [imitative]

château /'ʃatəʊ/ *noun* (PL. **châteaux**) 1 a large French castle or country seat. 2 a vineyard estate around a castle or house. [from French *château*]

châtelaine /'ʃatəlen/ *noun Hist.* 1 the mistress of a large house. 2 a chain or set of chains for attaching keys to, worn hanging from the belt by women. [from French *châtelaine*]

chat room or **chat site** *Comput.* an Internet site where users can type almost instantaneous messages to each other, usually on a particular topic.

chat show a television or radio programme in which well-known people are interviewed informally.

chattel *noun* a moveable possession, especially in the expression *goods and chattels*. [from Old French *chatel*, from Latin *capitale*, wealth]

chatter — *verb intrans.* (**chattered**, **chattering**) 1 to talk rapidly, noisily, unceasingly, and heedlessly, usually about trivial matters. 2 *said of the teeth* to keep knocking together as a result of cold or fear. 3 *said of eg monkeys and birds* to make high-pitched noises similar to chattering. — *noun* chattering talk or a sound similar to it. [imitative]

∎ *verb* 1 chat, prattle, *colloq.* babble, *colloq.* natter, *colloq.* rabbit (on), gossip. 2 rattle. *noun* chat, *colloq.* natter, tattle, prattle, *colloq.* babble, gossip.

chatterbox *noun derog.* a person who is inclined to chatter.

chatterer *noun* a person or thing that chatters.

chattily *adv.* in a chatty and amiable way.

chattiness *noun* a tendency to chat amiably.

chatty *adj.* (**chattier**, **chattiest**) *colloq.* 1 given to amiable chatting. 2 *said of writing* friendly and informal in style.

∎ 1 talkative, friendly, sociable, gossipy. 2 friendly, informal, colloquial, familiar, gossipy, newsy.

🄴 1 quiet, taciturn.

Chau *noun* a traditional theatre of E India, with three regional styles: *Mayurbhanj*, dance-drama without masks; *Seraikala*, dance with masks; and *Purulia*, dance-drama with masks.

chauffeur /'ʃəʊfə(r), ʃəʊ'fɜː(r)/ — *noun* a person employed to drive a car for someone else. — *verb* to act as a driver for (someone). [from French *chauffeur*, stoker]

chauffeuse /ʃəʊ'fɜːz/ *noun* a female chauffeur.

chauvinism /'ʃəʊvənɪzm/ *noun derog.* an unreasonable belief, especially if aggressively expressed, in the superiority of one's own nation, sex, etc. [named after Nicolas Chauvin (fl.1815), a fanatically patriotic soldier under Napoleon]

chauvinist — *noun* a person whose beliefs and actions are characterized by chauvinism. — *adj.* relating to or characteristic of chauvinism.

chauvinistic /ʃəʊvɪ'nɪstɪk/ *adj.* relating to or typical of chauvinism or a chauvinist.

chauvinistically *adv.* in a chauvinistic way.

ChB *abbrev.* Chirurgiae Baccalaureus (Latin), Bachelor of Surgery.

cheap — *adj.* 1 low in price; being, or charging, less than the usual price; being, or offering, good value for money. 2 low in price but of poor quality: *cheap plastic jewellery*. 3 of little worth; valueless: *war makes human life seem cheap*. 4 mean; unfair; unpleasant; nasty. — *adv. colloq.* cheaply: *good houses don't come cheap*. — **on the cheap** *derog.* cheaply; with minimal expense. [from Anglo-Saxon *ceap*, trade, price, bargain]

∎ *adj.* 1 inexpensive, reasonable, *colloq.* dirt-cheap, bargain, reduced, cut-price, knockdown, budget, economy, economical. 2 *colloq.* cheapo, *colloq.* tacky, *colloq.* trashy, *colloq.* tatty, shoddy. 3 inferior, *colloq.* low-rent, second-rate, worthless, tawdry, vulgar, common, poor, paltry. 4 mean, unfair, unpleasant, nasty, contemptible, despicable, low.

🄴 *adj.* 1 expensive, costly, dear, luxurious. 3 superior, noble, admirable. 4 fair, equitable, generous, pleasant, upright, honourable, proper.

cheapen *verb* (**cheapened**, **cheapening**) 1 to cause to appear cheap or not very respectable. 2 *trans., intrans.* to make or become cheaper.

∎ 1 devalue, degrade, lower, demean, belittle, disparage, denigrate. 2 depreciate, downgrade.

cheapjack — *noun derog.* a seller of cheap, poor-quality goods. — *adj.* of poor quality.

cheaply *adv.* at a low price; economically.

cheapness *noun* being cheap.

cheapskate *noun colloq., derog.* a mean, miserly person.

cheat — *verb* 1 to trick, deceive, swindle. 2 (**cheat someone of** or **out of something**) to deprive them of it by deceit or trickery. 3 *intrans.* to act dishonestly so as to gain an advantage: *cheat at cards*. 4 (**cheat on someone**) *colloq.* to be unfaithful to (a husband, wife, or partner), especially sexually. 5 to escape (something unpleasant) by luck or skill. — *noun* 1 a person who cheats. 2 a dishonest trick. [shortened from ESCHEAT]

∎ *verb* 1 defraud, swindle, diddle, *colloq.* do, *colloq.* rip off, *slang* fleece, *colloq.* con, double-cross, mislead, deceive, dupe, fool, trick, hoodwink. **2** defraud, trick, deceive, *colloq.* do. *noun* **1** cheater, dodger, fraud, swindler, deceiver, trickster, rogue, *colloq.* con man, *colloq.* shark, extortioner, double-crosser, impostor, charlatan. **2** fraud, swindle, deception, hoax, *slang* scam, *slang* sting.

. . . .

check — *verb* **1** *trans., intrans.* to establish that (something) is correct or satisfactory, especially by investigation or enquiry: *I need someone to check my work / will you check that I locked the front door?* **2** to hold back, prevent, stop: *he was about to complain, but checked himself.* **3** *North Amer.* to mark (something correct, etc) with a tick. **4** *North Amer.* to hand over or deposit for safekeeping. **5** *intrans.* said of information, etc to be consistent; to agree with other information: *that checks with the other boy's story.* **6** *Chess* to put (the opposing king) into check. — *noun* **1** (**check on**) an inspection or investigation made to find out about something or to ensure that something is as it should be. **2** a standard or test by means of which to check something. **3** a stoppage in, or control on, progress or development. **4** a pattern of squares: *cotton with a purple check.* **5** *North Amer., esp. US* a tick marked against something. **6** *North Amer., esp. US* a cheque. **7** *North Amer.* a restaurant bill. **8** *North Amer.* a ticket or token for claiming something left in safekeeping. **9** *Chess* the position of the king when directly threatened by an opposing piece. — **check in** to report one's arrival at an air terminal or hotel. **check something** or **someone in 1** to register or record the arrival of (especially guests at a hotel or passengers at an air terminal). **2** to hand in (luggage for weighing and loading) at an air terminal. See also CHECK-IN. **check something off** to mark an item on a list as dealt with. **check out 1** to register one's departure, especially from a hotel on paying the bill. **2** *chiefly North Amer., said of information, etc* to be satisfactory or consistent. See also CHECK-OUT. **check something** or **someone out** to investigate them thoroughly. [from Old French *eschec*, check in chess, from Persian *shah*, king]

▣ *verb* **1** examine, inspect, scrutinize, *colloq.* give the once-over, investigate, probe, test, monitor, study, research, compare, cross-check, confirm, verify. **2** hold back, prevent, stop, arrest, halt, curb, bridle, restrain, control, limit, retard, delay, repress, inhibit, damp, thwart, hinder, impede, obstruct, bar. **3** tick. **5** agree, correspond, accord, coincide, concur, square, tally. *noun* **1** inspection, investigation, examination, test, scrutiny, *colloq.* once-over, check-up, audit. **3** stoppage, control, curb, restraint, hindrance, impediment, obstruction, limitation, constraint, inhibition, damper, blow, disappointment, reverse, setback, frustration. **8** ticket, token, receipt, voucher, slip, docket.

. . . .

checkable *adj.* capable of being checked.

checked *adj.* having a squared pattern: *purple-checked cotton.*

checker[1] *noun* **1** a person who checks. **2** *North Amer.* a person who operates a checkout at a supermarket.

checker[2] see CHEQUER, CHEQUERS.

check-in *noun* at an air terminal, the desk at which passengers' tickets are checked and luggage weighed and accepted for loading.

checklist *noun* a list of things to be done or systematically checked.

checkmate — *noun* **1** *Chess* a winning position, putting one's opponent's king under inescapable attack. **2** frustration or defeat. — *verb* **1** *Chess* to put (the opposing king) into checkmate. **2** to foil or outwit. [from Persian *shah mata*, the king is dead]

checkout *noun* the pay desk in a supermarket.

checkpoint *noun* a place, eg at a frontier, where vehicles are stopped and travel documents checked.

check-up *noun* a thorough examination, especially a medical one.

cheek *noun* **1** either side of the face below the eye. **2** either of the two fleshy lateral walls of the mouth. **3** impudent speech or behaviour. **4** (*usually* **cheeks**) *colloq.* either of the buttocks. — **cheek by jowl** very close together. **turn the other cheek** to refuse to retaliate. [from Anglo-Saxon *ceace* or *cece*]

. . . .

▣ **3** impudence, impertinence, insolence, disrespect, effrontery, brazenness, temerity, audacity, *colloq.* nerve, *colloq.* gall.

. . . .

cheekbone *noun* either of a pair of bones that lie beneath the prominent part of the cheeks.

cheekily *adv.* in a cheeky way.

cheekiness *noun* a cheeky action, remark, or behaviour.

cheeky *adj.* (**cheekier, cheekiest**) impudent; disrespectful.

. . . .

▣ impudent, disrespectful, impertinent, insolent, brazen, pert, *colloq.* saucy, audacious, forward.
▣ respectful, polite.

. . . .

cheep — *verb intrans., said especially of young birds* to make high-pitched noises. — *noun* a sound of this sort. [imitative]

cheer — *noun* **1** a shout of approval or encouragement. **2** *old use* mood; spirits: *be of good cheer.* **3** *old use* merriment. **4** *old use* food and drink: *Christmas cheer.* — *verb trans., intrans.* to give approval or encouragement by shouting. — **cheer someone on** to encourage them by shouting. **cheer up** to become more cheerful. **cheer someone up** to make them more cheerful. [from Old French *chere*, face]

. . . .

▣ *noun* **1** acclamation, hurrah, bravo, applause, ovation. **2** mood, spirits, disposition, frame of mind, temper, humour. *verb* acclaim, hail, clap, applaud. **cheer up** take heart, rally, *colloq.* buck up, *colloq.* perk up, brighten up. **cheer someone up** comfort, console, gladden, warm, uplift, elate, exhilarate, encourage, hearten.
▣ *verb* boo, jeer. **cheer someone up** dishearten.

. . . .

cheerful *adj.* **1** happy; optimistic. **2** in a good mood. **3** bright and cheering. **4** willing; glad; ungrudging.

. . . .

▣ **1, 2** happy, optimistic, glad, contented, joyful, joyous, blithe, carefree, light-hearted, cheery, good-humoured, sunny, enthusiastic, hearty, genial, jovial, jolly, merry, lively, animated, bright, chirpy, breezy, jaunty, buoyant, sparkling. **4** willing, glad, ungrudging, agreeable, content, enthusiastic.
▣ **1, 2** sad, dejected, depressed.

. . . .

cheerfully *adv.* with a cheerful manner.

cheerfulness *noun* being cheerful.

cheerily *adv.* with a cheery manner.

cheeriness *noun* a cheery state.

cheering *adj.* bringing comfort; making one feel glad or happier.

cheerio *interj. Brit. colloq.* **1** goodbye. **2** cheers (sense 1). [from CHEER]

cheerleader *noun* in the USA, a person who leads organized cheering, especially at sports events.

cheerless *adj.* dismal, depressing, dreary or dull.

cheerlessly *adv.* in a cheerless way; miserably.

cheerlessness *noun* being cheerless.

cheers *interj. Brit. colloq.* **1** used as a toast before drinking. **2** thank you. **3** goodbye. [from CHEER]

cheery *adj.* (**cheerier, cheeriest**) cheerful; lively; jovial.

cheese[1] *noun* **1** a solid or soft creamy food that is prepared from the curds of milk. **2** a wheel-shaped solid mass of this substance. **3** a flavoured food with the consistency of soft cheese, eg lemon cheese. — **cheesed off** *Brit. slang* fed up or annoyed. **hard cheese** *Brit. old slang use* bad luck. [from Anglo-Saxon *cyse*, from Latin *caseus*]

Varieties of cheese include: Amsterdam, Bel Paese, Bleu d'Auvergne, Blue Cheshire, Blue Vinny, Boursin, Brie, Caboc, Caerphilly, Camembert, Carré, Cheddar, Cheshire, Churnton, cottage cheese, cream cheese, Crowdie, curd cheese, Danish blue, Derby, Dolcelatte, Dorset Blue, Double Gloucester, Dunlop, Edam, Emmental, Emmentaler, ewe-cheese, Feta, fromage frais, Gloucester, Gorgonzola, Gouda, Gruyère, Huntsman, Jarlsberg, Killarney, Lancashire, Leicester, Limburg(er), Lymeswold, mascarpone, mouse-trap, mozzarella, Neufchâtel, Orkney, Parmesan, Petit Suisse, Pont-l'Éveque, Port Salut, processed cheese, quark, Red Leicester, Red Windsor, ricotta, Roquefort, sage Derby, Saint-Paulin, Stilton, stracchino, vegetarian cheese, Vacherin, Wensleydale.

cheese[2] *noun slang* (**big cheese**) an important person. [perhaps from Urdu *chiz*, thing]

cheese board **1** a board on which to serve cheese. **2** the selection of cheeses served.

cheeseburger *noun* a hamburger served with a slice of cheese, usually in a bread roll.

cheesecake *noun* **1** a sweet food made with soft cheese. **2** *old colloq. use* photographs of partially clothed women, especially used to add sex appeal in advertising. See also BEEFCAKE.

cheesecloth *noun* **1** a type of thin cloth used for pressing cheese. **2** a loosely woven cloth used for shirts, etc.

cheeseparing *adj. derog.* mean with money.

cheese straw a long thin light cheese-flavoured biscuit.

cheesy *adj.* (**cheesier**, **cheesiest**) **1** of the nature of cheese; like cheese. **2** *colloq.* cheap, inferior.

cheetah /'tʃiːtə/ *noun* a large member of the cat family, found in Africa and SW Asia, and having a tawny or grey body covered with black spots, a small head, and very long legs. [from Hindi *cita*]

chef /ʃəf/ *noun* the chief cook, usually male, in a restaurant, etc. [from French *chef*, chief]

chef d'oeuvre /ʃeɪ 'dɜːvrə/ *noun* (PL. **chefs d'oeuvre**) an artist's or writer's masterpiece. [French, = chief work]

cheiromancy /'kaɪərəʊmansɪ/ see CHIROMANCY.

chelate /'kiːleɪt/ *noun Chem.* an organic chemical compound (eg haemoglobin) in which a central metal ion is attached to one or more rings of atoms. [from Greek *chele*, claw]

chemical /'kemɪkəl/ — *adj.* **1** relating to or used in the science of chemistry. **2** relating to a substance or substances that take part in or are formed by reactions in which atoms or molecules undergo changes. **3** relating to the properties of chemicals. — *noun* a substance that has a specific molecular composition, and takes part in or is formed by reactions (known as *chemical reactions*) in which atoms or molecules undergo changes. [from the earlier *chemic*, relating to alchemy or chemistry]

chemical element a substance that cannot be broken down into simpler substances by chemical means, and which is composed of similar atoms that all have the same atomic number (number of protons in the nucleus), which defines that substance and its position in the periodic table.

The chemical elements (with their symbols) are: actinium (Ac), aluminium (Al), americium (Am), antimony (Sb), argon (Ar), arsenic (As), astatine (At), barium (Ba), berkelium (Bk), beryllium (Be), bismuth (Bi), boron (B), bromine (Br), cadmium (Cd), caesium (Cs), calcium (Ca), californium (Cf), carbon (C), cerium (Ce), chlorine (Cl), chromium (Cr), cobalt (Co), copper (Cu), curium (Cm), dysprosium (Dy), einsteinium (Es), erbium (Er), europium (Eu), fermium (Fm), fluorine (F), francium (Fr), gadolinium (Gd), gallium (Ga), germanium (Ge), gold (Au), hafnium (Hf), hahnium (Ha), helium (He), holmium (Ho), hydrogen (H), indium (In), iodine (I), iridium (Ir), iron (Fe), krypton (Kr), lanthanum (La), lawrencium (Lr), lead (Pb), lithium (Li), lutetium (Lu), magnesium (Mg), manganese (Mn), mendelevium (Md), mercury (Hg), molybdenum (Mo), neodymium (Nd), neon (Ne), neptunium (Np), nickel (Ni), niobium (Nb), nitrogen (N), nobelium (No), osmium (Os), oxygen (O), palladium (Pd), phosphorus (P), platinum (Pt), plutonium (Pu), polonium (Po), potassium (K), praseodymium (Pr), promethium (Pm), protactinium (Pa), radium (Ra), radon (Rn), rhenium (Re), rhodium (Rh), rubidium (Rb), ruthenium (Ru), rutherfordium (Rf), samarium (Sm), scandium (Sc), selenium (Se), silicon (Si), silver (Ag), sodium (Na), strontium (Sr), sulphur (S), tantalum (Ta), technetium (Tc), tellurium (Te), terbium (Tb), thallium (Tl), thorium (Th), thulium (Tm), tin (Sn), titanium (Ti), tungsten (W), uranium (U), vanadium (V), xenon (Xe), ytterbium (Yb), yttrium (Y), zinc (Zn), zirconium (Zr).

chemical engineering the branch of engineering concerned with the design, manufacture, operation, and maintenance of machinery and other equipment used for chemical processing on an industrial scale.

chemically *adv.* **1** as regards chemistry or chemicals. **2** by a chemical process.

chemical reaction *Chem.* the process whereby one or more substances, known as *reactants*, react to form one or more different substances, known as *products*.

chemical symbol *Chem.* a single capital letter, or a combination of a capital letter and a small one, which is used to represent an atom of a particular chemical element in a chemical formula, eg the chemical symbol for copper is Cu.

chemical toilet a toilet in which human waste is treated with chemicals, used where running water is not available.

chemical warfare warfare involving the use of toxic chemical substances, eg mustard gas and tear gas, to kill or injure human beings (or to incapacitate them temporarily by causing confusion, stupor, etc) and to damage or render useless animals, plants, and non-living materials.

chemin de fer /ʃə'man də feə(r)/ *noun* a variation of the card game baccarat. [from French *chemin de fer*, railway]

chemise /ʃə'miːz/ *noun* a woman's shirt or loose-fitting dress. [from Old French, from Latin *camisa*, shirt]

chemist /'kemɪst/ *noun* **1** a scientist specializing in chemistry. **2** a person qualified to dispense medicines; a pharmacist. **3** a shop dealing in medicines, toiletries, cosmetics, etc. [formerly *chymist*, from Latin *alchimista*, alchemist]

chemistry /'kemɪstrɪ/ *noun* **1** the scientific study of the composition, properties, and reactions of chemical elements and their compounds. **2** *colloq.* emotional and psychological interaction experienced in a relationship.

chemo *noun colloq.* chemotherapy.

chemoreceptor /kemoʊrɪ'septə(r)/ *noun Biol.* any sense organ that responds to stimulation by chemical substances.

chemotaxis /kemoʊ'taksɪs/ *noun Biol.* the movement of a whole organism in response to chemical stimulus.

chemotherapeutic /kiːmoʊθerə'pjuːtɪk/ *adj.* relating to or involving chemotherapy.

chemotherapy /kiːmoʊ'θerəpɪ/ *noun Medicine* the treatment of a disease or disorder by means of drugs or other chemical compounds that are designed to destroy invading micro-organisms or specific areas of tissue, especially the treatment of cancer with cytotoxic drugs (as opposed to radiotherapy). [from CHEMICAL + THERAPY]

chenille /ʃə'niːl/ *noun* a soft shiny velvety fabric. [from French *chenille*, caterpillar]

cheque /tʃek/ *noun* a printed form on which to fill in instructions to one's bank to pay a specified sum of money from one's account to another account. [from CHECK]

chequebook *noun* a book of cheques ready for use, printed with one's own name and that of the bank issuing it.

chequebook journalism *derog.* the practice of paying enormous prices for exclusive rights to especially sensational material for newspaper stories.

cheque card a card issued to customers by a bank, guaranteeing payment of their cheques up to a stated amount.

chequer /ˈtʃekə(r)/ or, in N America, **checker** *noun* **1** a pattern of squares alternating in colour as on a chessboard. **2** one of the pieces used in the game of Chinese chequers. **3** *North Amer.* one of the round pieces used in the game of draughts. [Old French *escheker*, chessboard, from *eschec*, check in chess; see etymology for CHECK]

chequered *adj.* **1** patterned with squares or patches of alternating colour. **2** *said of a person's life, career, etc* eventful, with alternations of good and bad fortune.

chequered flag a black-and-white-checked flag waved in front of the winner and subsequent finishers in a motor race.

chequers or, in N America, **checkers** *sing. noun* the game of draughts.

cherish *verb* **1** to care for lovingly. **2** to take great care to keep (a tradition, etc) alive. **3** to cling fondly to (a hope, belief, or memory). [from Old French *cherir*, from *cher*, dear]

⊟ **1** foster, care for, look after, nurse, nurture, nourish, sustain, support. **2** foster, nurture, sustain. **3** harbour, shelter, entertain, hold dear, value, prize, treasure.

chernozem /ˈtʃɜːnəʊzem/ *noun Geol.* a dark highly fertile soil, rich in humus and soluble calcium salts, found in cool regions with low humidity, especially semi-arid grasslands. [from Russian *chernozëm* from *chernyl*, black + *zemlya*, earth]

cheroot /ʃəˈruːt/ *noun* a cigar that is cut square at both ends. [French *cheroute*, from Tamil *curuttu*, roll]

cherry *noun* (PL. **cherries**) **1** a small round red, purplish, or yellow fruit containing a small smooth stone surrounded by pulpy flesh, which may be sweet or sour, and a thin outer skin. **2** any of various small deciduous trees of the genus Prunus that are cultivated for this fruit, for their wood, or in the case of ornamental varieties for their attractive white or pink, single or double flowers. **3** the fine-grained reddish wood of this tree, which darkens on exposure to light, and is highly prized for cabinetwork, panelling, and fine furniture. **4** (*also* **cherry-red**) a bright red colour. — **two bites** or **another bite at the cherry** *colloq.* an unexpected further opportunity. [from Anglo-Saxon *ciris* (mistaken for a plural), from Greek *kerasion*]

cherry brandy a liqueur made with brandy in which cherries have been steeped.

cherry-picking *noun colloq.* **1** choosing the best people or things. **2** the business practice of rejecting insurance applications from those considered to be bad risks.

chert *noun Geol.* flint.

cherub *noun* **1** (PL. **cherubs, cherubim**) an angel, represented in painting and sculpture as a winged child. **2** a sweet, innocent, and beautiful child. [from Hebrew *k'rubh*, plural *k'rubhim*]

cherubic /tʃəˈruːbɪk/ *adj.* of the nature of a cherub.

cherubically *adv.* like a cherub.

chervil *noun* an annual plant (Anthriscus cerefolium), native to Europe and Asia, having hollow stems, divided leaves, small white flowers borne in flat-topped clusters, and smooth oblong fruits. It is widely cultivated for its aromatic leaves, which are used as a garnish and for flavouring salads, etc. [from Anglo-Saxon *cherfelle*, from Greek *chairephyllon*]

Ches. *abbrev.* Cheshire.

chess *noun* a board game for two people each with 16 playing-pieces, the most important pieces being the kings, and the object of the game to trap one's opponent's king. [from Old French *esches*, plural of *eschec*, check in chess, from Persian *shah*, king]

chessboard *noun* the board, divided into alternating black (or brown) and white squares, on which chess is played.

chessman *noun* one of the 32 figures used as playing-pieces in chess.

chest *noun* **1** the front part of the body between the neck and the waist; the non-technical name for the thorax. **2** a large strong box used for storage or transport. **3** a small cabinet, eg for medicines. — **get something off one's chest** *colloq.* to relieve one's anxiety about a problem, wrongdoing, etc by talking about it. [from Anglo-Saxon *cist, cest, cyst*, box, from Latin *cista*]

⊟ **2** trunk, crate, box, case, casket, coffer, strongbox.

chesterfield *noun* a heavily padded leather-covered sofa with arms and back of the same height. [named after a 19c Earl of Chesterfield]

chestily *adv.* in a chesty way.

chestiness *noun* being chesty.

chestnut /ˈtʃesnʌt/ *noun* **1** (**sweet chestnut**) a deciduous tree (Castanea sativa), native to S Europe and W Asia, and widely cultivated elsewhere, having spirally ridged bark, simple toothed glossy leaves, and erect catkins with yellow male flowers above and green female flowers below. **2** the large edible nut produced by this tree. **3** (**horse chestnut**) a large spreading deciduous tree (Aesculus hippocastanum), native to the Balkans and widely cultivated elsewhere, unrelated to the sweet chestnut, and having white-petalled flowers with yellow and pink spots, borne in pyramidal spikes. Its brown shiny inedible seeds, popularly known as *conkers*, are borne in prickly leathery capsules. **4** the hard timber of either of these trees. **5** a reddish-brown colour, especially of hair. **6** a reddish-brown horse. **7** an often-repeated joke or anecdote. — **pull someone's chestnuts out of the fire** *colloq.* to rescue them from difficulties. [from the earlier *chesten nut*, from Latin *castanea*, chestnut tree]

chest of drawers a piece of furniture fitted with drawers, especially for holding clothes.

chesty *adj.* (**chestier, chestiest**) *colloq.* **1** *Brit.* suffering from or displaying symptoms typical of chest disease or infection. **2** *said of a woman* having large breasts.

cheval glass /ʃəˈval/ *noun* a full-length mirror mounted on a stand with swivelling hinges that allow it to be positioned at any angle. [from French *cheval*, horse, support]

chevalier /ʃevəˈlɪə(r), ʃəˈvaljeɪ/ *noun* **1** in France, a member of a modern order such as the Legion of Honour, or of one of the historical knighthood orders. **2** *old use* a knight; a chivalrous man. [from French *chevalier*, from Latin *caballarius*, horseman]

chevron /ˈʃevrən/ *noun* a V-shaped mark or symbol, eg one worn on a military uniform to indicate rank. [from Old French *chevron*, rafter]

chevrotain /ˈʃevrəʊteɪn/ *noun* a ruminant mammal, native to tropical forests of Africa, India, Sri Lanka, and SE Asia, and having a small stocky body, short slender legs, and no horns or antlers. Also called MOUSE DEER.

chew — *verb* **1** *trans., intrans.* to use the teeth to break up (food) inside the mouth before swallowing. **2** *trans., intrans.* (**chew at** or **on something**) to keep biting or nibbling it. **3** (**chew something up**) to crush, damage, or destroy it by chewing, or as if by chewing. — *noun* **1** an act of chewing. **2** something for chewing, eg a chewy sweet. — **chew over** or **on something** *colloq.* to consider or discuss it at length. [from Anglo-Saxon *ceowan*]

⊟ *verb* **1** masticate, gnaw, munch, champ, crunch, grind.

chewiness *noun* being chewy.

chewing-gum *noun* a sticky sweet-flavoured substance for chewing without swallowing.

chewy *adj.* (**chewier, chewiest**) *colloq.* needing a lot of chewing.

Chianti /kɪˈantɪ/ *noun* a dry, usually red, Italian wine. [from Chianti in Italy, where the wine was first produced]

chiaroscuro /kɪˌrəʊˈskʊərəʊ/ *noun Art* an originally

Italian painting style in which strong highlighting and deep shadow are used to give figures their shape. [from Italian *chiaroscuro*, light-dark]

chiasma /'kaɪazmə/ or **chiasm** noun (PL. **chiasmata**) 1 *Genetics* during meiosis, any region where homologous chromosomes remain in contact after they have begun to separate from each other, and where mutual exchange of genetic material occurs as a result of crossing over. See also CROSSING OVER. 2 *Anat.* the point where the optic nerves cross each other in the brain. [from Greek *chiasma*, a cross-shaped mark]

chic /ʃiːk/ — *adj.* appealingly elegant or fashionable. — *noun* stylishness; elegance. [from French *chic*]

chicane /ʃɪ'keɪn/ — *noun* 1 an obstacle, eg a series of sharp bends, on a motor-racing circuit. 2 trickery; chicanery. — *verb* 1 (**chicane someone into** or **out of something**) *old use* to cheat them. 2 *intrans.* to use trickery or chicanery. [from French *chicane*, quibble]

chicanery /ʃɪ'keɪnərɪ/ noun (PL. **chicaneries**) 1 clever talk intended to mislead. 2 a dishonest argument. 3 trickery; deception. [from French *chicanerie*, from *chicane*, quibble]

chick noun 1 the young of a bird, especially a domestic fowl such as a chicken, that has just hatched or is about to hatch. 2 *old slang use* a young woman. [from Middle English *chike*, variant of *chiken*, chicken]

chicken — *noun* 1 the domestic fowl, bred virtually worldwide for its meat and eggs, and thought to be derived from the red jungle fowl of India and SE Asia. There are many commercial breeds as well as ornamental ones. Chickens have short wings and can only fly for very small distances. 2 the flesh of this animal used as food. 3 *derog. colloq.* a cowardly person. 4 *slang* a youthful person: *he's no chicken.* — *adj. derog. colloq.* cowardly. — *verb* (**chicken out of something**) to avoid or withdraw from an activity or commitment from lack of nerve or confidence. [from Middle English *chiken*]

chicken-and-egg situation a situation where one cannot tell which of two happenings is cause and which effect.

chickenfeed noun 1 food for poultry. 2 something small and insignificant, especially a paltry sum of money.

chicken-hearted or **chicken-livered** adj. derog. colloq. cowardly.

chickenpox noun an infectious viral disease that is transmitted by airborne droplets and mainly affects children. Its symptoms include a fever and an itchy rash of dark red spots.

chicken run a small strip of ground usually enclosed with wire netting, for keeping chickens.

chicken wire wire netting.

chickpea noun 1 a leafy branching annual plant (Cicer arietinum) with white or bluish flowers, native to Asia, and cultivated since antiquity for its wrinkled yellow pea-like edible seeds, which are borne in short swollen pods, generally containing two seeds each. 2 the edible seed of this plant, usually eaten boiled or roasted. [from earlier *chich pea*, from French *chiche*]

chickweed noun a low-growing sprawling annual plant (Stellaria media), native to Europe, having oval pointed leaves and tiny white flowers with deeply lobed petals that are about the same length as the sepals. [from CHICK + WEED, the leaves and seeds being enjoyed by birds]

chicly /'ʃiːklɪ/ adv. with a chic or stylish manner.

chicory noun 1 a perennial plant (Cichorium intybus), native to Europe, W Asia, and N Africa, and widely introduced elsewhere, having stiff stems, stalked lower leaves which may be toothed or lobed, stalkless upper leaves which clasp the stem, and a long stout tap root. 2 the dried root of this plant, which is often ground, roasted, and blended with coffee. 3 the leaves of this plant, which can be eaten raw as a salad vegetable. [from Greek *kichorion*]

chide verb (PAST TENSE **chided**, old use **chid**; PAST PARTICIPLE **chided**, old use **chidden**) to scold, rebuke. [from Anglo-Saxon *cidan*]

chiding noun a scolding or rebuke.

chief — *noun* 1 the head of a tribe, clan, etc. 2 a leader. 3 the person in charge of any group, organization, department, etc. — *adj.* 1 *used in titles, etc* first in rank; leading. 2 main; most important; principal. — **in chief** mainly; especially; most of all. [from Old French *chef*, from Latin *caput*, head]

▣ *noun* 1 ruler, chieftain. 2, 3 leader, head, principal, commander, captain, governor, boss, director, manager, superintendent, superior, ringleader, lord, master, supremo. *adj.* 2 main, principal, key, central, prime, leading, primary, major, supreme, premier, foremost, uppermost, highest, prevailing, predominant, pre-eminent, grand, arch, outstanding, vital, essential.

▣ *adj.* 2 minor, unimportant.

chief constable in the UK, the officer in charge of the police force of a county or region.

chief executive the director of a business, organization, etc.

chiefly adv. 1 mainly. 2 especially; above all.

▣ MAINLY, MOSTLY, FOR THE MOST PART, PREDOMINANTLY, PRINCIPALLY, PRIMARILY, ESSENTIALLY, ESPECIALLY, GENERALLY, USUALLY.

chief of staff (PL. **chiefs of staff**) the senior officer of each of the armed forces.

chief petty officer a senior non-commissioned officer in the Royal Navy and the navies of some other countries.

chieftain noun 1 the head of a tribe or clan. 2 a leader or commander. [from Old French *chevetaine*, from Latin *capitaneus*, captain]

chieftaincy or **chieftainship** noun (PL. **chieftaincies**) the position of chieftain.

chiffchaff noun a bird belonging to a group of Old World warblers, native to Europe, N Africa, and Asia, and inhabiting forest margins with thick undergrowth. It feeds on insects. [imitative of its call]

chiffon /'ʃɪfɒn/ noun 1 a very fine transparent silk or nylon fabric. 2 *Cookery* a light silkily frothy mixture, made with beaten whites of eggs. [from French *chiffon*, rag]

chiffonier or **chiffonnier** /ʃɪfə'nɪə(r)/ noun 1 a tall elegant chest of drawers. 2 a low wide cabinet with an open or grille front. [from French *chiffonnier*, a container for *chiffons*, scraps of fabric]

chigger or **chigoe** noun the bright red larval stage of a mite, often found in large numbers in damp fields in autumn. Also called HARVESTMITE. [from Carib (a W Indian language) *chigo*]

chignon /'ʃiːnjɒn/ noun a soft bun or coil of hair worn at the back of the neck. [from French *chignon*, from Old French *chaignon*, nape of the neck]

chigoe /'tʃɪgoʊ/ see CHIGGER.

chihuahua /tʃɪ'waːwə/ noun the smallest domestic breed of dog, only 18cm high and weighing about 0.8kg, having a tiny body and a disproportionately large head with a bulbous forehead, large widely spaced eyes, and large ears.

chilblain noun a painful red itchy swelling of the skin, especially on the fingers, toes, or ears, caused by abnormal constriction of the blood vessels of the skin on exposure to cold. [from CHILL + *blain*, blister]

child noun (PL. **children**) 1 a boy or girl between birth and puberty. 2 a baby or infant, or an unborn baby. 3 one's son or daughter. 4 someone lacking experience or understanding in something: *an absolute child in financial matters.* 5 *derog.* an innocent or naive person. 6 a person seen as a typical product of a particular historical period, movement, etc: *he was a child of his time.* — **child's play** *colloq.* a basic or simple task. **with child** *old use* pregnant. [from Anglo-Saxon *cild*]

▣ 1 youngster, girl, boy, *colloq.* kid, *colloq.* nipper, baby, infant, toddler, *colloq.* tot, *colloq.* brat, minor, juvenile. 2 baby, infant, fetus. **3** offspring, issue, descendant. **4** novice, amateur, *colloq.* greenhorn.

child abuse any form of physical, mental, or emotional maltreatment of a child, eg neglect or sexual abuse, by either of its parents or another adult.

childbearing — *noun* the process or state of carrying and giving birth to a child. — *adj.* relating to this process or state.

child benefit a regular state allowance to parents for the upbringing of children below a certain age.

childbirth *noun* the process whereby a mother gives birth to a child at the end of pregnancy.

childhood *noun* the state or time of being a child.

■ babyhood, infancy, boyhood, girlhood, schooldays, youth, adolescence, minority, immaturity.

childish *adj.* **1** *derog.* silly; immature. **2** relating to children or childhood; like a child.

■ IMMATURE, JUVENILE, BABYISH, INFANTILE, BOYISH, GIRLISH. **1** silly, foolish, frivolous, puerile.
■ MATURE. **1** sensible.

childishly *adv.* with a childish manner.
childishness *noun* being childish.
childless *adj.* having no children.
childlike *adj.* like a child; innocent.

■ innocent, naïve, ingenuous, artless, guileless, credulous, trusting, trustful, simple, natural.

child-lock *noun* a feature on a video recorder, etc which prevents settings on the equipment being altered by a child playing with it.
childminder *noun* a person, usually officially registered, who looks after children for payment, eg for working parents.
childproof or **child-resistant** *adj.* designed so as not to be able to be opened, operated, damaged, etc by a child.
Child Support Agency (ABBREV. **CSA**) a UK government body established in 1993 to administer the provisions of the Child Support Act by contacting and enforcing absent parents to pay child maintenance costs.
child welfare care of children's health and living conditions, as a branch of social work.
chili same as CHILLI.
chill — *noun* **1** a feeling of coldness: *a wintry chill in the air.* **2** a cold that causes shivering, chattering teeth, pale skin, and a sensation of coldness, often preceding a fever, and commonly caused by exposure to a cold damp environment. **3** a feeling, especially sudden, of depression or fear. **4** a coldness of manner; hostility. — *verb* **1** *trans., intrans.* to make or become cold; to cool. **2** to cause to feel cold. **3** to scare, depress, or discourage. **4** to preserve (food, etc) by cooling it. **5** to increase the hardness and density of (a molten metal) by pouring it into a (usually water-cooled) iron mould. *adj.* slightly cold. — **chill out** *slang* to relax, especially after a period of hard work or exercise. **take the chill off something** to warm it slightly. [from Anglo-Saxon *ciele*, cold]

■ *noun* **1** coolness, cold, coldness, rawness, bite, nip, crispness. **4** hostility, unfriendliness, coolness, iciness, aloofness, distance, antagonism, sourness, frigidity. *verb* **1**, **4** cool, refrigerate, freeze, ice. **2** freeze. **3** scare, frighten, terrify, depress, discourage, dismay, dishearten, dampen. *adj.* cool, chilling, cold, *colloq.* nippy, raw, fresh, brisk, wintry.
■ *noun* **1** warmth. **4** warmth, friendliness. *verb* **1**, **2** warm, heat. **3** hearten, encourage, cheer up.

chilled *adj.* **1** made cold. **2** hardened by chilling. **3** preserved by chilling.
chill factor a means of assessing the extent to which weather conditions, especially wind speed, increase the cooling effect of low temperatures.
chilli or **chili** *noun* (PL. **chillis**, **chillies**) **1** the fruit or 'pod' of one of the varieties of capsicum, which has a hot spicy flavour and is used in sauces, pickles, etc, or dried and ground to a powder, known as *cayenne pepper*, which is used as a spice. **2** (*in full* **chilli con carne**) a hot Mexican dish of minced meat and beans flavoured with chilli powder. [from Aztec *chilli*]
chilliness *noun* being chilly.
chilling *adj.* frightening.
chillingly *adv.* with a chilling manner.
chilly *adj.* (**chillier**, **chilliest**) **1** rather cold. **2** *colloq.* unfriendly; hostile.

■ **1** cold, fresh, brisk, crisp, *colloq.* nippy, wintry. **2** unfriendly, hostile, unwelcoming, cool, aloof, stony, frigid, unsympathetic.
■ **1** warm. **2** friendly.

chime — *noun* **1** a set of tuned bells; the sound made by them. **2** (**chimes**) a percussion instrument consisting of hanging metal tubes that are struck with a hammer. — *verb* **1** *intrans. said of bells* to ring. **2** *intrans., trans. said of a clock* to indicate (the time) by chiming. **3** *intrans.* to agree or harmonize: *that chimes with what others say.* — **chime in 1** to add a remark to a conversation, especially repeating or agreeing with something. **2** to agree with someone, or fit in with them. [formerly *chymbe belle*, probably from Anglo-Saxon *cimbal*, cymbal]

■ *verb* **1** ring, sound, strike, toll, peal, clang, dong, jingle, tinkle. **2** strike, dong, sound. **3** agree, harmonize, correspond.

chimera *noun* **1** in Greek mythology, a fire-breathing monster with the head of a lion, the body of a goat, and the tail of a serpent. **2** a wild or impossible idea. **3** *Biol.* an organism containing genetically different tissues as a result of mutation or grafting. [from Greek *khimaira*, she-goat]
chimerical /kaɪˈmɛrɪkəl/ *adj.* **1** of the nature of a chimera. **2** wild, fanciful.
chimney *noun* (PL. **chimneys**) **1** a vertical structure made of brick, stone, or steel, that carries smoke, steam, fumes, or heated air away from a fireplace, stove, furnace, or engine. **2** same as CHIMNEY STACK. **3** a vent in a volcano. **4** a glass funnel protecting the flame of a lamp. **5** a steep narrow cleft in a rock face, just large enough for a mountaineer to enter and climb. [from Old French *cheminee*, from Latin *camera caminata*, room with a fireplace]
chimney breast a projecting part of a wall built round the base of a chimney.
chimneypot *noun* a short hollow rounded fitting, usually made of pottery, that sits in the opening at the top of a chimney.
chimney stack 1 a stone or brick structure rising from a roof, usually carrying several chimneys. **2** a very tall factory chimney.
chimney-sweep *noun* a person who cleans soot out of chimneys, especially for a living.
chimp *noun colloq.* a chimpanzee.
chimpanzee *noun* the most intelligent of the great apes (Pan troglodytes), found in tropical rainforests of Africa, up to 1.5m in height, and having long coarse black hair, except for a white patch near the rump. The face, ears, hands, and feet are hairless. [from a W African language]
chin *noun* the projecting front part of the lower jaw, below the mouth. — **keep one's chin up** *colloq.* to stay cheerful in spite of misfortune or difficulty. **take it on the chin** *colloq.* to accept a difficulty or misfortune bravely. [from Anglo-Saxon *cinn*]

china — *noun* articles made from a fine translucent earthenware, originally from China; articles made from similar materials. — *adj.* made of china. [from Persian *chini*, Chinese]

∎ *noun* porcelain, pottery, earthenware, stoneware. *adj.* porcelain, ceramic.

china clay kaolin, a fine white clay used for making porcelain.

Chinaman *noun* (PL. **Chinamen**) 1 *old derog. use* a Chinese man. 2 *Cricket* a ball, spinning from the off to the leg side, bowled by a left-handed bowler to a right-handed batsman.

China tea a kind of smoke-cured tea grown in China.

Chinatown *noun* in any city outside China, a district where most of the inhabitants are Chinese.

chinchilla *noun* 1 a small mammal with a thick soft grey coat, a bushy tail, and large round ears, native to the Andes of S America. 2 the thick soft grey fur of this animal. 3 a breed of cats or of rabbits with grey fur. [from Spanish *chinchilla*]

chine [1] — *noun* 1 former name for the spine or backbone. 2 a cut, especially of pork, consisting of a piece of the backbone and adjoining meat. 3 the crest of a ridge. — *verb* to cut (the carcass of an animal) along the backbone. [from Old French *eschine*]

chine [2] *noun* a ravine or a deep cleft in the wall of a cliff. [from Anglo-Saxon *cinu*, crevice]

Chinese — *noun* (PL. **Chinese**) 1 a native or citizen of China, or a member of the main ethnic group of China. 2 the language of the main ethnic group of China. — *adj.* of China or its people or language.

Chinese cabbage or **Chinese leaves** a plant (Brassica rapa pekinensis), related to the cabbage, that produces a loose cylindrical head of crisp whitish leaves, eaten as a salad vegetable and used in Eastern cuisine.

Chinese chequers a game played by moving pegs or marbles on a star-shaped board.

Chinese gooseberry same as KIWI FRUIT.

Chinese lantern 1 a collapsible paper lantern that folds concertina-fashion. 2 a perennial plant (Physalis alkakengi), native to SE Europe and Asia, having white flowers with dark spots in the centre, each of which is surrounded by a persistent inflated calyx that encloses the developing fruit and eventually becomes orange-red in colour and papery in texture.

Chinese puzzle 1 a complex wooden puzzle, especially consisting of a series of boxes that fit one inside the next. 2 any highly complicated puzzle or problem.

Chink or **Chinkie** or **Chinky** *offensive slang* — *noun* (PL. **Chinkies**) a Chinese person. — *adj.* Chinese.

chink [1] *noun* 1 a small slit or crack. 2 a narrow beam of light shining through such a crack. [related to CHINE[2]]

∎ 1 slit, crack, crevice, fissure, cleft, rift, opening, aperture, gap, space.

chink [2] — *noun* a faint, short ringing noise; a clink. — *verb intrans., trans.* to make or cause to make this noise. [imitative]

chinless *adj. derog.* 1 having a small, weak, backwards-sloping chin. 2 having a weak, indecisive character.

chinoiserie /ʃiːnwɑːzəˈriː/ *noun* a European style of design and decoration which imitates or uses Chinese motifs and methods. [from French *chinois*, Chinese]

chinstrap *noun* a helmet strap, worn under the chin.

chintz *noun* a shiny cotton material originally imported from India, usually printed in bright colours on a light background, used especially for soft furnishings. [from *chints*, plural of *chint*, from Gujarati (an Indian language) *chi(n)t*]

chintzy *adj.* (**chintzier, chintziest**) *derog.* sentimentally or quaintly showy.

chinwag *noun colloq.* a chat.

chip — *verb* (**chipped, chipping**) 1 (**chip something** or **chip at something**) to knock or strike small pieces off a hard object or material. 2 *intrans.* to be broken off in small pieces; to have small pieces broken off. 3 to shape by chipping: *chip a design into the stone.* 4 to cut (potatoes) into strips for frying. 5 *trans., intrans. Golf, Football* to strike with, or play, a chip shot. — *noun* 1 a small piece chipped off. 2 a place from which a piece has been chipped off: *a big chip in the lid.* 3 *Brit.* (*usually* **chips**) a strip of potato, fried or for frying. 4 *North Amer.* (*also* **potato chip**) a potato crisp. 5 a plastic counter used as a money token in gambling. 6 *Electron.* same as SILICON CHIP. 7 a small piece of stone. — **chip in** *colloq.* 1 to interrupt: *chip in with a suggestion.* 2 to contribute. **a chip off the old block** *colloq.* a person very like one or other parent in personality or appearance. **have a chip on one's shoulder** *colloq.* to feel resentful about something, especially unreasonably. **have had one's chips** *colloq.* to have lost one's chance; to have failed or been killed. **when the chips are down** *colloq.* at the moment of crisis; when it comes to the point. [from Anglo-Saxon *cipp*, log, ploughshare, beam]

∎ *verb* 1 chisel, whittle, nick, notch, gash. 3 chisel, whittle. *noun* 1 fragment, scrap, wafer, sliver, flake, shaving, paring. 2 notch, nick, scratch, dent, flaw.

chipboard *noun* solid board made from compressed wood chips.

chipmunk *noun* any of several small ground squirrels found in N America and N Asia, with reddish-brown fur and a less bushy tail than that of tree squirrels. [from earlier *chitmunk*, from Ojibwa, a N American Indian language]

chipolata *noun* a small sausage. [from French *chipolata*, from Italian *cipollata*, onion dish]

chipped *adj.* 1 shaped or damaged by chipping. 2 shaped into chips.

Chippendale *adj.* denoting a graceful and elegant style of furniture made by, or imitating the style of, the 18c cabinet-maker Thomas Chippendale.

chipper *adj. North Amer. colloq.*, *said of a person* cheerful and lively. [perhaps from N English dialect]

chippy *noun* (PL. **chippies**) *Brit. colloq.* 1 a chip shop. 2 a carpenter or joiner.

chip shop a shop selling chips, fish, and other fried foods, for taking away to eat.

chip shot *Golf, Football* a short, high shot or kick.

chirography or **cheirography** /kaɪəˈrɒɡrəfɪ/ *noun* the study of the forms and styles of handwriting. [from Greek *cheir*, hand + *graphe*, writing]

chiromancy or **cheiromancy** /ˈkaɪərəʊmansɪ/ *noun* palmistry. [from Greek *cheir*, hand + *manteia*, divination]

chiropodist /ʃɪˈrɒpədɪst, kɪˈrɒpədɪst/ *noun* a person who specializes in the treatment of minor disorders of the feet, such as corns, bunions, and verrucas. Also called PODIATRIST. [from Greek *cheir*, hand + *pous*, foot; the original practitioners treated hands as well as feet]

chiropody /ʃɪˈrɒpədɪ, kɪˈrɒpədɪ/ *noun* the diagnosis, treatment, and prevention of disorders and diseases of the foot, especially in the elderly or disabled.

chiropractic /kaɪərəʊˈpraktɪk/ *noun* 1 a system of treatment based on the theory that nearly all bodily disorders are caused by abnormal nerve functioning, and so can be largely alleviated by manipulating the vertebrae of the spine. 2 a person who practises this treatment. Also called CHIROPRACTOR. [from Greek *cheir*, hand + *prattein*, to do]

chiropractor /ˈkaɪərəʊpraktə(r)/ *noun* a person who practises chiropractic. Also called CHIROPRACTIC.

chirp — *verb* 1 *intrans. said of birds, grasshoppers, etc* to produce a short high unmusical sound. 2 *trans., intrans.*

to chatter, or say (something), merrily. — *noun* a chirping sound. [imitative]

- -

▤ *verb* **1** chirrup, tweet, cheep, peep, twitter, warble, sing, pipe, whistle. **2** chatter, chirrup, pipe, babble, prattle. *noun* chirrup, tweet, cheep, peep, twitter, warble, whistle.

- -

chirpily *adv.* with a chirpy manner.

chirpiness *noun* being chirpy; cheeriness.

chirpy *adj.* (**chirpier, chirpiest**) *colloq.* cheerful and lively.

chirrup — *verb intrans.* (**chirruped, chirruping**) to chirp, especially in little bursts. — *noun* a burst of chirping. [imitative]

chirrupy *adj., said of a person* bright and cheerful.

chisel /ˈtʃɪzəl/ — *noun* a hand tool consisting of a flat steel blade with the end bevelled to a cutting edge, and a wooden handle, used for shaping or working wood, stone, or metal. — *verb* (**chiselled, chiselling**) **1** to shape or work (wood, stone, or metal) with a chisel. **2** *slang* to cheat. [from Old French *cisel*]

chit[1] *noun* a short note, especially an officially signed one, recording money owed or paid, an order for goods, etc. [from Hindi *citthi*]

chit[2] *noun derog.* a cheeky young girl; a mere child. [related to KITTEN]

chitarrone /kiːtəˈroʊneɪ/ *noun* (PL. **chitarroni**) a large lute or theorbo popular in the 16c and 17c, both as a solo instrument and in accompanying singing. [from Italian; related to GUITAR KITHARA]

chitchat *derog.* — *noun* chatter; gossip. — *verb intrans.* (**chitchatted, chitchatting**) to gossip idly. [reduplicated form of CHAT]

chitin /ˈkaɪtɪn/ *noun Zool.* a complex carbohydrate substance that serves to strengthen the tough outer covering or cuticle of insects and crustaceans, and the cell walls of many fungi. [from French *chitine*, from Greek *chiton*, tunic]

chitinous *adj.* consisting of or like chitin.

chitterlings *pl. noun* a pig's or other animal's intestines, prepared as a food. [from Middle English *cheterling*]

chitty same as CHIT[1].

chivalrous /ˈʃɪvlrəs/ *adj.* **1** showing chivalry; courteous towards, and concerned for, those weaker than oneself. **2** relating to medieval chivalry.

- -

▤ **1** polite, courteous, gentlemanly. **2** gallant, heroic, valiant, brave, courageous, bold, noble, honourable.

▣ **1** rude, ungentlemanly. **2** ungallant, cowardly.

- -

chivalrously *adv.* with a chivalrous manner.

chivalrousness *noun* being chivalrous.

chivalry /ˈʃɪvlrɪ/ *noun* **1** courtesy and protectiveness shown to the weak, or to women by men. **2** *Hist.* a code of moral and religious behaviour followed by medieval knights; the medieval system of knighthood. [from Old French *chevalerie*, from *chevalier*, knight]

- -

▤ **1** politeness, courtesy, gentlemanliness. **2** gallantry, bravery, courage, boldness.

- -

chive *noun* **1** a perennial plant (Allium schoenoprasum), native to Europe and Asia, having tufts of long narrow tubular leaves and dense flat-topped clusters of pink or purple flowers. **2** (**chives**) the leaves of this plant, which are chopped and used as a flavouring in salads, omelettes, etc. [from Old French *cive*]

chivvy or **chivy** *verb* (**chivvies, chivvied**) to keep urging on or nagging (someone), especially to hurry or to get some task done. [perhaps from the ballad Chevy Chase]

chlor- or **chloro-** *combining form* **1** green. **2** chlorine. [from Greek *chloros*, green]

chloral /ˈklɔːrəl/ *noun Chem.* (FORMULA CCl₃CHO) an oily colourless toxic liquid with a pungent odour, produced by the chlorination of acetaldehyde (ethanal). It is used in the manufacture of DDT and *chloral hydrate* (a sedative and hypnotic drug). Also called TRICHLOROETHANAL. [from CHLORINE + ALCOHOL]

chlorate /ˈklɔːreɪt/ *noun Chem.* any salt of chloric acid. Some chlorates are used in defoliant weedkillers.

chloric acid /ˈklɔːrɪk/ *Chem.* (FORMULA HClO₃) a strong acid with a pungent odour, that only occurs in aqueous solution and in the form of its salts, known as *chlorates*. It is used as a catalyst.

chloride /ˈklɔːraɪd/ *noun Chem.* **1** any compound containing chlorine and another chemical element or group, eg sodium chloride. **2** the negatively charged Cl⁻ ion, or any salt or ester of hydrochloric acid containing this ion. [from CHLORINE + -IDE]

chlorinate /ˈklɔːrɪneɪt/ *verb* **1** *Chem.* to introduce (chlorine) into an organic chemical compound. **2** to treat (a substance, especially water) with chlorine, usually in order to disinfect or bleach it. [from Greek *chloros*, green]

chlorinated *adj.* treated or combined with chlorine.

chlorination /klɔːrɪˈneɪʃən, klɒrɪˈneɪʃən/ *noun* **1** *Chem.* the formation of a chlorinated compound (an organic compound containing chlorine) as a result of a chemical reaction between chlorine and an organic compound. **2** the bleaching or disinfecting of a substance by treating it with chlorine.

chlorine /ˈklɔːriːn, ˈklɔːraɪn/ *noun Chem.* (SYMBOL Cl, ATOMIC NUMBER 17) a greenish-yellow poisonous gas with a pungent smell, that is obtained from deposits of sodium chloride (common salt) or potassium chloride, and from sea water, by electrolysis. It is widely used to purify water and as a bleach, and in the manufacture of chlorine-containing organic chemicals such as propellants.

chloro- see CHLOR-.

chlorofluorocarbon /klɔːrəflʊərəʊˈkɑːbən/ *noun Chem.* (ABBREV. **CFC**) a chemical compound composed of chlorine, fluorine, and carbon, used as an aerosol propellant, and in refrigeration systems to aid the circulation of cooling agents. It is also produced during the manufacture of plastic foam for containers.

chloroform /ˈklɒrəfɔːm, ˈklɔːrəfɔːm/ — *noun Chem.* (FORMULA CHCl₃) a colourless volatile sweet-smelling liquid, formerly used as an anaesthetic. It is used as a solvent, and in the manufacture of organic chemicals. Also called TRICHLOROMETHANE. — *verb* to anaesthetize with chloroform. [from CHLORINE + *formic* as in FORMIC ACID]

chlorophyll /ˈklɒrəfɪl, ˈklɔːrəfɪl/ *noun Bot.* the green pigment, found in the chloroplasts of all green plants, that absorbs light energy from the sun during photosynthesis, and converts it to chemical energy required for the manufacture of carbohydrates by the plant. [from CHLOR- + Greek *phyllon*, leaf]

chloroplast /ˈklɔːrəʊplast/ *noun Bot.* any of many specialized membrane-bound structures containing the green pigment chlorophyll, found within the cytoplasm of photosynthetic cells of all green plants that are regularly exposed to light. Photosynthesis takes place within these structures. [from CHLOR- + Greek *plastos*, moulded]

choc *noun colloq.* chocolate.

chocaholic /tʃɒkəˈhɒlɪk/ or **chocoholic** *noun* someone who is addicted to chocolate. [from CHOCOLATE by analogy with ALCOHOLIC]

chock — *noun* a heavy block or wedge used to prevent movement of a wheel, etc. — *verb* to wedge or immobilise with chocks.

chock-a-block *adj.* tightly jammed; crammed full: *a room chock-a-block with people.* [originally a nautical term, referring to a tackle with two blocks close together]

chock-full *adj.* absolutely full.

chocolate /ˈtʃɒklət, ˈtʃɒkələt/ — *noun* **1** a food product, made from cacao (cocoa) beans, that is usually sold in bars or blocks, and may be eaten on its own or used to flavour biscuits, cakes, ice cream, milk drinks, etc. **2** a sweet made from or coated with this substance. **3** a beverage made by dissolving a powder prepared from this substance in hot water or milk. **4** a dark-brown colour. — *adj.* **1** made from, or coated with, chocolate. **2** dark brown. [from Aztec *chocolatl*]

chocolate-box *adj. derog.* over-pretty or sentimental, like the designs on boxes of chocolates.

chocolaty *adj.* **1** made with or as if with chocolate. **2** tasting of or like chocolate. **3** coloured like chocolate.

choice — *noun* **1** the act or process of choosing. **2** the right, power, or opportunity to choose: *have no choice.* **3** something or someone chosen: *a good choice.* **4** a variety of things available for choosing between: *a wide choice.* — *adj.* of specially good quality. — **from choice 1** willingly. **2** if given a choice. **of one's choice** selected according to one's own preference. **take one's choice** to choose whatever one wants. [from Old French *chois*]

⊟ *noun* **1** choosing, opting, decision, election, discrimination, say, pick, preference. **2** say, decision. **3** option, alternative, selection. **4** selection, variety, range, assortment, mixture. *adj.* best, superior, prime, *colloq.* plum, excellent, fine, exquisite, exclusive, select, hand-picked, special, prize, valuable, precious.
⊡ *adj.* inferior, poor.

choiceness *noun* being choice.

choir /kwaɪə(r)/ *noun* **1** an organized group of trained singers, especially one that performs in church. **2** especially in a cathedral or large church, the area occupied by the choir; the chancel. [from Old French *cuer*, from Latin *chorus*]

choirboy or **choirgirl** *noun* a young boy or girl who sings in a church choir.

choirmaster or **choirmistress** *noun* the trainer of a choir.

choir stalls fixed wooden seats for the choir in the chancel of a church.

choke — *verb* **1** *trans., intrans.* to prevent or be prevented from breathing by an obstruction in the throat, fumes, emotion, etc. **2** to stop or interfere with breathing in this way. **3** *trans., intrans.* to make or become speechless from emotion: *choking with rage.* **4** to fill up, block, or restrict. **5** to restrict the growth or development of: *plants choked by weeds.* — *noun* **1** *Engineering* a valve in the carburettor of a petrol engine that reduces the air supply and so gives a richer fuel/air mixture while the engine is still cold. **2** (*in full* **choke coil**) *Electron.* a coil of wire that is included in a radio circuit in order to present a high impedance to the passage of audio-frequency or radio-frequency currents. — **choke something back** to suppress something indicative of feelings, especially tears, laughter, or anger. **choke someone off** to prevent them from continuing to speak. **choke something off** to put a stop to it; to prevent it. [from Anglo-Saxon *aceocian*, to suffocate]

⊟ *verb* **1** suffocate, throttle, strangle, asphyxiate, stifle, gag. **2** stifle. **4** fill up, block, obstruct, constrict, restrict, congest, clog, dam, bar, close, stop. **5** suppress, smother.

choker *noun* a close-fitting necklace or broad band of velvet, etc worn round the neck.

cholecalciferol /koʊlɪkalˈsɪfərɒl/ *noun* vitamin D₃. [from Greek *chole*, bile + CALCIFEROL]

choler /ˈkɒlə(r)/ *noun old use* anger; irritability. [earlier meaning, bile; from Greek *chole*, bile]

cholera /ˈkɒlərə/ *noun Medicine* an acute and potentially fatal bacterial infection of the small intestine, acquired by ingesting food or water contaminated with the bacterium, and often causing epidemics in areas with poor sanitation. [from Greek *chole*, bile]

choleric /ˈkɒlərɪk/ *adj.* irritable; bad-tempered.

cholesterol /kəˈlɛstərɒl, kɒˈlɛstərɒl/ *noun Biochem.* a sterol found mainly in animal tissues, especially in fat, blood, nervous tissue, bile, and the liver. [from Greek *chole*, bile + *stereos*, solid]

choline /ˈkoʊlɪn, ˈkoʊliːn/ *noun Biochem.* an organic compound that is a component of the neurotransmitter acetylcholine, and is also involved in the transport of fats in the body. [from Greek *chole*, bile]

chomp — *verb trans., intrans.* to munch noisily. — *noun* an act of chomping. [variant of CHAMP¹]

choose /tʃuːz/ *verb* (PAST TENSE **chose**; PAST PARTICIPLE **chosen**) **1** *trans., intrans.* to take or select (one or more things or persons) from a larger number, according to one's own preference or judgement. **2** to decide; to think fit. — **nothing** or **not much to choose between people** or **things** with little difference in quality, value, etc between them. [from Anglo-Saxon *ceosan*]

⊟ OPT FOR, PLUMP FOR, VOTE FOR, SETTLE ON, FIX ON, PREFER, ADOPT, ELECT. **1** pick, select, single out, designate. **2** wish, desire, see fit.

choosy *adj.* (**choosier, choosiest**) *colloq.* difficult to please; fussy.

⊟ particular, fussy, *colloq.* picky, finicky, fastidious, exacting, selective, discriminating.
⊡ undemanding.

chop¹ — *verb* (**chopped, chopping**) **1** (**chop something** or **chop at something**) to cut it with a vigorous downward or sideways slicing action, with an axe, knife, etc. **2** to hit (a ball) with a sharp downwards stroke. **3** *colloq.* to reduce or completely withdraw (funding, etc). — *noun* **1** a slice of pork, lamb, or mutton containing a bone, especially a rib. **2** a chopping action or stroke. **3** a sharp downward stroke given to a ball. **4** a short sharp blow. **5** (**the chop**) *colloq.* dismissal from a job: *get the chop.* **6** (**the chop**) *colloq.* the sudden stopping or closing down of something: *our project got the chop.* — **chop something off** to remove it by chopping. [variant of CHAP²]

⊟ *verb* **1** cut, hack, slice, hew, lop, sever, truncate, cleave, divide, split, slash. **3** cut, axe, decrease, trim, slash, withdraw, cancel. *noun* **2** cut, slice, slash, hack. **4** blow, clip, clout, punch, bash, knock, rap. **5** sack, *colloq.* push, *colloq.* boot. **6** axe.

chop² — **chop and change** to keep changing one's mind, plans, etc. **chop logic** to use over-subtle or complicated and confusing arguments. [from Anglo-Saxon *ceapian*, to bargain or trade]

chophouse *noun colloq.* a restaurant specialising in steak and chops.

chopper *noun* **1** *colloq.* a helicopter. **2** *colloq.* a motorcycle with high handlebars. **3** a short-handled axe-like tool. **4** (**choppers**) *colloq.* the teeth.

choppily *adv., said of water* roughly.

choppiness *noun, said of water* being rather rough.

chopping-board *noun* a board for chopping up vegetables, etc on.

choppy *adj.* (**choppier, choppiest**) *said of the sea, etc* rather rough, with small irregular waves.

⊟ rough, stormy, squally, ruffled, turbulent, tempestuous, wavy, uneven, broken.
⊡ calm, still.

chops *pl. noun* the jaws or mouth, especially an animal's. — **lick one's chops** *colloq.* to look forward to some pleasure with relish. [from *chap*, the lower half of the cheek]

chopsticks *pl. noun* a pair of slender wooden, plastic, or ivory sticks, operated in one hand like pincers, used for eating with in several Oriental countries. [from Pidgin English *chop*, quick + STICK¹]

chop suey /ˈsuːɪ/ a Chinese dish of chopped meat and vegetables fried in a sauce, usually served with rice. [from Chinese dialect *jaahp seui*, mixed bits]

choral /'kɔrəl/ *adj.* relating to, or to be sung by, a choir or chorus: *choral music.* [from Latin *choralis*, from *chorus*, choir]

chorale /kɒ'rɑːl/ *noun* **1** a hymn tune with a slow, dignified rhythm and strong harmonisation. **2** *North Amer., esp. US* a choir or choral society. [from German *Choral*, short for *Choralgesang*, choral singing]

chorally *adv.* **1** in the manner of a chorus. **2** for a choir.

choral society a group that meets regularly to practise and perform choral music.

chord[1] /kɔːd/ *noun Mus.* a combination of musical notes played together. [formerly *cord*, shortened from ACCORD]

chord[2] *noun* **1** *poetic* a string of a musical instrument. **2** *Anat.* same as CORD. **3** *Zool.* same as NOTOCHORD. **4** *Geom.* a straight line joining any two points on a curve or a curved surface. — **strike a chord** to prompt a feeling of recognition or familiarity. **touch the right chord** to get the desired emotional or sympathetic response from someone. [from Greek *chorde*, string, gut]

chordate /'kɔːdeɪt/ *noun Zool.* any animal belonging to the phylum Chordata, including animals that possess a notochord. [from Greek *chorde*, a string, intestine]

chore *noun* a piece of housework or other boring and laborious task. [see CHAR[2]]

.....

◩ job, task, errand, duty, burden.

.....

chorea /kɒ'rɪə/ *noun Medicine* either of two disorders of the nervous system that cause rapid involuntary movements of the limbs and sometimes of the face. *Sydenham's chorea* occurs mainly in children and is an allergic response to bacterial infection. *Huntingdon's chorea* is an inherited disorder in which degeneration of the nerve cells in the brain leads to progressive dementia. [from Greek *choreia*, dance]

choreograph /'kɒrɪəgraf/ *verb* to plan the choreography for (a dance, ballet, etc.).

choreographer /kɒrɪ'ɒgrəfə(r)/ *noun* a person who choreographs dance.

choreographic /kɒrɪə'grafɪk/ *adj.* relating to or involving dancing.

choreography /kɒrɪ'ɒgrəfɪ/ *noun* the arrangement of the sequence and pattern of movements in dancing. [from Greek *choreia*, dance + GRAPHY]

chorionic gonadotrophin *Physiol.* in mammals, a hormone produced during pregnancy. Its presence in the urine forms the basis of many types of pregnancy test.

chorister /'kɒrɪstə(r)/ *noun* a singer in a choir, especially a choirboy in a church or cathedral choir. [from Middle English *queristre*, from *quer*, choir, influenced by Latin *chorista*, singer in a choir]

choroid /'kɔːrɔɪd/ *adj. Anat.* the layer of cells, lying between the retina and the sclerotic, that lines the back of the eyeball in terrestrial vertebrates. It is rich in blood vessels, and contains a pigment that absorbs excess light, so preventing blurring of vision. [from Greek *chorion*, membrane]

chortle *verb intrans.* to give a half-suppressed, amused, or triumphant laugh. [word invented by Lewis Carroll in *Through the Looking-glass*, combining SNORT and CHUCKLE]

chorus /'kɔːrəs/ — *noun* **1** a set of lines in a song, sung after each verse. **2** a large choir. **3** a piece of music for such a choir. **4** the group of singers and dancers supporting the soloists in an opera or musical show: *a chorus girl.* **5** something uttered by a number of people at the same time: *a chorus of 'Nos'.* **6** *Theatr.* an actor who delivers an introductory or concluding passage to a play. **7** *Greek Theatr.* a group of actors, always on stage, who comment on the developments in the plot. — *verb* (**chorused, chorusing**) to say, sing, or utter together. — **in chorus** all together; in unison. [from Latin *chorus*, choir]

◩ *noun* **1** refrain. **2** choir, choristers, singers, vocalists, ensemble.

.....

chose /ʃəʊz/, **chosen** see CHOOSE.

chosen few a select, privileged group of people.

chough /tʃʌf/ *noun* either of two species of bird belonging to the crow family and native to Europe and Asia. [probably imitative of its cry]

choux pastry /ʃuː/ a very light pastry made with eggs. [from French *pâte choux*, cabbage pastry]

chow[1] /tʃaʊ/ *noun* a breed of dog, originally developed in China and introduced to Europe in the 18c, having a heavy body with a thick coat, a lion-like mane, and a blue tongue. Its tail is characteristically curved over its back. [probably from a Chinese dialect]

chow[2] *noun North Amer., esp. US slang* food. [from Pidgin English *chow-chow*, mixed fruit preserve]

chowder /'tʃaʊdə(r)/ *noun North Amer.* a thick soup containing clams or fish and vegetables, often made with milk. [from French *chaudière*, kettle]

chow mein /meɪn/ *noun* a Chinese dish of chopped meat and vegetables served with fried noodles. [from Chinese *chow mein*, fried noodles]

chrism /krɪzəm/ *noun* **1** holy oil used in the Roman Catholic and Orthodox Churches for anointing. **2** *Relig.* confirmation. [from Greek *chrisma*, anointing]

Christ /kraɪst/ — *noun* **1** the Messiah or 'anointed one' whose coming is prophesied in the Old Testament. **2** Jesus of Nazareth, or Jesus Christ, believed by Christians to be the Messiah. **3** a figure or picture of Jesus. — *interj. offensive* (to many) expressing surprise, anger, etc. [from Greek *christos*, anointed]

Christadelphian /krɪstə'dɛlfɪən/ *noun* a member of the Brothers of Christ, a Christian sect founded in the USA in 1848 by John Thomas, teaching a return to primitive Christianity and believing in the literal accuracy of the Bible. [from Greek *Christos*, Christ + *adelphos*, brother]

christen /'krɪsən/ *verb* (**christened, christening**) **1** to give (a person, especially a baby) a name, as part of the religious ceremony of receiving him or her into the Christian Church. **2** to give a name or nickname to. **3** *humorous* to use for the first time: *shall we christen the new wine glasses?* [from Anglo-Saxon *cristnian*, from *cristen*, Christian]

.....

◩ **1** baptize, name, call. **2** name, call, dub, title, style, term, designate. **3** inaugurate, use.

.....

Christendom /'krɪsndəm/ *noun* **1** all Christians. **2** the parts of the world in which Christianity is the recognized religion. [from Anglo-Saxon, from *cristen*, Christian + DOM]

christening *noun* the ceremony of baptism.

Christian /'krɪstʃən/ — *noun* **1** a person who believes in, and follows the teachings and example of, Jesus Christ. **2** *colloq.* a person of Christian qualities. — *adj.* **1** relating to Jesus Christ, the Christian religion, or Christians. **2** *colloq.* showing virtues associated with Christians, such as kindness, patience, tolerance, and generosity. [from Latin *Christianus*]

Christian era the period of time from the birth of Jesus Christ to the present.

Christianity /krɪstɪ'anɪtɪ/ *noun* **1** the religious faith based on the teachings of Jesus Christ. **2** the spirit, beliefs, principles, and practices of this faith. **3** Christendom.

christian name **1** the personal name given to a Christian at baptism. **2** anyone's first or given name; a forename.

Christian Scientist a follower of Christian Science.

Christmas /'krɪsməs/ *noun* **1** the annual Christian festival commemorating the birth of Christ, held on 25 December. **2** the period of celebration surrounding this date. [from Anglo-Saxon *Cristesmæsse*, Christ's Mass]

. . . .
⊟ Xmas, Noel, Yule, Yuletide.
. . . .

Christmas box a small gift of money given at Christmas to a postman or tradesman providing regular services.

Christmas cactus a hybrid cactus (Schlumbergera x buckleyi) that has spineless arching green stems consisting of flattened jointed segments, and magenta flowers, so called because it flowers in winter.

Christmas cake a large rich iced fruitcake, eaten at Christmas.

Christmas Day 25 December.

Christmas Eve 24 December, or the evening of this day.

Christmas pudding a rich steamed pudding containing dried fruit, spices, etc, eaten especially at Christmas.

Christmas rose an evergreen plant (Helleborus niger), native to S Europe and W Asia, having cup-shaped white or pink flowers, and so called because it blooms in winter or early spring.

Christmas stocking a long sock, traditionally hung up by children on Christmas Eve to be filled with presents.

Christmassy adj. of or suitable for Christmas.

Christmas tree a small fir tree, sometimes artificial, on which decorations, lights, and presents are hung at Christmas.

Christology /krɪˈstɒlədʒɪ/ noun Christianity the branch of theology which is concerned with the nature and person of Jesus Christ.

chromakey /ˈkrəʊməkiː/ noun Television a special effect in which an area of strong colour (usually a blue background) can be removed from an image and replaced by a picture or background from another source.

chromatic /krəʊˈmatɪk/ adj. 1 relating to colours; coloured. 2 Mus. relating to, or using notes from, the 12-note form of scale (chromatic scale) that includes semitones. See also DIATONIC. [from Greek chromatikos, from chroma, colour]

chromatically adv. in a chromatic way.

chromaticism /krəʊˈmatɪsɪzm/ noun an attribute in music which uses notes, intervals, and chords foreign to the prevailing mode or key. [from Greek chrōmatikos, coloured, embellished]

chromatid /ˈkrəʊmətɪd/ noun Genetics one of the two thread-like structures formed by the longitudinal division of a chromosome.

chromatin /ˈkrəʊmətɪn/ noun Biol. in a cell nucleus, the material that appears as a loose network of threads until the time of cell division, when it becomes organized into visible chromosomes. It consists of DNA and histone protein, and can be easily stained to allow study of cell division under the microscope. [from Greek chroma, colour]

chromato- see CHROMO-.

chromatography /krəʊməˈtɒgrəfɪ/ noun a technique for separating the components of a mixture of liquids or gases. It is widely used in biochemical and pharmaceutical research to detect minute quantities of a substance (eg a drug in blood), to separate and measure the quantities of several substances in a mixture, and to remove impurities. [from Greek chroma, colour + -GRAPHY]

chromatophore /krəʊˈmatəfɔː(r)/ noun Zool. a pigment-bearing cell or structure within a cell. In many animals, chromatophores are cells containing granules of pigment, and by dispersing or contracting the granules, the animal is able to change colour. [from Greek chroma, colour + -phore]

chrome /krəʊm/ — noun chromium or one of its compounds, especially when present in a dye or pigment, or used as a plating for other metals. — adj. denoting an object plated with chromium. — verb to plate (an object) with chromium, or to treat (it) with a chromium compound, especially in the form of a dye or pigment. [from Greek chroma, colour]

chrome yellow a yellow pigment consisting mainly of lead chromate.

chrominance /ˈkrəʊmɪnəns/ noun 1 Optics the difference between any given colour and a specified reference colour of equal brightness. 2 Electron. in colour television, the component controlling the colour of the picture as opposed to its brightness or luminance. [from CHROMO- + luminance]

chromite /ˈkrəʊmaɪt/ noun Geol. a mineral composed of chromium and iron oxides, that occurs as compact masses of black crystals with a metallic lustre. It is the main source of chromium.

chromium /ˈkrəʊmɪəm/ noun Chem. (SYMBOL Cr, ATOMIC NUMBER 24) a hard silvery metal that is resistant to corrosion, and is used in alloys with iron and nickel to make stainless steel. It is also used as an electroplated coating on other metals, especially steel, to give a shiny decorative finish and prevent rust. Several of its compounds are used in dyes and pigments. [a Latinized form of CHROME]

chromo- or **chromato-** combining form colour. [from Greek chroma, colour]

chromophore /ˈkrəʊməfɔː(r)/ noun Chem. that part of a molecule of a chemical compound that gives rise to the colour of the compound. Most chromophores in dyestuffs involve double bonds, which lower the energy of radiation absorbed by the molecule, so that visible light as well as ultraviolet radiation is absorbed by the compound.

chromosomal /krəʊməˈsəʊməl/ adj. relating to chromosomes.

chromosome /ˈkrəʊməsəʊm/ noun in the nucleus of a cell, any of a number of microscopic threadlike structures that become visible as small deeply staining rod-shaped bodies at the time of cell division, and which contain in the form of DNA all the genetic information that is needed for the development of the cell and the whole organism. [from Greek chroma, colour + soma, body]

chromosome map Genetics a diagram showing the positions (loci) of genes along an individual chromosome.

chromosphere or **chromatosphere** /ˈkrəʊməʊsfɪə(r)/ noun Astron. a layer of gas (mainly hydrogen) about 10,000km deep that lies above the Sun's visible surface (the photosphere). It can be seen as a thin crescent of pinkish-red light during a total eclipse of the Sun, when light from the photosphere is blocked by the Moon. [from Greek chroma, colour + SPHERE]

Chron. abbrev. Biblical Chronicles.

chron- or **chrono-** combining form time. [from Greek chronos, time]

chronic /ˈkrɒnɪk/ adj. 1 said of a disease or symptom of long duration, usually of gradual onset and often difficult to treat, eg chronic pain. It may or may not be severe. See also ACUTE. 2 Brit. colloq. very bad; severe; grave. 3 habitual. [from Greek chronikos, relating to time]

. . . .
⊟ 1 incurable, persistent, long-standing, long-term. 2 awful, severe, grave, terrible, dreadful, appalling, atrocious. 3 habitual, inveterate, confirmed, persistent, incessant, ingrained, deep-rooted, recurring.
⊟ 1 temporary.
. . . .

chronically adv. 1 in a chronic way. 2 Brit. colloq. badly; extremely.

chronic fatigue syndrome (ABBREV. CFS) same as MYALGIC ENCEPHALOMYELITIS.

chronicity /krɒˈnɪsɪtɪ/ noun a chronic condition or quality of a disease.

chronicle /ˈkrɒnɪkəl/ — noun (often chronicles) a record of historical events year by year in the order in which they occurred. — verb to record (an event) in a chronicle. [diminutive of Old French chronique, from Greek chronika, annals]

chronicle play a play based on recorded history, rather than myth or legend.

chronicler noun a person who compiles a chronicle.

chrono- see CHRON-.

chronogram /'krɒnəgram/ *noun* a date made up of the letters of Roman numerals (C, D, I, L, M, V, and X) hidden within the letters of a phrase or sentence, used eg in inscriptions on tombstones and foundation stones. [from Greek *chronos*, time + *gramma*, letter]

chronological /krɒnə'lɒɪkəl/ *adj.* **1** according to order of occurrence: *in chronological order.* **2** relating to chronology.

🞐 HISTORICAL. **1** consecutive, sequential, progressive, ordered.

chronologically *adv.* in a chronological way or order.

chronologist /krə'nɒləɪst/ *noun* a person who studies chronology.

chronology /krə'nɒlɒɪ/ *noun* (PL. **chronologies**) **1** the study or science of determining the correct order of historical events. **2** the arrangement of events in order of occurrence. **3** a table or list showing events in order of occurrence.

chronometer /krə'nɒmɪtə(r)/ *noun* an instrument that measures time extremely precisely, and is designed to remain accurate under all conditions of temperature and pressure, used especially for navigation at sea.

chrysalis /'krɪsəlɪs/ *noun* **1** the pupa of insects that undergo metamorphosis (transformation of a larva into a mature adult), eg butterflies, moths. **2** the protective case that surrounds the pupa. [from Greek *chrysallis*, from *chrysos*, gold]

chrysanthemum /krɪ'sanθəməm/ *noun* any of about 200 species of cultivated plants of the genus Chrysanthemum of the daisy family, having large yellow, deep gold, white, pink, or purple single or double flower-heads, and usually blooming in the autumn. [from Greek *chrysos*, gold + *anthemon*, flower]

chrysoberyl /'krɪsəbərɪl/ *noun Geol.* a green, yellow, or brown mineral, some varieties of which are used as gemstones. [from Greek *chrysos*, gold + *beryllos*, beryl]

chrysolite /'krɪsəlaɪt/ *noun Geol.* a light yellowish-green gemstone that is a variety of the mineral olivine. [from Greek *chrysos*, gold + *lithos*, stone]

chrysoprase /'krɪsoʊpreɪz/ *noun Geol.* a translucent bright green gemstone that is a variety of chalcedony. [from Greek *chrysos*, gold + *prason*, leek]

chub *noun* (PL. **chub**, **chubs**) **1** a freshwater fish of the carp family, native to Europe, having a cylindrical body up to 60cm in length, a greenish-grey back, silvery sides, and a white belly. **2** any of various N American fishes, eg certain minnows. [of uncertain origin]

chubbiness *noun* a chubby form or appearance.

chubby *adj.* (**chubbier**, **chubbiest**) plump, especially in a childishly attractive way. [perhaps from CHUB]

🞐 plump, podgy, tubby, fleshy, flabby, stout, portly, rotund, round, paunchy.
🞐 slim, skinny.

chuck[1] — *verb* **1** *colloq.* to throw or fling. **2** to give (a child, etc) an affectionate tap under the chin. **3** *slang* (**chuck something up**) to abandon or reject it. — *noun* **1** *colloq.* a toss, fling, or throw. **2** (**the chuck**) *slang* dismissal; rejection: *gave her boyfriend the chuck.* **3** an affectionate tap under the chin. — **chuck something out** *colloq.* to get rid of it; to reject it. **chuck someone out** *colloq.* to order them to leave.

chuck[2] or **chuck steak** *noun* beef cut from the area between the neck and shoulder. [variant of CHOCK]

chuck[3] *noun* a device for holding a piece of work in a lathe, or for holding the blade or bit in a drill. [a variant of CHOCK]

chuckle — *verb* **1** *intrans.* to laugh quietly, especially in a half-suppressed private way. **2** *trans.* to utter with a little laugh. — *noun* an amused little laugh. [from an old word *chuck*, to cluck like a hen]

🞐 *verb* LAUGH, GIGGLE, TITTER, SNIGGER, CHORTLE, SNORT.

chuff *verb intrans.*, *said of a steam train* to progress with regular puffing noises. [imitative]

chuffed *adj. Brit. colloq.* very pleased. [from dialect *chuff*, plump, swollen with pride]

chug — *verb intrans.* (**chugged**, **chugging**) *said of a motor boat, motor car, etc* to progress while making the typical quiet thudding noise of an unsophisticated engine. — *noun* this noise. [imitative]

chukka boot a leather ankle boot.

chukker or **chukka** *noun* one of the six seven-and-a-half-minute periods of play in the game of polo. [from Hindi *cakkar*, round]

chum — *noun colloq.* a close friend. — *verb* (**chummed**, **chumming**) (**chum up with someone**) to make friends with them. [perhaps from *chamber fellow*, a fellow student, etc sharing one's room]

chummy *adj.* (**chummier**, **chummiest**) *colloq.* friendly.

chump *noun* **1** *colloq.* an idiot; a fool. **2** the thick end of a loin cut of lamb or mutton: *a chump chop.* **3** a short thick heavy block of wood. — **off one's chump** *Brit. colloq.* crazy; extremely foolish. [perhaps a combination of CHUNK and LUMP]

chunder *Austral. slang* — *verb intrans.* to vomit; to be sick. — *noun* vomit. [origin unknown]

chunk *noun* **1** a thick, especially irregularly shaped, piece. **2** *colloq.* a large or considerable amount. [variant of CHUCK[3]]

🞐 **1** lump, hunk, *colloq.* wodge, wedge, block, slab, piece, portion. **2** hunk, *colloq.* wodge, mass.

chunky *adj.* (**chunkier**, **chunkiest**) **1** thick-set; stockily or strongly built. **2** *said of clothes, fabrics, etc* thick; bulky. **3** solid and strong. **4** containing chunks: *chunky marmalade.*

church *noun* **1** a building for public Christian worship. **2** the religious services held in a church: *go to church.* **3** (**Church**) the profession of a clergyman: *enter the Church.* **4** (**Church**) the clergy considered as an especially political group: *quarrels between Church and State.* **5** (**Church**) any of many branches of Christians with their own doctrines, style of worship, etc: *the Methodist Church.* **6** the whole Christian establishment: *studying church history.* [from Anglo-Saxon *cirice*, from Greek *kyriakon* (*doma*), the house of the Lord, from *kyrios*, lord]

🞐 **1** chapel, house of God, cathedral, minster, abbey, temple. **5** denomination, tradition.

churchgoer *noun* a person who attends church services, especially regularly.

churchman or **churchwoman** *noun* a member of the clergy or of a church.

Church of England the official state Church of England, a national Church that has both Protestant and Catholic features, is based on episcopal authority, and has the sovereign as its head.

church officer in some churches, a person acting as church caretaker, with certain other duties.

churchwarden *noun* **1** in the Church of England, one of two lay members of a congregation elected to look after the church's property, money, etc. **2** an old-fashioned long clay pipe.

churchyard *noun* the burial ground round a church.

churlish *adj.* bad-tempered; rude; ill-mannered. [from *churl*, surly person, peasant]

churlishly *adv.* with a churlish manner.

churlishness *noun* being churlish.

churn — *noun* **1** an apparatus used for making butter, in which cream or whole milk is repeatedly stirred and turned until the fat is separated from the liquid. **2** a large metal container for holding milk. **3** the rate at which television viewers change channels, satellite or cable television providers, etc. — *verb* **1** to stir and turn (cream or whole milk) in order to separate out the fat and produce butter. **2** (**churn something up**) to shake or agitate it violently. **3** *of brokers, financial advisers, etc* to encourage clients excessively to buy and sell (investments etc) and so generate commissions. — **churn something out** to keep producing things of tedious similarity in large quantities. [from Anglo-Saxon *cirin* or *cyrn*]

chute[1] /ʃuːt/ *noun* **1** a sloping channel down which to send water, rubbish, etc. **2** a slide in a children's playground or swimming-pool. [from French *chute*, fall]

chute[2] *noun colloq.* a parachute.

chutney *noun* an Indian type of pickle made with fruit, vinegar, spices, sugar, etc. [from Hindi *catni*]

chutzpah /'xʊtspə/ *noun chiefly North Amer. colloq.* self-assurance bordering on impudence; audacity; effrontery; nerve. [from Yiddish *chutzpah*]

chyle /kaɪl/ *noun Physiol.* a milky fluid, consisting of lymph containing fats that have been absorbed from the small intestine during digestion. [from Greek *chylos*, juice]

chyme /kaɪm/ *noun Physiol.* the partially digested food that passes into the duodenum and small intestine from the stomach. [from Greek *chymos*, juice]

CI *abbrev.* **1** Channel Islands. **2** *as an international vehicle mark* Côte d'Ivoire (French), Ivory Coast.

Ci *symbol* curie.

CIA *abbrev.* Central Intelligence Agency (USA).

ciabatta /tʃə'bɑːtə/ *noun* Italian bread with a sponge-like texture, made with olive oil. [Italian, = slipper]

CIB *abbrev.* Chartered Institute of Bankers.

cicada /sɪ'kɑːdə, sɪ'keɪdə/ *noun* a large hemipteran insect of mainly tropical regions that spends most of its life in trees, sucking sap from beneath the bark, against which it is well camouflaged. The males attract females with a high-pitched warbling whistle produced by vibrating tambourine-like membranes on either side of the body. [from Latin *cicada*]

cicatrix /'sɪkətrɪks, sɪ'keɪtrɪks/ or **cicatrice** *noun* (PL. **cicatrices**) **1** *Medicine* the scar tissue that lies over a healed wound. **2** *Bot.* a scar on a plant, especially one marking the former point of attachment of a leaf, branch, etc. [from Latin *cicatrix*]

CICB *abbrev. Brit.* Criminal Injuries Compensation Board.

cicely /'sɪsəlɪ/ *noun* any of various umbelliferous plants related to chervil, especially *sweet cicely*. [from Greek *seselis*, with spelling influenced by the name Cicely]

CID *abbrev.* Criminal Investigation Department, the detective branch of the British police force.

-cide *combining form* forming nouns denoting: **1** the act of killing; murder: *homicide*. **2** a person, substance, or thing that kills. [from Latin *cida*, killer, and *cidium*, killing]

cider *noun* an alcoholic drink made from apples. [from French *cidre*]

cigar *noun* a long slender roll of tobacco leaves for smoking. [from Spanish *cigarro*]

cigarette *noun* a tube of finely cut tobacco rolled in thin paper, for smoking. [from French *cigarette*, diminutive of *cigare*, cigar]

cigarette end or **cigarette butt** the unsmoked stub of a cigarette.

cigarette-holder *noun* a long slim mouthpiece into which a cigarette can be fitted for smoking.

cigarette-lighter *noun* a petrol- or gas-fuelled device with a flint, for lighting cigarettes.

cigar-shaped *adj.* having an elongated oval shape with pointed ends.

CII *abbrev.* Chartered Insurance Institute.

cilantro /sɪ'lɑːntroʊ/ *noun* coriander. [Spanish]

ciliary *adj. Anat.* denoting a muscle that controls the curvature of the lens of the eye, by contracting to make it thin (for viewing distant objects), or relaxing to make it thicker (for viewing nearby objects). [from Latin *cilium*, eyelash]

ciliate *noun Zool.* a microscopic single-celled organism that typically possesses short hair-like appendages, known as *cilia*, on its surface, which are used to aid locomotion. [from Latin *cilium*, eyelash]

cilium *noun* (PL. **cilia**) *Biol.* any of the short hair-like appendages that project from the surface of certain cells, and move rhythmically, usually to aid locomotion, or to cause movement of the water surrounding some single-celled aquatic organisms. [from Latin *cilium*, eyelash]

cimbalom /'tsɪmbələm/ *noun* a form of dulcimer used in Hungary and other E European countries. It consists of a wooden box with a series of metal strings strung on pegs, and is played by striking the strings with sticks. [Hungarian, from Italian *cembala*, cymbal]

C-in-C *abbrev.* Commander-in-Chief.

cinch *noun colloq.* **1** an easily accomplished task. **2** a certainty. [from Spanish *cincha*, saddle girth]

cinchona /sɪŋ'koʊnə/ *noun* **1** any tree of the Cinchona genus, yielding bark from which quinine and related by-products are obtained. **2** the dried bark of these trees.

cincture *noun literary* a belt or girdle. [from Latin *cinctura*]

cinder *noun* **1** a piece of burnt coal or wood. **2** (**cinders**) ashes. [from Anglo-Saxon *sinder*, slag]

Cinderella /sɪndə'relə/ *noun* someone or something whose charms or merits go unnoticed; a neglected member of a set or group. [from the fairy-tale character Cinderella]

cindery *adj.* of the nature of or composed of cinders.

cine /sɪnɪ/ *adj., combining form* relating to moving pictures: *a cinecamera / a cine projector*. [shortened from CINEMA]

cinema /'sɪnəmɑː/ *noun* **1** a theatre in which motion pictures are shown. **2** cinemas in general: *we don't go to the cinema much.* **3** (*usually* **the cinema**) motion pictures or films generally. **4** the art or business of making films. [from CINEMATOGRAPH]

. . . .

◫ **1** picture-house, picture-palace, *colloq.* fleapit. **2** *colloq.* pictures, *colloq.* movies, *colloq.* flicks. **3** films, pictures, *colloq.* movies, *colloq.* flicks, the screen, silver screen. **4** film, *colloq.* Hollywood.

. . . .

cinematic /sɪnɪ'matɪk/ *adj.* relating to or characteristic of the cinema.

cinematograph /sɪnə'matəgrɑːf/ *noun* an apparatus for taking and projecting moving pictures, ie a series of still photographs each representing an instant of time, in rapid succession.

cinematographer /sɪnəmə'tɒgrəfə(r)/ *noun* a person skilled in cinematography.

cinematographic /sɪnəmətə'graːfɪk/ *adj.* relating to or characteristic of cinematography.

cinematography /sɪnəmə'tɒgrəfɪ/ *noun* the art of making motion pictures. [from Greek *kinema*, motion + GRAPHY]

cinema vérité *Cinema* a style of film production characterized by documentary treatment, giving the appearance of real life even for fictional drama. [French, = cinema truth]

Cinerama /sɪnə'rɑːmə/ *trademark* one of the first systems of wide-screen cinema presentation (1952), using three synchronized projectors to cover a large curved screen in three blended panels. [from CINEMA + PANORAMA]

cineraria /sɪnə'reərɪə/ *noun* a dwarf shrub of the genus Senecio, native to Africa and Madagascar, having rounded lobed leaves, the undersurfaces of which are densely covered with white hairs, and numerous red, deep blue, violet, or variegated daisy-like flower-heads. [from Latin *cinerarius*, relating to ashes]

cinerary /ˈsɪnərərɪ/ adj. relating to ashes; for holding ashes: a cinerary urn. [from Latin cinerarius, relating to ashes]

cinnabar /ˈsɪnəbɑː(r)/ noun 1 Geol. a bright red transparent to translucent mineral form of mercury sulphide, that is the principal source of mercury, and is also used to make the orange-red pigment vermilion. 2 vermilion, an orange-red colour. 3 a moth with red and black wings. [from Greek kinnabari, from Persian]

cinnamon /ˈsɪnəmən/ noun 1 any of various small evergreen trees of the genus Cinnamomum, native to SE Asia, having ovoid to oblong leaves, greenish flowers, and black berries. 2 a spice obtained from the cured dried bark of this tree, used as a flavouring in bakery products and confectionery. 3 a brownish-orange colour. [from Greek kinnamon]

cinquecento /ˌtʃɪŋkweˈtʃentoʊ/ noun Italian art and literature of the 16c Renaissance. [from Italian, = 500, referring to the century 1500–99]

cinquefoil /ˈsɪŋkfɔɪl/ noun 1 any of various plants belonging to the genus Potentilla, native to north temperate regions, and typically having yellow, white, or purple flowers with five petals. 2 Heraldry a five-petalled flower. 3 Archit. a design composed of five petal-like arcs, found at the top of an arch, in a circular window, etc. [from Old French cincfoille, from Latin quinquefolium, five-leaved plant]

CIOB abbrev. Chartered Institute of Building.

CIPA abbrev. Chartered Institute of Patent Agents.

CIPFA abbrev. Chartered Institute of Public Finance and Accountancy.

cipher /ˈsaɪfə(r)/ — noun 1 a secret code. 2 something written in code. 3 the key to a code. 4 an interlaced set of initials; a monogram. 5 Maths. old use the symbol 0, used to fill blanks in writing numbers, but of no value itself. 6 a person or thing of little importance. 7 any Arabic numeral. — verb (ciphered, ciphering) to write (a message, etc) in code. [from Latin ciphra, from Arabic sifr, empty, zero]

circa prep., used especially with dates about; approximately: circa 1250. [from Latin circa]

circadian /sɜːˈkeɪdɪən/ adj. Biol. denoting a biological rhythm that is more or less synchronized to a 24-hour cycle, eg the pattern of sleeping and waking in adult humans. [from CIRCA + Latin dies, day]

circle — noun 1 a perfectly round plane (two-dimensional) figure that is bordered by a line, known as the circumference, which consists of all points that are an equal distance (the radius) from a fixed point within the figure (the centre). 2 anything in the form of a circle. 3 a circular route, eg the orbit of a planet, etc. 4 a curved upper floor of seats in a theatre, etc. 5 a series of events, steps, or developments, ending at the point where it began. See also VICIOUS CIRCLE. 6 a group of people associated in some way: his circle of acquaintances. — verb 1 trans., intrans. to move in a circle; to move in a circle round. 2 to draw a circle round. — come full circle 1 to complete a full cycle. 2 to reach or arrive back at the starting-point. go round in circles to be trapped in an endless and frustrating cycle of repetitive discussion or activity. run round in circles to rush around frantically, making little progress. [from Anglo-Saxon circul, from Latin circulust]

⊞ noun 1, 2 ring, hoop, loop, round, disc, sphere, globe, orb. 3 orbit, circuit, revolution, turn, cycle, circumference, perimeter, coil, spiral. 4 balcony. 5 circuit, ring, round, loop. 6 group, band, company, crowd, set, clique, coterie, club, society, fellowship, fraternity. verb 1 ring, loop, encircle, gird, surround, encompass, circumscribe, circumnavigate. 2 ring, encircle.

circlet noun 1 a simple band or hoop of gold, silver, etc worn on the head. 2 a small circle. [from Old French cerclet, diminutive of cercle, circle]

circotherm oven an oven with a fan to circulate internal hot air. It is designed to achieve uniformity of heating and to economize in heating and cooking time. Also popularly known as a fan oven.

circuit /ˈsɜːkɪt/ noun 1 a complete course, journey, or route round something. 2 a race track, running-track, etc. 3 (in full electric circuit) a path consisting of various electrical devices joined together by wires so that an electric current can flow continuously through it. 4 the places or venues visited in turn and regularly by entertainers, etc. 5 a round of places made by a travelling judge. 6 a group of cinemas, theatres, etc under common control, with shows moving on from one to the next. [from French circuit, from Latin circuitus, round trip, revolution]

⊞ 1 lap, orbit, revolution, tour, journey, course, route, track, round, beat, circumference, boundary, bounds, limit, range, compass, ambit. 2 track, course, route. 4 tour. 5 tour, district, area, region.

circuit-breaker noun in an electric circuit, a switch or other device that will automatically interrupt the circuit if the current exceeds a certain value, eg as a result of a short circuit caused by an insulation failure. It thus serves the same function as a fuse, but unlike a fuse it cannot be reset.

circuitous /səˈkjuːɪtəs/ adj. taking a long complicated route; indirect; roundabout.

⊞ roundabout, indirect, tortuous, winding, meandering, rambling, labyrinthine, periphrastic, oblique, devious. ⊞ direct, straight.

circuitously adv. in a circuitous or roundabout way.

circuitry /ˈsɜːkɪtrɪ/ noun (PL. circuitries) Electr. 1 a plan or system of circuits used in a particular electronic or electrical device. 2 the equipment or components making up such a system.

circuit training athletic training in the form of a repeated series of exercises.

circular /ˈsɜːkjʊlə(r)/ — adj. 1 having the form of a circle. 2 moving or going round in a circle, leading back to the starting-point. 3 said of reasoning, etc containing a fallacy, the truth of the conclusion depending on a point that depends on the conclusion being true. 4 said of a letter, etc addressed and copied to a number of people. — noun a circular letter or notice. [from Latin circularis]

⊞ adj. 1 round, annular, ring-shaped, hoop-shaped, disc-shaped. noun leaflet, pamphlet, notice, letter, handbill, announcement, advertisement.

circularity /ˌsɜːkjʊˈlarɪtɪ/ noun (PL. circularities) a circular form, position, or quality.

circularize or **circularise** verb to send circulars to.

circularly adv. in a circular way.

circular saw a power-driven saw with a rotating disc-shaped toothed blade.

circulate /ˈsɜːkjʊleɪt/ verb 1 trans., intrans. to move or cause to move round freely, especially in a fixed route: traffic circulating through the town centre. 2 trans., intrans. to spread; to pass round: circulate the report. 3 intrans. to move around talking to different people, eg at a party. [from Latin circulare, to encircle]

⊞ 1 move round, go round, flow, run. 2 spread, pass round, distribute, propagate, broadcast, publicize, publish, issue, diffuse. 3 mingle, socialize.

circulation /ˌsɜːkjʊˈleɪʃən/ noun 1 the act or process of circulating. 2 Anat. in all except very simple animals, the system of vessels that transports blood and other tissue fluids, eg lymph, to and from all the parts of the body via a regular circuitous course. 3 the distribution of a newspaper or magazine, or the number of copies of it that are sold. — **in** or **out of circulation 1** *said of money* being, or not being, used by the public. **2** taking part, or not taking part, in one's usual social activities.

....

🔲 **1** flow, motion, circling, spread, transmission, dissemination, distribution, publication. **2** blood-flow, bloodstream.

....

circulatory /ˈsɜːkjʊˈleɪtərɪ, ˈsɜːkjʊleɪtərɪ/ *adj.* relating to circulation, especially of the blood.

circum- *combining form* round about. [from Latin *circum*, about]

circumcise *verb* **1** to remove all or part of the foreskin of the penis of (a male). **2** to remove the clitoris, and sometimes the labia, of (a female). See also CIRCUMCISION. [from Latin *circum*, around + *caedere*, to cut round]

Circumcision /ˈsɜːkəmˈsɪʒən/ *noun Christianity* a festival (1 Jan) in honour of the circumcision of Christ, eight days after his birth.

circumcision *noun* **1** in males, the surgical removal of all or part of the foreskin of the penis, usually performed during early childhood for religious or ethnic reasons, or on medical grounds. **2** in females, the surgical removal of the clitoris (and sometimes the labia).

circumference /səˈkʌmfərəns/ *noun* **1** *Geom.* the length of the boundary of a circle or other closed curve, eg an ellipse, or the length of a path around a sphere at its widest point. **2** the boundary of an area of any shape. **3** the distance represented by any of these. [from Latin *circum*, around + *ferre*, to carry]

. . . .

🔲 **2** boundary, perimeter, rim, edge, outline, border, bounds, limits, extremity, margin, verge, fringe, periphery, circuit.

. . . .

circumferential /səkʌmfəˈrenʃəl/ *adj.* relating to or of the nature of a circumference.

circumflex *noun* a mark placed over a vowel (eg *ô, û*) in some languages as an indication of pronunciation, length, or the omission of a letter. [from Latin *circumflexus*, arch]

circumlocution /ˈsɜːkəmləˈkjuːʃən/ *noun* an unnecessarily long or indirect way of saying something. [from Latin *circum*, around + *loqui*, to speak]

circumlocutory /ˈsɜːkəmləˈkjuːtərɪ/ *adj.* given to or marked by circumlocution.

circumnavigate *verb* to sail or fly round (the world). [from Latin *circum*, around + *navigare*, to sail]

circumnavigation *noun* the process of circumnavigating the world.

circumnavigator *noun* a person who circumnavigates.

circumscribe *verb* **1** to put a boundary round or to draw a line round. **2** to limit or restrict. **3** *Geom.* to draw one geometrical figure round (another geometrical figure) so that they touch one another but do not intersect. See also INSCRIBE. [from Latin *circum*, around + *scribere*, to write]

circumscription /ˈsɜːkəmˈskrɪpʃən/ *noun* the act of circumscribing.

circumspect *adj.* cautious; prudent; wary. [from Latin *circum*, around + *specere*, to look]

circumspection /ˈsɜːkəmˈspekʃən/ *noun* caution; vigilance.

circumspectly *adv.* in a circumspect way.

circumstance *noun* **1** (*often* **circumstances**) a fact, occurrence, or condition, especially when relating to an act or event: *died in mysterious circumstances*. **2** (**circumstances**) one's financial situation. **3** events that one cannot control; fate: *a victim of circumstance*. **4** ceremony: *pomp and circumstance*. — **in** or **under no circumstances** never, not for any reason at all. **in** or **under the circumstances** the situation being what it is or was. **reduced circumstances** poverty. [from Latin *circum*, around + *stare*, to stand]

. . . .

🔲 **1** facts, factors, conditions, situation, position, state, state of

affairs. **2** means, resources, status, lifestyle. **3** fate, fortune, providence, chance, destiny.

....

circumstantial /ˈsɜːkəmˈstanʃəl/ *adj.* **1** *said of an account of an event* full of detailed description, etc. **2** *Legal, said of evidence* including details or facts that give a statement, etc the appearance of truth, but do not prove it.

circumstantially *adv.* in a circumstantial way.

circumvent *verb* **1** to find a way of getting round or evading (a rule, law, etc). **2** to outwit or frustrate (someone). [from Latin *circum*, around + *venire*, to come]

circumvention *noun* the act of circumventing; avoidance.

circus *noun* **1** a travelling company of performers including acrobats, clowns, and often trained animals, etc; a performance by such a company, traditionally in a circular tent. **2** *colloq.* a scene of noisy confusion. **3** a travelling group of professional sportspeople, etc who put on displays. **4** *often in place names* an open space, especially one roughly circular, at the junction of a number of streets; a circular terrace of houses. **5** in ancient Rome, an oval or circular open-air stadium for chariot-racing and other competitive sports. [from Latin *circus*, circle, ring, stadium]

cirque /sɜːk/ *noun Geog.* a deep semicircular hollow resembling an amphitheatre, with steep side and back walls, located high on a mountain slope and often containing a small lake. Cirques are formed as a result of the erosion of bedrock by a small glacier. Also called CORRIE, CWM. [from French *cirque*, circus]

cirrhosis /səˈroʊsɪs, sɪˈroʊsɪs/ *noun Medicine* a chronic disease of the liver, characterized by injury and death of some of its cells, followed by the abnormal growth of many strands of fibrous tissue between clusters of regenerating cells. It is usually caused by excessive alcohol consumption, but can also be a symptom of other disorders such as viral hepatitis. [from Greek *kirrhos*, tawny, from the colour of the diseased liver + -OSIS]

cirriped /ˈsɪrɪped/ *noun Zool.* any invertebrate animal belonging to the Cirripedia, a subclass of marine crustaceans which includes the barnacles. [from Latin *cirrus*, curl + *pes*, foot]

cirrocumulus /sɪroʊˈkjuːmjʊləs/ *noun* (PL. **cirrocumuli**) *Meteorol.* a type of high cloud, often referred to as a 'mackerel sky' because it consists of small masses of white clouds that form a rippled pattern. It is associated with warm fronts. [from CIRRUS + CUMULUS]

cirrostratus /sɪroʊˈstraːtəs/ *noun* (PL. **cirrostrati**) *Meteorol.* a type of high cloud that forms a thin whitish layer with a fibrous appearance, and which may cover most or all of the sky. It is associated with the approach of a depression. [from CIRRUS + STRATUS]

cirrus *noun* (PL. **cirri**) *Meteorol.* a common type of high cloud with a wispy fibrous or feathery appearance. It is composed of ice crystals, and is associated with fair weather. [from Latin *cirrus*, curl]

CIS *abbrev.* **1** Chartered Institute of Secretaries. **2** Commonwealth of Independent States.

cissy see SISSY.

cist *noun Archaeol.* a grave lined and covered with slabs of stone. [from Welsh *cist*, chest, from Latin *cista*]

Cistercian — *noun* a member of a religious order formed in 1098 in Cîteaux in France by Benedictine monks, following a strict rule. — *adj.* relating to the Cistercians. [from Latin *Cistercium*, Cîteaux]

cistern *noun* **1** a tank storing water, usually in the roof-space of a house, or serving a flushing toilet. **2** *Archaeol.* an underground reservoir. [from Latin *cisterna*, reservoir]

cistron *noun Genetics* that part of a chain of DNA that is functionally equivalent to a gene. [from *cis-trans test*, a test defining the unit of genetic function]

citadel /ˈsɪtədəl/ *noun* a stronghold or fortress close to, or dominating the centre of, a city, built for its protection and as a place of refuge. [from Italian *cittadella*, diminutive of *città*, city]

▤ stronghold, fortress, bastion, castle, keep, tower, fortification, acropolis.

citation /saɪˈteɪʃən/ *noun* **1** the quoting or citing of something as example or proof. **2** a passage quoted from a book, etc. **3** *Legal* an order to appear in court. **4** a special official commendation or award for merit, bravery, etc, or a list of the reasons for such an award.

cite *verb* **1** to quote (a book, its author, or a passage from it) as an example or proof. **2** to mention as an example or illustration. **3** *Legal* to summon (a person) to appear in court; to name (a person) as being involved in a case. **4** to mention (someone) in an official report by way of commendation: *cited for bravery*. [from Old French *citer*, to summon]

▤ **1** quote, mention, refer to. **2** quote, adduce, mention, enumerate, refer to, advance, bring up.

CITES *abbrev.* Convention on International Trade in Endangered Species (of Wild Fauna and Flora).

citizen /ˈsɪtɪzn/ *noun* **1** an inhabitant of a city or town. **2** a native of a country or state, or a naturalized member of it. [from Middle English *citesein*, from Old French *citeain*, from *cite*, city]

▤ **1** city-dweller, townsman, townswoman, inhabitant, denizen, resident, householder, taxpayer. **2** native, subject.

citizenry *noun* the citizens of a town, country, etc.

citizen's arrest an arrest, allowable in some countries, made by a member of the public.

Citizens' Band (ABBREV. **CB**) *in the USA and many European countries* a band of radio frequencies (around 27 MHz) that is used for personal or business communication over limited distances by members of the public, eg for motorists to send messages to each other.

citizens' charter an official document setting out the minimum acceptable standards of service in health care, education, etc, people's rights with regard to public bodies, compensation for unacceptably poor service, etc.

citizenship *noun* **1** the status or position of a citizen. **2** the rights and duties of a citizen.

citrate /ˈsɪtreɪt/ *noun Chem.* a salt or ester of citric acid.

citric *adj.* **1** derived from citric acid. **2** relating to or derived from citrus fruits. [see CITRUS]

citric acid *Chem.* (FORMULA $C_6H_8O_7$) an organic acid, present in the juice of citrus fruit, that plays an important role in the energy-generating biochemical reactions of the Krebs cycle in plant and animal cells. It is used as a food flavouring and antioxidant.

citrin *noun* vitamin P. [from CITRUS]

citron *noun* **1** a small thorny evergreen tree (Citrus medica), native to Asia, and cultivated in warm regions for its edible fruit. **2** the ovoid citrus fruit of this tree, which has a yellowish-orange rind and yellowish-green flesh. **3** the thick peel or rind of this fruit, candied and used for flavouring, cake decoration, etc. [from Italian *citrone*, from Latin *citrus*, the citron tree]

citrus *noun* (*also* **citrus fruit**) any of a group of edible fruits with a tough outer peel enclosing membranous segments filled with juicy flesh rich in vitamin C, citric acid, and water, obtained from trees or shrubs of the orange family (genus Citrus), eg orange, lemon, grapefruit, lime, tangerine, and kumquat. [from Latin *citrus*, the citron tree]

city *noun* (PL. **cities**) **1** any large town; in the UK, a town with a royal charter, and usually a cathedral. **2** the body of inhabitants of a city. **3** (**the City**) the business centre of a city, especially London. [from Old French *cite*, from Latin *civitas*, state]

▤ **1** town, municipality, conurbation, metropolis. **2** town, inhabitants, townsmen, townswomen, denizens, residents, householders.

city desk in a newspaper office, the department of the **city editor**, dealing with financial news.

city fathers the magistrates of a city, or members of its council.

city hall (*often* **City Hall**) the local government of a city, or the building in which it is housed.

city-state *noun Hist.* a city that possesses its own territory and forms an independent state.

civet *noun* **1** (*also* **civet cat**) a small carnivorous mammal related to the mongoose, native to forests of Africa and SE Asia, and having a long body and tail, a spotted and striped coat, a sharp muzzle, and special glands near the reproductive organs that secrete a strong-smelling substance known as *musk*, which is sometimes added to perfumes. **2** a yellowish-brown strong-smelling fatty substance secreted by glands near the reproductive organs of this animal, added to perfumes in order to prolong their scent. Also called MUSK. **3** the fur of this animal. [from French *civette*]

civic *adj.* relating to a city, citizen, or citizenship. [from Latin *civicus*, from *civis*, citizen]

▤ city, urban, municipal, borough, community, local, public, communal.

civically *adv.* in a civic way.

civic centre a place, sometimes a specially designed complex, where the administrative offices and chief public buildings of a city are grouped.

civics *sing. noun* the study of local government and of the rights and duties of citizenship.

civil *adj.* **1** relating to the community: *civil affairs*. **2** relating to or occurring between citizens: *civil disturbances*. **3** relating to ordinary citizens; not military, legal, or religious. **4** *Legal* relating to cases about individual rights, etc, not criminal cases. **5** polite; not discourteous. [from Latin *civilis*, relating to citizens, from *civis*, citizen]

▤ **1** domestic, home, national, internal, interior, municipal, civic. **2** domestic. **3** state, civilian, lay, secular. **5** polite, courteous, well-mannered, well-bred, polished, urbane, affable, civilized, courtly, refined.

▣ **1** international. **5** uncivil, discourteous, rude.

civil defence **1** the organization and training of ordinary citizens to assist the armed forces in wartime, especially during enemy attack. **2** the body of people involved in this.

civil disobedience the refusal to obey regulations, pay taxes, etc, as a form of non-violent protest.

civil engineer an engineer qualified to design and build roads, bridges, railways, canals, tunnels, docks, etc.

civil engineering the branch of engineering concerned with the design, construction, and maintenance of roads, bridges, railways, canals, tunnels, docks, and other large non-mechanical structures, as well as land drainage, water supply, and sewage treatment.

civilian /sɪˈvɪlɪən/ — *noun* anyone who is not a member of the armed forces or the police force. — *adj.* relating to civilians. [from Old French *civilien*, relating to civil law]

civility /sɪˈvɪlɪtɪ/ *noun* (PL. **civilities**) **1** politeness. **2** an act of politeness; a polite remark or gesture. [from Old French *civilite*]

▤ **1** politeness, courteousness, courtesy, graciousness, affability, urbanity, breeding, refinement, amenity. **2** courtesy, pleasantry.

▣ **1** discourtesy, rudeness.

civilization /sɪvɪlaɪˈzeɪʃən/ or **civilisation** *noun* **1** the state of being, or process of becoming, civilized; the act of civilizing. **2** a stage of development in human society that is socially, politically, culturally, and technologically advanced. **3** the parts of the world that have reached such a stage. **4** *usually Hist.* a people and their society and culture: *the Minoan civilization.* **5** built-up areas as opposed to wild, uncultivated, or sparsely populated parts. **6** intellectual or spiritual enlightenment, as opposed to brutishness or coarseness.

. . . .

⊟ **1, 2** progress, advancement, development, education, enlightenment. **4** age, era, culture. **6** enlightenment, culture, refinement, sophistication, urbanity.
⊟ **1, 2, 6** barbarity, primitiveness.

. . . .

civilize or **civilise** *verb* **1** to lead out of a state of barbarity to a more advanced stage of social development. **2** to educate and enlighten morally, intellectually, and spiritually. [from French *civiliser,* from Latin *civilis,* relating to political life]

. . . .

⊟ **1** tame, humanize, educate. **2** educate, enlighten, refine, polish, improve, cultivate.

. . . .

civilized or **civilised** *adj.* **1** socially, politically, and technologically advanced. **2** agreeably refined, sophisticated, or comfortable. **3** *facetious* trained to behave and speak politely.

. . . .

⊟ **1** advanced, developed, educated. **2** refined, sophisticated, enlightened, cultured, urbane, polite, sociable.
⊟ **1, 2** uncivilized, barbarous, primitive.

. . . .

civil law the part of a country's law that deals with its citizens' rights, etc, not with crimes.

civil liberty (*often in pl.*) personal freedom of thought, word, action, etc.

civil list in the UK, the annual Parliamentary allowance to the sovereign and the Royal family for household expenses.

civilly *adv.* with a civil manner.

civil rights the personal rights of any citizen of a country, especially to freedom and equality regardless of race, religion, sex, or sexuality.

civil servant a person employed in the civil service.

civil service the body of officials employed by a government to administer the affairs of a country.

civil war a war between citizens of the same state.

civvies *pl. noun colloq.* ordinary civilian clothes as opposed to a military uniform.

civvy street *colloq.* ordinary civilian life outside the armed forces.

CJD *abbrev.* Creutzfeldt-Jakob disease.

CL *abbrev.,* *as an international vehicle mark* Sri Lanka (formerly Ceylon).

Cl *symbol Chem.* chlorine.

clack — *noun* a sharp noise made by one hard object striking another. — *verb* **1** *trans., intrans.* to make or cause to make this kind of noise. **2** *intrans.* to talk noisily. [imitative]

clad — *adj. literary* **1** clothed: *clad in velvet.* **2** covered. — *verb* (**cladding**; PAST TENSE AND PAST PARTICIPLE **clad**) to cover (one material) with another, as protection, etc. [a past tense and past participle of CLOTHE]

cladding *noun Engineering* **1** a thin covering applied to the external surface of a building in order to improve its appearance or to increase its weather or fire resistance. **2** a thin layer of an expensive metal that is used to coat a cheaper metal. **3** in nuclear reactors, a thin layer of metal, eg zirconium or stainless steel, that covers the fuel elements and protects them from corrosion. It also prevents the release of fission products into the coolant. **4** the process whereby one material is covered with another, and the two are then bonded together under conditions of high temperature and pressure.

cladistics /kləˈdɪstɪks/ *sing. noun Biol.* a system of animal and plant classification in which organisms are grouped together on the basis of similarities due to recent origin from a common ancestor. [from Greek *klados,* branch]

claim — *verb* **1** to state (something) firmly, insisting on its truth. **2** to declare oneself (to be, to have done, etc). **3** to assert that one has. **4** *trans., intrans.* to demand or assert as a right. **5** to take, use up. **6** to need; to deserve; to have a right to. **7** to declare that one is the owner of. **8** to identify oneself as having (responsibility). — *noun* **1** a statement one insists on the truth of. **2** a demand, especially for something that one has, or believes one has, a right to: *lay claim to the throne / stake one's claim / make claims on someone's time.* **3** (**claim to**) a right to or reason for: *a claim to fame.* **4** something one has claimed, eg a piece of land or a sum of money. — **jump a claim** to claim land containing gold, oil, etc which already belongs to someone else. [from Latin *clamare,* to cry out]

. . . .

⊟ *verb* **1** allege, state, affirm, assert, maintain, contend, hold, insist. **2** pretend, profess. **4** demand, assert, require. **5** take, collect, exact, use (up). **6** require, need, deserve, have a right to, be entitled to. *noun* **1** allegation, pretension, affirmation, assertion, contention, insistence. **2** demand, call, application, petition, request, requirement. **3** right, privilege.

. . . .

claimant *noun* a person who makes a claim.

clairvoyance /kleəˈvɔɪəns/ *noun* the ability, claimed by some, to see into the future, or know things that cannot be discovered through the normal range of senses. [from French *clairvoyance,* from *clair,* clear + *voir,* to see]

clairvoyant /kleəˈvɔɪənt/ — *adj.* involving or claiming the power of clairvoyance. — *noun* a person who claims to have the power of clairvoyance.

. . . .

⊟ *adj.* psychic, prophetic, visionary, telepathic, extrasensory. *noun* psychic, telepathist, fortune-teller, visionary, prophet, prophetess, seer, soothsayer, augur, oracle, diviner.

. . . .

clam — *noun* **1** any of various edible bivalve molluscs. **2** *colloq.* an uncommunicative person. — *verb* (**clammed,** **clamming**) (**clam up**) *colloq.* to stop talking suddenly; to refuse to speak, answer questions, etc. [a shortening of *clamshell,* from *clam,* an old word related to CLAMP]

clamber — *verb intrans.* to climb, especially using hands as well as feet. — *noun* an act of clambering. [related to CLIMB]

clamminess *noun* the state or condition of being clammy.

clammy *adj.* (**clammier, clammiest**) moist or damp, especially unpleasantly so. [from Anglo-Saxon *clæman,* to smear]

. . . .

⊟ moist, damp, sweaty, sweating, sticky, dank, muggy, heavy, close.

. . . .

clamorous /ˈklamərəs/ *adj.* noisy, boisterous.

clamorously *adv.* in a clamorous or noisy way.

clamour /ˈklamə(r)/ — *noun* **1** a noise of shouting or loud talking. **2** an outcry; loud protesting or loud demands. **3** any loud noise. — *verb intrans.* (**clamour for something**) to demand it noisily. [from Latin *clamor,* shout]

clamp[1] — *noun* **1** a tool with adjustable jaws for gripping things firmly or pressing parts together. **2** a reinforcing or fastening device, used in woodwork, etc. **3** (*also* **wheel clamp**) a heavy metal device that can be fitted to the wheels of a car to prevent it being moved. — *verb* **1** to fasten together or hold with a clamp. **2** to fit a clamp to a wheel of (a parked car) to stop it being moved. **3** to hold, grip, shut, or press tightly. — **clamp down on something** or **someone**

---

to put a stop to it/them or control it/them strictly. [from Old Dutch *clampe*]

◆ noun 1 vice, grip, press. 2 brace, bracket, fastener. verb 1, 3 fasten, secure, hold, fix, clinch, grip, brace.

clamp² — noun a harvested root crop, silage, etc, piled into a mound, covered with straw and earth to protect it in cold weather, and stored in the open. — verb to store (a harvested root crop, silage, etc) in such a mound. [from Old Dutch *clamp*, heap]

clampdown noun a restriction; a suppression of activity.

clamper noun a person who clamps a car.

clan noun 1 a group of families, in Scotland or of Scots origin, generally with the same surname, and (especially formerly) led by a chief. 2 humorous one's family or relations. 3 a group of people who have similar interests, concerns, etc. 4 a division of a tribe. [from Gaelic *clann*, children]

◆ 1, 2 tribe, family, house, relatives. 3 sect, faction, group, band, set, clique, coterie, society, brotherhood, sisterhood, fraternity.

clandestine /klan'dɛstɪn, klan'dɛstaɪn/ adj. 1 concealed; kept secret. 2 furtive; sly; surreptitious. [from Latin *clandestinus*, from *clam*, secretly]

clandestinely adv. in a clandestine way.

clang — verb intrans., trans. to make or cause to make a loud deep ringing sound. — noun this sound. [from Latin *clangere*, to clang, resound]

clanger noun colloq. a tactless, embarrassing, and all too obvious blunder: *drop a clanger*.

clangour /'klaŋə(r)/ noun poetic a continuous, loud, confused, and intrusive noise. [from Latin *clangor*, noise]

clank — verb intrans., trans. to make or cause to make a sharp sound of metal striking metal or some other hard surface. — noun this sound. [imitative]

clannish adj. derog., said of a group of people closely united, with little interest or trust in people not belonging to the group.

clannishly adv. in a clannish way.

clannishness noun being clannish.

clansman or **clanswoman** noun (PL. clansmen, clanswomen) a member of a clan.

clap¹ — verb (clapped, clapping) 1 intrans., trans. to strike (especially the palms of one's hands) together with a loud noise, to applaud (someone), mark (a rhythm), gain attention, etc. 2 to strike (someone) with the palm of the hand, usually as a friendly gesture. 3 to place forcefully: *clapped the book on the table*. 4 colloq. to put suddenly (into prison, chains, etc). — noun 1 an act of clapping. 2 the sudden loud explosion of noise that thunder makes. — **clap eyes on** colloq. to see. **clapped out** colloq. 1 said of a machine, etc old, worn out, and no longer working properly. 2 said of a person exhausted. [from Anglo-Saxon *clæppan*]

◆ verb 1 applaud, acclaim, cheer. 2 slap, smack, pat, colloq. wallop, colloq. whack, bang. 3 colloq. plonk, dump, smack, slap. 4 throw, fling. noun 1 applause. 2 crack, crash, rumble.

clap² noun (often **the clap**) coarse slang venereal disease, especially gonorrhoea. [related to Old French *clapier*, brothel]

clapper noun 1 the dangling piece of metal inside a bell that strikes against the side to make it ring. 2 a device that produces a loud clattering noise, for scaring birds from crops, etc. — **like the clappers** colloq. very quickly.

clapperboard noun a pair of hinged boards clapped together in front of the camera before and after shooting a piece of film, so as to help synchronize sound and vision.

claptrap noun meaningless, insincere, or pompous talk. [from CLAP¹ + TRAP]

claque /klak/ noun 1 a group of people paid to applaud a speaker at a meeting or performer in a theatre, etc. 2 a circle of flatterers or admirers. [from French *claquer*, to clap]

claret /'klarət/ noun 1 a French red wine, especially from the Bordeaux district. 2 the deep reddish-purple colour of this wine. [from Old French *clare*, spiced wine]

clarification /klarɪfɪ'keɪʃən/ noun the process of making clear.

clarify /'klarɪfaɪ/ verb trans., intrans. (clarifies, clarified) 1 to make or become clearer or easier to understand. 2 said of butter, fat, etc to make or become clear by heating. [from Latin *clarus*, clear + *facere*, to make]

◆ 1 explain, illuminate, elucidate, gloss, define, simplify, resolve, clear up. 2 refine, purify, filter, clear.
◆ 1 obscure, confuse. 2 cloud.

clarinet /klarɪ'nɛt, 'klarɪnɛt/ noun a woodwind instrument, with a cylindrical tube and a single reed. [from French *clarinette*, diminutive of Old French *clarin*, clarion]

clarinettist /klarɪ'nɛtɪst/ noun a person who plays the clarinet.

clarion /'klarɪən/ noun an old kind of trumpet with a shrill sound, used to call men to arms, etc: *a clarion call*. [from Latin *clario*, from *clarus*, clear]

clarity /'klarɪtɪ/ noun 1 the quality of being clear and pure. 2 the quality of being easy to see, hear, or understand. 3 clearness and accuracy of thought, reasoning, and expression. [from Latin *claritas*]

◆ CLEARNESS. 1 transparency. 2 transparency, lucidity, simplicity, intelligibility, comprehensibility, unambiguousness, obviousness. 3 lucidity, explicitness, definition, accuracy, precision.
◆ 2 obscurity. 3 vagueness, imprecision.

clarsach /'klɑːrsəx/ noun a small harp strung with wire, played in Scotland and Ireland. [from Gaelic *clarsach*]

clash — noun 1 a loud noise, like that of metal objects striking each other. 2 a serious disagreement; a quarrel or argument. 3 a fight, battle, or match. 4 the coinciding in one's timetable of two or more events, both or all of which one ought to or would like to attend. — verb 1 intrans., trans. said of metal objects, etc to strike against each other noisily. 2 intrans. to fight; to have a battle. 3 intrans. (**clash with someone**) to disagree violently. 4 intrans. said of commitments, etc to coincide, usually fortuitously. 5 intrans. said of colours, styles, etc to be unpleasing or unharmonious together. [imitative]

◆ noun 1 crash, bang, jangle, clatter, noise. 2 disagreement, quarrel, argument, dispute, fight, altercation, confrontation, showdown, conflict. 3 fight, bout, brush, brawl, colloq. scrap, scuffle, tussle, skirmish, contest. 4 conflict. verb 1 crash, bang, clank, clang, jangle, clatter, rattle. 2 fight, grapple, colloq. scrap, war, feud. 3 disagree, quarrel, argue, fight, wrangle. 4 conflict. 5 jar, conflict.

clasp noun 1 a fastening on jewellery, a bag, etc made of two parts that link together. 2 a firm grip, or act of gripping. — verb 1 to hold, or take hold of, firmly. 2 to fasten or secure with a clasp.

◆ noun 1 fastener, buckle, clip, pin, hasp, hook, catch. 2 hold, grip, grasp, embrace, hug. verb 1 hold, grip, grasp, clutch, embrace, enfold, hug, squeeze, press. 2 fasten, secure, connect, attach, hook, clip, pin.

clasp knife a folding pocket knife, originally one held open by a catch.

class — noun 1 a lesson or lecture. 2 a number of pupils taught together. 3 the body of students that begin or finish university or school in the same year. 4 a category, kind, or type. **5** a grade or standard. **6** any of the social groupings into which people fall according to their job, wealth, etc. **7** the system by which society is divided into these groups. **8** *colloq.* stylishness in dress, behaviour, etc; good quality. — *verb* to regard as belonging to a certain class; to put into a category. — **in a class of its own** outstanding; with no equal. [from Latin *classis*, rank, class, division]

> **⊟** *noun* **1** lesson, lecture, seminar, tutorial, course. **2** form, group, set. **3** year, form, *North Amer.* grade. **4** category, kind, type, sort, genre, style, classification, group, order, league, set, species, genus, section, division. **5** grade, standard, quality, order, league. **6** rank, status, caste, sphere, grouping, order, league. **7** caste. **8** style, stylishness, quality, breeding, elegance. *verb* categorize, classify, group, sort, rank, grade, designate, brand.

> *Social classes / groups include*: aristocracy, nobility, gentry, landed gentry, gentlefolk, élite, *slang* nob, high society, *colloq.* top drawer, upper class, *slang* Sloane Ranger, ruling class, jetset, middle class, lower class, working class, bourgeoisie, proletariat, hoi-polloi, commoner, serf, plebeian, *colloq.* pleb.

class-conscious *adj. derog.* aware of one's own and other people's social class.

class-consciousness *noun* awareness of social classification.

classic — *adj.* **1** of the highest quality; established as the best. **2** entirely typical. **3** simple, neat, and elegant, especially in a traditional style: *a classic black suit.* — *noun* **1** an established work of literature. **2** an outstanding example of its type. **3** something, eg an item of clothing, always approved of and essential to have: *the little black dress, a classic of the 50s.* **4** (*also* **Classic**) a celebrated annual sporting event, especially a horse race. [from Latin *classicus*, relating to classes, especially the best]

> **⊟** *adj.* **1** model, exemplary, ideal, best, finest, first-rate, consummate, definitive, masterly, excellent, established. **2** typical, characteristic, archetypal. **3** traditional, time-honoured. *noun* **1** standard. **2** masterpiece, masterwork, pièce de résistance, exemplar, model, prototype.
> **⊟** *adj.* **1** second-rate. **2** atypical, unusual, unrepresentative.

classical — *adj.* **1** *said of literature, art, etc* of ancient Greece and Rome. **2** *said of architecture or the other arts* showing the influence of ancient Greece and Rome: *a classical façade.* **3** *said of music and arts related to it* having an established, traditional, and somewhat formal style and form: *classical music.* **4** *said of procedures, etc* following the well-known traditional pattern: *the classical method.* **5** *said of a shape, design, etc* simple; pure; without complicated decoration. **6** *said of a language* being the older, literary form. — *noun colloq.* classical music.

> **⊟** *adj.* **5** simple, pure, restrained, refined, traditional, well-proportioned, symmetrical.

classically *adv.* **1** in a classic or classical way. **2** so as to be classic.

classical revival a form of Western art characterized by a return to the classical orders in architecture, and interest in themes from classical literature, and an emphasis on the human form (with proportions based on Roman sculpture), as in central motif.

classicism /ˈklasɪsɪzm/ *noun* in art, architecture, prose, and poetry, a simple, elegant style typical in 18c and early 19c Europe.

classicist /ˈklasɪsɪst/ *noun* someone who has studied classics, especially as a university subject.

classics *sing. noun* (*often* **Classics**) the study of Latin and Greek and the literature and history of ancient Greece and Rome.

classifiable /ˈklasɪfaɪəbl/ *adj.* capable of being classified.

classification /klasɪfɪˈkeɪʃən/ *noun* **1** the arrangement and division of things and people into classes. **2** a group or class into which a thing or person is put.

> **⊟** **1** categorization, taxonomy, sorting, grading, arrangement, systematization, codification, tabulation, cataloguing.

classified *adj.* **1** arranged in groups or classes. **2** *said of information* kept secret by the government. **3** *said of a road* classed as a motorway or major route.

classified ad a small advertisement in a newspaper offering something for sale, advertising a job, etc.

classify /ˈklasɪfaɪ/ *verb* (**classifies**, **classified**) **1** to put into a particular class or group. **2** to declare (information) secret, and not for publication. [Latin *classis*, class, division + *facere*, to make]

> **⊟** **1** categorize, class, group, pigeonhole, codify, tabulate, file, catalogue, sort, grade, rank, arrange, dispose, distribute, systematize.

classless *adj.* **1** *said of a community* not divided into social classes. **2** not belonging to any particular social class.

classlessness *noun* **1** being without social classification. **2** not belonging to any class.

classmate *noun* a fellow pupil or student in one's class at school or college.

classroom *noun* a room in a school or college where classes are taught.

classy *adj.* (**classier**, **classiest**) *colloq.* stylish; fashionable; superior.

clatter — *noun* a loud noise made by hard objects striking each other, or falling on to a hard surface. — *verb intrans., trans.* (**clattered**, **clattering**) to make or cause to make this noise. [imitative]

clause *noun* **1** *Grammar* part of a sentence that has its own subject, verb, object, etc. **2** *Legal* a paragraph or section in a contract, will, or act of parliament. [from Latin *clausa*]

> **⊟** **2** paragraph, section, subsection, article, condition, proviso, provision, item, part, point, chapter, passage.

claustrophobia /klɔːstrəˈfoʊbɪə/ *noun* **1** an irrational fear of small or enclosed spaces such as tunnels or lifts. **2** an uncomfortable feeling of being shut in or confined. [from Latin *claustrum*, bolt, barrier + PHOBIA]

claustrophobic /klɔːstrəˈfoʊbɪk/ *adj.* relating to or of the nature of claustrophobia.

clavichord /ˈklavɪkɔːd/ *noun* an early keyboard instrument with a soft tone. [from Latin *clavis*, key + *chorda*, string]

clavicle /ˈklavɪkəl/ *noun Anat.* in vertebrates, either of two short slender bones linking the shoulder-blades with the top of the breastbone. [from Latin *clavicula*, diminutive of *clavis*, key]

claw — *noun* **1** a hard curved pointed nail on the end of each digit of the foot in birds, most reptiles, and many mammals. **2** the foot of an animal or bird, bearing a number of such nails. **3** any structure resembling a claw, eg the pincer of a crab or lobster, or a sharp curved structure at the tip of the leg of certain insects. **4** something with the shape or action of a claw, eg part of a mechanical device. — *verb trans., intrans.* (**claw at something**) to tear or scratch it with claws, nails, or fingers. — **claw something back 1** *said of a government* to recover money given in the form of benefits and allowances by imposing a new tax. **2** to regain a commercial advantage, etc with difficulty. [from Anglo-Saxon *clawu*]

⊟ *noun* **1** talon, nail. **2** talon. **3**, **4** pincer, nipper, gripper. *verb* scratch, scrabble, scrape, tear, rip, lacerate, maul, mangle.

clawback *noun* the process of clawing back; recovery of expenditure by taxation.

clawed frog or **clawed toad** an African or S American frog, so called because it has claws on three hind toes. It is aquatic, has no tongue, and catches its prey with its hands.

claw hammer a hammer with two points on one side of its head, that can be used for pulling out nails.

clay *noun* **1** *Geol.* a poorly draining soil with a very fine texture, consisting mainly of aluminium silicates. It is hard when dry, but can absorb large quantities of water, swelling to become soft, pliable, and sticky. It is used to make pottery, bricks, ceramics, etc. **2** earth or soil generally. **3** *Tennis* the hard surface of clay courts. **4** *poetic* the substance of which the human body is formed. — **have feet of clay** to lack moral courage. [from Anglo-Saxon *clæg*]

clay court a tennis court with a hard surface of clay or a similar substance.

clayey / ˈkleɪɪ/ *adj.* **1** like or made of clay. **2** covered with clay.

claymation /kleɪˈmeɪʃən/ *noun* animation using clay or plasticine figures.

clay mineral *Geol.* any of various silicates of aluminium that are the chief constituents of clay, and form fine flaky crystals which can absorb water, giving clay its characteristic plasticity when wet.

claymore *noun Hist.* a two-edged broadsword used by Scottish highlanders. [from Gaelic *claidheamh mór*, large sword]

clay pigeon a clay disc that is thrown up mechanically as a target in shooting.

clay pipe a tobacco pipe made of baked clay.

clean — *adj.* **1** free from dirt. **2** not containing anything harmful to health; pure. **3** pleasantly fresh: *a clean taste*. **4** hygienic in habits: *a clean animal*. **5** unused; unmarked: *a clean sheet of paper*. **6** neat and even: *a clean cut*. **7** simple and elegant: *a ship with good clean lines*. **8** clear of legal offences: *a clean driving licence*. **9** morally pure; innocent. **10** *said of humour, etc* not offensive or obscene. **11** fair: *a clean fight*. **12** *slang* not carrying drugs or offensive weapons. **13** *said of a nuclear installation, etc* not producing a harmful level of radioactive fallout or contamination. **14** *said of a wound* showing no signs of infection. **15** *said of an aeroplane's landing gear* in a retracted position. **16** *Relig.*, *said of certain animals* allowed for people to eat. **17** *said of musical sounds* pure and accurate. **18** absolute; complete: *make a clean break.* — *adv.* **1** *colloq.* completely: *get clean away / I clean forgot.* **2** straight; directly; encountering no obstruction: *sailed clean through the window.* — *verb* **1** *trans., intrans.* to make or become free from dirt. **2** *trans., intrans.* to dry-clean or be dry-cleaned. **3** *intrans.* to dust, polish floors and furniture, etc in a house or office, especially as a job. **4** to prepare (vegetables, etc) for cooking or eating by cutting away the inedible parts. — *noun* **1** an act of cleaning. **2** *Weight-lifting* a lift of the weight as far as the shoulders clean. **clean something out** to clean a room or cupboard, etc thoroughly. **clean someone out** *slang* to deprive or cheat them of money. **clean up 1** to clean a place thoroughly. **2** *slang* to make a large profit. **clean something up** to make a dirty place or person clean; to get rid of a mess. **clean up after someone** to clean up a mess, etc left by them. **come clean** *colloq.* to admit or tell the truth about something that one has previously concealed or lied about. **have clean hands** *colloq.* to have no connection with the crime, etc in question. **make a clean sweep 1** to make sweeping changes. **2** to win all the prizes at a sporting event, etc. **with a clean slate** or **sheet** with a fresh start, as though from the beginning again, especially after an error or misdeed. [from Anglo-Saxon *clæne*]

⊟ *adj.* **1** washed, immaculate, spotless, unspotted, unstained, unsoiled, laundered. **2** pure, purified, sterile, aseptic, antiseptic, hygienic, sanitary, sterilized, decontaminated, unadulterated, unpolluted, uncontaminated. **5** unused, unmarked, blank, fresh. **6** tidy, regular, straight, neat. **9** innocent, guiltless, virtuous, upright, moral, honest, honourable, respectable, decent, chaste, unsullied, perfect, faultless, flawless, unblemished. *adv.* **1** completely, utterly. **2** straight, directly, right. *verb* **1** wash, bath, rinse, wipe, sponge, scrub, scour, mop, swab, launder, sweep, vacuum, dust, freshen, deodorize, cleanse, purge, purify, decontaminate, disinfect, sanitize, sterilize, clear, filter. **3** *colloq.* skivvy.

⊟ *adj.* **1** dirty. **2** dirty, unhygienic, insanitary, polluted, contaminated. **6** rough. **9** guilty, dishonourable, indecent. **10** blue, dirty, coarse, offensive. *verb* **1** dirty, defile.

clean bill of health a declaration that a person is healthy, or that a machine or organization is working satisfactorily.

clean-cut *adj.* **1** pleasingly regular in outline or shape: *clean-cut features.* **2** neat; respectable.

cleaner *noun* **1** a person employed to clean inside buildings, offices, etc. **2** a machine or substance used for cleaning. **3** (*also* **cleaners**) a shop where clothes, etc can be taken for cleaning. — **take someone to the cleaners** *colloq.* to extort all or most of their money from them.

cleaning lady or **cleaning woman** a woman whose job is to clean inside a house, factory, office, etc.

clean-limbed *adj.* having a tall, slim, shapely body.

cleanliness / ˈklɛnlɪnəs/ *noun* habitual cleanness or purity.

clean-living *adj.* leading a decent, healthy existence.

cleanly [1] / ˈkliːnlɪ/ *adv.* **1** in a clean way. **2** tidily; efficiently; easily.

cleanly [2] / ˈklɛnlɪ/ *adj.* *old use* hygienic in one's personal habits.

cleanness / ˈkliːnnəs/ *noun* being clean.

clean-out *noun* **1** a thorough cleaning. **2** *colloq.* a swindle.

clean room 1 an area in a factory where rigorous standards of cleanliness are maintained, especially during the manufacture of computer components and other sensitive equipment. **2** a special facility for handling material, especially that destined for use in space exploration, in a sterile and dust-free environment.

cleanse / klɛnz/ *verb* **1** to clean or get rid of dirt from. **2** to purify; to remove sin or guilt from. [from Anglo-Saxon *clænsian*]

cleanser / ˈklɛnzə(r)/ *noun* a substance that cleans, eg a cream or liquid for cleaning the face.

⊟ soap, soap powder, detergent, cleaner, solvent, scourer, scouring powder, purifier, disinfectant.

clean-shaven *adj.* without a beard or moustache.

cleansing department / ˈklɛnzɪŋ/ the local-government department responsible for cleaning the streets and collecting rubbish.

clean-up *noun* a thorough cleaning.

clear — *adj.* **1** transparent; easy to see through. **2** *said of weather, etc* not misty or cloudy. **3** *said of the skin* healthy; unblemished by spots, etc. **4** easy to see, hear, or understand. **5** bright; sharp; well-defined: *a clear photograph.* **6** *said of vision* able to see well. **7** *said of musical sounds* pure and accurate. **8** certain; convinced; having no doubts or confusion: *are you clear about that point?* **9** definite; free of doubt, ambiguity, or confusion. **10** capable of, or resulting from, accurate observation, logical thinking, etc. **11** evident; obvious. **12** (**clear of something**) free of obstruction. **13** (**clear of something**) well away from it; out of range of or contact with it: *well clear of the rocks.* **14** (**clear of something**) free of it; no longer affected by it. **15** remaining after all charges, taxes, expenses, etc have been paid. **16** *said of the conscience, etc* free from guilt, etc. **17** entire; without interruption: *need a clear week to finish.* **18** free of appointments, etc. — *adv.* **1** in a clear manner. **2** completely: *get clear away.* **3** *North Amer.* all the way: *see* clear to the hills. **4** (**clear of something**) well away from it; out of the way of it: *keep / steer clear of trouble / stand clear.* — *verb* **1** *trans., intrans.* to make or become clear, free of obstruction, etc. **2** to remove or move out of the way. **3** to prove or declare to be innocent. **4** to get over or past without touching: *clear the fence.* **5** to make as profit over expenses. **6** to pass inspection by (customs). **7** to give or get official permission for (a plan, etc). **8** to approve (someone) for a special assignment, access to secret information, etc. **9** *trans., intrans.* to pass (a cheque), or (of a cheque) to pass from one bank to another through a clearing-house. **10** to decode. **11** to pay (a debt). — **clear the air** *colloq.* to get rid of bad feeling, suspicion, or tension, especially by frank discussion. **clear the decks** see DECK. **clear off** *colloq.* to go away. **clear something off** to finish paying debts, etc. **clear out** *colloq.* to go away. **clear something out** to rid it of rubbish, etc. **clear up** *said of the weather* to brighten after rain, a storm, etc. **clear something up 1** to tidy up a mess, room, etc. **2** to solve a mystery, etc. **3** to make something better. **in the clear** no longer under suspicion, in difficulties, or in danger. [from Old French *cler*]

. . . .

▤ *adj.* **1** transparent, limpid, crystalline, glassy, see-through, clean, unclouded, colourless. **2** cloudless, unclouded, fine, bright, sunny. **4** plain, distinct, comprehensible, intelligible, coherent, lucid, explicit, precise, unambiguous, pronounced, obvious, well-defined, manifest, conspicuous, unmistakable, unquestionable, recognizable, perceptible, evident, patent, audible. **6** good, undimmed. **7** pure, accurate, bright, sharp. **8** certain, sure, convinced, positive, definite. **9** certain, definite. **11** evident, obvious, plain, unmistakable, apparent, patent. **12** unobstructed, unblocked, open, free, empty, unhindered, unimpeded. **15** net. *adv.* **2** completely, utterly, clean, right. *verb* **1** unblock, unclog, decongest, free, rid, extricate, disentangle. **2** clean, wipe, erase, cleanse, refine, filter, tidy, empty, unload. **3** acquit, exculpate, exonerate, absolve, vindicate, excuse, justify. **7, 8** pass, approve. **clear something up 1** tidy, order, sort, rearrange, remove. **2** solve, resolve, answer, explain, unravel, clarify, elucidate.

▣ *adj.* **1** opaque, cloudy. **2** cloudy, dull, misty, foggy. **4** unclear, vague, indistinct, ambiguous, confusing, inaudible. **5** blurred, fuzzy. **6** poor, weak, dim. **7** flat, dull, dead. **8** unsure, muddled, doubtful. **11** unclear, uncertain. **12** blocked, obstructed. *verb* **1** block, dirty. **3** condemn.

. . . .

clearance *noun* **1** the act of clearing. **2** the distance between one object and another passing beside or under it. **3** permission, or a certificate granting this. **4** (*also* **security clearance**) official acknowledgement that one can be trusted not to pass secrets to an enemy.

. . . .

▤ **2** headroom, space, gap, margin, allowance. **3** permission, consent, authorization, sanction, endorsement, leave, *colloq.* OK, *colloq.* go-ahead, *colloq.* green light.

. . . .

clear blue water distance between political parties in terms of their policies.

clear-cut *adj.* clear; sharp.

clear-headed *adj.* capable of, or showing, clear, logical thought.

clearing *noun* an area in a forest, etc that has been cleared of trees, etc.

. . . .

▤ glade, space, gap, opening.

. . . .

clearing bank a bank using the services of a central clearing-house.

clearing-house *noun* **1** an establishment that deals with transactions between its member banks. **2** a central agency that collects, organizes, and distributes information.

clearly *adv.* **1** in a clear manner. **2** obviously: *clearly, he's wrong.*

clearness *noun* the quality of being clear.

clear-out *noun* a clearing out of rubbish, etc.

clear-sighted *adj.* capable of, or showing, accurate observation and good judgement.

clearway *noun* a stretch of road on which cars may not stop except in an emergency.

cleavage *noun* **1** a series of cell divisions of an ovum immediately after it has been fertilized, which transform it into a group of small cells called a blastula. **2** *Biochem.* the breakdown of a complex molecule, such as a protein, into simpler molecules by the splitting of chemical bonds within its structure. **3** *Geol.* the splitting of rocks into thin parallel sheets, or the splitting of a crystal in one or more specific directions to give smooth surfaces. **4** *colloq.* the hollow between a woman's breasts, especially as revealed by a dress with a low neck. [from CLEAVE[1]]

cleave[1] *verb* (PAST TENSE **clove**, **cleft**, **cleaved**; PAST PARTICIPLE **cloven**, **cleft**, **cleaved**) *trans., intrans. formal, literary* **1** to split or divide. **2** to cut or slice: *cleave a way through the undergrowth.* See also CLOVEN. [from Anglo-Saxon *cleofan*]

cleave[2] *verb intrans.* (PAST TENSE AND PAST PARTICIPLE **cleaved**) to cling or stick. [from Anglo-Saxon *cleofian*]

cleaver *noun* a knife with a large square blade, used by butchers for chopping meat. [from CLEAVE[1]]

clef *noun Mus.* each of three symbols placed on a stave to indicate the pitch of the notes written on it: the *treble clef* or G clef on the second line up, the *bass clef* or F clef on the second line down, and the *alto clef* or C clef on the middle line. [from French *clef*, key]

cleft[1] *noun* a split, fissure, wide crack, or deep indentation. [related to CLEAVE[1]]

cleft[2] *adj.* split; divided. — **in a cleft stick** in a difficult or awkward situation. [past participle of CLEAVE[1]]

cleft palate *Medicine* a deformity of the palate caused by failure of the two sides of the roof of the mouth to meet and fuse together in the developing fetus, resulting in an abnormal opening between the mouth cavity and nasal cavities at birth.

clematis /ˈklemətɪs, kləˈmeɪtɪs/ *noun* any woody climbing plant of the genus Clematis, native to north temperate regions, and having leaves divided into leaflets, leaf stalks that act as tendrils and twine around supports with which they come into contact, and flowers with long feathery styles. [from Greek *clematis*, periwinkle, convolvulus, or traveller's joy]

clemency *noun* **1** the quality of being clement. **2** mercy.

clement /ˈklemənt/ *adj.* **1** *said of the weather* mild; not harsh or severe. **2** merciful. [from Latin *clemens*, mild, calm, merciful]

clementine /ˈklemənti:n/ *noun* a citrus fruit (Citrus nobilis var. *deliciosa*) resembling a small orange, widely cultivated in Spain and N Africa, and considered to be either a variety of tangerine or the result of a cross between a tangerine and an orange. [from French *clementine*]

clemently *adv.* **1** mildly. **2** mercifully.

clench — *verb* **1** to close (one's teeth or one's fists) tightly, especially in anger. **2** to hold or grip firmly. — *noun* **1** the action of clenching. **2** a very tight grasp. [from Anglo-Saxon *beclencan*, to hold fast]

clerestory *or* **clearstory** /ˈklɪəstɔːrɪ/ *noun* (PL. **clerestories**) *Archit.* in a church, an upper row of windows in the nave wall, above the roof of the aisle. [from CLEAR (referring to the windows) + STOREY]

clergy /ˈklɜːdʒɪ/ *noun pl., or, sometimes, sing.* (PL. **clergies**) the ordained ministers of the Christian church, or the priests of any religion. [from French *clergé*]

. . . .

▤ clergymen, churchmen, clerics, the Church, the cloth, ministry, priesthood.

. . . .

clergyman *or* **clergywoman** *noun* a member of the clergy.

. . . .

▤ churchman, cleric, ecclesiastic, divine, man of God, minister, priest, reverend, father, vicar, pastor, padre, parson, rector, canon, dean, deacon, chaplain, curate, presbyter, rabbi.

....

cleric *noun* a clergyman. [from Latin *clericus*, priest]
clerical *adj.* **1** relating to the clergy. **2** relating to clerks, office workers, or office work.

....

▣ **1** ecclesiastical, pastoral, ministerial, priestly, episcopal, canonical, sacerdotal. **2** office, secretarial, white-collar, official, administrative.

....

clerical collar the stiff white collar, fastening at the back, worn by clergymen.
clerihew /ˈklɛrɪhjuː/ *noun* a humorous poem four lines long, especially about a famous person. [named after the inventor, E Clerihew Bentley]
clerk /klɑːk, klɜːrk/ *noun* **1** a person in an office or bank who deals with letters, accounts, records, files, etc. **2** in a law court, a person who keeps records or accounts. **3** a public official in charge of the records and business affairs of the town council. **4** an unordained or lay minister of the church. **5** *North Amer.* a shop assistant or hotel receptionist. **6** *old use* a scholar or clergyman. [from Anglo-Saxon *clerc*, variant of CLERIC]
clerkess /klɑːˈkes/ *noun* a female clerk.
clerk of works the person in charge of the construction and care of a building.
clever *adj.* **1** good or quick at learning and understanding. **2** skilful, dexterous, nimble, or adroit. **3** well thought out; ingenious. [from Middle English *cliver*, related to Anglo-Saxon *clifer*, claw]

....

▣ **1** intelligent, *colloq.* brainy, bright, smart, witty, gifted, expert, knowledgeable, quick, quick-witted, sharp, keen. **2** skilful, skilled, dexterous, nimble, talented, adroit, apt, able, capable, shrewd, knowing, discerning, sensible, rational. **3** cunning, ingenious, inventive, resourceful.
▣ **1** foolish, stupid, senseless, ignorant. **2** clumsy, awkward.

....

clever dick *derog. colloq.* a person who is over-sure of his or her cleverness.
cleverly *adv.* in a clever way.
cleverness *noun* the quality of being clever.
clew — *noun* **1** *Naut.* the corner of a ship's sail. **2** *old use* a ball of thread. **3** the arrangement of cords by which a hammock is suspended. — *verb* (**clew a sail up** or **down**) to haul it up or let it down. [from Anglo-Saxon *cliewen*, ball of thread]
cliché /ˈkliːʃeɪ/ *noun derog.* **1** a phrase or combination of words that was striking and effective when first used, but has become stale and feeble through repetition. **2** a too-frequently used idea or image; a stereotype. [from French *cliché*, a stereotype plate or stencil]

....

▣ **1** platitude, commonplace, banality, truism, bromide, old chestnut.

....

clichéd *adj.* of the nature of a cliché.
click — *noun* **1** a short sharp sound like that made by two parts of a mechanism locking into place. **2** *Mech.* a catch in a piece of machinery. **3** in some African languages, a click-like speech sound produced by a sucking action with the tongue. — *verb* **1** *trans., intrans.* to make or cause to make a click. **2** *intrans. colloq.* to meet with approval. **3** *intrans. colloq.* to become clear or understood. **4** *Comput.* to press and release one of the buttons on a mouse input device in order to send an instruction to the computer to which it is attached, eg to select a particular item from a menu displayed on the screen. — **click with someone** *colloq.* to become friendly with them. [imitative]
client /ˈklaɪənt/ *noun* **1** a person using the professional services of eg a lawyer, bank manager, architect, etc. **2** a cus-

tomer. **3** *Comput.* a computer used to contact and download data from a server. [from Latin *cliens*, dependant]

....

▣ **1** customer, patron, patient. **2** customer, patron, regular, buyer, shopper, consumer, user.

....

clientèle /kliːɒnˈtel/ *noun* the clients of a professional person, customers of a shopkeeper, etc, or people habitually attending a theatre. [from French *clientèle*]
cliff *noun* a high steep rock face, especially one that runs along the coast or the side of a mountain. [from Anglo-Saxon *clif*]

....

▣ bluff, face, rock face, scar, scarp, escarpment, crag, overhang, precipice.

....

cliffhanger *noun* **1** a story that keeps one in suspense up to the end. **2** the ending of an episode of a serial story which leaves the audience in suspense, as if with the hero clinging to a cliff edge. **3** an exciting situation, especially a contest, of which the conclusion is in doubt until the very last minute.
cliffhanging *adj.* of the nature of a cliffhanger; full of suspense.
climacteric /klaɪˈmaktərɪk/ *noun* **1** *Biol.* in living organisms, a period of changes, especially those associated with the menopause in women, and with a reduction in sexual desire in men. **2** *Bot.* in plants, an increase in respiration rate associated with the ripening of fruit. It can be artificially delayed so as to prevent the deterioration of fruit during transport and storage. [from Greek *klimakter*, rung of a ladder]
climactic /klaɪˈmaktɪk/ *adj.* of the nature of a climax.
climactically *adv.* in a climactic way.
climate *noun* **1** the average weather conditions of a particular region of the world over a long period of time, usually at least 50 years. These conditions include the average temperature, rainfall, air pressure, humidity, hours of sunshine, and wind speed and direction. **2** a part of the world considered from the point of view of its weather conditions: *move to a warmer climate.* **3** a current trend in general feeling, opinion, policies, etc. [from Greek *klima*, latitude, region]

....

▣ **1** weather, temperature. **3** trend, tendency, atmosphere, mood, feeling, environment, setting, milieu.

....

climatic /klaɪˈmatɪk/ *adj.* relating to climate.
climatically *adv.* as regards climate.
climatological /klaɪmətəˈlɒdʒɪkəl/ *adj.* relating to climatology.
climatologist /klaɪməˈtɒlədʒɪst/ *noun* a scientist who specializes in climatology.
climatology /klaɪməˈtɒlədʒɪ/ *noun* the scientific study of climate.
climax — *noun* **1** the high point or culmination of a series of events or of an experience. **2** a sexual orgasm. — *verb intrans., trans.* **1** to come or bring to a climax. **2** to experience (sexual orgasm). [from Greek *climax*, ladder, climax]

....

▣ *noun* **1** culmination, high point, height, highlight, acme, zenith, peak, summit, top, head. *verb* **1** peak, culminate.
▣ *noun* **1** nadir.

....

climax community *Biol.* a stable plant community representing the final stage in the colonization of a habitat, eg oak woodland in the UK.
climb /klaɪm/ — *verb* **1** *trans., intrans.* (*also* **climb up**) to go towards the top of (a hill, ladder, etc). **2** *intrans.* (**climb down** or **in** or **out**, etc) to reach somewhere with difficulty, especially by using hands and feet. **3** *intrans.* to rise or go

up. **4** *intrans.* to increase. — *noun* **1** an act of climbing. **2** a slope to be climbed. — **climb down** to concede one's position on some issue, etc, especially publicly or humiliatingly. [from Anglo-Saxon *climban*]

....

◨ *verb* **1** ascend, scale, shin up, clamber, mount. **2** scramble, crawl, creep. **3** rise, soar, mount, spiral, top. **4** increase, rise, mount, soar, escalate, spiral. *noun* **1** ascent. **2** slope, ascent, hill, incline, gradient. **climb down** concede, retract, *colloq.* eat one's words, back down, retreat.

....

climbable *adj.* capable of being climbed.

climb-down *noun* a dramatic or humiliating change of mind or concession.

climber *noun* **1** a climbing plant. **2** a mountaineer. **3** *derog.* a person who is too obviously trying to rise through the social ranks.

climbing *noun* the sport of climbing rock faces, especially with the help of ropes and other devices.

climbing-frame *noun* a strong framework of metal or wooden bars for children to climb around on.

climbing perch an Asiatic freshwater fish common in rivers, lakes, and canals, up to 25cm in length and having a special respiratory organ above the gills for breathing air. It is able to move overland by jerky thrusts of its tail fin.

climbing plant *Bot.* a plant which reaches toward the light by clinging to neighbouring plants, walls, or other supports. Also called VINE.

clime *noun poetic, humorous* a part of the world: *foreign climes*. [from Greek *klima*, region, latitude]

clinch — *verb* **1** to settle (an argument or bargain) finally and decisively. **2** *intrans. Boxing, Wrestling, said of contestants* to hold each other in a firm grip. **3** *intrans. colloq.* to embrace. **4** *Joinery* to bend over and hammer down the projecting point of (a nail or rivet that has been driven through a piece of wood, etc). — *noun* **1** an act of clinching. **2** *Boxing, Wrestling* an act of clinging to each other to prevent further blows, create a breathing space, etc. **3** *colloq.* an embrace. [variant of CLENCH]

clincher *noun* a point, argument, or circumstance that finally settles or decides a matter.

cline *noun Biol.* a gradual change in the form of an animal or plant species across different parts of its geographical or environmental range, so that the populations at either end of the cline may be very different from each other. [from Greek *klinein*, to lean]

cling — *verb intrans.* (PAST TENSE AND PAST PARTICIPLE **clung**) **1** to hold firmly or tightly; to stick. **2** to be emotionally over-dependent: *still clinging to his mother.* **3** to refuse to drop or let go. — *adj.* same as CLINGSTONE. [from Anglo-Saxon *clingan*]

....

◨ *verb* **1** clasp, clutch, stick, grasp, grip, adhere, cleave, fasten, embrace, hug.

....

clinger *noun* someone or something that clings.

clingfilm *noun* a thin, clear plastic material that adheres to itself, used for wrapping food, covering containers, etc.

clinginess *noun* being clingy.

clingstone *noun* a variety of peach or other fruit in which the flesh is firmly attached to the stone.

clingy *adj.* (**clingier, clingiest**) inclined to cling.

clinic *noun* **1** a private hospital or nursing home that specializes in the treatment and care of patients with particular diseases or disorders. **2** a department of a hospital or a health centre that specializes in the diagnosis, treatment, and medical care of one type of patient, or in one form of treatment, eg a family planning clinic. **3** a session during which patients are given medical treatment or advice in such a specialized department. **4** the instruction in examination and treatment of patients that is given to medical students, usually at the patient's bedside in a hospital

ward. **5** a session in which an expert is available for consultation. [from Greek *klinikos*, relating to the sickbed]

clinical *adj.* **1** relating to or resembling a clinic or hospital. **2** *said of medical studies* relating to or based on the direct observation and treatment of patients, as distinct from experimental or theoretical work. **3** *said of manner, behaviour, etc* cold; impersonal; unemotional; detached. **4** *said of surroundings, etc* severely plain and simple, with no personal touches.

clinical death same as BRAIN DEATH.

clinically *adv.* **1** in a clinical way. **2** in terms of direct medical observation and treatment, as distinct from experimental or theoretical work.

clinical psychology the practical application of psychological research findings to the diagnosis, treatment, and prevention of a wide range of mental disorders, including anxiety, depression, sexual and marital problems, childhood behavioural problems, eating disorders, drug and alcohol dependence, phobias, obsessions, schizophrenia, mental handicap, and dementia.

clinical thermometer a thermometer consisting of a calibrated glass tube with a narrow bulb at one end containing mercury, used for measuring body temperature. The mercury expands and rises up the tube until it reaches a level corresponding to the patient's body temperature, which continues to be indicated until the thermometer is reset by shaking.

clinician /klɪˈnɪʃən/ *noun* a doctor who works directly with patients in a clinic, etc, as opposed to conducting experimental or theoretical work.

clink[1] — *noun* a short sharp ringing sound. — *verb intrans., trans.* to make or cause to make a clink. [perhaps from Old Dutch *klinken*, to ring]

clink[2] *noun slang* prison. [originally the name of a prison in Southwark]

clinker *noun* **1** the combustible residue, consisting of a hard mass of fused ash, that is raked out from coal- or coke-fired furnaces. It is often used for road-making or as aggregate for concrete. **2** the jagged cindery crust on the surface of some lava flows. **3** a hard form of partially vitrified brick. [from Dutch *klinker*, hard brick]

clinker-built *adj., said of a boat* with a hull each of whose planks overlaps the one below it on the outside. See also CARVEL-BUILT. [from *clink*, a form of CLINCH, from the use of clinched nails]

clinometer /klɪˈnɒmɪtə(r)/ *noun* any of various hand-held surveying instruments used to measure vertical angles of slope. [from Greek *klinein*, to lean]

clint *noun Geol.* **1** one of a series of limestone blocks or ridges divided by fissures. **2** any exposed outcrop of hard flinty rock that forms a projection or ledge. [from Middle English, = cliff]

clip[1] — *verb* (**clipped, clipping**) **1** to cut (hair, wool, etc). **2** to trim or cut off the hair, wool, or fur of. **3** to punch out a piece from (a ticket) to show that it has been used. **4** to cut (an article, etc) from a newspaper, etc. **5** *colloq.* to hit or strike sharply. **6** to cut (a small amount) from something. — *noun* **1** an act of clipping. **2** a short sequence extracted from a film. **3** *colloq.* a sharp blow. **4** *colloq.* speed; rapid speed: *going at a fair clip.* **5** *Austral., New Zealand* the total amount of wool shorn from sheep, at one time, place, etc. — **clip someone's wings** to reduce their power or scope for activity. [from Norse *klippa*, to cut]

....

◨ *verb* **1** cut, trim, snip, crop, dock. **2** shear, dock. **6** prune, pare, truncate, curtail, shorten, abbreviate. *noun* **1** cut, snip, trim. **2** excerpt, extract.

....

clip[2] — *noun* **1** (*often in compounds*) any of various usually small devices for holding things together or in position. **2** (*also* **cartridge clip**) a container for bullets attached to a gun, that feeds bullets directly into it. **3** a piece of jewellery in the form of a clip, for attaching to clothing. — *verb trans., intrans.* (**clipped, clipping**) to fasten with a clip. [from Anglo-Saxon *clyppan*, to embrace, clasp]

. . . .

◼ *verb* pin, staple, fasten, attach, fix, hold.
. . . .

clipboard *noun* a board serving as a portable writing surface, with a clip at the top for holding paper, forms, etc.

clip joint *slang* a bar, restaurant, or nightclub charging excessively high prices.

clip-on *adj.*, *said eg of earrings* fastening with a clip.

clipped *adj.* **1** *said of the form of a word* shortened, eg *sec* from *second*. **2** *said of speaking style* tending to shorten vowels, omit syllables, etc.

clipper *noun Hist.* a fast sailing ship with large sails. [from CLIP¹]

clippers *pl. noun* (*often in compounds*) a clipping instrument.

clipping *noun* **1** a piece clipped off: *hair clippings*. **2** a cutting from a newspaper, etc.

. . . .

◼ **2** cutting, snippet, quotation, citation, passage, section, excerpt, extract.
. . . .

clique /kliːk/ *noun derog.* a group of friends, professional colleagues, etc who stick together and are hostile towards outsiders. [from French *clique*]

. . . .

◼ circle, set, coterie, faction, clan, group, gang, crowd, bunch.
. . . .

cliquey or **cliquish** *adj.* (**cliquier, cliquiest**) characteristic of a clique; socially exclusive.

cliquiness or **cliquishness** *noun* being cliquey.

clitoral /ˈklɪtərəl, ˈklaɪtərəl/ *adj.* relating to or in the region of the clitoris.

clitoridectomy /klɪtərɪˈdɛktəmɪ/ *noun Medicine* the surgical removal of the clitoris. See also CIRCUMCISION.

clitoris /ˈklɪtərɪs/ *noun Anat.* in female mammals, a small highly sensitive organ located in front of the opening of the vagina, which like the penis in males becomes erect when sexually stimulated. [from Greek *kleitoris*]

Cllr *abbrev.* Councillor.

cloaca /kloʊˈeɪkə/ *noun Zool.* in most vertebrates apart from mammals, the terminal region of the gut, into which the alimentary canal, urinary system, and reproductive system all open and discharge their contents, which are then expelled from the body via a single common aperture. [from Latin *cloaca*, from *cluere*, to purge]

cloak — *noun* **1** a loose outdoor garment, usually sleeveless, fastened at the neck so as to hang from the shoulders. **2** a covering: *a cloak of mist*. **3** a concealment or disguise: *use one's job as a cloak for spying activities*. — *verb* to cover up or conceal: *cloaked in mystery*. [from Old French *cloke*, from Latin *clocca*, bell, bell-shaped cape]

. . . .

◼ *noun* **1** cape, mantle, robe, wrap, coat. **2** mantle, pall, shroud. **3** concealment, disguise, cover, shield, mask, front, façade, pretext. *verb* cover (up), conceal, veil, mask, screen, hide, obscure, disguise, camouflage.
. . . .

cloak-and-dagger *adj.*, *said of stories, situations, etc* full of adventure, mystery, plots, spying, etc.

cloakroom *noun* **1** a room in a theatre, restaurant, etc where coats, hats, etc may be left. **2** a toilet, especially in a public building.

clobber¹ *verb* (**clobbered, clobbering**) *colloq.* **1** to hit. **2** to defeat completely. **3** to criticize severely.

clobber² *noun slang* **1** clothing. **2** personal belongings, equipment, etc.

cloche /klɒʃ/ *noun* **1** a transparent glass or (usually) plastic cover, formerly bell-shaped but now usually tunnel-shaped, placed over young plants, especially when these are grown in rows, in order to protect them from frost, etc. **2** a woman's close-fitting dome-shaped hat. [from French *cloche*, bell, bell jar, from Latin *clocca*, bell]

clock¹ — *noun* **1** an instrument for measuring and indicating time, usually by means of a digital display or pointers on a dial. **2** a device that controls the speed of the central processing unit in a computer. **3** a device that synchronizes the timing in switching circuits, transmission systems, etc. **4** a device in a vehicle for showing distance travelled or speed of travel. **5** (*in full* **time clock**) an instrument for recording employees' times of arrival and departure. **6** the downy seedhead of a dandelion. **7** *slang* the face. — *verb* **1** to measure or record time using such an instrument. **2** to record with a stopwatch the time taken by (a racer, etc) to complete a distance, etc. **3** *colloq.* to travel at (a speed as shown on a speedometer). **4** *slang* to hit (someone). — **against the clock** with a time deadline. **beat the clock** to finish before the set time limit or deadline. **clock in** or **on** to record one's time of arrival at a place of work. **clock out** or **off** to record one's time of departure from a place of work. **clock something up** to reach a particular speed, cover a particular distance, or achieve a particular score, etc. **put back the clock** to seek to return to the conditions of an earlier period. **round the clock** throughout the day and night. **watch the clock** to pay close attention to the time of day, especially in order not to exceed minimum working hours. [from Old Dutch *clocke*, bell, clock]

Types of clock or watch include: alarm clock, digital clock, mantel clock, bracket clock, carriage clock, cuckoo clock, longcase clock, grandfather clock, grandmother clock, speaking clock, *colloq.* Tim; wristwatch, fob watch, repeating watch, chronograph, pendant watch, ring-watch, stopwatch; chronometer, sundial.

clock² *noun* a decoration on the side of a sock.

clock tower a four-walled tower with a clock face on each wall.

clockwise *adj.*, *adv.* moving, etc in the same direction as that in which the hands of a clock move.

clockwork — *noun* a mechanism like that of a clock, working by means of gears and a spring that must be wound periodically. — *adj.* operated by clockwork. — **like clockwork** smoothly and with regularity; without difficulties.

clod *noun* **1** a lump of earth, clay, etc. **2** *colloq.* a stupid person. [from Middle English *clodde*]

cloddish *adj.* **1** like a clod or clods. **2** stupid.

cloddishly *adv.* in a cloddish way.

cloddishness *noun* being cloddish.

clodhopper *noun colloq.* **1** a clumsy person. **2** a large, heavy boot or shoe. [from CLOD + HOP¹]

clodhopping *adj. colloq.* like a clodhopper; large and clumsy.

clog — *noun* a shoe carved entirely from wood, or having a thick wooden sole. — *verb trans.*, *intrans.* (**clogged, clogging**) (*also* **clog up**) to obstruct or become obstructed so that movement is difficult or impossible. [from Middle English]

. . . .

◼ *verb* obstruct, block, choke, stop up, *colloq.* bung up, dam, congest, jam, impede, hinder, hamper, burden.
◼ *verb* unblock.
. . . .

cloisonné /ˈklwazɒneɪ/ *noun* a form of decoration for vases, etc, the pattern being formed in wire and filled in with coloured enamel. [from French = compartmented]

cloister — *noun* **1** a covered walk built against the wall of a church, college, etc with arches along its other side that open on to a garden, quadrangle, etc. **2** a place of religious retreat, eg a monastery or convent; the quiet secluded life of such a place. — *verb* (**cloistered, cloistering**) to keep (someone) away from the problems of normal life in the world. [from Old French *cloistre*]

cloistral *adj.* **1** relating to or like a cloister. **2** living in a cloister.

clonal *adj.* relating to or like a clone.

clone — *noun* **1** *Biol.* any of a group of genetically identical cells or organisms derived from a single parent cell or organism by asexual reproduction, eg vegetatively propagated plants. **2** *Biol.* any of a large number of identical copies of a gene produced by genetic engineering. **3** *Comput.* a usually cheaper imitation of an existing computer or software product, produced by a different manufacturer. **4** *colloq.* a person or thing that looks like a replica of someone or something else. **5** *colloq.* a mobile phone that has been given the identity of another phone, to which calls will be charged. — *verb trans., intrans.* to produce a set of identical cells or organisms from a single parent cell or organism, or to produce many identical copies of a gene by genetic engineering. [from Greek *klon*, twig]

clonk — *noun* a noise of a heavy, especially metal, object striking something. — *verb intrans., trans.* to make or cause to make this noise. [imitative]

clop — *noun* the hollow sound of a horse's hooves on hard ground. — *verb intrans.* (**clopped, clopping**) *said of a horse* to walk along making this noise. [imitative]

close[1] /kloʊs/ — *adj.* **1** near in space or time; at a short distance: *at close range.* **2** near in relationship, friendship, or connection. **3** touching or almost touching. **4** tight, not loose; dense or compact; with little space between. **5** near to the surface: *a close haircut.* **6** thorough; searching. **7** *said of a contest, etc* with little difference between entrants, etc. **8** (**close to something**) about to happen, do something, etc: *close to tears.* **9** similar to the original, or to something else: *a close translation / a close resemblance.* **10** uncomfortably warm; stuffy. **11** secretive. **12** mean: *close with money.* **13** heavily guarded: *under close arrest.* **14** *old use* shut; closed; confined. **15** *said of an organization, etc* restricted in membership. — *adv.* **1** (*often in compounds*) in a close manner; closely: *close-fitting / follow close behind.* **2** at close range. **3** (**close on** or **to** ...) nearly: *close on a thousand.* — **at close quarters 1** at close range; near to. **2** *said of fighting* hand-to-hand, one individual fighting another. **close at** or **to hand** close by; easily available. **a close call** or **shave** a narrow or lucky escape. **a close thing 1** a narrow escape. **2** something only just managed or achieved. **close to home** uncomfortably close to the truth, or to a sensitive matter. [from Old French *clos*, closed, from Latin *claudere*, to close]

· · · · · · · · · · · · · · · · · · · ·

☰ *adj.* **1** near, nearby, at hand, neighbouring, impending, imminent. **2** intimate, dear, familiar, attached, devoted, loving. **3** touching, adjacent, adjoining. **4** tight, dense, compact, solid, packed, crammed. **6** thorough, searching, concentrated, intense, keen. **8** near to, on the verge of. **9** accurate, exact, precise, strict, literal, faithful. **10** stuffy, oppressive, heavy, muggy, humid, sultry, sweltering, airless, stifling, suffocating, unventilated. **11** secretive, uncommunicative, taciturn, private, secret, confidential. **12** mean, miserly, parsimonious, *colloq.* tight, stingy, niggardly.

☷ *adj.* **1** far, distant. **2** cool, unfriendly, distant. **4** loose, open. **9** rough, loose. **10** fresh, airy. **11** open. **12** generous.

· · · · · · · · · · · · · · · · · · · ·

close[2] /kloʊz/ — *verb* **1** *trans., intrans.* to shut. **2** to block (a road, etc) so as to prevent use. **3** *trans., intrans., said of shops, etc* to stop or cause to stop being open to the public for a period of time. **4** *trans., intrans., said of a factory, business, etc* to stop or cause to stop operating permanently. **5** *trans., intrans.* to finish; to come or bring to an end; to stop discussion, etc of. **6** *trans., intrans.* to join up or come together; to cause edges, etc of something to come together. **7** to settle or agree on: *close a deal.* **8** *intrans. Econ., said of currency, shares, etc* to be worth at the end of a period of trading. **9** (**close on someone**) to catch them up: *the police were closing on him.* — *noun* an end or conclusion. — **close down 1** *said of a business* to close permanently. **2** *said of a television or radio station, etc* to stop broadcasting at the end of the day. **close something down** to close it permanently. **close one's eyes to something** to pretend not to notice it. **close in 1** *said of days* to become shorter in winter, while nights get longer.

close in on someone to approach and surround them: *the police were closing in on them.* **close up** to move closer together. **close something up** to bring closer together: *close up the gaps.* **close with someone 1** to strike a bargain with; to agree to (an offer, etc). **2** *old use* to begin fighting them. [from Latin *claudere*, to close]

· · · · · · · · · · · · · · · · · · · ·

☰ *verb* **1** shut, fasten, secure, lock, bar. **2** block, obstruct, clog, plug, cork, stop up. **3, 4** shut. **5** finish, end, complete, conclude, terminate, wind up, stop, cease. **6** join, unite, fuse, seal. *noun* end, finish, conclusion, completion, culmination, ending, finale, dénouement, termination, cessation, stop, pause.

☷ *verb* **1** open, unfasten, unlock, undo. **2** unblock, open, clear. **3, 4** open. **5** start, commence. **6** separate. *noun* start, beginning.

· · · · · · · · · · · · · · · · · · · ·

close[3] /kloʊs/ *noun* **1** in Scotland, a narrow passage leading from the street to the stair of a tenement building. **2** (**Close**) used as the name of a street, usually one closed to traffic at one end. **3** the land and buildings surrounding and belonging to a cathedral; a quadrangle. [from Middle English *clos*, enclosure, from Latin *claudere*, to close]

closed /kloʊzd/ *adj.* **1** shut; blocked. **2** *said of a community or society* with membership restricted to a chosen few. — **behind closed doors** privately, the public being excluded.

closed book a person or subject that one cannot understand.

closed circuit 1 a complete electrical circuit through which current flows when a voltage is applied. **2** a closed-circuit television.

closed-circuit television (ABBREV. **CCTV**) a television system that does not broadcast to the general public, but in which the transmission is restricted to a limited number of screens connected to a television camera over a relatively short distance by cables or telephone links.

closed-loop *adj. Comput.* denoting a computer system in which performance is controlled by comparing an amount of output with an expected standard in order to identify and reduce deviations.

closedown 1 the permanent closing of a business. **2** *Brit.* the closing of broadcasting at the end of the day.

closed shop a factory, etc in which only members of a trade union are employed. See also OPEN SHOP.

closed syllable a syllable ending in a consonant.

close-fisted *adj. colloq.* mean; miserly.

close harmony a style of singing in harmony with the voice parts nearly coinciding.

close-hauled *adj. Naut.* with sails set for sailing as nearly into the wind as possible.

close-knit *adj., said of a group, community, etc* closely bound together.

closely *adv.* in a close way; with close attention: *shall watch them closely.*

closeness *noun* a close quality or state.

close season 1 the time of year when it is illegal to kill certain birds, animals, or fish for sport. **2** an inactive period between seasons in particular sports, for example football.

closet /ˈklɒzɪt/ — *noun* **1** a cupboard. **2** *old use* a small private room. **3** *old use* same as WATER CLOSET. — *adj.* secret, not openly declared. — *verb* (**closeted, closeting**) (**closet someone** or **oneself away**) to shut them or oneself away in private, eg for confidential discussion. [from Old French diminutive of *clos*, enclosed place]

close-up *noun* **1** a photograph, television shot, etc taken at close range. **2** a detailed look at, or examination of, something.

closing date the last possible date on which something can be done, sent in, etc.

closing-time *noun* the time when pubs must stop serving drinks and close.

clostridium /klɒˈstrɪdɪəm/ *noun* (PL. **clostridia**) *Biol.* a rod-shaped Gram-negative bacterium of the genus Clostridium that occurs in soil and in the digestive tract of humans and animals. Species of Clostridium cause botulism (a severe form of food poisoning) and tetanus. [from Greek *kloster*, spindle]

closure — *noun* 1 the act of closing something, eg a business or a transport route. 2 a device for closing or sealing something. 3 a parliamentary procedure for cutting short a debate and taking an immediate vote. 4 the resolution of a problem or issue from a person's past. — *verb* to use this procedure for ending (a debate). [from Latin *clausura*, from *claudere*, to close]

clot — *noun* 1 a soft semi-solid mass, especially one formed during the coagulation of blood. 2 *colloq.* a fool. — *verb intrans., trans.* (**clotted**, **clotting**) to form or cause to form (a soft semi-solid mass). [from Anglo-Saxon *clott*, lump, mass]

. . . .

⊟ *noun* 1 lump, mass, thrombus, thrombosis, clotting, coagulation. 2 fool, idiot, *colloq.* dope, *slang* wally, *colloq.* nitwit, *colloq.* twit, *colloq.* chump. *verb* coalesce, curdle, coagulate, congeal, thicken, solidify, set, gel.

. . . .

cloth /klɒθ/ *noun* 1 woven, knitted, or felted material. 2 (*often in compounds*) *a piece of fabric for a special use: table-cloth.* 3 (**the cloth**) the clergy. [from Anglo-Saxon *clath*]

. . . .

⊟ 1 fabric, material, stuff, textile. 2 rag, face-cloth, flannel, dish-cloth, floor-cloth, duster, towel.

. . . .

cloth cap a flat cap, especially made of tweed, with a stiff brim.

clothe /kloʊð/ *verb* (PAST TENSE AND PAST PARTICIPLE **clothed**, **clad**) *old use* 1 to cover or provide with clothes. 2 to dress. 3 to cover, conceal, or disguise: *hills clothed in mist.* See also CLAD. [from Anglo-Saxon *clathian*]

. . . .

⊟ 1, 2 dress, attire. 3 cover, shroud, conceal, hide, disguise, drape.

⊟ 2 undress, strip, disrobe.

. . . .

clothes /kloʊðz, kloʊz/ *pl. noun* 1 articles of dress for covering the body, for warmth, decoration, etc. 2 same as BED-CLOTHES. [from Anglo-Saxon *clathas*, plural of *clath*, cloth]

. . . .

⊟ 1 clothing, garments, wear, attire, garb, *colloq.* gear, *colloq.* togs, outfit, *colloq.* get-up, dress, costume, wardrobe.

. . . .

Clothes include: suit, trouser suit, dress suit, catsuit, jumpsuit, tracksuit, shell suit, wet suit; dress, frock, evening dress, shirtwaister, caftan, kimono, sari; skirt, mini skirt, dirndl, pencil skirt, pinafore skirt, divided skirt, culottes, kilt, sarong; cardigan, jumper, jersey, sweater, polo neck, turtleneck, fleece, guernsey, pullover, twinset, shirt, dress shirt, sweatshirt, tee shirt, T-shirt, waistcoat, blouse, smock, tabard, tunic; trousers, jeans, *trademark* Levis, denims, slacks, cords, flannels, drainpipes, bell-bottoms, combat trousers, dungarees, leggings, pedal pushers, breeches, plus-fours, jodhpurs, Bermuda shorts, hot pants, shorts; bra, brassière, body stocking, camisole, liberty bodice, corset, girdle, garter, suspender belt, suspenders, shift, slip, petticoat, teddy, basque, briefs, pants, panties, French knickers, camiknickers, pantihose, tights, stockings; underpants, boxer shorts, Y-fronts, vest, string vest, singlet; swimsuit, bathing costume, bikini, swimming costume, swimming trunks, leotard, salopette; nightdress, *colloq.* nightie, pyjamas, bedjacket, bedsocks, dressing gown, housecoat, negligee; scarf, glove, mitten, muffler, earmuffs, legwarmers, sock, tie, bow tie, cravat, stole, shawl, belt, braces, cummerbund, veil, yashmak. *See also* **coat**; **footwear**; **hat**.

clothes horse a hinged frame on which to dry or air clothes indoors.

clothesline *noun* a rope suspended usually outdoors, on which to hang clothes to dry.

clothes moth a small drab moth, whose larvae feed on dried organic matter, including woollen materials and fur. It can be a serious household pest.

clothes peg a small clip-like or forked device for securing clothes to a clothesline.

clothes pole a fixed vertical pole for tying a clothesline to.

clothier /ˈkloʊðɪə(r)/ *noun old use* a person who makes, sells, or deals in cloth or especially men's clothing. [from Middle English *clothier*, altered from *clother*, from CLOTH]

clothing /ˈkloʊðɪŋ/ *noun* 1 clothes. 2 something forming a covering: *a clothing of snow.* [from CLOTHE]

cloth of gold a silk or woollen fabric interwoven with gold thread.

clotted cream thick cream made by slowly heating milk and taking the cream from the top.

cloud — *noun* 1 *Meteorol.* a visible floating mass of small water droplets or ice crystals suspended in the atmosphere above the Earth's surface. 2 a visible mass of particles of dust or smoke in the atmosphere. 3 a dark or dull spot. 4 a circumstance that causes anxiety. 5 a state of gloom, depression, or suspicion: *he left the firm under a cloud.* — *verb* 1 (*usually* **cloud over**) to become overcast with clouds. 2 *trans., intrans.* (*usually* **cloud over** or **cloud something over**) to make or become misty or cloudy. 3 (*also* **cloud over**) *said of the face* to develop a troubled expression. 4 to make dull or confused. 5 to spoil or mar. — **on cloud nine** *colloq.* extremely happy. **up in the clouds** *colloq.* out of touch with reality. **with one's head in the clouds** *colloq.* preoccupied with one's own thoughts. [from Anglo-Saxon *clud*, hill, mass of rock]

. . . .

⊟ *noun* 2 vapour, haze, mist, fog. 3 fog, haze, blur, shadow. 4 shadow. 5 gloom, darkness, suspicion. *verb* 2 mist, fog, blur. 4 dull, dim, veil, shroud, obscure, muddle, confuse, obfuscate. 5 shadow, overshadow, eclipse.

⊟ *verb* 1, 2 clear.

. . . .

cloud base *Meteorol.* the height above sea level of the lowest part of a cloud.

cloudburst *noun* a sudden heavy downpour of rain over a small area.

cloud chamber *Physics* a device for detecting subatomic particles, consisting of a chamber containing vapour prone to condensing to form a liquid. The movement of particles forms ions, which act as centres for the condensation of liquid, and the paths of the particles then become visible as trails of mist.

cloud-cuckoo-land *noun* a place where everything goes well, the apparent dwelling-place of over-optimistic people who refuse to see the problems of the real world.

cloudily *adv.* in a cloudy way.

cloudiness *noun* being cloudy.

cloudless *adj.*, *said especially of the sky* having no clouds; clear and bright.

cloudy *adj.* (**cloudier**, **cloudiest**) 1 full of clouds; overcast. 2 *said eg of a liquid* not clear; milky. 3 confused; muddled.

. . . .

⊟ 1 overcast, dull, sunless, leaden, lowering, dark, sombre. 2 milky, muddy, dim, murky, nebulous, hazy, misty, foggy, blurred, blurry, opaque, indistinct, obscure. 3 confused, muddled, hazy, foggy, blurred, blurry, indistinct, obscure.

⊟ CLEAR. 1 bright, sunny, cloudless. 2 transparent.

. . . .

clout — *noun* 1 *colloq.* a blow. 2 *colloq.* influence or power. 3 *dialect* a piece of clothing. — *verb colloq.* to hit. [from Anglo-Saxon *clut*, piece of cloth]

clove[1] *noun* 1 an evergreen tree (Eugenia caryophyllata) of the myrtle family, native to Indonesia and widely cultivated elsewhere, having lance-shaped leaves, and yellow flowers borne in terminal clusters. **2** a spice obtained from the dried flower buds of this tree, used as a flavouring in meat and bakery products. [from French *clou*, nail, from its shape]

clove[2] *noun* any of the segments into which a compound bulb, such as that of garlic, is divided. [from Anglo-Saxon *clufu*, bulb]

clove[3] see CLEAVE[1].

cloven *adj. old use, poetic* split; divided. [past participle of CLEAVE[1]]

cloven hoof 1 the partially divided hoof of any of various mammals, including cattle, pigs, goats, and deer. **2** in folklore, etc, the partly divided hoof of the Devil.

clover *noun* a small herbaceous plant of the genus Trifolium that grows wild in temperate regions. It has leaves divided into three leaflets (a four-leafed clover is sometimes considered lucky), and small dense red or white flowers. It is widely cultivated as a fodder crop for animal livestock, and is a good source of nectar for honey. — **in clover** *colloq.* in great comfort and luxury. [from Anglo-Saxon *clæfre*]

cloverleaf *noun* an arrangement of curving roads at the junction of two motorways, etc, having, from the air, the shape of a four-leaved clover.

clown — *noun* **1** a comic performer in a circus or pantomime, usually wearing ridiculous clothes and make-up. **2** someone who behaves comically. **3** *derog.* a fool. — *verb intrans.* (*usually* **clown about** or **around**) to behave ridiculously.

. . . .
▣ *noun* **1** jester, fool, pierrot, harlequin. **2** buffoon, comic, comedian, joker. **3** fool, idiot, *colloq.* nitwit. *verb* fool about or around.
. . . .

clownish *adj.* like a clown; foolish or playful.

clownishly *adv.* in a clownish way.

clownishness *noun* being like a clown.

cloy *verb intrans.* to become distasteful through excess, especially of sweetness. [variant of earlier *acloy*, originally meaning to nail, from Latin *clavus*, nail]

cloying *adj.* sickly sweet.

cloze testing a procedure used to establish a student's level of comprehension of a reading passage. The passage is presented with words omitted at regular intervals and the student must supply the missing words, or plausible substitutes. Cloze testing is mainly used in foreign language teaching. [formed from CLOSURE]

club — *noun* **1** a stick, usually thicker at one end, used as a weapon. **2** a stick with a specially shaped head, for playing golf or putting with. **3** (*also* **Indian club**) a bottle-shaped wooden object for swinging and throwing, for exercise. **4** a society or association. **5** the place where such a group meets. **6** a building with dining, reading, and sleeping facilities for members. **7** same as NIGHTCLUB. **8** (**clubs**) one of the four suits of playing-cards with black cloverleaf-shaped symbols. **9** one of the playing-cards of this suit. — *verb* (**clubbed, clubbing**) **1** to beat or strike with a club. **2** (**club together**) to contribute money jointly for a special purpose. — **in the club** or **pudding club** *colloq.* pregnant. [from Norse *klubba*, cudgel]

. . . .
▣ *noun* **1** cosh, truncheon, cudgel, mace, bludgeon. **2** stick, bat. **4** association, society, company, league, guild, order, union, fraternity, group, set, circle, clique. *verb* **1** hit, strike, beat, bash, clout, *slang* clobber, bludgeon, *colloq.* cosh, batter, pummel.
. . . .

clubbable *adj.* friendly; able to mix well socially.

clubbed *adj., said of the fingers* thickened at the tips.

clubbing — **go clubbing** to go dancing at a nightclub.

club foot a congenital deformity (present from birth), in the commonest form of which the sole of one or both feet is twisted downwards and inwards, so that the affected

person walks on the outer edge of the upper part of the foot.

clubhouse *noun* a building where a club meets, especially the premises of a sports club.

clubmoss *noun Bot.* a spore-bearing vascular plant of the genus Lycopodium, related to ferns and horsetails.

clubroot *noun Bot.* a disease of plants of the cabbage family (Cruciferae), characterized by gall-like swellings of the roots and discoloration of the leaves, caused by the parasitic slime mould Plasmodiophora brassicae.

cluck — *noun* the sound that a hen makes. — *verb intrans.* **1** *said of a hen* to make clucks. **2** to express disapproval by making a similar sound with the tongue. [imitative]

clue — *noun* **1** a fact or circumstance the discovery of which helps one to solve a mystery or to make progress in investigating something, eg a crime. **2** a word or words representing, in a more or less disguised form, something to be entered in a crossword. — *verb trans., intrans.* (**cluing**) (**clue someone in** or **up**) *colloq.* to inform them. — **not have a clue** *colloq.* to be completely ignorant about something. [variant of *clew*, ball of thread, from its use in finding the way out of a maze]

. . . .
▣ *noun* **1** hint, lead, pointer, tip, tip-off, suggestion, idea, notion, sign, indication, evidence, trace, suspicion, inkling, intimation.
. . . .

clueless *adj. derog.* stupid, incompetent, or ignorant.

clump — *noun* **1** a group of eg trees, plants, or people standing close together. **2** a dull heavy sound, eg of treading feet. — *verb* **1** *intrans.* to walk with a heavy tread. **2** *trans., intrans.* to form into clumps. [related to Dutch *klompe*, lump, mass]

. . . .
▣ *noun* **1** cluster, bundle, bunch, mass, tuft, thicket. **2** tramp, clomp, stamp, stomp, plod, thump, thud. *verb* **1** tramp, clomp, stamp, stomp, plod, lumber, thump, thud.
. . . .

clumpiness *noun* being clumpy.

clumpy *adj.* (**clumpier, clumpiest**) **1** large and heavy: *clumpy shoes.* **2** clumping.

clumsily *adv.* in a clumsy way.

clumsiness *noun* being clumsy.

clumsy *adj.* (**clumsier, clumsiest**) **1** unskilful with the hands or awkward and ungainly in movement. **2** badly or awkwardly made. [from Middle English *clumse*, to be numb with cold]

. . . .
▣ **1** awkward, ungainly, unco-ordinated, bungling, unskilful, *colloq.* ham-fisted, unhandy, inept, bumbling, blundering, lumbering, gauche, *colloq.* gawky, ungraceful, uncouth. **2** crude, ill-made, shapeless, rough, unwieldy, heavy, bulky, cumbersome.
▣ GRACEFUL, ELEGANT. **1** careful, skilful, dexterous.
. . . .

clung see CLING.

clunk — *noun* the sound of a heavy, especially metal, object striking something. — *verb intrans., trans.* to make or cause to make this sound. [imitative]

cluster — *noun* **1** a small group or gathering. **2** a number of flowers growing together on one stem. — *verb trans., intrans.* (**clustered, clustering**) to form into a cluster or clusters. [from Anglo-Saxon *clyster*, bunch]

. . . .
▣ *noun* **1** bunch, clump, batch, group, knot, mass, crowd, gathering, collection, assembly. *verb* bunch, group, gather, collect, assemble.
. . . .

clutch[1] — *verb* **1** to grasp tightly. **2** *intrans.* (**clutch at something**) to try to grasp it. — *noun* **1** (*usually* **clutches**) control or power. **2** any device for connecting and disconnecting two rotating shafts, especially the device in a motor vehicle that transmits or prevents the transmission of the driving force from the engine to the gearbox. **3** *in a motor vehicle* the pedal that controls such a device. The driver depresses the pedal in order to disconnect the engine from the gearbox when changing gear. — **clutch at straws** to try anything, however unlikely, in one's desperation. [from Anglo-Saxon *clyccan*]

▤ *verb* **1** grasp, hold, clasp, grip, hang on to, seize, snatch, grab, catch, grapple, embrace. **2** grasp at, snatch at.

clutch² *noun* **1** a collection of eggs laid in a single nest or at the same time. **2** a brood of newly hatched birds, especially chickens. [from Norse *klekja*, to hatch]

clutch bag a small handbag without handles, held in the hand or under the arm.

clutter — *noun* an untidy accumulation of objects, or the confused, overcrowded state caused by it. — *verb* (**cluttered, cluttering**) (**clutter something up**) to overcrowd it or make it untidy with accumulated objects. [variant of earlier *clotter*, from CLOT]

▤ *noun* litter, mess, jumble, untidiness, disorder, disarray, muddle, confusion. *verb* crowd, overcrowd, litter, encumber, fill, cover, strew, scatter.

Cm *symbol Chem.* curium.

cm *abbrev.* centimetre.

CMG *abbrev.* Companion of the Order of St Michael and St George.

CNAA *abbrev.* Council for National Academic Awards.

CNN *abbrev.* Cable News Network (USA).

CNR *abbrev.* Canadian National Railway.

CO *abbrev.* **1** *as an international vehicle mark* Colombia. **2** Colorado. **3** Commanding Officer.

Co¹ *abbrev.* **1** Company. **2** County.

Co² *symbol Chem.* cobalt.

co- *prefix* forming words meaning 'with, together, jointly': *co-star* / *co-exist* / *co-operate*.

c/o *abbrev.* care of.

coach — *noun* **1** a railway carriage. **2** a bus designed for long-distance travel. **3** *Hist.* a closed horse-drawn carriage. **4** a trainer or instructor in a sport, etc, or a private tutor, especially one who prepares pupils for examinations. — *verb trans., intrans.* to train in a sport, etc, or teach privately. — **drive a coach and horses through something** *colloq.* to ignore and therefore make nonsense of laws, regulations, existing arrangements, etc. [from Old French *coche*, from Hungarian *kocsi*, from Kocs in Hungary]

▤ *noun* **4** trainer, instructor, tutor, teacher. *verb* train, drill, instruct, teach, tutor, cram, prepare.

coachbuilder *noun* a person who builds the bodies of motor vehicles.

coaching *noun* **1** tutoring, instruction. **2** *Hist.* travelling by coach.

coachman *noun Hist.* the driver of a horse-drawn coach.

coachwork *noun* the painted outer bodywork of a motor or rail vehicle.

coagulant /koʊˈæɡjʊlənt/ *noun* any substance that causes or facilitates clotting, curdling, or the formation of a soft semi-solid mass, especially the clotting of blood.

coagulate /koʊˈæɡjʊleɪt/ — *verb intrans., trans.* **1** to cause (a liquid) to clot, curdle, or form a soft semi-solid mass. **2** *said of a liquid* to become clotted or curdled, or to form a soft semi-solid mass. — *noun* the soft semi-solid mass produced by this process. [from Latin *coagulare*]

▤ *verb* CLOT, CURDLE, CONGEAL, THICKEN, SOLIDIFY, GEL.

coagulation /koʊæɡjʊˈleɪʃən/ *noun* **1** the action or process of coagulating. **2** forming or uniting into a mass.

coal *noun* **1** a hard brittle generally brown or black combustible rock consisting mainly of carbon, and formed by the compaction of partially decomposed plant material. It is widely burned as a fuel, and is also used to make coke. **2** a piece of this. — **coals to Newcastle** something brought to a place where it is already plentiful. **haul someone over the coals** *colloq.* to scold them severely. **heap coals of fire on someone's head** to make them feel guilty by repaying evil with good. [from Anglo-Saxon *col*]

coalesce /koʊəˈlɛs/ *verb intrans.* to come together so as to form a single mass. [from Latin *co-*, together + *alescere*, to grow]

coalescence /koʊəˈlɛsəns/ *noun* growing into each other; fusion.

coalescent *adj.* **1** that coalesces. **2** coalescing. **3** growing together.

coalface *noun* **1** the exposed face in a coalmine from which coal is being cut. **2** the area where the essential practical work is carried on in any particular field of activity.

coalfield *noun* a district or area containing rich underground deposits of coal.

coal-fired *adj.* fuelled by coal.

coalfish *noun* same as COLEY.

coal gas a flammable gas, consisting mainly of hydrogen and methane, obtained by the destructive distillation of coal, or by heating coal in the absence of air. Formerly used as a domestic fuel, it has now been superseded by natural gas.

coalition /koʊəˈlɪʃən/ *noun Politics* **1** a combination or temporary alliance, especially between political parties. **2** (*in full* **coalition government**) government by, or a government made up of, representatives of two or more political parties. Coalition governments are more common in electoral systems using proportional representation. [from Latin *coalitio*]

▤ **1** combination, alliance, merger, amalgamation, association, affiliation, union, compact, league, bloc, federation, confederation, confederacy, integration, fusion.

coalmine *noun* a place where coal is mined.

coal tar a thick black liquid obtained as a by-product during the manufacture of coke. It was formerly a major source of organic compounds, eg benzene and phenol, for the manufacture of drugs, dyes, etc, but most of these compounds are now obtained from petroleum or natural gas.

coal tit a small bird belonging to the tit family, native to Europe, Asia, and Africa, and having a large head with a glossy black crown and white cheeks, and a characteristic white patch on the nape of its neck.

coaming *noun Naut.* the raised edging round the hatches on a ship, to keep out water.

coarse *adj.* **1** rough or open in texture. **2** rough or crude; not refined. **3** *said of behaviour, speech, etc* rude or offensive.

▤ **1** rough, bristly, scratchy. **2** rough, crude, unpolished, unfinished, uneven, lumpy, unpurified, unrefined, unprocessed. **3** rude, offensive, foul-mouthed, boorish, loutish, bawdy, ribald, earthy, smutty, vulgar, crude, impolite, indelicate, improper, indecent, immodest.
▤ **1, 2** smooth, fine. **3** refined, sophisticated, polite, genteel.

coarse fish any freshwater fish that does not belong to the salmon family.

coarse fishing the sport of fishing for coarse fish.

coarsely *adv.* with a coarse manner.

coarsen *verb trans., intrans.* (**coarsened, coarsening**) to make or become coarse.

coarseness *noun* being coarse.

coast — *noun* the zone of land that borders the sea; the seashore. — *verb intrans.* **1** to travel downhill, eg on a bicycle or in a motor vehicle, using no kind of propelling power, relying on gravity or momentum. **2** to progress smoothly and satisfactorily without much effort. — **the coast is clear** *colloq.* there is no danger of being spotted or caught. [from Old French *coste*]

◼ *noun* coastline, seaboard, shore, beach, seaside. *verb* **1** freewheel. **2** sail, cruise, glide, slide, drift.

coastal *adj.* **1** relating to the coast. **2** situated near a coast.

coaster *noun* **1** a vessel that sails along the coast taking goods to coastal ports. **2** a small mat or tray for slipping under a glass, bottle, decanter, etc to protect the table surface. [from COAST]

coastguard *noun* a person stationed on the coast to watch for ships or swimmers in difficulties, and to give help.

coastline *noun* the shape of the coast, especially as seen on a map or from the sea or air.

coat — *noun* **1** an outer garment with long sleeves, typically reaching to the knees. **2** a jacket. **3** the hair, fur, or wool of an animal. **4** a covering or application (of something, eg paint, dust, sugar, etc). — *verb* to cover with a layer of something. [from Old French *cote*]

◼ *noun* **3** fur, hair, fleece, pelt, hide, skin. **4** layer, coating, covering. *verb* cover, spread, paint.

Types of coat include: overcoat, greatcoat, car-coat, duffel coat, Afghan, blanket, frock coat, tailcoat, jacket, biker jacket, bomber jacket, dinner jacket, donkey jacket, hacking jacket, reefer, pea-jacket, shooting jacket, sports jacket, safari jacket, Eton jacket, matinee jacket, tuxedo, blazer, raincoat, trench coat, mackintosh, *colloq.* mac, Burberry, parka, anorak, cagoule, windcheater, jerkin, blouson, cape, cloak, poncho.

coat hanger a shaped piece of wood, plastic, or metal, with a hook, on which to hang garments.

coati /koʊˈɑːtiː, kəˈwɑːtiː/ *noun* a raccoon-like N and S American mammal, having reddish-brown fur, a long narrow muzzle with an overhanging tip, and a long banded tail. It lives in woodland and feeds on fruit and small animals. Solitary males are called *coatimundis* (or *koatimundis*). [from a S American name]

coating *noun* **1** a covering or outer layer. **2** material for making a coat or coating.

◼ **1** covering, layer, dusting, wash, coat, blanket, sheet, membrane, film, glaze, varnish, finish, veneer, lamination, overlay.

coat of arms a heraldic design consisting of a shield bearing the special symbols of a particular person, family, organization, or town.

coat of mail *Hist.* a protective garment made of interlinked metal rings, worn by soldiers.

coat-tails *pl. noun* two long pieces that hang down at the back of a man's tailcoat. — **on someone's coat-tails** enjoying undeserved success as a result of someone else's achievement.

co-author /koʊˈɔːθə(r), ˈkoʊɔːθə(r)/ — *noun* one's fellow author. — *verb* to write (a book, etc) with one or more others.

coax *verb* **1** (**coax someone into** or **out of something**) to persuade them, using flattery, promises, kind words, etc. **2** to get by coaxing. [from earlier *cokes*, fool]

◼ **1** persuade, cajole, wheedle, *colloq.* sweet-talk, *colloq.* soft-soap, flatter, beguile, allure, entice, tempt. **2** wheedle.

coaxial /koʊˈaksɪəl/ *adj.* **1** having or mounted on a common axis. **2** *Electr.* denoting a cable consisting of a conductor in the form of a metal tube surrounding and insulated from a second conductor. [from CO- + AXIS]

coaxingly *adv.* in a coaxing way.

cob *noun* **1** a short-legged sturdy horse used for riding. **2** a male swan. **3** a hazelnut or hazel tree. **4** same as CORN-COB.

cobaltic /koʊˈbɔːltɪk/ *adj.* **1** relating to or resembling cobalt. **2** denoting any of various cobalt compounds, especially those in which cobalt has a valency of three.

cobber *noun Austral., New Zealand colloq.* (often used as a form of address) a pal.

cobble [1] *noun* (*also* **cobblestone**) a rounded stone used especially formerly to surface streets. [from COB]

cobble [2] *verb* **1** *trans., intrans.* to mend (shoes). **2** (**cobble something together**) to construct or concoct it roughly or hastily. [back-formation from COBBLER]

cobbled *adj.* having a cobbled surface.

cobbler *noun* a person who mends shoes.

cobblers *noun slang* nonsense. [rhyming slang: *cobblers' awls*, ie *balls*]

COBOL /ˈkoʊbɒl/ *or* **Cobol** *noun* short for Common Business-Oriented Language, a high-level computer programming language, developed in the late 1950s for commercial data processing and other business applications, and still used on an international scale for this purpose. It requires large amounts of memory, but has the advantage of using terms that closely resemble normal English.

cobra /ˈkoʊbrə, ˈkɒbrə/ *noun* any of various species of venomous snake, usually about 2m long, found in Africa and Asia. When threatened, it rears up and movable ribs spread the skin behind the head to form a flattened hood. [from Portuguese, from Latin *colubra*, snake]

cobweb *noun* **1** a web formed of fine sticky threads spun by a spider. **2** a single thread of such a web. [from Middle English *coppeweb*, from Anglo-Saxon *atorcoppe*, spider]

cobwebby *adj.* **1** full of cobwebs. **2** like a cobweb.

coca *noun* **1** either of two shrubs (Erythroxylon coca or E.truxinense), native to S America, the leaves of which contain cocaine and are chewed as a stimulant. **2** the dried leaves of this plant, which are used as a source of cocaine. [from Spanish *coca*, from Quechua *kuka*]

cocaine *noun Medicine* an alkaloid drug obtained from the leaves of the coca plant, sometimes used medicinally as a local anaesthetic.

coccus *noun* (PL. **cocci**) *Biol.* a spherical bacterium. [from Greek *kokkos*, berry]

coccyx /ˈkɒksɪks/ *noun* (PL. **coccyges**, **coccyxes**) *Anat.*, *in humans and certain apes* a small triangular bone at the base of the spine. In humans it consists of four vestigial vertebrae fused together. [from Greek *coccyx*, cuckoo, from its triangular beak]

cochineal /ˈkɒtʃɪniːl, kɒtʃɪˈniːl/ *noun* **1** a bright red pigment widely used as a food colouring, eg in alcoholic drinks. **2** an insect found in Mexico and the West Indies, the dried body of which yields this dye. [from Spanish *cochinilla*]

cochlea /ˈkɒklɪə/ *noun* (PL. **cochleae**) *Anat.* in the inner ear of mammals, crocodiles, and birds, a hollow spirally coiled structure that converts the vibrations of sound waves into nerve impulses, which can then be interpreted by the brain as sound. [from Greek *cochlias*, snail with spiral shell]

cochlear *adj.* relating to or in the region of the cochlea.

cock [1] — *noun* **1** a male bird, especially an adult male chicken. **2** a stopcock for controlling the flow of liquid, gas, etc. **3** the hammer of a gun, raised and let go by the trigger. **4** *coarse slang* the penis. **5** *coarse slang* nonsense. **6** *slang* a pal, usually used as a form of address. — *verb* **1** *trans., intrans.* to lift; to stick up. **2** to turn in a particular direction: *cock an ear towards the door.* **3** to draw back the hammer of (a gun). **4** to set (one's hat) at an angle. — **go off at half cock** to begin too soon, without being fully prepared. [from Anglo-Saxon *cocc*]

cock² *noun* a small pile of hay, etc. [related to Norse *kökkr*, lump]

cockade *noun Hist.* a feather or a rosette of ribbon worn on the hat as a badge. [from COCK¹]

cock-a-hoop *adj. colloq.* jubilant; exultant.

cock-a-leekie *noun* soup made from chicken boiled with leeks. [from COCK¹ + LEEK]

cock-and-bull story *noun colloq.* an unlikely story, especially one used as an excuse or explanation.

cockatoo *noun* any of 16 species of the parrot family, usually found in woodland areas in Australasia, and resembling a parrot but with a large brightly coloured crest on its head that can be erected at will. [from Malay *kakatua*]

cockatrice /ˈkɒkətrɪs, ˈkɒkətraɪs/ *noun 1 Mythol.* a monster with the head, wings, and legs of a cock and the body and tail of a serpent. **2** *Biblical* a poisonous snake. [from Old French *cocatris*]

cockchafer *noun* a large brown beetle, native to Europe and Asia, having a black pointed hind end that projects beyond the rigid wing-cases or *elytra*. [from COCK¹ + *chafer*, beetle]

cock-crow *noun* dawn; early morning.

cocked hat *Hist.* a three-cornered hat with upturned brim. — **knock into a cocked hat** *colloq.* to surpass spectacularly or defeat utterly. [from COCK¹]

cocker (*in full* **cocker spaniel**) a breed of dog developed in the USA from the English cocker spaniel, recognized as a separate breed in 1941, and having a small compact body, a long white coat with black or brown markings, and long ears set low on its head. [from WOODCOCK, which it was bred to hunt]

cockerel /ˈkɒkərəl, ˈkɒkrəl/ *noun* a young cock. [a diminutive of COCK¹]

cock-eyed *adj.* **1** crooked; lopsided. **2** senseless; crazy; impractical. [from COCK¹]

cockfight *noun* a fight between cocks armed with sharp metal spurs.

cockfighting *noun* contests in which cocks are set to fight each other.

cockily *adv.* with a cocky manner.

cockiness *noun* a cocky manner.

cockle *noun* any of about 200 species of marine bivalve mollusc, especially Cardium edule, which has a white to mid-brown rounded shell consisting of two more or less equal valves with 22 to 26 coarse ribs. — **warm the cockles of one's heart** *colloq.* to delight and gladden one. [from French *coquille*, shell]

cockleshell *noun* **1** the shell of the cockle. **2** any tiny insubstantial boat.

cockney — *noun* (PL. **cockneys**) **1** (*often* **Cockney**) a native of London, especially of the East End. **2** the dialect used by Cockneys. — *adj.* relating to Cockneys or their dialect. [from Middle English *cokeney*, a cock's egg (ie a misshapen egg), contemptuous name for a towndweller]

cockpit *noun* **1** the compartment for the pilot and crew aboard an aircraft. **2** the driver's seat in a racing-car. **3** the part of a small yacht, etc containing the wheel and tiller. **4** *Hist.* a pit into which cocks were put to fight each other. **5** any scene of prolonged conflict, especially in war. [from COCK¹ + PIT¹]

cockroach *noun* a large insect with a flattened body, long slender antennae, and biting mouthparts, found mainly in the tropics, where it feeds nocturnally on decaying animal and vegetable matter. [from Spanish *cucaracha*]

cockscomb *noun* **1** the fleshy red crest on a cock's head. **2** (*also* **coxcomb**) *old derog. use* a conceited fellow. [from *cock's comb*]

cocksure *adj.* foolishly over-confident. [from COCK¹]

cocktail *noun* **1** a mixed drink of spirits and other liquors. **2** a mixed dish especially of seafood and mayonnaise. **3** a mixture of different things.

cocktail stick a short thin pointed wooden stick on which to impale small items of food for serving at parties, etc.

cock-up *noun slang* a mess or muddle resulting from incompetence. [from COCK¹]

cocky *adj.* (**cockier**, **cockiest**) *derog.* cheekily self-confident. [from COCK¹]

⊟ cocksure, over-confident, swaggering, brash, arrogant, bumptious, self-important, self-assured, conceited, vain, swollen-headed, egotistical.
⊞ humble, modest, shy.

coco see COCONUT.

cocoa /ˈkoʊkoʊ/ *noun* **1** the seed of the cacao tree (Theobroma cacao). **2** a powder prepared from the seeds of the cacao tree after they have been fermented, dried, and roasted. **3** a drink prepared by mixing this powder with hot milk or water. [a variant of CACAO]

cocoa bean one of the seeds from the cacao tree (cocoa plant) after it has been fermented, removed from the pod, and roasted. Cocoa beans form the raw material for chocolate manufacture.

cocoa butter a pale yellow fat obtained from cocoa beans, used as a base in the manufacture of chocolate and in cosmetics.

coconut *noun* **1** (*in full* **coconut palm**) a tropical palm tree (Cocos nucifera) with a characteristic curved trunk, up to 30m in height, with a crown of feathery leaves up to 6m long, probably native to Polynesia, and a characteristic tree of oceanic islands. **2** the large single-seeded fruit of this tree, with a thick fibrous outer husk and a hard woody inner shell enclosing a layer of white edible flesh and a central cavity, containing a clear sweet-tasting liquid known as coconut milk. [from Portuguese *coco*, grimace or ugly face, from the face-like markings on a coconut]

coconut shy a stall at a fair where contestants throw balls to knock coconuts off stands.

cocoon — *noun* the protective silky covering that many animals, eg spiders, earthworms, spin around their eggs; a similar covering that a larva spins around itself before it develops into a pupa. — *verb* **1** to wrap up as if in a cocoon. **2** to protect from the problems of everyday life. [from Provençal *coucoun*, eggshell]

cocooning *noun* the practice of choosing to spend one's spare time with a partner or one's family, rather than taking part in more social activities.

cocotte /kɒˈkɒt/ *noun* a small lidded pot for oven and table use, especially intended for an individual portion. [from French *cocotte*]

co-counselling *noun* a form of self-help therapy in which two or more people take turns at being client and counsellor.

cod¹ *noun* (PL. **cod**) a large soft-finned fish, found mainly in the N Atlantic Ocean, with a plump olive-green or brown body, covered with spots, and a silvery underside. It is second only in importance to the herring as a food fish in western countries. However cod populations are now becoming depleted by overfishing.

cod² *slang* — *noun* **1** a hoax. **2** a parody. — *verb* (**codded**, **codding**) **1** *intrans., trans.* to hoax (someone). **2** to parody.

cod³ *noun slang* nonsense. [from CODSWALLOP]

coda *noun Mus.* a passage added at the end of a movement or piece, to bring it to a satisfying conclusion. [from Italian *coda*, tail]

coddle *verb* **1** to cook (eggs) gently in hot, rather than boiling, water. **2** to pamper, mollycoddle, or over-protect. [variant of *caudle*, spiced egg drink for an invalid, from Latin *calidus*, warm]

code — *noun* **1** a system of words, letters, or symbols, used in place of those really intended, for secrecy's or brevity's sake. **2** a set of signals for sending messages, etc. **3** *Comput.* a set of symbols that represent numbers, letters, etc in binary form so that information can be stored or exchanged between different computer systems, eg the ASCII code. **4** *Comput.* the set of written instructions or statements that make up a computer program. **5** a group of numbers and letters used as means of identification. **6** a set of principles of behaviour. **7** a systematically organized set of laws. — *verb* **1** to put (a message, etc) into a code. **2** to generate a set of written instructions or statements that make up a computer program. [from Old French, from Latin *codex*, book]

■ *noun* **1** cipher, secret language. **6** principles, ethics, rules, regulations, system, custom, convention, etiquette, manners.

codeine /'koʊdi:n/ *noun Medicine* a morphine derivative that relieves mild to moderate pain, has a sedative effect, and suppresses the coughing reflex. It causes constipation, and is sometimes used to treat diarrhoea. [from Greek *kodeia*, poppy head]

co-dependency *noun* a condition in which an individual seeks to avoid facing his or her emotional or psychological problems by caring for or controlling a person who is dependent on alcohol, drugs, etc. Such an individual is considered to be 'addicted' to playing the role of helper.

code word a word or phrase of special and secret significance, agreed on by its users for a purpose.

codex *noun* (PL. **codices**) an ancient manuscript bound in book form. [from Latin *codex*, set of tablets, book]

codfish (PL. **codfish**, **codfishes**) *noun* a cod.

codger *noun colloq.* a man, especially an old and strange man. [perhaps a variant of CADGER]

codicil /'koʊdɪsɪl/ *noun Legal* a short addition to a will, added after the will has been written. [from Latin *codicillus*, diminutive of *codex*, book]

codification /koʊdɪfɪ'keɪʃən/ *noun* **1** the process of codifying. **2** the state of being codified.

codify /'koʊdɪfaɪ/ *verb* (**codifies**, **codified**) to arrange (laws, etc) into a systematic code.

codling¹ or **codlin** *noun* any of several varieties of apple with a long tapering shape. [from Middle English *querdling*]

codling² *noun* a cod, especially a young one.

cod-liver oil a pale yellow oil extracted from the liver of the cod and related fish, widely used medicinally as a source of vitamins A and D.

codon /'koʊdɒn/ *noun Genetics* in a molecule messenger of RNA, a set of three bases that is specific for one particular amino acid. The order of codons determines the order in which amino acids are added to form a chain during the manufacture of a protein molecule.

codpiece *noun Hist.* a flap of material attached to a man's breeches, covering his genitals. [from earlier *cod*, scrotum]

codswallop *noun slang* nonsense.

co-ed — *abbrev. colloq.* co-education or co-educational. — *noun North Amer., esp. US* a female student in a coeducational school or college.

co-education *noun* education of pupils of both sexes in the same school or college.

co-educational *adj.* teaching both sexes together.

coefficient /koʊɪ'fɪʃənt/ *noun* **1** *Maths.* in an algebraic expression, a number or other constant factor, which may be represented by a letter, placed before a variable to signify that the variable is to be multiplied by that factor, eg in the expression $3x^2$, the coefficient of x^2 is 3, and in the equation $ax^2 + bx + c = 0$, a is the coefficient of x^2 and b is the coefficient of x. **2** *Physics* a number or parameter that is a measure of a specified property of a particular substance under certain conditions, eg the coefficient of viscosity.

coelacanth /'si:ləkanθ/ *noun* a marine bony fish (Latimeria chalumnae), thought to have become extinct about 70 million years ago, until a specimen was caught off the coast of South Africa by a trawler in 1938. [from Greek *koilos*, hollow + *akantha*, spine]

coelenterate /sə'lentəreɪt/ *noun Zool.* any invertebrate animal of the phylum Coelenterata. They are mainly marine organisms, many of which possess stinging cells that are used for capturing prey, and for defence, eg jellyfish,

sea anemones, corals. [from Greek *koilos*, hollow + *enteron*, intestine]

coeliac or **celiac** /'si:lɪak/ — *adj.* **1** relating to or in the region of the abdomen. **2** relating to coeliac disease. — *noun* a person suffering from coeliac disease. [from Greek *koilia*, belly]

coeliac disease *Medicine* a condition in which the lining of the small intestine is abnormally sensitive to the protein gluten, found in wheat, rye, and barley. Food is not digested and absorbed properly, giving rise to symptoms of malnutrition, including deficiency disorders, as well as fatigue and breathlessness.

coelom /'si:loʊm/ *noun Zool.* the main body cavity in multicellular animals, which typically forms the cavity around the gut in annelids (eg earthworms), echinoderms (eg starfish), and vertebrates. [from Greek *koiloma*, cavity]

coenobite /'si:nəbaɪt/ *noun* a member of a monastic community. [from Greek *koinos*, common + *bios*, life]

coenobitic /si:nə'bɪtɪk/ *adj.* relating to, or characterized by, a coenobite or the monastic way of life.

co-enzyme *noun Biochem.* an organic molecule (such as a vitamin) that bonds with a specific enzyme only while a biochemical reaction is being catalysed. It is essential to, but remains unaffected by, the reaction.

coerce /koʊ'ɜ:s/ *verb* (**coerce someone into something**) to force or compel them, using threats, etc. [from Latin *coercere*, to restrain]

■ force, compel, drive, constrain, pressurize, bully, intimidate, browbeat, bludgeon, bulldoze, dragoon, pressgang.

coercible *adj.* capable of being coerced.

coercion *noun* **1** the action of coercing. **2** constraint, restraint, force.

■ **1** forcing, compulsion, bullying, intimidation, browbeating. **2** constraint, restraint, force, duress, pressure, threats.

coercive *adj.* **1** coercing. **2** of the nature of coercion.

coeval /koʊ'i:vəl/ *formal* — *adj.* of the same age or period of time. — *noun* someone of the same age or period of time. [from Latin *co-*, with + *aevum*, age]

co-exist *verb intrans.* **1** to exist together, or simultaneously. **2** to live peacefully side by side in spite of differences, etc.

co-existence *noun* a state of co-existing.

co-existent *adj.* existing together.

co-extensive *adj.* covering the same distance or time.

C of E *abbrev.* Church of England.

coffee *noun* **1** an evergreen tree or shrub of the genus Coffea. It belongs to the madder family (Rubiaceae), and has oval leaves, white fragrant flowers, and red fleshy fruits which typically contain two seeds (the coffee beans) rich in caffeine. **2** the seeds of this plant, roasted whole or ground to a powder. **3** a drink that contains the stimulant caffeine and is prepared from the roasted and ground 'beans' (the seeds) of the coffee plant, especially Coffea arabica. **4** the brown colour of the drink when mixed with milk. [from Turkish *kahveh*, from Arabic *qahwah*, coffee or wine]

coffee bar a place where coffee and snacks are sold at a counter.

coffee bean the seed of the coffee tree, rich in caffeine, often roasted and ground and used to make coffee.

coffee break a pause for a cup of coffee during working hours.

coffee house *Hist.* an establishment serving coffee, used by fashionable people especially in the 18c.

coffee mill a machine for grinding coffee beans.

coffee table a small low table.

coffee-table book *often derog.* a large expensive highly illustrated book, suitable for visitors to browse through.

coffer *noun* **1** a large chest for holding valuables. **2** (**cof-**

fers) a treasury or supply of funds. **3** *Archit.* a hollow or sunken section in the elaborate panelling or plasterwork of a ceiling. [from Old French *cofre*, from Greek *kophinos*, basket]

▤ **1** casket, case, box, chest, trunk, strongbox, repository.

cofferdam *noun* a caisson.

coffin *noun* a box in which to bury or cremate a corpse. [from Old French *cofin*, from Greek *kophinos*, basket]

cog *noun* **1** any of the projections along the rim of a toothed wheel, such as a gear wheel, that engage with the projections on another toothed wheel in order to transmit motion. **2** a small gear wheel. **3** a person unimportant in, though necessary to, a process or organization. [from Middle English *cogge*]

cogency /ˈkoʊdʒənsɪ/ *noun* convincing or persuasive force.

cogent /ˈkoʊdʒənt/ *adj., said of arguments, reasons, etc* strong; persuasive; convincing. [from Latin *cogere*, to drive]

cogently *adv.* in a cogent way.

cogitate /ˈkɒdʒɪteɪt/ *verb intrans.* to think deeply; to ponder. [from Latin *cogitare*, to think]

cogitation /kɒdʒɪˈteɪʃən/ *noun* deep thought; meditation.

cogitative /ˈkɒdʒɪtətɪv, ˈkɒdʒɪteɪtɪv/ *adj.* having the power of thinking; given to cogitating.

cognac /ˈkɒnjak/ *noun* a high-quality French brandy from Cognac in SW France.

cognate *adj.* **(cognate with someone** or **something) 1** descended from or related to a common ancestor. **2** *said of words or languages* derived from the same original form. **3** related; akin. [from Latin *co-*, with + *gnasci*, to be born]

cognition /kɒgˈnɪʃən/ *noun Psychol.* the combination of mental activities, which include perception, memory, reasoning, judgement, problem-solving, language, symbolism, and conceptual thought, that enable a person to experience and learn about his or her environment. [from Latin *cognitio*, study, knowledge]

▤ perception, comprehension, understanding, awareness, reasoning, knowledge, apprehension, discernment, insight, intelligence.

cognitive *adj.* relating to cognition or capable of cognition.

cognitively *adv.* in terms of cognition.

cognitive therapy *Psychol.* a form of psychotherapy based on the view that the manner in which people perceive themselves and the world about them strongly influences their feelings and emotions.

cognizance or **cognisance** /ˈkɒgnɪzəns, ˈkɒnɪzəns/ *noun* **1** knowledge; understanding; perception; awareness. **2** the range or scope of one's awareness or knowledge. **3** *Legal* the right of a court to deal with a particular matter. **4** *Heraldry* a distinctive mark or sign. — **take cognizance of something** to take it into consideration. [from Old French *conoisance*, from Latin *cognoscere*, to know; g added later under the influence of Latin]

cognizant or **cognisant** /ˈkɒgnɪzənt, ˈkɒnɪzənt/ *adj.* **(cognizant of something)** aware of it.

cognomen /kɒgˈnoʊmən/ *noun* **1** *Roman Hist.* a Roman's third name, often in origin an epithet or nickname. **2** a nickname or surname. [from Latin, *co-*, with + *nomen*, name]

cognoscenti /kɒnjoʊˈʃentiː/ *pl. noun* knowledgeable or refined people; connoisseurs. [Italian, from Latin *cognoscere*, to know]

cogwheel *noun* a wheel with cogs.

cohabit *verb intrans.* **(cohabited, cohabiting)** to live together as, or as if, husband and wife. [from Latin *cohabitare*, to live together]

cohabitation /koʊhabɪˈteɪʃən/ *noun* living together.

cohabiter or **cohabitee** *noun* a person who lives with another or others.

cohere *verb intrans.* **1** to stick together. **2** to be consistent; to have a clear logical connection or development. [from Latin *cohaerere*, to be connected]

▤ **1** stick, adhere, cling, fuse, unite, bind, combine, coalesce, consolidate. **2** be consistent, hold, hang together, square, agree, correspond.

▤ **1** separate.

coherence *noun* **1** a tendency to cohere. **2** a sticking together. **3** consistency.

coherence theory *Philos.* a theory of truth which maintains either that a proposition is true if it fits into a network of propositions, or that a necessary condition for justifying a belief is that it should fit with the believer's other beliefs.

coherent *adj.* **1** *said of a description or argument* logically and clearly developed; consistent. **2** speaking intelligibly. **3** sticking together; cohering. **4** *Physics* denoting two or more waves of electromagnetic radiation, such as light waves, that have the same frequency, and either the same phase (stage of wave motion) or a constant phase difference, eg the light waves produced by a laser. [from Latin *cohaerere*, to be connected]

▤ **1** logical, consistent, reasoned, rational, lucid, meaningful, sensible, orderly, systematic, organized. **2** articulate, intelligible, comprehensible.

▤ **1** incoherent, confused, illogical, inconsistent, irrational, meaningless. **2** incoherent, unintelligible, inarticulate, incomprehensible.

coherently *adv.* in a coherent way.

cohesion *noun* **1** the process or state of sticking together. **2** the tendency to stick together. **3** *Physics* the attraction between atoms or molecules of the same substance, eg water molecules, that produces surface tension effects such as the formation of droplets and thin films. See also ADHESION. [from Latin *cohaerere*, to stick together]

cohesive /koʊˈhiːsɪv/ *adj.* **1** having the power of cohering. **2** tending to unite into a mass. **3** *Physics* denoting the forces of attraction that exist between atoms or molecules of the same substance. See also COHESION.

cohort *noun* **1** *Hist.* in the ancient Roman army, one of the ten divisions of a legion. **2** a band of warriors. **3** a group of people sharing a common quality or belief. **4** *colloq.* a follower, supporter, or companion. [from Latin *cohors*]

COHSE *abbrev.* Confederation of Health Service Employees.

coif¹ /kɔɪf/ *noun* a close-fitting cap worn especially by women in medieval times or by nuns under a veil. [from Old French *coiffe*]

coif² — *noun* a hairstyle. — *verb* **(coiffed, coiffing)** to dress (hair); to dress the hair of. [probably from COIFFURE]

coiffeur /kwaˈfɜː(r)/ *noun* a male hairdresser. [from French *coiffeur*]

coiffeuse /kwaˈfɜːz/ *noun* a female hairdresser.

coiffure /kwaˈfʊə(r)/ — *noun* a hairstyle. — *verb* to dress (hair); to dress the hair of. [from French *coiffure*]

coil — *verb trans., intrans.* **(also coil up)** to wind round and round in loops to forms rings or a spiral. — *noun* **1** something looped into rings or a spiral. **2** a single loop in such an arrangement. **3** *Electr.* a conducting wire wound into a spiral, used to provide a magnetic field, to react mechanically (ie by moving) in response to a change in an existing magnetic field, or to introduce inductance into an electrical circuit. **4** an intrauterine device.

coin — *noun* **1** a small metal disc stamped for use as money. **2** coins generally. — *verb* **1** to manufacture (coins) from metal; to make (metal) into coins. **2** to invent (a new word or phrase). — **be coining it** *colloq.* to be making a lot of money. **the other side of the coin** the opposite way of looking at the issue under consideration. **pay someone**

back in their own coin to respond to their discourteous or unfair treatment with similar behaviour. **to coin a phrase** *ironic* used to introduce an over-used expression. [from Old French *coin*, wedge, die]

. . . .

▤ *noun* **1** piece, bit. **2** change, small change, loose change, silver, copper, cash, money. *verb* **1** mint, forge. **2** invent, make up, think up, conceive, devise, formulate, originate, create, fabricate, produce.

. . . .

coinage *noun* **1** the process of coining. **2** coins. **3** a newly invented word or phrase. **4** the official currency of a country.

coincide /kəʊɪn'saɪd/ *verb intrans.* **1** to happen at the same time. **2** to be the same; to agree. **3** to occupy the same position. [from Latin *co-*, together + *incidere*, to happen]

. . . .

▤ **1** co-exist, synchronize. **2** agree, concur, correspond, square, tally, accord, harmonize, match.

. . . .

coincidence /kəʊ'ɪnsɪdəns/ *noun* **1** the occurrence of events together or in sequence in a startling way, without any causal connection. **2** the fact of being the same.

. . . .

▤ **1** chance, accident, eventuality, *colloq.* fluke, luck, fortuity. **2** correspondence, correlation, conjunction, concurrence.

. . . .

coincident *adj.* **1** coinciding in space or time. **2** in agreement.

coincidental /kəʊɪnsɪ'dentəl/ *adj.* happening by coincidence.

. . . .

▤ chance, accidental, casual, unintentional, unplanned, *colloq.* fluky, lucky, fortuitous.

▣ deliberate, planned, intentional.

. . . .

coincidentally *adv.* by coincidence; at the same time.

coin-operated *adj.*, *said of a machine* operating on the insertion of a coin.

coir *noun* fibre from coconut shells, used for making ropes, matting, etc. [from Malayalam (a SW Indian language) *kayaru*, cord]

coital /'kɔɪtəl/ *adj.* involving or relating to sexual intercourse.

coition /kəʊ'ɪʃən/ or **coitus** /'kəʊɪtəs/ *noun* sexual intercourse. [from Latin *coire*, to unite]

coke[1] — *noun* a brittle greyish-black porous solid consisting of the residue of carbon and ash that remains after heating bituminous coal in the absence of air. It is used as a carbon source in the smelting of metal ores, and as a smokeless fuel for domestic heating. — *verb trans., intrans.* to convert coal into this material. [from dialect *colk*, core]

coke[2] *noun colloq.* cocaine.

Col. *abbrev.* **1** Colonel. **2** Colorado (US state). **3** (*also* **Col**) *Biblical* Colossians.

col /kɒl/ *noun* **1** *Geol.* in a mountain range, a pass between two adjacent peaks, or the lowest point in a ridge, often used for lines of communication, eg roads. **2** *Meteorol.* in a weather chart, a zone of low pressure and light winds between two anticyclones. [from French *col*, neck]

col- see CON-.

col. *abbrev.* **1** colour. **2** column.

cola or **kola** *noun* **1** an evergreen tree (Cola acuminata), native to Africa and cultivated in other tropical regions for its seeds (cola nuts), which are borne in pods and contain caffeine. **2** a soft-drink flavoured with the extract obtained from the seeds of this tree. [from W African *kolo*, nut]

colander /'kʌləndə(r)/ *noun* a perforated metal or plastic bowl in which to drain the water from cooked vegetables, etc. [from Latin *colare*, to strain]

cold — *adj.* **1** low in temperature; not hot or warm. **2** lower in temperature than is normal, comfortable, or pleasant. **3** *said of food* cooked, but not eaten hot: *cold meat.* **4** unfriendly. **5** comfortless; depressing. **6** *colloq.* unenthusiastic: *the suggestion left me cold.* **7** without warmth or emotion: *a cold, calculating person.* **8** sexually unresponsive. **9** *said of colours* producing a feeling of coldness rather than warmth. **10** *colloq.* unconscious, usually after a blow, fall, etc: *out cold.* **11** dead. **12** in trying to guess or find something, far from the answer or the hidden object. **13** *said of a trail or scent* not fresh; too old to follow. — *adv.* without preparation or rehearsal. — *noun* **1** lack of heat or warmth; cold weather. **2** a contagious viral infection, common in colder climates, that causes inflammation of the mucous membranes of the nose, throat, and bronchial tubes. Its symptoms are a sore throat, coughing and sneezing, a congested nose, headache, and sometimes fever, as well as a general feeling of fatigue. — **catch cold** to become ill with a cold. **get cold feet** *colloq.* to lose courage; to become reluctant to carry something out. **give someone the cold shoulder** *colloq.* to respond aloofly to them; to rebuff or snub them. **in cold blood** deliberately and unemotionally. **make someone's blood run cold** to terrify or horrify them. **out in the cold** *colloq.* ignored, disregarded, and neglected by others. **pour** or **throw cold water on something** *colloq.* to be discouraging or unenthusiastic about a plan, idea, etc. [from Anglo-Saxon *cald*]

. . . .

▤ *adj.* **1, 2** cool, chilled, chilly, chill, *colloq.* nippy, *colloq.* parky, raw, biting, bitter, wintry, frosty, icy, glacial, freezing, frozen, arctic, polar, shivery. **4** unfriendly, distant, aloof, stand-offish, reserved. **5** comfortless, depressing, cheerless, bleak, sombre, gloomy. **6** unenthusiastic, indifferent, lukewarm. **7** unfeeling, unsympathetic, undemonstrative, unresponsive, indifferent, lukewarm, stony, unmoved, cold-blooded. **8** frigid. **9** cool, icy, hard. *noun* **1** coldness, chill, chilliness, coolness, iciness. **2** chill.

▣ *adj.* **1, 2** hot, warm. **4** warm, friendly. **5** cheerful, bright. **7** warm, affectionate, responsive, passionate, hot-blooded. **8** passionate. **9** warm, hot, rich. **12** warm, close. *noun* **1** warmth, heat.

. . . .

cold-blooded *adj.* **1** *said of an animal* having a body temperature that varies with the temperature of the surrounding environment, eg reptiles, amphibians, fish. Also called POIKILOTHERMIC. **2** lacking emotion; callous; cruel.

. . . .

▤ **2** cold, callous, cruel, unfeeling, heartless, merciless, pitiless, inhuman, brutal, savage, barbaric, barbarous.

▣ **2** compassionate, emotional, merciful.

. . . .

cold boot *Comput.* a reboot activated by completely switching off and restarting a computer from the power source.

cold calling a marketing technique in which a sales representative contacts potential customers by telephone, without advance warning.

cold chisel a chisel for cutting cold metal, stone, etc.

cold comfort no comfort at all.

cold cream face cream for cleaning the skin and keeping it soft.

cold frame a glass-covered frame for protecting young plants growing outdoors.

cold front *Meteorol.* the leading edge of an advancing mass of cold air, moving under a retreating mass of warm air, and often associated with a fall in air temperature, brighter weather, and (in the northern hemisphere) the veering of the wind in a north-westerly direction.

cold-hearted *adj.* unkind.

coldly *adv.* with a cold or unfriendly manner; without warmth: *replied coldly that he did not know.*

coldness *noun* **1** a cold state or quality. **2** aloofness.

cold-shoulder *verb* to snub (someone); to give (someone) the cold shoulder.

cold sore a cluster of small blisters on or near the lips, caused by infection with the virus *herpes simplex*.

cold storage 1 the storage of food, etc under refrigeration. **2** the state of being put aside or saved till another time; postponement; abeyance.

cold sweat sweating from fear or nervousness.

cold turkey *slang* **1** the sudden complete withdrawal of drugs, used as a method of curing drug addiction. **2** the withdrawal symptoms (eg nausea, shivering) experienced by a drug addict when drug intake is stopped suddenly and completely.

cold war a state of hostility and antagonism between nations, without actual warfare.

cole *noun* a general name for any of various plants belonging to the cabbage family. [from Anglo-Saxon *cawl*, from Latin *caulis*]

colectomy /kə'lɛktəmɪ/ *noun Medicine* the surgical removal of the colon.

coleslaw *noun* a salad made with finely-cut raw cabbage and carrots. [from Dutch *koolsla*, cabbage salad]

coleus /'koʊlɪəs/ *noun* a perennial plant (Coleus blumei), native to Java. It has square stems, oval toothed leaves borne in opposite pairs, and slender spikes of small pale blue or white flowers. [from Greek *koleos*, sheath]

coley *noun* (PL. **coleys**) a large edible fish of the cod family, widely distributed in inshore waters of the N Atlantic Ocean, up to 1.2m long, with a dark green back and silvery-grey sides and belly.

colic /'kɒlɪk/ *noun Medicine* severe abdominal pain, common in infants and caused by wind in the intestines caused by swallowing air or overfeeding. In adults it is usually caused by constipation, or partial or complete obstruction of the intestine. [from Greek *kolon*, colon. See COLON[2]]

colicky *adj.* suffering from colic.

coliseum /kɒlə'sɪəm/ *noun Hist.* a large stadium or amphitheatre for sports and other entertainment. [a Latin variant of *Colosseum*, the largest Roman amphitheatre]

colitis /koʊ'laɪtɪs, kɒ'laɪtɪs/ *noun Medicine* inflammation of the colon, the main symptoms of which are diarrhoea and pain in the lower abdomen. [from COLON[2] + -ITIS]

collaborate /kə'labəreɪt/ *verb intrans.* **1** to work together with another or others on something. **2** *derog.* to co-operate with or help (an enemy occupying one's country). [from Latin *com-*, together + *laborare*, to work]

. . . .

▣ **1** work together, co-operate, join forces, team up, participate, conspire, collude.

. . . .

collaboration /kəlabə'reɪʃən/ *noun* the act of collaborating.

. . . .

▣ co-operation, alliance, partnership, teamwork, association, conspiring, collusion.

. . . .

collaborationism *noun* a policy of collaboration.

collaborationist *noun derog.* a supporter of collaboration.

collaborative /kə'labərətɪv/ *adj.* collaborating; involving or given to collaborating.

collaboratively *adv.* in a collaborative way.

collaborator /kə'labəreɪtə(r)/ *noun* a person who collaborates.

. . . .

▣ co-worker, associate, partner, team-mate, colleague, assistant, accomplice.

. . . .

collage /kɒ'lɑːʒ, 'kɒlɑːʒ/ *noun* **1** a design or picture made up of pieces of paper or cloth, or parts of photographs, etc fixed to a background surface. **2** the art of producing such works. [from French *collage*, pasting, gluing]

collagen /'kɒlədʒən/ *noun Biol.* a tough fibrous protein that is the main constituent of connective tissue found in skin, bones, teeth, cartilage, ligaments, etc. [from Greek *kolla*, glue + -GEN]

collapse — *verb usually intrans.* **1** to fall, give way, or cave in. **2** to drop unconscious; to faint; to drop exhausted or helpless. **3** to break down emotionally. **4** to fail suddenly: *several firms collapsed.* **5** *intrans., trans.* to fold up compactly for storage or space-saving. **6** *intrans., trans.* said *of the lungs or blood vessels, etc* to become or cause to become flattened. **7** *Stock Exchange* to suffer a sudden steep drop in value. — *noun* the process of collapsing. [from Latin *collabi*, to slide, fall]

. . . .

▣ *verb* **1** fall, give way, cave in, fall apart, disintegrate, crumble, sink, subside. **2** faint, pass out. **4** fail, founder, *colloq.* fold. **7** crash, plummet. *noun* fall, subsidence, cave-in, faint, exhaustion, failure, breakdown, disintegration, flop, debacle, downfall, ruin.

. . . .

collapsibility /kəlapsə'bɪlɪtɪ/ *noun* the quality of being collapsible.

collapsible *adj.* capable of collapsing or being collapsed.

collar — *noun* **1** a band or flap of any of various shapes, folded over or standing up round the neck of a garment; the neck of a garment generally. **2** something worn round the neck. **3** a band of leather, etc worn round the neck by a dog, etc. **4** a padded leather object, shaped to fit round a horse's neck, to ease the strain of pulling a vehicle. **5** a distinctively coloured ring of fur or feathers round the neck of certain mammals and birds. **6** a cut of meat from the neck of an animal. **7** a ring-shaped fitting for joining two pipes, etc together. **8** any collar-like part. — *verb* (**collared, collaring**) **1** to seize by the collar. **2** *colloq.* to catch or capture. **3** *colloq.* to grab for oneself. — **hot under the collar** *colloq.* angry or flustered. [from Old French *colier*, from Latin *collum*, neck]

collarbone *noun* either of two bones, the clavicles, linking the shoulder-blades with the top of the breastbone.

collarless *adj.* lacking a collar.

collate *verb* **1** to examine and compare (texts, evidence, etc). **2** to check and arrange in order (sheets of paper, pages of a book, etc) ready for fastening together. [from Latin *collatus*, past participle of *conferre*, to put together, compare]

collateral /kə'latərəl/ — *adj.* **1** descended from a common ancestor, but through a different branch of the family. **2** additional; secondary in importance; subsidiary. — *noun* (*also* **collateral security**) assets offered to a creditor as security for a loan. [from Latin *collateralis*, from Latin *com-*, with + *latus*, side]

collaterally *adv.* **1** side by side. **2** additionally. **3** with descent from a different family branch.

collation *noun* **1** the act of collating. **2** a light meal.

collator *noun* a person or device which collates.

colleague /'kɒliːg/ *noun* a fellow-worker, especially in a profession. [from Latin *collega*, partner, colleague]

. . . .

▣ fellow-worker, co-worker, workmate, team-mate, partner, associate, helper, assistant, aide, auxiliary, confederate, collaborator, ally, confrère, comrade, companion.

. . . .

collect /kə'lɛkt, 'kɒlɛkt/ — *verb* (with stress on *-lect*) **1** *trans., intrans.* to bring or come together; to gather; to accumulate. **2** to build up an assortment of (things of a particular type) out of enthusiasm for them: *collect stamps.* **3** to call for; to fetch; to pick up. **4** *trans., intrans.* to get (eg money owed or voluntary contributions) from people: *offered to collect for Oxfam.* **5** to calm or control (oneself); to get (one's thoughts, etc) under control. — *adj.* (with stress on *-lect*) *North Amer., esp. US, said of a telephone call* paid for by the person receiving it. — *adv.* (with stress on *-lect*) *North Amer., esp. US* reversing the charges. — *noun* (with stress on *coll-*) *Christianity* a short form of prayer used in the Anglican and Roman Catholic Churches. [from Latin *colligere*, to gather]

■ *verb* **1** gather, assemble, congregate, convene, muster, rally, converge, cluster, aggregate, accumulate, amass. **2** save, hoard, stockpile, accumulate, amass. *adj.* reverse-charge.

collectable *adj.* **1** capable of being collected. **2** desirable.

collected *adj.* **1** *said of a writer's works* all published together in a single volume or a uniform set of volumes. **2** cool; calm; self-possessed.

■ **2** cool, calm, composed, self-possessed, unruffled, unperturbed, placid, serene, imperturbable.
■ **2** anxious, worried, agitated, ruffled, perturbed.

collectedly *adv.* in a collected way.

collectedness *noun* self-possession; coolness.

collection *noun* **1** the act of collecting. **2** an accumulated assortment of things of a particular type. **3** an amount of money collected. **4** the removal of mail from a postbox at scheduled times.

■ **1** gathering, assembly, accumulation. **2** group, cluster, accumulation, conglomeration, assortment, mass, heap, pile, hoard, stockpile, store, set, assemblage, job lot, anthology, compilation, gathering, assembly, convocation, congregation, crowd.

collective *adj.* of, belonging to, or involving all the members of a group.

■ joint, common, shared, united, combined, corporate, concerted, co-operative, democratic, composite, aggregate, cumulative.
■ individual.

collective bargaining talks between a trade union and a company's management to settle questions of pay and working conditions.

collective farm *Agric.* a large state-owned farm run on co-operative principles, and formed by the merging of several smaller farms that were previously owned by individuals.

collectively *adv.* in a collective way; as a whole, together.

collective noun a noun standing for a group of people, animals, etc, usually taking a singular verb, eg *swarm / herd / gang / committee.*

Collective nouns (by animal) include: shrewdness of *apes,* cete of *badgers,* sloth of *bears,* swarm of *bees,* obstinacy of *buffaloes,* clowder of *cats,* drove of *cattle,* brood of *chickens,* bask of *crocodiles,* murder of *crows,* herd of *deer,* pack of *dogs,* school of *dolphins,* dole of *doves,* team of *ducks,* parade of *elephants,* busyness of *ferrets,* charm of *finches,* shoal of *fish,* skulk of *foxes,* army of *frogs,* gaggle/skein of *geese,* tribe of *goats,* husk of *hares,* cast of *hawks,* brood of *hens,* bloat of *hippopotamuses,* string of *horses,* pack of *hounds,* troop of *kangaroos,* kindle of *kittens,* exaltation of *larks,* leap of *leopards,* pride of *lions,* swarm of *locusts,* tittering of *magpies,* troop of *monkeys,* watch of *nightingales,* family of *otters,* parliament of *owls,* pandemonium of *parrots,* covey of *partridges,* muster of *peacocks,* rookery of *penguins,* nye of *pheasants,* litter of *pigs,* school of *porpoises,* bury of *rabbits,* colony of *rats,* unkindness of *ravens,* crash of *rhinoceroses,* building of *rooks,* pod of *seals,* flock of *sheep,* murmuration of *starlings,* ambush of *tigers,* rafter of *turkeys,* turn of *turtles,* descent of *woodpeckers,* gam of *whales,* rout of *wolves,* zeal of *zebras.*

collective security *Politics* the concept of maintaining

security and territorial integrity by the collective actions of nation states, especially through international organizations.

collectivism *noun* **1** the economic theory that industry should be carried on with a collective capital. **2** a system embodying this.

collectivization /kəlɛktɪvaɪˈzeɪʃən/ or **collectivisation** *noun* organization according to collectivism.

collectivize or **collectivise** *verb* to group (farms, factories, etc) into larger units and bring under state control and ownership.

collector *noun* (*often in compounds*) a person who collects, as a job or hobby: *stamp collector.*

Names of collectors and enthusiasts include: zoophile (*animals*), antiquary (*antiques*), tegestollogist (*beer mats*), campanologist (*bell-ringing*), ornithologist (*birds*), bibliophile (*books*), audiophile (*broadcast and recorded sound*), lepidopterist (*butterflies*), cartophilist (*cigarette cards*), numismatist (*coins/medals*), conservationist (*countryside*), comper (*competitions*), cruciverbalist (*crosswords*), environmentalist (*the environment*), xenophile (*foreigners*), gourmet (*good food*), gastronome (*good-living*), discophile (*gramophone records*), chirographist (*hand-writing*), hippophile (*horses*), entomologist (*insects*), phillumenist (*matches/matchboxes*), monarchist (*the monarchy*), deltiologist (*postcards*), arachnologist (*spiders/arachnids*), philatelist (*stamps*), arctophile (*teddy bears*), etymologist (*words*).

collector's item something that is a good specimen of its type and would interest a collector.

colleen /ˈkɒliːn, kɒˈliːn/ *noun* Irish a girl. [from Irish *cailffn,* girl]

college /ˈkɒlɪdʒ/ *noun* **1** an institution, either self-contained or part of a university, providing higher education, further education, or professional training. **2** one of a number of self-governing establishments that make up certain universities. **3** the staff and students of a college. **4** (*often* **College**) a name used by some larger secondary schools. **5** a body of people with particular duties and rights: *College of Cardinals.* **6** an official body of members of a profession, concerned with maintaining standards, etc. [from Latin *collegium,* group of associates, fellowship]

college of education *Brit.* a college specializing in the training of teachers, and usually offering degree courses. Since the 1970s, many colleges of education have merged with polytechnics and universities.

collegiate /kəˈliːdʒɪət/ *adj.* **1** of, relating to, or belonging to a college. **2** having the form of a college. **3** *said of a university* consisting of individual colleges. [from Latin *collegiatus,* from *collegium,* fellowship]

collegiate church 1 in Scotland, a church served by two clergymen of equal rank. **2** a church having a chapter of canons attached to it.

collide *verb intrans.* **1** to crash together, or crash into someone or something. **2** *said of people* to disagree or clash. [from Latin *collidere,* from *com-,* with + *laedere,* to strike]

■ **1** crash, bump, smash, clash. **2** disagree, clash, conflict, confront.

collie *noun* a medium-sized domestic dog, several breeds of which have been developed in Scotland as sheepdogs, usually having a brown and white coat and a long pointed muzzle. There are two forms: the long-haired *rough collie* and the rarer *smooth collie.* [perhaps from Scot. *colle,* coal, the breed having once been black]

collier *noun* **1** a coalminer. **2** a ship that transports coal. [from Middle English *coliere,* from Anglo-Saxon *col,* coal]

colliery *noun* (PL. **collieries**) a coalmine with its buildings.

collimator /ˈkɒlɪmeɪtə(r)/ *noun* **1** any device for obtaining a beam of parallel rays of light, used to test the focal lengths of lenses, etc. **2** any device (eg a diaphragm made of radiation-absorbing material) used to limit the size and angle of spread of a beam of radiation or radioactive particles. **3** a small fixed telescope that is attached to a larger optical instrument (eg an astronomical telescope) to assist in preliminary alignment (eg to fix the larger telescope's line of sight on a particular celestial body). [from Latin *collineare*, to bring into line with]

collinear /kɒ'lɪnɪə(r), koʊ'lɪnɪə(r)/ *adj. Maths.* lying on the same straight line.

collision *noun* **1** the violent meeting of objects; a crash. **2** a disagreement or conflict. [from Latin *collisio*]

▤ **1** crash, impact, bump, smash, accident, pile-up. **2** disagreement, conflict, clash, confrontation, opposition.

collision course a direction taken, or course of action begun, that is bound to result in collision with something or someone.

collocate /'kɒləkeɪt/ *verb intrans. Grammar, said of a word* to occur frequently alongside another word, often as part of the construction that relates it to its context: *'different' collocates with 'from' and 'to', and sometimes with 'than'*. [from Latin *collocare*, to place together]

collocation /kɒlə'keɪʃən/ *noun* **1** grouping together in a certain order. **2** *Grammar* the occurring of certain words together; grammatical interdependence: *the frequent collocation of 'different' and 'to'*.

colloid *noun Chem.* a state that is intermediate between a suspension and a true solution, in which fine particles of one substance are spread evenly throughout another substance. [from Greek *kolla*, glue]

colloquial /kə'loʊkwɪəl/ *adj., said of language or vocabulary* informal; used in conversation rather than in formal speech or writing. [from Latin *colloquium*, conversation]

▤ informal, conversational, familiar, everyday, vernacular, idiomatic.

▣ formal.

colloquialism *noun* a colloquial expression.

colloquially *adv.* in a colloquial or informal way.

colloquium /kə'loʊkwɪəm/ *noun* (PL. **colloquia**) an academic conference; a seminar. [from Latin *colloquium*, conversation]

colloquy /'kɒləkwɪ/ *noun* (PL. **colloquies**) a conversation; talk. [from Latin *colloquium*, conversation]

collusion *noun* secret and illegal co-operation for the purpose of fraud or other criminal activity, etc. [from Latin *collusio*]

▤ conspiracy, plotting, connivance, scheming, machination, intrigue.

collywobbles *pl. noun colloq.* **1** pain or discomfort in the abdomen. **2** nervousness; apprehensiveness. [probably from COLIC + WOBBLE]

Colo. *abbrev.* Colorado.

cologne /kə'loʊn/ *noun* eau-de-Cologne. [from Cologne, the place of manufacture]

colon¹ /'koʊlɒn/ *noun* a punctuation mark (:), properly used to introduce a list, an example, or an explanation. [from Greek *colon*, clause]

colon² /'koʊlən/ *noun* in vertebrates, the large intestine except for the rectum. Its main function is to reabsorb water from the indigestible remains of food, which are converted to solid faeces. [from Greek *kolon*, large intestine]

colonel /'kɜːnəl/ *noun* a senior army officer, in charge of a regiment, below a brigadier in rank. [from Italian *colonello*, leader of a column]

Colonel Blimp see BLIMP, COLONEL.

coloneley /'kɜːnəlsɪ/ *noun* (PL. **colonelcies**) the rank or office of colonel.

colonel-in-chief *noun* in the British army, an honorary rank and title often held by a member of the Royal family.

colonial /kə'loʊnɪəl/ — *adj.* **1** relating to, belonging to, or living in a colony or colonies. **2** possessing colonies: *colonial powers*. — *noun* an inhabitant of a colony. [from COLONY]

colonialism *noun often derog.* the policy of acquiring colonies, especially as a source of profit.

colonialist *noun* a supporter of colonialism.

colonially *adv.* as regards colonies or colonialism.

colonic *adj.* relating to or in the region of the colon (see COLON²).

colonization /kɒlənaɪ'zeɪʃən/ or **colonisation** *noun* **1** the act of colonizing or the process of being colonized. **2** setting up a colony or colonies.

colonize /'kɒlənaɪz/ or **colonise** *verb* **1** to establish a colony in (an area or country). **2** to settle (people) in a colony.

▤ **1** people, populate, occupy, settle.

colonnade /kɒlə'neɪd/ *noun* a row of columns, usually supporting a roof. [from French *colonnade*, from Latin *columna*, column]

colonnaded *adj.* having a colonnade.

colony /'kɒlənɪ/ *noun* (PL. **colonies**) **1** a settlement abroad founded and controlled by the founding country; the settlers living there; the territory they occupy. **2** a group of the same nationality or occupation forming a distinctive community within a city, etc. **3** a group of animals or plants of the same species living together in close proximity, sometimes with physical connections between individual members, eg sponges, corals, or a large number of animals living together in a highly organized social group, eg bees, ants, termites. **4** an isolated group of bacteria or fungi growing on a solid medium, and forming a visible mass. [from Latin *colonia*, farm, colony]

▤ **1** settlement, outpost, dependency, dominion, possession, territory, province.

colophon /'kɒləfɒn/ *noun* **1** an inscription at the end of a printed book or manuscript giving the name of the writer, printer, etc and place and date of production. **2** a publisher's ornamental mark or device. [from Greek *colophon*, summit, finishing touch]

Colorado beetle /kɒlə'rɑːdoʊ/ a small beetle that has a yellow back with 10 longitudinal black stripes on its wing cases. The females lay eggs on potato plants, and the larvae are reddish-yellow with black side spots. The Colorado beetle is a serious pest of potato crops.

colorant /'kʌlərənt/ *noun* a substance used for colouring. [from Latin *color*, colour]

coloration /kʌlə'reɪʃən/ *noun* arrangement or combination of colours; colouring. [from Latin *colorare*, to colour]

coloratura /kɒlərə'tʊərə, kɒlərə'tjʊərə/ *noun* **1** an elaborate and intricate passage or style in singing. **2** a soprano specializing in such singing. [from Italian *coloratura*, colouring]

colorimeter /kʌlə'rɪmɪtə(r), kɒlə'rɪmɪtə(r)/ *noun Chem.* an instrument for measuring the colour intensity of a solution, in order to determine the concentration of the coloured constituent. This is done by comparing the result with the colour intensities of standard solutions of known concentrations of the constituent.

colossal /kə'lɒsəl/ *adj.* **1** huge; vast. **2** *colloq.* splendid; marvellous. [from COLOSSUS]

▤ **1** huge, vast, enormous, immense, massive, gigantic, mammoth, monstrous, monumental. **2** splendid, marvellous, wonderful, *colloq.* brilliant, *colloq.* tremendous, *colloq.* great, enormous, huge.

▣ **1** tiny, minute.

colossally *adv.* immensely, hugely.

colossus /kə'lɒsəs/ *noun* (PL. **colossi, colossuses**) **1** a gigantic statue. **2** an overwhelmingly powerful person or organization. [from Greek *kolossos*]

colostomy /kə'lɒstəmɪ/ *noun* (PL. **colostomies**) *Surgery* a surgical operation in which part of the colon is brought to the surface of the body through an incision in the abdomen, forming an artificial anus through which the colon can be emptied. [from COLON² + Greek *stoma*, mouth]

colostrum /kə'lɒstrəm/ *noun Zool.* in mammals, the yellowish milky fluid secreted by the mammary glands immediately before and after giving birth. [from Latin *colostrum*]

colour /'kʌlə(r)/ — *noun* **1** the visual sensation produced in the brain as a result of nerve impulses relayed from the cones of the retina when they absorb light energy of a particular wavelength. Thus the colour of an object depends on the wavelength of the light it reflects. **2** any of these variations or colours, often with the addition of black and white. **3** *Photog., Art* the use of some or all colours, as distinct from black and white only: *in full colour.* **4** a colouring substance, especially paint. **5** the shade of a person's skin, as related to race; the darker skin shades. **6** pinkness of the face or cheeeks. **7** lively or convincing detail: *add local colour to the story.* **8** richness of quality in music, or its mood and quality generally. See also COLOURS. — *verb* **1** to put colour on; to paint or dye. **2** (*also* **colour something in**) to fill in an outlined area or a black and white picture with colour. **3** to influence: *feelings can colour one's judgement.* **4** *intrans.* to blush. — **off colour** *colloq.* unwell. [from Old French *color*]

. . . .

🔲 *noun* **2** hue, shade, tinge, tone, tincture, tint. **4** paint, pigment, pigmentation, dye. **5** colouring, coloration, complexion. **6** rosiness, ruddiness, glow. **7** vividness. **8** liveliness, animation, richness. *verb* **1** paint, crayon, dye, tint, stain, tinge. **3** influence, affect, bias, prejudice, distort, falsify, pervert, exaggerate. **4** blush, flush, redden.

. . . .

The range of colours includes: red, crimson, scarlet, vermilion, cherry, cerise, magenta, maroon, burgundy, ruby, orange, tangerine, apricot, coral, salmon, peach, amber, brown, chestnut, mahogany, bronze, auburn, rust, copper, cinnamon, chocolate, tan, sepia, taupe, beige, fawn, yellow, lemon, canary, ochre, saffron, topaz, gold, chartreuse, green, eau de nil, emerald, jade, bottle, avocado, sage, khaki, turquoise, aquamarine, cobalt, blue, sapphire, gentian, indigo, navy, violet, purple, mauve, plum, lavender, lilac, pink, rose, magnolia, cream, ecru, milky, white, grey, silver, charcoal, ebony, jet, black.

colour bar discrimination against coloured people.

colour-blindness *noun* any of various conditions characterized by an inability to distinguish between certain colours, due to a congenital defect (present from birth) in the light-sensitive cone cells of the retina that are responsible for colour perception. The commonest type is inability to distinguish between reds and greens.

colour-coded *adj.* marked by a system of colours for the purposes of identification or classification.

colour coding the systematic use of easily distinguishable colours as a means of identification or classification, eg for the identification of electric wires in plugs, etc.

coloured — *adj.* **1** (*also in compounds*) having colour, or a specified colour: *lemon-coloured.* **2** belonging to a dark-skinned race; non-white. **3** (**Coloured**) *South Afr.* of mixed white and non-white descent. — *noun* **1** a person of dark-skinned race. **2** (**Coloured**) *South Afr.* a person of mixed white and non-white descent.

colour-fast *adj., said of fabrics* dyed with colours that will not run when washed.

colour filter *Photog.* a transparent material which transmits light for only a selected portion of the visible spectrum, partially or completely absorbing the remainder.

colourful *adj.* **1** full of especially bright colour. **2** lively; vivid; full of interest or character.

. . . .

🔲 **1** multicoloured, kaleidoscopic, variegated, particoloured, vivid, bright, brilliant, rich, intense. **2** lively, vivid, graphic, picturesque, stimulating, exciting, interesting.
🔳 **1, 2** colourless, drab, dull.

. . . .

colourfully *adv.* in a colourful way.

colouring *noun* **1** a substance used to give colour, eg to food. **2** the applying of colour. **3** arrangement or combination of colour. **4** facial complexion, or this in combination with eye and hair colour.

colourist *noun* someone skilled in the use of colour; an artist.

colourization /kʌlərɑɪ'zeɪʃən/ or **colourisation** *noun Cinema* the process of adding colour to a motion picture originally made in black-and-white, now normally carried out by electronic means.

colourize or **colourise** *verb trans.* to add colour to (a cinema film made in black and white).

colourless *adj.* **1** without, or lacking, colour. **2** uninteresting; dull; lifeless. **3** pale.

. . . .

🔲 **1** transparent, neutral, bleached, *colloq.* washed-out, faded. **2** uninteresting, dull, lifeless, insipid, lacklustre, dreary, drab, plain, characterless, unmemorable, tame. **3** pale, ashen, sickly, anaemic.
🔳 **1** colourful. **2** bright, exciting, lively, interesting. **3** rosy, glowing, burning.

. . . .

colourlessly *adv.* in a colourless way.

colours *pl. noun* **1** the flag of a nation, regiment, or ship. **2** the coloured uniform or other distinguishing badge awarded to team-members in certain games. **3** a badge of ribbons in colours representing a particular party, etc, worn to show support for it. **4** the coloured dress of a jockey and horse, identifying the horse's owner. — **in one's true colours** as one really is. **nail one's colours to the mast** to announce openly one's support for something or someone. **with flying colours** with great success.

colour scheme a choice or combination of colours in house decoration, etc.

colour sergeant a sergeant who carries the company's colours.

colour supplement an illustrated magazine accompanying a newspaper.

colour television a television system in which separate signals corresponding to the three primary colours of light (red, blue, and green) are used to form a full-colour image on the screen of a specially designed television receiver.

colour therapy a form of therapy that involves the selection and use of appropriate colours that are said to promote healing and well-being.

colourway *noun* a combination of colours in patterned material, etc.

Colt *noun trademark* a type of small pistol. [named after Samuel Colt, the inventor]

colt *noun* **1** a male horse or pony less than four years old. **2** a thoroughbred horse or pony less than five years old. **3** an inexperienced young team-player or member of a junior team. [from Anglo-Saxon]

coltish *adj.* youthfully awkward in movement or behaviour.

coltishly *adv.* in a coltish or awkward way.

coltsfoot *noun* a perennial plant (Tussilago farfara), native to Europe, Asia, and N Africa, having flowering stems bearing large scales tinged with purple, and single bright yellow daisy-like flower-heads that appear before the large heart-shaped leaves. Coltsfoot was formerly used as a herbal remedy for chest complaints.

colugo /kə'lu:goʊ/ *noun* a nocturnal mammal, native to SE Asia, that has a lemur-like face, and a large membrane along each side of the body, extending to the tips of the fingers, toes, and long tail. It lives in trees, and glides through the air by extending the membrane. Also called FLYING LEMUR. [probably from a Malaysian word]

columbine /ˈkɒləmbaɪn/ *noun* (*in full* **common columbine**) a perennial plant (Aquilegia vulgaris), native to Europe, Asia, and N Africa, having erect slender stems, and long-stalked bluish-green leaves divided into three-lobed leaflets. [from Latin *columba*, dove, pigeon]

columbium /kɒˈlʌmbɪəm/ *noun Chem.* former name for niobium.

column /ˈkɒləm/ *noun* **1** *Archit.* a usually cylindrical pillar with a base and capital. **2** something similarly shaped; a long, more or less cylindrical mass. **3** a vertical row of numbers. **4** a vertical strip of print on a newspaper page, etc. **5** a regular section in a newspaper concerned with a particular topic, or by a regular writer. **6** a line of people or a troop of soldiers or vehicles standing or moving a few abreast. [from Latin *columna*, pillar]

🖿 **1, 2** pillar, post, shaft, upright, support. **3** list, line. **6** row, rank, file, procession, queue, string.

columnar /kəˈlʌmnə(r)/ *adj.* **1** relating to columns. **2** like a column. **3** arranged or formed in columns.

columnist /ˈkɒləmnɪst/ *noun* a person writing a regular section of a newspaper.

com- see CON-.

coma *noun* a prolonged state of deep unconsciousness from which a person cannot be awakened. It is usually caused by brain damage or infection, brain tumour, severe hypoglycaemia (low blood-sugar levels) due to diabetes, or poisoning, eg by alcohol. In deep coma there may be no response to painful or reflex stimuli. [from Greek *koma*, deep sleep]

comatose *adj.* **1** in a coma. **2** *facetious* sleepy; asleep. [from Greek *koma*, deep sleep]

comb /koʊm/ — *noun* **1** a rigid toothed device for tidying and arranging the hair, sometimes worn in the hair to keep it in place. **2** a toothed implement or part of a machine, used for cleaning, separating, and straightening wool, cotton, flax, etc. **3** an act of combing. **4** a honeycomb. **5** a fleshy serrated crest on the top of the head of certain male birds, especially chickens and other fowl. — *verb* **1** to arrange, smooth, or clean with a comb. **2** to search (a place) thoroughly. — **comb something out 1** to remove (dirt, etc) by combing. **2** to find and get rid of (unwanted elements). [from Anglo-Saxon *camb*]

🖿 *verb* **1** arrange, groom, smooth, neaten, tidy, untangle. **2** search, hunt, scour, sweep, sift, screen, rake, rummage, ransack.

combat /ˈkɒmbat, ˈkʌmbat, kəmˈbat/ — *noun* fighting; a struggle or contest: *single combat.* — *verb* (**combated**, **combating**) to fight against; to oppose. [from French *combat*]

🖿 *noun* fighting, war, warfare, hostilities, struggle, contest, action, battle, fight, skirmish, conflict, clash, encounter, engagement, bout, duel. *verb* fight, oppose, battle against, strive against, resist, withstand, defy.

combatant — *adj.* involved in a fight. — *noun* a combatant person.

combative *adj.* inclined to fight or argue.

combat trousers loose casual trousers with large external pockets on the upper legs. Also called CARGO PANTS.

combination /kɒmbɪˈneɪʃən/ *noun* **1** the process of combining or state of being combined. **2** two or more things, people, etc combined; the resulting mixture or union. **3** a set of numbers or letters for opening a combination lock. **4** a motorcycle with sidecar. **5** *Maths.* a set of numbers or objects selected from a given set of numbers or objects, re-

gardless of their order. **6** (**combinations**) an old-fashioned one-piece undergarment combining long-sleeved vest and long underpants.

🖿 **1** merger, amalgamation, unification, alliance, coalition, association, federation, confederation, union, integration, fusion, coalescence, connection. **2** blend, mix, mixture, union, compound, amalgam, composite, synthesis, alliance, coalition, association, federation, confederation, confederacy, combine, consortium, syndicate.

combination lock a lock with a numbered dial or rotating sections, which must be turned so as to register or line up a particular combination of numbers before it will open.

combinatory /ˈkɒmbɪnətərɪ/ *adj.* able to be or tending to be combined.

combine /kəmˈbaɪn, ˈkɒmbaɪn/ — *verb* (with stress on -*bine*) **1** *trans., intrans.* to join together; to unite. **2** to possess (two contrasting qualities, etc); to manage or achieve (two different things) at the same time. — *noun* (with stress on *com*-) **1** a group of people or businesses associated for a common purpose. **2** *colloq.* a combine harvester. [from Latin *combinare*, from *com*-, with + *bini*, two each]

🖿 *verb* **1** join, unite, unify, merge, amalgamate, blend, mix, integrate, incorporate, synthesize, compound, fuse, bond, bind, connect, link, marry, pool, associate, co-operate. *noun* **1** association, league, alliance, coalition, confederation, confederacy, consortium, syndicate, cartel, union, fellowship.

🖿 *verb* **1** divide, separate, detach.

combine harvester /ˈkɒmbaɪn/ *Agric.* a machine used to harvest cereals and other arable crops, so called because it is equipped both to reap (cut) the crop, and to thresh it by separating the grain or seed, which is lifted to a hopper, from the straw, which is left in a swathe on the ground.

combining form *noun Grammar* a word-form that occurs in combinations or compounds, eg *Anglo-* as in *Anglo-American* and *-lysis* in *electrolysis.*

combo *noun* (PL. **combos**) *colloq.* a small jazz dance band. [from COMBINATION]

comb-over *noun* a hairstyle in which the hair is combed from one side of the head over to the other, usually to hide a bald patch.

combustibility *noun* a combustible quality.

combustible /kəmˈbʌstəbəl/ — *adj.* **1** *said of a material* liable to ignite and burn. **2** easily exploding into violent passion. — *noun* a material that is liable to ignite or burn. [from Latin *combustibilis*]

combustion /kəmˈbʌstʃən/ *noun* **1** the process of catching fire and burning. **2** *Chem.* a chemical reaction in which a gas, liquid, or solid is rapidly oxidized, usually by oxygen, with the production of heat and often light. [from Latin *combustio*]

come /kʌm/ — *verb usually intrans.* (PAST TENSE **came**; PAST PARTICIPLE **come**) **1** to move in the direction of speaker or hearer. **2** to reach a place; to arrive. **3** (**come to an opinion, conclusion**, etc) to reach it after consideration. **4** (**come to** or **into something**) to reach a certain stage; to pass into a certain state: *come to power.* **5** (**come to harm**, etc) to suffer it. **6** (**come up to something**) to extend to or reach a level, standard, etc. **7** (**come to an amount**) to reach it in total: *that comes to £20 exactly.* **8** to travel or traverse (a distance, etc). **9** (**come from a place**) to have as a source or place of origin: *do you come from Australia?* **10** (**come to do** or **be something**) to happen: *how did you come to hurt yourself?* **11** to enter one's consciousness or perception: *come into view.* **12** to occupy a specific place in order, etc: *in 'ceiling', 'e' comes before 'i'.* **13** to be available; to exist or be found: *come in several sizes.* **14** to become: *come undone.* **15** to turn out: *come true.* **16** (**come

to something) to be a case of it: *when it comes to hard work, Jim's your man.* **17** to descend or result from: *come from healthy stock / this is what comes of being indulgent.* **18** (*with complement*) to act like; to pretend to be: *don't come the innocent.* **19** *colloq.* to have a sexual orgasm. **20** on the arrival of (a particular point in time): *come next Tuesday I'll be free.* — *interj.* used to reassure or admonish: *oh, come now, don't exaggerate.* — **come about 1** to happen. **2** *Naut.* to change direction. **come across** (*with complement*) to make a certain impression: *her speech came across well.* **come across something** or **someone** to discover them; to encounter them. **come across with something** *slang* to provide what is required. **come again?** *colloq.* could you repeat that? **come along 1** to progress; to improve. **2** to arrive. **3** to hurry up. **come and go** to reappear from time to time. **come apart** to fall to pieces. **come at something** or **someone 1** to attack them. **2** to approach them. **come away** to become detached. **come back 1** to be recalled to mind: *it's all coming back to me now.* **2** (*also* **come in**) to become fashionable again. **come back at someone** to answer them rudely. **come between people** to interfere or cause trouble between them. **come by something** to obtain it: *how did you come by that cut?* **come down 1** to lose one's social position: *come down in the world.* **2** *said of an heirloom, etc* to be inherited. **3** to leave university. **4** to decide. **come down on someone** or **something** to deal with them severely; to be very disapproving: *come down heavily on bullying.* **come down to something** to be equivalent to it, in simple terms: *it comes down to this.* **come down with something** to develop an illness. **come for someone** or **something 1** to attack them. **2** to call to receive something: *came for our subscription.* **come forward** to offer oneself: *several witnesses came forward.* **come in 1** to arrive; to be received. **2** to have a particular role, function, or use: *this is where you come in / come in useful.* **3** *said of the tide* to rise. **4** to become fashionable. **come in for something** to deserve or incur it: *came in for some criticism.* **come into something** to inherit money, etc. **come into one's own** to have the opportunity to display one's talents. **come it over** *slang* to put on an act: *don't come it over me.* **come off 1** to become detached. **2** to succeed. **3** to take place. **come off it!** *colloq.* stop talking nonsense! **come on 1** to start. **2** to develop successfully; make progress. **3** to hurry up, cheer up, not talk nonsense. **come one's way** to become available. **come out 1** *said of the sun or stars* to appear. **2** to become known. **3** to fade in the wash: *the mark won't come out.* **4** to strike: *come out in sympathy.* **5** to declare one's opinion openly: *come out in favour of the plan.* **6** to work out: *can't get the sum to come out.* **7** to emerge in a certain position or state: *come out well from the affair.* **8** *said of a photograph* to be developed: *come out nice and clear.* **9** *colloq.* to declare openly that one is a homosexual. **10** *old use, said of a girl* to be launched in society. **come out in something** to develop a rash, etc: *come out in spots.* **come out with something** to make a remark, etc: *what will she come out with next?* **come over 1** to change one's opinion or side: *come over to our side.* **2** to make a certain impression: *comes over well on television.* **3** (*with complement*) *colloq.* to feel or become: *come over a bit faint.* **come over someone** to affect them: *what came over them?* **come round 1** to regain consciousness. **2** to regain one's temper; to calm down. **3** to change one's opinion. **4** to recur in order or routine. **come through** to survive. **come through something** to survive it. **come to** to regain consciousness. **come to nothing** to fail. **come to oneself 1** to regain consciousness. **2** to calm down; to regain one's self-control. **come under something** or **someone 1** to belong to a category. **2** to be a specified responsibility: *swimming-pools come under the local authority.* **come up 1** to occur; to happen: *I'll contact you if anything comes up.* **2** to be considered or discussed: *the question didn't come up.* **3** to rise socially: *come up in the world.* **come up against someone** or **something** to be faced with them as an opponent, challenge, etc. **come up to someone** to approach them. **come up with something** to offer it; to put it forward: *come up with an idea.* **come upon something** or **someone** to discover it by chance. **have it coming to one** *colloq.* to deserve whatever unplea-

sant fate befalls one. **not know whether one is coming or going** to be in a dazed or bewildered state. **when it comes to** ... when it is a question of: *when it comes to hard work, he's your man.* [from Anglo-Saxon *cuman*]

⊞ *verb* **1** advance, move towards, approach, near, draw near. **2** reach, arrive, enter, appear. **4** reach, attain, achieve, pass into. **5** suffer, endure, experience, undergo. **6** reach, attain, achieve. **8** travel, traverse, cover, cross. **9** hail from. **come about 1** happen, occur, transpire, arise, result, come to pass. **come across something** or **someone** discover, find, encounter, chance upon, happen upon, *colloq.* bump into, meet, notice. **come along 1** progress, improve, develop, rally, mend, recover, recuperate. **2** arrive, happen. **come apart** fall to pieces, disintegrate, break, separate, split, tear. **come between** divide, split up, disunite, estrange, alienate, separate, part. **come by** obtain, acquire, get, gain, secure. **come in 1** arrive, enter, appear, *colloq.* show up. **come off 3** take place, happen, occur. **come on 1** start, begin. **2** develop, progress, improve, thrive, succeed. **come out with** say, state, affirm, declare, disclose, divulge. **come round 1** recover, wake, awake. **3** yield, relent, concede, accede. **come through** survive, endure, prevail, triumph, succeed. **come through something** survive, endure, withstand, accomplish, achieve. **come up 1** occur, happen, take place, transpire, arise. **2** arise, *colloq.* crop up. **come up with** put forward, offer, suggest, submit.

⊟ *verb* **1** go. **2** go, depart, leave.

comeback *noun* **1** a return to former success, or to the stage, etc after a period of retirement or obscurity: *stage a comeback.* **2** a retort. **3** an opportunity for redress or retaliation.

⊞ **1** return, reappearance, resurgence, revival, recovery.

comedian /kə'mi:dɪən/ *noun* **1** an entertainer who tells jokes, performs comic sketches, etc. **2** an actor in comedy. [from COMEDY]

⊞ **1** comic, clown, humorist, wit, joker, wag.

comedienne /kəmidɪ'en/ *noun* a female comedian.

comedo /'kɒmɪdoʊ/ *noun* (PL. **comedos, comedones**) *Medicine* technical name for a blackhead, a mass of fatty material forming a plug blocking one of the sebaceous ducts in the skin. Its black colour is caused by the oxidation of keratin in the plug. [from Latin *comedo,* glutton]

comedown *noun* **1** a decline in social status. **2** an anticlimax.

⊞ **1** decline, reverse, descent, demotion, humiliation, degradation. **2** anticlimax, let-down, disappointment, deflation, blow.

comedy /'kɒmədɪ/ *noun* (PL. **comedies**) **1** a light, amusing play or film. **2** drama of this type generally. **3** in earlier literature, a play with a fortunate outcome. **4** funny incidents or situations. [from Greek *komoidia,* from *komos,* comic chorus + *aoidos,* singer]

⊞ **1** farce, slapstick. **4** clowning, hilarity, drollery, humour, wit, joking, jesting, facetiousness.

come-hither *adj. colloq.* flirtatious: *a come-hither look.*

comeliness /'kʌmlɪnəs/ *noun* a comely or attractive quality.

comely /'kʌmlɪ/ *adj.* (**comelier, comeliest**) *said of a woman* wholesomely attractive. [from Anglo-Saxon *cymlic,* beautiful]

come-on *noun colloq.* sexual encouragement: *give someone the come-on.*

comer /'kʌmə(r)/ *noun* (*often in compounds*) a person who comes: *latecomers* / *a newcomer* / *challenge all comers*.

comestible /kə'mɛstɪbl/ *noun* (*usually in pl.*) something to eat. [from French *comestible*, from Latin *comedere*, to eat up]

comet /'kɒmɪt/ *noun Astron.* in the solar system, a small body composed mainly of frozen gases, ice, and dust, that follows an elliptical orbit around the Sun, and has a characteristic bright head (*coma*) and a streaming tail when its orbit takes it close to the Sun. [from Greek *kometes*, literally 'long-haired', from *kome*, hair]

come-uppance *noun colloq.* a well-deserved punishment or retribution: *get one's come-uppance*.

comfit /'kʌmfɪt/ *noun Hist.* an old type of sweet, usually a sugar-coated nut, etc. [from French *confit*]

comfort /'kʌmfət/ — *noun* **1** a state of physical and mental contentedness or wellbeing. **2** relief from suffering, or consolation in grief. **3** a person or thing that provides such relief or consolation. **4** (*usually* **comforts**) something that makes for ease and physical wellbeing. — *verb* to relieve from suffering; to console or soothe. [from French *conforter*]

⊟ *noun* **1** ease, relaxation, luxury, snugness, cosiness, wellbeing, satisfaction, contentment, enjoyment. **2** relief, alleviation, consolation, compensation, cheer, reassurance, encouragement. **3** help, aid, support. **4** luxury. *verb* soothe, console, ease, relieve, alleviate, assuage, cheer, gladden, reassure, hearten, encourage, strengthen.

⊠ *noun* **1** discomfort, distress. *verb* discomfort, distress.

comfortable *adj.* **1** in a state of especially physical wellbeing; at ease. **2** providing comfort. **3** *colloq.* financially secure. **4** *said of a hospital patient, etc* in a stable, more or less pain-free condition. **5** quite large: *win by a comfortable margin*. [from French *confortable*]

⊟ **1** snug, cosy, *colloq.* comfy, at ease, relaxed, contented, happy. **2** snug, cosy, *colloq.* comfy, relaxing, restful, easy, pleasant, enjoyable. **3** affluent, well off, well-to-do, prosperous. **5** easy, large, good.

⊠ **1** uncomfortable, uneasy, nervous. **2** uncomfortable, unpleasant. **3** poor. **5** narrow, slim, tight.

comfortably *adv.* **1** so as to be comfortable. **2** in a comfortable way. — **comfortably off** *colloq.* financially secure; able to live in comfort.

comforter *noun* **1** a person who comforts. **2** *old use* a warm scarf. **3** *old use* a baby's dummy. **4** *North Amer., esp. US* a quilt.

comfrey /'kʌmfrɪ/ *noun* (*in full* **common comfrey**) a robust perennial plant (Symphytum officinale), native to Europe except for the Mediterranean region, having upright stems bearing large spear-shaped bristly leaves, and tubular white, pink, or purple flowers borne in terminal clusters. [from Latin *conferva*, healing water plant]

comfy /'kʌmfɪ/ *adj.* (**comfier, comfiest**) *colloq.* comfortable.

comic /'kɒmɪk/ — *adj.* **1** characterized by or relating to comedy; intended to amuse. **2** funny. — *noun* **1** a comedian. **2** (*also* **comic book**) a paper or magazine, especially one aimed at children or teenagers, which includes strip cartoons, illustrated stories, etc. The term is now applied to the format rather than the content, which may be serious (and even horrific) as well as comic. [from Greek *komikos*, from *komos*, comic chorus]

⊟ *adj.* **1** humorous, funny, light. **2** funny, amusing, comical, droll, humorous, witty, hilarious, side-splitting, *colloq.* priceless, *colloq.* rich, farcical, ridiculous, ludicrous, absurd, laughable, facetious, entertaining, diverting. *noun* **1** comedian, joker, humorist, wit, wag, *colloq.* gagster, jester, clown, buffoon.

⊠ *adj.* **1** tragic, serious.

comical *adj.* funny; amusing; humorous; ludicrous.

comicality /kɒmɪ'kalɪtɪ/ *noun* a comical quality.

comically *adv.* in a comical way.

comic opera a lighthearted opera with spoken dialogue as well as singing.

comic strip a brief story or episode told through a short series of pictures, in a newspaper, etc.

coming /'kʌmɪŋ/ — *noun* an arrival; an approach: *await their coming*. — *adj.* **1** *colloq.* looking like a winner: *the coming man*. **2** approaching: *in the coming months*. — **comings and goings** *colloq.* bustle; activity; movement.

⊟ *noun* arrival, approach, advent, accession. *adj.* **1** up-and-coming, rising, aspiring. **2** forthcoming, approaching, future, next, impending, imminent, due, near.

comity /'kɒmɪtɪ/ *noun* civility; politeness; courtesy. [from Latin *comitas*, from *comis*, friendly]

comity of nations mutual respect between nations for one another's laws and customs.

comma *noun* a punctuation mark (,) indicating a slight pause or break made for the sake of clarity, etc. [from Greek *comma*, clause]

command — *verb* **1** to order formally. **2** to have authority over or be in control of. **3** to have at one's disposal. **4** to deserve or be entitled to. **5** to look down over: *the window commands a view of the bay.* — *noun* **1** an order. **2** control; charge; *second in command.* **3** knowledge of and ability to use. **4** a military unit, or a district, under one's command. **5** a specialized section of an army, air force, etc: *Bomber Command.* **6** a group of high-ranking army officers, etc: *the British High Command.* **7** *Comput.* an instruction to a computer to initiate a specific operation. [from French *commander*]

⊟ *verb* **1** order, bid, charge, enjoin, direct, instruct, require, demand, compel. **2** lead, head, rule, reign, govern, control, dominate, manage, supervise. *noun* **1** order, directive, direction, instruction, injunction, commandment, decree, edict, precept, mandate, bidding, charge, requirement. **2** control, charge, authority, leadership, domination, dominion, power, rule, sway, government, management.

commandant /'kɒmandant/ *noun* a commanding officer, especially of a prisoner-of-war camp or a military training establishment. [from French *commandant*, present participle of *commander*, to command]

command economy a centrally controlled economy in which the state takes all economic decisions. Most countries of the former communist bloc were command economies (see also MARKET ECONOMY).

commandeer /kɒmən'dɪə(r)/ *verb* **1** to seize (property) for military use in wartime, official use in an emergency, etc. **2** to seize without justification. [from Afrikaans *commandeer*, from French *commander*, to command]

commander *noun* **1** a person who commands. **2** in the British navy, an officer just below captain in rank. **3** a high-ranking police officer. **4** (*also* **knight commander**) a senior member in some orders of knighthood.

⊟ **1** leader, head, chief, boss, commander-in-chief, general, admiral, captain, commanding officer, officer.

commander-in-chief *noun* (PL. **commanders-in-chief**) the officer in supreme command of a nation's forces.

commanding *adj.* **1** powerful; leading; controlling. **2** in charge. **3** inspiring respect or awe. **4** giving good views all round: *a house with a commanding position*.

commandment *noun* (*usually* **Commandment**) a divine command, especially one of 10 given to Moses, listed in the Bible in Exodus 20.

command module in a spacecraft, the self-contained unit from which operations are directed, which also serves as living quarters for the crew.

commando /kə'mːndoʊ/ *noun* (PL. **commandos**) a member of a unit of soldiers specially trained to carry out dangerous and difficult attacks or raids. [from Afrikaans *commando*, originally from Portuguese *commandar*, to command]

command paper a government document presenting a report on some matter or outlining government policy. See also GREEN PAPER, WHITE PAPER.

command performance a special performance of a play, etc given at the request, and in the presence, of the head of state.

command post a temporary military headquarters.

commedia dell'arte /kə'mɛdʒə del'aːteɪ/ a 16c Italian form of comedy with stock characters and plots full of intrigue. [Italian, = comedy of the arts]

commemorate /kə'mɛməreɪt/ *verb* **1** to honour the memory of (a person or event) with a ceremony, etc. **2** to be a memorial to. [from Latin *commemorare*, to keep in mind]

⊟ **1** celebrate, remember, mark, honour, salute, observe, keep. **2** memorialize, celebrate, mark, honour, salute, immortalize.

commemoration /kəmɛmə'reɪʃən/ *noun* an act or ceremony of preserving the memory of some person or thing.

⊟ celebration, tribute, observance, remembrance, honouring.

commemorative /kə'mɛmərətɪv/ *adj.* tending or serving to commemorate.

commence *verb trans., intrans.* to begin. [from Old French *commencier*, from Latin *initiare*, to begin]

⊟ begin, start, embark on, originate, initiate, inaugurate, open, launch.
⊠ finish, end, cease.

commencement *noun* **1** a beginning. **2** *North Amer.* a graduation ceremony.

commend *verb* **1** to praise. **2** to entrust (someone or something) to someone. **3** to recommend or make acceptable: *if the idea commends itself to you.* [from Latin *commendare*]

⊟ **1** praise, compliment, acclaim, extol, applaud, approve, recommend. **2** entrust, commit, confide, consign, deliver, yield. **3** recommend, endorse, approve.
⊠ **1** criticize, censure.

commendable *adj.* praiseworthy; creditable.

commendably *adv.* in a commendable way.

commendation /kɒmən'deɪʃən/ *noun* **1** praise; approval. **2** an award or honour.

commendatory *adj.* commending; involving commendation.

commensalism /kə'mɛnsəlɪzm/ *noun Biol.* the partnership or association of two organisms of different species which does not affect or benefit either of them. [from COM- + Latin *mensa*, table]

commensurable /kə'mɛnʃərəbl/ *adj.* (*often* **commensurable with** or **to something**) **1** *Maths.* having a common factor. **2** denoting quantities whose ratio is a rational number (a number that can be expressed in the form of a fraction). **3** denoting two or more quantities that can be measured in the same units. [from Latin *com*, with + *mensurare*, to measure]

commensurate /kə'mɛnʃərɪt/ *adj.* (**commensurate with something**) **1** in proportion to it; appropriate to it. **2** equal to it in extent, quantity, etc. [from Latin *com*, with + *mensurare*, to measure]

commensurately *adv.* so as to be commensurate.

comment — *noun* **1** a remark or observation, especially a critical one. **2** talk, discussion, or gossip. **3** an explanatory or analytical note on a passage of text. — *verb trans., intrans.* (**comment on something**) to make observations about it. — **no comment** I decline to comment. [from Latin *commentum*, commentary]

⊟ *noun* **1** remark, observation, statement, criticism. **2** talk, discussion, gossip, commentary, criticism. **3** note, annotation, footnote, marginal note, explanation, elucidation, illustration. *verb* remark, observe, say, mention, interject, note, interpret, explain.

commentary /'kɒməntərɪ/ *noun* (PL. **commentaries**) **1** a continuous, especially broadcast, report on an event, match, etc as it actually takes place. **2** an explanation accompanying a film, etc. **3** a set of notes explaining or interpreting points in a text, etc. [from Latin *commentarium*, notebook]

⊟ **1, 2** narrative, narration, voice-over. **3** analysis, description, review, critique, explanation, notes, treatise.

commentate /'kɒmənteɪt/ *verb intrans.* to give a running commentary.

commentator *noun* **1** a broadcaster giving a commentary on a match, event, etc. **2** the writer of a textual commentary. [from Latin *commentator*, interpreter]

⊟ **1** broadcaster, sportscaster, reporter, narrator. **2** critic, annotator, interpreter.

commerce *noun* **1** the buying and selling of commodities and services; trade, including banking, insurance, etc. **2** *old use* social dealings or communication. [from French *commerce*, from Latin *commercium*, trade]

⊟ **1** trade, business, dealings, relations, dealing, traffic, trafficking, exchange, marketing, merchandizing.

commercial /kə'mɜːʃəl/ — *adj.* **1** relating to, engaged in, or used for commerce. **2** profitable; having profit as chief aim; exploited or exploitable for profit. **3** paid for by advertising. — *noun* a radio or television advertisement. [from Latin *commercium*, trade]

⊟ *adj.* **1** trade, trading, business, sales. **2** profitable, profit-making, sellable, saleable, popular, monetary, financial, mercenary.

Commercial Court a court within the Queen's Bench Division which hears major commercial cases in England and Wales. Cases often involve litigants from overseas, and are usually heard in private, with the judge in the role of arbitrator.

commercialism *noun* **1** commercial attitudes and aims. **2** undue emphasis on profit-making.

commerciality /kəmɜːʃɪ'alɪtɪ/ *noun* a commercial quality or nature.

commercialization or **commercialisation** /kəmɜːʃəlaɪ'zeɪʃən/ *noun* **1** exploitation for profit. **2** making commercial.

commercialize or **commercialise** *verb* **1** to exploit for profit, especially by sacrificing quality. **2** to make commercial.

commercially *adv.* in a commercial way; as regards commerce.

commercial traveller *noun* a person who travels around the country representing a business firm and selling their goods.

commie *colloq., derog.* — *noun* a communist. — *adj.* communist: *commie talk.*

comminute /'kɒmɪnjuːt/ *verb technical* to break (a solid, eg bone, minerals) into minute particles or fragments by crushing, grinding, or pulverizing. [from Latin *comminuere*]

comminution /kɒmɪ'njuːʃən/ *noun* the act of comminuting.

commis /'kɒmiː/ or **commis chef** *noun* (PL. **commis**, **commis chefs**) an assistant or trainee waiter or chef. [from French *commis*]

commiserate /kə'mɪzəreɪt/ *verb intrans.* (**commiserate with someone**) to express sympathy for them. [from Latin *com-*, with + *miserari*, to lament]

commiseration /kəmɪzə'reɪʃən/ *noun* pity, sympathy.

commissar /'kɒmɪsɑː(r)/ *noun* in the former Soviet Union, the head of a government department, or a Communist Party official responsible for the political education of military units. [from Russian *komisar*, from Latin *commissarius*, officer in charge]

commissarial /kɒmɪ'sɛərɪəl/ *adj.* relating to or associated with a commissary.

commissariat /kɒmɪ'sɛərɪət/ *noun* 1 a department in the army responsible for food supplies. 2 *formerly* a government department in the Soviet Union. [from French and Russian, from Latin *commissarius*, officer in charge]

commissary /'kɒmɪsərɪ/ *noun* (PL. **commissaries**) 1 an officer responsible for supplies and provisions in the army. 2 *North Amer.* a store supplying provisions and equipment to a military force. 3 *orig. North Amer., esp. US* a canteen serving a film studio, etc. [from Latin *commissarius*, officer in charge]

commission /kə'mɪʃən/ — *noun* 1 a formal or official request to someone to perform a task or duty; the authority to perform it; the task or duty. 2 a military rank above a certain level, or the document conferring this. 3 an order for a piece of work, especially a work of art. 4 a board or committee entrusted with a particular task. 5 a fee or percentage given to the agent arranging a sale. 6 the act of committing, eg a crime. — *verb* 1 to give a commission or authority to. 2 to grant military rank above a certain level to. 3 to request (someone to do something). 4 to place an order for (a work of art, etc). 5 to prepare (a ship) for active service. — **in** or **out of commission** in use, or not in use or working condition. [from Latin *commissio*, entrusting]

⬛ *noun* 1 assignment, mission, errand, task, job, duty, function, appointment, employment, order, mandate, warrant, authority, charge, trust. 4 board, committee, delegation, deputation, representative. 5 fee, percentage, *slang* cut, *slang* rake-off, allowance. *verb* 1 appoint, engage, employ, authorize, empower, delegate, depute, nominate, select, send, order. 3 request, ask, require, bid. 4 order, ask for.

commissionaire /kəmɪʃə'nɛə(r)/ *noun* a uniformed attendant at the door of a cinema, theatre, office, or hotel. [from French *commissionaire*]

commissioned officer a military officer who is holding a commission. See also NON-COMMISSIONED OFFICER.

commissioner *noun* 1 a representative of the government in a district, department, etc. 2 a member of a commission.

commissionership *noun* the position or office of a commissioner.

commit *verb* (**committed, committing**) 1 to carry out or perpetrate (a crime, offence, error, etc). 2 to have (someone) put in prison or a mental institution. 3 to promise or engage (especially oneself) for some undertaking, etc. 4 to dedicate (oneself) to a cause, etc from a sense of conviction: *a committed Christian.* 5 to entrust or give, eg facts to memory (ie memorize them), or thoughts to paper (ie write them down). 6 to send (a person) for trial in a higher court. — **commit oneself** to make a definite decision. [from Latin *committere*, to give, entrust, perpetrate]

⬛ 1 do, perform, execute, perpetrate, enact. 2 send, confine. 3 promise, undertake, pledge, bind, obligate, engage. 4 dedicate, bind, pledge. 5 entrust, confide, commend, consign, deliver, deposit. **commit oneself** decide, undertake, promise, pledge, bind oneself.

commitment *noun* 1 the act of committing someone or oneself; the state of being committed. 2 dedication or devotion; strong conviction. 3 an undertaking or responsibility: *taking on too many commitments.*

⬛ 2 dedication, devotion, conviction, involvement, adherence, loyalty, tie. 3 undertaking, responsibility, obligation, duty, guarantee, assurance, promise, word, pledge, vow, liability.
🔲 2 vacillation, wavering.

committal *noun* the action of committing someone to a prison or mental institution.

committee /kə'mɪtɪ/ *sing. or pl. noun* 1 a group of people selected by, and from, a larger body, eg a club, to undertake especially administrative work on its behalf. 2 a body specially appointed to undertake an investigation, enquiry, etc. [from earlier *committen*, to entrust + -EE]

⬛ COUNCIL, BOARD, PANEL, COMMISSION, TASK FORCE.

committee stage *Politics* the stage between the second and third readings of a parliamentary bill, when it is examined in detail by members sitting in committee.

commode *noun* 1 a chair with a hinged seat covering a chamber pot. 2 a chest of drawers. [from French *commode*, from Latin *commodus*, convenient]

commodious /kə'moʊdɪəs/ *adj.* comfortably spacious. [from Latin *commodus*, convenient]

commodiously *adv.* in a commodious way.

commodiousness *noun* the quality of being commodious.

commodity /kə'mɒdɪtɪ/ *noun* (PL. **commodities**) 1 something that is bought and sold, especially a manufactured product or raw material. 2 something, eg a quality, from the point of view of its value in society: *courtesy is a scarce commodity.* [from Latin *commoditas*, benefit]

commodity market or **commodity exchange** a market where buyers and sellers of commodities (eg wool, sugar, coffee, wheat, metals) trade. Often prices are fixed on a bargain-by-bargain basis. The London Commodity Exchange is one of the most important in the world and deals in many different commodities; some markets deal with only one commodity.

commodore /'kɒmədɔː(r)/ *noun* 1 in the British navy, an officer just below a rear admiral in rank. 2 the president of a yacht club. 3 the senior captain in charge of a fleet of merchant ships. [perhaps through Dutch from French *commandeur*, commander]

common — *adj.* 1 often met with; frequent; familiar. 2 shared by two or more people, things, etc: *characteristics common to both animals.* 3 publicly owned. 4 of a standard one has a right to expect: *common decency.* 5 widespread: *common knowledge.* 6 *derog.* lacking taste or refinement; vulgar. 7 of the ordinary type: *the common cold.* 8 not of high rank or class: *the common people.* 9 *Maths.* shared by two or more numbers: *highest common factor.* — *noun* 1 a piece of land that is publicly owned or available for public use. 2 *Legal* a right to something, or to do something, on someone else's land. 3 *slang* common sense. See also COMMONS. — **the common touch** an ability, in someone distinguished by accomplishment or rank, to relate sociably to ordinary people. **in common** 1 *said of interests, etc* shared: *they have little in common.* 2 in joint use or ownership: *a garden owned in common by the residents.* **make common cause** to co-operate to achieve a common aim. [from Latin *communis*]

▣ *adj.* **1** frequent, familiar, customary, habitual, usual, daily, everyday, routine, regular. **2** shared, mutual, joint, collective. **3** communal, public. **4** basic. **5** widespread, prevalent, general, universal. **6** vulgar, coarse, unrefined, tasteless, crude, inferior, low, ill-bred, loutish, plebeian. **7** ordinary, standard, average, plain, simple, workaday, run-of-the-mill, undistinguished, unexceptional, conventional, accepted, popular, commonplace. **8** ordinary, working-class.

▣ *adj.* **1** uncommon, unusual, rare, noteworthy. **6** tasteful, refined.

common denominator 1 *Maths.* a whole number that is a multiple of each of the denominators of two or more fractions, eg 15 (3 x 5) is a common denominator of $\frac{1}{3}$ and $\frac{2}{5}$. See also LOWEST COMMON DENOMINATOR. **2** something that enables comparison, agreement, etc between people or things.

commoner *noun* a person who is not a member of the nobility.

common era a culturally neutral term for the present era, reckoned since the birth of Christ. See also BCE, CE.

common gender *Grammar* the gender of such nouns as *doctor, scientist, baby,* that can refer to either sex.

common ground an area of agreement between people, as a starting-point for discussion.

common law in England, law based on custom and decisions by judges, as distinct from written law.

common-law *adj.* denoting a relationship of two people living together as husband and wife but not legally married: *common-law marriage.*

commonly *adv.* **1** usually, often; generally, ordinarily. **2** in a common way. **3** vulgarly.

Common Market the European Community.

commonness *noun* being common.

common noun *Grammar* a noun that is not a proper name and which can refer to any member of a class of things, eg *car, table, girl* as opposed to *Paris, John.* See also PROPER NOUN.

common-or-garden *adj.* of the ordinary, everyday kind.

commonplace — *adj.* **1** ordinary; everyday. **2** *derog.* unoriginal; lacking individuality; trite. — *noun* **1** *derog.* a trite comment; a cliché. **2** an everyday occurrence. [translation of Latin *locus communis*, an argument widely used]

▣ *adj.* **1** ordinary, everyday, common, humdrum, pedestrian, widespread, frequent. **2** unoriginal, trite, hackneyed, stock, stale, banal, obvious, worn out, boring, uninteresting, threadbare. *noun* **1** cliché, chestnut, platitude, banality.

▣ *adj.* **2** memorable, exceptional.

common room in a college, school, etc a sitting-room for general use by students or staff.

common rorqual See RORQUAL.

commons *noun* **1** *Hist.* (**the commons**) (*pl.*) the ordinary people. **2** (**the Commons**) the House of Commons. **3** *old use, facetious* shared food rations. — **on short commons** having reduced rations.

common seal a true seal native to the N Pacific and N Atlantic oceans, usually grey with dark blotches. It dives to depths of more than 90m, and feeds on fish, squid, and crabs.

common sense practical good sense.

common-sense or **commonsensical** *adj.* having or noted for common sense.

▣ sensible, practical, matter-of-fact, level-headed, down-to-earth, pragmatic, shrewd, astute, prudent, judicious, sane, sound, reasonable, realistic.

▣ foolish, unreasonable, unrealistic.

common time *Mus.* a rhythm with two or four beats to the bar.

commonwealth *noun* **1** a country or state. **2** an association of states that have joined together for their common good. **3** (**the Commonwealth**) **a** an English republican regime created by Oliver Cromwell. **b** same as COMMONWEALTH OF NATIONS. **4** a title used by certain US states. [from COMMON + WEALTH]

Commonwealth Day the second Monday in March, celebrated throughout the Commonwealth of Nations. Until 1946 it was celebrated, as Empire Day, on 24 May (Queen Victoria's birthday); from 1967 it was celebrated on the Queen's official birthday in June; and it was changed to its present day in 1977.

Commonwealth of Nations former name **British Commonwealth** a voluntary organization of autonomous states which had been imperial possessions of Britain. Its head is the reigning British monarch.

commotion /kə'moʊʃən/ *noun* **1** a disturbance; an upheaval; tumult. **2** noisy confusion; uproar; din. [from Latin *commotio*, from *movere*, to move]

▣ **1** disturbance, upheaval, tumult, turmoil, disorder, excitement, agitation, hurly-burly, ferment, fuss, bustle, ado, *colloq.* to-do, *colloq.* bust-up. **2** uproar, furore, *colloq.* ballyhoo, *colloq.* hullabaloo, racket, hubbub, rumpus, fracas.

communal /'kɒmjʊnəl, kə'mju:nəl/ *adj.* **1** relating to, or belonging to, a community. **2** shared; owned in common. **3** relating to a commune or communes. [from Latin *communalis*, from *communis*, common]

▣ **1, 2** public, community, shared, joint, collective, general, common.

▣ **1, 2** private, personal.

communally *adv.* as regards a community; collectively rather than individually.

commune[1] /'kɒmju:n/ *noun* **1** a number of unrelated families and individuals living as a mutually supportive community, with shared accommodation, supplies, responsibilities, etc. **2** in some European countries, the smallest local administrative unit. [from Latin *communa*, from *communis*, common]

▣ **1** collective, co-operative, kibbutz, community, fellowship, colony, settlement.

commune[2] /kɒ'mju:n/ *verb intrans.* **1** to communicate intimately or confidentially. **2** to get close to or relate spiritually to (eg nature). [from French *communer*, to share]

▣ **1** communicate, converse, discourse. **2** communicate, make contact.

communicable /kə'mju:nɪkəbl/ *adj.* **1** capable of being communicated. **2** *Medicine* denoting an infectious or contagious disease, such as the common cold, that can be transmitted from one organism to another by direct physical contact, infected airborne droplets, etc. The most serious communicable diseases are known as *notifiable diseases*, eg diphtheria, meningitis, rabies. [from Latin *communicabilis*, from *communicare*, to share or impart]

communicant /kə'mju:nɪkənt/ *noun* **1** a person who receives Communion. **2** an informant. [from Latin *communicare*, to partake, impart]

communicate /kə'mju:nɪkeɪt/ *verb* **1** *trans., intrans.* to impart (information, ideas, etc); to make (something) known or understood; to get in touch. **2** to pass on or transmit (a disease, feeling, etc). **3** *intrans.* to understand someone; to have a comfortable social relationship. **4** *intrans.*, *said of rooms, etc* to be connected: *a communicating door*. **5** *intrans.* in the Christian Church, to receive Communion. [from Latin *communicare*, to share]

. . . .

⊟ 1 announce, declare, proclaim, report, reveal, disclose, divulge, impart, inform, acquaint, intimate, notify, publish, talk, converse, commune, correspond, write, phone, telephone, contact. **2** pass on, transmit, convey, spread, disseminate, diffuse.

. . . .

communication /kəmjuːnɪ'keɪʃən/ *noun* **1** the process or act of communicating; the exchanging or imparting of ideas and information, etc. **2** a piece of information, a letter, or a message. **3** social contact. **4** (**communications**) the various electronic processes by which information is conveyed from one person or place to another, especially by means of wires, cables, or radio waves. **5** (**communications**) means or routes used for moving troops or supplies. **6** (**communications**) the science and activity of transmitting information, etc.

. . . .

⊟ 1 communicating, contact, transmission, dissemination, connection. **2** information, letter, message, intelligence, intimation, disclosure.

. . . .

Forms of communication include: broadcasting, radio, wireless, television, TV, cable TV, satellite, video, teletext; newspaper, press, news, newsflash, magazine, journal, advertising, publicity, poster, leaflet, pamphlet, brochure, catalogue; post, dispatch, correspondence, letter, postcard, aerogram, telegram, cable, *colloq.* wire, chain letter, junk mail, mailshot; conversation, word, message, dialogue, speech, gossip, *colloq.* grapevine; notice, bulletin, announcement, communiqué, circular, memo, note, report; telephone, intercom, answering machine, walkie-talkie, bleeper, tannoy, telex, teleprinter, facsimile, fax, computer, word processor, typewriter, dictaphone, megaphone, loudhailer; radar, Morse code, semaphore, Braille, sign language.

communication cord *Brit.* a chain or cord fitted in a railway carriage, to be pulled in an emergency to stop the train.

communications satellite *Astron.* an unmanned artificial satellite sent by rocket into orbit around the Earth, and used to relay radio, television, and telephone signals.

communication theory the application of information theory to human communication in general. Communication is seen as involving an information source which encodes a message to be transmitted through a channel to a receiver, where it is decoded and has an effect.

communicative /kə'mjuːnɪkətɪv/ *adj.* **1** sociable; talkative. **2** relating to communication: *communicative skills*.

. . . .

⊟ 1 sociable, talkative, voluble, expansive, informative, chatty, friendly, forthcoming, outgoing, extrovert, unreserved, free, open, frank, candid. **2** interpersonal.

⊟ 1 quiet, reserved, reticent, secretive, taciturn.

. . . .

communicatively *adv.* in a communicative way.

communion /kə'mjuːnɪən/ *noun* **1** the sharing of thoughts, beliefs, or feelings. **2** a group of people sharing the same religious beliefs. **3** (*also* **Holy Communion**) in the Christian Church, a service at which bread and wine are taken as symbols of Christ's body and blood; the consecrated bread and wine. [from Latin *communio*, mutual participation]

communiqué /kə'mjuːnɪkeɪ/ *noun* an official bulletin, communication, or announcement. [from French *communiqué*, something communicated]

communism /'kɒmjʊnɪzm/ *noun* **1** a political theory advocating that society should be classless, private property should be abolished, and land, factories, and other

sources of wealth should be collectively owned and controlled by the people. **2** (**Communism**) a political movement founded on the principles of communism set out by Karl Marx. **3** the political and social system established on these principles in the former Soviet Union and other countries of E Europe. [from French *communisme*, from *commun*, common]

communist — *noun* **1** a supporter of or believer in communism. **2** (*often* **Communist**) a member of a Communist party. — *adj.* **1** relating to communism. **2** believing in or favouring communism.

communistic /kɒmjʊ'nɪstɪk/ *adj.* **1** believing in or favouring communism. **2** involving or favouring communal living and ownership.

communitarian /kəmjuːnɪ'teərɪən/ *noun* **1** a member of a community. **2** an advocate of community life.

community /kə'mjuːnɪtɪ/ *noun* (PL. **communities**) **1** the group of people living in a particular locality. **2** a group of people bonded together by a common religion, nationality or occupation. **3** a religious or spiritual fellowship of people living together. **4** the quality or fact of being shared or common: *community of interests*. **5** a group of states with common interests. **6** the public; society in general. **7** *Biol.* a collection of different plant or animal species that occupy the same habitat and interact with each other. [from Latin *communitas*, fellowship]

. . . .

⊟ 1 district, locality, population, people, populace, public, residents. **2** population, people, populace, nation, state, colony, fellowship, brotherhood, fraternity. **3** commune, kibbutz, society, association, fellowship, brotherhood, fraternity. **5** federation, association. **6** public, people, population, populace, residents, nation.

. . . .

community centre a place where members of a community may meet for social, sporting, or educational activities.

community charge a tax levied on individuals to pay for local services; the poll tax. See also RATE[1] *noun* 6, COUNCIL TAX.

community home an institution in which young offenders are accommodated.

community school or **college** a school or college which is open to the whole community, not just to those of school age. Its facilities may be made available at evenings and at weekends, and in some cases children and adults may study in the same class or take part in the same recreational activities.

community service work of benefit to the local community, sometimes prescribed for offenders in place of a prison sentence.

community singing organized singing at a large gathering, with everyone taking part.

community work work that serves the social and economic needs of members of a community.

community worker a person who works to meet the needs of a community, eg a social worker.

commutable /kə'mjuːtəbl/ *adj.* capable of being commuted or exchanged.

commutation /kɒmjʊ'teɪʃən/ *noun* the act of being commuted or exchanged.

commutative /kə'mjuːtətɪv/ *adj. Maths.*, *said of an arithmetical process* performed on two quantities, the order of which does not affect the result, eg addition and multiplication, because $a + b$ is equal to $b + a$, and a is equal to b a. Subtraction and division are not commutative operations.

commutator /'kɒmjʊteɪtə(r)/ *noun* that part of a direct-current motor or generator that reverses the direction of flow of electric current in the armature windings, and also provides an electrical connection between the rotating armature windings and the stationary terminal.

commute *verb* **1** *intrans.* to travel regularly between two places, especially between home and work in a city, etc. **2**

to alter (a criminal sentence) to one less severe. **3** to substitute; to convert. **4** to exchange (a pension, etc) for another form of payment, especially a lump sum. [from Latin *commutare*, to alter or exchange]

⊟ **1** travel, journey. **2** reduce, decrease, shorten, curtail, lighten, soften, mitigate, remit, adjust, modify, alter, change. **3**, **4** convert, exchange, substitute.

commuter *noun* a person who travels regularly between home and work.

compact[1] /kəm'pakt, 'kɒmpakt/ — *adj.* (with stress on *-pact*) **1** firm and dense in form or texture. **2** small, but with all essentials neatly contained. **3** neatly concise. — *verb* (with stress on *-pact*) to compress. — *noun* (with stress on *com-*) a small case for women's face powder, usually including a mirror. [from Latin *compactus*, put together]

⊟ *adj.* **1** firm, dense, close, impenetrable, solid. **3** short, brief, terse, succinct, concise, condensed, compressed.
⊟ *adj.* **1** open, coarse, loose. **2** large, rambling. **3** rambling, diffuse, wordy.

compact[2] *noun* (with stress on *com-*) a contract or agreement. [from Latin *com-*, with + *pacisci*, to agree]

compact disc (ABBREV. **CD**) an aluminium disc that is used to store digital data, mainly recorded music, but also large collections of computer data, eg the text of catalogues and encyclopedias, especially using the CD-ROM (compact disc with read-only memory) format.

compact disc interactive (ABBREV. **CD-i**) *Comput.* a type of CD-ROM that responds intelligently to instructions given by the user, and is used in conjunction with a computerized reader. It can be used to store sound, text, graphics, animation, and video in a single unit.

compact disc read-only memory (ABBREV. **CD-ROM**) *Comput.* a facility that allows large amounts of data, such as the text of catalogues and encyclopedias, stored on compact disc, to be 'read' (but not altered) on a visual display unit by passing a low-power laser beam over the disc.

compaction /kəm'pakʃən/ *noun* the act of compacting or state of being compacted.

compactly *adv.* in a compact way; so as to be compact.

compactness *noun* the quality of being compact.

companion[1] *noun* **1** a friend, comrade, or frequent associate. **2** someone who accompanies one on a journey. **3** *Hist.* a woman paid to live or travel with, and be company for, another. **4** *especially as a title* a book of advice; a handbook or guide. **5** one of a pair of matching objects. **6** (**Companion**) an honourable title denoting a low-ranking member of any of various orders of knighthood. [from French *compagnon*, from Latin *companio*, literally foodsharer, from *panis*, bread]

⊟ **1** friend, comrade, *colloq.* buddy, *colloq.* crony, intimate, confidant(e), ally, confederate, colleague, associate, partner, mate. **2**, **3** escort, chaperone, attendant.

companion[2] *noun Naut.* a hatch admitting light to a cabin or lower deck. [from Dutch *kompanje*, quarterdeck]

companionable *adj.* friendly; sociable; comfortable as a companion.

companionably *adv.* in a companionable way.

companionship *noun* **1** fellowship, company. **2** a body of companions.

⊟ **1** fellowship, comradeship, camaraderie, esprit de corps, support, friendship, company, togetherness, conviviality, sympathy, rapport.

companionway *noun* a staircase between decks.

company /'kʌmpənɪ/ *noun* (PL. **companies**) **1** the presence of another person or other people; companionship. **2** the presence of guests or visitors, or the people involved: *expecting company.* **3** one's friends, companions, or associates: *get into bad company.* **4** a business organization. **5** a troupe of actors or entertainers. **6** a military unit of about 120 men. **7** a ship's crew. **8** a gathering of people, at a social function, etc. — **be good** or **bad company** to be an entertaining, or dreary, companion. **be in good company** to be not the only one in a situation. **in company with** ... together with ...; along with: *in company with other reasons.* **keep someone company** to act as their companion to. **part company with someone 1** to separate from them. **2** to disagree with them. [from Old French *compaignie*, from the same root as COMPANION]

⊟ **1** society, companionship, fellowship, support, attendance, presence. **2** guests, visitors, callers. **3** set, circle, crowd. **4** firm, business, concern, organization, association, corporation, establishment, house, partnership, syndicate, cartel, consortium. **5** troupe, group, band, ensemble. **8** gathering, crowd, throng, body, troop, *colloq.* crew, party, assembly.

company secretary a senior member of a business organization, in charge of financial and legal matters.

comparability /kɒmpərə'bɪlɪtɪ/ *noun* the fact or extent of being comparable.

comparable /'kɒmpərəbl, kəm'parəbl/ *adj.* **1** of the same or equivalent kind. **2** able to be compared; similar enough to allow comparison.

⊟ SIMILAR, ALIKE, RELATED, AKIN, COGNATE, CORRESPONDING, ANALOGOUS, EQUIVALENT, TANTAMOUNT, PROPORTIONATE, COMMENSURATE, PARALLEL, EQUAL.
⊟ DISSIMILAR, UNLIKE, UNEQUAL.

comparably *adv.* in a comparable way; so as to be comparable.

comparative /kəm'parətɪv/ — *adj.* **1** judged by comparison; as compared with others. **2** relating to, or using the method of, comparison. **3** as observed by comparing one another: *their comparative strengths.* **4** denoting a form of study that is concerned with the similarities and differences between various forms or cultures: *comparative history.* **5** *Grammar*, *said of adjectives and adverbs* in the form denoting a greater degree of the quality in question, either using the suffix *-er* as in *larger, faster* or the word *more*, as in *more usual, more usually.* — *noun Grammar* **1** a comparative adjective or adverb. **2** the comparative form of a word. [from Latin *comparare*, to match]

comparatively *adv.* **1** relatively; rather, somewhat: *the weather is comparatively mild.* **2** by way of comparison.

compare *verb* **1** (**compare one thing with another**) to examine (things of the same kind) to see what differences there are between them. **2** (**compare one person** or **thing to another**) to liken them: *compare her to an angel.* **3** (**compare with something** or **someone**) to stand comparison with them; to be comparable with them: *he can't compare with his predecessor in ability.* — **beyond compare** or **without compare** *formal* without equal; incomparable. **compare notes** to exchange ideas and opinions. [from Latin *comparare*, to match]

⊟ **1** contrast, juxtapose, balance, weigh, correlate. **2** liken, equate. **3** match, equal, parallel.

comparison /kəm'parɪsən/ *noun* **1** the process of, an act of, or a reasonable basis for, comparing: *it doesn't bear comparison with them / there can be no comparison between them.* **2** *Grammar* the positive, comparative, and superlative forms of adjectives and adverbs: *the degrees of comparison.* [from French *comparaison*]

⊟ **1** likeness, resemblance, similarity, comparability, analogy,

parallel, correlation, relationship, contrast, juxtaposition, distinction.
. . . .

compartment *noun* **1** a separated-off or enclosed section. **2** any of several enclosed sections into which a railway carriage is divided. [from French *compartiment*]
. . . .

⊞ **1** section, division, subdivision, category, pigeonhole, cubbyhole, niche, alcove, bay, area, stall, booth, cubicle, locker, carrel, cell, chamber, berth.
. . . .

compartmental /kɒmpɑːˈmentəl/ *adj.* involving or consisting of compartments.

compartmentalization or **compartmentalisation** *noun* the process or state of being compartmentalized.

compartmentalize or **compartmentalise** *verb* to divide, distribute, or force into categories.

compass /ˈkʌmpəs/ *noun* **1** any instrument for finding direction, especially one consisting of a magnetized needle that swings freely on a pivot and points to magnetic north, from which true north can be calculated. See also GYRO-COMPASS. **2** (*usually* **compasses** or **pair of compasses**) a V-shaped instrument consisting of two hinged arms, used for drawing circles, measuring distances on maps, etc. **3** range or scope. **4** *Mus.* the range, from highest to lowest possible note, of a voice or instrument. [from French *compas*, from *compasser*, to measure]

compassion *noun* a feeling of sorrow and pity for someone in trouble, usually inclining one to help, show mercy, etc. [from Latin *compassio*]
. . . .

⊞ sorrow, pity, sympathy, commiseration, tenderness, fellow feeling, humanity, mercy, condolence, kindness, concern, care.
⊟ cruelty, indifference.
. . . .

compassionate *adj.* inclined to pity or mercy; merciful.
. . . .

⊞ merciful, pitying, tender, caring, kind-hearted, kindly, tender-hearted, warm-hearted, sympathetic, understanding, supportive, lenient, humane, benevolent, humanitarian.
⊟ cruel, indifferent.
. . . .

compassionate leave special leave granted in cases of bereavement.

compassionately *adv.* in a compassionate way.

compassion fatigue progressive disinclination to show compassion because of continued or excessive exposure to deserving cases.

compatibility /kəmpatɪˈbɪlɪtɪ/ *noun* the quality of being compatible.

compatible /kəmˈpatɪbl/ *adj.* (*often* **compatible with something** or **someone**) **1** able to associate or co-exist agreeably. **2** *Comput.*, *said of a program or device* capable of being used with a particular computer system, especially one produced by another manufacturer. **3** *Engineering*, *said of a device or piece of machinery* capable of being used in conjunction with another, especially a newer version, without the need for special modification. [from Latin *compatibilis*]
. . . .

⊞ **1** harmonious, consistent, congruous, matching, consonant, accordant, suitable, reconcilable, adaptable, conformable, sympathetic, like-minded, wellmatched, similar.
⊟ INCOMPATIBLE. **1** antagonistic, contradictory.
. . . .

compatibly *adv.* in a way that is compatible; so as to be compatible.

compatriot /kəmˈpeɪtrɪət/ *noun* someone from one's own country; a fellow-citizen. [from Latin *compatriota*, from *com-* with + *patria*, one's country]

compeer /kəmˈpɪə(r)/ *noun* an equal; a companion or comrade. [from French *comper*, from Latin *com-* with + *par*, equal]

compel /kəmˈpɛl/ *verb* (**compelled, compelling**) **1** to force; to drive. **2** to arouse; to draw forth: *their plight compels sympathy*. [from Latin *compellere*, to force]
. . . .

⊞ **1** force, make, constrain, oblige, necessitate, drive, urge, impel, coerce, pressurize, browbeat, bully, *colloq.* strongarm, bulldoze, *facetious* pressgang, dragoon. **2** arouse, prompt, provoke, kindle.
. . . .

compelling *adj.* **1** powerful; forcing one to agree, etc. **2** irresistibly fascinating.
. . . .

⊞ **1** powerful, forceful, coercive, persuasive, convincing, conclusive, incontrovertible, irrefutable, imperative, urgent, pressing, overriding, cogent. **2** irresistible, fascinating, gripping, enthralling, spellbinding, mesmeric, compulsive.
⊟ **1** weak, unconvincing. **2** boring.
. . . .

compellingly *adv.* in a compelling or convincing way.

compendious /kəmˈpɛndɪəs/ *adj.* concise but comprehensive. [from Latin *compendiosus*, from *compendium*, summary]

compendiously *adv.* in a compendious way.

compendium /kəmˈpɛndɪəm/ *noun* (PL. **compendiums, compendia**) **1** a concise summary; an abridgement. **2** a collection of boardgames, puzzles, etc in a single container. [from Latin *compendium*, from *com-*, together + *pendere*, to weigh]

compensate *verb* **1** (**compensate someone for something**) to make amends to them for loss, injury, or wrong, especially by a suitable payment. **2** (**compensate for something**) to make up for a disadvantage, loss, etc. [from Latin *compensare*]
. . . .

⊞ **1** recompense, reward, remunerate, indemnify. **2** balance, counterbalance, cancel, neutralize, counteract, offset, redress, make good, repay, refund, reimburse, restore.
. . . .

compensation /kɒmpənˈseɪʃən/ *noun* **1** the process of compensating. **2** something that compensates. **3** a sum of money given to make up for loss, injury, etc.
. . . .

⊞ **1** reparation, reimbursement, indemnification, repayment, restoration, restitution, consolation, redress, comfort, requital. **2** amends, redress, satisfaction, requital. **3** repayment, refund, reimbursement, indemnification, indemnity, damages, reparation, recompense, reward, payment, remuneration, return.
. . . .

compensatory /kɒmpənˈseɪtərɪ/ *adj.* involving or giving compensation.

compère /ˈkɒmpeə(r)/ — *noun* a person who presents a radio or television show, introduces performers, etc. — *verb* to act as compère for (a show). [from French *compère*, godfather]

compete *verb intrans.* (*often* **compete with** or **against someone** or **something**) **1** to take part in a contest. **2** to strive or struggle: *compete with other firms*. **3** *said of a product, firm, etc* to give good value, be reasonably cheap, etc when compared to market rivals. [from Latin *competere*, to coincide, ask for, seek]
. . . .

⊞ **1** take part, participate. **2** vie, battle, struggle, strive.
. . . .

competence /ˈkɒmpɪtəns/ *noun* (*also occasionally* **competency**) **1** capability; efficiency. **2** legal authority or capability. **3** *old use* sufficient income to live comfortably.

competent /ˈkɒmpɪtənt/ *adj.* **1** efficient. **2** having sufficient skill or training to do something. **3** legally capable. [from Latin *competere*, to meet, be sufficient]

. . . .

☐ **1** efficient, capable, able, adept, well-qualified, experienced, skilled, proficient, expert, masterly. **2** trained, qualified, capable, able, equal, fit.
☒ **1** incompetent, inefficient. **2** incompetent, incapable, unable.

. . . .

competently *adv.* in a competent way; ably.

competition /kɒmpə'tɪʃən/ *noun* **1** an event in which people compete. **2** the process or fact of competing. **3** one's rivals, eg in business, or their products. **4** *Biol.* in a community of plants and animals, the simultaneous demand for the same limited resource, eg light, water, by two or more organisms or species, which leads to a struggle for continued survival. [from Latin *competitio*, meeting together]

. . . .

☐ **1** contest, championship, tournament, cup, event, race, match, game, quiz. **2** rivalry, opposition, challenge, contention, conflict, struggle, strife, competitiveness, combativeness. **3** competitors, rivals, opponents, challengers, field.

. . . .

competitive /kəm'pɛtɪtɪv/ *adj.* **1** involving rivalry. **2** enjoying rivalry; aggressive; ambitious. **3** *said of a price or product* reasonably cheap; comparing well with those of market rivals. [from Latin *competere*, to meet together]

. . . .

☐ **2** combative, contentious, antagonistic, aggressive, pushy, ambitious, keen, cut-throat. **3** cheap, good value.

. . . .

competitively *adv.* in a competitive way.
competitiveness *noun* the quality of being competitive.
competitor /kəm'pɛtɪtə(r)/ *noun* a person, team, firm, or product that competes; a rival. [from Latin *competitor*, from *competere*, to meet]

. . . .

☐ contestant, contender, challenger, opponent, adversary, antagonist, rival, emulator, entrant, candidate, competition, opposition.

. . . .

compilation /kɒmpɪ'leɪʃən/ *noun* **1** the process of compiling. **2** the book, etc compiled.
compile *verb* **1** to collect and organize (information, etc); to produce (a list, reference book, etc) from information collected. **2** *Comput.* to create (a set of instructions written in machine code) from a source program written in a high-level programming language, using a compiler. [from Latin *compilare*, to plunder]

. . . .

☐ **1** compose, put together, collect, gather, garner, cull, accumulate, amass, assemble, marshal, organize, arrange.

. . . .

compiler *noun* **1** a person who compiles information, etc. **2** *Comput.* a program that converts a source program written in a high-level programming language into a set of instructions written in machine code that can be acted on by a computer.
complacence or **complacency** *noun* being complacent.
complacent *adj.* **1** self-satisfied; smug. **2** too easily satisfied; disinclined to worry. [from Latin *complacere*, to be pleasing]

. . . .

☐ **1** self-satisfied, smug, gloating, triumphant, proud, self-righteous. **2** unconcerned, serene, self-assured, contented.
☒ **1** diffident, discontented. **2** concerned, anxious.

. . . .

complacently *adv.* with a complacent manner.
complain *verb intrans.* **1** to express one's dissatisfaction or displeasure. **2** (**complain of something**) to say that one is

suffering from a pain, disease, etc. [from Old French *complaindre*, to pity]

. . . .

☐ **1** protest, grumble, *colloq.* grouse, *colloq.* gripe, *slang* kvetch, *colloq.* beef, carp, fuss, lament, bemoan, bewail, moan, whine, groan, growl.

. . . .

complainant *noun Legal* a plaintiff.
complainer *noun* a person who complains.
complaint *noun* **1** the act of complaining. **2** an expression of dissatisfaction; a cause for this. **3** a disorder, illness, etc.

. . . .

☐ **1** protest, objection, fault-finding, criticism, censure, accusation. **2** protest, objection, *colloq.* grumble, *colloq.* grouse, *colloq.* gripe, *colloq.* beef, moan, accusation, dissatisfaction, charge, grievance, annoyance. **3** disorder, illness, ailment, sickness, disease, malady, malaise, indisposition, affliction, trouble, upset.

. . . .

complaisance /kəm'pleɪzəns/ *noun* **1** a desire to please, especially in excess. **2** an obliging manner or attitude.
complaisant /kəm'pleɪzənt/ *adj.* wanting to please; obliging; amenable. [from French *complaisant*, from *complaire*, to please]
complaisantly *adv.* in a complaisant way.
complement /'kɒmpləmənt/ — *noun* **1** something that completes or perfects; something that provides a needed balance or contrast. **2** the number or quantity required to fill something, eg the crew of a ship. **3** *Grammar* a word or phrase added to a verb to complete the predicate of a sentence, eg *dark* in *it grew dark*. **4** *Maths.* in set theory, all the members of a universal set that do not belong to a specified set S. For example, if the universal set represents all positive whole numbers, and set S represents all odd numbers, the complement of set S will represent all even numbers. **5** *Geom.* that amount by which an angle or arc falls short of a right angle or quadrant. **6** *Biol.* in blood serum, a group of proteins that combine with antibodies and participate in the destruction of foreign particles following an immune response. — *verb* to be a complement to. [from Latin *complementum*, from *complere*, to fill]
complementarily /kɒmplɪmen'tɑːrɪlɪ/ *adv.* in a complementary way; so as to complement.
complementary /kɒmplɪ'mentərɪ/ *adj.* **1** serving as a complement to something. **2** complementing each other. **3** *Physics* denoting either of a pair of coloured lights that, when mixed together in the correct intensities, produce the sensation of white light. **4** *Geom.* denoting one of a pair of angles whose sum is 90°. **5** denoting the treatments or techniques of alternative medicine.

. . . .

☐ **1** reciprocal, corresponding, matching, twin, fellow, companion. **2** interdependent, correlative, interrelated, corresponding, matching.
☒ **1** contradictory. **2** incompatible.

. . . .

complementary medicine *Medicine* alternative medicine.
complete — *adj.* **1** whole; finished; with nothing missing. **2** thorough; utter; absolute; total. — *verb* **1** to finish; to make complete or perfect. **2** to fill in (a form). — **complete with ...** having the additional feature of ... [from Latin *complere*, to fill up]

. . . .

☐ *adj.* **1** whole, finished, unabridged, unabbreviated, unexpurgated, entire, full, undivided, intact, ended, concluded, over, done, accomplished, achieved. **2** thorough, utter, absolute, total, downright, out-and-out, perfect. *verb* **1** finish, end, close, conclude, wind up, terminate, finalize, settle, clinch, perform, discharge, execute, fulfil, realize, accomplish, achieve, consummate, crown, perfect.
☒ *adj.* **1** partial, incomplete, abridged, damaged.

. . . .

completely *adv.* **1** so as to be complete: *completely full.* **2** to a full or extreme extent; without reserve: *was completely satisfied.*

completeness *noun* a complete state or quality.

completion *noun* **1** the fact or process of completing. **2** the state of being complete. **3** fulfilment.

⊟ **1, 2** conclusion, termination, finalization, settlement, discharge. **3** fulfilment, realization, accomplishment, achievement, attainment, fruition, culmination, consummation, perfection.

complex /'kɒmplɛks, kəm'plɛks/ — *adj.* **1** composed of many interrelated parts. **2** complicated; involved; tangled. **3** *Grammar, said of a sentence* having a main clause and one or more subordinate clauses. — *noun* **1** something made of interrelating parts, eg a multi-purpose building: *a leisure complex.* **2** *Psychol.* in psychoanalysis, a set of repressed thoughts and emotions that strongly influence an individual's behaviour and attitudes. **3** *colloq.* an obsession or phobia. [from Latin *complex*, closely connected]

⊟ *adj.* **1** composite, compound, mixed, varied, diverse, multiple, ramified. **2** complicated, involved, intricate, elaborate, tangled, convoluted, circuitous, tortuous, devious. *noun* **1** establishment, institute, development, network, structure, system, scheme, organization. **3** obsession, phobia, *colloq.* hang-up, fixation, preoccupation.

⊟ *adj.* SIMPLE. **2** easy.

complexion /kəm'plɛkʃən/ *noun* **1** the colour or appearance of the skin, especially of the face. **2** character or appearance: *that puts a different complexion on the matter.* [from Latin *complexio*, combination]

⊟ **1** skin, colour, colouring, pigmentation. **2** character, appearance, look, aspect, light, nature, type, kind.

complexity /kəm'plɛksɪtɪ/ *noun* (PL. **complexities**) **1** the quality of being complex. **2** a complication; an intricacy.

complex number *Maths.* the sum of a real and an imaginary number.

complex sentence a sentence comprising a main clause and one or more subordinate clauses. See also COMPOUND SENTENCE, SIMPLE SENTENCE.

compliance /kəm'plaɪəns/ *noun* **1** yielding. **2** agreement, assent. **3** submission.

compliant /kəm'plaɪənt/ *adj.* inclined to comply with or yield to the wishes of others; obedient; submissive.

compliantly *adv.* in a compliant way.

complicate *verb* to add difficulties or intricacies to; to make complex or involved. [from Latin *com-*, together + *plicare*, to fold]

⊟ compound, muddle, mix up, confuse, tangle, entangle, elaborate, involve.

⊟ simplify.

complicated *adj.* **1** difficult to understand or deal with. **2** intricate; complex. **3** *said of a fracture in a bone* accompanied by piercing of the overlying skin, and therefore susceptible to infection.

⊟ **1** difficult, problematic, puzzling, perplexing. **2** complex, intricate, elaborate, involved, convoluted, tortuous.

⊟ SIMPLE. **1** easy, straightforward.

complication *noun* **1** the process of becoming complicated. **2** a circumstance or element that causes difficulties. **3** *Medicine* a second and possibly worse disease or disorder that arises during the course of (and often as a result of) an existing disease or disorder.

⊟ **1** confusion, ramification, elaboration, convolution. **2** difficulty, drawback, snag, obstacle, problem, ramification, repercussion, complexity, intricacy, elaboration, convolution, tangle, web, confusion, mixture.

complicity /kəm'plɪsɪtɪ/ *noun* participation in a crime or wrongdoing. [from Latin *complex*, closely connected]

compliment /'kɒmplɪmənt/ — *noun* **1** an expression of praise, admiration, or approval. **2** a gesture implying approval: *paid her the compliment of dancing with her.* **3** (**compliments**) formal regards accompanying a gift, etc. — *verb* (**compliment someone on something**) to congratulate them for it. [from French *compliment*, from Italian *complimento*]

⊟ *noun* **1** praise, flattery, admiration, approval, favour, congratulations, tribute, commendation, eulogy. **2** honour, accolade, bouquet. *verb* congratulate, flatter, admire, commend, praise, applaud, salute.

⊟ *noun* **1** insult, criticism. *verb* insult, condemn.

complimentary /kɒmplɪ'mɛntərɪ/ *adj.* **1** paying a compliment; admiring or approving. **2** given free.

⊟ **1** flattering, admiring, favourable, approving, appreciative, congratulatory, commendatory, eulogistic. **2** free, gratis, honorary, courtesy.

⊟ **1** insulting, unflattering, critical.

compline /'kɒmplɪn/ *noun* in Roman Catholic liturgy, the seventh and last service of the day, at 9pm, completing the set hours for prayer. See also LAUDS, MATINS, NONE[2], SEXT, TERCE, VESPERS. [from French *complie*, from Latin *completa hora*, complete hour]

comply /kəm'plaɪ/ *verb intrans.* (**complies, complied**) (*often* **comply with something**) to act in obedience to an order, command, request, etc: *we had to comply / complied with their wishes.* [from Italian *complire*, to fulfil]

⊟ obey, agree, consent, assent, accede, yield, submit, defer, respect, fall in, conform, follow, oblige, observe, perform, discharge, fulfil, satisfy, accommodate, meet.

⊟ defy, disobey.

component — *noun* any of the parts that make up a machine, engine, instrument, etc. — *adj.* being one of the parts of something. [from Latin *componere*, to assemble into a whole]

⊟ *noun* part, constituent, ingredient, element, factor, item, unit, piece, bit, spare part.

componential /kɒmpoʊ'nɛnʃəl/ *adj.* involving or relating to the components or elements of something.

comport *verb* **1** (**comport oneself**) to behave in a specified way. **2** *intrans.* (**comport with something**) to suit or be appropriate to it. [from Latin *com-*, together + *portare*, to carry]

comportment *noun* behaviour, bearing.

compose *verb* **1** *trans., intrans.* to create (music). **2** to write (a poem, letter, article, etc). **3** to make up or constitute. **4** to arrange as a balanced, artistic whole: *compose a painting.* **5** to calm (oneself); to get (one's thoughts, etc) under control. **6** to settle (differences between people in dispute). **7** *Printing* to arrange (type) or set (a page, etc) in type ready for printing. [from Latin *com-*, together + *ponere*, to put]

⊟ **1, 2** create, invent, devise, write, arrange, produce, make, form, fashion, build, construct, frame. **3** constitute, make up, form. **5** calm, soothe, quiet, still, settle, quell, pacify, control.

composed *adj., said of a person* calm; controlled.

◼ calm, controlled, tranquil, serene, relaxed, unworried, unruffled, imperturbable, unflappable, placid, level-headed, cool, collected, self-possessed.

◪ agitated, worried, troubled.

composedly /kəm'poʊzɪdlɪ/ *adv.* with a composed manner.

composer *noun* someone who composes, especially music.

composite /'kɒmpəzɪt, kəm'pɒzɪt/ — *adj.* **1** made up of different parts, materials, or styles. **2** *Bot.* of or relating to the Compositae (a family of flowering plants). — *noun* **1** *Bot.* a member of a large family of flowering plants (Compositae) in which the flower head consists of many tiny florets crowded together and often surrounded by a circle of bracts, eg daisy, sunflower. **2** *Chem.* a combination of two or more materials which has superior properties to any of its individual components, eg carbon-fibre reinforced plastics, combinations of metal alloys. **3** *Archit.* (*often* **Composite**) the most decorative of the five main orders of architecture. It was introduced by the Romans and was characterized by the combination of the Corinthian acanthus with the Ionic volute, carved mouldings, and decorated entablature.

composition /kɒmpə'zɪʃən/ *noun* **1** something composed, especially a musical or literary work. **2** the process of composing. **3** *Art* arrangement, especially with regard to balance and visual effect: *photographic composition.* **4** *old use* a school essay. **5** what something consists of. **6** a synthetic material of any of various kinds. **7** *Printing* the arrangement of pages of type ready for printing.

◼ **1** work, opus, piece, study, exercise. **2** creation, writing, making, production, formation, formulation, compilation, invention, design. **3** arrangement, organization, form, structure, configuration, layout, harmony, consonance, balance, symmetry, proportion. **5** constitution, make-up, combination, mixture.

compositor /kəm'pɒzɪtə(r)/ *noun Printing* a person who sets or arranges pages of type ready for printing.

compos mentis /'kɒmpɒs 'mentɪs/ *adj. Legal* being of sound mind; perfectly rational. [Latin, = in control of the mind]

compost — *noun* a mixture of decaying organic matter such as rotting vegetation and manure, often piled into a *compost heap*, and kept for mixing into soil as a form of nutrient-rich fertilizer, much used by gardeners to nourish plants and improve their growth. — *verb* **1** to make (decaying organic matter) into compost. **2** to fertilize (a soil) with such a mixture. [from Latin *com-*, together + *ponere*, to put]

composure *noun* mental and emotional calmness; self-control. [from COMPOSE]

◼ calmness, calm, self-control, self-possession, tranquillity, serenity, coolness, aplomb, poise, dignity, imperturbability, placidity, equanimity, dispassion, impassivity, confidence, ease, assurance, selfassurance.

◪ agitation, nervousness, discomposure.

compound¹ /'kɒmpaʊnd, kəm'paʊnd/ — *noun* (with stress on *com-*) **1** (*in full* **chemical compound**) *Chem.* a substance that is composed of two or more chemical elements combined in fixed proportions. It differs from a mixture in that its constituents cannot be separated from each other by physical means. **2** something composed of two or more ingredients or parts. **3** a word made up of two or more words, eg *tablecloth*. See also DERIVATIVE. — *adj.* (with stress on *com-*) **1** composed of a number of parts or ingredients. **2** *Grammar, said of a sentence* made up of two or more main clauses. — *verb* (with stress on *-pound*)

1 to make (especially something bad) much worse; to complicate or add to (a difficulty, error, etc). **2** to mix or combine (ingredients); to make up (a mixture, etc) by doing this. **3** *Legal* to agree to overlook (an offence, etc) in return for payment. **4** *intrans.* (**compound with someone**) to come to an agreement (especially a financial agreement) with them. [from French *compoundre*, from Latin *componere*, to put together]

◼ *noun* **2** mixture, alloy, blend, medley, composite, amalgam, synthesis, fusion, composition, amalgamation, combination. *adj.* **1** composite, complex, multiple, mixed, complicated, intricate. *verb* **1** worsen, exacerbate, aggravate, complicate, intensify, heighten, magnify, increase, augment. **2** mix, combine, amalgamate, blend, mingle, intermingle, unite, fuse, coalesce, synthesize, alloy.

compound² /'kɒmpaʊnd/ *noun* **1** in China, India, etc, an area enclosed by a wall or fence and containing a house or factory. **2** an enclosed area in a prison, used for a particular purpose. **3** in S Africa, an enclosure in which labourers are housed. [from Malay *kampong*]

compound fracture *Medicine* a type of bone fracture in which one or both broken ends of the bone pierce the overlying skin. Also called OPEN FRACTURE.

compound interest interest on the original sum and on any interest already accumulated. See also SIMPLE INTEREST.

compound sentence a sentence comprising more than one main clause. See also COMPLEX SENTENCE, SIMPLE SENTENCE.

compound time *Mus.* with three, or a multiple of three, beats to a bar.

comprehend *verb* **1** to understand; to envisage. **2** to include. [from Latin *comprehendere*, to seize, understand]

◼ **1** understand, envisage, conceive, see, realize, appreciate, know, apprehend, perceive, discern, take in, assimilate, grasp, fathom, penetrate, *colloq.* tumble to. **2** include, comprise, encompass, embrace, cover.

◪ **1** misunderstand.

comprehensibility /kɒmprɪhensə'bɪlɪtɪ/ *noun* the quality of being comprehensible.

comprehensible /kɒmprɪ'hensəbəl/ *adj.* capable of being understood. [from Latin *comprehensibilis*]

◼ understandable, intelligible, coherent, explicit, clear, lucid, plain, simple, straightforward.

◪ incomprehensible, obscure.

comprehensibly *adv.* in a comprehensible way.

comprehension /kɒmprɪ'henʃən/ *noun* **1** the process or power of understanding; the scope or range of one's knowledge or understanding. **2** a school exercise for testing students' understanding of a passage of text. [from Latin *comprehensio*]

◼ **1** understanding, conception, grasp, realization, appreciation, knowledge, apprehension, perception, discernment, judgement, sense, intelligence.

◪ **1** incomprehension, unawareness.

comprehensive /kɒmprɪ'hensɪv/ — *adj.* **1** covering or including everything or a great deal. **2** *said of a school or education* providing teaching for children of all abilities between the ages of 11 and 18. — *noun* a comprehensive school. [from Latin *comprehendere*, to comprise, include]

◼ *adj.* **1** thorough, exhaustive, full, complete, inclusive, all-inclusive, all-embracing, broad, wide, extensive, sweeping, general, blanket, across-the-board, encyclopedic, compendious.

🔳 *adj.* **1** partial, incomplete. **2** selective.

. . . .

comprehensively *adv.* so as to include everything; completely.

comprehensiveness *noun* the quality of being comprehensive.

compress /kəm'pres, 'kɒmpres/ — *verb* **1** to press together, squeeze, or squash. **2** to reduce in bulk; to condense. **3** to pack (data) into the minimum possible space in computer memory. — *noun* a cloth or gauze pad, often previously soaked in hot or cold water, applied with firm pressure to some part of the body in order to reduce fever, relieve discomfort caused by swelling, etc. [from Latin *compressare*, to squeeze together]

. . . .

🔳 *verb* **1** press, squeeze, crush, squash, flatten, jam, wedge, cram, stuff. **2** condense, compact, concentrate, contract, telescope, shorten, abbreviate, summarize.

🔳 *verb* **2** expand, diffuse.

. . . .

compressibility /kəmpresɪ'bɪlɪtɪ/ *noun* the property of being reduced in volume by pressure.

compressible /kəm'presɪbəl/ *adj.* able to be compressed.

compression /kəm'preʃən/ *noun* **1** the process of compressing or the state of being compressed. **2** the process whereby the volume of a substance, especially a gas, is reduced as a result of an increase in pressure. **3** the stroke that compresses the gases in an internal combustion engine.

compressor /kəm'presə(r)/ *noun Engineering* a device that compresses a gas, especially air, by raising its pressure and decreasing its volume. Compressors are used as power sources for pneumatic tools, eg road drills, sprayers, tyre pumps.

comprise /kəm'praɪz/ *verb* **1** to contain, include, or consist of. **2** to go together to make up. [from French *compris*, included]

. . . .

🔳 **1** include, consist of, contain, incorporate, embody, involve, encompass, embrace, cover. **2** make up, constitute, compose, form.

. . . .

compromise /'kɒmprəmaɪz/ — *noun* something agreed on after concessions have been made on each side. — *verb* **1** *intrans.* to make concessions; to reach a compromise. **2** to endanger, or expose to scandal, by acting indiscreetly. **3** to settle (a dispute) by making concessions; to relax (one's principles, etc). [from Latin *compromittere*, to promise reciprocally]

. . . .

🔳 *noun* agreement, accommodation, bargain, trade-off, settlement, concession. *verb* **1** make concessions, concede, meet halfway, adapt, adjust, negotiate, bargain, arbitrate, settle, agree. **2** endanger, imperil, jeopardize, expose, risk, prejudice, dishonour, discredit, embarrass, involve, implicate, weaken, undermine. **3** settle, agree, negotiate.

🔳 *noun* disagreement, intransigence.

. . . .

compulsion *noun* **1** the act of compelling or condition of being compelled. **2** an irresistible urge to perform a certain action, especially an irrational one. **3** *Psychol.* a specific action or ritual that is repeated many times and usually represents a form of obsession, eg repetitive washing based on fear of contamination. [from Latin *compulsio*]

compulsive *adj.* **1** *said of an action* resulting from a compulsion. **2** *said of a person* acting on compulsion. **3** *said of a book, film, etc* holding one's attention. [from Latin *compulsivus*]

. . . .

🔳 **1** irresistible, overwhelming, overpowering, uncontrollable, compelling, driving, urgent. **2** obsessive, hardened,

incorrigible, irredeemable, incurable, hopeless. **3** compelling, fascinating, enthralling, spellbinding.

. . . .

compulsively *adv.* in a compulsive way.

compulsorily /kəm'pʌlsərɪlɪ/ *adv.* so as to be compulsory.

compulsory /kəm'pʌlsərɪ/ *adj.* required by the rules, law, etc; obligatory. [from Latin *compulsorius*]

. . . .

🔳 obligatory, mandatory, required, requisite, set, stipulated, binding, contractual, imperative, forced.

🔳 optional, voluntary, discretionary.

. . . .

compulsory purchase the purchase, against the will of the owner, of property or land needed for some public project, etc by a local authority.

compunction *noun* a feeling of guilt, remorse, or regret; scruples or misgivings. [from Latin *compungere*, to puncture]

computable /kəm'pjuːtəbl/ *adj.* able to be computed or calculated.

computation *noun* **1** the act or process of computing or calculating. **2** the result of computing, or the result of a calculation involving numbers or quantities.

computational *adj.* **1** involving or using computers. **2** involving calculation. **3** denoting an error caused by arithmetical rounding of figures.

computationally *adv.* by means of computer processes; with computers.

compute *verb trans., intrans.* **1** to calculate or estimate (a result), especially with the aid of a computer. **2** to carry out (a computer operation). [from Latin *computare*, to reckon]

computer *noun* an electronic device that is capable of accepting data, processing it at great speed according to a set of instructions (a program) stored within the device, and presenting the results.

. . . .

🔳 personal computer, PC, mainframe, laptop, notebook, processor, word processor, data processor.

. . . .

computer-aided design (ABBREV. **CAD**) the use of a computer system to create and edit design drawings, using an electronic 'drawing board' in the form of a computer screen, and incorporating many of the techniques of computer graphics. It is widely used in architecture, manufacturing, engineering (eg car design), and electronics.

computer game *Comput.* a game on cassette or disk for playing on a home computer, the player manipulating moving images on the screen by pressing certain keys, or using a control pad or joystick.

computer generation any of five broad groups used to denote the different eras of technological development of digital computers.

computer graphics the use of computers to display and manipulate information in graphical or pictorial form, either on a visual-display unit (VDU), or via a printer or plotter.

computerization or **computerisation** /kəmpjuːtəraɪ-'zeɪʃən/ *noun* **1** the use of a computer to perform or control a process, operation, or system of operations that was formerly done by manual or mechanical means. **2** the installation of a computer for this purpose. **3** the processing of information or data by a computer.

computerize or **computerise** *verb* **1** to transfer (a process, operation, or system of operations formerly done by manual or mechanical means) to control by a computer. **2** to organize (information, data, etc) by means of a computer. **3** to install (computers) for this purpose.

computer language a defined set of numbers, symbols, or words that is used to write a computer program. It translates the user's instructions into the machine code that is used by the computer, and converts the coded responses of the computer back into a form that can be understood by the user.

computer literacy the condition of being competent or fully versed in the use of computers.

computer memory the part of a computer system that stores programs and data, either temporarily or permanently, and is connected to the central processing unit (CPU) of the computer. Memory capacity is measured in bytes, kilobytes, or megabytes.

computer science the study of the development, operations, and applications of computers.

computer scientist a scientist who specializes in the development, operations, and applications of computers for data processing, information storage, etc.

comrade /ˈkɒmreɪd, ˈkɒmrəd/ *noun* **1** a friend or companion; an associate, fellow worker, etc. **2** a fellow communist or socialist. [from Spanish *camarada*, the soldiers sharing a billet, a room-mate, from Latin *camera*, room]

comrade-in-arms *noun* a fellow soldier or campaigner.

comradely *adj.* like a comrade.

comradeship *noun* **1** friendship, camaraderie. **2** the state or position of a comrade.

COMSAT or **comsat** *abbrev. North Amer.* Communications Satellite.

con[1] *colloq.* — *noun* a confidence trick; a deception, trick, or bluff. — *verb* (**conned, conning**) to swindle or trick (someone), especially after winning their trust.

· ·

∎ *noun* confidence trick, trick, *slang* sting, deception, bluff, swindle, fraud. *verb* swindle, trick, hoax, dupe, deceive, mislead, inveigle, hoodwink, *colloq.* bamboozle, cheat, double-cross, defraud, *colloq.* rip off, *colloq.* rook.

· ·

con[2] *verb trans., intrans.* (**conned, conning**) *old use* to read over and learn by heart. [from CAN[1]]

con[3] *verb* (**conned, conning**) *Naut.* to direct the steering of (a ship). [earlier *cond*, from French *conduire*, to conduct]

con- or **col-** or **com-** or **cor-** *prefix, found usually in words derived from Latin* with or together; sometimes used with emphatic or intensifying effect. [from Latin *com-*, form of *cum*, with]

conc. *abbrev.* concentrated.

concatenate /kənˈkatəneɪt/ *verb* to link up into a connected series. [from Latin *con-*, with + *catena*, chain]

concatenation /kənkatəˈneɪʃən/ *noun* a series of things, eg events, each linked to the one before in chain-like fashion.

concave /ˈkɒŋkeɪv, kɒŋˈkeɪv/ *adj., said of a surface or shape* inward-curving, like the inside of a bowl. See also CONVEX. [from Latin *concavus*, vaulted, from *cavus*, hollow]

· ·

∎ hollow, hollowed, cupped, scooped, excavated, sunken, depressed.

∎∎ convex.

· ·

concavity /kənˈkavɪtɪ/ *noun* (PL. **concavities**) **1** the quality of being concave. **2** a hollow.

conceal *verb* **1** to hide; to place out of sight. **2** to keep secret. [from Latin *concelare*]

· ·

∎ **1** hide, obscure, disguise, camouflage, mask, screen, veil, cloak, cover, bury, submerge, smother. **2** suppress, keep dark, keep quiet, hush up.

∎∎ REVEAL, DISCLOSE, UNCOVER.

· ·

concealment *noun* **1** keeping secret or hidden; secrecy. **2** a hiding place.

concede *verb* **1** to admit to be true or correct. **2** to give or grant. **3** to yield or give up. **4** to admit defeat in (a contest) before, or without continuing to, the end. — **concede defeat** to admit that one is beaten. [from Latin *concedere*, to yield]

· ·

∎ **1** admit, confess, acknowledge, recognize, own, grant, allow, accept. **2** give, grant, allow, confer, bestow. **3** yield, give up,

surrender, relinquish, forfeit, sacrifice. **4** give up, abandon.

∎∎ **1** deny.

· ·

conceit /kənˈsiːt/ *noun* **1** too good an opinion of oneself; vanity. **2** *old use* a witty, fanciful, or ingenious thought or idea. [from CONCEIVE]

· ·

∎ **1** conceitedness, vanity, pride, arrogance, self-love, self-importance, self-satisfaction, boastfulness, swagger, egotism, cockiness, complacency.

∎∎ **1** modesty, diffidence.

· ·

conceited *adj.* having too good an opinion of oneself.

· ·

∎ vain, boastful, swollen-headed, *colloq.* big-headed, egotistical, self-important, cocky, self-satisfied, complacent, smug, proud, arrogant, *colloq.* stuck-up, *colloq.* toffee-nosed.

∎∎ modest, self-deprecating, self-effacing, diffident, humble.

· ·

conceitedly *adv.* with a conceited manner.

conceivability /kənsiːvəˈbɪlɪtɪ/ *noun* a conceivable quality or state.

conceivable /kənˈsiːvəbl/ *adj.* imaginable; possible: *try every conceivable method.*

· ·

∎ imaginable, believable, thinkable, credible, tenable, possible, likely, probable.

∎∎ inconceivable, unimaginable.

· ·

conceivably *adv.* possibly; perhaps.

conceive /kənˈsiːv/ *verb* **1** *trans., intrans.* to become pregnant; to begin to form (a baby). **2** to form (an idea, etc). **3** *trans., intrans.* (**conceive of something**) to think of or imagine an idea, etc. [from French *concever*, from Latin *concipere*, to conceive or perceive]

· ·

∎ **2** form, formulate, devise, create, produce, develop, invent, design, originate. **3** imagine, envisage, comprehend, visualize, see, grasp, understand, realize, appreciate, believe, think, suppose.

· ·

concentrate — *verb* **1** (**concentrate on something** or **someone**) to give all one's attention and energy to them. **2** to focus: *concentrate our efforts.* **3** *trans., intrans.* to bring or come together in one place. **4** *Chem.* to increase the amount of a dissolved substance in a solution, either by adding more of it, or by evaporating the solvent in which it is dissolved. **5** *Chem.* to make a chemical substance denser or purer. — *noun* a concentrated liquid. [from Latin *con-*, together + *centrum*, centre]

· ·

∎ *verb* **1** apply oneself, think, pay attention. **2** focus, centre, direct. **3** converge, centre, cluster, crowd, congregate, gather, collect, accumulate. **4, 5** condense, evaporate, reduce, thicken, intensify.

∎∎ *verb* **3** disperse. **4, 5** dilute.

· ·

concentrated *adj.* **1** attentive, focused. **2** contracted. **3** condensed, compressed.

· ·

∎ **1** attentive, focused, intense, intensive, all-out, concerted, hard, deep. **3** condensed, compressed, evaporated, reduced, thickened, dense, rich, strong, undiluted.

∎∎ **1** feeble. **3** diluted.

· ·

concentration /kɒnsənˈtreɪʃən/ *noun* **1** intense mental effort devoted to something, especially for a sustained period. **2** the act of concentration, or state of being concentrated. **3** the number of molecules or ions of a substance present in unit volume or weight of a solution or mixture.

■ **1** attention, heed, absorption, application, single-mindedness, intensity. **2** convergence, centralization, grouping, collection, accumulation, agglomeration, conglomeration, compression, reduction, consolidation, denseness, thickness.

▣ **1** distraction. **2** dispersal, dilution.

concentration camp a prison camp for civilians who are not tolerated by the authorities.

concentric *adj. Geom.* denoting two or more circles of different sizes but with a common centre, or two or more cylinders with a common axis. [from Latin *con-*, same + *centrum*, centre]

concentrically *adv.* in a concentric way.

concentricity /kɒnsən'trɪsɪtɪ/ *noun* the quality of being concentric.

concept *noun* a notion; an abstract or general idea. [from Latin *conceptum*]

■ notion, idea, plan, theory, hypothesis, thought, abstraction, conception, conceptualization, visualization, image, picture, impression.

conception /kən'sɛpʃən/ *noun* **1** an idea or notion. **2** the origin or start of something, especially something intricate. **3** the act of conceiving. **4** *Biol.* the fertilization of an ovum (egg cell) by a sperm, representing the start of pregnancy. [from Latin *concipere*, to conceive]

■ **1** idea, notion, concept, thought, knowledge, understanding, appreciation, perception, visualization, image, picture, impression, inkling, clue. **2** origin, start, beginning, birth, outset, initiation, inauguration, formation, invention, design. **4** fertilization, impregnation, insemination.

conceptual /kən'sɛptjʊəl/ *adj.* relating to or existing as concepts or conceptions.

conceptualism *noun Philos.* any theory of universals (ie general terms and abstract objects, such as qualities, relations, and numbers) that maintains that these are formed and constructed in the mind, and therefore exist only in the mind. For example, there are many things in nature that are red, but redness is a concept that has no independent existence outside the mind.

conceptualization or **conceptualisation** /kənsɛptjʊəlaɪ'zeɪʃən, kɒnsɛptjʊəlaɪ'zeɪʃən/ *noun* **1** the process of conceptualizing. **2** something that is conceptualized.

conceptualize or **conceptualise** *verb* to form a concept of.

conceptually *adv.* in a conceptual way; as a concept.

concern — *verb* **1** to have to do with; to be about: *it concerns your son.* **2** (*often* **be concerned about something** or **someone**) to worry, bother, or interest. **3** to affect; to involve: *a perfectionist where food is concerned.* — *noun* **1** worry, or a cause of worry. **2** interest, or a subject of interest. **3** one's business or responsibility: *no concern of yours.* **4** an organization; a company or business. [from Latin *concernere*, to distinguish or relate to]

■ *verb* **1** relate to, refer to, regard, involve. **2** upset, distress, trouble, disturb, bother, worry. **3** affect, involve, interest, touch. *noun* **1** anxiety, worry, unease, disquiet, care, sorrow, distress. **2** interest, regard, consideration, attention, heed, thought. **3** business, responsibility, duty, charge, job, task, field, affair, matter, problem. **4** organization, company, business, firm, corporation, establishment, enterprise.

▣ *noun* **1** joy, indifference.

concerned *adj.* worried. — **concerned with something** or **someone** having to do with them; involving them.

■ worried, anxious, uneasy, apprehensive, upset, unhappy, distressed, troubled, disturbed, bothered. **concerned with** connected to, related to, involved with, implicated in, interested in.

▣ unconcerned, indifferent, apathetic.

concernedly /kən'sɜːnɪdlɪ/ *adv.* with a concerned manner.

concernedness *noun* the quality of being concerned.

concerning *prep.* about; regarding.

■ about, regarding, with regard to, as regards, respecting, with reference to, relating to, in the matter of.

concernment *noun* concern.

concert /'kɒnsət, kən'sɜːt/ — *noun* (with stress on *con-*) a musical performance given before an audience by singers or players. — *verb* (with stress on *-cert*) to endeavour or plan by arrangement. — **in concert 1** jointly; in cooperation. **2** *said of singers, etc* in a live performance. [from French *concert*, from Italian *concerto*, from *concertare*, to organize]

concerted /kən'sɜːtɪd/ *adj.* planned and carried out jointly.

■ combined, united, joint, collective, shared, collaborative, co-ordinated, organized, prearranged, planned.

▣ unco-ordinated, disorganized.

concertina /kɒnsə'tiːnə/ — *noun* a musical instrument like a small accordion. — *verb intrans., trans.* (**concertinaed**, **concertinaing**) to fold or collapse like a concertina. [made up by inventor]

concertino /kɒntʃə'tiːnəʊ/ *noun* (PL. **concertinos**) **1** a musical work for solo instrument(s) and orchestra, shorter than a concerto and usually with lighter accompaniment. **2** the passages in a concerto grosso for solo instrument(s), typically for two violins and a cello.

concerto /kən'tʃɛətəʊ/ *noun* (PL. **concertos**, **concerti**) a musical composition for one or more solo instruments and orchestra. [from Italian *concerto*, from *concertare*, to organize]

concerto grosso (PL. **concerti grossi**) *Mus.* an orchestral work, especially of the 18c, usually in four or more movements with passages for solo instruments (*concertino*) alternating with the full body of the orchestra (*ripieno*). [Italian, = large concerto]

concert pitch *Mus.* the standard pitch that instruments are tuned to for concert performances.

concession *noun* **1** the act of conceding. **2** something conceded or allowed. **3** the right, granted under government licence, to extract minerals, etc in an area; the right to conduct a business from within a larger concern. **4** a reduction in price, fare, etc for categories such as students, the elderly, the disabled, the unemployed. [from Latin *concessio*, yielding]

■ **1** compromise, admission, acknowledgement. **2** allowance, exception, privilege, favour, indulgence. **3** right, permit. **4** reduction, discount, rebate, grant.

concessionaire *noun* the holder of a mining or trading concession.

concessionary *adj.* involving or obtained by a concession, especially a reduction in price: *concessionary fares for students.*

concessive *adj. Grammar* expressing concession, especially by means of words such as *although*, *though*, and *even if*. [from Latin *concessivus*]

conch /kɒŋk, kɒntʃ/ *noun* **1** any of a family of large marine snails, native to warm shallow tropical waters, having a large colourful shell with a long narrow opening and an outer lip which is generally expanded to form a broad plate. Conches feed on seaweed and range in size from 14mm to 60cm, the largest being the *queen conch*, which is abundant in the Caribbean, and is collected for food and the curio trade. **2** the large brightly coloured shell of this animal, used as a trumpet or collector's item. [from Greek *konche*]

conchologist /kɒŋ'kɒlǝɪst/ *noun* a person who specializes in the study of the shells of molluscs.

conchology /kɒŋ'kɒlǝɪ/ *noun* the study of the shells of molluscs.

conciliate /kǝn'sɪlɪeɪt/ *verb* **1** to win over; to overcome the hostility of; to placate. **2** to reconcile (people in dispute, etc). [from Latin *conciliare*, to unite in friendship]

conciliation /kǝnsɪlɪ'eɪʃǝn/ *noun* the act or process of conciliating.

conciliator *noun* a person who tries to bring about conciliation.

conciliatory /kǝn'sɪljǝtǝrɪ/ *adj.* intended to conciliate: *conciliatory remarks.*

concise *adj.* brief, but covering essential points. [from Latin *concisus*, cut short]

⊟ brief, short, succinct, pithy, terse, compact, compressed, condensed, compendious, abridged, abbreviated, summary, synoptic.
⊞ diffuse, wordy.

concisely *adv.* in a concise way; briefly.

concision or **conciseness** *noun, said especially of writing* the quality of being concise or brief.

conclave *noun* **1** a private or secret meeting. **2** in the RC Church, the body of cardinals gathered to elect a new pope; their meeting-place. [from Latin *conclave*, a room that can be locked, from *clavis*, key]

conclude *verb* **1** *trans., intrans.* to come or bring to an end. **2** to reach an opinion based on reasoning. **3** to settle or arrange: *conclude a treaty with a neighbour state.* [from Latin *concludere*, from *claudere*, to close]

⊟ **1** end, close, finish, complete, cease, terminate, culminate. **2** infer, deduce, assume, surmise, suppose, reckon, judge. **3** settle, arrange, resolve, decide, establish, determine, clinch.
⊞ **1** start, commence.

conclusion *noun* **1** an end. **2** a reasoned judgement; an opinion based on reasoning: *come to / draw a conclusion.* **3** settling of terms, an agreement, etc. — **in conclusion** finally; lastly. **jump to conclusions** to presume something with inadequate evidence. [from Latin *conclusio*, from *concludere*, to end]

⊟ **1** end, close, finish, completion, consummation, termination, culmination, finale. **2** judgement, opinion, inference, deduction, assumption, conviction. **3** settlement, agreement, resolution, consequence, outcome, upshot, answer, solution, result, verdict, decision.

conclusive *adj., said of evidence, proof, etc* decisive, convincing; leaving no room for doubt. [from Latin *conclusivus*]

⊟ decisive, convincing, definitive, final, ultimate, clear, definite, undeniable, irrefutable, indisputable, incontrovertible, unarguable, unanswerable, clinching.
⊞ inconclusive, questionable.

conclusively *adv.* decisively, convincingly.

conclusiveness *noun* being conclusive or decisive.

concoct *verb* **1** to make, especially ingeniously from a variety of ingredients. **2** to invent (a story, excuse, etc). [from Latin *concoctus*, cooked together]

⊟ **1** devise, contrive, formulate, prepare, develop, plan, plot, hatch, brew. **2** invent, fabricate.

concoction *noun* **1** the act of concocting. **2** something that is concocted.

⊟ **1** creation, contrivance. **2** brew, potion, preparation, mixture, blend, compound, creation, contrivance.

concomitant /kǝn'kɒmɪtǝnt/ — *adj.* accompanying: *fever with concomitant headache, sore throat, etc.* — *noun* something that is concomitant. [from Latin *concomitare*, to accompany]

concomitantly *adv.* in a concomitant way.

concord *noun* **1** agreement; peace or harmony. **2** *Grammar* agreement between words, especially in number and gender, eg between verb and subject. **3** *Mus.* a chord with a harmonious sound, the opposite of a *discord.* **4** a treaty; a pact. [from Latin *concordia*, agreement]

concordance *noun* **1** a state of harmony. **2** an alphabetical index of words used by an author or in a book, giving the reference and usually meaning. [from Latin *concordantia*, from Latin *concordare*, to agree]

concordant *adj.* harmonious, united.

concordat *noun* an agreement, especially between church and state. [from French *concordat*, from Latin *concordare*, to agree]

concourse *noun* **1** a large open area for people, in a railway station, airport, etc. **2** a throng; a gathering. [from French *concours*, from Latin *concursus*, assembly]

concrete — *noun* a building material consisting of cement, sand, and gravel mixed with water, which forms a hard rock-like mass when allowed to dry. — *adj.* **1** relating to such a material. **2** able to be felt, touched, seen, etc, as opposed to abstract: *concrete objects.* **3** definite or positive, as opposed to vague or general: *concrete evidence.* **4** *Grammar, said of a noun* denoting a physical thing rather than a quality, condition, or action. **5** *said of music* produced from sounds and music already recorded. **6** *said of poetry* relying partly for its effect on the physical arrangement of words on the page. **7** *said of art* denoting a style of non-figurative art in which the picture is constructed from geometrical forms and simple planes. — *verb* **1** to cover with or embed in concrete. **2** *trans., intrans.* to solidify. [from Latin *concretus*, from *con-*, together + *crescere*, to grow]

⊟ *adj.* **2** real, actual, factual, solid, physical, material, substantial, tangible, touchable, perceptible, visible. **3** definite, positive, firm, specific, explicit.

concretely *adv.* in a concrete way.

concreteness *noun* being concrete; material existence.

concretion /kǝn'kriːʃǝn/ *noun* **1** *Medicine* a hard stony mass occurring in a body tissue or natural cavity. **2** *Geol.* a hard rounded nodule of mineral matter formed within the pores of a sedimentary or igneous rock as a result of precipitation of dissolved mineral salts. [from Latin *concretio*, from *con-*, together + *crescere*, to grow]

concubinage /kɒn'kjuːbɪnɪd / *noun* **1** the state of a man and a woman living together without being married to each other. **2** the status of a concubine.

concubine *noun usually Hist.* a woman who lives with a man and has sexual intercourse with him, without being married to him. [from Latin *concubina*, from *con-*, together + *cumbere*, to lie]

concupiscence /kǝn'kjuːpɪsǝns/ *noun* strong sexual desire. [from Latin *concupiscere*, to long for]

concupiscent /kǝn'kjuːpɪsǝnt/ *adj.* lustful.

concur *verb intrans.* (**concurred, concurring**) **1** to agree. **2** to happen at the same time; to coincide. [from Latin *con-*, together + *currere*, to run]

concurrence *noun* **1** agreement; consent. **2** the coinciding of events, etc.

concurrent *adj.* **1** running in parallel; happening or taking place simultaneously. **2** *said of lines* meeting or intersecting. **3** in agreement. [from Latin *con-*, together + *currere*, to run]

. . . .

▤ **1** simultaneous, synchronous, contemporaneous, coinciding, coincident, concomitant, coexisting, coexistent. **3** coinciding, coincident.

. . . .

concurrently *adv.* so as to be concurrent; at the same time.

concuss *verb* to cause concussion in. [from Latin *concutere*, to shake together]

concussion *noun* **1** a violent shaking or jarring of the brain, caused by injury to the head (eg as a result of a severe blow or fall), and usually resulting in temporary loss of consciousness. **2** a violent shock caused by the sudden contact of two bodies.

condemn /kən'dɛm/ *verb* **1** to declare to be wrong or evil. **2** to find guilty; to convict. **3** (**condemn someone to something**) **a** to sentence them to a punishment, especially death. **b** to be the cause of someone's disagreeable fate: *was condemned to a friendless existence by his own ill-temper.* **4** to betray the guilt of; to give away: *his obvious nervousness condemned him.* **5** to declare (a building) unfit to be used or lived in. [from Latin *condemnare*, to condemn]

. . . .

▤ **1** disapprove, reprehend, reprove, upbraid, reproach, castigate, blame, disparage, revile, denounce, censure, *colloq.* slam, *colloq.* slate. **3** damn, doom.
▣ **1** praise, approve.

. . . .

condemnation /kɒndəm'neɪʃən/ *noun* **1** the act of condemning. **2** the state of being condemned.

. . . .

▤ **1** disapproval, reproof, reproach, castigation, blame, disparagement, denunciation, censure, damnation, conviction. **2** damnation, conviction, castigation, disparagement, denunciation, censure, blame.
▣ praise, approval.

. . . .

condemnatory /kɒndəm'neɪtərɪ/ *adj.* expressing or implying condemnation.

condensation /kɒndən'seɪʃən/ *noun* **1** *Physics* the process whereby a gas or vapour turns into a liquid as a result of cooling. **2** *Chem.* a chemical reaction in which two or more small molecules combine to form a larger molecule, usually with the elimination of a molecule of water. **3** *Optics* in an optical instrument, the process of focusing a beam of light.

. . . .

▤ **1** distillation, liquefaction, precipitation, concentration, evaporation, reduction, consolidation.

. . . .

condensation reaction *Chem.* a reaction in which two or more relatively small molecules combine to form a larger one, with the elimination of a relatively simple byproduct, usually a molecule of water.

condense *verb* **1** to decrease the volume, size, or density of (a substance). **2** *said of a substance* to be reduced in volume, size, or density. **3** to concentrate. **4** *trans., intrans.* to undergo or cause to undergo (condensation). See also CONDENSATION. **5** to express more briefly; to summarize. [from Latin *condensare*, to compress]

. . . .

▤ **1** contract, compress, compact, shorten, curtail, abbreviate, abridge, précis, summarize, encapsulate. **2** evaporate, reduce, compact.
▣ **1** expand. **3** dilute.

. . . .

condensed milk milk that has been concentrated and thickened by evaporation, and to which sugar has been added as a preservative.

condenser *noun* **1** *Electr.* a capacitor. **2** *Chem.* an apparatus for changing a vapour into a liquid by cooling it and allowing it to condense. Condensers are standard equipment in chemistry laboratories, and are also built into steam engines, steam turbines, etc. **3** *Optics* in an optical instrument such as a microscope, a lens or series of lenses that is used to concentrate a light source.

condescend *verb intrans.* **1** to act in a gracious manner to those one considers one's inferiors. **2** to be gracious enough to do something, especially as though it were a favour: *they condescended to meet us.* [from Latin *condescendere*, from *descendere*, to descend]

. . . .

▤ **1** stoop, bend, lower oneself, patronize, talk down. **2** deign, see fit.

. . . .

condescending *adj.* **1** gracious. **2** offensively patronizing.

. . . .

▤ **2** patronizing, disdainful, supercilious, *colloq.* snooty, snobbish, haughty, lofty, superior, lordly, imperious.
▣ **2** humble.

. . . .

condescendingly *adv.* with a condescending manner.

condescension *noun* **1** the action of being condescending. **2** condescending behaviour.

condign /kən'daɪn/ *adj., said of praise, reward, punishment, etc* well-deserved. [from Latin *condignus*, from *dignus*, worthy]

condiment *noun* a seasoning, eg salt, pepper, mustard, etc, used at table to give flavour to food. [from Latin *condimentum*]

condition — *noun* **1** a particular state. **2** a state of health, fitness, or suitability for use: *out of condition.* **3** an ailment or disorder: *a heart condition.* **4** (**conditions**) circumstances: *poor working conditions.* **5** a requirement or qualification: *a necessary condition for membership.* **6** *Maths.* that which must be true for a further statement to be true. — *verb* (**conditioned**, **conditioning**) **1** to accustom or train to behave or react in a particular way; to influence. **2** to prepare or train (a person or animal) for a certain activity or for certain conditions of living. **3** to subject (a person or animal) to a particular stimulus in order to secure, by training, a certain behavioural response that was not initially associated with that stimulus. **4** to affect or control; to determine. **5** to improve (the physical state of hair, skin, fabrics, etc) by applying a particular substance. — **on condition that** ... only if: *will go on condition that you come too.* **on no condition** absolutely not. [from Latin *conditio*, from *condicere*, to agree]

. . . .

▤ *noun* **1** state, circumstances, position, situation, case, predicament, plight. **2** fitness, health, shape, form, fettle, *colloq.* nick. **3** disorder, ailment, complaint, disease, illness, defect, weakness, infirmity, problem. **4** circumstances, situation, state, surroundings, environment, milieu, setting, atmosphere, background, context. **5** requirement, qualification, obligation, prerequisite, terms, stipulation, proviso, limitation, restriction, rule. *verb* **1, 2** train, groom, accustom, influence, mould, educate, prepare, indoctrinate, brainwash, equip, prime. **4** affect, control, determine, influence, direct, ordain.

. . . .

conditional *adj.* (**conditional on something**) dependent on a particular condition, etc.

. . . .

▤ dependent on, contingent on, provisional, qualified, limited, restricted, tied, relative.
▣ unconditional, absolute.

. . . .

conditionally *adv.* in a conditional way; with conditions.
conditioned reflex *Physiol.* a type of reflex action in

which the response occurs not to a *sensory stimulus*, such as hunger, but to a *neutral stimulus* that has become firmly associated by learning with the sensory stimulus, eg the sound of a bell which is linked to the imminent presence of food.

conditioner *noun* (*often in compounds*) a substance for improving the condition of something.

conditioning *noun* **1** the process of making or becoming conditioned. **2** *Psychol.* a reflex response to a stimulus which depends upon the former experience of the individual, and can be modified, eg by rewarding or punishing a particular response so that it comes to occur more or less frequently.

condole /kən'dəʊl/ *verb intrans.* (**condole with someone**) to express one's sympathy to them. [from Latin *con-*, with + *dolere*, to grieve]

condolence *noun* (*often* **condolences**) sympathy, or an expression of sympathy: *offer one's condolences.*

condom *noun* a contraceptive device consisting of a thin rubber sheath worn on the penis during sexual intercourse, to prevent the release of sperm into the vagina and so avoid pregnancy, and to prevent the spread of disease.

▤ sheath, *slang* rubber, *slang* French letter, *slang* johnnie, protective.

condominium /kɒndə'mɪnɪəm/ *noun* **1** *North Amer.* a block of individually owned apartments. **2** joint control of a state by two or more other states. [from Latin *con-*, with + *dominium*, dominion, rule]

condonable /kən'dəʊnəbl/ *adj.* capable of being condoned.

condone /kən'dəʊn/ *verb* to pardon or overlook (an offence or wrong). [from Latin *condonare*, to present, overlook]

▤ pardon, overlook, forgive, excuse, ignore, disregard, tolerate, brook, allow.
▣ condemn, censure.

condor *noun* either of two species of large American vulture, with the largest wingspan of any living bird (up to 3m). The Andean condor is still relatively common, but the Californian condor is almost extinct. [from Spanish *cóndor*, from Quechua *kuntur*]

conduce *verb intrans.* (**conduce to something**) to help or tend towards a result, especially a desirable one. [from Latin *con-*, together + *ducere*, to lead]

conducive *adj.* (**conducive to something**) likely to achieve a desirable result.

▤ leading to, tending to, contributory, productive, advantageous, beneficial, favourable, helpful, encouraging.
▣ detrimental, adverse, unfavourable.

conduct /kən'dʌkt, 'kɒndʌkt/ — *verb* (with stress on *-duct*) **1** to lead or guide. **2** to manage; to control: *conduct the firm's business.* **3** *trans., intrans.* to direct the performance of an orchestra or choir by movements of the hands or a baton. **4** to transmit (heat or electricity) by conduction: *metal conducts heat.* **5** to direct, channel, or convey: *hot air conducted through pipes.* **6** (**conduct oneself**) to behave in a specified way: *one should always conduct oneself with dignity.* — *noun* (with stress on *con-*) **1** behaviour. **2** the managing or organizing of something: *the conduct of the war.* [from Latin *conductus*, guide]

▤ *verb* **1** lead, guide, usher, direct, pilot, steer, accompany, escort. **2** manage, control, run, handle, administer, organize, orchestrate, regulate, chair. **5** transmit, convey, carry, bear, direct, channel. **6** behave, act, acquit oneself, comport oneself. *noun* **1** behaviour, comportment, actions, ways, manners, bearing, attitude. **2** management,

organization, direction, running, administration, supervision, leadership, operation, control, guidance.

conductance *noun* the ability of a material to conduct heat or electricity. In a direct current circuit it is the reciprocal of resistance. The SI unit of conductance is the siemens. See also CONDUCTIVITY.

conduction *noun* **1** the transmission of heat through a material from a region of higher temperature to one of lower temperature, without any movement of the material itself. **2** the flow of electricity through a material under the influence of an electric field, without any movement of the material itself. **3** the passage of a nerve impulse along a nerve fibre.

conductivity /kɒndʌk'tɪvɪtɪ/ *noun* **1** (*in full* **electrical conductivity**) a measure of the ability of a material to conduct electricity. It is the reciprocal of resistivity. **2** (*in full* **thermal conductivity**) the ability of a material to conduct heat.

conductor *noun* **1** the director of a choir's or orchestra's performance. **2** (*in full* **thermal conductor**) a material that allows heat to flow through it by the process of conduction. **3** (*in full* **electrical conductor**) a material that allows electricity to flow through it by the process of conduction. **4** a person who collects the fares from passengers on a bus, etc.

conductress *noun* a woman who collects fares on a bus, etc.

conduit /'kɒndjʊɪt, 'kɒndɪt/ *noun* **1** a channel, pipe, tube, or duct through which a fluid (a liquid or a gas) may pass. **2** a rigid or flexible tube that houses electrical cables. [from French *conduit*, from Latin *conductus*, channel]

cone — *noun* **1** *Geom.* a solid (three-dimensional) figure with a flat base in the shape of a circle or ellipse, and a curved upper surface that tapers to a fixed point (the *vertex*). **2** something similar to this in shape, eg a pointed holder for ice cream, made of wafer biscuit, or a plastic object used to mark off temporary lanes for traffic, etc. **3** *Anat.* one of the two types of light-sensitive receptor cell in the retina of the eye of vertebrates. Cones are specialized for the detection of colour, and function best in bright light. **4** *Bot.* the reproductive structure of gymnosperms, eg conifers and cycads, consisting of a central axis bearing many overlapping sporophylls (modified leaves resembling scales) that in turn bear the reproductive organs. Most gymnosperms produce separate male and female cones. Also called STROBILUS. — *verb* (*usually* **cone something off**) to close off an area or part of a road with a line of traffic cones. [from Greek *konos*]

confab *colloq.* — *noun* a confabulation. — *verb intrans.* (**confabbed, confabbing**) to confabulate.

confabulate /kən'fabjʊleɪt/ *verb intrans.* *formal* to talk, discuss, or confer. [from Latin *confabulari*, to converse]

confabulation /kənfabjʊ'leɪʃən/ *noun* a discussion.

confection *noun* **1** any sweet food, eg a cake, sweet, biscuit, pudding. **2** *old use, facetious* a fancy or elaborate garment, eg a hat. [from Latin *confectio*, making]

confectioner *noun* a person who makes or sells sweets or cakes.

confectionery *noun* **1** sweets, biscuits, and cakes. **2** the art or business of a confectioner.

confederacy /kən'fɛdərəsɪ/ *noun* (PL. **confederacies**) **1** a league or alliance of states. **2** (**the Confederacy**) *Hist.* the union of 11 southern states that seceded from the USA in 1860–1, so causing the American Civil War. They were Virginia, North Carolina, South Carolina, Georgia, Florida, Tennessee, Alabama, Mississippi, Louisiana, Texas, and Arkansas. **3** a conspiracy; an association formed for illegal purposes. [from Latin *confoederatio*, league]

confederate /kən'fɛdərət, kən'fɛdəreɪt/ — *noun* (pronounced -rət) **1** a member of a confederacy. **2** a friend or an ally; an accomplice or a fellow conspirator. **3** (**Confederate**) *Hist.* a supporter of the Confederacy of American states that seceded in 1860–1. — *adj.* (pronounced -rət) **1** allied; united. **2** (**Confederate**) *Hist.* belonging to the Confederacy. — *verb* (pronounced -reɪt) to unite into a confederacy. [from Latin *confoederatus*, united in a league]

confederation /kənfədəˈreɪʃən/ *noun* **1** the uniting of states into a league. **2** the league so formed.

confer *verb* (**conferred, conferring**) **1** *intrans.* to consult. **2** (**confer something on someone**) to grant them an honour or distinction. [from Latin *con-*, together + *ferre*, to bring]

⊟ **1** consult, talk, converse, discuss, debate, deliberate. **2** grant, bestow, award, present, give, accord, impart, lend.

conference *noun* **1** a formally organized gathering for the discussion of matters of common interest or concern. **2** consultation; the formal exchanging of views: *in conference with the Prime Minister.* **3** an assembly of representatives of an association, church denomination, etc. [from Latin *conferentia*, from *con-*, together + *ferre*, to bring]

⊟ **1, 3** meeting, convention, congress, convocation, symposium, forum. **2** consultation, discussion, debate.

conferencing *noun* the practice of holding a business conference in which the participants are linked by telephone, video equipment, and/or computer.

conferment *noun* the bestowing of honours.

confess *verb* **1** *trans., intrans.* to own up to (a fault, wrongdoing, etc); to admit (a disagreeable fact, etc) reluctantly. **2** *trans., intrans.* to recount (one's sins) to a priest, in order to gain absolution. **3** *said of a priest* to hear the confession of (someone). [from Latin *confiteri*, to admit]

⊟ **1** admit, confide, own up (to), *colloq.* come clean, grant, concede, acknowledge, recognize, affirm, disclose, divulge, profess, expose.
⊞ **1** deny, conceal.

confessed *adj.* having openly admitted a weakness: *a confessed alcoholic.*

confessedly /kənˈfesɪdlɪ/ *adv.* admittedly, avowedly.

confession *noun* **1** the admission of a sin, fault, crime, distasteful or shocking fact, etc. **2** the formal act of confessing one's sins to a priest. **3** a declaration of one's religious faith or principles: *a confession of faith.* **4** a religious body with its own creed or set of beliefs.

⊟ **1** admission, acknowledgement, disclosure, divulgence, revelation, unburdening. **3** declaration, affirmation, assertion, profession.
⊞ **1** denial, concealment.

confessional *noun* the small enclosed stall in a church where a priest sits when hearing confessions.

confessor *noun* **1** a priest, especially one to whom members of the church go regularly, who hears confessions and gives spiritual advice. **2** *Hist.* a person whose holy life serves as a demonstration of his or her religious faith: *Edward the Confessor.* [from Latin *confessor*, martyr, witness]

confetti *noun* tiny pieces of coloured paper traditionally thrown at the bride and groom by wedding guests. [from Italian, plural of *confetto*, sweetmeat]

confidant or **confidante** /kɒnfɪˈdant, ˈkɒnfɪdant/ *noun* respectively a male or female friend with whom one discusses personal matters. [from French *confident(e)*, from Latin *confidere*, to trust]

confide *verb intrans., trans.* **1** (**confide in someone**) to speak freely with them about personal matters. **2** to tell (a secret, etc) to someone. **3** to entrust to someone's care. [from Latin *confidere*, to trust]

⊟ **1** tell, unburden oneself. **2** confess, admit, reveal, disclose, impart, divulge, whisper, breathe.
⊞ **2** hide, suppress.

confidence /ˈkɒnfɪdəns/ *noun* **1** trust in, or reliance on, a person or thing. **2** faith in one's own ability; self-assurance. **3** a secret, etc confided to someone. **4** a relationship of mutual trust: *took her into his confidence.* — **in confidence** in secret; confidentially. [from Latin *confidentia*]

⊟ **1** certainty, faith, credence, trust, reliance, dependence. **2** self-assurance, self-confidence, self-possession, self-reliance, assurance, composure, calmness, boldness, courage.
⊞ **1** distrust, doubt. **2** diffidence, self-consciousness, timidity, reserve, self-doubt.

confidence interval *Maths.* in statistical analyses, an interval that can with reasonable confidence be expected to contain the true value of an unknown parameter.

confidence trick a form of swindle in which the swindler first wins the trust of the victim.

confidence trickster a swindler.

confident /ˈkɒnfɪdənt/ *adj.* **1** certain; sure: *confident of success.* **2** self-assured.

⊟ **1** sure, certain, positive, convinced. **2** self-assured, self-confident, self-possessed, self-reliant, assured, composed, cool, bold, fearless, dauntless, unabashed.
⊞ **1** doubtful. **2** diffident, timid, reserved, self-conscious.

confidential /kɒnfɪˈdenʃəl/ *adj.* **1** secret; not to be divulged: *confidential information.* **2** trusted with private matters: *a confidential secretary.* **3** used for privacy's sake: *a confidential whisper.* [from Latin *confidentia*, confidence]

⊟ **1** secret, private, top secret, classified, restricted, *colloq.* hush-hush, off-the-record, personal, intimate.

confidentiality /kɒnfɪdenʃɪˈalɪtɪ/ *noun* a confidential quality or requirement.

confidentially *adv.* in a confidential way; in confidence.

confiding *adj.* trustful; not suspicious.

confidingly *adv.* with a confiding manner.

configuration /kənfɪgəˈreɪʃən/ *noun* **1** the positioning or distribution of the parts of something relative to each other. **2** an outline or external shape. **3** *Physics* the arrangement of atoms in a molecule, or the arrangement of electrons in orbitals around the nucleus of an atom. [from Latin *configurare*, to form, fashion]

confine /kənˈfaɪn/ *verb* **1** to restrict; to limit: *shall confine my remarks to the main points.* **2** to prevent the spread of (eg a fire). **3** to keep prisoner or keep from moving. **4** *old use* to keep (a woman about to give birth) indoors or in bed. [from Latin *confinis*, border]

⊟ **1** restrict, limit, constrain, circumscribe, bound, cramp, repress, inhibit. **3** imprison, incarcerate, intern, cage, shut up, enclose, bind, shackle, trammel, restrain.
⊞ **3** free, liberate.

confined *adj.* narrow; restricted.

confinement *noun* **1** the state of being shut up or kept in an enclosed space. **2** the period surrounding childbirth: *her fourth confinement.*

⊟ **1** imprisonment, incarceration, internment, custody, detention, house arrest. **2** childbirth, birth, labour, delivery.
⊞ **1** freedom, liberty.

confines /ˈkɒnfaɪnz/ *pl. noun* limits; boundaries; restrictions.

⊟ limits, boundaries, bounds, restrictions, borders, frontiers, circumference, perimeter.

confirm verb 1 to provide support for the truth or validity of (something): refused to confirm or deny the rumour. 2 to finalize or make definite (a booking, arrangement, etc). 3 (**confirm someone in an opinion**, etc) to make them more convinced about it: I was confirmed in my suspicion that he was cheating us. 4 to give formal approval to; to establish officially: confirm someone in his appointment. 5 to accept (someone) formally into full membership of the Christian Church. [from Latin confirmare]

■ 1 support, endorse, back, reinforce, strengthen, fortify, validate, authenticate, corroborate, substantiate, verify, prove. 2 finalize, fix, settle, clinch. 4 approve, authorize, establish, ratify, sanction, endorse, validate.
▨ 1 refute, deny.

confirmation noun 1 the act of confirming. 2 proof or support. 3 finalization. 4 the religious ceremony in which a person is admitted to full membership of the church.

■ 1 ratification, sanction, approval, assent, acceptance, agreement, endorsement, validation, authentication, verification. 2 proof, evidence, support, backing, corroboration, substantiation, verification, testimony.
▨ 1 denial.

confirmatory adj. 1 giving additional support to an argument, etc. 2 confirming.
confirmed adj. so settled into the state or condition mentioned as to be unlikely to change.

■ inveterate, entrenched, dyed-in-the-wool, rooted, established, long-established, long-standing, habitual, chronic, seasoned, hardened, incorrigible, incurable.

confiscate verb to take away (something) from someone, as a penalty. [from Latin confiscare, to transfer to the state treasury]

■ take away, seize, appropriate, expropriate, remove, impound, sequester, commandeer.
▨ return, restore.

confiscation noun the act of confiscating.
conflagration /kɒnfləˈɡreɪʃən/ noun a fierce and destructive blaze. [from Latin conflagrare]
conflate verb to blend or combine (eg two different versions of a text, story, etc) into a single whole. [from Latin conflare, to smelt or fuse]
conflation noun 1 the act of conflating. 2 a fusion or combination.
conflict /ˈkɒnflɪkt, kənˈflɪkt/ — noun (with stress on con-) 1 disagreement; fierce argument; a quarrel. 2 a clash between different aims, interests, ideas, etc. 3 a struggle, fight, battle, or war. — verb intrans. (with stress on -flict) to be incompatible or in opposition: the demands of a career often conflict with those of family life. [from Latin confligere, to dash together, clash]

■ noun 1 disagreement, argument, quarrel, dispute, feud, opposition, antagonism, hostility, friction, strife, unrest, confrontation, contention, dissension. 2 clash, difference, variance, discord. 3 fight, battle, war, warfare, combat, contest, engagement, skirmish, set-to, fracas, brawl, feud, encounter, clash. verb differ, clash, collide, disagree, war, strive, struggle, contend.
▨ noun 1 agreement. 2 harmony, concord. verb agree, harmonize.

conflict theory Sociol. the theory that conflict and social division are inevitable in all social structures because the mechanisms by which society integrates and exercises control over its members are never wholly successful.

confluence noun 1 the meeting and flowing together of two or more rivers, streams, glaciers, etc. 2 the place where this occurs. [from Latin con-, together + fluere, to flow]
confluent adj. 1 flowing together. 2 running into one. 3 uniting.
conform verb intrans. 1 to behave, dress, etc in obedience to some standard considered normal by the majority. 2 (**conform to something**) to obey rules, etc; to meet or comply with standards, etc. 3 (**conform to** or **with something**) to be in agreement with it; to match or correspond to it. [from Latin conformare, to shape]

■ 2 obey, comply, follow, adapt, adjust. 3 agree with, accord with, harmonize with, match, correspond to, tally with, square with.
▨ 1, 2 rebel. 3 differ, conflict.

conformable adj. 1 corresponding or matching. 2 compliant; agreeable. 3 Geol., said of rock strata arranged in a continuous sequence of parallel layers that have remained in their original relative positions since the time of their formation.
conformation noun a shape, structure, or arrangement.
conformist noun a person who conforms to the norm, obeys rules, does the expected thing, etc.
conformity noun 1 obedience to rules, normal standards, etc. 2 accordance; compliance: in conformity with safety standards.

■ 1 conventionality, orthodoxy, traditionalism. 2 accordance, agreement, compliance, observance, allegiance, affinity, harmony, correspondence.
▨ 1 nonconformity, rebellion.

confound verb 1 to puzzle; to baffle. 2 to defeat or thwart (one's enemies or their schemes). 3 to mix up or confuse (one thing with another). 4 as an exclamation of annoyance: confound it! [from Latin confundere, to pour together, throw into disorder, overthrow]

■ 1 puzzle, baffle, bewilder, confuse, perplex, mystify, colloq. bamboozle, nonplus, surprise, amaze, astonish, astound, colloq. flabbergast, dumbfound, stupefy. 2 defeat, thwart, upset, overwhelm, overthrow, destroy, demolish, ruin. 3 mix up, confuse, muddle, mistake.

confounded adj. used to indicate annoyance: a confounded nuisance.
confoundedly adv. 1 colloq. hatefully, shamefully. 2 cursedly.
confrère /ˈkɒnfreə(r)/ noun a fellow member of one's profession, etc; a colleague. [from Old French confrère, from Latin con-, with + frater, brother]
confront verb 1 to face, especially defiantly or accusingly: he confronted his accusers. 2 to prepare to deal firmly with: confront the problem. 3 (**confront someone with something**) to bring them face to face with a damning or revealing circumstance: decided to confront him with his error. 4 said of an unpleasant prospect to present itself to (someone): certain death confronted them. [from Latin confrontari, from frons, forehead, brow]

■ 1 face, meet, beard, brave, defy, accost, address. 2 face (up to), brave. 3 challenge.
▨ 1, 2 evade.

confrontation noun an act of confronting; a hostile meeting or exchange of words.

■ encounter, clash, collision, showdown, conflict, disagreement, fight, battle, quarrel, set-to, engagement, contest.

Confucian /kənˈfjuːʃən/ — noun a follower or supporter of Confucianism. — adj. of or belonging to Confucianism.

Confucianism noun the teachings of the Chinese philosopher Confucius (551–479 BC), with emphasis on morality, consideration for others, obedience, and good education.

Confucianist noun a follower of Confucius.

confuse verb 1 to put into a muddle or mess. 2 (**confuse one thing with another** or **several things**) to fail to distinguish; to mix up: confuse 'ascetic' with 'aesthetic' / tended to confuse the different brands. 3 to puzzle or bewilder. 4 to complicate. 5 to embarrass. [from Latin confundere, to mix]

⬛ 1 muddle, mix up, jumble, disarrange, disorder, tangle, entangle, involve, mingle. 2 muddle up, mix up, mistake. 3 puzzle, bewilder, baffle, perplex, mystify, confound, disorient. 5 embarrass, disconcert, fluster, discompose, upset, mortify.
🔁 1 enlighten, clarify.

confused adj. 1 perplexed, muddled. 2 disordered. 3 embarrassed.

⬛ 1 perplexed, muddled, puzzled, baffled, colloq. flummoxed, nonplussed, bewildered, disorientated. 2 disordered, disorderly, disorganized, muddled, jumbled, disarranged, untidy, colloq. higgledy-piggledy, chaotic.
🔁 2 orderly.

confusedly /kənˈfjuːzɪdlɪ/ adv. in a confused way.
confusing adj. causing confusion.
confusingly adv. in a confusing way.
confusion noun 1 the act of confusing or state of being confused. 2 disorder; muddle. 3 mental bewilderment. [from Latin confusio, from confundere, to mix]

⬛ 2 disorder, disarray, muddle, untidiness, mess, clutter, jumble, mix-up, disorganization, chaos, turmoil, commotion, upheaval. 3 bewilderment, puzzlement, perplexity, mystification, misunderstanding.
🔁 2 order. 3 clarity.

confutation noun 1 the action of confuting. 2 something that confutes a person or theory, etc.

confute verb to prove (a person) wrong, or (a theory, etc) false. [from Latin confutare, to pour cold water on]

conga — noun 1 an originally Cuban dance performed in single file, with three steps followed by a kick. 2 a large drum beaten with the fingers. — verb intrans. (**congaed, congaing**) to dance the conga. [from Spanish conga]

congé /ˈkɒnʒeɪ/ noun 1 permission to depart. 2 abrupt dismissal. [from French congé]

congeal /kənˈdʒiːl/ verb trans., intrans., said of liquid to change or cause to change from a liquid to a more solid state, especially as a result of cooling; to coagulate. [from Latin congelare, to freeze completely]

⬛ coagulate, coalesce, clot, thicken, stiffen, harden, solidify, set, curdle, gel.
🔁 dissolve, melt.

congealment or **congelation** noun 1 the act or process of congealing. 2 anything congealed.

congener /ˈkɒndʒənə(r)/ noun a plant or animal that is a member of the same genus as another plant or animal. [from Latin con-, same + genus, kind]

congenial /kənˈdʒiːnɪəl/ adj. 1 companionable; having a personality and interests that fit well with one's own. 2 pleasant or agreeable. [from Latin con-, same + genius, spirit]

congeniality /kəndʒiːnɪˈalɪtɪ/ noun being congenial.
congenially adv. with a congenial manner.
congenital /kənˈdʒɛnɪtəl/ adj. 1 said of a disease, defect, or deformity present at or before birth, and either inherited, or caused by injury, infection, or the presence of certain drugs or chemicals in the mother's body during pregnancy, eg spina bifida. 2 affected since birth by a particular condition: a congenital idiot. [from Latin con-, with + gignere, to give birth to]

congenitally adv. from birth.

conger noun (in full **conger eel**) a large marine eel, native to shallow waters of temperate and tropical coasts, and having a light to dark brown scaleless body, up to 2.75m long but usually much smaller, and weighing up to 45 kg, with well-developed pectoral fins, large eyes, strong jaws, and sharp close-set conical teeth. [from Latin conger, from Greek gongros]

congeries /kənˈdʒɛriːz/ noun (PL. **congeries**) a miscellaneous accumulation; a confused heap. [from Latin congeries, heap]

congested /kənˈdʒɛstɪd/ adj. 1 crowded; too full; obstructed. 2 said of a part of the body affected with an accumulation of blood, mucus, or some other fluid. [from Latin congerere, to heap together]

⬛ 1 crowded, clogged, blocked, jammed, packed, stuffed, crammed, full, overcrowded, overflowing, teeming. 2 blocked, clogged.
🔁 CLEAR.

congestion /kənˈdʒɛstʃən/ noun 1 an overcrowded condition, especially of traffic. 2 the accumulation of blood, mucus, or some other fluid within a particular part of the body. 3 fullness.

⬛ 1 overcrowding, clogging, blockage, jam, traffic jam, colloq. snarl-up, gridlock, bottleneck. 2 clogging, blockage.

conglomerate /kənˈglɒmərət, kənˈglɒməreɪt/ — noun (pronounced -rət) 1 a mass formed from things of different kinds. 2 Geol. a sedimentary rock consisting of small rounded pebbles embedded in a matrix of sand, silt, or some other fine-textured material. 3 a business group composed of a large number of firms merged together. — adj. (pronounced -rət) composed of things of different kinds formed into a mass. — verb intrans. (pronounced -reɪt) to accumulate to form a mass. [from Latin con-, together + glomus, ball of yarn]

conglomeration noun 1 the state of being conglomerated. 2 a collection or jumble of things.

⬛ 2 collection, jumble, agglomeration, aggregation, accumulation, assemblage, mass, composite, medley, hotchpotch.

congrats pl. noun (often as an exclamation) colloq. congratulations.

congratulate /kɒnˈgratʃʊleɪt/ verb (**congratulate someone on something**) 1 to express one's pleasure to someone at their success, good fortune, happiness, etc. 2 to consider (oneself) lucky or clever to have managed something: congratulated herself on her narrow escape. [from Latin congratulari, to wish one another joy]

⬛ 1 praise, felicitate, compliment, wish well.
🔁 COMMISERATE WITH.

congratulation /kɒngratʃʊˈleɪʃən/ noun 1 the action or an expression of congratulating. 2 (also **congratulations**) (often as an exclamation) an expression used to congratulate someone.

congratulatory /kənˈgratʃʊlətrɪ/ adj. expressing congratulations.

congregation /kɒŋgrəˈgeɪʃən/ noun 1 a gathering or assembly of people, especially for worship in church. **2** the people regularly attending a particular church.

. . . .

◫ FLOCK, PARISHIONERS, PARISH. **1** assembly, crowd, throng, multitude, host, fellowship.

. . . .

congregational *adj.* **1** relating to or administered by a congregation or separate congregations. **2** (**Congregational**) belonging to a Protestant denomination in which the affairs of each individual church are run by its own congregation.

Congregationalism *noun* a Christian movement established on congregational principles.

Congregationalist *noun* a member of a Congregational Church. *adj.* relating to the Congregationalists.

congress *noun* **1** a large, especially international assembly of delegates, gathered for discussion. **2** a name used for the law-making body in some countries, especially (**Congress**) that of the US. [from Latin *congredi*, to meet]

congressional /kənˈgreʃənəl/ *adj.* relating or belonging to a congress.

congressman and **congresswoman** *noun* respectively a male and female member of a congress.

congruence or **congruency** *noun* **1** suitability or appropriateness. **2** agreement. **3** *Geom.* the quality of being congruent. **4** *Maths.* the relationship between two integers having the same remainder when divided by a third integer.

congruent *adj.* **1** *Geom.* denoting two or more plane (two-dimensional) or solid (three-dimensional) figures that are identical in size and shape, and so can be made to fit exactly one on top of the other. **2** *Maths.* of or relating to two integers that have the same remainder when divided by a third integer. **3** (**congruent with something**) suitable or appropriate to it. [from Latin *congruere*, to meet together]

congruently *adv.* in a congruent way.

congruity /kənˈgruːɪtɪ/ *noun* **1** agreement between things. **2** consistency. **3** suitability.

congruous *adj.* (**congruous with something**) fitting; suitable; proper. [from Latin *congruus*, from *congruere*, to meet together]

congruously *adv.* in a congruous way.

conic /ˈkɒnɪk/ — *adj. Geom.* relating to or resembling a cone. — *noun* same as CONIC SECTION. [from Greek *konikos*, from *konos*, cone]

conical *adj.* cone-shaped. [from Greek *konikos*, cone-shaped]

. . . .

◫ cone-shaped, pyramidal, tapering, tapered, pointed.

. . . .

conic section *Geom.* the curved figure produced when a plane (flat surface) intersects a cone. Depending on the angle at which it cuts through the cone, it may be a circle, ellipse, hyperbola, or parabola.

conifer /ˈkɒnɪfə(r)/ *noun* any of various mostly evergreen trees and shrubs that have narrow needle-like leaves and produce their pollen and seeds in cones, eg pine, spruce (Christmas tree), cedar, and yew. [from Latin, *conus*, cone + *ferre*, to carry]

coniferous /kəˈnɪfərəs/ *adj.*, *said of a tree* being a conifer; bearing cones.

conj. *abbrev. Grammar* conjunction.

conjectural /kənˈdʒɛktʃərəl/ *adj.*, *said of an argument, conclusion, etc* based on conjecture.

conjecturally *adv.* with conjecture.

conjecture /kənˈdʒɛktʃə(r)/ — *noun* **1** an opinion based on incomplete evidence. **2** the process of forming such an opinion. — *verb intrans.* to make a conjecture. [from Latin *conjectura*, conclusion]

. . . .

◫ *noun* **1** speculation, theory, hypothesis, notion, guess, estimate, supposition, surmise, assumption, presumption,

conclusion, inference. **2** speculation, guesswork, inference, assumption, presumption, supposition, extrapolation, projection. *verb* spec-ulate, theorize, hypothesize, infer, guess, estimate, reckon, suppose, surmise, assume, imagine, suspect.

. . . .

conjoin *verb trans.*, *intrans.* to join together, combine, or unite. [from French *conjoindre*, to join together]

conjoined twins (*also* **Siamese twins**) twins born with a piece of flesh joining one to the other.

conjoint *adj.* joint; associated; united.

conjointly *adv.* in a united fashion.

conjugal /ˈkɒndʒʊgəl/ *adj.* relating to marriage, or to the relationship between husband and wife. [from Latin *conjugalis*, from *con-*, together + *jugum*, yoke]

conjugal family the family of one's husband or wife.

conjugality /kɒndʒʊˈgalɪtɪ/ *noun* the state or condition of being married.

conjugally *adv.* in a conjugal way.

conjugate /ˈkɒndʒʊgeɪt, ˈkɒndʒʊgət/ — *verb trans.*, *intrans.* (pronounced -geɪt) **1** *Grammar* **a** to give the inflected parts of (a verb), indicating number, person, tense, voice, and mood. **b** *intrans. said of a verb* to have inflected parts. **2** *Biol.* to reproduce by fusion of two cells, eg in protozoa, or by formation of a tube between two cells, eg in certain algae. — *adj.* (pronounced -gət) **1** joined, connected, or coupled. **2** *Chem.*, *said of an acid and base* related to each other such that the acid is converted into the base by losing a proton, and the base is converted into the acid by gaining a proton. **3** *Geom.* denoting a pair of angles whose sum is 360°. **4** *said of words* having a common origin. — *noun* (pronounced -gət) a conjugate word or thing. [from Latin *con-*, with + *jugum*, yoke]

conjugation /kɒndʒʊˈgeɪʃən/ *noun* **1** *Grammar* the inflection of a verb to indicate number, person, tense, voice and mood, or a particular class of verbs having the same set of inflections. See also DECLENSION. **2** a uniting, joining, or fusing.

conjunction *noun* **1** *Grammar* a word used to link sentences, clauses, or words, eg *and*, *but*, *if*, *or*, *because*. **2** a joining together; combination. **3** the coinciding of two or more events. **4** *Astrol.* the apparent meeting or passing of two or more heavenly bodies. — **in conjunction with something** together with it. [from Latin *con-*, with + *jungere*, to join]

conjunctiva /kɒndʒʌŋkˈtaɪvə/ *noun* (PL. **conjunctivas**, **conjunctivae**) *Anat.* in the eye of vertebrates, the delicate mucous membrane that lines the eyelids and covers the exposed surface of the cornea at the front of the eyeball. [from Latin *membrana conjunctiva*, conjunctive membrane]

conjunctival /kɒndʒʌŋkˈtaɪvəl/ *adj.* relating to or in the region of the conjunctiva.

conjunctive — *adj.* **1** connecting; linking. **2** *Grammar* used as a conjunction. — *noun Grammar* a word or phrase used as a conjunction. [from Latin *conjunctivus*, connecting]

conjunctively *adv.* as or like a conjunction.

conjunctivitis /kɒndʒʌŋktɪˈvaɪtɪs/ *noun* inflammation of the conjunctiva, caused by infection, allergy, or irritation of the eye. The main symptoms are redness, swelling, itching, and a watery discharge.

conjuncture *noun* a combination of circumstances, especially one leading to a crisis. [from Latin *conjungere*, to join]

conjure /ˈkʌndʒə(r)/ *verb* **1** *intrans.* to practise conjuring. **2** to summon (a spirit, demon, etc) to appear. **3** *old use* to beg (someone) earnestly to do something. — **conjure something up 1** to produce it as though from nothing. **2** to call up, evoke, or stir (images, memories, etc). **a name to conjure with** a name of great importance or significance. [from Latin *conjurare*, to swear together]

. . . .

◫ **2** summon, invoke, rouse, raise. **conjure up 1** produce, create. **2** call up, evoke, stir, excite, awaken, recollect, recall.

. . . .

conjurer or **conjuror** *noun* an entertainer who performs conjuring tricks.

conjuring *noun* the performing of tricks that deceive the eye or seem to defy nature, especially by adroit use of the hands.

conk[1] *noun slang* the nose.

conk[2] *verb slang* to hit (someone) on the head.

conk[3] *verb intrans. slang* (*usually* **conk out**) **1** *said of a machine, etc* to break down. **2** *said of a person* to collapse with fatigue, etc.

conker *noun colloq.* the brown shiny seed of the horse chestnut tree. [either dialect *conker*, snail shell, originally used in the game, or a form of CONQUER]

conkers *sing. noun* a children's game played with conkers on strings, in which players try to shatter each other's conkers by hitting them with their own.

con man *noun colloq.* a swindler using confidence tricks.

Conn. *abbrev.* Connecticut.

connect *verb* (*usually* **connect to** or **with something** or **someone**) **1** *trans., intrans.* to join; to link. **2** to associate or involve: *is connected with advertising*. **3** to associate or relate mentally. **4** to join by telephone. **5** to relate by marriage or birth. **6** *intrans. said of aeroplanes, trains, buses, etc* to be timed so as to allow transfer from one to another. **7** *intrans. humorous, said of the fist, etc* to strike. **8** *intrans. colloq.* to make sense. — **well connected** with important or aristocratic relatives. [from Latin *con-*, together + *nectere*, to fasten]

. . . .

🔲 **1** join, link, unite, couple, combine, fasten, affix, attach. **2** associate, involve, link, ally, mix up. **3** associate, relate, ally.

🔁 **1** disconnect, cut off, detach. **4** disconnect, cut off.

. . . .

connectable or **connectible** *adj.* capable of being connected.

connecting-rod *noun* in an engine, reciprocating pump, etc, a rod or bar that transmits motion from one part to another, especially a rod that connects the piston to the crankshaft in an internal combustion engine.

connection or **connexion** *noun* **1** the act of connecting or state of being connected. **2** something that connects; a link. **3** a relationship through marriage or birth. **4** an especially influential person whom one meets through one's job, etc; a contact. **5** a train, bus, etc timed so as to allow transfer to it from another passenger service; the transfer from one vehicle to another. — **in connection with something** to do with it; concerning it. **in this connection** with reference to the matter being considered.

. . . .

🔲 **1** junction, coupling, fastening, attachment, association, alliance, relationship, interrelation, correlation, correspondence. **2** link, coupling, fastening, attachment, bond, tie.

🔁 **1** disconnection.

. . . .

connective — *adj.* **1** serving to connect. **2** *Grammar* linking two sentences, clauses, etc. — *noun Grammar* a connective word.

connective tissue *Anat.* any of several widely differing tissues, usually containing collagen, that provide the animal body and its internal organs with structural support, eg bone, cartilage, tendons, ligaments.

connector *noun* that which joins or links one thing to another.

conning-tower *noun* **1** the raised part of a submarine containing the periscope. **2** the wheelhouse of a warship. [from CON[3]]

connivance *noun* the act or practice of conniving.

connive *verb intrans.* **1** (**connive at something**) to pretend not to notice a wrongdoing, and thereby share responsibility for it. **2** (**connive with someone**) to conspire. [from Latin *connivere*, to blink]

conniver *noun* a person who connives.

connoisseur /kɒnə'sɜː(r)/ *noun* a person who is knowledgeable about, and a good judge of, eg the arts, wine, food, etc. [from French *connoisseur*, from *connaître*, to know]

. . . .

🔲 authority, specialist, expert, judge, devotee, *colloq.* buff, gourmet, epicure.

. . . .

connotation *noun* **1** the act of connoting. **2** an idea, association, or implication additional to the main idea or object expressed.

. . . .

🔲 **2** implication, suggestion, hint, nuance, undertone, overtone, colouring, association.

. . . .

connotative /'kɒnəteɪtɪv, kə'noʊtətɪv/ *adj.* connoting; relating to connotation.

connote *verb formal* **1** *said of a word* to suggest, in addition to its literal meaning: *'portly' somehow connotes pomposity*. **2** to mean; to imply. [from Latin *connotare*, to mark in addition]

connubial /kə'njuːbɪəl/ *adj.* of or relating to marriage or to relations between a husband and wife. [from Latin *connubium*, marriage]

connubially *adv.* in a connubial way.

conquer /'kɒŋkə(r)/ *verb* (**conquered**, **conquering**) **1** to gain possession or dominion over (territory) by force. **2** to defeat. **3** to overcome or put an end to (a failing, difficulty, evil, etc). **4** to succeed in climbing, reaching, traversing, etc. **5** to become a celebrity in: *the singer who conquered America*. **6** *intrans.* to win; to succeed. [from Latin *conquirere*, to go in search of]

. . . .

🔲 **1** seize, take, annex, occupy, possess, win, acquire, obtain. **2** defeat, beat, overthrow, vanquish, rout, overrun, get the better of, best, worst, triumph over, prevail over, overpower, crush, subdue, quell, subjugate, humble. **3** get the better of, overcome, surmount, master, prevail over.

🔁 **2** surrender to, yield to, give in to. **3** give in to.

. . . .

conquering *adj.* victorious.

conqueror *noun* a person who conquers.

. . . .

🔲 victor, winner, champion, *colloq.* champ, hero, vanquisher.

. . . .

conquest *noun* **1** the act of conquering. **2** a conquered territory. **3** something won by effort or force. **4** a person whose affection or admiration one has won. [from French *conqueste*, from Latin *conquirere*, to seek out]

. . . .

🔲 **1** victory, triumph, defeat, overthrow, coup, rout, mastery, subjugation, subjection, invasion, occupation, capture, appropriation, annexation. **2, 3** acquisition.

. . . .

conquistador /kən'kwɪstədɔː(r)/ *noun* (PL. **conquistadores**, **conquistadors**) any of the 16th-century Spanish conquerors of Peru and Mexico. [from Spanish *conquistador*, conqueror]

consanguineous /kɒnsæŋ'gwɪnɪəs/ *adj.* descended from a common ancestor. [from Latin *con-*, same + *sanguis*, blood]

consanguinity /kɒnsæŋ'gwɪnɪtɪ/ *noun* descent from a common ancestor.

conscience /'kɒnʃəns/ *noun* the sense of moral right and wrong that affects a person and affects behaviour. — **in all conscience** by any normal standard of fairness. **on one's conscience** making one feel guilty. [from Latin *conscientia*]

. . . .

🔲 morals, principles, standards, ethics, scruples, qualms.

. . . .

conscience-stricken *adj.* feeling guilty over something one has done.

conscientious /kɒnʃɪˈɛnʃəs/ *adj.* **1** careful; thorough; painstaking. **2** guided by conscience. [from Latin *conscientiosus*]

⬛ **1** careful, thorough, painstaking, diligent, hard-working, responsible, scrupulous, punctilious, meticulous, particular, attentive. **2** upright, honest, faithful, dutiful.
⬛ **1** careless, irresponsible, unreliable.

conscientiously *adv.* in a conscientious way.

conscientiousness *noun* the quality of being conscientious.

conscientious objector a person who refuses on moral grounds to serve in the armed forces.

conscious /ˈkɒnʃəs/ — *adj.* **1** awake, alert, and aware of one's thoughts and one's surroundings. **2** aware, knowing. **3** deliberate: *a conscious effort to be polite.* **4** (*often in compounds*) concerned, especially too concerned, with: *class-conscious.* — *noun* the part of the human mind which is responsible for such awareness, and is concerned with perceiving and reacting to external objects and events. [from Latin *conscius*, from *scire*, to know]

⬛ *adj.* **1** awake, alert, responsive, sentient, sensible, rational, reasoning, alive. **2** aware, knowing, self-conscious, heedful, mindful. **3** deliberate, intentional, calculated, premeditated, studied, wilful, voluntary.
⬛ *adj.* **1** unconscious. **2** unaware.

consciously *adv.* in a conscious way; knowingly.

consciousness *noun* **1** the state of being conscious. **2** awareness. **3** *Psychol.* the physical and mental state of being awake and fully aware of one's environment, thoughts, and feelings.

⬛ **2** awareness, sentience, sensibility, knowledge, intuition, realization, recognition.
⬛ UNCONSCIOUSNESS.

conscript /kənˈskrɪpt, ˈkɒnskrɪpt/ — *verb trans.* (with stress on *-script*) to enrol for compulsory military service. — *noun* (with stress on *con*-) a person who has been conscripted. [from Latin *conscribere*, to enlist]

conscription *noun* the compulsory enrolment of recruits for military service.

consecrate *verb* **1** to set apart for a holy use; to make sacred; to dedicate to God. **2** to devote to a special use. [from Latin *consecrare*, from *sacer*, sacred]

⬛ **1** sanctify, hallow, bless, dedicate, ordain, venerate, revere, exalt. **2** devote, dedicate, ordain.

consecration /kɒnsəˈkreɪʃən/ *noun* the act or process of making holy.

consecutive /kənˈsɛkjʊtɪv/ *adj.* **1** following one after the other: *consecutive numbers.* **2** *Grammar* expressing result or consequence. [from Latin *consequi*, to follow]

⬛ **1** sequential, successive, continuous, unbroken, uninterrupted, following, succeeding, running.
⬛ **1** discontinuous.

consecutively *adv.* in a consecutive way; successively.

consensus *noun* general feeling or opinion; agreement; a majority view. [from Latin *consensus*, agreement, from *con*-, same + *sensus*, feeling]

consent — *verb* **1** *intrans.* (**consent to something**) to give one's permission for it; to agree to it. **2** to agree to do something. — *noun* agreement; assent; permission: *give one's consent.* — **by common consent** as is generally agreed. [from Latin *consentire*, to agree]

⬛ *verb* **1** agree, concur, accede, assent, approve, permit, allow, grant, admit. **2** agree, concur, accede, concede, acquiesce, yield, comply. *noun* agreement, concurrence, assent, approval, permission, *colloq.* go-ahead, *colloq.* green light, sanction, concession, acquiescence, compliance.
⬛ *verb* **1** refuse, oppose. **2** refuse, decline. *noun* disagreement, refusal, opposition.

consequence *noun* **1** something that follows from, or is caused by, an action or set of circumstances. **2** a conclusion reached from reasoning. **3** importance: *of no consequence.* — **in consequence of something** as a result of it. **take the consequences** to accept whatever results from one's decision or action. [from Latin *consequi*, to follow]

⬛ **1** result, outcome, issue, end, upshot, effect, side effect, repercussion. **3** importance, significance, concern, value, weight, note, eminence, distinction.
⬛ **1** cause. **3** unimportance, insignificance.

consequent *adj.* (**consequent on** or **upon something**) resulting from it.

⬛ resultant, resulting, ensuing, subsequent, following, successive, sequential.

consequential /kɒnsəˈkwɛnʃəl/ *adj.* **1** important. **2** *said of a person* self-important; pompous. **3** following as a result. [from Latin *consequentia*, consequence]

consequently *adv.* as a result; therefore.

conservable /kənˈsɜːvəbl/ *adj.* capable of being conserved.

conservancy /kənˈsɜːvənsɪ/ (PL. **conservancies**) *noun* **1** in the UK, a court or commission having authority to preserve a river, forest, port, or area of countryside. **2** the act of conservation, especially the official care of a river, forest, etc. [from Latin *conservare*, to preserve]

conservation *noun* **1** the act of conserving; the state of being conserved. **2** the management of the environment in such a way that its wildlife, natural resources, and quality are preserved and protected. **3** the preservation of historical artefacts, eg books, paintings, monuments, for future generations. **4** *Physics* (also **conservation law**) a law which states that the energy, mass, electrical charge, or some other physical property of a closed system will remain constant, eg energy cannot be created or destroyed, although it can be converted from one form to another. [from Latin *conservare*, to save]

⬛ **1** keeping, safe-keeping, custody, saving, economy, husbandry, maintenance, upkeep, preservation, protection, safeguarding. **2** ecology, environmentalism.
⬛ **1** destruction.

conservation area an area, especially in a village, town, or city, designated as being of special architectural or historic interest, and therefore protected from any alterations that may threaten its character.

conservationist *noun* **1** a person who is trained or qualified to manage the environment and natural resources. **2** a person who actively encourages or supports conservation, especially of the environment or natural resources.

conservation of energy *Physics* the law which states that the total energy of a closed (isolated) system remains constant, ie energy can be converted from one form to another, but it cannot be created or destroyed.

conservation of mass *Physics* the law which states that the total mass of the substances that take part in a chemical reaction (the reactants) is equal to the total mass of the products formed, ie mass cannot be created or destroyed.

conservatism /kənˈsɜːvətɪzm/ *noun* **1** the inclination to preserve the existing state of affairs and to avoid especially sudden or radical change. **2 (Conservatism)** the policies and principles of a Conservative Party.

conservative /kən'sɜːvətɪv/ — *adj.* **1** favouring the keeping of what is established or traditional; disliking change. **2** *said of an estimate or calculation* deliberately low, for the sake of caution. **3** *said of tastes, clothing, etc* restrained; not flamboyant. **4 (Conservative)** relating to the Conservative Party, a UK political party supporting free enterprise and private ownership of industry, or any other Conservative Party. — *noun* **1** a traditionalist. **2 (Conservative)** a member or supporter of a Conservative Party. [from Latin *conservare*, to preserve]

■ *adj.* **1** traditional, conventional, hidebound, die-hard, reactionary, establishmentarian, unprogressive, moderate, middle-of-the-road, cautious, guarded, sober. **4** Tory, right-wing. *noun* **1** traditionalist, diehard, *colloq.* stick-in-the-mud, reactionary, moderate. **2** Tory, right-winger.
E3 *adj.* **1** radical, innovative. **4** left-wing. *noun* **1** radical. **2** left-winger.

conservatively *adv.* in a conservative way.
conservatoire /kən'sɜːvətwɑː(r)/ *noun* a school specializing in music or any of the fine arts. [from French *conservatoire*, from Italian *conservatorio*, originally an orphanage]
conservatory /kən'sɜːvətrɪ/ *noun* (PL. **conservatories**) **1** a greenhouse for plants, or a similar room used as a lounge, attached to, and entered from, the house. **2** a conservatoire. [from Latin *conservare*, to conserve]

■ **1** greenhouse, glasshouse, hothouse.

conserve /kən'sɜːv, 'kɒnsɜːv/ — *verb* (with stress on *-serve*) to keep safe from damage, deterioration, loss, or undesirable change. — *noun* (with stress on *con-*) a jam made especially from fresh fruit. [from Latin *conservare*, to save]

■ *verb* keep, save, store up, hoard, maintain, preserve, protect, guard, safeguard. *noun* jam, preserve, jelly.
E3 *verb* use, waste, squander.

consider /kən'sɪdə(r)/ *verb* (**considered, considering**) **1** to go over in one's mind. **2** to look at thoughtfully. **3** to call to mind for comparison, etc. **4** to assess with regard to employing, using, etc: *consider someone for a job.* **5** to contemplate doing something. **6** to regard as. **7** to think; to have as one's opinion. **8** to take into account; to make allowances for. **9** *intrans.* to think carefully. — **all things considered** taking all the circumstances into account. [from Latin *considerare*, to examine]

■ **1** ponder, deliberate, reflect, contemplate, meditate, muse, mull over, *colloq.* chew over, examine, study, weigh, respect, remember, take into account. **2** regard as, examine, contemplate. **6** regard, deem, count. **7** think, believe, judge, rate, count.

considerable *adj.* **1** large; great. **2** having many admirable qualities: *a considerable person.* [from Latin *considerabilis*]

■ **1** large, great, big, sizeable, substantial, *colloq.* tidy, ample, plentiful, abundant, lavish, marked, noticeable, perceptible, appreciable, reasonable, tolerable. **2** noteworthy, distinguished, respectable, important, influential.
E3 **1** small, slight. **2** insignificant, unremarkable.

considerably *adv.* largely; to a large extent.
considerate *adj.* careful not to hurt or inconvenience others. [from Latin *consideratus*, careful]

■ kind, thoughtful, caring, attentive, obliging, helpful,

charitable, unselfish, altruistic, gracious, sensitive, tactful, discreet.
E3 inconsiderate, thoughtless, selfish.

considerately *adv.* with a considerate manner.
considerateness *noun* the quality of being considerate.
consideration *noun* **1** thoughtfulness on behalf of others. **2** careful thought. **3** a fact, circumstance, etc to be taken into account. **4** a payment, reward, or recompense. — **in consideration of something** in return for it: *a small fee in consideration of your efforts.* **take something into consideration** to allow for it. **under consideration** being considered. [from Latin *considerare*, to consider]

■ **1** kindness, thoughtfulness, care, attention, regard, respect. **2** thought, deliberation, reflection, contemplation, meditation, examination, analysis, scrutiny, review, attention, notice, regard.
E3 **1** thoughtlessness. **2** disregard.

considered *adj.* **1** carefully thought about: *my considered opinion.* **2** (*with an adverb*) thought of or valued in some way: *highly considered.*
considering — *conj.* taking into account: *still very active, considering her age.* — *adv.* taking the circumstances into account: *pretty good, considering.*
consign /kən'saɪn/ *verb* **1** to hand over; to entrust. **2** to send, commit, or deliver. **3** to send (goods). [from Latin *consignare*, to put one's seal to]

■ **1** hand over, entrust, commit, devote, transfer. **2** send, commit, deliver, transfer, convey, ship. **3** send, ship, transport.

consignee /kɒnsaɪ'niː/ *noun* the addressee or recipient of goods, etc.
consignment /kən'saɪnmənt/ *noun* **1** a load of goods, etc sent or delivered. **2** the act of consigning. — **on consignment** *said of retail goods* to be paid for only if sold, and returned if unsold.

■ **1** cargo, shipment, load, batch, delivery, goods. **2** shipment, delivery, transfer.

consignor /kən'saɪnə(r)/ *noun* the sender or deliverer of goods.
consist *verb intrans.* **1** (**consist of something**) to be composed or made up of several elements or ingredients: *the mixture consists of flour, eggs, and water.* **2** (**consist in** or **of something**) to have it as an essential feature: *their character consists in their heroism.* [from Latin *consistere*, to stand firm]

■ **1** be composed of, comprise, contain, include, incorporate, embody, embrace, involve.

consistency *noun* (PL. **consistencies**) **1** the texture or composition of something, with regard to density, thickness, firmness, solidity, etc. **2** the quality of being consistent. **3** agreement, harmony. [from Latin *consistere*, to stand together]

■ **1** density, viscosity, thickness, firmness. **2** regularity, evenness, uniformity, sameness, constancy, steadiness, steadfastness. **3** agreement, harmony, accordance, correspondence, congruity, compatibility.
E3 **2** inconsistency.

consistent *adj.* **1** (**consistent with something**) in agreement with it; in keeping with it: *injuries consistent with a heavy blow.* **2** unchanging, reliable, regular, steady. [from Latin *consistere*, to stand firm]

∷ **1** in agreement, consonant with, congruous with, compatible with, harmonious with. **2** unchanging, reliable, regular, steady, stable, uniform, undeviating, constant, persistent, unfailing, dependable.

✷ INCONSISTENT. **2** irregular, erratic.

consistently *adv.* in a consistent way.

consistory /kən'sɪstərɪ/ *noun* (PL. **consistories**) an ecclesiastical council, especially one composed of the pope and cardinals. [from Latin *consistorium*, meeting-place]

consolable /kən'soʊləbl/ *adj.* capable of being consoled.

consolation /kɒnsə'leɪʃən/ *noun* **1** a circumstance or person that brings one comfort. **2** the act of consoling.

consolation prize a prize given to someone who just fails to win a major prize.

consolatory /kən'sɒlətərɪ/ *adj.* comforting.

console[1] /kən'soʊl/ *verb* to comfort in distress, grief, or disappointment. [from Latin *consolari*, to comfort]

∷ comfort, soothe, calm, cheer, hearten, encourage, relieve.

✷ upset, agitate.

console[2] /'kɒnsoʊl/ *noun* **1** *Mus.* the part of an organ with the keys, pedals, and panels of stops. **2** a panel of dials, switches, etc for operating an electronic machine. **3** a freestanding cabinet for audio or video equipment. **4** an ornamental bracket for a shelf, etc. [from French *console*, from *consolateur*, comforter, supporter]

consolidate /kən'sɒlɪdeɪt/ *verb trans., intrans.* **1** to make or become solid or strong. **2** *said of businesses, etc* to combine or merge. [from Latin *consolidare*]

∷ **1** reinforce, strengthen, secure, stabilize, cement, condense, thicken, harden, solidify. **2** unite, combine, amalgamate, unify, join, fuse.

consolidation *noun* **1** making solid or strong. **2** the merging of businesses, etc.

consolidator *noun* a person or thing that consolidates.

consols *pl. noun Brit.* government securities. [from consolidated annuities]

consommé /kən'sɒmeɪ/ *noun* thin clear soup made from meat stock. [from French *consommé*, finished]

consonance *noun* **1** the state of agreement. **2** *Mus.* a pleasant-sounding combination of musical notes.

consonant[1] *noun* **1** any speech-sound produced by obstructing the passage of the breath in any of several ways. **2** a letter, used alone or in combination (as in *ch, ll, st*, etc), representing such a sound. [from Latin *consonans litera*, letter having the same sound]

consonant[2] *adj.* (**consonant with something**) in harmony or agreement with it. [from Latin *consonare*, to sound together]

consonantal /kɒnsə'nantəl/ *adj.* **1** characteristic of a consonant. **2** *said of an alphabet, etc* using only consonants, and usually marking vowels by means of accents.

consort[1] /'kɒnsɔːt, kən'sɔːt/ — *noun* (with stress on *con-*) **1** a wife or husband, especially of a reigning sovereign. **2** *Naut.* an accompanying ship. — *verb intrans.* (with stress on *-sort*) (**consort with someone**) to associate or keep company with them (usually with unfavourable implications). [from Latin *consors*, sharer]

consort[2] /'kɒnsɔːt/ *noun* a group of players, singers, or instruments, especially specialising in early music. [variant of CONCERT]

consortium /kən'sɔːtɪəm/ *noun* (PL. **consortia, consortiums**) an association or combination of several banks, businesses, etc. [from Latin *consortium*, partnership]

conspectus *noun* a survey or report; a summary. [from Latin *conspectus*, view, survey]

conspicuous /kən'spɪkjʊəs/ *adj.* **1** very noticeable or obvious. **2** notable; striking; glaring. [from Latin *conspicuus*, visible]

∷ **1** noticeable, obvious, apparent, visible, marked, clear, evident, patent, manifest. **2** notable, striking, glaring, prominent, blatant, flagrant, ostentatious, showy, flashy, garish.

✷ INCONSPICUOUS, CONCEALED, HIDDEN.

conspicuously *adv.* in a conspicuous or obvious way.

conspicuousness *noun* the quality of being conspicuous.

conspiracy /kən'spɪrəsɪ/ *noun* (PL. **conspiracies**) **1** the activity of conspiring. **2** a plot. **3** a group of conspirators. [from Latin *conspiratio*, plot]

∷ **1** intrigue, machination, collusion, treason. **2** plot, scheme, intrigue, machination, *colloq.* fix, *colloq.* frame-up.

conspiracy of silence an agreement to keep quiet about something.

conspirator /kən'spɪrətə(r)/ *noun* someone who plots, or joins a conspiracy. [from Latin *conspirator*, from *conspirare*, to plot]

∷ conspirer, plotter, schemer, intriguer, traitor.

conspiratorial /kənspɪrə'tɔːrɪəl/ *adj.* relating to or involving conspiracy.

conspiratorially *adv.* in a conspiratorial way.

conspire *verb intrans.* **1** to plot secretly together especially for an unlawful purpose. **2** *said of events* to seem to be working together to thwart one: *everything conspired to make me miss my train.* [from Latin *conspirare*]

∷ **1** plot, scheme, intrigue, manoeuvre, connive, collude.

constable /'kʌnstəbl, 'kɒnstəbl/ *noun* **1** a policeman or policewoman of the most junior rank. **2** *Hist.* the chief officer of a royal household. **3** the governor of a royal castle. [from French *conestable*, from Latin *comes stabuli*, count of the stable]

constabulary /kən'stabjʊlərɪ/ — *noun* (PL. **constabularies**) the police force of a district or county. — *adj.* of or relating to constables or the police. [from Latin *constabularius*, from Middle English *constablerie*, from French *conestable*, constable]

constancy *noun* **1** not stopping or changing. **2** being faithful or loyal.

∷ **1** stability, steadiness, permanence, firmness, regularity, uniformity. **2** loyalty, faithfulness, fidelity, devotion, resolution, perseverance, tenacity.

✷ **1** change, irregularity. **2** fickleness.

constant *adj.* **1** never stopping. **2** frequently recurring. **3** unchanging. **4** faithful; loyal. *noun Maths.* a symbol (usually a numeral) that remains unchanged, unlike a *variable*, for which one or more values may be substituted. For example, in the expression $3y^2 - 4$, y is a variable and the numbers 3 and 4 are constants. [from Latin *constare*, to be unchanging or steadfast]

∷ *adj.* **1** continuous, unbroken, never-ending, non-stop, endless, interminable, ceaseless, incessant, eternal, everlasting, perpetual, continual, unremitting, relentless, persistent, resolute, persevering, unflagging, unwavering, stable, steady. **3** unchanging, unvarying, changeless, immutable, invariable, unalterable, permanent, firm, even, regular, uniform. **4** faithful, loyal, staunch, steadfast, dependable, trustworthy, true, devoted.

✷ *adj.* **1** occasional, irregular, fitful. **3** variable. **4** disloyal, fickle.

constantly *adv.* in a constant way; steadily, regularly.

constellation /kɒnstəˈleɪʃən/ *noun* **1** any of 88 regions into which the sky is conceptually divided, each consisting of a group of stars that often form a distinctive shape in the sky, although their distances from the Earth may differ greatly, eg Ursa Major (great bear), Centaurus (centaur). **2** a group of associated people or things. [from Latin *constellatio*, from *stella*, star]

consternation /kɒnstəˈneɪʃən/ *noun* dismay, alarm, agitation or anxiety. [from Latin *consternatio*]

constipate *verb* to cause constipation in. [from Latin *con-*, together + *stipare*, to press]

constipated *adj.* suffering from constipation.

constipation /kɒnstɪˈpeɪʃən/ *noun* a condition in which the faeces become hard, and bowel movements occur infrequently or with pain or difficulty.

constituency /kənˈstɪtjʊənsɪ/ *noun* (PL. **constituencies**) **1** the district represented by a member of parliament or other representative in a legislative body. **2** the voters in that district. [from CONSTITUENT]

constituent /kənˈstɪtjʊənt/ — *adj.* **1** forming part of a whole. **2** having the power to create or alter a constitution: *a constituent assembly.* **3** having the power to elect. — *noun* **1** a necessary part; a component. **2** a resident in a constituency. [from Latin *constituere*, to establish]

▣ *adj.* **1** component, integral, essential, basic, intrinsic, inherent. *noun* **1** ingredient, element, factor, principle, component, part, bit, section, unit.

constitute *verb* **1** to be; to go together to make. **2** to establish; to appoint: *the recently constituted board of enquiry.* [from Latin *constituere*, to establish]

▣ **1** make up, represent, compose, comprise, form, create. **2** establish, appoint, set up, found.

constitution /kɒnstɪˈtjuːʃən/ *noun* **1** a set of rules governing an organization; the supreme laws and rights of a country's people, etc. **2** the way in which something is formed or made up. **3** one's physical make-up, health, etc. **4** the act of forming or constituting. [from Latin *constitutio*, arrangement, physical make-up]

constitutional — *adj.* **1** legal according to a given constitution. **2** relating to, or controlled by, the law of the land. **3** relating to one's physical make-up, health, etc. — *noun old use* a regular walk taken for the sake of one's health.

constitutionally *adv.* in a constitutional way; in terms of a constitution.

constrain *verb* **1** (*usually* **be constrained**) to force; to compel: *feel constrained to tell the truth.* **2** to limit the freedom, scope, or range of. [from French *constraindre*]

▣ **1** force, compel, oblige, necessitate, drive, impel, urge. **2** limit, confine, constrict, restrain, check, curb, bind.

constrained *adj.* awkward; embarrassed; forced.

▣ awkward, uneasy, embarrassed, forced, inhibited, reticent, reserved, guarded, stiff, unnatural.
▣ relaxed, free.

constraint *noun* **1** a limit or restriction. **2** force; compulsion. **3** awkwardness, unnaturalness, embarrassment, or inhibition.

▣ **1** limit, limitation, restriction, hindrance, restraint, check, curb, damper. **2** force, compulsion, duress, coercion, pressure, necessity, deterrent.

constrict *verb* **1** to squeeze or compress; to enclose tightly, especially too tightly; to cause to tighten. **2** to inhibit. [from Latin *constringere*, to bind]

▣ **1** squeeze, compress, pinch, cramp, narrow, tighten, contract, shrink, choke, strangle. **2** inhibit, limit, restrict.
▣ **1** expand.

constriction *noun* **1** the process of constricting. **2** something that is constricted. **3** contraction, tightness.

constrictive *adj.* causing a constriction.

constrictor *noun* **1** a snake that kills by coiling around its prey, then squeezing and suffocating it. **2** *Anat.* any muscle that compresses an organ or narrows an opening.

construct /kənˈstrʌkt, ˈkɒnstrʌkt/ — *verb* (with stress on -*struct*) **1** to build. **2** to form, compose, or put together. **3** *Geom.* to draw (a figure). — *noun* (with stress on *con-*) **1** something constructed, especially in the mind. **2** a complex idea or thought constructed from a number of simpler ideas or thoughts. [from Latin *construere*, to build, pile together]

▣ *verb* **1** build, erect, raise, elevate, make, manufacture, fabricate. **2** form, compose, assemble, put together, formulate, shape, fashion, model, design, engineer, create, found, establish.
▣ *verb* **1**, **2** demolish, destroy.

construction *noun* **1** the process of building or constructing. **2** something built or constructed; a building. **3** *Grammar* the arrangement of words in a particular grammatical relationship, to form a sentence, clause, etc. **4** interpretation: *put a wrong construction on someone's words.*

▣ **1** building, manufacture, fabrication, assembly, composition, constitution, formation, creation. **2** building, edifice, erection, structure, fabric, form, shape, figure, model.
▣ **1** destruction.

constructional *adj.* **1** involving construction. **2** used for structures. **3** using structures.

constructive *adj.* **1** helping towards progress or development; useful. **2** *Legal, said of facts* realized from what has been stated, rather than actually stated themselves. **3** relating to construction.

▣ **1** useful, helpful, valuable, beneficial, advantageous, productive, positive, practical.
▣ **1** destructive, negative, unhelpful.

constructively *adv.* in a constructive way.

constructor *noun* a person who constructs.

construe *verb* **1** to interpret or explain. **2** *Grammar* to analyse the grammatical structure of (a sentence, etc). **3** *Grammar* (**construe one word with another**) to combine them grammatically. **4** *Grammar* to translate word for word. **5** to deduce; to infer. [from Latin *construere*, to construct]

consubstantiation *noun Christianity* a doctrine attributed to Luther, describing the presence of Christ in the Eucharist 'under and with the elements of bread and wine'. See also TRANSUBSTANTIATION.

consul *noun* **1** an official repesentative of a state, stationed in a foreign country to look after eg the interests of fellow citizens living there. **2** *Hist.* either of the two joint chief magistrates in ancient Rome. [from Latin *consul*]

consular /ˈkɒnsjʊlə(r)/ *adj.* relating to the office or status of a consul.

consulate /ˈkɒnsjʊlət/ *noun* the post or official residence of a consul (see CONSUL 1).

consulship *noun* the office or position of a consul.

consult *verb* **1** to ask the advice of: *consult a lawyer.* **2** to refer to (a map, book, etc). **3** to consider (wishes, feelings, etc). **4** (**consult with someone**) to have discussions with them. **5** *intrans.* to give advice as a consultant: *the doctor's consulting hours.* [from Latin *consultare*]

▣ **2** refer to, look at. **4** confer with, discuss with, debate with, deliberate with.

consultancy *noun* **1** the post of consultant. **2** an agency offering professional advice.

consultant *noun* **1** a person who gives professional advice. **2** the most senior grade of doctor in a given speciality in a hospital or clinic, who accepts ultimate responsibility for the treatment and care of patients.

▣ **1** adviser, expert, authority, specialist.

consultation *noun* **1** the act or process of consulting. **2** a meeting for the obtaining of advice or for discussion.

▣ **2** discussion, deliberation, dialogue, conference, meeting, hearing, interview, examination, appointment, session.

consultative *adj.* available for consultation; advisory: *a consultative committee.*

consulting *adj.* acting as an adviser: *a consulting architect.*

consulting room the room in which a doctor sees patients.

consumable /kən'sjuːməbl/ *adj.* capable of being consumed.

consume /kən'sjuːm/ *verb* **1** to eat or drink. **2** to use up. **3** to destroy. **4** (**be consumed with something**) to be obsessed or overcome by a feeling, etc: *they are consumed with jealousy.* [from Latin *consumere*]

▣ **1** eat, drink, swallow, devour, gobble. **2** use (up), expend, exhaust, spend, deplete, drain, absorb. **3** destroy, demolish, annihilate, devastate, ravage.

consumer *noun* **1** the person who uses a product; any member of the public buying and using goods and services. **2** someone or something that consumes.

▣ **1** customer, user, end-user, buyer, purchaser, shopper.

consumer durable a product that does not need frequent replacement, eg an item of furniture, audio equipment, etc.

consumer goods goods bought to satisfy personal needs, as distinct from eg machinery and other equipment used in the production of goods.

consumerism *noun* **1** the protection of the interests of consumers. **2** *Econ.* the theory that steady growth in the consumption of goods is necessary for a sound economy.

consumer research the study of the needs and preferences of consumers.

consumer society the advanced stage of industrial society, in which there is a high availability and consumption of consumer goods and services.

consumer terrorism the deliberate contamination by harmful substances of certain food products, usually to reinforce demands made of the producers or retailers of the products.

consuming *adj.*, *said of an enthusiasm, etc* obsessive; overwhelming.

consummate /'kɒnsəmeɪt, kən'sʌmɪt/ — *verb* (with stress on *con-*) **1** to finish, perfect, or complete. **2** to make (a marriage) into a marriage in its full legal sense through the act of sexual intercourse. — *adj.* (with stress on *-summ-*) **1** supreme; very great; very skilled. **2** complete; utter: *a consummate idiot.* [from Latin *consummare*, to complete, perfect]

consummately /kən'sʌmɪtli/ *adv.* perfectly; with great skill.

consummation /kɒnsə'meɪʃən/ *noun* **1** the act of consummating. **2** perfection.

consumption *noun* **1** the act or process of consuming. **2** the amount consumed. **3** the buying and using of goods. **4** *old use* tuberculosis of the lungs. [from Latin *consumptio*]

▣ **1** use, utilization, depletion, exhaustion. **3** spending, expenditure.

consumptive — *adj.* **1** relating to consumption; wasteful or destructive. **2** suffering from tuberculosis of the lungs. — *noun* a person suffering from tuberculosis of the lungs.

cont. *abbrev.* continued.

contact /'kɒntakt, kən'takt/ — *noun* (with stress on *con-*) **1** the condition of touching physically. **2** communication, or a means of communication. **3** an acquaintance whose influence or knowledge may prove useful to one, especially in business. **4** in an electrical device, a connection made of a conducting material that allows the passage of a current by forming a junction with another conducting part, eg a switch that can be used to make or break a circuit. **5** an individual who has been exposed to and is therefore capable of transmitting an infectious disease. **6** a contact lens. — *verb* (with stress on *con-* or *-tact*) to get in touch with; to communicate with. [from Latin *contactus*, touching]

▣ *noun* **1** touch, impact, juxtaposition, contiguity, communication, meeting, junction, connection, union. **3** connection. *verb* get in touch with, get hold of, communicate with, approach, telephone, phone, ring, call, apply to, reach, notify.

contactable *adv.* able to be contacted.

contact lens a small lens, consisting of hard, soft, or gas-permeable plastic material, that is worn in direct contact with the front of the eyeball as an alternative to spectacles for the correction of visual defects.

contact process *Chem.* the process whereby sulphuric acid is manufactured on an industrial scale by the oxidation of sulphur dioxide to sulphur trioxide in the presence of a catalyst.

contagion /kən'teɪdʒən/ *noun* **1** the transmission of a disease by direct physical contact with the body of an infected person. **2** *old use* a disease that is transmitted in this way. **3** a spreading social evil; a corrupting influence. [from Latin *contagio*, touching, contact]

contagious /kən'teɪdʒəs/ *adj.* **1** formerly used to denote a disease that can only be transmitted by direct contact. **2** denoting a disease that can be transmitted by direct contact with or close proximity to an infected individual. Also called COMMUNICABLE. **3** denoting an organism that has been exposed to and is capable of transmitting such a disease. **4** *said of a mood, laughter, etc* spreading from person to person; affecting everyone in the vicinity.

▣ INFECTIOUS, CATCHING. **1**, **2**, **3** communicable, transmissible.

contain *verb* **1** to hold or have; to have in or inside; to consist of. **2** to control, limit, check, or prevent the spread of. **3** to control (oneself or one's feelings). **4** to enclose or surround. **5** *Maths.* to be divisible by (a number), without a remainder. [from Latin *continere*, to contain, restrain]

▣ **1** hold, include, comprise, incorporate, embody, accommodate, seat. **2**, **3** control, limit, check, curb, restrain, repress, stifle. **4** enclose, surround, embrace.

containable *adj.* able to be contained; controllable.

container *noun* **1** an object designed for holding or storing, such as a box, tin, carton, etc. **2** a huge sealed metal box of standard size and design for carrying goods by lorry or ship.

■ **1** receptacle, holder, vessel.

containerization or **containerisation** *noun* the process of containerizing goods.

containerize or **containerise** *verb* to put (cargo) into containers.

container ship a cargo ship designed to carry 6m or 12m containers in pre-determined positions, largely dispensing with the loading and stowage problems associated with traditional cargo.

containment *noun* the action of preventing the expansion of a hostile power, etc.

containment building a steel or concrete structure enclosing a nuclear reactor, designed to withstand high pressure and high temperature and, in emergency, to contain the escape of radiation.

contaminant /kən'tæmɪnənt/ *noun* something which contaminates.

contaminate /kən'tæmɪneɪt/ *verb* **1** to pollute or infect (a substance). **2** to make (a substance) radioactive by exposing it to radioactive material. [from Latin *contaminare*]

■ **1** pollute, infect, adulterate, taint, soil, sully, defile, corrupt, deprave, debase, stain, tarnish. **2** irradiate.
➡ **1** purify.

contamination /kəntæmɪ'neɪʃən/ *noun* **1** pollution caused by the presence of unwanted substances, infectious microorganisms, radioactivity, etc. **2** adulteration, corruption. **3** infection.

contd or **contd.** *abbrev.* continued.

contemn /kən'tɛm/ *verb literary* to despise, disdain, or scorn. [from Latin *contemnere*]

contemplate *verb* **1** *trans., intrans.* to think about; to go over (something) mentally; to meditate. **2** to look thoughtfully at. **3** to consider as a possibility. [from Latin *contemplari*, to survey, look at carefully]

■ **1** consider, reflect on, meditate, ponder, mull over, deliberate. **2** regard, view, survey, observe, study, examine, inspect, scrutinize. **3** expect, foresee, envisage, plan, design, propose, intend, mean.

contemplation /kɒntəm'pleɪʃən/ *noun* thought, meditation.

contemplative /kən'tɛmplətɪv/ — *adj.* **1** thoughtful; meditative. **2** relating to religious contemplation. — *noun* a person whose life is spent in religious contemplation.

contemplatively *adv.* in a contemplative way.

contemporaneity /kəntempərə'niːɪtɪ/ *noun* being contemporaneous.

contemporaneous /kəntempə'reɪnɪəs/ *adj.* (**contemporaneous with something**) existing or happening at the same time or period as something. [from Latin *contemporaneus*, from *con-*, same + *tempus*, time]

contemporaneously *adv.* at the same time or period.

contemporary /kən'tɛmpərərɪ/ — *adj.* **1** (**contemporary with something**) belonging to the same period or time as something. **2** (**contemporary with someone**) of the same age as them. **3** modern. — *noun* (PL. **contemporaries**) **1** a person who lives or lived, or thing that exists or existed, at the same time as another. **2** a person of about the same age as another. [from Latin *con*, same + *tempus*, time]

■ *adj.* **1** contemporaneous, co-existent, concurrent, synchronous, simultaneous. **3** modern, current, present, present-day, recent, latest, up to date, fashionable, up-to-the-minute, ultra-modern.
➡ *adj.* **3** out of date, old-fashioned.

contempt *noun* **1** scorn. **2** *Legal* disregard of, disrespect for, or disobedience to the rules of a court of law. — **hold someone in contempt** to despise them. [from Latin *contemnere*, to scorn]

■ **1** scorn, disdain, condescension, derision, ridicule, mockery. **2** disrespect, dishonour, disregard, neglect.
➡ **1** admiration. **2** regard.

contemptible /kən'tɛmptɪbl/ *adj.* **1** despicable; disgusting; vile. **2** worthless; paltry.

■ **1** despicable, disgusting, vile, shameful, ignominious, low, mean, detestable, loathsome. **2** worthless, paltry, abject, wretched, pitiful.
➡ **1** admirable, honourable.

contemptibly *adv.* in a contemptible way.

contemptuous /kən'tɛmptʃʊəs/ *adj.* (**contemptuous of someone** or **something**) showing contempt for them; scornful of them. [from Latin *contemnere*, to scorn]

■ scornful, disdainful, sneering, supercilious, condescending, arrogant, haughty, *colloq.* high and mighty, cynical, derisive, insulting, disrespectful, insolent.
➡ humble, respectful.

contemptuously *adv.* with a contemptuous manner.

contend *verb* **1** *intrans.* to struggle, strive, fight, or compete. **2** *intrans.* to argue earnestly. **3** to say, maintain, or assert. [from Latin *contendere*, to strive]

■ **1** struggle, strive, fight, compete, vie, contest, dispute, clash, wrestle, grapple. **3** maintain, hold, argue, allege, assert, declare, affirm.

contender *noun* a contestant or competitor.

content¹ /kən'tɛnt/ — *adj.* (**content with something**) satisfied about it; happy; uncomplaining. — *verb* **1** to satisfy. **2** (**content oneself with something**) to limit oneself to a particular choice, or course of action: *contented themselves with a cream tea.* — *noun* peaceful satisfaction; peace of mind. [from Latin *contentus*]

■ *adj.* satisfied, happy, uncomplaining, contented, untroubled, fulfilled, pleased, willing. *verb* **1** satisfy, please, delight, appease, pacify, placate. **2** satisfy oneself, indulge.
➡ *adj.* dissatisfied, troubled. *verb* **1** displease.

content² /'kɒntɛnt/ *noun* **1** the subject-matter of a book, speech, etc. **2** the proportion in which a particular ingredient is present in something: *a diet with a high starch content.* **3** (**contents**) the things contained in something. **4** (**contents**) the text of a book; a summary of the text by chapters, etc given at the beginning of a book. [from Latin *continere*, to contain]

■ **1** substance, matter, essence, gist, meaning, significance, text, subject matter, ideas, load, burden. **2** volume, measure, size, capacity. **3** constituents, parts, elements, ingredients, load, items. **4** text, subject matter, chapters, divisions, subjects, topics, themes, ideas.

contented *adj.* peacefully happy or satisfied.

■ happy, satisfied, content, glad, pleased, cheerful, comfortable, relaxed.
➡ discontented, unhappy, annoyed.

contentedly *adv.* in a contented way.

contentedness *noun* being contented.

contention *noun* **1** a point that one asserts or maintains in an argument. **2** argument or debate. [from Latin *contentio*, strife, controversy]

contentious *adj.* **1** likely to cause argument or quarrelling. **2** quarrelsome or argumentative. [from Latin *contendere*, to strive]

contentiously *adv.* in a contentious way.

contentment *noun* the quality of being content.
. . . .

■ contentedness, peace, peacefulness, serenity, equanimity, satisfaction, fulfilment, happiness, gladness, pleasure, gratification, comfort, ease, complacency.
F3 discontent, unhappiness, dissatisfaction.
. . . .

contest /'kɒntest, kən'test/ — *noun* (with stress on *con-*) **1** a competition. **2** a struggle. — *verb* (with stress on *-test*) **1** to enter the competition or struggle for. **2** to dispute (a claim, someone's will, etc). [from Latin *contestari*, to call to witness]
. . . .

■ *noun* **1** competition, game, match, tournament, encounter. **2** struggle, fight, battle, set-to, combat, conflict, dispute, debate, controversy. *verb* **1** compete, vie, contend, strive, fight. **2** dispute, challenge, question, refute, deny, oppose, argue against, doubt, debate, litigate.
F3 *verb* **2** accept.
. . . .

contestable /kən'testəbl/ *adj.* able to be contested.

contestant /kən'testənt/ *noun* a person who takes part in a contest; a competitor.
. . . .

■ competitor, participant, player, contender, entrant, candidate, aspirant, rival, opponent.
. . . .

context *noun* **1** the passage in a text or speech within which a particular word, statement, etc occurs. **2** circumstances, background, or setting. — **out of context** without reference to context. [from Latin *contextus*, connection]
. . . .

■ **2** background, setting, surroundings, framework, frame of reference, situation, position, circumstances, conditions.
. . . .

contextual /kən'tekstʃʊəl/ *adj.* relating to or depending on a context.

contiguity /kɒntɪ'gjuːɪtɪ/ *noun* being contiguous.

contiguous /kən'tɪgjʊəs/ *adj.* (**contiguous with** or **to something**) **1** touching it; neighbouring or adjacent to it. **2** near or next in order or time. [from Latin *contiguus*, touching]

contiguously *adv.* in a contiguous way.

continence *noun* **1** the ability to control one's bowels and bladder. **2** self-control; control over one's appetites and passions. [from Latin *continentia*, self-control]

continent[1] *noun* **1** any of the seven main land masses of the world, namely Europe, Asia, N America, S America, Africa, Australia, and Antarctica. **2** the mainland portion of one of these land masses. **3** (**the Continent**) the mainland of Europe, regarded from the British Isles. [from Latin *continere*, to contain]

continent[2] *adj.* **1** able to control one's bowels and bladder. **2** self-controlled.

continental — *adj.* **1** belonging or relating to the mainland of the continent of Europe. **2** relating to any of the continents of the world. — *noun old use* an inhabitant of the mainland of Europe.

continental breakfast a light breakfast, eg of rolls and coffee.

continental drift *Geol.* the theory that the continents were formed as a result of the breaking up of a single land mass into several smaller land masses which slowly drifted apart across the Earth's surface.

continental quilt a duvet.

continental shelf *Geol.* the gently sloping seabed, under-

lying an area of relatively shallow sea, that surrounds the continents.

contingency /kən'tɪndʒənsɪ/ *noun* (PL. **contingencies**) **1** something liable, but not certain, to occur; a chance happening. **2** something dependent on a chance future happening.

contingency plans plans made in case a certain situation should arise.

contingent — *noun* **1** a body of troops. **2** any identifiable body of people: *there were boos from the Welsh contingent*. — *adj.* **1** (**contingent on** or **upon something**) dependent on some uncertain circumstance. **2** liable, but not certain, to occur; accidental. [from Latin *contingere*, to touch, happen]
. . . .

■ *noun* **2** body, company, deputation, delegation, detachment, section, group, set, batch, quota, complement.
. . . .

continual /kən'tɪnjʊəl/ *adj.* **1** constantly happening or done; frequent. **2** constant; never ceasing. [from Latin *continualis*, from *continuus*, uninterrupted]
. . . .

■ CONSTANT, PERPETUAL, INCESSANT, INTERMINABLE, REGULAR, FREQUENT, RECURRENT, REPEATED.
F3 OCCASIONAL, INTERMITTENT, TEMPORARY.
. . . .

continually *adv.* repeatedly, persistently.

continuance /kən'tɪnjʊəns/ *noun* **1** the act or state of continuing. **2** duration. [from Latin *continuare*, to make continuous]

continuation *noun* **1** the act or process of continuing, often after a break or pause. **2** that which adds to something or carries it on, eg a further episode of or sequel to a story.
. . . .

■ **1** resumption, maintenance, prolongation. **2** extension, development, furtherance, addition, supplement.
F3 **1** cessation, termination.
. . . .

continue *verb* **1** *trans., intrans.* to go on; not to stop. **2** *trans., intrans.* to last or cause to last. **3** *trans., intrans.* to carry on or start again after a break. **4** *intrans.* (**continue with something**) to persist in it; to keep on with it. **5** *intrans.* to keep moving in the same direction: *continue up the hill.* [from Latin *continuare*]
. . . .

■ **1** go on, carry on, proceed, keep on. **2** last, endure, survive, remain, abide, stay, rest, pursue, sustain, maintain, lengthen, prolong, extend, project. **3** resume, recommence, carry on. **4** persist with, persevere with, keep on with, stick at.
F3 STOP. **1**, **2**, **3**, **4** discontinue.
. . . .

continuity /kɒntɪ'njuːɪtɪ/ *noun* **1** the state of being continuous, unbroken, or consistent. **2** *Television, Cinema* the arrangement of scenes so that one progresses smoothly from another. [from Latin *continuitas*, from *continuus*, unbroken]
. . . .

■ **1** flow, progression, succession, sequence, cohesion.
F3 **1** discontinuity.
. . . .

continuo /kɒn'tɪnjʊoʊ/ *noun* (PL. **continuos**) *Mus.* a bass part for a keyboard or stringed instrument; the instrument or instruments playing this. [from Italian *continuo*, continuous]

continuous /kən'tɪnjʊəs/ *adj.* **1** never ceasing. **2** unbroken; uninterrupted. **3** *Grammar, said of tense* formed with the verb *be* and the present participle, and representing continuing action or a continuing state, as in *I am waiting*, *they were dancing*, and *you will be needing this*. [from Latin *continuus*, unbroken]
. . . .

■ **1** ceaseless, non-stop, endless, unending, unceasing, constant, unremitting, prolonged, extended, continued,

lasting. **2** unbroken, uninterrupted, consecutive, seamless.
⊟ DISCONTINUOUS, BROKEN, SPORADIC.
. . . .

continuous assessment *Education* the judging of pupils' progress by means of frequent tests throughout the year, as an alternative to occasional examinations.
continuously *adv.* so as to be continuous; without stopping.
continuous representation *Art* the practice of illustrating several consecutive stages of a story in one picture. For example, in paintings of the Nativity, the shepherds may be shown in the foreground adoring the new-born Jesus and again in the background watching their flocks.
continuum /kən'tɪnjʊəm/ *noun* (PL. **continua, continuums**) a continuous sequence; an unbroken progression. [from Latin *continuus*, unbroken]
contort *verb trans., intrans.* to twist violently out of shape. [from Latin *contorquere*, to twist]
. . . .

⊟ twist, distort, warp, deform, misshape, convolute, wrench, disfigure, gnarl, knot, writhe, squirm, wriggle.

. . . .

contortion *noun* **1** a violent twisting. **2** a deformed shape.
contortionist *noun* an entertainer who is able to twist his body into spectacularly unnatural positions.
contour /'kɒntʊə(r)/ — *noun* **1** (*usually* **contours**) the distinctive outline of something. **2** (*also* **contour line**) a line on a map joining points of the same height or depth. — *verb* **1** to shape the contour of, or shape so as to fit a contour. **2** to mark the contour lines on (a map). [from French *contour*, from Italian *contornare*, to outline]
. . . .

⊟ *noun* **1** outline, silhouette, shape, form, figure, curve, relief, profile, character, aspect.

. . . .

contra- *prefix* **1** against: *contraception*. **2** opposite: *contraflow*. **3** contrasting: *contradistinction*. **4** *Mus.* lower in pitch: *contrabass*. [from Latin *contra*]
contraband — *noun* **1** the smuggling of goods prohibited from being imported or exported. **2** smuggled goods: *police found crates of contraband in the warehouse.* — *adj.* prohibited from being imported or exported; smuggled. [from Spanish *contrabanda*, from Latin *contra-* + *bandum*, ban]
contrabass /'kɒntrəbeɪs/ *noun* another name for the double bass.
contraception /kɒntrə'sɛpʃən/ *noun* the prevention of unwanted pregnancy by artificial or natural means. See also CONTRACEPTIVE. [from CONTRA- + CONCEPTION]
contraceptive /kɒntrə'sɛptɪv/ — *noun* a drug or device that prevents pregnancy following sexual intercourse; used to plan the timing and number of children in individual families, and so control population growth. Some contraceptives are also used to provide protection against sexually transmitted diseases. — *adj.* having the effect of preventing pregnancy.
contract /'kɒntrakt, kən'trakt/ — *noun* (with stress on *con-*) **1** an agreement, especially a legally binding one. **2** a document setting out the terms of such an agreement. — *verb* (with stress on -*tract*) **1** *intrans., trans.* to make or become smaller. **2** *intrans., trans. said of muscles* to make or become shorter, especially in order to bend a joint. **3** *intrans., trans. said of the brows* to draw together into a frown. **4** to catch (a disease). **5** to enter into (an alliance or marriage). **6** to incur or accumulate a debt). **7** *trans., intrans. said of a word, phrase, etc* to reduce to a short form: *'are not' is contracted to 'aren't'.* **8** *intrans., trans.* (**contract with someone**) to enter a legal contract concerning them. — **contract in** or **out** to arrange to participate, or not to participate, eg in a pension scheme. **contract something out** or **put something out to contract** *said of a business, company, etc* to arrange for part of a job to be done by another company. [from Latin *contractus*, contraction, agreement]

. . . .

⊟ *noun* **1** agreement, settlement, commitment, transaction, arrangement, compact, understanding, pact, treaty, convention, covenant, bargain, deal, bond, engagement. **2** agreement, treaty, convention, covenant, bond. *verb* **1** shrink, lessen, diminish, reduce, shorten, curtail, abbreviate, abridge, condense, compress, constrict, narrow, shrivel, wrinkle. **2** shorten, tighten, tense. **4** catch, get, go down with, develop. **8** agree, undertake, promise, pledge, stipulate, arrange, negotiate, bargain.
⊟ *verb* **1** expand, enlarge, lengthen.
. . . .

contractable /kən'traktəbl/ *adj., said especially of a disease or habit* able to be contracted.
contract bridge the usual form of the card game bridge, in which only tricks bid and won count in one's score.
contractible /kən'traktəbl/ *adj., said of muscles, etc* capable of being contracted or shortened.
contractile *adj. Zool.* able to contract or cause contraction.
contraction *noun* **1** the process of contracting or state of being contracted. **2** a decrease in length, size, or volume. **3** a tightening of the muscles caused by a shortening in length of the muscle fibres. **4** (**contractions**) the regular painful spasms of the muscles of the uterus that occur during labour. **5** a shortened form of a word or phrase: *'aren't' is a contraction of 'are not'.*
contractor *noun* a person or firm that undertakes work on contract, especially connected with building, installation of equipment, or the transportation of goods.
contractual /kən'traktjʊəl/ *adj.* relating to a contract or binding agreement.
contractually *adv.* on a contractual basis.
contradict *verb* **1** to assert the opposite of or deny (a statement, etc) made by (a person). **2** *said of a statement, etc* to disagree or be inconsistent with (another): *the two accounts contradict each other.* [from Latin *contra-*, opposite + *dicere*, to say]
. . . .

⊟ **1** deny, *formal* gainsay, disaffirm, dispute, confute, challenge, oppose, impugn. **2** negate, counter, *formal* gainsay.
⊟ AGREE WITH, CONFIRM, CORROBORATE.
. . . .

contradiction *noun* **1** the act of contradicting. **2** one statement contradicting another, etc. **3** denial. **4** inconsistency.
contradictory *adj.* **1** inconsistent. **2** denying. **3** contrary.
. . . .

⊟ **1** inconsistent, incompatible, irreconcilable, conflicting, discrepant, paradoxical. **2**, **3** opposed, opposite, contrary, antagonistic.
⊟ CONSISTENT.
. . . .

contradistinction *noun* a distinction made in terms of a contrast between qualities, properties, etc.
contraflow *noun* a form of traffic diversion used on dual carriageways, with vehicles moving in opposite directions sharing the same carriageway.
contraindicate *verb Medicine* to be a reason for not using (a treatment, operation, etc).
contraindication *noun Medicine* a contraindicating factor.
contralto *noun* (PL. **contraltos**) **1** the female singing voice that is lowest in pitch. **2** a singer with this voice. **3** a part to be sung by this voice. [from Italian *contralto*, lower than alto]
contraption *noun humorous, colloq.* a machine or apparatus.
. . . .

⊟ contrivance, device, gadget, apparatus, rig, machine, mechanism.
. . . .

contrapuntal /kɒntrə'pʌntəl/ *adj. Mus.* relating to, or arranged as, counterpoint. [from Italian *contrappunto*, counterpoint]

contrapuntally *adv.* in a contrapuntal way.

contrariety /kɒntrə'raɪətɪ/ or **contrariness** *noun* 1 opposition. 2 inconsistency, discrepancy.

contrarily /kən'trɛərɪlɪ/ *adv.* in a contrary way.

contrariwise /'kɒntrərɪwaɪz, kən'trɛərɪwaɪz/ *adv.* reversing the situation; the opposite way round.

contrary /'kɒntrərɪ, kən'trɛərɪ/ — *adj.* 1 (**contrary to something**) opposite; quite different; opposed. 2 *said of a wind* blowing against one; unfavourable. 3 obstinate, perverse, self-willed, or wayward. — *noun* (PL. **contraries**) 1 an extreme opposite. 2 either of a pair of opposites. 3 *Logic* either of two propositions that cannot both be true of the same thing. — **contrary to something** in opposition or contrast to it. **on the contrary** in opposition or contrast to what has just been said. **to the contrary** to the opposite effect; giving the contrasting position. [from Latin *contrarius*, from *contra*, opposite]

■ *adj.* 1 opposite, opposed, counter, reverse, conflicting. 3 obstinate, perverse, self-willed, wayward, awkward, disobliging, difficult, intractable, cantankerous, *colloq.* stroppy. *noun* 1, 2 opposite, converse, reverse.
🔁 *adj.* 1 like. 3 obliging.

contrast /'kɒntrɑːst, kən'trɑːst/ — *noun* (with stress on *con-*) 1 difference or dissimilarity between things or people that are being compared. 2 a person or thing that is strikingly different from another. 3 the degree of difference in tone between the colours, or the light and dark parts, of a photograph or television picture. — *verb* (with stress on *-trast*) 1 to compare so as to reveal contrasts. 2 (**contrast with something**) to be distinct from it; to show a contrast. — **in contrast to** or **with something** or **someone** as an opposite to them or something distinct from them. [from CONTRA-[1] + Latin *stare*, to stand]

■ *noun* 1 difference, dissimilarity, disparity, divergence, distinction, differentiation, opposition. 2 foil, antithesis. *verb* 1 compare, differentiate, distinguish, discriminate. 2 differ from, clash with, conflict with.
🔁 *noun* 1 similarity.

contravene *verb* to break or disobey (a law or rule). [from CONTRA-[1] + Latin *venire*, to come]

■ infringe, violate, break, breach, disobey, defy, flout, transgress.
🔁 uphold, observe, obey.

contravention *noun* (*usually* **in contravention**) infringement of a law, etc.

contretemps /'kɒntrətɑːn/ *noun* 1 an awkward or embarrassing moment, happening, etc. 2 a slight disagreement. [from French *contretemps*, from *contre*, against + *temps*, time]

contribute /kən'trɪbjuːt/ *verb* (*usually* **contribute to something**) 1 *trans., intrans.* to give for some joint purpose. 2 *intrans.* to be one of the causes of something. 3 to supply (an article, etc) for publication in a magazine, etc. [from Latin *contribuere*, to bring together]

■ 1 donate, subscribe, *colloq.* chip in, add, give, bestow, provide, supply, furnish. 2 help, lead, conduce.
🔁 1 withhold.

contribution /kɒntrɪ'bjuːʃən/ *noun* 1 the act of contributing. 2 something contributed, eg money, or an article for a magazine.

■ 1 donation, subscription, offering, addition, input. 2 donation, subscription, gift, gratuity, handout, grant, offering, input, addition.

contributor /kən'trɪbjutə(r)/ *noun* 1 a person or organization that contributes money. 2 a person who supplies an article, etc for publication in a magazine, etc.

■ 1 donor, subscriber, giver, patron, benefactor, sponsor, backer, supporter. 2 writer, journalist, reporter, correspondent, freelance.

contributory /kən'trɪbjutərɪ/ *adj.* 1 giving or given to a common purpose or fund. 2 having partial responsibility. 3 *said of a pension scheme* involving contribution from the employee as well as the employer.

con trick *colloq.* a confidence trick.

contrite *adj.* sorry for something one has done. [from Latin *contritus*, crushed]

■ sorry, regretful, remorseful, repentant, penitent, conscience-stricken, chastened, humble, ashamed.

contritely *adv.* with a contrite manner.

contrition *noun* 1 remorse. 2 *Christianity* deep sorrow for past sin and resolve to avoid future sin.

contrivance *noun* 1 the act or power of contriving. 2 a device or apparatus. 3 a scheme; a piece of cunning.

■ 2 device, apparatus, invention, contraption, gadget, implement, appliance, machine, mechanism, equipment, gear. 3 scheme, stratagem, ploy, trick, dodge, ruse, plot, expedient, design, intrigue, machination.

contrive *verb* 1 to manage or succeed. 2 to bring about: *contrive one's escape.* 3 to make or construct, especially with difficulty. [from Old French *controver*, to find]

contrived *adj.* forced or artificial: *a contrived ending to a play.*

■ forced, artificial, unnatural, false, strained, laboured, mannered, overdone, elaborate.
🔁 natural, realistic, genuine.

control — *noun* 1 authority or charge; power to influence or guide: *in control* / *take control* / *under control* / *out of control.* 2 a means of limitation: *impose strict controls on spending.* 3 (**controls**) a device for operating, regulating, or testing (a machine, system, etc). 4 the people in control of some operation: *mission control.* 5 the place where something is checked: *go through passport control.* 6 (**control experiment**) a scientific experiment in which the variable being tested in a second experiment is held at a constant value, in order to establish the validity of the results of the second experiment. 7 *Spiritualism* a dead person guiding a medium. — *verb* (**controlled, controlling**) 1 to have or exercise control over. 2 to operate, regulate, or test (a machine, system, etc). 3 to limit. 4 to establish validity of (the results of a scientific experiment) by performing another experiment in which the variable being tested is held at a constant value, in order to provide a standard of comparison. [from Old French *contrerolle*, duplicate account or register]

■ *noun* 1 authority, charge, power, command, mastery, government, rule, direction, management, oversight, supervision, superintendence, discipline, guidance. 2 restraint, check, limit, curb, repression. 3 dial, switch, button, knob, lever, instrument. *verb* 1 lead, govern, rule, command, direct, manage, oversee, supervise, superintend. 2 operate, regulate, test, run, adjust, monitor. 3 limit, restrain, check, curb, subdue, repress, hold back, contain.

control freak *colloq.* a person who is obsessed with gaining and exercising control.

controllability *noun* the quality of being controllable.

controllable *adj.* capable of being controlled.

controller *noun* **1** a person or thing that controls. **2** an official in charge of public finance. **3** a person in charge of the finances of an enterprise, etc.

control tower a tall building at an airport, providing a good view of the airport and surrounding airspace, and from which take-off and landing instructions are given to aircraft pilots by air-traffic controllers.

controversial /kɒntrə'vɜːʃəl/ *adj.* involving or causing controversy.

▣ contentious, polemical, disputed, doubtful, questionable, debatable, disputable.

controversially *adv.* in a controversial way.

controversy /'kɒntrəvɜːsɪ, kən'trɒvəsɪ/ *noun* (PL. **controversies**) a usually long-standing disagreement or dispute. [from CONTRA-¹ + Latin *vertere*, to turn]

▣ disagreement, dispute, argument, debate, discussion, war of words, polemic, quarrel, squabble, wrangle, strife, contention, dissension.
▣ accord, agreement.

contumacious /kɒntjʊ'meɪʃəs/ *adj.* **1** obstinately disobedient. **2** opposing lawful authority with contempt.

contumaciously *adv.* in a contumacious way.

contumacy /'kɒntjʊməsɪ/ *noun formal* obstinate refusal to obey; resistance to authority. [from Latin *contumacia*, stubbornness]

contumelious /kɒntjʊ'miːlɪəs/ *adj.* haughtily insolent.

contumely /'kɒntjuːmlɪ/ *noun* (PL. **contumelies**) *formal* scornful or insulting treatment or words. [from Latin *contumelia*, outrage, insult]

contuse /kən'tjuːz/ *verb Medicine* **1** to bruise (a part of the body). **2** to crush. [from Latin *contundere*, to beat, bruise]

contusion *noun technical* **1** the act of bruising or the state of being bruised. **2** a bruise.

conundrum *noun* **1** a confusing problem. **2** a riddle, especially involving a pun.

conurbation /kɒnɜː'beɪʃən/ *noun* an extensive built-up area, consisting of several towns whose outskirts have merged. [from CON- + Latin *urbs*, city]

convalesce /kɒnvə'les/ *verb intrans.* to recover one's strength after an illness, operation, or injury, especially by resting. [from Latin *convalescere*, to recover]

convalescence *noun* a period of recovery after illness or injury.

convalescent — *adj.* recovering from an illness. — *noun* a convalescent person.

convection *noun* the process whereby heat is transferred through a liquid or gas from a more dense region of lower temperature to a less dense region of higher temperature as a result of movement of molecules of the fluid itself. [from Latin *con-*, together + *vehere*, to carry]

convector *noun* an electrical device used to heat the surrounding air in rooms, etc, by convection. [from Latin *con-*, together + *vehere*, to carry]

convene *verb trans., intrans.* to assemble or summon to assemble: *convene a meeting.* [from Latin *con-*, together + *venire*, to come]

convener or **convenor** *noun* a person who convenes or chairs a meeting.

convenience /kən'viːnɪəns/ *noun* **1** the quality of being convenient. **2** something useful or advantageous. **3** *Brit.* a lavatory, especially a public one. — **at one's convenience** when and where it suits one.

▣ **1** accessibility, availability, handiness, usefulness, use, utility, serviceability, suitability, fitness. **2** service,

benefit, advantage, help, facility, amenity, appliance.
▣ **1, 2** inconvenience.

convenience food any food which has been partially or entirely prepared by the manufacturer, and needs only to be cooked, eg frozen, canned, and dried foods.

convenient *adj.* **1** fitting in with one's plans, etc; not causing trouble or difficulty. **2** useful; handy; saving time and trouble. **3** available; at hand. [from Latin *convenire*, to fit, be suitable]

▣ **1** suitable, appropriate, opportune, timely, well-timed, fitted, suited. **2** useful, handy, beneficial, helpful, labour-saving. **3** available, handy, nearby, at hand, accessible.
▣ **1, 2** inconvenient, awkward.

conveniently *adv.* in a convenient way.

convent *noun* **1** a community of nuns, or the building they occupy. **2** a school where the teaching is done by nuns. [from Latin *conventus*, assembly]

conventicle /kən'ventɪkəl/ *noun Hist.* a secret, especially unlawful, religious meeting. [from Latin *conventiculum*, assembly]

convention *noun* **1** a large and formal conference or assembly. **2** a formal treaty or agreement. **3** a custom or generally accepted practice, especially in social behaviour. [from Latin *conventio*, meeting, agreement]

▣ **1** conference, assembly, congress, meeting, council, delegates, representatives. **3** custom, tradition, practice, usage, protocol, etiquette, formality, matter of form, code.

conventional /kən'venʃənəl/ *adj.* **1** traditional; normal; customary. **2** conservative or unoriginal: *conventional attitudes.* **3** *said of weapons or warfare* non-nuclear.

▣ **1** traditional, customary, usual, normal, ordinary, regular, standard, common, routine, prevalent, prevailing, accepted, received, expected, straight, orthodox, formal, correct, proper, ritual. **2** conservative, unoriginal, stereotyped, hidebound, pedestrian, commonplace, run-of-the-mill.
▣ **1, 2** unconventional, unusual, exotic.

conventionality /kənvenʃə'nalɪtɪ/ *noun* (PL. **conventionalities**) **1** being conventional. **2** something which is established by use or custom.

conventionalize or **conventionalise** *verb* to make conventional.

conventionally *adv.* in a conventional way; by way of convention.

converge *verb intrans.* **1** (**converge on** or **upon something** or **someone**) to move towards or meet at one point. **2** *said eg of opinions* to tend towards one another; to coincide.

▣ **1** focus on, concentrate on, approach, gather. **2** coincide, meet, join, merge, combine.
▣ DIVERGE. **1** disperse.

convergence *noun* the act or point of converging.

▣ concentration, approach, merging, blending, meeting, coincidence, union, confluence, junction, intersection.
▣ divergence, separation.

convergent *adj.* **1** converging; coming together. **2** agreeing.

convergent evolution *Biol.* the tendency of unrelated species that inhabit a similar environment to develop superficially similar structures, eg the wings of birds and insects.

converging lens *Physics* a lens that causes light rays to converge to a focus, eg a convex lens.

conversant /kən'vɜːsənt/ adj. (**conversant with something**) having a thorough knowledge of it. [from Latin *conversari*, to associate with]

conversation /kɒnvə'seɪʃən/ noun informal talk between people. [from Latin *conversatio*]

▭ talk, chat, gossip, discussion, discourse, dialogue, exchange, communication.

conversational adj. **1** relating to conversation. **2** used in conversation rather than formal language. **3** communicative; talkative.

conversationalist noun a person fond of, or skilled in, conversation.

conversation piece 1 a striking object that stimulates conversation. **2** a group portrait, eg showing members of a family engaged in characteristic activities in their usual setting.

converse[1] /kən'vɜːs/ verb intrans. (**converse with someone**) *formal* to hold a conversation with them; to talk to them. [from Latin *conversari*, to associate with]

converse[2] /'kɒnvɜːs/ — adj. reverse; opposite. — noun opposite. [from Latin *conversus*, opposite]

▭ adj., noun OPPOSITE, REVERSE, CONTRARY. adj. counter, reversed, transposed. noun antithesis, obverse.

conversely adv. in a converse way; on the contrary.

conversion noun **1** the act of converting. **2** something converted to another use. **3** *Rugby* the scoring of one or two further points after a try by kicking the ball over the goal.

▭ **1** alteration, change, transformation, adaptation, modification, remodelling, reconstruction, reorganization, reformation, regeneration, rebirth.

convert /kən'vɜːt, 'kɒnvɜːt/ — verb (with stress on -*vert*) **1** *trans., intrans.* (**convert something into something else**) to change it in form or function. **2** *trans., intrans.* to win over, or be won over, to another religion, opinion, etc: *many were converted to Christianity / decided to convert to Judaism.* **3** to change into another measuring system or currency. **4** *Rugby* to achieve a conversion after (a try). — noun (with stress on *con*-) a person who has been converted to a new religion, practice, etc. [from Latin *convertere*, to change]

▭ verb **1** alter, change, turn, transform, adapt, modify, remodel, restyle, revise, reorganize. **2** win over, convince, persuade, proselytize.

converter or **convertor** noun **1** a person or thing that converts. **2** an electrical device for converting alternating current into direct current, or more rarely, vice versa. **3** a device for converting a signal from one frequency to another. **4** *Comput.* a device that converts coded information from one form to another, eg a device that converts the output of an analogue computer into a form that can be used by a digital computer. **5** a vessel in which air or oxygen is blown into a molten metal in order to refine it by oxidizing impurities.

convertible /kən'vɜːtəbəl/ adj. capable of being converted.

convex adj., *said of a surface or shape* outward-curving, like the surface of the eye. See also CONCAVE. [from Latin *convexus*, arched]

▭ rounded, bulging, protuberant.

▣ concave.

convexity /kɒn'veksɪtɪ/ noun (PL. **convexities**) **1** roundness of form on the outside. **2** a round form or figure.

convey /kən'veɪ/ verb **1** to carry; to transport. **2** to communicate: *difficult to convey exactly what I mean.* **3** *Legal* to transfer the ownership of (property). [from Old French *conveier*, from Latin *via*, way]

▭ **1** carry, transport, bear, bring, fetch, move, send, forward, deliver, transfer, conduct, guide, transmit. **2** communicate, impart, express, tell, relate, reveal.

conveyable adj. capable of being conveyed.

conveyance noun **1** the process of conveying. **2** a vehicle of any kind. **3** *Legal* the transfer of the ownership of property.

conveyancer noun a person who prepares deeds for the transfer of property.

conveyancing noun the act or process of transferring the ownership of property.

conveyer or **conveyor** noun a person or thing that conveys.

conveyor belt an endless moving rubber or metal belt for conveying articles, eg in a factory.

convict /kən'vɪkt, 'kɒnvɪkt/ — verb (with stress on -*vict*) (**convict someone of something**) to prove or declare them guilty of a crime. — noun (with stress on *con*-) a person serving a prison sentence. [from Latin *convincere*]

▭ verb condemn, sentence, imprison. noun criminal, felon, culprit, prisoner.

conviction noun **1** the act of convicting; an instance of being convicted. **2** the state of being convinced; a strong belief. — **carry conviction** to be convincing. [from Latin *convincere*, to overcome, convict]

▭ **1** persuasion. **2** certainty, firmness, assurance, confidence, fervour, earnestness, persuasion, view, opinion, belief, faith, creed, tenet, principle.

convince verb (**convince someone of something**) to persuade them of it; to cause them to believe it. [from Latin *convincere*, to overcome]

▭ persuade, assure, sway, win over, bring round, reassure, satisfy.

convinced adj. firm in one's belief: *a convinced atheist.*

convincing adj. **1** believable. **2** certain, positive. **3** *said of a victory* achieved by a significant margin.

▭ **1** persuasive, cogent, powerful, telling, impressive, credible, plausible, likely, probable. **2** incontrovertible, conclusive. **3** conclusive.

▣ **1** unconvincing, improbable.

convincingly adv. in a convincing way; so as to convince.

convivial /kən'vɪvɪəl/ adj. **1** lively, jovial, sociable, and cheerful. **2** festive. [from Latin *convivialis*, from *convivium*, feast]

conviviality /kənvɪvɪ'alɪtɪ/ noun **1** cheerful sociability. **2** festivity.

convivially adv. in a convivial way.

convocation /kɒnvə'keɪʃən/ noun **1** the act of summoning together. **2** an assembly. **3** (**Convocation**) *Church of E.* a gathering of clergy, originally in the provinces of Canterbury and York, to regulate affairs of the Church. **4** a formal assembly of graduates of a college or university. [from Latin *convocatio*, summoning together]

convoke verb to call together; to assemble: *convoke the committee.* [from Latin *convocare*]

convoluted /kɒnvə'luːtɪd/ adj. **1** coiled and twisted. **2** complicated: *convoluted reasoning.* [from Latin *convolvere*, to roll together]

▤ 1 twisting, winding, meandering, tortuous. **2** involved, complicated, complex, tangled, tortuous.
▣ 1 straight. **2** straightforward.

convolution /kɒnvə'luːʃən/ *noun* a twist or coil.
convolvulus /kən'vɒlvjʊləs/ *noun* any of a large number of trailing or twining plants of the genus Convolvulus, native to temperate regions and having funnel-shaped flowers, eg bindweed. [from Latin *convolvere*, to roll up]
convoy — *noun* a group of vehicles or merchant ships travelling together, or under escort. — *verb* to accompany for protection. [from Old French *convoier*, from Latin *con-*, with + *via*, way]

▤ *noun* fleet, escort, guard, train.

convulse *verb trans., intrans.* to jerk or distort violently by or as if by a powerful spasm. [from Latin *convellere*, to pull violently]
convulsion *noun* **1** the state of being convulsed. **2** (*often* **convulsions**) a violent involuntary contraction of the muscles of the body, or a series of such contractions, resulting in contortion of the limbs and face, and sometimes accompanied by loss of consciousness. **3** (**convulsions**) *colloq.* spasms of laughter. [from Latin *convulsio*]

▤ 2 fit, seizure, paroxysm, spasm, cramp, contraction, tremor.

convulsive *adj.* **1** causing or affected by convulsions. **2** violent and uncontrollable; spasmodic.

▤ 2 spasmodic, jerky, fitful, sporadic, uncontrolled, violent.

convulsively *adv.* in a convulsive way.
cony or **coney** /'kəʊnɪ, 'kʌnɪ/ *noun* (PL. **conies, coneys**) **1** a rabbit. **2** its fur used for clothing, etc. **3** *in the Bible* a hyrax. [from Old French *conil*]
coo[1] — *noun* the soft murmuring call of a dove. — *verb* (**cooed, cooing**) **1** *intrans.* to make this sound. **2** *intrans., trans.* to murmur affectionately. [imitative]
coo[2] *interj. colloq.* used to express amazement.
cooee /'kuːiː/ — *interj.* used to attract attention. — *verb intrans.* (**cooeed, cooeeing**) to call 'cooee'. [from an Australian Aboriginal language]
cook — *verb* **1** *trans., intrans.* to prepare or be prepared by heating. **2** *colloq.* to alter (accounts, etc) dishonestly. — *noun* a person who cooks or prepares food. — **cook something up** *colloq.* to concoct or invent it: *tried to cook up an excuse.* **what's cooking**? *colloq.* what's up?; what's the plan? [from Anglo-Saxon *coc*, from Latin *coquus*]

▤ cook something up concoct, invent, prepare, brew, fabricate, contrive, devise, plan, plot, scheme.

Ways of cooking include: bake, barbecue, boil, braise, broil, casserole, coddle, deep-fry, fry, grill, microwave, poach, pot-roast, roast, sauté, scramble, simmer, spit-roast, steam, stew, stir-fry, toast; prepare, heat.

cook-chill *adj. Food Science* denoting foods, especially individual meals, that are cooked, packaged, and stored in a refrigerated state, and require reheating before serving.
cooker *noun* **1** an apparatus, or special pot, for cooking food. **2** *colloq.* (*also* **cooking-apple**) an apple for cooking rather than eating raw.
cookery *noun* the art or practice of cooking food.
cookery book or **cookbook** a book of recipes.
cookie *noun* **1** *North Amer.* a biscuit. **2** *Scot.* a bun. **3** *colloq.* a person: *a smart cookie.* — **that's the way the cookie crumbles** *colloq.* that's how things usually turn out. [from Dutch *koekje*, little cake]

cool — *adj.* **1** between cold and warm; fairly cold. **2** pleasantly fresh; free of heat: *a cool breeze.* **3** calm: *keep a cool head.* **4** lacking enthusiasm; unfriendly: *a cool response.* **5** impudent; audacious; brazen. **6** *said of a large sum* at least: *made a cool million.* **7** *colloq.* admirable; excellent. **8** *said of colours* suggestive of coolness, typically pale and containing blue. — *noun* **1** a cool part or period; coolness: *in the cool of the evening.* **2** *colloq.* self-control; composure: *lose / keep one's cool.* — *verb trans., intrans.* (**cool down** or **off**) **1** to become cool. **2** to become less interested or enthusiastic. **3** (**to cool something down** or **off**) to make it cool. — **cool it** *colloq.* to calm down. **cool one's heels** to be kept waiting. **play it cool** to deal with a situation calmly but warily. [from Anglo-Saxon *col*]

▤ *adj.* **1** chilly, breezy, nippy, cold, chilled, iced. **2** refreshing, fresh. **3** calm, unruffled, unexcited, composed, self-possessed, level-headed, unemotional, quiet, relaxed, *colloq.* laid-back. **4** unenthusiastic, unfriendly, unwelcoming, cold, frigid, lukewarm, half-hearted, apathetic, uninterested, unresponsive, uncommunicative, reserved, distant, aloof, standoffish. *noun* **2** coolness, calmness, self-control, composure, collectedness, poise, control, self-possession, self-discipline, temper. *verb* **1** chill, freeze. **2** moderate, lessen, temper, dampen, quiet, abate, calm, allay, assuage. **3** chill, refrigerate, ice, freeze, fan.
▣ *adj.* **1, 2** warm, hot. **3** excited, angry. **4** warm, friendly, welcoming. *noun* **1** warm, heat. *verb* **1, 3** warm, heat. **2** excite.

coolant *noun* **1** a liquid or gas used as a cooling agent, especially to absorb and remove heat from its source in a system such as a car radiator, nuclear reactor, etc. **2** a liquid or gas that is used to cool the edge of a cutting tool during machining.
cooler *noun* **1** a container or device for cooling things. **2** *slang* prison.
coolie *noun offensive* **1** an unskilled native labourer in Eastern countries. **2** *South Afr.* an Indian. [from Tamil *kuli*, hired person]
cooling-off period an interval for reflection and negotiation before taking action.
cooling tower a tall structure resembling a tower, in which water heated in an industrial process is cooled for re-use.
coolly *adv.* **1** with a cool manner. **2** calmly, indifferently. **3** impudently.
coolness *noun* **1** being cool. **2** moderate cold. **3** loss of friendship. **4** lack of enthusiasm. **5** calmness.
coomb or **coombe** or **comb** or **combe** /kuːm/ *noun* **1** a short deep valley. **2** a deep hollow in a hillside. [from Anglo-Saxon *cumb*, valley]
coon *noun* **1** *offensive slang* a black person. **2** *North Amer. colloq.* a raccoon.
coop *noun* a cage for hens. — **coop someone** or **something up** to confine them in a small space. [related to Anglo-Saxon *cypa*, basket]
co-op /'kəʊɒp/ *noun colloq.* a co-operative society, or a shop run by one.
cooper *noun* a person who makes or repairs barrels. [from Latin *cuparius*, from *cupa*, cask]
co-operate /kəʊ'ɒpəreɪt/ *verb intrans.* **1** (**co-operate with someone**) to work together with them. **2** to be helpful, or willing to fit in with others' plans. [from CO- + OPERATE]

▤ 1 collaborate, work together, combine, unite, conspire, participate. **2** help, assist, aid, *colloq.* play ball, contribute.

co-operation /kəʊɒpə'reɪʃən/ *noun* **1** the act of cooperating. **2** willingness to help. **3** assistance.

▤ PARTICIPATION, COLLABORATION, CO-ORDINATION, GIVE-AND-TAKE, ASSISTANCE, TEAMWORK, UNITY, HELPFULNESS.

OPPOSITION, RIVALRY, COMPETITION.

. . . .

co-operative /koʊˈɒpərətɪv/ — adj. **1** relating to, or giving, co-operation. **2** helpful; willing to fit in with others' plans, etc. **3** said of a business or farm jointly owned by workers, with profits shared equally. — noun a co-operative business or farm.

. . . .

▣ adj. **1** collective, joint, shared, combined, united, concerted, co-ordinated. **2** helpful, supportive, obliging, accommodating, willing. **3** collective, joint, shared, combined.

▣ adj. **2** unco-operative, rebellious.

. . . .

co-operatively adv. in a co-operative way.

co-operative society a profit-sharing association for the cheaper purchase of goods.

co-operator /koʊˈɒpəreɪtə(r)/ noun a person who co-operates.

co-opt /koʊˈɒpt/ verb, said of the members of a body, etc to choose as an additional member. [from Latin cooptare, to appoint, admit as member]

co-option /koʊˈɒpʃən/ noun the act or process of co-opting.

co-optive /koʊˈɒptɪv/ adj. that is co-opted.

co-ordinate /koʊˈɔːdɪneɪt, koʊˈɔːdɪnət/ — verb (pronounced -neɪt) **1** to combine, integrate, and adjust (a number of different parts or processes) so as to relate smoothly one to another. **2** to bring (one's limbs or bodily movements) into a smoothly functioning relationship. — adj. (pronounced -nət) **1** relating to, or involving, coordination or co-ordinates. **2** Grammar, said of clauses equal in status, as when joined by and or but. — noun (pronounced -nət) **1** (usually **coordinate**) Geog. either of a pair of numbers taken from a vertical and horizontal axis which together establish the position of a fixed point on a map. **2** Geom. any of a set of numbers, especially either of a pair, that are used to define the position of a point, line, or surface by reference to a system of axes that are usually drawn through a fixed point at right angles to each other. **3** Chem. denoting a type of covalent bond between two atoms in which both members of the shared pair of electrons are provided by one atom. **4** (**co-ordinates**) garments designed to be worn together.

. . . .

▣ verb **1** integrate, organize, arrange, mesh, synchronize, harmonize, match, correlate, regulate, systematize, tabulate.

. . . .

coordinate geometry Geom. a system of geometry in which points, lines, and surfaces are located in two-dimensional or three-dimensional space by means of co-ordinates.

co-ordination /koʊɔːdɪˈneɪʃən/ noun **1** ordered action together. **2** balanced or skilful movement.

co-ordinator /koʊˈɔːdɪneɪtə(r)/ noun a person who co-ordinates an activity, etc.

coot noun **1** any of 10 species of aquatic bird belonging to the rail family and closely related to the moorhen, native to Europe and Asia, and having dark plumage, a characteristic white shield above the bill, and large feet with lobed toes. **2** old colloq. use a fool. [from Middle English cote]

cop[1] noun slang a policeman. [from COPPER[2]]

cop[2] verb (**copped, copping**) slang **1** to catch. **2** to grab; to seize. **3** to suffer (a punishment, etc). — **cop it** slang to be punished. **cop out** colloq. to escape or withdraw; to avoid a responsibility. **not much cop** colloq. of little use or interest. [from Old French caper, to seize]

cope[1] verb intrans. **1** (**cope with something**) to deal with a difficulty or problem, etc successfully. **2** to manage; to get by. [from Old French couper, to hit]

. . . .

▣ **1** deal with, contend with, handle, manage, weather.

2 manage, get by, carry on, survive, make do.

. . . .

cope[2] noun a long sleeveless cape worn by clergy on ceremonial occasions. [from Latin capa]

Copernican system /kəˈpɜːnɪkən/ Astron. a model of the Solar System, proposed by Copernicus in 1543, in which the Sun is regarded as the centre, with the Earth and other planets moving in perfectly circular orbits around it.

copier /ˈkɒpɪə(r)/ noun a machine for making copies, especially photocopies.

co-pilot noun the assistant pilot of an aircraft.

coping noun the top row of stones in a wall. [related to COPE[2]]

coping-stone noun one of the stones forming the top row in a wall, etc.

copious adj. plentiful. [from Latin copiosus]

. . . .

▣ plentiful, abundant, inexhaustible, overflowing, profuse, rich, lavish, bountiful, liberal, full, ample, generous, extensive, great, huge.

▣ scarce, meagre.

. . . .

copiously adv. in abundance, plentifully.

cop-out noun colloq. an avoidance of a responsibility; an escape or withdrawal.

copper[1] — noun **1** Chem. (SYMBOL **Cu**, ATOMIC NUMBER 29) a soft reddish-brown metal that occurs both as the free metal and in various ores, especially copper pyrites (chalcopyrite). It is an excellent conductor of heat and electricity, and is used to make electric cables, wire, pipes, and coins. Its main alloys are brass (copper and zinc) and bronze (copper and tin), and it is an important trace element in many plants and animals. **2** any coin of low value made of copper or bronze. **3** a large metal vessel for boiling water in. — adj. of the brownish-red colour of copper. [from Latin cuprum, from cyprium aes, brass of Cyprus]

copper[2] noun slang a policeman. [from COP[2]]

copper-bottomed adj. **1** said eg of ships or pans having the bottom protected by a layer of copper. **2** colloq. reliable, especially financially.

copperhead noun **1** a poisonous pit viper, native to the eastern USA, so called because the top of its head is reddish-brown. **2** a venomous snake, native to SE Australia, so called because there is a reddish-brown band at the back of its head.

copperplate noun **1** Printing a copper plate used for engraving or etching, or a print made from it. **2** fine regular handwriting of the style formerly taught in schools and used on copperplates.

copper pyrites Geol. chalcopyrite.

copper sulphate Chem. (FORMULA $CuSO_4$) a white compound that tends to absorb moisture from the atmosphere, forming a blue crystalline hydrate ($CuSO_4.5H_2O$). It is used in electroplating, and as an antiseptic, pesticide, and wood preservative.

coppery adj. like copper.

coppice /ˈkɒpɪs/ — noun Bot. an area of woodland in which trees are regularly cut back to ground level to encourage the growth of side shoots, which are then periodically harvested for firewood, fencing, etc. — verb to manage woodland in this way. [from Old French copeiz]

copra /ˈkɒprə/ noun the dried kernel or 'meat' of the coconut, rich in coconut oil, used to make soap, margarine, etc. [from Portuguese copra, from Malayalam (Indian language) koppara]

coprolalia /kɒprəʊˈleɪlɪə/ noun Psychol. the repetitive use of indecent language, which may be involuntary, eg as a symptom of Tourette's syndrome, a disorder characterized by severe nervous tics. [from Greek kopros, dung]

copse noun a coppice.

Copt noun **1** a member of the ancient Christian Church in Egypt. **2** an Egyptian descended from the ancient Egyptians.

Coptic — *noun* the language of the Copts, now used only in the Coptic Church. — *adj.* relating to the Copts or their language. [from Greek *Aigyptios*, Egyptian]

copula *noun Grammar* a verb that links subject and complement, eg is in *She is a doctor*. [from Latin *copula*, bond]

copulate *verb intrans.* to have sexual intercourse. [from Latin *copulare*, to bind, couple]

copulation /kɒpjʊˈleɪʃən/ *noun* sexual intercourse.

copy /ˈkɒpɪ/ — *noun* (PL. **copies**) **1** an imitation or reproduction. **2** one of the many specimens of a book, or of a particular issue of a magazine, newspaper, etc. **3** written material for printing, especially as distinct from illustrations, etc. **4** the wording of an advertisement. **5** material suitable for a newspaper article. — *verb* (**copies, copied**) **1** to imitate. **2** to make a copy of. **3** *trans., intrans.* to reproduce; to photocopy. **4** *trans., intrans.* to make a copy of another's work, pretending that it is one's own. **5** to give a copy to. [from Latin *copia*, transcript]

. . . .

▣ *noun* **1** imitation, reproduction, duplicate, carbon copy, photocopy, *trademark* Photostat, *trademark* Xerox, facsimile, print, tracing, transcript, transcription, replica, model, pattern, archetype, representation, image, likeness, counterfeit, forgery, fake, borrowing, plagiarism, crib. **3, 4, 5** text. *verb* **1** imitate, impersonate, mimic, ape, parrot, repeat, echo, mirror, follow, emulate. **2, 3** duplicate, photocopy, reproduce, print, trace, transcribe, forge, counterfeit, simulate. **4** plagiarize, crib.

▣ *noun* **1** original.

. . . .

copybook — *noun* a book of handwriting examples for copying. — *adj.* **1** *derog.* unoriginal. **2** faultless; perfect. — **blot one's copybook** to spoil one's good record by misbehaviour or error.

copycat *noun derog.* a mere imitator.

copyist *noun* **1** a person who makes copies in writing. **2** an imitator.

copyright *noun* the sole right to print, publish, translate, perform, film, or record a literary, dramatic, musical, or artistic work.

copywriter *noun* a person who writes advertising copy.

coquetry /ˈkoʊkɪtrɪ/ *noun* flirtation.

coquette /koʊˈkɛt/ *noun* a flirtatious woman. [from French *coquet*, diminutive of *coq*, cock]

coquettish *adj.* flirting; like a flirt.

coquettishly *adv.* with a coquettish manner.

coquettishness *noun* coquettish behaviour.

Cor. *abbrev. Biblical* Corinthians.

cor- see CON-.

coracle /ˈkɒrəkl/ *noun* a small, oval rowing-boat made of wickerwork covered with hides or other waterproof material. [from Welsh *corwgl*]

coral /ˈkɒrəl/ — *noun* **1** a tiny invertebrate marine animal, found mainly in tropical seas, belonging to the same class (Anthozoa) as sea anemones, and consisting of a hollow tube with a mouth, surrounded by tentacles, at the top. The tentacles trap small crustaceans and pass them to the mouth. **2** a hard chalky substance of various colours, formed from the skeletons of this animal. **3** a pinkish-orange colour. — *adj.* pinkish-orange in colour. [from Greek *korallion*]

coral island or **reef** a coral reef containing a central lagoon that has become raised above sea level, and has then drained to form a hollow, eventually becoming colonized by plants, insects, birds, etc. Coral islands are found mainly in the Indian and Pacific Oceans.

coralline /ˈkɒrəlaɪn/ — *adj.* of, like, or containing coral. — *noun* a common seaweed of a delicate pinkish or purplish colour.

coral snake a venomous snake native to the New World and E Asia, usually with bold alternating bands of black, yellow, and red. It produces strong venom, but is not aggressive. Its short fangs do not inject venom easily, and the snake either grips its prey in its mouth after striking it, or bites it several times.

cor anglais /kɔːˈrɒŋgleɪ/ (PL. **cors anglais**) a woodwind musical instrument similar to, but lower in pitch than, the oboe. [from French *cor anglais*, English horn]

corbel /ˈkɔːbəl/ *noun Archit.* a stone or timber projecting from a wall, taking the weight of eg a parapet, arch, or bracket. [from Old French *corbel*, crow]

corbelled *adj.* provided with corbels.

corbelling *noun* stone or brickwork made into corbels.

cord *noun* **1** a thin rope or string consisting of several separate strands twisted together. **2** *Anat.* any long flexible structure resembling this, eg spinal cord, umbilical cord. **3** *North Amer.* the cable of an electrical appliance. **4** a ribbed fabric, especially corduroy. **5** (**cords**) corduroy trousers. **6** a unit for measuring the volume of cut wood, equal to 128 cubic feet, so called because it was originally determined by use of a cord or string. It is now used mainly for measuring stacks of wood cut for fuel. [from Greek *chorde*, string]

. . . .

▣ **1** string, twine, rope, line, cable, flex. **3** cable, flex.

. . . .

corded *adj., said of fabric* ribbed.

cordial — *adj.* **1** warm and affectionate. **2** heartfelt; profound: *a cordial dislike*. — *noun* a fruit-flavoured drink. [from Latin *cordialis*, from *cor*, heart]

cordiality /kɔːdɪˈalɪtɪ/ *noun* warmth and friendliness; sincerity.

cordially *adv.* warmly, heartily.

cordite *noun* any of various smokeless explosive materials containing a mixture of cellulose nitrate and nitroglycerine, used as a propellant for guns, etc. [from CORD]

cordless *adj., said of an electrical appliance* operating without a flex; battery-powered.

cordon /ˈkɔːdən/ — *noun* **1** a line of police or soldiers, or a system of road blocks, encircling an area so as to prevent or control passage into or out of it. **2** a ribbon bestowed as a mark of honour. **3** a fruit tree trained to grow as a single stem. — *verb* (**cordon something off**) to close off an area with a cordon. [from French *cordon*, diminutive of *corde*, cord]

cordon bleu /kɔːdɒn ˈblɜː/ — *adj., said of a cook or cookery* of the highest standard. — *noun* (PL. **cordons bleus**) a cook of the highest standard. [from French *cordon bleu*, blue ribbon]

corduroy /ˈkɔːdərɔɪ/ *noun* **1** a thick ribbed cotton fabric. **2** (**corduroys**) trousers made of corduroy. **3** (*also* **corduroy road**) *North Amer.* a road made of logs lying side by side.

core — *noun* **1** the fibrous case at the centre of some fruits, eg apples and pears, containing the seeds. **2** the innermost, central, essential, or unchanging part. **3** the central region of a star or planet, especially the Earth. **4** *Archaeol.* the lump of stone left after flakes have been struck off it for shaping into tools. **5** the central part of a nuclear reactor, containing the fuel, where the nuclear reaction takes place. **6** *Electr.* a piece of magnetic material that, when placed in the centre of a wire coil through which an electric current is being passed, increases the intensity of the magnetic field and the inductance of the coil. Cores are used in transformers, electromagnets, electric engines, etc. **7** (*in full* **core memory**) the main memory of a computer, where instructions and data are stored in such a way that they are available for immediate use. **8** the inner part of an electric cable. **9** a cylindrical sample of rock, soil, etc, removed with a hollow tubular drill. — *verb* to remove the core of (an apple, etc).

. . . .

▣ *noun* **1** kernel. **2** centre, middle, heart, nucleus, kernel, nub, crux, essence, gist, *colloq.* nitty-gritty.

▣ *noun* **2** surface, exterior.

. . . .

core curriculum *Education* a basic central provision for all pupils, as opposed to a set of options taken only by some. The core curriculum usually includes mathematics, science, and the child's native language.

corer *noun* a knife with a hollow cylindrical blade for coring fruit.

co-respondent *noun Legal* in divorce cases, a person said to have committed adultery with the partner (called the *respondent*) against whom the case is being brought.

CORGI *abbrev.* Confederation for Registration of Gas Installers (UK).

corgi *noun* a small British breed of dog having a long body, very short legs, a pointed muzzle, and large erect ears. [from Welsh *cor*, dwarf + *ci*, dog]

coriander /kɒrɪˈandə(r)/ *noun* **1** an annual plant (Coriandrum sativum), native to Europe and Asia, having narrowly lobed leaves, small white, pink, or lilac flowers borne in flat-topped clusters, and globular aromatic fruits. **2** the dried ripe fruit of this plant, used as a spice in sausages and other meat products, curry powder, confectionery, tobacco, gin, and liqueurs, and widely used as a flavouring in cooking. [from Greek *koriannon*]

Corinthian /kəˈrɪnθɪən/ *adj.* **1** relating to ancient Corinth in Greece. **2** *Archit.* denoting an order of classical architecture characterized by a style of column with a fluted shaft and a heavily carved capital having a distinctive acanthus-leaf design. See also DORIC, IONIC.

Coriolis effect or **Coriolis force** /kɒrɪˈoʊlɪs/ *Physics* a hypothetical force that appears to act on objects moving across the Earth's surface, and results from the Earth's rotation. In the northern hemisphere, the path of an object appears to be deflected to the right, and in the southern hemisphere it appears to be deflected to the left. [named after the French physicist Gaspard Gustave de Coriolis]

cork — *noun* **1** *Bot.* a layer of tissue that forms below the epidermis in the stems and roots of woody plants, eg trees. It consists of dead cells coated with suberin, a waxy substance that renders them impermeable to air and water, and so protects the underlying cells from water loss and physical injury. Cork is particularly abundant in the bark layer of certain tree species, and is stripped from the cork oak for commercial use. **2** a piece of this used as a stopper for a bottle, etc. — *verb* (*usually* **cork up** or **cork something up**) **1** to stop (a bottle, etc) with a cork. **2** to suppress (one's feelings, etc). **3** *intrans.* to be quiet. [from Arabic *qurq*, from Latin *quercus*, oak]

corkage *noun* the fee charged by a restaurant for serving to customers wine that they have bought elsewhere.

corked *adj.*, *said of wine* spoilt as a result of having a faulty cork.

corker *noun, old slang use* something or someone marvellous.

cork oak an evergreen tree (Quercus suber), native to the Mediterranean region, that grows to a height of up to 20m, and has glossy leaves with spiny margins. Its bark produces a thick cork layer which can be removed in cylindrical sheets from the tree. It is cultivated as a commercial source of cork.

corkscrew — *noun* a tool with a spiral spike for screwing into bottle corks to remove them. — *adj.* shaped like a corkscrew. — *verb intrans.* to move spirally.

corm *noun Bot.* in certain plants, eg crocus, a swollen underground stem, rounded in shape and bearing roots on its lower surface. It functions primarily as a food store. [from Greek *kormos*, lopped tree trunk]

cormorant *noun* any of over 30 species of seabird with an upright stance, dark brown or black plumage, webbed feet, a long neck, and a slender bill, found along coasts or on inland waters almost worldwide. Cormorants are expert divers and swimmers, and feed mainly on fish. They breed in large colonies. [from French, from Latin *corvus marinus*, sea raven]

Corn. *abbrev.* Cornwall.

corn¹ *noun* **1** in the UK, the most important cereal crop of a particular region, especially wheat in England, and oats in Scotland and Ireland. **2** *North Amer.* maize. **3** a general term for the harvested seed of cereal plants; cereal grains.

4 *slang* something stale or old-fashioned. [from Anglo-Saxon]

corn² *noun* a small painful area of hard thickened skin, especially on or between the toes, caused by pressure or friction, eg as a result of wearing ill-fitting shoes. — **tread on someone's corns** *colloq.* to hurt their feelings. [from Latin *cornu*, horn]

corncob *noun* the woody core of an ear of maize, bearing many closely packed rows of kernels. — **corn on the cob** a corncob cooked and served as a vegetable.

corncrake *noun* a bird belonging to the rail family, native to Europe and W Asia and migrating to tropical Africa and Asia in winter, having light brown streaky plumage, chestnut wings, and a barred tail. [from CORN¹ + *crake*, from Norse *krakr*, crow]

corn dolly a figure made of plaited straw.

cornea /ˈkɔːnɪə/ (PL. **corneas, corneae**) *noun* the convex transparent membrane that covers the front of the eyeball in vertebrates. [from Latin *cornea tela*, horny tissue]

corneal *adj.* relating to or in the region of the cornea.

corned beef *adj.* beef that has been salted, cooked, and canned. [from CORN¹]

cornelian /kɔːˈniːlɪən/ or **carnelian** *noun Geol.* a red and white form of agate, used as a semi-precious stone and for making seals. [from Old French *corneline*]

corner — *noun* **1** a point or place where lines or surface-edges meet; the inside or outside of the angle so formed. **2** an intersection between roads. **3** a quiet or remote place. **4** an awkward situation: *in a tight corner*. **5** *Econ.* control of a particular market gained by buying up the total stocks of a commodity, to re-sell at one's own price. **6** *Boxing* either of the angles of the ring used as a base between bouts by contestants. **7** *Football* a free kick from a corner of the field. — *verb* (**cornered, cornering**) **1** to force into a place or position from which escape is difficult. **2** to gain control of (a market) by buying up total stocks of a commodity. **3** *intrans. said of a driver or vehicle* to turn a corner. — **cut corners** to spend less money, effort, time, etc on something than one should, especially to save time. **take a corner** to negotiate a corner in a motor vehicle: *took the corner too fast*. **turn the corner 1** to go round a corner. **2** to get past the most dangerous stage, eg of an illness. [from Old French *corne*, corner, horn]

• •

▣ *noun* **1** angle, joint, crook, bend, recess. **2** junction, intersection, turning. **3** nook, cranny, niche, hideout, hideaway, retreat.

• •

cornerstone *noun* **1** a stone built into the corner of the foundation of a building. **2** a crucial or indispensable part; a basis: *the cornerstone of his argument*.

cornet *noun* **1** a brass musical instrument similar to the trumpet. **2** a cone-shaped edible holder for ice cream; an ice-cream cone. [from Old French *cornet*, diminutive of Latin *cornu*, horn]

cornetist or **cornettist** *noun* a person who plays the cornet.

cornflakes *pl. noun* toasted maize flakes, eaten as a breakfast cereal.

cornflour *noun* a finely ground flour obtained from maize and consisting of purified starch, used in cooking to thicken sauces, custard, blancmange, etc.

cornflower *noun* an annual plant (Centaurea cyanus), native to SE Europe, having narrow lance-shaped leaves covered with grey hairs, and long-stalked solitary flowerheads consisting of bright blue outer florets surrounding the smaller reddish purple inner florets

cornice /ˈkɔːnɪs/ *noun* **1** a decorative border of moulded plaster round a ceiling. **2** *Archit.* the lower section of the horizontal layer of masonry surmounting a row of columns. **3** *Archit.* a projecting moulding at the top of an external wall. **4** *Art* the projecting top part of a pedestal. **5** *Mountaineering* an overhang formed of snow or ice. [from Italian *cornice*, crow]

cornichon /'kɔːnɪʃɔːn/ *noun* a type of small gherkin. [French]

cornily *adv.* in a corny way.

corniness *noun* being corny.

Cornish — *adj.* relating to Cornwall, its people, or language. — *noun* the Celtic language once spoken in Cornwall, related to Welsh.

Cornish pasty a semicircular folded pastry case containing meat and vegetables.

cornucopia /kɔːnjʊ'kəʊpɪə/ *noun Art* a horn full to overflowing with fruit and other produce, used as a symbol of abundance. [from Latin *cornu*, horn + *copia*, abundance]

cornucopian *adj.* 1 relating to a cornucopia. 2 abundant.

corny *adj.* (**cornier, corniest**) *colloq.* 1 *said of a joke* old and stale. 2 embarrassingly old-fashioned or sentimental. [from CORN¹]

corolla /kə'rɒlə/ *noun Bot.* the collective name for the petals of a flower, which may be separate, or partially or completely fused to form a tube. The corolla encloses the stamens and carpels, and is itself surrounded by the sepals of the calyx. [from Latin *corolla*, garland]

corollary /kə'rɒlərɪ/ *noun* (PL. **corollaries**) 1 something that follows from another thing that has been proved. 2 a natural or obvious consequence. [from Latin *corollarium*, gift of money, originally for a garland, from *corolla*, garland]

corona /kə'rəʊnə/ *noun* (PL. **coronae, coronas**) 1 *Astron.* the outer atmosphere of the Sun, consisting of a halo of hot luminous gases that boil from its surface, visible during a total solar eclipse. 2 *Bot.* in certain plants, eg daffodil, a trumpet-like outgrowth from the corolla of petals. 3 *Physics* the glowing region produced by ionization of the air surrounding a high-voltage conductor. [from Latin *corona*, crown]

coronary /'kɒrənərɪ/ — *adj.* 1 relating to a crown or a corona. 2 denoting structures that encircle in the manner of a crown or a corona, especially blood vessels, nerves, ligaments, etc, that encircle a body part or structure. 3 relating to the blood vessels of the heart, eg coronary arteries. — *noun* (PL. **coronaries**) a coronary thrombosis. [from Latin *coronarius*, encircling (the heart) like a wreath, from *corona*, wreath]

coronary thrombosis *Medicine* the formation of a blood clot (thrombus) in one of the two coronary arteries that supply blood to the heart.

coronation /kɒrə'neɪʃən/ *noun* the ceremony of crowning a king, queen, or consort. [from Latin *coronatio*, from *corona*, crown]

coroner /'kɒrənə(r)/ *noun* 1 an official who inquires into sudden or accidental deaths, and investigates cases of treasure trove. 2 the principal officer of one of the six ancient divisions of the Isle of Man. [from Old French *corouner*, supervisor of the Crown's pleas]

coronet /'kɒrənɪt/ *noun* 1 a small crown. 2 a circlet of jewels for the head. [from Old French *coronet*, diminutive of *corone*, crown]

corp. *abbrev.* 1 (*also* **Corp.**) corporal. 2 corporation.

corpora /'kɔːpərə/ see CORPUS.

corporal¹ *noun* an officer in the army or air force just below a sergeant in rank. [from Italian *caporale*, from *capo*, head]

corporal² *adj.* of or relating to the body. [from Latin *corporalis*, from *corpus*, body]

corporal punishment punishment inflicted on the body, such as spanking or caning.

corporate *adj.* 1 shared by members of a group; joint. 2 belonging, or relating, to a corporation: *corporate finance.* 3 formed into a corporation: *a corporate body.* [from Latin *corporare*, to form into a body]

corporately *adv.* in a corporate way.

corporate raider a company or individual who seeks to gain control of a business by acquiring a large proportion of its stock.

corporate state *Politics* a capitalist state which operates corporatism.

corporate strategy the broad aims and strategies that a company wishes to follow over a period of time, especially five years.

corporation /kɔːpə'reɪʃən/ *noun* 1 a body of people acting jointly eg for administration or business purposes. 2 the council of a town or city. 3 *facetious* a paunch. [from Latin *corporatio*, trade guild]

⊟ **1** association, society, organization, company, firm, combine, conglomerate. **2** council, local authority, authorities.

corporation tax a tax paid by companies on the profits they make.

corporatism or **corporativism** *noun Politics* the belief that the state should intervene in a capitalist economy in order to guarantee social harmony. Corporatism operates in many modern capitalist democracies.

corporatization or **corporatisation** *noun* the act of making or becoming more like a commercial business.

corporatize or **corporatise** *verb trans., intrans.* to make or become more like a commercial business.

corporeal /kɔː'pɔːrɪəl/ *adj.* relating to the body as distinct from the soul; bodily; physical; material. [from Latin *corpus*, body]

corporeality /kɔːpɔːrɪ'alɪtɪ/ *noun* being corporeal.

corporeally /kɔː'pɔːrɪəlɪ/ *adv.* in a corporeal way.

corps /kɔː(r)/ *noun* (PL. **corps**) 1 a military body or division: *the intelligence corps.* 2 a body of people engaged in particular work: *the diplomatic corps.* [from French *corps*, body]

corps de ballet /kɔː də baleɪ/ a company of ballet dancers, eg at a theatre. [from French *corps de ballet*]

corpse *noun* the dead body of a human being. [from Latin *corpus*, body]

⊟ body, *slang* stiff, carcase, skeleton, remains.

corpulence *noun* extreme fatness.

corpulent *adj.* fat; fleshy; obese. [from Latin *corpulentus*]

corpus /'kɔːpəs/ *noun* (PL. **corpora**) 1 a body of writings, eg by a particular author. 2 a body of written and/or spoken material for language research. 3 *Anat.* any distinct mass of body tissue that may be distinguished from its surroundings. [from Latin *corpus*, body]

corpus callosum /kə'lɒsəm/ (PL. **corpora callosa**) *Anat.* a thick bundle of about 300m nerve fibres in the centre of the brain, that serves to connect the left and right cerebral hemispheres. [from Latin *corpus*, body + *callosus* callous]

Corpus Christi /'krɪstɪ/ a Roman Catholic festival in honour of the Blessed Sacrament, held on the Thursday after Trinity Sunday

corpuscle /'kɔːpʌsəl/ *noun Anat.* any small particle or cell within a tissue or organ, especially a red or white blood cell. [from Latin *corpusculum*, diminutive of *corpus*, body]

corpuscular /kɔː'pʌskjʊlə(r)/ *adj.* 1 relating to corpuscles, especially red or white blood cells. 2 *Physics* denoting radiation that consists of a stream of subatomic particles, such as electrons or protons, as distinct from electromagnetic radiation.

corpus luteum /'luːtɪəm/ (PL. **corpora lutea**) *Anat.* in the ovary of female mammals, the mass of yellowish tissue that develops from a ruptured Graafian follicle after ovulation. It secretes the hormone progesterone. [from Latin *corpus*, body + *luteus*, yellow]

corral /kə'rɑːl/ *North Amer.* — *noun* 1 a pen or enclosure for cattle or horses. 2 an enclosure into which hunted animals can be driven. — *verb* (**corralled, corralling**) to herd or pen into a corral. [from Spanish *corral*]

correct — *verb* 1 to set or put right; to remove errors from. 2 to mark the errors in. 3 to adjust or make better. 4

old use to rebuke or punish. — *adj.* **1** free from error; accurate; not mistaken. **2** right; proper; appropriate. **3** conforming to accepted standards: *very correct in his behaviour.* — **stand corrected** acknowledge one's mistake. [from Latin *corrigere*]

. . . .

▣ *verb* **1** rectify, put right, right, emend, remedy, cure, debug. **3** adjust, improve, amend, regulate, reform. **4** rebuke, punish, discipline, reprimand, reprove. *adj.* **1** right, accurate, precise, exact, strict, true, truthful, word-perfect, faultless, flawless. **2** right, proper, acceptable, appropriate, fitting, *colloq.* OK, standard, regular, just.
▣ *adj.* **1** incorrect, wrong, inaccurate. **2** wrong, inappropriate, unacceptable, improper.

. . . .

correcting fluid a thick, usually white, liquid for covering up errors in writing or typing.

correction *noun* **1** the act of correcting. **2** an alteration that corrects something. **3** *old use* punishment.

. . . .

▣ **1** rectification, emendation, adjustment, alteration, modification, amendment, improvement. **2** alteration, modification, amendment, improvement.

. . . .

corrective — *adj.* having the effect of correcting or adjusting. — *noun* something that has this effect.

correctly *adv.* in a correct way; so as to be correct.

correctness *noun* being correct.

corrector *noun* someone or something that corrects.

correlate /'kɒrəleɪt/ *verb* **1** *intrans., trans. said of two or more things, or of one thing in relation to another* to have a connection or correspondence; to relate one to another: *smoking in pregnancy correlates with lower birth weight.* **2** to combine, compare, show relationships between (information, reports, etc). [from Latin *cor-*, with + *relatio*, carrying back]

correlation /kɒrə'leɪʃən/ *noun* **1** a connection or correspondence. **2** *Statistics* the strength of the relationship between two random variables.

correlative /kə'relətɪv/ *adj.* **1** mutually linked. **2** *Grammar, said of words* used as an inter-related pair, like *either* and *or.*

correspond *verb intrans.* **1** (**correspond to something**) to be similar or equivalent to it: *an increase in wages followed by a corresponding increase in prices.* **2** (**correspond with** or **to something** or **someone**) to be in agreement; to match. **3** (**correspond with someone**) to write and receive letters from them. [from Latin *cor-*, with + *respondere*, to answer]

. . . .

▣ **1** match, fit, conform to, tally with, square with. **2** agree, match, concur, coincide, correlate, accord, harmonize, dovetail, complement. **3** communicate, write.

. . . .

correspondence *noun* **1** similarity; equivalence. **2** agreement. **3** communication by letters; letters received or sent.

. . . .

▣ **1** similarity, equivalence, resemblance, congruity, harmony, match, coincidence, correlation, relation, analogy, comparison, comparability. **2** agreement, conformity, concurrence. **3** communication, writing, letters, post, mail.
▣ **1, 2** divergence.

. . . .

correspondence course a course of study conducted by post.

correspondent *noun* **1** a person with whom one exchanges letters. **2** a person employed by a newspaper, radio station, etc to send reports from a particular part of the world, or on a particular topic.

. . . .

▣ **2** journalist, reporter, contributor, writer.

. . . .

corridor *noun* **1** a passageway, esp. one off which rooms open or, on a train, one giving access to compartments. **2** a strip of land through foreign territory, giving access eg to a port. **3** a restricted route through the air that air traffic must follow. [from Italian *corridore*, corridor, place for running]

. . . .

▣ **1** passageway, passage, aisle, hallway, hall, lobby.

. . . .

corridors of power places where the people who make the important decisions are to be found.

corrie *noun* **1** in the Highlands of Scotland, a semicircular hollow on a hillside. **2** a deep semicircular hollow with steep sides, located high on a mountain slope and often containing a small lake, formed as a result of erosion of bedrock by a small glacier. Also called CIRQUE, CWM. [from Gaelic *coire*, pot]

corrigendum /kɒrɪ'gendəm/ *noun* (PL. **corrigenda**) an error for correction, eg in a book. [from Latin *corrigendum*, something to be corrected]

corroborate /kə'rɒbəreɪt/ *verb* to confirm (eg someone's statement): *corroborating evidence.* [from Latin *corroborare*, to strengthen]

. . . .

▣ confirm, prove, bear out, support, endorse, ratify, substantiate, validate, authenticate, document, underpin, sustain.
▣ contradict.

. . . .

corroboration /kərɒbə'reɪʃən/ *noun* confirmation.

corroborative *adj.* tending to confirm.

corroborator *noun* a person who corroborates.

corroboree /kə'rɒbəri/ *noun* Austral. **1** a ceremonial or warlike dance. **2** a noisy gathering. [from an Australian Aboriginal language]

corrode /kə'rəʊd/ *verb* **1** to subject (a material, especially a metal) to the process of corrosion. **2** *said of a material, especially a metal* to undergo the process of corrosion; to rust. **3** to destroy gradually or eat away by degrees: *a relationship corroded by mutual ill feeling.* [from Latin *corrodere*, to gnaw to pieces]

. . . .

▣ **2** rust, oxidize, corrode, deteriorate, crumble, disintegrate. **3** erode, wear away, eat away, consume.

. . . .

corrosion *noun* **1** the wearing away and eventual destruction of a metal or alloy as a result of its oxidation by air, water, or chemicals, eg the rusting of iron and steel, or the tarnishing of silver. **2** a corroded part or patch. [from Latin *corrodere*, to gnaw to pieces]

corrosive — *adj.* **1** tending to eat away or consume. **2** *said of a substance* tending to cause corrosion. **3** *said of language* hurtful, sarcastic. — *noun* any material that causes corrosion, eg a strong acid.

. . . .

▣ *adj.* **1** corroding, erosive, acid, caustic, abrasive. **3** hurtful, sarcastic, caustic, acid, cutting.

. . . .

corrugate *verb* to fold into parallel ridges, so as to make stronger: *corrugated iron.* [from Latin *corrugare*, to wrinkle]

. . . .

▣ ridge, flute, furrow.

. . . .

corrugation /kɒrə'geɪʃən/ *noun* **1** the act of wrinkling, or the state of being wrinkled. **2** a wrinkle.

corrupt /kə'rʌpt/ — *verb* **1** *trans., intrans.* to change for the worse, especially morally. **2** to spoil, deform, or make impure. **3** to bribe. **4** *intrans.* to decay or deteriorate. **5** *Comput.* to introduce errors into (a program or data), either accidentally or deliberately, so that it is no longer reliable. — *adj.* **1** morally evil. **2** accepting bribes. **3** dishonest. **4** *said of a text* so full of errors and alterations as to be unreliable. **5** *Comput.*, *said of a program or data* containing errors and therefore no longer reliable, eg as a result of a fault in the hardware or software. [from Latin *corrumpere*, to spoil]

....

◼ *verb* **1** pervert, deprave, lead astray, lure. **2** spoil, deform, contaminate, pollute, adulterate, taint, defile, debase. **3** bribe, suborn. *adj.* **1** immoral, depraved, degenerate, dissolute, unscrupulous, unprincipled, unethical, rotten. **3** fraudulent, *colloq.* shady, dishonest, *slang* bent, *colloq.* crooked, untrustworthy.

◪ *verb* **2** purify. *adj.* **1** ethical, virtuous, upright. **3** honest, trustworthy.

....

corruptibility /kərʌptə'bılıtı/ *noun* a tendency to be corrupted.

corruptible *adj.* capable of being or liable to be corrupted.

corruption *noun* **1** the process of corrupting or condition of being corrupt. **2** a deformed form of a word or phrase: *'Santa Claus' is a corruption of 'Saint Nicholas'.*

....

◼ **1** unscrupulousness, immorality, impurity, depravity, degeneration, degradation, perversion, distortion, dishonesty, *colloq.* crookedness, fraud, *colloq.* shadiness, bribery, extortion, vice, wickedness, iniquity, evil.

◪ **1** honesty, virtue.

....

corruptive *adj.* tending to corrupt.

corruptly *adv.* in a corrupt way.

corsage /kɔː'sɑː/ *noun* a small spray of flowers for pinning to the bodice of a dress. [from Old French *corsage*, bodily shape, later bodice, from Latin *corpus*]

corsair /'kɔːseə(r)/ *noun old use* **1** a pirate or pirate ship. **2** a privately owned warship. [from Old French *corsaire*]

corselet /'kɔːslɪt/ *noun* **1** (*also* **corslet**) *Hist.* a protective garment or piece of armour for the upper part of the body. **2** (*also* **corselette**) a woman's undergarment combining girdle and brassière. [from Old French diminutive of *cors*, body, bodice]

corset — *noun* **1** a tightly fitting undergarment stiffened by strips of bone or plastic, for shaping, controlling, or supporting the figure. **2** *Commerce* government restrictions on the lending power of banks. — *verb* (**corseted**, **corseting**) **1** to put a corset on. **2** to restrict. [from Old French diminutive of *cors*, body, bodice]

corsetry *noun* the making and selling of corsets.

cortège /kɔː'teʒ/ *noun* a procession, especially at a funeral. [from French *cortège*, from Italian *corteggio*, retinue]

cortex (PL. **cortices**) *noun Anat.* the outer layer of an organ or tissue, when this differs in structure or function from the inner region, eg the cerebral cortex (outer layer of grey matter) of the brain. [from Latin *cortex*, tree bark]

cortical *adj.* **1** relating to or in the region of the cortex. **2** external.

corticosteroid /kɔːtɪkoʊ'stɪərɔɪd/ or **corticoid** *noun Biochem.* any steroid hormone, eg cortisone, manufactured by the adrenal cortex.

cortisone /'kɔːtɪzoʊn/ *noun Biochem.* a naturally occurring steroid hormone that is isolated from the cortex (outer part) of the adrenal glands, and is used as an anti-inflammatory agent to treat rheumatoid arthritis, certain eye and skin disorders, and Addison's disease (in which there is a deficiency of corticosteroid hormones). [from *corticosterone*, a hormone secreted by the cortex of the adrenal gland]

corundum *noun Geol.* an extremely hard aluminium oxide mineral, used as an abrasive powder and as a constituent of emery. Its coloured crystalline forms include the gemstones ruby and sapphire. [from Tamil *kuruntam*]

coruscate /'kɒrəskeɪt/ *verb intrans.* to sparkle. [from Latin *coruscare*, to sparkle]

coruscation /kɒrəs'keɪʃən/ *noun* a glittering; a flash.

corvette /kɔː'vət/ *noun* **1** a small warship for escorting larger vessels. **2** *Hist.* a sailing warship with one tier of guns. [from Dutch *corver*, pursuit vessel]

cos[1] *noun* (*also* **cos lettuce**) a lettuce with slim crisp leaves. [from Cos, a Greek island where it originated]

cos[2] *abbrev.* cosine.

cosecant /koʊ'siːkənt/ *noun Maths.* (ABBREV. **cosec**) for a given angle in a right-angled triangle, the ratio of the length of the hypotenuse to the length of the side opposite the angle under consideration; the reciprocal of the sine of an angle.

cosh — *noun* a club, especially a rubber one filled with metal, used as a weapon. — *verb colloq.* to hit with a cosh or something heavy. [perhaps from Romany *koshter*, stick]

co-signatory *noun* a person or country etc that signs a document or treaty jointly with others.

cosily *adv.* with a cosy manner; comfortably.

cosine /'koʊsaɪn/ *noun Maths.* (ABBREV. **cos**) in trigonometry, a function of an angle in a right-angled triangle, defined as the length of the side adjacent to the angle divided by the length of the hypotenuse (the longest side).

cosiness *noun* a cosy state or condition; comfort.

cosmetic — *adj.* **1** used to beautify the face, body, or hair. **2** improving superficially, for the sake of appearance only. — *noun* a cosmetic application, especially for the face. [from Greek *kosmetikos*, of adornment]

....

◼ *adj.* **2** superficial, surface. *noun* make-up, greasepaint.

....

cosmetically *adv.* **1** by using cosmetics. **2** superficially.

cosmic *adj.* **1** relating to the Universe; universal. **2** coming from outer space: *cosmic rays.* **3** *colloq.* large or significant. [from Greek *kosmikos*, from *kosmos*, universe]

cosmically *adv.* **1** in a cosmic way. **2** *said of a star rising* with the sun.

cosmic rays or **cosmic radiation** *Astron.* radiation consisting of streams of high-energy particles from outer space, travelling at about the speed of light, most of which are thought to originate from supernovae.

cosmogony /kɒz'mɒgənɪ/ *noun* (PL. **cosmogonies**) the study of the origin and development of the Universe as a whole, or of specific celestial objects or systems, especially the Solar System. [from Greek *kosmos*, universe + *gonia*, giving birth to]

cosmological /kɒzmə'lɒdʒɪkəl/ *adj.* relating to or associated with cosmology.

cosmologist /kɒz'mɒlədʒɪst/ *noun* a scientist who specializes in cosmology.

cosmology /kɒz'mɒlədʒɪ/ *noun* **1** the scientific study of the origin, nature, structure, and evolution of the Universe. **2** a theory or model of the origin and structure of the Universe. [from Greek *kosmos*, universe + -LOGY]

cosmonaut *noun* a Russian astronaut. [from Greek *kosmos*, universe + *nautes*, sailor]

cosmopolitan /kɒzmə'pɒlɪtən/ — *adj.* **1** belonging to, or representative of, all parts of the world. **2** free of national prejudices; international in experience and outlook. — *noun* a person of this type; a citizen of the world. [from Greek *kosmos*, universe + *polites*, citizen]

....

◼ *adj.* **1** international, universal. **2** worldly, worldly-wise, well-travelled, sophisticated, urbane.

◪ INSULAR, PAROCHIAL.

....

cosmopolitanism *noun* belief in a cosmopolitan outlook.

cosmos *noun* the Universe seen as an ordered system. [from Greek *kosmos*, world order, universe]

Cossack — *noun* a member of a former warrior people of southern Russia. — *adj.* belonging or relating to this people. [from Ukrainian *kozak*, originally freebooter]

cosset *verb* (**cosseted**, **cosseting**) to treat too kindly; to pamper. [perhaps from Anglo-Saxon *kossetung*, kissing]

⊟ coddle, mollycoddle, pamper, indulge, spoil, cherish.

cost — *verb* (PAST TENSE AND PAST PARTICIPLE **cost**) **1** to be obtainable at a certain price. **2** to involve the loss or sacrifice of. **3** (**costed**) to estimate or decide the cost of. **4** *trans. intrans. colloq.* to put (someone) to some expense. — *noun* **1** what something costs. **2** loss or sacrifice. **3** (**costs**) *Legal* the expenses of a case. — **at all costs** no matter what the risk or effort may be. **cost someone dear** to prove costly to them. **count the cost 1** to consider all the risks before taking action. **2** to realize the bad effects of something done. **to one's cost** with some loss or disadvantage. [from Latin *constare*, to cost]

⊟ *noun* **1** price, rate, amount, charge, payment, figure, expense, outlay, disbursement, expenditure, worth. **2** loss, sacrifice, price, penalty, detriment, harm, injury, hurt, deprivation.

cost-accounting *noun* a branch of accountancy concerned with the analysis of costs for a product or operation.

costal *adj. Anat.* **1** relating to or in the region of the ribs. **2** relating to the side of the body. [from Latin *costa*, rib]

co-star — *noun* a fellow star in a film, play, etc. — *verb intrans.* (**co-starred**, **co-starring**) **1** *said of an actor* to appear alongside another star. **2** *said of a production* to feature as fellow stars: *co-starred Gielgud and Olivier*.

cost-benefit analysis a type of study which compares the cost of a particular course of action with the resulting benefits.

cost-effective *adj.* justifying its cost; giving acceptable value for money.

costermonger / 'kɒstəmʌŋgə(r)/ *noun Brit.* (*also* **coster**) a person who sells fruit and vegetables from a barrow. [from *costard*, an apple + -MONGER]

costive *adj.* constipated. [from Old French *costivé*]

costliness *noun* **1** being costly. **2** price.

costly *adj.* (**costlier**, **costliest**) **1** involving much cost; expensive. **2** lavish; sumptuous. **3** involving major losses or sacrifices.

⊟ **1** expensive, dear, *colloq.* pricey, exorbitant, excessive, precious, priceless. **2** lavish, sumptuous, rich, splendid, valuable. **3** loss-making, harmful, damaging, disastrous, catastrophic.
⊟ **1** cheap, inexpensive. **2** cheap.

cost of living the cost to the individual of ordinary necessities such as food and clothing.

cost price the price paid for something by the retailer, before resale at a profit.

costume *noun* **1** a set of clothing of a special kind, especially of a particular historical period or particular country. **2** a garment or outfit for a special activity: *a swimming costume*. **3** *old use* a woman's suit. [from Italian *costume*, habit, dress]

⊟ **1** dress, clothing. **2** outfit, garment, dress, clothing, uniform, livery, robes, vestments, *colloq.* get-up, fancy dress.

costume jewellery jewellery made of inexpensive or artificial materials.

costumier /kɒ'stjuːmɪə(r)/ *noun* a person who makes or supplies costumes.

cosy — *adj.* (**cosier**, **cosiest**) **1** warm and comfortable. **2** friendly, intimate, and confidential. — *noun* (PL. **cosies**) a warm cover to keep something warm, especially a teapot or boiled egg.

⊟ *adj.* **1** snug, comfortable, warm, *colloq.* comfy, sheltered,

secure, homely. **2** friendly, intimate, warm, personal.
⊟ *adj.* **1** uncomfortable, cold. **2** unfriendly, cold, impersonal.

cot[1] *noun* **1** a small bed with high sides for a child. **2** *North Amer., esp. US* a camp bed. [from Hindi *khat*, bedstead]

cot[2] *noun* **1** *poetic* a cottage. **2** a cote. [from Anglo-Saxon]

cot[3] *abbrev.* cotangent.

cotangent /koʊ'tandʒənt/ *noun Maths.* (ABBREV. **cot**) for a given angle in a right-angled triangle, the ratio of the length of the side adjacent to the angle under consideration to the length of the side opposite it; the reciprocal of the tangent of an angle.

cot death same as SUDDEN INFANT DEATH SYNDROME.

cote *noun* (*usually in compounds*) a small shelter for birds or animals: *dovecote*. [from Anglo-Saxon]

coterie / 'koʊtərɪ/ *noun* a small exclusive group of people with interests in common. [from Old French *coterie*, group of tenant farmers]

coterminous /koʊ'tɜːmɪnəs/ *adj.* having the same boundaries, duration, or range. [from Latin *con-*, same + *terminus*, boundary]

cotinga /koʊ'tɪŋgə/ *noun* a bird native to the New World tropics, that inhabits woodland. [from a S American name]

cotoneaster /kɒtoʊnɪ'astə(r)/ *noun* a deciduous or evergreen shrub or small tree of the genus Cotoneaster, native to north temperate regions, having arching branches that may be spreading or erect, small oval to rounded leaves, and clusters of white or pink flowers. [from Latin *cotonea*, quince]

cottage *noun* a small house, especially an old stone one, in a village or the countryside. [from COT[2]]

cottage cheese a type of soft white cheese made from sour milk.

cottage industry a craft industry such as knitting or weaving, employing workers in their own homes.

cottage loaf a loaf consisting of a round piece of dough with a smaller round piece on top of it.

cottager *noun* a person who lives in a cottage.

cottar or **cotter** *noun Hist. Scot.* a farm labourer occupying a cottage rent-free. [from COT[2]]

cotton — *noun* **1** a shrubby plant of the genus Gossypium, belonging to the mallow family (Malvaceae), and having broad lobed leaves, creamy-white, yellow, or reddish flowers, and egg-shaped seed pods. **2** the soft white fibre obtained from this plant, which is used to make textiles. **3** the cloth that is woven from fibres that have been obtained from this plant and spun into yarn. — *verb* (**cotton on to something**) *colloq.* to begin to understand it. [from Old French *coton*, from Arabic *qutun*]

cotton gin a machine for separating the seeds from raw cotton fibres.

cottongrass *noun* a genus (Eriophorum) of sedges, having long silky or cotton-like hairs around the ripened ovary.

cottonwool *noun* soft fluffy wadding used in treating injuries, applying cosmetics, etc, originally made from cotton fibre.

cottony *adj.* **1** made of or with cotton. **2** like cotton.

cotyledon /kɒtɪ'liːdən/ *noun Bot.* in flowering plants, one of the leaves produced by the embryo, and an important feature in the classification of plants. Monocotyledons and dicotyledons have one and two cotyledons, respectively, in each seed. [from Greek, from *kotyle*, cup]

couch[1] — *noun* **1** a sofa or settee. **2** a bed-like seat with a headrest, eg for patients to lie on when being examined or treated by a doctor or psychiatrist. **3** *poetic* a bed. — *verb* to express in words of a certain kind. [from French *coucher*, to lay down]

⊟ *noun* **1** sofa, settee, chesterfield, chaise longue, ottoman, divan. **2** bed.

couch[2] /kuːtʃ/ *noun* a perennial grass (Elymus repens), native to north temperate regions, having rough dull green or bluish-green leaves, normally slightly hairy on the upper surface, and spikelets each containing up to six flowers, arranged with their broader faces pressed against the stem axis. [from Anglo-Saxon *cwice*]

couchette /kuːˈʃet/ *noun* a sleeping-berth on a ship or train, converted from ordinary seating; a railway carriage with such berths. [from French *couchette*, diminutive of *couche*, bed]

couch potato *colloq.* someone who spends their leisure time sitting inactive in front of the television or video.

cougar /ˈkuːɡə(r)/ *noun* North Amer. a puma. Also called MOUNTAIN LION, PANTHER. [from French *couguar*, from a S American Indian word]

cough /kɒf/ — *verb intrans.* 1 to expel air, mucus, etc, violently from the lungs with a characteristic rough sound, usually in order to release foreign particles from the airways, or in response to irritation of the lining of the throat, etc. 2 *said of an engine, etc* to make a similar noise. — *noun* 1 the act or sound of coughing. 2 a condition of the lungs or throat that is characterized by frequent coughing. — **cough up** *slang* to provide money or information. **cough something up** 1 to bring up mucus, phlegm, blood, etc by coughing. 2 *slang* to provide money or information. [imitative]

cough mixture a liquid medicine that is used to relieve a cough.

could /kʊd/ *verb aux.* 1 past tense of CAN: *I found I could lift it.* 2 used to express a possibility or a possible course: *you could try telephoning her.* 3 used in making requests: *could you help me?* 4 to feel like doing something or able to do something: *I could have strangled him / I could not allow that.* — **could be** *colloq.* that may be the case.

couldn't /ˈkʊdənt/ *contr.* could not.

couldst *verb old use* the form of *could* used with *thou*.

coulis /ˈkuːliː/ *noun* a thin puree of fish, fowl, fruit, or vegetables. [French]

coulomb /ˈkuːlɒm/ *noun* (SYMBOL C) the SI unit of electric charge. It is equal to the amount of charge transported by a current of one ampere in one second.

council *noun* 1 a body of people whose function is to advise, administer, organize, discuss, or legislate. 2 the elected body of people that directs the affairs of a town, district, region, etc. [from Old French *concile*, from Latin *concilium*]

⊟ 1 committee, panel, board, cabinet, ministry, parliament, congress, assembly, convention, conference. 2 local authority, regional authority.

council house a house owned and rented out by a local council.

councillor *noun* a member of a council, especially of a town, etc.

council tax a UK local government tax based on and banded according to property values, introduced in 1993 to replace the community charge or poll tax.

counsel — *noun* 1 advice. 2 consultation, discussion, or deliberation: *take counsel with one's supporters.* 3 a lawyer or group of lawyers that gives legal advice and fights cases in court. — *verb* (**counselled, counselling**) to advise. — **keep one's own counsel** to keep one's opinions and intentions to oneself. [from Old French *conseil*, from Latin *consilium*, advice]

⊟ *noun* 1 advice, suggestion, recommendation, guidance, direction, information. 2 consultation, discussion, deliberation, consideration, forethought. 3 lawyer, advocate, solicitor, attorney, barrister. *verb* advise, warn, caution, suggest, recommend, advocate, urge, exhort, guide, direct, instruct.

counsellor or North Amer. **counselor** *noun* 1 an adviser. 2 a lawyer.

count[1] — *verb* 1 *intrans.* to recite (numbers) in ascending order up to a given value: *count to five.* 2 to add up (a series of numbers or items) in order to determine their sum or total amount. 3 to include. 4 *intrans.* to be important; to matter; to have an effect or value. 5 consider; regard: *count yourself lucky.* — *noun* 1 an act of counting. 2 the number reached by adding up a series of numbers or items. 3 a charge brought against an accused person. 4 a single response registered by an instrument used to detect or measure ionizing radiation. 5 the total number of responses registered by such an instrument. — **count someone** or **something in** to include them. **count me in** or **out** I am willing, or not willing, to be included. **count on someone** or **something** to rely on them. **count someone out** 1 to declare (a floored boxer) to have lost the match if he is unable to get up within a count of ten seconds. 2 to exclude them from consideration. **count something out** to lay down or present items one at a time while counting: *counted out five pounds each.* **keep** or **lose count** to keep, or fail to keep, a note of the running total. **out for the count** 1 *said of a boxer* unable to rise to his feet within a count of ten. 2 unconscious. 3 *facetious* fast asleep. [from Old French *cunter*, from Latin *computare*]

⊟ *verb* 1 number, enumerate, list. 2 add, total, tot up, reckon, calculate, compute, tell, check, score. 4 matter, signify, qualify. 5 consider, regard, deem, judge, think, reckon, hold. *noun* 1 numbering, enumeration, poll, reckoning, calculation, computation. 2 sum, total, tally. **count on** rely on, depend on, bank on, reckon on, expect, believe, trust.

count[2] *noun* a European nobleman equal in rank to a British earl. [from Latin *comes*, companion]

countable *adj.* 1 able to be counted. 2 *Grammar, said of a noun* capable of being used with *a* or *an*, or in the plural.

countdown *noun* a count backwards, with zero as the moment for action, used eg in launching a rocket.

countenance /ˈkaʊntənəns/ — *noun* face; expression or appearance. — *verb* to allow; to tolerate. — **give countenance to something** to support a proposal, etc. **keep one's countenance** to remained composed, manage not to laugh, etc. [from Old French *contenance*, from Latin *continentia*, self-control]

counter[1] *noun* 1 a long flat-topped fitting in a shop, cafeteria, bank, etc over which goods are sold, food is served, or business transacted. 2 a small flat disc used as a playing-piece in various board games. 3 a disc-shaped token used as a substitute coin. 4 a device for counting something. — **over the counter** by the normal method of sale in a shop, etc. **under the counter** by secret illegal sale, or by unlawful means. [from Latin *computare*, to reckon]

counter[2] — *verb trans., intrans.* (**countered, countering**) to oppose, act against, or hit back. — *adv.* (**counter to something**) in the opposite direction to it; in contradiction of it: *results ran counter to expectations.* — *noun* 1 a return blow; an opposing move. 2 an opposite or contrary. 3 something that can be used to one's advantage in negotiating or bargaining. 4 *Naut.* the curved, overhanging part of a ship's stern. [from Old French *contre*, against]

⊟ *verb* oppose, hit back, retaliate, respond, answer, retort, return, parry, resist, meet, offset. *adv.* against, in opposition.

counter- *prefix* 1 against: *counter-attack.* 2 in competition or rivalry: *counter-attraction.* 3 matching or corresponding: *counterpart.* [from Old French *contre*, against]

counteract *verb* to reduce or prevent the effect of.

⊟ neutralize, counterbalance, offset, countervail, negate, annul, invalidate, undo, act against, oppose, resist, hinder, check, thwart, frustrate, foil, defeat.
⊞ support, assist.

counteraction *noun* resistance, opposition.

counteractive *adj.* tending to counteract.

counter-attack — *noun* an attack in response to an attack. — *verb intrans.* to attack in return.

counter-attraction *noun* a rival attraction.

counterbalance — *noun* a weight, force, or circumstance that balances another and cancels it out. — *verb* to act as a counterbalance to; to neutralize or cancel out.

counterblast *noun* a vigorous and indignant verbal or written response.

counter-charge *noun* an accusation made in response to one made against oneself.

counter-claim *noun* a claim or assertion made in opposition to one made by someone else.

counter-clockwise *adj.*, *adv.* anticlockwise.

counter-culture *noun* a culture that rejects or opposes the values of the culture of the majority.

counter-espionage *noun* activities undertaken to frustrate spying by an enemy or rival.

counterfeit /'kaʊntəfiːt/ — *adj.* **1** made in imitation of a genuine article, especially with the purpose of deceiving; forged. **2** not genuine; insincere. — *verb* **1** to copy for a dishonest purpose; to forge. **2** to pretend: *counterfeit friendship.* [from Old French *contrefait*, copied, from Latin *contra-*, against + *facere*, to make]

. . . .

■ *adj.* forged, fake, imitation, artificial, false, *colloq.* phoney, copied, fraudulent, bogus, pseudo, sham. **2** insincere, false, fake, *colloq.* phoney, simulated, feigned, pretended, fraudulent, bogus, pseudo, sham, spurious. *verb* **1** fake, forge, impersonate. **2** pretend, feign, simulate.
■ *adj.* GENUINE. **1** authentic, real.
. . . .

counterfoil *noun* the section of a cheque, receipt, ticket, etc retained as a record by the person who issues it. [from Latin *folium*, leaf]

counter-insurgency *noun* military action taken against insurgents or rebels.

counter-intelligence *noun* counter-espionage.

countermand *verb* to cancel (an order or command). [from Old French *contremander*, from Latin *contra-*, against + *mandare*, to order]

counter-measure *noun* an action taken to counteract a threat, dangerous development, or move.

counter-offensive *noun* an aggressive move made in response to an initial attack.

counterpane *noun* a coverlet; a bedspread. [from Old French *coitepoint*, quilt, from Latin *culcita puncta*, quilted mattress]

counterpart *noun* the matching or corresponding person or thing elsewhere.

. . . .

■ twin, opposite number, equivalent, duplicate, copy, fellow, mate, match, complement, supplement.
. . . .

counterpoint *noun Mus.* **1** the combining of two or more melodies sung or played simultaneously into a harmonious whole. **2** a part or melody combined with another. See also CONTRAPUNTAL.

counterpoise *noun* **1** a state of balance between two weights. **2** something that counterbalances.

counter-productive *adj.* tending to undermine productiveness and efficiency; having the opposite effect to that intended.

counter-revolution *noun* a revolution to overthrow a system of government established by a previous revolution.

counter-revolutionary — *adj.* opposing revolution or a revolution. — *noun* a person involved in a counter-revolution.

countersign — *verb* to sign (a document, etc already signed by someone else) by way of confirmation. — *noun* a password or signal used in response to a sentry's challenge.

counter-signature *noun* a name countersigned on a document.

countersink *verb* (PAST TENSE **countersank**; PAST PARTICIPLE **countersunk**) **1** to widen the upper part of (a screw hole) so that the top of the screw when inserted will be level with the surrounding surface. **2** to insert (a screw) into such a hole.

counter-tenor *noun* an adult male singer who sings falsetto, using the same range as a female alto.

counterweight *noun* a counterbalancing weight.

countess *noun* **1** the wife or widow of an earl or count. **2** a woman with the rank of earl or count. [from Old French *contesse*, from Latin *comitissa*, feminine of *comes*, companion]

countless *adj.* so many as to be impossible to count.

. . . .

■ innumerable, myriad, numberless, unnumbered, untold, incalculable, infinite, endless, immeasurable, measureless, limitless.
▣ finite, limited.
. . . .

countrified /'kʌntrɪfaɪd/ *adj.* rural; rustic in appearance or style.

country /'kʌntrɪ/ *noun* (PL. **countries**) **1** the land of any of the nations of the world. **2** the population of such land. **3** one's native land. **4** open land, with moors, woods, hills, fields, etc, as distinct from towns, etc. **5** land having a certain character or connection: *Burns country.* **6** an area of knowledge or experience: *back in the familiar country of simple arithmetic.* — **across country** not keeping to roads. **go to the country** to dissolve parliament and hold a general election. [from Latin *contrata terra*, land lying in front of one]

. . . .

■ **1** state, nation, people, kingdom, realm, principality. **4** countryside, green belt, farmland, provinces, *colloq.* sticks, backwoods, wilds. **5** terrain, land, territory, region, area, district. **6** province, area, territory.
▣ **4** town, city.
. . . .

country-and-western — *adj.* denoting a style of music popular among white people of the Southern USA. — *noun* folk music or songs in this style.

country club a club in a rural area with facilities for sport and recreation.

country dance a traditional British dance in which partners face each other in parallel lines.

country dancing the performance of country dances.

country house or **country seat** a landowner's large house in the country.

countryman or **countrywoman** *noun* **1** a man or woman who lives in a rural area. **2** a man or woman belonging to the same country as oneself.

countryside *noun* land outside or away from towns.

. . . .

■ country, green belt, farmland, landscape, scenery.
. . . .

countrywide *adj.* all over the country.

county — *noun* (PL. **counties**) **1** any of the geographical divisions within England, Wales, and Ireland that form the larger units of local government. **2** in the USA, the main administrative subdivision within a state. — *adj. derog. colloq.* typical of the landed gentry. [from Old French *conte*]

. . . .

■ *noun* PROVINCE, SHIRE, REGION, AREA, DISTRICT.
. . . .

county court a local court for non-criminal cases.

county town the chief town of a county, acting as its seat of administration.

coup /ku:/ *noun* **1** a successful move. **2** a coup d'état. [from French *coup*, stroke or blow]

coup de grâce /ku: də 'grɑːs/ a final decisive blow. [French, = blow of mercy]

coup d'état /ku: deɪ'tɑː/ (PL. **coups d'état**) the sudden, usually violent, overthrow of a government. [French, = stroke of the state]

coupe /ku:p/ *noun* a dessert made with fruit and ice cream. [from French *coupe*, glass, cup]

coupé /ku:'peɪ/ *noun* a four-seated two-door car with a sloping rear. [from French *coupé*, from *couper*, to cut]

couple /'kʌpl/ — *noun* **1** a man and wife, boyfriend and girlfriend, or other pair of people romantically attached. **2** a pair of partners, eg for dancing. **3** two, or a few. **4** *Physics* a pair of equal but opposite forces that are applied to different points on the same object, producing a turning effect or *torque*. — *verb* **1** to link; to connect. **2** *intrans.* to have sexual intercourse.

▣ *noun* **1, 2** pair. **3** pair, brace, twosome, duo. *verb* **1** pair, unite, join, link, connect, fasten, hitch, clasp, buckle, yoke, match, marry, wed.

couplet /'kʌplɪt/ *noun* a pair of consecutive lines of verse, especially rhyming. [diminutive of COUPLE]

coupling /'kʌplɪŋ/ *noun* **1** a link for joining things together. **2** *derog.* the act of having sexual intercourse.

coupon /'ku:pɒn/ *noun* **1** a slip of paper entitling one to something, eg a discount. **2** a detachable order form, competition entry form, etc printed on packaging, etc. **3** a betting form for football pools. [from Old French *colpon*, piece cut off]

▣ **1** voucher, token, slip, check, ticket, certificate. **2** slip.

courage /'kʌrɪd/ *noun* **1** bravery. **2** cheerfulness or resolution in coping with setbacks. — **have the courage of one's convictions** to be brave enough to act in accordance with one's beliefs. **pluck up courage** or **take one's courage in both hands** to become resolved to meet a challenge. **take courage** to be resolute or cheerful in difficult circumstances. [from Old French *corage*, from Latin *cor*, heart]

▣ **1** bravery, pluck, *colloq.* guts, fearlessness, dauntlessness, heroism, gallantry, valour, boldness, audacity, nerve, daring. **2** resolution, fortitude, spirit, mettle.
▣ **1** cowardice, fear.

courageous /kə'reɪdʒəs/ *adj.* having or showing courage.

▣ brave, *colloq.* plucky, fearless, dauntless, indomitable, heroic, gallant, valiant, lion-hearted, hardy, bold, audacious, daring, intrepid, resolute.
▣ cowardly, afraid.

courageously *adv.* in a courageous way.
courageousness *noun* possession of courage.

courante /ku'rɑːnt/ *noun* a lively dance in triple time, originating in the 16c; also, a piece of music for it. [from French *danse courante*, running dance]

courgette /kɔː'ʒet/ *noun* a small variety of marrow, which can be cooked and eaten as a vegetable. Also called ZUC-CHINI. [from French *courgette*]

courier /'kʊrɪə(r)/ *noun* **1** a guide who travels with, and looks after, parties of tourists. **2** a messenger. [from Old French *courier*, from Latin *currere*, to run]

course /kɔːs/ — *noun* **1** the path that anything moves in. **2** a direction taken or planned: *go off course*. **3** the channel of a river, etc. **4** the normal progress of something. **5** the passage of a period of time: *in the course of the next hour*. **6** a line of action: *your best course is to wait*. **7** a series of lessons, etc. **8** a prescribed treatment, eg medicine to be taken, over a period. **9** any of the successive parts of a meal. **10** (*often in compounds*) the ground over which a game is played or a race run. **11** *Archit.* a single row of bricks or stones in a wall, etc. — *verb* **1** *intrans.* to move or flow. **2** *trans.* to hunt (hares, etc) using dogs. — **in the course of something** while doing it; during it. **in the course of time** eventually. **in due course** at the appropriate or expected time. **a matter of course** a natural or expected action or result. **of course 1** as expected. **2** naturally; certainly; without doubt. **3** admittedly. **stay the course** to endure to the end. [from Old French *cours*, from Latin *currere*, to run]

▣ *noun* **1, 2** path, direction, way, track, road, route, channel, trail, line, circuit, orbit, trajectory, flight path. **4** progress, advance, development, furtherance, flow, movement, order, sequence, series, succession, progression. **5** duration, time, period, term, passage. **6** plan, policy, schedule, programme, procedure, method, mode. **7** lessons, lectures, studies, classes, curriculum, syllabus. **10** track, ground.

coursebook *noun* a book to accompany a course of instruction.

courser *noun* **1** a person who courses hares, etc, or a hound used for this. **2** *poetic* a swift horse. **3** any of nine species of fast-running bird, native to Africa and S Asia, having pale sandy plumage, a long curved bill, short strong wings, long legs, and three forward-pointing toes on each foot.

coursing *noun* hunting hares with dogs.

court /kɔːt/ — *noun* **1** the judge, law officials, and members of the jury gathered to hear and decide on a legal case. **2** the room (*also* **courtroom**) or building (*also* **court-house**) used for such a hearing. **3** an area marked out for a particular game, or a division of this. **4** an open space or square surrounded by houses or by sections of a building. **5** (**Court**) a name used for a group of houses so arranged, or for a block of flats or for a country mansion. **6** the palace, household, attendants, and advisers of a sovereign. — *verb* **1** *trans., intrans. old use* to try to win the love of. **2** to try to win the favour of. **3** to seek (popularity, etc). **4** to risk or invite: *court danger.* — **the ball is in his** or **your,** etc **court** he, you, etc must make the next move. **go to court to take legal action. hold court** to be surrounded by a circle of admirers. **out of court** without legal action being taken: *settle out of court.* **pay court to someone** to pay them flattering attention. **put** or **rule something out of court** to prevent it from being heard or considered. **take someone to court** to bring a legal case against them. [from Old French *cort*, from Latin *cohors* or *cors*, yard]

▣ *noun* **1** lawcourt, bench, bar, tribunal, trial, session. **2** lawcourt. **4** courtyard, yard, quadrangle, square, cloister, forecourt, enclosure. **6** entourage, attendants, retinue, suite, train.

court card *Cards* the king, queen, or jack.

courteous /'kɜːtɪəs/ *adj.* polite; considerate; respectful. [from Old French *corteis*, from *cort*, court]

▣ polite, civil, considerate, respectful, well-mannered, well-bred, ladylike, gentlemanly, gracious, obliging, attentive, gallant, courtly, urbane, debonair, refined, polished.
▣ discourteous, impolite, rude.

courteously *adv.* with a courteous manner.
courteousness *noun* the quality of being courteous.

courtesan /'kɔːtɪzan/ *noun Hist.* a prostitute with wealthy or noble clients. [from Old French *courtisane*, from Italian *cortigiana*, woman of the court]

courtesy /'kɜːtəsɪ/ *noun* (PL. **courtesies**) **1** courteous behaviour; politeness. **2** a courteous act. — **by courtesy of someone 1** by their permission. **2** *colloq.* from them. [from Old French *corteisie*, from *corteis*, courteous]

▣ **1** politeness, civility, respect, manners, breeding, graciousness, consideration, attention, gallantry, urbanity. ▣ DISCOURTESY. **1** rudeness.

courtesy title a frequently used but legally invalid title, eg 'Lord' before the first name of a peer's younger son.
courtier / 'kɔːtɪə(r)/ *noun* **1** a person in attendance at a royal court. **2** an elegant flatterer. [from Old French *courteiour*, attendant at court]

▣ **1** noble, nobleman, noblewoman, lord, lady, steward, page, attendant, follower. **2** flatterer, sycophant, toady.

courtliness / 'kɔːtlɪnəs/ *noun* being courtly.
courtly / 'kɔːtlɪ/ *adj.* having fine manners.
court-martial — *noun* (PL. **courts-martial, court-martials**) a trial, by a group of officers, of a member of the armed forces, for a breach of military law. — *verb* to try by court-martial.
court order a direction or command of a judiciary court which, if not complied with, may lead to criminal proceedings against the offender or offenders.
courtroom *noun* a room in which a lawcourt is held.
courtship *noun* the courting or wooing of an intended spouse; the period for which this lasts.
court shoe a woman's shoe in a plain, low-cut style.
courtyard *noun* an open space surrounded by buildings or walls.

▣ yard, quadrangle, *colloq.* quad, area, enclosure, court.

couscous / 'kuskus/ *noun* a N African dish of crushed wheat steamed and served eg with meat. [from French *couscous*, from Arabic *kuskus*]
cousin / 'kʌzən/ *noun* (*also* **first cousin**) a son or daughter of one's uncle or aunt. [from Old French *cosin*, from Latin *con-*, with + *sobrinus*, cousin]
cousin once removed (*also* **first cousin once removed**) a son or daughter of one's cousin.
couture / kʊ'tjʊə(r)/ *noun* the designing, making, and selling of fashionable clothes. [from French *couture*, sewing]
couturier / kʊ'tjʊərɪeɪ/ *noun* a fashion designer.
couturière / kʊ'tjʊərɪeə(r)/ *noun* a female fashion designer.
covalent / koʊ'veɪlənt/ *adj. Chem.* denoting a chemical bond in which two atoms are held together by the sharing of a pair of electrons between them.
covariance / koʊ'veərɪəns/ *noun* **1** the property of varying concomitantly. **2** *Maths.* a statistic that is used to measure the agreement between two sets of random variables, and differs from correlation in that it is dependent on the scale used to measure the variables.
cove[1] *noun* a small and usually sheltered bay or inlet on a rocky coast. [from Anglo-Saxon *cofa*, room]

▣ bay, bight, inlet, estuary, firth, creek.

cove[2] *noun old colloq. use* a fellow.
coven / 'kʌvən/ *noun* a gathering of witches. [from Old French *covin*, from Latin *convenire*, to meet]
covenant / 'kʌvənənt/ — *noun* **1** a formal written promise to pay a sum of money regularly, eg to a charity. **2** *Legal* a formal sealed agreement. **3** *Biblical* God's agreement with the Israelites. — *verb trans., intrans.* to agree by covenant to do something.
covenanter / 'kʌvənəntə(r)/ *noun* **1** a person who makes a covenant. **2** (**Covenanter**) *Hist.* an adherent of either of two 17c religious covenants defending Presbyterianism in Scotland. [from Old French *covenir*, to agree]
Coventry / 'kɒvəntrɪ/ — **send someone to Coventry**

to refuse to speak to them or associate with them, especially as a punishment or protest. [perhaps from the imprisonment of Royalists in Coventry during the Civil War]

cover / 'kʌvə(r)/ — *verb* (**covered, covering**) **1** to form a layer over. **2** to protect or conceal by putting something over. **3** to clothe. **4** to extend over. **5** to strew, sprinkle, spatter, mark all over, etc. **6** (**be covered with a feeling**, etc) to be overwhelmed by it: *covered with embarrassment.* **7** to deal with (a subject). **8** *said of a reporter, etc* to investigate or report on (a story). **9** to have as one's area of responsibility. **10** to travel (a distance). **11** to be adequate to pay: *cover one's expenses.* **12** to insure; to insure against. **13** to threaten by aiming a gun at. **14** to keep (a building, its exits, etc) under armed watch. **15** to shield with a firearm at the ready or with actual fire. **16** *Sport* to protect (a fellow team-member) or obstruct (an opponent). **17** *said of a stallion, bull, etc* to mate with (a female). **18** *said of a bird* to sit on (eggs). — *noun* **1** something that covers. **2** a lid, top, protective casing, etc. **3** the covering of something: *plants that give good ground cover.* **4** (**covers**) the sheets and blankets on a bed. **5** the paper or board binding of a book, magazine, etc.; one side of this. **6** an envelope: *a first-day cover.* **7** shelter or protection: *take cover.* **8** insurance. **9** service: *Dr Brown will provide emergency cover.* **10** a pretence; a screen; a false identity: *his cover as a salesman was blown.* **11** armed protection; protective fire. **12** *Cricket* cover point. **13** in restaurants, etc, a place setting at table. — **cover for someone** to take over the duties of an absent colleague, etc. **cover something up** to conceal a dishonest act, a mistake, etc. **under cover 1** in secret. **2** within shelter. **under cover of something** using it as a protection or pretence. **under plain cover** in a plain envelope without tradename, etc. **under separate cover** in a separate envelope or parcel. [from Old French *covrir*]

▣ *verb* **1, 5** coat, spread, daub, plaster, encase, wrap, envelop, clothe, strew, sprinkle, spatter. **2** shroud, cloak, veil, screen, mask, disguise, camouflage, obscure, conceal, hide, protect. **4** encompass, embrace, incorporate, embody, involve, include, contain, comprise. **7** deal with, treat, consider, examine, investigate, embrace, encompass. **14, 15** shield, guard, protect, defend. *noun* **1** coating, covering, veil, screen, mask, case, envelope, clothing. **2** lid, top, cap, case, casing. **4** bedclothes. **5** jacket, wrapper. **7** shelter, protection, defence, refuge, shield, guard, concealment. **10** pretence, screen, front, façade, disguise, camouflage. **cover up** conceal, hide, whitewash, dissemble, suppress, *colloq.* hush up, keep dark, repress.

▣ *verb* **1, 3, 5** uncover, strip. **2** uncover, expose. **7** exclude. **cover up** disclose, reveal.

coverage *noun* an amount covered; the fullness of treatment of a news item in any of the media, etc.
coverall / 'kʌvərɔːl/ — *noun* (*usually* **coveralls**) a one-piece protective garment worn over normal clothes. — *adj.* serving many purposes.
cover charge a service charge made per person in a restaurant, etc.
cover girl a girl or woman whose photograph is shown on a magazine cover.
covering *noun* something that covers, especially a blanket, protective casing, etc.

▣ layer, coat, coating, blanket, casing, housing, wrapping, clothing, mask, overlay, cover, top, roof, crust, shell, film, veneer, skin, shelter, protection.

covering letter a letter accompanying and explaining documents or goods.
coverlet *noun* a thin top cover for a bed; a bedspread or counterpane. [from Old French *cuver-lit*, cover-bed]
cover note a temporary certificate of insurance.

cover point *Cricket* the fielding position forward and to the right of the batsman.

covert /'kʌvət/ — *adj.* secret; secretive; stealthy. — *noun* **1** a thicket or woodland providing cover for game. **2** a shelter for animals. **3** *Zool.* any of the small feathers that surround the bases of the large quill feathers of the wings and tail of a bird. [from Old French *covert*, past participle of *covrir*, to cover]

covertly *adv.* in a secretive way.

cover-up *noun* an act of concealing or withholding information about something suspect or illicit.

▣ concealment, whitewash, smokescreen, front, façade, pretence, conspiracy, complicity.

cover version an artist's version of a song, etc already recorded by someone else.

covet /'kʌvɪt/ *verb* (**coveted, coveting**) to long to possess (something belonging to someone else). [from Old French *coveitier*, from Latin *cupiditas*, longing, greed]

▣ envy, begrudge, crave, long for, yearn for, hanker for, want, desire.

covetous *adj.* envious, greedy.

covetously *adv.* in a covetous way.

covetousness *noun* jealous desire.

covey /'kʌvɪ/ *noun* (PL. **coveys**) **1** a small flock of game birds of one kind, especially grouse or partridge. **2** a small group of people. [from Old French *covee*, from *cover*, to hatch]

cow[1] *noun* **1** the mature female of any bovine animal, especially domesticated cattle. **2** the mature female of certain other mammals, such as the elephant, whale, and seal. **3** loosely used to refer to any domestic breed of cattle. **4** a term of abuse for a woman. — **till the cows come home** *colloq.* for an unforeseeably long time. [from Anglo-Saxon *cu*]

cow[2] *verb* to frighten into submission. [from Old Norse *kuga*, to subdue]

coward *noun* **1** someone easily frightened, or lacking courage to face danger or difficulty. **2** someone who acts brutally towards the weak or undefended. [from Old French *couard*, from Latin *cauda*, tail]

▣ *colloq.* chicken, *slang* yellow-belly, *colloq.* wimp, craven, faint-heart, renegade, deserter.
▣ hero.

cowardice /'kɑʊədɪs/ or **cowardliness** *noun* lack of courage.

▣ cowardliness, faint-heartedness, timorousness, spinelessness.
▣ bravery, courage, valour.

cowardly *adj.* like a coward.

▣ faint-hearted, craven, *colloq.* chicken, *colloq.* chicken-hearted, *colloq.* chicken-livered, *slang* yellow, *slang* yellow-bellied, *colloq.* spineless, weak, weak-kneed, timorous, soft, fearful, scared, unheroic.
▣ brave, courageous, heroic, bold.

cowbell *noun* a bell hanging from a cow's neck.

cowberry *noun* a small evergreen shrub (Vaccinium vitis-idaea), native to N temperate regions, up to 30cm tall, and having oval leaves (often notched at the tip), drooping bell-shaped pinkish-white flowers borne in terminal clusters, and edible red berries.

cowboy *noun* **1** in the western USA, a man in charge of cattle, especially as a character in films of the Wild West.

2 *derog.* someone who undertakes building or other work without proper training or qualifications; a dishonest businessman or entrepreneur.

cowcatcher *noun* a concave metal fender on the front of a railway engine for clearing cattle and other obstacles from the line.

cower *verb intrans.* (**cowered, cowering**) to shrink away in fear. [from Middle English *couren*]

▣ shrink, flinch, cringe, quail.

cowhand, cowherd same as COWMAN.

cowhide *noun* a cow's hide made into leather.

cowl *noun* **1** a monk's large loose hood or hooded habit. **2** a revolving cover for a chimney-pot for improving ventilation. **3** a cowling. [from Anglo-Saxon *cugele*, from Latin *cucullus*, hood]

cowlick *noun* a lock of hair standing up stiffly from the forehead.

cowling *noun* the streamlined metal casing, usually having hinged or removable panels, that houses the engine of an aircraft or other vehicle.

cowman or **cowhand** or **cowherd** *noun* a person who assists with cattle or has charge of them.

co-worker *noun* a fellow worker; a colleague.

cow parsley a biennial or perennial plant (Anthriscus sylvestris), native to Europe, Asia, and N Africa, and growing up to 1.5m tall. Also called QUEEN ANNE'S LACE.

cowpat *noun* a flat circular deposit of cow dung.

cow pea *Bot.* an annual plant (Vigna sinensis) that is a legume, cultivated in various parts of the world for its edible seeds.

cowpox *noun Medicine* a viral infection of the udders of cows that can be transmitted to humans by direct contact, and causes mild symptoms so similar to smallpox that an attack confers immunity. The virus is used as a smallpox vaccine.

cowrie or **cowry** *noun* **1** any of about 150 species of marine snail, found mainly in tropical waters, having a colourful egg-shaped shell, the opening of which is in the form of a narrow slit. **2** the brightly coloured glossy egg-shaped shell of this animal, often highly patterned, a popular collector's item, and even used as currency in parts of Africa and S Asia. [from Hindi *kauri*]

cowshed or **cowhouse** *noun* a building for housing cattle.

cowslip *noun* a perennial plant (Primula veris), native to Europe and Asia, found mainly on chalky soils, and having a rosette of oval, slightly crinkled leaves, and small deep yellow flowers borne in a drooping slightly one-sided cluster. [from Anglo-Saxon *cuslyppe*, cow dung]

cox — *noun* short for coxswain. — *verb trans., intrans.* to act as cox of (a boat).

coxcomb /'kɒkskoʊm/ *noun old derog. use* a foolishly vain or conceited man. [a contraction of *cock's comb*; originally applied to jesters from their comb-like headgear]

coxless *adj.*, *said of a rowing boat, especially in racing* having no cox.

coxswain /'kɒksən/ *noun* **1** the person who steers a small boat. **2** a petty officer in a small ship. [from *cock*, ship's boat + SWAIN]

coy *adj.* **1** shy; modest; affectedly bashful. **2** irritatingly uncommunicative about something. [from Old French *coi*, calm, from Latin *quietus*, quiet]

▣ **1** shy, modest, bashful, demure, shrinking, prudish, diffident, timid, backward, retiring, self-effacing, reserved, arch, flirtatious, coquettish, skittish, kittenish. **2** evasive.
▣ **1** bold, forward.

coyly *adv.* in a coy way.

coyness *noun* being coy.

coyote /kɔɪ'oʊtɪ/ *noun* (PL. **coyote, coyotes**) a small N

American wolf with a pointed face, tawny fur, and a black-tipped bushy tail, originally found mainly in deserts, prairies, and open woodland, but now increasingly known as an urban scavenger. Also called PRAIRIE WOLF. [from Aztec *coyotl*]

coypu /'kɔɪpuː/ *noun* (PL. **coypu**, **coypus**) a large aquatic rodent, native to S America and introduced to Europe and N America as a result of escape from captivity. It is related to the porcupine and resembles a giant rat, over 1m long, with a broad blunt muzzle and webbed hind feet. [from a S American Indian language]

CPAG *abbrev.* Child Poverty Action Group.

CPGB *abbrev.* Communist Party of Great Britain.

CPO *abbrev.* Chief Petty Officer.

CPR *abbrev.* Canadian Pacific Railway.

CPRE *abbrev.* Council for the Protection of Rural England.

CPSA *abbrev.* Civil and Public Services Association.

CPU *abbrev. Comput.* central processing unit.

CR *abbrev., as an international vehicle mark* Costa Rica.

Cr *symbol Chem.* chromium.

crab *noun* **1** any of about 4500 species of crustacean belonging to the order Decapoda, most of which have a hard flattened shell and five pairs of jointed legs. Most crabs are marine, although there are a number of freshwater species. Many crabs are used as food. **2** (**Crab**) the sign of the zodiac and constellation Cancer. **3** a the crab louse. b (**crabs**) infestation by this. — **catch a crab** in rowing, either to sink the oar too deeply or to miss the water. [from Anglo-Saxon *crabba*]

crab apple 1 a large deciduous shrub or small tree (Malus sylvestris), native to north temperate regions. **2** the hard round fruit of this tree, which has sour flesh surrounded by a yellowish-green skin, sometimes tinged with red when ripe. [from Middle English *crabbe*]

crabbed /'krabɪd/ *adj.* **1** bad-tempered. **2** *said of handwriting* cramped and hard to decipher. [from CRAB]

crabbedly *adv.* in a crabbed way.

crabbedness *noun* bad temper.

crabby *adj.* (**crabbier, crabbiest**) *colloq.* bad-tempered. [from CRAB]

crab louse a crab-shaped parasitic louse that infests the hair of the pubic region in humans.

crabwise *adj., adv.* moving sideways.

crack — *verb* **1** *trans., intrans.* to fracture partially without falling to pieces. **2** *trans., intrans.* to split. **3** *trans., intrans.* to make or cause to make a sudden sharp noise. **4** *trans., intrans.* to strike sharply. **5** *trans., intrans.* to give way or cause to give way: *crack someone's resistance.* **6** to force open (a safe). **7** to solve (a code or problem). **8** to tell (a joke). **9** *intrans., said of the voice* to change pitch or tone suddenly and unintentionally. **10** *Chem. trans., intrans.* to break down long-chain hydrocarbons produced during petroleum refining into lighter more useful short-chain products. — *noun* **1** a sudden sharp sound. **2** a fracture in a material produced by an external force or internal stress, often originating in a defective region of the material. **3** a narrow opening. **4** a resounding blow. **5** *colloq.* a joke. **6** *Irish colloq.* (also CRAIC) fun and entertainment: *It's good crack in here.* **7** *slang* a highly addictive derivative of cocaine, consisting of hard crystalline lumps that are heated and 'smoked' (inhaled) as a stimulant. Habitual use leads to physical and mental deterioration, and addiction to crack is a serious social problem in some countries. — *adj. colloq.* expert: *a crack shot.* — **at the crack of dawn** *colloq.* at daybreak; very early. **crack down on someone** or **something** *colloq.* to take firm action against them. **crack up** to suffer an emotional breakdown. **crack something up** *colloq.* to praise it extravagantly. **not all it's cracked up to be** not as good as people say it is. **a fair crack of the whip** a fair opportunity. **get cracking** *colloq.* to make a prompt start with a journey, undertaking, etc. **have a crack at something** *colloq.* to attempt it. [from Anglo-Saxon *cracian*, to resound]

⊟ *verb* **1, 2** fracture, break, split, snap. **3** explode, burst, pop,

crackle, snap, crash. **4** strike, hit, clap, slap, *colloq.* whack. **5** break, shatter. **7** solve, decipher, work out. **9** break. *noun* **1** burst, pop, snap, crash, explosion. **2** fracture, break. **3** split, gap, crevice, chink, line, flaw, rift. **4** blow, clap, smack, slap, *colloq.* whack. **5** joke, quip, witticism, *colloq.* gag, wisecrack, gibe, dig. *adj.* first-class, first-rate, *colloq.* top-notch, excellent, superior, choice, hand-picked. **crack down on** clamp down on, end, stop, put a stop to, crush, suppress, check, repress, act against. **crack up** break down, go to pieces, collapse, go mad.

crackbrained *adj. colloq.* mad; crazy.

crackdown *noun* a firm action taken against someone or something.

cracked *adj.* **1** *colloq.* crazy; mad. **2** *said of a voice* harsh; uneven in tone.

cracker *noun* **1** a thin crisp unsweetened biscuit. **2** a small noisy firework. **3** a party toy in the form of a gaudy paper tube usually containing a paper hat, gift, and motto, that pulls apart with an explosive bang. **4** *colloq.* an attractive or exciting person, especially a young woman. **5** *Comput.* someone who breaks into a system, especially with malicious intent.

crackers *adj. colloq.* mad.

cracking *colloq.* — *adj.* **1** very good. **2** very fast: *a cracking pace.* — *adv.* used for emphasis: *a cracking good story.* — *noun Chem.* same as CATALYTIC CRACKING.

crackling *noun* the crisp skin of roast pork. [from CRACK]

crackly *adj.* **1** producing a crackling sound. **2** brittle, crisp.

cracknel *noun* **1** a light brittle biscuit. **2** a hard nutty filling for chocolates. **3** (**cracknels**) *North Amer.* crisply fried pieces of fat pork. [from Middle English *krakenelle*]

crackpot *colloq.* — *adj.* crazy. — *noun* a crazy person.

-cracy *combining form* denoting rule, government, or domination by a particular group, etc: *democracy.* [from Greek *kratos*, power]

cradle — *noun* **1** a cot for a small baby, especially one that can be rocked. **2** a place of origin; the home or source of something: *the cradle of civilization.* **3** a suspended platform or cage for workmen engaged in the construction, repair, or painting of a ship or building. **4** the support for the receiver on an old-style telephone. — *verb* to rock or hold gently: *cradle a baby in one's arms.* — **from the cradle to the grave** throughout one's life. [from Anglo-Saxon *kradol*]

⊟ *noun* **1** cot, crib, bed. **2** source, origin, spring, wellspring, fount, fountainhead, birthplace, beginning. *verb* hold, rock, nurse, support, lull, nurture, tend.

cradle-snatcher *noun derog.* someone who chooses a much younger person as a lover or marriage partner.

craft — *noun* **1** (*also in compounds*) a skill or occupation, especially one requiring the use of the hands: *crafts such as weaving and pottery.* **2** skilled ability. **3** cunning. **4** (PL. **craft**) (*often in compounds*) a boat or ship, or an air or space vehicle. — *verb* to make skilfully. [from Anglo-Saxon *cræft*]

⊟ *noun* **1** skill, occupation, art, handicraft, handiwork, trade, job, work. **2** skill, expertise, mastery, talent, knack, ability, aptitude, dexterity. **3** craftiness, artfulness, shrewdness, cleverness. **4** boat, ship, vessel, aircraft, spacecraft, spaceship.

craftily *adv.* in a crafty way.

craftiness *noun* being crafty.

craftsman or **craftswoman** *noun* a man or woman skilled at a craft.

⊟ artisan, maker, wright, smith, technician, master.

craftsmanship *noun* the skill of a craftsman or craftswoman.

....

◨ skill, workmanship, expertise, mastery, artistry, technique, dexterity.

....

crafty *adj.* (**craftier, craftiest**) clever, shrewd, cunning, or sly.

....

◨ clever, shrewd, cunning, sly, artful, wily, devious, canny, sharp, astute, subtle, scheming, calculating, designing.
◲ artless, naïve.

....

crag *noun* a rocky peak or jagged outcrop of rock. [from Celtic *crag*, related to Welsh *craig* and Gaelic *creag*]

cragginess *noun* being craggy.

craggy *adj.* (**craggier, craggiest**) **1** full of crags. **2** rough. **3** rugged.

craic /krak/ see CRACK *noun* 6.

cram *verb* (**crammed, cramming**) **1** to stuff full. **2** (**cram something in** or **together**) to push or pack it tightly. **3** *intrans., trans.* to study intensively, or prepare (someone) rapidly, for an examination. [from Anglo-Saxon *crammian*, to stuff full]

....

◨ **1** stuff, pack, crowd, overfill, glut, gorge. **2** stuff, jam, ram, force, press, squeeze, crush, compress.

....

cram-full *adj.* full to bursting.

crammer *noun* a person or school that prepares pupils for examinations by rapid study.

cramp[1] — *noun* **1** an involuntary and prolonged painful contraction of a muscle or a group of muscles, usually caused by overexertion, fatigue, stress, heat, low temperatures, or an imbalance of salts in the body. It often results in temporary partial paralysis of a group of muscles, eg writer's cramp. **2** (**cramps**) severe abdominal pain. — *verb* to restrict tiresomely. — **cramp someone's style** to restrict their scope for creativity or individuality. [from Old French *crampe*]

....

◨ *noun* **1** pins and needles, stiffness. **2** stitch, pain, ache, twinge, pang, contraction, convulsion, spasm, crick. *verb* restrict, hinder, hamper, obstruct, impede, inhibit, handicap, thwart, frustrate, check, confine, shackle, tie.

....

cramp[2] — *noun* (*also* **cramp-iron**) a clamp for holding stone or timbers together. — *verb* to fasten with a cramp. [from Old Dutch *crampe*, hook]

cramped *adj.* **1** *said of a space* too small; overcrowded. **2** *said of handwriting* small and closely written.

....

◨ **1** narrow, tight, uncomfortable, restricted, confined, crowded, packed, squashed, squeezed, overcrowded, *colloq.* jam-packed, congested. **2** squashed.
◲ **1** spacious.

....

crampon *noun* a spiked iron attachment for climbing boots, to improve grip on ice or rock. [from French *crampon*]

cranberry *noun* (PL. **cranberries**) **1** a dwarf evergreen shrub (Vaccinium oxycoccus), native to north temperate regions, found only on boggy acidic soils, and having long slender stems, oval pointed leaves (dark green above and bluish-green beneath) with inrolled margins, and flowers with four pink petals curling backwards and prominent stamens. The fruit is a round red edible berry. **2** the fruit of this plant, a red berry with sour-tasting flesh, used to make sauces, jellies, etc. [from German dialect *kraanbeere*, crane berry]

crane *noun* **1** a machine with a long pivoted arm from which lifting gear is suspended, allowing heavy weights to be moved both horizontally and vertically. **2** a large wading bird with a long neck and long legs, found in marshlands and swamps in N America and throughout most of Europe, Asia, and Africa. [from Anglo-Saxon *cran*]

cranefly *noun* a large fly with a slender body, long slender legs, and narrow spotted wings that are often held well away from the body when the insect is at rest. Also called DADDY-LONG-LEGS.

cranesbill *noun* an annual or perennial plant of the genus Geranium, native to temperate regions, and having leaves with lobes radiating from a central point, and white, purple, or blue flowers with five petals.

cranial *adj.* relating to or in the region of the cranium (the skull).

cranial nerve *Anat.* in vertebrates, one of the ten to twelve pairs of nerves that arise directly from the brain.

craniosacral therapy (ABBREV. **CST**) a form of alternative therapy involving gentle manipulation in order to release tensions and imbalances which are said to arise in the bones and membranes of the skull [from CRANIUM + SACRUM]

cranium *noun* (PL. **crania, craniums**) **1** the dome-shaped part of the skull, consisting of several fused bones, that encloses and protects the brain. **2** the skull. [from Greek *kranion*]

crank *noun* **1** a device consisting of an arm connected to and projecting at right angles from the shaft of an engine or motor, used to communicate motion to or from the shaft, or to convert reciprocating motion into rotary motion or vice versa. **2** a handle bent at right angles and incorporating such a device, used to start an engine or motor by hand. Also called CRANK HANDLE, STARTING HANDLE. **3** *derog.* an eccentric person. — **crank something up 1** to rotate (a shaft) using a crank. **2** to start (an engine or motor) using a crank. [from Anglo-Saxon *crancstæf*, weaving implement]

crank handle a handle bent at right angles, that can be attached to a crank. Also called CRANK, STARTING HANDLE.

crankshaft *noun* the main shaft of an engine or other machine, bearing one or more cranks, used to transmit power from the cranks to the connecting rods to which they are attached.

cranky *adj.* (**crankier, crankiest**) *colloq.* eccentric or faddy.

crannied *adj.* having crannies or narrow openings.

cranny *noun* (PL. **crannies**) **1** a narrow opening; a cleft or crevice. **2** an out-of-the-way corner. [from Middle English *crany*]

crap *coarse slang* — *noun* **1** faeces. **2** nonsense. — *verb intrans.* (**crapped, crapping**) to defecate. [from Middle English *crap*, chaff]

crape see CRÊPE.

craps *sing. noun* a gambling game in which the player rolls two dice.

crapulence *noun* sickness caused by excessive drinking. [from Latin *crapula*, drunkenness]

crapulent or **crapulous** *adj.* suffering from crapulence.

crash — *verb* **1** *trans., intrans.* to fall or strike with a banging or smashing noise. **2** *trans., intrans.* (*usually* **crash into something**) *said of a vehicle* to collide with or cause it to collide with something. **3** *intrans.* to make a deafening noise. **4** *intrans.* to move noisily. **5** *intrans., said of a business or stock exchange* to collapse. **6** *intrans., Comput., said of a computer system or program* to break down completely, usually because of faulty software, failure of memory, or fluctuations in the mains electricity supply. **7** to cause (a computer system or program) to break down completely. **8** *slang* to gatecrash. **9** (*usually* **crash out**) *slang* to fall asleep; to sleep the night. — *noun* **1** a violent impact or breakage, or the sound of it. **2** a deafening noise. **3** a traffic or aircraft accident; a collision. **4** the collapse of a business or the stock exchange. **5** the sudden failure or complete breakdown of a computer system or program. — *adj.* concentrated or intensive, so as to produce results in minimum time: *a crash diet*. [imitative]

▤ *verb* **1** fall, topple, pitch, plunge, collapse, bang, bump, bash, smash, dash. **2** *colloq.* prang, collide, hit, bump. **3** rumble, thunder, boom, roar, blast. **4** lumber, stomp, charge, clatter. **5** collapse, fail, fold (up), go under, *colloq.* go bust. *noun* **1** bang, clash, clatter, clang, thud, thump. **2** boom, thunder, roar, blast, racket, din. **3** accident, collision, bump, *colloq.* smash, pile-up. **4** collapse, failure, ruin, downfall, bankruptcy.

crash barrier a protective metal barrier along the edge of a road or carriageway.

crash dive a rapid emergency dive by a submarine.

crash-dive *verb intrans.* to make a crash dive.

crash helmet a protective helmet worn eg by motorcyclists.

crashing *adj. colloq.* utter; great: *a crashing bore.*

crash-land *verb trans., intrans., said of an aircraft* to make an abrupt emergency landing, usually without lowering the undercarriage and with the risk of crashing.

crash-landing *noun* in an emergency, the abrupt landing of an aircraft, with resultant damage.

crass *adj.* **1** gross; downright. **2** colossally stupid. **3** utterly tactless or insensitive. [from Latin *crassus*, thick, stupid]

crassly *adv.* in a crass way.

crassness *noun* being crass.

-crat *combining form* forming nouns and adjectives corresponding to words in *-cracy: democrat.*

crate — *noun* **1** a strong wooden, plastic, or metal case with partitions, for carrying breakable or perishable goods. **2** *derog. slang* a decrepit vehicle or aircraft. — *verb* to pack in a crate. [from Latin *cratis*, wickerwork barrier]

▤ *noun* container, box, case, tea chest, packing-case.

crater *noun* **1** the bowl-shaped mouth of a volcano or geyser. **2** a bowl-shaped depression in the ground, usually having steep sides, formed by the impact of a falling body such as a meteorite, or by an exploding bomb, shell, or mine. **3** a circular rimmed depression in the surface of the moon. [from Greek *krater*, mixing-bowl]

-cratic *combining form* forming adjectives corresponding to nouns in *-cracy: democratic.*

craton *noun Geol.* a relatively rigid and immobile part of the Earth's crust that has been stable for at least 1500m years. [from Greek *kratos*, strength]

cravat /krə'vat/ *noun* a formal style of neckerchief worn by men instead of a tie. [from French *cravate*, an imitation of the neckwear of the Cravates (Croatians)]

crave *verb* **1** (**crave something** or **crave for** or **after something**) to long for it; to desire it overwhelmingly. **2** *old formal use* to ask for politely; to beg. [from Anglo-Saxon *crafian*]

▤ **1** long for, desire, want, hunger for, thirst for, yearn for, pine for, hanker after, fancy.

craven *old derog. use* — *adj.* cowardly; cringing. — *noun* a coward. [from Middle English *cravant*, defeated]

cravenly *adv.* in a cowardly or cringing way.

cravenness *noun* being craven.

craving *noun* an intense longing; an overwhelming desire.

▤ longing, desire, appetite, hunger, thirst, yearning, hankering, urge, lust.

craw *noun* **1** the crop of a bird or insect. **2** the stomach of a lower animal. — **stick in one's craw** *colloq.* to be difficult for one to swallow or accept. [from Middle English *crawe*]

crawfish *noun* (PL. **crawfish**) same as CRAYFISH.

crawl — *verb intrans.* **1** *said of insects, worms, etc* to move along the ground. **2** to move along on hands and knees, especially as a stage before learning to walk. **3** *said eg of traffic* to progress very slowly. **4** to be, or feel as if, covered with crawling insects. **5** (**crawl to someone**) *derog. colloq.* to behave in an over-humble way to someone whose approval one wants. — *noun* **1** a crawling motion. **2** a very slow pace. **3** a swimming-stroke with an alternate overarm action.

▤ *verb* **1** creep, inch, edge, slither, wriggle. **5** grovel, toady, fawn, *colloq.* suck up.

crawler *noun derog. colloq.* someone who behaves in an over-humble, ingratiating way to those in senior positions.

crayfish *noun* (PL. **crayfish**) a freshwater crustacean resembling a small lobster, found in lakes and rivers of all continents except Africa, and ranging in length from 2.5 to 40cm. The head and thorax are covered with a single shell, and the front pair of legs are modified to form a stout pair of pincers which are used to capture and hold prey. Most crayfish hunt nocturnally, and many species are exploited commercially for food. [from Old French *crevice*, from Old German *krebiz*, crab]

crayon /'kreɪən/ — *noun* a coloured pencil, or stick of coloured wax or chalk. — *verb trans., intrans.* (**crayoned**, **crayoning**) to draw or colour with a crayon. [from French *crayon*, from *craie*, chalk]

craze — *noun* an intense but passing enthusiasm or fashion. — *verb* **1** to make crazy: *a crazed look.* **2** *trans., intrans., said eg of a glazed or varnished surface* to develop or cause to develop a network of fine cracks. [probably from Norse]

▤ *noun* fad, novelty, enthusiasm, fashion, vogue, mode, trend, *colloq.* rage, *colloq.* thing, obsession, preoccupation, mania, frenzy, passion, infatuation.

crazily *adv.* in a crazy way.

craziness *noun* being crazy.

crazy *adj.* (**crazier**, **craziest**) **1** mad; insane. **2** foolish; absurd; foolhardy. **3** (**crazy about something** or **someone**) madly enthusiastic about them. — **like crazy** *colloq.* keenly; fast and furious.

▤ **1** mad, insane, lunatic, unbalanced, deranged, demented, crazed. **2** foolish, idiotic, absurd, ludicrous, ridiculous, silly, senseless, *colloq.* potty, *colloq.* barmy, *colloq.* daft, unwise, imprudent, *colloq.* half-baked, impracticable, irresponsible, wild, nonsensical, preposterous, outrageous. **3** enthusiastic, fanatical, zealous, ardent, passionate, infatuated, enamoured, smitten, *colloq.* mad, wild.
▣ **1** sane. **2** sensible. **3** apathetic, indifferent.

crazy paving paving made up of irregularly shaped slabs of stone or concrete.

creak — *noun* the squeaking noise made typically by an unoiled hinge or loose floorboard. — *verb intrans.* **1** to make this noise. **2** *facetious* to be in an unreliable or infirm condition. [imitative]

▤ *verb* **1** squeak, groan, grate, scrape, rasp, scratch, grind, squeal, screech.

creakily *adv.* **1** with a creaking sound. **2** stiffly.

creakiness *noun* being creaky.

creaky *adj.* (**creakier**, **creakiest**) **1** squeaky. **2** tending to creak. **3** badly made or performed. **4** stiff.

cream — *noun* **1** the yellowish fatty substance that rises to the surface of milk, and yields butter when churned. In the UK, single cream contains not less than 18% fat, and double cream contains 48% fat. **2** any food that resembles this substance in consistency or appearance, eg 'synthetic' cream, ice cream. **3** any cosmetic substance that resembles cream in texture or consistency, eg cold cream. **4** the best part of something; the pick. **5** a yellowish-white colour. — *verb* **1** to beat (eg butter and sugar) till creamy. **2** to remove the cream from (milk). — **cream something off** to select or take away the best part. [from Old French *cresme*]

⊟ *noun* **3** lotion, ointment, salve, emulsion, paste. **4** best, pick, élite, prime.

creamer *noun* **1** a powdered milk substitute, used in coffee. **2** *Antiq. North Amer., esp. US* a cream jug. **3** a device for separating cream from milk.

creamery *noun* (PL. **creameries**) **1** an establishment where butter and cheese are made from the milk and cream supplied by a number of producers. **2** a shop selling milk, butter, and other dairy products.

cream of tartar potassium hydrogen tartrate, a white powder used together with sodium bicarbonate in baking powder, which produces bubbles of carbon dioxide when water is added to it, lightening the texture of bakery products, eg cakes.

creamware *noun* a hard durable type of earthenware first produced in Staffordshire in the 18c, and usually having a cream-coloured glaze. Josiah Wedgwood produced a much-refined version of it around 1760.

creamy *adj.* (**creamier**, **creamiest**) **1** full of cream. **2** like cream in appearance or consistency.

⊟ **2** cream-coloured, off-white, yellowish-white, milky, buttery, oily, smooth, velvety, rich, thick.

crease /kriːs/ — *noun* **1** a line made by folding, pressing, or crushing. **2** *Cricket* a line marking the position of batsman or bowler. — *verb trans., intrans.* to make a crease or creases in; to develop creases. — **crease up** or **crease someone up** *trans., intrans. colloq.* to be or make incapable with laughter, pain, or exhaustion. [from Middle English *creeste*, connected with CREST]

⊟ *noun* **1** line, fold, pleat, tuck, wrinkle, pucker, ruck, crinkle, ridge, groove. *verb* fold, pleat, wrinkle, pucker, crumple, rumple, crinkle, crimp, ridge.

create /krɪ'eɪt/ *verb* **1** to form from nothing: *create the universe.* **2** to bring into existence: *create a system.* **3** to cause. **4** to produce or contrive. **5** *trans., intrans.* said of an artist, etc to use one's imagination to make. **6** *intrans. colloq.* to make a fuss. **7** said of an actor to be the first to play (a certain role). **8** to raise to an honourable rank: *was created a peer.* [from Latin *creare*]

⊟ **1, 2** make, form, invent, coin, formulate, compose, design, devise, concoct, hatch, introduce, originate, initiate, found, establish, set up, institute. **3** cause, occasion. **4** produce, contrive, generate, engender. **8** appoint, install, invest, ordain.
🔁 **1** destroy.

creatine or **creatin** /'kriːətɪn/ *noun Biochem.* an organic compound, found in muscle, whose phosphate serves as an important source of energy for muscle contraction. [from Greek *kreas kreatos*, flesh]

creation /krɪ'eɪʃən/ *noun* **1** the act of creating. **2** something created. **3** the universe; all created things.

⊟ **1** making, formation, constitution, invention, concoction, origination, foundation, establishment, institution, production, generation, procreation, conception. **2** invention, brainchild, concept, product, handiwork, chef d'oeuvre, achievement.
🔁 **1** destruction.

creative /krɪ'eɪtɪv/ *adj.* having or showing the ability to create; inventive or imaginative.

⊟ artistic, inventive, original, imaginative, inspired, visionary, talented, gifted, clever, ingenious, resourceful, fertile, productive.
🔁 unimaginative.

creatively *adv.* in a creative way.

creativity /kriːə'tɪvɪtɪ/ *noun* **1** being creative. **2** the ability to create.

creator /krɪ'eɪtə(r)/ *noun* **1** a person who creates. **2** (**the Creator**) God.

⊟ **1** maker, inventor, designer, architect, author, originator, initiator.

creature *noun* **1** a bird, beast, or fish. **2** a person: *a wretched creature.* **3** the slavish underling or puppet of someone. [from Latin *creatura*, act of creating]

⊟ **1** animal, beast, bird, fish, organism, being, mortal, individual. **2** person, man, woman, body, soul.

creature comforts comforts such as food, clothes, warmth, etc.

creature of habit **1** an animal with fixed, especially seasonal, behaviour patterns. **2** a person of unchanging routines.

crèche /krɛʃ/ *noun* a nursery where babies can be left and cared for while their parents are at work, shopping, exercising, etc. [from French *crèche*, manger]

cred *noun slang* credibility: *street cred.*

credence /'kriːdəns/ *noun* faith or belief placed in something: *give their claims no credence.* [from Latin *credentia*]

credentials *pl. noun* personal qualifications and achievements that one can quote in evidence of one's trustworthiness; documents or other evidence of these. [from Latin *credentia*, belief]

⊟ papers, documents, accreditation, authorization, permit, passport, identity card, diplomas, certificates, references, testimonials, recommendations.

credibility /krɛdə'bɪlɪtɪ/ *noun* the quality of being credible.

⊟ integrity, reliability, trustworthiness, plausibility, probability.
🔁 implausibility.

credibility gap in politics, the discrepancy between what is claimed and what is actually, or is likely to be, the case.

credible *adj.* **1** capable of being believed. **2** reliable; trustworthy. [from Latin *credibilis*]

⊟ **1** believable, imaginable, conceivable, thinkable, tenable, plausible, likely, probable, possible, reasonable, persuasive, convincing. **2** reliable, trustworthy, honest, dependable.
🔁 **1** incredible, unbelievable, implausible. **2** unreliable, untrustworthy, dishonest.

credibly *adv.* in a credible way.

credit — *noun* **1** faith placed in something. **2** honour, or a cause of honour: *to her credit, she didn't say anything / your loyalty does you credit.* **3** acknowledgement, recognition, or praise: *give him credit for trying / take credit for someone else's hard work.* **4** (**credits**) a list of acknowledgements to those who have helped in the preparation of a book or (*also* **credit titles**) film. **5** trust given to someone promising to pay later for goods already supplied: *buy goods on credit.* **6** one's financial reliability, especially as a basis for such trust. **7** the amount of money available to one at one's bank. **8** an entry in a bank account acknowledging a payment. **9** the side of an account on which such entries are made. See also DEBIT. **10** a certificate of completion of a course of instruction; a distinction awarded for performance on such a course. — *verb* (**credited, crediting**) **1** to believe; to place faith in. **2** (**credit something to someone** or **someone with something**) to enter a sum as a credit on someone's account, or allow someone a sum as credit. **3** (**credit someone with something**) to attribute a quality or achievement to them: *we credited you with more sense.* [from Old French *crédit*, from Latin *creditum*, loan]

⊟ *noun* **1** faith, trust, reliance, confidence. **2** glory, honour, acclaim, esteem, estimation. **3** acknowledgement, recognition, thanks, approval, commendation, praise, acclaim, tribute. *verb* **1** believe, trust, rely on, accept, *colloq.* swallow, subscribe to. **3** attribute, accredit, ascribe, assign.
⊟ *noun* **2** discredit, shame. *verb* **1** disbelieve.

creditable *adj.* praiseworthy; laudable.

⊟ praiseworthy, laudable, honourable, estimable, admirable, commendable, excellent, exemplary, good, worthy, deserving, reputable, respectable.
⊟ shameful, blameworthy.

creditably *adv.* in a creditable way.

credit account a financial arrangement with a shop that allows one to purchase goods on credit.

credit card a card authorizing one to purchase goods or services on credit.

credit note a form entitling one to a certain sum as credit, eg in place of returned or faulty goods.

creditor *noun* a person to whom one owes money. See also DEBTOR.

credit rating an assessment of a person's creditworthiness.

credit squeeze restrictions on borrowing imposed by the government.

credit transfer payment made directly from one bank account to another.

credit union a co-operative and non-profit-making savings association which makes loans to its members at a low rate of interest, often for consumer items.

creditworthiness *noun* entitlement to credit.

creditworthy *adj.* judged as deserving financial credit on the basis of earning ability and previous promptness in repaying debts.

credo /ˈkriːdoʊ/ *noun* (PL. **credos**) a creed. [from Latin *credo*, I believe]

credulity /krəˈdjuːlɪtɪ/ *noun* a tendency to believe something without proper proof.

credulous /ˈkredjʊləs/ *adj.* too trusting; too ready to believe. [from Latin *credulus*, trustful]

⊟ trusting, naïve, gullible, wide-eyed, unsuspecting, uncritical.
⊟ sceptical, suspicious.

credulously *adv.* in a credulous way.

creed *noun* **1** (*often* **Creed**) a statement of the main points of Christian belief. **2** any set of beliefs or principles, personal or religious. [from Anglo-Saxon *creda*, from Latin *credo*, I believe]

⊟ **2** belief, principles, faith, persuasion, credo, catechism, doctrine, tenets, articles, canon, dogma.

creek *noun* **1** a small narrow inlet or bay in the shore of a lake, river, or sea. **2** *North Amer., Austral., New Zealand* a small natural stream or tributary, larger than a brook and smaller than a river. — **up the creek** *colloq.* in desperate difficulties. [from Old Norse *kriki*, nook]

⊟ **1** inlet, estuary, cove, bay, bight.

creel *noun* a large basket for carrying fish. [from Middle English *crele*]

creep — *verb intrans.* (PAST TENSE AND PAST PARTICIPLE **crept**) **1** to move slowly, with stealth or caution. **2** to move with the body close to the ground; to crawl. **3** *said of a plant* to grow along the ground, up a wall, etc. **4** to enter barely noticeably: *anxiety crept into her voice.* **5** to develop little by little: *creeping inflation.* **6** *said especially of the flesh* to have a strong tingling sensation as a response to fear or disgust. — *noun* **1** *derog.* an unpleasantly sly or sinister person; also as a general term of abuse. **2** the slow deformation with time of a solid material, especially a metal, under stress. It usually occurs at high temperatures, although lead, zinc, and tin show this property at ordinary temperatures. Creep is taken into account during the design of machinery, vehicles, etc. **3** the slow movement of soil, broken rock, or mining ground downward under the influence of gravity. — **give one the creeps** *colloq.* to disgust or repel one. [from Anglo-Saxon *creopan*]

⊟ *verb* **1** inch, edge, tiptoe, steal, sneak, slink. **2** crawl, slither, worm, wriggle, squirm, grovel, writhe.

creeper *noun* **1** a creeping plant, eg ivy, Virginia creeper. **2** a tree creeper.

creepers *pl. noun* shoes with thick quiet soles.

creepily *adv.* in a creepy way.

creepy *adj.* (**creepier, creepiest**) *colloq.* slightly scary; spooky; eerie.

⊟ scary, spooky, eerie, sinister, threatening, frightening, terrifying, hair-raising, nightmarish, macabre, gruesome, horrible, unpleasant, disturbing.

creepy-crawly *noun* (PL. **creepy-crawlies**) *colloq.* any small creeping insect.

cremate *verb* to burn (a corpse) to ashes, as an alternative to burial. [from Latin *cremare*, to burn]

cremation *noun* the act or process of cremating a corpse.

crematorium /kreməˈtɔːrɪəm/ *noun* (PL. **crematoria, crematoriums**) a place where corpses are cremated.

crème /krem/ *noun* **1** cream, or a creamy food. **2** a liqueur. [from French *crème*, cream]

crème caramel /krem karəˈmel/ an egg custard baked in a dish lined with caramel.

crème de la crème /krem də la ˈkrem/ the cream of the cream; the very best.

crème de menthe /krem də ˈmɒnθ/ a green peppermint-flavoured liqueur.

crème fraîche /krem ˈfreʃ/ cream thickened with a culture of bacteria, used in cooking. [French, = fresh cream]

crenellated /ˈkrenɪleɪtɪd/ *adj.*, *said of a castle, wall, etc* having battlements. [from French *crenel*, the notch or space in battlements]

crenellation /krenɪˈleɪʃən/ *noun* battlements along the top of a castle wall.

creole /ˈkriːoʊl/ *noun* **1** a pidgin language that has become the accepted language of a region. **2** (**Creole**) the French-based creole spoken in the US states of the Caribbean Gulf. **3** (**Creole**) a native-born West Indian or Latin American of mixed European and Negro blood; a French or Spanish native of the US Gulf states. [from French *creole*, from Portuguese *crioulo*, native]

creosote or **creasote** — *noun* **1** a thick dark oily liquid with a penetrating odour, obtained by distilling coal tar, used as a wood preservative. **2** a colourless or pale yellow oily liquid with a penetrating odour, obtained by distilling wood tar, used as an antiseptic. — *verb* to treat (wood, etc) with creosote. [literally 'flesh-preserver', from Greek *kreas*, flesh + *soter*, saviour]

crêpe or **crepe** /kreɪp, krɛp/ *noun* **1** (*also* **crape**) a thin finely-wrinkled silk fabric, dyed black for mourning wear; a mourning armband made of this. **2** rubber with a wrinkled surface, used for shoe soles. **3** a thin pancake. [from French *crêpe*, from Latin *crispus*, crisp]

crêpe paper paper with a wrinkled, elastic texture, used for making decorations, etc.

crept see CREEP.

crepuscular /krɪˈpʌskjʊlə(r)/ *adj.* **1** of, or relating to, twilight; dim. **2** denoting animals that are active before sunrise or at dusk, eg bats, rabbits, deer. [from Latin *crepusculum*, twilight]

crêpy *adj.* (**crêpier, crêpiest**) **1** like crêpe. **2** *said especially of the skin* wrinkled.

Cres. *abbrev.* Crescent.

crescendo /krɪˈʃɛndəʊ/ — *noun* (PL. **crescendos**) **1** a gradual increase in loudness; a musical passage of increasing loudness. **2** a high point or climax. — *adj., adv. Mus.* played with increasing loudness. See also DIMINUENDO. [from Italian *crescendo*, from Latin *crescere*, to grow]

crescent /ˈkrɛsənt/ *noun* **1** the curved shape of the moon during its first or last quarter, when it appears less than half illuminated. **2** something similar in shape to this, eg a semicircular row of houses. [from Latin *crescere*, to grow]

cress *noun* **1** any of various plants of the cabbage family, especially Lepidum sativum, cultivated for its edible seed leaves. **2** a perennial aquatic plant (Nasturtium officinale), commonly known as *watercress*, cultivated for its pungent-tasting leaves which are used as a garnish, and in salads, soups, etc. [from Anglo-Saxon *cressa* or *cærse*]

crest *noun* **1** a comb or a tuft of feathers or fur on top of the head of certain birds and mammals. **2** a ridge of skin along the top of the head of certain reptiles and amphibians. **3** a plume on a helmet. **4** *Heraldry* the part of a coat of arms that appears above the shield. **5** the topmost ridge of a hill or mountain. **6** the foaming edge of a wave. [from Latin *crista*]

   ·

▣ **1** comb, tuft, tassel, plume, mane. **4** insignia, device, symbol, emblem, badge. **5** ridge, crown, top, peak, summit, pinnacle, apex, head.

   ·

crested *adj.* having a crest, or something like one.

crestfallen *adj.* dejected as a result of a blow to one's pride or ambitions. [from CREST]

Cretaceous /krɪˈteɪʃəs/ *adj.* **1** *Geol.* relating to the last period of the Mesozoic era, lasting from about 140m to 65m years ago. During this period the first flowering plants appeared, and dinosaurs and many other reptiles became extinct at the end of the period. Ammonites also died out at this time. **2** relating to rocks formed during this period. **3** (**cretaceous**) composed of or resembling chalk. [from Latin *creta*, chalk]

cretin *noun* **1** a person suffering from cretinism. **2** *offensive* an idiot. [from French dialect *crestin*, from Latin *christianus*, Christian, human creature]

cretinism *noun* a chronic condition caused by a congenital deficiency of thyroid hormone, the main symptoms of which are dwarfism and mental retardation.

cretinous *adj.* typical of a cretin.

cretonne /ˈkrɛtɒn/ *noun* a strong cotton material used for curtains, chair-covers, etc. [from French *cretonne*, from Creton in Normandy]

Creutzfeldt-Jakob disease /ˈkrɔɪtsfɛlt ˈjɑːkɒb/ (ABBREV. **CJD**) *Medicine* a degenerative condition of the brain thought to be caused by infection with a slow-acting virus, characterized by loss of muscle coordination and mental deterioration. [named after Hans G Creutzfeldt and Alfons M Jakob, German physicians]

crevasse /krɪˈvas/ *noun Geol.* a deep vertical crack in a glacier, formed by stresses that build up as different parts of the glacier move at different rates. [from French, from Old French *crevace*, crevice]

crevice /ˈkrɛvɪs/ *noun* **1** a narrow crack or fissure, especially in a rock. **2** a narrow opening. [from Old French *crevace*, from Latin *crepare*, to crack]

   ·

▣ **1** crack, fissure, split, rift, cleft, slit, chink, cranny, break. **2** gap, hole, opening, break.

   ·

crew [1] — *noun* **1** the team of people manning a ship, aircraft, space vehicle, etc. **2** a ship's company excluding the officers. **3** a team engaged in some operation: *camera crew.* **4** *colloq., usually derog.* a bunch of people: *a strange crew.* — *verb intrans.* to serve as a crew member on a yacht, etc. [from Middle English *creue*, reinforcements, from Old French *creu*, increase]

   ·

▣ *noun* **1** team, company. **3** team, party, squad, company, gang, band. **4** bunch, gang, crowd, mob, set, lot.

   ·

crew [2] see CROW.

crewcut *noun* a closely cropped hairstyle for men.

crewel *noun* thin, loosely twisted yarn for tapestry or embroidery.

crewelwork *noun* needlework using crewels.

crew neck a firm round neckline on a sweater.

crew-necked *adj.* having a crew-neck.

crib — *noun* **1** a baby's cot or cradle. **2** a manger. **3** a model of the nativity, with the infant Christ in a manger. **4** a literal translation of a text, used as an aid by students. **5** something copied or plagiarised from another's work. **6** the discarded cards in cribbage, used by the dealer in scoring. — *verb trans., intrans.* (**cribbed, cribbing**) to copy or plagiarize. [from Anglo-Saxon *cribb*, stall, manger]

cribbage *noun* a card game for two to four players, who each try to be first to score a certain number of points. [from CRIB, the discarded cards in the game]

crick *colloq.* — *noun* a painful spasm or stiffness, especially in the neck. — *verb* to wrench (eg one's neck or back).

cricket [1] *noun* an outdoor game played with a ball, bats, and wickets, between two sides of eleven players. — **not cricket** *colloq.* unfair; unsporting.

cricket [2] *noun* any of about 2,500 species of mainly nocturnal insect found worldwide, but primarily in tropical regions. It is closely related to the grasshopper, but can be distinguished from the latter by its long slender antennae. The males produce a distinctive chirping sound by rubbing their forewings together. [imitative]

cricketer *noun* a person who plays cricket.

cri de coeur /kri də ˈkɜː/ *noun* a cry from the heart; a sincere appeal. [French, = cry of the heart]

crier *noun Hist.* an official who announces news by shouting it out in public.

crikey *interj. old slang use* an expression of astonishment. [altered form of CHRIST]

crime *noun* **1** an illegal act; an act punishable by law. **2** such acts collectively. **3** an act gravely wrong morally. **4** *colloq.* a deplorable act; a shame. [from Latin *crimen*, charge, crime]

   ·

▣ **1** offence, felony, misdemeanour, misdeed, wrongdoing, transgression, violation. **2** law-breaking, lawlessness, delinquency, misconduct, wrongdoing, transgression, violation. **3** sin, iniquity, vice, villainy, wickedness. **4** shame, disgrace, atrocity, outrage.

   ·

Crimes include: theft, robbery, burglary, larceny, pilfering, mugging, poaching; assault, rape, grievous bodily harm, *colloq.* GBH, battery, manslaughter, homicide, murder, assassination; fraud, bribery, corruption, embezzlement, extortion, blackmail; arson, treason, terrorism, hijack, piracy, kidnapping, sabotage, vandalism, hooliganism, drug smuggling, forgery, counterfeiting, perjury, joyriding, drink-driving, drunk and disorderly conduct.

criminal — *noun* a person guilty of a crime. — *adj.* **1** against the law: *criminal activities.* **2** of, or relating to, crime or criminals or their punishment. **3** *colloq.* very wrong; wicked. [from Latin *criminalis*, from *crimen*, crime]

- *noun* law-breaker, crook, felon, delinquent, offender, wrongdoer, miscreant, culprit, convict, prisoner. *adj.* **1** illegal, unlawful, illicit, indictable. **2** lawless, dishonest, *colloq.* crooked, *slang* bent, corrupt, culpable, indictable, penal. **3** wrong, wicked, scandalous, deplorable.
- *adj.* **1** legal, lawful. **2** honest, upright.

criminality /krɪmɪˈnalɪtɪ/ *noun* **1** the condition of being a criminal. **2** guiltiness.

criminal law a branch of law that deals with unlawful acts which are offences against the public and society generally.

criminally *adv.* in a criminal way.

criminologist /krɪmɪˈnɒlədʒɪst/ *noun* a person who studies or is an expert in criminals and their crimes.

criminology /krɪmɪˈnɒlədʒɪ/ *noun* the study of crime and criminals. [from Latin *crimen*, crime]

crimp *verb* **1** to press into small regular ridges; to corrugate. **2** to wave or curl (hair) with curling-tongs. **3** to roll the edge of (sheet metal). **4** to seal by pinching together. [from Anglo-Saxon *crympan*, to curl]

Crimplene *noun* trademark **1** a thick polyester yarn. **2** a crease-resistant clothing material made from this.

crimson /ˈkrɪmzən/ — *adj.* of a deep purplish red colour. — *noun* this colour: *dressed in crimson.* — *verb* **1** to dye crimson. **2** *intrans.* to become crimson; to blush. [from Old French *cramoisin*, from Arabic *qirmizi*, a dye made from a Mediterranean insect]

cringe *verb intrans.* **1** to cower away in fear. **2** *derog.* to behave in a submissive, over-humble way. **3** *loosely* to wince in embarrassment, etc. [from Anglo-Saxon *cringan*, to fall in battle]

- **1** cower, shrink, recoil, shy, start, quail. **2** grovel, crawl, creep, stoop. **3** flinch, wince.

cringer *noun* a person who cringes.

crinkle — *verb trans., intrans.* to wrinkle or crease. — *noun* a wrinkle or crease; a wave. [related to Anglo-Saxon *crincan*, to yield]

crinkly *adj.* (**crinklier, crinkliest**) wrinkly.

crinoline /ˈkrɪnəlɪn, ˈkrɪnəliːn/ *noun Hist.* a hooped petticoat for making skirts stand out. [originally a stiff horsehair fabric, from Latin *crinis*, hair + *linum*, flax]

cripple — *verb* **1** to make lame; to disable. **2** to damage, weaken, or undermine. — *noun* **1** a person who is lame or badly disabled. **2** a person damaged psychologically: *an emotional cripple.* [from Anglo-Saxon *crypel*]

- *verb* **1** lame, disable, paralyse, handicap, injure, maim, mutilate. **2** damage, weaken, incapacitate, debilitate, undermine, impair, spoil, ruin, destroy, sabotage.

crisis /ˈkraɪsɪs/ *noun* (PL. **crises**) **1** a crucial or decisive moment. **2** a turning-point, eg in a disease. **3** a time of difficulty or distress. **4** an emergency. [from Greek *krisis*, decision, judgement]

- **1** *colloq.* crunch. **3** difficulty, trouble, dilemma, quandary, predicament, problem, extremity. **4** emergency, catastrophe, calamity, disaster.

crisis management the policy or practice, especially in politics and business, of dealing with problems as they arise, rather than by strategic planning.

crisp — *adj.* **1** dry and brittle: *crisp biscuits.* **2** *said of vegetables or fruit* firm and fresh. **3** *said of weather* fresh; bracing. **4** *said of a person's manner or speech* firm; decisive; brisk. **5** *said of fabric, etc* clean; starched. **6** *said of hair* springy. — *noun* (*also* **potato crisp**) a thin deep-fried slice of potato, sold in packets as a snack. — **to a crisp** *facetious* burnt till black and brittle. [from Latin *crispus*, curly]

- *adj.* **1** crispy, crunchy, brittle. **2** firm, fresh, crunchy, hard. **3** fresh, bracing, invigorating, refreshing, brisk. **4** firm, decisive, brisk, terse, pithy, snappy, brief, short, clear, incisive.
- *adj.* **1, 2** soft, soggy, limp. **3** muggy. **4** indecisive, wordy, vague.

crispbread *noun* a brittle unsweetened rye or wheat biscuit.

crisply *adv.* in a crisp way; sharply.

crispy *adj.* (**crispier, crispiest**) **1** crisp. **2** curling, wavy.

criss-cross — *adj.* **1** *said of lines* crossing one another in different directions. **2** *said of a pattern, etc* consisting of criss-cross lines. — *adv.* running or lying across one another. — *noun* a pattern of criss-cross lines. — *verb trans., intrans.* to form, mark with, or move in, a criss-cross pattern. [from Christ-Cross, a decorative cross introducing the alphabet in old learning-books]

criterion /kraɪˈtɪərɪən/ *noun* (PL. **criteria**) a standard or principle on which to base a judgement. [from Greek *kriterion*, from *krites*, judge]

- standard, principle, norm, touchstone, benchmark, yardstick, measure, gauge, rule, canon, test.

critic *noun* **1** a professional reviewer of literature, art, drama, or music. **2** a person who finds fault with or disapproves of something. [from Greek *kritikos*, discerning, from *krites*, judge]

- **1** reviewer, commentator, analyst, pundit, authority, expert, judge. **2** censor, carper, fault-finder, attacker, *colloq.* knocker.

critical *adj.* **1** fault-finding; disapproving. **2** relating to a critic or criticism. **3** involving analysis and assessment. **4** relating to a crisis; decisive; crucial. **5** *said of a patient* so ill or seriously injured as to be at risk of dying. **6** *Physics* denoting a state, level, or value at which there is a significant change in the properties of a system, eg critical mass, critical temperature. **7** *Nuclear Physics, said of a fissionable material, a nuclear reactor, etc* having reached the point at which a nuclear chain reaction is self-sustaining.

- **1** fault-finding, disapproving, uncomplimentary, derogatory, disparaging, censorious, carping, cavilling, nit-picking. **3** analytical, diagnostic, penetrating, probing, discerning, perceptive. **4** crucial, decisive, vital, essential, all-important, momentous, urgent, pressing, serious, grave, dangerous, perilous.
- **1** complimentary, appreciative. **4** unimportant.

critically *adv.* in a critical way.

critical mass *Physics* the smallest amount of a given fissile material (one that is able to undergo nuclear fission), formed into a given shape, that is needed to sustain a nuclear chain reaction, eg for a sphere of uranium-235, the critical mass is 52kg.

critical path analysis a procedure used to manage and produce a detailed schedule for a complex project so that it can be completed in the minimum time possible. It often involves the use of a specially written computer package.

critical temperature 1 *Physics* the temperature above which a gas cannot be liquefied by pressure alone. **2** the temperature above which a magnetic material loses its magnetic properties.

criticism *noun* **1** fault-finding. **2** reasoned analysis and assessment, especially of art, literature, music, or drama; the art of such assessment. **3** a critical comment or piece of writing.

. . . .

▤ **1** fault-finding, condemnation, disapproval, disparagement, censure, blame. **2** analysis, assessment, evaluation, appraisal, judgement, appreciation. **3** review, critique, assessment, evaluation, appraisal, analysis, commentary, appreciation, brickbat, *colloq.* flak.
▣ **1** praise, commendation.

. . . .

criticize or **criticise** *verb trans., intrans.* **1** to find fault; to express disapproval of. **2** to analyse and assess.

. . . .

▤ **1** find fault, censure, blame, condemn, disparage, *colloq.* slate, *colloq.* slam, *colloq.* knock, carp. **2** review, assess, evaluate, appraise, judge, analyse.
▣ **1** praise, commend.

. . . .

critique /krɪˈtiːk/ *noun* a critical analysis; a criticism. [from French *critique*, from Greek *kritike*, the art of criticism]

croak — *noun* the harsh throaty noise typically made by a frog or crow. — *verb* **1** *intrans.* to make this sound. **2** to utter with a croak. **3** *intrans., trans. slang* to die or kill. [imitative]

crochet /ˈkrəʊʃeɪ/ — *noun* decorative work consisting of intertwined loops, made with wool or thread and a hooked needle. — *verb intrans., trans.* (**crocheted**, **crocheting**) to work in crochet. [from French *crochet*, diminutive of *croche*, hook]

crock[1] *noun colloq.* an old decrepit person, vehicle, etc: *poor old crock*. [from Middle English *crok*, old ewe]

crock[2] *noun* an earthenware pot. [from Anglo-Saxon *crocc*, pot]

crockery *noun* earthenware or china dishes; plates, cups, etc.

. . . .

▤ dishes, tableware, china, porcelain, earthenware, stoneware, pottery.

. . . .

Items of crockery include: cup, saucer, coffee cup, mug, beaker, plate, side plate, dinner plate, bowl, cereal bowl, soup bowl, salad bowl, sugar bowl, jug, milk jug, basin, pot, teapot, coffee pot, percolator, cafetière, cakestand, meat dish, butter dish, tureen, gravy boat, cruet, teaset, dinner service.

crocket *noun Archit.* in Gothic architecture, a stylized leaf- or flower-shaped carved decoration.

crocodile *noun* **1** a large aquatic reptile belonging to the genus Crocodylus, found in rivers and estuaries in tropical regions of Africa, Asia, Australia, and America, and having a bulky body, short legs, powerful jaws that narrow to form a long snout (which may be slender or broad), and a thick scaly skin. **2** leather made from its skin. **3** a line of schoolchildren walking in twos. [from Greek *krokodeilos*]

crocodile tears a show of pretended grief.

crocus *noun* (PL. **crocuses**) a small perennial flowering plant of the genus Crocus of the iris family, that has an underground corm and thin spiky leaves. It is widely cultivated for its single yellow, purple, or white flowers, and as a source of saffron powder, a yellow dye obtained from the stigmas of Crocus sativus. [from Greek *krokos*, saffron]

croft — *noun* especially in the Scottish Highlands, a small piece of enclosed farmland attached to a house. — *verb intrans.* to farm a croft. [from Anglo-Saxon]

crofter *noun* a person who runs or farms a croft.

croissant /ˈkrwʌsɒŋ/ *noun* a crescent-shaped bread roll, made with a high proportion of fat, and flaky in consistency. [from French *croissant*, crescent]

cromlech /ˈkrɒmlək/ *noun Archaeol.* **1** a prehistoric circle of standing stones. **2** *loosely* a dolmen. [from Welsh *crom*, curved + *llech*, stone]

crone *noun offensive* an old woman. [from Old Dutch *croonie*, old ewe, from Old French *caronie*, carrion]

crony *noun* (PL. **cronies**) a close friend. [from Greek *chronios*, long-lasting]

crook — *noun* **1** a bend or curve: *carried it in the crook of his arm*. **2** a shepherd's or bishop's hooked staff. **3** any of various hooked fittings, eg on woodwind instruments. **4** *colloq.* a thief or swindler; a professional criminal. — *adj. Austral., New Zealand colloq.* **1** ill. **2** not working properly. **3** nasty; unpleasant. — *verb* to bend or curve. [from Old Norse *kraka*, hook]

. . . .

▤ *noun* **4** thief, swindler, criminal, robber, cheat, *colloq.* shark, rogue, villain.

. . . .

crooked /ˈkrʊkɪd/ *adj.* **1** bent, curved, angled, or twisted. **2** not straight; tipped at an angle. **3** *colloq.* dishonest.

. . . .

▤ **1** bent, curved, angled, twisted, hooked, bowed, warped, distorted, misshapen, deformed, tortuous, winding, zigzag. **2** askew, *colloq.* skew-whiff, awry, lopsided, tilted, slanting, asymmetric, irregular, uneven, off-centre. **3** dishonest, illegal, unlawful, *slang* bent, corrupt, fraudulent, *colloq.* shady, shifty, underhand, illicit, criminal, nefarious, deceitful, treacherous, unscrupulous, unprincipled, unethical.
▣ **1, 2** straight. **3** honest.

. . . .

crookedly *adv.* in a crooked way.

crookedness *noun* being crooked.

croon — *verb intrans., trans.* to sing in a subdued tone and reflective or sentimental style. — *noun* this style of singing. [from Old Dutch *cronen*, to lament]

crooner *noun* a person who croons.

crop — *noun* **1** *Agric.* a plant that is cultivated to produce food for man, fodder for animals, or raw materials, eg cereals, clover, barley. **2** *Agric.* the total yield produced by or harvested from such a plant, or from a certain area of cultivated land, such as a field. **3** a batch; a bunch: *this year's crop of graduates*. **4** a short style of haircut. **5** a whip handle; a horserider's short whip. **6** *Zool.* in the gullet of birds, the thin-walled pouch where food is stored before it is digested. — *verb* (**cropped**, **cropping**) **1** to trim; to cut short. **2** *said of animals* to feed on grass, etc. **3** to reap or harvest a cultivated crop. **4** *intrans. said of land* to produce a crop. — **crop up** *intrans. colloq.* to occur or appear unexpectedly. [from Anglo-Saxon *cropp*]

. . . .

▤ *noun* **2** yield, growth, produce, fruits, harvest, vintage, gathering. *verb* **1** trim, cut, snip, clip, shear, pare, prune, lop, shorten, curtail. **crop up** occur, happen, arise, appear, emerge, arrive.

. . . .

crop circle a swirled or flattened circular area in a field in which an arable crop is growing, especially in SE England, originally thought to be a natural phenomenon caused by particular meteorological conditions on an undulating landscape, but in many instances now proved to be man-made.

cropper — **come a cropper** *colloq.* **1** to fall heavily. **2** to fail disastrously.

crop rotation *Agric.* a system of farming in which two or more different crops are grown in succession on the same piece of land, in order to maintain the fertility of the soil.

croquet /ˈkrəʊkeɪ/ *noun* a game played on a lawn, in which mallets are used to drive wooden balls through a sequence of hoops. [from French *croquet*, diminutive of *croc*, hook]

croquette /krəʊˈket/ *noun* a ball or roll of eg minced meat, fish, or potato, coated in breadcrumbs and fried. [from French *croquette*, from *croquer*, to crunch]

crosier or **crozier** *noun* a bishop's hooked staff, carried as a symbol of office. [from Middle English *crocer* or *croser*, staff-bearer, from Old French *croce*, hooked staff]

cross — *noun* **1** a mark, structure, or symbol composed of two lines, one crossing the other in the form + or ×; the mark × indicating a mistake or cancellation, as distinct from a tick. **2 a** a vertical post with a horizontal bar fixed to it, on which criminals were crucified in antiquity. **b** (**the Cross**) *Christianity* the cross on which Christ was crucified, or a representation of it; this as a symbol of Christianity. **3** a burden or affliction: *have one's own cross to bear.* **4** a monument, not necessarily in the form of a cross; (as a place name) the site of such a monument. **5** a medal in the form of a cross. **6** a plant or animal produced by crossing two different strains, breeds, or varieties of a species in order to produce an improved hybrid offspring. **7** a mixture or compromise: *a cross between a bedroom and a living room.* **8** a movement across, eg of a football from wing to centre. — *verb* **1** *trans., intrans.* (*also* **cross over**) to move, pass, or get across. **2** to place one across the other: *cross one's legs.* **3** *intrans.* to meet; to intersect. **4** *intrans.* said of letters between two correspondents to be in transit simultaneously. **5** (**cross oneself**) to make the sign of the Cross. **6** to draw a line across: *cross one's t's.* **7** to make (a cheque) payable only through a bank by drawing two parallel lines across it. **8** (*also* **cross something out**, **off**, etc) to delete or cancel it by drawing a line through. **9** to cross-breed (two different strains, breeds, or varieties of a species of animal or plant): *cross a sheep with a goat.* **10** to frustrate or thwart. **11** to cause unwanted connections between (telephone lines). — *adj.* **1** angry; in a bad temper. **2** (*in compounds*) **a** across: *cross-Channel / cross-country.* **b** intersecting or at right angles: *crossbar.* **c** contrary: *cross purposes.* **d** intermingling: *cross-breeding.* — **be at cross purposes** *said of two or more people* to misunderstand or clash with one another. **cross one's fingers** or **keep one's fingers crossed** to appeal for good fortune, originally by crossing one's middle finger over one's index finger. **cross one's heart** to make a crossing gesture over one's heart as an indication of good faith. **cross someone's mind** to occur to them. **cross someone's palm** to put a coin in their hand. **cross someone's path** to encounter them. **cross swords with someone** to have a disagreement or argument with them. [from Anglo-Saxon *cros*, from Latin *crux*]

. . . .

▣ *noun* **2** crucifix. **3** burden, affliction, misfortune, trouble, worry, trial, tribulation, grief, misery, woe, load. **6** crossbreed, hybrid, mongrel. **7** mixture, compromise, blend, amalgam, combination. *verb* **1** go across, traverse, ford, bridge, span. **2** lace, intertwine, criss-cross, overlap. **3** meet, intersect, criss-cross. **9** cross-breed, interbreed, mongrelize, hybridize, cross-fertilize, cross-pollinate, blend, mix. **10** frustrate, thwart, foil, hinder, impede, obstruct, block, oppose. *adj.* **1** angry, annoyed, irritable, vexed, *colloq.* shirty, crotchety, grumpy, grouchy, irascible, crabby, snappy, snappish, surly, sullen, fractious, bad-tempered, illtempered, short, fretful, impatient. **2** transverse, crosswise, oblique, diagonal, intersecting, opposite, reciprocal.

▣ *adj.* **1** placid, pleasant.
. . . .

crossbar *noun* **1** a horizontal bar, especially between upright posts. **2** the horizontal bar on a man's bicycle.

crossbench *noun* a seat in parliament for members not belonging to the government or opposition.

crossbencher *noun* a member of parliament who sits on the crossbenches.

crossbill *noun* any of various birds belonging to the finch family, native to coniferous forests of Europe, Asia, and N America, having a large head, a stout body, and a short forked tail, and with the upper and lower parts of its bill crossed for extracting seeds.

crossbones *pl. noun* a pair of crossed femurs appearing beneath the skull in the skull-and-crossbones symbol eg used on pirate flags or gravestones.

crossbow *noun* a bow placed crosswise on a stock, with a crank to pull back the bow, and a trigger to release arrows.

cross-breed *Biol.* — *verb* to mate (two animals of different pure breeds) in order to produce offspring in which the best characteristics of both parents are combined. — *noun* an animal that has been bred from two different pure breeds.

cross-check — *verb* to check (information) from an independent source. — *noun* a check of this kind.

cross-country *adj.* across fields, etc rather than on roads.

cross cut a transverse or diagonal cut.

crosse *noun* a lacrosse stick. [from French *crosse*, hooked stick]

cross-examination *noun* the process of crossexamining.

cross-examine *verb* to question (especially a witness for the opposing side in a law case) so as to develop or throw doubt on his or her statement.

cross-examiner *noun* a person who makes a crossexamination.

cross-eyed *adj.* **1** squinting. **2** having an abnormal condition in which one or both eyes turn inwards towards the nose.

cross-fertilization or **cross-fertilisation** *noun* **1** in plants and animals, the fusion of a female gamete (egg) with a male gamete (sperm or pollen) of another individual, especially one of a different species or variety. **2** the fruitful interaction of ideas from different cultures, etc.

cross-fertilize or **cross-fertilise** *verb trans., intrans.* to fertilize by cross-fertilization.

crossfire *noun* **1** gunfire coming from different directions. **2** a bitter or excited exchange of opinions, arguments, etc.

cross-grained *adj.* **1** *said of timber* having the grain or fibres crossed or intertwined. **2** *said of a person* perverse; awkward to deal with.

crosshatch *verb trans., intrans. Art* to shade with intersecting lines.

crossing *noun* **1** a place for crossing a river, road, etc. **2** a journey across water: *a rough crossing.*

crossing over *Genetics* in meiosis, the exchange of genetic material that occurs as a result of the exchange of segments of homologous chromosomes, giving rise to genetic variation in the offspring.

cross-legged / ˈlɛgɪd, ˈlɛgd/ *adj., adv.* sitting with the ankles crossed and knees wide apart.

crosspatch *noun colloq.* a bad-tempered person.

cross-ply *adj., said of a tyre* having fabric cords that run diagonally in the outer casing, in order to stiffen and strengthen the side walls. See also RADIAL.

cross-pollination *noun Bot.* the transfer of pollen from the anther of the stamen of one flower to the stigma of another flower of the same species.

cross-question *verb* to cross-examine.

cross-refer *verb intrans., trans.* to direct (the reader) to refer from one part of a text to another.

cross-reference — *noun* a reference from one part of a text to another. — *verb* to supply with cross-references.

crossroads *sing. noun* **1** the point where two or more roads cross or meet. **2** a point at which an important choice has to be made.

cross section 1 a the surface revealed when a solid object is sliced through, especially at right angles to its length. **b** a diagram representing this. **2** a representative sample.

cross-sectional *adj.* in the form of a cross-section.

cross-stitch *noun* an embroidery stitch made by two crossing stitches.

cross-talk *noun* **1** unwanted interference between communication channels. **2** fast and clever conversation; repartee.

cross-training *noun* a method of exercise alternating the use of gymnasium equipment with aerobic floor exercises in the same session.

crosswind *noun* a wind blowing across the path of a vehicle or aircraft.

crosswise *adj.*, *adv.* lying or moving across, or so as to cross.

crossword *noun* a puzzle in which clues yield words that cross vertically and horizontally within a grid of squares.

crotch *noun* the place where the body or a pair of trousers forks into the two legs. [variant of CRUTCH]

crotchet *noun Mus.* a note equal to two quavers or half a minim in length. [from Old French *crochet*, hooked staff]

crotchetiness *noun* being crotchety.

crotchety *adj. colloq.* irritable; peevish. [from CROTCHET, in the sense of an odd fancy]

crouch — *verb intrans.* (*also* **crouch down**) **1** to bend low or squat with legs close to the chest and often also with one's hands on the ground. **2** *said of animals* to lie close to the ground ready to spring up. — *noun* a crouching position or action.

    ▣ *verb* **1** squat, kneel, stoop, bend, bow, hunch, duck, cower, cringe.

croup[1] /kru:p/ *noun* a condition characterized by inflammation and consequent narrowing of the larynx, occurring especially in young children, and usually caused by a viral infection. The main symptoms are a hoarse cough, difficulty in breathing, fever, and restlessness. [imitative]

croup[2] or **croupe** /kru:p/ *noun* **1** the rump or hindquarters of a horse. **2** the place behind the saddle. [from Old French *crope*, related to CROP]

croupier /'kru:pɪə(r)/ *noun* the person who presides over a gaming-table, collecting the stakes and paying the winners. [from French *croupier*, pillion passenger on a horse]

croupy /'kru:pɪ/ *adj.* (**croupier, croupiest**) suffering from or typical of croup.

croûton /'kru:tɒn/ *noun* a small cube of fried or toasted bread, served in soup, etc. [from French *croûton*, diminutive of *croûte*, crust]

crow /krəʊ/ — *noun* **1** any of about 100 species of large black bird, usually with a powerful black beak, including the carrion crow, rook, raven, jackdaw, and magpie. **2** the shrill and long-drawn-out cry of a cock. — *verb intrans.* (PAST TENSE **crowed, crew**) **1** *said of a cock* to cry shrilly. **2** *said of a baby* to make happy inarticulate sounds. **3** (**crow over someone** or **something**) to triumph gleefully over them; to gloat. — **as the crow flies** in a straight line. [from Anglo-Saxon *crawa*]

crowbar /'krəʊbɑ:(r)/ *noun* a heavy iron bar with a bent, flattened end, used as a lever.

crowd — *noun* **1** a large number of people gathered together. **2** the spectators or audience at an event. **3** (*usually* **crowds**) *colloq.* a large number of people. **4** a set or group of people. **5** the general mass of people: *don't just follow the crowd.* — *verb* **1** *intrans.* to gather or move in a large, usually tightly-packed, group. **2** to fill: *crowded streets.* **3** to pack; to cram. **4** to press round, or supervise (someone) too closely. — **crowd someone out** to overwhelm and force them out: *big businesses crowd out the small ones.* **crowd something out** to fill it completely: *the concert hall was crowded out.* [from Anglo-Saxon *crudan*, to press]

    ▣ *noun* **1** assembly, company, throng, multitude, host. **2** spectators, gate, attendance, audience. **3** horde, throng, swarm, flock, herd, pack, press, crush, squash. **4** set, group, bunch, gang, lot, circle, clique. **5** masses, mob, populace, people, public, riff-raff, rabble. *verb* **1** gather, congregate, muster, huddle, mass, throng, swarm, flock, surge, stream. **2** fill, pack, cram, congest. **3** fill, pack, cram, compress, press, squeeze, bundle, pile. **4** press, push, shove, elbow, jostle.

crowded *adj.* full of people, thronged.

    ▣ full, filled, packed, jammed, *colloq.* jam-packed, congested,

cramped, overcrowded, overpopulated, busy, teeming, swarming, overflowing.
    ▣ empty, deserted.

crown — *noun* **1** the circular, usually jewelled gold head-dress of a sovereign. **2** (**Crown**) the sovereign as head of state; the authority or jurisdiction of a sovereign or of the government representing a sovereign. **3** a wreath for the head, or other honour, awarded for victory or success. **4** a highest point of achievement; a summit or climax: *the crown of one's career.* **5** the top, especially of something rounded. **6** the part of a tooth projecting from the gum; an artificial replacement for this. **7** a representation of a royal crown used as an emblem, symbol, etc. **8** a British coin worth 25 pence (formerly 5 shillings). **9** the junction of the root and stem of a plant. **10** a UK paper size, 385x505 mm. — *verb* **1** to place a crown ceremonially on the head of; to make king or queen. **2** to be on or round the top of. **3** to reward; to make complete or perfect: *efforts crowned with success.* **4** to put an artificial crown on (a tooth). **5** *colloq.* to hit on the head. **6** *Draughts* to give a piece) the status of king. — **to crown it all** *colloq.* as the finishing touch to a series of especially unfortunate events. [from Old French *coroune*, from Latin *corona*, wreath, crown]

    ▣ *noun* **1** coronet, diadem, tiara, circlet, wreath, garland. **2** sovereign, monarch, king, queen, ruler, sovereignty, monarchy, royalty. **3** laurel, honour, prize, trophy, reward. **4** summit, climax, top, pinnacle, peak, acme. **5** top, tip, apex, crest, summit, pinnacle, peak. *verb* **1** enthrone, anoint. **2** top, cap. **3** reward, honour, dignify, complete, perfect, fulfil, consummate.

crown colony a colony under the direct control of the British government.

crowning *adj.* highest; greatest: *her crowning achievement.*

crown jewels the crown, sceptre, and other ceremonial regalia of a sovereign.

crown prince the male heir to a throne.

crown princess 1 the wife of a crown prince. **2** the female heir to a throne.

crow's feet the wrinkles at the outer corner of the eye.

crow's nest a platform for a lookout, fixed to the top of a ship's mast.

crozier see CROSIER.

CRT *abbrev.* cathode ray tube.

cruces /'kru:si:z/ see CRUX.

crucial *adj.* **1** decisive; critical. **2** very important; essential. **3** *slang* very good; great. [from Latin *crux*, cross]

    ▣ **1** decisive, critical, trying, testing, searching. **2** important, essential, vital, key, pivotal, central, momentous, urgent, pressing.
    ▣ **2** unimportant, trivial.

crucially *adv.* in a crucial way.

crucible *noun* an earthenware pot in which to heat metals or other substances. [from Latin *crucibulum*, lamp]

crucifix *noun* a representation, especially a model, of Christ on the cross. [from Latin *crucifixus*, man fixed to a cross]

crucifixion /kru:sɪ'fɪkʃən/ *noun* **1** execution by crucifying. **2** (**Crucifixion**) the crucifying of Christ, or a representation of this. [from Latin *crucifixio*, from *crux*, cross + *figere*, to fix]

cruciform *adj.* cross-shaped. [from Latin *crux*, cross]

crucify *verb* (**crucifies, crucified**) **1** to put to death by fastening to a cross by the hands and feet. **2** to torment, torture, or persecute. **3** *slang* to defeat or humiliate utterly. [from Old French *crucifier*, from Latin *crux*, cross + *figere*, to fix]

crude *adj.* **1** in its natural, unrefined state: *crude oil.* **2** rough or undeveloped: *a crude sketch.* **3** vulgar; tasteless. [from Latin *crudus*, raw]

■ **1** raw, natural, unprocessed, unrefined. **2** rough, unfinished, unpolished, primitive. **3** vulgar, tasteless, coarse, rude, indecent, obscene, gross, dirty, lewd.
☒ **1** refined. **2** finished, polished. **3** polite, decent.

crudely *adv.* in a crude way.

crudités /kruːˈdiːteɪ/ *pl. noun* raw fruit and vegetables served as an hors d'oeuvre. [French]

crudity *noun* **1** something crude. **2** rawness, unripeness.

cruel /ˈkruːəl/ *adj.* **1** deliberately and pitilessly causing pain or suffering. **2** painful; distressful. [from French *cruel*]

■ **1** brutal, inhuman, inhumane, unkind, malevolent, spiteful, callous, heartless, unfeeling, merciless, pitiless, savage, barbarous, bloodthirsty, murderous, cold-blooded, hard-hearted, stony-hearted, flinty, implacable, remorseless, unrelenting, ruthless, sadistic. **2** painful, distressing, inexorable, grim, hellish, atrocious, bitter, severe, cutting, excruciating, fierce, ferocious, vicious.
☒ **1** kind, compassionate, merciful.

cruelly *adv.* in a cruel way.

cruelty *noun* (PL. **cruelties**) a cruel act; cruel behaviour.

■ inhumanity, barbarity, brutality, bestiality, spite, venom, callousness, heartlessness, hard-heartedness, harshness, severity, mercilessness, ruthlessness, tyranny, bloodthirstiness, murderousness, violence, ferocity, viciousness, savagery, sadism.
☒ kindness, compassion, mercy.

cruet /ˈkruːɪt/ *noun* **1** a small container for salt, pepper, mustard, vinegar, etc, for use at table. **2** a stand for a set of such jars. [from Old French *cruet*, diminutive of *cruye*, jar]

cruise /kruːz/ *verb intrans.* **1** to sail about for pleasure, calling at a succession of places. **2** *said eg of a vehicle or aircraft* to go at a steady comfortable speed. [from Dutch *kruisen*, to cross]

cruise missile a low-flying, long-distance, computer-controlled winged missile.

cruiser *noun* **1** a large fast warship. **2** (*also* **cabin cruiser**) a motor boat with living quarters.

cruiserweight *noun, adj.* light heavyweight.

crumb /krʌm/ — *noun* **1** a particle of dry food, especially bread. **2** a small amount: *a crumb of comfort.* **3** the interior of a loaf of bread. **4** *slang* an obnoxious person. — *verb* to coat in breadcrumbs. [from Anglo-Saxon *cruma*]

crumble — *verb* **1** *trans., intrans.* to break into crumbs or powdery fragments. **2** *intrans.* to collapse, decay, or disintegrate. — *noun* a dish of cooked fruit covered with a crumbled mixture of sugar, butter, and flour. [from Middle English *kremelen*, from Anglo-Saxon *gecrymian*]

■ *verb* disintegrate, fragment, break up, decompose, decay, degenerate, deteriorate, collapse, crush, pound, grind, powder, pulverize.

crumbly *adj.* (**crumblier**, **crumbliest**) easily crumbled.

crumbs /krʌmz/ *interj. colloq.* an expression of surprise, dismay, etc. [altered form of CHRIST]

crumby /ˈkrʌmɪ/ *adj.* (**crumbier**, **crumbiest**) **1** full of or in crumbs. **2** soft like the inside of a loaf.

crumminess *noun* inferiority.

crummy *adj.* (**crummier**, **crummiest**) *colloq., derog.* shoddy, dingy, dirty, or generally inferior. [variant of CRUMBY]

crumpet *noun* **1** a thick round cake made of soft light dough, eaten toasted and buttered. **2** in Scotland, a type of large thin pancake. **3** *offensive slang* a girl; female company generally.

crumple *verb* **1** *trans., intrans.* to make or become creased or crushed. **2** *intrans., said of a face or features* to pucker in distress. **3** *intrans.* to collapse; to give away. [from Anglo-Saxon *crump*, crooked]

■ **1** crease, crush, wrinkle, pucker, crinkle, rumple. **2** pucker, fall. **3** collapse, give way, fold.

crunch — *verb* **1** *trans., intrans.* to crush or grind noisily between the teeth or under the foot. **2** *intrans.* to produce a crunching sound. **3** *intrans., trans. Comput. colloq.* to process (large quantities of data, numbers, etc) at speed. — *noun* **1** a crunching action or sound. **2** *colloq.* the moment of decision or crisis: *when it comes to the crunch.* [imitative]

■ *verb* **1** munch, chomp, champ, masticate, grind, crush. **2** chomp, champ.

crunchy *adj.* (**crunchier**, **crunchiest**) that can be crunched.

crusade — *noun* **1** a strenuous campaign in aid of a cause. **2** (**Crusade**) *Hist.* each of several medieval military expeditions made by European Christians to recover territory in the Holy Land from the Muslims. — *verb intrans.* to engage in a crusade; to campaign. [from French *croisade* and Spanish *cruzada*, from Latin *crux*, cross]

■ *noun* **1** campaign, drive, push, movement, cause, undertaking, expedition.

crusader *noun* a person who goes on a crusade.

crush — *verb* **1** to break, damage, bruise, injure, or distort by compressing violently. **2** to grind or pound into powder, crumbs, etc. **3** *trans., intrans.* to crumple or crease. **4** to defeat, subdue, or humiliate. — *noun* **1** violent compression. **2** a dense crowd. **3** a drink made from the juice of crushed fruit. **4** *colloq.* an amorous passion, usually unsuitable; an infatuation. [from Old French *cruisir*]

■ *verb* **1** break, damage, bruise, injure, distort, squash, smash, compress. **2** grind, pound, pulverize, crumble, pulp, press, squeeze. **3** crumple, crease, wrinkle. **4** defeat, subdue, humiliate, conquer, vanquish, put down, quash, quell, demolish, devastate, overpower, overwhelm, overcome.

crush barrier a barrier for separating a crowd, eg of spectators, into sections to prevent crushing.

crusher *noun* a person or thing that crushes.

crust — *noun* **1** the hard-baked outer surface of a loaf of bread; a piece of this; a dried-up piece of bread. **2** the pastry covering a pie, etc. **3** a crisp or brittle covering. **4** the solid outermost layer of the Earth, consisting mainly of sedimentary rocks overlying ancient igneous rocks, and varying in thickness from about 8km under the oceans to about 40km under the continents. — *verb trans., intrans.* to cover with, or form, a crust.

■ *noun* **3** covering, surface, exterior, outside, coat, coating, layer, shell, scab, encrustation, caking, concretion, skin, rind.

crustacean — *noun Zool.* any invertebrate animal belonging to the class Crustacea (one of the classes of arthropods) and typically possessing two pairs of antennae and a segmented body covered by a calcareous (chalky) external skeleton or *carapace*. — *adj.* of or relating to these creatures. [from Latin *crusta*, shell]

crustie or **crusty** *noun Brit. slang* a New-Age traveller. [from CRUST]

crustily *adv.* in a crusty way.

crusty *adj.* (**crustier, crustiest**) **1** having a crisp crust. **2** irritable, snappy, or cantankerous.

crutch *noun* **1** a long wooden or metal staff, usually one of a pair, used as an aid to walking by a lame or injured person, and having a padded crosspiece that fits under the armpit, or a grip for the elbow. **2** a support, help, or aid. **3** same as CROTCH. [from Anglo-Saxon *crycc*]

crux *noun* (PL. **crux, cruces**) **1** a decisive, essential, or crucial point. **2** a problem or difficulty. [from Latin *crux*, cross]

....

🔳 **1** nub, heart, core, essence.

....

cry — *verb usually intrans.* (**cries, cried**) **1** to shed tears; to weep. **2** (*also* **cry out**) to shout or shriek, eg in pain or fear, or to get attention or help. **3** *trans.* to exclaim. **4** *said of an animal or bird* to utter its characteristic noise. **5** *trans. old use, said of a street trader* to proclaim (one's wares). — *noun* (PL. **cries**) **1** a shout or shriek. **2** an excited utterance or exclamation. **3** an appeal or demand. **4** a rallying call or slogan. **5** a bout of weeping. **6** the characteristic utterance of an animal or bird. **7** a street trader's call: *street cries*. — **cry something down** to be critical of it; to scorn it. **cry one's eyes** or **heart out** to weep long and bitterly. **cry off** to cancel an engagement or agreement. **cry out for something** to be obviously in need of it: *an abuse crying out for justice.* **cry someone** or **something up** to praise them. **for crying out loud** *colloq.* an expression of impatience or annoyance. **in full cry** in keen pursuit of something.

....

🔳 *verb* **1** weep, sob, blubber, wail, bawl, whimper, snivel. **2** shout, call, exclaim, roar, bellow, yell, scream, shriek, screech. *noun* **1, 2** shout, shriek, call, exclamation, roar, bellow, yell, scream. **3** appeal, demand, call, plea. **5** weep, sob, blubber, wail, bawl, whimper, snivel.

....

crybaby *noun derog. colloq.* a person who weeps at the slightest upset.

crying *adj.* demanding urgent attention: *a crying need.*

cryogenics /kraɪəˈdʒɛnɪks/ *sing. noun* the branch of physics concerned with the study of techniques for the production of very low temperatures (approaching absolute zero), and of the phenomena that occur at such temperatures, eg superconductivity. [from Greek *kryos*, frost + GENIC]

cryolite *noun Geol.* a pale grey mineral, composed of sodium, aluminium, and fluorine (Na_3AlF_6), used in the smelting of aluminium ores. It is found mainly in Greenland and the former Soviet Union. [from Greek *kryos*, frost + *lithos*, stone]

cryopreservation /kraɪo-/ *noun Biol.* the preservation of living cells (eg blood, human eggs, and sperm) by freezing; cryonics. [from Greek *kryos*, frost]

crypt /krɪpt/ *noun* an underground chamber or vault, especially one beneath a church used for burials. [from Greek *krypte*, from *kryptein*, to hide]

cryptanalysis /krɪptəˈnalɪsɪs/ *noun* the deciphering of coded information or messages.

cryptic *adj.* **1** puzzling, mysterious, obscure, or enigmatic. **2** *said of a crossword puzzle* with clues in the form not of synonyms but of riddles, puns, anagrams, etc. [from Greek *kryptikos*, from *kryptein*, to hide]

....

🔳 **1** puzzling, mysterious, obscure, enigmatic, perplexing, ambiguous, equivocal, strange, bizarre, secret, hidden, veiled, abstruse, esoteric, dark, occult.
🔁 **1** straightforward, clear, obvious.

....

cryptically *adv.* in a cryptic way.

crypto- /krɪptoʊ/ *combining form* forming words meaning: **1** hidden or obscure: *cryptogram.* **2** secret or undeclared: *crypto-fascist.* [from Greek *kryptein*, to hide]

cryptogam *noun* **1** *Bot.* a general term for a plant such as a seaweed, moss, or fern that reproduces by means of

spores. **2** *Bot.* a term often used loosely to refer to a plant that lacks flowers. [from CRYPTO- + Greek *gamos*, marriage]

cryptogram *noun* something written in a code or cipher.

cryptographer /krɪpˈtɒɡrəfə(r)/ *noun* a person who writes in and deciphers codes.

cryptographic /krɪptəˈɡrafɪk/ *adj.* relating to or typical of codes.

cryptography /krɪpˈtɒɡrəfɪ/ *noun* the study of, or art of writing in and deciphering, codes.

crystal /ˈkrɪstəl/ — *noun* **1** (*in full* **rock crystal**) a mineral, colourless transparent quartz. **2** (*also* **crystal ball**) a globe of rock crystal or glass used for crystal-gazing. **3** a brilliant, highly transparent glass used for cut glass; cut-glass articles. **4** a small piece of a solid that has a regular three-dimensional shape, and whose plane (flat) faces are arranged in a regular order and meet each other at specific angles. **5** *Chem.* any solid substance consisting of a regularly repeating arrangement of atoms, ions, or molecules. **6** *Electr.* a crystalline element, made of piezoelectric or semiconductor material, that functions as a transducer, oscillator, etc, in an electronic device. — *adj.* like crystal in brilliance and clarity. — **crystal clear** as clear or obvious as can be. [from Greek *krystallos*, ice]

crystal-gazer *noun* a fortune-teller.

crystal-gazing *noun* **1** a fortune-teller's practice of gazing into a crystal ball long and hard enough to conjure up a vision, for interpreting as appropriate. **2** *derog.* guesswork about the future.

crystal healing the selection and use of crystals that are said to promote healing and well-being.

crystal lattice *Physics* the orderly three-dimensional arrangement of atoms or ions in a crystal.

crystalline /ˈkrɪstəlaɪn/ *adj.* **1** composed of, or having the clarity and transparency of, crystal. **2** *Chem.* displaying the properties or structure of crystals, eg with regard to the regular internal arrangement of atoms, ions, or molecules. **3** *said of rock, minerals, etc* consisting of or containing crystals.

crystallization or **crystallisation** *noun Chem.* the process whereby crystals are formed by cooling a molten mass, by allowing a solution of a crystalline solid to evaporate slowly, or by adding more of a crystalline solid to an already saturated solution. Crystallization occurs naturally, eg in many rocks, and is also used commercially in the manufacture of common salt, sugar crystals, synthetic gemstones, etc.

crystallize or **crystallise** *verb* **1** *trans., intrans.* to form crystals by the process of crystallization. **2** to coat or preserve (fruit) in sugar. **3** *trans., intrans., said of plans, ideas, etc* to make or become clear and definite.

crystallographer /krɪstəˈlɒɡrəfə(r)/ *noun* a scientist who specializes in crystallography.

crystallography /krɪstəˈlɒɡrəfɪ/ *noun* the scientific study of the structure, forms, and properties of crystals.

crystalloid — *noun* a substance that dissolves to form a true solution which can pass through a semi-permeable membrane. — *adj.* **1** relating to or resembling a crystalloid. **2** resembling a crystal.

Cs *symbol Chem.* caesium.

c/s *abbrev.* cycles per second.

CSA *abbrev. Brit.* Child Support Agency.

CSE *abbrev. Brit.* Certificate of Secondary Education (replaced in 1988 by GCSE).

CSEU *abbrev.* Confederation of Shipbuilding and Engineering Unions.

CS gas *noun* the irritant vapour produced by a white solid organic compound, which causes a burning sensation in the eyes, streaming of the eyes and nose, choking, nausea, and vomiting, and is used as an incapacitating agent for riot control. [named after the US inventors (1928), B Carson & R Staughton]

CSP *abbrev.* Council for Scientific Policy.

CSU *abbrev.* Civil Service Union.

CSYS *abbrev.* Certificate of Sixth Year Studies.

CT and **Ct**. *abbrev.* Connecticut.

CTOL *abbrev.* conventional take-off and landing.

Cu *symbol Chem.* copper. [from Latin *cuprum*]

cu. *abbrev.* cubic.

cub — *noun* **1** the young of certain carnivorous mammals, such as the fox, wolf, lion, and bear. **2** (**Cub** or **Cub Scout**) a member of the junior branch of the Scout Association. **3** *old use, derog.* an impudent young man. **4** *colloq.* a beginner; a novice: *a cub reporter.* — *verb intrans.* (**cubbed, cubbing**) to give birth to cubs.

cubbyhole *noun colloq.* **1** a tiny room. **2** a cupboard, nook, or recess in which to accumulate miscellaneous objects. [from dialect *cub*, stall, pen]

cube — *noun* **1** a solid figure having six square faces of equal area, in which the angle between any two adjacent sides is a right angle. **2** a block of this shape. **3** *Maths.* the product of any number or quantity multiplied by its square, ie the third power of a number or quantity. — *verb* **1** *Maths.* to raise (a number or quantity) to the third power. **2** to form or cut into cubes. [from French *cube*, from Greek *kybos*, dice]

cube root the number or quantity of which a given number or quantity is the cube, eg 3 is the cube root of 27, because $3^3 = 27$.

cubic or **cubical** — *adj.* **1** relating to or resembling a cube. **2** having three dimensions. **3** of or involving a number or quantity that is raised to the third power, eg a cubic equation (in which the highest power of the unknown variable is three). **4** *said of a unit of volume* equal to that contained in a cube of specified dimensions: *a cubic metre.* — *noun* a cubic equation, in which the highest power of the unknown variable is three. Cubic equations have the general formula $ax^3 + bx^2 + cx + d = 0$, where a, b, c, and d are constants and x is a variable.

cubical *adj.* same as CUBIC *adj.* 1, 2.

cubicle /ˈkjuːbɪkəl/ *noun* a small compartment for sleeping or undressing in, screened for privacy. [from Latin *cubiculum*, from *cubare*, to lie down]

Cubism /ˈkjuːbɪzm/ *noun* an early 20c movement in art, especially painting, with objects represented as geometrical shapes.

Cubist /ˈkjuːbɪst/ — *adj.* relating to or characteristic of Cubism. — *noun* an artist who works in the Cubist style.

cubit /ˈkjuːbɪt/ *noun* an old measure, equal to the length of the forearm from the elbow to the tip of the middle finger. [from Latin *cubitum*, elbow]

cuckold /ˈkʌkəld/ — *noun old use* a man whose wife is unfaithful. — *verb* to make a cuckold of. [from Middle English *cokkewold*, from Old French *cocu*, cuckoo]

cuckoldry *noun* **1** the state of being a cuckold. **2** making a cuckold.

cuckoo /ˈkuku/ — *noun* any of about 130 species of insectivorous bird, named after the distinctive two-note call of the male common cuckoo. The common cuckoo is found in Europe, Asia, and America, and lays its eggs in the nests of other birds. — *adj. colloq.* insane; crazy. [imitative]

cuckoo clock *noun* a clock from which a model cuckoo springs on the hour, uttering the appropriate number of cries.

cuckoo pint see LORDS-AND-LADIES.

cuckoo spit a small white frothy mass, often observed on the stems and leaves of plants, surrounding and secreted by the larvae of the froghopper. See also FROGHOPPER.

cucumber /ˈkjuːkʌmbə(r)/ *noun* **1** a creeping vine (Cucumis sativa), trailing or climbing by means of tendrils, probably native to Africa, and having heart-shaped leaves and yellow funnel-shaped flowers. **2** the long green cylindrical fruit of this plant, which has juicy white flesh and a thin green rind. — **cool as a cucumber** *colloq.* calm and composed. [from Latin *cucumis*]

cud *noun* in ruminant animals, eg cattle, the partially digested food that is regurgitated from the first stomach into

the mouth to be chewed again. — **chew the cud** *colloq.* to meditate, ponder, or reflect. [from Anglo-Saxon *cwudu*]

cuddle — *verb* **1** *trans., intrans.* to hug or embrace affectionately. **2** (**cuddle in** or **up**) to lie close and snug; to nestle. — *noun* an affectionate hug.

⬛ *verb* **1** hug, embrace, clasp, hold, nurse. **2** nestle, snuggle. *noun* hug, embrace.

cuddlesome *adj.* pleasant to cuddle; cuddly.

cuddly *adj.* (**cuddlier, cuddliest**) pleasant to cuddle; attractively soft and plump.

⬛ cuddlesome, huggable, lovable, soft, plump, warm, cosy.

cudgel /ˈkʌdʒəl/ — *noun* a heavy stick or club used as a weapon. — *verb* (**cudgelled, cudgelling**) to beat with a cudgel. — **cudgel one's brains** to struggle to remember or solve something. **take up the cudgels for someone** to fight for or defend them. [from Anglo-Saxon *cycgel*]

cue[1] /kjuː/ — *noun* **1** the final words of an actor's speech, or something else said or done by a performer, that serves as a prompt for another to say or do something. **2** anything that serves as a signal or hint to do something. — *verb* (**cued, cueing**) to give a cue to. — **on cue** at precisely the right moment. **take one's cue from someone** to follow their lead as regards behaviour, etc. [perhaps from *q* for *quando* (Latin, when), formerly written in actors' scripts]

⬛ *noun* **2** signal, sign, nod, hint, suggestion, reminder, prompt, incentive, stimulus.

cue[2] /kjuː/ — *noun* **1** a stick tapering to a point, used to strike the ball in billiards, snooker, and pool. **2** *old use* a tail of hair or plait at the back of the head. — *verb* (**cued, cueing**) to strike (a ball) with the cue. [from French *queue*, tail]

cuff[1] *noun* **1** a band or folded-back part at the lower end of a sleeve, usually at the wrist. **2** *North Amer.* the turned-up part of a trouser leg. **3** (**cuffs**) *slang* handcuffs. — **off the cuff** *colloq.* without preparation or previous thought. [from Middle English *cuffe*, mitten]

cuff[2] — *noun* a blow with the open hand. — *verb* to hit with an open hand. [probably from Norse]

⬛ *noun* hit, slap, smack, clout, *colloq.* belt, box, clip, knock, *slang* biff, *colloq.* whack. *verb* hit, slap, smack, strike, clout, *colloq.* clobber, *slang* belt, box, clip, knock, *slang* biff, *colloq.* whack.

cufflink *noun* one of a pair of decorative fasteners for shirt cuffs.

cuirass /kwɪˈras, ˈkjʊərəs/ *noun Hist.* a piece of armour, a breastplate with or without a back plate attached to it. [from French *cuirasse*]

cuisine /kwɪˈziːn/ *noun* **1** a style of cooking. **2** the range of food served at a restaurant, etc. [from French *cuisine*, kitchen]

cul-de-sac /ˈkʌldəsak/ *noun* (PL. **culs-de-sac**) a street closed at one end. [from French *cul-de-sac*, sack-bottom]

culinary /ˈkʌlɪnərɪ/ *adj.* relating to cookery or the kitchen. [from Latin *culina*, kitchen]

cull — *verb* **1** to gather or pick up (information or ideas). **2** to select and kill (weak or surplus animals) from a group, eg seals or deer, in order to keep the population under control. — *noun* an act of culling. [from Old French *cuillir*, to gather]

culm *noun Bot.* **1** the jointed hollow stem of a grass. **2** the solid stem of a sedge. [from Latin *culmus*, stalk]

culminate *verb intrans.* (**culminate in something**) to reach the highest point or climax. [from Latin *culmen*, top, summit]

. . . .
- ▣ climax, end (up), terminate, conclude, finish.
- ▣ start, begin.
. . . .

culmination /kʌlmɪ'neɪʃən/ *noun* the act or point of culminating; the top or climax.

. . . .
- ▣ climax, top, peak, pinnacle, summit, crown, height, perfection, consummation, finale, conclusion, completion.
- ▣ start, beginning.
. . . .

culottes /kʊ'lɒts/ *pl. noun* flared trousers for women, looking like a skirt. [from French *culottes*, breeches]

culpability /kʌlpə'bɪlɪtɪ/ *noun* being guilty; blameworthiness.

culpable *adj.* deserving blame. [from Latin *culpare*, to blame]

culpably *adv.* in a way that deserves blame.

culprit *noun* 1 a person guilty of a misdeed or offence. 2 *Legal* a person accused of a crime. [said to be from Old French *culpable*, guilty + *prest*, ready: in legal tradition, when a prisoner pleaded not guilty, the clerk of the court replied *culpable: prest daverrer notre bille*, ie 'guilty, ready to prove our charge']

. . . .
- ▣ 1 guilty party, offender, wrongdoer, miscreant, law-breaker, criminal, felon, delinquent.
. . . .

cult *noun* 1 a system of religious belief; the sect of people following such a system. 2 an especially extravagant admiration for a person, idea, etc. 3 a fashion, craze, or fad. [from Latin *cultus*, from *colere*, to worship]

. . . .
- ▣ 1 sect, denomination, school, movement, party, faction. 3 fashion, craze, fad, vogue, trend.
. . . .

cultivar /'kʌltɪvɑ:(r)/ *noun* (ABBREV. **cv**) a variety of a plant that does not occur naturally in the wild, but has been developed and maintained by cultivation using horticultural or agricultural techniques. [a shortening of *cultivated variety*]

cultivate *verb* 1 to prepare and use (soil or land) for growing crops. 2 to grow (a crop, plant, etc). 3 to develop or improve: *cultivate one's mind / cultivate a taste for literature*. 4 to try to develop a friendship with (someone), especially for personal advantage. [from Latin *cultivare*]

. . . .
- ▣ 1 farm, till, work, plough. 2 grow, sow, plant, tend, harvest. 3 develop, improve, foster, nurture, cherish, help, aid, support, encourage, promote, further, work on, train, prepare, polish, refine, enrich.
- ▣ 3 neglect.
. . . .

cultivated *adj.* 1 well bred and knowledgeable. 2 *said of plants* not wild; grown in a garden, etc. 3 denoting soil or land that has been prepared for growing crops.

cultivation /kʌltɪ'veɪʃən/ *noun* 1 the act of cultivating. 2 education, breeding, and culture. 3 the preparation of soil or land for growing crops.

cultivator *noun* 1 a farm implement used to break up the surface of the soil and remove weeds. 2 a person who cultivates.

cultural /'kʌltʃərəl/ *adj.* 1 relating to a culture or civilization. 2 relating to the arts.

. . . .
- ▣ 2 artistic, aesthetic, liberal, civilizing, humanizing, enlightening, educational, edifying, improving, enriching, elevating.
. . . .

cultural lag or **culture lag** a slower rate of cultural change found in one part of a society compared with the whole or majority, or a slower rate of change in a particular society compared to the world at large.

culturally *adv.* in a cultural way; as regards culture.

culture /'kʌltʃə(r)/ — *noun* 1 the customs, ideas, art, etc of a particular civilization, society, or social group. 2 appreciation of art, music, literature, etc. 3 improvement and development through care and training: *beauty culture*. 4 a population of micro-organisms (especially bacteria), cells, or tissues grown in a solid or liquid nutrient medium (known as a *culture medium*) under controlled conditions in a laboratory, usually for scientific study or medical diagnosis. 5 (*also in compounds*) the cultivation of plants or the rearing and breeding of animals, especially for commercial purposes: *silkworm culture / apiculture*. — *verb* to grow (micro-organisms, cells, or tissues) in a culture medium under controlled conditions in a laboratory. [from Latin *cultura*, from *colere*, to cherish, practise]

. . . .
- ▣ *noun* 1 civilization, society, lifestyle, way of life, customs, mores. 2 taste, education, enlightenment, breeding, gentility, refinement, politeness, urbanity.
. . . .

cultured *adj.* 1 well-educated; having refined tastes and manners. 2 *said of micro-organisms, cells, or tissues* grown in a solid or liquid nutrient medium under controlled conditions in a laboratory. 3 *said of a pearl* formed by an oyster round a foreign body deliberately inserted into its shell.

. . . .
- ▣ 1 educated, cultivated, civilized, refined, advanced, enlightened, well-read, well-informed, scholarly, highbrow, well-bred, polished, genteel, urbane.
- ▣ 1 uncultured, uneducated, ignorant.
. . . .

culture medium a solid or liquid nutrient medium, often containing agar or gelatin, in which micro-organisms, cells, or tissues can be grown under controlled conditions in a laboratory.

culture shock disorientation caused by a change from a familiar environment, culture, ideology, etc, to another that is wholly or radically different or alien.

culvert *noun* a covered drain or channel carrying water under a road or railway.

-cum- *combining form* combined with; also used as: *kitchen-cum-dining-room*. [from Latin *cum*, with]

cumbersome *adj.* heavy, awkward, unwieldy, clumsy, or unmanageable. [from Middle English *cummyrsum*]

. . . .
- ▣ heavy, awkward, unwieldy, clumsy, unmanageable, inconvenient, bulky, burdensome, onerous, weighty.
- ▣ convenient, manageable.
. . . .

cumin /'kʌmɪn/ *noun* 1 a slender annual plant (Cuminum cyminum), native to N Africa and SW Asia, having leaves divided into narrow thread-like lobes, and white or pink flowers with notched petals. 2 (**cumin seed**) the dried fruit of this plant, used as a spice in cooking, as an ingredient of curry powder, and for flavouring cordials. [from Greek *kyminon*]

cummerbund *noun* a wide sash, especially one worn with a dinner jacket. [from Hindi *kamarband*, loin band]

cumulative /'kjuːmjʊlətɪv/ *adj.* increasing in amount, effect, or strength with each successive addition. [from Latin *cumulare*, to pile up]

cumulatively *adv.* in a cumulative way.

cumulonimbus /kjuːmjʊloʊ'nɪmbəs/ *adj. Meteorol.* denoting clouds of the cumulus family that rise to heights of up to 10km, and are often dark and threatening when seen from below. They are associated with thunderstorms and the arrival of a cold front during the passage of a depression. [from Latin *cumulus*, heap]

cumulus /'kjuːmjʊləs/ *noun* (PL. **cumuli**) *Meteorol.* a fluffy heaped cloud with a rounded white upper surface and a flat horizontal base. It is composed of water droplets, and usually develops over a heat source, eg a volcano or hot land surface. [from Latin *cumulus*, heap, mass]

cuneiform /'kjuːnɪfɔ:m/ — *adj.* of, or in, any of several ancient Middle-Eastern scripts with impressed wedge-shaped characters. — *noun* cuneiform writing. [from Latin *cuneus*, wedge]

cunnilingus /ˌkʌnɪ'lɪŋɡəs/ *noun* the stimulation of a woman's genitals by licking, etc. [from Latin *cunnus*, vulva + *lingere*, to lick]

cunning — *adj.* **1** clever, wily, sly, crafty, or artful. **2** ingenious, skilful, or subtle. — *noun* **1** slyness; wiliness. **2** skill; expertise. [from Anglo-Saxon *cunnan*, to know]

. . . .

▣ *adj.* **1** clever, wily, sly, crafty, artful, guileful. **2** ingenious, skilful, tricky, devious, subtle, sharp, shrewd, astute. *noun* **1** craftiness, slyness, wiliness, artfulness, trickery, deviousness, subtlety, guile. **2** skill, expertise, sharpness, shrewdness, astuteness, ingenuity, cleverness, adroitness.

▣ *adj.* naïve, gullible.

. . . .

cunningly *adv.* in a cunning way; with cunning.

cunt *noun coarse slang* **1** the female genitals. **2** *offensive slang* used as an abusive term for a person. [from Middle English *cunte*]

cup — *noun* **1** a small round container with a handle, from which to drink especially hot liquids, eg tea or coffee. **2** the amount a cup will hold, used as a measure in cookery. **3** a container or something else shaped like a cup: *egg cups / bra cups.* **4** an ornamental, usually silver, vessel awarded as a prize in sports competitions, etc. **5** a competition in which the prize is a cup. **6** a drink based on wine, with added fruit juice, etc: *claret cup.* **7** *literary* something that one undergoes or experiences: *one's own cup of woe.* — *verb* (**cupped, cupping**) **1** to form (one's hands) into a cup shape. **2** to hold (something) in one's cupped hands. — **one's cup of tea** *colloq.* one's personal preference. [from Anglo-Saxon *cuppe*, from Latin *cupa*, cask]

. . . .

▣ *noun* **1** mug, tankard, beaker, goblet, chalice. **4** trophy.

. . . .

cupboard /'kʌbəd/ *noun* a piece of furniture, or a recess, fitted with doors, shelves, etc, for storing provisions or personal effects. [from Anglo-Saxon *cuppebord*, table for crockery]

. . . .

▣ cabinet, locker, closet, wardrobe.

. . . .

cupboard love an insincere show of affection towards someone from whom one wants something.

cup final the final match in a football contest or other competition for a cup.

cupful *noun* (PL. **cupfuls**) the amount a cup will hold.

cupid /'kjuːpɪd/ *noun* a figure of Cupid in art or sculpture. [from Latin *cupido*, desire, love]

cupidity /kjʊ'pɪdɪtɪ/ *noun* greed for wealth and possessions. [from Latin *cupiditas*]

cupola /'kjuːpələ/ *noun* **1** a small dome or turret on a roof; a domed roof or ceiling. **2** an armoured revolving gun turret. **3** a furnace used in iron foundries. [from Italian *cupola*, from Latin *cupula*, diminutive of *cupa*, cask]

cuppa *noun colloq.* a cup of tea. [altered form of *cup of*]

cupping *noun Medicine* the former practice of applying heated cups to the skin, which was thought to promote healing by drawing 'harmful' blood away from diseased organs to the surface of the skin.

cupric /'kjuːprɪk/ *adj. Chem.* denoting any compound of copper in which the element has a valence of two, eg cupric chloride (CuCl₂).

cuprite /'kjuːpraɪt/ *noun Geol.* a red copper oxide mineral (Cu₂O) that is an important source of copper. [from Latin *cupreus*, from *cuprum*]

cupro-nickel /kjuːprəʊ'nɪkəl/ *noun* an alloy of copper and nickel that is resistant to corrosion, used to make 'silver' coins in the UK.

cuprous /'kjuːprəs/ *adj. Chem.* denoting any compound of

copper in which the element has a valence of one, eg cuprous chloride (CuCl). [from Latin *cupreus*, from *cuprum*, copper]

cup tie one of a series of knockout matches in a competition for a cup.

cur *noun old derog. use* **1** a surly mongrel dog. **2** a surly fellow; a scoundrel. [from Middle English *curdogge*, related to Norse *kurra*, to grumble]

curability *noun* the property of being curable.

curable *adj.* capable of being cured.

curacy /'kjʊərəsɪ/ *noun* the office or benefit of a curate.

curare /kjʊ'rɑːrɪ/ or **curari** *noun* **1** a black resin containing a highly toxic mixture of alkaloids, extracted from the bark of certain S American trees, that acts on the central nervous system and causes muscular paralysis. **2** any of the trees, especially species of Strychnos and Chondodendron, native to tropical S America, from which this resin is obtained. [from Carib (S American Indian language) *kurari*]

curate /'kjʊərət/ *noun* a clergyman who acts as assistant to a vicar or rector in the Church of England. [from Latin *curatus*, from *cura*, care]

curative /'kjʊərətɪv/ — *adj.* able, or tending, to cure. — *noun* a substance that cures. [from Latin *curativus*, from *cura*, healing]

curator /kjʊ'reɪtə(r)/ *noun* a person who has responsibility for a museum or other collection. [from Latin *curator*, keeper, from *cura*, care]

curb — *noun* **1** something that restrains or controls. **2** a chain or strap passing under a horse's jaw, attached at the sides to the bit; a bit with such a fitting. **3** a raised edge or border. **4** *North Amer.* a kerb. — *verb* **1** to restrain or control. **2** to put a curb on (a horse). [from Old French *courb*, curved]

. . . .

▣ *noun* **1** restraint, check, control, constraint, limitation, hindrance, impediment. *verb* **1** restrain, control, check, constrain, restrict, contain, moderate, suppress, subdue, repress, inhibit, hinder, impede, hamper. **2** bridle.

▣ *verb* **1** encourage, foster.

. . . .

curd *noun* **1** (*often* **curds**) the clotted protein substance, as opposed to the liquid component (known as *whey*), formed when fresh milk is curdled by the action of acids or an enzyme such as rennin. Curds are used to make cheese, and are also eaten as food. **2** any of several substances of similar consistency. **3** the edible flowering head of cauliflower, broccoli, etc. [from Middle English *curden*, to congeal]

curdle *verb trans., intrans.* to turn into curds. — **make someone's blood curdle** to horrify or petrify them. [from CURD]

. . . .

▣ coagulate, congeal, clot, thicken, turn, sour, ferment.

. . . .

cure — *verb* **1** (**cure someone of something**) to restore them to health or normality; to heal them. **2** to get rid of (an illness, harmful habit, or other evil). **3** to preserve meat by soaking it in salt solution and then removing it in order to dehydrate it and prevent the growth of bacteria. **4** to preserve leather, tobacco, etc, by drying. **5** to vulcanize (rubber). — *noun* **1** something that cures or remedies. **2** restoration to health. **3** a course of healing or remedial treatment. **4** *Relig.* the responsibility of a minister for the souls of the parishioners. [from Latin *curare*, to care for, heal, and *cura*, healing]

. . . .

▣ *verb* **1** heal, restore. **2** remedy, correct, repair, mend, relieve, ease, alleviate, help. **3** preserve, dry, smoke, salt, pickle. *noun* **1** remedy, antidote, panacea, medicine, specific, corrective, restorative. **2** recovery, healing, treatment, therapy, alleviation.

. . . .

cure-all *noun* a universal remedy; a panacea.

curettage /kjʊˈrɛtɪd/ *noun* the process of using a curette.

curette or **curet** /kjʊəˈrɛt/ — *noun Medicine* a spoon-shaped instrument that is used to scrape a tissue sample from the inner surface of an organ or body cavity for diagnostic purposes, or to remove diseased tissue from such a cavity. — *verb* (**curetted**, **curetting**) to scrape with a curette. [from French, from *curer*, to clean, clear]

curfew /ˈkɜːfjuː/ *noun* **1** an order forbidding people to be in the streets after a certain hour. **2** the time at which such an order applies. **3** *Hist.* the ringing of a bell as a signal to put out fires and lights. [from Old French *covrefeu*, literally 'covers the fire']

curie /ˈkjʊərɪ/ *noun* (SYMBOL **Ci**) the former unit of radio-activity, equivalent to 3.7 x 10^{10} disintegrations of a radio-active source per second. It has now been replaced by the becquerel in SI units. [named after the French physicists Marie and Pierre Curie]

curio /ˈkjʊərɪoʊ/ *noun* (PL. **curios**) an article valued for its rarity or unusualness. [from CURIOSITY]

curiosity /kjʊərɪˈɒsɪtɪ/ *noun* (PL. **curiosities**) **1** eagerness to know; inquisitiveness. **2** something strange, odd, rare, exotic, or unusual. [from Latin *curiositas*]

....

■ **1** inquisitiveness, nosiness, prying, snooping, interest. **2** oddity, rarity, curio, novelty, objet d'art, antique, bygone, trinket, knick-knack, freak, phenomenon, spectacle.

....

curious /ˈkjʊərɪəs/ *adj.* **1** strange; odd. **2** eager or interested: *curious to see what happens.* **3** inquisitive. [from Latin *curiosus*, careful, inquisitive]

....

■ **1** strange, odd, queer, *colloq.* funny, peculiar, bizarre, mysterious, puzzling, extraordinary, unusual, rare, unique, novel, exotic, unconventional, unorthodox, quaint. **2** eager, keen, interested, questioning, inquiring. **3** inquisitive, nosy, prying, meddlesome.

◼ **1** ordinary, usual, normal. **2, 3** uninterested, indifferent.

curiously *adv.* in a curious way.

curium /ˈkjʊərɪəm/ *noun Chem.* (SYMBOL **Cm**, ATOMIC NUMBER **96**) a radioactive element formed by bombarding plutonium-239 with alpha particles. [named after Marie and Pierre Curie, the discoverers of radium]

curl — *verb* **1** *trans., intrans.* to twist, roll, or wind (hair) into coils or ringlets; to grow in coils or ringlets. **2** *intrans., trans.* to move in, or form into, a spiral, coil, or curve. **3** *intrans.* to take part in the game of curling. — *noun* **1** a small coil or ringlet of hair. **2** the tendency of hair to curl. **3** a twist, spiral, coil, or curve. — **curl up 1** to sit or lie with the legs tucked up. **2** *colloq.* to writhe in embarrassment, etc. [from Middle English *crull*, curly]

....

■ *verb* **1** wave, crimp, frizz. **2** curve, coil, spiral, turn, twist, bend, wind, loop, meander, wreathe, twine, corkscrew, scroll, ripple.

◼ *verb* **2** uncurl, straighten. *noun* **1, 3** twist, ringlet, coil, wave, kink, swirl, spiral, whorl.

....

curler *noun* a device for curling the hair.

curlew /ˈkɜːljuː/ *noun* a large wading bird, found on open plains, moors, and marshes across Europe and Asia, with a slender down-curved bill, long legs, and a two-syllable fluting call. [from Old French *corleu*, perhaps imitative]

curlicue /ˈkɜːlɪkjuː/ *noun* a fancy twist or curl; a flourish made with a pen. [from CURLY + CUE^2]

curliness *noun* being curly.

curling *noun* a team game played on ice with smooth heavy stones with handles, that are slid towards a circular target marked on the ice. [from CURL]

curly *adj.* (**curlier**, **curliest**) having curls; full of curls.

■ curling, curled, wavy, kinky, spiralled, corkscrew, crimped, permed, frizzy, fuzzy.
◼ straight.

....

curmudgeon /kəˈmʌdʒən/ *noun* a bad-tempered or mean person.

curmudgeonly *adj.* like a curmudgeon.

currant *noun* **1** a small dried seedless grape. **2** any of various deciduous shrubs of the genus Ribes, native to north temperate regions, eg blackcurrant, redcurrant. **3** (*in compounds*) any of the small soft edible berries, borne in clusters, produced by certain of these plants, and used to make jam, pies, etc. [from Old French *raisins de Corinthe*, grapes of Corinth, the place of export]

currency /ˈkʌrənsɪ/ *noun* (PL. **currencies**) **1** the system of money, or the coins and notes, in use in a country. **2** general acceptance or popularity, especially of an idea, theory, etc. **3** modernity; up-to-dateness. [from Latin *currere*, to run]

....

■ **1** money, legal tender, coinage, coins, notes, bills. **2** acceptance, popularity, vogue, circulation, prevalence, exposure.

....

Currencies of the world include: baht (*Thailand*), bolivar (*Venezuela*), cent (*US, Canada, Australia, NZ, S Africa, etc*), centavo (*Portugal, Brazil, Mexico, etc*), centime (*France, Belgium, Algeria, etc*), dinar (*Iraq, Jordan, etc*), dirham (*Morocco*), dollar (*US, Canada, Australia, NZ, etc*), dong (*Vietnam*), drachma (*Greece*), euro (*EU*), escudo (*Portugal*), fils (*Iraq, Jordan, etc*), guilder (*Netherlands*), franc (*France, Belgium, Switzerland, etc*), hryvna (*Ukraine*), kopeck (*Russia*), koruna (*Czech Republic, Slovakia*), krona (*Sweden*), króna (*Iceland*), krone (*Denmark, Norway*), kyat (*Myanmar*), lek (*Albania*), leu (*Romania*), lev (*Bulgaria*), lira (*Italy*), mark (*Germany*), pence (*UK*), peseta (*Spain*), peso (*Mexico, Chile, etc*), pfennig (*Germany*), piastre (*Egypt, Syria, etc*), pound (*UK, Egypt, etc*), punt (*Ireland*), rand (*SAfrica*), real (*Brazil*), rial (*Iran*), riyal (*Saudi Arabia*), rouble (*Russia*), rupee (*India, Pakistan, etc*), schilling (*Austria*), shekel (*Israel*), shilling (*Kenya, Uganda, etc*), som (*Uzbekistan*), sterling (*UK*), sucre (*Ecuador*), tolar (*Slovenia*), won (*N Korea, S Korea*), yen (*Japan*), yuan (*China*), zloty (*Poland*).

current — *adj.* **1** generally accepted: *according to the current view.* **2** of or belonging to the present: *current affairs.* — *noun* **1** the continuous steady flow of a body of water, air, heat, etc, in a particular direction. **2** (*in full* **electric current**) a flow of electric charge, carried by electrons, ions, etc, through a conductor. The SI unit of current is the ampere. **3** the rate of flow of electric charge through a conductor per unit of time. **4** a popular trend or tendency: *currents of opinion.*

....

■ *adj.* **1** widespread, prevalent, common, general, prevailing, reigning, accepted. **2** present, ongoing, existing, contemporary, present-day, modern, fashionable, up to date, up to the minute, *colloq.* trendy, popular. *noun* **1** draught, stream, jet, flow, drift, tide, course. **4** trend, tendency, undercurrent, tide, mood, feeling.

◼ *adj.* **2** obsolete, old-fashioned.

....

current account a bank account from which money can be drawn without notice, and on which little or no interest is paid.

currently *adv.* at the present time.

curriculum /kəˈrɪkjʊləm/ *noun* (PL. **curricula**) a course, especially of study at school or university. [from Latin *curriculum*, course, from *currere*, to run]

curriculum vitae /ˈviːtaɪ/ (PL. **curricula vitae**) a written summary of one's personal details and the main events of one's education and career, produced to accompany job applications, etc. [from Latin *vita*, life]

curry[1] *noun* (PL. **curries**) a dish, originally Indian, of meat, fish, or vegetables cooked with usually hot spices. [from Tamil *kari*, sauce]

curry[2] *verb* **1** to groom (a horse). **2** to treat (tanned leather) so as to improve its flexibility, strength, and waterproof quality. — **curry favour with someone** to use flattery to gain their approval; to ingratiate oneself with them. [from Old French *correier*, to make ready]

curry powder a selection of ground spices used in making curry.

curse — *noun* **1** a blasphemous or obscene expression, usually of anger; an oath. **2** an appeal to God or other divine power to harm someone. **3** the resulting harm suffered by someone: *under a curse.* **4** an evil; a cause of harm: *the curse of drugs.* **5** *colloq.* **(the curse)** menstruation; a woman's menstrual period. — *verb* **1** to utter a curse against; to revile with curses. **2** *intrans.* to use violent language; to swear. — **be cursed with something** to be burdened or afflicted with it. [from Anglo-Saxon *curs*]

⊟ *noun* **1** blasphemy, oath, swear-word, expletive, obscenity, profanity. **4** evil, bane, plague, anathema, scourge, affliction, trouble, torment, ordeal, calamity. *verb* **1** damn, condemn, denounce, fulminate against. **2** swear, blaspheme. **be cursed with** be blighted by, be plagued with, be troubled by, be tormented by.

⊞ *noun* **4** blessing, advantage. *verb* **1** bless.

cursed /'kɜːsɪd, kɜːst/ *adj.* **1** under a curse. **2** *offensive* damnable; hateful.

cursive — *adj.*, *said of writing* having letters joined up, not printed separately. — *noun* cursive writing. [from Latin *cursivus*, from *currere*, to run]

cursively *adv.* in a cursive style.

cursor *noun* **1** on the screen of a visual display unit, a special symbol or character used to indicate the point at which the next keyboard operation will apply. **2** the transparent movable part of a measuring instrument, especially a slide rule, which can be set at any point along the graduated scale. [from Latin *cursor*, runner]

cursorily /'kɜːsərəlɪ/ *adv.* in a cursory way.

cursory *adj.* hasty; superficial, not thorough. [from Latin *cursorius*]

cursus honorum in ancient Rome, the ordered career structure which was normal for anyone who aspired to high public office. [Latin, = the course of honours]

curt *adj.* rudely brief; dismissive; abrupt. [from Latin *curtus*, short]

curtail *verb* to reduce; to cut short; to restrict. [originally *curtal*, something docked or shortened, from Latin *curtus*, short]

⊟ reduce, shorten, restrict, truncate, cut, trim, abridge, abbreviate, lessen, decrease.

⊞ lengthen, extend, prolong.

curtailment *noun* **1** the act of curtailing. **2** shortening.

curtain /'kɜːtən/ — *noun* **1** a hanging cloth over a window, round a bed, etc for privacy or to exclude light, or in front of a stage to screen it from the auditorium. **2** the rise of the curtain at the beginning, or fall of the curtain at the end, of a stage performance, act, scene, etc. **3** something resembling a curtain: *a curtain of thick dark hair.* **4** (**curtains**) *colloq.* the end; death. — *verb* **1** (*usually* **curtain something off**) to surround or enclose it with a curtain. **2** to supply (windows, etc) with curtains. [from Old French *cortine*, from Latin *cortina*]

⊟ *noun* **1** blind, screen, backdrop, hanging, drapery, tapestry.

curtain call an audience's demand for performers to appear in front of the curtain after it has fallen, to receive further applause.

curtain-raiser *noun* **1** a short play, etc before the main performance. **2** any introductory event.

curtain wall 1 *Archit.* a wall that is not load-bearing. **2** *Fortification* a wall between two towers or bastions.

curtly *adv.* with a curt manner.

curtness *noun* being curt.

curtsy /'kɜːtsɪ/ — *noun* (PL. **curtsies**) a slight bend of the knees with one leg behind the other, performed as a formal gesture of respect by women. — *verb intrans.* (**curtsies**, **curtsied**) to perform a curtsy. [variant of COURTESY]

curvaceous /kɜːˈveɪʃəs/ *adj. colloq.*, *said of a woman* having a shapely figure.

curvature *noun* the condition of being curved; the degree of curvedness. [from Latin *curvatura*]

curve — *noun* **1** a line no part of which is straight, or a surface no part of which is flat, eg part of a circle or a sphere. **2** (**curves**) *colloq.* the roundness of a woman's body. **3** any line representing measurable data (eg birth-rate) on a graph. **4** *Maths.* any line (including a straight line) representing a series of points whose co-ordinates satisfy a particular equation. — *verb intrans., trans.* to form, or form into, a curve; to move in a curve. [from Latin *curvus*, crooked]

⊟ *noun* **1** bend, turn, arc, trajectory, loop, camber, curvature. *verb* bend, arch, arc, bow, bulge, hook, crook, turn, wind, twist, spiral, coil.

curvilinear /kɜːvɪˈlɪnɪə(r)/ *adj.* consisting of, or bounded by, a curved line. [from CURVE + RECTILINEAR]

curvy *adj.* (**curvier, curviest**) having curves or a curved shape.

cushiness /'kʊʃɪnəs/ *noun* a cushy state or condition.

cushion /'kʊʃən/ — *noun* **1** a stuffed fabric case used for making a seat comfortable, for kneeling on, etc. **2** a thick pad, or something having a similar function. **3** something that gives protection from shock, reduces unpleasant effects, etc. **4** the resilient inner rim of a billiard table. — *verb* **1** to reduce the unpleasant or violent effect of. **2** to protect from shock, injury, or the extremes of distress. **3** to provide with cushions. [from Old French *cuissin*, from Latin *coxa*, hip]

⊟ *noun* **1** bolster, pillow, headrest, hassock. **3** buffer, shock absorber. *verb* **1** soften, deaden, dampen, absorb, muffle, stifle, suppress, lessen, mitigate. **3** bolster, buttress, support.

Cushitic /kʊˈʃɪtɪk/ — *noun* a group of about 30 Afro-Asiatic languages, spoken by c.13m people in Somalia, Kenya, Sudan, and Ethiopia. The most widely spoken are Oromo (or Gassa), and Somali. — *adj.* relating to this group of languages. [from Cush, an ancient kingdom in the Nile valley]

cushy /'kʊʃɪ/ *adj.* (**cushier, cushiest**) *colloq.* comfortable; easy; undemanding. [from Hindi *khush*, pleasant]

cusp *noun* **1** *Geom.* a point formed by the meeting of two curves. **2** *Astron.* either point of a crescent moon. **3** *Anat.* a sharp raised point on the grinding surface of a molar tooth. **4** *Astrol.* the point of transition between one sign of the zodiac and the next. [from Latin *cuspis*, a point]

cuss *old colloq. use* — *noun* **1** a curse. **2** a person or animal, especially if stubborn. — *verb intrans., trans.* to curse. [from CURSE]

cussed /'kʌsɪd/ *adj.* **1** obstinate, stubborn, awkward, or perverse. **2** cursed.

cussedly *adv.* in a cussed way.

cussedness *noun* obstinacy, awkwardness.

custard *noun* **1** a sweet sauce made with milk and cornflour. **2** (*also* **egg custard**) a dish or sauce of baked eggs and milk. [formerly *custade*, altered from Middle English *crustade*, pie with a crust]

custodial /kʌˈstoʊdɪəl/ *adj.* relating to custody; involving custody.

custodian /kʌˈstoʊdɪən/ *noun* a person who has care of something, eg a public building or ancient monument; a guardian or curator. [from Latin *custodia*, watch, watchman]

custodianship *noun* the office of custodian.

custody /ˈkʌstədɪ/ *noun* 1 protective care; the guardianship of a child, awarded to someone by a court of law. 2 the condition of being held by the police; arrest or imprisonment. — **take someone into custody** to arrest them. [from Latin *custodia*, watch, vigil]

⊟ 1 care, guardianship, custodianship, trusteeship, protection, supervision, safekeeping, keeping, preservation, possession, charge. 2 detention, confinement, imprisonment, incarceration.

custom *noun* 1 a traditional activity or practice. 2 a personal habit. 3 the body of established practices of a community; convention. 4 an established practice having the force of a law. 5 the trade or business that one gives to a shop, etc by regular purchases.

⊟ 1 tradition, procedure, practice, convention, formality, ritual. 2 habit, routine, way, manner. 3 tradition, convention, etiquette, ritual, procedure, practice.

customarily /ˈkʌstəmərɪlɪ/ *adv.* usually, traditionally.
customary /ˈkʌstəmərɪ/ *adj.* usual; traditional; according to custom.

⊟ usual, traditional, conventional, accepted, established, habitual, routine, regular, normal, ordinary, everyday, familiar, common, general, popular, prevailing.
⊟ unusual, rare.

custom-built or **custom-made** *adj.* built or made to an individual customer's requirements.

customer *noun* 1 a person who purchases goods from a shop, uses the services of a business, etc. 2 *colloq.* a person with whom one has to deal (usually with unfavourable implications): *an awkward customer.* [from CUSTOM]

⊟ 1 client, patron, regular, *colloq.* punter, consumer, shopper, buyer, purchaser.

customs *noun* 1 (*pl.*) taxes or duties paid on imports. 2 (*sing.*) the government department that collects these taxes. 3 (*sing.*) the place at a port, airport, frontier, etc where baggage is inspected for goods on which duty must be paid. [from CUSTOM]

customs house the office at a port, etc where customs duties are paid or collected.

customs union an economic agreement where nations adopt common excise duties, thereby eliminating the need for customs checks along their common frontiers, and creating a free trade area. The European Union is a customs union.

cut — *verb* (**cutting**; PAST TENSE AND PAST PARTICIPLE **cut**) 1 (*also* **cut something off** or **out**) (of a sharp-edged instrument or person using it) to slit, pierce, slice, or sever it. 2 (*also* **cut something up**) to divide it by cutting. 3 to trim (hair, nails, etc), reap (corn), mow (grass), or detach (flowers). 4 (*also* **cut something out**) to make or form it by cutting. 5 to shape the surface of (a gem) into facets, or decorate (glass), by cutting. 6 to shape the pieces of (a garment): *badly cut clothes.* 7 to bring out (a record or disc). 8 to injure or wound with a sharp edge or instrument. 9 to hurt: *cut someone to the heart.* 10 to reduce (eg prices, wages, interest rates, working hours, etc). 11 to shorten (eg

a book or play). 12 to delete or omit. 13 to edit (a film). 14 *intrans.* to stop filming. 15 *intrans. Cinema, said of a film or camera* to change directly to another shot, etc. 16 *Maths.* to cross or intersect. 17 to reject or renounce: *cut one's links with one's family.* 18 to ignore or pretend not to recognize (a person). 19 to stop: *cut drinking.* 20 to absent oneself from: *cut classes.* 21 to switch off (an engine, etc). 22 *Cricket* to hit (a ball) with a slicing action, causing it to spin or swerve. 23 *said of a baby* to grow (teeth). 24 *intrans.* (**cut across** or **through**) to go off in a certain direction; to take a short route. 25 to dilute (eg an alcoholic drink) or adulterate (a drug). 26 to divide; to partition: *a room cut in half by a bookcase.* — *noun* 1 an act of cutting; a cutting movement or stroke. 2 a slit, incision, or injury made by cutting. 3 a reduction. 4 a deleted passage in a play, etc. 5 the stoppage of an electricity supply, etc. 6 *slang* one's share of the profits. 7 a piece of meat cut from an animal. 8 the style in which clothes or hair are cut. 9 a sarcastic remark. 10 a refusal to recognize someone; a snub. 11 a short cut. 12 a channel, passage, or canal. — **a cut above something** *colloq.* superior to it. **cut across something** 1 to go against (normal procedure, etc). 2 *said of an issue, etc* to be more important than, or transcend (the barriers or divisions between parties, etc). **cut and dried** decided; definite; settled beforehand. **cut and paste** 1 a method of arranging a newspaper or magazine page, by cutting and sticking down items with paste. 2 *Comput.* a technique for moving blocks of text from one place to another. **cut and run** *colloq.* to escape smartly. **cut and thrust** aggressive competition; quick verbal exchange or repartee. **cut back on something** to reduce spending, etc. **cut both ways** to have advantages and disadvantages; to bear out both sides of an argument. **cut someone dead** to ignore them completely. **cut something down** to fell a tree, etc. **cut down on something** to reduce one's use of it; to do less of it: *cut down on drinking.* **cut in 1** to interrupt. 2 *said of a vehicle* to overtake and squeeze in front of another vehicle. **cut it** *colloq.* to succeed or reach the required standard. **cut it fine** *colloq.* to leave barely enough time or space for something. **cut it out** *slang* to stop doing something bad or undesirable. **cut something off 1** to separate or isolate it. 2 to stop the supply of gas, electricity, etc. 3 to stop it or cut it short. **cut someone off** to disconnect them during a telephone call. **cut out** *said of an engine, etc* to stop working. **cut something out 1** to remove or delete it. 2 to clip pictures, etc out of a magazine, etc. 3 *colloq.* to stop doing it. 4 to exclude it from consideration. 5 to block out the light or view. **cut out for** or **to be something** having the qualities needed for it. **cut something short** to reduce or shorten it. **cut someone short** to silence them by interrupting. **cut up** *colloq.* distressed; upset. **cut up rough** *colloq.* to get angry and violent. **to cut a long story short** to come straight to the point. [from Middle English *cutten*]

⊟ *verb* 1 slit, pierce, slice, sever, chop, hack, hew, carve, split, dock, lop, prune, excise. 2 dissect, divide, carve, slice, chop, dice, mince. 3 trim, clip, crop, shear, mow, shave, pare, prune. 5 engrave, incise, chisel, score. 8 stab, wound, nick, slash, lacerate. 10 reduce, decrease, lower, shorten. 11 shorten, curtail, abbreviate, abridge, condense, précis, edit. 18 ignore, cold-shoulder, spurn, avoid, snub, slight, rebuff, insult. *noun* 2 slit, incision, wound, nick, gash, slash, rip, laceration. 3 reduction, decrease, lowering, cutback, saving, economy. 6 share, *colloq.* slice, quota, ration, *colloq.* whack. **cut down** fell, hew, lop, level, raze. **cut down on** reduce, decrease, lower, lessen, diminish. **cut in 1** interrupt, butt in, interject, interpose, intervene, intrude. 2 *slang* carve up. **cut something off** 1 separate, isolate, sever, amputate. 2 disconnect, block, obstruct, intercept. 3 stop, end, halt, suspend, discontinue. **cut out 1** remove, delete, excise, extract. 3 stop, cease. 4 exclude, eliminate, debar.

cutaway *adj.* 1 *said of a diagram, etc* having outer parts omitted so as to show the interior. 2 *said of a coat* with the front part cut away below the waist.

cutback *noun* a reduction in spending, use of resources, etc.
. . . .
▤ cut, saving, economy, retrenchment, reduction, decrease, lowering, lessening.
. . . .

cute *adj. colloq.* **1** attractive; pretty. **2** clever; cunning; shrewd. [from ACUTE]

cutely *adv.* in a cute way.

cuteness *noun* being cute.

cut glass glass with patterns cut into its surface.

cuticle *noun* **1** *Anat.* the epidermis or outer layer of the skin, including the outer layer of cells in a hair, and the hardened skin at the base of the fingernails and toenails. **2** *Bot.* the waxy waterproof protective layer that covers all the parts of a plant that are exposed to the air, except for the stomata. **3** *Zool.* the protective layer of horny non-cellular material that covers the surface of many invertebrates, and forms the *exoskeleton* of arthropods, eg insects and crustaceans. [from Latin *cuticula*, skin]

cutlass *noun Hist.* a short, broad, slightly curved sword with one cutting edge. [from French *coutelas*, from Latin *cultellus*, little knife]

cutler *noun* a person who manufactures cutlery. [from French *coutelier*, from Latin *culter*, knife]

cutlery *noun* knives, forks, and spoons for table use.

Items of cutlery include: knife, butter knife, carving knife, fish knife, steak knife, cheese knife, bread knife, vegetable knife, fork, fish fork, carving fork, spoon, dessertspoon, tablespoon, teaspoon, soup spoon, caddy spoon, salt spoon, apostle spoon, ladle, salad servers, fish slice, cake server, sugar tongs, chopsticks, canteen of cutlery.

cutlet *noun* **1** a small piece of meat with a bone attached; a rib or neck chop. **2** a slice of veal. **3** a rissole of minced meat or flaked fish. [from Old French *costelette*, little rib, from Latin *costa*, rib]

cut-off *noun* **1** the point at which something is cut off or separated. **2** a stopping of a flow or supply.

cut-out *noun* **1** something cut out of a newspaper, etc. **2** a safety device for breaking an electrical circuit.

cutter[1] *noun* a person or thing that cuts.

cutter[2] *noun* **1** a small, single-masted sailing ship. **2** a ship's boat. **3** a motor launch sometimes armed. [from CUT]

cut-throat — *adj.* **1** *said of competition, etc* very keen and aggressive. **2** *said of a card game* played by three people. — *noun* **1** a murderer. **2** a long-bladed razor with a handle.

cutting — *noun* **1** an extract, article, or picture cut from a newspaper, etc. **2** a piece cut from a plant for rooting or grafting. **3** a narrow excavation made through high ground for a road or railway. — *adj.* hurtful; sarcastic.
. . . .
▤ *noun* **1** clipping, extract, piece. *adj.* hurtful, sarcastic, wounding, stinging, biting, caustic, acid, scathing, bitter, mordant, piercing, malicious.
. . . .

cuttlefish *noun* (PL. **cuttlefish**, **cuttlefishes**) any of about 100 species of mollusc related to the squid and octopus, having a shield-shaped body, inside which is a chalky plate containing gas-filled cells which make the animal buoyant. [from Anglo-Saxon *cudele*]

cutwater *noun* **1** the sharp vertical front edge of a ship's prow. **2** a pointed projection at the base of a bridge support.

CV *abbrev.* curriculum vitae.

CVO *abbrev.* Commander of the (Royal) Victorian Order.

cwm /kuːm/ *noun* **1** the Welsh name for a valley or glen. **2** *Geog.* a cirque or corrie. [from Welsh *cwm*]

CWS *abbrev.* Co-operative Wholesale Society.

cwt *abbrev.* hundredweight. [from Latin *centum*, hundred + *wt*, weight]

CY *abbrev., as an international vehicle mark* Cyprus.

cyan /ˈsaɪən/ *noun* **1** a greenish blue. **2** a blue ink used as a primary colour in printing. [from Greek *kyanos*, blue]

cyanide *noun* **1** any of the poisonous salts of hydrocyanic acid, which contain the CN⁻ ion and smell of bitter almonds, especially potassium cyanide and sodium cyanide, which are extremely toxic and rapidly cause death. **2** the negatively charged CN⁻ ion, which is highly poisonous because of its ability to prevent uptake of oxygen by the respiratory pigment haemoglobin in the blood. [from Greek *kyanos*, blue (hydrocyanic acid having been first obtained from Prussian blue, a blue dye)]

cyanobacteria /saɪənoʊbakˈtɪərɪə/ *pl. noun* blue-green algae. [from Greek *kyanos*, blue]

cyanocobalamin /saɪənoʊkoʊˈbaləmɪn/ *noun* vitamin B12. [from CYANIDE + COBALT + VITAMIN]

cyanogen /saɪˈanədʒen/ *noun Chem.* (FORMULA **NCCN**) compound of carbon and nitrogen, consisting of a colourless inflammable poisonous gas with a smell of bitter almonds, formed by the action of acids on cyanides. [from Greek *kyanos*, blue]

cyanosed *adj., said of the skin* showing symptoms typical of cyanosis.

cyanosis /saɪəˈnoʊsɪs/ *noun Pathol.* a bluish-purple discoloration of the skin and mucous membranes, usually resulting from lack of oxygen in the blood, eg as a result of heart failure, lung disease, or inadequate levels of oxygen in the surrounding air. [from Greek *kyanos*, blue]

cyber- *combining form* forming words relating to electronic communications through computers: *cyberculture / cybersuit*.

cybernetic /saɪbəˈnetɪk/ *adj.* relating to or involving cybernetics.

cybernetics *noun* the comparative study of communication and automatic control processes in mechanical or electronic systems (eg machines or computers) and biological systems (eg the nervous system of animals, especially humans). [from Greek *kybernetes*, steersman]

cyberpunk *noun* a genre of science fiction depicting a society rigidly controlled by computer networks and the actions of hackers who rebel against it. [from CYBERNETIC + PUNK]

cyberspace *noun* **1** the three-dimensional artificial environment of virtual reality, generated by computer, that gives the user the impression of presence within the environment and of physically interacting with it. See also VIRTUAL REALITY. **2** the space in which electronic communication takes place over computer networks. [from CYBERNETIC + SPACE]

cycad /ˈsaɪkad/ *noun* a tropical or subtropical gymnosperm (cone-bearing plant), more closely resembling a palm than a conifer, and having an unbranched trunk covered with the remains of old leaf bases, and a crown of tough leathery leaves. [from Greek *koix*, palm, from a misreading of the plural *koikas*]

cyclamate /ˈsɪkləmeɪt/ *noun Chem.* either of two chemical compounds formerly used as artificial sweeteners and food additives. [from an invented chemical name]

cyclamen /ˈsɪkləmən/ *noun* **1** a perennial plant of the genus Cyclamen, native to Europe and Asia, having heart-shaped leaves growing directly from a fleshy corm, and nodding white, pink, purple, or red flowers, the outer petals of which are bent back. **2** the bright pink colour characteristic of this plant. [from Greek *kuklaminos*]

cycle /ˈsaɪkəl/ — *noun* **1** a constantly repeating series of events or processes. **2** *Physics* one of a regularly repeated set of similar changes, eg in the movement of a wave. The duration of one cycle is equal to the *period* of the motion, and the rate at which a cycle is repeated per unit of time is equal to its *frequency.* One hertz represents a frequency of one cycle per second. **3** a series of poems, songs, plays, etc centred on a particular person or happening. **4** a bicycle or motor cycle. — *verb intrans.* **1** to ride a bicycle. **2** to happen in cycles. [from Greek *kyklos*, circle]

◨ *noun* **1** circle, round, rotation, revolution, series, sequence.

cyclic /'saɪklɪk/ or **cyclical** *adj.* **1** relating to, containing, or moving in a cycle. **2** recurring in cycles. **3** arranged in a ring or rings. **4** *Chem.* denoting an organic chemical compound whose molecules contain one or more closed rings of atoms, eg benzene.

cyclically *adv.* in a cyclical way.

cyclist /'saɪklɪst/ *noun* the rider of a bicycle or motor cycle.

cyclo- /'saɪkloʊ/ *combining form* forming words meaning: **1** circle; ring; cycle. **2** *Chem.* cyclic compound. **3** bicycle. [from Greek *kyklos*, circle]

cyclo-cross *noun* a cross-country bicycle race in the course of which bicycles have to be carried over natural obstacles.

cyclometer /saɪ'klɒmɪtə(r)/ *noun* a device for recording the revolutions of a wheel, used on a bicycle to measure the distance travelled. [CYCLO + -METER]

cyclone /'saɪkloʊn/ *noun* **1** *Meteorol.* an area of low atmospheric pressure in which winds spiral inward towards a central low, blowing in an anticlockwise direction in the northern hemisphere and a clockwise direction in the southern hemisphere. Cyclones are often associated with stormy weather. Also called DEPRESSION, LOW. **2** a violent tropical storm caused by such an area of low atmospheric pressure, and accompanied by torrential rain and extremely strong winds, often causing widespread destruction and loss of life. [from Greek *kyklon*, a whirling round]

cyclonic /saɪ'klɒnɪk/ *adj.* relating to or characteristic of a cyclone.

cyclopedia /saɪkloʊ'piːdɪə/ or **cyclopaedia** *noun* an encyclopedia.

cyclostyle — *noun* a duplicating machine that reproduces from a stencil. — *verb* to reproduce by means of a cyclostyle. [from CYCLO- + Latin *stylus*, writing tool]

cyclotron *noun* *Physics* a circular type of particle accelerator. [from CYCLO- + *-tron*, denoting particle accelerator]

cygnet /'sɪgnɪt/ *noun* a young swan. [from Greek *kyknos*, swan]

cylinder /'sɪlɪndə(r)/ *noun* **1** *Geom.* a solid figure of uniform circular cross-section, in which the curved surface is at right angles to the base. **2** a container, machine part, or other object of this shape, eg a storage container for compressed gas. **3** *Engineering* in an internal combustion engine, the tubular cylinder within which the chemical energy of the burning fuel is converted to the mechanical energy of a moving piston. [from Greek *kylindros*, roller]

◨ **2** barrel, drum, reel, bobbin, spool, spindle, column.

cylindrical /sɪ'lɪndrɪkəl/ *adj.* having the shape of a cylinder.

cyma /'saɪmə/ or **cymatium** *noun* an S-shaped or ogee moulding of the cornice in classical orders of architecture. When concave above and convex below it is known as a *cyma recta*; when convex above and concave below it is known as a *cyma reversa*. [from Greek *kyma*, a billow]

cymbal /'sɪmbəl/ *noun* a plate-like brass percussion instrument, either beaten with a drumstick, or used as one of a pair that are struck together to produce a ringing clash. [from Greek *kymbalon*]

cymbalist *noun* a person who plays the cymbals.

cymbidium /sɪm'bɪdɪəm/ *noun* an orchid of the genus Cymbidium, native to tropical forests from Asia to Australia. It is widely cultivated for its large showy flowers, which are much used in floristry and as cut flowers. [from Latin *cymba*, boat]

cyme /saɪm/ *noun* *Bot.* an inflorescence (flowering shoot) in which the main stem and each of its branches ends in a flower, and all subsequent flowers develop from lateral buds arising below the apical flowers. [from Greek *kyma*, wave]

cymose *adj.* bearing cymes, or in the form of a cyme.

Cymric /'kɪmrɪk/ — *adj.* of or belonging to Wales, its people, or language. — *noun* the Welsh language. [from Welsh *Cymru*, Wales]

cynic /'sɪnɪk/ *noun* **1** a person who habitually doubts or questions human goodness or sincerity. **2** (**Cynic**) *Philos.* a member of a discontinuous group of philosophers, influential in Greece and Rome 4c BC–6c AD. [from Greek *kyon*, dog]

◨ **1** sceptic, doubter, pessimist, killjoy, *colloq.* spoilsport, scoffer.

cynical *adj.* characterized by habitual scepticism about human goodness.

◨ sceptical, doubtful, distrustful, pessimistic, negative, scornful, derisive, contemptuous, sneering, scoffing, mocking, sarcastic, sardonic, ironic.

cynically *adv.* in a cynical way.

cynicism /'sɪnɪsɪzm/ *noun* **1** the attitude, beliefs, or behaviour of a cynic. **2** a cynical act, remark, etc.

◨ **1** scepticism, doubt, disbelief, distrust, pessimism, scorn, sarcasm, irony.

cynosure /'saɪnəʃʊə(r)/ *noun* the focus of attention; the centre of attraction. [from Greek *Kynosoura*, dog's tail, ie the Little Bear constellation, used as a guide by sailors]

cypher /'saɪfə(r)/ another spelling of CIPHER.

cypress /'saɪprəs/ *noun* **1** a coniferous evergreen tree or shrub of the genus Cupressus, native to north temperate regions, and widely planted and naturalized throughout W Europe, having paired scale-like leaves, less than 1mm long, and rounded cones composed of many woody scales that sometimes remain on the branches for years. **2** the timber of this tree, which contains an aromatic resin and is insect-repellent. [from Greek *kyparissos*]

Cypriot /'sɪprɪət/ — *noun* **1** a native of Cyprus, an E Mediterranean island. **2** the dialect of Greek spoken in Cyprus. — *adj.* of or belonging to Cyprus, its people, or language.

Cyrillic /sɪ'rɪlɪk/ *adj.* of or in the alphabet used for Russian, Bulgarian, and related languages, said to have been invented by St Cyril.

cyst /sɪst/ *noun* **1** *Anat.* an abnormal sac or closed cavity that contains fluid, semi-solid material, or gas, eg an ovarian cyst, which forms spontaneously, or a sebaceous cyst, which forms in the skin when the duct of a sebaceous gland becomes blocked. **2** *Biol.* the dormant or resting stage in the life cycle of certain bacteria, protozoa, or other organisms which is surrounded by a tough outer layer that protects it from unfavourable environmental conditions. [from Greek *kystis*, bladder, pouch]

cysteine /'sɪstiːn/ *noun* *Biochem.* an amino acid that is found in proteins.

cystic *adj.* **1** relating to or resembling a cyst. **2** enclosed within or having a cyst. **3** of or relating to the gall bladder or urinary bladder.

cystic fibrosis *Medicine* a hereditary disease in which the exocrine glands (especially of the lungs, pancreas, mouth, and intestinal tract) produce abnormally thick mucus that blocks the bronchi, pancreas, and intestinal glands, causing recurring bronchitis and other respiratory problems, impaired absorption of food, and (in children) failure to gain weight.

cystine /'sɪstiːn/ *noun* *Biochem.* an amino acid that is found in proteins, especially keratin. [from CYST]

cystitis /sɪ'staɪtɪs/ *noun* *Medicine* inflammation of the urinary bladder, usually caused by bacterial infection, and more common in women than in men. The main symptoms are a desire to pass urine frequently, and pain or a burning sensation when passing urine.

-cyte, cyto- *combining forms* forming words denoting a cell: *erythrocyte, cytochrome.* [from Greek *kytos*, vessel]

cytochrome *noun Biochem.* in the cells of living organisms, any of a group of substances that play an important role in the breakdown of carbohydrates to release energy.

cytogenetics *noun Genetics* the scientific study of the relationship between inheritance and cell structure, especially the origin, structure, and function of chromosomes, and their effects on inheritance in populations.

cytokinesis *noun Genetics* during the last stages of cell division (when the nucleus has already divided), the division of the cytoplasm of the cell into two parts, resulting in the formation of two daughter cells which may or may not be equal in size.

cytokinin /saɪtoʊˈkaɪnɪn/ *noun Bot.* any of various plant hormones that control growth by stimulating the division of plant cells. [from CYTO- + Greek *kineein*, to move]

cytological /saɪtəˈlɒɪkəl/ *adj.* relating to cytology.

cytologist /saɪˈtɒləɪst/ *noun* a scientist who specializes in cytology.

cytology /saɪˈtɒləɪ/ *noun* **1** the scientific study of the structure and function of individual cells, especially as revealed by examination with a microscope. **2** the detailed structure of a particular plant or animal tissue as revealed by examination with a microscope.

cytoplasm *noun Biol.* that part of a living cell, excluding the nucleus, that is enclosed by the cell membrane. The cytoplasm contains a range of organelles (specialized structures with a specific function) such as mitochondria, ribosomes, and (in plants only) chloroplasts. [from CYTO- + Greek *plasma*, body]

cytosine /ˈsaɪtəsɪn/ *noun Biochem.* a base derived from pyrimidine, and one of the four bases found in nucleic acids (DNA and RNA).

cytoskeleton *noun Biol.* in the cytoplasm of a living cell, a network of protein filaments that forms the structural framework of the cell.

cytosol *noun Biol.* the soluble component of the cytoplasm.

cytotoxic *adj. Biol.* describing any agent, especially a drug, that destroys or prevents the division of cells, and is used in chemotherapy to treat various forms of cancer.

czar /zɑː(r)/ see TSAR.

Czech /tʃɛk/ — *noun* **1** a native of former Czechoslovakia or the Czech Republic (since its separation from Slovakia in 1993), or formerly of Bohemia or Moravia. **2** one of the two principal languages of the Czechs (the other being Slovak). — *adj.* of or relating to the Czechs or their language. [from the Polish spelling *czech*]

D

D¹ or **d** *noun* (PL. **Ds, D's, d's**) **1** the fourth letter of the English alphabet. **2** (*usually* **D**) the fourth highest grade or quality, or a mark indicating this. **3** (**D**) *Mus.* **a** the second note in the scale of C major. **b** a musical key with the note D as its base. **4** (**D**) the D-shaped mark on a billiards table.

D² *abbrev.* **1** *North Amer., esp. US* Democrat. **2** *as an international vehicle mark Deutschland*, Germany. **3** *Cards* diamonds. See also 3-D.

D³ *symbol* **1** the Roman numeral for 500. **2** *Chem.* deuterium.

d *abbrev.* **1** deci-. **2** a penny or pence (in the UK before 1971). See also s. [from Latin *denarius*]

d. *abbrev.* **1** daughter. **2** died.

'd *contr.* **1** would: *I'd go.* **2** had: *he'd gone.* **3** *colloq.* did: *where'd he go?*

DA *abbrev.* (PL. **DAs, DA's**) *North Amer., esp. US* District Attorney.

da *abbrev.* deca-.

dab¹ — *verb* (**dabbed, dabbing**) **1** *intrans., trans.* to touch lightly and usually repeatedly with a cloth, etc. **2** (**dab something on** or **off**) to spread it on or remove it with light touches of a cloth, etc. — *noun* **1** a small amount of something creamy or liquid. **2** a light, gentle touch. **3** a gentle blow. **4** (**dabs**) *slang* fingerprints. [from Middle English *dabben*; probably imitative]

· · · · · · · · · · · · · · · · · · · ·

▣ *verb* **1** pat, tap, daub, swab, wipe. *noun* **1** bit, *colloq.* dollop, drop, speck, spot, trace, smear, smudge, fleck. **2** touch, pat, stroke, tap.

· ·

dab² *noun* a small brown European flatfish with rough scales. [from Old French *dabbe*]

dab³ — **a dab hand** an expert.

dabble *verb* **1** *trans., intrans.* to move or shake (one's hand, foot, etc) about in water, especially playfully. **2** *intrans.* (**dabble at** or **in** or **with something**) to do it or study it without serious effort. [from DAB¹ 1 or Dutch *dabbelen*]

· · · · · · · · · · · · · · · · · · · ·

▣ **1** paddle, moisten, wet, sprinkle, splash. **2** trifle with, tinker with, toy with, dally with.

· ·

dabbler *noun* a person who dabbles in some activity.

· · · · · · · · · · · · · · · · · · · ·

▣ amateur, dilettante, trifler.

▣ professional, expert.

· ·

dabchick *noun* a small duck-like bird, the little grebe.

da capo /dɑː ˈkɑːpoʊ/ *Mus.* an indication to the performer to go back to the beginning of the piece. [from Italian *da capo*, from the beginning]

dace *noun* (PL. **dace, daces**) a small European river fish. [from Old French *dars*, dart]

dacha /ˈdatʃə/ *noun* a country house or cottage in Russia, especially one provided for the use of a person of importance. [from Russian *dach*, originally meaning 'gift' (especially from a ruler)]

dachshund /ˈdaksʌnd/ *noun* a breed of small dog with a long body and very short legs. [from German *Dachs*, badger + *Hund*, dog]

dacoit or **dakoit** /dəˈkɔɪt/ *noun* an armed robber or bandit, one of a gang in India or Burma, especially in the 18c and 19c. [from Hindi *dākait*, robber]

dactyl /ˈdaktɪl/ *noun Poetry* a foot consisting of one long or stressed syllable followed by two short or unstressed ones. [from Greek *daktylos*, finger, from the similarity between the lengths of the syllables in a dactyl and the lengths of the bones in a finger (one long and two short)]

dactylic /dakˈtɪlɪk/ *adj. Poetry* consisting of or written in dactyls.

dad *noun colloq.* a father. [from the sound *da da* made by a baby]

daddy *noun* (PL. **daddies**) *colloq.* **1** a father. **2** the oldest, biggest, best, worst, etc example of something: *a daddy of a thunderstorm.* [from DAD]

daddy-long-legs *noun Brit. colloq.* a cranefly.

dado /ˈdeɪdoʊ/ *noun* (PL. **dadoes, dados**) **1** the lower part of the wall of a room when decorated differently from the upper part. **2** *Archit.* the plain square part of the base of a column or pedestal. [from Italian *dado*, dice]

daemon /ˈdiːmən/ *noun* **1** a spirit occupying a position halfway between gods and men. **2** a spirit which guards a place or takes care of or helps a person. See also DEMON. [from Greek *daimon*]

daffodil /ˈdafədɪl/ — *noun* **1** a flowering plant of the genus *Narcissus* that has an underground bulb and produces a single bright yellow flower consisting of a central trumpet surrounded by six petals. **2** the flower of this plant. **3** a pale yellow. — *adj.* pale yellow. [from Middle English *affodille*; the initial *d* is unexplained]

daft *adj. Brit. colloq.* **1** silly or foolish. **2** insane or mad. **3** (**daft about** or **on someone** or **something**) enthusiastic about or keen on them. [from Anglo-Saxon *gedæfte*, meek, mild]

· · · · · · · · · · · · · · · · · · · ·

▣ **1** foolish, crazy, silly, stupid, absurd, *colloq.* dotty, idiotic, inane. **2** insane, mad, lunatic, simple, crazy, mental. **3** enthusiastic about, *colloq.* crazy about, infatuated with.

▣ **1** sensible. **2** sane.

· ·

dagger *noun* **1** *Hist.* a knife or short sword with a pointed end, used for stabbing. **2** *in books, etc* the symbol (†), used as a reference mark. — **at daggers drawn** openly showing anger or dislike and on the point of fighting. **look daggers at someone** to give them a fierce or angry look.

dago /ˈdeɪgoʊ/ *noun* (PL. **dagoes**) *offensive* a person of Spanish, Portuguese, Italian or S American origin. [probably from Spanish *Diego*, James]

daguerreotype /dəˈgerəʊtaɪp/ *noun* **1** an early type of photography invented by Louis Daguerre, which used mercury vapour to develop an exposure of silver iodide on a copper plate. **2** a photograph made by this method.

dahl see DAL.

dahlia /ˈdeɪlɪə/ *noun* a garden plant with large brightly coloured flowers, some varieties having ball-like heads with many petals. [named after the 18c Swedish botanist Anders Dahl]

Dáil or **Dáil Éireann** /dɔɪl ˈɛərən/ *noun* the lower house of the parliament of the Republic of Ireland. [from Irish *Dáil*, assembly of Ireland]

daily — *adj.* **1** happening, appearing, etc every day, or every day except Sunday, or now often every day except Saturday and Sunday. **2** relating to a single day. — *adv.* every day. — *noun* (PL. **dailies**) **1** a newspaper published every day except Sunday. **2** *Brit. colloq.* a person, usually a woman, who is paid to clean and tidy a house regularly, but not necessarily every day. [from DAY]

■ *adj.* **1** regular, routine, everyday, customary, common, commonplace, ordinary.

daily bread the money, food, etc one needs to live.

daily dozen *old use* physical exercises performed every day for the sake of one's health.

daintily *adv.* with a dainty or neat manner.

dainty — *adj.* (**daintier, daintiest**) **1** small, pretty, neat, and usually delicate. **2** *said of food* particularly nice to eat. **3** *often derog.* very, or excessively, careful and sensitive about what one does or says. — *noun* (PL. **dainties**) something small and nice to eat, especially a small cake or sweet. [from Old French *daintie*, worthiness]

■ *adj.* **1** delicate, elegant, exquisite, refined, fine, graceful, neat, charming. **3** fastidious, fussy, particular, scrupulous, nice.
☒ *adj.* **1** gross, clumsy.

daiquiri /'dakərı/ *noun* a drink made with rum, lime juice and sugar. [from *Daiquiri* in Cuba]

dairy *noun* (PL. **dairies**) **1** a farm building where milk is cooled and stored before being transported to a processing plant or factory. **2** a plant or factory that processes milk and milk products. [from Middle English *daierie*, from *daie*, dairymaid]

dairy cattle *Agric.* cows that are kept to produce milk, and to rear calves in order to maintain a dairy herd, eg Friesian and Jersey breeds.

dairy farm a farm which specializes in producing milk, etc.

dairy farmer a farmer working in dairy products.

dairymaid *noun Hist.* a milkmaid.

dairyman or **dairywoman** *noun* a person who looks after the dairy cows on a farm.

dais /'deɪɪs/ *noun* a raised platform in a hall, eg for speakers at a meeting. [from Old French *deis*]

daisy *noun* (PL. **daisies**) **1** any of various common wild and cultivated flowering plants belonging to the sunflower family (Compositae), eg ox-eye daisy, Michaelmas daisy. **2** the common daisy (*Bellis perennis*), which has a flowerhead with a yellow centre consisting of many tiny flowers (florets), surrounded by white bracts. [from Anglo-Saxon *dæges eage*, day's eye]

daisy-wheel *noun* in a typewriter, etc, a metal disc divided into separate spokes, each with a letter of the alphabet at the end, the disc rotating so that the letter printed corresponds to the letter struck on the keyboard.

dal or **dahl** or **dhal** /dɑːl/ *noun* **1** any of various edible dried split pea-like seeds. **2** a cooked dish made of any of these seeds. [from Hindi *dal*, to split]

Dalai Lama /dalaɪ 'lɑːmə/ the chief lama, and ruler of Tibet until 1959.

dale *noun* a valley, especially in the N of England. [from Anglo-Saxon *dæl*]

Dalit *noun* a member of the former Untouchable class in India. [Hindi]

dalliance *noun* idle wasting of time.

dally *verb intrans.* (**dallies, dallied**) **1** to waste time idly or frivolously. **2** (**dally with someone**) *old use* to flirt with them. [from Old French *dalier*, to chat]

Dalmatian /dal'meɪʃən/ *noun* a large short-haired dog, white with dark spots.

dal segno /dal 'senjoʊ/ *Mus.* an indication that the performer must go back to the sign. [from Italian *dal segno*, from the sign]

dalton /'dɔːltən/ *noun Chem.* an atomic mass unit. [named after the UK chemist John Dalton]

dam¹ — *noun* **1** a barrier built across a river to hold back the flow of water, eg in order to form a reservoir to store water for domestic or industrial use, or to provide a head of water for a hydroelectric power station. **2** the water confined behind such a structure, often forming a lake or reservoir. — *verb* (**dammed, damming**) to hold back with a dam. [probably from Old German dialect *Damm*]

■ *noun* **1** barrier, barrage, embankment, blockage, obstruction, hindrance. *verb* block, confine, restrict, check, barricade, staunch, stem, obstruct.

dam² *noun, said of horses, cattle, and sheep* a female parent. [from DAME]

damage — *noun* **1** harm or injury, or loss caused by injury. **2** (**damages**) *Legal* payment due for loss or injury caused by another person, organization, etc. — *verb* to cause harm, injury, or loss to. [from Old French *damage*, from Latin *damnum*, loss]

■ *noun* **1** harm, injury, hurt, destruction, devastation, loss, suffering, mischief, mutilation, impairment, detriment. **2** compensation, reimbursement, indemnity, restitution. *verb* harm, injure, hurt, spoil, ruin, impair, mar, wreck, deface, mutilate, weaken, tamper with, play havoc with, incapacitate.
☒ *noun* **1** repair. *verb* mend, repair, fix.

damaged *adj.* harmed, injured; broken.

damaging *adj.* harmful; having a bad effect, especially on a reputation.

damask /'daməsk/ — *noun* a type of cloth, originally silk, now usually linen, with a pattern woven into it, often used for tablecloths, curtains, etc. — *adj.* greyish-pink or greyish-red. [from *Damascus* in Syria, where such cloth was made]

damask rose a sweet-smelling pink or red variety of rose.

dame *noun* **1** a woman who has been awarded the highest or second-highest class of distinction in any of four British orders of chivalry, or honours for service or merit awarded by the Queen or the Government. See also KNIGHT. **2** *North Amer. slang* a woman. **3** a comic female character in a pantomime, usually played by a man. [from Old French *dame*, from Latin *domina*, lady]

damn — *verb* **1** *Relig.* to sentence to never-ending punishment in hell. **2** to declare to be useless or worthless. **3** to suggest or prove the guiltiness of. — *interj.* (**damn it**) an expression of annoyance or disappointment. — *adj. often colloq., for emphasis* annoying; hateful: *the damn cold.* — *adv. colloq.* used for emphasis: *it's damn cold.* — **as near as damn it** *colloq.* as accurately, closely, etc as possible; acceptably accurate, etc; very nearly. **be damned if one will do something** *colloq.* to refuse to do it. **damn all** *colloq.* nothing at all. **damn someone** or **something with faint praise** to praise them so unenthusiastically as to seem disapproving. **not give a damn** *colloq.* not to care at all. [from Latin *damnare*, to condemn]

■ *verb* **1** condemn, doom, curse, imprecate. **2** condemn, denounce, criticize, censure, *colloq.* slate, denounce, castigate, *colloq.* slam.
☒ *verb* **1** bless.

damnable /'damnəbl/ *adj.* **1** hateful; awful; deserving to be condemned. **2** annoying.

damnably *adv.* annoyingly; very.

damnation /dam'neɪʃən/ — *noun Relig.* **1** eternal punishment in hell. **2** the act of condemning or state of being condemned to such punishment. — *interj.* an expression of annoyance or disappointment.

▤ *noun* **1** hell, perdition. **2** condemnation, doom, denunciation, excommunication, anathema.

damned /damd/ — *adj.* **1** *Relig.* sentenced to damnation. **2** *colloq.* annoying, hateful, etc. — *adv. colloq.* extremely; very: *damned cold.* — **do one's damnedest** *colloq.* to do one's utmost.

damning /ˈdamɪŋ/ *adj.* **1** highly critical. **2** proving or suggesting guilt.

damp — *adj.* slightly wet. — *noun* slight wetness, eg in walls or the air, especially if cold and unpleasant. — *verb* **1** to make slightly wet. **2** *said of ardour, spirits, etc* to discourage; to deaden. **3** *Mus.* to press (the strings, or a string, of an instrument) to stop or lessen vibration. — **damp something down 1** to make (emotions, interest, etc) less strong. **2** to make (a fire) burn more slowly. [from Middle English *damp*, harmful vapour]

▤ *adj.* moist, wet, clammy, dank, humid, dewy, muggy, drizzly, misty, soggy. *noun* dampness, moisture, clamminess, dankness, humidity, wet, dew, drizzle, fog, mist, vapour. *verb* **1** moisten, wet, dampen, sprinkle, spray. **2** discourage, deter, dash, dull, deaden, restrain, check, depress, dismay. **damp down 1** subdue, moderate, quieten, diminish, reduce, lessen, calm, placate, allay.

▣ *adj.* dry, arid. *noun* dryness. *verb* **1** dry. **2** encourage, fire.

damp-course or **damp-proof course** *noun* a horizontal layer of material in a wall of a building, usually near the ground, which stops damp rising through the bricks.

dampen *verb* (**dampened, dampening**) **1** to make slightly wet. **2** *said of enthusiasm, ardour etc* to discourage; to deaden. — **dampen down** *said of emotions, interest, etc* to become less strong. **dampen something down 1** to make (emotions, interest, etc) less strong. **2** to make (a fire) burn more slowly.

▤ *verb* **1** moisten, wet, spray, sprinkle. **2** discourage, deter, dash, dull, deaden, restrain, check, depress, dismay, dishearten, reduce, lessen, moderate, decrease, diminish, muffle, stifle, smother. **dampen something down 1** reduce, lessen, moderate, decrease, diminish, subdue, calm, allay.

▣ *verb* **1** dry. **2** encourage.

dampener *noun* a person or thing that dampens or causes dampness.

damper *noun* **1** something which lessens enthusiasm, interest, etc. **2** a movable plate which allows the flow of air to a fire, etc to be controlled so that the amount of heat may be altered. — **put a damper on something** to lessen enthusiasm for it, or interest in it, etc.

damp-proof *adj.*, *said of a material or substance* not allowing wetness to get through.

damp-proof course see DAMP-COURSE.

damp squib a disappointingly uninteresting or unsuccessful event.

damsel /ˈdamzəl/ *noun old use, literary* a girl or young woman. [from Old French *dameisele*]

damselfly *noun* (PL. **damselflies**) a large insect with a long body and two pairs of slender wings, typically held together over the abdomen when at rest. Damselflies are powerful predators, both as aquatic larvae and as flying adults.

damson /ˈdamzən/ *noun* **1** a small deciduous tree (*Prunus domestica* var. *institia*), native to W Asia. **2** the oval blue-black fruit of this tree, resembling a small plum, and having a waxy bloom. [from Latin *Damascenus*, of Damascus in Syria]

Dan. *abbrev.* **1** (*also* **Dan**) *Biblical* the Book of Daniel. **2** Danish.

dan *noun* any of the grades of black belt awarded for particular levels of skill in judo, karate, etc. [from Japanese]

dance — *verb* **1** *intrans.* to make a usually repeated series of rhythmic steps or movements (usually in time to music). **2** to perform (a particular series of such steps or movements): *dance a waltz.* **3** (*usually* **dance about** or **around**) to move or jump quickly up and down or from side to side. **4** to bounce (a baby), usually on one's knee. — *noun* **1** a series of fixed steps, usually made in time to music. **2** a social gathering at which people dance. **3** a piece of music played for dancing. — **dance attendance on someone** *derog.* to follow them and do whatever they want. **dance to someone's tune** to do what they want or expect. **lead someone a merry dance** *Brit.* to involve them in unnecessary difficulties and exertions. [from Old French *danser*, to dance]

▤ *verb* **3** waltz, jig, caper, prance, frolic, frisk, cavort, rollick. *noun* **2** ball, *colloq.* hop, *colloq.* knees-up, social, *colloq.* shindig.

Dances include: waltz, quickstep, foxtrot, tango, polka, one-step, military two-step, valeta, Lancers, rumba, salsa, samba, lambada, mambo, bossanova, beguine, fandango, flamenco, mazurka, bolero, paso doble, can-can; rock 'n' roll, jive, twist, stomp, bop, jitterbug, mashed potato; black bottom, Charleston, cha-cha, turkey trot; Circassian circle, Paul Jones, jig, reel, quadrille, Highland fling, morris dance, clog dance, hoe-down, hokey-cokey, Lambeth Walk, conga, belly dance; galliard, gavotte, minuet.

Dance functions include: disco, dance, social, teadance, barn dance, ball, fancy dress ball, charity ball, hunt ball, *colloq.* hop, *colloq.* knees-up, *colloq.* shindig, *colloq.* rave, *US* prom, ceilidh.

dancer *noun* a person who dances, especially professionally.

dancing *noun* the activity or occupation of a dancer.

Types of dancing include: ballet, tap, ballroom, old-time, disco, folk, country, Irish, Highland, Latin-American, flamenco, clog-dancing, morris dancing, limbo-dancing, break-dancing, robotics.

D and C *abbrev.* dilatation and curettage.

dandelion /ˈdandɪlaɪən/ *noun* a perennial plant of the genus *Taraxacum*, found in most temperate regions, having a rosette of deeply notched leaves and a single yellow flowerhead. [from French *dent de lion*, lion's tooth]

dander — **get one's** or **someone's dander up** *colloq.* to become angry, or make someone angry.

dandle *verb* to bounce (usually a small child) on one's knee.

dandruff *noun* a common condition in which thin whitish flakes of dead skin are deposited on the scalp as a result of an increase in the normal loss of cells from the outermost layer of the skin.

dandy — *noun* (PL. **dandies**) a man who pays a lot of attention to his appearance, dressing very fashionably or elegantly. — *adj. colloq.* (**dandier, dandiest**) good; fine.

Dane *noun* **1** a native or citizen of Denmark. **2** *Hist.* any of the Vikings from Scandinavia who invaded Britain in the 9c–11c. See also DANISH. [from Danish *Daner*, Danes]

Danegeld /ˈdeɪngeld/ *noun* **1** a tax levied on land in England between 991 and 1012, to buy peace from the Danish invaders. **2** a bribe used to appease someone.

Danelaw /ˈdeɪnlɔː/ *noun* the part of England occupied by the Danes from the 9c to the 11c. [from Anglo-Saxon *Dena lagu*, Danes' law]

danger *noun* **1** a situation or state in which someone or something may suffer harm, an injury, or a loss: *in danger of falling.* **2** something that may cause harm, injury, or loss. **3** a possibility of something unpleasant happening. — **on**

the danger list *Medicine* so ill or seriously injured that there is a high risk of death. [from Old French *dangier*, power, especially to harm]

⊟ **1** peril, jeopardy, insecurity, precariousness, liability, vulnerability. **2** risk, threat, peril, hazard, menace.
⊟ **1** safety, security. **2** protection, safeguard.

danger money extra money paid to a person for doing a dangerous job.

dangerous *adj.* likely to or able to cause harm or injury.

⊟ unsafe, insecure, risky, threatening, hazardous, perilous, precarious, *colloq.* hairy, treacherous, vulnerable, exposed, menacing, alarming, critical, severe, serious, grave, nasty, reckless, breakneck, daring.
⊟ safe, secure, harmless.

dangle *verb* **1** *intrans., trans.* to hang loosely. **2** to offer or present (an idea, a possible reward, etc) to someone.

⊟ **1** hang, droop, swing, sway, flap, trail. **2** flaunt, flourish, wave, tempt, entice, lure, tantalize.

Danish — *adj.* **1** of Denmark or its inhabitants. **2** of the language spoken in Denmark. — *noun* **1** the language spoken in Denmark. **2** (**the Danish**) the people of Denmark. See also DANE. [from Old French *daneis*]

Danish blue a type of strong-tasting cheese, white with streaks of bluish mould through it.

Danish pastry a flat cake of rich, light pastry, with any of various types of sweet filling on the top.

dank *adj.*, *usually said of a place* unpleasantly wet and cold.

⊟ damp, moist, clammy, dewy, slimy, soggy.
⊟ dry.

Daphnia /ˈdafnɪə/ *noun* a common type of water flea, found in bodies of freshwater.

dapper *adj.*, *usually said of small men* neat and smart in appearance and lively in movement. [from Dutch *dapper*, brave]

dappled *adj.* marked with spots or rounded patches of a different, usually darker, colour.

⊟ speckled, mottled, spotted, stippled, dotted, flecked, freckled, variegated, bespeckled, piebald, checkered.

dapple-grey — *adj.*, *said of a horse* of a pale grey colour with darker spots. — *noun* a dapple-grey horse.

Darby and Joan an old man and old woman who have been happily married for many years. [from characters in an 18c song]

dare — *verb* **1** *aux. intrans.* to be brave enough to do something frightening, difficult or dangerous: *he wouldn't dare to leave / dare I tell him?* **2** to challenge (someone to do something frightening, difficult, dangerous, etc). **3** to be brave enough to risk facing: *dare his father's anger.* — *noun* a challenge (to do something dangerous, etc). — **how dare you!** an expression of anger or indignation at something someone has said or done. **I dare say** or **daresay** probably; I suppose: *I dare say you're right.* [from Anglo-Saxon *durran*]

⊟ *verb* **1** risk, venture, presume. **2** challenge, goad, provoke, taunt. **3** defy, brave. *noun* challenge, provocation, taunt.

daredevil — *noun* a person who does dangerous or adventurous things without worrying about the risks involved. — *adj.*, *said of actions, etc* daring and dangerous.

⊟ *noun* adventurer, desperado, madcap. *adj.* adventurous,

daring, intrepid, dangerous, hazardous, madcap, reckless, rash.
⊟ *noun* coward. *adj.* cautious.

daring — *adj.* **1** bold, courageous or adventurous. **2** designed or intended to shock or surprise. — *noun* boldness, courage.

⊟ *adj.* BOLD, ADVENTUROUS. **1** intrepid, fearless, brave, plucky, audacious, dauntless, reckless, rash, impulsive, valiant. **2** risqué, naughty. *noun* boldness, fearlessness, courage, bravery, nerve, audacity, *colloq.* guts, intrepidity, defiance, pluck, rashness, spirit, grit, gall, prowess.
⊟ *adj.* **1** cautious, timid, afraid. *noun* caution, timidity, cowardice.

dark — *adj.* **1** without light. **2** *said of a colour* not light or pale; closer to black than white. **3** *said of a person or the colour of their skin or hair* not light or fair. **4** sad or gloomy. **5** evil or sinister: *dark powers.* **6** mysterious and unknown: *a dark secret.* — *noun* **1** (*usually* **the dark**) the absence of light. **2** the time of day when night begins and there is no more light: *after dark.* **3** a dark colour. — **in the dark** not knowing or aware of something. **keep it dark** to keep something secret. [from Anglo-Saxon *deorc*, dark]

⊟ *adj.* **1** unlit, overcast, black, dim, unilluminated, shadowy, murky, cloudy, dusky, dingy. **4** sad, gloomy, cheerless, dismal, bleak, forbidding, sombre. **5** sinister, mournful, grim, ominous, menacing. **6** hidden, mysterious, obscure, secret, unintelligible, enigmatic, cryptic, abstruse. *noun* **1** darkness, dimness, gloom, murkiness, obscurity. **2** night, night-time, nightfall, dusk, twilight. **in the dark** ignorant, unaware, uninformed, unenlightened, uninitiated.
⊟ *adj.* **1** light. **4** bright, cheerful. **6** comprehensible. *noun* **1** light. **2** dawn.

Dark Ages the period of European history from about the 5c to the 11c, regarded as historically obscure and culturally uneventful.

darken *verb trans., intrans.* (**darkened, darkening**) to make or become dark or darker.

⊟ dim, blacken, cloud (over), dull.
⊟ lighten, brighten.

dark horse a person about whom little is known.

darkly *adv.* in a mysterious, gloomy, sinister or threatening way or tone of voice.

darkness *noun* being dark; a dark state.

⊟ dark, dimness, gloom, murkiness, obscurity, night, night-time, nightfall.

darkroom *noun* a room into which no ordinary light is allowed, used for developing photographs.

darky or **darkie** *noun offensive* a person with black or brown skin, especially a black.

darling — *noun* **1** *often used as a term of affection* a dearly loved person. **2** a lovable person or thing. — *adj.* **1** well loved. **2** *colloq.* delightful.

⊟ *noun* DEAR, SWEETHEART. **1** love, dearest, pet, beloved. *adj.* **1** dear, beloved, adored, cherished, precious, treasured. **2** delightful, lovely, adorable, sweet, *colloq.* cute.

darn [1] *verb* to mend by sewing with rows of stitches which cross each other.

darn [2] *interj.* a less offensive or emphatic substitute for **damn**.

darned *adj.* irritating; disliked.

darning *noun* **1** the work of darning clothes, etc. **2** clothes, etc which need to be darned or which have been darned.

dart — *noun* **1** a narrow, pointed weapon that can be thrown or fired. **2** a small sharp-pointed missile used in the game of darts. **3** a sudden quick movement. **4** a fold sewn into a piece of clothing to make it fit more neatly. — *verb* **1** *intrans.* to move suddenly and quickly. **2** *trans.* to send or give (a look or glance) quickly. [from Old French *dart*]

· · · · · · · · · · · · · · · · · · · ·

▣ *noun* **1** bolt, arrow, barb, shaft. **3** dash, rush, bound, spring, leap. *verb* **1** dash, bound, sprint, flit, flash, fly, rush, run, race, spring, tear. **2** throw, cast, hurl, fling, shoot, sling.

· ·

dartboard *noun* a circular target used in the game of darts.

darter *noun* a slender bird native to warm regions worldwide. It spears fish underwater with its long pointed bill, and swims with only its head and long neck above the water surface.

darting *adj.* moving suddenly and quickly.

darts *sing. noun* a game in which darts are thrown at a circular target (*dartboard*) divided into numbered sections, points being scored according to the section each dart hits.

Darwinism *noun Biol.* the theory of evolution by natural selection, proposed jointly by Charles Darwin and Alfred Russel Wallace.

dash[1] — *verb* **1** *intrans.* to run quickly; to rush. **2** *intrans.* to crash or smash. **3** to hurl or smash violently. **4** to destroy or put an end to (hopes, etc). — *noun* **1** a quick run or sudden rush. **2** a small amount of something added, especially a liquid. **3** a patch of colour. **4** a short line (-) used in writing to show a break in a sentence, etc. **5** in Morse code, the longer of the two lengths of signal element, written as a short line (see also DOT). **6** stylish confidence, energy, and enthusiasm. **7** *North Amer. Sport* a short race for fast runners. [from Middle English *daschen* or *dassen*, to rush or strike violently]

· · · · · · · · · · · · · · · · · · · ·

▣ *verb* **1** rush, dart, hurry, race, sprint, run, bolt, tear. **3** hurl, fling, throw, crash, smash. **4** discourage, disappoint, dampen, confound, blight, ruin, destroy, spoil, frustrate, smash, shatter. *noun* **1** sprint, dart, bolt, rush, spurt, race, run. **2** drop, pinch, touch, flavour, soupçon, suggestion, hint, bit, little. **3** splash, patch, spot, touch. **6** style, vigour, confidence, *literary* élan, verve, panache.

· ·

dash[2] *interj.* a milder and less offensive substitute for *damn.*

dashboard *noun Brit.* a panel with dials, switches and instruments in front of the driver's seat in a motor vehicle, boat, etc. [from DASH[1]; originally a board protecting the driver of a horse-drawn coach from splashes of mud]

dashing *adj.* **1** smart; stylish. **2** lively and enthusiastic.

· · · · · · · · · · · · · · · · · · · ·

▣ **1** smart, stylish, elegant, debonair, showy, flamboyant. **2** lively, vigorous, spirited, gallant, daring, bold, plucky, exuberant.

▣ **1** dowdy. **2** lethargic.

· ·

dastardly *adj. old use* cowardly, mean, and cruel. [probably connected with DAZED]

DAT /dat/ *abbrev.* digital audio tape.

dat. *abbrev.* dative.

data /ˈdeɪtə/ *noun originally pl* but now treated as *sing.* See also DATUM. **1** two or more pieces of information or facts, especially those obtained by scientific observation or experiment. **2** a collection of information in the form of numbers, characters, electrical signals, etc, that can be supplied to, stored, or processed by a computer. [from Latin *data*, things given]

▣ **1** information, documents, facts, input, statistics, figures, details, materials.

· ·

databank *noun Comput.* a collection of files or records containing bibliographic or textual data on a particular subject, stored in a computer so that a number of users may copy items of interest from it.

database *noun Comput.* an organized collection of computer data coded and stored in such a way that different categories of data in a wide variety of different forms can be accessed, often by many users and for a wide variety of applications.

data capture *Comput.* **1** any process by which information in the form of raw data is converted into a machine-readable form that can be processed by a computer. **2** the gathering or collecting of information, in the form of raw data, for this purpose.

data communications the sending of digitally encoded data between computers by means of communication lines.

dataglove *noun* an electronically wired glove which transmits the wearer's movements to a virtual reality monitor.

data processing the performance of operations on data by a computer system, especially the arrangement of large amounts of data into a more useful form according to specified rules and procedures.

date[1] — *noun* **1** the day of the month, and/or the year, recorded by a number or series of numbers. **2** a statement on a letter, document, etc giving usually the day, the month and the year when it was written, sent, etc. **3** a particular period of time in history: *costumes of an earlier date.* **4** *colloq.* a planned meeting or social outing, usually with a person of the opposite sex. **5** *North Amer. colloq.* a person of the opposite sex whom one is meeting or going out with. **6** *colloq.* an agreed time and place of performance. — *verb* **1** to put a date on. **2** to find, decide on, or guess the date of. **3** (**date back to** or **from a specified time**) to have begun or originated then. **4** to show the age of; to make (especially a person) seem old. **5** *intrans.* to become old-fashioned. **6** *trans., intrans. colloq.* to go out with (a person of the opposite sex), especially regularly. — **to date** up to the present time. [from Old French *date*, from Latin *datum*, given]

· · · · · · · · · · · · · · · · · · · ·

▣ *noun* **3** time, age, period, era, stage, epoch. **4** appointment, engagement, assignation, meeting, rendezvous. **5** escort, partner, friend, boyfriend, girlfriend.

· ·

date[2] *noun* **1** the date palm. **2** the yellowish to reddish-brown fruit of this tree, consisting of a large woody seed surrounded by sweet sticky flesh. [from French *datte*, from Greek *daktylos*, finger, date]

dated *adj.* no longer current or up to date.

· · · · · · · · · · · · · · · · · · · ·

▣ old-fashioned, out of date, outdated, outmoded, unfashionable, passé.

· ·

dateline *noun* **1** a line, usually at the top of a newspaper article, which gives the date and place of writing. **2** (*usually* **Date Line**) an imaginary line, based by international agreement on the meridian of 180°, running north to south across the middle of the Pacific. The date in countries to the west of it are one day ahead of the date in countries to the east.

date palm a tall tree with a crown of long spreading leaves, cultivated in N Africa and the Middle East for its yellowish to reddish-brown edible fruits.

date rape rape committed by someone known to the victim while both are on a date.

date-stamp — *noun* **1** a device, usually a rubber stamp, for printing the date on something. **2** the date printed by this. — *verb* to print with a date-stamp.

dative — *noun Grammar* in some languages, a case which

is mostly used to show that a noun or pronoun is the indirect object of a verb. — *adj. Grammar* of or in this case. [from Latin *dativus*, from *dare*, to give]

datum /'deɪtəm/ *noun* (PL. **data**) a piece of information. See also DATA. [from Latin *datum*, something given]

daub — *verb* 1 to spread roughly or unevenly on to or over a surface: *daubed paint on the walls.* 2 to cover (a surface) with a soft sticky substance or liquid. 3 *trans., intrans. derog.* to paint carelessly or without skill. — *noun* 1 soft, sticky material such as clay, often used as a covering for walls. See also WATTLE AND DAUB. 2 *derog. colloq.* an unskilful or carelessly done painting. [from Old French *dauber*, from Latin *dealbare*, to whitewash]

◨ *verb* 1 spread, dab, splash, spatter, splatter, splodge, splosh.

dauber *noun* a person or implement that daubs, especially in painting.

daughter /'dɔːtə(r)/ — *noun* 1 a female child considered in relation to her parents. 2 a woman closely associated with, involved with, or influenced by a person, thing, or place: *a faithful daughter of the Church.* — *adj.* derived by some process from and thought of as being like a daughter of: *French is a daughter language of Latin.* [from Anglo-Saxon *dohtor*]

daughterboard *noun Electron.* a printed circuit board that is plugged into a *motherboard* (a printed circuit board that can be interconnected with other circuit boards).

daughter-in-law *noun* (PL. **daughters-in-law**) the wife of one's son.

daughterly *adj.* like a daughter; befitting a daughter: *daughterly devotion.*

daunt *verb* to frighten, worry, or discourage. — **nothing daunted** not at all discouraged or less enthusiastic. [from Old French *danter*]

◨ discourage, dishearten, put off, dispirit, deter, intimidate, overawe, unnerve, alarm, dismay, frighten, scare.
◪ encourage.

daunting *adj.* intimidating; discouraging.

dauntless *adj.* fearless; not easily discouraged.

◨ fearless, undaunted, resolute, brave, courageous, bold, intrepid, daring, plucky, valiant.
◪ discouraged, disheartened.

dauphin /'dɔːfɪn/ *noun* the title of the eldest son of the reigning French monarch in the period 1350–1830. [from Old French, from Latin *Delphinus*, dolphin, a family name]

davenport /'davnpɔːt/ *noun* 1 *Brit.* a type of desk. 2 *North Amer.* a large sofa.

davit /'davɪt/ *noun* a curved device used as a crane on a ship, especially either one of a pair of such devices from which a lifeboat is hung and by means of which it can be lowered over the side of the ship. [from a form of the name *David*]

Davy Jones's locker the bottom of the sea, especially as the place where the bodies of drowned sailors lie. [from *Davy Jones*, a sailors' name for the evil spirit of the sea]

Davy lamp an oil-burning safety lamp, formerly widely used by coal miners, in which the flame is surrounded by a fine metal gauze. [named after the English chemist Sir Humphrey Davey]

dawdle *verb intrans.* 1 to walk more slowly than necessary or desirable. 2 to waste time, especially by taking longer than necessary to do something.

◨ DELAY, LINGER, *colloq.* DILLY-DALLY, DALLY. 1 loiter, lag, hang about, trail, potter along. 2 loaf, idle, potter about, *colloq.* mess about.
◪ HURRY.

dawdler *noun* a person who dawdles; an idler.

dawn — *noun* 1 the time of day when light first appears as the sun rises. 2 the beginning of (a new period of time, etc). — *verb* 1 *said of the day* to begin; to become light. 2 *said of an era, age, etc* to begin; to come into being. — **at the break of dawn** at the first light of day when the sun rises. **dawn on someone** to begin to be realized by them. [first recorded as *dawning*, probably from Old Norse, related to DAY]

◨ *noun* 1 sunrise, daybreak, morning, daylight. 2 beginning, start, emergence, onset, origin, birth, advent. *verb* 1 break, brighten, lighten, gleam, glimmer. 2 begin, appear, emerge, open, develop, originate, rise.
◪ *noun* 1 dusk. 2 end. *verb* CLOSE.

dawn chorus the singing of birds at dawn.

day *noun* 1 the period of 24 hours during which the Earth rotates once on its axis with respect to the Sun (*solar day*) or the stars (*sidereal day*). Ordinary time is expressed in terms of the solar day, which is divided into 24 hours, and is nearly four minutes longer than the sidereal day. 2 the period of time from sunrise to sunset. 3 the period of time in any 24 hours normally spent doing something, especially working: *the working day.* 4 (**day** or **days**) a particular period of time, usually in the past: *one's childhood days / it never happened in their day.* — **all in a** or **the day's work** a normal or acceptable part of one's work or routine. **day after day** continually and routinely for a long time. **day by day** as each day passes. **day in, day out** continuously and tediously without change. **have had one's day** to have passed the time of one's greatest success, influence, popularity, etc. **in this day and age** nowadays; in modern times. **make someone's day** to satisfy or delight them. **one of these days** at some time in the future. **one of those days** a day of difficulties or misfortunes. **that will be the day** *colloq.* that is unlikely to happen. **those were the days** that was a good or happy time. **win** or **carry the day** to win a victory. [from Anglo-Saxon *dæg*]

◨ 2 daytime, daylight. 4 age, period, time, date, era, generation, epoch. **day after day** regularly, continually, routinely, endlessly, persistently, monotonously, perpetually, relentlessly. **day by day** gradually, progressively, slowly but surely, steadily. **day in, day out** continuously, constantly, endlessly, persistently, monotonously, perpetually, relentlessly, unremittingly, non-stop.
◪ 2 night.

daybreak *noun* the time in the morning when light first appears in the sky; dawn.

day care supervision and care given by trained nurses or other staff to young children or elderly handicapped people during the day.

day centre or **day care centre** a place which provides supervision and care, and/or social activities, during the day for the elderly, the handicapped, people who have just left prison, etc.

daydream — *noun* pleasant thoughts which take one's attention away from what one is, or should be, doing. — *verb intrans.* to be engrossed in daydreams.

◨ *noun* fantasy, imagining, reverie, castles in the air, pipe dream, vision, musing, wish, dream, figment. *verb* fantasize, imagine, muse, dream.

daydreamer *noun* a person who daydreams, especially habitually.

daylight *noun* 1 the light given by the sun; natural light as opposed to electric light, etc. 2 the time in the morning when light first appears in the sky; dawn. — **beat the living daylights out of someone** *colloq.* to beat them severely. **in broad daylight** *said of a shocking or criminal act* 1 during the day. 2 openly, with no attempt to hide one's actions. **scare** or **frighten the living daylights out of someone** *colloq.* to frighten them greatly. **see daylight 1** to begin to understand. **2** to be near the end of a difficult or lengthy task.

daylight robbery *colloq.* greatly overcharging for something.

day nursery a place where young children are looked after during the day, eg while their parents are at work.

Day of Judgement or **Last Judgement** according to some beliefs, the time when the world will end, and God will judge all mankind.

day of reckoning a time when mistakes, failures, bad deeds, etc are punished.

day-release *noun Brit.* a system by which employees are given time off work (usually one day a week) to study at college, etc.

day return *Brit.* a reduced bus or train fare for a journey to somewhere and back again on the same day.

day shift 1 a period of working during the day. **2** the people who work during this period. See also BACK SHIFT, NIGHT SHIFT.

daytime *noun* the time when there is daylight, between sunrise and sunset.

day trading the practice of buying and selling shares on the stock exchange with the aim of making a profit over the period of a day, rather than over a longer term.

daze — *verb* to make (someone) feel confused or unable to think clearly (eg by a blow or shock). — *noun* a confused, forgetful or inattentive state of mind. [from Norse *dasask*, to be weary]

▪ *verb* stun, stupefy, shock, bewilder, confuse, baffle, dumbfound, amaze, surprise, startle, perplex, astonish, *colloq.* flabbergast, astound, stagger. *noun* bewilderment, confusion, stupor, trance, shock, distraction.

dazed *adj.* affected by a blow or shock; mentally confused.

▪ stunned, stupefied, bewildered, confused, baffled, dumbfounded, amazed, surprised, startled, astonished, *colloq.* flabbergasted, astounded.

dazzle — *verb* **1** to cause to be unable to see properly, with or because of a strong light. **2** to impress greatly by one's beauty, charm, skill, etc. — *noun* a splendid or blinding light. [from DAZE]

▪ *verb* **1** daze, blind, confuse, blur. **2** fascinate, impress, overwhelm, awe, overawe, amaze, astonish, bewitch, stupefy. *noun* sparkle, brilliance, magnificence, splendour, scintillation, glitter, glare.

dazzling *adj.* **1** temporarily blinding. **2** highly impressive; brilliant: *a dazzling display.*

▪ **1** blinding, glaring, blazing. **2** brilliant, superb, magnificent, impressive, awe-inspiring.

dB *abbrev.* decibel.

DBE *abbrev.* Dame Commander of the Order of the British Empire.

DBS *abbrev.* direct broadcasting by satellite.

DC *abbrev.* **1** *Mus.* da capo. **2** direct current. **3** data communications. **4** District Commissioner. **5** District of Columbia.

DCC *abbrev.* digital compact cassette, a digital audio tape in standard cassette format, played via a fixed-head tape recorder.

DCL *abbrev.* Doctor of Civil Law.

DCM *abbrev.* Distinguished Conduct Medal.

DCMG *abbrev.* Dame Commander of the Order of St Michael and St George.

DCVO *abbrev.* Dame Commander of the (Royal) Victorian Order.

DD *abbrev. Divinitatis Doctor* (Latin), Doctor of Divinity.

D-Day *noun* **1** 6 June 1944, the day the Allies invaded German-occupied Europe. **2** the day chosen for a major activity.

DDR *abbrev. Deutsche Demokratische Republik* (German), the former German Democratic Republic (East Germany).

DDS *abbrev.* Doctor of Dental Surgery.

DDT *abbrev.* a highly toxic chemical compound formerly widely used as an insecticide. [from the full name *dichlorodiphenyltrichloroethane*]

DE *abbrev.* Delaware.

de- *prefix* **1** down or away. **2** reversal or removal. **3** completely. [de-1 and de-3 from Latin *de*, off, from; de- 2 from Old French *des-*, from Latin *dis-* (see DIS-)]

deacon *noun* **1** a member of the lowest rank of clergy in the Roman Catholic and Anglican Churches. **2** in some other Churches, an official with financial and other duties. See also DIACONATE. [from Greek *diakonos*, servant]

deaconess *noun* **1** in some churches, a woman who has similar duties to those of a deacon. **2** in some churches, a woman whose duties are similar to those of a minister and who acts as an assistant to the minister.

deactivate *verb* **1** to reduce or remove (the reactivity of a chemical compound). **2** to reduce (the radioactivity of a substance). **3** to render (a bomb or other explosive device) harmless.

deactivation *noun* the act or process of deactivating.

dead — *adj.* **1** no longer alive. **2** without life. **3** no longer in existence; extinct. **4** *said of land, etc* without animals or plants. **5** denoting an electrical device, especially a battery, that has been drained of electric charge. **6** *said of coals, etc* no longer burning. **7** no longer in use: *a dead language.* **8** no longer of interest or importance: *a dead issue.* **9** having little or no excitement or activity; boring. **10** *said of a body part, especially a limb* lacking sensation; numb. **11** *said of leaves or flowers* dry and withered. **12** complete; absolute. **13** *colloq.* extremely tired. **14** *said of a sound* dull. **15** *Sport, said of a ball* in a position where it cannot be played until brought back into the game. — *noun* **1** (**the dead**) dead people. **2** (**the dead of night**) the middle of the night, when it is most intensely dark and still. **3** (**the dead of winter**) the middle of winter, when it is most intensely cold. — *adv. slang* quite; very. — **dead against** or **dead set against something** completely opposed to it. **dead from the neck up** *derog. colloq.* very stupid or of little intelligence. **dead set on something** determined or keen to do or acquire it. **dead to something** incapable of understanding it; not affected by it. **dead to the world** *colloq.* fast asleep. **one wouldn't be seen dead doing something, etc** *colloq.* one would not ever do it. **stop dead** to stop suddenly and abruptly.

▪ *adj.* **1** lifeless, deceased, defunct, departed, late, gone. **2** inanimate, inert, inorganic. **3** extinct, defunct, obsolete. **4** barren, desert, lifeless, uninhabited, unpopulated. **9** dull, boring, lifeless, dreary. **10** numb, frozen, unfeeling, insensible, anaesthetized. **12** complete, absolute, exact, perfect, unqualified, utter, outright, entire, total, downright. **13** exhausted, tired, worn out. **dead to something** unresponsive to, apathetic about, indifferent to, insensitive to.
▪ *adj.* **1** alive, living.

dead-beat *noun colloq.* a useless person. See also BEAT.

dead duck *colloq.* someone or something with no chance of success or survival.

deaden *verb* to lessen; to make weaker, less sharp, less strong, etc.

▣ reduce, lessen, diminish, weaken, blunt, dull, muffle, quieten, suppress, dampen, hush, mute, numb, anaesthetize, desensitize, smother, stifle, check, abate, allay, alleviate.
▣ heighten.

dead end 1 a road closed off at one end. 2 a situation or activity with no possibility of further progress or movement.

dead-end *adj.* allowing no progress.

dead-head *verb* to remove withered or dead flowers from (plants).

dead heat in a race, competition, etc, the result when two or more competitors produce equally good performances.

dead letter a rule or law no longer obeyed or in force.

deadline *noun* a time by which something must be done.

deadlock — *noun* a situation in which no further progress towards an agreement is possible. — *verb trans., intrans.* to cause or come to such a situation.

▣ *noun* standstill, stalemate, impasse, halt.

dead loss *colloq.* someone or something that is totally useless.

deadly — *adj.* 1 causing or likely to cause death. 2 *colloq.* very dull or uninteresting. 3 extremely accurate or effective. 4 very great: *in deadly earnest.* — *adv.* very; absolutely.

▣ *adj.* 1 lethal, fatal, mortal, murderous, venomous, destructive, pernicious, malignant. 2 dull, boring, uninteresting, tedious, monotonous. 3 unerring, accurate, *colloq.* spot-on, effective, telling, true.
▣ *adj.* 1 harmless. 2 exciting.

deadly nightshade a poisonous perennial plant (*Atropa belladonna*), native to Central and S Europe, having large oval leaves and brownish-purple or greenish bell-shaped flowers, and large shiny black berries. Also called BELLADONNA.

dead man's handle or **dead man's pedal** a safety device on a piece of machinery, etc, designed so that the machine only operates while the user is exerting pressure on a handle, foot pedal, or similar control, and stops when the pressure is released.

dead-nettle *noun* any of various annual and perennial plants of the genus *Lamium*, native to Europe and Asia, with leaves that resemble the stinging nettle, although they lack stinging hairs.

deadpan *adj., said of someone's expression, etc* showing no emotion or feeling, especially when joking but pretending to be serious.

▣ blank, emotionless, expressionless, impassive, poker-faced, straight-faced.

dead reckoning the estimating of the position of a ship, aircraft, etc from the distance and direction travelled, without looking at the position of the stars, sun, or moon.

deadweight *noun* 1 a heavy load. 2 *technical* (*also* **dead weight**) the difference in the weight of a ship when unloaded and loaded.

dead wood *colloq.* someone or something that is no longer useful or needed.

deaf — *adj.* 1 affected with partial or total loss of hearing in one or both ears. 2 (**deaf to something**) not willing to listen to advice, criticism, etc. — *pl. noun* (**the deaf**) deaf people. — **turn a deaf ear to someone** or **something** to ignore or refuse to pay any attention to them. [from Anglo-Saxon *dēaf*]

▣ *adj.* 1 hard of hearing, stone-deaf. 2 unconcerned about, indifferent to, unmoved by, oblivious to, heedless of, unmindful of.
▣ *adj.* 2 aware of, conscious of.

deaf-aid *noun Brit.* a hearing-aid.

deafen *verb* to make deaf or temporarily unable to hear.

deafening *adj.* 1 extremely loud. 2 causing deafness.

▣ 1 piercing, ear-splitting, booming, resounding, thunderous, ringing, roaring.
▣ 1 quiet, silent.

deaf-mute *noun often offensive* a person who is both deaf and unable to speak.

deafness *noun* partial or total loss of hearing in one or both ears.

deal[1] — *noun* 1 a bargain, agreement, or arrangement, especially in business or politics. 2 a particular form of treatment or behaviour towards someone: *a rough deal.* 3 the act of, the way of, or a player's turn of sharing out cards among the players in a card game. — *verb* (PAST TENSE AND PAST PARTICIPLE **dealt**) 1 *intrans.* (**deal in something**) to buy and sell it. 2 *trans., intrans.* (*also* **deal out**) to divide the cards among the players in a card game. 3 *trans.* (*also* **deal out**) to give (something) out to a number of people, etc. — **deal someone a blow** to hit or strike them. **deal with something** or **someone** 1 to take action regarding them. 2 to be concerned with them. **a good** or **great deal** 1 a large quantity. 2 very much or often: *she sees them a great deal.* [from Anglo-Saxon *dæl*, part]

▣ *noun* 1 agreement, arrangement, contract, understanding, pact, transaction, bargain, buy. 2 treatment, handling. 3 round, hand, distribution. *verb* 1 trade in, traffic in, handle. 3 apportion, distribute, share, dole out, divide, allot, dispense, assign, mete out, give, bestow. **deal with** 1 attend to, see to, manage, handle, cope with, treat, consider. 2 concern, relate to, refer to, involve. **a good** or **great deal** *colloq.* A LOT, *colloq.* LOTS.

deal[2] *noun* a plank, or planks, of fir or pine wood, or other soft wood, used for making eg furniture. [from Old German dialect *dele*]

dealer *noun* 1 a person or firm dealing in retail goods. 2 the player who deals in a card-game.

▣ 1 trader, merchant, wholesaler, marketer, merchandiser.

dealership *noun* 1 a business which buys and sells things. 2 a business licensed to sell a particular product by its manufacturer.

dealings *pl. noun* business, etc contacts.

dealt see DEAL[1].

dean *noun* 1 a senior clergyman in an Anglican cathedral. 2 a senior official in a university or college, sometimes with responsibility for student discipline. 3 the head of a university or college faculty. [from Old French *deien*]

deanery *noun* (PL. **deaneries**) 1 the house or office of a dean. 2 a group of parishes for which a rural dean has responsibility.

dear — *adj.* 1 high in price; charging high prices. 2 greatly loved, liked or admired. 3 lovable; attractive. 4 used in addressing someone at the start of a letter. 5 (**dear to someone**) a greatly loved by them. b very important or precious to them. — *noun* 1 a charming or lovable person. 2 *used especially as a form of address* a person one loves or likes. — *interj.* an expression of dismay, etc. — **cost someone dear** to cause or result in a lot of trouble or suffering. **dear knows** *colloq.* no one knows. [from Anglo-Saxon *deore*]

▣ *adj.* 1 expensive, high-priced, costly, overpriced, *colloq.*

pricey. **2** loved, beloved, darling, treasured, cherished, precious, favourite, valued, esteemed, intimate, close, familiar. **3** attractive, appealing, sweet, lovely. *noun* **1** treasure. **2** darling, sweetheart, precious, *colloq.* honey, beloved.

⊟ *adj.* **1** cheap. **2** disliked, hated.

dearly *adv.* **1** with fond or devoted affection. **2** very much. **3** at a high price or cost. — **pay dearly** to be made to suffer.

⊟ 1 fondly, affectionately, lovingly, devotedly, tenderly. **2** greatly, extremely, profoundly.

dearness *noun* being dear or expensive.

dearth /dɜːθ/ *noun* a scarceness or lack of something. [from DEAR + -TH²]

⊟ scarcity, shortage, insufficiency, inadequacy, deficiency, lack, want, absence, scantiness, sparsity, need, paucity, poverty, famine.

⊟ excess, abundance.

death *noun* **1** the time, act, or manner of dying, or the state of being dead. **2** *Biol.* the cessation of all the vital functions that are required to keep an organism alive. **3** *Medicine* the cessation of the heartbeat when this is accompanied by brain death (the functional death of the centres in the brain stem that control breathing and other vital reflexes). **4** the fact of killing or being killed. **5** something which causes a person to die: *be the death of someone.* **6** the end or destruction of something. **7** (**Death**) the figure of a skeleton, as a symbol of death. — **at death's door** near death; gravely ill. **in at the death 1** present when a hunted animal, eg a fox, is killed. **2** present at the end or destruction of an enterprise, undertaking, etc. **like death warmed up** *colloq.* having a sick or unhealthy appearance. **like grim death** very hard or tightly. **put someone to death** to kill or cause them to be killed; to execute them. **to death** very much; to an extreme or excess: *bored to death.* **to the death** until dead or until one's opponent is dead. [from Anglo-Saxon *dēath*]

⊟ 1 decease, end, finish, loss, demise, departure, passing. **4** fatality, casualty, loss, killing, murder, slaying. **6** end, cessation, dissolution, expiration, destruction, ruin, undoing, annihilation, downfall, extermination, extinction, obliteration, eradication.

⊟ 1 birth, life.

death-bed *noun* the bed in which a person dies or is about to die.

death blow an action, decision, etc which puts an end to or destroys (hopes, plans, etc).

death cap a poisonous mushroom (*Amanita phalloides*), having a smooth shiny yellowish-green cap with darker streaks.

death cell a prison cell in which a prisoner who is condemned to death is kept before the sentence is carried out.

death certificate a certificate, signed by a doctor, stating the time and cause of someone's death.

death duty *Brit.* formerly, a tax paid on the value of property left by a person after he or she has died (now replaced by *inheritance tax*).

death-knell *noun* **1** the ringing of a bell when someone has died. **2** an action, announcement, etc that heralds the end or destruction of (hopes, plans, etc).

deathless *adj. often ironic* immortal; unforgettable: *deathless prose.*

deathly — *adj.* **1** as in death. **2** deadly. — *adv.* as in death.

⊟ *adj.* **1** ashen, grim, haggard, pale, pallid, ghastly, wan. **2** fatal, deadly, mortal.

death-mask *noun* a mask made of a person's face after he or she has died.

death penalty punishment of a crime by death.

death-rate *noun* the number of deaths as a proportion of the total population, usually calculated as a percentage or rate per thousand.

death row *North Amer., esp. US* part of a prison where people who have been sentenced to death are kept.

death's-head *noun* a human skull, or a picture, mask, etc representing one.

deathtrap *noun* a building, vehicle, etc which is unsafe and likely to cause serious or fatal accidents.

death-warrant *noun* an official order that a death sentence is to be carried out.

deathwatch beetle a small brownish beetle, related to the furniture beetle, whose larvae bore into the mature timber of old buildings, especially oak.

death wish a desire to die, or that someone else should die.

deb *noun colloq.* a debutante.

debacle or **débâcle** /dɪ'bɑːkl/ *noun* total disorder, defeat, collapse of organization, etc. [from French *débâcle*]

⊟ collapse, defeat, rout, overthrow, downfall, fiasco, disaster, *colloq.* flop.

debar *verb* (**debarred**, **debarring**) to stop (someone) from joining, taking part in, doing, etc something.

⊟ stop, prevent, prohibit, bar, exclude, ban.

debarment *noun* exclusion from acting or taking part.

debase *verb* **1** to lower the value, quality, or status (of something). **2** to lower the value of (a coin) by adding metal of a lower value. [from DE- + ABASE]

⊟ 1 degrade, demean, devalue, disgrace, dishonour, lower, reduce, abase, defile, contaminate, pollute, corrupt, adulterate, taint.

⊟ 1 elevate, purify.

debased *adj.* lowered in value or status; spoiled.

debasement *noun* debasing; degradation.

debatable or **debateable** *adj.* doubtful; which could be argued about; uncertain.

⊟ doubtful, questionable, uncertain, disputable, contestable, controversial, arguable, open to question, contentious, undecided, unsettled, problematical, dubious, moot.

⊟ unquestionable, certain, incontrovertible.

debate — *noun* **1** a formal discussion, often in front of an audience, in which two or more people put forward opposing views on a particular subject. **2** any general discussion on a subject, not necessarily in one place or at one time. — *verb trans., intrans.* **1** to hold or take part in a formal discussion on a particular topic, often in front of an audience. **2** to consider the arguments for or against (something). — **open to debate** not certain or agreed; in doubt. [from Old French *debatre*, to discuss]

⊟ *noun* DISCUSSION, DISPUTATION. **1** meeting, conference, forum, symposium. **2** argument, controversy, deliberation, consideration, contention, dispute, reflection, polemic. *verb* **1** dispute, argue, discuss, contend. **2** consider, deliberate, ponder, reflect (on), meditate (on).

debater *noun* a person who takes part in a debate.

debating *noun* formal discussion of a question.

debauch /dɪ'bɔːtʃ/ — *verb* to corrupt; to cause or persuade (someone) to take part in immoral (especially sexual) activities or excessive drinking. — *noun* a period of debauched behaviour. [from Old French *desbaucher*, to corrupt]

debauched *adj.* corrupted; immoral.

debauchee /dɛbɔːˈtʃiː/ *noun* a person who likes sensual indulgence.

debauchery *noun* excessive sensual indulgence.

■ depravity, intemperance, overindulgence, dissipation, licentiousness, dissoluteness, excess, decadence, wantonness, lewdness, carousal, orgy, revel, lust, riot.
🗷 restraint, temperance.

debenture /dɪˈbɛntʃə(r)/ *noun* 1 a type of loan to a company or government agency which is usually made for a set period of time and carries a fixed rate of interest. 2 the document or bond acknowledging this loan. [from Latin *debentur*, there are due or owed]

debilitate /dɪˈbɪlɪteɪt/ *verb* to make weak or weaker. [from Latin *debilis*, weak]

■ weaken, enervate, undermine, sap, incapacitate, wear out, exhaust, impair.
🗷 strengthen, invigorate, energize.

debilitating *adj.* weakening; enervating.

debilitation /dɪbɪlɪˈteɪʃən/ *noun* a debilitating or weakening state or process.

debility /dɪˈbɪlɪtɪ/ *noun* weakness of the body or mind, especially as a result of illness or disease.

debit — *noun* 1 an entry in an account recording what is owed or has been spent. 2 a sum taken from a bank, etc account. 3 a deduction made from a bill or account. See also CREDIT. — *verb* (**debited**, **debiting**) 1 to take from (an account, etc). 2 to record in a debit entry: *debited £150 against them / debited them with £150*. [from Latin *debitum*, what is due]

debit card a plastic card which automatically transfers money from the purchaser's account to the retailer's at the point of sale.

debonair /dɛbəˈnɛə(r)/ *adj.*, *said especially of a man* cheerful, charming, and of elegant appearance and good manners. [from Old French *de bon aire*, of good manners]

debonairly *adv.* with a debonair or cheerful manner.

debouch /dɪˈbʊtʃ, dɪˈbuːʃ/ *verb intrans. technical, said of troops or a river, etc* to come out of a narrow place or opening into a wider or more open place. [from French *déboucher*, from *de*, from + *bouche*, mouth]

debouchment *noun* 1 coming out into an open place. 2 the outlet of a river, etc.

debrief *verb* to gather information from (a diplomat, astronaut, soldier, etc) after a battle, event, mission, etc.

debriefing *noun* interrogation after a completed mission, etc.

debris or **débris** /ˈdɛbriː/ *noun* 1 what remains of something crushed, smashed, destroyed, etc. 2 rubbish. 3 small pieces of rock. [from French *débris*]

■ 1 remains, ruins, wreck, wreckage, fragments, rubble, pieces, bits. 2 rubbish, waste, trash, litter, sweepings. 3 drift, scree.

debt /dɛt/ *noun* 1 something which is owed. 2 the state of owing something. [from Old French *dette*, from Latin *debitum*, what is owed]

■ OBLIGATION, LIABILITY, ARREARS. 1 debit, bill, claim, due, score. 2 indebtedness, duty, commitment.
🗷 CREDIT. 1 asset.

debt of honour a debt one is morally but not legally obliged to pay.

debtor *noun* someone owing money. See also CREDITOR.

■ borrower, mortgagor, bankrupt, insolvent, defaulter.
🗷 creditor.

debug *verb* (**debugged**, **debugging**) 1 to detect, locate, and remove (concealed microphones, etc) from a room, building, etc. 2 *Comput.* to detect, locate, and remove (errors in a computer program or faults in computer hardware, popularly known as bugs). 3 *colloq.* to remove insects from (a building, etc). 4 to detect, locate, and remove (flaws) from a plan.

debunk *verb* to show (a person's claims, good reputation, etc) to be false or unjustified. [from DE- + BUNK²]

■ expose, deflate, show up, ridicule, mock, explode, lampoon.

début or **debut** /ˈdeɪbjuː/ *noun* the first public appearance of a performer. [from French *début*]

■ introduction, launching, beginning, entrance, presentation, inauguration, première, appearance, initiation.

débutante /ˈdɛbjʊtɒnt/ *noun* a young woman making her first formal appearance as an adult in upper-class society, usually at a ball. [from French *débutante*, from *débuter*, to start off]

Dec or **Dec.** *abbrev.* December.

deca- *combining form* ten: *decahedron*. [from Greek *deka*, 10]

decade /ˈdɛkeɪd/ *noun* 1 a period of 10 years. 2 a group or series of 10 things, etc. [from DECA-]

decadence /ˈdɛkədəns/ *noun* 1 a falling from high to low standards in morals, art, etc. 2 the state of having low or immoral standards of behaviour, etc. [from French *décadence*, from Latin *de*, from + *cadere*, to fall]

■ 1 decay, decline, deterioration, degeneration, debasement. 2 corruption, immorality, degeneracy, dissoluteness, dissipation, depravity, degradation, self-indulgence, licence.

decadent *adj.* 1 having low moral standards. 2 typical of a period of decline.

■ 1 corrupt, debased, debauched, depraved, dissolute, immoral, degenerate, degraded, self-indulgent. 2 decaying, declining.
🗷 1 moral.

decadently *adv.* in a decadent or immoral way.

decaff or **decaf** *colloq.* — *adj.* decaffeinated. — *noun* decaffeinated coffee.

decaffeinate /diːˈkafɪneɪt/ *verb* to remove all or part of the caffeine from.

decaffeinated *adj.*, *said of coffee, etc* having all or part of the caffeine removed.

decagon /ˈdɛkəgɒn/ *noun* Geom. a plane (two-dimensional) figure with 10 sides and 10 angles. It is a type of polygon. [from DECA- + Greek *gonia*, angle]

decagonal /dɪˈkagɒnəl/ *adj.* having 10 sides and angles.

decahedral /dɛkəˈhiːdrəl/ *adj.*, *said of a solid figure* having 10 faces.

decahedron /dɛkəˈhiːdrən/ *noun* a solid figure with ten faces. [from DECA- + Greek *hedra*, seat]

Decalogue /ˈdɛkəlɒg/ *noun* (**the Decalogue**) *Biblical* the Ten Commandments given by God to Moses. [from DECA- + Greek *logos*, word]

decamp *verb intrans.* to go away suddenly, especially secretly. [from French *décamper*]

decanal /dɪˈkeɪnəl/ *adj. Relig.* 1 of or relating to a dean or deanery. 2 *said of part of a choir* positioned on the same side of the cathedral as the dean, ie the south side. [from late Latin *decanus*, dean]

decant /dɪ'kant/ verb **1** to pour (wine, etc) from one bottle or container to another, leaving any sediment behind. **2** to remove (people) from where they usually live to some other place. [from French *décanter*, from Latin *de*, from + *canthus*, spout]

decanter noun an ornamental bottle for wine, sherry, whisky, etc.

decapitate /dɪ'kapɪteɪt/ verb to cut off the head of. [from DE 1 + Latin *caput*, head]

decapitation /dɪkapɪ'teɪʃən/ noun beheading.

decapod /'dekəpɒd/ noun Zool. **1** any invertebrate animal belonging to the order Decapoda, including crabs, lobsters, prawns, shrimps, and crayfish, with five pairs of walking legs. **2** any invertebrate animal belonging to a suborder of cephalopod molluscs that have two long tentacles and eight shorter ones, eg squid, cuttlefish. [from DECA- + Greek *pous podos*, foot]

decarbonization or **decarbonisation** noun **1** the removal of carbon from steel. **2** the removal of carbon from an internal combustion engine.

decarbonize or **decarbonise** verb to remove carbon from (an internal-combustion engine).

decathlete /dɪ'kaθliːt/ noun a contestant in a decathlon.

decathlon /dɪ'kaθlɒn/ noun an athletic competition (usually for men) in which competitors take part in ten different events over two days. [from DECA- + Greek *athlon*, contest]

decay — verb **1** trans., intrans. to make or become rotten. **2** trans., intrans. to make or become weaker in health or power, etc. **3** intrans. Physics, *said of a radioactive substance* to break down spontaneously into one or more isotopes which may or may not be radioactive. — noun **1** the natural breakdown of dead organic matter. **2** a gradual decrease in health, power, quality, etc. **3** Physics the spontaneous breakdown of an unstable nucleus of a radioactive substance into one or more isotopes which may or may not be radioactive, with the emission of alpha or beta particles, or gamma rays. **4** rotten matter in a tooth, etc. [from Old French *decair*]

⊟ verb **1** rot, putrefy, decompose, spoil, perish. **2** deteriorate, disintegrate, corrode, crumble, waste away, degenerate, wear away, shrivel, wither, sink. noun **1** rot, decomposition, rotting, perishing. **2** decline, deterioration, disintegration, degeneration, collapse, decadence, wasting, failing, withering, fading.
Ⓔ verb **2** flourish, grow.

decease noun *formal Legal* death. [from Old French *deces*]

⊟ death, dying, demise, departure, passing, dissolution.

deceased *formal Legal* — adj. dead. — noun (**the deceased**) a dead person or dead people.

⊟ adj. dead, departed, former, late, lost, expired, gone, extinct. noun the dead, the departed.

deceit /dɪ'siːt/ noun **1** an act of deceiving or misleading. **2** dishonesty; deceitfulness; willingness to deceive. [from Old French *deceite*]

⊟ DECEPTION, PRETENCE, MISREPRESENTATION. **1** swindle, fraud, subterfuge, artifice, ruse, stratagem, wile, imposition, feint, abuse. **2** cheating, duplicity, trickery, fraudulence, double-dealing, underhandedness, guile, treachery, hypocrisy, cunning, slyness, craftiness.
Ⓔ **2** honesty, openness, frankness.

deceitful adj. **1** deceiving, especially as a general habit. **2** intended to deceive.

⊟ DISHONEST, DECEIVING, FALSE, INSINCERE,

FRAUDULENT, UNDERHAND, SNEAKY, CRAFTY, DUPLICITOUS, GUILEFUL, HYPOCRITICAL, TREACHEROUS. **1** untrustworthy, double-dealing, two-faced. **2** deceptive, misleading, counterfeit, illusory.
Ⓔ HONEST, OPEN, SINCERE.

deceitfully adv. in a deceitful or dishonest way.

deceive /dɪ'siːv/ verb **1** to mislead or lie to. **2** to convince (oneself) that something is true when it is not. See also DECEPTION. [from Old French *deceivre*]

⊟ MISLEAD, DELUDE, FOOL. **1** cheat, betray, take in, trick, hoax, *colloq.* con, *colloq.* have on, *colloq.* take for a ride, double-cross, dupe, *colloq.* kid, swindle, impose upon, *colloq.* bamboozle, *colloq.* two-time, lead on, outwit, hoodwink, beguile, ensnare, abuse, gull.

deceiver noun a person who deceives, especially habitually.

decelerate /diː'seləreɪt/ verb trans., intrans. to slow down or cause to slow down (especially a vehicle, machine, etc). [from DE-1 + ACCELERATE]

deceleration /diːselə'reɪʃən/ noun reduction in speed.

December noun the twelfth month of the year. [from Latin *December*, from *decem*, 10 (because it was at one time the tenth month of the Roman year)]

decency noun (PL. **decencies**) **1** decent behaviour or character. **2** (**decencies**) the generally accepted rules of respectable or moral behaviour.

⊟ **1** propriety, courtesy, modesty, decorum, respectability, civility, correctness, fitness, helpfulness. **2** proprieties, etiquette, courtesies, civilities.
Ⓔ **1** impropriety, discourtesy.

decennial /dɪ'senɪəl/ adj. **1** happening every 10 years. **2** consisting of 10 years. [from Latin *decem*, 10 + *annus*, year]

decent adj. **1** conforming to accepted or acceptable standards; modest, not vulgar or immoral. **2** kind, tolerant or likeable. **3** fairly good; adequate. [from Latin *decere*, to be fitting]

⊟ **1** respectable, proper, fitting, decorous, chaste, seemly, suitable, modest, appropriate, presentable, pure, fit, becoming, befitting, nice. **2** kind, obliging, courteous, helpful, generous, tolerant, polite, gracious. **3** adequate, acceptable, satisfactory, reasonable, sufficient, tolerable, competent.
Ⓔ **1** indecent. **2** disobliging.

decently adv. in a decent way; so as to be decent or reasonable: *cannot decently refuse.*

decentralization or **decentralisation** noun the process of decentralizing.

decentralize or **decentralise** verb trans., intrans., *said of a part of government, industry, etc* to alter or be altered by the transfer of organization, etc from one main central place to several smaller, less central positions.

deception /dɪ'sepʃən/ noun **1** an act of deceiving or the fact of being deceitful or deceptive. **2** something which deceives or misleads. **3** the state of being deceived. [from Latin *decipere*, to deceive]

⊟ **1, 2** deceit, pretence, trick, cheat, fraud, imposture, *colloq.* con, lie, subterfuge. **1** dissembling, deceptiveness, insincerity, hypocrisy, fraudulence, duplicity, treachery, craftiness, cunning. **2** sham, artifice, bluff, hoax, ruse, snare, stratagem, *colloq.* leg-pull, illusion, wile.
Ⓔ **1** openness, honesty.

deceptive *adj.* that deceives or misleads.

⊟ deceiving, misleading, dishonest, false, fraudulent, unreliable, illusive, illusory, fake, spurious, mock, fallacious, specious.
⊞ genuine, artless, open.

deceptively *adv.* so as to deceive or mislead: *deceptively simple.*

deci- *combining form* one-tenth: *decilitre.* [from Latin *decimus*, tenth]

decibel /ˈdɛsɪbɛl/ *noun* (SYMBOL **dB**) a unit equal to $\frac{1}{10}$ of a bel, used for comparing levels of power, especially sound, on a logarithmic scale.

decide *verb* **1 a** *intrans.* to reach a decision; to establish an intention. **b** (**decide about something** or **to do something** or **that**) to establish an intention regarding it or doing it or that: *decided to leave early.* **2** (**decide on something**) to choose it. **3** (**decide against something**) to reject it as an intention or course of action: *decided against making a donation.* **4** to settle (something); to make the final result of (something) certain. **5** to cause (someone) to decide in a certain way: *the weather decided them to stay.* **6** to make a formal judgement about something. [from Latin *decidere*, to cut down, settle]

⊟ **1** reach a decision, make up one's mind, come to a conclusion, determine, resolve. **2** choose, select, opt for, plump for, settle on, *colloq.* go for. **4** settle, conclude, fix, establish. **6** adjudicate, judge, rule on, arbitrate.
⊞ **1** waver, vacillate.

decided *adj.* **1** clear and definite; unmistakable. **2** determined; showing no doubt.

⊟ **1** definite, certain, unmistakable, undeniable, indisputable, absolute, clear-cut, undisputed, unquestionable, positive, unambiguous, categorical, distinct, emphatic. **2** determined, resolute, decisive, firm, unhesitating, deliberate, forthright.
⊞ **1** inconclusive. **2** irresolute.

decidedly *adv.* undoubtedly; definitely: *decidedly ugly.*

decider *noun* **1** someone or something that decides. **2** something that decides the result of something.

deciduous /dɪˈsɪdjʊəs/ *adj.* **1** *Bot.* denoting plants which shed all their leaves at a certain time of year, usually the autumn in temperate regions, eg horse chestnut. See also EVERGREEN. **2** *Biol.* denoting structures which are shed at maturity or after a period of growth, eg milk teeth. [from Latin *decidere*, to fall down]

decilitre *noun* a tenth of a litre.

decimal — *adj.* **1** based on the number 10; relating to powers of 10 or the base 10. **2** denoting a system of measurement, etc, with units that are related to each other by multiples of 10. — *noun* a decimal fraction. [from Latin *decimalis*, of tenths]

decimal currency a system of money in which each coin or note is either a tenth of or 10 times another in value.

decimal fraction a fraction which is expressed in the form of an integer followed by a decimal point, followed by a series of digits.

decimalization or **decimalisation** *noun* conversion to a decimal system of units, especially the metric system.

decimalize or **decimalise** *verb* to convert (numbers, a currency, etc) from a non-decimal to a decimal system, especially the metric system.

decimal system 1 a system of measurement with units that are related to each other by multiples of 10. **2** the number system in common use, in which the place values of the digits in a number correspond to multiples of powers of 10. **3** a system of library classification, based on the division of books into numbered classes, with further subdivision shown by numbers following a decimal point.

decimate *verb* to reduce greatly in number; to destroy a large part or number of. [from Latin *decimare*, to take a tenth person or thing, from *decem*, 10]

decimation *noun* destruction of a large number.

decipher *verb* (**deciphered, deciphering**) **1** to translate (a message or text in code or in an unfamiliar or strange form of writing) into ordinary, understandable language. **2** to work out the meaning of (something obscure or difficult to read).

⊟ **1** decode, unscramble, transliterate. **2** make out, figure out, understand, construe, interpret, crack.
⊞ **1** encode.

decipherable *adj.* capable of being deciphered.

decipherment *noun* deciphering; translation from a code.

decision *noun* **1** the act of deciding. **2** something decided. **3** the ability to make decisions and act on them firmly. [from Latin *decisio*, cutting off]

⊟ **2** result, conclusion, outcome, verdict, finding, settlement, judgement, arbitration, ruling. **3** determination, decisiveness, firmness, resolve, purpose.

decisive /dɪˈsaɪsɪv/ *adj.* **1** putting an end to doubt or dispute. **2** willing and able to make decisions quickly and with firmness. **3** of crucial significance for the outcome or future of something.

⊟ **1** conclusive, definite, definitive, absolute, final. **2** determined, resolute, decided, positive, firm, forceful, forthright, strong-minded. **3** significant, critical, crucial, influential, momentous, fateful.
⊞ **1** inconclusive. **2** indecisive. **3** insignificant.

decisively *adv.* in a decisive way; to a decisive degree; conclusively.

decisiveness *noun* the quality of being decisive, especially habitually.

deck[1] *noun* **1** a platform extending from one side of a ship to the other, and forming a floor or covering. **2** a floor in a bus, etc. **3** *North Amer., esp. US* a pack of playing-cards. **4** that part of a tape recorder or computer in which the magnetic tapes are placed, and the mechanism for running them. — **clear the decks** to clear away obstacles or deal with preliminary jobs in preparation for further activity. **hit the deck** *colloq.* to lie or fall down suddenly and quickly on the ground or floor. [from Old Dutch *dec*, roof, covering]

deck[2] *verb* (**deck something out**) to decorate or embellish it. [from Dutch *dekken*, to cover]

deckchair *noun Brit.* a light folding chair made of wood and canvas or other heavy fabric, usually used for sitting outside.

-decker *combining form* forming words meaning 'having a certain number of decks': *triple-decker.*

deck hand a person who does general work on the deck of a ship.

decko see DEKKO.

declaim /dɪˈkleɪm/ *verb* **1** *trans., intrans.* to make (a speech) in an impressive and dramatic manner. **2** (**declaim against something**) to protest about it loudly and passionately. [from Latin *declamare*]

declamation /dɛkləˈmeɪʃən/ *noun* an impressive or emotional speech, usually made in protest or condemnation. [from Latin *declamare*, to declaim]

declamatory /dɪˈklamətrɪ/ *adj., said of speech* impassioned; rhetorical.

declaration /dɛkləˈreɪʃən/ *noun* **1** the act of declaring. **2** a formal statement or announcement.

⊟ ANNOUNCEMENT, PRONOUNCEMENT, PROCLAMATION,

AFFIRMATION, ACKNOWLEDGEMENT, STATEMENT, ATTESTATION, NOTIFICATION. **1** disclosure, revelation, profession. **2** testimony, edict, manifesto.

....

declarative /dɪˈklarətɪv/ *adj. Grammar* making a statement.

declare *verb* **1** to announce publicly or formally: *declare war.* **2** to say firmly or emphatically. **3** to make known (goods on which duty must be paid, income on which tax should be paid, etc). **4** *intrans. Cricket* to end an innings before 10 wickets have fallen. **5** *intrans.* (**declare for** or **against something**) to state one's support or opposition regarding it. **6** *trans., intrans. Cards* to state or show that one is holding (certain cards). [from Latin *declarare*, from *clarus*, clear]

....

■ **1, 2** announce, proclaim, pronounce. **1** decree, attest, certify. **2** affirm, assert, claim, profess, maintain, state, confess, confirm, disclose, reveal, show, aver, swear, testify, witness, broadcast.

....

declassification *noun* removal of information from an official secret list.

declassify *verb* (**declassifies, declassified**) to take (an official document, etc) off a list of secret information and allow public access to it.

declension /dɪˈklɛnʃən/ *noun Grammar* **1** in certain languages, such as Latin, any of various sets of different forms taken by nouns, adjectives or pronouns to indicate case, number, and gender. **2** the act of stating these forms. See also CONJUGATION, DECLINE. **3** any group of nouns or adjectives showing the same pattern of forms. [from Latin *declinatio*, bending aside]

declination /dɛklɪˈneɪʃən/ *noun* **1** *technical* the angle between true north (geographical north) and magnetic north (north as indicated by a magnetic compass). It varies according to time and geographical location. **2** *Astron.* the angular distance of a star or planet north or south of the celestial equator. It is measured in degrees, and is the coordinate on the celestial sphere that corresponds to latitude on the Earth. [from Latin *declinatio*, bending aside]

decline /dɪˈklaɪn/ — *verb* **1** to refuse (an invitation, etc), especially politely. **2** *intrans.* to become less strong or less healthy. **3** *intrans.* to become less in quality or quantity. **4** *intrans.* to slope downwards. **5** *Grammar* to state the pattern of forms representing the various cases of (a noun, adjective, or pronoun). See also CONJUGATE, DECLENSION. — *noun* **1** a lessening of strength, health, quality, quantity, etc. **2** a downward slope. [from Latin *declinare*, to bend aside]

....

■ *verb* **1** refuse, reject, deny, forego, avoid, balk. **2** decay, deteriorate, worsen, degenerate. **3** diminish, decrease, dwindle, lessen, fall, sink, wane. **4** descend, sink, slope, dip, slant. *noun* **1** deterioration, decay, degeneration, weakening, worsening, failing, downturn, diminution, decrease, dwindling, lessen-ing, falling-off, recession, slump, abatement. **2** descent, dip, declivity, declination, hill, slope.

◼ *verb* **2** improve. **3** increase. **4** rise. *noun* **1** improvement. **2** rise.

....

declivity /dɪˈklɪvɪtɪ/ *noun* (PL. **declivities**) *formal* a downward slope. See also ACCLIVITY. [from DE- 1 + Latin *clivus*, sloping]

declutch *verb intrans.* to release (the clutch of a motor vehicle).

decoction *noun* a liquid obtained by boiling something in water, eg to extract its flavour. [from Latin *decoctio*, from *coquere*, to cook or boil]

decode *verb* to translate (a coded message) into ordinary language.

◻ decipher, interpret, unscramble, translate, transliterate, uncipher.

◼ encode.

....

decoder *noun* a person or device that decodes.

décolletage /deɪˈkɒltɑːʒ/ *noun* a low-cut neckline on a woman's dress, etc.

décolleté or **décolletée** /deɪˈkɒlteɪ/ *adj.* **1** *said of a woman's dress, etc* having the neckline cut low at the front. **2** *said of a woman* wearing such a dress, etc. [from French *décolleter*, to bare the neck and shoulders]

decommission *verb* (**decommissioned, decommissioning**) to take (eg a warship or atomic reactor) out of use or operation.

decompose *verb* **1** *intrans., said of a dead organism* to rot, usually as a result of the activity of fungi and bacteria. **2** *said of a chemical compound* to break down into simpler compounds or its constituent elements, eg as a result of heating, exposure to light, or electrolysis. **3** *trans., intrans. technical* to separate into smaller or simpler parts or elements. [from French *décomposer*]

....

■ **1** rot, disintegrate, decay, putrefy, spoil, fester. **2** break down, break up, crumble, dissolve, separate.

....

decomposition *noun* decaying; rotting; disintegration.

decompress *verb* **1** to release (an object, substance, etc) from pressure or the effects of pressure. **2** to release the air pressure on (a diver, construction worker, etc) gradually on returning to conditions of normal atmospheric pressure. **3** *said of a diver, construction worker, etc* to be subjected to a gradual decrease in air pressure on returning to conditions of normal atmospheric pressure.

decompression *noun* **1** the act of releasing pressure or its effects. **2** the gradual release of air pressure on a diver, construction worker, etc, as he or she returns to normal atmospheric conditions. **3** *Medicine* any surgical operation to relieve excessive pressure.

decompression chamber a sealed room in which the air pressure can be varied, used especially to enable deep-sea divers to return gradually and safely to normal air pressure after a dive.

decompression sickness a painful and sometimes fatal disorder that occurs when a person who has been breathing air under high pressure, eg a deep-sea diver, returns too suddenly to normal atmospheric pressure, eg by surfacing too rapidly. Also called THE BENDS.

decongestant *noun Medicine* a drug or other agent, usually taken in the form of a nasal spray or taken by mouth, that reduces or relieves nasal congestion by clearing mucus from the nasal cavities.

deconstruction or **deconstructive criticism** an approach to critical analysis which requires that readers should eradicate or 'deconstruct' all philosophical and other concepts when approaching a text.

decontaminate *verb* to render (an object, area, or person) harmless by removing or deactivating toxic substances, radioactivity, etc.

decontamination *noun* the removal or inactivation of toxic substances, radioactivity, etc, from an object, area, or person, in order to render them harmless.

décor /ˈdeɪkɔː(r)/ *noun* the style of decoration, furnishings, etc in a room or house. [from French *décor*, decoration]

....

◻ decoration, furnishings, colour scheme, ornamentation.

....

decorate /ˈdɛkəreɪt/ *verb* **1** to beautify with ornaments, etc. **2** to put paint or wallpaper on. **3** to give a medal or badge to as a mark of honour. [from Latin *decorare*, to beautify]

....

■ **1** ornament, adorn, beautify, embellish, trim, deck, *slang* tart up, grace, enrich, prettify. **2** renovate, *colloq.*

do up, paint, paper, colour, refurbish. **3** honour, crown, cite, garland.

. . . .

decorating *noun* painting of a building, etc.
decoration /dɛkə'reɪʃən/ *noun* **1** something used to decorate. **2** the act of decorating. **3** a medal or badge given as a mark of honour.

. . . .

▣ **1, 2** adornment, ornamentation, embellishment. **1** ornament, trimming, garnish, flourish, frill, scroll, bauble. **2** beautification, enrichment, elaboration. **3** award, medal, order, badge, garland, crown, colours, ribbon, laurel, star, emblem.

. . . .

decorative /'dɛkərətɪv/ *adj.* ornamental or beautiful (especially if not useful).

. . . .

▣ ornamental, fancy, adorning, beautifying, embellishing, non-functional, pretty, ornate, enhancing.
▣ plain.

decorative arts the applied arts, as distinct from the fine arts, including ceramics, metalwork, textiles, calligraphy, etc.
decorator *noun* a person who decorates buildings professionally.
decorous /'dɛkərəs/ *adj.*, *said of behaviour or appearance* correct or socially acceptable; showing proper respect. [from Latin *decorus*, becoming, fitting]

. . . .

▣ proper, correct, suitable, seemly, acceptable, respectable, decent, respectful, polite, well-bred.
▣ indecorous, improper.

. . . .

decorously *adv.* with a decorous or proper manner.
decorum /dɪ'kɔːrəm/ *noun* correct or socially acceptable behaviour. [from Latin *decorus*, becoming or fitting]

. . . .

▣ propriety, seemliness, etiquette, good manners, respectability, protocol, behaviour, decency, dignity, deportment, restraint, politeness, modesty, grace, breeding.
▣ impropriety, indecorum, bad manners.

. . . .

decoy /dɪ'kɔɪ, 'diːkɔɪ/ — *verb* (with stress on -*coy*) to lead or lure into a trap. — *noun* (with stress on *de*-) someone or something used to lead or lure (a person or animal) into a trap. [probably from Dutch *de kooi*, the cage]

. . . .

▣ *verb* lead, lure, entrap, entice, ensnare, allure, tempt, deceive, attract, seduce. *noun* lure, bait, trap, enticement, inducement, ensnarement, pretence, attraction.

. . . .

decrease /dɪ'kriːs, 'diːkriːs/ — *verb trans.*, *intrans.* (with stress on -*crease*) to make or become less. — *noun* (with stress on *de*-) a lessening or loss. [from Latin *decrescere*]

. . . .

▣ *verb* lessen, lower, diminish, reduce, abate, contract, drop, ease, shrink, taper, slim (down), slacken. *noun* lessening, reduction, decline, falling-off, dwindling, loss, abatement, cutback, contraction, downturn, ebb, shrinkage, subsidence, step-down.
▣ *verb* increase. *noun* increase.

. . . .

decreasingly *adv.* to a lessening extent.
decree /dɪ'kriː/ — *noun* **1** a formal order or ruling made by someone in high authority (eg a monarch) and which becomes law. **2** *Legal* a ruling made in a law court. — *verb* to order or decide (something) formally or officially. [from Latin *decretum*]

. . . .

▣ *noun* **1** order, command, law, ordinance, regulation, statute, act, enactment, edict, proclamation, mandate, precept. **2** ruling, order, injunction. *verb* order, command, rule, lay

down, dictate, decide, determine, ordain, prescribe, proclaim, pronounce, enact.

. . . .

decree absolute *Legal* a decree issued by a court in divorce proceedings which officially ends a marriage.
decree nisi /'naɪsaɪ/ *Legal* a decree issued by a court in divorce proceedings which will become a decree absolute after a period of time unless some reason is shown why it should not. [from Latin *nisi*, unless]
decrepit /dɪ'krɛpɪt/ *adj.* **1** weak or worn out because of old age. **2** in a very poor state because of age or long use. [from Latin *decrepitus*, very old]

. . . .

▣ WORN-OUT. **1** aged, feeble, frail, weak. **2** dilapidated, run-down, rickety, broken-down, tumbledown, ramshackle.

. . . .

decrepitude /dɪ'krɛpɪtjuːd/ *noun* a decrepit or worn out state.
decretal /dɪ'kriːtəl, 'dɛkrɪtəl/ *noun* a papal decree. [from Latin *decretalis*, of a decree]
decry *verb* (**decries**, **decried**) to express disapproval of; to criticize as worthless or unsuitable. [from French *décrier*]

. . . .

▣ deplore, condemn, denounce, criticize, censure.

. . . .

dedicate *verb* (*usually* **dedicate something to someone** or **something**) **1** to give or devote (oneself or one's time, money, etc) wholly or chiefly to some purpose. **2** to devote or address (a book, piece of music, etc) to someone as a token of affection or respect. **3** to set apart for some sacred purpose. [from Latin *dedicare*, to declare, dedicate]

. . . .

▣ **1** devote, commit, assign, give over to, pledge, present, offer, sacrifice, surrender. **2** inscribe, address. **3** consecrate, bless, sanctify, set apart, hallow.

. . . .

dedicated *adj.* **1** working very hard at or spending a great deal of one's time and energy on something. **2** *technical* denoting a device or system, especially a computer, designed to fulfil one particular function. **3** denoting a computer that has been built into and designed to control or supply information to another specific machine or device.

. . . .

▣ **1** devoted, committed, enthusiastic, single-minded, wholehearted, single-hearted, zealous, given over to, purposeful.
▣ **1** uncommitted, apathetic.

. . . .

dedication *noun* **1** the quality of being dedicated. **2** the act of dedicating. **3** the words dedicating a book, etc to someone.

. . . .

▣ **1, 2** commitment, devotion. **1** single-mindedness, wholeheartedness, allegiance, attachment, adherence, faithfulness, loyalty, self-sacrifice. **2** consecration, hallowing, presentation. **3** inscription, address.
▣ **1** apathy.

. . . .

dedicator *noun* a person who makes a dedication.
dedicatory /'dɛdɪkeɪtərɪ/ *adj.* serving as a dedication in a book, etc: *dedicatory remarks*.
deduce /dɪ'djuːs/ *verb* to think out or judge on the basis of what one knows or assumes to be fact. [from DE- 1 + Latin *ducere*, to lead]

. . . .

▣ derive, infer, gather, conclude, work out, reason, surmise, understand, draw, glean.

. . . .

deducible /dɪ'djuːsɪbl/ *adj.* capable of being deduced.
deduct *verb* to take away (a number, amount, etc). [from DE- 1 + Latin *ducere*, to lead]

. . . .
☰ subtract, take away, remove, *colloq.* knock off, withdraw.
☲ add.
. . . .

deductible *adj.* capable of being deducted; eligible for deduction: *expenses deductible from tax.*

deduction *noun* 1 the act or process of deducting. 2 something, especially money, which has been or will be deducted. 3 the act or process of deducing, especially of deducing a particular fact from what one knows or thinks to be generally true. See also INDUCTION. 4 something that has been deduced. [from DE- 1 + Latin *ducere*, to lead]
. . . .
☰ 1, 2 subtraction, reduction, decrease, diminution, abatement, withdrawal. 2 discount, allowance. 3, 4 inference. 3 reasoning, logic, thinking, thought. 4 finding, conclusion, corollary, assumption, result.
☲ 1, 2 addition, increase.
. . . .

deductive *adj.*, *said of a logical process of thought* deducing or involving deduction of particular facts from general truths. See also INDUCTIVE.

deed *noun* 1 something someone has done. 2 a brave action or notable achievement. 3 *Legal* a signed statement which records the terms of an agreement, especially about a change in ownership of a house or other property. [from Anglo-Saxon *dæd* or *ded*]
. . . .
☰ 1 action, act, performance, fact. 2 achievement, exploit, feat, accomplishment. 3 document, contract, record, title, transaction, indenture .
. . . .

deed poll *Brit. Legal* a deed made and signed by one person only, especially when changing his or her name.

deejay or **DJ** — *noun colloq.* a disc jockey. — *verb intrans.* to act as a deejay. [from the initials *DJ*]

deem *verb formal, old use* to judge, think or consider. [from Anglo-Saxon *deman*, to form a judgement]

deep — *adj.* 1 far down from the top or surface; with a relatively great distance from the top or surface to the bottom. 2 going or being far in from the outside surface or edge. 3 (*usually in a hyphenated compound*) going or being far down by a specified amount: *knee-deep in mud.* 4 in a specified number of rows or layers: *lined up four deep.* 5 coming from or going far down; long and full: *a deep sigh / a deep breath.* 6 very great; serious: *deep trouble.* 7 *said of a colour* strong and relatively dark; not light or pale. 8 (**deep in something**) fully occupied or involved with it: *deep in thought.* 9 low in pitch. 10 *said of emotions, etc* strongly felt. 11 perceptive; not superficial; hard to understand: *deep thoughts.* 12 *said of a person* mysterious; keeping secret thoughts. 13 *Cricket* not close to the wickets. 14 *Football* well behind one's team's front line of players. — *adv.* 1 deeply. 2 far down or into. 3 late on in or well into (a period of time). — *noun* 1 (**the deep**) the ocean. 2 (*also* **deeps**) *old use* a place far below the surface of the ground or the sea. See also DEPTH. — **deep down** in reality, although not in appearance. **go off (at) the deep end** *colloq.* to lose one's temper suddenly and violently. **in deep water** *colloq.* in trouble or difficulties. **jump in** or **dive in** or **be thrown in at the deep end** *colloq.* to begin or be given a difficult undertaking with little or no experience or preparation. [from Anglo-Saxon *deop*]
. . . .
☰ *adj.* 1 profound, bottomless, unplumbed, fathomless. 6 serious, extreme, grave, acute. 8 immersed in, absorbed in, engrossed in, preoccupied with. 9 low, bass, resonant, booming. 10 profound, intense, earnest, heartfelt, sincere. 11 profound, perceptive, discerning, wise, astute, learned, obscure, mysterious, difficult, recondite, abstruse, esoteric. 12 secretive, mysterious, enigmatic, strange.
☲ *adj.* 1 shallow. 6 slight. 9 high. 10, 11 shallow, superficial.
. . . .

deepen *verb trans.*, *intrans.* (**deepened, deepening**) 1 to make or become deeper. 2 to make or become greater, more intense, etc.
. . . .
☰ 2 intensify, increase, strengthen, reinforce, magnify.
. . . .

deep-freeze — *noun* a specialized refrigeration unit, or a compartment in a refrigerator, that is designed for storage of perishable material, especially food, in a frozen state at a temperature below -18°C (0°F). — *verb* (PAST TENSE **deep-froze**; PAST PARTICIPLE **deep-frozen**) to preserve perishable material, especially food, by storing it in a frozen state, so as to prevent the growth and reproduction of bacteria and other microorganisms.

deep-fry *verb* to fry (something completely submerged in hot fat or oil).

deeply *adv.* very greatly.
. . . .
☰ profoundly, intensely, greatly, extremely, powerfully.
. . . .

deep-rooted or **deep-seated** *adj.*, *said of ideas, habits, etc* deeply and firmly established in a person or group of people and not easily removed or changed.
. . . .
☰ ingrained, entrenched, permanent, ineradicable, indelible, fixed, confirmed, deep, settled.
☲ eradicable, temporary.
. . . .

deep-sea *adj.* of, for, working, etc in the deeper parts of the sea.

deep-seated see DEEP-ROOTED.

deep-set *adj.* (of the eyes) in relatively deep sockets.

Deep South (the Deep South) the SE part of the USA, roughly the states of South Carolina, Georgia, Louisiana, Mississippi, and Alabama.

deep space 1 the region of space beyond the gravitational and magnetic fields of the Earth. 2 the region of space outside the solar system. 3 formerly used to refer to the region of space outside the Moon's orbit.

deer *noun* (PL. **deer**) any of numerous ruminant mammals belonging to the family Cervidae, found throughout Europe, Asia, and N and S America, and distinguished by the presence of antlers, usually branched, in the male. [from Anglo-Saxon *deor*, animal, deer]

deerhound *noun* a breed of dog, developed in Scotland from Mediterranean ancestors, that has a tall slim body, a shaggy grey coat, long legs, a long tail, and a small head with short soft ears.

deerskin *noun* leather made from the skin of a deer.

deerstalker *noun* a kind of hat with peaks at the front and back and flaps at the side to cover the ears.

deface *verb* to deliberately spoil the appearance of (eg by marking or cutting). [from Old French *desfacier*]
. . . .
☰ damage, spoil, disfigure, blemish, impair, mutilate, mar, sully, tarnish, vandalize, deform, obliterate, injure, destroy.
☲ repair.
. . . .

defacement *noun* defacing; spoiling the appearance of something.

de facto /deɪ 'faktoʊ/ actual or actually, though not necessarily legally so. See also DE JURE. [from Latin *de facto*, in fact]

defamation /dɛfəˈmeɪʃən/ *noun* defaming; attacking someone's good reputation.
. . . .
☰ vilification, aspersion, slander, libel, disparagement, slur, smear, innuendo, scandal.
☲ commendation, praise.
. . . .

defamatory /dɪˈfamətrɪ/ *adj.*, *said of a remark, etc* attacking someone's good reputation.

⊟ vilifying, slanderous, libellous, denigrating, disparaging, pejorative, insulting, injurious, derogatory.
⊞ complimentary, appreciative.

defame *verb* to attack the good reputation of (someone) by saying something unfavourable about them. [from Latin *diffamare*, to spread bad reports about]

⊟ vilify, slander, libel, smear, insult, denigrate, disparage.

default /dɪˈfɒlt/ — *verb intrans.* (**default on something**) to fail to do what one should do, especially to fail to pay what is due. — *noun* **1** a failure to do or pay what one should. **2** a value that is automatically used or a course of action that is automatically taken, especially by a computer system, when no specific alternative instruction is given by the user. — **by default** because of someone's failure to do something which would have prevented or altered the situation. [from Old French *defaillir*, to fail]

⊟ *verb* fail, evade, neglect, dodge, swindle, backslide. *noun* **1** failure, absence, neglect, non-payment, omission, deficiency, lapse, fault, defect.

defaulter *noun* a person who defaults, especially in paying a debt.

⊟ non-payer, offender.

defeat — *verb* **1** to beat, win a victory over, eg in a war, competition, game or argument. **2** to cause (plans, etc) to fail. — *noun* the act of defeating or state of being defeated. [from Old French *desfait*, from *desfaire*, to ruin, undo]

⊟ *verb* **1** conquer, beat, overpower, subdue, overthrow, worst, repel, subjugate, overwhelm, rout, ruin, *colloq.* thump, quell, *literary* vanquish. **2** frustrate, confound, balk, get the better of, disappoint, foil, thwart, baffle, checkmate. *noun* conquest, beating, overthrow, rout, subjugation, frustration, failure, setback, reverse, disappointment, checkmate.

defeatism *noun* a state of mind in which one too readily expects or accepts defeat or failure.

defeatist — *adj.* too ready to accept defeat or failure. — *noun* a person who is defeatist.

⊟ *adj.* pessimistic, resigned, fatalistic, despondent, helpless, hopeless, despairing, gloomy. *noun* pessimist, quitter, prophet of doom.
⊞ *adj.* optimistic. *noun* optimist.

defecate /ˈdefəkeɪt/ *verb formal* **1** *intrans.* to expel faeces from the body through the anus. **2** *trans.* to remove impurities from. [from Latin *defaecare*]
defecation /defəˈkeɪʃən/ *noun formal* the expulsion of faeces from the body through the anus.
defect /ˈdiːfɛkt, dɪˈfɛkt/ — *noun* (with stress on *de-*) a flaw, fault or imperfection. — *verb intrans.* (with stress on *-fect*) to leave one's country, political party or group, especially to support or join an opposing one. [from Latin *deficere*, to fail]

⊟ *noun* imperfection, fault, flaw, deficiency, failing, mistake, inadequacy, blemish, error, *colloq.* bug, shortcoming, want, weakness, frailty, lack, spot, absence, taint. *verb* desert, break faith, rebel, *formal* apostatize, revolt, renegue.

defection *noun* defecting; abandoning a country, cause, etc.

defective *adj.* imperfect; having a defect or defects.

⊟ faulty, imperfect, out of order, flawed, deficient, broken, abnormal.
⊞ in order, operative.

defector *noun* a person who defects, or abandons a cause.
defence *noun* **1** the act of defending against attack. **2** the method, means, or equipment used to guard or protect against attack or when attacked. **3** the armed forces of a country. **4** (**defences**) fortifications. **5** a person's answer to an accusation, justifying or denying what he or she has been accused of. **6** (**the defence**) in a law court, the person or people on trial and the lawyer or lawyers acting for them. **7** *Sport* (**the defence**) the players in a team whose main task is to prevent their opponents from scoring. [from Latin *defendere*, to defend]

⊟ **1** protection, security, safeguarding, fortification, resistance, deterrence, immunity. **2** safeguard, shelter, cover, guard, shield, barricade, bastion, bulwark, rampart, buttress. **4** fortifications, earthworks, walls, ramparts, lines, trenches. **5** justification, explanation, excuse, argument, exoneration, plea, vindication, apologia, pleading, alibi, case.
⊞ **1** attack, assault. **5** accusation.

defenceless *adj.* unable to defend oneself if attacked.

⊟ unprotected, undefended, unarmed, unguarded, vulnerable, exposed, helpless, powerless.
⊞ protected, guarded.

defence mechanism **1** *Psychol.* any of various unconscious mental processes whereby a person avoids or blocks out ideas, experiences, or impulses that cause guilt, anxiety, shame, etc. **2** *Physiol.* a protective response of the body to invasion by disease-causing micro-organisms, allergens, etc.
defend *verb* **1** to guard or protect against attack or when attacked. **2** to explain, justify, or argue in support of, the actions of (someone accused of doing wrong). **3** *trans., intrans.* to be the lawyer acting on behalf of (the accused) in a trial. **4** *trans., intrans. Sport* to try to prevent one's opponents from scoring. **5** *Sport* to take part in a contest against a challenger for (a title, medal, etc one holds). [from Latin *defendere*]

⊟ **1** guard, protect, safeguard, shelter, fortify, secure, shield, screen, cover. **2** explain, justify, support, stand up for, stand by, uphold, endorse, vindicate, champion, argue for, speak up for, plead for.
⊞ **1** attack. **2** accuse.

defendant *noun* a person against whom a charge is brought in a law-court. See also PLAINTIFF.

⊟ accused, offender, prisoner, respondent.

defender *noun* a person who defends against attack, especially in military and sporting contexts, or against an accusation.

⊟ protector, guard, bodyguard, supporter, advocate, vindicator, champion, patron, sponsor, counsel.
⊞ attacker, accuser.

defensible *adj.* able to be defended or justified. [from Latin *defensibilis*]
defensibly *adv.* so as to be defended or justified.
defensive *adj.* **1** defending or ready to defend. **2** attempting to justify one's actions when criticized or when expecting criticism. — **on the defensive** defending oneself or

prepared to defend oneself against attack or criticism. [from Latin *defensivus*]

⬛ **1** protective, defending, safeguarding, opposing, wary, cautious, watchful. **2** self-justifying, apologetic.

defer[1] /dɪˈfɜː(r)/ *verb* (**deferred**, **deferring**) to put off or leave until a later time. [from Latin *differre*, to delay, postpone]

⬛ delay, postpone, put off, adjourn, hold over, shelve, suspend, prorogue, protract, waive.

defer[2] /dɪˈfɜː(r)/ *verb intrans.* (**deferred**, **deferring**) (**defer to someone**) to yield to their wishes, opinions, or orders. [from French *déférer*]

⬛ yield to, give way to, comply with, submit to, accede to, capitulate to, respect, bow to.

deference /ˈdefərəns/ *noun* **1** willingness to consider or respect the wishes, etc of others. **2** the act of deferring. — **in deference to someone** or **something** deferring to them; showing recognition of or respect for them.

⬛ **1** respect, regard, honour, esteem, reverence, courtesy, civility, politeness, consideration. **2** submission, submissiveness, compliance, acquiescence, obedience, yielding.
🔳 **1** contempt. **2** resistance.

deferential /defəˈrenʃəl/ *adj.* showing deference or respect.

⬛ respectful, polite, courteous, reverential, humble, obsequious, subservient, servile.

deferentially *adv.* with a deferential or respectful manner.
deferment or **deferral** *noun* deferring; postponement.

⬛ postponement, adjournment, suspension, delaying, putting off.

deferred payment payment for goods one has received by small sums of money over a period of time.
defiance *noun* an act of defying or of open disobedience; challenging or opposition, especially in a way that shows lack of respect.

⬛ opposition, confrontation, resistance, challenge, disobedience, rebelliousness, contempt, insubordination, disregard, insolence.
🔳 compliance, acquiescence, submissiveness.

defiant *adj.* openly disobedient or challenging.

⬛ challenging, resistant, antagonistic, aggressive, rebellious, insubordinate, disobedient, intransigent, bold, insolent, obstinate, unco-operative, provocative.
🔳 compliant, acquiescent, submissive.

defiantly *adv.* with a defiant or openly challenging manner.
deficiency /dɪˈfɪʃənsɪ/ *noun* (PL. **deficiencies**) **1** a shortage or lack in quality or amount. **2** the thing or amount lacking. **3** a fault or inadequacy.

⬛ **1, 2** shortage, lack. **1** inadequacy, scarcity, insufficiency, dearth, want, scantiness, absence. **2** deficit, shortfall. **3** imperfection, shortcoming, weakness, fault, defect,

flaw, failing, frailty, inadequacy, disadvantage.
🔳 **1, 2** excess, surfeit. **3** advantage, virtue, perfection.

deficiency disease *Medicine* any disease caused by lack of one or more specific nutrients, especially vitamins, in the diet, eg rickets, scurvy, beriberi.
deficient /dɪˈfɪʃənt/ *adj.* **1** insufficient; not having all that is needed. **2** not good enough. [from Latin *deficere*, to fail or be lacking]

⬛ **1** inadequate, insufficient, scarce, short, lacking, wanting, meagre, scanty, skimpy, incomplete. **2** imperfect, impaired, flawed, faulty, defective, unsatisfactory, inferior, weak.
🔳 **1** excessive. **2** perfect.

deficit /ˈdefɪsɪt/ *noun* the amount by which some quantity, especially a sum of money, is less than what is required (eg the amount by which expenditure is greater than income). [from Latin *deficere*, to fail or be lacking]

⬛ shortage, shortfall, deficiency, loss, arrears, lack, default.
🔳 excess.

defile[1] /dɪˈfaɪl/ *verb* **1** to make dirty or polluted. **2** to take away or spoil the goodness, purity, holiness, etc of. [from Old French *defouler*, to trample or violate; altered under the influence of the old word *befile*, from Anglo-Saxon *befylan*, to make foul]

⬛ POLLUTE, SOIL, STAIN, SULLY, TARNISH, TAINT, DEGRADE, DEBASE, CORRUPT. **1** contaminate, infect. **2** desecrate, violate, dishonour, profane, disgrace.

defile[2] /ˈdiːfaɪl, dɪˈfaɪl/ — *noun* (with stress on *de*-) a narrow valley or passage between mountains. — *verb intrans.* (with stress on -*file*) to march in file. [from French *défilé*, from *défiler*, to march in file]

⬛ *noun* valley, pass, col.

defilement *noun* making dirty; pollution.
defiler *noun* a person or thing that defiles or pollutes.
definable *adj.* capable of being defined or described precisely.
define *verb* **1** to fix or state the exact meaning of (a word, etc). **2** to fix, describe, or explain (opinions, duties, the qualities or limits of, etc). **3** to make clear the outline or shape of: *an ill-defined splodge on the canvas*. See also DEFINITION. [from Latin *definire*, to set boundaries to]

⬛ **2, 3** clarify. **2** explain, characterize, describe, interpret, expound, determine, designate, specify, spell out, detail. **3** bound, limit, delimit, demarcate, mark out.

definite /ˈdefɪnɪt/ *adj.* **1** fixed or firm; not liable to change. **2** sure; certain. **3** clear and precise. **4** having clear outlines. [from Latin *definire*, to set boundaries to]

⬛ **1** fixed, firm, settled, set, guaranteed, specific. **2** sure, certain, positive, confident, decided, determined, assured. **3** clear, clear-cut, exact, precise, specific, explicit, particular, obvious, marked.
🔳 INDEFINITE, VAGUE.

definite article *Grammar* a word (*the* in English) used before a noun, or before an adjective used absolutely, to denote a specific or known example, or a defined class, as in *the cat by the door*, *the government*, *the uninitiated*. See also INDEFINITE ARTICLE.
definitely *adv.* **1** as a definite fact; certainly. **2** in a definite way.

⊟ **1** certainly, positively, surely, unquestionably, absolutely, categorically, undeniably, clearly, unmistakably, plainly, obviously, indeed.

definiteness *noun* a definite state or quality.
definition /dɛfɪ'nɪʃən/ *noun* **1** a statement of the meaning of a word or phrase. **2** the act of defining a word or phrase. **3** the act of demarcating the extent or boundaries of something. **4** the quality of having clear, precise limits or form. **5** the degree of clearness and preciseness of limits or form. — **by definition** because of what something or someone essentially is or does: *a carpenter is by definition a craftsman.* [from Latin *definitio*]

⊟ **1** meaning, sense, explanation, description, interpretation. **2** explanation, description, interpretation, exposition, clarification, elucidation. **3** delineation, demarcation, delimitation. **4, 5** distinctness, clarity, precision, clearness, sharpness. **5** focus, contrast.

definitive /dɪ'fɪnɪtɪv/ *adj.* **1** settling a matter once and for all. **2** most complete or authoritative. [from Latin *definitivus*]

⊟ AUTHORITATIVE, CORRECT. **1** decisive, conclusive, final, reliable. **2** standard, ultimate, exhaustive, perfect, exact, absolute, complete.

definitively *adv.* in a definitive or decisive way.
deflate /dɪ'fleɪt/ *verb* **1** *trans., intrans.* to collapse or grow smaller by letting out gas. **2** to reduce or take away the hopes, excitement, feelings of importance or self-confidence, etc of. **3** *trans., intrans. Econ.* to cause or undergo deflation. See also INFLATE, REFLATE. [from DE- + INFLATE]

⊟ **1** flatten, puncture, collapse, squash, empty, contract, void, shrink, squeeze. **2** debunk, humiliate, put down, dash, dispirit, humble, mortify, disconcert. **3** decrease, devalue, reduce, lessen, lower, diminish, depreciate, depress.
⊞ **1** inflate. **2** boost. **3** increase.

deflated *adj.* **1** having the air or gas removed. **2** *said of a person* deprived of confidence.
deflation /dɪ'fleɪʃən/ *noun* **1** the act of deflating or the process of being deflated. **2** the state of being or feeling deflated. **3** *Econ.* a reduction in the amount of money available in a country, resulting in lower levels of economic activity, industrial output, and employment, and a lower rate of increase in wages and prices. See also INFLATION, REFLATION.
deflationary /dɪ'fleɪʃənrɪ/ *adj.* tending to cause deflation.
deflect /dɪ'flɛkt/ *verb trans., intrans.* to turn aside from the correct or intended course or direction. [from Latin *deflectere*]

⊟ turn (aside), divert, bend, twist, swerve, veer, sidetrack, glance off, ricochet.

deflection *noun* deflecting; deviation.
deflower *verb literary* to deprive (a woman) of her virginity. [from Latin *deflorare*, from *de*, from + *flos*, flower]
defoliant /dɪ'fouliənt/ *noun Chem.* a type of herbicide that causes the leaves to fall off plants.
defoliate /dɪ'foulieɪt/ *technical* — *verb* (**defoliated, defoliating**) to remove (the leaves) from a plant, or to cause (them) to fall, especially prematurely. — *adj.* denoting a plant that has shed its leaves, either naturally or as a result of disease, spraying with chemicals, etc. [from Latin *defoliare*, from *de*, off + *folium*, leaf]

defoliation /dɪfouli'eɪʃən/ *noun* the shedding or removal of leaves from a plant, especially prematurely, eg to prevent concealment of enemy troops behind foliage during warfare.
deforest *verb Agric.* to cut down forest trees for commercial use as timber, firewood, etc, or to clear land for agriculture, without replacing them, or without allowing the natural forest to regenerate.
deforestation *noun Environ.* the felling of all trees, usually over a large area, in a region that was previously natural forest, without planting more trees to replace those that have been lost.
deform *verb* to change the shape of (something) without breaking it, so that it looks ugly, unpleasant, unnatural, or spoiled. [from Latin *deformis*, ugly]

⊟ distort, contort, disfigure, warp, mar, pervert, ruin, spoil, twist.

deformed *adj.* put out of shape; made ugly.

⊟ distorted, misshapen, contorted, disfigured, crippled, crooked, bent, twisted, warped, buckled, defaced, mangled, maimed, marred, ruined, mutilated, perverted, corrupted.

deformity *noun* (PL. **deformities**) being deformed or misshapen.

⊟ distortion, misshapenness, malformation, disfigurement, abnormality, irregularity, misproportion, defect, ugliness, monstrosity, corruption.

defraud *verb* (**defraud someone of something**) to dishonestly prevent (someone) getting or keeping something which belongs to them or to which they have a right. [from Latin *defraudare*]

⊟ cheat, swindle, dupe, fleece, *slang* sting, *colloq.* rip off, *colloq.* do, *colloq.* diddle, rob, trick, *colloq.* con, *colloq.* rook, deceive, delude, embezzle, beguile.

defray /dɪ'freɪ/ *verb formal* to provide the money to pay (someone's costs or expenses). [from Old French *deffroier*, to pay costs]
defrayal or **defrayment** *noun* provision of money to meet a cost.
defrock *verb* to remove (a priest) from office, usually because of unacceptable conduct or beliefs.
defrost *verb trans., intrans.* **1** to remove (frost or ice) from an object. **2** *said of food, etc* to make or become free of ice, especially as a result of removal from a deep freeze.
deft *adj.* skilful, quick, and neat. [from Anglo-Saxon *gedæfte*, meek]

⊟ skilful, adept, handy, dexterous, quick, nimble, agile, adroit, expert, nifty, proficient, able, neat, clever.
⊞ clumsy, awkward.

deftly *adv.* in a deft or skilful way.
deftness *noun* being deft or skilful.
defunct /dɪ'fʌŋkt/ *adj. facetious, formal* no longer living, existing, active, usable, or in use. [from Latin *defungi*, to finish]

⊟ dead, deceased, departed, gone, expired, extinct, obsolete, invalid, inoperative, expired.
⊞ alive, live, operative.

defuse *verb* **1** to remove the fuse from (a bomb, etc). **2** to make (a situation, etc) harmless or less dangerous.
defy *verb* (**defies, defied**) **1** to resist or disobey boldly and

openly. **2** to dare or challenge (someone). **3** *formal* to make impossible or unsuccessful. See also DEFIANCE. [from Old French *defier*, from Latin *diffidare*, to renounce one's faith]

- **1, 2** challenge, confront, face. **1** resist, withstand, disobey, flout, disregard, brave, scorn, spurn, repel, defeat, thwart. **2** dare, beard, provoke. **3** resist, elude, frustrate, baffle, foil.
- **1** obey, respect. **3** permit.

degauss / diːˈgaʊs/ *verb Physics* to neutralize the magnetic field of (an object) by encircling it with an electric field. The process is used to protect ships from magnetically activated mines.

degeneracy / dɪˈdʒenərəsɪ/ *noun* a degenerate or degraded state.

degenerate / dɪˈdʒenərət, -reɪt/ — *adj.* (pronounced -rət) **1** physically, morally, or intellectually worse than before. **2** *Biol.* having lost former structure, or changed from a complex to a simpler form. — *noun* (pronounced -rət) a degenerate person or animal. — *verb intrans.* (pronounced -reɪt) **1** to go from a better, more moral, etc state to a worse one. **2** *Biol.* to lose former structure, or change from a complex to a simpler form. [from Latin *degenerare*, to become unlike one's kind]

- *adj.* **1** degraded, debased, base, low, mean, degenerated, perverted, deteriorated, dissolute, debauched, depraved, decadent, corrupt, fallen, immoral. *verb* **1** decline, deteriorate, sink, decay, rot, slip, worsen, regress, fall off, lapse, decrease.
- *adj.* **1** moral, upright. *verb* **1** improve.

degeneration / dɪdʒenəˈreɪʃən/ *noun* **1** the process or act of degenerating. **2** *Biol.* the breakdown, death, or decay of cells, nerve fibres, etc. **3** *Biol.* an evolutionary change from a complex structural form to an apparently simpler form, as in the wings of flightless birds such as the emu.

degenerative / dɪˈdʒenərətɪv/ *adj. Medicine* denoting a disease in which the normal structure and functioning of cells and tissues is impaired or lost.

degradable / dɪˈɡreɪdəbl/ *adj. technical* denoting a substance that is capable of being decomposed chemically or biologically.

degradation / deɡrəˈdeɪʃən/ *noun* **1** moral deterioration. **2** reduction in quality, rank or status. **3** *Chem.* the breakdown of a molecule of an organic compound into smaller molecules of simpler compounds, usually in a series of stages. **4** *Physics* an irreversible process whereby the amount of energy available to do work decreases. **5** *Geol.* the wearing down of land, rock surfaces, etc, by erosion.

- **1** abasement, humiliation, mortification, dishonour, disgrace, shame, ignominy, decadence. **2** deterioration, degeneration, debasement, decline, downgrading, demotion.
- **1** virtue. **2** enhancement.

degrade / dɪˈɡreɪd/ *verb* **1** to disgrace or humiliate. **2** to reduce in rank, status, etc. **3** *trans., intrans. Chem.* to cause (a molecule of an organic compound) to break down into smaller molecules of simpler compounds, usually in a series of stages; to decompose. **4** *said of a molecule of an organic compound* to break down in this way; to decompose. **5** *Geol.* to erode (land, rock surfaces, etc). [from Old French *degrader*, from Latin *de*, down + *gradus*, step]

- **1** disgrace, humiliate, dishonour, debase, abase, shame, humble, discredit, demean, lower, weaken, impair, deteriorate, cheapen, adulterate, corrupt. **2** demote, depose, downgrade, deprive, cashier.
- **1** exalt. **2** promote.

degrading / dɪˈɡreɪdɪŋ/ *adj.* humiliating; debasing.

degree *noun* **1** an amount or extent. **2** *Physics* (SYMBOL °) a unit of temperature used in the Celsius, Fahrenheit, and Kelvin scales. **3** *Geom.* (SYMBOL °) a unit by which angles are measured and direction is described. It is equal to the angle of one segment of a circle that has been divided into 360 equal parts. Degrees are subdivided into minutes and seconds. **4** an award or title given by a university or college, either earned by examination or research or given as a mark of honour. **5** a comparative amount of severity or seriousness (see FIRST-DEGREE, SECOND-DEGREE, THIRD-DEGREE). **6** a stage, level or category in an ascending scale. **7** *Grammar* any of the three categories of comparison (*positive*, *comparative*, and *superlative*) of an adjective or adverb. — **by degrees** gradually. **to a degree** to a certain or considerable extent. [from Old French *degre*, from Latin *de*, down + *gradus*, step]

- **1** amount, extent, measure, range, intensity. **2, 3** unit, mark, level. **6** grade, class, level, standard, stage, step, rank, order, position, standing, status. **by degrees** gradually, bit by bit, step by step, little by little.

dehiscent / dɪˈhɪsənt/ *adj. Bot.* denoting a fruit, or the anther of a stamen, that bursts open spontaneously at maturity to release the seeds or pollen, eg laburnum pod. [from Latin *dehiscere*, to gape, split open]

dehumanize or **dehumanise** *verb* to remove the human qualities from.

dehydrate / diːhaɪˈdreɪt/ *verb* **1** to remove water from (a substance or organism). **2** *trans., intrans.* to lose or cause to lose too much water from the body. [from DE- + Greek *hydor*, water]

dehydrated *adj.* deprived of water; with water removed.

dehydration / diːhaɪˈdreɪʃən/ *noun* **1** the removal of water from a substance. **2** a method of preserving food by greatly reducing its moisture content, eg sun-dried fruit, freeze-dried coffee. **3** *Medicine* a condition in which there is insufficient water in the body, eg as a result of diarrhoea or excessive sweating.

de-ice *verb* to dislodge or melt ice or frost from (a surface).

de-icer *noun* a device or agent for dislodging or melting ice.

deification / diːɪfɪˈkeɪʃən/ *noun* making into a god; treating as divine.

deify / ˈdiːɪfaɪ/ *verb* (**deifies, deified**) to regard or worship (someone or something) as a god. [from Old French *deifier*, from Latin *deus*, god + *facere*, to make]

- exalt, elevate, worship, glorify, idolize, extol, venerate, immortalize, ennoble, idealize.

deign / deɪn/ *verb intrans.* to do something reluctantly and in a way that shows that one considers the matter hardly important or beneath one's dignity: *didn't even deign to reply.* [from Old French *daigner*, from Latin *dignari*, to consider worthy]

- condescend, stoop, lower oneself, consent, demean oneself.

deionization *noun Chem.* an ion-exchange process that is used to purify or change the composition of a solution, especially to purify water obtained from the mains water supply.

deism / ˈdeɪɪzm/ *noun* belief in the existence of God without acceptance of any religion or message revealed by God to man. See also THEISM. [from Latin *deus*, god + -ISM]

deist / ˈdeɪɪst/ *noun* a person who believes in God but rejects established religions.

deity / ˈdiːɪtɪ/ *noun* (PL. **deities**) *formal* **1** a god or goddess. **2**

the state of being divine. **3 (the Deity)** God. [from Latin *deitas*, from *deus*, god]

....

◻ **1** god, goddess, divinity, godhead, idol, demigod, demigoddess, power, immortal.

....

déjà vu /ˈdeɪʒɑ: ˈvu:/ the feeling or illusion that one has experienced something before although one is actually experiencing it for the first time. [from French *déjà vu*, already seen]

dejected *adj.* sad; miserable. [from Latin *deicere*, to throw down, disappoint]

....

◻ sad, miserable, downcast, despondent, depressed, downhearted, disheartened, down, low, melancholy, disconsolate, cast down, gloomy, glum, crestfallen, dismal, wretched, doleful, morose, spiritless.
◼ cheerful, high-spirited, happy.

....

dejectedly *adv.* with a dejected or sad manner.
dejection *noun* being dejected or sad.

....

◻ sadness, misery, melancholy, depression, despondency, gloom.

....

de jure /deɪ ˈdʒuːreɪ/ *Legal* according to law; by right. See also DE FACTO. [from Latin *de jure*, by law]
dekko — **have** or **take a dekko** *Brit. slang* to take a look. [from Hindi *dekhna*, to see]
Del. *abbrev.* Delaware.
delay — *verb* **(delayed, delaying) 1** to slow down or cause to be late. **2** to put off to a later time. **3** *intrans.* to be slow in doing something; to linger. — *noun* **1** the act of delaying or state of being delayed. **2** the amount of time by which someone or something is delayed. [from Old French *delaier*]

....

◻ *verb* **1** slow down, hold up, hold back, set back, detain, check, hinder, impede, obstruct, stop, halt. **2** defer, put off, postpone, suspend, shelve, hold over, stall. **3** dawdle, linger, lag, loiter, *colloq.* dilly-dally, tarry. *noun* **1** hold-up, stoppage, hindrance, obstruction, impediment, check, setback, stay, deferment, postponement, suspension, dawdling, lingering, tarrying. **2** time lag, interval, wait, lull.
◼ *verb* **1** accelerate. **2** bring forward. **3** hurry. *noun* **1** hastening, hurry. **2** continuation.

....

delayed action the operation of a device, such as a camera shutter or the detonator of an explosive device, a short time after the mechanism has been set.
delectable /dɪˈlɛktəbl/ *adj.*, *said especially of food* delightful or enjoyable; delicious. [from Latin *delectare*, to delight]
delectably *adv.* delightfully; deliciously.
delectation /diːlɛkˈteɪʃən/ *noun formal* delight, enjoyment, or amusement.
delegate /ˈdɛləgeɪt, ˈdɛlɪgət/ *verb* (pronounced -geɪt) **1** to give (part of one's work, power, etc) to someone else. **2** to send or name (a person) as a representative, as the one to do a job, etc. *noun* (pronounced -gət) someone chosen to be the representative for another person or group of people eg at a conference or meeting. [from Latin *de*, away + *legare*, to send as ambassador]

....

◻ *verb* ASSIGN, DESIGNATE. **1** entrust, devolve, consign, hand over. **2** authorize, appoint, nominate, name, depute, charge, commission, empower. *noun* representative, agent, envoy, messenger, deputy, ambassador, commissioner.

....

delegation /dɛləˈgeɪʃən/ *noun* **1** a group of delegates. **2** the act of delegating or the state of being delegated.

◻ **1** deputation, commission, legation, mission, contingent, embassy. **2** assignment, designation, devolution, authorization, commissioning, appointment, nomination.

....

delete *verb* to rub out, score out, or remove (especially from something written or printed). [from Latin *delere*, to blot out]

....

◻ erase, remove, cross out, cancel, rub out, strike (out), obliterate, edit (out), blot out, efface.
◼ add, insert.

....

deleterious /dɛlɪˈtɪərɪəs/ *adj. formal* causing harm or destruction. [from Greek *deleterios*]

....

◻ harmful, destructive, detrimental, malign, malignant, noxious, injurious.

....

deletion /dɪˈliːʃən/ *noun* rubbing out; something rubbed out or removed.
delft or **delf** *noun* same as DELFTWARE.
Delftware *noun* a type of earthenware decorated with an opaque glaze containing oxide of tin, and produced in Holland (at Delft and elsewhere) and England in large quantities in the 17c. It is usually blue and white with motifs copied from Chinese porcelain.
deliberate /dɪˈlɪbərət, dɪˈlɪbəreɪt/ — *adj.* (pronounced -rət) **1** done on purpose; not accidental. **2** slow and careful. — *verb trans., intrans.* (pronounced -reɪt) to think about something carefully. [from Latin *deliberare*, to consider carefully]

....

◻ *adj.* **1** intentional, planned, calculated, prearranged, premeditated, willed, conscious, considered, advised. **2** careful, unhurried, thoughtful, methodical, cautious, circumspect, studied, prudent, slow, ponderous, measured, heedful. *verb* think (about or on), consider, ponder, reflect (on), cogitate, meditate, debate, discuss.
◼ *adj.* **1** unintentional, accidental. **2** hasty.

....

deliberately *adv.* intentionally; on purpose.
deliberation /dɪlɪbəˈreɪʃən/ *noun* **1** careful thought. **2 (deliberations)** formal and thorough thought and discussion. **3** slowness and carefulness.

....

◻ **1** consideration, reflection, thought, calculation, forethought, meditation, rumination, study, debate, discussion, consultation, speculation. **3** care, carefulness, caution, circumspection, prudence.

....

delicacy /ˈdɛlɪkəsɪ/ *noun* (PL. **delicacies**) **1** fineness and fragility. **2** the need for sensitivity and tact in the treatment of someone or something. **3** consideration and tact. **4** something considered particularly delicious to eat. [from DELICATE]

....

◻ **1** daintiness, fineness, elegance, exquisiteness, lightness, precision. **2** sensitivity, difficulty, awkwardness, ticklishness, trickiness. **3** tact, consideration, sensitivity, diplomacy, subtlety, refinement, finesse, discrimination, niceness. **4** titbit, dainty, taste, sweetmeat, savoury, relish.
◼ **1** coarseness, roughness. **3** tactlessness.

....

delicate /ˈdɛlɪkət/ *adj.* **1** easily damaged or broken. **2** not strong or healthy. **3** of fine texture or workmanship. **4** dainty; small and attractive. **5** small, neat, and careful: *delicate movements.* **6** requiring tact and careful handling: *a delicate situation.* **7** careful about what one says or does, so as not to offend others. **8** *said of colours, flavours, etc* light; not strong. [from Latin *delicatus*]

crime or misdeed. [from Latin *delinquere*, to fail in one's duty]

⊟ *noun* offender, criminal, wrongdoer, law-breaker, hooligan, culprit, *literary, old use* miscreant. *adj.* criminal, offending, law-breaking, lawless.

deliquesce /dɛlɪˈkwɛs/ *verb intrans. Chem., said of certain chemical salts* to absorb water from the atmosphere and gradually dissolve in it to form a solution. [from Latin *deliquescere*, to dissolve]

deliquescence *noun* the process whereby certain chemical salts absorb water from the atmosphere and gradually dissolve in it to form a solution.

deliquescent *adj.* denoting a chemical salt that changes from a powdery solid to a liquid on exposure to air, eg calcium chloride.

delirious /dɪˈlɪrɪəs/ *adj.* 1 *said of a person* displaying the symptoms of delirium, especially as a result of fever or other illness. 2 highly excited or happy. [from Latin *delirus*, from *delirare*, to rave, originally to go off a straight furrow, from *de*, from + *lira*, furrow]

⊟ 1 demented, raving, incoherent, beside oneself, deranged, frenzied, light-headed, wild, mad, frantic, insane, crazy. 2 ecstatic, euphoric, overjoyed, elated, jubilant, *colloq.* over the moon.
⊞ 1 sane.

delirium /dɪˈlɪrɪəm/ *noun* (PL. **deliriums, deliria**) 1 a disordered mental state characterized by wandering of the mind, incoherent speech, extreme excitement, fear, or anxiety, and occasionally hallucinations. 2 extreme excitement or joy. [from Latin *delirare*; see DELIRIOUS]

delirium tremens /ˈtrɛmɛnz/ (ABBREV. **DTs**) a severe psychotic disorder caused by excessive consumption of alcohol over a long period, especially when this is followed by withdrawal or a reduction in levels of consumption. [from Latin *tremere*, to tremble]

deliver /dɪˈlɪvə(r)/ *verb* (**delivered, delivering**) 1 *trans., intrans.* to carry (goods, letters, etc) to a person or place. 2 *formal* (**deliver something up**) to hand over. 3 to give or make (a speech, etc). 4 *formal, old use* (**deliver from**) to set free or rescue. 5 to help (a woman) at the birth of (a child). 6 *trans., intrans. colloq.* to keep or fulfil (a promise or undertaking). 7 *formal* to aim or direct (a blow, criticism, etc) towards someone or something. — **deliver the goods** *colloq.* to fulfil a promise or undertaking.

⊟ 1 convey, bring, send, give, carry, supply. 2 surrender, hand over, relinquish, yield, transfer, grant, entrust, commit. 3 utter, speak, proclaim, pronounce. 4 set free, liberate, release, emancipate. 7 administer, inflict, direct.

deliverance *noun formal, old use* the act of rescuing, freeing, or saving from danger or harm, or the state of being rescued, freed, or saved.

deliverer *noun* a person who delivers, especially a liberator.

delivery *noun* (PL. **deliveries**) 1 the carrying of goods, letters, etc to a person or place. 2 the thing or things being delivered. 3 the process or manner of giving birth to a child. 4 the act of making, or one's manner of making, a speech, etc. 5 the act or manner of throwing a ball, especially in some sports.

⊟ 1, 2 consignment, shipment. 1 conveyance, dispatch, carriage, transmission. 2 load, parcel, batch. 3 childbirth, labour, confinement. 4 articulation, enunciation, speech, utterance, intonation, elocution.

dell *noun* a small valley or hollow, usually with trees. [from Anglo-Saxon *dell*]

⊟ 1, 2 fragile, frail. 1 fine, dainty, flimsy. 2 weak, ailing, faint. 3 fine, sheer, translucent, transparent, gossamer, exquisite, intricate. 4 dainty, exquisite, petite, elegant, graceful. 5 neat, light, deft, skilful, careful, cautious, wary. 6 sensitive, tricky, awkward, ticklish, difficult. 7 sensitive, scrupulous, discriminating, careful, accurate, precise. 8 subtle, muted, pastel, soft.
⊞ 2 healthy. 3 coarse. 5 clumsy, awkward.

delicatessen /dɛlɪkəˈtɛsn/ *noun* a shop selling foods prepared ready for the table, especially cooked meats, cheeses, and unusual or imported foods. [from German *Delikatessen*, from French *délicatesse*, delicacy]

delicious /dɪˈlɪʃəs/ *adj.* 1 with a very pleasing taste or smell. 2 giving great pleasure. [from Old French *delicious*, from Latin *deliciae*, delight]

⊟ DELECTABLE. 1 appetizing, palatable, tasty, *colloq.* scrumptious, mouth-watering, succulent, savoury. 2 enjoyable, pleasant, agreeable, delightful, exquisite.
⊞ 1 unpalatable. 2 unpleasant.

delight /dɪˈlaɪt/ — *verb* 1 to please greatly. 2 *intrans.* (**delight in something**) to take great pleasure from it. — *noun* 1 great pleasure. 2 something or someone that gives great pleasure. [from Old French *deliter*, from Latin *delectare*; spelling influenced by LIGHT]

⊟ *verb* 1 please, charm, gratify, enchant, tickle, thrill, ravish. 2 enjoy, relish, like, love, appreciate, revel in, take pride in, glory in, savour. *noun* JOY, PLEASURE. 1 bliss, happiness, ecstasy, enjoyment, gladness, rapture, transport, gratification, jubilation.
⊞ *verb* 1 displease, dismay. 2 dislike, hate. *noun* 1 disgust, displeasure.

delighted *adj.* highly pleased; thrilled.

⊟ charmed, elated, happy, pleased, enchanted, captivated, ecstatic, thrilled, overjoyed, jubilant, joyous.
⊞ disappointed, dismayed.

delightful *adj.* giving great pleasure.

⊟ charming, enchanting, captivating, enjoyable, pleasant, thrilling, agreeable, pleasurable, engaging, attractive, pleasing, gratifying, entertaining, fascinating.
⊞ nasty, unpleasant.

delightfully *adv.* in a highly pleasing way.

delimit /diːˈlɪmɪt/ *verb* (**delimited, delimiting**) to mark or fix the limits or boundaries of (powers, etc). [from Latin *delimitare*]

delimitation /dɪlɪmɪˈteɪʃən/ *noun* fixing limits or boundaries.

delineate /dɪˈlɪnɪeɪt/ *verb* to show by drawing or by describing in words. [from Latin *delineare*, to sketch out]

⊟ draw, outline, sketch, portray, depict, describe.

delineation /dɪlɪnɪˈeɪʃən/ *noun* description in drawing or words.

delinquency /dɪˈlɪŋkwənsɪ/ *noun* minor crime, especially committed by young people.

⊟ crime, wrongdoing, misbehaviour, misconduct, law-breaking, misdemeanour, criminality.

delinquent — *noun* a person, especially a young person, guilty of a minor criminal offence. — *adj.* guilty of a minor

delphinium /dɛlˈfɪnɪəm/ *noun* (PL. **delphiniums, delphinia**) any of about 200 species of tall perennial plants of the genus *Delphinium*, native to north temperate regions, with lobed or finely divided leaves and blue flowers. [from Greek *delphis*, dolphin (from the shape of the flowers)]

delta *noun* **1** at the mouth of some rivers, an often triangular area of silt, sand, gravel, or clay, formed from sediment deposited by the river as it slows down on entering the relatively still waters of a sea or lake. **2** the fourth letter of the Greek alphabet (Δ,δ). [from Greek *delta*]

delude /dɪˈluːd/ *verb* to deceive or mislead. See also DELUSION. [from Latin *deludere*, to cheat]

■ deceive, mislead, beguile, dupe, take in, trick, hoodwink, hoax, cheat, misinform.

deluge /ˈdɛljuːdʒ/ — *noun* **1** a flood. **2** a downpour of rain. **3** a great quantity of anything coming or pouring in. — *verb* **1** (**deluge with something**) to overwhelm with it. **2** *formal* to flood; to cover in water. [from Old French *deluge*, from Latin *diluvium*, flood]

■ *noun* FLOOD, TORRENT. **1** inundation, spate, rush. **2** downpour, cloudburst. *verb* FLOOD (WITH), INUNDATE (WITH), OVERWHELM (WITH), SWAMP (WITH), SUBMERGE (IN). **2** drench, drown, soak, engulf.

delusion /dɪˈluːʒən/ *noun* **1** the act of deluding or being deluded. **2** a false or mistaken belief, especially because of mental illness. [from Latin *delusio*]

■ DECEPTION. **2** illusion, hallucination, fancy, misconception, misapprehension, misbelief, fallacy.

delusive or **delusory** *adj.* deluding or likely to delude.

de luxe /də lʌks, dɪ lʊks/ very luxurious or elegant; with special features or qualities. [from French *de luxe*, of luxury]

delve *verb intrans.* **1** (**delve into something**) to search it for information. **2** (**delve through something**) to search through it. [from Anglo-Saxon *delfan*, to dig]

Dem. *abbrev.* Democrat and Democratic.

demagnetize or **demagnetise** *verb* **1** to remove magnetic properties from (an object). **2** *intrans.*, *said of an object* to lose its magnetic properties.

demagogic /dɛməˈgɒgɪk/ *adj.* typical of a demagogue.

demagogue /ˈdɛməgɒg/ *noun derog.* a person who tries to win political power or support by appealing to people's emotions and prejudices. [from Greek *demos*, people + *agogos*, leading]

demagoguery /ˈdɛməgɒgərɪ/ or **demagogy** *noun* behaviour of a demagogue.

demand — *verb* **1** to ask or ask for firmly, forcefully or urgently. **2** to require or need. **3** to claim as a right. — *noun* **1** a forceful request or order. **2** an urgent claim for action or attention: *makes great demands on one's time.* **3** people's desire or ability to buy or obtain (goods, etc): *a slump in demand for coffee.* — **in demand** very popular; frequently asked for. **on demand** when asked for. [from Old French *demander*, to ask]

■ *verb* **1** ask, request, call for, insist on, solicit. **2** necessitate, need, require, involve, entail. **3** claim, exact, command, require, requisition. *noun* CALL. **1** request, order, command, requisition, desire, wish. **2** claim.

demanding *adj.* **1** requiring a lot of effort, ability, etc: *a demanding job.* **2** needing or expecting a lot of attention: *a demanding child.*

■ DIFFICULT. **1** hard, challenging, exacting, taxing, testing, arduous, tough, exhausting, wearing, backbreaking. **2** trying, attention-seeking.

■ UNDEMANDING. **1** easy. **2** easy-going.

demarcate /ˈdiːmɑːkeɪt/ *verb* to mark out the limits or boundaries of.

■ delimit, define, outline.

demarcation /diːmɑːˈkeɪʃən/ *noun* **1** the marking out of limits or boundaries. **2** the strict separation of the areas or types of work to be done by the members of the various trade unions in a factory, etc: *a demarcation dispute.* [from Spanish *demarcar*, to mark the boundaries of]

demean /dɪˈmiːn/ *verb* to lower the dignity of or lessen respect for (someone, especially oneself). [from MEAN[1]]

■ lower, humble, degrade, humiliate, debase, abase, descend, stoop, condescend.
□ exalt, enhance.

demeaning *adj.* humiliating; debasing.

demeanour /dɪˈmiːnə(r)/ *noun* manner of behaving; behaviour towards others. [from Old French *demener*, to treat]

■ bearing, manner, deportment, conduct, behaviour, air.

demented *adj.* mad; out of one's mind. [from Latin *de*, from + *mens*, mind]

■ mad, insane, lunatic, out of one's mind, crazy, *slang* loony, deranged, unbalanced, frenzied.
□ sane.

dementia /dɪˈmenʃə/ *noun Medicine* **1** a chronic or persistent mental disorder characterized by loss of memory and personality change. See also SENILE DEMENTIA. **2** Alzheimer's disease. [from Latin *de*, from + *mens*, mind]

demerara /dɛməˈrɛərə/ *noun* a form of brown sugar. [from *Demerara* in Guyana, S America]

demerit /diːˈmerɪt/ *noun formal* a fault or failing. [from Latin *demereri*, to deserve]

demi- *combining form* half or partly: *demigod.* [from French *demi*, half]

demigod /ˈdemɪgɒd/ *noun Mythol.* a person who is part human and part god.

demijohn /ˈdemɪdʒɒn/ *noun* a large bottle with a short narrow neck and one or two small handles, used eg for storing wine. [from French *dame-jeanne*, Dame Jane, influenced by DEMI and the name *John*]

demilitarization or **demilitarisation** *noun* removal of armed forces from a region.

demilitarize or **demilitarise** *verb* to remove armed forces from (an area) and not allow any military activity in it.

demise /dɪˈmaɪz/ *noun* **1** *formal* death. **2** a failure or end. [from Old French *demise*, from *desmettre*, to lay down]

■ **1** death, passing, decease, departure. **2** end, termination, expiration, fall, collapse, failure, ruin, downfall.

demisemiquaver *noun Mus.* a note equal in time to half a semiquaver.

demist *verb* to remove ice or condensation from (the windscreen of a motor vehicle) by means of a demister.

demister *noun* a device for blowing warm air over the windscreen of a motor vehicle in order to remove ice or condensation.

demo *noun* (PL. **demos**) *colloq.* demonstration.

demob *Brit. colloq.* — *verb* (**demobbed, demobbing**) short form of DEMOBILIZE. — *noun* short form of DEMOBILIZATION.

demobilization or **demobilisation** *noun* release from service in the armed forces.

demobilize or **demobilise** *verb* to release from service in the armed forces, eg after a war.

democracy /dɪˈmɒkrəsɪ/ *noun* (PL. **democracies**) **1** a form of government in which the people govern themselves or elect representatives to govern them. **2** a country, state, or other body with such a form of government. [from Greek *demos*, people + *kratos*, strength]

▣ **1** self-government, autonomy. **2** republic, commonwealth.

democrat /ˈdɛməkrat/ *noun* **1** a person who believes in democracy as a principle. **2** (**Democrat**) a member or supporter of the Democratic Party in the USA, or of any political party with *Democratic* in its title. See also REPUBLICAN.

democratic /dɛməˈkratɪk/ *adj.* **1** concerned with or following the principles of democracy. **2** believing in or providing equal rights and privileges for all. **3** (**Democratic**) relating to or belonging to the *Democratic Party*, one of the two chief political parties of the US.

▣ **1** self-governing, autonomous, representative, popular, populist, republican. **2** egalitarian.

democratically *adv.* in a democratic way; on democratic principles.

demodulate /diːˈmɒdjʊleɪt/ *verb Radio* to subject (a modulated carrier wave) to demodulation. See also DEMODULATION.

demodulation /diːmɒdjʊˈleɪʃən/ *noun Radio* in radio transmission, the process whereby information in the form of an audio or video signal is extracted from a modulated carrier wave. It is the reverse process to modulation.

demodulator *noun Radio* a device that extracts information from the modulated carrier wave of a radio broadcast.

demographer /dɪˈmɒgrəfə(r)/ *noun* a person who studies demography or the statistics of populations.

demographic /dɛməˈgrafɪk/ *adj.* relating to demography or populations.

demography /dɪˈmɒgrəfɪ/ *noun technical* the scientific study of population statistics, including births, deaths, etc. [from Greek *demos*, people + *graphein*, to write]

demolish /dɪˈmɒlɪʃ/ *verb* **1** to pull or tear down (a building, etc). **2** to destroy (an argument, etc). **3** *facetious* to eat up. [from Latin *demoliri*, to throw down]

▣ DESTROY. **1** dismantle, knock down, pull down, flatten, bulldoze, raze, tear down, level. **2** ruin, defeat, annihilate, wreck, overturn, overthrow.
▣ **1** build up.

demolition /dɛməˈlɪʃən/ *noun* the act of demolishing.

▣ destruction, dismantling, levelling, razing.

demon /ˈdiːmən/ *noun* **1** an evil spirit. **2** a cruel or evil person. **3** a person who has great energy, enthusiasm, or skill: *a demon at football*. **4** (*also* **daemon**) a good or friendly spirit. [from Greek *daimon*, spirit]

▣ **1, 2** devil, fiend. **1** evil spirit, fallen angel, imp. **2** villain, rogue, monster.

demoniac or **demoniacal** /dɪˈmoʊnɪak, -ˈaɪəkəl/ *adj.* **1** of or like a demon or demons. **2** influenced by or as if influenced by demons; frenzied or very energetic.

demonic /dɪˈmɒnɪk/ *adj.* **1** of or like a demon or demons. **2** possessed or as if possessed by a demon or demons; evil.

▣ FIENDISH, DEVILISH, DIABOLICAL.

demonically *adv.* like a demon; as if possessed.

demonize or **demonise** *verb* to treat or portray (someone or something) as evil or wrong.

demonstrable /dɪˈmɒnstrəbl, ˈdɛmənstrəbl/ *adj.* capable of being demonstrated.

▣ verifiable, provable, arguable, attestable, self-evident, obvious, evident, certain, clear, positive.
▣ unverifiable.

demonstrably /dɪˈmɒnstrəblɪ, ˈdɛmənstrəblɪ/ *adv.* in a demonstrable way; as can be demonstrated.

demonstrate /ˈdɛmənstreɪt/ *verb* **1** to show or prove by reasoning or providing evidence. **2** *trans., intrans.* to show how something is done, operates, etc. **3** *intrans.* to show one's support, opposition, etc by protesting, marching, etc in public. [from Latin *demonstrare*, to show, indicate]

▣ **1** show, display, prove, establish, exhibit, substantiate, manifest, testify to, indicate. **2** explain, illustrate, teach. **3** protest, march, parade, rally, picket, sit in.

demonstration /dɛmənˈstreɪʃən/ *noun* **1** showing or demonstrating. **2** a public display of opinion on a political or moral issue. **3** *Maths., Philos.* establishing as true or evident by argument or proof.

▣ **1** display, exhibition, manifestation, expression, explanation, illustration, description, exposition, presentation, test, trial, evidence, testimony. **2** protest, march, *colloq.* demo, rally, picket, sit-in, parade. **3** proof, confirmation, substantiation, validation.

demonstrative /dɪˈmɒnstrətɪv/ *adj.* **1** showing one's feelings openly. **2** (**demonstrative of something**) showing it or proving it to be so: *words demonstrative of anger*.

▣ **1** affectionate, expressive, expansive, emotional, open, loving. **2** expressive of, indicative of, suggestive of.
▣ **1** reserved, cold, restrained.

demonstratively *adv.* in a demonstrative or openly expressive way.

demonstrative pronoun and **adjective** *noun Grammar* a word indicating the person or thing referred to, ie *this, that, these, those.*

demonstrator /ˈdɛmənstreɪtə(r)/ *noun* **1** a person who demonstrates equipment, etc. **2** a person who takes part in a public demonstration.

demoralization or **demoralisation** *noun* demoralizing; being demoralized.

demoralize or **demoralise** *verb* to take away the confidence, courage, or enthusiasm of; to dishearten. See also MORALE. [from French *démoraliser*]

▣ discourage, dishearten, dispirit, undermine, depress, deject, crush, lower, disconcert.
▣ encourage, inspire.

demote /diːˈmoʊt/ *verb* to reduce to a lower rank or grade. [from DE- + PROMOTE]

▣ downgrade, degrade, relegate, reduce.
▣ promote, upgrade.

demotic /dɪˈmɒtɪk/ — *adj.*, *said especially of a language* used in everyday affairs; popular. — *noun* **1** colloquial language. **2** (**Demotic**) a form of modern Greek based on popular usage, as distinct from formal or literary language. **3** a simplified form of ancient Egyptian writing. [from Greek *demotikos*, from *demos*, people]

demotion /diːˈmoʊʃən/ *noun* reduction to a lower rank.

demur /dɪˈmɜː(r)/ — *verb intrans.* (**demurred, demurring**) to object mildly; to be reluctant to do something. — *noun* (**without demur**) without objecting. [from Old French *demorer*, to wait]

▪ *verb* disagree, dissent, object, take exception, refuse, protest, balk, hesitate.

demure /dɪˈmjʊə(r)/ *adj.*, *said of a person* quiet, modest, and well-behaved. [from Old French *demorer*, to wait, influenced by *meur*, ripe]

▪ modest, reserved, reticent, quiet, prim, coy, shy, retiring, prissy, grave, prudish, sober, strait-laced, staid.
▪ wanton, forward.

demurral *noun* mild objection or reluctance.

demutualize *verb intrans.*, *said of a building society or other financial institution* to change from a mutual financial institution to a public company.

demystification *noun* reduction of an irrational element.

demystify *verb* (**demystifies, demystified**) to remove the mystery from.

den *noun* **1** the lair of a wild animal. **2** a centre (often secret) of illegal or immoral activity. **3** a room in a house or a hut outside it, used as a place to retire to for solitude, work, or play. **4** *Scot.* a narrow wooded valley; a dean. [from Anglo-Saxon *denn*, cave, lair]

▪ **1** lair, hole, burrow, nest. **3** retreat, study, hideaway, hideout, shelter, sanctuary, haunt.

denarius /dɪˈnɛərɪəs/ *noun* (PL. **denarii**) an ancient Roman silver coin. [from Latin *denarius*, containing 10, because originally equal to 10 asses]

denationalization or **denationalisation** *noun* restoration of an industry to private ownership.

denationalize or **denationalise** *verb* to return or transfer (an industry) to private ownership from state ownership.

denature /diːˈneɪtʃə(r)/ *verb* **1** *Biol.* to change the structure of a protein, eg an enzyme, by exposing it to high temperatures, certain chemicals, or extremes of pH. **2** *Physics* to add another isotope to a material capable of nuclear fission, so that it is no longer suitable for use in a nuclear weapon. **3** to add a poisonous or unpalatable substance to alcohol, methylated spirits, etc, to render it unfit for human consumption.

dendrite *noun Zool.* any of a number of cytoplasmic projections that radiate outwards from the star-shaped cell body of a neurone (nerve cell). See also NEURONE. [from Greek *dendrites*, of a tree]

dendrochronology /ˌdɛndroʊkrəˈnɒlədʒɪ/ *noun* the analysis of the patterns of annual growth-rings found in trees and the fixing of dates by comparative study of timber from different periods. [from Greek *dendron*, tree + *chronos*, time]

dendrologist /dɛnˈdrɒlədʒɪst/ *noun* a scientist who specializes in dendrology.

dendrology /dɛnˈdrɒlədʒɪ/ *noun* the branch of forestry concerned with the natural history of trees, including their identification and classification. [from Greek *dendron*, tree + -LOGY]

dendron *noun Physiol.* a dendrite. [from Greek *dendron*, tree]

denial /dɪˈnaɪəl/ *noun* **1** an act of denying or declaring something not to be true. **2** an act of refusing something to someone. **3** an act of refusing to acknowledge connections with somebody or something.

▪ **1** contradiction, negation, dissent, repudiation, disavowal, disclaimer, dismissal, renunciation. **2** refusal, withdrawal, deprivation, rebuff, rejection, prohibition, veto. **3** repudiation, renunciation, disavowal, disownment.

denier /ˈdɛnɪə(r)/ *noun* the unit of weight of silk, rayon, or nylon thread, usually used as a measure of the fineness of stockings or tights. [from French *denier*; originally a small coin, from DENARIUS]

denigrate /ˈdɛnɪɡreɪt/ *verb* to scorn or criticize; to attack or belittle the reputation, character, or worth of. [from Latin *denigrare*, to blacken]

▪ disparage, run down, slander, revile, defame, malign, vilify, decry, besmirch, impugn, belittle, abuse, assail, criticize.
▪ praise, acclaim.

denigration /ˌdɛnɪˈɡreɪʃən/ *noun* defamation; disparagement.

denigrator /ˈdɛnɪɡreɪtə(r)/ *noun* a person who denigrates or disparages.

denim /ˈdɛnɪm/ *noun* **1** a kind of hard-wearing, usually blue, cotton cloth used for making jeans, overalls, etc. **2** (**denims**) trousers or jeans made of denim. [from French *de Nîmes*, of Nîmes in France]

denizen /ˈdɛnɪzn/ *noun* **1** *formal* an inhabitant (human or animal). **2** *Biol.* a species of animal or plant which has become well established after being introduced to an area to which it is not native. [from Old French *deinzein*, from *deinz*, within]

denominate /dɪˈnɒmɪneɪt/ *verb formal* to give a specific name or title to (something). [from Latin *denominare*, to name]

denomination /dɪˌnɒmɪˈneɪʃən/ *noun* **1** a religious group with its own particular beliefs, organization, and practices. **2** a particular unit of value of a postage stamp, coin, or banknote, etc. **3** a kind or class that has a particular name.

▪ **1** religion, persuasion, sect, belief, faith, creed, communion, school. **3** classification, category, class, kind, sort.

denominational *adj.* relating to or belonging to a religious denomination.

denominator /dɪˈnɒmɪneɪtə(r)/ *noun Maths.* the lower number in a fraction, indicating the parts into which the whole number is divided, eg the quantity 5 in the fraction ⅗. See also NUMERATOR.

denotation /ˌdiːnoʊˈteɪʃən/ *noun* denoting; marking by signs or symbols.

denote /dɪˈnoʊt/ *verb* **1** to mean; to be the name of or sign for. **2** to be a sign, mark, or indication of. [from Latin *denotare*, to mark out]

▪ **1** mean, signify, designate, represent, symbolize, stand for, express. **2** indicate, mark, show, imply, intimate, point to.

dénouement /deɪˈnuːmɒn/ *noun* the final part of a story or plot, in which uncertainties are explained and previously unresolved problems and mysteries are resolved. [from French *dénouement*, from *dénouer*, to untie a knot]

▪ climax, culmination, conclusion, outcome, upshot, *colloq.* pay-off, resolution, solution, finale, finish, close.

denounce /dɪˈnaʊns/ *verb* **1** to inform against or accuse publicly: *denounced them as traitors.* **2** to condemn (an action, proposal, idea, etc) strongly and openly. See also DENUNCIATION. [from Old French *dénoncier*, from Latin *denuntiare*, to announce]

▣ **1** inform against, accuse, betray, impugn, indict, arraign, impeach. **2** condemn, censure, revile, decry, attack, vilify, fulminate against.
▣ **2** acclaim, praise.

dense *adj.* **1** closely packed or crowded together. **2** thick. **3** *colloq.* stupid; slow to understand. [from Latin *densus*]

▣ **1** packed, crowded, teeming, congested. **2** compact, thick, compressed, condensed, close, close-knit, heavy, solid, opaque, impenetrable. **3** stupid, *colloq.* thick, crass, dull, slow, slow-witted.
▣ **1** sparse. **2** thin. **3** quick-witted, clever.

densely *adv.* in a dense or closely packed way; to a dense degree.

denseness *noun* a dense state; stupidity.

density *noun* (PL. **densities**) **1** the state of being dense or the degree of denseness. **2** the ratio of the mass of a substance to its volume. The SI units of density measurement are kg m^{-3}. **3** the number of items within a specific area or volume, eg population density. **4** *Comput.* the number of bits that can be stored on one track of a disk, or within a specific area of magnetic tape, etc.

dent — *noun* a hollow in the surface of something, especially something hard, made by pressure or a blow. — *verb* **1** to make a dent in. **2** *intrans.* to become dented. [from Anglo-Saxon *dynt*, blow]

▣ *noun* hollow, depression, dip, concavity, indentation, crater, dimple, dint, pit. *verb* **1** depress, gouge, push in, indent.

dental *adj.* **1** relating to a tooth or teeth. **2** relating to dentistry. [from Latin *dentalis*, from *dens*, tooth]

dental floss a soft thread used for cleaning between the teeth.

dental surgeon a dentist.

dentate *adj. technical* **1** having teeth. **2** having tooth-like projections. **3** *Bot.*, *said of a leaf* having a serrated margin.

dentifrice /'dɛntɪfrɪs/ *noun* paste or powder for cleaning the teeth. [from French *dentifrice*, from Latin *dens*, tooth + *fricare*, to rub]

dentil *noun Archit.* each of a series of small square or rectangular blocks or projections, especially those set beneath the cornice in classical orders. [from their resemblance to a row of teeth; from French *dentille*, from *dent*, tooth]

dentine or **dentin** /'dɛntiːn/ *noun Anat.* in vertebrates, a hard yellowish-white material that forms the bulk of the tooth. [from Latin *dens*, tooth]

dentist *noun* a person who is professionally trained and qualified to practise dentistry. [from French *dentiste*, from *dent*, tooth]

dentistry *noun* the branch of medicine concerned with the diagnosis, treatment, and prevention of diseases of the mouth and teeth.

dentition /dɛn'tɪʃən/ *noun technical* **1** the type, number, and arrangement of the teeth in the mouth of a human or animal, often represented diagrammatically by a dental formula. **2** the development or cutting of teeth; teething.

denture /'dɛntʃə(r)/ *noun* **1** (*usually* **dentures**) a plate or frame bearing one or more artificial teeth, used as a replacement for missing teeth. **2** a set of natural teeth. [from French *denture*, from *dent*, tooth]

denudation /diːnjuː'deɪʃən/ *noun* **1** denuding; making bare. **2** *Geol.* the process by which the surface of the land is progressively lowered as a result of weathering and erosion, so that the underlying rocks are laid bare.

denude /dɪ'njuːd/ *verb* to make completely bare; to strip. [from Latin *denudare*, to lay bare, uncover]

▣ strip, divest, expose, uncover, bare, deforest.
▣ cover, clothe.

denunciation /dɪnʌnsɪ'eɪʃən/ *noun* a public condemnation or accusation. See also DENOUNCE. [from Latin *denuntiare*, to announce]

▣ condemnation, denouncement, censure, accusation, incrimination, invective, criticism.
▣ praise.

deny *verb* (**denies**, **denied**) **1** to declare (something) not to be true. **2** to refuse to give or allow to (someone). **3** to refuse to acknowledge a connection with. — **deny oneself** to do without (things that one desires or needs). See also DENIAL. [from Old French *denier*, from Latin *denegare*]

▣ **1** contradict, oppose, refute, disagree with, disaffirm, disprove. **2** refuse, turn down, forbid, reject, withhold, rebuff, veto. **3** disown, disclaim, renounce, repudiate, recant. **deny oneself** do without, go without, abstain from, refrain from, forbear to, renounce, forego.
▣ **1** admit. **2** allow. **deny oneself** allow oneself, permit oneself, indulge in.

deodorant /dɪ'oʊdərənt/ *noun* a substance that prevents or conceals unpleasant smells, especially the smell of stale sweat on the human body. [from DE- + ODOUR]

deodorization or **deodorisation** /dɪoʊdəraɪ'zeɪʃən/ *noun* removal of an unpleasant smell.

deodorize or **deodorise** /dɪ'oʊdəraɪz/ *verb* to remove, conceal, or absorb the unpleasant smell of.

deoxyribonucleic acid /diː'rɒksɪ-/ see DNA.

depart *verb intrans.* **1** *somewhat formal* to leave. **2** (**depart from something**) to stop following or decline to follow a planned or usual course of action. [from Old French *departir*]

▣ **1** go, leave, withdraw, exit, make off, quit, decamp, take one's leave, absent oneself, set off, remove, retreat, migrate, escape, disappear, retire, vanish. **2** deviate from, digress from, differ from, diverge from, swerve from, veer away from.
▣ **1** arrive, return. **2** keep to.

departed *formal* — *adj.* dead. — *noun* (**the departed**) a person or people recently dead.

▣ *adj.* dead, deceased, gone, the late.

department *noun* **1** a section of an organization (eg a government or other administration, a university, an office, or shop), with responsibility for one particular aspect or part of the organization's work. **2** a subject or activity which is someone's special skill or particular responsibility. [from French *département*]

▣ **1** division, branch, subdivision, section, sector, office, station, unit, region, district. **2** sphere, realm, province, domain, field, area, concern, responsibility, speciality, line.

departmental /diːpɑːt'mɛntl/ *adj.* **1** of or concerning a department or departments. **2** divided into departments.

department store a large shop with many different departments selling a wide variety of goods.

departure *noun* **1** an act of going away or leaving. **2** (**departure from something**) a change from a planned or usual course of action. **3** a new activity, different from what one has been doing or normally does.

▣ **1** exit, going, leave-taking, removal, withdrawal, retirement,

exodus. **2** change from, shift from, deviation from, digression from, divergence from, branching (out) from, veering away from. **3** change, innovation, novelty, variation.
⊟ 1 arrival, return.

depend *verb intrans.* (**depend on** or **upon someone** or **something**) **1** to rely on; to be able to trust. **2** to rely on financial or other support from. **3** to be decided by or vary according to (something else). [from Old French *dependre*, from Latin *dependere*, to hang down]

⊟ 1, 2 rely on or upon, count on, bank on. **1** trust in, lean on, build on. **2** calculate on, reckon on, expect. **3** hang on, hinge on, rest on, turn on, revolve around, be dependent on, be contingent on.

dependability *noun* being dependable or reliable.

⊟ reliability, trustworthiness, steadfastness, honesty, responsibility, conscientiousness.

dependable *adj.* able to be trusted or relied on.

⊟ reliable, trustworthy, steady, trusty, responsible, faithful, unfailing, sure, honest, conscientious, certain.
⊟ unreliable, fickle.

dependably *adv.* in a dependable or reliable way.
dependant *noun* a person who is kept or supported financially by another.
dependence *noun* (**dependence on** or **upon something** or **someone**) **1** the state of being dependent on them. **2** trust and reliance.

⊟ RELIANCE ON or UPON. **1** subordination to, attachment to, subservience to, helplessness before, addiction to. **2** trust in, confidence in, faith in, need of, expectation of.
⊟ INDEPENDENCE OF or FROM.

dependency *noun* (PL. **dependencies**) **1** a country governed or controlled by another. **2** addiction to drugs, etc.
dependent *adj.* (**dependent on** or **upon something** or **someone**) **1** relying on it or them for financial or other support. **2** *said of an issue or outcome* to be decided or influenced by it or them: *success is dependent on all our efforts*.

⊟ RELIANT ON or UPON. **1** subject to, subordinate to, vulnerable to, helpless before. **2** contingent on, conditional on, determined by, relative to.
⊟ 1 independent of or from.

dependent clause same as SUBORDINATE CLAUSE.
depersonalize or **depersonalise** *verb Psychol.* to take away the characteristics or personality of; to make impersonal.
depict *verb* **1** to paint or draw. **2** to describe. [from Latin *depingere*, to paint]

⊟ PORTRAY, ILLUSTRATE, SKETCH, OUTLINE, DELINEATE. **1** draw, picture, paint, trace. **2** describe, characterize, detail.

depiction *noun* representation in drawing or words.
depilatory /dɪˈpɪlətərɪ/ *technical* — *noun* (PL. **depilatories**) a chemical substance used to remove unwanted hair from the body. — *adj.* able to remove hair. [from Latin *depilare*, to remove hair]
deplete *verb* to reduce greatly in number, quantity, etc; to use up (supplies, money, energy, resources, etc). [from Latin *deplere*, to empty]

⊟ empty, drain, exhaust, evacuate, use up, expend, run down, reduce, lessen, decrease.

depletion *noun* reduction or exhaustion in numbers or amount.
deplorable *adj.* **1** shockingly inadequate, unfit or unpleasant. **2** reprehensible or regrettable.

⊟ APPALLING, LAMENTABLE, SHOCKING. **1** grievous, pitiable, wretched, distressing, sad, miserable, heartbreaking, melancholy, disastrous, dire. **2** reprehensible, disgraceful, scandalous, shameful, dishonourable, disreputable, regrettable, unfortunate.
⊟ 1 excellent. **2** commendable.

deplorably *adv.* in a deplorable way; to a deplorable extent.
deplore *verb* **1** to feel or express great regret for. **2** to feel or express great disapproval of. [from French *déplorer*, from Latin *deplorare*, to weep for]

⊟ 1 grieve for, lament, mourn, regret, bemoan, rue. **2** disapprove of, deprecate, censure, condemn, denounce.
⊟ 2 extol.

deploy *verb* **1** to spread out and position (troops) ready for battle. **2** to organize and bring into use (resources, arguments, etc). [from French *déployer*]

⊟ ARRANGE. **1** spread out, dispose, position, station, draw up, align. **2** organize, marshal, muster, assemble, mobilize, use, utilize.

deployment *noun* positioning or organization of resources, etc.
depolarization or **depolarisation** *noun Chem.* the removal or prevention of electrical polarization (separation into positive and negative charges).
depopulate *verb* to reduce greatly the number of people living in (an area, country, etc). [from Latin *depopulari*, to lay waste, later understood as meaning to deprive of people]
depopulated *adj.*, *said of an area, etc* having a reduced population.
depopulation *noun* reduction of population.
deport[1] *verb* to legally remove or expel (a person) from a country. [from Latin *deportare*, to carry away]

⊟ expel, banish, exile, extradite, transport, expatriate, oust, ostracize.

deport[2] *verb* (**deport oneself**) *formal* to behave oneself in a particular way. [from Latin *deportare*, to carry away]
deportation *noun* legal expulsion of a person from a country.
deportee *noun* a person who is expelled from a country.
deportment *noun* **1** the way one holds or carries oneself; one's bearing. **2** behaviour.

⊟ 1 carriage, bearing, posture, stance.

depose *verb* to remove from a high office or powerful position. [from Old French *deposer*, to put down or away]

⊟ dethrone, unseat, topple, displace, oust, demote, downgrade, dismiss, disestablish.

deposit — *verb* (**deposited**, **depositing**) **1** to put or leave. **2** to put (money, etc) in a bank, etc for safekeeping or to earn interest. **3** to give (a sum of money) as the first part of the payment for something, so guaranteeing that one can complete the purchase later. **4** to pay (a sum of money) as a guarantee against loss or damage. **5** to lay down (material) as a coating, bed, vein, etc. — *noun* **1** a sum of money, etc deposited in a bank, etc. **2** a sum of money given as part payment for something or paid as a guarantee against loss or damage. **3** any accumulation of material that has been laid down as a coating. **4** *Geol.* any natural accumulation of sediments, minerals, etc, formed by the laying down of material as a coating, bed, vein, etc. **5** a layer of material formed in this way, eg coal deposit. [from Latin *depositum*, from *deponere*, to put down]

- *verb* **1** put, leave, lay, drop, place, settle, dump, park, sit, locate. **2** save, store, hoard, bank, amass, consign, entrust, lodge, file. **3** put down. *noun* **2** security, stake, down payment, pledge, retainer, instalment, part payment, money. **3** sediment, accumulation, dregs, precipitate, lees, silt.

deposit account a bank account on which one is paid interest and which cannot be used for the transfer of money to other people by eg cheque or standing order.

depositary *noun* (PL. **depositaries**) *formal* a person, etc to whom something is given for safekeeping.

deposition /depə'zɪʃən/ *noun* **1** the act of deposing or process of being deposed. **2** the act of depositing or process of being deposited. **3** *Legal* a written statement made under oath and used as evidence in a court of law when the witness cannot be present. **4** *Geol.* the laying down on the Earth's surface of eroded material that has been transported by wind, rivers, glaciers, avalanches, etc. [from Latin *depositio*, putting down]

- **1** dethronement, toppling, unseating, ousting, dismissal, demotion. **2** placing, lodging, lodgement, saving, banking, storage, precipitation. **3** affidavit, statement, testimony.

depositor *noun* a person who deposits money in a bank.

depository *noun* (PL. **depositories**) **1** a place where things such as furniture are stored. **2** a depositary.

depot /'depoʊ/ *noun* **1** a storehouse or warehouse. **2** a place where buses, trains, and certain types of vehicles are kept and repaired. **3** *North Amer.* a bus or railway station. **4** a military headquarters, or military post where stores are kept and recruits trained. [from French *dépôt*, from Latin *deponere*, to put down]

- **1** storehouse, store, warehouse, depository, repository, arsenal. **2** station, garage, terminus.

deprave *verb* to make evil or morally corrupt. [from Latin *depravare*, to pervert, distort]

- corrupt, debauch, debase, degrade, pervert, subvert, infect, demoralize, seduce.
- improve, reform.

depraved *adj.* morally corrupted.

- corrupt, debauched, degenerate, perverted, debased, dissolute, immoral, base, shameless, licentious, wicked, sinful, vile, evil.
- moral, upright.

depravity /dɪ'pravɪtɪ/ *noun* moral wickedness, evil, or corruption.

deprecate /'deprəkeɪt/ *verb* to express disapproval of; to deplore. [from Latin *deprecari*, to try to avert]

- deplore, condemn, censure, disapprove of, object to, protest at, reject.
- approve, commend.

deprecating *adj.* disapproving of something.

deprecatingly *adv.* with a disapproving manner.

deprecation /deprə'keɪʃən/ *noun* expression of disapproval.

deprecatory /'deprəkeɪtərɪ/ *adj.* **1** showing or expressing disapproval. **2** apologetic; trying to avoid disapproval.

depreciate /dɪ'priːʃɪeɪt/ *verb* **1** *trans., intrans.* to fall or cause to fall in value. **2** to be contemptuous of the worth of; to belittle. [from Latin *depretiare*, to lower the price of]

- **1** devalue, deflate, downgrade, decrease, reduce, lower, drop, lessen. **2** belittle, disparage, undervalue, underestimate, underrate, slight.
- **1** appreciate. **2** overrate.

depreciation /dɪpriːʃɪ'eɪʃən/ *noun* **1** *Econ.* a fall in value of a currency against the value of other currencies. **2** the reduction in the value of fixed assets such as buildings and equipment through use or age. **3** the act of depreciating.

- **1** devaluation, deflation, depression, slump, fall. **3** disparagement, belittlement, underestimation.

depreciatory /dɪ'priːʃɪətərɪ/ *adj.* belittling; contemptuous.

depredation /deprə'deɪʃən/ *noun* (*often* **depredations**) damage, destruction, or violent robbery. [from Latin *depraedatio*, from *praedari*, to plunder]

depress *verb* **1** to lower the spirits of (someone); to make gloomy. **2** to reduce the vigour or energy of. **3** to lower the price or value of. **4** *formal* to press down. [from Old French *depresser*]

- **1** deject, sadden, dishearten, discourage, oppress, upset, daunt, burden, overburden. **2** reduce, lessen, lower, weaken, undermine, sap, tire, drain, exhaust, weary, impair. **3** devalue, bring down, lower.
- **1** cheer. **2** fortify. **3** increase, raise.

depressant — *noun* **1** *Medicine* any drug that reduces the activity of the central nervous system or other body systems, eg barbiturates, alcohol. See also ANTIDEPRESSANT. **2** anything which lowers activity or spirits. — *adj.* denoting a drug that is a depressant. **2** depressing.

depressed *adj.* **1** low in spirits; gloomy. **2** *Psychol.* suffering from depression; dispirited, dejected. **3** suffering from high unemployment and low standards of living: *a depressed area.* **4** pressed down, lowered, or slightly hollowed. **5** *Biol.* flattened.

- **1** dejected, low-spirited, melancholy, dispirited, sad, unhappy, low, down, downcast, disheartened, *colloq.* fed up, miserable, moody, cast down, discouraged, glum, downhearted, distressed, despondent, morose, crestfallen, pessimistic. **3** poor, disadvantaged, deprived, destitute. **4** sunken, recessed, concave, hollow, indented, dented.
- **1** cheerful. **3** affluent. **4** convex, protuberant.

depressing *adj.* causing low spirits.

- dismal, bleak, gloomy, saddening, cheerless, dreary, disheartening, sad, melancholy, sombre, grey, black, daunting, discouraging, heartbreaking, distressing, hopeless.
- cheerful, encouraging.

depressingly *adv.* in a depressing way.

depression *noun* **1** *Psychol.* a mental state characterized by prolonged feelings of despair and low self-esteem. **2** a period of low business and industrial activity accompanied by a rise in unemployment. **3** (**the Depression**) the period of worldwide economic depression from 1929 to 1934. **4** an area of low atmospheric pressure. **5** a hollow, especially in the ground.

▣ **1** dejection, despair, despondency, melancholy, low spirits, sadness, gloominess, doldrums, blues, glumness, *colloq.* dumps, hopelessness. **2** recession, slump, stagnation, hard times, decline, inactivity. **4** cyclone, low. **5** indentation, hollow, dip, concavity, dent, dimple, valley, dint, bowl, cavity, basin, impression, dish.

▣ **1** cheerfulness. **2** prosperity, boom. **4** anticyclone. **5** convexity, protuberance.

depressive — *noun* a person who suffers from periods of depression. — *adj.* **1** of or relating to depression. **2** tending to depress. **3** *said of a person* suffering from periods of depression.

deprivation /dɛprɪˈveɪʃən/ *noun* **1** hardship, etc caused by being deprived of necessities, rights, etc. **2** the act of depriving or state of being deprived.

▣ **1** hardship, privation, poverty, want, need, penury, destitution. **2** denial, withdrawal, removal, lack.

deprive /dɪˈpraɪv/ *verb* (**deprive someone of something**) to take or keep it from them; to prevent them from using or enjoying it. [from Latin *deprivare*, to degrade]

▣ dispossess of, strip of, divest of, bereave of, rob of, deny, refuse, withhold, withdraw.
▣ endow with, provide with.

deprived *adj.* **1** (**deprived of something**) having had it kept or taken from one. **2** *said of a person* suffering from hardship through lack of money, reasonable living conditions, etc. **3** *said of a district, etc* lacking good housing, schools, medical facilities, etc.

▣ **1** lacking, bereft of, robbed of, stripped of, destitute of, wanting. **2, 3** poor, needy, underprivileged, disadvantaged, impoverished, destitute.
▣ **1** provided with. **2, 3** prosperous.

dept. *abbrev.* department.

depth *noun* **1** deepness; the distance from the top downwards, from the front to the back, or from the surface inwards. **2** *said of feelings or colours* intensity or strength. **3** extensiveness: *the depth of one's knowledge.* **4** (**depths, the depth**) somewhere far from the surface or edge of: *the depths of the ocean, of the country.* **5** (**depths, the depth**) an extreme feeling (of despair, sadness, etc) or great degree (of deprivation, etc). **6** (*often* **the depths**) the middle and severest part of (winter, etc). **7** (**depths**) serious aspects of a person's character that are not immediately obvious. **8** *said of sound* lowness of pitch. — **in depth** deeply and thoroughly. **out of one's depth 1** in water so deep that one would be below the surface even when standing up. **2** not able to understand information or an explanation, or in a situation which is too difficult for one to deal with. [from Anglo-Saxon *deop*, deep + -TH²]

▣ **1** deepness, profoundness, extent, measure, drop. **2** intensity, strength, profundity. **3** extent, extensiveness, scope, profundity, penetration, wisdom, insight, discernment. **4** the middle. **5** an abyss, a pit, the extremes.
▣ **1, 2, 3** shallowness. **2, 3** superficiality.

depth charge a type of bomb dropped from a ship which explodes underwater and is used to attack submarines.

deputation /dɛpjʊˈteɪʃən/ *noun* a group of people appointed to represent and speak on behalf of others. [from Latin *deputare*, to select]

▣ commission, delegation, embassy, mission, representatives, legation.

depute /dɪˈpjuːt/ *verb formal* **1** to formally appoint (someone) to do something. **2** (**depute something to someone**) to give (one's work, etc, or part of it) to someone else to do. [from Old French *deputer*, from Latin *deputare*, to select]

▣ ASSIGN. **1** appoint, commission, second, designate, nominate. **2** delegate, consign, hand over.

deputize or **deputise** /ˈdɛpjʊtaɪz/ *verb* **1** *intrans.* (**deputize for someone**) to act as their deputy. **2** *trans.* to appoint as a deputy.

▣ **1** represent, stand in for, substitute for, replace, understudy, double for. **2** delegate, commission.

deputy /ˈdɛpjʊtɪ/ — *noun* (PL. **deputies**) **1** a person appointed to act on behalf of or as an assistant to someone else. **2** in some countries, a person elected to the lower house of parliament. — *adj.* in some organizations, next in rank to the head and having the authority to act on his or her behalf. [from Old French *deputer*, to appoint, from Latin *deputare*, to select]

▣ *noun* REPRESENTATIVE, DELEGATE. **1** agent, proxy, substitute, second-in-command, ambassador, commissioner, lieutenant, surrogate, subordinate, assistant, locum.

derail *verb trans., intrans.* to leave or cause to leave the rails.
derailment *noun, said of a train* accidental separation from the rails.
derange *verb* **1** to make insane. **2** to disrupt or throw into disorder or confusion. [from French *déranger*, to disturb]
deranged *adj.* made insane; thrown into confusion.

▣ disordered, demented, crazy, mad, lunatic, insane, unbalanced, disturbed, confused, frantic, delirious, distraught, berserk.
▣ sane, calm.

derangement *noun* disturbance; mental disorder.
derby¹ /ˈdɑːbɪ/ *noun* (PL. **derbies**) **1** (**the Derby**) a horse race held annually at Epsom Downs in Surrey. **2** a race or a sports event or contest, especially (**local derby**) a contest between teams from the same area. [named after the Earl of *Derby*, one of the founders of the race in 1780]
derby² /ˈdɑːbɪ/ *noun* (PL. **derbies**) *North Amer.* a bowler hat. [from DERBY¹]
Derbys. *abbrev.* Derbyshire.
deregulate *verb* to remove controls and regulations from (a business or business activity).
deregulation *noun* removal of controls from a business, etc.
derelict /ˈdɛrəlɪkt/ — *adj.* abandoned and falling in ruins. — *noun* a tramp; a person with no home or money. [from Latin *derelinquere*, to abandon]

▣ *adj.* abandoned, neglected, deserted, forsaken, desolate, dilapidated, ruined.

dereliction /dɛrəˈlɪkʃən/ *noun* (*usually* **dereliction of duty**) neglect or failure.
derestrict *verb* to remove a restriction from (something), especially a speed limit from (a road).
derestriction *noun* removal of restrictions.
deride *verb* to laugh at or make fun of. See also DERISION. [from Latin *deridere*]

▣ ridicule, mock, scoff at, scorn, jeer at, sneer at, satirize, *colloq.* knock, gibe at, disparage, insult, belittle, disdain, taunt.
▣ respect, praise.

de rigueur /də rɪ'gɜː/ required by fashion, custom or the rules of politeness. [from French *de rigueur*, of strictness]

derision /dɪ'rɪʒən/ *noun* the act of deriding; scornful laughter. [from Latin *derisio*]

. . . .

◼ ridicule, mockery, scorn, contempt, scoffing, satire, sneering, disrespect, insult, disparagement, disdain.

◼ respect, praise.

. . . .

derisive /dɪ'raɪsɪv/ *adj.* expressing derision. [from DERISION]

. . . .

◼ mocking, scornful, contemptuous, disrespectful, irreverent, jeering, disdainful, taunting.

◼ respectful, flattering.

. . . .

derisively *adv.* in a derisive or scornful way.

derisory /dɪ'raɪsərɪ/ *adj.* ridiculous and insulting, especially ridiculously small. [from Latin *derisorius*]

. . . .

◼ ridiculous, contemptible, insulting, offensive, paltry, trifling, miserable, negligible, minute, minimal, worthless.

. . . .

derivation /derɪ'veɪʃən/ *noun* **1** the act of deriving or the state or process of being derived. **2** the source or origin (especially of a word). **3** *Grammar* the process of forming a word by adding one or more prefixes or suffixes to another word. [from Old French *deriver*, from Latin *de*, from + *rivus*, stream]

. . . .

◼ **2** source, origin, root, beginning, etymology, foundation, extraction, genealogy, ancestry, basis, descent.

. . . .

derivative /dɪ'rɪvətɪv/ — *adj.* not original; derived from or copying something else (especially someone else's work). — *noun* **1** something which is derived from something else. **2** *Grammar* a word formed by adding one or more prefixes or suffixes to another word, such as *happily* from *happy*, *decarbonize* from *carbon*. **3** *Chem.* a compound (usually organic) that is made from another compound. **4** *Maths.* the result of differentiation in order to calculate the changes in one variable produced by changes in another variable. **5** *Finance* a financial contract the value of which is largely determined by a variable asset to which it is linked, such as a commodity or currency.

. . . .

◼ *adj.* unoriginal, acquired, copied, borrowed, derived, imitative, obtained, second-hand, secondary, plagiarized, cribbed, hackneyed, trite. *noun* **1** derivation, offshoot, by-product, development, branch, outgrowth, spin-off, product, descendant.

. . . .

derive /dɪ'raɪv/ *verb* **1** (**derive from something**) to come or arise from it; to have it as a source. **2** (**derive one thing from another**) to obtain or produce one thing from another. **3** to obtain by reasoning or deduction. **4** to trace (something) back to a source or origin.

. . . .

◼ **1** originate from, arise from, spring from, flow from, emanate from, descend from, proceed from, stem from, issue from, follow from, develop from. **2** gain, obtain, get, draw, extract, receive, procure, acquire, borrow. **3** infer, deduce.

. . . .

dermatitis /dɜːmə'taɪtɪs/ *noun Medicine* inflammation of the skin, which becomes red and itchy and may develop small blisters.

dermato- or **dermat-** or **derma-** or **-derm** *combining form* denoting the skin: *dermatitis / ectoderm*. [from Greek *derma*, skin]

dermatologist /dɜːmə'tɒlədʒɪst/ *noun* a doctor who specializes in dermatology.

dermatology /dɜːmə'tɒlədʒɪ/ *noun* the branch of medi-

cine concerned with the diagnosis and treatment of skin diseases and disorders.

dermis *noun Anat.* the thick layer of skin that lies beneath the epidermis. [from Greek *derma*, skin]

derogate /'derəgeɪt/ *verb intrans.* (**derogate from something**) *formal* to cause it to appear inferior; to show one's low opinion of it. [from Latin *derogare*, to detract from]

derogation /derə'geɪʃən/ *noun* **1** reduction in power or authority. **2** deterioration.

derogatorily /dɪ'rɒgətərɪlɪ/ *adv.* in a derogatory or disapproving way.

derogatory /dɪ'rɒgətərɪ/ *adj.* showing, or intended to show, disapproval, dislike, scorn, or lack of respect. [from Latin *derogatorius*]

. . . .

◼ insulting, pejorative, offensive, disparaging, depreciative, critical, defamatory, injurious.

◼ flattering.

. . . .

derrick *noun* **1** a simple crane consisting of a lifting tackle slung from a movable boom, widely used on freight-carrying ships. **2** a towerlike framework erected over an oil well to support the drilling tools and to enable the drill pipes to be raised and lowered. [named after Derrick, a 17c hangman]

derring-do /'derɪŋdu:/ *noun old use, literary* daring deeds. [from a wrong understanding by Spenser, the 16c poet, of the phrase *derrynge do* (= daring to do) in the work of an earlier poet]

derris *noun* **1** any of various shrubs or woody climbing plants of the genus *Derris*, native to E India. **2** an insecticide made from the powdered roots of this plant. [from Greek *derris*, leather jacket]

derv *noun Brit.* **1** diesel engine road vehicle. **2** diesel engine fuel oil.

dervish *noun* a member of any of various Muslim religious groups vowed to poverty, some of whom perform spinning dances as part of their religious ritual. [from Turkish *dervis*, from Persian *darvish*, poor man, dervish]

DES *abbrev.* Department of Education and Science.

desalinate /di:'salɪneɪt/ *verb technical* to remove salts, especially sodium chloride from (sea water or other brines) by the process of desalination. [from DE- 2 + SALINE]

desalination /di:salɪ'neɪʃən/ *noun* the removal of salt, mainly sodium chloride, from sea water in order to produce fresh water for drinking, irrigation, etc.

descale *verb* to remove the scale from (a kettle etc).

descant /'deskant/ *Mus.* — *noun* a melody played or harmony sung above the main tune. — *adj.*, *said of a musical instrument* having a higher pitch than others of the same type. [from Old French, from DIS-, apart + *cantus*, song]

descend *verb* **1** *trans., intrans.* to go or move down from a higher to a lower place or position. **2** *intrans.* to lead or slope downwards. **3** (**descend on** or **upon someone** or **something**) to invade or attack them. **4** *intrans., said of titles, property, etc* to pass by inheritance from one generation to another. — **be descended from someone** to have them as an ancestor. **would not descend to something** or **to do something** would not demean oneself by resorting to unworthy or immoral behaviour. [from Old French *descendre*]

. . . .

◼ **1** move down, sink. **2** go down, dip, slope, drop, fall, plummet, plunge, tumble. **3** raid, invade, attack, fall on, force oneself on, impose on, waylay. **be descended from** originate from, proceed from, spring from, stem from.

◼ **1, 2** ascend. **2** rise.

. . . .

descendant *noun* a person, animal, etc that is the child, grandchild, great-grandchild, etc of another.

descending *adj.* from the highest to the lowest, the greatest to the least, or the best to the worst.

descent *noun* **1** the act or process of coming or going down. **2** a slope downwards. **3** family origins or ancestry; the fact of being descended from someone. **4** a sudden invasion or attack. [from Old French *descente*]

▤ **1, 2** drop. **1** fall, plunge. **2** dip, decline, incline, slope. **3** ancestry, parentage, heredity, family tree, genealogy, lineage, extraction, origin.
▣ **1, 2** ascent, rise.

describe *verb* **1** to say what (someone or something) is like. **2** (**describe oneself as something**) to call oneself, or claim to be, something. **3** *Geom.* to trace out or draw (a line or figure, eg a circle). **4** *formal* to move in the shape of: *skaters describing circles on the ice.* [from Latin *describere*]

▤ **1** portray, depict, delineate, illustrate, characterize, specify, draw, define, detail, explain, express, tell, narrate, outline, relate, recount, present, report, sketch. **3, 4** trace, mark out, draw.

description *noun* **1** the act of describing. **2** a statement of what someone or something is like. **3** *colloq.* a sort, type, or kind: *toys of every description.* [from Latin *descriptio*]

▤ **1, 2** portrayal, representation, characterization, delineation, depiction, presentation. **1** explanation, exposition, narration. **2** account, sketch, report, outline. **3** sort, type, kind, variety, specification, order.

descriptive *adj.* describing, especially describing well or vividly. [from Latin *descriptivus*]

▤ illustrative, explanatory, expressive, detailed, graphic, colourful, pictorial, vivid.

descriptively *adv.* in a descriptive way.

descry /dɪ'skraɪ/ *verb* (**descries, descried**) *formal* **1** to see or catch sight of. **2** to see or discover by looking carefully. [from Old French *descrier*, to announce and *descrire*, to describe]

desecrate /'desəkreɪt/ *verb* to treat or use (a sacred object) or behave in (a holy place) in a way that shows a lack of respect or causes damage. [from DE- 2 + CONSECRATE]

▤ violate, profane, defile, invade, pollute.

desecration /desə'kreɪʃən/ *noun* treating a holy place with violence or disrespect.

desecrator *noun* a person who treats a holy place with violence or disrespect.

desegregate /diː'segrəgeɪt/ *verb* to end (especially racial) segregation in (public places, schools, transport systems, etc).

desegregation /diːsegrə'geɪʃən/ *noun* abolition of segregation.

deselect *verb Brit.* **1** *said of a branch of a political party* to reject (the existing Member of Parliament or local councillor) as a candidate for the next election. **2** *said of a selection committee, etc* not to re-select (eg an athlete) for a place on a team, etc.

deselection *noun* failure to re-select the existing candidate in a political election.

desensitization or **desensitisation** *noun* making less sensitive.

desensitize or **desensitise** *verb* to make less sensitive to light, pain, suffering, etc.

desert¹ /dɪ'zɜːt/ *verb* **1** to leave or abandon (a place or person), intending not to return. **2** *intrans.* to leave, especially a branch of the armed forces, without permission. **3** to take away one's support from (a person, cause, etc). [from French *déserter*]

▤ **1, 3** abandon, forsake, leave, quit, disown. **1** maroon, strand, jilt, *colloq.* rat on. **2** decamp, defect, abscond. **3** give up, renounce, relinquish, recant, deny.
▣ **1, 3** stand by, support.

desert² /'dezət/ — *noun* **1** an arid area of land where vegetation is scarce or non-existent, especially because of low rainfall. **2** an area of inactivity or deprivation. — *adj.* infertile and unpopulated. [Old French, from Latin *deserere*, to abandon]

▤ *noun* wasteland, wilderness, wilds. *adj.* dry, arid, infertile, bare, barren, waste, wild, uninhabited, unpopulated, uncultivated, desolate, sterile, solitary.

deserted /dɪ'zɜːtɪd/ *adj., said of a building, etc* empty or abandoned.

▤ abandoned, forsaken, empty, unoccupied, vacant, underpopulated, derelict, desolate, godforsaken, neglected, isolated, lonely, solitary.
▣ populous.

deserter *noun* a person who deserts from military service.

▤ runaway, absconder, escapee, truant, renegade, defector, *colloq.* rat, traitor, fugitive, betrayer, apostate, backslider, delinquent.

desertification *noun* the process by which a new desert is formed, or an existing desert spreads across an area that was formerly moist and fertile.

desertion *noun* the act of or an instance of deserting, especially deserting one's husband or wife or deserting from military service.

deserts /dɪ'zɜːts/ *pl. noun* what one deserves, usually something unfavourable: *get one's just deserts.* [from Old French *desert*, from *deservir*, to deserve]

▤ due, rights, reward, return, recompense, payment, retribution, nemesis, *colloq.* come-uppance.

deserve *verb* to have earned, be entitled to, or be worthy of (a reward or punishment, etc). [from Old French *deservir*]

▤ earn, be worthy of, merit, be entitled to, warrant, justify, win, rate, incur.

deserved *adj.* justly and appropriately awarded.

▤ due, earned, merited, justifiable, warranted, right, rightful, well-earned, suitable, proper, fitting, fair, just, appropriate, apt, legitimate, apposite.

deservedly *adv.* as one rightly deserves.

▤ rightly, rightfully, fittingly, properly, justly, fairly, duly.

deserving *adj.* **1** worthy or suitable (to be given support, a reward, etc). **2** *formal* (**deserving of something**) worthy of it; meriting it.

▤ **1** worthy, estimable, exemplary, praiseworthy, admirable, commendable, laudable, righteous.
▣ **1** undeserving, unworthy.

déshabillé /deɪzaˈbiːeɪ/ *adj.* the state of being only partly dressed. [from French *déshabillé*, undressed]

desiccant /'desɪkənt/ *noun Chem.* a substance that absorbs water and so can be used as a drying agent to remove water from or prevent absorption of water by other substances. [from Latin *desiccare*, to dry up]

desiccate /'dɛsɪkeɪt/ *verb* **1** to dry (a substance) by removing the moisture from it. **2** to preserve (food) by removing the moisture from it. **3** *said of a substance* to dry up. [from Latin *desiccare*, to dry up]

desiccated *adj.*, *said of food and other substances* dried up as a result of losing moisture.

desiccation *noun* **1** the act or process of removing moisture from a substance, eg food. **2** the state of being dried up.

desiccator *noun Chem.* a device, usually a closed glass vessel containing a desiccant, that is used to remove water from or prevent the absorption of water by other substances.

desideratum /dɪzɪdə'rɑːtəm/ *noun* (PL. **desiderata**) *formal* something wanted or required. [from Latin *desiderare*, to long for]

design — *verb* **1** to develop or prepare a plan, drawing, or model of (something) before it is built or made. **2** to plan, intend, create or develop for a particular purpose. — *noun* **1** a plan, drawing, or model showing how something is to be made. **2** the art or job of making such drawings, plans, etc. **3** the way in which something has been made. **4** a picture, pattern, arrangement of shapes, etc used eg as decoration. **5** one's plan, purpose, or intention: *put there by design*. — **have designs on something** to have plans to appropriate it. [from French *désigner*]

☐ PLAN. *verb* **1** sketch, draft, outline, draw (up), blueprint. **2** intend, devise, invent, originate, conceive, think up, create, develop, construct, fashion, form, shape, model, fabricate, make, tailor, purpose, aim, project. *noun* **1** blueprint, draft, pattern, plan, prototype, sketch, drawing, outline, model, guide. **3** style, shape, form, structure, organization, arrangement, composition, construction. **4** motif, pattern, figure, ornament, ornamentation, decoration. **5** plan, purpose, intention, aim, goal, end, object, objective, scheme, plot, project.

designate /'dɛzɪgneɪt, -nət/ — *verb* (pronounced -neɪt) **1** to name, choose, or specify for a particular purpose or duty. **2** to mark or indicate. **3** to be a name or label for. — *adj.* (pronounced -nət) (*used after a noun*) having been appointed to some official position but not yet holding it: *editor-designate*. [from Latin *designare*, to plan or mark out]

☐ *verb* INDICATE. **1** choose, select, appoint, assign, name, nominate, specify, recommend, put forward. **2** mark, show, point out, identify. **3** denote, stand for, signify, label.

designation /dɛzɪg'neɪʃən/ *noun* **1** a name or title. **2** designating; the state of being designated.

☐ **1** name, title, label, epithet, nickname. **2** indication, specification, description, definition, classification, category, nomination, appointment, selection.

designedly /dɪ'zaɪnɪdlɪ/ *adv.* intentionally; on purpose.

designer *noun* **1** a person who makes designs, plans, patterns, drawings, etc, especially professionally. **2** (*attributive*) **a** designed by and bearing the name of a famous fashion designer: *designer dresses*. **b** especially made for a particular purpose or effect: *designer drugs*. **c** *colloq.* following current fashion.

☐ **1** deviser, originator, maker, inventor, creator, contriver, fashioner, architect, author.

designing *adj. derog.* using cunning and deceit to achieve one's purpose.

☐ artful, crafty, scheming, conspiring, devious, intriguing, plotting, tricky, wily, sly, deceitful, cunning, guileful, underhand, sharp, shrewd.
☐ artless, naïve.

desirability *noun* being desirable or wanted.

desirable *adj.* **1** pleasing; worth having. **2** sexually attractive.

☐ **1** good, pleasing, worthwhile, advantageous, profitable, advisable, appropriate, expedient, beneficial, preferable, sensible, eligible. **2** attractive, alluring, *colloq.* sexy, seductive, fetching, tempting.
☐ **1** undesirable. **2** unattractive.

desirably *adv.* according to what is desirable or wanted.

desire — *noun* **1** a longing or wish. **2** strong sexual interest and attraction. — *verb* **1** *formal* to want. **2** to long for or feel sexual desire for. **3** *old use, formal* to ask or command. [from Old French *desirer*]

☐ *noun* **1** wish, need, want, longing, yearning, craving, hankering, appetite, aspiration. **2** lust, passion, ardour, concupiscence. *verb* **1** want, wish for, covet. **2** long for, need, crave, hunger for, yearn for, *colloq.* fancy, hanker after, lust after. **3** ask, request, petition, solicit.

desirous /dɪ'zaɪərəs/ *adj. formal* (**desirous of something**) wanting it keenly.

desist /dɪ'zɪst/ *verb intrans. formal* (**desist from something**) to stop doing it. [from Old French *desister*]

☐ stop, cease, leave off, refrain, discontinue, end, break off, give up, halt, abstain, suspend, pause, forbear.
☐ continue, resume.

desk *noun* **1** a sloping or flat table, often with drawers, for sitting at while writing, reading, etc. **2** a place or counter in a public building where a service is provided. **3** a section of a newspaper, etc office with responsibility for a particular subject. [from Latin *discus*, disc, table]

deskilling /diː-/ *noun* the process of removing the element of human skill from a job, operation, etc, through automation, computerization, etc.

desktop *adj.* small enough to fit on the top of a desk.

desktop publishing (ABBREV. **DTP**) the process of preparing and producing typeset output as a basis for published text, using a microcomputer with specialist software and high resolution printers.

desolate /'dɛsələt, -leɪt/ — *adj.* (pronounced -lət) **1** *said of a place* deserted, barren and lonely. **2** *said of a person* very sad; in despair. **3** lacking pleasure or comfort: *a desolate life*. **4** lonely; alone. — *verb* (pronounced -leɪt) **1** to overwhelm with sadness or grief. **2** to make deserted or barren; to lay waste. [from Latin *desolare*, to forsake]

☐ *adj.* **1** deserted, uninhabited, abandoned, unfrequented, barren, bare, arid, bleak, gloomy, dismal, dreary, lonely, god-forsaken, forsaken, waste, depressing. **2** forlorn, bereft, depressed, dejected, forsaken, despondent, distressed, melancholy, miserable, gloomy, disheartened, dismal, downcast, wretched. **3** cheerless, comfortless, unpleasant, miserable, dismal, wretched. **4** alone, lonely, solitary. *verb* **2** devastate, lay waste, destroy, despoil, spoil, wreck, denude, depopulate, ruin, waste, ravage.
☐ *adj.* **1** populous. **2** cheerful.

desolated *adj.* made wretched; forlorn.

desolation /dɛsə'leɪʃən/ *noun* **1** laying waste; a state of ruin or barrenness. **2** a state of lonely wretchedness or misery.

⊟ 1 destruction, devastation, ravages, ruin, barrenness, bleakness, emptiness, wilderness, waste. **2** dejection, despair, despondency, gloom, misery, sadness, melancholy, sorrow, unhappiness, anguish, grief, distress, wretchedness.

despair /dɪ'spɛə(r)/ — verb intrans. (often **despair of something** or **despair of doing something**) to lose or lack hope. — noun **1** the state of having lost hope. **2** (**the despair**) someone or something that causes worry and despair: *he's the despair of his parents.* [from Old French *desperer*]

⊟ verb lose heart, lose hope, give up, give in. noun **1** despondency, gloom, hopelessness, desperation, anguish, inconsolableness, melancholy, misery, wretchedness.
⊟ verb hope. noun **1** hope, cheerfulness, resilience.

despairing adj. giving up hope; involving loss of hope: *he gave a despairing glance.*

⊟ despondent, distraught, inconsolable, desolate, desperate, heart-broken, suicidal, grief-stricken, hopeless, disheartened, dejected, miserable, wretched, sorrowful, dismayed, downcast.
⊟ cheerful, hopeful.

despairingly adv. in a despairing or hopeless way.
despatch see DISPATCH.
desperado /dɛspə'rɑːdoʊ/ noun (PL. **desperados**, **desperadoes**) a bandit or outlaw, especially in the western USA in the 19c. [probably a mock-Spanish word formed from DESPERATE]

⊟ bandit, criminal, brigand, gangster, hoodlum, outlaw, ruffian, thug, cut-throat, law-breaker.

desperate /'dɛspərət/ adj. **1** extremely anxious, fearful or despairing. **2** willing to take risks fearlessly because of hopelessness and despair. **3** very serious, difficult, dangerous, and almost hopeless: *a desperate situation.* **4** dangerous and likely to be violent: *a desperate criminal.* **5** extreme and carried out as a last resort because of the seriousness or hopelessness of the situation: *desperate measures.* **6** very great: *desperate need.* **7** (**desperate for something**) in great or urgent need of it: *desperate for supplies.* **8** extremely anxious or eager: *desperate to go to the concert.* [from Latin *desperare*, to despair]

⊟ 1 hopeless, inconsolable, wretched, despondent, abandoned. **2** reckless, rash, impetuous, audacious, daring, do-or-die, foolhardy. **3** critical, grave, dire, dangerous, hazardous. **4** wild, violent, frenzied, determined. **5** drastic, extreme, last-ditch, last-minute, eleventh-hour. **6** critical, acute, serious, severe, extreme, urgent.
⊟ 1 hopeful. **2** cautious.

desperately adv. **1** in a despairing or desperate manner. **2** very seriously: *desperately ill.* **3** extremely: *desperately sorry.*

⊟ 1 despairingly, hopelessly, frantically, furiously, recklessly, at all costs. **2** dangerously, critically, gravely, seriously, severely, badly. **3** dreadfully, fearfully, frightfully.

desperation /dɛspə'reɪʃən/ noun **1** a state of despair; extreme hopelessness. **2** extreme recklessness.

⊟ 1 despair, despondency, anguish, hopelessness, misery, agony, distress, pain, sorrow, trouble, worry, anxiety. **2** recklessness, rashness, frenzy, madness, hastiness.

despicable /dɪ'spɪkəbl/ adj. deserving one's contempt; mean. [from Latin *despicabilis*]

⊟ contemptible, vile, worthless, detestable, disgusting, mean, wretched, disgraceful, disreputable, shameful, reprobate.
⊟ admirable, noble.

despicably /dɪ'spɪkəblɪ/ adv. in a despicable or contemptible way.
despise verb to look down on with scorn and contempt. [from Old French *despire*, from Latin *despicere*]

⊟ scorn, deride, look down on, disdain, condemn, spurn, slight, revile, deplore, dislike, detest, loathe, belittle, undervalue, *colloq.* turn up one's nose at.
⊟ admire.

despite prep. in spite of. [from Old French *despit*, from Latin *despicere*, to despise]

⊟ in spite of, notwithstanding, regardless of, in the face of, undeterred by, against, defying.

despoil verb formal, literary to rob or steal everything valuable from (a place). [from Old French *despoiller*, from Latin *spolium*, plunder]
despoiler noun a person who robs a place of its valuables.
despoliation /dɪspoʊlɪ'eɪʃən/ noun plundering; robbing.
despondency noun a despondent state; low spirits.

⊟ dejection, depression, melancholy, gloom, sorrow, unhappiness, wretchedness, misery.

despondent adj. sad; dejected; in low spirits. [from Latin *despondere*, to lose heart]

⊟ depressed, dejected, disheartened, downcast, down, low, gloomy, glum, discouraged, miserable, melancholy, sad, sorrowful, doleful, despairing, heartbroken, inconsolable, mournful, wretched.
⊟ cheerful, heartened, hopeful.

despondently adv. with a despondent or sad manner.
despot /'dɛspɒt/ noun a person who has very great or total power, especially one who uses such power in a cruel or oppressive way. [from Greek *despotes*, master]

⊟ autocrat, tyrant, dictator, oppressor, absolutist.

despotic /dɪ'spɒtɪk/ adj. like a despot; tyrannical; overbearing.

⊟ autocratic, tyrannical, imperious, oppressive, dictatorial, authoritarian, domineering, absolute, overbearing, arbitrary, arrogant.
⊟ democratic, egalitarian, liberal, tolerant.

despotically adv. in a despotic or overbearing way.
despotism noun absolute power; tyranny.

⊟ autocracy, totalitarianism, tyranny, dictatorship, absolutism, oppression, repression.
⊟ democracy, egalitarianism, liberalism, tolerance.

dessert /dɪ'zɜːt/ noun **1** a sweet food served after the main course of a meal. **2** the course at or near the end of a meal, when such food is served. [from Old French, from *desservir*, to clear the table]
dessertspoon noun **1** a medium-sized spoon, about half the size of a tablespoon and twice the size of a teaspoon. **2** the amount a dessertspoon will hold.

dessertspoonful *noun* (PL. **dessertspoonfuls**) the amount a dessertspoon will hold.

destabilization or **destabilisation** *noun* destabilizing; making less stable.

destabilize or **destabilise** *verb* to make (a country, economy, etc) less stable.

destination /dɛstɪ'neɪʃən/ *noun* the place to which someone or something is going or being sent. [from Latin *destinatio*, purpose]

⊟ journey's end, terminus, station, stop, goal, aim, objective, object, target, end.

destine /'dɛstɪn/ *verb formal* (*usually* **be destined for something** or **to do something**) to have it as an arranged purpose. [from Old French *destiner*]

destined 1 *adj.* ordained or apparently ordained by fate (for something or to do something). **2** (**destined for**) having as one's or its destination.

⊟ **1** fated, doomed, predetermined, ordained, foreordained, inevitable, certain, unavoidable, inescapable, meant, appointed. **2** bound for, heading for, headed for, en route for, directed to, scheduled to, addressed to.

destiny *noun* (PL. **destinies**) **1** one's purpose or future as arranged by fate or God. **2** (*also* **Destiny**) fate; the power which appears or is believed to control events. [from Old French *destinee*, from Latin *destinare*, to appoint]

⊟ FATE. **1** doom, fortune, karma, lot, portion, predestiny, kismet.

destitute /'dɛstɪtjuːt/ *adj.* **1** lacking money, food, shelter, etc; extremely poor. **2** *formal* (**destitute of something**) completely lacking in something necessary or desirable. [from Latin *destitutus*]

⊟ **1** poor, needy, penniless, poverty-stricken, impoverished, down-and-out, distressed, bankrupt. **2** without, lacking, wanting, devoid of, bereft of, innocent of, deprived of, deficient in.
⊡ **1** prosperous, rich.

destitution *noun* being desititute; lack of money and food.

destroy *verb* **1** to knock down, break into pieces, completely ruin, etc. **2** to put an end to. **3** to defeat totally. **4** to ruin or seriously damage the reputation, health, financial position, etc of. **5** to kill (a dangerous, injured, or unwanted animal). [from Old French *destruire*, from Latin *de*, down + *struere*, to build]

⊟ **1, 2** ruin, wreck, shatter, sabotage. **1** demolish, devastate, smash, break, crush, undo, dismantle, waste, gut, level, ravage, raze. **2** extinguish, eradicate, eliminate, nullify, frustrate, thwart, torpedo, undermine. **3** annihilate, decimate, rout, trounce, thrash, wipe out, *slang* wipe the floor with. **4** ruin, break, bankrupt. **5** put down, put to sleep.
⊡ **1** build up. **2** create.

destroyer *noun* **1** a person or thing that destroys or causes destruction. **2** a type of small, fast warship.

destruct *verb trans., intrans. chiefly North Amer., esp. US, said of equipment, especially a missile in flight* to destroy or be destroyed, especially for safety reasons.

destructibility *noun* the capacity to be or the likelihood of being destroyed.

destructible *adj.* able to be destroyed.

destruction *noun* **1** the act or process of destroying or being destroyed. **2** something that destroys. [from Latin *destruere*, to destroy, from *de*, down + *struere*, to build]

⊟ **1** ruin, devastation, wreckage, demolition, defeat, downfall, overthrow, ruination, desolation, havoc, annihilation, extermination, eradication, elimination, extinction, slaughter, massacre, end, liquidation, nullification.
⊡ **1** creation.

destructive *adj.* **1** causing destruction or serious damage. **2** *said of criticism, etc* pointing out faults, etc without suggesting improvements.

⊟ **1** devastating, damaging, catastrophic, disastrous, deadly, harmful, fatal, lethal, disruptive, ruinous, detrimental, hurtful, malignant, mischievous. **2** adverse, hostile, negative, discouraging, disparaging, *colloq.* knocking, undermining, subversive, vicious.
⊡ **1** creative. **2** constructive.

destructively *adv.* in a destructive or seriously damaging way.

desultorily /'dɛsəltərɪlɪ/ *adv.* in a desultory or purposeless way.

desultory /'dɛsəltərɪ/ *adj.* jumping from one thing to another with no plan, purpose, or logical connection. [from Latin *desultorius*, from *desultor*, circus performer who jumped from horse to horse]

⊟ random, erratic, aimless, disorderly, haphazard, irregular, spasmodic, inconsistent, undirected, unco-ordinated, unsystematic, unmethodical, fitful, disconnected, loose, capricious.
⊡ systematic, methodical.

Det. *abbrev.* Detective.

detach *verb* **1** to unfasten or separate. **2** *Mil.* to select and separate (a group of soldiers, etc) from a larger group, especially to carry out a special task. [from Old French *destachier*, from *des-, dis- + atachier*, to attach]

⊟ **1** unfasten, separate, disconnect, disjoin, cut off, disengage, remove, undo, uncouple, sever, dissociate, isolate, loosen, free, unfix, unhitch, segregate, divide, disentangle, estrange.
⊡ **1** attach.

detachable *adj.* capable of being detached; removable.

detached *adj.* **1** not connected to or integrated into anything else. **2** *said of a building* not joined to another on either side. See also SEMI-DETACHED. **3** *said of a person* feeling no personal or emotional involvement; showing no prejudice or bias.

⊟ **1** separate, disconnected, dissociated, severed, free, loose, discrete. **3** aloof, dispassionate, impersonal, neutral, impartial, independent, disinterested, objective.
⊡ **1** connected. **3** involved.

detachedly *adv.* with a detached or uninvolved manner: *spoke detachedly about the war.*

detachment *noun* **1** the state of being emotionally detached or free from prejudice. **2** a group (eg of soldiers) detached from a larger group for a special purpose. **3** the act of detaching or state or process of being detached.

⊟ **1** aloofness, remoteness, coolness, unconcern, indifference, impassivity, disinterestedness, neutrality, impartiality, objectivity, fairness. **2** squad, unit, detail, patrol, force, corps, brigade, task force. **3** separation, disconnection, disunion, disengagement.

detail — *noun* **1** a small feature, fact, or item. **2** something considered unimportant. **3** all the small features and parts (of something) considered as a whole: *an artist's eye for detail*. **4** a part of a painting, map, photograph, etc considered separately, often enlarged to show small features. **5** *Mil.* a group of eg soldiers given a special task or duty. — *verb* **1** to describe or list fully. **2** to appoint (someone) to do a particular task. — **in detail** giving or looking at all the details. [from Old French *detailler*, to cut up]

▣ *noun* **1** particular, item, factor, element, aspect, component, feature, fact, point, specific, ingredient, attribute. **2** triviality, technicality, nicety, trifle. **3** intricacies, complications, minutiae. **5** detachment, squad, unit. *verb* **1** list, enumerate, itemize, specify, catalogue, recount, relate. **2** assign, appoint, charge, delegate, commission.

detailed *adj.* having or giving many details; thorough.

▣ thorough, comprehensive, exhaustive, full, blow-by-blow, minute, exact, specific, particular, itemized, intricate, elaborate, complex, complicated, meticulous, descriptive.
▣ cursory, general.

detain *verb* **1** to stop, hold back, keep waiting, or delay. **2** *said of the police, etc* to keep (someone) in a cell, prison, or elsewhere, especially before trial. See also DETENTION. [from Old French *detenir*, to hold]

▣ **1** delay, hold (up), hinder, impede, check, retard, slow, stay, stop. **2** confine, arrest, intern, hold, restrain, keep.
▣ **2** release.

detainee /diːteɪˈniː/ *noun* a person held under guard eg by the police, especially for political reasons.

detect *verb* **1** to see or notice. **2** to discover, and usually indicate, the presence or existence of (something which should not be there or whose presence is not obvious). [from Latin *detegere*, to uncover]

▣ **1** notice, ascertain, note, observe, perceive, recognize, discern, distinguish, identify, sight, spot, spy. **2** discover, uncover, catch, disclose, expose, find, track down, unmask, reveal.

detectable or **detectible** *adj.* capable of being detected.

▣ perceptible, discernible, noticeable, observable, apparent.

detection *noun* **1** the act or process of detecting or state of being detected. **2** the work of a detective, investigating and solving crime.

detective *noun* a police officer whose job is to solve crime by observation and gathering evidence. See also PRIVATE DETECTIVE.

▣ investigator, plain-clothes officer, sleuth.

detective story a story whose main theme is the solving of a crime.

detector *noun* an instrument or device used for detecting the presence of something.

détente /deɪˈtɒnt/ *noun* a lessening of tension, especially in the relationships between countries. [from French *détente*]

detention *noun* **1** the act of detaining or the state of being detained, especially in prison or police custody. **2** a punishment in which a pupil is kept in school after the other pupils have gone home. [from Latin *detinere*, to detain]

▣ **1** custody, confinement, imprisonment, restraint, incarceration, constraint, quarantine, detainment.
▣ **1** release.

detention centre a place where young criminals are kept for a short time by order of a court.

deter *verb* (**deterred**, **deterring**) to discourage or prevent (someone) from doing (something) because of fear of unpleasant consequences. [from Latin *deterrere*, to frighten off]

▣ discourage, put off, inhibit, intimidate, dissuade, daunt, *colloq.* turn off, check, caution, warn, restrain, hinder, frighten, disincline, prevent, prohibit, stop.
▣ encourage.

detergent — *noun* a soapless and usually water-soluble substance that is added to a liquid, especially water, in order to improve its cleaning properties. It acts by reducing surface tension and so allowing fats and oils that bind dirt to skin, clothing, etc, to dissolve in water. — *adj.* having the power to clean. [from Latin *detergere*, to wipe off]

deteriorate /dɪˈtɪərɪəreɪt/ *verb intrans.* to grow worse. [from Latin *deterior*, worse]

▣ worsen, decline, degenerate, depreciate, go downhill, fail, fall off, lapse, slide, relapse, slip.
▣ improve.

deterioration *noun* a worsening or decline.

determinant *noun* **1** a determining factor or circumstance. **2** *Maths.* a number obtained by multiplying and adding the elements of a square matrix according to certain rules. **3** *Biol.* in an antigen molecule, a region or regions that enable it to be recognized and bound by an antibody.

determinate /dɪˈtɜːmɪnət/ *adj.* having definite, fixed limits, etc.

determination *noun* **1** firmness or strength of will, purpose or character. **2** the act of determining or process of being determined.

▣ **1** resoluteness, tenacity, firmness, willpower, perseverance, persistence, purpose, backbone, *colloq.* guts, *colloq.* grit, steadfastness, single-mindedness, will, insistence, conviction, dedication, drive, fortitude. **2** decision, judgement, settlement, resolution, conclusion.
▣ **1** irresolution.

determinative /dɪˈtɜːmɪnətɪv/ *adj.* having the power to limit or determine.

determine *verb* **1** to fix or settle the exact limits or nature of. **2** to find out or reach a conclusion about by gathering facts, making measurements, etc. **3** *trans., intrans.* to decide or cause (someone) to decide. **4** to be the main influence on; to control. [from Old French *determiner*, from Latin *determinare*, to fix the limits of]

▣ **1** settle, fix, define, establish, lay down. **2** discover, establish, find out, ascertain, identify, check, detect, verify, conclude, resolve, clinch. **3** decide, resolve, make up one's or someone's mind. **4** affect, influence, control, govern, dictate, direct, guide, regulate, ordain.

determined *adj.* **1** (**determined to do something**) firmly intending to do it. **2** having or showing a strong will.

▣ **1** intent on, set on, bent on, resolved to. **2** resolute, firm, purposeful, strong-willed, single-minded, persevering, persistent, strong-minded, steadfast, tenacious, dogged, insistent, fixed, convinced, decided, unflinching.
▣ **2** irresolute, wavering.

determiner *noun Grammar* a word that comes before a noun or noun phrase, and limits its meaning in some way, eg *a, the, this, every, some*.

determinism *noun Philos.* the theory that every event has a cause, or that nature is uniform.

determinist *noun* a believer in determinism.

deterrence /dɪ'terəns/ *noun* discouragement by fear of the consequences.

deterrent /dɪ'terənt/ *noun* something which deters, especially a weapon intended to deter attack.

▪ hindrance, impediment, obstacle, repellent, check, bar, discouragement, obstruction, curb, restraint, difficulty.
▪ incentive, encouragement.

detest *verb* to dislike intensely; to hate. [from Old French *detester*]

▪ hate, abhor, loathe, abominate, *formal* execrate, dislike, recoil from, deplore, despise.
▪ adore, love.

detestable *adj.* causing or deserving intense dislike; hateful.

▪ hateful, loathsome, abhorrent, abominable, repellent, obnoxious, execrable, despicable, revolting, repulsive, repugnant, offensive, vile, disgusting, heinous, shocking, sordid.
▪ adorable, admirable.

detestably *adv.* in a detestable or hateful way.

detestation /diːtɛ'steɪʃən/ *noun* great dislike; hatred.

dethrone *verb* 1 to remove (a monarch) from the throne. 2 to remove from a position of power, influence, or authority.

▪ DEPOSE, OVERTHROW. 2 unseat, topple, demote, dismiss.

dethronement *noun* removal from the throne.

detonate *verb trans., intrans.* to explode or cause to explode. [from Latin *detonare*, to thunder down]

detonation *noun* detonating; explosion.

detonator *noun* a small explosive charge used to trigger off a larger explosion.

detour — *noun* a route away from and longer than a planned or more direct route. — *verb intrans.* to make a detour. [from French *détour*]

▪ *noun* deviation, diversion, indirect route, circuitous route, roundabout route, digression, byroad, byway, bypath, bypass.

detox *colloq.* — *noun* 1 short for DETOXIFICATION. 2 a treatment centre where detoxification takes place. — *verb* short for DETOXIFY.

detoxification *noun* the process of detoxifying or removing toxic substances.

detoxify *verb* (**detoxifies, detoxified**) 1 to rid (a person, object, etc) of toxic substances, or to neutralize the effects of such substances. 2 to subject (a person) to medical treatment in order to promote their recovery from the toxic effects of alcoholism or drug addiction. [from DE- + TOXIC]

detract *verb intrans.* (**detract from something**) to take away from it or lessen it. [from Latin *detrahere*, to pull away]

▪ reduce, lessen, lower, diminish, subtract from, take away from, depreciate, belittle, disparage.

detraction *noun* detracting from a person's reputation; defamation.

detractor *noun* a person who criticizes or belittles (someone, or someone's beliefs, achievements, etc), especially unfairly.

detriment /'detrɪmənt/ *noun* harm or loss: *to the detriment of her health.* [from Latin *detrimentum*]

▪ damage, harm, hurt, disadvantage, loss, ill, injury, disservice, evil, mischief, prejudice.
▪ advantage, benefit.

detrimental /detrɪ'mentl/ *adj.* causing harm or damage.

▪ damaging, harmful, hurtful, adverse, disadvantageous, injurious, prejudicial, mischievous, destructive.
▪ advantageous, favourable, beneficial.

detrimentally *adv.* in a detrimental or harmful way.

detritus /dɪ'traɪtəs/ *noun* 1 *Geol.* loose fragments of weathered rock, produced by disintegration or erosion, that have been transported some distance from their place of origin. 2 *Biol.* dead plants or animals, or any debris of living organisms, eg shed parts. 3 bits and pieces of rubbish left over from something. [from Latin *deterere*, to rub away]

de trop /də 'troʊ/ not wanted; in the way. [from French *de trop*]

deuce¹ /djuːs/ *noun* 1 *Tennis* a score of forty points each in a game or five games each in a match. 2 a card, dice throw, etc of the value two. [from Old French *deus*, two]

deuce² /djuːs/ *noun old use* (**the deuce**) said in exclamations the devil. [perhaps from DEUCE¹, two being an unlucky throw in dice]

deus ex machina /'deʊs ɛks 'makɪnə/ 1 in classical drama, a god lowered on to the stage by a mechanical device to resolve problems which have arisen in the course of the play or to decide the final outcome. 2 in any literary genre, someone or something introduced suddenly or unexpectedly to provide a contrived solution to a difficulty. [Latin, = god out of a machine]

Deut. or **Deut** *abbrev. Biblical* Deuteronomy.

deuterium /djuː'tɪərɪəm/ *noun Chem.* (SYMBOL **D**) one of the three isotopes of hydrogen, almost identical to hydrogen in its chemical properties, but with slightly different physical properties, eg boiling point. Its nucleus contains one proton and one neutron. [from Greek *deuteros*, second]

deuterium oxide *Chem.* (FORMULA D_2O) a compound analogous to water, consisting of deuterium (heavy hydrogen) and oxygen. Also called HEAVY WATER.

deuteron /'djuːtərɒn/ *noun Physics* the nucleus of an atom of deuterium (an isotope of hydrogen), composed of a proton and a neutron. [from Greek *deuteros*, second]

Deutschmark /'dɔɪtʃmɑːk/ or **Deutsche Mark** /'dɔɪtʃə mɑːk/ *noun* (ABBREV. **DM**) the standard unit of currency in Germany, equal to 100 pfennigs. [from German *Deutschmark*]

devaluation *noun* reduction in the value of a currency.

devalue *verb* 1 *trans., intrans.* to reduce the value of (a currency) in relation to the values of other currencies. 2 to make (a person, action, etc) seem less valuable or important.

▪ DEPRECIATE. 2 belittle, disparage, deride, run down, dismiss, underrate, undervalue.

devastate /'devəsteɪt/ *verb* 1 to cause great destruction in or to. 2 to overwhelm with grief; to shock greatly. [from Latin *devastare*, to lay waste]

▪ 1 destroy, desolate, lay waste, demolish, level, raze, wreck, ruin, ravage, waste, spoil, despoil, ransack, plunder, pillage, sack. 2 overwhelm, shock, confound, distress, dismay, shatter, upset, disconcert, take aback, nonplus, discomfit.

devastated *adj.* 1 *said of a person* overwhelmed with shock or grief. 2 *said of an area or country* extensively harmed or damaged.

devastating *adj.* **1** completely destructive. **2** shocking; overwhelming. **3** very effective, especially in a destructive way: *a devastating reply.* **4** *colloq.* extremely attractive.
. . . .
◼ **1** destructive, disastrous. **2** shattering, traumatic, distressing, disturbing, upsetting, shocking. **3** crushing, effective, incisive, overwhelming, shattering. **4** stunning, gorgeous.
. . . .

devastatingly *adv.* in a devastating or destructive way.

devastation /dɛvəˈsteɪʃən/ *noun* **1** destruction; causing great harm or damage. **2** a ruined or desolate scene or state.
. . . .
◼ **1** destruction, demolition, annihilation, pillage, plunder, spoliation, ravages. **2** desolation, havoc, ruin, wreckage.
. . . .

develop *verb* (**developed**, **developing**) **1** *trans., intrans.* to make or become more mature, more advanced, more complete, more organized, more detailed, etc. **2** *intrans.*, *said of a living organism, organ, tissue, or cell* to become transformed from a simple structure to a much more complex one, usually by passing through a number of stages. **3** to begin to have; to have an increasing amount of: *develop an interest in politics.* **4** *intrans., trans.* to appear and grow, or to have or suffer from something which has appeared and grown: *be developing a cold.* **5** to occur as a result of something. **6** to use chemical agents to convert an invisible image on exposed photographic film or paper into a visible image. **7** to bring into fuller use (the natural resources, etc of a country or region). **8** to build on (land) or prepare (land) for being built on. [from French *développer*]
. . . .
◼ **1** advance, evolve, expand, mature, elaborate, amplify, augment, enhance, unfold. **3** acquire, take up, begin, pursue, carry on. **5** result, come about, grow, ensue, arise, follow, happen. **7** exploit, use, utilize, capitalize on.
. . . .

developer *noun* **1** a liquid chemical compound that is used to render visible the image recorded on photographic film or paper. **2** a person who builds on land or improves and increases the value of buildings. **3** an apparatus for developing muscles.

developing *adj.*, *said of a country* having a low income per capita of population. The term is applied to most of the countries of Asia, Africa, and Latin America, predominantly agricultural economies, though including some with a well-developed industrial base (eg Brazil, India, and Pakistan) or with rich mineral wealth.

development *noun* **1** the act of developing or the process of being developed. **2** a new stage, event, or situation. **3** a result or consequence. **4** land which has been or is being developed, or the buildings built or being built on it.
. . . .
◼ **1** growth, evolution, advance, blossoming, elaboration, furtherance, progress, unfolding, expansion, extension, spread, increase, improvement, maturity, promotion, refinement. **2** occurrence, happening, phenomenon, event, change, situation. **3** result, consequence, outcome, issue, effect.
. . . .

development aid *Politics* financial and economic assistance given by rich industrial nations to developing countries. Official development aid is channelled through organizations such as the International Development Association (a UN agency) and the International Finance Corporation (an arm of the World Bank).

developmental *adj.* relating to or in the nature of development.

developmentally *adv.* in a developmental way.

developmental psychology *Psychol.* the branch of psychology concerned with the scientific study of human mental development and behaviour from birth to maturity.

development area *Brit.* an area of high unemployment into which the government encourages businesses and industry to move eg by offering grants.

deviance /ˈdiːvɪəns/ *noun* departure from normal standards or methods.

deviant /ˈdiːvɪənt/ — *adj.* not following the normal patterns, accepted standards, etc. — *noun* a person who does not behave in a normal or acceptable fashion, especially sexually. [from Latin *deviare*; see etymology at DEVIATE]

deviate /ˈdiːvɪeɪt/ *verb intrans.* to turn aside or move away, especially from what is considered a correct or normal course, standard of behaviour, way of thinking, etc. [from Latin *deviare*, to turn from the road, from *de*, from + *via*, road]
. . . .
◼ diverge, turn (aside), veer, swerve, yaw, vary, differ, depart, stray, wander, err, go astray, go off the rails, digress, drift, part.
. . . .

deviation /diːvɪˈeɪʃən/ *noun* **1** the act of deviating. **2** *Geog.* the existence of or the amount of a difference between north as shown on a compass and true north, caused by the magnetism of objects near the compass, etc.
. . . .
◼ **1** divergence, detour, deflection, departure, aberration, abnormality, irregularity, variance, variation, digression, eccentricity, anomaly, alteration, disparity, discrepancy, fluctuation, change, quirk, shift, freak.
▣ **1** conformity, regularity.
. . . .

deviationism *noun* a tendency to dissent from some aspects of a (usually political) belief or ideology.

deviationist *noun* a person given to deviationism.

device *noun* **1** a machine, tool, instrument, or component designed to perform a specific task. **2** *Comput.* in a computer system, one of a number of different parts designed for a specific function, eg peripheral device, input device. **3** a plan or scheme for doing something, sometimes involving trickery or deceit. **4** a sign, pattern, or symbol used eg on a crest or shield. See also DEVISE. — **be left to one's own devices** to be left alone and without supervision or help. [from Old French *devis* and *devise*, from Latin *divisa*, mark, device]
. . . .
◼ **1** machine, tool, instrument, implement, appliance, gadget, contrivance, *colloq.* contraption, apparatus, utensil. **3** scheme, ruse, strategy, plan, plot, gambit, manoeuvre, wile, trick, dodge, machination. **4** emblem, symbol, motif, logo, design, insignia, crest, badge, shield.
. . . .

devil — *noun* **1** (**the Devil**) *Relig.* the most powerful evil spirit; Satan. **2** any evil or wicked spirit. **3** *colloq.* a mischievous or bad person. **4** *colloq.* a person of a stated type: *lucky devil.* **5** someone or something difficult to deal with. **6** a person who excels at something. **7** (**the devil**) used for emphasis in mild oaths and exclamations: *what the devil is she doing?* — *verb* (**devilled**, **devilling**) to prepare or cook with a spicy seasoning. — **be a devil** *colloq.* said to encourage someone to do something they are hesitating to do. **between the devil and the deep blue sea** in a situation where the alternatives are equally undesirable. **devil take the hindmost** one should take care of one's own success, safety, etc with no thought for others. **the devil to pay** serious trouble as a consequence of an action, etc. **give the devil his due** to admit the good points of a person one dislikes. **go to the devil 1** to be ruined. **2** *usually said as a command, in anger* to go away. **like the devil** *colloq.* very hard. **speak** or **talk of the devil** said at the arrival of someone one has just been talking about. [from Anglo-Saxon *deofol*, from Greek *diabolos*, slanderer]
. . . .
◼ *noun* **1** Satan, Lucifer, the Evil One, the Prince of Darkness, the Adversary, *colloq.* Old Nick, archfiend, Beelzebub. **2** demon, fiend, evil spirit, imp,

Mephistopheles. **3** fiend, brute, rogue, monster, ogre.

devilish — *adj.* **1** of or like a devil; as if from, produced by, etc a devil. **2** very wicked. **3** *colloq.* very great or very difficult. — *adv. old use* very.

⊟ *adj.* FIENDISH, DIABOLICAL, INFERNAL, HELLISH. **1** demonic. **2** evil, wicked, monstrous, vile, inhuman.

devilishly *adv. old use* very; terribly.
devil-may-care *adj.* cheerfully heedless of danger, consequences, etc.
devilment *noun* mischievous fun.
devilry *noun* (PL. **devilries**) **1** mischievous fun. **2** wickedness or cruelty. **3** witchcraft; black magic.
devil's advocate a person who argues for or against something simply to encourage discussion or argument.
devious *adj.* **1** not totally open or honest; deceitful. **2** cunning; able to think up clever and usually deceitful ways of achieving things, etc. **3** not direct: *came by a devious route.* [from Latin *devius*, from *de*, from + *via*, road]

⊟ **1** underhand, deceitful, dishonest, disingenuous, double-dealing, scheming, tricky, insidious, insincere, treacherous. **2** cunning, calculating, evasive, wily, sly, slippery, surreptitious, misleading. **3** indirect, circuitous, rambling, roundabout, wandering, winding, tortuous, erratic.
⊟ STRAIGHTFORWARD.

deviously *adv.* in a devious or deceitful way.
deviousness *noun* being devious or deceitful.
devise *verb* **1** to invent, make up, or put together (a plan, etc) in one's mind. **2** *Legal* to leave (property such as land or buildings) to someone in a will. See also BEQUEATH. [from Old French *deviser*, from Latin *divisa*, division of goods]

⊟ **1** invent, contrive, plan, plot, design, conceive, arrange, formulate, imagine, scheme, construct, concoct, forge, frame, project, shape, form.

devoid *adj.* (**devoid of something**) free from it, lacking it, or empty of it. [from Old French *devoidier*, to take away]

⊟ lacking, wanting, without, free from or of, bereft of, destitute of, deficient in, deprived of, barren of, empty of, void of.
⊟ endowed with.

devolution /diːvəˈluːʃən/ *noun* the act of devolving, especially the giving of certain powers to a regional government by a central government. [from Latin *devolutio*, from *devolvere*, to roll down]
devolutionist *noun* an advocate of devolution.
devolve /dɪˈvɒlv/ *verb* (**devolve to** or **on** or **upon someone**) **1** *trans., intrans., said of duties, power, etc* to transfer (them) or be transferred to someone else. **2** *intrans. Legal* to pass by succession: *on his death, the title will devolve on his nephew.* [from Latin *devolvere*, to roll down]
Devonian /dɛˈvəʊnɪən/ **1** *Geol.* relating to the fourth period of the Palaeozoic era (between the Silurian and the Carboniferous), lasting from about 410 million to 360 million years ago, when the first amphibians appeared. **2** relating to the rocks formed during this period. [from *Devon* in SW England]
devote *verb* to use or give up (a resource such as time or money) wholly to some purpose: *devoted their time to writing letters.* [from Latin *devovere*, to consecrate]

⊟ dedicate, consecrate, commit, give, set apart, set aside, reserve, apply, allocate, allot, sacrifice, enshrine, assign, appropriate, surrender, pledge.

devoted *adj.* **1** loving and loyal. **2** (**devoted to something**) given up to it; totally occupied by it.

⊟ DEDICATED, COMMITTED. **1** ardent, loyal, faithful, devout, loving, staunch, steadfast, true, constant, fond, unswerving, tireless, concerned, attentive, caring.
⊟ INDIFFERENT (TO). **1** disloyal.

devotedly /dɪˈvəʊtɪdlɪ/ *adv.* in a devoted way; with devotion.
devotedness *noun* being devoted.
devotee /dɛvəʊˈtiː/ *noun* **1** a keen follower or enthusiastic supporter. **2** a keen believer in a religion or follower of a god.

⊟ **1** enthusiast, fan, fanatic, addict, aficionado, *colloq.* buff, freak, *slang* merchant, *colloq.* fiend, supporter, follower, admirer. **2** worshipper, disciple, zealot, adherent.

devotion /dɪˈvəʊʃən/ *noun* **1** great love or loyalty; enthusiasm for or willingness to do what is required by. **2** devoting or being devoted. **3** religious enthusiasm and piety. **4** (**devotions**) *Relig.* worship and prayers.

⊟ **1, 2** dedication, commitment. **1** love, passion, ardour, fervour, adoration, affection, fondness, attachment, faithfulness, loyalty, allegiance, adherence, reverence, zeal, support, steadfastness, regard. **2** consecration. **3** devoutness, piety, godliness, faith, holiness, spirituality. **4** prayer, worship.
⊟ **1** inconstancy. **3** irreverence.

devotional *adj.* relating to or in the nature of devotion.
devour *verb* **1** to eat up greedily. **2** to destroy thoroughly. **3** to read eagerly. **4** to look at with obvious pleasure. **5** (*usually* **be devoured**) to be taken over totally: *was devoured by guilt.* [from Latin *devorare*, to gulp down]

⊟ **1** eat, consume, guzzle, gulp, gorge, gobble, bolt, *colloq.* wolf down, swallow, stuff, cram, *colloq.* polish off, gormandize, feast on, relish, revel in. **2** destroy, consume, absorb, engulf, ravage, dispatch.

devout *adj.* **1** sincerely religious in thought and behaviour. **2** deeply-felt; earnest. [from Latin *devovere*, to consecrate]

⊟ FAITHFUL. **1** pious, godly, religious, reverent, prayerful, saintly, holy, orthodox. **2** sincere, earnest, fervent, genuine, steadfast, ardent, passionate, intense, heartfelt, serious, wholehearted, devoted, constant, zealous, unswerving, deep, profound.
⊟ **1** irreligious. **2** insincere.

devoutly *adv.* in a devout or sincere way.
devoutness *noun* being devout or sincere.
dew *noun* a form of precipitation consisting of tiny droplets of water that are deposited on objects close to the ground, eg leaves, on cool clear nights when air in contact with the ground becomes saturated. [from Anglo-Saxon *deaw*]
Dewar flask /ˈdjuːə/ *Physics* an insulated vessel with double walls, in which the inner space is surrounded by a vacuum and silvered to reduce heat loss. [named after the Scottish scientist Sir James Dewar (1842–1923)]
dewclaw *noun* **1** a rudimentary non-functional inner claw or toe on the foot of a dog. **2** a rudimentary non-functional hoof in certain animals, eg deer, pigs.
dewdrop *noun* a drop of dew.
dewlap *noun* **1** a loose fold of skin hanging from beneath the throat of certain cattle, dogs, and other animals. **2** a loose fold or folds of skin hanging from the neck of an elderly person. [probably from DEW + Anglo-Saxon *læppa*, loose hanging piece]

dewy *adj.* (**dewier, dewiest**) covered in dew.

dewy-eyed *adj.* naïve and too trusting.

dexterity /dɛkˈstɛrɪtɪ/ *noun* **1** skill in using one's hands. **2** quickness of mind. [from French *dextérité*, from Latin *dexter*, right, skilful]

dexterous or **dextrous** /ˈdɛkstrəs/ *adj.* having, showing, or done with dexterity.

> ▣ deft, adroit, agile, able, nimble, proficient, skilful, clever, expert, nifty, nippy, handy, facile, nimble-fingered, neat-handed.
>
> ▣ clumsy, inept, awkward.

dexterously or **dextrously** *adv.* with dexterity; agilely; skilfully.

dextral *adj.* **1** associated with or located on the right side, especially of the body. **2** right-handed, or favouring the right-hand side. **3** *said of flatfish* lying right-side up. **4** *said of the shells of some gastropod molluscs* turning in the normal manner, ie clockwise from the top. [from medieval Latin *dextralis*, from *dextra*, right hand]

dextrin *noun Biochem.* any of a group of short-chain polysaccharides produced during the partial breakdown of starch or glycogen. [from French *dextrine*]

dextrose see GLUCOSE. [from Latin *dexter*, right]

DF *abbrev.* Defender of the Faith.

DFC *abbrev.* Distinguished Flying Cross.

DFM *abbrev.* Distinguished Flying Medal.

DG *abbrev.* **1** *Dei gratia* (Latin), by the grace of God. **2** *Deo gratias* (Latin), thanks be to God. **3** Director General.

dhal see DAL.

dharma /ˈdɑːmə/ *noun* **1** *Buddhism* truth. **2** *Hinduism* the universal laws, especially the moral laws to be followed by each individual. [from Sanskrit *dharma*]

dhobi /ˈdoʊbɪ/ *noun Hist.* in India, Malaya, etc, a man who does washing. [from Hindi *dhobi*]

dhoti /ˈdoʊtɪ/ *noun* a garment worn by some Hindu men, consisting of a long strip of cloth wrapped around the waist and between the legs. [from Hindi *dhoti*]

dhow /daʊ/ *noun* a type of ship with one or more sails, used in countries around the Indian Ocean.

DI *abbrev. Medicine* donor insemination.

di- *prefix* two, twice, or double: *dicotyledon* / *dioxide*. [from Greek *dis*, twice]

diabetes /daɪəˈbiːtiːz/ *noun* any of various disorders, especially diabetes mellitus, that are characterized by thirst and excessive production of urine. [from Greek *diabetes*, siphon]

diabetic /daɪəˈbɛtɪk/ — *noun* a person suffering from diabetes. — *adj.* **1** relating to or suffering from diabetes. **2** *said of food, etc* intended for people who have diabetes.

diabolic /daɪəˈbɒlɪk/ *adj.* **1** of or like a devil; devilish. **2** very wicked or cruel. [from Greek *diabolos*, slanderer, devil]

diabolical /daɪəˈbɒlɪkəl/ *adj. Brit.* **1** of or like a devil; devilish. **2** *colloq.* very shocking, annoying, bad, etc.

> ▣ **1** devilish, fiendish, demonic, hellish, damnable, evil, infernal, wicked. **2** dreadful, awful, frightful, outrageous, shocking, disastrous, excruciating, atrocious, vile.

diabolically *adv.* **1** in a diabolical way; wickedly. **2** *colloq.* exceedingly; very: *it was diabolically funny.*

diabolism /daɪˈabəlɪzm/ *noun* the worship of the Devil or devils; witchcraft; black magic. [from Greek *diabolos*, devil + -ISM]

diachronic /daɪəˈkrɒnɪk/ *adj. Linguistics* concerned with the study of a language in terms of its origins and historical development: the opposite of *synchronic*.

diaconate /daɪˈakəneɪt/ *noun* **1** the position of deacon. **2** one's period of time as a deacon. **3** deacons as a group. [from Latin *diaconus*, deacon]

diacritic /daɪəˈkrɪtɪk/ — *noun* a mark written or printed over, under, or through a letter to show that that letter has a particular sound, as in *é, è, ç, ñ.* — *adj.* same as DIACRITICAL. [from Greek *diakritikos*, able to distinguish]

diacritical /daɪəˈkrɪtɪkəl/ *adj.* functioning as a diacritic; distinguishing.

diadem /ˈdaɪədɛm/ *noun* **1** a crown or jewelled headband, worn by a royal person. **2** royal power or authority. [from Old French *diademe*, from Greek *dia*, around + *deein*, to bind]

diaeresis /daɪˈɛrəsɪs/ *noun* (PL. **diaereses**) a mark (¨) placed over a vowel to show that it is to be pronounced separately from the vowel before it, as in *naïve*. [from Greek *diairesis*, separation]

diagenesis /daɪəˈdʒɛnəsɪs/ *noun Geol.* the physical and chemical processes whereby unconsolidated sediment is converted to solid rock.

diagnose /ˈdaɪəgnoʊz/ *verb* **1** to identify (a disease or disorder) provisionally on the basis of its symptoms and the patient's medical history. **2** to identify (a fault or problem).

> ▣ **2** identify, determine, recognize, pinpoint, distinguish, analyse, explain, isolate, interpret, investigate.

diagnosis /daɪəgˈnoʊsɪs/ *noun* (PL. **diagnoses**) **1** the process whereby a disease or disorder is provisionally identified on the basis of its symptoms and the patient's medical history. **2** *Biol.* in taxonomy, a formal description, eg of a plant, made on the basis of its distinguishing characteristics. **3** identification of problems in other areas, eg in mechanics and computing. [from Greek, from *diagignoskein*, to distinguish]

> ▣ **3** identification, explanation, interpretation, analysis, opinion, investigation, examination, scrutiny, conclusion, answer, verdict.

diagnostic /daɪəgˈnɒstɪk/ *adj.* relating to or useful in diagnosis.

diagonal /daɪˈagənəl/ — *noun Geom.* **1** a straight line joining any two non-adjacent vertices (corners) of a polygon, eg a line joining opposite vertices of a square. **2** a plane joining any two non-adjacent faces of a polyhedron. — *adj.* **1** denoting a straight line or a plane so drawn. **2** sloping or slanting. [from Greek *dia*, through + *gonia*, angle]

> ▣ *adj.* **2** oblique, slanting, cross, crosswise, sloping, crooked, angled.

diagonally *adv.* in a diagonal direction.

> ▣ obliquely, crosswise, at an angle, on the bias.

diagram *noun* a line drawing, often labelled with text, that does not show all the visible details of an object or process, but only the most important features of its structure, or the manner in which it functions. [from Greek *diagramma*, from *dia*, round + *graphein*, to write]

> ▣ plan, sketch, chart, drawing, figure, representation, schema, illustration, outline, graph, picture, layout, table.

diagrammatic /daɪəgrəˈmatɪk/ *adj.* having the form of a diagram; serving as a diagram.

diagrammatically *adv.* in the form of a diagram.

diakinesis /daɪəkɪˈniːsɪs/ *noun* during meiosis, the final stage of prophase, when the pairs of homologous chromosomes are almost completely separated from one another.

dial — *noun* **1** a disc or plate on a clock, radio, meter, etc with numbers or other scales or measurements marked on it and a movable pointer or indicator, used to indicate measurements of speed, time, etc or selected settings of time, temperature, radio frequency, etc. **2** the round numbered plate on some telephones and the movable disc fitted over it. — *verb trans., intrans.* (**dialled, dialling**) to use a telephone dial to call (a number). [from Latin *dialis*, daily]

. . . .

▣ *noun* **1** gauge, control, meter, indicator. **2** circle, disc, face, clock. *verb* phone, ring, call (up).

. . . .

dialect /ˈdaɪəlɛkt/ *noun* a form of a language spoken in a particular region or by a certain social group, differing from other forms in grammar, vocabulary, and in some cases pronunciation. [from Greek *dialektos*, manner of speech]

. . . .

▣ regional variant, idiom, language, patois, provincialism, vernacular, argot, jargon, accent, *colloq.* lingo, speech, diction.

. . . .

dialectal /daɪəˈlɛktəl/ *adj.* relating to or belonging to dialect: *dialectal forms of words.*

dialectic /daɪəˈlɛktɪk/ — *noun Philos.* **1** (*also* **dialectics**) the art or practice of establishing truth by discussion. **2** (*also* **dialectics**) a debate which aims to resolve the conflict between two opposing theories rather than to disprove either of them. **3** the art of reasoning and arguing logically. — *adj.* dialectical. [from Greek *dialektike* (*techne*), (the art) of debating]

. . . .

▣ *noun* **1** dialectics, debate, argumentation, disputation, contention, discussion, polemics. **3** logic, reasoning, analysis, deduction, induction.

. . . .

dialectical /daɪəˈlɛktɪkəl/ *adj. Philos.* of or by dialectic; depending on or proceeding by the resolving of the conflict between opposing factors, theories, etc.

. . . .

▣ logical, rational, argumentative, analytical, rationalistic, logistic, polemical, inductive, deductive.

. . . .

dialling code the part of a telephone number that represents a town or area.

dialogue /ˈdaɪəlɒg/ *noun* **1** a conversation, especially a formal one. **2** the words spoken by the characters in a play, book, etc. **3** a discussion or exchange of ideas and opinions, especially between two groups, with a view to resolving conflict or achieving agreement. [from Greek *dialogos*, conversation]

. . . .

▣ **1** conversation, talk, exchange, discussion, converse, debate, conference, interchange, discourse, communication. **2** lines, script, text.

. . . .

dialysis /daɪˈalɪsɪs/ *noun* (PL. **dialyses**) **1** *Chem.* the separation of particles of different sizes in a solution, based on the different rates at which the various substances diffuse through a semi-permeable membrane. **2** *Medicine* the removal of toxic substances from the blood by diffusion through a semi-permeable membrane in an artificial kidney machine, used in cases of kidney failure when a transplant is not available. Also called HAEMODIALYSIS. [from Greek *dialysis*, separation]

diamanté /dɪəˈmɒnteɪ/ — *adj., said of a fabric* decorated with small sparkling ornaments. — *noun* a diamanté fabric. [from French *diamanté*, decorated with diamonds]

diameter /daɪˈamɪtə(r)/ *noun Geom.* the length of a straight line drawn from one side of a circle to the other, and passing through its centre. It is equal to twice the radius of the circle. [from Greek *dia*, across + *metron*, measure]

diametric /daɪəˈmɛtrɪk/ or **diametrical** *adj.* **1** of or along a diameter. **2** *said of opinions, etc* directly opposed; very far apart.

. . . .

▣ **2** opposed, opposite, contrary, counter, contrasting.

diametrically *adv., said in relation to opposition* completely; utterly: *diametrically opposite opinions.*

diamond *noun* **1** a crystalline allotrope of carbon, colourless when pure, and the hardest known mineral, used as a gemstone. **2** a piece of this substance, used in cutting tools, etc. **3** (**diamonds**) one of the four suits of playing cards, with red symbols of this shape. **4** one of the playing cards of this suit. **5** a baseball pitch, or the part of it between the bases. [from Old French *diamant*, from Latin and Greek *adamas*, steel, diamond]

dianthus /daɪˈanθəs/ (PL. **dianthuses**) *noun* any of various herbaceous plants of the genus *Dianthus*, native to Europe and Asia, such as the carnation and pink. [from Latin *dianthus*, from Greek *Dios anthos*, Zeus's flower]

diapause /ˈdaɪəpɔːz/ *noun Zool.* in the life cycle of an insect, a period during which growth and development are arrested, often until environmental conditions become more favourable. [from Greek *diapausis*, pause]

diaper /ˈdaɪəpə(r)/ *noun* **1** a type of linen or cotton cloth with a pattern of small diamond or square shapes. **2** *North Amer.* a baby's nappy. [from Old French *diaspre*]

diaphanous /daɪˈafənəs/ *adj., said of cloth* light and fine, and almost transparent. [from Greek *dia*, through + *phanein*, to show]

. . . .

▣ sheer, fine, translucent, see-through, flimsy, gauzy.

. . . .

diaphragm /ˈdaɪəfram/ *noun* **1** *Anat.* in mammals, the sheet of muscle that separates the thorax (chest) from the abdomen. It is lowered during inhalation, when the lungs are filled with air, and raised during exhalation, when air is expelled from the lungs. **2** *Optics* an opaque disc, with a central aperture of adjustable diameter, that is used to control the amount of light entering an optical instrument such as a camera or microscope. **3** a thin vibrating disc or cone that converts sound waves to electrical signals in a microphone, or electrical signals to sound waves in a loudspeaker. **4** a contraceptive device consisting of a soft plastic or rubber cap that is fitted over the neck of the uterus before intercourse to prevent the entry of sperm. Also called DUTCH CAP. [from Greek *diaphragma*, partition]

diarist /ˈdaɪərɪst/ *noun* a person who writes a diary, especially one which is published.

diarrhoea or **diarrhea** /daɪəˈrɪə/ *noun* an intestinal disorder characterized by the frequent discharge of abnormally liquid faeces, caused by food poisoning, inflammation of the intestine, etc, or occurring as a symptom of various diseases, eg dysentery. [from Greek *dia*, through + *rhoia*, flow]

diary *noun* (PL. **diaries**) **1** a written record of daily events in a person's life, or a book containing this. **2** *Brit.* a book with separate spaces or pages for each day of the year in which appointments, daily notes, and reminders may be written. [from Latin *diarium*, from *dies*, day]

. . . .

▣ **1** journal, daybook, logbook, chronicle, yearbook. **2** appointment book, engagement book.

. . . .

Diaspora /daɪˈaspərə/ *noun* (**the Diaspora**) **1** the scattering of the Jewish people to various countries following their exile in Babylon in the 6c BC. **2** the new communities of Jews which arose in various countries as a result. **3** the Jews who do not live in the modern state of Israel. [from Greek *dia*, through + *speirein*, to scatter]

diastase /ˈdaɪəsteɪz/ see AMYLASE. [from Greek *diastasis*, division]

diastole /daɪˈastəlɪ/ *noun Physiol.* the period between two successive contractions of the heart, during which the heart muscles relax, allowing the ventricles to fill with blood. See also SYSTOLE. [from Greek *dia*, apart + *stellein*, to place]

diastolic /daɪəˈstɒlɪk/ *adj. Medicine* **1** relating to the phase of the heartbeat when the heart muscles relax and the ventricles fill with blood. **2** denoting the blood pressure measured during this phase of the heartbeat.

diatom /'daɪətɒm/ *noun* the common name for a member of the division Bacillariophyta, a group of microscopic one-celled algae found in vast numbers in plankton. Their characteristic ornately marked shells are strengthened with silica, and fit together like the two halves of a box. [from Greek *diatomos*, cut through]

diatomic /daɪə'tɒmɪk/ *adj. Chem.* denoting a molecule that consists of two identical atoms, eg O_2, H_2.

diatomite /daɪ'atəmaɪt/ *noun Geol.* kieselguhr. [from Greek *diatomos*, cut through]

diatonic /daɪə'tɒnɪk/ *adj. Mus.*, *said of a scale, etc* consisting of or involving only the basic notes proper to a particular key, with no additional sharps, flats or naturals. See also CHROMATIC. [from Greek *dia*, through + *tonos*, tone]

diatonicism /daɪə'tɒnɪsɪzm/ *noun* an attribute of a piece or section of music which uses, either exclusively or predominantly, notes belonging to a major or minor scale. See also CHROMATICISM.

diatribe /'daɪətraɪb/ *noun* a bitter or abusive critical attack in speech or writing. [from Greek *diatribe*, discourse]

⊟ tirade, invective, harangue, attack, onslaught, denunciation, criticism, insult.
⊞ praise, eulogy.

diazepam /daɪ'azəpam/ *noun Psychol.* a tranquillizing drug, sold under the trade name Valium, which relieves anxiety and also acts as a muscle relaxant. [from DI- + *azo-* denoting nitrogen + *ep-* as in EPOXY]

diazo compound /daɪ'azoʊ/ *Chem.* any of various organic compounds containing two adjacent nitrogen atoms, only one of which is attached to a carbon atom. Diazo compounds are used in the manufacture of many dyes and drugs.

dibasic /daɪ'beɪsɪk/ *adj. Chem.* denoting an acid that contains two replaceable hydrogen atoms, eg sulphuric acid (H_2SO_4).

dibble or **dibber** *noun* a short pointed hand-tool used for making holes in the ground for seeds, young plants, etc.

dice — *noun* (PL. **dice**) **1** a small cube with a different number of spots, from 1 to 6, on each of its sides or faces, used in certain games of chance. **2** a game of chance played with one or more dice. See also DIE[2]. — *verb* **1** to cut (vegetables, etc) into small cubes. **2** *intrans.* to play or gamble with dice. — **dice with death** to take a great risk. **no dice** *colloq.* used to indicate a negative answer or unsuccessful outcome. [originally the plural of DIE[2]]

dicey *adj.* (**dicier, diciest**) *colloq.* involving risk, danger or uncertainty.

⊟ risky, chancy, unpredictable, tricky, problematic, dangerous, difficult, *colloq.* iffy, dubious.
⊞ certain.

dichotomous /daɪ'kɒtəməs/ *adj.* divided into two parts; involving division into two parts.

dichotomy /daɪ'kɒtəmɪ/ *noun* (PL. **dichotomies**) a division or separation into two groups or parts, especially when these are sharply opposed or contrasted. [from Greek *dicha*, in two + *tome*, cut]

dichroism /'daɪkroʊɪzm/ *noun Physics* a property of some crystals, that reflect certain colours when viewed from one angle, and different colours when viewed from another angle. [from Greek *dichroos*, two-coloured]

dick *noun* **1** *coarse slang* the penis. **2** *slang* a detective. [from the name *Dick*]

dickens *noun colloq.* (**the dickens**) the devil, used especially for emphasis. [from the name *Dickon* or *Dicken*, from *Richard*]

Dickensian /dɪ'kɛnzɪən/ *adj.* resembling the 19c English social life depicted in the novels of Charles Dickens, especially the poor living and working conditions or the odd and often grotesque characters described.

dicker *verb intrans.* to argue about the price or cost of something.

dicky[1] or **dickie** or **dickey** *noun* (PL. **dickies, dickeys**) a false shirt front, especially when worn with evening dress.

dicky[2] *adj.* (**dickier, dickiest**) *colloq.* not in good condition.

dicky-bird *noun* a child's word for a small bird. [from the name *Dicky*, for *Richard*]

dicotyledon /daɪkɒtɪ'liːdən/ *noun Bot.* a flowering plant with an embryo that has two cotyledons (seed leaves), leaf veins arranged in a network, a ring of vascular bundles in the stem, and flower parts arranged in multiples of two or five, eg potato, rose.

dicta see DICTUM.

Dictaphone /'dɪktəfoʊn/ *noun trademark* a small tape-recorder for use especially when dictating letters.

dictate /dɪk'teɪt, 'dɪkteɪt/ — *verb* (with stress on -*tate*) *trans., intrans.* to say or read out (something) for someone else to write down. **2** to state or lay down (rules, terms, etc) forcefully or with authority. **3** (**dictate to someone**) *derog.* to give orders to or try to impose one's wishes on them. — *noun* (with stress on *dict-*) (*usually* **dictates**) **1** an order or instruction. **2** a guiding principle. [from Latin *dictare*]

⊟ *verb* **2** lay down, command, order, decree, decide, determine, direct. **3** dominate, rule, lay down the law to.
noun **1** order, command, decree, injunction, edict, ruling, ultimatum. **2** principle, rule, law, precept, requirement.

dictation /dɪk'teɪʃən/ *noun* **1** something read for another to write down. **2** the act of dictating.

dictator /dɪk'teɪtə(r)/ *noun* **1** a ruler with complete and unrestricted power. **2** a person who behaves in a dictatorial manner. **3** in ancient Rome, a person given complete authority in the state for a period of six months at a time of crisis.

⊟ **1, 2** despot, autocrat, tyrant, *colloq.* supremo, Big Brother.

dictatorial /dɪktə'tɔːrɪəl/ *adj.* of, like, or suggesting a dictator; fond of using one's power and authority and imposing one's wishes on or giving orders to other people.

⊟ tyrannical, despotic, totalitarian, authoritarian, autocratic, oppressive, imperious, domineering, *colloq.* bossy, absolute, repressive, overbearing, arbitrary, dogmatic.
⊞ democratic, egalitarian, liberal.

dictatorially *adv.* with a dictatorial or authoritarian manner.

dictatorship *noun* the status or position of a dictator.

diction *noun* **1** the way in which one speaks. **2** one's choice or use of words to express meaning. [from Latin *dicere*, to say]

⊟ **1** speech, articulation, language, elocution, enunciation, intonation, pronunciation, inflection, fluency, delivery, expression, phrasing.

dictionary /'dɪkʃənərɪ/ *noun* (PL. **dictionaries**) **1** a book containing the words of a language arranged alphabetically with their meanings. **2** an alphabetically arranged book of information. [from Latin *dictionarium*]

⊟ **1** lexicon, glossary, thesaurus, vocabulary, wordbook. **2** encyclopedia, concordance.

dictum *noun* (PL. **dictums, dicta**) **1** a formal or authoritative statement of opinion. **2** a popular saying or maxim. [from Latin *dictum*]

⊟ **1** pronouncement, ruling, decree, dictate, command, order, utterance, edict, fiat, precept. **2** saying, maxim, axiom, adage, proverb.

did see DO[1].

didactic /daɪˈdaktɪk/ *adj.* **1** intended to teach or instruct. **2** *derog.* too eager or too obviously intended to instruct, in a way resented by the reader, listener, etc. [from Greek *didaskein*, to teach]

▣ **1** instructive, educational, educative, pedagogic, prescriptive. **2** pedantic, moralizing, heavy-handed.

didactically *adv.* with a didactic or instructive manner.

didacticism /daɪˈdaktɪsɪzm/ *noun* didactic or instructive principles.

diddle *verb colloq.* to cheat or swindle. [probably from Jeremy *Diddler*, character in a 19c play]

diddler *noun colloq.* a cheat or swindler.

didgeridoo /dɪdʒərɪˈduː/ *noun* an Australian Aborigine wind instrument, consisting of a long wooden or bamboo tube which when blown into produces a low droning sound. [from an Australian Aboriginal language]

didn't *contr.* did not.

die [1] *verb intrans.* (**died, dying**) **1** to stop living; to cease to be alive. **2** to cease to exist, come to an end, or fade away. **3** *said of an engine, etc* to stop working suddenly and unexpectedly. **4** (**die of something**) to suffer or be overcome by the effects of it: *die of boredom.* — **be dying for something** or **to do something** *colloq.* to have a strong desire or need for it or to do it. **die away 1** to fade away from sight or hearing until gone. **2** to become steadily weaker and finally stop. **die back** *said of a plant's soft shoots* to die or wither from the tip back to the hard wood. **die down 1** to lose strength or force. **2** *said of a plant or its soft shoots* to wither back to the root without completely dying. **die hard** to be difficult to change or remove. **die off** to die one after another. **die out** to cease to exist anywhere; to become extinct. **never say die** never give up or give in. [from Middle English *dien*, from Norse *deyja*]

▣ **1** decease, perish, pass away, expire, depart, breathe one's last, *colloq.* peg out, *slang* snuff it, *colloq.* bite the dust, *slang* flatline, *slang* kick the bucket. **2** finish, end, lapse, disappear, vanish, decay. **3** stall, *slang* conk out. **be dying for** long for, pine for, yearn for, desire. **die away** FADE. **2** dwindle, ebb, sink, wane, wilt, wither, peter out. **die down 1** decline, subside, moderate, abate, diminish, quieten (down), slacken (off). **die out** disappear, vanish, perish.

◨ **1** live.

die [2] *noun* (PL. **dies** in sense 1, **dice** in sense 2) **1** a metal tool or stamp for cutting or shaping metal or making designs on coins, etc. **2** a dice. — **the die is cast** a decision has been made or an action taken which cannot be changed or gone back on. **straight as a die 1** completely straight. **2** completely honest. [from Old French *de*, from Latin *datum*, something given]

dieback *noun Bot.* the progressive death of the parts of a plant, starting at the tips of the shoots and progressing backwards to the main branches or stems.

die casting 1 *Engineering* a form of casting in which molten metal is forced under pressure into cooled *dies* (metal moulds), usually in order to produce large numbers of small items of a particular shape. **2** an object made in this way.

diehard *noun* a person who stubbornly refuses to accept new ideas or changes.

▣ reactionary, intransigent, hardliner, ultra-conservative, blimp, old fogey, *colloq.* stick-in-the-mud, rightist, fanatic.

dielectric *Physics* — *noun* a non-conducting material whose molecules align or polarize under the influence of applied electric fields. Dielectrics are an essential component of capacitors. — *adj.* denoting such a material.

dieresis /daɪˈɛrəsɪs/ *North Amer., esp. US* same as DIAERESIS.

diesel *noun* **1** diesel oil. **2** a diesel engine. **3** a train, etc driven by a diesel engine. [named after the 19c German engineer Rudolf *Diesel*]

diesel engine a type of internal combustion engine in which air in the cylinder is compressed until it reaches a sufficiently high temperature to ignite the fuel.

diesel fuel or **oil** a type of liquid fuel, composed mainly of hydrocarbons derived from petroleum, that is designed for use in a diesel engine.

diet [1] — *noun* **1** the food and drink habitually consumed by a person or animal. **2** a planned or prescribed selection of food and drink, especially one designed for weight loss, maintenance of good health, or the control of a medical disorder. **3** (*attributive*) denoting a food or drink, often with a brand name, that contains less sugar than the standard version. — *verb intrans.* (**dieted, dieting**) to restrict the quantity or type of food that one eats, especially in order to lose weight. [from Old French *diete*, from Greek *diaita*, way of life]

▣ *noun* **1** food, nutrition, provisions, sustenance, rations, foodstuffs, subsistence. **2** fast, abstinence, regimen. *verb* lose weight, slim, fast, reduce, abstain.

diet [2] *noun* **1** the legislative assembly of certain countries, eg Japan. **2** *Hist.* a conference held to discuss political or church affairs. [from Latin *dieta*, public assembly, from Greek *diaita*, way of life]

dietary /ˈdaɪətərɪ/ *adj.* of or concerning a diet.

dietary fibre indigestible plant material, found in unrefined carbohydrate foods such as wholemeal bread and cereals, fruit and vegetables, which keeps bowel movements regular. Also called ROUGHAGE.

dieter /ˈdaɪətə(r)/ *noun* a person who diets or is dieting.

dietetic /daɪəˈtɛtɪk/ *adj.* **1** relating to diet. **2** denoting food that has been processed or prepared so as to meet specific dietary requirements.

dietetics *sing. noun* the scientific study of diet, especially with regard to the regulation of food intake and methods of preparation so as to promote health and reduce the likelihood of disease.

dietician or **dietitian** /daɪəˈtɪʃən/ *noun* a scientist who specializes in dietetics, especially the application of the principles of nutrition to the regulation of food intake.

differ *verb intrans.* (**differed, differing**) **1** *said of two or more people or things* to be different or unlike each other in some way. **2** (**differ from something**) to be different from it or unlike it. **3** (**differ with someone**) to disagree with them. [from Old French *differer*]

▣ **1** vary, contrast, clash. **2** diverge from, deviate from, depart from, contradict, contrast with. **3** disagree with, argue with, conflict with, oppose, dissent from, be at odds with, clash with, quarrel with, fall out with, debate with, take issue with.

◨ **2** conform to. **3** agree with.

difference *noun* **1** what makes one thing or person unlike another. **2** the state of being unlike. **3** a change from an earlier state, etc. **4** the amount by which one quantity or number is greater or less than another. **5** a quarrel or disagreement. — **make a** or **no, etc difference** to have some or no, etc effect on a situation. [from Latin *differentia*]

▣ **1, 2** dissimilarity, variation, contrast, disparity. **1** discrepancy, divergence, distinction. **2** unlikeness, diversity, variety, distinctness, deviation, differentiation, singularity, exception. **3** change, alteration, transformation, variation, fluctuation. **4** remainder, rest. **5** quarrel, disagreement, clash, dispute, conflict, contention, controversy.

◨ **1, 2** similarity. **5** agreement.

different *adj.* **1** (**different from** or **to something** or **someone**) not the same; unlike. **2** separate; distinct; various. **3** *colloq.* unusual.

....

◫ **1** dissimilar to, unlike, contrasting with, divergent from, inconsistent with, deviating from, at odds with, clashing with, opposed to. **2** separate, distinct, individual, detached, varied, various, diverse, miscellaneous, assorted, disparate, many, numerous, several, sundry, other. **3** unusual, unconventional, unique, distinctive, extraordinary, individual, original, special, strange, peculiar, rare, bizarre, anomalous.

▣ **1** similar to, the same as. **3** conventional.
....

differential /dɪfəˈrenʃəl/ — *adj.* **1** of, showing or based on a difference. **2** *Maths.* an infinitesimal change in the value of one or more variables as a result of a similarly small change in another variable or variables. — *noun* **1** (*in full* **wage differential**) a difference in the rate of pay between one category of worker and another in the same industry or company. **2** a differential gear. [from Latin *differentialis*]

differential calculus a procedure for calculating the rate of change of one variable quantity produced by changes in another variable. It employs *differentiation* to determine rates of change, gradients of curves, maximum and minimum values, etc.

differential coefficient *Maths.* the ratio of the rate of change of a function to that of its independent variable.

differential gear an arrangement of gears that allows the wheels on either side of a vehicle to rotate at different speeds (the outer wheels rotating more rapidly) when the vehicle is being driven round a corner.

differentiate /dɪfəˈrenʃɪeɪt/ *verb* **1** *intrans., trans.* (**differentiate between things**, or **one thing from another**) to establish a difference between them; to be able to distinguish one from another. **2** to constitute a difference between (things) or in (one thing as against another): *the shape of its mouth differentiates a crocodile from an alligator.* **3** (**differentiate between people**) to treat one person, etc differently from another. **4** to become different. **5** *Maths.* to use the process of differentiation to calculate the changes in one variable quantity produced by changes in a related variable, ie to find the *derivative* of a function *f*. **6** *Biol.*, *said of an unspecialized cell or tissue* to become increasingly specialized in structure and function, eg during the development of a muscle fibre or a red blood cell. [from Latin *differentiare*]

....

◫ **1** distinguish between, tell apart, discriminate between, contrast, make a distinction between. **2** separate, mark off, individualize, particularize. **3** discriminate between, make a distinction between, segregate, separate.

....

differentiation *noun* **1** the process of differentiating. **2** *Maths.* a method used in calculus to calculate the rate of change of one variable quantity produced by changes in a related variable. **3** *Biol.* the process whereby unspecialized precursor cells or tissues develop into cells or tissues that have a highly specialized structure and function, eg the development of embryonic tissue into muscle cells, neurones (nerve cells), etc. **4** a change by which what is generalized or homogeneous becomes specialized or heterogeneous.

differently *adv.* in a different way.

difficult *adj.* **1** requiring great skill, intelligence, or effort. **2** *said of a person* not easy to please; awkward, uncooperative. **3** *said of a problem, situation, etc* potentially embarrassing; hard to resolve or get out of. [from Latin *difficultas*, difficulty]

....

◫ **1** hard, laborious, demanding, arduous, strenuous, tough, wearisome, uphill, formidable, complex, complicated, intricate, involved, abstruse, obscure, dark, knotty, thorny, problematical, perplexing, baffling, intractable. **2** awkward,

unmanageable, perverse, troublesome, trying, unco-operative, tiresome, stubborn, obstinate, intractable. **3** awkward, tricky, ticklish, delicate, embarrassing.

▣ **1** easy, straightforward. **2** manageable, easy-going.
....

difficulty *noun* (PL. **difficulties**) **1** the state or quality of being difficult. **2** a difficult thing to do or understand. **3** a problem, obstacle, or objection. **4** (*usually* **difficulties**) trouble or embarrassment, especially financial. **5** the effort, labour or trouble involved in doing something.

....

◫ **1** hardness, toughness, laboriousness, arduousness, painfulness, awkwardness, complexity, intricacy, intractability, thorniness. **2** problem, trial. **3** problem, complication, *colloq.* hiccup, gremlin, obstacle, hindrance, hurdle, pitfall, impediment, stumbling-block, objection, opposition. **4** problem, predicament, dilemma, quandary, perplexity, embarrassment, plight, distress, *colloq.* fix, mess, *colloq.* jam, *colloq.* spot. **5** trouble, labour, effort, stress, strain.

▣ **1** ease.
....

diffidence *noun* being diffident or shy; lack of confidence.

....

◫ unassertiveness, modesty, shyness, self-consciousness, self-effacement, timidity, insecurity, reserve, bashfulness, humility, inhibition, meekness, self-distrust, self-doubt, hesitancy, reluctance, backwardness.

▣ confidence.
....

diffident *adj.* lacking in confidence; too modest or shy. [from Latin *diffidere*, to distrust]

....

◫ unassertive, modest, shy, timid, self-conscious, self-effacing, insecure, bashful, abashed, meek, reserved, withdrawn, tentative, shrinking, inhibited, hesitant, reluctant, unsure, shamefaced.

▣ assertive, confident.
....

diffidently *adv.* with a diffident or shy manner.

diffract *verb* *Physics* **1** to cause (waves) to undergo diffraction. **2** *said of waves* to undergo diffraction. [from Latin *diffringere*, to shatter]

diffraction *noun* *Physics* the spreading out of waves (eg light or sound waves) as they emerge from a small opening or slit. Diffraction causes the bending of a beam of light around an obstruction.

diffraction grating *Physics* a device that contains many hundreds of slits per centimetre, and can be used to divide a light beam into its component colours, the pattern produced being known as a spectrum.

diffractive *adj.* causing diffraction.

diffuse /dɪˈfjuːz, -ˈfjuːs/ — *verb* (pronounced -ˈfjuːz) *trans., intrans.* to spread or send out in all directions. — *adj.* (pronounced -ˈfjuːs) **1** widely spread; not concentrated. **2** *said of a style of writing or speaking* using too many words; not concise. [from Latin *diffundere*, to pour out in various directions]

....

◫ *verb* spread, scatter, disperse, distribute, propagate, dispense, disseminate, circulate, dissipate. *adj.* **1** scattered, unconcentrated, diffused, dispersed, disconnected. **2** verbose, imprecise, wordy, rambling, long-winded, prolix, waffling, vague, discursive.

▣ *verb* concentrate. *adj.* **1** concentrated. **2** succinct.
....

diffused *adj.* widely spread; dispersed.

diffusely *adv.* in a diffuse or widely spread way.

diffuseness *noun* being diffuse or widely spread.

diffusion /dɪˈfjuːʒən/ *noun* **1** the act of diffusing or state of being diffused. **2** *Physics* the process whereby a fluid (a liquid or gas) gradually and spontaneously disperses from a region of high concentration to one of low concentration, as a result of the random movements of its constituent atoms, molecules, or ions.

dig — *verb* (**digging**; PAST TENSE AND PAST PARTICIPLE **dug**) 1 *trans., intrans.* to turn up or move (earth, etc), especially with a spade. 2 to make (a hole, etc) by digging. 3 *trans., intrans.* to poke. 4 *old slang use* to appreciate. 5 *trans., intrans. old slang use* to understand. — *noun* 1 a remark intended to irritate, criticize, or make fun of. 2 a place where archaeologists are digging, eg to uncover ancient ruins. 3 a poke. 4 an act of digging. — **dig in** 1 *colloq.* to start to eat. 2 to make a protected place for oneself. **dig something in** to mix it into the soil, etc by digging. **dig into something** 1 *colloq.* to start eating a meal, etc. 2 to examine or search through it for information. **dig in one's heels** to refuse to change one's mind. **dig one's own grave** to be the cause of one's own failure or downfall. **dig something or someone out** 1 to get them out by digging. 2 *colloq.* to find them by extensive searching. **dig something up** 1 to remove it from the ground by digging. 2 to find or reveal something buried or hidden by digging. 3 *colloq.* to search for and find information, etc. [from Middle English *dig-gen*]

⊟ *verb* **1, 2** excavate, burrow, quarry, mine, tunnel. **1** till. **2** gouge (out), scoop (out). **3** poke, prod. *noun* **1** gibe, jeer, sneer, taunt, crack, insinuation, insult, wisecrack. **dig into 2** investigate, probe, go into, research, search. **dig out 2** unearth, discover, uncover, disinter, find, retrieve, track down. **dig up 2, 3** discover, unearth, uncover, disinter, expose. **2** exhume.
⊟ *noun* **1** compliment. **dig up 2** bury, obscure.

digest¹ /daɪˈdʒɛst/ *verb trans., intrans.* to subject (food) to the process of digestion in the alimentary canal (stomach and intestines). See DIGESTION. 2 *Chem.* to soften by means of heat or moisture. 3 to hear and consider the meaning and implications of (information). [from Latin *digerere*, to dissolve]

⊟ **1** absorb, assimilate, incorporate, process, dissolve. **3** take in, absorb, understand, assimilate, grasp, study, consider, contemplate, meditate, ponder.

digest² /ˈdaɪdʒɛst/ *noun* 1 a usually regularly published collection of summaries or shortened versions (of news stories or current literature). 2 a summary or shortened version. 3 a systematically arranged collection of laws. [from Latin *digerere*, to arrange]

⊟ **2** summary, abridgement, abstract, précis, synopsis, résumé, reduction, abbreviation, compression, compendium.

digestible *adj.* able to be digested.

digestion /dɪˈdʒɛstʃən/ *noun* 1 the process whereby complex substances in food are broken down into simpler soluble compounds by enzymes, usually in the alimentary canal (stomach and intestines). 2 the process of absorbing information, etc.

digestive — *adj.* of or for digestion. — *noun Brit.* (*also* **digestive biscuit**) a type of plain slightly sweetened biscuit made from wholemeal flour.

digger *noun* 1 a machine used for digging and excavating. 2 a person who digs, especially a gold-miner. 3 *colloq.* an Australian or New Zealander, especially a soldier.

diggings *pl. noun* 1 a place where people dig, especially for gold or precious stones. 2 *Brit. old colloq. use* lodgings. See also DIGS.

digit *noun* 1 any numerical character used to represent a single number, especially one of the ten Arabic numerals 0 to 9, or either of the two binary numerals 0 and 1. 2 *Zool.* a finger or toe. Most digitate vertebrates have five digits on each limb. [from Latin *digitus*, finger, toe]

digital *adj.* 1 showing numerical information in the form of a set of digits, rather than by means of a pointer on a dial: *a digital watch.* 2 denoting a process or a device that operates by processing information that is supplied and stored in the form of a series of binary digits, eg digital recording, digital computer. 3 denoting an electronic circuit that responds to and produces signals which at any given time are in one of two possible states. 4 of or involving digits in any way. See also ANALOGUE.

digital/analog converter *Comput.* a device that converts digital signals into analog (continuously varying) signals for use by an analog computer.

digital audio tape *Electron.* (ABBREV. DAT) 1 a magnetic audio tape on which sound has been recorded after it has been converted into a digital code. 2 this form of recorded sound, affording greater clarity and compactness, and less distortion than conventional recording.

digitalis /dɪdʒɪˈteɪlɪs/ *noun* 1 *Bot.* any plant of the genus *Digitalis*, eg the purple foxglove (*D. purpurea*). 2 *Medicine* an extract from the dried leaves of the foxglove (genus *Digitalis*) that stimulates the heart muscle by increasing contractions of the heart. [from the Latin genus name of the foxglove]

digital television or **TV** 1 a television system by which signals are transmitted in digital form and decoded by a special receiver. 2 a television set which receives and decodes digital signals.

digitization or **digitisation** *noun* the conversion of data into a digital form for processing by a (usually digital) computer.

digitize or **digitise** *verb* to convert data into binary form, ie into a form that uses only the digits 0 and 1.

digitizer or **digitiser** *noun Comput.* a device that converts data into a digital form.

dignified *adj.* stately, serious, or showing dignity.

⊟ stately, solemn, imposing, majestic, noble, august, lordly, lofty, exalted, formal, distinguished, serious, grave, impressive, reserved, honourable.
⊟ undignified, lowly.

dignify *verb* (**dignifies, dignified**) 1 to make (something) impressive or dignified. 2 to make (something) seem more important or impressive than it is. [from Latin *dignus*, worthy + *facere*, to make]

dignitary *noun* (PL. **dignitaries**) a person of high rank or position, especially in public life. [from DIGNITY]

⊟ worthy, notable, *colloq.* VIP, high-up, personage, *colloq.* bigwig, grandee.

dignity *noun* 1 stateliness, seriousness, and formality of manner and appearance. 2 goodness and nobility of character. 3 calmness and self-control. 4 consciousness of one's own worth and status. 5 high rank or position. — **beneath one's dignity** not worthy of one's attention or time, etc. **stand on one's dignity** to demand to be treated with proper respect. [from Latin *dignitas*, from *dignus*, worthy]

⊟ **1** stateliness, grandeur, loftiness, majesty, solemnity, gravity, gravitas, seriousness, formality, courtliness, decorum. **2** nobility, nobleness, honour, worthiness, respectability. **3** calm, calmness, composure, self-control, self-discipline, self-possession, poise. **4** self-respect, self-esteem, self-worth, pride. **5** importance, status, standing, eminence, greatness.

digraph /ˈdaɪɡrɑːf/ *noun* a pair of letters that represent a single sound, as in the *ph* of *digraph*. [from Greek *di-*, twice + *graphe*, mark, character]

digress /daɪˈɡrɛs/ *verb intrans.* to wander from the point, or from the main subject in speaking or writing. [from Latin *digredi*, to move away]

▣ diverge, deviate, stray, wander, go off at a tangent, drift, depart, ramble, waffle.

digression *noun* departure from the main subject of discussion, etc.

digs *pl. noun Brit. colloq.* lodgings. See also DIGGINGS.

dihedral /daɪˈhiːdrəl/ *Geom.* — *noun* the angle formed by two intersecting planes, eg the angle between two faces of a polyhedron. Also called DIHEDRON. — *adj.* **1** relating to such an angle. **2** formed or bounded by two intersecting planes. [from Greek *di-*, twice + *hedra*, seat]

dike see DYKE.

diktat /ˈdɪktat/ *noun* **1** a forceful, sometimes unreasonable, order which must be obeyed. **2** a harsh settlement forced on the defeated or powerless. [from German *diktat*, something dictated]

dilapidated /dɪˈlapɪdeɪtɪd/ *adj.*, *said of furniture, buildings, etc* falling to pieces because of neglect or age; in great need of repair. [from Latin *dilapidare*, to demolish]

▣ ramshackle, shabby, broken-down, neglected, tumbledown, uncared-for, rickety, decrepit, crumbling, run-down, worn out, ruined, decayed, decaying.

dilapidation /dɪlapɪˈdeɪʃən/ *noun* a state or process of disrepair or ruin.

dilatation /daɪləˈteɪʃən/ or **dilation** /daɪˈleɪʃən/ *noun* dilating; becoming larger.

dilatation and curettage (ABBREV. **D and C**) *Medicine* a gynaecological operation, usually performed to remove small tumours or to obtain specimens of tissue in order to diagnose various disorders.

dilate /daɪˈleɪt/ *verb* **1** to widen, enlarge, or stretch (a body cavity, opening, or tubular structure such as a blood vessel, etc). **2** *said of a body cavity, opening, or tubular structure such as a blood vessel, etc* to widen, enlarge, or stretch. **3** *said of the cervix of the uterus* to stretch beyond its normal size during childbirth. **4** *intrans. formal* (**dilate on something**) to speak or write at great length about it. [from Latin *dilatare*, to spread out]

▣ **1, 2** distend, enlarge, expand, spread, broaden, widen, increase, extend, stretch, swell. **4** expatiate on, expand on.
▣ **1, 2** contract.

dilatorily /ˈdɪlətrɪlɪ/ *adv.* in a dilatory or delaying way.
dilatoriness /ˈdɪlətrɪnəs/ *noun* being dilatory; delaying.
dilatory /ˈdɪlətərɪ/ *adj.* slow in doing things; inclined to or causing delay. [from Latin *dilatorius*]

▣ delaying, procrastinating, slow, tardy, tarrying, sluggish, lingering, lackadaisical, slack.
▣ prompt.

dildo /ˈdɪldoʊ/ *noun* (PL. **dildos**) an object shaped like an erect penis, used for sexual pleasure.

dilemma /dɪˈlɛmə, daɪˈlɛmə/ *noun* **1** a situation in which one must choose between two (or more than two) courses of action, both (or all) equally undesirable. **2** *colloq.* a problem or difficult situation. [from Greek *di-*, twice + *lemma*, assumption]

▣ QUANDARY, PREDICAMENT. **1** catch-22, conflict. **2** problem, difficulty, puzzle, embarrassment, perplexity, plight.

dilettante /dɪləˈtantɪ/ *noun* (PL. **dilettantes**, **dilettanti**) *often derog.* a person who has an interest in a subject, especially art, literature, or science, but does not study it very seriously or in depth. [from Italian *dilettante*, from *dilettare*, to delight]

▣ dabbler, amateur, trifler.
▣ expert, connoisseur, practitioner.

dilettantism *noun* superficial interest in a subject, especially in the arts.

diligence *noun* careful and hard-working effort.

▣ industriousness, conscientiousness, assiduity, care, carefulness, pains, tirelessness, perseverance.

diligent *adj.* **1** hard-working and careful. **2** showing or done with care and serious effort. [from Latin *diligens*, careful]

▣ CONSCIENTIOUS, PAINSTAKING, CAREFUL, METICULOUS. **1** assiduous, industrious, hard-working, busy, attentive, tireless, persevering, persistent, studious.
▣ NEGLIGENT. **1** lazy.

diligently *adv.* in a diligent or hard-working way.

dill *noun* **1** a small aromatic annual plant (*Anethum graveolens*), native to S Europe and W Asia, having feathery leaves divided into narrow linear lobes, and yellow flowers borne in flat-topped clusters. **2** the dark brown aromatic fruit of this plant, either intact or ground to a powder, used as a food flavouring. **3** the aromatic leaves of this plant, used as a food flavouring. [from Anglo-Saxon *dile*]

dilly-dally *verb intrans.* (**dilly-dallies, dilly-dallied**) *colloq.* **1** to be slow or waste time. **2** to be unable to make up one's mind. [from DALLY]

▣ **1** delay, dally, dawdle, *colloq.* hang about, loiter, linger, lag.

diluent /ˈdɪljʊənt/ *noun Chem.* any solvent that is used to dilute a solution.

dilute /daɪˈljuːt/ — *verb* **1** to decrease the concentration of a solute (dissolved substance) in a solution by adding more solvent, especially water. **2** to reduce the strength, influence, or effect of (something). — *adj. Chem.*, *said of a solution* containing a relatively small amount of solute (dissolved substance) compared to the amount of solvent present. [from Latin *diluere*, to wash away]

▣ *verb* WEAKEN, WATER DOWN, ATTENUATE. **1** adulterate, thin (out). **2** diffuse, diminish, decrease, lessen, reduce, temper, mitigate.
▣ *verb* CONCENTRATE.

dilution *noun* making a liquid thinner or weaker.

diluvial /dɪˈluːvɪəl/ or **diluvian** /-vɪən/ *adj.* **1** relating to a flood, especially the flood mentioned in the Book of Genesis in the Bible. **2** caused by a flood. [from Latin *diluvium*, flood]

dim — *adj.* (**dimmed, dimming**) **1** not bright or distinct. **2** lacking enough light to see clearly. **3** faint; not clearly remembered: *a dim memory*. **4** *colloq.* not very intelligent. **5** *said of eyes* not able to see well. **6** *colloq.* not good; not hopeful: *dim prospects*. — *verb trans., intrans.* (**dimmed, dimming**) to make or become dim. — **take a dim view of something** *colloq.* to disapprove of it. [from Anglo-Saxon *dimm*]

▣ *adj.* **1, 2** dark, shadowy, dull. **1** indistinct, blurred, hazy, ill-defined, obscure, misty, unclear, foggy, fuzzy, vague, faint, dingy, lacklustre. **2** dusky, cloudy, gloomy, sombre. **3** vague, faint, hazy, misty. **4** unintelligent, dim-witted, dense, obtuse, dull, stupid, *colloq.* thick, doltish. **5** feeble, imperfect, weak. *verb* darken, dull, cloud, blur, fade, tarnish.
▣ *adj.* **1** bright, distinct. **2, 3** clear. **4** bright, intelligent. *verb* brighten, illuminate.

dime *noun* a coin of the USA and Canada worth ten cents or one tenth of a dollar. [from Old French *disme*, from Latin *decima*, tenth]

dime novel *North Amer.* a cheap popular novel.

dimension /daɪˈmenʃən, dɪ-/ *noun* **1** a measurement of length, width, or height. **2** any directly measurable physical quantity, eg mass, length, time, charge. **3** *Geom.* the number of parameters that are needed to specify the size of a geometrical figure, and the location of particular points on it, eg a triangle has two dimensions, whereas a pyramid has three dimensions. **4** (*often* **dimensions**) size or extent. **5** a particular aspect of a problem, situation, etc. [from Old French, from Latin *dimensio*, measuring]

▣ **1** measurement, length, width, height. **4** size, extent, measurements, scope, magnitude, largeness, capacity, mass, scale, range, bulk, importance, greatness. **5** aspect, facet, side, feature.

-dimensional *combining form* forming words meaning 'having a certain number of dimensions': *two-dimensional*.

dimer /ˈdaɪmə(r)/ *noun Chem.* a chemical compound composed of two similar units, known as *monomers*, which may combine during either an addition reaction or a condensation reaction.

diminish *verb* **1** *trans., intrans.* to make or become less or smaller. **2** to cause to seem less important, valuable, or satisfactory. [from an obsolete word *minish* combined with Middle English *diminue*, from Latin *deminuere*, to make less]

▣ **1** decrease, lessen, reduce, lower, contract, shrink, recede, taper off, weaken, abate, fade. **2** belittle, disparage, depreciate, devalue.
▣ **1** increase. **2** exaggerate.

diminished *adj.* **1** having become less, smaller, less important, etc. **2** *Mus.* reduced by a semitone.

diminishing returns (*in full* **law of diminishing returns**) *Econ.* a law or prediction that there is a point beyond which any additional input in the form of capital and labour, or additional taxation, results in progressively smaller output per unit of capital or labour, or smaller tax yields.

diminuendo /dɪmɪnjuˈendoʊ/ *Mus.* — *noun* (PL. **diminuendos**) **1** a gradual lessening of sound. **2** a musical passage with gradually lessening sound. — *adj., adv.* with gradually lessening sound. See also CRESCENDO. [from Italian *diminuendo*, from Latin *deminuere*, to make less]

diminution /dɪmɪˈnjuːʃən/ *noun* a lessening or decrease. [from Latin *diminutio*]

diminutive /dɪˈmɪnjʊtɪv/ — *adj.* very small. — *noun Grammar* **1** (*also* **diminutive suffix**) an ending added to a word to indicate smallness, eg *-let* in *booklet*. **2** a word formed in this way. [from Latin *deminuere*, to make less]

▣ *adj.* undersized, small, tiny, little, miniature, minute, infinitesimal, wee, petite, midget, *colloq.* mini, *colloq.* teeny, *colloq.* teeny-weeny, Lilliputian, *colloq.* dinky, *humorous* pint-size, pocket, pygmy.
▣ *adj.* big, large, oversized.

dimly *adv.* in a dim way; faintly: *we could dimly see the lighthouse in the distance*.

dimmer *noun* a switch used to vary the brightness of a light.

dimness *noun* being dim or faint; lack of light or brightness.

dimorphism /daɪˈmɔːfɪzm/ *noun* **1** *Biol.* the occurrence of two distinct forms within a species of living organism, eg the male and female in many animals. **2** *Chem.* the crystallization of a chemical element or compound into two different crystalline forms that have the same chemical composition.

dimple *noun* a small hollow, especially in the skin of the cheeks, chin or, in babies, at the knees and elbows.

dimpled *adj.* having slight hollows on the surface.

dimwit *noun colloq.* a stupid person.

dim-witted *adj.* stupid.

▣ unintelligent, dense, obtuse, dull, stupid, *colloq.* thick, doltish.

DIN *abbrev.* (German) *Deutsche Industrie-Norm*, German Industry Standard, a set of standards for electrical connections, paper sizes, etc.

din — *noun* a loud, continuous, and unpleasant noise. — *verb* (**dinned, dinning**) (**din something into someone**) to repeat (something) forcefully to someone over and over again so that it will be remembered. [from Anglo-Saxon *dyne*]

▣ *noun* noise, row, racket, clash, clatter, clamour, pandemonium, uproar, commotion, crash, *colloq.* hullabaloo, hubbub, outcry, shout, babble.
▣ *noun* quiet, calm.

dinar /ˈdiːnɑː(r)/ *noun* the standard unit of currency in Yugoslavia and several Arab countries. [from Arabic & Persian *dinar*]

dine *verb intrans. formal* **1** to eat dinner. **2** (**dine off** or **on** or **upon something**) to eat food for one's dinner. — **dine out** to have dinner somewhere other than one's own house, eg in a restaurant. [from Old French *disner*, from Latin *dis*, dis- + *jejunare*, to fast]

▣ **1** eat, feast, sup, lunch, banquet, feed.

diner *noun* **1** a person who dines. **2** a dining-car on a train. **3** *North Amer.* a small, cheap restaurant.

ding — *noun* a ringing sound. — *verb* to make a ding. [imitative]

ding-dong — *noun* **1** the sound of bells ringing. **2** *colloq.* a heated argument or fight. — *adj. colloq.*, *said of a fight, argument, etc* fierce or heated. [imitative]

dinghy /ˈdɪŋɪ, ˈdɪŋɡɪ/ *noun* (PL. **dinghies**) **1** a small open boat propelled by oars, sails, or an outboard motor. **2** a small collapsible rubber boat, especially one kept for use in emergencies. [from Hindi *dingi*, small boat]

dinginess *noun* being dingy or dirty.

dingo *noun* (PL. **dingoes**) a species of wild dog found only in Australia, standing about 50cm high at the shoulder, and having pointed ears and a bushy tail. [from Dharuk (Australian Aborigine language) *dinggu*]

dingy /ˈdɪndʒɪ/ *adj.* (**dingier, dingiest**) **1** faded and dirty-looking: *dingy clothes*. **2** dark and rather dirty: *a dingy room*.

▣ **1** drab, shabby, faded, worn, grimy, soiled, dirty, discoloured, colourless, seedy, run-down. **2** dark, murky, dull, dim, dreary, gloomy, sombre, obscure, dusky.
▣ **1** clean. **2** bright.

dining car a carriage on a train in which meals are served.

dining room a room in a house used mainly for eating in.

dinitrogen oxide /daɪ-/ *noun Chem.* nitrous oxide.

dinitrogen tetroxide /daɪ-/ *noun Chem.* (FORMULA N_2O_4) a colourless or pale-yellow liquid that is used as an oxidant in rocket fuel.

dinkum *adj. Austral., New Zealand colloq.* real; genuine; honest. [from dialect *dinkum*, fair share of work]

dinky *adj.* (**dinkier, dinkiest**) *colloq.* neat; dainty. [from Scot. *dink*, neat]

dinner *noun* **1** the main meal of the day, eaten in the middle of the day or in the evening. **2** a formal meal, especially in the evening, often held to honour a person or in celebration of an event. [same as DINE]

▣ MEAL. 2 banquet, feast, spread, *formal, old use* repast.

dinner-dance *noun* a social occasion consisting of a formal dinner followed by dancing.

dinner jacket a usually black jacket worn by men at formal social gatherings, especially in the evening.

dinner-service or **dinner-set** *noun* a complete set of plates and dishes for serving dinner to several people.

dinosaur /'daɪnəsɔː(r)/ *noun* any member of a large group of prehistoric reptiles that dominated life on land during the Mesozoic era, from about 225 million to 65 million years ago, becoming extinct at the end of the Cretaceous period. [from Greek *deinos*, terrible + *sauros*, lizard]

dint *noun* a hollow made by a blow; a dent. — **by dint of something** by means of it. [from Anglo-Saxon *dynt*, blow]

diocesan /daɪ'ɒsɪzən/ *adj.* relating to or concerning a diocese.

diocese /'daɪəsɪs, 'daɪəsiːs/ *noun* the district over which a bishop has authority. [from Greek *dioikesis*, housekeeping]

diode /'daɪəʊd/ *noun Electron.* an electronic device containing two electrodes (an anode and a cathode) that allows current to flow in one direction only. [from Greek *di-*, twice + *hodos*, way]

dioecious /daɪ'iːʃəs/ *adj.* denoting a plant in which the male and female flowers are borne on separate individuals of the same species, eg willow. See also MONOECIOUS. [from Greek *di-*, twice + *oikos*, house]

dioptre or **diopter** /daɪ'ɒptə(r)/ *noun Optics* (ABBREV. **dpt**) a unit that is used to express the power of a lens, the reciprocal of the focal length of the lens in metres. [from Greek *dioptron*, spyglass]

dioxide /daɪ'ɒksaɪd/ *noun Chem.* any oxide that contains two atoms of oxygen per molecule. [from Greek *di-*, twice + OXIDE]

dioxin /daɪ'ɒksɪn/ *noun* any of various highly toxic chlorinated organic chemicals produced as a by-product of the manufacture of certain herbicides and insecticides.

Dip. *abbrev.* Diploma.

dip — *verb* (**dipped, dipping**) **1** to dye, clean, or coat (an object) by immersing it in a liquid. **2** to immerse (wood) in a preservative solution. **3** to immerse (sheep) briefly in a liquid chemical to prevent or rid them of infestation by parasitic insects. **4** *intrans., trans.* to go or push briefly under the surface of a liquid. **5** *intrans.* to drop below a surface or level. **6** *intrans., trans.* to go or push down briefly and then up again. **7** *intrans.* to slope downwards. **8** *intrans., trans.* to put (one's hand, etc) into a dish, container, etc and take out some of the contents. **9** *Brit.* to lower the beam of (the headlights of a motor vehicle) so that it shines below the eye level of oncoming motorists. — *noun* **1** an act of dipping. **2** a downward slope or hollow (especially in a road). **3** a short swim or bathe. **4** (*in full* **magnetic dip**) at a particular point on the Earth's surface, the angle between the plane of the horizon and the direction of the Earth's magnetic field. **5** a liquid chemical in which sheep are dipped. **6** a liquid dye in which garments, etc, are dipped. **7** a type of thick sauce into which biscuits, raw vegetables, etc are dipped. **8** a candle made by dipping a wick into melted wax. — **dip into something 1** to take or use part of it. **2** to look briefly at a book or study a subject in a casual manner.[from Anglo-Saxon *dyppan*]

▣ *verb* 4 plunge, immerse, submerge, duck, dunk, bathe, douse. 5 descend, decline, drop, fall, sink, subside, slump. 7 descend, decline, drop, fall, sink. *noun* 1 immersion, submersion, soaking, drenching, infusion. 2 hollow, basin, decline, hole, concavity, incline, depression, fall, slope, slump, lowering. 3 bathe, plunge, swim, dive.

diphtheria /dɪf'θɪərɪə/ *noun Medicine* a highly contagious bacterial infection, now rare, in which a tough grey 'membrane' forms at the back of the throat, causing difficulty in breathing and swallowing. [from Greek *diphthera*, leather (from the leathery covering formed in the throat)]

diphthong /'dɪfθɒŋ/ *noun Grammar* **1** two vowel sounds pronounced as one syllable, as the sound represented by the *ou* in *sounds*. **2** a digraph. [from Greek *di-*, twice + *phthongos*, sound]

diploid /'dɪplɔɪd/ *adj. Genetics* denoting an organism, cell, or nucleus in which there are two sets of chromosomes, one set being derived from each of the parents. [from Greek *diploos*, double]

diploma *noun* a document certifying that one has passed a certain examination or completed a course of study. [from Latin *diploma*, official document, from Greek *diploma*, letter folded over]

diplomacy /dɪ'pləʊməsɪ/ *noun* **1** the art or profession of making agreements, treaties, etc between countries, or of representing and looking after the affairs and interests of one's country in a foreign country. **2** skill and tact in dealing with people.

▣ **1** statesmanship, politics, negotiation, manoeuvring. **2** tact, tactfulness, finesse, delicacy, discretion, savoir-faire, subtlety, skill, craft.

diplomat /'dɪpləmat/ *noun* **1** a government official or representative engaged in diplomacy. **2** a very tactful person. [from French *diplomate*, from Latin *diploma*, official document]

▣ **1** go-between, mediator, negotiator, ambassador, envoy, conciliator, peacemaker, moderator.

diplomatic /dɪplə'matɪk/ *adj.* **1** concerning or involved in diplomacy. **2** showing skill and tact in dealing with people.

▣ **2** tactful, politic, discreet, judicious, subtle, sensitive, prudent, discreet.

▣ **2** tactless.

diplomatically *adv.* with a diplomatic manner; in terms of diplomacy.

diplomatic bag a bag or other container for official letters, packages, etc sent to and from an embassy, not subject to customs inspection.

diplomatic corps all the diplomats and embassy staff of all the embassies in the capital of a country.

diplomatic immunity the privilege granted to members of the diplomatic corps by which they may not be taxed, arrested, etc by the country in which they are working.

dipole *noun Physics* a separation of electric charge, in which two equal and opposite charges are separated from each other by a small distance. Certain molecules act as dipoles.

dipper *noun* **1** a type of ladle. **2** any of four species of small perching water bird, native to Europe, Asia, and N America, having a stocky body, dense plumage, and a very short often slightly cocked tail.

dipsomania /dɪpsəʊ'meɪnɪə/ *noun Medicine* an extreme form of alcoholism, in which there is an insatiable craving for alcoholic drink. [from Greek *dipsa*, thirst + *mania*, madness]

dipsomaniac /dɪpsəʊ'meɪnɪak/ *noun* a person with an abnormal craving for alcohol.

dipstick *noun* **1** a stick used to measure the level of a liquid in a container, especially the oil in a vehicle engine. **2** *slang* a term of abuse for a person.

dipswitch *noun* a switch used to dip the headlights of a motor vehicle.

diptych /'dɪptɪk/ *noun* a work of art, especially on a church altar, consisting of a pair of pictures painted on hinged wooden panels which can be folded together like a book. See also TRIPTYCH. [from Greek *diptychos*, folded together]

dire *adj.* **1** dreadful; terrible. **2** extreme; very serious; very difficult. [from Latin *dirus*]

▣ **1** disastrous, dreadful, awful, appalling, calamitous, catastrophic. **2** desperate, urgent, grave, drastic, crucial, extreme, alarming, ominous.

direct /daɪə'rekt/ — *adj.* **1** straight; following the quickest and shortest path from beginning to end or to a destination. **2** *said of a person's manner, etc* open, straightforward and honest; going straight to the point. **3** with no other factors involved: *the direct cause of the accident.* **4** not working or communicating through other people, or ganizations, etc: *a direct link with the chairman.* **5** exact; complete: *a direct opposite.* **6** forming or being part of an unbroken line of descent from parent to child to grandchild, etc: *a direct descendant of Sir Walter Raleigh.* — *verb* **1** to point, aim or turn in a particular direction. **2** to show the way. **3** to order or instruct. **4** to control or manage; to be in charge of (something). **5** *trans., intrans.* to plan and supervise the production of (a play or film). **6** *formal* to put a name and address on (a letter). — *adv.* directly; by the quickest or shortest path. [from Latin *directus*]

▣ *adj.* **1** straight, undeviating, through, uninterrupted. **2** straightforward, outspoken, forthright, blunt, frank, unequivocal, sincere, candid, honest, explicit. **4** immediate, first-hand, face-to-face, personal. **5** exact, complete, total, diametric. *verb* **1** aim, point, focus, turn. **2** guide, lead, conduct, point. **3** instruct, command, order, charge. **4** control, manage, run, administer, organize, lead, govern, regulate, superintend, supervise.
▣ *adj.* **1** circuitous. **2** equivocal. **4** indirect.

direct action action taken by an individual or group, such as a trade union, in order to obtain some demand or concession from a government, employer, etc.

direct current (ABBREV. **d.c.**) electric current that always flows in the same direction, eg the current produced by a battery. See also ALTERNATING CURRENT.

direct debit an order to one's bank which allows someone else to withdraw sums of money from one's account, especially in payment of bills.

directed energy weapon *Mil.* a weapon using advanced laser beam, particle beams, plasma beams, or microwave beams, all of which travel at the speed of light, and which are theoretically capable of shooting down missiles in space.

direction *noun* **1** the place or point towards which one is moving or facing. **2** the way in which someone or something is developing. **3** (*usually* **directions**) information, instructions, or advice, eg on how to construct or operate a piece of equipment. **4** (**directions**) instructions about the way to go to reach a place. **5** management or supervision. **6** the act, style, etc of directing a play or film. [from Latin *directio*]

▣ **1** route, way, line, road, course, heading. **2** course, trend, tendency, drift. **3** instructions, information, guidance, guidelines, advice, tips, hints, pointers, indications. **5** control, administration, management, government, supervision, guidance, leadership.

directional *adj.* relating to direction in space.

direction-finder *noun Engineering* a radio receiver that is used in navigation to determine the direction from which an incoming radio signal is coming, and thus to establish the location of its source.

directive *noun* an official instruction issued by a higher authority, eg a government. [from Latin *directivus*]

▣ command, instruction, order, regulation, ruling, imperative, dictate, decree, charge, mandate,

injunction, ordinance, edict, fiat, notice.

directly *adv.* **1** in a direct manner. **2** by a direct path. **3** at once; immediately. **4** very soon. **5** exactly: *directly opposite.*

▣ **1** frankly, bluntly, candidly, honestly. **3** at once, immediately, instantly, promptly, right away, speedily, forthwith, instantaneously, quickly, straight away, straight. **4** soon, presently, in a minute, in a little while.

directness *noun* a direct or straightforward manner, especially of speech or thought: *they discusssed the matter with a welcome directness.*

▣ straightforwardness, forthrightness, candour, frankness, honesty, bluntness, explicitness.

direct object *noun Grammar* the noun, noun phrase or pronoun which is directly affected by the action of a transitive verb, as *the dog* in *The boy kicked the dog.* See also INDIRECT OBJECT.

director *noun* **1** any of the most senior managers of a business firm. **2** the person in charge of a college, organization, institution, or special activity. **3** the person directing a play, film, etc.

▣ **1** manager, head, boss, chief, controller, executive. **2** principal, provost, rector, governor, leader, organizer, supervisor, administrator.

directorate *noun* **1** the directors of a business firm. **2** the position or office of director.

directorial /dɪrek'tɔːrɪəl/ *adj.* relating to directors or management.

▣ managerial, executive, administrative, supervisory, decision-making.

directorship *noun* the office or status of a director.

directory *noun* (PL. **directories**) **1** a book with a (usually alphabetical) list of names and addresses of people or organizations. **2** *Comput.* a named grouping of files on a disk, usually with a common element, allowing a command to be applied to, or bypass, all the files it contains, etc. **3** (**Directory**) the government of the First Republic of France, with five executive Directors, ruling from 1795 to 1799. [from Latin *directorium*]

direct speech *noun Grammar* speech reported in the actual words of the speaker. See also INDIRECT SPEECH.

direct tax *noun* a tax paid directly on earnings rather than one levied on goods and services. See also INDIRECT TAX.

dirge *noun* **1** a funeral song or hymn. **2** *sometimes derog.* a slow, sad song or piece of music. [from Latin *dirige*, lead, the first word in a hymn sung in the Latin Office (religious service) for the Dead]

▣ LAMENT, THRENODY, REQUIEM, ELEGY.

dirigible /'dɪrɪdʒɪbl/ — *adj.* capable of being steered or propelled. — *noun technical* an air balloon or airship that is capable of being steered or propelled. [from Latin *dirigere*, to direct]

dirk *noun* a small knife or dagger. [from Scots *durk*]

dirndl *noun* **1** a traditional alpine peasant-woman's dress, tight-fitting at the top and waist, and wide and loose at the bottom. **2** a skirt that is tight at the waist and wide at the bottom. [from German dialect *dirndl*]

dirt *noun* **1** any unclean substance, eg mud or dust. **2** soil; earth. **3** a mixture of earth and cinders used to make road surfaces. **4** *euphemistic* excrement. **5** *colloq.* obscene speech or writing. **6** *colloq.* spiteful gossip; scandal: *got* *some dirt on him.* — **treat someone like dirt** to treat them with no consideration or respect. [from Norse *drit*, excrement]

. . . .

⊟ **1** filth, grime, muck, mire, stain, smudge, slime, tarnish. **2** earth, soil, clay, dust, mud. **5** smut, indecency, impurity, obscenity, pornography.

. . . .

dirt bike a motorcycle designed for scrambling over rough terrain.

dirt-cheap *adj., adv. colloq.* very cheap or cheaply.

dirtily *adv.* in a dirty way.

dirtiness *noun* a dirty state.

dirty — *adj.* (**dirtier, dirtiest**) **1** marked with dirt; soiled. **2** which involves one becoming soiled with dirt: *a dirty job*. **3** unfair; dishonest: *dirty tricks*. **4** obscene, lewd, or pornographic: *dirty films*. **5** for the purposes of having sex in secret: *a dirty weekend*. **6** *said of weather* rainy or stormy. **7** *said of a colour* dull. **8** showing dislike or disapproval: *a dirty look*. **9** unsportingly rough or violent: *a dirty tackle*. — *verb trans.* (**dirties, dirtied**) to make dirty. — *adv.* dirtily: *fight dirty*. — **do the dirty on someone** *colloq.* to cheat or trick them.

. . . .

⊟ *adj.* **1** filthy, grimy, grubby, mucky, foul, messy, muddy, soiled, polluted, miry, unwashed, scruffy, shabby, sullied, squalid. **3** unfair, foul, unethical, immoral, underhand, crafty, sneaky, devious, deceitful, crooked. **4** indecent, obscene, filthy, smutty, sordid, salacious, vulgar, pornographic, corrupt. *verb* pollute, soil, stain, foul, mess up, defile, smear, smirch, spoil, smudge, sully, muddy, blacken.

⊟ *adj.* **1** clean. **4** decent. *verb* clean, cleanse.

. . . .

dirty word 1 an indecent or vulgar word. **2** *colloq.* an unpopular concept or point of view: *ambition is a dirty word*.

dirty work *noun* **1** work that makes one dirty. **2** *colloq.* unpleasant or dishonourable duties.

dis- *prefix* forming words denoting: **1** the opposite of the simple word: *disagree / dislike*. **2** reversal of the action of the simple word: *disassemble*. **3** removal or undoing: *dismember / disrobe*. [from Latin *dis-*]

disability *noun* (PL. **disabilities**) **1** the state of being disabled. **2** a condition, such as a physical handicap, that results in partial or complete loss of a person's ability to perform social, occupational, or other everyday activities.

. . . .

⊟ INFIRMITY. **1** disablement, inability, incapacity, impairment, unfitness, disqualification. **2** handicap, defect, affliction, ailment, complaint, disorder, weakness.

. . . .

disable *verb* **1** to deprive of a physical or mental ability. **2** to make (eg a machine) unable to work; to make useless.

. . . .

⊟ CRIPPLE, DAMAGE, IMMOBILIZE, PARALYSE. **1** lame, incapacitate, handicap, impair, debilitate, disqualify, weaken, prostrate. **2** wreck, sabotage.

. . . .

disabled *adj.* **1** *said of a person* having a physical or mental handicap. **2** *said of a machine, etc* made unable to work.

. . . .

⊟ CRIPPLED, IMMOBILIZED, INCAPACITATED, PARALYSED. **1** handicapped, impaired, infirm, lame, maimed, weak, weakened. **2** wrecked.

⊟ **1** able, able-bodied.

. . . .

disablement *noun* disabling of a person or machine.

disabuse *verb* (**disabuse someone of something**) to rid them of a mistaken idea or impression.

disaccharide /daɪˈsakəraɪd/ *noun Biochem.* a carbohydrate that consists of two monosaccharides (simple sugars) joined together, with the elimination of a molecule of water.

disadvantage — *noun* **1** a difficulty, drawback or weakness. **2** detriment or harm. **3** an unfavourable situation. — *verb* to put at a disadvantage.

. . . .

⊟ *noun* **1** difficulty, problem, drawback, snag, hindrance, handicap, impediment, inconvenience, flaw, nuisance, weakness, trouble. **2** detriment, loss, prejudice, harm, damage, hurt, injury. *verb* handicap, hold back, hinder, impede, encumber, inconvenience, restrict.

⊟ *noun* ADVANTAGE. **1** benefit. *verb* favour, benefit.

. . . .

disadvantaged *adj.* in an unfavourable position, especially deprived of normal social or economic benefits.

. . . .

⊟ deprived, underprivileged, poor, handicapped, impoverished, struggling.

⊟ privileged.

. . . .

disadvantageous *adj.* having disadvantages or weaknesses.

. . . .

⊟ harmful, detrimental, inopportune, unfavourable, prejudicial, adverse, damaging, hurtful, injurious, inconvenient, ill-timed.

⊟ advantageous, auspicious.

. . . .

disaffected *adj.* dissatisfied and no longer loyal or committed. [from DIS- 2]

. . . .

⊟ disloyal, hostile, estranged, alienated, antagonistic, rebellious, dissatisfied, disgruntled, discontented.

⊟ loyal.

. . . .

disaffection *noun* loss of loyalty to, or satisfaction with, a person, organization, etc.

. . . .

⊟ disloyalty, hostility, alienation, discontent, discontentment, resentment, ill-will, dissatisfaction, animosity, coolness, unfriendliness, antagonism, disharmony, discord, disagreement, aversion, dislike.

⊟ loyalty, contentment.

. . . .

disagree *verb intrans.* **1** *said of two or more people* to have conflicting opinions. **2** (**disagree with someone**) to have a different opinion from them. **3** (**disagree with something**) to be opposed to something. **4** to conflict with each other: *the two theories disagree*. **5** *euphemistic* to quarrel. **6** (**disagree with someone**) *said of food* to cause digestive problems. [from Old French *desagreer*]

. . . .

⊟ **1, 4** conflict, diverge, differ, clash. **3** differ from, deviate from, contradict, run counter to, oppose, dissent from, quarrel with, argue with, dispute, contest, object to, counter. **5** quarrel, argue, bicker, fall out, wrangle, fight, squabble, contend, dispute.

⊟ **1, 4** agree. **2** agree with. **3** correspond with, tally with, agree with. **4** correspond.

. . . .

disagreeable *adj.* **1** unpleasant. **2** bad-tempered; unfriendly.

. . . .

⊟ **1** unpleasant, disgusting, offensive, repulsive, repellent, obnoxious, unsavoury, objectionable, nasty. **2** bad-tempered, unfriendly, ill-humoured, difficult, peevish, rude, surly, churlish, irritable, contrary, cross, brusque.

⊟ **1** agreeable. **2** amiable, pleasant.

. . . .

disagreeably *adv.* in a disagreeable or unpleasant way; to an unpleasant degree.

disagreement *noun* **1** the state of disagreeing. **2** *euphemistic* a quarrel.

. . . .

⊟ DIFFERENCE. **1** variance, unlikeness, disparity, discrepancy,

deviation, discord, dissimilarity, incompatibility, divergence, diversity, incongruity. **2** dispute, argument, conflict, altercation, quarrel, clash, dissent, falling-out, contention, strife, misunderstanding, squabble, tiff, wrangle.
🡒 AGREEMENT. **1** harmony, similarity.

disallow *verb* to formally refuse to allow or accept; to judge to be invalid. [from Old French *desalouer*]

🡒 refuse, reject, cancel, rescind, revoke, repeal, invalidate, nullify, void.

disallowance *noun* refusal to allow something.

disappear *verb intrans.* **1** to go out of sight; to vanish. **2** to cease to exist. **3** to go away or go missing. [from DIS- 1]

🡒 **1** vanish, wane, recede, fade, evaporate, dissolve, ebb. **2** end, expire, perish, pass. **3** go, depart, withdraw, retire, flee, fly, escape, *colloq.* scarper, hide, abscond, decamp.
🡒 **1** appear. **3** emerge.

disappearance *noun* disappearing; passing from sight.

🡒 vanishing, fading, evaporation, departure, loss, going, passing, desertion, flight.
🡒 appearance, manifestation.

disappoint *verb* **1** to fail to fulfil the hopes or expectations of. **2** *formal* to prevent (eg a plan) from being carried out. [from Old French *desapointer*]

🡒 **1** fail, dissatisfy, let down, disillusion, dismay, disenchant, sadden, dishearten, disgruntle, disconcert, vex. **2** dash, thwart, foil, hamper, hinder, frustrate, deceive, defeat, delude.
🡒 **1** satisfy, please, delight.

disappointed *adj.* having one's hopes or expectations frustrated.

🡒 let down, frustrated, thwarted, disillusioned, dissatisfied, *colloq.* miffed, upset, discouraged, disgruntled, disheartened, distressed, downhearted, saddened, despondent, depressed.
🡒 pleased, satisfied.

disappointing *adj.* causing disappointment; frustrating one's hopes or expectations.

🡒 unsatisfactory, dissatisfying, poor, mediocre, discouraging, disheartening, upsetting, dismaying, frustrating.

disappointment *noun* **1** the state of being disappointed. **2** something that disappoints.

🡒 **1** frustration, dissatisfaction, failure, disenchantment, disillusionment, displeasure, discouragement, distress, regret. **2** failure, let-down, setback, comedown, blow, misfortune, fiasco, disaster, calamity, *colloq.* washout, *colloq.* damp squib, *colloq.* swizz, *colloq.* swizzle.
🡒 **1** pleasure, satisfaction, delight. **2** success.

disapprobation *noun formal* disapproval, especially on moral grounds. [from DIS- 1]

disapproval *noun* thinking badly of someone or something.

🡒 censure, *formal* disapprobation, condemnation, criticism, displeasure, reproach, objection, dissatisfaction, denunciation, dislike.
🡒 approbation, approval.

disapprove *verb intrans.* (**disapprove of something** or **someone**) to have a low opinion of them; to think them bad or wrong.

🡒 censure, condemn, blame, take exception to, object to, deplore, denounce, disparage, dislike, reject, spurn.

disapproving *adj.* showing disapproval; thinking badly.

disarm *verb* **1** to take weapons away from. **2** *intrans.* to reduce or destroy one's own military capability. **3** to take the fuse out of (a bomb). **4** to take away the anger or suspicions of. [from Old French *desarmer*]

🡒 **1** disable, unarm, demilitarize, demobilize. **3** defuse, deactivate. **4** appease, conciliate, win over, mollify, persuade.
🡒 **1** arm.

disarmament *noun* the reduction or destruction by a nation of its own military forces.

disarming *adj.* taking away anger or suspicion; quickly winning confidence or affection.

🡒 conciliatory, mollifying, winning, charming, appealing, endearing.

disarmingly *adv.* with a disarming manner.

disarrange *verb* to make untidy or disordered.

🡒 disorder, disorganize, untidy, mess (up), confuse, muddle, jumble, tangle.

disarrangement *noun* lack of arrangement or order; putting things out of order.

disarray — *noun* a state of disorder or confusion. — *verb* throw into disorder.

🡒 *noun* disorder, confusion, chaos, mess, muddle, *colloq.* shambles, disorganization, clutter, untidiness, unruliness, jumble, indiscipline, tangle, upset.
🡒 *noun* order.

disassociate same as DISSOCIATE.

disaster *noun* **1** an event causing great damage, injury or loss of life. **2** a total failure. **3** extremely bad luck: *disaster struck.* [originally 'bad influence of the stars', from Old French *desastre*, from *des-*, dis- + *astre*, star]

🡒 CALAMITY, CATASTROPHE. **1** misfortune, reverse, tragedy, blow, accident, act of God, cataclysm, mishap. **2** failure, debacle, *colloq.* flop, fiasco. **3** trouble, mischance, ruination.
🡒 **1** success. **2** triumph.

disastrous *adj.* involving great damage or loss.

🡒 calamitous, catastrophic, cataclysmic, devastating, ruinous, tragic, unfortunate, dreadful, dire, terrible, destructive, ill-fated, fatal, miserable.
🡒 successful, auspicious.

disavow *verb formal* to deny knowledge of, a connection with, or responsibility for. [from Old French *desavouer*]

🡒 disown, deny, renounce.

disavowal *noun* refusal to acknowledge someone or something.

disband *verb trans., intrans.* to stop operating as a group; to break up. [from Old French *desbander*, to unbind]

🡒 disperse, break up, scatter, dismiss, demobilize, separate, dissolve.

▣ assemble, muster.

disbandment *noun* breaking up of a group; formal dispersal.

disbelief *noun* inability or refusal to believe something: *they looked at us in disbelief.*

▤ unbelief, incredulity, doubt, scepticism, suspicion, distrust, mistrust, rejection.
▣ belief.

disbelieve *verb* 1 to believe to be false or lying. 2 *intrans.* to have no religious faith.

▤ 1 discount, discredit, repudiate, reject, mistrust, suspect.
▣ BELIEVE. 1 trust.

disburse *verb* to pay out, especially from a fund. [from Old French *desbourser*]

disbursement *noun* payment from a fund.

disc *noun* 1 any flat thin circular object or structure. 2 any disc-shaped recording medium, such as a vinyl record, compact disc, or video disc. 3 *Anat.* any of the flat circular plates of cartilage situated between adjacent vertebrae of the spine, that act as shock absorbers. 4 (**slipped disc**) the slipping of one of these structures, usually caused by sudden twisting or bending, which results in painful pressure on adjacent spinal nerves. 5 *Comput.* same as DISK. 6 the circular shape of the sun, moon, or a planet when illuminated, especially as viewed through a telescope. 7 *Bot.* in composite plants such as the daisy and sunflower, the flat circular flower-head, consisting of many tiny florets crowded together. [from Greek *diskos*]

▤ 1 circle, face, plate, ring. 2 record, album, LP, CD.

discard *verb* 1 to get rid of as useless or unwanted. 2 *Cards* to put down (a card of little value) especially when unable to follow suit.

▤ 1 reject, abandon, dispose of, get rid of, jettison, dispense with, cast aside, *slang* ditch, dump, drop, scrap, shed, remove, relinquish.
▣ 1 retain, adopt.

disc brake a type of brake in which the rotating wheel of a vehicle is slowed down by means of special pads (known as *disc pads*) that are pressed against either side of a flat metal disc (known as a *brake disc*) attached to the wheel hub.

discern /dɪˈsɜːn/ *verb* to perceive, notice, or make out; to judge. [from Latin *discernere*]

▤ perceive, make out, recognize, see, ascertain, notice, determine, discover, descry, observe, detect, discriminate, distinguish, differentiate, judge.

discernible *adj.* capable of being seen or perceived: *no discernible difference.*

▤ perceptible, noticeable, detectable, appreciable, distinct, observable, recognizable, visible, apparent, clear, obvious, plain, patent, manifest, discoverable.
▣ imperceptible.

discerning *adj.* having or showing good judgement.

▤ discriminating, perceptive, astute, clear-sighted, sensitive, shrewd, wise, sharp, subtle, sagacious, penetrating, acute, piercing, critical, eagle-eyed.
▣ dull, obtuse.

discernment *noun* good judgement.

discharge /dɪsˈtʃɑːdʒ, ˈdɪstʃɑːdʒ/ — *verb* (with stress on -*charge*) 1 to allow (someone) to leave; to send away or dismiss, especially from employment. 2 to perform or carry out (eg duties). 3 *trans., intrans.* to flow out or cause to flow out or be released. 4 *Legal* to release from custody. 5 *trans., intrans.* to fire (a gun). 6 *Legal* to pay off (a debt). 7 *trans., intrans.* to unload (a cargo). 8 *trans., intrans. technical* to lose or cause (a device) to lose some or all electrical charge. — *noun* (with stress on *dis-*) 1 the act of discharging. 2 something discharged. 3 fulfilment or accomplishment. 4 *formal Legal* release or dismissal. 5 *Physics* the flow of electric current through a gas in a discharge tube, often resulting in luminescence of the gas. 6 *Electr.* the release of stored electric charge from a capacitor, battery, or accumulator. 7 *Electr.* a high-voltage spark of electricity produced when there is a large difference in electrical potential between two points, eg lightning. [from Old French *descharger*]

▤ *verb* 1 dismiss, *colloq.* sack, remove, *colloq.* fire, expel, oust, eject. 2 execute, carry out, perform, fulfil. 4 free, liberate, pardon, release, clear, absolve, exonerate, acquit. 5 fire, shoot, let off, detonate, explode. 6 pay off, liquidate, settle, clear. *noun* 1, 2 emission, secretion. 1 ejection, dismissal, firing. 3 execution, accomplishment, fulfilment, performance. 4 liberation, release, acquittal, exoneration.
▣ *verb* 1 appoint. 2 neglect. 4 detain. 6 default on. *noun* 1 absorption. 3 neglect. 4 confinement, detention.

disciple /dɪˈsaɪpl/ *noun* 1 a person who believes in, and follows, the teachings of another. 2 one of the twelve close followers of Christ. [from Latin *discipulus*, from *discere*, to learn]

▤ 1 follower, convert, proselyte, adherent, believer, devotee, supporter, learner, pupil, student. 2 apostle.

disciplinarian *noun* a person who enforces strict discipline on others.

▤ authoritarian, taskmaster, stickler, martinet, autocrat, despot, tyrant.

disciplinary *adj.* of, relating to, or enforcing discipline; intended as punishment.

discipline /ˈdɪsɪplɪn/ — *noun* 1 strict training, or the enforcing of rules, intended to produce ordered and controlled behaviour in oneself or others; the ordered behaviour resulting from this. 2 punishment designed to create obedience. 3 an area of learning, especially a subject of academic study. — *verb* 1 to train or force (oneself or others) to behave in an ordered and controlled way. 2 to punish. [from Latin *disciplina*]

▤ *noun* 1 training, exercise, drill, practice, strictness, restraint, regulation, self-control, orderliness. 2 punishment, chastisement, correction. *verb* 1 train, instruct, drill, educate, exercise, break in, check, control, correct, restrain, govern. 2 punish, chastise, chasten, penalize, reprimand, castigate.
▣ 1 indiscipline.

disc jockey *noun* a person who presents a programme of recorded popular music on the radio or at a disco.

disclaim *verb* 1 to deny (eg involvement with or knowledge of). 2 to give up a legal claim to. [from Old French *desclaimer*]

▤ 1 deny, disown, repudiate, abandon, renounce, reject, abjure.
▣ 1 accept, confess.

disclaimer *noun* **1** a written statement denying legal responsibility. **2** a denial.

disclose *verb* **1** to make known. **2** to show or make visible. [from Old French *desclore*]

....

■ **1** divulge, make known, reveal, tell, confess, let slip, relate, publish, communicate, impart, leak. **2** expose, reveal, uncover, lay bare, unveil, discover.

⊟ conceal.
....

disclosure *noun* the act of disclosing or making something known.

....

■ exposure, exposé, revelation, uncovering, publication, leakage, leak, discovery, admission, divulgence, acknowledgement, announcement, declaration.

....

disco — *noun* (PL. **discos**) **1** a discotheque. **2** a party with dancing to recorded music. **3** the mobile hi-fi and lighting equipment used for such a party. — *adj.* suitable for, or designed for, discotheques.

discoloration or **discolouration** *noun* change or loss of colour.

discolour *verb trans., intrans.* to stain or dirty; to change in colour. [from Old French *descolorer*]

discomfit /dɪsˈkʌmfɪt/ *verb* (**discomfited, discomfiting**) **1** to cause to feel embarrassed or uneasy; to perplex. **2** to frustrate the plans of. [from Old French *desconfire*]

discomfiture *noun* frustration; humiliating disappointment.

discomfort — *noun* slight physical pain or mental uneasiness. — *verb* to make physically uncomfortable or mentally uneasy. [from Old French *desconfort*]

....

■ *noun* ache, pain, uneasiness, malaise, trouble, distress, disquiet, hardship, vexation, irritation, annoyance.

⊟ *noun* comfort, ease.
....

discompose *verb* to upset, worry, or agitate.

discomposure *noun* a state of upset or agitation.

disconcert /dɪskənˈsɜːt/ *verb* to cause to feel anxious or uneasy; to fluster. [from obsolete French *disconcerter*]

....

■ disturb, confuse, upset, unnerve, alarm, startle, surprise, fluster, bewilder, embarrass, baffle, perplex, dismay.

....

disconcerting *adj.* causing anxiety or unease.

....

■ disturbing, confusing, upsetting, unnerving, alarming, bewildering, *colloq.* off-putting, distracting, embarrassing, awkward, baffling, perplexing, dismaying, bothersome.

....

disconnect *verb* **1** to break a connection, especially of an electrical nature, eg to separate an electrical device from a power supply, or to break a circuit. **2** to stop the supply of (a public service such as the gas supply or the telephone) to (a building, etc).

....

■ CUT OFF. **1** disengage, uncouple, sever, separate, detach, unplug, unhook, part, divide.

⊟ CONNECT (UP). **1** attach.
....

disconnected *adj.* **1** no longer connected. **2** *said especially of speech* not correctly constructed, and often not making sense.

....

■ **2** confused, incoherent, rambling, unco-ordinated, unintelligible, loose, irrational, disjointed, illogical, jumbled.

⊟ **2** coherent, connected.
....

disconnection *noun* a break in a connection or link.

disconsolate /dɪsˈkɒnsələt/ *adj.* deeply sad or disappointed; not able to be consoled. [from Latin *disconsolatus*]

....

■ desolate, dejected, dispirited, sad, melancholy, unhappy, wretched, miserable, gloomy, forlorn, inconsolable, crushed, heavy-hearted, hopeless.

⊟ cheerful, joyful.

disconsolately *adv.* with deep sadness or disappointment.

discontent *noun* dissatisfaction; lack of contentment.

....

■ uneasiness, dissatisfaction, disaffection, disquiet, restlessness, fretfulness, unrest, impatience, vexation, regret.

⊟ contentment.
....

discontented *adj.* dissatisfied; unhappy.

....

■ dissatisfied, *colloq.* fed up, disgruntled, unhappy, *colloq.* browned off, *Brit. slang* cheesed off, disaffected, miserable, exasperated, complaining.

⊟ contented, satisfied.
....

discontinuance or **discontinuation** *noun* discontinuing; breaking off.

discontinue *verb* **1** *trans., intrans.* to stop or cease. **2** to stop producing: *a discontinued line.* [from Old French *discontinuer*]

....

■ **1** stop, end, finish, cease, break off, terminate, halt.

⊟ **1** continue.
....

discontinuity *noun* lack of continuity; interruption.

discontinuous *adj.* having breaks or interruptions.

....

■ broken, interrupted, episodic, uneven, irregular, intermittent, spasmodic.

....

discord *noun* **1** disagreement; conflict; failure to get on. **2** *Mus.* an unpleasant-sounding combination of notes; lack of harmony. **3** uproarious noise. [from Latin *discordia*]

....

■ **1** dissension, disagreement, clashing, disunity, incompatibility, conflict, difference, dispute, contention, friction, division, opposition, strife, split, wrangling. **2** dissonance, disharmony, cacophony, jangle, jarring, harshness.

⊟ **1** concord, agreement. **2** harmony.
....

discordant *adj.* **1** marked by disagreement or conflict. **2** lacking harmony.

....

■ **1** disagreeing, conflicting, at odds, clashing, contradictory, incongruous, incompatible, inconsistent. **2** dissonant, cacophonous, grating, jangling, jarring, harsh.

⊟ HARMONIOUS.
....

discotheque /ˈdɪskətɛk/ *noun* a night-club with dancing to recorded pop music. See also DISCO. [from French *discotheque*]

discount /ˈdɪskaʊnt, dɪsˈkaʊnt/ — *noun* (with stress on *dis-*) an amount deducted from the normal price, eg for prompt payment. — *verb* (with stress on *-count*) to disregard as unlikely, untrue, or irrelevant. **2** (with stress on *dis-*) to make a deduction from (a price). — **at a discount** for less than the usual price. [from Old French *descompter*]

....

■ *noun* reduction, rebate, allowance, cut, concession, deduction, mark-down. *verb* **1** disregard, ignore, overlook, disbelieve, gloss over. **2** reduce, deduct, mark down, *colloq.* knock off.

....

discount house *Brit.* a financial institution which buys short-dated government stocks with money borrowed from commercial banks for short periods. Profit is derived from the difference between the borrowing rate and the lending rate.

discourage /dɪsˈkʌrɪdʒ/ *verb* **1** to deprive of confidence, hope, or the will to continue. **2** to seek to prevent (a person or an action) with advice or persuasion. [from Old French *descourager*]

■ **1** dishearten, dampen, dispirit, depress, demoralize, dismay, unnerve, deject, disappoint. **2** deter, dissuade, hinder, put off, restrain, prevent, advise against.
⊟ **1** hearten. **2** encourage.

discouragement *noun* **1** feeling discouraged. **2** dissuasion; something that dissuades.

■ **1** downheartedness, despondency, pessimism, dismay, depression, dejection, despair, disappointment. **2** deterrence, opposition, hindrance, deterrent, damper, setback, impediment, obstacle, restraint, rebuff.
⊟ **1** encouragement. **2** incentive.

discouraging *adj.* taking away one's courage or confidence; dissuading: *our first efforts had a discouraging response.*

discourse /ˈdɪskɔːs, dɪsˈkɔːs/ — *noun* (with stress on *dis-*) **1** a formal speech or essay on a particular subject. **2** serious conversation. — *verb intrans.* (with stress on *-course*) to speak or write at length, formally or with authority. [from Latin *discursus*]

■ *noun* **1** speech, address, lecture, oration, sermon, homily, essay, paper, dissertation, treatise. **2** conversation, dialogue, communication, talk, converse, discussion. *verb* converse, talk, discuss, debate, confer, lecture.

discourteous *adj.* showing a lack of courtesy; impolite. [from DIS- 1]

■ rude, bad-mannered, ill-mannered, impolite, boorish, disrespectful, ill-bred, uncivil, unceremonious, insolent, offhand, curt, brusque, abrupt.
⊟ courteous, polite.

discourteously *adv.* with a discourteous or impolite manner.

discourtesy *noun* lack of courtesy; impoliteness.

discover *verb* (**discovered**, **discovering**) **1** to be the first person to find. **2** to find by chance, especially for the first time. **3** to learn of or become aware of for the first time. [from Old French *descouvrir*]

■ FIND. **1, 2** uncover, unearth. **1** locate, originate, invent, pioneer. **2** dig up, light on, come upon, stumble on. **3** ascertain, determine, realize, notice, recognize, perceive, see, find out, spot, discern, learn, detect.
⊟ MISS.

discovery *noun* (PL. **discoveries**) **1** the act of discovering. **2** a person or thing discovered.

■ **1** breakthrough, finding, detection, disclosure, revelation, location, origination, introduction, exploration. **2** find, innovation, invention.

discredit — *noun* loss of good reputation, or the cause of it. — *verb* (**discredited, discrediting**) **1** to cause to be disbelieved or regarded with doubt or suspicion. **2** to damage the reputation of.

■ *noun* dishonour, disrepute, censure, aspersion, disgrace,

blame, shame, reproach, slur, smear, scandal. *verb* **1** challenge, undermine, cast doubt on. **2** disparage, dishonour, degrade, defame, disgrace, slander, slur, smear, reproach, vilify.
⊟ *noun* credit. *verb* **2** honour.

discreditable *adj.* bringing discredit.

■ dishonourable, disreputable, disgraceful, reprehensible, scandalous, blameworthy, shameful, infamous, degrading, improper.
⊟ creditable.

discreet *adj.* **1** careful to prevent suspicion or embarrassment, especially by keeping a secret. **2** avoiding notice; inconspicuous. See also DISCRETION. [from Latin *discretus*]

■ **1** tactful, careful, diplomatic, politic, prudent, cautious, delicate, judicious, reserved, wary, sensible. **2** inconspicuous, unobtrusive, low-key, low-profile, unostentatious, modest.
⊟ **1** tactless, indiscreet. **2** conspicuous, obtrusive, showy.

discrepancy /dɪsˈkrɛpənsɪ/ *noun* (PL. **discrepancies**) a failure (eg of sets of information) to correspond or be the same. [from Latin *discrepare*, to differ in sound]

■ difference, disparity, variance, variation, inconsistency, dissimilarity, discordance, divergence, disagreement, conflict, inequality.

discrepant *adj.* showing a discrepancy or failure to correspond.

discrete *adj.* separate; distinct. [from Latin *discretus*]

discretely *adv.* in a discrete or separate manner.

discreteness *noun* being discrete; separateness.

discretion /dɪsˈkrɛʃən/ *noun* **1** the quality of behaving in a discreet way. **2** the ability to make wise judgements. **3** the freedom or right to make decisions and do as one thinks best: *allowed to change the plans at our own discretion.* [from Latin *discretio*]

■ **1, 2** judiciousness, prudence, circumspection. **1** tact, diplomacy, caution, consideration, wariness, care, carefulness. **2** wisdom, discernment, judgement. **3** choice, freedom, preference, will, wish.
⊟ **1, 2** indiscretion.

discretionary *adj.* made, done, given, etc according to the wishes of a particular person or group; not compulsory or automatic.

discriminate /dɪsˈkrɪmɪneɪt/ *verb intrans.* **1** to recognize a difference between two people or things. **2** to give different treatment to different people or groups in identical circumstances, especially without justification and on political or religious grounds. [from Latin *discriminare*, to separate]

■ DIFFERENTIATE, MAKE A DISTINCTION. **2** be prejudiced, be biased.

discriminating *adj.* showing good judgement; able to recognize even slight differences.

■ discerning, critical, perceptive, tasteful, astute, sensitive, cultivated, particular, selective, fastidious.

discrimination /dɪskrɪmɪˈneɪʃən/ *noun* **1** unjustifiably different treatment given to different people or groups. **2** the ability to draw fine distinctions; good judgement, especially in matters of taste.

⊟ **1** bias, prejudice, intolerance, unfairness, bigotry, favouritism, inequity, racism, sexism. **2** discernment, judgement, acumen, perception, acuteness, insight, penetration, subtlety, keenness, refinement, taste.

discriminatory /dɪsˈkrɪmɪnətərɪ/ *adj.* displaying or representing unfairly different treatment.

discursive *adj.* **1** wandering from the main point. **2** *Philos.* based on argument or reason, rather than on intuition. [from DISCOURSE]

⊟ **1** rambling, digressing, wandering, long-winded, meandering, wide-ranging, circuitous.
⊠ **1** terse.

discus *noun* **1** a heavy metal disc, thicker at the centre than the edge, thrown in athletic competitions. **2** the competition itself. [from Greek *diskos*]

discuss *verb* to examine or consider in speech or writing. [from Latin *discutere*, to shake to pieces]

⊟ debate, talk about, confer about, argue, consider, deliberate, converse, consult, examine.

discussion *noun* a conversation or debate on a particular topic.

⊟ debate, conference, argument, conversation, dialogue, exchange, consultation, discourse, deliberation, consideration, analysis, review, examination, scrutiny, seminar, symposium.

disdain — *noun* dislike arising out of lack of respect; contempt. — *verb* **1** to refuse or reject out of disdain. **2** to regard with disdain. [from Old French *desdaigner*, from Latin *dignus*, worthy]

⊟ *noun* scorn, contempt, arrogance, haughtiness, derision, sneering, dislike, snobbishness. *verb* **1** spurn, reject, refuse, scorn, turn down, rebuff, repulse. **2** look down on, despise, slight, disregard, snub, cold-shoulder, ignore.
⊠ *noun* admiration, respect. *verb* **1** welcome. **2** admire, respect.

disdainful *adj.* showing disdain or contempt.

⊟ scornful, contemptuous, derisive, haughty, aloof, arrogant, supercilious, sneering, superior, proud, insolent.
⊠ respectful.

disdainfully *adv.* with a disdainful or contemptuous manner.

disease *noun* **1** any abnormal condition that impairs the structure or functioning of a living organism, that can be identified on the basis of specific signs and symptoms, and that is caused by factors other than injury, eg infection, genetic defects, exposure to toxic agents, or whose cause is unknown. **2** the general condition of illness or sickness. **3** any undesirable phenomenon. [from Old French *desaise*, unease]

⊟ **1, 2** illness, sickness, indisposition, infirmity. **1** complaint, disorder, ailment, malady, condition, affliction, infection, epidemic. **2** ill-health.
⊠ **2** health.

diseased *adj.*, *usually said of a part of the body* suffering from disease.

⊟ sick, ill, unhealthy, ailing, unsound, contaminated, infected.
⊠ healthy.

diseconomy *noun* (PL. **diseconomies**) an economic disadvantage, such as lower efficiency or higher costs.[from DIS- I]

disembark *verb trans., intrans.* to take or go from a ship on to land. [from Old French *desembarquer*]

⊟ land, unload, debark.
⊠ embark.

disembarkation *noun* departure or removal from a ship.

disembodied *adj.* **1** *said eg of a spirit or soul* separated from the body; having no physical existence. **2** seeming not to come from, or be connected to, a body: *a disembodied voice*.

⊟ GHOSTLY, PHANTOM. **1** bodiless, incorporeal, spiritual, immaterial, intangible.

disembowel /dɪsɛmˈbʊəl/ *verb* (**disembowelled, disembowelling**) to remove the internal organs of, as a punishment, torture, etc.

disembowelment *noun* forcible or violent removal of the internal organs.

disenchant *verb* **1** to free from illusion. **2** to make dissatisfied or discontented.

disenchanted *adj.* feeling dissatisfied or disappointed, especially after high expectations.

⊟ disappointed, dissatisfied, discontented, disillusioned, let down.

disenchantment *noun* a feeling of disappointment, especially after high expectations.

disenfranchise see DISFRANCHISE.

disengage *verb* **1** to release or detach from a connection. **2** *trans., intrans.* to withdraw (troops) from combat. [from Old French *desengager*]

⊟ WITHDRAW. **1** disconnect, detach, loosen, free, extricate, undo, release, liberate, separate, disentangle, untie.
⊠ ENGAGE. **1** connect.

disengagement *noun* release from a connection or commitment.

disentangle *verb* **1** to release from entanglement. **2** to free from complication, difficulty, or confusion. **3** to take the knots or tangles out of (eg hair).

⊟ UNTANGLE, UNRAVEL. **1** loose, free, extricate, disconnect, disengage, detach, separate, unfold. **2** resolve, clarify, simplify.
⊠ ENTANGLE.

disentanglement *noun* freeing from complication or entanglement.

disestablish *verb* to take away the official status or authority of.

disestablishment *noun* removal of official status or authority from an institution.

disfavour *noun* **1** a state of being disliked, unpopular, or disapproved of. **2** dislike or disapproval.

⊟ **1** unpopularity, discredit, disrepute. **2** dislike, disapproval, disapprobation, displeasure, distaste.
⊠ FAVOUR.

disfigure *verb* to spoil the beauty or general appearance of. [from Old French *desfigurer*]

⊟ deface, blemish, mutilate, scar, mar, deform, distort, damage, spoil.
⊠ adorn, embellish.

disfigurement *noun* spoiling the appearance of something; defacement.

disfranchise or **disenfranchise** *verb* to deprive of the right to vote.

disfranchisement or **disenfranchisement** *noun* the removal of rights, especially to vote in elections.

disgorge *verb* **1** to vomit. **2** to discharge or pour out. **3** to give up or relinquish, especially under pressure. [from Old French *desgorger*, from *gorge*, throat]

disgrace — *noun* shame or loss of favour or respect, or the cause of it. — *verb* to bring shame upon. [from French *disgrâce*]

⊟ *noun* shame, ignominy, disrepute, dishonour, disfavour, humiliation, defamation, discredit, scandal, reproach, slur, stain. *verb* shame, dishonour, abase, defame, humiliate, disfavour, stain, discredit, reproach, slur, sully, taint, stigmatize.
⊠ *noun* honour, esteem. *verb* honour, respect.

disgraceful *adj.* bringing shame; degrading.

⊟ shameful, dishonourable, disreputable, degrading, ignominious, scandalous, shocking, unworthy, dreadful, appalling.
⊠ honourable, respectable.

disgruntled *adj.* annoyed and dissatisfied; in a bad mood. [from DIS- + obsolete *gruntle*, to complain]

⊟ annoyed, irritated, angry, peevish, cross, displeased, dissatisfied, discontented.

disguise /dɪs'gaɪz/ — *verb* **1** to hide the identity of by a change of appearance. **2** to conceal the true nature of (eg intentions). — *noun* **1** a disguised state: *in disguise*. **2** something, especially a combination of clothes and make-up, intended to disguise. [from Old French *desguiser*]

⊟ *verb* CONCEAL, COVER, CAMOUFLAGE, MASK, HIDE, DRESS UP, CLOAK, SCREEN, VEIL, SHROUD. **2** falsify, deceive, dissemble, misrepresent, fake, fudge. *noun* **1** concealment, camouflage. **2** costume, mask, cloak, cover, front, façade, masquerade, deception, pretence, travesty, screen, veil.
⊠ *verb* REVEAL, EXPOSE.

disgust — *verb* to sicken; to provoke intense dislike or disapproval in. — *noun* intense dislike; loathing. [Old French *desgouster*]

⊟ *verb* offend, displease, nauseate, revolt, sicken, repel, outrage, put off. *noun* revulsion, repulsion, repugnance, distaste, aversion, abhorrence, nausea, loathing, detestation, hatred.
⊠ *verb* delight, please. *noun* delight, pleasure.

disgusted *adj.* having a feeling of intense dislike or revulsion.

⊟ repelled, repulsed, revolted, offended, appalled, outraged.
⊠ attracted, delighted.

disgusting *adj.* causing a feeling of intense dislike or revulsion.

⊟ repugnant, repellent, revolting, offensive, sickening, nauseating, odious, foul, unappetizing, unpleasant, vile, obscene, abominable, detestable, objectionable, nasty.
⊠ delightful, pleasant.

dish — *noun* **1** a shallow container in which food is served or cooked. **2** its contents, or the amount it can hold. **3** anything shaped like this. **4** a particular kind of food. **5** (**dishes**) the used plates and other utensils after the end of a meal. **6** a dish aerial. **7** *colloq.* a physically attractive person. — *verb* *colloq.* to ruin (especially chances or hopes). — **dish something out** *colloq.* **1** to distribute (food, books, leaflets, etc). **2** to give out (punishment, advice, etc). **dish something up** *colloq.* **1** to serve (food). **2** to offer or present (eg information). [from Anglo-Saxon *disc*, plate, bowl, table]

⊟ *noun* **1, 2** plate, bowl. **4** food, recipe. **dish out** DISTRIBUTE, GIVE OUT, HAND OUT, HAND ROUND, DOLE OUT, ALLOCATE. **2** mete out, inflict. **dish up** SERVE UP. **1** serve, ladle, spoon, scoop. **2** present, offer, supply, dispense.

dishabille /dɪsə'biːl/ same as DÉSHABILLÉ.

dish aerial a microwave aerial in the form of a large dish-shaped parabolic reflector, used in radar and radio telescopes, and as a receiver for satellite broadcasts.

disharmonious *adj.* lacking harmony; disagreeing.

disharmony *noun* disagreement; lack of harmony. [from DIS- 1]

⊟ discord, disunity, friction, contention, conflict, strife, dissonance.

dishearten *verb* (**disheartened**, **disheartening**) to dampen the courage, hope, or confidence of.

⊟ discourage, dispirit, dampen, cast down, depress, dismay, dash, disappoint, deject, daunt, crush, deter.
⊠ encourage, hearten.

disheartening *adj.* dispiriting; discouraging.

disheartenment *noun* being disheartened; discouragement.

dishevelled *adj.*, *said of clothes or hair* untidy; in a mess. [from Old French *descheveler*]

⊟ unkempt, uncombed, untidy, bedraggled, tousled, messy, ruffled, slovenly, disordered.
⊠ neat, tidy.

dishevelment *noun* a state of personal untidiness.

dishonest *adj.* not honest; likely to deceive or cheat; insincere. [from Old French *deshoneste*]

⊟ untruthful, fraudulent, deceitful, false, lying, deceptive, double-dealing, cheating, *colloq.* crooked, treacherous, unprincipled, swindling, *colloq.* shady, corrupt, disreputable.
⊠ honest, trustworthy, scrupulous.

dishonestly *adv.* in a dishonest way.

dishonesty *noun* lack of honesty; a dishonest act.

⊟ deceit, falsehood, falsity, fraudulence, fraud, criminality, insincerity, treachery, cheating, *colloq.* crookedness, corruption, unscrupulousness, trickery.
⊠ honesty, truthfulness.

dishonour — *noun* shame or loss of honour, or the cause of it. — *verb* **1** to bring dishonour on. **2** to treat with no respect. **3** *Commerce* to refuse to honour (a cheque). [from Old French *deshonneur*]

⊟ *noun* disgrace, abasement, humiliation, shame, degradation, discredit, disrepute, indignity, ignominy, reproach, slight, slur, scandal, insult, disfavour, outrage, aspersion, abuse, discourtesy. *verb*

1 disgrace, shame, humiliate, debase, defile, degrade, defame, discredit, demean.
⊞ HONOUR.

- -

dishonourable *adj.* bringing dishonour or disgrace.

⊟ disgraceful, shameful, ignoble, base, low, discreditable, disreputable, demeaning, degrading.

- -

dishwasher *noun* **1** a machine that washes and dries dishes. **2** a person employed to wash dishes, eg in a restaurant.

dishwater *noun* water in which dirty dishes have been washed.

dishy *adj.* (**dishier, dishiest**) *colloq.* sexually attractive.

disillusion *verb* (**disillusioned, disillusioning**) to correct the mistaken beliefs or illusions of.

⊟ disabuse, undeceive, enlighten, disappoint, let down, disenchant.

- -

disillusionment *noun* being disillusioned.

disillusioned *adj.* sad or disappointed at having discovered the unpleasant truth.

⊟ disenchanted, disabused, undeceived, disappointed.

- -

disincentive *noun* something that discourages or deters.

⊟ discouragement, deterrent, damper, *colloq.* turnoff.

- -

disinclination *noun* being disinclined or unwilling.

⊟ unwillingness, reluctance, hesitancy, resistance, opposition, aversion.

- -

disinclined *adj.* unwilling.

⊟ averse, reluctant, resistant, indisposed, loath, opposed, hesitant.
⊞ inclined, willing.

- -

disinfect *verb* to clean with a substance that kills germs.

⊟ sterilize, fumigate, sanitize, decontaminate, cleanse, purify, purge, clean.
⊞ contaminate, infect.

- -

disinfectant *noun* a germ-killing substance.

⊟ sterilizer, antiseptic, sanitizer.

- -

disinformation *noun* false information intended to deceive or mislead.

disingenuous *adj.* not entirely sincere or open; creating a false impression of frankness.

⊟ insincere, deceitful, devious, hypocritical.

- -

disingenuously *adv.* with a disingenuous or insincere manner.

disingenuousness *noun* a disingenuous or insincere manner.

disinherit *verb* (**disinherited, disinheriting**) to legally deprive of an inheritance.

disinheritance *noun* rejection of an heir; removal from inheritance.

disintegrate *verb trans., intrans.* **1** to break into tiny pieces; to shatter or crumble. **2** to break up. **3** to undergo or cause to undergo nuclear fission.

⊟ **1, 2** break up, splinter, disperse, dissolve. **1** decompose, crumble, rot, separate.

- -

disintegration *noun Physics* **1** the process or result of breaking down. **2** the breakdown of an atomic nucleus, either spontaneously by radioactive decay, or as a result of bombardment with high-energy particles.

⊟ **1** breakdown, splitting, decomposition, dispersal, dissolution, separation.

- -

disinter / dɪsɪn'tɜː(r) / *verb* (**disinterred, disinterring**) **1** to dig up (especially a body from a grave). **2** to discover and make known.

⊟ UNEARTH. **1** exhume. **2** discover, find, uncover, reveal.

- -

disinterest or **disinterestedness** *noun* lack of personal or subjective bias.

⊟ impartiality, objectivity, neutrality, detachment, unbiasedness, dispassionateness, fairness.

- -

disinterested *adj.* **1** not having an interest in a particular matter; impartial, objective. **2** *colloq.* showing no interest; uninterested.

⊟ **1** unbiased, neutral, impartial, unprejudiced, dispassionate, detached, uninvolved, open-minded, equitable, even-handed, unselfish.
⊞ **1** biased, concerned.

- -

disinterment *noun* removal of a body from a grave.

disjointed *adj.*, *said of speech* not properly connected; incoherent. [from Old French *desjoindre*]

⊟ disconnected, incoherent, aimless, confused, disordered, loose, unconnected, bitty, rambling, spasmodic.
⊞ coherent.

- -

disjunctive *adj.* marked by breaks; discontinuous. [from Old French *desjoindre*]

disk *noun Comput.* a magnetic disc-shaped medium used to record and store data in a computer. See also FLOPPY DISK, HARD DISK. [a variant of DISC]

⊟ disc, diskette, floppy disk, hard disk, CD-ROM.

- -

disk drive *Comput.* see DRIVE *noun* 10.

diskette *noun Comput.* **1** an alternative name for a floppy disk. **2** formerly used to refer to a 5.25in floppy disk.

dislike — *verb* to consider unpleasant or unlikeable. — *noun* **1** mild hostility; aversion. **2** something disliked.

⊟ *verb* hate, detest, object to, loathe, abhor, abominate, disapprove of, shun, despise, scorn. *noun* AVERSION, HATE. **1** hatred, repugnance, hostility, distaste, disinclination, disapproval, disapprobation, displeasure, animosity, antagonism, enmity, detestation, disgust, loathing.
⊞ *verb* like. *noun* **1** liking, favour.

- -

dislocate *verb* **1** to dislodge (a bone) from its normal position in a joint, eg by violently displacing it from the socket during a sports injury. The most common sites of dislocation include the shoulder and hip. **2** to disturb the order of; to disrupt. [from Latin *dislocare*]

⊟ **1** put out, dislodge, displace, disjoint. **2** disorder, disrupt, disturb, disunite.

- -

dislocation *noun* dislocating, especially of a bone in the body.

dislodge *verb* **1** to force out of a fixed or established position: *dislodge a stone*. **2** to drive from a place of rest, hiding, or defence. [from Old French *desloger*]

■ REMOVE, MOVE, UPROOT, DISPLACE, EXTRICATE, SHIFT. **2** eject, oust, evict.

dislodgement or **dislodgment** *noun* change from an established position.

disloyal *adj.* not loyal or faithful. [from Old French *desloyal*]

■ treacherous, faithless, false, traitorous, two-faced, unfaithful, apostate, unpatriotic.
▣ loyal, trustworthy, faithful.

disloyalty *noun* lack of loyalty; unfaithfulness.

■ treachery, unfaithfulness, infidelity, falseness, two-facedness, apostasy.

dismal /ˈdɪzməl/ *adj.* **1** not cheerful; causing or suggesting sadness. **2** *colloq.* third-rate; of poor quality. [from Old French, from Latin *dies mali*, unlucky days]

■ **1** dreary, gloomy, depressing, bleak, cheerless, dull, drab, low-spirited, melancholy, sad, sombre, lugubrious, forlorn, despondent, dark, sorrowful, long-faced, hopeless, discouraging. **2** second-rate, mediocre, lacklustre.
▣ **1** cheerful, bright.

dismally *adv.* in a dismal way; miserably: *dismally cold weather.*

dismantle *verb* **1** to take to pieces; to demolish. **2** to abolish or close down, especially bit by bit. [from Old French *desmanteller*]

■ **1** demolish, take apart, take to pieces, disassemble, strip (down). **2** phase out, wind down, run down, abolish, close down.
▣ **1** assemble, put together.

dismay — *noun* a feeling of sadness arising from deep disappointment or discouragement. — *verb* to cause this feeling in (someone). [from Old French *desmaiier*]

■ *noun* consternation, alarm, distress, apprehension, agitation, dread, fear, trepidation, fright, horror, terror, discouragement, disappointment. *verb* alarm, daunt, frighten, unnerve, unsettle, scare, put off, dispirit, distress, disconcert, dishearten, discourage, disillusion, depress, horrify, disappoint.
▣ *noun* boldness, encouragement. *verb* encourage, hearten.

dismember *verb* (**dismembered, dismembering**) **1** to tear or cut the arms and legs from. **2** to divide up (especially land). [from Old French *desmembrer*]

■ DIVIDE. **1** disjoint, amputate, dissect, dislocate, mutilate, sever. **2** parcel out.
▣ ASSEMBLE, JOIN.

dismemberment *noun* **1** forcible or violent removal of the arms and legs. **2** division of territory.

dismiss *verb* **1** to refuse to consider or accept. **2** to put out of one's employment. **3** to send away; to allow to leave. **4** to close (a court case). **5** *Cricket* to bowl out. [from Latin *dis-*, from, away + *mittere*, to send]

■ **1** discount, disregard, reject, repudiate, set aside, shelve, spurn. **2** *colloq.* sack, make redundant, lay off, *colloq.* fire, relegate. **3** discharge, free, let go, release, send away, remove, drop, discard, banish.
▣ **1** accept. **2** appoint. **3** keep.

dismissal *noun* dismissing, especially of a person from employment: *an offence that warrants instant dismissal.*

■ *colloq.* the sack, *colloq.* the boot, *colloq.* sacking, *colloq.* firing, lay-off, rejection, repudiation.

dismissive *adj.* (*often* **dismissive of something** or **someone**) giving no consideration or respect; showing no willingness to believe.

■ scornful, contemptuous, disdainful, haughty, arrogant, high-handed, cavalier.

dismount *verb* **1** *intrans.* to get off a horse, bicycle, etc. **2** to force (someone) off a horse, bicycle, etc. **3** to remove from a stand or frame. [from Old French *desmonter*]

■ **1** get off, alight, descend. **2** throw, unseat.

disobedience *noun* refusal to obey.

disobedient *adj.* refusing or failing to obey. [from DIS- 1]

■ rebellious, defiant, resistant, naughty, unmanageable, refractory.

disobey *verb* *trans., intrans.* to act contrary to the orders of; to refuse to obey. [from Old French *desobeir*]

■ contravene, infringe, violate, transgress, flout, disregard, defy, ignore, resist, rebel.
▣ obey.

disobliging *adj.* unwilling to help; disregarding, or tending to disregard, wishes or requests. [from DIS- 1]

■ unhelpful, unco-operative, inconsiderate, unfriendly.

disorder — *noun* **1** lack of order; confusion or disturbance. **2** unruly or riotous behaviour. **3** any malfunction of the body or mind. **4** an ailment or illness. — *verb* to put into a state of disorder. [from Old French *desordre*]

■ *noun* **1** confusion, chaos, muddle, disarray, mess, untidiness, *colloq.* shambles, clutter, disorganization, jumble. **2** disturbance, tumult, riot, confusion, commotion, uproar, fracas, brawl, fight, clamour, quarrel. **3** illness, complaint, disease, sickness, disability, ailment, malady, affliction. *verb* disturb, mess up, disarrange, mix up, muddle, upset, disorganize, confuse, confound, clutter, jumble, discompose, scatter, unsettle.
▣ *noun* **1** order, neatness. **2** law and order, peace. *verb* arrange, organize.

disordered *adj.* lacking order; put out of order.

disorderly *adj.* **1** not neatly arranged; disorganized. **2** causing trouble in public.

■ **1** disorganized, confused, chaotic, irregular, messy, untidy, unruly, undisciplined, unmanageable, obstreperous, rowdy, turbulent, rebellious, lawless.
▣ **1** neat, tidy. **2** well-behaved.

disorganization or **disorganisation** *noun* lack of organization; confusion.

■ disorder, confusion, muddle, chaos.

disorganize or **disorganise** *verb* to disturb the order or arrangement of; to throw into confusion.

■ disorder, disrupt, disturb, disarrange, muddle, upset, confuse, discompose, jumble, play havoc with, unsettle, break up, destroy.
⊟ organize.

disorientate or **disorient** *verb* to cause to lose all sense of position, direction, or time.

■ confuse, muddle, disconcert, put out, throw out.

disorientation *noun* confusion as to one's position, etc.
disown *verb* to deny having any relationship to or connection with; to refuse to recognize or acknowledge.

■ repudiate, renounce, disclaim, deny, cast off, disallow, reject, abandon.
⊟ accept, acknowledge.

disownment *noun* refusal to acknowledge someone; renunciation.
disparage /dɪsˈparɪdʒ/ *verb* to speak of with contempt. [from Old French *desparager*, to marry below one's class]

■ belittle, deride, run down, dismiss, underrate, undervalue.

disparagement *noun* speaking with contempt.
disparaging *adj.* contemptuous; showing disapproval.

■ contemptuous, derisive, derogatory, mocking, scornful, critical, insulting, snide.
⊟ flattering, praising.

disparate /ˈdɪsparət/ *adj.* completely different; too different to be compared. [from Latin *disparare*, to separate]

■ different, discrete, separate, opposite, contrasting, unlike, dissimilar.

disparity /dɪsˈparɪtɪ/ *noun* (PL. **disparities**) great or fundamental difference; inequality.

■ difference, dissimilarity, inequality, disproportion, discrepancy, contrast.

dispassionate *adj.* 1 calm; unemotional. 2 not influenced by personal feelings; impartial. [from DIS- 1]

■ 1 calm, composed. 2 detached, objective, impartial, neutral, disinterested, impersonal, fair.
⊟ 1 emotional. 2 biased.

dispatch or **despatch** — *verb* 1 to send to a place for a particular reason. 2 to finish off or deal with quickly: *dispatch a meal*. 3 *euphemistic* to kill. — *noun* 1 (*often* **dispatches**) an official (especially military or diplomatic) report. 2 a journalist's report sent to a newspaper. 3 the act of dispatching; the fact of being dispatched. 4 *old use* speed or haste. [from Old French *despeechier*, to set free]

■ *verb* 1 send, express, transmit, forward, consign, expedite. 2 dispose of, finish, perform, discharge, conclude. 3 kill, murder, execute. *noun* 1, 2 report, communication, message. 2 bulletin, communiqué, news, newsflash, account. 3 sending (off), forwarding, transmission. 4 speed, rapidity, swiftness, haste, *formal* celerity, *formal* expedition.

dispatch rider *noun* a person employed to deliver messages by motorcycle or, formerly, on horseback.
dispel /dɪˈspɛl/ *verb* (**dispelled**, **dispelling**) to drive away or banish (thoughts or feelings). [from Latin *dispellere*]

■ drive away, disperse, dissolve, break up, banish, remove.

dispensable *adj.* 1 that can be done without. 2 able to be dispensed.

■ 1 expendable, redundant, superfluous, unnecessary, unwanted.

dispensary *noun* (PL. **dispensaries**) a place where medicines are made up according to a doctor's prescription and dispensed to patients.
dispensation *noun* 1 special exemption from a rule, obligation or (especially religious) law. 2 the act of dispensing. 3 a religious or political system regarded as the chief governing force in a nation or during a particular time. 4 *Relig.* God's management of human affairs.
dispense *verb* 1 to give out (eg advice). 2 to prepare and distribute (medicine). 3 to administer (eg the law). — **dispense with something** to do without it. [from Latin *dispendere*, to weigh out]

■ 1 distribute, give out, apportion, allot, allocate, assign, share. 2 distribute, give out, supply. 3 administer, apply, implement, enforce, discharge, execute, operate. **dispense with** do without, forego, ignore, omit, disregard, waive, dispose of, get rid of, abolish, discard, cancel.

dispersal or **dispersion** *noun* dispersing; scattering.
disperse *verb trans., intrans.* 1 to spread out over a wide area. 2 to break up or cause (a crowd) to break up and leave. 3 to vanish or cause to vanish. 4 *Biol.* to scatter (seeds, etc) in all directions over a wide area. 5 *Physics* to split (a ray of white light) into its component wavelengths (all the colours of the spectrum) by passing it through a prism or diffraction grating. 6 *said of a ray of white light* to be split into its component wavelengths on passing through a prism or diffraction grating. 7 *Physics* to suspend (fine particles) in a liquid or gas. 8 *said of fine particles* to become evenly distributed throughout a liquid or gas. [from Latin *dispergere*, to scatter widely]

■ 1, 2, 3, 4 scatter, break up, separate. 1 spread, distribute. 2 disperse. 3 dispel, diffuse, dissolve.
⊟ 1, 2, 3, 4 gather.

dispirit *verb* (**dispirited**, **dispiriting**) to dishearten or discourage.
displace *verb* 1 to put or take out of the usual place. 2 to take the place of. 3 to remove from a post. [from Old French *desplacer*]

■ 1 dislodge, move, shift, misplace, disturb, dislocate. 2, 3 replace, supplant. 2 succeed, supersede. 3 depose, oust, remove, dismiss, discharge, eject, evict.

displaced person *noun* a person forced to leave his or her own country through war or persecution.
displacement *noun* 1 the act of displacing. 2 *technical* the weight or volume of fluid that is displaced by a body floating in that fluid. 3 the movement of a point or body from one position in space to another. 4 the position of a point or body relative to its previous position, or to the position of a second point or body, measured as the linear distance in a particular direction. 5 *Psychol.* the transfer of emo-

tional feelings from the person, object, or situation to which they were originally directed to a more socially acceptable substitute.

display — *verb* **1** to put on view. **2** to show or betray (eg feelings). — *noun* **1** the act of displaying. **2** an exhibition; a show of talent; an arrangement of objects on view. **3** the visual display unit linked to a computer, or the digital characters of a liquid-crystal display unit, used in watches, calculators, etc. **4** a pattern of animal behaviour, usually involving stereotyped sounds, movements, colour patterns, etc, that produces a specific response in another individual, especially of the same species. Displays are most frequently associated with courtship or the defence of territory. [from Old French *despleier*]

◼ *verb* SHOW, EXHIBIT, REVEAL, EXPOSE. **1** present, demonstrate, show off, flourish, parade, flaunt. **2** betray, disclose. *noun* **1, 2** exhibition, demonstration, presentation, parade. **1** showing, revelation. **2** show, spectacle.
◪ *verb* CONCEAL, DISGUISE. *noun* concealment.

displease *verb* to annoy or offend. [from Old French *desplaisir*]

◼ offend, annoy, irritate, anger, upset, put out, infuriate, exasperate, incense.
◪ please.

displeasure *noun* a feeling of annoyance or offence.

◼ offence, annoyance, disapproval, irritation, resentment, disfavour, anger, indignation, wrath.
◪ pleasure.

disport *verb trans., intrans. literary* to indulge (oneself) in lively amusement. [from Old French *se desporter*, to carry oneself away]

disposable *adj.* **1** intended to be thrown away or destroyed after use. **2** *said of income or assets* remaining after tax and other commitments are paid; available for use when needed.

◼ **1** throwaway, expendable.

disposal *noun* the act of getting rid of something. — **at the disposal of someone** available for use by them.

◼ removal, riddance, discarding, jettisoning. **at the disposal of** available to, for the use of, at the service of.

dispose *verb* **1** (**dispose of something**) to get rid of it. **2** (**dispose of something**) to deal with or settle it. **3** to place in an arrangement or order. [from Latin *disponere*, to set out]

◼ **1** get rid of, discard, scrap, destroy, dump, jettison. **2** deal with, decide, settle. **3** deploy, arrange, spread, distribute.

disposed *adj.* **1** (**disposed to**) inclined or willing to: *am not disposed to try.* **2** having a disposition of the kind specified: *ill-disposed towards us.*

◼ **1** inclined to, liable to, likely to, willing to, predisposed to, apt to, prone to, ready to, subject to.

disposition *noun* **1** temperament; personality; a tendency. **2** arrangement; position; distribution. **3** *Legal* the act of giving over (eg property).

◼ **1** character, nature, temperament, inclination, make-up, bent, leaning, predisposition, constitution, habit, spirit, tendency, proneness.

dispossess *verb* (**dispossess someone of something**) to take (especially property) away from them.

dispossession *noun* removal of property from a person.

disproof *noun* the act of disproving; something that disproves.

disproportion *noun* lack of balance or equality; failure to be in proportion.

disproportionate *adj.* unreasonably large or small in comparison with something else.

◼ unequal, uneven, incommensurate, excessive, unreasonable.
◪ balanced.

disproportionately *adv.* in a disproportionate way; to a disproportionate degree.

disprove *verb* to prove to be false or wrong. [from Old French *desprover*]

◼ refute, rebut, confute, discredit, invalidate, contradict, expose.
◪ confirm, prove.

disputable /dɪs'pjuːtəbl/ *adj.* liable to be disputed or argued about.

◼ contentious, moot.

disputation /dɪspjʊ'teɪʃən/ *noun* argument; debate; discussion.

disputatious /dɪspjuː'teɪʃəs/ *adj., said of a person* inclined to dispute or argue; contentious.

dispute /dɪ'spjuːt, 'dɪspjuːt/ — *verb* (with stress on *-spute*) **1** to question or deny the accuracy or validity of. **2** to quarrel over rights to or possession of: *disputed territory.* **3** *trans., intrans.* to argue about (something). — *noun* (with variable stress) an argument. [from Latin *disputare*, to discuss]

◼ *verb* **1** question, challenge, contend. **2** contest. **3** argue (about), debate, quarrel (about), clash, wrangle, squabble. *noun* argument, debate, disagreement, controversy, conflict, contention, quarrel, wrangle, feud, strife, squabble.
◪ *verb* **1** accept. **3** agree (on). *noun* agreement, settlement.

disqualification *noun* making or declaring someone ineligible, especially for infringing rules.

disqualify *verb* (**disqualifies, disqualified**) **1** to remove from a competition, especially for breaking rules. **2** to make unsuitable or ineligible.

◼ **1** debar, eliminate. **2** disentitle, rule out, preclude, incapacitate, disable, invalidate, prohibit.
◪ **2** qualify.

disquiet — *noun* a feeling of anxiety or uneasiness. — *verb* to cause this feeling in (someone).

◼ *noun* anxiety, worry, concern, nervousness, uneasiness, restlessness, alarm, distress, fretfulness, fear, disturbance, trouble. *verb* worry, concern, alarm, distress, fret, disturb, worry.
◪ *noun* calm, reassurance. *verb* calm.

disquieting *adj.* causing a feeling of anxiety or unease.

disquietude /dɪs'kwaɪətjuːd/ *noun* a feeling of disquiet or unease.

disquisition /dɪskwɪ'zɪʃən/ *noun formal* a long and detailed discussion of a subject in speech or writing. [from Latin *disquisitio*]

disregard — *verb* **1** to pay no attention to. **2** to dismiss as unworthy of consideration. — *noun* dismissive lack of attention or concern.

◨ *verb* DISCOUNT, IGNORE. **1** overlook, neglect, pass over, disobey, make light of, turn a blind eye to, brush aside. **2** slight, snub, despise, disdain, disparage. *noun* neglect, negligence, inattention, oversight, indifference, disrespect, contempt, disdain, *colloq.* brush-off.

◪ *verb* **1** heed, pay attention to. **2** respect. *noun* attention, heed.

disrepair *noun* bad condition or working order owing to a need for repair. [from DIS- 1]

◨ dilapidation, deterioration, decay, collapse, ruin, shabbiness.

◪ good repair.

disreputable /dɪsˈrɛpjʊtəbl/ *adj.* **1** suffering from, or leading to, a bad reputation. **2** *said of a person's appearance, clothes, etc* shabby, dirty and unprepossessing.

◨ **1** disgraceful, discreditable, dishonourable, unrespectable, notorious, scandalous, shameful, shady, base, contemptible, low, mean, shocking. **2** scruffy, shabby, seedy, unkempt.

◪ **1** respectable. **2** smart.

disreputably *adv.* in a way that causes discredit: *behave disreputably.*

disrepute /dɪsrɪˈpjuːt/ *noun* the state of having a bad reputation: *bring something into disrepute.* [from DIS- 1]

◨ disgrace, discredit, dishonour, notoriety, shame.

disrespect *noun* lack of respect; impoliteness; rudeness. [from DIS- 1]

◨ discourtesy, rudeness, impertinence, impoliteness, impudence, insolence, irreverence, cheek.

disrespectful *adj.* showing a lack of respect; impolite.

◨ rude, discourteous, impertinent, impolite, impudent, insolent, uncivil, unmannerly, cheeky, insulting, irreverent, contemptuous.

◪ polite, respectful.

disrespectfully *adv.* with a disrespectful or impolite manner.

disrobe *verb trans., intrans.* **1** *literary* to undress. **2** to take ceremonial robes off. [from DIS- 3]

disrupt *verb* to disturb the order or peaceful progress of. [from Latin *disrumpere*, to break into pieces]

◨ disturb, disorganize, confuse, interrupt, break up, unsettle, intrude, upset.

disruption *noun* disturbance to peace or order.

disruptive *adj.* causing disturbance to peace or order.

◨ disturbing, troublesome, vexatious, confusing, unsettling.

diss or **dis** *verb North Amer. slang* to insult or show disrespect for (someone). [shortened from DISRESPECT]

dissatisfaction *noun* being dissatisfied; a feeling of discontent.

◨ discontent, displeasure, dislike, discomfort, disappointment, frustration, annoyance, irritation, exasperation, regret, resentment.

◪ satisfaction.

dissatisfied *adj.* not satisfied.

◨ displeased, discontented, unhappy, *colloq.* fed up, disappointed, frustrated, annoyed, irritated, cross.

dissatisfy *verb* (**dissatisfies, dissatisfied**) to fail to satisfy; to make discontented.

◨ displease, discontent, disappoint, annoy, irritate.

dissect /dɪˈsɛkt/ *verb* **1** to cut apart; to cut into small pieces. **2** to cut open (an animal, plant, or human corpse) in order to expose and examine its internal structure for the purpose of scientific or medical study. **3** to examine in minute detail, especially critically. [from Latin *dissecare*, to cut into pieces]

◨ **1** dismember. **3** analyse, investigate, scrutinize, examine, inspect, pore over.

dissection *noun* cutting open or into pieces.

dissemble *verb trans., intrans.* to conceal or disguise (true feelings or motives); to assume a false appearance of (something). [from Latin *dissimulare*]

◨ pretend, feign, dissimulate, act, sham, fake.

disseminate /dɪˈsɛmɪneɪt/ *verb* to cause (eg news or theories) to be widely circulated or diffused. [from Latin *disseminare*, to sow widely]

◨ propagate, spread, broadcast, circulate, diffuse.

dissemination *noun* wide circulation of news, etc.

dissension *noun* disagreement leading to strife or violence.

◨ disagreement, discord, dissent, dispute, contention, conflict, strife, friction, quarrel.

◪ agreement.

dissent — *noun* **1** disagreement, especially open or hostile. **2** voluntary separation, especially from an established church. — *verb intrans.* (*often* **dissent from someone** or **something**) **1** to differ in opinion; to disagree. **2** to break away, especially from an established church. [from Latin *dissentire*, to disagree]

◨ *noun* **1** disagreement, difference, dissension, discord, resistance, opposition, objection. *verb* **1** disagree, differ, protest, object, refuse, quibble.

◪ *noun* **1** agreement, conformity. *verb* **1** assent.

dissenter *noun* a person who dissents or disagrees, especially in religious matters.

dissentient /dɪˈsɛnʃənt/ *formal* — *adj.* disagreeing with a majority or established view. — *noun* a dissentient person.

dissenting *adj.* disagreeing; differing in opinion.

dissertation /dɪsəˈteɪʃən/ *noun* **1** a long essay, especially forming part of a higher education degree course. **2** a formal lecture on a particular subject. [from Latin *disserere*, to discuss]

disservice *noun* a wrong; a bad turn. [from Old French *desservir*]

◨ wrong, bad turn, disfavour, injury, harm, unkindness, injustice.

◪ favour.

dissidence *noun* open or public disagreement.

dissident /ˈdɪsɪdənt/ — *noun* a person who disagrees publicly, esp with a government. — *adj.* disagreeing; dissenting. [from Latin *dissidere*, to sit apart]

▭ *noun* dissenter, protester, nonconformist, rebel, agitator, revolutionary, schismatic. *adj.* disagreeing, differing, dissenting, discordant, nonconformist, heterodox.
▣ *noun* assenter. *adj.* acquiescent, orthodox.

dissimilar *adj.* (*often* **dissimilar to something**) unlike; different.

▭ unlike, different, divergent, disparate, unrelated, incompatible, mismatched, diverse, various, heterogeneous.
▣ similar, like.

dissimilarity *noun* being unlike; difference.

▭ difference, unlikeness, diversity, variety, disparity, discrepancy, incompatibility.

dissimulate *verb trans., intrans.* to hide or disguise (especially feelings). [from Latin *dissimulare*]

▭ pretend, feign, dissemble, put on an act, sham, fake.

dissimulation *noun* hiding or disguising feelings.

▭ pretence, feigning, shamming, faking, dissembling, disguise, concealment, deception, hypocrisy, insincerity.

dissipate /ˈdɪsɪpeɪt/ *verb* **1** *trans., intrans.* to separate and scatter. **2** to use up carelessly; to squander. [from Latin *dissipare*]

▭ **1** disperse, dispel, diffuse, evaporate, dissolve. **2** spend, waste, squander, expend, consume, deplete, fritter away, burn up.
▣ **1** accumulate, gather. **2** save.

dissipated *adj.* over-indulging in pleasure and enjoyment; debauched.

▭ dissolute, debauched, wanton, abandoned, corrupt, immoral, licentious, lewd, wild, depraved.
▣ restrained, virtuous.

dissipation *noun* **1** the process of dissipating. **2** extravagant or debauched living.

▭ **1** dispersal, diffusion, evaporation, disappearance, squandering, expenditure, consumption, depletion. **2** extravagance, debauchery, licence, immorality.

dissociate /dɪˈsoʊʃɪeɪt/ *verb* **1** to regard as separate. **2** to declare (someone or oneself) to be unconnected with. **3** *Chem.*, *said of a chemical substance* to break down into its constituent molecules, atoms, or ions, eg when dissolved in water or exposed to electromagnetic radiation. [from Latin *dissociare*]

▭ separate, detach, divorce, isolate, segregate. **2** distance, disunite, disengage, disconnect, cut off.
▣ **1, 2** associate, join.

dissociation *noun* being separate; lack of connection.

dissoluble *adj.* **1** able to be disconnected. **2** soluble. [from Latin *dissolubilis*]

dissolute /ˈdɪsəluːt/ *adj.* indulging in pleasures considered immoral; debauched. [from Latin *dissolutus*, lax, loose]

▭ dissipated, debauched, degenerate, depraved, wanton, abandoned, corrupt, immoral, licentious, lewd, wild.
▣ restrained, virtuous.

dissoluteness *noun* indulgence in immoral pleasures.

dissolution *noun* **1** the breaking up of a meeting or assembly, eg Parliament; the ending of a formal or legal partnership, eg a marriage or business. **2** abolition, eg of the monarchy or an institution. **3** the process of breaking up into parts. [from DISSOLVE]

▭ **1** ending, termination, break-up, conclusion, suspension, discontinuation, divorce, annulment. **2** abolition, suppression, destruction, overthrow. **3** break-up, disintegration, decomposition, separation, resolution, division, dispersal, evaporation, disappearance.

dissolve — *verb* **1** *trans., intrans.* to cause (a substance) to go into solution. **2** *said of a substance* to go into solution. **3** to cause (a solid) to become liquid; to melt. **4** *said of a solid* to become liquid; to melt. **5** to bring (an assembly, eg Parliament) to a close; to end (a legal partnership, eg a business). **6** *trans., intrans.* to disappear or cause to disappear: *our support dissolved.* **7** *intrans.* (*often* **dissolve into laughter, tears**, etc) be overcome emotionally. **8** *intrans. technical, said of a film or television image* to fade out as a second image fades in. — *noun technical* a fading out of one film or television image as a second is simultaneously faded in. [from Latin *dissolvere*, to loosen]

▭ *verb* **1** blend, merge. **3, 4** liquefy, melt. **5** end, terminate, prorogue, suspend, sever, annul, cancel. **6** evaporate, disintegrate, disperse, break up, dissipate, crumble.

dissonance /ˈdɪsənəns/ *noun* **1** *Mus.* an unpleasant combination of sounds or notes; lack of harmony. **2** disagreement; incompatibility. [from Latin *dissonare*, to be discordant]

dissonant *adj.* lacking in harmony; harsh-sounding.

▭ discordant, clashing, jarring, harsh, grating, unmusical, unharmonious.

dissuade /dɪˈsweɪd/ *verb* (**dissuade someone from doing something**) to deter them with advice or persuasion. [from Latin *dissuadere*]

▭ deter, discourage, put off, disincline.
▣ persuade.

dissuasion /dɪˈsweɪʒən/ *noun* advice or persuasion meant to deter.

dissyllable same as DISYLLABLE.

distaff /ˈdɪstɑːf/ *noun* the rod on which a bunch of wool, flax, etc is held ready for spinning by hand. — **the distaff side** *old use* the wife's or mother's side of the family. [from Anglo-Saxon *distæf*]

distance — *noun* **1** the measured length between two points in space; the fact of being apart. **2** any faraway point or place; the furthest visible area. **3** coldness of manner. — *verb* **1** to put at a distance. **2** (*usually* **distance oneself**) to declare oneself to be unconnected or unsympathetic to something: *distanced themselves from government policy.* — **go the distance** *colloq.* to last out until the end, usually of a sporting (especially boxing) contest. **keep one's distance** to stay safely away, especially refusing involvement; to avoid friendship or familiarity. [from Latin *distancia*]

▭ *noun* **1** space, interval, gap, extent, range, reach, length, width. **3** aloofness, reserve, coolness, coldness, remoteness. *verb* **2** dissociate, separate.

▣ *noun* **1** closeness. **3** approachability.

distant *adj.* **1** far away or far apart in space or time. **2** not closely related. **3** cold and unfriendly. **4** appearing to be lost in thought.

▣ **1** far, faraway, far-flung, out-of-the-way, remote, outlying, abroad, dispersed. **3** aloof, cool, reserved, stand-offish, formal, cold, restrained, stiff.
▣ **1** close. **3** approachable.

distantly *adv.* in the distance; remotely in time or place: *they are distantly related.*

distaste *noun* dislike; aversion.

▣ dislike, aversion, repugnance, disgust, revulsion, loathing, abhorrence.
▣ liking.

distasteful *adj.* unpleasant or offensive.

▣ disagreeable, offensive, unpleasant, objectionable, repulsive, obnoxious, repugnant, unsavoury, loathsome, abhorrent.
▣ pleasing.

distemper[1] *noun* any of various infectious diseases of mammals, with a fever, loss of appetite, and discharge from the eyes and nose. [from Old French *destemper*, to derange]

distemper[2] — *noun* any water-based paint, especially when mixed with glue or size and used for poster-painting or murals. — *verb* (**distempered, distempering**) to paint with distemper. [from Latin *distemperare*, to soak]

distend /dɪsˈtend/ *verb trans., intrans.* to make or become swollen, inflated, or stretched. [from Latin *distendere*]

▣ swell, inflate, bloat, blow up, belly out, stretch, extend.

distensible *adj.* capable of being distended or stretched.

distension *noun* distending; stretching.

distil /dɪˈstɪl/ *verb* (**distilled, distilling**) **1** to purify a liquid by the process of distillation. **2** to produce alcoholic spirits in this way. **3** to create a shortened version of. [from Latin *destillare*, to drip down]

distillate /ˈdɪstɪleɪt/ *noun* the liquid that is formed by condensation of vapour during the process of distillation.

distillation *noun Chem.* a method of purifying a liquid by heating it to boiling point and condensing the vapour formed to a liquid.

distilled water *Chem.* water that has been purified by distillation.

distiller *noun* a person or company that makes alcoholic spirits.

distillery *noun* (PL. **distilleries**) a place where distilling, especially of alcoholic beverages such as whisky, is carried out.

distinct *adj.* **1** easily seen, heard, or recognized; clear or obvious. **2** noticeably different or separate. [from Latin *distinctus*, from *distinguere*, to distinguish]

▣ **1** clear, plain, evident, obvious, apparent, marked, definite, noticeable, recognizable. **2** separate, different, detached, individual, dissimilar, distinctive.
▣ **1** indistinct, vague.

distinction *noun* **1** exceptional ability or achievement, or an honour awarded in recognition of it. **2** the act of differentiating. **3** the state of being noticeably different. **4** a distinguishing feature.

▣ **1** renown, fame, celebrity, prominence, eminence,

importance, reputation, greatness, honour, prestige, repute, superiority, worth, merit, excellence, quality. **2** differentiation, discrimination, discernment, separation. **3** difference, dissimilarity, contrast. **4** characteristic, peculiarity, individuality, feature, quality, mark.
▣ **1** unimportance, obscurity.

distinctive *adj.* easily recognized because very individual.

▣ characteristic, distinguishing, individual, peculiar, different, unique, singular, special, original, extraordinary, idiosyncratic.
▣ ordinary, common.

distinctiveness *noun* the quality of being distinctive or individual.

distinctly *adv.* clearly; unmistakably.

distinguish /dɪˈstɪŋgwɪʃ/ *verb* **1** to mark as different from other things, people, etc. **2** *trans., intrans.* (**distinguish one thing from another, distinguish between things** or **people**) to see the difference between them. **3** to make out; to identify. **4** (**distinguish oneself**) to be considered outstanding because of some achievement. [from Latin *distinguere*]

▣ **1** categorize, characterize, classify, individualize, particularize, typify, mark, stamp. **2** differentiate, discriminate, tell the difference. **3** discern, perceive, identify, ascertain, make out, recognize, see.

distinguishable *adj.* capable of being distinguished or recognized as different.

▣ discernible, perceptible, identifiable, ascertainable, noticeable, recognizable, evident, clear.

distinguished *adj.* **1** famous (and usually well respected). **2** with a noble or dignified appearance.

▣ **1** famous, eminent, celebrated, well-known, acclaimed, illustrious, notable, noted, renowned, famed, honoured, outstanding. **2** striking, dignified, impressive, noble.
▣ UNIMPRESSIVE. **1** insignificant, obscure.

distinguishing *adj.* serving to identify.

distort *verb* **1** to twist out of shape. **2** to change the meaning or tone of by inaccurate retelling. **3** to alter the quality of (sound). [from Latin *distorquere*]

▣ **1** deform, contort, bend, misshape, disfigure, twist, warp. **2** falsify, misrepresent, pervert, slant, colour, garble.

distorted *adj.* **1** twisted out of shape. **2** wrongly changed in meaning.

distortion *noun* distorting; impaired quality of sound, etc.

distract *verb* **1** (**distract someone from something**) to divert their attention from it. **2** to entertain or amuse. **3** to confuse, worry, or anger. [from Latin *distrahere*, to draw apart]

▣ **1** divert, sidetrack, deflect. **2** amuse, occupy, divert, engross. **3** confuse, disconcert, bewilder, confound, disturb, perplex, puzzle.

distracted *adj.* **1** not concentrating on the matter in hand. **2** seriously confused or troubled.

▣ **1** abstracted, wandering, absent-minded, faraway, preoccupied, inattentive, dreaming, *colloq.* miles away, *colloq.* not with it. **2** confused, perplexed, bewildered, worried, troubled, disturbed, distraught, agitated, frantic.

distracting *adj.* diverting one's attention from the main topic.

distraction *noun* **1** something that diverts the attention. **2** an amusement; recreation. **3** anxiety; anger. **4** madness.

distrain *verb Legal* to seize (eg property) as, or in order to force, payment of a debt. [from Old French *destraindre*]

distraint *noun Legal* seizure of property or goods in order to meet a debt or obligation.

distrait /diˈstreɪ/ *adj. literary* thinking of other things. [from French *distrait*]

distraught /drˈstrɔːt/ *adj.* in an extremely troubled state of mind. [a form of DISTRACT]

⊟ agitated, anxious, overwrought, upset, distressed, distracted, beside oneself, worked up, frantic, hysterical, raving, mad, wild, crazy.
𝟻𝟹 calm, untroubled.

distress — *noun* **1** mental or emotional pain. **2** financial difficulty; hardship. **3** great danger; peril: *in distress.* — *verb* to cause distress to; to upset. [from Old French *destresse*]

⊟ *noun* **1** anguish, grief, misery, sorrow, heartache, affliction, suffering, torment, wretchedness, sadness, worry, anxiety, desolation, pain, agony. **2** adversity, hardship, poverty, need, privation, destitution, misfortune, trouble, difficulties, trial. *verb* upset, afflict, grieve, disturb, trouble, sadden, worry, torment, harass, harrow, pain, agonize, bother.
𝟻𝟹 *noun* **1** contentment. **2** comfort, ease. *verb* comfort.

distressed *adj.* **1** suffering distress. **2** *said of furniture or fabric* given an antique appearance; artificially aged.

distressing *adj.* causing distress or emotional pain.

distribute /drˈstrɪbjuːt, ˈdɪstrɪbjuːt/ *verb* **1** to give out. **2** to supply or deliver (goods). **3** to spread out widely; to disperse. [from Latin *distribuere*]

⊟ **1** dispense, allocate, dole out, dish out, share, deal, divide, apportion. **2** deliver, hand out, spread, issue, circulate. **3** diffuse, disperse, scatter.
𝟻𝟹 COLLECT.

distribution *noun* **1** the process of distributing or being distributed. **2** the location or pattern of things spread out. **3** *Statistics* a set of measurements or values, together with the observed or predicted frequencies with which they occur. Such information is often presented in the form of a graph.

⊟ **1** allocation, apportionment, division, sharing, circulation, spreading, scattering, delivery, dissemination, supply. **2** spread, deployment, arrangement, grouping, classification, organization.
𝟻𝟹 **1** collection.

distributive /drˈstrɪbjuːtɪv/ *adj.* **1** relating to distribution. **2** *Grammar, said of a word* referring individually to all members of a group, as do the words *each, every.*

distributor *noun* **1** a person or company that distributes goods. **2** a device in the ignition system of a car or other motor vehicle that directs pulses of high-voltage electricity from the induction coil to the spark plugs in the cylinders of the engine.

district *noun* an area or region, especially one forming an administrative or geographical unit. [from Latin *districtus,* jurisdiction]

⊟ region, area, quarter, neighbourhood, locality, sector, precinct, parish, locale, community, vicinity, ward.

district attorney *North Amer., esp. US* a lawyer employed by a district to conduct prosecutions.

district nurse in the UK, a nurse appointed to visit and treat patients in their own homes.

distrust — *verb* to have no trust in; to doubt. — *noun* suspicion; lack of trust.

⊟ *verb* mistrust, doubt, disbelieve, suspect, question. *noun* mistrust, doubt, disbelief, suspicion, misgiving, wariness, scepticism, question, qualm.
𝟻𝟹 *verb* trust. *noun* trust.

distrustful *adj.* having no trust in someone or something; suspicious.

disturb *verb* **1** to interrupt. **2** to inconvenience. **3** to upset the arrangement or order of. **4** to upset the peace of mind of. [from Latin *disturbare*]

⊟ **1, 2** bother. **1** disrupt, interrupt, distract. **2** inconvenience, trouble. **3** disarrange, disorder, disrupt, confuse, upset. **4** agitate, unsettle, upset, distress, worry, fluster, annoy.
𝟻𝟹 **3** order. **4** reassure.

disturbance *noun* **1** an outburst of noisy or violent behaviour. **2** an interruption. **3** an act of disturbing or process of being disturbed.

⊟ **1** disorder, uproar, commotion, tumult, turmoil, fracas, fray, brawl, riot. **2** interruption, intrusion. **3** disruption, agitation, upheaval, upset, confusion, annoyance, bother, trouble, hindrance.

disturbed *adj. Psychol.* confused, emotionally upset, or maladjusted.

disturbing *adj.* causing anxiety; unsettling.

⊟ worrying, unsettling, distressing, upsetting.

disunite *verb* to drive apart; to cause disagreement or conflict between or within.

⊟ divide, separate, estrange, alienate.

disunity *noun* lack of unity or agreement.

⊟ division, disunion, disagreement, dissent, contention, schism, faction.

disuse *noun* the state of no longer being used, practised, or observed; neglect.

⊟ neglect, abandonment, discontinuance, decay.
𝟻𝟹 use.

disused *adj.* no longer used; obsolete.

disyllabic /daɪ-/ *adj., said of a word* having two syllables.

disyllable *noun* a word of two syllables. [from Greek *di-*, twice + SYLLABLE]

ditch — *noun* a narrow channel dug in the ground for drainage or irrigation, or as a boundary. — *verb slang* to get rid of; to abandon. [from Anglo-Saxon *dic*]

⊟ *noun* trench, dyke, channel, gully, furrow, moat, drain, level, watercourse. *verb* abandon, dump, get rid of, throw away, scrap, jettison.

dither — *verb intrans.* (**dithered, dithering**) to act in a nervously uncertain manner; to waver. — *noun* a state of nervous indecision. [from Middle English *didderen*]

⊟ *verb* hesitate, shilly-shally, waver, vacillate.

ditherer *noun* a person who dithers or is indecisive.

dithery *adj.*, *said of a person* dithering; indecisive.

ditsy *adj. North Amer. colloq.* scatterbrained; flighty. [perhaps a mixture of DOTTY and DIZZY]

ditto — *noun* (PL. **dittos**) the same thing; the above; that which has just been said. — *adv.* likewise; the same. [from Latin *dictum*, said]

ditto marks marks (") written immediately below a word, etc in a list to mean 'same as above'.

ditty *noun* (PL. **ditties**) a short simple song or poem. [from Latin *dictare*, to dictate or compose]

diuretic /daɪjʊˈrɛtɪk/ — *noun Medicine* a drug or other substance that increases the volume of urine produced and excreted. — *adj.*, *said of a substance* increasing the production and excretion of urine. [from Greek *dia*, through + *ouron*, urine]

diurnal /daɪˈɜːnəl/ *adj. formal*, *technical* **1** daily. **2** denoting a phenomenon or event that occurs during the daytime. **3** *said of animals* at rest during the night and active during the day. **4** *said of flowers* closed at night and open during the day. **5** *Astron.*, *Biol.* denoting an event that recurs once every 24 hours. [from Latin *diurnus*]

diurnally *adv. formal*, *technical* during the day.

diva /ˈdiːvə/ *noun* (PL. **divas, dive**) a great female singer, especially in opera. [from Latin *diva*, goddess]

divalent /daɪˈveɪlənt/ *adj. Chem.*, *said of an atom of a chemical element* having a valency of two, and therefore capable of combining with two atoms of hydrogen or their equivalent. Also called BIVALENT. [from DI- + VALENCY]

Divali or **Diwali** /dɪˈvɑːliː, -ˈwɑːliː/ *noun* the Hindu festival of lights, held in October or November in honour of Lakshmi, goddess of wealth and good fortune. [from Hindi]

divan /dɪˈvan/ *noun* **1** a sofa with no back or sides. **2** a bed without a headboard or footboard. [from Persian *diwan*, long seat]

dive[1] — *verb intrans.* **1** to leap head first into water. **2** to become submerged. **3** to fall steeply through the air. **4** to throw oneself to the side or to the ground. **5** to move quickly and suddenly out of sight. — *noun* an act of diving. **2** *slang* any dirty or disreputable place, especially a bar or club. **3** *Boxing slang* a faked knockout: *take a dive*. — **dive into something 1** to plunge one's hands (eg into a bag). **2** to involve oneself enthusiastically in an undertaking. [from Anglo-Saxon *dyfan*]

⊟ *verb* **1, 3** plunge, plummet. **2** submerge. **3** nosedive, fall, drop, swoop, descend. *noun* **1** plunge, lunge, header, jump, leap, nosedive, swoop, dash, spring. **2** bar, club, saloon.

dive[2] see DIVA.

dive-bomb *verb trans.*, *intrans.* to bomb while diving in an aircraft.

dive-bomber *noun* an aircraft from which bombs are released while diving.

dive-bombing *noun* bombing from a diving aircraft.

diver *noun* **1** a person who dives. **2** a person who swims or works underwater. **3** a large diving bird, native to northern waters of the northern hemisphere, and having plumage with fine contrasting patterns. It feeds mainly on fish, and only comes ashore to breed.

diverge *verb intrans.* **1** to separate and go in different directions. **2** to differ. **3** (**diverge from something**) to depart or deviate (eg from a usual course). [from Latin *di-*, apart + *vergere*, to turn]

⊟ **1** divide, branch, fork, separate, spread, split. **2** differ, vary,

disagree, dissent, conflict. **3** deviate, digress, stray, wander.
⊞ **1** converge. **2** agree.

divergence *noun* separation; deviation.

divergent *adj.* separating; going in different directions.

diverging lens *Physics* a lens that causes light rays to diverge (spread out), eg a concave lens.

divers /ˈdaɪvəz/ *adj. old use*, *literary* various; many different. [etymology as for DIVERSE]

diverse /daɪˈvɜːs/ *adj.* **1** various; assorted. **2** different; dissimilar. [from Latin *diversus*, turned different ways]

⊟ **1** various, varied, varying, sundry, assorted, miscellaneous, several. **2** different, differing, dissimilar, discrete, separate, distinct.
⊞ SIMILAR, IDENTICAL.

diversification *noun* engaging in different activities; branching out.

diversify *verb* (**diversifies, diversified**) **1** *trans.*, *intrans.* to make or become diverse. **2** *intrans.* to engage in new and different activities; to branch out.

⊟ **1** vary, change, alter, mix. **2** expand, branch out, spread out.

diversion *noun* **1** the act of diverting; the state of being diverted. **2** a detour from a usual route. **3** something intended to draw attention away. **4** amusement. [from Latin *diversio*]

⊟ **1** deflection, redirection, rerouteing, switching. **2** detour, deviation. **4** amusement, entertainment, distraction, pastime, recreation, relaxation, play, game.

diversionary *adj.* intended to cause a diversion.

diversity *noun* variety in kind; being varied or different.

⊟ variety, dissimilarity, difference, variance, assortment, range, medley.
⊞ similarity, likeness.

divert /daɪˈvɜːt/ *verb* **1** to cause to change direction. **2** to draw away (especially attention). **3** to amuse. [from Latin *divertere*, to turn aside]

⊟ DISTRACT. **1** deflect, redirect, reroute, switch. **2** draw away, draw off, sidetrack, avert. **3** amuse, entertain, occupy, distract, interest.

diverticular /daɪvəˈtɪkjʊlə(r)/ *adj. Medicine* relating to diverticula.

diverticulitis /daɪvətɪkjʊˈlaɪtɪs/ *noun Medicine* inflammation of one or more diverticula.

diverticulum /daɪvəˈtɪkjʊləm/ *noun* (PL. **diverticula**) *Medicine* a pouch formed at a weak point in the muscular wall of the alimentary canal, especially the colon.

divertimento /dɪv-/ *noun* (PL. **divertimenti, divertimentos**) a light musical composition intended primarily for entertainment, especially in the 18c. [from Italian *divertimento*, entertainment, amusement]

divest /daɪˈvɛst/ *verb* **1** to undress (oneself or another). **2** (**divest someone of something**) to take it from them. [from Latin *de-*, away from + *vestire*, to clothe]

⊟ STRIP. **1** undress, disrobe. **2** deprive, dispossess, rob.

divestment *noun* divesting; depriving of possession.

divide — *verb* **1** *trans.*, *intrans.* to split up or separate into parts. **2** (*also* **divide something up**) to share. **3 a** to calculate how many times one number or quantity (the *divisor*) is contained in another number or quantity (the *dividend*), by performing the arithmetical operation of division. The result obtained is known as the *quotient*. **b** *intrans. said of a number* to divide exactly into another number without a remainder: *3 divides into 9*. **4** to cause disagreement among; to set at odds. **5** (*also* **divide something up**) to arrange it in different categories. **6** to serve as a boundary between. — *noun* **1** a disagreement; a gap or split. **2** *North Amer., esp. US* an area of relatively high ground separating two adjacent drainage basins. Also called WATERSHED. [from Latin *dividere*, to force apart]

⬛ *verb* **1** split, separate, part, cut, break up, detach, bisect, disconnect. **2** distribute, share, allocate, deal out, allot, apportion. **4** disunite, separate, estrange, alienate. **5** classify, group, sort, grade, segregate. **6** separate.
◨ **1** join. **2** collect. **4** unite.

dividend /'dɪvɪdɛnd/ *noun* **1** a portion of a company's profits paid to a shareholder. **2** a benefit: *meeting her would pay dividends*. **3** *Maths.* a number or quantity that is to be divided by another number or quantity (the *divisor*). [from Latin *dividendum*, what is to be divided]

dividers *pl. noun* a type of compass, consisting of a V-shaped device with two pointed arms, used for measuring or dividing lines.

divination /dɪvɪ'neɪʃən/ *noun* **1** the practice of foretelling the future (as if) by supernatural means. **2** insight. **3** a guess. [from DIVINE]

divine — *adj.* **1** of, from, or relating to God or a god. **2** *colloq.* extremely pleasant or beautiful; excellent. — *verb* **1** to foretell; to learn of by intuition; to guess. **2** *trans., intrans.* to search for (underground water) with a divining-rod. — *noun* a member of the clergy expert in theology. [from Latin *divinus*, from *divus*, a god]

⬛ *adj.* **1** godlike, superhuman, supernatural, celestial, heavenly, angelic, spiritual, holy, sacred, sanctified, consecrated, transcendent, exalted, religious, supreme. **2** excellent, wonderful, delightful, glorious, lovely, delicious. *verb* **1** foretell, predict, discern, intuit, guess, suspect. **2** dowse.
◨ *adj.* **1** human, mundane.

divinely *adv.* **1** in divine terms. **2** *colloq.* extremely finely or well: *she sang divinely*.

diving *noun* the activity or sport of plunging into water, especially from a platform or board at the side of a swimming-pool.

diving-bell *noun* a large hollow bottomless underwater container pumped full of air, to which an unequipped diver returns to take in oxygen.

diving-board *noun* a narrow platform from which swimmers can dive into a pool, etc.

diving-suit *noun* a diver's waterproof suit, especially one with a helmet and heavy boots for walking on the sea-bottom, etc.

divining-rod *noun* a stick, especially of hazel, held near the ground when divining for water, (allegedly) twitching when a discovery is made.

divinity /dɪ'vɪnɪtɪ/ *noun* (PL. **divinities**) **1** theology. **2** a god. **3** the state of being God or a god. [from DIVINE]

⬛ **2, 3** deity, godhead. **2** god, goddess, spirit.

divisible *adj.* able to be divided.

division *noun* **1** the act of dividing; the state of being divided. **2** the act of sharing out or distributing. **3** something that divides or separates; a gap or barrier. **4** something that disunites; a disagreement. **5** one of the parts into which something is divided; a major unit of an organization, eg an army or police force. **6** *Maths.* the process of determining how many times one number (the *divisor*) is contained in another (the *dividend*). **7** a formal vote in Parliament. **8** *Bot.* in the plant kingdom, one of the major groups used for classification, corresponding to a phylum

in the animal kingdom, and subdivided into classes, eg Bryophyta (mosses and liverworts).

⬛ **1** separation, detaching, detachment, parting, cutting. **2** distribution, sharing, allotment, apportionment, partitioning. **3** partition, barrier, gap, breach, divider. **4** disagreement, feud, breach, rupture, split, schism, disunion, estrangement. **5** section, sector, segment, part, department, category, class, compartment, branch.
◨ **1** union. **2** collection. **4** unity. **5** whole.

divisional *adj.* relating to or belonging to a division or section, especially of a business or organization: *divisional headquarters*.

division sign the symbol representing division in calculations.

divisive /dɪ'vaɪsɪv/ *adj.* tending to cause disagreement or conflict. [from DIVIDE]

divisiveness *noun* being divisive; a tendency to cause disagreement.

divisor *noun* *Maths.* **1** the number or quantity by which another number or quantity (the *dividend*) is to be divided. **2** a number that divides another number without a remainder; a factor. [from Latin *divisor*, divider]

divorce — *noun* **1** the legal ending of a marriage. **2** a complete separation. — *verb* **1** *trans., intrans.* to legally end marriage to (someone). **2** to separate. [from Latin *divortere*, to leave one's husband]

⬛ *noun* SEPARATION, BREACH. **1** dissolution, annulment, break-up, split-up. **2** disunion, rupture. *verb* SEPARATE, PART, SPLIT UP. **2** sever, dissolve, divide, dissociate.
◨ *verb* **1** marry. **2** unite.

divorcé /dɪvɔ:'seɪ/ *noun* a divorced man.

divorced *adj.*, *said of a partner in marriage* separated by divorce.

divorcée /dɪvɔ:'seɪ/ *noun* a divorced woman.

divot *noun* a clump of grass and earth removed, especially by the blade of a golf club. [from Scot. *divot*]

divulge /daɪ'vʌldʒ/ *verb* to make known; to reveal. [from Latin *divulgare*, to publish widely]

⬛ disclose, reveal, communicate, tell, leak, impart, confess, betray, uncover, let slip, expose, publish, proclaim.

divulgence *noun* making known; disclosing a secret, etc.

divvy *slang* — *noun* (PL. **divvies**) a dividend or share. — *verb* (**divvies, divvied**) (*also* **divvy up**) to divide or share.

Diwali see DIVALI.

dixie *noun* a large metal cooking-pot or kettle. [perhaps from Hindi *degci*]

DIY *abbrev.* do-it-yourself.

dizzily *adv.* in a dizzy or bewildered way.

dizziness *noun* a dizzy or bewildered state.

dizzy — *adj.* (**dizzier, dizziest**) **1** experiencing or causing a spinning sensation causing loss of balance: *feel dizzy / dizzy heights*. **2** *colloq.* silly; not reliable or responsible. **3** *colloq.* bewildered. — *verb* (**dizzies, dizzied**) **1** to make dizzy. **2** to bewilder. [from Anglo-Saxon *dysig*, foolish]

⬛ *adj.* **1** giddy, faint, light-headed, *colloq.* woozy, shaky, reeling. **2** silly, irresponsible, feather-brained, scatterbrained, *North Amer. colloq.* ditsy. **3** confused, bewildered, dazed, muddled.

DJ *abbrev.* **1** *slang* dinner jacket. **2** disc jockey.

djinn and **djinni** see JINNI.

DK *abbrev.*, *as an international vehicle mark* Denmark.

dl *abbrev.* decilitre.

DLitt or **DLit** *abbrev. Doctor litterarum litteraturae* (Latin), Doctor of Letters or of Literature.

DM *abbrev.* Deutschmark.

DMus *abbrev.* Doctor of Music.

DMZ *abbrev.* demilitarized zone.

DNA *abbrev.* deoxyribonucleic acid: the nucleic acid, containing the sugar deoxyribose, that forms the material of which the chromosomes and genes of almost all living organisms are composed, and contains coded instructions for the transmission of genetic information.

DNB *abbrev.* Dictionary of National Biography.

D-notice *noun* a notice sent by the government to newspapers asking them not to publish certain information for reasons of security. [from *defence* notice]

do¹ — *verb* (**does, doing**; PAST TENSE **did**; PAST PARTICIPLE **done**) **1** to carry out, perform, or commit. **2** to finish or complete. **3** *trans., intrans.* to be enough or suitable: *that will do for me / that will do me.* **4** to work at or study. **5** *intrans.* to be in a particular state: *Business is doing well.* **6** to put in order or arrange. **7** *intrans.* to act or behave. **8** to provide as a service: *do lunches.* **9** to bestow (honour, etc). **10** to cause or produce. **11** to travel (a distance); to travel at (a speed). **12** *colloq.* to be an improvement or enhancement to: *this dress doesn't do much for my figure.* **13** *colloq.* to cheat. **14** *colloq.* to copy the behaviour of; to mimic. **15** to visit as a tourist. **16** *colloq.* to ruin: *now he's done it!* **17** *colloq.* to assault or injure: *tell me, or I'll do you.* **18** *colloq.* to spend (time) in prison. **19** *colloq.* to convict. **20** *intrans. colloq.* to happen: *there was nothing doing.* **21** *slang* to take (drugs). — *verb aux.* **1** used in questions and negative statements or commands: *do you smoke? / I don't like wine / don't do that!* **2** used to avoid repetition of a verb: *she eats as much as I do.* **3** used for emphasis: *she does know you've arrived.* — *noun* (PL. **dos, do's**) *colloq.* **1** a party or other gathering. **2** something done as a rule or custom: *dos and don'ts.* **3** a violent scene; a fracas. — **be done for** to face ruin or death. **be** or **have done with something** or **someone** to have finished with or to have dealt with them. **could do with something** or **someone** would benefit from having them. **do away with someone** or **something 1** to murder them. **2** to abolish an institution, etc. **do someone** or **something down** to speak of them as if unimportant or not very good. **do for someone** *colloq.* to do household cleaning for them on a regular basis. **do someone in** *colloq.* **1** to kill them. **2** to exhaust them. **do something out** to clear out a room, etc; to decorate it. **do someone out of something** to deprive them of it, especially by trickery. **do someone over** *slang* **1** to rob them. **2** to attack or injure them. **do something up** *colloq.* **1** to repair, clean, or improve the decoration of a building, etc. **2** to fasten it; to tie or wrap it up. **do oneself up** to dress up. **do without something** to manage without it. **have** or **be to do with someone** or **something 1** *said of a thing, event, etc* to be related to or connected with something else: *that has a great deal to do with your question / it has nothing to do with me.* **2** *said of a person* to be partly or wholly responsible for something: *I had nothing to do with the arrangement.* [from Anglo-Saxon *don*]

⊟ *verb* **1** perform, carry out, execute, accomplish, achieve, fulfil, implement, undertake, work, put on, present.
   2 end, finish, conclude, complete. **3** suffice, satisfy, serve. **4** work on, work at, study, read. **6** fix, prepare, organize, arrange, deal with, look after, manage. **7** behave, act, conduct oneself. **8** provide, supply, sell, stock. **10** produce, make, create, cause. **13** cheat, *colloq.* rip off, *colloq.* have.
   noun **1** party, function, affair, event, gathering, occasion.
   do away with GET RID OF, DISPOSE OF, EXTERMINATE, ELIMINATE. **1** kill, murder. **2** abolish, discontinue, remove, destroy, discard. **do down** run down, belittle, disparage, deride, dismiss, underrate, undervalue. **do in 1** kill, murder, *slang* bump off. **2** exhaust, tire out, wear out, *colloq.* knacker. **do up 1** renovate, restore, decorate, redecorate, modernize, repair. **2** fasten, tie, lace, pack.
   do without dispense with, abstain from, forego, give up, relinquish.

do² same as DOH.

do. *abbrev.* ditto.

DOA *abbrev.* dead on arrival.

doable *adj.* able to be done.

⊟ possible, feasible, manageable, practicable, attainable, achievable, realizable.

Doberman or **Dobermann** *noun* (*in full* **Doberman** or **Dobermann pinscher**) a large breed of dog with a lean body, long neck and muzzle, pendulous ears, and a glossy black and tan coat. They are often used as guard dogs. [from *Dobermann*, the breeder's name + German *Pinscher*, terrier]

doc *noun colloq.* a doctor.

docile *adj.* easy to manage or control; submissive. [from Latin *docilis*, easily taught]

⊟ tractable, co-operative, manageable, submissive, obedient, amenable, controlled, obliging.
⊞ truculent, unco-operative.

docilely *adv.* with a docile or willing manner.

docility *noun* a docile manner.

dock¹ — *noun* **1** an artificially constructed basin or waterway for the berthing of ships and the loading and unloading of cargo. *Dry docks* are enclosed basins from which water can be pumped, enabling ships to be repaired. **2** (**docks**) the area surrounding this. **3** the waterway between two wharves or two piers. — *verb trans., intrans.* **1** to bring or come into a dock. **2** to equip with docks. **3** *said of space vehicles* to link up in space. — **in dock** being repaired. [from Old Dutch *docke*]

⊟ *noun* **1** harbour, wharf, quay, boatyard, pier, waterfront, marina. *verb* **1** anchor, moor, land, berth, tie up.

dock² *verb* **1** to cut off all or part of (an animal's tail). **2** to make deductions from (especially pay); to deduct (an amount). [from Middle English *dok*]

⊟ **1** crop, clip, cut, shorten, curtail. **2** deduct, reduce, lessen, withhold, decrease, subtract, diminish.

dock³ *noun* any of various perennial plants of the genus *Rumex*, related to buckwheat and rhubarb, and native to north temperate regions, especially the broad-leaved dock (*Rumex obtusifolia*). [from Anglo-Saxon *docce*]

dock⁴ *noun* the enclosure in a court of law where the accused sits or stands. [from Flemish *dok*, cage, sty]

docker *noun* a labourer who loads and unloads ships.

docket — *noun* any label or note accompanying a parcel, eg detailing contents or recording receipt. — *verb* (**docketed, docketing**) to fix a label to; to record the contents or delivery of.

dockyard *noun* a shipyard.

Doc Martens *trademark* a make of lace-up leather boots with light, thick resilient soles.

doctor — *noun* **1** a person trained and qualified to practise medicine. **2** *North Amer.* a dentist. **3** *North Amer.* a veterinary surgeon. **4** a person who has received a doctorate from a university. — *verb* (**doctored, doctoring**) **1** to falsify (eg information); to tamper with; to drug (food or drink). **2** *colloq.* to sterilize or castrate (an animal). **3** *often facetious* to give medical treatment to. [from Latin *doctor*, teacher]

⊟ *noun* **1** physician, general practitioner, GP, *colloq.* medic, medical officer, consultant, clinician. *verb* **1** alter, tamper with, falsify, misrepresent, pervert, adulterate, change, disguise, dilute. **2** sterilize, spay, castrate, neuter.

doctoral *adj.* relating to a doctorate.

doctorate *noun* a high academic degree, awarded especially for research.

doctrinaire /dɒktrɪˈnɛə(r)/ *adj. derog.* adhering rigidly to theories or principles, often regardless of practicalities or appropriateness.

doctrinal /dɒkˈtraɪnəl/ *adj.* relating to or consisting of doctrine.

doctrine /ˈdɒktrɪn/ *noun* a thing or things taught, especially (any one of) a set of religious or political beliefs. [from Latin *doctrina*, teaching]

⬛ dogma, creed, belief, tenet, principle, teaching, precept, conviction, opinion, canon.

docudrama *noun* a play or film based on real events and characters. [a contraction of *documentary drama*]

document — *noun* 1 any piece of writing of an official nature, eg a certificate. 2 *Comput.* a file of text produced and read by a computer, especially a word processor. — *verb* 1 to record, especially in written form. 2 to provide written evidence to support or prove. [from Latin *documentum*, lesson, proof]

⬛ *noun* 1 paper, certificate, deed, record, report, form, instrument. *verb* 1 record, report, chronicle, list, detail, cite. 2 support, prove, corroborate, verify.

documentary — *noun* (PL. **documentaries**) a film or television or radio programme presenting real people in real situations. — *adj.* 1 connected with, or consisting of, documents. 2 of the nature of a documentary; undramatised.

documentation *noun* documents or documentary evidence, or the provision or collection of these.

dodder *verb intrans.* (**doddered, doddering**) to move in an unsteady, trembling fashion as a result of old age. [variant of an old word *dadder*]

dodderer *noun* a doddering person.

doddery *adj.* tending to dodder; unsteady.

doddle *noun colloq.* something easily done or achieved.

dodecagon /dəʊˈdɛkəgɒn/ *noun* a plane (two-dimensional) figure with 12 sides and 12 angles. It is a type of polygon. [from Greek *dodeka*, twelve + *gonia*, angle]

dodecahedron /dəʊdɛkəˈhiːdrən/ *noun* a solid (three-dimensional) figure with 12 plane faces. It is a type of polyhedron. [from Greek *dodeka*, twelve + *hedra*, seat]

dodge — *verb* 1 to avoid by moving quickly away, especially sideways. 2 to escape or avoid by cleverness or deceit. — *noun* 1 a sudden movement aside. 2 a trick to escape or avoid something.

⬛ *verb* AVOID, ELUDE, EVADE. 1 swerve, side-step, jink, duck. 2 shirk, *colloq.* duck. *noun* 1 side-step, jink. 2 trick, ruse, ploy, wile, scheme, stratagem, machination, manoeuvre.

Dodgems *noun trademark* a fairground amusement consisting of a rink in which drivers of small electric cars try to bump each other.

dodger *noun* a shirker; a trickster.

dodgy *adj.* (**dodgier, dodgiest**) *colloq.* 1 difficult or risky. 2 untrustworthy; dishonest, or dishonestly obtained. 3 unstable; slightly broken.

⬛ *colloq.* IFFY. 1 dicey, risky, chancy. 2 disreputable, untrustworthy, dubious, dishonest, seedy, suspicious, suspect, *slang* hot. 3 unstable, unsteady, wobbly, shaky, rickety.

dodo *noun* (PL. **dodos, dodoes**) 1 a large flightless bird of the pigeon family, about the size of a turkey, that once lived on the island of Mauritius, and became extinct around the middle of the 17c. 2 *colloq.* any old-fashioned person or thing. 3 *colloq.* a stupid person. — **as dead as a dodo** *colloq.* 1 extinct. 2 out-of-date; obsolete. [from Portuguese *doudo*, silly]

DOE *abbrev.* Department of the Environment.

doe *noun* (PL. **does, doe**) the adult female of the deer, antelope, rabbit, hare, and certain other mammals. [from Anglo-Saxon *da*]

doer *noun* a person who does something; an active person.

does see DO.

doesn't *contr.* does not.

doff *verb old use, literary* to take off (a piece of clothing); to lift (one's hat) in greeting. [from DO¹ + OFF]

dog — *noun* 1 any carnivorous mammal belonging to the family Canidae, which includes the wolves, jackals, and foxes. Dogs have strong jaws and sharp teeth, and they are fast runners and good hunters. 2 any of many different breeds of a domestic species of this family (*Canis familiaris*). 3 the male of any such animal. 4 any of various mammals of other families, eg prairie dog. 5 a mechanical gripping device. 6 *offensive slang* an unattractive woman. 7 *colloq.* a fellow or rogue. — *verb* (**dogged, dogging**) 1 to follow very closely; to track. 2 to trouble or plague. — **a dog's breakfast** or **dinner** *colloq.* an untidy mess; a shambles. **a dog's life** a life of misery. **like a dog's dinner** *colloq.* dressed smartly or showily. [from Anglo-Saxon *docga*]

⬛ *noun* 1, 2 hound, cur, mongrel, canine, puppy, pup, bitch, *colloq.* mutt. *verb* 1 pursue, follow, trail, track, tail, shadow. 2 plague, hound, harry, haunt, trouble, worry.

Breeds of dog include: Afghan hound, alsatian, basset hound, beagle, Border collie, borzoi, bull mastiff, bulldog, bull terrier, cairn terrier, chihuahua, chow, cocker spaniel, collie, corgi, dachshund, Dalmatian, Doberman pinscher, foxhound, fox terrier, German Shepherd, golden retriever, Great Dane, greyhound, husky, Irish wolfhound, Jack Russell, King Charles spaniel, Labrador, lhasa apso, lurcher, Maltese, Old English sheepdog, Pekingese, pit bull terrier, pointer, poodle, pug, Rottweiler, saluki, *colloq.* sausage-dog, schnauzer, *colloq.* Scottie, Scottish terrier, Sealyham, setter, sheltie, shih tzu, springer spaniel, St Bernard, terrier, whippet, West Highland terrier, *colloq.* Westie, wolfhound, Yorkshire terrier.

dogcart *noun* a two-wheeled horse-drawn passenger carriage with seats back-to-back.

dog collar 1 a collar for a dog. 2 *colloq.* a close-fitting white collar worn by members of the clergy.

dog days the hottest period of the year, when the Dogstar rises and sets with the sun.

doge /dəʊdʒ/ *noun* the chief magistrate in the former republics of Venice and Genoa. [from Italian dialect *doge*, duke]

dog-eared *adj., said of a book* with its pages turned down at the corners; shabby; scruffy.

dog-end *noun slang* a cigarette end.

dogfight *noun* 1 a battle at close quarters between two fighter aircraft. 2 any fight between dogs. 3 any violent fight.

dogfish *noun* (PL. **dogfish, dogfishes**) 1 any of several species of small shark native to coastal waters of all temperate and tropical oceans. 2 any of various other small fishes, especially the bowfin.

dogged *adj.* persistent and determined in pursuing an objective.

⬛ determined, resolute, persistent, persevering, intent, tenacious, firm, steadfast, staunch, single-minded, indefatigable, steady, unshakable, stubborn, obstinate, relentless, unyielding. ⬛ irresolute, apathetic.

doggedly *adv.* in a dogged or resolute way.
doggedness *noun* being dogged or resolute.

doggerel — *noun* **1** badly written poetry. **2** poetry with an irregular rhyming pattern for comic effect. — *adj.* of poor quality. [from Middle English *dogerel*, worthless]

doggo — **lie doggo** *old colloq. use* to hide; to lie low. [probably from DOG]

doggy — *adj.* (**doggier, doggiest**) *colloq.* **1** like or relating to dogs. **2** fond of dogs. — *noun* (*also* **doggie**) (PL. **doggies**) a child's word for a dog.

doggy bag a bag in which a customer at a restaurant can take home uneaten food.

doggy-paddle or **dog-paddle** — *noun* a basic swimming stroke with short paddling movements like a dog's. — *verb intrans.* to swim using this stroke.

doghouse — **in the doghouse** *colloq.* out of favour.

dog in the manger a person who has no need of something and refuses to let others use it.

dog-in-the-manger *adj.* characteristic of a dog in the manger; possessively selfish.

dogleg *noun* a sharp bend, especially on a golf course.

dogma *noun* **1** a belief or principle laid down by an authority as unquestionably true; such beliefs or principles in general. **2** *colloq.* an opinion arrogantly stated. [from Greek *dogma*, opinion]

■ **1** doctrine, creed, belief, precept, principle, article (of faith), credo, tenet, conviction, teaching, opinion.

dogmatic /dɒgˈmatɪk/ *adj.* **1** *said of an opinion* forcefully and arrogantly stated as if unquestionable. **2** *said of a person* tending to make such statements of opinion.

■ CATEGORICAL, EMPHATIC, AUTHORITATIVE. **2** opinionated, assertive, positive, doctrinaire, dictatorial, overbearing.

dogmatism /ˈdɒgmətɪzm/ *noun* the quality of being, or the tendency to be, dogmatic.

dogmatist /ˈdɒgmətɪst/ *noun* a person who is dogmatic or given to positive assertions.

dogmatize or **dogmatise** /ˈdɒgmətaɪz/ *verb intrans.* to state one's opinions dogmatically.

do-gooder *noun colloq.* an enthusiastically helpful person, especially one whose help is unwanted or impractical.

dog rose a deciduous shrubby plant (*Rosa canina*), found in woodland and hedgerows, and having berry-like fruits, known as *hips*, which are a rich source of vitamin C.

dogs *pl. noun* (**the dogs**) *colloq.* greyhound racing. — **go to the dogs** *colloq.* to deteriorate greatly.

dogsbody *noun* (PL. **dogsbodies**) *colloq.* a person who does menial tasks for someone else.

Dog Star *Astron.* see SIRIUS.

dog-tired *adj. colloq.* extremely tired.

dogtrot *noun* a gentle trotting pace.

dogwood *noun* **1** any of about 90 species of small deciduous trees and shrubs of the genus *Cornus*, native to Europe, Asia, and N America, especially the common European dogwood (*Cornus sanguinea*), with oval pointed leaves and black waxy berries. **2** the wood of this tree.

doh *noun* the first note of the scale in the sol-fa system of music notation. [from Italian *doh*]

doily or **doyley** *noun* (PL. **doilies, doyleys**) a small decorative napkin of lace or lace-like paper laid on plates under sandwiches, cakes, etc. [named after *Doily*, London draper]

doings *sing. noun colloq.* the thing whose name cannot be remembered; a thingummy.

do-it-yourself *noun* (ABBREV **DIY**) the practice of doing one's own household repairs, etc without professional help.

Dolby or **Dolby system** a system of noise reduction in magnetic audio tape-recording. [named after the US engineer Raymond *Dolby*]

dolce /ˈdɒleɪ/ *adj., adv. Mus.* to be sung or played gently or sweetly. [Italian, = sweet, from Latin *dulcis*]

doldrums *pl. noun* (**the doldrums**) **1** a depressed mood; low spirits. **2** a state of inactivity. **3** (*also* **Doldrums**) *Meteorol.* a hot humid region on either side of the Equator, where there is generally little or no wind. [from obsolete *dold*, stupid]

dole — *noun colloq.* (**the dole**) unemployment benefit. — *verb intrans.* (**dole something out**) to hand it out or give it out. — **on the dole** *colloq.* unemployed; receiving unemployment benefit. [from Anglo-Saxon *dal*, share]

■ *noun Brit.* benefit, welfare. *verb* distribute, allocate, hand out, dish out, apportion, allot, mete out, share, divide, deal, issue, ration, dispense, administer, assign.

doleful *adj.* sad; expressing or suggesting sadness; mournful. [from Old French *doel*, grief + -FUL]

■ sad, sorrowful, mournful, woeful, miserable, melancholy, sombre, elegaic, funereal.

dolefully *adv.* with a doleful or melancholy manner.

dolefulness *noun* a doleful or melancholy manner.

doll — *noun* **1** a toy in the form of a model of a human being, especially a baby. **2** *derog. colloq.* a showy over-dressed woman. **3** *slang, often offensive* any girl or woman, especially when considered pretty. **4** *colloq.* a term of endearment, especially for a girl. — *verb* (**doll oneself up**) to dress smartly or showily. [from the name *Dolly*]

dollar *noun* (SYMBOL **$**) the standard unit of currency in the US, Canada, Australia, and several other countries, divided into 100 cents. [from German *Thaler*, short for *Joachimsthaler*, the name of silver coins from *Joachimsthal* in Bohemia]

dollop *noun colloq.* a small shapeless mass of any semi-solid substance, especially food.

dolly *noun* (PL. **dollies**) **1** *colloq.* a child's name for a doll. **2** *Cinema, Broadcasting* a frame with wheels on which a film or television camera is mounted for moving shots.

dolmen /ˈdɒlmən/ *noun* a simple prehistoric monument consisting of a large flat stone supported by several vertical stones. [perhaps from Breton *dol*, table + *men*, stone]

dolomite /ˈdɒləmaɪt/ *noun* **1** *Geol.* a mineral composed of calcium magnesium carbonate, formed by the replacement of limestone. **2** a sedimentary carbonate rock containing more than 50 per cent dolomite. [named after the Dolomites, in which it is found]

dolorous /ˈdɒlərəs/ *adj. literary* causing, involving, or suggesting sorrow or grief. [from DOLOUR]

dolour /ˈdɒlə(r)/ *noun poetic* sorrow or grief. [from Latin *dolor*, pain]

dolphin *noun* **1** a small toothed whale belonging to the family Delphinidae, and found in seas virtually worldwide, both in deep water and near to coasts. **2** a freshwater (or river) dolphin. [from Greek *delphinos*]

dolphinarium /dɒlfɪˈnɛərɪəm/ *noun* a large open-air aquarium in which dolphins are kept, both for study and to display to the public. [from DOLPHIN + AQUARIUM]

dolt *noun derog.* a stupid person. [from Anglo-Saxon *dol*, stupid]

doltish *adj.* dull; stupid.

DOM *abbrev., as an international vehicle mark* Dominican Republic.

-dom *suffix* forming words denoting: **1** a state or rank: *serfdom / dukedom*. **2** an area ruled or governed: *kingdom*. **3** a group of people with a specified characteristic: *officialdom*. [from Anglo-Saxon *dom*, judgement]

domain *noun* **1** the scope of any subject or area of interest. **2** a territory owned or ruled by one person or government. **3** *Maths.* the set of values specified for a given mathematical function. **4** *Physics* in a ferromagnetic substance, eg iron, nickel, a small region within which individual magnetic moments can be aligned, giving that substance permanent magnetic properties. **5** *Comput.* the country, network, etc where a computer on the Internet is located, as identified by the suffix (**domain name**) on the address. [from French *domaine*]

. . . .

⊟ **1** field, area, speciality, concern, department, sphere, discipline, jurisdiction. **2** dominion, kingdom, realm, territory, region, empire, land(s), province.

. . . .

dome *noun* **1** a roof in the shape of a hemisphere. **2** anything of similar shape. **3** *colloq.* a head. [from Latin *domus*, house]

domed *adj.*, *said of a building* having a dome.

Domesday Book or **Doomsday Book** a survey of all lands in England, ordered by William the Conqueror in 1086, detailing their value, ownership, etc. See also DOOMSDAY. [from Anglo-Saxon *dom*, judgement]

domestic /dəˈmestɪk/ — *adj.* **1** of or relating to the home, the family, or private life. **2** *said of animals* not wild; kept as a pet or farm animal. **3** within or relating to one's country; not foreign: *domestic sales and export sales.* **4** enjoying home life. — *noun* a household servant. [from Latin *domesticus*, from *domus*, house]

. . . .

⊟ *adj.* **1** home, family, household. **2** domesticated, tame, pet, house-trained. **3** internal, inland, indigenous, native. **4** home-loving, stay-at-home, domesticated. *noun* daily help, daily, au pair, servant, maid, charwoman, char.
⊟ *adj.* **2** wild. **3** foreign, overseas, international.

. . . .

domesticate *verb* **1** to train (an animal) for life in the company of people. **2** *often facetious* to make used to home life, especially to train in cooking, housework, etc.

. . . .

⊟ **1** tame, house-train, break, train, accustom, familiarize.

. . . .

domestication *noun* adaptation to home life.
domesticity *noun* home life, or a liking for it.
domestic science training in household skills, especially cooking; home economics.
domicile /ˈdomɪsaɪl/ — *noun* **1** *formal* a house. **2** a legally recognized place of permanent residence. — *verb* *Legal* to establish in a fixed residence. [from Latin *domicilium*, dwelling]
domiciliary /domɪˈsɪlɪərɪ/ *adj.* relating to people and their homes.
dominance *noun* dominant position; influence over others.

. . . .

⊟ primacy, pre-eminence, superiority, supremacy, influence, control, command, authority, leadership.

. . . .

dominant — *adj.* **1** most important, evident, or active; foremost. **2** tending or seeking to command or influence others. **3** *said of a building, etc* overlooking others from an elevated position. **4** *Biol.* denoting a gene, or the characteristics determined by it, whose phenotype (visible effect) is fully expressed in an individual whether there are two dominant alleles, or one dominant and one recessive allele. **5** denoting a characteristic determined by such a gene. **6** *Biol.* denoting the most prevalent plant or animal species in a particular community or during a particular period, or describing an animal that occupies a superior position within a group of its own kind. *noun* the fifth note on a musical scale. [from DOMINATE]

. . . .

⊟ *adj.* **1** foremost, principal, main, outstanding, chief, important, predominant, primary, prominent, leading, pre-eminent, prevailing, prevalent, commanding. **2** authoritative, controlling, governing, ruling, powerful, assertive, influential.
⊟ *adj.* **1** subordinate. **2** submissive.

. . . .

dominate *verb trans., intrans.* **1** to have command or influence over (someone). **2** to be the most important, evident, or active of (a group). **3** to enjoy an elevated position over (a place). [from Latin *dominari*, to be master]

. . . .

⊟ **1** control, domineer, govern, rule, direct, monopolize, master, lead, overrule, prevail, overbear, tyrannize. **3** command, overlook, overshadow, tower over, dwarf.

. . . .

dominating *adj.* tending to dominate.
domination *noun* dominating; absolute authority.

. . . .

⊟ command, control, mastery, supremacy, superiority, ascendancy, pre-eminence, predominance.

. . . .

domineer /domɪˈnɪə(r)/ *verb intrans.* to behave in an arrogantly dominant way.
domineering *adj.* overbearing; behaving arrogantly towards others.

. . . .

⊟ overbearing, authoritarian, imperious, autocratic, *colloq.* bossy, dictatorial, despotic, masterful, high-handed, oppressive, tyrannical, arrogant.
⊟ meek, servile.

. . . .

Dominican — *noun* a member of a Christian order of friars and nuns founded in 1216 by St Dominic in Italy to provide defenders of the Roman Catholic Faith. — *adj.* relating to this order.
dominion *noun* **1** rule; power; influence. **2** a territory or country governed by a single ruler or government; formerly, a self-governing colony within the British Empire. [from Latin *dominium*, ownership]

. . . .

⊟ **1** power, authority, influence, domination, command, control, rule, sway, jurisdiction, government, lordship, mastery, supremacy, sovereignty. **2** domain, country, territory, province, colony, realm, kingdom, empire.

. . . .

domino *noun* (PL. **dominoes**) **1** any of a set of small rectangular tiles marked, in two halves, with a varying number of spots. **2** a grouping of tiles with matching halves laid end to end in the game of *dominoes*. **3** a black cloak with a hood and mask attached, worn at masked balls. [perhaps from Italian *domino!*, master!, the winner's cry in dominoes]
domino effect the relation of political cause and effect implied by the *domino theory*.
domino theory the theory that a political event can cause a series of similar events in neighbouring areas, like a falling domino causing the others in a row to fall in turn.
Don *noun* the Spanish equivalent of Mr. [from Spanish *Don*, from Latin *dominus*, lord]
don[1] *noun* a university lecturer, especially at Oxford or Cambridge. [from Spanish *Don*, from Latin *dominus*, lord]
don[2] *verb* (**donned, donning**) to put on (clothing). [from DO + ON]
donate *verb* to give, especially to charity. [from Latin *donare*, to give]

. . . .

⊟ give, contribute, present, bequeath, *slang* cough up, *colloq.* fork out, bestow, confer, subscribe.
⊟ receive.

. . . .

donation *noun* a formal gift, usually of money; an amount given as a gift.

. . . .

⊟ gift, present, offering, grant, gratuity, largesse, contribution, presentation, subscription, alms, benefaction, bequest.

. . . .

done — *adj.* **1** finished. **2** *said of food* fully cooked. **3** socially acceptable. **4** used up. **5** *colloq.* exhausted. — *interj.* expressing agreement or completion of a deal. — **done for** *colloq.* facing ruin or death. **done with something** or **someone** *colloq.* finished with them; having dealt with them.

    adj. **1** finished, over, accomplished, completed, ended, concluded, settled, realized, executed. **2** cooked, ready. **3** conventional, acceptable, proper.

doner kebab /ˈdɒnə/ thin slices cut from a block of minced and seasoned lamb grilled on a spit and eaten on unleavened bread. [from Turkish *döner*, rotating]

dong[1] — *noun* a deep ringing sound. — *verb* to make this sound. [imitative]

dong[2] *noun coarse slang* a penis.

donjon /ˈdʌndʒən/ *noun* a heavily fortified central tower in a medieval castle. [old variant of DUNGEON]

Don Juan a man who is, or claims to be, a regular seducer of women.

donkey *noun* (PL. **donkeys**) **1** the domestic ass, a hoofed herbivorous mammal with a large head and long ears, related to but smaller than the horse. **2** *colloq.* a stupid person.

donkey jacket a heavy jacket made of a thick (usually black) woollen fabric.

donkey's years *colloq.* a very long time; ages.

donkey-work *noun* **1** heavy manual work. **2** preparation; groundwork.

donnish *adj.* of, typical of, or resembling a don; intellectual or bookish.

donor *noun* **1** a person who donates something, especially money. **2** a person or animal that provides blood, semen, living tissue, or organs for medical use. **3** *Electron.* an impurity in the form of a chemical element, such as antimony, that is deliberately added to a pure semiconductor material such as silicon. **4** *Chem.* an atom that donates a pair of electrons to an acceptor, resulting in the formation of a coordinate bond.

    1 giver, donator, benefactor, contributor, philanthropist, provider, *colloq.* fairy godmother.
    beneficiary.

donor card a card carried by a person who is willing, in the event of his or her death, to have (usually specified) healthy organs removed for use in transplant surgery.

donor insemination (ABBREV. **DI**) artificial insemination using semen from a donor.

don't — *contr.* do not. — *noun colloq.* something that must not be done: *dos and don'ts.*

don't-know *noun* a person undecided, especially as to whom to vote for.

donut same as DOUGHNUT.

doodah *noun colloq.* a thing whose name one cannot remember.

doodle — *verb intrans.* to scrawl or scribble aimlessly and meaninglessly. — *noun* a meaningless scribble.

doom — *noun* **1** inescapable death, ruin, or other unpleasant fate. **2** a judgement or sentence. — *verb* to condemn to death or some other dire fate. [from Anglo-Saxon *dom*, judgement]

    noun **1** fate, destiny, lot, destruction, catastrophe, downfall, ruin, death, death-knell. **2** condemnation, judgement, sentence, verdict. *verb* condemn, damn, consign, judge, sentence, destine.

doomsday *noun* the last day of the world; in Christianity, the day on which God will judge the human race. — **till doomsday** *colloq.* for ever.

door *noun* **1** a movable barrier opening and closing an entrance, eg to a room, cupboard, or vehicle. **2** an entrance. **3** a house considered in relation to others: *three doors away.* **4** a means of entry; an opportunity to gain access: *opened the door to stardom.* — **lay something at someone's door** to blame them for it. [from Anglo-Saxon *duru*]

    2 opening, entrance, entry, exit, doorway, portal, hatch.

doorbell *noun* a bell on or at a door, rung by visitors as a sign of arrival.

doorknocker SEE KNOCKER.

doorman *noun* a (usually uniformed) man employed to guard the entrance to a hotel, restaurant, theatre, etc and give assistance to guests or customers.

doormat *noun* **1** a mat for wiping shoes on before entering. **2** *colloq.* a person easily submitting to unfair treatment by others.

doorstep *noun* **1** a step positioned immediately in front of a door. **2** *slang* a thick sandwich or slice of bread. — **on one's doorstep** situated very close, especially to one's home.

doorstop *noun* a device, especially a wedge, for holding a door open.

door-to-door *adj., adv.* **1** going from house to house. **2** *said eg of a journey time* between precise points of departure and arrival.

doorway *noun* an entrance to a building or room; the space filled by a door.

dopa *noun Biochem.* an amino acid that plays an important role in the manufacture of adrenaline and noradrenaline, and the neurotransmitter dopamine. [from *dioxyphenylalanine*, a former name for the compound]

dopamine /ˈdoʊpəmiːn/ *noun Biochem.* a chemical compound known as a *catecholamine*, that functions as a neurotransmitter and is also an intermediate in the manufacture of adrenaline and noradrenaline. [from DOPA + AMINE]

dope — *noun* **1** *North Amer.* a thick liquid, semi-liquid, or pasty material. **2** an absorbent material. **3** a lubricant, in the form of a thick liquid or grease, applied to a surface. **4** a substance that is added to another substance in order to modify or improve its properties, eg antiknock compounds added to petrol. **5** *colloq.* any illegal drug, especially cannabis. **6** *colloq.* a drug that is illegally administered in order to improve performance, eg in an athlete or racehorse. **7** *colloq.* a stupid person. **8** (**the dope**) *slang* information, especially when confidential. — *verb* **1** to give or apply drugs to, especially dishonestly or furtively. **2** to add impurities to (a crystal of silicon, germanium, etc), in order to convert it into a semiconductor. [from Dutch *doop*, sauce]

    noun **5** cannabis, narcotic, drug, marijuana, opiate, hallucinogen. **7** fool, dolt, idiot, halfwit, dunce, simpleton, *colloq.* dimwit, *colloq.* clot, *colloq.* blockhead. **8** information, facts, *colloq.* low-down, details. *verb* **1** drug, sedate, anaesthetize, stupefy, medicate, narcotize, inject, doctor.

dopey or **dopy** *adj.* (**dopier, dopiest**) *colloq.* **1** sleepy or inactive, as if drugged. **2** stupid.

    DOZY. **1** sleepy, drowsy, nodding, somnolent, lethargic, torpid. **2** stupid, foolish, silly, daft.

dopiness *noun colloq.* a dopey or stupid manner or state.

doping *noun Physics* the addition of very small amounts of impurities (eg antimony, arsenic) to a crystal of silicon, germanium, etc, in order to convert it into a semiconductor.

doppelgänger /ˈdɒpəlɡɛŋə(r)/ *noun* an apparition or double of a person. [German, = double-goer]

Doppler effect *Physics* the change in wavelength observed as the distance between a source of waves and the observer changes, as with the changing pitch of the siren of a passing motor vehicle. [named after the Austrian physicist Christian *Doppler*]

Dorian /'dɔːrɪən/ — *noun* a member of a sub-group of Hellenic peoples, thought to have migrated into Greece about 1100 BC. — *adj.* relating or belonging to the Dorians.

Doric /'dɒrɪk/ *adj. Archit.* denoting an order of classical architecture, characterized by thick fluted columns. See also CORINTHIAN, IONIC. [from Greek *Dorikos*, from *Doris*, in ancient Greece]

dorm *noun colloq.* a dormitory.

dormancy *noun* a quiet or inactive state.

dormant *adj.* 1 temporarily quiet or inactive as if sleeping. 2 currently out of use or in abeyance. 3 *Biol.* denoting a living organism or a reproductive body such as a seed, spore, or cyst that is in a resting state, especially in order to survive a period of unfavourable environmental conditions, eg drought, low temperature. [from Latin *dormire*, to sleep]

⊟ 1 inactive, asleep, sleeping, inert, resting, slumbering, sluggish, torpid, hibernating, fallow, comatose. 2 latent, unrealized, potential, undeveloped, undisclosed.
⊟ 1 active, awake. 2 realized, developed.

dormer or **dormer window** *noun* a window fitted vertically into an extension built out from a sloping roof. [from DORMITORY, in which they were originally fitted]

dormitory /'dɔːmɪtərɪ/ *noun* (PL. **dormitories**) 1 a large bedroom for several people, especially in a school. 2 *North Amer., esp. US* a hall of residence in a college or university. [from Latin *dormitorium*, from *dormire*, to sleep]

dormitory town or **dormitory suburb** a town or suburb from which most residents travel to work elsewhere.

Dormobile *noun trademark* a van equipped for living and sleeping in. [from DORMITORY + AUTOMOBILE]

dormouse *noun* (PL. **dormice**) a small nocturnal rodent with rounded ears, large eyes, velvety fur, and a bushy tail, that spends the day asleep in nests in trees or on the ground. [connected with Latin *dormire*, to sleep, from its hibernating habits]

Dors. *abbrev.* Dorset.

dorsal *adj. Anat.* 1 denoting the upper surface of an organism, usually the surface furthest from the ground. In vertebrates it is the surface closest to the backbone: *dorsal fin.* 2 relating to or lying near the back of the body. [from Latin *dorsum*, back]

dory *noun* (PL. **dories**) (*also* **John Dory**) a marine fish of the mackerel family, native to the Atlantic Ocean and Mediterranean Sea, having spiny fins and a golden-yellow or grey body. It is a highly prized food fish. [from French *dorée*, golden]

DOS *abbrev. Comput.* disk-operating system, an operating system consisting of a series of programs that control the storage and retrieval of information on disk in a computer system.

dosage *noun* 1 a dose. 2 the administration of a drug or other therapeutic agent, eg X-rays, in prescribed amounts. 3 the optimum therapeutic dose for a particular patient or condition.

dose — *noun* 1 *Medicine* the measured quantity of medicine, ionizing radiation, eg X-rays, or some other therapeutic agent that is prescribed by a doctor to be administered to a patient at any one time, or at regular intervals over a period of time. 2 the amount of ionizing radiation to which a person is exposed over a specified period of time. 3 *colloq.* a bout, especially of an illness or something unpleasant: *a dose of the flu.* 4 *slang* any sexually transmitted disease, especially gonorrhoea: *catch a dose.* — *verb* (**dose someone (up) with something**) to give them medicine, especially in large quantities. — **like a dose of salts** *colloq.* extremely quickly and effectively. [from Greek *dosis*, giving]

⊟ *noun* 1 measure, dosage, amount, portion, quantity, draught, potion, prescription, shot. *verb* medicate with, administer, prescribe, dispense, treat with.

dosh *noun slang* money.

dosimeter /dəʊ'sɪmɪtə(r)/ *noun Physics* an instrument for measuring the dose of radiation received by a person, or by a laboratory or other area.

doss *verb intrans. slang* (**doss down**) to settle down to sleep, especially on an improvised bed. [perhaps *doss*, dialect for HASSOCK]

dosser *noun slang* 1 a homeless person sleeping on the street or in a doss-house. 2 a lazy person.

doss-house *noun slang* a very cheap lodging-house for homeless people.

dossier /'dɒsɪeɪ/ *noun* a file of papers containing information on a person or subject. [from French *dossier*]

dost /dʌst/ *verb old use* the form of *do* used with *thou*.

dot — *noun* 1 a small round mark; a spot; a point. 2 in Morse code, the shorter of the two lengths of signal element, written as a point. See also DASH. — *verb* (**dotted, dotting**) 1 to put a dot on. 2 to scatter; to cover with a scattering. — **dot the i's and cross the t's** 1 to pay close attention to detail. 2 to finish the last few details of something. **on the dot** exactly on time. **the year dot** *colloq.* a very long time ago. [from Anglo-Saxon *dott*, head of a boil]

⊟ *noun* 1 point, spot, speck, mark, fleck, atom, decimal point, full stop, iota, jot. *verb* 2 spot, sprinkle, stud, dab, punctuate.

dotage *noun* a state of feeble-mindedness owing to old age; senility: *in one's dotage.* [etymology as for DOTE]

dotard *noun* a person in his or her dotage. [from DOTE]

dotcom *noun* a company operating solely via the Internet. [from the suffix *.com* that ends many domain names on the Internet]

dote *verb intrans.* (**dote on** or **upon someone** or **something**) to show a foolishly excessive fondness for them. [from Old Dutch *doten*, to be silly]

⊟ adore, idolize, treasure, admire, indulge.

doth /dʌθ/ *old use* does.

doting *adj.* foolishly or excessively fond of someone.

dot matrix printer a type of non-impact printer that uses a rectangular matrix consisting of lines of pins, a selection of which is used to create characters and images by printing a pattern of very small dots.

dotty *adj.* (**dottier, dottiest**) *colloq.* 1 silly; crazy. 2 (**dotty about someone** or **something**) infatuated with them.

double — *adj.* 1 made up of two similar parts; paired; in pairs. 2 of twice the (usual) weight, size, etc. 3 for two people: *a double bed.* 4 ambiguous: *double meaning.* 5 *said of a musical instrument* sounding an octave lower: *double bass.* — *adv.* 1 twice. 2 with one half over the other: *folded double.* — *noun* 1 a double quantity. 2 a duplicate or lookalike. 3 an actor's stand-in, used especially in dangerous scenes. 4 a double measure of alcoholic spirit. 5 a racing bet in which any winnings from the first stake become a stake in a subsequent race. 6 a win in two events on the same racing programme. — *verb* 1 *trans., intrans.* to make or become twice as large in size, number, etc. 2 (**double something over**) to fold one half of it over the other. 3 *intrans.* to have a second use or function: *the spare bed doubles as a couch.* 4 *intrans.* (**double for someone**) to act as their substitute. 5 *intrans.* to turn round sharply. — **at** or **on the double** very quickly. **double back** to turn and go back, often by a different route. **double up 1** to bend sharply at the waist, especially through pain. 2 (*also* **double up with someone**) to share a bedroom. [from Latin *duplus*]

. . . .

■ *adj.* **1** dual, twofold, duplicate, twin, paired, doubled, coupled. *noun* **2** twin, duplicate, copy, clone, replica, doppelgänger, lookalike, *colloq.* spitting image, *colloq.* ringer, *colloq.* dead ringer, image, counterpart, impersonator. *verb* **1** enlarge, increase, repeat, multiply, magnify. **at the double** immediately, at once, quickly, without delay.
■ *adj.* **1** single, half.

. . . .

double agent a spy working for two governments with conflicting interests.

double-barrelled *adj.* **1** *said of a gun* having two barrels. **2** *said of a surname* made up of two names (eg *Lloyd-Jones*).

double bass the largest and lowest in pitch of the orchestral stringed instruments, having four (or five) strings which may be bowed or plucked.

double bill or **triple bill** two or three films or plays presented as a single entertainment, one after the other.

double bond *Chem.* a covalent bond formed by the sharing of two pairs of electrons between two atoms.

double-breasted *adj.*, *said of a coat or jacket* having overlapping front flaps.

double-check *verb trans.*, *intrans.* to check twice or again.

double chin a chin with an area of loose flesh underneath.

double cream thick cream with a high fat content.

double-cross — *verb* to cheat or deceive (especially a colleague or ally, or someone one is supposed to be helping). — *noun* such a deceit.

. . . .

■ *verb* cheat, swindle, defraud, trick, *colloq.* con, hoodwink, betray, *colloq.* two-time, mislead. *noun* cheat, swindle, fraud, trick, *colloq.* con.

. . . .

double-crosser *noun* a person who double-crosses or cheats another.

double-dealer *noun* a person who cheats or deceives.

. . . .

■ cheat, cheater, deceiver, trickster, swindler, *colloq.* shark, *colloq.* con man, double-crosser.

. . . .

double-dealing *noun* cheating; treachery.

double-decker *noun* **1** a bus with two decks. **2** *colloq.* anything with two levels or layers: *double-decker sandwich*.

double Dutch *colloq.* nonsense; incomprehensible jargon.

double-edged *adj.* **1** having two cutting edges. **2** having two possible meanings or purposes.

double entendre /ˈdʌblə ɑːnˈtɑːndrə/ *noun* a remark having two possible meanings, one of them usually sexually suggestive; the use of such remarks. [from Old French *double entendre*, double meaning]

double figures the numbers between 10 and 99 inclusive, especially the lower ones.

double-glazed *adj.* having double-glazing.

double glazing windows constructed with two panes separated by a vacuum, providing added heat insulation.

double-jointed *adj.* having extraordinarily flexible body joints.

double negative an expression containing two negative words where only one is needed, as in *He hasn't never asked me.*

double-park *verb trans.*, *intrans.* to park at the side of another vehicle parked alongside the kerb.

double-quick *adj.*, *adv.* very quick or quickly.

doubles *sing. noun* a competition in tennis, etc between two teams of two players each.

double standard (*also* **double standards**) a principle or rule applied firmly to one person or group and loosely or not at all to another, especially oneself.

double star *Astron.* **1** a binary star. **2** a pair of stars that appear close together when viewed through a telescope, but are in fact at very different distances from Earth.

doublet /ˈdʌblɪt/ *noun* **1** a close-fitting man's jacket, with or without sleeves, popular from the 14c to the 17c. **2** a pair of objects of any kind, or each of these. [from Old French *doublet*]

double take an initial inattentive reaction followed swiftly by a sudden full realisation, especially used as a comic device: *do a double take.*

double-talk *noun* ambiguous talk, or talk that seems relevant but is really meaningless, especially as offered up by politicians.

doublethink *noun* simultaneous belief in, or acceptance of, two opposing ideas or principles.

double time a rate of pay equal to double the basic rate.

doubloon /dʌˈbluːn/ *noun* a former gold coin of Spain and S America. [from Spanish *doblón*]

doubly *adv.* **1** to twice the extent; very much more. **2** in two ways.

doubt — *verb* **1** to feel uncertain about; to be suspicious, or show mistrust, of. **2** *trans.*, *intrans.* to be inclined to disbelieve. — *noun* **1** a feeling of uncertainty, suspicion, or mistrust. **2** an inclination to disbelieve; a reservation. — **no doubt** surely; probably. **without doubt** or **without a doubt** certainly. [from Latin *dubitare*]

. . . .

■ *verb* BE UNCERTAIN (ABOUT), BE DUBIOUS (ABOUT), BE SCEPTICAL (ABOUT), HAVE RESERVATIONS (ABOUT). **1** distrust, mistrust, query, question, suspect, fear. **2** disbelieve. *noun* UNCERTAINTY, SCEPTICISM, SUSPICION. **1** distrust, mistrust, apprehension, hesitation, indecision, perplexity, dilemma, quandary. **2** incredulity, reservation, misgiving, difficulty, problem. **no doubt** doubtless, certainly, surely, probably, most likely, presumably. **without doubt** certainly, surely, assuredly, undoubtedly, unquestionably, indisputably, infallibly.
■ *verb* BELIEVE. **1** trust. *noun* CERTAINTY, BELIEF, TRUST, FAITH.

. . . .

doubter *noun* a person who doubts, especially habitually.

doubtful *adj.* **1** feeling doubt. **2** uncertain; able to be doubted. **3** likely not to be the case.

. . . .

■ UNCERTAIN, UNSURE, UNDECIDED, DUBIOUS. **1** suspicious, irresolute, wavering, hesitant, vacillating, tentative, sceptical. **2** questionable, unclear, ambiguous, vague, obscure, debatable. **3** unlikely, improbable.
■ CERTAIN, DECIDED. **2**, **3** definite, settled.

. . . .

doubtfully *adv.* in a doubtful or uncertain way.

doubtless *adv.* probably; certainly.

. . . .

■ probably, presumably, most likely, seemingly, supposedly, certainly, without doubt, undoubtedly, unquestionably, indisputably, no doubt, clearly, surely, of course, truly.

. . . .

douche /duːʃ/ — *noun* **1** a powerful jet of water that is used to clean a body orifice, especially the vagina. **2** an apparatus for producing such a jet. — *verb* to apply a douche to. [from French *douche*]

dough /dəʊ/ *noun* **1** a mixture of flour, liquid (water or milk), and yeast, used in the preparation of bread, pastry, etc. It usually refers to such a mixture that has been kneaded but not baked. **2** *slang* money. [from Anglo-Saxon *dah*]

doughnut *noun* a spongy ring-shaped pastry, especially filled with cream or jam, usually with a hole in the middle.

doughnutting *noun* the surrounding of a speaker in parliament by members of the same party, to give the impression on television of a packed House.

doughtily *adv. literary* bravely.

doughtiness *noun literary* bravery.

doughty /ˈdaʊtɪ/ *adj.* (**doughtier, doughtiest**) *literary* brave; stout-hearted. [from Anglo-Saxon *dyhtig*]

doughy *adj.* (**doughier, doughiest**) like dough, or having the consistency of dough.

dour /dʊə(r)/ *adj.* **1** gloomy-looking; sullen. **2** stern, severe. [from Latin *durus*, hard]

⬛ **1** gloomy, dismal, forbidding, grim, sour, sullen, morose, unfriendly, dreary, austere. **2** stern, hard, inflexible, unyielding, rigid, severe, rigorous, strict, obstinate.
⊟ **1** cheerful, bright. **2** easy-going.

douse or **dowse** *verb* **1** to throw water over; to plunge into water. **2** to extinguish (a light or fire).

⬛ **1** soak, saturate, steep, submerge, immerse, immerge, dip, duck, drench, dunk, plunge. **2** extinguish, put out, blow out, smother, snuff.

dove *noun* **1** any of several smaller members of the pigeon family with a small head, stout body, and pointed tail. In fact there is no real difference between a pigeon and a dove. **2** *Politics* a person favouring peace rather than hostility. See also HAWK. [from Anglo-Saxon *dufe*]

dovecote or **dovecot** *noun* a shed in which domestic pigeons are kept.

Dover sole a flatfish, distributed from the Mediterranean to Norway, up to 50cm in length, and having both eyes on the right side of the body. Also called EUROPEAN SOLE.

dovetail — *noun* (*also* **dovetail joint**) a corner joint, especially in wood, made by fitting v-shaped pegs into corresponding slots. — *verb trans., intrans.* to fit or combine neatly.

dowager /ˈdaʊədʒə(r)/ *noun* **1** a title given to a nobleman's widow, to distinguish her from the wife of her husband's heir: *dowager duchess*. **2** *colloq.* a grand-looking old lady. [from Old French *douagiere*, from Latin *dotare*, to endow]

dowdiness *noun* a dowdy or dull manner or appearance.

dowdy *adj.* (**dowdier, dowdiest**) *said especially of a woman* dull, plain, and unfashionable. [from Middle English *dowd*, slut]

⬛ unfashionable, ill-dressed, frumpish, drab, shabby, *colloq.* tatty, dingy, old-fashioned, slovenly.
⊟ fashionable, smart.

dowel /daʊəl/ *noun* a thin cylindrical (especially wooden) peg, especially used to join two pieces by fitting into corresponding holes in each. [from Old German *dovel*]

dower *noun* a widow's share, for life, in her deceased husband's property. [from Old French *douaire*, from Latin *dotare*, to endow]

dower house a house smaller than, and within the grounds of, a large country house, originally one forming part of a dower.

down¹ — *adv.* **1** towards or in a low or lower position, level, or state; on or to the ground. **2** from a greater to a lesser size, amount or level: *scaled down / calm down*. **3** towards or in a more southerly place. **4** in writing; on paper: *take down notes*. **5** as a deposit: *put down five pounds*. **6** to an end stage or finished state: *hunt someone down / grind down*. **7** from earlier to later times: *handed down through generations*. **8** not vomited up: *keep food down*. — *prep.* **1** in a lower position on. **2** along; at a further position on, by, or through: *down the road*. **3** from the top to, or towards, the bottom. **4** *dialect* to or in (a particular place): *going down the town*. — *adj.* **1** sad; in low spirits. **2** going towards or reaching a lower position: *a down pipe*. **3** (**down by**) with a deficit (of): *down by three goals*. **4** made as a deposit: *a down payment*. **5** reduced in price. **6** (**down for**)

noted; entered in a list, etc: *Your name is down for the hurdles*. **7** *said of a computer, etc* out of action, especially temporarily. — *verb* **1** to drink quickly, especially in one gulp. **2** to force to the ground. — *noun* **1** an unsuccessful or otherwise unpleasant period: *ups and downs*. **2** (**downs**) an area of rolling (especially treeless) hills. — **down to the ground** *colloq.* completely; perfectly. **down tools** *colloq.* to stop working, as a protest. **down under** *colloq.* in or to Australia or New Zealand. **down with...!** let us get rid of...! **have a down on someone** *colloq.* to be ill-disposed towards them. [from Anglo-Saxon *of dune*, from the hill]

⬛ *adj.* **1** sad, depressed, blue, unhappy, miserable, dejected, downcast. *verb* **1** swallow, drink, gulp, *colloq.* swig, *colloq.* knock back. **2** knock down, fell, floor, prostrate, throw, topple.

down² *noun* soft fine feathers or hair. [from Norse *dunn*]

down-and-out — *adj.* homeless and penniless, with no hope of earning a living. — *noun* a down-and-out person.

⬛ *adj.* destitute, impoverished, penniless, derelict, ruined. *noun* tramp, vagrant, *slang* dosser.

down-at-heel *adj.* shabby.

⬛ shabby, ill-dressed, frayed, tattered, ragged, drab, *colloq.* tatty, frowsy, dowdy, *colloq.* tacky, dingy.

downbeat — *adj.* **1** taking a gloomy or pessimistic view. **2** calm; relaxed. — *noun Mus.* the first beat of a bar.

⬛ *adj.* **1** gloomy, pessimistic, negative, depressed, despondent, cheerless, cynical. **2** calm, relaxed, *colloq.* laid back, informal, casual, unhurried, unworried.

downcast *adj.* **1** glum; dispirited. **2** *said of eyes* looking downwards.

⬛ **1** dejected, depressed, despondent, sad, unhappy, miserable, down, low, disheartened, dispirited, *colloq.* blue, *colloq.* fed up, discouraged, disappointed, crestfallen, dismayed.
⊟ **1** cheerful, happy, elated.

downer *noun* **1** *colloq.* a state of depression: *be on a downer*. **2** *slang* a tranquillizing or depressant drug.

downfall *noun* failure or ruin, or its cause.

⬛ fall, ruin, failure, collapse, destruction, disgrace, debacle, undoing, overthrow.

downgrade *verb* to reduce to a lower grade.

⬛ degrade, demote, lower, humble.
⊟ upgrade, improve.

downhearted *adj.* sad; discouraged.

⬛ depressed, dejected, despondent, sad, downcast, discouraged, disheartened, dispirited, unhappy, gloomy, glum, dismayed.
⊟ cheerful, enthusiastic.

downhill — *adv.* **1** downwards. **2** to or towards a worse condition. — *adj.* **1** downwardly sloping. **2** becoming increasingly easier. **3** deteriorating.

down-in-the-mouth *adj.* unhappy; depressed.

download *verb Comput.* to transfer (data or a program) from the memory of one computer to that of another via communication channels such as a telephone line or radio link.

down-market *adj.* cheap, poor quality, or lacking prestige.

down payment a deposit.

downpour *noun* a very heavy fall of rain.

. . . .

🖃 cloudburst, deluge, rainstorm, flood, inundation, torrent.
. . . .

downright *adj.*, *adv.* utter or utterly.

. . . .

🖃 utter(ly), absolute(ly), outright, plain(ly), clear(ly), complete(ly), out-and-out, total(ly).
. . . .

downshift *verb intrans.* **1** to select a lower gear in a vehicle. **2** to choose a less affluent lifestyle in order to improve one's life in non-material ways.

downside *noun* **1** the lower or under side. **2** *colloq.* a negative aspect; a disadvantage.

downsizing *noun* the practice of reducing the size of a workforce, especially by redundancies.

Down's syndrome a congenital disorder which results in mental retardation, slow physical development, flattened facial features, and slight slanting of the eyes, formerly called *mongolism.* [named after the UK physician John Langdon Haydon Down]

downstage *adj.*, *adv.* at or towards the front of a theatre stage.

downstairs — *adv.* to or towards a lower floor; down the stairs. — *adj.* on a lower or ground floor. — *noun* a lower or ground floor.

downstream *adj.*, *adv.* further along a river towards the sea; with the current.

downtime *noun* **1** *Comput.* a period of time during which a computer system cannot be accessed. **2** a period when work is halted because of equipment failure, lack of materials, bad weather, etc.

down-to-earth *adj.* **1** sensible and practical. **2** not at all pretentious. **3** plain-speaking.

. . . .

🖃 **1** level-headed, sensible, practical, common-sense, commonsensical, sane, rational. **2** simple, straightforward, modest, ordinary, unpretentious, unassuming. **3** plain-speaking, blunt, frank, candid, forthright, explicit.
. . . .

downtown — *adj.*, *adv.* in or towards the lower part of the city, or the city centre. — *noun* this area of a city.

downtrodden *adj.* ruled or controlled tyrannically.

. . . .

🖃 oppressed, subjugated, subject, exploited, trampled on, abused, tyrannized, victimized, helpless, subservient.
. . . .

downturn *noun* a decline in economic activity.

downward — *adj.* leading or moving down; descending; declining. — *adv.* same as DOWNWARDS.

. . . .

🖃 *adj.* descending, declining, downhill, sliding, slipping.
🔁 *adj.* upward.
. . . .

downwardly *adv.* in a downward direction.

downwards *adv.* to or towards a lower position or level.

downwind — *adv.* **1** in or towards the direction in which the wind is blowing; with the wind blowing from behind. **2** behind in terms of wind direction; with the wind carrying one's scent away from (eg an animal one is stalking). — *adj.* moving with, or sheltered from, the wind.

downy *adj.* (**downier, downiest**) covered with or made of down; soft like down.

dowry *noun* (PL. **dowries**) an amount of wealth handed over by a woman to her husband on marriage. [from DOWER]

dowse[1] *verb intrans.* to search for underground water with a divining-rod.

dowse[2] see DOUSE.

dowser *noun* a person who searches for water with a divining-rod.

doxology *noun* (PL. **doxologies**) a Christian hymn, verse, or fixed expression praising God. [from Greek *doxa*, glory + *logos*, discourse]

doyen /ˈdɔɪən/ *noun literary* the most senior and most respected member of a group or profession. [from French *doyen*]

doyley see DOILY.

doz. *abbrev.* dozen.

doze — *verb intrans.* to sleep lightly. — *noun* a brief period of light sleep. — **doze off** to fall into a light sleep. [from Norse *dus*, lull]

. . . .

🖃 *verb* sleep, snooze, *colloq.* have forty winks, *slang* kip, *slang* zizz. *noun* nap, catnap, siesta, snooze, *colloq.* forty winks, *slang* kip, *slang* shuteye, *slang* zizz. **doze off** nod off, drop off, fall asleep.
. . . .

dozen *noun* (PL. **dozen** following a number, **dozens**) **1** a set of twelve. **2** (**dozens**) *colloq.* very many: *saw dozens of them.* [from Latin *duodecim*]

dozenth *adj.* **1** twelfth. **2** denoting an indeterminately high place in a sequence: *for the dozenth time.*

dozy *adj.* (**dozier, doziest**) **1** sleepy. **2** *colloq.* stupid; slow to understand; not alert.

. . . .

🖃 **1** sleepy, drowsy, tired. **2** stupid, unintelligent, *colloq. chiefly North Amer., esp US* dumb, *colloq.* dim, *colloq.* dense, *colloq.* thick.
. . . .

DPA *abbrev.* Data Protection Authority.

DPhil or **DPh** *abbrev.* Doctor of Philosophy. See also PHD.

DPP *abbrev.* Director of Public Prosecutions.

Dr *abbrev.* **1** Doctor. **2** drachma. **3** *in addresses* Drive.

drab *adj.* (**drabber, drabbest**) **1** dull; dreary. **2** of a dull greenish-brown colour. [perhaps from French *drap*, cloth]

. . . .

🖃 **1** dull, dingy, dreary, dismal, gloomy, flat, grey, lacklustre, cheerless, sombre, shabby.
🔁 **1** bright, cheerful.
. . . .

drably *adv.* drearily; dully.

drabness *noun* a dreary or dull state or appearance.

drachm /dram/ *noun* a measure equal to ⅛ of an ounce or fluid ounce, formerly used by pharmacists. [etymology as for DRACHMA]

drachma /ˈdrakmə/ *noun* (PL. **drachmas, drachmae**) (SYMBOL **Dr**) the standard unit of currency in Greece, divided into 100 lepta. [from Greek *drakhme*, handful]

draconian /drəˈkoʊnɪən/ *adj.*, *said of a law, etc* harsh, severe. [named after Draco, 7c Athenian lawgiver]

draft — *noun* **1** a written plan; a preliminary sketch. **2** a written order requesting a bank to pay out money, especially to another bank. **3** a group of people drafted. **4** *North Amer., esp. US* conscription. — *verb* **1** to set out in preliminary sketchy form. **2** to select and send off (personnel) to perform a specific task. **3** *North Amer., esp. US* to conscript. [a form of DRAUGHT]

. . . .

🖃 *noun* **1** outline, sketch, plan, delineation, abstract, rough, blueprint, protocol. **2** bill of exchange, cheque, money order, letter of credit, postal order. *verb* **1** draw (up), outline, sketch, plan, design, formulate, compose.
. . . .

drag — *verb* (**dragged, dragging**) **1** to pull roughly or violently; to pull along slowly and with force. **2** *trans., intrans.* to move or cause to move along scraping the ground. **3** *intrans., said of time, an event, etc* to seem to pass or take place at a very slow pace. **4** *colloq.* (*usually* **drag someone away**) to force or persuade them to come away. **5** to search (eg a lake) with a hook or dragnet. — *noun* **1** an act of dragging; a dragging effect. **2** a person or thing that makes progress slow. **3** *colloq.* a draw on a cigarette. **4** *colloq.* a dull or tedious person or thing. **5** *colloq.* women's clothes worn by a man. **6** the resistance to motion that is encountered by an object travelling through a fluid (a liquid or gas). Drag is counteracted by the forward thrust of the engines of aircraft, but causes a substantial increase in fuel consumption. The effects of drag are greatly reduced in aircraft, cars, and trains with a streamlined shape. — **drag on** *colloq.* to proceed or continue slowly and tediously. **drag one's feet** or **heels** *colloq.* to delay; to be deliberately slow to take action. **drag something out** *colloq.* to make it last as long as possible. **drag something up** *colloq.* to mention an unpleasant subject long forgotten. [from Anglo-Saxon *dragan*]

⊟ *verb* **1** draw, pull, haul, lug, tug, trail, tow. **2** trail. **3** go slowly, creep (by), crawl (by). *noun* **2** brake, curb, check, restraint. **3** draw, puff. **4** bore, annoyance, nuisance, *colloq.* pain, bother.

draggle *verb trans., intrans.* to make or become wet and dirty (as if) through trailing along the ground. [from DRAG]

dragnet *noun* a heavy net pulled along the bottom of a river, lake, etc in a search for something.

dragon *noun* **1** a large mythical fire-breathing reptile-like creature with wings and a long tail. **2** *colloq.* a frighteningly domineering woman. [from Greek *drakon*]

dragonfly *noun* (PL. **dragonflies**) any insect belonging to the order Odonata, with a fairly large slender brightly coloured body, often metallic in appearance, and gauzy translucent wings.

dragoon — *noun Hist.* a heavily armed mounted soldier. — *verb* to force or bully (someone) into doing something. [from French *dragon*]

drag race a contest in acceleration between specially designed cars over a short distance. See DRAGSTER.

drag-racing *noun* the activity or sport of competing in drag races.

dragster *noun* a car designed or adapted to be used in drag races.

drain — *verb* **1** (**drain liquid off** or **away**) to cause or allow it to escape. **2** (**drain something of liquid**) to remove liquid from it. **3** (**drain off**) *said of liquid, etc* to escape; to flow away. **4** to drink the total contents of (a glass, etc). **5** *trans., intrans.* (**drain away** or **drain something away**) to disappear or cause it to disappear: *our support drained away.* **6** to use up the strength, emotion, or resources of (someone). **7** *said of a river* to carry away surface water from (land). — *noun* **1** a device, especially a pipe, for carrying away liquid. **2** (**a drain on something**) anything that exhausts or seriously depletes a supply. — **down the drain** *colloq.* wasted; lost. [from Anglo-Saxon *dreahnian*]

⊟ *verb* **1**, **2** empty, evacuate, strain, milk, bleed. **1** remove, draw off. **3** discharge, trickle, flow out, empty, leak, ooze. **6** exhaust, consume, sap, use up, deplete, drink up, swallow. *noun* **1** pipe, channel, conduit, culvert, duct, outlet, trench, ditch, sewer. **2** strain.

⊟ *verb* **1** fill.

drainage *noun* **1** the act, process, or method of draining. **2** the system of drains and watercourses used to lead away water and waste from buildings, especially from baths, sinks, and lavatories. **3** the means of discharging water.

draining-board *noun* a sloping (especially channelled) surface at the side of a sink allowing water from washed dishes to drain away.

drainpipe *noun* **1** a pipe carrying water from a roof into a drain below ground. **2** (**drainpipes**) *colloq.* narrow tight-fitting trousers.

drake *noun* a male duck.

dram *noun* **1** *colloq.* a small amount of alcoholic spirit, especially whisky. **2** a unit of mass, formerly used in the UK, equal to $\frac{1}{16}$ of an ounce avoirdupois or 1.77g. **3** *North Amer.* a unit of mass used in the apothecaries' system of measurement, equal to $\frac{1}{8}$ of an ounce or 3.89g. [from etymology as for DRACHMA]

drama *noun* **1** a play; any work performed by actors. **2** plays in general, as an art form. **3** the art of producing, directing, and acting in plays. **4** excitement and emotion; an exciting situation. [from Greek *drama*]

⊟ **1** play, show, spectacle, scene, melodrama. **2** plays, theatre. **3** acting, dramatics, dramaturgy, stage-craft. **4** excitement, crisis, turmoil, tragedy.

dramatherapy *noun Psychol.* a form of therapy in which drama is used as a means of acting out different responses to real-life situations.

dramatic / drə'matɪk/ *adj.* **1** of or relating to plays, the theatre, or acting in general. **2** exciting. **3** sudden and striking; drastic. **4** *said of a person or behaviour* flamboyantly emotional.

⊟ **1** theatrical. **2** exciting, stirring, thrilling. **3** striking, marked, significant, expressive, impressive, drastic, momentous. **4** theatrical, histrionic, exaggerated, melodramatic, flamboyant.

dramatically *adv.* in a dramatic or exciting way.

dramatics *sing. noun* **1** activities associated with the staging and performing of plays. **2** exaggeratedly emotional behaviour.

dramatis personae /'dramatɪs pɜː'soʊnaɪ/ a list of the characters in a play. [from Latin *dramatis personae*, persons of the drama]

dramatist *noun* a writer of plays.

dramatization or **dramatisation** *noun* an adaptation of a literary work as a play or drama.

dramatize or **dramatise** *verb* **1** to make into a work for public performance. **2** to treat as, or cause to seem, more exciting or important.

⊟ **1** stage, put on, adapt. **2** exaggerate, overdo, overstate.

drank see DRINK.

drape *verb* **1** to hang (cloth) loosely over (something). **2** to arrange or lay loosely. [from Old French *draper*]

⊟ WRAP, HANG, FOLD, DROP, SUSPEND. **1** cover, shroud.

draper *noun* a person who sells fabric.

drapery *noun* (PL. **draperies**) **1** fabric; textiles. **2** curtains and other hanging fabrics. **3** a draper's business or shop.

drapes *pl. noun North Amer.*, *esp. US* curtains.

drastic *adj.* extreme; severe. [from Greek *drastikos*, from *draein*, to act]

⊟ extreme, radical, strong, forceful, severe, harsh, far-reaching, desperate, dire.

⊟ moderate, cautious.

drastically *adv.* extremely; severely.

drat *interj. colloq.* expressing anger or annoyance. [an alteration of *God rot*]

dratted *adj. colloq.* expressing annoyance: *the dratted handle's come off.*

draught / drɑːft/ — *noun* **1** a current of air, especially indoors. **2** a quantity of liquid swallowed in one go. **3** the amount of water required to float a ship. **4** any of the discs used in the game of draughts. **5** *colloq.* draught beer. **6** the act of pulling or drawing. **7** a dose of liquid medicine. — *adj.* **1** *said of beer* pumped direct from the cask to the glass.

2 *said of an animal* used for pulling loads. — **on draught** *said of beer* stored in casks from which it is served direct. [from Anglo-Saxon *draht*, from *dragan*, to draw]

◼ *noun* **1** puff, current, influx, flow. **2** drink, potion, quantity. **6** pulling, traction.

draughts *sing. noun* a game for two people played with 24 discs on a chequered board.

draughtsman *noun* **1** a person skilled in drawing. **2** a person employed to produce accurate and detailed technical drawings. **3** any of the discs used in the game of draughts.

draughtsmanship *noun* skill in drawing, especially in technical drawing.

draughty *adj.* (**draughtier, draughtiest**) prone to or suffering draughts of air.

Dravidian /drə'vɪdɪən/ — *adj.* **1** denoting a dark-skinned race of S India. **2** denoting a family of over 20 languages used mainly in India, SE Asia, Africa, and the Pacific. — *noun* the languages forming this family.

draw — *verb* (PAST TENSE **drew**; PAST PARTICIPLE **drawn**) **1** *trans., intrans.* to make a picture of (something or someone), especially with a pencil. **2** to pull along: *draw a cart.* **3** to pull out, take out, or extract: *draw water from a well / with swords drawn.* **4** *intrans.* to move or proceed steadily in a specified direction: *draw nearer.* **5** (**draw on something**) to make use of assets from a fund or source: *draw on reserves of energy.* **6** to open or close (curtains). **7** to attract (eg people, crowds, attention, or criticism). **8** *trans., intrans.* (*also* **draw with someone**) to end a game with neither side winning; to finish on equal terms with an opponent. **9** to choose or be given as the result of random selection. **10** (**be drawn on something**) to be persuaded to talk or give information: *he refused to be drawn on his plans.* **11** to arrive at or infer (a conclusion). **12** *intrans.* to suck air (eg through a cigarette); *said of a chimney* to cause air to flow through a fire, allowing burning. **13** *technical, said of a ship* to require (a certain depth of water) to float. **14** *intrans., said of tea* to brew or infuse. **15** to disembowel: *hanged, drawn, and quartered.* — *noun* **1** a result in which neither side is the winner; a tie. **2** the making of a random selection, eg of the winners of a competition; a competition with winners chosen at random. **3** the potential to attract many people, or a person or thing having this. **4** the act of drawing a gun. — **draw back from something** to refuse to become involved in it; to avoid commitment. **draw in** *said of nights* to start earlier, making days shorter. **draw the line** to fix a limit, eg on one's actions or tolerance. **draw something out 1** to make it last a long time or longer than necessary. **2** to make it longer. **draw someone out** to encourage to be less shy or reserved. **draw up** to come to a halt. **draw something up** to plan and write a contract or other document. **draw oneself up** to lift oneself into an upright position. [from Anglo-Saxon *dragan*]

◼ *verb* **1** delineate, map out, sketch, portray, trace, pencil, depict, design. **2** pull, drag, haul, tow, tug. **3** pull (out), take out, extract, remove, withdraw. **5** exploit, use, utilize, employ. **7** attract, allure, entice, bring in, influence, persuade, elicit. **8** tie. *noun* **1** tie, stalemate, dead heat. **2** lottery, raffle. **3** attraction, enticement, lure, appeal, bait, interest. **draw something out** EXTEND. **1** protract, prolong, drag out, spin out. **2** elongate, stretch, lengthen, string out. **draw up** pull up, stop, halt, arrive, *something* draft, compose, formulate, prepare, frame, write out.

◼ *verb* **2** push. **7** repel. **draw something out** SHORTEN.

drawback *noun* a disadvantage.

◼ disadvantage, snag, hitch, obstacle, impediment, hindrance, difficulty, flaw, fault, fly in the ointment, catch, stumbling-block, nuisance, trouble, defect, handicap, deficiency, imperfection.

◼ advantage, benefit.

drawbridge *noun* a bridge that can be lifted to prevent access across, or to allow passage beneath.

drawer *noun* **1** a sliding lidless storage box fitted as part of a desk or other piece of furniture. **2** a person who draws. **3** (**drawers**) *old use* knickers, especially when large and roomy. — **out of the top drawer** *colloq.* of the very best quality or the highest standard. [see DRAW]

drawing *noun* any picture made up of lines, especially one drawn in pencil.

◼ sketch, picture, outline, representation, delineation, portrayal, illustration, cartoon, graphic, portrait.

drawing-board *noun* a board to which paper is fixed for drawing. — **go back to the drawing-board** to return to the planning stage, to find a more successful approach.

drawing-pin *noun* a pin with a broad flat head, used especially for fastening paper to a board or wall.

drawing-room *noun* a sitting-room or living-room.

drawl *verb trans., intrans.* to speak or say in a slow lazy manner, especially with prolonged vowel sounds. [connected with DRAW]

drawn *adj.* showing signs of mental strain or tiredness.

-drawn *combining form* forming words meaning 'pulled by': *horse-drawn.*

drawn-out *adj.* tedious; prolonged.

drawstring *noun* a cord sewn inside a hem eg on a bag or piece of clothing, closing up the hem when pulled.

dray[1] *noun* a low horse-drawn cart used for heavy loads. [from Anglo-Saxon *dræge*, from *dragan*, to draw]

dray[2] same as DREY.

dread — *noun* great fear or apprehension. — *verb* to look ahead to (something) with dread. — *adj. literary* inspiring awe or great fear. [from Anglo-Saxon *ondrdan*]

◼ *noun* fear, apprehension, misgiving, trepidation, dismay, alarm, horror, terror, fright, disquiet, worry, qualm. *verb* fear, shrink from, quail at, cringe at, flinch from, shy from, shudder at, tremble at.

◼ *noun* confidence, security.

dreaded *adj.* **1** greatly feared. **2** *loosely* much disliked.

dreadful *adj.* **1** inspiring great fear; terrible. **2** *loosely* very bad, unpleasant, or extreme.

◼ AWFUL, TERRIBLE, FRIGHTFUL, HORRIBLE, APPALLING, DIRE, SHOCKING, GHASTLY, HORRENDOUS, TREMENDOUS, FEARSOME. **1** tragic, grievous, hideous.

◼ **2** wonderful.

dreadfully *adv.* **1** terribly. **2** *colloq.* extremely; very: *it's dreadfully late.*

dreadlocks *pl. noun* thin braids of hair tied all over the head, especially worn by Rastafarians.

dreadnought *noun* **1** a heavily armed battleship. **2** a fearless person.

dream — *noun* **1** a series of unconscious thoughts and mental images that are experienced during sleep, and may be pleasant, bizarre, or (in the case of nightmares) frightening. Most dreams are not remembered on waking. **2** a state of complete engrossment in one's own thoughts. **3** a distant ambition, especially unattainable. **4** *colloq.* an extremely pleasing person or thing. **5** *colloq.* (*attributive*) luxurious, ideal. — *verb* (PAST AND PAST PARTICIPLE **dreamed, dreamt**) **1** *trans., intrans.* to have thoughts and visions during sleep. **2** (*usually* **dream of something**) **a** to have a distant ambition or hope. **b** to imagine or conceive of something. **3** *intrans.* to have extravagant and unrealistic thoughts or plans. **4** *intrans.* to be lost in thought. — **dream something up** to devise or invent something unusual or absurd. **like a dream** *colloq.* extremely well, easily, or successfully. [from Middle English]

◼ *noun* **1** trance, fantasy, vision, nightmare, hallucination. **2** reverie, daydream. **3** aspiration, wish, hope, ambition, desire, pipe dream, ideal, goal, design, speculation. **4** *colloq.* dish, *colloq.* honey, *colloq.* peach. *verb* **2** imagine, envisage, fancy, visualize, conceive (of), conjure up. **3** fantasize, hallucinate. **4** daydream, muse. **dream up** invent, devise, conceive, think up, imagine, concoct, hatch, create, spin, contrive.

dreamboat *noun slang* an ideal romantic partner.

dreamer *noun* a person who dreams, especially of unrealistic schemes.

◼ idealist, visionary, fantasizer, romancer, daydreamer, *colloq.* stargazer, theorizer.
▣ realist, pragmatist.

dream ticket **1** *chiefly North Amer.* an ideal or optimum list of electoral candidates. **2** an ideal combination.

dreamy *adj.* (**dreamier, dreamiest**) **1** unreal, like in a dream. **2** having or showing a wandering mind. **3** *colloq.* lovely.

◼ **1** fantastic, unreal, imaginary, shadowy, vague, misty. **2** impractical, fanciful, daydreaming, romantic, visionary, faraway, absent, musing, pensive.
▣ **1** real. **2** practical, down-to-earth.

drearily *adv.* in a dreary or uninteresting way.

dreariness *noun* a dreary or uninteresting state or appearance.

dreary *adj.* (**drearier, dreariest**) **1** dull and depressing. **2** uninteresting. [from Anglo-Saxon *dreorig*, bloody, mournful]

◼ DULL. **1** gloomy, depressing, drab, dismal, bleak, sombre, sad, mournful. **2** boring, tedious, uneventful, humdrum, routine, monotonous, wearisome, commonplace, colourless, lifeless.
▣ **1** cheerful. **2** interesting.

dredge¹ — *verb trans., intrans.* to clear the bottom of or deepen (the sea or a river) by bringing up mud and waste. — *noun* a machine for dredging, with a scooping or sucking action. — **dredge something up** *colloq.* to mention or bring up something long forgotten.

dredge² *verb* to sprinkle (food), eg with sugar or flour. [from Old French *dragie*, sugar-plum]

dredger *noun* a barge or ship fitted with a dredge.

dregs *pl. noun* **1** solid particles in a liquid that settle at the bottom. **2** worthless or contemptible elements. [from Norse *dregg*]

◼ **1** sediment, deposit, residue, lees, grounds, scum, dross, trash, waste. **2** outcasts, rabble, riff-raff, scum, down-and-outs.

drench — *verb* **1** to make soaking wet. **2** to administer liquid medicine to (an animal). — *noun* a dose of liquid medicine for an animal. [from Anglo-Saxon *drencan*, to cause to drink]

◼ *verb* **1** soak, saturate, steep, wet, douse, souse, immerse, inundate, duck, flood, imbue, drown.

dress — *verb* **1** *intrans.* to put on clothes; to wear clothes (of a certain kind). **2** to put clothes on: *dress the baby.* **3** to treat and bandage (wounds). **4** to prepare, or add seasoning or a sauce to (food). **5** to arrange a display in (a window): *window dressing.* **6** to shape and smooth (especially stone). **7** to brush out and arrange (the hair). **8** *intrans.* to put on or have on formal evening wear. — *noun* **1** a woman's garment with top and skirt in one piece. **2** clothing; wear: *in evening dress.* — *adj.* formal; for wear in the evenings: *dress jacket.* — **dress down** to dress in casual clothes. **dress someone down** to scold them. **dress up 1** to put on fancy dress. **2** to dress in very smart or formal clothes. **dress something up** to make it appear more pleasant or acceptable by making additions or alterations. [from Old French *dresser*, to prepare]

◼ *verb* **2** clothe, garb, rig out, robe. **3** bandage, tend, treat. **4** season, spice, flavour, garnish. **5** decorate, deck, adorn, drape, trim. **7** arrange, groom, brush out, comb out. *noun* **1** frock, gown, robe. **2** clothes, clothing, garment(s), outfit, costume, garb, *colloq.* get-up, *colloq.* gear, togs. **dress someone down** scold, reprimand, rebuke, *colloq.* carpet, *colloq.* haul over the coals, *colloq.* tear a strip off, *colloq.* give an earful. **dress something up** beautify, adorn, embellish, improve, deck, doll up, *slang* tart up, gild, disguise.
▣ *verb* **1** strip, undress.

dressage / 'drɛsɑːʒ/ *noun* horses' training in, or performance of, set manoeuvres signalled by the rider. [from French *dressage*]

dress circle a balcony in a theatre, especially the first above the ground floor.

dresser *noun* **1** a free-standing kitchen cupboard with shelves above, for storing and displaying dishes, etc. **2** a theatre assistant employed to help stage actors with their costumes. **3** a person who dresses in a particular way.

dressily *adv.* with a dressy or stylish manner.

dressing *noun* **1** any sauce added to food, especially salad. **2** a covering for a wound. **3** *Agric.* **a** an application of fertilizer to the soil surface. **b** chemical treatment of seeds, especially those of cereal crops, before sowing in order to control fungal diseases.

dressing-down *noun* a reprimand.

dressing gown a loose robe worn informally indoors, especially over nightclothes.

dressing-table *noun* a piece of bedroom furniture typically with drawers and a large mirror.

dressmaker *noun* a person who makes women's clothes.

dressmaking *noun* the business of making women's clothes.

dress rehearsal **1** the last rehearsal of a play, with full costumes, lighting and other effects. **2** a practice under real conditions, or an event considered as such in relation to another more important.

dressy *adj.* (**dressier, dressiest**) **1** dressed or dressing stylishly. **2** *said of clothes* for formal wear; elegant. **3** *colloq.* fancy; over-decorated.

drew see draw.

drey /dreɪ/ *noun* a squirrel's nest.

dribble — *verb* **1** *intrans.* to fall or flow in drops. **2** *intrans.* to allow saliva to run slowly down from the mouth. **3** *trans., intrans.* to move along keeping (a ball) in close control with frequent short strokes. — *noun* **1** a small quantity of liquid, especially saliva. **2** an act of dribbling a ball. [from obsolete *drib*]

◼ *verb* **1** trickle, drip, leak, run, seep, drop, ooze. **2** drool, slaver, slobber, drivel.

driblet *noun* a very small amount, especially of liquid. [see DRIBBLE]

dribs and drabs very small quantities at a time. [see DRIBBLE]

drier or **dryer** *noun* a device or substance that dries hair, paint, etc.

drift — *noun* **1** a bank or mass (of snow, sand, etc) heaped up by the action of wind or current. **2** *Geol.* superficial deposits of rock material that have been carried from their place of origin by glaciers. **3** *Geol.* continental drift. **4** a general movement or tendency to move. **5** the movement of a stretch of sea in the direction of a prevailing wind. **6** degree of movement off course caused by wind or a current. **7** the general or essential meaning of something. — *verb intrans.* **1** to float or be blown along or into heaps. **2** to move aimlessly or passively from one place or occupation to another. **3** to move off course. [from Norse *drift*, snowdrift]

. . . .

◼ *noun* **1** accumulation, mound, pile, bank, mass, heap. **4** trend, tendency, course, direction, flow, movement, current, rush, sweep. **7** meaning, intention, implication, gist, tenor, thrust, significance, aim, design, scope. *verb* **1** gather, accumulate, pile up, drive. **2, 3** wander, stray. **2** waft, float, freewheel, coast. **3** deviate.

. . . .

drifter *noun* **1** a fishing boat that uses a drift-net. **2** a person who moves from place to place, settling in none.

drift-net *noun* a large fishing net allowed to drift with the tide.

driftwood *noun* wood floating near, or washed up on, a shore.

drill¹ — *noun* **1** a cutting tool with a rotating end that is used for boring or enlarging holes in metal, wood, and other solid materials. **2** a rotary instrument with a handpiece that is used for boring or enlarging holes in teeth or bones, especially in order to remove decayed material prior to filling a tooth. **3** a training exercise, or a session of it. **4** *colloq.* correct procedure; routine. — *verb* **1** *trans., intrans.* to make (a hole) with a drill; to make a hole in (a solid material) with a drill. **2** to exercise or teach through repeated practice. [probably from Dutch *drillen*, to bore]

. . . .

◼ *noun* **1** borer, awl, bit, gimlet. **3** instruction, training, practice, coaching, exercise, repetition, tuition, preparation, discipline. *verb* **1** bore, pierce, penetrate, puncture, perforate. **2** teach, train, instruct, coach, practise, rehearse, exercise.

. . . .

drill² *noun* thick strong cotton cloth. [from German *Drillich*, ticking]

drill³ — *noun* **1** a shallow furrow or series of holes in which seeds are sown. **2** a seed drill. **3** a row of seeds sown using a seed drill. — *verb* to sow (seeds) by means of a seed drill.

drill⁴ *noun* a forest-living baboon, native to W Africa, related to the mandrill but having a smaller body, a black face surrounded by a white ruff, and a short tail. [from a W African language]

drily *adv.* with a dry, especially mildly sarcastic, manner.

drink — *verb* (PAST TENSE **drank**; PAST PARTICIPLE **drunk**) **1** *trans., intrans.* to swallow (a liquid); to consume (a liquid) by swallowing. **2** *intrans.* to drink alcohol; to drink alcohol to excess. **3** to get (oneself) into a certain state by drinking alcohol: *drank himself silly / drank themselves into a stupor.* **4** *trans., intrans.* (**drink to someone** or **something**) to drink a toast to them. — *noun* **1** an act of drinking; a liquid suitable for drinking. **2** alcohol of any kind; the habit of drinking alcohol to excess. **3** a glass or amount of drink. **4** (**the drink**) *colloq.* the sea. — **drink something in** to listen to it eagerly. [from Anglo-Saxon *drincan*]

. . . .

◼ *verb* **1** imbibe, swallow, sip, gulp, *colloq.* swig, sup, quaff, absorb, guzzle, partake (of), swill. **2** get drunk, *slang* booze, *colloq.* tipple, indulge, carouse, revel, *slang* tank up. *noun* **1** beverage, liquid, refreshment, draught, sip, swallow, *colloq.* swig, gulp. **2** alcohol, spirits, *slang* booze, liquor, *colloq.* tipple, tot, *slang* the bottle.

. . . .

Alcoholic drinks include: ale, beer, cider, lager, shandy, stout, *trademark* Guinness; aquavit, Armagnac, bourbon, brandy, Calvados, Cognac, gin, gin and tonic, pink gin, sloe gin, rum, grog, rye, vodka, whisky, Scotch and soda, hot toddy; wine, red wine, vin rouge, vin rosé, white wine, vin blanc, Beaujolais, Beaune, Bordeaux, burgundy, claret, mulled wine, muscatel, Chianti, Graves, Rioja, Chablis, champagne, *colloq.* bubbly, hock, Moselle, Riesling, Sauterne, mead, perry, *colloq.* vino, *colloq.* plonk; absinthe, advocaat, Benedictine, Chartreuse, black velvet, bloody Mary, Buck's fizz, Campari, cherry brandy, cocktail, *trademark* Cointreau, crème de menthe, daiquiri, eggnog, ginger wine, kirsch, Marsala, *trademark* Martini, ouzo, *trademark* Pernod, pina colada, port, punch, retsina, sake, sangria, schnapps, sherry, snowball, tequila, Tom Collins, vermouth.

drinkable *adj.* fit to be drunk.

drink-driver *noun* a person who drives while under the influence of alcohol.

drink-driving *noun* the act or practice of driving while under the influence of alcohol.

drinker *noun* a person who drinks, especially alcohol.

drip — *verb* (**dripped, dripping**) **1** *trans., intrans.* to release or fall in drops. **2** *intrans.* to release a liquid in drops: *a dripping tap.* **3** *trans., intrans. colloq.* to bear or contain an impressive or excessive amount of something: *a film dripping with sentimentality.* — *noun* **1** the action or noise of dripping. **2** an amount of a liquid that has dripped from something. **3** same as DRIP-FEED. **4** *derog. colloq.* a person lacking spirit or character. [from Anglo-Saxon *dryppan*]

. . . .

◼ *verb* **1, 2** dribble, trickle, weep. **1** drop, plop, percolate, drizzle, splash, sprinkle. *noun* **1** trickle, dribble, leak. **2** drop, bead, tear. **4** weakling, *colloq.* wimp, *colloq.* softy, bore, wet, ninny.

. . . .

drip-dry — *adj., said of a garment* requiring little or no ironing if hung up to dry. — *verb trans., intrans.* to dry in this way.

drip-feed — *noun* a device for passing a liquid slowly and continuously into the body of a patient, especially via a vein; a drip. — *verb* (PAST TENSE AND PAST PARTICIPLE **drip-fed**) to feed (a patient) with liquid in this way.

dripping *noun* fat from roasted meat, especially when solidified.

drive — *verb* (PAST TENSE **drove**; PAST PARTICIPLE **driven**) **1** *trans., intrans.* to control the movement of (a vehicle); to be legally qualified to do so. **2** *intrans.* to travel in a vehicle. **3** to take or transport in a vehicle. **4** to urge or force to move. **5** to strike or cause to strike (more than one). **6** to produce motion in; to cause to function. **7** to motivate or compel into a particular frame of mind or course of action: *these delays are driving me mad / they were driven to steal by sheer hunger.* **8** to conduct or dictate: *drive a hard bargain.* — *noun* **1** a trip in a vehicle; travel by road. **2** (*also* **driveway**) a path for vehicles, leading from a private residence to the road outside. **3** energy and enthusiasm. **4** an organized campaign; a group effort: *economy drive.* **5** operating power, or a device supplying this. **6** an instinct; a psychological need or urge. **7** a forceful strike of a ball in various sports. **8** a united movement forward, especially by a military force. **9** a meeting to play a game, especially cards. **10** *Comput.* a device containing the mechanisms for rotating a magnetic disk at high speed. — **be driving at something** to intend or imply it as a meaning or conclusion: *what is he driving at?* **drive something home** to make it clearly understood. [from Anglo-Saxon *drifan*]

. . . .

◼ *verb* **1** steer. **2** ride, travel, motor. **3** transport, convey, carry. **4** force, compel, impel, coerce, constrain, press, push, urge, dragoon, goad, guide. **5** strike, hammer, knock, thump. **6** propel, impel, direct, control, manage, operate, run, handle. **7** motivate, force, compel, impel, lead, prompt, incite, provoke, persuade, move. *noun* **1** excursion, outing, journey, ride, spin, trip, jaunt. **3** energy, enterprise, ambition, initiative, *colloq.* get-up-and-go, vigour, motivation, determination. **4** campaign, crusade, appeal, effort, action. **5** power, thrust, propulsion, transmission, propeller shaft. **6** urge, instinct, impulse, need, desire. **drive at** imply, allude to, intimate, mean, suggest, hint, get at, intend, refer to, signify, insinuate, indicate.

· · · · · · · · · · · · · · · · · · · ·

drive-by shooting (*often* **drive-by**) a shooting that is carried out from a moving vehicle.

drive-in *noun adj.*, *said of a cinema, restaurant, etc* providing a service or facility for customers remaining seated in vehicles.

drivel — *noun* nonsense. — *verb intrans.* (**drivelled, drivelling**) **1** to talk nonsense. **2** to dribble or slaver. [from Anglo-Saxon *dreflian*, to dribble]

· · · · · · · · · · · · · · · · · · · ·

▤ *noun* nonsense, rubbish, gibberish, claptrap, *colloq.* twaddle, *old use* balderdash. *verb* **1** blather, jabber, witter on. **2** dribble, slaver, drool, slobber, salivate.

· ·

driver *noun* **1** a person who drives a vehicle. **2** a large-headed golf club for hitting the ball from the tee.

driving — *noun* the act, practice, or way of driving vehicles. — *adj.* **1** producing or transmitting operating power: *driving wheel.* **2** heavy and windblown: *driving rain.* **3** providing the motive for determined hard work.

· · · · · · · · · · · · · · · · · · · ·

▤ *adj.* **2** heavy, violent. **3** compelling, forceful, vigorous, dynamic, energetic, forthright.

· ·

driving licence an official licence to drive a motor vehicle.

driving seat — **in the driving seat** *colloq.* in a controlling or commanding position.

driving test a test of ability to drive safely, especially an official or obligatory test. In the UK, the official driving test is administered by the Department of Transport.

drizzle — *noun* fine light rain. — *verb intrans.* to rain lightly. [from Anglo-Saxon *dreosan*, to fall]

· · · · · · · · · · · · · · · · · · · ·

▤ *noun* mist, mizzle, rain, spray, shower. *verb* spit, spray, sprinkle, rain.

· ·

drizzly *adj.*, *said of the weather* inclined to drizzle.

droit de seigneur /drwa: də sen'jɜ:(r)/ **1** *Hist.* the alleged right of a feudal lord to take the virginity of a vassal's bride on her wedding night. **2** an excessive or unreasonable demand made of a subordinate. [French, = lord's right]

droll *adj.* oddly amusing or comical. [from French *drôle*]

· · · · · · · · · · · · · · · · · · · ·

▤ bizarre, odd, queer, peculiar, comical, amusing, humorous, ridiculous, ludicrous.

· ·

drollery *noun* droll or oddly amusing ideas or humour.

drolly /'drəʊlɪ/ *adv.* in a droll or oddly amusing way.

dromedary /'drɒmədərɪ/ *noun* (PL. **dromedaries**) a breed of single-humped camel that is capable of moving at speed across the desert, and is much used as a means of transport in N Africa, the Middle East, and India. [from Greek *dromados*, running]

drone — *verb intrans.* **1** to make a low humming noise. **2** (**drone on**) to talk at length in a tedious monotonous voice. — *noun* **1** a deep humming sound. **2** a male social insect, eg honeybee, ant, that does not contribute to the maintenance of the colony, and whose sole function is to mate with fertile females. See also WORKER. **3** a lazy person, especially one living off others. [from Anglo-Saxon *dran*, bee]

drool *verb intrans.* **1** to dribble or slaver. **2** (**drool over something**) to show uncontrolled admiration for it or pleasure at the sight of it. [alteration of DRIVEL]

· · · · · · · · · · · · · · · · · · · ·

▤ **1** dribble, slaver, drivel, slobber, salivate. **2** slobber over, slaver over, covet.

· ·

droop — *verb intrans.* **1** to hang loosely; to sag. **2** to be weak with tiredness. — *noun* drooping state. [from Norse *drupa*]

· · · · · · · · · · · · · · · · · · · ·

▤ *verb* SLUMP, SINK. **1** hang down, dangle, sag, bend. **2** languish, decline, flag, falter, lose heart, wilt, wither, drop, faint, fall down, fade, slouch.

▣ *verb* **1** straighten. **2** flourish, rise.

· ·

droopy *adj.* (**droopier, droopiest**) hanging loosely; drooping.

drop — *verb* (**dropped, dropping**) **1** *intrans.* to fall. **2** to allow to fall. **3** *trans., intrans.* to decline or cause to decline; to lower or weaken. **4** to give up or abandon (eg a friend or a habit); to stop doing temporarily. **5** to stop discussing (a topic). **6** (*also* **drop someone** or **something off**) to set them down from a vehicle; to deliver or hand them in. **7** to leave or take out: *they've dropped me from the team.* **8** to mention casually: *drop a hint.* **9** to fail to pronounce: *drop one's h's.* **10** *colloq.* to write informally: *drop me a line.* **11** *intrans.* (**drop into something**) to pass idly or passively (into a habit, etc). **12** *coarse slang* to give birth to. **13** *slang* to beat to the ground. — *noun* **1** a small round or pear-shaped mass of liquid, especially falling; a small amount (of liquid). **2** a descent; a fall. **3** a vertical distance. **4** a decline or decrease. **5** any small round or pear-shaped object, eg an earring or boiled sweet. **6** (**drops**) liquid medication administered in small amounts. **7** a delivery. — **at the drop of a hat** *colloq.* promptly; for the slightest reason. **drop back** or **behind** to get left behind others in a group. **drop in** or **by** to pay a brief unexpected visit. **drop off 1** *colloq.* to fall asleep. **2** to decline; to lessen. **drop out 1** to withdraw from an activity. **2** *colloq.* to adopt an alternative lifestyle as a reaction against traditional social values. **drop out of something** to withdraw eg from a prearranged activity. **let something drop** to make it known inadvertently or as if inadvertently. [from Anglo-Saxon *droppian*]

· · · · · · · · · · · · · · · · · · · ·

▤ *verb* **1** fall, sink, decline, plunge, plummet, tumble, dive, descend, droop. **2** lower, let fall, let go. **3** lower, lessen, weaken, diminish. **4, 5** leave, abandon, give up, relinquish, forsake. **4** desert, reject, jilt, renounce, throw over, repudiate. **5** cease, discontinue, quit. **6** set down, deliver, hand in. *noun* **1** droplet, bead, tear, drip, bubble, globule, trickle, dash, pinch, spot, sip, trace, dab. **3** fall, precipice, slope, chasm, abyss. **4** decline, falling-off, lowering, downturn, decrease, reduction, slump, plunge, deterioration. **drop back** fall behind, lag (behind), retreat, fall back. **drop in** call (round), come over, come round, visit. **drop off 1** nod off, doze, *colloq.* snooze, *colloq.* have forty winks. **2** decline, fall off, decrease, dwindle, lessen, diminish, slacken. **drop out 1** back out, cry off, withdraw, leave, quit. **drop out of** back out of, cry off from, withdraw from, leave, quit, abandon.

▣ *verb* **1** rise. **6** pick up. **drop off 1** wake up. **2** increase.

· ·

drop-kick — *noun Rugby* a kick in which the ball is released from the hands and struck as it hits the ground. — *verb* to kick (a ball) in this way.

droplet *noun* a tiny drop.

dropout *noun* **1** a person who rejects traditional social values. **2** a student who quits before completing a course of study. **3** *Electron.* a momentary loss of a recorded audio or video signal, due to the absence of a small area of magnetic coating on the recording tape. **4** *Comput.* a patch of magnetic tape which fails to record data properly. See also DROP OUT.

dropper *noun* a short narrow glass tube with a rubber bulb on one end, for applying liquid in drops.

droppings *pl. noun* animal faeces.

dropsical *adj.* affected with dropsy.

dropsy *noun* the former name for oedema (the abnormal

accumulation of fluid in the body tissues). [from Greek *hydrops*, from *hydor*, water]

dross *noun* **1** waste coal. **2** scum that forms on the surface of molten metal. **3** *derog. colloq.* rubbish; any worthless substance. [from Anglo-Saxon *dros*]

drought /draʊt/ *noun* a prolonged lack of rainfall. [from Anglo-Saxon *drugath*, dryness]

⊟ dryness, aridity, parchedness, dehydration, desiccation, shortage, want.

drove¹ see DRIVE.

drove² — *noun* **1** a herd of animal livestock, especially cattle, being driven together. **2** a broad-edged chisel for dressing stone. **3** a large moving crowd. — *verb* to drive (animal livestock, especially cattle) for a considerable distance. [from Anglo-Saxon *draf*, herd]

⊟ *noun* **1** herd, flock. **3** horde, gathering, crowd, multitude, swarm, throng, flock, herd, company, mob, press.

drover *noun Hist.* a person employed to drive animal livestock to and from market.

drown *verb* **1** *intrans.* to die by suffocation as a result of inhaling liquid, especially water, into the lungs. **2** to kill by suffocation in this way. **3** to apply an excessive amount of liquid to; to soak or flood. **4** (**drown something out**) to suppress the effect of one sound with a louder one. — **drown one's sorrows** *colloq.* to become drunk in order to forget one's troubles. [from Middle English *drounen*]

⊟ **3, 4** swamp, submerge. **3** immerse, inundate, flood, sink, deluge, engulf, drench. **4** overwhelm, extinguish.

drowse *verb intrans.* to sleep lightly for a short while; to be in a pleasantly sleepy state. [from Anglo-Saxon *drusian*, to be sluggish]

⊟ doze, nod (off), *colloq.* snooze, *colloq.* have forty winks.

drowsy *adj.* (**drowsier, drowsiest**) **1** sleepy; causing sleepiness. **2** lethargic. **3** quiet and peaceful.

⊟ SLEEPY. **1** tired, nodding, dreamy, dozy. **2** lethargic, sluggish, torpid, hibernating, inert, dormant, inactive.
⊟ **1, 2** alert, awake.

drub *verb* (**drubbed, drubbing**) **1** to defeat severely. **2** to beat; to thump. [from Arabic *daraba*, to beat]

drubbing *noun* a beating; a complete defeat.

drudge — *verb intrans.* to do hard, tedious, or menial work. — *noun* a servant; a labourer.

⊟ *verb* plod, toil, work, slave, *colloq.* plug away, *colloq.* grind, labour, *colloq.* beaver away. *noun* toiler, menial, *colloq.* dogsbody, hack, servant, slave, factotum, worker, *colloq.* skivvy, galley-slave, lackey.
⊟ *verb* idle, laze.

drudgery *noun* tedious or menial work.

⊟ labour, donkey-work, hack-work, *colloq.* slog, *colloq.* grind, slavery, sweat, sweated labour, toil, *colloq.* skivvying, chore.

drug — *noun* **1** a substance used to treat a disease. **2** any narcotic substance, especially an addictive one. **3** anything craved for. — *verb* (**drugged, drugging**) **1** to administer a drug to. **2** to poison or stupefy with drugs. **3** *said of food, etc* to mix or season with drugs. — **a drug on the market** a commodity in plentiful supply but not in demand. [from Old French *drogue*]

⊟ *noun* **1** medication, medicine, remedy, potion. *verb* **1** medicate, sedate, tranquillize, anaesthetize, dose. **2** dope, *colloq.* knock out, stupefy, deaden, numb.

Types of drug include: anaesthetic, analgesic, antibiotic, antidepressant, antihistamine, barbiturate, narcotic, opiate, hallucinogenic, sedative, steroid, stimulant, tranquillizer; chloroform, aspirin, codeine, paracetamol, morphine, penicillin, diazepam, temazepam, *trademark* Valium, cortisone, insulin, digitalis, laudanum, quinine, progesterone, oestrogen, cannabis, marijuana, smack, LSD, acid, ecstasy, *slang* E, heroin, opium, cocaine, crack, *colloq.* dope. *See also* **medicine**.

drug addict a person who is addicted to narcotic drugs.

drugget /'drʌgɪt/ *noun* thick coarse woollen fabric; a protective cover for a floor or carpet made from this. [from Old French *droguet*, waste fabric]

druggist *noun North Amer., esp. US* a pharmacist.

drugstore *noun North Amer., esp. US* a chemist's shop where medical prescriptions are made up and dispensed, and a variety of goods, usually including light refreshments, are sold.

druid /'druːɪd/ *noun* **1** a member of a Celtic order of priests in N Europe in pre-Christian times. **2** an eisteddfod official. [from Gaulish *druides*]

druidic or **druidical** *adj.* relating to or belonging to the druids.

drum — *noun* **1** a percussion instrument consisting of a hollow frame with a skin or other membrane stretched tightly across its opening, sounding when struck. **2** any object resembling this in shape, especially a cylindrical container. **3** an eardrum. — *verb* (**drummed, drumming**) **1** *intrans.* to beat a drum. **2** *trans., intrans.* to make continuous tapping or thumping sounds (with). — **drum something in** or **into someone** to force something into their mind through constant repetition. **drum someone out** to expel them. **drum something up** *colloq.* to achieve or attract it by energetic persuasion: *managed to drum up more support*. [from German *Trommel*, originally imitative]

⊟ *verb* **2** beat, tap, tattoo, rap. **drum out** throw out, expel, eject, dismiss, ban, bar. **drum up** obtain, round up, collect, gather, muster, marshal, solicit, canvass, petition, attract.

drumhead *noun* the part of a drum that is struck.

drumlin *noun Geol.* a small streamlined hill produced by the pressure of moving ice over glacial deposits. Drumlins often occur in groups, producing a 'basket of eggs' topography. [from Scottish and Irish Gaelic *druim*, back]

drum machine a synthesizer for simulating the sound of drums and other percussion instruments.

drum major the leader of a marching (especially military) band.

drum majorette see MAJORETTE.

drummer *noun* a person who plays drums.

drumstick *noun* **1** a stick used for beating a drum. **2** the lower leg of a cooked fowl, especially a chicken.

drunk — *verb* past participle of DRINK. — *adj.* **1** lacking control in movement, speech, etc through having drunk an excess of alcohol. **2** (**drunk with something**) intoxicated or overwhelmed with it: *drunk with self-pity*. — *noun* a drunk person, especially one regularly drunk.

⊟ *adj.* **1** inebriated, intoxicated, under the influence, drunken, *slang* stoned, *colloq.* legless, *colloq.* paralytic, *colloq.* sloshed, *colloq.* merry, *colloq.* tight, *colloq.* tipsy, *slang* tanked up, *colloq.* tiddly, *colloq.* plastered, *colloq.* loaded, *colloq.* lit up, *colloq.* sozzled, *colloq.* well-oiled, *slang* canned, *slang* blotto.

◨ adj. **1** sober, temperate, abstinent, teetotal.

drunkard noun a person who is often drunk.

◨ drunk, inebriate, alcoholic, dipsomaniac, slang boozer, slang wino, colloq. tippler, colloq. soak, slang lush.

drunken adj. **1** drunk. **2** relating to, or brought on by, alcoholic intoxication.

drupe noun Bot. a fleshy fruit containing one or more seeds that are surrounded by a stony protective layer or en-docarp, eg plum, cherry, peach, holly. Raspberries and blackberries are clusters of small drupes, and not true berries. [from Greek dryppa, olive]

Druze /druːz/ — noun (PL. **Druze**) a member of a Muslim people, mostly inhabiting a mountainous district in the south of Syria. — adj. relating to this people or their religion. [perhaps from Darazi, an early exponent of the religion]

dry — adj. (**drier, driest**) **1** free from moisture or wetness. **2** with little or no rainfall. **3** from which all the water has evaporated or been taken: a dry well. **4** thirsty. **5** said of an animal no longer producing milk. **6** said of wine, etc not sweet. **7** not buttered. **8** said of humour expressed in a quietly sarcastic or matter-of-fact way. **9** forbidding the sale and consumption of alcohol. **10** said of eyes without tears. **11** dull; uninteresting. **12** lacking warmth of character. **13** said of a cough not producing catarrh. — verb (**dries, dried**) **1** trans., intrans. to make or become dry. **2** trans. to preserve (food) by removing all moisture. — noun (PL. **dries**) colloq. a staunch right-wing Conservative politician. See also WET. — **dry out 1** to become completely dry. **2** colloq. to receive treatment to cure addiction to alcohol; to have one's addiction cured. **dry something out** to dry it completely. **dry up 1** colloq., said of a speaker or actor to run out of words; to forget lines while on stage. **2** slang to shut up or be quiet. **dry something up** to dry (dishes) after washing them. [from Anglo-Saxon dryge]

◨ adj. **2** arid, parched, barren. **3** dehydrated, desiccated. **8** ironic, cynical, droll, deadpan, sarcastic, cutting. **11** boring, dull, dreary, tedious, monotonous. verb **1** parch, drain, shrivel, wither. **2** dehydrate, desiccate.
◨ adj. **1** wet. **11** interesting. verb **1** soak.

dryad /ˈdraɪad/ noun Greek Mythol. a woodland nymph or fairy, often with demigod status. [from Greek dryados]

dry battery a battery composed of two or more dry cells, used in portable devices such as torches, radios, and calculators.

dry cell Chem. an electrolytic cell in which current is passed through an electrolyte that consists of a moist paste, eg ammonium chloride, instead of a liquid. Dry cells are used as portable energy sources in batteries for torches, radios, calculators, etc.

dry-clean verb to clean (especially clothes) with liquid chemicals, not with water.

dry-cleaner noun a business that dry-cleans clothes, etc.

dry-cleaning noun clothes, etc to be dry-cleaned.

dry dock a dock from which the water can be pumped out to allow work on a ship's lower parts.

dryer see DRIER.

dry ice solid carbon dioxide used as a refrigerating agent.

dry land land as opposed to sea or other water.

dryness noun a dry state.

dry rot 1 Bot. a timber decay caused by the fungus Serpula lacrymans, common in damp, poorly ventilated buildings. **2** Bot. several fungal diseases of plants, eg stored potatoes, fruit.

dry run a rehearsal or practice.

◨ dummy run, simulation, practice, rehearsal, test, trial, try-out.

dry-stone adj., said of a wall made of stones wedged together without mortar.

DSC abbrev. Distinguished Service Cross.

DSc abbrev. Doctor of Science.

DSM abbrev. Distinguished Service Medal.

DSO abbrev. Distinguished Service Order.

DST abbrev. daylight saving time.

DT or **DTs** abbrev. delirium tremens.

DTh or **DTheol** abbrev. Doctor of Theology.

DTI abbrev. Department of Trade and Industry.

DTP abbrev. desktop publishing.

dual adj. **1** consisting of or representing two separate parts. **2** double; twofold. [from Latin duo, two]

◨ **1** binary, combined, paired, twin, duplicate, duplex, matched. **2** double, twofold.

dual carriageway a road on which traffic moving in opposite directions is separated by a central barrier or strip of land.

dualism noun Philos. the belief that reality is made up of two separate parts, one spiritual and one physical, or influenced by two separate forces, one good and one bad.

duality /djuˈalɪtɪ/ noun the state of being double.

dub[1] verb (**dubbed, dubbing**) **1** to give a name, especially a nickname, to. **2** to confer the title of knight on by touching each shoulder with a sword. **3** to smear (leather) with grease. [from Anglo-Saxon dubbian]

dub[2] — verb (**dubbed, dubbing**) **1** to add a new soundtrack to (eg a film), especially one in a different language. **2** to add sound effects or music to (eg a film). — noun a type of reggae music. [contraction of DOUBLE]

dubbin noun a wax-like mixture of oil and tallow for softening and waterproofing leather. [from DUB[1]]

dubiety /djuˈbaɪɪtɪ/ noun formal dubiousness. [from Latin dubietas]

dubious adj. **1** feeling doubt; unsure; uncertain. **2** arousing suspicion; potentially dishonest or dishonestly obtained. [from Latin dubium, doubt]

◨ **1** doubtful, uncertain, undecided, unsure, wavering, unsettled, suspicious, sceptical, hesitant. **2** questionable, debatable, unreliable, ambiguous, suspect, obscure, colloq. fishy, colloq. shady.
◨ **1** certain. **2** trustworthy.

dubiously adv. in a dubious or suspicious way.

ducal /ˈdjuːkəl/ adj. relating to a duke. [from Latin ducalis]

ducat /ˈdʌkət/ noun a former European gold or silver coin of varying value. [from Latin ducatus, duchy]

duchess noun **1** the wife or widow of a duke. **2** a woman of the same rank as a duke in her own right. [from Old French duchesse]

duchy noun (PL. **duchies**) the territory owned or ruled by a duke or duchess. [from Old French duché]

duck[1] noun **1** any wild or domesticated water bird related to the swans and geese, and having short legs, webbed feet, and a large flattened beak, eg eider, teal, mallard. **2** the flesh of this animal used as food. **3** the female of such a bird, as opposed to the male drake. **4** colloq. a likeable person; a term of endearment or (loosely) of address. **5** Cricket a batsman's score of zero. — **break one's duck** colloq. to enjoy one's first success after several failures. **like water off a duck's back** colloq. having no effect at all. [from Anglo-Saxon duce]

duck[2] verb **1** intrans. to lower the head or body suddenly, to avoid notice or a blow. **2** to push briefly under water. **3** colloq. (**duck out of something**) to avoid something unpleasant or unwelcome. [from Middle English douken]

◨ **1** crouch, stoop, bob, bend, lower. **2** dip, immerse, plunge, dunk, dive, submerge, douse, souse, wet. **3** avoid, dodge, evade, shirk, sidestep.

....

duck[3] *noun* hard-wearing cotton fabric, used for tents, sails, etc. [from Dutch *doek*, linen cloth]

duck-billed platypus SEE PLATYPUS.

duckboard *noun* a narrow board laid across muddy ground to form a path.

ducking *noun* immersion of a person or animal in water.

ducking-stool *noun Hist.* a chair on a long wooden pole, used for ducking offenders into water as punishment.

duckling *noun* a young duck.

ducks and drakes the game of skimming stones across the surface of water. — **play ducks and drakes with something** *colloq.* to squander or waste it.

duckweed *noun* any of about 30 species of perennial floating aquatic plant, especially common duckweed (*Lemna minor*), found in most parts of the world except for polar and some tropical regions.

ducky *colloq.* — *noun* (PL. **duckies**) a term of endearment. — *adj.* (**duckier, duckiest**) excellent; attractive or pleasing.

duct *noun* **1** *Anat.* any tube in the body, especially for carrying glandular secretions away from a gland, eg tear duct. **2** in a building, a casing or shaft that accommodates pipes or electrical cables, or a tube used for ventilation and air conditioning. [from Latin *ducere*, to lead]

....

■ **2** conduit, shaft, tube, inlet, outlet.

....

ductile *adj.* **1** *Chem.* denoting certain metals, eg copper, that can be drawn out into a thin wire or thread without breaking or decreasing in strength. **2** easily influenced by others. [from Latin *ductilis*, from *ducere*, to lead]

ductility *noun* the capacity of metal to be stretched or pressed into shape.

dud *colloq.* — *noun* **1** a counterfeit article. **2** a bomb or other projectile that fails to go off. **3** any useless or ineffectual person or thing. **4** (**duds**) clothes. — *adj.* **1** useless. **2** counterfeit.

....

■ *noun* **1** fake, counterfeit, forgery, copy, imitation. *adj.* **1** useless, broken, *colloq.* duff, unworkable, impractical. **2** counterfeit, fake, sham, imitation.

....

dude *noun colloq. North Amer., esp. US* **1** a man. **2** a city man, especially an Easterner holidaying in the West. **3** a man preoccupied with dressing smartly.

dudgeon /'dʌdʒən/ — **in high dudgeon** very angry, resentful, or indignant.

due — *adj.* **1** owed; payable. **2** expected according to timetable or pre-arrangement. **3** proper, appropriate. — *noun* **1** what is owed; that which can be rightfully claimed or expected. **2** (**dues**) subscription fees. — *adv.* directly: *due north.* — **due to something** or **someone 1** caused by them. **2** because of them. **give someone his or her due** to acknowledge their qualities or achievements, especially when disapproving in other ways. [from Old French *deü*, from *devoir*, to owe]

....

■ *adj.* **1** owed, owing, payable, unpaid, outstanding, in arrears. **2** expected, scheduled. **3** rightful, fitting, appropriate, proper, merited, deserved, justified, suitable, adequate, enough, sufficient, ample, plenty of. *adv.* exactly, direct(ly), precisely, straight, dead.

F3 *adj.* **1** paid. **3** inappropriate, inadequate.

....

duel — *noun* **1** a pre-arranged fight to the death between two people, to settle a matter of honour. **2** any serious conflict between two people or groups. — *verb intrans.* (**duelled, duelling**) to fight a duel. [from Latin *duellum*, variation of *bellum*, war]

....

■ *noun* COMBAT, FIGHT, ENCOUNTER. **1** affair of honour. **2** contest, clash, competition, rivalry.

....

duellist *noun* a person who takes part in a duel.

duenna /dju'ɛnə/ *noun* an older woman acting as a chaperone to a girl or young woman (especially formerly) in Spanish and Portuguese society. [from Spanish *dueña*]

due process *Legal* a principle asserting the lawful judgement of an accused person.

duet *noun* a piece of music for two singers or players; a pair of musical performers. [from Italian *duetto*, from Latin *duo*, two]

duettist *noun* a performer in a duet.

duff[1] *noun* a heavy boiled or steamed pudding, especially containing fruit. [form of DOUGH]

duff[2] *adj. colloq.* useless; broken. [perhaps from DUFFER]

duff[3] *verb* — **duff someone up** *slang* to treat them violently; to beat them up. [perhaps from DUFFER]

duff[4] — *verb colloq.* **1** to bungle. **2** to misplay or mishit (a shot, especially in golf). — *adj.* bungled. [from DUFFER]

duffel or **duffle** *noun* a thick coarse woollen fabric. [from Dutch *duffel*, from *Duffel*, Belgian town]

duffel bag a cylindrical canvas shoulder bag with a drawstring fastening.

duffel coat a heavy (especially hooded) coat made of duffel, typically with toggle fastenings.

duffer *noun colloq.* a clumsy or incompetent person.

dug[1] past tense of **dig**.

dug[2] *noun* **1** an animal's udder or nipple. **2** *coarse slang* a woman's breast.

dugong /'du:gɒŋ/ *noun* an aquatic mammal, native to tropical waters of the Pacific and Indian Oceans and the Red Sea, having a large streamlined body, flipperlike forelimbs, no hindlimbs, and a notched tail that is held horizontally like that of the whale. [from Malay *duyong*]

dugout *noun* **1** a canoe made from a hollowed-out log. **2** a soldier's rough shelter dug into a slope or bank or in a trench. **3** a covered shelter at the side of a sports field, for the trainer, substitutes, etc.

duke *noun* **1** a nobleman of the highest rank outside the royal family. **2** the ruler of a small state or principality. **3** *old slang use* a fist. [from Latin *dux*, leader]

dukedom *noun* the title or property of a duke.

dulcet /'dʌlsɪt/ *adj. literary, said of sounds* sweet and pleasing to the ear. [from Latin *dulcis*, sweet]

dulcimer /'dʌlsɪmə(r)/ *noun* a musical instrument consisting of a flattish box with tuned strings stretched across, struck with small hammers. [from Latin *dulce melos*, sweet song]

dull — *adj.* **1** *said of colour or light* lacking brightness or clearness. **2** *said of sounds* deep and low; muffled. **3** *said of weather* cloudy; overcast. **4** *said of pain* not sharp. **5** *said of a person* slow to learn or understand. **6** uninteresting; lacking liveliness. **7** *said of a blade* blunt. — *verb trans., intrans.* to make or become dull. [from Anglo-Saxon *dol*, stupid]

....

■ *adj.* **1** dark, gloomy, drab, murky, indistinct, lack-lustre, opaque, dim. **2** low, deep, heavy, muffled, indistinct. **3** overcast, grey, cloudy. **5** unintelligent, dense, *colloq.* dim, *colloq.* dim-witted, *colloq.* thick, stupid, slow. **6** boring, uninteresting, unexciting, flat, dreary, monotonous, tedious, uneventful, humdrum, unimaginative, dismal, lifeless, plain, insipid, heavy. *verb* dim, obscure, fade, subdue, blunt, alleviate, mitigate, moderate, lessen, relieve, soften, deaden, numb, paralyse.

F3 *adj.* **1, 3, 5** bright. **5** intelligent, clever. **6** interesting, exciting.

....

dullard *noun old use* a dull person.

dullness *noun* a dull or uninteresting state.

dully /ˈdʌlɪ/ *adv.* in a dull or uninteresting way.

dulse /dʌls/ *noun* any of various red seaweeds, especially *Rhodymenia palmata*, found in the intertidal zone in northern latitudes, and having large tough edible fronds that are used as a food source. [from Gaelic *duileasg*]

duly *adv.* **1** in the proper way. **2** at the proper time. [from DUE]

dumb *adj.* **1** not having the power of speech. **2** *said of animals* not having human speech. **3** temporarily deprived of the power of speech, eg by shock. **4** silent; not expressed in words. **5** *colloq. chiefly North Amer.* foolish; unintelligent. **6** performed without words: *dumb show*. [from Anglo-Saxon]

▣ **1** mute. **3** speechless, tongue-tied, inarticulate, *colloq.* mum. **4** silent, soundless. **5** stupid, unintelligent, *colloq.* dim-witted, *colloq.* dim, *colloq.* dense, *colloq.* thick.

dumbbell *noun* **1** a weight used in pairs in muscle-developing exercises, consisting of a short metal bar with a heavy ball or disc on each end. **2** *colloq. chiefly North Amer.* a stupid person.

dumb down *usually derog.* to make or become much simpler or less complex.

dumbfound or **dumfound** *verb* to astonish or confound, originally so as to leave speechless.

▣ astonish, amaze, astound, overwhelm, leave speechless, take aback, *colloq.* throw, *colloq.* floor, confound, stagger, *colloq.* flabbergast, *colloq.* bowl over, startle.

dumbly *adv.* silently; without speaking.

dumbness *noun* inability to speak.

dumbo *noun* (PL. **dumbos**) *colloq.* a stupid person. [from DUMB]

dumbstruck *adj.* silent with astonishment or shock.

dumb waiter **1** a small lift for transporting laundry, dirty dishes, etc between floors in a restaurant or hotel. **2** a movable shelved stand for food, placed near a table. **3** a revolving food tray set in the middle of a table.

dumdum *noun* a bullet that expands on impact, causing severe injury. [from *Dum-Dum*, arsenal near Calcutta, India]

dumfound see DUMBFOUND.

dummy — *noun* (PL. **dummies**) **1** a life-size model of the human body, eg used for displaying clothes. **2** a realistic copy, especially one misleadingly substituted for the genuine article. **3** a baby's rubber teat sucked for comfort. **4** *colloq. chiefly North Amer.* a stupid person. **5** *Sport* an act of dummying with the ball. **6** a person or company acting seemingly independently, but really the agent of another. — *adj.* false; sham; counterfeit. — *verb trans., intrans.* (**dummies, dummied**) *Sport* to make as if to move one way before sharply moving the other, in order to deceive (an opponent). [from DUMB]

▣ *noun* **1** model, lay figure, mannequin, figure, form. **2** copy, duplicate, imitation, counterfeit, substitute. **3** teat, pacifier. *adj.* artificial, fake, imitation, false, bogus, mock, sham, *colloq.* phoney.

dummy run a practice; a try-out.

▣ dry run, simulation, practice, test, trial, try-out.

dump — *verb* **1** to put down heavily or carelessly. **2** *trans., intrans.* to dispose of (rubbish), especially in an unauthorized place. **3** *colloq.* to break off a romantic relationship with. **4** *Econ.* to sell (goods unsaleable domestically) abroad at a much reduced price, usually to keep the domestic price high. **5** *Comput.* to transfer computer data from one program to another using a dump, or to transfer a computer program or data on to disk or tape. — *noun* **1** a place where rubbish may be dumped. **2** a military store, eg of weapons or food. **3** *Comput.* a printed copy of the contents of a computer's memory, used to transfer data from one program to another, or to find the cause of an error in a program. **4** *colloq.* a dirty or dilapidated place. [from Middle English]

▣ *verb* **1** deposit, drop, offload, throw down, let fall, unload, empty out, discharge, park, *colloq.* plonk. **2** get rid of, scrap, throw away, dispose of, ditch, tip, jettison. **3** drop, leave, abandon, desert, reject, jilt, renounce, throw over, cast off. *noun* **1** rubbish tip, junk yard, rubbish heap, tip. **4** hovel, slum, shack, shanty, *colloq.* hole, *slang* joint, pigsty, mess.

dumping *noun Commerce* the sale of a commodity on a foreign market at a price below the cost of producing it.

dumpling *noun* **1** dough served with meat. **2** a rich fruit pudding. **3** *colloq.* a plump person. [from obsolete *dump*, lump]

dumps — **down in the dumps** *colloq.* in low spirits; depressed. [perhaps from German *dumpf*, gloomy]

dumpy *adj.* (**dumpier, dumpiest**) short and plump. [perhaps from DUMPLING]

dun[1] *noun* **1** a dark greyish brown colour. **2** a horse of this colour. [from Anglo-Saxon]

dun[2] — *verb* (**dunned, dunning**) to press persistently for payment. — *noun* a demand for payment.

dunce *noun* a stupid person; a slow learner. [from *Dunses*, followers of J *Duns* Scotus, 13c educationalist opposed to classical studies]

dunderhead *noun* a stupid person.

dunderheaded *adj.* stupid.

dune *noun* a ridge or hill formed by the accumulation of windblown sand, usually on a seashore or in a hot desert. [from Old Dutch *duna*]

dung *noun* animal excrement. [from Anglo-Saxon]

dungarees *pl. noun* loose trousers with a bib and shoulder straps attached, worn as casual wear or overalls. [from Hindi *dungri*]

dung-beetle *noun* a shiny dark coloured beetle whose larvae feed on the dung of herbivorous animals, eg cattle.

dungeon /ˈdʌndʒən/ *noun* a prison cell, especially underground. [from Old French *donjon*]

▣ cell, prison, jail, gaol, cage, lockup, keep, vault.

dunk *verb* **1** to dip (eg a biscuit) into tea or a similar beverage. **2** to submerge. [from Old German *dunkon*]

dunlin *noun* a small wading bird, native to the northern hemisphere, and having mottled brown plumage with pale underparts, and a slender probing bill. [a diminutive of DUN[1]]

duo *noun* (PL. **duos**) **1** a pair of musicians or other performers. **2** any two people considered a pair. [from Latin *duo*, two]

▣ **1** duet. **2** pair, couple, brace, twosome.

duodecimal — *adj.* **1** relating to the number 12. **2** denoting a number system that uses the number 12 as a base, now largely superseded by the decimal system. — *noun* a twelfth. [from Latin *duodecim*, twelve]

duodenal /djuːoʊˈdiːnəl/ *adj.* relating to or affecting the duodenum.

duodenum /djuːoʊˈdiːnəm/ *noun* (PL. **duodena, duodenums**) *Anat.* the first part of the small intestine, into which food passes after leaving the stomach. [from Latin, from *duodecim*, twelve, the portion being twelve fingers' breadth in length]

duologue /ˈdjuːoʊlɒg/ *noun* **1** a dialogue between two actors. **2** a play for two actors. [from Latin *duo*, two + Greek *logos*, discourse]

dupe — *verb* to trick or deceive. — *noun* a person who is deceived. [from French *dupe*]

. . . .

☒ *verb* deceive, delude, fool, trick, outwit, *colloq.* con, cheat, hoax, swindle, *colloq.* rip off, take in, hoodwink, defraud, *colloq.* bamboozle. *noun* victim, *colloq.* sucker, fool, gull, *colloq.* mug, *colloq.* pushover, *colloq.* fall guy, pawn, puppet, instrument, stooge, simpleton.

. . . .

duple *adj.* **1** double; twofold. **2** *Mus.* having two beats in the bar. [from Latin *duplus*]

duple time musical time with two main beats to the bar.

duplex — *noun* **1** a flat on two floors. **2** a semi-detached house. **3** *Biol.* a double-stranded region in a molecule of nucleic acid, especially DNA. — *adj.* **1** double; twofold. **2** *Electron.*, *Comput.* allowing communication and transmission of signals in both directions simultaneously. **3** *said of a machine* having two parts that work together or have a similar operating procedure. [from Latin *duplex*]

duplicate /ˈdjuːplɪkət, ˈdjuːplɪkeɪt/ — *adj.* (pronounced -kət) identical to another. — *noun* (pronounced -kət) **1** an exact (especially printed) copy. **2** another of the same kind; a subsidiary or spare. — *verb* (pronounced -keɪt) **1** to make or be an exact copy or exact copies of. **2** to repeat. — **in duplicate** in the form of two exact copies. [from Latin *duplicare*, to fold in two]

. . . .

☒ *adj.* identical, matching, twin, corresponding, matched. *noun* copy, replica, reproduction, photocopy, carbon (copy), match, facsimile. *verb* REPEAT. **1** copy, reproduce, photocopy, double, clone, echo.

. . . .

duplication *noun* duplicating; making an exact copy.
duplicator *noun* a machine for copying documents, etc.
duplicitous /djuːˈplɪsɪtəs/ *adj.* insincere; cheating.
duplicity *noun formal* deception. [from Latin *duplicis*, double]

. . . .

☒ deception, deceit, trickery, double-dealing, double-crossing, deviousness, insincerity, guile, treachery.

. . . .

Dur. *abbrev.* Durham.
durability *noun* the capacity to last a long time.

. . . .

☒ toughness, sturdiness, strength, reliability, dependability, permanence.

. . . .

durable — *adj.* **1** lasting a long time without breaking; sturdy. **2** long-lasting; enduring. — *noun* a durable item, especially one not frequently replaced. [from Latin *durare*, to last]

. . . .

☒ *adj.* LONG-LASTING, RELIABLE, DEPENDABLE, FIRM, FIXED, FAST. **1** hard-wearing, strong, sturdy, tough, rugged, substantial, sound, stable, resistant, persistent. **2** lasting, enduring, abiding, constant, permanent, unfading.
☒ *adj.* **1** perishable, weak, fragile. **2** short-lived, temporary.

. . . .

durably *adv.* in a durable or long-lasting way.
dura mater /ˈdjuːrə ˈmɑːtər/ *Anat.* the outermost and thickest of the three membranes (*meninges*) that surround the brain and spinal cord. [from Latin *duritia*, hardness + *mater*, mother]
duration *noun* the length of time that something lasts or continues. [from Latin *durare*, to last]
duress /djʊəˈres/ *noun* the influence of force or threats; coercion. [from Latin *duritia*, hardness]

. . . .

☒ constraint, coercion, compulsion, pressure, restraint, threat, force.

during *prep.* **1** throughout the time of. **2** in the course of. [from obsolete *dure*, to last, from Latin *durare*]
dusk *noun* twilight; the period of semi-darkness before night. [from Anglo-Saxon *dox*, dark]

. . . .

☒ twilight, sunset, nightfall, evening, sundown, gloaming, darkness, dark, gloom, shadows, shade.
☒ dawn.

. . . .

duskiness *noun* partial darkness or obscurity.
dusky *adj.* (**duskier, duskiest**) **1** dark; shadowy. **2** having a dark colour or skin.

. . . .

☒ **1** dark, shadowy, dim, gloomy, murky, twilit. **2** dark-coloured, dark-skinned, swarthy, tawny, black, brown.

. . . .

dust — *noun* **1** earth, sand, or household dirt in the form of a fine powder. **2** a cloud of this. **3** any substance in powder form. **4** *colloq.* an angry complaint; a commotion: *kick up a dust.* **5** *poetic* human remains; a dead body. — *verb* **1** *trans., intrans.* to remove dust from (furniture, etc.). **2** to sprinkle with a substance in powder form. — **let the dust settle** *colloq.* to wait until calm is restored before acting. **throw dust in someone's eyes** *colloq.* to deceive them. [from Anglo-Saxon]

. . . .

☒ *noun* **1** powder, particles, dirt, earth, soil, ground, grit, grime. *verb* **1** wipe, brush, sweep, clean, vacuum. **2** powder, sprinkle, dredge, pepper.

. . . .

dustbin *noun* a large (usually cylindrical) lidded container for household rubbish, especially one kept outside.
dust bowl an area of land that has been farmed without protection against the effects of soil erosion, and from which the topsoil has been removed as a result of strong winds and drought.
dustcart *noun* a vehicle in which household rubbish is collected.
dust cover **1** a dust jacket. **2** a dust sheet.
duster *noun* **1** a cloth for removing household dust. **2** a machine for spraying crops with fertilizer or other chemical preparations; a sprinkler.
dustily *adv.* curtly; rudely: *replied dustily that he didn't know.*
dust jacket a loose protective paper cover on a book, carrying the title and other information.
dustman *noun* a person employed to collect household rubbish.
dustpan *noun* a handled container into which dust is swept, like a flattish open-ended box with a shovel edge.
dust sheet a cloth sheet used to protect unused furniture from dust.
dust-storm *noun* a storm characterized by strong turbulent winds that whip up large whirling clouds of dust or sand and carry them over large areas of dry land, especially after a period of drought.
dust-up *noun colloq.* an argument or fight.
dusty *adj.* (**dustier, dustiest**) **1** covered with, or containing, dust. **2** like dust in appearance or consistency. **3** *said of a colour* dull. **4** old-fashioned; dated. **5** lacking liveliness; flat. **6** impolitely blunt.

. . . .

☒ **1** dirty, grubby, filthy. **2** powdery, granular, crumbly, chalky, sandy.
☒ **1** clean. **2** solid, hard.

. . . .

Dutch — *noun* **1** the language of the Netherlands. See also AFRIKAANS, FLEMISH. **2** (**the Dutch**) the people of the Netherlands. — *adj.* of the Netherlands, its people or their language. — **go Dutch** *colloq.* to each pay his or her own share of a meal, etc. [from Old Dutch *dutsch*]
Dutch auction an auction at which the price is gradually lowered until someone agrees to buy.

Dutch barn an open-sided barn with a curved roof.

Dutch cap a contraceptive cap worn over a woman's cervix.

Dutch courage artificial courage gained by drinking alcohol.

Dutch elm disease *Bot.* a serious disease of elm trees, caused by the fungus *Ceratocystis ulmi*, and spread by a bark beetle. Symptoms include wilting, yellowing of leaves, and death of individual branches or whole trees.

Dutchman or **Dutchwoman** *noun* a native or citizen of the Netherlands.

Dutch oven 1 an open-fronted metal box for cooking food in front of a fire. **2** a lidded earthenware or iron stewpot or casserole.

Dutch treat an amusement where each person pays for himself or herself.

Dutch uncle a person who openly criticizes or reprimands where appropriate, without sparing one's feelings.

duteous /ˈdjuːtɪəs/ *adj. literary* dutiful. [from DUTY + -OUS]

dutiable *adj.*, *said of goods* on which duty is payable.

dutiful *adj.* having or showing a sense of duty. [from DUTY + -FUL]

⊟ obedient, respectful, conscientious, devoted, filial, reverential, submissive.

dutifully *adv.* in a dutiful or respectful way.

duty *noun* (PL. **duties**) **1** something one is or feels obliged to do; a moral or legal responsibility, or the awareness of it. **2** a task to be performed, especially in connection with a job. **3** tax on goods, especially imports. **4** respect for elders or seniors. — **do duty for something** to serve in its place; to act as a substitute for it. **off duty** not working; not liable to be called upon to go into action. **on duty** working; liable to be called upon to go into action. [from Old French *dueté*]

⊟ **1** obligation, responsibility, requirement, calling, charge, role, business, function, work, office, service. **2** task, job, assignment, activity. **3** tax, toll, tariff, levy, customs, excise. **4** obedience, respect, loyalty. **do duty for** act as, stand in for, substitute for, replace. **off duty** resting, inactive. **on duty** at work, engaged, busy, on call, active.

duty-bound *adj.* obliged by one's sense of duty.

duty-free — *adj.*, *said of goods, especially imports* nontaxable. — *noun colloq.* a duty-free shop.

duty-free shop a shop, especially at an airport or on a ship, where duty-free goods are sold.

duvet /ˈduːveɪ/ *noun* a thick quilt filled with feathers or man-made fibres, for use on a bed instead of a sheet and blankets. [from French *duvet*]

DV *abbrev. Deo volente* (Latin) God willing.

DVD *abbrev.* digital video disk or digital versatile disk.

DVLA *abbrev.* Driver and Vehicle Licensing Agency (formerly Centre).

dwarf /dwɔːf/ — *noun* (PL. **dwarfs**, **dwarves**) **1** an abnormally small person. **2** an animal or plant that is much smaller or shorter than others of its species, usually as a result of selective breeding. **3** a mythical man-like creature with magic powers. — *adj.* much smaller or shorter than normal. — *verb* **1** to cause to seem small or unimportant. **2** to stunt the growth of. [from Anglo-Saxon *dweorg*]

⊟ **1** person of restricted growth, midget, pygmy, Tom Thumb, Lilliputian. **3** gnome, goblin. *adj.* miniature, small, tiny, pocket, *colloq.* mini, diminutive, petite, Lilliputian, baby. *verb* **1** overshadow, tower over, dominate. **2** stunt, retard, check.
⊞ *noun* GIANT. *adj.* giant, large, towering.

dwarfish *adj.* like a dwarf; very small.

dweeb *noun North Amer.*, *esp. US derog. slang* an idiot, a nerd. [perhaps a mixture of FEEBLE and WEED]

dwell *verb intrans.* (PAST TENSE AND PAST PARTICIPLE **dwelt, dwelled**) **1** *formal, literary* to reside. **2** (**dwell on** or **upon something**) to think or speak about it obsessively. [from Anglo-Saxon *dwellan*, to delay or tarry]

⊟ **1** live, inhabit, reside, stay, settle, lodge, rest, *old use* abide. **2** brood on or over, think about, meditate on, reflect on, ruminate on, harp on, return to, insist on, emphasize.

dweller *noun* a person who lives in a particular place or area: *a city-dweller*.

⊟ resident, inhabitant, occupant, native.

dwelling *noun formal, literary* a place of residence; a house.

⊟ house, residence, *formal* abode, *formal* domicile.

dwindle *verb intrans.* to shrink in size, number or intensity. [from Anglo-Saxon *dwinan*, to fade]

⊟ diminish, decrease, decline, lessen, subside, ebb, fade, weaken, taper off, tail off, shrink, peter out, fall, wane, waste away, die out, wither, shrivel, disappear.
⊞ increase, grow.

DY *abbrev.*, *as an international vehicle mark* Benin, formerly Dahomey.

Dy *symbol Chem.* dysprosium.

dybbuk /ˈdɪbək/ *noun* in Jewish folklore, an evil spirit or the soul of a dead person, which enters the body of a living person and controls their behaviour until exorcized by a religious rite. [from Hebrew *dibbuq*]

dye — *verb trans.*, *intrans.* (**dyeing**) to colour or stain permanently. — *noun* a coloured substance, either natural or synthetic, that is used in solution to impart colour to another material, eg paper, textiles, leather. It differs from a pigment, which is used in suspension. [from Anglo-Saxon *deagian*]

⊟ *verb* colour, tint, stain, pigment, tinge, imbue. *noun* colour, colouring, stain, pigment, tint, tinge.

dyed-in-the-wool *adj.* of firmly fixed opinions; out-and-out.

⊟ out-and-out, diehard, hardline, intransigent, unwavering, opinionated, dogmatic.

dyer *noun* a person who dyes cloth, etc, especially as a business.

dying — *verb* present participle of DIE¹. — *adj.* **1** that is about to die; that is about to end or disappear. **2** expressed immediately before death. **3** final: *dying seconds of the match*.

⊟ *adj.* **1** moribund, passing, going, mortal, not long for this world, perishing, failing, fading, vanishing.
⊞ *adj.* **1** reviving.

dyke¹ or **dike** — *noun* **1** a wall or embankment built to prevent flooding. **2** *Geol.* a vertical or semi-vertical sheet of igneous rock that cuts across the layering or bedding planes in the surrounding rock, formed when molten magma is forced under pressure into older rocks and then solidifies below the Earth's surface. **3** *Scot.* a wall, eg surrounding a field. — *verb* to protect or drain with a dyke. [from Anglo-Saxon *dic*, ditch]

dyke² *noun offensive slang* a lesbian.

dynamic /daɪˈnamɪk/ *adj.* **1** full of energy, enthusiasm, and new ideas. **2** relating to dynamics. [from Greek *dynamis*, power]

....

▣ **1** forceful, powerful, energetic, vigorous, *colloq.* go-ahead, high-powered, driving, self-starting, spirited, vital, lively, active.
▣ **1** inactive, apathetic.
....

dynamically *adv.* **1** with energy and enthusiasm. **2** in relation to dynamics or motion.

dynamics *noun* **1** (*sing.*) *Physics* the branch of mechanics that deals with the motion of objects and the forces that act to produce such motion. **2** (*pl.*) movement or change in any sphere; also, the forces causing this: *political dynamics*.

dynamism /ˈdaɪnəmɪzm/ *noun* limitless energy and enthusiasm.

dynamite /ˈdaɪnəmaɪt/ — *noun* **1** any of a group of powerful blasting explosives, formerly consisting of nitroglycerine absorbed into a porous material such as wood pulp or charcoal, but now usually containing ammonium nitrate or sodium nitrate. **2** *colloq.* a thrilling or dangerous person or thing. — *verb* to blow up with dynamite. [from Greek *dynamis*, power]

dynamo /ˈdaɪnəmoʊ/ *noun* (PL. **dynamos**) **1** *Electr.* an electric generator that converts mechanical energy into electrical energy, usually in the form of direct current. **2** *colloq.* a highly active or energetic person. [from Greek *dynamis*, power]

dynamometer /daɪnəˈmɒmɪtə(r)/ *noun Engineering* an instrument that is used to measure mechanical force, especially in order to determine the output power of a motor or engine.

dynastic /dɪˈnastɪk/ *adj.* relating to or associated with a dynasty: *a dynastic marriage*.

dynasty /ˈdɪnəstɪ/ *noun* (PL. **dynasties**) **1** a succession of rulers from the same family; their period of rule. **2** a succession of members of a powerful family or other connected group. [from Greek *dynasteia*, power, dominion]

....

▣ **1** house, line, succession, dominion, regime, government, rule, empire, sovereignty.
....

dyne /daɪn/ *noun* (SYMBOL **dyn**) the unit of force in the cgs system, equal to the force that will give a mass of one gram an acceleration of one centimetre per second per second. [from Greek *dynamis*, force]

dysarthria /dɪsˈɑːθrɪə/ *noun Psychol.* an impaired ability to enunciate speech clearly, caused by a disease or disorder of the tongue or other muscles associated with speech. [from Greek *dys-*, amiss + *arthron*, joint]

dysentery /ˈdɪsəntrɪ/ *noun Medicine* severe infection and inflammation of the intestines, characterized by violent diarrhoea containing blood and mucus, and severe abdominal pain. [from Greek *dysenteria*, bad bowels]

dysfunctional *adj. said of family* not functioning as it should, for example in providing mutual love and support.

dyslexia /dɪsˈlɛksɪə/ *noun* a disorder that develops in childhood, characterized by difficulty in reading and writing and in spelling correctly. [from Greek *dys-*, amiss + *lexis*, word]

dyslexic — *adj.* affected by dyslexia. — *noun* a person affected by dyslexia.

dysmenorrhoea or **dysmenorrhea** /dɪsmɛnəˈrɪə/ *noun Medicine* pain in the lower abdomen, associated with menstruation. [from Greek *dys-*, amiss + *men*, month + *rhoia*, flow]

dyspepsia /dɪsˈpɛpsɪə/ *noun Medicine* indigestion, the main symptoms of which are discomfort or pain in the abdomen and lower chest region after eating. [from Greek *dys-*, amiss + *pepsis*, digestion]

dyspeptic *adj.* **1** suffering from dyspepsia. **2** *colloq.* bad-tempered; liverish.

dysplasia /dɪsˈpleɪzɪə/ *noun Medicine* **1** abnormal development of a tissue, eg skin, bone. **2** an abnormal change in the size or shape of a mature cell. [from Greek *dys-*, amiss + *plasis*, moulding]

dyspnoea or **dyspnea** /dɪsˈpnɪə/ *noun Medicine* difficulty in breathing, often associated with serious disease of the heart or lungs. [from Greek *dyspnoia*, from *dys-*, amiss + *pnoe*, breathing]

dyspraxia /dɪsˈpraksɪə/ *noun* a disorder characterized by impaired motor function. [from Greek *dys-*, amiss + *praxis*, action]

dysprosium /dɪsˈprəʊzɪəm/ *noun* (SYMBOL **Dy**, ATOMIC NUMBER **66**) a soft silvery metallic element of the lanthanide series that is highly magnetic and a strong absorber of neutrons, used to make magnets, laser materials, some alloys, and phosphors. [from Greek *dysprositos*, difficult to reach]

dystrophy /ˈdɪstrəfɪ/ *noun Medicine* any of various disorders of organs or tissues, especially muscle, arising from an inadequate supply of nutrients. [from Greek *dys-*, amiss + *trophe*, nourishment]

DZ *abbrev., as an international vehicle mark* Barr al-Djaza'ir (Arabic), Algeria

E

E[1] or **e** *noun* (PL. **Es, E's, e's**) **1** the fifth letter of the English alphabet. **2** the fifth highest grade or quality. **3** *Mus.* the third note in the scale of C major. **4** a musical note with the key E as its base.

E[2] *abbrev.* **1** East. **2** Ecstasy. **3** *Physics* electromotive force. **4** (*also* **e**) electronic: *e-mail.* **5** *Physics* energy. **6** *as an international vehicle mark España*, Spain. **7** European: *E-number.*

e[1] *abbrev.* see E[2] 4.

e[2] *symbol* used with a number to mark any of several standard sizes of pack as set out in EC law.

each — *adj.* every one of two or more people or items considered separately. — *pron.* every single one of two or more people, animals or things. — *adv.* to, for, or from each one: *give them one each.* — **each other** used as the object of a verb or preposition when an action takes place between two (or more than two) people, etc: *they were talking to each other.* **each way** *said of a bet* winning if the horse, dog, etc on which the bet is placed finishes first, second, or third in a race. [from Anglo-Saxon *ælc*]

eager *adj.* (*often* **eager for something** or **to do something**) feeling or showing great desire or enthusiasm; keen to do or get something. [from Old French *aigre*]

⊟ keen, enthusiastic, fervent, intent, earnest, zealous, longing, yearning.
⊟ unenthusiastic, indifferent.

eager beaver *colloq.* a person who is exceptionally enthusiastic or willing.

eagerly *adv.* with an eager or enthusiastic manner.

eagerness *noun* being eager; enthusiasm.

eagle *noun* **1** any of various birds of prey having powerful hooked beaks, feathered legs, and strong curved talons. They are noted for their soaring graceful flight and keen eyesight. **2** a figure of an eagle, used as a national emblem by various countries. **3** *Golf* a score of two under par. [from Old French *aigle*, from Latin *aquila*]

eagle eye **1** exceptionally good eyesight. **2** careful supervision, with an ability to notice small details.

eagle-eyed *adj.* having exceptionally good eyesight.

eagle owl an owl native to the Old World, including a species that is the largest of all owls. It has eyelashes, an unusual feature in owls.

eaglet *noun* a young eagle.

EAK *abbrev.*, *as an international vehicle mark* Kenya (ie East Africa Kenya).

ear[1] *noun* **1** the sense organ, usually one of a pair situated on each side of the head (or in some animals on top of the head), that is concerned with hearing and the maintenance of balance in vertebrates. **2** the external part of the ear. **3** the sense or power of hearing, especially the ability to hear the difference between sounds. **4** anything like an ear in shape or position. **5** *formal, literary* attention; the act of listening: *lend an ear / give ear to.* — **be all ears** *colloq.* to listen attentively or with great interest. **have someone's ear** to have them willing to listen or pay attention. **have one's ear to the ground** to keep oneself well informed about what is happening around one. **in one ear and out the other** *colloq.* heard but quickly disregarded or forgotten. **make someone's ears burn** to talk, especially unfavourably, about them in their absence. **out on one's ear** *colloq.* dismissed swiftly and summarily. **play something by ear 1** to play a piece of music without the help of a score. **2** *colloq.* to do something without a fixed plan, as circumstances suggest. **up to one's ears in something** *colloq.* deeply involved in or occupied with it. [from Anglo-Saxon *eare*]

⊟ **3** hearing, perception, sensitivity, discrimination, appreciation, skill, ability. **5** attention, heed, notice, regard.

ear[2] *noun Bot.* the flowering head or spike of grasses, especially cereals, that contains the seeds. [from Anglo-Saxon *ēar*]

earache *noun* continuous or intermittent pain in the ear, caused by infection, disease, or disorders of the nose or mouth cavity.

eardrum *noun* the small membrane that separates the outer ear from the middle ear, and transmits vibrations made by external sound waves to the tiny bones or *ossicles* of the middle ear. Also called TYMPANUM.

earful *noun colloq.* (PL. **earfuls**) (*not usually in pl.*) a long complaint or telling-off.

earl / ɜːl/ *noun* a male member of the British nobility ranking below a marquess and above a viscount. See also COUNTESS. [from Anglo-Saxon *eorl*]

earldom *noun* the status or position of an earl.

Earl Marshal a hereditary British office of state, head of the College of Arms and responsible for organizing state ceremonies.

earlobe or **ear lobe** *noun* the soft fleshy lower part of the outer ear.

early (**earlier, earliest**) — *adj.* **1** occurring near the beginning of a period of time, period of development, etc. **2** occurring before the usual or expected time. **3** in the near future. **4** in the far-off past. — *adv.* **1** near the beginning of a period of time. **2** sooner than others, sooner than usual, or sooner than expected or intended. — **at the earliest** not before, and probably later than. **early on** at or near the beginning of a period of time, etc. **it's early days** *colloq.* it is too soon to be able to judge the outcome or expect a result. [from Anglo-Saxon *ærlice*]

⊟ *adj.* **1** first, initial, opening. **2** forward, advanced, premature, untimely, undeveloped. **4** primitive, ancient, primeval. *adv.* **2** ahead of time, in good time, beforehand, in advance, prematurely.
⊟ *adj.* **1, 2, 3** late. *adv.* LATE.

early bird *colloq.* **1** a person who gets out of bed early. **2** a person who arrives early.

early warning system a radar system designed to give the earliest possible warning of attack from enemy aircraft or missiles.

earmark *verb* to set aside or intend for a particular purpose.

⊟ reserve, set aside, set apart, select, single out, destine, intend.

earmuffs *pl. noun* coverings worn over the ears to protect them from cold or noise.

earn 1 to gain (money, wages, one's living) by working. 2 *intrans.* (**to be earning**) to be in paid employment. 3 to gain. 4 to deserve. See also WELL-EARNED. [from Anglo-Saxon *earnian*]

◼ **1** receive, obtain, make, get, draw, bring in, realize, gross, reap. **3** gain, win, acquire. **4** deserve, merit, warrant, rate.
◼ **1** spend, lose.

earner *noun* **1** a person who earns. **2** *slang* an easy and sometimes dishonest way of making money.

earnest¹ *adj.* **1** serious or over-serious. **2** showing determination, sincerity or strong feeling. — **in earnest** serious or seriously. [from Anglo-Saxon *eornust*]

◼ **1** serious, sincere, solemn, grave, heartfelt. **2** resolute, devoted, conscientious, intent, firm, fixed, steady, keen, fervent, ardent, eager, enthusiastic.
◼ **1** frivolous, flippant. **2** apathetic.

earnest² *noun literary, old use* **1** a part payment made in advance, especially to confirm an agreement. **2** a sign or foretaste of what is to come. [from Middle English *ernes*, from Old French *erres*, pledges]

earnings *pl. noun* money earned.

◼ pay, income, salary, wages, profits, gain, proceeds, reward, receipts, return, revenue, remuneration, stipend.
◼ expenditure, outgoings.

earphones same as HEADPHONES.

earpiece *noun* the part of a telephone or hearing-aid which is placed at or in the ear.

ear-piercing — *adj.*, *said of a noise* loud and sharp. — *noun* the piercing of the earlobe for the purpose of inserting an earring.

earplug *noun* a piece of wax, rubber, etc placed in the ear as a protection against noise, cold or water.

earring *noun* a piece of jewellery worn attached to the ear, especially to the earlobe.

earshot *noun* the distance at which sound can be heard: *out of earshot / within earshot.*

ear-splitting *adj.*, *said of a noise* extremely loud.

earth — *noun* **1** (*often* **Earth**) the third planet from the Sun and the fifth-largest planet in the solar system, the only planet in the solar system known to support life. **2** the material world, or human existence. **3** the land and sea as opposed to the sky. **4** dry land as opposed to the sea. **5** the soil, consisting of a mixture of loose fragmented rock and organic material, in which plants are rooted. **6** a burrow in which an animal, especially a fox, lives. **7** an electrical connection with the ground. **8** a wire that provides an electrical connection with the ground. **9** *Chem.* the old name for certain oxides of metals, eg alkaline earth, rare earth. — *verb* **1** *Electr.* to connect to the ground electrically. **2** (*also* **earth something up**) to heap soil around the lower part of a plant, eg as a protection against frost. — **come back** or **down to earth** to become aware of the realities of life. **cost the earth** *colloq.* to be extremely expensive. **go to earth** *said of an animal* to go into its hole or hiding-place. **on earth** used for emphasis: *what on earth is that?* **run someone** or **something to earth** 1 to chase or hunt an animal to its hole or hiding-place. 2 to find them after a long search. [from Anglo-Saxon *eorthe*]

◼ *noun* **1** world, planet, globe, sphere. **3**, **4** land, ground. **5** soil, clay, loam, sod, humus.

earthbound *adj.* **1** attached to the earth. **2** *said of a spacecraft, etc* moving towards the earth. **3** *sometimes derog.* unable to think beyond what is known or familiar; lacking imagination.

earthen *adj.* **1** *said of a floor, etc* made of earth. **2** *said of a pot, etc* made of baked clay.

earthenware *noun* pottery made of a kind of baked clay which is rather coarse to the touch.

◼ pottery, ceramics, crockery, pots.

earthling *noun* in science fiction, a native of the Earth.

earthly *adj.* **1** *literary* of or belonging to this world; not spiritual. **2** *colloq.* used for emphasis: *have no earthly chance.* — **not have an earthly** *colloq.* **1** not to have the slightest chance of success. **2** not to have the least idea. See also UNEARTHLY.

◼ **1** material, physical, human, worldly, mortal, mundane, fleshly, secular, sensual, profane, temporal. **2** possible, likely, conceivable, slightest.
◼ **1** spiritual, heavenly.

earthquake *noun* a series of shock waves which pass through the Earth, and may cause the ground to shake, sometimes resulting in major destruction and loss of life. It is caused by the movement of rocks under stress deep in the Earth's crust.

earth science each of a group of sciences concerned with the study of the Earth and its atmosphere, including geology, geography, and meteorology.

earth-shattering or **earth-shaking** *adj. colloq.* of great importance.

earthshine or **earthlight** *noun Astron.* a phenomenon often observable close to the time of a new moon, when sunlight reflected from the surface of the Earth on to the Moon causes the dark disc of the latter to be faintly illuminated.

earthstar *noun Biol.* a fungus, related to the puffball and found in woodland, that produces spores contained within a spherical fruit body that splits into segments resembling a star.

earth tremor a slight earthquake.

earthwork *noun technical* (*often in pl.*) a man-made bank of earth, used formerly as a fortification, or as a foundation in modern road-building.

earthworm *noun* the common name for various worms belonging to the class Oligochaeta and having a long slender body divided into segments.

earthy *adj.* (**earthier, earthiest**) **1** of or like earth or soil. **2** coarse or crude; lacking politeness.

◼ **2** crude, coarse, vulgar, bawdy, rough, *slang* raunchy, down-to-earth, ribald, robust.
◼ **2** refined, modest.

ear-trumpet *noun* an old-fashioned hearing-aid consisting of a small trumpet held up to the ear.

earwig *noun* any nocturnal insect belonging to the order Dermaptera, characterized by a large pair of pincers at the hind end of the body. [from Anglo-Saxon *eare*, ear + *wicga*, insect, from the former belief that it enters the ear of a sleeping person]

ease — *noun* **1** freedom from pain or anxiety. **2** absence of difficulty. **3** freedom from embarrassment. **4** absence of restriction. — *verb* **1** to free from pain, trouble or anxiety. **2** *trans., intrans.* (**ease off** or **up**) to become less intense; to relax. **3** (**ease something in** or **out**) to move (something heavy or awkward) gently or gradually in or out of position. — **at ease** **1** relaxed; free from anxiety or embarrassment. **2** *Mil.* (*often as a command*) standing with legs apart and hands clasped behind the back. **ill at ease** anxious or embarrassed. **take one's ease** *formal* to relax; to make oneself comfortable. [from Old French *aise*]

◼ *noun* **1** comfort, contentment, peace, affluence, repose, leisure, relaxation, rest, quiet, happiness. **2** facility, effortlessness, skilfulness, deftness, dexterity, naturalness, cleverness. *verb* **1, 2** moderate, lessen, lighten, abate, relax, diminish. **1** alleviate, relieve, mitigate, relent, allay, assuage, comfort, calm, soothe, facilitate, smooth. **3** inch, steer, slide, still.

🔄 *noun* **1** discomfort. **2** difficulty. *verb* **1** aggravate, intensify, worsen.

easel *noun* a stand for supporting a blackboard, an artist's canvas, etc. [from Dutch *ezel*, ass]

easement *noun Legal* the right of a landowner to use land which is not the landowner's own, or to prevent its owner from making an inconvenient use of it.

easily *adv.* **1** without difficulty. **2** clearly; beyond doubt; by far: *easily the best*. **3** very probably.

🔄 **1** effortlessly, comfortably, readily, simply. **2** by far, undoubtedly, indisputably, definitely, certainly, doubtlessly, clearly, far and away, undeniably. **3** probably, well.

🔄 **1** laboriously.

east — *noun* **1** (*also* **the east** or **the East**) the direction from which the sun rises; or any part of the earth, a country, a town, etc lying in that direction. **2** (**the East**) **a** the countries of Asia, east of Europe. **b** *Politics* the former communist countries of eastern Europe. — *adj.* **1** in the east; on the side which is on or nearest the east. **2** coming from the direction of the east: *an east wind*. — *adv.* towards the east. [from Anglo-Saxon *east*]

eastbound *adj.* going or leading towards the east.

Eastender *noun* an inhabitant of London's East End.

Easter *noun* **1** a Christian religious festival, held on the Sunday after the first full moon in spring, celebrating the resurrection of Christ. **2** the period during which the festival takes place, thought of as extending from Good Friday (the Friday before Easter Sunday) to the following Monday (Easter Monday). [from Anglo-Saxon *eastre*, perhaps from *Eostre*, a goddess associated with spring]

Easter Day or **Easter Sunday** the Sunday of Easter.

Easter egg an egg, traditionally a painted hard-boiled egg, but now more commonly a chocolate egg, given as a present at Easter.

easterly — *adj.* **1** *said of a wind, etc* coming from the east. **2** looking, lying etc towards the east. — *adv.* to or towards the east. — *noun* (PL. **easterlies**) an easterly wind.

eastern *adj.* **1** of or in the east. **2** facing or directed towards the east.

easterner *noun* a person who lives in or comes from the east, especially the eastern part of the USA.

easternmost *adj.* situated furthest east.

Easter Sunday see EASTER DAY.

eastward or **eastwards** *adv., adj.* towards the east.

easy — *adj.* (**easier, easiest**) **1** not difficult. **2** free from pain, trouble, anxiety, etc. **3** not stiff or formal; friendly. **4** not tense or strained; leisurely. **5** *colloq.* having no strong preference. — *adv. colloq.* in a slow, calm or relaxed way: *take it easy*. — **easy does it!** (be careful!; (in the performing of a physical task) don't strain yourself! **easy on the eye** or **ear** pleasant to look at or listen to. **go easy on** or **with something** to use, take, etc not too much of: *go easy on the wine*. **go easy on** or **with someone** to deal with them gently or calmly. **stand easy** *Mil.* (*often as a command*) to stand less stiffly than standing at ease. [from Old French *aisie*, from *aisier*, to ease]

🔄 *adj.* **1** effortless, simple, uncomplicated, undemanding, straightforward, manageable, painless, *colloq.* cushy, comfortable, calm, untroubled, unworried, leisured, well-off, affluent, prosperous, well-to-do. **3, 4** relaxed, carefree, easy-going, comfortable, informal, calm, natural, leisurely.

🔄 *adj.* **1** difficult, demanding, exacting. **3, 4** tense, uneasy, strained.

easy-care *adj., said of fabrics* easy to clean and requiring little or no ironing; usually made from synthetic fibres or from specially treated natural fibres.

easy chair a soft, comfortable chair, usually with arms.

easy-going *adj.* not strict, demanding, or dogmatic.

🔄 relaxed, tolerant, *colloq.* laid back, amenable, happy-go-lucky, carefree, calm, even-tempered, serene.

🔄 strict, intolerant, critical.

easy street *colloq.* a situation of comfort and financial well-being.

easy terms payment for goods in instalments over an agreed period.

EAT *abbrev., as an international vehicle mark* Tanzania (ie East Africa Tanganyika).

eat *verb* (PAST TENSE **ate**; PAST PARTICIPLE **eaten**) **1** *trans., intrans.* to bite, chew and swallow (food). **2** *intrans.* to take in food. **3** to take in as food. **4** (**eat something away** or **eat into something**) to destroy the material, substance, form, etc of, especially by chemical action. **5** (**eat into** or **through something**) to use it up gradually. **6** (**eat up** or **eat something up**) to finish one's food. **7** (**be eaten up by** or **with something**) *usually of a bad feeling* to be greatly affected by it: *be eaten up with jealousy*. **8** *colloq.* to trouble or worry: *what's eating you?* — **eat one's heart out** to suffer, especially in silence, from some longing or anxiety, or from envy. **eat humble pie** to lower oneself or lose dignity, eg by admitting a mistake. **eat in** to eat at home rather than in a restaurant. **eat out** to eat at a restaurant rather than at home. **eat out of someone's hand** *colloq.* to be very willing to follow, obey, or agree with them. **eat one's words** to admit that one was wrong. [from Anglo-Saxon *etan*]

🔄 **1** consume, swallow, devour, chew, *colloq.* scoff, munch. **2** feed, dine, lunch, breakfast. **4** erode, wear away, corrode, decay, rot, crumble, dissolve. **5** consume, use up, drain, sap, absorb, *colloq.* make a hole in.

eatable — *adj.* fit to be eaten. — *noun* (*usually* **eatables**) an item of food. See also EDIBLE.

🔄 *adj.* edible, palatable, good, wholesome, digestible, harmless.

🔄 *adj.* inedible, unpalatable.

eater *noun* **1** a person who eats: *a noisy eater*. **2** an eating apple, or any other fruit meant to be eaten raw.

eatery *noun* (PL. **eateries**) *colloq.* a small restaurant.

eating apple an apple for eating raw.

eats *pl. noun colloq.* food.

EAU *abbrev., as an international vehicle mark* Uganda (ie East Africa Uganda).

eau-de-cologne /oʊ də kəˈloʊn/ or **cologne** *noun* a mild type of perfume, originally made in Cologne in Germany. [from French *eau-de-cologne*, water of Cologne]

eaves *pl. noun* the part of a roof that sticks out beyond the wall, or the underside of it. [from Anglo-Saxon *efes*, the clipped edge of thatch]

eavesdrop *verb intrans.* (**eavesdropped, eavesdropping**) (**eavesdrop on someone**) to listen secretly to a private conversation. [from Anglo-Saxon *yfesdrype*, eavesdropper, a person who stands under the eaves to listen to conversations]

🔄 listen in to, spy on, overhear, snoop on, monitor, tap, *colloq.* bug.

eavesdropper *noun* a person who eavesdrops.

eavesdropping *noun* listening to another's conversation.

EAZ *abbrev., as an international vehicle mark* Zanzibar (ie East Africa Zanzibar).

ebb — *verb intrans.* **1** *said of the tide* to flow back from high to low water. **2** (*also* **ebb away**) to grow smaller or weaker. — *noun* **1** the flowing back or lowering of the tide. **2** the ebbing tide. **3** a growing smaller or weaker: *his health is on the ebb.* — **at a low ebb** in a poor or weak state (mentally or physically). [from Anglo-Saxon *ebba*]

◼ *verb* **2** weaken, lessen, fade away, wane, dwindle, diminish.

ebony /'ɛbənɪ/ — *noun* **1** a hard heavy jet-black wood that takes a high polish and is used to make carvings, piano keys, woodwind instruments, knife handles, and jewellery, and is also used in cabinetwork. **2** the tropical hardwood tree (*Diospyros ebenum*), found in Africa and Asia, from which this wood is obtained. — *adj.* **1** made from this wood. **2** *literary* black. [from Latin *ebeninus*]

EBU *abbrev.* European Broadcasting Union.

ebullience or **ebulliency** *noun* cheerfulness; enthusiasm.

ebullient /ɪ'bʌlɪənt/ *adj. formal* very high-spirited; full of cheerfulness or enthusiasm. [from Latin *ebullire*, to boil out]

◼ high-spirited, cheerful, exuberant, lively, vivacious, animated, enthusiastic, effervescent.

EC *abbrev.* **1** European Commission. **2** European Community (now European Union). **3** *as an international vehicle mark* Ecuador.

eccentric /ɪk'sɛntrɪk/ — *adj.* **1** *said of a person, behaviour, etc* odd; unusual. **2** *technical, said of a wheel, etc* not having the axis at the centre. **3** *Geom.* denoting two circles that do not have a common centre, ie that are not concentric. **4** denoting a moving body that deviates from a circular path or orbit. — *noun* **1** an eccentric person. **2** *technical* a device for converting rotating motion into backward and forward motion. [from Latin *eccentricus*, from Greek *ek*, out of + *kentros*, centre]

◼ *adj.* **1** odd, peculiar, abnormal, unconventional, strange, quirky, weird, *slang* way-out, queer, outlandish, idiosyncratic, bizarre, freakish, erratic, singular, *colloq.* dotty. *noun* **1** nonconformist, *colloq.* oddball, oddity, crank, freak, character.
◼ᴇ *adj.* **1** conventional, orthodox, normal. *noun* **1** conformist.

eccentrically *adv.* in an eccentric or unusual way.
eccentricity /ɛksɛn'trɪsɪtɪ/ *noun* (PL. **eccentricities**) an eccentric manner or characteristic.

◼ unconventionality, strangeness, peculiarity, nonconformity, abnormality, oddity, weirdness, idiosyncrasy, singularity, quirk, freakishness, aberration, anomaly, capriciousness.
◼ᴇ conventionality, ordinariness.

Eccl. or **Eccl** *abbrev. Biblical* Ecclesiastes.
ecclesiastic /ɪkliːzɪ'astɪk/ *noun formal* a clergyman. [from Latin *ecclesiasticus*, from Greek *ekklesia*, church]
ecclesiastical or **ecclesiastic** *adj.* of or relating to the Church or the clergy.

◼ church, churchly, religious, clerical, priestly, divine, spiritual.

ecclesiastically *adv.* as regards the Church or the clergy.
ecclesiology /ɪkliːzɪ'ɒlədʒɪ/ *noun Relig.* **1** the theological study of the nature of the Christian Church. **2** the science of church construction and decoration.

Ecclus. or **Ecclus** *abbrev.* Ecclesiasticus (Apocrypha).
ecdysis /'ɛkdɪsɪs/ *noun Zool.* in animals with a rigid exoskeleton, eg insects and crustaceans, the act of shedding the exoskeleton to allow growth to occur. [from Greek *ekdysis*, from *ek*, out of + *dyein*, to put on]

ECG *abbrev.* electrocardiogram or electrocardiograph.
echelon /'ɛʃəlɒn/ *noun* **1** *formal* a level or rank in an organization, etc, or the people at that level. **2** *technical* a roughly V-shaped formation, used by ships, planes, birds in flight, etc in which each member is in a position slightly to the outside of the one in front. [from French *échelon*, from *échelle*, ladder]
echidna /ɪ'kɪdnə/ *noun* (PL. **echidnas**, **echidnae**) any of five species of mainly nocturnal egg-laying mammals, native to Australia and New Guinea, slightly larger than a hedgehog, having a slender snout and a squat body covered with sharp spines. [from Greek *echidna*, viper]
echinacea /ɛkɪ'neɪsɪə/ *noun* a plant of the daisy family, native to North America, having flowers with a spiny, conelike centre. It is widely used in herbal medicine for its antibiotic and healing properties. [Latin, from Greek *ekhinos*, hedgehog]
echinoderm /ɪ'kaɪnoʊdɜːm/ *noun Zool.* any marine invertebrate animal belonging to the phylum Echinodermata, usually characterized by the possession of five-rayed symmetry in the adult, eg starfish, brittle star, sea urchin, sea lily, sea cucumber. [from Greek *echinos*, hedgehog, sea urchin + *derma*, skin]
echo /'ɛkoʊ/ — *noun* (PL. **echoes**) **1** the reflection of a sound wave by the surface of a nearby object so that a weaker signal is received a short time after the original signal. **2** a sound repeated in this way. **3** *often facetious* a person who imitates or repeats what others say or think. **4** an imitation or repetition (sometimes accidental). **5** (*often* **echoes**) a trace; something which brings to mind memories or thoughts of something else. **6** a reflected radio or radar beam, or the visual signal it produces on a screen. — *verb* (**echoes, echoed**) **1** *intrans.* to sound loudly with an echo. **2** to send back an echo of. **3** to repeat (a sound or a statement). **4** to imitate or in some way be similar to.

◼ *noun* **1, 2** reverberation, reiteration, repetition. **4** imitation, copy, reproduction, mirror image, image, parallel.
verb **1** reverberate, resound, ring. **2** reflect. **2, 3** repeat. **3** reiterate. **4** imitate, copy, reproduce, mirror, resemble, mimic.

echocardiography /ɛkoʊkɑːdɪ'ɒgrəfɪ/ *Medicine* a technique which involves the use of ultrasound waves to produce pictures of the internal structure and movements of the heart as it beats, used in the diagnosis of heart disease.
echoic /ɛ'koʊɪk/ *adj.* **1** *formal, said of a sound* of or like an echo. **2** *of a word* imitating the sound it represents; onomatopoeic: *'bump' is an echoic word.*
echolocation /ɛkoʊloʊ'keɪʃən/ *noun Physics* the perception of objects by means of reflected sound waves, usually after high-frequency sounds have been emitted.
echo-sounder *noun* a device for testing the depth of water by echo-sounding.
echo-sounding *noun* a method used to estimate the depth of water beneath a ship or other vessel, by sending out an ultrasound signal and measuring the time taken for its echo to return to a receiver.
éclair /ɪ'kleə(r)/ *noun* a long cake of light pastry, with a cream filling and chocolate or coffee icing. [from French *éclair*, flash of lightning, perhaps because it is quickly eaten]
eclampsia /ɪ'klampsɪə/ *noun Medicine* a disorder of late pregnancy, characterized by a sudden increase in blood pressure and convulsions. [from Greek *eklampsis*, from *eklampein*, to flash forth, to burst forth violently]
éclat /eɪ'klɑː/ *noun literary* **1** striking effect. **2** splendid success. **3** applause; praise. [from French *éclat*]
eclectic /ɪ'klɛktɪk/ *adj., said of a style of writing or art, or a set of beliefs* selecting material or ideas from a wide range of sources or authorities. [from Greek *ek*, from + *legein*, to choose]
eclectically *adv.* in an eclectic or widely selective manner or style.

eclecticism /ɪˈklɛktɪsɪzm/ *noun* an eclectic manner or style.

eclipse /ɪˈklɪps/ — *noun* **1** a phenomenon in which light from a celestial body, eg the Sun, is partly or totally obscured by another celestial body, eg a *solar eclipse* occurs when the Moon passes between the Earth and the Sun, and casts a shadow on the Earth, and a *lunar eclipse* occurs when the Earth passes between the Moon and the Sun, and casts a shadow on the Moon, which therefore reflects no sunlight. **2** a loss of fame or importance. — *verb* **1** to cause an eclipse of. **2** to surpass or outshine. [from Greek *ekleipsis*, failure to appear]

- *noun* **1** obscuration, overshadowing, darkening, shading, dimming. **2** decline, failure, fall, loss. *verb* **1** blot out, obscure, cloud, veil, darken, dim. **2** outdo, overshadow, outshine, surpass, transcend.

ecliptic /ɪˈklɪptɪk/ — *noun* (**the ecliptic**) *Astron.* the path that the Sun appears to follow through the stars (and therefore around the celestial sphere) each year as the Earth orbits around the Sun. — *adj.* relating to an eclipse or the ecliptic.

eclogue /ˈɛklɒg/ *noun* a short poem, or part of a longer one, in the form of a dialogue or soliloquy. [from Latin *ecloga*, from Greek *ekloge*, a selection]

eco- *combining form* forming words concerned with ecology or the environment: *ecology* / *ecotourism*. [from Greek *oikos*, house]

eco-friendly *adj.* denoting a product, policy, or practice that is ecologically acceptable and not harmful to the environment.

E.coli *abbrev.* Escherichia coli. See ESCHERICHIA.

ecological /iːkəˈlɒdʒɪkəl/ *adj.* **1** relating to or concerned with ecology. **2** using, concerned with, or relating to products, policies, or practices that are not harmful to the environment, or cause minimal damage to it.

- GREEN. **1** environmental. **2** eco-friendly, environment-friendly, non-polluting, recyclable, biodegradable.

ecologically *adv.* as regards ecology or the environment: *policies that are beneficial ecologically.*

ecologist /ɪˈkɒlədʒɪst/ *noun* a scientist who specializes in the study of ecology.

ecology /ɪˈkɒlədʒɪ/ *noun* the branch of biology that is concerned with the relationship between living organisms and their natural environment, including their relationship with each other. [from Greek *oikos*, house + -LOGY]

e-commerce *noun* commercial business conducted via the Internet.

econ. *abbrev.* economic, economics, or economy.

econometrics /ɪkɒnəˈmɛtrɪks/ *sing. noun* a specialized branch of economics which uses mathematical and statistical techniques to develop and test economic theories, make economic forecasts, etc.

economic /iːkəˈnɒmɪk/ *adj.* **1** of or concerned with the economy of a nation, etc. **2** *said of a business practice, etc* likely to bring a profit. **3** of economics.

- **1** commercial, business, industrial. **2** profitable, profit-making, money-making, productive, costeffective, viable. **3** financial, budgetary, fiscal, monetary.

economical *adj.* not wasting money or resources.

- thrifty, careful, prudent, saving, sparing, frugal, cheap, inexpensive, low-priced, reasonable, cost-effective, modest, efficient.
- wasteful, expensive, uneconomical.

economically *adv.* in an economical way.

economic growth the increase in a country's output of goods and services over a given period of time.

economics *sing. noun* **1** the study of the production, distribution, and consumption of money, goods and services. **2** financial aspects: *the economics of the situation.* See also HOME ECONOMICS.

economist /ɪˈkɒnəmɪst/ *noun* an expert in economics.

economization or **economisation** *noun* being economical; economizing.

economize or **economise** /ɪˈkɒnəmaɪz/ *verb intrans.* to cut down on spending or waste: *we need to economize* / *we decided to economize on coffee.*

- save, cut back, cut down, cut costs, make cuts, *colloq.* tighten one's belt.
- waste, squander.

economy /ɪˈkɒnəmɪ, ɛˈkɒnəmɪ/ — *noun* (PL. **economies**) **1** the organization of money and resources within a nation, etc, especially in terms of the production, distribution, and consumption of goods and services. **2** a system in which these are organized in a particular way: *a socialist economy.* **3** careful management of money or other resources, avoiding waste and cutting down on spending. **4** (*usually* **economies**) an instance of economizing; a saving. **5** efficient or sparing use: *economy of movement.* — *adj.* **1** *said of a class of travel, especially air travel* of the cheapest kind. **2** (*also* **economy-size** or **-sized**) *said of a packet of food, etc* larger than the standard or basic size, and proportionally cheaper. [from Greek *oikos*, house + *nomos*, law]

- *noun* **3, 4** saving. **3** thrift, restraint, prudence, frugality, parsimony, providence, husbandry. **4** cut, cutback, reduction.
- *noun* **3** extravagance.

ecosocialism *noun Politics* a branch of socialism which combines concern for environmental and ecological matters with the more established aims of socialism.

ecosphere *noun* same as BIOSPHERE.

ecosystem *noun Biol.* a self-contained community of plants and animals and the physical environment with which it interacts and exchanges materials, eg rainforest, grassland.

ecoterrorism *noun* action in which the natural environment is threatened for political or military ends.

ecotourism *noun* tourism in areas of natural beauty, organized so that visitors have minimum impact on the environment.

ecotype *noun Biol.* a variety or race of a plant species that is restricted to a particular habitat.

ECSC *abbrev.* European Coal and Steel Community.

ecstasy /ˈɛkstəsɪ/ *noun* (PL. **ecstasies**) **1** a feeling of immense joy. **2** *Psychol.* a mental state of extreme well-being and trance-like elation. **3** *slang* (*also* **Ecstasy**) methylenedioxymethamphetamine, a 'designer drug' taken for its stimulant and hallucinogenic properties. [from French *extasie*, from Greek *ekstasis*, standing outside oneself]

- **1** delight, rapture, bliss, elation, joy, euphoria, frenzy, exaltation, fervour.
- **1** misery, torment.

ecstatic /ɛkˈstatɪk/ *adj.* **1** of, showing, or causing ecstasy. **2** *colloq.* very happy or pleased.

- OVERJOYED, EUPHORIC, ELATED. **1** blissful, joyful, rapturous, delirious, frenzied, fervent. **2** delighted, pleased, happy.
- DOWNCAST.

ecstatically *adv.* in an ecstatic or intensely joyful way.

ECT *abbrev.* electro-convulsive therapy.

ecto- *combining form* forming words meaning 'outside': *ectomorph*. See also ENDO-, ENTO-, EXO-. [from Greek *ektos*, outside]

ectoderm /'ɛktoʊdɜːm/ *noun Zool.* in a multicellular animal that has two or more layers of body tissue, the outermost layer of cells of the embryo, which develops into the epidermal tissues such as skin, hair, tooth enamel, and sense organs. Also called EPIBLAST. [from ECTO- + Greek *derma*, skin]

ectomorph /'ɛktoʊmɔːf/ *noun* a person of slender build with long thin limbs and a relatively low body weight, sometimes said to be associated with a sensitive inhibited personality. [from ECTO- + Greek *morphe*, form]

-ectomy *combining form* (PL. **-ectomies**) *Medicine* denoting surgical removal, especially of an organ or body part: *appendectomy / hysterectomy*. [from Greek *ektome*, from *ektemnein*, to cut out]

ectopic /ɛk'tɒpɪk/ *adj. Medicine* situated or occurring in an abnormal position, especially denoting the development of a fertilized egg outside the uterus (an *ectopic pregnancy*). [from Greek *ek*, from + *topos*, place]

ectoplasm /'ɛktoʊplazm/ *noun* **1** *Biol.* in organisms such as the amoeba, the layer of clear non-granular and relatively rigid cytoplasm lying immediately below the cell membrane. **2** the substance thought by some people to be given off by the body of a spiritualistic medium during a trance. [from ECTO- + Greek *plasma*, something moulded]

ecu or **ECU** /'eɪkjuː/ *noun* European currency unit, a trading currency whose value is based on the combined values of several European currencies.

ecumenical /iːkjuˈmɛnɪkəl/ *adj.* **1** bringing together different branches of the Christian Church. **2** working towards the unity of the Christian Church. **3** of the whole Christian Church: *an ecumenical council*. [from Greek *oikoumenikos*, of the inhabited world]

ecumenicalism or **ecumenism** /iːˈkjuːmənɪzm/ *noun* the principles or practice of Christian unity.

ecumenically *adv.* as regards Christian unity or the whole Christian world.

eczema /'ɛksɪmə, ɪɡˈziːmə/ *noun Medicine* acute or chronic inflammation of the outer layer (epidermis) of the skin, usually consisting of a reddish itching rash accompanied by small blisters, followed by thickening, crusting, or discoloration of the skin. [from Greek *ekzema*, from *ek*, out of + *zeein*, to boil]

ed. *abbrev.* **1** edited. **2** edition. **3** editor. **4** educated. **5** education.

-ed *suffix* **1** used to form past tenses and past participles: *talked / waited*. **2** used to form adjectives from nouns: *bearded / bald-headed*.

Edam /'iːdam/ *noun* a type of mild yellow cheese, usually shaped into balls and covered with red wax. [from *Edam*, the town in the Netherlands where it was originally made]

edaphic /ɪˈdafɪk/ *adj.* denoting any physical or chemical property of a soil, eg acidity, texture, or water content, that influences plants growing in that soil. [from Greek *edaphos*, soil]

edaphology /ɛdəˈfɒlədʒɪ/ *noun* the scientific study of the soil, especially with regard to its interactions with living organisms. [from Greek *edaphos*, ground, soil + -LOGY]

eddy — *noun* (PL. **eddies**) **1** a circular or swirling movement that develops within a current of water or air when the continuity of flow is disturbed in some way. **2** a movement of air, smoke, fog, etc similar to this. — *verb intrans., trans.* (**eddies, eddied**) to move or cause to move in this way.

⊟ *noun* SWIRL. **1** whirlpool, vortex. *verb* swirl, whirl.

edelweiss /'eɪdlvaɪs/ *noun* (PL. **edelweiss**) a small alpine plant (*Leontopodium alpinum*), native to the mountains of S Europe, that grows up to 10cm high and is covered with dense grey or white hairs. [from German *edel*, noble + *weiss*, white]

Eden /'iːdən/ *noun* **1** (*also* **Garden of Eden**) a biblical place depicted as an earthly paradise, where Adam and Eve lived prior to their sin and expulsion (Genesis 2, 3). **2** a beautiful region; a place of delight. [from Hebrew *eden*, delight, pleasure]

edentate /iːˈdɛnteɪt/ *Biol.* — *adj.* lacking teeth. — *noun* an animal belonging to the order Edentata, a group of mammals that characteristically have few or no teeth, and well-developed claws, eg armadillos, anteaters, sloths. [from Latin *edentatus*, toothless]

edge — *noun* **1** the part farthest from the middle of something; a border or boundary. **2** the area beside a cliff or steep drop. **3** the cutting side of something sharp such as a knife. **4** *Geom.* the meeting point of two surfaces. **5** sharpness or severity: *a cold wind with an edge to it*. **6** bitterness: *there was an edge to his criticism*. **7** (**the edge on** or **over somebody** or **something**) an advantage over them. — *verb* **1** to form or make a border to: *edged with flowers*. **2** to shape the edge or border of. **3** *trans., intrans.* (**edge forward** or **in** or **out**) to move gradually and carefully. **4** to sharpen (a knife, etc). — **have the edge on** or **over someone** or **something** to have an advantage over them; to be better than them. **on edge** uneasy; nervous and irritable. **take the edge off something 1** to make it less unpleasant or less difficult. **2** to weaken or diminish it. [from Anglo-Saxon *ecg*]

⊟ *noun* **1** border, rim, boundary, limit, brim, lip, threshold, outline, line, perimeter, periphery. **2** brink, fringe, margin, side, verge. **5** sharpness, acuteness, keenness, incisiveness, pungency, zest. **6** bitterness, rancour, acerbity. **7** advantage, superiority, the upper hand. *verb* **1** border, trim, hem, fringe. **3** creep, inch, ease, sidle.

edgeways or **edgewise** *adv.* sideways. — **not get a word in edgeways** to be unable to contribute to a conversation because the others are talking continuously.

edging *noun* a decorative border.

edgy /'ɛdʒɪ/ *adj.* (**edgier, edgiest**) *colloq.* **1** easily annoyed; nervous or tense. **2** *said of a picture, film, etc* sharp and intense: *an edgy thriller*.

⊟ on edge, nervous, tense, anxious, ill at ease, keyed up, touchy, irritable.
⊟ calm.

EDI *abbrev.* electronic data interchange.

edibility *noun* the state of being edible.

edible *adj.* fit to be eaten; suitable to eat. [from Latin *edibilis*]

⊟ eatable, palatable, digestible, wholesome, good, harmless.
⊟ inedible.

edict /'iːdɪkt/ *noun* an order issued by a monarch or government. [from Latin *edicere*, to proclaim]

⊟ command, order, proclamation, law, decree, regulation, pronouncement, ruling, mandate, statute, injunction, manifesto.

edification *noun* improvement of the mind or morals.

edifice /'ɛdɪfɪs/ *noun formal* **1** a building, especially a large impressive one. **2** a large and complex organization. [from French *édifice*, from Latin *aedificare*, to build]

⊟ **1** building, construction, structure, erection.

edify /'ɛdɪfaɪ/ *verb* (**edifies, edified**) *formal* to improve the mind or morals of. [from French *édifier*, from Latin *aedificare*, to build]

⊟ build up, instruct, improve, enlighten, inform, guide, educate, nurture, teach.

edifying *adj.* intellectually or morally stimulating.

edit /'edɪt/ — *verb* 1 to prepare (a book, newspaper, programme, film, etc) for publication or broadcasting, especially by making corrections or alterations. 2 to be in overall charge of the process of producing (a newspaper, etc). 3 (*usually* **edit something out**) to remove (parts of a work) before printing, broadcasting, etc. 4 to prepare (a cinema film, or a television or radio programme) by putting together material previously photographed or recorded. 5 *Comput.* to add, delete, modify, or rearrange (data) in preparation for processing by a computer, or to enable it to be used by other programs. 6 *Comput.* to produce a new version of (a text or program file). — *noun* a period or instance of editing. [from French *éditer*, from Latin *edere*, to bring forth]

⊟ *verb* 1 correct, emend, revise, rewrite, reorder, rearrange, adapt, check, compile, rephrase, select, polish, annotate. 3 cut, censor, expurgate.

edited *adj.* prepared for publication or broadcasting by editing.

edition /ɛ'dɪʃən/ *noun* 1 a number of copies of a book, etc printed at one time, or at different times without alteration. 2 the form in which a book, etc is published: *paperback edition*. 3 a single copy of a particular printing or issue of a book, magazine, etc.

⊟ 1 impression, printing. 2 version. 3 copy, volume, number, issue.

editor /'ɛdɪtə(r)/ *noun* 1 a person who edits books, etc. 2 a person who is in charge of a newspaper, magazine or programme, or one section of it. 3 a person who puts together the various sections of a cinema film, etc.

editorial /ɛdɪ'tɔːrɪəl/ — *adj.* of or relating to editors or editing. — *noun* an article written by or on behalf of the editor of a newspaper or magazine, usually one offering an opinion on a current topic.

editorialize or **editorialise** *verb intrans.* 1 to write an editorial. 2 *derog.* in journalism, to introduce personal opinion into what is meant to be factual reporting.

editorship *noun* the status or position of an editor.

EDP *abbrev.* electronic data processing.

EDTA *abbrev. Chem.* ethylene diamine tetra-acetic acid.

educable /'ɛdjʊkəbl/ or **educatable** /'ɛdjʊkeɪtəbl/ *adj.* capable of being educated.

educate *verb* 1 to train and teach. 2 to provide school instruction for. 3 to train and improve (one's taste, etc). [from Latin *educare*, to bring up]

⊟ 1, 2 teach. 1 train, instruct, tutor, coach, school, drill, inform. 3 cultivate, edify, improve, discipline, develop.

educated *adj.* 1 having received an education, especially to a level higher than average. 2 produced by or suggesting a (good) education. 3 based on experience or knowledge: *an educated guess*.

⊟ 1 trained. 2 knowledgeable, well-informed, well-instructed, well-taught, well-schooled, learned, lettered, cultured, civilized, tutored, refined, well-bred. 3 informed, knowledgeable.
⊟ UNEDUCATED. 2 uncultured.

education /ɛdʒʊ'keɪʃən/ *noun* 1 the process of teaching and training, usually from infancy. 2 the instruction received. 3 the result of a process of teaching and training. 4 the process of training and improving (one's taste, etc).

⊟ 1, 2 teaching, training, schooling, tuition, tutoring, coaching, guidance, instruction. 2 knowledge, information. 4 cultivation, improvement, development.

educational *adj.* 1 relating to education. 2 having the function of educating: *educational television programmes*.

⊟ 2 educative, informative, instructive, enlightening, edifying, illuminating, helpful, useful.

Educational establishments include: kindergarten, nursery school, infant school, primary school, middle school, combined school, secondary school, secondary modern, upper school, high school, grammar school, grant-maintained school, preparatory school, public school, private school, boarding school, college, sixth-form college, polytechnic, poly, city technical college, CTC, technical college, university, adult education centre, academy, seminary, finishing school, business school, secretarial college, Sunday school, convent school, summer school.

educationalist /ɛdjʊ'keɪʃənəlɪst/ or **educationist** *noun* an expert in methods of education.

educational psychology *Psychol.* the branch of psychology concerned with the application of the findings of psychology to the understanding of the learning process.

educative /'ɛdʒʊkətɪv/ *adj.* educating.

educator *noun* 1 a person who educates. 2 an educating experience or circumstance.

⊟ 1 teacher, instructor, trainer, mentor.

educe /ɪ'djuːs/ *verb formal* to bring out or develop. [from Latin *e*, out + *ducere*, to lead]

educible *adj.* capable of being educed or developed.

eduction /ɪ'dʌkʃən/ *noun* the process of educing or developing.

edutainment /ɛdjʊ'teɪnmənt/ *noun* the presentation of educational material as entertainment.

Edwardian /ɛd'wɔːdɪən, ɛd'wɑːdɪən/ *adj.* characteristic of Britain in the years 1901–10, the reign of King Edward VII.

-ee *suffix* forming nouns denoting: 1 the person who is the object of the action of a verb: *payee* / *employee*. 2 a person in a stated condition: *absentee* / *escapee* / *refugee*. 3 a person with a stated association or connection: *bargee*. [from French *-é* or *-ée*]

EEC *abbrev.* European Economic Community, the former name of the European Community (now the European Union).

EEG *abbrev.* electroencephalogram or electroencephalograph.

eel *noun* any of several species of fish with a long slender snakelike body, small fins, and a smooth slimy skin, often without scales. [from Anglo-Saxon *æl*]

e'en /iːn/ *old use, poetic* — *adv.* even. — *noun* evening.

e'er /eə(r)/ *adv. old use, poetic* ever.

-eer *suffix* 1 forming nouns denoting a person concerned with or engaged in a stated activity: *auctioneer* / *mountaineer*. 2 forming verbs denoting actions or behaviour associated with a stated activity: *electioneer*. [from French *-ier*]

eerie *adj.* (**eerier, eeriest**) strange and disturbing or frightening. [perhaps from Anglo-Saxon *earg*, cowardly]

⊟ weird, strange, uncanny, *colloq.* spooky, creepy, frightening, *colloq.* scary, spine-chilling.

eerily *adv.* with a strange and disturbing manner.

eeriness *noun* being eery or strange.

efface /ɪ'feɪs, ɛ'feɪs/ *verb* 1 to rub or wipe out. 2 to block out (a memory, etc). 3 to avoid drawing attention to (oneself). See also SELF-EFFACING. 4 to surpass or outshine. [from French *effacer*]

⊟ 1, 2 erase, obliterate, expunge. 1 rub out, wipe away, wipe out, delete, cancel. 2 suppress, repress.

effacement *noun* the process of effacing or wiping out.

effect — *noun* **1** a result. **2** an impression given or produced. **3** operation; working state: *come, bring, put into effect*. **4** (*usually* **effects**) *formal* property. **5** (*usually* **effects**) devices, especially lighting and sound, used to create a particular impression in a film, on a stage, etc: *special effects*. — *verb formal* to do, cause to happen, or bring about. — **for effect** in order to make an impression on others. **give effect to something** *formal* to do it or bring it into operation. **in effect** in reality; practically speaking. **take effect** to begin to work; to come into force. **to the effect that** *formal* with the meaning or result that. **to good, some, no, effect** with much, some, no, etc success. **to that effect** *formal* with that meaning or intended result. **with effect from** ... *formal* coming into operation or becoming valid at the time stated. **with immediate effect** *formal* as from now. [from Old French, from Latin *effectus*]

. . . .

▣ *noun* **1** outcome, result, conclusion, consequence, upshot, aftermath, issue. **2** power, force, impact, efficacy, impression, strength. **4** belongings, possessions, property, goods, *colloq.* gear, movables, chattels, things, trappings. *verb* cause, execute, create, achieve, accomplish, perform, produce, make, initiate, fulfil, complete. **in effect** in fact, actually, really, in reality, to all intents and purposes, for all practical purposes, essentially, effectively, virtually. **take effect** be effective, become operative, come into force, come into operation, be implemented, begin, work.

. . . .

effective *adj.* **1** having the power to produce, or producing, a desired result. **2** producing a powerful or pleasing effect. **3** in, or coming into, operation; working; active. **4** actual, rather than theoretical.

. . . .

▣ **1** efficient, efficacious, productive, adequate, capable, useful. **2** forceful, cogent, powerful, persuasive, convincing, telling, striking, impressive, attractive, well-placed. **3** operative, in force, functioning, current, active. **4** actual, de facto.
▣ **1** ineffective, powerless.

. . . .

effectively *adv.* **1** in an effective way. **2** in reality; for all practical purposes.

. . . .

▣ **1** well, efficiently, competently, ably, capably, satisfactorily, adequately. **2** in fact, actually, really, in reality, to all intents and purposes, for all practical purposes, virtually, essentially, basically.

. . . .

effector *noun Biol.* in an animal, any structure, usually a muscle or gland, that causes the animal, or part of it, to respond to a particular stimulus, such as a nerve impulse.

effectual *adj.* **1** producing the intended result. **2** *said of a document, etc* valid. [from Latin *effectualis*]

effectuate *verb formal* to do; to carry out with success. [from Latin *effectuare*]

effectuation *noun* the process of causing something to happen.

effeminacy /ɪˈfɛmɪnəsɪ/ *noun* an effeminate state or manner.

effeminate /ɪˈfɛmɪnət/ *adj. sometimes derog.*, *said of a man* having features of behaviour or appearance more typical of a woman. [from Latin *effeminare*, to make like a woman]

. . . .

▣ unmanly, womanly, womanish, girlish, feminine, sissy, delicate.
▣ manly.

. . . .

effeminately *adv.* with an effeminate manner.

efferent /ˈɛfərənt/ *adj. Anat.* **1** denoting an anatomical structure, especially a nerve or blood vessel, that leads outwards or away from a central point. **2** denoting a nerve

or neurone that carries nerve impulses from the central nervous system (the brain and spinal cord) to the muscles, glands, etc. See also AFFERENT. [from Latin *efferre*, from *e*, from + *ferre*, to carry]

effervesce /ɛfəˈvɛs/ *verb intrans.* **1** to give off bubbles of gas. **2** to behave in a lively, energetic way. [from Latin *effervescere*, to boil up]

effervescence *noun* an effervescent state; giving off bubbles of gas.

effervescent *adj.* **1** effervescing; giving off bubbles of gas. **2** full of energy; vivacious.

. . . .

▣ **1** bubbly, sparkling, fizzy, frothy, carbonated, foaming. **2** lively, ebullient, vivacious, animated, buoyant, exhilarated, enthusiastic, exuberant, excited, vital.
▣ **1** flat. **2** dull.

. . . .

effete /ɪˈfiːt, ɛˈfiːt/ *adj. derog.* **1** *said of an institution, organization, etc* lacking its original power or authority. **2** *said of a person* lacking strength or energy; made weak by too much protection or refinement. [from Latin *effetus*, weakened by having given birth]

effeteness *noun* being effete or weak.

efficacious /ɛfɪˈkeɪʃəs/ *adj. formal* producing, or certain to produce, the intended result. [from Latin *efficax*]

. . . .

▣ effective, efficient, effectual, powerful, potent, convincing, compelling.

. . . .

efficacy /ˈɛfɪkəsɪ/ *noun* effectiveness; having the intended result.

efficiency *noun Physics* **1** the state or quality of being efficient. **2** a measure of the effectiveness of the performance of a machine, engine, etc. It is equal to the ratio of the useful energy output to the energy input, and is usually expressed as a percentage.

. . . .

▣ **1** effectiveness, competence, proficiency, skill, expertise, skilfulness, capability, ability, productivity.
▣ **1** inefficiency, incompetence.

. . . .

efficient *adj.* **1** producing satisfactory results with an economy of effort and a minimum of waste. **2** *said of a person* capable of competent work within a relatively short time. [from Latin *efficere*, to accomplish]

. . . .

▣ **1** effective, efficacious, powerful, productive, economical, cost-effective, energy-saving, labour-saving, time-saving, fast, swift, rapid. **2** competent, proficient, skilful, capable, able, well-organized, businesslike, well-conducted.
▣ **1** INEFFICIENT. **2** incompetent.

. . . .

effigy /ˈɛfɪdʒɪ/ *noun* (PL. **effigies**) **1** a crude doll or model representing a person, on which hatred or contempt for the person can be expressed, eg by burning. **2** *formal* a portrait or sculpture of a person used as an architectural ornament. [from Latin *effigies*]

effloresce /ɛfləˈrɛs/ *verb intrans.* **1** *Chem.*, *said of a crystalline salt* to undergo the process of efflorescence. **2** *Bot.*, *said of a plant* to produce flowers. [from Latin *efflorescere*, to blossom]

efflorescence *noun* **1** *Chem.* the process whereby certain crystalline salts, known as hydrates, lose water of crystallization and become powdery on exposure to air. **2** *Bot.* the production of flowers by a plant.

efflorescent *adj.*, *said of certain crystalline salts, known as hydrates* tending to lose water of crystallization and become dry and powdery on exposure to air.

effluent /ˈɛfluənt/ — *noun* **1** an outflow of sewage, agricultural fertilizers, industrial waste, etc, into a river, lake, or sea. **2** *Geog.* a stream or river flowing from a larger body of water. — *adj. formal, technical* flowing out. [from Latin *effluere*, to flow out]

effluvium /ɛˈfluːvɪəm, ɪˈfluːvɪəm/ *noun* (PL. **effluvia**) *formal* an unpleasant smell or vapour given off by something, eg decaying matter. [from Latin *effluere*, flow out]

efflux /ˈɛflʌks/ *noun* the act of flowing out; something that flows out. [from Latin *effluere*, to flow out]

effort *noun* **1** hard mental or physical work, or something that requires it. **2** an act of trying hard. **3** the result of an attempt; an achievement. [from Old French *esfort*, from Latin *fortis*, strong]

. . . .

■ **1** exertion, strain, application, struggle, trouble, energy, toil, striving, pains, travail. **2** attempt, try, go, endeavour, shot, stab. **3** achievement, accomplishment, feat, exploit, production, creation, deed, product, work.

. . . .

effortless *adj.* done without effort or apparent effort.

. . . .

■ easy, simple, smooth, nonchalant, casual, undemanding, facile, painless.
✦ difficult.

. . . .

effrontery /ɪˈfrʌntərɪ/ *noun* (PL. **effronteries**) shameless rudeness; impudence. [from French *effronterie*, from Latin *effrons*, shameless]

. . . .

■ audacity, impertinence, insolence, cheek, impudence, temerity, boldness, brazenness, cheekiness, gall, nerve, presumption, disrespect, arrogance, brashness.
✦ respect, timidity.

. . . .

effulgence /ɪˈfʌldʒəns/ *noun* an effulgent or bright quality; brilliance.

effulgent /ɪˈfʌldʒənt/ *adj. literary* shining brightly; brilliant. [from Latin *effulgere*, to shine out]

effusion /ɪˈfjuːʒən/ *noun* **1** a pouring or flowing out. **2** *derog.* an uncontrolled flow of speech or writing. [from Latin *effusio*, pouring out]

effusive /ɪˈfjuːsɪv/ *adj. derog.* expressing feelings, especially happiness or enthusiasm, in an excessive or very showy way. [from *effuse*, to pour out]

. . . .

■ fulsome, gushing, unrestrained, expansive, demonstrative, profuse, overflowing, enthusiastic, exuberant, extravagant, lavish, talkative, voluble.
✦ reserved, restrained.

. . . .

E-fit *noun* a system (largely replacing **Photofit**) used by the police for building up a likeness of someone to fit a witness's description, using computer-generated images.

EFL *abbrev.* English as a Foreign Language.

EFTA or **Efta** *abbrev.* European Free Trade Association.

EFTPOS *abbrev.* electronic funds transfer at point of sale.

EFTS *abbrev.* electronic funds transfer system.

eg or **e.g.** *abbrev. exempli gratia* (Latin), for example.

egalitarian /ɪɡalɪˈtɛərɪən/ — *adj.* relating to, promoting, or believing in the principle that all human beings are equal and should enjoy the same rights. — *noun* a person who upholds this principle. [from French *égalitaire*, from *égal*, equal]

egalitarianism *noun* egalitarian principles or beliefs.

egg[1] *noun* **1** *Biol.* in animals and plants, the unfertilized ovum or female gamete (reproductive cell) that is produced by the ovary. If fertilized by a sperm cell during the process of sexual reproduction, it forms a zygote, which then develops into an embryo. Also called OVUM. **2** *Zool.* in oviparous animals, eg birds, reptiles, amphibians, fish, and insects, a structure containing the ovum that is expelled from the body of the female either before or after fertilization. **3** the hard shell of an egg. **4** a hen's egg, used as food. **5** anything with the shape of a hen's egg. — **have** or **put all one's eggs in one basket** to depend entirely on a single plan, etc. **have** or **get egg on one's face** *colloq.* to be made to look foolish. **teach one's grandmother to suck**

eggs *colloq.* to try to show someone more experienced than oneself how to do something. [from Norse *egg*]

egg[2] *verb* — **egg someone on** *colloq.* to urge or encourage them. [from Norse *eggja*, edge]

egg-cup *noun* a small cup-shaped container for holding a boiled egg while it is being eaten.

egg custard see CUSTARD.

egg-flip see EGG-NOG.

egghead *noun colloq., sometimes derog.* a very clever person; an intellectual.

egg-nog or **egg-flip** *noun* a drink made from raw eggs, milk, sugar, and an alcoholic spirit, especially rum or brandy.

eggplant *noun North Amer.* an aubergine plant or its edible fruit.

eggshell — *noun* the hard, thin covering of an egg. — *adj.* **1** *said of paint or varnish* having a slightly glossy finish. **2** *said of articles of china* very thin and fragile.

egg-timer *noun* a device consisting of a sealed glass tube narrowed in the middle, containing sand or salt which, by trickling slowly from the top to the bottom of the tube through the narrow part, indicates the approximate time required to boil an egg.

egg tooth *Zool.* a hard point on the beak of an unhatched bird or reptile, which is used to break the shell of the egg.

eglantine /ˈɛɡləntaɪn/ *noun* a species of wild rose (*Rosa eglanteria*) that has aromatic sweet-smelling foliage. Also called SWEET BRIER. [from French *églantine*]

ego /ˈiːɡəʊ, ˈɛɡəʊ/ *noun* (PL. **egos**) **1** personal pride. **2** self-centredness or conceit. **3** *Psychol.* in psychoanalysis, the part of the mind that maintains conscious contact with the outside world, and is concerned with perception, memory, and reasoning. See also ID, SUPEREGO. [from Latin *ego*, I]

egocentric /iːɡəʊˈsɛntrɪk/ *adj. derog.* interested in oneself only.

. . . .

■ self-centred, self-absorbed, self-interested, narcissistic, egotistic, egoistic, selfish, self-seeking, self-serving.

. . . .

egocentrically *adv.* with interest in oneself only.

egocentricity /iːɡəʊsɛnˈtrɪsɪtɪ/ *noun* interest in oneself only.

egoism /ˈiːɡəʊɪzm, ˈɛɡəʊɪzm/ *noun* **1** *Philos.* the principle that self-interest is the basis of morality. **2** selfishness. **3** egotism.

. . . .

■ **2** selfishness, self-interest, self-serving, selfcentredness, egocentricity.

. . . .

egoist /ˈiːɡəʊɪst, ˈɛɡəʊɪst/ *noun* a person who believes in self-interest as a moral principle.

egoistic /iːɡəʊˈɪstɪk/ or **egoistical** *adj.* relating to or characterized by self-interest.

. . . .

■ self-interested, selfish, self-seeking, self-serving, self-centred, vain, conceited, *colloq.* swollen-headed, big-headed, self-important, egotistic.

. . . .

egoistically /iːɡəʊˈɪstɪkəlɪ/ *adv.* with self-interest.

egomania /iːɡəʊˈmeɪnɪə/ *noun Psychol.* obsessive love for or preoccupation with oneself.

egomaniac /iːɡəʊˈmeɪnɪak/ *noun* a person whose behaviour is governed by egomania.

egotism /ˈiːɡəʊtɪzm/ *noun derog.* **1** the habit of speaking too much about oneself. **2** the fact of having a very high opinion of oneself.

. . . .

■ **2** egoism, egomania, self-centredness, self-importance, conceitedness, self-regard, self-love, self-conceit, narcissism, self-admiration, vanity, big-headedness.
✦ HUMILITY.

. . . .

egotist /ˈiːgəʊtɪst/ *noun* a self-centred person.

egotistic /iːgəʊˈtɪstɪk/ or **egotistical** *adj.* speaking too much about oneself.

················

⊟ egoistic, egocentric, self-centred, self-important, conceited, vain, *colloq.* swollen-headed, big-headed, boasting, bragging.

🔁 humble.

················

egotistically *adv.* with too much reference to or interest in oneself.

ego trip *colloq.* an action or enterprise undertaken to enhance one's own reputation or standing.

egregious /ɪˈgriːdʒəs/ *adj. formal* outrageous; shockingly bad. [from Latin *egregius*, standing out from the herd, from *e*, out of + *grex*, herd]

egress /ˈiːgrɛs/ *noun formal Legal* **1** the act of leaving, or the right to leave, a building or other enclosed place. **2** an exit. [from Latin *egredi*, to go out]

egret /ˈiːgrət/ *noun* any of various species of wading bird resembling a heron but usually having white plumage, a long pointed bill, a long neck, and long lacy plumes developed by the male during the breeding season. [from French *aigrette*]

Egyptian /ɪˈdʒɪpʃən/ — *noun* **1** a native or citizen of Egypt. **2** the language of ancient Egypt. — *adj.* relating or belonging to Egypt.

Egyptologist /iːdʒɪpˈtɒlədʒɪst/ *noun* an expert in or student of Egyptology.

Egyptology /iːdʒɪpˈtɒlədʒɪ/ *noun* the study of the language, culture, and history of ancient Egypt.

eider /ˈaɪdə(r)/ *noun* (*also* **eider duck**) any of various large sea ducks, native to the Arctic coasts of Canada and Siberia, having a heavy body, a short neck, and a long sloping head. [from Icelandic *æthr*]

eiderdown *noun* **1** the down or soft feathers of the eider. **2** a quilt filled with this or some similar material.

eight — *noun* **1** the number or figure 8; any symbol for this number. **2** the age of 8. **3** something, eg a garment or a person, whose size is denoted by the number 8. **4** 8 o'clock. **5** a set of 8 people or things, eg the crew of an eight-oared boat. **6** a playing-card with 8 pips. **7** a score of 8 points. — *adj.* **1** 8 in number. **2** aged 8. — **be** or **have had one over the eight** *colloq.* to be slightly drunk. [from Anglo-Saxon *æhta*]

eighteen — *noun* **1** the number or figure 18; any symbol for this number. **2** the age of 18. **3** something, especially a garment, or a person, whose size is denoted by the number 18. **4** a set of 18 people or things. **5** a film classified as suitable for people aged 18 and over. — *adj.* **1** 18 in number. **2** aged 18. [from Anglo-Saxon *æhtatene*]

eighteenth *noun, adj.* the position in a series corresponding to 18 in a sequence of numbers.

eightfold — *adj.* **1** equal to eight times as much or as many. **2** divided into, or consisting of, eight parts. — *adv.* by eight times as much.

eighth *noun, adj.* **1** the position in a series corresponding to 8 in a sequence of numbers. **2** one of eight equal parts.

eighthly /ˈeɪtθlɪ/ *adv.* as eighth in a series.

eighties *pl. noun* **1** the period of time between one's eightieth and ninetieth birthdays. **2** the range of temperatures between eighty and ninety degrees. **3** the period of time between the eightieth and ninetieth years of a century.

eightieth *noun, adj.* the position in a series corresponding to 80 in a sequence of numbers.

eightsome reel 1 a lively Scottish dance for eight people. **2** the music for this dance.

eighty — *noun* (PL. **eighties**) **1** the number or figure 80. **2** the age of 80. **3** a set of 80 people or things. — *adj.* **1** 80 in number. **2** aged 80. [from Anglo-Saxon *æhtatig*]

einsteinium /aɪnˈstaɪnɪəm/ *noun* (SYMBOL **Es**, ATOMIC NUMBER **99**) a synthetic radioactive metallic element, produced by bombarding transuranic elements in a cyclotron. [named after US physicist Albert Einstein, 1879–1955]

EIS *abbrev.* Educational Institute of Scotland.

eisteddfod /aɪˈstɛdfəd, aɪˈstɛðvɒd/ *noun* (PL. **eisteddfods**, **eisteddfodau**) an annual Welsh arts festival during which competitions are held to find the best poetry, drama, songs, etc. [from Welsh *eisteddfod*, session]

either /ˈaɪðə(r), ˈiːðə(r)/ — *adj.* **1** any one of two. **2** each of two; both: *a garden with a fence on either side.* — *pron.* any one of two things, people, etc. — *adv.* **1** (*used in negative statements*) also; as well: *I thought him rather unpleasant, and I didn't like his wife either.* **2** (*used after a negative phrase*) what is more; besides: *he plays golf, and he's not bad, either.* — **either... or...** introducing two choices or possibilities: *I need either a pen or a pencil* / *either you come or I don't go.* **either way** or **in either case** in whichever of two cases. [from Anglo-Saxon *ægther*]

ejaculate /ɪˈdʒækjʊleɪt, ɪˈdʒækjʊlət/ — *verb* (pronounced -leɪt) *intrans., trans.* **1** *said of a man or male animal* to discharge (semen) from the penis. **2** to exclaim or cry suddenly. — *noun* (pronounced -lət) semen discharged from the penis. [from Latin *ejaculari*, to throw out]

················

⊟ *verb* **1** discharge, eject, spurt, emit. **2** exclaim, call, blurt (out), cry, shout, yell, utter, scream.

················

ejaculation *noun* **1** a sudden exclamation or cry. **2** discharge of semen.

ejaculatory /ɪˈdʒækjʊlətərɪ, ɪdʒakjʊˈleɪtərɪ/ *adj.* relating to ejaculation or discharge of fluid.

eject *verb* **1** to throw out with force. **2** to force to leave. **3** *intrans.* to leave (a moving aircraft) rapidly in an emergency by using an ejector seat. [from Latin *ejicere*, to throw out]

················

⊟ **1** emit, expel, discharge, spout, spew, evacuate, vomit. **2** oust, evict, throw out, drive out, turn out, expel, remove, banish, deport, dismiss, exile, *colloq.* kick out, *colloq.* fire, *colloq.* sack.

················

ejection *noun* ejecting; the process of being ejected.

ejective *adj.* that ejects or throws out.

ejector *noun* a person or device that ejects something or someone.

ejector seat a type of seat fitted to an aircraft, designed to eject the pilot from the cockpit in an emergency.

eke /iːk/ *verb* (**eke out**) **1** to make (a supply) last longer, eg by adding something else to it or by careful use. **2** to manage with difficulty to make (a living, etc). [from Anglo-Saxon *eacan*, to increase]

elaborate /ɪˈlabərət, ɪˈlabəreɪt/ — *adj.* (pronounced -rət) **1** complicated in design; complex. **2** carefully planned or worked out. — *verb* (pronounced -reɪt) **1** (**elaborate on** or **upon something**) to add detail to it. **2** to work out in great detail. **3** to make more ornate. [from Latin *elaborare*]

················

⊟ *adj.* **1** intricate, complex, complicated, involved, ornamental, ornate, fancy, decorated, ostentatious, showy, fussy. **2** detailed, careful, thorough, exact, extensive, painstaking, precise, perfected, minute, laboured, studied. *verb* **1** amplify, develop, enlarge on, expand, flesh out, improve on, refine, explain. **2** devise, work out, construct, evolve.

🔁 *adj.* **1** simple, plain. *verb* **1** précis, simplify.

················

elaboration *noun* the process of elaborating or explaining in detail.

élan /eɪˈlɑːn/ *noun literary* impressive and energetic style. [from French *élan*]

eland /ˈiːlənd/ *noun* (PL. **elands**, **eland**) a large antelope, found in Central and S Africa, having a fawn coat, a well-developed dewlap below the throat, and straight spirally twisted horns. [from Dutch]

elapse *verb intrans. formal, said of time* to pass. [from Latin *elabi*, to slide away]

▣ pass, lapse, go by, slip away.

elastic / ɪ'lastɪk / — *adj.* **1** *said of a material or substance* able to return to its original shape or size after being pulled or pressed out of shape. **2** *said of a force* caused by, or causing, such an ability. **3** able to be changed; flexible. **4** made of elastic. **5** *said of a person or feelings* able to recover quickly from a shock or upset. — *noun* stretchable cord or fabric woven with strips of rubber. [from Greek *elastikos*, from *elaunein*, to propel]

▣ *adj.* **1** stretchy, stretchable, springy, rubbery, pliant, pliable, flexible, supple, resilient, yielding, plastic, bouncy, buoyant. **3** adaptable, accommodating, flexible, tolerant, adjustable.
▣ *adj.* **1** rigid. **3** inflexible.

elastically *adv.* flexibly; so as to stretch easily.
elasticated *adj.*, *said of a fabric* having been made elastic by being interwoven with rubber.
elastic band a thin loop of rubber for holding papers or other items together or in place. Also called RUBBER BAND.
elasticity / iːla'stɪsɪtɪ/ *noun Physics* the property of certain materials that allows them to return to their original shape and size after the removal of a deforming force or *stress*.

▣ stretchiness, springiness, pliability, flexibility, resilience, suppleness, give, plasticity, bounce, buoyancy, adaptability, flexibility, tolerance, adjustability.
▣ rigidity, inflexibility.

elasticize or **elasticise** / ɪ'lastɪsaɪz/ *verb* to make elastic.
elastomer / ɪ'lastəmə(r)/ *noun Physics* a material that returns to its original shape after it has been deformed by stretching or compression, eg synthetic rubber.
elate *verb* to make intensely happy; to fill with optimism. [from Latin *elatus*, elevated, exalted]
elated *adj.* highly pleased; overjoyed.

▣ exhilarated, excited, euphoric, ecstatic, exultant, jubilant, overjoyed, joyful.
▣ despondent, downcast.

elatedly *adv.* with an elated or highly pleased manner.
elation *noun* an elated or highly pleased state.
elbow — *noun* **1** in humans, the angular joint between the upper arm and the forearm, where the arm bends. **2** the corresponding joint in other vertebrates. **3** the part of a coat, jacket, etc which covers this joint. **4** a sharp turn or bend resembling this joint, eg in a road, river, or pipe. — *verb* **1** to push or strike with the elbow. **2** to make (one's way through) by pushing with the elbows. — **at one's elbow** close to one. **give** or **get the elbow** *slang* to dismiss or be dismissed. **out at elbow** or **elbows 1** *said of a garment* no longer smart; worn out. **2** *said of a person* wearing worn-out clothes. [from Anglo-Saxon *elnboga*]

▣ *verb* PUSH, SHOVE. **1** jostle, nudge, bump, crowd, knock.

elbow-grease *noun colloq.* hard work, especially hard polishing.
elbow-room *noun* **1** space enough for moving or doing something. **2** freedom; lack of constraint.
elder [1] — *adj.* **1** older. **2** (**the elder**) used before or after a person's name to distinguish him or her from a younger person of the same name. — *noun* **1** a person who is older. **2** (*often* **elders**) an older person, especially when regarded as having authority. **3** in some Protestant Churches, a lay person who has some responsibility for administration. [from Anglo-Saxon *eldra*]

▣ *adj.* **1** older, senior, first-born, ancient.
▣ *adj.* YOUNGER.

elder [2] *noun* any of various deciduous shrubs or small trees of the genus *Sambucus*, native to north temperate regions, especially *Sambucus nigra*, which has small creamy-white fragrant flowers and purplish-black edible berry-like fruits. The flowers and fruits are used to make wine and preserves. [from Anglo-Saxon *ellærn*]
elderberry *noun* (PL. **elderberries**) the purplish-black edible berry-like fruit of the elder, used to make wine, preserves, and jellies.
elderly — *adj.* rather old. — *noun* (**the elderly**) old people.

▣ *adj.* ageing, aged, old, hoary, senile.
▣ *adj.* young, youthful.

elder statesman an old and very experienced member of a group, especially a politician, whose opinions are respected.
eldest — *adj.* oldest. — *noun* a person who is the oldest of three or more.
elec. *abbrev.* electric or electricity.
elect — *verb* **1** to choose by vote. **2** (**elect to do something**) to do it by choice. — *adj.* **1** (*following the noun*) elected to a position, but not yet formally occupying it. **2** specially chosen. **3** *Relig.* chosen by God for salvation. — *noun* (**the elect**) people chosen, for salvation or otherwise. [from Latin *eligere*, to choose]

▣ *verb* **1** choose, pick, opt for, select, vote for, prefer, adopt, designate, appoint, determine. **2** choose to, opt to, decide to. *adj.* **1** designate, to be, prospective.

electability *noun* capability of being elected.
electable *adj* capable of being elected, especially to political office.
elected *adj.* chosen by election.
election *noun* the process or act of choosing people for (especially political) office by taking a vote. See also GENERAL ELECTION.

▣ choice, selection, voting, ballot, poll, appointment, determination, decision, preference.

electioneer *verb intrans.* to take part in an (especially political) election campaign.
electioneering *noun* taking part in an election campaign.
elective *adj.* **1** *said of a position, office, etc* to which someone is appointed by election. **2** having the power to elect. **3** optional.
electively *adv.* by means of an election.
elector *noun* **1** a person who has the right to vote at an election. **2** (**Elector**) *Hist.* a German prince or archbishop in the Holy Roman Empire who had the right to elect the emperor.

▣ **1** selector, voter, constituent.

electoral / ɪ'lektərəl/ *adj.* of elections or electors.
electoral college in the US, the body of people who elect the President, having themselves been elected by popular vote.
electorally *adv.* as regards elections or voters.
electoral roll or **electoral register** the list of people in a particular area who are allowed to vote in local and general elections.
electorate *noun* (**the electorate**) all the electors of a city, country, etc.

electric — *adj.* **1** of or relating to electricity. **2** charged with or capable of being charged with electricity. **3** producing or produced by, conveying, powered by, or making use of electricity. **4** denoting a musical instrument that is amplified electronically: *electric guitar*. **5** having or causing great excitement, tension, or expectation. — *noun* (**electrics**) **1** electrical appliances. **2** *colloq.* electric circuits. [from Greek *elektron*, amber, which produces electricity when rubbed]

. . . .

▤ *adj.* **5** electrifying, exciting, stimulating, thrilling, charged, dynamic, stirring, tense, rousing.
▤ *adj.* **5** unexciting, flat.
. . . .

electrical *adj.* related to or operated by electricity.

electrical engineering the branch of engineering concerned with the practical applications of electricity and magnetism in the design and construction of machinery, and in power generation, distribution, and storage.

electrically *adv.* as regards electricity; by means of electricity.

electric arc *Electr.* a continuous electric discharge (of low voltage and high current), giving out heat and light, that is maintained across the space between two electrodes.

electric blanket a blanket for warming a bed, containing an electrical element controlled by a thermostat.

electric chair a chair used for executing criminals by sending a powerful electric current through them.

electric current the flow of electric charge, in the form of electrons, in the same direction through a conductor. The SI unit of electric current is the ampere (amp). A current of one amp corresponds to the flow of a charge of one coulomb every second.

electric eel a freshwater fish, native to shallow streams of the Amazon and Orinoco river basins of S America, that resembles but is not related to the eel. It can deliver a shock of 550 volts to its prey and predators.

electric eye *colloq.* a photoelectric cell.

electric fence an electrically charged wire fence that emits high-voltage low-current pulses as mild electric shocks when touched by humans or animal livestock.

electric field a region in space, surrounding an electrically charged particle, within which another charged particle experiences a force.

electric guitar a guitar with an electrical amplifier.

electrician /ɛlək'trɪʃən/ *noun* a person whose job is to install and repair electrical equipment.

electricity /ɛlək'trɪsɪtɪ/ *noun* **1** the manifestation of a form of energy associated with separation or movement of charged particles, especially electrons and protons. **2** the scientific study of this form of energy. **3** an electric charge or current, especially when supplied as a source of power for heating, lighting, running electronic equipment, etc. **4** excitement, tension, or expectation.

electric motor *Physics* any device for converting electrical energy into mechanical energy.

electric ray any of various bottom-dwelling marine fish, widespread in tropical and temperate seas, with electric organs that produce strong shocks to stun prey. Also called TORPEDO RAY.

electric shock therapy same as ELECTRO-CONVULSIVE THERAPY.

electrification *noun* **1** the adaptation of a system or device so that it can be operated by electrical power. **2** the process whereby a component or device is charged with electricity. **3** the process whereby a system, object, or person is subjected to electricity or its effects.

electrify /ɪ'lɛktrɪfaɪ/ *verb* (**electrifies, electrified**) **1** to adapt (a system or device, eg a railway system) so that it can be operated by electrical power. **2** to charge (a component or device) with electricity. **3** to subject (a system, object, or person) to electricity or its effects. **4** to cause great excitement in; to give a shock to.

▤ **4** thrill, excite, shock, invigorate, animate, stimulate, stir, rouse, fire, jolt, galvanize, amaze, astonish, astound, stagger.
▤ **4** bore.
. . . .

electrifying *adj.* extremely exciting.

electro- *combining form* forming words relating to electricity.

electrocardiogram *noun Medicine* (ABBREV. **ECG**) a recording of the electrical activity of the heart muscle, obtained by means of an electrocardiograph, and used in the diagnosis of heart disease.

electrocardiograph *noun Medicine* (ABBREV. **ECG**) a recording instrument, connected by leads to a number of electrodes taped to the chest wall and limbs, used to record the electrical activity of the heart muscle.

electrocardiography *noun Medicine* the branch of medicine concerned with the production and interpretation of electrocardiograms, whereby the electrical activity of the heart is recorded.

electro-convulsive therapy *Medicine* (ABBREV. **ECT**) a treatment for mental disorders, especially severe depression, in which a low-voltage electric current is passed through the brain while the patient is under anaesthesia. Formerly a common treatment, it has now been largely replaced by the use of drugs.

electrocute *verb* **1** to kill accidentally by electric shock. **2** to execute by means of electricity. [from ELECTRO- + EXECUTE]

electrocution *noun* the process of electrocuting or killing by electric shock.

electrode *noun Electr.* either of the two conducting plates through which an electric current enters or leaves a battery, thermionic valve, discharge tube, semiconductor device, etc. The cathode is the negative electrode and the anode is the positive electrode. [from ELECTRIC + Greek *hodos*, way]

electroencephalogram /ɪlɛktroʊɛn'sɛfələgram, ɪlɛktroʊɛn'kɛfələgram/ *noun Medicine* (ABBREV. **EEG**) a recording of the electrical activity of different parts of the brain, in the form of a tracing or graph produced by an electroencephalograph.

electroencephalograph /ɪlɛktroʊɛn'sɛfələgrɑːf, ɪlɛktroʊɛn'kɛfələgrɑːf/ *noun Medicine* an instrument for recording the electrical activity of different parts of the brain, usually by means of electrodes taped to the scalp. It is used to diagnose epilepsy and other disorders, and to detect brain tumours and brain damage.

electrolysis /ɪlɛk'trɒlɪsɪs/ *noun* **1** *Chem.* the process whereby the elements of a chemical compound are separated by passing an electric current through a solution or molten form of that compound, known as an *electrolyte*. **2** the removal of tumours, hair roots, etc, by means of an electric current.

electrolyte /ɪ'lɛktroʊlaɪt/ *noun Chem.* a chemical substance that can conduct electricity when in its molten state or when dissolved in water or some other solvent. [from ELECTRO- + Greek *lutos*, released]

electrolytic /ɪlɛktroʊ'lɪtɪk/ *adj.* relating to or involving electrolysis.

electrolytic cell *Chem.* any cell that consists of an electrolyte (a substance that when molten or in solution conducts electricity), in which electrodes (a positively charged anode and a negatively charged cathode) are immersed.

electromagnet *noun Physics* a temporary magnet consisting of a coil of insulated wire wrapped around a soft iron or steel core, which becomes strongly magnetized when an electric current flows through the wire.

electromagnetic *adj.* **1** relating to electromagnetism. **2** relating to electromagnetic radiation. **3** relating to or operated by an electromagnet.

electromagnetism *noun* **1** the branch of physics concerned with the study of the interaction between electric and magnetic fields, and the applications of the phenomena produced by this interaction. **2** magnetism that is produced by the flow of electric current, rather than by a permanent magnet.

electromotive *adj. Physics* relating to or producing an electric current.

electromotive force (ABBREV. **EMF**) *Electr.* **1** the energy supplied by a source of electrical power, such as a battery or generator, in order to drive an electric current around a circuit. **2** the potential energy difference that exists between an anode and a cathode immersed in the same electrolyte. Also called VOLTAGE.

electron *noun Physics* a fundamental particle (one that cannot be subdivided further) that carries a negative electric charge. The mass of an electron is 9.110×10^{-31}kg, and it carries a charge of -1.602×10^{-19} coulombs. The flow of electrons along a conductor constitutes an electric current.

electronegativity *noun Chem.* a measure of the ability of an atom within a molecule to attract electrons.

electron gun *Physics* a device that is used to produce a beam of electrons, eg a heated cathode. It is an essential component of television tubes, electron microscopes, and cathode-ray tubes.

electronic /iːlɛk'trɒnɪk/ *adj.* **1** *said of a device* operated by the movement of electrons in very small electric circuits containing semiconductors, etc, or in a vacuum or gas. **2** produced, operated, etc using electronic apparatus, especially computers: *electronic music, electronic publishing.* **3** relating to electronics.

electronically *adv.* by means of electronics.

electronic mail *noun* (ABBREV. **e-mail**) *Comput.* the sending of messages via computer systems. Messages are usually stored centrally until they are accessed by the recipient. E-mail facilities have the advantages of speed, flexibility, and low cost, and are provided by most computer networks. They are also available on a national and international basis.

electronic publishing *Comput.* the publishing of computer-readable texts on disk, CD-ROM, CD-I, etc.

electronics *noun* **1** (*sing.*) the scientific study of the conduction of electricity in a vacuum, in gases, and in semiconductors, and the design and applications of devices that control the movement of electrons. **2** (*pl.*) the electronic parts of a machine or system.

electronic tagging a monitoring system that allows the supervision of an offender outside prison, consisting of an electronic device fitted with a transmitter, usually worn on the wrist or ankle.

electron microscope *Biol.* a microscope that uses a beam of electrons instead of light rays to produce a highly magnified image of an object that is too small to be seen with a light microscope. Electron microscopes are used to examine and photograph cells, viruses, and large molecules.

electron volt or **electronvolt** (SYMBOL **eV**) *Physics* a unit of energy equal to the energy acquired by an electron when it accelerates through a potential difference of one volt. It is equal to 1.602×10^{-19} joules.

electrophoresis /ɪlɛktrəʊfə'riːsɪs/ *noun Chem.* the migration of charged particles in a solution under the influence of an electric field. It is used to separate individual amino acids from a mixture, by adjusting the pH of the solution so that some amino acids become positively charged and others become negatively charged. [from ELECTRO- + Greek *phoreein*, to bear]

electroplate — *verb* to plate or coat (a metal surface) with a thin layer of another metal by electrolysis, usually for decorative purposes, or to protect the underlying metal from corrosion. Metals commonly used for electroplating include silver, gold, copper, nickel, and chromium. — *noun* electroplated articles.

electroplated *adj., said of a metallic surface* plated or coated with another metal by the process of electrolysis.

electroplating *noun* the deposition of a thin layer of

metal on the surface of another metal by the process of electrolysis.

electroscope /ɪ'lɛktrəskoʊp/ *noun Physics* a device for detecting the presence of an electric charge and estimating its amount.

electrostatic field *Physics* an electric field associated with stationary electric charges.

electrostatics *sing. noun Physics* the scientific study of fields and potentials caused by stationary electric charges.

elegance /'ɛləgəns/ *noun* being elegant or graceful; refinement.

     . . . .

◫ style, chic, smartness, beauty, grace, gracefulness, delicacy, refinement, polish, taste, tastefulness, dignity, stateliness.

     . . . .

elegant /'ɛləgənt/ *adj.* **1** having or showing good taste in dress or style, combined with dignity and gracefulness. **2** *said of a movement* graceful. **3** *said of a plan, etc* simple and ingenious. [from Latin *elegans*]

     . . . .

◫ **1** stylish, chic, fashionable, modish, smart, refined, polished, genteel, tasteful, dignified, artistic, fine, exquisite, beautiful, handsome. **2** graceful, smooth, delicate, neat.

◫ **1, 2** inelegant. **1** unrefined, unfashionable.

     . . . .

elegantly *adv.* with an elegant or graceful manner.

elegiac /ɛlə'dʒaɪak/ *adj. literary* mournful or thoughtful; which is, or is like, an elegy.

elegiacally *adv.* by means of elegiacs; mournfully.

elegize or **elegise** *verb literary* **1** *intrans., trans.* to write an elegy about someone or something. **2** *intrans.* to produce mournful or thoughtful writings or songs.

elegy /'ɛlədʒɪ/ *noun* a mournful or thoughtful song or poem, especially one whose subject is death or loss. [from Latin *elegia*, from Greek *elegos*, lament]

     . . . .

◫ dirge, lament, requiem, plaint.

     . . . .

element /'ɛləmənt/ *noun* **1** a part of anything; a component or feature. **2** *Chem.* a chemical element. **3** a person or small group within a larger group. **4** a slight amount. **5** a high-resistance wire through which an electric current is passed in order to produce heat in an electric fire, kettle, or similar appliance. **6** one of a number of components in an electric circuit. **7** *Maths.* a single member of a set. **8** *Comput.* a single item in a set of computer data. **9** any one of the four basic substances (earth, water, fire, and air) from which, according to ancient philosophy, everything is formed. **10** (**elements**) weather conditions, especially when severe. **11** (**elements**) basic facts or skills. **12** (**elements**) *Relig.* bread and wine as the representation of the body and blood of Christ in the Eucharist. — **in one's element** in the surroundings that one finds most natural and enjoyable. [from Latin *elementum*]

     . . . .

◫ **1** factor, component, feature, constituent, ingredient, member, part, piece, fragment. **3** group, faction, set, party, clique. **4** trace, touch, hint, suspicion, soupçon. **11** basics, foundations, fundamentals, principles, rudiments, essentials.

◫ **1** whole.

     . . . .

elemental /ɛlə'mɛntəl/ *adj.* **1** basic or primitive; of the forces of nature, especially the four elements earth, air, fire, and water. **2** immense; of the power of a force of nature.

elementary /ɛlə'mɛntərɪ/ *adj.* dealing with simple or basic facts.

     . . . .

◫ basic, fundamental, rudimentary, principal, primary, clear, easy, introductory, straightforward, uncomplicated, simple.

◫ advanced.

     . . . .

elementary particle *Physics* any of a number of different types of subatomic particle that do not appear to be divisible into smaller units.

elementary school *North Amer., esp. US* primary school.

elephant *noun* (PL. **elephants, elephant**) the largest living land mammal, belonging to the family Elephantidae, and having an almost hairless grey skin, thick pillar-like legs with broad feet, large ears, and upper incisor teeth modified to form tusks. [from Latin *elephantus*, from Greek *elephas*]

elephantiasis /ɛləfən'taɪəsɪs/ *noun Medicine* a chronic disease, with thickening of the skin, that occurs mainly in the tropics, caused by infection with parasitic roundworms.

elephantine /ɛlə'fantaɪn/ *adj.* **1** of or like an elephant. **2** huge. **3** *derog.* large and awkward; not graceful.

elevate *verb* **1** to raise or lift. **2** to give a higher rank or status to. **3** to improve (a person's mind, etc) morally or intellectually. **4** to make more cheerful. [from Latin *elevare*]

■ **1** lift, raise, hoist, heighten, intensify, magnify. **2** exalt, advance, promote, aggrandize, upgrade. **3** uplift, edify, improve. **4** rouse, boost, brighten, lift.
▣ **1** lower. **2** downgrade.

elevated *adj.* **1** *said of a rank, position, etc* very high; important. **2** *said of thoughts, ideas, etc* intellectually advanced or very moral. **3** *said of land or buildings* raised above the level of their surroundings. **4** cheerful; elated.

■ **1, 2** lofty, exalted, high, grand, noble, dignified, sublime. **3** raised.
▣ **1** lowly.

elevating *adj.* improving the mind; morally uplifting.

elevation *noun* **1** the act of elevating or state of being elevated. **2** *technical* height, eg of a place above sea level. **3** *technical* a drawing or diagram of one side of a building, machine, etc. **4** *formal* a high place.

■ **1** rise, promotion, advancement, preferment, aggrandizement, exaltation, loftiness, grandeur, eminence, nobility. **2** height, altitude. **4** hill, rise.
▣ **1** demotion. **4** dip.

elevator *noun* **1** *North Amer.* a lift in a building. **2** a tall building in which grain is stored. **3** *Anat.* a muscle used to raise a part of the body. **4** *Aeron.* a movable flap at the tail of an aircraft, by means of which the aircraft climbs or descends.

elevatory /'ɛləveɪtərɪ/ *adj.* serving to elevate or bring to a higher position.

eleven — *noun* **1** the number or figure 11; any symbol for this number. **2** the age of 11. **3** something, eg a garment or a person, whose size is denoted by the number 11. **4** 11 o'clock. **5** a set of 11 people or things, especially a team of 11 players. **6** a score of 11 points. — *adj.* **1** 11 in number. **2** aged 11. — **at the eleventh hour** at the last possible moment; only just in time. [from Anglo-Saxon *endleofan*]

eleven-plus *noun* in the UK, an examination formerly taken at 11 or 12 to determine the type of secondary school a pupil will attend.

elevenses *noun colloq.* a snack, usually consisting of coffee, tea, biscuits, etc, taken at about eleven o'clock in the morning.

eleventh *noun, adj.* a position in a series corresponding to 11 in a sequence of numbers.

elf *noun* (PL. **elves**) **1** in folklore, a tiny fairy with a tendency to play tricks. **2** a mischievous child. [from Anglo-Saxon *ælf*]

elfin *adj.* **1** *said of physical features, etc* small and delicate. **2** elfish; small and mischievous, but charming.

elfish or **elvish** *adj.* characteristic of an elf; mischievous.

elicit /ɪ'lɪsɪt/ *verb* (**elicited, eliciting**) **1** (**elicit something from someone**) to succeed in getting information from them, usually with some effort or difficulty. **2** to cause or bring out. [from Latin *elicere*]

■ **1** draw out, extract, extort, obtain, derive. **2** cause, evoke, provoke, bring out, bring about.

elicitation *noun* the process of eliciting or drawing out a response.

elicitor *noun* a person who elicits or draws out a response.

elide *verb* **1** *Grammar* to omit (a vowel or syllable) at the beginning or end of a word. **2** to omit (a part of anything). See also ELISION. [from Latin *elidere*, to strike out]

eligibility *noun* the status of being eligible or suitable.

eligible /'ɛlɪdʒɪbəl/ *adj.* (*often* **eligible for something**) **1** suitable, or deserving to be chosen (for a job, as a husband, etc). **2** having a right: *eligible for compensation*. [from Latin *eligere*, to elect]

■ **1** qualified, fit, appropriate, suitable, acceptable, worthy, deserving, proper, desirable.
▣ INELIGIBLE.

eliminable /ɪ'lɪmɪnəbl/ *adj.* that may be eliminated.

eliminate *verb* **1** to get rid of or exclude. **2** to exclude from a later part of a competition by defeat in an earlier part. **3** *slang* to kill. [from Latin *eliminare*, to carry outside]

■ **1, 3** remove, get rid of, do away with, take out, dispose of. **1** cut out, exclude, delete, dispense with, rub out, omit, reject, disregard, drop, eradicate, expel, extinguish, stamp out, exterminate. **2** knock out, defeat. **3** kill, murder.
▣ **1** include, accept.

elimination *noun* the process of eliminating or getting rid of.

eliminator *noun* someone or something that eliminates, eg the first round of a competition.

elision /ɪ'lɪʒən/ *noun Grammar* the omission of a vowel or syllable, as in *I'm, we're*. See also ELIDE. [from Latin *elidere*, to strike out]

elite or **élite** /eɪ'liːt/ — *noun* **1** the best, most important, or most powerful people within society. **2** the best of a group or profession. **3** a size of letter in typewriting, twelve characters per inch. — *adj.* best, most important or most powerful. [from Old French *eslire*, to choose, from Latin *eligere*, to elect]

■ *noun* **1, 2** best, cream, crème de la crème, pick. **1** aristocracy, upper classes, nobility, gentry, establishment, high society. *adj.* choice, best, exclusive, select, first-class, aristocratic, noble, upper-class.

elitism or **élitism** /eɪ'liːtɪzm/ *noun* **1** the belief in the need for a powerful social elite. **2** the belief in the natural social superiority of some people. **3** *often derog.* awareness of, or pride in, belonging to an elite group in society.

elitist or **élitist** /eɪ'liːtɪst/ *noun* a supporter of elitism.

elixir /ɪ'lɪksə(r)/ *noun* **1** *Chem.* in alchemy, a chemical preparation that was formerly claimed to have the power to change ordinary metals into gold, or to be a universal remedy for illness (the elixir of life). **2** a panacea. **3** *Medicine* a clear sweetened liquid containing alcohol or glycerine, used to mask the taste of an unpalatable medicine that is dissolved in it. [from Arabic *al-iksir*, the philosopher's stone]

Elizabethan /ɪlɪzə'biːθən/ — *adj.* relating to or typical of the reign of Queen Elizabeth I of England (1558–1603). — *noun* a person who lived during this time.

elk *noun* (PL. **elks, elk**) **1** the largest of all deer, native to northern parts of Europe and Asia, and also found in N America, where it is called *moose*. **2** (*in full* **American elk**) a large deer, native to N America. Also called WAPITI. [probably from Anglo-Saxon *elhr*]

ellipse / ɪˈlɪps/ *noun Geom.* a plane (two-dimensional) curve joining all the points around two *foci* (fixed points) so that the sum of their distances from the foci remains constant. It is a conic section formed by slicing through a cone in a plane that is not parallel to and does not pass through its base. [from Latin *ellipsis*, from Greek *elleipsis*, omission]

ellipsis / ɪˈlɪpsɪs/ *noun* (PL. **ellipses**) /-siːz/ **1** *Grammar* a figure of speech in which a word or words needed for the sense or grammar are omitted but understood. **2** a set of three dots that indicate the omission of a word or words, eg in a lengthy quotation. [see ELLIPSE]

ellipsoid / ɪˈlɪpsɔɪd/ *noun Geom.* **1** a smooth closed surface formed by rotation of an ellipse about one of its axes. All plane sections of an ellipsoid will be ellipses or circles. **2** the solid (three-dimensional) figure enclosed by such a surface.

elliptical / ɪˈlɪptɪkəl/ or **elliptic** *adj.* **1** *Maths.* of or having the shape of an ellipse. **2** *said of speech or writing* containing an ellipsis; so concise as to be unclear or ambiguous. [from Greek *elleipsis*, omission]

elliptically *adv.* in an elliptical way; over-concisely.

elm *noun* any of various tall deciduous trees of the genus *Ulmus*, found mainly in the northern hemisphere, that have broad serrated leaves and produce clusters of small flowers which develop into winged fruits bearing a single seed [from Anglo-Saxon *elm*]

elocution *noun* the art of speaking clearly and effectively. [from Latin *eloqui*, to speak out]

▣ delivery, articulation, diction, enunciation, pronunciation, oratory, rhetoric, speech, utterance.

elocutionary *adj.* relating to elocution or clear speech.

elocutionist *noun* a teacher of, or an expert in, elocution.

elongate / ˈiːlɒŋgeɪt/ *verb* to lengthen or stretch out. [from Latin *elongare*]

▣ lengthen, extend, prolong, protract, stretch (out), draw out.

elongated / ˈiːlɒŋgeɪtɪd/ *adj.* long and narrow.

▣ lengthened, extended, prolonged, protracted, stretched, long.

elongation / iːlɒŋˈgeɪʃən/ *noun* the process of elongating; making longer.

elope / ɪˈloʊp/ *verb intrans.* to run away secretly, especially to get married. [from Old French *aloper*, probably from Middle English *alopen*]

▣ run off, run away, decamp, bolt, abscond, *slang* do a bunk, escape, steal away, leave, disappear.

elopement *noun* an act of eloping.

eloquence / ˈɛləkwəns/ *noun* **1** the art or power of using speech to impress, move, or persuade. **2** fine and persuasive language. [from Latin *eloqui*, to speak out]

▣ **1** oratory, rhetoric, articulacy, fluency, persuasiveness. **2** magniloquence, grandiloquence.

eloquent / ˈɛləkwənt/ *adj.* having or showing eloquence.

▣ articulate, fluent, well-expressed, expressive, vocal, voluble, persuasive, moving, forceful, graceful, plausible, stirring, vivid.
▣ inarticulate, tongue-tied.

eloquently *adv.* with eloquence.

else *adj., adv.* different from or in addition to something or someone known or already mentioned: *I'd like something else* / *where else can you buy it?* — **or else** ...**1** or if not ...; otherwise: *hurry up, or else we'll be late.* **2** *colloq.* or I will punish or harm you: *give me the money, or else!* [from Anglo-Saxon *elles*]

elsewhere *adv.* somewhere else.

ELT *abbrev.* English Language Teaching.

elucidate / ɪˈluːsɪdeɪt/ *verb* to make clear or explain; to shed light on. [from Latin *elucidare*]

▣ explain, clarify, clear up, interpret, spell out, illustrate, unfold.
▣ confuse.

elucidation *noun* elucidating; clear explanation.

elucidatory / ɪˈluːsɪdeɪtərɪ/ *adj.* serving to elucidate or make clear.

elude / ɪˈluːd/ *verb* **1** to escape or avoid by quickness or cleverness. **2** to fail to be understood by, discovered by, or found in the memory of. [from Latin *eludere*]

▣ **1** avoid, escape, evade, dodge, shirk, *colloq.* duck, flee. **2** puzzle, frustrate, baffle, confound, thwart, stump, foil.

elusive / ɪˈluːsɪv/ *adj.* **1** difficult to find or catch. **2** difficult to define or grasp. **3** avoiding the issue or the question. [from ELUDE]

▣ **1, 3** slippery, tricky. **2** indefinable, intangible, unanalysable, subtle, puzzling, baffling, transient, transitory. **3** evasive, shifty.

elusively *adv.* in an elusive way; so as to be difficult to catch or understand.

elusiveness *noun* being elusive or difficult to catch or understand.

elution / ɪˈluːʃən/ *noun Chem.* in chromatography, the removal of a substance that has been adsorbed on the surface of another substance, usually a column of resin, by passing a solvent down the column. [from Latin *elutio*, from *elure* to wash]

elver *noun* a young eel, especially one migrating back up a river. [from an old word *eelfare*, literally 'eel journey', a reference to the migration of young eels upstream]

elves see ELF.

elvish see ELFISH.

Elysian / ɪˈlɪzɪən/ *adj.* characteristic of the happiness associated with Elysium.

Elysium / ɪˈlɪzɪəm/ or **Elysian fields 1** in Greek and Roman mythology, the happy fields, often located on the borders of the Underworld, where the good remain after death in perfect happiness. **2** *poetic* a state or place of perfect happiness. [from Latin *elysium*, from Greek *elysion*]

em- *prefix* a form of en- used before b, m, and p.

'em / əm/ *contr. colloq.* them. [from Middle English *hem*, them]

emaciate / ɪˈmeɪsɪət/ *verb* to make extremely thin, especially through illness, starvation, etc. [from Latin *emaciare*]

emaciated / ɪˈmeɪsɪeɪtɪd/ *adj.* thin through malnutrition or starvation.

▣ thin, gaunt, lean, haggard, wasted, scrawny, skeletal, pinched, attenuated, meagre, lank.
▣ plump, well-fed.

emaciation *noun* extreme leanness or wasting of the body caused by malnutrition, parasitic worms, or diseases such as cancer or tuberculosis.

e-mail or **email** —*noun* **1** short for ELECTRONIC MAIL. — *verb* **2** to send (something) by e-mail or to e-mail (someone).

emanate /ˈɛmǝneɪt/ *verb intrans.* **1** *said of an idea, etc* to emerge or originate. **2** *said of light, gas, etc* to flow; to issue. **3** to send out or give off. [from Latin *emanare*, to flow out]

🔲 **1, 2** originate, proceed, issue, flow, come, emerge. **1** arise, derive, spring, stem. **3** discharge, send out, emit, give out, give off, radiate.

emanation *noun* emanating or originating.

emancipate /ɪˈmansɪpeɪt/ *verb* to set free from slavery, or from some other social or political restraint. [from Latin *emancipare*, to free]

🔲 free, liberate, release, set free, enfranchise, deliver, discharge, loose, unchain, unshackle, unfetter.
🔳 enslave.

emancipated *adj.* freed, especially from a social restraint.

🔲 free, freed, liberated, enlightened, sophisticated, broad-minded, tolerant.

emancipation *noun* the process of emancipating or freeing.

emasculate /ɪˈmaskjʊleɪt/ *verb* **1** to reduce the force, strength, or effectiveness of. **2** to remove the testicles of; to take away the masculinity of. [from Latin *e*, from + *masculus*, diminutive of *mas*, male]

emasculation *noun* emasculating; making feeble or ineffective.

emasculatory /ɪˈmaskjʊlǝtǝrɪ/ *adj.* serving to emasculate or make feeble.

embalm /ɛmˈbɑːm/ *verb* to preserve (a dead body) from decay, originally with oils and spices, but now by treatment with chemicals or drugs. [from Old French *embaumer*]

embalmment *noun* the process of embalming dead bodies.

embankment /ɛmˈbaŋkmǝnt/ *noun* **1** a bank or wall of earth made to enclose a waterway, or to carry a road or railway. **2** a slope of grass, earth, etc which rises from either side of a road or railway.

🔲 **1** causeway, dam, rampart, levee, earthwork.

embargo /ɪmˈbɑːgoʊ/ — *noun* (PL. **embargoes**) **1** an official order forbidding something, especially trade with another country. **2** the resulting stoppage, especially of trade. **3** any restriction or prohibition. — *verb* (**embargoes, embargoed**) **1** to place under an embargo. **2** to take for use by the state. [from Spanish *embargar*, to impede or restrain]

🔲 *noun* **1, 3** restriction, ban, prohibition, restraint, proscription, bar, barrier, interdict, impediment, check hindrance, blockage. **2** stoppage.

embark /ɛmˈbɑːk/ *verb* **1** *intrans.* to go on board ship: *embark for America.* **2** to place or take on board ship. **3** (**embark on something**) to begin a task, especially a lengthy one. [from French *embarquer*]

🔲 **1** board, go aboard, take ship. **3** begin, start, commence, set about, launch, undertake, enter, initiate.
🔳 **1** disembark. **3** complete, finish.

embarkation /ɛmbˈkeɪʃǝn/ *noun* embarking; boarding a ship.

embarrass /ɪmˈbarǝs/ *verb* **1** to cause to feel anxious, self-conscious, or ashamed. **2** *intrans.* to become anxious, self-conscious, or ashamed. **3** (**be embarrassed**) to be in financial difficulties. **4** to make more complicated. **5** to confuse or perplex. [from French *embarrasser*]

🔲 **1** disconcert, mortify, show up, discompose, fluster, humiliate, shame, distress.

embarrassed *adj.* feeling awkward or self-conscious.

🔲 awkward, self-conscious, uncomfortable, uneasy, ill at ease, disconcerted, flustered, abashed, ashamed, humiliated.

embarrassing *adj.*, *said of an incident, remark, etc* causing awkwardness or self-consciousness.

🔲 awkward, tricky, uncomfortable, disconcerting, distressing, shameful.

embarrassment *noun* **1** self-conscious awkwardness. **2** a cause of this: *he's an embarrassment to all of us.*

🔲 **1** discomposure, self-consciousness, chagrin, mortification, humiliation, shame, awkwardness, confusion, bashfulness.

embassy /ˈɛmbǝsɪ/ *noun* (PL. **embassies**) **1** the official residence of an ambassador. **2** an ambassador and his or her staff. **3** a diplomatic mission to a foreign country. [from Old French *ambassee*]

embattled /ɪmˈbatld/ *adj.* **1** prepared for battle. **2** troubled by problems or difficulties. [from Old French *embataillier*, to prepare or arm for battle]

🔲 **2** beleaguered, beset, harassed, bothered, persecuted.

embed /ɛmˈbɛd/ *verb* (**embedded, embedding**) to set or fix firmly and deeply.

embellish /ɪmˈbɛlɪʃ/ *verb* **1** to make (a story, etc) more interesting by adding details which may not be true. **2** to beautify with decoration. [from Old French *embellir*, to make beautiful]

🔲 EMBROIDER, DRESS UP. **2** adorn, ornament, decorate, deck, beautify, gild, garnish, festoon, elaborate, enrich, enhance, varnish, grace.
🔳 SIMPLIFY.

embellished *adj.* beautified with decoration.

embellishment *noun* **1** beautifying with decoration. **2** something which adorns or beautifies. **3** elaboration of a story, etc with details.

🔲 **1, 2** adornment, ornament, ornamentation, decoration, elaboration, trimming, gilding, enrichment, enhancement. **2** garnish. **3** embroidery, exaggeration.

ember *noun* (*usually* **embers**) **1** a piece of glowing or smouldering coal or wood in a dying fire. **2** *literary* what remains of a once strong feeling. [from Anglo-Saxon *æmyrge*]

Ember Days in the Christian Church, the Wednesday, Friday, and Saturday of the weeks (*Ember Weeks*) following the first Sunday in Lent, Whit Sunday, Holy Cross Day (14 Sep), and St Lucia's Day (13 Dec); formerly observed as special days of fasting and abstinence. [from Middle English *ymber*, from Old English *ymbren*, a period, circuit, rotation (as of the seasons)]

embezzle /ɛmˈbɛzl/ *verb* to take dishonestly (money with which one has been entrusted). [from Old French *embesiler*, to make away with]

🔲 appropriate, misappropriate, steal, pilfer, filch, *colloq.* pinch.

embezzlement *noun* the act of embezzling.

■ appropriation, misappropriation, pilfering, fraud, stealing, theft, filching.

embezzler *noun* a person who embezzles money.

embitter /ɛmˈbɪtə(r)/ *verb* (**embittered, embittering**) to cause (someone) to feel bitter.

embittered *adj.* made to feel bitter and resentful.

■ bitter, resentful, disaffected, aggrieved, sour, rancorous, disillusioned.

embittering *adj.* causing feelings of bitterness and resentment.

embitterment *noun* the process of causing bitter feelings.

emblazon /ɪmˈbleɪzən/ *verb* (**emblazoned, emblazoning**) 1 to decorate with a coat of arms or some other bright design. 2 to display in a very obvious or striking way. [from EM- + *blazon*, from French *blason*, shield]

emblazonment *noun* decoration or display, especially heraldic.

emblem *noun* an object chosen to represent an idea, a quality, a country, etc. [from Latin *emblema*]

■ symbol, sign, token, representation, logo, insignia, device, crest, mark, badge, figure.

emblematic /ɛmbləˈmatɪk/ *adj.* in the nature of an emblem; serving as an emblem.

embodiment *noun* 1 embodying; something that is embodied. 2 a typical example or representative of something: *the embodiment of evil.*

■ INCARNATION, PERSONIFICATION. 1 exemplification, expression, incorporation, realization, representation, manifestation, concentration. 2 epitome, example, model, type.

embody *verb* (**embodies, embodied**) 1 to be an expression or a representation of in words, actions, or form; to typify or personify. 2 to include or incorporate.

■ 1 personify, typify, exemplify, represent, stand for, symbolize, express, manifest. 2 include, incorporate, contain.

embolden /ɪmˈbəʊldn/ *verb* (**emboldened, emboldening**) to make bold.

embolism /ˈɛmbəlɪzm/ *noun Medicine* the blockage of a blood vessel (usually in the heart, lungs, or brain) by a blood clot, air bubble, or a fragment of tissue or some other material that has travelled through the bloodstream. [from Greek *embolismos*, from *emballein*, to insert]

embolus /ˈɛmbələs/ *noun* (PL. **emboli**) *Medicine* any material, especially a fragment of a blood clot, an air bubble, or a small piece of tissue, that travels through the bloodstream until it becomes lodged within a small blood vessel and blocks the circulation.

emboss /ɛmˈbɒs/ *verb* to carve or mould a raised design on (a surface). [from Old French *embocer*]

embossed *adj.* carved or moulded with a raised design.

embrace — *verb* 1 to hold closely in the arms, affectionately or as a greeting. 2 *intrans., said of two people* to hold each other closely in the arms, affectionately or as a greeting. 3 to take (eg an opportunity) eagerly, or accept (eg a religion) wholeheartedly. 4 to include. — *noun* 1 an act of embracing. 2 a loving hug. [from Old French *embracer*, from Latin *in*, in + *bracchium*, arm]

■ *verb* 1, 2 hug, cuddle. 1 clasp, hold, grasp, squeeze.

3 accept, take up, welcome. 4 include, encompass, incorporate, contain, comprise, cover, involve. *noun* 2 hug, cuddle, clasp, *colloq.* clinch.

embrasure /ɛmˈbreɪʒə(r)/ *noun* 1 an opening in the wall of a castle, etc for shooting through. 2 an opening in a thick wall for a door or window, with angled sides which make it narrower on the outside. 3 the sloping of these sides. [from French *embraser*, to splay]

embrocation *noun* 1 a lotion for rubbing into the skin as a treatment for sore or pulled muscles. 2 the act of rubbing in such lotion. [from Greek *embroche*, lotion]

embroider *verb* (**embroidered, embroidering**) 1 *trans., intrans.* to decorate (cloth) with sewn designs. 2 to make (a story, etc) more interesting by adding details, usually untrue. [from Old French *embroder*]

embroiderer *noun* a person who embroiders, especially professionally.

embroidery *noun* 1 the art or practice of sewing designs on to cloth. 2 articles decorated in this way. 3 *derog.* gaudy decoration. 4 the addition of (usually false) details to a story, etc.

embroil *verb* 1 (**embroil someone in something**) to involve them in a quarrel or in a difficult situation. 2 to throw into a state of confusion. [from French *embrouiller*]

■ 1 involve in, implicate in, entangle in, enmesh in, mix up in, incriminate.

embroilment *noun* embroiling; uproar; commotion.

embryo /ˈɛmbrɪəʊ/ *noun* (PL. **embryos**) 1 in animals, the developing young organism, from the first division of the zygote (fertilized ovum or egg) until hatching or birth. 2 in humans, the developing young organism during the first seven weeks after conception. Thereafter it is usually referred to as a fetus. 3 a plant structure in its early stage of development, prior to germination. 4 anything in its earliest stages. [from Greek *embryon*, from *en*, in + *bryein*, to swell]

■ 4 nucleus, germ, beginning, root.

embryological /ɛmbrɪəʊˈlɒdʒɪkəl/ *adj.* relating to embryology or the study of embryos.

embryologist /ɛmbrɪˈɒlədʒɪst/ *noun* a scientist who specializes in the study of embryology.

embryology /ɛmbrɪˈɒlədʒɪ/ *noun* the scientific study of the formation and development of embryos.

embryonic /ɛmbrɪˈɒnɪk/ *adj.* 1 relating to anything that is rudimentary, incomplete, or at an early stage of development. 2 relating to or resembling an embryo.

■ 1 undeveloped, rudimentary, immature, early, germinal, primary.
🔁 1 developed.

emend /ɪˈmend/ *verb* to edit (a text), removing errors and making improvements. See also AMEND. [from Latin *emendare*]

emendation *noun* a change or correction, especially to a text.

emerald *noun* 1 a deep green variety of beryl, containing chromium, found mainly in metamorphic rocks in Colombia, and highly valued as a gemstone. It can also be manufactured synthetically. 2 (*also* **emerald green**) the colour of this stone. [from Old French *esmeralde*, from Greek *smaragdos*]

Emerald Isle *poetic* Ireland, so called from its greenness.

emerge *verb intrans.* 1 to come out from hiding or into view. 2 to become known or apparent. 3 to survive a difficult or dangerous situation. [from Latin *emergere*]

■ 1 come out, come forth, emanate, issue, proceed, arise,

rise, surface, appear, develop, *colloq.* crop up, turn up, materialize. **2** appear, transpire, turn out.
F3 1 disappear.

emergence *noun* emerging; first appearance.

E appearance, rise, advent, coming, dawn, development, arrival, disclosure, issue.
F3 disappearance.

emergency *noun* (PL. **emergencies**) **1** an unexpected and serious happening which calls for immediate and determined action. **2** a serious injury needing immediate medical treatment; or a patient suffering such an injury.

E 1 crisis, danger, difficulty, *formal* exigency, predicament, plight, pinch, strait, quandary.

emergent *adj.* emerging; developing.
emeritus /ɪ'mɛrɪtəs, iː'merɪtəs/ *adj.* retired, but retaining a former title as an honour: *emeritus professor / professor emeritus.* [from Latin *mereri*, to earn]
emery /'ɛmərɪ/ *noun Geol.* an impure variety of corundum (aluminium oxide) containing oxides of iron and silica. It is used as an abrasive and polishing material. [from Greek *smyris*, polishing powder]
emery board a small flat strip of wood or card coated with emery powder or some other abrasive, used for filing one's nails.
emery paper or **emery cloth** paper or cloth coated with emery, used for cleaning or polishing metal.
emetic /ɪ'mɛtɪk/ *Medicine* — *adj.* denoting any drug or other agent that causes vomiting. — *noun* any drug or other agent that causes vomiting, used medicinally to induce vomiting after accidental consumption of poison, drug overdosing, etc. [from Greek *emeein*, to vomit]
EMF *abbrev.* **1** (*also* **emf**) electromotive force. **2** European Monetary Fund.
emigrant *noun* a person who emigrates or who has emigrated. [from Latin *emigrare*, to move from a place]
emigrate *verb intrans.* to leave one's native country and settle in another. See also IMMIGRATE. [from Latin *emigrare*, to move from a place]

E migrate, relocate, go abroad, move, depart.

emigration *noun* emigrating; departure to settle in another country.
émigré /'ɛmɪgreɪ/ *noun* a person who has emigrated, usually for political reasons. [from French *émigré*, from Latin *emigrare*, to move from a place]
eminence *noun* **1** honour, distinction, or prestige. **2** an area of high ground. **3** (**Your** or **His Eminence**) a title of honour used in speaking to or about a cardinal. [from Latin *eminere*, to stand out]

E 1 honour, distinction, fame, pre-eminence, prominence, prestige, renown, reputation, greatness, importance, esteem, note, rank.

éminence grise /'ɛmɪnɑ̃s 'griːz/ (PL. **éminences grises**) a person who has great influence over a ruler, government, etc, without occupying an official position of power. [French, = grey eminence, first applied to Cardinal Richelieu's private secretary, Father Joseph]
eminent *adj.* famous and admired.

E distinguished, famous, prominent, illustrious, outstanding, notable, pre-eminent, prestigious, celebrated, renowned, noteworthy, conspicuous, esteemed, admired, important, well-known, elevated, respected, great, high-ranking, grand, superior.

unknown, obscure, unimportant.

eminently *adv.* **1** very. **2** obviously.
emir /eɪ'mɪə(r)/ *noun* a title given to various Muslim rulers, especially in the Middle East or W Africa. [from Arabic *amir*, ruler]
emirate /'ɛmɪrət/ *noun* the position or authority of, or the territory ruled by, an emir.
emissary /'ɛmɪsərɪ/ *noun* (PL. **emissaries**) **1** a person sent on a mission, especially on behalf of a government. **2** a person sent with a message. [from Latin *emissarius*]

E 1 ambassador, agent, envoy, go-between, delegate, representative, scout, deputy, spy. **2** messenger, courier, herald, runner.

emission *noun* **1** the act of emitting. **2** something emitted, especially heat, light, or gas. [from Latin *emissio*, a sending out]

E DISCHARGE, ISSUE, EMANATION, EXHALATION, RADIATION, TRANSMISSION. **1** ejection, ejaculation, diffusion, release.

emissive *adj.* having the power to emit energy, eg heat, light.
emit /ɪ'mɪt, iː'mɪt/ *verb* (**emitted, emitting**) to give out (light, heat, a sound, a smell, etc). [from Latin *emittere*, to send out]

E discharge, give out, give off, emanate, exude, diffuse, radiate, release, issue, eject, shed, vent.
F3 absorb.

Emmental or **Emmenthal** /'ɛməntɑːl/ *noun* a mild hard Swiss cheese with holes in it. [from *Emmenthal*, a valley in Switzerland]
emollient — *adj.* **1** *Medicine* softening or soothing the skin. **2** *formal* advocating a calmer, more peaceful attitude. — *noun Medicine* a substance which softens or soothes the skin. [from Latin *emollire*, to soften]

E *adj.* **2** conciliatory, placatory, appeasing, calming, propitiatory.

emolument /ɪ'mɒljʊmənt/ *noun formal* (*often in pl.*) any money earned or otherwise gained through a job or position, eg salary or fees. [from Latin *emolumentum*, a corn-grinder's fee, from *molere*, to grind]
emote *verb intrans. derog. colloq.* to display exaggerated or insincere emotion.
emoticon *noun Comput.* (*also* **smiley**) a small image of a face created from keyboard characters and included in an electronic mail message to convey the feelings of the sender.
emotion *noun* **1** a strong feeling. **2** depth or intensity of feeling. [from Latin *emovere*, to stir up, disturb]

E FEELING, PASSION. **1** sensation, sentiment, reaction. **2** ardour, fervour, warmth, vehemence, excitement.

emotional *adj.* **1** of the emotions. **2** feeling or expressing emotion. **3** causing emotion. **4** *said of a person* tending to express emotions easily or excessively. **5** *often derog.* based on emotions, rather than rational thought: *an emotional response.*

E 2 feeling, passionate, sensitive, responsive, ardent, tender, warm, roused, enthusiastic, fervent, impassioned, moved, zealous, heated, tempestuous, fiery. **3** emotive, moving, poignant, thrilling, touching, stirring, heart-warming, exciting, pathetic. **4** demonstrative, sentimental, soft-

hearted, soft, *colloq.* soppy, excitable, highly-strung, hot-blooded, hot-tempered, hotheaded, overcharged, temperamental.
🔁 2 unemotional, cold, detached, calm.

emotionalism *noun often derog.* the tendency to be too easily affected or excited by the emotions.

emotive *adj.* tending, or designed, to excite emotion. [from Latin *emovere*, to stir, disturb]

🔁 emotional, sentimental, moving, pathetic, stirring, rousing, inflammatory, incendiary.

empanel *verb* (**empanelled, empanelling**) 1 to enter (the names of prospective jurors) on a list. 2 to select (a jury) from such a list.

empathetic *adj.* able to share others' feelings.

empathize or **empathise** *verb intrans.* (**empathize with someone**) to share their feelings.

empathy *noun* the ability to share and understand another person's feelings. [from Greek *empatheia*, passion, affection]

🔁 sympathy, fellow feeling, affinity, rapport, sensitivity.

emperor /ˈɛmpərə(r)/ *noun* the male ruler of an empire or of a country which was once the centre of an empire. See also EMPRESS. [from Old French *emperere*, from Latin *imperator*, commander]

emperor penguin the largest species of penguin, native to Antarctica, that stands about 1.2m high and has black plumage, a white belly, and a distinctive orange and yellow collar.

emphasis /ˈɛmfəsɪs/ *noun* (PL. **emphases**) 1 special importance or attention: *lay special emphasis on something.* 2 greater force or loudness on certain words or parts of words to show that they are important or have a special meaning. 3 force or firmness of expression. [from Greek *emphasis*, outward appearance, implied meaning]

🔁 1, 2 stress, accent. 1 weight, significance, importance, priority, underscoring, prominence, pre-eminence, attention. 3 intensity, strength, urgency, positiveness, insistence, force, power.

emphasize or **emphasise** *verb* to put emphasis on.

🔁 stress, accentuate, underline, highlight, accent, feature, dwell on, weight, point up, spotlight, play up, insist on, press home, intensify, strengthen, punctuate.
🔁 play down, understate.

emphatic /ɛmˈfatɪk/ *adj.* 1 expressed with or expressing emphasis. 2 *said of a person* speaking firmly and forcefully. [from Greek *emphatikos*]

🔁 FORCEFUL, POSITIVE, INSISTENT, DEFINITE. 1 marked, pronounced, significant, strong, striking, vigorous, distinct, energetic, forcible, impressive, powerful, telling, vivid, direct, unequivocal, absolute, categorical.
🔁 TENTATIVE, HESITANT. 1 understated.

emphatically *adv.* with emphasis or forceful expression: *replied emphatically that he was not going.*

emphysema /ɛmfɪˈsiːmə/ *noun Medicine* the presence of air in the body tissues. In *pulmonary emphysema*, the alveoli (air sacs) of the lungs become over-inflated and damaged, causing laboured breathing. [from Greek, from *emphysaein*, to swell]

empire *noun* 1 a group of nations or states under the control of a single ruler or ruling power, especially an emperor or empress. 2 the period of time during which such

control is exercised. 3 a large commercial or industrial organization controlling many separate firms, especially one headed by one person. 4 *often facetious* that part of an organization, a company, etc under the management of a particular person. 5 *formal, literary* supreme control or power. See also EMPEROR, EMPRESS, IMPERIAL. [from Old French *empire*, from Latin *imperium*, command, power]

🔁 1 domain, dominion, kingdom, realm, commonwealth, territory.

empire-builder *noun* a person who ambitiously seeks extra personal authority within an organization.

empire-building *noun colloq..* the practice of ambitiously acquiring extra personal authority within an organization.

empirical /ɪmˈpɪrɪkəl/ or **empiric** *adj.* 1 based on experiment, observation, or experience, rather than on theory. 2 regarding experiment and observation as more important than scientific law. [from Greek *empeiria*, experience]

empirically *adv.* by means of experiment rather than theory.

empiricism /ɪmˈpɪrɪsɪzm/ *noun* 1 *Philos.* the theory or philosophy stating that knowledge can only be gained through experiment and observation. 2 the application of empirical methods, eg to science.

empiricist /ɪmˈpɪrɪsɪst/ *noun* a person who believes in experiment as a basis of knowledge.

emplacement *noun* 1 *Mil.* a strongly defended position from which a field gun may be fired. 2 *formal* the act of putting, or the state of having been put, into place. [from French *emplacement*]

employ — *verb* 1 to give (usually paid) work to. 2 (**be employed in something**) to have one's time and attention devoted to it: *busily employed in writing letters.* 3 to use. — *noun formal* the state of being in paid work; employment. [from French *employer*]

🔁 *verb* 1 engage, hire, take on, recruit, enlist, commission, retain. 3 use, utilize, make use of, occupy, take up, apply, bring to bear, exercise.

employable *adj.*, *said of a person* suitable to be employed.

employed *adj.* having a job; working.

employee /ɛmˈplɔɪiː, ɪmˈplɔɪ/ *noun* a person who works for another in return for payment.

🔁 worker, member of staff, job-holder, hand, wage-earner.

employer *noun* a person or company that employs workers.

🔁 boss, proprietor, owner, manager, *colloq.* gaffer, management, company, firm, business, establishment.

employment *noun* 1 the act of employing or the state of being employed. 2 an occupation, esp regular paid work. See also UNEMPLOYMENT.

🔁 1 recruitment, enlistment, engagement, hiring, use, exercise, application, utilization. 2 job, work, occupation, situation, business, calling, profession, line, vocation, trade, pursuit, craft.
🔁 1 unemployment.

employment agency an organization which finds jobs for people, and workers for companies seeking them.

employment exchange *Brit.* the former name for a job centre.

emporium /ɛmˈpɔːrɪəm/ *noun* (PL. **emporiums, emporia**) *formal* a shop, especially a large one selling a wide variety of goods. [from Greek *emporion*, trading station]

empower *verb* (**empowered, empowering**) 1 (**empower someone to do something**) to give them authority or official permission to do it. 2 to give power to; to give the ability to make decisions and choices to.

◾ 1 authorize, warrant, enable, license, sanction, permit, entitle, commission, delegate, qualify. 2 enable, equip.

empress /ˈɛmprəs/ *noun* 1 the female ruler of an empire or of a country which was once the centre of an empire. 2 the wife or widow of an emperor. [from Old French *emperesse*, from *emperere*, emperor]

emptily *adv.* with an empty manner; without meaning: *replied emptily that he didn't know.*

emptiness *noun* 1 an empty state; being empty. 2 lack of substance or meaning.

◾ 1 vacuum, vacantness, void, hollowness, hunger, bareness, barrenness, desolation. 2 futility, meaninglessness, worthlessness, aimlessness, ineffectiveness, unreality.
◾ 1 fullness.

empty — *adj.* (**emptier, emptiest**) 1 having nothing inside. 2 not occupied, inhabited, or furnished. 3 having no purpose or value: *an empty existence.* 4 not likely to be satisfied or carried out: *empty promises.* 5 without expression; blank. 6 (**empty of something**) completely without it: *a life empty of meaning.* — *verb trans., intrans.* (**empties, emptied**) 1 to make or become empty. 2 to tip, pour, or fall out of a container. — *noun* (PL. **empties**) *colloq.* an empty container, especially a bottle. [from Anglo-Saxon *æmetig*, unoccupied]

◾ *adj.* 1 vacant, void, hollow, unfilled, blank, clear. 2 unoccupied, uninhabited, deserted, bare, desolate. 3, 4 meaningless, vain, worthless, useless. 3 futile, aimless, senseless, trivial. 4 insubstantial, ineffective, insincere. 5 vacuous, inane, expressionless, blank, vacant. 6 devoid of, without, deprived of, innocent of, lacking in. *verb* POUR OUT, POUR OFF, DRAIN, DISCHARGE. 1 exhaust, clear, evacuate, vacate, unload, void, gut.
◾ *adj.* 1 full. 3 meaningful. *verb* FILL.

empty-handed *adj.* 1 carrying nothing. 2 having gained or achieved nothing.

empty-headed *adj.* foolish; having no capacity for serious thought.

◾ inane, silly, frivolous, *colloq.* feather-brained, *colloq.* scatterbrained.

empyreal /ɛmpɪˈriːəl, ɛmˈpɪriəl/ *adj. literary* relating to the sky.

empyrean /ɛmpɪˈriːən/ *noun poetic* (*usually* **the empyrean**) the sky. [from Latin *empyreus*, from Greek *empyros*, fiery]

EMS *abbrev.* European Monetary System.

EMU *abbrev.* Economic and Monetary Union (between EC countries).

emu /ˈiːmjuː/ *noun* a large flightless but swift-running bird, almost 2m tall with coarse brown plumage, found in deserts, plains, and forests in Australia. [from Portuguese *ema*, ostrich]

emulate /ˈɛmjʊleɪt/ *verb* 1 to try hard to equal or be better than. 2 to imitate. [from Latin *aemulari*, to rival]

◾ 1 equal, match, come up to, compete with, contend with, rival, vie with. 2 copy, mimic, follow, imitate, echo.

emulation *noun* emulating; trying to equal someone else.

emulsifier /ɪˈmʌlsɪfaɪə(r)/ or **emulsifying agent** a chemical substance that coats the surface of droplets of one liquid so that they can remain dispersed throughout a second liquid, forming a stable emulsion. Emulsifiers are used in the food industry to prevent the coalescence of oil droplets in oil-water emulsions such as margarine, ice cream, and salad cream.

emulsify *verb trans., intrans.* (**emulsifies, emulsified**) to make or become an emulsion.

emulsion — *noun* 1 *Chem.* a colloid consisting of a stable mixture of two immiscible liquids (such as oil and water), in which small droplets of one liquid are dispersed uniformly throughout the other, eg salad cream, low-fat spreads. 2 *Photog.* the light-sensitive material that is used to coat photographic film, paper, etc. 3 emulsion paint. — *verb colloq.* to apply emulsion paint to. [from Latin *emulgere*, to drain out]

emulsion paint water-based paint.

EN *abbrev.* Enrolled Nurse.

en- *prefix* 1 forming verbs with the meaning 'put into, on, or on to': *entrust / enthrone.* 2 forming verbs with the meaning 'cause to be': *enrich / enfeeble.* 3 forming verbs with the meaning 'in, into' or with a meaning simply stronger than that of the base verb: *entangle / enliven.*

-en *suffix* 1 forming verbs with the meaning 'make or become (more)': *deepen / sadden.* 2 forming verbs with the meaning 'give, endow with': *strengthen.* 3 forming adjectives with the meaning 'made or consisting of': *wooden.*

enable *verb* 1 to make able; to give the necessary means, power, or authority to. 2 to make possible.

◾ ALLOW, PERMIT. 1 equip, qualify, empower, authorize, sanction, warrant, prepare, fit, license, commission. 2 facilitate.
◾ PREVENT, INHIBIT. 1 forbid.

enact *verb* 1 to act or perform, on stage or in real life. 2 to establish by law.

◾ 1 act out, perform, play, portray, represent, depict. 2 decree, ordain, order, authorize, command, legislate, sanction, ratify, pass, establish.
◾ 2 repeal, rescind.

enactment *noun formal* 1 the act of passing, or the passing of, a parliamentary bill into law. 2 that which is enacted; a law.

enamel /ɛˈnaməl, ɪˈnaməl/ — *noun* 1 the smooth extremely hard white material, rich in calcium salts, that covers and protects the crown of each tooth in vertebrates. 2 a coloured translucent or opaque ceramic coating that is fused to the surface of articles made of metal, pottery, or glass, for decoration or protection. 3 a paint or varnish that produces a coating resembling this. 4 a metal, pottery, or glass object decorated with enamel. — *verb* (**enamelled, enamelling**) to apply (a coloured translucent or opaque ceramic coating) to the surface of an article, for decoration or protection. [from Old French *enameler*, from *esmail*, enamel]

enamoured /ɪˈnaməd/ *adj.* 1 (**enamoured of someone**) *formal, literary* in love with them. 2 (**enamoured of something**) very fond of it, pleased with it, or enthusiastic about it. [from Old French *enamourer*, from *amour*, love]

◾ 1 infatuated with, in love with, smitten with. 2 fond of, enchanted with, charmed with *or* by, captivated by, entranced with, keen on, taken with, fascinated by.

en bloc /ɒn ˈblɒk/ *adv.* all together; as one unit. [from French *en bloc*, in a block]

enc. *abbrev.* 1 enclosed. 2 enclosure.

encamp *verb trans., intrans.* to settle in a camp.

encampment *noun* settlement in a camp.

encapsulate *verb* 1 to express concisely the main points or ideas of, or capture the essence of. 2 to enclose in, or as if in, a capsule.

⊟ **1** summarize, précis, sum up, epitomize, embody, render.

encapsulation *noun* encapsulating; precise expression of an idea.

encase *verb* **1** to enclose in, or as if in, a case. **2** to surround or cover.

⊟ ENCLOSE. **1** box in. **2** surround, cover, coat, blanket, envelop, wrap.

encasement *noun* enclosing in a case.

encash *verb* to convert into cash; to cash.

encaustic /ɛŋ'kɒstɪk/ — *adj.*, *said of ceramics* decorated using pigments melted in wax and burnt into the clay. — *noun* **1** the technique which uses pigments in this way. **2** a piece of pottery or any other article decorated using this technique. [from Greek *enkaustikos*, from *enkaiein*, to burn in]

-ence *suffix* forming nouns indicating: **1** a state or quality, or an action, etc which shows a state or quality: *confidence / diligence / impertinence*. **2** an action: *reference*. [from French *-ence*, from Latin *-entia*]

encephalin /ɛn'sɛfəlɪn/ or **enkephalin** /ɛn'kɛfəlɪn/ *noun Biochem.* either of two chemical compounds that occur naturally in the brain and spinal cord, and have pain-relieving properties similar to those of morphine and other opiates. [from Greek *en*, in + *kephale*, head]

encephalitis /ɛnsɛfə'laɪtɪs/ *noun Medicine* inflammation of the brain, usually as a result of a viral or bacterial infection, or an allergic reaction. [from Greek *enkephalos*, brain + -ITIS]

encephalo- or **encephal-** *combining form Anat.* forming words relating to the brain. [from Greek *enkephalos*, from *en*, in + *kephale*, head]

encephalogram /ɛn'sɛfələgram/, **encephalograph** /ɛn'sɛfələgrɑːf/ same as ELECTROENCEPHALOGRAM, ELECTROENCEPHALOGRAPH.

enchain *verb literary* **1** to put in chains. **2** to hold or fix (attention, etc). [from French *enchaîner*]

enchant *verb* **1** to charm or delight. **2** to put a magic spell on. [from French *enchanter*, from Latin *incantare*, to sing a magic spell over]

⊟ ENTRANCE, ENTHRAL, SPELLBIND, HYPNOTIZE, MESMERIZE. **1** captivate, charm, fascinate, enrapture, attract, allure, appeal, delight, thrill.

⊟ **1** repel.

enchanted *adj.* charmed; bewitched.

enchanter or **enchantress** *noun* **1** a person who casts spells. **2** a charming person, especially one who sets out to be so.

enchanting *adj.* extremely pleasant or attractive.

⊟ charming, entrancing, captivating, delightful, lovely, pleasant, attractive, appealing, endearing.

enchantment *noun* **1** the act of enchanting or state of being enchanted. **2** a magic spell. **3** charm; attraction.

enchilada /ɛntʃɪ'lɑːdə/ *noun* a Mexican dish consisting of a flour tortilla with a meat filling, served with a chilli-flavoured sauce. [from Spanish *enchilar*, to season with chilli]

encircle *verb* to surround, form a circle round.

⊟ surround, besiege, encompass, ring, circle, girdle, enclose.

encirclement *noun* encircling, especially of territory.

encl. *abbrev.* **1** enclosed. **2** enclosure.

enclave /'ɛŋkleɪv/ *noun* **1** a small country or state entirely surrounded by foreign territory. **2** a distinct racial or cultural group isolated within a country. [from French *enclave*, from Latin *inclavare*, to lock up]

enclose *verb* **1** to put inside a letter or its envelope. **2** to shut in or surround.

⊟ **1** insert, attach. **2** encircle, encompass, surround, fence, hedge, hem in, bound, encase, embrace, envelop, confine, hold, shut in, wrap, pen, cover, circumscribe.

enclosed *adj.* put inside something, especially an envelope.

enclosure /ɪŋ'kloʊʒə(r)/ *noun* **1** the process of enclosing or being enclosed, especially with reference to common land. **2** land surrounded by a fence or wall. **3** an enclosed space at a sporting event. **4** an additional paper or other item included with a letter.

⊟ **2, 3** paddock. **2** pen, pound, compound, fold, stockade, sty, corral, cloister. **3** arena, court, ring.

encode *verb* to express in or convert into code.

encomiastic /ɛŋkoʊmɪ'astɪk/ *adj. literary* serving as an encomium; flattering.

encomium /ɛŋ'koʊmɪəm/ *noun* (PL. **encomiums**, **encomia**) *formal* a formal speech or piece of writing praising someone. [from Greek *enkomion*, song of praise]

encompass /ɪŋ'kʌmpəs/ *verb* **1** to include or contain, especially contain a wide range or coverage of. **2** to surround. **3** to cause or bring about.

⊟ **1** include, cover, embrace, contain, comprise, admit, incorporate, involve, embody, comprehend. **2** encircle, circle, ring, surround, girdle, envelop, circumscribe, hem in, enclose, hold.

encore /'ɒŋkɔː(r)/ — *noun* a repetition of a performance, or an additional performed item, after the end of a concert, etc. — *interj.* an enthusiastic call from the audience for such a peformance. — *verb* to call for an extra performance of or from. [from French *encore*, again]

encounter — *verb* (**encountered**, **encountering**) **1** to meet, especially unexpectedly. **2** to meet with (difficulties, etc). **3** to meet in battle or conflict. — *noun* **1** a chance meeting. **2** a fight or battle. [from Old French *encontrer*, from Latin *contra*, against]

⊟ *verb* **1, 2** meet, come across, *colloq.* run into. **1** happen on, come upon, chance upon, run across. **2** confront, face, experience. **3** fight, clash with, combat, cross swords with, engage, grapple with, struggle with *or* against, strive with *or* against, contend with *or* against. *noun* **1** meeting, brush, confrontation. **2** clash, fight, combat, conflict, contest, battle, set-to, dispute, engagement, action, skirmish, collision.

encounter group *Psychol.* a group of people who meet together to discuss their feelings so as to establish greater self-awareness.

encourage *verb* **1** to give support, confidence, or hope to. **2** to urge someone to do something. **3** to promote or recommend. [from French *encourager*]

⊟ **1** inspire, hearten, stimulate, rouse, buoy up, cheer, reassure, rally, comfort, console. **2** urge, exhort, incite, *colloq.* egg on, spur on. **3** promote, advance, aid, boost, forward, further, foster, support, help, strengthen.

⊟ DISCOURAGE. **1** depress.

encouragement *noun* **1** support; a source of increased confidence. **2** urging. **3** promotion and support.

⊟ **1** support, reassurance, inspiration, cheer, pep talk,

stimulation, consolation. **2** urging, exhortation, incitement. **3** promotion, furtherance, support, sponsorship, help, aid, boost, *colloq.* shot in the arm, incentive, stimulus.
🔁 DISCOURAGEMENT. **1** disapproval.

encouraging *adj.* **1** giving support or courage. **2** giving hope of success or improvement.

🔁 **1** inspiring, heartening, reassuring, stimulating, uplifting, comforting, supportive. **2** promising, hopeful, auspicious, cheering, bright, rosy, cheerful, satisfactory.
🔁 DISCOURAGING.

encouragingly *adv.* so as to increase courage or confidence: *an encouragingly good response.*

encroach *verb intrans.* (*usually* **encroach on someone or something**) **1** to intrude or extend gradually or stealthily on someone else's land, etc. **2** to go beyond the fair limits of a right, etc. **3** to overstep proper or agreed limits. [from Old French *encrochier*, to seize]

🔁 **1** intrude on, invade, impinge on, trespass on, infringe on, make inroads into, *colloq.* muscle in on, usurp. **2, 3** overstep, infringe.

encroachment *noun* encroaching; intrusion on another's territory or rights.

encrust *verb* to cover with a thick hard coating, eg of jewels or ice. [from Latin *incrustare*]

encrustation *noun* encrusting; a hard crust or coating.

encumber /ɪŋˈkʌmbə(r)/ *verb* (**encumbered, encumbering**) **1** to prevent the free and easy movement of; to hamper or impede. **2** to burden with a load or debt. [from Old French *encombrer*, to block]

🔁 **1** hamper, hinder, impede, handicap, cramp, slow down, obstruct, inconvenience, prevent, retard. **2** burden, overload, weigh down, saddle, oppress.

encumbrance /ɪŋˈkʌmbrəns/ *noun* an impediment, hindrance or burden.

🔁 impediment, hindrance, handicap, obstruction, obstacle, inconvenience, difficulty, liability, burden, cumbrance, load, cross, millstone, albatross.

-ency *suffix* forming nouns indicating a state or quality, or something which shows a state or quality: *efficiency / inconsistency.* [from Latin *-entia*]

encyclical /ɛnˈsɪklɪkəl/ — *noun Relig.* a letter sent by the pope to all Roman Catholic bishops. — *adj. formal, said of a letter* for general or wide circulation. [from Greek *enkyklios*, from *en*, in + *kyklos*, circle]

encyclopedia or **encyclopaedia** /ɪnsaɪkləˈpiːdɪə/ *noun* a reference work containing information on every branch of knowledge, or on one particular branch, usually arranged in alphabetical order. [from Greek *enkyklios paideia*, general education]

encyclopedic or **encyclopaedic** /ɪnsaɪkləˈpiːdɪk/ *adj.* **1** *said of knowledge* full and detailed. **2** of, belonging to, or like an encyclopedia.

🔁 **1** detailed, thorough, extensive, comprehensive, exhaustive, all-embracing.

encyclopedist or **encyclopaedist** /ɪnsaɪkləˈpiːdɪst/ *noun* a compiler of encyclopedias.

end — *noun* **1** the point or part farthest from the beginning, or either of the points or parts farthest from the middle, where something stops. **2** a finish or conclusion: *come to an end.* **3** a piece left over: *a cigarette end.* **4** death or destruction: *meet one's end.* **5** an object or purpose: *the ends*

justify the means. **6** *Sport* one of the two halves of a pitch or court defended by a team, player, etc. **7** the part of a project, etc for which one is responsible: *they've had a few problems at their end.* — *verb* **1** *trans., intrans.* to finish or cause to finish; to reach a conclusion or cease to exist. **2** to put an end to; to destroy. — **at the end of the day** *colloq.* when everything has been taken into account. **end it all** *colloq.* to kill oneself. **the end of the road** the point beyond which one cannot continue or survive. **end on** or **end to end** with ends touching. **end up** ... *colloq.* **1** to arrive or find oneself ... eventually: *we ended up in Manchester.* **2** (**end up as** ...) to become ... finally: *they ended up as circus clowns.* **in the end** finally; after much discussion, work, etc. **keep** or **hold one's end up** *colloq.* to fulfil one's promises or obligations in spite of difficulties. **make ends meet** to live within one's income and avoid debts. **no end** *colloq.* very much; very many. **on end 1** vertical; standing straight up. **2** continuously; without a pause. [from Anglo-Saxon *ende*]

🔁 *noun* **1** extremity, boundary, edge, limit, tip. **2** finish, conclusion, termination, close, completion, cessation, culmination, dénouement. **3** remainder, tip, butt, left-over, remnant, stub, scrap, fragment. **4** death, demise, destruction, extermination, downfall, doom, ruin, dissolution. **5** aim, object, objective, purpose, intention, goal, point, reason, design. *verb* **1** finish, close, cease, conclude, stop, terminate, wind up. **2** destroy, annihilate, exterminate, extinguish, ruin, abolish, dissolve.
🔁 *noun* **2** beginning, start. **4** birth. *verb* **1** begin, start, commence.

endanger *verb* (**endangered, endangering**) to put in danger; to expose to possible loss or injury.

🔁 imperil, hazard, jeopardize, put at risk, expose, threaten, compromise.
🔁 protect.

endangered species any plant or animal species that is in danger of extinctions.

endear *verb* (**endear someone to someone** or **something**) to cause them to be beloved or liked.

endearing *adj.* arousing feelings of affection.

🔁 lovable, charming, appealing, attractive, winsome, delightful, enchanting.

endearingly *adv.* with an endearing or affectionate manner.

endearment *noun* **1** a word or phrase expressing affection. **2** affection or fondness.

endeavour /ɪnˈdɛvə(r)/ — *verb* (**endeavour to do something**) to try to do it, especially seriously and with effort. — *noun* a determined attempt or effort. [from Middle English *endeveren*, to exert oneself, from French *devoir*, duty]

🔁 *verb* attempt, try, strive, aim, aspire, undertake, venture, struggle, labour, take pains. *noun* attempt, effort, go, try, *colloq.* shot, *colloq.* stab, undertaking, enterprise, aim, venture.

endemic /ɛnˈdɛmɪk/ — *adj.* **1** *said of a disease, etc* present or regularly found within a particular population or geographical region. **2** *Biol., said of a species or population* confined to a particular geographical region. — *noun* an endemic disease or plant. [from Greek *endemos*, native]

ending *noun* **1** the end, especially of a story, poem, etc. **2** *Grammar* the end part of a word, especially an inflection.

🔁 **1** end, close, finish, completion, termination, conclusion, culmination, climax, resolution, consummation, dénouement, finale, epilogue.

■ **1** beginning, start.

....

endive /'endaɪv/ *noun* an annual or perennial plant (*Cichorium endivia*), native to Asia and widely cultivated elsewhere, that has crisp leaves with curly edges and a slightly bitter taste. The leaves are often used in salads, and are grown in the absence of sunlight for several weeks before harvesting in order to remove the bitter taste. [from French *endive*]

endless *adj.* having no end, or seeming to have no end.

....

■ infinite, boundless, unlimited, measureless, everlasting, ceaseless, perpetual, constant, continual, continuous, undying, eternal, interminable, monotonous.

■ finite, limited, temporary.

....

endlessly *adv.* without end, or seemingly without end.

endmost *adj.* farthest; nearest the end.

endo- *combining form* internal; inside. See also ECTO-, ENTO-, EXO-. [from Greek *endon*, within]

endocarditis /endəʊkɑː'daɪtɪs/ *noun Medicine* inflammation of the delicate membrane that lines the heart (the endocardium) and of the heart valves. [from Greek *endon*, within + *kardia*, heart]

endocrine /'endəʊkrɪn/ *adj.* **1** *Physiol.* relating to internal secretions, or to a pathway or structure that secretes internally. **2** *said of a gland* ductless and producing and secreting one or more hormones directly into the bloodstream. [from ENDO- + Greek *krinein*, to separate]

endocrinology /endəʊkrɪ'nɒlədʒɪ/ *noun Physiol.* the scientific study of those glands, known as endocrine glands, that produce and secrete hormones, and of the hormones themselves.

endoderm /'endəʊdɜːm/ *noun Zool.* the innermost layer of cells of the embryo in a multicellular animal that has two or more layers of body tissue. [from ENDO- + Greek *derma*, skin]

endodontics /endəʊ'dɒntɪks/ *noun Medicine* the branch of dentistry concerned with the diagnosis, treatment, and prevention of disorders of the tooth pulp, including root canal treatment.

endogamy /ɛn'dɒgəmɪ/ *noun Anthropol.* the practice or rule of marrying only within one's own group. [from ENDO- + Greek *gamos*, marriage]

endomorph *noun* a person of rounded or plump build, sometimes said to be associated with a calm, easy-going personality. [from ENDO- + Greek *morphe*, form]

endoplasm *noun Biol.* the central portion of the cytoplasm of a cell.

endorphin /ɛn'dɔːfɪn/ *noun Biochem.* any of a group of chemical compounds that occur naturally in the brain and have similar pain-relieving properties to morphine. [from ENDO- + MORPHINE]

endorse *verb* **1** to write one's signature on the back of (a document), especially on the back of (a cheque) to specify oneself or another person as payee. **2** to make a note of an offence on (a driving licence). **3** to state one's approval of or support for. [from Old French *endosser*, to put on the back, from Latin *dorsum*, back]

....

■ **1** sign, countersign. **3** approve, sanction, authorize, support, back, affirm, ratify, confirm, vouch for, advocate, warrant, recommend, subscribe to, sustain, adopt.

....

endorsement *noun* **1** endorsing or confirming. **2** a signature or other mark endorsing a document. **3** a record of a conviction entered on a driving licence.

....

■ **1** approval, sanction, authorization, support, backing, affirmation, ratification, confirmation, advocacy, warrant,

recommendation, commendation, seal of approval, testimonial, *colloq.* OK. **2** signature, countersignature.

....

endoscope /ɛndəʊ'skəʊp/ *noun Medicine* a long thin flexible instrument containing bundles of optical fibres and having a light at one end, used for viewing internal body cavities and organs.

endoscopic *adj. Medicine* involving the use of an endoscope.

endoscopy /ɛn'dɒskəpɪ/ *noun Medicine* examination of the internal organs by means of an endoscope.

endoskeleton *noun Zool.* in vertebrates (animals with backbones), such as mammals, birds, and fish, an internal skeleton made of bone or cartilage.

endothelium *noun* (PL. **endothelia**) *Zool.* a single layer of cells that lines the internal surfaces of the heart, blood vessels, and lymph vessels.

endothermic *adj. Chem.* involving the absorption of heat.

endow /ɛn'daʊ/ *verb* **1** to provide a source of income for (a hospital, place of learning, etc). **2** (**to be endowed with something**) to have a quality, ability, etc: *endowed with common sense*. [from Old French *endouer*, from Latin *dos*, dowry]

....

■ **1** bestow, bequeath, leave, will, give, donate, confer, grant, present, award, finance, fund, support, make over, furnish, provide, supply. **2** have, possess, enjoy, be endued with, be blessed with.

....

endowment /ɪn'daʊmənt/ *noun* **1** the act of endowing. **2** a sum endowed. **3** a natural talent or skill.

....

■ **1, 2** bequest, award, grant, gift, donation, provision, settlement. **1** bestowal. **2** legacy, fund, benefaction, dowry, income, revenue. **3** talent, attribute, faculty, gift, ability, quality, flair, genius, qualification.

....

endowment assurance or **endowment insurance** a form of insurance in which a set sum is paid at a certain date, or earlier in the event of death.

endpaper *noun* one of the two leaves at the front or back of a hardback book, fixed with paste to the inside of the cover, to give strength to the binding.

end-product *noun* the final product of a series of operations, especially industrial processes.

endue /ɪn'djuː/ *verb* (**endue someone with something**) to provide with a certain quality. [from Old French *enduire*, from Latin *inducere*, to lead in]

endurable *adj.* capable of being endured.

....

■ bearable, tolerable, supportable, withstandable, manageable.

....

endurance *noun* **1** the capacity for, or the state of, patient toleration. **2** the ability to withstand physical hardship or strain.

....

■ **1** fortitude, patience, resignation, stoicism, tenacity, perseverance, resolution, stability, persistence, toleration. **2** staying power, stamina, strength, toughness, durability.

....

endure *verb* **1** to bear patiently, put up with. **2** *intrans. formal* to continue to exist; to last. [from Old French *endurer*, from Latin *indurare*, to harden]

....

■ ABIDE. **1** bear, stand, put up with, tolerate, weather, brave, cope with, face, go through, experience, submit to, suffer, sustain, undergo, withstand, *colloq.* stick, *colloq.* stomach, allow, permit, support. **2** last, remain, live, survive, stay, persist, hold, prevail.

....

enduring *adj.* lasting.

▣ lasting, durable, permanent, perpetual, abiding, continuing, long-standing.

end-user *noun* a person, company, etc that will buy and use a product that is being sold.

endways *adv.* **1** with the end forward or upward. **2** end to end.

enema /ˈɛnəmə/ *noun* (PL. **enemas**, **enemata**) *Medicine* **1** a procedure whereby a quantity of liquid is injected into the rectum through a tube passed through the anus, usually for cleansing or medicinal purposes. **2** the liquid injected in this way. [from Greek *enienai*, to send in]

enemy — *noun* (PL. **enemies**) **1** a person who is actively opposed to someone else. **2** a hostile nation or force, or a member of it. **3** an opponent or adversary. **4** a person, thing, etc that opposes or acts against: *cleanliness is the enemy of disease.* — *adj.* hostile; belonging to a hostile nation or force. [from Old French *enemi*, from Latin *inimicus*]

▣ *noun* **1, 2, 3** adversary, opponent, foe. **1** antagonist, opposer. **2** the opposition, the other side. **3** rival, competitor.
▣ *noun* FRIEND, ALLY.

energetic *adj.* having or displaying energy; forceful; vigorous. [from Greek *energetikos*]

▣ lively, vigorous, active, animated, dynamic, spirited, tireless, zestful, brisk, strong, forceful, potent, powerful, strenuous, high-powered.
▣ lethargic, sluggish, inactive, idle.

energetically *adv.* with energy or vigour; forcefully.

energize or **energise** *verb* **1** to stimulate, invigorate, or enliven. **2** to provide energy for the operation of (a machine, etc).

energy *noun* (PL. **energies**) **1** the capacity for vigorous activity; liveliness or vitality. **2** force or forcefulness. **3** *Physics* the capacity to do work. Within a particular system, energy may be converted from one form to another, but is neither created nor destroyed, so the total energy content of the system remains constant (the law of conservation of energy). [from Greek *energeia*, from *en*, in + *ergon*, work]

▣ **1** liveliness, vigour, vivacity, vitality, animation, drive, dynamism, *colloq.* get-up-and-go, *colloq.* zip, life, spirit, verve, zest, zeal, ardour, fire, stamina. **2** force, forcefulness, strength, power, intensity.
▣ **1** lethargy, inertia. **2** weakness.

energy level *Physics* one of the fixed amounts of energy that an electron in an atom can possess at any given time.

enervate /ˈɛnəveɪt/ *verb* **1** to take energy or strength from. **2** to deprive of moral or mental vigour. [from Latin *enervare*, to weaken]

enervating *adj.* depriving of vigour.

enervation *noun* being enervated or deprived of vigour.

enfant terrible /ɒnfɒn təˈriːbl/ *noun* (PL. **enfants terribles**) a person with a reputation for indiscreet or embarrassing behaviour in public. [French, = dreadful child]

enfeeble *verb formal* to make weak.

enfeeblement *noun* making weak.

enfilade /ɛnfɪˈleɪd/ *Mil.* — *noun* a continuous burst of gunfire sweeping from end to end across a line of enemy soldiers. — *verb* to direct an enfilade at. [from French *enfiler*, to thread]

enfold *verb* **1** to wrap up, enclose. **2** to embrace.

▣ **1** wrap, wrap up, enclose, envelop, encase, shroud, swathe, surround. **2** embrace, clasp.

enforce *verb* **1** to cause (a law or decision) to be carried out. **2** (**enforce something on someone**) to impose (one's will, etc) on them. **3** to strengthen (an argument). **4** to persist in (a demand). [from Old French *enforcer*]

▣ **1** carry out, implement, apply, execute, administer, impose, prosecute. **2** impose (on), insist on, compel, require, urge. **3** reinforce, strengthen, back up.

enforceable *adj.* capable of being enforced.

enforcement *noun* the process of enforcing.

enfranchise /ɪnˈfrantʃaɪz/ *verb formal* **1** to give the right to vote in elections to. **2** to set free, especially from slavery. **3** to give (a town) the right to be represented in parliament. [from Old French *enfranchir*, to set free]

enfranchisement /ɪnˈfrantʃɪzmənt/ *noun* the conferring of rights, especially to vote in elections.

engage *verb* **1** to take on as a worker. **2** to book or reserve. **3** to attract or hold: *engage someone's attention.* **4** (**engage someone in something**) to involve or occupy them in it: *she engaged me in small talk.* **5** *intrans., trans. Mil.* to come or bring into battle: *engage the enemy / engage with the enemy.* **6** *trans., intrans.* to cause part of a machine, etc to fit into and lock with another part: *engage a gear / the gears engage.* — **engage in something** to take part in it. [from French *engager*]

▣ **1** employ, hire, appoint, take on, enlist, enrol, commission, recruit, contract. **3** attract, draw, catch, grip, occupy, hold, engross, absorb, busy. **4** involve in, draw into, occupy with. **5** fight, do battle (with), attack, encounter, combat. **6** interlock, mesh, interconnect, join, interact, attach. **engage in** participate in, take part in, embark on, take up, do, practise, involve oneself in, occupy onself with.
▣ **1** dismiss, discharge. **3** repel. **5, 6** disengage.

engagé /ɒngaˈʒeɪ/ *adj.* having or showing a political or moral commitment. [French, = engaged]

engaged *adj.* **1** (**engaged to someone**) bound by a promise to marry them. **2** (**engaged in something**) busy or occupied with it. **3** *said of a room, etc* not free or vacant; occupied; being used.

▣ **1** promised, *formal* betrothed, pledged, spoken for. **2** occupied in, busy with, engrossed in, immersed in, absorbed in, preoccupied with, involved in, employed in. **3** busy, in use, occupied, tied up, unavailable.

engagement *noun* **1** the act of engaging or state of being engaged. **2** a firm agreement between two people to marry. **3** an arrangement made in advance; an appointment. **4** *Mil.* a battle.

▣ **2** *formal* betrothal, vow, promise, pledge. **3** appointment, meeting, date, commitment, obligation, arrangement, assignation, fixture, rendezvous. **4** fight, battle, combat, conflict, action, encounter, confrontation, contest.

engaging *adj.* charming or attractive.

▣ charming, attractive, appealing, captivating, pleasing, delightful, winsome, lovable, likable, pleasant, fetching, fascinating, agreeable.
▣ repulsive, repellant.

engagingly *adv.* with a charming or attractive manner.

engender /ɪnˈdʒɛndə(r)/ *verb* (**engendered, engendering**) to produce or cause (especially feelings or emotions). [from French *engendrer*]

◨ cause, produce, occasion, bring about, create, inspire, generate, arouse, kindle.

engine *noun* **1** a machine that is used to convert some form of energy, especially the heat energy released by a burning fuel, into mechanical energy that can be used to perform useful work. **2** a railway locomotive. **3** *formal* a device or instrument: *an engine of destruction*. [from Old French *engin*, from Latin *ingenium*, device]

◨ **1** motor, machine, mechanism, dynamo, appliance, contraption, apparatus. **2** locomotive, diesel, shunter. **3** device, instrument, tool.

Types of engine include: diesel, donkey, fuel injection, internal combustion, jet, petrol, steam, turbine, turbojet, turboprop, V-engine.

engine driver a person who drives a railway locomotive.

engineer — *noun* **1** a person who is professionally qualified to design, construct, or maintain engines or machinery. **2** (*also* **civil engineer**) a person who is professionally qualified to design or construct roads, bridges, railways, canals, tunnels, docks, sewers, etc. **3** an officer in charge of a ship's engines. **4** a member of the armed forces who is trained to plan and construct military fortifications, roads, trenches, etc. **5** *formal* the person who devises or brings about something. — *verb* **1** *often derog.* to arrange or bring about by skill or deviousness. **2** to design or construct by engineering.

◨ *noun* **1** mechanic, technician, engine driver. **5** designer, originator, planner, inventor, deviser, mastermind, architect, author. *verb* **1** plan, contrive, plot, devise, mastermind, originate, cause, bring about, create, manipulate, control, orchestrate, effect.

engineering *noun* the application of scientific knowledge, especially that concerned with matter and energy, to the practical problems of design, construction, operation, and maintenance of devices encountered in everyday life.

English — *adj.* **1** relating to England or the people of England. **2** *chiefly North Amer.* relating to Great Britain or its inhabitants (this use is often offensive to non-English inhabitants of Britain). **3** of or using the English language. — *noun* **1** the main language of Britain, N America, a great part of the British Commonwealth, and some other countries. **2** (**the English**) the people of England. — **Middle English** English as spoken and written between about 1150 and 1500. **Old English** English as spoken and written until about 1150. [from Anglo-Saxon *Englisc*]

English breakfast a cooked breakfast, usually consisting of several dishes or courses.

English horn same as COR ANGLAIS.

Englishman or **Englishwoman** *noun* a native or citizen of England.

engorged *adj.* **1** crammed full. **2** *Physiol.* congested with blood. [from EN- + GORGE]

engrave *verb* **1** to carve (letters or designs) on stone, wood, metal, etc. **2** to decorate (stone, etc) in this way. **3** to fix or impress deeply (on the mind, etc). [from EN- + obsolete *grave*, to carve]

◨ **1, 2** inscribe, cut, carve, chisel, etch, chase. **3** imprint, impress, fix, stamp, lodge.

engraver *noun* a person who engraves letters or designs, especially professionally.

engraving *noun* **1** the art of carving designs on stone, etc. **2** a piece of stone, etc decorated in this way. **3** a print taken from an engraved metal plate.

◨ **1, 2** carving. **1** etching, cutting, chiselling, inscription. **3** print, etching, impression, woodcut, plate, block.

engross /ɪnˈgrəʊs/ *verb* to take up completely the attention and interest of. [from Old French *engrosser*, from *en gros*, completely]

◨ absorb, occupy, engage, grip, hold, preoccupy, rivet, fascinate, captivate, enthral, arrest, involve, intrigue.
⊟ bore.

engrossed *adj.* having one's attention fully occupied; mentally absorbed.

engrossing *adj.* engaging one's full attention; highly interesting.

engulf *verb* **1** to swallow up completely. **2** to overwhelm. [from EN- + *gulf*, to swallow]

◨ **1** swallow up, devour. **2** overwhelm, swamp, flood, submerge, overrun.

enhance *verb* to improve or increase the value, quality or intensity of (often something already good). [from Old French *enhauncer*]

◨ heighten, intensify, increase, improve, elevate, magnify, swell, exalt, raise, lift, boost, strengthen, reinforce, embellish.
⊟ reduce, minimize.

enhanced radiation weapon (ABBREV. **ERW**) a more precise term for NEUTRON BOMB.

enhancement *noun* increase in quality; improvement.

enigma /ɪˈnɪgmə/ *noun* **1** a puzzle or riddle. **2** a mysterious person, thing, or situation. [from Greek *ainigma*]

◨ MYSTERY, RIDDLE, PUZZLE. **1** problem, *colloq.* poser, brainteaser, conundrum.

enigmatic /ɛnɪgˈmatɪk/ *adj.* obscure; puzzling.

◨ mysterious, puzzling, cryptic, obscure, strange, perplexing.
⊟ simple, straightforward.

enigmatically *adv.* in an obscure or puzzling way.

enjoin *verb formal* **1** to order or command (someone) to do something. **2** (**enjoin something on someone**) to demand behaviour of a certain kind from them: *enjoin politeness on one's children*. **3** *Legal* (**enjoin someone from something**) to forbid them to do it, by means of an injunction. [from French *enjoindre*]

enjoy *verb* **1** to find pleasure in. **2** to have, experience, have the benefit of (something good): *the room enjoys sunlight all day*. — **enjoy oneself** to experience pleasure or happiness. [from Old French *enjoir*]

◨ **1** take pleasure in, delight in, appreciate, like, relish, revel in, rejoice in, savour. **enjoy oneself** have a good time, have fun, make merry.
⊟ **1** dislike, hate.

enjoyable *adj.* capable of being enjoyed; offering pleasure.

◨ pleasant, agreeable, delightful, pleasing, gratifying, entertaining, amusing, fun, delicious, good, satisfying.
⊟ disagreeable.

enjoyably *adv.* in an enjoyable or pleasurable way.

enjoyment *noun* **1** enjoying; deriving pleasure. **2** having or having the benefit of.

▤ 1 pleasure, delight, amusement, gratification, entertainment, relish, joy, fun, happiness, diversion, indulgence, recreation, zest, satisfaction. **2** possession, use, advantage, benefit.

▣ 1 displeasure.

enkindle *verb literary* **1** to set fire to. **2** to stir up (feelings), or arouse strong feelings in.

enlarge *verb* **1** *trans., intrans.* to make or become larger. **2** to reproduce (a photograph, etc) in a larger form. **3** *intrans.* (**enlarge on** or **upon something**) to speak or write about it at greater length or in greater detail.

▤ 1 increase, expand, augment, extend, magnify, inflate, swell, stretch, multiply, develop, amplify, widen, broaden, lengthen, heighten. **2** blow up. **3** elaborate on, *formal* expatiate on, *formal* dilate on.

▣ 1 diminish, shrink.

enlargement *noun* **1** something enlarged, esp a photographic print larger than the standard or original print. **2** the act of enlarging or the state of being enlarged. **3** the process of admitting new member countries to the European Union.

▤ 1 blow-up. **2** increase, expansion, augmentation, extension, magnification, inflation, swelling, stretching, multiplication, development, amplification.

enlighten *verb* (**enlightened, enlightening**) **1** to give more information to. **2** to free from ignorance or superstition.

▤ EDUCATE. 1 instruct, edify, inform, illuminate, teach, counsel, apprise, advise. **2** civilize, cultivate, convert.

▣ 1 confuse.

enlightened *adj.* having or showing awareness and understanding and a freedom from prejudice and superstition.

▤ informed, aware, knowledgeable, educated, civilized, cultivated, refined, sophisticated, conversant, wise, reasonable, liberal, open-minded, literate.

▣ ignorant, confused.

enlightening *adj.* providing information; freeing from ignorance or prejudice.

enlightenment *noun* **1** the act of enlightening or the state of being enlightened; freedom from ignorance or superstition. **2** (**Enlightenment**) a European philosophical movement of the 18c, founded in a belief in the superiority of reason.

enlist *verb* **1** *intrans.* to join one of the armed forces. **2** *trans.* to obtain the support and help of; to obtain (support and help).

▤ ENROL. 1 join (up), sign up, volunteer, enter. **2** engage, register, recruit, conscript, employ, gather, muster, secure, obtain, procure.

enlisted man or **enlisted woman** *North Amer., esp. US* a member of the armed forces below the rank of officer.

enlistment *noun* enlisting; joining one of the armed services.

enliven / ɪnˈlaɪvn, ɛnˈlaɪvn/ *verb* (**enlivened, enlivening**) to make (more) active, lively, or cheerful.

▤ liven up, put life into, animate, invigorate, revitalize, energize, brighten, cheer up, perk up, *colloq.* pep up.

enlivenment *noun* enlivening; making cheerful.

en masse / ɒn ˈmas/ all together; as a mass or group. [from French *en masse*]

enmesh *verb* to catch or trap in a net, or as if in a net; to entangle.

▤ catch, trap, snare, ensnare, entangle, tangle, embroil, mix up in.

enmity /ˈɛnmɪtɪ/ *noun* **1** the state or quality of being an enemy. **2** ill-will; hostility. [from Old French *enemistie*, from Latin *inimicus*, enemy]

▤ 2 animosity, hostility, antagonism, antipathy, discord, strife, feud, acrimony, bitterness, hatred, aversion, ill-will, bad blood, rancour, malevolence, malice, venom.

▣ FRIENDSHIP.

ennoble *verb* **1** to make (something) noble or dignified. **2** to make (someone) a member of the nobility.

▤ 1 dignify, uplift, elevate, raise, exalt, enhance.

ennoblement *noun* ennobling; making someone a member of the nobility.

ennui / ɒˈnwiː/ *noun literary* boredom or discontent caused by a lack of activity or excitement. [from French *ennui*, boredom]

ENO *abbrev.* English National Opera.

enormity *noun* (PL. **enormities**) **1** outrageousness or wickedness. **2** an outrageous or wicked act.

▤ INIQUITY, HORROR, EVIL. 1 wickedness, vileness, depravity, atrociousness, viciousness, monstrousness. **2** atrocity, outrage, crime, abomination, monstrosity.

enormous *adj.* extremely large; huge. [from Latin *enormis*, unusual]

▤ huge, immense, vast, gigantic, massive, colossal, tremendous, prodigious, gross, gargantuan, monstrous, mammoth, *colloq.* jumbo.

▣ small, tiny.

enormously *adv.* to a large extent; hugely: *enormously helpful.*

enough — *adj.* in the number or quantity needed: *enough food to eat.* — *adv.* **1** to the necessary degree or extent. **2** fairly: *she's pretty enough.* **3** quite: *oddly enough, I can't remember.* — *pron.* the amount needed. — **have had enough of something** to be able to tolerate no more of it. [from Anglo-Saxon *genoh*]

▤ *adj.* sufficient, adequate, ample, plenty, abundant. *adv.* **1** sufficiently, adequately, satisfactorily, amply. **2** reasonably, tolerably, passably, moderately, fairly. *noun* sufficiency, adequacy, plenty, abundance.

en passant / ɒn paˈsɒn/ in passing; by the way. [French, = in passing]

enquire, enquiry see INQUIRE, INQUIRY.

enrage *verb* to make very angry. [from Old French *enrager*]

▤ incense, infuriate, anger, madden, provoke, incite, inflame, exasperate, irritate, rile.

▣ calm, placate.

enraged *adj.* extremely angry.

▤ furious, angry, incensed, infuriated, beside oneself, fuming, *colloq.* boiling, *colloq.* livid, exasperated, irritated.

enrapture / ɪn'ræptʃə(r)/ *verb* to give intense pleasure or joy to.

▣ delight, entrance, enchant, captivate, fascinate, spellbind, charm, *colloq.* carry away.

enraptured or **enrapt** *adj.* intensely pleased or delighted.

enrich *verb* 1 to make rich or richer, especially better or stronger in quality, value, flavour, etc. 2 to make wealthy or wealthier.

▣ 1 enhance, improve, refine, develop, cultivate, augment, adorn, ornament, beautify, embellish, decorate, grace.
◪ IMPOVERISH.

enriched *adj.* made rich or richer.
enrichment *noun* making rich or richer; improvement in quality, etc.

enrol *verb* (**enrolled, enrolling**) 1 to add the name of (a person) to a list or roll, eg of members; to secure the membership or participation of. 2 *intrans.* to add one's own name to such a list; to become a member. [from Old French *enroller*]

▣ REGISTER, ENLIST, SIGN ON, SIGN UP. 1 recruit, engage, admit, record, list, note, inscribe. 2 join up.

enrolment *noun* enrolling; adding a name to a list.

▣ registration, recruitment, enlistment, admission, acceptance.

en route / ɒn 'ruːt/ on the way to a place. [French, = on the way]

ensconce *verb trans. literary, humorous* (*usually* **be ensconced**) to settle comfortably or safely. [from EN- + *sconce*, small fort]

ensemble / ɒn'sɒmbəl/ *noun* 1 a small group of musicians who regularly perform together. 2 a passage in opera, ballet, etc performed by all the singers, musicians, or dancers together. 3 a set of items of clothing worn together; an outfit. 4 all the parts of a thing considered as a whole. [from French *ensemble*, together]

▣ 1 group, band, orchestra, quartet, quintet, sextet, septet, octet, chorus, company, troupe. 3 outfit, costume, *colloq.* get-up, *colloq.* rig-out. 4 whole, total, entirety, sum, aggregate, set, collection.

enshrine *verb* 1 to enter and protect (a right, idea, etc) in the laws or constitution of a state, constitution of an organization, etc. 2 to place in a shrine.

enshroud / ɛn'ʃraʊd/ *verb* 1 to cover completely; to hide by covering up. 2 to cover in a shroud.

ensign / 'ɛnsaɪn, 'ɛnsən/ *noun* 1 the flag of a nation or regiment. 2 a coloured flag with a smaller union flag in one corner, especially the **White Ensign**, the flag of the Royal Navy and the Royal Yacht Squadron, or the **Red Ensign**, the flag of the Merchant Navy. 3 *Hist.* the lowest rank of officer in the infantry, or an officer of this rank. 4 *North Amer., esp. US* the lowest rank in the navy, or an officer of this rank. [from Old French *enseigne*, from Latin *insignia*, from *signum*, sign]

▣ 1 banner, standard, flag, colours, pennant, jack, badge.

ensilage / 'ɛnsɪlɪdʒ/ same as SILAGE.
enslave *verb* 1 to make into a slave. 2 to subject to a dominating influence.

▣ 2 subjugate, subject, dominate, bind, enchain, yoke.
◪ FREE, EMANCIPATE.

enslavement *noun* making into a slave.
ensnare / ɪn'snɛə(r)/ *verb* to catch in, or as if in, a trap; to trick or lead dishonestly (into doing something).

▣ catch, trap, snare, enmesh, entangle, tangle, embroil, mix up in.

ensue / ɪn'sjuː/ *verb intrans.* (**ensue from something**) 1 to follow it; to happen after it. 2 to result from it. [from Old French *ensuer*, from Latin *sequi*, to follow]

▣ 1 follow, succeed, happen, turn out. 2 result from, arise from, flow from, derive from, stem from, issue from, proceed from.
◪ 1 precede.

ensuing *adj.* 1 following. 2 happening as a result.

▣ 1 following, subsequent, later. 2 resulting, resultant, consequent.

en suite / ɒn 'swiːt/ forming, or attached as part of, a single unit or set: *an en suite bathroom.* [from French *en suite*, in sequence]

ensure *verb* 1 to make certain; to assure or guarantee. 2 to make safe and secure. [from Old French *enseurer*, from Latin *securus*, safe]

▣ 1 certify, guarantee, warrant, assure. 2 protect, guard, safeguard, secure.

ENT *abbrev. Medicine* ear, nose, and throat.
-ent *suffix* forming adjectives and nouns denoting an action, activity, or function: *resident / different.* [from the Latin ending *-ens, -entis*]

entablature / ɛn'tæblətʃə(r)/ *noun Archit.* in classical architecture, the part of a building directly supported by the columns, usually with a frieze and a cornice. [from Italian *intavolatura*]

entail — *verb* 1 to have as a necessary result or requirement. 2 *Legal* (**entail something on someone**) to bequeath property to one's descendants, not allowing them the option to sell it. — *noun Legal* 1 the practice of entailing (property). 2 property which has been entailed. 3 the successive heirs to property. [from EN- + TAIL²]

▣ *verb* 1 involve, necessitate, occasion, require, demand, cause, give rise to, lead to, result in.

entailment *noun* 1 the process of entailing property. 2 *Philos.* the necessity of a proposition being true as a result of another proposition.

entangle *verb* 1 to cause to get caught in some obstacle, eg a net. 2 to involve in difficulties. 3 to make knotted and ravelled. 4 to make complicated or confused.

▣ 1, 2 enmesh, ensnare, snare, tangle, entrap, trap, catch, mix up. 2 implicate, embroil, involve. 3 knot, ravel, tangle. 4 complicate, embroil, confuse, muddle.
◪ DISENTANGLE.

entanglement *noun* the process of entangling; complication.
entasis / 'ɛntəsɪs/ *noun* the slightly bulging outline of a column or similar structure, intended to counteract the illusion of concavity that a straight column would create. [from Greek *entasis*, from *en*, in + *tasis*, a stretch]

entente cordiale / ɒn'tɒnt kɔ:dɪ'ɑ:l/ a friendly agreement or relationship between nations or states.

enter *verb* (**entered, entering**) **1** *intrans., trans.* to go or come in or into. **2** *trans., intrans.* to register (another person, oneself, one's work, etc) in a competition. **3** to record in a book, diary, etc. **4** to join (a profession, society, etc). **5** to submit or present: *enter a complaint*. **6** (**enter into**) to begin to take part in. **7** (**enter into**) to agree to be associated in or bound by: *enter into an agreement*. **8** (**enter on** or **upon something**) to begin an undertaking, especially a lengthy one: *enter upon a new stage of life*.
. . . .
▣ **1** come in (to), go in (to), board, penetrate. **2, 3** register, inscribe. **3** record, log, note, take down, insert, introduce. **4** join, enrol in, enlist in, sign up for. **5** lodge, register, submit, place on record. **8** embark on, commence, start, begin, set about.
▣ **1** depart from. **3** delete.
. . . .

enteric / ɛn'tɛrɪk/ *adj. Medicine* of the intestines. [from Greek *enteron*, intestine]

enteritis / ɛntə'raɪtɪs/ *noun Medicine* inflammation of the intestines, especially the lining of the small intestine, which usually causes vomiting, diarrhoea, and abdominal pain.

entero- or **enter-** *combining form* forming words with the meaning 'intestine': *enteritis*. [from Greek *enteron*, intestine]

enterprise *noun* **1** a project, undertaking. **2** a project that requires boldness and initiative. **3** boldness and initiative. **4** a business firm. [from Old French *entreprendre*, to undertake]
. . . .
▣ **1, 2** venture, initiative. **1** undertaking, project, plan, effort, operation, programme, endeavour. **2** adventure, exploit, speculation. **3** initiative, resourcefulness, drive, adventurousness, boldness, *colloq.* get-up-and-go, push, energy, enthusiasm, spirit. **4** business, company, firm, establishment, concern.
▣ **3** apathy.
. . . .

enterprise zone an area offically designated as a site where industrial and commercial renewal is to be encouraged by financial and other incentives.

enterprising *adj.* showing enterprise and initiative; adventurous.
. . . .
▣ venturesome, adventurous, bold, daring, *colloq.* go-ahead, imaginative, resourceful, self-reliant, enthusiastic, energetic, keen, ambitious, aspiring, spirited, active.
▣ unenterprising, lethargic.
. . . .

entertain *verb* **1** to provide amusement or recreation for. **2** *intrans., trans.* to give hospitality to (a guest), especially in the form of a meal. **3** to consider or be willing to adopt (an idea, suggestion, etc). [from French *entretenir*, to maintain, to hold together]
. . . .
▣ **1** amuse, divert, please, delight, cheer. **2** receive, have (as) guests. **3** consider, contemplate, imagine, conceive, harbour, countenance.
▣ **1** bore. **3** reject.
. . . .

entertainer *noun* a person who provides amusement, especially professionally.

Entertainers include: acrobat, actor, actress, busker, chat show host, clown, comedian, comic, conjuror, dancer, disc jockey, *colloq.* DJ, escapologist, game show host, hypnotist, ice skater, impressionist, jester, juggler, magician, mime, mind-reader, minstrel, musician, presenter, singer, song-and-dance act, stand-up comic, striptease artist, *colloq.* stripper, trapeze artist, tightrope walker, ventriloquist; performer, artiste. *See also* **musician; singer.**

entertaining *adj.* interesting and amusing.
. . . .
▣ amusing, diverting, fun, delightful, interesting, pleasant, pleasing, humorous, witty.
▣ boring.
. . . .

entertainment *noun* **1** something that entertains, eg a theatrical show. **2** the act of entertaining. **3** amusement or recreation.
. . . .
▣ AMUSEMENT, DIVERSION. **1** play, show, spectacle, performance, extravaganza, pastime. **3** recreation, enjoyment, fun, sport, distraction, pleasure.
. . . .

Forms of entertainment include: cinema, cartoon show, video, radio, television, theatre, pantomime; dance, disco, discothèque, concert, recital, musical, opera, variety show, music hall, revue, karaoke, cabaret, nightclub, casino; magic show, puppet show, Punch and Judy show, circus, gymkhana, waxworks, laser light show, zoo, rodeo, carnival, pageant, fête, festival, firework party, barbecue.

enthalpy / 'ɛnθəlpɪ/ *noun Chem.* the amount of heat energy possessed by a substance, expressed per unit mass. It is measured as the heat change that occurs during a chemical reaction that takes place at constant pressure. [from Greek *enthalpein*, to warm in]

enthral / ɪn'θrɔ:l/ *verb* (**enthralled, enthralling**) to fascinate; to hold the attention or grip the imagination of. [from EN- + THRALL]
. . . .
▣ captivate, entrance, enchant, fascinate, charm, beguile, thrill, intrigue, hypnotize, mesmerize, engross.
▣ bore.
. . . .

enthralled *adj.* having one's attention absorbed; fascinated.
enthralling *adj.* absorbing one's attention; fascinating.
. . . .
▣ captivating, entrancing, enchanting, fascinating, thrilling, intriguing, mesmerizing, absorbing, engrossing.
. . . .

enthralment *noun* being enthralled; fascination.
enthrone *verb* to place on a throne.
enthronement *noun* installing of a monarch on the throne, especially as a ceremony.
enthuse *verb intrans., trans.* to be enthusiastic, or make (someone) enthusiastic.
enthusiasm *noun* **1** lively or passionate interest or eagerness. **2** something that someone is passionately interested in. [from Greek *enthousiasmos*, zeal inspired by a god, from *en*, in + *theos*, god]
. . . .
▣ CRAZE, MANIA, *colloq.* RAGE. **1** zeal, ardour, fervour, passion, keenness, eagerness, vehemence, warmth, frenzy, excitement, earnestness, relish, spirit, devotion. **2** hobby, thing.
▣ **1** apathy.
. . . .

enthusiast *noun* a person filled with enthusiasm, especially for a particular subject; a fan or devotee.
. . . .
▣ devotee, zealot, admirer, fan, supporter, follower, *colloq.* buff, freak, fanatic, *colloq.* fiend, lover, fancier.
. . . .

enthusiastic *adj.* showing lively interest.
. . . .
▣ keen, ardent, eager, fervent, vehement, passionate, warm, wholehearted, zealous, vigorous, spirited, earnest, devoted, avid, excited, exuberant.
▣ unenthusiastic, apathetic.
. . . .

enthusiastically *adv.* with lively interest or enthusiasm.

entice *verb* to tempt or persuade, by arousing hopes or desires or by promising a reward. [from Old French *enticier*]

⊟ tempt, lure, attract, seduce, lead on, draw, coax, persuade, induce, *colloq.* sweet-talk.

enticement *noun* enticing; something that allures or fascinates.

enticing *adj.* that allures or fascinates.

⊟ alluring, tempting, attractive, seductive, persuasive, appealing, mouth-watering, eye-catching, tantalizing.

enticingly *adv.* in an enticing or alluring way.

entire *adj.* 1 whole, complete. 2 absolute; total. [from Old French *entier*, from Latin *integer*, whole]

⊟ COMPLETE, TOTAL. 1 whole, full, perfect.
⊞ 1 incomplete, partial.

entirely *adv.* 1 fully or absolutely. 2 solely.

⊟ COMPLETELY, WHOLLY, TOTALLY. 1 fully, utterly, unreservedly, absolutely, in toto, thoroughly, altogether, perfectly. 2 solely, exclusively, every inch.
⊞ 1 partially.

entirety /en'taɪərətɪ/ *noun* (PL. **entireties**) completeness; wholeness. — **in its entirety** totally; taken as a whole.

entitle *verb* 1 (**entitle someone to something**) to give them a right to have or to do it. 2 to give a title or name to (a book, etc). [from Old French *entitler*]

⊟ 1 authorize, qualify, empower, enable, allow, permit, license, warrant. 2 name, call, term, title, style, christen, dub, label, designate.

entitlement *noun* having a right to something.

entity *noun* (PL. **entities**) 1 something that has a physical existence, as opposed to a quality or mood. 2 the essential nature (of something). 3 *Philos.* the fact or quality of existing. [from Latin *entitas*, from *ens*, thing that exists]

⊟ 1, 3 being, existence. 1 thing, body, creature, individual, organism, substance.

ento- *combining form* inside. See also ECTO-, ENDO-, EXO-. [from Greek *entos*, within]

entomb /ɪn'tuːm/ *verb* 1 to put in a tomb. 2 to cover, bury or hide as if in a tomb. [from Old French *entoumber*]

entombment *noun* being put in a tomb.

entomological *adj.* relating to entomology or the study of insects.

entomologist *noun* a person who studies entomology.

entomology *noun* the scientific study of insects. [from Greek *entomon*, insect, from *entomos*, cut into sections]

entourage /'ɒntʊərɑːʒ/ *noun* a group of followers or assistants, especially one accompanying a famous or important person. [from French *entourage*, from *entourer*, to surround]

entr'acte /ɒn'trakt/ *noun* 1 an interval between the acts of a play. 2 *formerly* entertainment provided during this interval. [from French *entr'acte*, from *entre*, between + *acte*, act]

entrails /'entreɪlz/ *pl. noun* 1 the internal organs of a person or animal. 2 *literary* the inner parts of anything. [from Old French *entrailles*, from Latin *intralia*, from *inter*, within]

entrance[1] /'entrəns/ *noun* 1 a way in, eg a door. 2 *formal* the act of entering: *gain entrance.* 3 the right to enter. [from ENTER + -ANCE]

⊟ 1 opening, way in, door, doorway, gate. 2 arrival, appearance, début, initiation, introduction, start. 3 access, admission, admittance, entry, entrée.
⊞ 1 exit. 2 departure.

entrance[2] /ɪn'trɑːns/ *verb* 1 to grip the attention and imagination of. 2 to put into a trance.

⊟ BEWITCH, SPELLBIND, HYPNOTIZE, MESMERIZE. 1 charm, enchant, enrapture, captivate, fascinate, delight, ravish, transport.
⊞ 1 repel.

entrancement *noun* enchantment; fascination.

entrancing *adj.* gripping the imagination; fascinating.

⊟ charming, enchanting, captivating, fascinating, delightful, ravishing, bewitching, spellbinding, mesmerizing.

entrant *noun* 1 a person who enters for something (especially an examination, a competition, or a sports event). 2 a newcomer to a group or activity.

⊟ 1 competitor, candidate, contestant, contender, entry, applicant, participant, player. 2 novice, beginner, newcomer, initiate, convert, probationer.

entrap *verb* (**entrapped, entrapping**) 1 to catch in, or as if in, a trap. 2 to trick (someone) into doing something. [from Old French *entraper*]

⊟ 1 catch, trap, snare, ensnare, entangle, enmesh, ambush. 2 trick, deceive, delude.

entrapment *noun* 1 the act of entrapping or process of being entrapped. 2 *Legal* the act or process of deliberately inducing someone to commit a crime in order to provide a reason for arresting and prosecuting him or her.

entreat *verb* to ask passionately or desperately; to beg. [from Old French *entraiter*]

⊟ beg, implore, plead with, beseech, crave, supplicate, pray, invoke, ask, petition, request, appeal to.

entreaty *noun* (PL. **entreaties**) a passionate or desperate request.

⊟ appeal, plea, prayer, petition, supplication, suit, invocation, cry, solicitation, request.

entrecôte /'ɒntrəkoʊt/ *noun* a boneless steak cut from between two ribs. [from French *entrecôte*, from *entre*, between + *côte*, rib]

entrée /'ɒntreɪ/ *noun* 1 a small dish served after the fish course and before the main course at a formal dinner. 2 a main course. 3 *formal* the right of admission or entry: *entrée into polite society.* [from French *entrée*, entrance]

entrench *verb* 1 to fix or establish firmly, often too firmly: *deeply entrenched ideas.* 2 to fortify with trenches dug around.

⊟ 1 establish, fix, embed, ensconce, install, lodge, root, settle, seat, plant, anchor, set.
⊞ 1 dislodge.

entrenchment *noun* establishing a firm position.

entrepôt /'ɒntrəpoʊ/ *noun* a port through which goods

are imported and exported, often without duty being paid on them. [from French *entrepôt*, warehouse]

entrepreneur /ɒntrəprə'nɜː(r)/ *noun* a person who engages in business enterprises, usually with some personal financial risk. [from French *entrepreneur*, one who undertakes]

⊟ businessman, businesswoman, capitalist, industrialist, tycoon.

entrepreneurial /ɒntrəprə'nɜːrɪəl/ *adj.* acting as an entrepreneur; undertaking business enterprises.

entropy /'entrəpɪ/ *noun* (PL. **entropies**) *Physics* a measure of the amount of disorder in a system, or of the unavailability of energy for doing work. [from German *Entropie*, from Greek *en*, in + *tropos*, turn, change]

entrust *verb* (**entrust something to someone**, or **someone with something**) to give it to them to take care of or deal with.

⊟ trust, commit, confide, consign, charge, assign, turn over, commend, depute, invest, delegate, deliver.

entry *noun* (PL. **entries**) **1** the act of coming or going in. **2** the right to enter. **3** a place of entering such as a door or doorway. **4** a person, or the total number of people, entered for a competition, etc. **5** an item written on a list, in a book, etc, or the act of recording an item in this way. [from Old French *entree*, from *entrer*, to enter]

⊟ **1, 2, 3** entrance. **1** appearance. **2** admittance, admission, access, entrée, introduction. **3** opening, door, doorway, access, threshold, way in, passage, gate. **4** entrant(s), competitor(s), contestant(s), candidate(s), participant(s), player(s). **5** record, item, minute, note, memorandum, statement, account.
⊟ **1, 3** exit.

entryism *noun derog.* the practice of joining a political party in large enough numbers to gain power and change the party's policies.

entryist *noun derog.* a person who engages in political entryism.

Entryphone *noun trademark* an intercom system fitted at the entrance to a building, especially a block of flats, by which visitors can identify themselves to specific occupants before being admitted to the building.

entwine *verb* **1** to wind or twist two things together. **2** to make by winding or twisting something together.

E-number *noun* any of various identification codes, consisting of the letter E (for European) followed by a number, that are used to denote all food additives, except flavourings, that have been approved by the European Union (EU).

enumerate *verb* **1** to list one by one. **2** to count. [from Latin *enumerare*, to count up]

⊟ **1** list, name, itemize, cite, detail, specify, relate, recount, spell out, tell, mention, quote, recite. **2** count, number, calculate, reckon.

enumeration *noun* enumerating; counting, listing.
enumerative /ɪ'njuːmərətɪv/ *adj.* serving to list or count.
enunciate /ɪ'nʌnsɪeɪt/ *verb* **1** *trans., intrans.* to pronounce words clearly. **2** to state formally. [from Latin *enuntiare*, to announce]

⊟ **1** articulate, pronounce, vocalize, speak, utter, sound. **2** state, declare, proclaim, announce, propound.

enunciation *noun* clear pronunciation of words.
enuresis /ɛnjʊ'riːsɪs/ *noun Medicine* involuntary urina-

tion, especially during sleep. [from Greek *en*, in + *ouresis*, urination]

enuretic /ɛnjʊ'retɪk/ *adj.* involving involuntary urination.
envelop /ɛn'vɛləp/ *verb* (**enveloped, enveloping**) **1** to cover or wrap completely. **2** to obscure or conceal: *an event enveloped in mystery.* [from Old French *envoloper*, from *en*, in + *voloper*, to wrap]

⊟ **1** wrap, enfold, enwrap, encase, cover, swathe, engulf, enclose, encircle, encompass, surround. **2** conceal, shroud, cloak, veil, blanket, obscure, hide.

envelope /'ɛnvələʊp, 'ɒn-/ *noun* **1** a thin flat sealable paper packet or cover, especially for a letter. **2** a cover or wrapper of any kind. **3** *Biol.* a plant or animal structure that contains or encloses something, eg the nuclear envelope, consisting of a double membrane that surrounds the nucleus of a cell. **4** *technical* the glass casing that surrounds an incandescent lamp. [from French *enveloppe*, from *envelopper*; related to ENVELOP]

⊟ **2** wrapper, wrapping, cover, case, casing, sheath, covering, shell, skin, jacket, coating.

envelopment *noun* enveloping or being enveloped; covering.
enviable /'ɛnvɪəbl/ *adj.* likely to cause envy; highly desirable.

⊟ desirable, privileged, favoured, blessed, fortunate, lucky, advantageous, sought-after, excellent, fine.
⊟ unenviable.

enviably *adv.* so as to cause envy or admiration: *they were enviably sure of themselves.*
envious *adj.* feeling or showing envy: *they were envious of our successes.*

⊟ covetous, jealous, resentful, green (with envy), dissatisfied, grudging, jaundiced.

environment /ɪn'vaɪərənmənt/ *noun* **1** the surroundings or conditions within which something or someone exists. **2** (*usually* **the environment**) the combination of external conditions that surround and influence a living organism, including light, temperature, availability of food and water, and climatic conditions. [from Old French *environnement*, from *environner*, to surround]

⊟ **1** surroundings, conditions, circumstances, milieu, atmosphere, habitat, situation, element, medium, background, ambience, setting, context, territory, domain.

environmental /ɪnvaɪərən'mɛntəl/ *adj.* concerning or connected with the environment: *environmental issues.*
environmentalism *noun* concern about the natural environment and its protection from pollution and other harmful effects of human activity.
environmentalist — *noun* a person who is concerned about the harmful effects of human activity on the environment. — *adj.* used to describe a group or organization whose aims are to protect the environment and to increase public awareness of environmental issues.
environmentally *adv.* as regards the environment.
environs /ɪn'vaɪərənz/ *pl. noun* surrounding areas, especially the outskirts of a town or city. [from Old French *environ*, around]

⊟ surroundings, vicinity, neighbourhood, district, suburbs.

envisage /ɪnˈvɪzɪdʒ/ *verb* **1** to picture in the mind. **2** to consider as likely in the future: *we envisage a payrise in the autumn.* [from French *envisager*, from *visage*, face]

▣ **1** visualize, imagine, picture, envision, conceive of, preconceive, see. **2** predict, anticipate, foresee, contemplate.

envoy *noun* **1** a diplomat ranking next below an ambassador. **2** a messenger or agent, especially on a diplomatic mission. [from French *envoyer*, to send]

▣ **2** agent, representative, ambassador, diplomat, messenger, legate, emissary, minister, delegate, deputy, courier, intermediary, go-between.

envy — *noun* **1** a feeling of resentment or regretful desire for another person's qualities, better fortune, or success. **2** anything that arouses envy: *a house that is the envy of his colleagues.* — *verb* (**envies, envied**) **a** to wish to have what someone else has: *envy someone's good fortune.* **b** (**envy someone something**) to feel envy against someone on account of their fortune, success, etc: *I envy them their good luck.* [from Old French *envie*]

▣ *noun* **1** covetousness, jealousy, resentfulness, resentment, dissatisfaction, grudge, ill-will, malice, spite. *verb* covet, resent, begrudge, grudge, crave.

enzyme /ˈɛnzaɪm/ *noun Biochem.* a specialized protein molecule that acts as a catalyst for the biochemical reactions that occur in living cells. [from Greek *en*, in + *zume*, leaven]

EOC *abbrev.* Equal Opportunities Commission.

Eocene /ˈiːəʊsiːn/ — *noun Geol.* the second epoch of the Tertiary period, lasting from about 54 million to 38 million years ago. During this time the first horses and elephants appeared, and most plants were similar to modern types. — *adj.* **1** relating to this epoch. **2** relating to rocks formed during this epoch. [from Greek *eos*, dawn + *kainos*, recent]

Eohippus /iːəʊˈhɪpəs/ *noun Zool.* the earliest stage in the evolution of the modern horse, about the size of a small dog, with four splayed front toes and three hind toes. [from Greek *eos*, dawn + *hippos* horse]

EOKA /eɪˈəʊkə/ *abbrev. Ethnike Organosis Kypriakou Agonos* (Greek) National Organization for the Cypriot Struggle.

eolian harp same as AEOLIAN HARP.

eolithic or **Eolithic** /iːəʊˈlɪθɪk/ *adj.* belonging to the early part of the Stone Age, when crude stone implements were first used by man. [from Greek *eos*, dawn + *lithos*, stone]

eon or **aeon** /ˈiːən, ˈiːɒn/ *noun* **1** a long period of time. **2** *Geol.* the largest unit of geological time, consisting of a number of eras. **3** *Astron.* a period of a thousand million years.

eosin /ˈiːəʊsɪn/ *noun Biol.* a red acidic dye used to stain thin sections of plant or animal tissue to be examined under an optical microscope. [from Greek *eos*, dawn]

EP *noun* an extended-play gramophone record.

EPA *abbrev.* Environmental Protection Agency (USA).

epaulette or **epaulet** /ˈɛpəlɛt/ *noun* a decoration on the shoulder of a coat or jacket, especially of a military uniform. [from French *épaulette*, from *épaule*, shoulder]

épée /ˈɛpeɪ/ *noun* a sword with a narrow flexible blade, used formerly in duelling and, with a blunted end, in modern fencing. [from French *épée*]

Eph. or **Eph** *abbrev. Biblical* Ephesians.

ephedrine /ˈɛfədrɪn, ɪˈfedrɪn/ *noun Medicine* an alkaloid drug, with similar effects to adrenaline, that constricts blood vessels and widens the bronchial passages. It is now mainly used as a nasal decongestant. [from Greek *ephedra*, horsetail (the plant)]

ephemera /ɪˈfɛmərə/ *pl. noun* things that are valid or useful for a short time, especially printed items. [from Greek *ephemeros*, living a day, from *epi*, for + *hemera*, day]

ephemeral /ɪˈfɛmərəl/ — *noun Biol.* a plant or animal that completes its life cycle within weeks, days, or even hours, eg mayfly, many desert plants. — *adj.* **1** *Biol.* denoting such a plant or animal. **2** lasting a short time.

▣ *adj.* **2** transient, transitory, fleeting, momentary, short-lived, temporary, brief, short.

ephemeris /ɪˈfɛmərɪs/ *noun* (PL. **ephemerides**) *Astron.* **1** a table that shows the predicted future positions of celestial bodies such as the Sun, Moon, planets, certain stars, and comets. **2** a book, usually published annually, containing a collection of such tables, together with other relevant information about predictable astronomical phenomena such as eclipses.

epi- *combining form* forming words meaning 'above, over, upon': *epicentre / epidural.* [from Greek *epi*, on, over]

epiblast /ˈɛpɪblast/ *noun Zool.* same as ECTODERM. [from EPI- + Greek *blastos*, shoot]

epic — *noun* **1** a long narrative poem telling of heroic acts, the birth and death of nations, etc. **2** a long adventure story, film, etc. — *adj.* of or like an epic, especially in being large-scale and imposing. [from Greek *epikos*, from *epos*, word, song]

▣ *adj.* heroic, grand, majestic, imposing, vast, colossal, huge.

epicene /ˈɛpɪsiːn/ *adj.* **1** having characteristics of both sexes, or of neither sex. **2** relating to or used by both sexes. **3** effeminate. **4** *Grammar, said of a noun* referring to people or animals of either sex, eg 'driver', as opposed to 'waiter' and 'waitress'. [from Greek *epikoinos*, common to many]

epicentre *noun* the point on the earth's surface which is directly above the focus (centre of activity) of an earthquake, or directly above or below a nuclear explosion. [from Greek *epi*, over + *kentron*, point]

epicure /ˈɛpɪkjʊə(r)/ *noun* a person who has refined taste, especially one who enjoys good food and drink. [from *Epicurus*, the ancient Greek philosopher]

Epicurean /ɛpɪkjʊˈriːən/ *noun* **1** a follower of the philosophy of Epicureanism. **2** (**epicurean**) a person who likes pleasure and good living. — *adj.* (**epicurean**) **1** given to luxury or to the tastes of an epicure. **2** relating to the philosophy of the Greek philosopher Epicurus (c.341–270 BC).

Epicureanism a philosophical school established by the Greek philosopher Epicurus in the 4c BC, surviving until the 3c AD. Its basic moral principle was that personal happiness is the supreme good, with freedom from fears (eg of death) and from pain.

epicurism /ˈɛpɪkjʊərɪzm/ *noun* **1** the pursuit of pleasure, especially as found in good food and drink. **2** the tendency to be critical and hard to please in matters of luxury.

epicycle *noun Maths.* a circle whose centre rolls around the circumference of another fixed circle. The curved path followed by a point on the circumference of the epicycle is known as an *epicycloid.*

epidemic — *noun* **1** a sudden outbreak of infectious disease (such as cholera and influenza) which spreads rapidly and affects a large number of people, animals, or plants in a particular area for a limited period of time. **2** a sudden and extensive spread of anything undesirable. — *adj.* of or like an epidemic; sometimes also used to describe a non-infectious condition such as malnutrition. See also ENDEMIC. [from Greek *epi*, among + *demos*, the people]

▣ *noun* PLAGUE, OUTBREAK. **2** spread, rash, upsurge, wave. *adj.* widespread, prevalent, rife, rampant, pandemic, sweeping, wide-ranging, prevailing.

epidemiology /ɛpɪdiːmɪˈɒlədʒɪ/ *noun Biol.* the study of the distribution, effects, and causes of diseases in populations, and the means by which they may be treated or prevented.

epidermal *adj.* relating to or in the region of the epidermis.

epidermis *noun Biol.* the outermost layer of a plant or animal, which serves to protect the underlying tissues from infection, injury, and water loss. [from Greek *epi*, upon + *derma*, the skin]

epididymis /ɛpɪˈdɪdɪmɪs/ *noun* (PL. **epididymides**) *Anat.* a long narrow highly coiled tube in the testis of mammals, birds, and reptiles, that conveys sperm from the seminiferous tubules of the testis to the vas deferens. [from EPI- + Greek *didymos*, twin, testicle]

epidural /ɛpɪˈdjʊərəl/ — *adj. Medicine* situated on or outside the *dura mater* (the outermost of the three membranes enveloping the brain and the spinal cord). — *noun Medicine* a local anaesthetic injected into the space outside the dura mater, especially during childbirth, in order to produce loss of sensation below the waist. [from EPI- + DURA MATER]

epiglottal *adj.* relating to or in the region of the epiglottis.

epiglottis *noun Anat.* in mammals, a moveable flap of cartilage which hangs at the back of the tongue. It closes the opening of the larynx (windpipe) when food or drink is being swallowed, so preventing obstruction of the air passages. [from Greek *epi*, over + *glottis*, glottis]

epigram *noun* a witty or sarcastic saying, or a short poem with such an ending. [from Greek *epigramma*, from *epi*, upon + *gramma*, writing]

epigrammatic *adj.* in the nature of an epigram; short and witty.

⊟ concise, succinct, brief, terse, laconic, pithy, incisive, witty, ironic.

epigraph *noun* **1** a quotation or motto at the beginning of a book or chapter. **2** an inscription on a building. [from Greek *epigraphe*, from *epi*, upon + *graphein*, to write]

epigraphy /ɛˈpɪɡrəfɪ/ *noun* the historical study of ancient inscriptions. [from Greek *epigraphe*, from *epi*, upon + *graphein*, to write]

epilepsy *noun* any of a group of disorders of the nervous system characterized by recurring attacks that involve impairment or sudden loss of consciousness. [from Greek *epilepsia*, from *epilambanein*, to seize]

epileptic — *adj.* relating to or suffering from epilepsy. — *noun* a person who suffers from epilepsy.

epilogue /ˈɛpɪlɒɡ/ *noun* **1** the closing section of a book, programme, etc. **2** a speech addressed to the audience at the end of a play. [from Greek *epilogos*, from *epi*, upon + *logos*, speech]

⊟ **1** afterword, postscript, coda, conclusion.
⊟ PROLOGUE. **1** foreword, preface.

epiphany /ɪˈpɪfənɪ/ *noun* (PL. **epiphanies**) **1** (*usually* **Epiphany**) a Christian festival on 6 January which, in the western churches, commemorates the showing of Christ to the three wise men, and, in the Orthodox and other eastern Churches, the baptism of Christ. **2** the sudden appearance of a god. **3** *literary* a sudden revelation or insight. [from Greek *epiphaneia*, manifestation]

epiphysis /ɪˈpɪfɪsɪs/ *noun* (PL. **epiphyses**) **1** *Anat.* the growing end of a long bone, which is initially separated from the long shaft of the bone by cartilage, and develops separately. **2** the pineal gland. [from Greek *epiphysis*, excrescence]

epiphyte /ˈɛpɪfaɪt/ *noun Bot.* a plant that grows on another plant, using it for support, but is not a parasite, eg moss. [from EPI- + Greek *phyton*, plant]

episcopacy /ɪˈpɪskəpəsɪ/ *noun* (PL. **episcopacies**) **1** the government of the church by bishops. **2** bishops as a group. **3** the position or period of office of a bishop. [from Greek *episkopos*, overseer]

episcopal /ɪˈpɪskəpl/ *adj.* relating to or governed by bishops.

episcopalian /ɪpɪskəˈpeɪlɪən/ — *adj.* relating to or advocating Church government by bishops. — *noun* a member of an episcopal (especially Anglican) Church.

episcopalianism /ɪpɪskəˈpeɪlɪənɪzm/ *noun* episcopalian principles.

episcopate /ɪˈpɪskəpət/ *noun* **1** the position or period of office of a bishop. **2** bishops as a group. **3** an area under the care of a bishop; a diocese or bishopric.

episiotomy /ɛpɪzɪˈɒtəmɪ/ *noun* (PL. **episiotomies**) *Medicine* a surgical cut made at the opening of the vagina during childbirth, to assist the delivery of the baby. [from Greek *epision*, pubic area + -TOMY]

episode *noun* **1** one of several events or distinct periods making up a longer sequence. **2** one of the separate parts in which a radio or television serial is broadcast or a serialized novel, etc published. **3** any scene or incident forming part of a novel or narrative poem, often one providing a digression from the main story. [from Greek *epeisodion*, from *epi*, upon + *eisodos*, a coming in]

⊟ **1** incident, event, occurrence, happening, occasion, circumstance, experience, adventure, matter, business. **2** instalment, part. **3** passage, chapter, section, scene.

episodic *adj.* **1** consisting of several distinct periods. **2** occurring at intervals; sporadic.

⊟ **2** broken, interrupted, discontinuous, irregular, intermittent, sporadic, occasional.

episodically *adv.* at intervals; sporadically.

epistemological /ɪpɪstəməˈlɒdʒɪkəl/ *adj.* relating to epistemology or the study of knowledge.

epistemology /ɪpɪstəˈmɒlədʒɪ/ *noun* the philosophical theory and study of knowledge and its functions. [from Greek *episteme*, knowledge]

epistle /ɪˈpɪsl/ *noun* **1** *literary* a letter, especially a long one dealing with important matters. **2** a novel or poem written in the form of letters. **3** (*usually* **Epistle**) each of the letters written by Christ's Apostles which form part of the New Testament. **4** a reading from one of the Epistles as part of a religious service. [from Latin *epistola*]

epistolary /ɪˈpɪstələrɪ/ *adj. formal* **1** relating to or consisting of letters. **2** *said of a novel* written in the form of a series of letters.

epitaph *noun* **1** an inscription on a gravestone. **2** a short commemorative speech or piece of writing in a similar style. [from Greek *epitaphion*, from *epi*, upon + *taphos*, tomb]

epithelial /ɛpɪˈθiːlɪəl/ *adj.* relating to the epithelium.

epithelium /ɛpɪˈθiːlɪəm/ *noun* (PL. **epithelia**) *Anat.* the layer of tissue covering all external and many internal surfaces of a multicellular animal. [from Greek *epi*, upon + *thele*, nipple]

epithet *noun* an adjective or short descriptive phrase which captures the particular quality of the person or thing it describes: *King Ethelred II was given the epithet 'The Unready'.* [from Greek *epitheton*, from *epi*, on + *tithenai*, to place]

epitome /ɪˈpɪtəmɪ/ *noun* **1** a miniature representation of a larger or wider idea, issue, etc. **2** a person or thing that is the embodiment of or a perfect example of (a quality, etc). **3** a summary of a written work. [from Greek *epi*, upon + *tome*, a cut]

⊟ **2** personification, embodiment, representation, model, archetype, type, essence. **3** summary, abstract, abridgement, digest.

epitomize or **epitomise** *verb* to be or make an epitome of.

▤ sum up, personify, embody, exemplify, typify, summarize.

EPNS *abbrev.* electroplated nickel silver.

epoch /ˈiːpɒk/ *noun* **1** a major division or period of history, a person's life, etc, usually marked by some important event. **2** *Geol.* an interval of geological time representing a subdivision of a period, and during which a particular series of rocks was formed, eg the Pleistocene epoch. [from Greek *epoche*, fixed point]

▤ **1** age, era, period, time, date.

epochal /ˈiːpɒkəl/ *adj.* relating to or lasting for an epoch.
epoch-making *adj.* highly significant or decisive.

▤ historic, momentous, decisive, critical, crucial, extraordinary, remarkable.

eponym /ˈɛpənɪm/ *noun* a person after whom something is named, especially the main character in a play, novel, etc whose name provides its title. [from Greek *epi*, upon + *onyma*, a name]
eponymous /ɛˈpɒnɪməs/ *adj.*, *said of a character in a story, etc* having the name from which the title is taken.
EPOS *abbrev.* electronic point of sale.
epoxy /ɪˈpɒksɪ/ *Chem.* — *adj.* consisting of an oxygen atom bonded to two carbon atoms. — *noun* (*in full* **epoxy resin**) any of a group of synthetic thermosetting resins, containing epoxy groups. [from Greek *epi*, upon + OXY-GEN]
EPROM *abbrev. Comput.* erasable programmable read-only memory, a read-only memory in which stored data can be erased by ultraviolet light, etc, and reprogrammed.
EPS *abbrev.* earnings per share (stock exchange).
Epsom salts or **Epsom salt** (FORMULA MgSO$_4$.7H$_2$O) hydrated magnesium sulphate crystals, used medicinally as a laxative and anti-inflammatory agent. [from *Epsom* in Surrey, where it occurs naturally in spring water]
EPSRC *abbrev.* Engineering and Physical Sciences Research Council.
equability *noun* an equable or even-tempered manner or condition.
equable /ˈɛkwəbl/ *adj.* **1** *said of a climate* never showing very great variations or extremes. **2** *said of a person* even-tempered. [from Latin *aequabilis*, from *aequus*, equal]

▤ **1** uniform, even, consistent, constant, regular, temperate, unvarying, steady, stable, smooth. **2** even-tempered, placid, calm, serene, unexcitable, tranquil, unflappable, composed, level-headed, easy-going.
▤ **1** variable. **2** excitable.

equably /ˈɛkwəblɪ/ *adv.* with an equable manner; calmly.
equal /ˈiːkwəl/ — *adj.* **1** the same in size, amount, value, etc. **2** evenly balanced; displaying no advantage or bias. **3** having the same status; having or entitled to the same rights. **4** (**equal to something**) having the necessary ability for it. — *noun* a person or thing of the same age, rank, ability, worth, etc. — *verb* (**equalled**, **equalling**) **1** to be the same in amount, value, size, etc as. **2** to be as good as; to match. **3** to achieve something which matches (a previous achievement or achiever). [from Latin *aequus*]

▤ *adj.* **1** identical, the same, alike, like, equivalent, corresponding, commensurate, comparable. **2** even, uniform, balanced, matched, fair, impartial, unbiased, neutral, non-partisan. **3** fit for, adequate for, capable of, suitable for. *noun* peer, counterpart, equivalent, coequal, match, parallel, twin, fellow. *verb* MATCH. **1** correspond to, balance, parallel, square with, tally with, coincide with, equalize, equate with.

2 rival, emulate, be on a par with, come up to.
▤ *adj.* UNEQUAL (TO). **1** different. **3** unsuitable for.

equality *noun* **1** an equal state; being equal. **2** equal rights; equal treatment.

▤ **1** uniformity, evenness, equivalence, correspondence, balance, parity, par, symmetry, proportion, identity, sameness, likeness. **2** impartiality, fairness, justice, egalitarianism.
▤ INEQUALITY.

equalization or **equalisation** *noun* making or becoming equal.
equalize or **equalise** *verb* **1** *trans., intrans.* to make or become equal. **2** *intrans.* to reach the same score as an opponent, after being behind.

▤ **1** level, even up, match, equate, balance (out), square. **2** draw level.

equalizer or **equaliser** *noun* a person or thing that equalizes, especially a goal or point scored which makes one equal to one's opponent. See also GRAPHIC EQUALIZER.
equally *adv.* in an equal way; to an equal extent.
equal opportunities the principle of equal treatment of all employees or candidates for employment, irrespective of race, religion, sex, etc.
equanimity /ɛkwəˈnɪmɪtɪ/ *noun* calmness of temper; composure. [from Latin *aequanimitas*, from *aequus*, equal + *animus*, mind]

▤ calmness, collectedness, composure, self-possession, imperturbability, *colloq.* unflappability, placidity, impassivity.

equate /ɪˈkweɪt/ *verb* **1** (**equate one thing to** or **with another**) to consider them as equivalent. **2** (**equate with something**) to be equivalent to it. [from Latin *aequare*, to make equal]

▤ **1** compare with, liken to, match with, pair with, juxtapose with. **2** correspond to, correspond with, balance, parallel, equalize, offset, square with, agree with, tally with.

equation /ɪˈkweɪʒən/ *noun* **1** *Maths.* a mathematical statement of the equality between two expressions involving constants and/or variables, used to find solutions to variables, or to describe a set of points, eg on a line or curve. **2** *Chem.* a chemical equation. **3** the act of equating.

▤ **3** balancing, pairing, comparison, matching, juxtaposition.

equator *noun* **1** (**the Equator**) the imaginary great circle that passes around the Earth at latitude 0 at an equal distance from the North and South Poles, and divides the Earth's surface into the northern and southern hemispheres. It is 40,076km/24,902mi in length. **2** *Astron.* same as CELESTIAL EQUATOR.
equatorial /ɛkwəˈtɔːrɪəl/ *adj.* of or near the equator.
equerry /ˈɛkwərɪ, ɪˈkwɛrɪ/ *noun* (PL. **equerries**) an official who serves as a personal attendant to a member of a royal family. [from Old French *esquierie*, company of squires, from *esquier*, squire]
equestrian *adj.* **1** of horse-riding or horses. **2** on horseback. [from Latin *equestris*, relating to horsemen]
equi- *combining form* equal or equally: *equidistant.* [from Latin *aequus*, equal]
equiangular /ɛkwɪˈæŋɡjʊlə(r)/ *adj. Geom.*, *said of a geometrical figure* having all angles equal.
equidistance /ɛkwɪˈdɪstəns, iːkwɪ-/ *noun* equality of distance.

equidistant /ɛkwɪˈdɪstənt, iːkwɪ-/ *adj.* equally distant.

equilateral /ɛkwɪˈlatərəl, iːkwɪ-/ *adj. Geom., said of a geometrical figure* having all sides of equal length: *equilateral triangle*. [from EQUI- + Latin *latus*, side]

equilibrium /ɛkwɪˈlɪbrɪəm, iːkwɪ-/ *noun* 1 *Physics* a state in which the various forces acting on an object or objects in a system balance each other, so that there is no tendency for any part of the system to move. 2 *Chem.* a reversible chemical reaction in which the rate of forward and backward reactions is the same, so that the concentrations of reactants and products remain unchanged. 3 a calm and composed state of mind. [from Latin *aequi librium*, from *aequus*, equal + *libra*, balance]

⊟ 1 balance, poise, symmetry, evenness, stability. 3 equanimity, self-possession, composure, calmness, coolness, serenity.
⊟ 1 imbalance.

equine /ˈɛkwaɪn/ *adj. formal* relating to or like a horse or horses. [from Latin *equinus*, from *equus*, horse]

equinoctial /ɛkwɪˈnɒkʃəl/ — *adj.* 1 relating to or occurring at one or both equinoxes. 2 of or relating to the time of the equinoxes, when day and night are of equal length. 3 *Astron.* of or relating to the celestial equator. — *noun* 1 a storm or gale occurring around the time of an equinox. 2 (*also* **equinoctial line**) *Astron.* the celestial equator.

equinox /ˈɛkwɪnɒks/ *noun* either of the two annual occasions when the Sun's path (the *ecliptic*) appears to cross the celestial equator, so that day and night are of equal length. The *vernal* (spring) equinox occurs around 21 Mar in the northern hemisphere and the *autumnal equinox* occurs around 23 Sep. [from Latin *a equi noctium*, from *aequus*, equal + *nox*, night]

equip *verb* (**equipped, equipping**) to fit out or provide with the necessary tools, supplies, abilities, etc. [from French *équiper*, from Old French *eschiper*, to fit out a ship, probably from Norse *skip*, ship]

⊟ provide, fit out, supply, furnish, prepare, arm, fit up, kit out, stock, endow, rig, dress, array, deck out.

equipage /ˈɛkwɪpɪdʒ/ *noun* 1 a horse-drawn carriage with its footmen. 2 *formerly* the equipment carried by a military unit.

equipment *noun* 1 the clothes, machines, tools, instruments, etc necessary for a particular kind of work or activity. 2 *formal* the act of equipping.

⊟ 1 apparatus, gear, supplies, tackle, tools, material, furnishings, baggage, outfit, paraphernalia, stuff, things, accessories, furniture.

equipoise /ˈɛkwɪpɔɪz/ *noun formal* 1 a state of balance. 2 a counterbalancing weight. [from EQUI- + POISE]

equitable /ˈɛkwɪtəbl/ *adj.* 1 fair and just. 2 *Legal* relating to, or valid according to, the concept of natural justice, or equity, as opposed to common law or statute law. [from French *équitable*: see EQUITY]

equitation *noun formal* the art of riding a horse. [from Latin *equitare*, to ride, from *equus*, horse]

equity *noun* (PL. **equities**) 1 fair or just conditions or treatment. 2 *Legal* the concept of natural justice, as opposed to common law or statute law, often invoked to support an interpretation, or the complete waiving, of a law. 3 the excess in value of a property over the mortgage and other charges held on it. 4 (*usually* **equities**) an ordinary share in a company. [from Old French *equite*, from Latin *aequitas*, equality]

equivalence *noun* the fact or state of being equivalent; having equal value.

⊟ identity, parity, correspondence, agreement, likeness, interchangeability, similarity, substitutability, correlation, parallel, conformity, sameness.
⊟ unlikeness, dissimilarity.

equivalent — *adj.* equal in value, power, meaning, etc. — *noun* an equivalent thing, amount, etc. [from Latin *aequus*, equal + *valere*, to be worth]

⊟ *adj.* equal, same, similar, substitutable, corresponding, alike, comparable, interchangeable, even, tantamount, twin. *noun* counterpart, equal, coequal, match, parallel, twin, fellow.
⊟ *adj.* unlike, different.

equivocal /ɪˈkwɪvəkəl/ *adj.* 1 ambiguous; of doubtful meaning. 2 of an uncertain nature. 3 questionable, suspicious, or mysterious. [from Latin *aequivocus*, from *aequus*, equal + *vox*, voice, word]

⊟ 1, 2 ambiguous, uncertain, obscure, vague, confusing, indefinite. 1 evasive, oblique, misleading. 3 questionable, dubious, supect, suspicious, mysterious, enigmatic.
⊟ 1, 2 unequivocal, clear.

equivocally *adv.* in an equivocal or ambiguous manner.

equivocate /ɪˈkwɪvəkeɪt/ *verb intrans.* to use ambiguous words in order to deceive or to avoid answering a question.

⊟ prevaricate, evade, dodge, fence, *colloq.* beat about the bush, hedge, mislead.

equivocation *noun* evasive ambiguity.

ER *abbrev.* 1 *Elizabeth Regina* (Latin), Queen Elizabeth. 2 *Edwardus Rex* (Latin), King Edward.

Er *symbol Chem.* erbium.

-er[1] *suffix* used to form the comparative of adjectives and adverbs: *happier* / *sooner*. [from Anglo-Saxon forms]

-er[2] *suffix* 1 used to form words meaning the person or thing performing the action of the verb: *driver* / *heater*. 2 used to form words meaning a person from a particular town or city: *Londoner* / *New Yorker*. [from Anglo-Saxon *-ere*]

ERA *abbrev.* Equal Rights Amendment.

era /ˈɪərə/ *noun* 1 a distinct period in history marked by or beginning at an important event. 2 *Geol.* the second largest interval of geological time, representing a subdivision of an eon, eg Mesozoic era. Each era is in turn divided into a number of periods. [from Latin *aera*, number]

⊟ 1 age, epoch, period, date, day, days, time, aeon. stage, century.

eradicate *verb* to get rid of completely. [from Latin *eradicare*, to root out]

⊟ eliminate, annihilate, get rid of, remove, root out, suppress, destroy, exterminate, extinguish, weed out, stamp out, abolish, erase, obliterate.

eradication *noun* getting rid of something; elimination.

⊟ elimination, annihilation, removal, suppression, destruction, exterminate, abolition, erasure, obliteration.

erase /ɪˈreɪz/ *verb* 1 to rub out (pencil marks, etc). 2 to remove all trace of. [from Latin *eradere*, to scratch out]

⊟ OBLITERATE, RUB OUT, EXPUNGE, DELETE, BLOT OUT, CANCEL, EFFACE. 2 get rid of, remove, eradicate.

eraser *noun* something that erases, especially a rubber for removing pencil or ink marks.

erasure *noun* **1** the act of rubbing out. **2** a place where something written has been erased.

erbium /ˈɜːbɪəm/ *noun Chem.* (SYMBOL **Er**, ATOMIC NUMBER **68**) a soft silvery metal, belonging to the lanthanide series, that absorbs neutrons and has a high electrical resistivity. It is used in alloys for nuclear reactors, and in lasers for medical applications. [from the name *Ytterby* in Sweden, where it was first discovered]

ere /ɛə(r)/ *prep.*, *conj. poetic* before. [from Anglo-Saxon *ær*]

erect — *adj.* **1** upright; not bent or leaning. **2** *said of the penis, clitoris, or nipples* enlarged and rigid through being filled with blood, usually as a result of sexual excitement. — *verb* **1** to put up or to build. **2** to set or put (a pole, flag, etc) in a vertical position. **3** to set up or establish. [from Latin *erigere*, to set upright]

■ *adj* **1** upright, straight, vertical, upstanding, standing, raised, rigid, stiff. *verb* **1** build, construct, put up, raise, assemble, pitch. **2** raise, rear, lift. **3** establish, set up, found, form, institute, initiate, create.

erectile *adj. Physiol.*, *said of tissues or organs, especially the penis, clitoris, or nipples* capable of becoming erect.

erection *noun* **1** the act of erecting or the state of being erected. **2** *sometimes derog.* a building or structure. **3** *said of a sexual organ, especially the penis* the process of becoming erect or the state of being erect. **4** an erect sexual organ, especially an erect penis.

■ **1**, **2** construction, building. **1** raising, elevation. **2** edifice, pile, structure, framework.

erg *noun Physics* a unit of work or energy defined as the amount of work done when a force of one dyne moves through a distance of one centimetre. It is used in the centimetre-gramme-second (c.g.s.) system of measurement, and one erg is equal to 10^{-7} joules. [from Greek *ergon*, work]

ergo *adv. formal Logic* therefore. [from Latin *ergo*]

ergonomic *adj.* relating to ergonomics or the study of people in their work environment.

ergonomically *adv.* in terms of people and their work environment: *an ergonomically sound practice.*

ergonomics *noun Engineering* the study of the relationship between people and their working environment. [from Greek *ergon*, work + *-nomics* as in ECONOMICS]

ergonomist *noun* a person who studies ergonomics, especially professionally.

ergot *noun* **1** a disease of rye and other cereals caused by the fungus *Claviceps purpurea*, which appears as hard purple structures (ergots) on the seedheads. **2** (**ergots**) the hard purple structures characteristic of this disease. **3** the fungus that produces this disease. [from French, from Old French *argot*, cock's spur, because of its appearance]

ergotism *noun Medicine* poisoning caused by the consumption of bread made from rye infected with the fungus *Claviceps purpurea* (ergot). Formerly known as *St Anthony's fire.*

Erin /ˈɪərɪn, ˈɛərɪn/ *noun old use, poetic* Ireland. [from Old Irish *Erinn*]

Erinyes /ɪˈrɪnɪːz/ in Greek mythology, spirits of vengeance, depicted as carrying torches and covered with snakes.

ERM *abbrev.* Exchange Rate Mechanism.

ermine /ˈɜːmɪn/ *noun* **1** the winter phase of the stoat, when its fur has turned white except for the tip of the tail, which remains dark. **2** the fur of this animal, which was highly prized by the fur trade and formerly reserved for royalty. [from Old French *hermine*, from Latin *Armenius mus*, Armenian mouse]

Ernie *noun* in the UK, a computer which applies the laws of chance to pick the prize-winning numbers of premium bonds. [from *E*lectronic *r*andom *n*umber *i*ndicator *e*quipment]

erode *verb trans.*, *intrans.* to wear away, destroy, or be destroyed gradually. See also EROSION. [from Latin *erodere*, to gnaw away]

■ wear away, wear down, corrode, consume, disintegrate, deteriorate, spoil.

erogenous /ɪˈrɒdʒɪnəs/ *adj.*, *said of part of the body* sensitive to sexual stimulation. [from Greek *eros*, love + *genes*, born]

erosion /ɪˈrəʊʒən/ *noun* **1** the loosening, fragmentation, and transport from one place to another of rock material by water, wind, ice (eg glaciers), gravity, or living organisms, including human activity. **2** the process of eroding or being eroded.

■ wear, corrosion, abrasion, attrition, denudation, disintegration, deterioration, destruction, undermining.

erosive *adj.* causing erosion.

erotic *adj.* of or arousing sexual desire, or giving sexual pleasure. [from Greek *erotikos*, from *eros*, love]

■ aphrodisiac, seductive, sexy, sensual, titillating, pornographic, lascivious, stimulating, suggestive, amorous, amatory, carnal, lustful, voluptuous.

erotica *pl. noun* erotic literature, pictures, etc.

erotically *adv.* with an erotic manner or sense.

eroticism /ɪˈrɒtɪsɪzm/ *noun* **1** the erotic quality of a piece of writing, a picture, etc. **2** interest in, or pursuit of, sexual sensations. **3** the use of erotic images and symbols in art, literature, etc.

err /ɜː(r)/ *verb intrans.* **1** to make a mistake, be wrong, or do wrong. **2** to sin. — **err on the side of** ... to run the risk of a particular fault, in order to avoid an opposite and greater fault: *err on the side of caution.* [from Old French *errer*, from Latin *errare*, to stray]

■ GO ASTRAY. **1** be wrong, miscalculate, mistake, misjudge, slip up, blunder, misunderstand, do wrong. **2** sin, offend, transgress, deviate, misbehave.

errand *noun* **1** a short journey made in order to get or do something, especially for someone else. **2** the purpose of such a journey. [from Anglo-Saxon *ærende*, mission]

■ **1** mission, assignment, message, commission, charge, task, job, duty.

errant *adj. literary* **1** doing wrong; erring. **2** wandering in search of adventure: *a knight errant.* [from Old French *errer*, in sense 1 from Latin *errare*, to stray, and in sense 2 from Latin *itinerare*, to make a journey]

errantry *noun literary* wandering in search of adventure.

errata see ERRATUM.

erratic *adj.* **1** irregular; having no fixed pattern or course. **2** unpredictable in behaviour. [from Latin *errare*, to stray]

■ CHANGEABLE, VARIABLE, INCONSISTENT, UNSTABLE, UNPREDICTABLE, UNRELIABLE, ABERRANT, ABNORMAL, ECCENTRIC, INCONSTANT. **1** irregular, fitful, fluctuating, shifting, desultory, meandering.
E3 STEADY, CONSISTENT, STABLE.

erratically *adv.* with no fixed pattern or course; unpredictably.

erratum /ɛˈrɑːtəm/ *noun* (PL. **errata**) *formal* an error in writing or printing. [from Latin *errare*, to stray]

erroneous *adj.*, *said of an impression, etc; not said of a person* wrong or mistaken. [from Latin *erroneus*, straying]

■ incorrect, wrong, mistaken, false, untrue, inaccurate, inexact, invalid, illogical, unfounded, faulty, flawed.
■ correct, right.

erroneously *adv.* in error; by mistake.

error *noun* **1** a mistake, inaccuracy, or misapprehension. **2** the state of being mistaken. **3** the possible discrepancy between an estimate and an actual value or amount: *a margin of error*. [from Latin *error*, a wandering or straying, error]

■ **1** mistake, inaccuracy, slip, slip-up, blunder, *colloq.* howler, gaffe, faux pas, solecism, lapse, miscalculation, misunderstanding, misconception, misapprehension, misprint, oversight, omission, fallacy, flaw, fault, wrong.

ersatz /ˈɜːzats/ *derog.* — *noun* a cheaper substitute, often used because the genuine article is unavailable. — *adj.* substitute; imitation. [from German *ersatz*]

Erse /ɛəs/ — *noun* the name formerly used by lowland Scots for the Gaelic language of the Scottish Highlands and Islands; now applied to the Gaelic language of Ireland. — *adj.* relating to or spoken or written in this language. [from Lowland Scots *Erisch*, Irish]

erstwhile *adj. formal, old use* former; previous. [from Anglo-Saxon *ærest*, from *ær*, before]

eructation *noun formal* a belch or the act of belching. [from Latin *eructare*, to belch out]

erudite *adj.* showing or having a great deal of knowledge; learned. [from Latin *erudire*, to instruct]

■ learned, scholarly, well-educated, knowledgeable, lettered, educated, well-read, literate, academic, cultured, wise, sagacious, highbrow, profound.
■ illiterate, ignorant.

erudition *noun* scholarly learning or knowledge.

■ learning, scholarship, knowledge, knowledgeability, education, wisdom, sagacity, culture.

erupt *verb intrans.* **1** *said of a volcano* to eject (lava, ash, gases, steam, or solid rock debris), often suddenly and violently, on to the Earth's surface. **2** to break out suddenly and violently. **3** *said of a rash, blemish, or spot* to appear (especially suddenly) on the surface of the skin. **4** *said of a developing tooth* to emerge through the gum. [from Latin *erumpere*, to break out]

■ **2** break out, explode, belch, discharge, burst, gush, spew, spout, flare up.

eruption *noun* **1** the process of erupting, especially of a volcano. **2** a sudden or violent breaking-out. **3** a rash or blemish on the skin.

■ **2** outburst, discharge, outbreak, outpouring, explosion, flare-up. **3** rash, outbreak, inflammation.

-ery or **-ry** *suffix* **1** indicating a place where work or an activity of the stated kind is carried out: *brewery*. **2** indicating a class, group, or type of the stated kind: *greenery / weaponry*. **3** indicating an art, skill, or practice of the stated kind: *dentistry*. **4** indicating behaviour of the stated kind: *bravery*. **5** indicating anything connected with the stated person or thing: *popery*. [from French *-erie*, from Latin *-arius*]

erysipelas /ɛrɪˈsɪpɪlas/ *noun* a contagious disease of the skin and underlying tissues, caused by infection with the bacterium *Streptococcus pyogenes*, characterized by inflammation of the face and scalp, fever, and the appear-

ance of raised red or purplish lesions. [from Greek, perhaps from *eruthros*, red + *pella*, skin]

erythema /ɛrɪˈθiːmə/ *noun Medicine* redness of the skin, caused by dilation of the blood capillaries. [from Greek *erythema*, from *erythros* red]

erythrocyte /eˈrɪθrəʊsaɪt/ *noun Medicine* a red blood cell. [from Greek *erythros*, red + *kytos*, hollow vessel]

erythromycin /ɛrɪθrəʊˈmaɪsɪn/ *noun Medicine* an antibiotic that is used to treat a wide range of bacterial infections, especially in patients who are allergic to penicillin. [from Greek *erythros* red]

erythropoietin /ɪrɪθrəʊpɔɪˈiːtɪn/ *noun Physiol.* a hormone, secreted mainly by the kidneys, that stimulates an increase in the rate of formation of red blood cells in bone marrow. It is produced in response to a decrease in the amount of oxygen in the tissues. [from Greek *erythros*, red + *poiesis*, making]

ES *abbrev., as an international vehicle mark* El Salvador.

Es *symbol Chem.* einsteinium.

-es *suffix* see -s.

ESA *abbrev.* **1** Environmentally Sensitive Area. **2** European Space Agency.

Esc. *abbrev.* escudo.

escalate *verb intrans., trans.* to increase or be increased rapidly in scale, degree, etc. [a back-formation from ESCALATOR]

■ increase, intensify, accelerate, step up, heighten, magnify, enlarge, expand, extend, amplify.
■ decrease, diminish.

escalation *noun* a rapid increase or intensification.

■ increase, intensification, stepping up, growth, acceleration, rise, spiral, enlargement, expansion, extension.

escalator *noun* a type of conveyor belt which forms a continuous moving staircase. [originally a trademark, probably from Spanish *escalada*, from Latin *scala*, ladder]

escalop *noun* same as SCALLOP.

escalope /ˈɛskalɒp/ *noun* a thin slice of boneless meat, especially veal. [from French *escalope*]

escapade *noun* a daring, adventurous, or unlawful act. [from French *escapade*]

■ adventure, exploit, fling, prank, caper, romp, spree, *colloq.* lark, antic, stunt, trick.

escape — *verb* **1** *intrans.* to gain freedom. **2** to manage to avoid (punishment, disease, etc). **3** not to be noticed or remembered by: *nothing escapes his notice*. **4** *intrans. said of a gas, liquid, etc* to leak out or get out. **5** *said of words, etc* to be uttered unintentionally by. — *noun* **1** an act of escaping. **2** a means of escape. **3** the avoidance of danger or harm: *a narrow escape*. **4** a leak or release. **5** something providing a break or distraction. [from Old French *escaper*, probably from Latin *excappare*, to remove one's cape]

■ *verb* **1** get away, break free, run away, bolt, abscond, flee, fly, decamp, break loose, break out, *slang* do a bunk, flit, slip away. **2** avoid, evade, elude, dodge, skip, shun, shake off, slip. **4** leak, seep, flow, drain, gush, issue, discharge, ooze, trickle, pour forth. *noun* **1** getaway, flight, bolt, *colloq.* flit, breakout, decampment, jailbreak. **3** avoidance, evasion. **4** leak, seepage, leakage, outflow, gush, drain, discharge, emission, spurt, outpouring, emanation. **5** escapism, diversion, distraction, recreation, relaxation, pastime, safety valve.

escape clause a clause in a contract stating the conditions under which the contract may be broken.

escapee /ɪskeɪˈpiː/ *noun* a person who has escaped, especially from prison.

escapement *noun* the mechanism in a clock or watch that transmits regular impulses from the moving parts (the toothed wheelwork) to a pendulum or balance wheel, and so regulates the ability of the timepiece to keep accurate time.

escape road a short side-road, eg at a bend on a hill, into which a driver can turn in order to stop if in difficulty.

escape velocity *Physics* the minimum velocity required for an object such as a space vehicle or rocket to escape from the pull of the gravitational field of the Earth, or of another planet or celestial body.

escapism /ɪˈskeɪpɪzm/ *noun* the means of escaping, or the tendency to escape, from unpleasant reality into daydreams or fantasy.

escapist /ɪˈskeɪpɪst/ — *adj.* characterized by escapism. — *noun* a person who indulges in escapism.

. . . .
🔳 *adj.* make-believe, fantasy, unrealistic, mindless, undemanding, *colloq.* ostrich-like. *noun* dreamer, daydreamer, fantasizer, wishful thinker, non-realist.
🔳 *noun* realist.
. . . .

escapologist *noun* a person who practises escapology, especially professionally.

escapology *noun* the art or practice of freeing oneself from chains and other constraints, especially as theatrical entertainment.

escarpment *noun Geol.* a more or less continuous line of very steep slopes, formed by faulting or erosion, and found, for example, around the margins of a plateau. [from French *escarper*, to cut steeply]

eschatological /ɛskətɒˈlɒdʒɪkəl/ *adj.* relating to eschatology or the theological last things.

eschatology /ɛskəˈtɒlədʒɪ/ *noun* the branch of theology dealing with last things, eg death, divine judgement, and life after death. [from Greek *eschatos*, last]

escheat /ɪsˈtʃiːt/ — *Legal noun* **1** *formerly* the handing over of property to the state or a feudal lord in the absence of a legal heir. **2** property handed over in this way. — *verb* **1** *intrans.* to be handed over in this way. **2** *trans.* to hand over, or confiscate (property). [from Old French *eschete*, from *escheoir*, to fall to someone]

Escherichia /ɛʃəˈrɪkɪə/ *noun* a genus of rod-shaped bacteria that occurs naturally in the intestines of vertebrates and is sometimes pathogenic (**Escherichia coli**). [named after Theodor Escherich, who first described E.coli]

eschew /ɪsˈtʃuː/ *verb formal* to avoid, keep away from, or abstain from. [from Old French *eschever*]

eschewal /ɪsˈtʃuːəl/ *noun* avoidance; abstinence.

escort /ˈɛskɔːt, ɪˈskɔːt/ — *noun* (with stress on *es-*) **1** one or more people, vehicles, etc accompanying another or others for protection, guidance, or as a mark of honour. **2** a person of the opposite sex asked or hired to accompany another at a social event. — *verb* (with stress on -*scort*) to accompany as an escort. [from French *escorte*]

. . . .
🔳 *noun* **1** attendant, aide, squire, chaperon(e), guide, bodyguard, protector, entourage, company, retinue, suite, train, guard, convoy, cortège. **2** companion, partner, *colloq.* date. *verb* accompany, partner, chaperon(e), guide, lead, usher, conduct, guard, protect.
. . . .

escritoire /ɛskrɪˈtwɑː(r)/ *noun* a writing-desk, usually ornamented and with drawers, compartments, etc. [from French *escritoire*, from Latin *scriptorium*, writing-room]

escudo /eˈskuːdoʊ/ *noun* (PL. **escudos**) (ABBREV **Esc.**) the standard unit of currency in Portugal. [from Portuguese *escudo*, from Latin *scutum*, shield]

esculent /ˈɛskjʊlənt/ *formal* — *adj.* edible. — *noun* any edible substance. [from Latin *esculentus*, from *esca*, food]

escutcheon /ɪˈskʌtʃən/ *noun* **1** a shield decorated with a coat of arms. **2** a small metal plate around a keyhole or doorknob. — **a blot on the escutcheon** *facetious* a stain on one's good reputation. [from Old French *escuchon*, from Latin *scutum*, shield]

-ese *suffix* forming nouns and adjectives: **1** relating to a stated country or place: *Japanese* / *Vietnamese*. **2** indicating the people or language of a stated country: *Chinese*. **3** *often derog.* the typical style or language of a particular group or profession: *journalese*. [from Old French *-eis*, from Latin *-ensis*]

esker *noun Geol.* a long narrow hill of gravel and sand which may wind for long distances along a valley floor, and is thought to be formed by water flowing in tunnels underneath glaciers. [from Irish *eiscir*, ridge]

Eskimo — *noun* (PL. **Eskimos**, **Eskimo**) **1** *now often offensive* a member of any of several peoples inhabiting N Canada, Greenland, Alaska, and E Siberia. **2** the family of languages spoken by these peoples. — *adj.* relating to these peoples or to their language. [from N American Indian *esquimantsic*, eaters of raw flesh]

Eskimo dog a large powerful breed of dog with a double coat of long thick hair and a curled tail, widely distributed in the Arctic region and used by Inuit (Eskimos) for pulling sledges and hunting.

ESL *abbrev.* English as a second language.

ESN *abbrev.* educationally subnormal.

esophagus same as OESOPHAGUS.

esoteric /ɛsoʊˈtɛrɪk, iːsoʊˈtɛrɪk/ *adj.* understood only by those few people who have the necessary special knowledge; secret; mysterious. [from Greek *esoterikos*, from *eso*, within]

. . . .
🔳 recondite, obscure, abstruse, cryptic, inscrutable, mysterious, mystic, mystical, occult, hidden, secret, confidential, private, inside.
🔳 well-known, familiar.
. . . .

esoterically *adv.* in an esoteric or mysterious way.

ESP *abbrev.* **1** English for special purposes. **2** extra-sensory perception.

esp. *abbrev.* especially.

espadrille /ɛspəˈdrɪl, ˈɛspədrɪl/ *noun* a light canvas shoe with a sole made of rope or other plaited fibre. [from French *espadrille*, from Provençal *espardillo*, from *espart*, esparto grass]

espalier /ɪˈspalɪə(r)/ *noun* **1** a trellis or arrangement of wires against which a shrub or fruit tree is trained to grow flat, eg against a wall. **2** such a shrub or tree. [from French *espalier*]

esparto *noun* (PL. **espartos**) any of various tufted perennial grasses native to S Europe and N Africa and naturalized elsewhere, especially *Stipa tenacissima*, the leaves of which are used to make paper, rope, twine, baskets, mats, etc. It also yields a hard wax that is used as an ingredient of varnishes and polishes. [from Spanish *esparto*, from Latin, from Greek *sparton*, kind of rope]

especial *adj.* special. [from Old French, from Latin *specialis*, individual]

especially *adv.* **1** principally. **2** more than in other cases.

. . . .
🔳 PARTICULARLY. **1** chiefly, mainly, principally, primarily, pre-eminently, above all. **2** specially, markedly, notably, exceptionally, outstandingly, expressly, supremely, uniquely, unusually, strikingly, very.
. . . .

Esperanto *noun* a language invented for international use, published in 1887. [from the pseudonym of its inventor, Dr Zamenhof, meaning 'the one who hopes']

espionage /ˈɛspɪənɑːʒ/ *noun* the activity of spying, or the use of spies to gather information. [from French *espionnage*, from *espion*, spy]

esplanade /ˈɛspləneɪd/ *noun* a long wide pavement next to a beach. [from French *esplanade*, from Spanish *esplanar*, make level]

espousal /ɪˈspaʊzəl/ *noun* **1** *formal* the act of espousing (a cause, etc). **2** *old use* a marriage or engagement.

espouse / ɪ'spaʊz/ *verb* **1** *formal* to adopt or give one's support to (a cause, etc). **2** *old use* to marry, or to give (eg a daughter) in marriage. [from Old French *espouser*, to marry]

espresso /ɛ'spresəʊ/ *noun* (PL. **espressos**) **1** coffee made by forcing steam or boiling water through ground coffee beans. **2** the machine for making it. [from Italian *espresso*, pressed out]

esprit / ɛs'priː/ *noun formal, literary* liveliness or wit. [from French *esprit*, spirit]

esprit de corps / ɛs'priː də kɔː(r)/ *noun* loyalty to, or concern for the honour of, a group or body to which one belongs. [French, = spirit of the group]

espy / ɪ'spaɪ/ *verb* (**espies, espied**) *literary* to catch sight of; to observe. [from Old French *espier*]

Esq. *abbrev.* esquire.

-esque *suffix* **1** in the style or fashion of: *Byronesque*. **2** like or similar to: *picturesque*. [from French]

esquire / ɪ'skwaɪə(r)/ *noun* **1** (*abbrev.* **Esq.**) a title used after a man's name when no other form of address, eg Mr, is used, especially when addressing letters. **2** a squire. [from Old French *esquier*, squire]

esquisse / ɛ'skiːs/ *noun* in art, a preliminary study: for a picture or design, usually a rapid sketch or rough drawing; for a sculpture, a model, often made smaller than the final work. [from French *esquisse*, sketch]

ESRC *abbrev.* Economic and Social Research Council.

-ess *suffix* indicating a female of the type or class: *lioness / duchess*. [from French *-esse*, from Latin *-issa*]

essay /'ɛseɪ, ɛ'seɪ/ — *noun* (with stress on *es-*) **1** a short formal piece of writing, usually dealing with a single subject. **2** *formal* an attempt. — *verb formal* (with stress on *-say*) to attempt. [from French *essayer*, to try]

◨ *noun* **1** composition, dissertation, paper, article, assignment, thesis, piece, commentary, critique, discourse, treatise, review, leader, tract.

essayist *noun* a writer of literary essays.

essence *noun* **1** the basic distinctive part or quality of something, determining its nature or character. **2** a liquid obtained from a plant, drug, etc and having its properties in concentrated form. — **in essence** basically or fundamentally. **of the essence** absolutely necessary or extremely important. [from French *essence*, from Latin *esse*, to be]

◨ **1** nature, being, quintessence, substance, soul, spirit, core, centre, heart, meaning, quality, significance, life, entity, crux, kernel, marrow, pith, character, principle. **2** concentrate, extract, distillation, spirits.

essential — *adj.* **1** absolutely necessary. **2** of the basic or inner nature, the essence, of something. — *noun* **1** something necessary. **2** a basic or fundamental element, principle, or piece of information.

◨ *adj.* **1** crucial, indispensable, necessary, vital, requisite, required, needed, important. **2** fundamental, basic, intrinsic, inherent, principal, main, key, characteristic, definitive, typical, constituent. *noun* **1** necessity, prerequisite, must, requisite, requirement, necessary, sine qua non. **2** basic, fundamental, foundation, principle.

▣ *adj.* INESSENTIAL. **1** dispensable. **2** incidental. *noun* INESSENTIAL.

essentiality *noun* being essential; an essential quality or nature.

essentially *adv.* **1** basically; most importantly. **2** necessarily.

◨ **1** fundamentally, basically, intrinsically, inherently, principally, in essence, in principle.

essential oil *Bot.* a mixture of volatile oils which have distinctive and characteristic odours, obtained from certain aromatic plants, eg rose, jasmine, juniper. They are widely used in cosmetics and aromatherapy.

est. *abbrev.* **1** established. **2** estimated.

-est *suffix* forming the superlative of adjectives and some adverbs: *quickest / soonest*. [from Anglo-Saxon *-est* and *-ost*]

establish *verb* **1** to settle (someone) firmly in a position, place, job, etc. **2** to set up (eg a university or a business). **3** to find, show, or prove. **4** to cause people to accept (eg a custom or a claim). [from Old French *establir*]

◨ **1** install, plant, settle, secure, lodge, entrench, ensconce. **2** set up, found, start, form, institute, create, organize, inaugurate, introduce. **3** prove, substantiate, demonstrate, authenticate, ratify, verify, validate, certify, confirm, affirm.

▣ **1** uproot. **3** refute.

established *adj.* **1** settled or accepted. **2** said of a Church, recognized as the official Church of a country.

establishment *noun* **1** the act of establishing. **2** a business, its premises, or its staff. **3** a public or government institution: *a research establishment*. **4** (**the Establishment**) the group of people in a country, society, or community who hold power and exercise authority, and are regarded as being opposed to change.

◨ **1** formation, setting up, founding, creation, foundation, installation, institution, inauguration. **2** business, company, firm, institute, organization, concern, institution, enterprise. **4** ruling class, the system, the authorities, the powers that be.

estancia / ɛ'stansɪə/ *noun* a large estate or cattle ranch in Spanish America. [from Spanish *estancia*, station, dwelling]

estate *noun* **1** a large piece of land owned by a person or group of people. **2** an area of land on which development of a particular kind has taken place, eg houses (a **housing estate**) or factories (an **industrial trading estate**). **3** *Legal* a person's total possessions (property, money, etc), especially at death. **4** a plantation. **5** *Hist.* any of various groups or classes within the social structure of society, eg the **first estate** or lords spiritual (ie bishops and archbishops), the **second estate** or lords temporal (ie the nobility) and the **third estate** (the common people). **6** *old use* a condition or state: *the holy estate of matrimony*. [from Old French *estat*]

◨ **1** land, manor, domain. **2** area, development, park. **3** possessions, effects, assets, belongings, holdings, property, goods, lands. **6** status, standing, class, place, condition, state, rank.

estate agent 1 a person whose job is the buying, selling, leasing, and valuation of houses and other property. **2** the manager of a private estate.

estate car a car with a large area behind the rear seats for luggage, etc, and a rear door.

estate duty same as DEATH DUTY.

esteem — *verb* **1** to value, respect, or think highly of. **2** *formal* to consider to be. — *noun* high regard or respect. [from Old French *estimer*, from Latin *aestimare*, to estimate the value of]

◨ *verb* **1** value, respect, appreciate, admire, venerate. **2** think, consider, *formal* deem. *noun* regard, respect, admiration, veneration, honour.

ester *noun Chem.* an organic chemical compound formed by the reaction of an alcohol with an organic acid, with the loss of a water molecule. [probably a contraction of German *Essigäther*, acetic ether]

Esth. *abbrev. Biblical* (Book of) Esther.

esthetic same as AESTHETIC.

estimable *adj.* highly respected; worthy of respect. [see ESTIMATE]

◼ esteemed, respected, worthy, creditable, admirable, commendable.

estimate /ˈɛstɪmeɪt, ˈɛstɪmət/ — *verb* (pronounced -meɪt) **1** to judge or calculate (size, amount, value, etc) roughly or without measuring. **2** to have or form an opinion (that); to think. **3** to submit to a possible client a statement of the likely cost of a piece of work. — *noun* (pronounced -mət) **1** a rough assessment (of size, etc). **2** a calculation of the probable cost of a job. [from Latin *aestimare*, to estimate the value of]

◼ *verb* **1** assess, reckon, evaluate, calculate, compute, gauge, guess, value, conjecture. **2** consider, judge, think, believe. *noun* **1** assessment, reckoning, valuation, judgement, guess, approximation, estimation, evaluation, computation, opinion.

estimation *noun* **1** judgement; opinion. **2** the act of estimating.

◼ **1** judgement, opinion, belief, consideration, estimate, view. **2** evaluation, assessment, reckoning, calculation, computation.

estimator *noun* a person who estimates values, etc.

estrange *verb* to cause (someone) to break away from a previously friendly state or relationship. [from Old French *estranger*, from Latin *extraneare*, to treat as a stranger]

estranged *adj.* no longer friendly or supportive: *his estranged wife.*

◼ separated, alienated, disaffected, antagonistic.
◱ reconciled, united.

estrangement *noun* separation; loss of friendship or affection.

estuary /ˈɛstjʊərɪ/ *noun* (PL. **estuaries**) the broad mouth of a river that flows into the sea, where fresh water mixes with sea water. Estuaries are affected by the tides, and are often used as harbours because they are relatively sheltered. [from Latin *aestus*, commotion, tide]

◼ inlet, mouth, firth, fjord, creek, arm, sea loch.

Estuary English a dialect of English influenced by Cockney, spoken in the Thames Estuary and surrounding areas.

ESU *abbrev.* English-Speaking Union.

ET *abbrev.*, *as an international vehicle mark* Egypt.

ETA *abbrev.* estimated time of arrival.

e-tailer *noun* a retail company that sells products on the Internet.

et al. *abbrev.* et alia or et alii (Latin), and other things or people.

etc or **etc.** *abbrev.* et cetera.

et cetera or **etcetera** /ɛt ˈsɛtərə/ (Latin) and the rest, and so on.

etceteras *pl. noun* additional things or people; extras.

etch *verb* **1** *trans., intrans.* to make designs on (metal, glass, etc) using an acid to eat out the lines. **2** to make a deep or irremovable impression. [from German *ätzen*, to etch, eat away with acid]

etcher *noun* a person who etches, especially professionally.

etching *noun* **1** the act or art of making etched designs. **2** a print made from an etched plate.

ETD *abbrev.* estimated time of departure.

eternal *adj.* **1** without beginning or end; everlasting. **2** unchanging; valid for all time. **3** *colloq.* frequent, endless. — **the Eternal** a name for God. [from Old French *eternel*, from Latin *aeternalis*]

◼ **1** unending, endless, ceaseless, everlasting, never-ending, infinite, limitless, immortal, undying, imperishable. **2** unchanging, timeless, enduring, lasting, perennial, abiding. **3** constant, continuous, perpetual, incessant, interminable. ◱ **1** ephemeral, temporary. **2** changeable.

eternally *adv.* for ever; without end; constantly.

eternal triangle a relationship, involving love and jealousy, between two men and a woman, or two women and a man.

eternity *noun* (PL. **eternities**) **1** time regarded as having no end. **2** the state of being eternal. **3** *Relig.* a timeless existence after death. **4** *colloq.* an extremely long time. [from Old French *eternite*]

◼ **1** everlasting, infinity. **2** everlastingness, endlessness, imperishability, timelessness, perpetuity, immutability. **3** afterlife, hereafter, immortality, heaven, paradise, next world, world to come. **4** ages, age, eons.

eternity ring a ring set with a circle of stones, as a symbol of lasting love.

ETH *abbrev.*, *as an international vehicle mark* Ethiopia.

ethane /ˈiːθeɪn, ˈɛθeɪn/ *noun Chem.* (FORMULA C_2H_6) a colourless odourless flammable gas belonging to the alkane series of hydrocarbons, and found in natural gas. It is used as a fuel and refrigerant, and in the synthesis of organic compounds. [from ETHER + -*ane*]

ethanedioic acid /iːθeɪndaɪˈoʊɪk/ *Chem.* oxalic acid.

ethanediol /iːθeɪnˈdaɪɒl/ *noun* ethylene glycol.

ethanoate /ɛˈθanoʊeɪt/ *noun Chem.* same as ACETATE.

ethanoic acid /ɛθəˈnoʊɪk/ *Chem.* same as ACETIC ACID.

ethanol /ˈɛθənɒl/ *noun Chem.* (FORMULA C_2H_5OH) a colourless volatile flammable alcohol that is produced by fermentation of the sugar in fruit or cereals, and is used as an intoxicant in alcoholic beverages, and as a fuel. Also called ETHYL ALCOHOL.

ethene /ˈɛθiːn/ *noun Chem.* same as ETHYLENE.

ether /ˈiːθə(r)/ *noun* **1** any of a group of organic chemical compounds that are volatile and highly flammable, and contain two hydrocarbon groups linked by an oxygen atom. They are formed by the dehydration of alcohols. **2** (**diethyl ether**) (FORMULA $C_2H_5OC_2H_5$) the commonest ether, widely used as a solvent, and formerly employed as an anaesthetic. **3** (*also* **aether**) *Physics* a hypothetical medium formerly believed to be necessary for the transmission of electromagnetic radiation. This concept was abandoned when the theory of relativity was accepted. **4** (*also* **aether**) *poetic* the clear upper air or a clear sky. [from Greek *aither*, the heavens]

ethereal /ɪˈθɪərɪəl/ *adj.* **1** of an unreal lightness or delicateness; fairy-like. **2** heavenly or spiritual. [see ETHER]

◼ INCORPOREAL. **1** airy, impalpable, intangible, immaterial, delicate, gossamer, gauzy. **2** heavenly, spiritual.

ethic *noun* the moral system or set of principles particular to a certain person, community, group, etc. [from Greek *ethikos*, from *ethos*, custom, character]

ethical *adj.* **1** of or concerning morals, justice, or duty. **2** morally right. **3** *said of a medicine or drug* not advertised to the general public, and available only on prescription.

◼ **1, 2** moral. **2** principled, just, right, proper, virtuous, honourable, fair, upright, righteous, seemly, honest,

good, correct, commendable, fitting, noble.
⊞ **2** unethical.

. . . .

ethically *adv.* as regards ethics or moral principles: *an ethically justifiable practice.*

ethics *noun* **1** (*sing.*) the study or the science of morals. **2** (*pl.*) rules or principles of behaviour: *medical ethics.*

. . . .

⊞ **1** moral philosophy. **2** moral values, morality, principles, standards, code, rules, beliefs, propriety, conscience, equity.

. . . .

ethnic *adj.* **1** relating to, or having, a common race or cultural tradition: *an ethnic group.* **2** associated with, or resembling, an exotic, especially non-European, racial or tribal group: *ethnic clothes.* **3** from the point of view of race, rather than nationality: *ethnic Asians.* **4** between or involving different racial groups: *ethnic violence.* [from Greek *ethnikos*, from *ethnos*, nation]

. . . .

⊞ **1, 4** racial. **1** cultural, national. **2** native, indigenous, traditional, tribal, folk, aboriginal.

. . . .

ethnically *adv.* as regards race; in terms of race.

ethnic cleansing genocide or forced removal inflicted by one ethnic group on all others in a particular area.

ethnicity /ɛθˈnɪsɪtɪ/ *noun* racial status or distinctiveness.

ethnocentric *adj.* relating to, or holding, the belief that one's own cultural tradition or racial group is superior to all others. [from Greek *ethnos*, nation + -CENTRIC]

ethnocentricity or **ethnocentrism** *noun* the policy or practice of being ethnocentric.

ethnography *noun* the detailed study of the culture of a particular society based on fieldwork and participation in the life of the society.

ethnological *adj.* relating to ethnology or the study of race.

ethnologist *noun* a person who studies ethnology or race.

ethnology *noun* the scientific study of different races and cultural traditions, and their relations with each other. [from Greek *ethnos*, nation]

ethology /iːˈθɒlədʒɪ/ *Zool.* the study of animal behaviour, especially by direct observation and monitoring (eg by radio-tracking) of animals in their natural habitats. [from Greek *ethos*, custom + -LOGY]

ethos /ˈiːθɒs/ *noun* the typical spirit, character, or attitudes (of a group, community, etc) [from Greek *ethos*, custom, culture]

. . . .

⊞ attitude, beliefs, standards, manners, ethics, morality, code, principles, spirit, tenor, rationale, character, disposition.

. . . .

ethyl /ˈiːθaɪl, ˈɛθɪl/ *noun Chem.* in organic chemical compounds, the (C_2H_5-) group, as for example in ethylamine $(C_2H_5NH_2)$. [from ETHER + Greek *hyle*, matter]

ethylene /ˈɛθɪliːn/ *noun* (FORMULA C_2H_4) a colourless flammable gas with a sweet smell, belonging to the alkene series of hydrocarbons. It is used in the manufacture of polythene. Also called ETHENE.

ethylene glycol *Chem.* a thick liquid alcohol used as an antifreeze. Also called ETHANEDIOL.

ethyne /ˈiːθaɪn, ˈɛθaɪn/ *noun Chem.* same as ACETYLENE.

etiolated /ˈiːtɪəʊleɪtɪd/ *adj.* **1** *Bot.*, *said of a plant* having foliage that has become yellow through lack of sunlight. **2** *formal literary, said of a person* pale and weak in appearance. [from French *étioler*, to become pale]

etiolation /iːtɪəʊˈleɪʃən/ *noun Bot.* the abnormal appearance of plants grown in darkness or severely reduced light, where the leaves appear yellow due to lack of chlorophyll and the stems are long and spindly.

etiology same as AETIOLOGY.

etiquette /ˈɛtɪkɛt/ *noun* **1** conventions of correct or polite social behaviour. **2** rules, usually unwritten, regarding the behaviour of members of a particular profession, etc towards each other. [from French *étiquette*, label]

. . . .

⊞ CODE, CONVENTIONS, RULES, PROTOCOL. **1** formalities, standards, correctness, customs, manners, politeness, courtesy, civility, decorum, ceremony, decency.

. . . .

Etruscan /ɪˈtrʌskən/ — *noun* **1** a member of an ancient people inhabiting Etruria in central Italy from the 8c BC. **2** their language. — *adj.* relating to this people or their language.

-ette *suffix* **1** indicating a female of the stated type: *usherette.* **2** indicating a small thing of the type: *cigarette / kitchenette.* **3** indicating an imitation: *leatherette.* [from Old French *-ette*]

étude /eɪˈtjuːd/ *noun Mus.* a short piece written for a single instrument, intended as an exercise or a means of showing talent. [from French *étude*, study]

ety. *abbrev.* etymology.

etymological *adj.* relating to etymology or the origin of words.

etymologist *noun* a person who studies etymology or the origin of words.

etymology *noun* (PL. **etymologies**) **1** the study of the origin and development of words and their meanings. **2** an explanation of the history of a particular word. [from Latin *etymologia*, from Greek *etymon*, the literal sense of a word, from *etymos*, true]

EU *abbrev.* European Union.

Eu *symbol Chem.* europium.

eucalyptus /juːkəˈlɪptəs/ *noun* (PL. **eucalyptuses**, **eucalypti**) **1** any of various evergreen trees of the genus *Eucalyptus*, native to Australia and grown widely elsewhere. Some species produce an oil, which is strongly antiseptic and used in medicines. **2** the hard durable wood of this tree, which contains strong-smelling resins, and is widely used as timber. **3** eucalyptus oil. [from Greek *eu*, well + *kalyptos*, covered]

Eucharistic /ˈjuːkərɪst/ *adj.* relating to the Eucharist.

euchre /ˈjuːkə(r)/ *noun* an American card-game for two, three, or four players, played with 32 cards.

Euclidean /juːˈklɪdɪən/ or **Euclidian** *adj.* relating to the three-dimensional geometrical system devised by Euclid, a Greek mathematician of the 3c BC.

eugenic /juːˈdʒɛnɪk/ *adj.* relating to eugenics or the science of improving human populations.

eugenics /juːˈdʒɛnɪks/ *sing. noun* **1** the science of dealing with human hereditary diseases and disorders by genetic counselling of parents who may be carriers of such conditions. **2** the principle or practice of trying to improve the human race by selective breeding. [from Greek *eugenes*, well-born, of good stock]

eukaryote or **eucaryote** /juːˈkarɪəʊt/ *Biol.* an organism in which the cells have a distinct nucleus containing the genetic material and separated from the cytoplasm by a nuclear membrane. See also PROKARYOTE. [from Greek *eu*, well + *karyon*, kernel]

eulogistic *adj.* expressing praise.

eulogistically *adv.* as an expression of praise.

eulogize or **eulogise** *verb* to praise highly.

eulogy /ˈjuːlədʒɪ/ *noun* (PL. **eulogies**) **1** a speech or piece of writing in praise of someone or something. **2** high praise. [from Latin *eulogium*, from Greek *eu*, well + *logos*, discourse]

. . . .

⊞ **1** panegyric, tribute, accolade.

. . . .

eunuch /ˈjuːnək/ *noun* **1** a man who has been castrated, especially one formerly employed as a guard of a harem in Eastern countries. **2** *derog.* a person who lacks power or effectiveness in some respect. [from Greek *eunouchos*]

euphemism /ˈjuːfəmɪzm/ *noun* **1** a mild or inoffensive term used in place of one considered offensive or unpleasantly direct, eg *pass on* instead of *die*. **2** the use of such terms. [from Greek *eu*, well + *phanai*, to speak]

⊟ **1** evasion, polite term, substitution, genteelism, politeness, understatement.

euphemistic *adj.*, *said of an expression* serving as a euphemism, or mild expression replacing a harsher one.
euphemistically *adv.* with a euphemistic manner; as a euphemism.
euphonious *adj.* pleasing to the ear.
euphonium *noun* a brass instrument of the tuba family.
euphony /ˈjuːfənɪ/ *noun* (PL. **euphonies**) **1** a pleasing sound, especially in speech. **2** pleasantness of sound, especially of pronunciation. [from Greek *eu*, well + *phone*, sound]
euphoria *noun* a feeling of wild happiness and well-being. In unjustified circumstances it may be a symptom of mania or the side-effect of certain drugs. [from Greek *euphoria*, ability to endure well]

⊟ elation, ecstasy, bliss, rapture, high spirits, well-being, *colloq.* high, exhilaration, exultation, joy, intoxication, jubilation, transport, glee, exaltation, enthusiasm, cheerfulness.
⊟ depression, despondency.

euphoric *adj.* feeling intense happiness.

⊟ elated, ecstatic, blissful, rapturous, exultant, joyful, intoxicated, jubilant, gleeful.

euphorically *adv.* with intense happiness.
euphuism /ˈjuːfjuːɪzm/ *noun* a pompous and affected style of writing. [from the style of John Lyly's romance *Euphues*]
euphuistic *adj.* having a pompous and affected style.
euphuistically *adv.* in a pompous and affected style.
Eur. *abbrev.* Europe.
Eurasian — *adj.* **1** of mixed European and Asian descent. **2** of, or relating to, Europe and Asia. — *noun* a person of mixed European and Asian descent.
Euratom *abbrev.* European Atomic Energy Community.
eureka /juəˈriːkə/ *interj.* an exclamation of triumph at finding something, solving a problem, etc. [from Greek *heureka*, I have found it]
eurhythmic /juəˈrɪðmɪk/ *adj.* **1** *Archit.* in harmonious proportion. **2** relating to eurhythmics.
eurhythmics *sing. noun* a system of training by rhythmic movement to music. [from Greek *eu*, well + *rhythmos*, rhythm]
euro *noun* (PL. **euros**) a common unit of currency in most parts of the European Union.
Euro- *combining form* Europe or European.
Eurocheque *noun* a cheque which may be drawn on the user's own account and exchanged for cash, goods, or services in a number of European (and non-European) countries.
Eurocrat *noun sometimes derog.* an official involved in the administration of any organization in the European Community.
Eurocurrency or **Euromoney** *noun* convertible currencies held in banks in W Europe outside the country of origin.
Eurodollars *pl. noun* US currency held in European banks to assist trade.
Eurocommunism *noun* a form of communism advocated by the western European communist parties.
European /juərəˈpɪən/ — *adj.* **1** relating to Europe. **2** showing or favouring a spirit of co-operation between the countries of Europe, especially those of the European

Community. — *noun* **1** a native or inhabitant of Europe. **2** a person who favours close political and economic contact between the countries of Europe.
European sole see DOVER SOLE.
europium /juəˈroʊpɪəm/ *noun Chem.* (SYMBOL **Eu**, ATOMIC NUMBER **63**) a soft silvery metal belonging to the lanthanide series, used as a neutron absorber in the control rods of nuclear reactors. [from the name *Europe*]
Euro-sceptic *noun* a person, especially a politician, who is sceptical about the value of links between the UK and the European Union.
Eustachian tube /juːˈsteɪʃɪən/ in terrestrial vertebrates, a narrow air-filled tube that links the middle ear to the pharynx at the back of the throat, and serves to ensure that the air pressure remains the same on both sides of the eardrum. [named after the Italian anatomist Bartolomeo Eustachio]
eustasy /ˈjuːstəsɪ/ *noun Geol.* worldwide change in sea-level caused by advancing or receding polar ice caps. This has caused a gradual rise in sea-level over the last century. [from Greek *eu*, well + *stasis*, standing]
euthanasia /juːəˈneɪzɪə/ *noun* the act or practice of ending the life of a person who is suffering from an incurable and often painful or distressing illness. [from Greek, from *eu*, well + *thanatos*, death]
eutrophic /juːˈtrɒfɪk/ *adj. Environ.* describing a body of water that has become over-enriched with nutrients, either naturally or as a result of pollution with artificial fertilizers, etc. [from Greek *eutrophia*]
eV *abbrev.* electronvolt.
evacuate *verb* **1** to leave (a place), especially because of danger. **2** to cause (people) to leave a place, especially because of danger. **3** *Biol.* to discharge (waste) from the body, especially by emptying the bowels. **4** *Physics* to create (a vacuum) in a bulb, flask, or other sealed vessel by removing all gases and vapours. **5** *Medicine* to suck (fluid) out of a cavity. [from Latin *evacuare*, to empty out]

⊟ **1** leave, vacate, depart from, withdraw from, quit, retire from, abandon, desert, forsake, relinquish. **2** clear, remove. **3** empty, eject, void, expel, discharge, eliminate, defecate, purge.

evacuation *noun* the process of evacuating, especially removing people from a place because of danger.

⊟ departure, withdrawal, retreat, retirement, exodus, removal, quitting, desertion, abandonment, relinquishment, clearance, vacation, emptying, expulsion, ejection, discharge, elimination.

evacuee *noun* an evacuated person.
evade *verb* **1** to escape or avoid by trickery or skill. **2** to avoid answering (a question). See also EVASION. [from Latin *evadere*, to go out]

⊟ AVOID, DODGE. **1** escape, elude, shirk, steer clear of, shun, sidestep, *colloq.* duck, *colloq.* skive off, *colloq.* chicken out of, *colloq.* cop out of. **2** parry, fend off.
⊟ **1** confront, face.

evaluate *verb* **1** to form an idea or judgement about the worth of. **2** *Maths.* to calculate the value of. [from French *évaluation*]

⊟ **1** value, assess, appraise, estimate, reckon, calculate, gauge, judge, rate, size up, weigh, compute, rank.

evaluation *noun* an estimate of value or worth.

⊟ valuation, appraisal, assessment, estimation, estimate, judgement, reckoning, calculation, opinion, computation.

evanesce /ɛvə'nɛs/ *verb intrans. literary* to disappear gradually; to fade from sight. [from Latin *evanescere*, to vanish]

evanescence /ɛvə'nɛsəns/ *noun* vanishing; gradual disappearance.

evanescent /ɛvə'nɛsənt/ *adj. literary* **1** quickly fading. **2** short-lived; transitory.

evangelical /i:va'ndʒelikəl/ — *adj.* **1** based on the Gospels of the New Testament. **2** denoting any of various groups within the Protestant church stressing the authority of the Bible and claiming that personal acceptance of Christ as saviour is the only way to salvation. **3** enthusiastically advocating a particular cause, etc. — *noun* a member of an evangelical movement, or a supporter of evangelical beliefs. [from Greek *eu*, well + *angellein*, to bring news]

evangelicalism /i:va'ndʒelikəlizm/ *noun* evangelical principles.

evangelism /ɪ'vandʒəlizm/ *noun* **1** the act or practice of evangelizing. **2** evangelicalism.

evangelist /ɪ'vandʒəlɪst/ *noun* **1** a person who preaches Christianity, especially at public meetings. **2** (*usually* **Evangelist**) each of the writers of the four Biblical Gospels: Matthew, Mark, Luke, or John.

evangelistic /ɪvandʒə'lɪstɪk/ *adj.* relating to evangelism.

evangelization or **evangelisation** /ɪvandʒəlaɪ'zeɪʃən/ *noun* evangelizing; promoting Christianity.

evangelize or **evangelise** /ɪ'vandʒəlaɪz/ *verb* **1** to preach Christianity to (someone). **2** *intrans.* to preach Christianity, especially by travelling from place to place. **3** *intrans., trans. often facetious* to attempt to persuade (someone) to adopt a particular principle or cause.

evaporate /ɪ'vapəreɪt/ *verb trans., intrans.* **1** to change or cause to change from a liquid into a vapour at a temperature below the boiling point of the liquid. **2** to disappear or cause to disappear. [from Latin *evaporare*, from *vapor*, steam, vapour]

▪ **1** dematerialize, melt (away), dissolve, disperse, dispel, dissipate, fade. **2** vaporize.

evaporated milk unsweetened milk that has been concentrated by evaporation. When tinned it has a long shelf-life, and is widely used in many tropical countries.

evaporation *noun* the process of evaporating; disappearance.

evaporite /ɪ'vapəraɪt/ *noun Geol.* a mineral deposit formed as a result of the evaporation of all or most of the water from a saline solution such as sea water or a salt lake.

evasion *noun* **1** the act of evading, especially a commitment or responsibility. **2** a trick or excuse used to evade (a question, etc). [from Latin *evasio*, from *evadere*, to go out]

▪ EQUIVOCATION, PREVARICATION. **1** avoidance, escape, shirking, trickery, subterfuge, fencing, hedging. **2** dodge, excuse, quibble.

evasive *adj.* **1** having the purpose of evading, especially trouble or danger. **2** not honest or open: *an evasive answer.*

▪ **2** equivocating, indirect, prevaricating, devious, shifty, unforthcoming, slippery, misleading, deceitful, deceptive, *colloq.* cagey, oblique, secretive, tricky, cunning.
🗗 **2** direct, frank.

eve *noun* **1** the evening or day before some notable event. **2** the period immediately before: *the eve of war.* [from EVEN²]

▪ **2** verge, brink, edge, threshold.

even¹ — *adj.* **1** smooth and flat. **2** constant or regular: *travelling at an even 50mph.* **3** *said of a number* divisible by 2,

with nothing left over. **4** designated or marked by such a number: *the even houses in the street.* **5** (**even with**) level; on the same plane or at the same height. **6** (**even with**) having no advantage or owing no debt. **7** *said of temper, character, etc* calm. **8** equal: *an even chance.* **9** level in terms of score or position. **10** fair. — *adv.* **1** used with a comparative to emphasize a comparison with something else: *he's good, but she's even better.* **2** used with an expression stronger than a previous one: *he looked sad, even depressed.* **3** used to introduce a surprising piece of information: *even John was there!* **4** used to indicate a lower extreme in an implied comparison: *even a child (let alone an educated adult) would have known that!* **5** (**even if, even though**) used to emphasize that whether or not something is or might be true, the following or preceding statement is or would remain true: *He'd be unhappy even if he did get the job. Even though he got the job, he's still unhappy. He got the job but, even so, he's still unhappy.* — *verb* **1** (**even something up**) to make it equal. **2** (**even something out** or **up**) to make it smooth or level. **3** (**even out**) to become level or regular. — *noun* **1** (*usually* **evens**) an even number, or something designated by one. **2** (**evens**) same as EVEN MONEY. — **even now** still; after all that has happened. **even then** after all that had happened, will have happened, or would have happened. **get even with someone** to be revenged on them. [from Anglo-Saxon *efen*]

▪ *adj.* **1** level, flat, smooth, horizontal, flush, parallel, plane. **2** steady, unvarying, constant, regular, uniform. **7** even-tempered, calm, placid, serene, tranquil, composed, unruffled. **8** equal, balanced, matching, same, similar, like, symmetrical, fifty-fifty. **9** level, side by side, neck and neck. **10** even-handed, balanced, equitable, fair, impartial. *verb* LEVEL. **1** balance, equalize, match, regularize, align, square. **2** smooth, flatten, straighten. **3** stabilize, steady.
🗗 *adj.* **1** uneven. **8** unequal.

even² *noun old use, poetic* evening. [from Anglo-Saxon *æfen*]

even-handed *adj.* fair.

▪ even, balanced, equitable, fair, impartial.

evening — *noun* **1** the last part of the day, usually from late afternoon until bedtime. **2** a party or other social gathering held at this time: *a poetry evening.* **3** *poetic* the latter part of anything: *the evening of his life.* — *adj.* of or during the evening. [from Anglo-Saxon *æfnung*]

▪ *noun* **1** nightfall, dusk, eve, eventide, twilight, sunset, sundown.

evening dress clothes worn on formal occasions in the evening.

evening primrose *Bot.* any of about 200 species of the genus *Oenothera*, a biennial with large scented yellow flowers that open at dusk.

evening star a planet, especially Venus, clearly visible in the west just after sunset.

evenly *adv.* **1** in an even way; uniformly. **2** in equal parts or shares: *evenly divided.*

even money gambling odds with the potential to win the same as the amount gambled.

evenness *noun* being even or uniform.

evensong *noun* the service of evening prayer in the Anglican Church. [from Anglo-Saxon *æfensang*, evening song]

event *noun* **1** something that occurs or happens; an incident, especially a significant one. **2** an item in a programme of sports, etc; a sports contest. — **at all events** or **in any event** in any case; whatever happens. **in either event** no matter which (of two things, possibilities, etc) happens. **in the event** in the end; as it happened, happens, or may happen. **in the event of something** if something occurs: *in the event of a power cut / in the event that there is* *a power cut.* **in that event** if that occurs. [from Latin *eventus*, result, event]

■ **1** happening, occurrence, incident, occasion, affair, circumstance, episode, eventuality, experience, matter, case, adventure, business, fact, possibility, milestone. **2** item, game, match, competition, contest, tournament, engagement.

even-tempered *adj.* unlikely to become angry or excited.

■ calm, placid, level-headed, stable, tranquil, serene, composed, collected, cool, steady, peaceful, peaceable. ☒ excitable, erratic.

eventer *noun* a person who takes part in eventing.
eventful *adj.* full of important or significant events.

■ busy, exciting, lively, active, full, *colloq.* action-packed, interesting, remarkable, significant, memorable, momentous, notable, noteworthy, unforgettable. ☒ dull, ordinary.

eventfully *adv.* with important or significant events.
eventide *noun poetic, old use* evening. [from Anglo-Saxon *æfentid*]
eventide home a home for old people.
eventing *noun* the practice of taking part in horse-riding events, especially the **three-day event**, a competition in jumping, cross-country riding, and dressage.
eventual *adj.* happening after or at the end of a period of time, a process, etc. [from French *éventuel*, from Latin *eventus*, result, event]

■ final, ultimate, resulting, concluding, ensuing, future, later, subsequent, prospective, projected, planned, impending.

eventuality *noun* (PL. **eventualities**) a possible happening or result: *plan for every eventuality.*

■ possibility, contingency, prospect, result, outcome, consequence, development.

eventually *adv.* after an indefinite period of time; in the end: *they came eventually.*

■ finally, ultimately, at last, in the end, at length, subsequently, after all, sooner or later.

eventuate *verb intrans. formal* to result; to turn out.
ever *adv.* **1** at any time. **2** *formal* always; continually. **3** *colloq.* used for emphasis: *She's ever so beautiful!* [from Anglo-Saxon *æfre*]

■ **1** at any time, in any case, in any circumstances, at all, on any account. **2** always, evermore, for ever, perpetually, constantly, at all times, continually, endlessly.

ever- *combining form* always, continually: *ever-hopeful.*
everglade *noun* **1** a large shallow lake or marsh. **2** (**Everglades**) a large expanse of these in S Florida in the USA.
evergreen — *adj.* **1** *Bot.* denoting plants that bear leaves all the year round, eg pines, firs. Individual leaves are shed independently of each other, and are often greatly reduced to prevent water loss. **2** always popular. — *noun* an evergreen tree or shrub.
everlasting — *adj.* **1** without end; continual. **2** lasting a long time, especially so long as to become tiresome. — *noun* **1** any of several kinds of flower that keep their shape and colour when dried. **2** eternity.

■ *adj.* ETERNAL, NEVER-ENDING, ENDLESS, CONSTANT, PERPETUAL. **1** undying, immortal, infinite, imperishable, permanent, indestructible, timeless. ☒ *adj.* **1** temporary, transient.

evermore *adv.* **for evermore** for all time to come; eternally.

■ eternally, always, for ever, perpetually, *formal* ever.

every — *adj.* **1** each single, omitting none. **2** the greatest or best possible: *we're making every effort to avoid war.* — *adv.* at, in, at the end of, each stated period of time, distance, etc: *every fourth week / every six inches.* — **every now and then** or **every now and again** or **every so often** occasionally; from time to time. **every other** ... or **every second** ... one of every two repeatedly (the first, third, fifth, etc or second, fourth, sixth, etc). [from Anglo-Saxon *æfre ælc*, ever each]
everybody *pron.* every person.
everyday *adj.* **1** happening, done, used, etc daily, or on ordinary days, rather than on special occasions. **2** common or usual: *an everyday occurrence.*

■ **1** daily, day-to-day. **2** ordinary, common, commonplace, familiar, run-of-the-mill, regular, plain, routine, usual, workaday, common-or-garden, normal, customary, stock, accustomed, conventional, habitual, simple, informal. ☒ **2** unusual, exceptional, special.

Everyman *noun* the ordinary or common person.
everyone *pron.* every person.

■ everybody, one and all, each one, all and sundry, the whole world.

everything *pron.* **1** all things; all. **2** the most important thing: *fitness is everything in sport.*
everywhere *adv.* in or to every place.

■ all around, all over, throughout, far and near, far and wide, high and low, ubiquitous, *colloq.* left, right and centre.

evict *verb* to put out of a house, etc or off land by force of law. [from Latin *evincere*, to overcome]

■ expel, eject, dispossess, put out, turn out, *colloq.* turf out, *colloq.* kick out, force out, remove, cast out, *colloq.* chuck out, oust.

eviction *noun* the process of evicting people, especially from a building.
evidence — *noun* **1** information, etc that gives grounds for belief; that which points to, reveals or suggests something. **2** written or spoken testimony used in a court of law. — *verb formal* to be evidence of; to prove. — **in evidence** easily seen; clearly displayed. [from Latin *evidentia*, clearness of speech]

■ *noun* **1** proof, verification, confirmation, affirmation, grounds, substantiation, documentation, data, indication, manifestation, suggestion, sign, mark, hint, demonstration, token. **2** testimony, declaration.

evident *adj.* clear to see or understand; obvious; apparent.

■ clear, obvious, manifest, apparent, plain, patent, visible, conspicuous, noticeable, clear-cut, unmistakable, perceptible, distinct, discernible, tangible, incontestable, indisputable, incontrovertible.

. . . .

evidential *adj. formal* relating to, based on, or providing evidence.

evidently *adv.* **1** obviously; apparently: *he is evidently drunk.* **2** as it appears; so it seems: *evidently they don't believe us.*

. . . .

◘ APPARENTLY. **1** clearly, plainly, patently, manifestly, obviously, undoubtedly, doubtless(ly), indisputably. **2** seemingly.

. . . .

evil — *adj.* **1** morally bad or offensive. **2** harmful. **3** *colloq.* very unpleasant: *an evil stench.* **4** bringing or marked by misfortune. — *noun* **1** wickedness or moral offensiveness, or the source of it. **2** harm, or a cause of harm; a harmful influence. **3** anything bad or unpleasant, eg crime, disease, etc. [from Anglo-Saxon *yfel*]

. . . .

◘ *adj* **1** wicked, wrong, sinful, bad, immoral, vicious, vile, malevolent, iniquitous, cruel, base, corrupt, heinous, malicious, malignant, devilish, depraved, mischievous. **2** harmful, pernicious, destructive, deadly, detrimental, hurtful, poisonous. **3** foul, offensive, noxious. **4** disastrous, ruinous, calamitous, catastrophic, adverse, dire, inauspicious. *noun* **1** wickedness, wrongdoing, wrong, immorality, badness, sin, sinfulness, vice, viciousness, iniquity, depravity, baseness, corruption, malignity, mischief, heinousness. **3** affliction, calamity, disaster, misfortune, suffering, sorrow, adversity, ruin, catastrophe, blow, curse, distress, hurt, harm, ill, injury, misery, woe.

. . . .

evildoer *noun* a person who does evil things.

. . . .

◘ wrongdoer, criminal, delinquent.

. . . .

evil eye (the evil eye) 1 the supposed power of causing harm by a look. **2** a glare, superstitiously thought to cause harm.

evilly / 'iːvɪlɪ/ *adv.* with an evil manner.

evince *verb formal* to show or display (usually a personal quality) clearly. [from Latin *evincere*, to overcome]

eviscerate / ɪ'vɪsəreɪt/ *verb formal* **1** to tear out the bowels of. **2** to take away the essential quality or meaning of. [from Latin *eviscerare*, to disembowel]

evisceration *noun formal* disembowelling.

evocation / ɛvə'keɪʃən/ *noun* bringing a feeling to mind.

evocative / ɪ'vɒkətɪv/ *adj.* bringing vividly to mind.

. . . .

◘ suggestive, expressive, indicative, reminiscent, redolent, vivid, graphic, memorable.

. . . .

evoke *verb* **1** to cause or produce (a response, a reaction, etc). **2** to bring into the mind. [from Latin *evocare*, to call out]

. . . .

◘ **1** elicit, arouse, stir, raise, stimulate, provoke, excite. **2** summon (up), call, call forth, call up, conjure up, invoke, awaken, recall.
◙ SUPPRESS.

. . . .

evolution *noun* **1** the process of evolving. **2** a gradual development. **3** *Biol.* the cumulative changes in the characteristics of living organisms or populations of organisms from generation to generation, resulting in the development of new types of organism over long periods of time. **4** *Chem.* the giving off of a gas. [from Latin *evolutio*, unrolling]

. . . .

◘ **1, 2** development, growth, progression, progress, expansion, increase, ripening, derivation, descent.

. . . .

evolutionary *adj.* relating to or as a part of evolution.

evolutionism *noun Anthropol., Biol.* the theory and principles of evolution.

evolutionist — *noun* a person who believes in the theory of evolution as a scientific principle. — *adj.* relating to or characterized by a theory of evolution.

evolve / ɪ'vɒlv/ *verb* **1** *trans., intrans.* to develop gradually. **2** *intrans. Biol.*, *said of living organisms* to change gradually from a more primitive into a more complex or advanced form. **3** *Chem.* to give off (heat, gas, etc). **4** *said of heat, gas, etc* to be given off. [from Latin *evolvere*, to roll out, unroll]

. . . .

◘ **1** develop, grow, increase, mature, unravel, expand, enlarge, derive, result, elaborate.

. . . .

ewe / juː/ *noun* a female sheep. [from Anglo-Saxon *eowu*]

ewer / 'juːə(r)/ *noun* a large water-jug with a wide mouth. [from Old French *eviere*, from Latin *aquarius*, of water]

ex [1] *noun* (PL. **ex's, exes**) *colloq.* a person who is no longer what he or she was, especially a former husband, wife, or lover.

ex [2] *prep. Commerce* **1** direct from: *ex warehouse.* **2** excluding: *ex dividend.* [from Latin *ex*, out of]

ex- *prefix* forming words meaning: **1** former: *ex-wife.* **2** outside: *ex-directory.* [from Latin *ex*, out of]

exacerbate / ɪg'zasəbeɪt/ *verb* to make (a bad situation, anger, pain, etc) worse. [from Latin *exacerbare*, to irritate]

. . . .

◘ aggravate, inflame, worsen, intensify, compound.

. . . .

exacerbation *noun* making something worse.

exact — *adj.* **1** absolutely accurate or correct. **2** insisting on accuracy or precision in even the smallest details. **3** dealing with measurable quantities or values: *psychology is not an exact science.* — *verb* **1** (**exact something from** or **of someone**) to demand payment from them. **2** to insist on (a right, etc). [from Latin *exigere*, to demand]

. . . .

◘ *adj.* **1** precise, accurate, correct, faithful, literal, flawless, faultless, right, true, veracious, definite, explicit, detailed, specific, strict, unerring, close, factual, identical, express, word-perfect, blow-by-blow. **2** careful, scrupulous, particular, rigorous, methodical, meticulous, orderly, painstaking. *verb* **1** extort from, extract from, wrest from, wring from, *colloq.* milk from. **2** claim, insist on, compel, demand, command, force, impose, require.
◙ *adj.* inexact, imprecise.

. . . .

exacting *adj.* making difficult or excessive demands.

. . . .

◘ demanding, difficult, hard, laborious, arduous, rigorous, taxing, tough, harsh, painstaking, severe, strict, unsparing.
◙ easy.

. . . .

exaction *noun formal* **1** the act of demanding payment, or the payment demanded. **2** illegal demands for money; extortion.

exactitude *noun formal* accuracy or correctness.

exactly *adv.* **1** just; quite; precisely; absolutely. **2** with accuracy; with attention to detail. **3** *said in reply* you are quite right.

. . . .

◘ PRECISELY. **1, 3** quite, indeed, absolutely, definitely, certainly. **1** truly, just, unequivocally. **2** accurately, literally, faithfully, correctly, specifically, rigorously, scrupulously, veraciously, verbatim, carefully, faultlessly, unerringly, strictly, to the letter, particularly, methodically, explicitly, expressly, *colloq.* dead.
◙ **2** inaccurately, roughly.

. . . .

exactness *noun* **1** being exact; accuracy. **2** close attention to detail.

exaggerate /ɪgˈzadʒəreɪt/ verb 1 trans., intrans. to regard or describe something as being greater or better than it really is. 2 to emphasize or make more noticeable: *the light exaggerated the contours of the hills.* 3 to do in an excessive or affected way. [from Latin *exaggerare*, to heap up]

⊞ 1 overstate, embellish, embroider, *colloq.* pile (it) on. 2 magnify, emphasize, enlarge, amplify. 3 overdo, overemphasize, oversell.
⊟ 1 understate.

exaggeration *noun* exaggerating; a statement or action that makes something seem greater than it is.

⊞ hyperbole, overstatement, embellishment, embroidery, overemphasis, magnification, enlargement, amplification.

exaggerator *noun* a person who exaggerates, especially habitually.

exalt /ɪgˈzɔːlt/ verb 1 to praise highly. 2 to fill with great joy. 3 to give a higher rank or position to. [from Latin *exaltare*, to raise]

⊞ 1 praise, laud, extol, glorify, magnify, acclaim, eulogize. 2 delight, elate, overjoy, transport. 3 promote, raise, prefer, elevate.

exaltation /ɛksɔːlˈteɪʃən/ *noun* 1 the act of exalting or state of being exalted. 2 a strong feeling of happiness.

exalted *adj.* 1 very senior or dignified: *exalted status.* 2 noble; very moral: *exalted ideals.* 3 exaggerated; too high: *an exalted opinion of one's own importance.*

⊞ LOFTY, HIGH, ELEVATED. 1 grand, regal, lordly, stately. 2 noble, idealistic, virtuous, moral. 3 exaggerated, inflated.

exam *noun colloq.* an examination (sense 1).

examination *noun* 1 a set of tasks, especially in written form, designed to test knowledge or ability. 2 *Medicine* a physical inspection of a patient carried out by a doctor, especially in order to assess the patient's state of health or to diagnose a disease. 3 the act of examining, or process of being examined. 4 *Legal* formal questioning in a court of law.

⊞ 1 test, exam, quiz, oral, viva. 2 scan, check, check-up. 3 inspection, inquiry, scrutiny, study, survey, search, analysis, exploration, investigation, probe, appraisal, observation, research, review, *colloq.* once-over, perusal, audit, critique. 4 questioning, cross-examination, cross-questioning, trial, inquisition, interrogation.

examine *verb* 1 to inspect, consider, or look into closely. 2 to inspect (a patient), especially in order to assess his or her state of health or diagnose a disease. 3 to test the knowledge or ability of (a person), especially in a formal examination. 4 *Legal* to question formally in a court of law. [from French *examiner*, from Latin *examinare*, to weigh or test, from *examen*, the pointer on a set of scales]

⊞ 1 inspect, investigate, scrutinize, study, survey, analyse, explore, inquire, consider, probe, review, scan, check (out), ponder, pore over, sift, vet, weigh up, appraise, assay, audit, peruse, *slang* case. 3 test, quiz. 4 question, cross-examine, cross-question, interrogate, *colloq.* grill, catechize.

examinee *noun* a candidate in an examination.

examiner *noun* a person who sets an examination.

example *noun* 1 something or someone that is a typical specimen. 2 something that illustrates a fact or rule. 3 a person, pattern of behaviour, etc as a model to be, or not to be, copied: *set a good example.* 4 a punishment given, or the person punished, as a warning to others: *make an example of someone.* — **for example** as an example or illustration. [from Old French *example*, from Latin *exemplum*]

⊞ 1 sample, specimen, exemplar, archetype, prototype. 2 instance, case, case in point, illustration, exemplification. 3 model, pattern, ideal, exemplar, standard, type, lesson.

exasperate *verb* to make (someone) annoyed and frustrated. [from Latin *exasperare*, to make rough]

⊞ infuriate, annoy, anger, incense, irritate, madden, provoke, *colloq.* get on someone's nerves, enrage, irk, rile, rankle, rouse, *colloq.* get to, goad, vex.
⊟ appease, pacify.

exasperation *noun* a feeling of angry frustration.

ex cathedra /ˌɛks kəˈθiːdrə/ — *adv.* with authority, especially the full authority of the Pope. — *adj.* (*usually* **ex-cathedra**) 1 *said of a papal pronouncement* stating an infallible doctrine. 2 made with, or as if with, authority. [from Latin *ex cathedra*, from the chair]

excavate *verb* 1 to dig up or uncover (especially historical remains). 2 to dig up (a piece of ground, etc) or to make (a hole) by doing this. [from Latin *excavare*, to make hollow]

⊞ DIG (OUT), DIG UP. 1 unearth, disinter, exhume, uncover. 2 hollow, burrow, gouge, scoop, tunnel, delve, mine, quarry.

excavation *noun* 1 the process of excavating or digging up ground, especially in archaeology. 2 an excavated area or site.

⊞ 2 hole, hollow, pit, quarry, mine, dugout, dig, diggings, burrow, cavity, crater, trench, trough, shaft, ditch, cutting.

excavator *noun* 1 a person who excavates or digs up ground. 2 a machine for digging.

exceed *verb* 1 to be greater in number or quantity than. 2 to go beyond; to do more than is required by. [from Old French *exceder*]

⊞ 1 be over, be above, pass, surpass, surpass, outdo, outstrip, beat, better, overtake. 2 overstep, transcend.

exceedingly *adv.* very; extremely.

excel *verb* (**excelled**, **excelling**) 1 *intrans.* (**excel in** or **at something**) to be exceptionally good at it. 2 *trans.* to be better than. — **excel oneself** *often ironic* to do better than usual or previously. [from Latin *excellere*, to rise up]

⊞ 1 be excellent at, be outstanding at, succeed at, shine at, predominate in. 2 surpass, outdo, beat, outclass, outperform, outrank, eclipse, better.

excellence *noun* great worth; very high or exceptional quality. [from Old French, from Latin *excellentia*]

⊞ superiority, pre-eminence, distinction, merit, supremacy, quality, worth, fineness, eminence, goodness, greatness, virtue, perfection, purity.

Excellency *noun* (PL. **Excellencies**) (*usually* **His** or **Her** or **Your Excellency** or **Their Excellencies**) a title of honour given to certain people of high rank, eg ambassadors.

excellent *adj.* of very high quality; extremely good.

⊞ superior, first-class, first-rate, prime, superlative, unequalled, outstanding, surpassing, remarkable, distinguished, great, good, exemplary, select, superb, admirable, commendable, *colloq.* top-notch, splendid,

noteworthy, notable, fine, wonderful, worthy.
■ inferior, second-rate.

except — *prep.* leaving out; not including. — *verb* to leave out or exclude: *present company excepted.* — **except for** apart from; not including or counting. [from Latin *excipere*, to take out]

■ *prep.* excepting, but, apart from, other than, save, omitting, not counting, leaving out, excluding, except for, besides, bar, minus, less. *verb* leave out, omit, bar, exclude, reject, rule out.

excepting *prep.* leaving out; not including or counting.
exception *noun* 1 a person or thing not included. 2 someone or something that does not, or is allowed not to, follow a general rule: *make an exception.* 3 an act of excluding. — **take exception to** to object to; to be offended by. [from Latin *excipere*, to take out]

■ 2 oddity, anomaly, deviation, abnormality, irregularity, peculiarity, inconsistency, rarity, special case, quirk.

exceptionable *adj.* 1 likely to cause disapproval, offence or dislike. 2 open to objection.
exceptional *adj.* 1 remarkable or outstanding. 2 being or making an exception.

■ 1 outstanding, remarkable, phenomenal, prodigious, notable, noteworthy, superior, unequalled, marvellous. 2 abnormal, unusual, anomalous, strange, odd, irregular, extraordinary, peculiar, special, rare, uncommon.
■ 1 mediocre. 2 normal.

exceptionally *adv.* in an exceptional way; to an exceptional or unusual degree: *it is exceptionally cold.*
excerpt /'ɛksɜːpt, ɪk'sɜːpt/ — *noun* (with stress on *ex*-) a short passage or part taken from a book, film, etc. — *verb* (with stress on *-cerpt*) to select extracts from (a book, etc). [from Latin *excerptum*, from *excerpere*, to pick]

■ *noun* extract, passage, portion, section, selection, quote, quotation, part, citation, scrap, fragment, clip.

excerption *noun* selection of extracts from a book, etc.
excess — *noun* 1 the act of going, or the state of being, beyond normal or suitable limits. 2 an amount or extent greater than is usual, necessary or wise. 3 the amount by which one quantity, etc exceeds another; an amount left over. 4 (*usually* **excesses**) an outrageous or offensive act. — *adj.* 1 greater than is usual, necessary or permitted. 2 additional; required to make up for an amount lacking: *excess postage.* — **in excess of** ... going beyond ...; more than: *in excess of 5 million.* [from Old French *exces*, from Latin *excessus*, departure, going beyond]

■ *noun* 1 overindulgence, dissipation, immoderateness, intemperance, extravagance, unrestraint, debauchery. 2 surfeit, overabundance, glut, plethora, superfluity, superabundance, surplus, overflow, overkill. 3 surplus, remainder, leftovers. *adj.* 1 extra, surplus, spare, redundant, remaining, residual, left-over, additional, superfluous, supernumerary.
■ *noun* 1 restraint. 2 deficiency. *adj.* 1 inadequate.

excessive *adj.* too great; beyond what is usual, right or appropriate.

■ immoderate, inordinate, extreme, undue, uncalled-for, disproportionate, unnecessary, unneeded, superfluous, unreasonable, exorbitant, extravagant, *colloq.* steep.
■ insufficient.

excessively *adv.* to an excessive degree.

■ immoderately, inordinately, extremely, unduly, disproportionately, unnecessarily, unreasonably, exorbitantly, extravagantly.

exchange — *verb* 1 (**exchange one thing for another**) to give, or give up, in return for something else. 2 to give and receive in return: *the two leaders exchanged gifts.* — *noun* 1 the giving and taking of one thing for another. 2 a thing exchanged. 3 a giving and receiving in return. 4 a conversation or argument, especially when brief. 5 the act of exchanging the currency of one country for that of another. 6 a place where shares are traded, or international financial deals carried out. 7 (*also* **telephone exchange**) a central telephone system where lines are connected, or the building housing this. — **in exchange for** in return for. [from Old French *eschangier*, from Latin *excambiare*, from EX- or *cambiare*, to barter]

■ *verb* 1 barter for, change for, trade for, swap for, switch for, replace with, interchange with, convert to, commute for, substitute for, bandy with. *noun* 1, 2 trade. 1 replacement, substitution, switching, swapping, barter, bargaining, dealing, traffic. 2 swap. 3 interchange, reciprocity. 4 conversation, discussion, chat.

exchangeable *adj.* that may be exchanged.
exchange rate or **rate of exchange** the value of the currency of one country in relation to that of another country or countries.
exchequer /ɪks'tʃɛkə(r)/ *noun* (*often* **Exchequer**) the government department in charge of the financial affairs of a nation. [from Old French *eschequier*, from Latin *scaccarium*, chessboard, from the practice of keeping accounts on a chequered cloth]
excise[1] /'ɛksaɪz/ — *noun* the tax on goods, etc produced and sold within a country, and on certain licences. — *verb* 1 to charge excise on (goods, etc). 2 to force (a person) to pay excise. [from Old Dutch *excijs*, from Old French *acceis*, tax]
excise[2] /ɛk'saɪz/ *verb* 1 to remove (eg a passage from a book). 2 to cut out or cut off (a tissue, organ, tumour, etc) by surgery. [from Latin *excidere*, to cut out]
excision *noun* 1 removal, especially of a passage from a text. 2 the cutting out or cutting off of a tissue, organ, tumour, etc, by surgery. 3 *Biochem.* the removal of a section of a molecule of DNA or RNA by means of enzymes.
excitability *noun* the capacity to become excited.
excitable *adj.* easily made excited, flustered, frantic, etc.

■ temperamental, volatile, passionate, emotional, highly-strung, fiery, hotheaded, hasty, nervous, hot-tempered, irascible, quick-tempered, sensitive, susceptible.
■ calm, stable.

excitation /ɛksɪ'teɪʃən/ *noun Physics* the addition of energy to an atom or molecule so that it becomes raised from its ground state (its lowest energy state) to an excited state (a higher energy state).
excite *verb* 1 to cause to feel lively expectation or a pleasant tension and thrill. 2 to arouse (feelings, emotions, sensations, etc). 3 to provoke (eg action). 4 to arouse sexually. [from Old French *exciter*]

■ 1 stir up, thrill, elate, *colloq.* turn on, impress, touch, move, agitate, disturb, upset. 2 arouse, rouse, animate, awaken, evoke, engender, inspire, kindle, fire, inflame, ignite. 3 provoke, motivate, stimulate, instigate, incite, induce, galvanize, generate, sway. 4 arouse, *colloq.* turn on.
■ 1 calm.

excited *adj.* aroused emotionally or sexually; thrilled.

⊟ aroused, roused, stimulated, stirred, thrilled, elated, enthusiastic, eager, moved, high, worked up, wrought-up, overwrought, restless, frantic, frenzied, wild.
⊟ calm, apathetic.

excitement *noun* **1** the state of being excited. **2** objects and events that produce such a state, or the quality they have which produces it: *the excitement of travel.* **3** behaviour, a happening, etc which displays excitement.

⊟ **1** passion, animation, elation, enthusiasm, exhilaration, intoxication, thrill, *colloq.* kick, *colloq.* buzz, restlessness, ferment, fever, eagerness, agitation. **2** thrill, stimulation. **3** unrest, ado, action, activity, commotion, fuss, tumult, flurry, furore, adventure.
⊟ **1** calm, apathy.

exciting *adj.* arousing a lively expectation or a pleasant tension and thrill.

⊟ stimulating, stirring, intoxicating, exhilarating, thrilling, rousing, moving, enthralling, electrifying, *colloq.* high-octane, *colloq.* nail-biting, cliffhanging, striking, sensational, provocative, inspiring, interesting.
⊟ dull, boring, unexciting.

exclaim *verb trans., intrans.* to call or cry out suddenly and loudly, eg in surprise or anger. [from Latin *exclamare*]

⊟ cry (out), declare, blurt (out), call, yell, shout, proclaim, utter.

exclamation *noun* **1** a word or expression uttered suddenly and loudly. **2** the act of exclaiming. [from Latin *exclamatio*]

⊟ INTERJECTION, EJACULATION, UTTERANCE. **1** cry, call, yell, shout, outcry.

exclamation mark the punctuation mark '!', used to indicate an exclamation.

exclamatory /ɪkˈsklamətrɪ/ *adj.* containing or expressing exclamation.

exclude *verb* **1** to prevent (someone) from sharing or taking part. **2** to shut out or keep out. **3** to omit or leave out of consideration. **4** to make impossible. **5** to dismiss (someone) permanently from a school. [from Latin *excludere*, to shut out]

⊟ **1, 4** rule out, preclude, forbid, prohibit, prevent, veto. **1** ban, bar, disallow, proscribe, blacklist, ostracize, excommunicate. **2** keep out, shut out, expel, eject, evict. **3** omit, leave out, refuse, reject, ignore, rule out, eliminate.
⊟ **1** admit. **3** include.

excluding *prep.* not counting; without including.

exclusion *noun* **1** the act of excluding, or the state of being excluded. **2** permanent dismissal of a child from a school. — **to the exclusion of** ... so as to leave out or make no time or room for ... [from Latin *exclusio*, from *excludere*, to shut out]

exclusive — *adj.* **1** involving the rejection or denial of something else or everything else: *mutually exclusive statements.* **2** not shared with anyone else: *exclusive rights.* **3** (**exclusive to someone or something**) limited to, given to, found in, etc only one place, group or person. **4** single; only. **5** not including (something mentioned). **6** not readily accepting others into the group, especially because of a feeling of superiority: *an exclusive club.* **7** fashionable and expensive: *an exclusive restaurant.* — *noun* a report or story published in only one newspaper or magazine. — **exclusive of** ... excluding ... [from Latin *exclusivus*]

⊟ *adj.* **1** incompatible, contradictory, irreconcilable. **2** sole, undivided, unshared, whole, total. **3** peculiar to, restricted to, limited to, **1** single, unique, only, **2** restrictive, closed, private, narrow, selective, discriminatory, cliquey, clannish, snobbish. **7** choice, select, chic, *colloq.* classy, elegant, fashionable, *colloq.* posh.

exclusively *adv.* to an exclusive degree; with exclusive right.

exclusiveness or **exclusivity** *noun* being exclusive; a tendency to exclude others.

excommunicate *verb Christianity* to remove (someone) from membership of a Church. [from Latin *excommunicare*, to exclude from the community]

excommunication *noun Christianity* removal from membership of a Church.

excoriate /ɛksˈkɔːrɪeɪt/ *verb* **1** *technical* to strip the skin from (a person or animal). **2** *formal* to criticize severely. [from Latin *excoriare*]

excoriation *noun technical* stripping of the skin.

excrement *noun* waste matter passed out of the body, especially faeces. [from Latin *excrementum*]

excremental *adj.* relating to or consisting of excrement or faeces.

excrescence /ɪksˈkrɛsəns/ *noun* **1** an abnormal outgrowth or protuberance on the surface of the body (eg a wart) or on an organ or body part (eg a tumour). **2** an unsightly addition. [from Latin *excrescere*, to grow up]

excreta /ɛksˈkriːtə/ *noun formal* any waste products, especially faeces, that are discharged from the body. [from Latin *excernere*, to sift out]

excrete *verb, said of a plant or animal* to eliminate (waste products). [from Latin *excernere*, to sift out]

excretion *noun Biol.* in plants and animals, the removal of excess, waste, or harmful material produced during the chemical reactions that take place within living cells.

excretory *adj.* relating to or having the function of excretion.

excruciating *adj.* **1** causing great physical or mental pain. **2** *colloq.* extremely bad or irritating. [from Latin *excruciare*, to torture]

⊟ AGONIZING, PAINFUL, UNBEARABLE, INTOLERABLE, INSUFFERABLE, ATROCIOUS. **1** severe, tormenting, acute, intense, sharp, piercing, extreme, racking, harrowing, savage, burning, bitter.

exculpate *verb formal* to remove from guilt or blame. [from EX- + Latin *culpa*, fault, blame]

exculpation *noun formal* removal from suspicion or blame.

excursion *noun* **1** a short trip, usually one made for pleasure. **2** a brief change from the usual course or pattern: *a novelist making an excursion into journalism.* [from Latin *excurrere*, to run out]

⊟ **1** outing, trip, jaunt, expedition, day trip, journey, tour, airing, breather, junket, ride, drive, walk, ramble.

excursive *adj. formal* tending to wander from the main point. [from Latin *excursus*, a running out]

excusable *adj.* that may be excused; forgivable.

⊟ forgivable, pardonable, understandable, slight, minor, venial.

excusably *adv.* in an excusable or forgivable way; to an excusable degree.

excuse — *verb* **1** to pardon or forgive. **2** to offer justification for (a wrongdoing). **3** to free (from an obligation, a duty, etc). **4** to allow to leave (a room, etc), eg in order to go to the lavatory. — *noun* **1** an explanation for a wrong-doing, offered as an apology or justification. **2** *derog.* a very poor example: *you'll never sell this excuse for a painting!* — **excuse me** an expression of apology, or used to attract attention. **excuse oneself** to leave after apologizing or asking permission. **make one's excuses** to apologize for leaving or not attending. [from Latin *excusare*, from *ex*, from, + *causa*, cause, accusation]

. . . .

▣ *verb* **1** forgive, pardon, overlook, absolve, acquit, exonerate, condone, tolerate, ignore, indulge. **2** explain, mitigate, justify, vindicate, defend, apologize for. **3** release, free, discharge, liberate, let off, relieve, spare, exempt. *noun* APOLOGY. **1** justification, explanation, grounds, defence, plea, alibi, reason, pretext, pretence, exoneration, evasion, *colloq.* cop-out, shift.

▣ *verb* **1** blame, condemn. **3** punish.
. . . .

ex-directory *adj.* **1** *said of a telephone number* not included in the directory at the request of the subscriber. **2** *said of a telephone subscriber* having such a number.

execrable *adj.* **1** detestable. **2** dreadful; of very poor quality. [from Latin *exsecrabilis*, detestable]

execrably *adv.* detestably; dreadfully.

execrate *verb formal* **1** to feel or express hatred or loathing of. **2** to curse. [from Latin *exsecrari*, to curse]

execration *noun formal* an expression of loathing; cursing.

execute *verb* **1** to put to death by order of the law. **2** to perform or carry out. **3** to produce, especially according to a design. **4** *Legal* to make valid by signing, etc. **5** *Legal* to carry out instructions contained in (a will or contract). See also EXECUTOR.

. . . .

▣ **1** put to death, kill, hang, electrocute, shoot, guillotine, decapitate, behead, *slang* liquidate. **2** carry out, perform, do, accomplish, achieve, fulfil, complete, discharge, effect, enact, deliver, enforce, finish, implement, administer, consummate, dispatch, expedite. **3** produce, realize. **4** sign, validate, serve, render.
. . . .

execution *noun* **1** the act, or an instance, of putting to death by law. **2** the act of carrying out, or the state of being carried out. **3** the manner or style in which something is carried out.

. . . .

▣ **1** death penalty, capital punishment, killing, hanging, electrocution, firing squad, shooting, guillotining, decapitation, beheading. **2** accomplishment, operation, performance, completion, achievement, administration, effect, enactment, implementation, realization, discharge, dispatch, consummation, enforcement. **3** performance, rendition, style, technique, delivery, manner, mode.
. . . .

executioner *noun* a person who carries out a sentence of death.

executive — *adj.* **1** in a business organization, etc, concerned with management or administration. **2** for the use of managers and senior staff. **3** *colloq.* expensive and sophisticated: *executive cars.* **4** *Legal, Politics* relating to the carrying out of laws: *executive powers.* — *noun* **1** a person or body of people in an organization, etc having power to direct or manage. **2** (**the executive**) *Legal, Politics* the branch of government that puts laws into effect. [from Latin *executivus*]

. . . .

▣ *adj.* **1, 2** administrative, managerial, directorial. **1** controlling, supervisory, regulating, decision-making, governing, organizing, directing, organizational, leading, guiding. *noun* **1** administrator(s), manager(s), organizer(s), leader(s), controller(s), director(s), governor(s), official(s), management, board, hierarchy. **2** administration, government, leadership.
. . . .

executive toy a gadget or object with little practical use, intended primarily as a diversion for executives.

executor /ɪgˈzɛkjʊtə(r)/ *noun Legal* a male or female person appointed to carry out instructions stated in a will.

executrix /ɛgˈzɛkjʊtrɪks, ɪg-/ *noun* (PL. **executrices**, **executrixes**) *Legal* a female executor.

exegesis /ɛksəˈdʒiːsɪs/ *noun* (PL. **exegeses**) a critical explanation of a text, especially of the Bible. [from Greek *exegesis*, explanation]

exegetic /ɛksəˈdʒɛtɪk/ or **exegetical** *adj.* critically explaining a text.

exemplar /ɪgˈzɛmplɑː(r)/ *noun* **1** a person or thing worth copying; a model. **2** a typical example. [from Latin *exemplum*, example]

exemplary /ɪgˈzɛmplərɪ/ *adj.* **1** worth following as an example. **2** serving as an illustration or warning. [from Latin *exemplaris*, from *exemplum*, example]

. . . .

▣ **1** model, ideal, perfect, admirable, excellent, faultless, flawless, correct, good, commendable, praiseworthy, worthy, laudable, estimable, honourable. **2** cautionary, warning.

▣ **1** imperfect, unworthy.
. . . .

exemplification *noun* provision of an example or examples; illustration.

exemplify *verb* (**exemplifies**, **exemplified**) **1** to be an example of. **2** to show an example of, show by means of an example. [from Latin *exemplum*, example + *facere*, to make]

. . . .

▣ ILLUSTRATE, DEMONSTRATE, SHOW. **1** represent, typify, manifest, embody, epitomize, exhibit, depict, display.
. . . .

exempt — *verb* to free from a duty or obligation that applies to others. — *adj.* free from some obligation; not liable. [from Latin *eximere*, to take out]

. . . .

▣ *verb* excuse, release, relieve, let off, free, absolve, discharge, dismiss, liberate, spare. *adj.* excused, not liable, immune, released, spared, absolved, discharged, excluded, free, liberated, clear.

▣ *adj.* liable.
. . . .

exemption *noun* release from a duty or obligation.

exercise — *noun* **1** physical training or exertion for health or pleasure. **2** an activity intended to develop a skill. **3** a task designed to test ability. **4** *formal* the act of using, putting into practice or carrying out: *the exercise of one's duty.* **5** (*usually* **exercises**) *Mil.* training and practice for soldiers. — *verb* **1** *intrans., trans.* to give exercise to (oneself, or someone or something else). **2** to use or bring into use: *exercise a skill* /right. **3** to trouble, concern, or occupy the thoughts of. [from Old French *exercice*, from Latin *exercere*, to keep busy]

. . . .

▣ *noun* **1, 2** training, drill, practice. **1** workout, aerobics, PE, PT, *colloq.* physical jerks, effort, exertion, discipline, activity, work, labour. **3** task, lesson, test, assignment. **4** use, utilization, employment, application, implementation, practice, operation, discharge, fulfilment, accomplishment. *verb* **1** train, drill, practise, work out, keep fit. **2** use, utilize, employ, apply, exert, practise, wield, try, discharge. **3** worry, disturb, trouble, upset, burden, distress, vex, annoy, agitate, afflict.
. . . .

exert *verb* to bring into use or action forcefully: *exert one's authority.* — **exert oneself** to make a strenuous, especially physical, effort. [from Latin *exserere*, to thrust out]

. . . .

▣ exercise, bring to bear, wield, assert, use, utilize, employ, apply, expend. **exert oneself** strive, struggle, strain, make an effort, take pains, toil, labour, work, sweat, endeavour, apply oneself.

....

exertion *noun* making a strenuous effort.

....

◪ effort, industry, labour, toil, work, struggle, diligence, assiduousness, perseverance, pains, endeavour, attempt, strain.

◪ idleness, rest.

exeunt /ˈɛksɪʌnt/ *verb intrans., as a stage direction* (they) leave the stage. — **exeunt omnes** all leave the stage. See also EXIT. [from Latin *exire*, to go out; *omnis*, all, every]

ex gratia /ɛks ˈgreɪʃɪə/ given as a favour, not in recognition of an (especially legal) obligation: *an ex gratia payment*. [from Latin *ex gratia*, as a favour]

exhalation /ɛkshaˈleɪʃən/ *noun* breathing out.

exhale /ɛksˈheɪl/ *verb trans., intrans.* **1** to expel (air, smoke, etc) from the lungs and out through the nose and mouth; to breathe out. **2** to give off or be given off. [from Old French *exhaler*]

exhaust — *verb* **1** to make very tired. **2** to use up completely. **3** to say all that can be said about (a subject, etc). **4** *Engineering* to remove (gas, etc) from a sealed vessel, especially in order to produce a vacuum. — *noun* **1** the discharge of waste gases, fumes, water vapour, etc, from the cylinders of an engine or turbine. **2** the waste gases, fumes, water vapour, etc, emitted in this way. **3** the duct, valve, or pipe through which waste gases, fumes, water vapour, etc, escape from an engine or turbine. [from Latin *exhaurire*, to draw off, drain away]

....

◪ *verb* **1** tire out, weary, fatigue, tax, strain, weaken, overwork, wear out, drain, sap. **2** use up, finish, consume, run through, drain dry, empty, deplete, spend, waste, squander, dissipate, impoverish, bankrupt. *noun* **1, 2** emission, exhalation, discharge. **2** fumes.

◪ *verb* **1** refresh. **2** renew.

....

exhausted *adj.* **1** made extremely tired; devoid of energy. **2** used up.

....

◪ **1** tired out, worn out, *colloq.* dog-tired, *colloq.* dead beat, *colloq.* all in, *colloq.* done (in), fatigued, weak, *colloq.* washed-out, *colloq.* washed-up, whacked, *colloq.* knackered, jaded, drained. **2** used up, finished, depleted, spent, empty, dry, void.

◪ **1** fresh, vigorous.

....

exhaustible *adj.* capable of being exhausted.

exhausting *adj.* extremely tiring or wearing.

....

◪ tiring, strenuous, taxing, gruelling, arduous, hard, laborious, backbreaking, draining, severe, testing, punishing, formidable, debilitating.

◪ refreshing.

....

exhaustion *noun* a state of being exhausted or devoid of energy.

....

◪ fatigue, tiredness, weariness, debility, feebleness, jet lag.

◪ freshness, liveliness.

....

exhaustive *adj.* complete; very thorough.

....

◪ comprehensive, all-embracing, all-inclusive, far-reaching, complete, extensive, encyclopedic, full-scale, thorough, full, in-depth, intensive, detailed, definitive, all-out, sweeping.

◪ incomplete, restricted.

....

exhaustively *adv.* thoroughly; completely.

exhibit — *verb* (**exhibited, exhibiting**) **1** to present or dis-

play for public appreciation. **2** to show or manifest (a quality, etc). — *noun* **1** an object displayed publicly, eg in a museum. **2** *Legal* an object or article produced in court as part of the evidence. [from Latin *exhibere*, to produce, show]

....

◪ *verb* DISPLAY, SHOW, PRESENT. **2** demonstrate, manifest, expose, reveal, express, disclose, indicate, air, parade, flaunt, offer. *noun* **1** display, show, illustration, model.

◪ *verb* **2** conceal.

....

exhibition *noun* **1** a display, eg of works of art, to the public. **2** the act, or an instance, of showing, eg a quality. **3** a scholarship awarded by a college or university. — **make an exhibition of oneself** to behave foolishly in public. [from Latin *exhibere*, to show]

....

◪ **1, 2** display, show, demonstration, presentation. **1** exhibit, spectacle, exposition, *colloq.* expo, fair, performance, representation, showcase. **2** showing, manifestation.

....

exhibitioner *noun* a student receiving an educational exhibition.

exhibitionism *noun* **1** *derog.* the tendency to behave so as to attract attention to oneself. **2** *Psychol.* the compulsive desire to expose one's sexual organs publicly.

exhibitionist *noun* a person who behaves so as to attract attention.

exhibitionistic *adj.* characterized by or given to exhibitionism.

exhibitor *noun* a person who provides an exhibit for a public display.

exhilarate /ɪgˈzɪləreɪt/ *verb* to fill with a lively cheerfulness. [from Latin *exhilarare*, from *hilaris*, cheerful]

....

◪ thrill, excite, elate, animate, enliven, invigorate, vitalize, stimulate.

◪ bore.

....

exhilaration *noun* a feeling of extreme cheerfulness.

exhort /ɪgˈzɔːt/ *verb* to urge or advise strongly and sincerely. [from Latin *exhortari*, to encourage]

....

◪ urge (on), encourage, implore, entreat, press, advise, counsel, prompt.

....

exhortation /ɛksɔːˈteɪʃən, ɛg-/ *noun* a strong appeal or urging.

exhumation *noun formal* digging up of a body from a grave.

exhume *verb formal* to dig up (a body) from a grave. [from French *exhumer*, from EX- + Latin *humus*, the ground]

exigency /ˈɛksɪdʒənsɪ/ *noun* (PL. **exigencies**) *formal* **1** an urgent need. **2** an emergency. [from Latin *exigere*, to drive out]

exigent /ˈɛksɪdʒənt/ *adj. formal* **1** pressing; urgent. **2** demanding.

exiguity /ɛksɪˈgjuːɪtɪ/ or **exiguousness** *noun* being scarce or meagre.

exiguous /ɪgˈzɪgjʊəs/ *adj. formal* scarce; meagre; insufficient. [from Latin *exiguus*, small, meagre]

exile — *noun* **1** enforced or regretted absence from one's country or town, especially for a long time, often as a punishment. **2** a person suffering such absence. — *verb* to send into exile. [from Old French *exil*, from Latin *exsilium*, banishment]

....

◪ *noun* **1** banishment, deportation, expatriation, expulsion, ostracism, transportation. **2** expatriate, refugee, émigré, deportee, outcast. *verb* banish, expel, deport, expatriate, drive out, ostracize.

....

exist *verb intrans.* **1** to be, especially to be present in the real world or universe rather than in story or imagination. **2** to occur or be found. **3** to manage to stay alive; to live with only the most basic necessities of life. [from Latin *exsistere*, to stand out]

. . . .

▣ **1** be, live, abide, continue, endure, have one's being, breathe, prevail. **2** be present, be found, occur, happen, be available, remain. **3** subsist, survive.

. . . .

existence *noun* **1** the state of existing. **2** a life, or a way of living. **3** everything that exists.

. . . .

▣ **1, 2** life. **1** being, reality, actuality, continuance, continuation, endurance, survival, breath, subsistence. **3** creation, the world.
▤ **1** death, non-existence.

. . . .

existent *adj.* having an actual being; existing.

existential /ˌɛgzɪˈstɛnʃəl/ *adj.* **1** relating to human existence. **2** *Philos.* relating to existentialism.

existentialism *noun* a philosophy emphasizing freedom of choice and personal responsibility for one's own actions, which create one's own moral values and determine one's future.

existentialist *adj., noun* a person who believes in existentialism.

exit — *noun* **1** a way out of a building, etc. **2** an act of going out or departing. **3** an actor's departure from the stage. **4** a place where vehicles can leave a motorway or main road. — *verb intrans.* (**exited, exiting**) **1** *formal* to go out, leave or depart. **2** *as a stage direction* (he or she) leaves the stage. See also EXEUNT. [from Latin *exire*, to go out]

. . . .

▣ *noun* **1** door, way out, doorway, gate, vent. **2** departure, going, retreat, withdrawal, leave-taking, retirement, farewell, exodus. *verb* **1** depart, leave, go, retire, withdraw, take one's leave, retreat, issue.
▤ *noun* **1, 2, 3** entrance. **2** arrival. *verb* **1** arrive, enter.

. . . .

exit poll a poll of a sample of voters in an election, taken as they leave a polling-station, and used to give an early indication of voting trends in a particular election.

exo- *combining form* out or outside. See also ECTO-, ENDO-, ENTO-. [from Greek *exo*, outside]

exobiology *noun Astron.* the study of living organisms that may exist elsewhere in the universe, methods of detecting them, and the possible effects of extraterrestrial conditions on terrestrial life forms.

Exocet /ˈɛksoʊsɛt/ *noun* a subsonic tactile missile, launched from a ship, aircraft, or submarine, and travelling at low altitude. [French, from modern Latin *Exocoetus volitans*, the flying fish]

exocrine /ˈɛksoʊkraɪn/ *noun* **1** *Physiol.* relating to external secretions, or to a pathway or structure that secretes externally. **2** *said of a gland* discharging its secretions through a duct which opens on to an epithelial surface, eg sweat gland, salivary gland. See also ENDOCRINE. [from EXO- + Greek *krinein*, to separate]

Exod. or **Exod** *abbrev. Biblical* Exodus.

exodus /ˈɛksədəs/ *noun* **1** a mass departure of people. **2** (**Exodus**) the departure of the Israelites from Egypt, probably in the 13c BC. [from Greek *exodos*, from *ex*, out + *hodos*, way]

ex officio /ɛks əˈfɪʃɪoʊ/ *adv.* by virtue of one's official position. [from Latin *ex officio*]

exogamy /ɛkˈsɒɡəmɪ/ *noun* the practice or rule of marrying only outside one's own group. [from EXO- + Greek *gamos*, marriage]

exogenous /ɛkˈsɒdʒənəs/ *adj. Biol.* **1** originating outside a cell, organ, or organism. **2** growing from near the surface of a living organism.

exonerate *verb* to free from blame, or acquit of a criminal charge. [from Latin *ex*, from + *onus*, burden]

. . . .

▣ absolve, acquit, clear, vindicate, *formal* exculpate, justify, pardon, discharge, exempt, excuse, spare, let off, release, relieve.
▤ **1** condemn, incriminate.

. . . .

exoneration *noun* freeing from blame or guilt.

exorbitance *noun* excessiveness of prices or demands.

exorbitant *adj., said of prices or demands* very high, excessive, or unfair. [from EX- + Latin *orbita*, track]

. . . .

▣ excessive, unreasonable, extortionate, unwarranted, unfair, undue, inordinate, immoderate, extravagant, enormous, preposterous.
▤ reasonable, moderate.

. . . .

exorcism /ˈɛksɔːsɪzm/ *noun, in some beliefs* driving away of an evil spirit or influence.

exorcist /ˈɛksɔːsɪst/ *noun, in some beliefs* a person who can drive away an evil spirit or influence.

exorcize or **exorcise** /ˈɛksɔːsaɪz/ *verb, in some beliefs* **1** to drive away (an evil spirit or influence) with prayer or holy words. **2** to free (a person or place) from the influence of an evil spirit in this way. [from Greek *exorkizein*]

exordium /ɪɡˈzɔːdɪəm/ *noun* (PL. **exordiums, exordia**) *formal* an introductory part, especially of a formal speech or piece of writing. [from Latin, beginning of a speech]

exoskeleton *noun Zool.* in some invertebrates, an external skeleton which forms a rigid covering that is external to the body.

exosphere *noun Astron.* the outermost layer of the Earth's atmosphere, which starts at an altitude of about 500km.

exothermic *adj. Chem.* denoting any process, especially a chemical reaction, that involves the release of heat.

exotic — *adj.* **1** introduced from a foreign, especially distant and tropical, country: *exotic plants.* **2** interestingly different or strange, especially colourful and rich, and suggestive of a distant land. — *noun* an exotic person or thing. [from Greek *exotikos*, from *exo*, outside]

. . . .

▣ *adj.* **1** foreign, alien, imported, introduced. **2** unusual, striking, different, unfamiliar, extraordinary, bizarre, curious, strange, fascinating, colourful, peculiar, outlandish.
▤ *adj.* **1** native. **2** ordinary.

. . . .

exotica *pl. noun* strange or rare objects.

exotically *adv.* in an exotic or colourfully strange way.

expand *verb* **1** *trans., intrans.* to make or become greater in size, extent, or importance. **2** *intrans.* (**expand on** or **upon something**) to give additional information; to enlarge on a description, etc. **3** *intrans. formal* to become more at ease, more open and talkative. **4** *intrans., trans. formal* to fold out flat or spread out. **5** to write out in full. **6** *Maths.* to express (a function or quantity) as the sum or product of a series of terms. [from Latin *expandere*, to spread out]

. . . .

▣ **1** increase, extend, enlarge, develop, spread, stretch, swell, widen, lengthen, thicken, magnify, multiply, inflate, broaden, open out, fill out, fatten, branch out, diversify. **2** elaborate on, amplify, expatiate on, flesh out.
▤ **1** contract.

. . . .

expandable *adj.* capable of being expanded or increased.

expanse *noun* a wide area or space. [from Latin *expansum*]

. . . .

▣ extent, space, area, breadth, range, stretch, sweep, field, plain, tract.

. . . .

expansible *adj.* able to expand or be expanded.

expansion *noun* **1** the act or state of expanding. **2** an increase in the volume of a body or substance, while its mass remains constant, caused by an increase in temperature, internal pressure, etc. **3** *Maths.* the expression of a function or quantity as the sum or product of a series of terms. [from Latin *expandere*, to spread out]

▤ **1** growth, increase, extension, enlargement, development, spread, widening, lengthening.

expansionism *noun* the act or practice of increasing territory or political influence or authority, usually at the expense of other nations or bodies.

expansionist — *noun* a person who supports expansionism. — *adj.* relating to or characterized by expansionism.

expansive *adj.* **1** ready or eager to talk; open; effusive. **2** wide-ranging. **3** able or tending to expand.

▤ **1** friendly, genial, outgoing, open, affable, sociable, talkative, warm, communicative, effusive. **2** extensive, broad, comprehensive, wide-ranging, all-embracing, thorough.

▣ **1** reserved, cold. **2** restricted, narrow.

expansively *adv.* in an expansive or wide-ranging way.

expansiveness *noun* an expansive or wide-ranging extent.

expat /ɛks'pat/ *noun colloq.* an expatriate.

expatiate /ɛks'peɪʃɪeɪt/ *verb intrans. formal* to talk or write at length or in detail. [from Latin *exspatiari*, to digress]

expatiation /ɛkspeɪʃɪ'eɪʃən/ *noun formal* lengthy writing or description.

expatriate /ɛks'patrɪət, ɛks'patrɪeɪt/ — *adj.* (pronounced -ət) **1** living abroad, especially for a long but limited period. **2** exiled. — *noun* (pronounced -ət) a person living or working abroad. — *verb* (pronounced -eɪt) **1** to banish or exile. **2** to deprive of citizenship. [from Latin *ex*, out of + *patria*, native land]

expect *verb* **1** to think of as likely to happen or come. **2 a** (**expect something from** or **of someone**) to require it of them; to regard it as normal or reasonable. **b** (**expect someone to do something** or **that someone will do something**) to require them to do it; to think it reasonable for them to do it. **3** *colloq.* to suppose: *I expect you're tired.* — **be expecting** *colloq.* to be pregnant. [from Latin *exspectare*, to look out for]

▤ **1** anticipate, await, look forward to, hope for, look for, bank on, bargain for, envisage, foresee, project, contemplate, predict, forecast. **2** require, want, wish, insist on, demand, rely on, count on. **3** suppose, surmise, assume, believe, think, presume, imagine, reckon, guess, trust.

expectancy *noun* (PL. **expectancies**) **1** the act or state of expecting. **2** a future chance or probability: *life expectancy.* [from Latin *exspectare*, to look out for]

▤ **1** anticipation, hope, eagerness, readiness, suspense, apprehension, anxiety.

expectant *adj.* **1** eagerly waiting; hopeful. **2** not yet, but expecting to be (especially a mother or father).

▤ **1** awaiting, anticipating, hopeful, in suspense, ready, apprehensive, anxious, watchful, eager, curious, agog. **2** pregnant, *colloq.* expecting, *old use* with child.

expectation *noun* **1** the state, or an attitude, of expecting. **2** (*often* **expectations**) something expected, whether good or bad. **3** (*usually* **expectations**) money, property, etc that one expects to gain, especially by inheritance.

▤ **1, 2** anticipation, hope. **1** confidence, assurance. **2** belief, assumption, presumption, surmise, forecast, prediction.

expectorant *Medicine* — *noun* **1** any medicine that promotes the ejection of mucus or phlegm from the air passages and lungs by coughing or spitting. **2** any medicine that is used to relieve a cough. — *adj.* promoting the ejection of phlegm or mucus by coughing or spitting.

expectorate *verb intrans., trans. Medicine* to cough up or spit out (mucus or phlegm) from the air passages and lungs. [from Latin *expectorare*, from EX- + *pectus*, the chest]

expedience /ɛk'spiːdɪəns/ or **expediency** (PL. expediencies) *noun* **1** suitability or convenience. **2** practical advantage or self-interest, especially as opposed to moral correctness. [from Latin *expedire*: see EXPEDITE]

expedient /ɛk'spiːdɪənt/ — *adj.* **1** suitable or appropriate. **2** practical or advantageous, rather than morally correct. — *noun* a suitable method or solution, especially one quickly thought of to meet an urgent need.

▤ *adj.* CONVENIENT. **1** suitable, appropriate, fitting, opportune. **2** politic, in one's own interest, advantageous, advisable, prudent, sensible, practical, pragmatic. *noun* stratagem, scheme, ploy, manoeuvre, plan, trick, shift, contrivance, device, stopgap.

expedite /'ɛkspədaɪt/ *verb* **1** to speed up, or assist the progress of. **2** to carry out quickly. [from Latin *expedire*, set free]

▤ **1** speed up, accelerate, hasten, hurry, further, facilitate, assist. **2** dispatch, discharge, hurry through.

expedition *noun* **1** an organized journey with a purpose, or the group making it. **2** *formal* speed, promptness. [from Latin *expeditio*]

▤ **1** journey, excursion, trip, voyage, tour, exploration, trek, safari, hike, sail, ramble, raid, quest, pilgrimage, mission, crusade. **2** promptness, speed, alacrity, haste.

expeditionary *adj.* of, forming, or for use on, an expedition.

expeditious *adj. formal* carried out with speed and efficiency.

expel *verb* (**expelled, expelling**) **1** to dismiss from or deprive of membership of (a club, school, etc), usually permanently as punishment for misconduct. **2** to get rid of; to force out. [from Latin *expellere*, to drive out]

▤ THROW OUT. **1** suspend, send down, ban, bar, deport, exile. **2** drive out, eject, evict, banish, oust, discharge, evacuate, void, cast out.

▣ **1** reinstate. **2** welcome.

expend *verb* to use or spend (time, supplies, effort, etc). [from Latin *expendere*, to weigh out]

▤ consume, use (up), dissipate, exhaust, employ, spend, pay, disburse, *colloq.* fork out.

▣ save, conserve.

expendable *adj.* **1** that may be given up or sacrificed for some purpose or cause. **2** not valuable enough to be worth preserving.

▤ DISPENSABLE, REPLACEABLE. **1** disposable, available. **2** inessential, unimportant, discardable.

expenditure *noun* 1 the act of expending. 2 an amount expended, especially of money.

⊟ EXPENSE, DISBURSEMENT, PAYMENT. 1 spending. 2 outlay, outgoings, output.
⊞ 2 income.

expense *noun* 1 the act of spending money, or money spent. 2 something on which money is spent. 3 (**expenses**) a sum of one's own money spent doing one's job, or this sum of money or an allowance paid by one's employer to make up for this. — **at the expense of something** or **someone** 1 with the loss or sacrifice of them. 2 causing damage to their pride or reputation. 3 with the cost paid by them. [from Latin *expensa*, from *expendere*, to weigh out]

⊟ 1 spending, expenditure, disbursement, outlay, payment, loss, cost, charge.

expensive *adj.* involving much expense; costing a great deal.

⊟ dear, high-priced, costly, exorbitant, extortionate, *colloq.* steep, extravagant, lavish.
⊞ cheap, inexpensive.

expensively *adv.* with much cost.

experience — *noun* 1 practice in an activity. 2 knowledge or skill gained through practice. 3 wisdom in all matters, gained through long and varied observation of life. 4 an event which affects or involves one. — *verb* 1 to have practical acquaintance with. 2 to feel or undergo. [from Latin *experientia*, from *experiri*, to try]

⊟ *noun* 1 practice, involvement, participation. 2, 3 knowledge, familiarity. 2 know-how, skill, training, technique, expertise, proficiency, competence. 3 wisdom, understanding, judgement, judiciousness, sense. 4 incident, event, episode, happening, encounter, occurrence, adventure. *verb* 2 undergo, go through, live through, suffer, feel, endure, encounter, face, meet, know, try, perceive, sustain.
⊞ *noun* 2, 3 inexperience.

experienced *adj.* having knowledge or skill gained from experience.

⊟ practised, knowledgeable, capable, competent, well-versed, expert, accomplished, qualified, skilled, tried, trained, professional, mature, seasoned, wise, veteran.
⊞ inexperienced, unskilled.

experiential /ɪkspɪərɪ'enʃəl/ *adj.*, *said of knowledge or learning* based on direct experience, as distinct from theoretical knowledge.

experiment — *noun* 1 a trial carried out in order to test a theory, a machine's performance, etc or to discover something unknown. 2 the carrying out of such trials. 3 an attempt at something original. — *verb intrans.* (**experiment on** or **with something**) to carry out such an experiment. [from Latin *experimentum*, from *experiri*, to try]

⊟ *noun* TRIAL. 1 test, investigation, examination, trial run, dry run, attempt, procedure, proof. 2 experimentation, research, trial and error. *verb* try, test, investigate, examine, research, sample, verify.

experimental *adj.* 1 of the nature of an experiment. 2 relating to, or used in, experiments. 3 trying out new styles and techniques.

⊟ 1, 2 trial, test. 1 exploratory, empirical, tentative, provisional, speculative, pilot, preliminary, trial-and-error.

experimentally *adv.* in an experimental way; on an experimental basis.

experimentation *noun* the process of experimenting; experimental procedure.

⊟ trial, testing, experiment, research, trial and error, practice.

experimenter *noun* a person who experiments, especially habitually.

expert — *noun* a person with great skill in, or extensive knowledge of, a particular subject. — *adj.* 1 highly skilled or extremely knowledgeable. 2 relating to or done by an expert or experts. [from Latin *expertus*, from *experiri*, to try]

⊟ *noun* specialist, connoisseur, authority, professional, *colloq.* pro, dab hand, ace, maestro, virtuoso. *adj.* PROFESSIONAL, SPECIALIST, QUALIFIED. 1 proficient, adept, skilled, skilful, knowledgeable, experienced, able, practised, masterly, virtuoso, *colloq.* ace.
⊞ *adj.* 1 amateurish, novice.

expertise *noun* special skill or knowledge.

⊟ expertness, proficiency, skill, skilfulness, know-how, knack, knowledge, mastery, dexterity, virtuosity.
⊞ inexperience.

expert system *Comput.* a computer program that is designed to solve problems by utilizing both knowledge and reasoning derived from human expertise in a particular field.

expiate /'ekspɪeɪt/ *verb* to make amends for (a wrong). [from Latin *expiare*, to atone for]

⊟ atone for, redeem, make up for, compensate for, make good, acquit.

expiation *noun* expiating; making amends for a wrong.

expiration *noun formal* 1 expiry. 2 the act of breathing out, in which the diaphragm rises and the ribcage contracts, forcing air rich in carbon dioxide out of the lungs.

expire *verb intrans.* 1 to come to an end, cease to be valid. 2 to breathe out. 3 to die. [from Latin *exspirare*, to breathe out]

⊟ 1 end, cease, finish, stop, terminate, close, conclude, discontinue, run out, lapse. 2 breathe out, exhale. 3 die, depart, decease, perish.
⊞ 1 begin.

expiry *noun* (PL. **expiries**) the ending of the duration or validity of something.

⊟ end, termination, conclusion, lapse.

explain *verb* 1 to make clear or easy to understand. 2 to give, or be, a reason for. 3 to justify (oneself or one's actions). — **explain something away** to dismiss it or lessen its importance, by explanation. [from Latin *explanare*, to make flat]

⊟ 1 interpret, clarify, describe, define, make clear, elucidate, simplify, resolve, solve, explicate, spell out, translate, unravel, untangle, illustrate, demonstrate, expound. 2 account for. 3 justify, excuse, rationalize, vindicate.
⊞ 1 obscure, confound.

explanation /eksplə'neɪʃən/ *noun* 1 the act or process of explaining. 2 a statement or fact that explains.

⊟ 1 interpretation, clarification, definition, elucidation, illustration, demonstration, description, exegesis, rationalization. **2** account, answer, meaning, motive, reason, key, justification, excuse, warrant, sense, significance.

explanatory /ɪkˈsplanətərɪ/ *adj.* serving to explain.

■ descriptive, clarifying, illustrative, interpretive, explicative, demonstrative, expository, justifying.

expletive /ɛkˈspliːtɪv/ — *noun* **1** a swear-word or curse. **2** a word added to fill a gap, eg in poetry. **3** a meaningless exclamation. — *adj.* being or of the nature of such a word or exclamation. [from Latin *explere*, to fill up]

explicable *adj.* able to be explained.

■ explainable, understandable, comprehensible, justifiable, clear, plain, obvious.

explicate *verb* to explain (especially a literary work) in depth, with close analysis of particular points. [from Latin *explicare*, to fold out]

explication *noun* detailed explanation or analysis.

explicit *adj.* **1** stated or shown fully and clearly. **2** speaking plainly and openly. [from Latin *explicitus*, straightforward]

■ CLEAR, OPEN, PLAIN, DIRECT, FRANK, STRAIGHTFORWARD, SPECIFIC, UNAMBIGUOUS, CATEGORICAL, POSITIVE. **1** distinct, exact, absolute, certain, express, declared, detailed, stated. **2** outspoken, unreserved.
🔁 **1** implicit, unspoken, vague.

explicitly *adv.* in an explicit or openly stated way.

explode *verb* **1** *intrans. said of a substance* to undergo an explosion. **2** to cause (something) to undergo an explosion. **3** *intrans.* to undergo a violent explosion as a result of a chemical or nuclear reaction. **4** *intrans.* to suddenly show a strong or violent emotion, especially anger. **5** to disprove (a theory, etc) with vigour. **6** *intrans. said especially of population* to increase rapidly. [from Latin *explodere*, to force off stage by clapping]

■ **1, 2** blow up, detonate. **1** burst, go off, erupt. **2** set off, discharge, blast. **4** erupt, *colloq.* boil (over), lose one's temper, lose control. **5** discredit, disprove, give the lie to, debunk, invalidate, refute, rebut, repudiate.
🔁 **5** prove, confirm.

exploded *adj.* **1** blown up. **2** *said of a theory, etc* no longer accepted; proved false. **3** *said of a diagram* showing the different parts (of something) relative to, but slightly separated from, each other.

exploit /ˈɛksplɔɪt, ɪkˈsplɔɪt/ — *noun* (with stress on *ex-*) (*usually* **exploits**) an act or feat, especially a bold or daring one. — *verb* (with stress on *-ploit*) **1** to take unfair advantage of so as to achieve one's own aims. **2** to make good use of: *exploit oil resources*. [from Old French *exploiter*]

■ *noun* deed, feat, adventure, achievement, accomplishment, attainment. *verb* **1** misuse, abuse, oppress, ill-treat, impose on, manipulate, *colloq.* rip off, *slang* fleece. **2** use, utilize, develop, capitalize on, profit by, turn to account, take advantage of, cash in on, make capital out of.

exploitation *noun* exploiting; making use of something.

■ use, development, misuse, abuse, oppression, ill-treatment, manipulation.

exploration *noun* **1** an exploring process or undertaking. **2** a journey into unknown territory.

■ **1** investigation, examination, inquiry, research, scrutiny, study, inspection, analysis, probe. **2** expedition, survey, reconnaissance, search, trip, tour, voyage, travels.

exploratory /ɛksˈplɔrətərɪ/ *adj.* **1** *said of talks, etc* serving to establish procedures or groundrules. **2** *Medicine* denoting surgery that aims to establish the nature of a complaint rather than treat it. **3** concerned with exploration or investigation.

■ **1** preliminary, preparatory, procedural. **2** diagnostic. **3** investigative, analytical, experimental, pilot, tentative.

explore *verb* **1** to search or travel through (a place) for the purpose of discovery. **2** to examine carefully: *explore every possibility*. [from Latin *explorare*, to search out]

■ **1** travel, tour, search, reconnoitre, prospect, scout, survey. **2** investigate, examine, inspect, research, scrutinize, probe, analyse.

explorer *noun* a person who explores unfamiliar territory, especially professionally or habitually.

explosion *noun* **1** *Chem.* a sudden and violent increase in pressure caused by an extremely rapid chemical or nuclear reaction, or a sudden change of state, that generates large amounts of heat and destructive shock waves that travel outward from the point of explosion and are heard as a loud bang. **2** a sudden display of strong feelings, etc. **3** a sudden great increase.

■ **1, 2** detonation, blast. **1** burst, discharge, eruption. **2** bang, report, clap, crack. **3** eruption, outburst, outbreak, fit. **4** increase, growth, escalation.

explosive — *adj.* **1** likely to, tending to, or able to explode. **2** likely to become marked by physical violence or emotional outbursts. **3** likely to result in violence or an outburst of feeling: *an explosive situation*. — *noun* any substance that is capable of producing an explosion, releasing large volumes of gas at high pressure when it is ignited or struck, eg gunpowder, dynamite, nitroglycerine, Semtex. Explosives are used in building and construction, mining, quarrying, and military warfare.

■ *adj.* UNSTABLE, VOLATILE. **2, 3** sensitive, tense, fraught, dangerous. **2** touchy, overwrought. **3** charged, hazardous, perilous, stormy.
🔁 *adj.* STABLE. **2, 3** calm.

expo *noun* (PL. **expos**) *colloq.* a large public exhibition. [from EXPOSITION]

exponent /ɪkˈspəʊnənt/ *noun* **1** a person able to perform some art or activity, especially skilfully. **2** a person who explains and promotes (a theory, belief, etc). **3** *Maths.* a number that indicates how many times a given quantity, called the *base*, is to be multiplied by itself. It is usually denoted by a superscript number or symbol immediately after the quantity concerned, eg $6^4 = 6 \times 6 \times 6 \times 6$. Also called POWER, INDEX.

■ **1** practitioner, adept, expert, master, specialist. **2** proponent, promoter, advocate, supporter, adherent, spokesman, spokeswoman, spokesperson, champion.

exponential *Maths.* — *adj.* **1** denoting a function that varies according to the power of another quantity, ie a function in which the variable quantity is an *exponent* (a symbol placed above and to the right of a mathematical expression). **2** denoting a logarithmic increase or decrease in numbers of a population, eg exponential growth of bacteria, exponential decay of radioactive isotopes. — *noun* (*also* **exponential function**) the function e^x, where e is a constant with a value of approximately 2.718. The inverse of this function, $\log_e x$, is the *natural logarithm* of x, ie natural logarithms use e as the base. [from Latin *exponere*, to set out]

exponentially *adv.* on an exponential basis; very rapidly.

export /ˈekspɔːt, eksˈpɔːt/ — *verb* (with variable stress) **1** to send or take (goods, etc) to another country, especially for sale. **2** *Comput.* to transfer (information) from one system or application to another. — *noun* (with stress on *ex-*) **1** the act or business of exporting. **2** something exported. [from Latin *exportare*, to carry away]

exportation *noun* the exporting of goods.

exporter *noun* a person or business that exports goods commercially.

exposé /eksˈpoʊzeɪ/ *noun* **1** a formal statement of facts, especially one introducing an argument. **2** an article or programme which exposes a public scandal, crime, etc. [from French *exposé*, from *exposer*, to expose]

exposed *adj.* **1** open to the wind and weather. **2** unprotected. **3** not covered or concealed.

⊟ BARE, OPEN, NAKED. **1** unsheltered, bleak, empty, desolate, windy, windswept, weatherbeaten, uninviting. **2** unprotected, vulnerable, susceptible, in danger, in peril, at risk. **3** uncovered, on show, on display, on view, manifest.

exposition *noun* **1** an in-depth explanation or account (of a subject). **2** the act of presenting such an explanation, or a viewpoint. **3** a large public exhibition. [from Latin *expositio*, a setting out]

expostulate *verb intrans.* (**expostulate with someone**) to argue or reason with them, especially in protest or so as to dissuade them. [from Latin *expostulare*, to demand]

expostulation *noun* expostulating; an argument or protest.

exposure *noun* **1** the act of exposing or the state of being exposed. **2** (**exposure to something**) being made liable to it, or put in danger from it. **3** (**exposure to something**) experience of it. **4** the harmful effects on the body of extreme cold. **5** the number or regularity of appearances in public, eg on television. **6** the act of exposing photographic film or paper to light. **7** the amount of light to which a film or paper is exposed, or the length of time for which it is exposed. **8** the amount of film exposed or to be exposed in order to produce one photograph.

⊟ **1** revelation, uncovering, disclosure, exposé, showing, unmasking, unveiling, display, airing, exhibition, presentation, manifestation, discovery, divulgence. **2** vulnerability to, susceptibility to. **3** familiarity with, experience of, knowledge of, contact with. **4** hypothermia. **5** publicity.

expound *verb* **1** to explain in depth. **2** *intrans.* (**expound on something**) to talk at length about it. [from Latin *exponere*, to set out]

⊟ **1** explain, explicate, analyse, dissect, unravel, untangle, clarify, illuminate, shed light on.

express — *verb* **1** to put into words. **2** to indicate or represent with looks, actions, symbols, etc. **3** to show or reveal. **4** to press or squeeze out. **5** to send by fast delivery service. — *adj.* **1** *said of a train* travelling especially fast, with few stops. **2** of or sent by a fast delivery service. **3** clearly stated: *his express wish.* **4** particular; clear: *with the express purpose of.* — *noun* **1** an express train. **2** an express delivery service. — *adv.* by express delivery service. — **express oneself** to put one's thoughts into words. [from Latin *exprimere*, to press out]

⊟ *verb* **1, 2, 3** communicate, convey, indicate, intimate, show.

1 articulate, verbalize, utter, voice, say, speak, state, pronounce, tell, assert, declare, put across, formulate, testify. **2** denote, depict, embody, symbolize, stand for, represent, signify, designate. **3** manifest, exhibit, disclose, divulge, reveal. *adj.* **1, 2** fast, high-speed. **2** speedy, rapid, quick. **3, 4** specific, explicit, particular, definite, unambiguous, clear, precise, distinct, clear-cut, certain, plain, manifest. **3** stated, exact, categorical.

⊟ *adj.* **3, 4** vague.

expressible *adj.* capable of being expressed.

expression *noun* **1** the act of expressing; something that expresses an idea, a feeling, a state, etc. **2** a look on the face that displays feelings. **3** a word or phrase. **4** the indication of feeling, eg in a manner of speaking or a way of playing music. **5** *Maths.* a set of one or more numbers or symbols, not usually including an 'equals' (=) sign, that represents a variable, function, etc, eg $3x^2$, $5x+4$. **6** *Genetics* the manifestation of a heritable trait (eg blue eye colour) in a living organism carrying the gene for that trait. **7** the act or process of forcing (a liquid) out by pressure.

⊟ **1** utterance, verbalization, communication, articulation, statement, assertion, announcement, declaration, pronouncement, speech, representation, manifestation, demonstration, indication, exhibition, embodiment, show, sign, symbol. **2** look, air, aspect, countenance, appearance, *literary* mien. **3** phrase, term, turn of phrase, saying, set phrase, idiom. **4** tone, intonation, delivery, diction, enunciation, modulation, wording, style.

Expressionism a movement in art, architecture, and literature which aims to communicate the internal emotional realities of a situation, rather than its external 'realistic' aspect.

Expressionist — *noun* a person, especially a painter, who practises Expressionism. — *adj.* relating to or characteristic of Expressionism.

expressionless *adj.*, *said of a face or voice* showing no feeling.

⊟ dull, blank, deadpan, impassive, straight-faced, poker-faced, inscrutable, empty, vacuous, glassy.

⊟ expressive.

expressive *adj.* **1** showing meaning or feeling in a clear or lively way. **2** (**expressive of something**) expressing a feeling or emotion: *words expressive of anger.*

⊟ **1** eloquent, meaningful, forceful, telling, revealing, informative, indicative, communicative, demonstrative, emphatic, moving, poignant, lively, striking, suggestive, significant, thoughtful, vivid, sympathetic.

expressly *adv.* **1** clearly and definitely. **2** particularly; specifically.

expropriate /eksˈproʊprɪeɪt/ *verb formal, Legal, said especially of the state* to take (property, etc) from its owner for some special use. [from Latin *expropriare*]

expropriation *noun* taking of property from its owner.

expropriator *noun* a person or body expropriating property.

expulsion *noun* **1** the act of expelling from school, a club, etc. **2** the act of forcing or driving out. [from Latin *expulsio*, a forcing out]

⊟ **2** ejection, eviction, exile, banishment, removal, discharge, exclusion, dismissal.

expulsive *adj.* having the power to expel or drive out.

expunge *verb* **1** to cross out or delete (eg a passage from a book). **2** to cancel out or destroy. [from Latin *expungere*, to mark for deletion]

. . . .

▣ CANCEL (OUT), ERASE, EFFACE, OBLITERATE. **1** delete, cross out, rub out. **2** destroy, eradicate, get rid of.

. . . .

expurgate *verb* **1** to revise (a book) by removing objectionable or offensive words or passages. **2** to remove (such words or passages). [from Latin *expurgare*, to purify]

expurgation *noun* removal from texts of items considered offensive.

exquisite *adj.* **1** extremely beautiful or skilfully produced. **2** able to exercise sensitive judgement; discriminating: *exquisite taste*. **3** *said of pain, pleasure, etc* extreme. [from Latin *exquisitus*]

. . . .

▣ **1** beautiful, attractive, dainty, delicate, charming, elegant, delightful, lovely, pleasing, perfect, flawless, fine, excellent, choice, precious, rare, outstanding. **2** refined, discriminating, meticulous, sensitive, impeccable. **3** intense, keen, sharp, poignant.

▣ **1** ugly. **2** flawed, unrefined.

. . . .

ex-serviceman and **ex-servicewoman** *noun* (PL. **ex-servicemen, ex-servicewomen**) a former male or female member of the armed forces.

ext. *abbrev.* **1** extension. **2** exterior. **3** external or externally.

extant /εk'stant/ *adj.* still existing. [from Latin *exstare*, to stand out]

extemporaneous /εkstεmpə'reɪnɪəs/ or **extempory** /εk'stεmpərɪ/ *adj.* **1** spoken, done, etc without preparation; impromptu. **2** makeshift; improvised. [from EX- + Latin *tempus*, time]

extemporaneously or **extemporarily** *adv.*, *said of speaking* without preparation.

extempore /εk'stεmpərɪ/ *adv.*, *adj.* without planning or preparation. [from EX- + Latin *tempus*, time]

. . . .

▣ *adv.* impromptu, ad lib, *colloq.* off the cuff, *colloq.* off the top of one's head, on the spur of the moment. *adj.* impromptu, improvised, ad-lib, unscripted, unrehearsed, unprepared, *colloq.* off-the-cuff.

. . . .

extemporization or **extemporisation** *noun* speaking or performing without preparation.

extemporize or **extemporise** *verb trans., intrans.* to speak or perform without preparation.

. . . .

▣ improvise, ad-lib, *colloq.* play (it) by ear.

. . . .

extend *verb* **1** to make longer or larger. **2** *intrans., trans.* to reach or stretch in space or time. **3** to hold out or stretch out (a hand, etc). **4** to offer (kindness, greetings, etc) to someone. **5** to increase in scope. **6** *intrans.* to include or go as far as: *their kindness did not extend to lending money.* **7** to exert to the physical or mental limit: *extend oneself.* [from Latin *extendere*, to stretch out]

. . . .

▣ **1** enlarge, increase, expand, develop, amplify, lengthen, widen, elongate, draw out, protract, prolong, spin out, unwind. **2** spread, stretch, reach, continue. **3, 4** offer, give, hold out, present, proffer. **4** impart, bestow, confer.

▣ **1** contract, shorten. **3** withhold.

. . . .

extendable or **extendible** *adj.* same as EXTENSIBLE.

extended family the family as a unit including all relatives. See also NUCLEAR FAMILY.

extended-play *adj.* (ABBREV. **EP**) *said of a gramophone record* with each side playing for about twice the length of a single.

extensible *adj.* capable of being extended or made longer.

extension *noun* **1** the process of extending, or the state of being extended. **2** an added part, making the original larger or longer. **3** a subsidiary or extra telephone, connected to the main line. **4** an extra period beyond an original time limit. **5** a scheme by which services, eg those of a university or library, are made available to non-members: *an extension course*. **6** range or extent. [from Latin *extensio*]

. . . .

▣ **1** enlargement, increase, stretching, broadening, widening, lengthening, expansion, elongation, development, enhancement, protraction, continuation. **2** addition, supplement, appendix, annexe, addendum. **4** delay, postponement.

. . . .

extensive *adj.* large in area, amount, range or effect. [from Latin *extensivus*, from *extendere*, to stretch out]

. . . .

▣ large, wide, broad, roomy, spacious, vast, huge, voluminous, long, lengthy, comprehensive, far-reaching, large-scale, thorough, widespread, universal, extended, all-inclusive, general, pervasive, prevalent.

▣ small, restricted, narrow.

. . . .

extensive farming a method of farming that employs only a relatively small amount of capital and labour to farm a relatively large area of land. See also INTENSIVE FARMING.

extensively *adv.* to an extensive degree; widely.

extensor *noun Medicine* any muscle that straightens or extends an arm, leg, or other body part. [from Latin *extendere*, to stretch out]

extent *noun* **1** the area over which something extends. **2** amount, scope, or degree. [from Old French *extente*, from Latin *extendere*, to stretch out]

. . . .

▣ **1** expanse, area. **2** amount, quantity, size, dimensions, magnitude, breadth, width, measure, duration, term, time, degree, spread, stretch, limit, scope, range, reach, compass, sweep.

. . . .

extenuate *verb* to reduce the seriousness of (an offence) by giving an explanation that partly excuses it. [from Latin *extenuare*, to make thin, to lessen]

. . . .

▣ mitigate, alleviate, excuse, qualify, moderate.

. . . .

extenuating *adj.*, *said especially of a circumstance* reducing the seriousness of an offence by partially excusing it.

extenuation *noun* lessening of an offence by extenuating circumstances.

exterior — *adj.* **1** on, from, or for use on the outside. **2** foreign, or dealing with foreign nations. — *noun* **1** an outside part or surface. **2** an outward appearance, especially when intended to conceal or deceive. **3** an outdoor scene in a film, etc. [from Latin *exterior*, from *exterus*, on the outside]

. . . .

▣ *adj.* **1** outer, outside, outermost, surface, external, superficial, surrounding, outward, peripheral, extrinsic. *noun* **1, 2** outside, surface, façade. **1** covering, coating, face, shell, skin, finish, externals, appearance.

▣ *adj.* **1** inside, interior. **2** domestic, inland. *noun* **1** inside, interior.

. . . .

exterminate *verb* to get rid of or completely destroy (something living). [from Latin *exterminare*, to drive away, from EX- + *terminus*, boundary]

. . . .

▣ annihilate, eradicate, destroy, eliminate, massacre, abolish, wipe out.

. . . .

extermination *noun* total destruction of something living.

■ annihilation, eradication, destruction, elimination, massacre,

exterminator *noun* a person or thing that destroys something living.

external — *adj.* **1** of, for, from, or on, the outside. **2** of the world, as opposed to the mind: *external realities*. **3** foreign; involving foreign nations: *external affairs*. **4** *said of a medicine* to be applied on the outside of the body, not swallowed, etc. **5** taking place, or coming from, outside one's school, university, etc: *an external examination*. — *noun* **1** (*often* **externals**) an outward appearance or feature, especially when superficial or insignificant. **2** *colloq.* an external examination or examiner. [from Latin *externus*, from *exterus*, on the outside]

■ *adj.* **1, 2** exterior, outer, visible.**1** surface, outside, superficial, outward, outermost, apparent, extraneous, extrinsic. **2** physical.
☒ *adj.* **1, 2** internal.

externalize or **externalise** *verb* to express (thoughts, feelings, ideas, etc) in words.

externally *adv.* outwardly; on the outside.

extinct *adj.* **1** denoting a plant or animal species that once existed but has now completely died out, either as a result of climatic or other major environmental changes in the past, or because of relatively recent human activity (eg hunting, pollution, or habitat destruction). **2** *said of a volcano* no longer active. **3** *formal, said of an emotion, etc* no longer felt; dead. [from Latin *exstinguere*, to extinguish]

■ **1** defunct, dead, gone, obsolete, ended, exterminated, terminated, vanished, lost, abolished. **2** inactive. **3** extinguished, quenched, dead.
☒ **1** living.

extinction *noun* **1** the process of making or becoming extinct; elimination, disappearance. **2** *Biol.* the total elimination or dying out of any plant or animal species, or a whole group of species, worldwide. Present-day extinctions are usually due to human activity, eg hunting, pollution, or destruction of natural habitats such as rainforests.

■ **1** annihilation, extermination, death, eradication, obliteration, destruction.

extinguish *verb* **1** to put out (a fire, etc). **2** *formal* to kill off or destroy (eg passion). **3** *Legal* to pay off (a debt). [from Latin *exstinguere*]

■ **1** put out, blow out, snuff out, stifle, smother, douse, quench. **2** annihilate, exterminate, eliminate, destroy, kill, eradicate, erase, expunge, abolish, remove, end, suppress.

extinguisher *noun* **1** a person or thing that extinguishes. **2** (*also* **fire extinguisher**) an apparatus filled with water or chemicals for putting out fires.

extirpate *verb* **1** *formal* to destroy completely. **2** *formal* to uproot. **3** to remove surgically. [from Latin *exstirpare*, to tear up by the roots]

extirpation *noun formal* total destruction.

extn. *abbrev.* extension.

extol *verb* (**extolled, extolling**) *somewhat formal* to praise enthusiastically. [from Latin *extollere*, to lift or raise up]

■ praise, laud, eulogize, glorify, exalt.

extolment *noun formal* enthusiastic praise.

extort *verb* to obtain (money, information, etc) by threats or violence. [from Latin *extorquere*, to twist or wrench out]

■ extract, wring, exact, coerce, force, *colloq.* milk, blackmail, squeeze, *colloq.* bleed, bully.

extortion *noun* the crime of obtaining money by threats.

extortionate *adj.* **1** *said of a price, demand, etc* unreasonably high or great. **2** using extortion.

■ **1** exorbitant, excessive, immoderate, unreasonable, inordinate. **2** grasping, exacting, rapacious, oppressive, *colloq.* bloodsucking, rigorous, severe, hard, harsh.

extortionately *adv.* to an extortionate or unreasonable degree.

extortionist *noun* a person who practises extortion.

extra — *adj.* **1** additional; more than is usual, necessary or expected. **2** for which an additional charge is made. — *noun* **1** an additional or unexpected thing. **2** an extra charge, or an item for which this is made. **3** an actor employed temporarily in a small, usually non-speaking, part in a film. **4** a special edition of a newspaper containing later news. **5** *Cricket* a run scored other than by hitting the ball with the bat. — *adv.* unusually or exceptionally. [probably a shortening of EXTRAORDINARY]

■ *adj.* **1** additional, added, auxiliary, supplementary, new, more, further, ancillary, fresh, other, excess, spare, superfluous, supernumerary, surplus, unused, unneeded, left-over, reserve, redundant. *noun* **1** addition, supplement, extension, acces-sory, appendage, bonus, complement, adjunct, addendum, attachment. *adv.* especially, exceptionally, extraordinarily, particularly, unusually, remarkably, extremely.
☒ *adj.* **1** integral, essential.

extra- *prefix* outside or beyond: *extra-curricular*. [from Latin *extra*, outside]

extracellular *Biol.* located or taking place outside a cell.

extract / ɪkˈstrakt, ˈɛkstrakt/ — *verb* (with stress on -*tract*) **1** to pull or draw out, especially by force or with effort. **2** to separate a substance from a liquid or solid mixture. **3** to derive (eg pleasure). **4** to obtain (money, etc) by threats or violence. **5** to select (passages from a book, etc). — *noun* (with stress on *ex-*) **1** a passage selected from a book, etc. **2** *Chem.* a substance that is separated from a liquid or solid mixture, usually by dissolving it in a suitable solvent and then evaporating the solvent by distillation. The active ingredients of many drugs are concentrated in this way. [from Latin *extrahere*, to draw out]

■ *verb* **1** remove, take out, draw out, uproot, withdraw. **3** derive, draw, distil, obtain, get, gather, glean, wrest, wring, elicit. **4** exact, extort, *colloq.* milk. **5** choose, select, cull, abstract, cite, quote. *noun* **1** excerpt, passage, selection, clip, cutting, quotation, abstract, citation. **2** distillation, essence, juice.
☒ *verb* **1** insert.

extraction *noun* **1** the act of extracting. **2** the process whereby a metal is obtained from its ore. **3** the removal of a tooth from its socket. **4** the use of a solvent to separate a substance from a liquid or solid mixture. **5** family origin; descent: *of Dutch extraction*.

extractor *noun* a person or thing that extracts, especially a device for ventilating a room: *extractor fan*.

extra-curricular *adj.* not belonging to, or offered in addition to, the subjects studied in a school's, college's, etc main teaching curriculum.

extraditable *adj., said of a person* liable to be extradited.

extradite *verb* to return (a person accused of a crime) for trial in the country where the crime was committed. [from EX- + Latin *tradere*, to deliver up]

extradition *noun* the procedure of returning a person accused of a crime to the country where it was committed.

extramarital *adj.*, *said especially of sexual relations* taking place outside marriage.

extramural *adj.* **1** *said of courses, etc* for people who are not full-time students at a college, etc. **2** outside the scope of normal studies. [from EXTRA- + Latin *murus*, wall]

extraneous /ɪkˈstreɪnɪəs/ *adj.* **1** not belonging; not relevant or related. **2** coming from outside. [from Latin *extraneus*, external]

· · · · · · · · · · · · · · · · · · · ·

▤ **1** superfluous, redundant, irrelevant, unrelated, unconnected, extra, peripheral.

· ·

extraneously *adv.* in an unrelated way; as a separate concern.

extraordinarily *adv.* in an extraordinary or unusual way; to an unusual degree.

extraordinary *adj.* **1** unusual; surprising; remarkable. **2** additional, not part of the regular pattern or routine: *extraordinary meeting*. **3** *formal* (often following the noun) employed to do additional work, or for a particular occasion: *ambassador extraordinary*. [from Latin *extra ordinem*, outside the usual order]

· · · · · · · · · · · · · · · · · · · ·

▤ **1** remarkable, unusual, exceptional, notable, noteworthy, outstanding, unique, special, strange, peculiar, rare, surprising, amazing, wonderful, unprecedented, marvellous, fantastic, significant, particular.

▣ **1, 2** ordinary. **1** commonplace.

· ·

extrapolate *verb trans.*, *intrans.* **1** *Maths.* to estimate (a value that lies outside a known range of values), on the basis of those values and usually by means of a graph. **2** to make (estimates) or draw (conclusions) from known facts. [from EXTRA- + INTERPOLATE]

extrapolation *noun* the process or result of extrapolating; a conclusion from known facts.

extrasensory *adj.* achieved using means other than the ordinary senses of sight, hearing, touch, taste and smell: *extrasensory perception.*

extraterrestrial — *adj.*, *said of a being, creature, etc* coming from outside the Earth or its atmosphere. — *noun* an extraterrestrial being.

extravagance *noun* excessive or indulgent spending; lack of restraint.

· · · · · · · · · · · · · · · · · · · ·

▤ overspending, profligacy, squandering, waste, excess, immoderation, recklessness, profusion, outrageousness, folly.

▣ thrift, moderation.

· ·

extravagant *adj.* **1** using, spending, or costing too much. **2** unreasonably or unbelievably great: *extravagant claims/ praise.* [from EXTRA- + Latin *vagari*, to wander]

· · · · · · · · · · · · · · · · · · · ·

▤ **1** profligate, prodigal, spendthrift, thriftless, wasteful, reckless, excessive, expensive, costly, overpriced, exorbitant. **2** immoderate, outrageous, pretentious, preposterous, lavish, ostentatious, flamboyant, ornate, *colloq.* flashy, fanciful, fantastic, wild.

▣ MODERATE. **1** thrifty, reasonable.

· ·

extravagantly *adv.* in an extravagant way; to an extravagant degree.

extravaganza /ɪkstrævəˈɡænzə/ *noun* a spectacular display, performance or production. [from Italian *estravaganza*, extravagance]

· · · · · · · · · · · · · · · · · · · ·

▤ spectacle, spectacular, gala, pageant, show.

· ·

extravert same as EXTROVERT.

extra virgin describing olive oil of the best quality.

extreme — *adj.* **1** very high, or highest, in degree or intensity. **2** very far, or furthest, in any direction, especially out from the centre. **3** very violent or strong. **4** not moderate; severe: *extreme measures.* **5** holding very radical or pronounced views; belonging to the far right or far left wing of a political party. — *noun* **1** either of two people or things as far, or as different, as possible from each other. **2** the highest limit; the greatest degree of any state or condition. — **go to extremes** to take action beyond what is thought to be reasonable. **in the extreme** to the highest degree. [from Latin *extremus*, from *exterus*, on the outside]

· · · · · · · · · · · · · · · · · · · ·

▤ *adj.* **1** intense, great, immoderate, inordinate, utmost, utter, out-and-out, maximum, acute, downright, extraordinary, exceptional, greatest, highest, unreasonable, remarkable. **2** farthest, far-off, faraway, distant, endmost, outermost, remotest, uttermost, final, last, terminal, ultimate. **4** harsh, drastic, dire, uncompromising, stern, strict, rigid, severe. **5** radical, zealous, extremist, fanatical. *noun* **2** extremity, limit, maximum, ultimate, utmost, top, pinnacle, peak, height, end, climax, depth, edge, termination.

▣ *adj.* **1** mild. **5** moderate.

· ·

extremely *adv.* to an extreme degree; very much: *the music was extremely loud.*

· · · · · · · · · · · · · · · · · · · ·

▤ exceptionally, extraordinarily, very, intensely, remarkably, unusually, unreasonably, immoderately, inordinately.

· ·

extreme sport a demanding sport, such as snowboarding or canyoning, that involves a high degree of physical risk.

extreme unction *RC Church* the act of anointing a sick or dying person with consecrated oil, now called the sacrament of the anointing of the sick.

extremism *noun* support for extreme opinions, especially in politics.

extremist — *noun* a person who has extreme opinions, especially in politics. — *adj.* relating to, or favouring, extreme measures.

· · · · · · · · · · · · · · · · · · · ·

▤ *noun* fanatic, zealot, militant, radical, revolutionary, diehard, fundamentalist. *adj.* fanatical, militant, radical, revolutionary, diehard, fundamentalist.

· ·

extremity *noun* (PL. **extremities**) **1** the farthest point. **2** an extreme degree; the quality of being extreme. **3** a situation of great danger. **4** (**extremities**) the hands and feet. [from Latin *extremitas*, end, farthest point]

· · · · · · · · · · · · · · · · · · · ·

▤ **1** extreme, pole, limit, boundary, brink, verge, margin, bound, border, apex, height, tip, top, edge, end, terminal, terminus. **2** acme, peak, pinnacle, ultimate, maximum, minimum. **3** crisis, danger, emergency, plight, hardship.

· ·

extricable *adj.* capable of being extricated or disentangled.

extricate *verb* to free from difficulties; to disentangle. [from Latin *extricare*, from EX- + *tricae*, hindrances]

· · · · · · · · · · · · · · · · · · · ·

▤ disentangle, clear, disengage, free, deliver, liberate, release, rescue, relieve, remove, withdraw.

▣ involve.

· ·

extrication *noun* extricating; disentangling.

extroversion or **extraversion** *noun Psychol.* a personality trait characterized by a tendency to be more concerned with the outside world and social relationships than with one's inner thoughts and feelings. See also INTROVERSION.

extrovert or **extravert** — *noun* **1** *Psychol.* a person who is more concerned with the outside world and social relationships than with his or her inner thoughts and feelings. **2** a person who is sociable, outgoing, and talkative. — *adj.* having the temperament of an extrovert; sociable, outgoing. See also INTROVERT. [from EXTRA- + Latin *vertere*, to turn]

....

■ *adj.* outgoing, friendly, sociable, amicable, amiable, exuberant.

◨ introvert.

....

extroverted *adj., said of a person* sociable and outgoing.

extrude *verb* **1** to squeeze or force out. **2** to force or press a semisoft solid material through a shaped hole or *die* in order to mould it into a continuous length of product. [from Latin *extrudere*, to push out]

extrusion *noun* **1** *Engineering* a manufacturing process in which hot or cold semisoft solid material, especially metal, plastic, or ceramic, is forced through a shaped hole or *die* in order to produce a continuous length of product. **2** *Geol.* an extrusive rock.

extrusive *adj. Geol.* denoting igneous rock formed from molten rock material, such as magma or volcanic lava, that has poured out on to the Earth's surface and then solidified, eg basalt.

exuberance *noun* high spirits; enthusiasm.

exuberant *adj.* **1** in very high spirits. **2** enthusiastic and energetic. **3** *said of health, etc* excellent. **4** *said of plants, etc* growing abundantly. [from Latin *exuberans*, from *uber*, rich]

....

■ **1, 2** lively, vivacious, spirited. **1** high-spirited, effervescent, ebullient, sparkling, excited, exhilarated, effusive, cheerful. **2, 3, 4** vigorous. **2** enthusiastic, zestful, energetic. **4** lush, rank.

◨ **1, 2** apathetic.

....

exuberantly *adv.* with an exuberant or high-spirited manner.

exudate /'ɛksjʊdeɪt/ *noun* **1** *Biol.* any substance released from an organ or cell of a plant or animal to the exterior through a gland, pore, or membrane, eg resin, sweat. **2** *Medicine* the fluid containing proteins and white blood cells that is discharged through small pores in membranes, usually as a result of inflammation.

exudation *noun* exuding; giving off odour or sweat.

exude *verb* **1** to give off or give out (an odour or sweat). **2** to show or convey by one's behaviour: *exude friendliness.* **3** *intrans.* to ooze out. [from Latin *exsudare*, to sweat out]

exult *verb intrans.* **1** (**exult in** or **at something**) to be intensely joyful about it. **2** (**exult over something**) to show or enjoy a feeling of triumph. [from Latin *exsultare*, to jump up and down]

....

■ **1** rejoice at, revel in, delight in, glory in, celebrate, relish. **2** crow over, gloat over, triumph over.

....

exultant *adj.* joyfully or triumphantly elated.

....

■ joyful, delighted, ecstatic, elated, overjoyed, jubilant, triumphant.

....

exultation *noun* a feeling or state of joyful elation.

eye — *noun* **1** the sense organ, usually one of a pair, that is responsible for vision. Various forms exist, including the simple eye (ocellus) of many annelid worms, the compound eye of insects, and the highly complex organ found in cephalopod molluscs (octopus and squid) and vertebrates, including man. **2** (*often* **eyes**) sight; vision: *surgeons need good eyes.* **3** attention, gaze, or observation: *keep one's eyes on/catch someone's eye/in the public eye.* **4** the ability to appreciate and judge: *an eye for beauty.* **5** judgement; opinion: *in the eyes of the law.* **6** a look or ex-

pression: *a hostile eye.* **7** *Bot.* the bud of a tuber such as a potato. **8** an area of calm and low pressure at the centre of a tornado, etc. **9** any rounded thing, especially when hollow, eg the hole in a needle or the small wire loop that a hook fits into. — *verb* (**eyed, eyeing**) **1** to look at carefully. **2** *colloq.* (*also* **eye someone** or **something up**) to assess their worth or attractiveness. — **be all eyes** *colloq.* to be vigilant. **cast** or **run an eye over something** to examine it cursorily. **clap** or **lay** or **set eyes on someone** or **something** *colloq.* to see it, especially for the first time. **close** or **shut one's eyes to something** to ignore or disregard it. **get** or **keep one's eye in** to become or remain familiar with the way in which a game or sport is played. **give an eye to something** *colloq.* to attend to it. **give someone the eye** or **the glad eye** *colloq.* to look at them in a sexually inviting way. **have one's eye on something** to be eager to acquire it. **have eyes for someone** to be interested in them. **have an eye to something** to have it as a purpose or intention. **keep one's eyes skinned** or **peeled** *colloq.* to watch out. **make eyes at someone** *colloq.* to look at them with sexual interest or admiration. **more than meets the eye** more complicated, difficult, etc than appearances suggest. **my eye!** *colloq.* nonsense! **one in the eye for someone** *colloq.* a harsh disappointment or rebuff for them. **see eye to eye with someone** to be in agreement with them. **be up to the** or **one's eyes in something** to be busy or deeply involved in work, a commitment, etc. **with an eye to something** having it as a purpose or intention. [from Anglo-Saxon *eage*]

....

■ *noun* **2** eyesight, vision, sight, perception. **3** attention, gaze, watch, observation, lookout. **4** appreciation, discrimination, discernment, perception, recognition. **5** viewpoint, opinion, judgement, mind. *verb* **1** look at, watch, regard, observe, stare at, gaze at, view, scrutinize, scan, examine, peruse, study, survey, inspect, contemplate. **2** look over, assess, appraise.

....

eyeball *noun* the body of the eye, which is almost spherical, and surrounded by a transparent cornea at the front and a white fibrous layer or *sclera* around the rest of the structure. — **eyeball to eyeball** *colloq., said of people* face to face and close together in a threatening confrontation.

eyebright *noun* a small annual plant belonging to the genus *Euphrasia*, so called because it is used in herbal medicine to treat sore eyes. The flowers have two lips and are usually white, with a yellow blotch and purple veins on the lower lip.

eyebrow *noun* the arch of hair on the bony ridge above each eye. — **raise an eyebrow** or **one's eyebrows** to show surprise, interest, or disbelief.

eye-catcher *noun* a strikingly attractive person or thing.

eye-catching *adj.* drawing attention, especially by being strikingly attractive.

....

■ conspicuous, noticeable, prominent, imposing, striking, attractive, good-looking, beautiful, stunning.

....

eyeful *noun colloq.* **1** an interesting or beautiful sight. **2** a look or view.

eyeglass *noun* **1** a single lens for aiding defective vision, especially a monocle. **2** an eyepiece. **3** (**eyeglasses**) *North Amer.* spectacles.

eyelash *noun* any of the short protective hairs that grow from the edge of the upper and lower eyelids.

eyelet *noun* a small hole through which a lace, etc is passed, or the metal ring reinforcing it. [from Old French *oillet*, diminutive of *oil*, eye]

eyelid *noun* in many terrestrial animals, including humans, a protective fold of skin and muscle, lined with membrane, that can be moved to cover or uncover the front of the eyeball.

eye-opener *noun colloq.* a surprising or revealing sight, experience, etc.

eyepiece *noun Optics* the lens or group of lenses in an optical instrument such as a telescope or microscope that is nearest to the eye of the observer.

eyesight *noun* the ability to see.

. . . .

▣ vision, sight, perception, observation, view.

. . . .

eyesore *noun* an ugly thing, especially a building.

. . . .

▣ blemish, monstrosity, blot on the landscape, disfigurement, horror, blight, atrocity.

. . . .

eye tooth one of the two upper canine teeth. — **give one's eye teeth for something** to go to any lengths to obtain it.

eyewash *noun* **1** liquid for soothing sore eyes. **2** *derog. colloq.* nonsense; insincere or deceptive talk.

eyewitness *noun* a person who sees something happen, especially a crime.

. . . .

▣ witness, observer, spectator, looker-on, onlooker, bystander, viewer, passer-by.

. . . .

eyrie or **eyry** or **aerie** or **aery** or **ayrie** / ˈɪərɪ, ˈaɪərɪ/ *noun* **1** the nest of a bird of prey, especially an eagle, built in a high inaccessible place. **2** any house, fortified place, etc perched high up. [from Old French *airie*]

Ez or **Ezr.** *abbrev. Biblical* Ezra.

Ezek. or **Ezek** *abbrev. Biblical* Ezekiel.

F

F¹ or **f** *noun* (PL: **Fs, F's f's**) **1** the sixth letter of the English alphabet. **2** (**F**) *Mus.* the fourth note in the scale of C major. **3** (**F**) a musical key with this note as its base.

F² *abbrev.* **1** Fahrenheit. **2** farad. **3** faraday. **4** Fellow (of a society, etc). **5** *on pencils* fine. **6** force. **7** franc.

F³ *symbol* **1** *Chem.* fluorine. **2** *Physics* force.

f *abbrev.* **1** femto- (a prefix denoting 10^{-15} in the metric system). **2** focal length. **3** *Mus.* forte. **4** frequency.

f. *abbrev.* **1** fathom. **2** female. **3** feminine. **4** folio. **5** following (page).

FA *abbrev.* Football Association.

Fa. *abbrev.* Florida.

fa same as FAH.

Fabian /ˈfeɪbɪən/ — *adj.* **1** cautious; inclined to use delaying tactics. **2** of the Fabian Society, a body founded in 1884 for the gradual establishment of socialism. — *noun* a member of this society. [named after the Roman general and statesman Quintus Fabius Maximus (c.260–203 BC)]

fable *noun* **1** a story with a moral, usually with animals as characters. **2** a lie; a false story. **3** a tale of wonder; myths and legends generally. [from Latin *fabula*, story]

⊟ **1, 3** allegory, parable, story, tale, yarn, myth, legend. **2** lie, fiction, fabrication, invention, untruth, falsehood, tall story, old wives' tale.

fabled *adj.* made famous by legend.

fabliau /ˈfæblɪəʊ/ *noun* (PL. **fabliaux**) a short comic poem or verse story popular in 12c France, and later in England. The plots usually involve deception and sex, and the subjects are amoral, frequently misogynist, and anticlerical. English examples include Chaucer's *The Miller's Tale* and *The Reeve's Tale*. [from Old French, a diminutive of FABLE]

fabric *noun* **1** woven, knitted or felted cloth. **2** quality; texture. **3** the walls, floor and roof of a building. **4** orderly structure: *the fabric of society.* [from Latin *fabrica*, craft]

⊟ **1** cloth, material, textile, stuff. **4** structure, framework, make-up, construction, constitution, organization, infrastructure, foundations.

Fabrics include: alpaca, angora, astrakhan, barathea, bouclé, cashmere, chenille, duffel, felt, flannel, fleece, *trademark* Harris tweed, mohair, paisley, serge, sheepskin, Shetland wool, tweed, vicuna, wool, worsted; brocade, buckram, calico, cambric, candlewick, canvas, chambray, cheesecloth, chino, chintz, cord, corduroy, cotton, crepe, denim, drill, jean, flannelette, gaberdine, gingham, jersey, lawn, linen, lisle, madras, moleskin, muslin, needlecord, piqué, poplin, sateen, seersucker, terry towelling, ticking, *trademark* Viyella, webbing, winceyette; grosgrain, damask, Brussels lace, chiffon, georgette, gossamer, voile, organza, organdie, tulle, net, crepe de Chine, silk, taffeta, shantung, velvet, velour; polycotton, polyester, rayon, nylon, *trademark* Crimplene, *trademark* Terylene, *trademark* Lurex, lamé; hessian, horsehair, chamois, kid, leather, leather-cloth, sharkskin, suede.

fabricate *verb* **1** to invent (a false story, etc). **2** to make, especially from whatever materials are available. **3** to forge (a document). [from Latin *fabricari*, to construct]

⊟ **1** invent, make up, trump up, concoct. **2** make, manufacture, construct, assemble, build, erect, form, shape, fashion, create, devise. **3** fake, falsify, forge.
⊟ **2** demolish, destroy.

fabrication *noun* **1** something that is fabricated or invented. **2** construction. **3** manufacture. **4** a story.

fabricator *noun* a person or business that fabricates.

fabulous *adj.* **1** *colloq.* marvellous. **2** immense; amazing. **3** legendary; mythical. [from Latin *fabulosus*]

⊟ **1** marvellous, wonderful, brilliant, fantastic, superb. **2** immense, amazing, breathtaking, spectacular, phenomenal, astounding, unbelievable, incredible, inconceivable. **3** legendary, mythical, fabled, fantastic, fictitious, invented, imaginary.
⊟ **3** real.

façade or **facade** /fəˈsɑːd/ *noun* **1** the front of a building. **2** a false appearance that hides the reality. [from French *façade*]

face — *noun* **1** the front part of the head, from forehead to chin. **2** the features or facial expression. **3** a surface or side, eg of a mountain, gem, geometrical figure, etc. **4** the important or working side, eg of a golf club head. **5** in a mine, the exposed surface from which coal, etc is mined. **6** the dial of a clock, watch, etc. **7** the side of a playing card marked with numbers, symbols, etc. **8** general look or appearance. **9** an aspect. **10** impudence; cheek. **11** *literary* someone's presence: *stand before his face*. **12** *Printing* a typeface. — *verb* **1** *trans., intrans.* to be opposite to. **2** to turn to look at or look in some direction. **3** to have before one (something unpleasant): *face ruin*. **4** to confront, brave or cope with (problems, difficulties, etc). **5** to accept (the unpleasant truth, etc). **6** to present itself to: *the scene that faced us*. **7** to cover with a surface: *bricks faced with plaster*. — **face someone down** to confront them boldly until they give way from embarrassment, shame, etc. **face to face** facing or confronting each other. **face up to something** or **someone** to deal with them bravely; to accept an unpleasant fact, etc. **fly in the face of something** to ignore a known circumstance or act contrary to it; to flout it. **in one's face** right in front of one. **in the face of something** in spite of a known circumstance, etc. **look someone in the face** to look directly at them without shame or embarrassment. **lose face** to suffer a loss of dignity or self-respect. **make** or **pull a face** to grimace, scowl, frown, etc. **on the face of it** at first glance. **put a good** or **brave face on something** to try to hide one's disappointment, fear, etc concerning it. **save one's face** to avoid losing one's dignity or self-respect. **set one's face against something** to oppose an idea, course of action, etc, firmly. **show one's face** to let oneself be seen. **to someone's face** directly; openly, in someone's presence. See also FACIAL. [from French *face*, from Latin *facies*]

⊟ *noun* **2** features, expression, countenance, look, visage, physiognomy. **3** surface, side, exterior, outside, façade. **4, 7** front. **8** look, appearance, air, aspect. *verb* **1** be opposite (to), give on to, front, overlook. **4** confront, brave, face up to, cope with, deal with, tackle, encounter, meet, experience, defy, oppose. **7** cover, coat, dress, clad, overlay, veneer. **face to face** opposite, eye to eye, *colloq.* eyeball to eyeball, in confrontation. **face up to** deal with, cope with, confront, meet head-on, stand up to, accept, come to terms with, acknowledge, recognize.

face card a court card.

faceless *adj.* lacking identity; impersonal; anonymous.

facelift *noun* **1** *Medicine* a surgical operation to rejuvenate the appearance of the face by tightening the skin, especially around the eyes or chin, and so removing facial wrinkles. It is a form of cosmetic surgery. **2** a procedure for improving the appearance of something.

face pack a liquid cosmetic preparation for cleaning the face, that hardens on the skin and is peeled or washed off.

facer *noun colloq.* a problem.

face-saving *noun, adj.* preserving one's reputation, credibility, etc, in difficult circumstances.

facet /ˈfasɪt, ˈfasət/ *noun* **1** any of the faces of a cut jewel. **2** an aspect, eg of a problem, topic, or personality. [from French *facette*, diminutive of *face*, face]

▣ **1** surface, plane, side, face. **2** aspect, angle, point, feature, characteristic.

facetious /fəˈsiːʃəs/ *adj.*, *said of a person or remark, etc* intending or intended to be amusing or witty, especially unsuitably so. [from Latin *facetus*, witty]

▣ flippant, frivolous, playful, jocular, jesting, tongue in cheek, funny, amusing, humorous, comical, witty.
▣ serious.

face value **1** the stated value on a coin, stamp, etc. **2** the apparent meaning or implication, eg of a statement.

facia /ˈfeɪʃə/ same as FASCIA.

facial /ˈfeɪʃl/ *adj.* of, relating to or belonging to, the face. [from Latin *facies*, face]

facile /ˈfasaɪl/ *adj.* **1** *derog.*, *of success, etc* too easily achieved. **2** *derog.*, *said of remarks, opinions, etc* oversimple; showing a lack of careful thought. **3** speaking or performing with fluency and ease. [from Latin *facilis*, easy]

▣ **1** easy, simple. **2** simplistic, glib, hasty, shallow, superficial. **3** fluent, smooth, slick, ready, quick.
▣ **1** complicated. **2** profound.

facilely *adv.* in a facile way.

facilitate *verb* to ease (a process, etc). [from FACILITY]

▣ ease, help, assist, further, promote, forward, expedite, speed up.

facilitation *noun* **1** the process of facilitating. **2** *Physiol.* in the nervous system, the process whereby signals are transmitted more effectively by each successive nerve impulse because of an increase in the amount of *neurotransmitter* released at the synapse (junction) between two adjacent neurones (nerve cells). **3** *Zool.* in animal behaviour, an improvement in the ability of an animal to respond to a specific stimulus.

facility *noun* (PL. **facilities**) **1** skill, talent, or ability. **2** fluency; ease. **3** an arrangement, feature, attachment, etc that enables something to do something. **4** (*usually* **facilities**) a building, service or piece of equipment for a particular activity. [from Latin *facilitas*, ease]

▣ **1** skill, skilfulness, talent, ability, proficiency, gift, knack. **2** fluency, ease, effortlessness, readiness, quickness. **3** amenity, convenience, service, resource, means, opportunity.

facing *noun* **1** an outer layer, eg of stone covering a brick wall. **2** a piece of material used to back and strengthen part of a garment. **3** (**facings**) the collar and cuffs of a jacket, etc, especially if in a contrasting colour.

facsimile /fakˈsɪmɪlɪ/ *noun* **1** an exact copy of a manuscript, drawing, map, photograph, etc. **2** electronic copying and telegraphic transmission of such material; fax. **3** a copy made by facsimile. [from Latin *fac simile*, make the same]

fact *noun* **1** a thing known to be true, to exist, or to have happened. **2** truth or reality, as distinct from mere statement or belief. **3** an assertion of fact; a piece of information. **4** *Legal* a crime, as in *after* or *before the fact.* — **as a matter of fact** or **in fact,** etc in reality; actually. **for a fact** with complete certainty. **in fact** *in summarizing* in short; that is to say. [from Latin *factum*, something done]

▣ **1, 3** information, datum, detail, particular, specific, point, item, circumstance, event, incident, occurrence, happening, act, deed, fait accompli. **2** truth, reality, actuality. **in fact** in short, that is to say, actually, in actual fact, in point of fact, as a matter of fact, in reality, really, indeed.
▣ **2** fiction.

faction¹ *noun* **1** an active or trouble-making group within a larger organization. **2** argument and fighting between members of a group. [from Latin *factio*, party, side]

▣ **1** splinter group, ginger group, division, section, minority, contingent, party, camp, set, clique, coterie, cabal, junta, lobby, pressure group.

faction² *noun* a docudrama. [from FACT + FICTION]

factional *adj.* **1** consisting of or relating to a faction. **2** causing faction.

factitious *adj.* deliberately contrived rather than developing naturally. [from Latin *facticius*]

fact of life **1** an unavoidable truth, especially if unpleasant. **2** (**facts of life**) basic information on sexual matters and reproduction.

factor *noun* **1** a circumstance that contributes to a result. **2** *Maths.* one of two or more numbers that will divide exactly into another given number, eg 2 and 4 are factors of 8. **3** in Scotland, the manager of an estate, or other property. [from Latin *factor*, person who acts]

▣ **1** cause, influence, circumstance, contingency, consideration, element, ingredient, component, part, point, aspect, fact, item, detail.

factor VIII or **factor 8** *Physiol.* one of the proteins present in the blood that controls the clotting process. Deficiency of this factor causes the disease haemophilia, in which the blood fails to clot.

factorial — *noun Maths.* the product of all the positive integers (positive whole numbers) from a given integer *n* down to one, written as *n*!, eg the factorial of five, written as 5!, which is equal to $5 \times 4 \times 3 \times 2 \times 1$, = 120. The factorial of zero, 0!, is equal to one. — *adj.* relating to a factor or factorial.

factoring *noun* (*in full* **debt factoring**) *Commerce* the selling of a company's list of debtors to an agent (*factor*) at a discount. The factor then retrieves the sums due. Factoring can be advantageous to a firm's cash flow and reduces overheads and costs associated with the collection of debts.

factorization or **factorisation** *noun* the process of factorizing.

factorize or **factorise** *verb Maths.* to resolve (an algebraic or numerical expression) into factors.

factory *noun* (PL. **factories**) a building or buildings with equipment for the large-scale manufacture of goods. [from Latin *factoria*]

- works, plant, mill, manufactory, assembly line, shop floor.

factory farm a farm in which large numbers of animals are reared by factory farming. Also called BATTERY FARM.

factory farming a highly intensive form of livestock farming in which large numbers of animals are reared indoors so that their environment and feeding regimes can be strictly controlled, resulting in a standardized product. Also called BATTERY FARMING.

factotum /fak'toʊtəm/ *noun* a person employed to do a large number of different jobs. [from Latin *fac totum*, do all]

factual *adj.* concerned with, or based on, facts.

- true, historical, actual, real, genuine, authentic, correct, accurate, precise, exact, literal, faithful, close, detailed, unbiased, objective.
- false, fictitious, imaginary, fictional.

facultative /'fakəltətɪv/ *adj. Biol.* able to live under different conditions, especially denoting a parasite able to live on dead or decaying organic matter as well as on its living host.

faculty /'fakəltɪ/ *noun* (PL. **faculties**) 1 any of the range of mental or physical powers. 2 a particular talent or aptitude for something. 3 a section of a university, comprising a number of departments. 4 *North Amer.* the staff of a college, school, or university. [from Latin *facultas*, capability]

- 1 power, ability, facility, capacity, sense. 2 talent, aptitude, ability, capability, knack, gift, skill, bent. 3 school.

fad *noun derog.* 1 a shortlived fashion; a craze. 2 an especially unreasonable prejudice or dislike, usually with regard to food.

- 1 craze, *colloq.* rage, mania, fashion, mode, vogue, trend, whim, fancy.

faddiness or **faddishness** *noun* being faddy.

faddy or **faddish** *adj.* (**faddier**, **faddiest**) 1 typical of a fad. 2 choosy, fussy, especially about food.

fade *verb* (*often* **fade away**) 1 *trans., intrans.* to lose or cause to lose strength, freshness, or colour. 2 *intrans. said of a sound or image* to disappear gradually. — **fade something in** or **out** *Cinema, Broadcasting* to cause a sound or picture to become gradually louder and more distinct, or to to become fainter and disappear. [from Old French *fade*, dull, pale]

- 1 discolour, bleach, blanch, blench, pale, whiten, dim, dull, decline, fall, diminish, dwindle, ebb, wane, flag, weaken, droop, wilt, wither, shrivel, perish, die.

fade-in *noun Cinema, Broadcasting* the process of fading in a picture or sound.

fade-out *noun Cinema, Broadcasting* the process of fading out a picture or sound.

faecal /'fiːkəl/ *adj.* of the nature of or containing faeces.

faeces /'fiːsiːz/ *pl. noun* the solid waste matter discharged from the body through the anus. [from Latin *faex*, dregs]

Faeroese or **Faroese** the N Germanic language spoken by inhabitants of the Faeroe Is. It is closely related to the other W Scandinavian languages, Norwegian and Icelandic.

faff *verb intrans. colloq.* (**faff about**) to act in a fussy, uncertain way; to dither.

fag [1] — *noun* 1 *colloq.* a cigarette. 2 *colloq.* a piece of drudgery; a bore. 3 in some schools, a young schoolboy who runs errands and does jobs for an older one. — *verb* (**fagged**, **fagging**) 1 to tire out; to exhaust. 2 *intrans. said of a schoolboy* to act as fag for an older boy. 3 *intrans.* to work hard; to toil.

fag [2] *noun North Amer. offensive slang* a male homosexual. [short for FAGGOT]

fag end *colloq.* 1 a cigarette end. 2 the last part of something.

faggot /'fagət/ *noun* 1 a ball or roll of chopped liver mixed with bread and herbs. 2 a bundle of sticks. 3 *North Amer. offensive slang* a male homosexual. 4 *derog. slang* an old woman. [from Old French *fagot*, bundle of sticks]

fag hag *offensive slang* a heterosexual woman who enjoys the company of gay men.

fah *noun* in tonic sol-fa, the fourth note of the major scale. [from the first syllable of the word *famuli* in a medieval Latin hymn, certain syllables of which were used in naming the notes of the scale]

Fahrenheit /'farənhaɪt/ *noun* relating to or measured by a temperature scale in which the freezing point of pure water under standard atmospheric pressure is 32° and its boiling point is 212°. It has now been largely superseded by the Celsius scale. [named after Gabriel Fahrenheit]

faience or **faïence** /faɪ'ɑːns/ *noun* glazed decorated pottery. [from French *faïence*, from *Faenza* in Italy, the place of manufacture]

fail *verb* 1 *intrans., trans.* (*often* **fail in something**) not to succeed; to be unsuccessful in an undertaking. 2 to judge (a candidate) not good enough to pass a test, etc. 3 *intrans. said of machinery, a bodily organ, etc* to stop working or functioning. 4 *intrans.* not to manage (to do something). 5 not to bother (doing something). 6 to let (someone) down; to disappoint. 7 *said of courage, strength, etc* to desert (one) at the time of need. 8 *intrans.* to become gradually weaker. 9 *intrans. said of a business, etc* to collapse. — **fail to see** to be unable to understand. **without fail** for certain; with complete regularity. [from Latin *fallere*, to deceive, disappoint]

- 1 go wrong, miscarry, misfire, flop, *slang* flunk, fall through, come to grief. 3 break down, go wrong, stop, *colloq.* pack up, *slang* conk out. 4, 5 omit, neglect. 7 desert, leave, abandon, forsake. 8 weaken, dwindle, fade, wane, sink, decline. 9 collapse, *colloq.* fold, go bankrupt, go bust, go under, founder, fall.
- 1 succeed. 2 pass. 9 prosper.

failing *noun* a fault; a weakness.

- fault, weakness, flaw, defect, imperfection, foible, blemish, drawback, deficiency, shortcoming, failure, lapse, error.
- strength, advantage.

fail-safe *adj. Engineering* denoting a mechanism which ensures that people operating a system, eg machinery, will not be placed at risk if that system ceases to function properly.

failure *noun* 1 the act of failing; lack of success. 2 a person or thing that is unsuccessful. 3 a stoppage in functioning. 4 a poor result. 5 the non-doing of something: *failure to turn up.*

- 1 defeat, downfall, decline, decay, deterioration, ruin, bankruptcy, miscarriage, loss, *colloq.* slip-up. 2 flop, *colloq.* washout, disappointment, fiasco. 3 stoppage, crash, collapse, breakdown. 5 neglect, omission, negligence.
- 1 success, prosperity.

fain *adv. old use* gladly; willingly. [from Anglo-Saxon *fægen*]

faint — *adj.* **1** pale; dim; indistinct; slight. **2** physically weak; on the verge of losing consciousness. **3** feeble; timid; unenthusiastic. — *verb intrans.* to lose consciousness; to collapse. — *noun* a sudden loss of consciousness. [from Old French *faindre*, to feign]

∎ *adj.* **1** pale, dim, indistinct, slight, weak, feeble, soft, low, hushed, muffled, subdued, faded, bleached, light, dull, hazy, vague. **2** dizzy, giddy, *colloq.* woozy, light-headed, weak, exhausted. **3** feeble, timid, unenthusiastic, weak, timorous, irresolute, spineless, nervous. *verb* black out, pass out, swoon, collapse, *colloq.* flake out, *colloq.* keel over, drop. *noun* blackout, swoon, collapse, unconsciousness.

E3 *adj.* **1** strong, clear.

faint-hearted *adj.* timid; cowardly.

faintly *adv.* in a faint way; weakly.

fair[1] — *adj.* **1** just; not using dishonest methods or discrimination. **2** in accordance with the rules. **3** *said of hair and skin* light-coloured; having light-coloured hair and skin. **4** *old use* beautiful. **5** quite good; reasonable. **6** sizeable; considerable. **7** *said of the weather* fine. **8** *said of the wind* favourable. **9** *said of words* insincerely encouraging. — *adv.* **1** in a fair way. **2** *dialect* completely. — **be fair game** to deserve to be attacked or criticized. **by fair means or foul** using any possible means, even if dishonest. **fair and square 1** absolutely; exactly. **2** honest and open. **fair enough** all right. **in a fair way to doing something** likely to achieve it. **to be fair** one ought to remember, if one is fair. [from Anglo-Saxon *fæger*, beautiful]

∎ *adj.* **1** just, equitable, square, even-handed, dispassionate, impartial, objective, disinterested, unbiased, unprejudiced, right, proper, lawful, legitimate, honest, trustworthy, upright, honourable. **3** fair-haired, fair-headed, blond(e), light. **5** satisfactory, adequate, acceptable, reasonable, passable, average, not bad, all right, *colloq.* OK, tolerable, moderate, middling, mediocre, *colloq.* so-so. **7** fine, dry, sunny, bright, clear, cloudless, unclouded.

E3 *adj.* **1** unfair. **3** dark. **5** excellent, poor. **7** inclement, cloudy, miserable.

fair[2] *noun* **1** a collection of sideshows and amusements, often set up temporarily on open ground and travelling from place to place. **2** *Hist.* a market for the sale of produce, livestock, etc, with or without sideshows. **3** an indoor exhibition of goods from different countries, firms, etc, held to promote trade. **4** a sale of goods to raise money for charity, etc. [from Old French *feire*, from Latin *feriae*, holiday]

∎ **1** funfair. **3** exhibition, show, exposition, *colloq.* expo, festival. **4** bazaar, fête, market.

fair copy a neat finished copy of a piece of writing.

fair dos or **fair do's** *colloq.* equal treatment for everyone.

fairground *noun* the piece of land on which sideshows and amusements are set up for a fair.

fairing *noun* an external structure fitted to an aircraft or vehicle to improve streamlining and reduce drag. [from *fair*, to make smooth, to streamline]

Fair Isle /ˈfɛər aɪl/ a complex multicoloured type of knitting pattern. [from *Fair Isle*, Shetland, where it was first developed]

fairly *adv.* **1** justly; honestly. **2** quite; rather. **3** *colloq.* absolutely.

fairness *noun* being fair. **in all fairness** one ought to remember, if one is fair.

fair play *noun* honourable behaviour; just treatment.

fair sex (**the fair sex**) *facetious* women.

fairway *noun* **1** *Golf* a broad strip of short grass extending from one tee to the next green. **2** a deep-water channel in a river, etc, used by shipping.

fair-weather friend a friend who deserts one when one is in trouble.

fairy *noun* (PL. **fairies**) **1** any of various supernatural beings with magical powers and more or less human shape, common in folklore. **2** *derog.* a male homosexual.

fairy godmother someone who comes unexpectedly or magically to one's aid.

fairyland *noun* **1** the home of fairies. **2** an entrancing place.

fairy lights small coloured lights used for decoration.

fairy ring a ring of darker coloured grass in a lawn or field, marking the outer edge of an underground fungal mycelium (a mass or network of threadlike filaments or *hyphae*), so called because it was formerly attributed to the dancing of fairies.

fairy tale or **fairy story 1** a story about fairies, magic, etc. **2** *euphemistic colloq.* a lie.

fait accompli /feɪt əkɒmˈpliː/ (PL. **faits accomplis**) something done and unalterable; an established fact. [from French *fait accompli*, accomplished fact]

faith *noun* **1** trust or confidence. **2** strong belief, eg in God. **3** a religion. **4** any set or system of beliefs. **5** loyalty to a promise, etc; trust: *keep/break faith with someone*. — **in good faith** from good or sincere motives. [from Old French *feid*]

∎ **1** trust, confidence, belief, credit, reliance, dependence, conviction, assurance. **3** religion, denomination, church. **4** belief, persuasion, creed, dogma. **5** loyalty, trust, faithfulness, fidelity, allegiance, honour, sincerity, honesty, truthfulness.

E3 **1** mistrust. **5** unfaithfulness, treachery.

faithful — *adj.* **1** having or showing faith. **2** loyal and true. **3** accurate. **4** loyal to one's sexual partner. **5** reliable; constant. — *noun* **1** (**the faithful**) the believers in a particular religion; loyal supporters. **2** a supporter: *party faithfuls*.

∎ *adj.* **2** loyal, true, devoted, staunch, steadfast, constant, trusty, reliable, dependable. **3** accurate, precise, exact, strict, close, true, truthful. **4** true. **5** reliable, constant, steadfast, trusty, dependable.

E3 *adj.* **2** disloyal, treacherous. **3** inaccurate, vague. **4** unfaithful.

faithfully *adv.* in a faithful way. — **yours faithfully** formal wording for ending a letter.

faith healer a person who claims or is reputed to heal others by the power of religion.

faith healing the curing of illness through religious faith rather than medical treatment.

faithless *adj.* **1** disloyal; treacherous. **2** having no religious faith.

fajitas /faˈhiːtas/ *pl. noun* a Mexican dish of seared strips of meat, chile, onions, etc served with flour tortillas. [from Spanish *fajitas*, a diminutive of *faja*, bundle]

fake — *noun* a person, thing, or act that is not genuine. — *adj.* not genuine; false. — *verb* **1** to alter dishonestly; to falsify or make up. **2** *trans., intrans.* to pretend to feel (an emotion) or have (an illness).

∎ *noun* forgery, copy, reproduction, replica, imitation, simulation, sham, hoax, fraud, *colloq.* phoney, impostor, charlatan. *adj.* false, forged, counterfeit, spurious, *colloq.* phoney, pseudo, bogus, assumed, affected, sham, artificial, simulated, mock, faux, imitation, reproduction. *verb* **1** forge, sham, counterfeit, falsify, make up, fabricate. **2** feign, pretend, put on, affect, sham, simulate, assume.

E3 *adj.* genuine.

faker *noun* a person who fakes.

fakery *noun* **1** the act of faking. **2** something that is faked.

fakir /ˈfeɪkɪə(r), faːˈkɪə(r)/ *noun* **1** a wandering Hindu or Muslim holy man depending on begging for survival. **2** a member of any Muslim religious order. [from Arabic *faqir*, poor man]

Falange Española /'falandʒ ɛspan'jɒlə/ a fascist movement, founded in Spain in 1933. [Spanish, = Spanish Falange]

falcon /'fɔːlkən/ *noun* any of several birds of prey with long pointed wings and notched beaks, capable of rapid graceful flight, eg peregrine, gyrfalcon, kestrel, merlin. They feed on the wing, taking birds, bats, and insects. [from Latin *falco*, hawk]

falconer *noun* 1 a person who breeds and trains hawks. 2 a person who takes part in the sport of hunting with hawks.

falconry *noun* the art or practice of breeding falcons, training them to return from flight, and using them to hunt small game.

fall — *verb intrans.* (PAST TENSE fell; PAST PARTICIPLE fallen) 1 to descend or drop by force of gravity, especially accidentally. 2 (*also* fall over or down) *said of a person, or something upright* to drop to the ground after losing balance. 3 *said of a building, bridge, etc* to collapse. 4 *said of rain, snow, etc* to come down. 5 *said eg of hair* to hang down. 6 *said of land* to slope down. 7 *said of a blow, glance, shadow, light, etc* to land. 8 to go naturally or easily into position: *fell open at page 61*. 9 to throw oneself; to move hurriedly or ungracefully. 10 *said of a government, etc* to lose power; to be no longer able to govern. 11 *said of a stronghold* to be captured. 12 *said of defences or barriers* to be lowered or broken down. 13 to die or be badly wounded in battle, etc. 14 to give in to temptation; to sin. 15 *said eg of value, temperature, etc* to become less. 16 *said of sound* to diminish. 17 *said eg of silence* to intervene. 18 *said of darkness or night* to arrive. 19 to pass into a certain state: *fall asleep*. 20 to be grouped or classified in a certain way: *falls into two categories*. 21 to occur at a certain time or place: *the accent falls on the first syllable*. 22 *said of someone's face* to show disappointment. — *noun* 1 an act or way of falling. 2 something, or an amount, that falls. 3 (**falls**) a waterfall. 4 a drop in eg quality, quantity, value, temperature, etc. 5 a defeat or collapse. 6 *Wrestling* a manoeuvre by which one pins one's opponent's shoulders to the ground. 7 (**the Fall**) *Biblical* the sinning of Adam and Eve. — **break someone's fall** to stop someone landing with the full impact of a free fall. **fall about** *colloq.* to be helpless with laughter. **fall apart** 1 to break in pieces. 2 to collapse. **fall away** 1 *said of land* to slope downwards. 2 to become fewer or less. 3 to disappear. **fall back** 1 to move back; to retreat. 2 (**fall back on something**) to make use of it in an emergency. **fall behind** to fail to keep up with someone, with one's work, etc. (**fall behind with something**) to be late in paying instalments or doing work. **fall down** *said of an argument, etc* to be shown to be invalid. (**fall down on something**) to fail in a task; to do it unsatisfactorily. **fall for someone** to become infatuated with them, or fall in love with them. **fall for something** to be deceived or taken in by it. **fall in** 1 *said eg of a roof* to collapse. 2 *said of a soldier, etc* to take one's place in a parade. (**fall in with someone**) to chance to meet or coincide with them. (**fall in with something**) to agree to; to support it. **fall into something** to become involved in it, especially by chance. **fall off** to decline in quality or quantity; to become less. **fall on or upon someone** 1 to attack them. 2 to embrace them passionately. **fall out** 1 *said of soldiers* to come out of military formation. 2 to happen in the end; to turn out. (**fall out with someone**) to quarrel with them. **fall over oneself** or **fall over backwards** *colloq.* to be strenuously or noticeably eager to please or help. **fall through** *said of a plan, etc* to fail; to come to nothing. **fall to** to begin eating. **fall to something** to start it; *fall to work*. **fall to someone** to become their job or duty: *it falls to me to deal with the matter*. **fall to pieces** or **bits** to break up; to disintegrate. [from Anglo-Saxon *feallan*]

· · · · · · · · · · · · · · · · · · · ·

▣ *verb* 1 descend, drop, go down, slope, slide, sink, dive, plunge, plummet, nosedive, pitch, tumble, stumble, trip, crash. 2 topple, *colloq.* keel over, collapse, slump. 3 collapse, topple. 6 drop. 10 collapse, tumble, topple. 15 decrease, lessen, decline, fall off, diminish, subside. 16

diminish, subside. *noun* 1 tumble, descent, dive, plunge, decrease, reduction, lessening. 3 cascade. 4 drop, decline, decrease, reduction, lessening, slump, crash, dive, plunge. 5 defeat, collapse, conquest, overthrow, downfall, surrender, capitulation. **fall apart** 1 break, shatter, disintegrate, crumble, decompose, decay, rot. 2 fail, collapse, founder, go wrong, go under, come to grief, go to pieces. **fall back on** resort to, have recourse to, use, turn to, look to. **fall behind** lag, trail, drop back. **fall in** 1 collapse, cave in, come down, give way, subside, sink. **fall in with something** go along with, agree to, assent to, accept, comply with, co-operate with. **fall off** decline, decrease, lessen, drop, slump, deteriorate, worsen, slow, slacken. **fall out with** quarrel with, argue with, squabble with, bicker with, fight with, clash with, disagree with, differ from. **fall through** fail, come to nothing, miscarry, founder, collapse.

▣ *verb* 1, 2, 6, 15 rise. 15 increase. **fall out with** agree. **fall through** come off, succeed.

· · · · · · · · · · · · · · · · · · · ·

fallacious /fə'leɪʃəs/ *adj.* 1 deceptive, misleading. 2 wrong. 3 disappointing.

fallacy /'faləsɪ/ *noun* (PL. **fallacies**) 1 a mistaken notion. 2 a mistake in reasoning that spoils a whole argument. [from Latin *fallax*, deceptive]

· · · · · · · · · · · · · · · · · · · ·

▣ MISCONCEPTION, DELUSION, MISTAKE, ERROR, FLAW, INCONSISTENCY, FALSEHOOD.

▣ TRUTH.

· · · · · · · · · · · · · · · · · · · ·

fallen *adj.* 1 *old use* having lost one's virtue, honour or reputation. 2 killed in battle. 3 having dropped or overturned.

fall guy *colloq.* 1 someone who is easily cheated. 2 someone who is left to take the blame for something.

fallible *adj.* capable of making mistakes. [from Latin *fallere*, to deceive]

falling-off *noun* a decline in quality or quantity.

falling star a meteor.

Fallopian tube or **fallopian tube** /fə'loʊpɪən/ in female mammals, either of a pair of long slender tubes through which the ova (egg cells) pass from either of the ovaries to the uterus. [named after the Italian anatomist Gabriello Fallopius]

fallout *noun* the particles of radioactive material that are released into the atmosphere and fall to the Earth's surface after a nuclear explosion.

fallow — *noun* the period during which arable farmland is not used to grow crops. — *adj.* denoting farmland that is ploughed but then left unplanted, usually for a season, to allow it to regain its natural fertility. [from Anglo-Saxon *fealga*]

· · · · · · · · · · · · · · · · · · · ·

▣ *adj.* uncultivated, unplanted, unsown, undeveloped, unused, idle, inactive, dormant, resting.

· · · · · · · · · · · · · · · · · · · ·

fallow deer a small deer with a reddish-brown coat, dappled with white spots in summer. [from Anglo-Saxon *fealu*, tawny]

false *adj.* 1 *said of a statement, etc* untrue. 2 *said of an idea, etc* mistaken. 3 artificial; not genuine. 4 *said of words, promises, etc* insincere. 5 treacherous; disloyal. 6 *Bot.*, *said of a plant* resembling, but wrongly so called: *false acacia*. — **play someone false** to cheat or deceive them. **under false pretences** by giving a deliberately misleading impression. [from Latin *falsus*]

· · · · · · · · · · · · · · · · · · · ·

▣ 1 untrue, wrong, fallacious, incorrect, erroneous, inaccurate. 2 mistaken, misleading, fallacious, faulty, invalid, inexact. 3 artificial, synthetic, imitation, simulated, unreal, mock, fake, counterfeit, forged, feigned, pretended, sham, bogus, assumed, fictitious. 4 insincere, hypocritical. 5

treacherous, disloyal, unfaithful, faithless, lying, deceitful, double-dealing, two-faced, unreliable. **E3** 1 true, right. 3 real, genuine. 4 sincere, genuine. 5 faithful, reliable.

false alarm an alarm given unnecessarily.

false fruit *Bot.* a fruit that is formed from other parts of the flower, in addition to the ovary. It may include the receptacle (eg strawberry, apple), or a complete inflorescence or flower head (eg pineapple). Also called PSEUDOCARP.

falsehood *noun* 1 lying; dishonesty. 2 a lie.

☐ UNTRUTH, FABRICATION. 1 dishonesty, untruthfulness, perjury, deceit, deception. 2 lie, fib, story, fiction. **E3** 1 truthfulness. 2 truth.

false memory syndrome (ABBREV. **FMS**) a condition of erroneous memory of childhood experiences, especially of sexual abuse, under hypnosis or other inducement.

false move a careless or unwise action that puts one in danger.

falseness or **falsity** *noun* being false.

false pregnancy *Medicine* a psychological disorder in which some of the physical symptoms of pregnancy, eg abdominal swelling, weight gain, morning sickness, and cessation of menstrual periods, occur in a woman who is not pregnant.

false start 1 a failed attempt to begin something. 2 an invalid start to a race, in which one competitor begins before the signal is given.

falsetto /fɔːlˈsetoʊ/ *noun* (PL. **falsettos**) an artificially high voice, especially produced by a tenor above his normal range. [from Italian *falsetto*]

falsification *noun* the act or process of falsifying.

falsify *verb* (**falsifies, falsified**) to alter dishonestly or make up, in order to deceive or mislead. [from Latin *falsus*, false + *facere*, to make]

☐ alter, *colloq.* cook, tamper with, doctor, distort, pervert, misrepresent, misstate, forge, counterfeit, fake.

falter /ˈfɔːltə(r)/ *verb* (**faltered, faltering**) 1 *intrans.* to move unsteadily; to stumble. 2 *intrans.* to start functioning unreliably. 3 *intrans.* to lose strength or conviction; to hesitate or break down in speaking. 4 to say hesitantly.

☐ 1 stumble, totter. 2 fail. 3 hesitate, waver, vacillate, flinch, quail, shake, tremble, flag. 4 stammer, stutter.

falteringly *adv.* in a faltering way.

fame *noun* 1 the condition of being famous. 2 *old use* repute. [from Latin *fama*, report, rumour]

☐ 1 renown, celebrity, stardom, prominence, eminence, reputation.

famed *adj.* famous.

familial *adj.* belonging to, typical of, or occurring in, a family.

familiar — *adj.* 1 well known or recognizable. 2 frequently met with. 3 (**familiar with something**) well acquainted with it; having a thorough knowledge of it. 4 friendly; close. 5 over-friendly; excessively informal. — *noun* 1 a close friend. 2 a demon or spirit especially in the shape of an animal, serving a witch. [from Latin *familiaris*, domestic, intimate]

☐ *adj.* 1 well-known, recognizable, ordinary, household. 2 everyday, routine, common. 3 acquainted with, aware of, abreast of, knowledgeable about, versed in, conversant in. 4 friendly, close, intimate, confidential, informal, free, free and easy, relaxed.

☐ *adj.* 1, 2 unfamiliar, strange. 3 unfamiliar with, ignorant of. 4 formal, reserved, unfriendly.

familiarity *noun* being familiar.

☐ awareness, acquaintance, experience, knowledge, understanding, grasp, intimacy, friendliness, closeness, informality, openness, naturalness, sociability.

familiarization or **familiarisation** *noun* the act or process of familiarizing.

familiarize or **familiarise** *verb* 1 (**familiarize someone with something**) to make (especially oneself) familiar with it. 2 to make well known or familiar.

☐ 1 accustom, acclimatize, school, train, coach, instruct.

family *noun* (PL. **families**) 1 a group consisting of a set of parents and children. 2 a set of relatives. 3 a person's children. 4 a household of people. 5 all those descended from a common ancestor. 6 a related group, eg of races, languages, words, etc. 7 a related group of plant or animal genera. — **in the family way** *colloq.* pregnant. [from Latin *familia*, household, family]

☐ 2 relatives, relations, kin, kindred, kinsmen, people, *colloq.* folk, ancestors, forebears. 3 children, offspring, issue, progeny, descendants. 5 clan, tribe, race, dynasty, house, pedigree, ancestry, parentage, descent, line, lineage, extraction, blood, stock, birth. 6 group, class, classification.

Members of a family include: ancestor, forebear, forefather, descendant, offspring, heir; husband, wife, spouse, parent, father, *colloq.* dad, *colloq.* daddy, *colloq.* old man, mother, *colloq.* mum, *colloq.* mummy, *colloq.* mom, grandparent, grandfather, grandmother, *colloq.* granny, *colloq.* nanny, grandchild, son, daughter, brother, half-brother, sister, half-sister, sibling, uncle, aunt, nephew, niece, cousin, godfather, godmother, godchild, stepfather, stepmother, foster parent, foster child.

family allowance *old use* child benefit.

family credit an allowance paid to families with low incomes.

family doctor a general practitioner.

family man a married man with children, especially one fond of home life.

family name 1 a surname. 2 the family honour: *a stain on the family name.*

family planning the use of contraceptive methods to control the number of children in a family.

family therapy *Psychol.* a form of psychotherapy that aims to resolve long-standing problems in communication within a family by discussing these difficulties with all family members present.

family tree the relationships within a family throughout the generations, or a diagram showing these.

☐ ancestry, pedigree, genealogy, line, lineage, extraction.

famine /ˈfamɪn/ *noun* 1 a severe general shortage of food, usually caused by a population explosion or failure of food crops. 2 the period during which this shortage occurs. 3 extreme hunger; starvation. [from Old French *famine*, from Latin *fames*, hunger]

☐ 1 scarcity. 3 hunger, starvation, destitution, want.

famished or **famishing** *adj.* very hungry; starving: *famished children.* [from Latin *fames*, hunger]

famous *adj.* **1** well known; celebrated; renowned. **2** great; glorious: *a famous victory.* [from Latin *famosus*, from *fama*, report, fame]

. . . .

▣ **1** well-known, famed, renowned, celebrated, noted. **2** glorious, great, distinguished, illustrious, eminent, honoured, acclaimed, legendary, remarkable, notable, prominent, signal.
▣ **1** unheard-of, unknown, obscure.

. . . .

famously *adv.* in a way that brings fame or notoriety.

fan[1] — *noun* **1** a hand-held device made of paper, silk, etc, usually semicircular and folding flat when not in use, for creating a current of air to cool the face. **2** any fan-shaped structure, eg a cone-shaped deposit of alluvium or sediment. **3** any structure that can be spread into the shape of a fan, eg the tail of certain birds. **4** any of various mechanical devices that can produce a current of air, usually by the rotation of one or more broad blades. **5** a small sail used to ensure that the vanes of a windmill face the direction of the wind. **6** a type of basket formerly used for winnowing grain by tossing it in the wind. — *verb* (**fanned, fanning**) **1** to cool (a person or object) by directing a moving current of air on it with or as if with a fan. **2** to kindle or stir up, with or as if with a moving current of air. **3** (**fan out**) to spread out in the shape of a fan. **4** to agitate (air), with or as if with a fan. **5** to winnow (grain). [from Anglo-Saxon *fann*]

. . . .

▣ *noun* **4** extractor fan, ventilator, air-conditioner, blower, propeller, vane. *verb* **1** cool, ventilate, air, air-condition, aircool, blow, refresh. **2** kindle, stir up, provoke, stimulate, rouse, arouse, excite, agitate, work up, whip up, increase.

. . . .

fan[2] *noun* an enthusiastic supporter or devoted admirer. [from FANATIC]

. . . .

▣ supporter, follower, adherent, devotee, enthusiast, admirer, lover, *colloq.* buff, *colloq.* fiend, freak.

. . . .

fanatic — *noun* someone with an extreme or excessive enthusiasm for something. — *adj.* excessively enthusiastic. [from Latin *fanaticus*, filled with a god, frenzied]

. . . .

▣ *noun* zealot, devotee, enthusiast, addict, *colloq.* fiend, freak, maniac, visionary, bigot, extremist, militant, activist.

. . . .

fanatical *adj.* fanatic.

. . . .

▣ overenthusiastic, extreme, passionate, zealous, fervent, burning, mad, wild, frenzied, rabid, obsessive, single-minded, bigoted, visionary.
▣ moderate, unenthusiastic.

. . . .

fanatically *adv.* in a fanatic way.

fanaticism /fəˈnatısızm/ *noun* wild and excessive enthusiasm, especially for a religion.

. . . .

▣ extremism, single-mindedness, obsessiveness, infatuation, bigotry, zeal, fervour, enthusiasm, dedication, monomania, madness.
▣ moderation.

. . . .

fan belt a tough rubber and fabric belt that drives the cooling fan in a vehicle engine.

fancier *noun especially in compounds* someone with a special interest in something, especially a breeder or grower of a certain kind of bird, animal, or plant.

fanciful *adj.* **1** indulging in fancies; imaginative or over-imaginative. **2** existing in fancy only; imaginary. **3** designed in a curious or fantastic way.

. . . .

▣ **2** imaginary, mythical, whimsical, airy-fairy, vaporous, wild,

extravagant. **3** fabulous, fantastic, visionary, romantic, fairy-tale.
▣ **2, 3** real, ordinary.

. . . .

fancily *adv.* in a fancy way.

fan club a club of admirers of a pop star, etc.

fancy — *noun* (PL. **fancies**) **1** one's imagination. **2** an image, idea, or whim. **3** a sudden liking or desire. — *adj.* **1** elaborate. **2** *colloq.* of special, unusual, or superior quality. **3** *colloq. facetious, said of prices* too high. — *verb* (**fancies, fancied**) **1** to think or believe. **2** to have a desire for. **3** *colloq.* to be sexually attracted to. **4** to consider likely to win or do well. **5** *trans., intrans.* to take in mentally; to imagine: *fancy him getting married at last!* **6** *colloq.* to think too well of (oneself). — **take a fancy to someone** or **something** to become fond of it. **take** or **tickle the fancy of someone** to appeal to them; to intrigue or attract them. [contracted from FANTASY]

. . . .

▣ *noun* **2** image, idea, whim, notion, thought, impression, dream, fantasy. **3** desire, liking, craving, hankering, urge, fondness, inclination, preference. *adj.* **1** elaborate, ornate, decorated, ornamented, rococo, baroque, elegant, extravagant, fantastic, fanciful. **3** extortionate, excessive. *verb* **1** think, believe, suppose, reckon, guess, conjecture, conceive, imagine, picture, dream of. **2** desire, like, be attracted to, take a liking to, take to, go for, prefer, favour. **3** be attracted to, take a liking to, desire, want.
▣ *noun* **1, 2** fact, reality. **3** dislike, aversion. *adj.* **1** plain. *verb* **2, 3** dislike.

. . . .

fancy dress clothes one dresses up in to represent a historical, fictional, etc character.

fancy-free *adj.* **1** not in love. **2** free to do as one pleases.

fancy goods small gifts, souvenirs, etc.

fancy man or **fancy woman** *old colloq. use* a lover.

fancywork *noun* fine decorative needlework.

fandango /fanˈdaŋɡoʊ/ *noun* (PL. **fandangos**) an energetic Spanish dance, or the music for it. [from Spanish *fandango*]

fanfare /ˈfanfeə(r)/ *noun* a short piece of music played on trumpets to announce an important event or arrival. [from French *fanfare*]

fang *noun* **1** one of the sharp pointed teeth by means of which a predator seizes and tears the flesh of its prey. **2** in poisonous snakes, one of the grooved teeth through which venom is injected into the prey. [from Anglo-Saxon *fang*, something caught]

fanlight *noun* a semicircular window over a door or window.

fan mail the admiring letters received by a celebrity.

fanny *noun* (PL. **fannies**) **1** *coarse slang* a woman's genitals. **2** *North Amer. slang* the buttocks.

fantail *noun* **1** a tail shaped like a fan. **2** a variety of domestic pigeon with tail feathers that can be spread out like a fan. **3** any of various small birds, native to Australia, New Zealand, and SE Asia, having a long tail that can be spread out like a fan.

fantasia /fanˈteɪzɪə, fantəˈzɪə/ *noun* **1** a musical composition that is free and unconventional in form. **2** a piece of music based on a selection of popular tunes. [from Italian *fantasia*, imagination]

fantasize or **fantasise** *verb intrans.* to indulge in pleasurable fantasies or daydreams.

fantastic *adj.* **1** *colloq.* splendid. **2** *colloq.* enormous; amazing. **3** *said of a story* absurd; unlikely; incredible. **4** strange, weird, or fanciful. [from Greek *phantastikos*, presenting to the mind]

. . . .

▣ **1** splendid, wonderful, marvellous, sensational, superb, excellent, first-rate, tremendous, terrific, great. **3** absurd, unlikely, incredible, unbelievable, extreme. **4** strange, weird, fanciful, odd, exotic, outlandish, fabulous, imaginative, visionary.

fantastically *adv.* in a fantastic way.

fantasy *noun* (PL. **fantasies**) **1** a pleasant daydream; a longed-for but unlikely happening. **2** a mistaken notion. **3** one's imaginings. **4** the activity of imagining. **5** a product of the imagination; a fanciful piece of writing, music, film-making, etc. [from Greek *phantasia*, image in the mind, imagination]

⊟ **1** dream, daydream, reverie, pipe dream, vision, hallucination, illusion, mirage, apparition. **2** misconception, delusion, unreality. **3** invention, fancy, flight of fancy. **4** imagination, invention.
⊟ **1** reality.

fanzine /'fanzi:n/ *noun* a magazine written, published, and distributed by and for supporters of football or by amateur enthusiasts of science fiction, pop music, etc; also, a television programme in magazine format for football fans. [from FAN² + MAGAZINE]

FAO *abbrev. Agric.* Food and Agriculture Organization (of the United Nations).

FAQ *abbrev.* frequently asked questions.

far (**farther, farthest** or **further, furthest**) — *adv.* **1** at, to, or from a great distance. **2** to or by a great extent: *my guess wasn't far out.* **3** at or to a distant time. — *adj.* **1** distant; remote. **2** the more distant of two. **3** extreme: *the far Right of the party.* — **as far as ...** up to (a certain place or point). **as** or **so far as ...** to the extent that .... **as** or **so far as I'm** *etc* **concerned** in my *etc* opinion. **as** or **so far as it goes** in its own limited way. **as** or **so far as that goes** or **is concerned** concerning that in particular. **by far** or **far and away** by a considerable amount; very much: *by far the most expensive item.* **far and wide** extensively. **far be it from me to do something** I am reluctant to do it: *far be it from me to criticize.* **a far cry from something** greatly different from it. **far from ...** the opposite of ...; not at all: *that is far from the truth.* **far from ...** or **so far from ...** not only not: *so far from winning, they finished last.* **far gone** in an advanced state, eg of illness or drunkenness. **go far** to achieve great things. **go so far** or **as far as to ...** to go to the extent of ...; to be prepared to ... . **go too far** to behave, speak, etc unreasonably. **in so far as ...** to the extent that ... [from Anglo-Saxon *feorr*]

⊟ *adv.* **1** a long way, a good way, *colloq.* miles. **2** much, greatly, considerably, extremely, *colloq.* miles. *adj.* **1** distant, far-off, faraway, far-flung, outlying, remote, out of the way, God-forsaken, removed, far-removed. **2** further. **3** extreme, radical.
⊟ *adv.* NEAR, CLOSE. *adj.* **1** nearby, close.

farad /'farəd/ *noun* (SYMBOL F) *Electr.* the SI unit of electrical capacitance, defined as the capacitance of a capacitor in which a charge of one coulomb produces a potential difference of one volt between its terminals. For most practical purposes the microfarad (10^{-6}F) is used.[named after the UK physicist Michael Faraday]

faraday /'farədeɪ/ *noun Physics* (SYMBOL F) a unit of electrical charge, defined as the charge on a mole (6.02×10^{23}) of electrons, which is equal to 9.65×10^4 coulombs. [named after the UK physicist Michael Faraday]

farandole /farən'doʊl/ *noun* (a piece of music for) a Provençal folk dance of ancient origin and usually in 6:8 time. [from Provençal *farandoula*]

faraway *adj.* **1** distant. **2** *said of a look or expression* dreamy; abstracted.

farce *noun* **1** a comedy involving a series of ridiculously unlikely turns of events; comedies of this type. **2** an absurd situation; something ludicrously badly organized. [from French *farce*, stuffing]

⊟ **1** comedy, slapstick, buffoonery, satire, burlesque. **2** absurdity, travesty, sham, parody, joke, mockery, ridiculousness, nonsense.

farcical *adj.* characteristic of farce; absurdly comic.

fare — *noun* **1** the price paid by a passenger to travel on a bus, train, etc. **2** a taxi passenger. **3** *old use, formal* food. — *verb intrans.* **1** to manage or make progress. **2** to be treated in a certain way: *fare badly.* [from Anglo-Saxon *faran*]

⊟ *noun* **1** price, charge, cost, fee, passage. **3** food, provisions, rations, sustenance, meals, diet, menu, board, table.

Far East a loosely used term which refers collectively to the region embraced by China, Japan, North Korea, South Korea, Mongolia, and East Siberia. More generally, it can include the Philippines, Vietnam, Laos, Cambodia, Thailand, Burma (Myanma), Malaysia, Singapore, and Indonesia.

Far-Eastern *adj.* of or from the Far East.

fare stage 1 each of the sections into which a bus route is divided, and for which a standard fare is charged. **2** a bus stop marking a fare stage.

farewell — *interj. old use* goodbye! — *noun* an act of saying goodbye. [from FARE *verb* + WELL¹]

far-fetched *adj.* unlikely; unconvincing.

⊟ unlikely, unconvincing, implausible, improbable, dubious, incredible, unbelievable, fantastic, preposterous, crazy, unrealistic.
⊟ plausible.

far-flung *adj.* **1** extensive. **2** distant.

farinaceous /farɪ'neɪʃəs/ *adj.* **1** consisting of or containing starch; having the texture of starch. **2** having a soft mealy texture. [from Latin *farina*, flour, meal]

farm — *noun* **1** an area of land and associated buildings owned by a farmer, or rented by a landlord and worked by a farmer, that is used to grow crops and/or to raise livestock. **2** a place that specializes in the breeding of particular animals: *fish farm/pig farm*. — *verb* **1** *trans., intrans.* to prepare and use land to grow crops, rear livestock, etc; to run a farm. **2** to collect and keep the proceeds from (taxes, etc) in return for a fixed sum. **3** (*also* **farm something** or **someone out**) to give (some of one's work) to others to do; to hand over (one's children) temporarily to a carer. [from Middle English *ferme*, rented land]

⊟ *noun* **1** ranch, farmstead, grange, homestead, station, land, holding, acreage, acres. *verb* **1** cultivate, till, work the land.

Types of farm include: arable farm, cattle ranch, dairy farm, fish farm, mixed farm, organic farm, pigfarm, sheep station, croft, smallholding, estate, plantation.

farmer *noun* a person who earns a living by managing a farm, either as owner or tenant.

⊟ agriculturist, crofter, smallholder, husbandman, yeoman.

farmer's lung *Medicine* a lung disease caused by an allergy to fungal spores that develop in hay baled while it is still damp.

farm hand a person employed to work on a farm.

farmhouse *noun* the farmer's house on a farm.

farming *noun* the business of running a farm by growing crops and raising livestock for sale.

⊟ agriculture, cultivation, husbandry, crofting.

farmstead *noun* a farmhouse and the buildings round it.

farmyard *noun* the central yard at a farm, surrounded by farm buildings.

far-off *adj.* distant; remote.

far-out *adj. colloq.* **1** strange; weird; outlandish. **2** excellent.

farrago /fə'rɑːgoʊ/ *noun* (PL. **farragos, farragoes**) a confused mixture; a hotchpotch. [from Latin *farrago*, mixed fodder]

far-reaching *adj.* having widespread effects.

. . . .

◨ widespread, broad, extensive, sweeping, important, significant, momentous.
◨ insignificant.

. . . .

farrier *noun* **1** a person who shoes horses. **2** *old use* a horse doctor. [from Old French *ferrier*, from Latin *ferrarius*, smith]

farrow — *noun* a sow's litter of piglets. — *verb trans., intrans.*, *said of a sow* to give birth to (pigs). [from Anglo-Saxon *fearh*]

Farsi /'fɑːsiː/ modern Persian. It is the official language of Iran, and belongs to the Indo-Iranian branch of the Indo-European family of languages. [from *Fars*, ('Persia'), a province of SW Iran]

far-sighted *adj.* **1** (*also* **far-seeing**) wise; prudent; forward-looking. **2** long-sighted.

fart *coarse slang* — *verb intrans.* **1** to emit wind from the anus. **2** (**fart about** or **around**) to fool about, waste time, etc. — *noun* **1** an act of farting. **2** a term of abuse for a person. [from Middle English *farten*]

farther same as FURTHER (with reference to physical distance).

farthest same as FURTHEST (with reference to physical distance).

farthing *noun formerly* one quarter of an old British penny, or a coin of this value. [from Anglo-Saxon *feortha*, quarter]

FAS *Medicine abbrev.* fetal alcohol syndrome.

fasces /'fasiːz/ *pl. noun Roman Hist.* a bundle of rods with an axe in the middle, carried before magistrates as a symbol of authority. [from Latin *fascis*, bundle]

Fasching a period of festivity held in Munich, S Germany between Epiphany (6 Jan) and the beginning of Lent. [from German *Fasching*, (Shrovetide) carnival]

fascia or **facia** /'feɪʃɪə/ (PL. **fasciae**) *noun* **1** the board above a shop entrance, bearing the shop name. **2** the dashboard of a motor vehicle. **3** *Archit.* a long flat band or surface. **4** *Anat.* any of the sheets of fibrous connective tissue that lie beneath the skin, enclose muscles or groups of muscle fibres, or surround any of the soft delicate organs of the body. [from Latin *fascia*, band]

fascial or **facial** /'faʃɪəl/ *adj.* relating to or located in a fascia.

fascinate *verb* **1** to interest strongly; to intrigue. **2** *said of a snake* to make unable to move, from fright. **3** to hold spellbound; to enchant irresistibly. [from Latin *fascinare*, to bewitch]

. . . .

◨ **1, 3** absorb, engross, intrigue, delight, charm, captivate, spellbind, enthral, rivet. **3** transfix, hypnotize, mesmerize.
◨ **1, 3** bore, repel.

. . . .

fascinating *adj.* that fascinates; intriguing.

fascination *noun* **1** the act of fascinating. **2** being fascinated.

. . . .

◨ **1** magnetism, lure, pull, charm, enchantment, spell, sorcery, magic. **2** interest, attraction.
◨ REPULSION. **2** boredom.

. . . .

fascioliasis /fasɪə'laɪəsɪs/ *noun Medicine* an infection of the bile ducts and liver of humans and other animals with the liver fluke (*Fasciola hepatica*).

fascism /'faʃɪzm/ *noun* **1** a political movement or system in which there is, typically, state control of all aspects of society, a supreme dictator, suppression of democratic bodies such as trade unions, and emphasis on nationalism and militarism. **2** (**Fascism**) this system in force in Italy from 1922 to 1943. [from Italian *fascismo*]

fascist /'faʃɪst/ — *noun* (*also* **Fascist**) a supporter of fascism. — *adj.* typical of or supporting fascism.

fashion — *noun* **1** style, especially the latest style, in clothes, etc. **2** a currently popular style or practice; a trend. **3** a manner of doing something. **4** the way something is made or constructed. — *verb* **1** to form or shape, especially with the hands. **2** to mould or influence. — **after a fashion** in a rather inexpert way. **in** or **out of fashion** currently (or no longer) fashionable. [from Old French *fachon*]

. . . .

◨ *noun* **1** custom, convention. **2** vogue, style, trend, mode, fad, craze, *colloq.* rage, *colloq.* latest. **3** manner, way, method, mode. **4** style, shape, form, pattern, line, cut, look, appearance. *verb* **1** form, shape, mould, model, create, design. **2** mould, influence, fit, tailor, adapt, suit, alter, adjust.

. . . .

fashionable *adj.* **1** *said of clothes or people* following the latest fashion. **2** used by, or popular with, wealthy, fashionable people.

. . . .

◨ **1** chic, smart, stylish, modish, à la mode, in vogue, *colloq.* trendy, in, *colloq.* all the rage. **2** popular, prevailing, current, latest, up-to-the-minute, contemporary, modern, up-to-date.
◨ UNFASHIONABLE.

. . . .

fashionably *adv.* in a fashionable way; so as to be fashionable.

fast[1] — *adj.* **1** moving, or able to move, quickly. **2** taking a relatively short time. **3** *said of a clock, etc* showing a time in advance of the correct time. **4** allowing or intended for rapid movement: *the fast lane*. **5** *said of a photographic film* requiring only brief exposure. **6** *colloq.* living a life of high excitement and expensive enjoyment. **7** *colloq.* tending to make sexual advances on rather brief acquaintance. **8** firmly fixed or caught. **9** *said of friends* firm; close. **10** *said of fabric colours* not liable to run or fade. — *adv.* **1** quickly; rapidly. **2** in quick succession: *coming thick and fast*. **3** firmly; tight. **4** deeply; thoroughly: *fast asleep*. — **fast and furious** fast and lively; frenzied or frantic in pace. **play fast and loose** to behave irresponsibly or unreliably. **pull a fast one on someone** *colloq.* to cheat or deceive them. [from Anglo-Saxon *fæst*, fixed, firm]

. . . .

◨ *adj.* **1, 2** quick, swift, rapid, brisk, accelerated, speedy, *colloq.* nippy, hasty, hurried, flying. **8** firm, fixed, fastened, secure, immovable, immobile, tight. *adv.* **1** quickly, swiftly, rapidly, speedily, like a flash, like a shot, hastily, hurriedly, presto. **2** quickly, swiftly, rapidly, speedily, apace.
◨ *adj.* **1** slow, unhurried. **8** loose. *adv.* **1, 2** slowly, gradually. **3** loosely, gently.

. . . .

fast[2] — *verb intrans.* to abstain from food completely or to restrict one's diet, eg as a religious discipline. — *noun* abstinence from food; the day or time of fasting. [from Anglo-Saxon *fæstan*]

. . . .

◨ *verb* go hungry, diet, starve, abstain. *noun* fasting, diet, starvation, abstinence.
◨ *noun* gluttony, self-indulgence.

. . . .

fast-breeder reactor a type of nuclear reactor in which the neutrons produced during nuclear fission are not slowed down by a moderator, but are used to produce (breed) more of the same nuclear fuel by converting uranium-238 to plutonium-239. At least as much fuel is produced as is consumed by the reactor.

fasten /ˈfɑːsən/ *verb trans., intrans.* (**fastened, fastening**) (*also* **fasten up**) to make or become firmly closed or fixed. — **fasten on** or **upon something** to concentrate on it eagerly; to dwell on it. [from Anglo-Saxon *fæstnian*]

■ close, seal, shut, lock, bolt, secure, fix, attach, clamp, grip, anchor, rivet, nail, tie, bind, chain, link, interlock, connect, join, unite, do up, button, lace, buckle.
⊟ unfasten, untie.

fastener /ˈfɑːsnə(r)/ or **fastening** *noun* a device that fastens something; a clasp or catch.

fast food food that is prepared, often by frying or microwaving, and served by means of a fast production line, eg hamburgers, pizzas.

fast-forward — *noun* a facility on an audio or video cassette player for advancing a tape quickly without playing it. — *verb* **1** *trans.* to advance (a tape) quickly by this means. **2** *intrans. colloq.* to pass or move on without delay.

fastidious *adj.* **1** particular in matters of taste and detail, especially excessively so. **2** easily disgusted. [from Latin *fastidium*, disgust]

fastness *noun* **1** the quality of being firmly fixed or, with reference to fabric colours, fast. **2** *old use* a stronghold.

fast neutron *Physics* a neutron with a very high energy content, produced by nuclear fission. Fast neutrons travel too fast to cause further fission, and are used to sustain nuclear chain reactions.

fast-track *colloq.* — *noun* **1** a routine for accelerating a proposal, etc through its formalities. **2** a quick but competitive route to advancement. — *verb* to process or promote speedily.

fat — *noun* **1** any of a group of organic compounds that occur naturally in animals and plants, and have twice the energy value of carbohydrates. Fats are solid at room temperature (20°C) and insoluble in water. **2** in mammals, a layer of white or yellowish tissue that lies beneath the skin and between various organs of the body. It is composed of cells filled with lipid substances, and serves both as an insulator to prevent heat loss, and as a means of storing energy. **3** any of various greasy or oily substances derived from animals or plants and used in liquid or solid form as food or in cooking. — *adj.* (**fatter, fattest**) **1** having too much fat on the body; plump; overweight. **2** containing a lot of fat. **3** thick or wide. **4** *colloq., said of a fee, profit, etc* large. **5** fertile; profitable. **6** *facetious slang* none at all: *a fat lot of good*. — *verb* (**fatted, fatting**) *old use* to fatten. — **the fat's in the fire** now there will be trouble. **kill the fatted calf** to prepare a feast for a homecoming. **live off the fat of the land** to live in luxury. [from Anglo-Saxon *fæt*, fatted]

■ *noun* **2** blubber, *colloq.* flab. *adj.* **1** plump, overweight, obese, tubby, stout, corpulent, portly, round, rotund, paunchy, pot-bellied, heavy, *colloq.* beefy, solid, chubby, podgy, fleshy, *colloq.* flabby, gross. **2** fatty, oily, greasy. **3** thick, wide, broad, heavy, solid. **4** large, handsome, considerable, generous, sizeable.
⊟ *adj.* **1** thin, slim. **2** low-fat. **3** narrow, slim, thin. **4** slim, meagre, miserable, poor.

fatal *adj.* **1** causing death; deadly. **2** bringing ruin; disastrous. **3** destined; unavoidable. [from Latin *fatalis*, from *fatum*, fate]

■ **1** deadly, lethal, mortal, killing, incurable, malignant, terminal. **2** disastrous, calamitous, catastrophic, destructive.
⊟ **1, 2** harmless.

fatalism *noun* the belief that fate controls everything, and humans cannot alter it.

fatalist *noun* a person who believes in fatalism.

fatalistic *adj.* characteristic of fatalism.

fatalistically *adv.* in a fatalistic way.

fatality /fəˈtælɪtɪ/ *noun* (PL. **fatalities**) **1** an accidental or violent death. **2** the quality of being fatal. **3** the quality of being controlled by fate.

■ **1** death, mortality, loss, casualty. **2** deadliness, lethality.

fatally /ˈfeɪtəlɪ/ *adv.* **1** so as to cause death. **2** unavoidably.

fate *noun* **1** (*also* **Fate**) the apparent power that determines the course of events, over which humans have no control. **2** the individual destiny or fortune of a person or thing; what happens to someone or something. **3** death, downfall, destruction, or doom. **4** (**the Fates**) *Mythol.* the three goddesses who determine the birth, life, and death of humans. — **a fate worse than death** *facetious* a frightful fate, especially *old use* a woman's loss of virginity before marriage. [from Latin *fatum*, fate]

■ **1** destiny, providence, chance. **2** destiny, future, fortune, horoscope, stars, lot. **3** death, downfall, destruction, doom, end, ruin.

fated *adj.* **1** destined or intended by fate. **2** doomed.

■ **1** destined, predestined, preordained, foreordained, unavoidable, inevitable, inescapable, certain, sure.
⊟ **1** avoidable.

fateful *adj.* **1** *said of a remark, etc* prophetic. **2** decisive; critical; having significant results. **3** bringing calamity or disaster.

■ **2** decisive, critical, crucial, important, momentous, significant. **3** fatal, lethal, calamitous, disastrous.
⊟ **2** unimportant.

fathead *noun colloq., offensive* a fool.

fat-headed *adj.* stupid.

fat hen an annual plant (*Chenopodium album*), widespread in Europe, that has diamond-shaped toothed lower leaves with mealy white covering, and tiny green flowers borne in densely branched clusters.

father — *noun* **1** a natural or adoptive male parent. **2** (**fathers**) one's ancestors. **3** a founder, inventor, originator, pioneer, or early leader. **4** (**Father**) a title, or form of address for a priest. **5** (**Father**) God. **6** (**fathers**) the leading or senior men of a city, etc. **7** (**Father**) used as a title in personifying something ancient or venerable: *Father Time*. — *verb* **1** to be the father of. **2** to invent or originate. **3** (**father a child on someone**) to claim that someone is the father of the child. [from Anglo-Saxon *fæder*]

■ *noun* **1** *colloq.* dad, *colloq.* daddy, *colloq.* old man, papa, patriarch, parent, begetter, procreator, progenitor, *formal* sire. **2** ancestors, forefathers, forebears, predecessors. **3** founder, inventor, originator, pioneer, creator, maker, architect, author, patron, leader, prime mover. **4** priest, padre. **6** elders. *verb* **1** beget, procreate, sire. **2** invent, originate, create, produce.

Father Christmas see SANTA CLAUS.

father figure an older man to whom one turns for help, support, advice, etc.

fatherhood *noun* being a father.

father-in-law *noun* (PL. **fathers-in-law**) the father of one's wife or husband.

fatherland *noun* one's native country.

fatherless *adj.* **1** without a living father. **2** without a known author.

fatherliness *noun* being fatherly.

fatherly *adj.* benevolent, protective, and encouraging, like a father.

Father's Day in some countries, the day on which fathers are honoured: in the USA and the UK, the third Sunday in June; in Australia, the first Sunday in September.

fathom — *noun* 1 in the imperial system, a unit of length equal to 6 feet (1.83m), used to measure the depth of water, especially at sea. 2 formerly used to denote a unit of length equal to the reach of a man's outstretched arms, from fingertip to fingertip. — *verb* (**fathomed, fathoming**) (*also* **fathom something out**) 1 to work out a problem; to get to the bottom of a mystery. 2 to measure the depth of (water). [from Anglo-Saxon *fæthm*]

⊟ *verb* 1 work out, get to the bottom of, understand, see, comprehend, grasp, interpret. 2 measure, gauge, plumb, sound, probe.

fathomless *adj.* 1 too deep to be measured. 2 too difficult or mysterious to understand.

fatigue /fə'ti:g/ — *noun* 1 a state of physical and mental tiredness, experienced as muscular weariness or discomfort, a decrease in energy and efficiency, and a strong desire for rest or sleep. It may be caused by prolonged or intense activity, inadequate food intake, disease, high temperatures, or stress. 2 permanent weakness in a material, eg a metal, due to changes in its properties resulting from repeated stresses placed on it. 3 *Mil.* a domestic task performed by a soldier. 4 (**fatigues**) uniform worn by soldiers in battle or for domestic tasks. — *verb trans., intrans.* to exhaust or become exhausted. [from French *fatigue*, from Latin *fatigare*, to weary]

⊟ *noun* 1 tiredness, weariness, exhaustion, lethargy, listlessness, lassitude, weakness, debility. *verb* exhaust, tire, wear out, weary, drain, weaken, debilitate.
⊟ *noun* 1 energy.

fatness *noun* 1 being fat. 2 richness.
fatten *verb trans., intrans.* (**fattened, fattening**) (*also* **fatten up**) to make or become fat.

⊟ build up, feed, nourish, overfeed, cram, stuff, bloat, swell, fill out, spread, expand, thicken.

fattening *adj.* that fattens.
fattiness *noun* the quality of being fat or containing fat.
fatty — *adj.* (**fattier, fattiest**) 1 containing fat. 2 greasy; oily. — *noun* (PL. **fatties**) *derog. colloq.* a fat person.
fatuity /fə'tju:ɪtɪ/ *noun* (PL. **fatuities**) 1 foolishness. 2 a fatuous act or remark; fatuous behaviour.
fatuous /'fatjʊəs/ *adj.* foolish, especially in a self-satisfied way; empty-headed. [from Latin *fatuus*]
fatwa or **fatwah** /'fatwə/ *noun* a formal legal opinion or decision issued by a Muslim authority, eg that someone should be killed. [Arabic, = decree]
faucet /'fɔ:sɪt/ *noun* 1 a tap fitted to a barrel. 2 *North Amer.* a tap on a washbasin, etc. [from Old French *fausset*, peg]
fault *noun* 1 a weakness or failing in character. 2 a flaw or defect in an object or structure. 3 responsibility for something wrong: *all my fault*. 4 *Geol.* a break or fracture in the Earth's crust where one rock face has been displaced relative to another in a horizontal, vertical, or oblique direction. Abrupt movements along faults cause earthquakes. 5 *Tennis* an incorrectly placed or delivered serve. 6 *Showjumping* a penalty for refusing or failing to clear a fence. — **at fault** blameworthy; to blame; wrong. **find fault with someone** or **something** to criticize them, especially excessively or unfairly. **to a fault** to too great an extent. [from Old French *faute*]

⊟ 1 weakness, failing, flaw, blemish, imperfection, deficiency, shortcoming, foible, misdeed, error, mistake, blunder, *colloq.* slip-up, slip, lapse, omission, oversight, offence, wrong, sin. 2 flaw, defect, blemish. 3 responsibility, accountability, liability, culpability. **at fault** blameworthy, to

blame, (in the) wrong, responsible, guilty, culpable. **find fault with** criticize, pick holes in, *colloq.* knock, impugn, censure, blame, call to account.
⊟ praise.

faultless *adj.* having no faults; perfect.

⊟ perfect, flawless, unblemished, spotless, immaculate, unsullied, pure, blameless, exemplary, model, correct, accurate.
⊟ faulty, imperfect, flawed.

faulty *adj.* (**faultier, faultiest**) having a fault or faults; not working correctly.

⊟ imperfect, defective, flawed, blemished, damaged, impaired, out of order, broken, wrong.
⊟ faultless, perfect.

faun *noun* a mythical creature with a man's head and body and a goat's horns, hind legs, and tail. [from Latin *Faunus*, a rural god]
fauna *noun* (PL. **faunas, faunae**) 1 the animals that are associated with a particular habitat, region, or geological period. 2 a book or list describing the animals of a certain area. See also FLORA. [from Latin *Fauna*, goddess of living creatures]
Fauvism /'foʊvɪzm/ *noun* an early 20c movement in French painting, using colour for its purely decorative qualities or as a means of communicating emotion, without regard to realism. [from French *fauve*, wild beast]
faux *adj.* false or imitation. [French]
faux pas /foʊ pɑ:/ *noun* (PL. **faux pas**) an embarrassing blunder. [French, = false step]
favour — *noun* 1 a kind or helpful action performed out of goodwill. 2 the liking, approval, or goodwill of someone. 3 unfair preference. 4 a knot of ribbons worn as a badge of support for a particular team, political party, etc. 5 *Hist.* something given or worn as a token of affection. 6 (**favours**) *old euphemistic use* a woman's consent to lovemaking or sexual liberties. — *verb* 1 to regard with goodwill. 2 to treat with preference, or over-indulgently. 3 to prefer; to support. 4 *said of circumstances* to give an advantage to. 5 *old use* to look like (eg one's mother or father). 6 *affected* to be wearing (a colour, etc). — **in favour of something** or **someone** 1 having a preference for them. 2 to their benefit. 3 in support or approval of them. **in** or **out of favour with someone** having gained or lost their approval. [from Latin *favor*, from *favere*, to favour]

⊟ *noun* 1 kindness, service, good turn, courtesy. 2 approval, goodwill, esteem, support, backing, patronage, sympathy. 3 preference, favouritism, partiality. *verb* 1 like, approve. 2 spoil, pamper. 3 prefer, support, choose, opt for, back, advocate, champion, encourage, promote. 4 help, assist, aid, benefit. **in favour of** 3 for, supporting, on the side of.
⊟ *noun* 2 disapproval. *verb* 1 dislike. 2 mistreat. **in favour of** against.

favourable *adj.* 1 showing or giving agreement or consent. 2 pleasing; likely to win approval. 3 (**favourable to someone**) advantageous or helpful to them; suitable. 4 *said of a wind* following.

⊟ 1 positive, sympathetic, agreeable, well-disposed, complimentary, enthusiastic, friendly, amicable, kind, understanding, encouraging, reassuring. 2 good, fair, promising, auspicious, hopeful. 3 advantageous, helpful, beneficial, suitable, fit, convenient, timely, opportune.
⊟ UNFAVOURABLE. 1 negative. 3 unhelpful.

favourite — *adj.* best-liked; preferred. — *noun* 1 a favourite person or thing. 2 someone unfairly preferred or particularly indulged. **3** a horse or competitor expected to win. [from Old French *favorit*]

■ *adj.* preferred, favoured, pet, best-liked, best-loved, dearest, beloved, esteemed, chosen. *noun* **1** preference, choice, pick. **2** pet, *colloq.* blue-eyed boy, teacher's pet, the apple of one's eye, darling, idol.
▣ *adj.* hated. *noun* **2** bête noire, pet hate.

favouritism *noun* the practice of giving unfair preference, help or support to someone or something.

■ nepotism, preferential treatment, preference, partiality, one-sidedness, partisanship, bias, injustice.
▣ impartiality.

fawn [1] — *noun* **1** a young deer of either sex. **2** the colour of a fawn, beige. — *verb*, *said of deer* to give birth to young. [from Old French *faon*]

fawn [2] *verb intrans.* (**fawn on someone**) **1** *said of a dog* to show affection for them by licking, nuzzling, etc. **2** to flatter them or behave over-humbly towards them, in order to win approval. [from Anglo-Saxon *fagnian*]

fawning *adj.* that fawns.

fax — *noun* **1** facsimile transmission, a system for transmitting exact copies of printed or handwritten documents, drawings, maps, photographs, etc, using telephone networks. **2** a document transmitted in this way. — *verb* **1** to send a document via this system. **2** to send a faxed communication to. [a shortening of FACSIMILE]

fay *noun poetic* a fairy. [from Old French *fae*]

FBI *abbrev.* Federal Bureau of Investigation (USA).

FC *abbrev.* football club.

FD *abbrev.* (on coins) *Fidei Defensor* (Latin), Defender of the Faith.

FDA *abbrev.* Food and Drug Administration (USA).

Fe *symbol Chem.* iron. [from Latin *ferrum*]

fealty *noun Hist.* the loyalty sworn by a vassal or tenant to his feudal lord. [from Old French *fealte*, from Latin *fidelitas*, loyalty]

fear — *noun* **1** anxiety and distress caused by the awareness of danger or expectation of pain. **2** a cause of this feeling. **3** religious awe or dread. **4** *colloq.* likelihood: *no fear of winning.* — *verb* **1** to be afraid of (someone or something). **2** *intrans.* (**fear for something**) to be frightened or anxious about it: *feared for their lives.* **3** to think or expect with dread. **4** to regret; to be sorry to say. — **for fear of something** or **someone** because of the danger they represent. **in fear of something** or **someone** frightened of them. **put the fear of God into someone** *colloq.* to terrify them. **without fear or favour** completely impartially. [from Anglo-Saxon *fær*, calamity]

■ *noun* **1** anxiety, distress, alarm, fright, terror, horror, panic, agitation, worry, consternation, concern, dismay, uneasiness, qualms, misgivings, apprehension, trepidation, dread, foreboding. *verb* **1** be afraid of, take fright at, shrink from, dread, shudder at. **2** be frightened about, be anxious about, worry about. **3** expect, foresee, suspect, anticipate.
▣ *noun* **1** courage, bravery, confidence.

fearful *adj.* **1** afraid. **2** frightening. **3** *colloq.* very bad.

■ **1** afraid, frightened, scared, alarmed, nervous, anxious, tense, uneasy, apprehensive, hesitant, nervy, panicky. **2** frightening, frightful, terrible, dreadful, awful, atrocious, shocking, appalling, monstrous, gruesome, hideous, ghastly, horrible. **3** dreadful, awful, atrocious, shocking, appalling, terrible, hideous, ghastly.
▣ **1** brave, courageous, fearless. **3** wonderful, delightful.

fearfully *adv.* **1** with fear. **2** in a frightening way. **3** *colloq.* very badly, terribly.

fearless *adj.* without fear; brave.

fearsome *adj.* frightening.

feasibility *noun* being feasible.

feasible *adj.* capable of being done or achieved. [from Old French *faisible*]

■ practicable, practical, workable, achievable, attainable, realizable, viable, reasonable, possible, likely.
▣ impossible.

feast — *noun* **1** a large rich meal, eg to celebrate some occasion. **2** a pleasurable abundance of. **3** *Relig.* a festival or saint's day. — *verb* **1** *intrans.* (**feast on** or **upon something**) to eat or experience it with enjoyment. **2** to honour with a feast. — **feast one's eyes on** or **upon something** to gaze at it with pleasure. [from Old French *feste*]

■ *noun* **1** banquet, dinner, spread, *colloq.* blow-out, *colloq.* binge, junket. **2** wealth. **3** festival, holiday, gala, fête, celebration, revels. *verb* **1** gorge on, eat one's fill of. **2** wine and dine, treat, entertain.

feat *noun* a deed or achievement, especially a remarkable one. [from Old French *fait*]

■ deed, achievement, exploit, act, accomplishment, attainment, performance.

feather — *noun* **1** a rigid outgrowth of the skin of a bird, consisting of a horny material called keratin which is extremely light, and highly specialized for flight, insulation, and display purposes. **2** condition; spirits: *in fine feather.* — *verb* **1** to provide, cover, or line with feathers. **2** to turn (one's oar) parallel to the water, to lessen air resistance. — **a feather in one's cap** something one can be proud of. **feather one's own nest** to accumulate money for oneself, especially dishonestly. **make the feathers fly** *colloq.* to cause a commotion. [from Anglo-Saxon *fether*]

feather bed a mattress stuffed with feathers.

feather-bed *verb* **1** to spoil or pamper. **2** *colloq.* to give financial inducements to.

feather-brained *adj. derog.* empty-headed.

feather duster a dusting implement consisting of a stick with a head made of feathers.

feathered *adj.* **1** containing or covered with feathers or something similar. **2** like feathers.

featherweight *noun* **1** a class for boxers, wrestlers, and weight-lifters of not more than a specified weight (57kg in professional boxing, similar weights in the other sports). **2** a boxer, etc of this weight. **3** someone who weighs very little. **4** *derog.* someone of little importance or influence.

feathery *adj.* resembling or covered with feathers, or something similar.

feature *noun* **1** any of the parts of the face, eg eyes, nose, mouth, etc; (in *pl*) the face. **2** a noticeable part or quality of something. **3** a non-news article in a newspaper. **4** a feature film. [from Old French *faiture*]

■ **2** aspect, quality, facet, point, factor, attribute, property, trait, characteristic, peculiarity, mark, hallmark, speciality, highlight. **3** article, report, story, piece, item, column, comment.

feature film a film that forms the main part of a cinema programme.

featureless *adj.* dull; with no points of interest.

Feb or **Feb.** *abbrev.* February.

febrile / ˈfiːbraɪl, ˈfɛbraɪl/ *adj.* relating to or caused by fever; feverish. [from Latin *febris*, fever]

February *noun* (PL. **Februaries**) the second month of the year. [from Latin *Februarius*, month of expiation]

feckless *adj.* helpless; clueless; irresponsible; aimless. [from Scot. *feck*, effect + LESS]

fecund /ˈfiːkənd, ˈfɛkənd/ adj. fruitful; fertile; richly productive. [from Latin fecundus]

fecundity /fɪˈkʌndɪtɪ/ noun fruitfulness, fertility, productiveness.

fed see FEED.

Fedayeen noun a term commonly used for a commando or guerilla fighter, trained by organizations such as the PLO (Palestine Liberation Organization). [from Arabic fidai, one who sacrifices oneself (for a cause or country)]

federal adj. 1 consisting of a group of states independent in local matters but united under a central government for other purposes, eg defence. 2 relating to the central government of a federal union. 3 (**Federal**) Hist. supporting the union government during the American Civil War. [from Latin foedus, treaty]

federalism noun Politics the principles and practice of federal government, especially a system in which constitutional powers are devolved to national and regional governments.

federalist noun an advocate or supporter of federal government.

Federalist Party a political party formed in the USA in the 1790s.

federalize or **federalise** verb trans., intrans. to make federal.

federate verb trans., intrans. to unite to form a federation. [from Latin foedus, treaty]

federation noun 1 a federal union of states. 2 a union of business organizations, etc. 3 the act of uniting in a league.

federative adj. relating to or constituted as a federation.

fee noun 1 a charge made for professional services, eg by a doctor or lawyer. 2 a charge for eg membership of a society, sitting an examination, entrance to a museum, etc. 3 (usually **fees**) a payment for school or college education, or for a course of instruction. 4 a payment made to a football club for the transfer of one of its players. 5 Legal an estate in the form of land that is inheritable with either restricted rights (fee tail) or unrestricted rights (fee simple). [from Old French fie]

▪ 1 charge, terms, bill, account, pay, remuneration, payment, retainer, reward, recompense, hire, toll. 2 charge, subscription. 3 charge.

feeble adj. 1 lacking strength; weak. 2 lacking power, influence, or effectiveness. [from Old French feible, from Latin flebilis, lamentable]

▪ 1 weak, faint, exhausted, frail, delicate, puny, sickly, infirm. 2 powerless, helpless, inadequate, lame, poor, thin, flimsy, ineffective, incompetent, indecisive.

Ⓔ STRONG, POWERFUL.

feeble-minded adj. 1 stupid. 2 mentally below normal.

feebly adv. in a feeble way.

feed — verb (PAST TENSE AND PAST PARTICIPLE **fed**) 1 intrans. (**feed on something**) said especially of animals to eat it, especially as a regular diet. 2 to give food to or prepare food for. 3 intrans. (**feed on something**) to be fuelled by it. 4 to give as food. 5 to supply (a machine, furnace, etc) with the raw materials, fuel, etc, that are required for its continued operation. 6 to strengthen or encourage (a feeling, etc). — noun 1 an act or session of feeding. 2 any of various types of food, eg hay, cereal grains, that are used as food for animal livestock. 3 an amount or allowance of food given to babies. 4 colloq. a meal, especially a hearty one. 5 the channel or mechanism by which a machine, furnace, etc, is supplied with raw materials, fuel, etc. — **fed up** colloq. bored and impatient. **feed someone up** to fatten them up with nourishing food. [from Anglo-Saxon fedan]

▪ verb 1 eat, dine (on), graze, pasture. 2 nourish, cater for, provide for, suckle, nurture, pasture. 3 live on, exist on, be

sustained by. 6 strengthen, foster, fuel, nurture. noun 2 food, fodder, forage, pasture, silage.

feedback noun 1 responses and reactions, eg customers' comments on a product or service, that provide guidelines for adjustment and development. 2 the process whereby part of the output of a system or device, or of a component of a living organism, is returned to the input in order to regulate or modify subsequent output. Positive feedback increases the output, whereas negative feedback decreases it. 3 in a public-address system, etc, the partial return to the microphone of the sound output, producing a whistle or howl.

feeder noun 1 a baby or animal with particular eating habits: a poor feeder. 2 a minor road, railway line, etc leading to a main one.

feeding frenzy 1 an occurrence of fish, especially sharks, attacking each other during feeding. 2 colloq. a period of intense activity over something, especially by the media.

feel — verb (PAST TENSE AND PAST PARTICIPLE **felt**) 1 to become aware of through the sense of touch. 2 trans., intrans. to have the sensation of; to sense. 3 trans., intrans. to find out or investigate with the hands, etc. 4 intrans., trans. to have (an emotion). 5 trans., intrans. to react emotionally to something: feels the loss very deeply. 6 intrans. to give the impression of being (soft, hard, rough, etc) when touched. 7 intrans. to be or seem. 8 to think, be of the opinion, or be under the impression that. 9 trans., intrans. to seem to oneself to be: feel a fool. — noun 1 a sensation or impression produced by touching. 2 an impression or atmosphere created by something. 3 an act of feeling with the fingers, etc. — **feel around for something** to search for it with the fingers, etc. **feel for someone** to feel sympathy for them. **feel for something** to try to find it by feeling. **feel like something** to have an inclination for it: feel like a walk. **feel one's way** to make one's way cautiously. **feel up to something** to feel fit enough for it. **get the feel of something** to become familiar with it or used to it. **have a feel for something** have a natural ability for, or understanding of, an activity, etc. **not feel oneself** to feel unwell. [from Anglo-Saxon felan]

▪ verb 1 sense. 2 sense, perceive, notice, observe, know. 3 touch, finger, handle, manipulate, hold, stroke, caress, fondle, paw, fumble, grope. 4 experience, go through, undergo, suffer, endure, enjoy. 6, 7 seem, appear. 8 think, believe, consider, reckon, judge. noun 1 texture, surface, finish. 2 impression, atmosphere, sense, feeling, quality.
feel for someone pity, sympathize (with), commiserate (with), be sorry for. **feel like** fancy, want, desire.

feeler noun 1 a tentacle. 2 either of a pair of long slender jointed structures, sensitive to touch, on the head of certain invertebrate animals, especially insects or crustaceans. Also called ANTENNA. — **put out feelers** colloq. to test for possible reactions, before taking action.

feelgood adj. colloq. reinforcing or associated with pleasant feelings of comfort, security, etc: the feelgood factor.

feeling — noun 1 a sensation or emotion. 2 (**feelings**) one's attitude to something: have strong feelings. 3 emotion as distinct from reason. 4 strong emotion: speak with feeling. 5 a belief or opinion. 6 (**have a feeling for something**) a natural ability for, or understanding of, an activity, etc. 7 affection. — adj. sensitive; sympathetic.

▪ noun 1 sensation, perception, sense, air, aura, atmosphere, mood, quality. 2 attitude, ideas, notions, opinions, views. 4 emotion, passion, intensity, susceptibility, sensibility, sensitivity. 5 belief, opinion, hunch, suspicion, inkling, impression. 6 talent for, gift for, appreciation of. 7 affection, warmth, fondness, sentiment, sentimentality, compassion, sympathy, understanding, concern, pity.

feelingly *adv.* with sincerity resulting from experience.

feet see FOOT.

feign /feɪn/ *verb* to pretend to have (eg an illness) or feel (an emotion, etc). [from Latin *fingere*, to contrive]

feigned *adj.* 1 pretended. 2 simulated. 3 imagined.

feint[1] *noun* in boxing, fencing or other sports, a movement, eg a mock attack, intended to deceive or distract one's opponent.

feint[2] *adj.*, *said of paper* ruled with faint lines. [variant of FAINT]

feisty /'faɪstɪ/ *adj.* (**feistier, feistiest**) *colloq.* 1 spirited; lively. 2 irritable; quarrelsome. [from US dialect *fist*, an aggressive small dog]

feldspar /'fɛldspɑː(r)/ or **felspar** /'fɛlspɑː(r)/ *noun Geol.* any of a large group of rock-forming minerals, mainly aluminium silicates, that represent about 60 per cent of the Earth's crust. Feldspar is found in most igneous and many metamorphic rocks, eg orthoclase, plagioclase. [from Swedish *Feldt*, field + *Spat*, spar]

feldspathic /fɛld'spaθɪk/ or **felspathic** /fɛl'spaθɪk/ *adj.* of the nature of or containing feldspar.

felicitate *verb* to congratulate. [from Latin *felicitas*, happiness]

felicitation *noun* 1 congratulation. 2 (*also* **felicitations**) an expression used to congratulate someone.

felicitous *adj.* 1 *said of wording* elegantly apt. 2 pleasant; happy. [from Latin *felicitas*, happiness]

felicity *noun* 1 happiness. 2 elegance or aptness of wording.

feline /'fiːlaɪn/ *adj.* of or like a cat. [from Latin *felis*, cat]

fell[1] see FALL.

fell[2] *verb* 1 to cut down (a tree). 2 to knock down. 3 *Needlework* to turn under and stitch down the edges of (a seam). [from Anglo-Saxon *fyllan*, to cause to fall]

⊞ 1 cut down, hew. 2 knock down, strike down, floor, level, flatten, raze, demolish.

fell[3] *noun* (*often* **fells**) a hill or moor. [from Norse *fjall*]

fell[4] *adj. old use* destructive; deadly. — **at** or **in one fell swoop** at a single deadly blow; in one quick operation. [from Old French *fel*, cruel]

fellatio /fɛ'leɪʃɪəʊ/ *noun* sexual stimulation of the penis by sucking or licking. [from Latin *fellare*, to suck]

fellow *noun* 1 a man or boy. 2 a companion or equal. 3 a person in the same situation or condition as oneself, or having the same status, etc: *a fellow citizen.* 4 a senior member of a college or university. 5 a postgraduate research student financed by a fellowship. 6 a member of any of many learned societies. 7 *colloq.* a boyfriend. 8 one of a pair: *one sock on the chair, its fellow on the floor.* [from Anglo-Saxon *feolaga*, partner]

⊞ 1 man, boy, *colloq.* chap, *colloq.* bloke, *colloq.* guy, individual, character, person. 2 companion, equal, peer, comrade, friend, counterpart, compeer, partner, associate, colleague, co-worker. 8 mate, twin, double, match.

fellow feeling sympathy for someone with experiences similar to one's own.

fellowship *noun* 1 friendly companionship. 2 commonness or similarity of interests between people. 3 a society or association. 4 the status of a fellow of a college, society, etc; a salary paid to a research fellow.

⊞ 1 companionship, camaraderie, communion, familiarity, intimacy. 3 association, league, guild, society, club, fraternity, brotherhood, sisterhood, order.

fellow traveller someone who sympathises with a political party, especially the Communist Party, without actually joining it.

felon *noun* a person guilty of a serious crime. [from Old French *felon*, from Latin *fello*, traitor]

felonious *adj.* relating to or of the nature of a felony.

felony *noun* (PL. **felonies**) *Legal* a serious crime.

felspar same as FELDSPAR.

felt[1] see FEEL.

felt[2] — *noun* a fabric formed by matting or pressing together wool fibres, etc. — *verb* 1 *trans.*, *intrans.* to form into felt; to mat. 2 to cover with felt. [from Anglo-Saxon *felt*]

felt-tip pen or **felt-tipped pen** a pen with a point made of felt.

fem. *abbrev.* 1 female. 2 feminine.

female — *adj.* 1 denoting the sex that gives birth to young, produces eggs, etc. 2 denoting the reproductive structure of a plant that contains an ovum (egg cell), such as the pistil of flowering plants. 3 of, relating to, or belonging to a woman. 4 *Engineering* denoting a piece of machinery into which another part (the male) fits. — *noun* 1 a woman or girl. 2 a female animal or plant. [from Latin *femella*, diminutive of *femina*, woman]

⊞ 1 *adj.* feminine, she-. 3 feminine, womanly, girlish.
🠴 *adj.* MALE.

Female terms include: girl, lass, maiden, woman, lady, daughter, sister, girlfriend, fiancée, bride, wife, mother, aunt, niece, grandmother, matriarch, godmother, widow, dowager, dame, madam, mistress, virgin, spinster, old maid, *slang* bird, *slang* chick, lesbian, *slang* bitch, prostitute, whore, harlot; cow, heifer, bitch, doe, ewe, hen, mare, filly, nanny-goat, sow, tigress, vixen.

female condom a form of contraception that first became available in 1992, consisting of a thin polyurethane pouch that fits inside the vagina.

female genital mutilation female circumcision.

feminine *adj.* 1 of, or typically belonging to, a woman. 2 having or denoting qualities considered suitable for a woman. 3 *Grammar, said of nouns in certain languages* belonging to the gender into which most words for females fall. [from Latin *feminina*, diminutive of *femina*, woman]

⊞ 1 female. 2 womanly, womanish, girlish, ladylike, graceful, gentle, tender.
🠴 1 male, masculine. 2 manly.

femininity *noun* being feminine.

feminism *noun* a belief or movement advocating the cause of women's rights and opportunities. [from Latin *femina*, woman]

⊞ women's movement, women's lib(eration), female emancipation, women's rights.

feminist — *noun* a person who advocates or supports feminism. — *adj.* relating to or characterized by feminism.

feminist criticism literary criticism approached from a feminist standpoint.

femme fatale /fam fə'tɑːl/ (PL. **femmes fatales**) a woman whose irresistible charms fascinate and destroy people, usually men. [French, = fatal woman]

femoral /'fɛmərəl/ *adj.* relating to the femur or thigh.

femto- *combining form* a thousand million millionth (10^{-15}). [from Danish or Norwegian *femten*, 15]

femur /'fiːmə(r)/ (PL. **femora, femurs**) *noun Anat.* 1 the longest and largest bone of the human skeleton, the upper end of which articulates with the hip joint, and the lower end of which articulates with the knee joint. Also called THIGH BONE. 2 the corresponding bone in the hind limb of four-limbed vertebrates. 3 the segment of an insect's leg that is closest to its body. [from Latin *femur*, thigh]

fen *noun* a waterlogged area of lowland dominated by

grasses, sedges, and rushes, and having an alkaline soil, in contrast to the acid peat of a bog. [from Anglo-Saxon *fenn*]

fence — *noun* **1** a barrier eg of wood or wire, for enclosing or protecting land. **2** a barrier of any of various designs for a horse to jump. **3** *slang* a person who receives and disposes of stolen goods. **4** a guard to limit motion in a piece of machinery. **5** a guiding device on a circular saw or plane. — *verb* **1** (**fence something in** or **off**) to enclose or separate it with a fence, or as if with a fence. **2** *intrans.* to practise the sport of fencing. **3** *intrans.* to avoid answering directly. — **sit on the fence** to avoid supporting either side in a dispute, etc. [from DEFENCE]

....

◼ *noun* **1** barrier, railing, paling, wall, hedge, windbreak, defence, barricade, stockade, rampart. *verb* **1** enclose, surround, encircle, bound, hedge, wall, pen, coop, confine, restrict, separate, protect, guard, defend, fortify. **3** hedge, equivocate, quibble, *colloq.* pussyfoot, stonewall.

....

fencer *noun* a person who fences.

fencing *noun* **1** the sport of fighting with swords. **2** material for constructing fences.

fend *verb* **1** (**fend something** or **someone off**) to defend oneself from (blows, questions, etc). **2** (**fend for someone**) to provide for (especially oneself). [from DEFEND]

....

◼ **1** ward off, beat off, parry, deflect, avert, resist, repel, repulse, hold at bay, keep off, shut out. **2** provide for, look after, take care of, shift for, support, maintain, sustain.

....

fender *noun* **1** *North Amer.* the wing or mudguard of a car. **2** a low guard fitted round a fireplace to keep ash, coals, etc within the hearth. **3** a bundle of rope or other object hanging from a ship's side to protect it when in contact with piers, etc. [from FEND]

feng shui /ˈfʌŋ ˈʃweɪ, ˈfɛŋ ˈʃuːɪ/ *noun* the process of making the correct decision about the siting of a building so as to ensure the optimum happiness for the occupants. [Chinese, = wind and water]

fennel *noun* a perennial plant (*Foeniculum vulgare*), native to SE Europe and widely cultivated elsewhere, having finely divided feathery leaves, and small yellow flowers. The leaves are used as a flavouring, the seeds are used as a spice, and the swollen leaf bases of certain cultivated forms, which have a flavour similar to aniseed, can be eaten raw in salads or cooked as a vegetable. [from Anglo-Saxon *finol*]

fenugreek /ˈfɛnjʊɡriːk/ *noun* an annual plant (*Trigonella foenum-graecum*) of the pea family, native to SW Asia and the Mediterranean region, and widely cultivated in India, having hairy stems and heavily scented yellowish-white flowers. It is grown as fodder for animal livestock, its edible seeds are used in curries, and its leaves are eaten raw in salads. [from Latin *fenum graecum*, Greek hay]

feoff /fiːf, fɛf/ same as FIEF.

feral /ˈfɛrəl, ˈfɪərəl/ *adj.*, *said of plants or animals* having reverted from a domesticated or cultivated state to a wild or uncultivated state; wild. [from Latin *fera*, wild beast]

fer-de-lance /fɛədəˈlɑːns/ *noun* either of two species of a New World pit viper, the commonest cause of human death by snakebite. [from French *fer de lance*, lance-head]

fermata /fɜːˈmɑːtə/ *noun* (PL. **fermatas**) *Mus.* a pause. [from Italian *fermata*, a stop, halt]

Fermat's principle the principle that light rays travel between two points in such a way that the time taken is a minimum. [from the French mathematician Pierre de Fermat (1601–65)]

ferment — *noun* **1** a substance that causes fermentation. **2** fermentation. **3** a state of agitation or excitement. — *verb* **1** *intrans., trans.* to cause the breakdown of organic compounds such as carbohydrates in the absence of oxygen, especially by yeast or bacteria, eg during the brewing of beer. **2** to be or cause to be in a state of excitement or instability. [from Latin *fermentum*, yeast]

....

◼ *noun* **3** agitation, excitement, unrest, stir, turbulence, turmoil, disruption, commotion, tumult, hubbub, uproar, furore, frenzy, fever, glow. *verb* **1** bubble, effervesce, froth, foam, boil, seethe, smoulder, fester, brew, rise. **2** rouse, stir up, excite, work up, agitate, foment, incite, provoke, inflame, heat.

◻ *noun* **3** calm. *verb* **2** calm.

....

fermentation *noun Chem.* a biochemical process in which micro-organisms such as bacteria, yeasts, or moulds are used to break down an organic compound, usually a carbohydrate, in the absence of oxygen.

fermium *noun Chem.* (SYMBOL **Fm**, ATOMIC NUMBER **100**) an artificially produced radioactive metallic element of the actinide series, produced by bombarding plutonium with neutrons, and having properties similar to those of erbium. [named after the Italian physicist Enrico Fermi]

fern *noun* any of several thousand species of seedless non-flowering plants belonging to the class Pteropsida, and related to clubmosses and horsetails. [from Anglo-Saxon *fearn*]

ferny *adj.* (**fernier, ferniest**) **1** relating to or resembling a fern. **2** covered with or full of ferns.

ferocious *adj.* fierce; cruel; savage. [from Latin *ferox*, wild]

....

◼ fierce, cruel, savage, vicious, wild, barbarous, barbaric, brutal, inhuman, sadistic, murderous, bloodthirsty, violent, merciless, pitiless, ruthless.

◻ gentle, mild, tame.

....

ferocity or **ferociousness** *noun* being ferocious; fierceness.

....

◼ fierceness, viciousness, cruelty, savagery, wildness, barbarity, brutality, inhumanity, sadism, bloodthirstiness, violence, ruthlessness.

◻ gentleness, mildness.

....

-ferous *combining form* bearing or containing: *carboniferous*. [from Latin *ferre*, to carry]

ferret — *noun* **1** a semi-domesticated albino variety of the European polecat having an almost cylindrical body, long coarse yellowish-white fur, and pink eyes, formerly widely used for flushing rabbits and rats out of their burrows. Ferrets are also kept as pets, or for show purposes. **2** an inquisitive and persistent investigator. — *verb* (**ferreted, ferreting**) *colloq.* **1** *intrans.* (**ferret about** or **around**) to search busily; to rummage. **2** (**ferret something out**) to find it out through persistent investigation. **3** to hunt (rabbits or rats) by using ferrets to drive them out of their burrows. [from Old French *furet*, from Latin *fur*, thief]

ferric *adj. Chem.* **1** of or relating to iron. **2** denoting a chemical compound that contains iron in its trivalent state. [from Latin *ferrum*, iron]

Ferris wheel *noun* a giant fairground wheel that turns vertically, with seats hanging from its rim. [named after the US engineer G W G Ferris (1859–96)]

ferrite /ˈfɛraɪt/ *noun Chem.* any of a class of ceramic materials composed of oxides of iron and some other metal, such as copper, nickel, or manganese. [from Latin *ferrum*, iron]

ferro- *combining form* **1** relating to or containing iron. **2** denoting a chemical compound that contains iron in its divalent state. [from Latin *ferrum*, iron]

ferrous *adj. Chem.* **1** of or relating to iron. **2** denoting a chemical compound that contains iron in its divalent state. [from Latin *ferrum*, iron]

ferrule /ˈfɛrəl/ *noun* **1** a metal ring or cap for protecting the tip of a walking-stick or umbrella. **2** a cylindrical fitting, threaded internally like a screw, for joining pipes, etc together. [from Latin *viriola*, little bracelet]

ferry — *noun* (PL. **ferries**) a boat that carries passengers and often cars across a river or strip of water, especially as a regular service. — *verb* (**ferries, ferried**) **1** *trans., intrans.* to transport or go by ferry. **2** to convey in a vehicle. [from Anglo-Saxon *ferian*, to convey]

■ *noun* ferry-boat, car ferry, ship, boat, vessel. *verb* **1** ship, transport, convey, carry. **2** transport, convey, carry, take, move, shift.

ferryman *noun* a person in charge of a ferry.

fertile *adj.* **1** *said of soil or land* containing the nutrients required to support an abundant growth of crops or other plants. **2** producing or capable of producing living offspring. **3** capable of bearing abundant fruit, seeds, etc. **4** *said of plants* capable of prolific growth. **5** *said of the mind* rich in ideas. **6** providing a wealth of possibilities: *fertile ground for research.* **7** *Physics, said of a chemical substance* capable of being converted into a fissile or fissionable material. [from Latin *fertilis*]

■ **1** fruitful, productive, rich. **2** generative. **3** fruitful, productive. **4, 6** prolific, teeming, abundant, plentiful, fruitful, productive, rich.

🔁 **1, 2, 3, 4, 6** infertile, barren. **2** sterile. **3** unproductive.

fertility *noun* **1** the state or quality of being fertile. **2** the ability of a living organism to produce offspring or large numbers of offspring. **3** the ability of soil or land to support an abundant growth of crops or other plants.

fertility drug *Medicine* a drug that is used to treat infertility in women by inducing ovulation.

fertilization or **fertilisation** *noun* the fusion of two unlike gametes (specialized reproductive cells) to form a zygote, as occurs during sexual reproduction. The gametes are typically male (a sperm) and female (an ovum or egg).

fertilize or **fertilise** *verb* **1** *said of a male gamete, especially a sperm cell* to fuse with a female gamete, especially an egg cell, to form a zygote. **2** *said of a male animal* to inseminate or impregnate (a female animal). **3** *said of flowering and cone-bearing plants* to transfer (pollen) by the process of pollination. See also POLLINATION. **4** to supply (soil or land) with extra nutrients in order to increase its fertility and improve the growth of crops or other plants on it.

■ **1, 2** impregnate, inseminate. **3** pollinate. **4** feed, enrich, dress, compost, manure, dung.

fertilizer or **fertiliser** *noun* any chemical substance containing plant nutrients, especially nitrogen, potassium salts, or phosphates, that is added to the soil in order to improve the yield, size, or quality of plants, especially food crops.

■ dressing, plant food, compost, manure, dung.

fervent *adj.* enthusiastic; earnest or ardent. [from Latin *fervere*, to boil]

■ enthusiastic, earnest, ardent, eager, wholehearted, excited, energetic, vigorous, fiery, spirited, intense, vehement, passionate, full-blooded, zealous, devout, impassioned, heartfelt, emotional, warm.

🔁 cool, indifferent, apathetic.

fervently *adv.* with fervour.

fervid *adj.* fervent; full of fiery passion or zeal. [from Latin *fervidus*, fiery]

fervour *noun* passionate enthusiasm; intense eagerness or sincerity. [from Latin *fervor*, violent heat]

■ enthusiasm, eagerness, ardour, vehemence, passion, sincerity, zeal, energy, vigour, spirit, verve, excitement, animation, intensity, warmth.

🔁 apathy.

fescue /ˈfeskjuː/ *noun* a tufted grass of the genus *Festuca* with inrolled bristle-like leaves. It grows in dense tufts, and forms much of the turf on chalk downs. [from Old French *festu*, from Latin *festuca*, straw]

-fest *suffix* forming ad hoc words meaning: **1** *colloq.* an indulgent spree or concentration on a particular activity or quality: *newsfest/horrorfest.* **2** a gathering for a specific purpose; a collection of articles, etc on a particular theme. [from German *Fest*, festival]

festal *adj.* relating to a festival; festive. [from Latin *festum*, holiday]

fester — *verb intrans.* (**festered, festering**) **1** *said of a wound* to form or discharge pus. **2** *said of an evil* to continue unchecked or get worse. **3** to rot, putrefy, or decay. **4** *said of resentment or anger* to smoulder; to become more bitter. **5** to be a continuing cause of resentment; to rankle. — *noun* a small sore discharging pus. [from Old French *festre*, from Latin *fistula*, kind of ulcer]

■ *verb* **1** ulcerate, gather, discharge. **3** rot, putrefy, decay.

festival *noun* **1** a day or period of celebration, especially one kept traditionally. **2** *Relig.* a feast or saint's day. **3** a programme of musical, theatrical, or other cultural events. [from Latin *festivalis dies*, festive day]

■ **1, 2** celebration, commemoration, anniversary, jubilee, holiday, feast. **3** festivities, entertainment, gala, fête, carnival, fiesta, merrymaking, party.

festive *adj.* of, or suitable for, a celebration; lively and cheerful. [from Latin *festivus*]

■ celebratory, festal, holiday, gala, carnival, lively, cheerful, joyful, merry, hearty, cheery, jolly, happy, jovial, cordial, convivial.

🔁 gloomy, sombre, sober.

festivity *noun* (PL. **festivities**) **1** celebration; merrymaking. **2** (**festivities**) festive activities.

■ **1** celebration, merrymaking, merriment, enjoyment, revelry, jollity, joviality, conviviality, jubilation, feasting, banqueting, sport. **2** celebrations, entertainment, fun, amusements.

festoon — *noun* a decorative chain of flowers, ribbons, etc looped between two points. — *verb* to hang or decorate with festoons. [from Italian *festone*, decoration for a feast]

■ *verb* garland, decorate, adorn, hang, drape, garnish.

feta /ˈfetə/ *noun* a soft crumbly white cheese, originally from Greece, made with ewe's or goat's milk. [from Modern Greek *pheta*, a slice]

fetal /ˈfiːtl/ or **foetal** relating to a fetus.

fetal alcohol syndrome (ABBREV. **FAS**) a condition characterized by mental retardation, etc in a newborn baby, caused by excessive alcohol intake by the mother during pregnancy.

fetch — *verb* **1** to go and get, and bring back. **2** to be sold for (a certain price). **3** to deal (someone a blow). **4** *old use* to utter (a sigh or groan). **5** to bring forth (tears or blood). — *noun* a trick or dodge. — **fetch and carry** to act as servant. **fetch up** *colloq.* to arrive; to turn up; to end up. **fetch something up** to vomit food. [from Anglo-Saxon *feccan*]

■ *verb* **1** get, collect, bring, carry, transport, deliver, escort. **2** sell for, go for, bring in, yield, realize, make, earn.

fetching *adj. colloq.* charming; attractive.

◪ charming, attractive, pretty, sweet, cute, enchanting, fascinating, captivating.
◪ repellent.

fête or **fete** /feɪt/ — *noun* an outdoor entertainment with competitions, stalls, etc usually to raise money for a charitable or other purpose. — *verb* to entertain or honour lavishly. [from French *fête*, feast]

◪ *noun* fair, garden party, gala, carnival, festival, bazaar, sale of work. *verb* entertain, honour, treat, regale, welcome.

fetid or **foetid** /'fiːtɪd, 'fetɪd/ *adj.* having a disgusting smell. [from Latin *fetere*, to stink]

fetish *noun* **1** in primitive societies, an object worshipped for its magical powers. **2** a procedure or ritual followed obsessively, or an object of obsessive devotion. **3** an object that is handled or visualized as an aid to sexual stimulation; a person's attachment to such an object. [from French *fétiche*, from Portuguese *feitiço*, magic]

fetishism *noun* **1** the worship of a fetish. **2** belief in charms. **3** compulsive attachment of sexual interest to an inanimate object.

fetishist *noun* a person who believes in or is influenced by fetishism.

fetishistic *adj.* relating to or affected by fetishism or a fetish.

fetlock *noun* **1** the thick projection at the back of a horse's leg, above its hoof. **2** the tuft of hair growing on this. [from Middle English *fetlak*]

fetter — *noun* **1** (*usually* **fetters**) a chain or shackle fastened to a prisoner's ankle. **2** (**fetters**) tiresome restrictions. — *verb* (**fettered, fettering**) **1** to put in fetters. **2** to restrict. [from Anglo-Saxon *fetor*]

fettle *noun* spirits or condition: *in fine fettle*. [from Anglo-Saxon *fetel*, belt]

fettuccine /fetʊ'tʃiːnɪ/ *noun* pasta in the form of flat wide ribbons. [Italian, a diminutive (plural) of *fettuccia*, tape]

fetus or **foetus** /'fiːtəs/ *noun* **1** *Zool.* the embryo of a viviparous mammal (one giving birth to live offspring) during the later stages of development in the uterus (womb), when it has started to resemble the fully formed animal. **2** specifically, the human embryo from about 8 weeks after conception until birth. [from Latin *fetus*, offspring]

fetwa /'fetwɑː/ same as FATWA.

feud /fjuːd/ — *noun* a long-drawn-out bitter quarrel between families, tribes, or individuals. — *verb intrans.* (**feud with someone**) to carry on a feud with them. [from Old French *feide*]

◪ *noun* quarrel, vendetta, row, argument, disagreement, dispute, conflict, strife, discord, animosity, ill-will, bitterness, enmity, hostility, antagonism, rivalry.
◪ *noun* agreement, peace.

feudal *adj.* relating to the social system of medieval Europe, in which vassals or tenants were obliged to serve under their lord in battle, and were in return protected by him. [from Latin *feudum*, fee]

feudalism *noun* the medieval feudal system, or a system reminiscent of it; feudal principles.

fever *noun* **1** any rise in body temperature above the normal level (37°C or 98.6°F), most commonly as a result of viral or bacterial infections, or infectious diseases such as malaria. It is usually accompanied by shivering, thirst, and headache. **2** any of many usually infectious diseases in which this is a marked symptom, eg scarlet fever, yellow fever. **3** agitation or excitement. [from Latin *febris*]

◪ **1** feverishness, (high) temperature, delirium. **3** excitement, agitation, turmoil, unrest, restlessness, heat, passion, ecstasy.

fevered *adj.* feverish; affected with fever.

feverfew *noun* an aromatic perennial plant (*Tanacetum parthenium*) having yellowish-green leaves and clusters of white and yellow flowers. It is grown for ornament and as a medicinal herb. [from medieval Latin *febrifugia*, plant for ridding fever]

feverish *adj.* **1** suffering from fever, or showing symptoms of fever. **2** agitated or restless.

◪ **1** delirious, hot, burning, flushed. **2** excited, agitated, restless, frenzied, frantic, hectic, hasty, hurried, overwrought, impatient, nervous.
◪ **1** cool. **2** calm.

fever pitch a state of high excitement.

few — *adj.* not many; hardly any. — *pron.* hardly any things, people, etc. — **a few** a small number; some. **as few as ...** no more than ... . **few and far between** *colloq.* rare; scarce. **a good few** or **quite a few** a fairly large number; several. **have had a few** *colloq.* to have drunk sufficient alcohol to affect one's behaviour. **no fewer than ...** as many as ... . **precious few** *colloq.* hardly any at all. **the few** the minority, or the discerning people, as distinct from *the many*. [from Anglo-Saxon *feawa*]

◪ *adj.* scarce, rare, uncommon, sporadic, infrequent, sparse, thin, scant, scanty, meagre, inconsiderable, inadequate, insufficient, in short supply. *pron.* not many, hardly any, one or two, a couple, a scattering, a sprinkling, a handful, some.
◪ *adj.* many. *pron.* many.

fey *adj.* **1** strangely fanciful. **2** able to foresee future events. **3** *Scot.* doomed to die early. [from Anglo-Saxon *fæge*, doomed to die]

feyness *noun* being fey.

fez *noun* (PL. **fezzes**) a hat shaped like a flat-topped cone, with a tassel, worn by some Muslim men. [from Turkish *fes*, from *Fez* in Morocco]

ff *abbrev. Mus.* fortissimo.

ff. *abbrev.* and the following (pages, etc).

fiacre /fɪ'ɑːkrə/ *noun Hist.* a small four-wheeled cab. [from French *fiacre*, from the Hôtel de St *Fiacre* in Paris, where such a vehicle was first used]

fiancé /fɪ'ɒnseɪ/ *noun* a man to whom a woman is engaged to be married. [from Old French *fiancier*, to betroth]

fiancée /fɪ'ɒnseɪ/ *noun* a woman to whom a man is engaged to be married.

fiasco /fɪ'askəʊ/ *noun* (PL. **fiascos, fiascoes**) **1** a ludicrous or humiliating failure. **2** a disgraceful or ludicrous affair. [from Italian *fiasco*, bottle]

fiat /'faɪət/ *noun* **1** an official command; a decree. **2** a formal authorization for some procedure. [from Latin *fiat*, let it be done]

fib *colloq.* — *noun* a trivial lie. — *verb intrans.* (**fibbed, fibbing**) to tell fibs.

fibber *noun* a person who fibs.

Fibonacci series or **Fibonacci sequence** /fɪbə'nɑːtʃɪ/ *Maths.* an infinitely long series of numbers in which each term is the sum of the two preceding terms, ie 1, 1, 2, 3, 5, 8, 13 ... .

fibre /'faɪbə(r)/ *noun* **1** a thin thread of a natural or artificial substance, eg cellulose, nylon. **2** an elongated cell, or a number of cells joined end to end to form a single strand of tissue, eg muscle fibre, nerve fibre. **3** *Bot.* in the stems of woody plants, a long narrow thick-walled cell that provides mechanical support. Stem fibres of many species, eg flax, jute, are economically important. **4** dietary fibre. **5** an optical fibre. **6** character; stamina. [from Latin *fibra*]

◪ **1** thread, filament, strand. **2** nerve, sinew. **6** character, stamina, calibre, backbone, resolution, determination, courage, strength, toughness.

fibreboard *noun* a strong board made of compressed wood chips or other organic fibres, used in the construction industry, and for making panelling, etc.

fibreglass *noun* a strong durable synthetic material consisting of fine flexible glass fibres. It is resistant to heat, fire, and corrosion, and is used as a strengthener in glass-reinforced plastics for boat hulls, car bodies, etc, and as an electrical insulator.

fibre-optic *adj.* containing or using fibre optics.

fibre optics *Optics* the branch of optics concerned with the behaviour of light in long thin flexible strands of glass or plastic (optical fibres), and the use of such systems to transmit telephone messages, television signals, computer data, etc, in the form of modulated light signals. See also OPTICAL FIBRE.

fibril /ˈfaɪbrɪl/ *noun* a small fibre. [from Latin *fibrilla*, diminutive of *fibra*, fibre]

fibrillate /ˈfaɪbrɪleɪt, ˈfɪ-/ *verb intrans. Medicine, said of the muscle fibres of the heart* to contract spontaneously, rapidly, and irregularly.

fibrillation /faɪbrɪˈleɪʃən, fɪ-/ *noun Medicine* the spontaneous rapid and irregular contraction of the individual muscle fibres in the muscular walls of the chambers of the heart (the atria and ventricles). [from Latin *fibrilla*, fibril]

fibrin /ˈfaɪbrɪn, ˈfɪ-/ *noun Biochem.* an insoluble protein that forms a network of fibres during the clotting of blood, sealing off the ruptured blood vessel.

fibrinogen /faɪˈbrɪnoʊdʒən, fɪ-/ *noun Biochem.* a protein, produced by the liver, that is present in blood plasma, and is converted to the insoluble protein fibrin during the clotting of blood.

fibroid /ˈfaɪbrɔɪd/ — *adj.* denoting a structure composed of fibrous tissue or resembling fibres. — *noun Medicine* a benign tumour consisting of fibrous tissue, one or more of which may develop in the muscular walls of the uterus.

fibrosis /faɪˈbroʊsɪs/ *noun* the formation of an abnormal amount of fibrous connective tissue over the surface of or in place of normal tissue of an organ or body part, usually as a result of inflammation or injury. See also CYSTIC FIBROSIS.

fibrositis /faɪbroʊˈsaɪtɪs/ *noun* inflammation of fibrous connective tissue, especially that which sheathes the muscles of the back. It causes pain and stiffness. [from *fibrose*, fibrous + -ITIS]

fibrous /ˈfaɪbrəs/ *adj.* consisting of, containing, or like, fibre.

fibula /ˈfɪbjʊlə/ *noun* (PL. **fibulae, fibulas**) *Anat.* 1 in the human skeleton, the outer and narrower of the two bones in the lower leg, between the knee and the ankle. 2 the corresponding bone in the hind limb of four-limbed vertebrates. [from Latin *fibula*, brooch]

fiche /fiːʃ/ *noun* a card or strip of film containing miniaturized data; a microfiche. [from French *fiche*, a slip of paper, etc]

fickle *adj. derog.* changeable, especially in one's loyalties. [from Anglo-Saxon *ficol*, cunning]

■ changeable, inconstant, disloyal, unreliable, unpredictable, capricious, mercurial, irresolute, vacillating, unfaithful, faithless, treacherous.
F3 constant, loyal, steady, stable.

fiction *noun* 1 literature concerning imaginary characters or events. 2 a pretence; a lie. 3 *Legal* a misrepresentation of the truth, accepted for convenience. [from Latin *fictio*, from *fingere*, to mould]

■ 1 novels, fantasy, romance, fable, parable, legend, myth. 2 pretence, lie, falsehood, untruth, *colloq.* fib, fabrication, concoction.
F3 1 non-fiction. 2 fact, truth.

fictional *adj.* relating to or of the nature of fiction.

■ literary, invented, made-up, imaginary, make-believe, legendary, mythical, mythological, fabulous, non-existent, unreal.
F3 factual, real.

fictitious *adj.* 1 imagined; invented; not real. 2 of, or occurring in, fiction. [from Latin *ficticius*]

■ 1 imagined, imaginary, invented, unreal, untrue, false, made-up, fabricated, apocryphal, non-existent, bogus, counterfeit, spurious, assumed, supposed.
F3 true, genuine.

fiddle — *noun* 1 *colloq.* a violin, especially when used to play folk music or jazz. 2 *colloq.* a dishonest arrangement; a fraud. — *verb* 1 *intrans.* to play about aimlessly; to tinker, toy, or meddle. 2 (**fiddle around** or **about**) to waste time. 3 *trans., intrans.* to falsify (accounts, etc); to manage or manipulate dishonestly. 4 *intrans., trans.* to play a violin, or play (a tune) on one. — **as fit as a fiddle** in excellent health. **fiddle while Rome burns** to be preoccupied with trifles in a crisis. **on the fiddle** *colloq.* making money dishonestly. **play second fiddle to someone** to be subordinate to them. [from Anglo-Saxon *fithele*]

■ *noun* 2 fraud, racket, sharp practice, swindle, *colloq.* con, *colloq.* rip-off, *slang* scam, *slang* graft. *verb* 1 toy, tinker, play, fidget, meddle, tamper, *colloq.* mess around, interfere. 2 *colloq.* mess about. 3 cheat, swindle, diddle, *colloq.* cook the books, racketeer, *slang* graft.

fiddler *noun* 1 a person who plays the fiddle. 2 a swindler. 3 (*in full* **fiddler crab**) any of various small burrowing crabs, so called because the movements of an enlarged pincer-like claw in the male resemble those of a fiddler.

fiddlesticks *interj. colloq.* nonsense.

fiddling *adj.* unimportant; trifling.

■ unimportant, trifling, petty, trivial, insignificant, negligible, paltry.
F3 important, significant.

fiddly *adj.* (**fiddlier, fiddliest**) awkward to handle or do, especially if the task requires delicate finger movements.

fideism /ˈfiːdeɪɪzm/ *noun* the doctrine that the principles of some area of inquiry cannot be established by reason, but must be accepted by faith.

fidelity *noun* 1 faithfulness; loyalty. 2 accuracy in reporting, describing, or copying something. 3 precision in sound reproduction. [from Latin *fidelitas*]

■ 1 faithfulness, loyalty, allegiance, devotion, constancy, reliability. 2 accuracy, exactness, precision, closeness, adherence.
F3 1 infidelity, disloyalty, inconstancy, treachery. 2 inaccuracy.

fidget — *verb* (**fidgeted, fidgeting**) 1 *intrans.* to move or fiddle restlessly. 2 to cause to feel nervous and uneasy. — *noun* 1 a person who fidgets. 2 (**the fidgets**) nervous restlessness. [from earlier *fidge*, to twitch]

■ *verb* 1 squirm, wriggle, shuffle, twitch, fret, fuss, fiddle, mess about.

fidgety *adj.* fidgeting, restless.

■ fidgeting, restless, impatient, uneasy, nervous, agitated, jittery, jumpy, twitchy, on edge.
F3 still, calm, composed.

fiduciary /fɪˈdjuːʃərɪ/ *Legal* — *adj.* held or given in trust.

— *noun* (PL. **fiduciaries**) a trustee. [from Latin *fiducia*, trust]

fie /faɪ/ *interj. old use* for shame!

fief /fiːf/ *noun Hist.* **1** under the feudal system, land granted to a vassal by his lord in return for military service, or on other conditions. **2** one's own area of operation or control. [from Old French *fie*]

field — *noun* **1** an area of land, usually enclosed by a fence, hedge, or ditch, that is used for growing crops, or as pasture for livestock. **2** an area marked off as a ground for a sport, etc. **3** (*in compounds*) **a** an area rich in a particular mineral, etc: *coalfield.* **b** an expanse: *snowfields.* **4** an area of knowledge, interest, or study. **5** the area included in something; the range over which a force, etc extends: *field of vision.* **6** the contestants, or a particular contestant's rivals, in a race, competition, etc. **7** a place of battle: *fell on the field.* **8** *Cricket* the fielding side. **9** the background to the design on a flag, coin, etc. — *verb* **1** *intrans., trans. Cricket* **a** to be the team whose turn it is to retrieve balls hit by the batting team. **b** *said of a fielder* to retrieve (the ball). **2** to put forward as (a team or player) for a match. **3** to deal with a succession of (inquiries, etc). — **hold the field** to remain supreme. **lead the field** to be in the foremost or winning position. **play the field** *colloq.* to try out the range of possibilities before making a choice. **take the field 1** *said of a team* to go on to the pitch ready for a match. **2** to go into battle; to begin a campaign.

. . . .

▣ *noun* **1** grassland, meadow, pasture, paddock. **2** ground, playing-field, pitch, green, lawn. **4** discipline, speciality, forte, department, line, domain, sphere, area, province, territory. **5** range, scope, bounds, limits, confines. **6** contestants, participants, entrants, applicants, competitors, contenders, candidates, runners, opponents, opposition, competition.

. . . .

field day 1 *Mil.* a day of exercises and manoeuvres. **2** *facetious* an occasion on which one has unusually wide scope for one's activities.

fielder *noun Cricket* a member of the fielding side.

field event *Athletics* a contest involving jumping, throwing, etc, as distinct from a track event. See also TRACK EVENT.

field glasses binoculars.

field gun a light cannon mounted on wheels.

field hockey *North Amer.* ordinary hockey as distinct from ice hockey.

field magnet *Physics* a permanent magnet or electromagnet that provides the magnetic field in an electric machine.

field marshal an army officer of the highest rank.

fieldmouse *noun* (PL. **fieldmice**) any of various species of small mouse, native to Europe, non-tropical Asia, and S America, having yellowish-brown fur, prominent ears, and a long tail. Fieldmice live among dense vegetation in woods, grassland, fields, and gardens, and feed mainly on seeds, but also eat berries, roots, insects, and grubs.

field officer an army officer between the ranks of captain and general.

field sports the sports of hunting, shooting, and line-fishing.

fieldwork *noun* **1** practical work or research carried out away from the laboratory or place of work. **2** *Mil.* a temporary fortification.

fieldworker *noun* a person who carries out fieldwork; a practical researcher.

fiend *noun* **1** a devil; an evil spirit. **2** *colloq.* a spiteful person. **3** *colloq.* an enthusiast. [from Anglo-Saxon *feond*]

. . . .

▣ **1** devil, evil spirit, demon, monster. **3** enthusiast, fanatic, *colloq.* addict, devotee, freak, *colloq.* nut.

. . . .

fiendish *adj.* **1** like or of a fiend. **2** devilishly cruel. **3** *colloq.* extremely difficult; most unpleasant.

▣ **1** devilish, diabolical, infernal, wicked, malevolent, cunning. **2** cruel, inhuman, savage, monstrous, unspeakable. **3** horrendous.

. . . .

fierce *adj.* **1** violent and aggressive. **2** intense; strong; severe; extreme. [from Old French *fers*, from Latin *ferus*, savage]

. . . .

▣ **1** ferocious, vicious, savage, cruel, brutal, merciless, aggressive, dangerous, murderous, frightening, menacing, threatening, stern, grim. **2** intense, strong, severe, extreme, relentless, raging, wild, passionate, powerful.

▣ GENTLE. **1** kind. **2** mild, weak.

. . . .

fierily *adv.* in a fiery way; angrily.

fiery *adj.* (**fierier, fieriest**) **1** consisting of fire; like fire. **2** easily enraged. **3** passionate; spirited; vigorous: *fiery oratory.* **4** *said of food* hot-tasting; causing a burning sensation.

. . . .

▣ **1** burning, afire, flaming, aflame, blazing, ablaze, red-hot, glowing, aglow, flushed, hot, torrid, sultry. **2** passionate, impatient, excitable, impetuous, impulsive, hotheaded. **3** passionate, spirited, vigorous, inflamed, heated, ardent, fervent, fierce. **4** hot, spicy.

▣ **1** cold. **2**, **3** impassive, calm, cool.

. . . .

fiesta /fɪˈɛstə/ *noun* especially in Spain or Latin America, a religious festival with dancing, singing, etc. [from Spanish *fiesta*, feast]

FIFA *abbrev. Fédération Internationale de Football Association* (French) International Association Football Federation.

fife *noun* a small type of flute played in military bands. [from Old German *pfifa*, pipe]

FIFO *abbrev.* first in, first out.

fifteen — *noun* **1** the number or figure 15; any symbol for this number. **2** the age of 15. **3** something, especially a garment, or a person, whose size is denoted by the number 15. **4** a set of 15 things or people, eg a Rugby team. **5** *Brit.* a film classified as suitable for people aged 15 and over. — *adj.* **1** 15 in number. **2** aged 15. [from Anglo-Saxon *fiftene*]

fifteenth *noun, adj.* **1** the position in a series corresponding to 15 in a sequence of numbers. **2** one of 15 equal parts.

fifth *noun, adj.* **1** the position in a series corresponding to 5 in a sequence of numbers. **2** one of five equal parts. **3** *Mus.* an interval of four diatonic degrees; a tone at that interval from another, or a combination of two tones separated by that interval.

fifth column a body of citizens prepared to co-operate with an invading enemy.

fifth columnist a person who sympathizes with and will support an enemy.

fifthly *adv.* as fifth in a series.

fifties *pl. noun* **1** the period of time between one's fiftieth and sixtieth birthdays. **2** the range of temperatures between fifty and sixty degrees. **3** the period of time between the fiftieth and sixtieth years of a century.

fiftieth *noun, adj.* **1** the position in a series corresponding to 50 in a sequence of numbers. **2** one of fifty equal parts.

fifty — *noun* (PL. **fifties**) **1** the number or figure 50; any symbol for this number. **2** the age of 50. **3** a set of 50 people or things. — *adj.* **1** 50 in number. **2** aged 50. [from Anglo-Saxon *fiftig*]

fifty-fifty — *adj., said of a chance* equal either way. — *adv., adj.* divided equally between two.

fig *noun* **1** a large shrub or small tree of the genus *Ficus* which has large shiny leaves and bears fleshy receptacles containing hundreds of tiny flowers. It is widely cultivated, especially in the Mediterranean region, for its edible fruit which contains hundreds of tiny seeds. Many fig. 476 file

species are cultivated as ornamental plants. **2** the green, brown, or purple pear-shaped fleshy fruit of this tree, which may be eaten fresh, but is usually canned or dried after harvesting. — **not give** or **care a fig** *colloq.* not to care in the least. [from Latin *ficus*]

fig. *abbrev.* figure (diagram or illustration).

fight — *verb* (PAST TENSE AND PAST PARTICIPLE **fought**) **1** *trans., intrans.* to attack or engage in combat. **2** (**fight for someone** or **something**) to struggle or campaign on their behalf. **3** to oppose vigorously. **4** *intrans.* to quarrel. **5** to take part in or conduct (a battle, campaign, etc). **6** to make (one's way) with a struggle. — *noun* **1** a battle; a physically violent struggle; a quarrel. **2** resistance. **3** the will or strength to resist: *lost all his fight.* **4** a contest. **5** a boxing match. **6** a campaign or crusade: *the fight for freedom.* — **fight back** to resist an attacker. **fight something back** or **down** to try not to show one's emotions, etc. **fighting fit** *colloq.* in vigorous health. **fight someone off** to repulse an attacker. **fight something off** to get rid of or resist an illness. **fight it out** to fight over something until one side wins. **fight shy of something** to avoid it. [from Anglo-Saxon *feohtan*, to fight]

. . . .

■ *verb* **1** wrestle, box, fence, joust, brawl, *colloq.* scrap, scuffle, tussle, skirmish, combat, battle, do battle, war, wage war, clash, cross swords, engage, grapple, struggle, strive, contend. **3** oppose, resist, withstand, defy, stand up to. **4** quarrel, argue, dispute, squabble, bicker, wrangle. **5** take part in, conduct, contest, campaign for or against. *noun* **1** battle, war, hostilities, combat, action, brawl, scrap, scuffle, tussle, struggle, skirmish, set-to, clash, engagement, brush, encounter, conflict, fray, free-for-all, fracas, riot, duel, quarrel, row, argument, dispute, dissension. **3** determination, willpower, tenacity, firmness, resoluteness, drive. **4** contest, competition, match, brush, encounter. **5** bout. **6** campaign, crusade, movement, drive, battle. **fight back** retaliate, defend oneself, resist, put up a fight, retort, reply. **fight something back** or **down** hold back, restrain, curb, control, repress, bottle up, contain, suppress. **fight off** *someone* hold off, keep at bay, ward off, stave off, resist, repel, rebuff, beat off, rout, put to flight; *something* hold off, keep at bay, ward off, stave off, resist, beat off.

. . . .

fighter *noun* **1** a person who fights; a professional boxer. **2** a person with determination. **3** an aircraft equipped to attack other aircraft.

. . . .

■ **1** combatant, contestant, contender, disputant, boxer, wrestler, pugilist, prize-fighter, soldier, trouper, mercenary, warrior, man-at-arms, swordsman, gladiator.

. . . .

fighting chance a chance to succeed dependent chiefly on determination.

fighting fish a small freshwater fish, native to Thailand, that feeds on aquatic insects, especially mosquito larvae, and is up to 6cm in length. It is renowned for its aggressive behaviour.

fig leaf 1 a fig-tree leaf. In art the traditional covering for the genitals in representations of nude figures. **2** any device used to cover up something embarrassing.

figment *noun* something imagined or invented. [from Latin *figmentum*]

figurative *adj.* **1** metaphorical, not literal. **2** *said of writing, etc* full of figures of speech, especially metaphor. **3** *said of art* not abstract; showing things as they look; representational; pictorial.

. . . .

■ **1, 2** metaphorical, symbolic, emblematic, allegorical, parabolic. **3** representational, pictorial, naturalistic.

■ **1** literal.

. . . .

figure — *noun* **1** an indistinctly seen or unidentified person. **2** the shape of one's body. **3** a symbol representing a number; a numeral. **4** a number representing an amount; a cost or price. **5** (**figures**) arithmetical calculations; statistics. **6** a well-known person: *a public figure.* **7** the impression that one makes: *cut a poor figure.* **8** a representation of the human form. **9** a diagram or illustration. **10** an image, design, or pattern. **11** a geometrical shape. **12** a set pattern of steps or movements in dancing or skating, or of notes in music. **13** a figure of speech. — *verb* **1** (**figure in something**) to play a part in a story, incident, etc. **2** *North Amer., esp. US* to think; to reckon. **3** to imagine; to envisage. **4** *intrans. colloq.* to be probable or predictable; to make sense: *that figures.* **5** to decorate (a surface) with a design; to add elaborations to (music). — **figure on something 1** to intend to do something. **2** to make plans that depend on something happening. **figure something out** to work it out; to begin to understand it. **keep one's figure** to remain slim. **lose one's figure** to become overweight. [from Latin *figura*, from *fingere*, to mould]

. . . .

■ *noun* **1** shape, form, outline, silhouette. **2** shape, physique, build. **3** number, numeral, digit, integer. **4** amount, sum, total, cost, price. **6** dignitary, celebrity, personality, character, person. **8** body, frame. **9** diagram, illustration, picture, drawing, sketch. **10** image, design, pattern, representation, symbol. *verb* **1** feature in, appear in, crop up in. **2** think, reckon, guess, estimate, judge, believe. **figure out** work out, calculate, compute, reckon, puzzle out, resolve, fathom, understand, see, make out, decipher.

. . . .

figured bass *Mus.* a bass part with numerals added to indicate the harmonies to be played above it, formerly known as the 'through bass' (from Italian *basso continuo*).

figurehead *noun* **1** a leader in name only, without real power. **2** *Hist.* a carved wooden figure fixed to a ship's prow.

. . . .

■ **1** mouthpiece, front man, name, dummy, puppet.

. . . .

figure of eight a pattern, movement, etc in the shape of an 8.

figure of fun someone whom others ridicule.

figure of speech any of many devices such as metaphors, similes, etc that enliven language.

figurine *noun* a little statue. [from Italian *figurina*, diminutive of *figura*, figure]

filament *noun* **1** a fine thread or fibre. **2** *Electr.* in electrical equipment, a fine wire with a high resistance that emits heat and light when an electric current is passed through it. Filaments are used in light bulbs, heaters in thermionic valves, etc. **3** *Bot.* in a flower, the stalk of a stamen, which bears the anther. **4** *Bot.* a long strand of cells joined end to end, as in certain algae and fungi. **5** *Zool.* any of the long slender barbs of a bird's feather. [from Latin *filum*, thread]

. . . .

■ **1** fibre, thread, strand, hair, whisker, wire, string.

. . . .

filch *verb* to steal (something small or trivial). [from Middle English *filchen*, to take as booty]

file[1] — *noun* a steel tool with a rough surface consisting of fine parallel grooves with sharp cutting edges, used to smooth metal, wood, or plastic items. — *verb* **1** to cut or smooth with, or as if with, a file. **2** to polish or improve (a literary style etc) [from Anglo-Saxon *fil*]

. . . .

■ *verb* **1** rub (down), sand, abrade, scour, scrape, grate, rasp, hone, whet, shave, plane. **2** smooth, polish.

. . . .

file[2] — *noun* **1** a folder or box in which to keep loose papers. **2** a collection of papers so kept, especially dealing with a particular subject. **3** *Comput.* an organized collection of data that is stored in the external memory of a computer, and can be accessed and manipulated as a single named unit. **4** a line of people or things moving one behind the other: *single file*. — *verb* **1** to put (papers, etc) into a file. **2** *intrans.* to make a formal application to a law court: *file for divorce*. **3** *intrans.* to move along one behind the other. **4** *said of a reporter* to submit (a story) to a newspaper. — **on file** retained in a file for reference; on record. [from Latin *filum*, a thread]

🔲 *noun* **1** folder, binder. **2** dossier, portfolio, record, documents, information, case. **4** line, queue, crocodile, string. *verb* **1** categorize, pigeonhole, catalogue, classify, process, store. **2** record, register, note, enter. **3** march, troop, parade, stream, trail.

file-server *noun* *Comput.* a computer which handles files from several computers linked in a network.

filial *adj.* of, or suitable to, a son or daughter. [from Latin *filius*, son, and *filia*, daughter]

filibuster — *noun* **1** the practice of making long speeches to delay the passing of laws. **2** a member of a law-making assembly who uses this practice. — *verb intrans.* (**filibustered**, **filibustering**) to obstruct legislation in this way. [from Spanish *filibustero*, freebooter]

filigree *noun* delicate work in gold or silver wire, used in jewellery, etc. [from Latin *filum*, thread + *granum*, grain]

filing cabinet a piece of furniture with drawers, etc for holding files.

filings *pl. noun* pieces of wood, metal, etc rubbed off with a file.

fill — *verb* **1** (*also* **fill something up**) to make it full. **2** to take up the space in; to occupy completely. **3** (**be filled with feelings**) to be profoundly affected by them. **4** *intrans.* (*also* **fill up**) to become full. **5** to satisfy (a need); to perform (a role) satisfactorily. **6** to occupy (time). **7** to appoint someone to (a position or post). **8** (**fill something in** or **up**) to put material into (a hole, cavity, etc) to level the surface. **9** *intrans. said of a sail* to billow out in the wind. — *noun* as much as satisfies one or as one can tolerate: *eat one's fill*. — **fill someone in** *slang* to hit or beat them. **fill something in** to write information as required on a form. **fill someone in on something** to inform them fully about it. **fill in for someone** to take over their work temporarily. **fill out** to become plumper. **fill something out** to enlarge it satisfactorily; to amplify it. **fill something out** or **up** to write information as required on a form. **have had one's fill of something** to have had too much of it. [from Anglo-Saxon *fyllan*]

🔲 *verb* **1** replenish, stock, pack, cram, stuff. **2** pack, crowd, cram, block, congest, clog. **5** satisfy, supply, furnish, meet, fulfil, discharge, suffice, serve. **6** take up. **8** plug, bung, cork, stop, close, seal. **fill something in** complete, fill out, answer. **fill someone in on something** brief, inform, advise, acquaint, bring up to date. **fill in for someone** stand in for, deputize for, understudy, substitute for, replace, represent, act for. **fill something out** or **up** complete, fill in, answer.

🔳 *verb* **1** empty, drain.

filler *noun* a substance used for filling cracks or holes.

fillet — *noun* **1** a boneless piece of meat or fish. **2** a broad ribbon or headband. **3** *Archit.* a narrow flat band. — *verb* (**filleted**, **filleting**) to remove the bones from; to divide into fillets. [from Latin *filum*, thread]

filling *noun* **1** a specially prepared substance, such as amalgam, gold, or composite resin, that is inserted into a cavity that has been drilled in a decayed tooth. **2** the process whereby such a material is inserted into a drilled tooth cavity. **3** food put inside a pie, sandwich, etc.

🔲 **3** inside, contents, stuffing, padding, wadding, filler.

filling station a place where one can get petrol for one's car.

fillip *noun* **1** something that has a stimulating or brightening effect; a boost. **2** a flick made with the nail of a finger. [from Middle English *philippe*]

filly *noun* (PL. **fillies**) **1** a young female horse or pony. **2** *old colloq.* use a young girl. [from Norse *fylja*]

film — *noun* **1** a strip of thin flexible plastic or other substance, coated so as to be light-sensitive and exposed inside a camera to produce still or moving pictures. **2** a motion picture for showing in the cinema, or on television or video. **3** (**films** or **the films**) the cinema in general. **4** a fine skin or coating. — *verb* **1** *trans.*, *intrans.* to photograph with or operate a cine camera. **2** (**film over**) *intrans.* to become covered with a film. [from Anglo-Saxon *filmen*, membrane]

🔲 *noun* **1** membrane, sheet, tissue. **2** motion picture, picture, *colloq.* movie, video, feature film, short, documentary. **4** skin, coating, layer, covering, dusting, coat, glaze, cloud, mist, haze. *verb* **1** photograph, shoot, video, videotape.

film festival any national or international gathering for the showing, promotion, and marketing of motion pictures. Among the most important international film festivals are those at Cannes in the S of France, and Montreux in Switzerland.

filminess *noun* being filmy.

filmsetting *noun* *Printing* typesetting by exposing type on to film which is then transferred by printing plates.

film star a celebrated film actor or actress.

film strip a series of photographs on a strip of film, for separate projection as slides.

filmy *adj.* (**filmier**, **filmiest**) *said of a fabric* thin, light, and transparent.

FILO *abbrev.* first in, last out.

filo or **phyllo** /'fiːloʊ/ *noun* a type of pastry, originally from Greece, made in thin sheets and layered with oil or butter for cooking. [from Greek *phyllon*, a leaf]

filoplume /'fɪloʊpluːm/ *noun* *Zool.* a small slender hair-like feather. [from Latin *filum*, thread]

filter — *noun* **1** *Chem.* a device consisting of a porous material through which a liquid or gas is passed in order to remove suspended solid particles, eg a funnel containing a cone of filter paper. **2** a plate of glass or other semi-transparent material placed over a camera lens, etc that allows only certain wavelengths of light to pass when it is placed in the path of a beam of radiation. **3** *Electr.* in electronics, a device that only allows signals of certain frequencies to pass. **4** a traffic signal at traffic lights that allows left- or right-turning vehicles to proceed while the main stream is halted. — *verb* **1** *trans.*, *intrans.* to pass through a filter. **2** *intrans.* to pass little by little. **3** *intrans.*, *said of a vehicle* to proceed left or right at a filter. — **filter out** or **through** *said of news or information* to leak out. **filter something out** to remove impurities, etc by filtering. [from Latin *filtrum*, felt used as a filter]

🔲 *noun* **1** strainer, sieve, sifter, mesh, gauze, membrane. *verb* **1** strain, sieve, sift, screen, refine, purify, clarify. **2** percolate, ooze, seep, leak, trickle, dribble.

filter paper porous paper through which a liquid can be passed in order to separate out any solid particles suspended in it.

filter tip a filter on the end of a cigarette that traps some of the smoke's impurities before the smoker inhales it.

filter-tipped *adj.* having a filter tip.

filth *noun* **1** repulsive dirt; disgusting rubbish. **2** obscene vulgarity. [from Anglo-Saxon *fylth*]

🔲 **1** dirt, rubbish, grime, muck, dung, excrement, faeces, sewage, refuse, garbage, trash, slime, sludge, effluent, pollution, contamination, impurity, uncleanness, foulness, sordidness, squalor. **2** obscenity, vulgarity,

smut, indecency, coarseness, pornography.
F3 1 cleanness, cleanliness, purity.

filthily *adv.* in a filthy way.
filthiness *noun* being filthy.
filthy — *adj.* (**filthier, filthiest**) **1** extremely dirty. **2** obscenely vulgar. — *adv. colloq.* used for emphasis, especially showing disapproval: *filthy rich*.

F3 *adj.* 1 dirty, soiled, unwashed, grimy, grubby, mucky, muddy, slimy, sooty, unclean, impure, foul, gross, sordid, squalid. 2 obscene, vulgar, smutty, bawdy, suggestive, indecent, offensive, foul-mouthed, coarse, corrupt, depraved, pornographic.
F3 *adj.* 1 clean, pure. 2 decent.

filthy lucre *derog.* or *humorous* money, profit.
filtrate — *noun Chem.* the clear liquid obtained after filtration. — *verb* to filter. [from Latin *filtrare*, to filter]
filtration *noun* the act or process of filtering.
fin *noun* **1** in fish, a wing-like projection consisting of a thin fold of skin supported by bone or cartilage, used for propelling the fish through the water, balancing, steering, display, and in some cases protection (eg the spines of the stickleback). **2** any structure of similar shape in other aquatic animals. **3** a fixed or adjustable aerofoil attached to the rear of an aeroplane, that provides increased stability. **4** a thin metal plate protruding from the cylinder of an air-cooled engine, that increases the surface area available for dissipation of heat. **5** a swimmer's flipper. [from Anglo-Saxon *finn*]
final — *adj.* **1** occurring at the end; last. **2** completed; finished. **3** *said of a decision, etc* definite; not to be altered; conclusive. — *noun* **1** the last round of a competition, or a round of deciding heats. **2** (**finals**) the examinations held at the end of a degree course, etc. [from Latin *finis*, end]

F3 *adj.* 1 last, latest, closing, concluding, finishing, end, ultimate, terminal, dying, last-minute, eventual, conclusive. 3 definite, definitive, decisive, incontrovertible.
F3 *adj.* 1 first, initial.

finale /fɪˈnɑːlɪ/ *noun* the grand conclusion to a show, etc. [from Italian *finale*, from Latin *finis*, end]

F3 conclusion, climax, dénouement, culmination, crowning glory, end, close, curtain, epilogue.

finalist *noun* a person who reaches the final round in a competition.
finality *noun* **1** being final. **2** completeness, conclusiveness. **3** something that is final.
finalization or **finalisation** *noun* making final; completion.
finalize or **finalise** *verb* **1** to decide on, or agree to, finally. **2** to complete; to finish.

F3 1 decide (on), agree to, resolve, settle, close, clinch. 2 conclude, finish, complete, round off, *slang* sew up, *colloq.* wrap up.

finally *adv.* **1** lastly. **2** at last. **3** to conclude. **4** conclusively; definitely.

F3 1 lastly, ultimately. 2 at last, at length, in the end, eventually. 3 in conclusion. 4 conclusively, definitely, once and for all, irreversibly, irrevocably, for ever.

finance /ˈfaɪnæns, faɪˈnæns/ — *noun* (with stress on *fin-*) **1** money affairs; their study or management. **2** the money needed or used to pay for something. **3** (**finances**) a person's financial resources. — *verb* (with stress on *-nance*)

to provide funds for. [from Old French *finer*, to settle]

F3 *noun* 1 money management, economics, accounting, banking, investment, stock market, business, commerce, trade. 2 money, funds, funding, sponsorship, subsidy. 3 income, resources, affairs, money, cash, funds, budget, revenue, assets, capital, wealth, liquidity, wherewithal.
verb fund, pay for, sponsor, back, support, underwrite, guarantee, subsidize, capitalize, float, set up.

financial /faɪˈnænʃəl, fɪˈnænʃəl/ *adj.* relating to finance.

F3 monetary, money, economic, fiscal, budgetary, commercial, pecuniary.

financial year the 12-month period, in Britain starting 6 Apr, used in accounting, annual taxation, etc.
financier /fɪˈnænsɪə(r), faɪ-/ *noun* **1** a person engaged in large financial transactions. **2** someone who finances an operation. [from French *financier*]

F3 1 banker, stockbroker, money-maker, investor, speculator. 2 backer.

finch *noun* any of several small usually colourful birds with short stout conical beaks adapted for cracking seeds, distributed worldwide, eg sparrow, crossbill, canary, chaffinch, goldfinch, bullfinch, linnet, bunting. [from Anglo-Saxon *finc*]
find — *verb* (PAST TENSE AND PAST PARTICIPLE **found**) **1** to discover through search, enquiry, mental effort, or chance. **2** to seek out and provide: *I'll find you a plumber.* **3** to realize or discover. **4** to experience as being: *find it hard to express oneself.* **5** to get or experience: *find pleasure in reading.* **6** to consider; to think. **7** to become aware of: *found her beside him.* **8** to succeed in getting (time, courage, money, etc) for something. **9** to see or come across: *a bird found only in Madagascar.* **10** to reach: *find one's best form.* **11** *trans., intrans. Legal* (**find for** or **against someone**) *said of a jury* to give a verdict in favour or not in favour of the accused. — *noun* something or someone found; an important discovery. — **all found** with food and housing provided. **find it in oneself** or **in one's heart** to be prepared (to do something hurtful, etc). **find oneself** to find the role, etc that satisfies one. **find oneself doing something** to discover or realize that one is doing it: *found themselves agreeing.* **find one's feet** to establish oneself in a new situation. **find out about something** to discover or get information about it. **find someone out** to detect them in wrongdoing; to discover the truth about them. [from Anglo-Saxon *findan*]

F3 *verb* 1 discover, locate, track down, trace, retrieve, recover, unearth, uncover, expose, reveal, come across, chance on, stumble on, meet, encounter. 2 get, obtain. 3 realize, discover, learn, notice, observe, perceive, recognise, detect. 5 get, experience, obtain, attain, achieve, win, reach, gain. 6 consider, think, judge, declare. **find out about** learn, ascertain, discover, detect, note, observe, perceive, realize, uncover, reveal, disclose, *colloq.* tumble to. **find someone out** unmask, expose, show up, catch out, *slang* suss out, *slang* rumble.
F3 *verb* 1 lose.

finder *noun* **1** a person or thing that finds. **2** a small telescope attached to a larger one, or a lens attached to a camera to help in positioning the apparatus.
finding *noun* (*usually* **findings**) a conclusion reached as a result of an investigation, etc.

F3 decision, conclusion, judgement, verdict, pronouncement, decree, recommendation, award.

fine[1] — *adj.* **1** of high quality; excellent; splendid. **2** beautiful; handsome. **3** *facetious* grand; superior: *her fine relations.* **4** *said of weather* bright; not rainy. **5** well; healthy. **6** quite satisfactory. **7** pure; refined. **8** thin; delicate. **9** close-set in texture or arrangement. **10** consisting of tiny particles. **11** intricately detailed: *fine embroidery.* **12** slight; subtle: *fine adjustments.* — *adv.* **1** *colloq.* satisfactorily. **2** finely; into fine pieces. — **cut** or **run it fine** *colloq.* to leave barely enough time for something. **fine something down** to make an activity, operation, etc more effective or efficient by cutting out inessentials. **get something down to a fine art** to find the most efficient way of doing it. **not to put too fine a point on it** to speak honestly or bluntly. [from Old French *fin*]

⊟ *adj.* **1** excellent, splendid, outstanding, exceptional, superior, magnificent, brilliant, good. **2** beautiful, handsome, attractive, elegant, lovely, exquisite. **4** bright, sunny, clear, cloudless, dry, fair. **6** satisfactory, acceptable, all right, *colloq.* OK. **8** thin, delicate, slender, sheer, gauzy, powdery, flimsy, fragile, dainty.
⊟ *adj.* **1** mediocre. **2** ugly. **4** cloudy, dull, wet. **6** poor. **8** thick, coarse. **9, 10** coarse.

fine[2] — *noun* an amount of money to be paid as a penalty. — *verb* to exact a fine from. — **in fine** in total; to sum up. [from Old French *fin*]

⊟ *noun* penalty, punishment, forfeit, forfeiture, damages.

fine arts painting, drawing, sculpture, and architecture, the arts that appeal to the sense of beauty.

finely *adv.* in a fine way; delicately or sensitively.

fineness *noun* **1** being fine. **2** *said of measuring gold or silver* the number of parts in a thousand.

finery *noun* splendid clothes, jewellery, etc.

fines herbes /finz 'erb/ a mixture of herbs for use in cooking. [French, = fine herbs]

finespun *adj.* delicate; over-subtle.

finesse /fɪ'nɛs/ *noun* **1** skilful elegance or expertise. **2** tact and poise in handling situations. **3** *Cards* an attempt by a player holding a high card to win a trick with a lower one. [from Old French *finesse*, fineness]

fine-tooth comb a comb with narrow close-set teeth. — **go over something with a fine-tooth comb** to search or examine it exhaustively.

fine-tune *verb* to make slight adjustments to (a machine, etc) to make it work perfectly.

finger — *noun* **1** one of the five jointed extremities of the hand; any of the four of these other than the thumb. **2** the part of a glove that fits over a finger. **3** anything similar to a finger in shape. **4** a measure of alcoholic spirits in a glass, equal to the breadth of a finger. — *verb* **1** to touch or feel with the fingers. **2** to play (a musical instrument) with the fingers. **3** *slang* to identify (a criminal) to the police, etc. — **be all fingers and thumbs** *colloq.* to be clumsy in handling or holding things. **keep one's fingers crossed** to hope (sometimes indicated by crossing the middle finger over the index finger). **get one's fingers burnt** *colloq.* to suffer for one's over-boldness or mistakes. **have a finger in every pie** *colloq.* to have an interest, or be involved, in everything. **not lay a finger on someone** *colloq.* not to touch or harm them. **not lift a finger** *colloq.* to make no effort. **point the finger** *colloq.* to blame or accuse someone. **pull** or **get one's finger out** *slang* to make an effort to work effectively. **put one's finger on something** *colloq.* to identify a point, difficulty, etc. **put the finger on someone** *slang* to identify a criminal, etc to the police. **slip through someone's fingers** to manage to escape from them. **twist someone round one's little finger** *colloq.* to be able to get what one wants from them. [from Anglo-Saxon *finger*]

⊟ *verb* **1** touch, handle, manipulate, feel, stroke, caress, fondle, paw, fiddle with, toy with, play about with, meddle with.

fingerboard *noun* the part of a violin, guitar, etc against which the strings are pressed by the fingers to change the note.

fingerbowl *noun* a small bowl of water for cleaning one's fingers at table.

fingering *noun* the correct positioning of the fingers for playing a particular musical instrument or piece of music.

fingermark *noun* a mark left on a surface by a finger.

fingernail *noun* the nail at the tip of one's finger.

fingerprint — *noun* **1** the print or inked impression made by the pattern of minute swirling ridges on the surface of the end joints of the fingers and thumbs, which is unique to each person. Fingerprints are used as a means of identification, especially of criminals. **2** any accurate and unique identifying feature or characteristic, especially that produced by analysis of a sample of a person's DNA, using a technique known as *DNA fingerprinting.* — *verb* to take an impression of the fingerprints of (a person).

fingerstall *noun* a sheath for an injured finger.

fingertip *noun* the tip of one's finger. — **have something at one's fingertips** to know a subject thoroughly. **to one's fingertips** absolutely; in all ways.

finial /'fɪnɪəl/ *noun Archit.* a decorative feature on the top of a gable, spire, or pillar, often in the form of a spike or carved foliage. [from Latin *finis*, end]

finicky *adj.* **1** too concerned with detail. **2** *said of a task* intricate; tricky. **3** fussy; faddy. [from *finical*, over-precise]

⊟ **1** particular, fussy, pernickety, nit-picking, fastidious, critical, hypercritical, meticulous. **2** intricate, tricky, fiddly, difficult, delicate. **3** fussy, faddy, particular, pernickety, *colloq.* choosy, fastidious.
⊟ **1, 3** easy-going. **2** easy.

finish — *verb* (*often* **finish off** or **up**) **1** *trans., intrans.* to bring or come to an end; to stop. **2** to complete or perfect. **3** to use, eat, drink, etc the last of. **4** *intrans.* (*often* **finish up**) to reach or end up in a certain position or situation. **5** (**finish something** or **someone off**) *colloq.* to exhaust them; to defeat or kill them. **6** *intrans.* (**finish with something** or **someone**) to end a relationship; to stop dealing with or needing. **7** to give a particular treatment to the surface of (cloth, wood, etc). — *noun* **1** the last stage; the end. **2** the last part of a race, etc. **3** perfecting touches put to a product. **4** the surface texture given to cloth, wood, etc. — **fight to the finish** to fight till one party is dead or too severely disabled to continue. [from Old French *finir*]

⊟ *verb* **1** end, terminate, stop, cease, conclude, close, wind up, settle, round off, culminate. **2** complete, perfect, accomplish, achieve, fulfil, discharge, deal with, do. **3** use (up), eat, drink, consume, devour, exhaust, drain, empty. **5** exhaust, defeat, destroy, overcome, rout, overthrow, ruin, exterminate, get rid of, annihilate. *noun* **1** end, termination, completion, conclusion, culmination, close. **2** ending, finale. **4** surface, appearance, texture, grain, polish, shine, gloss, lustre, smoothness.
⊟ *verb* **1** begin, start. *noun* **1** beginning, start, commencement.

finished *adj.* **1** *colloq.* no longer useful, productive, creative, wanted, or popular. **2** *said of a performer* accomplished. **3** (**finished with something** or **someone**) having reached the end of one's need for or interest in them.

finisher *noun* **1** a person or thing that finishes. **2** a person or thing that perfects or completes something.

finishing *noun* any of the final processes in the manufacture of a fibre, fabric, or garment.

finishing school a private school where girls are taught social skills and graces.

finite *adj.* **1** having an end or limit. **2** *Grammar, said of a verb* being of a form that reflects person, number, tense, etc, as distinct from being an infinitive or participle. [from Latin *finire*, to finish]

. . . .

⊟ **1** limited, restricted, bounded, demarcated, terminable, definable, fixed, measurable, calculable, countable, numbered.
⊟ **1** infinite.

. . . .

Finn *noun* a native or citizen of Finland. [from Anglo-Saxon *Finnas*, Finns]

finnan *noun* haddock cured in the smoke from peat, turf, or green wood. [probably from *Findon*, Kincardineshire]

Finnish — *adj.* **1** of Finland or its inhabitants. **2** of the language spoken in Finland. — *noun* **1** the language spoken in Finland. **2** (**the Finnish**) the people of Finland. See also FINN.

fiord / 'fiːɔːd/ same as FJORD.

fipple *noun* the piece of wood, etc that plugs the mouthpiece of a recorder or other similar wind instrument.

fir *noun* **1** any of various coniferous evergreen trees of the genus *Abies*, native to north temperate regions and Central America, and usually having silvery or bluish foliage, with leathery needle-like leaves that are borne singly, directly on the stems, and erect cones. **2** any of various related trees, such as the Douglas fir, which belongs to the genus *Pseudotsuga*. **3** the timber of any of these trees. [from Anglo-Saxon *fyrh*]

fire — *noun* **1** the flames, heat, and usually smoke produced by combustion (burning) of an inflammable material. **2** a destructive conflagration of a building, forest, etc. **3** a mass of burning material, eg wood, coal, burning in a grate, stove, boiler, etc. **4** a gas or electric room-heater. **5** the discharging of firearms. **6** the launching of a missile. **7** enthusiasm; passion; ardour. **8** fever; a burning sensation. **9** sparkle; brilliance (eg of a gem). — *verb* **1** *trans., intrans.* (**fire at, fire on**) to discharge (a firearm); to send off (a bullet or other missile) from a gun, catapult, bow, etc. **2** to cause to explode. **3** to launch (a rocket or missile). **4** to detonate (an explosive). **5** to direct (eg questions) in quick succession at someone. **6** *colloq.* to dismiss from employment. **7** *trans., intrans.* to start or cause to start burning. **8** *trans., intrans.* to glow or cause to glow. **9** *intrans. said of a vehicle engine* to ignite when a spark causes the fuel to burn. **10** *said of a firearm* to be discharged. **11** to inspire or stimulate. **12** to bake (bricks or pottery) in a kiln. — **catch fire** to begin to burn. **cease fire** to stop fighting. **draw someone's fire** to deliberately divert someone's gunfire, criticism, etc towards oneself. **fire away** *colloq.* to say or ask what one wants to. **fire and brimstone** the supposed condition or torment of hell; eternal damnation. **go through fire and water for someone or something** to suffer or undergo danger for their sake. **hold one's fire** to stop shooting. **in the line of fire** between the guns and the target, and therefore in danger of attack. **on fire 1** burning. **2** filled with enthusiasm, love, etc. **open fire on someone or something** to begin shooting at them. **play with fire** *colloq.* to take risks; to act recklessly. **pull something out of the fire** to rescue the situation at the last minute. **return someone's fire** to shoot back at them. **set fire to something** or **set something on fire** to cause it to begin burning. **set someone on fire** to fill them with enthusiasm, love, etc. **under fire 1** being shot at. **2** being criticized or blamed. [from Anglo-Saxon *fyr*]

. . . .

⊟ *noun* **1, 2** flames, blaze, bonfire, conflagration, inferno, burning, combustion. **7** enthusiasm, passion, ardour, excitement, spirit, intensity, heat, radiance, sparkle, feeling. *verb* **1, 3** shoot, launch, discharge, set off, let off. **6** dismiss, discharge, *colloq.* sack. **7** ignite, light, kindle, set fire to, set on fire, set alight. **10** go off. **11** inspire, stimulate, stir, arouse, rouse, incite, spark off, trigger off, excite, whet, enliven, galvanize, electrify. **on fire 1** burning, alight, ignited, flaming, in flames, aflame, blazing, ablaze, fiery.

. . . .

fire alarm a bell or other device activated to warn people of fire.

fire and brimstone see FIRE.

firearm *noun* a gun, pistol, revolver, or rifle.

fireball *noun* **1** a mass of hot gases at the centre of a nuclear explosion. **2** *colloq.* a lively person. **3** a ball-shaped flash of lightning. **4** a brilliant meteor.

firebomb *noun* an incendiary bomb.

firebrand *noun* **1** a piece of burning wood. **2** someone who stirs up unrest; a troublemaker.

firebreak *noun* a cleared strip in a forest to stop the spread of a fire.

firebrick or **fire brick** *noun* a refractory brick, made from fire clay, that can withstand high temperatures and is used to line furnaces, chimneys, fireplaces, etc.

fire brigade a team of people trained to prevent and extinguish fires.

firebug *noun colloq.* a person who deliberately sets fire to buildings, etc.

fireclay *noun Chem.* clay that contains large amounts of alumina and silica and can withstand high temperatures. It is used for making fire-resistant pottery, firebricks, and refractory materials for lining furnaces.

firecracker *noun* a small firework that bangs repeatedly.

-fired *combining form* fuelled by: *gas-fired central heating*.

firedamp *noun* a gaseous mixture of hydrocarbons, chiefly methane, that is explosive when mixed with air. It is formed in coal mines by the decomposition of coal.

firedog *noun* an andiron.

fire drill the routine to be followed in case of fire, or a practice of this routine.

fire-eater *noun* **1** a performer who pretends to swallow fire from flaming torches. **2** an aggressive or quarrelsome person.

fire engine a vehicle carrying fire-fighting equipment.

fire escape an external metal staircase or other device by which people can escape from a burning building.

fire extinguisher a portable device containing water, liquid carbon dioxide under pressure, foam, etc, for spraying on to a fire in order to put it out, either by cooling it or by excluding oxygen, eg by covering the fire with a thick layer of carbon dioxide gas.

firefighter *noun* a fireman or other person who puts out large fires.

fire fighting the act, process, or occupation of fighting fire.

firefly *noun* any of a number of species of small winged beetles, found mainly in tropical regions, that emit light in a series of brief flashes, the pattern of flashes being unique to a particular species, so that males and females can recognize and respond to their own kind.

fireguard *noun* a protective metal or wire-mesh screen for putting round an open fire.

fire hydrant same as HYDRANT.

fire irons a set of tools for looking after a household fire, including a poker, tongs, brush and shovel.

firelighter *noun* a block of flammable material used to help light a fire.

fireman *noun* a male member of a fire brigade.

fireplace *noun* a recess for a fire in a room, with a chimney above it; a hearth, grate, or the structure surrounding it.

firepower *noun Mil.* the destructive capacity of an artillery unit.

fireproof — *adj.* resistant to fire and fierce heat. — *verb* to make fireproof.

fire raiser an arsonist.

fire-raising *noun* arson.

fireside *noun* the area round a fireplace, especially as a symbol of home.

fire station a fire brigade's headquarters, housing its fire engines, etc.

firetrap *noun* **1** a building without adequate escape routes in case of fire. **2** a building likely to burn easily.

firewall *noun* **1** a partitition or wall designed to check the spread of fire. **2** *Comput.* software that protects a network against unauthorized users.

firewater *noun colloq.* alcoholic spirit.

firewood *noun* wood for burning as fuel.

firework *noun* **1** a device containing combustible chemicals, designed to produce spectacular coloured sparks, flares, etc, often with accompanying loud bangs, when ignited. **2** (**fireworks**) a show at which such devices are let off for entertainment. **3** (**fireworks**) *colloq.* a show of anger or bad temper.

firing line the front line of battle. — **in the firing line** in a prominent position, liable to get shot at or criticized.

firing squad a detachment of soldiers with the job of shooting a condemned person.

firm[1] — *adj.* **1** strong; steady. **2** solid; not soft or yielding. **3** definite: *a firm offer.* **4** determined; resolute. **5** *said of a mouth or chin* suggesting determination. — *adv.* firmly: *hold firm to one's promise.* — *verb* to make firm or secure. — **firm up** to become firm or firmer. **firm something up** to make it firmer or more definite: *can we firm up the plans for your visit?* [from Latin *firmus*]

⬛ *adj.* **1** strong, steady, stable, sturdy, fixed, embedded, fast, tight, secure, fastened, anchored, immovable, motionless, stationary. **2** solid, hard, unyielding, set, stiff, rigid, inflexible, dense, compressed, compact, concentrated. **3** definite, settled, committed. **4** determined, resolute, adamant, unshakable, dogged, unwavering, strict, constant, steadfast, staunch, dependable, true, sure, convinced.

⬛ *adj.* **1** unsteady. **2** soft, flabby. **4** hesitant.

firm[2] *noun* a business company. [from Spanish *firma*, signature]

⬛ company, corporation, business, enterprise, concern, house, establishment, institution, organization, association, partnership, syndicate, conglomerate.

firmament *noun old literary use* the sky. [from Latin *firmamentum*]

firmware *noun Comput.* software permanently held in a computer's read-only memory, eg the operating system, a particular programming language or word-processor.

first — *adj.* **1** earliest in time or order. **2** foremost in importance: *first prize.* **3** basic: *first principles.* **4** *Mus.* having the higher part. **5** denoting the lowest forward gear in a motor vehicle. — *adv.* **1** before anything or anyone else. **2** foremost: *got in feet first.* **3** before doing anything else: *first make sure of the facts.* **4** for the first time: *since I first saw her.* **5** rather; preferably: *I'd die first.* — *noun* **1** a first person or thing. **2** a first occurrence of something; something never done before. **3** first-class honours in a university degree. **4** the beginning: *from first to last.* — **at first** at the beginning. **at first hand** directly from the original source. **be the first to do something** to be most willing to do it. **first and last** essentially. **first thing** *colloq.* early; before anything else. **in the first place** firstly. **not have the first idea** or **know the first thing about something** *colloq.* to be completely ignorant about it. [from Anglo-Saxon *fyrest*]

⬛ *adj.* **1** earliest, earlier, original, prior, initial, opening, introductory, preliminary, primitive, primeval, oldest, eldest, senior. **2** chief, main, key, cardinal, principal, head, leading, ruling, sovereign, highest, uppermost, paramount, primary, prime, predominant, pre-eminent. **3** basic, fundamental, elementary, primary. *adv.* **1** initially, beforehand, originally. **3** to begin with, to start with, at the outset, initially. **4** originally, initially. **5** in preference, rather, sooner.

⬛ *adj.* **1** last, final.

first aid immediate emergency treatment given to an injured or ill person.

first-born — *noun* the eldest child in a family. — *adj.* eldest.

first class 1 the highest grade, eg of travelling accommodation, of academic performance, etc. **2** the category of mail most speedily delivered.

first-class — *adj.* **1** of the first class. **2** excellent. — *adv.* by first-class mail or transport.

first cousin see COUSIN.

first-day cover a stamped envelope postmarked with the stamp's date of issue.

first-degree *adj.* **1** *Medicine* denoting the least severe type of burn, in which only the outer layer of the skin is damaged. It is characterized by pain and reddening of the skin surface. **2** *North Amer. Legal* denoting the most serious of the three levels of murder.

first floor 1 the floor above the ground floor. **2** *North Amer.* the ground floor.

first foot the first person to enter one's house in the new year.

first-foot *verb trans., intrans.* to visit as first foot.

first fruits 1 the first produce of the season. **2** the first results or proceeds from an enterprise.

first-generation *adj.* denoting the first or earliest stage in technological development: *a first-generation missile.*

first-hand *adj.* direct; from the original source.

First Lady *North Amer., esp. US* the wife of the American President.

first light dawn.

firstly *adv.* first; in the first place; to begin with.

First Minister the chief minister of some governing bodies, such as the Northern Ireland Assembly and the Scottish Parliament.

first name one's personal name as distinct from one's family name or surname. — **be on first-name terms** to be friendly enough to address one another by first names.

⬛ forename, Christian name, baptismal name, given name.

first night the first public performance of a play, etc.

first offender a person found guilty for the first time of a crime.

first officer or **first mate** the officer second in command on a merchant ship.

first-past-the-post *adj.* of an election system in which voters have one vote only and whoever gets most votes wins.

first person see PERSON.

first-rate *adj.* **1** of the highest quality. **2** splendid; fine.

⬛ **1** first-class, A1, second-to-none, matchless, peerless, top, *colloq.* top-notch, top-flight, leading, supreme, superior, prime. **2** splendid, fine, superb, excellent, outstanding, superlative, exceptional, admirable.

⬛ INFERIOR.

first school a primary school.

first-strike capability *Mil.* the capability of a state to launch an initial nuclear attack with long-range missiles or aircraft.

First World the richest and technologically most developed countries of the world.

firth *noun* especially in Scotland, a river estuary or an inlet. [from Norse *fjörthr*]

FIS *abbrev.* Family Income Supplement.

fiscal — *adj.* **1** relating to government finances or revenue. **2** relating to financial matters generally. — *noun Scot.* the procurator fiscal. [from Latin *fiscus*, purse, state treasury]

fiscal drag *Econ.* the effect of inflation on tax revenues. If tax allowances are not kept in line with inflation, individuals pay relatively higher amounts of tax, thereby effectively reducing net incomes; this in turn reduces demand for goods and services.

fish — *noun* (**fish, fishes**) **1** any cold-blooded aquatic vertebrate that has no legs, and typically possesses paired fins, breathes by means of gills, and has a bony or cartilaginous skeleton and a body covered with scales. **2** (in compounds) any of various water-inhabiting creatures: *shellfish/jellyfish*. **3** the flesh of fish as food. **4** *derog. colloq.* a person: *an odd fish*. — *verb* **1** *intrans.* to try to catch (fish). **2** to try to catch fish in (a river, etc). **3** *intrans.* to search or grope: *fished in her bag for a pen*. **4** (*also* **fish something out**) to retrieve. **5** *intrans.* (**fish for something**) to seek information, compliments, etc by indirect means. — **drink like a fish** *colloq.* to be in the habit of drinking a lot of alcohol. **have other fish to fry** *colloq.* to have other, more important, things to do. **like a fish out of water** *colloq.* ill at ease in uncongenial company or surroundings. [from Anglo-Saxon *fisc*]

⊟ *verb* **1** angle, trawl. **3** delve, hunt. **4** retrieve, take out, extract, find, produce, come up with, dredge up, haul up. **5** seek, invite, solicit.

. . . .

Types of fish include: bloater, brisling, cod, coley, Dover sole, haddock, hake, halibut, herring, jellied eel, kipper, mackerel, pilchard, plaice, rainbow trout, salmon, sardine, sole, sprat, trout, tuna, turbot, whitebait; bass, Bombay duck, bream, brill, carp, catfish, chub, conger eel, cuttlefish, dab, dace, dogfish, dory, eel, goldfish, guppy, marlin, minnow, monkfish, mullet, octopus, perch, pike, piranha, roach, shark, skate, snapper, squid, stickleback, stingray, sturgeon, swordfish, tench, whiting; clam, cockle, crab, crayfish, *US* crawfish, king prawn, lobster, mussel, oyster, prawn, scallop, shrimp, whelk.

fishcake *noun* a breadcrumb-coated flat round cake of cooked fish and potato.

fisher *noun* **1** *old use* a fisherman. **2** an animal that catches fish.

fisherman *noun* a person who fishes as a job or hobby.

fishery *noun* (PL. **fisheries**) **1** an area of sea where fishing takes place. **2** the business of catching fish.

fish-eye lens a camera lens with an extremely wide angle and a small focal length, giving an angle of view of almost 180°.

fish finger an oblong, breadcrumb-coated piece of fish.

fish hook a hook with barbs for gripping the jaw of a fish taking the bait.

fishing *noun* the sport or business of catching fish.

. . . .

⊟ angling, trawling.

. . . .

fishing line a strong nylon, etc line with a fish hook.

fishing rod a long flexible rod to which a fishing-line is attached.

fishmonger *noun* a dealer in fish.

fishnet *adj.* having an open mesh like netting.

fish slice a kitchen tool with a flat slotted head, for lifting and turning food in a frying-pan, etc.

fishwife *noun* a woman who guts or sells fish, in tradition typically loud-voiced and coarse-mannered.

fishy *adj.* (**fishier, fishiest**) **1** of or like a fish. **2** *colloq.* odd; suspicious.

fissile *adj.* **1** *Physics, said of a chemical substance* capable of undergoing nuclear fission. **2** *Geol., said of certain rocks, eg shale* readily splitting along closely spaced parallel planes to form thin sheets. [from Latin *fissilis*, that can be split]

fission /ˈfɪʃən/ *noun* **1** a splitting or division. **2** *Biol.* a method of asexual reproduction in which a cell or a single-celled organism (eg an amoeba) divides into two or more equal parts which eventually develop into new individuals capable of independent existence. **3** *Physics*. See NUCLEAR FISSION. [from Latin *fissio*, splitting]

fissionable *adj.* capable of nuclear fission.

fissure /ˈfɪʃə(r)/ — *noun* **1** *Anat.* any narrow cleft or groove that divides the brain, liver, or certain other body organs into a number of lobes. **2** *Geol.* any long narrow crack or fracture, especially in a body of rock, the Earth's surface, or a volcano. — *verb* to crack, cleave, or divide. [from Latin *fissura*, split]

fist *noun* **1** a clenched hand. **2** *colloq.* a hand. **3** *colloq.* a person's handwriting. [from Anglo-Saxon *fyst*]

fistful *noun* (PL. **fistfuls**) an amount that can be held in a closed hand.

fisticuffs *pl. noun humorous* fighting with fists. [from *fisty*, of the fist + CUFF²]

fistula *noun Pathol.* an abnormal connection between two internal organs or body cavities, or between an internal organ or body cavity and the exterior, usually caused by infection or injury. Fistulas sometimes develop as a complication after surgery. [from Latin *fistula*, tube, ulcer]

fit¹ — *verb* (**fitted, fitting**) **1** *trans., intrans.* to be, or be made, the right shape or size for something. **2** *intrans.* (**fit in** or **into something**) to be small or few enough to be contained in it. **3** to be suitable or appropriate for: *a punishment that fits the crime.* **4** *trans., intrans.* to be consistent or compatible with something: *a theory that fits the facts.* **5** (**fit together** or **in**) to insert or place in position. **6** to fix or install. **7** to equip. **8** (**fit someone for something**) to make them suitable: *qualities that fit her for the job.* **9** to try clothes on (someone) to see where adjustment is needed. — *noun* the way something fits: *a good fit.* — *adj.* (**fitter, fittest**) **1** (**fit for something**) suited to it; good enough for it. **2** healthy, especially because of exercise; healthy enough. **3** about to do something, or apparently so: *looked fit to drop.* — *adv.* enough to do something: *laughed fit to burst.* — **fit in** to behave in a suitable or accepted way. **fit someone** or **something in** to find time to deal with them. **fit something out** to equip it as necessary: *fit out the ship.* **fit something up** to equip it. **fit someone up** *colloq.* to incriminate them. **see** or **think fit** *ironic* to choose to do something, especially unwise. [from Middle English *fitten*]

. . . .

⊟ *verb* **1** tailor, alter, modify, change, adjust, adapt, shape, fashion. **2** go. **3** match, correspond to, conform to, suit, harmonize, go, belong. **4** match, follow, agree with, concur with, tally with, correspond with, conform with. **5** dovetail, interlock, join. *adj.* **1** suitable, appropriate, apt, fitting, correct, right, proper, ready, prepared, able, capable, competent, qualified, eligible, worthy. **2** healthy, well, able-bodied, in good form, in good shape, sound, sturdy, strong, robust, hale and hearty. **3** ready. **fit out** equip, rig out, kit out, outfit, provide, supply, furnish, prepare, arm.

🗷 *adj.* **1** unsuitable, unworthy. **2** unfit.

. . . .

fit² *noun* **1** a sudden attack of one or more symptoms, usually of an involuntary and relatively violent nature, eg convulsions in grand mal epilepsy (epileptic fit), or paroxysms of coughing (coughing fit). **2** a burst, spell, or bout. — **by** or **in fits and starts** in irregular spells; spasmodically. **in fits** *colloq.* laughing uncontrollably.

. . . .

⊟ **1** seizure, attack, convulsion, spasm, paroxysm. **2** burst, spell, bout, outbreak, surge, outburst, eruption, explosion.

. . . .

fitful *adj.* irregular, spasmodic, or intermittent; not continuous. [from FIT²]

. . . .

⊟ irregular, intermittent, spasmodic, sporadic, erratic, occasional, uneven, broken, disturbed.

🗷 steady, regular.

. . . .

fitment *noun* a fixed piece of equipment or furniture.

fitness *noun* being fit.

fitted *adj.* **1** made to fit closely: *fitted sheets.* **2** *said of a carpet* covering a floor entirely. **3** fixed; built-in: *fitted cup-*

boards. **4** *said of a kitchen, etc* with built-in shelves, cupboards, etc.

. . . .

▣ **3** built-in, permanent.
▣ **3** free-standing.

. . . .

fitter *noun* a person who installs, adjusts, or repairs machinery, equipment, etc.

fitting — *adj.* suitable. — *noun* **1** (*usually* **fittings**) a piece of fitted furniture or equipment. **2** an act of trying on a specially made piece of clothing, to see where adjustment is necessary.

. . . .

▣ *adj.* suitable, appropriate, fit, apt, correct, right, proper, seemly, *old use* meet, desirable, deserved. *noun* **1** equipment, furnishings, furniture, fixture, installation, fitment, extra, connection, attachment, accessory, part, component, piece, unit.
▣ *adj.* unsuitable, improper.

. . . .

five — *noun* **1** the number or figure 5; any symbol for this number. **2** the age of 5. **3** something, especially a garment, or a person, whose size is denoted by the number 5. **4** 5 o'clock. **5** a set of 5 people or things. **6** a playing-card with 5 pips. **7** a score of 5 points. — *adj.* **1** 5 in number. **2** aged 5. [from Anglo-Saxon *fif*]

fivefold — *adj.* **1** equal to five times as much or many. **2** divided into, or consisting of, five parts. — *adv.* by five times as much.

fiver *noun colloq.* a five-pound note.

fives *sing. noun* a game like squash, in which a gloved hand or a bat is used to hit the ball.

fix — *verb* **1** to attach or place firmly. **2** to mend or repair. **3** to direct; to concentrate: *fixed his eyes on her.* **4** to transfix: *fixed him with a stare.* **5** to arrange or agree (a time). **6** to establish (the time of an occurrence). **7** *colloq.* to arrange the result of (a race, trial, etc) dishonestly. **8** *colloq.* to bribe or threaten into agreement. **9** *colloq.* to thwart, punish, or kill. **10** to make (a dye) or the image in (a photograph) permanent by the use of chemicals. **11** *North Amer.* to prepare (a meal, etc). **12** *North Amer.* to tidy. — *noun* **1** *colloq.* a difficulty; a spot of trouble. **2** *slang* an act of injecting a narcotic drug, etc. **3** a calculation of the position of a ship, etc. — **fix on something** to choose it. **fix something up 1** to arrange it (eg a meeting). **2** to get a place ready for some purpose. **3** to set it up, especially temporarily. **fix someone up with something** to provide them with what is needed. [from Latin *fixare*]

. . . .

▣ *verb* **1** attach, fasten, secure, tie, bind, join, connect, link, couple, anchor, pin, nail, rivet, stick, glue, cement, set, harden, solidify, stiffen, stabilize, plant, root, implant, embed, establish, install, locate, position. **2** mend, repair, correct, rectify, adjust, restore. **3** direct, concentrate, focus, turn. **5** arrange, set, specify, define, agree on, decide, determine, settle, resolve, finalize. **6** establish, determine. *noun* **1** dilemma, quandary, predicament, plight, difficulty, *colloq.* hole, corner, *colloq.* spot, mess, muddle. **fix up 1** arrange, organize, plan, settle, sort out, lay on, produce, bring about. **2** prepare, furnish, equip. **fix someone up with something** provide, supply.

. . . .

fixated *adj.* **1** affected by or engaged in fixation. **2** obsessively attached.

fixation *noun* **1** the act of fixing or state of being fixated. **2** an (often abnormal) attachment, preoccupation, or obsession. **3** *Psychol.* a strong attachment of a person to another person, an object, or a particular means of gratification during childhood. **4** *Biochem.* (**nitrogen fixation**) in the nitrogen cycle, the process whereby nitrogen in the atmosphere is converted into nitrogen-containing compounds, especially nitrates, by nitrifying bacteria and blue-green algae in the soil. **5** *Biol.* the procedure whereby cells or tissues are killed, hardened,

and their shape and structure preserved with suitable chemical agents before they are stained and examined under a microscope. **6** *Chem.* the conversion of a chemical substance into a form that does not evaporate, ie a non-volatile or solid form. **7** *Psychol.* inability to change a particular way of thinking or acting, which has become habitual as a result of repeated reinforcement or frustration. [from Latin *fixare*, to fix]

. . . .

▣ **2** preoccupation, obsession, mania, fetish, *colloq.* thing, infatuation, compulsion, *colloq.* hang-up, complex.

. . . .

fixative *noun* **1** a liquid sprayed on a drawing, painting, or photograph to preserve and protect it. **2** a liquid used to hold eg dentures in place. **3** a substance added to perfume to stop it evaporating. [from Latin *fixare*, to fix]

fixed *adj.* **1** fastened; immovable. **2** unvarying; set or established: *fixed ideas.* **3** *said of a gaze or expression* steady; concentrated; rigid. **4** *said of a point* stationary. **5** permanent: *a fixed address.* **6** *colloq.* supplied, especially financially: *how are you fixed for cash?*

. . . .

▣ **1** steady, secure, firm, fast, rooted. **2** unvarying, set, established, definite, rigid, inflexible. **3** steady, constant, unwavering, concentrated, rigid.
▣ **1** unsteady, insecure. **2** variable.

. . . .

fixedly *adv.* steadily.

fixed star the term formerly used to distinguish a star outside the solar system, which because of its distance from the earth appears to remain almost stationary in the sky, from a planet, which was referred to as a 'wandering star'.

fixer *noun* **1** *Photog.* a solution for fixing photographic images. **2** *slang* a person who arranges things, especially illegally.

fixity *noun* the quality of being fixed, steady, unchanging, unmoving, or immovable.

fixture *noun* **1** a permanently fixed piece of furniture or equipment. **2** a match or other event in a sports calendar; the date for this. [from Latin *fixura*, from *figere*, to fasten]

fizz — *verb intrans.* **1** *said of a liquid* to give off bubbles. **2** to hiss. — *noun* **1** a fizzing sound or sensation; fizziness. **2** vivacity; high spirits. **3** *old colloq. use* champagne. [from FIZZLE]

. . . .

▣ *verb* **1** effervesce, sparkle, bubble, froth, foam. **2** fizzle, hiss, sizzle, sputter, spit.

. . . .

fizziness *noun* being fizzy.

fizzle *verb intrans.* **1** to make a faint hiss. **2** (**fizzle out**) to come to a feeble end. [from Middle English *fysel*, to break wind]

fizzy *adj.* effervescent.

. . . .

▣ effervescent, sparkling, aerated, carbonated, gassy, bubbly, bubbling, frothy, foaming.

. . . .

fjord or **fiord** /ˈfiːɔːd, fjɔːd/ *noun* a long narrow steep-sided inlet of the sea in a mountainous coast, eg in Norway, Greenland, or New Zealand, formed by the flooding of a previously glaciated valley. [from Norse *fiörthr*]

FL or **Fla.** *abbrev.* Florida.

flab *noun colloq.* excess flesh or fat on the body. [from FLABBY]

flabbergast *verb colloq.* to amaze; to astonish.

. . . .

▣ amaze, astonish, confound, astound, stagger, dumbfound, overwhelm, *colloq.* bowl over.

. . . .

flabbily *adv.* in a flabby way.

flabbiness *noun* being flabby.

flabby *adj.* (**flabbier, flabbiest**) *derog.* **1** *said of flesh* sagging, not firm. **2** *said of a person* having excess or sagging flesh. **3** lacking vigour; feeble; ineffective. [altered form of FLAPPY]

🔳 **1** fleshy, soft, yielding, flaccid, limp, floppy, drooping, hanging, sagging, slack, loose, lax. **3** feeble, ineffective, weak.
🔳 **1** firm. **3** vigorous, effective, strong.

flaccid /ˈflaksɪd, ˈflasɪd/ *adj.* limp and soft, not firm. [from Latin *flaccidus*]

flaccidity *noun* being flaccid.

flag [1] — *noun* **1** a usually rectangular piece of cloth with a distinctive design, flown from a pole to represent a country, party, etc, or used for signalling. **2** national identity represented by a flag. **3** a small paper emblem with a pin, eg to wear in exchange for supporting a charity, or fixed as a marker to a map, etc. **4** a marker generally. **5** an adjustable plate in a taxi, raised to show that the taxi is for hire. — *verb* (**flagged, flagging**) **1** to mark with a flag, tag, or symbol. **2** (**flag someone** or **something down**) to signal a vehicle or driver to stop. **3** to signal a message using flags. — **fly the flag** or **keep the flag flying** to maintain a show of support for one's country or other affiliation. **with flags flying** with flying colours; triumphantly.

🔳 *noun* **1** ensign, pennant, colours, standard, banner, streamer, jack. *verb* **1** mark, label, tag, note. **2** signal, motion, hail.

flag [2] *verb intrans.* (**flagged, flagging**) to grow tired or feeble; to lose vigour or enthusiasm.

🔳 tire, weary, wilt, droop, sag, flop, weaken, slow, falter, lessen, diminish, decline, fall (off), abate, subside, sink, slump, dwindle, peter out, fade, fail, faint.
🔳 revive.

flag [3] — *noun* a flagstone. — *verb* (**flagged, flagging**) to pave with flagstones. [from Norse *flaga*, slab]

flag [4] *noun* any of various plants with long sword-shaped leaves, especially a species of iris (*Iris pseudacorus*), native to wet swampy areas of Europe, W Asia, and N Africa, that has yellow flowers.

flag day a day chosen by a charity for stationing collectors in the street who distribute flags or stickers in return for donations.

flagellant /ˈfladʒələnt/ *noun* a person who indulges in flagellation.

flagellate /ˈfladʒəleɪt, ˈfladʒələt/ — *verb* (pronounced -leɪt) to whip, as a means of religious discipline or for sexual stimulation. — *adj.* (pronounced -lət) **1** *Biol.* denoting a single-celled protozoan animal that has one or more long whip-like structures or flagella that are used to propel it through water. **2** of or relating to flagella. **3** whiplike. — *noun* (pronounced -lət) any of a group of single-celled protozoan animals, including free-living marine and freshwater species, as well as parasitic species, characterized by the possession of one or more flagella. [from Latin *flagellum*, whip]

flagellation *noun* the act of scourging or whipping, for religious or sexual purposes.

flagellum /fləˈdʒɛləm/ *noun* (PL. **flagella**) *Biol.* the long whip-like structure that projects from the cell surface of sperm, and certain bacteria, unicellular algae, and protozoans. The beating movement of the flagellum propels the cell through a liquid medium such as water. [from Latin *flagellum*, whip]

flageolet /fladʒoʊˈlɛt, ˈfladʒoʊlɛt/ *noun* a high-pitched woodwind instrument similar to the recorder. [from French *flageolet*]

flag of convenience the flag of a foreign country in which a ship is registered to avoid taxation, etc in its real country of origin.

flag of truce a white flag flown to show willingness to stop fighting.

flagon *noun* a large bottle or jug with a narrow neck, usually with a spout and handle. [from Old French *flacon*]

flagpole or **flagstaff** *noun* the pole from which a flag is flown.

flagrancy /ˈfleɪɡrənsɪ/ *noun* being flagrant; notoriety.

flagrant /ˈfleɪɡrənt/ *adj.*, *said of something bad* undisguised; glaring; brazen or barefaced: *a flagrant lie*. [from Latin *flagrare*, to blaze]

flagship *noun* **1** the ship that carries, and flies the flag of, the fleet commander. **2** the leading ship in a shipping-line. **3** a commercial company's leading product.

flagstone *noun* a large flat stone for paving.

flag-waving *noun* an excessive show of patriotic feeling.

flail — *noun* a threshing tool consisting of a long handle with a wooden or metal bar loosely attached to the end. — *verb* **1** (**flail about** or **around**) to wave about violently. **2** to beat with or as if with a flail. [from Anglo-Saxon *fligel*]

🔳 *verb* **1** thresh about, thrash about. **2** beat, whip, thresh, thrash.

flair *noun* **1** a natural ability or talent for something. **2** stylishness; dash. [from French *flair*, sense of smell]

🔳 **1** ability, talent, skill, aptitude, faculty, gift, facility, knack, mastery, genius, feel. **2** style, stylishness, dash, elegance, panache, taste, discernment, acumen.
🔳 **1** inability, ineptitude.

flak *noun* **1** anti-aircraft fire. **2** *colloq.* unfriendly criticism. [from German *Fliegerabwehrkanone*, flyer-defence-gun]

flake — *noun* (*often in compounds*) a small flat particle: *snowflakes/flakes of plaster*. — *verb* **1** *intrans.* to come off in flakes: *flaking paint*. **2** *trans.* to break (eg cooked fish) into flakes. — **flake out** *colloq.* to faint or fall asleep from exhaustion.

🔳 *noun* scale, sliver, wafer, chip, splinter, peeling, paring, shaving. *verb* **1** peel, chip, splinter, scale.

flak jacket a metal-reinforced jacket worn for protection by police or soldiers.

flaky *adj.* (**flakier, flakiest**) **1** made of or tending to form flakes. **2** *colloq.* crazy.

flambé /ˈflɑːmbeɪ/ — *adj.*, *said of food* soaked in brandy and set alight before serving. — *verb* (**flambéed, flambéing**) to serve (food) in this way. [from French *flamber*, to expose to flame]

flamboyance *noun* being flamboyant.

flamboyant *adj.* **1** *said of a person or behaviour* dashing, colourful, and exuberant. **2** *said of clothing or colouring* bright, bold, and striking. [from French *flamboyer*, to blaze]

🔳 SHOWY, OSTENTATIOUS, FLASHY, GAUDY, COLOURFUL, BRILLIANT, DAZZLING, STRIKING, EXTRAVAGANT, RICH, ELABORATE, ORNATE, FLORID.
🔳 MODEST, RESTRAINED.

flame — *noun* **1** any of the visible flickering streams of hot luminous gases or vapours produced by the rapid combustion of ignited material: *burst into flames/go up in flames*. **2** a strong passion: *the flame of love*. **3** a bright reddish-orange colour. **4** *colloq.* an insulting message sent by electronic mail. — *verb* **1** to apply a flame to (an object or substance). **2** *intrans.* to burn with flames; to blaze. **3** *intrans.* to shine brightly. **4** *intrans.* to explode with anger. **5** *intrans.* to get red and hot: *flaming cheeks*. **6** *colloq.* to send an insulting electronic mail message to (someone). — **fan the flames** or **add fuel to the flames** to stir up already existing feeling or unrest. [from Latin *flamma*]

◼ *noun* **1** fire, blaze, light, brightness, heat, warmth. **2** passion, ardour, fervour, intensity, zeal, intensity, radiance. *verb* **1** burn, blaze, flare. **2** shine, beam, glare, flash, flare. **4** glow, radiate.

flamenco /fləˈmɛŋkoʊ/ *noun* (PL. **flamencos**) a rhythmical, emotionally stirring type of Spanish gypsy music; the dance performed to it. [from Spanish *flamenco*, Flemish]

flameproof *adj.* not easily damaged by fire or fierce heat.

flame retardant a material that burns very slowly if at all, and is used to make clothing, etc.

flame-thrower *noun* a gun that discharges a stream of burning liquid, used as a weapon or to clear plants from ground.

flaming *adj.* **1** blazing. **2** bright; glowing. **3** *colloq.* very angry; furious; violent. **4** *colloq.* damned: *that flaming dog!*

◼ **1** blazing, burning, alight, aflame, fiery. **2** bright, glowing, red-hot, brilliant, scintillating. **3** furious, violent, aroused, impassioned, hot, raging, frenzied, intense, vivid.

flamingo *noun* (PL. **flamingos**, **flamingoes**) *noun* any of several large wading birds, found in flocks of many thousands on lakes and lagoons in tropical regions, with white or pinkish plumage, a long neck and long legs, webbed feet, and a broad down-curving bill. [perhaps from Spanish, as for FLAMENCO, or from Provençal *flamenc*, flaming]

flammable *adj.* liable to catch fire; inflammable. [from Latin *flammare*, to blaze]

◼ inflammable, ignitable, combustible.
◲ non-flammable, incombustible, flameproof, fire-resistant.

flan *noun* an open pastry or sponge case with a savoury or fruit filling. [from Old French *flaon*]

flange /flandʒ/ *noun* a broad flat projecting rim, eg round a wheel, added for strength or for connecting with another object or part. [from Old French *flanche*]

flank — *noun* **1** the side of an animal or human body, between ribs and hip. **2** the side of anything, especially of a body of troops or a fleet drawn up in formation. — *verb* to be or move beside. [from French *flanc*]

◼ *noun* **1** side, hip, loin. **2** side, edge, wing, quarter, thigh. *verb* edge, fringe, skirt, line, border, bound, confine, wall, screen.

flannel — *noun* **1** a soft woollen cloth used to make clothes. **2** (**flannels**) trousers made of flannel. **3** a small square of towelling for washing oneself with. **4** *colloq.* flattery, or meaningless talk intended to hide one's ignorance or true intentions. — *verb* (**flanneled**, **flanneling**) **1** *intrans.*, *trans.* to flatter, persuade by flattery, or talk flannel. **2** to rub with a flannel. [from Welsh *gwlanen*, from *gwlan*, wool]

flannelette *noun* cotton cloth with a soft brushed surface.

flap — *verb* (**flapped**, **flapping**) **1** *trans.*, *intrans.* to wave up and down or backwards and forwards. **2** *trans.*, *intrans.*, *said of a bird* to move (the wings) in this way; to fly with pronounced wing movements. **3** *intrans.* *colloq.* to get into a panic or flustered state. — *noun* **1** a broad piece or part of something attached along one edge and hanging loosely: *pocket flaps.* **2** an act, sound, or impact of flapping. **3** *colloq.* a panic; a flustered state. **4** a hinged section on an aircraft wing adjusted to control speed. [imitative]

◼ *verb* **1** wave, flutter, vibrate, agitate, shake, wag, swing, swish, thrash, beat. **2** flutter. *noun* **1** fold, fly, lapel, tab, lug, tag, tail, skirt, aileron. **3** panic, commotion, state, fuss, commotion, fluster, agitation, flutter, dither, *colloq.* tizzy.

flapjack *noun* **1** a thick biscuit made with oats and syrup. **2** *North Amer.* a pancake. [from FLAP + JACK]

flapper *noun* **1** a fashionable and frivolous young woman of the 1920s. **2** something or someone that flaps.

flappy *adj.* (**flappier**, **flappiest**) **1** tending to flap or wave up and down. **2** *colloq.* nervous, and likely to panic.

flare — *verb* **1** *intrans.* to burn with sudden brightness. **2** *intrans.* to explode into anger. **3** *trans.*, *intrans.* to widen towards the edge. — *noun* **1** a sudden blaze of bright light. **2** a device composed of combustible material that produces a sudden blaze of intense light, and is activated to give warning, emergency illumination (eg on an airfield), or a distress signal (eg at sea). **3** in chemical plants and oil refineries, a device for burning off superfluous combustible gas or oil, in order to ensure its safe disposal. **4** *Astron.* (*also* **solar flare**) a sudden brilliant eruption on the Sun, from which a stream of charged atomic particles is ejected into space, thought to be caused by the release of magnetic energy associated with a sunspot. **5** a flared edge. **6** (**flares**) *colloq.* flared trousers. — **flare up 1** to blaze suddenly. **2** to explode into anger.

◼ *verb* **1** flame, burn, blaze, glare, flash, flicker, burst. **2** explode, erupt, *colloq.* blow up. **3** broaden, widen, flare out, spread out, splay. *noun* **1** blaze, flame, glare, flash, flicker, burst. **5** broadening, widening, splay. **flare up 1** blaze, flame. **2** erupt, break out, explode, *colloq.* blow up.

flare-up *noun* **1** a sudden blaze. **2** an explosion of anger or feeling.

flash — *noun* **1** a sudden brief blaze of visible light or flame, eg when a weapon is fired. **2** an instant. **3** a brief but intense occurrence: *a flash of inspiration.* **4** a fleeting look on a face. **5** the brief brilliant light produced by a flashbulb or flashgun, used to illuminate a photographic subject. **6** a camera flashgun. **7** a brief news announcement on radio or television. **8** an emblem on a military uniform, etc indicating one's unit. **9** a sudden rush of water down a river. **10** a sudden and temporary increase in brightness and temperature of an evolving star. — *verb* **1** *intrans.*, *trans.* to shine briefly or intermittently. **2** *intrans.*, *trans.* to appear or cause to appear briefly; to move or pass quickly. **3** *intrans.*, *said of the eyes* to brighten with anger, etc. **4** to give (a smile or look) briefly. **5** to display briefly; to flourish, brandish, or flaunt. **6** to send (a message) by radio, satellite, etc. **7** *trans.*, *intrans.* to emit or cause to emit flashes of light, eg as a warning signal. **8** to sparkle brilliantly. **9** *intrans.* *colloq.*, *said of a man* to expose the genitals. — *adj.* **1** sudden and severe: *flash floods.* **2** quick: *flash freezing.* **3** *colloq.* smart and expensive. — **a flash in the pan** *colloq.* an impressive but untypical success, unlikely to be repeated. [imitative]

◼ *noun* **1** beam, ray, shaft, spark, blaze, flare, burst, streak, gleam, glint, flicker, twinkle, sparkle, shimmer. **2** instant, second, moment. **3** burst, spark, ray. **4** glimmer, flicker. *verb* **1** shine, glint, flicker, twinkle, sparkle, glitter, shimmer, gleam, beam, light up, flare, blaze. **2** streak, fly, dart, race, dash. **3** glare, gleam, light up, blaze. **8** sparkle, glitter, shimmer, twinkle, gleam.

flashback *noun* a return to the past, especially as a scene in a film, etc.

flashbulb *noun* an oxygen-filled glass bulb containing a flammable filament which may be ignited by a low-voltage current to produce a brief brilliant flash, used (especially formerly) as an artificial light source for illuminating a photographic subject.

flasher *noun* **1** a light that flashes; a device causing a light to do this. **2** *colloq.* a man who exposes his genitals in public.

flashgun *noun* **1** a device, attached to or incorporated within a camera, that holds and fires a flashbulb when the camera shutter opens. **2** any device that produces a brief brilliant flash of light for indoor or night photography.

flashily *adv.* in a flashy way.

flashiness *noun* being flashy.

flashlight *noun North Amer.* a torch.

flashpoint *noun* 1 a stage in a tense situation at which people lose their tempers and become angry or violent. 2 an area of political unrest where violence is liable to break out. 3 *Chem.* the lowest temperature at which the vapour above a volatile liquid, eg petrol or oil, will ignite momentarily on application of a small flame.

flashy *adj.* (**flashier, flashiest**) *colloq.* 1 ostentatiously smart. 2 cheap and showy.

. . . .

⊟ 1 showy, ostentatious, flamboyant, glamorous, bold, jazzy, *colloq.* flash. 2 loud, garish, gaudy, tawdry, cheap, vulgar, tasteless.
🔁 PLAIN, TASTEFUL.

. . . .

flask *noun* 1 (*also* **hip flask**) a small flat leather-cased pocket bottle for alcoholic spirits. 2 a vacuum flask. 3 a vessel with a long narrow neck, usually made of glass, used for holding liquids, especially in chemical experiments. 4 a wooden, iron, or steel box that is used to hold the mould in which a casting is made. [from Latin *flasco*]

flat — *adj.* (**flatter, flattest**) 1 level; horizontal; even. 2 without hollows or prominences. 3 lacking the usual prominence: *a flat nose.* 4 not bent or crumpled. 5 *said of shoes* not having a raised heel. 6 bored; depressed. 7 dull; not lively. 8 toneless and expressionless. 9 *colloq.* definite; downright; emphatic: *a flat refusal.* 10 *said of a tyre* having too little air in it. 11 *said of a drink* having lost its fizziness. 12 *said of a battery* having little or no electrical charge remaining. 13 *said of a price, rate, fee, etc* fixed; unvarying. 14 *Mus.* lower than the correct pitch. 15 *said of paint* matt, not glossy. — *adv.* 1 stretched out rather than curled up, etc. 2 into a flat compact shape: *folds flat for storage.* 3 exactly: *in two minutes flat.* 4 bluntly and emphatically: *I can tell you that flat.* 5 *Mus.* at lower than the correct pitch. — *noun* 1 a set of rooms for living in, especially all on one floor; an apartment. 2 something flat; a flat surface or part. 3 (**flats**) an area of flat land. 4 *colloq.* a flat tyre. 5 *Mus.* a note lowered by a semitone; a sign (♭) indicating this. 6 a flat upright section of stage scenery. 7 (**the flat**) *Racing* the season of flat racing. — **fall flat** *colloq.* to fail to achieve the hoped-for effect. **fall flat on one's face** *colloq.* to fail humiliatingly. **flat broke** *colloq.* completely without money. **flat out** *colloq.* with maximum speed and energy. **that's flat** *colloq.* that's certain or final. [from Norse *flatr*, flat]

. . . .

⊟ *adj.* 1 level, horizontal, even, plane, smooth, uniform, unbroken, outstretched, prostrate, prone, recumbent, reclining, low. 2 even, plane, smooth, uniform. 4 smooth. 7, 8 dull, boring, monotonous, tedious, uninteresting, unexciting, stale, lifeless, dead, spiritless, lacklustre, vapid, insipid, weak, watery, empty, pointless. 9 definite, downright, emphatic, absolute, utter, total, unequivocal, categorical, positive, unconditional, unqualified, point-blank, direct, straight, explicit, plain, final. 10 deflated, punctured, burst, collapsed. *noun* 1 apartment, penthouse, maisonette, tenement, flatlet, rooms, suite, *colloq.* bedsit(ter). 2 level. **flat out** at top speed, at full speed, all out, for all one is worth.
🔁 *adj.* 1 vertical, bumpy. 2 bumpy, lumpy, rough, hilly. 3 prominent, large, protruberant, protruding, bulbous. 5 high, heeled. 7, 8 exciting, full.

. . . .

flatfish *noun* (PL. **flatfish, flatfishes**) any of about 500 species of fishes living on the sea bed, widely distributed in shallow waters in cool temperate regions of the Atlantic, Pacific, and Indian Oceans, and having a body that is flat horizontally rather than vertically, with both eyes on the upper surface of the body. Flatfish include many com-

mercially important food fish, eg sole, halibut, turbot, plaice, dab, flounder, brill.

flat foot a condition in which the arch of the instep of the foot has fallen, so that the sole lies flat against the ground.

flat-footed *adj.* 1 having flat feet. 2 *derog.* clumsy or tactless.

flatiron /ˈflataɪən/ *noun Hist.* a clothes-pressing iron heated on the fire or stove.

flatlet *noun* a small flat.

flatline *verb intrans. slang* to die.

flatly *adv.* in a flat way; firmly, definitely.

flat race a horse race over a course without jumps.

flat racing the sport of racing horses on courses with no jumps.

flat spin 1 the uncontrolled rotation of an aircraft or projectile in a horizontal plane around a vertical axis. 2 *colloq.* a state of agitated bustle.

flatten *verb* (**flattened, flattening**) 1 *trans., intrans.* to make or become flat or flatter. 2 *colloq.* to knock to the ground. 3 *colloq.* to overcome, crush, or subdue utterly.

. . . .

⊟ 1 smooth, iron, press, roll, crush, squash, compress, level, even out. 2 knock down, prostrate, *colloq.* floor, fell, demolish, raze. 3 overcome, crush, subdue, overwhelm, defeat, *colloq.* floor, demolish.

. . . .

flatter *verb* (**flattered, flattering**) 1 to compliment excessively or insincerely. 2 *said of a picture or description* to represent (someone or something) over-favourably. 3 to show off well: *a dress that flatters the figure.* 4 to cause to feel honoured; to gratify. — **flatter oneself** to feel pleased, usually smugly and unjustifiably, about something concerning oneself. [from Middle English *flateren*, to fawn upon]

. . . .

⊟ 1 praise, compliment, *colloq.* sweet-talk, adulate, fawn, *colloq.* butter up, wheedle, humour, play up to, court, curry favour with.
🔁 1 criticize.

. . . .

flatterer *noun* a person who flatters.

flattery *noun* (PL. **flatteries**) excessive or insincere praise.

. . . .

⊟ adulation, eulogy, *colloq.* sweet talk, *colloq.* flannel, blarney, cajolery, fawning, toadyism, sycophancy, ingratiation, servility.
🔁 criticism.

. . . .

flatulence *noun* an accumulation of gas in the stomach or intestines, causing discomfort. [from Latin *flatus*, blowing]

flatulent *adj.* 1 suffering from or caused by flatulence. 2 causing flatulence.

flatworm *noun* a flattened worm-like animal with a definite head but without a true body cavity. Free-living flatworms typically feed on small invertebrates; parasitic forms include tapeworms and flukes.

flaunt *verb* to display or parade, in the hope of being admired.

flautist *noun* a flute-player. [from Italian *flautista*, from *flauto*, flute]

flavonoid /ˈfleɪvənɔɪd, ˈflavənɔɪd/ *noun Biochem.* any of a group of organic compounds containing a C_6-C_3-C_6 skeleton, where C_6 is a benzene ring. They include a large number of water-soluble plant pigments, and are responsible for most of the red, pink, and purple colours found in higher plants. [from Latin *flavus*, yellow]

flavour — *noun* 1 the taste of any particular food or drink. 2 a characteristic quality or atmosphere. — *verb* to give flavour to. [from Old French *flaour*]

. . . .

⊟ *noun* 1 taste, tang, smack, savour, relish, zest, *colloq.* zing. 2 quality, atmosphere, property, character, style, aspect, feeling, feel, hint, suggestion, touch, tinge, tone. *verb* season, spice, ginger up, infuse, imbue.

....

flavour enhancer *Food Science* any substance that improves the natural flavour of a food when added to it, without contributing any taste of its own, eg monosodium glutamate, small quantities of sugar, and salt.

flavouring *noun* any substance used to give food flavour.

....

🔲 seasoning, zest, essence, extract, additive.

....

flavourless *adj.* without flavour.

flavoursome *adj.* full of flavour.

flaw *noun* **1** a fault, defect, imperfection, or blemish. **2** a mistake, eg in an argument. [from Norse *flaga*, stone flag]

....

🔲 **1** fault, defect, imperfection, blemish, spot, mark, speck, crack, crevice, fissure, cleft, split, rift, break, fracture. **2** mistake, error, lapse, slip, weakness, shortcoming, failing, fallacy.

....

flawed *adj.* having flaws; imperfect.

....

🔲 imperfect, defective, faulty, blemished, marked, damaged, spoilt, marred, cracked, chipped, broken, unsound, fallacious, erroneous.
🔳 flawless, perfect.

....

flawless *adj.* without flaws; perfect.

....

🔲 perfect, faultless, unblemished, spotless, immaculate, stainless, sound, intact, whole, unbroken, undamaged.
🔳 flawed, imperfect.

....

flax *noun* an annual plant of the genus *Linum* that has blue flowers and is cultivated in many parts of the world for the fibre in its stem, which is used to make linen thread, and the linseed oil in its seeds, which is used as a solvent for paints and varnishes. [from Anglo-Saxon *fleax*]

flaxen *adj.*, *said of hair* very fair.

flay *verb* **1** to strip the skin from. **2** to whip or beat violently. **3** to criticize harshly. [from Anglo-Saxon *flean*]

flea *noun* any of about 1,800 species of wingless bloodsucking insects that live as parasites on mammals (including humans) and some birds. — **a flea in one's ear** *colloq.* a severe scolding. [from Anglo-Saxon]

fleabane *noun* a leafy perennial plant (*Pulicaria dysenterica*), native to marshes in Europe, N Africa, and Asia Minor, that has lance-shaped leaves with wavy margins, and yellow daisy-like flowers, so called because its dried leaves were formerly burned to repel insects.

flea bite 1 the bite of a flea, or an itchy swelling caused by it. **2** a trivial inconvenience.

flea-bitten *adj.* **1** bitten or infested with fleas. **2** dingy; squalid.

flea market *colloq.* a street market selling second-hand goods or clothes.

flea pit *colloq.* a drab cinema or other public building.

fleck *noun* a spot or speck. [from Norse *flekkr*]

....

🔲 spot, speck, speckle, dot, point, mark, streak.

....

flecked *adj.* spotted, dappled.

fled see FLEE.

fledged *adj* **1** *said of a young bird* able to fly. **2** qualified; trained: *a fully fledged doctor.* [from Anglo-Saxon *flycge*, able to fly]

fledgling or **fledgeling** *noun* **1** a young bird that has just grown its feathers and is still unable to fly. **2** a person who is inexperienced. [from *fledge*, ready to fly + -LING]

flee *verb* (PAST TENSE AND PAST PARTICIPLE **fled**) **1** *intrans.* to run away; to take to flight. **2** *trans.* to escape from (danger or a dangerous place). — **flee away** *poetic* to vanish. [from Anglo-Saxon *fleon*, to fly from]

....

🔲 **1** run away, bolt, fly, take flight, take off, make off, cut and run, escape, get away, decamp, abscond, leave, depart, withdraw, retreat, vanish, disappear.
🔳 **1** stay.

....

fleece — *noun* **1** the coat of wool covering the body of a sheep or similar animal. **2** the wool shorn from a single sheep at one time. **3** sheepskin or any soft fabric that resembles a fleece in appearance or texture, used to line garments, etc. **4** a casual jacket or pullover made from soft, thick, synthetic material. — *verb* **1** to shear the wool from (a sheep). **2** *slang* to rob, swindle, or overcharge. [from Anglo-Saxon *flies*]

fleecy *adj.* (**fleecier**, **fleeciest**) woolly, like a fleece.

fleet[1] *noun* **1** a number of ships under one command. **2** a navy. **3** a number of buses, taxis, under the same ownership or management. [from Anglo-Saxon *fleot*, ship]

....

🔲 **1** flotilla, armada, task-force, squadron.

....

fleet[2] *adj. poetic* swift: *fleet of foot.* [from Anglo-Saxon *fleotan*, to float]

fleeting *adj.* passing swiftly; brief; short-lived. [from Anglo-Saxon *fleotan*, to float]

....

🔲 brief, short-lived, short, flying, momentary, ephemeral, transient, transitory, passing, temporary.
🔳 lasting, permanent.

....

Fleming *noun* a native of Flanders or of the Flemish-speaking part of Belgium. [from Anglo-Saxon *Flæming*]

Flemish — *adj.* relating to or belonging to Flanders, or to the Flemings or their language. — *noun* the language of the Flemings; Dutch. See also WALLOON. [from Old Dutch *vlaemsch*]

flesh *noun* **1** the soft muscular tissue of the body of a human or animal, as opposed to the bones or body organs. **2** the soft tissue of an animal, especially that which covers the bones, used as food. **3** the meat of mammals, as distinct from that of fish and, sometimes, birds. **4** the soft edible tissue, or pulp, of a fruit or vegetable. **5** the body as distinct from the soul or spirit; bodily needs. **6** *poetic* mankind. **7** excess fat; plumpness. **8** a yellowish-pink colour. — **flesh and blood** bodily or human nature. **one's flesh and blood** one's family or relations. **flesh something out** to add descriptive detail to it. **in the flesh** in person. [from Anglo-Saxon *flæsc*]

....

🔲 **1** tissue, fat, muscle, brawn, skin.

....

flesh-coloured *adj.* yellowish pink.

fleshiness *noun* being fleshy.

fleshly *adj.* relating to the body as distinct from the soul; worldly.

fleshpots *pl. noun facetious* **1** luxurious living. **2** a place where bodily desires or lusts can be gratified.

flesh wound a superficial wound, not deep enough to damage bone or a bodily organ.

fleshy *adj.* (**fleshier**, **fleshiest**) **1** plump. **2** of or like flesh. **3** *said of leaves, etc* thick and pulpy.

fleur-de-lis or **fleur-de-lys** /flɜːdəˈliː, flɜːdəˈliːs/ *noun* (PL. **fleurs-de-lis**, **fleurs-de-lys**) a stylized three-petal representation of a lily or iris, used as a heraldic design. [from Old French *flour de lis*, lily flower]

flew see FLY[2].

flex[1] *verb* **1** to bend (a limb or joint). **2** to contract or tighten (a muscle) so as to bend a joint. [from Latin *flectere*, to bend]

⊟ **1** bend, bow, curve, angle, ply, double up. **2** tighten, contract, tense.

⊟ **1** straighten, extend. **2** relax.

flex[2] *noun* a flexible insulated electrical cable, especially one used for connecting an electrical appliance to the mains electricity supply. [from FLEXIBLE]

⊟ cable, wire, lead, cord.

flexibility *noun* the capacity to be flexible.

flexible *adj.* **1** bending easily; pliable. **2** readily adaptable to suit circumstances. [from Latin *flexibilis*]

⊟ **1** bendable, pliable, bendy, pliant, plastic, malleable, mouldable, elastic, stretchy, springy, yielding, supple, lithe, limber, double-jointed, mobile. **2** adaptable, adjustable, amenable, accommodating, variable, open.
⊟ INFLEXIBLE, RIGID.

flexibly *adv.* in a flexible way.

flexitime *noun* a system of flexible working hours operated in some organizations whereby employees may choose their time of arrival and departure, provided they work the agreed number of hours. [from FLEXIBLE]

flexor /ˈflɛksɔː(r)/ *noun Anat.* any muscle that causes bending of a limb or other body part.

flibbertigibbet /ˈflɪbətɪdʒɪbɪt/ *noun* a frivolous or over-talkative person. [imitative of fast talking]

flick — *verb* **1** *trans., intrans.* to move or touch with a quick light movement. **2** (**flick through something**) to look quickly through a book, etc. — *noun* a flicking action. [imitative]

⊟ *verb* **1** touch, tap, dab, flip, hit, strike, rap, jerk, whip. **2** look through, leaf through, thumb through, flip through, glance at, skim, scan. *noun* rap, tap, touch, dab, flip, jerk, click.

flicker — *verb* (**flickered, flickering**) **1** *intrans.* to burn or shine unsteadily. **2** *trans., intrans.* to move lightly to and fro; to flutter. — *noun* **1** a brief or unsteady light. **2** a fleeting appearance or occurrence. [from Anglo-Saxon *flicorian*, to flutter]

⊟ *verb* **1** flash, blink, wink, twinkle, sparkle, glimmer, shimmer, gutter. **2** flutter, vibrate, quiver, waver. *noun* **1** flash, gleam, glint, twinkle, glimmer, spark. **2** indication, glimpse, trace, drop, iota, atom.

flick knife a knife whose blade is concealed in its handle and springs out at the touch of a button.

flicks *pl. noun* (**the flicks**) *old colloq. use* the cinema. [from FLICK]

flight[1] *noun* **1** the art or the act of flying with wings or in an aeroplane or other vehicle. **2** the movement of a vehicle, bird, or insect through the air, supported by aerodynamic forces. **3** a flock of birds flying together. **4** a regular air journey, numbered and at a fixed time, made by an aircraft. **5** a journey of a spacecraft. **6** a group of aircraft involved in a joint mission. **7** a set of steps or stairs leading straight up or down. **8** a rather extreme example (of fancy, imagination, etc). **9** a feather or something similar attached to the end of a dart or arrow. — **in flight** flying. [from Anglo-Saxon *flyht*]

⊟ **1, 2** flying, aviation, aeronautics, air transport, air travel. **4, 5** journey, trip, voyage.

flight[2] *noun* the act of fleeing; escape. — **put someone to flight** to cause them to flee. **take flight** or **take to flight** to run away. [from Middle English]

⊟ fleeing, escape, getaway, breakaway, exit, departure, exodus, retreat.

flight attendant a member of the cabin crew on a passenger aircraft.

flight crew the members of an aircraft crew whose responsibility is operation and navigation, ie the pilot, engineer, navigator, etc; as distinct from the *cabin crew*.

flight deck 1 the upper deck of an aircraft carrier where planes take off and land. **2** the forward part of an aircraft, in which the pilot and crew sit.

flightless *adj.*, *said of certain birds and insects* unable to fly.

flight lieutenant the air force rank next below squadron leader.

flight recorder an electronic device fitted to an aircraft, that records information about the flight performance of the aircraft, the prevailing weather conditions, etc, and can be used to determine the cause of an air crash. Also called BLACK BOX.

flimsily *adv.* in a flimsy way.

flimsiness *noun* being flimsy.

flimsy *adj.* (**flimsier, flimsiest**) **1** *said of clothing, etc* light and thin. **2** *said of a structure* insubstantially made; frail. **3** *said of an excuse, etc* inadequate or unconvincing. [perhaps altered from FILM]

⊟ **1** light, thin, fine, slight, insubstantial, ethereal. **2** insubstantial, frail, fragile, delicate, shaky, rickety, makeshift. **3** inadequate, unconvincing, poor, implausible, weak, feeble, meagre, shallow, superficial, trivial.
⊟ **1, 2** strong, sturdy. **2** convincing, plausible.

flinch *verb intrans.* **1** to start or jump in pain or fright. **2** (**flinch from something**) to shrink from or avoid a task, duty, etc.

⊟ **1** start, jump, wince, cringe, cower, quail, tremble, shake, quake, shudder, shiver. **2** shrink from, recoil at, draw back from, balk at, shy away from, duck, shirk.

fling — *verb* (PAST TENSE AND PAST PARTICIPLE **flung**) **1** to throw, especially violently or vigorously. **2** *intrans.* (**fling off** or **out**) to rush angrily. — *noun* **1** *colloq.* a spell of enjoyable self-indulgence. **2** a lively reel: *the Highland fling*. — **fling something out** to throw it away or reject it. **have a fling at something** attempt it; have a try at it. [Middle English]

⊟ *verb* **1** throw, hurl, pitch, lob, toss, *colloq.* chuck, cast, *colloq.* sling, catapult, launch, propel, send, let fly, heave, jerk.

flint *noun* **1** *Geol.* a crystalline form of quartz, found in chalk and limestone, consisting of hard dark grey or black nodules encrusted with white, and used as an abrasive. In the Stone Age flint was used to make tools. Also called CHERT. **2** *Archaeol.* a trimmed piece of this used as a tool. **3** a piece of a hard metal alloy from which a spark can be struck, eg in a cigarette lighter. [from Anglo-Saxon]

flintlock *noun Hist.* a gun in which the powder was lit by a spark from a flint.

flinty *adj.* (**flintier, flintiest**) **1** made of or containing flint. **2** like flint.

flip — *verb* (**flipped, flipping**) **1** to toss (eg a coin) so that it turns over in mid air. **2** (**flip something over**) to toss or turn it with a light flick. **3** *intrans. colloq.* to go crazy. **4** (**flip through something**) to look quickly through a magazine, etc. — *noun* **1** a flipping action. **2** a somersault, especially performed in mid air. **3** an alcoholic drink made with beaten egg. **4** *colloq.* a short air trip. — *adj. colloq.* flippant; over-smart. — **flip one's lid** *colloq.* to lose one's temper. [imitative]

▤ *verb* **1** toss, flick, spin, throw. **2** turn, toss, flick, spin, twirl, twist, throw, cast, pitch, jerk. **4** flick through, thumb through, leaf through, glance at. *noun* **1** flick, spin, twirl, twist, turn, toss, jerk.

flip chart a large blank pad that is bound at the top and used in presentations, etc to write up and display information.

flip-flop *noun* **1** *colloq.* a rubber or plastic sandal consisting of a sole held on to the foot by a strap that separates the big toe from the other toes. **2** *Electron.*, *Comput.* an electronic circuit that remains in one of two stable states until it receives a suitable electric pulse, which causes it to switch to the other state. Flip-flops are widely used to store data in the form of binary digits in the integrated circuits of computers. Also called BISTABLE CIRCUIT. [from FLIP]

flippancy *noun* (PL. **flippancies**) **1** being flippant. **2** a flippant act or remark.

flippant *adj.* not serious enough about grave matters; disrespectful; irreverent; frivolous. [from FLIP]

▤ disrespectful, irreverent, frivolous, facetious, light-hearted, superficial, offhand, flip, glib, pert, *colloq.* saucy, *colloq.* cheeky, impudent, impertinent, rude.
▨ serious, respectful.

flipper *noun* **1** a limb adapted for swimming, eg in the whale, seal, penguin, etc. **2** a rubber foot-covering imitating an animal flipper, worn for underwater swimming. [from FLIP]

flipping *adj.*, *adv. colloq.* used to express annoyance: *that flipping cat!* [from FLIP]

flip side *colloq.* the side of a gramophone record not containing the principal item.

flirt — *verb intrans.* **1** (**flirt with someone**) to behave amorously towards them without serious intentions. **2** (**flirt with something**) to take a fleeting interest in it; to consider it briefly; to play riskily with it. — *noun* someone who flirts.

▤ *verb* **1** chat up, make up to, lead on, philander, dally with. **2** consider, entertain, toy with, play with, trifle with, dabble in, try.

flirtation *noun* **1** the act of flirting. **2** a brief light-hearted attachment or relationship.

flirtatious *adj.* **1** given to flirting. **2** *said of a remark, glance, etc* conveying a playful sexual invitation.

flit — *verb intrans.* (**flitted, flitting**) **1** to dart lightly from place to place. **2** *Scot.* & *N of England* to move house. **3** *Brit. colloq.* to move house to avoid paying debts. — *noun* an act of flitting. [from Norse *flytja*, to carry]

▤ *verb* **1** dart, speed, flash, fly, wing, flutter, whisk, skim, slip, pass, bob, dance.

flitch *noun* a salted and cured side of pork. [from Anglo-Saxon *flicce*]

FLN *abbrev.* Front de Libération Nationale.

float — *verb* **1** *trans., intrans.* to rest or move, or cause to rest or move, on the surface of a liquid. **2** *intrans.* to drift about or hover in the air. **3** *intrans.* to move about in an aimless or disorganized way. **4** to start up (a company, scheme, etc). **5** to offer (stocks) for sale. **6** to allow (a currency) to vary in value in relation to other currencies. — *noun* **1** a floating device fixed to a fishing-line, that moves to indicate a bite. **2** a low-powered delivery vehicle: *milk float*. **3** a vehicle decorated as an exhibit in a street parade. **4** an amount of money set aside for giving change, etc. [from Anglo-Saxon *flotian*]

▤ *verb* **1** sail, swim, bob, drift, hang. **2** drift, glide, waft, hover, hang. **3** hover, wander. **4** start up, launch, initiate, set up, promote.
▨ *verb* **1** sink.

floatation see FLOTATION.

floating *adj.* **1** not fixed; moving about: *a floating population*. **2** *said of a voter* not committed to supporting any one party. **3** *said of a currency* varying in value in relation to other currencies. **4** *said of a bodily organ, eg a kidney* moving about abnormally.

▤ **1** unattached, free, variable, fluctuating, movable, migratory, transitory, wandering. **2** uncommitted.
▨ **1** fixed.

flock¹ — *noun* **1** a group of creatures, especially birds or sheep. **2** a crowd of people. **3** a body of people under the spiritual charge of a priest or minister. — *verb intrans.* to gather or move in a crowd. [from Anglo-Saxon *flocc*]

▤ *noun* **1** herd, pack, swarm. **2** crowd, throng, multitude, mass, bunch, cluster, group, gathering, assembly. **3** parishioners, congregation. *verb* gather, herd, swarm, collect, congregate, crowd, converge, throng, mass, troop, bunch, cluster, huddle, group.

flock² *noun* **1** a tuft of wool, etc. **2** waste wool or cotton used for stuffing mattresses, etc. **3** fine particles of wool or nylon fibre applied to paper or cloth to give a velvety surface. [from Latin *floccus*, tuft of wool]

floe / floʊ/ *noun* a sheet of ice, other than the edge of an ice shelf or glacier, floating in the sea. [from Norwegian *flo*, layer]

flog *verb* (**flogged, flogging**) **1** to beat; to whip. **2** *colloq.* to sell. — **flog a dead horse** *colloq.* to waste time and energy on a lost cause. **flog something to death** *colloq.* to overuse (an idea, expression, etc) so that it becomes tedious and ineffective. [from Latin *flagellare*, to whip]

▤ **1** beat, whip, lash, flagellate, scourge, birch, cane, flay, drub, thrash, *colloq.* whack, chastise, punish.

flokati / flɒˈkɑːtɪ/ *noun* a hand-woven Greek rug with a thick shaggy wool pile. [from modern Greek *phlokate*, a peasant's blanket]

flood — *noun* **1** an overflow of water from rivers, lakes, or the sea on to dry land. **2** (**the Flood**) *Biblical* the deluge, described in the Old Testament, that covered the whole Earth, and from which Noah and his family and livestock escaped in the ark. **3** any overwhelming flow or quantity. **4** the rising of the tide. **5** *colloq.* a floodlight. — *verb* **1** to overflow or submerge (land). **2** to fill too full or to overflowing. **3** (*usually* **flood someone out**) to force them to leave a building, etc because of floods. **4** to supply (a market) with too much of a certain kind of commodity. **5** to supply (an engine) with too much petrol so that it cannot start. **6** *intrans.* to become flooded, especially frequently. **7** *intrans.* to move in a great mass: *crowds flooding through the gates.* **8** *intrans.* to flow or surge. — **in flood** overflowing. [from Anglo-Saxon *flod*]

▤ *noun* **1** deluge, downpour, torrent. **3** deluge, inundation, downpour, torrent, flow, tide, stream, rush, spate, outpouring, overflow, glut, excess, abundance, profusion. *verb* **1** overflow, submerge, immerse, drown, swamp, soak, drench, saturate. **2** fill, inundate, engulf, overwhelm, deluge. **4** saturate, swamp. **7, 8** pour, flow, surge, stream, rush, gush.
▨ *noun* **3** drought, trickle, dearth.

floodgate *noun* a gate that is used to control the flow of water through a sluice or lock. — **open the floodgates** to remove all restraints or controls.

floodlight — *noun* a powerful light used to illuminate extensive areas, especially sports grounds or the outside of buildings. — *verb* to illuminate with floodlights.

floodlit *adj.* lit by floodlights.

flood plain *Geol.* an extensive level area beside a river, corresponding to that part of the river valley which becomes covered with water when the river floods.

floor — *noun* **1** the lower interior surface of a room or vehicle. **2** all the rooms on the same level in a building. **3** the ground in a forest or cave; the bed of the sea, etc. **4** the debating area in a parliamentary assembly; the right to speak there: *have the floor.* — *verb* **1** to construct the floor of (a room, etc). **2** *colloq.* to knock (someone) down. **3** *colloq.* to baffle completely. — **hold the floor** to be the person who is talking while others listen. **take the floor 1** to rise to speak in a debate, etc. **2** to start dancing at a dance, etc. **wipe the floor with someone** *slang* to defeat them ignominiously; to humiliate them. [from Anglo-Saxon *flor*]

⊞ *noun* **1** flooring, ground, base. **2** storey, level, stage, landing, tier, deck. *verb* **3** baffle, puzzle, bewilder, confound, perplex, disconcert, throw, defeat, overwhelm, beat, *colloq.* stump, frustrate.

floorboard *noun* one of the boards forming a wooden floor.

flooring *noun* material for constructing floors.

floor show a series of performances at a nightclub or restaurant.

floosie or **floozie** *noun derog. colloq.* a woman or girl, especially a disreputable or immodestly dressed one.

flop — *verb intrans.* (**flopped, flopping**) **1** to fall, drop, move or sit limply and heavily. **2** *said of eg hair* to hang or sway about loosely. **3** *colloq., said of a play, etc* to fail. — *noun* **1** a flopping movement or sound. **2** *colloq.* a failure. — *adv.* with a flop. [a variant of FLAP]

⊞ *verb* **1** fall, drop, topple, tumble, slump, collapse, droop, hang, dangle, sag. **2** droop, hang, dangle. **3** fail, misfire, fall flat, founder, fold. *noun* **2** failure, non-starter, fiasco, debacle, *colloq.* washout, disaster.

floppily *adv.* in a floppy way.

floppiness *noun* being floppy.

floppy *adj.* (**floppier, floppiest**) tending to flop; loose and insecure.

⊞ droopy, hanging, dangling, sagging, limp, loose, baggy, soft, flabby.

⊟ firm.

floppy disk *Comput.* a portable flexible plastic disc-shaped medium, coated with magnetic material and enclosed in a plastic casing, which is used to store data. It is slower in operation than a hard disk, and has a smaller storage capacity. See also HARD DISK.

flora *noun* (PL. **floras, florae**) **1** *Bot.* the wild plants of a particular region, country, or time period. **2** *Bot.* a book or list giving descriptions of such plants. See also FAUNA. [from Latin *Flora*, goddess of flowers]

floral *adj.* **1** of or relating to flowers. **2** patterned with flowers: *floral material.* [from Latin *floralis*]

florally *adv.* like or with flowers.

floret *noun Bot.* **1** a small flower; one of the single flowers in the head of a composite flower, such as a daisy or sunflower. **2** each of the branches in the head of a cauliflower or of broccoli. [from Latin *flos, floris*, flower]

florid *adj.* **1** over-elaborate. **2** pink or ruddy in complexion. [from Latin *floridus*, blooming]

⊞ **1** over-elaborate, flowery, ornate, fussy, baroque, rococo,

flamboyant, grandiloquent. **2** pink, ruddy, red, purple.

⊟ **1** plain, simple. **2** pale.

florin *noun* a former name of the coin worth two shillings or 24 old pence, the equivalent of the modern ten-penny piece. [from Italian *fiorino*, a former gold coin from Florence]

florist *noun* a person who grows or sells flowers. [from Latin *flos*, flower]

floss — *noun* **1** loose strands of fine silk, for embroidery, tooth-cleaning, etc. **2** the rough silk on the outside of a silkworm's cocoon. — *verb* to clean (the teeth) with dental floss. [probably from Old French *flosche*, down]

flossy *adj.* (**flossier, flossiest**) made of or like floss.

flotation or **floatation** *noun* the launching of a commercial company with a sale of shares to raise money. [from FLOAT]

flotilla /flə'tɪlə/ *noun* a small fleet, or a fleet of small ships. [from Spanish *flotilla*, little fleet]

flotsam *noun* goods lost by shipwreck and found floating on the sea. — **flotsam and jetsam 1** odds and ends. **2** homeless people; vagrants. [from Old French *floteson*, from *floter*, to float]

⊞ jetsam, wreckage, debris. **flotsam and jetsam 1** odds and ends, oddments, junk, rubbish.

flounce[1] — *verb intrans.* to move in a way expressive of impatience or indignation. — *noun* a flouncing movement. [perhaps related to Norse *flunsa*, to hurry]

flounce[2] *noun* a deep frill on a dress, etc. [altered from *frounce*, plait, curl]

flounder[1] *verb intrans.* (**floundered, floundering**) **1** to thrash about helplessly, as when caught in a bog. **2** to be in difficulties or at a loss, from embarrassment, etc. [partly imitative, partly a blend of FOUNDER[2] + BLUNDER]

⊞ **1** thrash about, flail about, struggle, fumble, blunder, stagger, stumble, wallow.

flounder[2] *noun* any of various marine flatfish, closely related to the plaice and dab, native to shallow coastal waters of Europe, and having a flat body up to 50cm long, with both eyes on the upper surface. [from Old French *flondre*]

flour — *noun* **1** the finely ground meal of wheat or any other cereal grain. Wholemeal flour includes the bran (husk) and germ (embryo), whereas white flour contains less than 75% of the whole grain. Flour with a high gluten content is used to make bread and pasta. **2** a dried powdered form of any other vegetable material, eg potato flour. — *verb* to cover or sprinkle with flour. [from Middle English, a variant of FLOWER, in the sense 'best part']

flourish /'flʌrɪʃ/ — *verb* **1** *intrans.* to be strong and healthy; to grow well. **2** *intrans.* to do well; to develop and prosper. **3** *intrans.* to be at one's most productive, or at one's peak. **4** to wave or brandish. — *noun* **1** a decorative twirl in handwriting. **2** an elegant sweep of the hand. **3** a showy piece of music; a fanfare. **4** a piece of fancy language. [from Old French *florir*, to flower]

⊞ *verb* **1** thrive, grow. **2** do well, thrive, develop, prosper, get on, succeed, blossom, bloom, flower, boom, progress, wax, increase. **3** succeed, blossom, bloom, flower. **4** wave, brandish, shake, twirl, swing, display, wield, flaunt, parade, vaunt. *noun* **1** twirl, ornament, decoration. **2** sweep, gesture, wave.

⊟ *verb* **1** decline, languish. **2** decline, languish, fail.

floury *adj.* (**flourier, flouriest**) **1** covered with flour. **2** like flour.

flout *verb* to defy (an order, etc) openly; to disrespect (authority, etc). [from Middle English *flouten*, to play the flute]

⊟ defy, disrespect, disregard, disobey, violate, break, spurn, reject, scorn, jeer at, scoff at, mock, ridicule.
⊡ obey, respect, regard.

flow — *verb intrans.* **1** to move along like water. **2** *said of blood or electricity* to circulate. **3** to keep moving steadily. **4** *said of hair* to hang or ripple in a loose shining mass. **5** *said of words or ideas* to come readily to mind or in speech or writing. **6** *said of the tide* to rise. — *noun* **1** the action of flowing. **2** the rate of flowing. **3** a continuous stream or outpouring. **4** the rising of the tide. — **in full flow** speaking energetically. [from Anglo-Saxon *flowan*]

⊟ *verb* **1** run, pour, cascade, rush, gush, spill, stream, teem, flood, overflow, swirl, surge, well, spurt, squirt, trickle, ripple, bubble, ooze. **3** move, sweep, drift, slip, slide, glide, roll. **5** flood, pour, roll. *noun* **2** flux. **3** stream, outpouring, cascade, deluge, flood, current, spurt, gush.

flow chart a diagram representing the nature and sequence of operations to be carried out, especially in a computer program or an industrial process.

flower — *noun* **1** the structure in a flowering plant (angiosperm) that bears the reproductive organs, consisting of a leafy shoot in which the leaves are modified to form four distinct whorls of parts attached to a receptacle (the swollen apex of the flower stalk). **2** a plant bearing flowers, especially if cultivated for them. **3** the best part; the cream. — *verb intrans.* **1** to produce flowers; to bloom. **2** to reach a peak; to develop to full maturity. — **in flower** blooming or blossoming; with flowers fully out. [from Old French *flour*]

⊟ *noun* **1** bloom, blossom, bud, floret. **3** best, cream, pick, choice, elite. *verb* **1** bud, bloom, blossom, open, come out. **2** peak, develop, burgeon, blossom.

Flowers include: African violet, alyssum, anemone, aster, aubrietia, azalea, begonia, bluebell, busy lizzie (impatiens), calendula, candytuft, carnation, chrysanthemum, cornflower, cowslip, crocus, cyclamen, daffodil, dahlia, daisy, delphinium, forget-me-not, foxglove (digitalis), freesia, fuchsia, gardenia, geranium, gladioli, hollyhock, hyacinth, iris (flag), lily, lily-of-the-valley, lobelia, lupin, marigold, narcissus, nasturtium, nemesia, nicotiana, night-scented stock, orchid, pansy, petunia, pink (dianthus), phlox, poinsettia, polyanthus, poppy, primrose, primula, rose, salvia, snapdragon (antirrhinum), snowdrop, stock, sunflower, sweet pea, sweet william, tulip, verbena, viola, violet, wallflower, zinnia. *See also* **plant**; **shrub**.

flowerpecker *noun* a name loosely applied to many small woodland birds found from India to Australia, which have a tube-like tongue. They feed on nectar and berries, especially mistletoe.

flowerpot *noun* a clay or plastic container for growing plants in.

flower power a movement in the 1960s, which rejected materialism and advocated peace and universal love.

flowery *adj.* **1** decorated or patterned with flowers. **2** *said of language or gestures* excessively elegant or elaborate.

⊟ **2** elaborate, florid, ornate, fancy, baroque, rhetorical.
⊡ **2** plain, simple.

flown see FLY².
fl oz or **fl. oz.** *abbrev.* fluid ounce.
flu *noun colloq.* influenza.
fluctuate *verb intrans.* to vary in amount, value, level, etc; to rise and fall. [from Latin *fluctus*, wave]

⊟ vary, rise and fall, seesaw, ebb and flow, alternate, swing, sway, oscillate, vacillate, waver, change, alter, shift.

fluctuation *noun* **1** repeated rise and fall. **2** motion to and fro or a wave-like motion. **3** alternate variation.
flue *noun* **1** an outlet for smoke or gas, eg through a chimney. **2** a pipe or duct for conveying heat.
fluency *noun* being fluent.
fluent *adj.* **1** having full command of a language: *is fluent in French*. **2** spoken or written with ease: *speaks fluent German*. **3** speaking or writing in an easy flowing style. [from Latin *fluere*, to flow]

⊟ **3** flowing, smooth, easy, effortless, articulate, eloquent, ready, voluble, glib.
⊡ **1, 2** broken. **3** faltering, hesitant, inarticulate, tongue-tied.

fluently *adv.* in a fluent way.
fluff — *noun* **1** small bits of soft woolly or downy material. **2** *colloq.* a mistake, eg in speaking or reading aloud. — *verb* **1** (*usually* **fluff something out** or **up**) to shake or arrange it into a soft mass. **2** *trans., intrans., said eg of an actor* to make a mistake in (one's lines, etc); to bungle (something). [from earlier *flue*, down]

⊟ *noun* **1** down, nap, pile, fuzz, floss, lint, dust.

fluffiness *noun* being fluffy.
fluffy *adj.* (**fluffier, fluffiest**) **1** consisting of or resembling fluff. **2** covered with fluff or something similar.

⊟ **1** furry, fuzzy, downy, feathery, fleecy, woolly, hairy, shaggy, velvety, silky, soft.

flugelhorn *noun* a brass musical instrument, like a cornet but with a larger bell. It has three pistons and the same compass as a B flat cornet, though with a fuller tone. [from German *Flügelhorn*, from *Flügel*, wing]
fluid — *noun* any non-solid form of matter that can flow freely and has no fixed shape, such as a gas or liquid. The atoms or molecules of a fluid are free to move past each other, unlike those of a solid, which are rigidly held together by the forces between them. — *adj.* **1** capable of flowing freely and readily changing shape. **2** *said eg of movements* smooth and graceful. **3** altering easily; adaptable. [from Latin *fluidus*, flowing]

⊟ *noun* liquid, solution, liquor, juice, gas, vapour. *adj.* **1** liquid, liquefied, aqueous, watery, running, runny, melted, molten. **2** smooth, graceful, flowing. **3** variable, adaptable, shifting, mobile, changeable, unstable, inconstant, adjustable, flexible, open.
⊡ *noun* solid. *adj.* **1** solid. **2** awkward, jerky, clumsy. **3** stable.

fluidics *sing. noun* *Physics* the study of systems based on the movement of jets of fluid in pipes, used as an alternative to electronic devices to control instruments, industrial processes, etc, in cases where low sensitivity to high temperatures, radiation, and strong magnetic fields is required.
fluidity *noun* being fluid.
fluid ounce (ABBREV. **fl oz, fl. oz.**) a unit of liquid measurement, equal to 28.41cm³ or 0.05 of a British pint.
fluke¹ *noun* a success achieved by accident.
fluke² *noun* **1** any of thousands of species of parasitic flatworm belonging to the class Trematoda and having a complex life cycle which may involve several different hosts. **2** a flounder. [from Anglo-Saxon *floc*, plaice]
fluky *adj.* (**flukier, flukiest**) accidentally lucky.
flume *noun* **1** a narrow artificial channel made of plastic, reinforced concrete, steel, or wood, designed to carry

water for use in industry (eg for providing power, floating logs, etc), or used at swimming baths, leisure centres, etc, as a chute for riding (usually in special boats) or sliding down. **2** a ravine with a stream flowing through it. [from Old French *flum*, from Latin *flumen*, river]

flummery *noun* (PL. **flummeries**) **1** a jelly made with oatmeal, milk, egg, and honey. **2** pompous nonsense; empty flattery. [from Welsh *llymru*]

flummox /ˈflʌməks/ *verb colloq.* to confuse; to bewilder.

flung see FLING.

flunk *verb North Amer. colloq.* **1** *trans., intrans.* to fail (a test, examination, etc). **2** *said eg of an examiner* to fail (a candidate).

flunkey or **flunky** *noun* (PL. **flunkeys**, **flunkys**) **1** a uniformed manservant. **2** *derog.* a slavish follower. **3** *North Amer.* a person doing a humble or menial job.

fluor /ˈfluə(r), ˈfluːɔ:(r)/ *noun* **1** a material that absorbs electrons or radiation, especially ultraviolet light, and converts these into radiation of a different wavelength, usually visible light, which it then emits. **2** same as FLUORSPAR.

fluoresce /fluəˈrɛs/ *verb intrans.* to be or become fluorescent. [from FLUOR]

fluorescence *noun Physics* the emission of radiation, usually light, by an object after it has absorbed electrons, or radiation of a different wavelength, especially ultraviolet light. It ceases as soon as the energy source is removed, and is a type of luminescence. Fluorescence is exploited in dyes and in the coating of fluorescent light tubes.

fluorescent *adj., said of a material* having the property of fluorescence.

fluorescent light or **fluorescent lamp** *Electr.* a type of electric light consisting of a glass discharge tube containing mercury vapour or a chemically inert gas. The inner surface of the tube is coated with phosphors that absorb ultraviolet radiation produced by the electrical discharge, and then emit visible light (by the process of fluorescence). Also called STRIP LIGHT.

fluoridate or **fluoridize** or **fluoridise** *verb* to add (small amounts of fluoride salts) to drinking water supplies to help prevent tooth decay.

fluoridation or **fluoridization** or **fluoridisation** *noun* the addition of small amounts (about one part per million) of fluoride salts to drinking water supplies to help prevent tooth decay, a policy adopted by certain water authorities.

fluoride *noun Chem.* any chemical compound consisting of fluorine and another element, especially sodium fluoride, which is added to drinking water supplies and toothpaste to prevent tooth decay in children.

fluorine /ˈfluəri:n/ *noun Chem.* (SYMBOL **F**, ATOMIC NUMBER **9**) a poisonous pale yellow gas (one of the halogens) that is highly corrosive and causes severe skin burns. It is the most electronegative and reactive chemical element, and has been used as a rocket fuel and in the manufacture of organic compounds such as fluorocarbons, which are used as refrigerants and aerosol propellants. [from FLUOR]

fluorite /ˈfluərait/ *noun Geol.* same as FLUORSPAR.

fluorocarbon *noun Chem.* any of various compounds of carbon and fluorine that are highly resistant to heat and chemical action, and very stable over long periods, formerly widely used as aerosol propellants and refrigerants. Recent concern about their damaging effect on the ozone layer has led many countries to sign international agreements banning their use. [from Latin *fluor*, flow]

fluorspar /fluːəˈspaː(r)/ *noun Geol.* (FORMULA CaF_2) calcium fluoride, a mineral that is transparent when pure, but commonly occurs as blue or purple crystals. It is used in glass and some cements, and in the manufacture of hydrofluoric acid for the plastic industry. Also called FLUORITE. [from Latin *fluor*, flow (from the use of fluorspar as a flux) + SPAR²]

flurry — *noun* (PL. **flurries**) **1** a sudden gust; a brief shower of rain, snow, etc. **2** *colloq.* a commotion; a bustle or rush. — *verb* (**flurries**, **flurried**) to agitate or confuse. [imitative]

· · · · · · · · · · · · · · · · · ·

▣ *noun* **1** gust, blast, squall, burst, outbreak, spell, spurt. **2** commotion, bustle, rush, hurry, tumult, whirl, disturbance, fluster, fuss, stir, *colloq.* to-do, *colloq.* flap.

· · · · · · · · · · · · · · · · · ·

flush¹ — *verb* **1** *intrans., trans.* to blush or cause to blush or go red. **2** to clean out (especially a lavatory pan) with a rush of water; to wash (something) down the lavatory. **3** (**be flushed with pride**) to be visibly affected by it, eg by blushing. — *noun* **1** a redness or rosiness, especially of the face; a blush. **2** a rush of water that cleans a lavatory pan, or the mechanism that controls it. **3** high spirits: *in the first flush of enthusiasm.* **4** freshness; bloom; vigour: *in the first flush of youth.* [perhaps from FLUSH⁴]

· · · · · · · · · · · · · · · · · ·

▣ *verb* **1** blush, go red, redden, crimson, colour, burn, glow. **2** cleanse, wash, rinse, hose, swab, clear, empty, evacuate.

· · · · · · · · · · · · · · · · · ·

flush² — *adj.* **1** level with an adjacent surface. **2** *colloq.* having plenty of money. — *adv.* so as to be level with an adjacent surface. [perhaps from FLUSH¹]

· · · · · · · · · · · · · · · · · ·

▣ *adj.* **1** level, even, square, true, flat, plane. **2** rich, wealthy, moneyed, prosperous, well off, *colloq.* well-heeled, well-to-do.

· · · · · · · · · · · · · · · · · ·

flush³ *noun Cards* a hand made up of cards from a single suit. [from Latin *fluxus*, flow]

flush⁴ *verb* **1** *Hunting* to startle (game birds) so that they rise from the ground. **2** (**flush someone** or **something out**) to drive them out of a hiding-place. [from Middle English *flusshen*]

· · · · · · · · · · · · · · · · · ·

▣ **2** drive out, force out, expel, eject, run to earth, discover, uncover.

· · · · · · · · · · · · · · · · · ·

fluster — *noun* a state of confused agitation. — *verb* (**flustered, flustering**) to agitate or confuse. [related to Norse *flaustr*, hurry]

· · · · · · · · · · · · · · · · · ·

▣ *noun* agitation, *colloq.* flap, dither, *colloq.* tizzy, *colloq.* state, confusion, embarrassment, flurry, bustle, commotion, disturbance, turmoil. *verb* agitate, confuse, ruffle, discompose, confound, unnerve, disconcert, *colloq.* rattle, put off, bother, upset, embarrass, disturb, perturb, distract. ▣ *noun* calm. *verb* calm.

· · · · · · · · · · · · · · · · · ·

flute — *noun* **1** a woodwind instrument that is held horizontally out to the side of the head. **2** *Archit.* a rounded groove in wood or stone. **3** a tall, slender drinking glass with a stem, used for champagne. — *verb* **1** *intrans., trans.* to speak or utter in high shrill tones. **2** *intrans., trans.* to play the flute or play (a tune, etc) on it. **3** *Archit.* to make grooves in (wood or stone). See also FLAUTIST. [from Old French *flahute*]

· · · · · · · · · · · · · · · · · ·

▣ *noun* **2** groove, furrow, channel, rib, ridge.

· · · · · · · · · · · · · · · · · ·

fluting *noun* parallel grooves cut into wood or stone.

flutter — *verb* (**fluttered, fluttering**) **1** *trans., intrans.* to flap lightly and rapidly; to fly with a rapid wing movement or drift with a twirling motion. **2** *intrans.* to move about in a restless, aimless way. **3** *old use* to cause agitation in: *must have fluttered a few hearts in his time.* **4** *intrans., trans.* said of the heart to race, from excitement or some disorder. — *noun* **1** agitation; excitement. **2** *colloq.* a small bet. **3** in a record-player, etc, a regularly recurring variation in loudness and pitch. [from Anglo-Saxon *floterian*, to flutter]

· · · · · · · · · · · · · · · · · ·

▣ *verb* **1** flap, wave, beat, bat, flicker, vibrate, tremble, quiver, shiver, ruffle, ripple, twitch. **3** agitate, alarm, ruffle, disconcert, shake. **4** palpitate.

· · · · · · · · · · · · · · · · · ·

fluty *adj.* (**flutier, flutiest**) like a flute.

fluvial *adj.* of, relating to, or found in rivers. [from Latin *fluvialis*]

flux *noun* **1** constant change; instability. **2** any substance added to another in order to aid the process of melting. **3** in the smelting of metal ores, any substance that is added so that it will combine with impurities which can then be removed as a flowing mass of slag. **4** any substance, such as a resin, that is used to remove oxides from the surfaces of metals that are to be soldered, welded, or brazed. **5** *Physics* the rate of flow of particles, energy, mass, or some other quantity per unit cross-sectional area per unit time. **6** magnetic flux. **7** luminous flux. [from Latin *fluxus*, flow]
. . . .
☲ 1 fluctuation, instability, change, alteration, modification, fluidity, flow, movement, motion, transition, development.
☲ 1 stability, rest.
. . . .

fly¹ *noun* (PL. **flies**) **1** the common name for any of at least 90,000 species of small flying insects, the *true flies*, belonging to the order Diptera, found worldwide, and characterized by the possession of only one pair of functional wings. **2** (*in compounds*) any of various flying insects superficially resembling but unrelated to true flies: *mayfly/firefly/butterfly.* **3** a fish hook, used in fly-fishing, tied with coloured feathers, tinsel, etc, so as to resemble any of various flies or nymphs. — **drop like flies** *colloq.* to fall ill or die in large numbers. **a fly in the ointment** a drawback in an otherwise satisfactory state of affairs. **a fly on the wall** the invisible observer that one would like to be on certain occasions. **no flies on someone** *colloq.* no lack of alertness in them. **he etc wouldn't harm a fly** he, etc has a gentle nature. [from Anglo-Saxon *fleoge*]

fly² — *verb* (**flies**; PAST TENSE **flew**; PAST PARTICIPLE **flown**) **1** *intrans.* said of birds, insects, bats, and certain other animals to travel through the air, especially on wings or on structures resembling wings. **b** said of an aircraft or spacecraft to travel through the air or through space. **2** *intrans., trans.* to travel or convey in an aircraft. **3** to operate and control (an aircraft, kite, etc). **4** to cross (an area of land or sea) in an aircraft. **5** *trans., intrans.* to raise (a flag), or (of a flag) to blow in the wind. **6** *intrans.* to move or pass rapidly: *fly into a temper/rumours flying around.* **7** *intrans. colloq.* to depart quickly: *I must fly.* **8** *intrans.* (**fly at, fly out at**) to attack angrily. **9** *intrans., trans.* to escape; to flee (a country, etc). **10** *intrans.* to vanish: *darkness has flown.* — *noun* (PL. **flies**) **1** (**flies**) a zip or set of buttons fastening a trouser front, or the flap covering these. **2** a flap covering the entrance to a tent. **3** (**flies**) the space above a stage from which scenery is lowered. — **fly high** to be ambitious. **let fly at someone** or **something** to attack them. **send someone** or **something flying** to knock them down or knock them over with considerable force. [from Anglo-Saxon *fleogan*, to fly]
. . . .
☲ *verb* **1** soar, glide, float, hover, wing. **6** race, sprint, dash, tear, rush, hurry, speed, zoom, shoot, dart, career. **7** dash. **8** attack, go for, fall upon.
. . . .

fly³ *adj. colloq.* cunning; smart.

fly agaric a mushroom (*Amanita muscaria*) with a flattened scarlet cap covered with concentric rings of small white scales. The gills on the underside of the cap are crowded and whitish, and the stem is also white with a swollen base. It contains poisonous (though not deadly) substances and mild hallucinogens.

flyblown *noun* **1** said of food covered with blowfly eggs, and therefore unfit to eat; contaminated. **2** shabby, dirty, or dingy.

fly-by-night *adj. derog.*, said of a business, etc not reliable or trustworthy.

flycatcher *noun* **1** a name applied to birds of three distinct groups, New World or tyrant flycatchers, Old World flycatchers, and silky flycatchers, all of which usually eat insects caught in flight. **2** any of various birds of other families.

fly-drive *noun* a package holiday that includes the rental of a car to be collected at the destination.

flyer or **flier** *noun* **1** a creature that flies; someone or something that moves fast; an aviator or pilot. **2** an advertising leaflet.

fly fish to fish using artificial flies.

fly fishing the sport of fishing using artificial flies.

fly half *Rugby* a stand-off half.

flying — *noun* **1** flight. **2** the act of piloting, navigating, or travelling in an aircraft or spacecraft. — *adj.* **1** hasty; brief. **2** designed or organized for fast movement. **3** relating to, adapted for, or capable of flight. **4** said of birds, insects, bats, and certain other animals able to fly, or to glide for long distances: *flying fish.* **5** said eg of hair or a flag streaming; fluttering.

flying boat a seaplane with a fuselage shaped like the hull of a boat.

flying buttress a structure supporting, and forming an arch against, the outside wall of a large building, especially a church.

flying doctor a doctor who can be contacted by radio and who travels by light aircraft to visit patients in remote villages or on farms in sparsely populated areas of countryside, especially the Australian outback.

flying fish any of various small surface-living fishes, native to tropical and warm temperate seas, having stiff greatly enlarged pectoral fins, superficially resembling wings, that enable the fish to leap from the water and glide for considerable distances above the surface at speeds of up to 50km per hour.

flying fox any of about 60 species of large fruit-eating bat, native to S Asia, N Australia, Madagascar, and a few S Pacific islands, so called because in many species the animal's body is covered with reddish-brown fur, and its head resembles that of a fox, having small ears, large eyes, and a long muzzle.

flying leap a jump from a running start.

flying lemur see COLUGO.

flying lizard, flying dragon a species of lizard native to SE Asia. It is able to glide between trees by using a semicircular membrane, which is supported by moveable ribs on either side of its body. The membrane may be folded back when not in use.

flying officer a Royal Air Force rank immediately below flight lieutenant.

flying picket a picket travelling from place to place to support local pickets during any strike.

flying saucer any of a number of unidentified circular flying objects reported in the sky from time to time, believed by some to be craft from outer space.

flying snake a snake from SE Asia that glides between trees by launching itself in the air and then flattening its body and forming several S-shaped curves. Several regions of the body are then broadside to the direction of travel and act like wings. It can glide in this manner for distances of 20m or more.

flying squad a body of police specially trained for fast movement or action, or available for duty wherever the need arises.

flying squirrel any of various species of squirrel, most of which are found in SE Asia, with a large flap of skin between its front and hind legs, which it uses to glide between trees for distances of up to 450m.

flying start a start to a race in which the contestants are already travelling at full speed when they cross the starting-line. — **get off to a flying start** to begin promisingly or with a special advantage.

flyleaf *noun* a blank page at the beginning or end of a book.

Flymo *noun trademark* a type of lawnmower which hovers on a cushion of air.

flyover *noun* a bridge that takes a road or railway over another.

flypaper *noun* a strip of paper with a sticky poisonous coating that attracts, traps and kills flies.

flypast *noun* a ceremonial flight of military aircraft over a particular place.

flysheet *noun* **1** a protective outer sheet for a tent. **2** a single-sheet leaflet.

flyspray *noun* a liquid poisonous to flies, sprayed from an aerosol can.

fly-tipping *noun* unauthorized disposal of waste materials.

flyweight *noun* **1** a class for boxers, wrestlers and weight-lifters of not more than a specified weight (50.8kg in professional boxing, similar weights in the other sports). **2** a boxer, etc of this weight.

flywheel *noun* a heavy wheel attached to the rotating shaft of an engine. Its momentum tends to keep the shaft rotating at a constant speed, and so smooths the power output of the engine.

FM *abbrev.* frequency modulation.

Fm *symbol Chem.* fermium.

FMS *abbrev.* false memory syndrome.

f-number *noun Photog.* the relative aperture of a camera lens representing its light transmission, particularly when the lens is stopped down to increase the depth of field and/or exposure time. It expresses the diameter of the lens diaphragm as a fraction of its focal length, eg f/8 or f:8 or f8.

FO *abbrev.* **1** Flying Officer. **2** *Hist.* Foreign Office.

foal — *noun* the young of a horse or of a related animal. — *verb intrans.* to give birth to a foal. — **in foal** *said of a mare* pregnant. [from Anglo-Saxon *fola*]

foam — *noun* **1** a mass of small bubbles on the surface of a liquid, formed by shaking, aeration, or the addition of a detergent to the liquid. **2** frothy saliva produced as a symptom of certain diseases, eg rabies. **3** the frothy perspiration of a horse or other animal. **4** any of various light cellular solids, used as insulation and as packaging and padding materials (eg in upholstery), formed by blowing bubbles of gas through a liquid and then solidifying it. **5** a colloid consisting of gas bubbles dispersed evenly throughout a liquid, eg shaving foam. **6** *poetic* the sea. — *verb* **1** to gather, produce, or be full of foam. **2** to fill or cover with foam or froth. — **foam at the mouth 1** to produce frothy saliva. **2** *colloq.* to be furiously angry. [from Anglo-Saxon *fam*]

▣ *noun* **1** froth, lather, suds, head, bubbles, effervescence. **3** lather. **5** mousse. *verb* **1** froth, lather, bubble, effervesce, fizz. **foam at the mouth 2** boil, seethe.

foam rubber rubber in cellular form, used chiefly in upholstery.

foamy *adj.* (**foamier, foamiest**) frothy.

fob[1] *verb* (**fobbed, fobbing**) **1** (**fob someone off with something**) to provide them with something inferior, eg a poor substitute, or an inadequate explanation, usually in the hope that they will be satisfied. **2** (**fob something off on someone**) to manage to sell or pass off something inferior. **3** (**fob someone off**) to dismiss or ignore them: *tried to fob off his critics.* [related to German *foppen*, to delude]

▣ **1** deceive, put off. **2** foist, pass off, *colloq.* palm off, get rid of, dump, unload, inflict, impose.

fob[2] *noun* **1** a chain attached to a watch. **2** a decorative attachment to a key ring or watch chain. **3** *Hist.* a small watch pocket in a waistcoat or trouser waistband. [perhaps related to German dialect *fuppe*, pocket]

fob watch *noun* a watch for keeping in a fob.

focaccia /fə'katʃɪə/ *noun* a flat round of Italian bread topped with olive oil and herbs or spices. [from Italian *focaccia*, cake]

focal *adj.* relating to, or at, a focus.

focal length or **focal distance** *Optics* the distance from the centre of a lens or curved mirror to its focal point (the point at which parallel rays of light converge or appear to diverge after they have been reflected or refracted). The shorter the focal length of a lens, the greater its power.

focal point 1 *Optics* the point on the axis of a lens or curved mirror at which all incident parallel rays of light converge or appear to diverge after they have been reflected or refracted. Also called FOCUS. **2** a centre of attraction.

fo'c'sle /'fouksl/ *noun* a spelling of **forecastle** suggested by its pronunciation.

focus — *noun* (PL. **focuses, foci**) **1** *Optics* the point on the axis of a lens or curved mirror at which parallel rays of light meet, or from which they appear to diverge. Also called **FOCAL POINT**. **2** *Geol.* in seismology, the location of the centre of an earthquake, where the subterranean fracture takes place and from which the elastic waves radiate outward. **3** a centre of interest or attention. **4** special attention paid to something: *a shift of focus.* — *verb* (**focused, focusing** or **focussed, focussing**) **1** *trans., intrans.* to bring or be brought into focus; to (cause to) meet or converge at a focus. **2** to adjust the thickness of the lens of the eye or to move the lens of an optical instrument so as to obtain the sharpest possible image of a particular object. **3** to cause electron beams to converge or diverge by varying the voltage or current that controls the magnetic or electric fields through which they pass. **4** *trans., intrans.* to concentrate (one's attention). [from Latin *focus*, hearth, as the centre of the home]

▣ *noun* **3** focal point, target, centre, heart, core, nucleus, kernel, crux, hub, axis, linchpin, pivot, hinge. *verb* **1** converge, meet, join, centre. **4** concentrate, aim, direct, fix, spotlight, home in, zoom in, *colloq.* zero in.

focus group a group of people gathered together to discuss particular issues, products, etc and contribute ideas for their development.

fodder — *noun* **1** any bulk feed, especially hay or straw, that is given to cattle or other animal livestock. **2** *colloq.* something that is made use of to feed a constant need: *stories about royalty are fodder for the popular press.* — *adj.* denoting any crop that is grown for use as feed for animal livestock, eg kale. — *verb* to supply (animal livestock) with fodder. [from Anglo-Saxon *fodor*]

foe *noun old use, poetic* an enemy. [from Anglo-Saxon *fah*, hostile]

foetal /'fiːtl/ same as FETAL.

foetid /'fiːtɪd, 'fetɪd/ same as FETID.

foetus /'fiːtəs/ same as FETUS.

fog — *noun* **1** a suspension of tiny water droplets or ice crystals forming a cloud close to the ground surface, reducing visibility to less than 1km (if visibility is greater than this it is known as mist). Fog containing smoke is often called 'smog'. **2** *Photog.* a blurred patch on a negative, print, or transparency. **3** a blur; cloudiness. **4** a state of confusion or bewilderment. — *verb* (**fogged, fogging**) **1** *trans., intrans.* to obscure or become obscured (as if) with fog or condensation. **2** to confuse or perplex. — **not have the foggiest idea** *colloq.* not to know at all. [perhaps from Norse]

▣ *noun* **1** mist, haze, cloud, gloom, murkiness, smog, *colloq.* pea-souper. **4** confusion, bewilderment, perplexity, puzzlement, daze, trance, vagueness, obscurity. *verb* **1** mist, steam up, cloud, dull, dim, darken, obscure, blur. **2** confuse, muddle.

fog bank a distant and well-defined mass of dense fog, especially at sea, so called because it resembles a bank of land.

fogbound *adj.* brought to a standstill by fog.

fogey or **fogy** *noun* (PL. **fogeys, fogies**) *noun derog.* someone with boring, old-fashioned ideas.

foggy *adj.* (**foggier, foggiest**) **1** covered with fog. **2** not clear; confused.

☰ **1** misty, hazy, smoggy, cloudy, murky, dark, shadowy, dim, indistinct, obscure. **2** confused, muddled.

☒ CLEAR.

foghorn *noun* a horn that sounds a warning at regular intervals to ships in fog.

fog lamp a powerful lamp used by vehicles in fog.

foible *noun* a slight personal weakness or eccentricity. [from Old French *foible*, variant of *faible*, feeble]

foil[1] *verb* to prevent, thwart, or frustrate (a person or attempt). [from Old French *fuler*, to trample or full cloth]

☰ prevent, thwart, frustrate, stop, check, obstruct, block, counter, nullify, defeat, outwit, baffle, circumvent, elude.

☒ abet.

foil[2] *noun* **1** metal beaten or rolled out into thin sheets. **2** a thing or person that acts as a contrast to, and brings out, the superior or different qualities of another. [from Old French *foil*, leaf, from Latin *folium*]

☰ **2** contrast, complement, balance, setting, background, relief.

foil[3] *noun* a long slender sword with its point protected by a button, used in the sport of fencing.

foist *verb* (**foist something on someone**) **1** to inflict something unwanted on them. **2** to palm off something inferior on them. [perhaps from Dutch *vuist*, fist]

fold[1] — *verb* **1** (*also* **fold something over, back, up**) to double it over so that one part lies on top of another. **2** *intrans.* to be able to be folded: *it folds away for storage.* **3** to intertwine (one's arms) across one's chest or bend up (one's legs). **4** *said of an insect, etc* to bring in (wings) close to its body. **5** *intrans., said of flower petals* to close. **6** to wrap up. **7** to clasp (someone) in one's arms, etc. **8** to stir (an ingredient) gently into a mixture with an action like folding. **9** *intrans.* (*also* **fold up**) *colloq., said of a business, etc* to collapse; to fail. — *noun* **1** a doubling of one layer over another. **2** a rounded or sharp bend made by this; a crease. **3** a hollow in the landscape. **4** *Geol.* a buckling, bending, or contortion of stratified (layered) rocks as a result of movements of the Earth's crust. [from Anglo-Saxon *faldan*, to fold]

☰ *verb* **1** bend, double, ply, overlap, tuck, pleat, crease, crumple, crimp, crinkle. **3** cross, intertwine, entwine. **7** enfold, embrace, hug, clasp, envelop, wrap (up), enclose, entwine, intertwine. **9** fail, *colloq.* go bust, shut down, collapse, crash. *noun* **1** bend, turn, layer, ply, overlap, tuck, pleat. **2** crease, knife-edge, line, wrinkle, furrow, corrugation.

fold[2] *noun* **1** a walled or fenced enclosure for sheep or cattle. **2** the body of believers within the protection of a church. [from Anglo-Saxon *falod*]

-fold *suffix* **1** multiplied by a stated number: *increased threefold.* **2** having a certain number of parts: *a twofold benefit.* [from Anglo-Saxon *feald*]

folder *noun* a cardboard or plastic cover in which to keep loose papers.

☰ file, binder, folio, portfolio, envelope, holder.

foliaceous /fəʊlɪ'eɪʃəs/ *adj.* **1** consisting of or resembling leaves. **2** *Geol.* composed of thin leaflike or platelike layers of minerals; laminated. [from Latin *foliaceus*, from *folium*, leaf]

foliage /'fəʊli:ɪʤ/ *noun* the leaves on a tree or plant. [from Old French *fueillage*, from *feuille*, leaf]

foliate /'fəʊlɪət/ *adj.* leaf-like, or having leaves. [from Latin *foliatus*, leafy]

foliation *noun* **1** *Metall.* the process of beating metal into thin sheets. **2** *Bot.* the development of leaves.

folic acid /'fəʊlɪk/ *Biochem.* a member of the vitamin B complex that is found in many foods, especially liver and green leafy vegetables, and is required for the manufacture of DNA and RNA and the formation of red blood cells. Deficiency of the vitamin causes anaemia and retarded growth. [from Latin *folium*, leaf]

folio *noun* (PL. **folios**) **1** a leaf of a manuscript, etc, numbered on one side. **2** *Printing* a page number in a book. **3** *Hist.* a sheet of paper folded once; a book of the largest size, composed of such sheets: *a folio edition.* **4** *old use* a folder. [from Latin *in folio*, on (a certain numbered) leaf]

folk /fəʊk/ — *noun* **1** (*with pl. verb*) people. **2** (*with pl. verb*) (*also* **folks**) *colloq.* one's family. **3** a people or tribe. **4** *colloq.* folk music. — *adj.* traditional among a people; of popular origin: *folk music /a folksong.* [from Anglo-Saxon *folc*]

☰ *noun* **2** family, people, kin, kindred. **3** people, tribe, clan, race, nation, society. *adj.* traditional, ethnic, national, native, indigenous, tribal, ancestral.

folk art traditional handicrafts, especially pottery, woodcarvings, textiles, and basketware, produced by local craftsmen with no formal training, usually employing techniques, patterns, and designs that have been handed down from generation to generation. The products may be functional or decorative, or have religious significance.

folklore *noun* the customs, beliefs, stories, traditions, etc of particular peoples, or the study of these.

folk music traditional music in Europe, N America, India, and Asia, evolved from oral transmission and usually of ancient rural or peasant origins, evoking the events of daily life.

folksy *adj.* (**folksier, folksiest**) simple and homely, especially in an over-sweet way.

follicle *noun* **1** *Anat.* a small cavity or sac within a tissue or organ, eg hair follicle, Graafian follicle. **2** *Bot.* a fruit formed from a single carpel, containing several seeds, which splits along one side when mature, eg columbine fruit. [from Latin *folliculus*, diminutive of *follis*, bellows]

follicle-stimulating hormone (ABBREV. **FSH**) *Physiol.* a hormone, secreted by the pituitary gland in vertebrates, that plays an important role in reproduction. In mammals it stimulates the growth of the ovarian follicles (in females) and the production of sperm (in males).

follow *verb* **1** (**follow someone** or **something** or **follow after someone** or **something**) to go or come after them. **2** to accompany. **3** to pursue stealthily. **4** to accept as leader or authority. **5** *intrans.* to result; to be a consequence. **6** to go along (a road, etc), alongside (a river, etc) or on the path marked by (signs). **7** to watch (someone or something) as he, she, or it moves: *her eyes followed him up the street.* **8** to pass or practise: *follow a life of self-denial /follow a trade.* **9** to conform to: *follows a familiar pattern.* **10** to obey (advice, etc). **11** *trans., intrans.* to copy: *follow her example.* **12** *trans., intrans.* to understand. **13** to read (a piece of writing or music) while listening to a performance of it. **14** to take a keen interest in (a sport, etc). — **as follows** as announced after this or shown below. **followed by ...** with ... next. **follow on 1** to continue. **2** *Cricket, said of a side* to have to bat a second innings immediately after the first. **follow through** *Tennis, Golf* to continue the action of a stroke after hitting the ball. **follow something through** or **up** to investigate or test it. **follow something up** to take the next step after a particular procedure: *followed up their investigations with a detailed report.* [from Anglo-Saxon *folgian*]

☰ **1** come after, succeed, come next, replace, supersede, supplant. **2** accompany, go (along) with, escort, attend. **3** pursue, track, trail, shadow, tail, hound, chase, go after, hunt. **5** result, ensue, develop, emanate, arise. **10** obey, comply with, adhere to, heed, mind, observe, conform to, carry out, practise. **12** understand, grasp, comprehend, fathom. **follow through** or **up** investigate, check out, test, continue, pursue, reinforce, consolidate.

▣ **1** precede. **4** abandon, desert. **10** disobey.

. . . .

follower *noun* **1** a person who comes after. **2** a person who copies. **3** a supporter. **4** an attendant.

. . . .

▣ **2** imitator, emulator. **3** supporter, adherent, hanger-on, believer, convert, backer, admirer, fan, devotee, freak, *colloq.* buff. **4** attendant, retainer, helper, companion, *colloq.* sidekick, disciple, pupil.

▣ **3** opponent.

. . . .

following — *noun* a body of supporters. — *adj.* **1** coming after; next. **2** about to be mentioned: *need to deal with the following points.* **3** *said of a wind* blowing in the direction in which a ship, etc is travelling. — *prep.* after.

. . . .

▣ *noun* supporters, followers, suite, retinue, entourage, circle, fans, support, backing, patronage, audience, public, clientèle. *adj.* **1** subsequent, next, succeeding, successive, resulting, ensuing, consequent, later.

▣ *adj.* **1**, **2** previous.

. . . .

follow-on *noun Cricket* following on, the batting of a second innings by the same side immediately after the first.

follow-through *noun* following through; further investigation or testing.

follow-up *noun* following up; further action or investigation.

folly *noun* (PL. **follies**) **1** foolishness; a foolish act. **2** a mock temple, castle, etc built as a romantic addition to a view. [from Old French *folie*, madness]

. . . .

▣ **1** foolishness, stupidity, senselessness, rashness, recklessness, irresponsibility, indiscretion, craziness, madness, lunacy, insanity, idiocy, imbecility, silliness, absurdity, nonsense.

▣ **1** wisdom, prudence, sanity.

. . . .

foment /fəʊˈmɛnt/ *verb* to encourage or foster (ill-feeling, etc). [from Latin *fomentum*, poultice]

fomentation *noun* the act or process of fomenting.

fond *adj.* **1** (**fond of someone** or **something**) having a liking for them. **2** loving. **3** *said of wishes, hopes, etc* foolishly impractical. [from Middle English *fonnen*, to act foolishly]

. . . .

▣ **1** partial to, attached to, enamoured of, keen on, addicted to, *colloq.* hooked on. **2** affectionate, warm, tender, caring, loving, adoring, devoted, doting, indulgent.

. . . .

fondant *noun* a soft sweet or paste made with sugar and water. [from French *fondant*, from *fondre*, to melt]

fondle *verb* to touch, stroke, or caress affectionately. [from earlier *fond*, to handle]

. . . .

▣ caress, stroke, pat, pet, cuddle.

. . . .

fondly *adv.* in a fond way.

fondness *noun* being fond.

fondue /ˈfɒnduː/ *noun* **1** an originally Swiss dish of hot cheese sauce into which bits of bread are dipped. **2** a steak dish, the pieces of meat being cooked at table by dipping briefly into hot oil. [from French *fondu(e)*, from *fondre*, to melt]

font *noun* the basin in a church that holds water for baptisms. [from Anglo-Saxon *fant*, from Latin *fons*, fountain]

fontanelle or **fontanel** /fɒntəˈnɛl/ *noun* a soft membrane-covered gap between the immature bones of the skull of a fetus or young infant, or a young animal. [from Old French *fontanele*]

food *noun* **1** a substance taken in by a living organism that provides it with energy and materials for growth, maintenance, and repair of tissues. The human body requires proteins, fats, carbohydrates, vitamins, minerals, and water in order to carry out these processes. **2** solid as distinct from liquid nourishment: *food and drink.* **3** something that provides stimulation: *food for thought.* [from Anglo-Saxon *foda*]

. . . .

▣ **1** foodstuffs, comestibles, *colloq.* eatables, provisions, stores, rations, refreshment, sustenance, nourishment, nutrition, nutriment, subsistence, feed, fodder, diet, fare, cooking, cuisine, menu, board, table. **2** *colloq.* eats, *slang* grub, *slang* nosh.

. . . .

Kinds of food include: soup, broth, minestrone, bouillabaisse, borsch, cockaleekie, consommé, gazpacho, goulash, vichyssoise; chips, French fries, ratatouille, sauerkraut, bubble and squeak, nut cutlet, cauliflower cheese, chilladas, hummus, macaroni cheese; pasta, cannelloni, fettuccine, ravioli, spaghetti bolognese, tortellini, lasagne; fish and chips, fishcake, fish finger, fisherman's pie, kedgeree, gefilte fish, kipper, pickled herring, scampi, calamari, prawn cocktail, caviar; meat, casserole, cassoulet, hotpot, shepherd's pie, cottage pie, chilli con carne, biryani, chop suey, moussaka, paella, samosa, pizza, ragout, risotto, tandoori, vindaloo, Wiener schnitzel, smörgåsbord, stroganoff, Scotch woodcock, welsh rarebit, faggot, haggis, sausage, frankfurter, hot dog, fritter, hamburger, *trademark* McDonald's, *trademark* Big Mac, *trademark* Wimpy, bacon, egg, omelette, quiche, tofu, *trademark* Quorn, Yorkshire pudding, toad-in-the-hole; ice cream, charlotte russe, egg custard, fruit salad, fruit cocktail, gateau, millefeuilles, pavlova, profiterole, Sachertorte, soufflé, summer pudding, Bakewell tart, trifle, yogurt, sundae, syllabub, queen of puddings, Christmas pudding, tapioca, rice pudding, roly-poly pudding, spotted dick, zabaglione; doughnut, Chelsea bun, Eccles cake, éclair, flapjack, fruitcake, Danish pastry, Genoa cake, Battenburg cake, Madeira cake, lardy cake, hot cross bun, ginger nut, gingerbread, shortbread, ginger snap, macaroon, Garibaldi biscuit; bread, French bread, French toast, pumpernickel, cottage loaf, croissant; gravy, fondue, salad cream, mayonnaise, French dressing; sauces: tartare, Worcestershire, bechamel, white, barbecue, tomato ketchup, hollandaise, *trademark* Tabasco, apple, mint, cranberry, horseradish, pesto. *See also* **cheese; fish; fruit; meat; nut; sweets; vegetable**.

. . . .

food additive see ADDITIVE.

food chain a sequence of organisms arranged in such a way that each feeds on the organism below it in the chain, and serves as a source of food for the organism above it.

foodie *noun colloq.* a person who is greatly or excessively interested in the preparation and eating of food.

foodism *noun* interest in, or concern over, food.

food poisoning any of various illnesses that result from eating food or drinking water containing toxins or microorganisms, especially species of the bacterium *Salmonella.*

food processor an electrical domestic appliance that is used for automatically processing food by chopping, blending, mincing, etc.

foodstuff *noun* a substance used as food.

food technology the application of scientific methods and engineering technology to the commercial processing, preparation, packaging, storage, and distribution of foodstuffs.

food value the nutritional value of a particular food, expressed in terms of its protein, carbohydrate, fat, fibre, and energy content. In many countries it is a legal requirement for such information to be displayed on food packaging.

food web *Biol.* the interlocking patterns formed by a series of interconnected food chains.

fool[1] — *noun* **1** a person lacking common sense or intelligence. **2** someone made to appear ridiculous. **3** *Hist.* a person employed by kings, nobles, etc to amuse them; a jester. — *verb* **1** deceive (someone) so that they appear foolish. **2** (**fool someone into** or **out of something**) to persuade them by deception to do something or not to do it. **3** (**fool about** or **around**) to behave stupidly or playfully. — **make a fool of someone** to trick them, or make them appear ridiculous. **make a fool of oneself** to appear foolish. **nobody's fool** too wary to be tricked or deceived. **play the fool** deliberately to act in a comically foolish manner. [from Old French *fol*]

....

■ *noun* **1** *colloq.* blockhead, *colloq.* fathead, nincompoop, *colloq.* ass, *colloq.* chump, ninny, *colloq.* clot, *slang* divvy, *colloq.* dope, *slang* dork, *slang* wally, *colloq.* twit, *colloq.* nitwit, *slang* nit, dunce, *colloq.* dimwit, simpleton, halfwit, idiot, imbecile, *colloq.* moron. **2** dupe, *colloq.* sucker, *colloq.* mug, stooge. **3** jester, clown, buffoon. *verb* **1** deceive, take in, delude, mislead, dupe, gull, hoodwink, put one over on, trick, hoax, *colloq.* con, cheat, swindle, *colloq.* diddle, string along, *colloq.* have on, *colloq.* kid, tease. **3** lark about, *colloq.* horse around, play about, *colloq.* mess about, *colloq.* mess around.

....

fool[2] *noun* a dessert of puréed fruit mixed with cream or custard. [perhaps from FOOL[1]]

foolery *noun* (PL. **fooleries**) stupid or ridiculous behaviour.

foolhardiness *noun* **1** being foolhardy. **2** a foolhardy act or foolhardy behaviour.

foolhardy *adj.* taking foolish risks; rash; reckless. [from Old French *fol hardi*, foolish-bold]

....

■ rash, reckless, imprudent, ill-advised, irresponsible.
🔁 cautious, prudent.

....

foolish *adj.* **1** unwise; senseless. **2** ridiculous.

....

■ **1** stupid, senseless, unwise, ill-advised, ill-considered, short-sighted, *colloq.* half-baked, daft, crazy, mad, insane, idiotic, moronic, hare-brained, halfwitted, simple-minded, simple, unintelligent, inept, inane. **2** ridiculous, ludicrous, silly, absurd, nonsensical.
🔁 **1** wise, prudent.

....

foolproof *adj.* **1** *said of a plan, etc* unable to go wrong. **2** *said of a machine, etc* unable to be misunderstood or misused; simple to use.

....

■ **1** infallible, sure, certain, *colloq.* sure-fire, guaranteed. **2** idiot-proof, fail-safe.
🔁 **1** unreliable.

....

foolscap *noun* a large size of printing or writing-paper, measuring 17x13in (432x343mm). [from the jester's cap used as a watermark]

fool's errand a pointless or unprofitable task or venture.

fool's gold same as PYRITE.

fool's paradise a state of confidence based on false expectations.

foot *noun* (PL. **feet**) **1** the part of the leg on which a human being or animal stands or walks. **2** in molluscs, a muscular organ used for locomotion, which can be retracted into the animal's shell. **3** the part of a sock, stocking, etc that fits over the foot. **4** the bottom or lower part of something. **5** the end of a bed where the feet go. **6** (PL. **feet, foot**) in the imperial system, a measure of length equal to 12in (30.48cm). **7** a unit of rhythm in verse containing any of various combinations of stressed and unstressed syllables. **8** (*pl.*) *old use* infantry. — **fall on one's feet** to be unexpectedly or undeservedly lucky. **foot it 1** *colloq.* to walk. **2** *old use* to dance. **foot the bill** to pay the bill. **get a foot in**

the door to gain entry into, or get accepted for the first time in, an organization, profession, etc. **get off on the wrong foot** to make a bad start. **get** or **rise to one's feet** to stand up. **have a foot in both camps** to be connected with both of two opposed parties. **have one's feet on the ground** to have plenty of common sense. **have one foot in the grave** *colloq.* to be very old or near death. **my foot!** *colloq.* used to express derisive disbelief. **not put a foot right** to make many mistakes. **not put a foot wrong** to make no mistakes. **on foot** walking. **put one's best foot forward** to set off with determination. **put one's feet up** to take a rest. **put one's foot down** to be firm about something. **put one's foot in it** *colloq.* to cause offence or embarrassment. **set foot in** or **on something** to arrive in or on it. **under foot** beneath one's feet. **under one's feet** in one's way; hindering one.

footage *noun* **1** measurement or payment by the foot. **2** the length of exposed cine film measured in feet.

foot-and-mouth disease a notifiable and highly contagious viral disease of sheep, cattle, pigs, and goats, characterized by the development of blisters in the mouth and around the hooves, by weight loss, and in dairy cattle by a decline in milk yield. In the UK all diseased herds are slaughtered.

football *noun* **1** any of several team games played with a large ball that players try to kick or head into the opposing team's goal or carry across their opponents' goal line. **2** the ball used in the game.

footbridge *noun* a bridge for pedestrians.

footfall *noun* the sound of a footstep.

foothill *noun* a lower hill on the approach to a high mountain or range.

foothold *noun* a place to put one's foot when climbing.

footing *noun* **1** the stability of one's feet on the ground: *lose one's footing.* **2** basis or status. **3** relationship: *on a friendly footing.*

....

■ **1** foothold, balance. **2** basis, status, base, foundation, ground, state, standing, grade, rank, terms, conditions, position. **3** relationship, relations.

....

footlights *pl. noun* in a theatre, a row of lights set along the front edge of a stage to illuminate it.

footloose *adj.* free to go where, or do as, one likes.

footman *noun* a uniformed male attendant.

footnote *noun* a note at the bottom of a page.

footpath *noun* **1** a path or track for walkers. **2** a pavement.

footplate *noun* in a steam train, a platform for the driver and fireman.

footprint *noun* **1** the mark or impression of a foot or shoe. **2** *Comput.* the amount of space taken up by a computer and its hardware on a desk, etc.

....

■ **1** footmark, track, trail, trace.

....

footsie *noun* *colloq.* secret foot-touching with someone under the table, etc, especially as an indication of sexual interest.

footslog *verb intrans., trans.* to go on foot; to trudge.

footsore *adj.* having painful feet from prolonged walking.

footstep *noun* **1** the sound of a step in walking. **2** a footprint. — **follow in the footsteps of someone** to do as was done earlier by them; to copy or succeed them.

footstool *noun* a low stool for supporting the feet while sitting.

footway *noun* a passage for pedestrians.

footwear *noun* shoes, boots, socks, etc.

Types of footwear include: shoe, court shoe, brogue, casual, *colloq.* lace-up, *colloq.* slip-on, slingback, sandal, espadrille, stiletto heel, platform heel, moccasin, *trademark* Doc Martens, slipper, *colloq.* flip-flop, boot, bootee, wellington boot, *colloq.* welly, galosh, gumboot, football boot, rugby boot, tennis shoe, plimsoll, pump, sneaker, trainer, ballet shoe, clog, sabot, snowshoe, *slang* beetle-crushers, *slang* brothel creepers.

footwork *noun* the agile use of the feet in dancing or sport.

fop *noun* a man who is too consciously elegant in his dress and manners; a dandy.

foppery or **foppishness** *noun* (PL. **fopperies**) the behaviour, the concerns, or the clothes of a fop.

foppish *adj.* relating to or characteristic of a fop.

for — *prep.* **1** intended to be given or sent to. **2** towards: *heading for home.* **3** throughout (a time or distance). **4** in order to have, get, etc: *meet for a chat/fight for freedom.* **5** at a cost of. **6** as reward, payment or penalty appropriate to: *got seven months for stealing/charge for one's work.* **7** with a view to: *train for the race.* **8** representing; on behalf of: *the MP for Greenfield/speaking for myself.* **9** to the benefit of: *what can I do for you?* **10** in favour of: *for or against the proposal.* **11** proposing to oneself: *I'm for bed.* **12** because of: *couldn't see for tears.* **13** on account of: *famous for its confectionery.* **14** suitable to the needs of: *books for children.* **15** having as function or purpose: *scissors for cutting hair.* **16** on the occasion of: *got it for my birthday.* **17** meaning: *the German word for 'lazy'.* **18** in place of; in exchange with: *replacements for the breakages/translated word for word.* **19** in proportion to: *one woman for every five men.* **20** up to: *it's for him to decide.* **21** as being: *took you for someone else/know for a fact.* **22** with regard to: *can't beat that for quality.* **23** considering what one would expect: *serious for his age/warm for winter.* **24** about; aimed at: *proposals for peace/a desire for revenge.* **25** in spite of: *quite nice for all his faults.* **26** available to be disposed of or dealt with by: *not for sale.* **27** *with reference to time* **a** at or on: *an appointment for 12.00 on Friday.* **b** so as to be starting by: *7.30 for 8.00.* — *conj.* because. — **be for it** *colloq.* to be about to receive a punishment, etc. **for ever** for all time. **if it hadn't been for someone** or **something** had they not intervened or occurred. **O for** if only I had. [from Anglo-Saxon *for*]

forage /ˈfɒrɪdʒ/ — *noun* **1** (*also* **forage crop**) *Agric.* a crop grown for consumption by livestock, eg grass, clover, kale, turnip, swede, and maize. **2** the activity of foraging. — *verb* **1** *intrans.* to search around, especially for food. **2** to gather forage or provisions from (an area). **3** to find by searching. [from Old French *fourrage*]

⊟ *noun* **1** fodder, pasturage, feed, food, foodstuffs. *verb* **1** hunt, scavenge, scour around. **3** rummage, search, cast about, hunt, scour around, ransack, plunder, raid.

forasmuch as *conj.* *old use Legal* since; seeing that.

foray *noun* **1** a raid or attack. **2** a venture; an attempt. [from Middle English *forrayen*, to pillage]

forbade /fəˈbad, fɔːˈbad/ see FORBID.

forbear[1] /fɔːˈbeə(r)/ *verb trans., intrans.* (PAST TENSE **forbore**; PAST PARTICIPLE **forborne**) (**forbear from something** or **to do something**) to stop oneself going as far as that; to refrain from it: *forbear from answering/forbear to mention it.* [from Anglo-Saxon *forberan*]

forbear[2] /ˈfɔːbeə(r)/ same as FOREBEAR.

forbearance *noun* patience and self-control.

forbearing *adj.* patient and tolerant.

forbid *verb* (**forbidding**; PAST TENSE **forbade**, **forbad**; PAST PARTICIPLE **forbidden**) **1** to order (someone) not to do something. **2** to prohibit. **3** to refuse access to: *had forbidden them the orchard/forbidden territory.* **4** *trans., intrans.* to prevent or not allow: *time forbids a longer stay.* [from Anglo-Saxon *forbeodan*]

⊟ **1, 2** prohibit, disallow, ban, proscribe, interdict, veto, refuse, deny, outlaw, debar, exclude, rule out, preclude, prevent, block, hinder, inhibit.

⊞ **1, 2** allow, permit, approve.

forbidding *adj.* threatening; grim.

⊟ threatening, grim, stern, formidable, awesome, daunting, *colloq.* off-putting, uninviting, menacing, ominous, sinister, frightening.
⊞ approachable, congenial.

forbore, forborne see FOREBEAR.

force — *noun* **1** strength; power; impact or impetus. **2** compulsion, especially with threats or violence. **3** military power. **4** passion or earnestness. **5** strength or validity: *the force of her argument/come into force.* **6** meaning. **7** influence: *by force of habit.* **8** a person or thing seen as an influence: *a force for good.* **9** *Physics* any external agent that produces a change in the speed or direction of a moving object, or that causes a stationary object to move. **10** any irresistible power or agency: *the forces of nature.* **11** the term used in specifying wind speed: *a force 10 gale.* **12** a military body. **13** (**forces**) a nation's armed services. **14** any organized body of workers, etc. **15** (**the force**) the police force. — *verb* **1** to make or compel. **2** (**force someone** or **something back** or **out**) to drive them back or out, especially meeting resistance. **3** to obtain by effort, strength, threats, violence, etc: *forced an admission from them.* **4** (**force one's way**) to make progress by effort or ruthless determination. **5** to produce with an effort. **6** to inflict: *force one's opinions on people.* **7** to cause (a plant) to grow or (fruit) to ripen unnaturally quickly. **8** to strain: *force one's voice.* — **force someone's hand** to compel them to act in a certain way. **in force 1** *said of a law, etc* valid; effective. **2** in large numbers. **join forces** to come together or unite for a purpose. [from Old French, from Latin *fortia*, strength]

⊟ *noun* **1** strength, power, impact, impetus, might, intensity, effort, stress, emphasis. **2** compulsion, coercion, constraint, pressure, duress, influence, violence, aggression. **4** passion, earnestness, energy, vigour, drive, dynamism, determination, fervour, heat, vehemence. **6** meaning, sense, substance, gist. **8** power, influence. **12** army, troop, body, corps, regiment, squadron, battalion, division, unit, detachment, patrol. *verb* **1** make, compel, oblige, necessitate, urge, coerce, constrain, press, pressurize, *colloq.* lean on, *facetious* pressgang, bulldoze. **2** drive, propel, push, thrust. **3** wrench, wrest, extort, exact, wring, prise. **4** push, battle. **6** inflict, impose, press.
⊞ *noun* **1** weakness.

forced *adj.* **1** *said of a smile, laugh, etc* unnatural; unspontaneous. **2** done or provided under compulsion: *forced labour.* **3** carried out as an emergency: *a forced landing.* **4** done with great and long effort: *forced marches.*

⊟ **1** unnatural, stiff, wooden, stilted, laboured, strained, false, artificial, contrived, feigned, affected, insincere. **3** emergency.
⊞ **1** spontaneous, sincere.

force-feed *verb* to feed (a person or animal) forcibly, especially by passing liquid food through a soft rubber tube into the stomach via the mouth or nostril.

forceful *adj.* powerful; effective; influential.

⊟ powerful, effective, strong, mighty, potent, compelling, convincing, persuasive, cogent, telling, weighty, urgent, emphatic, vehement, forcible, dynamic, energetic, vigorous.
⊞ weak, feeble.

force majeure /fɔːs maˈʒɜː(r)/ *noun Legal* any irresistible force or compulsion which will excuse a party from carrying out or completing its part of the contract. [French, = superior force]

forcemeat *noun* a mixture of sausage meat, herbs, etc used as stuffing. [from earlier *farce*, stuffing]

forceps /ˈfɔːsɛps/ *pl. noun* (PL. **forceps**) a pincer-like instrument with two blades, used for grasping objects so that they can be held firmly in position, lifted, or removed. Forceps are widely used in surgery and dentistry, and for handling sterile material, and they are sometimes used to grip the baby's head during childbirth. [from Latin *forceps*, perhaps from *formus*, warm + *capere*, to take]

forcible *adj.* **1** done by, or involving, force. **2** powerful: *a forcible reminder*. [from Old French, from *force*, force]

forcibly *adv.* by force.

ford — *noun* a shallow crossing place in a river. — *verb* to ride, drive, or wade across (a stream, etc). [from Anglo-Saxon *ford-faran*, to go]

fordable *adj.* capable of being forded.

fore — *adj.* towards the front. — *noun* the front part. — *interj. Golf* ball coming! — **fore and aft** at front and rear; at bow and stern; from bow to stern. **to the fore** at or to the front; prominent; conspicuous. [from Anglo-Saxon *fore*]

fore- *prefix* **1** before or beforehand: *forewarn*. **2** in front: *foreleg*. [from Anglo-Saxon *fore*]

fore-and-aft *adj. Naut.*, *said of a sail or rigging* set lengthways, pointing to the bow and stern.

forearm[1] *noun* (with stress on *fore-*) the lower part of the arm between wrist and elbow.

forearm[2] *verb* (with stress on *-arm*) to prepare or arm beforehand.

forebear or **forbear** *noun* (with stress on *fore-*) an ancestor. [from FORE- + BE + -ER]

■ ancestor, forefather, father, predecessor, forerunner, antecedent.
🔁 descendant.

forebode *verb* to foretell; to be a sign of (especially something bad).

foreboding *noun* a feeling of approaching trouble.

■ misgiving, anxiety, worry, apprehension, dread, fear, intuition, feeling, omen, sign, token, premonition, warning, prediction.

forebrain *noun Anat.* the largest part of the vertebrate brain, consisting of the left and right cerebral hemispheres, thalamus, and hypothalamus. In the human brain it is the region that is most strikingly different to the brain of other animals.

forecast — *verb* (PAST TENSE AND PAST PARTICIPLE **forecast**, **forecasted**) to give warning of; to predict; to gauge or estimate (weather, statistics, etc) in advance. — *noun* a warning, prediction, or advance estimate.

■ *verb* predict, prophesy, foretell, foresee, anticipate, expect, gauge, estimate, calculate. *noun* warning, prediction, prophecy, estimate, expectation, prognosis, outlook, projection, guess, *colloq.* guesstimate.

forecastle /ˈfəʊksl, ˈfɔːkɑːsl/ *noun* the bow section of a ship, formerly the quarters of the crew.

foreclose /fɔːˈkləʊz/ *verb intrans.*, *said of a bank, etc* to repossess a property because of failure to pay back the loan used.

foreclosure /fɔːˈkləʊʒə(r)/ *noun* the act or process of foreclosing.

forecourt *noun* a courtyard or paved area in front of a building, eg a filling station.

forefather *noun* an ancestor.

forefinger *noun* the finger next to the thumb; the index finger.

forefoot *noun* either of the two front feet of a four-legged animal.

forefront *noun* **1** the very front. **2** the most prominent or active position.

■ FRONT, FRONT LINE, FIRING LINE, VAN, VANGUARD, LEAD, FORE.
🔁 REAR.

foregather /fɔːˈgaðə(r)/ *verb intrans.* (**foregathered**, **foregathering**) to meet together; to assemble.

forego /fɔːˈgoʊ, fəˈgoʊ/ or **forgo** *verb* (PAST TENSE **forewent**; PAST PARTICIPLE **foregone**) to do without; to sacrifice or give up.

■ do without, sacrifice, give up, yield, surrender, relinquish, forfeit, waive, renounce, abandon, resign, pass up, abstain from, refrain from.
🔁 claim, indulge in.

foregoing /ˈfɔːgoʊɪŋ, fɔːˈgoʊɪŋ/ — *adj.* just mentioned. — *noun* the thing or person just mentioned.

■ *adj.* preceding, antecedent, above, previous, earlier, former, prior.
🔁 *adj.* following.

foregone *adj.* **foregone conclusion** a predictable result; a certainty.

foreground *noun* **1** the part of a view or picture nearest to the viewer. **2** a position where one is noticeable.

forehand *noun Tennis, etc* a stroke made with palm facing forward. See also BACKHAND[1].

forehead /ˈfɔːhɛd, ˈfɒrɪd/ *noun* the part of the face between the eyebrows and hairline; the brow.

foreign /ˈfɒrɪn, ˈfɒrən/ *adj.* **1** of, from, relating, or belonging to another country. **2** concerned with relations with other countries: *foreign affairs*. **3** not belonging where found: *a piece of grit or other foreign body in the eye*. **4** (**foreign to someone**) **a** unfamiliar: *the technique was foreign to them.* **b** uncharacteristic: *envy was foreign to his nature.*

■ **1** alien, immigrant, imported, international, external, outside, overseas, exotic, faraway, distant, remote. **4** strange, unfamiliar, unknown, uncharacteristic, incongruous.
🔁 **1** native, indigenous. **2** domestic.

foreign aid *Politics* financial or other aid given by richer to poorer nations. Foreign aid may be in the form of grants, gifts, special trading deals, cheap loans or credit terms, expertise, or goods.

foreign correspondent a newspaper or broadcasting correspondent working in a foreign country in order to report news, etc.

foreigner *noun* **1** a person from another country. **2** an unfamiliar person; a person who doesn't belong.

■ **1** alien, immigrant. **2** stranger, newcomer, incomer, visitor.
🔁 **1** native.

foreign exchange *Commerce* the amount of currency of foreign origin held in a country. It is derived from exporting and from overseas investment.

foreign minister or **foreign secretary** the government minister responsible for a country's foreign affairs.

foreign office the department of a government dealing with foreign affairs.

foreknowledge *noun* knowledge about something before it happens.

foreleg *noun* either of the two front legs of a four-legged animal.

forelock *noun* a lock of hair growing or falling over the brow.

foreman or **forewoman** *noun* **1** a man or woman in charge of a body of fellow workers. **2** the spokesman or spokeswoman of a jury.

foremost — *adj.* leading; best. — *adv.* leading; coming first. — **first and foremost** essentially; most importantly. [from Anglo-Saxon *formest*, from *forma*, first]

⊞ *adj.* first, leading, front, chief, main, principal, primary, cardinal, paramount, central, highest, uppermost, supreme, prime, pre-eminent.

forenoon *noun Scot.* the morning.

forensic /fəˈrɛnsɪk, fəˈrɛnzɪk/ *adj.* **1** relating to or belonging to courts of law, or to the work of a lawyer in court. **2** concerned with the scientific aspect of legal investigations. [from Latin *forensis*, of the *forum*, where law courts were held in Rome]

forensically *adv.* in a forensic way.

forensic medicine the branch of medicine concerned with the production of evidence to be used in civil or criminal law cases. It is an important means of determining the cause of death in unexplained or suspicious circumstances.

foreordain /fɔːrɔːˈdeɪn/ *verb* to determine (events, etc) in advance; to destine.

foreplay *noun* sexual stimulation leading up to sexual intercourse.

forerunner *noun* **1** a person or thing that goes before; a predecessor; an earlier type or version. **2** a sign of what is to come. **3** an advance messenger or herald.

⊞ **1** predecessor, ancestor, antecedent, precursor. **2** sign, token, precursor, harbinger. **3** herald, envoy.
⊟ **1** successor, follower.

foresee *verb* (PAST TENSE **foresaw**; PAST PARTICIPLE **foreseen**) to see or know in advance.

⊞ envisage, anticipate, expect, forecast, predict, prophesy, foretell, forebode.

foreseeable *adj.* capable of being foreseen.

foreshadow *verb* to be an advance sign or indication of.

⊞ predict, prophesy, signal, promise, indicate, presage, augur, prefigure.

foreshore *noun* the area of a beach or shore that lies between the high and low tide marks, and so is regularly covered and uncovered by the tide.

foreshorten *verb* (**foreshortened**, **foreshortening**) in photographic or artistic perspective, to give a shortening effect to: *foreshortened limbs*.

foresight *noun* **1** the ability to foresee. **2** consideration taken or provision made for the future. **3** the front sight on a gun.

⊞ **2** anticipation, planning, forethought, far-sightedness, vision, caution, prudence, circumspection, care, readiness, preparedness, provision, precaution.
⊟ **2** improvidence.

foreskin *noun Anat.* the fold of skin that covers the end (glans) of the penis. It may be surgically removed by circumcision very early in childhood for religious or other reasons.

forest *noun* **1** *Bot.* a plant community extending over a large area and dominated by trees, the crowns of which form an unbroken covering layer or canopy. **2** a tract of country formerly owned, and used for hunting, by a sovereign. **3** a dense arrangement of objects. [from Latin *forestis silva*, unfenced woodland]

forestall *verb* to prevent by acting in advance: *issue an announcement to forestall the inevitable questions*. [from Middle English *forstallen*, to waylay]

⊞ pre-empt, anticipate, preclude, obviate, avert, head off, ward off, parry, balk, frustrate, thwart, hinder, prevent.

forestation *noun Bot.* the planting of trees on land that was formerly used for other purposes.

forested *adj.* covered with, or as if with, trees.

forester *noun* a person in charge of a forest or trained in forestry.

forestry *noun* the management of forest and woodland for the commercial production of timber.

foretaste *noun* a brief experience of what is to come.

⊞ preview, trailer, sample, specimen, example, whiff, indication, warning, premonition.

foretell *verb* (PAST TENSE AND PAST PARTICIPLE **foretold**) to tell about beforehand; to predict or prophesy.

⊞ predict, prophesy, forecast, foreshadow, forewarn, augur, presage, signify.

forethought *noun* consideration taken, or provision made, for the future.

⊞ preparation, provision, planning, forward planning, precaution, anticipation, foresight, far-sightedness, circumspection, prudence, caution.
⊟ improvidence, carelessness.

foretold see FORETELL.

forever *adv.* **1** always; eternally. **2** continually: *forever whining*.

⊞ **1** eternally, always, evermore, for all time, permanently. **2** continually, constantly, persistently, incessantly, perpetually, endlessly.

forewarn *verb* to warn beforehand.

forewoman see FOREMAN.

foreword *noun* an introduction to a book, often by a writer other than the author.

⊞ introduction, preface, prologue.
⊟ appendix, postscript, epilogue.

forfeit /ˈfɔːfɪt/ — *noun* something that one must surrender as a penalty. — *adj.* surrendered or liable to be surrendered as a penalty. — *verb* **1** to hand over as a penalty: *forfeit one's passport*. **2** to give up or do without voluntarily. [from Old French *forfait*, from Latin *foris-factum*, penalty]

⊞ *noun* penalty, fine, damages. *verb* **1** hand over, surrender, give up, relinquish. **2** lose, give up, surrender, relinquish, sacrifice, forego, renounce, abandon.

forfeiture *noun* **1** the act of forfeiting. **2** the state of being forfeited. **3** something that is forfeited.

forgave see FORGIVE.

forge [1] — *noun* **1** a special furnace for heating metal, especially iron, prior to shaping it. **2** the workshop of a blacksmith, where metal is heated and shaped into horseshoes, tools, etc. — *verb* **1** to shape metal by heating and hammering, or by heating and applying pressure more gradually. **2** to make an imitation of (a signature, document, banknote, etc) for a dishonest or fraudulent purpose. [from Old French, from Latin *fabrica*, workshop]

⊞ *verb* **1** shape, form, fashion, beat out, hammer out, work, make, mould, cast, create, invent. **2** fake, counterfeit, falsify, copy, imitate, simulate, feign.

• •

forge² *verb intrans.* to move steadily. — **forge ahead 1** to progress swiftly. **2** to take the lead.

forgery *noun* (PL. **forgeries**) **1** imitating pictures, documents, signatures, etc for a fraudulent purpose. **2** a copy made for a fraudulent purpose.

• • • • • • • • • • • • • • • • • • • •

🔳 **2** fake, counterfeit, copy, replica, reproduction, imitation, *colloq.* dud, *colloq.* phoney, sham, fraud.
🔳 **2** original.

• •

forget *verb trans., intrans.* (**forgetting**; PAST TENSE **forgot**; PAST PARTICIPLE **forgotten**) (*usually* **forget something** or **forget about something**) **1** (*also* **forget to do something**) to fail to remember it or be unable to remember it. **2** to stop being aware of: *forgot his headache in the excitement.* **3** to neglect or overlook (something). **4** to leave behind accidentally. **5** *colloq.* to dismiss from one's mind: *you can forget your proposed skiing trip.* **6** to lose control over (oneself). — **forget it** *colloq.* it doesn't matter. **not forgetting** ... and also ...; including ... . [from Anglo-Saxon *forgietan*]

• • • • • • • • • • • • • • • • • • • •

🔳 **1** omit to, fail to. **3** neglect, overlook, let slip, disregard, lose sight of, ignore. **5** dismiss, think no more of.
🔳 **1** remember, recall, recollect.

• •

forgetful *adj.* inclined to forget.

• • • • • • • • • • • • • • • • • • • •

🔳 absent-minded, dreamy, inattentive, oblivious, negligent, lax, heedless.
🔳 attentive, heedful.

• •

forget-me-not *noun* a low-growing annual or perennial plant of the genus *Myosotis*, native to temperate regions, and bearing one-sided clusters of small tubular flowers with five spreading lobes, often pink in bud and turning blue as they open. [a translation of Old French *ne m'oubliez mye*]

forgivable *adj.* able or likely to be forgiven.

forgive *verb* (PAST TENSE **forgave**; PAST PARTICIPLE **forgiven**) **1** to stop being angry with (someone who has done something wrong) or about (an offence). **2** to pardon. **3** to spare (someone) the paying of (a debt). [from Anglo-Saxon *forgiefan*]

• • • • • • • • • • • • • • • • • • • •

🔳 **1, 2** pardon, absolve, excuse, exonerate, exculpate, acquit, remit, condone, let off, overlook. **3** let off, overlook, absolve from, excuse, remit.
🔳 **1, 2** punish, censure.

• •

forgiveness *noun* **1** the act of forgiving or state of being forgiven. **2** readiness to forgive.

• • • • • • • • • • • • • • • • • • • •

🔳 **1** pardon, absolution, exoneration, acquittal, remission, amnesty. **2** mercy, clemency, leniency.
🔳 **1** punishment, censure, blame.

• •

forgiving *adj.* ready to forgive; patient and tolerant.

• • • • • • • • • • • • • • • • • • • •

🔳 merciful, clement, lenient, patient, tolerant, forbearing, indulgent, kind, humane, compassionate, soft-hearted, mild.
🔳 merciless, censorious, harsh.

• •

forgot, forgotten see FORGET.

fork — *noun* **1** an eating or cooking implement with prongs, for spearing and lifting food. **2** a pronged digging or lifting tool. **3** the division of a road, etc into two branches; one such branch. **4** something that divides similarly into two parts, eg the wheel support of a bicycle. — *verb* **1** *intrans.*, *said of a road etc* to divide into two

branches. **2** *intrans.*, *said of a person or vehicle* to follow one such branch: *fork left.* **3** to lift or move with a fork. — **fork something out** or **up** *colloq.* to pay, under pressure rather than voluntarily. [from Anglo-Saxon *forca*, from Latin *furca*]

• • • • • • • • • • • • • • • • • • • •

🔳 *verb* **1** divide, branch (off), split, part, separate, diverge. **2** bear.

• •

forked *adj.* **1** dividing into two branches or parts. **2** *said of lightning* forming a zigzag.

fork-lift truck a vehicle equipped with two horizontal prongs that can be raised or lowered to move or stack goods.

forlorn *adj.* **1** pathetically unhappy or alone. **2** deserted; forsaken. **3** desperate. [from Anglo-Saxon *forloren*, lost]

• • • • • • • • • • • • • • • • • • • •

🔳 **1, 2** unhappy, miserable, wretched, alone, deserted, forsaken, abandoned, forgotten, bereft, friendless, lonely, lost, homeless, destitute, desolate. **3** desperate, hopeless, miserable, wretched, helpless, pathetic, pitiable.
🔳 **1** cheerful.

• •

forlorn hope 1 a desperate but impractical hope. **2** a hopeless undertaking. [from Dutch *verloren hoop*, lost troop]

forlornness *noun* being forlorn.

form — *noun* **1** shape. **2** figure or outward appearance. **3** kind, type, variety, or manifestation. **4** a printed document with spaces for the insertion of information. **5** a way, especially the correct way, of doing or saying something. **6** structure and organization in a piece of writing or work of art. **7** one's potential level of performance, eg in sport: *soon find your form again.* **8** any of the ways that a word can be spelt or grammatically inflected. **9** a school class. **10** a bench. **11** *slang* a criminal record. **12** a hare's burrow. — *verb* **1** to organize or set up. **2** *intrans.* to come into existence; to take shape. **3** to shape; to make (a shape). **4** to take on the shape or function of. **5** to make up; to constitute. **6** to develop: *form a relationship.* **7** to influence or mould: *the environment that formed him.* **8** to construct, inflect grammatically, or pronounce (a word). — **good** or **bad form** polite or impolite social behaviour. **in good form** in good spirits or health. **a matter of form** a case of a procedure being gone through for the sake of legality or convention. **on** or **off form** performing well or badly. **take form** to come into existence; to begin to have shape. **true to form** in the usual, typical, or characteristic way. [from Latin *forma*, shape, model]

• • • • • • • • • • • • • • • • • • • •

🔳 *noun* **1, 2** shape, figure, appearance, mould, cast, cut, outline, silhouette, build, frame. **3** kind, type, sort, variety, manifestation, order, species, genre, style, manner, nature, character. **4** questionnaire, document, paper, sheet. **6** structure, format, model, pattern, design, arrangement, organization, system. **7** health, fitness, fettle, condition, spirits. **9** class, year, grade, stream. *verb* **1** organize, set up, create, found, establish, build, construct, arrange, put together, assemble. **2** take shape, materialize, appear, crystallize, grow, develop. **3** shape, mould, model, fashion, make, manufacture, produce. **5** make up, constitute, comprise, compose.

• •

-form *combining form* **1** having the appearance or structure of: *cuneiform.* **2** in so many forms or varieties: *multiform.* [from Latin *formis*]

formal *adj.* **1** relating to or involving etiquette, ceremony, or conventional procedure generally: *formal dress.* **2** stiffly polite rather than relaxed and friendly. **3** valid; official; explicit: *a formal agreement/proof, etc.* **4** *said of language* strictly correct with regard to grammar, style, and choice of words, as distinct from conversational. **5** organized and methodical: *the formal approach to teaching.* **6** precise and symmetrical in design: *a formal garden*. **7** relating to outward form as distinct from content. [from Latin *formalis*]

▣ **1** official, ceremonial, stately, solemn, conventional, orthodox, correct, fixed, set, regular. **2** stiff, prim, starchy, strict, rigid, precise, exact, punctilious, ceremonious, stilted, reserved.
▣ **1, 2, 3, 4, 5** informal. **1, 2** casual.

formaldehyde /fɔː'maldəhaɪd/ *noun Chem.* (FORMULA HCHO) a colourless pungent gas, the simplest of the aldehydes, which is commercially available as a 40% solution known as formalin. It is widely used as a disinfectant and preservative for biological specimens, and in the manufacture of synthetic resins, eg Bakelite. Also called METHANAL. [from FORMIC + ALDEHYDE]

formalin /'fɔːməlɪn/ *noun* a solution of formaldehyde (methanal) in water, widely used as a disinfectant and antiseptic, and as a preservative for biological specimens. [from FORMALDEHYDE; originally a trademark]

formalism *noun* concern, especially excessive concern, with outward form.

formalist *noun* a person who promotes formalism.

formality *noun* (PL. **formalities**) **1** a procedure gone through as a requirement of etiquette, ceremony, the law, etc. **2** a procedure gone through merely for the sake of correctness or legality: *the interview was a formality, as she had already been promised the job.* **3** strict attention to the rules of social behaviour.

▣ **1** custom, convention, ceremony, ritual, procedure, matter of form. **2** technicality. **3** protocol, etiquette, form, correctness, propriety, decorum, politeness.
▣ **3** informality.

formalization or **formalisation** *noun* **1** the act or process of formalizing. **2** something that is formalized.

formalize or **formalise** *verb* to make official, eg by putting in writing, etc; to give definite or legal form to.

formally *adv.* in a formal way.

format — *noun* **1** the size and shape of something, especially a book or magazine. **2** the style in which a television programme etc is organized and presented. **3** *Comput.* a specific arrangement of data in tracks and sectors on a disk. — *verb* (**formatted, formatting**) **1** to design, shape, or organize in a particular way. **2** to organize (data for input) into a particular computer. **3** to prepare a new disk for use by marking out the surface into tracks and sectors, so that it is capable of receiving data. [from Latin *formatus*, shaped (in a certain way)]

formation *noun* **1** the process of forming, making, developing or establishing. **2** a particular arrangement, pattern or order. **3** a shape or structure. [from Latin *formatio*, shape]

▣ **1** creation, construction, generation, production, manufacture, development, establishment, organization. **2** arrangement, pattern, order, configuration, format, design, structure, organization, grouping, construction, composition, constitution.

formative *adj.* **1** relating to development or growth. **2** having an effect on development. [from Old French *formatif*]

form criticism *Relig.* a method of analysing New Testament Gospel traditions, in which individual stories and sayings are studied in isolation from their Gospel contexts, and in terms of the stereotyped forms of oral folklore, in the belief that they were originally transmitted orally and individually before being strung together and given a context by Gospel writers.

former *adj.* **1** belonging to an earlier time. **2** previous; earlier. — **the former** the first of two things mentioned. [comparative of Anglo-Saxon *forma*, first, earliest]

▣ **1** old, old-time, ancient, bygone, past, ex-, one-time,

sometime, late, departed. **2** previous, earlier, prior, preceding, antecedent, foregoing, above.
▣ **1** current, present, future. **2** following.

formerly *adv.* previously; in the past.

▣ previously, once, earlier, before, at one time, lately.
▣ currently, now, later.

Formica /fɔː'maɪkə/ *noun trademark* a hard heat-resistant plastic, used for making easy-to-clean work surfaces in kitchens, laboratories, etc.

formic acid *Chem.* (FORMULA HCOOH) a colourless pungent liquid that is toxic and corrosive, and is largely responsible for the stinging sensation produced by ant bites and stinging nettles. It is the simplest carboxylic acid, and is used in the dyeing of textiles, and as a fumigant and insecticide. Also called METHANOIC ACID. [from Latin *formica*, ant]

formidable /'fɔːmɪdəbl, fə'mɪdəbl/ *adj.* **1** awesomely impressive. **2** *said of problems, etc* enormous; difficult to overcome. [from Latin *formidabilis*, causing fear]

▣ DAUNTING, CHALLENGING, INTIMIDATING, THREATENING, FRIGHTENING, TERRIFYING, TERRIFIC, FRIGHTFUL, FEARFUL, GREAT, HUGE, TREMENDOUS, PRODIGIOUS, IMPRESSIVE, AWESOME, OVERWHELMING, STAGGERING.

formless *adj.* lacking a clear shape or structure.

form of address the word or words used as a title before a person's name; the form of words used in speaking to someone on a formal or ceremonial occasion.

formula *noun* (PL. **formulas, formulae**) **1** a combination of chemical symbols that represents the chemical composition of a particular substance. Subscript numbers are used to denote the number of atoms of each element that are present in a molecule of the substance, eg the formula for water is H_2O. **2** a mathematical equation or expression, or a physical law, that represents the relationship between various quantities, and is usually expressed in numerical figures and letters. **3** the combination of ingredients used in a product, etc. **4** a method or rule of procedure, especially a successful one. **5** an established piece of wording used eg in religion or law. **6** a term used for classifying racing cars according to engine size: *Formula 1 racing.* **7** *North Amer.* powdered milk for babies. [from Latin *formula*, a diminutive of *forma*, form]

▣ **4** method, way, rule, procedure, technique, recipe, prescription, principle, form, proposal, blueprint. **5** wording, rubric, code.

formulaic /fɔːmjʊ'leɪɪk/ *adj.* relating to or typical of a formula or formulae.

formulary /'fɔːmjʊlərɪ/ *noun* (PL. **formularies**) a book or collection of especially legal or religious formulas. [from Old French *formulaire*]

formulate *verb* **1** to express in terms of a formula. **2** to express precisely and clearly.

▣ **2** express, state, specify, detail, frame, define, develop, evolve, create, invent, originate, found, form, devise, work out, plan, design, draw up.

formulation *noun* **1** the act or process of formulating. **2** something that is formulated.

fornicate *verb intrans.* to have sexual intercourse outside marriage. [from Latin *fornicari*, from *fornix*, brothel]

fornication *noun* voluntary sexual intercourse outside marriage.

forsake *verb* (PAST TENSE **forsook**; PAST PARTICIPLE **for-**

saken) to desert; to abandon. [from Anglo-Saxon *forsacan*]

....

■ desert, abandon, jilt, throw over, discard, jettison, reject, disown, leave, quit, give up, surrender, relinquish, renounce, forego.

....

forswear *verb* (PAST TENSE **forswore**; PAST PARTICIPLE **forsworn**) *old use* **1** to give up or renounce (one's foolish ways, etc). **2** to perjure (oneself). [from Anglo-Saxon *forswerian*, to swear falsely]

forsythia /fɔː'saɪθɪə/ *noun* a fast-growing deciduous shrub of the genus *Forsythia*, native to China, Japan, and SE Europe, and widely cultivated elsewhere, having yellow bell-shaped flowers, borne in clusters that appear in spring before the leaves. [named after W *Forsyth* (1737–1804), British botanist]

fort *noun* a fortified military building, enclosure, or position. — **hold the fort** to keep things running in the absence of the person normally in charge. [from Latin *fortis*, strong]

....

■ fortress, fortification, castle, tower, citadel, stronghold, garrison, station, camp.

....

forte[1] /'fɔːteɪ/ *noun* something one is good at; a strong point. [from French *fort*, strong]

forte[2] /'fɔːteɪ/ *Mus.* — *adj.* played loud. — *adv.* loudly. [from Italian *forte*]

forth *adv. old use* except in phrases **1** into existence or view: *bring forth children.* **2** forwards: *swing back and forth.* **3** out: *set forth on a journey.* **4** onwards: *from this day forth.* — **and so forth** and so on. **hold forth** to speak, especially at length. [from Anglo-Saxon *forth*]

forthcoming *adj.* **1** happening or appearing soon. **2** *said of a person* willing to talk; communicative. **3** available on request.

....

■ **1** impending, imminent, approaching, coming, prospective, projected, expected, future. **2** communicative, talkative, *colloq.* chatty, conversational, sociable, informative, expansive, open, frank, direct.
🔁 **2** reticent, reserved.

....

forthright *adj.* firm, frank, straightforward and decisive. [from Anglo-Saxon *forthriht*]

....

■ firm, frank, straightforward, decisive, direct, blunt, candid, plain, open, bold, outspoken.
🔁 devious, secretive.

....

forthwith *adv.* immediately.

forties *pl. noun* **1** the period of time between one's 40th and 50th birthdays. **2** the range of temperatures between 40 and 50. **3** the period of time between the 40th and 50th years of a century. — **roaring forties** the area of stormy west winds south of latitude 40°S, or north of latitude 40°N in the Atlantic.

fortieth *noun, adj.* **1** the position in a series corresponding to 40 in a sequence of numbers. **2** one of forty equal parts.

fortification *noun* **1** the process of fortifying. **2** (**fortifications**) walls and other defensive structures built in preparation for an attack.

fortify *verb* (**fortifies**, **fortified**) **1** to strengthen (a building, city, etc) in preparation for an attack. **2** to add extra alcohol to (wine): *sherry is a fortified wine.* **3** give fresh energy and determination to (a person). [from Latin *fortis*, strong + *facere*, to make]

....

■ **1** strengthen, reinforce, brace, shore up, buttress, garrison, defend, protect, secure. **3** invigorate, sustain, support, boost, encourage, hearten, cheer, reassure.

🔁 **1** weaken. **3** dishearten, discourage.

....

fortissimo /fɔː'tɪsɪmoʊ/ *Mus.* — *adj.* played very loud. — *adv.* very loudly. [from Italian *fortissimo*]

fortitude *noun* uncomplaining courage in pain or misfortune. [from Latin *fortitudo*, strength]

....

■ courage, bravery, valour, *colloq.* grit, pluck, resolution, determination, perseverance, firmness, strength of mind, willpower, endurance, stoicism.
🔁 cowardice, fear.

....

fortnight *noun* a period of 14 days. [from Anglo-Saxon *feowertiene niht*, 14 nights]

fortnightly *adj., adv.* occurring, appearing, etc once every fortnight.

FORTRAN *noun* a high-level computer programming language widely used for mathematical, scientific, and engineering programs in the 1950s and 1960s. Many of its general principles have been absorbed into BASIC. [from *formula translation*]

fortress *noun* a fortified town, or large fort or castle. [from Old French *forteresse*, from Latin *fortis*, strong]

fortuitous /fɔː'tjuːɪtəs/ *adj.* happening by chance; accidental. [from Latin *fortuitus*]

....

■ chance, accidental, random, arbitrary, casual, incidental, unforeseen, lucky, fortunate, providential.
🔁 intentional, planned.

....

fortunate *adj.* **1** lucky; favoured by fate. **2** timely; opportune. [from Latin *fortunatus*]

....

■ **1** lucky, providential, happy, felicitous, prosperous, successful, well-off. **2** timely, well-timed, opportune, convenient, propitious, advantageous, favourable, auspicious.
🔁 UNFORTUNATE. **1** unlucky, unhappy.

....

fortunately *adv.* in a fortunate way; by good luck.

fortune *noun* **1** chance as a force in human affairs; fate. **2** luck. **3** (**fortunes**) unpredictable happenings that swing affairs this way or that: *the fortunes of war.* **4** (**fortunes**) the state of one's luck. **5** one's destiny. **6** a large sum of money. — **make one's fortune** to become prosperous. **a small fortune** a large amount of money. **tell someone's fortune** to tell someone what their destiny is. [from Latin *fortuna*]

....

■ **1** chance, fate, luck, accident, providence. **5** destiny, doom, lot, portion, life, history, future. **6** wealth, riches, treasure, *colloq.* mint, *colloq.* pile, income, means, assets, estate, property, possessions.

....

fortune-teller *noun* a person who claims to be able to tell people their destinies.

forty — *noun* (PL. **forties**) **1** the number or figure 40; any symbol for this number. **2** the age of 40. **3** a set of 40 people or things. — *adj.* **1** 40 in number. **2** aged 40. [from Anglo-Saxon *feowertig*]

forty winks *colloq.* a short sleep.

forum *noun* **1** *Hist.* a public square or market place, especially that in ancient Rome where public business was conducted and law courts held. **2** a place, programme, or publication where opinions can be aired and discussed. [from Latin *forum*]

forward — *adv.* **1** (*also* **forwards**) in the direction in front or ahead of one. **2** (*also* **forwards**) progressing from first to last. **3** on or onward; to a later time: *put the clocks forward.* **4** to an earlier time: *bring the wedding forward a month.* **5** into view or public attention: *put forward suggestions.* — *adj.* **1** in the direction in front or ahead of one. **2** at the front. **3** advanced in development: *how far forward are the* plans? **4** concerning the future: *forward planning*. **5** *derog.* inclined to push oneself forward; over-bold in offering one's opinions. — *noun Football, Hockey* a player whose task is to score rather than defend the goal. — *verb* **1** to send (mail) on to another address. **2** to help the progress of. [from Anglo-Saxon *foreweard*]

················

▣ *adv.* **1** ahead, on, onward, out. **2** on, onward. **3** on, onward, ahead. **4** ahead. *adj.* **2** front, head, first, leading, fore, foremost. **3** on, ahead, onward, advanced, well-advanced, well-developed, progressive, go-ahead, forward-looking, enterprising, precocious. **4** future. **5** assertive, *colloq.* pushy, bold, audacious, brazen, brash, barefaced, *colloq.* cheeky, impudent, impertinent, *colloq.* fresh, familiar, presumptuous. *verb* **1** send (on), post, transport, ship, dispatch. **2** assist, aid, facilitate, advance, promote, further, foster, encourage, support, back, favour, help, accelerate, speed, hurry, hasten, expedite.

▣ *adj.* **3** backward, retrograde, retarded. **5** shy, modest. *verb* **2** impede, obstruct, hinder, slow.

·································

forward-looking *adj.* planning ahead; progressive, enterprising, or go-ahead.

forwent see FOREGO.

fossil *noun* **1** *Geol.* the petrified remains, impression, or cast of an animal or plant preserved within a rock. Most fossils consist of hard parts, eg the internal skeleton of vertebrates, the shells of molluscs and crustaceans. **2** a relic of the past. **3** *colloq.* a curiously antiquated person. **4** (*attributive*) **a** like, or in the form of, a fossil. **b** formed naturally through the decomposition of organic matter, and dug or otherwise got from the earth: *fossil fuels*. [from Latin *fossilis*, dug up]

fossil fuel any fuel derived from the fossilized remains of plants and animals, such as coal, petroleum, and natural gas.

fossilization or **fossilisation** /fɒsɪlaɪˈzeɪʃən/ *noun* a complex process whereby the remains of all or part of a plant or animal are preserved, sometimes in minute detail, as solid structures formed by the gradual conversion of bones, teeth, or shells into a type of mineral rock that differs from the surrounding material. Other types of fossil include casts (eg of footprints), and the remains of mammoths and other animals that have been preserved by refrigeration in ice.

fossilize or **fossilise** *verb trans., intrans.* **1** to convert (the remains of all or part of an animal or plant) into a fossil. **2** *said of the remains of all or part of an animal or plant* to be converted into a fossil. **3** *colloq.* to look for fossils.

foster — *verb* (**fostered, fostering**) **1** to bring up (a child that is not one's own). **2** to encourage the development of (ideas, feelings, etc). — *adj.* **1** concerned with, or offering, fostering. **2** (*in compounds*) in a specified family relationship through fostering rather than by birth: *foster-mother, brother*. [from Anglo-Saxon *fostrian*, to feed]

················

▣ *verb* **1** raise, rear, bring up, nurse, care for, take care of, nourish, feed, sustain. **2** encourage, support, promote, advance, stimulate, cultivate, nurture, cherish, entertain, harbour.

▣ *verb* **1** neglect. **2** discourage.

·································

fought see FIGHT.

foul — *adj.* **1** disgusting: *a foul smell.* **2** soiled; filthy. **3** contaminated: *foul air.* **4** *colloq.* very unkind or unpleasant. **5** *said of language* offensive or obscene. **6** unfair or treacherous: *by fair means or foul.* **7** *said of weather* stormy. **8** clogged. **9** entangled. — *noun Sport* a breach of the rules. — *verb* **1** *intrans., trans. Sport* to commit a foul against (an opponent). **2** to make dirty. **3** to contaminate or pollute. **4** *trans., intrans.* **a** (*also* **foul up**) to become entangled. **b** to become entangled with (something) so as to hinder its movement or functioning. — **fall foul of** to get into trouble or conflict with. **foul something up 1** to clog it. **2** *colloq.* to mess it up; to bungle it. [from Anglo-Saxon]

▣ *adj.* **1** disgusting, revolting, repulsive, nauseating, squalid, nasty, disagreeable. **2, 3** soiled, filthy, dirty, contaminated, unclean, tainted, polluted, rank, fetid, stinking, smelly, putrid, rotten. **4** unkind, unpleasant, awful, terrible, dreadful, bad, nasty. **5** offensive, obscene, lewd, smutty, indecent, coarse, vulgar, gross, blasphemous, abusive. **6** unfair, treacherous, wicked, vicious, vile, base, abhorrent, disgraceful, shameful. **7** stormy, bad, unpleasant, rainy, wet, rough. *verb* **2, 3** dirty, soil, contaminate, taint, pollute, stain, sully, defile. **4** entangle, catch, snarl, twist, ensnare, block, obstruct, clog, choke.

▣ *adj.* **1, 2** clean. **7** fine. *verb* **2, 3** clean. **4** clear, disentangle.

·································

foul-mouthed *adj.* using offensive or obscene language.

foulness *noun* **1** being foul. **2** something that is foul or fouled.

foul play 1 treachery or criminal violence, especially murder. **2** *Sport* a breach of the rules.

foul-up *noun colloq.* a bungled situation; a failure or disaster.

found[1] see FIND.

found[2] *verb* **1** to start or establish (an organization, institution, city, etc), often with a provision for future funding. **2** to base or establish conceptually: *a well-founded argument.* **3** to lay the foundation of (a building). [from Latin *fundare*]

················

▣ **1** start, establish, originate, create, initiate, institute, inaugurate, set up, endow, organize, raise, build, erect, construct. **2** base, establish, ground, bottom, rest, settle, fix, plant.

·································

found[3] *verb* **1** to cast (metal or glass) by melting and pouring into a mould. **2** to produce (articles) by this method. See also FOUNDRY. [from Latin *fundere*, to pour]

foundation *noun* **1** the act of founding or establishing an institution, etc; the institution, etc founded or the fund providing for it. **2** (*usually* **foundations**) the underground structure on which a building is supported. **3** the basis on which a theory, etc rests or depends. **4** a cream, etc smoothed into the skin as a base for additional cosmetics.

················

▣ **1** setting up, establishment, institution, inauguration, endowment, organization, groundwork. **2** base, foot, bottom, ground, bedrock. **3** basis, substance, footing.

·································

foundation course an introductory course, usually followed as a preparation for more advanced studies.

foundation stone a stone laid ceremonially as part of the foundations of a new building.

founder[1] *noun* a person who founds or endows an institution, etc.

················

▣ originator, initiator, father, mother, benefactor, creator, author, architect, designer, inventor, maker, builder, constructor, organizer.

·································

founder[2] *verb intrans.* (**foundered, foundering**) **1** *said of a ship* to sink. **2** *said of a vehicle, etc* to get stuck in mud, etc. **3** *said of a horse* to go lame. **4** *said of a business, scheme, etc* to fail. [from Old French *fondrer*, to submerge]

················

▣ **1** sink, go down, submerge, subside. **4** fail, collapse, fall, fall through, come to nothing, come to grief, break down, misfire, miscarry, abort.

·································

foundling *noun* an abandoned child of unknown parents. [from FOUND[1] + -LING]

foundry *noun* (PL. **foundries**) **1** the art of founding or casting of metal or glass. **2** a place where metal or glass castings are produced. [from FOUND³]

fount¹ *noun* **1** a spring or fountain. **2** a source of inspiration, etc. [from FOUNTAIN]

fount² *noun Printing* a set of printing type of the same design and size. [from Old French *fonte*, casting]

fountain *noun* **1** a jet or jets of water for drinking or for ornamental effect, or a structure supporting this. **2** a spring of water. **3** a source of wisdom, etc. [from Old French *fontaine*, from Latin *fons*, fountain]

....

▤ **1** jet, spray, spout. **2** spring, well, wellspring, reservoir. **3** source, origin, fount, font, fountainhead, wellhead.

....

fountainhead *noun* **1** a spring from which a stream flows. **2** the principal source of something.

fountain pen a metal-nibbed pen equipped with a reservoir of ink.

four — *noun* **1** the number or figure 4; any symbol for this number. **2** the age of 4. **3** something, especially a garment, or a person, whose size is denoted by the number 4. **4** 4 o'clock. **5** a set of 4 things or people, eg the crew of a 4-oared boat. **6** a playing-card with 4 pips. **7** a score of 4 points. — *adj.* **1** 4 in number. **2** aged 4. — **on all fours** on hands and knees. [from Anglo-Saxon *feower*]

four by four a vehicle with four-wheel drive.

fourfold — *adj.* **1** equal to four times as much. **2** divided into or consisting of four parts. — *adv.* by four times as much.

four-letter word any of several short English words referring to sex or excretion, usually considered offensive.

four-poster *noun* a large bed with a post at each corner to support curtains and a canopy.

fourscore *adj., noun* eighty.

foursome *noun* **1** a set of four people. **2** *Golf* a game between two pairs.

four-square — *adj.* **1** strong; steady; solidly based. **2** *said of a building* square and solid-looking. — *adv.* steadily; squarely.

fourteen — *noun* **1** the number or figure 14; any symbol for this number. **2** the age of 14. **3** something, especially a garment, or a person, whose size is denoted by the number 14. **4** a set of 14 people or things. — *adj.* **1** 14 in number. **2** aged 14. [from Anglo-Saxon *feowertiene*]

fourteenth *noun, adj.* **1** the position in a series corresponding to 14 in a sequence of numbers. **2** one of 14 equal parts.

fourth *noun, adj.* **1** the position in a series corresponding to four in a sequence of numbers. **2** one of four equal parts; a quarter. **3** *Mus.* an interval of three diatonic degrees; a tone at that interval from another, or a combination of two tones separated by that interval.

fourth dimension **1** time regarded as a dimension, as complementing the three dimensions of space (length, width, and depth). **2** anything which is beyond ordinary experience.

Fourth Estate the Press regarded as a political force. It was first coined in 1828 by Macaulay, who described the gallery of the house of Commons in which the reporters sit as 'the fourth estate of the realm', the traditional *three estates* being the lords spiritual, the lords temporal, and the commons.

fourthly *adv.* as fourth in a series.

Fourth of July a public holiday in the USA, commemorating the adoption of the Declaration of Independence in 1776.

four-wheel drive a system where all four wheels in a motor vehicle are powered.

Fourth World the poorest and technologically least developed countries of the world.

fovea /'fouviə/ *noun* (PL. **foveae**) **1** *Anat.* a shallow depression in the retina at the back of the eye in birds, lizards, and primates. It is formed only of cones, and is required

for acute vision. Also called YELLOW SPOT. **2** any small hollow or depression in a body structure. [from Latin *fovea*]

fowl — *noun* (PL. **fowls, fowl**) **1** a farmyard bird, eg a chicken or turkey. **2** *old use* (*in compounds*) any bird, especially if eaten as meat or hunted as game: *wildfowl*. — *verb intrans.* to hunt or trap wild birds. [from Anglo-Saxon *fugel*, bird]

fowler *noun* a person who hunts wild birds.

fox — *noun* **1** any of various carnivorous mammals belonging to the dog family (Canidae), especially species of the genus *Vulpes*, found in most parts of the world, and having a pointed muzzle, large pointed ears, and a long bushy tail. The fox is noted for its cunning. **2** the fur of this animal. **3** *colloq.* a cunning person. — *verb* **1** to puzzle, confuse, or baffle. **2** to deceive, trick, or outwit. **3** *trans., intrans., said of paper* to become or cause it to become discoloured with brown spots. [from Anglo-Saxon]

foxglove *noun* a biennial or perennial plant, belonging to the genus *Digitalis*, that produces tall spikes bearing many thimble-shaped purple or white flowers. The leaves are a source of digitalis, a drug that stimulates heart muscle and is used to treat heart failure.

foxhole *noun* a hole in the ground from which a soldier may shoot while protected from the enemy's guns.

foxhound *noun* either of two large breeds of dog, developed and kept for hunting foxes, and having a short brown, black, and white coat and soft ears. The *English foxhound* is smaller than its descendant, the *American foxhound*.

foxhunting *noun* the sport of hunting foxes on horseback, with a pack of foxhounds.

foxily *adv.* in a foxy way.

foxiness *noun* **1** being foxy. **2** foxy behaviour.

foxing *noun* discoloration in the form of brownish marks on paper that has been allowed to become damp.

fox terrier either of two small breeds of dog, the *wire-haired fox terrier* and the *smooth-haired fox terrier*, having a white coat with black and tan markings, a deep chest, a pointed muzzle, and soft folded ears. Originally bred for unearthing foxes, it is now a popular pet.

foxtrot — *noun* a ballroom dance with gliding steps, alternating between quick and slow, or the music for this. — *verb intrans.* (**foxtrotted, foxtrotting**) to perform this dance.

foxy *adj.* (**foxier, foxiest**) **1** like a fox. **2** *North Amer. colloq.*, *said of a woman* sexually attractive. **3** cunning; sly.

foyer /'fɔɪeɪ, 'fɔɪə(r)/ *noun* **1** the entrance hall of a theatre, hotel, etc. **2** *North Amer.* the hallway of a house or apartment. [from French *foyer*, fireplace]

FP *abbrev.* **1** fire plug, ie a hydrant. **2** former pupil.

FPA *abbrev.* Family Planning Association.

Fr¹ *abbrev.* **1** Father, as the title of a priest. **2** (**fr**) franc. **3** French. **4** Friday.

Fr² *symbol Chem.* francium.

fracas /'fraka:/ *noun* (PL. **fracas**) a noisy quarrel; a fight or brawl. [from French *fracas*]

fractal *noun Maths.* an irregular curve or surface produced by repeated subdivision, eg a *snowflake curve* (resembling a snowflake in outline) produced by repeatedly dividing the sides of an equilateral triangle into three segments and adding another triangle to the middle segment. Fractals generated on a computer screen are used to construct models for processes such as coastline erosion and crystal growth, and are also used in computer art. [from Latin *fractus*, broken]

fraction *noun* **1** *Maths.* an expression that indicates one or more equal parts of a whole, usually represented by a pair of numbers separated by a horizontal or diagonal line. **2** a portion; a small part. **3** *Chem.* a group of chemical compounds whose boiling points fall within a very narrow range. The components of such a mixture can be separated by *fractional distillation*. [from Latin *fractio*, breaking]

fractional *adj.* **1** of a fraction or fractions. **2** of the nature of a fraction. **3** tiny, insignificant.

fractional distillation *Chem.* the separation by distillation of the various constituents of a mixture of liquids with different boiling points.

fractionally *adv.* to a fractional or minute degree; barely: *the train is fractionally faster.*

fractionation *noun Chem.* the separation of the components of a mixture, eg by distillation.

fractious *adj.* inclined to quarrel and complain. [from FRACTION, with its earlier meaning of rupture or dissension]

fracture /'fraktʃə(r)/ — *noun* the breakage or cracking of anything hard, especially a bone, rock, or mineral. — *verb trans., intrans.* 1 to break or crack (a bone, rock, mineral, etc). 2 *said of a bone, rock, mineral, etc* to break or crack. [from Latin *fractura*]

⊟ *noun* break, crack, fissure, cleft, rupture, split, rift, rent, schism, breach, gap, opening. *verb* BREAK, CRACK, RUPTURE, SPLIT, SPLINTER, CHIP.
⊟ *verb* JOIN.

fragile *adj.* 1 easily broken. 2 easily damaged or destroyed. 3 delicate: *fragile beauty.* 4 in a weakened state of health. [from Latin *fragilis*, breakable]

⊟ 1, 2 brittle, breakable, frail, delicate, flimsy. 3 delicate, flimsy, dainty, fine, slight, insubstantial. 4 weak, frail, feeble, infirm.
⊟ 1, 2 strong, robust, tough, durable.

fragility *noun* being fragile.

fragment /'fragmənt, frag'mεnt/ — *noun* (with stress on *frag-*) 1 a piece broken off; a small piece of something that has broken. 2 something incomplete; a small part remaining. — *verb* (usually with stress on *-ment*) 1 *trans., intrans.* to break into pieces. 2 *intrans. Comput., said of a file to* split into sections on different parts of a floppy disk, making access slower. [from Latin *fragmentum*]

⊟ *noun* PIECE, BIT, PART, PORTION, REMNANT. 1 particle, crumb, morsel, scrap, shred, chip, splinter, shiver, sliver. *verb* 1 break, shatter, splinter, shiver, crumble, disintegrate, come to pieces, come apart, break up, divide, split (up), disunite.
⊟ *verb* 1 hold together, join. 2 defragment.

fragmentarily *adv.* in a fragmentary way; into fragments.

fragmentariness *noun* being fragmentary.

fragmentary *adj.* consisting of small pieces, not usually amounting to a complete whole.

⊟ bitty, piecemeal, scrappy, broken, disjointed, disconnected, separate, scattered, sketchy, partial, incomplete.
⊟ whole, complete.

fragmentation *noun* division into fragments.

fragrance *noun* 1 sweetness of smell. 2 a scent or odour.

⊟ 1 perfume, bouquet. 2 scent, smell, odour, aroma, perfume.

fragrant *adj.* having a pleasant smell. [from Latin *fragrare*, to give out a smell]

⊟ perfumed, scented, sweet-smelling, sweet, balmy, aromatic, odorous.
⊟ unscented.

frail *adj.* 1 easily broken or destroyed; delicate; fragile. 2 in poor health; weak. 3 morally weak; easily tempted. [from Old French *fraile*, from Latin *fragilis*, fragile]

⊟ 1 delicate, fragile, brittle, breakable, flimsy, insubstantial, slight. 2 weak, feeble, infirm, puny, vulnerable.

⊟ STRONG. 1, 2 tough, robust.

frailness *noun* being frail.

frailty *noun* (PL. **frailties**) 1 physical or moral weakness. 2 a moral failing or weakness.

⊟ 1 weakness, imperfection, fallibility, susceptibility. 2 failing, weakness, foible, deficiency, shortcoming, fault, defect, flaw, blemish, imperfection.
⊟ 1 strength, robustness, toughness.

frame — *noun* 1 a hard main structure round which something is built or to which other parts are added. 2 a structure that surrounds and supports. 3 something that surrounds: *her face with its frame of dark hair.* 4 a body, especially a human one, as a structure of a certain size and shape: *eased his tall frame into the chair.* 5 one of the pictures that make up a strip of film. 6 a single television picture. 7 one of the pictures in a comic strip. 8 a glass structure for protecting young plants growing out of doors. 9 a framework of bars for some purpose. 10 *Snooker* a triangular structure for confining the balls at the start of a round; a round. — *verb* 1 to put a frame round. 2 to be a frame for. 3 to compose or design. 4 *colloq.* to dishonestly direct suspicion for a crime, etc at (someone innocent). [from Anglo-Saxon *framian*, to benefit]

⊟ *noun* 1 structure, framework, skeleton, carcase, chassis, construction. 2 structure, framework, shell, casing, construction. 3 border, surround, edge, setting, mount, mounting. 4 body, build, form. *verb* 1 surround, enclose, mount, box in. 2 surround, enclose. 3 compose, design, formulate, conceive, devise, contrive, concoct, *colloq.* cook up, plan, map out, sketch, draw up, draft, shape, form, model, fashion, mould, forge, assemble, put together, build, construct, fabricate, make. 4 *slang* set up, *colloq.* fit up, trap.

frame of mind a mood.

⊟ mood, state of mind, humour, temper, attitude, outlook, disposition, spirit.

frame of reference 1 a set of facts, beliefs, or principles that serves as the context within which specific actions, events, or behaviour patterns can be analysed or described, or on the basis of which opinions can be formed and decisions made. 2 *Maths.* a set of points, lines, or planes, especially three geometrical axes, used to define and locate the position of a point in space.

frame-up *noun colloq.* a plot to make an innocent person appear guilty.

framework *noun* 1 a basic supporting structure. 2 a basic plan or system. 3 a structure composed of horizontal and vertical bars or shafts.

⊟ 1 structure, skeleton, bare bones, frame, shell, fabric. 2 plan, outline, foundation, groundwork, skeleton, bare bones.

franc /fraŋk/ *noun* the standard unit of currency in France, Belgium, Switzerland, and several other French-speaking countries. [from Old French *Francorum rex*, king of the Franks, the inscription on the first such coins]

franchise — *noun* 1 the right to vote, especially in a parliamentary election. 2 a right, privilege, exemption from a duty, etc, granted to a person or organization. 3 an agreement by which a business company gives someone the right to market its products in an area; the area concerned. — *verb* to grant a franchise to. [from Old French *franchir*, to set free]

⊟ *noun* 1 suffrage, vote. 2 right, privilege, exemption, immunity, freedom, liberty. 3 concession, licence, charter, authorization.

Franciscan /fran'sɪskən/ — *noun* a member of a Christian order of nuns and friars founded by St Francis of Assisi in the early 13c. It constitutes the largest religious order in the Roman Catholic Church, and is noted for its missionary and social work. — *adj.* relating to the Franciscans. [from Latin *Franciscus*, Francis]

francium /'fransɪəm/ *noun Chem.* (SYMBOL **Fr**, ATOMIC NUMBER **87**) the heaviest of the alkali metals, obtained by bombarding thorium with protons. It has several radioactive isotopes. [from the name *France*, where it was discovered]

Franco- /'fraŋkoʊ/ *combining form* forming words meaning 'French, French and ...': *Franco-German*. [from Latin *Francus*, Frank]

francophone *noun* a French-speaking person, especially in a country where other languages are spoken. [from FRANCO- + Greek *phone*, voice]

frangipani /frandʒɪ'paːnɪ/ *noun* **1** a shrub or small tree (*Plumeria rubra*), native to tropical America, which grows up to 6m tall, and has oval leaves and large clusters of highly fragrant white, yellow, or pink flowers. **2** (*also* **frangipane**) a perfume made from this, or imitating it. [from Frangipani, the name of the inventor of the perfume]

Frank *noun* a member of a Germanic people that invaded Gaul in the late 5cAD, founding a kingdom that included much of the country. Its greatest ruler was Charlemagne. [from Anglo-Saxon *Franca*]

frank — *adj.* **1** open and honest in speech or manner. **2** bluntly outspoken. **3** undisguised; openly visible. — *verb* to mark (a letter) to show that postage has been paid. — *noun* a franking mark. [from Latin *francus*, free]

◼ *adj.* **1** open, honest, truthful, sincere, candid, free. **2** blunt, outspoken, plain, direct, forthright, straight, straightforward, downright.
◪ *adj.* **1, 2** insincere, evasive.

Frankenstein or **Frankenstein's monster** a name for a creation or creature that destroys its creator. [named after *Frankenstein* in Mary Shelley's novel]

Frankenstein food *derog.* a foodstuff that has been genetically modified.

frankfurter *noun* a type of spicy smoked sausage. [from German *Frankfurter Wurst*, Frankfurt sausage]

frankincense *noun* a sweet-smelling gum resin obtained from any of various trees of the genus *Boswellia*, native to Asia and Africa. It is used as incense (eg in religious ceremonies), and as an ingredient of perfumes and pharmaceutical preparations. [from Old French *franc encens*, pure incense]

Frankish — *adj.* of the Franks or their language. — *noun* the W Germanic language of the Franks.

frankly *adv.* in a frank way.

◼ honestly, candidly, bluntly, openly, freely, plainly, directly, straight, to be frank, to be honest, in truth.
◪ insincerely, evasively.

frankness *noun* **1** being frank. **2** frank talk.

frantic *adj.* **1** desperate, eg with fear or anxiety. **2** hurried; rushed: *a frantic rush to meet the deadline*. [from Old French *frenetique*, from Greek *phrenetikos*, mad]

◼ **1** desperate, agitated, overwrought, fraught, beside oneself, raging, raving, berserk. **2** hurried, rushed, frenzied, hectic, furious, mad, wild.
◪ CALM, COMPOSED.

frantically *adv.* in a frantic way.

fraternal *adj.* **1** concerning a brother; brotherly. **2** *said of twins* developed from separate ova; not identical. [from Latin *fraternus*, from *frater*, brother]

fraternity *noun* (PL. **fraternities**) **1** a religious brotherhood. **2** a group of people with common interests. **3** the fact of being brothers; brotherly feeling. **4** *North Amer.* a social club for male students. See also SORORITY. [from Latin *fraternitas*, from *frater*, brother]

fraternization or **fraternisation** *noun* associating as brothers; comradeship.

fraternize or **fraternise** *verb intrans.* (**fraternize with someone**) to meet or associate together as friends. [from Latin *fraternus*, brotherly]

◼ mix with, mingle with, socialize with, consort with, associate with, unite with, sympathize with.
◪ shun, ignore.

fratricidal *adj.* relating to or of the nature of fratricide.

fratricide *noun* **1** the murder of a brother. **2** a person who murders his or her brother. [from Latin *frater*, brother + *caedere*, to kill]

fraud *noun* **1** an act of deliberate deception. **2** someone who dishonestly pretends to be something they are not. [from Latin *fraus*, trick]

◼ **1** deception, deceit, guile, cheating, swindling, double-dealing, sharp practice, fake, counterfeit, forgery, sham, hoax, *slang* sting, trick. **2** charlatan, impostor, pretender, *colloq.* phoney, bluffer, hoaxer, cheat, swindler, double-dealer, *colloq.* con man.

fraudulence *noun* being fraudulent.

fraudulent *adj.* involving deliberate deception; intended to deceive. [from Latin *fraudulentus*, from *fraus*, trick]

◼ dishonest, *colloq.* crooked, criminal, deceitful, deceptive, false, bogus, *colloq.* phoney, sham, counterfeit, swindling, double-dealing.
◪ honest, genuine.

fraught [frɔːt] *adj.* **1** (**fraught with danger**) full of danger, difficulties, problems, etc. **2** *colloq.* causing or feeling anxiety or worry. [from Dutch *vracht*, freight]

fray[1] *verb intrans., trans.* **1** *said of cloth or rope* to wear away along an edge or at a point of friction, so that the threads come loose. **2** *said of tempers, nerves, etc* to make or become edgy and strained. [from French *frayer*, from Latin *fricare*, to rub]

fray[2] *noun* **1** a fight, quarrel, or argument. **2** any scene of lively action. [from AFFRAY]

◼ **1** fight, quarrel, argument, brawl, scuffle, *colloq.* dust-up, free-for-all, set-to, clash, conflict, combat, battle, row, rumpus, disturbance, riot.

frazzle — *noun* **1** a state of nervous and physical exhaustion. **2** a scorched and brittle state: *burnt to a frazzle*. — *verb* to tire out physically and emotionally.

FRCP *abbrev.* Fellow of the Royal College of Physicians.

FRCS *abbrev.* Fellow of the Royal College of Surgeons.

freak — *noun* **1** a person or animal of abnormal shape. **2** someone or something odd or unusual. **3** someone highly enthusiastic about something. **4** a drug addict: *an acid freak*. **5** a whim or caprice: *a freak of fancy*. — *adj.* abnormal. — *verb* (**freak out** or **freak someone out**) *colloq.* **1** to become or make mentally or emotionally over-excited, especially by taking hallucinatory drugs. **2** to become or make angry.

◼ *noun* **1** mutant, monster, monstrosity. **2** abnormality, aberration, oddity, curiosity, anomaly, irregularity. **3** enthusiast, fanatic, addict, devotee, fan, *colloq.* buff, *colloq.* fiend, *colloq.* nut. **5** whim, caprice, quirk, vagary, twist, turn. *adj.* abnormal, atypical, unusual, exceptional, odd, queer, bizarre, aberrant, capricious, erratic, unpredictable, unexpected, surprise, chance, fortuitous, fluky.

⊟ adj. normal, common.

freakish or **freaky** adj. (**freakier, freakiest**) **1** very unusual; odd. **2** apt to change the mind suddenly.

freckle — noun a small yellowish-brown benign spot on the skin, especially of fair-skinned people, commonly formed as a result of excessive production of the pigment melanin after exposure to sunlight. — verb trans., intrans. to mark, or become marked, with freckles. [from Norse *freknur*, freckles]

freckly adj. (**frecklier, freckliest**) having many freckles.

free — adj. (**freer, freest**) **1** allowed to move as one pleases; not shut in. **2** not tied or fastened. **3** allowed to do as one pleases; not restricted, controlled, or enslaved. **4** said of a country independent. **5** costing nothing. **6** open or available to all. **7** not working, busy, engaged or having another appointment. **8** not occupied; not being used. **9** (**free of, free from**) without; not, or no longer, having or suffering (especially something harmful, unpleasant or not wanted). **10** (**free with**) generous, lavish, or liberal. **11** said of a translation not precisely literal. **12** smooth and easy: *free and relaxed body movement*. **13** without obstruction: *given free passage*. **14** derog., said of a person's manner disrespectful, over-familiar, or presumptuous. **15** Chem. not combined with another chemical element: *free nitrogen*. — adv. **1** without payment: *free of charge*. **2** without restriction: *wander free*. — verb (**free someone of something**) **1** to make them free from it; to release them. **2** to rid or relieve them of something. — **feel free** you have permission (to do something). **for free** colloq. without payment. **free and easy** cheerfully casual or tolerant. **a free hand** scope to choose how best to act. **it's a free country** colloq. there's no objection to acting in the way mentioned. **make free with something** to make too much, or unacceptable, use of something not one's own. [from Anglo-Saxon *freo*]

⊟ adj. **1** at liberty, at large. **2** loose, unattached, unrestrained. **3** liberated, emancipated. **4** independent, self-governing, democratic. **5** gratis, without charge, free of charge, complimentary, on the house. **7** unoccupied, unemployed, idle, available. **8** spare, unoccupied, available, vacant, empty. **9** without, lacking, devoid of, unaffected by, immune to, exempt from, safe from. **10** generous, lavish, liberal, open-handed, charitable, hospitable. **11** loose, rough. **12** smooth, easy, relaxed, fluid. **13** clear, unobstructed, unimpeded, open. verb **1** release, let go, loose, turn loose, set free, untie, unbind, unchain, unleash, liberate, emancipate, rescue, deliver, save, ransom, disentangle, disengage, extricate, clear. **2** rid, relieve, unburden, exempt, absolve, acquit, clear.

⊟ adj. **1** imprisoned, confined. **3** restricted. **7** busy, occupied, employed, engaged. **8** occupied, in use, engaged, busy. verb **1** imprison, confine. **2** burden.

-free combining form **1** not paying: *rent-free*. **2** not having; not affected or troubled by: *fat-free/pain-free*.

freebase slang — noun cocaine refined for smoking by being heated with ether. — verb to smoke this.

freebie noun colloq. something given or provided without charge.

freeboard noun the distance between the top edge of the side of a boat and the surface of the water.

freebooter noun Hist. a pirate. [from Dutch *vrijbuiter*, from *vrij*, free + *buit*, booty]

freeborn adj. born as a free citizen, not a slave.

Free Church in the UK, a Protestant Church other than an established Church.

freedman or **freedwoman** noun a freed slave.

freedom noun **1** the condition of being free to act, move, etc without restriction. **2** liberty or independence. **3** a right or liberty: *freedom of speech*. **4** the state of being without, or exempt from, something: *freedom from pain*. **5** unrestricted access to or use of: *give someone the freedom of one's*

house. **6** honorary citizenship of a place, entitling one to certain privileges. **7** frankness; candour. **8** over-familiarity; presumptuous behaviour.

⊟ **1** liberty, emancipation, deliverance, release, exemption, immunity, impunity, leeway, free rein, free hand. **2** liberty, independence, autonomy, self-government, home rule. **3** right, liberty, privilege, prerogative, authority, power, licence, opportunity.

⊟ **1** captivity, confinement, restriction.

freedom of conscience the right to hold religious or other beliefs without persecution.

free enterprise business done without government interference or control.

free fall 1 the fall of something acted on by gravity alone. **2** the part of a descent by parachute before the parachute opens.

free-falling noun **1** the process of falling by force of gravity alone. **2** in skydiving, the part of a descent before the parachute opens (at a height of c.600m).

Freefone noun trademark a British Telecom service whereby calls made to a business or organization are charged to that organization rather than to the caller.

free-for-all noun a fight, argument, or discussion in which everybody feels free to join.

freehand adj. adv., said of a drawing, etc done without the help of a ruler, compass, etc.

freehold — adj., said of land, property, etc belonging to the owner for life and without limitations. — noun ownership of such land, property, etc. See also LEASEHOLD.

freeholder noun an owner of property by freehold.

free house a hotel or bar not owned by a particular beer-producer and therefore free to sell a variety of beers.

free kick Football a kick allowed to one side with no tackling from the other, as a penalty to the latter.

freelance — noun a self-employed person offering his or her services where needed, not under contract to any single employer. — adj., adv. of, or as, a freelance. — verb intrans. to work as a freelance. [term for a mercenary medieval soldier, first used by Sir Walter Scott]

freelancer noun a freelance.

freeload verb intrans. to eat, live, enjoy oneself, etc at the expense of someone else.

freeloader noun a sponger.

free love the practice of having sexual relations with people regardless of marriage.

freely adv. in a free way; openly, without restraint.

⊟ readily, willingly, voluntarily, spontaneously, easily, generously, liberally, lavishly, extravagantly, amply, abundantly, frankly, candidly, unreservedly, openly, plainly.

⊟ unwillingly, grudgingly, evasively, cautiously.

freeman noun a respected person who has been granted the freedom of a city.

Freemason noun (also **Mason**) a member of an international secret male society, having among its purposes mutual help and brotherly fellowship.

Freemasonry noun the institutions of the Freemasons.

free pardon an unconditional pardon given, eg as a result of fresh evidence, to someone convicted of a crime.

free port a port, or a free-trade zone adjacent to a port or airport, where goods may be imported free of tax or import duties, provided they are re-exported or used to make goods to be re-exported.

Freepost noun trademark a Royal Mail service whereby postage costs for letters sent to a business or organization are charged to that organization rather than being prepaid by the sender.

free radical Chem. a group of atoms, containing at least one unpaired electron, that is capable of initiating a wide range of chemical reactions. Free radicals can have very damaging effects if they are formed in living organisms.

free-range *adj.* **1** *said of animal livestock, especially poultry* able to move about freely and graze or feed naturally, as opposed to being kept in a barn or battery. **2** denoting eggs laid by free-range hens.

freesia / ˈfriːzɪə, ˈfriːʒə/ *noun* a plant belonging to the genus *Freesia* of the iris family, which has an underground bulb and is widely cultivated for its fragrant trumpet-shaped white, yellow, purple, or crimson flowers. It is very popular as a cut flower. [named after the Swedish botanist Elias Magnus Fries]

free speech the right to express any opinion freely.

free-standing *adj.* not attached to, or supported by, a wall or other structure.

freestyle *Sport* — *adj.*, *said of a competition or race* in which competitors are allowed to choose their own style or programme. — *noun* a freestyle competition or race.

freethinker *noun* someone who forms religious or other ideas by original thought, rather than accepting the view of an authority.

free trade trade with foreign countries without customs, taxes, etc.

free verse poetry with no regular pattern of rhyme, rhythm, or line length.

freeware *noun Comput.* software which is in the public domain, allowing it to be copied legally, but not resold commercially.

freeway *noun North Amer., esp. US* a motorway.

freewheel *verb intrans.* **1** to travel, usually downhill, on a bicycle, in a car, etc without using mechanical power. **2** to act or drift about unhampered by responsibilities.

free will 1 the power of making choices without the constraint of fate or some other uncontrollable force, regarded as a human characteristic. **2** a person's independent choice.

Free World (**the Free World**) formerly, the name used by non-communist countries for themselves.

freeze — *verb* (PAST TENSE **froze**; PAST PARTICIPLE **frozen**) **1** *trans., intrans.* to change (a liquid) into a solid by cooling it to below its freezing point, eg to change water into ice. **2** *said of a liquid* to change into a solid when it is cooled to below its freezing point. **3** (**freeze over** or **freeze something over**) to become covered or cover with ice. **4** (**freeze up** or **freeze something up**) to become blocked up or stop operating because of frost or ice. **5** *trans., intrans.* (*often* **freeze together**) to stick or cause to stick together by frost. **6** *intrans. said of the weather, temperature, etc* to be at or below the freezing point of water. **7** *trans., intrans. colloq.* to be or make very cold: *frozen hands.* **8** *intrans.* to die of cold: *freeze to death.* **9** *trans., intrans., said of food* to preserve (food) by freezing it and storing it below the freezing point of water. **10** *trans., intrans.* to make or become motionless or unable to move, because of fear, etc. **11** to fix (prices, wages, etc) at a certain level. **12** to prevent (money, shares, etc) from being used. **13** to stop (a moving film or videotape) at a particular frame. **14** to anaesthetize (a part of the body). — *noun* **1** (*also* **freeze-up**) a period of very cold weather with temperatures below freezing-point. **2** a period of control of wages, prices, etc. — **freeze someone out** to exclude them from an activity, conversation, etc by persistent unfriendliness or unresponsiveness. [from Anglo-Saxon *freosan*]

⊟ *verb* **2** solidify. **3** ice over, glaciate. **4** ice up. **7** chill, numb. **9** deep-freeze, ice, refrigerate, chill, cool. **10** stop, stand still, immobilize. **11** fix, hold. **12** suspend. *noun* **1** freeze-up, frost. **2** stay, embargo, moratorium, stoppage, halt, standstill, shutdown, suspension, interruption.

freeze-dry *verb* (PAST TENSE AND PAST PARTICIPLE **freeze-dried**) to preserve (perishable material, especially food and medicines), by rapidly freezing it and then drying it under high-vacuum conditions so that ice is forced out of the material as water vapour without melting. Food

preserved in this way, eg coffee and soft fruit, keeps much of its original flavour and texture.

freeze-frame *noun* **1** a single frame of film that is isolated and then repeated as a continuous series in order to give an effect like a still photograph. **2** a facility on a video recorder that allows a single frame on a video tape to be viewed as a still picture by stopping the tape.

freezer *noun* a refrigerated cabinet or compartment in which to preserve food at below freezing-point.

freezing point (ABBREV. **fp, f.p.**) **1** the temperature at which the liquid form of a particular substance turns into a solid. **2** (*also* **freezing**) the freezing point of water (0°C at sea level).

freight / freɪt/ — *noun* **1** transport of goods by rail, road, sea, or air. **2** the goods transported in this way. **3** the cost of such transport. — *verb* **1** to transport (goods) by freight. **2** to load with goods for transport. [from Old Dutch *vrecht*]

⊟ *noun* **1** shipment, transportation, conveyance, carriage, haulage. **2** goods, cargo, load, lading, payload, contents, merchandise, consignment, shipment. **3** carriage, haulage.

freighter *noun trademark* a ship or aircraft that carries cargo rather than passengers.

freightliner *noun trademark* a train designed for the rapid transport of goods.

French — *adj.* **1** relating or belonging to France or its inhabitants. **2** relating to the language of the French. — *noun* **1** the Romance language spoken in France, parts of Belgium, Luxembourg, Switzerland, and elsewhere. **2** (**the French**) the people of France.

French bean a widely cultivated species of bean plant (*Phaseolus vulgaris*). Its edible seeds can be cooked and eaten as a vegetable while unripe and still in the pod, or they can be left to ripen on the plant, and the mature seeds, known as *haricot beans*, can be dried, or processed to form baked beans, etc.

French bread white bread in the form of long narrow loaves.

French Canadian a native of the French-speaking part of Canada.

French-Canadian *adj.* relating to French Canadians or their language.

French chalk a form of the mineral talc used to mark cloth or remove grease marks.

French dressing a salad dressing made from oil, spices, and lemon juice or vinegar.

French fries potato chips.

French horn see HORN.

French leave leave taken without permission from work or duty.

French letter *slang* a condom.

Frenchman or **Frenchwoman** *noun* a man or woman of French nationality.

French polish a varnish for furniture.

French-polish *verb* to apply French polish to.

French windows a pair of glass doors that open on to a garden, balcony, etc.

frenetic *adj.* frantic, distracted, hectic, or wildly energetic. [from Old French *frenetique*, from Greek *phrenitis*, delirium]

frenetically *adv.* in a frenetic way.

frenzied *adj.* in or as if in a frenzy; wild.

⊟ frantic, frenetic, wild, hectic, feverish, desperate, furious, uncontrolled, mad, demented, hysterical.
⊞ calm, composed.

frenzy *noun* (PL. **frenzies**) **1** a state of violent mental disturbance. **2** wild agitation or excitement. **3** a frantic burst of activity. [from Greek *phrenesis*, madness]

....

⊟ **1, 2** turmoil, agitation, distraction, derangement, madness, lunacy, mania, hysteria, delirium. **3** burst, fit, spasm, paroxysm, convulsion, seizure, outburst, transport, passion, rage, fury.

⊟ **1** calm, composure.

....

frequency *noun* (PL. **frequencies**) **1** the condition of happening often. **2** the rate at which a happening, phenomenon, etc, recurs. **3** *Physics* a measure of the rate at which a complete cycle of wave motion is repeated per unit time. The SI unit of frequency is the hertz. **4** *Radio* the rate of sound waves per second at which a particular radio signal is sent out. **5** *Statistics* the number of items, values, etc, that occur within a specified category. [from Latin *frequens*, happening often]

frequency distribution *Maths.* a set of data that includes numerical values for the frequencies of different scores or results, ie the number of times that each particular score or result occurs.

frequency modulation *Radio* (ABBREV. **FM**) a method of radio transmission in which the frequency of the carrier wave (the signal-carrying wave) increases or decreases instantaneously in response to changes in the amplitude of the signal being transmitted. It gives a better signal-to-noise ratio than amplitude modulation (AM).

frequent *adj.* (with stress on *fre-*) **1** recurring at short intervals. **2** habitual. — *verb* (with stress on *-quent*) to visit or attend often.

....

⊟ *adj.* **1** recurring, repeated, regular, incessant, persistent, constant, continual, numerous, countless. **2** habitual, common, commonplace, everyday, familiar, usual, customary. *verb* visit, haunt, patronize, attend, *colloq.* hang out at, associate with, *colloq.* hang about with, *colloq.* hang out with.

⊟ *adj.* **1** infrequent.

....

frequently *adv.* often.

fresco *noun* (PL. **frescoes, frescos**) a picture painted on a wall, usually while the plaster is still damp. [from Italian *fresco*, fresh]

fresh — *adj.* **1** newly made, gathered, etc. **2** having just arrived from somewhere, just finished doing something or just had some experience, etc: *fresh from university.* **3** other or another; different; clean: *a fresh sheet of paper.* **4** new; additional: *fresh supplies.* **5** original: *a fresh approach.* **6** *said of fruit or vegetables* not tinned, frozen, preserved, etc. **7** not tired; bright and alert. **8** cool; refreshing: *a fresh breeze.* **9** *said of air* cool and uncontaminated. **10** *said of water* not salt. **11** *said of the face or complexion* youthfully healthy; ruddy. **12** *colloq., said of behaviour* offensively informal. — *adv.* recently; newly: *fresh-baked bread.* [from Anglo-Saxon *fersc*, fresh, not salt]

....

⊟ *adj.* **1** new. **3** new, other, another, different, clean, blank. **4** new, additional, supplementary, extra, more, further, other. **5** original, new, novel, different, innovative, unconventional, modern, up-to-date, recent, latest. **6** raw, natural, unprocessed, crude. **7** bright, alert, energetic, vigorous, lively, refreshed, revived, restored, renewed, rested, invigorated. **8** cool, refreshing, bracing, invigorating, brisk, crisp, keen, fair, bright. **9** cool, clear, pure. **12** pert, *colloq.* saucy, *colloq.* cheeky, disrespectful, impudent, insolent, bold, brazen, forward, familiar, presumptuous.

⊟ *adj.* **1, 4** old. **5** old, hackneyed. **6** tinned, frozen, preserved, processed. **7** tired, stale. **9** stale, foul.

....

freshen *verb* (**freshened, freshening**) **1** to make fresh or fresher. **2** *trans., intrans.* (*also* **freshen up** or **freshen someone up**) to get washed and tidy; to wash and tidy (oneself). **3** *intrans. said of a wind* to become stronger.

....

⊟ **1** refresh, restore, revitalize, reinvigorate, liven, enliven, air, ventilate, purify. **2** spruce up, *slang* tart up.

....

fresher or **freshman** *noun* a first-year college or university student.

freshet *noun* **1** a stream of fresh water flowing into the sea. **2** the sudden overflow of a river. [a diminutive of FRESH]

freshly *adv.* newly; with freshness.

freshwater *adj.* denoting water that contains less than 0.2% dissolved salts, such as that found in most rivers and lakes.

fret[1] *verb* (**fretted, fretting**) **1** *intrans.* to worry, especially unnecessarily; to show or express anxiety. **2** to worry or agitate. **3** to wear away or consume by rubbing or erosion. [from Anglo-Saxon *fretan*, to gnaw]

....

⊟ **1** worry, agonize, brood, pine. **2** worry, agitate, vex, irritate, nettle, bother, trouble, torment.

....

fret[2] *noun* any of the narrow metal ridges across the neck of a guitar or similar musical instrument.

fret[3] — *noun* an ornamental repeated pattern used as a border, etc. — *verb* (**fretted, fretting**) to decorate with a fret, or carve with fretwork. [from Old French *frete*, interlaced design]

fretful *adj.* anxious and unhappy; tending to fret.

fretfulness *noun* **1** being fretful. **2** fretful behaviour.

fretsaw *noun* a narrow-bladed saw for cutting designs in wood or metal.

fretwork *noun* decorative carved openwork in wood or metal.

Freudian /ˈfrɔɪdɪən/ — *adj.* relating to or characteristic of the ideas of Sigmund Freud (1856–1939). — *noun* a person who supports or applies the theories of Sigmund Freud, especially his methods of psychoanalysis.

Freudian slip a slip of the tongue taken as revealing an unexpressed thought.

Fri or **Fri.** *abbrev.* Friday.

friability /fraɪəˈbɪlɪtɪ/ *noun* being friable.

friable /ˈfraɪəbl/ *adj.* easily broken; easily reduced to powder. [from Latin *friare*, to crumble]

friar /ˈfraɪə(r)/ *noun* a member of any of various religious orders who, especially formerly, worked as teachers of the Christian religion and lived by begging. [from Old French *frere*, brother]

friar's balsam a strong-smelling compound containing benzoin and aloes mixed with hot water, used as an inhalant for relieving the symptoms of colds.

friary *noun* (PL. **friaries**) *Hist.* a building inhabited by a community of friars.

fricassee /ˈfrɪkəsiː/ *noun* a cooked dish usually of pieces of meat or chicken served in a sauce. [from Old French *fricasser*, to cook chopped food in its own juice]

fricative — *adj., said of a sound* produced partly by friction, the breath being forced through a narrowed opening. — *noun* a fricative consonant, eg *f* and *th*. [from Latin *fricare*, to rub]

friction *noun* **1** the rubbing of one thing against another. **2** *Physics* the force that opposes the relative motion of two bodies or surfaces that are in contact with each other. **3** quarrelling; disagreement; conflict. [from Latin *frictio*, from *fricare*, to rub]

....

⊟ **1** rubbing, chafing, irritation, abrasion, scraping, grating, rasping, erosion, wearing away, resistance. **3** quarrelling, disagreement, conflict, dissension, dispute, disharmony, antagonism, hostility, opposition, rivalry, animosity, ill-feeling, bad blood, resentment.

....

frictional *adj.* relating to or causing friction.

Friday *noun* the sixth day of the week. [from Anglo-Saxon *Frigedæg*, (the goddess) Frig's day]

fridge *noun colloq.* a refrigerator.

friend *noun* **1** a person whom one knows and likes. **2** a person who gives support or help: *a friend of the poor.* **3** an ally as distinct from an enemy. **4** a person or thing already encountered or mentioned: *our old friend the woodworm.* **5** (**Friend**) a member of the Religious Society of Friends; a Quaker. **6** a member of an organization giving voluntary financial support to an institution, etc: *Friends of the National Gallery.* — **be** or **make friends with someone** to be, or become, their friend. [from Anglo-Saxon *freond*]

▣ **1** *colloq.* mate, *colloq.* pal, *colloq.* chum, *colloq.* buddy, *colloq.* crony, intimate, confidant(e), bosom friend, soul mate, comrade, ally, partner, associate, companion, playmate, acquaintance. **2** supporter, well-wisher.
▣ **3** enemy, opponent.

friendless *adj.* lacking friends.

friendliness *noun* being friendly.

friendly — *adj.* (**friendlier, friendliest**) **1** kind; behaving as a friend. **2** (**friendly with someone**) on close or affectionate terms with them. **3** relating to, or typical of, a friend. **4** being a colleague, helper, partner, etc rather than an enemy: *friendly nations.* **5** *Sport, said of a match, etc* played for enjoyment or practice and not as part of a formal competition. — *noun* (PL. **friendlies**) *Sport* a friendly match.

▣ *adj.* **1** kind, kindly, amiable, affable, genial, neighbourly, helpful, sympathetic. **2** fond of, affectionate towards, familiar with, intimate with, close to, *colloq.* matey with, *colloq.* pally with. **3** companionable, comradely, sociable, amicable, peaceable, well-disposed, convivial, congenial, cordial, welcoming, warm, favourable, approachable, receptive, outgoing.
▣ *adj.* **1, 3** hostile, unsociable, cold.

-friendly *combining form* denoting things that are made easy or convenient for those for whom they are intended: *user-friendly.*

friendly fire *Mil.* accidental firing on one's own or one's allies' forces instead of the enemy.

friendly society an organization giving support to members in sickness and old age, in return for regular contributions.

friendship *noun* **1** the having and keeping of friends. **2** a particular relationship between two friends.

▣ **1** alliance, fellowship, comradeship. **2** closeness, intimacy, familiarity, affinity, rapport, attachment, affection, fondness, love, harmony, concord, goodwill, friendliness.
▣ ENMITY, ANIMOSITY.

frier another spelling of FRYER.

Friesian /ˈfriːʒən/ *noun Agric.* a breed of black and white dairy cattle, originating in the Netherlands, and now the most important dairy breed in the UK on account of its very high milk yields. [variant of FRISIAN]

frieze *noun* **1** a decorative strip running along a wall. **2** *Archit.* a horizontal band between the cornice and capitals of a classical temple, or the sculpture filling it. [from Old French *frise*]

frigate /ˈfrɪɡət/ *noun* **1** a naval escort vessel, smaller than a destroyer. **2** *Hist.* a small fast-moving sailing warship. [from Old French *fregate*]

frigate bird a large bird, native to tropical seas, the male having an inflatable coloured pouch on the throat. It steals fish from other birds, and is unable to take off from level ground, but is a good flier, covering long distances.

fright *noun* **1** sudden fear; a shock. **2** *colloq.* a person or thing of ludicrous appearance. — **take fright** to become scared. [from Anglo-Saxon *fyrhto*]

▣ **1** shock, scare, alarm, consternation, dismay, dread, apprehension, trepidation, fear, terror, horror, panic.

frighten *verb* (**frightened, frightening**) **1** to make afraid. **2** (**frighten someone away** or **off**) to scare them away. **3** (**frighten someone into** or **out of something**) to persuade or dissuade them by threats.

▣ **1** alarm, daunt, unnerve, dismay, intimidate, terrorize, scare, startle, terrify, petrify, horrify, appal, shock. **2** scare off.
▣ **1** reassure, calm.

frightened *adj.* afraid; scared.

frightful *adj.* **1** ghastly; frightening. **2** *colloq.* bad; awful. **3** *colloq.* great; extreme.

▣ **1** ghastly, frightening, harrowing, grisly, macabre, terrible, appalling, shocking, unspeakable, grim, hideous, horrible, horrid, gruesome. **2** bad, awful, unpleasant, disagreeable, dreadful, fearful, terrible, appalling, shocking, dire, grim, ghastly, hideous, horrible, horrid. **3** dreadful, fearful, terrible, awful.
▣ **1, 2** pleasant, agreeable.

frightfully *adv. colloq.* very.

frigid /ˈfrɪdʒɪd/ *adj.* **1** cold and unfriendly. **2** *said of a woman* not sexually responsive, especially to sexual intercourse. **3** *Geog.* intensely cold. [from Latin *frigidus*, cold]

▣ **1** cold, unfriendly, unfeeling, unloving, cool, aloof. **2** unresponsive, passionless. **3** frozen, icy, frosty, glacial, arctic, cold, chill, chilly, wintry.
▣ **1** friendly, warm, loving. **2** passionate, responsive. **3** hot.

frigidity *noun* **1** being frigid. **2** frigid behaviour.

frill *noun* **1** a gathered or pleated strip of cloth attached along one edge to a garment, etc as a trimming. **2** (*usually* **frills**) something extra serving no very useful purpose.

frilly *adj.* (**frillier, frilliest**) with frills.

▣ ruffled, crimped, gathered, frilled, trimmed, lacy, fancy, ornate.
▣ plain.

fringe — *noun* **1** a border of loose threads on a carpet, tablecloth, garment, etc. **2** hair cut to hang down over the forehead. **3** the outer area; the edge; the part farthest from the main area or centre. **4** the area of activity of people who have moved away from the conventional practices of their group, profession, etc: *fringe medicine.* — *verb* **1** to decorate with a fringe. **2** to form a fringe round. [from Old French *frenge*, from Latin *fimbriae*, threads, fringe]

▣ *noun* **1** border, edging, trimming, tassel, frill, valance. **3, 4** margin, periphery, outskirts, edge, perimeter, limits, borderline.

fringe benefits things that one gets from one's employer in addition to wages or salary, eg a house, a car, etc.

frippery *noun* (PL. **fripperies**) showy and unnecessary finery or adornment. [from Old French *freperie*, from *frepe*, a rag]

Frisbee *noun trademark* a light plastic saucer-shaped object that spins when thrown, used for playing games. [perhaps from the surname *Frisbie*]

Frisian /ˈfrɪziən/ — *noun* **1** the language of Friesland in NW Netherlands. **2** a native of Friesland. — *adj.* belonging or relating to Friesland, its people, or their language. See also FRIESIAN. [from Latin *Frisii*, a tribe of NW Germany]

frisk — *verb* **1** *intrans.* to jump or run about happily. **2**

friskily *trans. slang* to search (a person) for eg weapons or drugs. — *noun* **1** a spell of prancing about. **2** an act of searching a person for weapons, etc. [from Old French *frisque*, lively]

■ *verb* **1** jump, run, leap, skip, hop, bounce, caper, dance, gambol, frolic, romp, play, sport.

friskily *adv.* in a frisky way.
friskiness *noun* being frisky.
frisky *adj.* (**friskier, friskiest**) lively; playful.

■ lively, playful, ludic, spirited, high-spirited, frolicsome, romping, rollicking, bouncy.
E3 quiet.

frisson / 'fri:sɒn/ *noun* a shiver of fear or excitement. [from French *frisson*]

fritillary /frɪ'tɪlərɪ/ *noun* **1** *Bot.* a perennial plant (*Fritillaria meleagris*), widespread in central Europe, with a drooping head bearing a single bell-shaped flower, composed of broad segments chequered pink and dull purple. **2** *Zool.* any of many species of a colourful butterfly having yellowish-brown wings with black markings. [from Latin *fritillus*, dice-box]

fritter¹ *noun* a piece of meat, fruit, etc coated in batter and fried. [from French *friture*]

fritter² *verb* (**frittered, frittering**) (**fritter something away**) to waste time, money, etc on unimportant things. [from earlier *fitter*, fragment]

■ waste, squander, dissipate, idle, misspend, *colloq.* blow.

frivolity *noun* frivolous behaviour; being frivolous.

■ fun, gaiety, flippancy, facetiousness, jest, lightheartedness, levity, triviality, superficiality, silliness, folly, nonsense.
E3 seriousness.

frivolous *adj.* **1** silly; not sufficiently serious. **2** trifling or unimportant, not useful and sensible. [from Latin *frivolus*]

■ SILLY, FOOLISH, TRIFLING, TRIVIAL, UNIMPORTANT, SHALLOW, SUPERFICIAL, LIGHT, IDLE, VAIN, POINTLESS, FLIPPANT, JOCULAR, LIGHT-HEARTED, JUVENILE, PUERILE.
E3 SERIOUS, SENSIBLE.

frizz — *noun* a mass of tight curls. — *verb trans., intrans.* to form or cause to form a frizz. [from French *friser*, to curl, or from FRIZZLE²]

frizzle¹ *verb trans., intrans., said of food* to fry till scorched and brittle.

frizzle² — *verb* to frizz (hair). — *noun* **1** a curl. **2** a frizz. [perhaps related to Anglo-Saxon *fris*, curly]

frizzy *adj.* (**frizzier, frizziest**) tightly curled.

fro *adv. old use* back or from, as in **to and fro**, forwards and backwards. [from Norse *fra*, from]

frock *noun* **1** a woman's or girl's dress. **2** a priest's or monk's long garment. **3** a loose smock. [from Old French *froc*, monk's garment]

frock coat *noun Hist.* a man's knee-length coat, closefitting round the waist.

frog¹ *noun* **1** a tailless amphibian belonging to the family Ranidae of the order Anura (which also includes toads), found worldwide except in Arctic and Antarctic regions, and having a moist smooth skin, protruding eyes, powerful hind legs for swimming and leaping, and webbed feet. **2** *offensive colloq.* a French person. — **a frog in one's throat** an accumulation of phlegm on the vocal cords that interferes with one's speech. [from Anglo-Saxon *frogga*]

frog² *noun* a decorative looped fastener on a garment.

frog³ *noun* **1** a V-shaped plate of iron or steel that allows a train or tram to cross from one set of rails to another at the point where they intersect. **2** a triangular mass of tough elastic horny material in the centre of the sole of the foot of a horse or similar animal. **3** a depression made in one or more of the larger faces of a brick, in order to reduce its weight.

frogging *noun* a set of fasteners, especially on a military uniform (see FROG²).

froghopper *noun* a small hopping insect that feeds by sucking the sap of plants.

frogman *noun* an underwater swimmer wearing a protective rubber suit and using breathing equipment.

frog march — *verb* **1** to force (someone) forward, holding them firmly by the arms. **2** to carry in a face-downward position. — *noun* a face-downward carrying position, with all four limbs held.

frogspawn *noun* the mass of fertilized eggs, surrounded by protective nutrient jelly, deposited in water by a frog.

frolic — *verb intrans.* (**frolicked, frolicking**) to frisk or run about playfully. — *noun* **1** a spell of happy playing or frisking. **2** something silly done as a joke. [from Dutch *vrolijk*, merry]

■ *verb* frisk, gambol, caper, romp, play, lark around, rollick, make merry, prance, dance. *noun* **1** fun, amusement, sport, gaiety, jollity, merriment, revel, romp, high jinks, antics. **2** prank, lark, caper.

frolicsome *adj.* playful.

from *prep.* indicating **1** a starting-point in place or time: *from London to Glasgow/crippled from birth.* **2** a lower limit: *tickets from £12 upwards.* **3** repeated progression: *trail from shop to shop.* **4** movement out of: *took a letter from the drawer.* **5** distance away: *16 miles from Dover.* **6** a viewpoint: *can see the house from here.* **7** separation; removal: *took it away from her.* **8** point of attachment: *hanging from a nail.* **9** exclusion: *omitted from the sample.* **10** source or origin: *made from an old curtain.* **11** change of condition: *translate from French into English/from being a close friend, he turned very hostile.* **12** cause: *ill from overwork.* **13** deduction as a result of observation: *see from her face she's angry.* **14** distinction: *can't tell one twin from the other.* **15** prevention, protection, exemption, immunity, release, escape, etc: *safe from harm/excused from attending/exempted from tax/released from prison.* [from Anglo-Saxon *fram*]

fromage frais / 'frɒmɑ:ʒ 'freɪ/ *noun* a creamy low-fat cheese with the consistency of whipped cream. [French, = fresh cheese]

frond *noun Bot.* a large compound leaf, especially of a fern or palm. [from Latin *frons*]

front — *noun* **1** the side or part of anything that is furthest forward or nearest to the viewer; the most important side or part, eg the side of a building where the main door is. **2** any side of a large or historic building. **3** the part of a vehicle or vessel that faces, or is closest to, the direction in which it moves. **4** the auditorium of a theatre, etc. **5** the cover or first pages of a book. **6** a road in a town that runs beside the sea. **7** in war, the area where the soldiers are nearest to the enemy. **8** a matter of concern or interest: *no progress on the job front.* **9** *Meteorol.* the boundary between two air masses that have different temperatures, eg a *warm front* is the leading edge of a mass of warm air. Much weather forecasting is based on the interpretation of fronts, which are associated with changeable weather. **10** an outward appearance. **11** (*usually* **Front**) a name given to some political movements. **12** *slang* an organization or job used to hide illegal or secret activity. — *verb* **1** *trans., intrans. said of a building* to have its front facing or beside something specified: *the house fronts on to the main road.* **2** to be the leader or representative of (a group, etc). **3** to be the presenter of (a radio or television programme). **4** (**front for something**) to provide a cover or excuse for an illegal activity, etc. **5** to cover the front of (a building, etc):

the house was fronted with grey stone. — **in front** on the forward-facing side; ahead. **in front of someone** or **something 1** at or to a position in advance of them. **2** to a place towards which a vehicle, etc is moving: *ran in front of a car.* **3** ahead of them: *pushed in front of her.* **4** facing or confronting them: *stood up in front of an audience.* **5** in their presence: *dare not say so in front of my mother.* **out front** *colloq.* in the audience, from the performer's standpoint. **up front** *colloq., said of money* paid before work is done or goods received, etc. [from Latin *frons*, forehead]

. . . .

▤ *noun* **1** face, top, head, lead, vanguard, forefront, foreground, cover, obverse. **2** side, face, aspect, frontage, façade, outside, exterior. **3** forepart, bow, nose. **6** esplanade, promenade. **7** front line. **10** appearance, look, show, air, manner, expression, façade, pretence, cover, mask, disguise, pretext, cover-up. *verb* **1** face. **2** lead, head. **3** present. **in front of someone** or **something 1** ahead of, leading, in advance of, preceding. **2, 4** before.

▨ *noun* **1** back, rear. *verb* **1** back on to. **in front of someone** or **something 1** behind.

. . . .

frontage *noun* the front of a building, especially in relation to the street, etc along which it extends.

frontal *adj.* **1** relating to the front. **2** aimed at the front; direct: *a frontal assault.* **3** *Anat.* relating to the forehead. [from FRONT; sense 3 is from Latin *frontalis*, from *frons*, forehead]

frontal lobe *Anat.* the front part of each cerebral hemisphere of the brain. It includes the motor cortex, which is responsible for the control of voluntary movement, and the prefrontal lobe, which is concerned with personality, behaviour, and learning.

frontal system *Meteorol.* a system of fronts on a weather chart.

frontbench *adj.* **1** holding a position in the government or the opposition. **2** relating to this position.

frontbencher *noun* a member of Parliament holding an official position in the government or the opposition. See also BACKBENCHER.

frontier *noun* **1** a boundary between countries. **2** (**frontiers**) limits: *the frontiers of knowledge.* **3** *North Amer. Hist.* the furthest edge of civilization, habitation or cultivation, beyond which the country is wild and deserted. [from Old French *frontier*, from *front*, opposite side]

. . . .

▤ **1** border, boundary, borderline, limit, edge, perimeter, marches. **2** limits, confines, bounds.

. . . .

frontispiece /ˈfrʌntɪspiːs/ *noun* a picture at the beginning of a book, facing the title page. [from Latin *frons*, front + *specere*, to see]

front line 1 that area in any concern where the important pioneering work is going on. **2** in a war, the area where soldiers are closest to the enemy.

front man 1 the leader or representative of an organization. **2** the presenter of a radio or television programme.

front-page *adj.* published on the front page of a newspaper, or suitable for publication there: *front-page news.*

front projection *Cinema* the projection of an image on to an opaque screen to be viewed from the same side as the projector; the normal practice for cinema and audiovisual presentation.

front-runner *noun* the person most likely to win a competition, etc.

frost — *noun* **1** a white feathery or powdery deposit of ice crystals formed when water vapour comes into contact with a surface whose temperature is below the freezing point of water. **2** an air temperature below freezing point: *12 degrees of frost.* — *verb* **1** *trans., intrans.* (*also* **frost up** or **over**) to cover or become covered with frost. **2** to damage (plants) with frost. [from Anglo-Saxon]

frostbite *noun* damage to the body tissues, usually of the extremities (eg fingers or toes), caused by exposure to very low temperatures. The affected parts become pale and numb as a result of lack of oxygen due to narrowing of the blood vessels, and amputation may be necessary if the tissues are irreparably damaged by the formation of ice crystals within them.

frostbitten *adj.* suffering from frostbite; affected by frost.

frosted *adj., said of glass* patterned or roughened as though with frost, so as to be difficult to see through.

frostily *adv.* in a frosty way.

frostiness *noun* being frosty.

frosting *noun North Amer.* cake icing.

frosty *adj.* (**frostier, frostiest**) **1** covered with frost. **2** cold enough for frost to form. **3** *said of a person's behaviour or attitude* cold; unfriendly.

. . . .

▤ **1** frosted. **2** icy, frozen, freezing, frigid, wintry, cold, chilly. **3** cold, unfriendly, unwelcoming, cool, aloof, standoffish, stiff, discouraging.

▨ **2** mild, warm. **3** friendly, warm.

. . . .

froth — *noun* **1** a mass of tiny bubbles forming eg on the surface of a liquid, or round the mouth in certain diseases. **2** writing, talk, etc that has no serious content or purpose. **3** showy glamour. — *verb intrans., trans.* to produce or cause to produce froth. [from Norse *frotha*]

. . . .

▤ *noun* **1** bubbles, effervescence, foam, lather, suds, head, scum. *verb* foam, lather, ferment, fizz, effervesce, bubble.

. . . .

frothy *adj.* (**frothier, frothiest**) **1** full of or like froth. **2** insubstantial.

frottage /frɒˈtɑːʒ/ *noun Art* a technique, analogous to brass-rubbing, used by some modern artists, notably Max Ernst. Paper is placed over a textured surface, such as wood or fabric, and rubbed with a soft pencil or crayon to produce an impression. [from French *frottage*]

frown — *verb intrans.* **1** to wrinkle one's forehead and draw one's eyebrows together in worry, disapproval, deep thought, etc. **2** (**frown on** or **at something**) to disapprove of it. — *noun* a disapproving expression or glance. [from Old French *froignier*]

. . . .

▤ *verb* **1** scowl, glower, glare, grimace. **2** disapprove of, object to, dislike, discourage. *noun* scowl, glower, *colloq.* dirty look, glare, grimace.

▨ *verb* **2** approve of.

. . . .

frowningly *adv.* with a frown.

frowsiness or **frowziness** *noun* being frowsy.

frowstiness *noun* being frowsty.

frowsty *adj.* (**frowstier, frowstiest**) stuffy; stale-smelling. [from FROWSY]

frowsy or **frowzy** /ˈfrɒzɪ/ *adj.* (**frowsier, frowsiest**) **1** *said of someone's appearance* untidy, dishevelled, or slovenly. **2** *said of an atmosphere* stuffy; stale-smelling.

froze, frozen see FREEZE.

FRS *abbrev. Brit.* Fellow of the Royal Society.

fructification *noun* **1** *Bot.* the fruit of a plant or the fruiting body (spore-producing structure) of a fungus. **2** *Bot.* the process of forming a fruit or a fruiting body. [from Latin *fructus*, fruit + *facere*, to make]

fructose *noun Biochem.* (FORMULA $C_6H_{12}O_6$) a six-carbon sugar (hexose) found in fruit, honey, and combined with glucose in sucrose (cane sugar). Its derivatives, in the form of fructose phosphates, play an important role in the chemical reactions that take place in living cells. Also called FRUIT SUGAR. [from Latin *fructus*, fruit]

frugal *adj.* **1** thrifty; economical; not generous. **2** not large; costing little: *a frugal meal.* [from Latin *frugalis*]

. . . .

▤ **1** thrifty, penny-wise, parsimonious, careful, provident, saving, economical, sparing. **2** meagre.

▣ **1** wasteful, generous. **2** generous.

frugality noun **1** being frugal. **2** economy, thrift.

fruit — noun **1** the fully ripened ovary of a flowering plant, containing one or more seeds that have developed from fertilized ovules, and sometimes including associated structures such as the receptacle. Many so-called 'vegetables' are in fact fruits, eg tomato, marrow. **2** an edible part of a plant that is generally sweet and juicy, especially the ovary containing one or more seeds, but sometimes extended to include other parts, eg the leaf stalk in rhubarb. **3** plant products generally: *the fruits of the land.* **4** (*also* **fruits**) whatever is gained as a result of hard work, etc. **5** offspring; young: *the fruit of her womb.* **6** *old colloq. use* a person: *old fruit.* — verb intrans. to produce fruit. — **bear fruit 1** to produce fruit. **2** to produce good results. **dried fruit** fruit such as currants, raisins, sultanas, preserved by drying in the sun to remove moisture. **in fruit** *said of a tree* bearing fruit. **soft fruit** small fruits and berries such as blackcurrants, redcurrants, strawberries, and raspberries. [from Old French *fruict*, from Latin *fructus*]

Varieties of fruit include: apple, Bramley, Cox's Orange Pippin, Golden Delicious, Granny Smith, crab apple; pear, William, Conference; orange, Jaffa, mandarin, mineola, clementine, satsuma, tangerine, Seville; apricot, peach, plum, nectarine, cherry, sloe, damson, greengage, grape, gooseberry, *colloq.* goosegog, rhubarb, tomato; banana, pineapple, olive, lemon, lime, ugli fruit, star fruit, lychee, date, fig, grapefruit, kiwi fruit, mango, avocado; melon, honeydew, cantaloupe, watermelon; strawberry, raspberry, blackberry, bilberry, loganberry, elderberry, blueberry, boysenberry, cranberry; redcurrant, blackcurrant.

fruitcake noun **1** a cake containing dried fruits, nuts, etc. **2** *colloq.* a slightly mad person.

fruiterer noun a person who sells fruit.

fruit fly any of various tiny brown or yellowish flies with red eyes, mainly of tropical regions, especially those belonging to the genus *Drosophila*. They feed on sap and fermenting fruit, and can be a minor pest of orchards and stored fruit.

fruitful adj. producing good or useful results.

▣ productive, rewarding, profitable, advantageous, beneficial, worthwhile, well-spent, useful, successful, fertile, rich, teeming, plentiful, abundant, prolific.
▣ fruitless, barren.

fruitily adv. in a fruity way.

fruitiness noun being fruity.

fruition /frʊˈɪʃən/ noun **1** the achievement of something that has been aimed at and worked for. **2** the bearing of fruit. [from Old French *fruition*, from Latin *frui*, to enjoy]

▣ **1** realization, fulfilment, attainment, achievement, completion, maturity, ripeness, consummation, perfection, success, enjoyment.

fruitless adj. useless; unsuccessful; done in vain.

▣ useless, unsuccessful, vain, abortive, futile, pointless, idle, hopeless, barren, sterile.
▣ fruitful, successful, profitable.

fruit machine a coin-operated gambling-machine with symbols in the form of fruits, that may be made to appear in winning combinations.

fruit salad a dish of mixed chopped fruits, usually eaten as a dessert.

fruit sugar same as FRUCTOSE.

fruity adj. (**fruitier, fruitiest**) **1** full of fruit; having the taste or appearance of fruit. **2** *said of a voice* deep and rich in tone. **3** *colloq., said of a story, etc* containing humorous and slightly shocking references to sexual matters. **4** *colloq.* sexually aroused.

frump noun *derog. colloq.* a woman who dresses in a dowdy, old-fashioned way.

frumpish or **frumpy** adj. (**frumpier, frumpiest**) dowdy, unattractive.

frustrate verb **1** to prevent (someone) from doing or getting something; to thwart or foil (a plan, attempt, etc). **2** to make (someone) feel disappointed, useless, lacking a purpose in life, etc. [from Latin *frustrari*, to deceive or disappoint]

▣ **1** thwart, foil, balk, baffle, block, check, defeat, circumvent, forestall, counter, nullify, neutralize, inhibit. **2** disappoint, discourage, dishearten, depress.
▣ **1** further, promote. **2** encourage.

frustrated adj. **1** disappointed; unhappy; dissatisfied. **2** unfulfilled in one's ambitions for oneself. **3** not sexually satisfied.

frustration noun being frustrated.

fry[1] — verb trans., intrans. (**fries, fried**) to cook in hot oil or fat. — noun (PL. **fries**) **1** a dish of anything fried, eg the offal of a pig or lamb. **2** *colloq.* (*also* **fry-up**) a mixture of fried foods; the cooking of these. [from Old French *frire*]

fry[2] noun **1** the young of certain species of fish, especially those that have just spawned. **2** young salmon in their second year. See also SMALL FRY. [Middle English, = seed or descendant]

fryer or **frier** noun **1** a frying-pan. **2** a chicken for frying.

frying pan or **frypan** a shallow long-handled pan for frying food in. — **out of the frying pan into the fire** from a bad situation into a worse one.

FT abbrev. Financial Times.

ft abbrev. foot or feet.

FTP abbrev. Comput. file transfer protocol.

fuchsia /ˈfjuːʃə/ noun **1** any of various evergreen or deciduous shrubs of the genus *Fuchsia*, native to Central and S America, New Zealand, and the Pacific region, having drooping purple, red, or white flowers. **2** the reddish-purple colour of this flower. [named after the German physician and herbalist Leonhard Fuchs]

fuck *coarse slang* — verb trans., intrans. to have sexual intercourse. — noun an act of, or partner in, sexual intercourse. — interj. an expression of anger, frustration, etc. — **fuck about** or **around** to behave foolishly or waste time. **fuck all** nothing; no. **fuck off** *offensive* to go away. **fuck something up** to ruin or spoil it. [a 16c word of unknown origin]

fucking adj. *coarse slang, as a general term of abuse* damned; bloody.

fuck-up noun *coarse slang* a bungled or spoilt situation or mess.

fuddle — verb to muddle the wits of; to stupefy. — noun a state of confusion or intoxication.

fuddy-duddy *colloq.* — adj. quaintly old-fashioned or prim. — noun (PL. **fuddy-duddies**) a fuddy-duddy person.

fudge[1] noun **1** a soft toffee made from butter and sugar. **2** *colloq.* nonsense.

fudge[2] verb *colloq.* **1** intrans. to avoid stating a clear opinion. **2** to invent or concoct (an excuse, etc). **3** to distort or deliberately obscure (figures, etc). **4** to dodge or evade. [perhaps from earlier *fadge*, to succeed or turn out]

fuel — noun **1** any material that releases energy when it is burned, and can be used as a source of heat or power for machines, engines, etc. The most widely used fuels are fossil fuels such as coal, oil, and natural gas. **2** any fissile material that is used to release energy by nuclear fission in a nuclear reactor, eg uranium-235. **3** food, as a source of energy and a means of maintaining bodily processes. **4** something that feeds or inflames passions, etc. — verb (**fuelled, fuelling**) **1** to fill or supply with fuel. **2** intrans. to take on fuel. **3** to inflame (anger or other passions). [from Old French *feuaile*, from Latin *focus*, hearth]

■ *noun* **1** combustible, propellant, motive power. **4** provocation, incitement, encouragement, ammunition, material. *verb* **3** incite, inflame, fire, encourage, fan, feed, nourish, sustain, stoke up.

⊟ *verb* **3** discourage, damp down.

Fuels include: gas, *trademark* calor gas, propane, butane, methane, acetylene, electricity, coal, coke, anthracite, charcoal, oil, petrol, gasoline, diesel, derv, paraffin, kerosine, methylated spirit, wood, logs, peat, nuclear power.

fuel cell *Chem.* a device in which chemical energy released by the oxidation of a liquid or gaseous fuel, eg methanol, is converted directly into electrical energy. It is more efficient than a heat engine.

fuel injection in a petrol or diesel engine, a system that injects pure fuel under pressure directly into the cylinder, the timing and amount of fuel injected being under electronic control. This eliminates the need for a carburettor and produces improved running performance.

fug *noun* a stale-smelling stuffy atmosphere.

fuggy *adj.* (**fuggier**, **fuggiest**) stuffy; suffocatingly hot and airless.

fugitive — *noun* a person who is fleeing someone or something. — *adj.* **1** fleeing away. **2** lasting only briefly; fleeting: *a fugitive smile.* [from Latin *fugitivus*]

■ *noun* escapee, runaway, deserter, refugee. *adj.* **2** fleeting, transient, transitory, passing, short, brief, flying, temporary, ephemeral, elusive.

⊟ *adj.* **2** permanent.

fugue /fjuːg/ *noun Mus.* a style of composition in which a theme is introduced in one part and developed as successive parts take it up. [from French *fugue*, from Italian *fuga*, flight]

-ful *combining form* **1** (PL. **-fuls**) forming nouns, denoting an amount held by a container, or something thought of as one: *an armful of books/two mugfuls of coffee.* **2** forming adjectives meaning. **a** full of: *meaningful/eventful.* **b** characterized by: *merciful/graceful.* **c** having the qualities of: *youthful.* **d** in accordance with: *lawful.* **e** showing an inclination to: *forgetful.* [from Anglo-Saxon *ful*, as in *handful*]

fulcrum /ˈfʊlkrəm/ *noun* (PL. **fulcrums**, **fulcra**) the fixed point about which a lever moves or pivots. [from Latin *fulcrum*, prop]

fulfil *verb* (**fulfilled**, **fulfilling**) **1** to carry out or perform (a task, promise, etc). **2** to satisfy (requirements). **3** to achieve (an aim, ambition, etc). — **fulfil oneself** to realize one's potential through the full use of one's talents. [from Anglo-Saxon *fullfyllan*]

■ **1** carry out, perform, execute, discharge, implement, comply with, observe, keep, obey, complete, finish, conclude. **2** satisfy, conform to, fill, answer. **3** achieve, realize, accomplish, consummate.

⊟ **1** fail, break.

fulfilment *noun* **1** being fulfilled. **2** performance. **3** achievement.

⊟ **2** performance, completion, execution, discharge, implementation, observance. **3** achievement, realization, accomplishment, consummation, success.

full[1] — *adj.* **1** (*also* **full of something**) holding, containing, or having as much as possible, or a large quantity. **2** complete: *do a full day's work.* **3** detailed; thorough; including everything necessary: *a full report.* **4** occupied: *my hands are full.* **5** having eaten till one wants no more. **6** plump; fleshy: *the fuller figure/full lips.* **7** *said of clothes*

made with a large amount of material: *a full skirt.* **8** rich and strong: *a full-flavoured wine.* **9** rich and varied: *a full life.* **10** having all possible rights, etc: *a full member.* **11** maximum: *at full speed.* **12** *said of the moon* at the stage when it appears as a complete disc. **13** *said of a brother or sister* having the same parents or (*of a cousin*) the same grandparents, as oneself. — *adv.* **1** completely; at maximum capacity: *is the heater full on?* **2** exactly; directly; *hit him full on the nose.* — **full of something** unable to talk about anything but it. **full of oneself** having too good an opinion of oneself and one's importance. **full well** perfectly well. **in full 1** completely. **2** at length; in detail: *reported in full.* **to the full** to the greatest possible extent. [from Anglo-Saxon *full*]

■ *adj.* **1** filled, loaded, packed, crowded, crammed, stuffed, jammed, abundant, plentiful, copious, profuse. **2** complete, entire, whole, intact, total, unabridged, unexpurgated. **3** detailed, thorough, comprehensive, exhaustive, all-inclusive, broad, vast, extensive. **4** occupied, busy. **5** satisfied, replete. **6** plump, generous, ample, generous, large. **8** rich, strong, resonant, loud, deep, clear, distinct. **11** maximum, top, highest, greatest, utmost.

⊟ *adj.* **1** empty. **2** partial, incomplete. **3** superficial.

full[2] *verb* to shrink and beat (cloth) to thicken it. [from Latin *fullo*, fuller]

full back *Hockey, Football, Rugby* a defence player positioned towards the back of the field to protect the goal.

full-blooded *adj.* **1** of pure breed, not mixed blood. **2** enthusiastic; whole-hearted.

full-blown *adj.* **1** having all the features of: *a full-blown war.* **2** *said of a rose, etc* completely open.

full board the provision of all meals at a hotel, etc.

full-bodied *adj.* having a rich flavour or quality: *a full-bodied wine.*

full dress the style of dress to be worn on formal or ceremonial occasions.

full-dress *adj.* relating to or wearing full dress.

full employment a situation in which all those seeking work in a community or country are able to find suitable work fairly readily, and in which the number of unfilled vacancies exceeds the number of people seeking work.

fuller *noun* a person who fulls cloth.

fuller's earth *Geol.* a green, blue, or yellowish-brown clay, composed mainly of montmorillonite, with a high adsorptive capacity. It is used to decolourize fats and oils, to remove grease from fabrics, as a filter, and a base for paper and cosmetics. It was formerly used to remove grease from and to bleach raw wool.

full-frontal *adj.* exposing the genitals completely to view.

full house 1 a theatre or cinema audience of maximum size. **2** *Cards* especially in poker, a set of five cards consisting of three cards of one kind and two of another.

full-length *adj.* **1** complete; of the usual or standard length. **2** showing the whole body: *a full-length mirror.* **3** of maximum length; long: *a full-length skirt.*

fullness *noun* the condition of being full or complete. — **in the fullness of time** when the proper time has elapsed.

full-on *adj. colloq.* explicit or unrestrained.

full-scale *adj.* **1** *said of a drawing, etc* of the same size as the subject. **2** using all possible resources, means, etc; complete or exhaustive.

full stop a punctuation mark (.) used to indicate the end of a sentence or to mark an abbreviation. Also called PERIOD.

full time the end of the time normally allowed for a sports match, etc.

full-time *adj., adv.* occupying the whole period of working time.

fully *adv.* **1** to the greatest possible extent. **2** completely: *fully qualified.* **3** in detail: *deal with it more fully next week.* **4** quite; at least: *stayed for fully one hour.*

▤ **1** completely, totally, utterly, wholly, entirely, thoroughly, altogether, quite, positively, without reserve, perfectly. **2** thoroughly.
▣ **1, 2** partly.

fully-fashioned *adj.*, *said of knitwear or stockings* shaped so as to give a close fit.

fully-fledged *adj.* **1** *said of a person* completely trained or qualified. **2** *said of a bird* old enough to have grown feathers.

fulmar /ˈfʊlmɑː(r), ˈfʊlmə(r)/ *noun* any of various seabirds of the petrel family, native to Arctic and sub-Arctic regions, having a hooked bill, a short stocky body, long narrow wings, webbed feet, and a short tail. Like many other members of the petrel family, both adults and young defend themselves from predators by spitting out a stream of oily foul-smelling liquid. [from Icelandic *ful*, foul, stinking + *mar*, gull]

fulminate /ˈfʊlmɪneɪt/ *verb intrans.* to utter angry criticism or condemnation. [from Latin *fulminare*, to hurl lightning]

fulmination *noun* **1** the act of fulminating. **2** denunciation.

fulsome *adj.*, *said of praise, compliments, etc* so overdone as to be distasteful. [from FULL¹]

fumble — *verb* **1** *intrans.* to handle things, or grope, clumsily. **2** to fail to manage, because of clumsy handling: *the fielder fumbled the catch.* — *noun* an act of fumbling.

▤ *verb* **1** grope, feel, scrabble. **2** bungle, *colloq.* botch, mishandle, mismanage.

fume — *noun* (**fumes**) **1** smoke, gases, or vapours, especially those that are strong-smelling or toxic, emanating from heated materials, operating engines or machinery, etc. **2** the pungent toxic vapours given off by solvents or concentrated acids. — *verb* **1** *intrans.* to be furious; to fret angrily. **2** *intrans.* to give off smoke, gases, or vapours. **3** *intrans. said of gases or vapours* to come off in fumes, especially during a chemical reaction. **4** to treat (clothing, etc) with fumes; to fumigate. [from Latin *fumus*, smoke]

▤ *noun* **1** smoke, gas, vapour, exhaust, haze, fog, smog, pollution. *verb* **1** rage, storm, rant, rave, seethe. **2** smoke, smoulder, boil, steam.

fumigant *noun* a chemical compound in the form of a gas or vapour that is used to destroy germs, insect pests, animal parasites, etc. [from Latin *fumigare*, to smoke]

fumigate *verb* to expose (clothing, buildings, etc) to a chemical compound in the form of a gas or vapour in order to destroy germs, insect pests, animal parasites, etc.

▤ deodorize, disinfect, sterilize, purify, cleanse.

fumigation *noun* the act or process of fumigating.

fumitory *noun* (*also* **common fumitory**) an annual plant (*Fumaria officinalis*) with slender stems and bluish-green leaves. Each flower has four pink petals with blackish-purple tips. It is a common weed on cultivated ground. [from Old French *fume-terre*, from Latin *fumus*, smoke + *terra*, earth]

fun — *noun* **1** enjoyment. **2** a source of amusement or entertainment. — *adj. colloq.* intended for amusement. — **figure of fun** someone whom others ridicule. **for fun** as a joke; for amusement. **fun and games 1** amusement; excitement. **2** *ironic* trouble. **in fun** as a joke; not seriously. **make fun of** or **poke fun at someone** or **something** to laugh at them, especially unkindly; to tease or ridicule them. [from earlier *fon*, to make a fool of]

▤ *noun* **1** enjoyment, pleasure, amusement, entertainment, diversion, distraction, recreation, play, sport, foolery, tomfoolery, horseplay, skylarking, romp, merrymaking, mirth, jollity, jocularity, joking, jesting. **2** amusement, entertainment, diversion, distraction, game. **make fun of** tease, ridicule, rag, *colloq.* rib, jeer at, laugh at, mock, taunt.

function — *noun* **1** the special purpose or task of a machine, person, bodily part, etc. **2** an organized event such as a party, reception, meeting, etc. **3** *Maths.* a mathematical procedure that relates one or more variables to one or more other variables, eg in the algebraic expression $y = x + 4$, the variable y is a function of the variable x, usually written as $y = f(x)$, and a change in x will produce a change in y. — *verb intrans.* **1** to work; to operate. **2** to serve or act: *a torch that functions as a screwdriver.*

▤ *noun* **1** purpose, task, job, role, duty, charge, responsibility, concern, office, occupation, business, activity, part, use. **2** party, reception, meeting, gathering, affair, *colloq.* do, dinner, luncheon. *verb* **1** work, operate, run, go. **2** serve, act, perform, behave.

functional *adj.* **1** designed for efficiency rather than decorativeness; plain rather than elaborate. **2** in working order; operational.

▤ **1** practical, useful, utilitarian, utility, plain, hard-wearing. **2** working, operational.
▣ **1** useless, decorative.

functional food a food which is designed to enhance certain areas of health, especially by means of additives.

functional group *Chem.* in a molecule of a substance, a combination of two or more atoms that are bonded together and tend to act as a single unit in chemical reactions, eg the hydroxyl (-OH) group. The functional group determines the chemical properties of the molecule.

functionalism *noun* the policy or practice of the practical application of ideas.

functionality *noun* the capacity a thing, idea, etc has to be functional or practical.

functionary *noun* (PL. **functionaries**) *derog.* a person who works as a minor official in the government, etc.

function key *Comput.* any of the keys marked with an 'F' and a following numeral on a keyboard, pressed alone or in combination with other keys to perform a specific task within a program.

fund — *noun* **1** a sum of money for a special purpose. **2** a large store or supply: *a fund of jokes.* **3** (**funds**) *colloq.* money available for spending. — *verb* **1** to provide money for: *fund the project.* **2** to make (a debt) permanent, with fixed interest. — **in funds** *colloq.* having plenty of cash. [from Latin *fundus*, bottom]

▤ *noun* **1** pool, kitty. **2** store, supply, reserve, stock, hoard, cache, stack, mine, well, source, treasury, repository, storehouse. **3** money, cash, capital, finance, resources, backing, savings, wealth. *verb* **1** finance, capitalize, endow, subsidize, underwrite, sponsor, back, support, promote, float.

fundamental — *adj.* **1** basic; underlying: *fundamental rules of physics/her fundamental honesty.* **2** large; important: *fundamental differences.* **3** essential; necessary. — *noun* **1** (*usually* **fundamentals**) a basic principle or rule. **2** *Mus.* the lowest note of a chord. [from Latin *fundamentum*, foundation]

▤ *adj.* **1** basic, underlying, primary, first, rudimentary, elementary, integral, central, principal, cardinal, prime, main. **2** large, important, significant, key, crucial. **3** essential, necessary, indispensable, vital, crucial.

....

fundamentalism *noun* in religion, politics, etc, unquestioning faith in the traditional teachings; especially, in the Protestant church, belief in the literal interpretation of the Bible.

fundamentalist *noun* a person who believes in fundamentalism.

fundamentally *adv.* in a fundamental way.

fundamental particle *Physics* an elementary particle.

fundamental unit *Physics* each of the units of length, mass, and time from which all other units of measurement are derived.

fundholder *noun* a general practitioner or medical practice that is assigned a budget.

fundholding *adj.* describing a general practitioner or medical practice that is assigned a budget.

funeral — *noun* **1** the ceremonial burial or cremation of a dead person. **2** *colloq.* one's own problem. — *adj.* of or relating to funerals. [from Latin *funeralia*, funeral rites]

....

▣ *noun* **1** burial, interment, entombment, cremation, obsequies, wake. **2** problem, *colloq.* pidgin, affair.

....

funeral director an undertaker.

funeral parlour an undertaker's place of business.

funerary /'fjuːnərərɪ/ *adj.* belonging to or used for funerals. [from Latin *funerarius*]

funereal /fjʊˈnɪərɪəl/ *adj.* **1** associated with or suitable for funerals. **2** mournful; dismal. **3** extremely slow. [from Latin *funereus*]

funfair *noun* a collection of sideshows and amusements, often set up temporarily on open ground.

fungal or **fungous** *adj.* **1** relating to or resembling a fungus. **2** caused by a fungus.

fungicidal /fʌŋgɪˈsaɪdəl, fʌndʒɪ-/ *adj.* **1** destroying or limiting the growth of fungi. **2** relating to a fungicide.

fungicide /'fʌŋgɪsaɪd, 'fʌndʒɪ-/ *noun Chem.* a chemical that kills or limits the growth of fungi.

fungoid /'fʌŋgɔɪd/ *adj. Bot.* resembling a fungus in nature or consistency.

fungus *noun* (PL. **fungi**) any organism that superficially resembles a plant, but does not have leaves and roots, and lacks chlorophyll, so must obtain its nutrients from other organisms, by living either as a parasite on living organisms, or as a saprophyte on dead organic matter. Most fungi reproduce by means of spores. [from Latin *fungus*, mushroom, fungus]

funicular /fjʊˈnɪkjʊlə(r)/ — *adj.*, *said of a mountain railway* operating by a machine-driven cable, with two cars, one of which descends while the other ascends. — *noun* a funicular railway. [from Latin *funiculus*, diminutive of *funis*, rope]

funk[1] — *noun colloq.* **1** (*also* **blue funk**) a state of fear or panic. **2** a coward. -- *verb* to avoid doing (something) from panic.

funk[2] *noun colloq.* jazz or rock music with a strong rhythm and repeating bass pattern. [from French dialect *funquer*, to give off smoke]

funky *adj.* (**funkier, funkiest**) *colloq.* **1** *said of jazz or rock music* strongly rhythmical and emotionally stirring. **2** trendy; good. **3** earthy; smelly.

funnel — *noun* **1** a cone-shaped utensil with a wide mouth that tapers to a narrow spout, used for directing poured liquids into narrow-necked bottles or containers. **2** a large vertical exhaust pipe on a steamship or steam engine, through which smoke and exhaust gases escape. — *verb* (**funnelled, funnelling**) **1** *intrans.* to rush through a narrow space: *wind funnelling through the streets*. **2** to transfer (liquid, etc) from one vessel to another using a funnel. [from Old Provençal *fonil*, from Latin *infundere*, to pour in]

▣ *verb* **2** channel, direct, convey, move, transfer, pass, pour, siphon, filter.

....

funnily *adv.* in a funny way.

funny *adj.* (**funnier, funniest**) **1** amusing; causing laughter. **2** strange; odd; mysterious. **3** *colloq.* dishonest; shady; involving trickery. **4** *colloq.* ill. **5** *colloq.* slightly crazy. [from FUN]

....

▣ **1** amusing, humorous, entertaining, comic, comical, hilarious, witty, facetious, droll, farcical, laughable, ridiculous, absurd, silly. **2** strange, odd, mysterious, peculiar, curious, queer, weird, unusual, remarkable, puzzling, perplexing. **3** dishonest, *colloq.* shady, suspicious, dubious, doubtful, underhand. **4** queer. **5** crazy, *colloq.* dotty, *slang* loopy, *colloq.* potty.

🔁 **1** serious, solemn, sad. **2** normal, ordinary, usual.

....

funny bone the area near the elbow where the ulnar nerve runs close to the skin surface. If struck, it sends a tingling sensation down the forearm to the fingers.

funny farm *colloq.* a mental hospital.

fun run a long-distance race that people run in for amusement, to raise money for a charity, etc.

fur — *noun* **1** the thick soft fine hairs covering the body of many mammals. **2** the dressed skin of such an animal with the hair attached, used to make, line, or trim garments; a synthetic imitation of this. **3** a coat, cape, jacket, or other garment made of or trimmed with fur, or an imitation of it. **4** a whitish coating on the tongue, caused by illness, excessive smoking, etc. **5** a whitish-grey deposit lining the inside of hot-water pipes, kettles, boilers, etc, and formed by the precipitation of calcium or magnesium salts from hard water. — *verb intrans., trans.* (**furred, furring**) (**fur up** or **fur something up**) to coat or become coated with a fur-like deposit. — **make the fur fly** *colloq.* to cause a commotion; to upset people. [from Old French *fuerre*, sheath]

furbelow *noun* **1** a dress trimming in the form of a ruched or pleated strip, ruffle, or flounce. **2** (**furbelows**) fussy ornamentation. [from French and Italian *falbala*]

furbish *verb* (*also* **furbish something up**) to restore, decorate, or clean. [from French *fourbir*, to polish]

furcate — *adj.* forked. — *verb intrans.* to fork or divide. [from Latin *furca*, fork]

furcation *noun* a forking; a fork-like division.

Furies /'fjʊərɪz/ see ERINYES.

furioso /fjʊərɪˈoʊsoʊ, fʊərɪ-/ *adj., adv. Mus.* to be played furiously. [Italian, = furious]

furious *adj.* **1** violently or intensely angry. **2** raging; stormy: *furious winds*. **3** frenzied; frantic: *furious activity*. [from FURY]

....

▣ **1** angry, *colloq.* mad, *colloq.* up in arms, livid, enraged, infuriated, incensed, raging, fuming, *colloq.* boiling. **2** raging, stormy, tempestuous, wild, violent, fierce. **3** frenzied, frantic, intense, vigorous, boisterous.

🔁 **1** calm, pleased. **2, 3** calm, quiet.

....

furl *verb trans., intrans., said of flags, sails, or umbrellas* to roll up. [from Old French *fer*, firm (from Latin *firmus*) + *lier*, to bind (from Latin *ligare*)]

furlong *noun* a measure of distance equal to 201.2m (220 yards or ⅛ mile), defined in medieval times as the length of a furrow in a common field, but now generally only used in horse racing. [from Anglo-Saxon *furh*, furrow + *lang*, long]

furlough /'fɜːloʊ/ *noun* leave of absence, especially from military duty abroad. [from Dutch *verlof*]

furnace *noun* **1** an enclosed chamber in which a fuel such as coal or coke is burned in order to generate intense heat for any of various industrial purposes, eg smelting or refining ores, destroying refuse, or producing hot water or steam. **2** a blast furnace. **3** *colloq.* a very hot place. [from Latin *fornax*, kiln, oven]

furnish *verb* **1** to provide (a house, etc) with furniture. **2** (**furnish someone with something**) to supply or equip them with what they require. **3** to supply (what is necessary). [from Old French *furnir*, to provide]

⊟ **2** supply, equip, fit out, provide, rig, stock, afford, grant, give, offer, present. **3** supply, provide.
⊟ **2** divest.

furnishings *pl. noun* furniture, fittings, carpets, curtains, etc.

furniture *noun* **1** movable household equipment such as tables, chairs, beds, etc. **2** the equipment needed on board ship or in a factory. **3** door fittings such as locks and handles. [from French *fourniture*, from *fournir*, to provide]

⊟ **1** furnishings, equipment, appliances, household goods, fittings, fitments, movables, possessions, effects, things. **3** fittings, fitments.

Types of furniture include: table, dining table, gateleg table, refectory table, lowboy, side table, coffee table, card table; chair, easy chair, armchair, rocking chair, recliner, dining chair, carver, kitchen chair, stool, swivel chair, high chair, suite, settee, sofa, couch, studio couch, chesterfield, pouffe, footstool, bean bag; bed, four-poster, chaise longue, daybed, bed settee, divan, camp bed, bunk, water bed, cot, cradle; desk, bureau, secretaire, bookcase, cupboard, cabinet, china cabinet, Welsh dresser, sideboard, buffet, dumb waiter, fireplace, overmantel, fender, firescreen, hallstand, umbrella stand, magazine rack; wardrobe, armoire, dressing-table, vanity unit, washstand, chest of drawers, tallboy, chiffonier, commode, ottoman, chest, coffer, blanket box.

furore /fjʊˈrɔːrɪ, fʊəˈrɔːreɪ/ *noun* a general outburst of excitement or indignation in reaction to something. [from Italian *furore*, from Latin *furor*, frenzy]

furrier *noun* a person who makes or sells furs.

furrow — *noun* **1** a groove or trench cut into the earth by a plough; a rut. **2** a wrinkle, eg in the forehead. — *verb* **1** to plough (land) into furrows. **2** *intrans.* to become wrinkled. [from Anglo-Saxon *furh*]

⊟ *noun* **1** groove, trench, channel, hollow, rut, track. **2** wrinkle, line, crease. *verb* **2** crease, wrinkle, draw together, knit.

furry /ˈfɜːrɪ/ *adj.* (**furrier**, **furriest**) **1** covered with fur. **2** made of, or like, fur.

further — *adj.* **1** more distant or remote. **2** more extended: *further delay.* **3** additional: *no further clues.* — *adv.* **1** at or to a greater distance or more distant point. **2** to or at a more advanced point: *further developed.* **3** to a greater extent or degree: *modified even further.* **4** moreover; furthermore. **5** (**further to ...**) following on from ... . — *verb* (**furthered**, **furthering**) to help the progress of. See also FARTHER. [from Anglo-Saxon *furthra*]

⊟ *adj.* **2** additional, more. **3** additional, more, supplementary, extra, fresh, new, other. *verb* help, advance, forward, promote, champion, push, encourage, foster, aid, assist, ease, facilitate, speed, hasten, accelerate, expedite.
⊟ *verb* stop, frustrate.

furtherance *noun* the furthering, advancement or continuation of something.

further education education for school-leavers not in higher education at a university or polytechnic.

furthermore *adv.* in addition; moreover.

⊟ in addition, moreover, what's more, further, besides, also, too, as well, additionally.

furthermost *adj.* most distant or remote; farthest.

furthest — *adj.* most distant or remote. — *adv.* **1** at or to the greatest distance or most distant point. **2** at or to the most advanced point; to the greatest extent or degree. See also FARTHEST. [superlative formed from FURTHER]

⊟ *adj.* farthest, furthermost, remotest, outermost, outmost.
⊟ *adj.* nearest.

furtive *adj.* secretive; stealthy; sly. [from Latin *furtivus*, stolen, clandestine]

⊟ secretive, stealthy, sly, surreptitious, underhand, hidden, covert, secret.
⊟ open.

fury *noun* (PL. **furies**) **1** violent or frenzied anger; an outburst of this. **2** violence: *the fury of the wind.* **3** a frenzy: *a fury of activity.* — **like fury** *colloq.* fast; eagerly; powerfully; like mad. [from French *furie*, from Latin *furere*, to rage]

⊟ **1** anger, rage, wrath, frenzy, madness, passion, vehemence. **2** violence, fierceness, ferocity, wildness, turbulence, power.
⊟ **1, 2** calm, peacefulness.

furze *noun* same as GORSE. [from Anglo-Saxon *fyrs*]

fuse[1] — *noun Electr.* a safety device designed to protect an electric circuit against surges of excess current, caused by overloading of the circuit, that would otherwise damage equipment or constitute a fire risk. It consists of a length of wire (usually enclosed by a small glass or ceramic tube with metal ends) that melts and breaks the circuit when the current exceeds a certain value. — *verb trans., intrans.* **1** to melt as a result of the application of heat. **2** to join by, or as if by, melting together. **3** *said of an electric circuit or appliance* to cease to function as a result of the melting of a fuse. — **blow a fuse** *colloq.* to lose one's temper. [from Latin *fusus*, melted]

fuse[2] — *noun* a cord or cable containing combustible material, used for detonating a bomb or explosive charge. — *verb* to fit with such a device. [from Latin *fusus*, spindle]

fuselage /ˈfjuːzəlɑːʒ, -lɪdʒ/ *noun* the main body of an aircraft, carrying the crew and passengers. [from French *fuselé*, spindle-shaped]

fusilier *noun* **1** *Hist.* an infantryman armed with a *fusil* or light musket. **2** a member of any of several British regiments formerly armed with these. [from French *fusilier*]

fusillade /fjuːsɪˈleɪd, -ˈlɑːd/ *noun* **1** a simultaneous or continuous discharge of firearms. **2** an onslaught, eg of criticism. [from French *fusillade*, from *fusiller*, to shoot]

fusilli /fjuːˈzɪlɪ/ *noun* pasta shaped into short thick spirals. [from Italian]

fusion *noun* **1** *Chem.* the process of melting, whereby a substance changes from a solid to a liquid. **2** the act of joining together. **3** *Physics* the process whereby two light atomic nuclei combine to form a heavier nucleus, with the release of large amounts of energy. Also called NUCLEAR FUSION. [from Latin *fusio*, melting]

⊟ **1** melting, smelting. **2** welding, union, synthesis, blending, coalescence, amalgamation, integration, merger, federation.

fusional language *Linguistics* a language type in which words vary in their internal structure, usually by inflectional endings, which may express several grammatical meanings at once. Fusional languages include Latin,

Greek, and Arabic. Also called *inflecting or synthetic language*. See also AGGLUTINATING LANGUAGE, ANALYTIC LANGUAGE.

fuss — *noun* **1** agitation and excitement, especially over something trivial. **2** a commotion, disturbance or bustle. — *verb intrans.* **1** to worry needlessly. **2** to concern oneself too much with trivial matters. **3** to agitate. — **fuss over something** or **someone** to display a fond concern for them. **make a fuss** to complain. **make a fuss of someone** *colloq.* to give them a lot of attention. [origin unknown]

■ *noun* BOTHER, TROUBLE, *colloq.* HASSLE, PALAVER, *colloq.* TO-DO, *colloq.* HOO-HA, FURORE, ROW, COMMOTION, STIR, FLUSTER, CONFUSION, UPSET, WORRY, AGITATION, *colloq.* FLAP, EXCITEMENT, BUSTLE, FLURRY. *verb* **1** worry, fret. **3** *colloq.* flap, bother.
■ *noun* CALM.

fussily *adv.* in a fussy way.
fussiness *noun* being fussy.
fusspot *noun derog. colloq.* a person who worries excessively, especially over trifles.
fussy *adj.* (**fussier, fussiest**) **1** choosy; discriminating. **2** over-concerned with details or trifles. **3** bustling and officious. **4** *said of clothes, etc* over-elaborate.

■ **1** *colloq.* choosy, discriminating, particular, hard to please. **2** particular, fastidious, scrupulous, finicky, pernickety, difficult. **4** over-elaborate, fancy, ornate, cluttered.
■ **2** casual, uncritical. **4** plain.

fustiness *noun* being fusty.
fusty *adj.* (**fustier, fustiest**) **1** stale-smelling; old and musty. **2** old-fashioned. [from Middle English *fust*, wine cask]
futhark /ˈfuːθɑːk/ or **futhork** /ˈfuːθɔːk/ *noun* the runic alphabet, so called from the names of the first six symbols: *f, u, (th), a or o, r, k.*
futile *adj.* unproductive, unavailing, foolish, vain or pointless. [from Latin *futilis*, easily pouring out, unreliable]

■ unproductive, unavailing, foolish, vain, pointless, useless, worthless, idle, wasted, fruitless, profitless, unsuccessful, abortive, unprofitable, barren, empty, hollow, forlorn.
■ fruitful, profitable.

futilely *adv.* in a futile way.
futility *noun* uselessness.

■ uselessness, meaninglessness, pointlessness,

worthlessness, vanity, emptiness, hollowness, aimlessness.
■ use, purpose.

futon *noun* a cloth-filled mattress designed to be used on the floor and rolled up when not in use. [from Japanese]
future — *noun* **1** the time to come; events that are still to occur. **2** *Grammar* the future tense. **3** prospects: *must think about one's future.* **4** likelihood of success: *no future in that.* **5** (**futures**) *Stock Exchange* commodities bought or sold at an agreed price, to be delivered at a later date. The price agreed on at the earlier date remains the same whether the market price of the particular commodity has fallen or risen in the meantime. — *adj.* **1** yet to come or happen. **2** about to become: *my future wife.* **3** *Grammar, said of the tense of a verb* indicating actions or events yet to happen. — **in future** from now on. [from Latin *futurus*, about to be]

■ *noun* **3** prospects, expectations, outlook. *adj.* **1** to come, forthcoming, in the offing, impending, coming, approaching, expected, planned, later, subsequent, eventual, unborn. **2** prospective, designate, to be, fated, destined.
■ *noun* **1, 2, 3** past. *adj.* **1, 3** past. **2** ex-.

Futurism *noun* a modern art movement founded by the poet Marinetti in Milan in 1909.
futurist *noun* **1** a person whose chief interest is what will happen in the future. **2** a person who believes in futurism.
futuristic *adj.* **1** relating to futurism. **2** *said of design, etc* so modern or original as to seem appropriate to the future.
futuristically *adv.* in a futuristic way.
futurity *noun* (PL. **futurities**) **1** the future. **2** a future event.
futurology *noun* the forecasting of future events from present tendencies.
fuzz[1] *noun* a mass of fine fibres or hair.
fuzz[2] *noun slang* the police.
fuzzily *adv.* in a fuzzy way.
fuzzy *adj.* (**fuzzier, fuzziest**) **1** covered with fuzz. **2** forming a mass of tight curls. **3** indistinct; blurred.

■ **1** fluffy, furry, woolly, fleecy, downy, velvety, napped. **2** frizzy. **3** indistinct, blurred, unfocused, unclear, vague, faint, hazy, shadowy, woolly, muffled, distorted, ill-defined.
■ **3** clear, distinct.

fuzzy logic *Comput.* a form of logic or reasoning that is a central part of artificial intelligence, and resembles human thinking in that it is used to process information that cannot be defined precisely because it is dependent on its context. Although difficult to program, fuzzy logic is widely used in expert systems.

G

G¹ or **g** *noun* (PL. **Gs, G's, g's**) **1** the seventh letter of the English alphabet. **2** (**G**) *Mus.* the fifth note on the scale of C major. **3** (**G**) the musical key having this note as its base.

G² *abbrev.* **1** German. **2** *North Amer. slang* a grand, 1000 dollars.

g *abbrev.* **1** gallon(s). **2** gram(s) or gramme(s). **3** (acceleration due to) gravity.

G7 *abbrev.* the Group of Seven, the name given to the seven countries (the UK, the USA, Canada, France, Italy, Germany, and Japan) which try to pursue a policy of co-operation on economic matters. Their heads of state and of government have met at an annual summit since 1976.

GA or **Ga** *abbrev.* Georgia.

Ga *symbol Chem.* gallium.

gab *colloq.* — *noun* idle talk; chat. — *verb intrans.* (**gabbed, gabbing**) (*also* **gab on** or **away**) to talk idly, especially at length. — **the gift of the gab** *colloq.* the ability to speak with ease, especially persuasively. [probably from Irish Gaelic *gob*, beak, mouth]

gabardine *noun* **1** a closely woven twill fabric, especially of wool or cotton. **2** a coat or loose cloak made from this. [from Old French *gauvardine*, pilgrim's garment]

gabble — *verb intrans., trans.* to talk or say quickly and unclearly. — *noun* fast indistinct talk. [from Dutch *gabbelen*]

gabbro *noun Geol.* a coarse-grained crystalline igneous rock with a low silica content. [from Italian *gabbro*]

gaberdine same as GABARDINE.

gable *noun* **1** the triangular upper part of a side wall between the sloping parts of a roof. **2** a triangular canopy above a door or window. [from Norse *gafl*]

gabled *adj.* having a gable or gables.

Gaboon viper one of the largest vipers, up to 2m in length, with the longest fangs of any viper.

gad¹ *verb intrans.* (**gadded, gadding**) *colloq.* (**gad about** or **around**) to go from place to place busily, especially in the pursuit of amusement or pleasure. [back-formation from Anglo-Saxon *gædeling*, companion]

gad² *interj. old use* an expression of surprise or affirmation. [a form of *God*]

gadabout *noun derog. colloq., humorous* a person who gads about.

gadfly *noun* (PL. **gadflies**) **1** any of various large flies, eg horsefly, that suck the blood of cattle and other animal livestock, inflicting painful bites. **2** *old derog. use* a person who deliberately and persistently annoys others. [from Anglo-Saxon *gad*, goad]

gadget *noun* any small device or appliance, especially one more ingenious than necessary.

⊟ tool, appliance, device, contrivance, contraption, thing, invention, novelty, gimmick.

gadgetry *noun* gadgets collectively.

gadolinium *noun Chem.* (SYMBOL **Gd**, ATOMIC NUMBER 64) a soft silvery-white metal, belonging to the lanthanide series, which is highly magnetic at low temperatures, and also behaves as a superconductor. [named after the Finnish chemist Johan *Gadolin*]

gadwall *noun* (PL. **gadwalls, gadwall**) a dabbling duck related to the mallard, native to inland waters in the northern hemisphere.

Gael /geɪl/ *noun* a Gaelic-speaking person from the Scottish Highlands, Ireland or the Isle of Man. [from Gaelic *Gaidheal*]

Gaelic /'geɪlɪk, 'galɪk/ — *noun* any of the closely related Celtic languages spoken in Ireland, Scotland, and the Isle of Man. — *adj.* of or relating to these languages, the people who speak them, or their customs.

gaff¹ — *noun* **1** a long pole with a hook, for landing large fish. **2** a vertical spar to which the tops of certain types of sail are attached. — *verb* to seize (a fish) with a gaff. [from Provençal *gaf*, boathook]

gaff² — **blow the gaff** *slang* to give away a secret.

gaffe *noun* a socially embarrassing action or remark. [from French *gaffe*]

gaffer *noun* **1** *colloq.* a boss or foreman. **2** the senior electrician on a film or television set. **3** *dialect, often as a form of address* an old man. [perhaps from GODFATHER]

gag¹ — *verb* (**gagged, gagging**) **1** to silence (someone) by putting something in or over their mouth. **2** to deprive of free speech. **3** *intrans.* to retch. **4** *intrans.* to choke. — *noun* something put into or over a person's mouth to impose silence. [from Middle English *gaggen*, to suffocate]

⊟ *verb* **2** muzzle, silence, quiet, censor, muffle, stifle, suppress, curb, check.

gag² *colloq.* — *noun* a joke or trick, especially as used by a professional comedian. — *verb intrans.* (**gagged, gagging**) to tell jokes.

⊟ *noun* joke, jest, quip, crack, wisecrack, one-liner, pun, witticism.

gaga *adj. colloq.* **1** weak-minded through old age; senile. **2** silly; foolish. **3** wildly enthusiastic. [from French *gaga*]

gage¹ *noun* **1** an object given as security or a pledge. **2** *Hist.* something thrown down to signal a challenge, eg a glove. [from Old French *guage*]

gage² same as GREENGAGE.

gaggle *noun* **1** a flock of geese. **2** *colloq.* a group of noisy people. [imitative]

Gaia theory /'gaɪə, 'geɪə/ the proposal that Earth has a self-regulating control system called Gaia, made up from all living things and their environment.

gaiety *noun* **1** the condition of being merry or gay. **2** attractively bright appearance. **3** fun; merrymaking. [from French *gaieté*]

⊟ **1** happiness, glee, cheerfulness, joie de vivre, jollity, merriment, mirth, hilarity, joviality, good humour, high spirits, liveliness. **2** brightness, brilliance, sparkle, colour, colourfulness, show, showiness. **3** fun, merrymaking, revelry, festivity, celebration.
⊟ **1** sadness. **2** drabness.

gaily *adv.* **1** in a light-hearted, merry way. **2** brightly; colourfully.

▣ **1** happily, joyfully, merrily, blithely. **2** brightly, brilliantly, colourfully, flamboyantly.

▣ **1** sadly. **2** dully.

gain — *verb* **1** to get, obtain, or earn. **2** *intrans.* (**gain by** or **from something**) to benefit or profit from it. **3** to have or experience an increase in: *gain speed.* **4** *trans., intrans.* *said of a clock, etc* to go too fast by (an amount of time). **5** to reach (a place), especially after difficulties. **6** *intrans.* (**gain on someone** or **something**) to come closer to them; to catch them up. — *noun* **1** (*often* **gains**) something gained, eg profit. **2** an increase, eg in weight. **3** an instance of gaining. — **gain ground** to make progress or win an advantage. **gain time** to get extra time for something through a delay or postponement. [from Old French *gaaignier*, to earn, gain, or till (land)]

▣ *verb* **1** get, obtain, acquire, earn, make, gross, net, clear, reap, win, secure, attain, achieve, realize. **3** increase, pick up, gather. **5** reach, arrive at, come to, get to. **6** approach, close on, catch up, level with, overtake, outdistance, leave behind. *noun* **1** earnings, proceeds, income, revenue, profit, return, yield, dividend, winnings, acquisition, attainment, achievement. **2** growth, increase, increment, rise, advance, progress, headway, improvement.

▣ *verb* **1**, **3**, **4** lose. *noun* **1**, **2** loss.

gainful *adj.* **1** profitable. **2** *said of employment* paid.

gainsay *verb* (PAST TENSE AND PAST PARTICIPLE **gainsaid**) *formal* to deny or contradict. [from Anglo-Saxon *gean*, against + *sayen*, to say]

gait *noun* **1** a way of walking. **2** an animal's leg-movements at a particular speed, eg trotting. [variation of obsolete *gate*, manner of doing]

gaiter *noun* a leather or cloth covering for the lower leg and ankle, often with a strap fitting under the shoe. [from French *guêtre*]

gal *noun old colloq. use* a girl.

gal. *abbrev.* gallon.

gala *noun* **1** an occasion of special entertainment or a public festivity of some kind, eg a carnival. **2** a meeting for sports, especially swimming, competitions. [from Old French *galer*, to make merry]

▣ **1** festivity, celebration, festival, carnival, jubilee, jamboree, fête, fair, pageant, procession.

galactic *adj.* relating to a galaxy or the Galaxy. [from GALAXY]

galactosaemia /gəlaktoʊˈsiːmɪə/ *noun Medicine* a disorder characterized by inability to convert the sugar galactose to glucose, resulting in the accumulation of galactose in the blood, which can lead to mental retardation. [from Greek *galaktos*, milk]

galactose *noun Biochem.* a monosaccharide (simple sugar) that occurs together with glucose in lactose (milk sugar). See also GALACTOSAEMIA. [from Greek *galaktos*, milk]

galantine /ˈɡaləntiːn/ *noun* a dish of boneless cooked white meat or fish served cold in jelly. [from Old French]

galaxy *noun* (PL. **galaxies**) **1** *Astron.* a huge collection of stars, dust, and gas, held together by mutual gravitational attraction. **2** (**the Galaxy**) the vast spiral arrangement of stars to which our Sun belongs, known as the Milky Way, which contains about 100,000 million stars, together with vast clouds of gas and dust called nebulae. **3** a fabulous gathering or array, eg of famous people. [from Greek *galaktos*, milk]

gale *noun* **1** a wind that blows with a speed of 63 to 87 km per hour on the Beaufort scale. **2** a very strong wind. **3** (*usually* **gales**) a sudden loud burst, eg of laughter.

▣ **2** wind, squall, storm, hurricane, tornado, typhoon, cyclone. **3** burst, outburst, outbreak, fit, eruption, explosion, blast.

galena /gəˈliːnə/ *noun Geol.* a mineral that occurs as compact masses of very dense dark grey crystals, consisting mainly of lead sulphide. It is the most important ore of lead. [from Latin *galena*, lead-ore]

Galilean telescope /galɪˈliːən/ *Physics* a refracting telescope that produces an upright image using a converging (convex) lens as the objective (which collects light) and a diverging (concave) lens as the eyepiece (which magnifies the image formed).

gall[1] /ɡɔːl/ *noun* **1** *colloq.* impudence; cheek. **2** bitterness or spitefulness. **3** something unpleasant. **4** *old medical use* a bitter liquid produced in the liver to aid digestion; bile. [from Anglo-Saxon *gealla*, bile]

gall[2] /ɡɔːl/ *noun Bot.* a round abnormal growth on the stem or leaf of a plant, usually caused by invading parasitic fungi or bacteria, or by the presence of insects, eg gall wasps. [from Latin *galla*]

gall[3] /ɡɔːl/ — *noun* **1** a sore or painful swelling on the skin, especially of horses, caused by chafing. **2** something annoying or irritating. **3** a state of being annoyed. — *verb* **1** to chafe (the skin). **2** *said of the skin* to become chafed. **3** to annoy. [from Anglo-Saxon *gealla*, sore on a horse]

gall. *abbrev.* gallon.

gallant — *adj.* **1** brave. **2** *old use, literary* splendid, grand or fine. **3** *said of a man* courteous and attentive to women. — *noun old use* **1** a woman's lover. **2** a handsome young man who pursues women. [from Old French *galer*, to make merry]

▣ *adj.* **1** brave, courageous, valiant, heroic, fearless, dauntless, bold, daring. **3** chivalrous, gentlemanly, courteous, polite, gracious.

▣ *adj.* **1** cowardly. **3** ungentlemanly.

gallantry *noun* (PL. **gallantries**) **1** bravery. **2** *old use* politeness and attentiveness to women; an action or phrase demonstrating this.

gall bladder or **gall-bladder** or **gallbladder** *noun* a small muscular pear-shaped sac, present in most vertebrates and usually lying beneath the right lobe of the liver, in which bile produced by the liver is stored. The gall bladder is stimulated by certain hormones to release bile into the duodenum to aid the breakdown of fats during the digestion of food.

galleon *noun* a large three-masted Spanish ship used for war or trade from the 15th to the 18th century. [from Spanish *galeón*]

gallery *noun* (PL. **galleries**) **1** a room or building used to display works of art. **2** a balcony along an inside upper wall, eg of a church or hall, providing extra seating or reserved for musicians, etc: *minstrels' gallery.* **3** the upper floor in a theatre, usually containing the cheapest seats; the part of the audience seated there. **4** a long narrow room or corridor. **5** an underground passage in a mine or cave. **6** a covered walkway open on one or both sides. **7** the spectators in the stand at a golf, tennis, etc tournament. — **play to the gallery** to seek mass approval or favour by crudely appealing to popular taste. [from Latin *galeria*]

▣ **3** balcony, circle, *colloq.* gods. **6** arcade, passage, walk.

galley *noun* (PL. **galleys**) **1** a long single-deck ship propelled by sails and oars. **2** the kitchen on a ship. **3** a rectangular tray holding arrangements of individual metal letters, from which a preliminary printing of part of a book, etc is made. **4** a galley proof. [from Greek *galaia*]

galley proof a preliminary printing of part of a book, etc in the form of a continuous sheet, on which corrections are marked.

galley slave 1 a slave forced to row a galley. **2** *colloq.* a person given menial tasks; a drudge.

galliard / 'galɪəd/ *noun* a lively dance in triple time; also, a piece of music for it. See also PAVAN(E). [from French *galliard*, merry]

Gallic *adj.* **1** typically or characteristically French. **2** of ancient Gaul or the Gauls. [from Latin *gallicus*, Gaulish]

Gallicism / 'galɪsɪzm/ *noun* a French word or expression used in another language.

gallinaceous / galɪ'neɪʃəs/ *adj. Zool.* of, relating to, or belonging to the Galliformes, an order of birds that includes domestic fowl, turkeys, pheasants, grouse, quail, etc. [from Latin *gallus*, cock]

galling / 'gɔːlɪŋ/ *adj.* irritating.

gallinule *noun* a water bird of the rail family, native to the Old World and much of S America. [from Latin *gallinula*, chicken]

gallium *noun Chem.* (SYMBOL **Ga**, ATOMIC NUMBER **31**) a soft silvery metal found in zinc blende, bauxite, and kaolin, and used in alloys with low melting points, and in luminous paints. Gallium arsenide is widely used as a semiconductor. [from Latin *gallus*, cock, from the name of its French discoverer, Le *coq* de Boisbaudran (1838–1912)]

gallivant *verb intrans. humorous colloq., derog.* to spend time idly or in search of amusement. [perhaps from GALLANT]

gallon *noun* **1** a unit of liquid measurement equal to four quarts or eight pints. It is equivalent to 4.546 litres (an *imperial gallon*) in the UK, and 3.785 litres in the USA. **2** (**gallons of something**) *colloq.* a large amount of liquid. [from Old French *galon*]

gallop — *noun* **1** the fastest pace at which a horse moves, with all four legs leaving the ground together. **2** a period of riding at this pace. **3** an unusually fast speed. — *verb* (**galloped, galloping**) **1** *intrans. said of a horse* to move at a gallop. **2** to cause (a horse) to move at a gallop. **3** *intrans. colloq.* to move, progress or increase very quickly: *galloping inflation*. [from Old French *galoper*]

⊟ *verb* **3** run, sprint, race, career, dash, tear, speed, shoot, rush, hurry.

gallows *sing. noun* **1** a wooden frame on which criminals are put to death by hanging. **2** (**the gallows**) death by hanging. [from Anglo-Saxon *gealga*]

gallows humour humour derived from unpleasant subjects like death and illness; black humour.

gallstone *noun* a small hard mass, usually consisting of cholesterol crystals, bile pigments, and calcium salts, that is formed in the gall bladder or one of its ducts.

Gallup poll / 'galəp/ a survey of the views of a representative group of people, used to assess overall public opinion, especially with regard to voting intentions. [named after the US public opinion expert George Gallup (1901–84)]

galop *noun* a lively 19c dance for couples, or a piece of music for this. [from GALLOP]

galore *adv.* in large amounts or numbers: *books galore*. [from Irish Gaelic *go leór*, to sufficiency]

galosh or **golosh** *noun* a waterproof overshoe. [from Old French *galoche*, from Latin *gallicula*, small Gaulish shoe]

galumph *verb intrans. colloq.* **1** to stride along triumphantly. **2** to walk in a heavy ungainly manner. [coined by Lewis Carroll, perhaps from GALLOP + TRIUMPH]

galvanic *adj.* **1** *Physics* **a** relating to or producing an electric current, especially a direct current, by chemical means. **b** *said of an electric current, especially a direct current* produced by chemical means. **2** *said of behaviour, etc* sudden, or startlingly energetic, as if the result of an electric shock. [from GALVANISM]

galvanism *noun* **1** *Medicine* formerly used to refer to any form of medical treatment involving the application of pulses of electric current to body tissues. **2** *Electr.* old use electric current produced by chemical means, eg by means of a cell or battery. [named after the Italian anatomist Luigi Galvani (1737–98)]

galvanization or **galvanisation** *noun* galvanizing or being galvanized.

galvanize or **galvanise** *verb* **1** *technical* to coat (a metallic surface, usually iron or steel) with a thin layer of zinc, in order to protect it from corrosion. **2** to stimulate by applying an electric current. **3** (**galvanize someone into something**) to stimulate or rouse them to action.

⊟ **3** jolt, prod, spur, stimulate, rouse, stir, move, arouse, excite, fire, electrify.

galvanized or **galvanised** *adj.* **1** *said of a metal* coated with a thin layer of zinc. **2** coated with metal by using galvanism.

galvanometer *noun* an instrument for detecting or measuring small electric currents, by measuring the mechanical movements that result from the electromagnetic forces produced by the current. [from GALVANISM + METER]

gambit *noun* **1** a chess move made early in a game, in which a pawn or other piece is sacrificed in order to gain an overall advantage. **2** an initial action or remark inviting others or establishing a point of view. **3** a piece of trickery; a stratagem. [from Italian *gambetto*, a tripping up]

gamble — *verb* **1** to bet (usually money) on the result of a card game, horse-race, etc. **2** *intrans.* to make bets or play games of chance, especially on a regular basis. **3** (**gamble on something**) to take a chance or risk on it: *gamble on the weather being fine*. **4** (*also* **gamble something away**) to lose money or other assets through gambling. — *noun* **1** an act of gambling; a bet. **2** a risk, or a situation involving risk: *take a gamble*. [from Anglo-Saxon *gamen*, to play]

⊟ *verb* **1** bet, wager, stake, chance, risk, hazard. **2** bet, game, speculate. *noun* **1** bet, wager, *colloq.* flutter. **2** chance, risk, venture, speculation, lottery.

gambler *noun* a person who gambles.

⊟ better, punter.

gambling *noun* **1** making a bet. **2** playing a game of chance. **3** taking a risk.

gamboge / gam'boudʒ/ *noun* **1** a gum resin obtained from any of various tropical Asian trees, especially *Garcinia morella*, and used as a source of a yellow pigment, and as a purgative. **2** the yellow pigment derived from this gum resin. [from *Cambodia* in SE Asia]

gambol — *verb intrans.* (**gambolled, gambolling**) to jump around playfully. — *noun* an act of leaping around playfully; a frolic. [from Italian *gamba*, leg]

⊟ *verb* caper, frolic, frisk, skip, jump, hop. *noun* caper, frolic, skip, jump.

gambrel roof 1 *Brit.* a hipped roof in which the upper parts of the hipped ends take the form of a small vertical gable end. **2** *North Amer.* a roof with the lower part at a steeper pitch than the upper part (see also MANSARD).

game[1] — *noun* **1** an amusement or pastime; the equipment used for this, eg a board, cards, dice, etc. **2** a competitive activity with rules, involving some form of skill. **3** an occasion on which individuals or teams compete at such an activity; a match. **4** in some sports, a division of a match. **5** (**games**) an event consisting of competitions in various (especially sporting) activities. **6** *colloq., often derog.* a type of activity, profession, or business: *the game of politics*. **7** a person's ability or way of playing: *her backhand game*. **8** *derog.* an activity undertaken lightheartedly: *war is just a game to him*. **9** certain birds and animals which are killed for sport; also the flesh of these creatures. **10** *colloq., derog.* a scheme, trick or intention:

give the game away / what's your game? **11 (the game)** slang prostitution: be on the game. — adj. colloq. **1** (usually **game for something**) ready and willing to undertake it: game for a try / I'm game! **2** old use having plenty of fighting spirit; plucky. — verb intrans. to gamble. — **make game of something** old use to make fun of or laugh at it. **play the game** to behave fairly. [from Anglo-Saxon gamen, play, amusement]

▣ noun **1** pastime, amusement, diversion, distraction, entertainment, fun, recreation, play, sport. **3** match, round, event, meeting, competition, contest, tournament. adj. **1** willing, ready, prepared, eager. **2** spirited, plucky, bold, daring, intrepid, brave, courageous, fearless, resolute.
▣ adj. **1** unwilling. **2** cowardly.

game[2] adj. old use lame. [perhaps from Irish Gaelic cam, crooked]

gamecock noun a cock trained for cock-fighting.

gamekeeper noun a person employed to take care of wildlife, eg on a country estate.

gamelan /'gaməlan/ noun **1** a musical instrument of SE Asia, resembling a xylophone. **2** (also **gamelan orchestra**) an orchestra of SE Asia, specifically Indonesia, usually made up of about 30 players each performing on several instruments which include xylophones, marimbas, drums, and gongs. [from Javanese]

gamesmanship noun derog. the art or practice of winning games by trying to disturb or upset one's opponent.

gamete /'gamiːt, gə'miːt/ noun Biol. a specialized sex cell, especially an ovum (egg cell) or sperm, formed by meiosis in sexually reproducing organisms. It fuses with another gamete of the opposite type during fertilization to form a zygote that will develop into a new individual. [from Greek gamete, wife]

game theory Maths. the branch of mathematics that is concerned with the analysis of choices and strategies available in a range of activities involving decision-making, such as games of chance (eg chess, roulette), business conflicts, and military strategies. It attempts to predict outcomes by assuming that each 'player' will try to adopt strategies that maximize his or her chance of winning. Game theory is also used in training and selection procedures.

gametophyte noun Bot. in plants whose life cycle shows alternation of generations, a plant of the generation that produces gametes and reproduces sexually. [from Greek gamete, wife + phyton, plant]

gamey see GAMY.

gamine /'gamiːn/ noun a girl or young woman with a mischievous, boyish appearance. [from French gamin(e)]

gaminess noun being gamey or high.

gamma noun **1** the third letter of the Greek alphabet (Γ, γ). **2** a mark indicating the third highest grade or quality.

gamma globulin Biol. any of various proteins in blood plasma that confer passive immunity to certain diseases, as well as disorders resulting from blood incompatibility.

gamma rays or **gamma radiation** Physics electromagnetic radiation of very high frequency, consisting of high-energy photons, often produced during radioactive decay.

gammon noun **1** cured meat from the upper leg and hindquarters of a pig, usually cut into thick slices. **2** the back part of a side of bacon including the whole back leg and hindquarters. [from Old French gambon, from gambe, leg]

gammy adj. (**gammier, gammiest**) old colloq. use lame; permanently injured. [related to GAME[2]]

gamp noun colloq. an umbrella. [named after Mrs Gamp, a character in Dickens's novel Martin Chuzzlewit]

gamut /'gamət/ noun **1** the whole range of anything, eg a person's emotions. **2** a scale of notes in music; the range of notes produced by a voice or instrument. [from gamma, the lowest note on a medieval six-note scale + ut, the first note (now doh) of an early sol-fa notation system]

▣ RANGE. **1** sweep, scope, compass, spectrum, field, area. **2** scale, series.

gamy or **gamey** adj. (**gamier, gamiest**) said of meat having the strong taste or smell of game which has been kept for a long time.

gander noun **1** a male goose. **2** colloq. a look: have a gander. [from Anglo-Saxon gandra]

gang — noun **1** a group, especially of criminals or troublemakers. **2** a group of friends, especially children. **3** an organized group of workers. **4** a set of tools arranged so as to be used together. — verb to arrange (tools) for simultaneous use. — **gang up on someone** to act as a group against them. **gang up with someone** to join in or form a gang with them. [from Anglo-Saxon gangan, to go]

▣ noun **1** group, band, ring, pack, herd, mob, crowd. **2** group, lot, mob, crowd, circle, clique, coterie, set. **3** team, crew, shift, squad, party.

gang-bang noun slang an occasion on which several men successively have sexual intercourse with one woman.

ganger noun colloq. the foreman of a group of workers.

gangland noun the world of organized crime.

gangling or **gangly** adj. (**ganglier, gangliest**) tall and thin, and usually awkward in movement. [from Anglo-Saxon gangan, to go]

ganglion noun (PL. **ganglia, ganglions**) **1** Anat. a group of nerve cell bodies, usually enclosed by a sheath or capsule, in the central nervous system. **2** Pathol. a cyst or swelling that forms on the tissue surrounding a tendon, eg on the back of the hand. **3** literary a centre of energy or activity. [from Greek ganglion, cystic tumour]

gangplank noun a movable plank, usually with projecting cross-pieces fixed to it, serving as a gangway for a ship.

gangrene noun the death and subsequent decay of part of the body due to failure of the blood supply to that region as a result of disease, injury, frostbite, severe burns, arteriosclerosis, etc. [from Greek gangraina]

gangrenous adj. **1** affected with gangrene. **2** of the nature of gangrene.

gangsta noun **1** a style of rap music characterized by violent lyrics or subject matter. **2** a rapper who performs in this style. [representing a colloquial pronunciation of GANGSTER]

gangster noun a member of a gang of usually armed criminals.

▣ mobster, desperado, hoodlum, ruffian, rough, tough, thug, slang heavy, racketeer, robber, criminal, colloq. crook.

gangue /gaŋ/ noun Geol. rock and mineral deposits that are associated with an ore. [from French gangue, from German Gang, vein]

gangway — noun **1** a small movable bridge used for getting on and off a ship; the opening on the side of a ship into which this fits. **2** a passage between rows of seats, eg on a plane or in a theatre. — interj. make way!

ganja noun slang marijuana. [from Hindi ganjha]

gannet noun **1** any of several large seabirds, closely related to the booby, native to temperate regions of the N Atlantic Ocean, S Africa, Australia, and New Zealand. **2** derog. colloq. a greedy person. [from Anglo-Saxon ganot, seabird]

gantry noun (PL. **gantries**) a large metal supporting framework, eg overhead for railway signals or a travelling crane, or at the side of a rocket's launch-pad.

gaol /dʒeɪl/ and **gaoler** see JAIL.

gap noun **1** a break or open space, eg in a fence. **2** a break in time; an interval. **3** a difference or disparity: the generation gap. **4** a ravine or gorge. [from Norse gap, chasm]

◫ **1** space, blank, void, hole, opening, crack, chink, cleft, break, breach. **2** break, recess, pause, lull, interval, interlude, intermission, interruption, hiatus. **3** difference, disparity, divergence, rift, divide.

gape — *verb intrans.* **1** to stare with the mouth open, especially in surprise or wonder. **2** to be or become wide open. **3** to open the mouth wide. — *noun* **1** a wide opening. **2** an open-mouthed stare. **3** the extent to which the mouth can be opened. [from Norse *gapa*, to open the mouth]

◫ *verb* **1** stare, gaze, *colloq.* gawp, *colloq.* gawk, goggle. **2** open, yawn, part, split, crack.

gaping *adj.* **1** that gapes. **2** astonished.

◫ **1** open, yawning, broad, wide, vast, cavernous. ◲ **1** tiny.

gappy *adj.* (**gappier, gappiest**) full of gaps.

gap year same as YEAR OUT.

garage /'gærɪdʒ, gə'rɑːʒ/ *noun* **1** a building in which motor vehicles are kept. **2** an establishment where motor vehicles are bought, sold and repaired, often also selling petrol, etc. **3** a style of pop music played in a loud, energetic, and unpolished style. [from Old French *garer*, to shelter]

◫ **2** petrol station, service station.

garam masala /'gærəm mə'sɑːlə/ a mixture of ground spices used to make curry. See also MASALA. [from Hindi, = hot mixture]

garb *literary* — *noun* **1** clothing, especially as worn by people in a particular job or position. **2** outward appearance. — *verb* to dress or clothe. [from Italian *garbo*, grace]

garbage *noun* **1** *North Amer., esp. US* domestic waste; refuse. **2** *derog.* worthless or poor quality articles or matter. **3** *derog.* nonsense. **4** *Comput.* erroneous, irrelevant, or meaningless data, especially that which cannot be recognized by a computer program. **5** any object or objects, discarded from a spacecraft, orbiting in space. — **garbage in, garbage out** *Comput.* an expression which emphasizes the fact that no matter how reliable or sophisticated computer software may be, the data output can only be as valid and accurate as the data input will allow.

garble *verb* **1** to unintentionally mix up the details of. **2** to deliberately distort the meaning of, eg by making important omissions. [from Arabic *ghirbal*, sieve]

◫ SCRAMBLE. **1** confuse, muddle, jumble, mix up. **2** twist, distort, pervert, slant, misrepresent, falsify. ◲ **2** decipher.

garçon /'gɑːsɒn/ *noun* a waiter in a French restaurant or café. [from French *garçon*]

garda /'gɑːdə/ *noun* (PL. **gardai**) a police officer in the Irish Republic. [from Irish Gaelic *garda*, guard]

garden — *noun* **1** an area of land, usually adjoining a house, on which grass, trees, ornamental plants, herbs, fruit, vegetables, etc, are cultivated. **2** (*usually* **gardens**) such an area of land, usually of considerable size, with flower beds, lawns, trees, walks, etc, laid out for enjoyment by the public: *botanical gardens*. **3** a similar smaller place where food and drinks are served outdoors: *tea garden*. **4** a fertile region. — *adj.* **1** *said of a plant* cultivated, not wild. **2** for use in a garden, or in gardening. — *verb intrans.* (**gardened, gardening**) to cultivate, work in, or take care of a garden, especially as a hobby. — **lead someone up the garden path** *colloq.* to mislead or deceive them deliberately. [from Old French *gardin*]

◫ *noun* **1** yard, backyard, plot, allotment. **2** park.

garden centre a place where plants, seeds, and garden tools are sold.

garden city a spacious modern town designed to have private gardens and numerous public parks.

gardener *noun* a person who gardens; a person employed to tend a garden.

gardenia *noun* **1** an evergreen shrub or small tree of the genus *Gardenia*, native to tropical and subtropical regions of Africa and Asia, having elliptical glossy leaves and flattened rosettes of large (usually white) fragrant flowers. **2** the flower produced by this plant. [named after the US physician and botanist Alexander Garden]

gardening *noun* the laying out and cultivation of gardens.

garden party a formal party held in a large private garden.

gargantuan *adj.* enormous; colossal. [named after *Gargantua*, the greedy giant in Rabelais' novel *Gargantua and Pantagruel*]

gargle — *verb intrans., trans.* to cleanse the mouth and throat by blowing air from the lungs through (a liquid) held there. — *noun* **1** an act of gargling, or the sound produced. **2** the liquid used. [from Old French *gargouille*, throat]

gargoyle *noun* a grotesque carved open-mouthed head or figure acting as a rainwater spout from a roof-gutter, especially on a church. [from Old French *gargouille*, throat]

garish *adj. derog.* unpleasantly bright or colourful; very gaudy. [from obsolete *gaurish*, from *gaure*, to stare]

◫ gaudy, lurid, loud, glaring, flashy, showy, tawdry, vulgar, tasteless. ◲ quiet, tasteful.

garland — *noun* **1** a circular arrangement of flowers or leaves worn round the head or neck, or hung up. **2** a collection of short poems or pieces of prose. — *verb* to decorate with a garland. [from Old French *garlande*]

◫ *noun* **1** wreath, festoon, decoration, flowers, laurels, honours. *verb* wreathe, festoon, deck, adorn, crown.

garlic *noun* **1** a perennial plant (*Allium sativum*) that is widely cultivated for its underground bulb, which is divided into segments (cloves) covered with white scale leaves. **2** the bulb of this plant, which contains a pungent oil and is widely used as a flavouring, especially in the form of powder or flakes, in cooking and food processing. [from Anglo-Saxon *gar*, spear + *leac*, leek]

garlicky *adj.* like garlic.

garment *noun* an article of clothing. [from Old French *garniment*, from *garnir*, to furnish]

garner *verb* (**garnered, garnering**) *formal, literary* to collect and usually store (information, knowledge, etc). [from Latin *granarium*, granary]

garnet *noun Geol.* any of a group of silicate minerals found mainly in metamorphic rocks. Garnet is used as an abrasive, and many of the coloured varieties are used as semi-precious stones, the best known form being deep red. [from Latin *granatum*, pomegranate]

garnish — *verb* to decorate (especially food to be served). — *noun* a decoration, especially one added to food. [from French *garnir*, to furnish]

◫ *verb* decorate, adorn, ornament, trim, embellish, enhance, grace, set off. *noun* decoration, ornament, trimming, embellishment, enhancement.

garret *noun* an attic room, often a dingy one. [from Old French *garite*, refuge]

garrison *noun* **1** a body of soldiers stationed in a town or fortress in order to defend it. **2** the building they occupy. [from Old French *garison*, from *garir*, to protect]

garrotte or **garotte** /gə'rɒt/ — *noun* **1** a wire loop or metal collar tightened around the neck to cause strangulation. **2** this method of execution. — *verb* to execute or kill with a garrotte. [from Spanish *garrote*]

garrulous *adj.* **1** tending to talk a lot, especially about trivial things. **2** *derog.*, *said of a speech, etc* long and wordy. [from Latin *garrire*, to chatter]

garrulousness or **garrulity** *noun* being garrulous; talkativeness.

garter *noun* a band of tight material, usually elastic, worn on the leg to hold up a stocking or sock. [from Old French *gartier*]

garter stitch a plain stitch in knitting.

gas — *noun* **1** a form of matter that has no fixed shape, and will expand to occupy all the space available, because its molecules are in constant rapid motion, and can move around freely and independently of each other. **2** a substance or mixture of substances which is in this state at ordinary temperatures, eg hydrogen, air. **3** natural gas used as a source of fuel for heating, etc. **4** firedamp, a mixture of gases occurring naturally in coalmines, explosive in contact with air. **5** a poisonous gas used as a weapon in war. **6** *colloq. esp. North Amer., esp. US* gasoline; petrol. **7** *colloq.* an amusing or enjoyable event or situation. **8** *colloq., derog.* foolish talk; boasting. — *verb* (**gassed, gassing**) **1** to poison or kill with gas. **2** *intrans. derog. colloq.* to chat, especially at length, boastfully or about trivial things. [coined by J B van Helmont, Belgian chemist (1577–1644), after Greek *khaos*, chaos]

gasbag *noun derog. colloq.* a person who talks a lot or too much.

gas chamber a sealed room which can be filled with poisonous gas, used for killing people or animals.

gas chromatography *Chem.* a form of chromatography that is used to identify the components of a mixture of gases, and is often also used to separate them.

gas constant *Chem.* the constant, usually denoted as R, that relates the volume, pressure, and temperature of a mass of gas in the equation $pV = nRT$, where p is the pressure exerted by n moles of the gas contained in a volume V at an absolute temperature T. The gas constant has a value of about 8.3 joules per mole per kelvin.

gas-cooled reactor *Physics* a nuclear reactor in which the cooling medium is carbon dioxide or some other gas.

gas engine a specially adapted or designed internal combustion engine which uses gas as its fuel.

gaseous /'gasɪəs/ *adj.* of the nature of gas; like gas.

gas exchange *Biol.* the uptake and output of gases, especially of carbon dioxide and oxygen in photosynthesis and respiration.

gash — *noun* a deep open cut or wound. — *verb* to make a gash in. [from Old French *garser*, to scratch or wound]

. . . .

◙ *noun* cut, wound, slash, slit, incision, laceration, tear, split, score, gouge. *verb* cut, wound, slash, slit, incise, lacerate, tear, split, score, gouge.

. . . .

gasholder *noun* **1** a large metal tank used for storing coal gas or natural gas before it is distributed to consumers. Its top section can move freely up and down to adjust to the volume of gas stored. Also called GASOMETER. **2** any vessel that is used for holding and measuring gas, especially for the purpose of chemical analysis, eg to measure the volume of gas evolved during a chemical reaction. Also called GASOMETER.

gasification *noun* any process whereby a substance is converted into a gas, especially the conversion of coal into a gaseous hydrocarbon fuel.

gasify *verb* (**gasifies, gasified**) **1** to convert into gas. **2** to produce gas, especially from coal.

gasket *noun* a thin flat shaped ring or sheet of rubber or paper fitting tightly in the join between two metal surfaces to form an airtight seal. — **blow a gasket 1** *said of an engine, etc* to cause a gasket to burst or break. **2** *colloq.* to lose one's temper. [perhaps from French *garcette*, end of a rope]

gaslight *noun* a lamp powered by gas, or the light from it.

gas mask a mask, covering the full face, which filters out poisonous gas, allowing the wearer to breathe clean air.

gas meter an instrument which measures and records the amount of gas used.

gasohol or **gasahol** *noun* a mixture of eight or nine parts petrol (gasoline) and one or two parts ethanol (ethyl alcohol, which must be water-free), useful as a high-octane rating fuel in internal combustion engines.

gasoline or **gasolene** *noun chiefly North Amer.* petrol.

gasometer *noun* a gasholder.

gasp — *verb* **1** *intrans.* to take a sharp breath in, through surprise, sudden pain, etc. **2** *intrans.* to breathe in with difficulty, eg because of illness. **3** (**gasp something out**) to say it breathlessly. **4** *intrans.* (**gasp for something**) *colloq.* to want or need it very much. — *noun* a sharp intake of breath. [from Norse *geispa*, to yawn]

. . . .

◙ *verb* **2** pant, puff, blow, wheeze, choke.

. . . .

gassiness *noun* being gassy.

gassy *adj.* (**gassier, gassiest**) **1** like gas; full of gas. **2** *derog. colloq.* talking a lot, especially about unimportant things.

gastarbeiter /'gastɑːbaɪtə(r)/ *noun* an immigrant worker granted a work permit by the host country, especially in Germany (originally in West Germany). [German, = guest-worker]

gasteropod same as GASTROPOD.

gastrectomy *noun Medicine* the surgical removal of all or part of the stomach. [from Greek *gaster*, stomach + -ECTOMY]

gastric *adj.* relating to or affecting the stomach. [from Greek *gaster*, belly]

gastric flu *colloq.* a popular term for any of several disorders of the stomach and intestinal tract, the main symptoms of which are nausea, diarrhoea, abdominal cramps, and fever.

gastric juice a strongly acidic fluid produced by the gastric glands of the stomach wall during digestion of food. It is composed primarily of hydrochloric acid, mucin (the main component of mucus), and the enzymes pepsin and rennin.

gastric ulcer *Medicine* an ulcer on the lining of the stomach wall.

gastritis *noun Medicine* inflammation of the lining of the stomach. [from Greek *gaster*, stomach + -ITIS]

gastro- or **gastr-** *combining form* the stomach. [from Greek *gaster*, belly]

gastroenteritis *noun Medicine* inflammation of the lining of the stomach and intestine, usually caused by bacterial or viral infection, food poisoning, or excessive alcohol consumption. Its main symptoms are vomiting and diarrhoea. [from GASTRO- + Greek *enteron*, intestine]

gastronome or **gastronomer** or **gastronomist** *noun* a person who enjoys, and has developed a taste for, good food and wine. [from GASTRO- + Greek *nomos*, law]

gastronomic *adj.* relating to gastronomy.

gastronomy *noun* **1** the enjoyment of good food and wine. **2** the style of cooking typical of a particular country or region: *French gastronomy.*

gastropod *noun Zool.* an invertebrate animal belonging to the class Gastropoda, eg snails, slugs, whelks, and winkles, typically possessing a large flattened muscular foot. When present, the shell is in one piece and usually spirally coiled, and the head and foot can be withdrawn into it for safety. [from GASTRO- + Greek *pous podos*, foot]

gastroscope *noun Medicine* an instrument that is used to inspect the interior of the stomach.

gastrula *noun Zool.* in the embryonic development of animals, the stage following the blastula, during which the cells of the embryo move into the correct position for development into the various organ systems of the adult.

gas turbine an engine that passes the products of the combustion of a mixture of fuel and air over the blades of a turbine. The turbine drives an air compressor, which in turn provides the energy for the combustion process.

gasworks *sing. noun* a place where gas is manufactured from coal.

gate — *noun* 1 a usually hinged door or barrier, moved to open or close an entrance in a wall, fence, etc leading eg into a garden, field or city; the entrance itself. 2 any of the numbered exits at an airport via which passengers can board or leave a plane. 3 the total number of people attending a sports event or other entertainment. 4 (*also* **gate money**) the total money paid in admission fees. 5 any of the pairs of posts that a slalom skier passes through. 6 (*in full* **logic gate**) *Electron.* an electronic circuit that produces a single output signal when one or more input signals fulfil certain conditions. The logical operations of a digital computer are based on the use of such circuits within the integrated circuits of a microprocessor or central processing unit. 7 the part of a projector or camera that holds the film flat and momentarily stationary behind the lens. 8 an H-shaped series of slots for controlling the movement of a gear lever in the gearbox of a motor vehicle. 9 *Biol.* a selective barrier in a membrane, that regulates the passage of molecules of different sizes through the membrane. — *verb* to confine (pupils) to school after hours. [from Anglo-Saxon *geat*, a way]

⊟ *noun* 1 barrier, door, doorway, gateway, opening, entrance, exit, access.

-gate *combining form* attached to the name of a person or place to refer to an associated scandal: *Irangate*. [by analogy with WATERGATE, a US political scandal (1972–4) that led to the resignation of President Nixon]

gateau *or* **gâteau** /ˈɡatoʊ/ *noun* (PL. **gateaux, gateaus, gâteaux**) a large rich cake, especially filled with cream and decorated with fruit, nuts, etc. [from French *gâteau*]

gatecrash *verb trans., intrans. colloq.* to gain entry to (a party, meeting, etc) uninvited or without paying.

gatecrasher *noun* a person who gatecrashes.

gatehouse *noun* a building at or above the gateway to a city, castle, etc, often occupied by the person who guards it.

gateleg *adj.*, *said of a table* having a hinged or framed leg that can swing inwards to let down a leaf.

gateway *noun* 1 an entrance, especially to a city, park, etc, with a gate across it. 2 (**gateway to a place**) a way to or into it. 3 (**gateway to something**) a means of acquiring it: *a gateway to success.* 4 *Comput.* a connection between computer networks, or between a computer network and a telephone line.

gather — *verb* (**gathered, gathering**) 1 *trans., intrans.* (*also* **gather together**) to bring or come together in one place. 2 (*often* **gather something in**) to collect, pick, or harvest it. 3 to increase in (speed or force). 4 to accumulate or become covered with (eg dust). 5 to learn or understand from information received. 6 to pull, and often stitch, (material) into small folds. 7 to pull (a garment) closely round the body. 8 to embrace: *she gathered the child into her arms.* 9 to wrinkle (the brow). 10 (**gather something together**) to draw together or muster (strength, courage, etc) in preparation for something. 11 *intrans.*, *said of a boil, etc* to form a head. — *noun* a small fold in material, often stitched. [from Anglo-Saxon *gaderian*]

⊟ *verb* 1 assemble, convene, muster, rally, collect, group, amass, accumulate, heap, pile up. 2 collect, pick, pluck, cut, harvest, reap, glean. 3 increase, pick up, gain, build up. 5 learn, hear, understand, infer, deduce, conclude,

surmise, assume. 6 fold, pleat, tuck, pucker.
⊟ *verb* 1 scatter, dissipate.

gathering *noun* 1 a meeting or assembly. 2 a series of gathers in material.

⊟ 1 meeting, assembly, convocation, convention, round-up, rally, get-together, jamboree, party, group, congregation, mass, crowd, turn-out.

GATT *abbrev.* General Agreement on Tariffs and Trade, an international treaty to promote trade and economic benefits, signed in 1947. Its aim is to encourage free trade by the imposition of trade rules and reduction of tariffs among its nations (now numbering 117).

gauche /ɡoʊʃ/ *adj.* ill-at-ease, awkward in social situations. [from French *gauche*, left, left-handed]

gaucherie /ˈɡoʊʃərɪ/ *noun* social awkwardness, or an instance of this.

gaucho /ˈɡaʊtʃoʊ/ *noun* (PL. **gauchos**) a modern cowboy of the S American plains. [from Spanish *gaucho*]

gaudily *adv.* in a gaudy way.

gaudiness *noun* being gaudy.

gaudy *adj.* (**gaudier, gaudiest**) *derog.* coarsely and brightly coloured or decorated. [from Middle English *gaude*, trinket]

⊟ bright, brilliant, glaring, garish, loud, flashy, showy, ostentatious, tinselly, *slang* glitzy, tawdry, vulgar, tasteless.
⊟ drab, plain.

gauge *or* **gage** /ɡeɪdʒ/ — *verb* 1 to measure accurately. 2 to estimate or guess (a measurement, size, etc). 3 to judge. — *noun* 1 any of various instruments that are used to measure a quantity such as weight, volume, pressure, etc: *pressure gauge.* 2 each of a series of standard sizes, eg of knitting needles. 3 a standard measurement, such as the diameter of a wire, the diameter of the barrel of a gun, or the thickness of sheet metal. 4 the distance between the inner faces of the rails of a railway or tramway track. 5 the width of magnetic tape. 6 a standard against which other things are measured or judged. [from Old French *gauge*]

⊟ *verb* 1 measure, count, calculate, compute. 2 estimate, guess, reckon, figure. 3 judge, assess, evaluate, value, rate, weigh, determine, ascertain. *noun* 1 meter, indicator, measure. 3 measurement, size, magnitude, capacity, bore, calibre, thickness, width, height, depth. 6 standard, norm, criterion, benchmark, yardstick, rule, guideline, sample, example, model, pattern.

Gaul /ɡɔːl/ *noun* an inhabitant of ancient Gaul, especially Transalpine Gaul. [from Latin *Gallus*]

Gaulish — *noun* the language of the Gauls. — *adj.* of the Gauls or their language.

gaunt *adj.* 1 thin or thin-faced; lean, haggard. 2 *said of a place* barren and desolate.

⊟ 1 haggard, hollow-eyed, angular, bony, thin, lean, lank, skinny, scraggy, scrawny, skeletal, emaciated, wasted. 2 bleak, stark, bare, barren, desolate, forlorn, dismal, dreary, grim.
⊟ 1 plump.

gauntlet¹ *noun* 1 a metal or metal-plated glove worn by medieval soldiers. 2 a heavy protective leather glove loosely covering the wrist. — **take up the gauntlet** to accept a challenge. **throw down the gauntlet** to make a challenge. [from Old French *gantelet*, diminutive of *gant*, glove; the idioms are derived from the former practice of throwing a gauntlet on the ground when issuing a challenge to a duel]

gauntlet[2] — **run the gauntlet 1** *Hist.* to suffer the military punishment of having to scramble along between two rows of men while receiving hard blows from them. **2** to expose oneself to hostile treatment or criticism. [altered from *gantlope*, from Swedish *gatlopp*, from *gata*, lane + *lopp*, course]

gauss /gaʊs/ *noun Physics* the cgs unit of magnetic flux density. In the SI system it has been replaced by the tesla (one gauss is equal to 10^{-4} tesla). [named after the German mathematician, astronomer, and physicist Carl Friedrich Gauss (1777–1855)]

gauze *noun* **1** thin transparent cloth, especially cotton as used to dress wounds. **2** thin wire mesh. [from French *gaze*]

gauzy *adj.* (**gauzier, gauziest**) like gauze.

gave see GIVE.

gavel *noun* a small hammer used by a judge, auctioneer, etc to call attention.

gavotte *noun* an old lively French country dance, or a piece of music for this. [from French *gavotte*]

gawk *colloq.* — *verb intrans.* to stare blankly or stupidly; to gawp. — *noun derog.* an awkward, clumsy or stupid person. [from obsolete *gaw*, to stare]

gawkiness *noun* being gawky; awkwardness.

gawky *adj.* (**gawkier, gawkiest**) *colloq., derog.* awkward-looking, ungainly, and usually tall and thin.

. . . .

◨ awkward, clumsy, gauche, oafish, ungainly, gangling, uncoordinated, graceless.
◪ graceful.

. . . .

gawp *verb intrans. colloq.* to stare stupidly, especially open-mouthed; to gape. [from obsolete *gaw*, to stare]

gay — *adj.* **1** happily carefree. **2** bright and attractive. **3** fun-loving or pleasure-seeking. **4** homosexual. **5** frequented by, or intended for, homosexuals: *a gay bar.* — *noun* a homosexual. [from Old French *gai*]

. . . .

◨ *adj.* **1** happy, joyful, jolly, merry, cheerful, blithe, sunny, carefree, debonair. **2** bright, brilliant, sparkling, festive, colourful, vivid, rich, gaudy, showy, flamboyant. **3** fun-loving, pleasure-seeking, lively, animated, playful, light-hearted. **4** homosexual, lesbian, *slang* queer. *noun* homosexual, *slang* queer, *slang* poof, lesbian, *slang* dyke.
◪ *adj.* **1** sad, gloomy. **4** heterosexual, *slang* straight. *noun* heterosexual.

. . . .

gayness *noun* the state of being gay, especially homosexual.

gaze — *verb intrans.* to stare fixedly, usually for a long time. — *noun* a fixed stare. [from Middle English *gasen*]

. . . .

◨ *verb* stare, contemplate, regard, watch, view, look, gape, wonder. *noun* stare, look.

. . . .

gazebo /gə'ziːbəʊ/ *noun* (PL. **gazebos, gazeboes**) a small summerhouse or open hut, especially in a garden, from which a fine view can be admired. [perhaps coined from GAZE]

gazelle *noun* (PL. **gazelles, gazelle**) a fawn-coloured antelope with a white rump and belly, and black and white face markings, found in arid plains, eg savanna, in Africa and Asia. [from French, from Arabic *ghazal*, wild goat]

gazette — *noun* **1** an official newspaper giving lists of government, military and legal notices. **2** *often facetious* a newspaper. — *verb formal* to announce or publish in an official gazette. [from Venetian dialect *gazeta*, from *gazet*, a small coin, the cost of an early news-sheet]

gazetteer *noun* a dictionary of place-names, with descriptions of the places. [from GAZETTE]

gazpacho /ga'spaːtʃoʊ/ *noun* a Spanish vegetable soup, served cold. [Spanish]

gazump /gə'zʌmp/ *verb colloq.* to go back on a verbal agreement to sell one's house to (a prospective buyer), and accept a better offer from another buyer. [perhaps from Yiddish *gezumph*, to swindle]

gazumper *noun* a person who gazumps.

gazumping *noun* **1** the act or process of gazumping. **2** being gazumped.

gazunder /gə'zʌndə/ *verb trans., intrans. colloq., said of a buyer* to lower the sum offered to (the seller of a property) just before contracts are due to be signed. [from GAZUMP + UNDER]

GB *abbrev.* Great Britain.

GBE *abbrev.* Knight or Dame Grand Cross of the British Empire.

GBH or **gbh** *abbrev.* grievous bodily harm.

GC *abbrev.* George Cross, an award for bravery.

GCB *abbrev.* Knight or Dame Grand Cross of the Order of the Bath.

GCE — *abbrev.* General Certificate of Education. — *noun* a subject in which an examination is taken at this level.

GCHQ *abbrev.* Government Communications Headquarters.

GCMG *abbrev.* Knight or Dame Grand Cross of the Order of St Michael and St George.

GCSE *abbrev.* the General Certificate of Secondary Education, introduced in England and Wales in 1988. It merged what had previously been two separate examinations (the General Certificate of Education, GCE, and the Certificate of Secondary Education, CSE) for pupils aged about 16 or older.

GCVO *abbrev.* Knight or Dame Grand Cross of the Royal Victorian Order.

Gd *symbol Chem.* gadolinium.

Gdns *abbrev.* Gardens, especially in street names.

GDP *abbrev.* gross domestic product.

GDR *abbrev.* German Democratic Republic, the former republic of East Germany.

Ge *symbol Chem.* germanium.

gear — *noun* **1** *Engineering* a toothed wheel or disc that engages with another wheel or disc having a different number of teeth, and turns it, so transmitting motion from one rotating shaft to another, the second shaft rotating at a different speed from the first one (the drive shaft). **2** the actual combination of such wheels or discs that is currently in use, eg first gear (bottom gear) in a car. **3** *colloq.* the equipment or tools needed for a particular job, sport, etc. **4** *colloq.* clothes. — *verb* **1** to adapt or design to suit a particular need. **2** to supply with or connect by gears. **3** (**gear up** or **gear something up**) to become or make it ready or prepared. — **in gear** *said of a motor vehicle* with a gear selected. **out of gear 1** *said of a motor vehicle* with no gear selected. **2** not working properly. [from Middle English *gere*, from Norse *gervi*]

. . . .

◨ *noun* **1** gearwheel, cogwheel. **2** gearing, mechanism, machinery, works. **3** equipment, kit, outfit, tackle, tools, instruments, accessories, paraphernalia, things, stuff. **4** clothes, clothing, garments, attire, dress, garb, *colloq.* togs, *colloq.* get-up.

. . . .

gearbox *noun* **1** the set or system of gears that transmits power from an engine (especially of a motor vehicle) to the road wheels, and allows the road speed to be varied while maintaining the engine speed at a constant high level. **2** the metal casing that encloses a system of gears.

gear lever or *North Amer.* **gear shift** a lever or similar device for engaging and disengaging gears, especially in a motor vehicle, by moving the gearwheels in relation to each other.

GEC *abbrev.* General Electric Company.

gecko /'gekoʊ/ *noun* (PL. **geckos, geckoes**) any of a large family of mainly nocturnal lizards found in all warm countries, and best known for the ease with which some species can climb smooth walls, even glass, clinging by means of the hooked ridges on the underside of their toes. [from Malay *gekoq*, imitative of its cry]

gee[1] *interj.* (*usually* **gee up**) used to encourage a horse to move, or go faster. — **gee someone up** *colloq.* to encourage them to work or perform better, more quickly, etc.

gee[2] *interj. colloq.* (*also* **gee whiz**) an expression of surprise, admiration, or enthusiasm. [a form of *Jesus*]

gee-gee *noun colloq., used especially to or by small children* a horse.

geek *noun slang* a socially inept or unprepossessing person, although often (especially in computers) knowledgeable. [from English dialect *geck*, fool]

geese see GOOSE.

geezer *noun colloq.* a man, especially an old man, often odd in some way. [from a dialect pronunciation of *guiser*, masked actor in mime]

gegenschein /ˈgeɪgənʃaɪn/ *noun Astron.* an elliptical patch of faint light that is sometimes observed in the sky directly opposite the Sun. It is caused by the reflection of sunlight from minute dust particles in space. Also called COUNTERGLOW. [from German *gegen* opposite + *Schein* glow, shine]

Geiger counter /ˈgaɪgə(r)/ an instrument that is used to detect and measure the intensity of ionizing radiation by counting the number of electrical pulses generated by the electrons released by ionized gas atoms. [named after the German physicist Hans Wilhelm Geiger (1882–1945)]

geisha /ˈgeɪʃə/ *noun* (PL. **geisha, geishas**) (*also* **geisha girl**) a female companion for Japanese men, trained in music, dancing, and the art of conversation. [from Japanese *gei*, art + *sha*, person]

gel — *noun* **1** *Chem.* a colloid (a state midway between a suspension and a true solution) consisting of a solid and a liquid that are dispersed evenly throughout a material and have set to form a jelly-like mass, eg gelatine. **2** (*also* **hair gel**) such a substance used to fix the hair in place. — *verb* (**gelled, gelling**) **1** *intrans., trans.* to form a colloid consisting of a solid and a liquid that are dispersed evenly throughout a material and have set to form a jelly-like mass. **2** *intrans.* to take on a definite form; to jell. [from GELATINE]

☐ *verb* **1** set, congeal, coagulate, harden, thicken, solidify. **2** materialize, take shape, form, jell, come together.

gelatine or **gelatin** *noun* a clear tasteless protein, formed by the partial breakdown of collagen, and extracted from animal bones and hides. It forms a stiff jelly when dissolved in water, and is used in adhesives, photographic materials, pharmaceutical capsules, and foods, eg table jellies. [from Italian *gelatina*, jelly]

gelatinize or **gelatinise** *verb trans., intrans. technical* **1** to make (a substance) gelatinous. **2** to coat (paper, glass, etc) with gelatine or jelly. **3** *said of a substance* to become gelatinous.

gelatinous *adj.* like gelatine or jelly.

☐ jelly-like, jellied, congealed, rubbery, glutinous, gluey, *colloq.* gooey, sticky, viscous.

geld *verb* to castrate (a male animal, especially a horse) by removing its testicles. [from Norse *geldr*, barren]

gelding *noun* a castrated male animal, especially a horse.

gel filtration *Chem.* a form of chromatography in which the components of a mixture of liquids are separated on the basis of differences in the size of their molecules.

gelignite *noun* a powerful explosive, used especially in mining, made from a mixture of nitroglycerine, cellulose nitrate, sodium nitrate, and wood pulp. [from GELATINE + Latin *ignis*, fire]

gem *noun* **1** a precious or semi-precious stone or crystal, especially one that has been cut and polished for use in jewellery and other ornaments, eg diamond, ruby, sapphire, and emerald. **2** *colloq.* a person or thing that one values, admires or likes very much. [from Latin *gemma*, bud, precious stone]

☐ **1** gemstone, precious stone, stone, jewel. **2** treasure, prize, masterpiece, pièce de résistance.

Gems and gemstones include: diamond, white sapphire, zircon, cubic zirconia, marcasite, rhinestone, pearl, moonstone, onyx, opal, mother-of-pearl, amber, citrine, fire opal, topaz, agate, tiger's eye, jasper, morganite, ruby, garnet, rose quartz, beryl, cornelian, coral, amethyst, sapphire, turquoise, lapis lazuli, emerald, aquamarine, bloodstone, jade, peridot, tourmaline, jet.

geminate *technical* — *adj.* (pronounced -nət) *said especially of leaves* arranged in pairs. — *verb trans., intrans.* (pronounced -neɪt) to arrange, or be arranged, in pairs. [from Latin *geminus*, twin]

gemination *noun* doubling, repetition.

Gemini *noun* **1** *Astron.* the Twins, a conspicuous zodiacal constellation that lies to the north-east of Orion. Its two brightest stars are Castor and Pollux. **2** a person born between 21 May and 20 June, under this sign. [from Latin *geminus*, twin]

gemstone *noun* same as GEM.

Gen. *abbrev.* **1** General. **2** (*also* **Gen**) Genesis.

gen *colloq.* — *noun* (**the gen**) the required information. — *verb* (**genned, genning**) (**gen up on something**) *colloq.* to obtain information about it. [from *general information*]

gen. *abbrev.* genitive.

-gen or **-gene** *combining form* denoting something that causes or produces: *carcinogen*. [from Greek *genes*, born]

gendarme /ˈʒɒndɑːm/ *noun* a member of an armed police force in France and other French-speaking countries. [from French *gens d'armes*, armed people]

gender *noun* **1** *Grammar* in some languages, the system of dividing nouns and pronouns into different classes. **2** *Grammar* any of these classes, usually two or three (masculine, feminine, and neuter) in European languages. **3** the condition of being male or female; sex. [from Latin *genus*, kind]

gender-bender *noun colloq.* someone who adopts a sexually-ambiguous image and style of dress, etc.

gene *noun* the basic unit of inheritance, consisting of a sequence of DNA that occupies a specific position or *locus* on a chromosome. Each gene is responsible for the passing on of one or more specific characteristics from parents to offspring. [from German *Gen*, from Greek *genes*, born]

genealogical *adj.* relating to or involving genealogy.

genealogist *noun* a person who studies or traces genealogies.

genealogy *noun* (PL. **genealogies**) **1** a person's direct line of descent from an ancestor or ancestors. **2** the pedigree of a particular person or animal, or a chart showing this, often in the form of a tree with branches. **3** the study of the history and lineage of families. **4** the study of the development of plants and animals from more primitive forms into present-day forms by the process of evolution. [from Greek *genea*, race + *logos*, discourse]

☐ **1** lineage, ancestry, descent, derivation, extraction, family, line. **2** family tree, pedigree.

gene probe *Genetics* a fragment of DNA that is labelled with a radioactive isotope (so that it can be easily recognized), and used to identify or isolate a gene.

genera see GENUS.

general — *adj.* **1** of, involving, or applying to all or most parts, people or things; widespread, not specific, limited, or localized: *the general opinion* / *general rule.* **2** not detailed or definite; rough; vague: *general description* / *in general terms.* **3** not specialized: *general knowledge.* **4** chief: *general manager.* — *noun* **1** a senior army officer of the rank next below Field Marshal. **2** the commander of a whole army. **3** any leader, especially when regarded as competent. **4** the head of a religious order, eg the Jesuits. **— in general** usually; mostly. [from Latin *generalis*, from *genus*, race, kind]

. . . .

◩ *adj.* **1** broad, sweeping, blanket, all-inclusive, comprehensive, universal, global, total, across-the-board, widespread, prevalent, extensive, overall, usual, regular, standard, normal, typical, ordinary, common, public. **2** vague, ill-defined, indefinite, imprecise, inexact, approximate, loose, unspecific.

◲ *adj.* **1** particular, specific, limited. **2** detailed, specific, precise. **3** specialized.
. . . .

General Certificate of Education *noun* see GCSE.

General Certificate of Secondary Education (ABBREV. **GCSE**) in England and Wales, a school-leaving qualification in one or more subjects, which replaced the GCE Ordinary level and CSE qualifications in 1988.

general election a national election in which the voters of every constituency in the country elect a member of parliament.

generalissimo /dʒenərəl'ɪsɪmoʊ/ *noun* (PL. **generalissimos**) a supreme commander of the combined armed forces in some countries, often also having political power. [from Italian *generalissimo*, superlative of *generale*, general]

generality *noun* (PL. **generalities**) **1** the quality of being general. **2** a general rule or principle. **3** the majority.

generalization or **generalisation** *noun* **1** the act of generalizing. **2** an example of generalizing.

generalize or **generalise** *verb* **1** *intrans.* to speak in general terms or form general opinions, especially too general to be applied to all individual cases. **2** *trans.* to make more general, especially applicable to a wider variety of cases.

generally *adv.* **1** usually. **2** without considering details; broadly. **3** as a whole; collectively.

. . . .

◩ **1** usually, normally, as a rule, by and large, on the whole, mostly, mainly, chiefly.
. . . .

general practitioner (ABBREV. **GP**) a doctor who does not specialize in any one area of medicine, and is the first point of contact for people seeking medical treatment. A general practitioner treats most illnesses and complaints, and refers appropriate cases to specialists.

general staff the officers assisting a military commander.

general strike a strike by workers in all or most of the industries in a country at one time.

generate *verb* to produce or create. [from Latin *generare*, from *genus*, a kind]

. . . .

◩ produce, engender, arouse, cause, bring about, give rise to, create, originate, initiate, make, form, breed, propagate.

◲ prevent.
. . . .

generation *noun* **1** *said of living organisms* the act or process of producing offspring. **2** the act of producing electricity, heat, etc. **3** all the individuals produced at a particular stage in the natural descent of humans or animals: *the younger generation*. **4** the average period between the birth of a person or animal and the birth of their offspring, considered to be about 35 years for humans: *three generations ago*. **5** *Comput.* any of five successive stages of digital computers, each stage marking a significant technological development over the last: *a fourth-generation computer*. See also COMPUTER GENERATION.

. . . .

◩ **1** procreation, reproduction, propagation, breeding. **2** production, creation, formation. **3** age group. **4** age, era, epoch, period, time.
. . . .

generation gap the difference in the ideas and ways of living of people from different (especially successive) generations.

Generation X people who grew up in the 1980s and 1990s who are thought to be sceptical about traditionally held values, especially those relating to work and the family. [popularized by the novel *Generation X* (1991) by Douglas Coupland]

generative *adj. formal* **1** able to produce or generate. **2** relating to production or creation.

generative grammar *Linguistics* a description of a language in terms of a finite set of grammatical rules able to generate an infinite number of grammatical sentences (and none of the ungrammatical ones). See also TRANSFORMATIONAL GRAMMAR.

generator *noun Electr.* a machine that converts mechanical energy into electrical energy, eg a dynamo. A generator that produces alternating current, eg in a power station, is called an alternator.

generic *adj.* **1** of or relating to any member of a general class or group. **2** *said of a drug name* not protected by a trademark and sold as a specific brand; non-proprietary: *generic aspirin*. **3** *Biol.* of, relating to, or belonging to a genus: *a generic name*. **4** *said of computers, computer software, etc* belonging to the same family; interchangeable. [from GENUS]

generosity *noun* (PL. **generosities**) **1** the quality of being generous. **2** a generous act. [from GENEROUS]

. . . .

◩ **1** liberality, munificence, open-handedness, bounty, charity, magnanimity, philanthropy, kindness, benevolence.

◲ **1** meanness, selfishness.
. . . .

generous *adj.* **1** giving or willing to give or help unselfishly. **2** *said eg of a donation* large and given unselfishly. **3** large; ample; plentiful: *generous portions*. **4** kind; willing to forgive: *of generous spirit*. [from Latin *generosus*, of noble birth]

. . . .

◩ **1** liberal, bountiful, free, lavish, open-handed, unstinting, unsparing, magnanimous, charitable, philanthropic, public-spirited, unselfish. **3** large, ample, full, plentiful, abundant, copious. **4** kind, big-hearted, benevolent, good, high-minded, noble.

◲ **1** mean, miserly, stingy, selfish. **3** meagre.
. . . .

genesis /'dʒenəsɪs/ *noun* (PL. **geneses**) a beginning or origin. [from Greek *genesis*]

gene therapy *Genetics* the notion that genetic engineering techniques could be used to introduce a normal gene into a cell in order to alter or replace a defective gene. It is hoped that it will eventually be possible to prevent hereditary diseases such as haemophilia using such techniques.

genetic or **genetical** *adj.* **1** of or relating to genes or genetics; inherited: *a genetic defect*. **2** of or relating to origin: *a genetic study of American folk music*. [from GENE]

genetically *adv.* **1** with respect to genetics. **2** by genes; according to genetics: *a disease inherited genetically*.

genetic code the code in which genetic instructions for the manufacture of proteins in the cells of living organisms are written.

genetic counselling advice given to prospective parents by a genetics specialist in cases where there is some likelihood of their conceiving children with hereditary disorders, and the options available for their prevention or management.

genetic engineering a form of biotechnology in which the genes of an organism are deliberately altered by a method other than conventional breeding in order to change one or more characteristics of the organism.

genetic fingerprinting *Biol.* the analysis of samples of DNA from body tissues such as blood, saliva, or semen in order to establish a person's identity in criminal investigations, paternity disputes, etc.

geneticist /dʒəˈnɛtɪsɪst/ *noun* a person who studies or is an expert in genetics.

genetic labelling the labelling of food products in supermarkets, etc to indicate the use of gene technology in their manufacture.

genetic modification the deliberate alteration of the genes of an organism, esp a food plant, in order to improve characteristics such as its flavour or size.

genetics *sing. noun* the scientific study of heredity, and of the mechanisms whereby characteristics are transmitted from one generation to the next.

genetic variation a measure of the variation between individuals of a population due to differences in their genetic make-up.

genial *adj.* **1** cheerful; friendly; sociable. **2** *said of a climate* pleasantly warm or mild. [from Latin *genialis*, from *genius*, guardian spirit or deity]

▣ AGREEABLE, PLEASANT, WARM. **1** affable, friendly, sociable, convivial, cordial, hearty, jovial, jolly, cheerful, happy, good-natured, easy-going, kind, warm-hearted. **2** mild, equable.
▣ COLD.

geniality *noun* being genial.

-genic *combining form* forming words meaning 'causing or producing': *carcinogenic*.

genie *noun* (PL. **genies**, **genii**) in fairy stories, a spirit with the power to grant wishes. [from French *génie*]

genital *adj.* **1** relating to or affecting the genitals or the region of the genitals. **2** connected with or relating to reproduction.

genitals or **genitalia** *pl. noun* the external sexual organs. [from Latin *genitalis*, from *gignere*, to beget]

genitive *Grammar* — *noun* **1** the form, or case, of a noun, pronoun or adjective which shows possession or association, eg 'John's'. **2** a noun, etc in this case. — *adj.* of or belonging to this case. [from Latin *genitivus*]

genius *noun* (PL. **geniuses**, **genii** in sense 4) **1** a person of outstanding creative or intellectual ability. **2** such ability. **3** a person who exerts a powerful (good or bad) influence on another. **4** in Roman mythology, a guardian spirit. **5** *formal* a quality or attitude with which something (eg a country or a period of time) is identified or typically associated: *rational inquiry was the genius of the century.* [from Latin *genius*, guardian spirit or deity]

▣ **1** virtuoso, maestro, master, expert, adept, intellectual, *colloq.* egghead, mastermind, brain, intellect. **2** intelligence, brightness, brilliance, ability, faculty, aptitude, gift, talent, flair, knack, bent, inclination, propensity, capacity.

genocidal *adj.* relating to or involving genocide.

genocide *noun* the deliberate and systematic killing of a whole nation or people. [from Greek *genos*, race + Latin *caedere*, to kill]

genome /ˈdʒiːnəʊm/ *noun* the complete set of genetic material in the cell of a living organism. [from GENE + CHROMOSOME]

genotype *noun* the particular set of genes possessed by an organism, ie its genetic make-up.

genre /ˈʒɒnrə/ *noun* **1** a particular type or kind of literature, music or other artistic work. **2** *Art* a type of painting featuring scenes from everyday life. [from French *genre*]

gent *noun colloq.* a gentleman.

genteel *adj.* **1** *derog.* polite or refined in an artificial, affected way approaching snobbishness. **2** well-mannered. **3** *old use, facetious* of, or suitable for, the upper classes. [from French *gentil*, well-bred]

gentian /ˈdʒɛnʃən/ *noun* **1** any of numerous species of mostly low-growing perennial plants of the genus *Gentiana*, native to Europe, Asia, N and S America, and New Zealand, having erect funnel-shaped or bell-shaped flowers, usually deep blue in colour, but white, yellow, or red in some species. **2** a tonic prepared from the bitter-tasting roots of this plant. [from Latin *gentiana*]

gentile — *adj.* **1** (*often* **Gentile**) not Jewish. **2** relating to a nation or tribe. — *noun* (*often* **Gentile**) a person who is not Jewish. [from Latin *gentilis*, from *gens*, nation, clan]

gentility *noun* **1** good manners and respectability. **2** *derog.* artificial politeness. **3** *old use* noble birth; the people of the upper classes. [from Old French *gentilite*]

gentle *adj.* **1** mild-mannered, not stern, coarse or violent. **2** light and soft; not harsh, loud, strong, etc: *a gentle caress / a gentle breeze*. **3** moderate; mild: *a gentle reprimand*. **4** *said of hills, etc* rising gradually. **5** *old use* noble; of the upper classes. [from French *gentil*, well-bred]

▣ **1** kind, kindly, merciful, mild, tender, soft-hearted, compassionate, sympathetic. **2** light, soft, quiet, soothing, peaceful, serene, calm, tranquil. **3** moderate, slight, imperceptible, mild. **4** gradual, slow, easy.
▣ **1** unkind, stern, rough. **2** harsh, strong. **4** steep.

gentlefolk *pl. noun old use* people of good breeding; members of the upper classes.

gentleman *noun* **1** a polite name for a man, used especially as a form of address. **2** a polite, well-mannered, respectable man. **3** a man from the upper classes, especially one with enough private wealth to live on without working.

gentlemanly *adj.* **1** polite and well-mannered. **2** suitable for, or typical of, a gentleman.

gentlemen's agreement or **gentleman's agreement** an unwritten agreement to which each participant is bound only by an informal commitment not binding in law.

gentlewoman *noun old use* **1** a woman from the upper classes. **2** her female servant or attendant.

gently *adv.* in a gentle way.

gentrification *noun derog.* the change in the character of a traditionally working-class area following an influx of new middle-class residents. [from GENTRY]

gentrify *verb* (**gentrifies**, **gentrified**) **1** to convert or renovate (housing) to conform to middle-class taste. **2** to make (an area) middle-class.

gentry *pl. noun* **1** people belonging to the class directly below the nobility. **2** *derog. colloq.* people generally. [from Old French *genterise*, nobility]

gents *sing. noun* a men's public toilet.

genuflect *verb intrans.* to bend the knee, especially in worship or as a sign of respect. [from Latin *genu*, knee + *flectere*, to bend]

genuflection or **genuflexion** *noun* the act of genuflecting.

genuine *adj.* **1** authentic, not artificial or fake. **2** honest; sincere. [from Latin *genuinus*, natural]

▣ **1** real, actual, natural, pure, original, authentic, veritable, true, bona fide, legitimate. **2** honest, sincere, frank, candid, earnest.
▣ **1** artificial, false. **2** insincere.

genuineness *noun* **1** being genuine. **2** honesty.

genus *noun* (PL. **genera**) **1** *Biol.* in plant and animal classification, a group of closely related species. Related genera are in turn grouped into families. **2** a class divided into several subordinate classes. [from Latin *genus*, race or kind]

geo- *combining form* forming words associated with the Earth. [from Greek *ge*, earth]

geocentric *adj.* **1** denoting a system, especially the universe or the solar system, regarded by some as having the Earth as its centre. **2** measured from the centre of the Earth.

geochemistry *noun Geol.* the branch of geology concerned with the scientific study of the chemical composition of the Earth.

geode *noun Geol.* a hollow cavity within a rock, lined with crystals that point inward towards its centre. [from Greek *geodes*, earthy]

geodesic *Maths.* — *noun* (*also* **geodesic line**) a line on a surface that represents the shortest distance between two points, eg a straight line on a plane, or a great circle on a sphere. — *adj.* denoting an artificial structure made up of a large number of identical components, eg a dome whose surface is composed of a large number of identical small triangles. [from GEO- + Greek *daisis*, division]

geodesy *noun Geol.* the scientific study of the Earth's surface by surveying (especially by satellite) and mapping in order to determine its exact shape and size, and to measure its gravitational field. It has applications in map-making, navigation, civil engineering, and geophysics.

geog. *abbrev.* geographical; geography.

geographer *noun* a person who studies or is an expert in geography.

geographical *adj.* relating to or involving geography.

geography *noun* 1 the scientific study of the earth's surface, especially its physical features, climate, and population. 2 *colloq.* the layout of a place.

geol. *abbrev.* geological; geology.

geological *adj.* relating to or involving geology.

geological survey *Geol.* a survey of the geology of a particular area, especially in order to locate economically important rocks and minerals such as coal and oil, or to determine the past history of the area (eg its climate, or the fossil organisms associated with it).

geological time scale *Geol.* a scale in which the Earth's history is subdivided into units of time known as *eons*, which are further subdivided into *eras*, *periods*, and *epochs*.

geologist *noun* a person who studies or is expert in geology.

geology *noun* 1 the scientific study of the Earth, including its origin, history, structure, and composition, and the changes it undergoes, especially in terms of the rocks of which it is made. 2 the history, composition, and structure of the rocks of a particular region which are relevant to such study.

geomagnetism *noun Physics* the Earth's magnetic field.

geometric or **geometrical** *adj.* 1 relating to geometry, or using the principles of geometry. 2 *said of a pattern, design, etc* using or consisting of lines, points, or simple geometrical figures such as circles or triangles.

geometric mean *Maths.* see MEAN³ 2c.

geometric progression *Maths.* a sequence of numbers in which the ratio between one term and the next remains constant, eg 1, 2, 4, 8..., where each successive term is obtained by multiplying its predecessor by 2.

geometric series *Maths.* any series of numbers or terms that forms a geometric progression.

geometry *noun* the branch of mathematics that is concerned with the properties of sets of points that form plane (two-dimensional) or solid (three-dimensional) figures in space.

geomorphology *noun Geol.* the scientific study of the nature and history of the landforms on the surface of the Earth and other planets, and of the processes that create them.

geophysics *sing. noun Physics* the study of the physical properties of the Earth, and the physical processes that determine its structure. Major subjects include seismology, geomagnetism, meteorology, and geophysical surveys to prospect for oil, gas, and mineral reserves.

geopolitics *sing. noun Politics* the study of geographical factors as a basis of the power of nations. It is a combination of political geography and political science, and its considerations include territory, resources, climate, population, social and political culture, and economic activity.

Geordie /'dʒɔːdɪ/ *colloq.* — *noun* 1 a person from Tyneside. 2 the Tyneside dialect. — *adj.* of or relating to Tyneside, its people, or their dialect. [diminutive of the name *George*]

George Cross (ABBREV. **GC**) in the UK, an award instituted in 1940 and named after George VI. It is bestowed on civilians for acts of great heroism or conspicuous bravery, or on members of the armed forces for actions in which purely military honours are not normally granted.

georgette *noun* a kind of thin silk material. [named after Georgette de la Plante, French dressmaker]

Georgian /'dʒɔːdʒən/ — *adj.* 1 *said of architecture, painting, or furniture* from the reign of King George I, II, III, and IV, 1714–1830. 2 *said of literature* from the reign of King George V, especially 1910–20. 3 of the E European republic of Georgia, its people, or their language. 4 of the US state of Georgia, or its people. — *noun* 1 a native of Georgia in E Europe, or the official language of Georgia. 2 a native of the US state of Georgia.

geosphere *noun* 1 *Geol.* the non-living part of the Earth, including the lithosphere, hydrosphere, and atmosphere. 2 the solid part of the Earth, as opposed to the atmosphere and hydrosphere.

geostationary *adj.* denoting the orbit of an artificial satellite above the Earth's equator, at an altitude of 35,900km, at which distance it takes exactly 24h to complete one orbit (the same time that it takes the Earth to rotate once on its own axis), and so appears to remain stationary above a fixed point on the Earth's surface.

geosynchronous /dʒiːoʊ'sɪŋkrənəs/ *adj. Astron.* same as GEOSTATIONARY.

geotaxis *noun Biol.* a change in the direction of movement of a living organism, usually an animal, in response to the force of gravity. [from GEO- + Greek *taxis*, arrangement]

geothermal *adj.* 1 *Geol.* relating to the internal heat of the Earth. 2 relating to or using the energy that can be extracted from this heat. See also GEOTHERMAL ENERGY.

geothermal energy *technical Geol.* the energy that can be extracted from the internal heat of the Earth, produced as a result of radioactive decay within rocks, and the slow cooling of the planet with time.

geotropism *noun Bot.* the growth of the roots or shoots of plants in response to gravity. Roots show positive geotropism, ie they grow in the direction of gravity, whereas shoots show negative geotropism, ie they grow in the opposite direction to gravity. [from GEO- + Greek *tropos*, a turning]

Ger. *abbrev.* German.

geranium *noun* 1 the name commonly used to refer to any of various plants of the subtropical genus *Pelargonium*, native to South Africa, having hairy stems, fragrant leaves, and conspicuous scarlet, pink, or white flowers. 2 *Bot.* strictly, any of many plants of the genus *Geranium*, including the cranesbills, which have divided leaves and (often large) flowers with five pink or purplish petals. [from Greek *geranos*, crane]

gerbil *noun* any of numerous small burrowing rodents, native to desert and semi-desert regions of Asia and Africa, having long hind legs and a long furry tail, and capable of moving in long bounds like a tiny kangaroo. [from Latin *gerbillus*, little jerboa]

geriatric — *adj.* 1 relating to or concerning old people; for or dealing with old people. 2 *derog. colloq.* very old. — *noun* an old person.

geriatrician *noun* a specialist in geriatrics.

geriatrics *sing. noun Medicine* the branch of medicine concerned with the care of the elderly, and with the diagnosis and treatment of diseases and disorders associated with ageing. [from Greek *geras*, old age + *iatros*, physician]

germ *noun* 1 an imprecise term for a pathogen, ie any micro-organism, such as a bacterium or virus, that causes disease. 2 formerly used to refer to any living structure that is capable of developing into a complete organism, eg a seed or a fertilized egg. 3 the embryo of a plant, especially wheat. 4 an origin or beginning: *the germ of a plan*. [from Latin *germen*, bud, sprout]

. . . .

▣ 1 micro-organism, microbe, bacterium, virus, *colloq.* bug.

4 beginning, start, origin, source, cause, spark, rudiment, nucleus, root, seed, embryo.

....

German — *noun* **1** a native or citizen of Germany. **2** the official language of Germany, Austria, and parts of Switzerland. — *adj.* of Germany, its people, or their language. [from Latin *Germanus*]

german *adj.* (*following the noun*) **1** having both parents the same: *brother german*. **2** having both grandparents the same on one side of the family: *cousin german*. [from Latin *germanus*, having the same parents]

germane / dʒɜːˈmeɪn/ *adj.*, *said of ideas, remarks, etc* relevant; closely related. [see GERMAN]

Germanic — *noun* a branch of the Indo-European family of languages that includes German, English, Dutch, and the Scandinavian languages (see GERMANIC LANGUAGES). — *adj.* **1** of these languages. **2** typical of Germany or the Germans.

Germanic languages the languages, making up a branch of the Indo-European family, with a common ancestry in the language of early N European Germanic tribes.

germanium *noun Chem.* (SYMBOL **Ge**, ATOMIC NUMBER **32**) a hard greyish-white metalloid element obtained mainly as a by-product of zinc smelting, and widely used as a semiconductor in electronic devices. [from the name *Germany*, the native country of its discoverer, C A Winkler (1838–1904)]

German measles same as RUBELLA.

German shepherd an Alsatian dog.

germ cell *Biol.* a gamete, usually a sperm or ovum (egg cell).

germicidal *adj.* relating to or involving an agent that destroys germs.

germicide *noun* any agent that destroys germs (disease-causing micro-organisms, such as bacteria and viruses).

germinal *adj.* **1** *technical* of or relating to germs. **2** in the earliest stage of development. [from Latin *germen*, bud, sprout]

germinate *verb* **1** *intrans. Bot.*, *said of a seed or spore* to show the first signs of development into a new individual. **2** *Bot.* to cause a seed or spore to show such signs. **3** *trans.*, *intrans.* to cause an idea to begin to grow. [from Latin *germinare*]

....

⊟ DEVELOP, GROW. **1** bud, sprout, shoot.

....

germination *noun Bot.* the first stages in the development of an embryo into a seedling, involving the emergence of the radicle (embryonic root) and plumule (embryonic shoot) from the seed.

germ layer *Biol.* in a multicellular animal that has two or more layers of body tissue, any of the three embryonic layers of cells, ie the ectoderm, mesoderm, or endoderm.

germ warfare the use of germs to inflict disease on an enemy in war.

gerontological *adj.* relating to gerontology.

gerontologist *noun* a person who studies or is expert in gerontology.

gerontology *noun* the scientific study of old age, the ageing process, and the problems of elderly people. [from Greek *geron*, old man + LOGY]

gerrymander / dʒerɪˈmændə(r)/ *derog.* — *verb* (**gerrymandered**, **gerrymandering**) to arrange or change the boundaries of (an electoral constituency) so as to favour one political party. — *noun* a constituency arranged in such a way. [named after Massachusetts Governor Elbridge Gerry (1744–1814) and SALAMANDER, from the shape on the map of one of his electoral districts after manipulation]

gerrymandering *noun* the act or process of arranging the boundaries of one or more electoral constituencies to favour one political party.

gerund / 'dʒerənd/ *noun Grammar* a noun formed from a verb, in English ending in -ing, and describing an action, eg 'the *baking* of bread' and '*Smoking* damages your health.' [from Latin *gerundium*, from *gerere*, to bear]

Gesamtkunstwerk / gəˈzamtkʊnstvɜːk/ *noun* a term denoting the totality of art. It was applied by Wagner to his operatic productions, in which music was combined with costume and visual effects to create a complete unified work. [from German, = total art work]

gesso / 'dʒesoʊ/ *noun* plaster used as a medium for sculpture or as a surface for painting. [from Italian *gesso*, from Latin *gypsum*; see GYPSUM]

Gestalt psychology / gəˈʃtalt/ *Psychol.* a school of psychology based on the concept that the whole is greater than the sum of its parts.

Gestalt therapy *Psychol.* a form of psychotherapy, derived from Gestalt psychology, which aims to make people 'whole' by increasing their awareness of aspects of their personality which have been denied or disowned.

Gestapo / gəˈstɑːpoʊ/ *noun* the political police of the German Third Reich, founded by Göring in 1933 on the basis of the Prussian political police. [a contraction of German *Geheime Staatspolizei*, secret state police]

gestate *verb trans., intrans.* **1** *Zool.*, *said of a viviparous mammal* to carry or be carried in the uterus (womb), and to undergo physical development, during the period between fertilization and birth. In humans the gestation period corresponds to the duration of pregnancy (266 days on average). **2** to develop (an idea, etc) slowly in the mind. [from Latin *gestare*, to carry]

gestation *noun* in mammals that bear live young, the period between fertilization of the egg and birth, during which the embryo develops in the uterus (womb) of the mother.

gesticulate *verb* **1** *intrans.* to make (bold) gestures, especially when speaking. **2** *trans.* to express in this way. [from Latin *gesticulare*, from *gestus*, gesture]

....

⊟ GESTURE, SIGNAL. **1** wave. **2** indicate.

....

gesticulation *noun* **1** the act of gesticulating. **2** the use of gestures.

gestural *adj.* **1** relating to or involving gestures. **2** by or using gestures.

gesture — *noun* **1** a movement of a part of the body as an expression of meaning, especially when speaking. **2** something done to communicate (especially friendly) feelings or intentions. **3** *derog.* something done simply as a formality: *asking our opinion was merely a gesture*. — *verb* **1** *intrans.* to make gestures. **2** *trans.* to express with gestures. [from Latin *gestus*]

....

⊟ *noun* **1** movement, motion, sign, signal, wave, gesticulation. **2** act, action, indication, sign. *verb* GESTICULATE, SIGNAL, BECKON. **1** wave, point. **2** indicate, motion.

....

get — *verb* (**getting**; PAST TENSE AND PAST PARTICIPLE **got**) **1** to receive or obtain. **2** to have or possess. **3** (**get across**, or **get someone across**, **away**, **to**, **through**, etc) to go or cause them to go, move, travel, or arrive as specified: *tried to get past him* / *will you get him to bed at 8?* / *got to Paris on Friday*. **4** (*usually* **get something down**, **in**, **out**, etc) to fetch, take, or bring it as specified: *get it down from the shelf* / *I'll get you a drink of water*. **5** to put into a particular state or condition: *don't get it wet* / *got him into trouble*. **6** *intrans.* to become: *got angry*. **7** to catch (a disease, etc). **8** to order or persuade: *get him to help us*. **9** *colloq.* to receive (a broadcast, etc): *unable to get the World Service*. **10** *colloq.* to make contact with, especially by telephone: *never get him at home*. **11** *colloq.* to arrive at by calculation. **12** *intrans.* (**get to do something**) *colloq.* to receive permission to do it: *can you get to stay out late?* **13** *colloq.* to prepare (a meal). **14** *colloq.* to buy or pay for: *got her some flowers for her birthday*. **15** *colloq.* to suffer: *got a broken arm*. **16** *colloq.* to receive as punishment: *got ten* years for armed robbery. **17** *colloq.* (**get** someone or **get** someone **back**) to attack, punish, or otherwise cause harm to: *I'll get you back for that!* **18** *trans., intrans. colloq.* (**get to** someone) to annoy them: *you shouldn't let him get to you.* **19** *colloq.* to understand. **20** *colloq.* to hear: *I didn't quite get his name.* **21** *colloq.* to affect emotionally. **22** *colloq.* to baffle: *you've got me there.* — *noun derog. slang* a stupid or contemptible person; a git. — **be getting on for**... *colloq.* to approach a certain time or age. **get about** or **around** *colloq.* **1** to travel; to go from place to place. **2** *said of a rumour, etc* to circulate. **get across to** make it understood. **get along with** someone *colloq.* to be on friendly terms with them. **get at** something **1** to reach or take hold of it. **2** *colloq.* to suggest or imply it: *what are you getting at?* **get at** someone *colloq.* **1** to criticize or victimize them persistently. **2** *colloq.* to influence them by dishonest means, eg bribery. **get away 1** to leave, or be free to leave. **2** to escape. **3** *colloq., as an exclamation* an expression of disbelief. **get away with** something to commit an offence or wrongdoing without being caught or punished. **get back at** someone *colloq.* to take revenge on them. **get by 1** *colloq.* to manage to live. **2** *colloq.* to be acceptable. **get** someone **down** *colloq.* to make them sad or depressed. **get** something **down 1** to manage to swallow it. **2** to write it down. **get down to** something to apply oneself to a task or piece of work. **get in 1** *said of a political party* to be elected to power. **2** to be accepted for entry or membership. **get** something **in 1** to gather or harvest it. **2** *colloq.* to succeed in doing or making it before something else occurs: *tried to get some work in before dinner.* **get in on** something *colloq.* to take part in it or share in it. **get into** something *colloq.* to develop a liking or enthusiasm for. **have got into** someone *colloq.* to affect their behaviour: *what's got into him?* **get in with** someone *colloq.* to become friendly with them, often for selfish reasons. **get it** *slang* to be punished. **get it together** *colloq.* to use one's energies and abilities effectively. **get nowhere** *colloq.* to make no progress, or produce no results. **get off** or **get** someone **off** *colloq.* to escape or cause to escape with no punishment, or with the stated punishment: *was charged but got off | managed to get him off with a warning.* **get off** something *colloq.* to stop discussing it or dealing with it: *let's get off this subject.* **get off on** something *colloq.* to get excitement from it. **get off with** someone *colloq.* to begin a casual sexual relationship with them. **get on** *colloq.* **1** to make progress or be successful. **2** *said of a person* to grow old. **3** *said of time, etc* to grow late. **get on at** someone *colloq.* to pester or criticize them continually. **get on to** someone to make contact with them; to begin dealing with them. **get on with** someone to have a friendly relationship with them. **get on with** something to continue working on it or dealing with it. **get out** *said of information* to become known. **get** something **out** to manage to say, usually with difficulty. **get out of** something to avoid having to do it. **get over** someone to be no longer emotionally affected by them. **get over** something to recover from an illness, disappointment, etc. **get** something **over** to explain it successfully; to make it understood. **get** something **over with** to deal with something unpleasant as quickly as possible. **get** one's **own back** *colloq.* to have one's revenge. **get round** *colloq., said of information, a rumour, etc* to become generally known. **get round** someone *colloq.* to persuade them, or win their approval or permission. **get round** something to successfully pass by or negotiate a problem, etc. **get round to** something or someone to deal with them eventually. **get somewhere** *colloq.* to make progress. **get there** *colloq.* to make progress towards, or achieve, one's final aim. **get through** something **1** to complete a task, piece of work, etc. **2** to use it steadily until it is finished: *managed to get through a pound of butter in a day.* **3** *colloq.* to pass a test or examination. **get through to** someone **1** to make contact with them by telephone. **2** to make them understand something: *we can't get through to him how important this is.* **get together** to meet, gather, or unite, usually for social or business purposes. **get up 1** to get out of bed. **2** *said of the wind, etc* to become strong. **get** someone **up** to make them get out of bed. **get** something **up** to arrange, orga-

nize, or prepare it: *decided to get up a celebration.* **get up speed** to increase and maintain a speed. **get up to** something *colloq.* to do or be involved in something bad or unwelcome. [from Norse *geta*, to obtain or beget]

. . . .

🔲 *verb* **1** obtain, acquire, procure, come by, receive, earn, gain, win, secure, achieve, realize. **2** have, possess, own, hold. **3** move, go, come. *get down* descend, dismount, disembark, alight. *get off* alight, land, disembark, dismount. *get on* board, embark, mount. *get to* reach, arrive at. *get up* stand (up), rise, ascend, climb. **4** take, bring, fetch, collect, pick up. **6** become, turn, go, grow. **7** catch, pick up, go down with, contract, develop. **8** persuade, coax, induce, influence, urge, order. **get across** communicate, transmit, convey, impart, put across, bring home. **get along with** get on with, hit it off with, agree with, harmonize with. **get at** something **1** reach, attain, find, discover. **2** suggest, imply, insinuate, hint, mean, intend. **get at** someone **1** criticize, find fault with, pick on, victimize, attack, make fun of. **2** bribe, suborn, corrupt, influence. **get away 1** leave, depart. **2** escape, get out, break out, break away, run away, flee. **get by 1** cope, manage, get along, survive. **get** someone **down** sadden, depress, dishearten, dispirit. **get in 2** enter, penetrate, infiltrate, arrive. **get on 1** advance, progress, fare, get along, cope, manage, succeed, prosper, thrive, flourish, get ahead, make good, make it, *colloq.* get there. **get on with** someone get along with, hit it off with, agree with, harmonize with. *something* proceed with, continue with, press on with. **get out of** avoid, evade, escape, extricate oneself from, free oneself from. **get over** something recover from, shake off, survive, surmount, overcome, defeat, deal with. **get** something **over** explain, put over, communicate, get across, convey, impart. **get round** someone persuade, win over, talk round, coax, prevail upon. **get round** something circumvent, bypass, evade, avoid. **get together** gather, assemble, congregate, rally, meet, join, unite, collaborate. **get up 1** rise. **2** increase, strengthen.

🔲 *verb* **1, 2** lose. **get** someone **down** encourage. **get on 1** fail.

. . . .

get-at-able /gɛtˈatəbl/ *adj. colloq.* able to be easily reached.

getaway *noun* an escape, especially after committing a crime.

get-together *noun colloq.* an informal meeting.

get-up *noun colloq.* outfit or clothes, especially when considered strange or remarkable.

get-up-and-go *noun colloq.* energy.

geum /ˈdʒiːəm/ *noun Bot.* a perennial plant with lobed leaves and brilliant yellow, orange, or scarlet flowers on slender stalks, often grown in rock gardens. [from Latin *geum*]

gewgaw /ˈgjuːgɔː/ *noun old derog. use* a brightly-coloured trinket.

Gewürztraminer /gəˈvʊətstramɪnə(r)/ *noun* **1** a variety of white grape grown especially in the Alsace region. **2** a medium-dry aromatic wine made from this grape. [from German, from *Gewürz*, spice, and *Traminer*, a grape variety (after *Tramin*, a wine-growing region in S Tyrol)]

geyser /ˈgiːzə(r)/ *noun* **1** *Geol.* in an area of volcanic activity, a type of hot spring that intermittently spouts hot water and steam into the air. **2** a domestic appliance for heating water rapidly. [from Icelandic *geysa*, from Norse *göysa*, to gush]

gharial /ˈgʌrɪəl/ or **gavial** /ˈgeɪvɪəl/ *noun Zool.* a large narrow-snouted crocodile found in parts of N India. [from Hindi *ghariyal*, crocodile]

ghastliness *noun* being ghastly.

ghastly — *adj.* (**ghastlier, ghastliest**) **1** extremely frightening; hideous; horrific. **2** *colloq.* very bad. **3** *colloq.* very ill. — *adv. colloq.* extremely; unhealthily: *ghastly pale.* [from Middle English *gasten*, to terrify]

. . . .
■ *adj.* AWFUL, DREADFUL, TERRIBLE. **1** grim, gruesome, hideous, horrible, frightening, horrific, loathsome, repellent. **2** shocking, appalling. **3** rotten, *slang* lousy.
. . . .

ghat /gɔːt/ *noun India and Pakistan* **1** a mountain pass. **2** a set of steps leading down to a river. [from Hindi *ghat*, descent]

ghee /giː/ *noun* butter made from cow's or buffalo's milk, purified by heating, used in Indian cooking. [from Hindi *ghi*]

gherkin *noun* **1** a variety of cucumber that bears very small fruits. **2** a small or immature fruit of any of various varieties of cucumber, used for pickling. [from Dutch *augurkje*]

ghetto *noun* (PL. **ghettos**, **ghettoes**) **1** *derog.* a poor area densely populated by people from a deprived social group, especially a racial minority. **2** *Hist.* a part of a European city to which Jews were formerly restricted. [perhaps from Italian *ghetto*, foundry, after one on the site of the first Jewish ghetto, in Venice]

ghetto-blaster *noun colloq.* a large portable radio-cassette recorder, especially one playing pop music at high volume.

ghost — *noun* **1** the spirit of a dead person when visible in some form to a living person. **2** a suggestion, hint, or trace. **3** a faint shadow attached to the image on a television screen. — *verb intrans., trans.* to be a ghost writer for (someone), or of (some written work). — **give up the ghost** *colloq.* to die. [from Anglo-Saxon *gast*]
. . . .
■ *noun* **1** spectre, phantom, apparition, *colloq.* spook, spirit, soul, wraith.
. . . .

ghostly *adj.* **1** like a ghost or ghosts. **2** relating to or suggesting the presence of ghosts.
. . . .
■ **1** ghostlike, spectral, phantom, illusory. **2** eerie, *colloq.* spooky, creepy, supernatural.
. . . .

ghost town a deserted town, especially one formerly thriving.

ghost writer a person who writes books, speeches, etc on behalf of another person who is credited as their author.

ghoul /guːl/ *noun* **1** in Arab mythology, a demon that robs graves and eats dead bodies. **2** a person interested in morbid or disgusting things. [from Arabic *ghul*]

ghoulish *adj.* like or typical of a ghoul.

GHQ *abbrev.* General Headquarters.

ghyll same as GILL[3].

GI *noun* (PL. **GIs**) *colloq.* a soldier in the US army, especially during World War II. [from Government Issue]

giant — *noun* **1** in fairy stories, a huge, extremely strong, often cruel creature of human form. **2** *colloq.* an unusually large person or animal. **3** a person, group, etc of exceptional ability or importance: *literary giants.* — *adj.* **1** *colloq.* huge: *giant portions.* **2** of a particularly large species, in implied contrast to smaller ones: *giant tortoise.* [from Greek *gigas*]
. . . .
■ *noun* **1** ogre. **2** monster, titan, colossus, goliath. **3** colossus, goliath. *adj.* **1** huge, enormous, immense, gigantic, colossal, mammoth, *colloq.* jumbo, king-size.
. . . .

giantess *noun* a female giant.

giant-killer *noun colloq.* a person or team that unexpectedly defeats a superior opponent.

giant panda a large bear-like mammal (*Ailuropoda melanoleuca*), about 1.8m in height, and having thick white fur, with black legs, shoulders, ears, and patches round the eyes.

giant star *Astron.* a highly luminous star that is much larger than the Sun, and is reaching the end of its life. Giant stars lie above the main sequence on the right-hand side of the Hertzsprung-Russell diagram.

gibber *verb intrans.* (**gibbered**, **gibbering**) **1** to talk so fast that one cannot be understood. **2** *derog.* to talk foolishly. [imitative]

gibberellin /dʒɪbəˈrɛlɪn/ *noun Bot.* any of a group of plant hormones that stimulate rapid growth by the elongation of cells as opposed to cell division. They also promote fruit and seed formation, and delay ageing in leaves. [from a fungus genus-name *Gibberella*, from Latin *gibber*, hump]

gibbering *adj.* that gibbers.

gibberish *noun* **1** fast unintelligible talk. **2** foolish talk; nonsense.

gibbet — *noun Hist.* **1** a gallows-like frame on which the bodies of executed criminals were hung as a public warning. **2** a gallows. — *verb* (**gibbeted**, **gibbeting**) **1** *Hist.* to hang on a gibbet. **2** to expose to public ridicule. [from French *gibet*, gallows]

gibbon *noun* the smallest of the apes, and the only one to walk upright habitually, found in SE Asia. [from French *gibbon*]

gibbous /ˈgɪbəs/ *adj. technical* **1** *said of the moon or a planet* not fully illuminated but more than half illuminated. **2** humpbacked. **3** swollen; bulging. [from Latin *gibbus*, hump]

gibe or **jibe** — *verb intrans.* to mock, scoff, or jeer. — *noun* a jeer. [from Old French *giber*, to treat roughly]
. . . .
■ *verb* mock, poke fun, scoff, jeer, sneer. *noun* jeer, sneer, taunt, dig, quip.
. . . .

giblets /ˈdʒɪblɪts/ *pl. noun* the heart, liver, and other edible internal organs of a chicken or other fowl. [from Old French *gibelet*, game stew, from *gibier*, game]

giddily *adv.* in a giddy way.

giddiness *noun* being giddy.

giddy *adj.* (**giddier**, **giddiest**) **1** suffering an unbalancing spinning sensation. **2** causing such a sensation. **3** *literary* overwhelmed by feelings of excitement or pleasure. **4** light-hearted and carefree; frivolous. [from Anglo-Saxon *gidig*, insane]
. . . .
■ DIZZY. **1** faint, light-headed, unsteady, reeling. **2** vertiginous. **4** light-hearted, carefree, frivolous, flighty.
. . . .

gift — *noun* **1** something given; a present. **2** a natural ability. **3** the act of giving: *the gift of a book.* **4** *colloq.* something easily obtained, or made easily available. — *verb formal* to give (something) as a present to (someone). — **in someone's gift** *formal* able to be given away by someone if they wish. **look a gift-horse in the mouth** to find fault with a gift or unexpected opportunity. [from Norse *gipt*]
. . . .
■ *noun* **1** present, offering, donation, contribution, bounty, largesse, gratuity, tip, bonus, *colloq.* freebie, legacy, bequest, endowment. **2** talent, flair, genius, aptitude, ability, knack, power, faculty, attribute.
. . . .

gifted *adj.* having a great natural ability.
. . . .
■ talented, adept, skilful, expert, masterly, skilled, accomplished, able, capable, clever, intelligent, bright, brilliant.
. . . .

giftedness *noun* exceptional cleverness or ability. In children, giftedness is often defined as exceptional natural ability in a particular subject or area, such as music, art, or mathematics; or, more generally, as high intelligence.

gift tax a tax formerly levied in the UK on gifts having a substantial value.

gift-wrap *verb* (**gift-wrapped**, **gift-wrapping**) to wrap attractively, especially for presentation as a gift.

gig[1] *noun* **1** *Hist.* a small open two-wheeled horse-drawn carriage. **2** a small rowing boat carried on a ship. **3** a long lightweight rowing boat used for racing. [from Middle English *gigge*, whirling thing]

gig[2] *colloq.* — *noun* **1** a pop concert. **2** a musician's booking to play, especially for one night only. — *verb* (**gigged, gigging**) to play a gig or gigs.

giga- /ˈdʒaɪgə, gaɪgə, dʒɪgə, gɪgə/ *combining form* (ABBREV. **G**) **1** used in the metric system to denote ten to the power of nine (10^9), ie one thousand million: *gigahertz.* **2** *Comput.* two to the power of thirty (2^{30}): *gigabyte.* [from Greek *gigas*, giant]

gigantic /dʒaɪˈgantɪk/ *adj.* huge; enormous. [from Greek *gigantikos*, from *gigas*, giant]

. . . .

◨ huge, enormous, immense, vast, giant, colossal, titanic, *colloq.* seismic, mammoth, gargantuan.

◪ tiny, Lilliputian.

. . . .

gigantically *adv.* hugely, enormously.

giggle — *verb intrans.* to laugh quietly in short bursts or in a nervous or silly way. — *noun* **1** such a laugh. **2** (**the giggles**) a fit of giggling. **3** *colloq.* a funny person, situation, or activity. [imitative]

. . . .

◨ *verb* titter, snigger, chuckle, chortle, laugh. *noun* **1** titter, snigger, chuckle, chortle, laugh.

. . . .

giggly *adj.* (**gigglier, giggliest**) tending or likely to giggle.

GIGO *abbrev. Comput.* garbage in, garbage out (see GARBAGE).

gigolo /ˈdʒɪgəloʊ/ *noun* (PL. **gigolos**) **1** *derog.* the paid male companion and lover of a rich (usually older) woman. **2** a hired professional dancing partner. [from French *gigolo*]

gigot /ˈdʒɪgət/ *noun* a leg of lamb or mutton. [from French *gigot*]

gigue /ʒiːg/ *noun* a lively dance, usually in 16:8 or 12:8 time; also, a piece of music for it. [from French *gigue*, probably related to English JIG]

gila monster /ˈhiːlə, xiːlə/ a venomous lizard, native to America, up to 60cm in length, dark with yellow mottling, and having bead-like scales, a blunt head, and a fat tail. [from the Gila River in Arizona]

gild *verb* (PAST TENSE AND PAST PARTICIPLE **gilded, gilt**) to cover with a thin coating of gold or something similar. — **gild the lily** to try to improve something which is already beautiful enough, often spoiling it. [from Anglo-Saxon *gyldan*, gold]

gilder same as GUILDER.

gill[1] *noun* (pronounced as in *gilt*) **1** in all fishes and many other aquatic animals, a respiratory organ that extracts dissolved oxygen from the surrounding water. **2** each of many thin vertical spore-bearing structures on the underside of the cap of mushrooms and toadstools. **3** (**gills**) *colloq.* the flesh under the ears and jaw. — **green about the gills** *colloq.* looking or feeling sick. [perhaps from Norse *gil*]

gill[2] *noun* (pronounced as in *jilt*) **1** in the UK, a unit of liquid measure equal to 142.1ml (a quarter of a pint). **2** *colloq.* an alcoholic drink. [from Old French *gelle*]

gill[3] *noun* (pronounced as in *gilt*) **1** a deep wooded ravine. **2** a mountain stream. [from Norse *gil*]

gillie or **ghillie** *noun* a guide or assistant to a game-hunter or fisherman, especially in Scotland. [from Gaelic *gille*, boy]

gilt[1] — *adj.* covered with a thin coating of gold; gilded. — *noun* **1** gold or a gold-like substance used in gilding. **2** (**gilts**) gilt-edged securities.

. . . .

◨ *adj.* gilded, gold, golden, gold-plated.

. . . .

gilt[2] *noun* a young female pig, especially one that has not produced a litter. [from Norse *gyltr*]

gilt-edged securities government securities with a fixed rate of interest, able to be sold at face value.

gimbals /ˈdʒɪmbəlz/ *pl. noun* a device consisting of a frame with two mutually perpendicular axes of rotation, which allows a navigation instrument (such as a gyroscope or compass) that is mounted on it to rotate freely about two perpendicular axes, and so to remain in a horizontal position at sea or in the air. [from Old French *gemel*, double ring for a finger]

gimcrack /ˈdʒɪmkrak/ *derog.* — *adj.* cheap, showy, and badly made. — *noun* a cheap and showy article. [from Middle English *gibecrake*, little ornament]

gimlet /ˈgɪmlət/ *noun* **1** a T-shaped hand-tool for boring holes in wood. **2** a cocktail of lime juice and gin or vodka. [from Old French *guimbelet*]

gimlet-eyed *adj.* having a piercing look or stare.

gimmick *noun derog.* a scheme or object used to attract attention or publicity, especially to bring in customers.

. . . .

◨ attraction, ploy, stratagem, ruse, scheme, trick, stunt, device, contrivance.

. . . .

gimmickry *noun* gimmicks, or the use of gimmicks.

gimmicky *adj.* **1** involving a gimmick or gimmicks. **2** designed to catch attention.

gimp *noun* a strip of silk with a wire core, used as a decoration in dressmaking, etc. [from French *guimpe*]

gin[1] *noun* an alcoholic spirit made from barley, rye, or maize, flavoured with juniper berries. [from Dutch *genever*, juniper]

gin[2] — *noun* **1** a wire noose laid as a snare or trap for catching game. **2** a machine that is used to remove the seeds from raw cotton. Also called COTTON GIN. **3** the building in which such machinery is housed. **4** a hoisting machine, especially one equipped with a windlass, pulleys, and ropes. — *verb* (**ginned, ginning**) **1** to snare or trap game in a gin. **2** to remove (the seeds) from raw cotton using a gin. [from Old French *engin*, engine]

ginger — *noun* **1** an aromatic spicy swollen root or rhizome, usually dried and ground to a yellow powder that is used as a flavouring in biscuits, cakes, curries, chutneys, etc, although it can also be eaten fresh or preserved in syrup. Ginger is used in some medicines. **2** the perennial plant (*Zingiber officinalis*), cultivated in many tropical regions, from which this root is obtained. **3** a reddish-brown colour. **4** *colloq.* energy; liveliness. — *adj.* **1** flavoured with ginger. **2** *said of hair* reddish-brown in colour. — *verb* (**ginger someone up**) *colloq.* to urge them to become more lively, active, or efficient. [from Latin *zingiber*, from Sanskrit *srnga*, horn + *vera*, body, from the shape of the root]

ginger ale or **ginger beer** a non-alcoholic fizzy drink flavoured with ginger.

gingerbread *noun* cake flavoured with treacle and ginger.

ginger group a small group within a larger (especially political) group, which urges stronger or more radical action.

gingerly *adv.* showing delicate caution. [perhaps from Old French *gensor*, delicate]

. . . .

◨ tentatively, hesitantly, warily, cautiously, carefully, delicately.

◪ boldly, carelessly.

. . . .

ginger nut or **ginger snap** a ginger-flavoured biscuit.

gingery *adj.* **1** ginger. **2** *said of remarks* critical.

gingham /ˈgɪŋəm/ *noun* striped or checked cotton cloth. [from Malay *ginggang*, striped]

gingivitis /dʒɪndʒɪˈvaɪtɪs/ *noun Medicine* inflammation of the gums (gingiva), which become swollen and painful and tend to bleed, usually caused by the accumulation of plaque in the region where the gums meet the teeth. [from Latin *gingiva*, gum + -ITIS]

ginkgo /ˈgɪŋkoʊ/ *noun* a deciduous gymnosperm (cone-bearing plant), *Ginkgo biloba*, native to SW China. Its leaves are similar to the fan-shaped leaves of the maiden-hair fern. Also called MAIDENHAIR TREE. [from Japanese, = silver apricot]

ginormous adj. colloq. exceptionally huge. [from GIGANTIC + ENORMOUS]

gin rummy colloq. **gin** a version of rummy allowing a finish by a player whose unmatched cards total 10 points or less.

ginseng /'dʒɪnseŋ, dʒɪn'seŋ/ noun **1** either of two plant species belonging to the genus *Panax*, with yellowish-green flowers and round red fruits, cultivated in China and N America for its aromatic root, which is widely used as a tonic and aphrodisiac. **2** a medicinal preparation made from the root of this plant. [from Chinese *jen-shen*, image of man, from the shape of the root]

gin sling an iced drink of sweetened gin.

gintrap noun a powerful animal trap with teeth.

gip same as GYP.

gippy tummy colloq. a severe stomach upset, especially as suffered by visitors to hot countries. [from EGYPTIAN]

Gipsy same as GYPSY.

giraffe noun a very tall mammal (*Giraffa camelopardalis*), and the tallest living animal, reaching a height of up to 5.5m. [from Arabic *zarafah*]

gird verb (PAST TENSE AND PAST PARTICIPLE **girded, girt**) *literary* to encircle or fasten with a belt or something similar. — **gird up one's loins** *literary* to prepare oneself for action. [from Anglo-Saxon *gyrdan*]

girder noun a large beam of wood, iron, or steel used to support a floor, wall, road, or bridge. [from Anglo-Saxon *gyrdan*, to gird]

girdle[1] — noun **1** a woman's close-fitting undergarment worn to reshape the figure from waist to thigh. **2** a belt or cord worn round the waist. **3** a surrounding part, especially such a part of the body: *pelvic girdle*. — verb **1** to put a girdle on. **2** *literary* to surround. [from Anglo-Saxon *gyrdan*, to gird]

.....

▣ noun **1** corset. **2** belt, sash, band, waistband.

.....

girdle[2] same as GRIDDLE.

girl noun **1** a female child. **2** a daughter. **3** *often offensive* a young woman, especially unmarried. **4** *often offensive* a woman of any age. **5** *colloq.* a woman's female friend or colleague. **6** a female employee, especially formerly a maid. [from Middle English *gerle, girle,* and *gurle,* child]

Girl Friday a young woman who does general office work.

girlfriend noun **1** a female sexual or romantic partner. **2** a female friend, especially of a woman.

girlhood noun the period of life when a person is a girl.

girlie or **girly** adj. *colloq.*, *said of a magazine, picture, etc* featuring naked or nearly naked young women in erotic poses.

girlish adj. with a girlish manner; like a girl.

giro noun (PL. **giros**) **1** a banking system by which money can be transferred from one account directly to another. **2** *colloq.* a social security benefit received in cheque form. [from Italian *giro,* turn or transfer]

girt see GIRD.

girth noun **1** distance round something, eg a tree or a person's waist. **2** the strap round a horse's belly that holds a saddle in place. [from Norse *gjörth,* belt]

.....

▣ **1** circumference, perimeter. **2** strap, band.

.....

gist /dʒɪst/ noun general meaning; main point. [from Old French *gist,* from *gesir,* to lie, consist in, or reside in]

.....

▣ pith, essence, substance, matter, meaning, significance, import, sense, idea, drift, point, nub, core.

.....

git noun *derog. slang* a stupid or contemptible person. [variant of GET]

gittern /'gɪtən/ noun a medieval musical instrument of the guitar family. It resembled a lute (but with a shorter neck which curved smoothly into the body of the instrument), and had three or four courses of strings played with a plectrum. [from Old French *guitern,* related to Greek *kithara*]

give — verb (PAST TENSE **gave**; PAST PARTICIPLE **given**) **1** to transfer ownership of; to transfer possession of temporarily: *gave him my watch* / *give me your bags.* **2** to provide or administer: *give advice* / *give medicine.* **3** to produce: *cows give milk.* **4** to perform (an action, service, etc): *give a smile, a lecture on beetles.* **5** to pay: *gave £20 for it.* **6** *intrans.* to make a donation: *please give generously.* **7** (*also* **give something up**) to sacrifice: *give one's life.* **8** to be the cause or source of: *gives me pain.* **9** *intrans.* to yield or break: *give under pressure.* **10** to organize at one's own expense: *give a party.* **11** to have as a result: *four into twenty gives five.* **12** to reward or punish by: *was given 20 years.* **13** *colloq.* to agree to or admit: *I'll give you that.* **14** to offer a toast to. **15** *Sport* to declare to be: *gave him offside.* **16** (**give into** or **on to something**) *said of a passage, etc* to lead or be an opening to it: *a terrace giving on to the lawn.* **17** *colloq.* used to state a preference: *give me jazz any day.* — noun capacity to yield; flexibility. — **give as good as one gets** *colloq.* to respond to an attack with equal energy, force, and effect. **give someone away** to present a bride to a bridegroom at a wedding ceremony. **give something away 1** to hand it over as a gift. **2** to allow a piece of information to become known, usually by accident. **give in to someone** or **something** to yield to them; to admit defeat. **give something off** to produce or emit eg a smell. **give or take something** *colloq.* allowing for a (stated) margin of error: *we have all the money, give or take a pound.* **give out** *colloq.* to break down or come to an end: *their resistance gave out.* **give something out 1** to announce or distribute it. **2** to emit a sound, smell, etc. **give something over 1** to transfer it. **2** to set it aside or devote it to some purpose: *the morning was given over to discussing the budgets.* **give over doing something** *colloq., usually as a command* to stop doing it: *give over shouting.* **give up** to admit defeat. **give someone up** to surrender a wanted person. **give something up** to renounce or quit a habit, etc: *give up smoking.* **give up doing something** to stop making the effort to achieve it: *gave up trying to talk sense to them.* **give someone up for dead** or **lost** to assume that they are dead or lost, etc, after abandoning hope. **give way 1** to give priority. **2** to collapse under pressure. **give way to something** to allow oneself to be affected by it: *give way to tears.* **what gives?** what is happening? [from Anglo-Saxon *gefan*]

.....

▣ verb **1** hand over, present, award, confer, lend, donate, contribute, grant, bestow, endow, gift, make over, deliver, entrust, commit, devote. **2** provide, supply, furnish, administer, offer, communicate, transmit, impart. **3** make, produce. **4** do, perform. **8** cause, occasion. **9** yield, give way, sink, bend, break, collapse, fall. **13** concede, allow, admit, agree to. **give something away 2** betray, expose, uncover, divulge, let slip, disclose, reveal, leak, let out. **give in to** yield to, submit to, give way to, surrender to, capitulate to. **give off** produce, emit, discharge, release, give out, send out, throw out, pour out, exhale, exude. **give something out 1** announce, declare, broadcast, publish, disseminate, communicate, transmit, distribute, hand out, dole out, deal out. **give up** surrender, capitulate, give in.**give something up** stop, cease, quit, abandon, renounce, relinquish, waive.

▣ verb **1** take, withhold. **9** withstand. **give something up** start.

.....

give-and-take noun **1** mutual willingness to accept the other's point of view. **2** a useful exchange of views.

give-away noun *colloq.* **1** an act of accidentally revealing secrets, etc. **2** something obtained extremely easily or cheaply: *the goal was a give-away.* **3** a free gift.

given — adj. **1** stated or specified. **2** (**given to something**) prone to it; having it as a habit: *given to biting his nails.* — prep. accepting as a basis for discussion; assuming.

☰ *adj.* **1** stated, specified, particular, definite. **2** prone to, inclined to, disposed to, likely to, liable to.

gizzard /ˈgɪzəd/ *noun* **1** *Zool.* in certain animals, a muscular chamber specialized for grinding up indigestible food. In birds (where it is situated behind the crop) and earthworms, it contains grit or small stones, and in insects it is lined with spines that form a tough grinding surface. **2** *colloq.* the stomach. [from Old French *guisier*, fowl's liver]

glacé /ˈglaseɪ/ *adj.* **1** coated with a sugary glaze; candied: *glacé cherries.* **2** frozen, or covered with ice. [from French *glacé*]

glacial /ˈgleɪsɪəl, ˈgleɪʃəl/ — *adj.* **1** *Geol., Geog.* relating to or resembling a glacier; caused by the action of a glacier. **2** of or relating to ice or its effects. **3** *said of a geological time period, etc* characterized by the presence of glaciers or large masses of ice. **4** *Chem.*, *said of a chemical compound* tending to form crystals that resemble ice: *glacial acetic acid.* **5** *colloq.* extremely cold. **6** hostile: *a glacial stare.* — *noun* a glacial period; an ice age. [from Latin *glacialis*, icy]

glacially *adv.* **1** by glacial action. **2** in an icy way, icily.

glacial period 1 any interval of geological time during which a large part of the Earth's surface was covered with ice, due to one or more major advances of glaciers towards the equator. **2** (**the Glacial Period**) the Ice Age (the Pleistocene epoch), or any ice age.

glaciate *verb Geol., Geog.* **1** *said of land, etc* to become covered with glaciers or ice sheets. **2** to subject (land, etc) to the eroding action of moving glaciers or ice sheets. **3** to polish by the action of ice. [from Latin *glaciare*, to freeze]

glaciation *noun Geol.* the process whereby part of the Earth's surface is covered and shaped by glaciers or ice sheets, resulting in the production of characteristic landforms after the ice has melted, eg U-shaped valleys, moraines (ridges of rock debris), and cirques.

glacier /ˈglasɪə(r), ˈgleɪsɪə(r)/ *noun* a large body of ice, formed by the compaction of snow, that occurs on land, and slowly moves down a gradient (bending under its own weight) or outward in all directions until it reaches a point where it melts or breaks up into icebergs. [from French, from *glace*, ice]

glad *adj.* (**gladder, gladdest**) **1** happy or pleased: *I'm glad you like it / she'll be glad to see you.* **2** (**glad of something**) grateful for it: *I was glad of your support.* **3** very willing: *we are glad to help.* **4** *old use* bringing happiness: *glad tidings.* [from Anglo-Saxon *glæd*]

☰ 1 pleased, delighted, happy, contented. **3** willing, eager, keen, ready, inclined, disposed. **4** joyful, merry, cheerful.
☒ 1, 4 sad, unhappy. **3** unwilling, reluctant.

gladden *verb* (**gladdened, gladdening**) to make happy or pleased.

glade *noun literary* an open space in a wood or forest.

glad eye (**the glad eye**) *old slang use* a sexually inviting look: *giving me the glad eye.*

gladiator *noun* in ancient Rome, a man trained to fight against other men or animals in an arena. [from Latin *gladiator*, swordsman]

gladiatorial *adj.* relating to or involving gladiators.

gladiolus *noun* (PL. **gladiolus, gladioli, gladioluses**) **1** a perennial plant of the genus *Gladiolus*, native to S Europe and Africa, having a large fibrous corm, upright sword-shaped leaves, and spikes of funnel-shaped flowers in a variety of bright colours. **2** any of the one-sided spikes of flowers produced by this plant. [from Latin *gladiolus*, diminutive of *gladius*, sword]

gladly *adv.* with gladness, willingly.

glad rags *colloq.* one's best clothes, worn for special occasions.

glair *noun* egg-white, or a similar substance, used as a glaze or an adhesive. [from Old French *glaire*, perhaps from Latin *clarus*, clear]

glamorize or **glamorise** *verb* **1** to make glamorous. **2** to romanticize.

glamorous *adj.* full of glamour.

☰ smart, elegant, attractive, beautiful, gorgeous, enchanting, captivating, alluring, appealing, fascinating, exciting, dazzling, glossy, colourful.
☒ plain, drab, boring.

glamour *noun* **1** the quality of being fascinatingly, if perhaps falsely, attractive. **2** great beauty or sexual charm, especially created by make-up, clothes, etc. [a variant of GRAMMAR, arising from the medieval association of magic with learning]

☰ 1 attraction, allure, appeal, fascination, magic, glitter, prestige. **2** beauty, elegance, charm.

glance — *verb usually intrans.* **1** (*often* **glance at something** or **someone**) to look quickly or indirectly. **2** (**glance off something**) to be deflected by it. **3** *trans. said of a weapon* to hit (its target) obliquely. **4** to shine in flashes; to glint: *the sunlight glanced off the table.* — *noun* **1** a brief look, often indirect. **2** a deflection. **3** *literary* a brief flash of light. — **at a glance** at once; from one brief look: *could see at a glance that it was wrong.* **glance at** or **over something** to read or look at it cursorily. [from Middle English *glenten*]

☰ *verb* **1** peep, peek, look. *noun* **1** peep, peek, glimpse, look. **glance at** or **over** scan, skim, leaf through, dip into.

gland *noun* **1** *Zool.* in animals, an organ that produces a specific chemical substance, eg a hormone, for use inside the body (by direct release into the bloodstream, or into a tubular organ via a duct), or for release to the exterior. **2** *Bot.* in plants, a specialized cell or group of cells involved in the secretion of plant products such as nectar, oils, resins, and tannins. [from Latin *glans*, acorn]

glanders *sing. noun* a highly infectious disease of horses, donkeys, and mules, sometimes transmitted to humans, caused by the bacterium *Actinobacillus mallei*. [from Latin *glans*, acorn]

glandular or **glandulous** *adj.* relating to, containing, or affecting a gland or glands. [from French *glandulaire*]

glandular fever infectious mononucleosis.

glare — *verb intrans.* **1** to stare angrily. **2** to be unpleasantly bright or shiny. — *noun* **1** an angry stare. **2** dazzling light. **3** brash colour or decoration. [from Old Dutch *glaren*, to gleam]

☰ *verb* **1** stare, glower, look daggers, frown, scowl. **2** blaze, flame, flare, shine, reflect. *noun* **1** stare, look, black look, *colloq.* dirty look, frown, scowl. **2** brightness, brilliance, blaze, flame, dazzle, spotlight.

glaring *adj.* **1** unpleasantly bright. **2** obvious.

☰ 1 dazzling, bright, brilliant, blazing, flaming. **2** blatant, flagrant, conspicuous, manifest, patent, obvious, outrageous, gross.
☒ 1 dull. **2** hidden, concealed.

glasnost /ˈglaznɒst/ *noun* openness and willingness to provide information on the part of governments. [from Russian *glasnost*, speaking aloud, openness; originally used of the Soviet government under Mikhail Gorbachev]

glass — *noun* **1** a hard brittle non-crystalline material that is usually transparent or translucent. **2** an article made from this, eg a mirror, a lens, or especially a drinking cup. **3** the amount held by a drinking glass. **4** articles made of glass: *a collection of glass.* **5** (**glasses**) spectacles. — *adj.*

made of glass. — *verb* to supply or cover with glass. [from Anglo-Saxon *glæs*]

glass-blower *noun* a person who is skilled at glass-blowing.

glass-blowing *noun* the process of shaping molten glass by blowing air into it through a tube.

glass ceiling a barrier on the career ladder beyond which certain categories of employee, especially women, can see but not progress.

glass ceramic a type of strong hard glass, composed of lithium and magnesium aluminium silicates, that has a high level of heat and shock resistance, and is used to make moulded electrical and mechanical parts, and ovenware.

glass fibre glass melted and then drawn out into extremely fine fibres. Glass fibres set in plastic resin are used to make strong lightweight structures, eg some vehicle bodies.

glasshouse *noun* **1** a building with walls and roof constructed mainly or entirely of glass, inside which the temperature is usually maintained at a constant predetermined level, used for growing young or tender plants, and for growing plants out of season. Also called GREENHOUSE. **2** *slang* a military prison.

glasspaper *noun* paper coated with finely ground glass, used as an abrasive.

glass wool glass that has been spun into fine thread-like fibres, forming a wool-like mass, used in air filters, insulation, and packaging, and for making fibreglass.

glasswort /ˈglɑːswɜːt/ *noun* a fleshy annual plant (*Salicornia europaea*), widespread in salt marshes on European coasts, with scalelike leaves, and tiny greenish flowers, borne near the tip of the stem.

glassy *adj.* (**glassier, glassiest**) **1** like glass. **2** expressionless: *glassy eyes*.

⊟ **1** glasslike, smooth, slippery, icy, shiny, glossy, transparent, clear. **2** expressionless, blank, empty, vacant, dazed, fixed, glazed, cold, lifeless, dull.

Glaswegian /glɑːˈziːwiːdʒən, glazˈwiːdʒən/ — *noun* a native or citizen of Glasgow. — *adj.* of Glasgow or its inhabitants. [after *Norwegian*]

glaucoma /glɔːˈkəʊmə, glaʊˈkəʊmə/ *noun* any of various eye diseases in which increased pressure within the eyeball damages the optic nerve and the nerve fibres of the retina, causing impaired vision. If left untreated, it can lead to blindness. [from Greek *glaukoma*, cataract]

glaucous *adj.* **1** of a dull green or blue colour. **2** *Bot.* having a pale bluish-green waxy coating that can be rubbed off, eg the bloom of grapes. [from Greek *glaukos*, bluish-green or grey]

glaze — *verb* **1** to fit glass panes into (a window, door, etc). **2** to give a hard shiny transparent coating to (pottery, etc). **3** (*usually* **glaze over**) *said of the eyes* to become fixed and expressionless. **4** to apply a shiny coating of milk, eggs, or sugar to (eg pastry). — *noun* **1** a hard glassy coating on pottery, etc. **2** a shiny coating of milk, eggs, or sugar on food. [originally a variant of GLASS]

⊟ *verb* **2** coat, enamel, gloss, varnish, lacquer, polish. *noun* COAT, COATING. **1** enamel, varnish, lacquer, polish, shine, lustre, gloss, finish.

glazed *adj.* **1** fitted or covered with glass. **2** covered with a glaze. **3** stupefied: *a glazed look*.

glazier *noun* a person employed to glaze windows, doors, etc.

GLC *abbrev.* Greater London Council, abolished in 1986.

gleam — *noun* **1** a gentle glow. **2** a brief flash of (especially reflected) light. **3** a brief appearance or sign: *a gleam of excitement in his eyes*. — *verb intrans.* **1** to glow gently. **2** to shine with brief flashes of light. **3** *said of an emotion, etc* to be shown briefly. [from Anglo-Saxon *glæm*]

⊟ *noun* **1** glow, shimmer. **2** glint, flash, beam, ray, sparkle, glitter. **3** flicker, glimmer. *verb* **1** glow, shimmer, glimmer. **2** glint, flash, glance, flare, shine, glitter, sparkle.

gleaming *adj.* shining.

glean *verb* **1** to collect (information, etc) bit by bit, often with difficulty. **2** *trans., intrans.* to collect (loose grain and other useful remnants of a crop left in a field) after harvesting. [from Old French *glener*]

gleanings *pl. noun* things gleaned, especially bits of information.

glebe *noun* **1** a piece of church-owned land providing income in rent, etc for the resident minister. **2** *poetic* land; a field. [from Latin *gleba*, clod]

glee *noun* **1** great delight; joy. **2** a song with different parts for three or four unaccompanied (especially male) voices. [from Anglo-Saxon *gleo*, mirth]

glee club especially in the US, a society of singers of glees.

gleeful *adj.* joyful; merry.

glen *noun* a long narrow valley, especially in Scotland. [from Gaelic *gleann*]

glengarry *noun* (PL. **glengarries**) a narrow brimless cap creased along its middle and usually with two ribbons hanging at the back. [from *Glengarry* in Inverness-shire]

glib *adj.* (**glibber, glibbest**) *derog.* speaking or spoken readily and persuasively, but neither sincere nor reliable: *glib politicians* / *glib explanations*. [from Old German *glibberich*, slippery]

⊟ facile, easy, quick, ready, talkative, plausible, persuasive, insincere, smooth, slick, suave, fluent.
⊟ tongue-tied, implausible.

glide — *verb intrans.* **1** to move smoothly: *glide along the ice*. **2** *said of a bird* to travel through the air without beating its wings. **3** *said of an aircraft* to travel through the air or to land without engine power. **4** to travel through the air by glider. **5** to pass gradually: *glide into sleep*. — *noun* **1** a gliding movement. **2** the controlled descent of an aircraft without engine power. **3** *Mus.* movement from one note to another with no break in sound. [from Anglo-Saxon *glidan*, to slip]

⊟ *verb* **1** slide, slip, skate, skim, fly, float, drift, sail, coast, roll, run, flow.

glider *noun* **1** an aircraft with fixed wings, designed to glide and soar in air currents without using any form of engine power. **2** any of various small marsupials native to Australia, capable of gliding through the air for long distances by extending a membrane of skin attached to the sides of the body.

glimmer — *verb intrans.* (**glimmered, glimmering**) to glow faintly. — *noun* **1** a faint glow; a twinkle. **2** a hint or trace: *a glimmer of hope*. [from Middle English *glemern*]

⊟ *verb* glow, shimmer, glisten, glitter, sparkle, twinkle, wink, blink, flicker, gleam, shine. *noun* **1** glow, shimmer, sparkle, twinkle, glint. **2** trace, hint, suggestion, flicker, gleam.

glimpse — *noun* a very brief look. — *verb* to see momentarily. [from Middle English *glymsen*]

⊟ *noun* peep, peek, squint, glance, look, sight, sighting, view. *verb* spy, espy, spot, catch sight of, sight, view.

glint — *verb intrans.* to give off flashes of bright light. — *noun* a brief flash of light. [from Middle English *glent*]

⊟ *verb* flash, gleam, shine, reflect, glitter, sparkle, twinkle, glimmer. *noun* flash, gleam, shine, reflection, glitter, sparkle, twinkle, glimmer.

....

glissade /glɪ'seɪd, glɪ'sɑːd/ — *noun* **1** a sliding ballet step. **2** *Mountaineering* an act of sliding down a snowy or icy slope. — *verb intrans.* to perform a glissade. [from French *glissade*, from *glisser*, to slide]

glissando /glɪ'sandoʊ/ (ABBREV. **gliss.**) *noun* (PL. **glissandi**, **glissandos**) *Mus.* a sliding from one note to another. The term is found on musical scores and the effect is produced on different instruments by a variety of methods. [from Italian *glissando*, from French *glissant*, sliding]

glisten *verb intrans.* (**glistened**, **glistening**) *usually said of something wet, icy, etc* to shine or sparkle. [from Middle English *glistnen*]

....

▣ *verb* shine, gleam, glint, glitter, sparkle, twinkle, glimmer, shimmer.

....

glitch *noun colloq.* a sudden brief irregularity or failure to function, especially in electronic equipment. [perhaps from Yiddish *glitsh*, slip]

glitter — *verb intrans.* (**glittered**, **glittering**) **1** to shine with bright flashes of light; to sparkle. **2** *colloq.* to be sparklingly attractive or resplendent: *a party glittering with famous film stars.* — *noun* **1** sparkle. **2** *colloq.* bright attractiveness, often superficial. **3** tiny pieces of shiny material, especially silvery paper, used for decoration. [from Middle English *gliteren*]

....

▣ *verb* **1** sparkle, spangle, scintillate, twinkle, shimmer, glimmer, glisten, glint, gleam, flash, coruscate, shine. *noun* **1** sparkle, scintillation, twinkle, shimmer, glimmer, glint, gleam, flash, coruscation, shine, lustre, sheen, brightness, radiance. **2** brilliance, splendour, showiness, glamour, tinsel.

....

glitterati *pl. noun colloq.* famous, fashionable, and beautiful people. [from GLITTER, after LITERATI]

glittering *adj.* shining brightly; sparkling.

glitz *noun* showiness, garishness.

glitzy *adj.* (**glitzier**, **glitziest**) *derog. slang* extravagantly showy; flashy. [perhaps from German *glitzern*, to glitter]

gloaming *noun poetic, Scot.* dusk; twilight. [from Anglo-Saxon *glomung*]

gloat — *verb intrans.* (*often* **gloat over something**) to feel or show smug or vindictive satisfaction, especially in one's own success or in another's misfortune. — *noun* an act of gloating. [perhaps from Norse *glotta*, to grin]

....

▣ *verb* triumph, glory, exult, rejoice, crow, boast, *colloq.* rub it in.

....

glob *noun colloq.* a small amount of thick liquid; a blob or dollop. [perhaps from BLOB]

global *adj.* **1** affecting the whole world. **2** total; including everything. **3** globe-shaped.

....

▣ **1** worldwide, international, universal. **2** general, total, all-inclusive, all-encompassing, thorough, exhaustive, comprehensive, encyclopedic, wide-ranging.
▣ **1** local. **2** limited, restricted.

....

globalize or **globalise** *verb trans., intrans.* to make or become international, especially with regard to economic and trade links.

global warming a gradual increase in the average temperature of the Earth's surface and its atmosphere, attributed to the greenhouse effect.

globe *noun* **1** (**the globe**) the earth. **2** a sphere with a map of the world on it. **3** any ball-shaped object, eg a glass lampshade. [from Latin *globus*]

....

▣ **1** the world, the earth. **3** sphere, ball, orb, round.

globe artichoke 1 a tall perennial plant (*Cynara scolymus*) with deeply divided leaves and large purplish-blue flowers, native to the Mediterranean region, and widely cultivated in temperate regions for the edible fleshy bracts that form the base of the unopened flower-heads. It is also grown as an ornamental plant. **2** the fleshy base of the immature flower-head of this plant, eaten as a vegetable.

globeflower *noun* a poisonous, perennial plant (*Trollius europaeus*), native to Europe and N America, having large (usually solitary) almost spherical flowers borne on long stalks.

globetrotter *noun colloq.* a person who travels all over the world.

globetrotting *noun* travelling the world as a sightseer.

globin /'gloʊbɪn/ *noun Biochem.* in animals, any of a group of soluble proteins that are present in the iron-containing pigments haemoglobin (in red blood cells) and myoglobin (in muscle cells). [from Latin *globus*, sphere]

globular *adj.* **1** shaped like a globe or globule. **2** consisting of globules. [from Latin *globulus*, diminutive of *globus*, globe]

globular cluster *Astron.* a spherical or nearly spherical dense cluster of hundreds of thousands to millions of very old stars that formed at an early stage in the development of the galaxies.

globule *noun* a small drop, especially of liquid.

globulin *noun Biol.* any of a group of single proteins, found in blood plasma, eggs, and milk, and as storage proteins in plant seeds, that are soluble in certain salt solutions and coagulated by heat.

glockenspiel /'glɒkənspiːl, 'glɒkənʃpiːl/ *noun* a musical instrument consisting of tuned metal plates in a frame, played with two small hammers. [from German *Glocke*, bell + *Spiel*, play]

glom *verb North Amer. slang* (**glomming**, **glommed**) to snatch or steal (something). — **glom on to** to become attached or catch on to. [possibly from Scots *glaum*]

glomerulus /glɒ'merjʊləs/ *noun* (PL. **glomeruli**) *Anat.* in the kidney, a small ball of blood capillaries surrounded by the cup-shaped end (*Bowman's capsule*) of a kidney tubule. [from Latin *glomus, glomeris*, a ball of yarn]

gloom — *noun* **1** near-darkness. **2** sadness or despair. — *verb* **1** (*intrans.*) *said of the sky* to be dark and threatening. **2** (*intrans.*) to behave in a sad or depressed way. **3** to make dark. **4** to make depressed or depressing. [from Middle English *gloumbe*]

....

▣ *noun* **1** dark, darkness, shade, shadow, dusk, twilight, dimness, obscurity, cloud, cloudiness, dullness. **2** sadness, unhappiness, glumness, low spirits, despondency, dejection, depression, melancholy, misery, desolation, despair.
▣ *noun* **1** brightness. **2** happiness, cheerfulness.

....

gloomily *adv.* in a gloomy way.

gloomy *adj.* (**gloomier**, **gloomiest**) **1** dark, dimly lit. **2** causing gloom. **3** sad, depressed.

....

▣ **1** dark, sombre, shadowy, dim, obscure, overcast, dull. **2** cheerless, dreary, dismal, depressing. **3** sad, miserable, glum, morose, depressed, down, low, despondent, dejected, downcast, downhearted, dispirited, pessimistic.
▣ **1** bright. **2, 3** cheerful.

....

glorification *noun* the act of glorifying or the state of being glorified.

glorified *adj. derog.* given a fancy name or appearance.

glorify *verb* (**glorifies**, **glorified**) **1** to exaggerate the beauty, importance, etc of. **2** to praise or worship (God). **3** to make glorious. [from Latin *gloria*, glory + *facere*, to make]

glorious *adj.* **1** having or bringing glory. **2** splendidly beautiful. **3** *colloq.* excellent. **4** *humorous colloq.* very bad: *glorious mess*.

⊟ **1** illustrious, eminent, distinguished, famous, renowned, noted, great, noble, grand, majestic, triumphant. **2** splendid, magnificent, fine, bright, radiant, shining, brilliant, dazzling, beautiful, gorgeous. **3** excellent, superb, wonderful, marvellous, delightful, heavenly.

glorious twelfth (**the glorious twelfth**) 12 Aug, the opening day of the grouse-shooting season.

glory — *noun* (PL. **glories**) **1** great honour and prestige. **2** great beauty or splendour. **3** praise and thanks given to God. **4** a greatly admired asset: *patience is her crowning glory*. — *verb intrans.* (**glories**, **gloried**) (**glory in something**) to feel or show great delight or pride in it. [from Latin *gloria*]

⊟ *noun* **1** honour, prestige, kudos, triumph, fame, renown, celebrity, illustriousness, greatness, eminence, distinction. **2** brightness, radiance, brilliance, beauty, splendour, resplendence, magnificence, grandeur, majesty, dignity. **3** praise, homage, tribute, worship, veneration, adoration, exaltation, blessing, thanksgiving, gratitude.

glory-hole *noun colloq.* a room or cupboard where odds and ends are kept, especially in a disorganized way. [perhaps from Middle English *glory*, to defile]

Glos. *abbrev.* Gloucestershire.

gloss[1] — *noun* **1** shiny brightness on a surface. **2** a superficial pleasantness or attractiveness. **3** (*also* **gloss paint**) paint which produces a shiny finish. **4** a substance which adds shine: *lip gloss*. — *verb* **1** to give a shiny finish to. **2** to paint with gloss. — **gloss over** to conceal, especially by treating briefly and dismissively.

⊟ *noun* **1** polish, varnish, lustre, sheen, shine, brightness, brilliance. **2** show, semblance, surface, front, façade, veneer, window-dressing. **gloss over** conceal, hide, veil, mask, disguise, camouflage, cover up, whitewash, explain away.

gloss[2] — *noun* a short explanation of a difficult word, phrase, etc in a text, eg in the margin. — *verb* to provide a gloss of (a word, etc), or add glosses to (a text). [from Latin *glossa*, word requiring explanation]

⊟ *noun* annotation, note, footnote, explanation, elucidation, interpretation, translation, definition, comment, commentary. *verb* annotate, explain, elucidate, interpret, construe, translate, define, comment.

glossary *noun* (PL. **glossaries**) a list of glosses, often at the end of a book.

glossily *adv.* with a gloss.

glossiness *noun* being glossy.

glossolalia /glɒsoʊˈleɪlɪə/ *noun* 'speaking in tongues': the phenomenon of spontaneously uttering unintelligible sounds believed to form part of an unknown language or languages, and considered by certain Christians, especially Pentecostalists and charismatic Catholics, to be a manifestation of the Holy Spirit in believers and converts. See also XENOGLOSSIA. [from Greek *glossa*, tongue + *laleein*, to talk]

glossopharyngeal /glɒsoʊfarənˈdʒiːəl/ *adj. Anat.* denoting the ninth cranial nerve of vertebrates, which contains motor nerve fibres that supply two triangular salivary glands (known as *parotid glands*) and part of the pharynx, and sensory nerve fibres that supply the back of the tongue and the soft palate. [from Greek *glossa*, tongue + PHARYNGEAL]

glossy *adj.* (**glossier**, **glossiest**) **1** smooth and shiny. **2** superficially attractive. **3** *said of a magazine* printed on glossy paper.

⊟ **1** shiny, lustrous, sleek, silky, smooth, glassy, polished, burnished, glazed, enamelled, bright, shining, brilliant.
⊟ **1** matt.

glottal *adj. technical* of or produced by the glottis.

glottal stop *Linguistics* a sound produced when the glottis is closed and then opened sharply, eg the sound substituted for a 't' in words such as 'bottle' in some pronunciations of English.

glottis *noun* (PL. **glottises**, **glottides**) *Anat.* the opening through which air passes from the pharynx (back of the throat) to the trachea (windpipe), including the space between the vocal cords. [from Latin *glotta*, tongue]

glottochronology *noun Linguistics* a statistical study of vocabulary to determine the degree of relationship between two languages, how far and at what rate the languages may have diverged from a common source over the centuries, and the time-scale of their independent development. [from Greek *glotta*, tongue + *chronos*, time]

glove — *noun* a covering for the hand, usually with a separate sheath for each finger. — *verb* to cover with a glove or gloves. — **fit like a glove** to fit perfectly. **the gloves are off** *colloq.* the serious argument, fight, etc is about to begin. [from Anglo-Saxon *glof*]

glover *noun* a glove-maker.

glow — *verb intrans.* **1** to give out a steady heat or light without flames. **2** to shine brightly, as if very hot: *cheeks glowing with health*. **3** to feel or communicate a sensation of intense contentment or well-being: *glow with pride*. — *noun* **1** a steady flameless heat or light. **2** bright, shiny appearance. **3** intensity of (especially pleasant) feeling. [from Anglo-Saxon *glowan*]

⊟ *verb* **1** shine, radiate, gleam, glimmer, burn, smoulder. **2** flush, blush, colour, redden. *noun* **1** light, gleam, glimmer, radiance, luminosity. **2** brightness, vividness, brilliance, splendour. **3** intensity, warmth, ardour, fervour, passion, enthusiasm, excitement.

glower — *verb intrans.* (**glowered**, **glowering**) to stare angrily. — *noun* an angry stare; a scowl.

⊟ *verb* stare, glare, look daggers, frown, scowl. *noun* stare, glare, black look, *colloq.* dirty look, frown, scowl.

glowing *adj.* **1** which glows. **2** full of praise: *glowing report*.

⊟ **1** bright, luminous, vivid, vibrant, rich, warm, flushed, red, flaming. **2** complimentary, enthusiastic, ecstatic, rhapsodic, *colloq.* rave.
⊟ **1** dull.

glow-worm *noun* **1** a small nocturnal beetle belonging to the same family as the fireflies, and found mainly in warm climates. At night the wingless female attracts the winged male by giving out a bright greenish light from organs on the underside of her abdomen. **2** in N America, any of various luminous insect larvae.

gloxinia *noun* any of various species of plant belonging to the genus *Siningia*, native to Brazil, and having large velvety funnel-shaped white, pink, red, or purple flowers. [from Gloxin, the name of a German botanist]

glucagon /ˈɡluːkəɡɒn/ *noun Biochem.* a hormone secreted by the pancreas which accelerates the conversion of glycogen to glucose in the liver, so increasing blood glucose levels. [from Greek *glykys*, sweet]

glucose *noun* **1** *Biochem.* (FORMULA $C_6H_{12}O_6$) the most abundant six-carbon sugar (hexose) in living cells. In animals it is the main form in which energy obtained from the digestion of carbohydrates is transported around the bloodstream, and in plants it is the initial product of photosynthesis. **2** (*also* **glucose syrup**) a concentrated solution of the products of breakdown of starch, used in the confectionery industry, for canning fruit, etc. [from Greek *glykys*, sweet]

glucoside *noun Biochem.* any of various derivatives of glucose, in which the first hydroxyl (–OH) group is replaced by another group, and which on treatment with enzymes or acids yields glucose.

glue — *noun* any adhesive obtained by extracting natural substances, especially bone, in boiling water, or by dissolving synthetic substances such as rubber or plastic in a suitable solvent. — *verb* (**glueing, gluing**) **1** to use such an adhesive to stick two materials together. **2** *colloq.* to put or stay very close to; to fix on: *eyes glued to the window.* [from Latin *glus*]

■ *noun* adhesive, gum, paste, size, cement. *verb* **1** stick, affix, gum, paste, seal, bond, cement.

glue-sniffer *noun* a person who practises glue-sniffing.
glue-sniffing *noun* the practice of breathing in fumes from some types of glue to produce hallucinatory or intoxicating effects.
gluey *adj.* (**gluier, gluiest**) containing glue; like glue, sticky.
glum *adj.* (**glummer, glummest**) in low spirits; sullen. [from Middle English *glome*, to frown]

■ sullen, gloomy, sad, miserable, despondent.

glume *noun Bot.* an outer sterile bract which, alone or with others, encloses the spikelet in grasses and sedges. [from Latin *gluma*, husk]
gluon *noun Physics* a hypothetical particle with no mass, the carrier of the force that is believed to hold quarks together.
glut — *noun* **1** an excessive supply of goods, etc. **2** an act of eating an unreasonably or unnecessarily large amount of food. — *verb* (**glutted, glutting**) **1** to feed or supply to excess. **2** to block or choke up. [from Latin *glutire*, to swallow]

■ *noun* **1** surplus, excess, superfluity, surfeit, overabundance, superabundance, saturation, overflow.
☒ *noun* **1** scarcity, lack.

glutamine *noun Biochem.* an amino acid found in proteins.[from Latin *gluten*, glue]
gluten *noun Biochem.* a mixture of two plant storage proteins, *gliadin* and *glutenin*, that occurs in wheat flour. When mixed with water and kneaded, these proteins give bread dough elastic properties, and also allow it to rise as gas bubbles are trapped by the gluten. [from Latin *gluten*, glue]
glutinous *adj.* like glue; sticky.
glutton[1] *noun* **1** *derog.* a person who eats too much. **2** a person whose behaviour suggests an eagerness (for something unpleasant): *a glutton for hard work.* — **a glutton for punishment** a person who is eager to undertake difficult or arduous tasks. [from Latin *gluttire*, to swallow]

■ **1** gourmand, guzzler, gorger, gobbler, pig.

glutton[2] same as **WOLVERINE**.
gluttonous *adj.* greedy.
gluttony *noun derog.* the habit or practice of eating too much.

■ greed, greediness, voracity, insatiability, piggishness.

glyceride *noun Chem.* an ester of glycerol and up to three fatty acid molecules. Triglycerides are the main components of fats and oils.
glycerine or **glycerin** see GLYCEROL.
glycerol *noun Chem.* a colourless viscous liquid with a sweet taste, soluble in water, that is an important constituent of fats and oils, and can be obtained from all vegetable and animal fats and oils by hydrolysis. It is used in various foodstuffs and medicines, and in the manufacture of the explosive nitroglycerine. Also called GLYCERINE. [from Greek *glykeros*, sweet]
glycine or **glycin** *noun Biochem.* an amino acid found in proteins. [from Greek *glykys*, sweet]
glycogen *noun Biochem.* in vertebrates, the main form in which carbohydrate is stored, especially in the liver and muscles. It is also found in invertebrates, and in some algae and fungi. Also called ANIMAL STARCH, AMYLUM. [from Greek *glykys*, sweet + -GEN]
glycogenic *adj.* **1** of or relating to glycogen. **2** of or relating to the biochemical processes whereby carbohydrates are produced, or glucose is converted into glycogen.
glycolysis *noun Biochem.* during respiration in the cells of living organisms, the conversion of glucose to pyruvic acid, with the release of energy in the form of ATP.
GM *abbrev.* **1** genetically modified. **2** George Medal.
gm *abbrev.* gram or gramme.
GMBATU *abbrev.* General, Municipal, Boilermakers and Allied Trades Union.
GMC *abbrev.* General Medical Council.
GMO *abbrev.* genetically modified organism.
GMT *abbrev.* Greenwich Mean Time.
GMWU *abbrev.* General and Municipal Workers Union.
gnarled /nɑːld/ or **gnarly** /'nɑːlɪ/ *adj.*, *said of tree trunks, branches, human hands, etc* twisted, with knotty swellings, usually as a result of age. [from Middle English *knarre*, knob-like protuberance]

■ knotted, knotty, twisted, contorted, distorted, rough, rugged, weather-beaten.

gnash /naʃ/ *verb trans.*, *intrans.* to grind (the teeth) together, especially in anger. [from Middle English *gnasten*]
gnashers /'naʃəz/ *pl. noun humorous slang* teeth.
gnat /nat/ *noun* **1** any of various small fragile biting flies. **2** (*in full* **winter gnat**) a small delicate fly, found at most times of year, and particularly noticeable on winter afternoons when the males dance up and down in conspicuous swarms low over water or in woodland clearings. **3** a mosquito. [from Anglo-Saxon *gnætt*]
gnaw /nɔː/ *verb* (PAST PARTICIPLE **gnawed, gnawn**) **1** (**gnaw something** or **gnaw at something**) to bite it with a scraping action, causing a gradual wearing away. **2** to make (eg a hole) in this way. **3** *trans.*, *intrans.* (**gnaw someone** or **gnaw at someone**) *said of pain, anxiety, etc* to trouble them persistently: *is gnawed by guilt.* [from Anglo-Saxon *gnagan*]

■ **1** bite, nibble, munch, chew, eat, devour, consume, erode, wear. **3** trouble, plague, haunt, nag, worry, niggle.

gnawing *adj.* that gnaws.
gneiss /naɪs/ *noun Geol.* a coarse-grained metamorphic rock that contains bands of quartz and feldspar alternating with bands of mica. [from German *Gneis*]
gnocchi /'njɒkɪ/ *pl. noun* an Italian dish of small dumplings made with flour, cooked potato, or semolina, poached and served with various sauces. [from Italian *gnocchi*, lumps]
gnome /noʊm/ *noun* **1** a fairy-tale creature, a small misshapen man, who lives underground, often guarding treasure. **2** a statue of such a creature, especially as a garden ornament. **3** *colloq.* a person with a secret powerful influence, especially in finance: *gnomes of Zurich.* [from Latin *gnomus*, dwarf]

gnomic /'nəʊmɪk/ *adj. formal, said of speech or writing* **1** expressing generally held views or principles. **2** *often derog.* moralizing. [from Greek *gnome*, opinion]

gnomish /'nəʊmɪʃ/ *adj.* like a gnome.

gnostic /'nɒstɪk/ — *adj.* **1** relating to knowledge, especially mystical or religious knowledge. **2** (*usually* **Gnostic**) relating to Gnosticism. — *noun* (*usually* **Gnostic**) an early Christian heretic believing in redemption of the soul from the world of matter through special religious knowledge. [from Greek *gnosis*, knowledge]

Gnosticism /'nɒstɪsɪzm/ *noun* a system of belief prominent within 2c Christianity, but which may have had earlier, non-Christian roots. It emphasized salvation through the acquisition of secret revealed knowledge about cosmic origins and the true destiny of the spirit within people; in later forms, this knowledge was imparted by a heavenly redeemer figure.

GNP *abbrev.* gross national product.

gnu /nuː/ *noun* (PL. **gnus, gnu**) either of two species of large grazing antelope, native to grasslands of Africa. Also called WILDEBEEST. [from Hottentot]

go[1] — *verb usually intrans.* (**goes**; PAST TENSE **went**; PAST PARTICIPLE **gone**) **1** (*often* **go about, by, down**, etc) to walk, move, or travel in the direction specified. **2** to lead or extend: *a path going across the field* / *the road goes all the way to the farm.* **3** (**go to somewhere**) to visit or attend it, once or regularly: *go to the cinema* / *go to school.* **4** to leave or move away. **5** to be destroyed or taken away; to disappear: *the old door had to go* / *the peaceful atmosphere has gone.* **6** to proceed or fare: *the scheme is going well.* **7** to be used up: *money going on drink.* **8** to be given or sold for a stated amount: *went for £20.* **9** to leave or set out for a stated purpose: *go for a ride* / *go on holiday* / *gone fishing.* **10** *intrans., trans.* to perform (an action) or produce (a sound): *go like this* / *go bang.* **11** to break, break down, or fail: *the old TV finally went* / *his eyes have gone.* **12** to work or be in working order: *get it going.* **13** to become; to pass into a certain condition: *go mad.* **14** to belong; to be placed correctly: *where does this go?* **15** to fit, or be contained: *my foot won't go into the shoe* / *four into three won't go.* **16** to continue in a certain state: *go hungry.* **17** *said of time* to pass. **18** to run in words or notes: *as the story goes.* **19** (*often* **go for someone** or **something**) to apply to them; to be valid or accepted for them: *the same goes for you* / *in this office, anything goes.* **20** *colloq.* to carry authority: *what she says goes.* **21** (*often* **go with something**) *said of colours, etc* to match or blend. **22** (**go with something**) to co-exist with it: *goodness doesn't always go with beauty.* **23** (**go by something**) to be guided by it: *don't go by what he says.* **24** to subject oneself: *go to much trouble.* **25** to adopt a system: *go metric.* **26** *trans.* to bet, especially at cards: *went five pounds.* **27** *colloq.* to be in general, for the purpose of comparison: *as girls go, she's quite naughty.* **28** to exist or be on offer: *the best offer going at the moment.* **29** *trans. colloq.* to welcome or enjoy: *I could go a cup of tea.* **30** *trans. colloq., usually with quoted speech* to say. — *noun* (PL. **goes**) **1** a turn or spell: *it's my go.* **2** an attempt: *have a go.* **3** energy; liveliness: *she lacks go.* **4** a verbal attack: *really had a go at me.* **5** *colloq.* busy activity: *it's all go.* **6** *colloq.* a success: *make a go of it.* — *adj. colloq.* working properly; in operation: *all systems go.* — **be going on for (a stated age)** *colloq.* to be approaching it: *she's going on for 60.* **go about 1** to circulate: *a rumour going about.* **2** *Naut.* to change course. **go about something 1** to busy oneself with it. **2** to attempt or tackle it: *how to go about doing this.* **go against something** to be contrary to it. **go against someone** to be decided unfavourably for them: *the court case went against him.* **go ahead** to proceed. **go all out for something** to make a great effort to obtain or achieve it. **go along with someone** or **something** to agree with and support them. **go and ...** to be so unwise or unfortunate as to: *they've gone and got lost.* **go back on something** to break an agreement, etc. **go down 1** to decrease. **2** *colloq.* to be accepted or received: *the joke went down well.* **go down with something** to contract an illness. **go for someone** or **something** *colloq.* **1** to attack them. **2** to be attracted by them. **3** to choose them: *went for the red shoes instead.* **go**

in for something *colloq.* **1** to take up a profession. **2** to enter a contest. **3** to be interested or attracted by something, as a rule. **go into something 1** to take up or join a profession. **2** to discuss or investigate something: *cannot go into that now.* **go it alone** *colloq.* to manage or try to manage without help, especially in difficulties. **go off 1** to explode. **2** *said of perishables, eg food* to become rotten. **3** to proceed or pass off: *the party went off well.* **go off someone** or **something** to stop liking them. **go on 1** to continue or proceed. **2** *colloq.* to talk too much. **3** to happen or take place: *what's going on?* / *find out what went on at the meeting.* **go on at someone** *colloq.* to criticize them or complain to them persistently. **go out 1** *said of a fire or light* to become extinguished. **2** to be broadcast. **3** to no longer be fashionable. **go out to someone** to feel sympathy for them: *my heart went out to him.* **go out with someone** to spend time with someone socially or especially romantically. **go over** to pass off or be received: *the play went over well.* **go over something 1** to examine it. **2** to revise or rehearse it. **go over to someone** to transfer support or allegiance: *go over to the enemy.* **go round** to be enough for all. **go slow** to work slowly so as to encourage an employer to negotiate or meet a demand. **go through** to be approved. **go through something 1** to use it up. **2** to revise or rehearse it. **3** to examine it. **4** to suffer from it: *went through hell.* **5** to search it: *went through all our bags.* **go through with something** to carry it out to the end. **go under** *colloq.* to fail or be ruined. **go up 1** to increase. **2** *said of a building, etc* to be erected. **3** *colloq.* to be destroyed by fire or explosion. **go with someone** *colloq.* to have a close romantic friendship with them. **go with something** to agree with or support it. **go without something** to suffer a lack of an essential thing or things. **have something going for one** *colloq.* to have as an attribute or advantage: *you have a lot going for you.* **no go** *colloq.* not possible; in vain. **on the go** *colloq.* busily active. **to be going on with** *colloq.* for the moment: *enough to be going on with.* [from Anglo-Saxon *gan*]

....

⊟ *verb* **1** move, pass, travel, journey. *go down* descend, sink, set, fall, drop. *go up* ascend, climb, scale, mount. **2** lead, extend, spread, stretch, reach, span. **4** depart, leave, retreat, withdraw, go away, set out, start, begin. **5** disappear, vanish. **6** proceed, fare, get on, advance, progress. **12** operate, function, work, run. **13** become, turn, get, grow. **17** pass, elapse, lapse, roll on, go by. **21** match, harmonize, co-ordinate, blend, complement, suit, fit, correspond. **23** heed, observe, follow, comply with. *noun* **2** attempt, try, *colloq.* shot, *colloq.* bash, *colloq.* stab. **3** energy, *colloq.* get-up-and-go, vitality, life, spirit, dynamism. **go about something 2** tackle, approach, address, begin, set about, attend to, undertake, engage in. **go ahead** proceed, carry on, continue, advance, progress. **go along with** agree with, support, back, endorse. **go down 1** decrease, fall, drop, diminish, decline, deteriorate, degenerate. **go for 1** attack, assail, set about, lunge at. **2** like, admire, enjoy. **3** choose, opt for, prefer, favour. **go in for 1** take up, embrace, adopt, undertake, practise, pursue, follow. **2** enter, take part in, participate, engage in. **go into 2** discuss, consider, examine, study, investigate, inquire into, check out, probe, delve into, analyse. **go off 1** explode, blow up, detonate. **2** deteriorate, turn, sour, go bad, rot. **go on 1** continue, carry on, proceed, persist, stay, endure, last. **2** chatter, *colloq.* rabbit, *colloq.* witter, ramble on. **3** happen, occur, take place. **go over something 1** examine, peruse, study, read, inspect, check. **2** revise, rehearse, practise, repeat. **go through something 1** use, consume, exhaust, spend, squander. **3** examine, study, investigate, check. **4** suffer, undergo, experience, endure, withstand. **5** search, look through, rummage through, rifle. **go under** fail, founder, collapse, *colloq.* fold. **go up 1** increase, rise, mount, soar, escalate. **go without** lack, want, need, do without, forego, abstain from.

go *verb* **1** stop. **4** arrive. **12** break down, fail. **21** clash. **go down 1** increase. **go up 1** decrease.

go² *noun* a Japanese board game for two players, played with black and white pieces. The object is to capture one's opponent's pieces and control the larger part of the board. [from Japanese]

goad — *verb* (**goad someone into something** or **to do something**) to urge or provoke. — *noun* **1** a sharp-pointed stick used for driving cattle, etc. **2** anything that provokes or incites. [from Anglo-Saxon *gad*]

verb provoke, incite, instigate, stimulate, prompt, urge, spur, impel, push, drive, nag, hound, harass, annoy, irritate, vex.

go-ahead *colloq.* — *adj.* energetically ambitious and far-sighted. — *noun* (**the go-ahead**) permission to start.

adj. ambitious, up-and-coming, dynamic, energetic, enterprising, far-sighted, pioneering, progressive. *noun* permission, authorization, clearance, *colloq.* green light, sanction, assent, consent, *colloq.* OK, agreement. *adj.* unenterprising, sluggish. *noun* ban, veto, embargo.

goal *noun* **1** a set of posts with a crossbar, through which the ball is struck to achieve a score in various sports, especially football; also more generally, the area in which the goal stands. **2** an act of scoring in this way; the point or points scored. **3** an aim or purpose: *one must have a goal in life.* [perhaps from Middle English *gol*, boundary]

3 aim, intention, object, purpose, target, mark, objective, end, ambition, aspiration.

goalie *noun colloq.* a goalkeeper.

goalkeeper *noun* the player guarding the goal in various sports, with the task of preventing the opposition from scoring.

goal-line *noun* the line marking each end of the field of play in some sports.

goalpost *noun* each of two upright posts forming the goal in some sports. — **move the goalposts** to change the accepted rules or aims of an activity during its course, to suit new conditions.

goat *noun* **1** any of a number of species of herbivorous mammal (*Capra hircus*) belonging to the family Bovidae, related to the sheep, and characterized by the presence of a beard in the male. **2** *derog. colloq.* a man, especially if old, who makes unwanted sexual advances to women. **3** *derog. colloq.* a foolish person. — **get someone's goat** *colloq.* to annoy or irritate them. [from Anglo-Saxon *gat*]

goatee /goʊˈtiː/ *noun* a pointed beard growing on the front of the chin only, like a goat's.

goatherd *noun* a person who looks after goats.

goatish *adj.* **1** like a goat. **2** stupid. **3** lustful.

gob — *noun* **1** *coarse slang* the mouth. **2** a soft wet lump. **3** *coarse slang* spit. — *verb intrans.* (**gobbed, gobbing**) *coarse slang* to spit. [from Old French *gober*, to gulp down]

gobbet *noun* **1** a lump or chunk. **2** *colloq.* an extract from a text. [from Old French *gobet*, diminutive of *gobe*, mouthful]

gobble — *verb* **1** (*usually* **gobble something up** or **down**) to eat it hurriedly and noisily. **2** *intrans.* to eat in this manner. **3** *intrans.*, *said of a male turkey* to make a loud gurgling sound in the throat. — *noun* the loud gurgling sound made by a male turkey. [from Old French *gober*, to gulp down]

verb **1** bolt, guzzle, devour, consume, *colloq.* put away, swallow, gulp.

gobbledygook or **gobbledegook** /ˈgɒbldɪguːk/ *noun colloq, usually derog.* **1** official jargon, meaningless to ordinary people. **2** nonsense; rubbish. [imitative, after GOBBLE]

gobbler *noun North Amer., esp. US* a male turkey.

go-between *noun* a messenger between two people or sides; an intermediary.

messenger, intermediary, mediator, liaison, contact, middleman, broker, dealer, agent, medium.

goblet *noun* a drinking-cup with a base and stem but no handles, often made from metal or glass. [from Old French *gobelet*, diminutive of *gobel*, cup]

goblin *noun* in folk-tales, an evil or mischievous spirit in the form of a small man. [from Old French *gobelin*, perhaps from Greek *kobalos*, mischievous spirit]

gobsmacked *adj. colloq.* astonished; dumbfounded.

gobstopper *noun colloq.* a large round sweet for sucking.

goby /ˈgoʊbɪ/ *noun* (PL. **goby, gobies**) any of about 2,000 species of small usually colourful marine fish, most of which are native to shallow waters of temperate and tropical seas and estuaries (although a few inhabit fresh water), having an elongated tapering scaly body, large eyes, and fleshy lips. [from Latin *gobius*, gudgeon]

go-by *noun* — **give someone the go-by** *colloq.* to ignore or snub them.

god *noun* **1** in many beliefs, a divine or superhuman being with power over nature and the human race, and often an object of worship. **2** (**God**) in the Christian and other religions, the supreme being and creator of the universe and the human race, an object of worship. **3** a man greatly admired, especially for his fine physique or wide influence. **4** *often derog.* an object of excessive worship or influence: *he made money his god.* — **the gods** the area of the balcony or upper circle in a theatre. [from Anglo-Saxon *god*]

1 deity, divinity, idol, spirit, power. **2** Supreme Being, Creator, Providence, Lord, Almighty, Holy One, Jehovah, Yahweh, Allah, Brahma, Zeus.

godchild *noun* a child for whom a godparent is responsible.

goddaughter *noun* a female godchild.

goddess *noun* **1** a superhuman feminine being with power over nature and man, an object of worship. **2** a woman greatly admired for her great beauty or wide influence.

1 deity, divinity, idol, spirit, power.

godfather *noun* **1** a male godparent. **2** the head of a criminal group, especially in the Mafia.

God-fearing *adj.* respectful of God's laws; pious.

God-forsaken *adj. derog.* remote and desolate.

remote, isolated, lonely, bleak, desolate, abandoned, deserted, forlorn, dismal, dreary, gloomy, miserable, wretched.

godhead *noun* **1** the divine state attributed to God or a god. **2** (**the Godhead**) God.

godless *adj.* **1** not religious; not believing in God. **2** wicked; immoral.

1 ungodly, atheistic, heathen, pagan, irreligious, unholy, impious, sacrilegious, profane, irreverent. **2** wicked, evil, bad, sinful, immoral.
1 godly, pious. **2** good.

godlessness *noun* **1** wickedness. **2** lack of faith.

godlike *adj.* like a god.

godliness *noun* piety.

godly *adj.* (**godlier**, **godliest**) religious; pious.

▪ ◨ religious, holy, pious, devout, God-fearing, righteous, good, virtuous, pure, innocent.
◪ godless, impious.

godmother *noun* a female godparent.

godparent *noun* a person with responsibility for the religious education of another, especially a child, or, loosely, for a child's upbringing in the event of the death of its parents.

godsend *noun* a person or thing whose arrival is unexpected but very welcome.

◨ blessing, boon, stroke of luck, windfall, miracle.
◪ blow, setback.

godson *noun* a male godchild.

Godspeed *interj. old use* an expression of wishes for a person's safety on a journey.

godwit *noun* any of various wading birds, found in most parts of the world, having grey-brown plumage in winter and bright chestnut plumage (on the neck and underparts) in summer, a long straight or slightly upcurved bill, and long legs.

goer *noun* **1** (*usually in compounds*) a person who makes (especially regular) visits: *cinema-goer*. **2** *colloq.* a sexually energetic person, especially a woman. **3** *colloq.* something that travels fast, or makes fast progress.

gofer *noun North Amer., esp. US* an office junior who runs errands. [from *go for*]

go-getter *noun colloq.* an ambitious, enterprising person.

go-getting *adj.* ambitious, pushy.

goggle — *verb* **1** *intrans.* to look with wide staring eyes. **2** to roll (the eyes). **3** *intrans., said of the eyes* to stick out. — *noun* a wide-eyed stare. [perhaps Middle English *gogelen*, to look aside]

goggle-box *noun colloq.* a television set.

goggles *pl. noun* protective spectacles with edges fitting closely against the face.

go-go dancer a female erotic dancer, especially in a club or bar. [from French *gogo*, galore, aplenty]

Goidelic /gɔɪˈdɛlɪk/ *noun* one of two distinct branches of the early Celtic language of Britain. See also BRYTHONIC, CELTIC, GAELIC.

going — *noun* **1** an act of leaving; a departure. **2** the condition of the track in horse-racing. **3** progress: *made good going*. **4** *colloq.* general situation or conditions: *when the going gets tough*. **5** (*in compounds*) the act or practice of making (especially regular) visits to: *theatre-going*. — *adj.* **1** working, especially bringing in business: *a going concern*. **2** usual or accepted: *the going rate*.

going-over *noun colloq.* **1** a beating. **2** a close inspection.

goings-on *pl. noun colloq.* events or happenings, especially if strange or disapproved of.

goitre /ˈgɔɪtə(r)/ *noun Medicine* abnormal enlargement of the thyroid gland, often resulting in a large swelling in the neck. [from French *goître*, from Latin *guttur*, throat]

go-kart *noun* a low racing vehicle consisting of a frame with wheels, engine, and steering gear.

gold — *noun* **1** (SYMBOL **Au**, ATOMIC NUMBER **79**) a soft dense yellow precious metal that is chemically unreactive, so does not tarnish, and highly malleable, so can be beaten into very thin sheets known as *gold leaf*. **2** articles made from it, especially jewellery and coins. **3** its value, used as a standard for the value of currency. **4** its deep yellow colour. **5** *colloq.* a gold medal. **6** precious or noble quality: *heart of gold*. **7** monetary wealth. — *adj.* **1** made of gold. **2** gold-coloured. [from Anglo-Saxon]

gold-digger *noun* **1** a person who digs for gold. **2** *derog. slang* a person who starts love affairs with rich people in order to get at their money.

gold dust gold in the form of a very fine powder.

golden *adj.* **1** gold-coloured. **2** made of or containing gold. **3** happy; prosperous or thriving: *golden years/golden age*. **4** excellent; extremely valuable: *golden opportunity*. **5** greatly admired or favoured: *golden girl*. **6** denoting a 50th anniversary.

◨ **1** yellow, blond(e), fair. **2** gold, gilt, gilded, gold-plated. **3** happy, joyful, prosperous, thriving, flourishing, successful, glorious. **4** excellent, favourable, auspicious, promising, rosy.

golden eagle a large eagle found in mountainous regions of the northern hemisphere, with dark brown plumage, a golden nape, and a wingspan of up to 2m.

golden goal in football, the first goal scored by either side in extra time, which wins the match for that side.

golden handshake *colloq.* a large sum received from an employer on retirement, or in compensation for compulsory redundancy.

golden jubilee the 50th anniversary of a significant event.

golden mean the midpoint between two extremes.

goldenrod or **golden rod** *noun* any of various plants of the genus *Solidago*, native to Europe, Asia, and N America, especially *S. canadensis*, a late-flowering perennial native to N America, which has long pointed lance-shaped leaves, and numerous spikes of tiny golden yellow flowers.

golden rule 1 any essential principle or rule. **2** the name given to Christ's command concerning one's duty to others: 'Do to others as you would have them do to you' (Luke 6.31; Matthew 7.12), a rule also found in earlier Jewish and Greek ethical teaching.

golden share a large share in a company held by an institution, or often a government, which prevents takeover by another company.

golden syrup light golden-coloured treacle.

goldfield *noun* an area where gold is mined.

goldfinch *noun* any of a number of species of finch, found in Europe and Asia, so called because of the broad yellow bar across each wing, only clearly visible when the bird is in flight.

goldfish *noun* (PL. **goldfishes**, **goldfish**) a freshwater fish belonging to the carp family, which is green or brown in its wild form, although most of the varieties that have been bred from it are yellow, orange, or golden-red in colour.

Goldilocks economy an well-balanced economy. [with allusion to the fairy tale *Goldilocks and the Three Bears*, in which Goldilocks finds things in the bears' house that are 'just right']

gold leaf gold rolled or beaten into very thin sheets used to decorate books, etc.

gold medal a medal awarded to the winner of a sporting contest, or in recognition of excellence, eg of a wine.

gold mine 1 a place where gold is mined. **2** *colloq.* a source of great wealth.

gold plate 1 a thin coating of gold, especially on silver. **2** articles, eg spoons and dishes, made of gold.

gold-plate *verb* to coat (another metal) with gold.

gold-plated *adj.* plated with gold.

gold rush a frantic settlement of masses of people in a newly-discovered goldfield.

goldsmith *noun* a person who makes articles out of gold.

gold standard *Finance* a monetary standard or system according to which the unit of currency has a precise value in gold.

golem /ˈgəʊlɛm/ *noun* in Jewish folklore, an image or automaton endowed with life, typically the servant and protector of a rabbi. [from Hebrew *golem*, a shapeless or embryonic thing]

golf — *noun* a game played on a large outdoor course, the object being to hit a small ball into each of a series of (nine or eighteen) holes using a set of long-handled clubs, taking as few strokes as possible. — *verb intrans.* to play golf. [perhaps from Old Dutch *colf*, club]

golf club 1 any of the set of long-handled clubs used to play golf. **2** an association of players of golf, or its premises with a golf course attached.

golfer *noun* a person who plays golf.

golf links a golf course, especially by the sea.

Golgi apparatus /'gɔːldʒɪ apə'reɪtəs/ *Biol.* any of various structures found within plant and animal cells, consisting of a stack of flattened discs, each of which is surrounded by a membrane. It is involved in the storage and transport of secretory products such as enzymes and hormones. [named after the Italian histologist Camillo Golgi (1843–1926)]

goliard /'gouliɑːd/ *noun* any of a band of wandering scholars and students of the 12–13c, renowned for their riotous behaviour, and for the satirical Latin verses lampooning the Church which they wrote and performed. [from Old French *golart, golard*, drunkard and glutton, from Latin *gula*, gluttony]

goliath /gə'laɪəθ/ *noun colloq.* **1** an unusually large or tall person. **2** a person or organization of great importance or influence. [named after *Goliath*, the Old Testament Philistine giant killed by David]

golliwog or **gollywog** *noun* a child's cloth doll with a black face and bristling hair and bright clothes. [from *Golliwogg*, the name of a character in children's books in the US, published from 1895]

golly [1] *interj. old use* an expression of surprise or admiration. [a euphemistic form of *God*]

golly [2] *noun* (PL. **gollies**) *colloq.* a golliwog.

golosh see GALOSH.

-gon *combining form Maths.* forming words denoting a geometrical figure having a specified number of sides and angles: *polygon* / *hexagon*. [from Greek *gonia*, angle]

gonad /'gounad/ *noun Biol.* an organ in which gametes (eggs or sperm) are produced, especially the ovary or testis. It may also secrete sex hormones. [from Greek *gone*, generation]

gonadotrophic hormone /gounədou'trouf ɪk/ *Physiol.* any of various hormones that stimulate the gonads (the ovaries and testes), and are responsible for the production of sex hormones, the onset of sexual maturity, and the control of the menstrual cycle in humans. [from Greek *gone*, generation]

gonadotrophin /gounədou'trouf ɪn/ *noun Physiol.* gonadotrophic hormone.

gondola /'gɒndələ/ *noun* **1** a long narrow flat-bottomed boat with pointed upturned ends, used on the canals of Venice. **2** a passenger cabin suspended from an airship, balloon, or cable-railway. **3** a (free-standing) shelved unit for displaying goods in a supermarket, etc. [from Venetian dialect]

gondolier /gɒndə'lɪə(r)/ *noun* a person who rows a gondola on a canal.

Gondwanaland /gɒnd'wɑːnəland/ *noun Geol.* the hypothetical southern supercontinent thought to have broken away from the single land mass Pangea about 200 million years ago. It is believed to have drifted apart to form parts of the present continents of Africa, Australia, S America, India, and Antarctica.

gone — *verb* past participle of GO. — *adj.* **1** departed. **2** lost. **3** dead. **4** *colloq.* pregnant: *four months gone*. **5** *colloq.* in ecstasy. **6** *colloq.* (**gone on someone** or **something**) infatuated or obsessed with them.

goner /'gɒnə/ *noun colloq.* a person or thing beyond hope of recovery.

gonfalon /'gɒnfələn/ *noun* a banner hung from a horizontal bar. [from Italian *gonfalone*, from Old German *gund*, battle + *fano*, flag]

gong *noun* **1** a hanging metal plate which sounds when struck. **2** *slang* a medal. [from Malay]

gonorrhoea /gɒnə'rɪə/ *noun Medicine* a sexually transmitted disease characterized by inflammation of the geni-

tal mucous membranes as a result of infection with the bacterium *Neisseria gonorrhoeae*. [from Greek *gonos*, seed, semen + *rhein*, to flow]

gonzo *adj. colloq., esp. US* bizarre or absurd, especially describing journalism that is eccentric and subjective. [possibly from Italian *gonzo*, simpleton or Spanish *ganso*, = goose]

goo *noun colloq.* **1** any sticky substance. **2** *derog.* excessive sentimentality.

good — *adj.* (**better**, **best**) **1** having desirable or necessary (positive) qualities; admirable. **2** (*usually* **good at something**) competent with it; talented. **3** morally correct; virtuous. **4** (**good for someone** or **something**) beneficial to them. **5** kind and generous. **6** bringing happiness or pleasure: *good news*. **7** well-behaved. **8** wise; advisable: *a good buy*. **9** thorough. **10** finest among others: *my good cups*. **11** adequate; satisfactory: *a good supply*. **12** enjoyable: *having a good time*. **13** valid. **14** well-respected. **15** sound; giving use; serviceable: *the roof is good for another winter*. **16** considerable; at least: *waited a good while* / *lasted a good month*. **17** certain to provide the desired result: *good for a laugh*. — *noun* **1** moral correctness; virtue. **2** benefit; advantage: *do you good* / *£20 to the good*. **3** (**the good**) good people. — *interj.* an expression of approval or satisfaction. — *adv. colloq. North Amer., esp. US* well. — **as good as** ... almost ...; virtually... **for good and all** for ever; permanently. **good and ...** *colloq.* very ...; completely or absolutely: *good and ready*. **good for** or **on someone** an expression of approval or congratulation. **good morning, afternoon** expressions of greeting or farewell. **make good** to be successful. **make something good 1** to repair it. **2** to carry it out or fulfil it. [from Anglo-Saxon *god*]

. . . .

▣ *adj.* **1** pleasing, commendable, admirable, excellent, *colloq.* great, *colloq.* super, first-class, first-rate, acceptable, satisfactory. **2** competent, proficient, skilled, accomplished, expert, professional, skilful, clever, talented, gifted, fit, able, capable. **3** virtuous, exemplary, moral, upright, honest, trustworthy, worthy, righteous. **4** advantageous to, beneficial to, helpful to, useful to, appropriate to, suitable to. **5** kind, considerate, gracious, benevolent, generous, charitable, philanthropic. **6** favourable, auspicious. **7** well-behaved, obedient, well-mannered. **9** thorough, comprehensive, complete, total. **12** enjoyable, nice, pleasant, agreeable. *noun* **1** virtue, morality, goodness, righteousness. **2** benefit, welfare, interest, sake, behalf, advantage, profit, gain, worth, merit, use, purpose, avail, usefulness, service.

▣ *adj.* **1** bad, poor. **2** bad, incompetent. **3** bad, wicked, immoral. **4** bad for. **5** unkind, inconsiderate. **6** bad, unfavourable. **7** bad, naughty, disobedient.

. . . .

goodbye — *interj.* an expression of farewell. — *noun* an act of saying goodbye.

. . . .

▣ *interj.* farewell, adieu, au revoir, *colloq.* bye. *noun* farewell, adieu, au revoir, valediction, leave-taking, parting.

. . . .

good-for-nothing — *adj.* lazy and irresponsible. — *noun* a lazy and irresponsible person.

Good Friday a Christian festival on the Friday before Easter, in memory of Christ's crucifixion.

goodies *pl. noun colloq.* things considered pleasant or desirable. See also GOODY.

goodliness *noun* being goodly.

good-looking *adj., said of a person* physically attractive.

. . . .

▣ attractive, handsome, beautiful, pretty, personable, presentable.

▣ ugly, plain.

. . . .

goodly *adj.* (**goodlier**, **goodliest**) *old use* **1** quite large. **2** physically attractive; fine.

goodness — *noun* **1** the state or quality of being good; generosity; kindness; moral correctness. **2** *euphemistic, used in exclamations* God: *goodness knows.* **3** nourishing quality: *all the goodness of the grain.* — *interj.* an expression of surprise or relief.

. . . .

▣ *noun* **1** virtue, uprightness, rectitude, kindness, compassion, graciousness, goodwill, benevolence, generosity, friendliness, helpfulness.
▣ *noun* **1** badness, wickedness.

. . . .

goods *pl. noun* **1** articles for sale; merchandise. **2** freight: *goods train.* **3** *colloq.* the required result: *deliver the goods.* **4** *old use* personal possessions. — **have the goods on someone** *colloq.* to have proof of wrongdoings or crimes committed by them.

. . . .

▣ **1** merchandise, wares, commodities, stock. **4** property, chattels, effects, possessions, belongings, paraphernalia.

. . . .

goodwill *noun* **1** a feeling of kindness towards others. **2** the good reputation of an established business, seen as having an actual value.

. . . .

▣ **1** benevolence, kindness, generosity, favour, friendliness.
▣ **1** ill-will.

. . . .

goody *noun* (PL. **goodies**) *colloq.* a hero in a film, book, etc. See also GOODIES.

goody-goody *colloq.* — *adj.* virtuous in an ostentatious or self-satisfied way. — *noun* an ostentatiously virtuous person.

gooey *adj.* (**gooier, gooiest**) sticky.

goof *chiefly North Amer. colloq.* — *noun* **1** a silly or foolish person. **2** a stupid mistake. — *verb intrans.* **1** to make a stupid mistake. **2** (**goof around**) to spend time idly or foolishly. [perhaps from Old French *goffe*, clumsy]

goofy *adj.* (**goofier, goofiest**) *colloq.* silly; crazy.

googly *noun* (PL. **googlies**) *Cricket* a ball bowled so as to change direction unexpectedly after bouncing.

goon *noun* **1** *colloq.* a silly person. **2** *slang* a hired thug. [from US cartoon character Alice the *Goon*, created by E C Segar (1894–1938)]

goosander *noun* a large duck, native to N America and northern regions of Europe and Asia, that migrates south in winter. Also called COMMON MERGANSER. [perhaps from GOOSE + Norse *ander*, plural of *önd*, duck]

goose — *noun* (PL. **geese**, **gooses** sense 5) **1** any of numerous species of large wild or domesticated waterfowl related to ducks and swans, with a stout body, long neck, webbed feet, and a broad flat bill, found in all parts of the world except Antarctica. **2** the female of this bird, as opposed to the gander, which is the male. **3** the flesh of a goose cooked as food. **4** *old colloq. use* a silly person. **5** *colloq.* a poke or pinch on the buttocks. — *verb colloq.* to poke or pinch (someone) on the buttocks. — **cook someone's goose** *colloq.* to ruin their plans or chances. [from Anglo-Saxon *gos*]

gooseberry /'gʊzbərɪ/ *noun* (PL. **gooseberries**) **1** a low-growing deciduous shrub (*Ribes uva-crispa*), native to cool temperate regions of Europe and Asia, having greenish flowers tinged with purple, followed by oval yellowish-green or reddish edible berries. **2** one of the small acidic berries produced by this plant, often used to make jam, pies, etc. — **play gooseberry** *colloq.* to be an unwanted third person in a group or social activity.

goosefish *noun* same as ANGLERFISH.

goose pimples or **goose flesh** or **goose bumps** a condition of the skin caused by cold or fear, in which the body hairs become erect, causing pimples to appear on the surface and causing a bristling feeling.

goose-step — *noun* a military marching step in which the legs are kept rigid and swung very high. — *verb intrans.* to march with this step.

gopher or **pocket gopher** *noun North Amer.* any of various hamster-like burrowing rodents found only in N America, and having two external fur-lined cheek pouches. [said to be from French *gaufre*, honeycomb (a reference to its burrows)]

gore[1] *noun* blood from a wound, especially when clotted. [from Anglo-Saxon *gor*, filth]

gore[2] *verb* to pierce with horn or tusk. [from Anglo-Saxon *gar*, spear]

. . . .

▣ pierce, penetrate, stab, spear, stick, impale, wound, injure.

. . . .

gore[3] — *noun* a triangular piece of material, eg a section of an umbrella or a tapering piece in a garment. — *verb* to construct from, or shape with, gores. [from Anglo-Saxon *gara*, triangular piece of land]

gorge — *noun* **1** a deep narrow valley, usually containing a river. **2** the contents of the stomach. **3** a spell of greedy eating. **4** *old use* the throat or gullet. — *verb* **1** *intrans., trans.* to eat or swallow greedily. **2** (*usually* **gorge oneself**) to stuff oneself with food. — **make one's gorge rise** to disgust or sicken one; to fill one with resentment. [from Old French *gorge*, throat]

. . . .

▣ *noun* **1** canyon, ravine, gully, defile, chasm, abyss, cleft, fissure, gap, pass. *verb* **1** guzzle, gobble, swallow, gulp. **2** stuff, cram, fill, sate.

. . . .

gorgeous *adj.* **1** extremely beautiful or attractive; magnificent. **2** *colloq.* excellent; extremely pleasant. [from Old French *gorgias*, fine, elegant]

. . . .

▣ **1** attractive, beautiful, handsome, good-looking, magnificent, splendid, grand, glorious, superb, fine, rich, sumptuous, luxurious, brilliant, dazzling, showy, glamorous. **2** excellent, delightful, pleasing, lovely, enjoyable, pleasant.
▣ **1** plain.

. . . .

Gorgonzola /gɔːgən'zəʊlə/ *noun* a blue-veined Italian cheese with a sharp flavour. [from *Gorgonzola*, a town near Milan]

gorilla *noun* **1** the largest of the apes (*Gorilla gorilla*), native to the rainforests of W and Central Africa, and reaching a height of up to 1.8m. **2** *colloq.* a brutal-looking man, especially a hired thug. [from Greek *Gorillai*, a tribe of hairy African women]

gormless *adj. derog. colloq.* stupid; dim. [variant of obsolete *gaumless*, from *gaum*, understanding]

gorse *noun* a highly branched evergreen shrub (*Ulex europaeus*), native to heaths and grassland of Europe and NW Africa, having upright main stems, leaves reduced to very sharp deeply furrowed spines, and bright yellow flowers. Also called FURZE, WHIN.

gorsy *adj.* covered with gorse.

gory *adj.* (**gorier, goriest**) **1** causing or involving bloodshed. **2** *colloq.* unpleasant: *gory details.* **3** covered in gore. [from GORE]

. . . .

▣ **1** bloody, sanguinary, grisly, brutal, savage, murderous. **3** bloody, bloodstained, blood-soaked.

. . . .

gosh *interj. colloq.* a mild expression of surprise. [euphemistic form of GOD]

goshawk /'gɒshɔːk/ *noun* a large hawk, native to Europe, Asia, and N America, resembling but much larger than a sparrowhawk. [from Anglo-Saxon *gos*, goose + *hafoc*, hawk]

gosling *noun* a young goose. [from Anglo-Saxon *gos*, goose + -LING]

go-slow *noun* working slowly to encourage an employer to negotiate.

gospel *noun* **1** the life and teachings of Christ: *preach the gospel.* **2** (*usually* **Gospel**) each of the New Testament books describing the life of Christ ascribed to Matthew, Mark, Luke, and John. **3** (**gospel truth**) *colloq.* the absolute truth. **4** a set of closely followed principles or rules. **5** (*also* **gospel music**) lively religious music of Black American origin. [from Anglo-Saxon *godspel*, from *god*, good + *spel*, story]

gossamer /'gɒsəmə/ *noun* **1** fine filmy spider-woven threads seen on hedges or floating in the air. **2** any soft fine material. [from Middle English *gossomer*, goose summer, a period in November when goose was traditionally eaten, and these cobwebs often seen]

gossip — *noun* **1** *derog.* talk or writing about the private affairs of others, often spiteful and untrue. **2** *derog.* a person who engages in or spreads such talk. **3** casual and friendly talk. — *verb intrans.* (**gossiped, gossiping**) **1** to engage in, or pass on, malicious gossip. **2** to chat. [from Anglo-Saxon *godsibb*, godparent, hence a familiar friend one chats to]

. . . .

◼ *noun* **1** rumour, hearsay, scandal, idle talk, tittle-tattle. **2** gossipmonger, scandalmonger, whisperer, prattler, babbler, tattler, *colloq.* nosy parker, busybody, talebearer, telltale. **3** talk, chat, chitchat, prattle. *verb* TALK. **1** whisper, tittle-tattle, tell tales. **2** chat, natter, chatter, gabble, prattle.

. . . .

gossipy *adj.* **1** involving gossip. **2** likely to gossip.

got see GET.

Goth *noun* **1** a member of a Scandinavian people who invaded parts of the Roman Empire between the 3c and 5c AD. They expanded into the Black Sea region and split into two confederations, Ostrogoths and Visigoths. **2** a crude or uncivilized person. [from Anglo-Saxon *Gotan*]

Gothic — *adj.* **1** of the Goths or their language. **2** of a style of architecture featuring high pointed arches, popular in Europe between the 12c and 16c. **3** of a type of literature dealing with mysterious or supernatural events in an eerie setting, popular in the 18c. **4** of a modern style of literature, films, etc which imitates this. **5** of various styles of heavy black printed letter. — *noun* **1** Gothic architecture or literature. **2** Gothic lettering. **3** the extinct Germanic language of the Goths.

gotten *North Amer., esp. US* past participle of GET.

gouache /gʊ'ɑːʃ/ *noun* **1** a painting technique using a blend of watercolour and a glue-like substance, giving an opaque matt surface. **2** a painting done in this way. [from French *gouache*]

Gouda /'gaʊdə/ *noun* a flat round mild Dutch cheese. [from *Gouda* in Holland]

gouge — *noun* **1** a chisel with a rounded hollow blade, used for cutting grooves or holes in wood. **2** a groove or hole made using this. — *verb* **1** to cut it out with or as if with a gouge. **2** (*also* **gouge something out**) to force or press it out of position: *gouged his eye out.* [from Old French, from Latin *gubia*, chisel]

. . . .

◼ *verb* **1** chisel, cut, incise, score, groove, scratch, claw, gash, slash, dig, scoop, hollow.

. . . .

goujons /'guːdʒɒnz/ *pl. noun* small strips of fish or chicken coated in seasoned flour, egg, and breadcrumbs, and deep-fried. [from French *goujon*, gudgeon (the fish)]

goulash *noun* a thick meat stew heavily seasoned with paprika, originally from Hungary. [from Hungarian *gulyas hus*, herdsman's meat]

gourd *noun* **1** any of various mostly climbing plants belonging to the cucumber family (Cucurbitaceae) that produce a large fruit with a hard woody outer shell, which varies widely in colour and is usually pear- or bottle-shaped. **2** the hard durable shell of the fruit of such a plant, which can be hollowed out, dried, and used as an ornament, cup, bowl, or other utensil. [from Old French *gourde*]

gourmand /'gʊəmənd/ *noun* **1** a greedy eater; a glutton. **2** a gourmet. [from French *gourmand*]

gourmandise /gʊəmən'diːz/ or **gourmandism** *noun* **1** indulgence in good eating. **2** discerning appreciation of good food and wines.

gourmet /'gʊəmeɪ/ *noun* a person with expert knowledge of, and a passion for, good food and wine. [from French *gourmet*]

. . . .

◼ gastronome, epicure, connoisseur, bon vivant, gourmand.

. . . .

gout *noun* a disease in which excess uric acid accumulates in the bloodstream and is deposited as crystals of sodium urate in the joints. It causes recurrent attacks of acute arthritis, most commonly of the big toe. [from Old French *goute*, a drop, the disease having formerly been thought of as caused by drops of humours]

gouty *adj.* afflicted with gout.

Gov. or **gov.** *abbrev.* **1** government. **2** governor.

govern *verb* **1** *trans., intrans.* to control and direct the affairs of (a country, state, or organization). **2** to guide or influence; to control or restrain: *govern his temper.* **3** *Grammar* to determine the form, or case, taken by (a word). [from Latin *gubernare*, from Greek *kybernaein*, to steer]

. . . .

◼ **1** rule (over), reign (over), lead, head, direct, manage, superintend, supervise, oversee, preside over, conduct. **2** guide, influence, steer, pilot, dominate, master, control, regulate, curb, check, restrain, contain, quell, subdue, tame, discipline.

. . . .

governable *adj.* capable of being governed.

governance *noun* **1** the act of governing. **2** a system of government. **3** authority or control.

governess *noun Hist.* a woman employed to teach, and perhaps look after, children, usually resident in their home.

governing *adj.* that governs.

government *noun* **1** (*often* **the Government**) a body of people, usually elected, with the power to control the affairs of a country or state. **2** the way in which this is done; the particular system used. **3** the act or practice of ruling. **4** *Grammar* the power of one word to determine the form, or case, of another.

. . . .

◼ **1** administration, executive, ministry, Establishment, authorities, powers that be, state, regime. **3** rule, sovereignty, sway, direction, management, superintendence, supervision, surveillance, command, charge, authority, power, domination, dominion, control.

. . . .

Government systems include: absolutism, autocracy, commonwealth, communism, democracy, despotism, dictatorship, empire, federation, hierocracy, junta, kingdom, monarchy, plutocracy, puppet government, republic, theocracy, triumvirate. *See also* **parliaments and political assemblies.**

governmental *adj.* relating to or involving government.

governor *noun* **1** (*also* **Governor**) the elected head of a US state. **2** the head of an institution, eg a prison. **3** a member of a governing body of a school, hospital, college, etc. **4** (*also* **Governor**) the head of a colony or province, especially the monarch's representative. **5** *colloq.* (*often* **guvnor** or **guv'nor** or **guv**) one's boss or father; a respectful form of address used to any man. **6** a device for maintaining or controlling uniform speed in an engine or vehicle.

. . . .

◼ **2** director, manager, head. **4** commissioner, administrator, leader, head, chief.

. . . .

Governor-General *noun* (PL. **Governors-General, Governor-Generals**) the official representative of the

British monarch in a Commonwealth country or British colony.

Govt. *abbrev.* Government.

gown *noun* **1** a woman's long formal dress. **2** an official robe worn by clergymen, lawyers and academics. **3** a protective overall worn by a surgeon and surgical staff in a hospital. **4** *formal* the members of a university, especially as opposed to *town*, the residents of the university town. [from Latin *gunna*, garment made of fur or leather]

◫ **1** dress, frock. **2** robe, vestment.

goy *noun* (PL. **goys, goyim**) *slang* a Jewish word for a non-Jewish person. [from Hebrew *goy*, people, nation]

GP *abbrev.* **1** Gallup poll. **2** general practitioner.

GPO *abbrev.* General Post Office.

Gr *abbrev.* Greek.

gr or **gr.** *abbrev.* **1** grain. **2** gram or gramme. **3** gross.

Graafian follicle /ˈgrɑːfɪən/ *Anat.* in the ovary of female mammals, one of many small spherical sacs within which an ovum (egg cell) develops. Also called OVARIAN FOLLICLE. [named after the Dutch anatomist Regnier de Graaf]

grab — *verb* (**grabbed, grabbing**) **1** *trans., intrans.* (**grab something** or **grab at something**) to seize it suddenly and often with violence. **2** to take greedily. **3** to take hurriedly or without hesitation: *grab a snack* / *grab an opportunity*. **4** *colloq.* to impress or interest: *how does that grab you?* — *noun* **1** an act of taking suddenly or greedily. **2** a mechanical device with scooping jaws, used eg for excavation. — **up for grabs** *colloq.* available, especially easily or cheaply. [from Old German dialect or Old Dutch *grabben*]

◫ *verb* **1** seize, snatch, take, *colloq.* nab, grasp, clutch, grip, catch, *colloq.* collar.

graben /ˈgrɑːbən/ *noun* *Geol.* a rift valley, usually a very large one, formed when a block of the Earth's crust, usually much longer than it is wide, drops down between two faults. [from German *Graben*, ditch]

grace — *noun* **1** elegance and beauty of form or movement. **2** decency; politeness: *had the grace to offer.* **3** a short prayer of thanks to God said before or after a meal. **4** a delay allowed, especially to a debtor, as a favour. **5** a pleasing or attractive characteristic: *social graces* / *a saving grace.* **6** *Relig.* the mercy and favour shown by God to mankind. **7** *Relig.* the condition of a person's soul of being made free from sin and evil by God. **8** (**His Grace** or **Your Grace**) a title used of or to a duke, duchess, or archbishop. **9** (**the Graces**) *Greek Mythol.* three daughters of Zeus and Hera, embodying beauty and social accomplishments. — *verb* **1** *often facetious* to honour, eg with one's presence. **2** to add beauty or charm to. — **airs and graces** behaviour meant to impress others or to show that one considers oneself superior to them. **with a good** or **bad grace** willingly or unwillingly. [from Latin *gratia*, favour]

◫ *noun* **1** gracefulness, poise, beauty, attractiveness, loveliness, shapeliness, elegance, tastefulness, refinement, polish, breeding, charm. **2** decency, politeness, courtesy, manners, kindness, consideration, goodness, benevolence, graciousness. **3** blessing, benediction, thanksgiving, prayer. **4** delay, remission, reprieve. **5** virtue. **6** mercy, favour, forgiveness, pardon, goodwill. *verb* **1** favour, honour. **2** enhance, set off, embellish, trim, garnish, decorate, ornament, adorn.

◧ *noun* **1** clumsiness, ugliness. **2** rudeness, cruelty. *verb* **2** spoil, detract from.

grace-and-favour *adj. Brit., said of a property* owned by the monarch and let rent-free.

graceful *adj.* having or showing elegance and beauty of form or movement.

◫ easy, flowing, smooth, supple, agile, lithe, lissom, slender, fine, tasteful, elegant, beautiful, charming, suave.

◧ graceless, awkward, clumsy, ungainly.

graceless *adj.* **1** awkward in form or movement. **2** bad-mannered.

gracious — *adj.* **1** kind and polite. **2** *said of God* merciful. **3** having qualities of luxury, elegance, comfort, and leisure. **4** *formal* used out of polite custom to describe a royal person or their actions. — *interj.* an expression of surprise. [from Latin *gratiosus*]

◫ *adj.* **1** kind, considerate, sweet, kindly, benevolent, generous, magnanimous, charitable, hospitable, obliging, accommodating, polite, courteous, well-mannered. **2** merciful, forgiving, indulgent, lenient, mild, clement. **3** elegant, refined, luxurious, comfortable.

◧ *adj.* **1** ungracious.

gradate *verb* **1** to shade off; to change imperceptibly. **2** to arrange according to grades.

gradation *noun* **1** a series of gradual and successive stages or degrees, or one step in this. **2** the act or process of forming grades or stages. **3** the gradual change or movement from one state, musical note, colour, etc to another. [from GRADE]

gradational *adj.* involving or characterized by gradation.

grade — *noun* **1** a stage or level on a scale of quality, rank, size, etc. **2** a mark indicating this. **3** *North Amer., esp. US* a particular class or year in school, or the level of work taught in it. **4** a slope or gradient. — *verb* **1** to arrange in different grades. **2** to award a mark indicating grade to. **3** to produce a gradual blending or merging of (especially colours). — **make the grade** *colloq.* to succeed; to reach the required or expected standard. [from Latin *gradus*, step]

◫ *noun* **1** rank, status, standing, station, place, position, level, stage, degree, step, rung, notch, mark, brand, quality, standard, condition, size, order, group, class, category. *verb* **1** sort, arrange, order, categorize, group, class, size, rank, range, classify, brand, label, pigeonhole. **2** evaluate, assess, rate, mark.

gradient *noun* **1** the steepness of a slope. **2** *formal* a slope. **3** *Maths.* the slope of a line, or the slope of a tangent to a curve at a particular point. **4** *Physics* the rate of change of a variable quantity over a specified distance, eg the temperature gradient in a metal bar is the rate of change of temperature along the bar. [from Latin *gradiens*, stepping]

◫ **2** slope, grade, incline, hill, bank, rise, declivity.

gradual *adj.* **1** developing or happening slowly, by degrees. **2** *said of a slope* not steep; gentle. [from Latin *gradualis*, from *gradus*, step]

◫ **1** slow, leisurely, unhurried, moderate, regular, even, steady, progressive, step-by-step. **2** easy, gentle.

◧ **1** sudden. **2** steep.

gradualism *noun* the process of, or support for, gradual progress or change, especially in politics.

gradualist — *noun* a supporter of gradual action. — *adj.* involving gradualism.

gradually *adv.* in a gradual way, slowly, steadily.

◫ little by little, bit by bit, inch by inch, step by step, progressively, by degrees, piecemeal, slowly, gently, cautiously, gingerly, moderately, evenly, steadily.

graduand /ˈgradjʊənd/ *noun* a person who is about to be awarded a higher-education degree. [from Latin *graduare*, to take a degree]

graduate — *verb* (pronounced -eɪt) **1** *intrans.* to receive an academic degree from a higher-education institution. **2** *intrans. North Amer.* to receive a diploma at the end of one's course of study at a high school. **3** *intrans.* to move up from a lower to a higher level, often in stages. **4** to mark (eg a thermometer) with units of measurement or other divisions. **5** to arrange into regular groups, according to size, type, etc. — *noun* (pronounced -ət) a person with a higher-education degree or *North Amer.* a high-school diploma. [from Latin *graduare*, to take a degree, from *gradus*, step]

▤ *verb* **1** pass, qualify. **4** calibrate, mark off. **5** grade, arrange, range, order, rank, sort, group, classify.

graduation *noun* **1** the act of receiving a higher-education degree or *North Amer.* a high-school diploma. **2** the ceremony marking this. **3** a unit of measurement or other division marked on a ruler, thermometer, etc; the process of marking such divisions.

Graeco- /ˈɡriːkoʊ/ *combining form* forming words relating to Greece or Greek: *Graeco-Roman.*

graffiti *pl. noun* (SING. **graffito**) words or drawings, usually humorous or political slogans, scratched or painted on walls, etc in public places. [from Italian *graffiti*]

graffito 1 *Art* same as SGRAFFITO. **2** See GRAFFITI.

graft[1] — *noun* **1** *Bot.* a piece of plant tissue (the *scion*) that is inserted into a cut in the outer stem of another plant (the *stock*), resulting in fusion of the tissues and growth of a single plant. **2** *Medicine* the transfer or transplantation of an organ or tissue from one individual to another, or to a different site within the same individual, usually to replace diseased or damaged tissue, eg skin graft, kidney transplant. — *verb* **1** to attach a graft in; to attach as a graft. **2** *intrans.* to attach grafts. [from Old French *graffe*, from Greek *graphein*, to write]

▤ *noun* **1** scion, shoot, sprout, bud. **2** implant, implantation, transplant, transplantation. *verb* **1** engraft, implant, insert, transplant, join, splice.

graft[2] — *noun* **1** *colloq.* hard work. **2** *slang* the use of illegal or unfair means to gain profit, especially by people in the public eye; the profit gained. — *verb intrans.* **1** *colloq.* to work hard. **2** *slang* to gain profit through corruption.

grafter *noun colloq.* a hard worker.

Graham's law *Chem.* a law which states that the rate of diffusion of a gas is inversely proportional to the square root of its density, ie a light gas will diffuse more rapidly than a heavy one.

grain — *noun* **1** a single small hard fruit, resembling a seed, produced by a cereal plant or other grass. **2** such fruits referred to collectively. **3** any of the cereal plants that produce such fruits, eg wheat, corn. **4** a small hard particle of anything. **5** a very small amount: *a grain of truth.* **6** the smallest unit of avoirdupois weight, equal to 0.065g, so called because it was formerly said to be the average weight of a grain of wheat. There are 7,000 grains in one pound avoirdupois. **7** a similar unit of weight used in the troy system. There are 5,760 grains in one pound troy. **8** the arrangement, size, and direction of the fibres or layers in wood, leather, etc, or the pattern formed as a result of this arrangement. **9** the arrangement and size of the constituent particles of rock, or the pattern formed as a result of this arrangement. **10** the main direction of the fibres in paper or the threads in a woven fabric. **11** any of the small particles of metallic silver that form the dark areas of the image on a developed photograph. — *verb* **1** *trans., intrans.* to form into grains. **2** to give a rough appearance or texture to. **3** to paint or stain with a pattern like the grain of wood or leather. — **go against the grain** to be against

one's principles or natural character. [from Latin *granum*, seed]

▤ *noun* **1** seed, kernel. **4** granule, particle, piece, fragment. **5** bit, scrap, crumb, atom, jot, iota, mite, modicum, speck, trace. **8** texture, fibre, pattern, marking, surface. **10** fibre, weave.

grainy *adj.* (**grainier, grainiest**) *said of a photograph* having a large grain size, and therefore not sharp or distinct.

gram or **gramme** *noun* (ABBREV. **g, gr**) the basic unit of mass in the metric system, equal to 10^{-3} (one thousandth) of a kilogram. It is also the fundamental unit of mass in the centimetre-gramme-second (cgs) system of measurement. [from Greek *gramma*, small weight]

gram. *abbrev.* grammar or grammatical.

-gram *combining form* denoting something written or recorded in a specified way: *diagram / telegram.* [from Greek *gramma*, letter]

grammar *noun* **1** the accepted rules by which words are formed and combined into sentences. **2** the branch of language study dealing with these. **3** a description of these rules as applied to a particular language; a book containing this. **4** a person's understanding or use of these rules: *bad grammar.* [from Greek *gramma*, letter]

grammarian *noun* an expert on grammar.

grammar school especially formerly, a secondary school emphasising the study of academic rather than technical subjects.

grammatical *adj.* **1** relating to grammar. **2** correct according to the rules of grammar. [from Greek *grammatikos*, from *gramma*, letter]

grammatically *adv.* in a grammatical way; as regards grammar.

gramme see GRAM.

gramophone *noun* a record player, especially an old-fashioned one. [from Greek *gramma*, letter, record + *phone*, sound]

grampus *noun* (PL. **grampuses**) **1** a grey dolphin, native to deeper waters of temperate and tropical seas, up to 4m in length, and having a bulbous forehead, no beak, relatively short flippers, and a tall fin. Also called RISSO's DOLPHIN. **2** a killer whale. **3** a person who breathes heavily. [from Old French *graspois*, from *gras*, fat + *pois*, fish]

Gram's stain *Biol.* an important staining procedure used to distinguish between two major groups of bacteria. Gram-positive bacteria stain deep purple and Gram-negative bacteria stain red, owing to differences in cell wall structure. [named after the Danish bacteriologist Hans Christian Joachim Gram (1853–1938)]

gran *noun colloq.* a grandmother.

granary — *noun* (PL. **granaries**) **1** a building where grain is stored. **2** a region that produces large quantities of grain. — *adj., said of bread* containing whole grains of wheat. [from Latin *granarium*, from *granum*, grain]

grand — *adj.* **1** large or impressive in size, appearance or style. **2** *sometimes derog.* dignified; self-important. **3** intended to impress or gain attention: *a grand gesture.* **4** complete; in full: *grand total.* **5** *colloq.* very pleasant; excellent. **6** greatest; highest ranking: *Grand Master.* **7** highly respected: *grand old man.* **8** main; principal: *the grand entrance.* — *noun* **1** *slang* a thousand dollars or pounds. **2** *colloq.* a grand piano. [from French *grand*, from Latin *grandis*, great]

▤ *adj.* **1** impressive, imposing, striking, monumental, large, majestic, regal, noble, stately, splendid, magnificent. **2** dignified, lordly, lofty, self-important, pompous, pretentious, grandiose. **5** excellent, outstanding, first-rate, superb, glorious, fine. **6** greatest, supreme, pre-eminent, leading, head, chief, arch, highest, senior. **7** great, illustrious, eminent, distinguished, venerable, revered.

▣ *adj.* **1, 2** humble, lowly.

grand- *combining form* indicating a family relationship that is one generation more remote than that of the base word.

grandad *noun colloq.* **1** a grandfather. **2** *offensive* an old man.

grandchild *noun* a child of one's son or daughter.

granddaughter *noun* a daughter of one's son or daughter.

grand duchess 1 the wife or widow of a grand duke. **2** a high-ranking noblewoman who rules a grand duchy.

grand duchy a small European country or state having a grand duke or grand duchess as its sovereign.

grand duke a high-ranking nobleman who rules a grand duchy.

grandee *noun* **1** a Spanish or Portuguese nobleman of the highest rank. **2** any well-respected or high-ranking person. [from Spanish *grande*]

grandeur /'grandjə(r)/ *noun* **1** greatness of character, especially dignity or nobility. **2** impressive beauty; magnificence. **3** *derog.* self-importance; pretentiousness. [from French *grandeur*]

■ **1** greatness, illustriousness, dignity, nobility, importance. **2** magnificence, splendour, majesty, stateliness, pomp, state.
■ **1** humbleness, lowliness. **2** simplicity.

grandfather *noun* the father of one's father or mother.

grandfather clock a clock built into a tall free-standing wooden case, operated by a long pendulum.

grandiloquence /gran'dɪləkwəns/ *noun* being grandiloquent.

grandiloquent /gran'dɪləkwənt/ *adj. derog.* speaking, or spoken, or written, in a pompous, self-important style. [from Latin *grandis*, great + *loqui*, to speak]

grandiose *adj.* **1** splendid; magnificent; impressive. **2** *derog.* exaggeratedly impressive or imposing, especially on a ridiculously large scale. [from Italian *grandioso*, from *grande*, great]

■ **1** grand, majestic, stately, magnificent, splendid, impressive, imposing, monumental. **2** pompous, pretentious, high-flown, lofty, ambitious, extravagant, ostentatious, showy, flamboyant.
■ UNPRETENTIOUS.

grand jury in the US, a jury which decides whether there is enough evidence for a person to be brought to trial.

grandma *noun colloq.* a grandmother.

grand mal /grɒn 'mal/ *Medicine* a serious form of epilepsy, commonly known as an epileptic fit, in which there is sudden loss of consciousness followed by convulsions, which subside after a period of a few seconds to several minutes. [French, = great illness]

grandmother *noun* the mother of one's father or mother.

Grand National a British horserace, generally viewed as the most famous steeplechase in the world, first held at Maghull near Liverpool in 1836, and now held at Aintree.

grand opera serious opera of the 19c, based on grand themes and using large forces and elaborate staging, with all the dialogue usually sung.

grandpa *noun colloq.* a grandfather.

grandparent *noun* either parent of one's father or mother.

grand piano a large piano in which the strings are arranged horizontally, used especially for concerts.

Grand Prix /grɒn 'pri:/ (PL. **Grands Prix**) the name applied to automobile racing on closed circuits, which began in France in 1906, and is controlled by the FIA (Fédération Internationale de l'Automobile). The premier class of Grand Prix racing-car is Formula One. The term 'Grand Prix' is also used in other sports (eg horse-racing, tennis) in which a series of events decides the overall champion. [from French *grand prix*, great prize]

grand slam 1 *Sport* the winning in one season of every part of a competition, or of all major competitions. **2** *Cards* especially in bridge, the winning of all thirteen tricks by one player or side, or the contract to do so.

grandson *noun* a son of one's son or daughter.

grandstand *noun* the largest covered stand at a sports ground, providing the best view.

grandstand finish 1 a close and rousing finish to a sporting contest. **2** a supreme effort to win at the close of a sporting contest.

grand tour 1 a tour of the major cities of Europe, considered essential to the education of a rich young person, especially in the 18c. **2** *colloq.* any extended tour or inspection.

grange *noun* a country house with farm buildings attached. [from Old French *grange*, barn]

granite /'granɪt/ *noun Geol.* a hard coarse-grained igneous rock, generally grey, pink, yellow, or green in colour, consisting mainly of quartz and feldspar, with small amounts of mica. It is widely used in the construction of buildings and roads. [from Italian *granito*, grained]

granny or **grannie** *noun* (PL. **grannies**) *colloq.* a grandmother.

granny flat *colloq.* a flat for an elderly relative or parent, built on to or contained in a house.

granny knot a reef knot with the ends crossed the wrong way, allowing it to slip or undo easily.

Granny Smith a crisp green variety of eating apple, originally Australian.

grant — *verb* **1** to give, allow, or fulfil. **2** to admit to be true. **3** (**granted**) an admission that something is true or valid: *granted you gave it back later.* — *noun* **1** something granted, especially an amount of money from a public fund for a specific purpose. **2** *Legal* the transfer of property by deed. — **take someone for granted** to treat them casually and without appreciation. **take something for granted** to assume it to be true or valid; to accept it without question. [from Old French *granter* or *greanter*, variant of *creanter*, to promise]

■ *verb* ALLOW. **1** give, donate, present, award, confer, bestow, impart, apportion, assign, allot, allocate, provide, supply, fulfil, permit, consent to, agree to, accede to. **2** admit, acknowledge, concede. *noun* **1** allowance, subsidy, concession, award, bursary, scholarship, gift, donation, annuity, pension, honorarium. **2** endowment, bequest.
■ *verb* DENY. **1** withhold.

Granth /grʌnt/ *noun* (also **Granth Sahib**) the sacred scripture of the Sikh religion. [from Hindi *granth*, book]

granular *adj. technical* **1** made of, or containing, tiny particles or granules. **2** *said of appearance or texture* rough. [see GRANULE]

■ **1** grainy, granulated, gritty, sandy, lumpy, crumbly, friable. **2** rough, coarse.

granularity *noun* being granular.

granulate *verb* **1** to break down into small particles or granules. **2** to give a rough appearance or texture to.

granulation *noun* **1** forming into grains. **2** a granulated texture.

granule *noun* a very small particle or grain. [from Latin *granulum*, diminutive of *granum*, grain]

grape *noun* **1** a pale green or purplish-black juicy edible berry, which may be eaten fresh, pressed to make wine, or dried to form currants, raisins, and sultanas. **2** a perennial climbing vine of the genus *Vitis*, widely cultivated in warm temperate regions for these edible berries, which are borne in clusters. **3** *literary* (**the grape**) wine. [from Old French *grape*, bunch of grapes]

grapefruit *noun* (PL. **grapefruit**, **grapefruits**) **1** an evergreen tree (*Citrus paradisi*), native to tropical and warm temperate regions, widely cultivated for its large yellow edible fruits, which are borne in clusters. **2** the large round edible citrus fruit produced by this tree, having juicy acidic pale yellow or pink flesh that is rich in vitamin C, and enclosed by a bitter pale yellow rind.

grape hyacinth a plant belonging to the genus *Muscari*, native to Europe, and having grass-like leaves, and dense spikes of drooping urn-shaped blue flowers, each with six small lobes.

grapeshot *noun* ammunition in the form of small iron balls, spreading when fired in bunches from a cannon.

grape sugar *Biochem.* glucose.

grapevine *noun* **1** a vine on which grapes grow. **2** (**the grapevine**) *colloq.* informal conversation between people, regarded as a network by which information is spread: *I heard on the grapevine that she's leaving.*

graph — *noun* **1** a diagram that illustrates the way in which one quantity varies in relation to another. It usually consists of two axes, one horizontal and the other vertical, which cross each other at a point called the origin. Points representing different sets of data are plotted in the areas between the axes. **2** a symbolic diagram. — *verb* to represent with a graph. [from Greek *graphein*, to write]

⊟ *noun* **2** diagram, chart, table, grid.

-graph *combining form* forming words denoting: **1** an instrument that writes or records: *telegraph.* **2** something written or recorded: *autograph.* [from Greek *graphein*, to write]

grapheme *noun Linguistics* **1** the letters or combination of letters used together to form a phoneme. **2** a letter of an alphabet. [from Greek *graphema*, letter]

graphic *adj.* **1** described or shown vividly and in detail. **2** denoting the branch of the arts concerned with drawing, printing, and lettering: *graphic design.* **3** relating to graphs; shown using a graph.

⊟ **1** vivid, descriptive, expressive, striking, telling, lively, realistic, explicit, clear, lucid, specific, detailed, blow-by-blow. **2** visual, pictorial. **3** diagrammatic, illustrative.

⊞ **1** vague, impressionistic.

-graphic or **-graphical** *combining form* forming adjectives corresponding to nouns in *-graph* and *-graphy*: *telegraphic / geographical.*

graphically *adv.* in a graphic way.

graphic equalizer *Electron.* in a sound system, a type of sliding control that enables the listener to regulate the tone by adjusting the output signal in each of a series of specific frequency bands.

graphic novel a full-length story, often of science fiction or some other form of fantasy, told in comic strip form and published as a book.

graphics *noun* **1** (*sing.*) the art or science of drawing according to mathematical principles, especially the drawing of three-dimensional objects on a two-dimensional surface using geometric methods. **2** (*pl.*) **a** the photographs and illustrations used in a magazine. **b** the non-acted visual parts of a film or television programme, eg the credits. **3** (*pl.*) *Comput.* the use of computers to display and manipulate information in graphical or pictorial form, either on a visual-display unit, or via a printer or plotter. See also COMPUTER GRAPHICS.

graphics tablet *Comput.* an input device which translates the movements of a pen over a sensitive pad to a corresponding pattern on the screen.

graphic user interface (ABBREV. GUI) *Comput.* a system of program management that uses *icons* (small pictures) on the screen to represent programs, files, and menu choices.

graphite *noun* a soft black allotrope of carbon that is a good conductor of heat and electricity, and is greasy and slippery to the touch. Also called BLACK LEAD, PLUMBAGO. [from Greek *graphein*, to write]

graphologist *noun* a person skilled in or practising graphology.

graphology *noun* the study of handwriting, especially as a way of analysing the writer's character. [from Greek *graphein*, to write + -LOGY]

graph paper paper printed with a grid of small squares, used for drawing graphs.

-graphy *combining form* **1** a type of writing or method of representing: *biography / lithography.* **2** a descriptive science or art: *geography / choreography.* [from Greek *graphein*, to write]

grapnel *noun* **1** a large multi-pointed hook on the end of a rope, used for securing a heavy object on the other end. **2** a light anchor for small boats. [from Old French *grapin*, diminutive of *grape*, hook]

grappa *noun* a brandy distilled from the fermentable residue (grape skins and stalks) from a wine-press. Originally Italian, it is now made in California, Uruguay, and elsewhere. [from Italian *grappa*, grape stalk]

grapple — *verb* **1** (**grapple with someone**) to grasp and struggle or fight. **2** (**grapple with something**) to struggle mentally with a difficult problem. **3** to secure with a hook, etc. — *noun* **1** a hook or other device for securing. **2** an act of gripping, as in wrestling; a way of gripping. [from Old French *grappelle*, diminutive of *grape*, hook]

⊟ *verb* **1** grasp, seize, grab, grip, clutch, clasp, hold, wrestle with, tussle with, struggle with, contend with, fight, combat. **2** struggle with, wrestle with, face, confront, tackle, deal with, cope with. **3** secure, hold, attach, fix.

⊞ *verb* **1, 3** release. **2** avoid.

grappling-iron or **grappling-hook** *noun* a grapnel.

graptolite *noun Geol.* any of a group of extinct marine animals that were common in the Palaeozoic era, and are thought to be related to present-day coelenterates (eg jellyfish, corals). [from Greek *graptos*, written + *lithos*, stone]

grasp — *verb* **1** to take a firm hold of; to clutch. **2** (**grasp at something**) to make a movement as if to seize it. **3** to understand. — *noun* **1** a grip or hold. **2** power or control; ability to reach, achieve, or obtain: *in one's grasp.* **3** ability to understand: *beyond their grasp.* [from Middle English *graspen*]

⊟ *verb* **1** hold, clasp, clutch, grip, seize. **2** snatch, grab. **3** understand, comprehend, *colloq.* get, follow, see, realize. *noun* **1** grip, hold, clasp, embrace. **2** power, control, possession, clutches, reach. **3** understanding, comprehension, mastery, familiarity, knowledge.

grasping *adj. derog.* greedy, especially for wealth.

⊟ greedy, avaricious, rapacious, acquisitive, mercenary, mean, selfish, miserly, close-fisted, tight-fisted, parsimonious.

⊞ generous.

grass — *noun* **1** any flowering plant belonging to the family Gramineae, typically having long narrow leaves with parallel veins, a jointed upright hollow stem, and flowers with no petals borne alternately on both sides of an axis known as a spikelet, eg wheat, maize, rye, sugar-cane, bamboo. **2** an area planted with or growing such plants, eg a lawn or meadow. **3** lawn or pasture. **4** *slang* marijuana. **5** *slang* a person who betrays others, especially to the police. — *verb* **1** to plant with grass or turf. **2** to feed with grass; to provide pasture for. **3** *slang* (*often* **grass on someone**) to inform, especially to the police. — **let the grass grow under one's feet** to delay or waste time. **put something** or **someone out to grass 1** to give a life of grazing to an old animal, eg a racehorse. **2** *colloq.* to put someone into retirement. [from Anglo-Saxon *gærs, græs*]

⊟ *noun* **2** lawn, green, field, meadow. **3** turf, lawn, grassland, pasture, prairie, pampas, savanna, steppe.

grasshopper *noun* a large brown or green jumping insect belonging to the same order (Orthoptera) as the crickets, but distinguished from them by its short antennae.

grass roots 1 ordinary people, as opposed to those in a position of (especially political) power. **2** bare essentials; fundamental principles.

grass-roots *adj.* relating to or involving ordinary people.

grass snake 1 a non-venomous snake, native to Europe (except for Ireland, the Isle of Man, and the far north), Asia, and N Africa, up to about 150cm long, and varying in colour from greenish-grey to olive-brown, with black and yellow patches on the back of its neck. **2** any of various related European snakes, such as the non-venomous common ringed snake.

grass widow or **grass widower** a person whose husband or wife is absent from home for long periods of time.

grassy *adj.* (**grassier**, **grassiest**) like or covered with grass.

grate[1] *noun* **1** a framework of iron bars for holding coal, etc in a fireplace or furnace. **2** the fireplace or furnace itself. [from Latin *grata*]

grate[2] *verb* **1** to cut into shreds by rubbing against a rough surface. **2** *trans., intrans.* to make or cause to make a harsh grinding sound by rubbing. **3** (**grate on someone**) to irritate or annoy them. [from Old French *grater*, to scrape]

▣ **1** grind, shred, mince, pulverize. **2** rub, grind, rasp, scrape. **3** annoy, irritate, *colloq.* aggravate, vex, irk, exasperate.

grateful *adj.* **1** feeling thankful; showing or giving thanks. **2** *formal* pleasant and welcome: *grateful sleep*. See GRATITUDE. [from Latin *gratus*, pleasing, thankful]

▣ **1** thankful, appreciative, indebted, obliged, beholden.
▣ **1** ungrateful.

gratefully *adv.* in a grateful way; with gratitude.

grater *noun* a device with a rough surface for grating food.

gratification *noun* **1** a pleasing. **2** that which pleases. **3** satisfaction.

gratify *verb* (**gratifies**, **gratified**) **1** to please. **2** to satisfy or indulge (eg a desire). [from Latin *gratus*, pleasing, thankful + *facere*, to make]

▣ **1** please, gladden, delight, thrill. **2** satisfy, fulfil, indulge, pander to, humour, favour.
▣ **1** displease. **2** frustrate, thwart.

grating[1] *noun* a framework of metal bars fixed into a wall eg over a window, or into a pavement eg over a drain. [from GRATE[1]]

▣ grate, grille, grid, lattice, trellis.

grating[2] — *adj.* **1** *said of sounds, etc* harsh. **2** irritating. — *noun* a grating sound.

▣ *adj.* **1** harsh, rasping, scraping, squeaky, strident, discordant, jarring. **2** annoying, irritating, *colloq.* aggravating, exasperating.
▣ *adj.* **1** harmonious. **2** pleasing.

gratis /ˈgratɪs/ *adv., adj.* free; without charge. [from Latin *gratis*, from *gratia*, favour]

gratitude *noun* the state or feeling of being grateful; thankfulness. [from Latin *gratus*, thankful]

▣ gratefulness, thankfulness, thanks, appreciation, acknowledgement, recognition, indebtedness, obligation.
▣ ingratitude, ungratefulness.

gratuitous /grəˈtjuːɪtəs/ *adj.* **1** done without good reason; unnecessary or unjustified. **2** given or received without charge; voluntary. [from Latin *gratuitas*, from *gratia*, favour]

▣ **1** wanton, unnecessary, needless, unwarranted, unjustified, groundless, undeserved, unprovoked, uncalled-for, unsolicited. **2** voluntary, free, gratis, complimentary.
▣ **1** justified, provoked.

gratuity /grəˈtjuːɪtɪ/ *noun* (PL. **gratuities**) **1** a sum of money given as a reward for good service; a tip. **2** a sum of money given to a soldier, etc on retirement, in recognition of long service. [from Latin *gratus*, thankful]

▣ **1** tip, bonus, *colloq.* perk, gift, present, donation, reward, recompense.

grave[1] *noun* **1** a deep trench dug in the ground for burying a dead body. **2** the site of an individual burial. **3** (**the grave**) *literary* death. — **dig one's own grave** to be the cause of one's own downfall. **turn in one's grave** *said of a dead person* to be thought likely to be distressed or offended when alive by circumstances such as those in question. [from Anglo-Saxon *græf*, grave or trench, from *grafan*, to dig]

▣ **2** burial-place, tomb, sepulchre, mausoleum, pit, barrow, tumulus, cairn.

grave[2] *adj.* **1** giving cause for great concern; very dangerous. **2** very important; serious. **3** solemn and serious in manner. [from Latin *gravis*]

▣ SERIOUS. **1** acute, severe, dangerous, hazardous. **2** important, significant, weighty, momentous, critical, vital, crucial, urgent. **3** solemn, dignified, sober, sedate, thoughtful, pensive, grim, long-faced, quiet, reserved, subdued, restrained.
▣ **2** trivial. **3** cheerful.

grave[3] *noun* (pronounced as in *halve*) (*also* **grave accent**) a mark placed over a vowel (eg à, è) in some languages to indicate a particular pronunciation or extended length of the vowel. [from French *grave*]

gravel — *noun* **1** a mixture of small loose or unconsolidated rock fragments and pebbles that is coarser than sand, found on beaches, in the beds of rivers, streams, and lakes, and also quarried for use in road building, and as an aggregate in concrete. **2** *Pathol.* small stones formed in the kidney or bladder, often causing severe pain. — *verb* (**gravelled**, **gravelling**) to cover (eg a path) with gravel. [from Old French *gravele*]

gravelly *adj.* **1** full of, or containing, small stones. **2** *said of a voice* rough and usually deep.

graven *adj.* **1** *old use* carved or engraved. **2** firmly fixed in the mind. [from old word *grave*, to carve or engrave]

graven image *Biblical* a carved idol used in worship.

gravestone *noun* a stone marking a grave, usually having the dead person's name and dates of birth and death engraved.

graveyard *noun* a burial place; a cemetery.

▣ cemetery, burial-ground, churchyard.

gravid /ˈgravɪd/ *adj. Medicine* pregnant. [from Latin *gravis*, heavy]

gravimeter *noun Geol.* an instrument for measuring variations in the magnitude of the gravitational field at different points on the Earth's surface. It is used to prospect for mineral deposits, eg petroleum, which produce local variations in the force of gravity. [from Latin *gravis*, heavy + Greek *metron*, measure]

gravimetric *adj.* **1** relating to or based on measurement by weight, especially for the purpose of chemical analysis. **2** denoting the techniques used to measure the properties of the Earth's gravitational field.

gravimetry *noun* **1** the scientific measurement of the Earth's gravitational field at different points on its surface, especially in order to map structures beneath the surface, such as high-density rock formations. **2** the chemical analysis of substances by separating their constituents and determining their relative proportions by weight.

gravitas /ˈgrav ɪtaːs/ *noun literary* seriousness of manner; solemnity. [from Latin *gravitas*]

gravitate *verb intrans.* **1** to fall or be drawn under the force of gravity. **2** to move or be drawn gradually, as if attracted by some force. [from GRAVITY[1]]

gravitation *noun* **1** *Physics* the force of attraction that exists between any two bodies on account of their mass. It is directly proportional to the product of their masses, and inversely proportional to the square of the distance between them. **2** the process of moving or being drawn, either by this force or some other attracting influence.

gravitational *adj.* relating to or caused by gravitation.

gravitational field *Physics* that region of space in which one object, by virtue of its mass, exerts a force of attraction on another object.

graviton *noun Physics* the hypothetical carrier of gravitational force.

gravity[1] *noun* **1** the observed effect of the force of attraction that exists between two massive bodies. The magnitude of the force is proportional to the product of the masses of the two bodies, and inversely proportional to the square of the distance between them. **2** the name commonly used to refer to the force of attraction between any object that is situated within the Earth's gravitational field, and the Earth itself. Objects feel heavy, and are pulled down towards the ground, because of this force. [from Latin *gravitas*, heaviness]

⊟ **2** gravitation, attraction, pull, weight, heaviness.

gravity[2] *noun* **1** seriousness; dangerous nature. **2** serious attitude; solemnity. [from Latin *gravitas*, seriousness]

⊟ SERIOUSNESS. **1** importance, significance, urgency, acuteness, severity, danger. **2** solemnity, dignity, sobriety, thoughtfulness, sombreness, reserve, restraint.
⊠ **1** triviality. **2** levity.

gravlax or **gravadlax** *noun* a Scandinavian dish of salmon dry-cured with herbs (usually dill), sugar, salt, and pepper, sliced on the slant to serve. [from Swedish *gravlax*, Norwegian *gravlaks*, buried salmon]

gravure /grəˈvjʊə(r)/ *noun* **1** a form of intaglio printing in which the image is engraved or etched into the surface of a metal cylinder; after inking, surplus ink is removed from the surface of the cylinder, and the ink retained in the engraved recesses is transferred to paper. **2** an image produced by this process (see also PHOTOGRAVURE).

gravy *noun* (PL. **gravies**) **1** the juices released by meat as it is cooking. **2** a sauce made by thickening and seasoning these juices; a similar sauce made with an artificial substitute. **3** *slang* easily obtained money. [perhaps from French *gravé*, mistaken reading of *grané*, cooking spice]

gravy boat a small boat-shaped container with a handle, for serving gravy and other sauces.

gravy train *slang* a job or scheme from which a lot of money is gained for little effort.

gray[1] *North Amer., esp. US* same as GREY.

gray[2] *noun Physics* (ABBREV. **Gy**) the SI unit used to express the amount of radiation absorbed, equal to one joule of energy per kilogram. [named after the UK radiobiologist Louis H Gray]

grayling *noun* (PL. **grayling, graylings**) **1** any of various butterflies, native to Europe (except for the far north), having grey or greyish-brown wings with eyespots, and front legs reduced to small brush-like appendages. **2** any of several freshwater fish related to the salmon, native to N America and northern parts of Europe and Asia, and having a long muscular body with large silvery scales and a greenish-gold sheen, dark zigzag lines running along its length, a small mouth, and a large dorsal fin that is purplish in colour. [from GREY]

graze[1] *verb* **1** *intrans. said of animals* to eat grass. **2** *trans.* to feed (animals) on grass. [from Anglo-Saxon *grasian*, from *græs*, grass]

graze[2] — *verb* **1** to suffer a break in the skin of (eg a limb), through scraping against a hard rough surface. **2** to brush against lightly in passing. — *noun* **1** an area of grazed skin. **2** the action of grazing skin.

⊟ *verb* **1** scratch, scrape, skin, abrade, rub, chafe. **2** brush, skim, touch. *noun* **1** scratch, scrape, abrasion.

grazing *noun* **1** the act of feeding by animal livestock on growing vegetation. **2** the grass or other growing vegetation that is available for animal livestock to feed on. **3** the land on which such vegetation grows.

grease — *noun* **1** animal fat softened by melting or cooking. **2** any thick oily substance, especially a lubricant for the moving parts of machinery. — *verb* **1** to lubricate or dirty with grease. **2** to ease the progress of. — **grease someone's palm** or **hand** *colloq.* to bribe them. **grease the wheels** *colloq.* to make progress easier. [from Old French *graisse*]

⊟ *noun* **1** fat, lard, dripping, tallow. **2** oil, lubrication. *verb* **1** lubricate, oil.

greasepaint *noun* waxy make-up used by actors.

greaser *noun* **1** a person whose job it is to grease machinery. **2** *slang* a member of a gang of usually long-haired motorcyclists. **3** *North Amer. offensive slang* a Mexican or Spanish American.

greasiness *noun* being greasy.

greasy *adj.* (**greasier, greasiest**) **1** containing, or covered in, grease. **2** having an oily appearance or texture. **3** slippery, as if covered in grease. **4** *colloq.* insincerely friendly or flattering.

⊟ OILY. **1** fatty, lardy, buttery, smeary. **2** smooth, waxy. **3** slippery, slimy. **4** smooth, smarmy, unctuous.

great — *adj.* **1** outstandingly talented, and much admired and respected. **2** very large in size, quantity, intensity, or extent. **3** (*also* **greater**) *Biol.* larger in size than others of the same kind, species, etc. **4** *colloq.* very enjoyable; excellent or splendid. **5** *colloq.* (**great at something**) clever at it; talented. **6** *colloq.* (**great for something**) very suitable or useful for it. **7** most important: *the great advantage of it*. **8** enthusiastic; keen: *a great reader*. **9** *colloq.* used to emphasize other adjectives describing size, especially big: *a great big dog*. **10** (**the Great**) in names and titles, indicating an importance or reputation of the highest degree: *Alfred the Great*. **11** *old use* used in various expressions of surprise: *Great Scott!* — *noun* a person who has achieved lasting fame, deservedly or not: *all-time greats*. [from Anglo-Saxon *great*]

⊟ *adj.* **1** famous, renowned, celebrated, illustrious, eminent, distinguished, prominent, noteworthy, notable, remarkable, outstanding, grand. **2** large, big, huge, enormous, massive, colossal, gigantic, mammoth, immense, vast, considerable, pronounced, extreme, excessive, inordinate. **4** excellent, first-rate, superb, wonderful, marvellous, tremendous, terrific, fantastic, fabulous. **7** important, significant, major, principal, primary, main, chief, leading.
⊠ *adj.* **1** unknown. **2** small, slight. **7** unimportant, insignificant.

great- *combining form* indicating a family relationship that is one generation more remote than that of the base word: *great-grandmother* / *great-great-grandson*. [from Anglo-Saxon *great*]

great-aunt *noun* an aunt of one's father or mother.

Great Britain a name for the combined kingdoms of England and Scotland, and the principality of Wales, which, together with Northern Ireland, make up the United Kingdom.

greatcoat *noun* a heavy overcoat.

Great Dane one of the largest breeds of dog, with a short smooth coat, usually pale brown in colour with dark flecks, long powerful legs, and a square head with a deep muzzle and small erect ears.

greatly *adv.* in a great way, much, very.

great-nephew *noun* a son of one's nephew or niece.

greatness *noun* being great.

great-niece *noun* a daughter of one's nephew or niece.

Great Red Spot *Astron.* the Red Spot of Jupiter.

great-uncle *noun* an uncle of one's father or mother.

Great War (**the Great War**) World War I, 1914–18.

greave *noun* (*usually* **greaves**) armour for the legs below the knee. [from Old French *greve*, shin]

grebe *noun* any of a family of large waterfowl with short wings, long individually webbed toes, a pointed bill, vestigial tail, and in most species colourful plumes on the head. [from French *grèbe*]

Grecian /'griːʃən/ *adj.*, *said of a design, etc* in the style of ancient Greece. [from Latin *Graecus*, Greek]

Grecian nose an uncurved nose forming a straight line with the forehead.

Greco- same as GRAECO-.

greed *noun* **1** an excessive desire for, or consumption of, food. **2** selfish desire in general, eg for money. [back-formation from GREEDY]

. . . .

⊟ HUNGER. **1** ravenousness, gluttony, voracity, insatiability. **2** acquisitiveness, covetousness, desire, craving, longing, eagerness, avarice, selfishness.
⊟ ABSTEMIOUSNESS.

. . . .

greedily *adv.* in a greedy way; with greed.

greedy *adj.* (**greedier**, **greediest**) filled with greed. [from Anglo-Saxon *grædig*]

. . . .

⊟ hungry, starving, ravenous, gluttonous, voracious, insatiable, acquisitive, covetous, desirous, craving, eager, impatient, avaricious, grasping, selfish.
⊟ abstemious.

. . . .

Greek — *noun* **1** the official language of Greece. **2** a native or inhabitant of Greece. **3** *colloq.* any language, jargon, or subject one cannot understand. — *adj.* of Greece, its people, or their language. [from Latin *Graecus*]

green — *adj.* **1** of the colour of the leaves of most plants, between yellow and blue in the spectrum. **2** covered with grass, bushes, etc: *green areas of the city.* **3** consisting mainly of leaves: *green salad.* **4** *said of fruit* not yet ripe. **5** *colloq.*, *said of people* young, inexperienced, or easily fooled. **6** showing concern for, or designed to be harmless to, the environment. **7** *said of a person's face* pale; showing signs of nausea. **8** not dried or dry: *green bacon* / *green timber.* **9** extremely jealous or envious. **10** healthy, vigorous, or flourishing: *green old age.* — *noun* **1** the colour of the leaves of most plants, between yellow and blue in the spectrum. **2** something of this colour. **3** an area of grass, especially in a public place. **4** an area of specially prepared turf: *bowling-green.* **5** (**greens**) vegetables with edible green leaves and stems. **6** (*often* **Green**) a person who supports actions or policies designed to protect or benefit the environment, especially one belonging to or supporting a green party — *verb trans.*, *intrans.* to make or become green. [from Anglo-Saxon *grene*]

. . . .

⊟ *adj.* **2** grassy, leafy, verdant. **4** unripe, immature. **5** young, immature, naïve, unsophisticated, credulous, gullible, ignorant, inexperienced, untrained, raw, new, recent, fresh. **6** ecological, environmental, environmentally friendly, eco-friendly. **8** unseasoned. **9** jealous, envious, covetous, resentful. **10** vigorous, flourishing, thriving, budding, blooming. *noun* **3** common, lawn, g rass, turf.

. . . .

green alga *Bot.* any alga belonging to the class Chlorophyceae, characterized by possession of the green pigment chlorophyll, the storage of starch as a food reserve, and the presence of cell walls composed of cellulose.

green audit *Environ.* an investigation of a company's accounts in order to determine the effects on the environment of that company's activities, eg the effects of a particular process, or of a product that is being manufactured, the possibility of recycling raw materials, etc.

greenback *noun colloq.* a US currency note (often printed in green on the back), first issued in 1862.

green bean any variety of bean, such as the French bean (*Phaseolus vulgaris*), the narrow green unripe pod and contents of which can be eaten whole.

green belt open land surrounding a town or city, where building or development is strictly controlled.

green card an official US work and residence permit (originally green) issued to foreign nationals.

greenery *noun* green plants or their leaves, either when growing or when cut for decoration.

green-eyed *adj. colloq.* jealous or envious.

greenfinch *noun* a bird belonging to the finch family, native to S Europe and S Asia, that inhabits forests and cultivated land, and feeds on seeds and insects.

green fingers *colloq.* natural skill at growing plants successfully.

greenfly *noun* (PL. **greenfly**, **greenflies**) any of various species of aphid that have a soft pear-shaped body and feed by sucking plant sap.

greengage *noun* **1** any of several cultivated varieties of a tree, sometimes regarded as a subspecies of the plum, but often considered to be a separate species, widely cultivated for its edible fruit. **2** the small round edible fruit produced by this tree, resembling a plum, but having greenish-brown flesh enclosed by greenish-yellow skin, used to make jam, etc.

greengrocer *noun* a person or shop selling fruit and vegetables.

greengrocery *noun* the produce sold by a greengrocer.

greenhorn *noun colloq.* an inexperienced person; a novice.

greenhouse *noun* a glasshouse, especially one with little or no artificial heating, used for growing young or tender plants, or for growing plants out of season. Also called GLASSHOUSE.

. . . .

⊟ glasshouse, hothouse, conservatory, pavilion, vinery, orangery.

. . . .

greenhouse effect the warming of the Earth's surface as a result of the trapping of long-wave radiation by carbon dioxide, ozone, and certain other gases in the Earth's atmosphere, so called because the atmosphere has a similar effect to the glass panels of a greenhouse.

greenhouse gas any of various gases such as carbon dioxide, methane, or chlorofluorocarbons, which are present in the lower atmosphere and act like a pane of glass in a greenhouse, trapping solar radiation reflected from the Earth's surface and redirecting it back towards the Earth. Increased emissions of greenhouse gases from burning fossil fuels are causing a slow increase in the average temperature of the Earth's surface, resulting in the so-called *greenhouse effect.*

greenkeeper *noun* a person responsible for the maintenance of a golf course or bowling-green.

green light 1 a signal to move forward. **2** *colloq.* (**the green light**) permission to proceed: *we've got the green light.*

greenmail *noun* the practice of buying sufficient shares in a company to threaten takeover and force the company to buy back its shares at a premium. [from GREEN (of paper money) + BLACKMAIL]

green paper (*often* **Green Paper**) in the UK, a written statement of the Government's proposed policy on a particular issue, for discussion. See also COMMAND PAPER, WHITE PAPER.

green party (*also* **Green Party**) a political party concerned with promoting policies for the protection and benefit of the environment.

green pepper a green unripe sweet pepper, eaten as a vegetable. See also RED PEPPER.

green pound the pound's value compared with that of the other European currencies used in trading EC farm produce.

Green Revolution a popular term for the recent improvements in agricultural productivity in some Third World countries that resulted from the development of new high-yielding strains of cereal crops, and the use of fertilizers and pesticides.

greenroom *noun* a backstage room in a theatre where actors, musicians, etc can relax and receive visitors.

greensand *noun Geol.* a greenish sand or sandstone, consisting mainly of grains of glauconite (a green mineral closely related to the micas).

greenstick fracture *Medicine* an incomplete fracture of a long bone, in which the bone is bent but only part of it is broken, most common in children, whose bones are more flexible than those of adults.

green tea a sharp-tasting light-coloured tea made from leaves that have been dried quickly without fermenting.

Greenwich Mean Time /ˈgrenɪdʒ/ (ABBREV. **GMT**) the local time at the line of 0° longitude, passing through Greenwich in England, used to calculate times in most other parts of the world.

greet[1] *verb* **1** to address or welcome, especially in a friendly way. **2** to react to in a certain way: *remarks greeted with dismay.* **3** to be immediately noticeable to: *smells of cooking greeted me.* [from Anglo-Saxon *gretan*]

◨ **1** address, accost, hail, acknowledge, welcome, receive, meet. **2** react to, respond to, receive, meet.

◧ **1** ignore.

greet[2] *Scot. & N of England dialect.* — *verb intrans.* (PAST TENSE **grat**; PAST PARTICIPLE **grutten**) to cry. — *noun* a spell of crying. [from Anglo-Saxon *gretan*]

greeting *noun* **1** a friendly expression or gesture used on meeting or welcoming someone. **2** (**greetings**) a good or fond wish; a friendly message.

◨ **1** salutation, acknowledgement, wave, hello, address, welcome, reception. **2** good wishes, best wishes, regards, respects, compliments, salutations.

greetings card a decorated card used to send greetings.

gregarious /grəˈgeərɪəs/ *adj.* **1** *said of a person* liking the company of other people; sociable. **2** *said of an animal* tending to live in groups. [from Latin *gregarius*, from *grex*, flock]

◨ **1** sociable, outgoing, extrovert, friendly, affable, convivial, cordial.

◧ **1** unsociable.

Gregorian calendar the system introduced by Pope Gregory XIII in 1582, and still widely in use, in which an ordinary year is divided into 12 months or 365 days, with a leap year of 366 days every four years. See also JULIAN CALENDAR.

gremlin *noun* an imaginary mischievous creature blamed for faults in machinery or electronic equipment. [origin unknown; there are many anecdotal accounts, but none is historically sound]

grenade *noun* a small bomb thrown by hand or fired from a rifle. [from Spanish *granada*, pomegranate]

grenadier /grenəˈdɪə(r)/ *noun* a member of a regiment of soldiers formerly trained in the use of grenades.

grenadine /ˈgrenədiːn/ *noun* a syrup made from pomegranate juice, used to flavour (especially alcoholic) drinks. [related to GRENADE]

grew see GROW.

grey — *adj.* **1** of a colour between black and white, the colour of ash and slate. **2** *said of the weather* dull and cloudy. **3** a *said of a person's hair* turning white. b *said of a person* having grey hair. **4** *derog.* anonymous or uninteresting; having no distinguishing features: *a grey character.* **5** *literary* aged, mature, or experienced. — *noun* **1** a colour between black and white. **2** grey material or clothes: *dressed in grey.* **3** dull light. **4** an animal, especially a horse, that is grey or whitish in colour. — *verb trans., intrans.* to make or become grey. [from Anglo-Saxon *græg*]

◨ *adj.* **1** neutral, colourless, pale, ashen, leaden. **2** dull, cloudy, overcast, dark, murky, gloomy, dismal, dreary, bleak.

grey area an unclear situation or subject, often with no distinct limits or identifiable characteristics.

Grey Friar a Franciscan friar.

greyhound *noun* a tall breed of dog with a slender body, short coat, arched back, long powerful legs, a long tail, and a long pointed muzzle. [from Anglo-Saxon *grighund*, probably bitch-dog]

greylag goose a goose native to Europe and Asia, where it is the most numerous and widespread goose species. [*lag* may be because of its lateness in migrating]

grey matter 1 *Anat.* the tissue of the brain and spinal cord that consists mainly of nerve cell bodies which give it a grey colour, especially the cerebral cortex of the brain. **2** *colloq.* intelligence or common sense.

grey squirrel a species of squirrel, native to N America, having fine grey fur which becomes tinged with russet in summer, a bushy tail with light-coloured fringes, and no ear tufts.

greywacke or **graywacke** *noun Geol.* a type of hard sandstone, dark grey or greenish-grey in colour, and composed of angular grains of quartz and feldspar embedded in a matrix of clay. [from German *Grauwacke*, partly translated and partly adopted]

grid *noun* **1** a network of evenly spaced horizontal and vertical lines that can be superimposed on a map, chart, building plan, etc, in order to identify or locate specific points, or to determine the direction or distance of one point from another. **2** such a network used for constructing a graph. **3** (**the grid**) the network of power transmission lines, consisting of overhead wires and underground cables, by means of which electricity is distributed from power stations across a region or country. **4** a network of underground pipes by which gas, water, etc, is distributed across a region or country. **5** a framework of metal bars, especially one covering the opening to a drain. **6** an arrangement of lines marking the starting-points on a motor racing track. **7** *Electron.* an electrode, usually consisting of a perforated wire screen or a spiral of wire, that controls the flow of electrons from the cathode to the anode of a thermionic valve or vacuum tube. [back-formation from GRIDIRON]

griddle or **girdle** *noun* a flat iron plate, either loose with a handle or set into the top of a stove, heated for baking or frying. [from Old French *gridil*]

gridiron /ˈgrɪdaɪən/ *noun* **1** a frame of iron bars used for grilling food over a fire. **2** the field of play in American football. [from Middle English *gredire*]

gridlock noun **1** chiefly North Amer. a traffic jam. **2** a situation in which no progress is possible.

grief noun **1** great sorrow and unhappiness, especially at a person's death. **2** an event causing this. **3** colloq. trouble or bother. — **come to grief** colloq. to end in failure; to have an accident. [from Old French grever, to grieve]

▤ TROUBLE. **1** sorrow, sadness, unhappiness, dejection, desolation, distress, misery, woe, heartbreak, mourning, bereavement, heartache, anguish, agony, pain, suffering, affliction, regret, remorse.
▨ **1** happiness, delight.

grievance noun **1** a real or perceived cause for complaint, especially unfair treatment at work. **2** a formal complaint, especially made in the workplace. [from Old French grevance]

▤ **1** wrong, injustice, injury, damage, trouble, hardship. **2** complaint, colloq. moan, colloq. grumble, objection, protest, charge.

grieve verb **1** intrans. to feel grief, especially at a death. **2** trans. to upset or distress. [from Old French grever, to grieve, from Latin gravare, to burden]

▤ **1** sorrow, mope, lament, mourn, wail, cry, weep. **2** sadden, upset, dismay, distress, afflict, pain, hurt, wound.
▨ **1** rejoice. **2** please, gladden.

grievous adj. **1** very severe or painful. **2** causing or likely to cause grief. **3** showing grief. **4** extremely serious or evil. [from Old French grevos]

grievous bodily harm (ABBREV. **GBH**) Legal severe injury caused by a physical attack; the criminal charge of causing such injury.

griffin or **gryphon** noun Mythol. a winged monster with an eagle's head and a lion's body. [from Old French grifon]

griffon noun **1** any of various small breeds of dog, originally developed in Belgium, having a square body with a rounded head, a short muzzle, and a coarse wiry reddish, black, or black and tan coat. **2** a large vulture, native to S Europe, Africa, and S Asia, having a large heavy body, brownish-black wings with a span of almost 3m, and a bald head with a neck ruff. [variant of GRIFFIN]

grill — verb **1** to cook under radiated heat. **2** colloq. to interrogate, especially at length. — noun **1** a device on a cooker which radiates heat downwards. **2** a metal frame for cooking food over a fire; a gridiron. **3** a dish of grilled food. **4** (also **grillroom**) a restaurant or part of a restaurant specializing in grilled food. [from French griller, to grill]

grille or **grill** noun a protective framework of metal bars or wires, eg over a window or a car radiator. [from French gril]

grilling noun colloq. an interrogation.

grilse noun (PL. **grilses**, **grilse**) a young salmon returning from the sea to fresh water for the first time.

grim adj. (**grimmer**, **grimmest**) **1** stern and unsmiling. **2** terrible; horrifying. **3** resolute; dogged: grim determination. **4** depressing; gloomy. **5** colloq. unpleasant. **6** colloq. ill. [from Anglo-Saxon grimm]

▤ **1** stern, severe, harsh, forbidding, dour, unsmiling, surly, sullen, morose. **2** terrible, horrifying, fearsome, frightening, sinister, grisly, gruesome. **3** resolute, determined, dogged, tenacious, persistent, stubborn. **4** depressing, cheerless, dismal, sombre, gloomy, dreary. **5** unpleasant, unattractive, horrible, horrid, ghastly.
▨ **5** pleasant, attractive.

grimace — noun an ugly twisting of the face, expressing pain or disgust, or for amusement. — verb intrans. to make a grimace. [from French grimace]

▤ noun frown, scowl, pout, smirk, sneer, face. verb make a face, pull a face, frown, scowl, pout, smirk, sneer.

grime — noun thick ingrained dirt or soot. — verb to soil heavily; to make filthy. [from Middle English]

▤ noun dirt, muck, filth, soot, dust.

griminess noun being grimy.

grimy adj. (**grimier**, **grimiest**) covered with grime, dirty.

▤ dirty, mucky, grubby, soiled, filthy, sooty, smutty, dusty.
▨ clean.

grin — verb (**grinned**, **grinning**) **1** intrans. to smile broadly, showing the teeth. **2** trans. to express (eg pleasure) in this way. — noun a broad smile, showing the teeth. — **grin and bear it** colloq. to endure something unpleasant without complaining. [from Anglo-Saxon grennian]

grind — verb (PAST TENSE AND PAST PARTICIPLE **ground**) **1** to crush into small particles or powder between two hard surfaces. **2** to sharpen or polish by rubbing against a hard surface. **3** trans., intrans. to rub together with a jarring noise. **4** to press hard with a twisting action: ground his heel into the dirt. **5** to operate by turning a handle: organ-grinding. **6** (**grind down**) to crush the spirit of; to oppress. — noun **1** colloq. steady, dull, and laborious routine. **2** the act or sound of grinding. **3** the size or texture of crushed particles. **4** colloq. an erotic circling movement of the hips in dancing. — **grind something out** to produce it mechanically or routinely. **grind to a halt** to stop completely and abruptly. [from Anglo-Saxon grindan]

▤ verb **1** crush, pound, pulverize, powder, mill. **2** sharpen, whet, smooth, polish, sand, file, rub, abrade. **3** grate, scrape.

grinder noun **1** a person or machine that grinds. **2** a molar tooth.

grindstone noun a revolving stone wheel used for sharpening and polishing. — **have** or **keep one's nose to the grindstone** colloq. to work hard and with commitment.

gringo /ˈɡrɪŋɡoʊ/ noun (PL. **gringos**) derog. an English-speaking foreigner in Latin America, especially Mexico. [from Spanish gringo, from griego, a Greek, a foreigner]

grinningly adv. with a grin.

grip — verb (**gripped**, **gripping**) **1** to take or keep a firm hold of. **2** to capture the imagination or attention of. — noun **1** a firm hold; the action of taking a firm hold. **2** a way of gripping. **3** a handle or part that can be gripped. **4** a U-shaped wire pin for keeping the hair in place. **5** North Amer., esp. US a holdall. **6** colloq. understanding. **7** colloq. control; mastery: lose one's grip of the situation. **8** technical a stagehand who moves scenery. **9** technical a person who manoeuvres a film camera. — **get to grips with something** to begin to deal successfully with it. [from Anglo-Saxon gripe, a grasp]

▤ verb **1** hold, grasp, clasp, clutch, seize, grab, catch. **2** fascinate, thrill, enthral, spellbind, mesmerize, hypnotize, rivet, engross, absorb, involve, engage. noun **1** hold, grasp, clasp, embrace, clutches. **7** control, mastery, power.

gripe — verb **1** intrans. colloq. to complain persistently. **2** trans., intrans. to feel or cause to feel intense stomach pain. — noun **1** colloq. a complaint. **2** (usually **gripes**) old colloq. use a severe stomach pain. [from Anglo-Saxon gripan]

Gripe Water trademark medicine given to babies to relieve colic and stomach complaints.

gripping adj. holding the attention.

grisaille / grɪˈzeɪl/ *noun* a painting executed in shades of grey. The term applies to a style of painting, in imitation of sculpture or bas-relief, used as a decorative feature on walls, pottery, or glass; and to a method of painting by Renaissance painters, in which the subject was modelled in light grey before colour was applied. [from French *grisaille*, from *gris*, grey]

griseofulvin / grɪziːoʊˈfʌlvɪn/ *noun Medicine* an antibiotic obtained from the fungus *Penicillium griseofulvum*, administered by mouth as a treatment for fungal infections of the skin, hair, and nails. [from Latin *griseus*, grey + *fulvus*, reddish yellow]

grisliness *noun* being grisly.

grisly *adj.* (**grislier, grisliest**) horrible; ghastly; gruesome. [from Anglo-Saxon *grislic*]

. . . .

◧ gruesome, gory, grim, macabre, horrible, ghastly, awful, frightful, terrible, dreadful, abominable, appalling, shocking.
◩ delightful.

. . . .

grist *noun* **1** cereal grain that is to be, or that has been, ground into flour in a mill. **2** malt that has been crushed in preparation for brewing. — **grist to the mill** anything useful or profitable; a useful contribution. [from Anglo-Saxon]

gristle /ˈgrɪsl/ *noun* cartilage, especially in meat. [from Anglo-Saxon *gristle*]

gristly /ˈgrɪslɪ/ *adj.* full of gristle.

grit — *noun* **1** *Geol.* small particles or grains of a rock or mineral, especially sand. **2** *colloq.* courage and determination. — *verb* (**gritted, gritting**) **1** to spread grit on (icy roads, etc). **2** to clench (the teeth), eg to overcome pain. [from Anglo-Saxon *greot*]

. . . .

◧ *noun* **1** gravel, pebbles, shingle, sand, dust. **2** courage, determination, resolve, *colloq.* guts. *verb* **2** clench, gnash, grate, grind.

. . . .

grits *noun* **1** (*pl.*) coarsely ground grain, especially oats, with the husks removed. **2** (*sing.*) a dish of these, boiled and eaten for breakfast in the southern USA. [from Anglo-Saxon *grytta*]

gritty *adj.* (**grittier, grittiest**) **1** full of or covered with grit. **2** of the nature of grit. **3** determined.

grizzle *verb intrans. colloq.* **1** *especially of a young child* to cry fretfully. **2** to sulk or complain.

grizzled *adj. literary* **1** *said of the hair* grey or greying. **2** *said of a person* having such hair. [from Middle English *grisel*, from Old French *gris*, grey]

grizzly — *adj.* (**grizzlier, grizzliest**) grey or greying; grizzled. — *noun* (PL. **grizzlies**) *colloq.* a grizzly bear. [etymology as for GRIZZLED]

grizzly bear the largest of the bears, so called because its dark brown fur is frosted with white. It is found in Alaska, Canada, and western USA.

groan — *verb* **1** *intrans., trans.* to make, or utter with, a long deep sound in the back of the throat, expressing pain, distress, disapproval, etc. **2** *intrans.* to creak loudly. **3** *intrans.* to be weighed down or almost breaking: *a table groaning under heaps of food / a system groaning under inefficiency.* — *noun* an act, or the sound, of groaning. [from Anglo-Saxon *granian*]

. . . .

◧ *verb* **1** moan, sigh, cry, wail, whine, complain, protest. *noun* moan, sigh, cry, wail, whine, lament, complaint, objection, protest, outcry.
◩ *noun* cheer.

. . . .

groat *noun* an obsolete British silver coin worth four old pennies. [from Old Dutch *groot*, thick]

groats *pl. noun* crushed grain, especially oats, with the husks removed. [from Anglo-Saxon *grot*, particle]

grocer *noun* **1** a person selling food and general household goods. **2** a grocer's shop. [from Middle English *grosser*, wholesale merchant, from French *grossier*]

grocery *noun* (PL. **groceries**) **1** the trade or business of a grocer. **2** (**groceries**) merchandise, especially food, sold in a grocer's shop.

grog *noun* **1** a mixture of alcoholic spirit, especially rum, and water, as formerly drunk by sailors. **2** *Austral., New Zealand colloq.* any alcoholic drink. [from Old Grog, nickname of British admiral Edward Vernon, who in 1740 issued the naval ration of rum diluted with water]

groggily *adv.* in a groggy way.

grogginess *noun* being groggy.

groggy *adj.* (**groggier, groggiest**) *colloq.* weak, dizzy and unsteady on the feet, eg from the effects of illness or alcohol.

grogram /ˈgrɒgrəm/ *noun* a coarse fabric made from a mix of silk and wool or mohair. [from Old French *gros grain*, coarse grain]

groin — *noun* **1** the part of the body where the lower abdomen joins the upper thigh. **2** *euphemistic* the male sex organs. **3** *Archit.* the edge formed by the joining of two vaults in a roof. — *verb Archit.* to build with groins. [perhaps from Anglo-Saxon *grynde*, abyss]

grommet same as GRUMMET.

groom — *noun* **1** a person who looks after horses and cleans stables. **2** a bridegroom. **3** a title given to various officers in a royal household. — *verb* **1** to clean, brush, and generally smarten (animals, especially horses). **2** to keep (a person) clean and neat, especially regarding clothes and hair. **3** to train or prepare for a specific purpose or job. [from Middle English *grom*, manservant]

. . . .

◧ *verb* **1** clean, brush, curry, preen. **2** smarten, neaten, tidy, spruce up. **3** prepare, train, school, drill.

. . . .

groove — *noun* **1** a long narrow channel, especially cut with a tool. **2** the long spiral cut in a gramophone record. **3** *colloq.* a set routine, especially when monotonous. **4** *colloq.* a state of performing excellently; top form: *the champion is really in the groove.* — *verb* **1** to cut a groove in. **2** *intrans. old slang use* to enjoy oneself. [from obsolete Dutch *groeve*, furrow]

. . . .

◧ *noun* **1** furrow, rut, track, slot, channel, gutter, hollow, indentation, score.
◩ *noun* **1** ridge.

. . . .

groovy *adj.* (**groovier, grooviest**) **1** *old slang use* excellent, attractive, or fashionable. **2** *slang* no longer fashionable; dated.

grope — *verb* **1** *intrans.* to search by feeling about with the hands, eg in the dark. **2** *intrans.* to search uncertainly or with difficulty: *groping for answers.* **3** to find (one's way) by feeling. **4** *colloq.* to touch or fondle (someone) sexually. — *noun colloq.* an act of sexual fondling. [from Anglo-Saxon *grapian*]

. . . .

◧ *verb* **1** feel, fumble, scrabble. **2** search, cast about, fish, probe.

. . . .

grosbeak /ˈgrəʊsbiːk/ *noun* **1** any of various finches having a stout conical beak, found mainly in N America, although a few species occur in Europe and Asia. **2** any of various unrelated birds with a stout conical beak, eg certain weavers. [from French *grosbec*, thick beak]

gross — *adj.* **1** total, with no deductions, as opposed to net: *gross weight.* **2** very great; flagrant; glaring: *gross negligence.* **3** *derog.* vulgar; coarse. **4** *derog.* unattractively fat. **5** *derog. colloq. chiefly North Amer.* very unpleasant. **6** dense; lush: *gross vegetation.* **7** *derog.* dull; lacking sensitivity or judgement. **8** solid; tangible; concrete; not spiritual or abstract. — *noun* **1** (PL. **gross**) 12 dozen, 144. **2** (PL. **grosses**) the total amount or weight, without deductions.

— *verb* to earn as a gross income or profit, before tax is deducted. [from French *gros*, large, fat]

. . . .

🔲 *adj.* **1** inclusive, all-inclusive, total, aggregate, entire, complete, whole. **2** serious, grievous, blatant, flagrant, glaring, obvious, plain, sheer, utter, outright, shameful, shocking. **3** vulgar, coarse, crude, rude, obscene, lewd, improper, indecent, offensive. **4** fat, obese, overweight, big, large, huge, colossal, hulking, bulky, heavy.

🔲 *adj.* **1** net. **4** slight.

. . . .

gross domestic product (ABBREV. **GDP**) the total value of all goods produced and all services provided by a nation in one year.

grossly *adv.* extremely and flagrantly.

gross national product (ABBREV. **GNP**) gross domestic product plus the value of income from investments abroad.

grossness *noun* extreme rudeness or vulgarity.

grotesque — *adj.* **1** very unnatural or strange-looking, so as to cause fear or laughter. **2** exaggerated; ridiculous; absurd. — *noun* **1** (**the grotesque**) a 16c style in art which features animals, plants, and people mixed together in a strange or fantastic manner. **2** a work of art in this style. [from Italian *pittura grottesca*, cave painting, from *grotta*, cave]

. . . .

🔲 *adj.* **1** bizarre, weird, odd, strange, unnatural, freakish, monstrous, hideous, ugly, unsightly, misshapen, deformed, distorted, fanciful, surreal, macabre. **2** exaggerated, extravagant, ridiculous, absurd.

🔲 *adj.* **1** normal.

. . . .

grottiness *noun* being grotty.

grotto *noun* (PL. **grottos**, **grottoes**) **1** a cave, especially small and picturesque. **2** a man-made cave-like structure, especially in a garden or park. [from Italian *grotta*, cave]

grotty *adj.* (**grottier**, **grottiest**) *colloq.* **1** *derog.* unpleasantly dirty or shabby. **2** ill. [short form of GROTESQUE]

grouch *colloq.* — *verb intrans.* to grumble or complain. — *noun* **1** a complaining person. **2** a bad-tempered complaint; the cause of it. [from Old French *grouchier*, to complain]

grouchy *adj.* (**grouchier**, **grouchiest**) bad-tempered, likely to grumble.

ground ¹ — *noun* **1** the solid surface of the earth, or any part of it; soil; land. **2** (*often* **grounds**) an area of land, usually extensive, attached to or surrounding a building. **3** an area of land used for a specific purpose: *football ground*. **4** the substance of discussion: *cover a lot of ground*. **5** a position or standpoint, eg in an argument: *stand/shift one's ground*. **6** progress relative to that made by an opponent; advantage: *lose/gain ground*. **7** (*usually* **grounds**) a reason or justification. **8** background colour in a painting. **9** (**grounds**) sediment or dregs, especially of coffee. **10** the bottom of the sea. — *verb* **1** to base (an argument, complaint, etc): *an argument grounded on logic.* **2** (**ground someone in something**) to give basic instruction to them. **3** *trans., intrans.* to hit or cause (a ship) to hit the seabed or shore and remain stuck. **4** to refuse to allow (a pilot or aeroplane) to fly. **5** to lay (eg weapons) on the ground. — *adj.* on or relating to the ground: *ground forces.* — **cut** or **take the ground from under someone's feet** to act in anticipation of someone's plan, etc, destroying its effect. **down to the ground** *colloq.* absolutely; completely: *suits me down to the ground.* **get something off the ground** to make a start on it. **go to ground 1** *said of an animal* to go into a burrow to escape from hunters. **2** to go into hiding, eg from the police. **into the ground** to the point of exhaustion; to a position of total defeat. **on the ground** amongst ordinary people: *opinion on the ground.* [from Anglo-Saxon *grund*]

. . . .

🔲 *noun* **1** earth, soil, clay, loam, dirt, dust, surface, land, dry land, terra firma, bottom, foundation. **2** land, terrain, holding,

estate, property, territory, domain, gardens, park, campus. **3** field, pitch, stadium, arena, park. **7** foundation, justification, excuse, vindication, base, reason, motive, inducement, cause, occasion, call. *verb* **1** base, found, establish, set, fix. **2** introduce to, initiate into, familiarize with, acquaint with, inform about, instruct in, teach about, train in, coach in, tutor in.

. . . .

ground ² see GRIND.

ground bait bait which drops to the river bed, attracting fish to a general area.

ground bass *Mus.* a short bass part constantly repeated throughout a changing melody.

ground-breaking *adj.* innovative, breaking new ground.

ground control 1 the control and monitoring from the ground of the flight of aircraft or spacecraft, especially by continuous transmission of radio instructions, based on information obtained by radar, computer systems, etc, to pilots or astronauts. **2** at an airport, the personnel, radar, radio equipment, computer systems, etc, by means of which air traffic controllers monitor the progress of approaching aircraft and issue detailed instructions to pilots during landing and take-off.

ground elder a perennial plant (*Aegopodium podagraria*), widespread in Europe, with white flowers and creeping underground stems that send up new shoots some distance from the parent plant.

ground floor the floor of a building at or nearest to the level of the ground outside. — **be** or **get in on the ground floor** *colloq.* to be or become involved at the beginning of an enterprise or undertaking.

Groundhog Day in the USA, a name given to 2 Feb (Candlemas) when, according to popular tradition, the groundhog or woodchuck (American marmot) is supposed to emerge from hibernation, marking the end of winter.

grounding *noun* a foundation of basic knowledge or instruction.

groundless *adj.* having no reason or justification.

. . . .

🔲 baseless, unfounded, unsubstantiated, unsupported, empty, imaginary, false, unjustified, unwarranted, unprovoked, uncalled-for.

🔲 well-founded, reasonable, justified.

. . . .

groundling *noun* **1** any of various small freshwater fishes, especially loaches, that live close to the bottom of a river or lake. **2** a low-growing or creeping plant. **3** *colloq.* a person on the ground as opposed to one in an aircraft. **4** *Hist.* a person standing in the pit, the cheapest area, of an Elizabethan theatre. **5** *derog.* a person of inferior tastes.

groundnut *noun* **1** any of various climbing plants of the pulse family, native to N America, that produce small edible underground tubers, seed pods, etc, eg the peanut plant (*Arachis hypogaea*). **2** one of the underground tubers produced by such a plant. **3** *North Amer.* a peanut.

ground plan 1 a plan of the ground floor of a building. **2** any general, undetailed plan.

ground rent rent paid to the owner of land leased for building on.

ground rule a basic principle.

groundsel *noun* an annual plant (*Senecio vulgaris*), native to Europe, Asia, and N Africa, and widely introduced elsewhere, having weak, highly branched stems, bright green irregularly toothed oblong leaves, and numerous small cylindrical flower-heads consisting of clusters of yellow florets surrounded by narrow black-tipped bracts. [from Anglo-Saxon *gundeswilge*, from *gund*, pus + *swelgan*, to swallow, from its use in poultices]

groundsheet *noun* a waterproof sheet spread on the ground, eg in a tent, to give protection against damp.

groundsman *noun* a person who maintains a sports field.

ground squirrel any of various species of burrowing rodent, mostly native to N America, although some are found in Europe and Africa, including certain marmots, chipmunks, susliks, and gophers. Most ground squirrels have yellowish-brown fur, small ears, short legs, and larger feet and less bushy tails than tree squirrels.

ground state *Physics* the lowest energy state of an atom. If an atom in its ground state absorbs energy, one of its electrons will be raised to a higher energy level, and the atom is then said to be in an excited state.

groundswell or **ground swell** *noun* **1** a broad high swell of the sea, increasing in height rapidly as it passes through the water, often caused by a distant storm or earthquake. **2** a sudden and rapid growth, especially of public opinion.

groundwater *noun Geol.* water which is distributed in the rocks beneath the surface of the Earth, and provides water for many springs.

groundwork *noun* essential preparatory work.

group — *noun* **1** a number of people or things gathered, placed, or classed together. **2** a number of business companies under single ownership and central control. **3** a band of musicians and singers, especially playing pop music. **4** a subdivision of an air force, consisting of two or more wings. **5** *Chem.* in the periodic table, a vertical column representing a series of chemical elements with similar chemical properties, eg the rare (noble) gases. **6** (*in full* **functional group**) *Chem.* a combination of two or more atoms that are bonded together and tend to act as a single unit in chemical reactions, eg the hydroxyl (–OH) group. The group determines the chemical properties of the molecule to which it is attached. **7** a blood group. — *verb* **1** *intrans.* to form a group; to gather in a group. **2** to sort into groups; to place in a group: *group them according to size.* [from French *groupe*]

▣ *noun* **1** band, gang, team, crew, troop, squad, detachment, party, faction, set, circle, clique, club, society, association, company, gathering, crowd, bunch, clump, cluster, batch, lot, combination, grouping, class, category. *verb* **1** gather, collect, assemble, congregate, mass, cluster, clump, bunch. **2** sort, range, arrange, marshal, organize, order, class, classify, categorize, band, link, associate.

group captain an air force officer of the rank above wing commander and below air commodore, equivalent to an army colonel.

groupie *noun colloq., often derog.* an ardent follower of a touring pop star or group, often a young woman seeking a sexual relationship with them.

group theory *Maths.* the study of the properties of mathematical groups, ie sets of elements (such as real numbers) that can be combined by an operation (such as addition).

group therapy a form of psychotherapy that involves the joint participation of several people (under the guidance of a trained therapist) who discuss their problems and possible ways of overcoming them or changing undesirable mental states or behaviour, eg alcoholism.

grouse[1] *noun* (PL. **grouse**, **grouses**) any of a family of mainly ground-living gamebirds found in the colder regions of the N hemisphere, with a plump body, short wings, feathered legs, and a short curved bill, eg red grouse, black grouse, ptarmigan, capercaillie.

grouse[2] *colloq.* — *verb intrans.* to complain. — *noun* a complaint or spell of complaining.

grout — *noun* thin mortar applied to the joints between bricks or especially ceramic tiles, as a decorative finish. — *verb* to apply grout to the joints of. [from Anglo-Saxon *grut*]

grove *noun* **1** *literary* a small group of trees. **2** an area planted with fruit trees. [from Anglo-Saxon *graf*]

grovel *verb intrans.* (**grovelled**, **grovelling**) **1** to act with exaggerated (and usually insincere) respect or humility, especially to gain the favour of a superior. **2** to lie or crawl face down, in fear or respect. [back-formation from Middle English *groveling*, prone]

▣ CRAWL, CREEP. **1** toady, *colloq.* suck up, ingratiate oneself, fawn, cringe, cower, kowtow, defer, demean oneself.

groveller *noun* a person who grovels.

grow *verb* (PAST TENSE **grew**; PAST PARTICIPLE **grown**) **1** *intrans., said of a living thing* to develop into a larger more mature form. **2** *intrans., trans., said of hair, nails, etc* to increase or allow to increase in length. **3** *intrans.* to increase in size, intensity, or extent. **4** to cultivate (plants). **5** (**grow into something**) to develop to become that form: *tadpoles grow into frogs.* **6** to become gradually: *over the years they grew very lazy.* **7** (**grow to do something**) to come gradually: *grew to hate him.* **8** (**grow from** or **out of something**) to originate in it: *the scheme grew from an idea they had at school.* — **grow into something** to become big enough to wear clothes that were originally too large. **grow on someone** to gradually come to be liked by them. **grow out of something 1** to become too big to wear clothes that were originally the right size. **2** to lose a liking for it, or the habit of doing it, with age: *grew out of reading comics.* **grow up 1** to become, or be in the process of becoming, an adult. **2** to behave in an adult way. **3** to come into existence; to develop. [from Anglo-Saxon *growan*]

▣ **1** germinate, shoot, sprout, bud, flower, mature, develop, · progress, thrive, flourish. **3** increase, rise, expand, enlarge, swell, spread, extend, stretch, develop, proliferate, mushroom. **4** cultivate, farm, produce, propagate, raise. **6** become, get, go, turn. **8** originate in, arise from, issue from, spring from.
▣ **3** decrease, shrink.

growing pains 1 muscular pains, especially in the legs, sometimes experienced by growing children. **2** temporary problems or difficulties encountered in the early stages of a project or enterprise.

growl — *verb* **1** *intrans., said of animals* to make a deep rough sound in the throat, showing hostility. **2** *intrans., trans., said of people* to make a similar sound showing anger or displeasure; to speak or say angrily. — *noun* an act or the sound of growling. [from Old French *grouller*, to grumble]

▣ *verb* SNARL, SNAP. **1** rumble, roar.

grown *adj.* **1** mature: *grown woman.* **2** developed to a certain degree: *fully grown.*

grown-up *colloq.* — *adj.* adult. — *noun* an adult.

▣ *adj.* adult, mature, of age, full-grown, fully-fledged. *noun* adult, man, woman.
▣ *adj.* young, immature. *noun* child.

growth *noun* **1** the process or rate of growing; specifically, the increase in size, weight, and complexity of a living organism, associated with cell division, that takes place as it develops to maturity. **2** an increase. **3** an increase in economic activity or profitability: *a growth industry.* **4** a benign or malignant tumour formed as a result of the uncontrolled multiplication of cells.

▣ **1** development, evolution. **2** increase, rise, extension, enlargement, expansion, spread, proliferation. **3** advance, progress, improvement, expansion, development, success, prosperity, boom. **4** tumour, lump, swelling, protuberance, outgrowth.
▣ **2** decrease. **3** decline, failure.

growth hormone *Biochem.* **1** a hormone, secreted by the anterior lobe of the pituitary gland, that controls growth and development in vertebrates. Also called SOMA-

TOTROPHIN. **2** any artificially manufactured substance used for the same purpose.

growth industry 1 *Commerce* an industry or branch of industry which is developing and expanding. **2** an area of human activity which is not necessarily a commercial enterprise but which is expanding in a similar way.

groyne *noun* a low broad wall built like a pier from a shore to reduce the force of waves and so check land erosion. [from Old French *groign*, snout]

grub — *noun* **1** the worm-like larva of an insect, especially a beetle. **2** *colloq.* food. — *verb* (**grubbed, grubbing**) **1** (*usually* **grub about**) to dig or search in the soil. **2** to search generally. **3** to clear (ground) by digging up roots and stumps. [from Middle English *grobe*]

⊟ *noun* **1** maggot, worm, larva, pupa, caterpillar, chrysalis. *verb* **1** dig, burrow, delve, root, forage. **2** search, hunt, ferret, rummage.

grubbily *adv.* in a grubby way.
grubbiness *noun* being grubby.
grubby *adj.* (**grubbier, grubbiest**) *colloq.* dirty. [from GRUB]

⊟ dirty, soiled, unwashed, mucky, grimy, filthy, squalid, seedy, scruffy.
⊟ clean.

Grub Street *slang* the profession, lifestyle, or standards of writers of low-grade literature.

grudge — *verb* **1** to feel a sense of unfairness or resentment at. **2** to be unwilling to do or give; to do or give unwillingly. — *noun* a long-standing feeling of resentment: *bear a grudge*. [from Old French *grouchier*, to grumble]

⊟ *verb* BEGRUDGE, MIND. **1** resent, envy, covet, dislike, take exception to, object to. *noun* resentment, bitterness, envy, jealousy, spite, malice, enmity, antagonism, hate, dislike, animosity, ill-will, hard feelings.
⊟ *noun* favour.

grudging *adj.* **1** resentful. **2** unwilling.

⊟ **1** resentful, envious, jealous. **2** reluctant, unwilling, hesitant, half-hearted, unenthusiastic.
⊟ **2** willing.

gruel *noun* thin porridge. [from Old French *gruel*, groats]
gruelling *adj.* exhausting; punishing. [from old word *gruel*, to punish]

⊟ hard, difficult, taxing, demanding, punishing, tiring, exhausting, laborious, arduous, strenuous, backbreaking, harsh, severe, tough.
⊟ easy.

gruesome *adj.* inspiring horror or disgust; sickening; macabre. [from dialect *grue*, shiver, shudder + -SOME]

⊟ horrible, disgusting, repellent, repugnant, repulsive, hideous, grisly, macabre, grim, ghastly, awful, terrible, horrific, shocking, monstrous, abominable.
⊟ pleasant.

gruff *adj.* **1** *of a voice* deep and rough. **2** rough, unfriendly, or surly in manner. [from Dutch *grof*, coarse]

⊟ ROUGH. **1** harsh, rasping, deep, guttural, throaty, husky, hoarse. **2** surly, sullen, grumpy, bad-tempered, unfriendly, curt, brusque, abrupt, blunt, rude.
⊟ **2** friendly, courteous.

grumble — *verb intrans.* **1** to complain in a bad-tempered way. **2** to make a low rumbling sound. — *noun* **1** a complaint. **2** a rumbling sound. [from Old German *grommelen*]

⊟ *verb* **1** complain, moan, whine, *colloq.* grouch, *colloq.* grouse, *colloq.* gripe, *North Amer. slang* kvetch, mutter, murmur, carp, find fault. *noun* **1** complaint, moan, *colloq.* grouch, *colloq.* grouse, *colloq.* gripe.

grumbler *noun* a person who grumbles.
grumbling *adj.*, *said of the human appendix* intermittently painful.
grummet *noun* a rubber or plastic ring around a hole in metal, to protect a tube or insulate a wire passing through. [perhaps Old French *grommette*, jaw strap on a bridle]
grump *noun colloq.* **1** a grumpy person. **2** a fit of bad temper or sulking.
grumpily *adv.* in a grumpy way.
grumpiness *noun* being grumpy.
grumpy *adj.* (**grumpier, grumpiest**) surly; bad-tempered. [from old word *grump*, surly remark]

⊟ bad-tempered, crotchety, crabbed, cantankerous, cross, irritable, grouchy, surly, sullen, sulky, discontented.
⊟ contented.

grunge *noun colloq.* **1** dirt, grime, trash. **2** any unpleasant or nasty substance. **3** a crude style of dress, rejecting current fashions. [probably imitative]
grunt — *verb* **1** *intrans.*, *said of animals, especially pigs* to make a low rough sound in the back of the throat. **2** *intrans. said of people* to make a similar sound, eg indicating disgust or unwillingness to speak fully. **3** to express with this sound. — *noun* an act or the sound of grunting. [from Anglo-Saxon *grunian*]
Gruyère /ˈɡruːjeə(r)/ *noun* a pale yellow cheese with holes, originally made in *Gruyère*, in Switzerland.
gryke or **grike** *noun Geol.* any of the clefts or fissures formed by the widening of joints between the blocks of limestone in limestone pavement (a flat expanse of exposed limestone). See also CLINT. [from Old Norse *kriki*, a crack]
gryphon see GRIFFIN.
G-string or **gee-string** *noun* a thin strip of cloth covering the genital area, attached with a string round the waist.
G-suit or **g-suit** *noun* a close-fitting garment, worn by astronauts and the pilots of high-speed aircraft, that can be inflated so that it exerts pressure on the abdomen and lower parts of the body, thereby preventing blackout caused by the accumulation of blood below the chest under conditions of high acceleration.
GT *noun* a name given to certain fast but comfortable sports cars. [abbreviation of Italian *gran turismo*, grand touring]
Gt *abbrev. in place-names* Great.
guacamole /ɡwækəˈmoʊlɪ/ *noun* a traditional Mexican dish of mashed avocado, tomatoes, and onions, eaten cold. [from Aztec *ahuacatl*, avocado + *molli*, sauce]
guanine /ˈɡwɑːnɪn/ *noun Biochem.* a base derived from purine that occurs in the nucleic acid DNA. [from GUANO]
guano /ˈɡwɑːnoʊ/ *noun* the accumulated droppings of large colonies of bats, fish-eating seabirds, or seals. It is rich in nitrogen and used as a fertilizer. [from Spanish *guano*, *huano*, from Quechua *huanu*, dung]
guarantee — *noun* **1** a formal and usually written promise, especially by a manufacturer, to repair or replace an article found to be faulty within a stated period of time. **2** (*also* **guaranty**) an agreement, usually written, to take on another person's responsibility or debt if they neglect it. **3** a person making such an agreement; a guarantor. **4** (*also* **guaranty**) something undertaken to be handed over if a contract or agreement is broken; a security or pledge.

— *verb* **1** to act as, or give, a guarantee for. **2** to promise; to state as unquestionably true. **3** to ensure. [from Old French *garantie*, from *garant*, warrant]

. . . .

◼ *noun* **1** warranty, insurance, assurance, promise, bond. **4** security, collateral, surety, pledge. *verb* **1** vouch for, answer for, warrant, certify, underwrite, endorse, secure, protect, insure. **2** promise, pledge, swear, assure. **3** ensure, make sure, make certain.

. . . .

guarantor *noun* a person who gives a guarantee.

guaranty / 'garǝntɪ/ *noun* (PL. **guaranties**) a guarantee (see GUARANTEE 2, 4).

guard — *verb* **1** to protect from danger or attack. **2** to prevent from escaping. **3** (**guard against something**) to take precautions to prevent it. **4** to control or check: *guard your tongue.* — *noun* **1** a person or group whose job is to provide protection, eg from danger or attack, or to prevent escape. **2** a person in charge of a railway train. **3** a state of readiness to give protection or prevent escape: *on guard / keep guard.* **4** on alert or in a wary state: *on one's guard against thieves / caught you off guard.* **5** a defensive position, eg in boxing or cricket. **6** (*especially in compounds*) anything that gives protection from something: *fireguard.* **7** the act or duty of protecting. **8** (*often* **Guard**) a soldier in any of certain army regiments originally formed to protect the sovereign. — **stand guard** to act as a guard or sentry. [from Old French *garder*, to protect]

. . . .

◼ *verb* **1** protect, safeguard, defend, save, preserve, shield, screen, shelter, cover, patrol, police. **2** escort, watch, supervise, oversee, mind. *noun* **1** protector, defender, custodian, warder, escort, bodyguard, *colloq.* minder, watchman, lookout, sentry, picket, patrol, security. **6** protection, safeguard, defence, wall, barrier, screen, shield, bumper, buffer, pad. **7** protection, defence, preservation, supervision.

. . . .

guard cell *Bot.* either of two semicircular cells that surround each of the specialized pores, known as stomata, present on the aerial parts of a plant, especially the undersurface of the leaves. The guard cells control the opening and closing of the stomata in response to the plant's need to conserve water.

guarded *adj.* cautious; reluctant to reveal information, one's feelings, etc.

. . . .

◼ cautious, wary, careful, watchful, discreet, non-committal, reticent, reserved, secretive, *colloq.* cagey.

◧ frank.

. . . .

guardhouse or **guardroom** *noun* a building or room for guards on duty, especially at the gate of a military camp, often also housing prisoners.

guardian *noun* **1** a person legally responsible for the care of another, especially an orphaned child. **2** a guard, defender or protector. [from Old French *gardein*]

. . . .

◼ **2** guard, escort, attendant, defender, champion, protector, preserver, trustee, curator, custodian, keeper, warden.

. . . .

guardianship *noun* the position or state of being a guardian.

guardsman *noun* **1** a member of a regiment of guards. **2** a guard.

guava / 'gwɑːvǝ/ *noun* **1** any of various small tropical trees of the genus *Psidium*, especially *P. guajava*, native to Central America. **2** the yellow pear-shaped fruit of this tree, which has sweet juicy pink, white, or yellow pulp rich in vitamin C, enclosed by a yellow skin. [from Spanish *guayaba*]

gubbins *sing. noun colloq.* **1** *derog.* a worthless object. **2** a device or gadget. **3** *derog.* rubbish. [from old word *gobbon*, portion]

gubernatorial / ˌɡʌbǝnǝ'tɔːrɪǝl/ *adj. formal* of or relating to a governor. [from Latin *gubernator*, steersman]

gudgeon[1] *noun* **1** a small freshwater fish belonging to the carp family, widespread in slow-flowing to moderately fast European rivers, and sometimes also found in lakes. **2** *colloq.* a gullible person. [from Old French *goujon*]

gudgeon[2] *noun* **1** a pivot or pin of any kind. **2** the socket part of a hinge or rudder, into which the pin part fits. [from Old French *goujon*, pin of a pulley]

guelder rose / 'ɡɛldǝ(r)/ a deciduous shrub (*Viburnum opulus*) belonging to the honeysuckle family, native to Europe and Asia, having white flowers, and glossy red berrylike fruit which is poisonous. [from *Gelder* land, province of the Netherlands]

guernsey *noun* (PL. **guernseys**) **1** a tight-fitting woollen pullover, especially worn by sailors. **2** (**Guernsey**) *Agric.* a breed of dairy cattle, similar to Jersey cattle but larger, that has a golden-red coat, often with distinct white markings, and short curved horns.

guerrilla or **guerilla** / ɡǝ'rɪlǝ/ *noun* a member of a small, independent, often politically motivated armed force making surprise attacks, eg against government troops. [from Spanish *guerrilla*, diminutive of *guerra*, war]

guess — *verb* **1** *intrans.* to make an estimate or form an opinion, based on little or no information. **2** to make such an estimate or form such an opinion about (something). **3** to estimate correctly. **4** *chiefly North Amer.* to think or suppose. — *noun* an estimate based on little or no information. — **anybody's guess** *colloq.* something impossible to know or determine. [from Middle English *gessen*]

. . . .

◼ *verb* **1** speculate, conjecture, theorize, hypothesize. **2** estimate, judge, reckon, predict, surmise, suspect. **4** think, believe, suppose, assume, imagine, fancy. *noun* estimate, prediction, speculation, conjecture, theory, hypothesis, supposition, assumption, belief, opinion, idea, notion, feeling, suspicion, intuition.

. . . .

guesstimate or **guestimate** *colloq.* — *noun* (pronounced -mǝt) a rough estimate, based on scant knowledge. — *verb* (pronounced -meɪt) to make such an estimate of. [from GUESS + ESTIMATE]

guesswork *noun* the process or result of guessing.

. . . .

◼ speculation, conjecture, estimation, reckoning, supposition, assumption, surmise, intuition.

. . . .

guest — *noun* **1** a person who receives hospitality in the home of, or at the expense of, another. **2** a person staying at a hotel, boarding-house, etc. **3** a person specially invited to take part: *guest star / guest speaker.* — *verb intrans.* to appear as a guest, eg on a television show. [from Anglo-Saxon *gest*]

. . . .

◼ *noun* **1** visitor, caller. **2** boarder, lodger, resident, patron, regular.

. . . .

guesthouse *noun* a private home offering accommodation to paying guests; a boarding-house.

guff *noun colloq., derog.* nonsense.

guffaw — *noun* a loud coarse laugh. — *verb intrans.* to make this sound. [imitative]

GUI *abbrev. Comput.* graphic user interface.

guidance *noun* **1** help, advice, or counselling; the act of guiding. **2** direction or leadership. **3** any process whereby a missile or an unmanned air or space vehicle is directed along a specific flight path to its target: *guidance system.*

. . . .

◼ **1** advice, counsel, counselling, help, instructions, directions, guidelines, pointers, recommendations. **2** leadership, direction, management, control.

. . . .

guide — *verb* **1** to lead, direct, or show the way to. **2** to control or direct the movement or course of: *guided missile.* **3** to advise or influence: *be guided by your parents.* — *noun* **1** a person who leads the way for eg tourists or mountaineers. **2** any device used to direct movement. **3** same as GUIDEBOOK. **4** (**Guide**) a member of a worldwide youth organization for girls, similar to the Scouts. **5** a person or thing, especially a quality, which influences another person's decisions or behaviour: *let truth be your guide.* [from Old French, *guider*]

⊟ *verb* DIRECT. **1** lead, conduct, point, steer, pilot, usher, escort, accompany. **2** control, steer, manoeuvre, navigate, point, head. **3** advise, counsel, influence, educate, teach, instruct, train. *noun* **1** leader, courier, navigator, pilot, usher, escort. **3** guidebook, handbook, manual, directory, catalogue. **5** adviser, counsellor, mentor, guru, teacher, instructor, example, model, standard, criterion, guideline, pointer, signpost, sign.

guidebook *noun* a book containing information on a particular subject or place.

guide dog a dog specially trained to guide a blind person safely.

guideline *noun* (*also* **guidelines**) an indication of what future action is required or recommended.

guild *noun* **1** a medieval association of merchants or craftsmen, maintaining standards and providing mutual support. **2** a name used by various modern societies, clubs, and associations. [from Anglo-Saxon *gield*]

guilder /ˈɡɪldə(r)/ *noun* **1** (PL. **guilder, guilders**) the standard unit of currency of the Netherlands, divided into 100 cents. **2** (PL. **guilders**) an old German and Dutch gold coin. [from Dutch *gulden*]

guildhall *noun* **1** a hall where members of a guild or other association meet. **2** a town hall.

guile /ɡaɪl/ *noun* the ability to deceive or trick; craftiness or cunning. [from Old French *guile*, deceit]

⊟ craftiness, cunning, deceit, trickery.

guileful *adj.* crafty, deceitful.

guileless *adj.* without guile.

guillemot /ˈɡɪlɪmɒt/ *noun* any of several seabirds belonging to the auk family, found only in the northern hemisphere, and having black and white plumage, a long narrow bill, short narrow wings, and short legs set far back on its body. [from French *Guillaume*, William, perhaps from Breton *gwelan*, gull]

guilloche /ɡɪˈloʊʃ/ *noun* an ornamental border or moulding in the form of interlacing or plaited bands in a continuous repeated pattern enclosing roundels. [from French, a tool used to make a curved line, said to be from the proper name *Guillot*]

guillotine /ˈɡɪlətiːn/ — *noun* **1** an instrument for beheading, consisting of a large heavy blade sliding rapidly down between two upright posts. **2** a device with a large blade moved lever-like to cut paper or metal. **3** a time limit set to speed up discussion of, and voting on, a parliamentary bill. — *verb* to behead, cut, or speed up progress of, with a guillotine. [named after the French physician and revolutionary Joseph Guillotin (1738–1814) who suggested using such an instrument as a means of execution]

guilt *noun* **1** a feeling of shame or remorse resulting from a sense of having done wrong. **2** the state of having done wrong or having broken a law. **3** blame. [from Anglo-Saxon *gylt*]

⊟ **1** shame, regret, remorse, contrition, self-reproach, self-condemnation, guilty conscience. **2** culpability, responsibility, disgrace.
⊟ **1** shamelessness. **2** innocence.

guiltily *adv.* in a guilty way.

guiltiness *noun* being guilty.

guiltless *adj.* innocent.

guilty *adj.* (**guiltier, guiltiest**) (*often* **guilty of something**) **1** responsible for a crime or wrongdoing, or judged to be so. **2** feeling, showing, or involving guilt: *a guilty look.* **3** able to be justly accused of something: *guilty of working too hard.*

⊟ **1** culpable, responsible, blameworthy, offending, wrong, sinful, criminal, convicted. **2** conscience-stricken, ashamed, shamefaced, sheepish, sorry, regretful, remorseful, contrite, penitent, repentant.
⊟ **1** innocent, guiltless, blameless. **2** shameless.

guinea /ˈɡɪnɪ/ *noun* **1** an obsolete British gold coin worth 21 shillings (£1.05). **2** its value, still used as a monetary unit in some professions, especially horse-racing. [named after Guinea in W Africa, where the gold for the coin was obtained]

guinea fowl (PL. **guinea fowl**) any of a family of ground-living birds related to pheasants and chickens, with a naked head and greyish plumage speckled with white.

guinea pig 1 a domesticated species of cavy, a small burrowing S American rodent unrelated to the pig, with a rounded body, short legs and ears, and a large head. **2** (*in full* **human guinea pig**) a person used as the subject of an experiment.

guipure /ɡɪˈpjʊə(r)/ *noun* heavy lace having a large open pattern with no background. [from French *guipure*, from *guiper*, to cover with cloth]

guise /ɡaɪz/ *noun* **1** assumed appearance; pretence: *under the guise of friendship.* **2** external appearance in general. [from Old French *guise*]

guiser /ˈɡaɪzə(r)/ *noun Scot.* a person, especially a child, who goes from house to house in disguise, especially at Hallowe'en, entertaining with songs, etc and receiving small gifts in return.

guitar *noun* a musical instrument with a body generally shaped like a figure of eight, a long fretted neck, and (usually six) strings that are plucked or strummed. [from French *guitare*]

guitar fish a bottom-dwelling ray-like fish with a flattened head, broad pectoral fins, and a slender body resembling a guitar or violin.

guitarist *noun* a person who plays the guitar.

Gujarati or **Gujerati** /ɡʊdʒəˈrɑːtɪ/ — *noun* an Indo-Aryan language spoken in the state of Gujarat, NW India, and surrounding areas. — *adj.* relating to or spoken or written in Gujarati.

gulag /ˈɡuːlæɡ/ *noun* **1** a network of political prisons or labour camps that existed formerly in the Soviet Union; one of these prisons or camps. **2** the government department responsible for their administration. [from Russian *glavnoe upravlenie ispravitelno-trudovykh lagerei*, main administration for corrective labour camps]

gulch *noun North Amer., esp. US* a narrow rocky ravine with a fast-flowing stream running through it.

gulden same as GUILDER.

gulf *noun* **1** a very large inlet of the sea extending far into the land, much more deeply indented and more enclosed than a bay. **2** a vast difference or separation, eg between viewpoints. **3** a deep hollow in the ground; a chasm. [from Old French *golfe*, from Greek *kolpos*, bosom]

⊟ **2** gap, opening, separation, rift, split, breach. **3** chasm, gorge, abyss, void.

Gulf States 1 the oil-producing countries around the Persian Gulf, ie Iran, Iraq, Kuwait, Bahrain, Saudi Arabia, Oman, Qatar, and the United Arab Emirates. **2** the US states around the Gulf of Mexico, ie Florida, Texas, Alabama, Mississippi, and Louisiana.

Gulf War Syndrome a nervous disorder suffered by servicemen who had served in the Gulf War of 1991, thought by some to be due to their exposure to harmful chemicals.

gull [1] *noun* any of various omnivorous seabirds, found almost worldwide, usually near the sea, and having a stout body, predominantly white or greyish plumage, sometimes with dark upper parts, a hooked bill, long pointed wings, and webbed feet. [probably from Welsh *gwylan*]

gull [2] *old use* — *verb* to cheat or deceive. — *noun* an easily fooled person. [perhaps from dialect *gull*, unfledged bird]

gullet *noun* the oesophagus or throat. [from Old French *goule*, throat, from Latin *gula*]

gullibility *noun* being gullible.

gullible *adj.* easily tricked or fooled. [from GULL [2]]

. . . .

▣ credulous, suggestible, impressionable, trusting, unsuspecting, foolish, naïve, green, unsophisticated, innocent.

▣ astute.

. . . .

gully or **gulley** *noun* (PL. **gullies**, **gulleys**) **1** a small channel or cutting with steep sides, formed by running water, especially after heavy rainstorms in tropical and semiarid regions. **2** *Cricket* a position around 9m from the batsman and at a level slightly behind the wicket; also, a fielder in this position.

. . . .

▣ **1** channel, watercourse, gutter, ditch.

. . . .

gulp — *verb* **1** *trans., intrans.* (*also* **gulp down**) to swallow (food, drink, etc) eagerly or in large mouthfuls. **2** *intrans.* to make a swallowing motion, eg because of fear. **3** (**gulp something back** or **down**) to stifle (tears, etc). — *noun* **1** a swallowing motion. **2** an amount swallowed at once; a mouthful. [from Old Dutch *gulpen*]

. . . .

▣ *verb* **1** swallow, swig, bolt, gobble, guzzle. *noun* SWALLOW. **2** swig, draught, mouthful.

▣ *verb* **1** sip, nibble.

. . . .

gum [1] *noun Anat.* the firm fibrous flesh surrounding the roots of the teeth. [from Anglo-Saxon *goma*, palate]

gum [2] — *noun* **1** *Bot.* one of various substances found in the stems and branches of certain plants, mainly trees, that produce a sticky solution or gel when added to water. Gums are widely used in confectionery, and in stationery items, eg gummed envelopes. **2** this or any similar substance used as glue. **3** same as GUMDROP. **4** *colloq.* chewing-gum. — *verb* (**gummed**, **gumming**) to glue with gum. — **gum up the works** *colloq.* to prevent a machine, scheme, etc from working properly. [from Old French *gomme*, from Latin *gummi*]

. . . .

▣ *noun* **2** adhesive, glue, paste, cement. *verb* stick, glue, paste, fix, cement, seal.

. . . .

gum arabic a thick sticky water-soluble gum exuded by certain acacia trees native to Africa and Australia, especially *Acacia senegal*. It is used as an adhesive and emulsifier.

gumbo *noun* (PL. **gumbos**) **1** a thick soup or stew made from meat or fish, okra, and other vegetables. **2** okra. [from Louisiana French *gombo*, from a Bantu language]

gumboil *noun* a small abscess on the gum.

gumboot *noun* a long rubber waterproof boot, a wellington boot.

gumdrop *noun* a sweet made from transparent hard jelly.

gummy [1] *adj.* (**gummier**, **gummiest**) having prominent gums; toothless.

gummy [2] *adj.* (**gummier**, **gummiest**) **1** sticky. **2** producing gum.

gumption *noun colloq.* **1** common sense; initiative. **2** courage.

gumshoe *noun* **1** a rubber overshoe, a galosh. **2** *slang* a detective, especially a private detective.

gum tree the common name for any of various evergreen trees that yield gum, especially those of the genus *Eucalyptus*. See also EUCALYPTUS. — **up a gum tree** *colloq.* in a difficult position, especially with no chance of escape.

gun — *noun* **1** any weapon which fires bullets or shells from a metal tube. **2** any instrument which forces something out under pressure: *spray gun.* **3** *colloq.* a gunman. **4** a member of a party of hunters. **5** the signal to start, eg a race. — *verb* (**gunned**, **gunning**) (**gun someone down**) to shoot them with a gun. — **go great guns** *colloq.* to function or be carried out with great speed or success. **be gunning for someone** to be searching determinedly for them, usually with hostile intent. **be gunning for something** to try to obtain it: *we're gunning for a pay rise.* **jump the gun** to do something before the proper time. **stick to one's guns** to maintain one's position firmly, in an argument, etc. [from Middle English *gonne*]

. . . .

▣ *noun* **1** firearm, handgun, pistol, revolver, *colloq.* shooter, rifle, shotgun, bazooka, howitzer, cannon.

. . . .

gunboat *noun* a small warship with large mounted guns.

gunboat diplomacy diplomacy consisting of threats of military attack.

guncotton or **gun cotton** *noun* any of various highly explosive materials containing a relatively high proportion of nitrogen, formed by treating clean cotton with nitric acid and sulphuric acid. Guncotton is used mainly in the manufacture of propellants and smokeless gunpowder.

gun dog **1** any dog specially trained to flush birds or small mammals, or to retrieve them when they have been shot by a gamekeeper or hunter. **2** any breed of dog that is used for this type of work.

gunfire *noun* **1** the act of firing guns. **2** the bullets fired. **3** the sound of firing.

gunge *colloq.* — *noun* any messy, slimy, or sticky substance. — *verb* (*also* **gunge something up**) to cover or block it with gunge. [perhaps from GOO + SPONGE]

gung-ho *adj. derog.* excessively or foolishly eager, especially to attack an enemy. [from Chinese *gong*, work + *he*, together]

gungy *adj.* (**gungier**, **gungiest**) of or like gunge.

gunk *noun colloq.* any slimy or oily semi-solid substance. [originally a trademark of a grease-solvent]

gunman *noun* **1** an armed criminal. **2** an assassin.

gunmetal or **gun metal** *noun* **1** any of several dark grey alloys, usually containing 88% to 90% copper, together with small amounts of tin and zinc, so called because it was formerly used to make cannons. **2** any of various other alloys that are used to make guns. **3** a dark grey colour.

gunnel see GUNWALE.

gunner *noun* **1** any member of an armed force who operates a heavy gun. **2** a soldier in an artillery regiment.

gunnery *noun* **1** the use of guns. **2** the science of designing guns.

gunny *noun* (PL. **gunnies**) **1** thick coarse jute cloth, used especially for sacking. **2** a sack made from this. [from Hindi *goni*]

gunpoint — **at gunpoint** threatening, or being threatened, with a gun.

gunpowder *noun* the oldest known explosive, consisting of a mixture of potassium nitrate, sulphur, and charcoal. It is still used in fireworks and for quarry blasting.

gunrunner *noun* a person who smuggles guns.

gunrunning *noun* the act of smuggling arms into a country, often to help terrorists, etc.

gunshot *noun* **1** bullets fired from a gun. **2** the distance over which a gun can fire a bullet: *within gunshot.* **3** a sound of firing.

gunslinger *noun slang* an armed fighter in the lawless days of the American West.

gunwale or **gunnel** /'gʌnl/ *noun* the upper edge of a ship's side. — **full to the gunwales** completely full. [from GUN + WALE]

guppy *noun* (PL. **guppies**) a small brightly coloured fresh-water fish, native to tropical waters of northern S America and the Caribbean Islands, up to 3cm long. [named after R J L Guppy, who sent the first specimens to the British Museum in the 19c]

gurdwara /gɜːdˈwɑːrə/ *noun Relig.* a Sikh place of worship which includes a place where the scripture is housed. In addition, it should include a hostel and an area for serving meals. [from Punjabi *gurduara*, from Sanskrit *guru*, teacher + *dvara*, door]

gurgle — *verb* 1 *intrans., said of water* to make a bubbling noise when flowing. 2 *intrans., trans.* to make, or express with, a bubbling noise in the throat. — *noun* the sound of gurgling. [from Latin *gurgulare*]

....

■ *verb* 1 bubble, babble, burble, murmur, ripple, lap, splash. *noun* babble, murmur, ripple.

....

Gurkha /'gɜːkə/ *noun* a member of a Hindu people of Nepal, from whom whole regiments in the British and Indian armies are formed.

Gurkhali /gɜːˈkɑːlɪ/ *noun* the Indo-European language spoken by Gurkhas.

guru /'gʊruː/ *noun* 1 a Hindu or Sikh spiritual leader or teacher. 2 *sometimes facetious* any greatly respected and influential leader or adviser. [from Hindi *guru*, from Sanskrit, venerable]

gush — *verb* 1 *intrans., said of a liquid* to flood out suddenly and violently. 2 to cause (a liquid) to flood out suddenly and violently. 3 *intrans. derog. colloq.* to speak or act with an affected and exaggerated emotion or enthusiasm. — *noun* 1 a sudden violent flooding-out. 2 *derog. colloq.* exaggerated emotion or enthusiasm. [from Middle English *gosshe* or *gusche*]

....

■ *verb* 1 flood, surge, burst, spurt, spout, jet, flow, run, pour, stream, cascade. 2 spurt, spout, jet. 3 enthuse, chatter, babble, *colloq.* go on. *noun* flood, burst, outburst, spurt, spout, jet, flow, outflow, stream, torrent, cascade.

....

gusher *noun* an oil-well from which oil flows without the use of pumps.

gushing *adj.* that gushes.

gusset *noun* a piece of material sewn into a garment for added strength, or to allow for freedom of movement, eg at the crotch. [from Old French *gousset*]

gust — *noun* 1 a sudden blast or rush, eg of wind or smoke. 2 an emotional outburst. — *verb intrans., said of the wind* to blow in gusts. [from Norse *gustr*, blast]

....

■ *noun* 1 blast, burst, rush, flurry, blow, puff, breeze, wind, gale, squall.

....

gusto *noun* enthusiastic enjoyment; zest; vigour. [from Italian *gusto*, from Latin *gustus*, taste]

....

■ zest, relish, appreciation, enjoyment, pleasure, delight, enthusiasm, exuberance, vigour, verve, zeal.
■ distaste, apathy.

....

gusty *adj.* (**gustier, gustiest**) 1 blowing in gusts, stormy. 2 fitfully irritable or upset.

gut — *noun* 1 the alimentary canal, or part of it. 2 (**guts**) *colloq.* the insides of a person or animal. 3 *colloq.* the stomach or abdomen. 4 *colloq.* a fat stomach; a paunch. 5 (**guts**) *colloq.* courage or determination. 6 (**guts**) *colloq.* the inner or essential parts: *the guts of the scheme.* 7 a

strong thread made from animal intestines, used for violin and racket strings; catgut. — *verb* (**gutted, gutting**) 1 to take the guts out of (especially fish). 2 to destroy the insides of; to reduce to a shell: *fire gutted the building.* — *adj.* 1 based on instinct and emotion, not reason: *a gut reaction.* 2 essential; basic: *the gut problem.* — **hate someone's guts** *colloq.* to have a violent dislike for them. **work, sweat, slave,** etc **one's guts out** *colloq.* to work extremely hard. [from Anglo-Saxon *gutt*]

....

■ *noun* 2 intestines, bowels, viscera, entrails, insides, *colloq.* innards. 3 stomach, abdomen, belly. 4 paunch, pot, *colloq.* pot-belly, *facetious* corporation. 5 courage, bravery, pluck, grit, *colloq.* nerve, *slang* bottle, determination, resolve. *verb* 1 disembowel, draw, clean (out). 2 strip, clear, empty, ransack, plunder, loot, sack, ravage. *adj.* 1 instinctive, impulsive, intuitive, emotional, visceral.

....

gutless *adj. derog.* cowardly; lacking determination.

gutsy *adj.* (**gutsier, gutsiest**) *colloq.* 1 courageous and determined. 2 gluttonous.

gutta-percha *noun* a whitish rubbery substance, obtained from the milky latex of certain evergreen Malaysian trees, that is hard at room temperature but becomes soft and elastic when heated, and if deformed will retain its new shape when subsequently cooled. Gutta-percha is used in dentistry to form the core of root fillings, and is also used to make golfballs. [from Malay *getah*, gum + *percha*, the tree producing it]

gutted *adj. colloq.* extremely shocked or disappointed.

gutter — *noun* 1 a channel for carrying away rainwater, fixed to the edge of a roof or built between a pavement and a road. 2 (**the gutter**) a state of poverty and social deprivation, or of coarse and degraded living. 3 *Printing* the inner margins between two facing pages. — *verb* (**guttered, guttering**) 1 *intrans., said of a candle* to melt away with wax forming channels down the side. 2 to wear away channels in. 3 *intrans.* to trickle. [from Old French *goutiere*, from *goute*, drop]

....

■ *noun* 1 drain, sluice, ditch, trench, trough, channel, duct, conduit, pipe, tube.

....

guttering *noun* 1 gutters collectively. 2 material for making roof-gutters.

gutter press *derog.* newspapers dealing largely with scandal and gossip reported in a sensational style.

guttersnipe *noun old derog. use* a raggedly dressed or ill-mannered person, especially a child.

guttural /'gʌtərəl/ *adj.* 1 *said of sounds* produced deep in the throat. 2 *said of a language or style of speech* having or using such sounds; harsh-sounding. [from Latin *guttur*, throat]

guv, guvnor and **guv'nor** see GOVERNOR.

guy[1] — *noun* 1 *colloq.* a man or boy. 2 a crude model of Guy Fawkes, burnt on a bonfire on Guy Fawkes Day. — *verb* to make fun of. [named after Guy Fawkes, leader of a plot to blow up Parliament in 1605, who was caught and hanged]

....

■ *noun* 1 fellow, *colloq.* bloke, *colloq.* chap, man, boy, person, individual.

....

guy[2] — *noun* a rope or wire used to hold something, especially a tent, firm or steady. — *verb* to secure with guys. [named after Old French *guie*, guide]

Guy Fawkes Day 5 Nov, the anniversary of the discovery of the Gunpowder Plot, a plot to blow up Parliament in 1605 of which Guy Fawkes was the leader, celebrated with firework displays.

guzzle *verb trans., intrans.* to eat or drink greedily. [perhaps from French *gosier*, throat]

guzzler *noun* a person who guzzles.

gybe /dʒaɪb/ — *verb trans., intrans. Naut. (also* **gibe**) **1** *said of a sail* to swing or cause it to swing over from one side of a boat to the other. **2** *said of a boat* to change or cause it to change course in this way. — *noun* an act of gybing. [from JIB]

gym *noun colloq.* **1** gymnastics. **2** a gymnasium.

gymkhana *noun* **1** a local public event consisting of competitions in various sports, especially horse-riding. **2** formerly, in India under British rule, an athletics meeting, or a public place providing athletics facilities. [from Hindi *gend-khana*, racket-court, remodelled on GYMNASIUM]

gymnasium *noun* (PL. **gymnasiums, gymnasia**) **1** a building or room with equipment for physical exercise. **2** in various European countries, a top-grade secondary school preparing pupils for university. [from Greek *gymnasion*, from *gymnazein*, to exercise naked]

gymnast *noun* a person skilled in gymnastics. [from Greek *gymnastes*, trainer of athletes]

gymnastic *adj.* relating to or involving gymnastics.

gymnastics *sing. noun* **1** physical exercises designed to strengthen the body and improve agility, usually using special equipment. **2** difficult exercises that test or demonstrate ability of any kind: *mental gymnastics*.

gymnosperm *noun Bot.* any plant belonging to the subdivision Gymnospermae, a large group of woody plants which produce seeds that are not enclosed in an ovary or fruit, but are usually borne on the surface of overlapping scale-like leaves (*sporophylls*) in cones, eg conifers, cycads. [from Greek *gymnos*, naked + *sperma*, seed]

gym shoe a light, canvas, usually rubber-soled, shoe.

gym slip a belted sleeveless dress or tunic, worn (especially formerly) by schoolgirls as part of their uniform.

gynaecium or **gynoecium** /gaɪnɪ'siːəm, dʒɪnɪ'siːəm/ *noun Bot.* the female reproductive parts of a flower, consisting of the carpels. [from Greek *gynaikeion*, women's apartments]

gynaecological /gaɪnəkə'lɒdʒɪkəl/ *adj.* relating to or involving gynaecology.

gynaecologist /gaɪnə'kɒlədʒɪst/ *noun* a doctor who specializes in gynaecology.

gynaecology /gaɪnə'kɒlədʒɪ/ *noun* the branch of medicine concerned with the diagnosis and treatment of diseases and disorders that affect the reproductive organs of the female body, eg cervical cancer, menstrual disorders, and the effects of the menopause. [from Greek *gyne*, woman + -LOGY]

gyp[1] /dʒɪp/ — **give someone gyp** *slang* to cause them pain or discomfort. [perhaps a contraction of *gee up*; see GEE[1]]

gyp[2] /dʒɪp/ *slang* — *verb* (**gypped, gypping**) to cheat or swindle. — *noun* a cheat. [a back-formation from GYPSY]

Gyproc /'dʒɪprɒk/ *noun trademark* a type of plasterboard. [from GYPSUM]

gypsophila /dʒɪp'sɒfɪlə/ *noun Bot.* an annual or perennial plant with dainty branching heads of small flowers, usually white, but sometimes pink or crimson. It is widely used by florists. [from Greek *gypsos*, chalk + *phileein*, to love]

gypsum /'dʒɪpsəm, 'gɪpsəm/ *noun Geol.* a soft mineral composed of calcium sulphate, used to make plaster of Paris, cement, rubber, and paper. Alabaster is a fine-grained variety of gypsum. [from Latin, from Greek *gypsos*, chalk]

Gypsy or **Gipsy** *noun* (PL. **Gypsies, Gipsies**) **1** a member of a dark-skinned travelling people, originally from NW India, now scattered throughout Europe and N America. See also ROMANY. **2** (**gypsy**) a person resembling or living like a Gypsy. [from *Egyptian*, because they were originally thought to have come from Egypt]

. . . .

⊟ **2** traveller, wanderer, nomad, tinker.

. . . .

gyrate *verb intrans.* to move with a circular or spiralling motion. [from Greek *gyros*, circle]

. . . .

⊟ turn, revolve, rotate, twirl, pirouette, spin, whirl, wheel, circle, spiral.

. . . .

gyration *noun* **1** a whirling motion. **2** a whirl or twist. **3** a whorl.

gyre /dʒaɪə(r)/ *noun Geol.* a circular movement of water that occurs in all of the major ocean basins, and is caused by the Earth's rotation, convection currents of warm surface water, and the prevailing winds. [from Latin *girus*, from Greek *gyros*, circle, ring]

gyrfalcon or **gerfalcon** /'dʒɜːfɔːlkən/ *noun* the largest of all the falcons, found only in N Europe, Scandinavia, Siberia, and N Canada. [from Old French *gerfaucon*]

gyrocompass *noun* a non-magnetic compass, widely used for navigation, operated by means of a spinning disc like a gyroscope powered by an electric motor. The axle of the disc always points in the same direction, and can be set to point North.

gyroscope *noun Engineering* a device consisting of a small flywheel with a heavy rim, mounted in such a way that it can rotate at high speed in any direction, but once in motion it resists any changes in the direction of rotation. Gyroscopes are used in ship stabilizers, and in the automatic steering systems of aircraft, missiles, etc. [from Greek *gyros*, circle + -SCOPE]

gyroscopic *adj.* relating to or of the nature of a gyroscope.

H

H¹ or **h** *noun* (PL. **Hs, H's, h's**) the eighth letter of the English alphabet.

H² *abbrev.* **1** *on a pencil* hard. **2** hospital.

H³ *symbol Chem.* hydrogen.

h *abbrev.* **1** hecto-. **2** height.

ha or **ha.** *abbrev.* hectare.

ha! *interj.* an expression of surprise, happiness, triumph, etc.

habeas corpus /ˈheɪbɪəs ˈkɔːpəs/ *noun Legal* a writ requiring a prisoner to be brought into court for a judge to decide if his or her imprisonment is legal. [from Latin *habeas corpus*, have the body (brought before the judge)]

haberdasher /ˈhabədaʃə(r)/ *noun* a person who deals in small items used for sewing, such as ribbons, needles, buttons, etc. [from Old French *hapertas*]

haberdashery *noun* (PL. **haberdasheries**) **1** a haberdasher's shop, business or department. **2** the ribbons, etc sold by a haberdasher.

Haber process or **Haber-Bosch process** /ˈhɑːbə/ *Chem.* an industrial process by which ammonia is manufactured from hydrogen and atmospheric nitrogen under conditions of high temperature and pressure, and in the presence of a catalyst consisting of powdered iron. [named after the German chemist Fritz Haber who developed the method]

habit *noun* **1** a usual or regular practice or tendency. **2** *Psychol.* a learned action or behaviour pattern that is practised in response to a particular situation, with little voluntary control. **3** mental attitude or constitution: *habit of mind*. **4** a long loose garment worn by monks and nuns. **5** *Bot.* the general appearance or method of growth of a plant: *creeping habit*. [from Latin *habitus*, practice]

▣ **1** custom, usage, practice, routine, rule, second nature, way, manner, mode, wont, inclination, tendency, bent. **2** addiction, dependence, weakness, fixation, obsession, mannerism, quirk.

habitability *noun* being habitable.

habitable *adj.* suitable for living in. [from Latin *habitabilis*]

habitat *noun Biol.* that part of the environment in which a particular plant or animal species (either an individual or a population) normally lives. It is usually defined in terms of its physical features or the dominant plant types, eg stream, pond, woodland, grassland. [from Latin *habitat*, it inhabits]

▣ home, abode, domain, element, environment, surroundings, locality, territory, terrain.

habitation *noun* **1** the act of living in a building, etc. **2** a house or home. [from Latin *habitatio*]

habitat loss *Environ.* the loss of distinct parts of the environment in which plants or animals normally live. Destruction or disturbance of such areas by human activity, eg the widespread felling of rainforest, may threaten the continued existence of wildlife, and result in the extinction of some species.

habit-forming *adj.*, *said of a drug, activity, etc* likely to become a habit or addiction.

habitual *adj.* **1** seen, done, etc regularly. **2** done, or doing something, by habit. [from Latin *habitualis*, from *habitus*, habit]

▣ **1** customary, traditional, wonted, routine, usual, ordinary, normal, standard, regular, recurrent, established, familiar. **2** confirmed, inveterate, hardened, addicted, dependent.

▣ **1** occasional, infrequent.

habituate *verb* (**habituate to**) to make (someone) used to something. [from Latin *habituare*]

habituation *noun* accustoming or becoming accustomed.

habitué /həˈbɪtjʊeɪ/ *noun* a regular or frequent visitor to a place, eg a restaurant. [from French *habitué*]

Habsburg Dynasty a major European dynasty whose origins lie in the Upper Rhine region. From the medieval period they were the sovereign rulers of Austria, and extended their territories and influence to secure the title of Holy Roman Emperor (1452–1806). [from German *Habichtsburg*, Hawk's Castle (in what is now Switzerland)]

hachure /haˈʃʊə(r)/ *noun* **1** (**hachures**) a system of parallel lines on a map to show the contours of hills, the closeness of the lines indicating steepness. **2** any of these lines. [from French *hachure*]

hacienda /hasɪˈɛndə/ *noun* in Spanish-speaking countries, a ranch or large estate with a house on it. [from Spanish *hacienda*]

hack¹ — *verb* **1** (*often* **hack something down, away**, etc) to cut or chop roughly. **2** (*often* **hack something out**) to cut (a path, etc) roughly. **3** *colloq.* (**hack into something**) to obtain access to computer files without authority. **4** *slang* to be able to bear or suffer. **5** *intrans.* to cough. **6** to kick (an opponent) on the shins, especially in football. — *noun* **1** a kick on the shins. **2** a wound or rough cut, especially from a kick. **3** a miner's pick. [from Anglo-Saxon *tohaccian*]

▣ *verb* **1** cut, chop, hew, slash, lacerate, mutilate, mangle.

hack² — *noun* **1** a horse kept for general riding, especially one for hire. **2** a ride on horseback. **3** a writer, journalist, etc who produces dull, mediocre or routine work. — *verb intrans.* to travel on horseback at a leisurely pace, usually for pleasure. [abbreviation of HACKNEY]

▣ *noun* **3** scribbler, writer, journalist, drudge, slave.

hacker *noun colloq.* **1** a skilled computer user whose main interest is in defeating password systems and gaining unauthorized access to other computer systems, especially large commercial or government databases, for fraudulent or malicious purposes, or for amusement. **2** formerly used to refer to a computer enthusiast or a skilled computer programmer.

hacking — *noun colloq.* the act of gaining access to computer files without permission. — *adj.*, *said of a cough* rough and dry.

hacking jacket a tweed jacket with slits at the sides, worn when riding.

hackles *pl. noun* the hairs on the back of the neck and the back of a dog or cat, which rise when it is angry or alarmed. — **make someone's hackles rise** to make them angry or indignant. [from Middle English *hechele*]

hackney *noun* (PL. **hackneys**) a horse for general riding. [named after Hackney in E London, where horses used to be pastured]

hackney cab or **hackney carriage 1** *Hist.* a horse-drawn carriage for public hire. **2** *formal* a taxi.

hackneyed *adj.*, *said of a word, phrase, etc* meaningless and trite through too much use. [from HACKNEY, in the sense of 'for general use']

....

▣ trite, commonplace, stale, overworked, tired, worn-out, threadbare, clichéd, stereotyped, stock, banal, common, pedestrian, uninspired, unoriginal, *colloq.* corny.

▣ new, fresh, original.

....

hacksaw *noun* a hand-held or power-driven saw having a narrow fine-toothed blade held under tension in a steel frame, used for cutting metal.

had see HAVE.

haddock *noun* (PL. **haddock**) a commercially important food fish related to but smaller than the cod, found close to the sea-bed on both sides of the North Atlantic. [from Middle English *haddok*]

hadj, hadji same as HAJJ, HAJJI.

hadn't *contr.* had not.

hadron /ˈhadrɒn/ *noun Physics* one of a class of subatomic particles, including baryons and mesons, that interact strongly with other subatomic particles. [from Greek *hadros*, heavy]

hadst *verb old use* the form of the past tense of the verb *have* used with *thou*.

haem /hiːm/ *noun Medicine* the iron compound which is combined with the protein globin in the respiratory pigment haemoglobin, and which gives the red blood cells their colour.

haem- or **haemato-** or **haemo-** *combining form Medicine* forming words relating to blood. [from Greek *haima*, blood]

haematite or **hematite** /ˈhɛmətaɪt/ *noun Geol.* a dense and relatively hard mineral containing iron oxide (Fe_2O_3), often occurring as dark brown nodules, that is the most important ore of iron.

haematology /hiːməˈtɒlədʒɪ/ *noun Medicine* the branch of medicine concerned with the diagnosis and treatment of diseases and disorders of the blood, and of the tissues in which the blood cells are formed.

haematuria /hiːməˈtjʊərɪə/ *noun Medicine* the presence of blood in the urine. [from HAEM- + Greek *ouron*, urine]

haemodialysis /hiːmoʊdaɪˈalɪsɪs/ *noun Medicine* the purification of the blood by means of an artificial kidney machine that removes waste products such as urea or excess salts, while blood cells and proteins are retained. It is used in cases of kidney failure. See also DIALYSIS.

haemoglobin /hiːmoʊˈgloʊbɪn/ *noun Biol.* the oxygen-carrying pigment that is the main constituent of the red blood cells (erythrocytes) in all vertebrates and some invertebrates, and contains the iron compound *haem* combined with the protein *globin*. Haemoglobin takes up oxygen in the lungs and combines with it to form *oxyhaemoglobin*, which is transported via the bloodstream to the body tissues, where the oxygen is released for use by the cells. [from HAEM- + Latin *globus*, ball]

haemolysis /hɪmˈɒlɪsɪs/ *noun Biol.* the abnormal destruction of red blood cells, accompanied by the release of the pigment haemoglobin, eg as a result of malaria, poisoning, the presence of abnormal types of haemoglobin or red blood cells, or mis-matching of blood groups in a blood transfusion.

haemophilia /hiːmoʊˈfɪlɪə/ *noun* an inherited disorder in which normal blood clotting is impaired, owing to a deficiency of factor VIII, one of the proteins that is essential for clotting. [from HAEM- + Greek *philia*, friendship]

haemophiliac /hiːmoʊˈfɪlɪak/ — *noun* a person who suffers from haemophilia. — *adj.* affected with haemophilia.

haemorrhage or **hemorrhage** /ˈhɛmərɪdʒ/ — *noun* the escape of blood from a ruptured blood vessel or vessels, especially profuse bleeding occurring over a short period of time. — *verb intrans.* **1** *said of a ruptured blood vessel* to bleed profusely. **2** to suffer a haemorrhage. [from HAEM- + Greek *rhegnynai*, to burst]

haemorrhoid /ˈhɛmərɔɪd/ *noun* (*usually* **haemorrhoids**) a swollen vein around the inside or outside of the anus. Haemorrhoids often cause itching or bleeding, and may be painful. [from HAEM- + Greek *rheein*, to flow]

hafnium *noun Chem.* (SYMBOL **Hf**, ATOMIC NUMBER **72**) a silvery metal found mainly in zirconium minerals, and used in tungsten alloys for light bulb filaments and electrodes. It is also a strong neutron absorber and is used to make control rods for nuclear reactors. [from Latin *Hafnia*, Copenhagen, where it was discovered]

haft /hɑːft/ *noun* a handle of a knife, sword, axe, etc. [from Anglo-Saxon *hæft*]

hag *noun* **1** *offensive* an ugly old woman. **2** a witch. [from Anglo-Saxon *hægtes*]

....

▣ **1** crone, *colloq.* battle-axe, shrew, termagant.

....

hagfish *noun* a primitive marine fish lacking true jaws, vertebrae, paired fins, and scales, and having an eel-like body covered in copious slime.

haggard /ˈhagəd/ *adj.* looking very tired and thin-faced, because of pain, worry, etc. [from Old French *hagard*]

....

▣ drawn, gaunt, careworn, thin, wasted, shrunken, pinched, pale, wan, ghastly.

▣ hale.

....

haggis *noun* a Scottish dish made from sheep's or calf's offal mixed with suet, oatmeal and seasonings and then boiled in a bag made from the animal's stomach, or something similar. [from Old Scot. *haggeis*]

haggle *verb intrans.* (*often* **haggle over** or **about something**) to bargain over or argue about a price, etc. [from Norse *höggva*, to hew]

....

▣ bargain, negotiate, barter, wrangle, squabble, bicker, quarrel, dispute.

....

haggler *noun* a person who haggles.

hagiographer /hagɪˈɒgrəfə(r)/ *noun* **1** a writer of saints' lives. **2** one of the writers of certain parts of the Old Testament.

hagiography *noun* (PL. **hagiographies**) the writing of the stories of saints' lives. [from Greek *hagios*, holy + -GRAPHY]

hagiology /hagɪˈɒlədʒɪ/ *noun* (PL. **hagiologies**) literature about the lives of, and legends about, saints. [from Greek *hagios*, holy + -LOGY]

hag-ridden *adj.* troubled or unhappy, as if cursed by a witch.

ha-ha[1] or **ha ha** *interj.* a standardized way of representing the sound of laughter. [imitative]

ha-ha[2] *noun* a ditch, often with a low wall inside it, which divides areas of land and forms a barrier or obstacle without interrupting the view. [from French; possibly from the supposed cry made when discovering one]

haiku /ˈhaɪkuː/ *noun* (PL. **haiku**) a Japanese poem with three lines of three, five and three syllables. [from Japanese]

hail[1] — *noun* **1** a form of precipitation that consists of roughly spherical pellets of ice, with diameters ranging from 5mm to several centimetres in some cases. **2** a large number or amount of words, questions, missiles, etc. — *verb* **1** *intrans.*, *said of hail* to fall. **2** *intrans.*, *said of words, questions, missiles, etc* to come in great numbers. **3** to shower with words, questions, missiles, etc. [from Anglo-Saxon *hagol*]

▤ *noun* **2** barrage, bombardment, volley, torrent, shower, rain. *verb* **2** shower, rain, pelt. **3** shower, pelt, bombard, batter, attack, assail.

hail² — *verb* **1** to call out to in order to attract attention, eg to signal to (a taxi) to stop. **2** to greet. **3** to recognize or describe as being or representing: *was hailed as emperor/was hailed a hero.* **4** *intrans.* to come from or belong to a place: *hails from Manchester.* — *interj. old use* expressing greeting. — **within hail** or **within hailing distance** close enough to hear when called to. [from Norse *heill*, healthy]

▤ *verb* **1** signal to, flag down, wave at, call out to. **2** greet, address, acknowledge, salute. **3** acclaim, applaud, honour, welcome.

hail-fellow-well-met *adj.* overpoweringly hearty and friendly.

hailstone *noun* a single grain of hail.

hailstorm *noun* a storm during which hail falls heavily.

hair *noun* **1** each of many long threadlike structures that grow out from the skin of mammals, including humans. Hairs contain the fibrous protein keratin, and are produced from bulb-shaped hair follicles within the dermis of the skin. **2** a mass of these, especially on a person's head. **3** anything resembling a hair. **4** a thread-like cell growing from the surface of a plant. **5** a hair's-breadth. — **get in someone's hair** *colloq.* to annoy or irritate them. **a hair of the dog** *colloq.* an alcoholic drink taken as a cure for a hangover. **keep one's hair on** *colloq.* to remain calm and not get angry. **let one's hair down** *colloq.* to enjoy oneself without restraint. **make someone's hair curl** *colloq.* to shock them. **make someone's hair stand on end** *colloq.* to terrify them. **not turn a hair** to remain calm. **split hairs** to make small or unimportant distinctions or quibbles. [from Anglo-Saxon *hær*]

▤ **2** locks, tresses, down, fur, fleece, wool.

hairbrush *noun* a brush for smoothing and arranging one's hair.

haircut *noun* the cutting of a person's hair; the shape or style in which it is cut.

hairdo *noun* (PL. **hairdos**) *colloq.* a style or process of hairdressing; a woman's haircut or style.

hairdresser *noun* **1** a person who cuts, washes and styles hair. **2** a hairdresser's shop.

▤ **1** hairstylist, stylist, barber, coiffeur, coiffeuse.

hairdressing *noun* the art or occupation of a hairdresser.

hairdrier or **hairdryer** *noun* an electrical apparatus which dries a person's hair by blowing hot air over it.

hair-grip *noun* a small wire clasp for holding the hair in place.

hairiness *noun* being hairy.

hairless *adj.* **1** having no hair. **2** *colloq.* very angry.

▤ **1** bald, bald-headed, shorn, shaven, clean-shaven, beardless.
▤ **1** hairy, hirsute.

hairline *noun* the line along the forehead where the hair begins to grow.

hairnet *noun* a fine-meshed net, usually with an outer band of elastic for fitting around the head, worn to keep the hair in place.

hairpiece *noun* a piece of false hair worn over a bald area on one's head, or to make one's own hair appear thicker.

hairpin *noun* a thin flat U-shaped piece of wire for keeping the hair in place.

hairpin bend a sharp and often U-shaped bend, especially on a mountain road.

hair-raising *adj.* extremely frightening.

▤ frightening, scary, terrifying, horrifying, shocking, bloodcurdling, spine-chilling, startling, thrilling, *colloq.* hairy.

hair's-breadth *noun* a very small distance or margin.

hair shirt a shirt made of a thick, coarse, uncomfortable cloth woven from hair, worn by religious people as a penance.

hair-slide *noun* a small metal or plastic clip, used to keep the hair in place.

hair-splitting *noun* the act of insisting on considering small, unimportant distinctions.

hairspray *noun* liquid sprayed from a can as a fine mist, used to keep the hair in place.

hairspring *noun* a fine spiral spring that regulates the movement of some clocks and watches.

hairstyle *noun* the way in which a person's hair is cut or shaped.

▤ style, coiffure, *colloq.* hairdo, cut, haircut, set, *colloq.* perm.

hairy *adj.* (**hairier, hairiest**) **1** covered in hair. **2** *colloq.* dangerous, frightening and exciting.

▤ **1** hirsute, bearded, shaggy, bushy, fuzzy, furry, woolly.
▤ **1** bald, clean-shaven.

Hajj /had3/ *noun* one of the Five Pillars of Islam, it is a formal pilgrimage to the holy city of Mecca during the Islamic month of Dhu-ul-Hijja. [from Arabic *hajj*, pilgrimage]

hajji /'had31/ *noun* a Muslim who has been on pilgrimage to Mecca.

hake *noun* (PL. **hake, hakes**) a marine fish, closely related to the cod, widely distributed near the continental shelf in temperate areas of the Atlantic and Pacific Oceans, up to 1m long, with a bluish-grey back, silvery-white underside, a large head, and heavily toothed jaws.

Halakhah *noun* the complete body of laws and decrees contained in the Talmudic and Rabbinic literature of Judaism, which governs religious or civil practice in the Jewish community. [Hebrew, = the way]

halal /ha'lal/ *noun* meat from an animal which has been killed in a way approved of by Muslim holy law. [from Arabic *halal*, lawful]

halation *noun* **1** *Photog.* the spread and blurring of a photographic image of a bright object, caused by light scattered in the photographic emulsion and reflected from the rear surface of the base material. In some films, this rear surface is coated with a thin black layer to reduce the effect. **2** a bright area around a bright spot on a fluorescent screen. [from HALO]

halberd /'halbəd/ *noun* *Hist.* a long spear with an axe-blade and a pick at one end. [from Old German *helm*, handle + *barde*, hatchet]

halcyon /'hals1ən/ *adj.* peaceful, calm, and happy: *halcyon days.* [from Greek *halkyon*, kingfisher, from the ancient belief that it nested on the sea and that the sea remained calm while it did so]

hale *adj.* strong and healthy: *hale and hearty.* [from Anglo-Saxon *hal*]

half — *noun* (PL. **halves**) **1** one of two equal parts which together form a whole. **2** the fraction equal to one divided by two. **3** *colloq.* a half pint, especially of beer. **4** one of two equal periods of play in a match. **5** a half-price ticket, especially for a child or old person. — *adj.* forming or equal to half. — *adv.* **1** to the extent or amount of one half: *half finished.* **2** almost; partly; to some extent: *half dead with exhaustion.* **3** 30 minutes past the hour stated. — ... **and a half** *colloq.* a very good: *she's a singer and a half.* **by half** *colloq.* excessively: *too clever by half.* **by halves** without being thorough. **go halves** to share the cost or expenses. **not half** *colloq.* very; very much. **one's better half** *colloq.* one's husband, wife, or partner. [from Anglo-Saxon *healf*]

▣ *noun* **1** fifty per cent, hemisphere, semicircle, section, segment, portion, share. *adj.* semi-, halved, divided, part, partial, incomplete, moderate, limited. *adv.* **2** partly, partially, incompletely, almost, nearly, moderately, slightly.
▣ *noun* **1** whole. *adj.* whole. *adv.* **2** completely.

half-and-half *adv., adj.* in equal parts.

halfback *noun* in football, hockey, etc, a player or position immediately behind the forwards.

half-baked *adj. colloq.*, *said of an idea, scheme, etc* not properly or completely thought out; hasty and unrealistic.

half-board *noun Brit.* the provision of a bed, breakfast, and one other meal in a hotel or boarding house.

half-breed *often offensive* — *noun* a person having parents of different races, especially one black parent and one white. — *adj.* concerning or relating to half-breeds. See also HALF-CASTE.

half-brother or **half-sister** *noun* a brother or sister with whom one has only one parent in common.

half-caste *often offensive* — *noun* a person having parents of different races, especially an Indian mother and a European father. — *adj.* concerning or relating to half-castes. See also HALF-BREED.

half-cell *noun Chem.* half of an electrolytic cell, consisting of one electrode (a positively charged anode or a negatively charged cathode) immersed in an electrolyte consisting of a solution of ions.

half-crown or **half-a-crown** *noun Hist.* a British coin worth two shillings and sixpence ($12\frac{1}{2}$p).

half-cut *adj. slang* drunk.

half-day *noun* a day on which one only works, etc in the morning or in the afternoon.

half-hearted *adj.* not eager; without enthusiasm.

▣ lukewarm, cool, weak, feeble, passive, apathetic, uninterested, indifferent, neutral.
▣ wholehearted, enthusiastic.

half-hitch *noun* a simple knot or noose formed by passing the end of the rope through a loop made in the rope.

half-hour *noun* a period of thirty minutes.

half-hourly *adj., adv.* done, occurring, etc every half-hour.

half-life *noun Physics* the period of time required for half the original number of atoms of a radioactive substance to undergo spontaneous radioactive decay. Some materials have half-lives of a few seconds, whereas others (eg some isotopes of plutonium) have half-lives of millions of years.

half-light *noun* dull light, especially at dawn or dusk.

half-marathon *noun* a long-distance race over 21km (13mi), half the distance of a modern marathon.

half mast the position halfway up a flagpole, where flags are flown as a mark of respect for a dead person.

half measures actions which are not sufficient or thorough enough to deal with a problem.

half-moon *noun* **1** the moon in its first or last quarter, when half of its disc is illuminated. **2** the time when this occurs. **3** anything shaped like a half-moon.

half nelson a hold in wrestling in which one puts one's arm under one's opponent's arm from behind, and pushes on the back of his or her neck with one's palm.

halfpenny or **ha'penny** /'heɪpnɪ/ *noun Hist.* a British coin worth half a penny.

halfpennyworth /'heɪpnɪwɜ:θ/ or **hap'orth** /'heɪpəθ/ *noun Brit.* **1** *Hist.* an amount of something costing a halfpenny. **2** *colloq.* a very small amount: *not make a hap'orth of difference.*

half-price *adj., adv.* at half the usual price.

half-sister see HALF-BROTHER.

half-term *noun Brit.* a short holiday halfway through a school term.

half-timbered *adj., said of a house, etc* built with a timber frame with brick or plaster filling.

half-time *noun* an interval between the two halves of a match.

half-tone *noun* an illustration produced using a method of printing in which black and white dots of different sizes create various shades of grey.

half-track *noun* a usually military vehicle with wheels in front and caterpillar tracks behind.

half-truth *noun* a statement which is only partly true.

half volley *Cricket, Tennis* a stroke in which the ball is hit immediately after it bounces or as it bounces.

halfway — *adv.* **1** at or to a point equally far from two others: *halfway between France and England.* **2** in, of, or into an incomplete manner. — *adj.* of or at a point equally far from two others. — **meet someone halfway** to compromise with someone.

▣ *adv.* **1** midway, in the middle, centrally. *adj.* middle, central, equidistant, mid, midway, intermediate.

halfway house 1 *Hist.* an inn where one can rest halfway through a journey. **2** *colloq.* something which is between two extremes, and which has some features of each. **3** a home where former prisoners or patients with mental illnesses stay so they may get used to life outside the prison or hospital.

halfwit *noun* a foolish or stupid person.

halfwitted *adj.* foolish, stupid.

half-yearly *adj., adv.* done, occurring, etc every six months.

halibut *noun* (PL. **halibut**) either of two species of very large flatfish found in the cold deep waters of the North Atlantic and North Pacific, respectively. [from Middle English *halybutte*, from *haly*, holy + *butt*, flat fish, so called because it was eaten on holy days]

halide /'halaɪd/ *noun Chem.* a chemical compound consisting of a halogen and another chemical element (eg hydrogen) or functional group (eg a hydrocarbon group). Halides may be fluorides (containing fluorine), chlorides (containing chlorine), bromides (containing bromine), or iodides (containing iodine). [from Greek *hals*, salt]

halite /'halaɪt/ *noun Geol.* the mineral form of sodium chloride. Also called ROCK SALT.

halitosis /halɪ'toʊsɪs/ *noun* unpleasant-smelling breath. [from Latin *halitus*, breath + -OSIS]

hall *noun* **1** a room or passage just inside the entrance to a house, usually allowing access to other rooms and the stairs. **2** a building or large room, used for concerts, public meetings, etc. **3** a large country house. **4** *Brit.* (**hall of residence**) a building where university or college students live. **5** *Brit.* the dining-room in a college or university; dinner in such a dining-room. [from Anglo-Saxon *heall*]

▣ **1** hallway, corridor, passage, passageway, entrance hall, foyer, vestibule, lobby. **2** concert-hall, auditorium, chamber, assembly room.

hallelujah see ALLELUIA.

Halley's comet *Astron.* a large bright comet that takes about 76 years to orbit the Sun (in the opposite direction to the planets). [named after Edmund Halley]

halliard see HALYARD.

hallmark — *noun* **1** an official mark on a gold or silver article guaranteeing its quality. **2** a typical or distinctive feature, especially of quality. — *verb* to stamp with a hall-mark.

◦◦◦◦◦◦◦◦◦◦◦◦◦◦◦◦◦◦◦◦

▣ *noun* STAMP, MARK. **2** sign, indication, symbol, emblem, badge, trademark.

◦◦◦◦◦◦◦◦◦◦◦◦◦◦◦◦◦◦◦◦◦◦◦◦◦◦◦◦◦◦

hallo see HELLO.

halloo — *noun, interj.* a cry encouraging hunting dogs or calling for attention. — *verb intrans.* to cry halloo, especially to dogs at a hunt. [imitative]

hallow — *verb* to make or regard as holy. — *noun old use* a saint. See HALLOWE'EN. [from Anglo-Saxon *halgian*]

hallowed *adj.* holy, revered.

Hallowe'en /haloʊˈiːn/ *noun* the evening of 31 October, the eve of All Saints' Day. [from *all hallow even*, all saints' eve]

hallstand *noun* a piece of furniture in the hall of a house, on which coats, hats, etc are hung.

hallucinate /həˈluːsɪneɪt/ *verb intrans.* to experience hallucinations. [from Latin *hallucinari*, to wander in the mind]

◦◦◦◦◦◦◦◦◦◦◦◦◦◦◦◦◦◦◦◦

▣ dream, see things, daydream, fantasize.

◦◦◦◦◦◦◦◦◦◦◦◦◦◦◦◦◦◦◦◦◦◦◦◦◦◦◦◦◦◦

hallucination *noun* the apparent perception of something that is not actually present, ie that has no objective reality. Hallucinations may involve any of the senses, and may be caused by mental disorders (eg schizophrenia), drugs (eg LSD or cannabis), extreme fatigue, fever, hypothermia, or sensory deprivation.

◦◦◦◦◦◦◦◦◦◦◦◦◦◦◦◦◦◦◦◦

▣ illusion, mirage, vision, apparition, dream, daydream, fantasy, figment, delusion.

◦◦◦◦◦◦◦◦◦◦◦◦◦◦◦◦◦◦◦◦◦◦◦◦◦◦◦◦◦◦

hallucinatory /həˈluːsɪneɪtərɪ/ *adj.* characterized by or involving hallucinations.

hallucinogen /həˈluːsɪnədʒɛn/ *noun* a drug that causes hallucinations. [from HALLUCINATE + -GEN]

hallucinogenic /həluːsɪnəˈdʒɛnɪk/ *adj.* causing hallucinations.

hallway *noun* an entrance hall.

halma /ˈhalmə/ *noun* a game for two players played on a board of 256 squares, in which each player attempts to move pieces into vacant squares immediately behind the opposing pieces. [from Greek *halma*, jump, leap]

halo /ˈheɪloʊ/ — *noun* (PL. **halos, haloes**) **1** a ring of light around the head of a saint, angel, etc in paintings, etc. **2** the glory or glamour attaching to a person or thing. **3** *Astron.* a luminous white or rainbow-coloured ring sometimes seen around a celestial body, especially the Sun or Moon, caused by the reflection or refraction of light by ice crystals in the Earth's atmosphere. — *verb* (**haloes, haloed**) to put a halo round. [from Greek *halos*, circular threshing floor]

halogen /ˈhalədʒɛn/ *noun Chem.* any of the five chemical elements in group VII of the periodic table, ie fluorine, chlorine, bromine, iodine, or astatine. [from Greek *hals*, salt + -GEN]

halogenation *noun Chem.* any chemical reaction in which an atom of a halogen (fluorine, chlorine, bromine, iodine, or astatine) is introduced into a compound.

halophyte /ˈhaloʊfaɪt/ *noun Bot.* a plant that can tolerate a very salty environment, such as a salt marsh or mudflat. [from Greek *hals*, salt]

halt — *noun* **1** a short or temporary stop. **2** *Brit.* a small railway station without a building. — *verb* **1** (*intrans.*) to stop. **2** to cause to stop. — **call a halt to something** to put an end to it. [from German *Halt*, stoppage]

◦◦◦◦◦◦◦◦◦◦◦◦◦◦◦◦◦◦◦◦

▣ *noun* **1** stop, stoppage, interruption, break, pause, rest, standstill, end, close, termination. *verb* STOP, CEASE, BREAK OFF, DISCONTINUE, END, TERMINATE. **1** draw up, pull up, pause, wait, rest. **2** check, curb, stem, arrest, obstruct, impede.

▣ *noun* **1** start, continuation. *verb* START, CONTINUE.

◦◦◦◦◦◦◦◦◦◦◦◦◦◦◦◦◦◦◦◦◦◦◦◦◦◦◦◦◦◦

halter — *noun* a rope or strap for holding and leading a horse by its head. — *verb* to put a halter on. [from Anglo-Saxon *hælfter*]

halterneck *noun* a woman's top or dress held in place by a strap which goes round her neck, leaving the shoulders and back bare.

halting *adj.* pausing a lot; hesitant. [from Anglo-Saxon *healt*, lame]

◦◦◦◦◦◦◦◦◦◦◦◦◦◦◦◦◦◦◦◦

▣ hesitant, stuttering, stammering, faltering, stumbling, broken, imperfect, laboured, awkward.

▣ fluent.

◦◦◦◦◦◦◦◦◦◦◦◦◦◦◦◦◦◦◦◦◦◦◦◦◦◦◦◦◦◦

haltingly *adv.* **1** hesitatingly. **2** lamely.

halva or **halvah** /ˈhalvə/ *noun* a sweetmeat, of E Mediterranean and Middle Eastern origin, containing sesame seeds, honey, nuts, rosewater, and saffron. [from Yiddish *halva*; ultimately from Arabic *halwa*, sweetmeat]

halve *verb* **1** to divide into two equal parts or halves. **2** to reduce (costs, problems, etc) by half. **3** *Golf* to draw a hole or match with one's opponent.

◦◦◦◦◦◦◦◦◦◦◦◦◦◦◦◦◦◦◦◦

▣ **1** bisect, cut in half, split in two, divide, split, share. **2** cut down, reduce, lessen.

◦◦◦◦◦◦◦◦◦◦◦◦◦◦◦◦◦◦◦◦◦◦◦◦◦◦◦◦◦◦

halves see HALF.

halyard or **halliard** /ˈhaljəd/ *noun* a rope for raising or lowering a sail or flag on a ship. [from Middle English *halier*]

ham[1] *noun* **1** the top part of the back leg of a pig, salted and smoked and used as food. **2** the back of the thigh. [from Anglo-Saxon *hamm*]

ham[2] *colloq.* — *noun* **1** a bad actor, especially one who overacts and exaggerates. **2** an amateur radio operator. — *verb intrans., trans.* (**hammed, hamming**) (*also* **ham something up**) to overact or exaggerate. [from *hamfatter*, a third-rate minstrel]

hamadryad /haməˈdraɪəd/ *noun* **1** *Greek and Roman Mythol.* a nymph who lives in a tree and dies when it dies. **2** a king cobra. [from Greek *hama*, together + *drys*, oak tree]

hamadryas baboon /haməˈdraɪəs/ a baboon native to NE Africa and SW Arabia, having silver-brown fur (which is long and thick over the male's head and shoulders), a naked face, and a long tail. Also called SACRED BABOON.

Hamas /ˈhamas/ *noun* a Palestinian Islamic fundamentalist organization. [from Arabic *harakat al-Muqawama al-Islamiyya*, Islamic Resistance Movement; also Arabic *hamas*, enthusiasm]

hamburger *noun* a flat, round cake of finely chopped beef, usually fried and served in a soft roll. [named after Hamburg in Germany]

ham-fisted or **ham-handed** *adj. colloq.* clumsy.

Hamitic /haˈmɪtɪk/ — *noun* a group of N African languages, including ancient Egyptian and Berber. — *adj.* relating to this group of languages. [named after *Ham*, one of Noah's sons, supposed founder of a race of people in N Africa]

hamlet *noun* a small village. [from Old French *hamelet*]

hammer — *noun* **1** a tool with a heavy metal head on the end of a handle, used for driving nails into wood, breaking hard substances, etc. **2** the part of a bell, piano, clock, etc that hits against some other part, making a noise. **3** the part of a gun, attached to the trigger, which causes the bullet to be fired. **4** a metal ball on a long, flexible steel chain, thrown in competitions; the sport of throwing this. **5** an auctioneer's gavel. — *verb* (**hammered, hammering**) **1** *trans., intrans.* to hit with a hammer. **2** *trans., intrans.* (**hammer something** or **hammer at** or **on something**) to strike it loudly and repeatedly. **3** (**hammer something in**) to drive or force it in with, or as if with, a hammer. **4** *Brit. colloq.* to criticize or beat severely. **5** *colloq.* to defeat. **6** *in-*

trans. (**hammer at** or **away at something**) to work constantly at it: *hammer away at the problem.* — **come** or **go under the hammer** to be sold at auction. **hammer and tongs** *colloq.* with a lot of noise and violence. **hammer something out** to produce an agreement, etc with a great deal of effort and discussion. [from Anglo-Saxon *hamor*]

....

◼ *verb* **2** hit, strike, beat, drum, bang, bash, pound, batter, knock. **hammer out** settle, sort out, negotiate, thrash out, produce, bring about, accomplish, complete, finish.

....

hammer and sickle the sign of a hammer and a sickle laid across each other, used as a symbol of communism.

hammer-beam roof *Archit.* a type of timber roof consisting of arched ribs, supported on hammer beams at their feet, and carrying the principal rafters. Hammer beams are short cantilevered beams projecting inwards from the junction of wall and roof and strengthened by curved struts underneath.

hammerhead *noun* **1** (**hammerhead shark**) any of several species of shark, native to temperate and tropical seas, so called because its head is drawn out into two flattened protuberances in the shape of the head of a hammer. The eyes are located on the extremities of these protuberances, and the nostrils are located on the front edge. The hammerhead shark grows to a length of up to 6m, and weighs up to a tonne. **2** a tropical wading bird, native to Africa, having dark plumage, a long backward-pointing crest, and a thick bill.

hammering *noun Brit. colloq.* a severe beating.

hammertoe *noun* a deformity of one of the toes, usually the second, which is permanently bent in a claw-like arch.

hammock /ˈhamək/ *noun* a piece of canvas or a net hung by the corners and used as a bed, eg in a ship. [from Spanish *hamaca*]

hamper[1] *verb* (**hampered, hampering**) to hinder the progress or movement of. [from Middle English *hampren*]

....

◼ hinder, impede, obstruct, slow down, hold up, frustrate, thwart, prevent, handicap, hamstring, shackle, cramp, restrict, curb, restrain.

◲ aid, facilitate.

....

hamper[2] *noun* **1** a large basket with a lid, used especially for carrying food. **2** *Brit.* the food and drink packed in such a basket. [from Middle English *hanypere*, wicker basket]

hamster *noun* any of a family of short-tailed burrowing nocturnal rodents native to Europe and Asia, similar to voles and gerbils, with large cheek pouches in which they store food before returning to their underground burrows. [from Old German *hamstra*, weevil]

hamstring — *noun Anat.* any of the tendons at the back of the knee which are attached to muscles in the thigh. — *verb* (PAST TENSE AND PAST PARTICIPLE **hamstringed, hamstrung**) **1** to make powerless or hinder. **2** to lame by cutting the hamstring. [from HAM[1]]

hand — *noun* **1** in humans, the extremity of the arm below the wrist, consisting of a thumb, four fingers and a palm; any corresponding member in the higher vertebrates. **2** (*often* **hands**) control, agency, or influence. **3** help; assistance. **4** a part or influence in an activity: *had a hand in the victory.* **5** a needle or pointer on a clock, watch, or gauge. **6** *colloq.* applause. **7** a manual worker or assistant, especially in a factory, on a farm, or on board ship. **8** a person skilful in some activity: *a dab hand at baking.* **9** a way of doing something: *have a light hand at pastry.* **10** the cards dealt to a player in one round of a card game. **11** one round of a card game. **12** a position in relation to an object or (*in compounds*) to a point in time: *on the right hand/ behind-hand.* **13** a source of information considered in terms of closeness to the original source: *hear the news at first hand.* **14** a person's handwriting or its style. **15** a promise or agreement to marry: *ask for her hand.* **16** a unit of measurement, equal to four inches, used for measuring the

height of horses. — *verb* (**hand something back, out, round,** *etc*) to deliver or give it using the hands. — **at hand** near by; about to happen. **by hand 1** with a person's hand or tools held in the hands. **2** delivered by messenger, not by post. **from hand to mouth** with only enough money and food for one's immediate needs. **get one's hands on something** or **someone** *colloq.* to catch or find someone or obtain something. **hand something down** to pass an heirloom, tradition, etc on to the next generation. **hand something in** to deliver something to someone entitled to hold it, eg lost property. **hand in glove** very closely associated. **hand in hand 1** holding a person's hand. **2** in close association. **hand it to someone** *colloq.* to give them due credit. **hand something on** to give it to the next person in succession. **hand something out** to give or distribute it to a number of people. **hand something over** to give possession of it to someone else, especially to someone entitled to it. **hand over fist** *colloq.* in large amounts and very quickly. **have one's hands full** *colloq.* to be very busy. **in hand 1** under control. **2** being done or prepared. **keep one's hand in** *colloq.* to practise a skill, etc so as to remain competent at it. **off one's hands** *colloq.* no longer one's responsibility. **on hand** near; available for use. **on one's hands** *colloq.* **1** left over; not sold or used. **2** remaining as one's responsibility. **on one's hands and knees 1** in a position with one's hands, knees and feet on the ground. **2** begging. **on the one hand... on the other hand ...** from one point of view... from another point of view... **out of hand 1** *said of a person, especially a child* unable to be controlled. **2** immediately and without thinking. **to hand** within reach. **the upper hand** the advantage or position of greatest power or strength. [from Anglo-Saxon *hand*]

....

◼ *noun* **1** fist, palm, *colloq.* paw, *colloq.* mitt. **2** control, power, authority, influence, command, charge, care, custody, possession. **3** help, assistance, aid, support. **4** part, share, participation, influence. **7** worker, employee, operative, labourer, hireling, helper, assistant. *verb* give, pass, offer, submit, present, distribute, deliver, transmit. **at hand** near, close, to hand, handy, accessible, available, ready, imminent. **hand down** pass on, bequeath, will, transfer, give, grant. **hand out** distribute, deal out, give out, share out, *colloq.* dish out, mete out, dispense. **hand over** yield, relinquish, surrender, turn over, deliver, give, donate, present.

◲ **hand over** keep, retain.

....

handbag *noun* a woman's small bag, often with a strap for carrying, for money, make-up, etc.

handball *noun* a game in which players hit a small ball with their hands.

handbill *noun* a small printed notice or advertisement given out by hand.

handbook *noun* a short manual or guidebook.

....

◼ manual, instruction book, guide, guidebook, companion.

....

handbrake *noun* **1** a brake, usually applied by means of a hand-operated lever, used to prevent the rolling of a motor vehicle while it is parked. **2** the lever that is used to operate this brake.

handcart *noun* a small light cart which can be moved by hand.

handclap *noun* a clap of the hands.

handcrafted *adj.* made by handicraft.

handcuff — *verb* to put handcuffs on (a person). — *noun* (**handcuffs**) a pair of steel rings, joined by a short chain, for locking round the wrists of prisoners.

handful *noun* (PL. **handfuls**) **1** as much as can be held in one hand. **2** a small amount or number. **3** *colloq.* a person who is difficult to control; a difficult task.

....

◼ **2** few, sprinkling, scattering, smattering.

◲ **2** lot, many.

....

hand grenade a grenade to be thrown by hand.

handgun *noun* a gun that can be held and fired in one hand, eg a pistol.

handicap — *noun* 1 a physical or mental disability that results in partial or total inability to perform social, occupational, or other normal everyday activities. 2 a disadvantage given to a superior competitor in a contest, race, etc. 3 a race or competition in which some competitors are given a handicap. 4 the number of strokes by which a golfer usually exceeds par for the course. 5 any disadvantage, drawback, or obstacle to success. — *verb* (**handicapped, handicapping**) 1 to give a handicap to. 2 to make something difficult for (someone). [from *hand i' cap*, an old sporting lottery]

■ *noun* 1 disability, impairment, defect, impediment, shortcoming, limitation. 2 disadvantage, restriction, penalty. 5 disadvantage, drawback, hindrance, impediment, obstacle, barrier, block, stumbling-block. *verb* 1 disadvantage, restrict, limit, disable. 2 impede, hinder, hold back, hamper, burden, encumber.

■ *noun* 5 advantage. *verb* 2 help, assist.

handicapped — *adj.* physically or mentally disabled. — *pl. noun* handicapped people.

handicraft *noun* 1 an activity which requires skilful use of the hands, eg pottery or model-making. 2 (*usually* **handicrafts**) any object produced by such craft. [from Anglo-Saxon *handcræft*]

■ 1 craft, art, craftwork, handiwork.

handily *adv.* in a handy way or position.

handiness *noun* being handy.

handiwork *noun* 1 work, especially skilful, done by the hands. 2 something bad done or caused by a particular person. [from Anglo-Saxon *handgeweorc*]

■ WORK. 1 creation, production, skill, workmanship, craftsmanship, artisanship. 2 doing, responsibility, product, result.

handkerchief *noun* (PL. **handkerchiefs, handkerchieves**) a small, usually square piece of cloth or soft paper used for wiping one's nose, face, etc. [from HAND + KERCHIEF]

handle — *noun* 1 the part of an object by which it is held so that it may be used or operated. 2 an advantage or opening given to an opponent. 3 *slang* a person's name. — *verb* 1 to touch, hold, move or operate with the hands. 2 to deal with or manage, especially successfully or in the correct way. 3 to buy, sell, or deal in (goods). 4 to write about or discuss (a subject). 5 *intrans.* to respond to control in the way stated. — **fly off the handle** *colloq.* to become suddenly angry. [from Anglo-Saxon *handle*]

■ *noun* 1 grip, handgrip, knob, stock, shaft, hilt. *verb* 1 touch, finger, feel, fondle, pick up, hold, grasp, move, drive, operate, work. 2 tackle, treat, deal with, manage, cope with, control.

handlebar moustache a wide, thick moustache which curls up at the ends.

handlebars *pl. noun* a usually curved metal bar with handles at each end, for steering a bicycle or motorcycle.

handler *noun* 1 a person who trains and controls an animal, especially a dog. 2 a person who handles something: *a baggage handler.*

handless *adj. old use* awkward or clumsy.

handling *noun* 1 touching, moving, holding, or turning with the hand. 2 packaging and transportation of goods. 3 treatment or management.

handmade *adj.* made with a person's hands or with tools held in the hands, not by machine.

handmaiden or **handmaid** *noun old use* a female servant.

hand-me-down *noun colloq.* a second-hand garment, toy, etc.

handout *noun* 1 money, food, etc given to people who need it. 2 a leaflet or statement containing information, etc, given eg to students before a lecture, to newspaper reporters, etc.

■ 1 charity, alms, dole, largesse, free sample, *colloq.* freebie. 2 leaflet, circular, bulletin, statement, press release.

handover *noun* the transfer of power from one person or group of people to another.

hand-pick *verb* to choose carefully, especially for a particular purpose.

hand-picked *adj.* carefully chosen.

handrail *noun* a narrow rail running along stairs, etc for support.

handsaw *noun* a saw worked by hand, especially one with a handle at one end.

handset *noun* a telephone mouthpiece and earpiece together in a single unit.

handshake *noun* the act of holding or shaking a person's hand, especially as a greeting.

hands-off *adj.* not touched or operated by the hands.

handsome *adj.* 1 *said of a man* good-looking. 2 *said of a woman* attractive in a strong, healthy, imposing way. 3 *said of a building* large and imposing. 4 substantial; generous: *a handsome donation.* [from HAND + -SOME; originally meaning 'easy to handle']

■ 1 good-looking, attractive, personable, elegant. 4 generous, liberal, large, considerable, substantial, ample.

■ 1 ugly, unattractive. 4 mean.

hands-on *adj.* involving practical experience rather than just information or theory.

handspring *noun* a somersault or cartwheel in which one lands first on one's hands and then on one's feet.

handstand *noun* an act of balancing one's body upside down on one's hands.

hand-to-hand *adj., said of fighting* involving direct physical contact with the enemy.

handwriting *noun* 1 writing with a pen or pencil. 2 the characteristic way a person writes.

■ WRITING, SCRIPT. 1 penmanship, calligraphy. 2 hand, *colloq.* fist.

handwritten *adj.* written using a pen or pencil, not printed or typed.

handy *adj.* (**handier, handiest**) 1 ready to use and conveniently placed. 2 easy to use or handle. 3 clever with one's hands.

■ PRACTICAL. 1 available, to hand, ready, at hand, near, accessible, convenient. 2 useful, helpful. 3 skilful, proficient, expert, skilled, clever, practical.

■ 1 inconvenient. 3 clumsy, awkward.

handyman *noun* a person skilled at, or employed to do, odd jobs around the house.

hang — *verb* (PAST TENSE AND PAST PARTICIPLE **hung, hanged** in senses 4 and 13) 1 *intrans.* to be fastened from above, especially with the lower part free. 2 to fasten from above. 3 *trans., intrans., said eg of a door* to fasten or be fastened with hinges so that it can move freely. 4 *trans., intrans.* to suspend or be suspended by a rope or something similar around the neck until dead. 5 (**hang over**) to remain without moving, especially in the air or in a threatening way. 6 *trans., intrans.* to droop or cause to droop: *hang one's head in shame*. **7** to fix (wallpaper) to a wall. **8** *trans., intrans., said of a painting, etc* to place or be placed in an exhibition. **9** to decorate (a room, wall, etc) with pictures or other hangings. **10** (**hang something on someone**) *colloq*. to blame them for it. **11** (**hang on something**) to depend on it: *it all hangs on the weather*. **12** (**hang on something**) to listen closely to it: *hanging on her every word*. **13** *trans., intrans. colloq*. to damn. **14** *intrans., said of a piece of clothing* to sit in a stated way when worn: *a coat which hangs well*. **15** to suspend (game) from a hook until it is mature. — *noun* the way something hangs, falls, or droops. — **get the hang of something** *colloq*. to learn or begin to understand how to do it. **hang about** or **around** *colloq*. **1** to stand around doing nothing. **2** (**hang about** or **around with someone**) to spend a lot of time with them. **hang back** to be unwilling or reluctant to do something. **hang fire 1** to delay taking action. **2** to cease to develop or progress. **hang in the balance** to be uncertain or in doubt. **hang loose** *North Amer. colloq*. to stay calm and in control of oneself. **hang on** *colloq*. **1** to wait. **2** to carry on bravely, in spite of problems or difficulties. **hang on to something** to keep a hold or control on it. **hang out 1** to lean or bend out. **2** *colloq*. to spend much time in a place: *hangs out in local bars*. **hang together 1** to be united and support each other. **2** *said of ideas, etc* to be consistent. **hang up** to finish a telephone conversation by replacing the receiver. **hang something up** to hang it on a hook or hanger. **let it all hang out** *colloq*. to be totally uninhibited and relaxed. [from Anglo-Saxon *hangian*]

. . . .

◫ *verb* **1** dangle, swing, drop, droop, sag, trail. **2** suspend, dangle, drape, fasten, attach, fix, stick. **5** remain, linger, hover, float, drift. **11** depend on, hinge on, turn on. **hang about** or **around 1** linger, loiter, dawdle, idle. **hang back** hold back, hesitate, shy away, demur, recoil. **hang on 1** wait, hold on. **2** carry on, continue, persevere, persist, endure, hold out. **hang on to** hold, grip, grasp, clutch.

◫ **hang on 2** give up.
. . . .

hangar /'haŋə(r)/ *noun* a building in which aircraft or spacecraft are housed and maintained. [from French *hangar*]

hangdog *adj*. ashamed or guilty.

hanger *noun* **1** a metal, wooden or plastic frame on which jackets, dresses, etc are hung up to keep their shape. **2** a person who hangs something.

hanger-on *noun* (PL. **hangers-on**) a fan or follower, especially one who is not wanted.

. . . .

◫ fan, supporter, follower, minion, lackey, toady, sycophant, parasite, sponger, dependant.
. . . .

hang-glider *noun* **1** an unpowered aircraft consisting of a small glider with a light metal or plastic framework from which the operator is suspended in a harness, used for gliding from cliff tops, etc, for sport. **2** the pilot of a hang-glider.

hang-gliding *noun* the sport of flying supported by a hang-glider.

hanging *noun* **1** an execution by hanging. **2** (*usually* **hangings**) curtains, tapestries, etc hung on walls for decoration.

hangman *noun* an official who hangs criminals.

hangnail *noun* a piece of loose skin that has been partly torn away from the base or side of a fingernail.

hang-out *noun slang* a place one lives in or spends much time in.

hangover *noun* **1** a collection of unpleasant physical symptoms that may follow a period of heavy drinking, such as headache, nausea, excessive thirst, dizziness, fatigue, and sensitivity to light and noise. Many of these effects are caused by dehydration. **2** something which remains from an earlier time.

hang-up *noun colloq*. an emotional or psychological problem.

. . . .

◫ inhibition, difficulty, problem, obsession, preoccupation, *colloq*. thing, block, mental block.
. . . .

hank *noun* a length of wool, string, rope, etc gathered in a loop. [from Old Norse *hanki*, a hasp]

hanker *verb intrans*. (**hankered, hankering**) (**hanker after** or **for something**) to long for or crave it.

. . . .

◫ long for, yearn for, pine for, itch for, crave, hunger for, thirst for, want, wish for, desire, covet.
. . . .

hankering *noun* a craving, a yearning.

. . . .

◫ craving, hunger, thirst, wish, desire, yearning, longing, itch, urge.
. . . .

hankie or **hanky** *noun* (PL. **hankies**) *colloq*. a handkerchief. [abbreviation]

hanky-panky *noun colloq*. **1** slightly improper sexual behaviour. **2** dishonest dealing.

Hanoverian /hanə'vɪərɪən/ — *adj*. of British sovereigns from George I (1714) to Victoria (1901), George I being also the Elector of Hanover in N Germany. — *noun* a member of this dynasty.

hansom or **hansom cab** *noun Hist*. a small, two-wheeled, horse-drawn carriage with a fixed roof and the driver's seat high up at the back, used as a taxi. [named after J A Hansom (1803–82), its inventor]

Hants. *abbrev*. Hampshire.

Hanukkah /'hɑːnəkə/ *noun* an eight-day Jewish festival held annually in December, commemorating the rededication of the Temple at Jerusalem in 165 BC. [from Hebrew *hanukkah*, consecration]

ha'penny see HALFPENNY.

haphazard /hap'hazəd/ *adj*. done by chance; random. — *adv*. at random. [from Norse *happ*, good luck + HAZARD]

. . . .

◫ *adj*. random, chance, casual, arbitrary, hit-or-miss, unsystematic, disorganized, disorderly, careless, slapdash, slipshod.

◫ *adj*. methodical, orderly.
. . . .

hapless *adj*. unlucky; unfortunate. [from Norse *happ*, good luck]

haploid *adj*. **1** describing a cell nucleus that contains only a single set of chromosomes. **2** describing a living organism, or stage of its life cycle, that has only a single set of chromosomes in its cell nuclei. [from Greek *haploos*, single, simple]

hap'orth see HALFPENNYWORTH.

happen — *verb intrans*. (**happened, happening**) **1** to take place or occur. **2** (**happen to someone**) *said especially of something unwelcome* to be done to them, or be experienced by them. **3** to have the good or bad luck to: *happened to meet him on the way*. **4** (**happen on something**) to discover or encounter it, especially by chance. — *adv. dialect* perhaps. [from Norse *happ*, good luck]

. . . .

◫ *verb* **1** occur, take place, arise, crop up, develop, come about, result, ensue, follow, turn out, transpire. **4** find, discover, encounter, come across, chance on.
. . . .

happening *noun* **1** an event or occurrence; something that happens. **2** a public performance, especially one which takes place in the street, which has not been fully planned, and in which the audience is invited to take part.

. . . .

◫ **1** occurrence, phenomenon, event, incident, episode, adventure, experience.
. . . .

happily *adv.* **1** in a happy way. **2** luckily.

happiness *noun* a happy state or feeling; pleasure, contentment.

⊞ joy, joyfulness, gladness, cheerfulness, contentment, pleasure, delight, glee, elation, bliss, ecstasy, euphoria.
⊠ unhappiness, sadness.

happy *adj.* **(happier, happiest) 1** feeling or showing pleasure or contentment: *a happy smile.* **2** causing pleasure: *a happy day for the company.* **3** suitable; fortunate: *a happy coincidence.* [from Norse *happ*, good luck]

⊞ **1** joyful, jolly, merry, cheerful, glad, pleased, delighted, elated, satisfied, contented. **3** lucky, fortunate, felicitous, favourable, suitable, appropriate, apt, fitting.
⊠ **1** unhappy, sad, discontented. **3** unfortunate, inappropriate.

happy-clappy *adj. colloq., usually derog.* denoting any form of Christian worship that involves hand-clapping and chanting.

happy event *euphemistic* the birth of a child.

happy-go-lucky *adj.* carefree.

happy medium a reasonable middle course between two extreme positions.

hara-kiri /harəˈkɪrɪ/ *noun* ritual suicide by cutting one's belly open with a sword, formerly practised in Japan to avoid dishonour. [from Japanese *hara*, belly + *kiri*, cut]

harangue /həˈraŋ/ — *noun* a loud, forceful speech either to attack people or to try to persuade them to do something. — *verb* to address such a speech to. [from Old French *arenge*]

⊞ *noun* diatribe, tirade, lecture, speech, address. *verb* lecture, preach to, hold forth to, address.

harass /ˈharəs, həˈras/ *verb* **1** to annoy or trouble (a person) constantly or frequently. **2** to make frequent sudden attacks on (an enemy). [from Old French *harasser*, to harry]

⊞ **1** pester, badger, harry, plague, torment, persecute, vex, annoy, irritate, bother, disturb, *colloq.* hassle, trouble, worry, tire, exhaust.

harassed /ˈharəst, həˈrast/ *adj.* troubled, worried, overburdened.

harassment /ˈharəsmənt, həˈrasmənt/ *noun* **1** harassing. **2** being harassed.

harbinger /ˈhɑːbɪndʒə(r)/ *noun* a person or thing which is a sign of something that is to come. [from Old French *herbergere*, host]

harbour — *noun* **1** a place of shelter for ships. **2** a refuge. — *verb* **1** to give shelter or protection to (eg a criminal). **2** to have (thoughts) in one's head: *harbour a grudge.* [from Anglo-Saxon *herebeorg*, lodgings]

⊞ *noun* HAVEN, SHELTER. **1** port, dock, quay, wharf, marina, mooring, anchorage. **2** refuge, sanctuary, asylum. *verb* **1** hide, conceal, protect, shelter. **2** hold, entertain, foster, nurse, nurture, cherish, retain, cling to.

harbour master a person officially in charge of a harbour.

hard — *adj.* **1** *said of a substance* resistant to scratching or indentation. **2** difficult to do, understand, solve or explain. **3** using, needing, or done with a great deal of effort. **4** harsh; cruel. **5** *said of weather* severe. **6** causing or suffering hardship: *hard times.* **7** harsh and unpleasant to the senses: *a hard light.* **8** *said of information, etc* proven and reliable. **9** *said of water* containing calcium or magnesium salts, and tending to produce an insoluble scum instead of a lather with soap. **10** *said of a drug* highly addictive. **11** *said of an alcoholic drink* strong; being a spirit rather than beer or wine. **12** politically extreme: *hard right.* **13** *said of the sounds of certain letters* produced as a stop rather than a fricative, as eg the *c* in *cat* and the *g* in *got.* **14** *said of currency* with a stable value and exchange rate. **15** *said of pornography* sexually explicit. — *adv.* **1** with great effort or energy: *work hard.* **2** with difficulty; as a result of great effort: *a hard-won victory/hard-earned results.* — **be hard going** to be difficult to do. **be hard put to do something** to have difficulty doing it. **go hard with someone** to be unpleasant or difficult for them. **hard at it** working hard. **hard by** close by. **hard done by** *colloq.* unfairly treated. **hard of hearing** partially deaf. **hard on someone** or **something** close behind them. **hard up** *colloq.* short of something, especially money. [from Anglo-Saxon *heard*]

⊞ *adj.* **1** solid, firm, unyielding, tough, strong, dense, impenetrable, stiff, rigid, inflexible. **2** difficult, complex, complicated, involved, knotty, baffling, puzzling, perplexing. **3** difficult, arduous, strenuous, laborious, tiring, exhausting, backbreaking. **4** harsh, severe, strict, callous, unfeeling, unsympathetic, cruel, pitiless, merciless, ruthless, unrelenting. **6** distressing, painful, unpleasant. *adv.* **1** industriously, diligently, assiduously, doggedly, steadily, earnestly, intently, energetically, vigorously, strenuously. **hard up** short, lacking, poor, *colloq.* broke, penniless, in the red, bankrupt.
⊠ *adj.* **1** soft, yielding. **2** easy, simple. **4** kind, merciful. **hard up** rich.

hard-and-fast *adj., said of a rule or principle* permanent or absolute; that can never be changed.

hardback — *noun* a book with a hard cover. — *adj.* having a hard cover.

hard-bitten *adj. colloq., said of a person* tough and ruthless, especially through difficult experience.

hardboard *noun* light, strong board made by compressing wood pulp.

hard-boiled *adj.* **1** *said of eggs* boiled until the yolk is solid. **2** *said of a person* tough; cynical.

hard case *colloq.* a tough, often violent person.

hard cash coins and bank-notes, as opposed to cheques and credit cards.

hard copy any form of computer output that is printed on paper, as opposed to material that is displayed on the screen of a visual display unit, or stored on magnetic disc or tape; a printout.

hardcore *noun* **1** pieces of broken brick, stone, etc used as a base for a road. **2** (*also* **hard core**) the central, most important group within an organization.

hard-core *adj.* **1** having long-lasting, strong, unchanging beliefs. **2** denoting pornography that is sexually explicit.

hard currency 1 money in the form of coins or notes. **2** a currency with a high, stable, or improving exchange rate, not subject to depreciation. **3** a currency backed by bullion.

hard disk *Comput.* a rigid aluminium disk, coated with magnetic material and normally permanently sealed within the disk drive, that is used to store data. It is much faster in operation than a floppy disk, and can store large amounts of data. See also FLOPPY DISK.

harden *verb* (**hardened, hardening**) **1** *trans., intrans.* to make or become hard or harder. **2** *trans., intrans.* to become or make less sympathetic or understanding: *hardened his heart to her tears.* **3** *intrans., said of prices* to stop falling.

⊞ **1** solidify, set, freeze, bake, stiffen, strengthen, toughen.
⊠ **1** soften, weaken.

hardened *adj.* toughened through experience and not likely to change: *a hardened criminal.*

hardening of the arteries same as ARTERIOSCLEROSIS.

hard-headed *adj.* clever and not influenced by emotion.

☲ shrewd, astute, businesslike, level-headed, clear-thinking, sensible, realistic, pragmatic, practical, hard-boiled, tough, unsentimental.

hard-hearted *adj.* feeling no pity or kindness.

☲ callous, unfeeling, cold, hard, stony, heartless, unsympathetic, cruel, inhuman, pitiless, merciless.
☲ soft-hearted, kind, merciful.

hard-hitting *adj.* direct; frankly critical.

☲ critical, condemnatory, unsparing, no-holds-barred, direct, vigorous, forceful, tough.
☲ mild.

hardihood *noun* courage and daring.

hardiness *noun* being hardy.

hard labour heavy physical work, eg breaking rocks, especially as a punishment in prison.

hardline *adj.* **1** *said of an attitude or policy* definite and unyielding. **2** having such an attitude or policy.

hard line a strong opinion, decision, or policy which is not likely to be changed.

hardliner *noun* a person who supports or promotes a hardline attitude or policy.

hardly *adv.* **1** only with difficulty; scarcely: *could hardly keep her eyes open*. **2** probably not: *they'll hardly come now*. **3** harshly.

☲ **1** barely, scarcely, just, only just.

hard-nosed *adj. colloq.* determined; influenced by reason, not emotion.

hard nut *colloq.* a person or thing that is tough or difficult to deal with.

hard-on *noun coarse slang* an erection of the penis.

hardpad *noun* a disorder of dogs, so called because it is characterized by an abnormal thickening of the skin of the foot pads and nose. It is one of the symptoms of distemper.

hard palate /'palət/ *Anat.* the bony front part of the palate, which separates the mouth from the nasal cavities.

hard-pressed or **hard-pushed** *adj.* having problems; in difficulties.

hard sell an aggressive and insistent way of promoting, selling, or advertising.

hardship *noun* severe suffering and pain, or a cause of this.

☲ misfortune, adversity, trouble, difficulty, affliction, distress, suffering, trial, tribulation, want, need, privation, austerity, poverty, destitution, misery.
☲ ease, comfort, prosperity.

hard shoulder a hard verge along the side of a motorway, on which vehicles can stop if in trouble.

hardtack *noun* hard biscuits formerly given to sailors as food on long journeys.

hardtop *noun* **1** a rigid roof on a motor vehicle. **2** a vehicle, especially a motor car, with such a roof.

hardware *noun* **1** metal goods such as pots, cutlery, tools, etc. **2** *Comput.* the electronic, electrical, magnetic, and mechanical components of a computer system, as opposed to the programs that form the software. See also SOFTWARE. **3** heavy military equipment, eg tanks.

hard water *Chem.* water that contains dissolved calcium or magnesium salts, which prevent it forming a lather with soap, and are responsible for the 'furring up' of hot-water pipes and kettles. Hard water forms a scum with soap.

hard-wearing *adj.* that will last a long time and stay in good condition.

☲ durable, lasting, strong, tough, sturdy, stout, rugged, resilient.
☲ delicate.

hard-wired *adj.* **1** *said of a computer* having functions which are controlled by hardware and cannot be altered by software programs. **2** *colloq.* seemingly inalterably set to act in a particular way.

hardwood *noun* **1** *Bot.* the wood of a slow-growing deciduous tree, eg oak, mahogany, teak. It is dense and has a fine grain. **2** *Bot.* any tree which produces such wood. See also SOFTWOOD.

hardy *adj.* (**hardier, hardiest**) **1** tough; strong; able to bear difficult conditions. **2** *said of a plant* able to survive outdoors in winter. [from Old French *hardi*, made bold]

☲ **1** strong, tough, sturdy, robust, vigorous, fit, healthy, sound.
☲ **1** weak, unhealthy.

hare — *noun* a herbivorous mammal belonging to the same family as the rabbit, found in Europe, Asia, Africa, and N and Central America, and having a brown or greyish coat which becomes white during the winter in northern species. — *verb intrans. colloq.* to run very fast. [from Anglo-Saxon *hara*]

harebell *noun* a slender perennial plant (*Campanula rotundifolia*), native to north temperate regions, having heart-shaped basal leaves, much narrower stem leaves and drooping bell-shaped pale blue (or rarely white) flowers, borne singly or in loose clusters on long slender stalks. In Scotland it is known as the bluebell.

hare-brained *adj.*, *said of people, actions, etc* foolish; done without considering the consequences.

Hare Krishna movement a religious movement founded (1965) in the USA and based on the ancient Vedic texts of India.

hare lip *Medicine* a deformity of the upper lip, present from birth, in which there is a cleft on one or both sides of the centre, caused by incomplete merging of the embryonic tissues beneath one or both nostrils. It is often associated with a cleft palate, and can be corrected by plastic surgery during childhood.

hare-lipped *adj.* having a hare lip.

harem /ha:'ri:m/ *noun* **1** a separate part of a traditional Muslim house in which the women live. **2** the women living in this. [from Arabic *harim*, forbidden]

haricot /'harɪkoʊ/ *noun* (*also* **haricot bean**) the mature seed, especially a light-coloured ellipsoid form, of a widely cultivated species of bean plant (*Phaseolus vulgaris*) (French bean), which after ripening on the plant can be dried, or processed to form baked beans, etc. [from French *haricot*]

hark *verb intrans. literary* (**hark at** or **to something** or **someone**) to listen to them attentively. — **hark back to something** to refer to or remind one of past experiences: *hark back to one's childhood*. [from Anglo-Saxon *heorcnian*, to hearken]

harken same as HEARKEN.

harlequin /'ha:ləkwɪn/ — *noun* (*also* **Harlequin**) a humorous character from traditional Italian plays who wears a black mask and a brightly coloured, diamond-patterned costume. — *adj.* in varied bright colours. [from French *harlequin*, probably from Old French *Hellequin*]

harlot /'ha:lət/ *noun old use* a prostitute. [from Old French *herlot*, rascal]

harlotry /'ha:lətrɪ/ *noun* prostitution.

harm — *noun* physical, mental, or moral injury or damage. — *verb* to cause harm to. — **out of harm's way** in a safe place, not able to be harmed or cause harm. [from Anglo-Saxon *hearm*]

☲ *noun* damage, loss, injury, hurt, detriment, ill, misfortune,

wrong, abuse. *verb* damage, impair, blemish, spoil, mar, ruin, hurt, injure, wound, ill-treat, maltreat, abuse, misuse.
☒ *noun* benefit. *verb* benefit, improve.

harmful *adj.* causing harm.

☐ damaging, detrimental, pernicious, noxious, unhealthy, unwholesome, injurious, dangerous, hazardous, poisonous, toxic, destructive.
☒ harmless.

harmless *adj.* not able or likely to cause harm.

☐ safe, innocuous, non-toxic, inoffensive, gentle, innocent.
☒ harmful, dangerous, destructive.

harmonic — *adj.* of or relating to harmony; harmonious. — *noun* a note produced on a stringed instrument by touching one of the strings lightly at one of the points which divide the string into exact fractions. [from Greek *harmonikos*, from *harmos*, joint]

harmonica *noun* **1** a mouth organ; a small, rectangular, musical instrument with metal reeds along one side, played by being held against the mouth, blown through, and moved from side to side to change the notes. **2** (*in full* **glass harmonica**) a musical instrument consisting of drinking-glasses (or revolving glass bowls in Benjamin Franklin's mechanized version) filled to different levels with water, and touched on the rims with a damp finger to produce sounds of different pitch. **3** a musical instrument made up of a sound-box with hanging strips of glass or metal, struck with a hammer.

harmonic motion *Physics* same as SIMPLE HARMONIC MOTION.

harmonic progression *Maths.* a series of terms in which there is a constant difference between the reciprocals of the terms, eg $\frac{1}{1}, \frac{1}{2}, \frac{1}{3}, \frac{1}{4}, \dots$

harmonics *sing. noun* the science of musical sounds.

harmonic series *Mus.* the combination or series of notes produced when a string or column of air is vibrated. A principal note, eg C, has a complex of such notes known as overtones or partials, which have the effect of enriching the quality of the principal note. The tone quality of musical instruments depends on the presence or absence of these overtones and their relative intensity.

harmonious *adj.* **1** pleasant-sounding and tuneful. **2** forming a pleasing whole: *a harmonious arrangement of colours.* **3** without disagreement or bad feeling. [from HARMONY]

☐ **1** melodious, tuneful, musical, sweet-sounding. **2** matching, co-ordinated, balanced. **3** agreeable, cordial, amicable, friendly, compatible, like-minded.
☒ **1** discordant.

harmonium *noun* a musical instrument with a keyboard, in which air from bellows pumped by the feet makes the reeds vibrate to produce sound. [from HARMONY]

harmonization or **harmonisation** *noun* the act of harmonizing.

harmonize or **harmonise** *verb* **1** *intrans., trans.* to be or bring into musical harmony. **2** *intrans.* to form a pleasing whole. **3** to cause to form a pleasing whole. **4** to add notes to (a simple tune) to form harmonies.

☐ **2** match, tone, co-ordinate, balance, correspond, agree. **3** co-ordinate, balance, blend, arrange, compose.
☒ **2** clash.

harmony *noun* (PL. **harmonies**) **1** *Mus.* a pleasing combination of notes or sounds produced simultaneously. **2** a pleasing arrangement of parts or things: *harmony of colour.* **3** agreement in opinions and feelings. [from Greek *harmonia*, from *harmos*, joint]

☐ **1** tunefulness, tune, melody, euphony. **2** coordination, balance, symmetry, correspondence. **3** agreement, unanimity, like-mindedness, accord, concord, unity, peace, goodwill, rapport, sympathy, understanding, compatibility, amicability, friendliness, co-operation.
☒ **1** discord. **3** discord, conflict.

harness — *noun* **1** a set of leather straps used to attach a cart to a horse, and to control the horse's movements. **2** a similar set of straps for attaching to a person's body, eg to hold a child who is just learning to walk. — *verb* **1** to put a harness on (a horse, person, etc). **2** to control and make use of (especially natural resources), especially to produce power. — **in harness** occupied with one's daily work or routine. [from Old French *herneis*, equipment]

☐ *noun* **1** straps, reins, tack, tackle, gear, equipment. *verb* **2** control, channel, use, utilize, exploit, make use of, employ, mobilize, apply.

harp — *noun* a large three-sided musical instrument with a series of strings stretched vertically across it, played by plucking the strings with the fingers. — *verb* (**harp on about something**) *colloq.* to talk or write repeatedly and tediously about it. [from Anglo-Saxon *hearpe*]

harpist *noun* a person who plays the harp.

harpoon — *noun* a barbed spear fastened to a rope, used for catching whales. — *verb* to strike (a whale, etc) with a harpoon. [from Greek *harpe*, hook]

harpsichord /'hɑːpsɪkɔːd/ *noun* a keyboard instrument in which the strings are plucked mechanically (and not struck with hammers as in a piano) when the player presses the keys. [from Latin *harpa*, harp + *chorda*, string]

harpy *noun* (PL. **harpies**) **1** an evil creature in Greek mythology with the features of a woman and the wings and claws of a bird. **2** a cruel, grasping woman. [from Greek *harpyia*, snatcher]

harridan /'harɪdən/ *noun* a bad-tempered, scolding old woman.

harrier[1] *noun* **1** a cross-country runner. **2** a hound used originally for hunting hares. [from HARE]

harrier[2] *noun* **1** any of various hawks, found worldwide except in polar regions, and having an owl-like head, a small beak, broad wings, and long legs and tail. **2** any person or thing which harries. [from HARRY]

harrow — *noun* *Agric.* a farm implement consisting of a heavy metal frame bearing a row of spikes or discs, which is dragged over the surface of ploughed soil in order to level it and reduce the soil to fine particles prior to seed sowing. It is also used to cover the seeds with soil after sowing. — *verb* **1** to level the surface of ploughed soil, or to cover seeds with soil after sowing, using such an implement. **2** (*usually* **be harrowing**) to distress greatly. [from Middle English *harwe*]

harrowing *adj.* extremely distressing.

☐ distressing, upsetting, heart-rending, disturbing, alarming, frightening, terrifying, nerve-racking, traumatic, agonizing, excruciating.

harry *verb* (**harries, harried**) **1** to ravage or destroy. **2** to annoy or worry (a person). See also HARRIER[2]. [from Anglo-Saxon *hergian*]

☐ **2** annoy, vex, worry, trouble, bother, disturb, *colloq.* hassle, badger, pester, nag, chivvy, harass, plague, torment, persecute.

harsh *adj.* **1** rough; grating; unpleasant to the senses. **2** strict, cruel or severe. [from Middle English *harsk*]

☐ **1** rough, coarse, rasping, croaking, guttural, grating, jarring, discordant, strident, raucous, sharp, shrill, unpleasant, bright, dazzling, glaring. **2** severe, strict, draconian, hard, cruel, unfeeling, pitiless, austere, spartan, bleak, grim, comfortless.

🔄 **1** soft. **2** lenient.
....

hart *noun* a male deer, especially a red deer more than five years old. [from Anglo-Saxon *heorot*]

hartebeest /ˈhɑːtəbiːst/ *noun* (PL. **hartebeest**) any of three species of large antelope, native to the open plains and desert regions of sub-Saharan Africa, having lyre-shaped horns (present in both sexes), a long narrow face, a reddish, pale brown, or yellowish-brown coat, with varying amounts of black on the limbs, a long bushy tail, and a small hump on its back. [from Afrikaans *hartebeest*, hart beast]

hart's tongue fern *Bot.* a fern belonging to the genus *Asplenium*, and having bright green strap-shaped undivided fronds.

harum-scarum /ˌhɛərəmˈskɛərəm/ — *adj.* wild and thoughtless; reckless. — *adv.* recklessly. — *noun* a wild, thoughtless person.

haruspex /həˈrʌspeks/ *noun* (PL. **haruspices**) in ancient Rome, a practitioner of the Etruscan system of divination foretelling events by examination of the entrails of sacrificial animals. Though less prestigious than the augurs, they were widely employed, and their art survived well into the Christian era. [perhaps from an Etruscan word + Latin *specere*, to view]

harvest — *noun* **1** the gathering in of ripened crops, usually in late summer or early autumn. **2** the season when this takes place. **3** the crops gathered. **4** the product or result of some action. — *verb* **1** *trans., intrans.* to gather as a harvest; to reap. **2** *trans.* to collect human organs for transplantation. [from Anglo-Saxon *hærfest*]
....

🔄 *noun* **1** reaping, gathering, collection. **3** crops, produce, fruits, yield. **4** product, result, consequence, yield, return. *verb* reap, mow, pick, gather, collect, accumulate, amass.
....

harvester *noun Agric.* a machine that harvests a crop, eg a combine harvester or potato lifter.

harvest festival or **harvest thanksgiving** a Christian religious service to thank God for the crops gathered in the harvest.

harvestman *noun* an extremely long-legged arthropod, having a compact body and four pairs of long legs, typically a predator of small insects, molluscs, or worms. Some are scavengers.

harvest moon the full moon nearest to the autumnal equinox, usually 22 or 23 September.

harvest mouse a small mouse, native to Europe and E Asia, having a reddish-brown coat, white underparts, and tiny ears, and growing to a length of up to 13cm, half of which is accounted for by its tail. It is the smallest European rodent.

has see HAVE.

has-been *noun colloq.* a person who is no longer successful, important or influential.

hash[1] — *noun* **1** a dish of cooked meat and vegetables chopped up together and recooked. **2** a re-using of old material. **3** *colloq.* a mess: *make a hash of something.* — *verb* to make into a hash. — **settle someone's hash** *colloq.* to silence or subdue them. [from Old French *hacher*, to chop]
....

🔄 *noun* **3** mess, botch, muddle, mix-up, jumble, confusion.
....

hash[2] *noun colloq.* hashish. [abbreviation]

hash browns a dish of potato (sometimes mixed with onion) cut into thin strips, fried to form a flat, browned cake, and eaten hot.

hashish /ˈhaʃɪʃ/ or **hasheesh** /ˈhaʃiːʃ/ *noun* a drug in the form of a resin derived from the dried flowers of the hemp plant (*Cannabis sativa*), smoked or chewed for its intoxicating effects. It is much more potent than marijuana. [from Arabic *hashish*, dry leaves]

Hasidim or **Chasidim** or **Hasideans** *pl. noun* originally, those Jews in the 2c BC who resisted Greek and pagan influences on Israel's religion and adhered strictly to the Jewish law. [Hebrew, = faithful ones]

Hasidism *noun* a movement of Jewish mysticism that began in 18c Poland, characterized by an ascetic pattern of life, strict observance of the commandments and loud ecstatic forms of worship and prayer.

hasn't *contr.* has not.

hasp *noun* a metal fastening for a door, box, etc consisting of a flat metal strip with a narrow slit in it, which fits over a small curved metal bar and is held shut by a pin or padlock fastened through the bar. [from Anglo-Saxon *hæpse*]

hassle *colloq.* — *noun* **1** trouble, annoyance, or inconvenience, or a cause of this. **2** a fight or argument. — *verb* **1** to annoy or bother, especially repeatedly. **2** *intrans.* to argue or fight.

hassock /ˈhasək/ *noun* **1** a firm cushion for kneeling on in church. **2** a tuft of grass. [from Anglo-Saxon *hassuc*]

hast /hast/ *verb old use* the form of the present tense of the verb *have* used with *thou*.

haste *noun* **1** urgency of movement. **2** too much speed. — **in haste** in a hurry; quickly. **make haste** to hurry. [from Old French *haste*]
....

🔄 **1** hurry, rush, hustle, bustle, urgency, speed, rapidity, swiftness, quickness, briskness. **2** rashness, recklessness, impetuosity.

🔄 **1** slowness.
....

hasten /ˈheɪsn/ *verb* **1** *intrans.* to move with speed. **2** to cause to move or happen more quickly. **3 (hasten to do something)** to do it eagerly and promptly: *he hastened to admit we were right.*
....

🔄 **1** hurry, rush, make haste, run, dash, tear, race, fly, accelerate, speed (up). **2** hurry, rush, accelerate, speed (up), quicken, step up, advance, expedite, dispatch, precipitate.

🔄 **1** dawdle. **2** delay.
....

hastily *adv.* in a hasty way.

hastiness *noun* **1** hurry. **2** rashness. **3** irritability.

hasty *adj.* (**hastier, hastiest**) **1** hurried; done or acting too quickly. **2** done without enough thought or preparation.
....

🔄 HURRIED, RUSHED, HEADLONG. **1** fast, quick, rapid, swift, speedy, brisk, short, brief, cursory. **2** rash, reckless, heedless, thoughtless, impetuous, impulsive, hotheaded.

🔄 DELIBERATE. **1** slow. **2** careful.
....

hat *noun* **1** a covering for the head, usually worn out of doors. **2** *colloq.* a role or capacity: *wearing her vet's hat.* — **keep something under one's hat** *colloq.* to keep it secret. **old hat** *colloq.* so well-known, familiar, etc as to be tedious and uninteresting. **pass the hat round** to collect money for a cause. **take one's hat off to someone** *colloq.* to admire or praise them, especially for some achievement. **talk through one's hat** *colloq.* to talk nonsense. [from Anglo-Saxon *hæt*]

Hats include: trilby, bowler, fedora, top-hat, Homburg, *US* derby, pork-pie hat, flat cap, beret, bonnet, tam o'shanter, tammy, deerstalker, hunting-cap, stovepipe hat, stetson, ten-gallon hat, boater, sunhat, panama, straw hat, picture-hat, pill-box, cloche, *US* beanie, poke-bonnet, mob-cap, turban, fez, sombrero, sou'wester, glengarry, bearskin, busby, peaked cap, sailor-hat, baseball cap, balaclava, hood, snood, toque, helmet, mortar-board, skullcap, yarmulka, mitre, biretta.

hatband *noun* a band of cloth or ribbon around a hat just above the brim.

hatbox *noun* a large, rounded, cardboard box for storing or carrying hats.

hatch¹ *noun* 1 a narrow or confined doorway or opening in a ship, aircraft, or spacecraft; the lid or cover of this opening. 2 a hatchway. 3 an opening in a wall between a kitchen and dining-room, used especially for serving food. [from Anglo-Saxon *hæc*]

hatch² — *verb* 1 (*also* **hatch out**) *said of the young of various animals, especially birds* to break out of an egg. 2 *intrans.*, *said of an egg* to break open, allowing the young of various animals, especially birds, to emerge. 3 to cause (the young of various animals, especially birds) to emerge from an egg. 4 (*also* **hatch something up**) to plan or devise a plot, scheme, etc, especially in secret. — *noun* 1 the act of hatching. 2 a group of newly hatched animals, especially birds. [from Middle English *hacchen*]

■ *verb* 3 incubate, brood. 4 devise, contrive, plan, plot, scheme, concoct, formulate, originate, think up, dream up, conceive.

hatch³ *verb* to shade (eg the surface of a map, drawing, or engraving) with close parallel or crossed lines. [from Old French *hacher*, to chop]

hatchback *noun* a car with a sloping door at the back which opens upwards, allowing access to the rear compartment.

hatchery *noun* (PL. **hatcheries**) a place where eggs, especially fish eggs, are hatched in controlled conditions.

hatchet *noun* a small axe held in one hand. [from Old French *hachette*, from *hacher*, to chop]

hatchet-faced *adj.* with a long thin face and sharp profile.

hatchet job *colloq.* a severe written or spoken critical attack on a person or his or her good reputation.

hatchet man *colloq.* a person employed to injure, kill, or ruin a person, his or her reputation, or something.

hatching *noun* shading with fine lines.

hatchway *noun* an opening in a ship's deck for loading cargo through.

hate — *verb* 1 to dislike very much. 2 *colloq.* to regret: *I hate to bother you.* — *noun* 1 great dislike. 2 *colloq.* a greatly disliked person or thing. [from Anglo-Saxon *hatian*]

■ *verb* 1 dislike, detest, loathe, abhor, abominate, *formal* execrate. *noun* 1 hatred, aversion, dislike, loathing, abhorrence.
▢ *verb* 1 like, love. *noun* 1 liking, love.

hateful *adj.* causing or deserving great dislike.

hate mail correspondence containing an abusive or threatening message, especially sent to a celebrity or person in the news.

hatpin *noun* a long metal pin, often decorated, pushed through a woman's hat and hair to keep the hat in place.

hatred *noun* great dislike or ill-will. [from Middle English]

■ hate, aversion, dislike, detestation, loathing, repugnance, revulsion, abhorrence, abomination, *formal* execration, animosity, ill-will, antagonism, hostility, enmity, antipathy.
▢ liking, love.

hatstand *noun* a piece of furniture with pegs for hanging hats, coats, umbrellas, etc on.

hatter *noun* a person who makes or sells hats. — **mad as a hatter** extremely mad or eccentric.

hat trick 1 the taking of three wickets in cricket with three balls following each other. 2 the scoring of three points, goals, etc in a single period of time or match. 3 the winning of three victories in a row.

hauberk /ˈhɔːbɜːk/ *noun Hist.* a long coat of chain-mail. [from Old French *hauberc*]

haughtily *adv.* in a haughty way.

haughtiness *noun* being haughty.

haughty /ˈhɔːtɪ/ *adj.* (**haughtier, haughtiest**) very proud; arrogant. [from Latin *altus*, high]

■ proud, arrogant, lofty, imperious, high and mighty, superior, supercilious, *colloq.* snooty, contemptuous, disdainful, scornful, snobbish, *colloq.* stuck-up.
▢ humble, modest.

haul — *verb* 1 *trans.*, *intrans.* to pull with great effort or difficulty. 2 to transport by road, eg in a lorry. — *noun* 1 the distance to be travelled: *a short haul.* 2 the act of pulling with effort or difficulty. 3 an amount gained at any one time, eg of fish caught in a single net or of something stolen. [from Old French *haler*, to drag]

■ *verb* 1 pull, heave, tug, draw, tow, drag, trail. 2 move, transport, convey, carry. *noun* 3 loot, booty, plunder, spoils, takings, gain, yield, catch, find.
▢ *verb* 1 push.

haulage *noun* 1 the business of transporting goods by road, especially in lorries. 2 the money charged for this.

haulier /ˈhɔːlɪə(r)/ *noun* a person or company which transports goods by road, especially in lorries.

haulm /hɔːm/ *noun Bot.* the stalk or stem of potatoes, peas, beans, or grasses. [from Anglo-Saxon *healm*]

haunch *noun* 1 the fleshy part of the human hip and buttock. 2 the leg and loin, especially of venison, as a cut of meat. [from Old French *hanche*]

haunt *verb* 1 *said of a ghost or spirit* to be present in (a place) or visit (a person or place) regularly. 2 *said of unpleasant thoughts, etc* to keep coming back to a person's mind: *haunted by the memory of his death.* 3 *colloq.* to visit (a place) frequently. [from Old French *hanter*]

■ 2 plague, torment, trouble, disturb, prey on, beset, obsess. 3 frequent, patronize, visit.

haunted *adj.* 1 frequented or infested by ghosts, etc. 2 worried.

haunting *adj.*, *said of a place, memory, piece of music, etc* making a very strong and moving impression.

■ memorable, unforgettable, persistent, recurrent, evocative, nostalgic, poignant.
▢ unmemorable.

hautboy /ˈoʊbɔɪ/ *noun old use* an oboe. [from French *haut*, high + *bois*, wood]

haute couture /oʊt kʊˈtjʊə(r)/ the most expensive and fashionable clothes available; the leading fashion designers or their products. [from French *haute couture*]

haute cuisine /oʊt kwɪˈziːn/ cookery (especially French) of a very high standard. [from French *haute cuisine*]

hauteur /oʊˈtɜː(r)/ *noun* haughtiness; arrogance. [from French *hauteur*]

have — *verb* (**has**; PAST TENSE AND PAST PARTICIPLE **had**) 1 to possess. 2 to receive, obtain, or take: *have a drink/have a look.* 3 to think of or hold in the mind: *have an idea.* 4 to experience, enjoy, or suffer: *have a good time/have a headache/had my car stolen.* 5 to be in a state: *have a page missing.* 6 to take part in or hold: *have a party.* 7 to cause, order, or invite someone to do something or something to be done: *have your hair cut/had him fired.* 8 (**have to be** or **do something**) to be required to be or do it: *had to run fast/had to be gentle.* 9 to gain an advantage over: *you have me on that point.* 11 *colloq.* to cheat or deceive: *you've been had.* 12 to show or feel: *have pity/have the goodness to leave.* 13 to accept or tolerate: *I won't have* *any of that!* **14** to receive as a guest: *have people to dinner.* **15** to be pregnant with or give birth to: *be having a baby.* **16** *coarse slang* to have sexual intercourse with. — *verb aux.* used with past participles of verbs to show that an action has been completed: *have made the cake/has been there many times.* — *noun* **1** (**haves**) *colloq.* people who have wealth and the security it brings: *the haves and the have-nots.* **2** *slang* a trick or swindle. — **have had it** *colloq.* **1** to be dead, ruined, or exhausted. **2** to have missed one's opportunity. **have it coming** *colloq.* to deserve the bad luck, punishment, etc that one will get. **have it in for someone** *colloq.* to feel hostile towards them. **have it off** or **away with someone** *coarse slang* to have sexual intercourse with them. **have someone on** *colloq.* to trick or tease them. **have something on 1** to be wearing it. **2** to have an engagement or appointment. **have something on someone** to have information about them, especially when adverse or incriminating. **have it out** to settle a disagreement by arguing or discussing it frankly. **have someone up** *Brit. colloq.* to bring them to court to answer a charge. **have what it takes** *colloq.* to have the required qualities or ability. [from Anglo-Saxon *habban*]

∷∷∷∷∷∷∷∷∷∷∷∷∷∷

▣ *verb* **1** own, possess, keep, hold, contain, include, comprise, incorporate, consist of. **2** take, accept, receive, get, obtain, gain, acquire, procure, secure. **4** feel, experience, enjoy, suffer, undergo, endure. **6** hold, arrange, organize, take part in, participate in. **8** must, be forced to, be compelled to, be obliged to, be required to, ought to, should. **11** deceive, dupe, fool, trick, cheat, swindle. **13** tolerate, put up with, take, accept. **15** give birth to, bear.

▣ *verb* **1** lack.

∷∷∷∷∷∷∷∷∷∷∷∷∷∷∷∷∷∷∷∷∷∷∷∷∷∷∷∷

haven *noun* **1** a place of safety or rest. **2** a harbour. [from Anglo-Saxon *hæfen*]

∷∷∷∷∷∷∷∷∷∷∷∷∷∷∷∷

▣ **1** shelter, refuge, sanctuary, asylum, retreat. **2** harbour, port, anchorage.

∷∷∷∷∷∷∷∷∷∷∷∷∷∷∷∷∷∷∷∷∷∷∷∷∷∷∷∷

haven't *contr.* have not.

haversack *noun* a canvas bag carried over one shoulder or on the back. [from German *Habersack*, from *Haber*, oats + *Sack*, bag]

havoc *noun* **1** great destruction or damage. **2** *colloq.* chaos. — **play havoc with something** to cause damage or confusion to it. [from Old French *havot*, plunder]

∷∷∷∷∷∷∷∷∷∷∷∷∷∷∷∷

▣ **1** damage, destruction, ruin, wreck, rack and ruin, devastation. **2** chaos, confusion, disorder, disruption.

∷∷∷∷∷∷∷∷∷∷∷∷∷∷∷∷∷∷∷∷∷∷∷∷∷∷∷∷

haw[1] *verb* — **hum and haw** see HUM.

haw[2] *noun* the fruit of the hawthorn. [from Anglo-Saxon *haga*]

hawfinch *noun* one of the larger finches, native to Europe, Asia, and N Africa, having a stocky body, a large head, a thick neck, a short white-tipped tail, broad white wing bars that are distinctive in flight, and a stout powerful beak which it uses to crack open hard seeds.

hawk[1] — *noun* **1** a relatively small bird of prey with short rounded wings and very good eyesight, belonging to the family Accipitridae. Hawks include sparrowhawks, harriers, kites, and buzzards (as opposed to eagles, the large members of this family). **2** in the USA, any of various falcons. **3** *Politics* a person favouring force and aggression rather than peaceful means of settling disputes. See also DOVE. — *verb intrans.* to hunt with a hawk. — **watch someone like a hawk** to watch them closely. [from Anglo-Saxon *hafoc*]

hawk[2] *verb* to carry (goods) round, usually from door to door, trying to sell them. [from Old German *haker*, retail dealer]

hawk[3] *verb* **1** *intrans.* to clear the throat noisily. **2** *trans.* to bring (phlegm) up from the throat. [imitative]

hawker[1] *noun* a person who hunts with a hawk.

hawker[2] *noun* a person who goes from house to house offering goods for sale from his or her vehicle.

hawk-eyed *adj.* having very keen eyesight.

hawkish *adj.* like a hawk.

hawk moth a medium to large moth, most abundant in the tropics, typically with long triangular wings and an elongated body. It is a fast flier, capable of hovering flight.

hawkweed *noun Bot.* a perennial plant, belonging to the genus *Hieracium*, found mainly in the northern hemisphere, having leaves arranged spirally around the stem, or forming a rosette at the base, and yellow flower heads that may be solitary or borne in loose clusters.

hawser *noun* a thick rope or a steel cable for tying ships to the quayside. [from Old French *haucier*]

hawthorn *noun* a spiny deciduous shrub or small tree (*Crataegus monogyna*), native to north temperate regions. It has white sweetly scented flowers borne in clusters, and scarlet berry-like fruits, called *haws*. Also called MAY. [from Anglo-Saxon *haguthorn*]

hay *noun* grass that has been cut and allowed to dry in the field before being baled and stored for use as winter fodder for animal livestock. — **hit the hay** *slang* to go to bed. **make hay while the sun shines** to take advantage of an opportunity while one has the chance. [from Anglo-Saxon *hieg*]

haycock *noun* a small, cone-shaped pile of hay in a field.

hay fever an allergic response to the pollen of grasses, trees, or other plants, characterized by sneezing, itching and watering of the eyes, and a running or blocked nose.

hayfork *noun* a fork with a long handle and long prongs, used for tossing and lifting hay.

haystack or **hayrick** *noun* a large firm stack of hay built in the open field and protected by plastic sheets or, more rarely, by thatching. Haystacks tend to be confined to small farms and hilly areas. — **look for a needle in a haystack** to try to find something which is lost or hidden in a pile of things and so is almost impossible to find.

haywire *adj. colloq.* out of order; in a state of confusion.

∷∷∷∷∷∷∷∷∷∷∷∷∷∷∷∷

▣ wrong, out of control, mad, wild, chaotic, confused, disordered, disorganized, topsy-turvy.

∷∷∷∷∷∷∷∷∷∷∷∷∷∷∷∷∷∷∷∷∷∷∷∷∷∷∷∷

hazard /ˈhazəd/ — *noun* **1** a risk of harm or danger. **2** something which is likely to cause harm or danger. **3** an obstacle on a golf course. — *verb* **1** to put forward (a guess or suggestion). **2** to risk. [from Old French *hasard*]

∷∷∷∷∷∷∷∷∷∷∷∷∷∷∷∷

▣ *noun* **1** risk, danger, peril, jeopardy. **2** danger, peril, threat, menace, deathtrap. *verb* VENTURE. **1** offer, put forward, suggest. **2** risk, endanger, jeopardize, expose, chance, gamble, stake.

▣ *noun* **1** safety.

∷∷∷∷∷∷∷∷∷∷∷∷∷∷∷∷∷∷∷∷∷∷∷∷∷∷∷∷

hazardous *adj.* damaging to safety or health; dangerous.

∷∷∷∷∷∷∷∷∷∷∷∷∷∷∷∷

▣ risky, dangerous, harmful, unsafe, perilous, precarious, insecure.

▣ safe, secure.

∷∷∷∷∷∷∷∷∷∷∷∷∷∷∷∷∷∷∷∷∷∷∷∷∷∷∷∷

hazardous substance any chemical substance that is potentially damaging to health, and that can cause pollution of the environment.

haze — *noun* **1** a thin mist, vapour, or shimmer which obscures visibility. **2** a feeling of confusion or not understanding. — *verb intrans.* (*also* **haze over**) to become covered in a thin mist.

∷∷∷∷∷∷∷∷∷∷∷∷∷∷∷∷

▣ *noun* **1** mist, fog, cloud, steam, vapour, shimmer, dimness, obscurity.

∷∷∷∷∷∷∷∷∷∷∷∷∷∷∷∷∷∷∷∷∷∷∷∷∷∷∷∷

hazel — *noun* **1** a deciduous shrub or small tree (*Corylus avellana*), native to north temperate regions. **2** the small rounded edible nut produced by this plant. **3** the timber of this tree. — *adj.* of a greenish-brown colour. [from Anglo-Saxon *hæsel*]

hazelnut *noun* the small rounded edible nut produced by the hazel tree.

hazily *adv.* **1** in a hazy way. **2** dimly, not clearly.

haziness *noun* being hazy.

hazy *adj.* (**hazier, haziest**) **1** misty. **2** vague; not clear.

. . . .

◨ UNCLEAR, INDISTINCT, FUZZY, DIM. **1** misty, foggy, smoky, cloudy, milky, blurred, ill-defined, obscure. **2** vague, faint, indefinite, uncertain.

◪ CLEAR. **1** bright. **2** definite.

. . . .

HB *abbrev., on a pencil* hard black.

H-bomb *noun* a hydrogen bomb.

HDTV *abbrev.* high-definition television.

HE *abbrev.* **1** His Eminence. **2** high explosive. **3** His or Her Excellency.

He *symbol Chem.* helium.

he — *pron.* **1** a male person or animal already referred to. **2** a person or animal of unknown or unstated sex. — *noun* (PL. **hes**) a male person or animal: *a he-goat*. [from Anglo-Saxon *he*]

head — *noun* **1** the uppermost or foremost part of an animal's body, containing the brain and the organs of sight, smell, hearing, and taste. **2** the head thought of as the seat of intelligence, imagination, ability, etc: *use your head/a good head for heights*. **3** something like a head in form or function, eg the top of a tool. **4** the person with the most authority in an organization, country, etc. **5** the position of being in charge. **6** *colloq.* a headmaster, headmistress, or principal teacher. **7** the top or upper part of something, eg a table or bed. **8** the front or forward part of something, eg a queue. **9** the foam on top of a glass of beer. **10** the top part of a plant which produces leaves or flowers. **11** a crisis: *come to a head.* **12** the pus-filled top of a boil or spot. **13** (PL. **head**) a person, animal, or individual considered as a unit: *600 head of cattle.* **14** *colloq.* a headache. **15** the source of a river, lake, etc. **16** the height or length of a head, used as a measurement: *win by a head.* **17** a headland: *Beachy Head.* **18** the amount of pressure produced by water or steam in an enclosed space. **19** an electromagnetic device in a tape recorder, video recorder, computer, etc for converting electrical signals into the recorded form on tapes or disks, or vice versa, or for erasing recorded material. **20** the side of a coin bearing the head of a monarch, etc. **21** a headline. — *verb* **1** to be at the front of or top of: *head the queue.* **2** to be in charge of. **3** *intrans.* to move in a certain direction: *head for home.* **4** to put or write (a title or headline) at the beginning of a chapter, top of a letter, etc. **5** *Football* to hit (the ball) with the head. — **above one's head** too difficult for one to understand. **give someone his** or **her head** to allow someone to act freely and without restraint. **go to one's head 1** *said of alcoholic drink* to make one slightly intoxicated. **2** *said of praise, success, etc* to make one conceited. **have one's head in the clouds 1** to be inattentive to what is said. **2** to have impractical or unrealistic thoughts, ideas, etc. **head someone off** to get ahead of them so as to intercept them and turn them back. **head over heels 1** rolling over completely with the head first. **2** completely. **head and shoulders** by a considerable degree; to a considerable degree: *is head and shoulders above his competitors.* **keep one's head** to remain calm and sensible in a crisis. **lose one's head** to become angry or excited or act foolishly in a crisis. **not make head or tail of** to not understand. **off one's head** *colloq.* mad, crazy. **off the top of one's head** *colloq.* without much thought or calculation. **on your own head be it** you, etc will bear the full responsibility for your actions. **over one's head 1** to a higher authority. **2** too difficult for one to understand. **put our** or **your** or **their heads together** to consult together. **take it into one's head 1** to decide to do something, usually foolishly. **2** to come to believe something, usually wrongly. **turn someone's head** to make them vain and conceited. [from Anglo-Saxon *heafod*]

◨ *noun* **1** skull, cranium. **2** brain, mind, mentality, intellect, intelligence, understanding, thought. **4** ruler, leader, chief, captain, commander, boss, director, manager, superintendent. **6** principal, head teacher, headmaster, headmistress. **7** top, peak, summit, crown, tip, apex. **8** front, fore, lead. **11** crisis, climax, culmination, height. *verb* **2** lead, rule, govern, command, direct, manage, run, control, superintend, oversee, supervise. **3** move, go, aim, point, turn. **head off** intercept, forestall, deflect, divert, fend off, ward off.

◪ *noun* **1** foot, tail. **7** base, foot.

. . . .

headache /ˈhedeɪk/ *noun* **1** any continuous pain felt deep inside the head, usually caused by fatigue or anxiety, but sometimes associated with migraine, ear infections, eye disorders, toothache, alcohol consumption, drug abuse, head injury (eg concussion), serious disorders such as meningitis, or brain disease. **2** *colloq.* a person or thing that causes worry or annoyance.

headachy /ˈhedeɪkɪ/ *adj.* **1** suffering or tending to suffer from headaches. **2** likely to cause a headache.

headband *noun* a band worn round the head, especially for decoration.

headbanger *noun slang* **1** a young person who shakes violently to the beat of pop or rock music. **2** a stupid or fanatical person.

headboard *noun* a board at the top end of a bed.

head cold a cold that affects various parts of the head, such as the eyes or nasal passages, rather than the throat and chest.

head count a count of people present.

headdress *noun* a covering for the head, especially one which is highly decorative and is used in ceremonies.

headed *adj.* having a heading: *headed notepaper.*

header *noun* **1** *colloq.* a fall or dive forwards. **2** *Football* the hitting of the ball with the head.

headfirst *adv.* **1** moving especially quickly with one's head in front or bent forward. **2** without thinking; rashly.

headgear *noun* anything worn on the head.

headhunter *noun* a person whose occupation is headhunting.

headhunting *noun* **1** the practice of taking the heads of one's dead enemies as trophies. **2** the practice of trying to attract people away from their present jobs to work for one's own company, by offering them more money.

heading *noun* **1** a title at the top of a page, letter, section of a report, etc. **2** a horizontal tunnel in a mine.

. . . .

◨ **1** title, name, headline, rubric, caption.

. . . .

headlamp same as HEADLIGHT.

headland *noun* **1** a high steep area of land jutting out into the sea. **2** an unploughed strip of land along the edge of a field, used to allow machinery to turn.

. . . .

◨ **1** promontory, cape, head, point, foreland.

. . . .

headless *adj.* lacking a head.

headlight *noun* a powerful light on the front of a vehicle.

headline *noun* **1** the title or heading of a newspaper article, written above the article in large letters. **2** (**headlines**) the most important points in a television or radio news broadcast. — *verb* to appear as the star act in a show. — **hit the headlines** *colloq.* to be an important or dramatic item of news.

headliner *noun* an act that is appearing as the star of a show.

headline rate a basic rate of inflation etc before adjustments are made.

headlong — *adj.* **1** moving especially quickly with one's head in front or bent forward. **2** hasty; rash; impulsive. —

adv. **1** moving especially quickly with one's head in front or bent forward. **2** quickly and usually without thinking.

. . . .

◼ *adj.* HURRIED, HASTY. **1** fast, quick, rapid, swift, breakneck. **2** rash, reckless, precipitate, impetuous, impulsive. *adv.* HEADFIRST, HURRIEDLY, HASTILY. **1** fast, quickly, rapidly, swiftly. **2** rashly, recklessly, precipitately, heedlessly, thoughtlessly, wildly.

. . . .

headman *noun* a tribal chief or leader.

headmaster or **headmistress** *noun* the principal teacher in charge of a school.

head-on *adv.*, *adj.* **1** head to head; with the front of one vehicle hitting the front of another: *a head-on crash*. **2** in direct confrontation.

headphones *pl. noun* a pair of small sound-receiving devices, each containing a miniature loudspeaker, which are worn over the ears and usually held in place by a flexible metal strap that passes over the head, and connected to a radio, cassette player, etc, so that the sound is confined or mainly confined to the person wearing the headphones. Also called EARPHONES.

headquarters *sing. or pl. noun* the centre of an organization or group, eg in the army, from which activities are controlled.

. . . .

◼ HQ, base, head office, nerve centre.

. . . .

headrest *noun* a cushion which supports the head, fitted to the top of a car seat, etc.

headroom *noun* the space between the top of a vehicle and the underside of a bridge.

headscarf *noun* a scarf worn over the head and tied under the chin.

headset *noun* a pair of headphones, often with a microphone attached, used in radio communication.

headship *noun* the position of, or time of being, head or leader of an organization, especially a school.

headshrinker *noun colloq.* a psychiatrist.

headstall *noun* the part of a bridle which fits round a horse's head.

head start an advantage at the beginning of a race or competition.

headstone *noun* an inscribed stone at the head of a grave.

headstrong *adj.*, *said of a person* difficult to persuade; determined; obstinate.

. . . .

◼ stubborn, obstinate, intractable, perverse, contrary, wilful, self-willed, determined, resolute.

◼ tractable, docile.

. . . .

head teacher a headmaster or headmistress.

headwaters *pl. noun* the highest part of a stream or river, closest to its source, and before it receives tributaries.

headway *noun* **1** progress: *make no headway with the backlog*. **2** a ship's movement forwards. **3** same as HEADROOM.

. . . .

◼ **1** advance, progress, improvement.

. . . .

headwind *noun* a wind blowing directly against the course of a ship, aircraft, etc.

headword *noun* a word forming a heading, especially for a dictionary or encyclopedia entry.

heady *adj.* (**headier, headiest**) **1** tending to make one drunk quickly. **2** very exciting. **3** rash; impetuous.

. . . .

◼ **1** intoxicating, strong. **2** exciting, thrilling, stimulating, exhilarating. **3** rash, reckless, impetuous, impulsive.

. . . .

heal *verb* **1** to cause (a person, wound, etc) to become healthy again. **2** *intrans.* (*also* **heal up** or **over**) *said of a*

wound to become healthy again. **3** to make (sorrow) less painful. **4** to settle or put right (disputes, etc). [from Anglo-Saxon *hælan*]

. . . .

◼ **1** cure, remedy, restore, treat, salve, soothe. **4** settle, reconcile, patch up.

. . . .

healer *noun* a person who heals another.

healing *noun* the action or process of restoring to a healthy state.

health *noun* **1** a state of physical, mental, and social well-being accompanied by freedom from illness or pain. **2** a person's general mental or physical condition: *be in poor health*. **3** the soundness, especially financial, of an organization, country, etc: *the economic health of the nation*. [from Anglo-Saxon *hælth*]

. . . .

◼ **1** healthiness, fitness, good condition. **2** constitution, form, shape, trim, fettle, condition, state. **3** soundness, robustness, strength, vigour, welfare.

◼ **1** illness, infirmity.

. . . .

health centre in the UK, a clinical and administrative centre that provides health care for a local community, and usually houses a group practice of general practitioners, community nurses, a child-health clinic, etc.

health education teaching, advice, and the provision of information to schoolchildren and the population at large, on healthy living.

health farm a place, usually in the country, where people go to improve their health through diet and exercise.

health food any food that is considered to be natural, free of additives, and particularly beneficial to one's health, eg whole-grain cereals, honey, organically grown fruit and vegetables.

healthful *adj.* causing or bringing good health.

healthily *adv.* in a healthy way.

healthiness *noun* being healthy.

health screening *Medicine* the performance of various tests on a large population of apparently healthy people in order to identify the presence of certain diseases or disorders, eg cervical smears to detect early stages of cancer of the cervix (neck of the womb).

health service a public service providing medical care, usually without charge.

health visitor a nurse trained in midwifery, preventive medicine, and health education, who is notified of all births in his or her area, and is responsible for visiting pre-school children and educating parents and relatives about childcare, as well as visiting the elderly and chronically ill on a regular basis.

healthy *adj.* (**healthier, healthiest**) **1** having or showing good health. **2** causing good health. **3** in a good state: *a healthy economy*. **4** wise: *a healthy respect for authority*.

. . . .

◼ **1** fit, well, in condition, in good shape, in fine fettle, sturdy, robust, strong, vigorous, hale and hearty, blooming, flourishing, thriving. **2** wholesome, nutritious, nourishing, bracing, invigorating, healthful. **3** sound, robust, strong, vigorous.

◼ **1** ill, sick, infirm.

. . . .

heap — *noun* **1** a collection of things in an untidy pile or mass. **2** (*usually* **heaps**) *colloq.* a large amount or number. **3** *colloq.* something, especially a motor vehicle, that is very old and not working properly. — *verb* **1** (*also* **heap something up**) to collect it together in a heap. **2** *intrans.* (*also* **heap up**) to be collected together in a heap. **3** (**heap something on someone**) to give it to them in large amounts: *heaped insults on his ex-wife*. [from Anglo-Saxon *heap*]

. . . .

◼ *noun* **1** pile, stack, mound, mountain, mass, accumulation, collection, hoard, stockpile, store. *verb* **1** pile, stack, amass, accumulate, collect, gather, hoard, stockpile. **2** pile up, build up, amass, accumulate, collect, gather.

heaped *adj.* denoting a spoonful that forms a rounded heap on the spoon.

heaps *adv. colloq.* very much: *heaps better.*

hear *verb* (PAST TENSE AND PAST PARTICIPLE **heard**) **1** *trans., intrans.* to perceive (sounds) with the ear. **2** to listen to. **3** (*often* **hear about** or **of something**) to be told about it or informed of it: *heard about his problems/heard that she had lost her job.* **4** (**hear from someone**) to be contacted by them, especially by letter or telephone. **5** *said of a judge* to listen to and judge (a case). — **hear! hear!** an expression of agreement or approval. **hear someone out** to allow them to finish speaking or explaining. **not hear of something** not to allow it to happen: *they would not hear of it.* [from Anglo-Saxon *hieran*]

2 listen to, overhear, eavesdrop on, heed, pay attention. **3** learn, find out, discover, ascertain, understand, gather. **5** judge, try, examine, investigate.

hearer *noun* a person who hears.

hearing *noun* **1** the sense that involves the perception of sound. The main organ of hearing is the cochlea of the inner ear, which relays nerve impulses via the auditory nerve to the brain, where they are interpreted as sound. **2** the distance within which something can be heard. **3** an opportunity to state one's case: *give him a hearing.* **4** a court case.

1 ear, perception. **2** earshot, range, reach, sound. **3** audience, interview, audition. **4** trial, inquiry, investigation, inquest.

hearing aid a small electronic device, consisting of a miniature sound receiver, an amplifier, and a power source, worn in or just behind the ear to aid the hearing of a person who is totally or partially deaf.

hearken /ˈhɑːkən/ *verb intrans.* (**hearken to something** or **someone**) *old use* to listen or pay attention to them. [from Anglo-Saxon *heorcnian*]

hearsay *noun* rumour; gossip.

rumour, word of mouth, talk, gossip, tittle-tattle, report.

hearse /hɜːs/ *noun* a car used for carrying a coffin at a funeral. [from Latin *hirpex*, harrow]

heart *noun* **1** in vertebrates, the hollow muscular organ that contracts and pumps blood through the blood vessels of the body. **2** this organ considered as the centre of a person's thoughts, emotions, conscience, etc. **3** ability to feel tenderness or pity: *have no heart.* **4** courage and enthusiasm: *take heart/lose heart.* **5** the central or most important part: *the heart of the problem.* **6** the breast: *hold her to her heart.* **7** the compact inner part of some vegetables, eg cabbages and lettuces. **8** a usually red symbol representing the heart, with two rounded lobes at the top curving down to meet in a point at the bottom. **9 a** a playing-card with a red heart-shaped symbol on it. **b** (**hearts**) a suit of cards with such shapes on them. — **at heart** really; basically. **break someone's heart** to cause them great sorrow. **by heart** by or from memory. **change of heart** a change of decision, attitude, etc, usually to a kinder one. **have one's heart in one's mouth** to be very frightened, worried, or anxious. **heart and soul** completely; with all one's attention and energy. **lose heart** to become discouraged. **lose one's heart to someone** to fall in love with them. **not have the heart to do something** to be too kind (to do something unpleasant). **set one's heart on something** to want it very much. **take heart** to become encouraged or more confident. **take something to heart** to pay great attention to it or be very affected by it. **to one's heart's content** as much as one wants. **wear one's heart on one's sleeve** to show one's deepest feelings openly. **with all one's heart** very willingly or sincerely. [from Anglo-Saxon *heorte*]

2 soul, mind, character, disposition, nature, temperament. **3** feeling, emotion, sentiment, love, tenderness, compassion, sympathy, pity. **4** courage, bravery, boldness, spirit, resolution, determination, enthusiasm, encouragement. **5** centre, middle, core, kernel, nucleus, nub, crux, essence. **by heart** by rote, parrot-fashion, pat, off pat, word for word, verbatim.

4 cowardice. **5** periphery.

heartache /ˈhɑːteɪk/ *noun* great sadness or mental suffering.

heart attack a sudden severe chest pain, which may spread to the left arm, caused by death of part of the heart muscle (known as *myocardial infarction*) after its blood supply has been interrupted by blockage of a coronary artery, usually by a blood clot (*coronary thrombosis*).

heartbeat *noun* **1** the regular throb or pulsation of the heart, measured as the pulse, caused by the alternate contraction and relaxation of the heart muscle as it pumps blood around the body. **2** a single pumping action of the heart.

heartbreak *noun* very great sorrow or grief.

heartbreaking *adj.* causing great sorrow or grief.

distressing, sad, tragic, harrowing, heart-rending, agonizing, grievous, bitter, disappointing.

heart-warming, heartening.

heartbroken *adj.* grieving; severely disappointed.

broken-hearted, desolate, sad, miserable, dejected, despondent, downcast, crestfallen, disappointed, dispirited, crushed.

delighted, elated.

heartburn *noun* a burning sensation felt beneath the breastbone or rising towards the throat, usually caused by irritation of the oesophagus or indigestion.

hearten *verb* (**heartened, heartening**) **1** to make happier, more cheerful or encouraged. **2** *intrans.* to become happier, more cheerful or encouraged.

CHEER (UP), *colloq.* BUCK UP. **1** comfort, console, reassure, encourage, boost, inspire, stimulate, rouse, *colloq.* pep up.

1 dishearten, depress, dismay.

heartening *adj.* cheering, encouraging.

heart failure a condition in which the ventricles of the heart fail to pump enough blood to meet the requirements of the body.

heartfelt *adj.* sincere.

deep, profound, sincere, honest, genuine, earnest, ardent, fervent, wholehearted, warm.

insincere, false.

hearth *noun* **1** the floor of a fireplace, or the area surrounding it. **2** the home. [from Anglo-Saxon *heorth*]

hearthrug *noun* a rug placed on the floor in front of the hearth.

heartily *adv.* in a hearty way.

heartiness *noun* being hearty.

heartland *noun* a central or vitally important area or region.

heartless *adj.* cruel; very unkind.

cruel, inhuman, brutal, pitiless, merciless, unfeeling, uncaring, cold, hard, hard-hearted, callous, unkind.

kind, considerate, sympathetic, merciful.

heart-lung machine an apparatus used to take over the functions of the heart and lungs temporarily during heart surgery. It consists of a pump which maintains the circulation of the blood around the body, and a device for oxygenating the blood.

heart-rending *adj.* causing great sorrow or pity.

. . . .

▣ harrowing, heartbreaking, agonizing, pitiful, piteous, pathetic, tragic, sad, distressing, moving, poignant.

. . . .

heart-searching *noun* the close examination of one's deepest feelings and conscience.

heartsease /ˈhɑːtsiːz/ *noun* an annual, biennial, or perennial plant (*Viola tricolor tricolor*), native to Europe, with tufted stems, heart-shaped to lance-shaped leaves, and multicoloured flowers, usually yellow, violet, and white. Also called WILD PANSY.

heartsick *adj.* very sad or disappointed.

heartstrings *pl. noun* deepest feelings of love, sympathy, or pity: *tug at her heartstrings.*

heart-throb *noun colloq.* a person whom a lot of people find very attractive, especially a male actor or singer.

heart-to-heart — *adj., said of a conversation* intimate, sincere, and candid. — *noun* an intimate and candid conversation.

heart-warming *adj.* pleasing; emotionally moving.

. . . .

▣ pleasing, gratifying, satisfying, cheering, heartening, encouraging, touching, moving, affecting.
▣ heartbreaking.

. . . .

heartwood *noun Bot.* the hard wood at the centre of a tree trunk or branch, which provides structural support. It consists of dead cells containing oils, gums, and resins which give it a distinct dark colour.

hearty *adj.* (**heartier, heartiest**) **1** very friendly and warm in manner. **2** strong, vigorous, or enthusiastic: *hale and hearty.* **3** *said of a meal, or an appetite* large.

. . . .

▣ **1** friendly, cordial, jovial, cheerful, warm, heartfelt, sincere, genuine, enthusiastic, wholehearted, unreserved. **2** strong, hardy, vigorous, energetic, boisterous, ebullient, exuberant, enthusiastic. **3** large, sizeable, substantial, filling, ample, generous.
▣ **1** cold, cool, half-hearted.

. . . .

heat — *noun* **1** a form of energy that is stored as the energy of vibration or motion (kinetic energy) of the atoms or molecules of a material. The amount of vibration determines the temperature, and large objects contain more heat energy than smaller ones at the same temperature. **2** a high temperature. **3** hot weather. **4** warmth of feeling, especially anger or excitement: *the heat of the argument.* **5** the most intense part of: *in the heat of the battle.* **6** *colloq.* pressure. **7** in a sports competition, etc, a preliminary race or contest which eliminates competitors. **8** oestrus, a period of sexual receptivity in some female mammals: *on heat.* **9** redness of the skin, especially when sore, with a feeling of heat: *prickly heat.* — *verb trans., intrans.* to make or become hot or warm. [from Anglo-Saxon *hætu*]

. . . .

▣ *noun* **1** hotness, warmth. **3** sultriness, closeness. **4** ardour, fervour, fieriness, passion, vehemence, fury, excitement, impetuosity, earnestness, zeal. *verb* warm, boil, toast, cook, bake, reheat, warm up.
▣ *noun* **1** cold, coldness, coolness. *verb* cool, chill.

. . . .

heat capacity or **specific heat capacity** *Physics* the quantity of heat that is required to raise the temperature of unit mass of a substance by one kelvin (or 1 °C). Loosely, it measures the ability of a substance to get hot while it is absorbing energy.

heated *adj.* **1** having been made hot or warm. **2** angry or excited.

▣ **1** hot, warm, warmed. **2** angry, furious, raging, passionate, excited, animated, fiery, stormy, tempestuous, bitter, fierce, intense, vehement, violent, frenzied.
▣ COOL. **1** cold. **2** calm.

. . . .

heatedly *adv.* angrily, passionately.

heat engine *Engineering* any device that transforms heat energy into useful mechanical work.

heater *noun* an apparatus for heating a room, building, water in a tank, etc.

heat exchanger *Physics* a device that transfers heat from one stream of fluid (gas or liquid) to another, without allowing the two fluids to come into contact, eg a car radiator.

heath *noun* **1** an area of open land, usually with dry sandy acidic soil, dominated by low-growing evergreen shrubs, especially heathers. **2** a low evergreen shrub of the genus *Erica*, with needle-like leaves and white, pink, or yellow bell-shaped flowers, found in northern and alpine regions, especially on open moors and heaths with acid soil. [from Anglo-Saxon *hæth*]

heathen — *noun* **1** a person who is not a Christian, Jew, or Muslim, but who follows another religion, especially one with many gods. **2** *colloq.* an ignorant or uncivilized person. **3** (**the heathen**) heathens as a group. — *adj.* of heathens; having no religion. [from Anglo-Saxon *hæthen*]

heathenish *adj.* involving or characteristic of heathens.

heather *noun* **1** a low evergreen shrub of the genus *Calluna*, with many side shoots bearing small scale-like leaves, and small pink or purple bell-shaped flowers, found in northern and alpine regions, and usually the predominant plant on open moors and heaths with acid soil. Also called LING. **2** loose term for a heath. [from Middle English *hathir*]

Heath-Robinson *adj., said of a machine or device* peculiarly or ludicrously complicated and impractical in design, especially in relation to its function. [named after William Heath Robinson (1872–1944), the cartoonist who drew such machines]

heating *noun* any of various systems for maintaining the temperature inside a room or building at a level higher than that of the surroundings.

heat pump *Engineering* a device that is used to transfer heat from a cooler object or space to a warmer one, ie in the opposite direction to the natural flow of heat, so that an input of energy is required. Heat pumps are used to maintain low temperatures in refrigerators and freezers.

heat-seeking *adj.* denoting a guided missile, etc, containing an infra-red device that enables it to home in on machinery or installations that radiate heat, eg aircraft engines.

heat shield any protective coating of heat-resistant material, such as metal sheeting, or quartz fibres embedded in a plastic resin, especially when used to prevent overheating of a spacecraft caused by friction when it re-enters the Earth's atmosphere.

heatstroke *noun* a severe and sometimes fatal condition in which continuous exposure to unaccustomed heat results in failure of the mechanism that regulates the internal temperature of the body. The main symptoms are a high body temperature (without sweating), exhaustion, headache, nausea, and eventual loss of consciousness. Also called SUNSTROKE.

heatwave *noun* a prolonged period of unusually hot dry weather.

heave — *verb* (PAST TENSE AND PAST PARTICIPLE **heaved, hove** in sense 6 and for *heave to*) **1** to lift or pull with great effort. **2** *colloq.* to throw (something heavy). **3** to utter: *heave a sigh.* **4** *intrans.* to rise and fall heavily or rhythmically. **5** *intrans.* to retch or vomit. **6** *intrans., said of a ship* to move: *heave into sight.* — *noun* an act of heaving. — **get the heave** *colloq.* to be dismissed or rejected. **give someone the heave** *colloq.* to dismiss or reject them. **heave to** *said of a ship* to stop or cause it to stop while at sea. [from Anglo-Saxon *hebban*]

▣ *verb* **1** pull, haul, drag, tug, lift, raise, hitch, hoist, lever. **2** throw, fling, hurl, cast, toss, *colloq.* chuck. **4** rise, surge. **5** retch, vomit, spew, *colloq.* throw up.

heaven *noun* **1** the place believed to be the abode of God, angels, and the righteous after death. **2** (*usually* **heavens**) the sky. **3** great happiness or bliss. **4** *often used in exclamations* God or Providence: *heaven forbid*. [from Anglo-Saxon *heofon*]

▣ **1** next world, hereafter, afterlife, paradise, utopia. **2** sky, firmament. **3** ecstasy, rapture, bliss, happiness, joy.
▣ **1** hell.

heavenliness *noun* being heavenly.

heavenly *adj.* **1** *colloq.* very pleasant; beautiful. **2** of or from heaven or the sky.

▣ SUBLIME. **1** lovely, delightful, wonderful, blissful, out of this world, glorious, beautiful. **2** celestial, unearthly, supernatural, spiritual, divine, godlike, angelic, immortal, blessed.
▣ INFERNAL. **1** hellish.

heavenly bodies *pl. noun* the sun, moon, planets, stars, etc.

heavens *interj.* an expression of surprise, anger, dismay, etc.

heaven-sent *adj.* very lucky or convenient; timely.

heavily *adv.* **1** in a heavy way; with or as if with weight. **2** intensely, severely, violently.

heaviness *noun* being heavy.

Heaviside layer *Physics* in the Earth's atmosphere, a layer of the ionosphere that reflects medium-frequency radio waves, and is most effective during daylight hours. [from Oliver Heaviside]

heavy — *adj.* (**heavier, heaviest**) **1** having great weight. **2** having a great or relatively high density: *a heavy metal.* **3** great in size, amount, force, power, etc: *heavy traffic/a heavy crop.* **4** severe, intense, or excessive: *heavy fighting/a heavy sleep.* **5** hard to bear or endure: *a heavy fate.* **6** *said of the sky* dark and cloudy. **7** needing a lot of physical or mental effort. **8** *said of literature* serious in tone and content. **9** *said of food* difficult to digest. **10** *said of breathing* loud, because of excitement, exhaustion, etc. **11** striking or falling with force; powerful: *heavy rain/a heavy sea.* **12** sad or dejected: *with a heavy heart.* **13** ungraceful and coarse: *heavy features.* **14** physically and mentally slow. **15** fat; solid. **16** *said of soil* wet and soft because containing a lot of clay. **17** *colloq.* strict; severe: *don't be heavy on him.* **18** *said of guns* large and powerful. **19** *said of cakes and bread* dense through not having risen enough. — *noun* (PL. **heavies**) **1** *slang* a large, violent, and usually not very intelligent man. **2** a villain in a play, film, etc. **3** *Scot.* a beer like bitter but darker in colour and gassier. **4** (*usually* **heavies**) a serious newspaper. — *adv.* heavily: *time hangs heavy on my hands.* — **heavy going** difficult or slow progress. **make heavy weather of something** to exaggerate the difficulties involved in it. [from Anglo-Saxon *hefig*]

▣ *adj.* **1** weighty, hefty, ponderous, burdensome. **2** solid, dense. **3** massive, large, bulky. **4** severe, intense, extreme, excessive. **5** hard, harsh, severe, oppressive. **6** dark, cloudy, overcast, dull. **7** hard, difficult, tough, arduous, laborious, strenuous, demanding, taxing. **8** serious, dull, tedious. **9** stodgy, indigestible.
▣ *adj.* **1, 2, 3, 4, 8, 9, 12** light. **6** bright. **7** easy.

heavy-duty *adj.* made to resist very hard wear or use.

heavy-handed *adj.* **1** clumsy. **2** too severe or strict.

▣ **1** clumsy, awkward, unsubtle, tactless, insensitive. **2** oppressive, overbearing, domineering, autocratic.

heavy-hearted *adj.* sad.

heavy hydrogen same as DEUTERIUM.

heavy industry any industry or the industries involving the use of large or heavy machines or producing large or heavy products, such as coal-mining, ship-building, etc.

heavy metal 1 loud, repetitive rock music with a strong beat. **2** large guns.

heavy water see DEUTERIUM OXIDE.

heavyweight — *noun* **1** the class for the heaviest competitors in boxing, wrestling, and weight-lifting. **2** (**light heavyweight**) a class between heavyweight and middleweight. **3** a boxer, etc of this weight. **4** *colloq.* an important, powerful, or influential person. **5** a person who is heavier than average. — *adj.* of the specified weight.

hebdomadal /hɛbˈdɒmədəl/ *adj.* weekly. [from Greek *hebdomas*, week]

Hebraic /hɪˈbreɪɪk/ *adj.* of Hebrews or the Hebrew language. [from Greek *hebraikos*]

Hebrew /ˈhiːbruː/ — *noun* **1** the ancient Semitic language of the Hebrews, revived and spoken in a modern form by Jews in Israel. **2** a member of an ancient Semitic people, originally based in Palestine. — *adj.* of the Hebrew language or people. [from Greek *Hebraios*, from Aramaic *Ibhraij*, one from the other side of the river]

heck *interj. colloq.* a mild exclamation of anger, annoyance, surprise, etc; hell.

heckle *verb trans., intrans.* to interrupt (a speaker) with critical or abusive shouts, especially at a public meeting. [from Middle English *hekelen*]

heckler *noun* a person who heckles.

hectare /ˈhɛktɛə(r)/ *noun* (ABBREV. **ha**) a unit of area in the metric system, most commonly used for land measurement, equal to 100 ares or 10,000 square metres (2.47 acres). [from HECTO- + ARE²]

hectic *adj.* very busy, confused, and excited. [from Greek *hektikos*, habitual]

▣ busy, frantic, frenetic, chaotic, fast, feverish, excited, heated, furious, wild.
▣ leisurely.

hectically *adv.* in a hectic way.

hecto- *combining form* one hundred: *hectometre*. [from Greek *hekaton*, one hundred]

hector — *verb* (**hectored, hectoring**) to bully, intimidate, or threaten. — *noun* a bully. [named after Greek *Hektor*, the Trojan hero in Homer's *Iliad*]

he'd *contr.* **1** he had. **2** he would.

hedge — *noun* **1** a fence or boundary formed by bushes and shrubs planted close together. **2** a barrier or protection against loss, criticism, etc. — *verb* **1** *intrans.* to avoid making a decision or giving a clear answer. **2** to enclose (an area of land) with a hedge. **3** to protect oneself from possible loss or criticism (eg in a bet or argument) by backing both sides: *hedge one's bets*. [from Anglo-Saxon *hecg*]

▣ *noun* BARRIER. **1** hedgerow, screen, windbreak, fence, boundary. *verb* **1** stall, temporize, equivocate, dodge, sidestep. **2** surround, enclose, hem in, confine, restrict.

hedge accentor same as HEDGE-SPARROW.

hedgehog *noun* an insectivorous mammal belonging to the family Erinaceidae, native to Europe, Africa, and Asia, and having a body covered with spines, and a short tail.

hedge-hop *verb intrans.* (**hedge-hopped, hedge-hopping**) to fly at a very low altitude, eg when crop-spraying.

hedgerow *noun* a hedge composed mainly of shrubs or small trees, especially one that borders a field or road.

hedge-sparrow *noun* a small bird, native to Europe and W Asia, having greyish-brown plumage, in fact more closely related to thrushes and warblers, but so called because it resembles a sparrow, although it can be distinguished by its grey face and slender finely pointed bill. Also called DUNNOCK, HEDGE ACCENTOR.

hedonism /ˈhɛdənɪzm/ *noun* the belief that pleasure is the most important aim in life. [from Greek *hedone*, pleasure]

hedonist *noun* a person whose chief concern is pleasure.

hedonistic *adj.* relating to hedonists or hedonism.

heebie-jeebies *pl. noun colloq.* feelings of nervousness or anxiety. [origin unknown]

heed — *verb* to pay attention to or take notice of (advice, a warning, etc). — *noun* attention; notice: *take heed of what she says*.

. . . .

▤ *verb* listen to, pay attention to, mind, note, observe, follow, obey. *noun* attention, notice, regard, thought.

▣ *verb* ignore, disregard.

. . . .

heedful *adj.* (**heedful of something** or **someone**) paying careful attention to a warning, advice, etc.

heedless *adj.* (*usually* **heedless of something** or **someone**) careless; taking no notice of a warning, advice, etc. [from Anglo-Saxon *hedan*]

. . . .

▤ oblivious, unthinking, thoughtless, careless, negligent, rash, reckless, inattentive, unobservant, regardless, unconcerned.

▣ heedful, mindful, attentive.

. . . .

hee-haw — *noun* the bray of a donkey. — *verb intrans.* to bray. [imitative]

heel¹ — *noun* **1** the rounded back part of the foot. **2** the part of a sock, stocking, etc that covers the heel. **3** the part of a shoe, boot, etc which supports the heel. **4** anything shaped or functioning like the heel, eg that part of the palm near the wrist. **5** *slang* a person very much disliked, or not considered trustworthy. — *verb* **1** to put a new heel on (a shoe, etc). **2** *intrans. Rugby* to kick the ball backwards with the heel. **3** *intrans., said of a dog* to walk at, or go to, a person's side. **4** *intrans.* to touch the ground with the heel, eg in dancing. — **cool** or **kick one's heels** to be kept waiting indefinitely. **dig one's heels in** to behave stubbornly. **down at heel** untidy; in poor condition. **lay** or **set someone by the heels** *old colloq. use* to put them in prison. **on the heels of someone** following close behind. **take to one's heels** to run away. **to heel** close behind; under control. **turn on one's heel** to turn round suddenly or sharply. [from Anglo-Saxon *hela*]

heel² *verb intrans.* (*often* **heel over**) *said of a ship* to lean over to one side. [from Anglo-Saxon *hieldan*, to slope]

heelball *noun* a black waxy substance used for blacking the heels and soles of shoes and doing brass rubbings.

heftily *adv.* in a hefty way, vigorously, strongly.

heftiness *noun* being hefty.

hefty *adj.* (**heftier, heftiest**) *colloq.* **1** *said of a person* big and strong. **2** *said of an object, blow, etc* large, heavy, or powerful. **3** large in amount: *a hefty sum of money*. [from HEAVE]

. . . .

▤ LARGE. **1** big, strapping, burly, hulking, beefy, brawny, strong, powerful, vigorous, robust. **2** heavy, weighty, powerful, solid, substantial, massive, colossal, bulky, unwieldy. **3** considerable, substantial, generous, ample.

▣ SMALL. **1** slight.

. . . .

hegemony /hɪˈgemənɪ/ *noun* (PL. **hegemonies**) leadership or control by one state within a group of states or alliance. [from Greek *hegemonia*, from *hegemon*, leader]

Hegira /ˈhedʒɪrə/ *noun Relig.* the flight of the Prophet Muhammad from Mecca to Yathrib (thereafter known as Medina, 'The City of the Prophet'), in Jul 622. The departure marks the beginning of the Muslim era. [from Arabic *hejira*, flight]

heifer /ˈhefə(r)/ *noun* a female cow over one year old that has not calved, or that has calved only once. [from Anglo-Saxon *heahfore*]

height *noun* **1** the distance from the bottom of something to the top. **2** a distance above the ground from a recognized point, especially above sea level. **3** relatively great altitude. **4** a high place or rising ground. **5** the highest point; the summit. **6** the most intense part: *the height of battle*. **7** a very good, bad, or serious example: *the height of stupidity*. [from Anglo-Saxon *hiehthu*]

. . . .

▤ **1** tallness, stature. **2** altitude, elevation. **3** highness, loftiness. **5** top, summit, peak, pinnacle, apex, crest, crown, zenith, apogee, maximum, limit, ceiling. **6** climax, culmination, heart, depth.

▣ **1** drop. **2** depth. **5** foot.

. . . .

heighten *verb trans., intrans.* (**heightened, heightening**) to make or become higher, greater, stronger, brighter, etc.

. . . .

▤ increase, magnify, intensify, strengthen, sharpen.

▣ lower, decrease, diminish, weaken.

. . . .

heinous /ˈheɪnəs, ˈhiːnəs/ *adj.* very evil or wicked. [from Old French *haineus*, from *hair*, to hate]

. . . .

▤ atrocious, abominable, abhorrent, detestable.

. . . .

heir /ɛə(r)/ *noun* a person who by law receives wealth, a title, etc when the owner or holder dies. [from Latin *heres*]

heir apparent (PL. **heirs apparent**) **1** *Legal* an heir whose claim cannot be set aside by the birth of another heir. **2** *colloq.* the probable next leader of an organization, especially a political party.

heiress /ˈɛərɪs/ *noun* a female heir, especially a woman who has inherited or will inherit great wealth when some person dies.

heirloom /ˈɛəluːm/ *noun* an object that has been handed down in a family from parents to children over many years.

heir presumptive (PL. **heirs presumptive**) *Legal* an heir whose claim can be set aside by the birth of another heir whose claim is more valid.

heist /haɪst/ *noun North Amer. slang* a robbery. [variant of HOIST]

Hejira same as HEGIRA.

held see HOLD¹.

helical *adj.* of or like a helix; coiled. [from HELIX]

helical scan 1 a type of radar scan in which pulses of radio waves from a transmitting antenna are directed in a narrow beam or *antenna beam* that rotates continuously about the vertical axis, while the elevation angle gradually changes from horizontal to vertical, so that the path of any given point on the radar beam is a distorted helix. **2** *Electron.* a system of magnetic tape recording in which the tape is wrapped in a partial helix around a drum carrying two or more rotating heads which trace a series of tracks diagonally across its width.

helicopter *noun* a powered wingless aircraft with two or more overhead rotary blades that provide lift, serving as both propeller and wings. Helicopters are capable of taking off and landing vertically, flying in any direction, and hovering in one position above the ground. [from Greek *helix*, screw + *pteron*, wing]

heliocentric /hiːlɪoʊˈsentrɪk/ *adj. Astron.* denoting a system with the Sun at its centre. [from Greek *helios*, sun + *kentron*, centre]

heliograph /ˈhiːlɪoʊgrɑːf/ *noun* **1** an instrument that is used for sending signals and messages by reflecting the sun's rays from a mirror. **2** an instrument that is used for photographing the sun. **3** an instrument that records the intensity and duration of sunshine. [from Greek *helios*, sun + GRAPH]

heliosphere /ˈhiːlɪoʊsfɪə(r)/ *noun Astron.* a spherical region of space surrounding the Sun, whose outer boundary (the *heliopause*), thought to lie about 100 astronomical units from the Sun, represents the zone where the solar wind merges with the interstellar gas. [from Greek *helios*, sun + SPHERE]

heliotrope /'hi:lɪoʊtroʊp/ *noun* **1** any plant belonging to the genus *Heliotropium*, especially *H.peruvianum*, a small evergreen shrub native to Peru, which has lance-shaped to oblong hairy leaves, and small tubular bluish-violet flowers with spreading lobes, borne in terminal clusters. It is widely cultivated as a garden plant for its fragrant flowers. **2** the colour of these flowers. [from Greek *helios*, sun + *trepein*, to turn]

helipad *noun* a landing place for a helicopter, usually a square marked with a cross or a large H.

heliport *noun* a place where helicopters take off and land. [contraction of HELICOPTER + AIRPORT]

helium *noun Chem.* (SYMBOL **He**, ATOMIC NUMBER **2**) a colourless odourless inert gas found in uranium and thorium ores and some natural gas deposits, and formed in stars by nuclear fusion. It is one of the rare or noble gases, and is used to fill balloons and airships, to provide inert atmospheres for welding, and is also used together with oxygen in 'air' mixtures for divers. [from Greek *helios*, sun, so called because it was first identified in the sun's atmosphere]

helix /'hi:lɪks/ *noun* (PL. **helices, helixes**) **1** a spiral or coiled structure, eg the thread of a screw. **2** *Geom.* a spiral-shaped curve that lies on the lateral surface of a cylinder or cone. [from Greek *helix*]

hell — *noun* **1** the abode of evil spirits and the place or state of punishment for the wicked after death. **2** the abode of the dead. **3** any place or state which causes pain and misery. — *interj. colloq.* an exclamation of annoyance. — **beat** or **knock the hell out of someone** *colloq.* to beat them severely. **come hell or high water** *colloq.* in spite of whatever problems or difficulties may arise. **for the hell of it** *colloq.* just for fun. **from hell** *colloq.* of the worst possible kind: *neighbours from hell.* **give someone hell** *colloq.* **1** to scold or punish them severely. **2** to make things extremely difficult for them. **hell for leather** *colloq.* extremely fast. **a hell** or **one hell of a ...** *colloq.* a very great or significant: *one hell of a row.* [from Anglo-Saxon *hel*]

▣ *noun* **1** underworld, Hades, inferno, lower regions, nether world, abyss. **3** suffering, anguish, agony, torment, ordeal, nightmare.
▣ *noun* **1** heaven.

he'll *contr.* he will; he shall.

hell-bent *adj.* (**hell-bent on something**) *colloq.* determined about it.

hellebore /'hɛləbɔː(r)/ *noun* any perennial plant of the genus *Helleborus*, native to Europe and Asia, having glossy deeply divided leaves and clusters of large flowers consisting of five green, white, or pinkish-purple petal-like segments. The plant contains alkaloids and is highly poisonous. [from Greek *helleboros*]

Hellene /'hɛli:n/ *noun* a Greek. [from Greek *Hellen*]

Hellenic /hɛ'lɛnɪk/ *adj.* Greek.

Hellenism /'hɛlənɪzm/ *noun* Greek character or culture, especially that of ancient Greece.

Hellenist /'hɛlənɪst/ *noun* an admirer of or expert in Greek language and culture.

Hellenistic *adj.* relating to the people, language, or culture of the ancient Greek world after the death of Alexander the Great in 323BC.

hell-fire *noun* the fire of, or punishment in, hell.

hellish *adj. colloq.* very bad; very unpleasant.

▣ infernal, diabolical, fiendish, accursed, damnable, monstrous, abominable, atrocious, dreadful.
▣ heavenly.

hello or **hallo** or **hullo** *interj.* a word used as a greeting, to attract attention, to start a telephone conversation, or to express surprise.

hell's angel a member of a motorcycle gang, especially one whose behaviour is violent and anti-social.

helm *noun* the wheel or tiller by which a ship is steered. — **at the helm** in a controlling position; in charge. [from Anglo-Saxon *helma*]

▣ tiller, wheel. **at the helm** in the driving seat, in the saddle, in charge, in command, in control.

helmet *noun* a hard, protective covering for the head. [from Anglo-Saxon *helm*]

helmsman *noun* a person who steers a ship.

helot /'hɛlət/ *noun* a serf, especially in ancient Sparta. [from Greek *heilotes*, inhabitants of *Helos*, a town in ancient Laconia (the area around Sparta)]

help — *verb* **1** *trans., intrans.* to assist. **2** to contribute towards making (difficulties, pain, etc) less severe; to improve (a situation). **3** *intrans.* to make such a contribution or improvement. **4** *trans., intrans.* to refrain from: *couldn't help laughing.* **5** to prevent or control: *I can't help the bad weather.* **6** (**help someone to something**) to serve a person: *help him to potatoes.* — *noun* **1** an act of helping. **2** a person or thing that helps. **3** a domestic servant; servants in general. **4** a remedy or relief. — **cannot help oneself** is not able to refrain from doing something. **help oneself to something** **1** to take (food, etc) for oneself, without being served. **2** to take something without authority or permission. **help out** or **help someone out** to offer help, usually for a short time, and especially by sharing a burden or the cost of something. [from Anglo-Saxon *helpan*]

▣ *verb* **1** assist, aid, lend a hand, serve. **2** improve, ameliorate, relieve, alleviate, mitigate, ease, facilitate. *noun* **1** aid, assistance, collaboration, co-operation, support, advice, guidance, service, use, avail, benefit. **2** aid, helper, assistant.
verb **1** hinder. **2** worsen. *noun* **1, 2** hindrance.

helpdesk *noun* a department of an organization that provides a support service by telephone.

helper *noun* a person who helps.

▣ assistant, auxiliary, subsidiary, attendant, aide, PA, mate, partner, associate, colleague, collaborator, accomplice, ally, supporter, second.

helpful *adj.* **1** *said of a person* giving help. **2** *said of an action, a suggestion, advice, etc* useful.

▣ **1** co-operative, obliging, neighbourly, friendly, caring, considerate, kind, sympathetic, supportive. **2** useful, practical, constructive, worthwhile, valuable, beneficial, advantageous.
▣ **2** useless, futile.

helping *noun* a single portion of food.

▣ serving, portion, share, ration, amount, plateful, piece, *colloq.* dollop.

helpless *adj.* **1** unable to do anything for oneself. **2** weak and defenceless.

▣ FEEBLE, POWERLESS. **1** dependent, disabled, paralysed, incapable, incompetent. **2** weak, defenceless, unprotected, vulnerable, exposed, abandoned, friendless, destitute, forlorn.
▣ **1** independent. **2** strong.

helpmate *noun* a friend or partner, especially a husband or wife.

helter-skelter — *adj.* careless and confused. — *adv.* in a careless and confused manner. — *noun Brit.* a spiral slide down the outside of a tower in an amusement park.

hem[1] — *noun* a bottom edge of a piece of clothing, folded over and sewn down. — *verb* (**hemmed, hemming**) to make a hem on. — **hem something** or **someone in** to surround them closely, preventing movement. [from Anglo-Saxon *hemm*]

. . . .

◼ *noun* edge, border, margin, fringe. **hem in** surround, enclose, box in, confine, restrict.

. . . .

hem[2] — *interj.* a slight clearing of the throat or coughing to show hesitation or call for attention. — *noun* such a sound. — *verb intrans.* (**hemmed, hemming**) to clear the throat or cough slightly. [imitative]

he-man *noun colloq.* a very strong, virile man.

hem-, hemat-, hemo- *North Amer., esp. US.* same as HAEM-, HAEMAT-, HAEMO-.

hemi- *combining form* forming words meaning 'half': *hemisphere.* [from Greek *hemi*]

hemipterous /hɪˈmɪptərəs/ *adj. Zool.* denoting an insect that belongs to the order Hemiptera, members of which have an oval flattened body and mouthparts modified into a beak for piercing and sucking. [from HEMI- + Greek *pteron*, wing]

hemisphere *noun* 1 one half of a sphere. 2 each half of the Earth's sphere, traditionally divided by the equator into the northern hemisphere and the southern hemisphere.

hemispherical *adj.* having the shape of a hemisphere.

hemline *noun* the level at which the bottom of a garment or its hem hangs.

hemlock *noun* 1 a tall, poisonous, biennial plant (*Conium maculatum*), native to Europe, Asia, and N Africa. 2 a poisonous drug derived from this plant, used as a poison since classical times. 3 (**hemlock spruce**) an evergreen coniferous tree belonging to the genus *Tsuga*, native to north temperate regions. 4 a poisonous potion made from this. [from Anglo-Saxon *hymlic*]

hemp *noun* 1 a tall annual plant (*Cannabis sativa*) that bears clusters of tiny green flowers, native to Asia. 2 the common name for any narcotic drug obtained from this plant, eg cannabis or marijuana. 3 the coarse tough fibre obtained from the stem of this plant, and used to make rope, cord, coarse cloth, etc. [from Anglo-Saxon *hænep*]

hemstitch *noun* a decorative stitch used when sewing hems.

hen *noun* 1 the female of any bird species, especially the domestic fowl. 2 the female of certain aquatic animals, such as the lobster and certain fishes. [from Anglo-Saxon *henn*]

henbane *noun* a poisonous plant (*Hyoscyamus niger*) belonging to the nightshade family, native to Europe and W Asia, so called because its poison is particularly toxic to domestic fowl. [from HEN + BANE]

hence *adv.* 1 for this reason. 2 from this time. 3 *old use* from this place. [from Middle English *hennes*]

henceforth or **henceforward** *adv.* from now on.

henchman *noun* (PL. **henchmen**) a faithful supporter, especially one who obeys without question. [from Anglo-Saxon *hengest*, horse + *man*, man]

henge *noun* a circular, prehistoric monument consisting of large upright stones or wooden posts. [from *Stonehenge*, a famous stone circle in S England]

henna — *noun* reddish-brown dye obtained from a tropical shrub, used for colouring the hair and decorating the skin. — *verb* (**hennaed, hennaing**) to dye or stain using henna. [from Arabic *hinna*]

hen party a party for a group of women only, especially one to celebrate the future marriage of one woman in the group.

henpecked *adj. colloq., usually said of a man* constantly harassed and criticized, especially by a wife, girlfriend, etc.

. . . .

◼ dominated, subjugated, browbeaten, bullied, intimidated, harassed, nagged, meek, timid.

◼ dominant.

. . . .

henry *noun* (SYMBOL **H**) (PL. **henries**) the SI unit of electrical inductance, defined as the inductance that produces an electromotive force of one volt when the electric current in a closed circuit changes at the rate of one ampere per second. [named after Joseph Henry, the US physicist who independently discovered electrical induction]

heparin /ˈhɛpərɪn/ *noun Biochem.* a chemical substance that prevents the clotting of blood, and in an extracted and purified form is used as an anticoagulant drug in medicine, eg to prevent thrombosis (formation of clots in blood vessels). [from Greek *hepar, hepatos*, liver]

hepatic /hɪˈpatɪk/ *adj.* 1 *Anat.* relating to or affecting the liver. 2 *Bot.* of or relating to liverworts.

hepatitis /hɛpəˈtaɪtɪs/ *noun* inflammation of the liver, usually caused by a viral infection, but sometimes occurring as a reaction to toxic substances such as alcohol or drugs, or as a complication of diseases such as amoebic dysentery. Typical symptoms include jaundice (yellowing of the skin), weakness, fever, loss of appetite, and nausea. [from Greek *hepar*, liver + -ITIS]

hepta- *combining form* forming words meaning 'seven'. [from Greek *hepta*, seven]

heptagon *noun* a plane (two-dimensional) figure with seven sides and seven angles. It is a type of polygon. [from Greek *hepta*, seven + *gonia*, angle]

heptagonal *adj.* having seven angles and seven sides.

heptarchy /ˈhɛptɑːkɪ/ *noun* (PL. **heptarchies**) 1 government by a group of seven, or a country governed in this way. 2 *Hist.* a once supposed system of seven English kingdoms, Wessex, Sussex, Kent, Essex, East Anglia, Mercia, and Northumbria.

heptathlon *noun* an athletic contest consisting of seven events, 100 metres hurdles, shotput, javelin, high jump, long jump, and races over 200 and 800 metres. [from HEPTA- + Greek *athlon*, contest]

her — *pron.* the form of *she* used as the object of a verb or after a preposition: *we all like her/send it to her.* — *adj.* of or belonging to a female person or animal, or a thing personified or thought of as female, eg a ship: *went to her house/give the cat her milk.* — **be her** *colloq.* to be suited to her: *that hat isn't her at all.* [from Anglo-Saxon *hire*]

herald — *noun* 1 a person who announces important news. 2 a person or thing that is a sign of what is to come. 3 *Hist.* an officer responsible for keeping a record of the genealogies and coats of arms of noble families. — *verb* to be a sign of the approach of; to proclaim: *dark clouds heralding a storm.* [from Old French *herault*]

. . . .

◼ *noun* 1 messenger, courier. 2 harbinger, forerunner, precursor, omen, token, signal, sign, indication. *verb* announce, proclaim, broadcast, advertise, publicize, trumpet, pave the way for, precede, usher in, indicate, presage.

. . . .

heraldic *adj.* of or concerning heraldry.

heraldry *noun* the art of recording genealogies and studying and preparing coats of arms.

Heraldic terms include: shield, crest, mantling, helmet, supporters, field, charge, compartment, motto, dexter, centre, sinister, annulet, fleur-de-lis, martlet, mullet, rampant, passant, sejant, caboched, statant, displayed, couchant, dormant, urinant, volant, chevron, pile, pall, saltire, quarter, orle, bordure, gyronny, lozenge, impale, escutcheon, antelope, camelopard, cockatrice, eagle, griffin, lion, phoenix, unicorn, wivern, addorsed, bezant, blazon, canton, cinquefoil, quatrefoil, roundel, semé, tierced, undee, urdé.

herb *noun* 1 *Bot.* a flowering plant in which the stems contain very little permanent woody tissue, and the aerial parts die back at the end of the growing season. 2 any flowering plant that has aromatic leaves or other parts, used for flavouring food, or as a source of essential oils for use in herbal medicine or perfumery, eg mint, parsley, thyme, sage. [from Latin *herba*, grass, green plant]

Herbs and spices include: angelica, anise, basil, bay, bergamot, borage, camomile, catmint, chervil, chives, comfrey, cumin, dill, fennel, garlic, hyssop, lavender, lemon balm, lovage, marjoram, mint, oregano, parsley, rosemary, sage, savory, sorrel, tarragon, thyme; allspice, caper, caraway seeds, cardamon, cayenne pepper, chilli, cinnamon, cloves, coriander, curry, ginger, mace, mustard, nutmeg, paprika, pepper, saffron, sesame, turmeric, vanilla.

herbaceous /hɜːˈbeɪʃəs/ *adj.* **1** relating to or resembling herbs. **2** denoting a flowering plant that contains little or no woody tissue. The aerial parts of herbaceous plants die back at the end of the growing season, and the plants survive the winter as bulbs, tubers, or other underground organs, containing little or no woody tissue. [from Latin *herba*, grass, green plant]

herbaceous border a flower bed composed mainly of perennial flowering plants as opposed to annuals.

herbage *noun* herbaceous vegetation covering the ground, especially the edible parts available for cattle, sheep, and other grazing animals to feed on. [from Latin *herba*, grass, green plant]

herbal — *adj. Bot.* relating to herbs. — *noun Bot.* a book describing the use of plants, or substances extracted from them, to treat medical disorders. [from Latin *herbalis*]

herbalism *noun Medicine* the use of herbs for medicinal purposes.

herbalist *noun* a person who prescribes and uses plant extracts and their derivatives for medical purposes.

herbarium /hɜːˈbɛərɪəm/ *noun* (PL. **herbaria**) **1** *Bot.* a collection of dried pressed plants, mounted on sheets of card labelled with the plant's name, the place and date of collection, and usually the collector's name. The larger herbaria are centres for research on the classification of plants. **2** a room or building housing such a collection.

herbicide *noun* a chemical that kills plants, either non-selectively, destroying all vegetation, or selectively, eg killing only weeds and leaving crops unharmed. [from Latin *herba*, grass, green crops]

herbivore *noun* an animal that feeds exclusively or mainly on plants, eg rabbit, cow, horse. [from Latin *herba*, grass, green plant + *vorare*, to swallow]

herbivorous *adj.*, *said of an animal* feeding exclusively or mainly on plants.

herculean /hɜːkjʊˈliːən/ *adj.* having, showing or needing great strength or effort: *a herculean task*. [named after Greek *Heracles* (in Latin *Hercules*), mythical Greek hero famous for his great strength]

herd — *noun* **1** a group of animals, especially cattle, that are kept together on a farm. **2** a person who looks after a herd. **3** a large group of people, especially when behaving noisily. **4** (**the herd**) the mass of people in general when seen as behaving in an unthinkingly conventional way. — *verb* **1** *intrans.* to gather or be gathered together in a group or herd. **2** to gather or cause to move in a group or herd. **3** *trans.* to look after a herd of animals, or to group animals together. [from Anglo-Saxon *heord*]

⊟ *noun* **1** drove, flock. **3** drove, flock, swarm, pack, press, crush, mass, horde, throng, multitude, crowd, mob. **4** the masses, the rabble, the mob, the common people. *verb* **1** flock, congregate, gather, collect, assemble, rally. **2** gather, round up, lead, guide, shepherd, drive, force.

herd instinct the instinct to associate with and act like a group of similar people or animals.

herdsman *noun* a person who looks after a herd of animals.

here — *adv.* **1** at, in, or to this place. **2** at this time; at this point in an argument. **3** used after a noun for emphasis: *this book here*. **4** *colloq.*, *dialect* used between a noun and *this*, *that*, etc for emphasis: *this here book*. — *noun* this place. — *interj.* **1** calling for someone's attention. **2** calling attention to one's own presence. — **here and now** at this time; immediately. **here and there** in, or to, various places. **here goes!** an expression used when about to start something difficult or challenging. **here's to …** an expression used as a toast when drinking: *here's to the President*/ *here's to gambling*. **neither here nor there** of no importance. [from Anglo-Saxon *her*]

hereabouts or **hereabout** *adv.* near this place.

hereafter — *adv. formal* after this; from now on. — *noun* (**the hereafter**) the future; life after death.

hereby *adv. formal* by means of; as a result of this.

hereditable /hɪˈredɪtəbl/ *adj.* that may be inherited. [from Latin *hereditas*, inheritance]

hereditarily /hɪˈredɪtərəlɪ/ *adv.* in a hereditary way; in terms of heredity.

hereditary /hɪˈredɪtərɪ/ *adj.* **1** relating to or determined by heredity. **2** denoting a characteristic that can be genetically transmitted from parents to offspring. **3** passed on by inheritance or descent: *a hereditary title*. [from Latin *hereditas*, inheritance]

⊟ **1** inborn, inbred, innate, natural, congenital. **3** inherited, bequeathed, handed down, family, ancestral.

heredity /hɪˈredɪtɪ/ *noun* (PL. **heredities**) **1** the transmission of genetically based characteristics from one generation to the next. **2** the genetic constitution of a living organism. [from Latin *hereditas*]

Hereford cattle a breed of cattle with a white face and a red coat, originating in Herefordshire.

herein /hɪəˈrɪn/ *adv. Legal formal* in this place, document, or matter.

hereinafter /hɪərɪnˈɑːftə(r)/ *adv. Legal formal* from this point on.

hereof /hɪərˈɒv/ *adv. Legal formal* of or concerning this.

heresy /ˈhɛrəsɪ/ *noun* (PL. **heresies**) **1** an opinion or belief which is contrary to official doctrine held by the religious community to which one belongs. **2** an opinion contrary to that which is normally accepted. [from Greek *hairesis*, choice]

⊟ HETERODOXY, UNORTHODOXY, FREETHINKING, APOSTASY, SCHISM. **1** blasphemy. **2** dissidence.
⊞ ORTHODOXY.

heretic *noun* a person who is guilty of especially religious heresy.

⊟ freethinker, nonconformist, apostate, dissident, dissenter, revisionist, separatist, sectarian, renegade.
⊞ conformist.

heretical *adj.* of heresy or heretics.

⊟ heterodox, unorthodox, freethinking, rationalistic, schismatic, impious, irreverent, iconoclastic, blasphemous.
⊞ orthodox, conventional, conformist.

hereto /hɪəˈtuː/ *adv. Legal formal* to this place, document, or matter.

heretofore /hɪətuːˈfɔː(r)/ *adv. Legal formal* before this time; formerly.

hereupon /hɪərəˈpɒn/ *adv. Legal formal* after or as a result of this.

herewith /hɪəˈwɪð/ *adv. Legal formal* with this; enclosed with this letter.

heritable *adj.* **1** *said of property* that may be passed on from parent to child. **2** *said of people* able to inherit property. **3** denoting a characteristic that can be transmitted from one generation to the next. [from Old French *heriter*, to inherit]

heritage *noun* **1** that which is inherited. **2** the characteristics, qualities, property, etc that one inherits at birth. **3** a nation's historic buildings, countryside, cultural traditions, etc seen as the nation's wealth to be passed on to future generations. [from Old French *heritage*]

■ **1** inheritance, legacy, bequest, endowment, lot, portion, share, due. **3** history, past, tradition, culture.

hermaphrodite /hɜːˈmæfrədaɪt/ — *noun* **1** a plant or animal possessing both male and female reproductive organs, eg earthworm, many plants. **2** an animal, especially a mammal, possessing both male and female reproductive organs as a result of an abnormality in development. — *adj.* possessing both male and female reproductive organs. [from Greek *Hermaphroditos*, in Greek mythology the son of Hermes and Aphrodite, who grew into one person with the nymph Salmacis]

hermaphroditic /hɜːmæfrəˈdɪtɪk/ *adj.* **1** belonging to or typical of a hermaphrodite. **2** combining two opposites.

hermeneutics /hɜːməˈnjuːtɪks/ *sing. noun* **1** the theory of the interpretation and understanding of texts. Its origins lie in ancient Greek philosophy, and it received fresh impetus in 18c discussion of the problems of biblical interpretation. **2** *Psychol.* methods which go beyond mere experimentation in an attempt to understand the reason behind human actions. [from Greek *hermēneutikos*, from *hermēneus*, an interpreter, from *Hermēs*]

hermetic /hɜːˈmɛtɪk/ *adj.* closed very tightly so that no air gets in or out. [named after Greek *Hermes Trismegistos*]

hermetically *adv.* in a hermetic way.

hermit *noun* a person who lives alone, especially for religious reasons. [from Greek *eremos*, solitary]

■ recluse, solitary, anchorite, ascetic.

hermitage *noun* **1** the place where a hermit lives. **2** any retreat or secluded place.

hermit crab a small crab, common in shallow coastal waters, with a soft, unprotected abdomen, that inhabits the cast-off shells of other animals, from which only the hard front end of its body protrudes. When it has outgrown its shell it searches for a larger one and moves into it.

hernia *noun* (PL. **hernias, herniae**) the abnormal protrusion of an organ or other body part through the wall of the body cavity in which it normally lies, especially the protrusion of part of the intestine through a weak part of the abdominal wall. Hernias are usually repaired surgically. [from Latin *hernia*]

hero *noun* (PL. **heroes**) **1** a person who is admired for bravery, courage, noble qualities, etc. **2** the main male character in a story, play, etc. See also HEROINE. [from Greek *heros*]

■ **1** idol, champion, conqueror, celebrity. **2** protagonist, lead, star, *colloq.* goody.

heroic — *adj.* **1** very brave. **2** of or about heroes or heroines. — *noun* (**heroics**) over-dramatic speech or behaviour.

■ *adj.* **1** brave, courageous, fearless, dauntless, undaunted, valiant, bold, daring, intrepid, adventurous, gallant, chivalrous, noble, selfless.
■ *adj.* **1** cowardly, timid.

heroically *adv.* in a heroic way.

heroic couplet *Poetry* a pair of rhymed 10-syllable lines, usually in iambic pentameters; one of the commonest metrical forms in English poetry.

heroin /ˈhɛroʊɪn/ *noun* a white crystalline powder with a bitter taste, derived from morphine, formerly used as a powerful narcotic analgesic drug. It is highly addictive, causing physical dependence, and heroin addiction is a major social problem. Unauthorized possession of the drug is illegal in most countries, but it is still used medicinally (although not in the USA) for treatment of severe pain, eg in terminal illness. [from German *Heroin*, from Greek *heros*, hero]

heroine /ˈhɛroʊɪn/ *noun* **1** a woman admired for her bravery, courage, noble abilities, etc. **2** the main female character in a play, story, etc. [from Greek *heros*, hero]

heroism /ˈhɛroʊɪzm/ *noun* the qualities of a hero, especially great bravery.

■ bravery, courage, valour, boldness, daring, intrepidity, gallantry, chivalry, selflessness.
■ cowardice, timidity.

heron *noun* any of various large wading birds, found mainly in tropical and subtropical regions, although some species live in temperate zones, having a slender body, soft (usually grey or white) plumage, broad wings, long legs, a long neck, and a long pointed bill. [from Old French *hairon*]

hero-worship — *noun* **1** the worship of heroes in antiquity. **2** great or excessive fondness and admiration for someone. — *verb* to have a great fondness and admiration for (someone).

herpes /ˈhɜːpiːz/ *noun* any of several infectious skin diseases caused by a virus, and characterized by inflammation of the skin and the formation of clusters of small blisters. *Herpes simplex* can affect the face, often causing watery blisters or *cold sores* on the lips, or it can cause *genital herpes*, a sexually transmitted disease, the main symptoms of which are painful blisters in the genital region. [from Greek *herpein*, to creep]

herring *noun* (PL. **herring, herrings**) the most important of all food fishes, found in very large shoals in the surface waters of the Atlantic and Pacific Oceans, and migrating north in the summer. It is eaten fresh, and also cured for marketing as kippers, bloaters, rollmops, etc. [from Anglo-Saxon *hæring*]

herringbone *noun* a zigzag pattern woven into cloth.

herring gull a large gull, native to northern regions of Europe, Asia, and N America, and the largest and most common species of gull in these areas, having white plumage with grey upper parts, black wingtips, a yellow bill with a red spot, and pink legs (yellow in the Mediterranean race).

hers *pron.* the one or ones belonging to her. — **of hers** of or belonging to her.

herself *pron.* **1** the reflexive form of *her* and *she*: *she made herself a dress*. **2** used for emphasis: *she did it herself*. **3** her normal self: *she isn't feeling herself*. **4** (*also* **by herself**) alone; without help. [from Anglo-Saxon *hire self*]

Herts. *abbrev.* Hertfordshire.

hertz *noun* (PL. **hertz**) (ABBREV. **Hz**) the SI unit of frequency, equal to one cycle per second. One kilohertz (kHz) is equal to 1000 hertz, and one megahertz (MHz) is equal to 1,000,000 hertz. Radio waves have frequencies in the range 200kHz to 100MHz. [named after the German physicist Heinrich Hertz]

Hertzsprung-Russell diagram /ˈhɜːtssprʌŋ ˈrʌsl/ *Astron.* a graph in which the surface temperature (or the colour) of stars (on the horizontal axis) is plotted against their luminosity (on the vertical axis). The temperature is always shown decreasing from left to right along the horizontal axis. [named after the Danish astronomer Ejnar Hertzsprung and the US astronomer Henry Norris Russell]

he's *contr.* **1** he is. **2** he has.

hesitance or **hesitancy** *noun* hesitating, doubt, delay.

hesitant *adj.* uncertain; holding back; hesitating.

■ hesitating, reluctant, uncertain, unsure, indecisive, irresolute, vacillating, wavering, tentative, wary, shy, timid, halting, stammering, stuttering.

◨ decisive, resolute, confident, fluent.
. . . .

hesitate *verb intrans.* **1** to be slow in speaking or acting, especially because of uncertainty. **2** to be unwilling to do or say something, eg because one is not sure it is right. [from Latin *haesitare*, to remain stuck]
. . . .

◨ **1** pause, wait, delay, hold back, falter, stumble, stammer, stutter. **2** be reluctant, be unwilling, think twice, scruple, boggle, demur, vacillate, waver, dither, shilly-shally.
. . . .

hesitation *noun* hesitating, doubt, delay.
. . . .

◨ hesitance, pause, delay, reluctance, unwillingness, scruple(s), qualm(s), misgivings, doubt, second thoughts, vacillation, uncertainty, indecision, irresolution, faltering, stumbling, stammering, stuttering.
◨ eagerness, readiness, willingness, certainty, assurance.
. . . .

hessian — *noun* a coarse cloth similar to sacking, made from jute. — *adj.* made of hessian. [from *Hesse*, in Germany]

het — **het up** *colloq.* angry; over-anxious; over-excited. [dialect for *heated*]

hetero- *combining form* forming words meaning 'other, different': *heterosexual*. [from Greek *heteros*, other]

heterodox *adj.* having a religious or other belief that is different from the one commonly accepted. [from Greek *heteros*, other + *doxa*, opinion]

heterogeneity /hɛtəroʊdʒəˈniːɪtɪ/ *noun* **1** being heterogeneous. **2** something which is heterogeneous.

heterogeneous /hɛtəroʊˈdʒiːnɪəs/ *adj.* made up of parts, people, things, etc of very different kinds. [from Greek *heteros*, other + *genos*, sort]

heteromorphic *adj.* **1** *Biol.* denoting an organism that has different forms at different stages of its life cycle, eg many insects, or whose form differs from one season to the next, or from one generation to the next, eg fern. **2** *Genetics* denoting a pair of chromosomes that differ in size and shape, eg the X and Y chromosome pair. [from HETERO- + Greek *morphe*, form]

heteromorphism *noun* a heteromorphic state or process.

heterosexual — *adj.* **1** sexually attracted to people of the opposite sex. **2** *said of a relationship* between a man and a woman. — *noun* a heterosexual person.

heterosexuality *noun* being heterosexual.

heterotrophic *adj. Biol.* describing a living organism that must obtain nutrients by taking in organic material from the environment, because it is unable to manufacture such material from simple compounds. All animals, fungi, and many bacteria, and a few flowering plants are heterotrophic.

heterozygous /hɛtəroʊˈzɪɡəs/ *adj.* describing an individual that contains two different alleles for a particular gene, and may therefore produce offspring that differ from the parent with respect to that gene. [from HETERO- + Greek *zygon*, yoke]

heuristic /hjʊəˈrɪstɪk/ *adj.* **1** *said of a teaching method* encouraging learners to find their own solutions. **2** denoting any of various problem-solving techniques that involve the use of trial and error, subjective knowledge, and exploration of possibilities, rather than following formal theoretical rules. **3** *Comput.* denoting a computer program that can modify itself or 'learn' from its mistakes or the response of a user. [from Greek *heuriskein*, to find]

heuristically *adv.* in a heuristic way.

hew *verb* (PAST TENSE **hewed**; PAST PARTICIPLE **hewn**) **1** to cut or hit (a person or thing) with an axe, sword, etc. **2** to carve or shape (figures, etc) out of wood or stone. [from Anglo-Saxon *heawan*]
. . . .

◨ **1** cut, fell, axe, lop, chop, hack, sever, split. **2** carve, sculpt,

sculpture, shape, form, model, fashion, make.
. . . .

hexa- *combining form* forming words meaning 'six'. [from Greek *hex*, six]

hexadecane /ˈhɛksədekeɪn/ *Chem.* same as CETANE.

hexadecimal *adj. Comput.* denoting a number system having 16 as its base. The numbers 0 to 9 are represented by the symbols used in the decimal system, and the numbers 10 to 16 are represented by the letters A to F. Hexadecimal numbers are widely used to represent the internal binary codes of digital computers because they are more compact than binary numbers, and so can be more easily keyed and checked.

hexagon *noun* a plane (two-dimensional) figure with six sides and six angles. It is a type of polygon. [from Greek *hex*, six + *gonia*, angle]

hexagonal *adj.* having six sides and angles.

hexagram *noun* a star-shaped figure formed by extending the lines of a hexagon until they meet at six points. [from HEXA- + Greek *gramma*, line]

hexameter *noun Poetry* a line or verse with six measures or feet. [from Greek *hex*, six + *metron*, measure]

hexane *noun Chem.* (FORMULA C_6H_{14}) a toxic flammable colourless liquid belonging to the alkane series of hydrocarbons, used as a solvent. [from Greek *hex*, six]

hexose *noun Biochem.* a sugar that has a molecule consisting of six carbon atoms, and has the general formula $C_6H_2O_6$, eg glucose, fructose. Hexoses belong to the simplest group of carbohydrates, known as monosaccharides.

hey *interj. colloq.* a shout expressing joy, surprise, a question, dismay, or used to attract attention. — **hey presto!** a conjuror's phrase, usually used at the successful completion of a trick. [from Middle English *hei*]

heyday *noun* a time of most success, power, importance, strength, popularity, etc. [from Old German *heida*, hey there]
. . . .

◨ peak, prime, flush, bloom, flowering, golden age.
. . . .

Hf *symbol Chem.* hafnium.

Hg *symbol Chem.* mercury. [from Latin *hydrargyrum*]

HGV *abbrev.* heavy goods vehicle.

HH *abbrev.* **1** *on a pencil* double hard. **2** His Holiness. **3** His or Her Highness.

HI *abbrev.* Hawaii.

hi *interj.* a word used as a greeting or to attract attention. [from HEY]

hiatus /haɪˈeɪtəs/ *noun* (PL. **hiatuses**) **1** a break or gap in something which should be continuous. **2** a break between two vowels coming together but not in the same syllable. [from Latin *hiare*, to gape]

hibernate /ˈhaɪbəneɪt/ *verb intrans.*, *said of many small mammals* to pass the winter in a state of hibernation, especially in cold climates. [from Latin *hibernare*, from *hibernus*, wintry]

hibernation *noun* a dormant sleep-like state in which many small mammals, such as hedgehogs, squirrels, and bats, pass the winter, especially in cold climates, so avoiding the need to maintain a high body temperature at a time when temperatures are low and food is scarce.

Hibernia /haɪˈbɜːnɪə/ *noun literary* Ireland. [from Latin *Hibernia*]

Hibernian /haɪˈbɜːnɪən/ *literary* — *adj.* of Ireland. — *noun* a native of Ireland.

hibiscus /hɪˈbɪskəs/ *noun* (PL. **hibiscuses**) any of various herbaceous plants, shrubs, and small trees of the genus *Hibiscus*, native to tropical and subtropical regions, and having lobed or dentate leaves, and large brightly coloured (usually red or white) flowers. [from Greek *hibiskos*, marsh-mallow]

hiccup or **hiccough** /ˈhɪkʌp/ — *noun* **1** a repeated involuntary contraction and lowering of the diaphragm, followed by sudden closure of the glottis, resulting in a sharp intake of air which produces a characteristic sound. **2** (**hiccups**) the condition characterized by such involuntary contractions, which are repeated at intervals of a few seconds. It is often caused by indigestion, but is sometimes associated with more serious disorders, such as alcoholism. **3** *colloq.* a minor and usually temporary problem or interruption. — *verb* (**hiccuped**, **hiccuping**) **1** *intrans.* to make a hiccup or hiccups. **2** *trans.* to say with a hiccup. [imitative]

hick *noun chiefly North Amer. colloq.* an unsophisticated person from the country. [a familiar form of *Richard*]

hickory *noun* (PL. **hickories**) **1** any of various tall deciduous trees of the genus *Carya*, belonging to the walnut family, native to eastern N America and E Asia, and having small green flowers lacking petals. The nut-like fruit has a hard smooth shell, and in some species the kernel is sweet and edible. **2** the hard heavy pliable timber of this tree, used to make furniture, tool handles, and sports equipment. [from an American Indian language]

hidden *adj.* difficult to see or find.

⊟ concealed, covered, shrouded, veiled, disguised, camouflaged, unseen, secret, covert, occult, cryptic, abstruse, latent, ulterior.
⊞ showing, apparent, obvious.

hidden agenda a set of motions or goals kept secret from those who might object to them or until it is too late to object.

hide[1] — *verb* (PAST TENSE **hid**; PAST PARTICIPLE **hidden**) **1** to put (a person, thing, etc) in a place where one cannot easily see or find him, it, etc. **2** *intrans.* to go to or be in a place where one cannot be seen or found easily. **3** to keep (information, feelings, etc) secret. **4** to make (something) difficult to see; to obscure: *trees hiding the house.* — *noun* a concealed shelter used for watching birds and wild animals. [from Anglo-Saxon *hydan*]

⊟ *verb* **1** conceal, cover, cloak, shroud, veil, screen, bury, *slang* stash, secrete. **2** take cover, shelter, lie low, go to ground, *colloq.* hole up. **3** withhold, keep dark, suppress. **4** obscure, shadow, eclipse, disguise, camouflage.
⊞ *verb* **1** reveal, uncover, unveil. **3** reveal, disclose, show, display.

hide[2] *noun* **1** the skin of an animal, either raw or tanned. **2** *colloq.* the human skin. — **not** or **neither hide nor hair** not the slightest trace. [from Anglo-Saxon *hyd*]

⊟ SKIN. **1** pelt, fell, fur, leather.

hide-and-seek *noun* a children's game in which one child searches for the others who have hidden themselves.

hideaway or **hideout** *noun* a hiding-place or refuge.

hidebound /ˈhaɪdbaʊnd/ *adj.* unwilling to accept new ideas or opinions, especially because of a petty or conservative attitude. [from HIDE[2] + BOUND[1]]

⊟ set, rigid, inflexible, entrenched, narrow-minded, strait-laced, conventional, ultra-conservative.
⊞ liberal, progressive.

hideous *adj., said of a person or thing* repulsively ugly or unpleasant. [from Old French *hideus*]

⊟ ugly, repulsive, grotesque, monstrous, horrid, ghastly, dreadful, terrible, shocking, appalling, grim, gruesome, macabre, horrible, disgusting, revolting.
⊞ beautiful, attractive.

hiding[1] *noun* the state of being hidden or concealed.

⊟ concealment, cover, disguise, camouflage.

hiding[2] *noun colloq.* a severe beating. [from HIDE[2]]

⊟ beating, flogging, whipping, caning, spanking, thrashing.

hiding-place *noun* a place of concealment.

⊟ cache, hideaway, hideout, lair, den, hide, cover, refuge, haven, sanctuary, retreat.

hie /haɪ/ *verb intrans.* (**hieing**, **hying**) *old use* to go quickly. [from Anglo-Saxon *higian*]

hierarchical /haɪəˈrɑːkɪkəl/ *adj.* relating to or involving a hierarchy.

hierarchy /ˈhaɪərɑːkɪ/ *noun* (PL. **hierarchies**) **1** an arrangement (especially of people or things in a group) in order of rank or importance. **2** the people who control an organization. [from Greek *hieros*, sacred + *archein*, to rule]

⊟ **1** pecking order, ranking, grading, scale, ladder.

hieroglyph /ˈhaɪərəglɪf/ *noun* a picture or symbol used to represent a word, syllable, or sound, especially in ancient Egyptian. [from Greek *hieros*, sacred + *glyphein*, to carve]

hieroglyphic *adj.* relating to or written in hieroglyphs or hieroglyphics.

hieroglyphics *pl. noun* **1** a form of writing using hieroglyphs, used in ancient Egypt. **2** *colloq.* writing that is difficult to read.

hi-fi /ˈhaɪfaɪ/ — *adj. colloq.* high fidelity. — *noun* an electronic system that gives such faithful reproduction of recorded music or speech that it is virtually indistinguishable from the original sound, with minimal distortion and background noise. Modern hi-fi systems often include a compact disc player, tape deck, record turntable, radio tuner, amplifier, and loudspeakers. [a shortening of *high fidelity*]

higgledy-piggledy /ˈhɪgldɪˈpɪgldɪ/ *adv., adj. colloq.* in confusion; in a muddle.

high — *adj.* **1** reaching up to a relatively great distance from the bottom: *high buildings.* **2** of a particular height: *three feet high.* **3** situated at a relatively great distance from the ground or from sea level: *a high branch.* **4** great; intense: *a high wind.* **5** greater than average height: *a high-necked sweater.* **6** at its peak: *high summer.* **7** very important or exalted: *high art.* **8** *said of sound* acute in pitch. **9** extremely emotional: *high drama.* **10** *said of meat* beginning to go bad. **11** elated. **12** *colloq.* under the influence of drugs or alcohol. — *adv.* at or to a height; in or into a raised position. — *noun* **1** a high point. **2** an area of high pressure; an anticyclone. **3** *colloq.* a state of great excitement or happiness, often produced by drugs or alcohol: *on a high.* — **high and dry 1** *said of boats* out of the water. **2** stranded or helpless. **high and low** everywhere. **high and mighty** *colloq.* arrogant. **on high** at or to a high place or position; in or to heaven. **on one's high horse** *colloq.* behaving arrogantly or condescendingly. [from Anglo-Saxon *heah*]

⊟ *adj.* **1** tall, lofty, soaring, towering. **4** great, strong, intense, extreme. **7** important, influential, powerful, eminent, distinguished, chief, leading, senior, elevated, exalted. **8** high-pitched, soprano, treble, sharp, shrill, piercing.
⊞ *adj.* **1** low, short. **7** unimportant, lowly, junior. **8** low, deep.

high altar the main altar in a large church which has more than one altar.

highball *noun North Amer.* an alcoholic drink of spirits and soda served with ice in a long glass.

high-born *adj.* of noble birth.

⊟ noble, aristocratic, blue-blooded, thoroughbred.
⊞ low-born.

highbrow *often derog.* — *noun* an intellectual or cultured person. — *adj., said of art, literature, etc* intellectual or cultured.

▪ *noun* intellectual, *colloq.* egghead, scholar, academic. *adj.* intellectual, sophisticated, cultured, cultivated, academic, bookish, deep, serious, classical.
▪ *noun* lowbrow. *adj.* lowbrow.

high chair a baby's or young child's tall chair, used especially at mealtimes.

High Church a section of the Church of England which places great importance on ceremony and priestly authority.

high-class *adj.* of high quality or high social class.

▪ upper-class, *colloq.* posh, *colloq.* classy, top-class, *colloq.* top-flight, high-quality, quality, de luxe, superior, excellent, first-rate, choice, select, exclusive.
▪ ordinary, mediocre.

High Commission an embassy representing one member country of the Commonwealth, situated in another.

High Commissioner the senior diplomat at the head of such an embassy.

High Court the supreme court for civil cases in England and Wales.

high-definition television (ABBREV. **HDTV**) an advanced television system in which the image is composed of more than 1,000 scanning lines, nearly twice the number in the standard system, which affords much improved picture quality.

higher education education beyond secondary-school level, eg at university or college.

high explosive — *noun* any of a group of extremely powerful explosives in which the active agent is so readily detonated that the explosion occurs virtually instantaneously, eg TNT, gelignite. — *adj.* (**high-explosive**) exploding with very great effect.

high-falutin or **high-faluting** /haɪfə'luːtɪn, haɪfə'luːtɪŋ/ *adj. colloq.* pompous or pretentious.

high fidelity see HI-FI.

high-five *noun* a sign of greeting or celebration, consisting of slapping together raised palms.

high-flier or **high-flyer** *noun* 1 an ambitious person who is likely to be successful. 2 a person with great ability in his or her career.

high-flown *adj., usually said of language* sounding grand but lacking real substance; rhetorical, extravagant.

▪ florid, extravagant, exaggerated, elaborate, flamboyant, ostentatious, pretentious, high-sounding, *colloq.* high-falutin, lofty, grandiose, pompous, bombastic, turgid, rhetorical, artificial, stilted, affected.

high-flying *adj.* extremely ambitious.

high frequency a radio frequency between 3 and 30 megahertz.

High German the standard form of the German language.

high-handed *adj.* acting or done without thought or consideration for others.

▪ overbearing, domineering, *colloq.* bossy, imperious, dictatorial, autocratic, arbitrary.

highjack same as HIJACK.

high jinks *colloq.* boisterous fun; mischief.

high jump 1 an athletic event in which competitors jump over a bar which is raised higher as the event progresses. 2 *colloq.* a severe punishment: *be for the high jump.*

highland — *noun* 1 (*often* **highlands**) a high mountainous area. 2 (**the Highlands**) the mountainous area of northern and western Scotland. — *adj.* of highlands or (**Highland**) the Scottish Highlands.

Highland cattle a small breed of beef cattle, so called because it originated in the Highlands of Scotland, having a thick shaggy fawn, reddish-brown, or black coat and very long horns.

highlander *noun* a person who comes from a mountainous area, especially (**Highlander**) that of Scotland.

Highland fling a lively solo dance from the Scottish Highlands.

high-level *adj.* conducted by or involving people at a high level of management, etc: *high-level discussions.*

high-level language *Comput.* a programming language that allows the user to write programs using English-like commands, mathematical equations, etc, rather than actual computer instructions. The programs produced are relatively slow because each statement corresponds to several computer instructions. See also LOW-LEVEL LANGUAGE.

highlight — *noun* 1 the best or most memorable event, experience, part of something, etc. 2 a lighter patch in one's hair, usually made artificially. 3 the brightest part of a photograph. — *verb* to draw attention to or emphasize.

▪ *noun* 1 high point, high spot, peak, climax, best, cream. *verb* underline, emphasize, stress, accentuate, point up, spotlight, show up, set off, focus on, feature.

highlighter *noun* a broad-tipped felt pen run over parts of a text to highlight the content.

highly *adv.* 1 very: *highly gratified.* 2 with approval: *speak highly of her.*

▪ 1 very, greatly, considerably, decidedly, extremely, immensely, tremendously, exceptionally, extraordinarily. 2 well, warmly, enthusiastically.

highly-strung *adj.* very nervous and easily upset or excited.

▪ sensitive, nervy, jumpy, edgy, temperamental, excitable, restless, nervous, neurotic, tense.
▪ calm.

High Mass especially in the Roman Catholic Church, an elaborate and usually sung form of the mass.

high-minded *adj.* having or showing noble ideals and principles, etc.

▪ lofty, noble, moral, ethical, principled, idealistic, virtuous, upright, righteous, honourable, worthy.
▪ immoral, unscrupulous.

highness *noun* 1 (**Highness**) a title used when addressing or speaking about a member of a royal family: *Your Highness.* 2 the state or quality of being high.

high-octane *adj.* 1 *said of petrol* having a high octane rating, and therefore good antiknock qualities. 2 *colloq.* dynamic or thrilling.

high-pitched *adj.* 1 *said of sounds, voices, etc* high in tone. 2 *said of a roof* steeply angled.

high point the best state reached.

high-powered *adj.* very powerful or energetic; very efficient.

▪ powerful, forceful, driving, aggressive, dynamic, *colloq.* go-ahead, enterprising, energetic, vigorous.

high-pressure *adj.* 1 having, using, etc air, water, etc at a high pressure. 2 *colloq.* very forceful and persuasive. 3 involving considerable effort or stress.

high priest or **high priestess** the priest or priestess who is the head of a cult.

high-rise *adj.*, *said of a building* having many storeys.

high-risk *adj.* dangerous: *high-risk sports.*

high road a main road.

high school a secondary school.

high seas the open sea not under the control of any country.

high season the busiest time of year at a holiday resort or destination.

high-sounding *adj.* pretentious; pompous.

high-spirited *adj.* lively, cheerful and vivacious.
. . . .

☐ boisterous, lively, energetic, spirited, exuberant, ebullient, effervescent, sparkling, bubbly, vivacious, happy, cheerful, bouncy, frolicsome, frisky.

☐ quiet, sedate.
. . . .

high street the main shopping street of a town.

high tea *Brit.* a meal consisting usually of cooked food with bread, cakes, and tea, served in the late afternoon.

high tech or **hi-tech** *colloq.* **1** involving or using advanced, especially electronic equipment. **2** *said of interior decoration, designs, etc* based on styles or elements found in industry. [a shortening of *high technology*]

high-tension *adj.* (ABBREV. **HT**) **1** *said of cables, etc* carrying high-voltage electric currents. **2** operating at or requiring a high voltage, usually hundreds or thousands of volts.

high tide **1** the highest level reached by a rising tide. Also called HIGH WATER. **2** the time when this occurs.

high time *colloq.* the time by which something ought to have been done.

high treason treason against one's sovereign or country.

high water **1** same as HIGH TIDE. **2** the time at which a stretch of water, eg floodwater, is at its highest level.

high-water mark the highest level reached by the tide or by any other stretch of water, eg floodwater.

highway *noun North Amer.* a public road that everyone may use, especially a large or main road.

Highway Code *Brit.* an official booklet containing rules and guidance for road-users.

highwayman *noun Hist.* a robber, usually on horseback, who attacks and robs people travelling on public roads.

high wire a tightrope high above the ground.

hijack *verb* **1** to take control of (a moving vehicle, especially an aircraft) and force it to go to a different destination. **2** to stop and rob (a vehicle). **3** to steal (goods) in transit. **4** *colloq.* to seize control of (an organization, event, etc).

hijacker *noun* a person who hijacks.

hijacking *noun* **1** being attacked or taken over by a hijacker. **2** the action of a hijacker.

hike — *noun* a long walk, usually in the country, often carrying equipment on one's back. — *verb* **1** *intrans.* to go on a hike. **2** (**hike something up**) to pull up or raise it with a jerk. **3** to increase (prices) suddenly. [originally a dialect word, of unknown origin]
. . . .

☐ *noun* ramble, walk, trek, tramp, march. *verb* **1** ramble, walk, trek, tramp, trudge, plod.
. . . .

hiker *noun* a person who walks long distances for pleasure.

hilarious *adj.* very funny. [from Greek *hilaros*, cheerful]
. . . .

☐ funny, amusing, comical, side-splitting, *colloq.* hysterical, *colloq.* killing, uproarious, merry, jolly.

☐ serious.
. . . .

hilarity *noun* merriment, laughter.
. . . .

☐ merriment, jollity, mirth, laughter, fun, amusement, levity,

frivolity, high spirits, boisterousness, exuberance.

☐ seriousness, gravity.
. . . .

hill *noun* **1** any natural elevation of the Earth's surface, lower and less steep than a mountain. **2** a slope on a road. **3** a heap or mound. — **over the hill** *colloq.* past one's best; too old. [from Anglo-Saxon *hyll*]
. . . .

☐ **1** hillock, knoll, prominence, eminence, elevation, foothill, down, fell. **2** slope, incline, gradient, ramp, rise, ascent, acclivity, drop, descent, declivity. **3** heap, pile, mound.
. . . .

hillbilly *noun* (PL. **hillbillies**) *North Amer., esp. US* **1** *derog.* an unsophisticated person from a remote, mountainous country area. **2** country and western music.

hilliness *noun* being hilly.

hillock *noun* a small hill.

hillside *noun* the sloping side of a hill.

hilly *adj.* (**hillier, hilliest**) having many hills.

hilt *noun* the handle of a sword, dagger, knife, etc. — **up to the hilt** completely; thoroughly. [from Anglo-Saxon *hilte*]

hilum / 'haɪləm/ *noun* (PL. **hila**) *Bot.* a scar on the seed or ovule of a plant marking the point at which it was attached to the wall of the fruit or ovary, respectively. [from Latin *hilum*, a little thing]

him *pron.* a male person or animal, the object form of *he.* — **be him** *colloq.* to be suited to him: *jackets and ties aren't really him.* [from Anglo-Saxon *him*]

himself *pron.* **1** the reflexive form of *him* and *he*: *he taught himself to dance.* **2** used for emphasis: *he did it himself.* **3** his normal self: *be feeling himself again after the operation.* **4** also **by himself** alone; without help.

hind[1] *noun* a female deer, especially a red deer more than three years old. [from Anglo-Saxon *hind*]

hind[2] *adj.* at the back: *hind legs.* [from Middle English *hinde*]

hinder[1] / 'hɪndə(r)/ *verb* (**hindered, hindering**) to delay or keep back; to prevent progress. [from Anglo-Saxon *hindrian*]
. . . .

☐ hamper, obstruct, impede, encumber, handicap, hamstring, hold up, delay, retard, slow down, hold back, check, curb, stop, prevent, frustrate, thwart, oppose.

☐ help, aid, assist.
. . . .

hinder[2] / 'haɪndə(r)/ *adj.* at the back: *the hinder part.*

Hindi / 'hɪndɪ/ *noun* **1** one of the main languages of India, a literary form of Hindustani. **2** a group of languages spoken in N India, including Hindustani. [from Persian *Hind*, India]

Hindlish or **Hinglish** — *noun* a language consisting of a mixture of Hindi and English. — *adj.* written or spoken in this language. [from HINDI + ENGLISH]

hindmost *adj.* last; farthest behind.

hindquarters *pl. noun* the back legs and buttocks of a four-legged animal.

hindrance *noun* **1** a person or thing that hinders. **2** the act of hindering. [from HINDER[1]]
. . . .

☐ OBSTRUCTION, RESTRAINT, RESTRICTION, LIMITATION. **1** impediment, handicap, encumbrance, obstacle, stumbling-block, barrier, bar, check, difficulty, snag, hitch, drawback, disadvantage, inconvenience, nuisance.

☐ HELP, AID. **2** assistance.
. . . .

hindsight *noun* wisdom or knowledge after the event.

Hindu / 'hɪndu:/ — *noun* a person who practises Hinduism. — *adj.* of Hindus or Hinduism. [from Persian *Hind*, India]

Hinduism / 'hɪndʊɪzm/ *noun* the main religion of India, which includes worship of many gods, a belief in reincarnation, and the arrangement of people in society in social castes.

Hindustani /hɪndʊˈstɑːnɪ/ — noun a form of Hindi with elements from Arabic and Persian, used as a lingua franca in much of the Indian subcontinent. — adj. relating to or spoken or written in Hindustani.

hinge — noun 1 the movable joint by means of which a door is fastened to a door-frame, a lid is fastened to a box, etc and on which the door, lid, etc turns when it opens or closes. 2 a principle or fact on which anything depends. — verb 1 intrans. to hang or turn on. 2 intrans. (**hinge on something**) to depend on it: *it all hinges on their decision.* 3 to fit with a hinge. [from Middle English *henge*]

. . . .
🔲 verb 1 hang, turn, revolve, pivot. 2 depend on, rest on, hang on, turn on.
. . . .

hinged adj. having a hinge or hinges.

hinge joint Anat. in vertebrates, a joint between two or more bones that allows free movement in one plane only, eg elbow and knee joint.

hinny noun (PL. **hinnies**) the sterile hybrid offspring of a male horse and a female donkey. [from Greek *hinnos*, mule]

hint — noun 1 a statement that passes on information without giving it openly or directly. 2 a helpful piece of advice. 3 a very small amount; a slight impression or suggestion of: *a hint of perfume.* — verb intrans. (*often* **hint at something**) to suggest or imply it, especially slightly or indirectly. — **take a hint** colloq. to understand what a person is hinting at, and do what that person wants. [from Anglo-Saxon *hentan*, to seize]

. . . .
🔲 noun SUGGESTION. 1 clue, tip-off, indication, sign, pointer, mention, allusion, intimation, insinuation, implication, innuendo. 2 tip, advice, help, reminder. 3 touch, trace, tinge, taste, dash, soupçon, suspicion, inkling. verb suggest, indicate, imply, insinuate, intimate, mention.
. . . .

hinterland noun 1 the land, often remote or undeveloped, that lies behind a coast, the banks of a river, or a folded mountain range. 2 the region lying inland from and served by a port. 3 the region near to, and dependent on, a commercial centre, etc. [from German *hinter*, behind + *Land*, land]

hip¹ noun the haunch, or upper fleshy part of the thigh just below the waist; the joint of the femur (thigh bone) with the pelvis. [from Anglo-Saxon *hype*]

hip² noun the large red cup-shaped fruit produced by members of the genus *Rosa*, eg dog-rose and other roses. [from Anglo-Saxon *heope*]

hip³ interj. an exclamation used to call for a united cheer: *hip, hip hooray!*

hip⁴ adj. (**hipper, hippest**) colloq. interested in, knowing about, and following current fashions in music, fashion, etc.

hip bath noun a portable bath for sitting in.

hip-hop noun a popular culture movement originating in the USA in the 1980s, incorporating rap music, breakdancing, and graffiti, and the wearing of characteristically baggy clothing. [from HIP⁴]

hipped roof Archit. a pitched roof consisting of two or more sloping roof ends with the walls finishing at the eaves instead of forming an angled gable.

hippie or **hippy** noun (PL. **hippies**) colloq. especially in the 1960s, a young person typically wearing brightly coloured casual clothes and long hair, advocating freedom of thought and expression, and rejecting many of the more conservative standards and values of society.

hippo noun (PL. **hippos**) colloq. a hippopotamus. [abbreviation]

hippocampus (PL. **hippocampi**) noun 1 Anat. in the vertebrate brain, a structure consisting of two ridges, one over each of the fluid-filled cavities in the cerebral hemi-

spheres. It it thought to be associated with short-term memory in human beings. 2 (*Hippocampus*) a genus of small fishes with a horse-like head and neck. Also called SEA HORSE. [from Greek *hippokampos*, from *hippos* a horse, and *kampos* a sea-monster]

Hippocratic oath an oath taken by a doctor, binding him or her to observe the code of medical ethics, duties, and obligations contained within it. [named after the Greek physician Hippocrates]

hippodrome noun 1 a variety theatre or circus. 2 in ancient Greece and Rome, an open-air racecourse for horses and chariots. [from Greek *hippos*, horse + *dromos*, course]

hippopotamus noun (PL. **hippopotamuses, hippopotami**) either of two species of mammal, especially *Hippopotamus amphibius*, which is found in rivers and lakes in certain parts of Africa, and having a thick hairless body, massive head, and short stout legs. Its enormous mouth contains large canine tusks which may be over 1.5m long. [from Greek *hippos*, horse + *potamos*, river]

hippy See HIP⁴.

hipsters pl. noun trousers which hang from the hips rather than the waist. [from HIP¹]

hiragana see KANA.

hire — verb 1 to get the temporary use of (something which belongs to someone else) in exchange for payment. 2 (**hire something out**) to give someone the temporary use of it for payment. 3 to employ (a servant, workman, etc) for wages. — noun 1 an act of hiring. 2 payment for hiring something. — **for hire** ready for hiring. **on hire** hired out. [from Anglo-Saxon *hyr*]

. . . .
🔲 verb 1 rent, lease, charter, commission, book, reserve. 2 rent, let, lease, charter. 3 employ, take on, sign up, engage, appoint, retain. noun RENTAL. 1 letting, charter. 2 rent, fee, charge, cost, price.
🔳 verb 3 dismiss.
. . . .

hireling noun derog. a person who works for another for payment. [from Anglo-Saxon *hyrling*]

hire-purchase noun Brit. a way of buying an article by paying for it in several weekly or monthly parts after one has taken possession of it.

hirsute /ˈhɜːsjuːt/ adj. hairy; shaggy. [from Latin *hirsutus*]

his — adj. of or belonging to a male person or animal. — pron. the one or ones belonging to him. [from Anglo-Saxon *his*]

Hispanic /hɪˈspanɪk/ — adj. of Spain, the Spanish, or other Spanish-speaking countries and peoples, eg Mexican. — noun North Amer., esp. US a Spanish-speaking American of Latin-American descent. [from Latin *Hispania*, Spain]

Hispanic American any person resident in the USA who comes from, or whose parents came from, Spanish-speaking countries in Central and S America, including the Caribbean.

hiss — noun a sharp sound like that of a prolonged *s*. — verb 1 intrans., *said of a person or animal, eg a snake* to make a hiss, especially as a sign of disapproval or anger. 2 trans. to show one's disapproval (of a person, etc) by hissing. [imitative]

. . . .
🔲 verb 2 deride, mock, ridicule, boo, hoot.
🔳 verb 2 applaud, cheer.
. . . .

histamine /ˈhɪstəmiːn/ noun Biochem. a chemical compound present in most body tissues, and released from connective tissue during allergic or inflammatory reactions. It causes dilation of capillaries and contraction of the smooth muscle of the bronchi, and is responsible for many of the symptoms in conditions such as hay fever and asthma. [from Greek *histos*, web + AMINE]

histidine /ˈhɪstɪdiːn/ noun Biochem. an amino acid found in proteins. [from Greek *histos*, web]

histogram *noun* a chart in which vertical rectangles of differing sizes are used to represent the class intervals (eg age range) and relative frequencies of a given variable, eg height. [from Greek *histos*, web + -GRAM]

histology *noun* the scientific study of the structure and organization of cells and tissues of living organisms by light and electron microscopy combined with special staining techniques. [from Greek *histos*, web + -LOGY]

histone *noun Biochem.* any of the soluble basic proteins that tend to form complexes with nucleic acids (DNA and RNA), and are present in large amounts in chromosomes. [from Greek *histos*, web]

historian *noun* a person who studies or writes about history.

historiated *adj.* decorated with elaborate ornamental designs and figures of humans and animals. [related to HISTORY]

historic *adj.* famous or important in history; significant.
. . . .
⊟ important, significant, consequential, momentous, epochmaking, notable, remarkable, outstanding, famous, famed, renowned, celebrated.
⊞ unimportant, insignificant, unknown.
. . . .

historical *adj.* 1 of or about history; of or about people or events from history. 2 *said of the study of a subject* based on its development over a period of time. 3 that actually happened or existed; authentic.
. . . .
⊟ 3 real, actual, authentic, factual, documented, recorded, attested, verifiable.
⊞ 3 legendary, fictional.
. . . .

historically *adv.* in a historical way.

historical novel a fictional prose narrative based on historical characters and/or events. Sir Walter Scott's series of romantic adventures, beginning with *Waverley*, greatly enhanced the appeal of the historical novel.

historicism /hɪˈstɒrɪsɪzm/ *noun* 1 the belief that historical events are governed by natural laws. 2 too much emphasis on or respect for the past, past styles, etc.

historicity /hɪstəˈrɪsɪtɪ/ *noun* historical truth or authenticity.

historiographer /hɪstɔːrɪˈɒɡrəfə(r)/ *noun* a writer of history, especially the official historian of a group.

historiography /hɪstɔːrɪˈɒɡrəfɪ/ *noun* the study of the writing of history.

history *noun* (PL. **histories**) 1 a the past; events, etc that happened in the past. b the study of such events, etc. 2 a record or account of past events and developments: *a history of the computer*. 3 everything that is known about past events connected with a particular nation, the world, a person, etc: *kings and queens are part of our history*. 4 a past full of events and of more than usual interest: *a house with an interesting history*. 5 a play which represents historical events. — **make history** to do something important or memorable, especially to be the first person to achieve something. [from Greek *historia*, from *histor*, knowing]
. . . .
⊟ 1 past, antiquity. 2 chronicle, record, annals, archives, chronology, account, biography. 3 past, heritage, life.
. . . .

histrionic — *adj.* 1 *said of behaviour, etc* theatrical; showing too much emotion. 2 of actors or acting. — *noun* (**histrionics**) theatrical or dramatic behaviour which shows excessive emotion and is insincere. [from Latin *histrionicus*, from *histrio*, actor]

histrionically *adv.* in a histrionic way.

hit — *verb* (**hitting**; PAST TENSE AND PAST PARTICIPLE **hit**) 1 to strike (a person or thing) with a blow, missile, etc. 2 to knock (something) against something, especially hard or violently: *hit one's head on the door*. 3 to cause to suffer or affect badly: *the bad news hit her hard*. 4 *intrans.* to direct a blow; to strike: *hit as hard as you can*. 5 *colloq.* to find

(especially an answer) by chance: *you've hit it!* 6 to reach or arrive at: *hit an all-time low*. 7 to drive (a ball) with a stroke of a bat, etc. — *noun* 1 a blow, stroke or shot. 2 a shot that is successful. 3 *colloq.* something which is popular or successful. 4 a single visit to an Internet website. — **hit back** to retaliate. **hit it off with someone** to get on well with them. **hit on** or **upon something** to think of an idea or find an answer, etc by chance. **hit out at** or **against something** or **someone** to attack them physically or verbally. **make** or **score a hit with someone** to be successful or popular with them. [from Anglo-Saxon *hittan*]
. . . .
⊟ *verb* 1 strike, smack, slap, thrash, *colloq.* whack, bash, thump, clout, punch, *colloq.* belt, *colloq.* wallop, beat, batter. 2 strike, knock, tap, bump, bash, thump, bang, crash, smash. *noun* 1 stroke, shot, blow, knock, tap, slap, smack, bash, bump, collision, impact, crash, smash. 3 success, triumph. **hit back** retaliate, reciprocate, counter-attack, strike back. **hit on** or **upon** chance on, stumble on, light on, discover, invent, arrive at, guess. **hit out at** attack, assail, lash out at, rail at, denounce, condemn, criticize.
⊞ *noun* 3 failure, flop.
. . . .

hit-and-miss or **hit-or-miss** *adj. colloq.* without any system, planning or care; random.

hit-and-run *adj.*, *said of a motor-vehicle accident* in which the driver leaves the scene immediately, without stopping, reporting the accident, or helping the victim.

hitch — *verb* 1 to fasten with a piece of rope, etc; to tether. 2 (*also* **hitch something up**) to pull it up with a jerk: *hitched up his trousers*. 3 *intrans., trans. colloq.* to hitchhike; to obtain (a lift) by hitchhiking: *hitch a ride*. — *noun* 1 a minor, temporary delay or difficulty. 2 a slight jerk. 3 a knot for attaching two pieces of rope together. — **get hitched** *colloq.* to get married. [from Middle English *hytchen*]
. . . .
⊟ *verb* 1 fasten, attach, tie, tether, harness, yoke, couple, connect, join, unite. 2 pull, heave, *colloq.* yank, tug, jerk, hoist, *colloq.* hike (up). *noun* 1 delay, hold-up, trouble, problem, difficulty, setback, *colloq.* hiccup, drawback, snag, catch, impediment, hindrance. 2 jerk, tug, pull.
⊞ *verb* 1 unhitch, unfasten.
. . . .

hitchhike *verb intrans.* to travel by means of free rides in other people's vehicles. [from HITCH + HIKE]

hitchhiker *noun* a person who hitchhikes.

hi-tech SEE HIGH TECH.

hither *adv. old use* to this place. — **hither and thither** in different directions. [from Anglo-Saxon *hider*]

hitherto /ˈhɪðəˈtuː/ *adv.* up to this or that time.

hit list *colloq.* a list of people, organizations, etc to be killed, closed down, etc.

hit man *colloq.* a hired assassin.

hit parade the best-selling records.

Hittites *pl. noun* a people of uncertain origin who inhabited central Asia Minor in the first part of the second millennium BC.

HIV *abbrev.* human immunodeficiency virus, the virus responsible for the disease AIDS.

hive *noun* 1 a box, basket, or other container designed to house a colony of social bees, especially honeybees. 2 a colony of social bees, especially honeybees. 3 a place where people are working very busily: *a hive of activity*. — **hive something off** 1 to separate (a company, etc) from a larger group or organization. 2 to transfer (the assets, especially of a nationalized company) to other ownership, especially private ownership. 3 to give (work) to another, subsidiary, company. 4 to collect (bees) into a hive. 5 *said of bees* to enter or take possession of a hive. [from Anglo-Saxon *hyf*]

hives *pl. noun* the popular name for a chronic or acute skin condition characterized by the formation of red or whitish raised weals that vary in size and shape and itch intensely.

They are usually caused by an allergic reaction, but are sometimes associated with other factors, such as stress or exposure to cold.

HIV-positive *adj. Medicine* denoting a person who has tested positively for the presence of the human immunodeficiency virus (HIV), and may therefore be assumed to be carrying the virus.

Hizbullah or **Hezbollah** or **Hizbollah** *noun* the umbrella organization in S Beirut of militant Shiite Muslims with Iranian links. [from Arabic, = party of God]

HM *abbrev.* Her or His Majesty or Majesty's, used in the titles of some British government organizations.

HMI *abbrev.* Her or His Majesty's Inspector, a British government official who checks on schools.

HMS *abbrev.* Her or His Majesty's Ship.

HMSO *abbrev.* Her or His Majesty's Stationery Office.

HNC *abbrev.* Higher National Certificate, a qualification in a technical subject recognized by many professional institutions.

HND *abbrev.* Higher National Diploma, a qualification in a technical subject, recognized by many professional institutions as equivalent to a degree.

Ho *symbol Chem.* holmium.

hoar *adj.* white or greyish-white, especially with age. [from Anglo-Saxon *har*]

hoard — *noun* an often secret store of money, food, treasure, usually hidden away for use in the future. — *verb* 1 to store (food, money, etc), often in secret and especially for use in the future. 2 *intrans.* to collect or keep food, money, etc in this way. [from Anglo-Saxon *hord*]

> ▣ *noun* store, stockpile, cache, treasure-trove, fund, reservoir, supply, reserve, collection, accumulation, heap, pile. *verb* 1 store, stockpile, *colloq.* stash away, keep, save, put by, lay up, collect, gather, amass, accumulate.
> ▣ *verb* 1 use, spend, squander.

hoarder *noun* a person who hoards.

hoarding *noun* 1 a temporary fence of light boards, especially round a building site. 2 a large, flat, wooden surface on which advertisements, posters, etc are displayed. [from Old French *hourd*, palisade]

hoar-frost *noun* the white frost on grass, leaves, etc in the morning after a cold night.

hoariness *noun* being hoary.

hoarse *adj.* 1 *said of the voice* rough and croaking, especially because of a sore throat or too much shouting. 2 *said of a person* having a hoarse voice. [from Anglo-Saxon *has*]

> ▣ 1 husky, croaky, rough, harsh, throaty, guttural, gravelly, gruff, growling, rasping, grating, raucous.

hoary *adj.* (**hoarier, hoariest**) 1 white or grey with age. 2 ancient.

hoax /hoʊks/ — *noun* a trick played to deceive people, done either humorously or spitefully. — *verb* to trick or deceive with a hoax. [probably from *hocus*, to trick]

> ▣ *noun* trick, prank, practical joke, *colloq.* put-on, joke, *colloq.* leg-pull, spoof, fake, fraud, deception, bluff, swindle, *colloq.* con. *verb* trick, deceive, take in, fool, dupe, delude, *colloq.* have on, swindle, *colloq.* con, *colloq.* take for a ride, cheat, hoodwink.

hoaxer *noun* a person who hoaxes.

hob *noun* 1 the flat surface for heating pots, etc on top of a cooker. 2 a small shelf next to a fireplace on which pots, etc may be kept hot.

hobble *verb* 1 *intrans.* to walk with difficulty, taking short unsteady steps. 2 *trans.* to tie the legs of (a horse) together loosely, to stop it straying. [from Middle English *hobelen*]

> ▣ 1 limp, stumble, falter, stagger, totter, dodder, shuffle.

hobby *noun* (PL. **hobbies**) 1 an activity or occupation done in one's spare time for pleasure or relaxation. 2 any of various small falcons, native to Europe, Asia, and Africa, having long wings and a short tail. Hobbies usually hunt at dusk, feeding on insects and small birds caught in flight or taken from their roosts. [from Middle English *hobyn*, a pet form of the name *Robin*]

> ▣ 1 pastime, diversion, recreation, relaxation, activity, pursuit, sideline.

hobby-horse *noun* 1 a child's toy consisting of a long stick with a horse's head at one end. 2 a figure of a horse used in Morris dancing. 3 a subject which a person talks about frequently.

hobgoblin *noun* a mischievous or evil spirit. [from Middle English *Hob*, pet form of *Robin* + GOBLIN]

hobnail *noun* a short nail with a heavy head for protecting the soles of boots and shoes: *hobnail boots.* [from an old meaning of HOB, peg or pin]

hobnailed *adj.* fitted with hobnails.

hobnob *verb intrans.* (**hobnobbed, hobnobbing**) (**hobnob with someone**) to spend time with them socially. [from the phrase *hab or nab*, have or have not]

hobo *noun* (PL. **hobos, hoboes**) *North Amer.* a tramp; a wandering worker.

HOBS *abbrev. Brit.* home and office banking service or system.

Hobson's choice the choice of taking what is offered, or nothing at all. [named after Thomas Hobson (died 1631), a Cambridge carrier who hired out his horses on the basis that customers had to take the one nearest the door]

hock¹ *noun* in horses and other hoofed mammals, the joint corresponding to the ankle bone on the hind leg. [from Anglo-Saxon *hoh*, heel]

hock² *noun* a German white wine from the Rhine valley. [from German *Hochheimer*, from *Hochheim*, a town on the Main]

hock³ *verb colloq.* to pawn. — **in hock** *colloq.* 1 in pawn. 2 in debt. 3 in prison. [from Dutch *hok*, prison, debt]

hockey *noun* 1 a game for two teams of eleven players in which each team tries to score goals, played with long clubs which are bent at one end and a small, hard ball. 2 *North Amer.* same as ICE HOCKEY.

hocus-pocus *noun colloq.* trickery; words, actions, etc which are intended to deceive or mislead; a formula used in conjuring. [sham Latin]

hod *noun* 1 a V-shaped box on a pole, used for carrying bricks. 2 a container for coal used in the home, usually near a fireplace. [from Middle English *hot*, basket]

hodgepodge *noun North Amer.* same as HOTCHPOTCH.

Hodgkin's disease or **Hodgkin's lymphoma** /ˈhɒdʒkɪn ... lɪmˈfəʊmə/ *Medicine* a malignant disease of the lymphatic tissue, which causes painless progressive enlargement of the lymph nodes, and may then spread to the spleen, liver, bones, and bone marrow. [named after Thomas Hodgkin, who first described the disease]

hoe — *noun* 1 a farm implement pulled by a tractor and consisting of horizontal blades that turn the soil between rows of a crop, in order to destroy weeds. 2 a long-handled tool with a metal blade at one end, used to loosen soil, control weeds, etc. — *verb* 1 to use a hoe to loosen soil and remove weeds from (crops, flower-beds, etc). 2 *intrans.* to use a hoe. [from Old French *houe*]

hog — *noun* 1 any domesticated pig, especially a castrated male reared for slaughter. 2 *North Amer., esp. US* a pig. 3 a young sheep that has not yet been sheared. 4 *colloq.* a greedy, and often bad-mannered or dirty person. — *verb* (**hogged, hogging**) *colloq.* to take, use, or occupy selfishly. [from Anglo-Saxon *hogg*]

Hogmanay /hɒgmə'neɪ/ *noun Scot.* New Year's Eve, the last day of the year, when children traditionally demanded gifts or *hogmanay* of oatcake or white bread. [possibly from Old French *aguillaneuf*, a gift at New Year]

hogshead *noun* a large cask.

hogwash *noun colloq.* nonsense.

hogweed *noun* a robust perennial plant (*Heracleum sphondylium*), native to north temperate regions, with ribbed hairy stems, large coarse leaves and white or pinkish flowers.

Hohenstaufen /'hoʊənʃtʊfən/ *noun* a German dynasty, dukes of Swabia from 1079, who ruled as German kings, or Holy Roman Emperors (1138–1254), and as kings of Sicily (1194–1266).

Hohenzollerns *pl. noun* the German ruling dynasty of Brandenburg-Prussia (1415–1861) and Imperial Germany (1871–1918).

ho! ho! *interj.* an expression used to show amusement or disbelief.

hoi same as HOY.

hoick /hɔɪk/ *verb colloq.* to lift up sharply.

hoi polloi /hɔɪ pə'lɔɪ/ (*usually* **the hoi polloi**) the masses; the common people. [from Greek *hoi polloi*]

hoisin *noun* a thick sweet slightly hot Chinese sauce made with soya beans, sugar, vinegar, chilli, and sesame oil. [from Chinese]

hoist — *verb* **1** to lift or heave up (especially something heavy). **2** to raise or lift using ropes and pulleys. — *noun* **1** equipment for hoisting heavy objects. **2** *colloq.* an act of hoisting. — **hoist with one's own petard** caught in the trap one set to catch someone else. [past tense of the old verb *hoise*, to hoist; *petard*, small bomb]

⊟ *verb* LIFT, RAISE. **1** heave up, jack up. **2** elevate, erect, winch up. *noun* **1** jack, winch, crane, tackle, lift, elevator.

hoity-toity *adj. colloq.* arrogant; haughty. [from old word *hoit*, to romp]

Hokan languages /'hoʊkən/ a group of about 30 N American Indian languages spoken by small numbers in W and SW USA, and E Mexico; the only Hokan language with more than 20,000 speakers is Tlapanec.

hokum /'hoʊkəm/ *noun North Amer. slang* **1** nonsense. **2** over-sentimental and over-sensational material in a play, film, etc. [probably from HOCUS-POCUS + BUNKUM]

hold[1] — *verb* (PAST TENSE AND PAST PARTICIPLE **held**) **1** to have or keep in one's hand, or in something else stated. **2** (**hold something down, up,** etc) to support or keep in a particular position. **3** *trans., intrans.* to keep or stay in a particular state: *hold firm.* **4** *intrans.* to remain in position, fixed and unbroken, especially when under pressure. **5** to detain or restrain. **6** to contain or be able to contain: *a bottle holding three pints.* **7** to cause to take place; to conduct: *hold a conversation/hold a meeting.* **8** to have (a position of responsibility, job, etc): *hold office.* **9** to have or possess: *hold the world record.* **10** to keep (a person's attention). **11** *intrans., said of good weather* to continue. **12** to consider to be; to think or believe. **13** *intrans.* to continue to be valid or apply. **14** (**hold someone to something**) to compel them to keep a promise, etc: *hold him to his word.* **15** to defend from the enemy. **16** to be able to drink (alcohol) without feeling any bad effects. **17** to stop: *hold fire.* **18** to continue to sing or play (a musical note). **19** *intrans., said of a telephone caller* to wait without hanging up while the person being called comes to the telephone. **20** *trans., intrans., said of the future, regarded as a force* to have in readiness: *no knowing what the future holds.* — *noun* **1** the act of holding; a grasp. **2** power; influence: *have a hold over him.* **3** a way of holding someone, especially in certain sports. **4** a thing to hold on to. — **get hold of someone** *colloq.* to manage to speak to them. **get hold of something** to buy or obtain it. **hold something against someone** to regard them as responsible for it, especially to their discredit. **hold back** to hesitate; to restrain oneself. **hold someone back** to restrain them from doing something. **hold some-**thing back to keep it in reserve. **hold court** to be surrounded by a group of admirers. **hold someone down** to control their freedom; to repress them. **hold something down** to manage to keep it: *hold down a job.* **hold forth** to give one's opinions about something, usually loudly and at great length. **hold good** or **hold true** to be true or valid; to apply. **hold something in** to restrain or check it. **hold off** or **hold off doing something** to delay or not begin: *I hope the rain holds off/hold off making a start.* **hold someone off** to keep an attacker at a distance. **hold on** *colloq.* to wait, especially during a telephone conversation. **hold on to something 1** to keep it. **2** to keep a firm hold on it. **hold out 1** to continue to stand firm, resist difficulties, etc: *held out against the enemy.* **2** to last. **hold something out** to offer it, especially as a promise or inducement: *held out the prospect of a pay rise.* **hold out for something** to continue to demand or fight for it. **hold out on someone** *colloq.* to keep back money, information, etc from them. **hold something over** to postpone or delay it. **hold someone up** to stop and rob them. **hold something up 1** to support it. **2** to delay or hinder it. **hold something up** or **someone up as something** to exhibit it or point to it, as an example of some quality, attribute, etc: *held them up as models of integrity.* **keep hold of something** or **someone** to continue to hold on to them. **no holds barred** not observing any rules; with no restrictions. **not hold with something** to decline to endorse or approve of it. [from Anglo-Saxon *healdan*]

⊟ *verb* **1** grip, grasp, clutch, clasp, embrace. **2** support, sustain, bear, carry. **4** stay, remain, cling, stick, adhere. **5** detain, imprison, stop, arrest, check, curb, restrain. **6** contain, accommodate, carry. **7** conduct, carry on, continue, call, convene. **9** have, possess, own. **10** keep, retain. **12** consider, regard, deem, judge, reckon, think, believe, maintain. *noun* **1** grip, grasp, clasp, embrace. **2** influence, power, sway, mastery, dominance, authority, control, leverage. **hold back** hesitate, delay, desist, refrain, shrink, refuse. **hold someone back** restrain, curb, check, control, repress, inhibit. **hold something back** retain, withhold, suppress, stifle. **hold forth** speak, talk, lecture, discourse, orate, preach, declaim. **hold off** put off, postpone, defer, delay. **hold someone off** fend off, ward off, keep off, repel, rebuff. **hold on** wait, hang on. **hold out 1** resist, stand firm, stand fast. **2** last, continue, persist, endure. **hold something out** offer, give, present, extend. **hold something up 1** support, sustain, brace, shore up, lift, raise. **2** delay, retard, slow, hinder, impede. **not hold with** disagree with, disapprove of, dislike, object to, condemn.

◨ *verb* **1** release, drop. **5** release, free, liberate. **hold out 1** give in, yield.

hold[2] *noun* the place where cargo is stored in ships and aeroplanes. [variant of HOLE]

holdall *noun* a large, strong bag for carrying clothes, etc when travelling.

holder *noun* **1** a person who holds. **2** a thing that holds.

⊟ **1** bearer, owner, possessor, keeper, occupant, incumbent. **2** container, receptacle, case, housing, cover, sheath, rest, stand.

holding *noun* **1** land held by lease. **2** the amount of land, shares, etc which a person or company owns.

holding company a company which owns and controls all or part of at least one other company.

hold-up *noun* **1** a delay or setback. **2** an attack with a view to robbery.

⊟ **1** delay, wait, setback, hitch, snag, difficulty, trouble, obstruction, stoppage, traffic jam, log jam, bottleneck. **2** robbery, *slang* heist, *slang* stick-up.

hole — *noun* **1** an opening or gap in or through something: *a hole in the wall.* **2** a hollow area in something solid. **3** an animal's burrow. **4** *colloq.* an unpleasant or gloomy place. **5** *colloq.* an awkward or difficult situation. **6** *colloq.* a fault or mistake: *a hole in the argument.* **7** *Golf* a round can-shaped hollow in the middle of each green, into which the ball is hit; also, each of the (usually 18) sections of a golf course extending from the tee to the green. — *verb* **1** to make a hole in. **2** to hit (a ball, etc) into a hole. — **hole up** *colloq.* to hide. **make a hole in something** *colloq.* to use a large amount of a resource, eg money. **pick holes in something** to find fault with it. [from Anglo-Saxon *hol*]

⊟ *noun* **1** aperture, opening, gap, orifice, pore, puncture, perforation, eyelet, tear, split, crack, fissure, vent, outlet, shaft, slot. **2** dent, dimple, depression, hollow, cavity, pit, cave, cavern, chamber, pocket, recess. **3** burrow, nest, lair, den. **6** fault, mistake, error, defect, flaw.

hole-and-corner *adj.* secretive; underhand.

hole in the heart a congenital defect (present from birth) in which there is a hole in the wall dividing the left and right sides of the heart, as a result of which too much blood flows into the lungs. If this abnormal flow is excessive, heart failure may occur, and large holes in the heart are repaired surgically, but a small hole does not usually require treatment.

holey *adj.* (**holier, holiest**) full of holes.

Holi /ˈhoʊliː/ *noun* the Hindu 'Festival of Fire' in honour of Krishna, held in February or March and characterized by boisterous revelry, including the throwing of coloured water over people. It is also celebrated by Sikhs with sports competitions. [from Hindi *hōl*, from Sanskrit *holikā*]

holiday — *noun* **1** (*often* **holidays**) a period of time taken as a break from work, etc and during which one may go away from home. **2** a day when one does not have to work, eg a religious festival. — *verb intrans.* to spend a holiday. [from Anglo-Saxon *haligdæg*, holy day]

⊟ *noun* **1** vacation, recess, leave, time off, day off, break, rest, half-term. **2** bank holiday, feast day, festival, celebration, anniversary.

holiday camp a place, usually near the sea, which organizes games and other activities for the people staying there on holiday.

holidaymaker *noun* a person who is on holiday away from home.

holier-than-thou *adj. derog.* thinking oneself to be morally superior.

holily *adv.* in a holy way.

holiness *noun* **1** the state of being holy. **2** (**Holiness**) a title of the Pope and certain other religious leaders.

⊟ **1** sacredness, sanctity, spirituality, divinity, piety, devoutness, godliness, saintliness, virtuousness, righteousness, purity.
⊟ **1** impiety.

holism /ˈhoʊlɪzm/ *noun Philos.* the thesis that some wholes cannot be fully understood solely by reference to the self-sufficient elements which make up their parts. The doctrine is found in such disparate fields as political philosophy, social science, psychology, and biology. [from Greek *holos*, whole]

holistic /hɒˈlɪstɪk/ *adj.* denoting an approach to medical treatment that considers a person as a whole, and takes social and psychological factors into account as well as the physical symptoms. [from Greek *holos*, whole]

holistically *adv.* in a holistic way.

holland *noun* a smooth, hard-wearing linen cloth, usually unbleached or dyed brown. [originally made in Holland]

holler — *verb intrans., trans.* (**hollered, hollering**) *colloq.* to shout or cry loudly. — *noun* a shout. [from French *holà*, stop!]

hollow — *adj.* **1** containing an empty space; not solid. **2** sunken: *hollow cheeks.* **3** *said of a sound* echoing as if made in a hollow place. **4** worthless; insincere. — *noun* **1** hollow or sunken space in something. **2** a small valley or depression in the land. — *adv. colloq.* completely: *beat the other team hollow.* — *verb* (*usually* **hollow something out**) to make a hole or hollow in it; to form it by making a hollow. [from Anglo-Saxon *holh*]

⊟ *adj.* **1** empty, vacant, unfilled, cavernous. **2** sunken, concave, depressed. **3** deep, echoing, resounding. **4** insincere, false, artificial, deceptive, meaningless, empty, worthless, vain, futile, fruitless. *noun* DEPRESSION. **1** hole, cavity, pit, cave, concavity, dimple, dent, indentation, groove, channel, trough. **2** crater, basin, valley. *verb* excavate, burrow, tunnel, scoop, gouge, groove, furrow, pit, dent, indent.
⊟ *adj.* **1** solid. **4** genuine, sincere.

hollow-eyed *adj.* having sunken eyes, usually because of tiredness.

hollowly *adv.* **1** in a hollow way. **2** with a hollow sound.

hollowness *noun* **1** being hollow. **2** a cavity. **3** insincerity.

holly *noun* (PL. **hollies**) **1** any of numerous species of shrubs or small trees of the genus *Ilex*, especially *I. aquifolium*, an evergreen shrub, native to Europe, having silvery-grey bark and leathery leaves, usually with wavy spiny margins. The fruit, borne on female trees, is a small bright red poisonous berry that persists throughout the winter. **2** the ornamental foliage of this plant, used in many countries as a traditional Christmas decoration. **3** the hard white timber of this plant, used for carving and cabinet-making. [from Anglo-Saxon *holen*]

hollyhock *noun* a tall biennial or perennial plant of the genus *Althaea*, especially *A. rosea*, native to China, which has stout hairy stems that grow up to 3m high in the plant's second year, rounded shallowly lobed leaves, and long spikes of white, yellow, purple, or red flowers. [from Middle English *holi*, holy + *hoc*, mallow]

holmium /ˈhoʊlmɪəm/ *noun* (SYMBOL **Ho**, ATOMIC NUMBER 67) a soft silvery metallic element of the lanthanide series, that occurs naturally in apatite and some other rare-earth minerals. Its compounds are highly magnetic. [from Latin *Holmia*, Stockholm]

holocaust /ˈhɒləkɔːst/ *noun* **1** large-scale destruction and loss of life. **2** (**Holocaust**) the attempt by Nazi Germany to systematically destroy European Jews. [from Greek *holos*, whole + *kaustos*, burnt]

Holocene /ˈhɒləsiːn/ *adj. Geol.* relating to the most recent epoch of the Quaternary period, from 10,000 years ago to the present time. During this epoch modern human beings appeared and civilization began. [from Greek *holos*, whole + *kainos*, new]

hologram *noun Photog.* a three-dimensional image of an object recorded on a photographic plate by the process of holography. [from Greek *holos*, whole + -GRAM]

holograph — *adj., said of a document* completely in the handwriting of the author. — *noun* a holograph document. — *verb* to make a hologram of or to record as a hologram. [from Greek *holos*, whole + *graphein*, to write]

holographic *adj.* relating to or involving holographs.

holographically *adv.* **1** in a holographic way. **2** by means of holography.

holography *noun Photog.* a photographic technique that uses beams of laser light to produce a three-dimensional image of an object.

holophrase *noun* a one-word utterance used by young children in the earliest stages of language-learning to express meaning which in more mature speech would normally be contained in a more complex grammatical structure, such as a phrase or sentence. [from Greek *holos*, whole + PHRASE]

hols *pl. noun colloq.* holidays. [abbreviation]

holster *noun* a leather case for a pistol, usually worn attached to a belt round a person's hips. [from Dutch *holster*]

holt *noun* the lair of an animal, especially an otter or fish. [from HOLD¹]

holy *adj.* (**holier, holiest**) **1** belonging to or associated with God or gods; sacred. **2** morally pure and perfect; saintly. [from Anglo-Saxon *halig*]

▪ ▪ ▪ ▪ ▪ ▪ ▪ ▪ ▪ ▪ ▪ ▪ ▪ ▪ ▪ ▪ ▪ ▪

  ◨ **1** sacred, hallowed, consecrated, sanctified, dedicated, blessed, venerated, revered, spiritual, divine, evangelical. **2** pious, religious, devout, godly, God-fearing, saintly, virtuous, good, righteous, faithful, pure, perfect.

  ◪ **1** unconsecrated, unsanctified. **2** unholy, impious, irreligious.

· ·

Holy Communion see COMMUNION.

Holy Ghost see HOLY SPIRIT.

Holy Grail 1 in medieval legend, the platter or cup used by Christ at the Last Supper, that became the object of quests by King Arthur's knights. **2** a cherished ambition or goal. [from Old French *graal* or *grael*, a flat dish]

Holy Innocents' Day a Christian festival on 28 Dec commemorating the massacre ordered by Herod the Great of the male children of Bethlehem at the time of the birth of Christ.

Holy Land W Palestine, especially Judaea; the scene of Christ's ministry in the New Testament.

holy of holies any place or thing regarded as especially holy.

holy orders the office of an ordained member of the Christian clergy: *take holy orders.*

Holy See the see of Rome, the pope's see.

Holy Spirit a term used to denote the presence or power of God, often imbued with quasi-personal characteristics; in Christian thought, considered the third person of the Trinity, alongside the Father and the Son.

holy war *Relig.* a war waged for the eradication of heresy or a rival religion, eg Christian Crusades and jihad (in defence of Islam).

Holy Week in the Christian Church, the week before Easter Sunday, beginning on Palm Sunday and including Maundy Thursday and Good Friday.

Holy Writ holy writings, especially the Bible.

homage *noun* **1** a display of great respect towards someone or something. **2** *Hist.* a vassal's formal public acknowledgement that he is his feudal lord's servant. [from Old French *homage*]

· ·

  ◨ **1** recognition, acknowledgement, tribute, honour, praise, adulation, admiration, regard, esteem, respect, deference, reverence, awe, veneration, worship, devotion.

· ·

home — *noun* **1** the place where one lives. **2** the country or area one originally comes from. **3** a place where a thing first occurred or was first invented. **4** an institution where people who need care or rest live, eg orphans, the aged, etc. **5** a match won by a team playing on their own ground. **6** the finishing point in some games and races. — *adj.* **1** of one's home, country, or family. **2** made or done at home or in one's own country. **3** *said of a sporting event* played on one's own ground. — *adv.* **1** at or to a person's home. **2** to the place, position, etc aimed at: *hit the point home.* **3** as far as possible: *hammer the nail home.* **4** *said of a sporting event* on one's own ground, etc. — *verb intrans.* **1** *said of a bird* to return home safely. **2** (**home in on something**) to be directed towards a destination or target. — **at home 1** in one's home, country, sports ground, etc. **2** feeling at ease or familiar with a place. **3** prepared to receive visitors. **bring something home to someone** to make it clear or obvious to them. **home and dry** having arrived home or achieved one's goal. **home from home** a place where one feels as comfortable, relaxed, and happy as one feels at home. **make oneself at home** to behave as one would in one's own home. **nothing to write home about** *colloq.* not very exciting or attractive. [from Anglo-Saxon *ham*]

· ·

  ◨ *noun* **1** residence, domicile, dwelling-place, abode, house, pied-à-terre, base, habitat, element. **2** birthplace, home town, homeland. *adj.* **1** domestic, household, family, internal, local, national. **at home 2** at ease, comfortable, relaxed, familiar, knowledgeable, experienced.

  ◪ *adj.* **1** foreign, international.

· ·

home alone *said of a child* left alone in a house without supervision.

home banking a banking service allowing customers to access information about their account, transfer funds, etc using a computer link from their home or office to the bank's own system.

homecoming *noun* the return home of a person who has been away for a long time.

home farm a farm, especially formerly, attached to and providing food for a large country house or estate.

Home Guard *Brit. Hist.* a volunteer army formed to defend Britain from invasion during World War II.

home help *Brit.* a person who is paid, often by the local authority, to help people who are ill or old with their cleaning, cooking, etc.

homeland *noun* **1** the country where a person is born, or from where his or her ancestors come. **2** in South Africa, land set aside by the government for the native black population.

· ·

  ◨ **1** native land, native country, fatherland, motherland.

· ·

homeless — *adj.*, *said of people* without a home; having nowhere to live. — *pl. noun* (**the homeless**) people without a place to live.

· ·

  ◨ *adj.* itinerant, travelling, nomadic, wandering, vagrant, rootless, unsettled, displaced, dispossessed, evicted, exiled, destitute, down-and-out. *noun* travellers, vagabonds, vagrants, tramps, down-and-outs, *slang* dossers, squatters.

· ·

homeliness *noun* being homely.

homely *adj.* (**homelier, homeliest**) **1** simple but pleasant. **2** making someone feel at home. **3** *North Amer., esp. US, said of a person* plain and unattractive.

· ·

  ◨ **1** plain, simple, modest, unassuming, unpretentious, unsophisticated, natural, everyday, ordinary, domestic. **2** homelike, homy, comfortable, cosy, snug, relaxed, informal, friendly, welcoming, intimate, familiar.

  ◪ **1** grand. **2** formal, unwelcoming.

· ·

home-made *adj.*, *said of food, clothes, etc* made at home.

home movie a motion picture made by an amateur, using equipment such as a cine camera or a camcorder, and usually intended for domestic viewing.

Home Office *Brit.* the government department which deals with law and order within the country, immigration, etc.

homeopath or **homoeopath** /ˈhoʊmɪəpaθ/ *noun* a person who practises homeopathy.

homeopathic or **homoeopathic** /hoʊmɪəˈpaθɪk/ *adj.* relating to or involving homeopathy.

homeopathically or **homoeopathically** *adv.* in a homeopathic way; by means of homeopathy.

homeopathy or **homoeopathy** /hoʊmɪˈɒpəθɪ/ *noun* a system of alternative medicine developed by the German physician Samuel Hahnemann (1755–1843). It is based on the principles that like cures like, and that the activity of a drug is enhanced by dilution. Thus a drug that in large doses would induce particular symptoms of an illness is used in minute doses to cure the same symptoms. The emphasis is on treatment of the patient as a whole, rather than the eradication of a single symptom. [from Greek *homoios*, similar + *patheia*, suffering]

homeostasis or **homoeostasis** /hoʊmɪoʊˈsteɪsɪs/ *noun Biol.* the maintenance by a living organism, usually a higher animal, of a constant internal environment that is independent of fluctuations in the external environment, eg constant body temperature, blood sugar levels, etc. [from Greek *homos*, same + *stasis*, a standing still]

home page the first or main page of an Internet website.

Homeric /hoʊˈmɛrɪk/ *adj.* **1** relating to Homer or the poems attributed to him. **2** relating to Bronze Age Greece.

home rule government of a country by its own citizens.

Home Secretary *Brit.* the government minister in charge of the Home Office.

homesick *adj.* sad and depressed at being away from one's home and family.

homespun *adj.* **1** *said of advice, thinking, etc* simple and straightforward. **2** *old use, said of cloth* woven at home.

homestead *noun* **1** a house, especially a farmhouse, with the land and other buildings which belong to it. **2** *North Amer., esp. US* an area of land (usually 65ha) granted to a settler for development as a farm.

home straight or **home stretch** the last part of a racecourse just before the finish.

home truth (*usually* **home truths**) frank but unwelcome information about oneself, usually told directly.

homeward — *adj.* going home. — *adv.* (*also* **homewards**) towards home.

homework *noun* work or study done at home, especially by school pupils.

homicidal /hɒmɪˈsaɪdl/ *adj.*, *said of a person* psychologically disposed to commit murder.

homicide /ˈhɒmɪsaɪd/ *noun* **1** the killing of one person by another. **2** a person who kills another person. [from Latin *homo*, man + -CIDE]

· · · · · · · · · · · · · · · · · · · ·

◼ **1** manslaughter, murder, assassination, killing. **2** murderer, assassin, killer.

· ·

homiletic *adj.* **1** relating to or involving a homily or sermon. **2** characteristic of the art of writing or giving sermons.

homily *noun* (PL. **homilies**) **1** a sermon. **2** a long, boring talk, usually telling someone how to behave. [from Greek *homilia*, assembly, sermon]

homing *adj.* **1** *said of a pigeon* able to find its way home after being released a long way away. **2** *said of a missile* able to guide itself to its target.

homing instinct *Biol.* the navigational behaviour that occurs in a number of animal species, ranging from returning home after daily foraging and other excursions, to the more complex navigational task involved in large migrations.

hominid *noun, adj.* a primate belonging to the primate family Hominidae, which includes modern man (*Homo sapiens*) and his fossil ancestors. [from Latin *homo*, man]

hominoid — *noun* any member of the family of primates that includes modern man and man's close, now extinct, bipedal ancestors. — *adj.* **1** of or belonging to this family. **2** of or resembling man; manlike. [from Latin *homo*, man + -OID]

hominy *noun North Amer., esp. US* coarsely ground maize, boiled with milk or water to make porridge. [an American Indian word]

homo- *combining form* forming words meaning 'same': *homosexual*. [from Greek *homos*, same]

homoeopathy See HOMEOPATHY.

homogeneity /hɒmoʊdʒəˈniːɪti/ *noun* being homogeneous.

homogeneous /hɒməˈdʒiːnɪəs/ *adj.* made of parts that are all of the same kind. [from Greek *homos*, same + *genos*, kind]

· · · · · · · · · · · · · · · · · · · ·

◼ uniform, consistent, unvarying, identical, similar, alike, analogous, comparable, harmonious, compatible.
◰ heterogeneous.

· ·

homogenize or **homogenise** /həˈmɒdʒənaɪz/ *verb* **1** to break up the fat droplets of a liquid, especially milk, into smaller particles that are evenly distributed throughout the liquid. **2** to make homogeneous. [from Greek *homos*, same + *genos*, kind]

homogenous /həˈmɒdʒənəs/ *adj.* similar owing to common descent.

homogeny /həˈmɒdʒənɪ/ *noun Biol.* similarity of structure due to common descent or origin. [from Greek *homos*, same + *genos*, kind]

homograph *noun* a word with the same spelling as another, but with a different meaning and origin and sometimes a different pronunciation, eg *like* (similar) and *like* (be fond of), and *entrance* (a way in; stressed on *en-*) and *entrance* (to bewitch; stressed on *-trance*). [from Greek *homos*, same + GRAPH]

homoiothermic /hoʊmɔɪəˈθɜːmɪk/ *adj. Zool.* denoting an animal that maintains its internal body temperature at a relatively constant level, independent of fluctuations in the temperature of its environment. Higher vertebrates, such as mammals and birds, are homoiothermic. Also called WARM-BLOODED.

homologous /hoʊˈmɒləgəs/ *adj.* **1** having a related or similar function or position. **2** *Biol.* denoting plant or animal structures that have a common origin, but that have evolved in such a way that they may no longer perform the same functions or resemble each other in appearance, eg human arm and bird's wing. See also ANALOGOUS. **3** *Biol.* denoting two chromosomes in a cell, usually of the same size and shape, that contain genes for the same set of characteristics, but are derived from different parents. [from Greek *homos*, same + *logos*, proportion]

homologous series *Chem.* a series of organic chemical compounds that have the same functional group, each member of the series differing from the next by the presence of an extra -CH_2 group in its molecules. For example, the alkane series of hydrocarbons includes methane (CH_4), ethane (C_2H_6), propane (C_3H_8), etc.

homology *noun* a homologous state or condition.

homonym /ˈhɒmənɪm/ *noun* a word having the same sound and spelling as another word, but a different meaning, eg *kind* (helpful) and *kind* (sort). [from Greek *homos*, same + *onoma*, name]

homophobia /hoʊmoʊˈfoʊbɪə/ *noun* an intense dislike or fear of homosexuals. [from HOMOSEXUAL + PHOBIA]

homophone /ˈhɒməfoʊn/ *noun* a word which has the same sound as another word but has a different spelling and meaning, eg *bear/bare*. [from Greek *homos*, same + *phone*, voice]

homophony /hɒˈmɒfənɪ/ *noun Mus.* a style of musical composition in which one part or voice carries the melody with other parts or voices adding texture with simple chordal accompaniment. See also POLYPHONY. [from Greek *homos*, same + *phone*, a voice, sound]

Homo sapiens /hɒmoʊ ˈsapɪənz/ *noun* the scientific name for the present-day human species, a large omnivorous bipedal primate that first appeared about 100,000 years ago as Neanderthal man, and is the only living representative of the genus *Homo*. [from Latin *homo sapiens*, wise man]

homosexual /hoʊməˈsɛkʃʊəl/ — *noun* a person who is sexually attracted to people of the same sex. — *adj.* of or concerning a homosexual or homosexuals. [from Greek *homos*, same]

· · · · · · · · · · · · · · · · · · · ·

◼ *noun* gay, *slang* queer, *slang* poof, lesbian, *slang* dyke. *adj.* gay, *slang* queer, lesbian.
◰ *noun* heterosexual, *slang* straight. *adj.* heterosexual, *slang* straight.

· ·

homosexuality *noun* **1** being homosexual. **2** a homosexual character or nature. **3** homosexual activity or behaviour.

homozygous /hoʊmoʊˈzaɪɡəs/ *adj. Genetics* describing an individual that contains two identical alleles for a particular gene, and will therefore produce offspring that are identical to the parent with respect to that gene.

homy *adj.* (**homier, homiest**) like a home, especially in being warm and comfortable.

Hon. *abbrev.* Honourable.

hone — *noun* a smooth stone for sharpening tools and knives. — *verb* to sharpen with or as if with a hone. [from Anglo-Saxon *han*]

■ *verb* sharpen, whet, point, edge, grind, file.

honest — *adj.* **1** truthful; trustworthy; not likely to steal, cheat, or lie. **2** just or fair: *an honest wage.* **3** sincere and respectable: *an honest attempt.* **4** ordinary and undistinguished: *an honest wine.* — *adv. colloq.* honestly: *I do like it, honest.* [from Latin *honestus*]

■ *adj.* **1** truthful, sincere, frank, candid, blunt, direct, forthright, straightforward, open, trustworthy, reliable, law-abiding, upright, ethical, moral, legitimate, legal, lawful, aboveboard, *slang* on the level. **2** just, fair, impartial, objective. **3** sincere, genuine, real, true, respectable, reputable, honourable. **4** plain, simple, ordinary, undistinguished.

■ *adj.* **1** dishonest. **3** dishonourable.

honestly *adv.* **1** in an honest way. **2** truly.

■ **1** truthfully, sincerely, frankly, directly, outright, plainly, openly, legitimately, legally, lawfully, justly, fairly, objectively, honourably, in good faith. **2** truly, really, truthfully, sincerely.

■ **1** dishonestly, dishonourably.

honesty *noun* **1** the state of being honest and truthful. **2** a biennial plant (*Lunaria annua*), native to SE Europe, having heart-shaped leaves and cross-shaped reddish-purple flowers (rarely white). Its flat oval seed pods have a persistent silvery central dividing wall or *septum*, and are much used in dried flower decorations.

■ **1** truthfulness, veracity, sincerity, frankness, candour, bluntness, plain-speaking, openness, trustworthiness, uprightness, honour, integrity, morality, legitimacy, legality, justness, fairness, objectivity.

■ **1** dishonesty.

honey *noun* (PL. **honeys**) **1** a sweet viscous fluid, white to dark yellow in colour, manufactured by bees from the nectar of flowers, and stored in honeycombs as food for the developing larvae. It consists mainly of simple sugars such as glucose and fructose, and is used as a food and sweetener. **2** a dark dull yellow colour resembling that of honey. **3** *North Amer. colloq.* a word used when speaking to a person one loves. **4** *colloq.* a person or thing which is excellent of its kind. [from Anglo-Saxon *hunig*]

honey bee a species of bee (*Apis mellifera*), native to tropical Asia, that has been semi-domesticated for centuries in most parts of the world as a source of honey.

honeycomb *noun* **1** a regular structure consisting of a mass of adjacent hexagonal cells made of beeswax, built by a colony of bees and used mainly for storing honey. Also called COMB. **2** anything resembling this, eg a cellular metallic material.

honeyed *adj., said of a voice, words, etc* pleasing, flattering, or soothing.

honey guide *Bot.* any of various markings on the petal of a flower, said to show the way to the nectaries.

honeymoon — *noun* **1** a holiday taken by a newly married couple. **2** a period of goodwill and enthusiasm at the beginning, eg of a new business relationship. — *verb intrans.* to spend a honeymoon.

honeymooner *noun* a person taking a honeymoon, a newly married person.

honeysuckle *noun* **1** any of various evergreen or deciduous shrubs and woody climbing plants, native to temperate regions, so called because they produce large amounts of nectar. It is most commonly used to refer to species belonging to the genus *Lonicera*, native to Europe and N America, which have tubular white, yellow, or pink flowers. The flowers often produce a sweet scent at night. The fruit is a bright red or purplish-black berry. **2** any of various trees or shrubs of the genus *Banksia*, native to Australia, which bear dense spikes of flowers that are pollinated by marsupials. [from Anglo-Saxon *hunigsuge*]

honeytrap *noun* a scheme to entrap someone using sex as a bait.

honk — *noun* **1** the sound made by a car horn. **2** the cry of a wild goose. — *verb trans., intrans.* to make or cause to make a honking noise. [imitative]

honky or **honkie** *noun* (PL. **honkies**) *North Amer. Black slang* a white person.

honky-tonk *noun colloq.* **1** a style of popular piano music based on ragtime. **2** a cheap, seedy nightclub.

honorarium *noun* (PL. **honorariums, honoraria**) a gift, usually money, given to someone in return for professional services which would normally be free. [from Latin *honorarium*, honorary]

honorary *adj.* **1** given to a person as a mark of respect, and without the usual functions, etc. **2** *said of an official position* not having any payment. [from Latin *honorarius*]

■ **1** titular, nominal, honorific, formal. **2** unpaid.

■ **2** paid.

honorific *adj.* showing or giving respect. [from Latin *honor*, honour + *facere*, to do]

honour — *noun* **1** great respect or public regard. **2** the quality of doing what is right and having a high standard of moral behaviour. **3** fame or glory; distinction for bravery, etc. **4** a source of fame, glory, or distinction (for one's country, etc). **5** a pleasure or privilege. **6** *old use* a woman's chastity or her reputation for this. **7** (**honours**) *said of a university degree* a higher grade of distinction for specialized or advanced work. **8** (**Honour**) a title of respect given to judges, mayors, etc. **9** (**honours**) a mark of respect, especially at a funeral. **10** in some card games, any of the top four or five cards. **11** *Golf* the right to play from the tee first. — *verb* **1** to respect greatly. **2** to give (someone) an award, title, or honour as a mark of respect for (an ability or achievement, etc). **3** to pay (a bill, debt, etc) when it falls due. **4** to keep (a promise). — **do the honours** to perform the task of host towards one's guests, eg offering them drinks, etc. **on one's honour** under a moral obligation. **word of honour** a solemn promise. [from Latin *honor*]

■ *noun* **1** respect, admiration, reverence, worship, esteem, regard, credit, reputation, good name, dignity, pride, self-respect. **2** integrity, probity, morality, decency, rectitude. **3** fame, repute, renown, distinction, glory, praise, acclaim, homage, tribute, award, accolade, commendation, acknowledgement, recognition. *verb* **1** respect, revere, worship, admire, esteem, prize, value. **2** acknowledge, recognize, pay homage to, praise, acclaim, exalt, glorify, decorate, crown, celebrate, commemorate, remember. **4** keep, observe, respect, fulfil, carry out, discharge, execute, perform.

■ *noun* **1** dishonour, disgrace. *verb* **1** dishonour, disgrace.

honourable *adj.* **1** deserving or worthy of honour. **2** having high moral principles. **3** (**Honourable**) a courtesy title, given to some high officials, the children of some peers, and MPs. See also RIGHT HONOURABLE.

....

■ **1** great, eminent, distinguished, renowned, respected, worthy, reputable, respectable. **2** upright, honest, trustworthy, sincere, noble, high-minded, principled, moral, ethical, just, fair, decent.

◨ **1** dishonourable, unworthy. **2** dishonest.
....

honourably *adv.* in an honourable way.

honour-bound *adj.* obliged to do something not by law, but from duty or from moral considerations.

hooch *noun North Amer. colloq.* strong alcoholic drink, especially when distilled illegally. [from a Native American word]

hood¹ *noun* **1** a usually loose covering for the whole head, often attached to a coat at the collar. **2** a folding, usually removable, roof or cover on a car, cooker, push-chair, etc. **3** *North Amer.* a car bonnet. **4** a piece of cloth worn as part of academic dress. [from Anglo-Saxon *hod*]

hood² *noun slang* a hoodlum.

-hood *suffix* **1** denoting a state or condition: *manhood*. **2** denoting a collection or group: *priesthood*. [from Anglo-Saxon *-had*]

hooded *adj.* having, covered with, or shaped like a hood.

hooded crow a subspecies of crow, native to Europe and Asia, having a grey body and a black head, wings, and tail. It interbreeds with the carrion crow, and is regarded as the same species by some authorities.

hoodlum *noun* **1** *North Amer., esp. US* a criminal. **2** a young, violent, destructive, or badly behaved person.

hoodoo — *noun* **1** voodoo. **2** bad luck, or the thing or person which brings it. — *verb* to bring bad luck to. [variant of VOODOO]

hoodwink *verb* to trick or deceive (someone): *hoodwinked into buying stolen goods*. [from HOOD¹ + WINK]
....

■ trick, deceive, dupe, fool, take in, mislead, hoax, cheat, swindle, *colloq.* con.
....

hooey *noun slang* nonsense.

hoof — *noun* (PL. **hoofs, hooves**) in horses and other mammals that walk on the tips of their digits (toes), the horny structure that grows beneath and covers the ends of the digits. — *verb* (**hoof it**) *slang* to go on foot. — **on the hoof** *said of cattle, horses, etc* alive.

hoo-ha *noun colloq.* excited and noisy talk; a commotion. [probably from Yiddish *hu-ha*, uproar]

hook — *noun* **1** a small piece of metal, etc shaped like a J, used for catching and holding things. **2** a curved tool for cutting grain, branches, etc. **3** a sharp bend or curve, eg in land or a river. **4** *Boxing* a swinging punch with the elbow bent. **5** *Cricket, Golf* a shot that sends the ball to the right-handed player's left. — *verb* **1** to catch with or as if with a hook. **2** *trans., intrans.* (*also* **hook up** or **hook something up**) to fasten or be fastened to something else by means of a hook or hooks. **3** *Golf, Cricket* to hit (the ball) out round the other side of one's body, ie to the left if one is right-handed. **4** in a rugby scrum, to catch (the ball) with the foot and kick it backwards. **5** to make into the shape of a hook. — **by hook or by crook** by some means or another. **hook and eye** a small metal hook and the loop it fits into, used to fasten clothes. **hook, line, and sinker** *colloq.* completely. **off the hook 1** *colloq.* no longer in trouble; excused of the blame for something. **2** *said of a telephone receiver* not on its rest so not able to receive incoming calls. [from Anglo-Saxon *hoc*]
....

■ *noun* **1** peg, barb, catch, fastener, clasp, hasp. **2** sickle, scythe. **3** bend, curve, crook, elbow. *verb* **1** catch, grab, trap, snare, ensnare, entangle. **5** bend, crook, curve, curl.
....

hookah /ˈhʊkə/ *noun* an oriental tobacco-pipe consisting of a tube which passes through water, used for cooling the smoke before it is drawn into the mouth. [from Arabic *huqqah*, bowl]

hooked *adj.* **1** curved like a hook. **2** (**hooked on something**) *colloq.* addicted to a drug or activity; obsessively interested in something or committed to it.

hooker *noun* **1** *colloq.* a prostitute. **2** *Rugby* the forward whose job is to hook the ball out of a scrum.

Hooke's law /hʊks/ *Physics* the law which states that, for an elastic material within its elastic limit, the extension produced by stretching the material is proportional to the force that is producing the extension (above the elastic limit permanent deformation occurs). [named after the UK physicist Robert Hooke]

hookey or **hooky** /ˈhʊkɪ/ *noun* — **play hookey** *North Amer. colloq.* to be absent from school without permission.

hook-up *noun* **1** the temporary linking up of separate broadcasting stations for the transmission of a special programme. **2** an arrangement of circuits or other components for a particular purpose.

hookworm *noun* any of various parasitic roundworms that suck the blood of mammals, including humans, causing various diseases. The adult hookworm attaches itself to the lining of the small intestine by means of its hooked mouthparts, and can cause serious loss of blood. It is an important cause of anaemia and ill health in tropical and subtropical regions.

hooligan *noun* a violent, destructive or badly-behaved young person.
....

■ ruffian, rowdy, hoodlum, mobster, thug, tough, lout, *slang* yob, vandal, delinquent.
....

hooliganism *noun* **1** characteristic behaviour of hooligans. **2** an instance of such behaviour.

hoop — *noun* **1** a thin ring of metal, wood, etc, especially those used round casks. **2** a large ring, especially one made of light wood or plastic, rolled along the ground as a toy, whirled round the body, or for circus performers, etc to jump through. **3** an iron arch that the ball is hit through in croquet. — *verb* to bind or surround with a hoop or hoops. — **go** or **be put through the hoops** *colloq.* to undergo a thorough and difficult test. [from Anglo-Saxon *hop*]
....

■ *noun* **1** ring, circle, round, loop, band, girdle.
....

hoop-la *noun* a fairground game in which small rings are thrown at objects, with the thrower winning any objects he or she manages to throw a hoop over.

hoopoe /ˈhuːpuː/ *noun* a ground-dwelling bird, native to Europe, Asia, and Africa, that has pinkish-brown plumage with conspicuous black and white bars on the lower back and wings, and a long curved bill. When excited, it raises a fan-like crest of chestnut, black-tipped feathers on top of its head. [from Latin *upupa*, imitative of its cry]

hooray or **hoorah** same as HURRAH.

Hooray Henry *noun slang* a young middle- or upper-class man with a loud voice and immature and ineffectual manner.

hoot — *noun* **1** the call of an owl. **2** the sound of a car horn, siren, steam whistle, etc. **3** a loud shout of laughter, scorn, or disapproval. **4** *colloq.* an amusing person, event, or thing. — *verb* **1** *intrans.* to make a hoot. **2** to sound (a car horn, etc). **3** *intrans.* to shout or laugh loudly expressing disapproval, scorn, etc. **4** to force (a performer) off stage by hooting. — **not care** or **give a hoot** or **two hoots** *colloq.* not to care at all. [from Middle English *houten*, perhaps imitative]
....

■ *noun* **1** call, cry. **2** toot, beep, whistle. **3** shout, shriek, whoop, howl, sneer, jeer, boo. *verb* **1** call, cry. **2** toot, beep. **3** shout, shriek, whoop, howl, sneer, jeer, boo.
....

hooter *noun* **1** an instrument which makes a hooting sound. **2** *Brit. colloq.* a nose.

Hoover — *noun trademark* a vacuum cleaner. — *verb trans., intrans.* (**hoover**) (**hoovered, hoovering**) to clean (a carpet, etc) with a vacuum cleaner.

hooves see HOOF.

hop¹ — *verb* (**hopped, hopping**) **1** *intrans., said of a person* to jump on one leg, especially repeatedly as a form of movement. **2** *intrans., said of certain small birds, animals, and insects* to jump on both or all legs simultaneously. **3** to jump over. **4** *intrans.* (**hop in, out,** etc) *colloq.* to move in a sprightly or lively way. **5** (*usually* **hop over**) *colloq.* to make a short journey, especially by air. — *noun* **1** an act of hopping; a short jump. **2** *colloq.* a distance travelled in an aeroplane without landing; a short journey by air. **3** *old colloq.* use an informal dance. — **catch someone on the hop** *colloq.* to catch them unprepared or unawares. **hop it** *Brit. colloq.* to go away. **hopping mad** *colloq.* very angry. **keep someone on the hop** to keep someone busy, active, or alert. [from Anglo-Saxon *hoppian*, to dance]

▣ *verb* **2** jump, leap, spring, bound, skip, prance, frisk, frolic. **3** jump, leap, vault. *noun* **1** jump, leap, spring, bound, vault.

hop² — *noun* **1** a tall perennial climbing plant (a vine) of the genus *Humulus*, widely cultivated for its green cone-shaped female flowers, which are used to give a bitter flavour to beer. **2** (*usually* **hops**) the female flower of this plant, which contains bitter resins and essential oils used in brewing. — *verb* (**hopped, hopping**) **1** *intrans.* to pick hops. **2** to flavour (beer) with hops. [from Middle English *hoppe*]

hope — *noun* **1** a desire for something, with some confidence of obtaining it. **2** a person, thing, or event that one is relying on for help, or that gives one a good reason for hope. **3** a reason for believing that the thing desired will still happen. **4** that which is desired or hoped for. — *verb* **1** *trans., intrans.* to wish or desire that something may happen, especially with some reason to believe that it will: *hope for good weather / hoping to catch the early train / I hope you like it.* **2** *intrans. old use* to have confidence. — **hope against hope** to continue hoping when all reason for it has gone. **some hope** *colloq.* no hope at all. [from Anglo-Saxon *hopa*]

▣ *noun* **1** hopefulness, optimism, belief, confidence, assurance, conviction. **4** wish, desire, longing, dream, ambition, aspiration, expectation, anticipation, prospect, promise. *verb* **1** wish, desire, long, expect, believe.
▣ *noun* **1** pessimism, despair. *verb* **1** despair.

hopeful — *adj.* **1** feeling hope. **2** giving a reason for hope; likely to succeed. — *noun* a person, especially a young person, who is ambitious or expected to do well.

▣ *adj.* **1** optimistic, bullish, confident, assured, expectant, sanguine, cheerful, buoyant. **2** encouraging, heartening, reassuring, favourable, auspicious, promising, rosy, bright.
▣ *adj.* **1** pessimistic, despairing. **2** discouraging.

hopefully *adv.* **1** in a hopeful way. **2** *colloq.* it is to be hoped.

hopeless *adj.* **1** not likely to be successful. **2** *colloq.* (**hopeless at something**) not competent to do it. **3** unable to be stopped or cured. **4** lacking hope; despairing.

▣ **1** unattainable, unachievable, impracticable, impossible, vain, futile, useless, pointless. **3** lost, irremediable, irreparable, incurable. **4** pessimistic, defeatist, negative, despairing, demoralized, downhearted, dejected, despondent.
▣ **1** attainable, achievable. **3** remediable, curable. **4** hopeful, optimistic.

hopper¹ *noun* **1** a person, animal, or insect which hops. **2** *Agric.* a large container with a hole in the bottom that is used to feed grain, fertilizer, etc, into another container below it, into seed drills, or on to the ground.

hopper² *noun* **1** a machine used for picking hops. **2** a funnel-shaped container with sloping sides, into which solid materials such as grain or coal can be temporarily loaded and then discharged through a valve-like opening in the bottom into a truck or other receptacle. **3** a railway wagon with doors on its underside, through which its cargo can be discharged. **4** a long-legged hopping or leaping insect, especially a grasshopper or young locust.

hopscotch *noun* a children's game in which players take turns at throwing a stone into one of a series of squares drawn on the ground and hopping in the others around it.

horde *noun* **1** *often derog.* a crowd or large group, especially one which is noisy. **2** a group of nomads. [from Turkish *ordu*, camp]

▣ **1** band, gang, pack, herd, drove, flock, swarm, crowd, mob, throng, multitude, host.

horizon *noun* **1** the line at which the earth or sea and the sky appear to meet. **2** the limit of a person's knowledge, interests, or experience. **3** a layer of soil or rock that can be distinguished from adjacent layers, or dated, by its specific physical composition, by the presence of a particular fossil or fossils, or by artefacts characteristic of a particular culture or period. [from Greek *horizein*, to limit]

▣ **1** skyline, vista, prospect. **2** compass, range, scope.

horizontal — *adj.* **1** at right angles to vertical; parallel to the horizon; level or flat. **2** applying equally to all members of a group or aspects of a situation. — *noun* a horizontal line or position.

hormonal *adj.* **1** relating to or produced by the action of a hormone or hormones. **2** that is or behaves as a hormone.

hormone *noun* **1** a substance that is manufactured and secreted in minute amounts by a specialized gland, known as an endocrine gland, in one part of the body, and carried via the bloodstream to organs or tissues located elsewhere in the body, where it causes specific biological changes. Examples of hormones include insulin, adrenaline, thyroxine, and the sex hormones (androgens and oestrogens). **2** an artificially manufactured chemical compound which has the same effects as such a substance. **3** a plant growth substance that influences the growth and development of plant tissue. [from Greek *horman*, to stimulate]

hormone replacement therapy (ABBREV. **HRT**) *Medicine* a treatment for post-menopausal women that involves the administration (either by mouth or by injection) of the oestrogenic hormones that are not produced naturally after the menopause, in order to relieve some of the more undesirable menopausal symptoms, such as hot flushes, vaginal dryness, osteoporosis (thinning of the bones), and emotional disturbances.

horn — *noun* **1** one of a pair of hard hollow structures, usually pointed, that grow on the head of many ruminant animals, eg cattle, sheep. In male deer the horns are known as antlers. **2** any similar structure growing on the head of another animal, eg rhinoceros, or one of the two tentacles borne on the head of a snail. **3** the bony substance of which horns are made. **4** something which looks like a horn in shape. **5** a musical wind instrument originally made from horn but now usually made of brass. **6** (*in full* **French horn**) a coiled brass wind instrument. **7** an apparatus for making a warning sound, especially on a vehicle. — *verb* **1** to fit with a horn or horns. **2** to injure or gore with horns. — **horn of plenty** cornucopia. **on the horns of a dilemma** having to make a choice between two equally unwelcome alternatives. [from Anglo-Saxon]

hornbeam *noun* **1** a deciduous tree (*Carpinus betulus*), native to Europe and Asia, having grey fissured bark, oval leaves with pointed tips and sharply serrated margins, and tiny flowers borne in pendulous male and female catkins. **2** the smooth hard close-grained white timber of this tree, which is very durable, and is used in woodworking, and to make tool handles.

hornbill *noun* any of various large birds, native to tropical forests of Africa, Asia, and the Philippine and Solomon Islands, having black, brown, and white plumage, and so called because there is often a large bony ornamental outgrowth or *casque* on top of its long slightly curved red or yellow bill.

hornblende *noun Geol.* a dark green or black mineral that is a major component of many metamorphic and igneous rocks, including granite. [from German]

horned *adj.* having a horn or horns or something shaped like a horn.

hornet *noun* any of several large social wasps, similar in habits and life cycle to the common wasp, but with a brown and yellow striped body (as opposed to black and yellow), and up to 3.5cm in length. The sting of some tropical species can be fatal. — **stir up a hornet's nest** to cause a strong or hostile reaction. [from Anglo-Saxon *hyrnet*]

hornfels *noun Geol.* any of various hard fine-grained metamorphic rocks that originate from sedimentary rocks. [from German *Hornfels*, from *Horn*, horn + *Fels*, rock]

hornpipe *noun* **1** a lively, solo, sailor's jig. **2** the music for this dance.

horntail *noun* a large member of the wasp family, typically with a long cylindrical body without a distinct waist, black in colour and banded with yellow or red.

horny *adj.* (**hornier**, **horniest**) **1** of or like horn, especially in being hard. **2** *slang* sexually excited.

horological *adj.* **1** relating to horology. **2** measuring time.

horologist *noun* an expert in horology; a maker of clocks and watches.

horology *noun* the art of measuring time or making clocks and watches. [from Greek *hora*, hour + -LOGY]

horoscope *noun* **1** a description of a person's future based on the position of the stars and planets at the time of his or her birth. **2** a diagram showing the positions of the stars and planets at a particular moment in time, eg at the time of a person's birth. [from Greek *hora*, hour + *skopein*, to observe]

horrendous *adj.* causing great shock, fear, or terror; horrifying. [from Latin *horrere*, to shudder]

horrible *adj.* **1** causing horror, dread, or fear. **2** *colloq.* unpleasant. [from Latin *horribilis*]

⊟ DREADFUL, FRIGHTFUL, FEARFUL, TERRIBLE. **1** horrific, shocking, appalling, horrifying, terrifying, frightening, scary. **2** unpleasant, disagreeable, nasty, unkind, horrid, disgusting, revolting, offensive, ghastly, awful, abominable.

⧉ **2** pleasant, agreeable, lovely.

horribly *adv.* **1** in a horrible way. **2** badly, very: *the plot went horribly wrong.*

horrid *adj.* **1** revolting; detestable. **2** *colloq.* unpleasant; disagreeable. [from Latin *horridus*]

horrific *adj.* **1** causing fear, disgust, or horror; terrible. **2** *colloq.* very bad. [from Latin *horror*, horror + *facere*, to make]

⊟ SHOCKING, APPALLING, TERRIBLE. **1** horrifying, terrifying, frightening, scary, bloodcurdling, spine-chilling. **2** awful, dreadful, frightful, ghastly.

horrifically *adv.* in a horrific way.

horrify *verb* (**horrifies**, **horrified**) to shock greatly. [from Latin *horror*, horror + *facere*, to make]

⊟ shock, outrage, scandalize, appal, disgust, sicken, dismay, alarm, startle, scare, frighten, terrify.

⧉ please, delight.

horrifying *adj.* causing horror.

horror *noun* **1** great fear, loathing, or disgust. **2** great dislike. **3** a person or thing causing horror. **4** *colloq.* a bad or ridiculous person or thing. **5** (*attributive*) *said of literature, films, etc* based on horrifying or frightening themes. — **the horrors** *colloq.* a fit of anxiety and fear. [from Latin *horror*, a shudder with fear]

⊟ **1** shock, outrage, disgust, revulsion, repugnance, abhorrence, loathing, dismay, consternation, alarm, fright, fear, terror, panic, dread, apprehension.

⧉ **1** approval, delight.

horror-stricken or **horror-struck** *adj.* shocked; horrified.

hors d'oeuvre /ɔː ˈdɜːvrə/ a savoury appetizer served at the beginning of a meal. [from French *hors d'œuvre*]

horse *noun* **1** any of many domestic and wild breeds of a large hoofed mammal of the genus *Equus* belonging to the same family (Equidae) as asses and zebras, and having a slender head, a long neck covered with a mane of hair, and long legs. Horses are used in many countries for pulling loads, carrying goods, and for riding. **2** an adult male horse. **3** cavalry. **4** a piece of apparatus used for vaulting over and other gymnastic exercises. **5** (*also* **clothes-horse**) a frame on which clothes, etc are hung to dry. — **horse about** or **around** *colloq.* to fool about. **straight from the horse's mouth** directly from a well-informed and reliable source. [from Anglo-Saxon *hors*]

horseback *noun* — **on horseback** on the back of a horse.

horsebox *noun* a closed trailer fixed to or pulled by a motor vehicle and used for carrying horses.

horse chestnut SEE CHESTNUT 3.

horseflesh *noun* **1** the meat of a horse. **2** horses as a group.

horsefly *noun* (PL. **horseflies**) any of numerous species of large fly, the female of which sucks the blood of horses, cattle, deer, and other large mammals, including humans, inflicting painful bites, and using its sharp blade-like mouthparts to pierce the skin. Also called GADFLY.

horse laugh a loud, coarse laugh.

horseman or **horsewoman** *noun* **1** a rider. **2** a skilled rider.

⊟ **1** rider, cavalryman. **2** equestrian, jockey.

horsemanship *noun* the art of riding, training, and managing horses.

horseplay *noun* rough and noisy play.

⊟ skylarking, pranks, capers, high jinks, fun and games, rough-and-tumble, clowning, buffoonery, foolery, tomfoolery.

horsepower *noun* (ABBREV. **HP, hp**) the imperial unit of power, which in the SI system has been replaced by the watt. One horsepower is equal to 745.7 watts.

horseracing *noun* racing of horses against each other, each ridden by a jockey.

horseradish *noun* **1** a perennial plant (*Armoracia rusticana*), native to SE Europe and W Asia, widely cultivated for its thick white fleshy root, which has a strong flavour and is used to prepare a pungent seasoning. **2** a pungent seasoning prepared from the root of this plant, which is ground and mixed with vinegar to make a sauce usually eaten with beef.

horse sense plain good sense.

horseshoe *noun* **1** a piece of curved iron nailed to the bottom of a horse's hoof to protect the foot. **2** something in the shape of a horseshoe, especially as a symbol of good luck.

horsetail *noun* **1** the tail of a horse. **2** a primitive spore-bearing plant of the genus *Equisetum*, related to the ferns and clubmosses, and having a hollow green jointed stem bearing whorls of small scale-like leaves at regular intervals.

horse-trading *noun* hard bargaining.

horse trials a training competition combining the three main equestrian disciplines: dressage, showjumping, and cross-country.

horsewhip — *noun* a whip for encouraging horses. — *verb* (**horsewhipped, horsewhipping**) to whip, especially severely, and usually as a punishment.

horsewoman See HORSEMAN.

horsey or **horsy** *adj.* (**horsier, horsiest**) 1 of or relating to horses. 2 like a horse. 3 *Brit. colloq.* very interested in or devoted to horses.

hortative or **hortatory** *adj.* encouraging. [from Latin *hortari*, to incite to action]

horticultural *adj.* relating to or involving horticulture.

horticulture *noun* the intensive cultivation of fruit, vegetables, flowers, and ornamental shrubs, usually conducted on a smaller scale than agriculture. [from Latin *hortus*, garden + *cultura*, cultivation]

horticulturist *noun Bot.* a person who specializes in horticulture; an expert gardener.

hosanna *noun, interj.* a shout of adoration or praise to God. [from Hebrew *hoshiah nna*, save now, I pray]

hose — *noun* 1 (*also* **hosepipe**) a flexible tube for directing water, eg for watering plants. 2 (*as pl.*) stockings, socks, and tights. 3 *Hist.* breeches. — *verb* (**hose something down**) to direct water at or clean with a hose. [from Anglo-Saxon *hosa*]

hosepipe *noun* a flexible tube for directing water, eg for watering plants.

hosier *noun* a person who makes or sells hosiery.

hosiery /'hoʊzɪərɪ/ *noun* stockings, socks, tights and knitted underwear. [from HOSE]

hospice /'hɒspɪs/ *noun* 1 an institution that specializes in the care of the terminally ill and provides support for their families. 2 *old use* a house offering lodging for travellers, especially one kept by a religious order. [from Latin *hospes*, guest]

hospitable *adj.* showing kindness to guests or strangers. [from Latin *hospes*, guest]

■ welcoming, receptive, cordial, amicable, congenial, convivial, friendly, sociable, kind, gracious, generous, liberal.

ᴇ inhospitable, hostile, unfriendly.

hospital *noun* an institution, staffed by doctors and nurses, for the treatment and care of people who are sick or injured, either as *in-patients*, who receive treatment while residing at the hospital, or as *out-patients*, who attend clinics in various areas of speciality. Some hospitals cater for the needs of a single category of patient, eg psychiatric, maternity, or paediatric hospitals. General hospitals accept all categories of patient, but treat them in specialized wards or units. [from Latin *hospes*, guest]

hospitality *noun* a friendly welcome for guests or strangers, which usually includes offering them food and drink. [from Latin *hospes*, guest]

■ welcome, accommodation, entertainment, conviviality, friendliness, sociability, warmth, kindness, generosity, open-handedness.

ᴇ hostility, unfriendliness.

hospitalization or **hospitalisation** *noun* admission of a patient into hospital.

hospitalize or **hospitalise** *verb* to admit or send (a person) into a hospital for treatment.

hospitaller *noun* a member of a religious order which does work for charity, especially in hospitals. [from Latin *hospes*, guest]

hospital trust a self-governing trust set up with national funding to run a hospital or group of hospitals within the National Health Service.

host[1] — *noun* 1 a person who receives and entertains guests or strangers in his or her own home. 2 *old use* an innkeeper. 3 *Biol.* a plant or animal on which a parasite lives and feeds for all or part of its life. 4 a person who introduces performers, etc on a television or radio show. 5 *Medicine* the recipient of a tissue graft or organ transplant. 6 *Comput.* a computer in control of a number of computers in a network. — *verb* to act as a host to (people) or be the host of (an event or programme). [from Latin *hospes*, guest]

■ *noun* 2 publican, innkeeper, landlord, proprietor. 4 compère, master of ceremonies, presenter, announcer, anchorman, anchorwoman, linkman. *verb* present, introduce, compère.

host[2] *noun* 1 a very large number. 2 *old use* an army. [from Latin *hostis*, enemy]

■ 1 multitude, myriad, array, horde, crowd, throng, swarm.

host[3] *noun* the bread or wafer used in a Holy Communion service. [from Latin *hostia*, victim]

hosta /'hɒstə/ *noun* a perennial plant of the genus *Hosta*, native to China and Japan, and having conspicuous lance-shaped or broadly oval leaves, often variegated or bluish in colour, and spikes of tubular white or violet flowers. [named after the Australian botanist N T Host]

hostage *noun* a person who is held prisoner as a guarantee that demands, the conditions of an agreement, etc will be carried out. [from Latin *obses*]

■ prisoner, captive, pawn, surety, security, pledge.

hostel *noun* 1 a building which provides overnight accommodation as a charity, especially for the homeless. 2 a residence for students or nurses. 3 a youth hostel. 4 *old use* an inn. [from Old French *hostel*, from Latin *hospes*, guest]

■ 1 *slang* doss-house, boarding-house, guesthouse. 2 residence, home. 4 inn, hotel.

hostelry *noun* (PL. **hostelries**) *old use, facetious* an inn or public house.

hostess *noun* 1 a female host. 2 a woman employed to act as a man's companion for the evening at a night club. 3 an air hostess.

hostile *adj.* 1 unfriendly; aggressive. 2 of or belonging to an enemy. 3 (**hostile to something**) strongly opposed to it. [from Latin *hostis*, enemy]

■ 1 unfriendly, inimical, antagonistic, aggressive, belligerent, warlike, ill-disposed, unsympathetic, inhospitable, unfavourable.

ᴇ 1 friendly, welcoming, favourable.

hostility *noun* (PL. **hostilities**) 1 unfriendliness; opposition; aggression. 2 (**hostilities**) acts of war; battles.

■ 1 unfriendliness, antagonism, opposition, aggression, belligerence, enmity, animosity, ill-will, malice, hate, hatred, dislike, aversion. 2 war, warfare, battles, fighting, conflict, strife, bloodshed.

ᴇ 1 friendliness, friendship. 2 peace.

hot — *adj.* (**hotter, hottest**) 1 having a relatively high temperature, or a higher temperature than is normal or desirable. 2 producing or giving off heat. 3 highly radioactive. 4 *said of an electrical conductor or terminal* live or connected. 5 *said of food* causing a burning sensation on the tongue; spicy. 6 *said of a metal-working process* occurring at a high temperature so that metal can be rolled, shaped, etc, while it is soft. 7 easily made angry; excitable. 8 feeling intense emotion or sexual desire. **9** *said of a contest or fight* intense; animated. **10** *said of news* recent; fresh. **11** strongly favoured: *a hot favourite.* **12** *said of music* having strong and exciting rhythms. **13** *said of red colours* bright and fiery. **14** *slang, said of goods* stolen, especially recently stolen. **15** *said of a scent in hunting* fresh and strong, suggesting the quarry is not far ahead. **16** *slang, said of information* up to date and reliable: *a hot tip.* **17** *colloq., said of a situation* difficult, unpleasant, or dangerous: *make life hot for him.* **18** in a game, etc, very close to guessing correctly or finding the thing sought. — *adv.* hotly. — *verb* (**hotted, hotting**) — **hot up** or **hot something up** to become or make gradually hotter, more exciting, more dangerous, etc. **have** or **get the hots for someone** *coarse slang* to have a strong sexual desire for them. **hot and bothered** *colloq.* anxious and confused. **hot on something** very interested in or well informed about it. **in hot pursuit** chasing as fast or as closely as one can. [from Anglo-Saxon *hat*]

⬛ *adj.* **1** warm, heated, fiery, burning, scalding, blistering, scorching, roasting, baking, boiling, steaming, sizzling, sweltering, sultry, torrid, tropical. **5** spicy, peppery, piquant, sharp, pungent, strong.
🔲 *adj.* **1** cold, cool. **5** mild, bland.

hot air *colloq.* empty or boastful talk, promises that will not be kept, etc.

hotbed *noun* a place which allows something, especially something bad, to grow quickly: *a hotbed of discontent.*

hot-blooded *adj.* having strong, especially sexual, feelings.

hot button *Politics* a sensitive issue; an emotive topic.

hotchpotch *noun* **1** a confused mass or jumble. **2** a mutton stew with many different vegetables in it. [from Old French *hochepot*, from *hocher*, to shake + *pot*, pot]

⬛ **1** mishmash, medley, miscellany, collection, mixture, jumble.

hot cross bun a fruit bun marked with a cross on top, traditionally eaten on Good Friday.

hot desking the business practice of having no permanent desks for employees, who instead occupy whichever desk is available on that day.

hot dog a hot sausage in a long, soft, bread roll.

hotel *noun* a large house or building providing accommodation, meals, and other services, usually with a high level of comfort, to visitors for payment. [from Old French *hostel*, hostel, from Latin *hospes*, guest]

⬛ boarding-house, guesthouse, motel, inn, hostel.

hotelier /hoʊˈtɛljeɪ/ *noun* a person who owns or manages a hotel.

hotfoot *colloq.* — *adv.* in haste. — *verb* (**hotfoot it**) to rush.

hothead *noun* a person who is easily made angry.

hotheaded *adj.* easily angered, impetuous.

⬛ fiery, volatile, hot-tempered, quick-tempered, headstrong, impetuous, impulsive, hasty, rash, reckless.
🔲 cool, calm.

hothouse — *noun* **1** a greenhouse in which the temperature is maintained at a fixed and relatively high level for the cultivation of tropical or tender plants, or for growing plants out of season. **2** (*attributive*) *said of a plant* suitable for growing in a greenhouse. — *verb* to subject (a young child) to intensive education to boost its intellectual or artistic development.

⬛ *noun* **1** greenhouse, glasshouse, conservatory, orangery, vinery.

hot key *Comput.* a key which activates a terminate-and-stay-resident program when pressed, either alone or in combination with other keys.

hot line **1** a direct exclusive telephone line, especially for use in emergencies by political leaders. **2** an emergency telephone number for inquiries about a particular incident or accident.

hotly *adv.* **1** with great heat. **2** excitedly, keenly, passionately.

hot money money transferred from one country to another to take advantage of exchange rates and trading conditions, and make a quick profit.

HOTOL *abbrev.* horizontal take-off and landing.

hotplate *noun* **1** the flat top surface of a cooker on which food is cooked and kept warm. **2** a portable heated metal surface for keeping food, dishes, etc hot.

hotpot *noun* meat and vegetables, with a layer of sliced potato on top, cooked slowly in a closed pot.

hot potato *colloq.* a difficult problem or situation.

hot rod a motor car stripped of all non-essential parts and having a greatly modified engine to give high power and speed.

hot seat **1** *colloq.* an uncomfortable or difficult position. **2** *North Amer. slang* the electric chair.

hot spot **1** *colloq.* an area where there is likely to be trouble, especially political or military. **2** *Geol.* a heat source deep within the Earth's mantle, associated with an area of high volcanic activity. **3** a small region in a body or in space with a higher temperature, a higher level of radioactivity, or a higher concentration of a harmful chemical or mineral than its surroundings.

hot spring *Geol.* a spring of hot or warm groundwater that emerges from the Earth's surface and often contains dissolved minerals or sulphur. Very hot springs emerge as geysers, and are sometimes used as sources of geothermal energy.

hot stuff *colloq.* **1** a person who has outstanding ability. **2** a person who is sexually exciting.

hot-tempered *adj.* quick to get angry.

Hottentot *noun* **1** a member of a pale-brown-skinned race of people in SW Africa. **2** the language spoken by this people. [from Afrikaans *Hottentot*]

hotting *noun slang* the performing of stunts and skilful manoeuvres at high speed in a stolen car.

hot water *colloq.* trouble; bother: *get into hot water.*

hot-water bottle a rubber container for hot water, used to warm beds.

hot-wire *verb slang* to restart (a vehicle engine) by touching together electrical wires, rather than using the ignition switch.

hound — *noun* **1** (*often in compounds*) any of various breeds of domestic dog developed for hunting, especially those which track by scent: *wolfhound.* **2** sometimes used to refer to any hunting dog, including those which track by sight, eg greyhounds, borzois. **3** (**hounds**) a pack of foxhounds. **4** *colloq.* a man one despises or feels contempt for. — *verb* to chase or bother relentlessly. [from Anglo-Saxon *hund*]

⬛ *verb* chase, pursue, hunt, drive, nag, pester, badger, harry, harass, persecute.

hour *noun* **1** a unit of time equal to 60 minutes or 3600 seconds. There are 24 hours in one calendar day. **2** any of the points on a clock or watch that shows the hour. **3** a point in time: *an early hour.* **4** the time allowed or fixed for some activity: *office hours.* **5** the distance travelled in an hour: *two hours away from the airport.* **6** a special occasion: *his finest hour.* **7** a time for action: *the hour has come.* **8** (**hours** or **canonical hours**) *Relig.* seven set times for prayer during the day and night, or the prayers to be said at these times. — **after hours** after closing-time. **at all hours** at irregular times, especially late at night. **out of hours** before or after usual working hours. [from Greek *hora*]

hourglass — *noun* an instrument that measures time in hours, consisting of one glass container on top of and joined to another by a narrow glass tube, filled with as much sand as will pass from one container into the other in the space of one hour. — *adj.* curving in at the waist or middle like an hourglass.

houri / ˈhʊərɪ/ *noun* a beautiful young woman, especially in the Muslim Paradise. [from Arabic *haura*, gazelle-eyed]

hourly — *adj.* 1 happening or done every hour. 2 measured by the hour. 3 frequent; continual: *live in hourly fear of discovery.* — *adv.* 1 every hour. 2 at any hour: *expect news hourly.* 3 by the hour. 4 frequently.

house — *noun* 1 a building in which people, especially a single family, live. 2 the people living in such a building. 3 (*in compounds*) a building used for a particular purpose: *an opera-house.* 4 (**House**) the body of people who govern a country and make laws, or the place where they meet. 5 a business firm: *a publishing house.* 6 the audience in a theatre, a theatre, or a performance given there. 7 a family, especially an important or noble one: *the House of Hanover.* 8 *Astrol.* one of the twelve divisions of the heavens. 9 *Brit.* one of several divisions of pupils at a large school. 10 a building in which students or members of a religious community live. 11 a style of dance music produced electronically, incorporating edited fragments of other recordings. — *verb* 1 to provide with a house or similar shelter. 2 to store. 3 to protect (a part) by covering. — **bring the house down** *colloq.* to produce loud applause in a theatre. **keep house** to manage a household. **like a house on fire** *colloq.* 1 very well. 2 very quickly. **on the house** *said of food, drink, etc* free; paid for by the manager or owner. **put** or **set one's house in order** to organize or settle one's affairs. [from Anglo-Saxon *hus*]

⊟ *noun* 1 building, dwelling, residence, home. 2 household, family. 5 firm, company, corporation, association, organization, establishment, business. 7 dynasty, family, clan, tribe. *verb* 1 lodge, quarter, billet, board, accommodate, put up, take in, shelter, harbour. 2 store, keep, place, hold, contain. 3 protect, cover, sheathe, case.

Types of house include: semi-detached, *colloq.* semi, detached, terraced, town-house, council house, cottage, thatched cottage, *colloq.* prefab, pied-à-terre, bungalow, chalet bungalow; flat, bedsit, apartment, studio, maisonette, penthouse, grannyflat, *US* duplex, *US* condominium; manor, hall, lodge, grange, villa, mansion, rectory, vicarage, parsonage, manse, croft, farmhouse, homestead, ranchhouse, chalet, log cabin, shack, shanty, hut, igloo, hacienda.

house agent a person who arranges the buying, selling, or renting of houses.

house arrest confinement in one's own home rather than in prison.

houseboat *noun* a boat, usually with a flat bottom and usually stationary, which is built to be lived in.

housebound *adj.* unable to leave one's house because of illness, young children, etc.

housebreaker *noun* a person who breaks into a house to steal.

housebreaking *noun* unlawful breaking into a building to steal.

housecoat *noun* a woman's long, loose garment like a dressing-gown, worn at home.

housefly *noun* any of various small dark flies that commonly live in and around human dwellings, especially the common housefly, distributed worldwide, which has sponge-like mouthparts adapted for sucking up surface liquids.

household — *noun* the people who live together in a house and make up a family. — *adj.* of the house or family living there.

⊟ *noun* family, family circle, house, home, ménage,

establishment, set-up. *adj.* domestic, home, family, everyday, common, ordinary, plain.

householder *noun* 1 the person who owns a house or pays the rent for it. 2 the head of a family.

⊟ 1 resident, tenant, occupier, occupant, owner, freeholder, leaseholder, proprietor, landlord, landlady.

household name or **household word** a name or saying known to everyone.

house husband a husband who does the work usually done by a housewife.

housekeeper *noun* a person who is paid to look after the management of a usually large house and household.

housekeeping *noun* 1 the management of a house and household. 2 money set aside to pay for the expenses of running a house.

house lights the lights in the part of a cinema, theatre, etc where people sit.

housemaid *noun* a maid employed to keep a house clean and tidy.

housemaid's knee inflammation and swelling of a small fluid-filled sac of fibrous tissue, known as the *bursa*, in front of the kneecap, often resulting from prolonged kneeling on a hard surface.

houseman *noun* a recent graduate in medicine holding a junior resident post in a hospital.

house martin a bird belonging to the swallow family, that breeds in Europe and Asia, and has a streamlined body, glossy bluish-black upper parts, white underparts, a distinctive white rump, and a short forked black tail. It is agile in flight, and catches flying insects in the wide gape of its bill.

housemaster or **housemistress** *noun* in Britain, a teacher in charge of a house in a school, especially a boarding-school.

House of Commons in the UK, the lower elected assembly in parliament, or the building where this meets.

House of Keys in the Isle of Man, the elected chamber of the Manx parliament, the Tynwald.

House of Lords in the UK, the upper assembly in parliament, made up of peers and bishops.

house party a group of guests staying in a country house for several days.

house-proud *adj.* taking a lot of, often too much, pride in the condition and appearance of one's house.

housetop *noun* (*usually* **housetops**) the roofs of houses, especially seen as a row against the skyline. — **shout something from the housetops** to announce it loudly and publicly.

housetrain *verb* to train (a pet) to be clean in the house and to urinate and defecate outside or in a special tray, etc.

house-warming *noun* a party given to celebrate moving into a new house.

housewife *noun* 1 a woman who looks after her house, her husband, and her family, and who sometimes does not have a job outside the home. 2 a pocket sewing-kit.

housewifely *adj.* 1 thrifty and neat and tidy. 2 like or suitable for a housewife.

housework *noun* the work of keeping a house clean and tidy.

housing *noun* 1 houses as a group. 2 the act or job of providing housing for people. 3 the hard cover round a machine.

⊟ 1 accommodation, houses, homes, dwellings, habitation, shelter. 3 covering, cover, sheath, casing, case, container, holder.

hove See HEAVE.

hovel *noun* a small, dirty, dismal dwelling. [from Middle English *hovell*]

▣ shack, shanty, cabin, hut, shed, *colloq.* dump, *colloq.* hole.

hover — *verb intrans.* (**hovered, hovering**) **1** *said of a bird, helicopter, etc* to remain in the air without moving in any direction. **2** to move around while still remaining near a person or thing. **3** (*often* **hover between**) to be undecided. — *noun* an act or state of hovering or waiting to make a decision. [from Middle English *hoveren*]

▣ *verb* **1** hang, float, drift, fly, flutter, flap. **2** linger, hang about. **3** hesitate, waver, fluctuate, seesaw.

hovercraft *noun* a vehicle that is able to move over land or water, supported by a cushion of air.

hoverfly *noun* a medium to large fly often found hovering over flowers. The adults resemble wasps, and feed on pollen and nectar.

how — *adv.* **1** in what way; by what means: *how did it happen?* **2** to what extent: *how old is he?* **3** in what condition, especially of health: *how is she feeling now?* **4** to what extent is something good, successful, etc: *how was your holiday?* **5** using whatever means are necessary: *do it how best you can.* — *conj. colloq.* that: *told me how he'd done it on his own.* — *noun* a manner or means of doing something: *the how and why.* — **and how** *colloq.* very much indeed. **how about?** would you like?; what do you think of?: *how about another piece of cake?* **how come?** *colloq.* for what reason? **how do you do?** a formal greeting, especially to a person one is meeting for the first time. **how's that? 1** what is your opinion of that? **2** an appeal to the umpire in cricket to give the batsman out. [from Anglo-Saxon *hu*]

howdah /ˈhaʊdə/ *noun* a seat, usually with a sun-shade, used for riding on an elephant's back. [from Arabic *hawdaj*]

howdy *interj. North Amer. slang* hello. [a corrupt form of *how do you do?*]

however *adv.* **1** in spite of that; nevertheless. **2** *colloq.*, *especially implying surprise* in what way?; by what means?: *however did you do that?* **3** by whatever means: *do it however you want to.* **4** to no matter what extent: *you must finish this however long it takes.* [from Middle English]

▣ *adv.* **1** nevertheless, nonetheless, still, yet, even so, notwithstanding, though, anyhow.

howitzer /ˈhaʊɪtsə(r)/ *noun* a short heavy gun which fires shells high in the air. [from Czech *houfnice*, sling, catapult]

howl — *noun* **1** the long, loud, sad cry of a wolf or dog. **2** a long, loud cry made eg by the wind. **3** a cry of pain or distress. **4** a loud yell of laughter. — *verb* **1** (*intrans.*) to make a long, loud, sad cry or similar wailing noise. **2** (*intrans.*) to cry or laugh loudly. **3** to shout or shriek (instructions, orders, etc). — **howl someone down** to prevent a speaker from being heard by shouting loudly and angrily. [from Middle English *houlen*]

▣ *noun* **1** wail, cry, bay, yelp. **2** wail, cry, roar, moan, groan. **3** wail, cry, shriek, scream, yell, yelp, moan, groan. **4** shriek, scream, shout, yell, roar, bellow, hoot. *verb* CRY. **1** wail, bay, yelp, moan, groan. **2** wail, moan, groan, scream, roar, hoot. **3** shout, shriek, scream, yell, roar, bellow.

howler *noun colloq.* a glaring mistake.

howler monkey the largest of the S American monkeys, having black, brown, or reddish fur, and so called because it often howls at dawn in order to warn others off its territory.

howling *adj. colloq.* very great.

howsoever *adv.* in whatever way; to whatever extent. [from Middle English]

howzat /haʊˈzat/ *interj.* an appeal to the umpire in cricket to give the batsman out. [a contraction of *how's that?*]

hoy *interj.* a word used to attract someone's attention. [a variant of HEY]

hoyden *noun* a wild, lively girl. [from Dutch *heyden*, boor]

hoydenish *adj.* like a hoyden; boisterous.

HP or **hp** *abbrev.* **1** high pressure. **2** *Brit.* hire purchase. **3** horsepower.

HQ or **hq** *abbrev.* headquarters.

hr *abbrev.* hour.

HRH *abbrev.* His or Her Royal Highness.

HRT *abbrev.* hormone replacement therapy.

HTML *abbrev. Comput.* hypertext mark-up language, the language used to create World Wide Web documents.

HTTP *abbrev. Comput.* hypertext transfer protocol, the system by which hypertext documents are transferred over the Internet.

hub *noun* **1** the cylindrical centre of a wheel, propeller, fan, or other circular rotating part, to which the axle, blades, spokes, etc, are attached. **2** the main point of activity, interest, etc. [perhaps a variant of HOB]

▣ **2** centre, middle, focus, focal point, axis, pivot, linchpin, nerve centre, core, heart.

hubble-bubble *noun* **1** a bubbling sound. **2** confusion; confused talk. **3** a simple type of hookah. [a fanciful elaboration of BUBBLE]

Hubble's constant or **Hubble constant** *Astron.* a constant that describes the rate at which the universe is expanding by relating the speed at which a galaxy is moving away from us to its distance. [named after the US astronomer Edwin Hubble]

Hubble's law *Astron.* the law which states that the speed at which a galaxy is moving away increases as it becomes more distant (as measured by the red shift), due to the uniform expansion of the universe.

Hubble space telescope an optical telescope that was launched into orbit around the Earth in Apr 1990 in the space shuttle *Discovery*, as a joint project of the European Space Agency and NASA.

hubbub *noun* **1** a confused noise of many sounds, especially voices. **2** uproar. [probably of Irish origin]

▣ **1** noise, racket, din, clamour, commotion, disturbance. **2** uproar, hullabaloo, rumpus, confusion, disorder, tumult, hurly-burly, chaos, pandemonium.
▣ **1** peace, quiet.

hubby *noun* (PL. **hubbies**) *colloq.* a husband. [abbreviation]

hub-cap *noun* the metal cover over the hub of a wheel.

hubris /ˈhjuːbrɪs/ *noun* arrogance or over-confidence, especially when likely to end in disaster or ruin. [from Greek *hybris*]

huckleberry *noun Bot.* **1** either of two species of plant belonging to the genus *Gaylussacia*, native to woodlands and swamps of eastern N America. **2** the round fruit of this plant, which is either bluish or black, depending on the species. **3** sometimes used incorrectly to refer to blueberry.

huckster *noun* **1** *old use* a street trader. **2** an aggressive seller. [from Middle English *huccstere*]

huddle — *verb* **1** *intrans.* (**huddle together** or **up**) to heap or crowd together closely. **2** *intrans.* to sit curled up. **3** to curl (oneself) up. — *noun* **1** a confused mass or crowd. **2** a secret or private conference: *go into a huddle.* [probably related to HIDE[1]]

▣ *verb* **1** cluster, converge, meet, gather, congregate, flock, crowd, throng, press, snuggle, nestle. *noun* **1** mass, crowd, muddle, jumble, knot, clump, cluster. **2** conclave, conference, meeting.
▣ *verb* **1** disperse.

hue¹ *noun* **1** a colour or shade. **2** the feature of a colour which makes it different from other colours. **3** aspect. [from Anglo-Saxon *hiw*]

⊟ **1** colour, shade, tint, dye, tinge, tone, nuance. **3** aspect, light, complexion.

hue² *noun* — **hue and cry** a loud public protest. [from Old French *huer*]

huff — *noun* a fit of anger or annoyance: *in a huff.* — *verb* **1** *intrans.* to blow or puff loudly. **2** *trans., intrans.* to give or take offence. **3** *Draughts* to remove an opponent's man for failing to capture one's own man. — **huffing and puffing** loud empty threats. [imitative]

⊟ *noun* pique, mood, bad mood, temper, bad temper, anger, rage.

huffily *adv.* in a huffy way.

huffiness *noun* being huffy.

huffy or **huffish** *adj.* (**huffier, huffiest**) **1** offended. **2** easily offended; touchy.

hug — *verb* (**hugged, hugging**) **1** to hold tightly in one's arms, especially to show love. **2** to keep close to: *a ship hugging the shore.* **3** to hold (a belief, etc) very firmly. — *noun* a tight grasp with the arms, especially to show love. [perhaps from Norse *hugga*, to soothe]

⊟ *verb* **1** embrace, cuddle, squeeze, enfold, hold, clasp, clutch. *noun* embrace, cuddle, squeeze, clasp, hold, grasp, clinch.

huge *adj.* very large. [from Old French *ahuge*]

⊟ immense, vast, enormous, massive, colossal, titanic, giant, gigantic, mammoth, monumental, *colloq.* seismic, tremendous, great, big, large, bulky, unwieldy.
🗲 tiny, minute.

hugely *adv.* very; very much.

hugger-mugger — *noun* **1** secrecy. **2** confusion. — *adj., adv.* **1** secret; in secret. **2** confused; in confusion or disorder. [from Middle English *hokeren*, to hoard]

Huguenot /ˈhjuːɡənəʊ/ *Hist.* — *noun* one of the French Calvinist Protestants whose political rivalry with Catholics led to the French Wars of Religion (1562–98). — *adj.* relating to the Huguenots. [from French *Huguenot*]

huh *interj. colloq.* an expression of disgust, disbelief or inquiry. [imitative]

hula /ˈhuːlə/ *noun* a Hawaiian dance in which the dancer sways his or her hips and moves his or her arms gracefully. [from Hawaiian *hula*]

hulk *noun* **1** the body of an old ship from which everything has been taken away. **2** a ship which is or looks difficult to steer. **3** *derog. colloq.* a large, awkward person or thing. **4** *Hist.* the body of an old ship used as a prison. [from Anglo-Saxon *hulc*]

hulking *adj. derog. colloq.* large and awkward.

⊟ large, heavy, bulky, unwieldy, awkward, ungainly.
🗲 small, delicate.

hull¹ — *noun* the frame or body of a ship or airship. — *verb* to pierce the hull of. [perhaps from HULL²]

⊟ *noun* body, frame, framework, structure.

hull² — *noun* **1** the (often hard) outer covering or husk of a fruit or seed. **2** the calyx at the base of certain fruits, such as the strawberry and raspberry. **3** the floating body of a ship, not including the masts, sails, and rigging. **4** the outer casing of a guided missile, rocket, etc. — *verb* to remove

(the outer casing) from a fruit or seed. [from Anglo-Saxon *hulu*, husk]

hullabaloo /hʌləbəˈluː/ *noun colloq.* an uproar. [from Scot. *baloo*, lullaby]

⊟ fuss, palaver, *colloq.* to-do, uproar, outcry, furore, hue and cry, pandemonium, rumpus, disturbance, commotion, hubbub.
🗲 calm, peace.

hullo see HELLO.

hum — *verb* (**hummed, humming**) **1** *intrans.* to make a low, steady murmuring sound like a bee. **2** *trans., intrans.* to sing (a tune) with one's mouth shut. **3** *intrans.* to speak indistinctly or stammer, especially through embarrassment. **4** *intrans. colloq.* to be full of activity. **5** *intrans. slang* to give off an unpleasant smell. — *noun* **1** a humming sound. **2** *slang* a bad smell. — *interj.* an expression of hesitation. — **hum and haw** to make sounds which express doubt, uncertainty, or hesitation; to hesitate.

⊟ *verb* **1** buzz, whirr, purr, drone, thrum. **3** murmur, mumble. **4** throb, pulse. *noun* **1** buzz, whirr, purr, drone, murmur, mumble.

human — *adj.* **1** of or belonging to people. **2** having or showing the qualities, especially the weaknesses, of people as opposed to God, animals, or machines. **3** having the better qualities of people, eg in being kind, thoughtful, etc. — *noun* a human being. [from Latin *humanus*, from *homo*, man]

⊟ *adj.* **2** mortal, fallible, susceptible, reasonable, rational. **3** kind, considerate, thoughtful, understanding, humane, compassionate. *noun* human being, mortal, man, woman, child, person, individual, body, soul, homo sapiens.
🗲 *adj.* **3** inhuman.

human being *noun* a person.

humane *adj.* **1** kind; sympathetic. **2** *said of a killing* done with as little pain and suffering as possible. **3** *said of a branch of learning* likely to civilize or make more elegant. [a variant of HUMAN]

⊟ **1** kind, compassionate, sympathetic, understanding, kind-hearted, good-natured, gentle, tender, mild, lenient, merciful, forgiving, kindly, benevolent, charitable, humanitarian.
🗲 **1** inhumane, cruel.

humanism *noun* a non-religious system of thought which holds that humans are responsible and intelligent beings, capable by themselves of solving the problems of the world and deciding what is or is not correct moral behaviour.

humanist — *noun* **1** a follower of humanism. **2** *Hist.* a student of Greek and Roman culture during the Renaissance. — *adj.* of humanism or humanists.

humanistic *adj.* relating to or involving humanism.

humanitarian — *adj.* concerned about improving, or likely to improve, people's lives: *humanitarian aid for the war-zone.* — *noun* a person who tries to improve the quality of people's lives by means of reform, charity, etc.

⊟ *adj.* benevolent, charitable, philanthropic, public-spirited, altruistic, unselfish, compassionate, humane. *noun* philanthropist, benefactor, good Samaritan, do-gooder, altruist.
🗲 *adj.* selfish, self-seeking. *noun* egoist, self-seeker.

humanitarianism *noun* humanitarian principles, system, or practice.

humanity *noun* (PL. **humanities**) **1** the human race. **2** the nature of human beings. **3** the qualities of human beings, especially in being kind or showing mercy. **4 (humanities)** subjects involving the study of human culture, especially language, literature, and philosophy.

⊟ **1** human race, humankind, mankind, womankind, people. **3** humaneness, kindness, compassion, fellow feeling, sympathy, understanding, mercy, benevolence, generosity, goodwill.
⊟ **3** inhumanity.

humanization or **humanisation** *noun* the act or process of humanizing.

humanize or **humanise** *verb* to make more caring, more thoughtful, less brutal, etc.

⊟ civilize, cultivate, educate, enlighten, edify, improve, better, polish, refine, domesticate, tame.

humankind *noun* human beings as a race.

humanly *adv.* within human power.

humanoid — *noun* an animal or machine with human characteristics. — *adj.*, *said of an animal or machine* having human characteristics. [from HUMAN + -*oid*, from Greek *eidos*, form]

human resources 1 the workforce of an organization. **2** a department within an organization dealing with matters concerning employees.

human rights the rights of every person to justice and freedom.

human shield *Mil.* a non-combatant person or group of people deployed in strategic sites during hostilities, in order to deter enemy attack on those sites.

humble ¹ — *adj.* **1** having a low opinion of oneself and one's abilities, etc; not proud. **2** having a low position in society. **3** lowly; modest. — *verb* to make humble, modest, or of less importance. [from Latin *humilis*, low]

⊟ *adj.* **1** meek, submissive, unassertive, self-effacing, modest, polite, respectful, deferential, servile, subservient, sycophantic, obsequious. **2** lowly, low, mean, insignificant, unimportant. **3** lowly, low, mean, ordinary, plain, simple, modest, unassuming, unpretentious, unostentatious. *verb* bring down, lower, abase, demean, discredit, disgrace, shame, humiliate, mortify, chasten, crush, deflate, subdue.
⊟ *adj.* **1** proud, haughty, arrogant. **2** important. **3** pretentious. *verb* exalt.

humble ² *noun* — **eat humble pie** to be forced to make a humble apology. [a variant of *numbles*, the offal of a deer]

humbly *adv.* in a humble way.

humbug *noun* **1** a trick; something done to deceive. **2** nonsense; rubbish. **3** a person who pretends to be something he or she is not. **4** *Brit.* a hard, stripy, peppermint-flavoured sweet.

⊟ **1** trick, hoax, deception, deceit, trickery, pretence, sham, fraud, swindle, *colloq.* con. **2** nonsense, rubbish, *slang* baloney, *colloq.* bunkum, claptrap, *colloq.* eyewash, bluff, cant, hypocrisy. **3** fraud, charlatan, cheat, swindler, *colloq.* con man.

humdinger *noun slang* an exceptionally good person or thing. [a fanciful elaboration of HUM + DING]

humdrum *adj.* dull; ordinary. [probably from HUM]

⊟ boring, tedious, monotonous, routine, dull, dreary, uninteresting, uneventful, ordinary, mundane, everyday, commonplace.
⊟ lively, unusual, exceptional.

humeral *adj.* of or relating to the humerus.

humerus *noun* (PL. **humeri**) **1** the bone of the upper arm, extending from the shoulder to the elbow in humans. **2** the corresponding bone in the front limb of four-limbed vertebrates. [from Latin *umerus*, shoulder]

humid *adj.* damp; moist. [from Latin *humidus*]

⊟ damp, moist, dank, clammy, sticky, muggy, sultry, steamy.
⊟ dry.

humidifier *noun* a device for adding moisture to dry air in order to increase the humidity or maintain it at a desirable level, especially in a home or office. Most humidifiers work by trickling water over a material with a large surface area, enabling the maximum volume of water to come into contact with the dry air and evaporate into it.

humidify *verb* (**humidifies**, **humidified**) to make (the air or atmosphere) damp or humid.

humidity *noun* **1** *Meteorol.* a measure of the amount of water vapour in the atmosphere, usually expressed as a percentage. **2** dampness.

humiliate *verb* to make (someone) feel ashamed or look foolish, especially in the presence of others. [from Latin *humilis*, humble]

⊟ mortify, embarrass, confound, crush, deflate, chasten, shame, disgrace, discredit, degrade, demean, humble, bring down, lower.
⊟ dignify, exalt.

humiliating *adj.* shaming, humbling, embarrassing.

humiliation *noun* **1** the act of humiliating. **2** being humiliated.

⊟ MORTIFICATION, EMBARRASSMENT, DISGRACE, ABASEMENT. **1** *colloq.* put-down, snub, rebuff, affront. **2** shame, dishonour, ignominy.
⊟ EXALTATION.

humility *noun* **1** the state or quality of being humble. **2** lowliness of mind; modesty. [from Latin *humilis*, humble]

⊟ **1** humbleness, meekness, submissiveness, deference, self-abasement, servility. **2** lowliness, modesty, unpretentiousness.
⊟ PRIDE, ARROGANCE. **1** assertiveness.

hummingbird *noun* a small bird with brilliant plumage, often with iridescent patches, found mainly in the forests of S America, and so called because its wings beat so rapidly that they produce a low humming sound.

hummock *noun* a low hill.

hummus or **hoummos** or **houmus** /ˈhʊməs/ *noun* a Middle Eastern hors d'oeuvre or dip consisting of puréed cooked chickpeas and tahini paste, flavoured with lemon juice and garlic. [from Turkish *humus*]

humongous or **humungous** /hjuːˈmʌŋɡəs/ *adj. colloq.* huge, enormous. [perhaps a mixture of HUGE and MONSTROUS]

humorist *noun* a person who writes or tells humorous stories, jokes, etc.

⊟ wit, satirist, comedian, comic, joker, wag, jester, clown.

humorous *adj.* containing humour; funny; amusing.

⊟ funny, amusing, comic, entertaining, witty, satirical, jocular, facetious, playful, waggish, droll, whimsical, comical, farcical, zany, ludicrous, absurd, hilarious, side-splitting.
⊟ serious, humourless.

humour — *noun* **1** the quality of being amusing. **2** the ability to amuse or be amused. **3** a state of mind: *good humour.* **4** writing, plays, speech, etc that are amusing or funny. **5** any of various fluids in the body. **6** *Hist.* any of the four bodily fluids (blood, choler, melancholy, and phlegm) which were formerly believed to govern a person's physical health and character. — *verb* to please (someone) by doing what they wish. [from Latin *humor*]

- ◻ *noun* **1** wit, drollery, facetiousness, comedy, amusement, fun. **3** mood, temper, frame of mind, spirits, disposition, temperament. **4** comedy, satire, farce, jokes, jesting, badinage, repartee. *verb* please, comply with, go along with, accommodate, gratify, indulge, pamper, spoil, favour, mollify, flatter.

humourless *adj.* without humour.

- ◻ solemn, serious, dull, dry, boring, tedious, glum, morose.
- ◪ humorous, witty.

hump — *noun* **1** a large rounded lump of fat on the back of a camel that serves as an energy store when food is scarce. **2** an abnormal outward curvature of the spine, giving the back a hunched appearance, caused by a deformity of the spine, in some cases present at birth. **3** a rounded lump, especially one on the surface of a road. **4** *Brit. colloq.* a feeling of unhappiness or annoyance. — *verb* **1** (**hump something about** or **around**) to carry (especially something awkward or heavy) with difficulty. **2** *trans., intrans. coarse slang* to have sexual intercourse with (someone).

- ◻ *noun* **2** hunch. **3** lump, bump, knob, projection, protuberance, bulge, swelling, mound, prominence.

humpback — *noun* **1** a back with a hump. **2** a hunchback. **3** a large whale with a hump-like dorsal fin and long flippers. **4** a species of salmon, native to the Pacific Ocean, so called because the male has a humped back. — *adj.* (*also* **humpbacked**) rising and falling in the shape of a hump; having a hump.

humpback bridge a bridge with steep slopes on either side.

humph *interj.* an expression of doubt or displeasure. [imitative]

humus /ˈhjuːməs/ *noun* dark brown organic material that is produced in the topmost layer of soil as a result of the decomposition of plant and animal matter by fungi and bacteria. [from Latin *humus*, soil]

Hun *noun* **1** *Hist.* a member of a powerful and warlike Asiatic people who invaded Europe in the 4c and 5c and were feared throughout the Empire for their brutality. **2** *offensive colloq.* a German. [from Anglo-Saxon *Hune*]

hunch — *noun* **1** an idea or belief based on one's feelings, suspicions, or intuition rather than on clear evidence. **2** a hump. — *verb* **1** to bend or arch. **2** (*intrans.*) (*also* **hunch up**) to sit with one's body curled up or bent.

- ◻ *noun* **1** premonition, presentiment, intuition, suspicion, feeling, impression, idea, guess. *verb* **1** bend, curve, arch. **2** stoop, crouch, squat, huddle, curl up.

hunchback *noun* **1** a person whose spine is curved outward to an abnormal degree, resulting in a hunched posture. **2** such an abnormal curvature of the spine.

hunchbacked *adj.* having a deformed back.

hundred — *noun* (PL. **hundreds**, **hundred** after another number) **1** the number which is 10 times 10. **2** a numeral, figure, or symbol representing this, eg *100C*. **3** a set of 100 people or things: *one hundred pounds*. **4** a score of 100 points. **5** (*usually* **hundreds**) *colloq.* very many: *hundreds of people*. **6** (**hundreds**) (*in compounds*) the 100 years of a particular century: *the thirteen-hundreds*. **7** *Hist.* a division of an English county. — *adj.* totalling 100. [from Anglo-Saxon *hundred*]

hundredfold — *adj.* **1** equal to 100 times as much. **2** divided into or consisting of 100 parts. — *adv.* by 100 times as much.

hundreds and thousands tiny balls of coloured sugar used to decorate cakes.

hundredth *noun, adj.* **1** the position in a series corresponding to 100 in a sequence of numbers. **2** one of 100 equal parts.

hundredweight *noun* (ABBREV. **cwt**) (PL. **hundredweight**, **hundredweights**) **1** (*also* **long hundredweight**) *Brit.* an imperial unit of weight equal to 112 pounds (50.8kg). **2** (*also* **short hundredweight**) *North Amer.* a unit of weight equal to 100 pounds (45.4kg). **3** (*also* **metric hundredweight**) a metric unit of weight equal to 50kg.

hung — *verb* see HANG. — *adj.*, *said of a parliament or jury* with no one side having a majority. — **hung over** *colloq.* suffering from a hangover. **hung up on something** *colloq.* extremely anxious about it, especially needlessly.

Hungarian — *adj.* of Hungary or its official language. — *noun* **1** a citizen of or person from Hungary. **2** the official language of Hungary.

hunger — *noun* **1** the desire or need, especially very great, for food. **2** a strong desire: *hunger for affection.* — *verb intrans.* (**hungered**, **hungering**) (**hunger for** or **after something**) to have a strong desire for it. [from Anglo-Saxon *hungor*]

- ◻ *noun* **1** hungriness, ravenousness, emptiness, starvation, malnutrition, famine, appetite, voracity, greed, greediness. **2** desire, craving, longing, yearning, itch, thirst. *verb* want, wish for, desire, crave, hanker after, long for, yearn for, ache for, thirst for.

hunger strike a prolonged refusal to eat, usually by a prisoner as a form of protest.

hunger striker a person protesting by means of a hunger strike.

hungrily *adv.* **1** in a hungry way. **2** eagerly.

hungriness *noun* being hungry.

hungry *adj.* (**hungrier**, **hungriest**) **1** wanting or needing food. **2** (**hungry for something**) having a great desire for it. **3** greedy; eager: *hungry eyes*. [from Anglo-Saxon *hungrig*]

- ◻ **1** starving, ravenous, famished, underfed, undernourished, *colloq.* peckish, empty, hollow. **2** craving, longing for, aching for, thirsty for. **3** greedy, eager, avid.
- ◪ **1** satisfied, full.

hunk *noun* **1** a lump broken or cut off from a larger piece. **2** *colloq.* a strong, muscular, sexually attractive man. [perhaps a variant of HAUNCH]

- ◻ **1** chunk, lump, piece, block, slab, wedge.

hunky *adj.* (**hunkier**, **hunkiest**) *colloq., said of a man* strong, muscular, and sexually attractive.

hunky-dory *adj. colloq., said of a situation* quite satisfactory; excellent.

hunt — *verb* **1** *trans., intrans.* to chase and kill (animals) for food or for sport. **2** *intrans. Brit.* to hunt foxes using hounds, and on horseback. **3** *intrans.* (**hunt for something**) to search for it: *hunt for a new house.* **4** (**hunt someone** or **something down** or **out**) to search for them and find or capture them. — *noun* **1** an act or instance of hunting. **2** a group of people meeting together on horses to hunt foxes. **3** the area where such a group of people hunts. [from Anglo-Saxon *huntian*]

- ◻ *verb* **1** chase, pursue, stalk, track. **3** seek, look for, search for, forage for. *noun* **1** chase, pursuit, search, quest.

hunter *noun* **1** a person who hunts. **2** an animal that hunts, usually other animals for food. **3** a horse used in hunting, especially fox-hunting. **4** a watch with a hinged metal cover to protect the glass over its face.

hunting *noun* the activity or sport of pursuing and capturing or killing wild animals.

Huntington's chorea /-kə'rɪə/ or **Huntington's disease** *Medicine* an inherited brain disorder, which appears in early adulthood, characterized by slowly developing dementia accompanied by uncontrolled jerking or slow writhing movements. [named after the US physician George Summer Huntington (d.1916), who described it]

huntress *noun* a female hunter.

huntsman *noun* **1** a person who hunts. **2** an official who manages the hounds during a fox-hunt.

hurdle — *noun* **1** one of a series of light frames or hedges to be jumped in a race. **2** (**hurdles**) a race with hurdles. **3** a problem or difficulty. **4** a light frame with bars or wire across it, used as a temporary fence. — *verb trans., intrans.* to jump (hurdles) in a race. [from Anglo-Saxon *hyrdel*]

⊟ *noun* **1** jump, fence, wall, hedge, barrier, barricade, obstacle, obstruction. **3** problem, snag, difficulty, complication, stumbling-block, hindrance, impediment, handicap.

hurdler *noun* **1** a person or horse that runs hurdle races. **2** a person who makes hurdles.

hurdling *noun* racing over hurdles.

hurdy-gurdy *noun* (PL. **hurdy-gurdies**) a musical instrument with strings which make a droning sound when they are sounded by a wheel turned by a handle. [a variant of Scot. *hirdy-girdy*, uproar]

hurl *verb* **1** to throw violently. **2** to speak (especially words of abuse or insults) with force and spite. [from Middle English *hurlen*]

⊟ throw, toss, fling, sling, catapult, project, propel, fire, launch.

hurling or **hurley** *noun* a traditional Irish game resembling hockey, played by two teams of 15 players each. [from HURL]

hurly-burly *noun* the noisy activity of crowds of people; uproar. [from obsolete *hurling*, uproar]

hurrah *noun, interj.* a shout of joy, enthusiasm, or victory. [from German *hurra*]

hurricane *noun* an intense, often devastating, cyclonic tropical storm with average wind speeds in excess of 118kph, or force 12 on the Beaufort scale. The winds spiral around a central calm area (the 'eye') of low pressure and light winds. [from West Indian *hurakán*]

⊟ gale, tornado, typhoon, cyclone, whirlwind, squall, storm, tempest.

hurricane lamp an oil lamp in which the flame is enclosed in glass to protect it from the wind.

hurried *adj.* done or forced to act quickly, especially too quickly.

⊟ rushed, hasty, precipitate, speedy, quick, swift, rapid, brief, short, cursory, superficial, careless, slapdash.
⊞ leisurely.

hurry — *verb* (**hurries, hurried**) **1** *intrans.* to move or act quickly. **2** to cause to move or act quickly. **3** to cause to move or progress too quickly. — *noun* **1** great haste or speed. **2** the need for haste or speed. **3** eagerness. — **hurry up** or **hurry someone up** to move or cause to move more quickly than before. **in a hurry 1** hurrying; rushed. **2** readily; willingly: *they won't eat all that in a hurry/I shan't do that again in a hurry.* [probably imitative]

⊟ *verb* RUSH. **1** dash, fly, *colloq.* get a move on, hasten, speed up. **2** hasten, speed up. **3** hustle, push. *noun* **1** haste, speed, swiftness, rapidity, hustle, bustle, flurry. **2** rush, urgency.
⊞ *verb* slow down. *noun* **1** slowness, leisureliness.

hurt — *verb* (PAST TENSE AND PAST PARTICIPLE **hurt**) **1** to injure or cause physical pain to. **2** to upset or cause mental or emotional pain to. **3** *intrans.* to be injured or painful. — *noun* **1** an injury or wound. **2** mental pain or suffering. — *adj.* **1** injured. **2** upset; distressed. [from Old French *hurter*, to knock against]

⊟ *verb* **1** injure, wound, cut, scratch, bruise, burn, maim, disable, maltreat, ill-treat, harm, damage. **2** upset, sadden, grieve, distress, afflict, pain, wound, injure, offend, annoy. **3** ache, throb, sting. *noun* **1** injury, wound, cut, scratch, bruise, burn. **2** pain, suffering, distress, sorrow, grief, offence. *adj.* INJURED, WOUNDED. **1** cut, bruised, scarred, maimed. **2** upset, sad, saddened, distressed, aggrieved, annoyed, offended, affronted.

hurtful *adj.* causing mental or emotional pain.

⊟ upsetting, wounding, vicious, cruel, mean, unkind, nasty, malicious, spiteful, catty, derogatory, scathing, cutting.
⊞ kind.

hurtle *verb* **1** (*intrans.*) to move or be thrown very quickly and violently. **2** to throw or cause to move very quickly and violently. [from Middle English *hurtlen*]

⊟ DASH. **1** tear, race, fly, shoot, speed, rush, charge, plunge, dive. **2** hurl, fling.

husband — *noun* a man to whom a woman is married. — *verb* to use (money, resources, etc) wisely and with economy. [from Anglo-Saxon *husbonda*]

⊟ *noun* spouse, partner, mate, better half, *colloq.* hubby, groom, married man.

husbandry *noun* **1** the art, science, or business of farming. **2** the economical management of resources. **3** (*in full* **animal husbandry**) the breeding, rearing, and management of domesticated animals for the use of humans.

hush — *interj.* be quiet; be still. — *noun* silence, especially after noise. — *verb* **1** to make quiet, calm, or still. **2** (*intrans.*) to become quiet, calm, or still. — **hush something up** to prevent it becoming known; to keep it secret. [imitative]

⊟ *interj.* quiet, hold your tongue, shut up, not another word. *noun* silence, quiet, quietness, peace, stillness, calm, calmness, tranquillity, serenity. *verb* QUIETEN, SETTLE, CALM. **1** silence, still, soothe, subdue. **hush up** keep dark, conceal, cover up, suppress, stifle.
⊞ *noun* noise, clamour. *verb* **1** disturb, rouse. **hush up** publicize.

hushed *adj.* silent, very quiet, still.

hush-hush *adj. colloq.* secret.

⊟ secret, top-secret, confidential, classified, restricted, *colloq.* under wraps.
⊞ open, public.

hushkit *noun colloq.* a device fitted to an aircraft engine to reduce noise.

hush money *colloq.* money paid to someone in return for his or her agreeing to keep certain facts secret.

husk — *noun* the dry often green or membranous outer covering of certain fruits and seeds. — *verb* to remove (the husk or outer covering) from a fruit or seed. [from Middle English *huske*]

⊟ *noun* covering, case, shell, pod, hull, bran, chaff.

huskily *adv.* in a husky way.

huskiness *noun* being husky.

husky[1] *adj.* (**huskier, huskiest**) **1** *said of a voice* rough and dry in sound. **2** *colloq., usually said of a man* big and strong. [from HUSK]

⊟ **1** hoarse, croaky, rough, harsh, rasping, low, throaty, guttural, gruff.

husky[2] *noun* (PL. **huskies**) any of various breeds of dog with a powerful body, a thick double-layered insulating coat, and a curled tail, traditionally used in the Arctic region to pull sledges. [from Inuit]

hussar /hə'zɑː(r)/ *noun* a soldier in a cavalry regiment who carries only light weapons. [from Hungarian *huszar*]

hussy /'hʌsɪ/ *noun* (PL. **hussies**) *derog.* an immoral or immodest girl or woman. [a contraction of HOUSEWIFE]

hustings *pl. noun* **1** the platform, etc from which speeches are made during a political election campaign. **2** the speeches, etc made during an election campaign. [from Anglo-Saxon *husting*, tribunal, from *hus*, house + *thing*, assembly]

hustle — *verb* **1** to push quickly and roughly; to jostle. **2** *colloq.* to coerce (someone) to act or deal with something quickly: *hustled us into agreeing*. **3** *intrans. slang* to work as a prostitute. — *noun* **1** lively activity. **2** *slang* a swindle. [from Dutch *huselen*, to shake]

⊟ *verb* **1** push, shove, thrust, jostle, elbow. **2** hasten, rush, hurry, coerce, force, drive.

hustler *noun slang* **1** a swindler. **2** a prostitute.

hut *noun* a small house or shelter, usually made of wood. [from Old German *hutta*]

⊟ cabin, shack, shanty, booth, shed, lean-to, shelter, den.

hutch *noun* a box with a wire front in which small animals, eg rabbits, are kept. [from Old French *huche*]

hyacinth /'haɪəsɪnθ/ *noun* **1** any plant of the genus *Hyacinthus* of the lily family, native to the Mediterranean region, that grows from a bulb and has narrow leaves and fragrant bell-shaped flowers, usually pink, blue, or white in colour, borne in large cylindrical clusters. **2** the flower or bulb produced by this plant. **3** any of various related or similar plants, eg grape hyacinth. **4** a reddish-orange transparent variety of the mineral zircon, used as a gemstone. Also called JACINTH. [named after Greek *Hyakinthos*, in Greek mythology a youth from whose blood sprang a blue flower when he was killed by Apollo]

hyaena same as HYENA.

hybrid — *noun* **1** an animal or plant produced by crossing two species, varieties, or breeds. **2** anything produced by combining elements from different sources. — *adj.*, *said of an animal or plant* produced by crossing two species, varieties, or breeds.

⊟ *noun* **1** cross, crossbreed, half-breed, mongrel. **2** composite, combination, mixture, amalgam, compound. *adj.* crossbred, mongrel, composite, combined, mixed.

🔁 *adj.* pure-bred.

hybridism *noun* a hybrid state or condition.

hybridization or **hybridisation** *noun* **1** the formation of a hybrid or hybrids by the crossing of animals or plants that belong to genetically different populations or differ-

ent species. **2** the pairing of a strand of DNA from one source with a complementary strand of DNA or RNA from a genetically different source.

hybridize or **hybridise** *verb* **1** to cause (different species, etc) to produce hybrids; to crossbreed. **2** (*intrans.*) to produce hybrids.

hybrid vigour the increased size and vigour relative to its parents often found in a hybrid.

hydr- see HYDRO-.

hydra *noun* **1** any of various species of freshwater invertebrate animal belonging to the phylum Coelenterata, having a cylindrical tube-like body and six to twelve hollow tentacles surrounding the single body opening, through which food is taken in and waste material is ejected. It lacks a head and true sense organs, although its body contains a simple network of nerves. **2** anything which it is hard to finish, get rid of, or destroy.

hydrangea /haɪ'dreɪndʒə/ *noun* an evergreen or deciduous shrub of the genus *Hydrangea*, native to Asia and America, and widely cultivated elsewhere, having opposite pairs of oval leaves, and large showy white, pink, or blue flowerheads, usually composed of small fertile and large sterile flowers. [from HYDR- + Greek *angeion*, vessel]

hydrant /'haɪdrənt/ *noun* a pipe connected to the main water supply especially in a street, with a nozzle for attaching a hose when fighting fires. [from Greek *hydor*, water]

hydrate — *noun* (with stress on *hyd-*) *Chem.* any crystalline chemical compound that contains a fixed number of molecules of water of crystallization. — *verb* (with stress on *-drate*) **1** to form such a compound. **2** to cause a substance to absorb water. See also WATER OF CRYSTALLIZATION. [from Greek *hydor*, water]

hydration *noun Chem.* the process whereby water molecules become attached to the constituent ions of a solute (a soluble compound) as it is being dissolved in water.

hydraulic /haɪ'drɒlɪk/ *adj.* **1** of, relating to, or using a liquid or liquids in motion. **2** of or relating to the pressure generated when a liquid, such as water or oil, is forced through a pipe. **3** of or relating to a machine or device that is operated by this pressure: *hydraulic brakes*. **4** relating to hydraulics. [from HYDRO- + Greek *aulos*, pipe]

hydraulically *adv.* with hydraulic power or equipment.

hydraulics *sing. noun Engineering* the branch of engineering concerned with the mechanical properties of fluids, especially water, at rest or in motion, and their practical applications, eg the flow of liquids in pipes, the effects of water pressure on dams.

hydride /'haɪdraɪd/ *noun Chem.* any compound containing hydrogen and another chemical element: *lithium hydride (LiH)*. [from Greek *hydor*, water]

hydro[1] *noun* (PL. **hydros**) in the UK, especially formerly, a hotel or resort with special baths, etc, often situated near a spa, where guests can receive hydropathic treatment. [from HYDROPATHIC]

hydro[2] *noun* (PL. **hydros**) *North Amer.* a plant producing hydroelectric power. [from HYDROELECTRIC]

hydro- or **hydr-** *combining form* forming words meaning: **1** of or by means of water: *hydroelectricity.* **2** combined with hydrogen. [from Greek *hydor*, water]

hydrocarbon *noun Chem.* any of a very large group of organic chemicals that contain only carbon and hydrogen, eg methane, natural gas, kerosene. The main source of hydrocarbons is unrefined petroleum (crude oil).

hydrocephalic /haɪdrəʊsɪ'falɪk/ *adj.* **1** relating to or characteristic of hydrocephalus. **2** suffering from hydrocephalus.

hydrocephalus /haɪdrəʊ'sefələs, haɪdrəʊ'kefələs/ *noun Medicine* an abnormal condition in which excessive amounts of cerebrospinal fluid are present within the ventricles (hollow cavities) of the brain. In children it causes enlargement of the head, and in adults (who have rigid skulls) it causes compression of the brain, leading to drowsiness, vomiting, mental deterioration, and convulsions. [from HYDR- + Greek *kephale*, head]

hydrochloric acid /haɪdrou'klɒrɪk/ *Chem.* (FORMULA HCl) a strong corrosive acid that is formed by dissolving hydrogen chloride in water. It reacts with most metals, releasing hydrogen and forming the metal salt, which is known as a *chloride*.

hydrocyanic acid /haɪdrousaɪ'anɪk/ (FORMULA HCN) a highly poisonous volatile acid, consisting of a solution of hydrogen cyanide in water, that smells of bitter almonds. Its salts, known as cyanides, are highly toxic. Also called PRUSSIC ACID.

hydrodynamics *sing. noun* the scientific study of the motion of non-viscous incompressible fluids, especially liquids such as water and alcohol, and of the interactions that take place between such fluids and their boundaries.

hydroelectric *adj.* **1** relating to or operated by the generation of electricity by means of the pressure of falling water: *hydroelectric dam.* **2** of or relating to electric power generated in this way.

hydroelectrically *adv.* by means of hydroelectricity.

hydroelectricity *noun* (*also* **hydroelectric power**) electricity produced by generators linked to turbines that are driven by the force of falling water. About 20 per cent of the world's electricity is generated in this way.

hydrofoil *noun* **1** a device on a boat which lifts it out of the water as its speed accelerates. **2** a boat fitted with such a device. [from HYDRO- + AEROFOIL]

hydrogen /'haɪdroudʒən/ *noun* (SYMBOL **H**, ATOMIC NUMBER **1**) a colourless, odourless, tasteless gas that burns readily in air. It is the first and lightest element in the periodic table, and by far the most abundant element in the universe. [from HYDR- + Greek *gennaein*, to produce]

hydrogenate *verb Chem.* **1** *said of hydrogen* to combine with another substance. **2** to cause (a substance) to undergo a reaction with hydrogen.

hydrogenation *noun Chem.* any chemical reaction in which hydrogen is combined with another substance, especially in many industrial processes, such as the formation of solid fats, eg margarine, from liquid oils, eg vegetable oil.

hydrogen bomb *Mil.* the most powerful form of nuclear bomb, that releases vast amounts of energy as a result of the nuclear fusion of deuterium and tritium, which are isotopes of hydrogen. Also called H-BOMB. See also THERMONUCLEAR BOMB.

hydrogen bond *Chem.* a strong chemical bond that is formed when a hydrogen atom that is already bonded to another atom in a molecule forms an additional bond with an atom in the same or another molecule.

hydrogencarbonate *noun Chem.* a salt of carbonic acid that contains the HCO3− ion. Also called BICARBONATE.

hydrogen chloride *Chem.* (FORMULA HCl) a fuming poisonous colourless gas that is prepared by treating a chloride with concentrated sulphuric acid. It readily dissociates in water to form hydrochloric acid, and is used in the manufacture of polyvinyl chloride (PVC).

hydrogen ion /-'aɪɒn/ *Chem.* a hydrogen atom carrying a positive charge. Also called PROTON.

hydrogenous *adj.* relating to or consisting of hydrogen.

hydrogen peroxide *Chem.* (FORMULA H_2O_2) an unstable colourless viscous liquid that is a strong oxidizing agent and soluble in water. It is used as an oxidant in rocket fuel, and in antiseptics, disinfectants, and bleaches for hair and textiles. Also called PEROXIDE.

hydrogen sulphide *Chem.* (FORMULA H_2S) a colourless poisonous gas with a characteristic smell of bad eggs, produced by decaying organic matter, and also found in natural gas (from which it is removed) and volcanic emissions. It is used as a source of sulphur, in the purification of certain acids, and in stink bombs.

hydrographer *noun* an expert in hydrography.

hydrographic *adj.* relating to or involving hydrography.

hydrography *noun* the science of charting seas, rivers, and lakes. [from HYDRO- + -GRAPHY]

hydrology *noun* the scientific study of the occurrence, movement, and properties of water on or near the Earth's surface, and in the atmosphere. Its practical applications include flood control, irrigation schemes, control of industrial and domestic water supplies, and the generation of hydroelectric power.

hydrolysis /haɪ'drɒlɪsɪs/ *noun Chem.* the chemical decomposition or alteration of a compound as a result of its reaction with water. [from HYDRO- + Greek *lysis*, a loosening]

hydrometer /haɪ'drɒmɪtə(r)/ *noun Physics* a floating instrument, consisting of a weighted glass bulb with a long calibrated stem, that is used to measure the density of a liquid as indicated by the depth of immersion of the bulb. Hydrometers are widely used in brewing.

hydropathic /haɪdrou'paθɪk/ *adj.* relating to or involving hydropathy.

hydropathy /haɪ'drɒpəθɪ/ *noun* the treatment of disease by the use of water, both internally and externally. [from HYDRO- + Greek *patheia*, suffering]

hydrophilic *adj. Chem.* denoting a substance that has an affinity for, absorbs, or attracts water.

hydrophobia *noun* **1** an irrational fear of water. **2** the inability to swallow water and other liquids due to painful spasms of the throat, especially as a symptom of rabies. **3** rabies.

hydrophobic *adj.* **1** *Chem.* denoting a substance that repels or does not absorb water. **2** relating to or suffering from hydrophobia.

hydroplane — *noun* **1** a small light flat-bottomed motorboat that skims along the surface of the water when driven at high speed. **2** a movable horizontal fin on the hull of a submarine, that can be angled upward or downward and is used to control vertical movements of the vessel. **3** erroneously used to refer to a seaplane. — *verb, said of a boat* to skim along the surface of the water like a hydroplane.

hydroponic *adj.* relating to or involving hydroponics.

hydroponics *sing. noun Bot.* a technique for growing certain commercially important plants (especially glasshouse crops) without soil, by immersing the roots in water that contains essential nutrients, and using an inert substance such as sand or gravel to provide support. [from HYDRO- + Greek *ponos*, work]

hydrosphere *noun* that part of the Earth that is composed of water, including the oceans, seas, lakes, and rivers, groundwater, ice, and water vapour in the atmosphere.

hydrostatic *adj.* relating to or involving hydrostatics.

hydrostatics *sing. noun* the scientific study of the properties and behaviour of fluids at rest, including practical applications such as the design of dams, tanks, and hydraulic machinery. [from HYDRO- + Greek *-states*, causing to stand]

hydrotherapy *noun Medicine* the treatment of diseases and disorders by the external use of water, especially as a comparatively weightless form of exercise in physiotherapy, such as the rehabilitation of partially paralysed patients in remedial swimming pools.

hydrous /'haɪdrəs/ *adj., said of a substance* containing water. [from Greek *hydor*, water]

hydroxide *noun Chem.* any chemical compound that contains the hydroxide (OH−) ion or the hydroxyl (−OH) group.

hydroxyl group /haɪ'drɒksɪl/ *Chem.* in a chemical compound, the (−OH) group, consisting of a hydrogen atom and an oxygen atom bonded together, as for example in alcohols, organic acids, phenols, and hydroxides. [from HYDROGEN + OXYGEN + Greek *hyle*, matter]

hyena /haɪ'iːnə/ *noun* a mainly nocturnal dog-like mammal with strong shoulders that are higher than its hindquarters, powerful jaws, and strong teeth. Hyenas are known for their shrill cries which resemble maniacal laughter. [from Greek *hys*, pig]

hygiene *noun* **1** the science of preserving health and preventing the spread of disease, especially by the promotion of cleanliness. **2** sanitary principles and practices. [from Greek *hygieia*, health]

....

⊟ **2** sanitariness, cleanliness, sanitation, disinfection, sterilization, sterility.

⊡ **2** insanitariness.

....

hygienic *adj.* promoting and preserving health, sanitary.

....

⊟ sanitary, sterile, aseptic, germ-free, disinfected, clean, pure, salubrious, healthy, wholesome.

⊡ unhygienic, insanitary.

....

hygienically *adv.* in a hygienic way.

hygrometer *noun Meteorol.* an instrument for measuring the relative humidity of the air, ie the amount of water vapour in the atmosphere. [from Greek *hygros*, wet + -METER]

hygroscope *noun* an instrument which indicates changes in air humidity without measuring it. [from Greek *hygros*, wet + -SCOPE]

hygroscopic *adj.* **1** of or relating to a hygroscope. **2** *said of a substance* tending to absorb moisture from the air. **3** *said of the parts of certain plants* sensitive to or moving in response to changes in moisture.

Hyksos *noun* a tribe of desert nomads from Palestine, who founded a dynasty in ancient Egypt in c.1670BC.

hymen *noun Anat.* a thin membrane that covers the opening of the vagina at birth. It may be broken the first time a woman has sexual intercourse, but is usually at least partially ruptured before puberty. [from Greek *hymen*, membrane]

hymenopterous /haɪmɪˈnɒptərəs/ *adj.* denoting an insect that belongs to the order Hymenoptera, including ants, bees, wasps, and sawflies. [from Greek *hymen*, membrane + *pteron*, wing]

hymn /hɪm/ *noun* a song of praise, especially to God. [from Greek *hymnos*]

hymnal /ˈhɪmnəl/ or **hymnary** /ˈhɪmnərɪ/ (PL. **hymnaries**) *noun* a book containing hymns.

hymnody *noun* **1** the writing of hymns. **2** hymns as a group.

hymnologist *noun* a person who composes or studies hymns.

hymnology *noun* the study or writing of hymns.

hype[1] *colloq.* — *noun* intensive, exaggerated, and usually misleading publicity or advertising. — *verb* (**hype something up**) to promote or advertise it intensively.

hype[2] *verb intrans. slang* (usually **hype up**) to inject oneself with a drug. — **hyped up** *slang* highly excited, especially as if by drugs. [abbreviation of HYPODERMIC]

hyper *adj. colloq.*, *said of a person* over-excited; over-active. [abbreviation of HYPERACTIVE]

hyper- *combining form* forming words meaning 'over, beyond, more than normal': *hyperactive.* [from Greek *hyper*, over]

hyperactive *adj.*, *said especially of a child* abnormally or excessively active.

hyperactivity *noun Psychol.* a condition characterized by overactive, poorly controlled behaviour and lack of concentration, most frequently seen in children.

hyperbola /haɪˈpɜːbələ/ *noun* (PL. **hyperbolas**, **hyperbolae**) *Geom.* the curve produced when a plane (flat surface) cuts through a cone in such a way that the angle between the base of the cone and the plane is greater than the angle between the base and the sloping side of the cone. It is one type of *conic section.* [from Greek *hyperbole*, excess]

hyperbole /haɪˈpɜːbəlɪ/ *noun* the use of an overstatement or exaggeration to produce an effect. [from Greek *hyperbole*, excess]

....

⊟ overstatement, exaggeration, magnification, extravagance.

⊡ understatement.

....

hyperbolic[1] /haɪpəˈbɒlɪk/ *adj.* relating to or in the form of a hyperbola.

hyperbolic[2] /haɪpəˈbɒlɪk/ or **hyperbolical** /haɪpəˈbɒlɪkəl/ *adj.* involving hyperbole.

Hyperboreans *pl. noun* in Greek mythology, an unvisited people of fabled virtue and prosperity who lived in a land beyond the North Wind (Boreas).

hypercritical *adj.* over-critical.

hyperglycaemia /haɪpəglaɪˈsiːmɪə/ *noun Medicine* a condition in which the glucose (sugar) concentration in the blood is abnormally high. It is most commonly associated with diabetes mellitus. [from HYPER- + Greek *glykys*, sweet]

hyperlink *noun Comput.* a form of cross-reference in computer-readable text which allows instant access to related material, as used on the Internet.

hypermarket *noun* a very large supermarket. [a translation of French *hypermarché*]

hypermetropia /haɪpəməˈtrəʊpɪə/ *noun Medicine* the condition of being long-sighted, in which parallel rays of light entering the eye are brought to a focus behind the retina, so that nearby objects appear blurred. It usually occurs because the distance between the lens and the retina is too short, and is corrected by wearing contact lenses or spectacles with convex (converging) lenses. [from HYPER- + Greek *metron*, measure + *ops*, eye]

hyperon /ˈhaɪpərɒn/ *noun Physics* any of a class of elementary particles with masses greater than that of a neutron.

hypersensitive *adj.* very sensitive, or more sensitive than is normal.

hypersensitivity *noun* being hypersensitive.

hypersonic *adj.* **1** *Aeron.* denoting a speed greater than Mach number 5 (about five times the speed of sound in the same medium). **2** denoting an aircraft or rocket capable of flying at such speeds. **3** denoting sound waves with a frequency greater than 1000 million hertz.

hypertension *noun Medicine* a condition in which the blood pressure is abnormally high. It may be caused by obesity, stress, ageing, disease of the heart, arteries, or kidneys, or hormonal disorders, or it may have no identifiable cause. Hypertension itself may increase the risk of heart failure, atherosclerosis, kidney failure, or stroke.

hypertext *noun Comput.* computer-readable text in which cross-reference links have been inserted, enabling the user to call up relevant data from other files, or parts of the same file, by clicking on a coded word or symbol, etc.

hyperthyroidism /haɪpəˈθaɪrɔɪdɪzm/ *noun Medicine* overproduction of thyroid hormones by the thyroid gland, which may result in goitre (swelling of the neck due to enlargement of the thyroid gland), weight loss, rapid heartbeat, tremor, and increased appetite.

hypertonic *adj. Chem.* denoting a solution that has a higher osmotic pressure than another solution with which it is being compared.

hypertrophy /haɪˈpɜːtrəfɪ/ *noun* (PL. **hypertrophies**) *Biol.* an abnormal increase in the size of an organ as a result of the enlargement of its individual cells, rather than an increase in the total number of cells. Muscles undergo hypertrophy in response to a long-term increase in exercise. [from HYPER- + Greek *-trophia*, nutrition]

hyperventilation *noun Medicine* a condition in which breathing while at rest becomes abnormally rapid and deep, causing dizziness, a feeling of suffocation, and sometimes loss of consciousness. It is usually caused by anxiety, but may also occur when oxygen uptake is impaired by shallow breathing, eg in pneumonia.

hypha *noun Biol.* in fungi, any of many thread-like filaments that form a dense network known as a mycelium. [from Greek *hyphe*, web]

hyphen — *noun* a punctuation mark (-) used to join two words to form a compound (*booby-trap*, *double-barrelled*) or, especially in printing, to split a word between the end of one line and the beginning of the next. — *verb* (**hy-**

phened, **hyphening**) to hyphenate. [from Greek *hypo*, under + *hen*, one]

hyphenate *verb* to join (two words or parts of words) with a hyphen.

hyphenation *noun* the use of a hyphen or hyphens.

hypnosis *noun* (PL. **hypnoses**) a sleep-like state in which a person is deeply relaxed and unusually receptive to external suggestion, and may by questioning be induced to recall memories of past events, thought to have been forgotten. It is used to treat mental illness, addictions, and psychosomatic disorders, and for the relief of pain, eg during childbirth or dental treatment. [from Greek *hypnos*, sleep]

hypnotherapy *noun* the use of hypnosis to treat emotional or psychological disorders, or to cure habits such as smoking or nail-biting. [from *hypno*, of hypnosis]

hypnotic — *adj.* **1** of, relating to, causing, or produced by hypnosis. **2** causing sleep. — *noun* **1** any of various drugs that induce sleep, eg barbiturates. **2** a person who is susceptible to hypnosis. **3** a person in a state of hypnosis.

■ *adj.* **1** hypnotizing, mesmerizing, spellbinding, fascinating, irresistible, magnetic. **2** soporific, sleep-inducing.

hypnotically *adv.* in a hypnotic way.

hypnotism *noun* **1** the science of hypnosis. **2** the art or practice of inducing hypnosis. **3** hypnosis.

hypnotist *noun* a person who practises hypnotism.

hypnotize or **hypnotise** *verb* **1** to put (someone) in a state of hypnosis. **2** to fascinate or bewitch.

■ *verb* MESMERIZE. **2** spellbind, bewitch, enchant, entrance, fascinate, captivate, magnetize.

hypo *noun* (PL. **hypos**) *colloq.* a hypodermic syringe or injection. [abbreviation of HYPODERMIC]

hypo- *combining form* forming words meaning 'under, beneath, inadequate': *hypotension*. [from Greek *hypo*, under]

hypocaust *noun* a hollow space under a floor or between double walls in ancient Roman houses, into which hot air was passed as a form of heating. [from Latin *hypocaustum*, from Greek *hypo*, under + *kaiein*, to burn]

hypochlorite *noun Chem.* a salt of hypochlorous acid (a weak acid that is only stable in solution), containing the ClO^- ion, and used as a disinfectant and bleach.

hypochondria /haɪpəˈkɒndrɪə/ *noun* a condition, often associated with anxiety or depression, characterized by excessive concern about one's health. It often involves belief in the existence of a serious illness, for which treatment is sought, and may become a handicapping neurosis that dominates a person's life. [from Greek *hypochondrion*, abdomen, formerly believed to be the source of melancholy]

hypochondriac — *noun* a person suffering from hypochondria. — *adj.* of or relating to hypochondria or hypochondriacs.

hypochondriacal *adj.* relating to or affected by hypochondria.

hypocrisy /hɪˈpɒkrɪsɪ/ *noun* (PL. **hypocrisies**) the act or state of pretending to have feelings or beliefs which one does not actually have, or of hiding one's true character. [from Greek *hypokrisis*, play-acting]

■ insincerity, double-talk, double-dealing, falsity, deceit, deception, pretence.

F3 sincerity.

hypocrite /ˈhɪpəkrɪt/ *noun* a person who pretends to have feelings or beliefs he or she does not actually have, or who hides his or her true character.

hypocritical *adj.* **1** practising hypocrisy. **2** of the nature of hypocrisy.

■ INSINCERE. **1** two-faced, double-dealing, deceitful, dissembling, pharisaic, self-righteous. **2** false, hollow, deceptive, spurious.

F3 SINCERE.

hypodermic — *adj.*, *said of an instrument or drug* for injecting under the skin. — *noun* **1** a hypodermic syringe. **2** an injection of a drug under the skin. [from HYPO- + Latin *dermis*, skin]

hypodermic syringe a syringe with a fine hollow needle, used for injecting drugs under the skin or taking blood samples.

hypoglycaemia or **hypoglycemia** /haɪpəʊɡlaɪˈsiːmɪə/ *noun Medicine* an abnormal reduction in glucose (sugar) content of the blood, most commonly occurring in diabetics after an overdose of insulin. Symptoms include muscular weakness, sweating, mental confusion, faintness, and even coma in severe cases. It is treated by giving glucose by mouth.

hyponym /ˈhaɪpənɪm/ *noun Linguistics* one of a group of specific terms whose meanings are included in a more general term: for example, *oak* and *cedar* are hyponyms of *tree* and of *wood*, and *dog* and *alligator* are hyponyms of *animal*. [from HYPO- + Greek *onyma*, *onoma*, a name]

hypotension *noun* abnormally low blood pressure.

hypotenuse /haɪˈpɒtənjuːz/ *noun Maths.* the longest side of a right-angled triangle, opposite the right angle. [from Greek *hypoteinousa*, subtending]

hypothalamus /haɪpəʊˈθaləməs/ *noun Anat.* the region of the vertebrate forebrain that lies below the thalamus and above the pituitary gland. It is linked to both, and so acts as a centre for co-ordination of nervous system and hormonal activity. In mammals it is involved in the control of body temperature, heartbeat, breathing rate, blood pressure, water balance, hunger, thirst, and sleep patterns. It also influences emotional activity and libido in humans.

hypothermia *noun* **1** *Medicine* a condition in which the body temperature falls below normal as a result of exposure to cold. It most commonly occurs in babies and the elderly, especially during a long spell of exceptionally cold weather. **2** a decrease in body temperature that is deliberately induced, eg to reduce a patient's oxygen requirements during heart surgery. [from HYPO- + Greek *therme*, heat]

hypothesis /haɪˈpɒθəsɪs/ *noun* (PL. **hypotheses** /haɪˈpɒθəsiːz/) a statement or proposition assumed to be true and on which an argument, etc may be based. [from Greek *hypothesis*, supposition]

■ theory, thesis, premise, postulate, proposition, supposition, conjecture, speculation.

hypothesize or **hypothesise** *verb* **1** (*intrans.*) to form a hypothesis. **2** (*trans.*) to assume as a hypothesis.

hypothetical *adj.* based on hypothesis; assumed.

■ theoretical, imaginary, supposed, assumed, conjectural, speculative.

F3 real, actual.

hypothyroidism /haɪpəʊˈθaɪrɔɪdɪzm/ *noun Medicine* a deficiency in the production of thyroid hormones by the thyroid gland, which may result in slowing of the heartbeat, extreme sensitivity to cold, an increase in weight, and a slowing down of physical and mental activity. If present at birth and left untreated it can lead to cretinism.

hypotonic *adj. Chem.* describing a solution that has a lower osmotic pressure than another solution with which it is being compared.

hypsometer /hɪpˈsɒmɪtə(r)/ *noun* **1** any instrument used to measure altitude by determining the boiling point of water, which is directly dependent on atmospheric pressure (and so on height above sea level). **2** any instrument used to calibrate a thermometer at the boiling point of water. **3** any instrument used to calculate the heights of trees by triangulation. [from Greek *hypsos*, height + -METER]

Hyracotherium *noun* same as EOHIPPUS.

hyrax *noun* a mammal, native to Africa and Arabia, related to the elephant and aardvark, and superficially resembling a large guinea pig, with a pointed muzzle and round ears. [from Greek *hyrax*, shrew]

hyssop *noun* a small shrubby perennial plant (*Hyssopus officinalis*), native to S Europe and W Asia, and having narrow leaves and long loose one-sided spikes of two-lipped bluish-violet flowers. It was formerly cultivated as a medicinal herb. [from Greek *hyssopos*]

hysterectomy *noun* (PL. **hysterectomies**) the surgical removal of the uterus (womb), after which menstruation ceases and pregnancy is no longer possible. The operation is usually performed to treat conditions such as cancer or fibroids, and has no effect on the libido. [from Greek *hystera*, womb + -ECTOMY]

hysteresis /hɪstə'riːsɪs/ *noun Physics* the delay or lag between the cause of an effect, and the appearance of that effect. It occurs, for example, when a magnetic material becomes magnetized. [from Greek *hysteresis*, deficiency, delay]

hysteria *noun* **1** *Psychol.* a mental disorder characterized by mental and physical symptoms such as hallucinations, uncontrolled weeping, amnesia, or paralysis. This condition is a form of neurosis. **2** any uncontrolled emotional state caused by acute stress or a traumatic experience. [from Greek *hystera*, womb, from the former belief that disturbances in the womb caused emotional imbalance]
. . . .

▬ HYSTERICS. **1** neurosis, mania. **2** agitation, frenzy, panic.
▭ **2** calm, composure.
. . . .

hysteric *noun* a person suffering from hysteria.

hysterical *adj.* **1** of or suffering from hysteria. **2** *colloq.* very funny.
. . . .

▬ **1** frantic, frenzied, berserk, mad, raving, crazed, demented, overwrought, neurotic. **2** hilarious, uproarious, side-splitting, *colloq.* priceless, *colloq.* rich.
▭ **1** calm, composed, self-possessed.
. . . .

hysterics *pl. noun* **1** a fit of hysteria. **2** *colloq.* uncontrollable laughter.

Hz *abbrev.* hertz.

I

I[1] or **i** *noun* (PL. **Is**, **I's**, **i's**) the ninth letter of the English alphabet.

I[2] *pron.* used by the speaker or writer to refer to himself or herself as the subject of an actual or implied verb. [from Anglo-Saxon *ic*]

I[3] *abbrev.* **1** Institute. **2** Island. **3** Isle.

I[4] *symbol* **1** *Chem.* iodine. **2** the Roman numeral for one.

IA or **Ia** *abbrev.* Iowa.

IAAF *abbrev.* International Amateur Athletic Federation.

IAEA *abbrev.* International Atomic Energy Agency.

-ial *suffix* **1** forming adjectives meaning 'of, relating to': *managerial*. **2** forming nouns meaning 'the action of': *tutorial*. [from Latin *-ialis*]

iambic — *adj.* of or using iambuses. — *noun* an iambus.

iambus /aɪˈæmbəs/ or **iamb** /ˈaɪæm/ *noun* (PL. **iambuses**, **iambi**) *Poetry* a metrical foot containing one short or unstressed syllable followed by one long or stressed one. [from Greek *iambos*, from *iaptein*, to lampoon, this verse form being first used by satirists]

-ian *suffix* **1** forming adjectives meaning 'relating to, similar to': *Dickensian*. **2** forming nouns meaning 'a person interested or skilled in': *historian*.

ib. *abbrev.* ibidem.

IBA *abbrev. Brit.* Independent Broadcasting Authority.

Iberian /aɪˈbɪərɪən/ — *adj.* relating to the Iberian Peninsula, or its inhabitants, languages, and culture. — *noun* a person from the Iberian Peninsula; a Spaniard or Portuguese. [from Latin *Iberia*]

ibex /ˈaɪbɛks/ *noun* (PL. **ibex**, **ibexes**, **ibices**) a wild mountain goat with large, ridged, backward-curving horns, found in Europe, N Africa and Asia. [from Latin *ibex*]

ibid. *abbrev.* ibidem.

ibidem /ˈɪbɪdəm/ *adv.* in the same place in a book, article, passage, etc previously mentioned or cited. [from Latin *ibidem*, in the same place]

-ibility *suffix* forming nouns corresponding to adjectives in *-ible*: *possibility*.

ibis /ˈaɪbɪs/ *noun* (PL. **ibis**, **ibises**) a wading bird with a long slender downward-curving beak. [from Greek *ibis*, from Egyptian]

-ible *suffix* forming adjectives meaning 'that may be or is capable of being': *possible/expressible*. See also -ABLE. [from Latin *-ibilis*]

-ibly *suffix* forming adverbs corresponding to adjectives in *-ible*: *possibly/inexpressibly*.

IBRD *abbrev.* International Bank for Reconstruction and Development (World Bank).

IBS *Medicine abbrev.* irritable bowel syndrome.

-ic *suffix* **1** (*also* **-ical**, often with some difference in meaning) forming words meaning 'relating to': *historic/historical/photographic/political*. **2** *Chem.* forming words meaning 'formed with an element in its higher valency': *sulphuric*. See also -ICS. [from French *-ique*]

-ically *suffix* forming adverbs corresponding to adjectives in *-ic* or *-ical*: *historically/graphically*.

ICBM *abbrev.* intercontinental ballistic missile.

ICD *abbrev.* interactive compact disc; CD-i.

ice — *noun* **1** water in its solid frozen state. Pure water freezes at 0°C (32°F), and unlike other liquids it expands and becomes less dense when it freezes. For this reason it floats on water, and frozen water may cause pipes to burst. **2** a sheet of frozen water, eg on the surface of a road. **3** ice cream or water ice, or a portion of this. **4** *slang* diamonds. **5** *slang* an illicit drug, a highly synthesized form of metamphetamine. **6** coldness of manner; reserve. — *verb* **1** to cool with ice. **2** *intrans.* (*usually* **ice over** or **up**) to become covered with ice; to freeze. **3** to cover (a cake) with icing. — **break the ice** to relax feelings of reserve, shyness, or formality, especially between strangers. **cut no ice** to count for nothing. **on ice** in readiness or reserve, either to be used later, or awaiting further attention. **skate on thin ice** to be in a difficult, delicate, or potentially embarrassing situation. [from Anglo-Saxon *is*]

⊟ *noun* **1** frost, rime, icicle, glacier. **6** iciness, frostiness, coldness, coolness, reserve, aloofness. *verb* **1** cool, chill, refrigerate, freeze. **3** frost, glaze.

Ice Age 1 any of several periods of time in the Earth's history when the average temperature of the atmosphere decreased to such an extent that ice sheets and glaciers advanced from polar regions to cover large areas of the Earth that had previously had a temperate climate. **2** (**the Ice Age**) a popular name for the Pleistocene epoch.

ice-axe *noun* an axe used by mountain climbers to cut holes in the ice for their hands and feet.

iceberg *noun* a huge mass of ice floating in the sea, only a small part of which projects above the surface. Icebergs are broken off from a glacier or polar ice sheet, and commonly drift for up to two years before melting. — **the tip of the iceberg** the initial visible or perceived part of a much larger problem or commitment which remains to be discovered.

iceberg lettuce a crisp, light-green type of lettuce.

icebox *noun* **1** a refrigerator compartment where food is kept frozen and ice is made. **2** a container packed with ice, for keeping food cold. **3** *North Amer.* a refrigerator.

icebreaker *noun* a ship designed to cut channels through floating ice.

ice-bucket *noun* a small bucket for ice cubes, used for keeping bottles of wine cold.

icecap *noun* a permanent covering of ice, eg on top of a mountain, or at the North or South Poles.

ice cream a sweet, creamy frozen dessert, made either from cream or a substitute, and flavoured.

ice cube a small block of ice used for cooling drinks, etc.

iced *adj.* **1** covered with or affected by ice. **2** *said of a cake, etc* covered with icing.

ice field a large flat area of land covered with ice, or an area of sea covered with floating ice.

ice floe a large sheet of ice floating on the sea.

ice hockey a form of hockey played on ice by skaters, and with a puck instead of a ball.

Icelandic — *adj.* of Iceland or the Germanic language spoken in Iceland. — *noun* the language of Iceland.

Iceland spar *Geol.* a pure transparent form of calcite, noted for its ability to split a single incident ray of light into two refracted rays.

ice lolly *Brit. colloq.* flavoured water or ice cream, frozen on a small stick.

ice pack 1 a bag packed with crushed ice, used in medicine eg to reduce a swelling or to reduce a patient's temperature. **2** an area of pack ice.

ice pick 1 a tool with a pointed end used by rock and mountain climbers for splitting ice. **2** a similar smaller tool for breaking ice into small pieces for drinks.

ice skate a skate with a metal blade for use on ice.

ice-skate *verb intrans.* to skate on ice.

ice skater a person who skates on ice.

ice skating skating on ice.

ICFTU *abbrev.* International Confederation of Free Trade Unions.

ichneumon / ɪkˈnjuːmən/ *noun* **1** any of several winged insects which lay their larvae in or on the larvae of other insects, especially caterpillars. **2** a mongoose, especially the Egyptian species which destroys crocodile eggs. [from Greek *ichneumon*, tracker]

ichthyological / ɪkθɪoʊˈlɒdʒɪkəl/ *adj.* relating to or involving ichthyology.

ichthyologist / ɪkθɪˈɒlədʒɪst/ *noun* an expert in ichthyology.

ichthyology / ɪkθɪˈɒlədʒɪ/ *noun* the study of fishes. [from Greek *ichthys*, fish + -LOGY]

ICI *abbrev.* Imperial Chemical Industries.

icicle /ˈaɪsɪkl/ *noun* a long hanging spike of ice, formed by water freezing as it drops. [from Anglo-Saxon *isgicel*]

icily *adv.* in an icy way.

iciness *noun* being icy.

icing *noun* **1** a mixture of sugar, egg whites, water and sometimes lemon juice or other flavouring, used to form a hard coating on cakes. **2** the forming of ice on a ship or aircraft. — **the icing on the cake** *colloq.* a desirable although unnecessary addition to something which is already satisfactory.

icing sugar sugar in the form of a very fine powder used to make icing, sweets, etc.

ICL *abbrev.* International Computers Ltd.

icon or **ikon** /ˈaɪkɒn/ *noun* **1** an image of Christ, the Virgin Mary or a saint, usually painted on wood or done as a mosaic, especially in the Orthodox church. **2** a picture, image or representation. **3** *Comput.* an image on a computer screen which represents a function, operation, file, etc which is available, and which may be selected using the cursor rather than a typed command. [from Greek *eikon*, image]

. . . .

☰ **2** idol, picture, portrait, image, representation, symbol.

. . . .

iconoclasm *noun* the beliefs or actions of an iconoclast.

iconoclast *noun* **1** a person who destroys religious images and is opposed to their use in worship. **2** a person who is opposed to and attacks traditional and cherished beliefs and superstitions. [from Greek *eikon*, image + *klastes*, breaker]

iconoclastic *adj.* relating to iconoclasts or iconoclasm.

iconography *noun* the branch of art history that is concerned with the form and representation of the subject. [from Greek *eikon*, an image + -GRAPHY]

iconology *noun* **1** the historical study of the social, political, and religious meanings of works of art. **2** the study of icons. [from Greek *eikon*, an image + -LOGY]

iconostasis /aɪkoʊˈnɒstəsɪs/ *noun* a screen dividing the sanctuary from the main part of a Greek Orthodox or Byzantine church. It is usually covered with icons arranged in rows. [from Greek *eikon*, an image + *stasis*, placing]

icosahedron /aɪkɒsəˈhiːdrən/ *noun* (PL. **icosahedrons**, **icosahedra**) a solid figure with twenty faces. [from Greek *eikosi*, twenty + *hedra*, seat]

-ics *suffix* forming singular or plural nouns denoting subjects of study or activities: *acoustics/athletics/mathematics*. [from French *-iques*, from Greek *-ika*]

ICU *abbrev.* intensive care unit.

icy *adj.* (**icier, iciest**) **1** very cold. **2** covered with ice. **3** *said of someone's manner, behaviour, etc* unfriendly; hostile.

. . . .

☰ FROSTY. **1** ice-cold, arctic, polar, glacial, freezing, frozen, wintry, raw, bitter, biting, cold, chill, chilly. **2** slippery, glassy, frozen, icebound, frostbound. **3** unfriendly, hostile, cold, stony, cool, aloof, distant, formal.

☲ **1** hot. **3** friendly, warm.

. . . .

ID *abbrev.* **1** (*also* **Id**) Idaho. **2** identification.

I'd *contr.* **1** I had. **2** I would.

id *noun Psychol.* in psychoanalysis, the part of the unconscious mind that is regarded as the source of primitive biological instincts and urges for survival and reproduction. It governs the unconscious. The effects of the id on behaviour are limited by the *ego* and *superego*. See also EGO, SUPEREGO. [from Latin *id*, it]

'Id-al-Adha *noun* the Muslim 'Feast of Sacrifice' celebrating the faith of Abraham who was willing to sacrifice his son, Isaac, at Allah's request. Sheep and goats are killed as a reminder of the sheep Allah provided as a substitute for the boy, and the meat is shared with the poor. [from Arabic *'Id al-Adha*]

'Id-al-Fitr *noun* a Muslim festival, the 'Feast of Breaking Fast' on the first day ofter Ramadan, celebrated with festive meals, the wearing of new clothes, and giving gifts to charity. [from Arabic *'Id al-Fitr*]

IDD *abbrev.* International Direct Dialling.

-ide *suffix Chem.* denoting a compound of an element with some other element, etc, eg *chloride*, a compound of chlorine. See also -ATE, -ITE.

idea *noun* **1** a thought, image, notion or concept formed by the mind. **2** a plan or intention. **3** a main aim, purpose, or feature: *the idea of the game is to win as many cards as possible*. **4** an opinion or belief: *he's got the idea that no one likes him*. **5** a vague notion or fancy: *have no idea of the work required*. **6** a person's conception of what is the best or perfect example of something: *not my idea of fun*. **7** in Plato's philosophy, a universal model of which all existing examples are imperfect copies. — **get ideas** *colloq.* to have ideas which are over-ambitious or undesirable. **put ideas into someone's head** to cause them to have over-ambitious or impractical ideas. [from Latin and Greek *idea*, form, pattern]

. . . .

☰ **1** thought, concept, notion, image, vision, impression, perception, theory, hypothesis, guess, conjecture. **2** plan, scheme, design, intention, brainwave, suggestion, proposal, proposition, recommendation. **3** aim, intention, purpose, reason, point, object. **4** belief, opinion, view, viewpoint. **5** conception, notion, fancy, inkling, suspicion, clue. **6** conception, notion, understanding, interpretation.

. . . .

ideal — *adj.* **1** perfect; highest and best possible. **2** existing only in the mind; imaginary; visionary. — *noun* **1** the highest standard of behaviour, perfection, beauty, etc. **2** a person or thing considered to be perfect. [from Latin *idealis*]

. . . .

☰ *adj.* **1** perfect, dream, utopian, best, optimum, optimal, supreme, highest, model, archetypal. **2** unreal, imaginary, theoretical, hypothetical, impractical, unattainable, idealistic, visionary. *noun* MODEL, EXAMPLE. **1** perfection, acme, criterion, standard, pattern, archetype, prototype, image. **2** paragon, exemplar, epitome.

. . . .

ideal gas *Physics* a hypothetical gas in which atoms do not interact with one another. Such a gas would obey the gas laws, such as Boyle's law and Charles's law, exactly. Also called PERFECT GAS.

idealism *noun* **1** a tendency to show or present things in an ideal or idealized form rather than as they really are. **2** the practice of forming, and living according to, ideals. **3** *Phi-*

los. the theory that material objects and the external world do not really exist but are products of the mind. See also REALISM.

idealist *noun* **1** a person who lives or tries to live according to ideals. **2** an impractical person. **3** *Philos.* a believer in idealism.

▣ **1** perfectionist. **2** romantic, visionary, dreamer, optimist.
▣ **2** realist, pragmatist.

idealistic *adj.* involving or characterized by idealism.

▣ perfectionist, utopian, visionary, romantic, quixotic, starry-eyed, optimistic, unrealistic, impractical, impracticable.
▣ realistic, pragmatic.

idealistically *adv.* in an idealistic way.

idealization or **idealisation** *noun* idealizing or being idealized.

idealize or **idealise** *verb* **1** to regard or treat (a person, etc) as perfect or ideal. **2** *intrans.* to form ideas.

▣ **1** romanticize, glamorize, utopianize, glorify, exalt, worship, idolize.
▣ **1** caricature.

ideally *adv.* in an ideal way; in ideal circumstances.

idée fixe /iːˈdeɪ ˈfiːks/ *noun* (PL. **idées fixes**) an idea which dominates the mind; an obsession. [French, = fixed idea]

idem /ˈɪdem/ — *pron.* the same author, place, etc as previously mentioned. — *adv.* in the same place as previously mentioned. [from Latin *idem*, the same]

identical *adj.* **1** being very similar or exactly alike in every respect. **2** being the very same. **3** *said of twins* developed from a single fertilized egg which subsequently divided into equal halves to give two separate fetuses. [from Latin *identicus*, from *idem*, the same]

▣ **1** similar, like, alike, twin, duplicate, indistinguishable, interchangeable, corresponding, matching, equal, equivalent. **2** same, selfsame.
▣ **1, 2** different.

identifiable *adj.* capable of being identified.

identification *noun* **1** an act of identifying or process of being identified. **2** something which allows a person or thing to be identified. **3** (*usually* **identification with someone**) sympathy and understanding for a real or fictional person because of shared personal characteristics or experiences.

▣ **1** recognition, detection, diagnosis, naming, labelling, classification. **2** identity card, documents, papers, credentials. **3** sympathy, understanding, fellow feeling, empathy, rapport, relationship, association, involvement.

identification parade *Brit.* a line of people containing one person who is suspected of a crime and others who are innocent of it, from which a witness will try to identify the criminal.

identify *verb* (**identifies, identified**) **1** to recognize (someone or something) as being a particular person or thing; to establish the identity of. **2** to associate (one person, thing or group) with another. **3** (**identify with someone**) to feel sympathy and understanding for a real or fictional person because of shared personal characteristics or experiences. **4** to see clearly or pinpoint (a problem, method, solution, etc). [from Latin *idem*, the same + *facere*, to make]

▣ **1** recognize, know, pick out, single out, distinguish, perceive, make out, discern, detect, diagnose, name, label. **2** asso-

ciate, place, classify, catalogue. **3** sympathize with, feel for, empathize with, respond to, relate to, associate with.

Identikit *noun trademark* a series of transparent strips, each one showing a different typical facial feature, from which an impression or rough picture of a criminal or suspect can be put together from witnesses' descriptions.

identity *noun* (PL. **identities**) **1** the state or quality of being a specified person or thing; who or what a person or thing is: *the winner's identity is not yet known.* **2** the individual characteristics by which a person or thing can be identified; individuality; personality. **3** the state of being exactly the same. **4** *Maths.* **a** same as IDENTITY ELEMENT. **b** an equation which remains true whichever way it is written or expressed, and whichever values are substituted for the letters used. [from Latin *identitas*, from *idem*, the same]

▣ **2** individuality, particularity, singularity, uniqueness, self, personality, character. **3** sameness, likeness.

identity card a card bearing information about, and often a photograph of, the holder, taken as proof of a person's identity.

identity crisis *Psychol.* a mental conflict involving loss of a person's sense of self, and inability to accept or adopt the role he or she believes is expected by society. Typical symptoms include withdrawal or rebelliousness.

identity element *Maths.* an element which when combined with another element in a certain mathematical operation gives that second element as the product of the operation, *0* in addition (as $a + 0 = a$) and *1* in multiplication (as $a \times 1 = a$).

identity parade same as IDENTIFICATION PARADE.

ideogram or **ideograph** /ˈɪdɪoʊ-/ *noun* a written symbol designed to convey an abstract concept, or which stands for a real object without being a direct representation of it. See also LOGOGRAPH, PICTOGRAPH. [from Greek *idea*, idea + *gramma*, drawing]

ideograph *noun* an ideogram. [from Greek *idea*, idea + GRAPH]

ideographic *adj.* of the nature of or made up of ideographs.

ideographically *adv.* in an ideographic way.

ideological /aɪdɪə-/ *adj.* relating to or involving ideology.

ideologist *noun* **1** a person who supports a particular ideology. **2** a theorist. **3** a person who studies or is an expert in ideologies.

ideology *noun* (PL. **ideologies**) **1** the body of ideas and beliefs which form the basis for a social, economic, or political system. **2** the opinions, beliefs, and way of thinking characteristic of a particular person, group of people or nation. [from Greek *idea*, idea + -LOGY]

▣ IDEAS, PRINCIPLES, DOCTRINE(S), BELIEF(S). **2** philosophy, world-view, tenets, convictions, faith, creed, dogma.

Ides *pl. noun* (in the ancient Roman calendar) the fifteenth day of March, May, July, and October and the thirteenth day of the other months. [from Latin *idus*]

idiocy *noun* (PL. **idiocies**) **1** the state of being an idiot or extremely retarded mentally. **2** a foolish action or foolish behaviour.

▣ FOOLISHNESS, STUPIDITY, LUNACY. **2** folly, silliness, senselessness.
▣ WISDOM, SANITY.

idiolect *noun* a person's individual and distinctive way of speaking. [from Greek *idios*, own + dia*lect*]

idiom *noun* **1** an expression with a meaning which cannot be guessed at or derived from the meanings of the individual words which form it. **2** the syntax, grammar and forms of expression peculiar to a language or a variety of language. **3** the language, vocabulary, forms of expression, etc used by a particular person or group of people. **4** the characteristic style or forms of expression of a particular artist, musician, artistic or musical school, etc. [from Greek *idios*, own]

■ **1** phrase, expression, colloquialism. **3** language, vocabulary, phraseology, turn of phrase, usage, jargon, vernacular.

idiomatic *adj.* **1** characteristic of a particular language. **2** tending to use idioms.
idiomatically *adv.* in an idiomatic way.
idiosyncrasy /ˌɪdɪoʊˈsɪŋkrəsɪ/ *noun* (PL. **idiosyncrasies**) any personal way of behaving, reacting or thinking; a personal peculiarity or eccentricity. [from Greek *idios*, own + *syn*, together + *krasis*, mixing]

■ characteristic, peculiarity, singularity, oddity, eccentricity, freak, quirk, habit, mannerism, trait, feature.

idiosyncratic *adj.* involving idiosyncrasy; individual, eccentric.

■ personal, individual, characteristic, distinctive, peculiar, singular, odd, eccentric, quirky.
E3 general, common.

idiosyncratically *adv.* in an idiosyncratic way.
idiot *noun* **1** *colloq.* a foolish or stupid person. **2** a person who is severely mentally retarded. [from Greek *idiotes*, person lacking skill or expertise]

■ IMBECILE, MORON. **1** fool, blockhead, *colloq.* ass, *colloq.* nitwit, *colloq.* dimwit, *colloq.* halfwit, *slang* divvy, *slang* dork. **2** simpleton, dunce, ignoramus.

idiotic *adj.* stupid, foolish.

■ foolish, stupid, silly, absurd, senseless, *colloq.* daft, lunatic, insane, mad, crazy, foolhardy, hare-brained, halfwitted, moronic.
E3 sensible, sane.

idiotically *adv.* in an idiotic way.
idle — *adj.* **1** not in use; not being used; unoccupied; not working. **2** not wanting to work; lazy; indolent. **3** having no effect, result, purpose or value: *idle gossip*. **4** without cause, basis or good reason; unnecessary: *idle rumour*. — *verb* **1** (*usually* **idle away time**, etc) to spend time doing nothing or being idle. **2** *intrans.* to do nothing or be idle. **3** *intrans.*, *said of an engine, machinery, etc* to run gently without doing any work. **4** to cause (an engine, etc) to idle. [from Anglo-Saxon *idel*, worthless]

■ *adj.* **1** inactive, inoperative, unused, unoccupied, unemployed, jobless, redundant. **2** lazy, work-shy, indolent. **3** empty, trivial, casual, futile, vain, pointless, unproductive. **4** baseless, groundless, uncalled-for, unnecessary. *verb* **1** fritter, waste. **2** do nothing, laze, lounge, take it easy, kill time, potter, loiter, dawdle, loaf, slack, *colloq.* skive.
E3 *adj.* **1** active, busy. **2** industrious. *verb* **2** work.

idler *noun* a person who wastes time or is reluctant to work.
idly *adv.* in an idle way.
idol *noun* **1** an image or symbol, especially of a god, used as an object of worship. **2** an object of excessive love, honour or devotion. [from Greek *eidolon*]

■ **1** icon, effigy, image, graven image, god, deity, fetish. **2** favourite, darling, hero, heroine, pin-up.

idolater /aɪˈdɒlətə(r)/ *noun* **1** a person who worships idols. **2** a person who is a passionate and devoted admirer of someone or something.
idolatress /aɪˈdɒlətrɪs/ *noun* a female idolater.
idolatrous /aɪˈdɒlətrəs/ *adj.* relating to or involving worship of idols.
idolatry /aɪˈdɒlətrɪ/ *noun* (PL. **idolatries**) **1** the worship of idols. **2** excessive, love, honour, admiration or devotion.
idolization or **idolisation** *noun* idolizing or being idolized.
idolize or **idolise** *verb* **1** to love, honour, admire, etc (a person) too much. **2** to make an idol of.

■ **1** hero-worship, lionize, exalt, glorify, worship, venerate, revere, admire, love, adore, dote on.
E3 **1** despise.

idolizer or **idoliser** *noun* a person who idolizes.
idyll or **idyl** /ˈɪdɪl/ *noun* **1** a short poem or prose work describing a simple, pleasant, usually rural or pastoral scene. **2** a story, episode or scene suitable for such a work, eg one of happy innocence or love. [from Greek *eidyllion*]
idyllic /ɪˈdɪlɪk/ *adj.* **1** relating to or typical of an idyll. **2** charming, picturesque.

■ **1** pastoral, rustic, peaceful, happy, perfect, idealized. **2** charming, picturesque, unspoiled, delightful, heavenly.
E3 UNPLEASANT.

idyllically *adv.* in an idyllic way.
ie or **i.e.** *abbrev.* for Latin *id est*, that is to say.
if — *conj.* **1** in the event that; on condition that; supposing that. **2** although; even though. **3** whenever. **4** whether. **5** used to express a wish: *if only it would stop raining*. **6** used to make a polite request or suggestion: *if you wouldn't mind stopping just a minute*. **7** used to express surprise or annoyance: *well, if it isn't that book I'd thought I'd lost!* — *noun* a condition or supposition: *too many ifs and buts*. — **if anything** perhaps; on the contrary. [from Anglo-Saxon *gif*]
iffy *adj.* (**iffier**, **iffiest**) *colloq.* uncertain; doubtful; dubious.
igloo *noun* a dome-shaped Inuit house built with blocks of snow and ice. [from Inuit *iglu*, house]
igneous /ˈɪɡnɪəs/ *adj.* **1** of or like fire. **2** *Geol.* denoting any of a group of rocks that are formed by the solidification of molten magma either beneath the Earth's surface, producing *intrusive* (plutonic) rocks, eg granite, or after it has been extruded on to the surface, producing *extrusive* (volcanic) rocks, eg basalt. See also METAMORPHIC, SEDIMENTARY. [from Latin *ignis*, fire]
ignis fatuus /ˈɪɡnɪs ˈfatjʊəs/ (PL. **ignes fatui**) a will-o'-the-wisp. [from Latin *ignis fatuus*, foolish fire]
ignitable or **ignitible** *adj.* capable of being ignited.
ignite *verb* **1** to set fire to. **2** *intrans.* to catch fire. **3** to heat to the point at which combustion occurs. **4** to excite (feelings, emotions, etc). [from Latin *ignis*, fire]

■ **1** set fire to, set alight. **2** catch fire, flare up, burn, conflagrate. **4** fire, kindle, touch off, spark off.
E3 **1** extinguish, quench.

ignition *noun* **1** *Chem.* the point at which combustion of a chemical substance begins. **2** *Engineering* a system that initiates such combustion, especially by producing a spark which ignites an explosive mixture of fuel and air in an internal combustion engine, such as the petrol engine of a car.
ignition temperature *Chem.* the temperature to which a substance must be heated before it will burn in air.
ignobility or **ignobleness** *noun* being ignoble.
ignoble *adj.* **1** causing shame; dishonourable; mean. **2** of humble or low birth. [from Latin *ignobilis*]

▣ LOW, MEAN. **1** contemptible, despicable, base, vile, heinous, infamous, shameful, disgraceful, dishonourable. **2** humble, low-born.

▣ NOBLE. **1** worthy, honourable.

ignobly *adv.* in an ignoble way.

ignominious /ɪgnə'mɪnɪəs/ *adj.* causing shame or dishonour; humiliating.

▣ humiliating, mortifying, degrading, undignified, shameful, dishonourable, disgraceful, despicable, scandalous.

▣ triumphant, honourable.

ignominy /'ɪgnəmɪnɪ/ *noun* **1** public shame, disgrace or dishonour. **2** dishonourable conduct. [from Latin *ignominia*]

ignoramus /ɪgnə'reɪməs/ *noun* (PL. **ignoramuses**) an ignorant person. [from Latin *ignoramus*, we do not know]

ignorance *noun* **1** lack of knowledge or awareness. **2** being ignorant.

▣ **1** unawareness, unconsciousness, oblivion, unfamiliarity, inexperience, innocence, naïvety. **2** unintelligence, illiteracy.

▣ KNOWLEDGE. **1** awareness.

ignorant *adj.* **1** knowing very little; uneducated. **2** (*usually* **ignorant of something**) knowing little or nothing about it. **3** rude; ill-mannered. [from Latin *ignorare*, not to know]

▣ **1** uneducated, illiterate, unread, untaught, untrained, stupid, *derog.* clueless. **2** unenlightened, uninformed, unaware, unwitting, unconscious, oblivious.

▣ **1** educated, knowledgeable, clever, wise. **2** informed, aware.

ignore *verb* to take no notice of deliberately; to refuse to pay attention to. [from Latin *ignorare*, not to know]

▣ disregard, shut one's eyes to, overlook, pass over, neglect, omit, reject, snub, cold-shoulder, *slang* blank.

▣ notice, observe.

iguana /ɪ'gwɑːnə/ *noun* (PL. **iguanas**, **iguana**) any of a family of large insectivorous lizards with a crest of spines along its back. The common iguana is bright green and lives in tree branches in tropical Central and S America. [from Carib (S American Indian language) *iwana*]

ikebana /ɪkɪ'bɑːnə/ *noun* the Japanese art of flower arranging, in which blooms (or a single bloom), leaves, and other materials, are arranged formally and in careful relationship with one another to create a correct balance. [Japanese, = living flowers]

ikon see ICON.

IL *abbrev.* Illinois.

il- a form of *in-* used before words beginning in *l*: *illogical*.

ileostomy /ɪlɪ'ɒstəmɪ/ *noun* (PL. **ileostomies**) *Medicine* a surgical operation in which the ileum (the lowest part of the small intestine) is brought through an artificial opening in the abdominal wall, so that the contents of the ileum can be discharged directly to the outside of the body, bypassing the colon.

ileum /'ɪlɪəm/ *noun* (PL. **ilea**) the lower part of the small intestine leading into the large intestine. [from Latin *ilia*, groin, guts]

iliac *adj.* relating to or in the region of the ilium.

ilium *noun* (PL. **ilia**) one of a pair of large bones that form the upper part of each side of the pelvis; commonly called the hip bone. [from Latin *ilia*, groin, guts]

ilk — *noun* type; kind; class. — *adj. Scot.* same. — **of that ilk 1** of that type or kind. **2** *Scot.* of that same, ie of the estate or place of the same name (as the person's family name). [from Anglo-Saxon *ilca*]

Ill. *abbrev.* Illinois.

I'll *contr.* I will or I shall.

ill — *adj.* (**worse, worst**) **1** not in good health; sick. **2** *said of health* not good. **3** bad or harmful: *ill effects/ill-treatment*. **4** hostile; unfriendly: *ill-will*. **5** causing bad luck: *an ill omen*. **6** *said of manners* incorrect; improper. — *adv.* (**worse, worst**) **1** not easily; with difficulty. **2** hardly, scarcely: *be ill able to afford the money*. **3** badly; wrongly: *ill-matched*. **4** unfavourably: *it went ill with them*. **5** harshly: *speak ill of someone*. — *noun* **1** evil; harm. **2** injury; ailment. — **ill at ease** uneasy; embarrassed. **ill become one** to do one no credit; not to be to one's advantage. **take it ill** to be offended. [from Norse *illr*]

▣ *adj.* **1** sick, unwell, poorly, indisposed, laid up, ailing, off-colour, *colloq.* out of sorts, *colloq.* under the weather, seedy, queasy, unhealthy, infirm, frail. **3** bad, evil, damaging, harmful, injurious, detrimental, adverse. **4** hostile, antagonistic, unfriendly, unkind. **5** unlucky, unfortunate, unfavourable, inauspicious, sinister, ominous, threatening. *adv.* **2** hardly, barely, scarcely, only just.

▣ *adj.* **1** well. **3** good. **4** friendly. **5** fortunate, favourable.

ill-advised *adj.* foolish; done, or doing things, with little thought or consideration.

▣ imprudent, injudicious, unwise, foolish, ill-considered, thoughtless, hasty, rash, short-sighted, misguided.

▣ wise, sensible, well-advised.

ill-assorted *adj.* badly matched; not going well together.

ill-bred *adj.* badly brought up or educated; rude.

▣ bad-mannered, ill-mannered, discourteous, impolite, rude, coarse, indelicate.

▣ well-bred, polite.

ill-considered *adj.* badly thought out; not well planned.

ill-disposed *adj.* unfriendly; unsympathetic; unwilling to be supportive or helpful.

illegal *adj.* against the law; not legal. [from Latin *illegalis*]

▣ unlawful, illicit, criminal, wrong, forbidden, prohibited, banned, outlawed, unauthorized, under-the-counter, black-market, unconstitutional, wrongful.

▣ legal, lawful.

illegality *noun* (PL. **illegalities**) an illegal state or action.

illegibility *noun* being illegible.

illegible *adj.* difficult or impossible to read; not legible.

▣ unreadable, indecipherable, scrawled, obscure, faint, indistinct.

▣ legible.

illegitimacy *noun* being illegitimate.

illegitimate *adj.* **1** born of parents not married to each other at the time of birth. **2** unacceptable or not allowed, especially illegal. **3** *Logic* not properly inferred or reasoned. **4** improper.

▣ **1** natural, bastard. **2** illegal, unlawful, illicit, unauthorized, unacceptable, inadmissible. **3** invalid, unsound, spurious. **4** improper, incorrect.

▣ LEGITIMATE. **2** legal. **4** proper, correct.

ill-equipped *adj.* poorly provided with the necessary tools, abilities, etc.

ill-fated *adj.* ending in or bringing bad luck or ruin.

· · · · · · · · · · · · · · · · · · · ·

▤ doomed, ill-starred, ill-omened, unfortunate, unlucky, luckless, unhappy.

▣ lucky.

· ·

ill-favoured *adj.* not attractive, especially in appearance; objectionable.

ill-feeling *noun* bad or hostile feeling; animosity.

ill-founded *adj.*, *said of an argument, theory, suspicion, etc* having no sound basis or reason.

ill-gotten *adj.* obtained dishonestly: *ill-gotten gains.*

ill-humoured *adj.* bad-tempered; quick-tempered.

illiberal *adj.* **1** having strict opinions about morality, behaviour, etc; narrow-minded; prejudiced. **2** not generous; mean. **3** uncultured; unrefined. [from Latin *illiberalis*]

illiberality *noun* being illiberal.

illicit *adj.* not permitted by law or by social custom. [from Latin *illicitus*]

· · · · · · · · · · · · · · · · · · · ·

▤ illegal, unlawful, criminal, wrong, illegitimate, improper, forbidden, prohibited, unauthorized, unlicensed, black-market, contraband, under-the-counter, furtive, clandestine.

▣ legal, permissible, allowed.

· ·

ill-informed *adj.* lacking knowledge or information.

illiteracy *noun* being illiterate; the inability to read and write.

illiterate — *adj.* **1** unable to read and write. **2** uneducated or ignorant, especially in a particular field or subject. — *noun* an illiterate person. [from Latin *illiteratus*]

ill-judged *adj.* poorly advised; done without proper consideration.

ill-mannered *adj.* having bad manners; rude; uncouth.

ill-natured *adj.* spiteful; mean; surly.

illness *noun* **1** a disease. **2** the state of being sick or unwell.

· · · · · · · · · · · · · · · · · · · ·

▤ SICKNESS, INDISPOSITION, INFIRMITY. **1** disease, disorder, complaint, ailment, malady, affliction. **2** ill health.

· ·

illogical *adj.* **1** not based on careful thinking or reason. **2** not following the principles of logic.

· · · · · · · · · · · · · · · · · · · ·

▤ IRRATIONAL. **1** unreasonable, senseless, meaningless, absurd, inconsistent, unscientific. **2** invalid, unsound, faulty, fallacious, specious, sophistical.

▣ LOGICAL.

· ·

illogicality *noun* (PL. **illogicalities**) being illogical, or an instance of this.

ill-omened *adj.*, *said of a plan, course of action, etc* likely to end badly.

ill-starred *adj.* marked by bad luck; bound to fail.

ill-tempered *adj.* bad-tempered; spiteful and surly.

ill-timed *adj.* said or done at an unsuitable time; inopportune.

ill-treat *verb* to treat badly or cruelly; to abuse.

· · · · · · · · · · · · · · · · · · · ·

▤ maltreat, abuse, injure, harm, damage, neglect, mistreat, mishandle, misuse, wrong, oppress.

· ·

ill-treatment *noun* abuse, cruelty, misuse.

illuminant — *noun* something that gives off light. — *adj.* giving off light. [from Latin *illuminare*, from *lumen*, light]

illuminate *verb* **1** to light up or make bright. **2** to decorate with lights. **3** to decorate (a manuscript) with elaborate designs and initial letters in gold, silver or bright colours. **4** to make clearer and more easily understood. **5** to enlighten spiritually or intellectually. [from Latin *illuminare*, from *lumen*, light]

· · · · · · · · · · · · · · · · · · · ·

▤ **1** light, light up, brighten. **3** decorate, ornament, illustrate. **4** explain, clarify, clear up, elucidate, illustrate. **5** enlighten, edify, instruct.

▣ **1** darken. **5** mystify.

· ·

illuminating *adj.* that clarifies, explains, or informs.

illumination *noun* **1** the act of illuminating or state of being illuminated. **2** any source of light; lighting. **3** (**illuminations**) coloured decorative lights hung in streets and towns. **4** the art or skill of decorating manuscripts with elaborate designs and initial letters in gold, silver and bright colours. **5** such a design or initial letter in a manuscript.

· · · · · · · · · · · · · · · · · · · ·

▤ **2** light, lights, lighting, beam, ray, brightness, radiance. **4, 5** decoration, ornamentation, illustration.

· ·

illuminative *adj.* illuminating, lighting.

illumine *verb poetic*, *literary* to illuminate. [from Old French *illuminer*]

illusion *noun* **1** a deceptive or misleading appearance. **2** a false or misleading impression, idea, belief or understanding; delusion. **3** *Psychol.* a false perception of an object or experience due to misinterpretation by the mind of evidence relayed to it by the senses, eg the overheard conversations of others may be interpreted as voices conspiring to destroy the listener. [from Latin *illusio*, irony, mocking]

· · · · · · · · · · · · · · · · · · · ·

▤ **1** apparition, mirage, hallucination, figment, fantasy, fancy. **2** delusion, misapprehension, misconception, error, fallacy.

▣ **1** reality. **2** truth.

· ·

illusionism *noun Art* the use of perspective, foreshortening, light and shade, and other pictorial devices to produce an illusion of reality. Ancient Roman wall-paintings (such as at Pompeii), Renaissance stage-scenery, and Baroque ceiling-decoration are examples of illusionism.

illusionist *noun* a conjurer who plays tricks on the eyes.

illusive or **illusory** *adj.* **1** seeming to be or having the characteristics of an illusion. **2** deceptive; unreal.

· · · · · · · · · · · · · · · · · · · ·

▤ UNREAL. **1** apparent, seeming, hallucinatory, fanciful, unsubstantial. **2** deceptive, misleading, deluding, delusive, false, fallacious.

▣ REAL.

· ·

illustrate *verb* **1** to provide (a book, text, lecture, etc) with pictures and diagrams. **2** to make (a statement, etc) clearer, especially by providing examples. **3** to be an example of. [from Latin *illustrare*, to light up]

· · · · · · · · · · · · · · · · · · · ·

▤ **1** decorate, ornament, adorn. **2** explain, clarify, elucidate, illuminate. **3** exemplify, demonstrate, exhibit, show, depict.

· ·

illustrated *adj.* having or using illustrations.

illustration *noun* **1** a picture or diagram that helps make a text, book, lecture, etc clearer, or decorates it. **2** an example which makes something clear. **3** the act of illustrating or state of being illustrated.

· · · · · · · · · · · · · · · · · · · ·

▤ **1** picture, plate, half-tone, photograph, drawing, sketch, figure, diagram. **2** example, specimen, instance, case, analogy. **3** explanation, clarification, exemplification, demonstration.

· ·

illustrative *adj.* being or acting as an illustration, explanation or example.

illustrator *noun* a person who provides illustrations.

illustrious *adj.* distinguished; renowned; celebrated; noble. [from Latin *illustris*, bright, lustrous]

■ great, eminent, distinguished, celebrated, famous, famed, renowned, noted, prominent, outstanding, remarkable, notable, brilliant, splendid, magnificent, glorious, noble. ⊟ ignoble, inglorious, unknown.

illustriously *adv.* famously.

ill-will *noun* bad or unfriendly feeling; the urge or wish to do harm: *bear him no ill-will.*

■ hostility, antagonism, bad blood, enmity, unfriendliness, malevolence, malice, spite, animosity, ill-feeling, resentment, hard feelings, grudge, dislike, aversion, hatred. ⊟ goodwill, friendship.

ilmenite *noun Geol.* a black or dark brown mineral composed of iron, titanium, and oxygen, found in igneous rocks, and in metamorphic rocks such as gneiss and schist. It is the principal ore of titanium. [named after the Ilmen Mountains in the Urals]

I'm *contr.* I am.

im- a form of *in-* (see IN-^{1}, IN-^{2}) used before words beginning in *b*, *m*, and *p*: *immature/implode.*

image — *noun* 1 a likeness of a person or thing, especially in the form of a portrait or statue. 2 a person or thing that resembles another person or thing closely. 3 an idea or picture in the mind. 4 an optical reproduction of a physical object formed by light reflected in a mirror or refracted through a lens. It may be upright or inverted, and magnified or reduced in size. 5 *Physics* any reproduction of a physical object formed by sound waves or electromagnetic radiation originating from or reflected by the object, eg ultrasound scan, X-ray photograph. 6 the visual display reproduced by a television receiver. 7 *Psychol.* a mental view of another person, eg a child's image of its mother. 8 (*in full* **public image**) the impression that people in general have of someone's character, behaviour, etc. 9 a typical example or embodiment. 10 a simile or metaphor. — *verb* 1 to form an image of. 2 to form a likeness of in the mind; to imagine. 3 to mirror. 4 to be a typical example of. [from Latin *imago*]

■ *noun* 1 representation, likeness, picture, portrait, icon, effigy, figure, statue, model, replica. 3 idea, notion, concept, impression, perception. 4 reflection.

imagery *noun* (PL. **imageries**) 1 the use of figures of speech in writing, literature, etc. 2 the making of images, especially in the mind. 3 mental images. 4 statues, carvings, etc.

imaginable *adj.* capable of being imagined.

■ conceivable, thinkable, believable, credible, plausible, likely, possible. ⊟ unimaginable.

imaginary *adj.* existing only in the mind or imagination; not real.

■ imagined, fanciful, illusory, hallucinatory, pretend, make-believe, unreal, non-existent, fictional, fabulous, legendary, mythological, made-up, invented, fictitious, assumed, supposed, hypothetical. ⊟ real.

imaginary number *Maths.* the square root of a negative number.

imagination *noun* 1 a the ability to form or the process of forming mental images of things, etc one has not seen or of which one has no direct perception or knowledge. b the part of the mind where this takes place. 2 the creative ability of the mind. 3 the ability to cope resourcefully with unexpected events or problems.

■ 1 fancy, mind's eye. 2 imaginativeness, creativity, inventiveness, originality, inspiration, insight, vision. 3 ingenuity, resourcefulness, enterprise. ⊟ 2 unimaginativeness.

imaginative *adj.* 1 showing, done with or created by imagination. 2 having a lively imagination.

■ CREATIVE, INVENTIVE, VISIONARY, INGENIOUS. 1 innovative, original, inspired, fanciful, fantastic. 2 resourceful, enterprising. ⊟ UNIMAGINATIVE.

imagine *verb* 1 to form a mental picture of (something). 2 to see or hear, etc something which is not true or does not exist: *imagine things.* 3 to think, suppose, or guess: *I can't imagine where she's got to.* 4 *intrans.* to use the imagination. 5 *intrans., trans.* used as an exclamation of surprise: *imagine that!* [from Latin *imaginari*, from *imago*, image]

■ 1 picture, visualize, envisage, conceive, think up, dream up, invent, devise, create. 2 fancy, conjure up. 3 think, believe, suppose, guess, conjecture, assume, take it, gather. 4 fantasize, pretend, make believe. 5 fancy.

imaginings *pl. noun* things seen or heard which do not exist; fancies, fantasies.

imago /ɪˈmeɪɡoʊ/ *noun* (PL. **imagos**, **imagines**) the final stage in the life cycle of an insect, when it is a sexually mature adult. [from Latin *imago*, image]

imam /ɪˈmɑːm/ *noun* 1 a leader of prayers in a Mosque. 2 (**Imam**) a title given to various Muslim leaders, eg a Shiite religious leader believed to be a direct successor of the prophet Mohammed, or a learned Muslim theologian. [from Arabic *imam*, chief, leader]

IMAX *noun trademark* a system of large wide-screen motion-picture presentation, developed in Canada in 1968, using 70mm film running horizontally with a frame size 70 x 46 mm. It is projected on a screen, usually 18–23m wide and 14–18m high; the audience is seated comparatively close to the screen so that the picture fills their field of vision. [from IMAGE + MAXIMUM]

imbalance *noun* a lack of balance or proportion; inequality.

■ disproportion, unevenness, inequality, disparity, unfairness, partiality, bias. ⊟ balance, parity.

imbecile — *noun* 1 a person of very low intelligence, especially someone who is capable only of keeping himself or herself out of danger and of performing simple tasks under supervision. 2 a stupid person; a fool. — *adj.* mentally weak; stupid; foolish. [from Latin *imbecillus*]

■ *noun* IDIOT, MORON, CRETIN. 1 simpleton. 2 fool, blockhead, halfwit.

imbecility *noun* (PL. **imbecilities**) 1 being an imbecile. 2 extreme stupidity, or an instance of this.

imbed *verb* (**imbedded**, **imbedding**) same as EMBED.

imbibe *verb* 1 *trans., intrans.* to drink (especially alcoholic drinks). 2 to take in or absorb (ideas, etc). [from Latin *imbibere*]

imbricate *adj. Biol.*, *said of fish scales, leaves, layers of tissue, teeth, etc* overlapping like roof tiles. [from Latin *imbricare*, to cover with overlapping tiles, from *imbrex*, a tile]

imbroglio /ɛmˈbroʊlɪoʊ/ *noun* (PL. **imbroglios**) 1 a confused mass or heap. 2 a confused and complicated situation. 3 a misunderstanding or disagreement. [from Italian *imbroglio*, confusion]

imbue / ɪmˈbjuː / *verb* **1 (imbue someone with something)** to fill or inspire them, especially with ideals or principles. **2** to soak or saturate, especially with dye. [from Latin *imbuere*, to saturate]

▣ SATURATE, PERMEATE, SUFFUSE. **1** fill, inspire. **2** soak, steep, impregnate, tint, tinge.

IMF *abbrev*. International Monetary Fund.
imitable *adj*. capable of being imitated.
imitate *verb* **1** to copy the behaviour, manners, appearance, etc of; to take as a model. **2** to mimic. **3** to make a copy of; to reproduce or duplicate. [from Latin *imitari*]

▣ COPY. **1** emulate, follow. **2** mimic, ape, impersonate, take off, caricature, parody, *colloq.* send up, spoof, parrot, repeat, echo, mirror. **3** duplicate, reproduce, simulate, counterfeit, forge.

imitation — *noun* **1** an act of imitating. **2** that which is produced by imitating; a copy or counterfeit. **3** *Mus.* the repeating of a passage, phrase, theme, etc which has already been heard, often at a different pitch or in a different voice. — *adj*. cheaply made to look or function like something which is more expensive.

▣ *noun* **1** mimicry, impersonation, impression, take-off, caricature, parody, *colloq.* send-up, spoof, mockery, travesty. **2** copy, duplicate, reproduction, replica, simulation, counterfeit, fake, forgery, likeness, resemblance, reflection. *adj.* artificial, synthetic, man-made, ersatz, fake, faux, *colloq.* phoney, mock, sham, pseudo, reproduction, simulated.
▣ *adj.* genuine.

imitative *adj*. **1** imitating, copying, or mimicking. **2** copying a better or more expensive original. **3** *said of a word* imitating the sound (eg *sizzle*) or trying to represent the appearance, movement or general impression (eg *flash*) of a thing or action.

▣ **1** copying, mimicking. **2** unoriginal, derivative, plagiarized, simulated, mock.

imitator *noun* a person or creature that imitates.

▣ mimic, impersonator, impressionist, parrot, *derog.* copycat, copier, emulator, follower.

immaculate *adj*. **1** perfectly clean and neat; perfectly groomed. **2** free from blemish, flaw or error; pure. [from IM- + Latin *macula*, spot, stain]

▣ **1** spotless, clean, spick and span, neat, tidy, well-groomed. **2** perfect, unblemished, flawless, faultless, impeccable, pure, unsullied, undefiled, untainted, stainless, blameless, innocent.
▣ **1** dirty, untidy. **2** imperfect, blemished, flawed.

immanence or **immanency** *noun* the concept of a supreme being present throughout the universe.
immanent *adj*. **1** existing or remaining within; inherent. **2** *said of a supreme being or power* present everywhere. [from IM- + Latin *manere*, to remain]
immaterial *adj*. **1** not important. **2** not formed of matter. [from Latin *immaterialis*]

▣ **1** irrelevant, insignificant, unimportant, minor, trivial, trifling, inconsequential.
▣ **1** relevant, important.

immature *adj*. **1** not fully grown or developed; not ripe. **2** not fully developed emotionally or intellectually and therefore childish. [from Latin *immaturus*]

▣ JUVENILE. **1** young, under-age, adolescent, callow, inexperienced, green, unripe. **2** childish, puerile, infantile, babyish.
▣ MATURE.

immaturity *noun* being immature.
immeasurable *adj*. too great to be measured; very great; immense.

▣ vast, immense, infinite, limitless, unlimited, boundless, unbounded, endless, bottomless, inexhaustible, incalculable, inestimable.
▣ limited.

immediacy *noun* (PL. **immediacies**) **1** the quality of being immediate or appealing directly to the emotions, understanding, etc. **2** an immediate problem, requirement, or necessity.
immediate *adj*. **1** happening or done at once and without delay. **2** nearest or next in space, time or relationship: *the immediate family / the immediate vicinity*. **3** of the current time; urgent: *deal with the immediate problems first*. **4** having a direct effect and without anything coming in between: *the immediate cause of death*. [from Latin *immediatus*]

▣ **1** instant, instantaneous, direct, prompt, swift. **2** nearest, next, adjacent, near, close, recent. **3** current, present, existing, urgent, pressing.
▣ **1** delayed. **2** distant.

immediately — *adv.* at once or without delay; without anything coming in between. — *conj.* as soon as.

▣ *adv.* now, straight away, right away, at once, instantly, directly, forthwith, without delay, promptly, unhesitatingly.
▣ *adv.* eventually, never.

immemorial *adj*. extending far back in time beyond anyone's memory or written records: *a custom since time immemorial*. [from Latin *immemorialis*]
immemorially *adv.* far back in time.
immense *adj*. **1** very or unusually large or great. **2** *colloq.* very good. [from Latin *immensus*, immeasurable]

▣ **1** vast, great, huge, enormous, massive, giant, gigantic, tremendous, monumental.
▣ **1** tiny, minute.

immensely *adv.* very greatly.
immenseness or **immensity** *noun* great size, immeasurable extent.

▣ magnitude, bulk, expanse, vastness, greatness, hugeness, enormousness, massiveness.
▣ minuteness.

immerse *verb* **1** to dip into or under the surface of a liquid completely. **2** to baptize by submerging the whole body in water. **3** (**be immersed in something**) to be occupied or involved deeply in it; to be absorbed: *became immersed in the book*. [from Latin *immergere*, to dip]

▣ **1** plunge, submerge, submerse, sink, duck, dip, douse, bathe.

immersible *adj*. capable of being immersed.
immersion *noun* **1** immersing or being immersed. **2** baptism.

immersion heater an electric heating element that is immersed directly in a tank of water, and controlled by a thermostat. Immersion heaters are used to provide a supply of hot water for domestic purposes.

immigrant — *noun* **1** a person who immigrates. **2** *Biol.* an animal or plant which becomes established in an area where it was previously not found. — *adj.* **1** *said of a person* having recently immigrated. **2** concerning or relating to immigrants. See also EMIGRANT.

∙∙∙∙∙∙∙∙∙∙∙∙∙∙∙∙∙∙∙

⊟ *noun* **1** incomer, settler, newcomer, alien.
⊞ *noun* **1** emigrant.

∙∙∙∙∙∙∙∙∙∙∙∙∙∙∙∙∙∙∙∙∙∙∙∙∙∙∙∙∙∙∙∙∙∙∙

immigrate *verb intrans.* to come to a foreign country with the intention of settling in it. See also EMIGRATE. [from Latin *immigrare*]

immigration *noun* immigrating; settling in a foreign country.

imminence *noun* **1** being imminent. **2** something imminent.

imminent *adj., said especially of something unwelcome* likely to happen in the near future. [from Latin *imminere*, to project over]

∙∙∙∙∙∙∙∙∙∙∙∙∙∙∙∙∙∙∙∙∙∙

⊟ impending, forthcoming, in the offing, approaching, coming, near, close, looming, menacing, threatening, brewing, in the air.
⊞ remote, far-off.

∙∙∙

immiscible *adj. Chem.* denoting two or more liquids that when shaken together form separate layers and do not mix, eg oil and water.

immobile *adj.* **1** not able to move or be moved. **2** not moving; motionless. [from Latin *immobilis*]

∙∙∙∙∙∙∙∙∙∙∙∙∙∙∙∙∙∙∙∙

⊟ FROZEN, RIGID, STIFF. **1** static, immovable, rooted, fixed. **2** stationary, motionless, unmoving, still, stock-still.
⊞ MOBILE. **2** moving.

∙∙∙

immobility *noun* being immobile; stability, lack of movement.

immobilization or **immobilisation** *noun* immobilizing or being immobilized.

immobilize or **immobilise** *verb* to make or keep immobile.

∙∙∙∙∙∙∙∙∙∙∙∙∙∙∙∙∙∙∙

⊟ stop, halt, fix, freeze, transfix, paralyse, cripple, disable.
⊞ mobilize.

∙∙∙∙∙∙∙∙∙∙∙∙∙∙∙∙∙∙∙∙∙∙∙∙∙∙∙∙∙∙∙∙∙∙∙

immoderacy *noun* lack of restraint.

immoderate *adj.* going far beyond normal or reasonable limits; extreme; excessive. [from Latin *immoderatus*]

immoderately *adv.* extravagantly, without restraint.

immodest *adj.* **1** lacking modesty; shameful; indecent; improper. **2** boastful and conceited; forward. [from Latin *immodestus*]

∙∙∙∙∙∙∙∙∙∙∙∙∙∙∙∙∙∙∙∙∙∙∙

⊟ **1** indecent, revealing, improper, immoral, obscene, risqué. **2** boastful, *colloq.* big-headed, vain, conceited, cocky, forward.
⊞ MODEST.

∙∙∙

immodesty *noun* lack of modesty, indecency.

immolate *verb* to kill or offer in sacrifice. [from Latin *immolare*, to sprinkle with meal before sacrificing]

immolation *noun* **1** an act of immolating, a sacrifice. **2** something that is sacrificed.

immoral *adj.* **1** morally wrong or bad; evil. **2** not conforming to the sexual standards of society; promiscuous. See also AMORAL.

∙∙∙∙∙∙∙∙∙∙∙∙∙∙∙∙∙∙∙∙∙∙∙

⊟ CORRUPT. **1** unethical, wrong, bad, sinful, evil, wicked, unscrupulous, unprincipled. **2** depraved, degenerate,

dissolute, promiscuous, indecent, pornographic, obscene, impure.
⊞ **1** moral, right, good. **2** pure, chaste.

immorality *noun* (PL. **immoralities**) **1** being immoral. **2** an immoral act or activity. **3** promiscuity.

immortal — *adj.* **1** living forever and never dying. **2** lasting forever; perpetual. — *noun* **1** a person who will live forever, or who will always be remembered. **2** (**the immortals**) the ancient Greek and Roman gods. [from Latin *immortalis*]

∙∙∙∙∙∙∙∙∙∙∙∙∙∙∙∙∙∙∙∙∙∙

⊟ *adj.* UNDYING. **2** eternal, everlasting, perpetual, endless, ceaseless, imperishable, lasting, enduring, abiding, timeless, ageless.
⊞ *adj.* **1** mortal.

∙∙∙

immortality *noun* being immortal.

immortalize or **immortalise** *verb* to make (a person, event, etc) famous for ever, especially by inclusion in a work of art.

∙∙∙∙∙∙∙∙∙∙∙∙∙∙∙∙∙∙∙∙∙∙

⊟ celebrate, commemorate, memorialize, perpetuate, enshrine.

∙∙∙

immovability *noun* being immovable.

immovable *adj.* **1** impossible to move; not meant to be moved. **2** steadfast; unyielding. **3** incapable of feeling or showing emotion, especially sorrow or pity. **4** *Legal, said of property* consisting of land or houses.

∙∙∙∙∙∙∙∙∙∙∙∙∙∙∙∙∙∙∙∙∙∙

⊟ **1** fixed, rooted, immobile, stuck, fast, secure, stable, firm. **2** steadfast, constant, set, determined, resolute, adamant, unyielding, unshakable, obstinate.
⊞ **1** movable.

∙∙∙

immune *adj.* **1** (*usually* **immune to something**) protected by inoculation from, or having a natural resistance to, a particular disease: *is immune to German measles*. **2** (*usually* **immune from something**) free, exempt, or protected from it: *was immune from prosecution*. [from Latin *immunis*]

∙∙∙∙∙∙∙∙∙∙∙∙∙∙∙∙∙∙∙∙∙∙

⊟ PROTECTED, SAFE. **1** invulnerable, unsusceptible, resistant, proof. **2** exempt, free.
⊞ **1** susceptible.

∙∙∙

immune response *Physiol.* the response of the body to the introduction of an antigen (a foreign substance), especially the formation of antibodies, but also including the development of cellular immunity, hypersensitive reactions, etc.

immune system *Physiol.* the tissues and cells of the body that recognize and attack the antigens (foreign substances) associated with different diseases.

immunity *noun* (PL. **immunities**) an immune state; protection.

∙∙∙∙∙∙∙∙∙∙∙∙∙∙∙∙∙∙∙∙∙∙

⊟ resistance, protection, exemption, indemnity, impunity, exoneration, freedom, liberty, licence, franchise, privilege, right.
⊞ susceptibility.

∙∙∙

immunization or **immunisation** *noun* making immune, especially to a disease.

immunize or **immunise** *verb* to produce artificial immunity to a disease in (a person) by injecting an antiserum (containing antibodies formed in another organism), which confers *passive immunity*, or a treated antigen (eg dead or weakened viruses or bacteria), which confers *active immunity* by stimulating the body to produce its own antibodies.

∙∙∙∙∙∙∙∙∙∙∙∙∙∙∙∙∙∙∙∙∙∙

⊟ vaccinate, inoculate, protect, safeguard.

∙∙∙

immunodeficiency *noun* (PL. **immunodeficiencies**) a deficiency or breakdown in the body's ability to fight infection.

immunoglobulin *noun Biol.* one of a group of proteins found in blood plasma, acting as antibodies.

immunological *adj.* relating to or involving immunology.

immunologist *noun* an expert in immunology.

immunology *noun* the scientific study of resistance to, and protection against, infection.

immunosuppressive or **immunosuppressant** — *noun Medicine* a drug or other agent that suppresses the body's normal immune response and so lowers its resistance to infection. Immunosuppressive drugs are used to ensure that transplanted organs and tissues are not rejected. — *adj.* denoting such a drug or agent.

immure *verb* **1** to enclose or imprison within, or as if within, walls. **2** to shut (someone or oneself) away. [from IM- + Latin *murus*, wall]

immutability *noun* being unchangeable.

immutable *adj.* that cannot be changed or will not change. [from Latin *immutabilis*]

immutably *adv.* unalterably.

imp *noun* **1** a small mischievous or evil spirit. **2** a mischievous or annoying child. [from Anglo-Saxon *impa*, shoot]

impact — *noun* (with stress on *im-*) **1** the act of an object hitting or colliding with another object; a collision. **2** the force of such a collision. **3** a strong effect or impression. — *verb* (with variable stress) **1** to press (two objects) together with force or to force (one object) into (another). **2** *intrans.* to come into contact with force. **3** *intrans.* to have an impact or effect on someone or something. [from Latin *impingere*, to strike against]

⊟ *noun* **1** collision, crash, smash, bang, bump, blow, knock, contact. **2** force, brunt, shock, jolt. **3** effect, consequences, repercussions, impression, power, influence, significance, meaning.

impacted *adj.* **1** *said of a tooth* unable to grow because of being wedged between the jawbone and another tooth. **2** *said of a fracture* with the two broken ends of bone crushed together.

impair *verb* to damage or weaken, especially in quality or strength. [from Old French *empeirer*]

⊟ damage, harm, injure, mar, spoil, worsen, undermine, weaken, reduce, lessen, diminish, blunt.
⊟ improve, enhance.

impairment *noun* damage, weakening.

impala *noun* (PL. **impalas**, **impala**) a graceful African antelope with lyre-shaped horns, capable of long high leaps. [from Zulu]

impale *verb* **1** to pierce with or as if with a long pointed object or weapon. **2** to put (two coats-of-arms) on a shield divided vertically into two. [from IM- + Latin *palus*, stake]

⊟ **1** pierce, puncture, perforate, run through, spear, lance, spike, skewer, spit, stick, transfix.

impalement *noun* impaling or being impaled.

impalpability *noun* being impalpable.

impalpable *adj.* **1** not able to be felt or perceived by touch. **2** difficult to understand or grasp. [from Latin *impalpabilis*]

impanel *verb* (**impanelled**, **impanelling**) same as EMPANEL.

impart *verb* **1** to make (information, knowledge, etc) known; to communicate (news, etc). **2** to give or transmit (a particular quality). [from Latin *impartire*]

⊟ **1** tell, relate, communicate, make known, disclose, divulge, reveal, convey, pass on. **2** give, transmit, grant, confer, contribute, lend.
⊟ WITHHOLD.

impartation *noun* imparting, communication.

impartial *adj.* not favouring one person, etc more than another; fair and unbiased; not partial.

⊟ objective, dispassionate, detached, disinterested, neutral, non-partisan, unbiased, unprejudiced, open-minded, fair, just, equitable, even-handed.
⊟ partial, biased, prejudiced.

impartiality *noun* being impartial, fairness.

impassability or **impassableness** *noun* being impassable.

impassable *adj.* not able to be passed through or travelled along.

impasse /am'pas/ *noun* a situation in which progress is impossible and from which there is no way out. [from French *impasse*]

⊟ deadlock, stalemate, dead end, cul-de-sac, blind alley, halt, standstill.

impassion *verb* (**impassioned**, **impassioning**) to move with or fill with passion. [from Italian *impassionare*]

impassioned *adj.* moved by or showing very strong feelings.

impassive *adj.* **1** incapable of feeling and expressing emotion. **2** showing no feeling or emotion.

⊟ **1** unfeeling, unemotional, imperturbable, unexcitable, stoical, dispassionate. **2** expressionless, calm, composed, unruffled, unconcerned, unmoved.
⊟ **1** responsive, emotional. **2** concerned, moved.

impassiveness or **impassivity** *noun* being impassive.

impasto /im'pastoʊ/ *noun* in painting and pottery, the technique of laying the paint or pigment on thickly. [from Italian *impasto*]

impatience *noun* lack of patience or tolerance.

⊟ restlessness, agitation, anxiety, nervousness, irritability, intolerance, brusqueness, haste, rashness, eagerness, keenness.
⊟ patience.

impatiens /im'peɪʃɪɛnz/ *noun* any of 500 to 600 species of annual and perennial plants belonging to the genus *Impatiens*, native to Europe, Asia, most of Africa, and N America, and having translucent stems and oval toothed leaves. The flowers hang from a slender stalk, and either have five flat petals and a slender curved spur, or are two-lipped with a funnel-shaped tube and spur.

impatient *adj.* **1** unwilling to wait or delay. **2** intolerant. **3** restlessly eager and anxious. [from Latin *impatiens*]

⊟ **1** impetuous, hasty, precipitate, headlong. **2** intolerant, brusque, irritable, snappy, hot-tempered, quick-tempered. **3** eager, keen, restless, fidgety, fretful, anxious, nervous.
⊟ PATIENT.

impeach *verb* **1** *Brit.* to charge with a serious crime, especially a crime against the state or treason. **2** *North Amer.* to accuse (a public or government official) with misconduct while in office. **3** to call into question; to cast doubt upon (eg a person's honesty). [from Latin *impedicare*, to fetter]

⊟ **1, 2** accuse, charge, indict, arraign, denounce. **3** impugn, disparage, criticize, censure.

impeachable *adj.* **1** capable of being impeached. **2** *said of an offence* making a person liable to be impeached.
impeachment *noun Politics* the legal process of removing an undesirable person from office.
impeccable *adj.* **1** free from fault or error. **2** not liable to sin. [from Latin *impeccabilis*]

◻ **1** perfect, faultless, precise, exact, flawless, unblemished, stainless, immaculate, pure, irreproachable, blameless, innocent.
▣ **1** faulty, flawed, corrupt.

impecunious *adj.* having little or no money; poor; penniless. [from IM- + obsolete *pecunious*, wealthy]
impedance / ɪmˈpiːdəns/ *noun* (SYMBOL Z) **1** *Electr.* the effective resistance of an electric circuit or circuit component to the passage of an electric current. For an ac circuit it is due to the combined effect of resistance and reactance, and for a dc circuit it is due to the resistance alone. **2** anything that impedes.
impede *verb* to prevent or delay the start or progress of (an activity, etc); to obstruct or hinder. [from Latin *impedire*, to snare the foot]

◻ hinder, hamper, obstruct, block, clog, slow, retard, hold up, delay, check, curb, restrain, thwart, disrupt, stop, prevent.
▣ aid, promote, further.

impediment *noun* **1** a thing or person that delays or prevents the start or progress of something; an obstacle or hindrance. **2** a minor defect in a person's speech, eg a lisp. [from Latin *impedimentum*]

◻ **1** hindrance, obstacle, obstruction, barrier, bar, block, stumbling-block, snag, difficulty, check, curb, restraint, restriction. **2** defect, handicap.
▣ **1** aid.

impedimenta *pl. noun* any objects which impede progress or movement, especially military baggage and equipment.
impel *verb* (**impelled**, **impelling**) **1** to push, drive or urge forward; to propel. **2** to force or urge into action. [from Latin *impellare*]

◻ URGE, FORCE, DRIVE, PUSH, SPUR, GOAD, MOVE. **1** propel. **2** oblige, compel, constrain, prompt, stimulate, motivate, inspire.
▣ **2** deter, dissuade.

impend *verb intrans.* **1** to be about to happen. **2** *said of a danger, etc* to threaten; to hover threateningly. [from Latin *impendere*, to hang over]
impending *adj.* about to happen.

◻ imminent, forthcoming, approaching, coming, close, near, looming, menacing, threatening.
▣ remote.

impenetrability *noun* being inpenetrable.
impenetrable *adj.* **1** incapable of being entered or passed through. **2** not capable of receiving or being touched by intellectual ideas and influences. **3** impossible or very difficult to understand. [from Latin *impenetrabilis*]

◻ **1** solid, thick, dense, impassable. **3** unintelligible, incomprehensible, unfathomable, baffling, mysterious, cryptic, enigmatic, obscure, dark, inscrutable.
▣ **3** accessible, understandable.

impenitence *noun* being impenitent.

impenitent *adj.* not sorry for having done something wrong; unrepentant. [from Latin *impaenitens*]
imperative — *adj.* **1** absolutely essential; urgent. **2** having or showing authority; commanding. **3** *Grammar* of or being the mood of a verb used to give orders. — *noun* **1** *Grammar* the imperative mood. **2** a verb in the imperative mood. **3** that which is imperative, especially a command or order. [from Latin *imperativus*, from *imperare*, to command]

◻ *adj.* **1** essential, vital, crucial, urgent, pressing, compulsory, obligatory.
▣ *adj.* **1** optional, unimportant.

imperceptibility *noun* being imperceptible.
imperceptible *adj.* **1** too small or slight to be seen, heard, noticed, etc. **2** not able to be perceived by the senses. [from Latin *imperceptibilis*]

◻ **1** faint, slight, negligible, inappreciable, indiscernible, infinitesimal, microscopic, minute, tiny, small, fine, subtle, gradual. **2** invisible, inaudible.
▣ PERCEPTIBLE.

imperfect — *adj.* **1** having faults; spoilt; not perfect. **2** lacking the full number of parts; incomplete. **3** *Grammar* of or being the verb tense expressing a continuing state or incomplete action, usually in the past. — *noun Grammar* **1** the imperfect tense. **2** a verb in the imperfect tense. [from Latin *imperfectus*]

◻ *adj.* **1** faulty, flawed, defective, damaged, broken, chipped. **2** deficient, lacking, short, incomplete.
▣ *adj.* **1, 2** perfect.

imperfection *noun* **1** the state of being imperfect. **2** a fault, weakness or blemish.

◻ **2** fault, flaw, defect, blemish, deficiency, shortcoming, weakness, failing.
▣ **1** perfection.

imperial *adj.* **1** of or suitable for an empire, emperor, or empress. **2** having supreme authority. **3** commanding; august. **4** regal; magnificent. **5** *Brit.*, *said of the non-metric measure or system* conforming to standards fixed by parliament. [from Latin *imperialis*]

◻ **2** sovereign, supreme. **4** regal, majestic, grand, magnificent, great, noble.

imperialism *noun* **1** rule by an emperor or empress. **2** the policy or principle of having and extending control over the territory of other nations, or of extending one's country's influence through trade and diplomacy, etc.
imperialist — *noun* a believer in or supporter of imperialism. — *adj.* relating to or characterized by imperialism.
imperialistic *adj.* **1** involving imperialism. **2** according to an imperial system.
imperil *verb* (**imperilled**, **imperilling**) to put in peril or danger.

◻ endanger, jeopardize, risk, hazard, expose, compromise, threaten.

imperilment *noun* endangering, being imperilled.
imperious *adj.* arrogant, haughty and domineering. [from Latin *imperiosus*]

◻ arrogant, haughty, overbearing, domineering, autocratic, despotic, tyrannical, dictatorial, high-handed.
▣ humble.

imperishable *adj.* which will not decay and will last forever.

impermanence or **impermanency** *noun* lack of permanence.

impermanent *adj.* not lasting or remaining; transient.

impermeability *noun* being impermeable.

impermeable *adj.* not allowing especially liquids to pass through or penetrate. [from Latin *impermeabilis*]

impermissible *adj.* not permitted or allowed.

impersonal *adj.* **1** having no reference to any particular person; objective. **2** without or unaffected by personal or human feelings, warmth, sympathy, etc; cold. **3** without personality. **4** *Grammar, said of a verb* used without a subject, or with a formal one, usually *it*, as in *it's snowing*. **5** *Grammar, said of a pronoun* not referring to a definite person; indefinite. [from Latin *impersonalis*]

⊟ **1** neutral, objective, dispassionate. **2** cold, formal, official, aloof, remote, distant, detached, unemotional, unfeeling.
⊟ **2** informal, friendly.

impersonality *noun* being impersonal, lack of personality.

impersonate *verb* to pretend to be, or copy the behaviour and appearance of (another person), especially to entertain or deceive. [from IM- + Latin *persona*, person]

⊟ imitate, mimic, take off, parody, caricature, masquerade as, pose as, act, portray.

impersonation *noun* impersonating.

impersonator *noun* a person who impersonates.

impertinence *noun* **1** impertinent language or behaviour. **2** an impertinent act.

⊟ **1** rudeness, impoliteness, disrespect, insolence, impudence, *colloq.* cheek, *colloq.* brass, effrontery, *colloq.* nerve, audacity, boldness, brazenness, forwardness, presumption.
⊟ **1** politeness, respect.

impertinent *adj.* **1** rude; not showing respect where it is due; insolent. **2** *old use Legal* not relevant. [from Latin *impertinens*]

⊟ **1** rude, impolite, ill-mannered, discourteous, disrespectful, insolent, impudent, *colloq.* cheeky, *colloq.* saucy, pert, bold, brazen, forward, presumptuous.
⊟ **1** polite, respectful.

imperturbability *noun* being imperturbable.

imperturbable *adj.* not easily worried or upset; always calm. [from Latin *imperturbabilis*]

⊟ unexcitable, *colloq.* unflappable, calm, tranquil, composed, collected, self-possessed, cool, unmoved, unruffled.

impervious *adj.* **1** not allowing fluids to pass through or penetrate. **2** (**impervious to something**) not influenced or affected by it: *they seem impervious to criticism*. [from Latin *impervius*]

⊟ **1** impermeable, waterproof, damp-proof, watertight, hermetic, sealed, impenetrable. **2** unaffected by, untouched by, unmoved by, resistant to, immune to, invulnerable to.
⊟ **1** porous, pervious. **2** responsive to, vulnerable to.

impetigo / impɪˈtaɪɡoʊ/ *noun* a contagious skin disease causing pustules and yellow sores. [from Latin *impetigo*, from *impetere*, to attack]

impetuosity or **impetuousness** *noun* **1** being impetuous. **2** an impetuous act.

impetuous *adj.* **1** acting or done hurriedly and without thinking. **2** moving or acting forcefully or with great energy. [from Latin *impetuosus*]

⊟ **1** impulsive, spontaneous, unplanned, unpremeditated, hasty, precipitate, rash, reckless, thoughtless, unthinking.
⊟ **1** cautious, wary, circumspect.

impetus /ˈɪmpətəs/ *noun* (PL. **impetuses**) **1** the force or energy with which something moves. **2** a driving force. **3** an incentive or encouragement. [from Latin *impetus*, attack]

⊟ **1** force, energy, power, impulse, momentum. **2** drive, boost, push, thrust. **3** incentive, encouragement, motivation, stimulus, spur.
⊟ **3** deterrent.

impi *noun* (PL. **impis**, **impies**) a group of Zulu warriors. [from Zulu]

impiety / ɪmˈpaɪətɪ/ *noun* (PL. **impieties**) **1** lack of piety or devotion. **2** an act of impiety: *committed many impieties*. [from Latin *impietas*]

impinge *verb intrans.* (**impinge against** or **on something** or **someone**) **1** to interfere with or encroach on them. **2** to come into contact with them. **3** to make an impression on them. [from Latin *impingere*]

⊟ **1** interfere with, encroach on, infringe, intrude on, invade. **2** touch, hit, strike, collide with. **3** influence, affect, touch, move.

impingement *noun* impinging.

impious / ˈɪmpaɪəs/ *adj.* lacking respect or proper reverence, especially for a divine being. [from Latin *impius*]

impish *adj.* like an imp; mischievous.

impishness *noun* being impish; mischief.

implacability or **implacableness** *noun* being implacable.

implacable *adj.* not able to be calmed, satisfied or appeased. [from Latin *implacabilis*]

⊟ inexorable, relentless, remorseless, merciless, pitiless, cruel, ruthless, intransigent, inflexible.

implant — *verb* (with stress on -*plant*) **1** to fix or plant securely. **2** to fix (ideas, beliefs, etc) permanently in a person's mind. **3** to put (tissue, hormones, etc) permanently into the body. — *noun* (with stress on *im*-) anything implanted, especially tissue, a capsule containing a hormone, etc in the body.

⊟ *verb* **1** fix, sow, plant, root, embed. **2** fix, sow, plant, root, instil, inculcate. **3** insert, engraft, graft, transplant.

implantation *noun* the process of implanting or being implanted.

implausibility *noun* being implausible.

implausible *adj.* not plausible or easy to believe; not likely to be true.

⊟ improbable, unlikely, far-fetched, doubtful, dubious, suspect, unconvincing, weak, flimsy, thin.
⊟ plausible, likely, reasonable.

implement — *noun* a tool or utensil; a necessary piece of equipment. — *verb* to carry out, fulfil or perform. [from Latin *implementum*]

⊟ *noun* tool, instrument, utensil, gadget, device, apparatus, appliance. *verb* carry out, execute, discharge, perform, do, fulfil, complete, accomplish, realize, bring about, effect, enforce.

implementation *noun* implementing, performance, fulfilment.

implicate *verb* **1** to show or suggest that (a person) is involved, especially in a crime. **2** to imply. [from Latin *implicare*, to interweave]

‧‧‧‧‧‧‧‧‧‧‧‧‧‧‧‧‧‧‧‧‧

⊟ **1** involve, embroil, entangle, incriminate, *slang* stich up, compromise, connect, associate.
⊞ **1** exonerate.

implication *noun* **1** the act of implicating or state of being implicated. **2** the act of implying or state of being implied. **3** that which is implied. — **by implication** by suggestion and without being stated directly.

‧‧‧‧‧‧‧‧‧‧‧‧‧‧‧‧‧‧‧‧

⊟ **1** involvement, entanglement, incrimination, connection, association. **2** inference, insinuation, suggestion. **3** inference, insinuation, suggestion, meaning, significance, ramification, repercussion.

implicit *adj.* **1** implied or meant, although not stated directly. **2** present, although not explicit or immediately discernible: *there was a disappointment implicit in her words.* **3** unquestioning; complete. [from Latin *implicitus*, involved]

‧‧‧‧‧‧‧‧‧‧‧‧‧‧‧‧‧‧‧‧

⊟ **1** implied, insinuated, indirect, unspoken, tacit, understood, inferred, meant. **3** unquestioning, utter, total, full, complete, absolute, unqualified, unreserved, wholehearted.
⊞ **1** explicit. **3** half-hearted.

implied *adj.* hinted at, suggested.

implode *verb intrans., trans. Physics* to undergo or cause to undergo a sudden reduction in pressure as a result of a chemical reaction, or to collapse or burst inward in a violent manner. [from IM- + EXPLODE]

implore *verb* **1** to entreat or beg (a person). **2** to beg for earnestly. [from Latin *implorare*]

imploring *adj.* begging, pleading.

implosion *noun Physics* a violent collapse or bursting inward, eg when the seal of a vacuum-filled glass vessel is broken, or when material capable of nuclear fission is compressed by ordinary explosives in a nuclear weapon; the opposite of an explosion.

implosive *adj.* formed by implosion.

imply *verb* (**implies, implied**) **1** to suggest or express indirectly; to hint at. **2** to suggest or involve as a necessary result or consequence. [from Latin *implicare*, to interweave]

‧‧‧‧‧‧‧‧‧‧‧‧‧‧‧‧‧‧‧‧

⊟ SUGGEST. **1** insinuate, hint, intimate. **2** involve, require, indicate, mean, signify.
⊞ **1** state.

impolite *adj.* not polite; rude, disrespectful.

‧‧‧‧‧‧‧‧‧‧‧‧‧‧‧‧‧‧‧‧

⊟ rude, discourteous, bad-mannered, ill-mannered, ill-bred, disrespectful, insolent, coarse, vulgar, curt, abrupt.
⊞ polite, courteous.

impoliteness *noun* being impolite, rudeness.

impolitic *adj.* unwise; not to be advised.

imponderable — *adj.* having an influence or importance which cannot be measured or determined. — *noun* something that is imponderable. [from Latin *imponderabilis*]

import — *verb* (with variable stress) **1** to bring (goods, etc) in from another country. **2** to signify, imply, or portend. **3** *Comput.* to load (a file) into an application other than the one in which it was created. — *noun* (with stress on *im-*) **1** something imported. **2** the act or business of importing goods. **3** importance. **4** meaning. [from Latin *importare*]

importance *noun* being important, significance.

⊟ significance, momentousness, consequence, substance, matter, concern, interest, usefulness, value, worth, weight, influence, prominence, eminence, distinction, esteem, prestige, status, standing.
⊞ unimportance, insignificance.

important *adj.* **1** having great value, influence or effect. **2** (**important to someone**) of great significance or value to them: *their happiness is important to me.* **3** of high social rank or status; eminent. **4** pompous. [from Latin *importare*, to be of consequence]

‧‧‧‧‧‧‧‧‧‧‧‧‧‧‧‧‧‧‧‧

⊟ **1** significant, momentous, consequential, far-reaching, meaningful, relevant, material, salient, essential, vital, key, primary, major, substantial, valuable, seminal, weighty, serious, grave, urgent, crucial. **3** leading, foremost, high-level, high-ranking, influential, powerful, prominent, eminent, distinguished, noted.
⊞ UNIMPORTANT. **1** insignificant, trivial.

importation *noun* **1** importing. **2** something that is imported.

importer *noun* a person or organization that imports.

importunate *adj.* **1** persistent or excessively demanding. **2** extremely urgent. [from Latin *importunus*, inconvenient]

importune *verb trans., intrans.* **1** to make persistent and usually annoying requests (of someone). **2** to solicit for immoral purposes, eg prostitution. [from Latin *importunus*, inconvenient]

importunity *noun* (PL. **importunities**) being importunate.

impose *verb* **1** (*usually* **impose something on** or **upon someone**) to make payment of a tax, fine, etc or performance of a duty compulsory; to enforce it. **2** (**impose oneself on** or **upon someone**) to force oneself, one's opinions and company, etc on them. **3** (**impose on** or **upon someone**) to take advantage of them; to set unreasonable burdens or tasks on them: *it's easy to impose on his good nature.* **4** (**impose something on** or **upon someone**) to palm it off on them surreptitiously or dishonestly. **5** to arrange (pages) in the proper order for printing. [from Old French *imposer*]

‧‧‧‧‧‧‧‧‧‧‧‧‧‧‧‧‧‧‧‧

⊟ **1** enforce, introduce, exact, levy, set, fix, put, place, lay, inflict. **2** force oneself on, intrude on, butt in on, encroach on, trespass on.

imposing *adj.* impressive, especially because of large size, dignity, handsome appearance, etc.

‧‧‧‧‧‧‧‧‧‧‧‧‧‧‧‧‧‧‧‧

⊟ impressive, striking, grand, stately, majestic, dignified.
⊞ unimposing, modest.

imposition *noun* **1** the act of imposing or process of being imposed. **2** something imposed, especially a tax, or an unfair or excessive demand or requirement. **3** *Brit.* work given as a punishment at school. **4** the arranging of pages in the proper order for printing. [from Latin *impositio*]

‧‧‧‧‧‧‧‧‧‧‧‧‧‧‧‧‧‧‧‧

⊟ **1** enforcement, introduction, exaction, levying, infliction, intrusion, encroachment. **2** tax, levy, demand, burden, charge, duty, task.

impossibility *noun* (PL. **impossibilities**) **1** the state of being impossible. **2** something which is impossible.

impossible *adj.* **1** that cannot be done or cannot happen. **2** that cannot be true; difficult to believe. **3** *colloq.* unacceptable, unsuitable, or difficult to bear; intolerable. [from Latin *impossibilis*]

‧‧‧‧‧‧‧‧‧‧‧‧‧‧‧‧‧‧‧‧

⊟ **1** impracticable, unworkable, unattainable, unachievable, unobtainable, insoluble. **2** inconceivable, unthinkable,

preposterous, absurd, ludicrous, ridiculous, unbelievable, incredible, unlikely, improbable. **3** unacceptable, unreasonable, intolerable, unbearable.
1, 2 possible.

impostor or **imposter** *noun* a person who pretends to be someone else in order to deceive others. [from Latin *imponere*, to impose]

fraud, fake, *colloq.* phoney, quack, charlatan, impersonator, *colloq.* con man, swindler, cheat, rogue.

imposture *noun* **1** deception, especially by pretending to be someone else. **2** an act of imposture.
impotence *noun* **1** weakness. **2** *usually said of men* inability to perform sexual intercourse.
impotent /ˈɪmpətənt/ *adj.* **1** powerless; lacking the necessary strength. **2** *said of a man* unable to sustain a sexual erection and therefore unable to perform sexual intercourse. [from Latin *impotentia*, lack of self-control]

1 powerless, helpless, unable, incapable, ineffective, inadequate, weak, feeble, frail, infirm, disabled, incapacitated.
1 potent, strong.

impound *verb* **1** to shut (eg an animal) up in, or as if in, a pound; to confine. **2** to take legal possession of; to confiscate. **3** *said of a reservoir, dam, etc* to collect and hold (water).
impoverish *verb* **1** to make poor. **2** to reduce the quality or fertility of (eg soil). [from Middle English *empoverishen*]
impoverished *adj.* **1** made poor. **2** weakened, in poor condition.

1 poor, needy, impecunious, poverty-stricken, destitute, bankrupt, ruined.
1 rich.

impoverishment *noun* **1** impoverishing. **2** being impoverished. **3** loss of wealth.
impracticability *noun* being impracticable.
impracticable *adj.* not able to be done, put into practice or used.

unworkable, unfeasible, unattainable, unachievable, impossible, impractical, unusable, useless, unserviceable, inoperable.
practicable.

impractical *adj.* lacking common sense; not practical. See also UNPRACTICAL.

unrealistic, idealistic, romantic, starry-eyed, impracticable, unworkable, impossible, awkward, inconvenient.
practical, realistic, sensible.

impracticality *noun* (PL. **impracticalities**) being impractical.
imprecate *verb formal* **1** to call down by prayer (especially something evil). **2** to call down evil upon (someone); to curse. [from Latin *imprecari*, to pray to or for]
imprecation *noun* **1** imprecating. **2** a curse.
imprecatory *adj.* expressing or using imprecation, cursing.
imprecise *adj.* not precise; inaccurate.

inexact, inaccurate, approximate, estimated, rough, loose, indefinite, vague, woolly, hazy, ill-defined, ambiguous, equivocal.
precise, exact.

imprecision *noun* lack of precision.
impregnability *noun* being impregnable.
impregnable *adj.* **1** not able to be seized, defeated, or taken by force. **2** not able to be affected by criticism, doubts, etc. [from Old French *imprenable*, from Latin *prehendere* to take]

1 unassailable, impenetrable, unconquerable, invincible, unbeatable, indestructible, fortified, strong, solid, secure, safe, invulnerable.
1 vulnerable.

impregnate *verb* **1** to permeate completely or saturate. **2** to fill or imbue. **3** to make pregnant or fertilize. [from Latin *impraegnare*, to fertilize]

1 soak, steep, saturate, permeate. **2** fill, permeate, suffuse, imbue. **3** inseminate, fertilize.

impregnation *noun* impregnating or being impregnated.
impresario /ɪmprəˈsɑːrɪəʊ/ *noun* (PL. **impresarios**) an organizer of public entertainments, eg concerts, or the manager of an opera or theatre company. [from Italian *impresario*]
impress — *verb* (with stress on *-press*) **1** to produce a strong, lasting and usually favourable impression on (someone). **2** *intrans.* to produce such an impression. **3** (**impress on** or **upon someone**) to make very clear or emphasize to them. **4** to make or stamp (a mark) on by applying pressure. **5** (**impress something on** or **upon someone**) to fix a fact, etc firmly in their mind or memory. — *noun* (with stress on *im-*) **1** the act of impressing. **2** that which is made by impressing or being impressed, such as a mark or impression. [from Latin *imprimere*, to press into or on]

verb **1** strike, move, touch, affect, influence, stir, inspire, excite, *colloq.* grab. **4** stamp, imprint, mark, indent.

impression *noun* **1** an (especially favourable) idea or effect produced in the mind or made on the senses. **2** a vague or uncertain idea, notion or belief. **3** an act of or the process of impressing. **4** a mark or stamp produced by, or as if by, impressing or pressure. **5** an imitation, especially a caricature, of a person, or an imitation of a sound, done for entertainment. **6** the number of copies of a book, newspaper, etc printed at one time. **7** the pressing of a prepared inked plate or type on to the paper, etc being printed, or a copy made in this way.

1 effect, impact. **2** feeling, awareness, consciousness, sense, idea, notion, opinion, belief, suspicion, hunch, memory, recollection. **4** stamp, mark, print, imprint, dent, outline. **5** impersonation, imitation, take-off, parody, caricature, *colloq.* send-up.

impressionability *noun* susceptibility to being influenced by impressions.
impressionable *adj.* easily impressed or influenced.

naïve, gullible, susceptible, vulnerable, sensitive, responsive, open, receptive.

Impressionism *noun* a 19c style of art, music, or literature which aims to give a general impression of feelings and events rather than a formal or structural treatment of them.
Impressionist — *noun* **1** a painter, writer, or composer in the style of Impressionism. **2** (**impressionist**) a person who imitates or gives impressions of others. — *adj.* relating to or characteristic of Impressionism.
impressionistic *adj.* based on impressions or personal observation as distinct from definite facts or particular knowledge.

impressionistically *adv.* in an impressionistic way.

impressive *adj.* capable of making a deep impression on a person's mind, feelings, etc; causing admiration, wonder or approval.

⊟ striking, imposing, grand, powerful, effective, stirring, exciting, moving, touching.
⊟ unimpressive, uninspiring.

imprimatur / ɪmprɪˈmeɪtə(r)/ *noun* **1** a licence or permission to print or publish a book, granted especially by the Roman Catholic church. **2** approval; permission. [from Latin *imprimatur*, let it be printed]

imprint — *noun* (with stress on *im-*) **1** a mark or impression made by pressure. **2** a permanent effect, eg on the mind, produced by some experience or event. **3** a publisher's name and address, printed at the bottom of a book's title page. — *verb* (with stress on *-print*) **1** to mark or print an impression of (something). **2** to fix firmly in the mind.

⊟ *noun* **1** print, mark, stamp, impression. *verb* STAMP, IMPRESS. **1** print, mark, brand, engrave, etch.

imprinting *noun Zool.* the process by which animals rapidly learn the appearance, sound, or smell of significant individual members of their own species (eg parents, offspring, suitable mates) through being exposed to them. Imprinting to parent or offspring usually results in attachment or following behaviour.

imprison *verb* (**imprisoned, imprisoning**) to put in prison.

⊟ jail, incarcerate, intern, detain, *colloq.* send down, *colloq.* put away, lock up, cage, confine, shut in.
⊟ release, free.

imprisonment *noun* being imprisoned; imprisoning.

⊟ incarceration, internment, detention, custody, confinement.
⊟ freedom, liberty.

improbability *noun* (PL. **improbabilities**) **1** being improbable. **2** something that is improbable.

improbable *adj.* **1** unlikely to happen or exist; not probable. **2** hard to believe.

⊟ UNLIKELY. **1** uncertain, doubtful, dubious. **2** implausible, unconvincing, far-fetched, preposterous, absurd, unbelievable, incredible.
⊟ PROBABLE, LIKELY. **2** convincing.

improbity / ɪmˈprəʊbɪtɪ/ *noun* (PL. **improbities**) dishonesty; wickedness. [from IM- + PROBITY]

impromptu / ɪmˈprɒmptjuː/ — *adj.* made or done without preparation; improvised; spontaneous. — *adv.* without preparation; spontaneously. — *noun* **1** something that is impromptu. **2** a piece of music which suggests improvisation. [from Latin *in promptu*, in readiness]

⊟ *adj.* improvised, extempore, ad-lib, off the cuff, unscripted, unrehearsed, unprepared, spontaneous. *adv.* extempore, ad lib, off the cuff, off the top of one's head, spontaneously, on the spur of the moment.
⊟ *adj.* rehearsed.

improper *adj.* **1** not conforming to accepted standards of modesty and moral behaviour; unseemly; indecent. **2** not correct; wrong. **3** not suitable. [from Latin *improprius*]

⊟ **1** unseemly, unbecoming, indecorous, indecent, rude, vulgar, shocking. **2** wrong, incorrect, irregular. **3** unsuitable, inappropriate, inopportune.
⊟ PROPER. **1** decent. **2** correct. **3** suitable, appropriate.

improper fraction a fraction in which the numerator (upper part) has a value which is equal to or higher than that of the denominator (lower part), eg $\frac{5}{1}$. Therefore it is always equal to or greater than 1. See also PROPER FRACTION.

impropriety *noun* (PL. **improprieties**) **1** an improper act or improper use of a word. **2** the state of being improper; indecency. [from Latin *improprietas*]

improve *verb* **1** to make better, of higher quality or value; to cause to make progress. **2** *intrans.* to become better, of higher quality or value; to make progress. **3** (**improve on something**) to produce something better, of higher quality or value than a previous example. **4** to increase the value or beauty of (land or property) by cultivation, laying out gardens, building, etc. [from Old French *emprower*, from *prou*, profit]

⊟ **1** better, ameliorate, enhance, polish, refine, touch up, mend, rectify, correct, amend, reform, upgrade, increase, raise, develop, advance, further. **2** mend one's ways, turn over a new leaf, reform, increase, rise, pick up, look up, develop, advance, progress, get better, recover, recuperate, rally.
⊟ **1** worsen. **2** worsen, deteriorate, decline.

improvement *noun* **1** the act of improving or state of being improved. **2** something that adds beauty, quality, value, etc. **3** something which has been improved.

⊟ **1** betterment, amelioration, enhancement, rectification, correction, amendment, reformation, increase, rise, development, advance, progress, furtherance, recovery, rally. **2** enhancement, development.
⊟ **1** deterioration, decline.

improvidence *noun* being improvident.

improvident *adj.* **1** not provident; not considering or providing for likely future needs; lacking foresight. **2** careless; thoughtless.

improvisation *noun* **1** the process of improvising. **2** an instance of improvising.

improvise *verb* **1** *trans., intrans.* to compose, recite or perform (music, verse, etc) without preparing it in advance. **2** to make or provide quickly, without preparing in advance and using whatever materials are to hand. [from Latin *improvisus*, not foreseen]

⊟ **1** extemporize, ad-lib, play by ear, vamp. **2** throw together, concoct, contrive, devise, invent.

improviser *noun* a person who improvises.

imprudence *noun* **1** being imprudent. **2** an instance of this.

imprudent *adj.* not having or showing good sense or caution; rash; heedless. [from Latin *imprudens*, rash]

⊟ unwise, ill-advised, foolish, short-sighted, rash, reckless, hasty, careless, heedless, thoughtless, impolitic, indiscreet.
⊟ prudent, wise, cautious.

impudence *noun* **1** being impudent. **2** impudent behaviour or language.

⊟ RUDENESS, INSOLENCE, IMPERTINENCE, *colloq.* CHEEK, EFFRONTERY, *colloq.* NERVE, BOLDNESS, PRESUMPTION.
⊟ POLITENESS.

impudent *adj.* rude, insolent, or impertinent. [from Latin *impudens*, shameless]

⊟ impertinent, rude, insolent, *colloq.* cheeky, *colloq.* saucy, bold, forward, cocky, presumptuous.
⊟ polite.

impugn / ɪmˈpjuːn/ *verb* to call into question or raise doubts about (a person's honesty, integrity, a claim, etc); to criticize. [from Latin *impugnare*, to attack]

impugnable / ɪmˈpjuːnəbl/ *adj.* capable of being questioned or criticized.

impugnment / ɪmˈpjuːnmənt/ *noun* questioning, criticizing.

impulse *noun* 1 a sudden push forwards; a force producing sudden movement forwards. 2 the motion or movement produced by such a force or push. 3 a sudden desire or urge to do something without thinking of the consequences: *bought the dress on impulse.* 4 an instinctive or natural tendency. 5 *Physiol.* (*also* **nerve impulse**) an electrical signal that travels along a nerve fibre, and in turn causes excitation of other nerve, muscle, or gland cells, so relaying information throughout the nervous system. 6 *Physics* for two objects that briefly collide with each other, the product of the force produced and the time for which it acts. It is equal to the change in momentum of either object. [from Latin *impulsus*, pressure]

⊟ 1 impetus, momentum, force, pressure, drive, thrust, push, stimulus. 3 urge, wish, desire, whim, notion. 4 instinct, feeling, tendency, inclination.

impulse buying the buying of goods on the basis of an impulse or whim.

impulsion *noun* 1 an act of urging, forcing, or pushing forwards, into motion or into action, or the state of being so urged. 2 a force which urges, etc forwards, into motion, etc. 3 a sudden desire or urge.

impulsive *adj.* 1 likely to act suddenly and without considering the consequences. 2 done without such consideration. 3 having the power to urge or push forwards, into motion or into action.

⊟ 1 impetuous, rash, reckless. 2 impetuous, rash, reckless, hasty, spontaneous, automatic, instinctive, intuitive.
⊞ 1 cautious. 2 premeditated.

impulsiveness *noun* 1 being impulsive. 2 impulsive behaviour.

impunity *noun* freedom or exemption from punishment, injury, loss, or other ill consequences. — **with impunity** without having to suffer the normal consequences. [from Latin *impunitas*]

⊟ incapability, incapacity, powerlessness, impotence, inadequacy, weakness, handicap, disability.
⊞ ability.

impure *adj.* 1 mixed with something else; adulterated. 2 dirty. 3 immoral; not chaste. 4 ritually unclean. [from Latin *impurus*]

⊟ 1 unrefined, adulterated, diluted, contaminated, polluted, tainted. 2 dirty, foul, soiled, unwashed. 3 immoral, corrupt, indecent, obscene, immodest.
⊞ PURE. 1 refined, unadulterated. 2, 4 clean. 3 chaste, decent.

impurity *noun* (PL. **impurities**) 1 the state of being impure. 2 an impure or unclean thing or constituent.

⊟ 1 adulteration, contamination, pollution, dirtiness, corruption. 2 contaminant, dirt, filth, foreign body, mark, spot.
⊞ 1 purity.

imputation *noun* the act of imputing; something imputed.

impute *verb* (**impute something to someone**) 1 to regard something unfavourable or unwelcome as being brought about by them. 2 to believe something to be caused by a person or thing: *imputed his failure to laziness.*

IN *abbrev.* Indiana.

In *symbol Chem.* indium.

in — *prep.* 1 used to express the position of a person or thing with regard to what encloses, surrounds or includes it, him, etc. 2 into: *get in the car.* 3 after (a period of time): *come back in an hour.* 4 during; while: *lost in transit.* 5 used to express arrangement or shape: *in a square/in alphabetical order.* 6 from; out of: *two in every eight.* 7 by the medium or means of; using: *sung in Italian/in code.* 8 wearing. 9 used to describe a state or manner: *in a hurry.* 10 used to state an occupation: *a job in local government.* 11 used to state a purpose: *a party in his honour.* — *adj.* 1 to or towards the inside; indoors. 2 at home or work. 3 so as to be added or included: *beat in the eggs.* 4 so as to enclose or conceal, or be enclosed or concealed. 5 in or into political power or office. 6 in or into fashion. 7 in a good position; in favour. 8 *in certain games* batting. 9 into a proper, required or efficient state: *run a new car in.* 10 *said of the tide* at its highest point; as close to the shore as it gets. 11 (*in compounds*) expressing prolonged activity, especially by large numbers of people: *a sit-in.* — *adj.* 1 internal; inside; inward. 2 fashionable. 3 in power or office. 4 used for receiving things coming in: *an in-tray.* 5 (*also in compounds*) shared by a group of people: *an in-joke.* — **be in for it** *colloq.* to be likely to experience some trouble or difficulty. **have it in for someone** *colloq.* to cause them trouble, especially because of dislike. **in as far as** or **in so far as ...** to the degree that ... **in as much as ...** because ...; considering that ... **in on something** *colloq.* knowing about it and sharing in it. **ins and outs** the complex and detailed facts of a matter. **in with someone** *colloq.* friendly with them. [from Anglo-Saxon *in*]

in-¹ *prefix* (*also* **il-** before words beginning in *l*, **im-** before words beginning in *b*, *m*, and *p*, **ir-** before words beginning in *r*) forming words that are the negative or opposite of the root word, or that denote a lack of the quality implied by the root word: *inhospitable/illogical/immature/irrelevant.* [from Latin *in-*]

in-² *prefix* (*also* **il-** before words beginning with *l*, **im-** before words beginning with *b*, *m*, and *p*, **ir-** before words beginning with *r*) forming words meaning 'in, on, towards': *intrude/imprison.* [from Latin *in-* and Old French *en-*, in, into]

in. *abbrev.* inch.

inability *noun* (PL. **inabilities**) the lack of sufficient power, means or ability. [from Latin *inhabilitas*]

⊟ incapability, incapacity, powerlessness, impotence, inadequacy, weakness, handicap, disability.
⊞ ability.

in absentia / ɪn abˈsɛntɪə/ in his, her, or their absence. [Latin, = in absence]

inaccessibility *noun* 1 being inaccessible. 2 unapproachability.

inaccessible *adj.* 1 difficult or impossible to approach, reach, or obtain. 2 *said of a person* difficult to understand or influence; unapproachable. [from Latin *inaccessibilis*]

⊟ UNAPPROACHABLE. 1 isolated, remote, unfrequented, unreachable, *colloq.* unget-at-able, unattainable.
⊞ ACCESSIBLE.

inaccuracy *noun* (PL. **inaccuracies**) 1 the state of being inaccurate. 2 a mistake or error.

⊟ 1 imprecision, inexactness, unreliability, unfaithfulness. 2 mistake, error, miscalculation, slip, blunder, fault, defect.
⊞ 1 accuracy, precision.

inaccurate *adj.* containing errors; not correct or accurate.

⊟ incorrect, wrong, erroneous, mistaken, faulty, flawed, defective, imprecise, inexact, unreliable, unfaithful, untrue.
⊞ accurate, correct.

inaction *noun* lack of action; sluggishness.

▣ inactivity, immobility, inertia, rest, idleness, lethargy, torpor, sluggishness, stagnation.
▣ action.

inactive *adj.* **1** taking little or no exercise; idle. **2** no longer operating or functioning. **3** *said of members of a group, especially members of the armed forces* not taking part in or available for eg military duties. **4** *Chem.* showing little or no reaction.

▣ **1** immobile, inert, passive, sedentary, idle, lazy, lethargic, sluggish, torpid. **2** idle, unused, inoperative, dormant.
▣ ACTIVE. **1** busy. **2** working.

inactively *adv.* not actively, passively.
inactivity *noun* **1** being inactive. **2** lack of activity.
inadequacy *noun* (PL. **inadequacies**) **1** insufficiency. **2** not being competent or able to cope: *a feeling of inadequacy.* **3** a defect or shortcoming: *the inadequacies of the system.*

▣ **1** insufficiency, shortage, dearth, want, lack, deficiency, scantiness, meagreness. **2** incompetence, inability, ineffectiveness. **3** shortcoming, failing, weakness, fault, defect, imperfection.
▣ **1, 2** adequacy.

inadequate *adj.* **1** not sufficient or adequate. **2** *said of a person* not able to cope; not competent or capable.

▣ **1** insufficient, short, wanting, lacking, deficient, scanty, sparse, meagre. **2** incompetent, incapable, unequal, ineffective, unsatisfactory.
▣ ADEQUATE. **1** sufficient. **2** competent, capable, satisfactory.

inadmissibility *noun* being inadmissible.
inadmissible *adj.* not allowable or able to be accepted.

▣ unacceptable, irrelevant, immaterial, inappropriate, disallowed, prohibited.
▣ admissible.

inadvertence *noun* negligence, oversight.
inadvertent *adj.* **1** *said of an act* not done deliberately; unintentional. **2** not paying proper attention; heedless. [from Latin *inadvertentia*, inadvertence]

▣ **1** accidental, chance, unintentional, unintended, unplanned, unpremeditated. **2** careless, heedless.
▣ **1** deliberate, conscious. **2** careful.

inadvertently *adv.* unintentionally, carelessly.
inadvisability *noun* being inadvisable.
inadvisable *adj.* not wise; not to be advised.

▣ unwise, imprudent, injudicious, foolish, silly, ill-advised.
▣ advisable, wise.

inalienable *adj.* not capable of being taken or given away (eg to another person).
inamorata / ɪnaməˈrɑːtə/ *noun* (PL. **inamoratas**) a woman who is in love or who is beloved. [from Italian *inamorata*, from *innamorare*, to inflame with love]
inamorato / ɪnaməˈrɑːtoʊ/ *noun* (PL. **inamoratos**) a man who is in love or who is beloved.
inane *adj.* without meaning or point; silly. [from Latin *inanis*]

▣ senseless, foolish, stupid, silly, idiotic, fatuous, frivolous, trifling, mindless, vapid, empty, vacuous, vain, worthless, futile.

▣ sensible.

inanimate *adj.* **1** without life; not living: *inanimate objects.* **2** dull; spiritless. [from Latin *inanimatus*]

▣ LIFELESS. **1** unconscious, dead, defunct, extinct, dull, spiritless, listless, lethargic, inert, inactive.
▣ **1** animate, living, alive. **2** animated, lively.

inanition *noun* emptiness or exhaustion, especially physical from lack of food. [from Latin *inanitio*]
inanity *noun* (PL. **inanities**) **1** the state of being inane. **2** an inane remark, action, etc.
inapplicability *noun* **1** being inapplicable. **2** unsuitability.
inapplicable *adj.* not applicable or suitable.
inapplicably *adv.* not applicably, unsuitably.
inapposite *adj.* not suitable or appropriate; out of place.
inappropriate *adj.* not suitable or appropriate.

▣ unsuitable, ill-suited, inapt, irrelevant, incongruous, out of place, untimely, ill-timed, tactless, improper, unseemly, unbecoming.
▣ appropriate, suitable.

inappropriateness *noun* **1** being inappropriate. **2** unsuitability.
inapt *adj.* **1** not suitable or appropriate. **2** lacking skill; unqualified.
inarticulate *adj.* **1** unable to express oneself clearly or to speak distinctly. **2** badly expressed; not spoken or pronounced clearly. **3** not jointed or hinged. [from Latin *inarticulatus*]

▣ **1** incoherent, hesitant, faltering, halting, tongue-tied, speechless, dumb, mute. **2** incoherent, unintelligible, incomprehensible, unclear, indistinct.
▣ **1, 2** articulate.

inarticulateness *noun* **1** being inarticulate. **2** lack of clarity of sound or expression in speaking.
inartistic *adj.* **1** not following the rules or principles of art. **2** not able to appreciate art.
inartistically *adv.* in an inartistic way.
inasmuch as see IN.
inattention or **inattentiveness** *noun* lack of attention.

▣ carelessness, negligence, disregard, absent-mindedness, forgetfulness, daydreaming, preoccupation.
▣ attention, attentiveness.

inattentive *adj.* not paying proper attention; neglectful.

▣ distracted, dreamy, daydreaming, preoccupied, absent-minded, forgetful, unmindful, heedless, regardless, careless, negligent, neglectful.
▣ attentive.

inattentively *adv.* in an inattentive way; without attention.
inaudibility *noun* being inaudible.
inaudible *adj.* not audible; not loud enough to be heard.

▣ silent, noiseless, imperceptible, faint, indistinct, muffled, muted, low.
▣ audible, loud.

inaudibly *adv.* so that nothing is heard.
inaugural — *adj.* **1** relating to or describing a ceremony officially marking the beginning of something. **2** *said of a speech, lecture, etc* given by a person on taking office. — *noun* an inaugural speech or lecture. [from Latin *inaugurare*, to inaugurate]

inaugurate *verb* **1** to place (a person) in office with a formal ceremony. **2** to mark the beginning of (some activity) with a formal ceremony. **3** to mark the opening of (a new building or service), especially by being the first person to try it out. [from Latin *inaugurare*]

◼ **1** install, invest, induct, ordain. **2** open, launch, introduce, institute, set up, begin, commence, start.

inauguration *noun* **1** being inaugurated, especially formally into office. **2** inaugurating.
inaugurator *noun* a person who inaugurates.
inauspicious *adj.* not promising future success; not auspicious; unlucky.

◼ unfavourable, bad, unlucky, unfortunate, unpromising, discouraging, threatening, ominous, black.
◼ auspicious, promising.

in-between *adj.* coming between in space, time, style, etc; neither one thing nor the other.
inboard *adj., adv.* **1** *said of a boat's motor or engine* situated inside the hull. **2** situated within or close to an aircraft's fuselage. See also OUTBOARD.
inborn *adj.*, *said of a human attribute or characteristic* possessed or apparently possessed by a person from birth; innate or hereditary.

◼ innate, inherent, natural, native, congenital, inbred, hereditary, inherited, instinctive, intuitive.
◼ learned.

inbound *adj.*, *said of a vehicle, flight, etc* coming towards its destination; arriving.
inbred *adj.* **1** inborn. **2** denoting a plant or animal that is the result of inbreeding.
inbreed *verb* (PAST TENSE AND PAST PARTICIPLE **inbred**) to allow reproduction between closely related plants or animals within a species.
inbreeding *noun* breeding within a closely related group. Inbreeding eventually results in an increase in the frequency of abnormalities, eg certain mental defects in humans.
Inc. *abbrev. North Amer., esp. US* Incorporated.
incalculability *noun* being incalculable.
incalculable *adj.* **1** not able to be estimated or reckoned in advance; unpredictable. **2** too great to be measured.

◼ **1** inestimable, unpredictable. **2** vast, immense, unlimited, limitless, countless, untold.
◼ **2** limited, restricted.

in camera /ɪnˈkamərə/ *adv.* **1** *Legal* in a judge's private room. **2** in secret; in private. [Latin, = in a chamber]
incandesce /ɪnkənˈdɛs/ *verb trans., intrans.* to glow or cause to glow white with intense heat.
incandescence *noun* the light produced by a body that is being heated, or the production of such light.
incandescent *adj.* **1** white or glowing with intense heat. **2** shining brightly. **3** of, relating to, or being light produced by heating a substance until it glows white with intense heat. **4** *colloq.* extremely angry. [from Latin *incandescere*, to glow]
incandescent lamp *Electr.* an electric lamp consisting of an evacuated glass bulb containing an inert gas and a filament of highly resistive wire (usually tungsten) that becomes white hot and emits visible light when a current passes through it.
incantation *noun* **1** words said or sung as a spell; a magical formula. **2** the use of spells and magical formulae. [from Latin *incantare*, to put a spell on]
incantatory *adj.* of the nature of or using incantation.
incapability *noun* being incapable.

incapable *adj.* (*usually* **incapable of something**) **1** not capable of doing it. **2** lacking the necessary ability to do it. **3** unable or unfit to do anything, especially look after one's own affairs. [from Latin *incapabilis*]

◼ **2** unfit, unsuited, unqualified, incompetent, inadequate, ineffective. **3** unable, unfit, powerless, impotent, helpless, weak, feeble.
◼ CAPABLE. **1** able. **2** qualified, competent.

incapacitate *verb* **1** to take away (a person's) strength, power, or ability; to make (someone) unfit (for). **2** to disqualify legally. [from INCAPACITY]

◼ **1** disable, cripple, paralyse, immobilize, put out of action, lay up.

incapacitated *adj.* **1** disabled; deprived of power or strength. **2** disqualified by law.
incapacitation *noun* **1** being incapacitated. **2** incapacitating.
incapacity *noun* (PL. **incapacities**) **1** a lack of the necessary strength, power, or ability. **2** legal disqualification. [from Latin *incapacitas*]

◼ **1** incapability, inability, powerlessness, impotence, weakness, feebleness, disability, ineffectiveness, inadequacy, incompetence.
◼ **1** capability.

incapsulate same as ENCAPSULATE.
incapsulating language same as POLYSYNTHETIC LANGUAGE.
incarcerate *verb* to shut in or keep in prison. [from Latin *incarcerare*]
incarceration *noun* **1** being incarcerated. **2** incarcerating.
incarnate — *adj.* **1** in bodily, especially human, form: *God incarnate.* **2** personified; typified. — *verb* **1** to give bodily, especially human, form to. **2** to personify or typify. [from Latin *incarnare*, to make flesh]
incarnation *noun* **1** the bodily, especially human, form taken by a spirit or god. **2** a person who personifies, or thing that typifies, a quality or idea. **3** the taking of bodily, especially human, form by a spirit or god. **4** any of a succession of periods spent in a particular bodily form or state.

◼ **1, 3** manifestation. **2** personification, embodiment.

incautious *adj.* acting or done without thinking; heedless.

◼ careless, imprudent, injudicious, unthinking, thoughtless, inconsiderate, heedless, rash, reckless, hasty, impulsive.
◼ cautious, careful.

incendiarism *noun* arson.
incendiary — *adj.* **1** of or relating to the deliberate and illegal burning of property or goods. **2** *said eg of a bomb* designed to start fires. **3** tending to cause trouble or violence. — *noun* (PL. **incendiaries**) **1** a person who deliberately and illegally sets fire to buildings or property. **2** a device, eg a bomb, for starting fires. **3** a person who stirs up trouble or violence. [from Latin *incendere*, to kindle]
incense¹ (with stress on *in-*) — *noun* **1** a spice or other substance which gives off a pleasant odour when burned, used especially during religious services. **2** the odour or smoke given off by burning spices, etc. — *verb* **1** to offer incense to (a god). **2** to perfume or fumigate with incense. [from Latin *incensum*, thing burnt, from *incendere*, to kindle]
incense² *verb* (with stress on *-cense*) to make (someone) very angry. [from Latin *incendere*, to kindle]

◰ anger, enrage, infuriate, madden, exasperate, irritate, rile, provoke, excite.
◳ calm.

....

incentive — *noun* something that motivates or encourages an action, work, etc, such as extra money paid to workers to increase output. — *adj.* serving to motivate or encourage. [from Latin *incentivus*, provocative]

....

◰ *noun* encouragement, inducement, bait, lure, enticement, *colloq.* carrot, reward, *colloq.* sweetener, reason, motive, impetus, spur, stimulus, motivation.
◳ *noun* disincentive, discouragement, deterrent.

....

inception *noun* a beginning. [from Latin *incipere*, to begin]

incertitude *noun* uncertainty; doubt. [from Latin *incertitudo*]

incessant *adj.* going on without stopping; continual. [from Latin *in*, not + *cessare*, to cease]

....

◰ ceaseless, unceasing, endless, never-ending, interminable, continual, persistent, constant, perpetual, eternal, everlasting, continuous, unbroken, unremitting, non-stop.
◳ intermittent, sporadic, periodic, temporary.

....

incessantly *adv.* without stopping, endlessly.

incest / ˈɪnsest/ *noun* sexual intercourse between people who are too closely related to be allowed to marry, eg between brother and sister. [from Latin *incestum*, from *in-*, not + *castus*, chaste]

incestuous / ɪnˈsestjʊəs/ *adj.* 1 of, guilty of, or involving incest. 2 *said of a relationship or group of people* closed to outside influences or other people.

incestuousness *noun* 1 being incestuous. 2 incestuous behaviour.

inch — *noun* 1 a measure of length equal to one twelfth of a foot (2.54 centimetres). 2 the amount of rain or snow that will cover a surface to the depth of one inch. 3 a small amount or distance. 4 (**inches**) stature. — *verb trans., intrans.* to move or be moved slowly, carefully, and by degrees. — **every inch** completely; in every way. **inch by inch** gradually; by small degrees. **within an inch of something** almost as far as it. **within an inch of one's life** almost as far as death; thoroughly: *beat him within an inch of his life.* [from Anglo-Saxon *ynce*]

-in-chief *combining form* highest in rank; supreme: *commander-in-chief.*

inchoate / ˈɪŋkoʊeɪt/ *adj.* 1 at the earliest stage of development; just beginning. 2 not fully developed; unfinished; rudimentary. [from Latin *inchoare*, to begin]

incidence *noun* 1 the frequency with which something happens or the extent of its influence. 2 the way in which something moving in a line, eg a ray of light, comes into contact with a surface. [from Latin *incidentia*]

....

◰ 1 frequency, commonness, prevalence, extent, range, amount, degree, rate.

....

incident — *noun* 1 an event or occurrence. 2 an event or occurrence which is dependent on, related to, or a consequence of something else. 3 a relatively minor event or occurrence which might have serious consequences. 4 a brief violent conflict or disturbance, eg a bomb explosion. — *adj.* 1 (**incident to something**) belonging naturally to it or being a natural consequence of it. 2 *Legal* (**incident to something**) dependent on it. 3 *Physics, said of light rays, etc* falling or striking. [from Latin *incidens*, from *in*, on + *cadere*, to fall]

....

◰ *noun* 1 event, occurrence, happening, episode, adventure, affair. 4 clash, confrontation, fight,

skirmish, commotion, disturbance, scene.

incidental — *adj.* 1 happening, etc by chance in connection with something else, and of secondary or minor importance: *incidental expenses.* 2 occurring or likely to occur as a minor consequence. — *noun* 1 anything that occurs incidentally. 2 (**incidentals**) minor expenses.

....

◰ *adj.* 1 accidental, chance, random, minor, secondary, subordinate, subsidiary, ancillary, accompanying, attendant, related, contributory.
◳ *adj.* 1 major, primary.

....

incidentally *adv.* 1 by the way; parenthetically. 2 in an incidental manner.

incidental music music which accompanies the action of a film, play, etc.

incinerate *verb* to burn to ashes. [from Latin *in*, in + *cinis*, ashes]

....

◰ burn, cremate, reduce to ashes.

....

incineration *noun* burning completely; reduction to ashes.

incinerator *noun* a furnace or machine for burning rubbish, etc to ashes.

incipience or **incipiency** *noun* 1 being incipient. 2 a beginning.

incipient *adj.* beginning to exist; in an early stage. [from Latin *incipere*, to begin]

incise *verb* 1 to cut into. 2 to engrave (an inscription, stone, etc). [from Latin *incidere*, to cut into]

incision *noun* 1 a cut, especially one made by a surgeon. 2 an act of cutting, especially by a surgeon.

....

◰ 1 cut, opening, slit, gash.

....

incisive *adj.* clear and sharp; to the point; acute.

....

◰ sharp, keen, acute, penetrating, cutting, trenchant, biting, caustic, astute, perceptive.
◳ vague.

....

incisor *noun* one of the eight (in humans) sharp cutting teeth in the front of the mouth.

incite *verb* (*usually* **incite someone to something**) to stir them up or provoke them, eg to action. [from Latin *incitare*, to urge forward]

....

◰ prompt, instigate, rouse, stir up, work up, excite, animate, provoke, stimulate, spur, goad, impel, drive, urge, encourage, *colloq.* egg on.
◳ restrain.

....

incitement *noun* 1 inciting. 2 something which incites, a stimulus.

....

◰ MOTIVATION, ENCOURAGEMENT, INDUCEMENT.
1 prompting, instigation, agitation, provocation.
2 stimulus, impetus, spur, goad, incentive.
◳ DISCOURAGEMENT.

....

incivility *noun* (PL. **incivilities**) 1 rudeness. 2 a rude act or remark. [from Latin *incivilitas*]

incl. *abbrev.* 1 included. 2 including. 3 inclusive.

inclemency *noun* severity of weather.

inclement *adj., said of the weather* stormy or severe; harsh. [from Latin *inclemens*]

....

◰ intemperate, harsh, severe, stormy, tempestuous, rough.
◳ fine.

....

inclination *noun* **1** a particular tendency or disposition, especially a liking. **2** an act of inclining or bowing (the head, etc); a bow or nod. **3** a slope. **4** the degree at which an object slopes away from a horizontal or vertical line or plane.

▤ 1 liking, fondness, taste, predilection, preference, favour, partiality, bias, tendency, trend, disposition, propensity, leaning. **2** bend, bow, nod. **3** slope, gradient, incline. **4** angle, pitch, slant, tilt.
▣ 1 disinclination, dislike.

incline — *verb* (with stress on -*cline*) **1** (**incline someone to** or **towards something**) to cause (someone) to lean towards a particular opinion or conduct; to make (someone) disposed towards it. **2** *intrans.* (**incline to** or **towards something**) to lean towards a particular opinion or conduct; to be disposed towards it. **3** *trans.*, *intrans.* to slope or cause to slope from a horizontal or vertical line or direction. **4** to bow or bend (the head, one's body) forwards or downwards. — *noun* (with stress on *in-*) a slope; an inclined plane. [from Latin *inclinare*, to bend towards]

▤ *verb* **1** dispose, persuade, influence, affect, bias, prejudice. **2** lean, tend. **3** slope, slant, tilt, tip. **4** bend, bow, nod. *noun* slope, gradient, ramp, hill, ascent, acclivity, descent, declivity.

inclined *adj.* **1** disposed; given: *inclined to forget / if you feel so inclined.* **2** sloping.

▤ 1 disposed, given, apt, liable, likely, of a mind, willing.
▣ 1 disinclined.

inclined plane a plane surface at an angle to a horizontal surface, used especially as a mechanism for lessening the force needed to raise or lower heavy objects.

include *verb* **1** to take in or consider along with others as part of a group. **2** to contain or be made up of. [from Latin *includere*]

▤ 1 take in, subsume, add, insert, cover, encompass, embrace, comprehend, allow for, consider, take into account, involve, rope in. **2** contain, comprise, incorporate, embody.
▣ 1 exclude, omit.

inclusion *noun* **1** the act of including or state of being included. **2** something which is included.

▤ ADDITION, INSERTION. **1** incorporation, involvement.
▣ EXCLUSION.

inclusive *adj.* **1** comprehensive; including everything. **2** including the stated limits: *March to August inclusive.*

▤ 1 comprehensive, full, all-in, all-inclusive, all-embracing, catch-all, blanket, across-the-board, general, overall, sweeping.
▣ EXCLUSIVE.

incognito / ɪŋkɒgˈniːtəʊ/ — *adv.* keeping one's identity a secret, eg using a disguise and a false name. — *adj.* keeping one's identity a secret, eg using a disguise and a false name. — *noun* (PL. **incognitos**) **1** a person who is incognito. **2** the disguise and false name of a person who wishes to keep his or her identity secret. [from Latin *incognitus*, unknown]

▤ *adj.* in disguise, disguised, masked, unrecognizable, unmarked, unidentified, unknown.
▣ *adj.* undisguised.

incognizance or **incognisance** *noun* failure to recognize.

incognizant or **incognisant** *adj.* not aware; not knowing.

incoherence *noun* **1** being incoherent. **2** lack of clarity in speech or writing. **3** difficulty in expressing oneself.

incoherent *adj.* **1** *said of speech or writing* not expressed clearly or logically; difficult to understand and follow. **2** *said of a person* unable to speak clearly and logically.

▤ INARTICULATE, CONFUSED, MUDDLED. **1** unintelligible, incomprehensible, rambling, unconnected, disconnected, broken, garbled, scrambled. **2** stammering, stuttering.
▣ COHERENT. **1** intelligible.

incombustible *adj.* incapable of being set alight or burned. [from Latin *incombustibilis*]

income *noun* money received over a period of time as payment for work, etc or as interest or profit from shares or investment. [from Middle English *income*, that which has come in]

▤ revenue, returns, proceeds, gains, profits, interest, dividend, takings, receipts, earnings, pay, salary, wages, means.
▣ expenditure, expenses.

incomer *noun* a person who comes to live in a place, not having been born there.

incomes policy a government policy designed to curb inflation by controlling wages. Full legal backing is necessary if the policy is to be effective, and this step is opposed by some economists (who see it as interfering with market mechanisms), and trade unionists.

income support a state benefit paid to people on low incomes and to the unemployed.

income tax a personal tax levied on income.

incoming *adj.* **1** which is coming in; approaching. **2** next or following.

▤ 1 arriving, entering, approaching, coming, homeward, returning. **2** next, following, succeeding, ensuing.
▣ 1 outgoing.

incommensurability *noun* being incommensurable.

incommensurable *adj.* (**incommensurable with something**) having no common standard or basis and not able to be compared. [from Latin *incommensurabilis*]

incommensurate *adj.* **1** (**incommensurate with** or **to something**) out of proportion to it; inadequate for it. **2** incommensurable.

incommode *verb* to cause bother, trouble, or inconvenience to. [from Latin *incommodare*]

incommodious *adj.* inconvenient or uncomfortable, especially because too small. [from Latin *incommodus*]

incommunicado / ɪŋkəmjuːnɪˈkɑːdəʊ/ *adv.*, *adj.* not allowed to communicate with other people, especially because of being in solitary confinement. [from Spanish *incomunicado*]

incomparability or **incomparableness** *noun* inability to be compared; an incomparable state or standard.

incomparable *adj.* **1** without equal. **2** not to be compared. [from Latin *incomparabilis*]

▤ 1 matchless, unmatched, unequalled, unparalleled, unrivalled, peerless, supreme, superlative, superb, brilliant.
▣ 1 ordinary, run-of-the-mill, poor.

incompatibility *noun* being incompatible.

incompatible *adj.* **1** *said of people* unable to live and work together in harmony. **2** (**incompatible with something**) *said of statements, etc* not in agreement; inconsistent. **3** *said eg of drugs* not able to be combined; mutually intolerant. [from Latin *incompatibilis*]

⊞ **1** mismatched, unsuited. **2** irreconcilable with, conflicting with, at variance with, inconsistent with.
🔳 COMPATIBLE.

incompetence *noun* being incompetent.
incompetent *adj.* **1** lacking the necessary skill, ability, or qualifications. **2** not legally qualified. [from Latin *incompetens*]

⊞ **1** incapable, unable, unfit, inexpert, unskilful, bungling, useless, ineffective, inefficient.
🔳 COMPETENT. **1** able, skilful, efficient.

incomplete *adj.* not complete or finished. [from Latin *incompletus*]

⊞ unfinished, deficient, lacking, short, abridged, partial, part, fragmentary, broken, imperfect, defective.
🔳 complete, exhaustive.

incomprehensibility *noun* being incomprehensible.
incomprehensible *adj.* difficult or impossible to understand. [from Latin *incomprehensibilis*]

⊞ unintelligible, impenetrable, unfathomable, above one's head, puzzling, perplexing, baffling, mysterious, inscrutable, obscure, opaque.
🔳 comprehensible, intelligible.

incomprehension *noun* inability or failure to understand.
inconceivability *noun* being inconceivable.
inconceivable *adj.* unable to be imagined, believed, or conceived by the mind.

⊞ unthinkable, unimaginable, *colloq.* mind-boggling, staggering, unheard-of, unbelievable, incredible, implausible.
🔳 conceivable.

inconclusive *adj.* not leading to a definite conclusion, result, or decision.

⊞ indecisive, ambiguous, vague, unconvincing, unsatisfying, unsettled, undecided, open.
🔳 conclusive.

incongruity *noun* (PL. **incongruities**) **1** the state of being incongruous. **2** something which is incongruous.
incongruous *adj.* out of place; unsuitable; inappropriate. [from Latin *incongruus*]

⊞ inappropriate, unsuitable, out of place, out of keeping, inconsistent, conflicting, incompatible, irreconcilable, contradictory, contrary.
🔳 consistent, compatible.

inconsequent *adj.* **1** not following logically or reasonably; illogical. **2** irrelevant. **3** not connected or related. [from Latin *inconsequens*]
inconsequential *adj.* **1** of no importance or value. **2** illogical.

⊞ **1** minor, trivial, trifling, unimportant, insignificant, immaterial.
🔳 **1** major, important.

inconsequentiality *noun* an inconsequential character or quality.
inconsiderable *adj.* not worth considering; small in amount, value, etc. [from Latin *inconsiderabilis*]

⊞ small, slight, negligible, trivial, petty, minor, unimportant, insignificant.
🔳 considerable, large.

inconsiderably *adv.* insignificantly.
inconsiderate *adj.* thoughtless, especially in not considering the feelings, rights, etc of others. [from Latin *inconsideratus*]

⊞ thoughtless, uncaring, unconcerned, selfish, self-centred, unkind, insensitive, tactless, rude, unthinking, careless, heedless.
🔳 considerate.

inconsiderateness or **inconsideration** *noun* lack of consideration.
inconsistency *noun* (PL. **inconsistencies**) lack of consistency, or an instance of this.
inconsistent *adj.* **1** (**inconsistent with something**) not in agreement or accordance with it. **2** *said of a single thing* having contradictory or incompatible elements. **3** *said of a person* not always thinking, speaking, behaving, etc in accordance with the same principles; not consistent in thought, speech, behaviour, etc.

⊞ **1** conflicting with, at variance with, at odds with, incompatible with, irreconcilable with, discordant with, contrary to. **3** changeable, variable, unpredictable, varying, inconstant, fickle.
🔳 CONSISTENT.

inconsolable *adj.* not able to be comforted. [from Latin *inconsolabilis*]

⊞ heartbroken, broken-hearted, devastated, desolate, despairing, wretched.

inconspicuous *adj.* not easily noticed; attracting little attention. [from Latin *inconspicuus*]

⊞ hidden, concealed, camouflaged, plain, ordinary, unobtrusive, discreet, low-key, modest, unassuming, quiet, retiring.
🔳 conspicuous, noticeable, obtrusive.

inconstancy *noun* changeability.
inconstant *adj.* **1** *said of a person* having feelings which change frequently; fickle; unfaithful. **2** subject to frequent change; variable. [from Latin *inconstans*]
incontestability *noun* being incontestable.
incontestable *adj.* too clear or definite to be disputed. [from Latin *incontestabilis*]
incontinence or **incontinency** *noun* being incontinent.
incontinent *adj.* **1** unable to control one's bowels or bladder or both. **2** unable to control oneself, especially one's sexual desires. **3** (**incontinent of something**) lacking control over it. [from Latin *incontinens*]
incontrovertible *adj.* not able to be disputed or doubted. [from IN-[1] + *controvert*, to oppose]

⊞ indisputable, unquestionable, indubitable, irrefutable, undeniable, certain, clear, self-evident.
🔳 questionable, uncertain.

inconvenience — *noun* trouble or difficulty, or a cause of this. — *verb* to cause trouble or difficulty to. [from Latin *inconvenientia*]

⊞ *noun* trouble, difficulty, awkwardness, annoyance, nuisance, hindrance, drawback, bother, fuss, upset, disturbance, disruption. *verb* trouble, bother, disturb,

disrupt, put out, upset, annoy.
■ *noun* convenience. *verb* convenience.

inconvenient *adj.* not convenient, especially causing trouble or difficulty.

■ awkward, ill-timed, untimely, inopportune, unsuitable, troublesome, difficult, embarrassing, annoying, unwieldy, unmanageable.
■ convenient.

inconveniently *adv.* in an inconvenient way; at an inconvenient time.

incorporate — *verb* (pronounced -reit) **1** to contain or include as part of a whole. **2** *intrans.* to be included as part of a whole. **3** *trans., intrans.* to combine or be united thoroughly in a single mass. **4** to admit to membership of a legal corporation. **5** to form into a legal corporation. **6** *intrans.* to form a legal corporation. — *adj.* (pronounced -rət) (*also* **incorporated**) **1** united in one body or as a single whole. **2** forming or formed into a legal corporation. [from Latin *incorporare*, from *in*, in + *corpus*, body]

■ *verb* **1** contain, embody, include, subsume, take in, absorb, assimilate. **3** combine, unite, integrate, merge, blend, mix, fuse, coalesce, consolidate.
■ *verb* **1** exclude. **3** separate.

incorporating language same as POLYSYNTHETIC LANGUAGE.
incorporation *noun* **1** incorporating. **2** being incorporated.
incorporeal *adj.* **1** without bodily or material form or substance. **2** *Legal* having no material existence or value in itself, but attached as a right or profit to something else.[from Latin *incorporeus*, from *in-*, not + *corpus*, body]
incorporeity *noun* being incorporeal.
incorrect *adj.* **1** not accurate; wrong. **2** not in accordance with normal or accepted standards; improper. [from Latin *incorrectus*]

■ WRONG. **1** mistaken, erroneous, inaccurate, imprecise, inexact, false, untrue, faulty, ungrammatical. **2** improper, illegitimate, inappropriate, unsuitable.
■ CORRECT, RIGHT.

incorrigibility *noun* being incorrigible.
incorrigible *adj.*, *said of a person, behaviour, or habit* not able to be improved, corrected, or reformed, usually because too bad. [from Latin *incorrigibilis*]

■ irredeemable, incurable, inveterate, hardened, hopeless.

incorruptibility *noun* being incorruptible.
incorruptible *adj.* **1** incapable of being bribed or morally corrupted. **2** that cannot decay. [from Latin *incorruptibilis*]

■ **1** honest, straight, upright, moral, honourable, trustworthy, unbribable.
■ **1** corruptible.

increase — *verb* (with stress on -*crease*) **1** to make greater in size, intensity, or number. **2** *intrans.* to become greater in size, intensity, or number. — *noun* (with stress on *in-*) **1** the act or process of increasing or becoming increased; growth. **2** the amount by which something increases or is increased. — **on the increase** increasing in number, size, or frequency. [from Latin *increscere*, to grow]

■ *verb* **1** raise, boost, add to, improve, enhance, advance, further, step up, intensify, strengthen, heighten, develop, build up, enlarge, magnify, extend, prolong, expand, spread.

2 rise, mount, soar, improve, advance, progress, grow, develop, build up, intensify, strengthen, heighten, extend, expand, spread, swell, multiply, proliferate, escalate. *noun* RISE, GAIN, ADDITION. **1** surge, upsurge, upturn, boost, intensification, growth, development, enlargement, extension, expansion, spread, proliferation, escalation. **2** increment.
■ *verb* DECREASE, REDUCE. **2** fall, decline. *noun* DECREASE, REDUCTION. **1** decline.

increasingly *adv.* so as to increase; more and more.
incredibility *noun* being incredible.
incredible *adj.* **1** difficult or impossible to believe. **2** *colloq.* amazing; unusually good. [from Latin *incredibilis*]

■ **1** unbelievable, improbable, implausible, far-fetched, preposterous, absurd, impossible, inconceivable, unthinkable, unimaginable. **2** amazing, astonishing, astounding, extraordinary, remarkable, exceptional.
■ **1** credible, believable.

incredulity /ɪŋkrəˈdjuːlɪtɪ/ *noun* **1** being incredulous. **2** disbelief.

■ **1** scepticism, doubt, distrust, mistrust. **2** disbelief, unbelief.
■ **1** credulity.

incredulous /ɪŋˈkrɛdjʊləs/ *adj.* **1** unwilling to believe or accept something as true. **2** showing or expressing disbelief. [from Latin *incredulus*]

■ **1** disbelieving, unbelieving, unconvinced, sceptical, doubting, uncertain, doubtful, dubious, suspicious, distrustful, mistrustful.
■ **1** credulous.

incredulously *adv.* in an incredulous way; sceptically.
incredulousness *noun* **1** being incredulous. **2** being unbelieving or sceptical.
increment /ˈɪŋkrəmənt/ *noun* **1** an increase, especially of one point or level on a fixed scale, eg a regular increase in salary. **2** the amount by which something is increased. **3** *Maths.* a small increase in the value of a variable quantity. [from Latin *incrementum*]
incremental *adj.* involving or based on increments.
incriminate *verb* **1** to show that (someone) was involved in especially a crime. **2** to involve in especially a crime. **3** to charge with a crime or fault. [from Latin *incriminare*, to accuse of a crime]

■ **1** inculpate, implicate, *slang* stich up. **2** involve, embroil. **3** charge, accuse, impeach, indict, point the finger at, blame.
■ **1, 3** exonerate.

incriminating or **incriminatory** *adj.* that incriminates; implying or suggesting guilt.
incrimination *noun* **1** incriminating. **2** being incriminated.
incrust same as ENCRUST.
incubate *verb* **1** *trans., intrans., said of birds* to hatch (eggs) by sitting on them to keep them warm. **2** to cause (germs, bacteria, etc) to develop by creating favourable and controlled conditions, eg in a laboratory. **3** *intrans., said of germs, bacteria, etc* to develop gradually and slowly before signs of disease begin to appear. [from Latin *incubare*, to lie on]
incubation *noun* **1** an act of incubating. **2** the period between infection with bacteria, germs, etc and the appearance of the actual disease these cause.
incubative or **incubatory** *adj.* relating to or involving incubation.

incubator *noun* **1** a transparent box-like container in which a prematurely born baby can be reared under controlled conditions and protected from infection. **2** a cabinet or room that can be maintained at a constant preset temperature, used for culturing bacteria and other micro-organisms, hatching eggs, etc.

incubus *noun* (PL. **incubuses, incubi**) **1** an evil male spirit which is supposed to have sexual intercourse with sleeping women. See also SUCCUBUS. **2** something which oppresses or weighs heavily upon one, especially a nightmare. [from Latin *incubus*, nightmare]

inculcate *verb* (**inculcate something in** or **upon someone**) to teach or fix ideas, habits, a warning, etc firmly in their mind by constant repetition. [from Latin *inculcare*, to tread in]

inculcation *noun* inculcating.

inculpate *verb* to blame or show to be guilty of a crime; to incriminate. [from Latin *inculpare*, to blame]

incumbency *noun* (PL. **incumbencies**) the period of office of an incumbent.

incumbent — *adj.* **1** (**incumbent on** or **upon someone**) imposed as a duty on them. **2** occupying a specified position. — *noun* a holder of an office, especially a church office or benefice. [from Latin *incumbere*, to lie on]

incunabulum /ɪŋkjʊˈnabjʊləm/ *noun* (PL. **incunabula**) an early printed book, especially one printed before 1501. [from Latin *incunabula*, swaddling-clothes]

incur *verb* (**incurred, incurring**) to bring (something unpleasant) upon oneself; to become liable for (debts, etc). [from Latin *incurrere*, to run into]

⊟ suffer, sustain, provoke, arouse, meet with, run up, gain, earn.

incurability *noun* being incurable.

incurable — *adj.* **1** unable to be cured. **2** incorrigible; unable to change or be changed: *an incurable romantic*. — *noun* an incurable person or thing. [from Latin *incurabilis*]

⊟ *adj.* HOPELESS. **1** terminal, fatal, untreatable, inoperable. **2** incorrigible, inveterate, hardened, dyed-in-the-wool.
⊟ *adj.* curable.

incurious *adj.* showing no interest; lacking a normal curiosity; indifferent.

incuriously *adv.* without curiosity; in an uninterested way.

incursion *noun* **1** a brief or sudden attack made into enemy territory. **2** a using up of something: *unexpected expenses which made an incursion into their savings*. [from Latin *incursio*]

incursive *adj.* aggressive, invasive.

incus /ˈɪŋkəs/ *noun* (PL. **incudes**) *Anat.* a small anvil-shaped bone in the middle ear. Together with two other bones, the malleus and stapes, it transmits sound waves from the eardrum to the inner ear. [from Latin *incus*, anvil]

Ind. *abbrev.* **1** Independent. **2** India; Indian. **3** Indiana.

indaba /ɪnˈdɑːbə/ *noun* **1** an important conference or discussion between members of South African tribes. **2** *colloq.* a concern or problem for discussion. [from Zulu, = affair]

indebted /ɪnˈdɛtɪd/ *adj.* (*often* **indebted to someone**) **1** having reason to be grateful or obliged to them. **2** owing them money.

⊟ **1** obliged, grateful, thankful.

indecency /ɪnˈdiːsənsɪ/ *noun* (PL. **indecencies**) **1** indecent behaviour or character. **2** an indecent act.

⊟ **1** immodesty, impurity, obscenity, pornography, lewdness, vulgarity, coarseness, crudity, foulness, grossness.
⊟ **1** decency, modesty.

indecent /ɪnˈdiːsənt/ *adj.* **1** offensive against accepted standards of morality or sexual behaviour. **2** in bad taste; improper; unseemly. [from Latin *indecens*]

⊟ VULGAR, COARSE, CRUDE. **1** immodest, impure, indelicate, offensive, obscene, pornographic, X-rated, lewd, licentious, dirty, filthy, foul, gross, outrageous, shocking. **2** improper, unseemly, indecorous, unbecoming.
⊟ DECENT. **1** modest, pure. **2** proper, decorous.

indecent assault a sexual attack which falls short of being rape.

indecent exposure the crime of indecently showing parts of one's body, especially one's sexual organs, in public.

indecipherability *noun* being indecipherable.

indecipherable /ɪndɪˈsaɪfərəbl/ *adj.* that cannot be read or understood.

indecision *noun* the state of not being able to decide; uncertainty.

⊟ indecisiveness, irresolution, uncertainty, doubt, hesitation, hesitancy, vacillation, wavering, ambivalence.
⊟ decisiveness, resolution.

indecisive *adj.* **1** not producing a clear or definite decision or result. **2** unable to make a firm decision; hesitating.

⊟ **1** inconclusive, indefinite, indeterminate, unclear. **2** undecided, irresolute, uncertain, unsure, doubtful, vacillating, wavering, in two minds, hesitating, faltering, tentative.
⊟ DECISIVE.

indecorous /ɪnˈdɛkərəs/ *adj.* not decorous; in bad taste; improper. [from Latin *indecorus*]

indecorum /ɪndɪˈkɔːrəm/ *noun* improper or unseemly behaviour; lack of decorum.

indeed — *adv.* **1** without any question; in truth. **2** in fact; actually. **3** used for emphasis: *very wet indeed*. — *interj.* an expression of irony, surprise, disbelief, etc or acknowledgement. [from Middle English]

⊟ *adv.* **1** certainly, positively, truly, undeniably, undoubtedly. **2** really, actually, in fact.

indefatigable /ɪndɪˈfatɪgəbl/ *adj.* **1** never becoming tired. **2** never stopping; unremitting. [from Latin *indefatigabilis*]

indefensibility *noun* being indefensible.

indefensible *adj.* that cannot be defended or justified.

⊟ unjustifiable, inexcusable, unforgivable, unpardonable, insupportable, untenable, wrong.
⊟ defensible, excusable.

indefinable *adj.* that cannot be clearly, fully, or exactly defined or described.

indefinite *adj.* **1** without fixed or exact limits. **2** uncertain; vague; imprecise. [from Latin *indefinitus*]

⊟ **1** undefined, unspecified, unlimited. **2** uncertain, unsettled, unresolved, undecided, vague, ill-defined, indistinct, unclear, ambiguous, imprecise, inexact, loose.
⊟ DEFINITE. **1** limited. **2** clear.

indefinite article *Grammar* a word (*a* or *an* in English) used before a noun to denote an example that is not definite or specific: *a cat in the road/a new government/half a pound*. See also DEFINITE ARTICLE.

indefinitely *adv.* in an indefinite way; without limit.

⊟ for ever, eternally, endlessly, continually, ad infinitum.

indehiscent /ˌɪndɪˈhɪsənt/ *adj. Bot.* denoting a fruit that does not split open but is dispersed intact.

indelible *adj.* 1 *said of a mark, writing, etc* unable to be removed or rubbed out. 2 *said of a pen, etc* making indelible marks. 3 *said of an impression, a memory, etc* unable to be destroyed or forgotten. [from Latin *indelebilis*]

⊞ 1 permanent, fast. 3 lasting, enduring, indestructible, unforgettable.
⊟ 1 erasable.

indelibly *adv.* so as to be indelible; permanently.

indelicacy *noun* (PL. **indelicacies**) embarrassing or offensive language or behaviour.

indelicate *adj.* 1 tending to embarrass or offend; in poor taste; immodest. 2 slightly coarse; rough.

indemnification *noun* the process of indemnifying; protection against loss or misfortune.

indemnify *verb* (**indemnifies**, **indemnified**) 1 (**indemnify someone against something**) to provide them with security against loss or misfortune. 2 (**indemnify someone for something**) to pay them money in compensation for especially loss or damage; to reimburse them. [from Latin *indemnis*, without loss, unhurt]

indemnity *noun* (PL. **indemnities**) 1 compensation for loss or damage, or money paid in compensation. 2 security from loss or damage. 3 legal exemption from liabilities or penalties incurred.

⊞ 1 compensation, reimbursement, remuneration, reparation. 2 insurance, guarantee, security, protection. 3 exemption, immunity, impunity, amnesty.

indent[1] — *verb* (with stress on *-dent*) 1 *trans., intrans.* to begin (a line or paragraph) in from the margin. 2 to divide (a document drawn up in duplicate in two columns) along a zigzag line. 3 to draw up (a document, deed, etc) in duplicate. 4 *trans., intrans. Brit.* to make out a written order (for especially foreign goods). 5 to indenture as an apprentice. 6 to make a notch in. — *noun* (with stress on *in-*) 1 *Brit.* a written order for especially foreign goods. 2 an indented line or paragraph. 3 a notch. 4 an indenture. [from Latin *indentatus*]

indent[2] *verb* (with stress on *-dent*) to form a dent in or mark with dents.

indentation *noun* 1 a cut or notch. 2 a deep inward curve or recess, eg in a coastline. 3 the act of indenting.

⊞ 1 notch, nick, cut, dent, groove, furrow, hollow, pit, dimple.

indention *noun* 1 the indenting of a line or paragraph. 2 the blank space at the beginning of a line caused by indenting a line or paragraph.

indenture — *noun* 1 (*usually* **indentures**) a contract binding an apprentice to a master. 2 an indented document, agreement, or contract. — *verb* to bind (eg an apprentice) by indentures or by an indented contract or agreement.

independence *noun* an independent state or condition.

⊞ freedom, liberty, individualism, autonomy, self-government, self-determination, self-rule, home rule, sovereignty.
⊟ dependence.

Independence Day a public holiday celebrating the anniversary of a country's declaration of independence, eg held on 4 July in the USA.

independent *adj.* 1 not under the control or authority of others, especially (of a country or state) self-governing. 2 not relying on others for financial support, care, help, or guidance. 3 thinking and acting for oneself and not under an obligation to others. 4 not dependent on something else for value, purpose, or function. 5 *said of two or more people or things* not related to or affected by the others. 6 *said of*

private income or resources large enough to make having to work for a living unnecessary: *independent means*. 7 not belonging to a political party. 8 *said of a school or broadcasting company* not paid for with public money.

⊞ 1 autonomous, self-governing, self-determining, sovereign, absolute, non-aligned, neutral, impartial, unbiased. 2 self-sufficient, self-supporting, self-reliant, unaided. 3 free, liberated, unconstrained, individualistic, unconventional. 4 individual, self-contained. 5 separate, unconnected, unrelated.
⊟ 1, 2, 3, 4 dependent.

independent clause *Grammar* a clause which is grammatically correct and complete and has meaning even when it is taken out of the sentence in which it is found, eg *she picked it up* in *she picked it up and ran off*; a main clause.

in-depth *adj.* thorough, exhaustive: *an in-depth study of the problem.*

indescribable *adj.* that cannot be described, often because too extreme or too vague.

⊞ indefinable, inexpressible, unutterable, unspeakable.
⊟ describable.

indestructibility *noun* being indestructible.

indestructible *adj.* that cannot be destroyed.

⊞ unbreakable, durable, tough, strong, lasting, enduring, permanent, everlasting, imperishable.
⊟ breakable, perishable.

indeterminable *adj.* 1 not able to be fixed, decided, or measured. 2 *said of an argument, etc* that cannot be settled. [from Latin *indeterminabilis*]

indeterminacy *noun* being indeterminate.

indeterminate *adj.* 1 not precisely or exactly fixed, determined, or settled. 2 doubtful; vague. 3 *Maths.* not having a fixed or definite value. [from Latin *indeterminatus*]

⊞ 1 unspecified, unstated, undefined, unfixed, imprecise, inexact, indefinite, open-ended, undecided, undetermined, unresolved, unsettled. 2 vague, indefinite, doubtful, uncertain.
⊟ 1 specified, fixed.

indeterminateness *noun* 1 being indeterminate. 2 lack of determination. 3 absence of direction.

index — *noun* (PL. **indexes**, **indices**) *technical* 1 an alphabetical list of names, subjects, etc dealt with in a book, usually given at the end of that book, and with the page numbers on which each item appears. 2 a catalogue or set of reference cards, eg in a library, which lists each book, magazine, etc alphabetically, usually by author or title, and gives details of where it is shelved. 3 anything which points to, identifies, or highlights a particular trend or condition. 4 a scale of numbers which shows changes in price, wages, rates of interest, etc: *retail price index.* 5 a hand or pointer on a dial or scale. 6 *Maths.* an exponent or power, usually denoted by a superscript number or symbol which indicates the number of times a given value is to be multiplied by itself (see also EXPONENT). 7 *Physics* a numerical quantity, usually lacking units, that indicates the magnitude of a particular physical effect, eg refractive index. 8 *Geol.* a fossil or mineral that characterizes a particular type of rock. 9 (**Index**) *RC Church* an official list of prohibited books. — *verb* 1 to provide (a book) with an index. 2 to list in an index. 3 to relate (prices, wages, etc) to the cost-of-living index, so that they may rise or fall accordingly. [from Latin *index*, informer]

⊞ *noun* 1 list, table, key. 2 catalogue, file, directory, guide. 3

indicator, pointer, sign, token, mark, indication. **5** indicator, pointer, needle, hand.

. . . .

indexation or **indexing** *noun* the linking of prices, wages, rates of interest, etc to changes in an index showing the cost of living.

indexer *noun* a person who compiles an index.

index finger the finger next to the thumb; the forefinger.

index-linked *adj., said of prices, wages, rates of interest, etc* calculated so as to rise or fall by the same amount as the cost of living.

Indiaman *noun* (PL. **Indiamen**) *Hist.* a merchant ship trading with India or the East Indies.

Indian — *noun* **1** a native or citizen of India. **2** a person whose ancestors were born in India. **3** a member of any of the various native peoples of N, Central, and S America (but not including the Inuit). **4** any of the languages spoken by the native peoples of America. — *adj.* **1** relating to India or the Indian subcontinent (India, Bangladesh, and Pakistan), or its inhabitants, languages, and culture. **2** relating to the native peoples of America, or their languages and culture. [from Greek *India*, from *Indos*, the Indus river]

Indian club one of a pair of heavy, bottle-shaped clubs swung to develop the arm muscles.

Indian corn same as MAIZE.

Indian file single file.

Indian hemp same as HEMP 1.

Indian ink or *North Amer.* **India ink** black ink made from lampblack.

Indian summer 1 a period of unusually warm, dry weather in late autumn or early winter. **2** a period of happiness and success towards the end of a person's life.

India paper 1 a thin, soft, absorbent paper originally made in China and Japan. **2** a very thin, strong, opaque paper, used eg for printing Bibles.

India rubber same as RUBBER[1] 2.

Indic — *adj.* of the Indian branch of the Indo-European languages, made up of Sanskrit, and modern languages such as Hindi, Gujarati and Urdu. — *noun* the languages forming this group. [from Greek *Indikos*, Indian]

indicate *verb* **1** to point out or show. **2** to be a sign or symptom of. **3** *said of a gauge, dial, etc* to show as a reading. **4** to state briefly. **5** to point to as a suitable treatment or desirable or required course. [from Latin *indicare*]

. . . .

▪ **1** point out, show, point to, designate, specify. **2** show, reveal, display, manifest, mark, signify, mean, denote, express, suggest, imply. **3** register, record, read, show.

. . . .

indication *noun* **1** an act of indicating. **2** something which serves to indicate; a sign. **3** something which is indicated. **4** a reading on a gauge, dial, etc.

. . . .

▪ **2** sign, manifestation, evidence, symptom, mark, token, signal, warning, omen, suggestion, hint, clue.

. . . .

indicative — *adj.* **1** (**indicative of something**) being a sign or indication of it. **2** *Grammar* being the mood, or in the mood, used to state facts, describe events, or ask questions. — *noun* **1** the indicative mood. **2** a verb in the indicative mood.

indicator *noun* **1** an instrument, or a needle or pointer on a device, that shows the level of temperature, fuel, pressure, etc. **2** any of the flashing lights on a motor vehicle which show that the vehicle is about to change direction. **3** any sign, condition, situation, etc which shows or illustrates something. **4** a board or diagram giving information, eg in a railway station. **5** *Chem.* a substance, eg litmus, that changes colour reversibly depending on the pH of a solution, and that indicates when a chemical reaction is complete, eg during chemical titrations. **6** *Biol.* (*also* **indicator species**) a plant or animal species whose presence or absence indicates the levels of a particular environmental factor in an area, eg certain lichens are sensitive to air pollutants.

. . . .

▪ **1** pointer, marker, needle, hand, dial, gauge, meter. **3** sign, symbol, token, signal, indication, manifestation. **4** display, board, guide, signpost.

. . . .

indicatory *adj.* giving a sign or symptom.

indices see INDEX.

indict /ɪnˈdaɪt/ *verb* to accuse of or charge formally with a crime, especially in writing. [from Old French *enditer*, with spelling influenced by Latin *indicere*, to announce]

. . . .

▪ charge, accuse, arraign, impeach, summon, summons, prosecute, incriminate.

▪ exonerate.

. . . .

indictable /ɪnˈdaɪtəbl/ *adj.* **1** *said of a person* liable to be indicted for a crime. **2** *said of a crime* liable to cause a person to be indicted.

indictment /ɪnˈdaɪtmənt/ *noun* **1** a formal written accusation or charge. **2** an act of indicting. **3** something which deserves severe criticism or censure.

indie *noun colloq.* a small, independent, and usually non-commercial record or film company. [abbreviation of INDEPENDENT]

indifference *noun* **1** being indifferent. **2** lack of quality. **3** lack of importance.

. . . .

▪ **1** apathy, unconcern, coldness, coolness, inattention, disregard, neutrality, disinterestedness.

▪ **1** interest, concern.

. . . .

indifferent *adj.* **1** (*often* **indifferent to something** or **someone**) showing no interest in them or concern for them. **2** neither good nor bad; average; mediocre. **3** fairly bad; inferior. **4** without importance. **5** neutral. [from Latin *indifferens*]

. . . .

▪ **1** uninterested, unenthusiastic, unexcited, apathetic, unconcerned, uncaring, unmoved, unsympathetic, cold, cool, distant, aloof. **2** mediocre, average, middling, passable, moderate, fair. **5** neutral, disinterested, detached, uninvolved.

▪ **1** interested, enthusiastic, concerned, caring. **2** excellent.

. . . .

indigence /ˈɪndɪdʒəns/ *noun* poverty.

indigenous /ɪnˈdɪdʒɪnəs/ *adj.* belonging naturally to or occurring naturally in a country or area; native. [from Latin *indigena*, original inhabitant]

. . . .

▪ native, aboriginal, local, home-grown.

▪ foreign.

. . . .

indigent /ˈɪndɪdʒənt/ *adj.* very poor; needy. [from Latin *indigens*]

indigestibility *noun* being indigestible.

indigestible *adj.* **1** *said of food* difficult or impossible to digest. **2** not easily understood; complicated. [from Latin *indigestibilis*]

indigestion *noun* discomfort or pain in the abdomen or lower region of the chest, especially after eating, caused by difficulty in digesting or inability to digest food.

indignant *adj.* feeling or showing anger or a sense of ill-treatment. [from Latin *indignans*]

. . . .

▪ annoyed, angry, irate, heated, fuming, livid, furious, incensed, infuriated, exasperated, outraged.

▪ pleased, delighted.

. . . .

indignation *noun* anger caused by a feeling of having been ill-treated.

■ annoyance, anger, ire, wrath, rage, fury, exasperation, outrage.
☒ pleasure, delight.

indignity *noun* (PL. **indignities**) **1** any act or treatment which causes someone to feel shame; disgrace or dishonour. **2** a feeling of shame, disgrace, or dishonour. [from Latin *indignitas*]

indigo — *noun* (PL. **indigos, indigoes**) **1** a violet-blue dye either obtained naturally from a plant or made synthetically. **2** any of several leguminous plants whose leaves yield a violet-blue dye. **3** the violet-blue colour of this dye. — *adj.* violet-blue. [from Greek *indikon*, Indian]

indirect *adj.* **1** *said of a route, course, line, etc* not straight or direct. **2** not going straight to the point; devious. **3** not directly aimed at or intended: *indirect consequences.* [from Latin *indirectus*]

■ **1** roundabout, circuitous, wandering, rambling, winding, meandering, zigzag, tortuous. **2** roundabout, tortuous, devious, oblique. **3** secondary, incidental, unintended, subsidiary, ancillary.
☒ DIRECT. **1** straight. **3** primary.

indirect object *Grammar* a noun, noun phrase, or pronoun which is affected indirectly by the action of a verb, usually standing for the person or thing to whom something is given or for whom something is done, eg *him* in *give him a kiss.* See also DIRECT OBJECT.

indirect speech *Grammar* a speaker's words reported by another person with change of person and tense, eg *we will come* becomes *they said they would come* in indirect speech.

indirect tax a tax levied on goods and services as opposed to a person's income. See also DIRECT TAX.

indirect taxation see TAXATION.

indiscernible *adj.* that cannot be noticed or recognized as being distinct, especially because too small: *indiscernible differences.*

indiscipline *noun* lack of discipline.

indisciplined *adj.* lacking discipline.

indiscreet *adj.* **1** giving away too many secrets or too much information; not discreet. **2** not wise or cautious; injudicious. [from Latin *indiscretus*]

■ **1** tactless, undiplomatic. **2** impolitic, injudicious, imprudent, unwise, foolish, rash, reckless, hasty, careless, heedless, unthinking.
☒ **1** discreet. **2** cautious.

indiscretion *noun* **1** lack of discretion or caution; rashness. **2** an act or remark showing this.

■ **1** tactlessness, rashness, recklessness, foolishness, folly. **2** mistake, error, slip, *colloq.* boob, faux pas, gaffe.
☒ **1** discretion, caution.

indiscriminate *adj.* **1** making no distinctions; not making or showing careful choice and discrimination. **2** confused; not differentiated.

■ **1** general, sweeping, wholesale, random, haphazard, hit-or-miss, aimless, unsystematic, unmethodical. **2** mixed, motley, miscellaneous.
☒ **1** selective, specific.

indispensability *noun* being indispensable.

indispensable *adj.* essential; that cannot be done without. [from Latin *indispensabilis*]

■ vital, essential, basic, key, crucial, imperative, required, requisite, necessary, needed.

☒ dispensable, unnecessary.

indisposed *adj.* **1** slightly ill. **2 (indisposed to do something)** reluctant or unwilling to do it.

■ **1** ill, sick, unwell, poorly, ailing, laid up. **2** reluctant to, unwilling to, loath to, disinclined to, hesitant to.
☒ **1** well. **2** disposed to, inclined to.

indisposition *noun* being indisposed.

indisputable *adj.* certainly true; beyond doubt.

■ incontrovertible, unquestionable, indubitable, irrefutable, undeniable, undisputed, definite, positive, certain, sure.
☒ doubtful.

indisputably *adv.* as cannot be disputed or denied; unquestionably: *indisputably the finest singer in Italy.*

indissolubility *noun* being indissoluble.

indissoluble *adj.* incapable of being dissolved or broken; permanent; lasting. [from Latin *indissolubilis*]

indissolubly *adv.* so as to be lasting; permanently.

indistinct *adj.* not clear to a person's eye, ear or mind; confused; dim. [from Latin *indistinctus*]

■ unclear, ill-defined, blurred, fuzzy, misty, hazy, shadowy, obscure, dim, faint, muffled, confused, unintelligible, vague, woolly, indefinite, ambiguous.
☒ distinct, clear.

indistinguishable *adj.* not able to be distinguished or told apart.

indium *noun Chem.* (SYMBOL **In**, ATOMIC NUMBER **49**) a soft silvery-white metal that is used in the manufacture of mirrors, semiconductor devices, metal bearings, and certain alloys. [from Latin *indicium*, indigo, because of the indigo-coloured lines in its spectrum]

individual — *adj.* **1** intended for or relating to a single person or thing. **2** particular to one person; showing or having a particular person's unique qualities or characteristics. **3** separate; single. — *noun* **1** a particular person, animal, or thing, especially in contrast to the group to which it belongs. **2** *colloq.* a person: *a most offensive individual.* [from Latin *individualis*, from *individuus*, indivisible]

■ *adj.* **1** exclusive, special, personal, personalized, own, proper, respective, several. **2** distinctive, particular, specific, characteristic, idiosyncratic, peculiar, singular, unique. **3** separate, distinct, discrete, single. *noun* PERSON. **1** being, creature, party, body, soul. **2** character, fellow.
☒ *adj.* **1** collective, shared. **2** general.

individualism *noun* **1** behaviour governed by the belief that individual people should lead their lives as they want and should be independent. **2** the theory that the state should in no way control the actions of the individual. **3** self-centredness; egoism.

individualist — *noun* **1** a person who thinks and acts with independence or great individuality, sometimes for the sake of being different. **2** a person who supports individualism. — *adj.* (also **individualistic**) of individualists or individualism.

individualistically *adv.* in an individualistic way.

individuality *noun* (PL. **individualities**) **1** the qualities and character which distinguish one person or thing from others. **2** a separate and distinct existence.

■ **1** character, personality, distinctiveness, peculiarity, singularity, uniqueness.
☒ **1** sameness.

individualization or **individualisation** *noun* making individual.

individualize or **individualise** *verb* **1** to give (someone or something) a distinctive character or personality. **2** to make suitable for a particular person, thing, or situation.

individually *adv.* in an individual way; one by one.

indivisibility *noun* being indivisible.

indivisible *adj.* **1** not able to be divided or separated. **2** *Maths.* leaving a remainder. [from Latin *indivisibilis*]

Indo- *combining form* Indian; India: *Indo-European*. [from Greek *Indos*]

Indo-Aryan / ɪndoʊˈɛərɪən/ *noun* a group of some 500 languages, also known as Indic languages, spoken by c.500 million people in the N and central region of the Indian subcontinent. They form a subgroup of the Indo-Iranian branch of the Indo-European family, and include Hindu and Urdu, Assamese and Bengali, Punjabi, and Romany.

indoctrinate *verb* to teach (an individual or group) to accept and believe a particular teaching or set of beliefs uncritically. [from Latin *indoctrinare*, to teach]

☰ brainwash, teach, instruct, school, ground, train, drill.

indoctrination *noun* the process of indoctrinating or being indoctrinated.

Indo-European — *adj.* denoting the family of languages which are spoken throughout Europe and in many parts of Asia, including most of the European languages and many Asian ones, such as Hindi and Persian. — *noun* **1** the languages forming this family. **2** the hypothetical language which all of the languages in the Indo-European family come from.

Indo-Iranian *noun* the easternmost branch of the Indo-European family of languages made up of two major subgroups, the Indo-Aryan (or Indic) languages and the Iranian languages.

indolence *noun* laziness, idleness.

indolent *adj.* **1** lazy; disliking and avoiding work and exercise. **2** *Medicine* causing no pain. [from Latin *indolens*, not suffering pain]

indomitability *noun* being indomitable.

indomitable *adj.* that cannot be conquered or defeated. [from Latin *indomitabilis*]

Indonesian — *noun* **1** a native or citizen of Indonesia or the Malay archipelago. **2** the languages spoken in the Malay archipelago, especially the official language of the Republic of Indonesia. — *adj.* relating to Indonesia or its people, languages, and culture. [from Greek *Indos*, Indian + *nesos*, island]

indoor *adj.* used, belonging, done, happening, etc inside a building. [earlier *within-door*]

indoors *adv.* in or into a building.

Indo-Pacific — *adj.* denoting a group of c.700 languages spoken in New Guinea and nearby islands to the W and E. — *noun* the languages forming this group.

indorse same as ENDORSE.

indrawn *adj.* **1** *said especially of the breath* drawn or pulled in. **2** *said of a person* aloof.

indri or **indris** *noun* a leaping lemur, the largest primitive primate, having a dark coat with white legs and hindquarters, fluffy round ears, a very short tail, and a loud far-reaching cry. It inhabits tree tops and feeds on leaves. [from Malagasy *indry!*, look!; the exclamation was mistaken for the animal's name]

indubitable *adj.* that cannot be doubted; certain. [from Latin *indubitabilis*]

induce *verb* **1** to persuade, influence, or cause to do something. **2** to cause to happen or appear. **3** *Medicine* to cause (labour) to begin, especially by the use of drugs; to cause labour in (a pregnant woman). **4** to produce or transmit (an electrical current or magnetism) by induction. **5** *Logic* to infer or come to (eg a general conclusion) from particular cases. [from Latin *inducere*, to lead in]

☰ **1** persuade, talk into, coax, prevail upon, encourage, press, move, influence, draw, tempt. **2** cause, effect, bring about, occasion, give rise to, lead to, incite, instigate, prompt, provoke, produce, generate.
☲ **1** discourage, deter.

inducement *noun* that which induces, especially something which is persuasive or which influences or encourages certain behaviour.

☰ lure, bait, attraction, enticement, encouragement, incentive, reward, spur, stimulus, motive, reason.
☲ disincentive, deterrent.

inducible *adj.* capable of being induced.

induct *verb* **1** to place (eg a priest) formally and often ceremonially in an official position. **2** to initiate as a member of eg a society or profession. **3** *North Amer., esp. US* to enrol for military service or training. [from Latin *inducere*, to lead in]

inductance *noun* the property of an electric circuit or circuit component that causes an electromotive force to be generated in it in the presence of a changing current.

induction *noun* **1** the act or process of inducting or being inducted, especially into office. **2** *Medicine* during childbirth, the initiation of labour by artificial means, often involving the use of drugs such as oxytocin. **3** *Logic* the process of forming or coming to a general conclusion from particular cases. See also DEDUCTION. **4** *Electr.* the production of an electric current in a conductor as a result of its close proximity to a varying magnetic field. **5** *Electr.* the production of magnetization in an unmagnetized material as a result of its close proximity either to a magnetic field, or to the electromagnetic field of a current-carrying conductor. **6** *Engineering* the drawing in of steam or an explosive mixture of fuel and air into the cylinder of an engine.

induction coil a type of transformer that can produce a high-voltage alternating current from a low-voltage direct current source. Induction coils are used to produce short bursts of high voltages, eg to form a spark across the terminals of a spark plug in the internal combustion engine of a motor vehicle.

induction motor *Engineering* an alternating-current motor in which an electric current is supplied to a stationary coil, which creates a magnetic field and induces an electric current in a moving coil (known as the *rotor*). The magnetic field interacts with the induced current, causing the rotor to turn.

inductive *adj.* **1** *Logic* of or using induction. **2** of electric or magnetic induction. See also DEDUCTIVE.

inductively *adv.* by an inductive method or process.

inductor *noun* **1** *Electr.* a component of an electrical circuit that shows the property of inductance. **2** *Chem.* any substance that accelerates a reaction between two or more chemical substances by reacting rapidly with one of them.

indue same as ENDUE.

indulge *verb* **1** *trans., intrans.* (**indulge in something** or **indulge someone in something**) to allow oneself or someone else pleasure or the particular pleasure of something. **2** to allow (someone) to have anything they want; to pamper or spoil. **3** not to restrain or ignore (a desire, taste, wish, etc): *indulge a whim*. **4** *intrans. colloq.* to drink alcohol, especially freely or without restraint. [from Latin *indulgere*, to be kind or indulgent to]

☰ **2** humour, pander to, go along with, give in to, yield to, pamper, spoil, treat, regale, favour, pet, cosset, mollycoddle. **3** gratify, satisfy.

indulgence *noun* **1** an act of indulging a person, desire, etc. **2** the state of being indulgent; generosity; favourable or tolerant treatment. **3** a pleasure that is indulged in. **4** in the Roman Catholic Church, remission from the punishment which remains due after the sin has been absolved.

. . . .

■ **2** generosity, favour, lenience, tolerance. **3** extravagance, luxury, excess, immoderation, intemperance.

. . . .

indulgent *adj.* too quick to overlook or forgive faults or gratify the wishes of others; too tolerant or generous.

. . . .

■ permissive, lenient, tolerant, easy-going, generous, liberal, kind, fond, tender, understanding, forgiving, patient.
⊟ strict, harsh.

. . . .

industrial *adj.* **1** relating to or concerned with industry. **2** used in industry. **3** *said of a country, city, etc* having highly developed industry.

industrial action *Brit.* action, eg strikes, taken by workers as a protest.

industrial democracy a form of industrial management in which workers' representatives are appointed to the board of a company, or actively participate in the management in some other capacity.

industrial design a term referring to the design of anything made by machine or by an industrial process, from Coke bottles to Volkswagens. Early examples included Wedgwood pottery and Sheffield plate.

industrial espionage /ˈɛspɪənɑːʒ/ the practice of obtaining or attempting to obtain trade secrets or other confidential information about a company's activities by underhand or dishonest means. The information so obtained may be used, for example, to negate a company's competitive advantage, or to deal in the company's shares.

industrial estate an area in a town which is developed for industry and business.

industrialism *noun* a social system in which industry (rather than agriculture) is dominant and forms the basis of commerce and the economy.

industrialist *noun* a person who owns a large industrial organization or who is involved in its management at a senior level.

. . . .

■ manufacturer, producer, magnate, tycoon, baron, captain of industry, capitalist, financier.

. . . .

industrialization or **industrialisation** *noun* the process of industrializing.

industrialize or **industrialise** *verb trans., intrans.* to make or become industrially developed; to introduce industry, or have industry introduced.

industrially *adv.* in an industrial way; as regards industry: *industrially advanced nations.*

industrial relations relations between management and workers, especially in manufacturing industries.

Industrial Revolution the rapid development of a country's industry characterized by a change from small-scale production to increased mechanization and mass production in factories, especially in 18c Britain.

industrial tribunal *Industry* a tribunal set up to hear complaints and make judgements in disputes between employers and employees on matters such as industrial relations and alleged unfair dismissal.

industrious *adj.* busy and hard-working; diligent.

. . . .

■ busy, productive, hard-working, diligent, assiduous, conscientious, zealous, active, energetic, tireless, persistent, persevering.
⊟ lazy, idle.

. . . .

industriously *adv.* diligently; busily.

industry *noun* (PL. **industries**) **1** the business of producing goods; all branches of manufacturing and trade. **2** a branch of manufacturing and trade which produces a particular product: *the coal industry.* **3** organized commercial

exploitation or use of natural or national assets, such as historical buildings, famous people, etc: *the tourist industry.* **4** hard work or effort; diligence. [from Latin *industria*]

. . . .

■ **1, 2** business, trade, commerce, manufacturing, production. **4** industriousness, diligence, application, effort, labour, toil, persistence, perseverance.

. . . .

-ine *suffix* forming words meaning 'like, relating to': *crystalline/Alpine.* [from Latin *-inus*]

inebriate /ɪnˈiːbrɪeɪt/ — *verb* (pronounced -eɪt) **1** to make drunk. **2** to exhilarate greatly. — *adj.* (pronounced -ət) drunk, especially habitually. — *noun* (pronounced -ət) a person who is drunk, especially habitually. [from Latin *inebriare*]

inebriation or **inebriety** *noun* drunkenness, intoxication.

inedibility *noun* being inedible.

inedible *adj.* not fit or suitable to be eaten; not edible.

. . . .

■ uneatable, unpalatable, indigestible, harmful, noxious, poisonous, deadly.
⊟ edible.

. . . .

ineducability *noun* being ineducable.

ineducable /ɪnˈɛdjʊkəbl/ *adj.* not capable of being educated, especially because mentally retarded.

ineffability *noun* being ineffable.

ineffable *adj.* **1** that is too great to be described or expressed in words. **2** that should not be said or uttered. [from Latin *ineffabilis*]

ineffective *adj.* **1** having no effect; not producing a result or the result intended. **2** *said of a person* incapable of achieving results.

. . . .

■ INEFFECTUAL. **1** unavailing, fruitless, unproductive, unsuccessful, vain, idle, futile, useless, worthless. **2** inadequate, weak, feeble, powerless, impotent, inept, incompetent.
⊟ EFFECTIVE, EFFECTUAL.

. . . .

ineffectual *adj.* **1** not producing any result or the intended result. **2** *said of a person* lacking the ability and confidence needed to achieve results; weak. [from Latin *ineffectualis*]

inefficacious *adj., said especially of a medicine* not having the desired or intended effect.

inefficacy *noun* lack of efficacy.

inefficiency *noun* (PL. **inefficiencies**) lack of efficiency; an inefficient practice.

inefficient *adj.* not working or producing the required results, etc in the best way, thus wasting time, energy, resources, etc; not efficient.

. . . .

■ uneconomic, wasteful, incompetent, inexpert, slipshod, sloppy, careless, negligent.
⊟ efficient.

. . . .

inelegance *noun* lack of grace or refinement.

inelegant *adj.* not graceful; awkward; lacking elegance or good taste. [from Latin *inelegans*]

. . . .

■ graceless, ungraceful, clumsy, awkward, laboured, ugly, unrefined, crude, unpolished, rough, unsophisticated, uncultivated, uncouth.
⊟ elegant.

. . . .

ineligibility *noun* being ineligible.

ineligible *adj.* (**ineligible for something**) not qualified, not worthy, or not allowed.

. . . .

■ disqualified, ruled out, unacceptable, undesirable,

unworthy, unsuitable, unfit, unqualified, unequipped.
🔳 eligible.

. . . .

ineluctable *adj.* that cannot be avoided, resisted, or escaped from. [from Latin *ineluctabilis*]

ineluctably *adv.* unavoidably.

inept *adj.* **1** awkward; done without, or not having, skill. **2** not suitable or fitting; out of place. **3** silly; foolish. [from Latin *ineptus*]

. . . .

🔳 **1** awkward, clumsy, bungling, incompetent, unskilful, inexpert. **3** silly, foolish, stupid.
🔳 **1** competent, skilful.

. . . .

ineptitude or **ineptness** *noun* **1** awkwardness, incapacity. **2** silliness.

inequable *adj.* not fair or just. [from Latin *inaequabilis*, uneven]

inequality *noun* (PL. **inequalities**) **1** a lack of equality, fairness, or evenness. **2** an instance of this. **3** any dissimilarity or disparity. **4** *Maths.* a statement that two quantities or expressions are not equal. [from Latin *inaequalitas*]

. . . .

🔳 **1** unequalness, unevenness, disproportion, bias, prejudice, discrimination, unfairness, injustice, inequity. **3** difference, diversity, dissimilarity, disparity.
🔳 **1, 3** equality.

. . . .

inequitable *adj.* not fair or just.

inequitably *adv.* in an unfair or unjust way.

inequity *noun* (PL. **inequities**) **1** lack of fairness. **2** an unjust action.

ineradicable *adj.* not able to be removed completely or rooted out. [from IN-[1] + Latin *eradicare*, to root out]

inert *adj.* **1** without the power to move. **2** not wanting to move, act, or think; indolent; sluggish. **3** without active chemical, biological, etc properties. [from Latin *iners*, unskilled, idle]

. . . .

🔳 **1** immobile, motionless, unmoving, still, inactive, inanimate, lifeless, dead, dormant, passive, unresponsive. **2** apathetic, idle, lazy, indolent, lethargic, sluggish, torpid, sleepy.
🔳 **1** mobile, active. **2** lively, animated.

. . . .

inert gas *Chem.* same as NOBLE GAS.

inertia /ɪˈnɜːʃə/ *noun* **1** the tendency of an object to remain at rest, or to continue to move in the same direction at constant speed unless it is acted on by an external force. The magnitude of an object's inertia is determined by its mass. **2** the state of not wanting to move, act, or think; indolence; sluggishness. [from Latin *iners*, unskilled, idle]

. . . .

🔳 **2** apathy, idleness, laziness, indolence, lethargy, sluggishness, torpor, inactivity, passivity.
🔳 **2** activity, liveliness.

. . . .

inertial *adj.* relating to or involving inertia.

inertial control guidance or **navigation** an automatic gyroscope guidance system for aircraft, submarines, missiles, etc, which depends on the tendency of an object to continue in a straight line (*inertia*). Any changes in the direction and magnitude of motion are sensed, using data computed from the rate of acceleration and the physical properties of the Earth, and corrected automatically. The system dispenses with the magnetic compass and is independent of ground-based radio aids.

inertia-reel seat belt a vehicle seat belt on a reel which allows the wearer to move freely in normal conditions but which locks tight under impact or sudden movement.

inertia selling *Brit.* the illegal practice of sending unrequested goods to people followed by a bill if the goods are not returned.

inertly *adv.* in an inert way; idly, inactively.

inescapable *adj.* that cannot be avoided.

. . . .

🔳 inevitable, unavoidable, destined, fated, certain, sure, irrevocable, unalterable.
🔳 escapable.

. . . .

inescapably *adv.* unavoidably.

inessential — *adj.* not essential or necessary. — *noun* an inessential thing.

inestimable *adj.* too great, or of too great value, to be estimated, measured, or fully appreciated. [from Latin *inaestimabilis*]

inestimably *adv.* to an inestimable degree; certainly.

inevitability *noun* being inevitable.

inevitable — *adj.* **1** that cannot be avoided; certain to happen. **2** *colloq.* tiresomely regular or predictable. — *noun* that which is certain to happen and is unavoidable. [from Latin *inevitabilis*]

. . . .

🔳 *adj.* **1** unavoidable, inescapable, ineluctable, necessary, definite, certain, sure, decreed, ordained, destined, fated, automatic, assured, fixed, unalterable, irrevocable, inexorable.
🔳 *adj.* **1** avoidable, uncertain, alterable.

. . . .

inevitably *adv.* so as to be inevitable; certainly.

inexact *adj.* not quite correct, exact, or true.

inexactitude or **inexactness** *noun* lack of exactitude, or an instance of this.

inexcusable *adj.* too bad to be excused, justified, or tolerated. [from Latin *inexcusabilis*]

. . . .

🔳 indefensible, unforgivable, unpardonable, intolerable, unacceptable, outrageous, shameful, blameworthy, reprehensible.
🔳 excusable, justifiable.

. . . .

inexhaustibility *noun* being inexhaustible.

inexhaustible *adj.* **1** incapable of being used up (especially because too big) or exhausted. **2** incapable of becoming tired or exhausted. [from Latin *inexhaustus*, not exhausted]

. . . .

🔳 **1** unlimited, limitless, boundless, unbounded, infinite, endless, never-ending, abundant. **2** indefatigable, tireless, untiring, unflagging, unwearied, unwearying.
🔳 **1** limited.

. . . .

inexorability *noun* being inexorable.

inexorable /ɪnˈɛksərəbl/ *adj.* **1** that cannot be moved by entreaty or persuasion; unrelenting. **2** that cannot be altered or avoided. [from Latin *inexorabilis*]

inexpedience or **inexpediency** *noun* being inexpedient.

inexpedient *adj.* not wise, suitable, or appropriate.

inexpensive *adj.* not costing much; cheap.

. . . .

🔳 cheap, low-priced, reasonable, modest, bargain, discount, budget, low-cost, economical.
🔳 expensive, dear.

. . . .

inexpensively *adv.* without great expense; cheaply.

inexperience *noun* lack of experience, or of skill or knowledge gained from experience. [from Latin *inexperientia*]

. . . .

🔳 inexpertness, ignorance, unfamiliarity, strangeness, newness, naïvety, innocence.
🔳 experience.

. . . .

inexperienced *adj.* lacking experience; unskilled.

▣ inexpert, unskilled, untrained, unqualified, amateur, probationary, apprentice, unacquainted, unfamiliar, unaccustomed, new, fresh, raw, callow, young, immature, naïve, unsophisticated, innocent.
▣ experienced, mature.

inexpert *adj.* not skilled; not expert. [from Latin *inexpertus*]

inexplicability *noun* being inexplicable.

inexplicable *adj.* impossible to explain, understand or account for. [from Latin *inexplicabilis*]

▣ unexplainable, unaccountable, strange, mystifying, puzzling, baffling, mysterious, enigmatic, unfathomable, incomprehensible, incredible, unbelievable, miraculous.
▣ explicable.

inexplicit *adj.* not clearly and exactly stated. [from Latin *inexplicitus*, not straightforward]

inexpressible *adj.* that cannot be expressed or described, especially because too strong.

inexpressibly *adv.* as cannot be expressed in words; indescribably.

inexpressive *adj.*, *said especially of a person's face* expressing little or no emotion.

▣ expressionless, deadpan, blank, vacant, empty, impassive, emotionless, unemotional, inscrutable.
▣ expressive.

inextinguishable *adj.* that cannot be put out or destroyed.

in extremis / ɪn ɛk'striːmiːs/ in desperate or extreme circumstances, especially at or as if at the point of death. [Latin, = in the last]

inextricable *adj.* 1 that cannot be escaped from. 2 that cannot be disentangled or untied. [from Latin *inextricabilis*]

infallibility *noun* being infallible.

infallible *adj.* 1 *said of a person* never making a mistake; incapable of error. 2 *RC Church, said of the pope* unable to err when pronouncing officially on dogma. 3 always successful; not likely to fail. [from Latin *infallibilis*]

▣ 1 unerring, unfailing, perfect, faultless, impeccable. 3 foolproof, fail-safe, *colloq.* sure-fire, certain, sure, reliable, dependable, trustworthy, sound.
▣ FALLIBLE.

infamous *adj.* 1 having a very bad reputation; notoriously bad. 2 evil; vile. [from Latin *infamis*]

▣ EVIL, WICKED. 1 notorious, ill-famed, disreputable, dishonourable, ignominious. 2 vile, heinous, iniquitous, shocking, outrageous, scandalous.
▣ 1 illustrious.

infamously *adv.* notoriously.

infamy *noun* (PL. **infamies**) 1 bad reputation; notoriety; shame. 2 an infamous act.

▣ 1 notoriety, disrepute, disgrace, shame, dishonour, discredit, ignominy, wickedness.
▣ 1 glory.

infancy *noun* (PL. **infancies**) 1 the state or time of being an infant. 2 an early period of existence, growth, and development. 3 *Legal* the state of being under the legal age of maturity (in Britain, usually eighteen).

▣ 1 babyhood, childhood, youth. 2 beginning, start, inception,

outset, birth, dawn, genesis, emergence, origins, early stages.
▣ 1, 3 adulthood.

infant *noun* 1 a very young child in the first period of life. 2 *Legal* a person who is under the legal age of maturity (in Britain, usually eighteen). 3 *Brit.* a schoolchild under the age of seven or eight. [from Latin *infans*, not able to speak, from *in*, not + *fari*, to speak]

▣ 1 baby, *old use* babe, babe in arms, toddler, *colloq.* tot, child.
▣ 1, 2 adult.

infanta *noun Hist.* 1 the eldest daughter of the king of Spain or Portugal. 2 the wife of an infante.

infante / ɪn'fanteɪ/ *noun Hist.* a son of the king of Spain or Portugal who is not heir to the throne. [from Spanish and Portuguese *infante*, from Latin *infans*, infant]

infanticide / ɪn'fantɪsaɪd/ *noun* 1 the murder of a young child or infant. 2 a person who murders a young child or infant. [from Latin *infans*, infant + *caedere*, to kill]

infantile *adj.* 1 of infants or infancy. 2 very childish; immature. [from Latin *infantilis*]

▣ 2 babyish, childish, puerile, juvenile, immature.
▣ ADULT, MATURE.

infantile paralysis *old medical use* poliomyelitis.

infantilism / ɪn'fantɪlɪzm/ *noun* the presence of childish characteristics in an adult or older child.

infantry — *noun* (PL. **infantries**) a body of soldiers trained and equipped to fight on foot. — *adj.* relating to or for the infantry. [from Italian *infanteria*]

infantryman *noun* a soldier in the infantry.

infant school *Brit.* a school for children aged between five and seven or eight.

infarction *noun Medicine* the death of a localized area of tissue as a result of the blocking of its blood supply, usually by a blood clot (thrombus), air bubble, or fragment of tissue or foreign material. [from Latin *infarcire*, to stuff]

infatuate *verb* to cause to feel a passionate, foolish, and unreasonable love or admiration. [from Latin *infatuare*]

infatuated *adj.* (**infatuated with someone**) filled with passion for them; besotted with them.

▣ besotted with, obsessed with, enamoured with, *colloq.* smitten by, *colloq.* crazy about, captivated by, fascinated by.

infatuation *noun* 1 being infatuated. 2 someone or something one is infatuated with.

▣ LOVE. 1 besottedness, obsession, fixation, passion, *colloq.* crush, fondness.

infect *verb* 1 to contaminate (a living organism) with a pathogen, such as a bacterium, virus, or fungus, and thereby cause disease. 2 to pass a feeling or opinion, especially an adverse or negative one, to (someone). [from Latin *inficere*, to stain]

▣ 1 contaminate, pollute, defile, taint, blight, poison. 2 corrupt, pervert, influence, affect, touch, inspire.

infection *noun* 1 the process of infecting or state of being infected. 2 the invasion of a human, animal, or plant by pathogenic (disease-causing) micro-organisms, such as bacteria, viruses, fungi, or protozoa, which then multiply rapidly and usually cause symptoms of disease, sometimes after an *incubation period* during which no symptoms appear. 3 a disease caused by such a micro-organism. 4 the passing on of feelings, opinions, etc.

▣ **1** contagion, contamination, pollution, defilement, taint, blight. **3** illness, disease, epidemic.

infectious *adj.* **1** *said of a disease* capable of being transmitted by air, water, etc. **2** causing infection. **3** *said of a feeling, opinion, etc* likely to be passed on to others.

▣ **1** contagious, communicable, transmissible, catching, spreading, epidemic, virulent, deadly. **2** contaminating, polluting, defiling, corrupting.

infectious mononucleosis *Medicine* an infectious disease, mainly affecting adolescents, caused by the Epstein-Barr virus (a herpes virus). Its symptoms include swelling of the lymph nodes, fever, a sore throat, and headache. Also called GLANDULAR FEVER.

infelicitous *adj.* **1** not happy, fortunate, or lucky. **2** not suitable, fitting, or apt.

infelicity *noun* (PL. **infelicities**) **1** bad luck; misfortune; unhappiness. **2** something, especially an expression, phrase, choice of word, etc, that is not suitable or fitting. [from Latin *infelicitas*]

infer *verb* (**inferred, inferring**) **1** to conclude or judge from facts, observation, and deduction. **2** *colloq.* to imply or suggest. [from Latin *inferre*, to bring in]

▣ **1** deduce, conclude, derive, extrapolate, assume, presume, surmise, gather, understand.

inferable or **inferrable** *adj.* capable of being inferred or deduced.

inference *noun* **1** an act of inferring, especially of reaching a conclusion from facts, observation and careful thought. **2** that which is inferred, especially a conclusion.

▣ DEDUCTION, CONCLUSION, ASSUMPTION, PRESUMPTION. **1** surmise, conjecture, extrapolation, construction, interpretation, reading. **2** corollary, consequence.

inferential *adj.* of or based on inference.

inferior — *adj.* (*often* **inferior to something** or **someone**) **1** poor or poorer in quality. **2** low or lower in value, rank, or status. **3** low or lower in position. **4** *said of letters or figures* printed or written slightly below the line. **5** *said of a planet* revolving within the Earth's orbit; nearer the Sun. — *noun* a person who is inferior in some way to another. [from Latin *inferior*, lower]

▣ *adj.* **1** substandard, second-rate, *colloq.* low-rent, mediocre, bad, poor, unsatisfactory, slipshod, shoddy. **2** lower, lesser, minor, secondary, junior, subordinate, subsidiary, second-class, low, humble, lowly, menial. *noun* subordinate, junior, *derog.* underling, minion, vassal, menial.
▣ *adj.* **1** superior, excellent. **2** superior, senior. **3** superior, higher. *noun* superior, senior.

inferiority *noun* the state of being inferior.

▣ subordination, subservience, humbleness, lowliness, unimportance, insignificance, mediocrity, imperfection, inadequacy.
▣ superiority, excellence.

inferiority complex *Psychol.* a constant feeling that one is not as good as others in some way, which may lead to shyness or, in an attempt to compensate for this feeling, aggressive behaviour.

inferior planet *Astron.* a planet whose orbit around the Sun lies within the orbit of the Earth, ie Mercury or Venus.

infernal *adj.* **1** of hell. **2** wicked; evil. **3** *colloq.* extremely annoying or unpleasant. [from Latin *infernalis*, from *inferus*, low]

▣ DEVILISH, DIABOLICAL, FIENDISH. **1** hellish, satanic. **3** accursed, damned.
▣ **1, 3** heavenly.

infernally *adv.* **1** in an infernal way. **2** *colloq.* dreadfully.

inferno *noun* (PL. **infernos**) **1** (*often* **Inferno**) hell. **2** a place or situation of horror and confusion. **3** a raging fire. [from Italian *inferno*, from Latin *infernus*, hell]

infertile *adj.* **1** *said of soil, etc* not fertile or producing good crops. **2** *said of a person or animal* unable to have young. [from Latin *infertilis*]

▣ BARREN, STERILE. **1** unproductive, unfruitful, arid, parched, dried-up. **2** childless.
▣ FERTILE. **1** fruitful.

infertility *noun* the inability to produce offspring.

infest *verb, said of parasites such as fleas, lice, and certain fungi* to be present in large numbers on the surface of or within an animal or plant. [from Latin *infestare*, to disturb]

▣ overrun, invade, infiltrate, penetrate, permeate, pervade, ravage.

infestation *noun* **1** infesting. **2** an attack, especially by parasites.

infidel — *noun* **1** a person who rejects a particular religion, especially Christianity or Islam. **2** a person who rejects all religions; an unbeliever. **3** a person who rejects a theory. — *adj.* of unbelievers; unbelieving. [from Latin *infidelis*]

infidelity *noun* (PL. **infidelities**) **1** unfaithfulness to someone, especially a husband, wife, or partner. **2** an instance of this. **3** lack of belief in a religion. [from Latin *infidelitas*]

▣ **1** adultery, unfaithfulness, faithlessness, disloyalty, duplicity, treachery, betrayal, cheating, falseness. **3** unfaithfulness, faithlessness.
▣ **1, 3** fidelity, faithfulness.

infield *noun* **1** *Cricket* the area of the field close to the wicket, or the players positioned here. **2** *Baseball* the diamond-shaped area of the pitch formed by the four bases, or the players positioned here. See also OUTFIELD.

infielder *noun* a player who stands in the infield.

in-fighting *noun* fighting or competition between members of the same group, company, or organization.

infill — *noun* (*also* **infilling**) **1** the act of filling or closing gaps, holes, etc. **2** the material used to fill a gap, hole, etc. — *verb* to fill in (a gap, hole, etc).

infiltrate *verb* **1** *trans., intrans., said of troops, agents, etc* to pass into (territory or an organization held by the enemy or rivals) secretly, to gain influence, control, or information. **2** to filter (eg liquid or gas) through (a substance). **3** *intrans., said eg of liquid or gas* to filter in. **4** *trans., intrans.* to permeate gradually in (a substance). [from IN-² + FILTRATE]

▣ **1** penetrate, enter. **2, 3** filter, percolate.

infiltration *noun* infiltrating or being infiltrated.

infiltrator *noun* someone who infiltrates a group or organization.

infinite — *adj.* **1** having no boundaries or limits in size, extent, time, or space. **2** too great to be measured or counted. **3** very great; vast. **4** *Maths.* having an unlimited number of elements, digits, or terms. — *noun* anything which has no limits, boundaries, etc, especially (**the Infinite**) God. [from Latin *infinitus*]

▭ *adj.* **1** limitless, unlimited, boundless, unbounded, endless, never-ending, inexhaustible, bottomless. **2** uncountable, countless, innumerable, numberless, untold, incalculable, inestimable, immeasurable, unfathomable. **3** vast, immense, enormous, huge.
▣ *adj.* **1** finite, limited.

infinitely *adv.* to an infinite degree; without limit.
infiniteness *noun* **1** being infinite. **2** infinity. **3** vastness.
infinitesimal — *adj.* **1** infinitely small; with a value close to zero. **2** *colloq.* extremely small. — *noun* an infinitesimal amount. [from Latin *infinitesimus*]

▭ *adj.* **2** tiny, minute, microscopic, minuscule, inconsiderable, insignificant, negligible, inappreciable, imperceptible.
▣ *adj.* **2** great, huge, enormous.

infinitive — *noun Grammar* a verb form which expresses an action but which does not refer to a particular subject or time, in English often used with *to*, eg *tell him to go*, but used without *to* after certain verbs, eg *let her go*. — *adj.*, *said of a verb* having this form. [from Latin *infinitivus*]
infinitude *noun* **1** the state or quality of being infinite. **2** something infinite, especially an infinite quantity, degree, amount. [from INFINITE + MAGNITUDE]
infinity *noun* **1** the quality or state of being infinite. **2** space, time, distance, or quantity that is without limit or boundaries, or *loosely* is too great to be measured. **3** *Maths.* a number that is larger than any finite value, symbol α, that can be approached but never reached, because the sequence of natural numbers continues indefinitely. It is considered to be the reciprocal of zero, ie $\frac{1}{0}$. [from Latin *infinitas*]

▭ **1** limitlessness, boundlessness, endlessness, inexhaustibility, countlessness, immeasurableness, vastness, immensity. **2** eternity, perpetuity.
▣ **1** finiteness, limitation.

infirm *adj.*, *said of a person* weak or ill, especially from old age. [from Latin *infirmus*]

▭ weak, feeble, frail, ill, sickly, failing, faltering, unsteady, shaky, wobbly, doddery.
▣ strong, healthy.

infirmary *noun* (PL. **infirmaries**) **1** a hospital. **2** a room or ward where the sick and injured are treated, especially in a school or monastery. [from Latin *infirmaria*]
infirmity *noun* (PL. **infirmities**) **1** the state or quality of being sick, weak, or infirm. **2** a disease or illness.
infix — *verb* (with stress on -*fix*) **1** to fix firmly in (something, the mind, etc). **2** *Grammar* to insert (an affix) into the main part of a word as opposed to adding it as a prefix or suffix. — *noun* (with stress on *in*-) an affix inserted into the main part of a word, as opposed to a prefix or suffix. [from Latin *infigere*]
infixation *noun* the process of infixing or being infixed.
in flagrante delicto / ɪn flə'ɡræntɪ dɪ'lɪktoʊ/ in the very act of committing a crime. [Latin, = in the blazing crime]
inflame *verb* **1** to arouse strong or violent emotion in. **2** *intrans.* to begin to feel strong or violent emotion; to become excited or angry. **3** *trans., intrans.* to burst or cause to burst into flames. **4** to make more heated or intense; to exacerbate. **5** *trans., intrans.* to cause (part of the body) to become, or (of part of the body) to become, affected by inflammation. [from Latin *inflammare*, to kindle]

▭ **1** anger, enrage, infuriate, incense, exasperate, madden, provoke, stimulate, excite, rouse, arouse, agitate. **3** kindle, ignite, fire. **4** heat, fan, fuel, increase, intensify, exacerbate, aggravate.

▣ **1, 4** cool.

inflamed *adj.*, *said of part of the body* affected by inflammation.

▭ sore, painful, tender, swollen, septic, infected, poisoned, red, hot, heated, angry.

inflammability *noun* an inflammable quality.
inflammable — *adj.* **1** easily set on fire. **2** easily excited or angered. — *noun* an inflammable substance. [from Latin *inflammabilis*]

▭ *adj.* **1** flammable, combustible.
▣ *adj.* **1** non-flammable, incombustible, flameproof, fireproof.

inflammation *noun* **1** a protective response of the body tissues to disease, injury, infection, or the presence of an allergen. The affected part becomes red, heated, swollen, and painful. **2** an act of inflaming or state of being inflamed. [from Latin *inflammatio*]

▭ **1** soreness, painfulness, tenderness, swelling, abscess, infection, redness, heat, rash, irritation.

inflammatory *adj.* **1** likely to cause strong or violent emotion, especially anger. **2** of, causing, or caused by inflammation of part of the body. [from Latin *inflammare*, to kindle]
inflatable — *adj.*, *said of a cushion, ball, etc* that can be filled with air for use. — *noun* an inflatable object.
inflate *verb* **1** to cause to swell or expand with air or gas. **2** *intrans.* to swell or expand with air or gas. **3** to exaggerate the importance or value of. **4** to increase (prices generally) artificially or to increase (the volume of money in circulation). See also DEFLATE, REFLATE. [from Latin *inflare*, to blow into]

▭ **1** blow up, pump up, distend, bloat, expand, enlarge. **2** swell, puff out, expand, enlarge. **3** exaggerate, overstate, overrate, overestimate. **4** increase, raise, *colloq.* hike up, boost.
▣ DEFLATE.

inflated *adj.* **1** *said of prices* artificially increased to a high level. **2** *said especially of language or opinions* showing too great a sense of one's importance. **3** blown up or filled with air or gas; distended.
inflation *noun* **1** the process of inflating or being inflated. **2** a general increase in the level of prices accompanied by a fall in the purchasing power of money, caused by an increase in the amount of money in circulation and credit available. See also DEFLATION, REFLATION, STAGFLATION.

▭ **1** expansion, enlargement. **2** increase, rise, escalation, hyperinflation.
▣ DEFLATION.

inflationary *adj.* relating to or involving inflation.
inflect *verb* **1** *Grammar* to change the form of (a word) to show eg tense, number, gender, grammatical case, etc. **2** *intrans. Grammar, said of a word* to change, or be able to be changed, to show tense, number, gender, grammatical case, etc. **3** to vary the tone or pitch of (the voice). **4** to bend inwards. [from Latin *inflectere*, to curve]
inflection or **inflexion** *noun* **1** an act of inflecting or state of being inflected. **2** *Grammar* **a** the change in the form of a word which shows tense, number, gender, grammatical case, etc. **b** an inflected form of a word. **c** a suffix which is added to a word to form an inflected form, eg -*s*, -*ing*. **3** a change in the tone, pitch, etc, of the voice. **4** a change in a curve from being convex to concave, or vice versa.
inflectional or **inflexional** *adj. Grammar* relating to or involving inflection.

inflective *adj. Grammar* of or subject to inflection.

inflexibility or **inflexibleness** *noun* being inflexible.

inflexible *adj.* **1** incapable of being bent; rigid. **2** *said of a person* never giving way; unyielding; obstinate. **3** that cannot or may not be changed; fixed. [from Latin *inflexibilis*]

- **1** rigid, stiff, hard, solid. **2** unbending, unyielding, adamant, resolute, relentless, uncompromising, stubborn, obstinate, intransigent, entrenched, dyed-in-the-wool. **3** set, fixed, firm, strict, stringent.
- FLEXIBLE. **1** pliable. **2** yielding. **3** adaptable.

inflexion see INFLECTION.

inflict *verb* (*usually* **inflict something on someone**) to impose on or cause to suffer something unpleasant, eg a blow, defeat, or pain. [from Latin *infligere*, to strike against]

- impose, enforce, perpetrate, wreak, administer, apply, deliver, mete out, lay, exact, levy.

infliction *noun* **1** an act of inflicting. **2** something that is inflicted.

in-flight *adj.* provided during an aircraft flight.

inflorescence *noun* **1** *Bot.* the complete flower-head of a flowering plant, including the stem. **2** *Bot.* any of a number of different arrangements of the flowers on the main stem of a flowering plant. [from Latin *inflorescere*, to begin to blossom]

inflow *noun* **1** the act or process of flowing in. **2** something that flows in.

inflowing — *noun* the process of flowing in. — *adj.* that flows in.

influence — *noun* (*often* **influence on** or **over someone** or **something**) **1** the power that one person or thing has to affect another. **2** a person or thing that has such a power: *be a good influence on him*. **3** power resulting from political or social position, wealth, ability, standards of behaviour, etc. — *verb* to have an effect, especially an indirect or unnoticed one, on (a person, events, etc). — **under the influence** *colloq.* affected by alcohol; drunk. [from Latin *influentia*, from *influere*, to flow into]

- *noun* **1** power, sway, rule, authority, mastery, hold, control, direction, guidance, pull, pressure, effect, impact. **3** importance, prestige, standing. *verb* dominate, control, direct, guide, change, alter, modify, affect, move, stir, rouse, sway, persuade, induce, prompt, motivate, dispose, incline, bias, prejudice.

influential *adj.* **1** having influence or power. **2** (**influential in something**) making an important contribution to it.

- **1** dominant, controlling, leading, authoritative, charismatic, persuasive, convincing, compelling, inspiring, moving, powerful, potent, effective, telling, strong, weighty, important, significant. **2** instrumental in.
- **1** ineffective, unimportant.

influenza *noun* an infectious illness caused by a virus, whose symptoms include headache, fever, a sore throat, catarrh and muscle pains. See also FLU. [from Italian *influenza*, influence, from the belief that stars caused epidemics]

influx *noun* **1** a continual stream or arrival of large numbers of people or things. **2** a flowing in. [from Latin *influere*, to flow into]

- **1** arrival, stream, flow, rush, flood, inundation. **2** inflow, inrush.

info *noun colloq.* information. [abbreviation]

infomercial *noun* a short informational film promoted for commercial purposes.

inform *verb* **1** (*often* **inform someone about** or **of something**) to give them knowledge or information on it. **2** *intrans.* (**inform against** or **on someone**) to give incriminating evidence about them to the authorities. **3** to animate, inspire, or give life to. **4** to give an essential quality to. [from Latin *informare*, to give form to]

- **1** tell, notify, advise, warn, tip off, acquaint, *colloq.* fill in, brief, instruct, enlighten. **2** betray, incriminate, inculpate, denounce, *slang* shop, *slang* grass on, *colloq.* tell on.

informal *adj.* **1** without ceremony or formality; relaxed and friendly. **2** *said of language, clothes, etc* suitable for and used in relaxed, everyday situations.

- CASUAL. **1** unofficial, unceremonious, relaxed, easy, free, natural, simple, unpretentious, friendly, familiar, colloquial.
- FORMAL.

informality *noun* (PL. **informalities**) lack of formality, or an instance of this.

informant *noun* someone who informs, eg against another person, or who gives information.

information *noun* **1** knowledge gained or given; facts; news. **2** the communicating or receiving of knowledge. **3** an accusation made before a court or magistrate. **4** a signal or character which represents data, especially in telecommunications and computing.

- **1** knowledge, facts, data, *colloq.* gen, *colloq.* SP, intelligence, news, report, statement, communiqué, message, word, advice, notice. **2** briefing, instruction, enlightenment.

informational *adj.* relating to or involving information.

information retrieval the storing, sorting, and finding of information stored especially in a computer.

information technology *Comput.* (ABBREV. **IT**) the use of a range of technologies, especially computer systems, digital electronics, and telecommunications, to store, process, and transmit information.

information theory *Maths.* the mathematical analysis of the efficiency of communication channels, especially with regard to the coding and transmission of information. It uses statistical methods to determine the quantity and speed of information transmission that can be achieved by computers and telecommunication systems.

informative *adj.* giving useful or interesting information; instructive.

- educational, instructive, edifying, enlightening, illuminating, revealing, forthcoming, communicative, chatty, newsy, helpful, useful, constructive.
- uninformative.

informed *adj.* having or showing knowledge, especially in being educated and intelligent.

- knowledgeable, well-informed, authoritative, expert, well-read, erudite, learned, well-researched.
- ignorant.

informer *noun* a person who informs against another, especially to the police and usually for money or some other reward.

- informant, *slang* grass, *slang* supergrass, betrayer, traitor, Judas, telltale, sneak, spy, *colloq.* mole.

infotainment *noun* the presentation of serious subjects or current affairs as entertainment.

infra *adv.* below; lower down on the page or further on in the book. [from Latin *infra*]

infra- *combining form* forming words meaning 'below, beneath'. [from Latin *infra*, below]

infraction *noun* the breaking of a law, rule, etc. [from Latin *infringere*, to break]

infra dig *colloq.* abbreviation of Latin *infra dignitatem*, beneath one's dignity.

infrared — *adj.* of, using, producing, or sensitive to radiation with a wavelength just beyond the red end of the visible spectrum, usually felt as heat. — *noun* infrared radiation.

infrared astronomy *Astron.* the study of infrared radiation produced by celestial bodies, or by gas or dust in space, used to detect comets, star formation in galaxies, dust clouds, etc.

infrasonic *adj.* of or having a frequency below the range which can normally be heard by the human ear.

infrasound *noun Physics* sound having a frequency of less than 20Hz. Such sound waves cannot be heard by humans, but may be felt. Infrasound waves are produced by explosions and by an unsteady airflow past an object.

infrastructure *noun* **1** the basic structure of a society, organization or system. **2** the permanent services and equipment, eg the roads, railways, bridges, factories, and schools needed for a country to be able to function properly. **3** the permanent services and equipment, eg roads, railways and bridges, needed for military purposes.

infrequency *noun* **1** being infrequent. **2** rarity.

infrequent *adj.* not frequent; occurring rarely or only occasionally. [from Latin *infrequens*]

infringe *verb* **1** to break or violate (eg a law or oath). **2** to interfere with (a person's rights). **3** *intrans.* **(infringe on or upon something)** to affect a person's rights, freedom, etc in such a way as to limit or reduce them; to encroach or trespass. [from Latin *infringere*, to break]

◻ **1** break, violate, contravene, transgress, disobey, defy, flout, ignore. **3** intrude on, encroach on, trespass on, invade.
◪ **1** keep, obey.

infringement *noun* **1** infringing. **2** a breach.

infuriate *verb* to make very angry. [from Latin *infuriare*]

◻ anger, enrage, incense, exasperate, madden, provoke, rouse, annoy, irritate, antagonize.
◪ calm, pacify.

infuriating *adj.* causing great anger or annoyance.

infuse *verb* **1** **(infuse something into someone** or **infuse someone with something)** to inspire them with a positive feeling, quality, etc. **2** *trans., intrans.* to soak or cause (leaves, eg tea) to be soaked in hot water to release their flavour or other qualities. [from Latin *infundere*, to pour into]

infusion *noun* **1** the act of infusing. **2** being infused.

-ing[1] *suffix* forming nouns, especially from verbs, usually expressing the action of the verb, its result or product, etc: *building/driving*. [from Anglo-Saxon *-ing*, *-ung*]

-ing[2] *suffix* used to form the present participle of verbs: *charming/walking*. [from Anglo-Saxon *-ende*]

-ing[3] *suffix* forming nouns meaning 'one belonging to' or 'one of the same kind of': *gelding*. [from Anglo-Saxon *-ing*]

ingenious *adj.* marked by, showing or having skill, originality and inventive cleverness. [from Latin *ingenium*, common sense, cleverness]

◻ clever, skilful, masterly, imaginative, creative, inventive, resourceful, original, innovative, cunning, crafty.

◪ unimaginative.

ingénue /ˈanʒeɪˈnjuː/ *noun* **1** a naïve and unsophisticated young woman. **2** an actress playing the role of an ingénue. [French, from Latin *ingenuus*, native]

ingenuity *noun* inventive cleverness, skill or originality; ingeniousness. [from Latin *ingenuitas*, ingenuousness]

ingenuous *adj.* innocent and childlike, especially in being frank, honest, and incapable of deception. [from Latin *ingenuus*, native]

◻ artless, guileless, innocent, honest, sincere, frank, open, plain, simple, unsophisticated, naïve, credulous, trusting.
◪ artful, sly.

ingest *verb* **1** to take (eg food or liquid) into the body. **2** *said of a jet engine* to suck in (an object, eg a bird). [from Latin *ingerere*, to carry in]

ingestible *adj.* capable of being ingested.

ingestion *noun* **1** ingesting. **2** being ingested.

inglenook *noun* a corner or alcove in a large open fireplace. [from Scots Gaelic *aingeal*, fire + NOOK]

inglorious *adj.* **1** ordinary; not glorious or noble. **2** bringing shame. [from Latin *inglorius*]

ingoing *adj.* going in; entering.

ingot *noun* a brick-shaped mass of metal, especially of gold or silver. [from Middle English *ingot*, something poured in, from Anglo-Saxon *goten* cast in metal]

ingrained *adj.* fixed firmly; difficult to remove or wipe off or out. [from the phrase *dyed in grain*]

◻ fixed, rooted, deep-rooted, deep-seated, entrenched, ineradicable, permanent, inbuilt, inborn, inbred.

ingrate — *noun* an ungrateful person. — *adj.* ungrateful. [from Latin *ingratus*]

ingratiate *verb* **(ingratiate oneself with someone)** to gain or try to gain their favour or approval. [from Latin *in*, into + *gratia*, favour]

◻ curry favour with, flatter, crawl to, grovel to, toady to, *colloq.* suck up to, get in with.

ingratiating *adj.* trying to gain favour.

ingratitude *noun* the quality of being ungrateful; lack of proper gratitude. [from Latin *ingratitudo*]

◻ ungratefulness, thanklessness, unappreciativeness, ungraciousness.
◪ gratitude, thankfulness.

ingredient *noun* one of several things that goes into a mixture, especially in cooking. [from Latin *ingrediens*, going into]

◻ constituent, element, factor, component, part.

ingress *noun* the act of going in or entering, or power or right to do so. [from Latin *ingredi*, to go into]

ingrowing *adj.*, *said especially of a toenail* growing inwards, usually into the flesh.

ingrown *adj.* that has grown inwards.

inhabit *verb* **(inhabited, inhabiting)** to live in or occupy (a place). [from Latin *inhabitare*, to live in]

◻ live in, dwell in, reside in, occupy, possess, colonize, settle, people, populate.

inhabitable *adj.* fit to be lived in.

inhabitant *noun* a person or animal that lives permanently in a place.

⊟ resident, dweller, citizen, native, occupier, occupant, inmate, tenant, lodger.

inhalant / ɪn'heɪlənt/ *noun* a medicine (eg one for relieving congestion in the chest) which is inhaled.

inhalation / ɪnhə'leɪʃən/ *noun* the act of breathing in, or that which is breathed in.

inhale / ɪn'heɪl/ *verb trans., intrans.* to breathe in (air, gas, etc). [from Latin *inhalare*]

inhaler *noun* a small portable device used for inhaling certain medicines.

inharmonious *adj.* 1 not sounding well together; lacking harmony. 2 not agreeing or going well together; not compatible.

inhere *verb intrans.* (*often* **inhere in something** or **someone**) *said of character, a quality, etc* to be an essential or permanent part. [from Latin *inhaerere*, to stick in]

inherent / ɪn'hɪərənt/ *adj.* (*often* **inherent in someone** or **something**) *said of a quality, etc* belonging naturally or being an essential or permanent part.

⊟ inborn, inbred, innate, natural, inbuilt, intrinsic, ingrained, essential, fundamental, basic.

inherently / ɪn'hɪərəntlɪ/ *adv.* by virtue of being an essential part; in its nature: *an inherently difficult topic.*

inherit *verb* (**inherited**, **inheriting**) 1 to receive (property, a title, position, etc) from a member of one's family on his or her death, or through legal descent from a predecessor. 2 *intrans.* to receive property, a title, etc in such circumstances. 3 to receive genetically transmitted characteristics from the previous generation. [from Latin *inhereditare*]

⊟ 1 succeed to, accede to, assume, come into, be left, receive.

inheritable *adj.* 1 capable of being passed by heredity from one generation to another. 2 capable of being inherited.

inheritance *noun* 1 something (eg property, a title, physical or mental characteristics) that is or may be inherited. 2 the act of inheriting or right to inherit. 3 heredity.

⊟ 1 legacy, bequest, heritage, birthright. 2 succession, accession. 3 heredity, ancestry, descent.

inheritance tax a tax levied on inheritors according to their relationship to the person from whom they have inherited.

inheritor *noun* an heir.

⊟ heir, heiress, successor, beneficiary, recipient.

inhibit *verb* (**inhibited**, **inhibiting**) 1 to hold back, restrain or prevent (an action, desire, progress, etc). 2 to make (a person) feel nervous or frightened about acting freely or spontaneously, eg by causing him or her to doubt his or her abilities. 3 to prohibit or forbid (someone) from doing something. 4 *Chem.* to decrease the rate of a chemical reaction, or to stop it altogether, by means of a substance known as an inhibitor. [from Latin *inhibere*, to keep back]

⊟ 1 hold back, suppress, restrain, curb, check, hinder, impede, obstruct, frustrate, thwart, prevent, stop. 2 discourage, repress.
🔁 1 assist. 2 encourage.

inhibited *adj.* held back by inhibition.

⊟ repressed, self-conscious, shy, reticent, withdrawn, reserved, guarded, subdued.

🔁 uninhibited, open, relaxed.

inhibition *noun* 1 a feeling of fear or embarrassment, caused by emotional or psychological factors, which prevent one from acting, thinking, etc freely or spontaneously in some way: *sexual inhibitions.* 2 an act of inhibiting or process of being inhibited. 3 something which inhibits, prevents progress, holds back or forbids, etc. 4 *Chem.* a decrease in the rate of a chemical reaction, or of a biochemical reaction (catalyzed by enzymes) in living cells, that is brought about by a substance known as an inhibitor.

⊟ 1 *colloq.* hang-up, problem, mental block. 2 repression, self-consciousness, shyness, reticence, reserve. 3 restraint, curb, check, hindrance, impediment, obstruction, bar.

inhibitor or **inhibiter** *noun* 1 something that inhibits. 2 *Biochem.* a substance that interferes with a chemical or biological process.

inhospitable *adj.* 1 *said of a person* not friendly or welcoming. 2 *said of a place* offering little shelter (eg from harsh weather); barren. [from Latin *inhospitabilis*]

inhuman *adj.* 1 without human feeling; cruel and unfeeling; brutal. 2 not human. [from Latin *inhumanus*]

⊟ 1 barbaric, barbarous, animal, bestial, vicious, savage, sadistic, cold-blooded, brutal, cruel, unfeeling, inhumane.
🔁 HUMAN.

inhumane *adj.* showing no kindness, sympathy, or compassion; cruel; unfeeling. [a variant of INHUMAN]

⊟ unkind, insensitive, callous, unfeeling, heartless, cold-hearted, hard-hearted, pitiless, merciless, cruel, brutal, inhuman.
🔁 humane, kind, compassionate.

inhumanity *noun* (PL. **inhumanities**) 1 the state of being inhuman or inhumane; cruelty; lack of feeling or pity. 2 an inhuman, inhumane, cruel, etc act.

inimical *adj.* (*often* **inimical to someone**) 1 tending to discourage; unfavourable. 2 not friendly; hostile. [from Latin *inimicalis*]

inimitable *adj.* too good, skilful, etc to be satisfactorily imitated by others; unique. [from Latin *inimitabilis*]

iniquitous *adj.* 1 grossly unjust or unreasonable. 2 wicked.

iniquity *noun* (PL. **iniquities**) 1 the state of being unfair, unjust, wicked, or sinful. 2 an unfair, unjust, wicked, or sinful act. [from Latin *iniquitas*]

initial — *adj.* of or at the beginning. — *noun* the first letter of a word, especially of a proper name. — *verb* (**initialled**, **initialling**) to mark or sign with the initials of one's name, especially as a sign of approval. [from Latin *initialis*]

⊟ *adj.* first, beginning, opening, introductory, original, primary, early, formative.
🔁 *adj.* final, last.

initially *adv.* 1 as a beginning. 2 at first.

⊟ 1 first, firstly, first of all. 2 at first, at the beginning, to begin with, to start with, originally.
🔁 1 finally. 2 in the end.

Initial Teaching Alphabet (**i.t.a.** or **ITA**) an alphabet of 44 characters devised in 1959 by James Pitman (1901–85), in which each character corresponds to a single sound or phoneme in English. It has been used in the teaching of reading, though its popularity has declined in recent years.

initiate — *verb* (pronounced -eɪt) 1 to cause to begin. 2 (**initiate someone into something**) to accept a new member into a society, organization, etc, especially with secret ceremonies. **3 (initiate someone in something)** to give them instruction in the basics or rudiments of a skill, science, etc. — *noun* (pronounced -ət) a person who has recently been or is soon to be initiated. — *adj.* (pronounced -ət) having been recently initiated or soon to be initiated. [from Latin *initiare*]

▪ *verb* **1** begin, start, commence, originate, pioneer, institute, set up, introduce, launch, open, instigate, activate, trigger, prompt, cause.

initiation *noun* **1** initiating or being initiated. **2** the formal introduction of a new member into an organization or society.

▪ **2** admission, reception, entrance, entry, début, introduction, enrolment, induction, investiture, installation, inauguration.

initiation rites ceremonies effecting or marking a transition from one social condition or role to another, especially from childhood to adulthood: one of a number of rites of passage or *passage rites*.

initiative — *noun* **1** the ability or skill to initiate things, take decisions or act resourcefully. **2** a first step or move towards an end or aim. **3** the right or power to begin something. **4** the right of voters to originate legislation. — *adj.* serving to begin; introductory. — **on one's own initiative** as a result of one's own action; without needing to be prompted by others.

▪ *noun* **1** energy, drive, dynamism, *colloq.* get-up-and-go, enterprise, resourcefulness, inventiveness, originality. **2** first move, first step, lead, action.

initiator *noun* **1** someone who initiates. **2** *Chem.* a substance which starts a chain reaction.

inject *verb* **1** to introduce (a liquid, eg medicine) into the body of (a person or animal) using a hypodermic syringe. **2** to force (fuel) into an engine. **3** to introduce (a quality, element, etc): *inject a note of optimism.* [from Latin *injicere*, to throw in]

▪ **1** insert, inoculate, vaccinate, *slang* shoot. **3** introduce, add, bring, infuse, instil.

injection *noun* **1** an act of injecting or forcing in or the process of being injected. **2** that which is injected, eg a liquid medicine.

▪ **1** insertion, inoculation, vaccination, *colloq.* jab, *colloq.* shot. **2** dose, *slang* fix.

injection moulding *Engineering* a process used in the manufacture of plastics, in which plastic is heated until it is soft enough to inject through a nozzle into a mould in the shape of the desired articles.

injudicious *adj.* not wise; showing poor judgement.

injunction *noun* **1** *Legal* an official order from a court forbidding something, or commanding that something should be done. **2** any authoritative order or warning. [from Latin *injungere*, to enjoin]

▪ **2** command, order, directive, ruling, mandate, direction, instruction, warning.

injunctive *adj.* enjoining.

injure *verb* **1** to do physical harm or damage to. **2** to harm, spoil, or weaken. **3** to do an injustice or wrong to. [from Latin *injuria*, injury]

▪ **1** hurt, harm, ill-treat, maltreat, abuse, wound, cut, disfigure, mutilate, break, fracture, maim, disable, cripple, lame.

2 harm, damage, impair, spoil, mar, ruin, weaken, undermine. **3** offend, wrong, upset, put out.

injurious *adj.* causing injury or damage; harmful.

injuriously *adv.* so as to harm or injure.

injury *noun* (PL. **injuries**) **1** physical harm or damage. **2** a wound. **3** a wrong or injustice.

▪ **1** hurt, harm, damage, impairment, disfigurement, mutilation, ill-treatment, abuse. **2** wound, cut, lesion, fracture. **3** wrong, injustice, offence, insult.

injury time playing time added to the end of a football, rugby, etc match to make up for time taken to treat injured players during the match.

injustice *noun* **1** unfairness or lack of justice. **2** an unfair or unjust act. — **do someone an injustice** to judge them unfairly. [from Latin *injustitia*]

▪ **1** unfairness, inequity, inequality, discrimination, bias, prejudice, one-sidedness, partisanship, partiality, favouritism. **2** wrong, injury.
▪ **1** justice, fairness.

ink — *noun* **1** a liquid, paste, or powder, consisting of a pigment or a dye, that is used for writing, drawing, or printing on paper and other materials. **2** a dark liquid ejected by certain cephalopods, eg octopus, squid, in order to confuse predators by forming a smokescreen. — *verb* **1** to mark with ink. **2** to cover (a surface to be printed) with ink. — **ink something in** to write over a rough design in pencil using ink. [from Old French *enque*]

Inkatha *noun* a South African Zulu cultural and political movement, originally a paramilitary organization, which sought liberation from white minority rule. [from Zulu, = a plaited grass coil used for carrying loads on the head]

inkblot test same as RORSCHACH TEST.

inkiness *noun* being inky.

inkjet printer *Comput.* a printer which produces characters on paper by spraying a fine jet of ink which is vibrated, electrically charged, and deflected by electrostatic fields.

inkling *noun* a hint; a vague or slight idea or suspicion. [from Middle English *inclen*, to hint]

▪ suspicion, idea, notion, hunch, clue, hint, intimation, suggestion, allusion, indication, sign, pointer.

inkpad *noun* a pad of inked cloth inside a box, used for putting ink on rubber stamps.

inkstand *noun* a container for ink bottles and pens on a desk.

inkwell *noun* a small container for ink, especially one which fits into a hole in a desk.

inky *adj.* (**inkier, inkiest**) **1** covered with ink. **2** like ink, especially in being black or very dark.

INLA *abbrev.* Irish National Liberation Army.

inlaid *adj.* **1** *said of a design* set into a surface. **2** *said of an object* having a design set into its surface.

inland — *adj.* **1** of or in that part of a country which is not beside the sea. **2** *Brit.* done, operating, etc inside one country and not abroad; domestic. — *noun* those parts of a country that are not beside the sea. — *adv.* in or towards the inner regions of a country away from the sea. [from Anglo-Saxon *inland*, domain]

Inland Revenue *Brit.* the government department responsible for assessing and collecting taxes.

in-law *noun* (PL. **in-laws**) *colloq.* a relative by marriage.

inlay — *verb* (PAST TENSE AND PAST PARTICIPLE **inlaid**) **1** to set in or embed (eg pieces of wood, metal, etc in another material) so that the surfaces are flat. **2** to decorate (eg a piece of furniture) by setting flat pieces of different coloured wood, ivory, metal, etc in the surface. — *noun* **1** a decoration or design made by inlaying. **2** the pieces used to create an inlaid design. **3** a filling shaped to fit a cavity in a tooth.

inlaying *noun* a method of decorating furniture and other wooden objects by cutting away part of the surface of the solid material and replacing it with a thin sheet of wood in another colour or texture. Occasionally, slivers of ivory, bone, or shell are used in this way.

inlet *noun* **1** a narrow arm of water running inland from a sea-coast or lake-shore, or forming a passage between two islands. **2** a place of entry, eg for liquid or gas in a machine. **3** an extra piece of material sewn into a garment to make it larger. [from Middle English]

⊟ **1** bay, cove, creek, fjord. **2** opening, entrance, entry, passage.

in-line skates roller skates on which the wheels are arranged in single line along the middle of the sole.

in loco parentis / ɪn ˈloʊkoʊ pəˈrɛntɪs/ *said of those responsible for children* in the role or position of a parent. [Latin, = in the place of a parent]

inmate *noun* any of several people living in an institution, especially a prison or a hospital.

inmost *adj.* **1** farthest in; most in towards the centre. **2** most secret or private. [from Middle English]

inn *noun* a public house or small hotel providing food and accommodation, especially (*formerly*) one for travellers. [from Anglo-Saxon *inn*, dwelling]

⊟ public house, *colloq.* pub, *colloq.* local, tavern, hostelry, hotel.

innards /ˈɪnədz/ *pl. noun colloq.* **1** the inner organs of a person or animal, especially the stomach. **2** the inner workings of a machine. [a variant of INWARDS]

innate *adj.* belonging to or existing in a person from birth; natural rather than learnt or acquired; inherent. [from Latin *innatus*]

⊟ inborn, inbred, inherent, intrinsic, native, natural, instinctive, intuitive.
🗷 acquired, learnt.

innateness hypothesis *Linguistics* a controversial hypothesis which claims that a child is born with an inbuilt knowledge of at least some of the structures of language, and that it is this genetic predisposition which enables the child to acquire language with such speed and efficiency in its early years.

inner *adj.* **1** further in; situated inside or close to the centre. **2** *said of thoughts, feelings, etc* secret, hidden, and profound. [from Anglo-Saxon *innera*]

⊟ INNERMOST. **1** internal, interior, inside, inward, central, middle. **2** hidden, concealed, secret, private, personal, intimate, deep, profound.
🗷 **1** outer, external, exterior.

inner child the part of the mind or personality which remains childlike in adulthood.

inner city the central area of a city, often densely populated and very poor, with bad housing, roads, etc.

inner ear *Anat.* the innermost part of the ear in vertebrates, located in a bony cavity in the skull. It contains the cochlea and the semicircular canals, which are responsible for the sense of hearing and the maintenance of balance, respectively.

inner man or **inner woman 1** the mind or soul. **2** *humorous* the stomach.

innermost *adj.* **1** furthest within. **2** most secret or hidden.

inner tube an inflatable rubber tube inside a tyre.

inning *noun North Amer., esp. US* a division of a baseball match during which each team has an opportunity to bat. [see INNINGS]

innings *pl. noun* **1** *Cricket* a team's or a player's turn at batting. **2** *Cricket* the runs scored, or the quality of batting, during such a turn. **3** *Brit.* a period during which a person has an opportunity for action or achievement. — **have had a good innings** *colloq.* to have lived a long and eventful life. [from Anglo-Saxon *innung*, contents]

innkeeper *noun* a person who owns or manages an inn.

innocence *noun* **1** being free from guilt or sin. **2** artlessness; guilelessness; lack of experience or sophistication.

⊟ **1** guiltlessness, blamelessness, honesty, virtue, righteousness, purity, chastity, virginity, incorruptibility. **2** artlessness, guilelessness, ingenuousness, naïvety, credulity, gullibility, trustfulness, inexperience, ignorance, naturalness, simplicity, unworldliness.
🗷 **1** guilt, sin. **2** experience, sophistication.

innocent — *adj.* (*often* **innocent of something**) **1** free from sin; pure. **2** not guilty (eg of a crime). **3** not intending to cause or not causing harm. **4** lacking, free, or deprived of something. **5** simple and trusting; guileless; artless. — *noun* an innocent person, especially a young child or simple and trusting adult. [from Latin *innocens*, harmless]

⊟ *adj.* **1** virtuous, righteous, sinless, faultless, impeccable, stainless, spotless, immaculate, unsullied, untainted, pure, chaste, virginal. **2** guiltless, blameless, irreproachable, unimpeachable, honest, upright. **3** harmless, innocuous, inoffensive. **5** natural, simple, unsophisticated, unworldly, childlike, credulous, gullible, trusting, artless, guileless, ingenuous, naïve, green, inexperienced, ignorant.
🗷 *adj.* **1** sinful. **2** guilty. **3** harmful. **5** experienced, sophisticated.

innocuous *adj.* harmless; inoffensive. [from Latin *innocuus*]

⊟ harmless, safe, inoffensive, unobjectionable, innocent.
🗷 harmful.

Inn of Court *Brit. Legal* **1** any of the four societies which call lawyers to the bar. **2** any of the sets of buildings that these societies occupy.

innovate *verb* **1** (*intrans.*) to make changes; to introduce new ideas, methods, etc. **2** (*trans.*) to introduce (something) as new. [from Latin *innovare*, to renew]

innovation *noun* **1** an act of innovating. **2** something new which is introduced.

⊟ REFORM, CHANGE, ALTERATION, VARIATION, DEPARTURE. **1** modernization, progress. **2** novelty, neologism.

innovative or **innovatory** *adj.* innovating; new and usually imaginative or original.

⊟ new, fresh, ground-breaking, original, creative, imaginative, inventive, resourceful, enterprising, *colloq.* go-ahead, progressive, reforming, bold, daring, adventurous.
🗷 old, stale, unimaginative, conservative.

innovator *noun* a person who innovates.

innuendo /ɪnjʊˈɛndoʊ/ *noun* (PL. **innuendos**, **innuendoes**) **1** an indirect, and usually slightly unpleasant, critical, spiteful or rude remark, especially about someone's reputation or character; an oblique allusion or insinuation. **2** the act of making such remarks. [from Latin *innuendo*, by nodding at]

⊟ INSINUATION, IMPLICATION. **1** aspersion, slur, hint, intimation, suggestion.

Innuit same as INUIT.

innumerable *adj.* too many to be counted; a great many. [from Latin *innumerabilis*]

. . . .

▣ numberless, unnumbered, countless, uncountable, untold, incalculable, infinite, myriad, numerous, many.

. . . .

innumerably *adv.* to an innumerable extent.

innumeracy *noun* being innumerate.

innumerate *adj.* having no knowledge or understanding of mathematics or science. [from IN-[1] + NUMERATE, modelled on *illiterate*]

inoculate *verb* 1 to produce a mild form of a particular infectious disease in (a person or animal), followed by immunity to it, by injecting a harmless form of an antigen (eg dead or weakened viruses or bacteria) which stimulates the body to produce its own antibodies (same as VACCINATE). 2 to introduce a micro-organism, eg a bacterium or virus, into (a sterile medium) in order to start a culture, or into another organism, eg a rabbit, in order to produce antibodies to that micro-organism. 3 to imbue or instil (someone) with ideas. [from Latin *inoculare*, to graft a tree bud]

inoculation *noun* the process of inoculating against a disease.

. . . .

▣ vaccination, immunization, protection, injection, *colloq.* shot, *colloq.* jab.

. . . .

inoffensive *adj.* harmless; not likely to offend.

. . . .

▣ harmless, innocuous, innocent, peaceable, mild, unobtrusive, unassertive, quiet, retiring.
▣ offensive, harmful, provocative.

. . . .

inoperable *adj.* 1 *said of a disease or condition* unable to be removed by surgery or operated on successfully. 2 *said of a plan, idea, etc* not workable.

inoperative *adj.* not working or functioning; having no effect.

inopportune *adj.* not suitable or convenient; badly timed. [from Latin *inopportunus*]

inopportunely *adv.* in an inopportune way, at a bad time.

inordinate *adj.* greater than is reasonable; beyond acceptable limits. [from Latin *inordinatus*]

. . . .

▣ excessive, immoderate, unwarranted, undue, unreasonable, disproportionate.
▣ moderate, reasonable.

. . . .

inordinately *adv.* to an inordinate degree.

inorganic *adj.* 1 not made of or found in living (ie animal or plant) material; mineral. 2 not caused by natural growth. 3 not produced naturally.

inorganically *adv.* in an inorganic way.

inorganic chemistry the branch of chemistry concerned with the properties and reactions of the elements, and of compounds that do not contain chains or rings of carbon atoms. It therefore deals mainly with compounds of mineral origin, and includes only the simpler compounds of carbon. See also ORGANIC CHEMISTRY.

inorganic fertilizer *Agric.* a fertilizer containing a mixture of chemical compounds, mainly of nitrogen, potassium, and phosphorus, that are added to the soil in order to improve its fertility.

in-patient *noun* a patient temporarily living in hospital while receiving treatment there.

input — *noun* 1 *Comput.* the data that is transferred from a disk, tape, or input device, such as the keyboard, into the main memory of a computer. 2 something which is put or taken in, eg a contribution to a discussion. 3 an act or process of putting something in. 4 the money, power, materials, labour, etc required to produce something, especially the power put into a machine. — *verb* (**inputting**; PAST TENSE AND PAST PARTICIPLE **input**, **inputted**) to transfer (data) from a disk, tape, or input device into the main memory of a computer.

input device *Comput.* any piece of equipment used to transfer data into memory, such as a keyboard, mouse, or light pen.

input-output analysis *Econ.* an analysis which demonstrates how materials and goods flow between industries, and identifies where additional value is created. It enables economists to examine how the various sectors of an economy interrelate.

inquest *noun* 1 an official investigation into an incident, especially an inquiry into a sudden and unexpected death in a coroner's court before a jury. 2 *colloq.* any discussion after an event, game, etc, especially one which analyses its result and discusses mistakes made. [from Latin *inquesta*]

inquietude *noun* physical or mental restlessness or uneasiness. [from Latin *inquietudo*]

inquire or **enquire** *verb* 1 to ask. 2 *intrans.* to ask for information about something. 3 (**inquire after someone**) to ask about their health or happiness. 4 (**inquire for someone**) to ask to see or talk to them. 5 (**inquire for something**) to ask for goods, a service, etc. 6 (**inquire into something**) to try to discover the facts of a crime, etc, especially formally. 7 (**inquire of someone**) to ask them for information. [from Latin *inquirere*]

. . . .

▣ 1, 2 ask, query. 6 investigate, look into, probe, examine, inspect, explore. 7 ask, question, quiz.

. . . .

inquirer or **enquirer** *noun* a person who inquires; an investigator, a questioner.

inquiring or **enquiring** *adj.* 1 eager to discover or learn things. 2 *said eg of a look* appearing to be asking a question.

inquiringly or **enquiringly** *adv.* with an inquiring manner.

inquiry or **enquiry** *noun* (PL. **inquiries**) 1 an act of asking for information or inquiring. 2 an investigation, especially a formal one.

. . . .

▣ 1 question, query. 2 investigation, inquest, hearing, inquisition, examination, inspection, study, survey, poll, search, probe, exploration.

. . . .

inquisition *noun* 1 a searching or intensive inquiry or investigation. 2 an official or judicial inquiry. 3 (**Inquisition**) a papal tribunal for the prosecution of heresy, and such things as witchcraft and alchemy, originally of the medieval Christian Church. [from Latin *inquisitio*]

inquisitional *adj.* relating to or in the nature of inquiry.

inquisitive *adj.* 1 over-eager to find out things, especially about other people's affairs. 2 eager for knowledge or information. [from Latin *inquisitivus*]

. . . .

▣ CURIOUS. 1 nosy, prying, snooping, interfering, meddlesome, intrusive. 2 inquiring, questioning, searching, probing.

. . . .

inquisitor *noun* 1 a person carrying out an inquisition or inquiry, especially harshly or intensively. 2 (**Inquisitor**) a member of the Spanish Inquisition. [from Latin *inquisitor*]

inquisitorial *adj.* 1 of or like an inquisitor. 2 unnecessarily or offensively curious about other people's affairs. 3 *Legal, said of a trial or legal system* in which the judge is also the prosecutor.

in re *formal* in the matter of; about. [Latin, = in the matter]

inroad *noun* 1 (*usually* **inroads into something**) a large or significant using up or consumption: *make inroads into my savings.* 2 a hostile attack or raid.

inrush *noun* a sudden crowding or rushing in.

insalubrious *adj.*, *said of a place* unhealthy; sordid. [from Latin *insalubris*]

insane — *adj.* **1** not of sound mind; mentally ill. **2** extremely foolish; stupid. **3** of or for the mentally ill. — *noun* people who are insane. [from Latin *insanus*]

⊟ *adj.* **1** mad, crazy, lunatic, mentally ill, disturbed, demented, deranged, unhinged. **2** foolish, stupid, mad, crazy, lunatic, senseless, impractical.
⊟ *adj.* **1** sane. **2** sensible.

insanely *adv.* in an insane way; to an insane degree.
insanitariness *noun* an insanitary state or condition.
insanitary *adj.* so dirty as to be dangerous to health.
insanity *noun* (PL. **insanities**) **1** the state of being insane. **2** extreme folly or stupidity.

⊟ MADNESS, CRAZINESS, LUNACY. **1** mental illness, neurosis, psychosis, mania, dementia, derangement. **2** folly, stupidity, senselessness, irresponsibility.
⊟ SANITY.

insatiability *noun* being insatiable.
insatiable *adj.* not able to be satisfied; extremely greedy. [from Latin *insatiabilis*]

⊟ unquenchable, unsatisfiable, ravenous, voracious, immoderate, inordinate.

inscribe *verb* **1** to write, print, or engrave (words) on (paper, metal, stone, etc), often as a lasting record. **2** to enter (a name) on a list or in a book; to enrol. **3** (**inscribe something to someone**) to dedicate or address a book, etc to them, usually by writing in the front of it. **4** *Geom.* to draw (a figure) within another figure so as to touch all or some of its sides or faces. See also CIRCUMSCRIBE. [from Latin *in*, on + *scribere*, to write]

⊟ **1** write, print, engrave, etch, carve, cut, imprint, impress, stamp. **3** sign, autograph, dedicate, address.

inscription *noun* **1** words written, printed, or engraved, eg as a dedication in the front of a book or as an epitaph on a gravestone. **2** the act of inscribing, especially of writing a dedication in the front of a book or of entering a name on a list. [from Latin *inscriptio*, from *inscribere*, to inscribe]

⊟ WRITING, ENGRAVING, DEDICATION. **1** words, lettering, caption, legend, epitaph, signature, autograph. **2** printing, etching, carving, signing.

inscriptional *adj.* relating to or characteristic of inscriptions.
inscrutability *noun* being inscrutable.
inscrutable *adj.* hard to understand or explain; mysterious; enigmatic. [from Latin *inscrutabilis*]

⊟ incomprehensible, unfathomable, impenetrable, deep, inexplicable, unexplainable, baffling, mysterious, enigmatic, cryptic, hidden.
⊟ comprehensible, explicable.

insect *noun* **1** *Zool.* any invertebrate animal belonging to the class Insecta, the largest and most diverse class of living organisms, containing more than a million species, eg fly, beetle, ant, bee, wasp, butterfly. **2** *loosely* any other small invertebrate, eg a spider. **3** an insignificant or worthless person. [from Latin *insectum*, cut, notched]

Insects include: fly, gnat, midge, mosquito, tsetse-fly, locust, dragonfly, cranefly, *colloq.* daddy longlegs, horsefly, mayfly, butterfly, red admiral, cabbage-white butterfly, moth, tiger moth, bee, bumblebee, wasp, hornet, aphid, blackfly, greenfly, whitefly, froghopper, ladybird, water boatman, lacewing; beetle, cockroach,

US roach, earwig, stick insect, grasshopper, cricket, cicada, flea, louse, nit, leatherjacket, termite, glowworm, woodworm, weevil, woodlouse. *Arachnids include*: spider, black widow, tarantula, scorpion, mite, tick.

insecticidal *adj.* that kills insects.
insecticide *noun* any naturally occurring or artificially manufactured substance that is used to kill insects, usually to protect crops and animal livestock on farms, but also used in homes, hospitals, restaurants, etc.
insectivore *noun* **1** a living organism that feeds mainly or exclusively on insects, eg anteater. **2** an animal belonging to the order Insectivora, a group of small placental mammals that feed mainly although not necessarily exclusively on insects, eg moles, hedgehogs. [from Latin *insectum*, insect + *vorare*, to devour]
insectivorous *adj.* feeding on insects.
insecure *adj.* **1** not firmly fixed; unstable. **2** *said of a person* lacking confidence; anxious about possible loss or danger. **3** under threat or in danger or likely to be so. [from Latin *insecurus*]

⊟ **1** loose, unstable, unsteady, shaky, precarious, unsafe, dangerous, hazardous, perilous. **2** anxious, worried, nervous, uncertain, unsure, afraid. **3** unprotected, defenceless, exposed, vulnerable, unsafe, dangerous, hazardous, perilous.
⊟ SECURE. **1** stable, steady, safe. **2** confident, self-assured. **3** protected, safe.

insecurity *noun* (PL. **insecurities**) **1** being insecure. **2** anxiety, lack of confidence.
inseminate *verb* **1** to introduce semen into (a female) by a natural or artificial method. **2** to sow (seeds, ideas, etc). [from Latin *inseminare*]
insemination *noun* inseminating or being inseminated.
insensate *adj.* **1** not able to perceive physical sensations or experience consciousness; inanimate. **2** insensitive and unfeeling. **3** having little or no good sense; stupid. [from Latin *insensatus*]
insensibility *noun* being insensible.
insensible *adj.* **1** not able to feel pain or experience consciousness; unconscious. **2** (**insensible of** or **to something**) unaware of it; not caring about it. **3** not capable of feeling emotion; callous. **4** too small or slight to be noticed; imperceptible. [from Latin *insensibilis*]

⊟ **1** insensate, numb, anaesthetized, dead, unconscious, senseless, unresponsive, insensitive. **2** unaware of, oblivious of, unmindful of, blind to, deaf to. **3** cold, insensitive, unfeeling, callous.
⊟ **1** conscious. **2** aware of. **3** sensitive.

insensitive *adj.* (*often* **insensitive to something**) **1** not aware of or not capable of responding sympathetically, especially to other people's feelings. **2** not reacting to stimulation, eg touch or light.

⊟ **1** hardened, thick-skinned, immune, unsusceptible, unfeeling, impassive, indifferent, unaffected, unmoved, untouched, uncaring, unconcerned, callous, thoughtless, tactless, crass.
⊟ SENSITIVE.

insensitivity *noun* **1** being insensitive. **2** insensitive behaviour or language.
inseparability *noun* being inseparable.
inseparable *adj.* **1** incapable of being separated. **2** *said of friends, siblings, etc* unwilling to be apart and constantly together. [from Latin *inseparabilis*]

⊟ **1** indivisible, indissoluble, inextricable. **2** close,

intimate, bosom, devoted.
 ⊟ 1 separable.
....

inseparably *adv.* in an inseparable way; so as not be separated.

insert — *verb* (with stress on *-sert*) **1** to put or fit (something) inside something else. **2** to introduce (text, words, etc) into the body of other text, words, etc. — *noun* (with stress on *in-*) something inserted, especially a loose sheet in a book or magazine, or piece of material in a garment. [from Latin *inserere*]

 ⊟ *verb* **1** put, place, put in, stick in, push in, introduce, implant, embed, engraft, set, inset, let in. **2** interleave, intercalate, interpolate, interpose. *noun* insertion, enclosure, inset, supplement, addition.

....

insertion *noun* **1** an act of inserting. **2** something inserted, especially a piece of lace or embroidery inserted in a garment or an advertisement in a newspaper. **3** *Medicine* the place where, or the way in which, a muscle is attached to a bone.

in-service *adj.* carried on while a person is employed.

inset — *noun* (with stress on *in-*) **1** something set in or inserted, eg a piece of lace or cloth set into a garment, or a leaf or leaves set in into a book. **2** a small map or picture put in the corner of a larger one. — *verb* (with stress on *-set*) (**insetting**; PAST TENSE AND PAST PARTICIPLE **inset**) to put in, add, or insert.

inshore *adv., adj.* in or on the water but near or towards the shore.

inside — *noun* **1** the inner side, surface, or part of something. **2** the part of a path away from the road. **3** the lower part of a double-decker bus. **4** the lane of a running track that is nearest the centre; the equivalent part of any racetrack. **5** (**insides**) *colloq.* the inner organs, especially the stomach and bowels. **6** *colloq.* a position which gains one the confidence of and otherwise secret information from people in authority. — *adj.* **1** being on, near, towards, or from the inside. **2** *colloq.* coming from, provided by, or planned by someone within an organization: *the robbery was an inside job.* — *adv.* **1** to, in, or on the inside or interior. **2** indoors. **3** *colloq.* in or into prison. — *prep.* (*also* **inside of**) *colloq.* **1** to or on the side of; within. **2** in less than: *be back inside an hour.* — **inside out 1** with the inside surface turned out. **2** *colloq.* thoroughly; completely: *knows it all inside out.* [from Middle English]

 ⊟ *noun* **1** interior, middle, centre, heart, core, contents. **5** entrails, guts, intestines, bowels, *colloq.* innards, organs, viscera, belly, stomach. *adj.* **1** interior, internal, inner, innermost, inward. *adv.* **1** within, internally, inwardly.
 ⊟ *noun* **1** outside, exterior. *adj.* OUTSIDE. **1** exterior, external. *adv.* OUTSIDE.

....

insider *noun* a recognized or accepted member of an organization or group who has access to secret information about it.

insider dealing or **insider trading** the illegal buying and selling of shares by people who work on the stock exchange, based on their having access to information which has not been made public.

inside track 1 the inside lane of a race track, slightly shorter than the other lanes because of the curve. **2** a position of strength, power or advantage.

insidious *adj.* **1** developing gradually without being noticed but causing very great harm. **2** attractive but harmful; treacherous. [from Latin *insidiae*, ambush]

 ⊟ 1 gradual, subtle, sly, crafty, devious, stealthy, surreptitious, furtive, sneaking. **2** deceptive, treacherous.

....

insight *noun* **1** the ability to gain a relatively rapid, clear, and deep understanding of the real, often hidden, and usually complex nature of a situation, problem, etc. **2** an instance or example of this. [from Middle English]

....

 ⊟ PERCEPTION, INTUITION, OBSERVATION, VISION. **1** sensitivity, discernment, judgement, acumen, penetration, wisdom, intelligence. **2** awareness, knowledge, comprehension, understanding, grasp.

....

insightful *adj.* characterized by insight.

insignia *noun* (PL. **insignia**, **insignias**) badges or emblems of office, honour, or membership. [from Latin *insignia*, badges]

insignificance *noun* being insignificant.

insignificant *adj.* **1** of little or no meaning, value, or importance. **2** relatively small in size or amount.

....

 ⊟ 1 unimportant, irrelevant, meaningless, inconsequential, minor, trivial, trifling, petty. **2** small, tiny, paltry, insubstantial, inconsiderable, negligible.
 ⊟ SIGNIFICANT. **1** important. **2** considerable.

....

insincere *adj.* not sincere or genuine; false; hypocritical. [from Latin *insincerus*]

 ⊟ hypocritical, two-faced, double-dealing, lying, untruthful, dishonest, deceitful, unfaithful, faithless, untrue, false, feigned, pretended, hollow, empty.
 ⊟ sincere.

....

insincerity *noun* (PL. **insincerities**) being insincere, or an instance of this.

insinuate *verb* **1** to suggest or hint (something unpleasant) indirectly. **2** to introduce (eg an idea) in an indirect or devious way. **3** (**insinuate someone into something**) to gain acceptance or favour for (especially oneself) by gradual, careful, and often cunning means. [from Latin *insinuare*]

 ⊟ 1 imply, suggest, hint, intimate, *colloq.* get at.

....

insinuation *noun* **1** an unpleasant, devious or indirect suggestion, reference or hint. **2** an act of insinuating.

insipid *adj.* **1** without interest or liveliness; boring. **2** without taste or flavour. [from Latin *insipidus*]

....

 ⊟ 1 colourless, drab, dull, monotonous, boring, uninteresting, tame, flat, lifeless, spiritless, characterless. **2** tasteless, flavourless, unsavoury, unappetizing, watery, weak, bland, *colloq.* wishy-washy.
 ⊟ 2 tasty, spicy, piquant, appetizing.

....

insist *verb* **1** *trans., intrans.* to maintain, state, or assert firmly: *insisted that we were right.* **2** (**insist on** or **upon something**) to demand it firmly: *insisted on a fair hearing.* [from Latin *insistere*]

 ⊟ 1 maintain, claim, contend, hold, swear, assert, stress, emphasize, repeat, reiterate. **2** demand, require.

....

insistence *noun* insisting; determination.

....

 ⊟ demand, exhortation, claim, contention, assertion, stress, emphasis, repetition, reiteration, persistence, determination, resolution, firmness.

....

insistent *adj.* **1** making continual, forceful demands; insisting. **2** demanding attention; compelling.

....

 ⊟ 1 demanding, importunate, emphatic, forceful, pressing, urgent, dogged, tenacious, persistent, persevering, relentless, unrelenting, unremitting, incessant.

....

in situ / ɪn 'sɪtjuː/ done, carried out, etc while remaining in place; in the natural or original position. [Latin, = in the place]

insofar as see IN.

insole *noun* **1** a loose inner sole which can be put in a shoe or boot for extra warmth, or to make it slightly smaller. **2** a fixed inner sole in a shoe or boot.

insolence *noun* being insolent; insolent behaviour or language.

insolent *adj.* rude or insulting; showing a lack of respect. [from Latin *insolens*, departing from custom]

⊟ rude, abusive, insulting, disrespectful, *colloq.* cheeky, impertinent, impudent, *colloq.* saucy, bold, forward, presumptuous, arrogant, defiant, insubordinate.
⊟ polite, respectful.

insolubility *noun* being insoluble.

insoluble *adj.* **1** *said of a substance* not able to be dissolved in a particular solvent, especially water, to form a solution. **2** *said of a problem or difficulty* not able to be resolved. [from Latin *insolubilis*]

⊟ **2** unsolvable, unexplainable, inexplicable, incomprehensible, unfathomable, mystifying, puzzling, perplexing, baffling.
⊟ SOLUBLE.

insolvency *noun* being insolvent.

insolvent — *adj.* **1** not having enough money to pay one's debts. **2** of or relating to insolvent people or the state of being insolvent. — *noun* an insolvent person.

⊟ *adj.* **1** bankrupt, bust, failed, ruined, *colloq.* broke, penniless.
⊟ *adj.* **1** solvent.

insomnia *noun* regular or habitual inability to sleep. [from Latin *insomnia*, from *in-*, not + *somnus*, sleep]

insomniac — *noun* a person who suffers from insomnia. — *adj.* **1** suffering from insomnia. **2** causing or caused by insomnia.

insomuch *adv.* (**insomuch that ... or as ...**) **1** to such an extent. **2** given that; because of the fact that.

insouciance / ɪn'suːsɪəns/ *noun* lack of concern; indifference; carelessness.

insouciant / ɪn'suːsɪənt/ *adj.* without cares or worries; light-hearted. [from French *insouciant*, from *in*, not + *soucier*, to worry]

inspect *verb* **1** to look at or examine closely, often to find faults or mistakes. **2** to look at or examine officially or ceremonially. [from Latin *inspicere*, to look into]

⊟ **1** check, vet, look over, examine, scrutinize, study, scan, survey, search, investigate, superintend, supervise, oversee.

inspection *noun* inspecting, examination.

⊟ check, check-up, examination, scrutiny, scan, study, survey, review, search, investigation, supervision, surveillance.

inspector *noun* **1** a person employed to inspect something, especially officially. **2** *Brit.* a police officer below a superintendent and above a sergeant in rank.

⊟ **1** supervisor, superintendent, overseer, surveyor, controller, scrutineer, checker, tester, examiner, investigator.

inspectorate *noun* **1** a body of inspectors. **2** the office or post of inspector.

inspiration *noun* **1** a supposed power which stimulates the mind, especially to artistic activity or creativity. **2** a si-milar supposed divine power or influence which leads to the writing of Scripture. **3** a person or thing that inspires, or the state of being inspired. **4** a brilliant or inspired idea. **5** the act of drawing breath into the lungs, or a breath so taken.

⊟ **1** imagination, creativity, genius. **3** influence, encouragement, spur, stimulus, stimulation, motivation, Muse. **4** idea, brainwave, insight, illumination, revelation.

inspirational *adj.* involving or arising from inspiration; inspiring, inspired.

inspire *verb* **1** to stimulate (a person) to activity, especially artistic or creative activity. **2** to fill (a person) with a feeling of confidence, encouragement and exaltation. **3** (**inspire someone with something** or **something into someone**) to create a particular feeling in them. **4** to be the origin or source of (a poem, piece of music, etc). **5** *said of supposed divine power or influence* to guide (someone). **6** *trans.*, *intrans.* to breathe (air, etc) in. [from Latin *inspirare*, to breathe into]

⊟ **1** prompt, spur, stimulate, motivate, animate, enliven, galvanize, fire, kindle, stir, arouse. **2** encourage, hearten, influence, impress, enthuse, excite, exhilarate, thrill, enthral. **3** imbue, infuse.

inspired *adj.* so good, skilful, accurate, etc as to seem to be the result of inspiration, especially divine inspiration.

inspiring *adj.* that inspires.

⊟ encouraging, heartening, uplifting, invigorating, stirring, rousing, stimulating, exciting, exhilarating, thrilling, enthralling, moving, affecting, memorable, impressive.
⊟ uninspiring, dull, boring.

inst. *abbrev.* instant (= in the current month).

instability *noun* lack of physical or mental steadiness or stability. [from Latin *instabilitas*]

⊟ unsteadiness, shakiness, vacillation, wavering, irresolution, uncertainty, unpredictability, changeableness, variability, fluctuation, volatility, capriciousness, fickleness, inconstancy, unreliability, insecurity.
⊟ stability.

install *verb* **1** to put (equipment, machinery, etc) in place and make it ready for use. **2** to place (a person) in office with a formal ceremony. **3** to place (something, oneself, etc) in a particular position, condition or place. [from Latin *installare*]

⊟ **1** fix, fit, lay. **2** inaugurate, invest, induct, ordain. **3** put, place, position, locate, site, situate, station, settle, establish, set up.

installation *noun* **1** the act or process of installing. **2** a piece of equipment, machinery, etc that has been installed ready for use. **3** a military base.

instalment *noun* **1** one of a series of parts into which a debt is divided for payment. **2** one of several parts published, issued, broadcast, etc at regular intervals. [from Old French *estaler*, to fix, set, probably influenced by IN-STALL]

⊟ PART. **1** payment, repayment, portion. **2** episode, chapter, section, division.

instalment plan payment for goods purchased by instalments; hire-purchase.

instance *noun* **1** an example, especially of a particular condition or circumstance. **2** a particular stage in a process or a particular situation: *in this instance*. **3** *formal* request; urging: *at the instance of*. **4** *Legal* a process or suit.

— **for instance** for example. [from Latin *instantia*, from *instare*, to be present]

instant — *adj.* **1** immediate. **2** *said of food, etc* quickly and easily prepared. **3** urgent; pressing. **4** of or occurring in the current month. **5** present; current. — *noun* **1** a particular moment in time, especially the present: *this instant.* **2** a very brief period of time. [from Latin *instare*, to be present]

◼ *adj.* **1** immediate, instantaneous, direct, prompt, unhesitating, quick, fast, rapid, swift. *noun* MOMENT. **1** time, occasion. **2** flash, twinkling, trice, *colloq.* tick, split second, second, minute.

instantaneous *adj.* done, happening, or occurring at once, very quickly or in an instant; immediate. [from Latin *instantaneus*, from *instare*, to be present]

◼ immediate, instant, direct, on the spot.

instantaneously *adv.* in an instant; immediately.

instantly *adv.* at once; immediately.

instar *noun Zool.* the form of an insect at any stage of its physical development between two successive moults, before it has become fully mature. [from Latin *instar*, image]

instead *adv.* as a substitute or alternative; in place of something or someone. — **instead of something** or **someone** in place of them or as an alternative to them. [from Middle English *in stead*, in place]

◼ alternatively, preferably, rather. **instead of** in place of, in lieu of, on behalf of, in preference to, rather than.

instep *noun* **1** the inside of the arched middle section of the human foot. **2** the part of a shoe, sock, etc that covers this.

instigate *verb* **1** to urge on or incite (someone) especially to do something wrong or evil. **2** to set in motion or initiate (eg an inquiry). [from Latin *instigare*, to goad on]

◼ **1** encourage, urge, spur, prompt, provoke, stimulate, incite, rouse, stir, move, inspire, influence. **2** initiate, start, begin, cause.

instigation *noun* **1** instigating; inciting. **2** something that instigates, a stimulus.

instigator *noun* a person who instigates, an inciter.

instil *verb* (**instilled, instilling**) **1** (**instil something into someone**) to impart ideas, feelings etc gradually into a person's mind. **2** to pour (a liquid) into something drop by drop. [from Latin *instillare*, to drip into]

◼ **1** infuse, insinuate, introduce, implant, inculcate, impress.

instillation or **instilment** *noun* **1** instilling. **2** something that is instilled or infused.

instiller *noun* a person who instills or infuses.

instinct *noun* **1** in animal behaviour, an inherited and usually fixed pattern of response to a particular stimulus, common to all members of a particular species, that has not been learned but is based on a biological need, especially for survival or reproduction, eg the alarm call of a bird. **2** in humans, a basic drive that urges a person towards a specific goal such as survival or reproduction. **3** intuition. [from Latin *instinctus*, prompting]

◼ **2** impulse, urge, drive, faculty, ability, aptitude, predisposition. **3** intuition, sixth sense, feeling, hunch, *colloq.* gut reaction.

instinctive *adj.* prompted by instinct or intuition; involuntary; automatic.

◼ natural, native, inborn, innate, inherent, intuitive, *colloq.* gut, visceral, impulsive, involuntary, automatic, mechanical, reflex, spontaneous, unthinking, unpremeditated.

◪ voluntary, deliberate.

institute — *noun* **1** a society or organization which promotes research, education or a particular cause. **2** a building or group of buildings used by an institute. **3** an established law, principle, rule, or custom. **4** (**institutes**) a book of laws or principles. — *verb* **1** to set up, establish, or organize. **2** to initiate or cause to begin. **3** to appoint to or install in a position or office. [from Latin *instituere*, to establish]

◼ *noun* **1** school, college, academy, conservatory, foundation, institution. *verb* **1** set up, establish, organize, found, inaugurate, open, launch, introduce, enact. **2** initiate, begin, start, cause, instigate, originate, create. **3** appoint, install, invest, induct, ordain.

◪ *verb* **1** cancel, discontinue, abolish.

institution *noun* **1** an organization or public body founded especially for charitable or educational purposes, or as a hospital. **2** *derog.* a hospital, old people's home, etc, regarded as an impersonal or bureaucratic organization. **3** a custom or tradition. **4** a familiar and well-known object or person. **5** the act of instituting or process of being instituted. [from Latin *instituere*, to establish]

◼ **1** organization, association, society, guild, corporation, foundation, establishment, institute. **2** hospital, home. **3** custom, tradition, usage, practice, ritual, convention, rule, law. **5** initiation, beginning, inception, creation, establishment, formation, foundation, inauguration, launch, introduction, enactment.

institutional *adj.* of or like an institution, especially in being dull or regimented.

institutionalism *noun* **1** the characteristics or system of institutions, or life in institutions. **2** belief in the merits of such a system.

institutionalize or **institutionalise** *verb* **1** to place in an institution. **2** to cause (someone) to lose his or her individuality and ability to cope with life by keeping him or her in an institution (eg a long-stay hospital or prison) for too long. **3** to make into an institution.

instruct *verb* **1** to teach or train (a person) in (a subject or skill). **2** to direct or order. **3** *Legal* to give (a lawyer) the facts concerning a case. **4** *Legal* to engage (a lawyer) to act in a case. [from Latin *instruere*, to equip, train]

◼ **1** teach, educate, tutor, coach, train, drill, ground, school. **2** direct, order, command, tell.

instruction *noun* **1** (*often* **instructions**) a direction, order, or command. **2** (**instructions**) a set of detailed guidelines, eg on how to operate a machine or piece of equipment. **3** a command or code in a computer program that activates a particular function. **4** teaching.

◼ **1** direction, order, command, injunction, mandate, directive, ruling. **2** directions, guidelines, recommendations, advice, guidance, information. **4** education, schooling, lessons, classes, tuition, teaching, training, coaching, drilling, grounding, preparation.

instructive *adj.* giving knowledge or information.

◼ informative, educational, edifying, enlightening, illuminating, helpful, useful.

instructiveness *noun* an instructive quality.

instructor *noun* **1** a person who gives instruction. **2** *North Amer.* a college or university teacher ranking below a professor.

▱ TEACHER. **1** tutor, coach, trainer, demonstrator, adviser, mentor, guide, guru.

instructress *noun* a female instructor.

instrument — *noun* **1** a tool, especially one used for delicate scientific work or measurement. **2** (*also* **musical instrument**) any of several devices which can be made to produce sounds and music. **3** any thing or person used as a means of achieving or doing something. **4** any of several devices inside a vehicle or aircraft which measure, show, and control speed, temperature, direction, etc. **5** a formal or official legal document. — *verb* **1** to arrange (music). **2** to equip with instruments for measuring, etc. [from Latin *instrumentum*, equipment, tool]

▱ *noun* **1** tool, implement, utensil, appliance, gadget, contraption, device, contrivance, apparatus, mechanism. **3** agent, agency, vehicle, organ, medium, factor, channel, way, means.

instrumental — *adj.* **1** (*often* **instrumental in** or **to something**) being responsible for it or an important factor in it. **2** performed by or written or arranged for musical instruments (as opposed to voices). **3** of or done with an instrument or tool. **4** *Grammar* denoting the grammatical case which shows how or by what means an action is performed. — *noun* **1** a piece of music performed by or written or arranged for musical instruments. **2** *Grammar* the instrumental case.

▱ *adj.* **1** active, involved, contributory, conducive, influential, useful, helpful.

instrumentalist *noun* a person who plays a musical instrument.

instrumental learning *Psychol.* an elementary learning process in which an individual comes to perform a certain action more or less frequently or intensively than before, by virtue of the action having produced positive or negative consequences.

instrumently *adv.* **1** in an instrumental way, or with an instrument. **2** on or with a musical instrument. **3** *Grammar* in the instrumental case.

instrumentation *noun* **1** the particular way in which a piece of music is written or arranged to be played by instruments. **2** the instruments used to play a particular piece of music. **3** the use, design or provision of instruments or tools.

insubordinate *adj.* disobedient; refusing to take orders.

insubordination *noun* being insubordinate; defiance of authority.

insubstantial *adj.* **1** not solid, strong, or satisfying; flimsy. **2** not made up of solid material; not real. [from Latin *insubstantialis*]

insubstantiality *noun* being insubstantial, lack of substance.

insufferable *adj.* too unpleasant, annoying, etc to bear; intolerable.

▱ intolerable, unbearable, detestable, loathsome, dreadful, impossible.
▱ pleasant, tolerable.

insufferably *adv.* in an insufferable way, unbearably.

insufficiency *noun* **1** being insufficient. **2** *Pathol.* the failure of an organ to function.

▱ **1** inadequacy, shortage, deficiency, lack, scarcity, dearth, want, need.
▱ **1** sufficiency, excess.

insufficient *adj.* not enough or not adequate; not sufficient. [from Latin *insufficientia*]

▱ inadequate, short, deficient, lacking, sparse, scanty, scarce.
▱ sufficient, excessive.

insufficiently *adv.* inadequately; so as to be insufficient.

insular /ˈɪnsjələ(r)/ *adj.* **1** of or belonging to an island or the inhabitants of an island. **2** (*said of a person, opinions, etc*) not influenced by or responsive to contact with other people, cultures, etc; narrow-minded; prejudiced. [from Latin *insularis*, from *insula*, island]

▱ **2** parochial, provincial, cut off, detached, isolated, remote, withdrawn, inward-looking, blinkered, narrow-minded, narrow, limited, petty.
▱ **2** cosmopolitan, broad-minded.

insularity *noun* being insular.

insulate *verb* **1** to prevent the passing of heat, sound, electricity, etc from (a body), especially by covering it with some special material. **2** to remove or set (someone or something) apart; to isolate. [from Latin *insula*, island]

▱ **1** cushion, pad, lag, cocoon, protect, shield. **2** isolate, separate, cut off, set apart.

insulating tape adhesive tape used to cover bare or exposed electrical wires, to protect people from electric shocks.

insulation *noun* **1** material used in insulating, especially material which does not conduct heat or electricity. **2** the process of insulating or being insulated.

insulator *noun* any material that is a poor conductor of heat and electricity, eg plastics, glass, ceramics, and most non-metallic elements except for carbon.

insulin /ˈɪnsjʊlɪn/ *noun* a hormone produced in the pancreas which controls the amount of sugar in the blood, a lack of this hormone being the cause of diabetes. [from Latin *insula*, island, because it is obtained from a part of the pancreas known as the islets of Langerhans]

insult — *verb* to behave rudely or offensively to; to speak rudely or offensively to or about. — *noun* **1** a rude and offensive remark or action. **2** an affront. **3** *Medicine* injury or damage to the body, or a cause of this. — **add insult to injury** to treat with further discourtesy someone one has already harmed. [from Latin *insultare*, to jump on]

▱ *verb* abuse, call names, disparage, denigrate, revile, slander, libel, slight, snub, injure, affront, offend, outrage. *noun* **1** abuse, rudeness, slander, libel, slight, snub. **2** affront, indignity, offence, outrage.
▱ *verb* compliment, praise. *noun* **1** compliment, praise.

insulting *adj.* that insults.

insuperability *noun* being insuperable.

insuperable *adj.* too difficult to be overcome, defeated, or dealt with successfully. [from Latin *insuperabilis*]

insupportable *adj.* **1** that is too unpleasant, severe, annoying, etc to be tolerated. **2** that cannot be justified. [from Latin *insupportabilis*]

insurable *adj.* capable of being insured.

insurance *noun* **1** an agreement by which one party promises to pay another party money in the event of loss, theft, or damage to property, personal injury or death, etc. **2** (*also* **insurance policy**) the contract for such an agreement. **3** the protection offered by such a contract. **4** money, usually paid regularly, in return for such a contract; an insurance premium. **5** the sum which will be paid in the event of loss, theft, or damage to property, personal injury or death, etc. **6** the business of providing such contracts for clients. **7** anything done, any measure taken, to try to prevent possible loss, disappointment, problems, etc. **8** an act or instance of insuring.

▣ **1** assurance, indemnity, guarantee, warranty. **3** cover, provision, protection, safeguard, security.

insure verb **1** to arrange for the payment of an amount of money in the event of the loss or theft of or damage to (property) or injury to or the death of (someone), etc by paying regular amounts of money to an insurance company. **2** intrans. (**insure against something**) to take measures to try to prevent (an event leading to loss, damage, difficulties, etc). **3** intrans. chiefly North Amer. to provide insurance; to underwrite. [from Old French enseurer, to ensure]

▣ **1** cover, protect, assure, indemnify, guarantee.

insured adj. (**the insured**) a person whose life, health, or property is covered by insurance.

insurer noun a person or company that provides insurance.

insurgence or **insurgency** noun an uprising or rebellion.

insurgent — adj. opposed to and fighting against the government of the country; rebellious. — noun a rebel. [from Latin insurgere, to rise up]

insurmountability noun being insurmountable.

insurmountable adj. too difficult to be dealt with successfully; impossible to overcome.

▣ insuperable, unconquerable, invincible, overwhelming, hopeless, impossible.
▣ surmountable.

insurrection noun an act of rebellion against authority. [from Latin insurgere, to rise up]

▣ rising, uprising, insurgence, riot, rebellion, mutiny, revolt, revolution, coup, putsch.

insurrectionist noun a person who takes part in or supports an insurrection.

int. abbrev. **1** interior. **2** internal. **3** international.

intact adj. whole; not broken or damaged; untouched. [from Latin intactus]

▣ unbroken, all in one piece, whole, complete, integral, perfect, sound, undamaged, unharmed, unhurt, uninjured.
▣ broken, incomplete, damaged.

intaglio / ɪnˈtɑːliəʊ/ noun (PL. **intaglios**) **1** a stone or gem which has a design engraved in its surface (cf. CAMEO). **2** the art or process of engraving designs into the surface of objects, especially jewellery; also, an engraved design. **3** a technique of printmaking in which the design is incised into a metal plate, ink is forced into the cut lines and wiped off the rest of the surface, damp paper is laid on top, and both plate and paper are rolled through a press. [from Italian intaglio, from intagliare, to cut into]

intake noun **1** a thing or quantity taken in or accepted. **2** an opening through which liquid or gas enters a pipe, engine, etc. **3** an act of taking in.

intangibility noun being intangible.

intangible adj. **1** not able to be felt or perceived by touch. **2** difficult to understand or for the mind to grasp. **3** said of part of a business, eg an asset not having a solid physical existence, but having some value or worth. [from Latin intangibilis]

▣ **2** elusive, fleeting, airy, shadowy, vague, indefinite, abstract, unreal.
▣ TANGIBLE.

integer /ˈɪntɪdʒə(r)/ noun any of the positive or negative whole numbers, or zero, eg 0, 8, −12. [from Latin integer, untouched]

integral — adj. **1** being a necessary part of a whole. **2** forming a whole; supplied or fitted as part of a whole. **3** whole; complete. **4** Maths. denoting a number that is an integer. — noun Maths. the result of integrating a function. [from Latin integralis]

▣ adj. **1** intrinsic, constituent, basic, fundamental, necessary, essential, indispensable. **3** whole, undivided, complete, entire, full.

integral calculus Maths. the branch of calculus concerned with integration, ie the summing of a very large number of extremely small quantities. It can be used to solve differential equations, and to calculate the area enclosed by a curve, or the volume enclosed by an irregular surface.

integrand /ˈɪntɪgrand/ noun Maths. a function that is to be integrated. [from Latin integrandus]

integrate verb **1** to fit (parts) together to form a whole. **2** trans., intrans. to mix or cause to mix freely with other groups in society, etc. **3** to end racial segregation in. **4** Maths. **a** to find the integral of. **b** to find the total or mean value of. [from Latin integrare, to renew]

▣ **1** join, unite, combine, amalgamate, merge, fuse, knit, mesh. **2** mix, mingle, merge, blend.
▣ **1** divide, separate.

integrated circuit Electron. a miniature solid-state circuit formed on a single paper-thin chip of semiconductor material, usually silicon, and ranging in size from about one millimetre to one centimetre square. Also called SILICON CHIP.

integration noun **1** the process of integrating. **2** Maths. a method used in calculus to sum the effects of a continuously varying quantity or function, by treating it as a very large number of infinitely small quantities that represent the difference between two values of a given function.

integrity noun **1** strict adherence to moral values and principles; uprightness. **2** the quality or state of being whole and unimpaired. [from Latin integritas]

▣ **1** honour, morality, uprightness, probity, honesty, incorruptibility, purity, virtue, goodness, righteousness. **2** completeness, wholeness, unity, coherence, cohesion.
▣ **1** dishonesty. **2** incompleteness.

integument /ɪnˈtɛgjʊmənt/ noun any natural outer covering, eg a shell, skin, husk, etc. [from Latin integumentum]

integumental or **integumentary** adj. relating to or in the region of the integument.

intellect noun **1** the part of the mind that uses both memory and intelligence in order to think, reason creatively, and understand concepts. **2** a person who has a highly developed intellect and great mental ability. [from Latin intelligere, to understand]

▣ **1** mind, brain, intelligence, genius, reason, understanding, sense, wisdom.

intellectual — adj. **1** of, involving or appealing to the intellect. **2** having a highly developed ability to think, reason and understand. — noun a person with a highly developed intellect and great mental ability.

▣ adj. ACADEMIC, SCHOLARLY, HIGHBROW. **1** cerebral,

mental, cultural. **2** intelligent, studious, thoughtful. *noun* thinker, academic, highbrow, *colloq.* egghead, mastermind, genius.

☒ *adj.* LOWBROW. *noun* lowbrow.

intellectualize or **intellectualise** *verb* **1** to think about or analyse (eg a problem) intellectually or rationally. **2** *intrans.* to think rationally or intellectually; to philosophize.

intellectually *adv.* in an intellectual way; as regards intellect (as distinct from emotion).

intelligence *noun* **1** the ability to use memory, knowledge, experience, understanding, reasoning, imagination, and judgement in order to solve problems and adapt to new situations. **2** news or information. **3** the gathering of secret information about an enemy. **4** the government department or group of people, eg in the army, responsible for gathering such information. [from Latin *intelligentia*, from *intelligere*, to understand]

☒ **1** intellect, reason, wit(s), brain(s), brainpower, cleverness, brightness, quickness, alertness, discernment, perception, understanding, comprehension. **2** information, facts, data, *colloq.* low-down, news, report, warning, tip-off.
☒ **1** stupidity, foolishness.

intelligence quotient (ABBREV. **IQ**) a measure of a person's intellectual ability in relation to that of the rest of the population. It is expressed as the ratio of mental age to actual age, multiplied by 100, and is based on the scores achieved in an *intelligence test*.

intelligence test *Psychol.* any standardized assessment procedure to determine an individual's intellectual ability, or the age at which his or her ability would be normal. The score produced is usually expressed as an *intelligence quotient*.

intelligent *adj.* **1** having or showing highly developed mental ability; clever. **2** *said of a machine, computer, weapon, etc* able to vary its behaviour according to the situation.

☒ **1** clever, bright, smart, *colloq.* brainy, quick, alert, quickwitted, sharp, acute, knowledgeable, well-informed, thinking, rational, sensible.
☒ **1** unintelligent, stupid, foolish.

intelligentsia / ɪntelɪ'dʒentsɪə/ *noun* (*usually* **the intelligentsia**) the most highly educated and cultured people in a society, especially when considered as a political class. [from Russian, from Latin *intelligentia*]

intelligibility *noun* being intelligible.

intelligible *adj.* **1** able to be understood; clear. **2** only able to be understood by the intellect and not by the senses or feelings. [from Latin *intelligibilis*]

intemperance *noun* excess, lack of moderation.

intemperate *adj.* **1** going beyond reasonable limits; not controlled or restrained. **2** habitually drinking too much alcohol. **3** *said of a climate or region* having extreme and severe temperatures. See also TEMPERATE. [from Latin *intemperatus*]

intemperately *adv.* in an intemperate way; severely, excessively.

intend *verb* **1** to plan or have in mind as one's purpose or aim. **2** (**intend something for someone** or **something**) to set it aside or destine it to some specified person or thing. **3** to mean. [from Latin *intendere*, to stretch towards]

☒ MEAN. **1** plan, have in mind, contemplate, propose, project, aim, purpose, resolve, determine. **2** set apart, earmark, mark out, destine.

intended — *adj.* meant, done on purpose or planned. — *noun colloq.* one's future husband or wife.

intense *adj.* **1** very great or extreme. **2** feeling or expressing emotion deeply. **3** very deeply felt: *intense happiness.* [from Latin *intendere*, to stretch towards]

☒ **1** great, extreme, strong, powerful, forceful, fierce, harsh, severe, violent, intensive, concentrated, heightened. **2** ardent, fervent, passionate, vehement. **3** deep, profound, acute, sharp.
☒ **1** moderate, mild, weak.

intensely *adv.* in an intense way; deeply, extremely.

intensification *noun* **1** intensifying. **2** being intensified.

intensifier *noun Grammar* an adverb or adjective which adds emphasis to or intensifies the word or phrase which follows it.

intensify *verb trans., intrans.* (**intensifies, intensified**) to make or become intense or more intense.

☒ increase, heighten, strengthen, sharpen, deepen, concentrate.
☒ reduce, weaken.

intensity *noun* (PL. **intensities**) **1** the quality or state of being intense. **2** *Physics* the measurable amount of some force or quality, eg heat, light or sound.

intensive — *adj.* **1** (*often in compounds*) using, done with, or requiring considerable amounts of thought, effort, time, etc within a relatively short period: *labour-intensive.* **2** thorough; intense; concentrated. **3** using large amounts of capital and labour (rather than more land or raw materials) to increase production. **4** *Grammar, said of an adverb or adjective* adding force or emphasis, eg *extremely, quite.* — *noun Grammar* an intensive adverb or adjective. [from Latin *intensivus*, from *intendere*, to stretch towards]

☒ *adj.* **2** concentrated, intense, thorough, exhaustive, comprehensive, detailed, in-depth, thoroughgoing, all-out.
☒ *adj.* **2** superficial.

intensive care **1** the care of critically ill patients who require continuous attention, eg following severe injury or major surgery. **2** (*in full* **intensive-care unit**) a hospital unit that specializes in intensive care.

intensive farming farming in which the use of high levels of chemicals, and manufactured or supplementary feedstuffs, produces a higher level of yield per hectare, thus enabling the farmer to generate an acceptable income from a limited area. See also EXTENSIVE FARMING, FACTORY FARMING.

intent — *noun* **1** something which is aimed at or intended; a purpose. **2** the intent of committing a crime: *loitering with intent.* — *adj.* **1** (**intent on** or **upon something**) firmly determined to do it. **2** (**intent on something**) having one's attention firmly fixed on it; concentrating hard on it. **3** showing concentration; absorbed: *an intent look.* — **to all intents and purposes** in every important respect; virtually. [from Latin *intendere*, to stretch towards]

☒ *adj.* **1** determined to, resolved to, set on, bent on, eager to, keen to, committed to. **3** attentive, alert, concentrating, fixed, absorbed, occupied, wrapped up, engrossed, preoccupied.

intention *noun* **1** that which one plans or intends to do; an aim or purpose. **2** (**intentions**) *colloq.* someone's, especially a man's, purpose with regard to marriage. **3** *RC Church* (*also* **special** or **particular intention**) the purpose or reason for prayers being said or mass celebrated. [from Latin *intendere*, to stretch towards]

☒ **1** aim, purpose, object, end, point, target, goal, objective, idea, plan, design, view, intent, meaning.

intentional *adj.* said, done, etc on purpose; deliberate.

⊞ intended, meant, deliberate, conscious, planned, prearranged, premeditated, calculated, studied, wilful.
⊟ unintentional, accidental.

intentionally *adv.* so as to be intentional; deliberately.

intently *adv.* earnestly, diligently.

intentness *noun* 1 being intent. 2 close attention.

inter / ɪn'tɜ:(r)/ *verb* (**interred, interring**) to bury (a dead person, etc) in the earth or a tomb. [from Latin *in*, into + *terra*, earth]

inter- *combining form* forming words meaning: 1 between or among. 2 mutual or reciprocal. [from Latin *inter*, among]

interact *verb intrans.* to act with or on one another.

interaction *noun* action or influence of people or things on each other.

interactive *adj.* 1 in which the people, things, etc interact. 2 involving or allowing a continuous exchange of information between a computer and its user.

inter alia / ɪntə'reɪlɪə/ among other things. [Latin]

interbreed *verb intrans., trans.* (PAST TENSE AND PAST PARTICIPLE **interbred**) to breed or cause to breed with an animal or plant that is a member of a different variety or species.

interbreeding *noun* breeding together.

intercalary *adj.* 1 *said of a day* added to a calendar month to make the calendar year match the solar year, eg the day added to February every leap year. 2 *said of a year* containing such a day or days. 3 coming between two layers; intervening. [from Latin *intercalarius*]

intercede *verb intrans.* 1 to act as a peacemaker between (two parties, countries, etc). 2 (**intercede for someone**) to plead or make an appeal on their behalf. See also INTERCESSION. [from Latin *inter*, between + *cedere*, to move]

⊞ 1 mediate, arbitrate, conciliate, intervene. 2 plead for, speak for.

intercellular *adj. Biol.* situated or occurring between cells.

intercept — *verb* 1 to stop or catch (eg a person, missile, aircraft, etc) on his, its, etc way from one place to another; to prevent (a missile, etc) from arriving at its destination, often by destroying it. 2 *Maths.* to mark off (a space, line, curve, etc) between two points. — *noun Maths.* that part of a line that is intercepted. [from Latin *inter*, between + *capere*, to seize]

⊞ *verb* 1 head off, ambush, interrupt, cut off, stop, arrest, catch, seize, check, block, obstruct, delay, frustrate, thwart.

interception *noun* intercepting.

interceptive *adj.* intercepting.

interceptor *noun* a person or thing that intercepts, especially a small light aircraft used to intercept approaching enemy aircraft.

intercession *noun* 1 an act of interceding or making an appeal on behalf of another. 2 *Christianity* a prayer or request to God on behalf of someone else. [from Latin *intercessio*]

intercessional *adj.* relating to or involving intercession.

intercessor *noun* a person who intercedes; a mediator.

interchange — *verb intrans., trans.* to change or cause to change places with something or someone. — *noun* 1 an act of interchanging; an exchange. 2 a road junction, especially leading to or from a motorway, consisting of a series of roads and bridges designed to prevent streams of traffic from directly crossing one another. [from Middle English *entrechaungen*]

interchangeability *noun* being interchangeable.

interchangeable *adj.* capable of being interchanged.

⊞ reciprocal, equivalent, similar, identical, the same, synonymous, standard.
⊟ different.

intercity *adj. Brit.*, *said of transport* denoting an express service between major cities.

intercom *noun* a system consisting of microphones and loudspeakers which allow communication within a building, aircraft, ship, etc. [abbreviation of INTERCOMMUNICATION]

intercommunicate *verb intrans.* 1 to communicate mutually or together. 2 *said of adjoining rooms* to have a connecting door; to interconnect. [from Latin *intercommunicatus*, intercommunicating]

intercommunication *noun* mutual communication.

interconnect *verb trans., intrans.* to connect (two things) or be connected together or with one another.

interconnection *noun* mutual connection.

intercontinental *adj.* travelling between or connecting different continents.

intercontinental ballistic missile a ballistic missile which can travel great distances and which can therefore be fired at a target in another continent.

intercourse *noun* 1 sexual intercourse. 2 communication, connection or dealings between people, groups of people, countries, etc. 3 communion, eg between people and God. [from Latin *intercursus*, a running between, communication]

intercropping *noun Agric.* the practice of growing two or more crops in a field at the same time, in alternate rows.

interdenominational *adj.* happening between or involving (members of) different religious denominations.

interdepartmental *adj.* happening between or involving (members of) different departments within a single organization, etc.

interdependence *noun* mutual dependence.

interdependent *adj.* depending on one another.

interdict — *noun* 1 an official order forbidding someone to do something. 2 *RC Church* a sentence or punishment removing the right to most sacraments (including burial but not communion) from the people of a place or district. — *verb* to place under an interdict; to forbid or prohibit. [from Latin *interdictum*, prohibition]

interdiction *noun* 1 interdicting. 2 being interdicted.

interdictory *adj.* interdicting.

interdisciplinary *adj.* involving two or more subjects of study.

interest — *noun* 1 the desire to learn or know about someone or something; curiosity. 2 the power to attract a person's attention and curiosity. 3 something which arouses a person's attention and curiosity; a hobby or pastime. 4 money paid as a charge for borrowing money or using credit, usually in the form of a percentage of what is borrowed or owed. 5 (*often* **interests**) advantage, benefit, or profit, especially financial: *it is in your own interests to be truthful.* 6 a share or claim in a business and its profits, or a legal right to property. 7 (*also* **interest group**) a group of people or organizations with common, especially financial, aims and concerns: *the banking interest.* — *verb* 1 to attract the attention and curiosity of. 2 (**interest someone in something**) to cause them to take a part in or be concerned about some activity. — **in the interest** or **interests of something** in order to achieve or contribute to an objective: *in the interests of good industrial relations.* [from Latin *interest*, it concerns]

⊞ *noun* 1 curiosity, concern, care, attention, notice. 2 importance, significance, note. 3 activity, pursuit, pastime, hobby, diversion, amusement. 5 advantage, benefit, profit, gain. 6 share, claim, involvement, participation. *verb* 1 concern, affect, touch, move, attract, appeal to, divert, amuse, occupy, engage, involve, absorb, engross, fascinate, intrigue.

◨ *noun* **1** indifference. *verb* **1** bore.

interested *adj.* **1** (*often* **interested in something** or **someone**) showing or having a concern or interest in them. **2** personally involved and therefore not impartial or disinterested. See also DISINTERESTED, UNINTERESTED.

▣ **1** curious, attentive, absorbed, engrossed, fascinated, intrigued, enthusiastic, keen. **2** concerned, involved, affected.
◨ **1** uninterested, indifferent, apathetic. **2** disinterested, unaffected.

interesting *adj.* attracting interest; holding the attention.

▣ fascinating, intriguing, compelling, gripping, stimulating, thought-provoking, curious, unusual, attractive, appealing, entertaining, engaging, absorbing, engrossing.
◨ uninteresting, boring, monotonous, tedious.

interface — *noun* **1** a surface forming a common boundary between two regions, things, etc which cannot be mixed, eg oil and water. **2** a common boundary or meeting-point between two different systems or processes. **3** *Physics* the boundary between two adjacent phases, ie between gas and liquid, gas and solid, liquid and liquid, liquid and solid, or solid and solid. **4** *Comput.* a device consisting of hardware together with software programs to drive it, that links a computer to a peripheral device such as a printer. **5** *Comput.* the physical connection between a computer and the user. — *verb trans., intrans.* to connect (a piece of equipment, etc) with another by means of an interface.

interfacing *noun* a piece of stiff fabric sewn between two layers of material to give shape and stiffness.

interfere *verb intrans.* **1** (*often* **interfere in** or **with something**) to involve oneself in matters which do not concern one and where one is not wanted. **2** (**interfere with something**) to get in the way of a process; to slow down or hinder the progress of something. **3** (**interfere with someone**) *euphemistic* to assault or molest them sexually. **4** *Physics, said of sound waves, rays of light, etc* to combine together to cause disturbance or interference. [from Old French *s'entreferir*, to strike each other]

▣ **1** intrude, poke one's nose in, pry, butt in, interrupt, intervene, meddle. **2** hinder, hamper, obstruct, block, impede, handicap, cramp, inhibit, conflict with, clash with.
◨ **2** assist.

interference *noun* **1** the act of interfering. **2** *Physics* the interaction between two or more waves of the same frequency. If the peaks of two such waves arrive at the same point together, they will combine to give a larger wave, but if a peak of one wave coincides with a trough of the other, the waves cancel each other out and there is no wave motion. With light of a single wavelength, interference produces patterns of light and dark bands. **3** *Telecomm.* the distortion of transmitted radio or television signals by an external power source, eg machinery near to the receiver.

▣ **1** intrusion, prying, interruption, intervention, meddling, obstruction, opposition, conflict.

interfering *adj.* that interferes.

interferometer *noun Physics* an instrument that splits a beam of light into two or more parts which are then recombined to form an interference pattern. Interferometers are used to measure wavelengths, to test optical surfaces, and to measure accurately small angles and distances, eg the distance between two close stars.

interferon /ɪntəˈfɪərɒn/ *noun* any of various proteins, secreted by animal cells that have been infected with a virus,

which are capable of preventing the multiplication of that virus in non-infected cells. [from INTERFERE]

interfuse *verb* **1** to mix (with something). **2** *trans., intrans.* to blend or fuse together. [from Latin *interfundere*, to pour between]

interfusion *noun* **1** interfusing. **2** being interfused.

intergalactic *adj.* happening or situated between different galaxies.

interim *adj.* not intended to be final or to last; provisional, temporary. — **in the interim** in the time between two events; in the meantime. [from Latin *interim*, in the meantime]

▣ temporary, provisional, stopgap, makeshift, improvised, stand-in, acting, caretaker.

interior — *adj.* **1** on, of, suitable for, happening or acting in, or coming from the inside; inner. **2** away from the shore or frontier; inland. **3** concerning the domestic or internal, rather than foreign, affairs of a country. **4** of or existing in the mind or spirit; of mental or spiritual life. — *noun* **1** an internal or inner part; the inside. **2** the part of a country or continent that is furthest from the coast. **3** the internal or home affairs of a country. **4** a picture or representation of the inside of a room or building, especially with reference to its decoration or style: *a typical southern French interior.* [from Latin *interior*, further inward, from *inter*, inward]

▣ *adj.* **1** internal, inside, inner, central, inward. **2** inland, up-country. **3** home, domestic, internal. **4** mental, spiritual, private, secret, hidden. *noun* **1** inside, centre, middle, core, heart.
◨ *adj.* **1** exterior, external. **3** foreign, international. *noun* **1** exterior, outside.

interior angle an angle between two adjacent sides of a polygon.

interior decoration or **interior design** **1** the decoration, design and furnishings of a room or building. **2** the art or job of designing the insides of rooms, including selecting colours and furnishings.

interior decorator or **interior designer** a person whose occupation is interior decoration or design.

interj. *abbrev.* interjection.

interject *verb* to say or add abruptly; to interrupt with. [from Latin *interjicere*, to throw between]

interjection *noun* **1** a word, phrase or sound used as an exclamation to express surprise, sudden disappointment, pain, etc. **2** an act of interjecting.

▣ **1** exclamation, ejaculation, cry, shout, call.

interjectional *adj.* of the nature of an interjection.

interlace *verb* **1** *trans., intrans.* to join by lacing or by crossing over. **2** to mix or blend with: *a story interlaced with graphic descriptions.* [from Middle English *entrelacen*]

interlacement *noun* **1** interlacing. **2** being interlaced.

interlard *verb* to add foreign words, quotations, unusual phrases, etc to (a speech or piece of writing), often excessively. [from Old French *entrelarder*]

interleaf *noun* (PL. **interleaves**) a usually blank leaf of paper inserted between the leaves of a book.

interleave *verb* to insert a usually blank leaf of paper between.

interleukin /ɪntəˈljuːkɪn/ *noun* a protein produced by white blood cells which fights infection. [from INTER- + LEUCOCYTE]

interline¹ *verb* to insert (words) between the lines of (a document, book, etc). [from Latin *interlineare*]

interline² *verb* to put an extra lining between the first lining and the fabric (of a garment), especially for stiffness.

interlinear *adj., said of words* inserted between the lines of a document, book, etc.

interlineation *noun* **1** inserting a word or words between lines or writing. **2** the word or words inserted.

interlining *noun* a piece of material used as an extra lining.

interlink *verb trans., intrans.* to join or connect together.

interlock — *verb trans., intrans.* to fit, fasten or connect together, especially by means of teeth or parts which fit into each other. — *noun* a device or mechanism that connects and co-ordinates the functions of the parts or components of eg a machine. — *adj., said of a fabric or garment* knitted with closely locking stitches.

interlocking *adj.* that interlocks.

interlocution *noun* dialogue, conversation.

interlocutor / ɪntəˈlɒkjʊtə(r)/ *noun* a person who takes part in a conversation or dialogue. [from Latin *interloqui*, to speak between]

interlocutory / ɪntəˈlɒkjʊtərɪ/ *adj.* **1** of conversation or dialogue. **2** *Legal, said of a decree* given during legal proceedings and only provisional.

interloper /ˈɪntəloʊpə(r)/ *noun* a person who meddles or interferes with other people's affairs, or goes to places where he or she has no right to be; an intruder.

interlude *noun* **1** a short period of time between two events, or a short period of a different activity. **2** a short break between the acts of a play or opera, or between items of music. **3** a short piece of music, or short item of entertainment, played during such a break. [from Latin *interludium*]

intermarriage *noun* **1** intermarrying. **2** marriage between people of different groups, races, or nations etc. **3** marriage of people closely related.

intermarry *verb intrans.* (**intermarries, intermarried**) *said of different races, social and religious groups, etc* to become connected by marriage. **2** to marry someone from one's own family.

intermediary *noun* (PL. **intermediaries**) **1** a person who mediates between two people or groups, often to try to settle a dispute between them or bring them into agreement. **2** any intermediate person or thing. [from Latin *intermedium*, intervening place]

    ▣ **1** mediator, arbitrator, negotiator, go-between. **2** middleman, broker, agent.

intermediate — *adj.* (pronounced -ət) in the middle; placed between two points, stages, or extremes in place or time or skill. — *noun* (pronounced -ət) **1** an intermediate thing. **2** *Chem.* a short-lived chemical compound that is formed during one of the middle stages of a complex series of chemical reactions. **3** *Chem.* a chemical compound that is the precursor of a particular end-product, eg a dye, and must undergo a number of chemical changes to give the finished product. — *verb intrans.* (pronounced -eɪt) to act as an intermediary. [from Latin *intermediatus*, from *intermedium*, intervening place]

    ▣ *adj.* midway, halfway, in-between, middle, mid, median, mean, intervening, transitional.
    ▣ *adj.* extreme.

intermediately *adv.* in an intermediate position or condition.

intermediate technology technology involving the adaptation of highly sophisticated scientific inventions and techniques for use in the Third World, using local materials and methods of manufacture in order to reduce overhead costs and minimize environmental damage.

intermediation *noun* intermediating.

interment *noun* a burial.

intermezzo / ɪntəˈmɛtsoʊ/ *noun* (PL. **intermezzi, intermezzos**) *Mus.* a short instrumental piece usually performed between the sections of a symphonic work, opera, or other dramatic musical entertainment. [from Italian, from Latin *intermedium*, intervening place]

interminable *adj.* having or seeming to have no end, especially because of being extremely dull and tedious. [from Latin *interminabilis*]

    ▣ endless, never-ending, ceaseless, perpetual, limitless, unlimited, long, long-winded, long-drawn-out, boring, tedious.
    ▣ limited, brief.

interminably *adv.* endlessly, on and on.

intermingle *verb trans., intrans.* to mingle or mix together.

intermission *noun* a short pause between two things, eg between two parts of a film, play, etc or between two serious attacks of disease. [from Latin *intermissio*, interruption]

    ▣ interval, interlude, entr'acte, break, recess, rest, respite, pause, lull, *colloq.* let-up, remission, suspension, interruption, halt, cessation.

intermittence *noun* intermitting.

intermittent *adj.* happening occasionally; stopping for a while and then starting again; not continuous. [from Latin *intermittere*, to leave a space between]

    ▣ occasional, periodic, sporadic, spasmodic, fitful, erratic, irregular, broken.
    ▣ continuous, constant.

intermittently *adv.* in an intermittent way; at intervals.

intern ¹ *verb* (with stress on -*tern*) to confine within a country, restricted area or prison, especially during a war. [from French *interner*]

intern ² or **interne** *noun* (with stress on *in*-) *North Amer.* an advanced student or graduate who is gaining practical professional experience by working, especially a medical graduate working as an assistant physician or surgeon in a hospital. [from Latin *internus*, internal]

internal *adj.* **1** of, on, in, or suitable for the inside; inner. **2** of, on, in, or suitable for the inside of the body. **3** of a nation's domestic affairs as opposed to its relations with foreign countries. **4** of, for, or coming from within an organization. **5** of the inner nature or feelings or of the mind or soul. [from Latin *internalis*, from *internus*, inward]

    ▣ **1** inside, inner, interior, inward. **3** home, domestic, interior. **4** inside, in-house. **5** private, personal, intimate.
    ▣ **1** external, outer. **3** foreign, international.

internal combustion engine an engine that produces power by the combustion (burning) of a mixture of fuel and air within an enclosed space inside the engine. The hot gas produced is used to drive a moving piston, rotor, or turbine.

internalization or **internalisation** *noun* internalizing or being internalized.

internalize or **internalise** *verb* **1** to make (a type of behaviour, characteristic, etc) part of one's personality. **2** to keep (an emotion) inside oneself rather than express it.

internally *adv.* **1** in, on, or concerned with the inside or interior. **2** with respect to the inner state of anything, especially the internal affairs of a state or country.

international — *adj.* involving, affecting, used by, or carried on between two or more nations. — *noun* **1** a sports match between two national teams. **2** a player who takes part in, or has taken part in, such a match.

    ▣ *adj.* global, worldwide, intercontinental, cosmopolitan, universal, general.
    ▣ *adj.* national, local, parochial.

International Atomic Energy Agency an international agency, founded in 1957, which promotes research into and development of the non-military uses of nuclear energy, and oversees a system of safeguards and controls that restrict the use of nuclear materials for military purposes.

International Date Line an imaginary line on the earth's surface running N to S across the middle of the Pacific Ocean, the date in countries on the W of it being one day ahead of the date in countries on the E.

internationalism *noun* the view that the nations of the world should co-operate politically, economically, culturally, etc and work towards greater mutual understanding.

internationalist *noun, adj.* **1** a person who favours internationalism. **2** a person chosen to represent a country at international level in sport.

internationality *noun* the state of being international.

internationalization or **internationalisation** *noun* making international.

internationalize or **internationalise** *verb* to make international, especially to bring under the control of two or more countries.

international law the law that governs relationships between states (*public international law*), or the law that determines which nation's law shall in any particular case govern the relations of private persons (*private international law*). There is no worldwide international legislature and international law is principally based on custom.

internationally *adv.* **1** in an international way. **2** among or between nations.

International Monetary Fund an international financial organization set up to promote trade by keeping currencies stable and having a fund of money from which member states may borrow.

International Phonetic Alphabet (ABBREV. **IPA**) a system of signs and letters able to represent all of the speech sounds of every language.

interne see INTERN².

internecine / ɪntəˈniːsaɪn/ *adj.* **1** *said of a fight, war, etc* destructive and damaging to both sides. **2** involving or being a conflict or struggle within a group or organization: *an internecine feud.* [from Latin *internecinus*, murderous]

internee *noun* a person who is interned.

Internet *noun* an international computer network linking both business and private users.

internment *noun* interning or being interned.

internode *noun Bot.* the part of a plant stem that lies between two successive nodes (points where leaves are attached, or may develop from buds). [from Latin *internodium*, from *inter*, between + *nodus*, knot]

internship *noun* the position of an intern.

interpellate / ɪnˈtɜːpəleɪt/ *verb* to question (eg a government minister) about policy during the course of, and as an interruption to, a debate. [from Latin *interpellare*, to disturb by speaking]

interpellation *noun* a question raised during a debate, especially in parliament.

interpellator *noun* a person who interpellates.

interpenetrate *verb* **1** to penetrate thoroughly. **2** *intrans.* to penetrate mutually.

interpenetration *noun* penetrating among or in; thorough penetration.

interpersonal *adj.* concerning or involving the relationships between people.

interphase *noun Biol.* the period between successive divisions of a living cell by mitosis.

interplanetary *adj.* **1** relating to the solar system. **2** happening or existing in the space between the planets.

interplanetary matter *Astron.* matter in the solar system other than the planets and their satellites (moons). It includes dust particles, and gas that flows continuously outward from the Sun as the solar wind, consisting of streams of charged particles, mainly protons and electrons.

interplay *noun* the action and influence of two or more things on each other.

⊟ interaction, reciprocation, exchange, interchange, give-and-take.

Interpol *noun* an international organization through which police forces in different countries can communicate and co-operate with each other in fighting crime. [from *Inter*national Criminal *Pol*ice Organization]

interpolate *verb* **1** to add (words) to a book or manuscript, especially so as to make the text misleading or corrupt. **2** to alter (a text) in this way. **3** to interrupt a conversation, a person speaking, etc with (a remark or comment). **4** *Maths.* to estimate (values) from others in the same series which are already known. [from Latin *interpolare*, to refurbish or touch up]

interpolation *noun* **1** interpolating. **2** something that is interpolated.

interpose *verb* **1** to put (something) between two other things. **2** *intrans.* to come between two other things. **3** to interrupt a conversation or argument with (a remark, comment, etc). **4** *intrans.* to act as mediator; to intervene. [from Old French *interposer*]

⊟ **1** insert, introduce. **3** interpolate, put in. **4** intervene, step in, mediate.

interposition *noun* **1** the act of placing something or oneself between others. **2** intervention. **3** interference.

interpret *verb* (**interpreted, interpreting**) **1** to explain the meaning of (a foreign word, dream, etc). **2** *intrans.* to act as an interpreter. **3** to consider or understand (behaviour, a remark, etc): *interpret her silence as disapproval.* **4** to bring out one's idea of the meaning of (eg a dramatic role, piece of music) in one's performance. [from Latin *interpretari*]

⊟ **1** explain, expound, elucidate, clarify, define, paraphrase, translate, render, decode, decipher, solve. **3** consider, regard, understand, construe, read, take.

interpretation *noun* **1** an act of interpreting or the sense given as a result. **2** the representing of one's idea of the meaning of a dramatic role, piece of music, etc in one's performance.

⊟ **1** explanation, clarification, analysis, translation, rendering, version, understanding, reading, sense, meaning. **2** performance, rendering, version, reading, take, representation.

interpretative or **interpretive** *adj.* **1** interpreting, explanatory. **2** of or using interpretation.

interpretatively or **interpretively** *adv.* in an interpretative way.

interpreter *noun* **1** a person who translates speech in a foreign language as the words are spoken, relaying the translation orally as it is done. **2** a computer program that translates instructions one by one and executes them immediately.

interracial *adj.* between different races of people.

interregnum *noun* (PL. **interregnums, interregna**) **1** the time between two reigns when the throne is unoccupied, eg between the death of one monarch and the coronation of the next. **2** the period between the end of rule by one government and the beginning of rule by the next. **3** any interval or pause in a continuous sequence of events. [from Latin *inter*, between + *regnum*, reign]

interrelate *verb trans., intrans.* to be in or be brought into a mutually dependent or reciprocal relationship.

interrelated *adj.* mutually related or connected.

interrelation *noun* being interrelated.

interrelationship *noun* mutual relationship.

interrogate *verb* **1** to question closely and thoroughly, or examine by asking questions and sometimes with threatening behaviour. **2** *said of a radar set, etc* to send out signals to (a radio beacon) to work out a position. [from Latin *interrogare*]

   ▣ **1** question, quiz, examine, cross-examine, grill, give the third degree, pump, debrief.

interrogation *noun* **1** the act or process of interrogating. **2** a question.

   ▣ **1** questioning, examination, cross-examination, grilling, third degree, inquisition.

interrogative — *adj.* **1** like a question; asking or seeming to ask a question. **2** *Grammar, said of an adjective or pronoun* used to ask a question. — *noun* an interrogative word, sentence or construction. [from Latin *interrogativus*]

interrogator *noun* **1** a person who interrogates. **2** a transmitter used to send out interrogating signals.

interrogatory — *adj.* being or expressing a question. — *noun* (PL. **interrogatories**) a question or inquiry. [from Latin *interrogatorius*]

interrupt *verb* **1** *intrans.* to break into a conversation or monologue by asking a question or making a comment. **2** to break into (a conversation, etc) in this way or stop (someone) speaking. **3** to make a break in the continuity of (an event, a supply, etc). **4** to destroy (a view eg of a clear sweep of land) by getting in the way. [from Latin *interrumpere*, to break apart]

   ▣ **1** butt in, *colloq.* barge in, intrude, break in, heckle. **2** break into, disturb, heckle. **3** disturb, disrupt, hold up, stop, halt, suspend, discontinue, cut off, disconnect, break, punctuate. **4** obstruct, block, disturb, interfere with.

interrupter or **interruptor** *noun* **1** a person who interrupts. **2** a device for interrupting, especially for opening and closing an electric circuit.

interruption *noun* **1** the act of interrupting or state of being interrupted. **2** something that interrupts, such as a question or remark. **3** a short pause or break.

   ▣ **1** intrusion, disturbance, disruption, suspension, disconnection. **2** question, remark, interpolation, interjection, obstruction, impediment, obstacle, hitch. **3** pause, break, halt, stop.

interruptive *adj.* tending to interrupt.

intersect *verb* **1** to divide (lines, an area, etc) by passing or cutting through or across. **2** *intrans., said especially of lines, roads, etc* to run through or cut across each other. [from Latin *intersecare*, to cut through]

   ▣ **1** divide, bisect, cut across. **2** cross, criss-cross.

intersection *noun* **1** a place where things meet or intersect, especially a road junction. **2** the act of intersecting. **3** *Geom.* the point or line where two lines or plane surfaces intersect. **4** *Maths.* the set of elements which two or more sets have in common.

   ▣ **1** junction, interchange, crossroads, crossing.

intersectional *adj.* relating to or involving intersection.

interspace — *noun* a space between two things; an interval. — *verb* to put a space or intervals between.

intersperse *verb* **1** to scatter or insert (something) here and there. **2** *intrans.* to diversify or change slightly with scattered things. [from Latin *interspergere*, to strew here and there]

interspersion *noun* **1** interspersing. **2** being interspersed. **3** dispersion.

interstate — *adj.* between two or more states, especially in the USA or Australia. — *noun North Amer., esp. US* a major road crossing a state boundary.

interstellar *adj.* happening or existing in the space between individual stars within galaxies.

interstice / ɪnˈtɜːstɪs/ *noun* **1** a very small gap or space between two things. **2** *Physics* any of the spaces between atoms in a crystal. [from Latin *interstitium*]

intertwine *verb trans., intrans.* to twist or be twisted together.

   ▣ entwine, interweave, interlace, interlink, twist, twine, cross, weave.

interval *noun* **1** a period of time between two events. **2** a space or distance between two things. **3** *Brit.* a short break between the acts of a play or opera, or between parts of a concert or long film. **4** *Mus.* the difference in pitch between two notes or tones. — **at intervals 1** here and there; now and then. **2** with a stated distance in time or space between: *at intervals of ten minutes*. [from Latin *intervallum*, space between palisades]

   ▣ **1** interlude, intermission, break, rest, pause, delay, wait, period, spell, time, interim, meantime, meanwhile. **2** gap, opening, space, distance. **3** interlude, intermission, entr'acte, break.

intervene *verb intrans.* **1** (*often* **intervene in something**) to involve oneself in something which is happening in order to affect the outcome. **2** (*often* **intervene in something** or **between people**) to involve oneself or interfere in a dispute between other people in order to settle it or prevent more serious conflict. **3** to come or occur between two things in place or time. **4** *Legal* to become involved in a lawsuit as a third party. [from Latin *intervenire*, to come between]

   ▣ **1** interfere, step in, interrupt, intrude. **2** interfere, step in, mediate, arbitrate, intercede. **3** occur, happen, elapse, pass.

intervention *noun* an act of intervening, especially in the affairs of other people or other countries.

   ▣ involvement, interference, intrusion, mediation, arbitration, intercession.

interventionism *noun* the belief that the government of a country should be allowed to interfere, or should interfere, in the economic affairs of the country or in the internal affairs of other countries or states.

interventionist — *noun* a person who supports interventionism. — *adj.* relating to or characteristic of interventionism.

interview — *noun* **1** a formal meeting and discussion with someone, especially one at which an employer meets and judges a prospective employee. **2** a conversation or discussion which aims at obtaining information, especially one in which a journalist asks questions of a famous or important person and which is broadcast or published. — *verb* to hold an interview with. [from Old French *entrevue*, from *entrevoir*, to glimpse]

   ▣ *noun* AUDIENCE, CONSULTATION, TALK, DIALOGUE, DISCUSSION. **1** meeting, conference, oral, viva. **2** conversation, press conference. *verb* question, interrogate, examine, vet.

interviewee *noun* a person who is interviewed.

interviewer *noun* a person who interviews.

interweave *verb trans., intrans.* (PAST TENSE **interwove**; PAST PARTICIPLE **interwoven**) to weave or be woven together.

intestacy *noun* the state of dying without making a valid will.

intestate / ɪnˈtesteɪt/ *Legal* — *adj.*, *said of a person* dying without having made a valid will. — *noun* a person who dies without making a valid will. [from Latin *intestatus*]

intestinal / ɪnˈtestɪnəl, ɪnteˈstaɪnəl/ *adj.* relating to or in the region of the intestines.

intestine / ɪnˈtestɪn/ *noun* the tube-like part of the alimentary canal leading from the stomach to the anus, divided into the *small intestine* (comprising the duodenum, jejunum, and ileum) and the *large intestine* (comprising the caecum, colon, and rectum). [from Latin *intestinus*, internal]

⊟ bowel, gut.

intifada / ɪntɪˈfɑːdə/ *noun* the name for the Palestinian uprising against the Israelis in Gaza which began in Dec 1987, and also for the militant group of Palestinians involved in it. [Arabic, = shaking off]

intimacy *noun* (PL. **intimacies**) **1** a warm, close personal friendship. **2** an intimate or personal remark. **3** sexual intercourse. **4** the state or quality of being intimate.

⊟ **4** friendliness, informality, familiarity, closeness, confidentiality, privacy.
⊟ **4** distance.

intimate [1] (pronounced -mət) — *adj.* **1** marked by or sharing a close and affectionate friendship. **2** very private or personal. **3** *said of a place* small and quiet with a warm, friendly atmosphere promoting close personal relations. **4** (**intimate with someone**) sharing a sexual relationship with them. **5** *said of knowledge* deep and thorough. — *noun* a close friend. [from Latin *intimus*, innermost]

⊟ *adj.* **1** friendly, familiar, affectionate, dear, bosom, close, near. **2** confidential, secret, private, personal. **3** friendly, informal, cosy, warm. **5** deep, penetrating, detailed, exhaustive, thorough. *noun* friend, bosom friend, confidant(e).
⊟ *adj.* **3** unfriendly, cold. *noun* stranger.

intimate [2] *verb* (pronounced -meɪt) **1** to announce or make known. **2** to hint or suggest indirectly. [from Latin *intimare*, to impress upon]

⊟ **1** announce, declare, state, communicate, impart. **2** hint, insinuate, imply, suggest, indicate.

intimation *noun* **1** an indication, a hint. **2** an announcement.

intimidate *verb* (**intimidate someone into something**) to coerce or frighten them into doing what one wants, especially with threats. [from Latin *intimidare*, from *timidus*, frightened]

⊟ daunt, cow, overawe, dismay, alarm, scare, frighten, terrify, threaten, menace, terrorize, bully, browbeat, bulldoze, coerce, pressure, pressurize.

intimidating *adj.* that intimidates.

intimidation *noun* **1** intimidating. **2** being intimidated.

intimism or **intimisme** *noun Art* a genre of French Impressionist painting that flourished c.1890. The term was applied to the representation of everyday subjects, such as domestic interiors, portrayal of close family members and friends in their home or working environment, and small-scale landscapes of local areas.

into *prep.* **1** to or towards the inside or middle of. **2** against; into contact or collision with. **3** *expressing a change of state or condition* so as to be: *change into a suit/get into difficulties/form into groups.* **4** up to a certain point in time. **5** *Maths.* used to express division: *divide four into twenty.* **6** *colloq.* involved with, interested in or enthusiastic about. [from Anglo-Saxon]

intolerable *adj.* which is too bad, difficult, painful, etc to be put up with. [from Latin *intolerabilis*]

⊟ unbearable, unendurable, insupportable, insufferable, unacceptable, impossible.
⊟ tolerable.

intolerably *adv.* in an intolerable way; to an intolerable degree.

intolerance *noun* **1** being intolerant. **2** an inability to tolerate.

intolerant *adj.* (*often* **intolerant of something**) refusing or unwilling to accept ideas, beliefs, behaviour, etc different from one's own. [from Latin *intolerans*, impatient]

⊟ bigoted, prejudiced, narrow-minded, small-minded, opinionated, dogmatic, illiberal, uncharitable.
⊟ tolerant.

intonate *verb trans., intrans.* to intone. [from Latin *intonare*, to intone]

intonation *noun* **1** the rise and fall of the pitch of the voice in speech. **2** the opening phrase of a plainsong melody. **3** an act of intoning. **4** the correct pitching of musical notes.

⊟ **1** modulation, tone, accentuation, inflection.

intone *verb trans., intrans.* **1** to recite (a prayer, etc) in a solemn, monotonous voice or in singing tones. **2** to say (something) with a particular intonation or tone. [from Latin *intonare*]

in toto / ɪnˈtoʊtoʊ/ totally, completely; in sum. [Latin, = in total]

intoxicant — *noun* something that causes intoxication, especially an alcoholic drink. — *adj.* intoxicating. [from Latin *intoxicare*, to poison]

intoxicate *verb* **1** to make drunk. **2** to excite or elate to the point at which self-control is lost.

⊟ **1** make drunk, inebriate. **2** excite, elate, exhilarate, thrill.

intoxicating *adj.* having the power to intoxicate.

⊟ alcoholic, strong, heady, stimulating, exciting, exhilarating, thrilling.
⊟ sobering.

intoxication *noun* a condition in which certain centres in the brain are affected as a result of poisoning by ingestion of alcohol (or other drugs), gases, heavy metals, or other toxic substances. It is characterized by impaired intellectual ability and confusion, and alcoholic intoxication also causes severe dehydration.

⊟ drunkenness, inebriation.
⊟ sobriety.

intra- *prefix* forming words meaning 'within, inside, on the inside'. [from Latin *intra*, within]

intracellular *adj. Biol.* situated or occurring within cells.

intractability *noun* being intractable.

intractable *adj.* **1** *said of a person* difficult to control or influence; obstinate. **2** *said of a problem, illness, etc* difficult to solve, cure, or deal with. [from Latin *intractabilis*]

⊟ **1** unmanageable, uncontrollable, wild, unruly,

obstinate, stubborn, disobedient.

. . . .

intramural *adj.* **1** within or amongst the people in an institution, especially a school, college, or university. **2** within the scope of normal studies. **3** situated within walls. [from INTRA- + Latin *murus*, wall]

intramurally *adv.* within the boundaries or walls; inside a particular community or organization, etc.

intranet *noun Comput.* a local private network created with Internet software. [from INTRA-, modelled on INTERNET]

intransigence *noun* being intransigent.

intransigent — *adj.* holding firmly to one's (often extreme) beliefs and refusing to change or compromise; stubborn. — *noun* an intransigent person. [from Spanish *intransigente*, from Latin *in-*, not + *transigere*, to come to an agreement]

intransitive *adj. Grammar, said of a verb* not having a direct object, such as the verb *run* in the phrase *run as fast as you can.* See also TRANSITIVE. [from Latin *intransitivus*]

intrapreneur *noun* someone who initiates commercial ventures within a large organization. [from INTRA- + ENTREPRENEUR]

intrauterine / ɪntrəˈjuːtəraɪn/ *adj.* within the uterus.

intrauterine device or **intrauterine contraceptive device** (ABBREV. **IUD, IUCD**) a contraceptive device consisting of a plastic or metal coil, loop, or other shape that is inserted into the uterus (womb) to prevent implantation of a fertilized egg (and thus pregnancy) by causing mild inflammation of the lining of the uterus. Also called COIL.

intravenous *adj.* in or into a vein or veins.

intravenously *adv.* into or through a vein or veins.

intrepid *adj.* bold and daring; fearless; brave. [from Latin *intrepidus*]

. . . .

   ◼ bold, daring, brave, courageous, plucky, valiant, fearless, dauntless, undaunted, gallant, heroic.
   ◪ cowardly, timid.

. . . .

intrepidity *noun* being intrepid, courage.

intricacy /ˈɪntrɪkəsɪ/ *noun* (PL. **intricacies**) **1** being intricate, complexity. **2** a complication.

intricate *adj.* full of complicated, interrelating, or tangled details or parts and therefore difficult to understand, analyse, or sort out. [from Latin *intricare*, to perplex]

. . . .

   ◼ elaborate, fancy, ornate, rococo, complicated, complex, sophisticated, involved, convoluted, tortuous, tangled, entangled, knotty, perplexing.
   ◪ plain, simple, straightforward.

. . . .

intrigue — *noun* **1** secret plotting or underhand scheming. **2** a secret plot or plan. **3** a secret illicit love affair. — *verb* **1** to arouse the curiosity or interest of; to fascinate. **2** *intrans.* to plot secretly. [from French *intrigue*]

. . . .

   ◼ *noun* **1** plotting, scheming, conspiracy, collusion, trickery, double-dealing, sharp practice. **2** plot, scheme, conspiracy, machination, manoeuvre, stratagem, ruse. **3** romance, liaison, affair, amour. *verb* **1** fascinate, rivet, puzzle, tantalize, attract, charm. **2** plot, scheme, conspire, connive, machinate, manoeuvre.
   ◪ *verb* **1** bore.

. . . .

intriguing *adj.* arousing curiosity or interest.

intrinsic *adj.* (**intrinsic to something**) **1** belonging to it as an inherent and essential part of its nature. **2** *Anat.* denoting a muscle that is entirely contained within the organ or body part on which it acts, eg the muscles of the tongue. [from Latin *intrinsecus*, inwardly]

intrinsically *adv.* in an intrinsic way.

intro *noun* (PL. **intros**) *colloq.* an introduction. [abbreviation]

intro- *prefix* forming words meaning 'within, into, inwards'. [from Latin *intro*, to the inside]

introduce *verb* **1** (**introduce one person to another**) to make them known by name to each other, especially formally. **2** to announce or present (eg a radio or television programme) to an audience. **3** to bring (especially something new) into a place, situation, etc for the first time. **4** to bring into operation, practice, or use. **5** to put forward or propose (a possible law or bill) for attention, consideration, or approval. **6** (**introduce someone to something**) to cause (a person) to experience or discover something for the first time. **7** to start or preface: *introduce the play with a brief analysis of the plot.* **8** (**introduce one thing into another**) to insert or put (something) into something else. [from Latin *introducere*]

. . . .

   ◼ **3** initiate, begin, start, institute, bring in, establish, found. **4** open, launch, inaugurate, begin, start. **5** put forward, advance, submit, offer, propose, suggest. **6** acquaint with, familiarize with. **7** begin, start, preface, precede.
   ◪ **3, 4, 7** end. **5** withdraw.

. . . .

introducible *adj.* capable of being introduced.

introduction *noun* **1** the act of introducing or process of being introduced. **2** a presentation of one person to another or others. **3** a section at the beginning of a book which explains briefly what it is about, why it was written, etc. **4** a book which outlines the basic principles of a subject. **5** a short passage of music beginning a piece or song, or leading up to a movement. **6** something which has been introduced.

. . . .

   ◼ **1** presentation, début, initiation, beginning, start, institution, establishment, opening, launch, inauguration. **3** foreword, preface, preamble, prologue. **5** overture, prelude, lead-in.
   ◪ **3** appendix, epilogue.

. . . .

introductorily *adv.* in an introductory way.

introductory *adj.* giving or serving as an introduction; preliminary.

. . . .

   ◼ preliminary, preparatory, opening, inaugural, first, initial, early, elementary, basic.

. . . .

introit /ˈɪntrɔɪt/ *noun* a hymn, psalm, or anthem sung at the beginning of a service or, in the RC Church, as the priest approaches the altar to celebrate Mass. [from Latin *introitus*]

intron *noun Genetics* any segment of a gene that does not carry coded instructions for the manufacture of a protein. [from *inter*vening sequence + *-on, combining form* indicating a molecular unit]

introspection *noun* the (sometimes excessive or morbid) examination of one's own thoughts, feelings, and intuitions, etc. [from Latin *introspicere*, to look within]

introspective *adj.* looking within oneself; examining one's own emotions, thoughts, and intuitions, or having a tendency to do so.

. . . .

   ◼ inward-looking, contemplative, meditative, pensive, thoughtful, brooding, introverted, withdrawn, reserved, self-centred, egocentric.
   ◪ outward-looking.

. . . .

introversion *noun* a personality trait characterized by a tendency to be more interested in the self and inner feelings than in the outside world and social relationships. See also EXTROVERSION.

introvert or **intravert** — *noun* **1** *Psychol.* a person who is more concerned with his or her thoughts and inner feelings than with the outside world and social relationships. **2** a person who tends not to socialize and who is uncommunicative and withdrawn. — *adj.* (*also* **introverted**) concerned more with one's own thoughts and feelings than with other people and outside events. — *verb* **1** to turn (one's thoughts) inward to concentrate on oneself. **2** to withdraw (eg a part of the body) into the main part, eg as a tortoise can withdraw its head into its shell. See also EXTROVERT. [from Latin *intro*, within + *vertere*, to turn]

■ *adj.* introspective, inward-looking, withdrawn, shy, reserved, quiet.
🔁 *adj.* extrovert.

intrude *verb intrans.* (*often* **intrude on someone** or **something**) to force or impose oneself or one's presence where it is unwanted and unwelcome. [from Latin *intrudere*, to thrust in]

■ interrupt, butt in, meddle, interfere, violate, infringe, encroach on, trespass on.
🔁 withdraw, stand back.

intruder *noun* a person who enters premises secretly or by force, usually in order to commit a crime.

■ trespasser, prowler, burglar, raider, invader, infiltrator, interloper, gatecrasher.

intrusion *noun* **1** an act of intruding. **2** *Geol.* the forcing of molten magma under pressure into pre-existing rock. **3** a mass of igneous rock formed by the solidification of molten magma beneath the Earth's surface, after it has been forced into pre-existing rock. [from Latin *intrusio*, from *intrudere*, to thrust in]

■ **1** interruption, interference, violation, infringement, encroachment, trespass, invasion, incursion.
🔁 **1** withdrawal.

intrusive *adj.* **1** tending to intrude. **2** *said of rock* being an intrusion.

intrusive rock *Geol.* igneous rock formed by the cooling and solidification of magma beneath the Earth's surface, eg granite.

intrust same as ENTRUST.

intuit /ɪnˈtjuːɪt/ *verb* (**intuited**, **intuiting**) to become aware of (something) by intuition.

intuition *noun* **1** the power of understanding or realizing something without conscious rational thought or analysis. **2** something understood or realized in this way. **3** immediate, instinctive understanding or belief. [from Latin *intuitio*, from *in*, in + *tueri*, to look]

■ **1** perception, discernment, insight. **2** hunch, feeling, *colloq.* gut feeling. **3** instinct, sixth sense.
🔁 **1** reasoning.

intuitive *adj.* having, showing or based on intuition.

■ instinctive, spontaneous, involuntary, innate, untaught.
🔁 reasoned, taught.

Inuit /ˈɪnjuːɪt/ *noun* a native people of the Arctic and sub-Arctic regions of Canada, Greenland, Alaska, and Siberia (also known as Eskimos), closely related to the Aleut.

Inuktitut /ɪˈnʊktɪtʊt/ *noun* the form of the Inuit language spoken in the Canadian Arctic. [Inuit, from *inuk*, person]

inundate *verb* to overwhelm with or as if with water. [from Latin *inundare*, to flow over]

■ flood, deluge, swamp, overwhelm, engulf, submerge, immerse, drown.

inundation *noun* **1** a flood. **2** an act of inundating.

inure *verb* (**inure someone to something**) to accustom someone or oneself to something unpleasant or unwelcome. [from Old French *en ure*, in use]

inurement *noun* **1** inuring. **2** being inured.

invade *verb* **1** *trans., intrans.* to enter (a country) by force with an army. **2** to attack or overrun. **3** to interfere with (a person's rights, privacy, etc). See also INVASION. [from Latin *invadere*]

■ **1** enter, penetrate, infiltrate. **2** attack, raid, seize, occupy, overrun, swarm over, infest, pervade. **3** intrude on, encroach on, trespass on, infringe, violate.

invader *noun* a person who invades.

invalid[1] (with stress on *in-*) — *noun* a person who is constantly ill or who is disabled. — *adj.* **1** being an invalid. **2** suitable for an invalid. — *verb* (**invalided**, **invaliding**) (**invalid someone out**) to discharge (a soldier, etc) from service because of illness. [from French *invalide*, from Latin *invalidus*, weak]

■ *adj.* **1** sick, ill, ailing, sickly, weak, feeble, frail, infirm, disabled, bedridden.
🔁 *adj.* **1** healthy.

invalid[2] *adj.* (with stress on *-val-*) **1** *said of a document, agreement, etc* having no legal force. **2** *said of an argument, reasoning, etc* based on false reasoning or a mistake and therefore not valid, correct, or reliable. [from Latin *invalidus*, weak]

■ **1** illegal, null, void, worthless. **2** false, fallacious, unsound, ill-founded, unfounded, baseless, illogical, irrational, unscientific, wrong, incorrect.
🔁 VALID. **1** legal. **2** sound.

invalidate *verb* to make (a document, agreement, argument, etc) invalid.

invalidation *noun* invalidating or being invalidated.

invalidity[1] *noun* being an invalid.

invalidity[2] *noun* being invalidated.

invalidly *adv.* so as to be invalid.

invaluable *adj.* having a value that is too great to be measured.

■ priceless, inestimable, incalculable, precious, valuable, useful.
🔁 worthless.

invariable *adj.* which does not change and is always the same. [from Latin *invariabilis*]

■ fixed, set, unvarying, unchanging, unchangeable, permanent, constant, steady, unwavering, uniform, rigid, inflexible.
🔁 variable.

invariably *adv.* consistently, constantly.

■ consistently, always, without exception, without fail, unfailingly, constantly, habitually, regularly.
🔁 never.

invariant *noun Maths.* a property of a mathematical equation, geometric figure, etc, that is unaltered by a particular procedure.

invasion *noun* an act of invading or process of being invaded, eg by a hostile country or by something harmful. [from Latin *invasio*]

■ attack, offensive, onslaught, raid, incursion, foray, breach,

penetration, infiltration, intrusion, encroachment, infringement, violation.
🔄 withdrawal, evacuation.

invasive *adj.* **1** invading, aggressive. **2** entering, penetrating.

invective *noun* **1** angry attacking words, often including abuse and swearing. **2** an attack using such words. [from Latin *invectivus*, abusive]

inveigh / ɪn'veɪ/ *verb intrans.* to speak strongly or passionately against someone or something, especially in criticism or protest. [from Latin *invehi*, to attack with words]

inveigle / ɪn'viːgəl/ *verb* (**inveigle someone into something**) to trick or deceive them into doing something. [from Old French *enveogler*, to blind]

inveiglement *noun* trickery, enticement.

invent *verb* **1** to be the first person to make or use (a machine, game, method, etc). **2** to think or make up (an excuse, false story, etc). [from Latin *invenire*, to find]

🔲 THINK UP. **1** conceive, design, discover, create, originate, formulate, frame, devise, contrive. **2** make up, concoct, cook up, trump up, fabricate, imagine, dream up.

invention *noun* **1** something invented, especially a device, machine, etc. **2** the act of inventing. **3** the ability to create and invent things; inventiveness. **4** *colloq.* a lie. **5** *Mus.* a short piece of keyboard music based on a single, simple idea.

🔲 **1** design, creation, brainchild, discovery, development, device, gadget. **2** design, creation, discovery, development. **3** inventiveness, imagination, creativity, innovation, originality, ingenuity, inspiration, genius. **4** lie, falsehood, deceit, fabrication, fiction, tall story, fantasy, figment.
🔄 **4** truth.

inventive *adj.* skilled at inventing; creative; resourceful.

🔲 imaginative, creative, innovative, original, resourceful, ingenious, inspired, gifted, clever.

inventiveness *noun* the quality of being inventive; creativity.

inventor *noun* a person who invents.

🔲 designer, discoverer, creator, originator, author, architect, maker, scientist, engineer.

inventory — *noun* (PL. **inventories**) **1** a formal and complete list of the articles, goods, etc found in a particular place, eg of goods for sale in a shop, or of furniture and possessions in a house. **2** the items included in such a list. **3** the making of such a list of articles, goods, etc. — *verb* (**inventories, inventoried**) to make an inventory of; to list in an inventory. [from Latin *inventorium*, list of things found]

inverse — *adj.* **1** opposite or reverse in order, sequence, direction, effect, etc. **2** *Maths.* describing a mathematical function that is opposite in effect or nature to another function. — *noun* **1** a direct opposite. **2** the state of being directly opposite or reversed. [from Latin *inversus*, from *invertere*, to invert]

🔲 *adj.* **1** inverted, upside down, transposed, reversed, opposite, contrary, reverse, converse. *noun* **1** opposite, contrary, reverse, converse.

inversely *adv.* **1** in an inverse way, condition, or state. **2** by inversion.

inversion *noun* **1** the act of turning upside down or inside out, or otherwise inverting. **2** the state of being turned up-

side down, inside out, or otherwise inverted. **3** a reversal of position, order, direction, form, effect, etc. **4** something achieved by inverting. [from Latin *inversio*]

invert *verb* **1** to turn upside down or inside out. **2** to reverse in order, sequence, direction, effect, etc. **3** *Mus.* to change (eg a chord) by placing the lowest note an octave higher. [from Latin *invertire*]

🔲 **1** upturn, up-end, overturn, capsize, upset. **2** reverse, transpose.
🔄 **1** right.

invertase / ɪn'vɜːteɪs/ *noun Biochem.* an enzyme found in plants that breaks down sucrose to form glucose and fructose.

invertebrate — *noun Zool.* any animal that does not possess a backbone, such as an insect, worm, snail, or jellyfish. — *adj.* **1** relating to an animal that does not possess a backbone. **2** having no strength of character. [from Latin *in-*, no + *vertebra*, spinal joint]

inverted comma same as QUOTATION MARK.

invert sugar *Biochem.* a mixture of glucose and fructose, found in many fruits, and formed as a result of the breakdown of sucrose (cane-sugar).

invest *verb* **1** *trans., intrans.* to put (money) into a company or business, eg by buying shares in it, in order to make a profit. **2** (**invest in something**) *colloq.* to buy it: *decided to invest in some new socks*. **3** to devote (time, effort, energy, etc) to something: *invested all their energies in animal welfare*. **4** (**invest someone with something**) to give them the symbols of power, rights, rank, etc officially. See also INVESTITURE. **5** (**invest something in someone**) to place power, rank, a quality or feeling, etc in someone. **6** to clothe or adorn. **7** *Mil.* to besiege (a stronghold). [from Latin *investire*, to clothe]

🔲 **3** spend, put in, devote, dedicate. **5** vest in, empower with, give to, bestow on, endow with.

investigate *verb* **1** to carry out a thorough, detailed and often official inquiry into or examination of (something or someone). **2** *intrans.* to carry out such an inquiry or examination. [from Latin *investigare*, to track down]

🔲 **1** inquire into, look into, consider, examine, study, inspect, scrutinize, analyse, go into, probe, explore, search.

investigation *noun* the act or process of investigating.

🔲 inquiry, inquest, hearing, examination, study, research, survey, review, inspection, scrutiny, analysis, probe, exploration, search.

investigative or **investigatory** *adj.* relating to or involving investigation.

investigative journalism journalism involving the investigation and exposure of corruption, crime, inefficiency, etc.

investigator *noun* a person who investigates.

🔲 examiner, researcher, detective, *colloq.* sleuth, private detective, *colloq.* private eye.

investiture *noun* a formal ceremony giving a rank or office to someone. See also INVEST. [from Latin *investitura*]

investment *noun* **1** a sum of money invested. **2** something, such as a business, house, etc in which one invests money, time, effort, etc. **3** the act of investing.

🔲 **1** stake, contribution, outlay, expenditure. **2** asset, speculation, venture.

investment bank a US bank handling new share issues, often in a syndicate with others. It may buy all the shares on offer and then resell them to the general public, in effect underwriting the issue. Its function is similar to that of a British merchant bank.

investment company or **investment trust** a company which holds a portfolio of shares in other companies, aimed at obtaining a reasonable dividend yield, growth, and balanced risk. Such companies are often of value to inexperienced investors who wish to invest in the stock market.

investment trust an organization which invests money in different companies or financial concerns on behalf of its members.

investor *noun* a person who invests.

inveterate *adj.* **1** *said of a habit, practice, etc* firmly established. **2** *said of a person* firmly fixed in a habit by long practice. [from Latin *inveteratus*, long continued]

invidious *adj.* likely to cause envy, resentment, or indignation, especially by being or seeming to be unfair. [from Latin *invidia*, envy]

invigilate *verb trans., intrans. Brit.* to keep watch over people sitting (an examination), especially to prevent cheating. [from Latin *invigilare*, to keep watch over]

invigilation *noun* invigilating.

invigilator *noun* a person who invigilates.

invigorate *verb* to give fresh life, energy, and health to; to strengthen or animate. [from Latin *in*, in + *vigor*, strength]

■ vitalize, energize, animate, enliven, liven up, quicken, strengthen, fortify, brace, stimulate, inspire, exhilarate, perk up, refresh, revitalize, rejuvenate.

◨ tire, weary, dishearten.

invigorating *adj.* having the power to invigorate.

invigoration *noun* being invigorated.

invincibility or **invincibleness** *noun* being invincible.

invincible *adj.* that cannot be defeated. [from Latin *invincibilis*]

■ unbeatable, unconquerable, insuperable, unsurmountable, indomitable, unassailable, impregnable, impenetrable, invulnerable, indestructible.

◨ beatable.

inviolability *noun* being inviolable.

inviolable / ɪnˈvaɪələbl/ *adj.* that must not be broken or violated; sacred. [from Latin *inviolabilis*]

inviolate / ɪnˈvaɪələt/ *adj.* which has not been broken, violated, or injured. [from Latin *inviolatus*, unhurt]

invisibility *noun* being invisible.

invisible *adj.* **1** not able to be seen. **2** unseen. **3** *Econ.* relating to services (eg insurance, tourism) rather than goods: *invisible earnings/invisible exports.* **4** not shown in regular statements: *invisible assets.* [from Latin *invisibilis*]

■ **1** out of sight, hidden, concealed, disguised, inconspicuous, indiscernible, imperceptible, imaginary, non-existent. **2** unseen, unnoticed, unobserved.

◨ **1, 2** visible.

invisibly *adv.* without being seen.

invitation *noun* **1** a request to a person to come or go somewhere, eg to a party, meal, etc. **2** the form such a request takes, either verbally or written on a card. **3** an act of inviting. **4** encouragement; enticement; inducement.

■ **1** request, call, summons. **4** encouragement, inducement, temptation, enticement, allurement, provocation, incitement, challenge.

invite — *verb* **1** to request the presence of (someone) at one's house, at a party, etc, especially formally or politely. **2** to ask politely or formally for (eg comments, advice, etc). **3** to bring on or encourage (something unwanted or undesirable). **4** to attract or tempt. — *noun colloq.* (with stress on *in*-) an invitation. [from Latin *invitare*]

■ *verb* **1** ask, call, summon, welcome. **2** ask for, request, solicit, seek. **3** ask for, bring on, provoke, encourage. **4** attract, draw, tempt, entice, allure.

inviting *adj.* attractive or tempting.

■ welcoming, attractive, appealing, tempting, seductive, enticing, alluring, pleasing, delightful, captivating, fascinating.

◨ uninviting, unappealing.

in vitro / ɪn ˈviːtroʊ/ *Biol.*, *said of biological techniques or processes* performed outside a living organism in an artificial environment created by means of scientific equipment, eg in a test-tube: *in-vitro fertilization.* See also IN VIVO. [Latin, = in glass]

in-vitro fertilization (ABBREV. IVF) a technique whereby a human embryo is conceived outside the mother's body. A mature ovum (egg cell) is removed from the ovary of a woman who is unable to conceive normally, and it is placed in a culture medium in a laboratory and fertilized with sperm from the father. After an egg has been fertilized and has divided several times, it is reimplanted in the mother's uterus (womb), and the pregnancy proceeds in the normal manner thereafter.

in vivo / ɪn ˈviːvoʊ/ *Biol.*, *said of biological techniques or processes* performed within a living organism. See also IN VITRO. [Latin, = in a living thing]

invocation *noun* **1** an act of invoking. **2** a prayer calling on God, a saint, etc for blessing or help. **3** an opening prayer at the beginning of a public service or sermon. **4** any appeal to supernatural beings, spirits, etc, such as an appeal to a Muse for inspiration at the beginning of a poem. [from Latin *invocatio*]

invocatory / ɪnˈvɒkətərɪ/ *adj.* making an invocation.

invoice — *noun* a list of goods supplied, delivered with the goods and giving details of price and quantity, usually treated as a request for payment. — *verb* **1** to send an invoice to (a customer). **2** to provide an invoice for (goods). [from obsolete *invoyes*, from Old French *envoyer*, to send]

invoke *verb* **1** to make an appeal to (God, some deity, a Muse, authority, etc) for help, support, or inspiration. **2** to appeal to (a law, principle, etc) as an authority or reason for eg one's behaviour. **3** to make an earnest appeal for (help, support, inspiration, etc). **4** to conjure up (a spirit) by reciting a spell. **5** to put (a law, decision, etc) into effect. See also INVOCATION. [from Latin *invocare*]

■ **1** call upon, conjure, appeal to, petition, implore, entreat, supplicate. **3** appeal for, solicit, beg, beseech, pray for.

involuntarily *adv.* in an involuntary way.

involuntary *adj.*, *said of an action, movement, muscle action, etc* done without being controlled by the will; not able to be controlled by the will; unintentional. [from Latin *involuntarius*]

■ automatic, mechanical, reflex, instinctive, conditioned, spontaneous, impulsive, unthinking, unconscious, uncontrolled, unintentional.

◨ voluntary, deliberate, intentional.

involuntary muscle *Anat.* muscle that is not under conscious control, eg muscle of the heart, blood vessels, stomach, and intestines. Also called SMOOTH MUSCLE.

involve *verb* **1** to require as a necessary part. **2** (**involve someone in something**) to cause them to take part or be implicated in it. **3** to have an effect on. **4 (involve oneself in something)** to become emotionally concerned in it. **5** to complicate. [from Latin *involvere*, to roll up]

■ **1** require, necessitate, mean, entail, include, incorporate, embrace, cover, take in. **2** implicate in, incriminate in, draw in, mix up in, embroil in. **3** affect, concern. **4** engage oneself in, occupy oneself with, absorb oneself in, preoccupy oneself with.

🗷 **1** exclude.

involved *adj.* **1** concerned, implicated. **2** complicated.

■ **1** concerned, implicated, mixed up, caught up, *colloq.* in on, participating. **2** complicated, complex, intricate, elaborate, tangled, knotty, tortuous, confusing.

🗷 **1** uninvolved. **2** simple.

involvement *noun* **1** involving. **2** being involved.

■ IMPLICATION, ENTANGLEMENT. **2** concern, interest, responsibility, association, connection, participation.

invulnerability *noun* being invulnerable.

invulnerable *adj.* that cannot be hurt, damaged, or attacked. [from Latin *invulnerabilis*]

■ safe, secure, unassailable, impenetrable, invincible, indestructible.

🗷 vulnerable.

invulnerably *adv.* in an invulnerable way or condition.

inward — *adj.* **1** placed or being within. **2** moving towards the inside. **3** of or relating to the mind, inner thoughts, or soul. — *adv.* (*also* **inwards**) **1** towards the inside or the centre. **2** into the mind, inner thoughts, or soul. [from Anglo-Saxon *inweard*]

■ *adj.* **1** inside, interior, internal, inner. **2** incoming, entering. **3** personal, private, secret, confidential, inmost, innermost.

🗷 *adj.* OUTWARD. **1** external.

inwardly *adv.* **1** on the inside; internally. **2** in one's thoughts; secretly.

inwards see INWARD.

in-your-face *adj. colloq., of a style, production, etc* aggressively assertive; demanding attention.

IOB *abbrev.* Institute of Building.

IOC *abbrev.* International Olympic Committee.

iodide *noun* a chemical compound containing iodine.

iodine /ˈaɪədiːn/ *noun* **1** *Chem.* (SYMBOL **I**, ATOMIC NUMBER 53) a non-metallic element consisting of dark violet crystals that sublime to a violet vapour when heated. It is used as an antiseptic, in the production of dyes, and as a catalyst and chemical reagent. Silver iodine is used in photography. Iodine is essential for the normal functioning of the thyroid gland. **2** *Medicine* (*also* **tincture of iodine**) a solution of iodine in ethanol (alcohol), used as an antiseptic. [from Greek *ioeides*, violet-coloured]

iodize or **iodise** *verb* to treat with iodine.

IOM *abbrev.* Isle of Man.

ion /aɪən/ *noun Chem.* an atom or group of atoms that has acquired a net positive charge as a result of losing one or more electrons, or a net negative charge as a result of gaining one or more electrons. [from Greek, = going]

-ion *suffix* forming nouns denoting a process, state, result, etc: *completion/contrition/pollution.* See also -ATION. [from French *-ion*]

ion engine *Engineering* an engine, used to propel spacecraft or satellites, in which the thrust is produced by a stream of ionized (charged) particles.

ion exchange *Chem.* a chemical reaction in which ions which have the same charge are exchanged between a solution and a porous granular solid, such as a synthetic resin, in contact with the solution. It is used to remove undesirable salts during the processes of water softening and sugar refining.

Ionic /aɪˈɒnɪk/ *adj.* denoting an order of classical architecture, characterized by slim and usually fluted shafts and capitals with spiral scrolls known as *volutes*. See also CO-RINTHIAN, DORIC. [from Greek *Ionikos*]

ionic *adj.* relating to or using ions.

ionic bond *Chem.* a chemical bond formed by the transfer of one or more electrons from one atom to another, resulting in the conversion of electrically neutral atoms to positively and negatively charged ions.

ion implantation *Electron.* the introduction of impurities into a semiconductor crystal, in order to modify its electronic properties, by directing a beam of ions at its surface.

ionization or **ionisation** /aɪənaɪˈzeɪʃən/ *noun Chem.* the formation of ions from atoms as a result of chemical reactions, dissociation of atoms of a molecule in solution, electrolysis, exposure to ionizing radiation (eg alpha particles) or short-wavelength electromagnetic radiation (eg X-rays), or passage through a discharge tube. Very high temperatures can also cause ionization.

ionize or **ionise** *verb trans., intrans. Chem.* to produce or cause to produce ions.

ionizer or **ioniser** *noun* a device that produces negatively charged ions, considered to relieve headaches, fatigue, and other symptoms said to be caused by the accumulation of positive ions in rooms and buildings where electrical machinery, computers, etc, are in frequent use.

ionizing radiation *Physics* any radiation that can cause ionization (formation of ions).

ionomer /aɪˈɒnəmə(r)/ *noun Chem.* a thermoplastic polymer which has both organic components (mainly ethylene) and inorganic components (such as sodium, potassium, magnesium, or zinc). Ionomers are tough, resilient, and highly transparent, and are used to make goggles, shields, etc.

ionosphere *noun Meteorol.* the layer of the Earth's atmosphere that extends from about 50km to about 500km above the Earth's surface. It contains many ions and free electrons produced by the ionizing effects of solar radiation, and it plays an important role in the transmission of radio waves. [from ION + SPHERE]

ionospheric *adj.* relating to the ionosphere.

iota /aɪˈoʊtə/ *noun* **1** the ninth letter of the Greek alphabet (I, ι). **2** a very small amount. [from Greek *iota*]

■ **2** scrap, bit, mite, jot, speck, trace, hint, grain, particle, atom.

IOU *noun* (PL. **IOUs, IOU's**) *colloq.* a written and signed note of a debt. [pronunciation of *I owe you*]

IOW *abbrev.* Isle of Wight.

IPA *abbrev.* International Phonetic Alphabet.

IPCS *abbrev.* Institution of Professional Civil Servants.

ipecacuanha /ɪpɪkakjʊˈɑːnə/ *noun* the dried root of several Latin American plants, used as a purgative or emetic. [from Portuguese *ipecacuanha*, from Tupi (S American Indian language) *ipekaaguene*, from *ipeh*, low + *kaa*, leaves + *guene*, vomit]

IPM *abbrev.* Institute of Personnel Management.

IPPF *abbrev.* International Planned Parenthood Federation.

ipso facto /ˈɪpsoʊ ˈfaktoʊ/ by or because of that very fact; thereby. [Latin, = by the fact itself]

IQ (PL. **IQs, IQ's**) *colloq.* intelligence quotient.

Ir *symbol Chem.* iridium.

ir- *prefix* a form of *in-* used before words beginning in *r*: *irrelevant.*

IRA *abbrev.* Irish Republican Army.

Iranian — *noun* **1** a native or citizen of Iran. **2** a branch of the Indo-European family of languages. — *adj.* relating to the Iranians or their language, history, or culture.

irascibility *noun* being irascible.

irascible *adj.* easily made angry; irritable. [from Latin *irascibilis*, from *ira*, anger]

irascibly *adv.* with an irascible manner.

irate *adj.* very angry; enraged. [from Latin *iratus*, from *ira*, anger]

. . . .

◨ annoyed, indignant, up in arms, angry, enraged, *colloq.* mad, furious, infuriated, incensed, fuming, livid, exasperated.
◧ calm, composed.

. . . .

irately *adv.* furiously, angrily.

irateness *noun* being irate, fury.

ire /aɪə(r)/ *noun* anger. [from Latin *ira*]

ireful *adj.* **1** angry. **2** resentful.

iridescence *noun* an iridescent quality.

iridescent /ɪrɪˈdɛsənt/ *adj.* having many bright rainbow-like colours which seem to shimmer and change constantly. [from Greek *iris*, rainbow]

iridium /ɪˈrɪdɪəm/ *noun Chem.* (SYMBOL **Ir**, ATOMIC NUMBER 77) a silvery metal that is resistant to corrosion, and is mainly used in hard alloys with platinum or osmium to make surgical instruments, pen nibs, bearings, electrical contacts, and crucibles. [from Greek *iris*, rainbow, from the colourful appearance of some solutions of its salts]

iris /ˈaɪrɪs/ *noun* **1** (PL. **irises**, **irides**) a perennial plant of the genus *Iris*, having an underground rhizome or corm, flattened sword-shaped leaves, and large brilliantly coloured flowers. **2** *Anat.* an adjustable pigmented ring of muscle, lying in front of the lens of the eye and surrounding the pupil. It controls the amount of light entering the eye by increasing or decreasing the size of the pupil. **3** (**iris diaphragm**) a device consisting of a series of thin overlapping crescent-shaped plates surrounding a central circular aperture. By adjustment of the plates the diameter of the aperture can be continuously varied, eg to control the amount of light entering the lens of a camera. [from Greek *iris*, rainbow]

Irish — *adj.* **1** of Ireland, its inhabitants, history, culture, Celtic language, or dialect of English. **2** *colloq.* amusingly contradictory or inconsistent. — *noun* **1** (**the Irish**) the people of Ireland as a group. **2** (*in full* **Irish Gaelic**) the Celtic language of Ireland. **3** whiskey made in Ireland. [from Anglo-Saxon *Iras*, people of Ireland]

Irish coffee coffee served with a dash of Irish whiskey and cream on top.

Irish elk a giant fossil deer that ranged through open woodland from Ireland to Siberia and China during the Pleistocene epoch.

Irishman *noun* a man who is Irish by birth or descent.

Irish moss an edible red seaweed found in the N Atlantic Ocean, used for making soup.

Irish stew a stew made from mutton, potatoes, and onions.

Irish wolfhound the tallest domestic breed of dog, a very old breed, used for hunting by the Celts, and having a long, usually grey, coat, and soft ears.

Irishwoman *noun* a woman who is Irish by birth or descent.

irk *verb* to annoy or irritate, especially persistently. [from Middle English *irken*]

irksome *adj.* annoying, irritating, or boring.

iron /aɪən/ — *noun* **1** (SYMBOL **Fe**, ATOMIC NUMBER 26) a strong hard silvery-white metallic element that is naturally magnetic, and is thought to be the main component of the Earth's core. **2** a tool, weapon, or other implement made of iron. **3** a triangular, flat-bottomed, now usually electrical, household tool used for smoothing the creases out of and pressing clothes. **4** a golf club with an angled iron head. **5** (*in full* **branding-iron**) a metal instrument with a long handle and shaped end which can be heated and used to mark animals for identification. **6** great physical or mental strength. **7** (**irons**) chains; fetters. **8** (**irons**) supports for a weak or lame leg or legs. — *adj.* **1** made of iron. **2** like iron, especially in being very strong, inflexible, unyielding, etc. — *verb* (**ironed**, **ironing**) **1** to smooth the creases out of or press (eg clothes) with an iron. **2** (*also* **iron something out**) to remove creases in it by ironing. **3** *intrans.*, *said of clothing or fabric* to react or respond in the way specified to being ironed: *shiny material which irons badly.* — **iron something out** to remove or put right difficulties, problems, etc so that progress becomes easier. **have several** or **too many irons in the fire** to have several or too many commitments at the same time. **strike while the iron is hot** to act while the situation is to one's advantage. [from Anglo-Saxon *isen*]

. . . .

◨ *adj.* **2** rigid, inflexible, adamant, determined, hard, steely, tough, strong. *verb* **1** press, smooth, flatten. **iron out** resolve, settle, sort out, straighten out, clear up, put right, deal with, get rid of, eradicate, eliminate.
◧ *adj.* **2** pliable, weak.

. . . .

Iron Age the period in history following the Bronze Age, when weapons and tools were made of iron, from about 1000 BC.

ironclad — *adj.* covered with protective iron plates. — *noun Hist.* a 19c warship covered with protective iron plates.

Iron Curtain from 1945 to 1989, a notional barrier between countries in W Europe and the communist countries of E Europe, which hindered trade and communications.

iron-grey *adj.* dark grey.

ironic or **ironical** *adj.* **1** containing, characterized by, or expressing irony. **2** *said of a person* given to frequent use of irony.

. . . .

◨ SARCASTIC, SARDONIC. **1** mocking, satirical, wry, paradoxical.

. . . .

ironically *adv.* in an ironic way.

ironing *noun* clothes and household linen, etc which need to be or have just been ironed.

ironing board a collapsible, narrow wooden or metal table with a thick fitted cover, used for ironing clothes.

iron lung an apparatus consisting of a long metal case which covers the body up to the neck and which by means of rhythmically varying air pressure helps the person in it to breathe.

ironmaster *noun* the owner of an ironworks.

ironmonger *noun Brit.* a person who sells articles made of metal, eg tools, locks, etc and other household hardware.

ironmongery *noun* (PL. **ironmongeries**) *Brit.* the business of, or the goods sold by, an ironmonger.

iron pyrites see PYRITE.

iron rations small quantities of food with a high energy value, carried for emergencies by climbers, walkers, military personnel, etc.

Ironsides *pl. noun Hist.* Oliver Cromwell's cavalry during the English Civil War (1642–9).

ironstone *noun* **1** *Geol.* a sedimentary rock, at least 15 per cent of which comprises iron minerals such as haematite and pyrite. **2** hard, white earthenware.

ironware *noun* things made of iron, especially household hardware.

ironwork *noun* **1** things made of iron, especially iron which has been specially shaped for decoration, such as gates and railings. **2** (**ironworks**) a factory where iron is smelted and made into goods.

irony *noun* (PL. **ironies**) **1** a linguistic device or form of humour that takes its effect from stating or implying the opposite of what is the case or what is intended; eg *you have done well* might be used to refer to someone who has done badly. **2** a dramatic device by which information is given to the audience that is not known to all the participants in the drama, or in which the same words are meant to convey different meanings to the audience and to other participants; eg the fact that one of the characters being discussed in the drama is actually dead. **3** awkward or perverse circumstances applying to a situation that is in itself satisfactory or desirable. [from Greek *eironeia*, dissimulation]

....

▣ **1** sarcasm, mockery, satire, paradox, incongruity. **3** perversity, contrariness.

....

Iroquois *noun* a Native American people of the NE region, concentrated in the Great Lakes area.

irradiate *verb* **1** to expose a part of the body to electromagnetic radiation or a radioactive source for diagnostic or therapeutic purposes. **2** to preserve food by exposing it to electromagnetic radiation or a radioactive source in order to destroy bacteria and other micro-organisms. **3** to shed light on; to light up. **4** to make bright or clear intellectually or spiritually. [from Latin *irradiare*]

irradiation *noun* **1** *Medicine* exposure of part of the body to electromagnetic radiation, eg X-rays, or a radioactive source, for diagnostic or therapeutic purposes, eg the use of certain radioactive isotopes to treat cancerous tumours. **2** *Optics* an optical illusion that causes bright objects to appear larger than their actual size when viewed against a dark background. It is a result of spreading of excitation of the retina. **3** a highly effective method of preserving food by exposing it to either ultraviolet radiation, which sterilizes the food surface, or ionizing radiation from radioactive isotopes, which destroys micro-organisms. **4** the use of microwaves (high-energy electromagnetic radiation) to heat food.

irrational — *adj.* **1** not the result of clear, logical thought. **2** not able to think logically and clearly. **3** *Maths.*, *said of a root, expression, etc* involving irrational numbers. — *noun* an irrational number. [from Latin *irrationalis*]

....

▣ *adj.* **1** illogical, unsound, unreasonable, absurd, crazy, wild, foolish, silly, senseless.
▣ *adj.* RATIONAL.

....

irrationality *noun* being irrational.

irrational number *Maths.* a real number that cannot be expressed as a fraction in the form m/n, where m and n are integers. Irrational numbers can be expressed to any degree of accuracy, but their exact value can never be calculated, eg π (the ratio of the circumference of a circle to its diameter, equal to approximately 3.141592...), and surds such as $\sqrt{2}$.

irreconcilability *noun* being irreconcilable.

irreconcilable *adj.* **1** not agreeing or able to be brought into agreement; inconsistent; incompatible. **2** hostile and opposed; unwilling to be friendly.

....

▣ OPPOSED. **1** incompatible, conflicting, clashing, contradictory, inconsistent. **2** hostile, unfriendly.
▣ **1** reconcilable.

....

irreconcilably *adv.* so as to be irreconcilable.
irrecoverable *adj.* not able to be recovered.
irrecoverably *adv.* so as to be irrecoverable.
irredeemable *adj.* **1** *said of a person* too evil to be saved; beyond help. **2** incapable of being recovered, repaired, or cured. **3** *said of shares, etc* which the issuing company does not have the right to buy back from the shareholder for the sum originally paid. **4** *said of paper money* which cannot be exchanged for coin.
irredeemably *adv.* so as to be irredeemable.
irredentism / ɪrɪˈdɛntɪsm/ *noun* the policy or activities of the irredentists.
irredentist / ɪrɪˈdɛntɪst/ *noun* a person, especially in 19c Italy, who is in favour of his or her country recovering ter-

ritory which belonged to it in the past. [from Italian *Italia irredenta*, unredeemed Italy]

irreducible *adj.* **1** that cannot be reduced or made simpler. **2** that cannot be brought from one state into another, usually desired, state.

irreducibly *adv.* so as to be irreducible.

irrefutable / ɪrɪˈfjuːtəbl/ *adj.* not able to be denied or proved false. [from Latin *irrefutabilis*]

....

▣ undeniable, incontrovertible, indisputable, incontestable, unquestionable, certain, sure.
▣ questionable.

....

irregular — *adj.* **1** not happening or occurring at regular or equal intervals. **2** not smooth, even, or balanced. **3** not conforming to rules, custom, accepted or normal behaviour, or to routine. **4** *Grammar, said of a word, especially a verb or noun* not changing its form (eg to show tenses or plurals) according to the usual patterns in the language. **5** *said of troops* not belonging to the regular army. — *noun* an irregular soldier. [from Latin *irregularis*]

....

▣ *adj.* **1** intermittent, sporadic, spasmodic, occasional, erratic, fitful, variable, fluctuating, wavering, random, haphazard, disorderly, unsystematic. **2** rough, bumpy, uneven, crooked. **3** unconventional, unorthodox, improper, unusual, exceptional, anomalous, abnormal.
▣ *adj.* REGULAR. **2** smooth, even. **3** conventional, orthodox, standard, normal.

....

irregularity *noun* (PL. **irregularities**) **1** being irregular. **2** an act or behaviour not conforming to expected standards. **3** a bump or patch of roughness on an otherwise smooth surface.

irrelevance or **irrelevancy** *noun* (PL. **irrelevancies**) being irrelevant, lack of relevance.

irrelevant *adj.* not connected with or applying to the subject in hand; not relevant.

....

▣ immaterial, beside the point, inapplicable, inappropriate, unrelated, unconnected, peripheral, tangential.
▣ relevant.

....

irreligion *noun* **1** lack of religion. **2** lack of respect for or opposition or hostility towards religion.

irreligious *adj.* **1** lacking a religion. **2** lacking in respect for or hostile or opposed to religion. [from Latin *irreligiosus*]

irremediable *adj.* which cannot be made better, cured, or corrected. [from Latin *irremediabilis*]

irremediably *adv.* so as to be irremediable.

irremovable *adj.* not able to be removed.

irremovably *adv.* so as to be irremovable, permanently.

irreparability *noun* being irreparable.

irreparable / ɪˈrɛpərəbl/ *adj.* not able to be restored or put right. [from Latin *irreparabilis*]

irreparably *adv.* so as to be irreparable.

irreplaceable *adj.* not able to be replaced, especially because too rare or valuable.

....

▣ unique, peerless, matchless, priceless, indispensable, essential, vital.
▣ replaceable, dispensable.

....

irreplaceably *adv.* so as to be irreplaceable.

irrepressibility *noun* being irrepressible.

irrepressible *adj.* not able to be controlled, restrained, or repressed, especially because of being too lively and full of energy or strength.

....

▣ uncontrollable, ungovernable, boisterous, ebullient, bubbly, buoyant, resilient.

....

irreproachable *adj., said especially of behaviour* free from faults; blameless.

⊟ irreprehensible, blameless, unimpeachable, faultless, impeccable, perfect, unblemished, immaculate, stainless, spotless, pure.
⊟ blameworthy, culpable.

irresistibility or **irresistibleness** *noun* being irresistible.
irresistible *adj.* too strong, tempting, or attractive to be resisted; overpowering. [from Latin *irresistibilis*]

⊟ overwhelming, overpowering, uncontrollable, unavoidable, inevitable, inescapable, powerful, potent, compelling, imperative, pressing, urgent, tempting, enticing, seductive, ravishing.
⊟ resistible, avoidable.

irresolute *adj.* hesitating or doubtful; not able to take firm decisions; showing that no firm decision has been taken.
irresoluteness or **irresolution** *noun* being irresolute.
irrespective *adj.* (**irrespective of something**) without considering or taking it into account.
irresponsibility *noun* 1 being irresponsible. 2 lack of responsibility.
irresponsible *adj.* 1 done without or showing no concern for the consequences; reckless; careless. 2 not able to bear responsibility; not reliable or trustworthy.

⊟ CARELESS, NEGLIGENT, WILD. 1 ill-considered, rash, reckless, thoughtless, heedless. 2 unreliable, untrustworthy, flighty, fickle, immature.
⊟ RESPONSIBLE.

irretrievable *adj.* not able to be recovered or put right.
irretrievably *adv.* so as to be irretrievable.
irreverence *noun* 1 lack of reverence, disrespect. 2 a disrespectful act or remark.
irreverent *adj.* lacking respect or reverence (eg for things considered sacred, or important people). [from Latin *irreverentia*]

⊟ sacrilegious, blasphemous, disrespectful, discourteous, rude, impudent, impertinent, mocking, flippant.
⊟ reverent, respectful.

irreversible *adj.* not able to be changed back to a former or original state; permanent.

⊟ irrevocable, final, permanent, lasting, irreparable, irremediable, irretrievable.
⊟ reversible, revocable, reparable, remediable.

irreversible reaction *Chem.* a chemical reaction which takes place in one direction only, and therefore proceeds to completion.
irreversibly *adv.* so as to be irreversible.
irrevocability *noun* being irrevocable.
irrevocable /ɪˈrɛvəkəbl/ *adj.* that cannot be changed, stopped, or undone. [from Latin *irrevocabilis*]

⊟ unalterable, unchangeable, invariable, immutable, final, fixed, settled, predetermined, irreversible.
⊟ revocable, alterable, reversible.

irrigable /ˈɪrɪgəbl/ *adj.* capable of being irrigated.
irrigate *verb* 1 *said of a river, etc* to provide (land) with a supply of water. 2 to supply water to (agricultural land) by channels or other artificial means. 3 *Medicine* to wash out (the eye, or a wound, body cavity, or hollow organ, eg the colon), with a continuous flow of water or antiseptic solution. [from Latin *irrigare*]

irrigation *noun* the supply of water to agricultural land by artificial means, such as channels, dams, or sprinklers, especially to enable crops to be grown in dry regions.
irritability or **irritableness** *noun* being irritable.
irritable *adj.* 1 easily annoyed, angered, or excited. 2 extremely or excessively sensitive. 3 *Biol.* denoting a living organism that is capable of responding to an external stimulus, such as light, heat, or touch.

⊟ 1 cross, bad-tempered, ill-tempered, crotchety, crusty, cantankerous, crabby, testy, short-tempered, snappy, impatient, touchy, edgy, peevish, fretful, fractious. 2 hypersensitive, thin-skinned.
⊟ 1 good-tempered.

irritable bowel syndrome *Medicine* a condition in which the mucous membrane lining the colon becomes inflamed, causing abdominal pain, with constipation or diarrhoea.
irritant — *noun* 1 any chemical, physical, or biological agent that causes irritation of a tissue, especially inflammation of the skin or eyes, eg nettles. 2 something that causes physical or mental irritation. — *adj.* irritating.
irritate *verb* 1 to make angry or annoyed. 2 to make (part of the body, an organ, etc) sore and swollen or itchy. 3 *Biol.* to stimulate (eg an organ) to respond. [from Latin *irritare*]

⊟ 1 annoy, *colloq.* aggravate, bother, harass, nettle, *colloq.* needle, provoke, rile, anger, enrage, infuriate, incense, exasperate. 2 inflame, chafe, rub, tickle, itch.
⊟ 1 please.

irritating *adj.* that irritates.
irritation *noun* 1 something that irritates. 2 irritating. 3 being irritated.

⊟ 1 irritant, nuisance. 2 provocation. 3 annoyance, *colloq.* aggravation, displeasure, dissatisfaction, anger, vexation, indignation, fury, exasperation, crossness, testiness, snappiness, impatience.
⊟ 3 pleasure, delight.

irrupt *verb intrans.* (**irrupt into a place**) to burst into it or enter it suddenly with speed and violence. [from Latin *irrumpere*]
irruption *noun* entering violently, violent entry.
irruptive *adj.* 1 irrupting or tending to irrupt. 2 relating to or causing irruption.
IRS *abbrev.* Internal Revenue Service (USA).
is see BE.
ISA *abbrev. Finance* Individual Savings Account.
ISBN *abbrev.* International Standard Book Number.
ischaemia or **ischemia** /ɪˈskiːmɪə/ *noun Medicine* an inadequate flow of blood to a part of the body, caused by blockage or constriction of a blood vessel. [from Greek *ischein*, restrain + *haima*, blood]
ISDN *abbrev.* integrated services digital network, an advanced telecommunications network.
-ise see -IZE.
-ish *suffix* forming adjectives meaning: 1 slightly; fairly; having a trace of: *reddish/autumnish*. 2 like; having the qualities of: *childish*. 3 having as a nationality: *Swedish*. 4 approximately; about; roughly: *fiftyish*. [from Anglo-Saxon *-isc*]
isinglass /ˈaɪzɪŋglɑːs/ *noun* 1 the purest form of animal gelatine, made from the dried swim bladders of certain fish, eg sturgeon. It has strong adhesive properties. 2 thin transparent sheets of mica used in furnace and stove doors. [from Old Dutch *huizenblas*, sturgeon's bladder]
ISIS *abbrev.* Independent Schools Information Service.
Islam *noun* the religion that originated in Arabia during the 7c AD through the prophet Muhammad. Followers of

Islam are known as Muslims, or Moslems, and their religion embraces every aspect of life.

Islamic *adj.* relating to Islam, Muslim.

Islamicist /ɪzˈlamɪsɪst/ a person who studies Islam, Islamic law or Islamic culture.

Islamicize or **Islamicise** /ɪzˈlamɪsaɪz/ *verb* to Islamize.

Islamization or **Islamicization** *noun* the process of making Islamic.

Islamize or **Islamise** *verb* to cause to become a follower of or conform to Islam.

island *noun* **1** a piece of land completely surrounded by water. **2** anything which is like an island, especially in being isolated or detached. **3** (*in full* **traffic island**) a small raised traffic-free area in the middle of a street on which people may stand when crossing the road. [from Anglo-Saxon *iegland*, with the *s* from Old French *isle*]

island arc *Geol.* an arc-shaped (curved) chain of oceanic islands, eg the islands of Japan, that usually contain active volcanoes.

islander /ˈaɪləndə(r)/ *noun* a person who lives on an island.

isle /aɪl/ *noun* an island, especially a small one. [from Old French *isle*]

islet /ˈaɪlət/ *noun* **1** a small island. **2** a small area of tissue which has a different nature and structure to the tissue surrounding it.

islets of Langerhans /ˈaɪləts əv ˈlɑːŋəhɑːns/ *Anat.* in vertebrates, small groups of specialized cells scattered throughout the pancreas. They control the level of glucose (sugar) in the blood by secreting the hormones insulin and glucagon. [named after the German anatomist Paul Langerhans, who described them in 1869]

ism *noun colloq., usually derog.* a distinctive and formal set of ideas, principles, or beliefs. [from -ISM, regarded as a separate word]

-ism *suffix* forming nouns meaning: **1** a formal set of beliefs, ideas, principles, etc: *feminism*. **2** a quality or state: *heroism*. **3** an activity or practice, or its result: *criticism*. **4** discrimination or prejudice on the grounds of: *ageism*. **5** an illness caused by, causing resemblance to, or named after (something or someone stated): *alcoholism/dwarfism*. **6** a characteristic of (a specified language or type of language): *regionalism*. [from Greek *-ismos* or *-isma*]

isn't *contr.* is not.

ISO *abbrev.* **1** Imperial Service Order. **2** International Standards Organization.

iso- *combining form* forming words meaning 'same, equal'. [from Greek *isos*, equal]

isobar /ˈaɪsoʊbɑː(r)/ *noun* **1** a line drawn on a weather chart connecting points that have the same atmospheric pressure at a given time. They can be used to make forecasts, eg closely packed isobars are associated with strong winds. **2** *Physics* either of two atoms which have the same total number of protons and neutrons in their nuclei, but have different numbers of protons and therefore different atomic numbers and chemical properties. [from Greek *isobares*, of equal weight]

isobaric *adj.* **1** relating to or measured in isobars. **2** having equal atmospheric pressure.

isochronal /aɪˈsɒkrənəl/ or **isochronous** /aɪˈsɒkrənəs/ *adj.* **1** having the same length of time. **2** performed or happening at the same time. **3** happening at equal or regular intervals. [from Greek *isochronos*, equal in age or time]

isolate *verb* **1** to separate from others; to cause to be alone. **2** to place in quarantine. **3** to separate or detach, especially to allow closer examination: *isolate a problem*. **4** to separate so as to obtain in a pure or uncombined form. [from Italian *isolare*, from Latin *insula*, island]

⊞ **1** set apart, sequester, seclude, cut off, separate, keep apart, segregate, alienate, shut out, ostracize, exclude. **3** separate, detach, remove, cut off, disconnect.

⊟ **1** integrate, incorporate, assimilate.

isolated *adj.* **1** placed or standing alone or apart. **2** separate. **3** solitary; single: *an isolated occurrence*.

⊞ **1** secluded, cut off, lonely, remote, out-of-the-way. **2** separate, detached, disconnected. **3** solitary, single, unique, special, exceptional, atypical, anomalous.

isolation *noun* **1** isolating. **2** being isolated. **3** separation.

⊞ **1** separation, segregation. **2** quarantine, solitude, loneliness, remoteness, seclusion, retirement, exile. **3** separation, detachment, disconnection.

isolationism *noun* the policy of not joining with other countries in international political and economic affairs.

isolationist — *noun* a person who supports or promotes isolationism. — *adj.* relating to isolationism or isolationists.

isoleucine /aɪsoʊˈljuːsiːn/ *noun Biochem.* an essential amino acid found in proteins.

isomer /ˈaɪsəmə(r)/ *noun* **1** *Chem.* one of two or more chemical compounds that have the same chemical formula, ie the same molecular composition, but different three-dimensional structures. As a result they may have different physical and chemical properties. **2** *Physics* one of two or more atomic nuclei with the same atomic number and mass number, but with different energy states and radioactive properties, eg different half-lives. [from Greek *isomeres*, having equal parts]

isomeric *adj. Chem.* identical in every way except in the arrangement of atoms.

isometric *adj.* **1** having equal size or measurements. **2** *said of muscle movement* with the muscle tense and with an increase of muscle strength and tone but without the muscle being contracted or shortened (eg without causing a limb to bend). **3** *said of a three-dimensional drawing* in which the three faces shown are drawn at the same angle to the drawing surface so that all of the lines are equally foreshortened. [from ISO- + Greek *metron*, measure]

isometrics *sing. or pl. noun* a system of physical exercises for strengthening and toning the body in which the muscles are pushed either together or against an immovable object and are not contracted or flexed or made to bend limbs.

isomorph *noun* an individual, chemical, or set, etc in an isomorphic relation with another.

isomorphic or **isomorphous** *adj.* showing isomorphism.

isomorphism *noun* **1** *Biol.* apparent similarity of form between individuals belonging to different races or species. **2** *Chem.* the existence of two or more chemical compounds with the same crystal structure. **3** *Maths.* a one-to-one correspondence between the elements of two or more sets and between the sums or products of the elements of one set and those of the equivalent elements of the other set or sets. [from ISO- + Greek *morphe*, form]

isoprene *noun Chem.* (FORMULA C_5H_8) a colourless liquid hydrocarbon that is the basic unit of natural rubber, and can be polymerized to form synthetic rubber. [from ISO- + *propyl*, the name of an alkyl group, + *-ene*]

isosceles /aɪˈsɒsəliːz/ *adj., said of a triangle* having two sides of equal length. [from Greek *isos*, equal + *skelos*, leg]

isostasy /aɪˈsɒstəsɪ/ *noun Geol.* a theoretical state of equilibrium in which the Earth's crust, which is considered to consist of large blocks of material of relatively low density, floats on the surface of the much denser semi-solid material of the Earth's mantle. [from Greek *isos*, equal + *stasis*, setting]

isotherm *noun* a line on a weather map connecting places where the temperature is the same at a particular time or where the average is the same for a particular period of time. [from Greek *isos*, equal + *therme*, heat]

isotonic *adj.* **1** *Chem.* denoting a solution that has the same osmotic pressure as another solution with which it is being compared. **2** denoting a drink designed to replace the salts and minerals lost from the body in sweat. [from ISO- + Greek *tonos*, tension, tone]

isotope *noun Chem.* one of two or more atoms of the same chemical element that contain the same number of protons but different numbers of neutrons in their nuclei. Isotopes of an element have the same atomic number and chemical properties, but different mass numbers and physical properties. [from ISO- + Greek *topos*, place (ie on the periodic table)]

isotopic *adj.* relating to or involving an isotope or isotopes.

isotropic *adj., said of a substance, material, etc* having physical properties (eg magnetism and elasticity) which do not vary with direction. [from ISO- + Greek *tropos*, turn]

ISP *abbrev. Comput.* Internet Service Provider, a company that provides access to the Internet.

Israeli / ɪzˈreɪliː/ — *adj.* of the modern state of Israel or its inhabitants. — *noun* a person born or living in the modern state of Israel. [from Hebrew *Yisrael*, God perseveres]

Israelite /ˈɪzrəlaɪt/ — *noun Hist.* a person born or living in the ancient kingdom of Israel (922 BC–721 BC), especially a Jew claiming descent from Jacob. — *adj.* of the ancient kingdom of Israel or its inhabitants.

issue — *noun* **1** the giving out, publishing, or making available of something, eg stamps, a magazine, etc. **2** that which is given out, published, or made available, eg stamps, a magazine, book, etc. **3** one item in a regular series: *the December issue of the magazine.* **4** a subject for discussion or argument. **5** a result or consequence. **6** *formal* children; offspring. **7** an act of going or flowing out. **8** a way out, outlet, or outflow, eg where a stream begins. — *verb* **1** to give or send out, distribute, publish, or make available, especially officially or formally. **2** (**issue someone with something**) to supply them with something required, eg an official document. **3** *intrans.* (often **issue forth** or **out**) to flow or come out, especially in large quantities. **4** (**issue in something**) to end or result in it. **5** (**issue from someone** or **something**) to come or descend from them; to be produced or caused by them. — **at issue 1** in dispute or disagreement. **2** under discussion. **force the issue** to act so as to force a decision to be taken. **join** or **take issue with someone** to disagree with them. **make an issue of something** to make it the explicit subject of an argument or disagreement. [from Old French *issue*, from Latin *exitus*, exit]

. . . .

▤ *noun* **1** publication, release, distribution, supply, delivery, circulation, promulgation, broadcast, announcement. **3** copy, number, instalment, edition. **4** subject, topic, question, matter, affair, concern, problem, debate, argument, dispute, controversy. *verb* **1** publish, release, distribute, deliver, give out, send out, circulate, promulgate, broadcast, announce, put out, emit. **2** supply, provide. **3** emerge, burst forth, gush, flow. **5** come from, originate from, stem from, spring from, proceed from, arise from.

. . . .

issuing house a merchant bank which specializes in the issue of shares and bonds on the stock market.

-ist *suffix* forming words denoting: **1** a believer in some formal system of ideas, principles or beliefs: *feminist.* **2** a person who carries out some activity or practises some art: *novelist.* [from Greek *-istes*]

isthmus /ˈɪsməs/ *noun* (PL. **isthmuses**) **1** a narrow strip of land, bounded by water on both sides, joining two larger areas of land. **2** *Anat.* a narrow or constricted region of an organ or tissue. [from Greek *isthmos*]

IT *abbrev.* information technology.

it[1] — *pron.* **1** the thing, animal, small baby, or group already mentioned. **2** the person in question: *who is it?* **3** used as the subject with impersonal verbs and when describing the weather or distance or telling the time. **4** used as the grammatical subject of a sentence when the real subject comes later: *it's not a very good idea running away.*

5 used to refer to a general situation or state of affairs: *how's it going?* **6** used to emphasize a certain word or phrase in a sentence: *when is it her train is due to arrive?* **7** exactly what is needed, suitable or available: *that's it!* **8** used with many verbs and prepositions as an object with little meaning: *run for it.* — *noun* **1** the person in a children's game who has to oppose all the others, eg by trying to catch them. **2** *old colloq. use* sex appeal. **3** *colloq.* sexual intercourse. [from Anglo-Saxon *hit*]

it[2] *noun old colloq. use* Italian vermouth. [abbreviation]

ITA *abbrev.* Independent Television Authority (now IBA).

i.t.a. or **ITA** *abbrev.* Initial Teaching Alphabet.

Italian — *adj.* of Italy, its inhabitants, culture, history, or the Romance language spoken there. — *noun* **1** a person born or living in Italy. **2** the Romance language spoken in Italy and in parts of Switzerland. [from Latin *Italianus*, from *Italia*, Italy]

Italianate *adj.* of or in an Italian style, especially of decoration, architecture, or art.

italic — *adj.* **1** of or in a typeface with characters which slope upwards to the right. **2** (**Italic**) of ancient Italy. — *noun* (*usually* **italics**) a typeface, first used in Italy, with characters which slope upwards to the right or a letter printed or written in this typeface. [from Greek *Italikos*]

italicization or **italicisation** *noun* putting or being in italics.

italicize or **italicise** *verb* to print or write in italics.

Italo- *combining form* of Italy, the Italians, etc.

ITC *abbrev.* Independent Television Commission.

itch — *noun* **1** an unpleasant irritation on the surface of the skin which makes one want to scratch. **2** *colloq.* a strong or restless desire. **3** a skin disease or condition which causes a constant unpleasant irritation, especially scabies. — *verb* **1** *intrans.* to have an itch and want to scratch. **2** *trans., intrans.* to cause (someone) to feel an itch. **3** *intrans. colloq.* to feel a strong or restless desire. [from Anglo-Saxon *giccan*]

. . . .

▤ *noun* **1** itchiness, tickle, irritation, prickling. **2** eagerness, keenness, desire, longing, yearning, hankering, craving. *verb* **2** tickle, prickle.

. . . .

itchiness *noun* being itchy.

itchy *adj.* (**itchier, itchiest**) causing or affected with an itch or itching.

itchy feet *colloq.* the strong desire to leave, move, or travel.

itchy palm or **itching palm** greed for money.

it'd *contr.* **1** it had. **2** it would.

-ite *suffix* forming nouns denoting: **1** a place, origin, or national group: *Israelite.* **2** a follower of or believer in: *pre-Raphaelite/anti-Semite.* **3** a fossil: *ammonite.* **4** a mineral: *graphite.* **5** a salt of a certain formula: *nitrite.* So also -ATE, -IDE. **6** an explosive: *dynamite.* [from Greek *-ites*]

item *noun* **1** a separate item, object, or unit, especially one on a list. **2** a separate piece of information or news. [from Latin *item*, likewise]

. . . .

▤ PIECE. **1** object, article, thing, entry, component, ingredient, element, factor, consideration, matter. **2** article, piece, report, account, notice, point, detail, particular.

. . . .

itemization or **itemisation** *noun* listing or being listed item by item.

itemize or **itemise** *verb* to list (things) separately, eg on a bill.

iterate *verb* to say or do again; to repeat. [from Latin *iterare*, from *iterim*, again]

iteration *noun* repetition.

iterative *adj.* repeating.

itinerant — *adj.* travelling from place to place, eg on business. — *noun* an itinerant person. [from Latin *iter*, journey]

. . . .

◨ *adj.* travelling, peripatetic, roving, roaming, wandering, rambling, nomadic, migratory, rootless, unsettled.
◨ *adj.* stationary, settled.

. . . .

itinerary *noun* (PL. **itineraries**) **1** a plan of one's route for a journey or trip. **2** a diary or record of a journey. **3** a guidebook. [from Latin *iter*, journey]

. . . .

◨ **1** route, course, journey, tour, circuit, plan, programme, schedule.

. . . .

-itis *combining form* **1** *in the names of diseases* denoting inflammation: *appendicitis*. **2** *colloq.* in ad hoc formations, denoting distress or suffering caused by an excess: *jazzitis*. [from Greek *-itis*]

it'll *contr.* **1** it will. **2** it shall.

ITN *abbrev.* Independent Television News.

its — *adj.* belonging to it. — *pron.* the one or ones belonging to it.

it's *contr.* **1** it is. **2** it has.

itself *pron.* **1** the reflexive form of *it.* **2** used for emphasis. **3** (*also* **by itself**) alone; without help.

itsy-bitsy or **itty-bitty** *adj. colloq.* very small. [a rhyming compound based on *little bit*]

ITT *abbrev.* International Telephone and Telegraph Corporation.

ITU *abbrev.* International Telecommunication Union.

ITV *abbrev. Brit.* Independent Television.

-ity *suffix* forming words denoting a state or quality, or an instance of it: *authority/irregularity.* [from French *-ité*]

IUD *abbrev.* intrauterine device.

I've *contr.* I have.

-ive *suffix* forming words denoting a quality, action, etc, or a person associated with it: *creative/detective.* [from French *-if*]

IVF *abbrev.* in-vitro fertilization.

ivory — *noun* **1** a hard white material that forms the tusks of the elephant, walrus, etc, formerly used to make ornaments, art objects, and piano keys. **2** the creamy-white colour of this substance. **3** an article made from this substance. **4** (**ivories**) *colloq.* the keys on a piano. — *adj.* of or resembling this material, especially in colour. [from Latin *ebur*]

ivory tower a place where one can be secluded from the unpleasant realities of life.

ivy *noun* (PL. **ivies**) **1** an evergreen shrub with dark leaves with five points which climbs on walls and trees. **2** any of several other climbing plants, such as poison ivy.

Ivy League a group of long-established colleges and universities in NE USA, formally established in 1956 to oversee inter-collegiate sports.

ixia *noun* a plant of the iris family with large showy flowers, originally found in S Africa. [from Greek *ixos*, mistletoe]

-ization or **-isation** *suffix* forming nouns of action corresponding to verbs in *-ize or -ise.*

-ize or **-ise** *suffix* forming verbs meaning: **1** to make or become: *equalize.* **2** to treat or react to (in a stated way): *criticize.* **3** to engage in (a stated activity): *theorize.* [from Latin *-izare*]

J

J¹ or **j** *noun* (PL. **Js, J's, j's**) the tenth letter of the English alphabet.

J² *abbrev.* joule.

jab — *verb trans., intrans.* (**jabbed, jabbing**) (**jab something** or **jab at something**) to poke or prod it. — *noun* **1** a poke or prod. **2** *colloq.* an injection or inoculation. **3** *Boxing* a short straight punch. [from Middle English *jobben*]

....

◨ *verb* poke, prod, stab, dig, nudge, elbow, push, thrust, lunge, punch.

....

jabber — *verb intrans., trans.* (**jabbered, jabbering**) to talk or utter rapidly and indistinctly. — *noun* rapid indistinct speech. [imitative]

jabot /ˈʒaboʊ/ *noun* a lace ruffle for a shirt front, worn especially with full Highland dress. [from French *jabot*]

jack — *noun* **1** a device for raising heavy objects off the ground. **2** *Cards* the court card of least value, bearing a picture of a page (Also called KNAVE). **3** *Bowls* the small white ball that players aim at. **4** a small national flag flown at the bows of a ship. **5** one of the playing-pieces used in the game of jacks. **6** *Electr.* (also **jack socket**) a socket taking a single-pronged plug (see JACK PLUG). **7** the male of certain animals, eg the donkey. — *verb* (often **jack something up**) to raise it with a jack. — **every man jack** everybody. **jack something in** or **up** *slang* to give it up. [from the name *Jack*]

jackal *noun* a mainly nocturnal carnivorous mammal, closely related to the dog and wolf, that lives in deserts, grassland, and woodland in Asia and Africa. [from Persian *shagual*]

jackanapes /ˈdʒakəneɪps/ *noun old use* a mischievous or impertinent person. [from Middle English *Jakken apes*, or 'jack of the apes', ie the Duke of Suffolk (1396–1450), whose badge was an ape's ball and chain]

jackass *noun* **1** a male ass. **2** *colloq.* a foolish person.

jackboot *noun* a tall leather knee-high military boot, especially as a symbol of oppressive military rule.

jackdaw *noun* a bird of the crow family having a reputation for stealing bright objects. [from JACK + old word *daw*, jackdaw]

jacket *noun* **1** a short coat, especially a long-sleeved hip-length one. **2** something worn over the top half of the body: *a life jacket*. **3** same as DUST JACKET. **4** an outer casing for a boiler, etc, for preventing heat loss; any protective casing. **5** the skin of a potato that has been cooked without being peeled. **6** an animal's natural coat. [from Old French *jaquet*]

Jack Frost in story books, etc, a being personifying frost.

jack-in-office *noun derog.* a self-important minor official.

jack-in-the-box *noun* (PL. **jack-in-the-boxes**) a box containing a doll attached to a spring, that leaps out when the lid is opened.

jackknife /ˈdʒaknaɪf/ — *noun* **1** a large pocket knife with a folding blade. **2** a dive in which the body is bent double and then straightened before entering the water. — *verb intrans., said of an articulated vehicle* to go out of control in such a way that the trailer swings round against the cab.

jack-of-all-trades *noun* (PL. **jacks-of-all-trades**) a handyman used to a variety of jobs.

jack plug *Electr.* an electrical plug with a single prong.

jackpot *noun* the maximum win, especially consisting of the accumulated stakes, to be made in a lottery, card game, etc. — **hit the jackpot** *colloq.* to have a remarkable financial win or stroke of luck.

....

◨ prize, award, winnings, kitty, pool, stakes, *colloq.* big time, bonanza.

....

jack rabbit a long-eared N American hare.

Jack Robinson — **before you can say Jack Robinson** *colloq.* very suddenly or quickly; in a trice. [18c; various origins have been suggested, but none is certain]

jacks or **jackstones** *noun* a game in which playing-pieces (originally small bones or pebbles) are tossed and caught on the back of the hand.

Jack tar *old use* a sailor.

Jacobean /dʒakəˈbɪən/ *adj.* **1** relating or belonging to the reign of James I of England (VI of Scotland) (1603–25). **2** *said of furniture, drama, etc* typical of the style current in his reign. **3** denoting a style of English architecture characterized by a symmetry of façades, large windows and, in the case of manor houses such as Hatfield (1608–12), E- or H-shaped plans. [from Latin *Jacobus*, James]

Jacobins *pl. noun* a radical political group in the French Revolution.

Jacobite *Brit. Hist.* — *noun* a member or supporter of the Jacobites, supporters of the claim of the Catholic James II and VII, and his successors, to the British throne. — *adj.* relating to the Jacobites. [from Latin *Jacobus*, James]

Jacuzzi /dʒəˈkuːzɪ/ *noun trademark* a large bath equipped with underwater jets that massage and invigorate the body.

jade¹ *noun* **1** *Geol.* a very hard green, white, brown, or yellow semi-precious stone consisting of either of two minerals, *jadeite* and *nephrite*, used to make vases and carved ornaments. **2** the intense green colour of jade. [from Spanish *piedra de ijada*, colic(-curing) stone]

jade² *noun old use* **1** a disreputable or ill-natured woman. **2** a worn-out old horse.

jaded *adj.* fatigued; dull and bored.

....

◨ fatigued, exhausted, spent, tired out, tired, weary, bored.

◪ fresh, refreshed.

....

jadeite /ˈdʒeɪdaɪt/ *noun Geol.* a tough fibrous mineral with a slightly greasy lustre, consisting of a silicate of aluminium and sodium that forms in compact waxy masses, principal sources occurring in Myanmar (Burma) and Guatemala.

jag¹ — *noun* **1** a sharp projection. **2** *Scot.* an injection or inoculation. — *verb* (**jagged, jagging**) to prick, sting, or pierce.

jag² *noun slang* **1** a bout of heavy drinking or drug-taking. **2** a bout of indulgence in anything.

jagged *adj.* having a rough or sharp uneven edge. [from JAG¹]

. . . .

▣ uneven, irregular, rough, ragged, notched, indented, serrated, toothed, pointed, ridged, craggy, broken.
▣ even, smooth.

jaguar *noun* the largest of the American cats, with a deep yellow or tawny coat covered with black spots, more heavily built than a leopard and with larger spots, found mainly in tropical forests, especially near water. [from S American Indian (Tupí) *jaguara*]

jail or **gaol** — *noun* prison. — *verb* to imprison. [from Old French *gaole*]

. . . .

▣ *noun* prison, custody, lock-up, penitentiary, guardhouse, *colloq.* nick, *slang* clink. *verb* imprison, incarcerate, lock up, *colloq.* put away, *colloq.* send down, detain, intern, impound, confine, immure.

. . . .

jailbird or **gaolbird** *noun colloq.* a person in prison, especially regularly so.
jailbreak or **gaolbreak** *noun* an escape, especially by several prisoners, from jail.
jailer or **gaoler** *noun* a person who is in charge of prisoners in a jail.

. . . .

▣ prison officer, warden, warder, guard, *slang* screw, keeper, captor.

. . . .

Jain /dʒaɪn/ *noun* an adherent of Jainism, an indigenous religion of India.
jalapeño or **jalepeño pepper** /halə'peɪnjəʊ, halə'piːnəʊ/ *noun* an especially hot type of capsicum pepper used in Mexican cooking. [Mexican Spanish]
jalopy /dʒə'lɒpɪ/ *noun* (PL. **jalopies**) *colloq.* a worn-out old car.
jam¹ *noun* a thick sticky food made from fruit boiled with sugar, used as a spread on bread, etc. — **jam tomorrow** *colloq.* something agreeable constantly promised but never provided. **money for jam** *colloq.* money easily made. **want jam on it** *colloq.* to expect more than is reasonable. [perhaps from JAM²]

. . . .

▣ conserve, preserve, jelly, spread.

. . . .

jam² *verb* (**jammed**, **jamming**) **1** to stick or wedge so as to be immovable. **2** *trans., intrans., said of machinery, etc* to stick or cause it to stick and stop working. **3** to push or shove; to cram, press, or pack. **4** (*also* **jam something up**) to fill (eg a street) so full that movement comes to a stop. **5** *trans.* to cause interference to (a radio signal, etc), especially deliberately. **6** *intrans. colloq.* to play jazz in a jam session. [probably imitative]

. . . .

▣ **1** stick, lodge, wedge, trap. **3** push, shove, ram, stuff, cram, pack, wedge, squash, squeeze, press, force. **4** block, clog, obstruct, congest, crowd.

. . . .

jamb /dʒam/ *noun* the vertical post at the side of a door, window, or fireplace. [from Old French *jambe*, leg]
jamboree *noun* **1** *colloq.* a large and lively gathering. **2** a large rally of Scouts, Guides, etc.
jammy *adj.* (**jammier**, **jammiest**) **1** covered, or filled, with jam. **2** *colloq., said of a person* lucky. **3** *colloq., said of a job, etc* profitable, especially at little cost in effort.
jam-packed *adj. colloq.* packed tight.
jam session *slang* a session of live, especially improvised, jazz or popular music.
Jan or **Jan.** *abbrev.* January.
JANET *abbrev.* Joint Academic Network, a computer network linking UK universities and research bodies.

jangle *verb* **1** (*trans., intrans.*) to make or cause to make a discordant ringing noise. **2** to upset or irritate. [from Old French *jangler*]

. . . .

▣ **1** clang, clank, clash, clatter, jingle, rattle, jar.

. . . .

jangly *adj.* (**janglier**, **jangliest**) making a jangling sound.
janissary or **janizary** *noun* (PL. **janissaries**, **janizaries**) *Hist.* a soldier of the Turkish sultan's personal guard. [from Turkish *yeniçeri*, new troops]
janitor *noun* **1** *North Amer., Scot.* a caretaker. **2** a doorkeeper. [from Latin *janitor*, from *janua*, door]
January *noun* the first month of the year. [from Latin *Januarius mensis*, month of the god Janus]
japan — *noun* a hard glossy black lacquer, originally from Japan, used to coat wood and metal. — *verb* (**japanned**, **japanning**) to lacquer with japan. [from *Japan*, the country]
Japanese — *noun* **1** (PL. **Japanese**) a native or citizen of Japan. **2** the language of Japan. — *adj.* relating or belonging to Japan, or its people or language.
jape *noun old use* a trick, prank, or joke. [from Middle English *japen*]
japonica /dʒə'pɒnɪkə/ *noun* **1** a red-flowered shrub of the quince family, originally from Japan. **2** another name for the oriental plant camellia. [from Latin *japonica*, Japanese]
jar¹ *noun* **1** a wide-mouthed cylindrical container, usually of glass; the contents of this. **2** *colloq.* a glass of beer. [from Old French *jarre*, from Arabic *jarrah*, earthenware vessel]

. . . .

▣ **1** pot, container, receptacle, crock, urn, vase, pitcher, jug.

. . . .

jar² — *verb* (**jarred**, **jarring**) **1** *intrans.* to have a harsh effect; to grate. **2** *trans., intrans.* to jolt or vibrate. **3** *trans., intrans.* to make or cause to make a harsh sound. **4** *intrans.* (**jar with something**) to clash or conflict with it: *buildings that jar with the environment.* — *noun* a jarring sensation, shock, or jolt. [imitative]

. . . .

▣ *verb* **1** grate, annoy, irritate. **2** jolt, rattle, shake, vibrate, rock. **3** jangle, clang, clank, clatter. **4** clash, conflict, disagree.

. . . .

jardinière /ʒɑːdɪ'njɛə(r)/ *noun* **1** an ornamental pot or stand for flowers. **2** *Cookery* an accompaniment of mixed vegetables for a meat dish. [from French *jardinière*, feminine of *jardinier*, gardener]
jargon *noun* **1** the specialized vocabulary of a particular trade, profession, group, or activity. **2** *derog.* confusing or meaningless talk. [from Old French *jargon*]

. . . .

▣ **1** parlance, cant, slang, argot, vernacular, idiom. **2** nonsense, *colloq.* gobbledygook, *colloq.* mumbo-jumbo, gibberish.

. . . .

jarring *adj.* that jars.

. . . .

▣ discordant, jangling, cacophonous, strident, harsh, rasping, grating, irritating, upsetting, disturbing, clashing, conflicting.

. . . .

jarringly *adv.* **1** harshly. **2** with a shock or jolt.
jasmine /'dʒazmɪn/ *noun* a shrub or vine of the genus *Jasminium* with fragrant white or yellow flowers, native to Asia. [from Persian *yasmin*]
jasper *noun Geol.* a usually red semi-precious gemstone that is an impure form of chalcedony (a variety of the mineral quartz) containing iron oxides, used to make jewellery and ornaments. [from Greek *iaspis*]
jaundice /'dʒɔːndɪs/ *noun* a condition in which there is an excess of the bile pigment *bilirubin* in the blood, as a result of which the skin and the whites of the eyes take on a yel-

lowish appearance. [from Old French *jaunisse*, from *jaune*, yellow]

jaundiced *adj.* 1 suffering from jaundice. 2 *said of a person or attitude* bitter or resentful; cynical.

- - - - - - - - - - - - - - - - - -

■ 2 bitter, resentful, envious, jealous, cynical, pessimistic, sceptical, disbelieving, distrustful, suspicious, hostile.

- -

jaunt — *noun* a short journey for pleasure. — *verb intrans.* to go for a jaunt.

jauntily *adv.* with a jaunty manner.

jauntiness *noun* being jaunty.

jaunty *adj.* (**jauntier, jauntiest**) 1 *said of a person's manner or personality* breezy and exuberant. 2 *said of dress, etc* smart; stylish. [from French *gentil*, noble, gentle]

- - - - - - - - - - - - - - - - - -

■ 1 breezy, airy, buoyant, high-spirited, exuberant, carefree, perky, lively, sprightly. 2 smart, stylish, debonair, dapper, spruce.

✷ 1 depressed. 2 dowdy.

- -

Java *noun* 1 a large island that is part of Indonesia. 2 *Comput. trademark* a programming language.

Javanese *noun* 1 the largest ethnic group of Java. 2 a language of the Indo-Pacific family, spoken throughout Java and in parts of Indonesia.

javelin *noun* 1 a light spear for throwing as a weapon or in sport. 2 throwing the javelin as an athletic event. [from Old French *javeline*]

jaw — *noun* 1 either of the two hinged parts of the skull in which the teeth are set. 2 the lower part of the face round the mouth and chin. 3 (**jaws**) the mouth, especially of an animal. 4 (**jaws**) a threshold, especially of something fearful: *the jaws of death*. 5 (**jaws**) the gripping parts of a tool, etc. 6 *colloq.* a long conversation; a talking-to; talk; chatter. — *verb intrans. colloq.* to chatter, gossip, or talk. [from Old French *joue*, cheek]

- - - - - - - - - - - - - - - - - -

■ *noun* 6 talk, gossip, chat, conversation, discussion, *colloq.* chinwag, *colloq.* natter. *verb* chat, chatter, gossip, *colloq.* natter, talk, *colloq.* rabbit (on), gabble, babble.

- -

jawbone *noun* the bone that forms the lower jaw.

jay *noun* a noisy bird of the crow family, with pinkish-brown plumage and blue, black, and white bars on its wings. [from Old French *jai*]

jaywalk *verb intrans.* to cross streets at will, without regard to traffic. [from JAY, with the meaning 'fool']

jaywalker *noun* a pedestrian who jaywalks.

jaywalking *noun* crossing the road carelessly, or disregarding pedestrian crossing signals.

jazz — *noun* 1 popular music of Black American origin, with strong, catchy rhythms, performed with much improvisation. 2 *colloq.* talk; nonsense; business, stuff, etc. — *verb* (*usually* **jazz something up**) *colloq.* 1 to enliven or brighten it. 2 to give it a jazzy rhythm. — **... and all that jazz** *colloq.* ... and all that sort of thing: *philosophy and all that jazz*.

jazzily *adv.* in a jazzy way.

jazz poetry poetry which is recited to the accompaniment of jazz music, popular in the 1960s in Britain (especially London) and the USA.

jazzy *adj.* (**jazzier, jazziest**) 1 in the style of, or like, jazz. 2 *colloq.* showy; flashy; stylish.

JCB *noun* a vehicle or machine used in the building industry, with a hydraulic shovel at the front and a digging arm at the back. [named after Joseph Cyril Bamford, the manufacturer]

JCR *abbrev.* junior common room.

J-curve *noun Econ.* a J-shaped curve on graphs showing balance-of-trade statistics over a period of time after a currency has been devalued.

jealous *adj.* (*often* **jealous of someone** or **something**) 1 envious of someone else, his or her possessions, success, talents, etc. 2 suspicious and resentful of possible rivals; possessive. 3 anxiously protective of something one has. 4 *Biblical, said of God* intolerant of unfaithfulness. 5 caused by jealousy: *a jealous fury*. [from Old French *gelos*, from Greek *zelos*, rivalry, jealousy]

- - - - - - - - - - - - - - - - - -

■ 1 envious, covetous, bitter, resentful, *colloq.* green, *colloq.* green-eyed. 2 suspicious, wary, distrustful, resentful, possessive.

✷ 1 contented, satisfied.

- -

jealously *adv.* in a jealous way.

jealousy *noun* (PL. **jealousies**) 1 the emotion of envy or suspicious possessiveness. 2 (*usually* **jealousies**) an occurrence of this.

- - - - - - - - - - - - - - - - - -

■ 1 envy, covetousness, bitterness, resentment, ill-will, suspicion, distrust, possessiveness.

- -

jeans *pl. noun* casual denim trousers, especially blue. [from *jean*, a strong cotton from *Gênes* (French, Genoa)]

Jeep *noun trademark* a light military vehicle capable of travelling over rough country. [from *GP*, general-purpose vehicle]

jeer — *verb* 1 to mock or deride (a speaker, performer, etc). 2 *intrans.* (**jeer at**) to laugh unkindly: *jeered at his accent*. — *noun* a taunt, insult, or hoot of derision.

- - - - - - - - - - - - - - - - - -

■ *verb* 1 mock, ridicule, deride, scoff at, sneer at, barrack, heckle. 2 laugh at, make fun of. *noun* taunt, gibe, sneer, insult, abuse, catcall, hoot, boo, hiss.

- -

jehad see JIHAD.

Jehovah's Witness a member of a fundamentalist sect of Christians.

jejune /dʒɪˈdʒuːn/ *adj. derog.* 1 *said of writing, ideas, etc* dull, banal, unoriginal, and empty of imagination. 2 childish; naïve. [from Latin *jejunus*, hungry, empty]

jejunum /dʒɪˈdʒuːnəm/ *noun Anat.* the part of the small intestine between the duodenum and the ileum. [from Latin *jejunum intestinum*, empty intestine]

Jekyll and Hyde /ˈdʒɛkɪl ənd ˈhaɪd/ a person with two distinct personalities, one good, the other evil. [from the novel *The Strange Case of Dr Jekyll and Mr Hyde* (1886) by Robert Louis Stevenson]

jell or **gel** *verb intrans.* 1 to become firm; to set. 2 to take definite shape. [from JELLY]

- - - - - - - - - - - - - - - - - -

■ CRYSTALLIZE. 1 set, congeal, coagulate, thicken, harden, solidify. 2 take shape, come together, form, materialize.

- -

jellied *adj.* set in jelly: *jellied eels*.

jelly *noun* (PL. **jellies**) 1 a wobbly, transparent, fruit-flavoured dessert set with gelatine. 2 a clear jam made by boiling and straining fruit. 3 meat stock or other savoury medium set with gelatine. 4 any jelly-like substance. 5 *slang* a temazepam capsule. [from Old French *gelee*, from Latin *gelare*, to freeze]

jelly baby or **jelly bean** a soft fruit-flavoured sweet in the shape of a baby or a bean, made with gelatine.

jellyfish *noun* (PL. **jellyfish, jellyfishes**) the common name for the free-swimming stage (medusa) of invertebrate animals belonging to the phylum Coelenterata.

jelly shoe a shoe made from transparent, often brightly coloured plastic.

jemmy *noun* (PL. **jemmies**) a small crowbar used by burglars for forcing open windows, etc. [from the name *James*]

jenny *noun* (PL. **jennies**) 1 a name given to the female of certain birds, eg the wren, or animals, eg the donkey. 2 a spinning-jenny. [from the name *Jenny*]

jeopardize or **jeopardise** /'dʒɛpədaɪz/ *verb* to put at risk of harm, loss, or destruction.

....

⊟ endanger, imperil, risk, hazard, venture, stake, gamble, chance, threaten, menace, expose.

⊠ protect, safeguard.

jeopardy /'dʒɛpədɪ/ *noun* danger of harm, loss, or destruction. [from Old French *jeu parti*, a divided or even (ie uncertain) game]

....

⊟ danger, peril, risk, hazard, endangerment, exposure, vulnerability, insecurity.

⊠ safety, security.
....

jerbil same as GERBIL.

jerboa /dʒɜː'bouə/ *noun* a small rat-like animal of N Africa and Asia, with long hind legs adapted for jumping. [from Arabic *yarbu*]

jeremiad /dʒɛrə'maɪəd/ *noun colloq.* a lengthy and mournful tale of woe. [from French *jérémiade*, from *The Lamentations of Jeremiah* in the Old Testament]

jerk — *noun* 1 a quick tug or pull. 2 a sudden movement; a jolt. 3 *derog. slang* a stupid person. — *verb* 1 to pull or tug sharply. 2 *intrans.* to move with sharp suddenness.

....

⊟ *noun* 1 tug, twitch, pluck, pull, yank, wrench. 2 jolt, jar, jog, lurch, throw. *verb* 1 tug, twitch, pluck, pull, yank, wrench. 2 jolt, jog, lurch, bounce, jiggle.
....

jerkily *adv.* in a jerky way.

jerkin *noun* a short close-fitting especially sleeveless jacket.

jerky *adj.* (**jerkier, jerkiest**) moving in or with jerks.

....

⊟ fitful, spasmodic, convulsive, twitchy, jumpy, bumpy, bouncy, shaky, rough, disconnected, unco-ordinated, uncontrolled, incoherent.

⊠ smooth.
....

jeroboam /dʒɛrə'bouəm/ *noun* a large wine bottle holding the equivalent of six standard bottles (or four of champagne). [from *Jeroboam* in the Old Testament, I Kings 11.28]

Jerry *noun* (PL. **Jerries**) *Brit. war slang* a German or German soldier; the Germans collectively. [alteration of GERMAN]

jerry *noun* (PL. **jerries**) *old colloq. use* a chamber pot. [from JEROBOAM]

jerry-builder *noun* a person who puts up flimsy buildings cheaply and quickly.

jerry-building *noun* the act or process of putting up cheap and flimsy buildings.

jerry-built *adj.*, *said of buildings, etc* built cheaply, hastily and incompetently.

jerry can a flat-sided can used for carrying water, petrol, etc. [from JERRY]

jersey *noun* (PL. **jerseys**) 1 a knitted garment worn on the upper part of the body, pulled on over the head; a pullover. 2 a fine knitted fabric used for clothing. 3 (**Jersey**) a breed of dairy cattle. [named after *Jersey* in the Channel Islands]

Jerusalem artichoke a plant related to the sunflower; its potato-like roots can be eaten as a vegetable. [a corruption of Italian *girasole*, sunflower]

jest *noun* a joke or prank. — **in jest** as a joke; not seriously. [from Old French *geste*, deed, from Latin *gesta*, things done]

....

⊟ joke, quip, witticism, *colloq.* crack, *colloq.* gag, banter, prank, trick, hoax, *colloq.* leg-pull.
....

jester *noun Hist.* a colourfully dressed professional clown employed by a king or noble to amuse the court. [from Middle English *gester*, from *gest*, exploit]

jestingly *adv.* as a joke, with jesting.

Jesuit /'dʒɛzjʊɪt/ — *noun* a member of the Jesuits, in full the Society of Jesus, a male religious order founded in 1540. — *adj.* relating to the Jesuits.

jesuitical *adj.* 1 *said of an argument* over-subtle; cleverly misleading. 2 *said of a plan* crafty; cunning.

jesuitically *adv.* in a jesuitical way.

Jesus 1 see JESUS CHRIST. 2 *offensive* an exclamation of surprise, anger, etc. [from Hebrew *Yeshua*]

Jesus Christ or **Jesus of Nazareth** (1c AD) the central figure of the Christian faith, which is based on the fundamental belief that he was the Son of God who was sacrificed and raised from the dead to redeem humanity from the consequences of sin and death.

jet[1] *noun Geol.* a hard black variety of lignite (a low-grade coal) that can be cut and polished and was formerly a popular gemstone, used to make jewellery and ornaments. [from Old French *jaiet*]

jet[2] — *noun* 1 a strong fast stream (of liquid, gas, etc), forced under pressure from a narrow opening. 2 the opening through which a jet is forced. 3 (*also* **jet aircraft**) an aircraft powered by a jet engine. — *verb* (**jetted, jetting**) 1 *intrans., trans. colloq.* to travel or transport by jet aircraft. 2 *intrans.* to come out in a jet; to spurt. [from French *jeter*, to throw]

....

⊟ *noun* 1 gush, spurt, squirt, stream, spout, spray, fountain. *verb* 2 gush, spurt, squirt, stream, spout, spray.
....

jet-black *adj.* deep glossy black.

....

⊟ pitch-black, ebony, sable, sooty.
....

jet engine a type of gas turbine engine used in aircraft, in which air taken in from outside is compressed to a high pressure, mixed with fuel, and ignited.

jetfoil *noun* an advanced form of hydrofoil propelled by waterjets.

jet lag the tiredness and lethargy that result from the body's inability to adjust to the rapid changes of time zone that go with high-speed, long-distance air travel.

jet-lagged *adj.* affected by jet lag.

jet plane an aircraft powered by a jet engine.

jet-propelled *adj.* 1 driven by jet propulsion. 2 *colloq.* fast.

jet propulsion the forward thrust effected as air sucked into the front of an engine is forced out behind.

jetsam /'dʒɛtsəm/ *noun* goods jettisoned from a ship and washed up on the shore. See also FLOTSAM. [contracted from JETTISON]

jet set *colloq.* (**the jet set**) wealthy people who lead a life of fast travel and expensive enjoyment.

jet-setter *noun* a member of the jet set.

jet-setting — *noun* the lifestyle of a jet-setter. — *adj.* relating to jet-setters, or their way of life.

jet stream *Geol.* a narrow current of rapidly moving air blowing in a westerly direction at speeds ranging from 60kph in summer to 125kph in winter, and found in both hemispheres at or just below the top of the troposphere.

jettison *verb* (**jettisoned, jettisoning**) 1 to throw (cargo) overboard to lighten a ship, aircraft, etc in an emergency. 2 to abandon, reject, or get rid of. [from Old French *getaison*, from Latin *iactatio*, a tossing]

jetty *noun* (PL. **jetties**) 1 a stone or wooden landing-stage. 2 a stone barrier built out into the sea to protect a harbour from currents and high waves. [from Old French *jetee*, from *jeter*, to throw]

....

⊟ MOLE. 1 pier, landing-stage, quay, wharf. 2 breakwater, groyne.
....

Jew noun 1 a member of the Hebrew race. 2 someone who practises Judaism. 3 old offensive use a miser; an unrelenting bargainer. [from Old French Juiu, from Latin Judaeus]

jewel noun 1 a precious stone. 2 a personal ornament made with precious stones and metals. 3 a gem used in the machinery of a watch. 4 someone or something greatly prized. [from Old French joel]

▣ 1 gem, gemstone, precious stone, slang rock. 4 treasure, prize, find, rarity, paragon, pearl.

jewelled adj. set or decorated with jewels.

jeweller noun a person who deals in, makes or repairs jewellery, watches, and objects of gold and silver.

jewellery or North Amer., esp. US **jewelry** noun articles worn for personal adornment, eg bracelets, necklaces, brooches, rings, etc.

Types of jewellery include: bangle, bracelet, charm bracelet, anklet, cufflink, tiepin, hatpin, brooch, cameo, earring, nose-ring, ring, signet-ring, solitaire ring, necklace, necklet, choker, pendant, locket, chain, beads, amulet, torque, tiara, coronet, diadem.

Jewess noun offensive a Jewish woman or girl.

Jewish adj. relating or belonging to the Jews or to Judaism.

Jewry noun old use Jews collectively.

Jew's harp a tiny lyre-shaped musical instrument held between the teeth, with a narrow metal tongue that is twanged with the finger.

Jezebel noun derog. a shameless or scheming woman. [named after Ahab's wife in the Old Testament, 1 Kings 21; 2 Kings 9.30]

jib[1] — noun a small three-cornered sail in front of the mainsail of a yacht. — verb (**jibbed, jibbing**) (often **jib at something**) 1 intrans., said of a horse to refuse a jump, etc. 2 intrans., said of a person to object to it. 3 intrans., trans. Naut. to gybe. [17c, origin unknown]

jib[2] noun the projecting arm of a crane from which the lifting gear hangs. [from GIBBET]

jib boom Naut. an extension to the bowsprit on which the jib is spread.

jibe another spelling of GIBE or GYBE.

jiffy or **jiff** noun (PL. **jiffies**) colloq. a moment.

Jiffy bag trademark a padded envelope.

jig — noun 1 a lively country dance or folk dance; music for this. 2 Mech. a device that holds a piece of work in position and guides the tools being used on it. — verb (**jigged, jigging**) 1 intrans. to dance a jig. 2 intrans. to jump up and down. 3 Mech. to work on (something under construction) using a jig.

▣ verb 2 jump, prance, caper, hop, skip, bounce, bob.

jigger[1] noun 1 a small quantity of alcoholic spirits, or a glass for measuring this. 2 Billiards colloq. a cue rest. 3 Golf an iron-headed club. 4 North Amer. colloq. an all-purpose term for a gadget when its name is not known or not remembered. [from JIG noun]

jigger[2] noun a variant of CHIGGER.

jiggered adj. colloq. exhausted. — **I'll be jiggered** colloq. an expression of astonishment. [possibly euphemistic for buggered]

jiggery-pokery noun colloq. trickery or deceit. [from Scot. joukery-pawkery, from jouk, to dodge + pawk, trick]

jiggle — verb trans., intrans. to jump or cause to jump up and down or jerk about. — noun a jiggling movement. [from JIG 1]

jigsaw noun 1 (also **jigsaw puzzle**) a picture mounted on wood or cardboard and sawn into irregularly shaped interlocking pieces, taken apart for later re-assembly into the picture. 2 a fine-bladed saw for cutting intricate patterns. [from JIG + SAW[2]]

jihad or **jehad** /dʒɪˈhɑːd/ noun a holy war fought by Muslims on behalf of Islam. [from Arabic jihad, struggle]

jilt verb old use to discard (a lover). [contracted from jillet, a flirt]

▣ abandon, desert, reject, discard, slang ditch, drop.

Jim Crow North Amer. slang 1 offensive a black person. 2 the policy of segregating blacks from whites. [from the title of a black minstrel song]

jimjams pl. noun 1 colloq. a state of nervous excitement. 2 slang delirium tremens. 3 colloq. pyjamas.

jingle — noun 1 a ringing or clinking sound, as of small bells, coins, or keys. 2 a simple rhyming verse or song. — verb trans., intrans. to make or cause to make a ringing or clinking sound. [imitative]

▣ noun 1 ring, tinkle, clink, chink, jangle, clatter, rattle. 2 rhyme, verse, song, ditty, doggerel, poem, chant, chorus, slogan. verb ring, tinkle, clink, chink, jangle, clatter, rattle.

jingoism noun over-enthusiastic or aggressive patriotism. [from 'By jingo!' (ie by God!), from a chauvinistic British song of 1878]

▣ chauvinism, flag-waving, patriotism, nationalism, imperialism.

jingoist noun an over-enthusiastic patriot.

jingoistic adj. characteristic of jingoism.

jinja noun Relig. a Shinto shrine or sanctuary.

jink — verb intrans., trans. to dodge. — noun a dodge. See also HIGH JINKS. [imitative]

jinni or **jinnee** or **djinni** /dʒɪˈniː/ noun (PL. **jinn, djinn**) in Muslim folklore, a supernatural being able to adopt human or animal form. [from Arabic jinni]

jinx — noun an evil spell or influence, held responsible for misfortune. — verb to put a jinx on. [from jynx, the wryneck, a bird used in spells; hence a spell or charm]

▣ noun spell, curse, evil eye, hex, voodoo, hoodoo, black magic. verb curse, bewitch, bedevil, doom, plague.

jitter colloq. — verb intrans. (**jittered, jittering**) to shake with nerves. — noun (**jitters**) an attack of nervousness. [variant of chitter, to shiver]

jitterbug — noun 1 an energetic dance like jive, popular in the 1940s. 2 an alarmist or scaremonger. — verb intrans. (**jitterbugged, jitterbugging**) to dance the jitterbug. [from JITTER]

jittery adj. nervous.

jive — noun a lively style of dancing to jazz music, popular in the 1950s. — verb to dance in this style.

Jnr abbrev. Junior.

job — noun 1 a person's regular paid employment. 2 a piece of work. 3 a completed task: made a good job of the pruning. 4 a function or responsibility. 5 colloq. a problem; difficulty: had a job finding it. 6 a crime, especially a burglary: an inside job. 7 an underhand scheme: a put-up job. 8 colloq. a do, affair, business, etc: the wedding was a proper church job. 9 colloq. a surgical operation, usually involving plastic surgery: a nose job. 10 colloq. a manufactured product, or other object: smart little jobs, these calculators. — verb (**jobbed, jobbing**) 1 intrans. to do casual jobs. 2 trans., intrans. to buy and sell (stocks) as a stockjobber; to act as stockjobber. 3 trans., intrans. to bring about by, or practise, jobbery. 4 to hire or let out for a period or a job. — **do the job** to succeed in doing what is required. **give something up as a bad job** to abandon a task, etc as impossible or not worthwhile. **a good job** colloq. fortunate; lucky: it's a good job I was early. **jobs for the boys** derog. superfluous work created as employment for one's supporters and friends. **just the job** exactly what is required. **make the best of a bad job** to do one's best in difficult circumstances. [16c, origin unknown]

- - - - - - - - - - - - - - - - - - - -

■ *noun* **1** work, employment, occupation, position, post, office, situation, profession, career, calling, vocation, trade, business, livelihood. **2** task, chore, commission, assignment, project, enterprise, under taking, venture, mission, errand. **4** duty, responsibility, province, department, function, capacity, role, part, place, share, contribution. **8** affair, concern.

- -

jobber *noun Stock Exchange* a stockjobber. [from JOB]

jobbery *noun* the abuse of public office for private gain. [from JOB]

job centre or **Jobcentre** *Brit.* a government office displaying information on available jobs.

job club or **Jobclub** an association aimed at helping the jobless find work through learning and using the necessary skills of presentation, etc.

job description *Industry* a systematic and detailed listing of all the duties, responsibilities, activities, etc necessary to a specific job.

job evaluation *Industry* a method of assessing the relative position and appropriate salary for the different jobs in an organization by allocating points for the various aspects of each job as listed in a job description.

jobless *adj.* having no paid employment; unemployed. — *noun* (**the jobless**) unemployed people.

- - - - - - - - - - - - - - - - - - - -

■ *adj.* unemployed, out of work, on the dole, laid off, redundant.
■ *adj.* employed.

- -

job lot a mixed collection of objects sold as one item at an auction, etc.

Job's comforter a person whose attempts at sympathy have the effect of adding to one's distress. [from *Job* in the Old Testament]

jobseeker's allowance a regular payment made through the national insurance scheme to an unemployed person who is looking for work.

job-sharing *noun* the practice of sharing the tasks of one full-time job between two or more part-time workers.

Jock *noun colloq.* a Scotsman, especially a soldier. [Scots form of *Jack*]

jockey — *noun* (PL. **jockeys**) a rider, especially professional, in horse races. — *verb* **1** to ride (a horse) in a race. **2** *trans., intrans.* (**jockey someone into something, out of something**, etc) to manipulate them deviously. — **jockey for position** to seek an advantage over rivals, especially unscrupulously. [diminutive of JOCK]

jockstrap *noun* a garment for supporting the genitals, worn by male athletes. [from dialect *jock*, penis]

jocose /dʒə'kəʊs/ *adj.* playful; humorous. [from Latin *jocosus*]

jocosely *adv.* in a humorous way, merrily.

jocosity /dʒəʊ'kɒsɪtɪ/ *noun* being playful or humorous.

jocular *adj.* **1** given to joking; good-humoured. **2** *said of a remark* intended as a joke. [from Latin *joculus*, a little joke]

- - - - - - - - - - - - - - - - - - - -

■ JOCOSE. **1** jocund, jovial, jolly, merry, good-humoured, joking, jesting. **2** humorous, funny, amusing, teasing, facetious, droll, witty.
■ SERIOUS.

- -

jocularity *noun* merriment, being jocular.

jocund *adj.* cheerful; merry; good-humoured. [from Latin *jocundus*, agreeable]

jocundity *noun* a cheerful condition or state.

jodhpurs /'dʒɒdpəz/ *pl. noun* riding-breeches that are loose-fitting over the buttocks and thighs and tight-fitting from knee to calf. [from *Jodhpur* in India]

jog — *verb* (**jogged, jogging**) **1** to knock or nudge slightly. **2** to prompt (the memory). **3** *intrans.* (**jog along**) to progress slowly and steadily; to plod. **4** *intrans.* to run at a gentle, steady pace, for exercise. — *noun* **1** a spell of jogging. **2** a nudge, knock, or jolt. [variant of *shog*, to shake]

- - - - - - - - - - - - - - - - - - - -

■ *verb* **1** jolt, jar, bump, knock, jerk, joggle, shake, rock, nudge, poke, prod, push. **2** prompt, stir, arouse, stimulate, activate. **4** run, trot. *noun* **1** run, trot. **2** jolt, bump, knock, jerk, shake, nudge, poke, prod, push, shove.

- -

jogger *noun* a person who jogs, especially on a regular basis.

joggers or **jog pants** *pl. noun* loose trousers of a warm material, fitting tightly round the waist and ankles.

jogger's nipple *colloq.* painful inflammation of the nipples caused by friction against clothing while running or jogging.

jogging *noun* running at a gentle or steady pace.

joggle — *verb trans., intrans.* to jolt, shake, or wobble. — *noun* a shake or jolt. [from JOG]

jog-trot *noun* an easy pace like that of a horse between walking and trotting.

john *noun North Amer. colloq.* (*usually* **the john**) a lavatory. [from the name JOHN]

johnny *noun* (PL. **johnnies**) *colloq.* a chap; a fellow. [diminutive of *John*]

joie de vivre /ʒwɑː də 'viːvrə/ enthusiasm for living; exuberant spirits. [French, = joy of life]

join — *verb* **1** (*often* **join one thing to another**, or **join things up**) to connect, attach, link, or unite. **2** to become a member of (a society, firm, etc). **3** *intrans.* to become a member, employee, etc. **4** *intrans., trans., said of roads, rivers, etc* to meet. **5** to come together with; to enter the company of: *joined them for supper.* **6** *trans., intrans.* (*also* **join on**) to add oneself: *join the queue.* **7** to take part in. **8** to do the same as, for companionship: *who'll join me in a drink?* — *noun* a seam or joint. — **join in** to participate in; to take part. **join up** to enlist as a member of an armed force. **join up with someone** to come together for joint action, etc. [from Old French *joindre*]

- - - - - - - - - - - - - - - - - - - -

■ *verb* **1** connect, link, attach, fasten, tie, unite, combine, amalgamate, merge, marry, couple, yoke, splice, knit, cement, add, annex. **3** enrol, enlist, sign up, enter. **4** meet, touch, abut, adjoin.
■ *verb* **1** divide, separate. **3** leave.

- -

joined-up *adj.* **1** *said of handwriting* having all the letters linked, with no spaces in between. **2** *said of political policies* well-balanced and complementary with each other.

joiner *noun* **1** a craftsman who makes and fits wooden doors, window frames, stairs, shelves, etc. **2** *colloq.* a sociable person who likes joining clubs and being a member of a group.

joinery *noun* the trade or work of a joiner.

joint — *noun* **1** the place where two or more pieces join. **2** in vertebrates, the point of contact or articulation between two or more bones, together with the ligaments that surround it. **3** a piece of meat, usually containing a bone, for cooking or roasting. **4** *slang* a cheap, shabby cafe, bar, nightclub, etc. **5** *slang* a cannabis cigarette. **6** *Geol.* a crack in a mass of rock. — *verb* **1** connect by joints. **2** to divide (a bird or animal) into, or at, the joints, for cooking. — *adj.* **1** owned, done, etc in common; shared. **2** working together. — **case the joint** *slang* to look over premises with a view to burgling them. **out of joint 1** *said of a bone* dislocated. **2** in disorder. [from Old French *joint(e)*, from *joindre*, to join]

- - - - - - - - - - - - - - - - - - - -

■ *noun* **1** join, connection, link, union, junction, intersection, hinge, articulation, knot, seam. *adj.* **1** common, mutual, communal, shared, collective, united, combined, amalgamated, consolidated, co-operative, co-ordinated, concerted.

- -

jointly *adv.* together; in combination.

joint-stock company a business whose capital is owned jointly by the shareholders.

jointure — *noun* property settled on a woman by her husband for her use after his death. — *verb* to provide with a jointure. [from Old French, from Latin *junctura*, joining]

joint venture a business activity undertaken by two or more companies acting together, sharing the costs, risks, and profits.

joist *noun* any of the beams supporting a floor or ceiling. [from Old French *giste*, from *gesir*, to lie]

jojoba /hoʊˈhoʊbə/ *noun* a N American shrub whose seeds contain a wax similar to spermaceti and which is used as a substitute for it in cosmetics, etc. [from Mexican Spanish *jojoba*]

joke — *noun* **1** a humorous story: *crack a joke.* **2** anything said or done in jest. **3** an amusing situation. **4** something or someone ludicrous. — *verb intrans.* **1** to make jokes. **2** to speak in jest, not in earnest. — **the joke's on him, her, etc** *colloq.* he, she, etc has become the victim of his or her own joke. **joking apart** or **aside** to be serious; seriously. **no joke** *colloq.* a serious matter. **play a joke on someone** to trick them. **see the joke** *colloq.* to see the funny side of a situation. **take a joke** to be able to laugh at a joke played on one. [from Latin *jocus*, joke]

⊟ *noun* **1** jest, quip, *colloq.* crack, *colloq.* gag, witticism, pun, *colloq.* one-liner. **2** trick, prank, jape, lark. *verb* **1** jest, quip, *colloq.* gag, pun, clown, fool. **2** tease, *colloq.* kid, banter.

joker *noun* **1** *Cards* an extra card in a pack, usually bearing a picture of a jester, used in certain games. **2** a cheerful or amusing person, always full of jokes. **3** *colloq.* an irresponsible or incompetent person. **4** *colloq.* a person. — **joker in the pack** a person or thing whose effect on a situation is unpredictable.

⊟ **2** comedian, comic, wit, humorist, wag, jester, clown, buffoon.

jokey *adj.* **1** given to joking, good-humoured. **2** as or in a joke.

jokiness *noun* being jokey.

jokingly *adv.* as a joke.

jollification *noun* **1** merriment; fun. **2** (**jollifications**) cheerful celebrations. [a fanciful elaboration of JOLLY]

jolliness *noun* being jolly.

jollity *noun* (PL. **jollities**) **1** merriment. **2** (**jollities**) festivities. [from Middle English *jolite*, from Old French *jolif*, pretty, merry]

jolly — *adj.* (**jollier, jolliest**) **1** good-humoured; cheerful. **2** happy; enjoyable; convivial. — *adv. Brit. colloq.* very. — *verb* (**jollies, jollied**) **1** (*also* **jolly someone up**) to make them more cheerful. **2** (**jolly someone into** or **out of something**) to coax or cajole them. **3** (*also* **jolly someone along**) to keep them cheerful and co-operative. — **jolly well** *Brit. colloq.* used for emphasis: *you jolly well deserved it.* [from French *jolif*, pretty, merry]

⊟ *adj.* MERRY. **1** jovial, hearty, good-humoured, cheerful. **2** happy, enjoyable, convivial, festive.
⊟ *adj.* SAD.

jollyboat *noun* a small boat carried on a larger ship.

Jolly Roger *Hist.* the black flag of a pirate ship bearing a white skull-and-crossbones.

jolt — *verb* **1** *intrans.* to move along jerkily. **2** *trans.* to shake, jog, or jar. — *noun* **1** a jarring shake. **2** an emotional shock. [blend of dialect *jot* and *joll*, to bump]

⊟ *verb* JERK, BUMP. **1** bounce, lurch. **2** shake, jar, jog, knock, jostle, push. *noun* BLOW. **1** jar, shake, jerk, lurch, jog, bump, impact. **2** shock, start, surprise, setback.

Jonah /ˈdʒoʊnə/ *noun* a person who seems to bring bad luck. [named after Jonah in the Old Testament, who almost brought disaster on the ship on which he was sailing]

jonquil *noun* a European and Asian plant of the narcissus family, with sweet-smelling white or yellow flowers. [from French *jonquille*]

josh *North Amer. colloq.* — *verb trans., intrans.* to tease. — *noun* a bit of teasing.

joss-stick *noun* a stick of dried scented paste, burnt as incense. [from *joss* (pidgin Chinese), household god, from Portuguese *deos*, god]

jostle *verb* **1** *intrans.* to push and shove, especially in a crowd. **2** to push against (someone) roughly. **3** *intrans.* to compete aggressively. [formed from JOUST]

⊟ **1** push, shove, hustle, crowd, throng. **2** push, shove, jog, bump, elbow, shoulder.

jot — *noun* (*usually* **not** or **never a jot**) the least bit: *not a jot of sympathy.* — *verb* (**jotted, jotting**) (*often* **jot something down**) to write it down hastily. [from *iota*, the Greek letter *i*]

⊟ *verb* write down, take down, scribble, note, record, register, enter.

jotter *noun Scot.* a school notebook for rough work and notes.

jotting *noun* (*usually* **jottings**) something jotted down.

joule /dʒuːl/ *noun Physics* (ABBREV. **J**) the SI unit of work and energy, equal to the work done when a force of one newton moves through a distance of one metre in the direction of the force. [named after James Joule]

journal *noun* **1** a magazine or periodical, eg one dealing with a specialized subject. **2** a diary in which one recounts one's daily activities. **3** *Mech.* the part of an axle or rotating shaft within the bearing. [from Latin *diurnalis*, daily]

⊟ **1** magazine, periodical, newspaper, paper, publication, weekly, monthly. **2** diary, gazette, chronicle, daybook, log, record, register.

journalese *noun derog.* the language, typically shallow and full of clichés and jargon, used by less able journalists.

journalism *noun* the profession of writing for newspapers and magazines, or for radio and television.

journalist *noun* a person whose profession is journalism.

⊟ reporter, hack, correspondent, columnist, editor, commentator, newscaster.

journalistic *adj.* relating to or involving journalism or journalists.

journey — *noun* (PL. **journeys**) **1** a process of travelling from one place to another. **2** the distance covered by, or time taken for, a journey. — *verb intrans.* (**journeys, journeyed**) to make a journey. [from Old French *journee*, day]

⊟ *noun* **1** voyage, expedition, passage, trip, outing, tour, trek, safari. *verb* travel, voyage, go, proceed, tour, roam, rove, wander, trek, tramp.

journeyman *noun* **1** a craftsman qualified in a particular trade and working for an employer. **2** an experienced and competent but not outstanding worker. [from JOURNEY, in the old sense of a day's work]

journo *noun* (PL. **journos, journoes**) *colloq.* a journalist.

joust — *noun Hist.* a contest between two knights on horseback armed with lances. — *verb* to take part in a joust. [from French *jouster*, to joust, from Latin *juxta*, near]

Jove — **by Jove!** *Brit. old colloq. use* an exclamation of surprise or emphasis.

jovial *adj.* good-humoured; merry; cheerful. [from Latin *jovialis*, of the planet Jupiter, believed to be a lucky influence]

. . . .

▣ jolly, good-humoured, cheerful, merry, cheery, affable, cordial, genial.

▣ gloomy.

. . . .

joviality *noun* being cheerful.

jovially *adv.* in a cheerful way.

jowl[1] *noun* **1** the lower jaw. **2** the cheek. [from Anglo-Saxon *ceafl*, jaw]

jowl[2] *noun* (*usually* **jowls**) **1** loose flesh under the chin; a heavy double chin. **2** an animal's dewlap. [from Anglo-Saxon *ceole*, throat]

joy *noun* **1** a feeling of happiness. **2** a cause of this. **3** *Brit. colloq.* satisfaction; success: *any joy at the enquiry desk?* [from Old French *joie*]

. . . .

▣ **1** happiness, gladness, pleasure, delight, joyfulness, exultation, elation, bliss, ecstasy, rapture.

▣ **1** despair, grief.

. . . .

joyful *adj.* **1** happy; full of joy. **2** expressing or causing joy.

. . . .

▣ HAPPY, GLAD, EXULTANT, TRIUMPHANT. **1** pleased, delighted, elated, ecstatic.

▣ SAD, SORROWFUL.

. . . .

joyfully *adv.* with joy; gladly.

joyless *adj.* without joy, not giving joy.

joyous *adj.* filled with, causing, or showing joy.

joyride — *noun* a jaunt, especially a reckless drive in a stolen vehicle. — *verb intrans.* to go for such a jaunt.

joyrider *noun* a person who joyrides, especially in a stolen vehicle.

joystick *noun colloq.* a controlling lever, eg for a computer or an aircraft.

JP *abbrev.* Justice of the Peace.

Jr *abbrev.* (*used after a name*) Junior: *John Smith, Jr.*

jubilant *adj.* showing and expressing triumphant joy. [from Latin *jubilare*, to shout for joy]

. . . .

▣ joyful, delighted, thrilled, elated, overjoyed, rejoicing, exultant, triumphant.

. . . .

jubilantly *adv.* with great joy.

jubilation *noun* **1** triumphant rejoicing. **2** (**jubilations**) celebrations. [from Latin *jubilatio*]

jubilee *noun* a special anniversary, especially the 25th (*silver jubilee*), 50th (*golden jubilee*), or 60th (*diamond jubilee*) of a significant event, eg the succession of a monarch. [from Old French *jubile*, from Latin *jubilaeus annus*, the Jewish celebration of emancipation and restoration held every 50 years; ultimately from Hebrew *yobhel*, the ram's horn or trumpet used to announce this]

. . . .

▣ celebration, commemoration, anniversary, festival, festivity, gala, carnival.

. . . .

Jud. *abbrev. Biblical* **1** Judges. **2** Judith (Apocrypha).

Judaeo- or **Judeo-** *combining form* forming words meaning 'Jewish, Jewish and ...': *Judaeo-Hispanic.*

Judaic /dʒʊˈdeɪɪk/ *adj.* relating to the Jews or Judaism.

Judaism *noun* the religion of the Jews, central to which is the belief in one God, the transcendent creator of the world who delivered the Israelites out of their bondage in Egypt and chose them to be a light to all humankind.

Judas *noun* a traitor, especially to one's friends. [named after Judas Iscariot, the Apostle who betrayed Christ]

judder — *verb intrans.* (**juddered**, **juddering**) *said of a vehicle* to jolt, shake, shudder, or vibrate. — *noun* a shuddering vibration. [perhaps from SHUDDER + JAR[2]]

judge — *noun* **1** a public officer who hears and decides cases in a law court. **2** a person appointed to decide the winner of a contest. **3** someone who assesses something; a connoisseur: *a good judge of character.* **4** the person who decides or assesses: *let me be the judge of that.* — *verb* **1** to try (a legal case) in a law court as judge. **2** to decide the winner of (a contest). **3** to act as judge or adjudicator. **4** to assess. **5** *intrans.* to form an opinion. **6** to estimate. **7** to consider or state: *judged her fit to travel.* **8** to criticize, especially severely; to condemn. [from Old French *juge*]

. . . .

▣ *noun* **1** justice, magistrate, *slang* beak, arbiter, arbitrator, mediator, moderator. **2** adjudicator, referee, umpire. **3** connoisseur, authority, expert, arbiter, evaluator, assessor, reviewer, critic. *verb* **1** try, examine, arbitrate, mediate, moderate, decree, rule, find, sentence. **2** decide, determine, ascertain. **3** adjudicate, referee, umpire. **4** assess, appraise, evaluate, value, rate. **6** estimate, gauge, guess. **7** consider, deem, reckon, think, believe. **8** criticize, condemn, doom.

. . . .

judgement or **judgment** *noun* **1** the decision of a judge in a court of law. **2** the act or process of judging. **3** the ability to make wise or sensible decisions; good sense. **4** an opinion: *in my judgement.* **5** (*usually* **judgement on someone**) *old use* punishment regarded as sent by divine providence: *his sickness was a judgement on him.* — **against one's better judgement** contrary to what one believes to be the sensible course. **pass judgement on someone** to condemn them. **pass judgement on someone** or **something** to give an opinion or verdict about them. **reserve judgement** to postpone one's verdict. **sit in judgement on someone** to assume the responsibility of judging another person. [from Old French *jugement*]

. . . .

▣ **1** verdict, sentence, ruling, decree, order, finding, decision, conclusion. **2** adjudication, arbitration, mediation, moderation. **3** discernment, discrimination, wisdom, shrewdness, common sense, intelligence, taste, appreciation. **4** opinion, view, belief, estimate, assessment, evaluation, appraisal. **5** punishment, retribution, doom, fate.

. . . .

judgemental or **judgmental** *adj.* **1** involving judgement. **2** apt to pass judgement.

judicature *noun* **1** the administration of justice by legal trial. **2** the office of judge. **3** a body of judges. **4** a court or system of courts. [from Latin *judicare*, to judge]

judicial /dʒuːˈdɪʃəl/ *adj.* of, or relating to, a court of law, judges, or their decisions. [from Latin *judicialis*, from *judicium*, judgement]

. . . .

▣ legal, judiciary, judicatory, forensic.

. . . .

judiciary /dʒuːˈdɪʃərɪ/ *noun* (PL. **judiciaries**) **1** the branch of government concerned with the legal system and the administration of justice. **2** a country's body of judges. [from Latin *judiciarius*, of the law courts]

judicious /dʒuːˈdɪʃəs/ *adj.* shrewd, sensible, wise or tactful. [from Latin *judicium*, judgement]

. . . .

▣ wise, prudent, careful, cautious, shrewd, astute, discerning, reasonable, sensible, sound, well-judged, well-advised.

▣ injudicious.

. . . .

judo *noun* a Japanese form of wrestling using minimum physical effort, developed from jujitsu. [from Japanese *ju*, gentleness + *do*, art]

jug — *noun* **1** a deep container for liquids with a handle and a shaped lip for pouring. **2** the amount that a jug can hold. **3** *slang* prison. — *verb* (**jugged, jugging**) to stew (hare) in an earthenware container.

◨ *noun* **1** pitcher, ewer, carafe, flagon, urn, jar, vessel, container.

jugful *noun* (PL. **jugfuls**) the amount a jug will hold.

juggernaut *noun* **1** a mighty force sweeping away and destroying everything in its path. **2** *Brit. colloq.* a large articulated commercial road vehicle. [named after the gigantic chariot of the Hindu god JAGANNATHA]

juggle *verb* **1** *intrans.* to keep several objects simultaneously in the air by skilful throwing and catching. **2** *trans., intrans.* (**juggle something** or **juggle with something**) to adjust (facts, figures, etc) to create a misleading impression. [from Old French *jogler*, to act as jester]

◨ **2** alter, change, rearrange, manipulate, rig, falsify, doctor.

juggler *noun* a person who juggles.

jugular — *adj.* relating to the neck or throat. — *noun Anat.* (*in full* **jugular vein**) any of several veins that carry deoxygenated blood from the head to the heart in vertebrates. [from Latin *jugulum*, throat]

juice *noun* **1** liquid from fruit or vegetables. **2** (*usually* **juices**) the body's natural fluids: *digestive juices.* **3** *slang* power or fuel, especially electricity or petrol. [from Old French *jus*]

◨ **1** liquid, extract, essence, sap, nectar. **2** fluid, secretion.

juiciness *noun* being juicy.

juicy *adj.* (**juicier, juiciest**) **1** full of juice; rich and succulent. **2** *colloq., said of a problem, etc* challenging; meaty. **3** *colloq., said of gossip* intriguing; spicy. **4** *colloq.* profitable; lucrative.

◨ **1** succulent, moist, rich, lush. **3** interesting, intriguing, sensational, spicy, racy, risqué.

◧ **1** dry.

jujitsu or **jiu-jitsu** /dʒuːˈdʒɪtsuː/ *noun* a martial art founded on the ancient Japanese system of combat and self-defence without weapons, developed by the Samurai. [from Japanese *ju*, gentleness + *jutsu*, art]

juju *noun* **1** a charm or fetish used by W African tribes. **2** the magic contained in such a charm. [from Hausa (W African language) *djudju*, fetish]

jujube /ˈdʒuːdʒuːb/ *noun* **1** a soft fruit-flavoured sweet made with gelatine. **2** *Hist.* the fruit of a spiny shrub of the buckthorn family, dried and eaten as a sweet. [from Latin *jujuba*, from Greek *zizyphon*]

jukebox *noun* a coin-operated machine that plays whatever gramophone record one selects. [from Gullah (W African language) *juke*, disorderly]

Jul or **Jul.** *abbrev.* July.

julep /ˈdʒuːlɪp/ *noun* especially in N America, an iced drink of spirits and sugar, flavoured especially with mint. [from Persian *gulab*, rosewater]

Julian calendar the calendar introduced by Julius Caesar in 46BC, with a year of 365 days and 366 every leap year or centenary year. See also GREGORIAN CALENDAR.

July *noun* the seventh month of the year. [from *Julius mensis*, the month of Julius Caesar]

jumble — *verb* (*often* **jumble things up** or **together**) **1** to mix or confuse them, physically or mentally. **2** to throw them together untidily. — *noun* **1** a confused mass. **2** unwanted possessions collected, or suitable, for a jumble sale. [probably imitative]

◨ *verb* **1** mix (up), confuse, muddle, shuffle, disarrange, disorganize. *noun* **1** mess, chaos, mix-up, confusion, disorder, disarray, muddle, clutter, mixture, hotchpotch, *colloq.* mishmash.

jumble sale a sale of unwanted possessions, eg used clothing, usually to raise money for charity.

jumbo *colloq.* — *adj.* extra-large. — *noun* (PL. **jumbos**) a jumbo jet. [origin unknown; popularized as the name of an elephant exhibited in London in the 1880s]

jumbo jet *colloq.* the largest size of passenger jet airliner.

jump — *verb* **1** *intrans.* to spring off the ground, pushing off with the feet. **2** *intrans.* to leap or bound. **3** to get over or across by jumping. **4** to make (especially a horse) leap. **5** *intrans. said of prices, levels, etc* to rise abruptly. **6** *intrans.* to make a startled movement. **7** *intrans.* to twitch, jerk, or bounce. **8** (*intrans.*) to pass directly from one point to another, omitting intermediate matter or essential steps: *jump straight to the mad scene/jump to conclusions.* **9** to omit; to skip: *jump the next chapter.* **10** *colloq.* to pounce on. **11** *North Amer. colloq.* to board and travel on (especially a train) without paying. — *noun* **1** an act of jumping. **2** an obstacle to be jumped, especially a fence by a horse. **3** the height or distance jumped. **4** a jumping contest: *the high jump/the long jump.* **5** a sudden rise in amount, cost, or value. **6** an abrupt change or move. **7** a startled movement; a start: *gave a jump of surprise.* — **be** or **stay one jump ahead of someone** *colloq.* to anticipate the moves of rivals, and so maintain an advantage over them. **have the jump on someone** *colloq.* to have an advantage over them. **jump at something** to take or accept it eagerly. **jump down someone's throat** *colloq.* to snap at them impatiently. **jump on someone** to attack them physically or verbally. **jump to it** to hurry up.

◨ *verb* **1** spring, leap, bound, bounce, skip, hop. **2** leap, bound, prance, frolic, gambol. **3** leap, vault, clear. **5** rise, mount, increase, escalate, spiral. **6** start, flinch, wince, recoil. **9** omit, leave out, skip, miss, pass over, disregard, ignore, avoid, bypass. *noun* **1** spring, leap, bound, vault, bounce, skip, hop, prance, frolic. **2** hurdle, fence, gate, hedge, obstacle. **5** rise, increase, escalation, spiral, upsurge, upturn. **7** start, jerk, jolt, lurch, twitch, spasm, quiver, shiver.

jumped-up *adj. derog. colloq.* having an inflated view of one's importance; cocky, arrogant.

jumper[1] *noun* **1** a knitted garment for the top half of the body. **2** *North Amer.* a pinafore dress. [from old word *jump*, a short coat]

jumper[2] *noun* **1** a person or animal that jumps. **2** *Electr.* a wire used to make a temporary connection.

jumpily *adv.* in a nervous way.

jumpiness *noun* nervousness.

jump jet a jet aircraft that can take off and land vertically.

jump lead one of the two electric cables used to recharge one battery from another.

jump-off *noun Showjumping* an extra round held in the event of a tie.

jump start the act of jump-starting a vehicle.

jump-start *verb* to start the engine of (a motor vehicle) that has a weak or flat battery by using leads to attach it to a charged battery.

jumpsuit *noun* a one-piece garment combining trousers and top.

jumpy *adj.* (**jumpier, jumpiest**) **1** nervy; anxious. **2** moving jerkily.

◨ **1** nervy, nervous, anxious, agitated, jittery, shaky, tense, edgy, fidgety.

◧ **1** calm, composed.

Jun or **Jun.** *abbrev.* **1** June. **2** Junior.

junction *noun* **1** a place where roads or railway lines meet; an intersection. **2** a point of exit from, and access to, a motorway. **3** *Electr.* a point at which wires or cables are connected. **4** the process, an instance, or a point, of joining. [from Latin *junctio*, joining]

⊞ **1** intersection, meeting-point, confluence. **4** joint, join, connection, union, linking, coupling.

junction box the casing for an electrical junction.

juncture *noun* a point in time, especially if critical. [from Latin *junctura*, connection]

June *noun* the sixth month of the year. [from *Junius mensis*, the month of the goddess Juno]

jungle *noun* **1** an area of dense vegetation in an open area of tropical rainforest, eg on the site of former tree clearings, along a river bank, or at the forest edge. **2** a popular name for a tropical rainforest. **3** a mass of complexities difficult to penetrate: *the jungle of building regulations.* **4** a complex or hostile environment where toughness is needed for survival: *the blackboard jungle.* **5** a style of dance music with a strong and fast electronic drum beat. [from Hindi *jangal*]

junglefowl *noun* a pheasant native to E India and SE Asia, that inhabits forest and scrub, and feeds on grain, shoots, berries, and insects.

jungly *adj.* (**junglier, jungliest**) characteristic of or like jungle.

junior — *adj.* **1** (*often* **junior to someone**) **a** low or lower in rank. **b** younger. **2** of or for schoolchildren aged between 7 and 11: *junior schools.* **3** *North Amer., esp. US* of third-year college or university students. **4** younger; used after the name of a person with the same name as his or her parent. — *noun* **1** a person of low, or lower, rank in a profession, organization, etc. **2** a pupil in a junior school. **3** *North Amer., esp. US* a third-year college or high-school student. **4** a person younger than the one in question: *she's three years his junior.* **5** (**Junior**) a name used for referring to the son of a family: *have you seen Junior?* [from Latin *junior*, younger]

⊞ *adj.* **1** younger, minor, lesser, lower, subordinate, secondary, subsidiary, inferior.
⊟ *adj.* SENIOR.

juniper *noun* an evergreen shrub of northern regions with purple berries used as a medicine and for flavouring gin. [from Latin *juniperus*]

junk¹ — *noun colloq.* **1** worthless or rejected material; rubbish. **2** old or second-hand articles sold cheaply: *a junk shop.* **3** nonsense. **4** *slang* narcotic drugs, especially heroin. — *adj.* cheap and worthless: *junk jewellery.* [from Middle English *jonke*, pieces of old rope]

⊞ *noun* **1** rubbish, refuse, trash, garbage, waste, scrap, litter, clutter, wreckage, debris.

junk² *noun* a Far-Eastern flat-bottomed square-sailed boat. [from Portuguese *junco*, from Malay *jong*]

Junkers *pl. noun* Prussian aristocrats whose power rested on their large estates and on their traditional role as army officers and civil servants.

junket *noun* **1** a dessert made from sweetened and curdled milk. **2** a feast or celebration. **3** a trip made by a government official and paid for out of public funds. — *verb intrans.* (**junketed, junketing**) to feast, celebrate, or make merry. [from Old French *jonquette*, a rush basket for holding cheeses, etc]

junk food food with little nutritional value.

junkie or **junky** *noun* (PL. **junkies**) *slang* a drug addict or drug-pusher. [from JUNK¹ 4]

junta /'dʒʌntə, 'hʊntə/ *noun derog.* a group, clique or faction, usually of army officers, in control of a country after a coup d'état. [from Spanish *junta*, meeting]

Jupiter *noun Astron.* the fifth planet from the Sun, and the largest planet in the solar system. Its orbit lies between those of Mars and Saturn.

Jurassic — *noun Geol.* in the Mesozoic era, the period of geological time between the Triassic and Cretaceous periods, lasting from about 210 to 140 million years ago. — *adj.* belonging or relating to this period. [from the name *Jura*, a limestone mountain range in E France]

juridical *adj.* of or relating to the law or the administration of justice. [from Latin *juridicus*, of justice]

jurisdiction *noun* **1** the right or authority to apply laws and administer justice. **2** the district or area over which this authority extends. **3** authority generally. [from Latin *jurisdictio*, administration of justice]

⊞ **1** right, prerogative, power, authority, control, influence, dominion, command, sovereignty, rule, sway. **2** area, district, province, field, scope, range, reach, bounds, sphere, orbit. **3** power, authority, control, influence, dominion, command.

jurisprudence *noun* **1** the science and philosophy of law. **2** a speciality within law: *medical jurisprudence.* [from Latin *jurisprudentia*, from *jus*, law + *prudentia*, wisdom]

jurisprudential *adj.* relating to or involving jurisprudence.

jurist *noun* an expert in law. [from French *juriste*]

juristic *adj.* **1** relating to jurists. **2** relating to law or the study of it.

juror *noun* **1** a member of a jury in a court of law. **2** a person taking an oath. [from Latin *jurare*, to swear]

jury¹ *noun* (PL. **juries**) **1** a body of usually 12 people sworn to give an honest verdict on the evidence presented to a court of law on a particular case. **2** a group of people selected to judge a contest. [from Old French *juree*, something sworn]

jury² *adj. Naut.* makeshift; temporary: *a jury mast.*

jury-box *noun* the enclosure in which the jury sit in a law court.

just¹ *adj.* **1** fair; impartial. **2** reasonable; based on justice. **3** deserved. [from Latin *justus*, just, upright, equitable]

⊞ **1** fair, equitable, even-handed, impartial, unbiased, unprejudiced, objective, upright, honourable, honest, irreproachable. **2** reasonable, rightful, lawful, legitimate. **3** deserved, merited, fitting, appropriate, suitable, proper, due.
⊟ UNJUST. **1** unfair. **2** unreasonable. **3** undeserved.

just² *adv.* **1** exactly; precisely. **2** a short time before: *he had just gone.* **3** at this or that very moment: *was just leaving.* **4** and no earlier, more, etc: *only just enough.* **5** barely; narrowly: *just missed his ear.* **6** only; merely; simply: *just a brief note.* **7** *colloq.* used for emphasis: *just not true.* **8** *colloq.* absolutely: *just marvellous.* — **just about** almost: *am just about ready.* **just about to do something** on the point of doing it. **just as well** fortunate; lucky: *it's just as well you came.* **2** advisable: *it would be just as well to wait.* **just in case** as a precaution. **just a minute** or **second**, etc an instruction to wait a short while. **just now** at this particular moment. **just so 1** a formula of agreement. **2** neat and tidy: *they like everything just so.* **just then 1** at that particular moment. **2** in the next moment. **just the same** nevertheless. **not just yet** not immediately, but soon. [from Latin *justus*, right, proper]

justice *noun* **1** the quality of being just; just treatment; fairness. **2** the quality of being reasonable. **3** the law, or administration of or conformity to the law: *a miscarriage of justice.* **4** (**Justice**) the title of a judge. **5** a justice of the peace. **6** *North Amer., esp. US* a judge. — **bring someone to justice** to arrest and try them. **do justice to someone** or **something 1** to treat them fairly or properly. **2** to show their full merit, etc. **do justice to oneself** to fulfil one's potential. **in justice to someone** or **something** to be fair to them. [from Latin *justitia*, from *justus*, just]

▣ **1** fairness, impartiality, objectivity, equity, equitableness, justness, legitimacy, legality, honesty, rectitude. **2** reasonableness, justifiableness, right, rightness, rightfulness. **3** law, punishment, penalty, recompense, reparation.
▣ **1** injustice, unfairness.

justice of the peace (PL. **justices of the peace**) a person authorized to judge minor criminal cases.
justiciary /dʒʌˈstɪʃɪərɪ/ *noun* (PL. **justiciaries**) an administrator of justice; a judge. [from Latin *justiciarius*]
justifiable *adj.* that can be justified.

▣ defensible, excusable, forgivable, pardonable, understandable, reasonable, justified, warranted, lawful, legitimate, acceptable, tenable, valid, right, proper, fit.
▣ unjustifiable.

justifiably *adv.* in a justifiable way.
justification *noun* **1** justifying. **2** something which justifies.

▣ DEFENCE, VINDICATION, EXPLANATION. **1** mitigation, rationalization. **2** plea, apology, excuse, warrant, reason, grounds.

justify *verb* (**justifies, justified**) **1** to prove or show to be right, just, or reasonable. **2** *Printing* to arrange (text) so that the margins are even-edged. [from Latin *justus*, just + *facere*, to make]

▣ defend, vindicate, mitigate, exonerate, warrant, excuse, forgive, pardon, acquit, absolve, explain, rationalize, substantiate, validate, uphold, sustain, support, maintain.

jut *verb intrans.* (**jutted, jutting**) (*also* **jut out**) to stick out; to project. [variant of JET²]

▣ project, protrude, stick out, overhang, extend.

Jute *noun* a member of a Germanic people whose original homeland was the northern part of the Danish peninsula (Jutland). [from Anglo-Saxon *Iotas*, the Jutes]
jute *noun* fibre from certain tropical barks used for making sacking, ropes, etc. [from Bengali *jhuta*]
juvenile — *adj.* **1** young; youthful. **2** suitable for young people. **3** *derog.* childish; immature. — *noun* **1** a young person. **2** a young animal. **3** an actor playing youthful parts. [from Latin *juvenilis*, youthful]

▣ *adj.* **1** young, youthful, adolescent. **3** immature, childish, puerile, infantile, babyish. *noun* **1** child, youngster, young person, minor, youth, adolescent, teenager, boy, girl, *colloq.* kid.
▣ *adj.* **1** adult. **3** mature. *noun* **1** adult.

juvenile delinquency criminal or antisocial acts or behaviour of juvenile delinquents.
juvenile delinquent a young person who is guilty of a crime.
juvenile hormone *Zool.* a hormone that is required for growth and development of the immature stages in the life cycle of an insect, but inhibits development into the adult form.
juvenilia *pl. noun* the works produced by a writer or artist during his or her youth. [from Latin *juvenilis*, youthful]
juxtapose *verb* to place side by side. [from Latin *juxta*, beside + POSITION]
juxtaposition *noun* placing or being placed together.

▣ contact, contiguity, proximity, nearness, closeness, vicinity.

K

K¹ or **k** *noun* (PL. **Ks**, **K's**, **k's**) the eleventh letter of the English alphabet.

K² *noun* (PL. **K**) **1** *colloq.* one thousand, especially £1000. **2** *Comput.* a unit of memory equal to 1024 bits, bytes, or words. [from KILO-]

K³ *abbrev.* **1** kelvin. **2** kilo. **3** *Chess, Cards* king. **4** *Knitting* knit (a plain stitch). **5** krona, króna, or krone.

K⁴ *symbol Chem.* potassium. [from Latin *kalium*]

kabaddi /kə'badı/ *noun* an Asian version of tag played barefoot by two teams of seven.

kachina /kə'tʃiːnə/ *noun Relig.* any of the ancestral spirits invoked by the Pueblo Indians of N America at ritual ceremonies; also, a dancer representing one of these. [from Hopi *qachina*, supernatural]

Kaffir /'kafə(r)/ *noun* **1** *South Afr. offensive* a black African. **2** *old use* the Xhosa language, a Bantu language of South Africa. [from Arabic *kafir*, unbeliever]

kaftan see CAFTAN.

kaiser /'kaɪzə(r)/ *noun Hist.* the emperor of Germany, Austria or the Holy Roman Empire. [from German *Kaiser*, from *Caesar*, family name of the earliest Roman emperors]

kakemono /kakı'mɒnoʊ/ *noun* a Japanese wall hanging made of silk or paper with a roller at the bottom. [from Japanese *kake*, to hang + *mono*, thing]

kalanchoe /kalən'koʊı/ *noun* a succulent herb or shrub of the genus *Kalanchoe*, native to tropical Africa and Madagascar. [from Mandarin]

kalashnikov /kə'laʃnıkɒf/ *noun* a type of submachine-gun manufactured in the Soviet Union. [from Russian *Kalashnikov*, the name of the inventor]

kale *noun* **1** a variety of cabbage that does not form a head, and has loose wrinkled or curled leaves, widely cultivated in Europe as a vegetable and fodder crop. **2** *Scot.* cabbage. [from Anglo-Saxon *cawl*]

kaleidoscope *noun* **1** a tubular device inside which loose fragments of coloured glass, etc are reflected in mirrors, usually two set at 45° or 60°, so as to form constantly changing symmetrical patterns as the tube is shaken or rotated. **2** any colourful and constantly changing scene or succession of events. [from Greek *kalos*, beautiful, *eidos*, form + -SCOPE]

kaleidoscopic *adj.* **1** relating to or characteristic of a kaleidoscope. **2** showing constant change.

kaleidoscopically *adv.* in a kaleidoscopic way.

kalends same as CALENDS.

kaleyard *noun Scot.* a vegetable garden.

kamikaze /kamı'kɑːzı/ — *noun* in World War II, a Japanese plane loaded with explosives deliberately crashed by its pilot on an enemy target; the pilot himself. — *adj. colloq., said of exploits, missions, etc* suicidally dangerous. [from Japanese, = divine wind]

Kan. *abbrev.* Kansas.

kana /'kɑːnə/ *noun* either of two Japanese syllabic writing systems (*katagana* and *hiragama*) based on spoken language, as distinguished from the form of Japanese writing based on Chinese characters known as *Kanji*. See also SYLLABARY.

kangaroo *noun* any of various herbivorous marsupials native to Australia, Tasmania, and New Guinea, and hav-

ing strong hind legs with elongated feet, short front legs, and a thick muscular tail. [from *gangurru*, an Australian Aboriginal word]

kangaroo court an unofficial court of eg strikers to try strikebreakers, or prisoners to try fellow prisoners.

Kans. *abbrev.* Kansas.

KANU *abbrev.* Kenya African National Union.

kaolin /'keɪəlɪn/ *noun* china clay, a fine white clay used for making pottery, and medically in poultices and medicines. [named after Chinese *Kao-ling* or *Gao-ling* ('high ridge'), a mountain where it was mined]

kaolinite *noun Geol.* a white, grey, or yellowish clay mineral consisting of hydrated aluminium silicate formed as a result of the alteration of feldspars by heated water or weathering. [from the mountain Kao-ling (high ridge) in China]

kapok /'keɪpɒk/ *noun* a light cotton-like fibre obtained from the pods of a tropical tree and used as padding or as stuffing for toys, etc. [from Malay *kapoq*]

kappa *noun* the tenth letter of the Greek alphabet (κ).

kaput /kə'pʊt/ *adj. colloq.* **1** broken. **2** ruined; destroyed. [from German *kaputt*]

karakul /'kɑːrəkuːl/ *noun* an Asian sheep whose lambs have a dark curly fleece; fur made from, or in imitation of, this fleece. [named after *Kara-Kul*, a lake in Tajikistan, central Asia, near which the sheep were originally bred]

karaoke /kɑːrə'oʊkı/ *noun* an originally Japanese form of entertainment in which amateur performers sing pop songs to the accompaniment of pre-recorded music from a machine. [from Japanese, = 'empty orchestra']

karate /kə'rɑːtı/ *noun* an originally Japanese system of unarmed self-defence, using blows and kicks. [from Japanese, = empty hand]

karate chop a sharp downward blow with the side of the hand.

karbovanets /kɑːbə'vɑːnɪts/ *noun* (PL. **karbovantsi**) the unit of currency of the Republic of the Ukraine. [Ukrainian]

karma /'kɑːmə/ *noun Buddhism, Hinduism* one's lifetime's actions, seen as governing one's fate in one's next life. [from Sanskrit *karma*, act, deed]

kart *noun colloq.* a go-kart.

karyotype /'karıətaɪp/ *noun Genetics* **1** the number, size, and structure of the chromosomes in the nucleus of a cell, characteristic of all the diploid cells of a particular individual, strain, or species. **2** the representation of this in a diagram or photograph. [from Greek *karyon*, kernel]

kasbah /'kazbɑː/ *noun* a castle or fortress in a N African town or the area around it, especially in Algiers. [from Arabic dialect *kasba*]

Kassites *pl. noun* a people, possibly of Iranian origin, who were the dominant power in Babylonia and Lower Mesopotamia after the Hittite destruction of Babylon in 1595 BC.

katydid /'keɪtıdıd/ *noun* a large N American grasshopper. [imitative]

kauri /'kaʊərı/ *noun* a coniferous tree of New Zealand grown for its wood and resin. [from Maori]

kayak *noun* **1** a sealskin-covered canoe used by the Inuit. **2** a similar canvas-covered or fibreglass craft used in the sport of canoeing. [from Inuit *qayaq*]

kazoo /kə'zu:/ *noun* a crude wind instrument consisting of a short metal tube into which one hums, causing a strip of parchment, etc stretched across a hole in its upper surface, to vibrate with a buzzing effect. [imitative]

KB *abbrev.* King's Bench.

KBE *abbrev.* Knight Commander of the British Empire.

KBS *abbrev. Comput.* knowledge-based systems, software systems which aim to store and effectively utilize large amounts of specialist knowledge.

KC *abbrev.* King's Counsel.

KCB *abbrev.* Knight Commander of (the Order of) the Bath.

KCMG *abbrev.* Knight Commander of (the Order of) St Michael and St George.

KCVO *abbrev.* Knight Commander of the (Royal) Victorian Order.

kebab /kə'bab/ *noun* a dish of small pieces of meat and vegetable, especially (*shish kebab*) grilled on a skewer. [from Arabic *kabab*; from Turkish *sis*, skewer]

kedge — *verb trans., intrans., said of a ship* to manoeuvre by means of a hawser attached to a light anchor. — *noun* a light anchor used for kedging. [related to Middle English *caggen*, to fasten]

kedgeree /'kɛdʒəri:/ *noun* an originally E Indian dish, now usually a mixture of rice, fish and eggs. [from Hindi *khichri*]

keek *Scot.* — *noun* a peep. — *verb intrans.* to take a peep. [from Middle English *kiken*]

keel — *noun* the timber or metal strut extending from stem to stern along the base of a ship, from which the hull is built up. — *verb* (**keel over**) **1** *said of a ship* to tip over sideways. **2** *colloq.* to fall over, eg in a faint. — **on an even keel** calm and steady. [from Middle English *kele*, from Old Dutch *kiel*, ship]

∙∙∙∙∙∙∙∙∙∙∙∙∙∙∙∙∙∙∙∙

⊟ *verb* **1** overturn, capsize, founder, collapse. **2** faint, pass out, fall, drop, fall over, topple over.

∙∙

keelhaul *verb* to drag (someone) under the keel of a ship from one side to the other, as a naval punishment.

keelson same as KELSON.

keen[1] *adj.* **1** eager; willing. **2** (**keen on someone** or **something**) enthusiastic about them; fond of them. **3** *said of competition, rivalry, etc* fierce. **4** *said of the wind* bitter. **5** *said of a blade, etc* sharp. **6** *said of the mind or senses* quick; acute. **7** *said of prices* low; competitive. [from Anglo-Saxon *cene*, bold, fierce]

∙∙∙∙∙∙∙∙∙∙∙∙∙∙∙∙∙∙∙∙∙

⊟ **1** eager, avid, ardent, fervent, enthusiastic, earnest, diligent, industrious. **3** fierce, intense. **4** bitter, piercing, penetrating. **5** sharp, razor-sharp, edged, knife-edged, pointed. **6** quick, acute, sharp, astute, shrewd, perceptive, discerning, sensitive.

E3 **1** apathetic. **5** blunt. **6** dull.

∙∙

keen[2] — *verb intrans., trans.* especially in Ireland, to lament or mourn in a loud wailing voice. — *noun* a lament for the dead. [from Irish *caoine*, lament]

keenly *adv.* in a keen way; with enthusiasm.

keenness *noun* being keen.

keep[1] — *verb* (PAST TENSE AND PAST PARTICIPLE **kept**) **1** to have; to possess. **2** to continue to have; not to part with; to save. **3** to maintain or retain: *keep one's temper.* **4** to store. **5** *trans., intrans.* to remain or cause to remain in a certain state, position, place, etc. **6** *intrans.* to continue or be frequently (doing something): *keep smiling/kept fainting.* **7** *said of a shopkeeper, etc* to have regularly in stock. **8** to own (an animal, etc) for use or pleasure: *keep hens.* **9** to own or run (a shop, boarding-house, etc). **10** to look after: *keep house/keep this for me.* **11** *intrans., said of food* to remain fit to be eaten. **12** to maintain (a record, diary, accounts, etc). **13** (**keep from something**) to hold back or delay doing it. **14** to obey (the law, etc). **15** to preserve (a se-

cret). **16** to stick to (a promise or appointment). **17** to celebrate (a festival, etc) in the traditional way; to follow (a custom). **18** to support financially. **19** to protect: *keep them from harm.* **20** to guard (the goal) in football or (the wicket) in cricket. **21** to remain firm on: *managed to keep his feet despite the strong wind.* **22** to delay or hold up: *don't let me keep you/I wonder what's keeping them.* — *noun* the cost of one's food and other daily expenses: *earn one's keep.* — **for keeps** *colloq.* permanently; for good. **keep at something** to persevere at or persist in it. **keep something back 1** to conceal information, etc. **2** to suppress laughter, tears, etc. **keep someone down** to oppress them; to prevent their development, progress, etc. **keep something down 1** to control or limit prices, etc. **2** to manage not to vomit food, etc. **keep someone from something** to prevent them from doing something. **keep something from someone** to prevent it from reaching them: *tried to keep the news from him.* **keep going** to persevere in spite of problems. **keep someone going** to help them survive difficulties, etc. **keep in with someone** to remain on good terms with them, especially to avoid a harmful food, awkward topic, etc. **keep on doing something** to continue with it. **keep someone on** to continue to employ them. **keep something on 1** to continue renting or using it: *we had a flat in town but decided not to keep it on.* **2** to continue to wear a piece of clothing. **keep on about something** or **someone** to talk continually and repetitively about them. **keep on at someone** to nag or harass them. **keep to something** not to leave it: *keep to the path.* **keep someone to something** to make them adhere to a promise, decision, etc: *I'll keep you to that.* **keep to oneself** to avoid the company of others. **keep something to oneself** not to reveal it to others. **keep someone under** to subdue, repress, or crush them. **keep something up 1** to prevent eg spirits, morale, etc from falling. **2** to maintain a habit, friendship, pace, etc. **3** to go on making payments, etc. **4** to maintain a house, garden, etc in good condition. **keep up with someone** not to be left behind; to maintain the pace or standard set by someone else. **keep up with the Joneses** *colloq.* to compete with one's neighbours in a display of material prosperity. [from Anglo-Saxon *cepan*, to guard, observe, watch]

∙∙∙∙∙∙∙∙∙∙∙∙∙∙∙∙∙∙∙∙∙

⊟ *verb* **1** have, possess, own, hold. **2** retain, hold on to, hang on to, save, reserve, conserve, preserve. **4** store, collect, amass, accumulate, heap, pile, stack. **6** continue, carry on, remain. **7** stock, sell, retail, handle, deal in. **9** own, run, manage. **10** look after, tend, care for, have custody of, mind, watch (over). **14** obey, respect, comply with, observe, follow. **16** fulfil, stick to, adhere to. **17** celebrate, commemorate, mark, honour, observe, follow, perpetuate. **18** maintain, provide for, subsidize, support, sustain, feed, nurture. **19** protect, shelter, shield, safeguard. **20** guard, defend. **22** delay, detain, slow down, hold up. *noun* living, livelihood, maintenance, support, upkeep, subsistence, board. **keep back** HOLD BACK, SUPPRESS, STIFLE. **1** conceal, hide, withhold, hush up, censor. **2** contain, restrict, restrain, check, curb, control, stop. **keep someone from something** prevent from, deter from, restrain from, inhibit from. **keep on doing something** continue, carry on, endure, persist in, persevere at, keep at. **keep up with** keep pace with, compete with, contend with, vie with, rival, match, equal, emulate.

E3 *verb* **1, 2, 3** lose. **14, 16** break.

∙∙

keep[2] *noun* the central tower or stronghold in a Norman castle. [from KEEP[1]]

∙∙∙∙∙∙∙∙∙∙∙∙∙∙∙∙∙∙∙∙∙

⊟ tower, citadel, stronghold, fort, fortress, castle.

∙∙

keeper *noun* **1** a person who looks after something, eg animals in a zoo or a collection in a museum. **2** *colloq.* a goalkeeper or wicketkeeper.

∙∙∙∙∙∙∙∙∙∙∙∙∙∙∙∙∙∙∙∙∙

⊟ **1** guardian, custodian, curator, caretaker, attendant,

steward, warden, guard, jailer, warder, supervisor, overseer.

keep-fit *noun* a series or system of exercises, especially for women, intended to improve suppleness, stamina, etc.

keeping *noun* care or charge. — **in** or **out of keeping with something** in, or not in, harmony with it.

keepsake *noun* something kept in memory of the giver.

■ memento, souvenir, remembrance, reminder, relic, token, pledge, emblem.

keg *noun* a small barrel for transporting and storing beer. [from Old Norse *kaggi*]

kelp *noun* **1** the common name for any large brown seaweed that grows below the low-tide mark. **2** the ash obtained by burning kelp, used as an agricultural fertilizer and a source of iodine. [a variant of Middle English *culp*]

kelpie *noun Scot. Folklore* a malignant water spirit in the form of a horse.

kelson or **keelson** *noun* a timber fixed along a ship's keel for strength. [from Old German *kielswin*, keel swine]

Kelt same as CELT.

kelt *noun* a salmon or sea trout that has just spawned.

kelvin *noun Physics* the SI unit of thermodynamic temperature, equal to one degree Celsius. [named after William Thomson Kelvin, who introduced the absolute (Kelvin) scale of temperature (1848)]

Ken. *abbrev.* Kentucky.

ken — *verb* (**kenning**; PAST TENSE AND PAST PARTICIPLE **kent, kenned**) *Scot. dialect* to know. — *noun* one's range of knowledge: *beyond/within one's ken*. [from Anglo-Saxon *cennan*]

kendo *noun* a Japanese form of fencing using bamboo swords. [from Japanese *kendo*, sword way]

kennel — *noun* **1** a small shelter for a dog. **2** (**kennels**) an establishment where dogs are boarded or bred. — *verb* (**kennelled, kennelling**) to put or keep in a kennel. [from Latin *canis*, dog]

kepi /'keɪpi:/ *noun* a French military cap with a flat circular crown and horizontal straight-edged peak. [from French *képi*, from Swiss German *Käppi*, diminutive of German *Kappe*, cap]

kept — *verb* past tense and past participle of KEEP. — *adj. said of a man or woman* supported financially by someone in return for being available to them for sexual relations.

keratin /'kerətɪn/ *noun Biol.* a tough fibrous protein produced by the outer layer of the skin (the epidermis) of vertebrates. It is the main component of hair, nails, claws, horns, feathers, and the dead outer layers of skin cells. [from Greek *keras -atos*, horn]

kerb *noun* the row of stones forming the edging of a pavement. [variant of CURB]

kerb-crawler *noun* a person who practises kerb-crawling.

kerb-crawling *noun* the practice of driving slowly alongside the kerb in order to lure potential sexual partners into one's car.

kerbstone *noun* one of the stones forming a kerb.

kerchief /'kɜːtʃɪf/ *noun old use* **1** a cloth or scarf for wearing over the head or round the neck. **2** a handkerchief. [from Old French *cuevrechief*, from *covrir*, to cover + *chef*, head]

kerfuffle /kə'fʌfl/ *noun colloq.* a commotion or fuss. [from Gaelic prefix *car-* + Scot. *fuffle*, to disorder]

Kermit *noun Comput.* a public-domain computer program used to transfer files between different computer systems, eg between a PC and a mainframe. [named after *Kermit the Frog*, a character in the US television show 'The Muppet Show']

kernel *noun* **1** *Bot.* the inner part of a seed, eg the edible part of a nut. **2** *Bot.* in cereal plants such as corn, the entire grain or seed. **3** the important, essential part of anything. [from Anglo-Saxon *cyrnel*, diminutive of *corn*, a grain]

■ **1** nucleus, heart, core. **2** grain, seed. **3** essence, nub, marrow, substance, gist, *colloq.* nitty-gritty, nucleus, heart, core.

kerosene /'kerəsiːn/ *noun* **1** paraffin oil distilled from petroleum or obtained from coal or shale, used for heating and lighting, and as an aircraft fuel. **2** *North Amer.* paraffin. [from Greek *keros*, wax]

kerygma /kə'rɪgmə/ *noun Relig.* the preaching of the Christian gospel, especially in the way of the early Christian Church, specifically the apostles' announcement of the saving nature of Christ's death and resurrection, so that Christ becomes not just the proclaimer of salvation but that which is proclaimed. [from Greek *kerygma*, proclamation, that which is announced]

kestrel *noun* a small type of falcon. [from Old French *quercerelle*]

ketch *noun* a small two-masted sailing boat. [from Middle English *cache*, related to CATCH]

ketchup *noun* a thick sauce made from tomatoes, vinegar, spices, etc. [from Malay *kechap*]

ketone /'kiːtəʊn/ *noun Chem.* any member of a class of organic chemical compounds that are formed by the oxidation of secondary alcohols, and contain a carbonyl (C=O) group attached to two hydrocarbon groups, eg acetone. [from German *Keton*, from *Aketon*, acetone]

kettle *noun* a kitchen vessel with a spout, lid and handle, for boiling water. — **a different kettle of fish** *colloq.* an entirely different matter. **a pretty kettle of fish** *colloq.* an awkward situation. [from Anglo-Saxon *cetel*]

kettledrum *noun* a large copper or brass cauldron-shaped drum mounted on a tripod.

key¹ — *noun* **1** an instrument designed to turn a lock, wind a clock, grip and turn a nut, etc. **2** one of a series of buttons or levers pressed to sound the notes on a musical instrument, or to print or display a character on a computer, typewriter, calculator, etc. **3** a system of musical notes related to one another in a scale. **4** pitch, tone or style: *spoke in a low key*. **5** something that provides an answer or solution. **6** a means of achievement: *the key to success*. **7** a set of answers, eg at the back of a book of puzzles, exercises, etc. **8** a table explaining signs and symbols used on a map, etc. **9** *Electr.* a switch for completing or breaking a circuit. **10** the winged seed of the sycamore or ash tree. **11** roughness given to a surface by sandpapering, etc, so as to take paint, etc more readily. **12** a fret pattern. **13** a pin or wedge for fixing something. — *adj.* centrally important: *key questions*. — *verb* **1** to enter (data) into a computer by operating keys. **2** to fasten or fix with a key. **3** (**key one thing to another**) to adjust or harmonize it. — **keyed up** *colloq.* excited; tense; anxious. **under lock and key 1** safely stored. **2** in prison. [from Anglo-Saxon *cæg*]

■ *noun* **5** clue, indicator, pointer, sign, cue, answer, solution, interpretation, explanation. **6** means, secret. **7** index, glossary. **8** table, legend. *adj.* important, essential, vital, crucial, necessary, central, chief, main, principal, major, leading, basic, fundamental.

key² or **cay** *noun* a small low island or reef formed of sand, coral, rock, or mud, especially such islands off the coast of Florida. [Spanish *cayo*]

keyboard — *noun* **1** the set of keys on a piano, etc or the bank of keys for operating a typewriter or computer. **2** especially in jazz, a musical instrument with a keyboard, eg a synthesizer. — *verb* **1** *intrans.* to operate the keyboard of a computer. **2** *trans.* to set (text) using a computer keyboard.

keyboarder *noun* a person who enters data, especially text, by means of a keyboard.

keyboardist *noun* **1** a person who plays music on a keyboard. **2** same as KEYBOARDER.

keyhole *noun* the hole through which a key is inserted into a lock.

keyhole surgery *Medicine* surgery using miniature instruments, performed through tiny holes in the outer tissue.

Keynesian /ˈkeɪnzɪən/ *adj.* relating to the economic theories of J M Keynes, advocating government funding of public works to maintain full employment.

keynote *noun* **1** the note on which a musical scale or key is based. **2** a central theme of a speech, feature of an occasion, etc.

. . . .

▣ **2** theme, gist, substance, essence, centre, heart, core, emphasis, accent, stress.

. . . .

key pad a small panel of keys or buttons. eg for dialling a telephone number, operating a calculator, adjusting a television, etc.

key punch a device operated by a keyboard for transferring data on to punched cards.

key-ring *noun* a ring for keeping keys on.

key signature *Mus.* the sharps and flats shown on the stave at the start of a piece of music, indicating its key.

keystone *noun* **1** the central supporting stone at the high point of an arch. **2** the point in a theory or argument on which the rest depends.

. . . .

▣ **2** cornerstone, linchpin, crux, base, basis, foundation, root, source.

. . . .

keystroke *noun* a single press of a key on a typewriter, computer, etc.

keyword *noun* **1** in text, a word that sums up or gives an indication of the nature of the passage in which it occurs. **2** a word indexed or highlighted in a concordance or VDU display.

KG *abbrev.* Knight of the Order of the Garter.

kg *abbrev.* kilogram.

KGB *abbrev. Komitet Gosudarstvennoi Bezopastnosti* (Russian) (Committee of State Security), the Russian and former Soviet secret police.

khaki /ˈkɑːkɪ/ *noun* **1** a brownish-green colour. **2** cloth of this colour, or military uniforms made of it. [from Urdu and Persian *khaki*, dusty]

khalif see CALIPH.

khan /kɑːn/ *noun* **1** the title of a ruler or prince in central Asia. **2** in ancient Persia, a governor. [related to Turkish *kagan*, ruler]

Khmer /kmɛə(r)/ *— noun* the official language of Cambodia (formerly Kampuchea and the Khmer Republic): also known as Cambodian. *— adj.* relating to or spoken or written in Khmer.

Khoisan *pl. noun* a collective term for the San (Bushmen) and Khoi (Hottentot) peoples of southern Africa.

KHz *abbrev.* kilohertz.

kibbutz /kɪˈbʊts/ *noun* (PL. **kibbutzim**) in Israel, a farm or other concern owned and run jointly by its workers. [from Modern Hebrew *kibus*]

kibosh /ˈkaɪbɒʃ/ *noun —* **put the kibosh on something** *colloq.* to put an end to it; to ruin it.

kick *— verb* **1** to hit (a person, etc) or propel (a ball, etc) with the foot. **2** *intrans., trans.* to swing or jerk (the leg) vigorously. **3** *intrans., said of a gun* to recoil when fired. **4** *intrans.* (**kick against something**) to resist it: *kick against discipline.* **5** to get rid of (a habit, etc). **6** to score (a goal) with a kick. *— noun* **1** a blow with the foot. **2** a swing of the leg: *high kicks.* **3** *Swimming* any of various leg movements. **4** the recoil of a gun after firing. **5** *colloq.* a thrill of excitement. **6** *colloq.* a strong effect; power: *a drink with quite a kick.* **7** *colloq.* a brief enthusiasm: *we're on a culture kick.* *—* **kick about** or **around** *colloq.* **1** to lie around unused. **2** to be idle; to go about aimlessly. **kick someone about** or **around** *colloq.* to treat them badly or roughly. **kick something about** or **around** *colloq.* to discuss an idea, etc informally among several people. **kick in** *colloq.*

to start working or being effective. **a kick in the teeth** *colloq.* a humiliating snub. **kick someone in the teeth** *colloq.* to inflict a snub on them. **kick off 1** to start a football game by kicking the ball away from the centre. **2** *colloq.* to begin a discussion or other activity involving several people. **kick something off** *colloq.* to begin a discussion. **kick something** or **someone out** *colloq.* to dismiss or get rid of them, especially using force. **kick up a fuss** or **stink** *colloq.* to complain or disapprove strongly. **kick someone upstairs** *colloq.* to promote them to a position of higher rank but less influence. [from Middle English *kiken*]

. . . .

▣ *verb* **1** boot, hit, strike, propel. **5** give up, quit, stop, leave off, desist from, break. *noun* **5** thrill, excitement, stimulation. **kick off 2** start, begin, commence, set the ball rolling. **kick something off** start, begin, commence, open. **kick out** eject, evict, expel, oust, dismiss, discharge, *colloq.* sack, get rid of, throw out, *colloq.* chuck out.

. . . .

kickback *noun* money paid for help or favours, especially if illegally given.

kicker *noun* a person or animal that kicks.

kick-off *noun* **1** the start or re-start of a football match. **2** *colloq.* the start of anything. *—* **for a kick-off** *colloq.* for a start.

kick pleat a small pleat at the back of a skirt.

kick-start *— noun* **1** (*also* **kick-starter**) a pedal on a motor cycle that is kicked vigorously downwards to start the engine. **2** the starting of an engine with this. *— verb* **1** to start (a motor cycle) using this. **2** to get something moving or give it a sudden impulse.

kid[1] *— noun* **1** *colloq.* a child; a young person. **2** a young goat. **3** soft leather made from its skin. *— adj. colloq.* younger: *my kid sister. —* **handle someone with kid gloves** to treat them with special care or caution. *— verb intrans.* (**kidded, kidding**) *said of a goat* to give birth to young. [related to Norse *kith*, young goat]

. . . .

▣ *noun* **1** child, youngster, *colloq.* nipper, boy, girl, youth, teenager, infant, *colloq.* tot.

. . . .

kid[2] *verb* (**kidded, kidding**) *colloq.* **1** to fool or deceive, especially light-heartedly or in fun. **2** *intrans.* to bluff; to pretend. **3** *trans., intrans.* to tease. *—* **kid oneself** to fool oneself about something: *kidding himself all was well.* [perhaps from KID[1]]

. . . .

▣ **1** tease, fool, deceive, *colloq.* have on, hoax, trick, delude, dupe, hoodwink, *colloq.* con. **2** bluff, pretend, joke, jest.

. . . .

kidder *noun* a person who deceives, a joker.

kiddie or **kiddy** *noun* (PL. **kiddies**) *colloq.* a small child. [from KID[1]]

kidnap *verb* (**kidnapped, kidnapping**) to seize and hold (someone) prisoner illegally, usually demanding a ransom for his or her release. [from KID[1] + NAP, variant of *nab*]

. . . .

▣ abduct, hold to ransom, capture, seize, snatch, hijack, steal.

. . . .

kidney *noun* (PL. **kidneys**) **1** in vertebrates, one of a pair of organs that are concerned with the removal of waste products, especially nitrogenous compounds, from the blood, and the excretion of such waste material, usually in the form of urine. **2** animal kidneys as food. [from Middle English *kidnei*; *-ei* is perhaps related to EGG (from the shape of the organ)]

kidney bean a dark red kidney-shaped bean eaten as a vegetable.

kidney machine an apparatus used, when the kidney has failed, to remove harmful substances from the blood by dialysis.

kieselguhr /ˈkiːzlɡʊə(r)/ *noun Geol.* a soft whitish powdery deposit containing silica, and consisting mainly of the remains of cell walls of diatoms. Also called DIATOMITE. [from German *Kieselguhr*, from *Kiesel*, flint + *Ghur*, fermentation]

kill — *verb* **1** to cause the death of. **2** *colloq.* to cause pain to: *my feet are killing me.* **3** *colloq.* to cause to fail; to put an end to: *how to kill a conversation.* **4** to defeat (a parliamentary bill). **5** *colloq.* to destroy the effect of: *the turquoise kills the green.* **6** *colloq.* to deaden (pain, noise, etc). **7** to pass (time), especially aimlessly or wastefully, while waiting for some later event. **8** *colloq., usually ironic* to exhaust or put a strain on: *don't kill yourself.* — *noun* **1** an act of killing. **2** the prey killed by any creature. — **be in at the kill** *colloq.* to be present at someone's dramatic downfall, or some other kind of confrontation. **dressed to kill** *facetious* captivatingly or impressively dressed. **kill someone** or **something off** to destroy them completely, or on a large scale. **kill oneself** *colloq.* to be reduced to helpless laughter. [from Middle English *cullen* or *killen*]

▤ *verb* **1** slaughter, put to death, destroy, put down, murder, slay, assassinate, do to death, *colloq.* do in, *colloq.* knock off, *slang* bump off, exterminate, annihilate, massacre, butcher, execute, *slang* eliminate, *slang* liquidate, *North Amer. slang* rub out. **6** deaden, smother, stifle, suppress, quell.

killer *noun* **1** a person who kills. **2** a substance or thing that can cause or has caused death. **3** *colloq.* a gruelling activity or task.

▤ murderer, assassin, executioner, exterminator, slaughterer, butcher, cut-throat, gunman, *colloq.* hit man, *colloq.* hatchet man.

killer whale a toothed whale found worldwide in cool coastal waters, 9m to 10m in length, black with white underparts, and having white patches on its head, and a narrow vertical dorsal fin.

killifish *noun* a small colourful carp-like freshwater fish widespread in tropical and warm temperate regions, and having jaws bearing small teeth. [from dialect *kill*, stream]

killing *colloq.* — *noun* an act of slaying. — *adj.* **1** exhausting. **2** highly amusing. — **make a killing** *colloq.* to make a large amount of money, especially unexpectedly or in a quick transaction.

▤ *noun* **1** slaughter, manslaughter, murder, homicide, assassination, execution, extermination, massacre, carnage, bloodshed, *slang* elimination, *slang* liquidation. *adj.* **1** exhausting, taxing, arduous, hard. **2** hilarious, side-splitting, *colloq.* hysterical, *colloq.* rich, *colloq.* priceless, funny, comical, amusing. **make a killing** *slang* clean up, make a fortune, have a windfall, have a lucky break.

killingly *adv.* overpoweringly, exhaustingly.

killjoy *noun* someone who spoils others' pleasure.

kiln *noun* an oven for baking pottery or bricks or for drying grain. [from Anglo-Saxon *cylen*, from Latin *culina*, kitchen]

kilo *noun* (PL. **kilos**) a kilogram or kilometre.

kilo- *combining form* forming words meaning 'one thousand'. [from Greek *chilioi*, thousand]

kilobyte *noun Comput.* a unit of 1024 bytes.

kilocalorie *noun* (ABBREV. **kcal**) the amount of heat required to raise the temperature of one kilogram of water by 1°C (1K). It is often used to express the energy content of food, but has been replaced in SI units by the joule (1kcal = 4.18kJ). Also called CALORIE, LARGE CALORIE.

kilocycle *noun old use* a kilohertz.

kilogram or **kilogramme** *noun* (ABBREV. **kg**) the SI unit of mass, equal to 1000 grams (2.2 pounds).

kilohertz *noun* (PL. **kilohertz**) a unit of frequency of sound and radio waves equal to 1000 cycles per second.

kilolitre *noun* a unit of liquid measure equal to 1000 litres.

kilometre *noun* a unit of distance equal to 1000 metres.

kiloton or **kilotonne** *noun* a unit of explosive force equal to that of 1000 tons of TNT.

kilowatt *noun* a unit of electrical power equal to 1000 watts.

kilowatt hour (ABBREV. **kWh**) a unit of electricity consumption, equal to the energy used when an electrical appliance with a power of one kilowatt is run for one hour.

kilt *noun* a pleated tartan knee-length skirt, traditionally worn by men as part of Scottish Highland dress. [related to Danish *kilte*, to tuck up]

kilted *adj.* wearing a kilt.

kimono /kɪˈmoʊnoʊ/ *noun* (PL. **kimonos**) **1** a long loose wide-sleeved Japanese garment fastened by a sash at the waist. **2** a dressing-gown imitating this. [from Japanese *kimono*, clothing]

kin — *noun* one's relations. — *adj.* related: *kin to the duke.* — **next of kin** one's nearest relative. [from Anglo-Saxon *cynn*]

-kin *suffix* indicating a diminutive: *catkin/lambkin.* [from Old Dutch]

kind[1] *noun* **1** a group, class, sort, or type. **2** nature, character, or distinguishing quality: *differ in kind.* — **a kind of ...** something like a: *a kind of magazine.* **in kind 1** *said of payment* in goods instead of money. **2** *said of repayment or retaliation* in the same form as the treatment received. **kind of ...** *colloq.* somewhat ...; slightly: *kind of old-fashioned.* **nothing of the kind** not at all; completely the reverse. **of a kind 1** of the same sort: *three of a kind.* **2** *derog.* of doubtful worth: *an explanation of a kind.* [from Anglo-Saxon *gecynd*, nature]

▤ **1** sort, type, group, class, category, set, variety, genus, species, family, breed, race. **2** nature, character, temperament, manner, description, stamp, brand, genre, style.

kind[2] *adj.* **1** friendly, helpful, well-meaning, generous, benevolent, or considerate. **2** warm; cordial: *kind regards.* — **be so kind as to ...** or **be kind enough to ...** a polite formula of request. [from Anglo-Saxon *gecynde*, natural]

▤ **1** friendly, amiable, congenial, neighbourly, helpful, obliging, benevolent, kindly, kind-hearted, good-natured, generous, charitable, warm-hearted, thoughtful, considerate, compassionate, tender-hearted, soft-hearted, sympathetic, understanding, indulgent, lenient, mild, gentle, humane.

▣ **1** unkind, cruel, inconsiderate.

kindergarten *noun* a school for young children, usually ones aged between four and six. [from German *Kindergarten*, children's garden]

kind-hearted *adj.* kind; generous; good-natured.

kindle *verb* **1** *trans., intrans.* to start or cause to start burning. **2** to stir (feelings, etc). **3** *intrans., said of feelings* to be stirred. [related to Norse *kyndill*, torch]

▤ **1** light, ignite, fire. **2** inflame, fire, stir, rouse, arouse, awaken, stimulate, excite, thrill, incite, provoke, spark off.

kindliness *noun* **1** being kindly. **2** a kindly act.

kindling *noun* dry wood, leaves, etc for starting a fire.

kindly — *adv.* **1** in a kind manner. **2** please. — *adj.* (**kindlier, kindliest**) kind, friendly, generous, or good-natured. — **look kindly on someone** or **something** to approve of them. **not take kindly to something** to be unwilling to put up with it. **think kindly of someone** or **something** to have a good opinion of it.

▤ *adj.* kind, friendly, benevolent, charitable, generous, good-natured, helpful, warm, cordial, favourable, pleasant, compassionate, sympathetic, tender, gentle, mild,

indulgent, patient, polite, courteous.
E3 *adj.* cruel, uncharitable.

kindness *noun* **1** being kind. **2** a kind act.

E **1** benevolence, kindliness, charity, magnanimity, generosity, hospitality, friendliness, compassion, gentleness, humanity, goodwill, goodness, grace, indulgence, tolerance, understanding. **2** favour, good turn, help, service.
E3 **1** unkindness, cruelty, inhumanity. **2** disservice.

kindred — *noun* **1** one's relations. **2** relationship by blood. — *adj.* **1** related. **2** having qualities in common: *kindred arts.* [from Anglo-Saxon *cynred*]

kindred spirit someone who shares one's tastes, opinions, etc.

kine *pl. noun* old use cattle. [from Anglo-Saxon *cyna*, of cows]

kinematic *adj.* relating to or involving kinematics.

kinematics *sing. noun Physics* the branch of mechanics that deals with the motion of objects, but unlike dynamics is not concerned with the forces that act to produce such motion. [from Greek *kinema*, movement]

kinesics /kɪ'niːzɪks/ *sing. noun Psychol.* the study of visual body language as communication. [from Greek *kinesis*, movement]

kinesiology /kɪniːzɪ'ɒlədʒɪ/ *noun* the scientific study of human movement and posture, used to diagnose blockages and other physical problems by means of light finger pressure. [from Greek *kinesis*, movement + -OLOGY]

kinesis /kɪ'niːsɪs/ *noun Zool.* the movement of a living organism or cell in response to a simple stimulus (eg light, humidity), the rate of movement being dependent on the intensity as opposed to the direction of the stimulus.

kinetic /kɪ'netɪk/ *adj.* of or relating to motion. [from Greek *kinetikos*, from *kineein*, to move]

kinetically *adv.* in a kinetic way.

kinetic art or **kinetic sculpture** art or sculpture of which movement (produced by air currents, electricity, etc) is an essential feature.

kinetic energy *Physics* the energy possessed by an object because of its motion. The kinetic energy of an object of mass m moving with velocity v is equal to $\frac{1}{2}mv^2$.

kinetics *sing. noun* **1** *Chem.* the scientific study of the rates of chemical reactions. **2** *Physics* the branch of mechanics concerned with the relationship between moving objects, their masses, and the forces acting on them.

kinetic theory *Physics* a theory which attempts to account for the physical properties of matter, especially gases, in terms of the movement of the atoms or molecules of which they are composed.

king *noun* **1** a male, especially hereditary, ruler of a nation. **2** a ruler or chief. **3** a creature considered supreme in strength, fierceness, etc: *the lion, king of beasts.* **4** a large, or the largest, variety of something: *king penguins/king prawns.* **5** a leading or dominant figure in some field, eg a wealthy manufacturer or dealer: *the diamond king.* **6** *Cards* the court card bearing a picture of a king. **7** *Chess* the most important piece, which must be protected from checkmate. **8** *Draughts* a piece that, having crossed the board safely, has been crowned, and may move both forwards and backwards. — **live like a king** *colloq.* to live in great luxury. [from Anglo-Saxon *cyning*]

E **1** monarch, sovereign, ruler, prince, emperor. **2** ruler, chief, chieftain. **5** supremo, leading light.

King Charles spaniel a small black and tan spaniel, made popular by Charles II.

king cobra the world's largest venomous snake, up to 5.5m in length, native to India and SE Asia. Also called HAMADRYAD.

kingcup *noun* the marsh marigold.

kingdom *noun* **1** a country or organized community ruled by a king or queen. **2** *Biol.* the highest rank in the classification of plants and animals. **3** the domain in which something is thought of as existing or operating: *the kingdom of the imagination.* — **to kingdom come** *colloq.* as if into the next world: *blow them all to kingdom come.* **till kingdom come** for ever; indefinitely: *wait till kingdom come.*

E **1** monarchy, sovereignty, realm, empire, dominion, commonwealth, principality, nation, state, country, land, territory. **3** domain, province, sphere, realm.

kingfisher *noun* any of a large family of brightly coloured birds with long stout bills, often found by rivers and streams, where it catches fish with a single swooping dive. [originally *king's fisher*]

kingliness *noun* with a kingly manner.

kingly *adj.* (**kinglier, kingliest**) **1** suitable for a king. **2** royal.

kingmaker *noun* someone who has influence over the choice of people for high office.

king of arms or **king at arms** the most senior rank in heraldry; the chief herald.

kingpin *noun* **1** the most important person in an organization, team, etc. **2** *Mech.* a bolt serving as a pivot.

kingpost *noun Archit.* a perpendicular beam in the frame of a roof rising from the tie-beam to the ridge and shaped near the base to bear struts, one on either side, which support the principal rafters.

King's Bench SEE QUEEN'S BENCH.

King's English SEE QUEEN'S ENGLISH.

King's evidence SEE QUEEN'S EVIDENCE.

King's evil old use scrofula, ie tuberculosis of the neck glands, once believed curable by the touch of a monarch.

kingship *noun* the position and authority of a king; royalty.

king-size or **king-sized** *adj.* of a large, or larger-than-standard, size.

kinin /'kaɪnɪn/ *noun* **1** *Physiol.* any of a group of peptides, found in blood, that are associated with inflammation (eg as a result of insect stings), and cause contraction of smooth muscles and dilation of blood vessels. **2** *Bot.* any of a group of plant growth substances that stimulate cell division. Also called CYTOKININ. [from Greek *kinesis*, movement]

kink — *noun* **1** a bend or twist in a string, rope, wire, etc. **2** *colloq.* an oddness of personality; an eccentricity; a strange sexual preference. — *verb trans., intrans.* to develop or cause to develop a kink. [from Dutch *kink*]

E *noun* **1** curl, twist, bend, loop, coil, tangle, knot, wrinkle. **2** quirk, eccentricity, idiosyncrasy, foible, fetish, perversion.

kinkiness *noun* being kinky.

kinky *adj.* (**kinkier, kinkiest**) *colloq.* intriguingly odd or eccentric, especially in some sexual way.

kinnor *noun* a musical instrument of the ancient Hebrews: a type of lyre plucked with a plectrum or the fingers. The word is also the modern Hebrew name for the violin.

kinsfolk *noun* one's relations.

kinship *noun* family relationship.

E kin, family, blood, relationship, tie, bond, connection, association, affinity, similarity.

kinsman or **kinswoman** *noun* one's male or female relation.

kiosk *noun* **1** a booth or stall for the sale of sweets, newspapers, etc. **2** a public telephone box. [from French *kiosque*, stand in a public park, from Turkish *kösk*, villa]

E BOOTH, BOX. **1** stall, stand, news stand, bookstall, counter.

kip *slang* — *noun* **1** sleep or a sleep. **2** somewhere to sleep; a bed. — *verb intrans.* (**kipped, kipping**) **1** to sleep. **2** (**kip down**) to go to bed; to doss down. [originally 'brothel']

kipper — *noun* **1** a herring split open, salted, and smoked. **2** a male salmon in the spawning season. — *verb* (**kippered, kippering**) to cure (herring) by salting and smoking. [from Anglo-Saxon *cypera*, spawning salmon]

Kirbigrip *noun trademark* a hair-grip. [named after *Kirby*, the manufacturer's name]

kirk *noun Scot.* **1** a church. **2** (**the Kirk**) the Church of Scotland. [from Old Norse *kirkja*]

kirk session the governing body of a Presbyterian congregation, consisting of the minister and elders.

kirsch /kɪəʃ/ *noun* a clear liqueur distilled from black cherries. [from German *Kirschwasser*, cherry water]

kismet *noun* **1** fate. **2** one's destiny. [from Turkish *qismet*]

kiss — *verb* **1** to touch with the lips, as a greeting or sign of affection. **2** *intrans.* to kiss each other on the lips. **3** to express by kissing: *kissed them goodbye*. **4** *poetic* to pass over with a gentle touch; to caress: *sun-kissed peaches*. — *noun* **1** an act of kissing. **2** a gentle touch. — **kiss hands** to kiss the sovereign's hands on acceptance of high office. [from Anglo-Saxon *cyssan*]

....

◨ *verb* **1** peck, *colloq.* smooch, *colloq.* neck, *slang* snog. **4** touch, caress, glance, brush, graze, scrape. *noun* **1** peck, *colloq.* smacker.

....

kissable *adj.* **1** that can be kissed. **2** desirable.

kiss curl a flat curl pressed against the cheek or forehead.

kisser *noun* **1** one who kisses. **2** *slang* the mouth or face.

kiss of death *colloq.* something that brings failure or ruin on some enterprise; a fatal move.

kiss of life **1** in first aid, a mouth-to-mouth method of restoring the breathing. **2** a means of restoring vitality or vigour.

kissogram or **kissagram** *noun* **1** a greetings service by means of which one may employ someone to deliver a kiss to someone else on a special occasion. **2** the kiss or greeting thus delivered. **3** the person delivering it. [from KISS + TELEGRAM]

kit¹ — *noun* **1** a set of instruments, equipment, etc needed for a purpose, especially if kept in a container. **2** a set of special clothing and personal equipment, eg for a soldier, footballer, etc. **3** a set of parts ready for assembling. — *verb* (**kitted, kitting**) (*also* **kit someone out**) to provide them with the clothes and equipment necessary for a particular occupation, assignment, etc. [from Old Dutch *kitte*, tankard]

....

◨ *noun* **1** set, outfit, equipment, gear, tackle, rig, apparatus, tools, implements, instruments, utensils, supplies, provisions. **2** outfit, clothes, gear, rig, equipment, trappings, effects, luggage, baggage, paraphernalia. *verb* equip, fit out, provide, supply, furnish, fix up, prepare, arm, rig out, dress.

....

kit² *noun* a kitten. [shortened form]

kitbag *noun* a soldier's or sailor's bag, usually cylinder-shaped, for holding kit.

Kit-cat *noun* a portrait painted on a canvas 36 x 28 in (c.90 x 70 cm) or, more generally, any canvas of this size. [from the series of life-size, half-length portraits of members of the Kit-cat dining-club, London, painted by Kneller c.1700–17 and now in the National Portrait Gallery in London]

kitchen *noun* a room where food is prepared and cooked. [from Anglo-Saxon *cycene*, from Latin *coquina*]

kitchen cabinet an informal unelected group of advisors to a political office-holder, particularly a US president.

kitchenette *noun* a small kitchen, or a section of a room serving as a kitchen.

kitchen garden a garden, or a section of one, in which vegetables are grown.

Kitchen-Sink *adj.* a term coined in the 1950s and used, often in a derogatory sense, to describe a style of British contemporary drama and painting which dealt with domestic themes.

kite *noun* **1** a long-tailed bird of prey of the hawk family. **2** a light frame covered in paper or some other light material, with a long holding string attached to it, for flying in the air for fun, etc. — **fly a kite** to spread a rumour or suggestion intended to provoke reaction and so test public opinion. **high as a kite** *colloq.* in an elated state brought on by drugs or alcohol. [from Anglo-Saxon *cyta*]

Kitemark *noun* a kite-shaped mark on goods indicating that they conform to the specification of the British Standards Institution.

kith *noun* friends, as in **kith and kin**, friends and relations. [from Anglo-Saxon *cythth*, from *cunnan*, to know]

kithara /ˈkɪθərə/ *noun* a musical instrument of classical antiquity: the national instrument of the ancient Greeks, resembling a lyre. [from Greek *kithara*]

kitsch *noun* sentimental or vulgar tastelessness in art, design, writing, film-making, etc. [from German *kitsch*]

kitschy *adj.* (**kitschier, kitschiest**) like kitsch; bright and gaudy.

kitten *noun* **1** a young cat. **2** the young of any of several small furry mammals, eg the rabbit. — **have kittens** *colloq.* to become extremely agitated.

kittenish *adj.* like a kitten, playful.

kittiwake *noun* a long-winged type of seagull. [imitative of its cry]

kitty¹ *noun* (PL. **kitties**) **1** a fund contributed to jointly, for communal use by a group of people. **2** *Cards* a pool of money used in certain games.

kitty² *noun* (PL. **kitties**) an affectionate name for a cat or kitten.

kiwi *noun* **1** any of three species of nocturnal flightless bird about the size of a chicken, found only in pine forests in New Zealand. **2** *colloq.* a New Zealander. [from Maori]

kiwi fruit an oval edible fruit with pale green juicy flesh, rich in vitamin C, enclosed by a brown hairy skin, produced by a climbing plant (*Actinidia chinensis*) native to China, and so called because the fruit is exported to Europe and the USA from New Zealand.

kJ *abbrev.* kilojoule.

KKK *abbrev.* Ku-Klux Klan.

kl *abbrev.* kilolitre.

klaxon *noun* a loud horn used as a warning signal on ambulances, fire engines, etc. [originally a tradename]

kleptomania *noun Psychol.* an irresistible urge to steal, especially objects that are not desired for themselves, and are of little monetary value. [from Greek *kleptein*, to steal + -MANIA]

kleptomaniac — *noun* a person suffering from kleptomania. — *adj.* relating to or affected by kleptomania.

klipspringer *noun* a dwarf antelope, native to Africa south of the Sahara, and having a thick yellowish-grey speckled coat, short vertical horns, rounded ears with dark radiating lines, and black feet. [from Dutch *klip*, rock + *springer*, jumper]

KLM *abbrev.* *Koninklijke Luchtvaart Maatschappij* (Dutch), Royal Dutch Airlines.

KM *abbrev.* Knight of Malta.

km *abbrev.* kilometre.

kn *abbrev. Naut.* knot.

knack *noun* **1** the ability to do something effectively and skilfully: *has a knack of tying knots*. **2** a habit or tendency. [probably related to *knack*, sharp blow or sound]

....

◨ **1** flair, faculty, facility, aptitude, skill, talent, gift, genius, forte, trick, *colloq.* hang, ability, expertise, skilfulness, dexterity. **2** habit, disposition, tendency, inclination, bent, propensity.

....

knacker — *noun* a buyer of worn-out old horses for slaughter. — *verb* (**knackered, knackering**) *colloq.* to exhaust.

knapsack *noun* a hiker's or traveller's canvas bag for food, clothes, etc, carried on the back or over the shoulder. [from Old German *knappen*, eat + *Sack*, bag]

☰ bag, pack, haversack, rucksack, backpack.

knapweed *noun* a plant of the daisy family, with purple thistle-like flowers. [from Middle English *knopwed*]

knave *noun old use* **1** *Cards* the jack. **2** a mischievous young man; a scoundrel. [from Anglo-Saxon *cnafa*]

knavery *noun* (PL. **knaveries**) mischief; trickery.

knavish *adj. old use* rascally.

knead *verb* **1** to work (dough) with one's fingers and knuckles. **2** to massage (flesh) with firm finger movements. [from Anglo-Saxon *cnedan*]

☰ **1** work, ply, manipulate, press, squeeze, shape, form, mould. **2** massage, rub.

knee — *noun* **1** the joint between the femur (thigh bone) and the tibia (shin bone). It is protected by the patella (kneecap). **2** the upper surface of a sitting person's thigh; the lap: *sat with the child on her knee*. **3** the part of a garment covering the knee. — *verb* (**kneed**) to strike or nudge with the knee. — **at one's mother's knee** as a small child. **bring someone to his** or **her knees** to defeat, prostrate or ruin someone utterly. **go weak at the knees** *colloq.* to be overcome by emotion. **on one's knees 1** kneeling. **2** exhausted; prostrated. [from Anglo-Saxon *cneow*]

knee-breeches *pl. noun* knee-length breeches.

kneecap — *noun* a triangular plate of bone covering the front of the knee joint. — *verb* (**kneecapped, kneecapping**) to shoot or otherwise damage the kneecaps of (a person) as a form of revenge or unofficial punishment.

kneecapping *noun* being kneecapped.

knee-deep *adj., adv.* up to the knees.

knee-high *adj.* tall enough to reach the knees: *knee-high grass*.

knee-jerk — *noun* an involuntary kick of the lower leg, a reflex response to a tap on the tendon below the knee. — *adj.*, *said of a response or reaction* automatic; unthinking.

kneel *verb intrans.* (PAST TENSE **knelt**; PAST PARTICIPLE **kneeled**) (*also* **kneel down**) to support one's weight on, or lower oneself on to, one's knees. [from Anglo-Saxon *cneowlian*]

knee-length *adj.* coming down, or up, as far as the knees.

kneeler *noun* a cushion for kneeling on, especially in church.

knees-up *noun colloq.* a party or dance.

knell — *noun* **1** the tolling of a bell announcing a death or funeral. **2** something that signals the end of anything. — *verb* to announce or summon by or as if by tolling. [from Anglo-Saxon *cnyll*]

☰ *noun* **1** toll, tolling, ringing, chime, peal.

knelt see KNEEL.

Knesset *noun* the Israeli parliament, which has a four-year term of office, and which elects the country's president.

knew see KNOW.

knickerbockers *pl. noun* baggy trousers tied just below the knee or at the ankle. [named after Diedrich *Knickerbocker*, the supposed author of Washington Irving's *History of New York*, 1809]

knickers *pl. noun* an undergarment for women and girls, covering the lower abdomen and buttocks, with separate legs or leg holes. [short for KNICKERBOCKERS]

knick-knack *noun* a little trinket or ornament. [from KNACK, with the old meaning 'toy']

☰ trinket, ornament, trifle, bauble, gewgaw, gimcrack, bric-à-brac.

knife — *noun* (PL. **knives**) a cutting instrument or weapon, typically in the form of a blade fitted into a handle. — *verb* to stab or kill with a knife. — **have one's knife into someone** *colloq.* to be constantly spiteful to them. **the knives are out** *colloq.* the argument has taken a savage turn. **twist the knife in the wound** to deliberately increase someone's distress or embarrassment by constant reminders of the circumstances that caused it. **under the knife** *colloq.* having a surgical operation. [from Anglo-Saxon *cnif*]

☰ *noun* blade, cutter, carver, dagger, penknife, pocket knife, switchblade, jackknife, flick knife. *verb* stab, pierce, wound, cut, rip, slash.

knife-edge *noun* the cutting edge of a knife. — **on a knife-edge** in a state of extreme uncertainty.

knife pleat a flat narrow pleat.

knight — *noun* **1** *Hist.* a man-at-arms of high social standing, usually mounted, serving a feudal lord. **2** *Hist.* the armed champion of a lady, devoted to her service. **3** a man who has been awarded the highest or second highest class of distinction in any of the four British orders of chivalry, ie honours for service or merit awarded by the Queen or the Government. See also DAME. **4** *Chess* a piece shaped like a horse's head. — *verb* to confer a knighthood on. [from Anglo-Saxon *cniht*, boy, servant, warrior]

knight errant (PL. **knights errant**) *Hist.* a knight travelling about in search of opportunities for daring and chivalrous deeds.

knighthood *noun* the rank of a knight, just below that of a baronet, conferring the title 'Sir'.

knightly *adj.* (**knightlier, knightliest**) relating to or suitable for a knight.

knit *verb* (**knitting**; PAST TENSE AND PAST PARTICIPLE **knitted**, *old use* **knit**) **1** *trans., intrans.* to produce a fabric composed of interlocking loops of yarn, using a pair of knitting-needles or a machine; to make (garments, etc) by this means. **2** to make (a stitch) in plain knitting. **3** to unite: *a close-knit family/a loosely-knit alliance*. **4** *trans., intrans. said of broken bones* to grow or cause them to grow together again. **5** to draw (one's brows) together in a frown. **6** *poetic* to intertwine. [from Anglo-Saxon *cnyttan*, to tie]

☰ **3** join, unite, tie, fasten, connect, link. **5** wrinkle, furrow. **6** intertwine, interlace, interweave.

knitter *noun* a person who knits (by hand or machine).

knitting *noun* knitted work or the art of producing it.

knitting-needle *noun* an implement like a long stout pin, made of wood, plastic or metal.

knitwear *noun* knitted garments.

knives see KNIFE.

knob *noun* **1** a hard rounded projection. **2** a handle, especially rounded, on a door or drawer. **3** a button on mechanical or electrical equipment, pressed or rotated to operate it. **4** a small roundish lump: *a knob of butter*. [from Old German *knobbe*, knot in wood]

knobbly *adj.* (**knobblier, knobbliest**) covered with knobs. [from KNOB]

knobby *adj.* (**knobbier, knobbiest**) having or full of knobs.

knock — *verb* **1** *intrans.* to tap or rap with the knuckles or some object. **2** (**knock something down, over,** etc) to strike and so push it, especially accidentally. **3** to put into a certain condition by hitting: *knocked him senseless*. **4** to make by striking. **5** *trans., intrans.* (**knock against** or **into something** or **someone**) to strike, bump, or bang against them. **6** *colloq.* to find fault with or criticize, especially unfairly. **7** *intrans. Engineering, said of an internal combustion engine* to make a metallic knocking sound caused by the explosion of an unburned mixture of fuel vapour and air before it is ignited by the spark. See also PINK³. — *noun* **1** an act of knocking. **2** a tap or rap. **3** *colloq.* a personal misfortune, blow, setback, calamity, etc. **4** a metallic knocking sound caused by the explosion of an unburned mixture of fuel vapour and air before it is ignited by the spark. — **knock about** or **around** *colloq.* **1** *said of a person* to wander about casually or aimlessly; to be idle. **2** *said of a thing* to lie about unused or not needed. **knock someone about** or **around** to treat them roughly; to hit or batter them. **knock about with someone** *colloq.* to associate or go about with them. **knock something back** *colloq.* **1** to eat or drink it rapidly and with relish. **knock someone back 1** to cost them a specified amount: *knocked them back twenty pounds.* **2** to surprise, dismay, or disappoint them. **knock someone down** to strike them to the ground. **knock something down 1** to demolish a building, etc. **2** *colloq.* to reduce a price. **knock something down to someone** *colloq.* to sell them goods at an auction. **knocking on ...** *colloq.* nearly..., especially with reference to a person's age: *must be knocking on 60 by now.* **knock something into someone** *colloq.* to teach it to them vigorously: *has had some sense knocked into him.* **knock off** *colloq.* to stop working. **knock off doing something** to stop doing it. **knock someone off** *colloq.* to kill them. **knock something off** *colloq.* **1** to produce it quickly or in large quantities. **2** to deduct it from a price or charge: *knocked £15 off.* **3** to steal it. **knock on** *Rugby* to commit the foul of sending the ball forward with the hand. **knock something on the head** *colloq.* to put an end to it. **knock someone out 1** to hit them unconscious; in boxing, to hit an opponent so as to be incapable of rising in the required time. **2** to defeat an opponent in a knockout competition. **3** *colloq.* to amaze them; to impress them hugely. **knock something out** *colloq.* to cause it to stop functioning. **knock someone sideways** *colloq.* to come as a severe shock to them. **knock something together** *colloq.* to assemble it hurriedly. **knock up** *Tennis* to exchange practice shots with one's opponent before a match. **knock someone up 1** *colloq.* to wake or disturb them suddenly, especially by loud knocking. **2** *colloq.* to exhaust them. **3** *North Amer. coarse slang* to make someone pregnant. **knock something up** *colloq.* to assemble it hurriedly. [from Anglo-Saxon *cnucian*]

- -

☐ *verb* **1** tap, rap, thump, pound, hammer, bang. **2** hit, strike. **5** hit, strike, bump into, bang into, collide with. *noun* **1** blow, slap, smack, cuff, clip, thump, pounding, hammering, bump, bang, collision. **2** tap, rap, thump, bang. **knock about** or **around 1** wander, roam, rove, ramble, range, travel. **knock someone about** hit, beat, batter, abuse, ill-treat, maltreat, manhandle. **knock about with** associate with, fraternize with, hang about with, go about with. **knock something down 1** demolish, destroy, smash, wreck, raze, level. **knock off** stop, cease, finish, terminate, clock off, clock out. **knock someone off** kill, murder, assassinate, *colloq.* do in, *slang* bump off. **knock something off 2** deduct, subtract, take away. **3** steal, pilfer, filch, *colloq.* pinch, *slang* nick.

- -

knockabout *adj., said of comedy, etc* boisterous; slapstick.

knockdown *adj. colloq.* **1** low; cheap: *knockdown prices.* **2** *said of furniture* able to be taken to pieces easily. **3** *said of an argument* overwhelmingly strong.

knocker *noun* **1** (*also* **door knocker**) a heavy piece of metal, usually of a decorative shape, fixed to a door by a hinge and used for knocking. **2** (**knockers**) *coarse slang* a woman's breasts.

knocking-shop *noun slang* a brothel.

knock-kneed *adj.* having knock knees.

knock knees a condition of the legs in which the knees are close together but the feet splayed out.

knock-on *noun Rugby* the foul of sending the ball forward with the hand.

knock-on effect a secondary or indirect effect of some action, etc.

knockout *noun* **1** *colloq.* someone or something stunning. **2** a competition in which the defeated competitors are dropped after each round. **3** *Boxing* the act of knocking out.

- -

☐ **1** success, triumph, sensation, hit, *colloq.* smash, *colloq.* smash hit, winner, *colloq.* stunner.
☐ **3** flop, loser.

- -

knoll *noun* a small round hill. [from Anglo-Saxon *cnoll*]

knot — *noun* **1** a join or tie in string, etc made by looping the ends around each other and pulling tight. **2** a bond or uniting link. **3** a coil or bun in the hair. **4** a decoratively tied ribbon, etc. **5** a tangle in hair, string, etc. **6** a difficulty or complexity. **7** a hard mass in a tree trunk where a branch has grown out from it; the resultant crossgrained patch in timber. **8** a small gathering or cluster of people, etc. **9** a unit of speed at sea, a nautical mile (1.85km) an hour. **10** a tight feeling, eg in the belly, caused by nervousness. — *verb* (**knotted, knotting**) **1** to tie in a knot. **2** *trans., intrans.* to tangle. **3** *intrans.* to become tight with nervousness, etc. — **at a rate of knots** *colloq.* very fast. **get knotted** *offensive slang* an expression of disagreement, refusal, or dismissiveness. **tie someone in knots** to confuse or perplex them. **tie the knot** *colloq.* to get married. [from Anglo-Saxon *cnotta*]

- -

☐ *noun* **1** tie, fastening, hitch, splice, join. **2** bond, link, connection. **4** loop, bow. **8** bunch, cluster, clump, group. *verb* **1** tie, fasten, secure, bind, join, splice. **2** tangle, entangle, ravel, entwine, weave.

- -

knotgrass or **knotweed** *noun* an annual plant (*Polygonum aviculare*), widespread throughout most of Europe, that has tiny white or pink flowers and usually forms low mats up to 100cm across.

knothole *noun* a hole left in a piece of wood where a knot has fallen out.

knotty *adj.* (**knottier, knottiest**) **1** full of knots. **2** *said of a problem, etc* difficult, complex or intricate.

know *verb* (PAST TENSE **knew**; PAST PARTICIPLE **known**) **1** *trans., intrans.* (**know something** or **know of** or **about something**) to be aware of it; to be certain about it. **2** to have learnt and remember. **3** to have an understanding or grasp of. **4** to be familiar with: *know her well.* **5** to be able to recognize or identify. **6** to be able to distinguish or tell apart: *wouldn't know him from Adam.* **7** *intrans.* to have enough experience or training: *knew not to question him further.* **8** to think of (someone or something) in a certain way: *knew him as a kindly man.* **9** to experience or be subject to: *know poverty/happiness knew no bounds.* **10** *old use* to have sexual intercourse with. — **be known as ...** be called ...; have ... as one's name. **Heaven** or **God knows** *colloq.* a formula admitting ignorance. **in the know** *colloq.* having information not known to most. **know a thing or two** *colloq.* to be pretty shrewd. **know something backwards** *colloq.* to know it thoroughly. **know what's what** to be shrewd, wise, or hard to deceive. **let it be known** to reveal, especially indirectly. **make oneself known** to introduce oneself. **there's no knowing** it's impossible to predict. **what do you know?** *colloq.* an expression of surprise. **you never know** *colloq.* it's not impossible. [from Anglo-Saxon *cnawan*]

- -

☐ **1** be aware of, perceive, see, realize. **3** understand, comprehend, grasp, fathom. **4** be acquainted with, be familiar with. **5** recognize, identify. **6** distinguish, discriminate, differentiate, discern, make out, tell. **9** experience, undergo.

- -

knowable *adj.* that can be known.

know-all *noun derog.* a person who seems, or claims, to know more than others.

know-how *noun colloq.* skill; ability; adroitness.

knowing *adj.* **1** shrewd; canny; clever. **2** *said of a glance, etc* signifying secret awareness.

knowingly *adv.* **1** in a knowing manner. **2** on purpose; deliberately.

knowingness *noun* being knowing, cunning.

knowledge *noun* **1** the fact of knowing; awareness; understanding. **2** what one knows; the information one has acquired through learning or experience. **3** learning; the sciences: *a branch of knowledge*. — **to the best of one's knowledge** as far as one knows. [from Middle English *knouleche*]

. . . .

☒ **1** awareness, consciousness, cognizance, cognition, understanding, comprehension, grasp, judgement, discernment, recognition, acquaintance, familiarity, intimacy. **2** information, enlightenment, wisdom, *colloq.* know-how, education, schooling, instruction, tuition. **3** learning, scholarship, erudition, science.
☒ **1** ignorance.

. . . .

knowledgeable *adj.* well-informed.

. . . .

☒ well-informed, educated, scholarly, learned, experienced, conversant, familiar, acquainted, aware, conscious, informed, *colloq.* in the know, *colloq.* sussed.
☒ ignorant.

. . . .

known see KNOW.

knuckle *noun* **1** a joint of a finger, especially the one at its base. **2** the knee or ankle joint of an animal, especially with the surrounding flesh, as food. — **knuckle down to something** to begin to work hard at it. **knuckle under** *colloq.* to submit, yield, or give way. **near the knuckle** *colloq.* bordering on the indecent or obscene. [from Middle English *knokel*]

knuckle-duster *noun* a set of metal links or other metal device worn over the knuckles as a weapon.

KO *colloq.* — *noun* a knockout. — *verb* (**KO's, KO'd, KO'ing**) to knock out. [abbreviation]

koala *noun* (*also* **koala bear**) a nocturnal marsupial found only in Australia and resembling a very small bear, with thick grey fur, whitish underparts, no tail, large ears, and a black nose. [from Aboriginal *koolah*]

kohl /koʊl/ *noun* an oriental cosmetic in the form of a powder, used to darken the eyelids. [from Arabic *koh'l*]

kohlrabi /koʊl'rɑːbɪ/ *noun* a kind of cabbage whose thick turnip-like stem is eaten as a vegetable. [from Italian *cavolrape*, cabbage turnip]

kolkhoz /kɒl'xɒz/ *noun* a large-scale collective farm in the former Soviet Union. [from Russian]

Komodo dragon or **Komodo lizard** a rare SE Asian monitor lizard, native to the islands of Komodo, Flores, Pintja and Padar (Indonesia). It is the world's largest lizard, up to 3m in length

kook *noun North Amer. colloq.* a crazy or eccentric person. [perhaps from CUCKOO]

kookaburra /'kʊkəbʌrə/ *noun* either of two species of large bird of the kingfisher family, found in Australia and New Guinea. It is known for its chuckling cry. Also called LAUGHING JACKASS. [from Aboriginal *gugubarra*]

kooky or **kookie** /'kʊkɪ/ *adj.* (**kookier, kookiest**) *North Amer., esp. US* crazy, eccentric, foolish.

kopeck or **kopek** /'koʊpɛk/ *noun* a coin or unit of currency of the former Soviet Union worth a hundredth of a rouble. [from Russian *kopeika*]

Koran /kə'rɑːn/ *noun* the holy book of Islam, believed by Muslims to be composed of the revelations of Allah to Muhammad. [from Arabic *qur'an*, book]

Koranic /kə'ranɪk/ *adj.* relating to the Koran.

kore /'kɔːreɪ/ *noun* (PL. **korai**) *Art* a term conventionally applied by art historians to the draped, standing, female figure commonly represented by Greek sculptors working in the Archaic style. See also KOUROS. [from Greek *kore*, maiden]

Korean /kə'rɪən/ — *noun* **1** a native or citizen of N or S Korea. **2** a language spoken in North and South Korea (where it is the official language), and parts of China, Japan, and the former USSR. — *adj.* relating to Korea or its people or language.

kosher /'koʊʃə(r)/ — *adj.* **1** in accordance with Jewish law. **2** *said of food* prepared as prescribed by Jewish dietary laws. **3** *colloq.* genuine; legitimate. — *noun* kosher food, or a shop selling it. [from Yiddish *kosher*, from Hebrew *kasher*, right, fit]

kouros /'kuːrɒs/ *noun* (PL. **kouroi**) *Art* a term conventionally applied by art historians to the naked, standing, youthful male figure commonly represented by Greek sculptors working in the Archaic style (7c–5c BC). See also KORE. [from Greek *kouros*, young man]

kowtow /kaʊ'taʊ/ — *verb* **1** *intrans.* (*usually* **kowtow to someone**) *colloq.* to defer to them, especially in an oversubmissive or obsequious way. **2** to touch the forehead to the ground in a gesture of submission. — *noun* an act of kowtowing. [from Chinese *k'o t'ou*, strike the head]

. . . .

☒ *verb* **1** defer, pander, fawn, grovel, cringe, toady, flatter, *colloq.* suck up.

. . . .

KP *abbrev.* Knight of (the Order of) St Patrick.

kph *abbrev.* kilometres per hour.

Kr *symbol Chem.* krypton.

kraal /krɑːl/ *noun* **1** in S Africa, a village of huts surrounded by a fence. **2** *South Afr.* an enclosure for cattle, sheep, etc. [from Afrikaans *kraal*, from Portuguese *curral*, pen]

kremlin *noun* **1** the citadel of a Russian town, especially (**Kremlin**) that of Moscow. **2** (**Kremlin**) the government of the former Soviet Union. [from Russian *kreml*]

krill *noun* a tiny shrimp-like shellfish, eaten by whales, etc. [from Norwegian *kril*, fry, ie young fish]

kris /kriːs/ *noun* a Malay or Indonesian dagger with a wavy blade. [from Malay]

krona /'kroʊnə/ *noun* **1** (PL. **kronor**) the standard unit of Swedish currency. **2** (PL. **kronur**) the standard unit of Icelandic currency. [from Swedish and Icelandic *krona*, crown]

krone /'kroʊnə/ *noun* (PL. **kroner**) the standard unit of Danish and Norwegian currency. [from Danish and Norwegian *krone*, crown]

krugerrand /'kruːɡərand/ *noun* a South African one-ounce (or 28-gram) gold coin bearing a portrait of Paul Kruger, Boer statesman. [from RAND]

krummhorn or **krumhorn** /'krʊmhɔːn/ *noun* a musical instrument used widely throughout Europe in the Middle Ages and the Renaissance. [from German *Krummhorn*, curved horn]

krypton /'krɪptɒn/ *noun Chem.* (SYMBOL **Kr**, ATOMIC NUMBER **36**) a colourless odourless gas, representing 0.0001% of the air by volume. [from Greek *kryptos*, hidden, secret]

KS or **Ks.** *abbrev.* Kansas.

KT *abbrev.* Knight of the Thistle.

Kt *abbrev.* Knight.

kudos /'kjuːdɒs/ *noun colloq.* credit, honour or prestige. [from Greek *kudos*, glory]

Ku Klux Klan the name of successive secret societies in the USA. The first was founded after the American Civil War (1861–5) to oppose Reconstruction and the new rights being granted to blacks. [probably from Greek *kyklos*, circle + *klan* as a variant of clan]

kukri /'kʊkrɪ/ *noun* a heavy curved knife or short sword used by Gurkhas. [from Hindi *kukri*]

kulak /'kuːlak/ *noun Hist.* a wealthy, property-owning Russian peasant. [from Russian *kulak*, literally 'fist']

kulfi /'kʊlfiː/ *noun* an Indian dessert made from frozen concentrated milk with nuts and cardamom seeds.

kümmel /'kʊml/ *noun* a German liqueur flavoured with cumin and caraway seeds. [from German *Kümmel*, from *kumin*, cumin]

kumquat /ˈkʌmkwɒt/ *noun* a citrus fruit resembling a miniature orange. [from Chinese dialect *gamgwat*, golden citrus fruit]

kung fu /kʌŋˈfuː/ a Chinese martial art with similarities to karate and judo. [from Chinese]

Kurds *pl. noun* a nationalistic West Iranian-speaking ethnic group settled in neighbouring mountainous areas of Anatolia, Iraq, Iran and Turkey (including some in Syria and Armenia), an area which they themselves call Kurdistan.

kvass /kvɑːs/ *noun* a weak rye beer made in countries of E Europe. [from Russian *kvas*]

kW *abbrev.* kilowatt.

kwashiorkor /kwaʃiˈɔːkɔː(r)/ *noun* a disease of children caused by lack of protein in the diet. [a Ghanaian name]

kWh *abbrev.* kilowatt hour.

KWIC *abbrev.* keyword in context, with reference to a concordance or VDU text display in which a selected keyword is highlighted.

KWOC *abbrev.* keyword out of context.

KY or **Ky** *abbrev.* Kentucky.

kyle *noun Scot.* a channel, strait or sound. [from Gaelic *caol*, narrow]

L

L¹ or **l** *noun* (PL. **Ls, L's, l's**) the twelfth letter of the English alphabet.

L² *abbrev.* **1** lake. **2** learner driver. **3** Liberal. **4** licentiate. **5** lira or lire.

L³ *symbol* the Roman numeral for 50.

l *abbrev.* **1** left. **2** length. **3** line. **4** lira or lire. **5** litre.

LA *abbrev.* **1** Los Angeles. **2** Louisiana.

La *symbol Chem.* lanthanum.

La. *abbrev.* Louisiana.

la or **lah** *noun Mus.* in tonic sol-fa, the sixth note of the major scale. [from the first syllable of the word *labii* in a medieval Latin hymn, certain syllables of which were used in naming the notes of the scale]

Lab *abbrev.* Labour.

lab *noun colloq.* a laboratory.

label — *noun* **1** a small written note attached to a parcel, object, etc, giving details of its contents, owner, destination, etc. **2** a word or short phrase which describes only part of a person's or thing's character but which comes to be used as a general description. **3** a small strip of material inside a garment, giving the maker's or designer's name. **4** a record company's trademark. — *verb* (**labelled, labelling**) **1** to attach a label to. **2** to call by a certain name or describe in a certain way: *were labelled as rebels.* [from Old French *label*, ribbon]

∷ *noun* **1** tag, ticket, docket, mark, marker, sticker, badge, identification. **2** description, characterization, categorization, classification. *verb* **1** tag, mark, identify. **2** define, describe, classify, categorize, characterize, brand, stamp, designate, call, dub, name.

labial — *adj.* **1** relating to the lips. **2** *said of a sound* made with the lips almost or completely closed. — *noun* a sound made with the lips almost or completely closed, eg *b, m.* [from Latin *labium*, lip]

labiate / 'leɪbɪət/ *Bot.* — *noun* any flowering plant belonging to the family Labiatae, in which the stems are usually square, and the corolla of petals is divided into two lips, eg various aromatic herbs, including mint and thyme. — *adj.* **1** of this family of plants. **2** *Anat.* having or resembling lips. [from Latin *labium*, lip]

labile *adj.* **1** unstable. **2** *Chem.* denoting a chemical compound that can be readily altered by heat, etc. [from Latin *labilis*, from *labi*, to slip]

labium *noun* (PL. **labia**) a lip or lip-like structure, especially one of the folds of the vulva. [from Latin *labium*, lip]

laboratory *noun* (PL. **laboratories**) a room or building specially equipped for scientific experiments, research, the preparation of drugs, etc. [from Latin *laborare*, to work]

laborious *adj.* **1** requiring hard work or much effort. **2** not looking or sounding natural; not fluent. [from Latin *laboriosus*]

∷ **1** hard, difficult, tough, arduous, strenuous, backbreaking, exhausting, tiring, uphill, onerous, heavy. **2** laboured, stilted, unnatural, artificial.

▣ **1** easy, effortless. **2** natural, fluent.

laboriously *adv.* in a laborious way; at tedious length.

labour — *noun* **1** strenuous and prolonged physical or mental work. **2** (*usually* **labours**) a difficult task or job. **3** working people or their efforts regarded collectively as a resource or as a political force. **4** the process of giving birth, especially from the point where contractions of the uterus begin. **5** (**Labour**) in the UK, a shortened name for the Labour Party: *Labour won the seat with an increased majority.* — *verb* **1** *intrans.* to work hard or with difficulty. **2** *intrans.* to progress or move slowly and with difficulty: *the old man laboured slowly up the path.* **3** *intrans.* to strive earnestly to do something: *laboured hard to get results.* **4** *trans.* to deal with (a subject or issue) at excessive length or in too much detail, especially tediously and repetitively: *I have no wish to labour the point.* — **labour under a misapprehension** to persist in some activity or notion while unknowingly mistaken about it. [from Latin *labor*]

∷ *noun* **1** work, toil, effort, exertion, drudgery, *colloq.* grind, *colloq.* slog, *colloq.* sweat. **2** task, job, chore. **3** workers, employees, workforce, labourers. **4** childbirth, birth, contractions, confinement, delivery. *verb* **1** work, toil, drudge, slave, *colloq.* slog. **2** plod, trudge, tramp, lumber. **3** struggle, strive, endeavour. **4** overdo, overemphasize, overstress, dwell on, elaborate.

▣ *noun* **1** ease, leisure. **3** management, *colloq.* bosses. *verb* **1** idle, laze, lounge.

labour camp a prison camp where prisoners are made to do hard labour.

Labour Day a public holiday in honour of working people, often celebrated with marches. It is held on 1 May in many countries and on the first Monday in September in the USA and Canada.

laboured *adj.* **1** showing signs of effort or difficulty. **2** not natural or spontaneous.

labourer *noun* a worker employed to do heavy and usually unskilled physical work.

∷ worker, manual worker, blue-collar worker, navvy, hand, drudge, hireling.

labour exchange *Brit.* a former term for a job centre, still used informally.

labour force the body of people available for work, especially in a particular company or area, or in a country as a whole.

labour-intensive *adj.*, *said of an industry or enterprise* requiring a large resource of people as distinct from machinery. See also CAPITAL-INTENSIVE.

labour of love an undertaking made mainly for personal satisfaction or pleasure rather than for profit or material advantage.

Labour Party in the UK, a political party originally formed in 1900 as the Labour Representation Committee to represent the interests of working people.

labour-saving *adj.* serving to reduce the amount of work or effort needed: *labour-saving devices.*

Labrador *noun* a breed of large dog with a short black or golden coat. [named after *Labrador* in Canada]

laburnum *noun* a small garden tree of the pea family, with hanging yellow flowers and poisonous seeds. [from Latin *laburnum*]

labyrinth *noun* **1** a complicated network of passages through which it is very difficult to find one's way. **2** a complicated arrangement. **3** *Anat.* in the inner ear of vertebrates, the complex arrangement of membranous and bony structures that form the organs of hearing and balance. [from Greek *labyrinthos*]

labyrinthine *adj.*, *said of an arrangement or system* extremely complex and confusing.

lac *noun* a resinous substance produced by certain Asian insects, used in making varnish. [from Hindi *lakh*]

lace — *noun* **1** a delicate material made from fine thread woven into net-like patterns. **2** a string or cord drawn through holes, used for fastening shoes, etc. — *verb* **1** *trans.*, *intrans.* (*also* **lace up**) to fasten or be fastened with a lace or laces. **2** to flavour or strengthen with alcohol: *bitter lemon laced with gin.* **3** to trim with lace. **4** to weave in and out of; to intertwine. — **lace into** *colloq.* to attack them physically or with words. [from Latin *laqueus*, noose]

lacerate *verb* **1** to tear or cut (flesh) roughly. **2** to wound or hurt (a person's feelings). [from Latin *lacerare*, to tear]

laceration *noun* the process or an act of lacerating or cutting.

lace-up — *noun* a shoe fastened with a lace. — *adj.*, *said of shoes* fastened with a lace or laces.

lachrymal *adj. literary* relating to or producing tears. [from Latin *lacrima*, tear]

lachrymal gland the tear-producing gland at the outer edge of the eye.

lachrymose *adj. literary* **1** crying very easily and very often. **2** very sad; likely to make a person cry. [from Latin *lacrima*, tear]

lack — *noun* something missing or in short supply; a deficiency or want. — *verb* **1** to be completely without or to have too little of. **2** (**lack for something**) to be in need of something: *did not lack for money.* — **no lack of something** a plentiful supply of it. [from Middle English *lak*]

lackadaisical *adj.* **1** without energy, interest, or enthusiasm. **2** sentimental in a feeble dreamy way. [from archaic *alack the day*, alas the day]

lackadaisically *adv.* without energy; feebly.

lackey *noun* (PL. **lackeys**) **1** *derog.* a grovelling or servile follower. **2** *old use* a male servant. [from Old French *laquais*]

lacking *adj.* absent; deficient: *is lacking in energy.*

lacklustre *adj.* lacking in energy or brightness; dull.

laconic *adj.* using few words; terse, concise. [from Greek *lakonikos*, of Laconia or Sparta in ancient Greece, so called from the Spartans' reputedly terse style of speech]

laconically *adv.* tersely; with few words.

lacquer — *noun* **1** a usually clear substance made by dissolving natural or man-made resins in alcohol, used to form a hard, shiny covering on wood and metal. **2** the sap from some trees, used as a varnish for wood. **3** a clear, sticky substance sprayed on to hair to keep it place. — *verb* (**lacquered, lacquering**) to cover with lacquer. [from Portuguese *laca*, lac]

lacrimal same as LACHRYMAL.

lacrosse *noun* a game in which two teams use long sticks with rigid triangular nets at one end to throw a small ball into their opponents' goal-net. [from French *la*, the + *crosse*, hooked stick]

lactate — *verb intrans.* (with stress on *-tate*) *Zool.*, *said of the mammary glands of a mammal* to secrete milk. — *noun* (with stress on *lac-*) *Biochem.* a salt or ester of lactic acid. [from Latin *lac*, milk]

lactation *noun Zool.* in mammals, the secretion of milk by the mammary glands, under the control of hormones, in order to feed a baby or young animal until it is weaned.

lactic *adj.* of or derived from milk. [from Latin *lac*, milk]

lactic acid *Biochem.* (FORMULA $CH_3CH(OH)COOH$) an organic acid produced during the souring of milk by bacterial fermentation of lactose (milk sugar), a process that is of commercial importance in the manufacture of cheese, yoghurt, and other dairy products.

lactose *noun Biochem.* (FORMULA $C_{12}H_{22}O_{11}$) a white crystalline disaccharide sugar, found only in milk, consisting of a molecule of glucose and a molecule of galactose. Also called MILK SUGAR. [from Latin *lac*, milk]

lactovegetarian or **lactarian** *noun* a vegetarian whose diet includes milk and other dairy products. — *adj.* relating to such a person or diet.

lacuna *noun* (PL. **lacunae, lacunas**) a gap or a space where something is missing, especially in printed text. [from Latin *lacuna*, pool]

lacy *adj.* (**lacier, laciest**) of or like lace, especially in being fine and delicate.

lad *noun* **1** a boy or youth. **2** (*usually* **the lads**) *colloq.* a group of regular male acquaintances: *one of the lads.* **3** *Brit.* a person working in stables, regardless of age or sex. [from Middle English *ladde*]

ladder — *noun* **1** a piece of equipment consisting of a set of horizontal rungs or steps between two long vertical supports, used for climbing up or down. **2** a long narrow flaw, especially in a stocking or tights, where a row of stitches has broken. **3** a means or route of progress or advancement: *the social ladder.* **4** anything like a ladder in arrangement, eg a list of names of players in a competition on which names are moved up or down depending on whether the players win or lose. — *verb* (**laddered, laddering**) **1** *intrans.*, *said of stockings, etc* to develop a ladder. **2** to cause a ladder in stockings, etc. [from Anglo-Saxon *hlæder*]

laddie *noun dialect*, *colloq.* a young boy or lad.

laddish *adj. said of young men* boisterous or aggressive.

laden *adj.* **1** *said of a ship* loaded with cargo. **2** *said of a person, animal, or vehicle, or something comparable* heavily loaded: *trees heavily laden with fruit.* **3** *said of one's mind, conscience, etc* oppressed with guilt, worry, etc. [from Anglo-Saxon *hladan,* to load]

ladette *noun* a young woman who enjoys social behaviour of a kind associated with young men.

la-di-da or **lah-di-dah** *adj. colloq.* behaving or speaking in a pretentious or affected way. [imitating an affected manner of speech]

ladies *sing. noun* a women's public lavatory.

lading *noun* **1** a cargo or load carried. **2** the act of loading cargo or goods. See also BILL OF LADING. [from Anglo-Saxon *hladan,* to load]

ladle — *noun* a large spoon with a long handle and deep bowl, for serving or transferring liquid. — *verb* to serve or transfer with a ladle. — **ladle something out** to serve or distribute praise, blame, etc generously or excessively. [from Anglo-Saxon *hlædel*]

ladleful *noun* (PL. **ladlefuls**) the amount held in a ladle.

lady *noun* (PL. **ladies**) **1** a woman regarded as having good manners and elegant or refined behaviour. **2** a polite word for a woman generally. **3** *Hist.* a woman belonging to the upper classes by birth. **4** (**Lady**) in the UK, a title of honour used for peeresses (but not duchesses), the wives and daughters of peers and knights, and for some women of importance, eg mayoresses. **5** a woman in a position of authority or control: *lady of the house.* **6** (*attributive*) female: *a lady doctor.* — **Our Lady** *RC Church* the Virgin Mary. [from Anglo-Saxon *hlæfdige,* kneader of bread]

ladybird *noun* any of thousands of species of small beetle with an oval body that is usually bright red or yellow with black spots.

Lady Chapel *RC Church* a chapel dedicated to the Virgin Mary. It is usually built behind the main altar, and forms an extension to the main building.

Lady Day 25 Mar, the feast of the Annunciation.

lady-in-waiting *noun* (PL. **ladies-in-waiting**) a woman attending a queen or princess.

lady-killer *noun colloq.* a man who habitually pursues or seduces women.

ladylike *adj.* like or appropriate to a lady in manners, appearance, or behaviour, especially in being polite and elegant.

Ladyship *noun* (*usually* **Your** or **Her Ladyship**) a title used to address peeresses (but not duchesses) and the wives and daughters of peers and knights.

lady's-slipper *noun* an orchid with a large yellow slipper-like lip.

lag¹ — *verb intrans.* (**lagged, lagging**) (*often* **lag behind**) to move or progress too slowly and become left behind. — *noun* **1** a lagging behind; a delay. **2** the amount by which one thing is delayed behind another. [origin uncertain: perhaps a corruption of *last* in a children's game]

⊟ *verb* dawdle, saunter, loiter, linger, straggle, trail, hang back, delay, tarry.
⊟ *verb* hurry, lead.

lag² — *verb* (**lagged, lagging**) to cover (a boiler, water pipes, etc) with a thick covering to keep the heat in. — *noun* same as LAGGING.

lag³ *noun slang* a convict or former convict. [origin unknown]

lager *noun* a light beer. [from German *Lagerbier,* beer for storing]

lager lout a man, especially a youth, who behaves in a boorish, aggressive, or unruly manner after drinking lager, beer, etc.

laggard /ˈlagəd/ *noun* a person or thing that lags behind.

lagging *noun* an insulating cover for pipes, boilers, etc.

lagoon *noun* a relatively shallow body of water, often brackish, that is more or less separated from the open sea by a barrier such as a reef or a narrow bank of sand or shingle. [from Italian *laguna*]

lah see LA.

laid past participle of LAY¹. — **laid back** *colloq.* relaxed. **laid up 1** *colloq.* confined to bed because of illness. **2** *said of a boat* in dock or on shore.

laid paper paper with fine lines running across the surface.

lain past participle of LIE².

lair *noun* **1** a wild animal's den. **2** *colloq.* a place of refuge or hiding. [from Anglo-Saxon *leger*]

⊟ **1** den, hole, burrow, earth, form, set. **2** retreat, refuge, sanctuary, hiding-place, hideout.

laird *noun Scot.* a landowner, especially of a large estate.

laissez-faire or **laisser-faire** /ˌlɛseɪˈfɛə(r)/ *noun* a policy of not interfering in what others are doing. [from French *laissez faire,* let do]

laity /ˈleɪɪtɪ/ *noun* (*usually* **the laity**) ordinary people who are not members of a particular profession, especially people who are not members of the clergy. [from LAY³]

lake¹ *noun* a large area of still fresh or salt water, surrounded by land and lying in a depression in the Earth's surface, which receives water from rivers, streams, springs, direct rainfall, or melting snow. [from Middle English *lac*]

⊟ lagoon, reservoir, mere, tarn, loch, lough.

lake² *noun* **1** a reddish dye, originally obtained from lac. **2** a substance made from dye and a mordant, used in dyeing fabrics to make the dye insoluble. [from LAC]

lake dwellings *Archaeol.* Stone Age villages built on supports on marshy ground around lakes, or on piling driven into the bottom of lakes.

Lakota — *noun* **1** a Native American people comprising the westernmost branch of the Sioux. **2** a member of this people. **3** the Siouan language of this people. — *adj.* relating to this people or their language. [a native American name]

lam *verb* (**lammed, lamming**) *slang* to beat or thrash. [from Norse *lemja,* to beat until lame]

lama *noun* a Buddhist priest or monk in Tibet or Mongolia. [from Tibetan *blama*]

Lamarckism /lɑːˈmɑːkɪzm/ *noun Biol.* one of the earliest theories of evolution, proposed by Jean-Baptiste Lamarck during the early 19c, suggesting that characteristics acquired during the lifetime of an organism could be transmitted from parents to offspring.

lamb — *noun* **1** a young sheep. **2** the flesh of a lamb or sheep, eaten as food. **3** a person who is kind, gentle, and good. **4** (**the Lamb** or **the Lamb of God**) a name for Christ (John 1.29). — *verb intrans.* **1** *said of a ewe* to give birth to a lamb or lambs. **2** *said of a shepherd* to tend lambing ewes. [from Anglo-Saxon *lamb*]

lambada *noun* a style of dance with sinuous hip movements to salsa-like music, originating in Brazil and popularized in the late 1980s. [from Portuguese *lambada,* whip-crack]

lambaste or **lambast** /lamˈbast/ *verb* **1** to thrash or beat severely. **2** to scold severely. [from LAM + BASTE³]

lambency *noun* a state of sparkling or flickering.

lambent *adj.* **1** *said of a flame or light* flickering over a surface. **2** *said of eyes, etc* gently sparkling. **3** *said of wit* light and brilliant. [from Latin *lambere,* to lick]

lambing *noun* the time when ewes give birth to lambs.

lambskin *noun* the skin of a lamb, usually with the wool left on it, used to make slippers, coats, etc.

lambswool *noun* fine wool obtained from a lamb.

LAMDA *abbrev.* London Academy of Music and Dramatic Art.

lame — *adj.* **1** not able to walk properly, especially because of an injury or defect. **2** *said of an excuse, etc* not convincing; weak. — *verb* to make lame. [from Anglo-Saxon *lama*]

◼ *adj.* **1** crippled, limping, hobbling, disabled, handicapped. **2** weak, feeble, flimsy, inadequate, unsatisfactory, poor.
◪ *adj.* **1** able-bodied. **2** convincing.

lamé /ˈlɑːmeɪ/ *noun* a fabric which has gold and silver threads woven into it. [from French *lamé*]

lame duck 1 a person who can do nothing without the help of others. **2** an official in the final months of office, after the election of a successor. **3** a company with financial problems.

lamella *noun* (PL. **lamellae**) **1** *Anat.* a thin sheet or plate of tissue, especially one of the many thin layers of which compact bone is formed. **2** *Bot.* any of the thin sheet-like membranes that are present within the chloroplasts of plant cells. **3** *Biol.* in a mushroom or toadstool, any of the vertical spore-bearing structures or gills that radiate outwards from the stalk on the underside of the cap. [from Latin *lamella*]

lamely *adv.* in a weak or ineffectual manner; feebly.

lameness *noun* a lame state; weakness.

lament — *verb* **1** *intrans.* to feel or express regret or sadness. **2** to feel or express regret or sadness about (something). — *noun* **1** an expression of sadness, grief, regret, etc. **2** a poem, song, etc which expresses great grief, especially following someone's death. [from Latin *lamentum*]

◼ *verb* MOURN. **1** grieve, sorrow, weep, wail, bewail, bemoan, complain. **2** regret, deplore. *noun* LAMENTATION. **1** wail, moan, complaint. **2** dirge, elegy, threnody, requiem.
◪ *verb* REJOICE (IN), CELEBRATE.

lamentable *adj.* (with stress on *lam-*) regrettable, shameful, deplorable.

◼ regrettable, shameful, disgraceful, deplorable, disappointing, unsatisfactory, inadequate, insufficient, pitiful, miserable, unfortunate, distressing, tragic.

lamentably *adv.* (with stress on *lam-*) regrettably; shamefully: *they are lamentably behind the times.*

lamentation *noun* an act of lamenting; a lament.

lamented *adj.*, *said of a dead person* mourned for.

lamina *noun* (PL. **laminae**) **1** a thin plate or layer of a material of uniform thickness, eg bone, rock, or metal. **2** *Bot.* the flattened part of a leaf blade. [from Latin *lamina*]

laminate — *verb* (pronounced -neɪt) **1** to beat (metal) into thin sheets. **2** to make by bonding thin sheets of material on top of each other. **3** to cover with a thin sheet of plastic or other material. **4** *trans.*, *intrans.* to split or be split into layers. — *noun* (pronounced -ət) material or a structure made by bonding thin layers of material together. — *adj.* (pronounced -ət) in thin plates or layers. [from Latin *lamina*, thin plate]

laminated *adj.*, *said of metal* beaten into thin sheets; made into laminate.

lamination *noun* the process of laminating or making metal into thin sheets.

Lammas /ˈlaməs/ *noun* 1 Aug, an old feast celebrating the first crops from the harvest. [from Anglo-Saxon *hlafmæsse*, from *hlaf*, loaf + *mæsse*, mass]

lammergeyer /ˈlaməgaɪə(r)/ *noun* a large rare vulture, found in the remote mountain regions of Europe, Africa, and Asia (especially the Himalayas), that has a wingspan of nearly 3m, a feathered neck, and dark tufts of feathers on either side of its beak. [from German *Lämmergeier*, lamb vulture]

lamp *noun* **1** an appliance for producing a steady light, especially in the form of bulb-holder and shade. **2** an appliance with a glass case covering a flame produced by burning oil, etc, as a source of light. **3** an appliance produc-

cing ultraviolet or infrared radiation for treating certain medical complaints. [from Greek *lampe*, torch]

lampblack *noun* soot obtained from burning carbon, used as a pigment.

lampoon — *noun* a personal satirical attack. — *verb* to attack or laugh at in lampoons. [from French *lampon*, thought to be from *lampons*, let us drink, the refrain of a drinking-song]

◼ *noun* satire, skit, caricature, parody, *colloq.* send-up, take-off, spoof, burlesque. *verb* satirize, caricature, parody, *colloq.* send up, take off, spoof, make fun of, ridicule, mock, burlesque.

lampooner or **lampoonist** *noun* a person who composes lampoons.

lamppost *noun* a tall post supporting a street-lamp.

lamprey /ˈlamprɪ/ *noun* (PL. **lampreys**) *Zool.* any of about 30 species of primitive jawless fish, resembling an eel in shape, and belonging to the same class (Agnatha) as the hagfish. Lampreys lack scales, and have a skeleton of cartilage. [from Old French *lampreie*, from medieval Latin *lampreda*]

lampshade *noun* a shade placed over a lamp or light-bulb to soften or direct the light coming from it.

LAN *abbrev. Comput.* local area network, a computer network operating over a small area, such as an office or group of offices.

Lancastrian — *noun* **1** a person from Lancaster or Lancashire. **2** *Hist.* a supporter of the House of Lancaster in the Wars of the Roses. See also YORKIST. — *adj.* relating to Lancaster, the House of Lancaster, or Lancashire.

lance — *noun usually Hist.* a long spear with a hard pointed head at one end and sometimes a small flag at the other, used as a weapon by charging horsemen. — *verb* **1** to cut open (a boil, etc) with a lancet. **2** to pierce with, or as if with, a lance. [from Latin *lancea*]

lance corporal in the British army, a soldier holding the lowest rank of non-commissioned officer, between private and corporal.

lanceolate /ˈlɑːnsɪəleɪt/ *adj.* shaped like a spearhead, being much longer than it is wide, and tapering to a point at each end. [from Latin *lanceola*, small lance]

lancer *noun Hist.* a cavalry soldier belonging to a regiment armed with lances.

lancers *sing. noun* a set of quadrilles, or the music for it.

lancet *noun* **1** a small surgical knife with a point and both edges sharpened. **2** (*in full* **lancet arch** or **window**) *Archit.* a high and narrow pointed arch or window, typical of Early English architecture of the 13c. [from Old French *lancette*, a small lance]

Lancs. *abbrev.* Lancashire.

land — *noun* **1** the solid part of the earth's surface, not covered by water. **2** the ground or soil, especially in terms of its use or quality: *building land.* **3** land used for agriculture; farmland: *work on the land.* **4** a country, state, or region: *one's native land.* **5** (**lands**) estates. — *verb* **1** *intrans.* to come to rest on the ground or water, or in a particular place, after flight through the air. **2** to bring to rest after flight through the air. **3** to bring on to land from a ship. **4** (**land someone** or **oneself in something**) *colloq.* to put someone or find oneself in a given position or situation, usually unwelcome or unfavourable: *landed themselves in trouble.* **5** (**land someone with something**) *colloq.* to give or pass something unpleasant or unwanted to someone: *landed us with all the bills to pay.* **6** to bring (a fish caught on a line) to land. **7** *colloq.* to succeed in acquiring (a job, prize, etc). **8** *colloq.* to give (a blow) to (someone): *landed him one on the ear.* — **land up** *colloq.* to come to be in a given position or situation: *likely to land up married.* **see how the land lies** to find out what the situation is, especially before making a decision. [from Anglo-Saxon *land*]

◼ *noun* **1** earth, ground, terra firma. **2** soil, earth, ground.

3 farmland, countryside, country. **4** country, nation, state, region, territory. **5** property, grounds, estate, *North Amer.* real estate. *verb* **1** touch down, arrive, alight, come to rest, settle. **3** disembark, unload, drop, deposit. **7** secure, gain, get, obtain, acquire, net, capture, achieve, win. **land up** wind up, end up.

land agent a person who manages a large estate for the owner.

landau /ˈlandɔ/ *noun* a four-wheeled, horse-drawn carriage with a removable front cover and a back cover which folds down. [from *Landau* in Germany, where they were first made]

landed *adj.* **1** owning land or estates: *landed gentry.* **2** consisting of or derived from land: *landed estates.*

landfall *noun* an approach to land, or the land approached, after a journey by sea or air.

landfill *noun* **1** the disposal of refuse by burying it under the soil. **2** a place where refuse has been buried.

land girl a woman who works on a farm, especially during a war.

landing *noun* **1** the process of coming to shore or to ground. **2** a place for disembarking, especially from a ship. **3** the level part of a staircase between flights of steps, or at the very top.

landing-craft *noun* (PL. **landing-craft**) *Mil.* a low open vessel for landing troops and equipment on beaches.

landing-gear *noun* the wheels and supporting structure which allow an aircraft to land and take off.

landing-stage *noun* a platform, either fixed or floating, for disembarking passengers and goods from a ship.

landlady *noun* **1** a woman who owns property which is let to a tenant. **2** a woman who keeps a public house or hotel.

landlocked *adj.*, *said of a country* almost or completely enclosed by land.

landlord **1** a man who owns property which is let to a tenant. **2** a man who keeps a public house or hotel.

▣ **1** owner, proprietor, leaseholder, freeholder. **2** host, publican, innkeeper, hotelier, restaurateur.
▣ **1** tenant.

landlubber *noun derog. Naut.* a person who lives and works on the land and has no experience of the sea.

landmark *noun* **1** a conspicuous or well-known object on land, especially one that serves as a guide to sailors and travellers. **2** an event of importance, especially in marking a significant stage in the history or development of something.

▣ **1** feature, monument, beacon, cairn. **2** milestone, watershed, turning-point.

landmass *noun* a large area of land unbroken by seas.

landmine *noun* a mine laid on or near the surface of the ground, detonated when disturbed from above.

landowner *noun* a person who owns extensive areas of land.

landrace *noun* a type of domestic pig, originating from Denmark, that has a long pale body, white hair, and large pendulous ears.

Landrover *noun trademark* a strong motor vehicle used for driving over rough ground.

landscape *noun* **1** the area and features of land that can be seen in a broad view. **2** a picture showing a view of the countryside. **3** the genre of landscape painting.

▣ **1** scene, scenery, view, panorama, outlook, vista, prospect, countryside.

landscape gardener a person who practises landscape gardening, especially professionally.

landscape gardening the art or business of planning and laying out gardens and parks, especially on a large scale and so as to resemble natural scenery.

landslide *noun* **1** (*also* **landslip**) the sudden downward movement of a mass of soil and rock material, especially in mountainous areas, eg as a result of heavy rain or snow, earthquakes, or blasting operations. **2** a victory in an election by an overwhelming majority.

landslip same as LANDSLIDE 1.

landward — *adj.* lying or facing towards the land. — *adv.* (**landward** or **landwards**) towards land: *then turned landward.*

lane *noun* **1** a narrow road or street. **2** a division of a road for a single line of traffic. **3** a regular course across the sea taken by ships, or through the air by aircraft. **4** a lengthways division of a running track or swimming pool, for one competitor. **5** a passage through a crowd. [from Anglo-Saxon *lanu*]

language *noun* **1** the system of human communication, both spoken and written, using words in combinations according to established principles. **2** the speech and writing of a particular nation or social group. **3** the faculty of speech. **4** a style of speech or expression with words: *elegant language.* **5** any other way of communicating or expressing meaning: *sign language.* **6** professional or specialized vocabulary: *legal language.* **7** (**language** or **bad language**) the use of rude and offensive words: *mind one's language.* **8** a system of signs and symbols used to write computer programs. — **speak the same language** to have the same way of thinking or similar tastes. [from Old French *langage*]

▣ **1** communication, speech, utterance, talk, conversation, discourse. **2** tongue, *colloq.* lingo, dialect, patois, slang. **4** style, wording, phrasing, phraseology, expression. **6** vocabulary, terminology, parlance, jargon.

Language terms include: brogue, dialect, idiom, patois, tongue, pidgin, creole, lingua franca, vernacular, argot, cant, jargon, doublespeak, gobbledegook, buzzword, journalese, *colloq.* lingo, patter, slang, cockney rhyming slang; etymology, lexicography, linguistics, phonetics, semantics, syntax, usage, grammar, orthography, sociolinguistics.

Languages of the world include: Aborigine, Afghan, Afrikaans, Arabic, Balinese, Bantu, Basque, Bengali, Burmese, Belorussian, Catalan, Celtic, Chinese, Cornish, Czech, Danish, Dutch, English, Esperanto, Estonian, Ethiopian, Farsi, Finnish, Flemish, French, Gaelic, German, Greek, Haitian, Hawaiian, Hebrew, Hindi, Hindustani, Hottentot, Hungarian, Icelandic, Indonesian, Inuit, Iranian, Iraqi, Irish, Italian, Japanese, Kurdish, Lapp, Latin, Latvian, Lithuanian, Magyar, Malay, Maltese, Mandarin, Manx, Maori, Nahuatl, Navajo, Norwegian, Persian, Polish, Portuguese, Punjabi, Quechua, Romanian, Romany, Russian, Sanskrit, Scots, Serbo-Croat, Siamese, Sinhalese, Slavonic, Slovak, Slovenian, Somali, Spanish, Swahili, Swedish, Swiss, Tamil, Thai, Tibetan, Tupi, Turkish, Ukrainian, Urdu, Vietnamese, Volapük, Welsh, Yiddish, Zulu.

language laboratory a room with separate cubicles equipped with tape recorders and pre-recorded tapes, used for language learning.

languid *adj.* **1** lacking in energy or vitality; listless. **2** slow-moving; sluggish. [from Latin *languere*, to languish]

languidly *adv.* in a listless or sluggish way.

languish *verb intrans.* **1** to grow weak; to lose energy or vitality. **2** to look sorrowful. **3** to pine: *the old dog was languishing for its master.* [from Latin *languere*, to be faint]

🔲 **1** wilt, droop, fade, fail, flag, weaken, sink, decline, wither, waste away. **2** mope, grieve, sorrow, sigh. **3** pine, yearn, long, wish, desire, hanker, hunger, thirst, ache.
🔳 **1** flourish.

languishing *adj.* growing weak; pining.

languor /ˈlaŋgə(r)/ *noun* **1** a feeling of dullness or lack of energy. **2** tender softness or sentiment. **3** a stuffy suffocating atmosphere or stillness. [from Latin *languor*]

languorous *adj.* lacking in energy; dull, idle.

lank *adj.* **1** long and thin. **2** *said of hair* long, straight, and limp. [from Anglo-Saxon *hlanc*]

lankiness *noun* being lanky.

lankness *noun* a lank state; being long and thin.

lanky *adj.* (**lankier, lankiest**) thin and tall, especially in an awkward and ungainly way.

🔲 gangling, tall, thin, gaunt, scraggy, scrawny, weedy.
🔳 squat, dumpy.

lanolin *noun* fat obtained from sheep's wool, used in ointments and cosmetics. [from Latin *lana*, wool + *oleum*, oil]

lantern *noun* **1** a lamp or light contained in a transparent case, usually of glass, so that it can be held or carried. **2** a fixed lamp or light in this style. **3** the top part of a lighthouse, where the light is kept. **4** a structure with windows or open sides, built over an opening in the top of a roof or dome, for letting in light or air. [from Old French *lanterne*]

lantern-jawed *adj.*, *said of the face* hollow and drawn.

lantern jaws long thin jaws giving the face a hollow drawn appearance.

lanthanide series *Chem.* any of a group of 15 chemical elements in the periodic table with atomic numbers ranging from 57 (lanthanum) to 71 (lutetium). They are silvery, highly reactive metals that share similar chemical properties. Also called RARE EARTHS.

lanthanum *noun Chem.* (SYMBOL **La**, ATOMIC NUMBER **57**) a silvery-white metal (one of the lanthanide series) that ignites spontaneously in air, and is used in rocket propellants, electronic devices, and as a catalyst for the cracking of petroleum. [from Greek *lanthanein*, to escape notice, because it was hidden in rare minerals until 1839]

lanyard *noun* **1** a cord for hanging a knife, whistle, etc round the neck, worn especially by sailors. **2** *Naut.* a short rope for fastening rigging, etc. [from Old French *laniere*]

lap[1] — *verb* (**lapped, lapping**) **1** *usually said of an animal* to drink (liquid) by scooping it up with the tongue. **2** *trans., intrans., said of water* to wash or flow against a shore or other surface with a light splashing sound. — *noun* **1** the act of lapping or the amount lapped up. **2** the sound of waves gently splashing or lapping. — **lap something up 1** to drink something eagerly, especially eagerly or greedily. **2** to listen eagerly to (praise, gossip, information, etc). [from Anglo-Saxon *lapian*]

🔲 *verb* **1** drink, sip, sup, lick.

lap[2] *noun* **1** the front part of the body, from waist to knees, when sitting. **2** the part of clothing, especially of a skirt or dress, which covers this part of the body. — **drop** or **land in someone's lap** to make or become someone's responsibility, especially suddenly or unexpectedly. **in the lap of the gods** *said of a situation* beyond human control. **in the lap of luxury** in very luxurious conditions. [from Anglo-Saxon *læppa*]

lap[3] — *noun* **1** one circuit of a racecourse or other track. **2** one section of a journey. **3** a part which overlaps or the amount it overlaps by. **4** the amount of thread or material wound once round a reel, etc. — *verb* (**lapped, lapping**) **1** to get ahead of (a competitor) in a race by one or more laps. **2** (**lap something round someone**) to fold a piece of clothing etc round someone. **3** (**lap someone in some-**

thing) to wrap a person in clothing etc, especially protectively. **4** to cause to overlap. **5** *intrans.* to lie with an overlap. [from Middle English *lappen*]

🔲 *noun* **1** circuit, round, orbit, tour, loop, course. **2** leg, stage. *verb* **2** wrap, fold. **3** wrap, envelop, enfold, swathe, swaddle, cover.

laparoscope *noun Medicine* a surgical instrument, consisting of a narrow flexible illuminated tube with an eye-piece, that is inserted through a small incision in the abdominal wall, enabling the abdominal cavity to be examined. [from Greek *lapara*, flank + -SCOPE]

lapdog *noun* a small pet dog.

lapel *noun* the part of a coat or jacket joined to the collar and folded back across the chest. [a diminutive of LAP[2]]

lapidary /ˈlapɪdərɪ/ — *noun* (PL. **lapidaries**) a person who cuts and polishes gemstones. — *adj.* **1** relating to stones. **2** engraved on stone. **3** *said of writing* concise and to the point, as in inscriptions. [from Latin *lapis*, stone]

lapis lazuli /ˈlapɪs ˈlazjʊlɪ/ **1** *Geol.* a deep blue gemstone, consisting of *lazurite* (a deep blue mineral) embedded in a matrix of white calcite, together with dark specks of pyrite. It is used as a semi-precious stone and ornamental material. **2** the bright blue colour of this material. [from Latin *lapis*, stone + *lazuli*, azure]

lap joint a joint formed in rails, timbers, etc, by reducing their thickness at the ends and overlapping them.

lap of honour a ceremonial circuit of a racecourse or sports pitch by the winner to acknowledge the applause of the audience.

Lapp — *noun* **1** a member of a nomadic people living in N Scandinavia. **2** (**Lapp** or **Lappish**) the language spoken by this people. — *adj.* (**Lapp** or **Lappish**) relating to this people or their language or culture.

lappet *noun* **1** a small flap or fold in material, a piece of clothing, etc. **2** a piece of loose hanging flesh. [a diminutive of LAP[2]]

Lapplander same as LAPP *noun* 1.

lapse — *noun* **1** a slight mistake or failure: *a lapse of memory*. **2** a decline in standards of behaviour. **3** a passing of time: *after a lapse of two years*. **4** *Legal* the loss of a right or privilege by failing to renew a claim to it. — *verb intrans.* **1** to fail to behave properly or in a morally sound way. **2** (*often* **lapse into something**) to pass into or return to a bad or less welcome state: *showed signs of lapsing into carelessness*. **3** to turn away from a faith or belief. **4** *Legal*, *said of a right or privilege* to be no longer valid because the claim to it has not been renewed. [from Latin *lapsus*, slip]

🔲 *noun* **1** mistake, error, slip, failure, omission, oversight, fault, failing, aberration, indiscretion. **2** decline, drop, fall, deterioration, relapse, backsliding. **3** break, gap, interval, lull, pause. *verb* **2** decline, sink, drop, fall, slip, slide, backslide, worsen, deteriorate, degenerate, fail. **4** expire, run out, end, stop.

lapsed *adj.* **1** having fallen into error or former bad ways. **2** no longer practising a religion, etc: *a lapsed Catholic*. **3** no longer used or valid.

laptop *noun Comput.* a portable personal computer that is small enough to be used on a person's lap and can be operated from batteries or mains power.

lapwing *noun* a plover with greenish-black and white feathers and a crest. [from Anglo-Saxon *hleapewince*]

larcenist *noun old use Legal* a person who committed larceny.

larceny *noun* (PL. **larcenies**) *old use Legal* theft of personal property. [from Old French *larcin*]

larch *noun* **1** a coniferous tree with needle-like leaves and cones, which loses its leaves in the winter. **2** the wood of this tree. [from Latin *larix*]

lard — *noun* soft white fat from pigs, used in cooking. — *verb* **1** to put lard on. **2** to stuff (meat) with bacon or pork. **3** to fill (a piece of writing, etc) with details, technical or elaborate words, etc. [from Latin *laridum*, bacon fat]

larder *noun* **1** a cool room or cupboard for storing food. **2** a store of food kept for winter by a wild animal. [from Old French *lardier*, from Latin *laridum*, bacon fat]

Lares *pl. noun* in Roman mythology, minor Roman gods. Lares included the guardians of the household, of the crossroads, and of the state.

large — *adj.* **1** occupying much space; great in size, extent, or amount. **2** broad; wide-ranging. **3** generous. **4** in a big way; extensive. — *adv.* importantly; prominently. — **at large 1** *said of prisoners, etc* free and threatening. **2** in general; as a whole: *people at large.* **3** at length and with full details. **large it** *slang* to have a good time, especially by going to a nightclub. [from Latin *largus*, plentiful]

. . . .

▤ *adj.* **1** big, great, huge, enormous, immense, massive, vast, giant, gigantic, king-sized, bulky, sizeable, considerable, substantial. **2** broad, wide, wide-ranging, sweeping. **3** generous, liberal, plentiful, ample, roomy, spacious. **4** grand, grandiose, extensive, full. **at large 1** free, at liberty, on the loose, on the run.

▣ *adj.* **1** small, tiny.
. . . .

largely *adv.* **1** mainly or chiefly. **2** to a great extent.
. . . .

▤ **1** mainly, chiefly, principally, primarily, predominantly, mostly, generally, by and large. **2** greatly, considerably, widely, extensively.
. . . .

largeness *noun* a large state or size.

largesse or **largess** /lɑːˈdʒɛs/ *noun* **1** generosity. **2** gifts, money, etc given generously. [from Old French *largesse*, from Latin *largus*, plentiful]

largo *Mus.* — *adv.* slowly and with dignity. — *adj.* slow and dignified. — *noun* (PL. **largos**) a piece of music to be played in this way. [from Italian *largo*, broad]

lariat *noun* a lasso or rope used for tethering animals. [from Spanish *la reata*, the lasso]

lark¹ *noun* any of several kinds of songbirds, especially the skylark. [from Anglo-Saxon *lawerce*]

lark² *noun colloq.* **1** a joke or piece of fun. **2** *Brit.* a job or activity. — *verb intrans.* (**lark about** or **around**) *colloq.* to play or fool about frivolously. [origin uncertain]
. . . .

▤ *noun* **1** joke, prank, mischief, escapade, antic, fling, revel, romp, frolic, caper, game. *verb* play about, fool about, clown around, skylark.

. . . .

larkspur *noun* a plant with spur-like calyces and blue, white, or pink flowers. [from LARK¹ + SPUR]

larva *noun* (PL. **larvae**) *Zool.* in the lifecycle of many insects, amphibians, and fish, the immature stage which hatches from the fertilized egg and is capable of independent existence, eg the caterpillar of butterflies, the tadpole of frogs. [from Latin *larva*, ghost, mask]

larval *adj.* like or in the form of a larva.

laryngeal *adj.* relating to the larynx.

laryngitis *noun* inflammation of the larynx, causing pain and making it difficult to speak.

larynx *noun* a hollow organ in the throat, forming the upper end of the windpipe and containing the vocal cords. [from Greek *larynx*]

lasagne *noun* pasta in the form of thin flat sheets, often cooked in layers with a mixture of meat and tomatoes, and a cheese sauce. [from Italian *lasagne* (plural)]

lascivious *adj.* feeling, expressing, or causing sexual desire. [from Latin *lascivus*, playful, wanton]

laser *noun* a device that produces a very powerful narrow beam of coherent light of a single wavelength by stimulating the emission of photons from atoms, molecules, or ions. [from *light amplification by stimulated emission of radiation*]

laser printer *Comput.* a fast high-quality printer that projects a laser beam on to a rotating drum coated with a material that becomes electrically charged and attracts a metallic powder. The powder image is then transferred to paper and fixed to it by heat.

lash — *noun* **1** a stroke or blow with a whip. **2** the flexible part of a whip. **3** (*usually* **lashes**) an eyelash. — *verb* **1** to hit or beat with a lash. **2** *trans., intrans.* (of waves or rain) to beat or strike with great force: *waves lashing the shore/rain lashing against the window.* **3** (*often* **lash something down** or **together**) to fasten with a rope or cord. **4** *intrans., said of something resembling a whip* to make a sudden whip-like movement. **5** *said of an animal* to move (the tail) with a sudden or restless movement. **6** to attack with harsh scolding words or criticism. **7** to urge on as if with a whip. — **lash out** to hit out or complain violently. **lash out on something** *colloq.* to spend money extravagantly on it. [from Middle English *lashe*]
. . . .

▤ *noun* **1** whip, stroke, blow, swipe, hit. *verb* **1** whip, flog, scourge, beat, hit, strike, thrash. **3** tie, bind, fasten, secure, make fast, join, rope, strap, tether. **6** attack, lay into, criticize, scold.
. . . .

lashing *noun* **1** a rope for tying things fast. **2** a beating with a whip.

lashings *pl. noun colloq.* a large amount.

lass *noun dialect, poetic* a girl or young woman (now often used as a general term of affection). [from Middle English *lasce*, from Old Norse *laskwa*, unmarried]

lassi *noun* an Indian cold drink of yoghurt mixed with water, flavoured with salt or sugar. [from Hindi]

lassie *noun Scot.* a young girl.

lassitude *noun* a feeling of physical or mental tiredness; lack of energy and enthusiasm. [from Latin *lassus*, tired]

lasso /ləˈsuː/ — *noun* (PL. **lassos**, **lassoes**) a long rope with a loop which tightens when the rope is pulled, used for catching animals, etc. — *verb* (**lassoes**, **lassoed**) to catch with a lasso. [from Spanish *lazo*, from Latin *laqueus*, noose]

last¹ — *adj.* **1** coming at the end of a series or after all others. **2** most recent; next before the present: *last week.* **3** coming or remaining after all the others. **4** least likely or suitable: *the last person to expect help from.* **5** lowest in rank; worst. **6** (used for emphasis) single: *broke every last one of the plates.* — *adv.* **1** after all others. **2** most recently. **3** lastly. — *noun* **1** the person or thing that is last. **2** the end or last moment. **3** (**the last**) the final appearance or mention: *we haven't heard the last of him.* — **at long last** in the end, especially after a long delay. **last thing** after doing everything else, especially before leaving or going to bed. **on one's last legs** worn out; exhausted. **to the last** until the very end, especially until death. [from Anglo-Saxon *latost*, *latest*]
. . . .

▤ *adj.* **1** final, ultimate, closing, concluding, conclusive, definitive, end, terminal, rearmost, furthest, remotest, utmost, extreme. **2** latest, previous. *adv.* **1** after, behind. **3** lastly, finally, ultimately. **at long last** eventually, finally, in the end, at length.

▣ *adj.* **1** first, initial. *adv.* **1** before. **3** first, firstly.
. . . .

last² *verb* **1** *intrans.* to continue for a long time, or for a specified time: *the journey lasts for three days.* **2** *intrans.* to remain adequate or in good condition: *enough water to last us a week/but the bread will only last one more day.* — **last out** to survive for a given or implied length of time. [from Anglo-Saxon *læstan*]
. . . .

▤ **1** continue, endure, abide, stay, remain, persist, keep on, carry on. **2** keep, wear. **last out** survive, hold out.

▣ **1** stop, end, cease.
. . . .

last[3] *noun* a foot-shaped piece of wood or metal on which shoes are made and repaired. — **stick to one's last** to avoid interfering in things one does not understand. [from Anglo-Saxon *læste*]

last-ditch *adj.* done as a last resort.

lasting *adj.* existing or continuing for a long time or permanently.

◾ enduring, abiding, permanent, unchanging, continuing, unending, unceasing, perpetual, lifelong, long-standing, long-term.

◪ brief, fleeting, short-lived.

Last Judgement see DAY OF JUDGEMENT.

lastly *adv.* as the last item; finally; at the end.

last-minute *adj.* made, done, or given at the latest possible moment: *a last-minute birthday present*.

last name a surname.

last rites (**the last rites**) religious rites for a dying person.

last straw (**the last straw**) an often insignificant addition to a mounting difficulty or burden, which finally makes all of it intolerable: *losing my keys was the last straw*.

last word (**the last word**) **1** the final or definitive remark in an argument or debate. **2** the final decision. **3** the most up-to-date or fashionable thing: *the last word in elegance*.

Lat or **Lat**. *abbrev.* Latin.

lat. *abbrev.* latitude.

latch — *noun* **1** a door-catch consisting of a bar which is lowered or raised from its notch by a lever or string. **2** a door-lock by which a door may be opened from the inside using a handle, and from the outside by using a key. — *verb trans., intrans.* to fasten or be fastened with a latch. — **latch on** *colloq.* to understand: *took them a moment to latch on*. **latch on to someone** *colloq.* to follow or observe them closely. **on the latch** *said of a door* shut but not locked; able to be opened by the latch. [from Anglo-Saxon *læccan*]

◾ *noun* **1** fastening, catch, bar, bolt.

latchkey *noun* a key for an outer door with a latch.

latchkey child a child who returns home from school while the parents are still out at work.

late — *adj.* **1** coming, arriving, etc after the expected or usual time. **2** far on in the day or night; nearly at the end: *late afternoon*. **3** occurring, ripening, etc at a relatively advanced time in the season: *late potatoes*. **4** having died, especially recently: *his late father*. **5** former: *the late prime minister*. **6** most recent. — *adv.* **1** after the expected or usual time. **2** far on in the day or night. **3** at an advanced time: *flower late in the season*. **4** recently: *the letter was sent as late as this morning*. **5** formerly, but no longer: *late of Glasgow*. — **late in the day** at a late stage, especially too late to be of any use. **of late** lately; recently. [from Anglo-Saxon *læt*]

◾ *adj.* **1** overdue, behind, behindhand, delayed, slow, unpunctual. **2** advanced, latter, last-minute. **4** dead, deceased. **5** former, previous, past, old. **6** recent, up-to-date, current, fresh, new.

◪ *adj.* **1** early, punctual.

lateen /lə'ti:n/ *adj. Naut., said of a ship* having a triangular sail on a long, sloping yard. [from French *voile latine*, Latin sail: so called because they are common on the Mediterranean]

lately *adv.* in the recent past; not long ago.

◾ recently, of late, latterly.

latency *noun* the state of being latent or hidden.

lateness *noun* a late state or time.

latent *adj.* present but hidden and not yet developed. [from Latin *latere*, to lie hidden]

◾ potential, dormant, undeveloped, unrealized, hidden, concealed, veiled, underlying, lurking, unexpressed, secret, unseen, invisible.

◪ active, conspicuous.

latent heat *Physics* the amount of heat energy that is required to change a solid to a liquid, or a liquid to a gas, without a change in temperature.

latent image the invisible image formed in a photographic emulsion by its exposure to light. It is made visible in the development process.

latent period 1 *Biol.* the period of time between a stimulus and a response. **2** *Medicine* the time between the contracting of a disease and the appearance of symptoms.

later — *adj.* more recent; coming after. — *adv.* at some time after, or in the near future: *they are coming here later*.

◾ *adj.* next, subsequent. *adv.* after, afterwards, next, subsequently.

◪ *adj.* earlier. *adv.* earlier.

lateral — *adj.* at the side; to or from the side. — *noun* a side part, especially a branch. [from Latin *latus*, side]

◾ *adj.* side, oblique, sideward, sideways, edgeways, marginal, flanking.

laterality or **lateralization** *noun* **1** the state of being lateral or to the side; physical one-sidedness, either right or left. **2** *Physiol.* a characteristic of the human brain, in which the left and right cerebral hemispheres are specialized for different functions.

lateral line *Zool.* in fishes, a line of specialized receptor cells along the sides of the body that is sensitive to vibrations and water pressure.

laterally *adv.* on or to a side.

lateral thinking a form of thinking which seeks new and unusual ways of approaching and solving problems, and does not merely proceed by logical steps from the starting point of what is known or believed.

laterite *noun Geol.* a deposit of soft porous soil or hard dense rock, often occurring as a thick reddish layer, and formed as a result of the weathering of igneous rocks in humid tropical climates. It is composed mainly of hydroxides of iron and aluminium. [from Latin *later*, brick]

latest — *adj.* most recent. — *noun* (**the latest**) the most recent news, occurrence, fashion, etc. — **at the latest** not later than a time stated: *be home by 10 at the latest*.

latex *noun* (PL. **latexes**, **latices**) **1** a thick milky juice of some plants, especially of the rubber tree, used in commercial applications. **2** a rubber-like synthetic product. [from Latin *latex*, liquid]

lath /lɑːθ/ *noun* a thin narrow strip of wood, especially one of a series used to support plaster. [from Anglo-Saxon *lætt*]

lathe *noun* a machine tool that is used to cut, drill, or polish a piece of metal, wood, or plastic, which is rotated against the cutting edge of the lathe. [from Middle English, = frame, stand]

lather — *noun* **1** a foam made by mixing water and soap. **2** foamy sweat, especially of a horse. — *verb* (**lathered**, **lathering**) **1** *intrans.* to form a lather. **2** to cover with lather. **3** *colloq.* to beat or thrash. — **in a lather** *colloq.* extremely agitated or excited. [from Anglo-Saxon *leathor*, soap]

◾ *noun* **1** foam, suds, soap suds, froth, bubbles. *verb* **1** foam, froth. **2** soap, shampoo. **in a lather** agitated, flustered, *colloq.* in a state, *colloq.* in a flap.

lathery *adj.* like lather; foamy.

Latin — *noun* 1 the language of ancient Rome and its empire. 2 an inhabitant of ancient Latium in Central Italy. — *adj.* 1 relating to or in the Latin language. 2 *said of a language* ultimately derived from Latin, as Italian and Spanish are. 3 *said of a person* having a passionate or excitable character. 4 relating to the Roman Catholic Church. [from Latin *latinus*, of Latium]

Latin American *noun* an inhabitant of Latin America. — *adj.* relating to Latin America.

Latino or **Latina** *noun* a man or woman of Latin American descent, especially in N America.

latitude *noun* 1 any of a series of imaginary circles drawn around the Earth parallel to the Equator. All points on the Equator have a latitude of 0°, and the distance between the Equator and the poles is divided into 90° of latitude, ie the North and South Poles correspond to 90°N and 90°S, respectively. Latitude is used together with longitude to specify any position on the Earth's surface. See also LONGITUDE. 2 (*usually* **latitudes**) a region or area in terms of its distance from the equator or its climate: *warm latitudes*. 3 scope for freedom of action or choice. [from Latin *latus*, broad]

⊟ **3** scope, range, room, space, clearance, play, leeway, freedom, liberty, licence.

latitudinal *adj.* relating to latitude; measured by latitude.
latitudinally *adv.* as regards latitude; in terms of latitude.
latrine *noun* a communal lavatory, especially in a barracks. [from Latin *lavatrina*, bath]
latte /ˈlɑteɪ/ *noun* (PL. **lattes**) coffee made by adding a shot of espresso to hot milk. [from Italian *latte*, milk]
latter — *adj.* 1 (**the latter**) nearer to the end: *the latter part of the holiday*. 2 being the second of two people or things mentioned, or (loosely) the last of several mentioned. 3 recent; modern. — *noun* (**the latter**) the second of two people or things mentioned, or (loosely) the last of several mentioned. [from Anglo-Saxon *lætra*]

⊟ *adj.* 1 late, later, closing, concluding. 2 second, last-mentioned, last.
⊟ *adj.* 2 former.

latter-day *adj.* recent or modern.
Latter-day Saints the Mormons' preferred name for themselves.
latterly *adv.* 1 recently. 2 towards the end.
lattice *noun* 1 (*also* **lattice-work**) an open frame made from crossed narrow strips of wood or metal, used especially for gates and fences. 2 (*also* **lattice window**) a window with small diamond-shaped panels of glass formed by strips of lead. 3 *Chem.* the regular three-dimensional arrangement of atoms, ions, or molecules that forms the structure of a crystalline solid. [from Old French *lattis*, from *latte*, lath]
latticed *adj.* containing or made up of lattice.
Latvian — *noun* 1 a native or citizen of Latvia. 2 the Baltic language of Latvia. — *adj.* relating to Latvia or its people or language.
laud — *verb formal* to praise (a deity), especially in hymns. — *noun formal* praise for a deity. See also LAUDS. [from Latin *laus*, praise]
laudability *noun* being laudable or praiseworthy.
laudable *adj.* worthy of praise; commendable.
laudably *adv.* in a worthy or commendable way.
laudanum /ˈlɔːdnəm/ *noun Medicine* a solution of morphine in alcohol, prepared from raw opium, and formerly often taken by mouth as a painkiller. [a Latinized name used by Paracelsus (16c) for an expensive medicine containing opium]
laudatory /ˈlɔːdətərɪ/ *adj.* containing or expressing praise. [from Latin *laus*, praise]

lauds *pl. noun RC Church* the customary first morning prayers.
laugh — *verb* 1 *intrans.* to make spontaneous sounds associated with happiness, amusement, scorn, etc. 2 (**laugh oneself silly**, etc) to bring oneself into a certain state (often figuratively) through laughing. 3 to express by laughing: *laughed his contempt.* — *noun* 1 an act or sound of laughing. 2 *colloq.* a person or thing that is amusing or causes laughter. — **have the last laugh** to win or succeed in the end, especially after setbacks, or be finally proved right. **laugh at someone** or **something** to make fun of or ridicule them. **laugh something off** to treat (an injury, embarrassment, etc) trivially. **laugh up one's sleeve** to be secretly or gleefully amused. [from Anglo-Saxon *hlæhhan*]

⊟ *verb* 1 chuckle, giggle, snigger, titter, chortle, guffaw, split one's sides, *colloq.* fall about. *noun* 1 chuckle, giggle, snigger, titter, chortle, guffaw. 2 joke, lark, *colloq.* hoot, *colloq.* scream. **laugh at** mock, ridicule, make fun of, scoff at, deride, jeer, taunt.

laughable *adj.* deserving to be laughed at; absurd, ludicrous.

⊟ funny, amusing, comical, humorous, hilarious, farcical, absurd, ludicrous, ridiculous, preposterous, nonsensical, derisory, derisive.
⊟ serious.

laughably *adv.* in a laughable or absurd way.
laughing *noun* laughter. — **no laughing matter** a very serious matter.
laughing gas nitrous oxide used as an anaesthetic. It can cause a feeling of exhilaration when inhaled without oxygen.
laughing jackass see KOOKABURRA.
laughingly *adv.* in a laughing or derisory manner.
laughing-stock *noun* someone who is laughed at or ridiculed.

⊟ figure of fun, butt, target, fair game.

laughter *noun* the act or sound of laughing.

⊟ laughing, chuckling, giggling, sniggering, tittering, chortling, guffawing, mirth, amusement, merriment, hilarity.

launch¹ — *verb* 1 to send (a boat or ship) into the water, especially for the first time. 2 to send (a spacecraft, missile, etc) into the air. 3 to start (a person, project, etc) off on a course. 4 to bring (a new product) on to the market, especially with promotions and publicity. 5 (**launch into something**) a to begin an undertaking with vigour and enthusiasm. b to begin a story or speech, especially a long one. — *noun* a launching of a ship or spacecraft. [from Latin *lanceare*, to wield a lance]

⊟ *verb* 1 float. 2 throw, fire, discharge, project, propel. 3 start, begin, send off, dispatch, initiate, set in motion, establish, found, open, inaugurate. 4 introduce, bring out. 5 start, begin, commence, embark on.

launch² *noun* 1 a large powerful motorboat. 2 *Hist.* the largest boat carried by a man-of-war. [from Spanish *lancha*, perhaps from a Malay word meaning 'swift']
launcher *noun* a device used for launching a spacecraft or missile.
launching-pad or **launch pad** *noun* a platform for launching a spacecraft or rocket.
launch vehicle *Astron.* a rocket-propelled vehicle that is used to carry a spacecraft (eg a satellite or space probe) from the Earth's surface into space.

launch window *Astron.* the period of time during which the launching of a spacecraft must take place if it is to put a satellite, space probe, etc, in the right orbit or on the right flight path.

launder *verb* (**laundered, laundering**) **1** to wash and iron (clothes or linen). **2** *colloq.* to transfer (money obtained illegally) through banks or legitimate businesses to hide its origins. [from Latin *lavanda*, things to be washed, from *lavare*, to wash]

launderette or **laundrette** *noun* an establishment with coin-operated machines for customers to wash and dry clothes. [originally a trademark]

laundress *noun* a woman who washes and irons clothes and linen, especially professionally.

laundry *noun* (PL. **laundries**) **1** a place where clothes and linen are washed. **2** clothes and linen for washing or newly washed.

Laurasia *noun Geol.* the ancient landmass or 'supercontinent' that is thought to have existed in the N hemisphere during the Mesozoic era. It subsequently split to form the present-day landmasses of N America, Greenland, Europe, and N Asia. [named after Laurentia, the ancient N American landmass, from Laurentian strata of the Canadian Shield, and Eurasia]

laureate /ˈlɒrɪət/ *adj.* crowned with laurel leaves as a sign of honour or distinction. — *noun* a person honoured for artistic or intellectual achievement, especially a poet laureate. [from Latin *laureatus*, from *laurus*, laurel]

laurel *noun* **1** a small evergreen tree with smooth, dark, shiny leaves used for flavouring in cooking. **2** a crown of laurel leaves worn as a symbol of victory or mark of honour. **3** (**laurels**) honour; praise. — **look to one's laurels** beware of losing one's reputation by being outclassed. **rest on one's laurels** to be satisfied with past successes and not try to achieve anything more. [from Latin *laurus*]

LAUTRO *abbrev.* Life Assurance and Unit Trust Regulatory Organization.

lav *noun colloq.* a lavatory.

lava *noun* **1** *Geol.* hot molten rock material (*magma*) that has erupted from a volcano or fissure and flowed on to the Earth's surface or the ocean floor. **2** the solid rock that forms as a result of cooling and solidification of this material. [from Italian *lava*, from Latin *labes*, a sliding down]

lavatorial *adj., said especially of humour* relating to lavatories and excretion.

lavatory *noun* (PL. **lavatories**) **1** a piece of equipment for receiving urine and faeces, and with a mechanism for flushing this away into a sewer. **2** a room containing one or more of these. [from Latin *lavare*, to wash]

☰ TOILET, *Brit. colloq.* LOO, WC, *Brit. slang* BOG, *North Amer. slang* JOHN. **2** bathroom, cloakroom, washroom, powder room, public convenience, ladies, gents.

lavender *noun* **1** a plant or shrub with sweet-smelling pale bluish-purple flowers. **2** the dried flowers from this plant, used to perfume clothes or linen. **3** the pale bluish-purple colour of the flowers. [from Latin *lavendula*]

lavender water a light perfume containing lavender oil.

laver *noun* any of several edible seaweeds. [from Latin *laver*, water plant]

laver bread a Welsh dish made from boiled laver dipped in oatmeal and fried.

lavish — *adj.* **1** *said of a person* spending or giving generously. **2** gorgeous or luxurious: *lavish decoration.* **3** too generous; extravagant or excessive. — *verb* to spend (money) or give (praise, etc) freely or generously: *lavished all kinds of honours on them.* [from Old French *lavasse*, deluge of rain]

☰ *adj.* **1** generous, liberal, open-handed, unstinting. **2** gorgeous, splendid, luxurious, rich, lush, luxuriant, abundant, plentiful, profuse. **3** extravagant, prodigal, thriftless, immoderate, intemperate, excessive, fulsome.

☰ *adj.* **1** miserly, mean. **3** frugal, thrifty.

law *noun* **1** a customary rule recognized as allowing or prohibiting certain actions. **2** a collection of such rules according to which people live or a country or state is governed. **3** the control which such rules exercise: *law and order.* **4** a controlling force: *their word is law.* **5** a collection of laws as a social system or a subject for study. **6** a group of laws relating to a particular activity: *commercial law.* **7** (**the law**) **a** people skilled in law, especially professionally. **b** *colloq.* the police or a member of the police. **8** (**laws**) jurisprudence. **9** the legal system as a recourse; litigation: *go to law.* **10** a rule in science, philosophy, etc, based on practice or observation, which says that under certain conditions certain things will always happen. **11** (**the Law**) the first five books of the Old Testament, which contain Jewish law. — **be a law unto oneself** to act as one wants and not according to laws or custom. **have the law on someone** *colloq.* (usually as a threat) to ensure that legal action is taken against them. **lay down the law** to assert one's opinions and orders forcefully and domineeringly. **take the law into one's own hands** to get justice in one's own way, without involving the law or the police. [from Anglo-Saxon *lagu*]

☰ **1** rule, regulation, canon, act, statute, ordinance, decree, edict, order, command. **2** charter, constitution. **10** rule, principle, axiom, criterion, standard, formula, code.

law-abiding *adj.* obeying the law.

☰ lawful, honest, honourable, upright, orderly, decent, good, obedient.

☰ lawless.

law centre *Brit.* a legal advisory service available to the public free of charge.

lawcourt *noun* (*also* **court of law**) a place where people accused of crimes are tried and legal disagreements settled.

lawful *adj.* **1** allowed by or according to law. **2** just or rightful.

☰ **1** legal, legitimate, authorized, warranted, permissible, allowable, valid. **2** just, fair, rightful, proper.

☰ **1** unlawful, illegal, illicit.

lawfully *adv.* justly; in accordance with the law.

lawfulness *noun* being lawful or just; a just state.

lawless *adj.* **1** ignoring or breaking the law, especially violently. **2** having no laws.

☰ ANARCHIC. **1** disorderly, unruly, riotous, mutinous, rebellious. **2** chaotic, wild.

☰ **1** law-abiding.

lawlessly *adv.* without regard to the law.

lawlessness *noun* a lawless state; lack of laws.

Law Lord **1** a peer in the House of Lords who holds or has held high legal office, and who sits in the highest court of appeal. **2** *Scot.* a judge of the Court of Session.

lawn[1] *noun* an area of smooth mown grass, especially as part of a garden. [from Middle English *launde*, glade]

lawn[2] *noun* fine linen or cotton. [probably from *Laon* in France, where linen-making was once important]

lawnmower *noun* a machine for cutting grass on lawns.

lawn tennis the usual form of tennis, played on grass-covered or hard courts. See also REAL TENNIS.

law of averages the theory that if something happens, its opposite is likely to happen also, so that balance may be maintained.

law of the jungle the principle that one should protect one's own interests ruthlessly and competitively.

lawrencium *noun Chem.* (SYMBOL **Lr**, ATOMIC NUMBER 103) a synthetic radioactive metallic element formed by bombarding californium with boron ions. [named after Ernest Orlando Lawrence]

lawsuit *noun* an argument or disagreement taken to a court of law to be settled.

. . . .
⊟ suit, action, case, cause, dispute, argument, contest, litigation, proceedings, process, trial.

. . . .

lawyer *noun* a person whose work it is to know about the law, and give legal advice and help, especially a solicitor.

. . . .
⊟ solicitor, barrister, QC, counsel, advocate, attorney.

. . . .

lax *adj.* **1** lacking care or concern in one's behaviour or morals. **2** loose, slack, or flabby. [from Latin *laxus*, loose]

. . . .
⊟ LOOSE, SLACK. **1** casual, easy-going, lenient, permissive, negligent, careless, remiss.
▣ **1** strict. **2** tight.

. . . .

laxative *noun* a medicine or food that stimulates movement of the bowels. — *adj.* having this effect. [from Latin *laxare*, to loosen]

laxity or **laxness** *noun* being lax; a lax state.

laxly *adv.* in a lax or slack way.

lay[1] — *verb* (PAST AND PAST PARTICIPLE **laid**) **1** to place on a surface, especially in a lying or horizontal position: *laid the letter on the table*. **2** to put or bring into the proper or stated position or condition: *laid her hand on his arm*. **3** to design, arrange, or prepare: *lay plans*. **4** to put plates and cutlery, etc on (a table) ready for a meal. **5** to prepare (a fire) by putting coal, etc in the grate. **6** *trans., intrans., said of a female bird* to produce (eggs). **7** to present: *lay one's case before the court*. **8** to deal with or remove: *lay a fear*. **9** to locate or attribute: *laid the blame on his friends*. **10** *trans., colloq.* to place (a bet). **11** *offensive, slang* to have sexual intercourse with (especially a woman). — *noun* **1** the way or position in which something is lying. **2** *offensive, slang* **a** a partner in sexual intercourse. **b** an act of sexual intercourse. — **lay about one** to strike blows in all directions. **lay something aside 1** to put it to one side, especially for later use or treatment. **2** to discard or abandon it. **lay something bare** to reveal or explain a plan or intention that has been kept secret. **lay something by** to put it away for future use. **lay something down 1** to put it on the ground. **2** to give up or sacrifice something: *lay down one's life*. **3** to formulate or devise something: *lay down a plan*. **4** to store (wine) in a cellar. **5** to begin to build (a ship or railway). **lay one's hands on something** *colloq.* **1** to find or be able to get it. **2** to catch something. **lay something in** to get and store a supply of it. **lay into someone** *colloq.* to attack or scold them severely. **lay someone low 1** *said of an illness* to affect them severely. **2** to make them feel humble. **lay people off** to dismiss (employees) when there is no work available. See also LAY-OFF. **lay off doing something** *colloq.* to stop doing something annoying or unwelcome. **lay something on** to provide a supply of something: *we'll bring the food if you'll lay on some drinks*. **lay it on thick** *colloq.* to exaggerate, especially praise or flattery. **lay oneself open** to expose oneself to criticism or attack. **lay something open 1** to uncover or reveal something. **2** to cut or wound something. **lay someone out 1** *colloq.* to knock them unconscious. **2** to prepare a dead body for burial. **lay something out 1** to plan and arrange (land or natural features): *the next stage was to lay out the new park*. **2** to spread out or display something. **3** *colloq.* to spend (money). See also LAYOUT. **lay someone to rest** to bury a dead body. **lay someone up** *colloq., said of an illness* to force them to stay in bed or at home. **lay something up 1** to keep or store something. **2** to put a ship out of use, especially for repairs. **lay waste** to destroy or devastate completely. [from Anglo-Saxon *lecgan*]

. . . .
⊟ *verb* **1** put, place, set, position, locate, deposit, put down,

set down, leave, spread, stretch. **3** arrange, set out, devise, work out, prepare. **7** present, submit. **9** attribute, ascribe, assign, charge. **lay in** store, stock up with, gather, collect, amass, accumulate, hoard, stockpile. **lay into** attack, assail, set about, criticize, scold. **lay people off** dismiss, discharge, *colloq.* sack, let go, make redundant. **lay off doing something** stop, cease, quit, give up, drop, desist from, leave off. **lay on** provide, supply, furnish, give, arrange, organize. **lay someone out 1** knock out, fell, *colloq.* floor. **lay something out 1** plan, design. **2** arrange, set out, spread out, display, exhibit. **3** spend, pay, *colloq.* shell out, *colloq.* fork out, give, invest. **lay something up 1** keep, save, put away, store, hoard, accumulate, amass.

. . . .

lay[2] see LIE[2].

lay[3] *adj.* **1** relating to or involving people who are not members of the clergy. **2** not having specialized or professional knowledge of a particular subject. [from Greek *laos*, the people]

. . . .
⊟ **1** laic, secular. **2** amateur, non-specialist.
▣ **1** clergy. **2** professional, expert.

. . . .

lay[4] *noun* a short narrative or lyric poem, especially one intended to be sung. [from Old French *lai*]

layabout *noun* a lazy or idle person.

lay-by *noun* (PL. **lay-bys**) *Brit.* an area at the side of a road for drivers to stop out of the way of the traffic.

layer — *noun* **1** a thickness or covering, especially one of several on a surface. **2** a person or thing that lays: *carpet-layer*. **3** a hen regularly laying eggs. **4** a shoot from a plant which is fastened into the soil to root while still attached to the parent plant. — *verb* **1** to arrange or cut in layers. **2** to produce (a new plant) by preparing a layer from the parent plant.

. . . .
⊟ *noun* **1** thickness, coat, coating, cover, covering, film, blanket, mantle, sheet, ply, tier, stratum, seam, bed.

. . . .

layette *noun* a complete set of clothes, blankets, etc for a baby. [from Old French *laiete*, small chest]

lay figure 1 a jointed adjustable model of the human body, used as a guide by painters and sculptors. **2** a person or a character in a novel who lacks individuality or is unrealistic. [from Dutch *leeman*, from *led*, jointed + *man*, man]

layman or **layperson** or **laywoman** *noun* **1** a person who is not a member of the clergy. **2** a person who does not have specialized or professional knowledge of a particular subject. See also LAITY.

. . . .
⊟ **2** amateur, non-specialist, outsider.
▣ **1** clergyman, clergywoman. **2** professional, specialist, expert.

. . . .

lay-off *noun* a dismissal of employees when there is no work available.

layout *noun* **1** an arrangement or plan of how land, buildings, pages of a book, etc are to be set out. **2** the things displayed or arranged in this way. **3** the general appearance of a printed page.

. . . .
⊟ **1** arrangement, design, plan, sketch, draft, outline, map, chart.

. . . .

lay reader an unordained person licensed to undertake some religious duties.

laze — *verb intrans.* to be idle or lazy. — *noun* a period of time spent lazing. — **laze around** to spend one's time doing nothing. [a back-formation from LAZY]

. . . .
⊟ *verb* idle, loaf, lounge, sit around, loll, sprawl.

. . . .

lazily *adv.* in a lazy or idle manner.

laziness *noun* a lazy state; a spell of idleness.

lazy *adj.* (**lazier, laziest**) **1** disinclined to do work or anything requiring effort; idle. **2** of or causing idleness. **3** *said of a river* slow-moving, sluggish.

▣ **1** idle, slothful, slack, work-shy, inactive, lethargic.

▨ **1** industrious.

lazy-bones *noun colloq.* a lazy person.

lb *abbrev.* pound (weight). [from Latin *libra*]

lbw or **l.b.w.** *abbrev. Cricket* leg before wicket.

lc or **l.c.** *abbrev.* **1** *loco citato* (Latin), in the place cited. **2** *Printing* lower case.

LCD *abbrev.* **1** liquid crystal display. **2** (*also* **lcd**) lowest common denominator.

LCDT *abbrev.* London Contemporary Dance Theatre.

LCM or **lcm** *abbrev.* lowest common multiple.

L/Cpl *abbrev.* Lance Corporal.

LEA *abbrev. Brit.* Local Education Authority.

lea /liː/ *noun poetic* a field, meadow, or piece of arable or pasture land. [from Anglo-Saxon *leah*]

leach *verb* **1** *Chem.* to wash a soluble substance out of a solid by allowing a suitable liquid solvent to percolate through it. **2** to make liquid seep through (bark, ash, or soil) to remove certain substances from (the bark, etc). **3** *trans., intrans.* (*also* **leach away** or **out**) to remove (soluble substances) or be removed by having liquid seep through. [probably from Anglo-Saxon *leccan*, to water]

leaching *noun* **1** *Chem.* the process of washing a soluble substance out of a solid by allowing a suitable liquid solvent to percolate through it. **2** *Geol.* the natural removal of soluble substances, eg certain mineral salts, from a layer of soil or rock as a result of the action of water percolating through it.

lead¹ (pronounced *leed*) — *verb* (PAST AND PAST PARTICIPLE **led**) **1** *trans., intrans.* to guide by going in front. **2** to guide or cause to go in a certain direction by holding or pulling with the hand, etc. **3** *intrans.* to direct or be in control. **4** to direct or be in control of. **5** to cause to act, feel, or think in a certain way: *what led you to say that?* **6** to pass or experience: *lead a miserable existence.* **7** *trans., intrans.* to go or take in a certain direction: *the road leads to the village.* **8** *intrans.* to have as an end or consequence: *this will lead to problems.* **9** *trans., intrans.* to be foremost or first; to be the most important or influential person (in a group) in a particular field: *they lead the world in engineering.* **10** *intrans. said of a newspaper* to have a particular story as its most important article: *the tabloids all lead with the royal separation.* **11** *Brit.* to play the principal violin in (an orchestra). **12** to conduct (liquid) along a channel or course. **13** *trans., intrans.* to begin a round of cards by playing (the first card, especially of a particular suit). — *noun* **1** an instance of guidance given by leading: *we're waiting for you to give a lead.* **2** the first, leading, or most prominent place; leadership. **3** the amount by which a person, etc is in front of others in a race, contest, etc. **4** a strap or chain for leading or holding a dog, etc. **5** a clue or piece of information, especially at the beginning of an inquiry, which might help solve a problem, mystery, etc. **6** the principal part in a play, film, etc, or the actor playing this role. **7** the most important story in a newspaper. **8** an act of playing the first card in a card game, or the first card played. **9** a wire or conductor taking electricity from a source to an appliance. — **lead off** to begin. **lead someone on 1** to persuade them to go further than intended. **2** to deceive or mislead them. **lead up to something 1** to prepare to do something, for something to happen, etc by gradual steps or stages: *all that flattery was leading up to a request for money.* **2** to be an underlying cause of something. **lead the way** to go first, especially to guide others. [from Anglo-Saxon *lædan*]

▣ *verb* **2** guide, steer, pilot, conduct, escort, usher. **3** rule, govern. **4** head, direct, control, preside over, rule, govern. **5** cause, influence, persuade, incline. **6** pass, spend, live, experience, undergo. **9** excel, transcend. *noun* **1** guidance, direction, example, model. **2** first place, head, front, van, vanguard, forefront, priority, precedence. **3** advantage, edge, margin. **5** clue, hint, indication, guide, tip, suggestion. **6** title role, principal, star. **lead off** begin, start, commence, open, initiate, get going, *colloq.* kick off. **lead on 1** persuade, entice, tempt, lure, seduce. **2** deceive, trick, mislead, string along. **lead up to** prepare for, pave the way for, approach, introduce.

▨ *verb* **1** follow.

lead² (pronounced *led*) — *noun* **1** (SYMBOL **Pb**, ATOMIC NUMBER **82**) a soft heavy bluish-grey metallic element that is highly toxic, malleable, ductile, resistant to corrosion, and a poor conductor of heat and electricity. **2** graphite. **3** a thin stick of graphite, or some other coloured substance, used in pencils. **4** a lump of lead used for measuring the depth of the water, especially at sea. **5** (*usually* **leads**) a sheet of lead for covering roofs; a roof covered with lead sheets. **6** a lead frame for a small window-pane, eg in stained glass windows. **7** a lead weight or piece of lead shot used at the end of a fishing line and in cartridges. **8** (**leading**) a thin strip of metal used formerly in printing to produce a space between lines. — *adj.* made of lead. — *verb* to cover, weight, fit, or surround with lead. [from Anglo-Saxon *lead*]

leaded *adj.*, *said of petrol* having added lead, which acts as an antiknock agent.

leaden *adj.* **1** made of lead. **2** dull grey in colour. **3** heavy or slow. **4** depressing; dull.

leader *noun* **1** a person, animal, or thing that leads or guides others. **2** a person who organizes or is in charge of a group. **3** *Brit.* the principal violinist in an orchestra. **4** *Brit.* (*also* **leading article**) an article in a newspaper, etc written to express the opinions of the editor. **5** *Brit.* (**Leader** or **Leader of the House**) a member of the government officially responsible for introducing business in Parliament. **6** *Photog.* a short blank strip at the beginning and end of a film or tape, used for loading the film or tape on to a spool. **7** a horse or dog in front place in a team or pair. **8** *Bot.* a long shoot growing from the stem or branch of a plant.

▣ **1** guide, courier, escort, usher. **2** head, chief, ruler, director, commander, captain, boss, superior, ringleader.

▨ **1, 2** follower.

leadership *noun* **1** the state of being a leader. **2** the ability to lead others. **3** leaders as a group.

▣ **1** direction, control, command, authority, domination, pre-eminence, premiership, directorship, management, administration, guidance.

lead-in *noun* **1** an introduction to an article, discussion, piece of music, etc. **2** a cable connecting a television or radio with an outside aerial.

leading — *adj.* acting as leader; guiding; directing. — *noun* guidance, leadership.

▣ *adj.* chief, ruling, governing, principal, primary, first, number one, supreme, outstanding, dominant, pre-eminent, foremost, greatest, highest, guiding, leading.

▨ *adj.* subordinate.

leading aircraftman or **leading aircraftwoman** a man or woman with the rank above aircraftman or aircraftwoman.

leading article see LEADER 4.

leading light a very important and influential person in a particular field or subject.

leading note *Mus.* the seventh note of the diatonic scale in any key.

leading question a question asked in such a way as to suggest the answer wanted.

lead pencil a pencil with a thin stick of graphite in the middle.

lead poisoning poisoning caused by the absorption of lead into the body.

lead time 1 the time necessary between the conception or design of a product and its production. **2** the time taken for delivery of goods after an order has been placed.

lead-up *noun* something that introduces or causes something else, or the process involved.

leaf — *noun* (PL. **leaves**) **1** an expanded outgrowth, usually green and flattened, from the stem of a plant, that contains the pigment chlorophyll and is the main site of photosynthesis in green plants. **2** anything like a leaf. **3** leaves as a group. **4** the condition of having leaves: *in leaf.* **5** a single sheet of paper forming two pages in a book. **6** a metal, especially gold, that has been beaten into very thin sheets, usually so that it can be stamped on to another material, such as a book cover: *gold leaf.* **7** a hinged or sliding extra part or flap on a table, door, etc. — *verb* **1** *trans., intrans.* to turn the pages of a book quickly, and usually only glancing at the contents. **2** *intrans., said of plants* to produce leaves. — **turn over a new leaf** to resolve to do or behave better. [from Anglo-Saxon *leaf*]

leafage *noun* the leaves of plants.

leafcutter bee a solitary bee that cuts pieces of leaf to line or close its nest.

leafless *adj.* without leaves.

leaflet — *noun* **1** a single sheet of paper, or several sheets of paper folded together, giving information, advertising products, etc. **2** *Bot.* a small leaf. **3** *Bot.* one of the individual leaf-like parts of a compound leaf. — *verb trans., intrans.* (**leafleted, leafleting**) to distribute leaflets to.

$\square$ *noun* **1** pamphlet, booklet, brochure, circular, handout.

leaf mould earth formed from rotted leaves, used as a compost for plants.

leafy *adj.* (**leafier, leafiest**) **1** having or covered with leaves. **2** like a leaf.

league[1] — *noun* **1** a union of persons, nations, etc formed for the benefit of the members. **2** a group of sports clubs which compete over a period for a championship. **3** a class or group, considered in terms of ability, importance, etc: *they're not in the same league.* — *verb trans., intrans.* to form or be formed into a league. — **in league with someone** acting in concert with them, usually for some unfavourable purpose. [from Latin *ligare*, to bind]

$\square$ *noun* **1** union, syndicate, guild, fellowship, association, confederation, alliance, coalition, consortium, cartel, combine, partnership. **3** group, category, class, level. **in league** allied, collaborating, conspiring.

league[2] *noun old use* a unit for measuring distance travelled, usually about 4.8km/3mi. [from Latin *leuga*, a Gaulish unit of distance]

league table 1 a table in which clubs in a league are placed according to their performance. **2** any grouping made to reflect relative success, importance, etc.

leak — *noun* **1** an unwanted crack or hole in a container, pipe, etc which allows liquid or gas to pass in or out. **2** liquid or gas which has escaped in this way: *can you smell a leak?* **3** a loss of electricity from a conductor, etc, usually because of faulty insulation. **4** a divulging of secret information, especially when unauthorized. **5** *slang* an act of urinating. — *verb* **1** *intrans., said of liquid, gas, etc* to pass accidentally in or out of an unwanted crack or hole. **2** to allow (liquid, gas, etc) to leak. **3** to divulge (secret information) without authorization. **4** *intrans., said of secret in-*

formation to become known. [from Anglo-Saxon *hlec*, leaky]

$\square$ *noun* **1** opening, hole, puncture, crack, crevice, chink. **2** leakage, seepage, oozing, drip. **4** divulgence, disclosure. *verb* **1** escape, drip, trickle, seep, ooze, exude, percolate. **3** divulge, disclose, reveal, let slip, make known, make public, tell, give away, pass on.

leakage *noun* **1** an act or instance of leaking. **2** something that enters or escapes through a leak.

leakiness *noun* a leaky state.

leaky *adj.* (**leakier, leakiest**) **1** having a leak or leaks. **2** habitually divulging secrets.

$\square$ **1** leaking, holey, perforated, punctured, split, cracked, porous, permeable.

lean[1] — *verb* (PAST AND PAST PARTICIPLE **leant, leaned**) **1** *intrans.* to slope or be placed in a sloping position. **2** to place (something) in a sloping position. **3** *intrans.* to rest or be rested against something for support. **4** to rest (something) against something else for support. **5** (**lean towards something**) to have an inclination or preference for or tendency towards: *they were leaning towards the moderate view.* — *noun* an act or condition of leaning. — **lean on someone** or **something 1** to rely on or be supported by them. **2** *colloq.* to put pressure on someone to persuade them to act in a certain way. [from Anglo-Saxon *hlinian*]

$\square$ *verb* **1** slant, slope, incline, bend, tilt, list. **2** slant, incline, bend, tilt. **3** rest, recline. **4** rest, prop. **5** be inclined towards, be disposed towards, favour, prefer.

lean[2] *adj.* **1** *said of a person or animal* thin; having no superfluous fat. **2** *said of meat* containing little or no fat. **3** producing very little food, money, etc; unfruitful: *lean years.* [from Anglo-Saxon *hlæne*]

$\square$ **1** thin, slim, skinny, bony, gaunt, angular, scraggy, scrawny, emaciated. **3** barren, unproductive, unfruitful.

$\square$ **1** fat.

leaning *noun* a liking or preference.

$\square$ liking, preference, partiality, bias, tendency, inclination, propensity, disposition, bent, aptitude.

leanness *noun* a lean state; thinness.

lean production the business practice of cutting costs and improving efficiency by streamlining production lines, keeping only minimum stocks, etc.

leant see LEAN[1].

lean-to *noun* (PL. **lean-tos**) a shed or light construction built against another building or wall.

leap — *verb* (PAST AND PAST PARTICIPLE **leapt, leaped**) **1** *intrans.* to jump suddenly or with force. **2** to jump over: *then they must leap the fence.* **3** (**leap at something**) to accept it eagerly. **4** *intrans., said of prices* to go up suddenly and quickly. — *noun* **1** an act of leaping or jumping. **2** the distance leaped. **3** a sudden increase or advance. — **by leaps and bounds** extremely rapidly and successfully. **a leap in the dark** an action, decision, etc whose results cannot be guessed in advance. [from Anglo-Saxon *hleapan*]

$\square$ *verb* **1** jump, bound, spring, bounce, hop, skip, caper, gambol. **2** jump over, vault, clear. **4** soar, rocket, escalate, increase, rise. *noun* **1** jump, bound, spring, vault, hop, skip, caper. **3** surge, upsurge, upswing, escalation, increase, rise.

$\square$ *verb* **4** plummet, drop.

leap-frog — *noun* a game in which one player bends over for another player to vault over with legs parted. — *verb trans., intrans.* **1** to jump over a person's back in this way. **2** *said of two or more people, vehicles, etc* to move forward by passing each other one after the other.

leap year a year of 366 days, with 29 Feb being taken as the extra day.

learn *verb* (PAST AND PAST PARTICIPLE **learnt, learned**) **1** *intrans.* to gain knowledge or skill through study, teaching, or experience. **2** to gain knowledge of or skill in (something) in this way. **3** to get to know by heart; to memorize. **4** (*usually* **learn of** or **about something**) to acquire information about something: *we've learned of a new plan to increase efficiency.* **5** *old use or slang* to teach. [from Anglo-Saxon *leornian*]

     ▪ **2** master, acquire, pick up, assimilate, gather, grasp, understand, comprehend. **3** memorize, learn by heart, commit to memory, remember. **4** discover, find out, hear, ascertain.

learned *adj.* (pronounced as two syllables) **1** having great knowledge or learning, especially through years of study. **2** showing or needing great learning. **3** of or relating to learned people; scholarly.

     ▪ SCHOLARLY, ERUDITE, ACADEMIC, INTELLECTUAL. **1** well-informed, well-read, cultured, lettered, educated, literate.
     ▪ **1** uneducated, illiterate.

learnedly *adv.* in a learned or scholarly way.

learner *noun* **1** a person who is learning or being taught something. **2** a person who is learning to drive a motor vehicle, and has not passed a driving test.

     ▪ **1** novice, beginner, student, trainee, pupil, scholar, apprentice.

learning *noun* knowledge gained through study.

     ▪ scholarship, erudition, study, education, schooling, tuition, knowledge, wisdom, information, edification, culture.

learning curve **1** a graph used in education and research to represent progress in learning. **2** the rate at which knowledge and practical skill is acquired (over a given period or time) by an individual or group: *a steep learning curve.*

learning support teaching intended to help pupils with learning difficulties. See also REMEDIAL.

lease — *noun* a contract by which the owner of a house, land, etc agrees to let another person use it for a stated period of time in return for payment. — *verb* to give or borrow (a building or land) on lease. — **a new lease of life** the prospect of renewed life or health, or of use of something after repair. [from Old French *lais*]

     ▪ *verb* let, rent, hire, charter.

leaseback *noun Commerce* a method of converting property into cash while still being able to use it. For example, a business may sell a property and lease it back from the buyer. The cost of leasing is a permitted business expense for which tax relief can be obtained, and the business also benefits from the cash it receives for the sale.

leasehold — *noun* **1** the holding of land or buildings by lease. **2** the land or building held by lease. — *adj.* held by lease. See also FREEHOLD.

leaseholder *noun* a holder of a lease.

leash — *noun* a strip of leather or chain used for leading or holding a dog or other animal. — *verb* **1** to put a leash on. **2** to control or restrain. — **straining at the leash** impatient or eager to begin. [from Old French *laisser*, to let a dog run on a leash]

least — *adj.* smallest; slightest. — *adv.* in the smallest or lowest degree. — *pron.* the smallest amount. — **at least 1** at all events; anyway. **2** not less than. **at the least** as a minimum. **not in the least** or **not the least bit** not at all. [from Anglo-Saxon *læst*]

     ▪ *adj.* smallest, slightest, lowest, minimum, fewest.
     ▪ *adj.* most.

leather — *noun* **1** the skin of an animal made smooth by tanning. **2** a small piece of leather for polishing or cleaning. **3** the leather part of something. — *verb trans.* (**leathered, leathering**) **1** to cover or polish with leather. **2** *colloq.* to thrash. [from Anglo-Saxon *lether*]

leather-jacket *noun* a grub of the crane-fly, with a skin which is tough like leather.

leathery *adj.* tough like leather.

leave[1] *verb* (PAST AND PAST PARTICIPLE **left**) **1** *intrans.* to go away; to move out; to begin a journey. **2** to go away (from); to move out (of); to begin a journey (from). **3** (*also* **leave behind**) to go without taking; to cause to remain behind. **4** to allow to remain in a particular state or condition: *leave the window open.* **5** *trans., intrans.* to stop going to, belonging to, or working at: *decided to leave the company.* **6** to deliver to or deposit with: *I'll leave the keys with a neighbour.* **7** (**leave something to someone**) to allow or cause someone to do something without help: *leave the cleaning to me.* **8** to have as a remainder: *three minus one leaves two.* **9** to make a gift of (something) in one's will when one dies. **10** to cause: *it may leave a scar.* — **leave someone** or **something alone** to avoid disturbing, upsetting, worrying, or interfering with them. **leave off doing something** to stop doing it; to come or bring to an end. **leave something out** to exclude or omit it. [from Anglo-Saxon *læfan*]

     ▪ **1** depart, go, set out, set off, go away, move out, quit, retire, withdraw, exit, decamp, *colloq.* do a bunk. **3** abandon, desert, forsake, give up, drop, relinquish, renounce. **6** deliver, hand over, entrust, consign, deposit. **9** bequeath, will, hand down. **leave off** stop, cease, halt, break off, quit, lay off, desist from, abstain from, refrain from. **leave out** exclude, count out, except, bar, omit, overlook, neglect, ignore, disregard, pass over, cut (out), eliminate, reject, cast aside.
     ▪ **1** arrive.

leave[2] *noun* **1** permission to be absent, especially from work or military duties. **2** the length of time this lasts. **3** permission to do something. — **on leave** officially absent from work. **take one's leave of** to say goodbye to. [from Anglo-Saxon *leaf*]

     ▪ **1** holiday, time off, vacation, sabbatical, furlough. **2** holiday, vacation. **3** permission, authorization, sanction, consent, allowance, concession, dispensation, indulgence, liberty, freedom.
     ▪ **3** refusal.

leaven — *noun* (*also* **leavening**) **1** a substance, especially yeast, added to dough to make it rise. **2** anything which is an influence and causes change. — *verb* **1** to cause (dough) to rise with leaven. **2** to influence or cause change in. [from Latin *levare*, to lift]

leaves see LEAF.

leavings *pl. noun colloq.* things which are left; rubbish.

Lebensraum *noun* an expansionist concept developed by the Nazis from the early 1920s to explain the planned extension of German control into E Europe. Hitler argued that Germany needed more agriculturally productive land to guarantee future food supplies for an expanded German population. [from German *Lebensraum*, living space]

lecher *noun* a lustful or lecherous man. [from Old French *lecheor*, from *lechier*, to lick]

lecherous *adj.* having or showing great or excessive sexual desire, especially in ways which are offensive.

lechery *noun* excessive sexual desire.

lecithin *noun Biochem.* a chemical compound that is a major component of cell membranes in higher animals and plants. Lecithin is used in foods, pharmaceuticals, cosmetics, and paints. [from Greek *lekithos*, egg-yolk]

lectern *noun* a stand with a sloping surface for holding a book to be read from, especially in a lecture-hall or church. [from Latin *legere*, to read]

lecture — *noun* 1 a formal talk on a particular subject given to an audience. 2 a long and tedious scolding or warning. — *verb* 1 *intrans.* to give or read a lecture. 2 to give or read a lecture to (a group of people). 3 to scold (someone) at length. [from Latin *legere*, to read]

⬛ *noun* 1 speech, talk, discourse, address, lesson, instruction. 2 harangue, *colloq.* talking-to, *colloq.* telling-off, *colloq.* dressing-down, scolding, reprimand, rebuke, reproof. *verb* 1 speak, talk, hold forth, expound, teach. 2 address, speak to, talk to, teach. 3 harangue, scold, chide, *colloq.* tell off, reprimand, reprove, admonish.

lecturer *noun* a person who lectures, especially to students at a college or university.

lectureship or **lecturership** *noun* a position or post held by a lecturer.

LED *abbrev.* light-emitting diode.

led see LEAD[1].

ledge *noun* a narrow horizontal shelf or shelf-like part. [from Middle English *legge*, perhaps from *leggen*, to lay]

⬛ shelf, sill, ridge, projection, step.

ledger *noun* the chief book of accounts of an office or shop, in which details of all transactions are recorded. [probably from Middle English *leggen*, to lay]

ledger line a short line added above or below a musical stave on which to mark a note higher or lower than the stave allows for.

lee *noun* 1 shelter given by a neighbouring object. 2 (*also* **lee side**) the sheltered side, away from the wind. [from Anglo-Saxon *hleo*, shelter]

leech *noun* 1 any of various annelid worms, having a sucker at each end of the body, and feeding on the blood and tissue of other animals. 2 a person who befriends another in the hope of personal gain. [from Anglo-Saxon *læce*]

leek *noun* a long thin vegetable with broad flat dark green leaves and a white base, closely related to the onion. [from Anglo-Saxon *leac*]

leer — *noun* a lecherous grin or sneer. — *verb intrans.* to grin or sneer lecherously at someone. [from Anglo-Saxon *hleor*, face, cheek]

leering *adj.* grinning lecherously.

leery *adj.* (**leerier, leeriest**) 1 sly; cunning. 2 (**leery of someone**) not having great trust in them; suspicious of them.

lees *pl. noun* the sediment that settles at the bottom of wine. [from Old French *lie*]

leet *noun Scot.* a selected list of candidates for an office.

leeward *Naut.* — *adj., adv.* in or towards the direction in which the wind blows. — *noun* the sheltered side.

leeway *noun* 1 *Naut.* a ship's drift sideways, away from its true course. 2 scope for freedom of movement or action. — **make up leeway** to make up for lost progress or time.

⬛ 2 latitude, scope, play, space, room, elbow-room.

left[1] see LEAVE[1].

left[2] — *adj.* 1 relating to the side of a person or thing which is towards the west when that person or thing is facing north. 2 on or close to a spectator's left side: *stage left.* 3 *said of a river bank* on the left hand of a person going downstream. 4 relating to the political left. — *adv.* on or towards the left side. — *noun* 1 the left side, part, direction, etc. 2 the members of any political party holding the most socialist views (from the practice of European parliaments in which members holding the most radical views sat on the president's left). 3 (**the Left**) people, political parties, etc, in favour of socialism. 4 *Boxing* the left hand, or a punch with this. [from Anglo-Saxon *left*, weak]

⬛ *adj.* 1 left-hand, port, sinistral. 4 left-wing, socialist, communist, *colloq.* red, revolutionary, radical, progressive.

⬛ *adj.* RIGHT. 1 right-hand. 4 right-wing.

left-field *adj. colloq.* out of the ordinary, bizarre. [from the area so designated on a baseball field, to the left facing from the plate]

left-hand *adj.* 1 on or towards the left. 2 done with the left hand.

left-handed *adj.* 1 having the left hand stronger and more skilful than the right. 2 for use by left-handed people, or the left hand. 3 awkward, clumsy. 4 *said of compliments, etc* dubious, ambiguous; only seeming to be sincere.

left-handedly *adv.* with the left hand; awkwardly.

left-handedness *noun* being left-handed; awkwardness.

left-hander *noun* a left-handed person.

left-hand rule *Physics* in an electric motor, a rule which relates the direction of movement, the direction of the magnetic field, and the direction of flow of electric current, so called because it can be represented by holding the left hand with the thumb and first and second fingers at right angles. See also RIGHT-HAND RULE.

leftism *noun* the principles and policies of the political left.

leftist *noun* a supporter of the political left, a socialist. — *adj.* relating to or characteristic of the political left.

left-luggage office an office at a railway or coach station where travellers may leave luggage in return for payment.

left-over *adj.* not used up, eaten, etc.

leftovers *pl. noun* food that remains uneaten at the end of a meal.

⬛ leavings, scraps, remnants, remains, remainder, surplus, excess, residue, dregs, refuse.

left wing 1 the members of a political party who hold the most socialist opinions. 2 a the left side of a team in a field game. b a player playing on this side. 3 the left side of an army.

left-wing *adj.* relating to or supporting the political left.

left-winger *noun* a member of a political left wing.

lefty *noun* (PL. **lefties**) *colloq.* a left-winger.

leg — *noun* 1 one of the limbs on which animals, birds, and people walk and stand. 2 an animal's or bird's leg used as food. 3 the part of a piece of clothing that covers one of these limbs. 4 a long narrow support of a table, chair, etc. 5 one stage in a journey. 6 a section of a competition or lap of a race. 7 *Cricket* a the side of the field that is to the left of a right-handed batsman facing the bowler or to the right of a left-handed batsman. b a fielder on this side of the field. 8 a branch or limb of a forked object. — *verb* (**legged, legging**) (*usually* **leg it**) *colloq.* to walk or run quickly. — **a leg up** *colloq.* help in climbing up or over something. **leg before wicket** *Cricket, said of a batsman* given out because of stopping with any part of the body other than the hand a ball which would otherwise have hit the wicket. **not have a leg to stand on** *colloq.* to have no way of excusing one's behaviour or supporting one's arguments with facts. **on its** or **one's last legs** near to being no longer usable; near to death or total collapse. **pull someone's leg** *colloq.* to try to make them believe something which is not true, especially as a joke. **shake a leg** *colloq.* to hurry up. [from Norse *leggr*]

⊟ *noun* **1** limb, member, *colloq.* pin, *colloq.* stump. **4** upright, support, prop, brace. **5** stage, part, section, segment, portion, stretch, lap.

legacy *noun* (PL. **legacies**) **1** an amount of property or money left in a will. **2** something handed on or left unfinished by a past owner or predecessor: *a legacy of mismanagement*. [from Latin *legare*, to leave by will]

⊟ **1** bequest, endowment, inheritance, gift, heritage, birthright, estate, heirloom.

legal *adj.* **1** lawful; allowed by the law. **2** of or relating to the law or lawyers. [from Latin *legalis*]

⊟ **1** lawful, legitimate, licit, permissible, allowed, authorized, sanctioned, legalized, constitutional, valid, honest, above-board, rightful, proper. **2** judicial, judiciary, forensic.

⊟ **1** illegal.

legal aid financial assistance from public funds given to people who cannot afford to pay for legal advice.

legalism *noun* strict adherence to the law.

legalist *noun* a person who adheres strictly to the law.

legalistic *adj.* adhering strictly to the law.

legality *noun* the state of being legal; lawfulness.

legalization or **legalisation** *noun* the process of making legal or lawful.

legalize or **legalise** *verb* to make legal or lawful.

⊟ legitimize, validate, approve, permit, allow, sanction, authorize, license, warrant.

legally *adv.* in accordance with or as regards the law: *they were not acting legally/legally, you are entitled to compensation*.

legal tender currency which legally must be accepted in payment.

legate *noun* an ambassador or representative, especially from the pope. [from Latin *legare*, to send a commission]

legatee *noun* a person who is left a legacy by the terms of a will. [from Latin *legare*, to leave by will]

legation *noun* **1** a diplomatic mission or group of delegates. **2** the official residence of such a mission or group. [from Latin *legare*, to send a commission]

legato *Mus.* — *adv.* smoothly, with the notes running into each other. — *adj.* smooth and flowing. — *noun* (PL. **legatos**) **1** a piece of music to be played in this way. **2** a legato style of playing. [from Italian *legato*, bound]

legend *noun* **1** a traditional story which is popularly regarded as true but is not confirmed as such. **2** such stories collectively: *the realm of legend*. **3** a famous person about whom popularly believed stories are told: *a legend in her own lifetime*. **4** words accompanying a map or picture, etc, which explain the symbols used. **5** an inscription on a coin, medal, or coat of arms. [from Latin *legenda*, to be read]

⊟ **1** myth, story, tale, fable, fiction. **2** myth, mythology. **4** key, caption. **5** inscription, motto.

legendary *adj.* **1** relating to or in the nature of legend. **2** described or spoken about in legend. **3** *loosely* very famous.

⊟ **1** mythical, mythological, fictional, traditional. **2** mythical, mythological, fabulous, story-book, fictional. **3** famous, celebrated, renowned, well-known, illustrious.

legerdemain /lɛdʒədə'meɪn/ *noun* **1** skill to deceive or conjure with the hands. **2** trickery. [from French *léger*, light + *de*, of + *main*, hand]

leger line same as LEDGER LINE.

leggings *pl. noun* outer coverings for the lower legs.

leggy *adj.* (**leggier, leggiest**) **1** *said especially of a woman* having attractively long slim legs. **2** *said of a plant* having a long stem.

legibility *noun* being legible; the capacity to be read.

legible *adj.* (especially of handwriting) clear enough to be read. [from Latin *legibilis*]

⊟ readable, decipherable, intelligible, clear, distinct, neat.

⊟ illegible.

legibly *adv.* so as to be readable: *please write legibly*.

legion — *noun* **1** *Hist.* a unit in the ancient Roman army, containing between 3000 and 6000 soldiers. **2** a very great number. **3** the name of certain military forces: *the French Foreign Legion*. — *adj.* great in number: *books on this subject are legion*. [from Latin *legere*, to choose]

legionary — *noun* (PL. **legionaries**) *Hist.* a soldier in an ancient Roman legion. — *adj.* relating to legions.

legionnaire *noun* a member of a legion, especially of the French Foreign Legion.

Legionnaires' disease *Medicine* a severe and sometimes fatal disease caused by infection of the lungs with the bacterium *Legionella pneumonophila*. [named after the American Legion Convention in Philadelphia, Pennsylvania, where an outbreak of the disease occurred in 1976]

legislate *verb intrans.* **1** to make laws. **2** (**legislate for something**) make provision for it. [from Latin *lex*, law + *latio*, bringing, proposing]

legislation *noun* **1** the process of legislating. **2** a law or group of laws.

⊟ **1** law-making, law-giving, enactment, codification. **2** law, statute, bill, act, charter, ruling, measure.

legislative *adj.* **1** relating to or concerned with law-making. **2** having the power to make laws: *a legislative assembly*.

⊟ LAW-MAKING, LAW-GIVING, JUDICIAL. **2** parliamentary, congressional, senatorial.

legislator *noun* a person who makes laws, especially a member of a legislative body.

⊟ law-maker, law-giver, member of parliament, parliamentarian.

legislature *noun* the part of the government which has the power to make laws.

⊟ assembly, chamber, house, parliament, congress, senate.

legitimacy *noun* being legitimate; a legitimate state.

legitimate — *adj.* (pronounced -mət) **1** lawful. **2** born to parents who are married to each other. **3** *said of an argument or conclusion, etc* reasonable or logical. **4** *said of a sovereign* ruling according to strict hereditary right. — *verb* (pronounced -meɪt) to make lawful or legitimate. [from Latin *legitimus*]

⊟ *adj.* **1** lawful, legal, licit, authorized, statutory, rightful, proper, correct. **3** reasonable, rational, logical, sensible, admissible, acceptable, justifiable, warranted, well-founded, valid, true.

⊟ *adj.* **1** unlawful, illegal. **3** unreasonable, invalid.

legitimately *adv.* lawfully; with justification: *they felt they could legitimately complain.*

legitimization or **legitimisation** *noun* making legitimate or lawful.

legitimize or **legitimise** *verb* **1** to make lawful or legal. **2** to make (an illegitimate child) the legal heir to its parents.

legless *adj.* **1** having no legs: *a legless amphibian.* **2** *colloq.* very drunk.

Lego *noun trademark* a children's toy construction system consisting of small plastic bricks which can be fastened together. [from Danish *lege*, to play]

leg-pull *noun colloq.* a joking attempt to make someone believe something which is not true.

legroom *noun* space for one's legs, especially in a vehicle, aircraft, etc.

legume *noun Bot.* **1** any plant belonging to the pulse family (Leguminosae), which produces a dry dehiscent fruit in the form of a pod, including many important vegetable crops (eg pea, bean), several fodder crops (eg clover), and ornamental plants (eg sweet pea). **2** the dry dehiscent fruit of this plant, containing one to many often edible seeds rich in protein. **3** the edible seed of this plant, which may be cooked and eaten when green and immature (eg pea, bean), or harvested when mature and then dried (eg chickpea, lentil). [from Latin *legumen*, that which is picked by hand]

leguminous *adj. Bot.* producing fruit or seeds in pods.

lei *noun* a Polynesian garland of flowers worn round the neck. [from Hawaiian *lei*]

Leics. *abbrev.* Leicestershire.

leisure *noun* time when one is free to relax and do as one wishes. — **at leisure 1** not occupied. **2** without hurrying. **at one's leisure** at a time convenient to one. [from Latin *licere*, to be allowed]

....

⊟ relaxation, rest, ease, recreation, spare time, time off, holiday, vacation, freedom, liberty.

⊞ work.
....

leisure centre a centre providing a wide variety of recreational facilities.

leisured *adj.* having ample leisure time.

leisurely — *adj.* not hurried; relaxed. — *adv.* without hurrying and taking plenty of time.

....

⊟ *adj.* unhurried, slow, relaxed, comfortable, easy, restful, tranquil, gentle, carefree, *colloq.* laid-back, lazy.

⊞ *adj.* rushed, hectic.
....

leitmotiv or **leitmotif** /ˈlaɪtmouːtiːf/ *noun* a theme associated with a particular person, idea, etc which recurs throughout a piece of music, novel, etc. [from German *Leitmotiv*, from *leiten*, to lead + *Motiv*, motif]

lemming *noun* a northern and Arctic rodent, reputed to rush into the sea in large numbers and drown during migration. [from Norwegian *lemming*]

lemon — *noun* **1** a small oval citrus fruit with pointed ends and a tough yellow outer skin or rind enclosing membranous segments filled with sour-tasting acidic juicy flesh rich in vitamin C. **2** *Bot.* the small evergreen tree (*Citrus limon*) that bears this fruit, widely cultivated in S Europe, California, and Florida. **3** a pale yellow colour. **4** *colloq.* a person or thing thought of as worthless. — *adj.* **1** pale yellow in colour. **2** tasting of or flavoured with lemon. [from Persian *limun*]

lemonade *noun* a fizzy or still drink flavoured with or made from lemons.

lemon curd or **lemon cheese** a thick creamy paste made from lemons, sugar, butter, and egg.

lemon sole a European flatfish used as food. [from French *limande*]

lemon squash a concentrated drink made from lemons.

lemur /ˈliːmə(r)/ *noun* any of various species of nocturnal tree-dwelling primate, related to but more primitive than monkeys, and once widespread but now confined to Madagascar. [from Latin *lemures*, ghosts]

lend *verb* (PAST TENSE AND PAST PARTICIPLE **lent**) **1** to give (someone) the use of (something) on the understanding that it is to be returned. **2** to allow (someone) the use of (money), especially in return for interest paid on it. **3** to give or add (interest, beauty, etc) to (something or someone). — **lend a hand** to help. **lend an ear** to listen. **lend itself to something** to be suitable for a purpose. **lend oneself to something** to adapt oneself to a purpose or policy. [from Anglo-Saxon *lænan*]

....

⊟ **2** loan, advance. **3** give, grant, bestow, confer, impart, contribute.

⊞ **1, 2** borrow.
....

lender *noun* a person who lends, especially money.

length *noun* **1** the distance from one end of an object to the other, normally the longest dimension. **2** the distance a thing extends: *an arm's length.* **3** a period of time. **4** the quality of being long. **5** a long piece of something or a stated amount of something long, eg cloth, hair, or tubing. **6** the extent from end to end of a horse, boat, etc, as a unit by which a lead in a race is measured. **7** (*usually* **lengths**) trouble or effort; action taken: *go to great lengths.* **8** *Phonetics, Mus.* the amount of time a vowel, syllable, note, etc sounds. — **at length 1** in detail. **2** at last. [from Anglo-Saxon *lengthu*]

....

⊟ **1** extent, measure. **2** distance, reach, span. **3** duration, term, stretch, period, spell. **5** piece, portion, section, segment.
....

lengthen *verb* **1** to make longer. **2** *intrans.* to become longer.

....

⊟ STRETCH, EXTEND, DRAW OUT, INCREASE, EXPAND. **1** elongate, prolong, protract, spin out, pad out.

⊞ SHORTEN, REDUCE.
....

lengthily *adv.* at great length; tediously: *spoke lengthily about the war.*

lengthiness *noun* a lengthy state; being excessively long.

lengthways or **lengthwise** *adv., adj.* in the direction of a thing's length; longways.

lengthy *adj.* (**lengthier, lengthiest**) **1** of great, often excessive, length. **2** *said of speech, etc* long and tedious.

....

⊟ LONG. **1** prolonged, protracted, extended, overlong, long-drawn-out. **2** long-winded, rambling, diffuse, verbose, tedious, interminable.

⊞ SHORT. **1** brief. **2** concise.
....

lenience or **leniency** *noun* being lenient or mild.

lenient *adj.* mild and tolerant, especially in punishing; not severe. [from Latin *lenis*, soft]

....

⊟ mild, gentle, tolerant, forbearing, sparing, merciful, forgiving, indulgent, soft-hearted, kind, compassionate.

⊞ strict, severe.
....

leniently *adv.* mildly; with tolerance.

lenity *noun literary* mildness; mercifulness. [from Latin *lenis*, soft]

lens *noun* **1** an optical device consisting of a piece of glass, clear plastic, etc, curved on one or both sides, that changes the direction of a beam of light by the process of refraction. Biconvex lenses cause parallel rays to converge, and biconcave lenses cause them to diverge, in both cases producing an image of an object. **2** any similar device that focuses a beam of electrons, eg an electromagnet in an electron microscope. **3** in the eyes of many vertebrates, including humans, a transparent biconvex structure lying between the iris and the vitreous humour. It focuses light from an object on to the retina, forming an image. [from Latin *lens*, lentil (because of the shape)]

Lent *noun* in the Christian Church, the weeks before Easter; a period of prayer, penance, and abstinence commemorating Christ's 40-day fast in the wilderness. In Western Churches, it begins on Ash Wednesday; in Eastern Orthodox Churches, it begins eight weeks before Easter. [from Anglo-Saxon *lencten*, spring]

lent see LEND.

Lenten *adj.* relating to or during Lent.

lenticel /'lentɪsel/ *noun Bot.* a small pore, on the surface of a woody stem or root, that allows gases to pass to and from tissues. [from Latin *lenticula*, a diminutive of *lens, lentis*, lentil]

lentil *noun* a small orange, brown, or green seed from a pod-bearing plant, used as food. [from Latin *lens, lentis*]

lento *Mus.* — *adv.* slowly. — *adj.* slow. — *noun* (PL. **lentos**) a piece of music to be performed in this way. [from Italian *lento*]

Leo *noun* **1** *Astron.* the Lion, a large conspicuous northern constellation of the zodiac, lying between Cancer and Virgo. **2** *Astrol.* the fifth sign of the zodiac, the Lion. **3** a person born between 21 July and 22 August, under this sign. [from Latin *leo*, lion]

leonine *adj.* of or like a lion. [from Latin *leo*, lion]

leopard *noun* **1** a large cat (*Panthera pardus*) belonging to the same family (Felidae) as the lion, tiger, and jaguar, having tawny yellow fur covered with small black spots, and whitish underparts. **2** the male of this animal, as opposed to the female. [from Greek, *leon*, lion + *pardos*, panther]

leopardess *noun* a female leopard.

leotard *noun* a tight-fitting one-piece garment worn for dancing and exercise. [from Jules Léotard (1830–70), French trapeze artist]

leper *noun* **1** a person who has leprosy. **2** a person who is avoided, especially on moral grounds.

lepidopterist *noun* a person who studies butterflies and moths.

lepidopterous *adj.* relating to the order Lepidoptera, including butterflies and moths.

leprechaun /'leprəkɔːn/ *noun* a small mischievous elf in Irish folklore. [from Old Irish *lúchorpán*, from *lú*, small + *corp*, body]

leprosy *noun Medicine* an infectious disease of the skin, mucous membranes, and nerves. It occurs mainly in tropical regions, and is caused by infection with the bacterium *Mycobacterium leprae*.

leprous *adj.* suffering from leprosy.

lepton *noun* **1** *Physics* any subatomic particle that participates only in weak interactions with other particles. Leptons include electrons, muons, and tau particles, and their respective neutrinos and antiparticles. **2** *Physics* originally used to refer to any light particle (eg an electron), as opposed to a heavy one. [from Greek *leptos*, small, thin]

leptotene *noun Biol.* the first stage of prophase in the first cell division of meiosis, during which the chromosomes become visible as thin threads. [from Greek *leptos*, slender]

lesbian — *noun* a woman who is sexually attracted to other women. — *adj.* relating to lesbians. [from *Lesbos*, Aegean island and home of the 7cBC Greek poetess Sappho, whose works deal with homosexual relations between women]

lesbianism *noun* female homosexuality.

lese-majesty /leɪz'madʒəsti/ *noun* an insult to a sovereign; treason. [from French *lèse-majesté*, from Latin *laesa majestas*, injured majesty]

lesion /'liːʒən/ *noun* **1** an injury or wound. **2** *Medicine* an abnormal change in the structure of an organ or tissue as a result of disease or injury, eg a scar, ulcer, or abscess. [from Latin *laesio*, from *laedere*, to injure]

less — *adj.* **1** smaller in size, duration, etc. **2** *colloq.* fewer in number: *smoke less cigarettes.* — *adv.* not so much; to a

smaller extent. — *noun* a smaller amount or number. — *prep.* without; minus. [from Anglo-Saxon *læssa* (adj.), *læs* (adv.)]

-less *combining form* forming words meaning: **1** free from; lacking; without: *heartless/godless.* **2** not subject to the action of the verb: *countless.* [from Anglo-Saxon *leas*]

lessee *noun* (with stress on second syllable) a person granted the use of property by lease.

lessen *verb trans., intrans.* to make or become less.

....
⊟ decrease, reduce, diminish, lower, ease, abate, moderate, lighten, weaken, shrink, shorten, narrow.
⊞ increase.
....

lesser *adj.* smaller in size, quantity, or importance.

....
⊟ smaller, slighter, lower, inferior, secondary, subordinate, minor.
⊞ greater.
....

lesson *noun* **1** an amount taught or learned at one time. **2** a period of teaching. **3** (**lessons**) instruction in a particular subject given over a period of time: *have singing lessons.* **4** an experience or example which one should take as a warning or encouragement: *let that be a lesson to you.* **5** a passage from the Bible read during a church service. [from French *leçon*, from Latin *legere*, to read]

....
⊟ **1** assignment, task, exercise, drill. **2** period, class, lecture, seminar, tutorial. **3** instruction, teaching, coaching. **4** example, model, warning, deterrent, encouragement, inspiration.
....

lessor *noun* a person who rents out property by lease.

lest *conj. formal, literary* **1** for fear that: *speak quietly lest they hear us.* **2** that: *worried lest we are late.* [from Anglo-Saxon *thy læs the*, the less that]

let[1] *verb* (**letting**; PAST TENSE AND PAST PARTICIPLE **let**) **1** to allow, permit, or cause to do something. **2** (**let someone** or **something in** or **out**) to allow or cause them to pass in or out: *will someone let the cat in?* **3** *Brit.* to give the use of (rooms, a building, or land) in return for payment. **4** (*usually in imperative*) to give orders, requests, warnings, permission, etc and to show assumptions: *let him go* / *let him just try!/let 'D' be the distance travelled.* — **let alone** not to mention; without considering: *they have no radio, let alone a television.* **let someone alone** or **let someone be** to avoid disturbing or worrying them. **let someone** or **something down 1** to lower them. **2** to disappoint or fail to help someone when necessary. **3** to allow the air to escape from something inflated: *let down the tyres.* **4** to make longer: *let the hem down.* **let something drop** to make secret information, etc known, especially unintentionally. **let fly at someone** to attack them physically or verbally. **let go of something** to release or stop holding it. **let someone in for something** *colloq.* to involve them in something difficult or unpleasant. **let someone in on something** *colloq.* to share a secret, etc with them. **let something loose** to release it. **let someone off 1** to allow them to go without punishment, etc. **2** to release them from work, duties, etc. **let something off 1** to fire a gun or explode a bomb. **2** to release liquid or gas. **let up 1** to become less strong or violent. **2** to stop or relax. **to let** *said of property* available for rent. [from Anglo-Saxon *lætan*, to permit]

....
⊟ **1** permit, allow, give leave, authorize, sanction, consent to, agree to, cause, enable. **2** *let in* admit, receive, take in, accept, welcome. *let out* free, release, let go, discharge. **3** rent, lease, hire. **let someone off** EXEMPT, SPARE.
1 excuse, pardon, forgive, absolve, acquit, exonerate.
2 release, free, liberate. **let something off 1** discharge, fire, detonate, explode. **2** release, emit. **let up 1** abate, subside, ease, moderate, slacken, diminish, decrease.
2 stop, cease, halt, rest, relax.

▣ **1** prohibit, forbid. **2** *let in* keep out. *let out* keep in. **let someone off 1** punish. **let up 2** continue.

let² *noun Tennis, Squash* an obstruction of the ball (eg by the net), requiring the ball to be served again. — **without let or hindrance** without anything hindering or preventing action or progress. [from Anglo-Saxon *lettan*, to hinder]

-let *suffix* denoting a small or young example of the thing specified: *piglet/leaflet*.

let-down *noun* a disappointment.

▣ disappointment, disillusionment, anticlimax, *colloq.* washout, betrayal, desertion.

lethal *adj.* causing or enough to cause death. [from Latin *letum*, death]

▣ fatal, deadly, mortal, dangerous, noxious, poisonous, toxic, destructive, devastating.
▣ harmless, safe.

lethally *adv.* so as to cause death.
lethargic *adj.* lacking in energy or vitality.
lethargically *adv.* without energy or vitality.
lethargy *noun* **1** lack of interest, enthusiasm, or energy. **2** *Medicine* a state of abnormal drowsiness and inactivity caused by inadequate rest, insomnia, boredom, depression, anxiety, anaemia, lack of food, recent illness, or any of various disorders (eg diabetes mellitus). [from Greek *lethargos*, drowsy]

▣ **1** lassitude, listlessness, sluggishness, torpor, dullness, slowness, apathy, inertia, inaction, sleepiness, drowsiness, stupor.
▣ **1** liveliness.

letter — *noun* **1** a conventional mark, usually part of an alphabet, used to express a speech sound. **2** a written or printed message normally sent by post in an envelope. **3** (**the letter**) the strict, literal meaning of words: *the letter of the law.* **4** (**letters**) literature; knowledge of books: *a woman of letters.* — *verb* (**lettered**, **lettering**) to write or mark letters on. — **to the letter** exactly; in every detail. [from Latin *littera*, letter of the alphabet]

▣ *noun* **1** character, symbol, sign, grapheme. **2** note, message, line, *literary* missive, *literary* epistle, dispatch, communication, acknowledgement.

letter bomb a device concealed in an envelope that explodes when the envelope is opened.
letter box *Brit.* **1** a slot in a door, sometimes with a box behind it, by which letters are delivered to a building. **2** a large metal box with a slot in the front, for people to post letters.
letterboxing *noun* the screening of films on television in their original wide-screen format, producing a black band at the top and bottom of the screen.
lettered *adj.* **1** well educated; literary. **2** marked with letters.
letterhead *noun* a printed heading on notepaper, giving a person's or company's name, address, etc.
lettering *noun* **1** the act of forming letters or the way in which they are formed. **2** letters which have been written, painted, or inscribed.
letter of credit a letter authorizing a bank to issue credit or money to the bearer.
letterpress *noun* **1** the printed words in an illustrated book. **2** a technique of printing by which ink on raised surfaces is pressed onto paper.
letters patent an official document giving a patent to an inventor, etc.

lettuce *noun* a green plant with large edible leaves used as a salad vegetable. [from Latin *lactuca*, from *lac*, milk, because of the milky juice from the leaves]
leucine or **leucin** /'lu:si:n/ *noun Biochem.* an essential amino acid found in proteins. [from Greek *leukos*, white]
leucocyte or **leukocyte** /'lu:kəsaɪt/ *noun Anat.* a white blood cell. [from Greek *leukos*, white + -CYTE]
leukaemia /lju'ki:mɪə/ *noun Medicine* any of a group of malignant diseases which affect the bone marrow and other blood-forming organs so that there is a permanent increase in the number of white blood cells produced. It tends to be progressive and fatal. [from Greek *leukos*, white + *haima*, blood]
Levantine *adj.* **1** of the Levant. **2** *said of ships* trading to the Levant.
levee¹ /'levɪ/ *noun* **1** *Hist.* a sovereign's official meeting on rising from bed. **2** *old use* an official reception of guests or visitors in the morning or relatively early in the day. [from French *levée*, from *lever*, to raise]
levee² /'levɪ/ *noun* **1** the natural embankment of silt and sand that is deposited along the banks of a river or stream during flooding. **2** an artificial embankment constructed along a water course in order to protect the surrounding land from flooding, or to control the flow of water in irrigation channels. **3** a quay. [from French *levée*, raised, from *lever*, to raise]
level — *noun* **1** a horizontal plane or line. **2** a height, value, or extent. **3** position, status, or importance in a scale of values: *discussions at government level.* **4** a stage or degree of progress. **5** an aspect or way: *provide help on a practical level.* **6** a flat area of land. **7** same as SPIRIT LEVEL. — *adj.* **1** having a flat smooth even surface. **2** horizontal. **3** having the same height (as something else): *a chair level with the bed.* **4** having the same standard (as something else); equal to it. **5** steady; constant; regular: *keep one's body temperature level.* **6** denoting a spoonful that forms a flat heap on the spoon. — *verb* (**levelled**, **levelling**) **1** to make flat, smooth, or horizontal. **2** to make equal. **3** (**level something at someone**) to point (a gun, etc) at them. **4** to pull down or demolish. **5** (**level something at** or **against someone**) to direct (an accusation, criticism, etc). **6** *intrans.* (**level with someone**) *colloq.* to speak honestly to them. — **do one's level best** *colloq.* to make the greatest possible effort. **find one's level** to find one's proper place, rank, etc among others, or a comfortable rate of work, etc. **level off** or **something off** to make or become flat, even, steady, regular, etc. **level out** or **level something out** to make or become level. **level pegging** equality of scores and accomplishments among rivals. **on the level** *slang* fair; honest; genuine. [from Latin *libella*, little scale]

▣ *noun* **1** plane, line, layer, stratum, floor, storey. **2** height, elevation, altitude, value, amount, extent, degree. **3** position, rank, echelon, status, standing, class. **4** stage, degree, grade, standard. *adj.* **1** flat, smooth, even, plane. **2** horizontal, flat. **3** aligned, flush. **4** equal, even, on a par, neck and neck, balanced, matching. **5** steady, stable, constant, unchanging, regular, uniform. *verb* **1** flatten, smooth, plane. **2** equalize, even out. **3** point at, aim at. **4** pull down, knock down, tear down, demolish, destroy, devastate, raze, flatten, bulldoze. **5** direct at, aim at.
▣ *adj.* **1** uneven. **2** vertical. **4** unequal.

level crossing *Brit.* a place where a road crosses a railway on the same level.
level-headed *adj.* sensible; well-balanced.

▣ sensible, reasonable, sane, well-balanced, balanced, steady, dependable, reliable, calm, cool, composed, self-possessed, *colloq.* unflappable.

Levellers *pl. noun* members of a radical political movement during the English Civil Wars and the Commonwealth, which called for the extension of manhood franchise to all but the poorest, religious toleration, and the abolition of the monarchy and the House of Lords.

levelness *noun* a level state; being level.

level pegging equality of scores or accomplishments among rivals.

level playing field a position of equality from which rivals may compete without either having an unfair advantage.

lever — *noun* **1** a rigid bar that is supported by and pivots about a fulcrum at some point along its length, so that an *effort* applied at one point can be used to move an object (the *load*) at another point. **2** a strong bar for moving heavy objects, prising things open, etc. **3** a handle for operating a machine. **4** anything that can be used to gain an advantage. — *verb* (**levered**, **levering**) to move or open using a lever. [from Latin *levare*, to raise]

■ *noun* **2** bar, crowbar, jemmy. **3** handle, joystick. *verb* jemmy, force, prise, raise, dislodge, shift, move.

leverage *noun* **1** the mechanical power or advantage gained by using a lever. **2** the action of a lever. **3** power or advantage over someone.

leveret *noun* a young hare. [from Latin *lepus*, hare]

leviathan /lə'vaɪəθən/ *noun* anything which is large or powerful.

Levis /'liːvaɪz/ *pl. noun trademark* heavy, close-fitting jeans with points of particular strain made stronger by rivets.

levitate *verb trans., intrans.* to float or cause to float in the air, especially through supernatural power or spiritualism. [from Latin *levis*, light, on the model of *gravitate*]

levitation *noun* the act or process of levitating; floating in the air.

levity *noun* light-heartedness; flippancy.

■ light-heartedness, frivolity, facetiousness, flippancy, irreverence, triviality, silliness.

🅴 seriousness.

levy — *verb* (**levies**, **levied**) to raise or collect, especially an army or a tax. — *noun* **1** the act of levying. **2** soldiers or money collected by order. [from Latin *levare*, to raise]

■ *verb* raise, collect, impose, exact, demand, charge. *noun* **2** tax, duty, toll, subscription, contribution, fee, tariff, charge.

lewd *adj.* feeling or expressing crude sexual desire or lust; obscene, indecent. [from Anglo-Saxon *læwede*, unlearned]

■ obscene, indecent, smutty, bawdy, pornographic, salacious, licentious, lascivious, lustful, rude, vulgar, impure, unchaste.

🅴 decent, chaste.

lewdly *adv.* in a lewd or indecent way.

lewdness *noun* being lewd; indecency.

lexeme *noun Linguistics* a word or other essential unit of vocabulary in a language which represents the constant semantic element in a set of related forms, as in *buy, buyer, buying, bought*. [from LEXICON + *-eme* as in PHONEME]

lexical *adj.* **1** relating to the words of a language. **2** relating to a lexicon. [from Greek *lexis*, word]

lexically *adv.* as regards words; in terms of words.

lexicographer *noun* a writer or editor of dictionaries.

lexicographic *adj.* relating to lexicography or to dictionaries.

lexicography *noun* the writing of dictionaries. [from Greek *lexis*, word]

lexicology *noun* the study of the vocabulary of a language, both historical and modern, and the investigation of the similarities and differences between vocabularies of different languages.

lexicon *noun* **1** a dictionary. **2** the vocabulary of an individual person, branch of knowledge, or language. [from Greek *lexikon*, from *lexis*, word]

lexis *noun* **1** the way in which a piece of writing is expressed in words; diction. **2** the total stock of words in a language. [from Greek *lexis*, word]

ley or **lea** /leɪ, liː/ *noun Agric.* an area of arable land that is temporarily under grass (eg for hay or silage production) or pasture, and will eventually be ploughed and used to grow crops.

Leyden jar a glass jar coated inside and out with layers of metal foil, used as an early form of electricity condenser. [from the name *Leyden* in the Netherlands, where it was invented in the 18th century]

Li *symbol Chem.* lithium.

liability *noun* (PL. **liabilities**) **1** the state of being legally liable or responsible for something. **2** a debt or obligation. **3** a person or thing one is responsible for. **4** a person or thing which is or causes a problem.

■ **1** accountability, responsibility, obligation, onus. **2** debt, arrears, duty, obligation. **4** hindrance, impediment, problem, disadvantage, drawback.

liable *adj.* **1** legally bound or responsible. **2** (**liable to something**) likely to have, get, suffer from it, etc. **3** (**liable to do something**) likely to do it: *they are liable to act childishly*. [from Old French *lier*, to bind]

■ **1** responsible, answerable, accountable, amenable, bound, obliged. **2** susceptible to, prone to. **3** likely to, apt to, inclined to, disposed to, prone to.

liaise *verb intrans.* (**liaise between** or **with**) to have or establish a close working relationship with or between other people. [back-formation from LIAISON]

liaison *noun* **1** communication or co-operation between groups. **2** a sexual or romantic relationship which is kept secret, especially when illicit or adulterous. [from French *liaison*]

■ **1** communication, contact, connection, link, cooperation, collaboration. **2** affair, romance, intrigue, amour.

liana *noun* a climbing, twisting plant found in tropical forests. [from French *liane*]

liar *noun* a person who tells lies, especially habitually.

Lib *abbrev.* Liberal.

lib *noun colloq.* liberation, used especially in the names of movements: *gay lib*.

libation *noun* **1** the pouring out of wine, etc in honour of a god. **2** the drink poured. [from Latin *libare*, to pour]

Lib Dem *abbrev.* Liberal Democrat.

libel — *noun* **1** *Legal* the publication of a false statement which damages a person's good reputation (see also SLANDER). **2** any false, damaging, or unflattering description of a person. — *verb* (**libelled**, **libelling**) **1** *Legal* to commit a libel against (someone). **2** to accuse wrongly and spitefully. [from Latin *libellus*, little book]

■ *noun* **1** defamation, vilification, slander, calumny. **2** slur, smear, aspersion. *verb* **1** defame, vilify, slander, calumniate, malign, slur, smear.

libellous *adj.* containing or forming a libel; damaging to a person's reputation.

■ defamatory, vilifying, slanderous, derogatory, injurious, scurrilous, untrue.

libellously *adv.* in a libellous way; so as to damage a person's reputation.

liberal — *adj.* **1** given or giving generously, freely, or abundantly. **2** tolerant of different opinions; open-minded. **3** in favour of social and political reform. **4** (**Liberal**) of the Liberal Party. **5** *said of education* aiming at developing general cultural interests and broadening the mind. **6** free from restraint: *a liberal translation*. **7** free from dogma, etc. — *noun* **1** a liberal person. **2** (**Liberal**) a member or supporter of the Liberal Party in the UK; a member or supporter of any other Liberal Party. [from Latin *liberalis*, from *liber*, free]

◻ *adj.* **1** generous, bountiful, lavish, ample, plentiful, abundant. **2** open-minded, broad-minded, tolerant, lenient. **3** progressive, reformist.

◼ *adj.* **1** mean, miserly. **2** narrow-minded, intolerant. **3** conservative.

liberalism *noun* liberal moral, religious, or political views.

liberality *noun* **1** the quality of being generous. **2** the quality of being open-minded and free from prejudice.

liberalization or **liberalisation** *noun* the act or process of liberalizing.

liberalize or **liberalise** *verb trans., intrans.* to make or become more liberal or less strict.

liberally *adv.* freely, generously.

Liberal Party 1 a British political party which, in 1988, combined with the Social Democrats to form the Social and Liberal Democrats (later to be known as the Liberal Democrats). **2** in Australia, the largest conservative political party.

liberate *verb trans.* **1** to set free. **2** to free (a country) from enemy occupation. **3** *Chem.* to give off (a gas).

◻ **1** free, emancipate, release, let go, discharge, let out, loose, set free, untie, unchain, deliver, rescue, ransom. **2** free, deliver.

◼ **1** imprison, enslave.

liberated *adj.* **1** not bound by traditional ideas about sexuality and morality. **2** freed from enemy occupation.

liberation *noun* the act or process of liberating.

liberation theology a development of Christian doctrine which emphasizes a commitment to liberation from social, political, and economic oppression.

liberator *noun* a person who liberates, especially from oppression.

libertarianism *noun* **1** a metaphysical doctrine, held by Jean-Paul Sartre and others, which attempts to vindicate free will and responsibility of action by denying causal determinism in respect of many human actions and responses. **2** a political philosophy, held by Russo-US novelist Ayn Rand (1905–82) and others, which claims that the only justified function of the state is to provide protection; the promotion of other goals is an intrusion on individual rights.

libertine — *noun old use* a person, especially a man, who leads a life not bound by the generally accepted rules of morality. — *adj.* leading such a life; dissolute; promiscuous. [from Latin *libertinus*, freed-man]

liberty *noun* (PL. **liberties**) **1** freedom from captivity or from slavery. **2** freedom to act and think as one pleases. **3** (*usually* **liberties**) a natural right or privilege. **4** an action or utterance thought of as over-familiar or presumptuous. — **at liberty 1** free from prison or control. **2** allowed or permitted (to). **take liberties with someone** to treat them with too much freedom or familiarity. **take the liberty** to do or venture to do something, usually without permission. [from Latin *libertas*]

◻ **1** freedom, emancipation, release, deliverance, independence, autonomy. **2** freedom, licence, permission, sanction, authorization, dispensation. **3** right, privilege, prerogative, entitlement. **4** over-familiarity, presumption,

impertinence, impudence, disrespect. **at liberty 1** free, unrestricted, unconstrained.

◼ **1** imprisonment. **4** respect.

libidinal *adj.* concerning or characteristic of libido.

libidinous *adj.* lustful. [from Latin *libido*, desire]

libido *noun* (PL. **libidos**) **1** the intensity of sexual desire, which varies from one person to another, and even within the same person at different times. **2** *Psychol.* in psychoanalysis, the sexual drive which, like the death instinct, is said to be a fundamental source of energy for mental events and behaviour. [from Latin *libido*, desire]

Libra *noun* **1** *Astron.* the Balance, a dim southern constellation and one of the least conspicuous in the zodiac, lying between Virgo and Scorpius. **2** the seventh sign of the zodiac, the Scales. **3** a person born between 23 Sep and 22 Oct, under this sign. [from Latin *libra*, pound weight]

Libran — *noun* a person born under the sign Libra. — *adj.* relating to this sign.

librarian *noun* a person who is employed in or in charge of a library.

librarianship *noun* the business of a librarian.

library *noun* (PL. **libraries**) **1** a collection of books, either for public or private use. **2** the room or rooms or building housing a collection of books. **3** a similar collection of films, records, etc, or the place where it is kept. **4** a group of books published as a series. **5** *Comput.* a collection of related computer files. **6** *Comput.* a collection of programs that can be accessed by a computer programmer when required. [from Latin *librarium*, book-case]

library science the study of all aspects of library functions, including selection and acquisition policy, classification systems, cataloguing, bibliography, and library administration.

librettist *noun* the writer of an opera libretto.

libretto *noun* (PL. **libretti, librettos**) the words or text of an opera, oratorio, or musical. [from Italian *libretto*, little book]

lice see LOUSE.

licence or *North Amer., esp. US* **license** *noun* **1** a document giving official permission to own a gun, television, etc, or to do something such as sell alcohol. **2** permission or leave. **3** excessive freedom of action or speech. **4** a departure from a rule or convention, especially by writers and artists, for effect: *poetic licence.* [from Latin *licentia*, from *licere*, to be allowed]

◻ **1** permit, warrant, authority, certificate, charter, imprimatur. **2** permission, leave, authorization, right, privilege, freedom, liberty, carte blanche, dispensation, exemption. **3** freedom, liberty, indulgence, excess, immoderation, dissipation, debauchery, abandon, lawlessness, anarchy, irresponsibility.

◼ **2** prohibition, restriction. **3** moderation, decorum.

license *verb* to give a licence or permit for (something) or to (someone).

◻ permit, allow, sanction, authorize, certify, warrant, entitle, empower, commission, accredit.

◼ ban, prohibit.

licensed *adj., said of a shop, hotel, etc* legally allowed to sell alcohol.

licensee *noun* (with stress on *-see*) a person to whom a licence is given, especially to sell alcohol.

licentiate *noun* **1** a person who holds a certificate of competence to practise a profession. **2** a person licensed to preach in the Presbyterian church. [from Latin *licentia*, licence]

licentious *adj.* immoral or promiscuous. [from Latin *licentia*, licence]

⊟ debauched, dissolute, lascivious, lewd, lustful, immoral, promiscuous, wanton, abandoned, impure, unchaste.
⊡ moral, pure, chaste.

lichee same as LYCHEE.

lichen / 'laɪkən/ *noun Bot.* the common name for any plant belonging to the division Lichenes, consisting of composite organisms formed by the symbiotic association between a fungus and a green or blue-green alga. [from Greek *leichen*]

lichgate *noun* a gate with a roof over it in a wall around a church, where originally a coffin would wait for the arrival of a member of the clergy. [from Anglo-Saxon *lic*, corpse + GATE]

licit *adj.* lawful; permitted. [from Latin *licitus*]

lick — *verb* **1** to pass the tongue over to moisten, taste, or clean. **2** to flicker over or around. **3** *colloq.* to defeat. **4** *colloq.* to beat or hit repeatedly. — *noun* **1** an act of licking with the tongue. **2** *colloq.* a small amount. **3** *colloq.* a quick speed: *at a lick.* **4** *colloq.* a sharp blow. — **a lick and a promise** *colloq.* a short and not very thorough wash. **lick into shape** *colloq.* to make more efficient or satisfactory. **lick one's wounds** to recover after having been thoroughly defeated or humiliated. [from Anglo-Saxon *liccian*]

⊟ *verb* **1** tongue, wet, moisten, lap, taste, wash, clean. **2** flicker, dart. **3** defeat, beat, thrash, *colloq.* hammer.

licorice / 'lɪkərɪʃ/ *North Amer., esp. US* same as LIQUORICE.

lictor *noun* in ancient Rome, an officer who attended a magistrate, and whose duties included binding the hands and feet of criminals before sentence was executed. [from Latin *ligo*, I bind or tie]

lid *noun* **1** a removable or hinged cover for a pot, box, etc. **2** an eyelid. [from Anglo-Saxon *hlid*, covering]

lidded *adj.* having a lid.

lido / 'liːdoʊ/ *noun* (PL. **lidos**) **1** a fashionable beach. **2** a public open-air swimming pool. [from Italian *Lido*, an island in the Venice lagoon which has a fashionable beach]

lie¹ — *noun* **1** a false statement made with the intention of deceiving. **2** anything misleading; a fraud: *live a lie.* — *verb intrans.* (**lying**) **1** to say things which are not true with the intention of deceiving. **2** to give a wrong or false impression: *the camera never lies.* — **give the lie to someone** or **something 1** to accuse someone of lying. **2** to show a statement, etc to be false. See also LIAR. [from Anglo-Saxon *lyge*]

⊟ *noun* **1** falsehood, untruth, *colloq.* fib, *colloq.* whopper, fabrication, invention, fiction, deceit, perjury. *verb* **1** *colloq.* fib, perjure oneself, equivocate, prevaricate.
⊡ *noun* **1** truth.

lie² — *verb intrans.* (**lying**; PAST TENSE **lay**; PAST PARTICIPLE **lain**) **1** to be in or take on a flat or more or less horizontal position on a supporting surface. **2** *said of subjects for discussion* to remain undiscussed: *let matters lie.* **3** to be or remain in a particular, especially hidden, state: *lie dormant.* **4** (**lie with someone**) to apply to or rest with them: *the responsibility lies with you.* **5** to be situated. **6** to stretch or be spread out to view: *the harbour lay before us.* **7** (**lie in something**) to consist in or have as an essential part: *success lies in hard work.* — *noun* **1** the way or direction in which something is lying. **2** an animal's or bird's hiding-place. — **lie back** to lean back on a support. **2** to rest, especially after a period of hard work. **lie down** to take a flat or horizontal position, especially to sleep or have a short rest. **lie in 1** to stay in bed later than usual in the morning. **2** *old use* to be in bed giving birth to a child. **lie in wait** or **lie in wait for someone** to wait in ambush. **lie low** to stay quiet or hidden. **the lie of the land** the current state of affairs. **see how the land lies** to find out all the facts before taking a decision which will affect one. **take**

something lying down to accept a rebuke or disappointment, etc meekly and without protest (usually in uses with *not, refuse,* etc): *refused to take it lying down.* [from Anglo-Saxon *licgan*]

⊟ *verb* **1, 6** extend, stretch, sprawl. **3** be, remain, stay, keep. **lie down** recline, stretch out, rest, repose, lounge, laze.

lied / liːt/ *noun* (PL. **lieder** / 'liːdə(r)/) a German song, usually romantic in theme, for solo voice and piano. [from German *Lied*, song]

lie detector a machine which is connected to a person's body during questioning to measure changes in blood pressure and pulse. These symptoms are thought to indicate an internal discomfort caused by lying.

lie-down *noun* a short rest taken lying down.

liege / liːdʒ/ *Hist.* — *adj.* **1** entitled to receive feudal service or homage from a vassal. **2** bound to give feudal service or homage to a superior. — *noun* **1** (*also* **liege lord**) a feudal superior, lord, or sovereign. **2** a feudal subject or vassal. [from Old French *lige*]

lie-in *noun* a long stay in bed in the morning.

lien / lɪ ən, liːn/ *noun Legal* a right to keep another person's property until the owner pays a debt. [from Old French *loien*, from Latin *ligamen*, bond]

lieu / ljuː, luː/ — **in lieu of** in place of or instead of. [from French *lieu*, place]

Lieut or **Lieut.** *abbrev.* Lieutenant.

lieutenancy / lefˈtenənsɪ/ *noun* (PL. **lieutenancies**) the rank of lieutenant.

lieutenant / lefˈtenənt/ *noun* **1** a deputy acting for a superior. **2** an officer in the British army with the rank next below captain. **3** an officer in the British navy with the rank next below lieutenant commander. **4** *North Amer., esp. US* / luːˈtenənt/ a police officer or fireman with the rank next below captain. [from French *lieutenant*, from *lieu*, place + *tenant*, holding]

lieutenant colonel an officer with the rank next below colonel.

lieutenant commander an officer with the rank next below commander.

lieutenant general an officer with the rank next below general.

life *noun* (PL. **lives**) **1** the quality or state which distinguishes living animals and plants from dead ones and from matter such as rocks, stones, etc which have never been alive, including the ability to grow, develop, and change. **2** the period between birth and death, between birth and the present time, or between the present time and death. **3** the length of time a thing exists or is able to function: *a battery with a long life.* **4** living things as a group: *marine life.* **5** the condition of being alive as a living person: *many lives lost in war.* **6** a way or manner of living: *a joyless life.* **7** an aspect of one's life: *love-life.* **8** liveliness; energy; high spirits: *full of life.* **9** a source of liveliness, energy, or high spirits: *the life and soul of the party.* **10** a written account of a person's life. **11** *colloq.* a prison sentence for life, now usually taken to mean about 15 years. **12** any of a number of opportunities of remaining in a game: *each player starts with four lives.* — **as large as life** *colloq.* in person; real and living. **bring to life** to make lively or interesting. **come to life** to become lively or interesting. **for life** until death. **a matter of life and death** an extremely important or urgent matter. **not on your life** *colloq.* on no account. **take one's life in one's hands** to take a very important decision which will have serious consequences for oneself; to put one's life at risk. **to the life** exactly like the original. [from Anglo-Saxon *lif*]

life-and-death *adj.* extremely serious or critical, deciding or as if deciding whether someone will live or die.

life assurance or **life insurance** insurance which will be paid to the policy-holder on reaching a certain age, or to the policy-holder's dependants in the case of his or her death.

lifebelt *noun* a ring or belt which floats in water, used to support people in danger of drowning.

lifeblood *noun* 1 the blood necessary for life. 2 anything which is an essential part or factor.

lifeboat *noun* 1 a boat for rescuing people in trouble at sea. 2 a small boat, usually one of several, carried on a larger ship for use in emergencies.

lifebuoy *noun* a float for supporting a person in the water until help is available.

life cycle 1 the sequence of different stages through which a living organism passes, from the fusion of male and female gametes (specialized reproductive cells) to form a zygote (fertilized egg), until the same stage is reached in the next generation. 2 in vertebrates, the sequence of stages between the fusion of male and female gametes to form a zygote, and the eventual death of the organism.

life expectancy 1 the average length of time for which a person from a particular location might be expected to live if general health and living standards are not affected by disease, dietary factors, stress, war, famine, etc. 2 the length of time for which any living organism can reasonably be expected to remain alive.

lifeguard *noun* an expert swimmer employed at a swimming-pool or beach to rescue people in danger of drowning.

Life Guards a British army regiment which guards the monarch, especially on ceremonial occasions.

life imprisonment a sentence in which the convicted person is to be imprisoned for the remainder of his or her life. In practice, the sentence is often not for life; in the UK a prisoner may be released on licence by the Home Secretary on the recommendation of a Parole Board, after serving 10 or 15 years.

life interest an interest in property that entitles the holder to income (eg rents, interest, and dividends) only; the capital or land is preserved for the benefit of those that follow.

life-jacket *noun* an inflatable sleeveless jacket for supporting a person in the water until help is available.

lifeless *adj.* 1 dead. 2 unconscious. 3 having no energy or vivacity; dull.

▪ 1 dead, deceased, defunct, inanimate. 2 unconscious, insensible, inanimate. 3 lethargic, listless, sluggish, slow, apathetic, passive, dull, colourless, insipid, arid, barren, empty.
▪ 1 alive. 2 conscious. 3 lively.

lifelessly *adv.* with no sign of life: *lay lifelessly on the floor.*

lifelessness *noun* being without signs of life; lack of vitality.

lifelike *adj.*, *said of a portrait etc* very like the person or thing represented.

▪ realistic, true-to-life, vivid, graphic, natural, authentic, real, true, faithful, exact.
▪ unrealistic, unnatural.

lifeline *noun* 1 a rope for support in dangerous operations or for saving lives. 2 a vital means of communication or support.

lifelong *adj.* lasting the whole length of a life: *their lifelong wish.*

▪ long-lasting, long-standing, lasting, enduring, abiding, permanent, constant, persistent.
▪ temporary.

life peer or **life peeress** a peer whose title is not hereditary.

lifer *noun slang* a person sent to prison for life.

life raft a raft kept on a ship, for use in emergencies.

life-saver *noun* a person or thing that saves lives, or that saves a person from difficulty.

life-saving *noun* the act or skill of rescuing people who are in danger of drowning.

life sciences the sciences concerned with living animals, plants, or organisms, such as biology and zoology.

life-size or **life-sized** *adj.*, *said of a copy, drawing, etc* as large as the original.

lifestyle — *adj.* relating to or suggestive of a desirable way of living: *lifestyle magazines.* — *noun* a person's or group's way of living.

life-support *adj.*, *said of equipment* allowing a person to remain alive, eg in an unfavourable environment such as space, or when seriously ill.

life-support machine a device or system designed to keep a person alive in adverse conditions, as in space, or to maintain vital functions such as breathing and heartbeat in a seriously ill person.

lifetime *noun* the duration of a person's life.

LIFO *abbrev.* last in, first out.

lift — *verb* 1 to raise to a higher position. 2 *intrans.* to rise to a higher position. 3 to move (especially one's eyes or face) upwards. 4 to take and carry away. 5 to raise to a better or more agreeable level: *lift one's spirits.* 6 *intrans.*, *said of cloud, fog, etc* to clear. 7 to remove (a barrier or restriction). 8 to dig up (crops growing in the ground, eg potatoes). 9 *colloq.* to plagiarize from someone else's work or from published material. — *noun* 1 an act of lifting. 2 the upward force of the air on an aircraft, etc. 3 *Brit.* a device for moving people and goods between floors of a building, consisting of a compartment which moves up and down in a vertical shaft. 4 a ride in a person's car or other vehicle. 5 a boost to the spirits or sudden feeling of happiness. — **lift off** *said of a spacecraft* to rise, especially vertically, from the ground. [from Norse *lypta*]

▪ *verb* 1 raise, elevate, hoist. 5 raise, uplift, exalt, buoy up, boost. 7 remove, revoke, cancel, relax. 9 plagiarize, copy, crib, steal.
▪ *verb* 1 drop, lower. 2 drop, fall. 3, 4 lower.

lift-off *noun* the vertical launching of a spacecraft or rocket.

lig *verb intrans.* (**ligging**, **ligged**) *slang* to be a freeloader, especially in the entertainment industry. [originally dialect = LIE[1]]

ligament *noun Anat.* a band of tough fibrous connective tissue that holds two bones together at a joint, thereby limiting the number of directions in which it can move. [from Latin *ligare*, to bind]

ligature — *noun* 1 anything that binds or ties. 2 a thread, etc for tying, especially for sealing blood vessels during surgery. 3 *Mus.* a smooth link between a sequence of notes. 4 *Printing* a character formed from two or more characters joined together. — *verb* to bind with a ligature. [from Latin *ligare*, to bind]

light[1] — *noun* 1 a form of electromagnetic radiation that travels freely through space, especially visible light, which is that part of the electromagnetic spectrum that can be seen, and that has wavelengths ranging from about 390 to 780 nanometres. 2 any source of light, such as the sun, a lamp, a candle, etc. 3 an appearance of brightness; a shine or gleam: *see a light away in the distance.* 4 daylight; dawn. 5 a particular quality or amount of light: *a good light for taking photographs.* 6 (*usually* **lights**) a traffic light: *turn left at the lights.* 7 a flame or spark for igniting. 8 a means of producing a flame for igniting, such as a match. 9 a way in which something is thought of or regarded: *see the problem in a new light.* 10 a glow in the eyes or on the face as a sign of energy, liveliness, happiness, or excitement. 11 sudden understanding or spiritual insight: *see the light.* 12 an eminent person: *a leading light.* 13 (**lights**) a person's mental ability, knowledge, or understanding: *act according to one's lights.* 14 an opening in a wall that lets in light, such as a window. — *adj.* 1 having light; not dark. 2 *said of a colour* pale; closer to white than black. — *verb* (PAST TENSE AND PAST PARTICIPLE **lit**, **lighted**) 1 to bring light to: *light the stage.* **2** *trans., intrans.* to begin or cause to begin to burn: *light the fire.* **3** to guide or show (someone) the way, or (someone's) way, using a light or torch. — **bring something to light** to make it known or cause to be noticed. **come to light** to be made known or discovered. **in the light of something** taking it into consideration. **light up 1** to become bright. **2** *said of a person* to become lively and excited. **3** *colloq.* to light a cigarette, etc and begin smoking. **light something up** to illuminate it or make it bright. **2** to light (a cigarette, etc). **see the light of day 1** to be born, discovered, or produced. **2** to come to public notice. **shed** or **throw light on something** to make it clear or help to explain it. [from Anglo-Saxon *leoht*]

⊟ *noun* **1** illumination, brightness, brilliance, radiance, luminescence, glow, ray, beam. **2** lamp, lantern, torch, candle, bulb, beacon. **3** shine, gleam, glint, flash, glare, blaze. **4** daylight, day, daytime, daybreak, dawn, sunrise. **7** flame, spark. **8** match, lighter. **11** understanding, insight, enlightenment, explanation, elucidation. *adj.* **1** illuminated, bright, brilliant, radiant, luminous, glowing, shining, well-lit, sunny. **2** pale, pastel, fair, blond(e), bleached, faded, faint. *verb* **1** illuminate, brighten, lighten, switch on, turn on, put on. **2** ignite, kindle, fire.

⊞ *noun* **1** dark. **4** darkness, night. *adj.* DARK. *verb* **1** darken.

light² — *adj.* **1** of little weight; easy to lift or carry. **2** low in weight, amount, or density: *light rain.* **3** easy to bear, suffer, or do: *light work.* **4** of less weight than is correct or proper. **5** having only light weapons or equipment: *light infantry.* **6** without problems, sorrow, etc; cheerful: *a light heart.* **7** graceful and quick; nimble: *a light skip.* **8** not serious or profound, but for amusement only: *light reading.* **9** thoughtless or trivial: *a light remark.* **10** not thinking clearly or seriously; giddy: *a light head.* **11** *said of food* easily digested. **12** *technical, said of wine* with an alcohol content of between 5.5% and 15% by volume. **13** *loosely, said of wine* with a delicate, fresh flavour. **14** *said of cakes, etc* spongy and well risen. **15** *said of soil* loose and sandy. **16** *said of a vehicle or ship* designed to carry light loads only. **17** *said of a ship* unloaded. — *adv.* **1** in a light manner. **2** with little luggage: *travel light.* — **make light of something** to treat it as unimportant or trivial. [from Anglo-Saxon *leoht*]

⊟ *adj.* **1** lightweight, insubstantial, flimsy, delicate, airy, buoyant, weightless. **2** slight, inconsiderable. **6** cheerful, cheery, carefree, blithe, merry, lively. **8** entertaining, amusing, humorous, frivolous. **9** trivial, trifling, inconsequential, flippant.

⊞ *adj.* **1** heavy, weighty. **6** heavy, solemn. **8** heavy, serious, deep, profound. **9** serious.

light³ *verb* (PAST TENSE AND PAST PARTICIPLE **lit, lighted**) **1** (**light on** or **upon**) to come upon or find by chance. **2** *said especially of birds* to come to rest after flight. [from Anglo-Saxon *lihtan*, to alight]

light bulb an airtight glass envelope surrounding the electric filament of an incandescent lamp. The filament becomes white hot and emits visible light when a current is passed through it.

light-emitting diode *Electron.* (ABBREV. LED) a semiconductor diode that gives out light when an electric current is passed through it, used to display numerals and letters in calculators, watches, and other electronic instruments that require a self-luminous display.

lighten¹ *verb* **1** *trans., intrans.* to make or become brighter. **2** to cast light on. **3** *intrans.* to shine or glow.

⊟ **1** brighten, light up. **2** illuminate, light. **3** shine, glow, radiate, beam, flash.

⊞ **1, 2** darken.

lighten² *verb* **1** to make less heavy. **2** *intrans.* to become less heavy. **3** *trans., intrans.* to make or become happier

or more cheerful. **4** to make (a problem, unhappy mood, etc) less: *tried to lighten her sadness.*

⊟ **1** lessen, reduce, ease, relieve, unload. **2** lessen, ease. **3** brighten, cheer, hearten, revive, *colloq.* perk up.

⊞ **1** burden.

lighter¹ *noun* a device for lighting cigarettes, etc.

lighter² *noun* a large, open boat used for transferring goods between ships, or between a ship and a wharf. [from Anglo-Saxon *lihtan*, to relieve of a weight]

lighter-than-air *adj., said of an aircraft* weighing less than the air it displaces.

light-fingered *adj.* having a tendency to steal habitually.

light-headed *adj.* **1** having a dizzy feeling in the head. **2** thoughtless and silly; frivolous.

⊟ **1** faint, dizzy, giddy, *colloq.* woozy. **2** silly, foolish, scatterbrained, frivolous, flighty, feather-brained, empty-headed.

⊞ **2** level-headed, solemn.

light-hearted *adj.* **1** *said of a person* happy and carefree. **2** not serious; cheerful and amusing: *a light-hearted entertainment.*

⊟ CHEERFUL, MERRY, JOLLY. **1** happy, joyful, elated, happy-go-lucky, carefree, untroubled, bright, sunny, playful, high-spirited. **2** light, entertaining, amusing.

⊞ **1** unhappy, sad. **2** serious.

lighthouse *noun* a building on the coast with a flashing light to guide ships or warn them of rocks, etc.

lighting *noun* **1** equipment for providing light. **2** the quality or type of light produced.

lighting-up time the time of day at which road vehicles must have their lights turned on.

lightly *adv.* in a light or frivolous manner. — **get off lightly** to escape without serious rebuke or punishment.

light meter a meter for measuring the amount of light present, used especially when taking photographs.

lightness *noun* being light; lack of weight.

lightning — *noun* a gigantic spark produced by the discharge of static electricity from a charged cloud to the Earth's surface, from one charged cloud to another, or between different parts of the same cloud. It is accompanied by a bright flash of light, and thunder resulting from the sudden expansion of air that has been rapidly heated by the flash. — *adj.* very quick and sudden.

lightning conductor a metal rod, usually projecting above the roof of a building, that is connected by a wire or cable to another rod buried beneath the ground. It prevents structural damage to tall buildings by diverting lightning directly to earth.

light pen 1 *Comput.* a light-sensitive device resembling a pen that can be used to select objects on a computer screen to which it is connected, or to draw shapes and move them about on the screen using a suitable graphics program. Light pens are used when great precision is needed, eg in computer-aided design. **2** a loose term for a bar code reader.

light pollution an excessive amount or degree of artificial lighting, especially in large cities.

lights *pl. noun* the lungs of an animal, used for food. [a Middle English use of LIGHT² as a noun]

lightship *noun* a ship with a beacon, which acts as a lighthouse.

lightweight — *adj.* **1** light in weight. **2** having little importance or authority. — *noun* **1** a person or thing having little importance or authority. **2** a person or thing of little physical weight. **3** a class for boxers, wrestlers, and weightlifters of not more than a specified weight (61.2kg in professional boxing, different but similar weights in amateur boxing and the other sports). **4** a boxer, etc of this class.

light-year *noun* the distance light travels in a year, nearly 10 million million miles.

ligneous *adj. technical* made of or like wood. [from Latin *lignum*, wood]

lignin *noun Biochem.* a complex polymer that cements together the fibres of cellulose within the cell walls of plants, making them woody and rigid. [from Latin *lignum*, wood]

lignite *noun Geol.* a soft brown low-grade form of coal, intermediate between peat and bituminous coal, with a high moisture content. Also called BROWN COAL. [from Latin *lignum*, wood]

like¹ — *adj.* **1** similar; resembling. **2** typical of: *it's just like them to forget.* **3** in the correct state or mood for: *we feel like a drink.* — *prep.* in the same manner as; to the same extent as: *run like a deer.* — *adv.* **1** *old use, dialect* likely: *she'll be on time, like as not.* **2** *old use* in the same manner. — *conj.* **1** *colloq.* as if: *look like you've been awake all night.* **2** as: *not pretty like you are.* — *noun* the equal of a person or thing: *compare like with like.* — **the like** a thing or things of the same kind: *hills, mountains, and the like.* **the likes of** people or things such as. [from Anglo-Saxon *gelic*, alike]

⊟ *adj.* **1** similar, resembling, alike, akin, same, identical, equivalent, analogous, corresponding, parallel, related, allied.
⊟ *adj.* **1** unlike, dissimilar.

like² — *verb* **1** to be pleased with; to find pleasant or agreeable. **2** to be fond of. **3** to prefer: *she likes her tea without sugar.* **4** to wish, or wish for: *would you like to help?* — *noun* (usually **likes**) a thing liked: *likes and dislikes.* [from Anglo-Saxon *lician*, to please]

⊟ *verb* **1** enjoy, relish, delight in, revel in, admire, appreciate, care for, approve of. **2** love, adore, cherish, hold dear, esteem, prize. **3** prefer, favour, choose, select. **4** wish, want, desire, feel inclined.
⊟ *verb* **1** dislike. **2** hate. **3** reject.

-like *combining form* forming words meaning 'resembling, suitable for, or characteristic of': *childlike.*

likeable or **likable** *adj.* easy to like; lovable; pleasant.

⊟ pleasing, attractive, appealing, charming, lovable, pleasant, agreeable, amiable, congenial, sympathetic.
⊟ disagreeable, unpleasant.

likelihood *noun* probability. — **in all likelihood** very probably.

⊟ likeliness, probability, possibility, chance, prospect.
⊟ unlikeliness, improbability.

likely — *adj.* **1** probable. **2** suitable or useful for a particular purpose: *a likely spot for a picnic.* — *adv.* probably. — **as likely as not** probably. **not likely!** *colloq.* an exclamation of refusal or denial.

⊟ *adj.* **1** probable, odds-on, expected, anticipated, liable, prone, inclined, foreseeable, predictable, possible, feasible, plausible, believable, credible. **2** suitable, appropriate, promising, hopeful. *adv.* probably, no doubt, doubtless, presumably.
⊟ *adj.* **1** unlikely. **2** unsuitable.

like-minded *adj.* having similar opinions, tastes, or purpose.

liken *verb* (**likened, likening**) (**liken one thing to another**) to think or speak of them as comparable.

⊟ compare, equate, match, parallel, relate, associate, juxtapose.

likeness *noun* **1** a similarity. **2** a person or thing which is like someone or something else. **3** a portrait: *have one's likeness taken.*

⊟ **1** similarity, resemblance, affinity, correspondence. **2** copy, reproduction, replica, facsimile, counterpart, twin, double, image. **3** portrait, picture, photograph, image, effigy.
⊟ **1** unlikeness, dissimilarity.

likewise *adv.* **1** in the same or a similar manner. **2** also.

⊟ **1** similarly. **2** also, too, in addition, besides, furthermore, moreover, by the same token.

liking *noun* **1** a taste or preference: *a liking for chocolates.* **2** satisfaction.

⊟ **1** taste, appreciation, predilection, penchant, inclination, partiality, preference, desire, fancy, weakness, soft spot, fondness, love.
⊟ **1** dislike, aversion, hatred.

lilac — *noun* a small tree or shrub which has bunches of white or pale pinkish-purple, sweet-smelling flowers. — *adj.* pale pinkish-purple in colour. [from Persian *nilak*, bluish, from *nil*, blue]

Lilliputian — *noun* a very small person or thing. — *adj.* very small.

LILO *abbrev.* last in, last out.

Lilo /'laɪloʊ/ *noun trademark* a type of inflatable mattress.

lilt — *noun* **1** a light, graceful, swinging rhythm. **2** a tune, song, or voice with such a rhythm. **3** a springing, swinging quality when walking. — *verb intrans.* to speak, sing, or move with a lilt. [from Middle English *lulte*]

lilting *adj.*, *said of a tune* graceful and with a gentle rhythm.

lily — *noun* (PL. **lilies**) **1** any of various perennial plants belonging to the genus *Lilium*, native to north temperate regions, that have underground bulbs, narrow leaves, and white or brightly coloured flowers, often spotted, with long protruding stamens, borne on a tall stem, eg Easter lily, tiger lily. **2** any of a large number of perennial plants belonging to the family Liliaceae, which in addition to true lilies of the genus *Lilium* includes the hyacinth, bluebell, tulip, onion, etc. **3** any flowering plant that superficially resembles a lily, eg water lily. **4** any person or thing considered exceptionally pure. — *adj.* pale; white. [from Latin *lilium*]

lily-livered *adj.* morally feeble; cowardly.

lily-of-the-valley *noun* a spring plant with small white bell-shaped flowers having a sweet smell.

lily-white *adj.* pure white; faultless.

lima bean /'liːmə/ a flat white edible bean from tropical America. [named after Lima in Peru]

limb¹ *noun* **1** an arm, leg, or wing. **2** a main branch on a tree. **3** a branch or section of a larger organization. — **out on a limb** exposed or isolated, especially as regards an opinion or attitude. [from Anglo-Saxon *lim*]

⊟ **1** arm, leg, wing, member, appendage, extremity. **2** branch, bough, offshoot, projection, extension. **3** branch, department, section, part.

limb² *noun* **1** an edge of the disk of the sun or moon or a planet as specified: *the northern limb.* **2** *Bot.* the expanded, blade-like part of a leaf or petal. [from Latin *limbus*, border]

limbed *adj.* having limbs.

limber¹ — *adj.* flexible and supple. — *verb* (**limbered, limbering**) (**limber up**) *trans., intrans.* to stretch and warm up (oneself or a part of the body) before exercise. [perhaps from LIMB¹]

⊟ *verb* loosen up, warm up, exercise, prepare.

limber[2] — *noun* the detachable front part of a gun carriage, consisting of an axle, pole, and two wheels. — *verb* (**limbered, limbering**) to attach (a gun) to a limber. [from Middle English *lymour*, the pole of a vehicle]

limbic system *Physiol.* that part of the central nervous system, including the hippocampus and parts of the midbrain, that is associated with emotions such as fear, pleasure, and memory, and with various autonomic functions. [from Latin *limbus*, border]

limbless *adj.* having no limbs.

limbo[1] *noun* (PL. **limbos**) **1** an area between heaven and hell, reserved for the unbaptized dead. **2** a state of uncertainty or waiting: *in limbo.* **3** a place of oblivion or neglect. [from Latin *in limbo,* from *in,* in + *limbus,* border]

limbo[2] *noun* (PL. **limbos**) a West Indian dance in which the dancer leans backwards to dance under a rope or bar which is moved lower and lower towards the floor. [from Jamaican English *limba,* to bend]

lime[1] — *noun Chem.* a loose term for calcium oxide (quicklime) or calcium hydroxide (slaked or hydrated lime), also often used incorrectly to refer to limestone. — *verb* to apply ground limestone as a fertilizer to soil in order to reduce its acidity and increase its calcium content. [from Anglo-Saxon *lim*]

lime[2] *noun* **1** a small round green citrus fruit having a sour taste. **2** (*also* **lime green**) the green colour of this fruit. [from Persian *limun*]

lime[3] *noun* **1** a tree with rough bark, heart-shaped leaves and sweet-smelling yellow blossom. Also called LINDEN. **2** the wood from this tree. [from Anglo-Saxon *lind,* linden]

limekiln *noun* a kiln for heating limestone to produce lime.

limelight *noun* **1** a bright white light produced by heating a block of lime in a flame, used formerly in theatres. **2** the glare of publicity: *in the limelight.*

⊟ **2** spotlight, public eye, publicity, attention, recognition, prominence, fame, renown, celebrity, stardom.

limerick *noun* a humorous poem of five lines with an *aabba* rhyme-scheme. [said to be from the refrain *Will you come up to Limerick?,* sung between comic verses at a party]

limescale *noun* same as SCALE 4.

limestone *noun Geol.* any of a group of sedimentary rocks composed mainly of calcium carbonate and in most cases of organic origin, eg chalk, which is formed from the calcareous skeletons and shell fragments of marine invertebrates. Limestone is used as a building material, and in iron smelting and the manufacture of cement.

lime water *Chem.* an alkaline solution of calcium hydroxide in water, sometimes used as an antacid.

limey *noun* (PL. **limeys**) *North Amer. slang* a British person, originally a British sailor or ship. [from LIME[2] because of the use of lime-juice on British navy ships to prevent scurvy]

limit — *noun* **1** a point, degree, or amount beyond which something does not or may not pass. **2** (*often* **limits**) the boundary or edge of an area. **3** the greatest or smallest extent, degree, etc allowed. **4** (**the limit**) *colloq.* an intolerable or extremely annoying person or thing. **5** *Maths.* in calculus, a value that is approached more and more closely, but never reached. — *verb* (**limited, limiting**) to be a limit or boundary to; to restrict. — **within limits** with a moderate degree of freedom only. [from Latin *limes,* boundary]

⊟ *noun* **1** limitation, restriction, restraint, ceiling, cut-off point, saturation point, deadline, terminus, end, termination. **2** boundary, border, frontier, bounds, confines, perimeter, edge, brink, verge, threshold, brim, rim. **3** utmost, ultimate,

extreme, maximum, minimum. *verb* check, curb, control, restrain, hinder, hem in, confine, demarcate, delimit, bound, ration, restrict, specify, define.

limitation *noun* **1** an act of limiting or the condition of being limited. **2** (*often* **limitations**) a person's weakness, lack of ability, etc which sets a limit on what he or she can achieve: *know one's limitations.* **3** *Legal* a period of time within which an action must be brought.

⊟ **1** check, curb, control, restraint, demarcation, delimitation, restriction, condition, qualification, reservation. **2** weakness, shortcoming, inadequacy, disadvantage, drawback.

⊞ **1** extension. **2** strength.

limited *adj.* **1** having a limit or limits. **2** restricted; incomplete: *a limited understanding of the problem.*

⊟ RESTRICTED. **1** controlled, confined, circumscribed, specified, defined, finite, fixed. **2** incomplete, imperfect, narrow, inadequate, insufficient.

⊞ **1** unlimited, limitless.

limited company or **limited liability company** a business company owned by shareholders who are responsible for its debts only to the extent of the money they have put into it.

limited edition an edition of a book, art print, etc of which only a certain number of copies are printed or made.

limitless *adj.* having no limit; endless.

⊟ unlimited, unbounded, boundless, infinite, endless, never-ending, unending, inexhaustible, immeasurable, incalculable, countless, untold, vast, unspecified, undefined.

⊞ limited.

limning *noun* a term applied by the Elizabethans to the technique of painting 'pictures in little', ie miniature paintings, especially portraits. [from Old French *eluminer,* to illuminate (a manuscript)]

limo /ˈlɪmoʊ/ *noun* (PL. **limos**) *colloq.* a limousine.

limonite /ˈlaɪmənaɪt/ *noun Geol.* any of a group of brown or yellowish-brown amorphous iron oxides, formed by the oxidation of iron minerals, or by direct precipitation from water in bogs, shallow seas, or lagoons. It is a minor source of iron, and is also used as the pigment yellow ochre. [from Greek *leimon,* a meadow]

limousine /ˈlɪməziːn/ *noun* a large, luxurious motor car, especially one with a screen separating the driver and passengers. [from French *limousine:* originally a cloak worn in *Limousin,* a province in France]

limp[1] — *verb intrans.* **1** to walk with an awkward or uneven step, because one leg is weak or injured. **2** *said of a damaged ship or aircraft* to move with difficulty. — *noun* the walk of a person who limps. [from Anglo-Saxon *lemphealt*]

⊟ *verb* **1** hobble, falter, stumble, hop, shuffle, shamble.

limp[2] *adj.* **1** not stiff or firm; hanging loosely. **2** without energy or vitality; drooping. **3** *said of a book* with a soft cover not stiffened by boards.

⊟ **1** flabby, drooping, flaccid, floppy, loose, slack, relaxed, lax, soft, flexible, pliable. **2** tired, weary, worn out, exhausted, weak, failing, flagging, drooping, lethargic, listless, debilitated, enervated.

⊞ **1** stiff, firm. **2** energetic, vigorous.

limpet *noun* **1** a small shellfish with a cone-shaped shell, which fastens itself very firmly to rocks. **2** a person it is difficult to get rid of. [from Anglo-Saxon *lempedu*]

limpet mine a mine which attaches itself to its target with a magnet.

limpid *adj.*, *said of water, the air, eyes, etc* clear, transparent. [from Latin *limpidus*]

limpidity or **limpidness** *noun* a limpid state; clarity.

limpidly *adv.* clearly, transparently.

limping *noun, adj.* involving a limp; halting: *a limping walk.*

limpingly *adv.* with a limp.

limply *adv.* **1** flexibly. **2** feebly: *answered limply that he didn't know.*

limpness *noun* being limp; lacking firmness or vitality.

limy[1] *adj.* (**limier, limiest**) like or having the consistency of lime (calcium oxide).

limy[2] *adj.* (**limier, limiest**) tasting of lime (the fruit).

linage /ˈlaɪnɪdʒ/ *noun* **1** the number of lines to a page. **2** payment by the line.

linchpin *noun* **1** a pin-shaped rod passed through an axle to keep a wheel in place. **2** a person or thing essential to a business, plan, etc. [from Anglo-Saxon *lynis*]

Lincs. *abbrev.* Lincolnshire.

linctus *noun* (PL. **linctuses**) *Brit.* a syrup-like medicine which helps soothe a sore throat. [from Latin *linctus*, licking]

linden same as LIME[3].

Linde process *Chem.* a process for the liquefaction of air and the subsequent extraction of liquid oxygen and liquid nitrogen from it. [named after the German engineer Carl von Linde]

line[1] — *noun* **1** a long narrow mark, streak, or stripe. **2** the use of such lines in art. **3** a length of thread, rope, wire, etc, especially for a specified purpose: *a fishing-line.* **4** a wrinkle or furrow, especially on the skin. **5** the path which a moving object is considered to leave behind it, having length but no breadth. **6** (often **lines**) an outline or shape, especially as part of the design: *a car noted for its clean lines.* **7** a number of things or people side by side or one behind the other; a row, file, or series. **8** a row of words. **9** (**lines**) the words of an actor's part. **10** (**lines**) an amount of text to be written as a punishment at school. **11** any one of the five horizontal marks forming a musical stave. **12** a series of notes forming a melody. **13** *colloq.* a short letter or note: *drop him a line.* **14** a series or group of people which come one after the other, especially in the same family or profession: *come from a long line of doctors.* **15** a field of activity, interest, study, or work: *one's line of business.* **16** a course or way of acting, behaving, thinking, or reasoning: *think along different lines.* **17** the rules or limits of acceptable behaviour: *toe the line.* **18** a group or class of goods for sale. **19** the manufacturing process: *a production line.* **20** *North Amer., esp. US* a boundary: *the county line.* **21** a point of change or development: *the dividing line between genius and madness.* **22** one of several white marks showing a pitch, race-track, etc on a field. **23** a single track for a railway or trams; a branch or route of a railway system. **24** a route, track, or direction of movement: *line of fire.* **25** a continuous system, eg of telephone cables, connecting one place with another. **26** a telephone connection: *trying to get a line to Manchester.* **27** a company running regular services of ships, buses, or aircraft between two or more places. **28** an arrangement of troops or ships side by side and ready to fight. **29** a connected series of military defences: *behind enemy lines.* **30** the regular army. **31** one of several narrow horizontal bands forming a television picture. **32** *North Amer.* a queue. **33** (**lines, marriage lines**) a marriage licence. — *verb* **1** to mark or cover with lines. **2** to form a line along. — **all along the line** at every point. **get a line on** *colloq.* to get information about. **hard lines!** *colloq.* bad luck! **in line for** likely to get: *in line for promotion.* **lay it on the line** to speak frankly. **lay or put (something) on the line** to risk one's reputation or career on. **line up 1** to bring into or cause to form a line. **2** *intrans.* to come into

or form a line. **3** *trans., intrans.* to organize or arrange: *lined herself up a new job.* **4** *intrans.* (**line up for** or **against** something) to make a stand in support of or against it. **read between the lines** to understand something implied but not actually stated. [from Old French *ligne*, combined with Anglo-Saxon *line*, rope]

····················

◾ *noun* **1** stroke, band, strip, bar, stripe, rule, dash, underline, mark, streak, score, scratch. **3** string, rope, cord, cable, wire, thread, filament, strand. **4** crease, wrinkle, furrow, groove, corrugation. **6** outline, contour, profile, silhouette, shape, figure, formation, configuration. **7** row, rank, file, queue, procession, column, series, chain, sequence, progression. **14** ancestry, descent, family, extraction, lineage, pedigree, stock, race, breed. **15** business, trade, profession, vocation, calling, job, occupation, activity, interest, pursuit, department, field, province, area, specialty, specialism, speciality, forte. **16** approach, avenue, path, course, practice, procedure, method, system, scheme, policy, belief, ideology. **20** limit, boundary, border, frontier. **21** borderline, border, frontier, demarcation. **24** course, path, route, track, direction. **line up 1** align, range, straighten, marshal, assemble, array, order. **2** queue up, fall in. **3** organize, arrange, prepare, lay on, procure, secure, obtain.

····················

line[2] *verb* **1** to cover the inside of (a garment, box, etc) with some other material. **2** to cover as if with a lining: *line the walls with books.* **3** *colloq.* to fill, especially with large amounts. [from Anglo-Saxon *lin*, flax]

····················

◾ **1** cover, pad, reinforce. **3** fill, stuff, cram.

····················

lineage /ˈlɪnɪɪdʒ/ *noun* ancestry. [from Latin *linea*, LINE[1]]

····················

◾ ancestry, descent, succession, extraction, genealogy, line, pedigree, stock, race, breed, birth, heredity, family, ancestors, forebears, descendants, offspring.

····················

lineal /ˈlɪnɪəl/ *adj.* **1** *said of family descent* in a direct line. **2** of or in lines. [from Latin *linealis*, from *linea*, LINE[1]]

lineally *adv.* in a direct line.

lineament /ˈlɪnɪəmənt/ *noun* (*usually* **lineaments**) a feature or distinguishing mark, especially of the face. [from Latin *linea*, LINE[1]]

linear *adj.* **1** of, consisting of, or like a line or lines. **2** relating to length. **3** *Maths.* involving one dimension only. **4** *Maths.* denoting an equation of a graph that is a straight line, of the general form $y = mx + c$, where x and y are variables, m is the gradient of the line, and c is the value of y at the point where the line crosses the vertical axis. [from Latin *linea*, line]

Linear A a syllabic script used for writing an as yet undeciphered pre-Greek language in Minoan Crete.

Linear B a syllabic script found on clay tablets at Mycenaean palace sites, adapted from Minoan Linear A and used by the Mycenaeans to write an early form of Greek.

linearity *noun* a linear state.

linear momentum *Physics* the product of the mass m and the velocity v of a moving object.

linear motor *Engineering* a type of induction motor in which the stator (the stationary part of the motor) and the rotor are straight and parallel to each other, rather than being cylindrical and one inside the other. Linear motors are used in automatic sliding doors, in which the rotor travels along a rail that acts as the stator.

lineation *noun* **1** the act of marking with lines. **2** an arrangement of lines.

lined *adj.* **1** having or marked with lines. **2** having creases or wrinkles.

🄴 **1** ruled, feint. **2** creased, wrinkled, furrowed, wizened.
🄵 **1** unlined. **2** smooth.

line dancing a type of dancing to country and western music, in which the dancers perform set steps while standing without partners in a line.

line drawing a drawing in pen or pencil using lines only.

line-engraving *noun* a technique used in intaglio printmaking, in which the metal plate is cut with a burin.

linen — *noun* **1** cloth made from flax. **2** household articles such as sheets, tablecloths, tea-towels, etc originally made from linen, now more likely to be made from cotton, nylon, etc. **3** underclothes, originally made from linen. — *adj.* of or like linen. — **wash one's dirty linen in public** to let one's personal problems and quarrels become generally known. [from Anglo-Saxon, from *lin*, flax]

line printer a printer attached to a computer which prints a line at a time rather than a character at a time.

liner [1] *noun* a large passenger ship or aircraft.

liner [2] *noun* something used for lining: *bin-liner*.

linesman or **lineswoman** *noun* an official at a boundary line in some sports, whose job is to indicate when the ball has gone out of play.

line-up *noun* **1** an arrangement of things or people in line. **2** a list of people selected for a sports team, or appearing in a show. **3** an identity parade.

🄴 **1** array, arrangement, row, queue. **2** selection, team, cast, bill.

ling [1] *noun* (PL. **ling**, **lings**) a fish of the cod family with a long, slender body. [Middle English]

ling [2] *noun* heather. [from Norse *lyng*]

-ling *suffix* forming words meaning: **1** a young, small, or minor person or thing: *duckling/princeling*. **2** *sometimes derog.* a person: *weakling/earthling*.

linga or **lingum** *noun* the principal symbolic representation of the Hindu deity Shiva, a phallic emblem. The female equivalent is the *yoni*, the shaped image of the female genitalia. [from Sanskrit]

linger *verb intrans.* **1** to be slow to depart; to delay. **2** *said of a dying person* to die very slowly. **3** (**linger over something**) to spend a long time with it or doing it. [from Anglo-Saxon *lengan*, to lengthen]

🄴 **1** loiter, tarry, wait, remain, stay, hang on, lag, dawdle, *colloq.* dilly-dally, delay, procrastinate. **2** hold out, last, endure, persist, survive.
🄵 **1** rush.

lingerer *noun* a person who lingers or delays unduly.

lingerie *noun* women's underwear and nightclothes. [from French *lingerie*, from Latin *linum*, flax]

lingering *adj.*, *said especially of a memory or thought* staying in the mind, persisting.

lingeringly *adv.*, *said especially of a memory or thought* persistently.

lingo *noun* (PL. **lingos**) *colloq.*, often *derog.* **1** language. **2** the specialized vocabulary used by a particular group of people or profession: *medical lingo*. [from Latin *lingua*, tongue, language]

lingua franca /ˈlɪŋɡwə ˈfraŋkə/ (PL. **lingua francas**) **1** a language, or often a simplified form of it, used as a means of mutual communication by speakers of other languages. **2** any system or set of conventions which are readily and easily understood. **3** *Hist.* Italian with a mixture of French, Spanish, Greek, and Arabic words, used in the eastern part of the Mediterranean for trade. [from Italian *lingua franca*, Frankish language]

lingual *adj.* **1** of the tongue; pronounced using the tongue. **2** of speech or languages. [from Latin *lingua*, tongue, language]

lingually *adv.* **1** with the tongue. **2** as regards speech or language.

linguist *noun* **1** a person who has a good knowledge of languages. **2** a person who studies linguistics, especially professionally. [from Latin *lingua*, tongue, language]

linguistic *adj.* of language or linguistics.

linguistically *adv.* as regards language or linguistics.

linguistics *sing. noun* the scientific study of language.

liniment *noun* a kind of thin oily cream for rubbing into the skin to ease muscle pain. [from Latin *linimentum*]

lining *noun* a piece of material used to line garments, boxes, etc.

🄴 padding, backing, interfacing, stiffening.

link — *noun* **1** a ring of a chain. **2** any person or thing that connects. **3** a means of communication or travel. **4** a cufflink. **5** a unit of measurement, equal to one hundredth of a surveyor's chain, 7.92in (c.20cm). — *verb* **1** to connect or join. **2** *intrans.* to be or become connected. — **link up** or **link something up** to join or be joined closely or by a link. [from Norse *link*]

🄴 *noun* **2** connection, bond, tie, joint, association, relationship, liaison, communication, element, member, constituent, component, part, piece. *verb* CONNECT, JOIN, UNITE, AMALGAMATE, MERGE. **1** couple, yoke, tie, fasten, attach, associate, relate, bracket, identify. **2** join forces, team up.
🄵 *verb* SEPARATE.

linkage *noun Genetics* the association between two or more genes that occur close together on the same chromosome and therefore tend to be inherited together.

linkage politics *Politics* a method of analysis which attempts to explain the behaviour of a political system by reference to phenomena occurring in a wider international context.

links *noun* **1** (*pl.*) a stretch of more or less flat ground along a shore near the sea. **2** (*sing., pl.*) a golf course by the sea. [from Anglo-Saxon *hlinc*, ridge]

link-up *noun* a connection or union, especially of two different systems.

linnet *noun* a small brown songbird. [from Old French *linette*, from Latin *linum*, flax, so called because it feeds on flax seeds]

lino /ˈlaɪnoʊ/ *noun* (PL. **linos**) *colloq.* linoleum.

linocut *noun* **1** a design cut in relief in linoleum. **2** a print made from this.

linoleum /lɪˈnoʊlɪəm/ *noun* a smooth hard-wearing covering for floors, made of canvas coated with linseed oil and cork. [from Latin *linum*, flax + *oleum*, oil]

linseed *noun* the seed of flax. [from Anglo-Saxon *linsæd*]

linseed oil a pale yellow oil, extracted from flax seed, which hardens on exposure to air, and is used in paints, varnishes, enamels, etc.

lint *noun* **1** linen or cotton with a raised nap on one side, for dressing wounds. **2** fine, very small pieces of wool, cotton, etc; fluff. [from Middle English *lynt*]

lintel *noun* a horizontal wooden or stone beam placed over a doorway or window. [from Old French *lintel*, threshold, from Latin *limes*, boundary, border]

lion *noun* **1** a large carnivorous cat (*Panthera leo*) with a tawny coat and tufted tail, belonging to the same family (Felidae) as the leopard, jaguar, and tiger. **2** the male of this animal, as opposed to the female. **3** a brave or celebrated person. **4** (**the Lion**) the constellation and sign of the zodiac Leo. — **the lion's share** the largest share. [from Greek *leon*]

lioness *noun* **1** a female lion. **2** a brave or celebrated woman.

lion-hearted *adj.* very brave.

lionize or **lionise** *verb* to treat as a celebrity or hero.

lip *noun* **1** either of the folds of flesh which form the edge of the mouth. **2** the edge or rim of something, especially a container for liquid. **3** *slang* insolence. — **bite one's lip** to control or smother one's feelings, tears, anger, etc. **curl one's lip** to sneer scornfully. **keep a stiff upper lip** to show no emotion or worry when faced with difficulties. **lick** or **smack one's lips** to lick or part one's lips noisily as a sign of relish or in anticipation of pleasure. [from Anglo-Saxon *lippa*]

⊟ **2** edge, rim, brim, brink, border, margin.

lipase *noun Biochem.* an enzyme that catalyses the breakdown of lipids (fats and oils) in living cells. [from Greek *lipos*, fat]

lipid *noun Biochem.* any of a group of organic compounds, mainly oils and fats, that occur naturally in living organisms, and are generally insoluble in water. [from Greek *lipos*, fat]

lipogram *noun* a composition in words from which a specific letter of the alphabet (and any word containing it) has been intentionally omitted, usually made to demonstrate the author's verbal ingenuity. [from Greek *leipein*, to want, leave + *gramma*, a letter]

liposculpture *noun* the practice of using liposuction to reshape the body. [from Greek *lipos*, fat + SCULPTURE]

liposome *noun Biol.* **1** a droplet of fat in a living cell. **2** a microscopic spherical vesicle or sac, surrounded by a membrane, that is made artificially in a laboratory, and can be incorporated into living cells and used to study the transport of substances across membranes, or to deliver relatively toxic drugs to diseased cells, eg to treat cancer. [from Greek *lipos*, fat + *soma*, body]

liposuction *noun* a process for removing excess fat from the body by sucking it out mechanically through an incision in the skin. [from Greek *lipos*, fat]

lipped *adj.*, *said especially of a container* having a lip.

lip-read *verb intrans.*, *said especially of a deaf person* to understand what a person is saying by watching the movement of the lips.

lip-reader *noun* a person who lip-reads or is lip-reading.

lip-reading *noun* the process by which a person lip-reads.

lip-service — **pay lip-service to someone** or **something** to pretend to agree with (someone) or approve of (an idea, etc) without really doing so.

lipstick *noun* a stick of cosmetic colouring for the lips.

liquefaction *noun* the process of liquefying.

liquefy *verb trans.*, *intrans.* (**liquefies**, **liquefied**) to make or become liquid. [from Latin *liquere*, to be liquid + *facere*, to make]

liqueur /lɪˈkjʊə(r)/ *noun* any of several strong sweet heavily perfumed alcoholic drinks, drunk especially at the end of a meal. [from French *liqueur*, liquor]

liquid — *noun* **1** a substance in a water-like state. **2** *Phonetics* the sound of *l* or *r*. — *adj.* **1** *said of a substance* able to flow and change shape; in a state between solid and gas, like water. **2** like water in appearance, especially in being clear: *liquid blue eyes*. **3** flowing and smooth. **4** *said of sounds* harmonious. **5** *said of assets* able to be easily changed into cash. [from Latin *liquidus*, liquid, clear]

⊟ *noun* **1** fluid, juice, sap, drink, liquor, solution, lotion. *adj.* **1** fluid, flowing, runny, liquefied, melted, molten, thawed. **2** watery, clear, wet. **3** fluid, flowing, smooth.
⊟ *noun* **1** solid. *adj.* **1** solid.

liquidate *verb* **1** to bring the trading of (a person or company) to an end, and have its debts and assets calculated. **2** to turn (assets) into cash. **3** to pay off (a debt). **4** *slang* to get rid of by violence; to kill. [from Latin *liquidare*, to make clear]

⊟ **1** close down, wind up, dissolve, terminate. **2** sell, realize. **3** pay off, clear, discharge, settle. **4** kill, murder, assassinate,

destroy, exterminate, annihilate, *slang* eliminate, *slang* rub out.

liquidation *noun* **1** the bringing to an end of a company's trading. **2** *slang* killing. — **go into liquidation** *said of a company, etc* to stop trading and have its debts and assets calculated.

liquidator *noun* an official called in to wind up a company's trading.

liquid crystal *Chem.* a chemical compound that flows like a liquid but resembles solid crystalline substances in its optical properties, because large clusters of its molecules retain some order in their arrangement.

liquid crystal display *Electron.* (ABBREV. **LCD**) a display unit with a very low power consumption and requiring an external light source, used in digital watches, calculators, laptop computers, etc.

liquidize or **liquidise** *verb* to make (food, etc) into a liquid or purée.

liquidizer or **liquidiser** *noun* a machine used in cookery to liquidize food.

liquor /ˈlɪkə(r)/ *noun* **1** strong alcoholic, especially distilled, drink. **2** water or liquid produced in cooking. **3** a solution of a drug or chemical in water. [from Latin *liquor*, from *liquere*, to be liquid]

⊟ **1** alcohol, intoxicant, spirits, *slang* hard stuff, drink, *slang* booze.

liquorice /ˈlɪkərɪs, ˈlɪkərɪʃ/ *noun* **1** a Mediterranean plant with sweet roots used in medicine and confectionery. **2** a black sticky sweet made from the juice of the roots of this plant. [from Greek *glykys*, sweet + *rhiza*, root]

lira /ˈlɪərə/ *noun* (PL. **lire**, **liras**) the standard unit of currency in Italy and Turkey. [from Italian *lira*, from Latin *libra*, pound]

lira organizzata an 18c musical instrument, a development of the medieval hurdy-gurdy incorporating a set or sets of organ pipes. It was also known by the French name *vielle organisée*.

lisle /laɪl/ *noun* fine smooth cotton thread used for making gloves, stockings, and underwear. [from *Lisle* (now Lille), a town in N France where it was first made]

LISP *noun Comput.* a high-level computer programming language, designed to manipulate complex lists of operations and data, and used mainly in artificial intelligence research. [a contraction of *list processing*]

lisp — *verb* **1** *intrans.* to pronounce *s* as *th* in *thin* and *z* as *th* in *this*, as a speech defect. **2** to say or pronounce in this way. — *noun* the act or habit of lisping. [from Anglo-Saxon *wlisp*, lisping]

lispingly *adv.* with a lisp.

lissom or **lissome** *adj.* graceful and supple in shape and movement. [from LITHE + -SOME]

list [1] — *noun* **1** a series of names, numbers, prices, etc written down or said one after the other: *shopping list*. **2** (**lists**) *Hist.* the barriers enclosing an area used for jousting and tournaments. **3** (**lists**) any scene of combat or conflict. — *verb* **1** to make a list of. **2** to add to a list. — **enter the lists** to give or accept a challenge; to start or become involved in a fight or controversy. [from Anglo-Saxon *liste*, border]

⊟ *noun* **1** enumeration, listing, catalogue, directory, inventory, index, tabulation, table, roll, register, record, schedule, series, sequence. *verb* NOTE, WRITE DOWN. **1** itemize, enumerate, register, record, catalogue, index, tabulate. **2** enter, book.

list [2] — *verb intrans.*, *said especially of ships* to lean over to one side. — *noun* the act of listing or a listing position.

⊟ *verb* lean, tilt, tip, heel (over), incline, slope.

listed building a building of particular architectural or historical interest, which may not be destroyed or changed.

listen — *verb intrans.* (**listened, listening**) 1 (*also* **listen out**) to give attention so as to hear something: *will you listen out for the milkman.* 2 to follow advice: *I warned him but he wouldn't listen.* — *noun* an act or period of listening. — **listen in** 1 to listen deliberately to a telephone conversation, radio message, etc intended for someone else. 2 to listen to a radio broadcast. [from Anglo-Saxon *hlysnan*]

. . . .

■ *verb* **1** pay attention, attend, hearken, lend an ear, prick up one's ears, eavesdrop, overhear. **2** heed, take notice.

. . . .

listener *noun* a person who listens, especially to radio programmes.

listeria *noun* a bacterium sometimes found in certain foods, eg chicken and soft cheese, which if not killed in cooking may cause *listeriosis*, a serious disease which can cause death and miscarriage. [named after the English surgeon, Joseph Lister]

listless *adj.* restlessly tired and lacking energy or interest. [from Middle English *listen*, to please]

. . . .

■ lethargic, languid, torpid, sluggish, heavy, enervated, limp, lifeless, spiritless, inert, inactive, lazy, indolent, apathetic, uninterested, indifferent, bored, depressed.

F3 energetic, enthusiastic.

. . . .

listlessly *adv.* in a listless way; without energy or interest.

listlessness *noun* being listless; lack of energy or interest.

list price a price for an article recommended by the maker.

lit see LIGHT¹, LIGHT².

litany *noun* (PL. **litanies**) **1** a series of prayers or supplications with a response which is repeated several times by the congregation. **2** a long tedious list: *a litany of jobs to be done.* [from Greek *litaneia*, prayer]

litchi same as LYCHEE.

lite *adj.* **1** *in food and drink names* low in calories, alcoholic content, etc. **2** *colloq.* not particularly intense or authentic. [simplification of LIGHT²]

liter *North Amer., esp. US.* same as LITRE.

literacy *noun* the ability to read and write.

literal — *adj.* **1** following the exact meaning of words or a text (ie without allegorical or metaphorical interpretation). **2** *said of a translation* exactly following the words of the original. **3** *said of a person* unimaginative and matter-of-fact. **4** true; exact: *the literal truth.* — *noun Printing* a misprint of one letter. [from Latin *literalis*, from *litera*, letter]

. . . .

■ *adj.* **1** strict, exact, precise, accurate. **2** verbatim, word-for-word, strict, close, faithful, exact, precise, accurate. **3** unimaginative, uninspired, prosaic, matter-of-fact, down-to-earth. **4** true, genuine, actual, factual, exact, precise, accurate. *noun* misprint, typo, error, mistake.

F3 *adj.* **1** figurative, metaphorical, allegorical. **2** loose. **3** imaginative.

. . . .

literalism *noun* strict adherence to the literal meaning of words.

literalist *noun* an advocate of literalism.

literally *adv.* **1** in a literal interpretation of the words. **2** as an intensifying word in figurative contexts: *they literally flew down the road.*

literalness *noun* being literal; direct interpretation.

literary *adj.* **1** of, relating to, or concerned with literature or the writing of books. **2** *said of a person* knowing a great deal about literature. **3** *said of a word* formal; used in (especially older) literature. [from Latin *literarius*, from *litera*, letter]

. . . .

F3 **2** well-read, bookish, educated, learned, erudite,

scholarly, lettered, literate, cultured, cultivated.

F3 **2** illiterate.

. . . .

literate *adj.* **1** able to read and write. **2** (*in combination*) competent and experienced in something specified: *computer-literate.* [from Latin *literatus*, from *litera*, letter]

literati /lɪtə'rɑːtiː/ *pl. noun* learned people; those who are knowledgeable about literature. [from Latin *literatus*, literate]

literature *noun* **1** written material of high quality, valued for its language and content, such as novels, poems and plays. **2** the whole body of written works of a particular country or period in time: *Elizabethan literature.* **3** the whole body of information published on a particular subject: *the literature on growing vegetables.* **4** the art or works produced by a writer. **5** *colloq.* any printed matter, especially advertising leaflets. [from Latin *literatura*, from *litera*, letter]

. . . .

■ **4** writings, works, books. **5** leaflets, pamphlets, brochures, circulars, hand-outs, *colloq.* bumf.

. . . .

Types of literature include; fiction, novel, story, novella, crime story, thriller, love story, *trademark* Mills & Boon, historical novel, *formal* belles-lettres, science fiction, *colloq.* sci-fi, ghost story, fairy tale, fable, folk tale, *colloq.* whodunit, *colloq.* blockbuster; non-fiction, biography, autobiography; prose, poetry. *See also* **poem**.

litharge /'lɪθɑːdʒ/ *noun Chem.* lead monoxide, a bright yellow solid compound, insoluble in water, used in pigments and paints, and in the manufacture of glass and ceramics. [from Greek *lithargyros*, from *lithos*, stone + *argyros*, silver]

lithe /laɪð/ *adj.* bending easily; supple and flexible. [from Anglo-Saxon *lithe*, gentle, soft]

lithification *noun Geol.* the process whereby an unconsolidated sediment is converted into solid rock, eg as a result of compaction, desiccation, or crystallization. [from Greek *lithos*, stone]

lithium *noun Chem.* (SYMBOL **Li**, ATOMIC NUMBER **3**) a soft silvery reactive metal, and the lightest of all solid chemical elements, used in batteries and certain alloys. Its compounds are used in lubricants, glass, ceramics, and drugs. [from Greek *lithos*, stone]

litho /'laɪθoʊ/ — *noun* (PL. **lithos**) **1** a lithograph. **2** lithography. — *adj.* lithographic. — *verb* (**lithoes, lithoed**) to lithograph.

lithograph /'lɪθəɡrɑːf/ — *noun* a picture or print made using lithography. — *verb* to print (images, etc) using lithography.

lithographer /lɪ'θɒɡrəfə(r)/ *noun* a person who makes lithographs.

lithographic /lɪθə'ɡrafɪk/ *adj.* relating to or using lithography.

lithographically *adv.* by means of lithography.

lithography /lɪ'θɒɡrəfɪ/ *noun* a method of printing using a stone or metal plate which has been treated so that the ink adheres only to the design or image to be printed. [from Greek *lithos*, stone + *graphein*, to write]

lithosphere /'lɪθoʊsfɪə(r)/ *noun Geol.* the rigid outer layer of the Earth, consisting of the crust and the solid outermost layer of the upper mantle, and extending to a depth of about 100km. It is composed of a wide range of different rock types. [from Greek *lithos*, stone + *sphaira*, sphere]

Lithuanian — *noun* **1** a native or citizen of Lithuania. **2** the Baltic language of Lithuania. — *adj.* relating to Lithuania or its people or language.

litigant *noun* a person involved in a lawsuit.

litigate *verb* **1** *intrans.* to be involved in a lawsuit; to go to law. **2** to contest (a point, claim, etc) in a lawsuit. [from Latin *litigare*, from *lis*, lawsuit + *agere*, to do]

litigation *noun* action at law; legal contest.

◻ action, lawsuit, suit, case, process, prosecution.

litigious *adj.* **1** relating to litigation or lawsuits. **2** often taking legal action over arguments, problems, etc. **3** disputable in a court of law. [from Latin *litigium*, quarrel]

litigiously *adv.* **1** as regards litigation. **2** with frequent recourse to legal action.

litmus — *noun Chem.* a dye obtained from certain lichens, widely used as an indicator to distinguish between acid solutions, in which it turns red, and alkaline ones, in which it turns blue. — *adj.* relating to this dye. [from Norse *litmosi*, dyeing-moss]

litmus paper paper treated with litmus, used to test liquids for acidity and alkalinity.

litmus test 1 a chemical test using litmus paper. **2** a definitive test or trial of something.

litotes /'laɪtoʊtiːz/ *noun* understatement used for effect, as in *not a little angry* meaning *furious*. [from Greek *litotes*, simplicity]

litre *noun* (ABBREV. l) the basic unit of volume in the metric system, equal to 1dm^3 (1000 cm^3) or 1.76 pints, and formerly defined as the volume of 1kg of distilled water at 4°C. [from Greek *litra*, pound]

litter — *noun* **1** a mess of paper, rubbish, etc in a public place. **2** a scattered or confused collection of objects. **3** straw, hay, etc used as bedding for animals. **4** a number of animals born to the same mother at the same time. **5** a framework consisting of cloth stretched tight between two long poles, used to carry the sick or wounded. **6** a framework consisting of a couch covered by curtains, with poles on either side, for transporting a single passenger. — *verb* (**littered**, **littering**) **1** to make (a place) untidy by spreading litter or objects: *they seemed to have littered the room with books and sweet wrappings.* **2** *said of objects* to lie untidily around (a place): *books littered the room.* **3** *trans.*, *intrans.*, *said of animals* to give birth to (a number of young). **4** to give bedding litter to (animals). [from Old French *litiere*, from Latin *lectus*, bed]

◻ *noun* **1** rubbish, refuse, waste, debris. **2** mess, clutter, jumble, junk, confusion, disorder, disarray, untidiness. **4** offspring, young, progeny, brood. *verb* **1** strew, scatter, clutter, mess up. **2** clutter, mess up.
◼ *verb* **1** tidy.

litterbug *noun North Amer. colloq.* same as LITTER-LOUT.

litter-lout *noun* a person who drops litter in public places.

little — *adj.* (usually having connotations of affection or emotion not present in *small*) **1** small in size, extent, or amount. **2** young or younger: *a little girl/her little brother.* **3** small in importance; trivial; petty: *funny little ways.* **4** small-minded or mean: *he's a little liar.* — *noun* anything small in size, amount, or extent: *do a little to help out.* — *adv.* **1** (**a little**) to a small degree or extent: *run around a little to keep warm.* **2** not much or at all: *they little understood the implications.* — **in a little** soon, shortly: *he'll be here in a little.* **little by little** gradually or by degrees. **make little of something 1** to treat it as unimportant or trivial. **2** to understand only a little of it. **think little of something** or **someone** to have a low opinion of them; to disapprove of them. [from Anglo-Saxon *lytel*]

◻ *adj.* **1** *size* small, short, tiny, *colloq.* teeny, *colloq. esp. Scot.* wee, minute, microscopic, infinitesimal, mini, miniature, diminutive, *colloq.* pint-sized, petite, slender, *extent* short-lived, brief, fleeting, passing, transient, *amount* insufficient, sparse, scant, meagre, paltry, skimpy. **3** insignificant, unimportant, inconsiderable, negligible, trifling, trivial, petty. *noun* bit, spot, dash, pinch, drop, dab, touch, trace, hint, speck, particle, fragment, modicum, trifle. *adv.* **2** hardly, barely, scarcely, not much, rarely, seldom, infrequently.

◻ *adj.* **1** *size* big, *extent* lengthy, *amount* ample. **3** significant, important, considerable. *noun* lot. *adv.* **2** much, frequently.

little end the smaller end of a main connecting rod in a car engine.

little people a fanciful name for fairies.

little slam *Cards, especially in Bridge* the winning of all but one trick, or the contract to do so.

littoral — *adj.* on or near the shore of a sea or lake. — *noun* an area of land on a shore or coast. [from Latin *littoralis*, from *litus*, shore]

liturgical *adj.* relating to liturgy or public worship.

liturgically *adv.* as regards the liturgy or public worship: *a concept that is not liturgically sound.*

liturgy *noun* (PL. **liturgies**) **1** the standard form of service in a church. **2** the service of Holy Communion in the Eastern Orthodox Church. [from Greek *leitourgia*, public service]

live [1] /lɪv/ *verb usually intrans.* **1** to have life; to be alive. **2** to continue to be alive; to survive or to escape death. **3** (**live on**) to continue or last: *memories live on.* **4** (**live with something**) to continue to suffer from or be haunted by the memory of; to put up with: *will live with the mistake for the rest of his life.* **5** to have a home or dwelling: *we live in a small flat.* **6** to lead one's life in a certain way: *live well.* **7** (**live by** or **on** or **off**) to support one's life; to get a living: *live by farming/live on rice/live off the land.* **8** to pass or spend: *live a happy life in the country.* **9** to enjoy life passionately or to the full: *they really know how to live.* **10** (*trans.*) to express in one's life or live according to: *live a lie/live one's religion.* — **live and let live** to be tolerant and expect toleration from others. **live something down** to cause (a mistake, guilt, etc in one's past) to be forgotten by living a normal and blameless life: *a blunder he could never live down.* **live in** to have one's home where one works. See also LIVE-IN. **live it up** *colloq.* to fill one's life with excitement and pleasure, often excessively. **live together** *said of an unmarried couple* to live as man and wife. **live up to someone** to behave in a manner worthy of them: *could never live up to her parents' expectations.* [from Anglo-Saxon *lifian*, *libban*]

◻ *verb* **1** be, exist, breathe, draw breath. **2** survive, endure, escape, pull through. **3** last, continue, remain, persist. **5** dwell, reside, lodge. **8** pass, spend, lead.
◼ **1**, **2** die. **3** cease.

live [2] /laɪv/ — *adj.* **1** having life; not dead. **2** *said of a radio or television broadcast* heard or seen as the event takes place and not from a recording. **3** *said of a record, etc* recorded during a performance. **4** *said of a wire* connected to a source of electrical power. **5** *said of coal, etc* still glowing or burning. **6** *said of a bomb, etc* still capable of exploding. **7** *said of an issue, etc* of current or topical interest. — *adv.* at, during, or as a live performance: *they had to perform live on stage.*

◻ *adj.* **1** alive, living, existent. **5** burning, glowing, lit, ignited. **7** current, topical, relevant, pertinent, controversial.
◼ *adj.* **1** dead.

liveable *adj.* **1** *said of a house, etc* fit to live in. **2** *said of a person* friendly and easy to live with. **3** *said of life* worth living.

lived-in *adj.* **1** *said of a room, etc* having a comfortable homely feeling. **2** *said of a face* showing a life's experiences by its expression.

live-in *adj.* **1** *said of a worker* living where one works. **2** *said of a sexual partner* living in the same house, etc as one's partner.

livelihood *noun* a means of living, especially of earning enough money for the basic requirements of life. [from Anglo-Saxon *liflad*, from *lif*, life or *lad*, course]

◻ living, means, income, work, employment, occupation, job,

maintenance, support, subsistence, sustenance.

liveliness *noun* being lively or full of energy.

livelong *adj. poetic, said of the day or night* in all its pleasant or excessive length. [from Middle English *lief*, dear + *longe*, long]

lively *adj.* (**livelier, liveliest**) **1** active and full of life, energy, and high spirits. **2** brisk. **3** vivid, bright. [from Anglo-Saxon *liflic*]

■ **1** animated, alert, active, energetic, vigorous, spirited, feisty, vivacious, sprightly, spry, agile, nimble, quick, keen, frisky, perky, *colloq.* chirpy. **2** brisk, busy, bustling, crowded, eventful, exciting. **3** vivid, bright, colourful, sparkling, stirring, stimulating, invigorating, refreshing.
➤ **1** moribund, inactive. **2** slow, sluggish. **3** dull.

liven *verb trans., intrans.* (**livened, livening**) (*usually* **liven up**) to make or become lively.

■ enliven, vitalize, rouse, animate, energize, invigorate, stir (up), *colloq.* buck up, *colloq.* perk up, *colloq.* pep up, *colloq.* hot up.

liver[1] *noun* a person who lives life in a specified way: *a fast liver.*

liver[2] — *noun* **1** in vertebrates, the largest gland in the body, a dark red flattened organ situated in the abdominal cavity just below the diaphragm. Its main function is to regulate the chemical composition of the blood. **2** this organ in certain animals used as food. — *adj.* dark reddish-brown in colour. [from Anglo-Saxon *lifer*]

liver fluke a leaf-like parasitic flatworm with a mouth-sucker on its cone-shaped front end.

liveried *adj.* wearing or covered in livery.

liverish *adj.* **1** *old use* suffering from a disordered liver. **2** easily annoyed or made angry.

Liverpudlian — *noun* a native or citizen of Liverpool. — *adj.* relating to Liverpool or its inhabitants.

liver sausage a sausage containing liver.

liverwort *noun Bot.* the common name for any plant belonging to the class Hepaticae, which consists of small spore-bearing bryophytes without a vascular system, closely related to mosses, and typically growing in moist shady conditions, eg on damp ground, rocks, or tree trunks. [from LIVER[2] + WORT]

livery *noun* (PL. **liveries**) **1** a distinctive uniform worn by male servants belonging to a particular household or the members of a trade guild. **2** *literary* distinctive markings or outward appearance: *the trees in their autumn livery.* **3** the distinctive colours and decoration used to identify the buses, aircraft, etc operated by a particular company. **4** the feeding, care, stabling, and hiring out of horses for money. [from Old French *livree*, from Latin *liberare*, to free]

■ **1** uniform, costume, regalia, vestments, dress, clothes, clothing, attire, garb, habit.

livery company any of several trade guilds in the City of London whose members formerly wore distinctive clothes.

liveryman *noun* a member of a livery company.

livery stable a place where people may keep their horses or where horses may be hired.

lives see LIFE.

livestock *noun* domesticated animals, especially sheep, cattle, horses, pigs, and poultry, that are kept for the production of meat, milk, wool, etc, or for breeding purposes.

liveware *noun* the users and controllers of a computer system; personnel as distinct from hardware or software.

live wire *colloq.* a person who is full of energy and enthusiasm.

livid *adj.* **1** having the greyish colour of lead. **2** *said of a bruise* black and blue. **3** white or very pale. **4** *colloq.* extremely angry. [from Latin *lividus*, lead-coloured]

■ **1** greyish, leaden. **2** black-and-blue, purple, bruised, discoloured. **3** white, blanched, ashen, pale, pallid, wan, waxy, pasty. **4** angry, irate, *colloq.* mad, furious, infuriated, enraged, raging, fuming, incensed.
➤ **4** calm.

living — *adj.* **1** having life; alive. **2** currently in existence, use, or activity. **3** *said of a likeness* exact. — *noun* **1** livelihood or means of subsisting. **2** a manner of life: *riotous living.* **3** *Church of E.* a position as a vicar or rector which has an income or property attached to it. **4** (**the living**) people who are alive. — **within living memory** within a period of time remembered by people who are still alive.

■ *adj.* **1** alive, live, animate, breathing, existing. **2** current, extant, operative. *noun* **1** livelihood, income, maintenance, support, subsistence, sustenance, work, job, occupation, profession. **2** way of life, lifestyle, life, existence.
➤ *adj.* **1** dead.

living-room *noun* a room in a house, etc for sitting and relaxing in.

living stone a perennial plant of the genus *Lithops*, native to Southern Africa, and adapted to dry desert conditions. Each species is associated with a particular kind of rock, which its leaves resemble in colour.

living wage a wage which can support a wage-earner and family.

living will a document drawn up to state what kind of medical care the signatory would prefer if he or she became terminally ill.

lizard *noun* any of numerous small and very active reptiles belonging to the same order (Squamata) as snakes, but differing from them in having an outer ear opening, movable eyelids, much less flexible jaws, and four well-developed limbs. Lizards include the iguanas, geckos, skinks, chameleons, monitor lizard, and Komodo dragon. [from Latin *lacerta*]

ll or **ll.** *abbrev.* lines.

'll *contr.* (usually with a pronoun) shall; will: *I'll/they'll.*

llama *noun* a domesticated hoofed mammal of S America, related to the camel, and having a long shaggy white, brown, or black coat, a long neck, and large ears. [from Quechua *llama*]

LLB *abbrev.* Bachelor of Laws. [from Latin *legum baccalaureus*]

LLD *abbrev.* Doctor of Laws. [from Latin *legum doctor*]

lo *interj. old use* look, see. — **lo and behold** an expression indicating surprise, etc at something unexpected. [from Anglo-Saxon *la*]

loach *noun* a slender-bodied freshwater fish found in rivers and lakes throughout Europe and Asia, usually less than 10cm in length. [from French *loche*]

load — *noun* **1** something that is carried; a burden. **2** something that is or can be carried at one time: *a coach-load of children.* **3** (**loads**) *colloq.* a large amount: *loads of money.* **4** work, duties, feelings, etc which are oppressive and heavy to bear. **5** an amount or number of things to be dealt with at one time, especially of clothes to be washed. **6** the power carried by an electric circuit. **7** the power produced by an engine. — *verb* **1** to put (a load of something) on or in (a ship, vehicle, washing-machine, etc). **2** *intrans.* (**load up**) to take or pick up a load. **3** to be a weight on or burden to; to oppress. **4** (**load someone with something**) to give something lavishly or in great amounts to someone. **5** to put (film, audio or video tape, etc) into a (camera, tape or video recorder, etc). **6** *Comput.* **a** to put (a disk, computer tape, etc) into a drive, so that it may be used. **b** to transfer (a program or data) to a main memory, so that it may be used. **7** to put (ammunition) into (a gun). **8** to give weight or bias to (dice, a roulette wheel, etc). — **get a load**

of something *slang* to pay attention to, listen to, or look at it. **load the dice against someone** to deprive someone of a fair chance. [from Anglo-Saxon *lad*, course, journey]

◼ *noun* **1** cargo, freight, lading, consignment, shipment, burden, encumbrance, weight, pressure. **2** consignment, shipment. **4** burden, onus, responsibility, millstone. *verb* **1** pack, fill, stack, pile, heap, freight. **3** burden, weigh down, encumber, saddle, oppress, trouble.
◼ *verb* **1** unload, unpack.

loaded *adj.* **1** carrying a load; with a load in place. **2** *said of a gun* containing bullets. **3** *said of a camera* containing film. **4** *said of a person colloq.* having much money; rich. **5** *said of a question* intended to elicit a particular response by the way it is phrased or by an implicit assumption contained in it.

◼ **1** laden, full, charged, burdened, weighted. **3** rich, wealthy, well-off, affluent.

loader *noun* (*in combination*) a gun or machine, etc loaded in a specified way: *front-loader*.
loadstar same as LODESTAR.
loadstone same as LODESTONE.
loaf¹ *noun* (PL. **loaves**) **1** a mass of bread for baking or when baked. **2** a quantity of food formed into a regular shape, eg meat or sugar. **3** *slang* the head or brains: *use one's loaf*. [from Anglo-Saxon *hlaf*]
loaf² *verb* **1** *intrans.* (**loaf about** or **around**) to pass time or stand about idly. **2** *trans.* (**loaf away**) to spend or pass idly: *loaf away one's life.*
loafer *noun* **1** a person who loafs about. **2** a light casual shoe like a moccasin.

◼ **1** idler, layabout, shirker, *colloq.* skiver, wastrel, ne'er-do-well, lounger, *colloq.* lazy-bones, sluggard.

loam *noun* a dark fertile easily worked soil consisting of sand, silt, small amounts of clay, and humus. [from Anglo-Saxon *lam*]
loamy *adj.* (**loamier, loamiest**) containing much loam.
loan — *noun* **1** anything lent, especially money lent at interest. **2** the act of lending or state of being lent. — *verb* to lend (especially money). — **on loan** given as a loan. [from Norse *lan*]

◼ *noun* **1** advance, credit, mortgage, allowance. *verb* lend, advance, credit, allow.

loan shark *colloq.* a person who lends money at exorbitant rates of interest.
loanword *noun* a word taken into one language from another.
loath *adj.* unwilling; reluctant: *were loath to admit it.* — **nothing loath** willing or willingly. [from Anglo-Saxon *lath*, hated]
loathe *verb* to feel intense dislike or disgust for. [from Anglo-Saxon *lathian*, to hate]

◼ hate, detest, abhor, abominate, dislike, despise.
◻ adore, love.

loathing *noun* intense dislike or disgust.

◼ hatred, detestation, abhorrence, abomination, dislike, aversion, disgust, horror, repugnance, revulsion.
◻ affection, love.

loathsome *adj.* causing intense dislike or disgust.

◼ hateful, detestable, abhorrent, abominable, odious,

repugnant, repulsive, repellent, offensive, horrible, nasty, disgusting, revolting, vile.

loaves see LOAF¹.
lob — *noun* **1** *Tennis* a ball hit in a high overhead path. **2** *Cricket* a slow high underhand ball. — *verb trans.* (**lobbed, lobbing**) to hit or throw (a ball) in this way. [from Anglo-Saxon *lobbe*, spider]
lobar *adj.* relating to or affecting a lobe, especially in the lungs.
lobate *adj.* having lobes.
lobby — *noun* (PL. **lobbies**) **1** a small entrance-hall, passage, or waiting-room from which several rooms open. **2** *Brit.* either of two corridors in the House of Commons which members pass into when they vote. **3** *Brit.* a hall in the House of Commons where members of the public may meet politicians. **4** a group of people who try to influence the government, politicians, etc in favour of a particular cause. — *verb* (**lobbies, lobbied**) **1** to try to influence (the government, politicians, etc) in favour of a particular cause. **2** *intrans.* to campaign on behalf of a particular cause. [from Latin *lobia*]

◼ *noun* **1** vestibule, foyer, porch, entrance-hall, hall, hallway, corridor, passage, waiting-room, anteroom. **4** pressure group, ginger group. *verb* **1** influence, persuade, urge, push, press, pressure. **2** campaign, press, push, call, appeal, petition.

lobbying *noun Politics* the process by which attempts are made to influence elected representatives through personal contacts in the 'lobbies' of legislative buildings.
lobbyist *noun* a person employed to lobby politicians, etc on behalf of a particular cause.
lobe *noun* **1** the soft, broad, lower part of the ear. **2** a division of an organ or gland in the body, especially the lungs or brain. **3** a broad, usually rounded division or projection of a larger object. [from Greek *lobos*]
lobed *adj.* having a lobe or lobes.
lobelia *noun* a garden plant with red, white, purple, blue, or yellow flowers. [from Matthias de *Lobel* (1538–1616), Flemish botanist]
lobotomy *noun* (PL. **lobotomies**) *Medicine* the surgical operation of cutting into an organ or gland, especially the front lobes in the brain to cure certain mental disorders. [from Greek *lobos*, lobe + *tomia*, cutting]
lobster *noun* **1** any of various large crustaceans belonging to the order Decapoda, and typically having four pairs of walking legs, and a pair of large claws or pincers that reach out in front and are used for capturing prey. **2** the flesh of this animal used as food. [from Anglo-Saxon *loppestre*]
lobster pot a basket for catching lobsters.
local — *adj.* **1** of or belonging to a particular place. **2** of or belonging to one's home area or neighbourhood. **3** *said of a train or bus* stopping at all the stations or stops in a neighbourhood or small area. **4** *Medicine* affecting or confined to a small area or part: *a local anaesthetic.* — *noun* **1** a person living in a particular area. **2** one's nearest and most regularly visited public house. **3** a local bus or train. **4** an anaesthetic affecting only a particular part of the body. [from Latin *localis*, from *locus*, place]

◼ *adj.* **1** regional, provincial, area, district, community, neighbourhood, limited, restricted. *noun* **1** inhabitant, citizen, resident, native.
◻ *adj.* **1** national.

local authority the elected local government body in an area.
local colour details in a story, etc which are characteristic of the time or place in which it is set.
locale *noun* the scene of some event or occurrence. [from French *local*, local]

local education authority (LEA) a regional government organization responsible for education in its area.

local government government of town or county affairs by a locally elected authority, as distinct from national or central government.

Local Group *Astron.* the name of the group of about 30 galaxies to which our own Galaxy, the Milky Way, belongs.

locality *noun* (PL. **localities**) **1** a district or neighbourhood. **2** the scene of an event. **3** the position of a thing. [from Latin *localitas*, from *locus*, place]

⊟ **1** neighbourhood, vicinity, district, area, region. **2** scene, locale, site, spot. **3** position, location, place.

localization or **localisation** *noun* the act of process of localizing.

localize or **localise** *verb* **1** to restrict to a place or area. **2** to mark with the characteristics of a particular place.

localized or **localised** *adj.* restricted to or characterized by a particular place.

locally *adv.* within or in terms of a particular area or the people living in it: *important issues to be decided locally.*

locate *verb* **1** to set in a particular place or position. **2** to find the exact position of. **3** to establish in its proper place or position. **4** to describe or state the position of (something). **5** *intrans., North Amer.* to establish oneself in business or residence in an area. [from Latin *locare*, from *locus*, place]

⊟ **1** situate, place, put, set, fix. **2** find, discover, track down, detect, identify, pinpoint. **3** establish, settle.

location *noun* **1** a position or situation. **2** the act of locating or process of being located. **3** an authentic place or natural setting for making a film or broadcast, as distinct from an artificial setting in a studio: *made on location in Spain.* **4** *South Afr.* any of the townships or other areas where black or coloured people were obliged to live. **5** *Comput.* a position in a memory which can hold a unit of information.

⊟ **1** position, situation, place, spot, site, venue, locale, whereabouts, bearings.

loc.cit. *abbrev.* for *loco citato* (Latin), in the passage just quoted.

loch /lɒx/ *noun Scot.* **1** a lake. **2** (*also* **sea loch**) a long narrow arm of the sea surrounded by land on three sides. [from Gaelic *loch*]

loci /ˈloʊsaɪ/ see LOCUS.

lock[1] — *noun* **1** a mechanical device that provides security by fastening a door, lid, machine, item of movable property, etc. Most locks consist of a cylinder containing a sliding bolt that is moved by turning a key, dial, or some other device. **2** an enclosed section of a canal or river in which the water level can be raised or lowered by means of gates, enabling boats to move from a higher section of the waterway to a lower one, or vice versa. **3** a state of being jammed or locked together, and completely immovable. **4** the part of a gun which explodes the charge. **5** *Wrestling* a tight hold which prevents one's opponent from moving. **6** the full amount by which the front wheels of a vehicle will turn. **7** (*in full* **lock forward**) a Rugby player in the second row of a scrum. **8** an airlock. — *verb* **1** to fasten (a door, box, bag, etc) with a lock. **2** *intrans., said of a door, etc* to become locked or have the means of becoming locked. **3** to shut up or secure (a building) by locking all the doors and windows. **4** *trans., intrans.* to jam or cause to jam. **5** *trans., intrans.* to fasten or cause to be fastened so as to prevent movement. **6** to hold closely in an embrace or tussle. — **lock someone in** to prevent them from leaving a building or room by locking the doors while they are inside. **lock someone out 1** to prevent them from entering a building or room by locking the doors while they are out-

side. **2** to prevent employees from entering a factory, etc during industrial action. **lock, stock, and barrel** completely; the whole thing. **lock up** to lock all the doors and windows of a building, especially when leaving it empty or unoccupied. **lock someone up** to confine them or prevent them from leaving by locking them in somewhere; to put them in prison. **lock something up** to lock a building, etc securely. **under lock and key** securely locked up; in prison. [from Anglo-Saxon *loc*]

⊟ *noun* **1** fastening, bolt, hasp, latch, padlock. *verb* **1** fasten, secure, bolt, latch, padlock. **3** secure, seal, shut up. **5** engage, link, mesh, entangle, entwine, clench. **6** hold, clasp, hug, embrace, grasp, clutch. **lock out** shut out, keep out, exclude, bar, debar. **lock someone up** imprison, jail, incarcerate, intern, confine, shut in, cage, pen. **lock something up** secure, shut up, close up.

⊟ *verb* **1** unlock. **lock someone up** free, release.

lock[2] *noun* **1** a section or curl of hair. **2** (**locks**) hair. [from Anglo-Saxon *locc*]

lockable *adj.*, *said especially of a room or building* able to be locked.

locker *noun* a small lockable cupboard for personal, temporary use, eg for sports equipment.

locket *noun* a small ornamental case for holding a personal photograph or memento, worn on a chain round the neck. [from Old French *loquet*, latch]

lockjaw *noun* **1** tetanus. **2** difficulty in opening the mouth caused by spasm of the jaw muscles. It may be a symptom of tetanus, or associated with hysteria or dental disease.

lockout *noun* the exclusion of employees by the management from their place of work during an industrial dispute, as a means of imposing certain conditions. See also LOCK OUT.

locksmith *noun* a person who makes and mends locks.

lockup *noun* **1** a cell for locking up prisoners. **2** *Brit.* a small shop with no living quarters attached. **3** the action or time of locking up a building, etc. **4** (*attributive*) *Brit.* denoting a building, etc that can be locked up: *a lockup garage.*

loco[1] /ˈloʊkoʊ/ *noun* (PL. **locos**) *colloq.* a locomotive.

loco[2] /ˈloʊkoʊ/ *adj. slang* crazy; mad. [from Spanish *loco* insane]

locomotion *noun* the process or capacity of moving from one place to another. [from Latin *locus*, place + *motio*, motion]

locomotive — *noun* a railway engine for pulling trains. — *adj.* relating to or causing locomotion.

locomotory or **locomotor** *adj.* relating to or involving locomotion.

locum *noun* (*in full* **locum tenens**) a person who temporarily takes the place of someone else, especially a doctor or dentist. [from Latin *locus*, place + *tenere*, to hold]

locus *noun* (PL. **loci**) **1** an exact place or location. **2** *Maths.* the set of points or values that satisfy an equation or a particular set of conditions. **3** *Biol.* the position of a particular gene on a chromosome. [from Latin *locus*, place]

locust *noun* **1** any of various large grasshoppers belonging to the same family (Acrididae) as ordinary grasshoppers, but distinguished from them by their tendency to form dense swarms and migrate, eating all the vegetation in their path and causing extensive destruction of crops. **2** (*in full* **locust tree**) an alternative name for the carob (*Ceratonia siliqua*), an evergreen tree native to the Mediterranean region. See CAROB. **3** (*in full* **locust bean**) a carob pod. [from Latin *locusta*, lobster, locust]

locution *noun* **1** a style of speech. **2** a word, phrase, or sentence. [from Latin *locutio*, from *loqui*, to speak]

lode *noun* a thin band or strip of rock containing metallic ore. [from Anglo-Saxon *lad*, course, journey]

lodestar *noun* **1** a star used as a guide by sailors and astronomers, especially the Pole Star. **2** any guide or guiding principle.

lodestone or **loadstone** *noun* **1** (FORMULA Fe₃O₄) a black naturally occurring variety of the mineral magnetite (iron oxide), which has strong magnetic properties. **2** an elongated piece of this material used as a magnet. **3** any person or thing that attracts.

lodge — *noun* **1** a small house at the gate to the grounds of a large house. **2** a small house in the country for sportsmen: *a hunting-lodge*. **3** a porter's room in a university or college. **4** the meeting-place of a local branch of some societies, or the members of this branch. **5** a beaver's nest, made of sticks that are usually plastered with mud, and having an underwater entrance. — *verb* **1** *intrans.* to live in rented accommodation, especially in someone else's home and usually temporarily. **2** to provide with rented, usually temporary accommodation, especially in one's home. **3** to bring (a charge or accusation) against someone; to make (a complaint) officially. **4** (**lodge something in** or **with someone**) to deposit money or valuables for safety with them. **5** to cause to become firmly fixed. **6** *intrans.* to become firmly fixed. **7** (**be lodged in** or **with someone**) *said of power, authority, etc* to be attributed to them. [from Old French *loge*, shelter]

▣ *noun* **1** house, gatehouse, cottage. **2** hut, cabin, chalet, shelter, retreat. *verb* **1** accommodate, put up, board, quarter, billet, shelter. **2** live, stay, board, put up, reside, dwell. **3** submit, register. **4** deposit, place, put. **5** fix, embed, implant, stick.

lodger *noun* a person who rents accommodation in someone else's home, often temporarily.

▣ boarder, paying guest, guest, resident, inmate, tenant.

lodging *noun* **1** (*usually* **lodgings**) a room or rooms rented in someone else's home. **2** temporary accommodation.

▣ **1** rooms, billet. **2** accommodation, *colloq.* digs, quarters, residence, dwelling, abode.

loess /ˈloʊɪs, lɜːs/ *noun Geol.* a loose fine-grained highly fertile soil consisting of particles of quartz, feldspar, hornblende, mica, and clay, thought to have been deposited by the wind during the Pleistocene period. [from Swiss German *lösch*, loose]

loft — *noun* **1** a room or space under a roof. **2** a gallery in a church or hall. **3** a room used for storage, especially one over a stable for storing hay. **4** a loft in a house used for keeping pigeons in. **5** a backward slope on the head of a golfclub. **6** a stroke that causes a golfball to rise up high. — *verb* to strike, kick, or throw (a ball, etc) high up in the air. [from Anglo-Saxon, from Norse *lopt*, sky, upper room]

loftily *adv.* imposingly; proudly, haughtily.

loftiness *noun* **1** great height. **2** haughtiness.

lofty *adj.* (**loftier, loftiest**) **1** of great or imposing height. **2** of high or noble character: *lofty ideals.* **3** haughty or proud.

log¹ — *noun* **1** part of a tree trunk or thick bare branch, especially when cut for firewood. **2** a detailed record of events occurring during the voyage of a ship or aircraft, etc. **3** a logbook. **4** a float attached by a line to a ship, used for measuring its speed. — *verb* (**logged, logging**) **1** to record (distances covered on a journey, events, etc) in a book or logbook. **2** to cut (trees, etc) into logs. **3** *intrans.* to cut logs. — **log in** or **on** *Comput.* to gain access to a computer system by keying in an appropriate command. **log out** or **off** *Comput.* to relinquish access to a computer system by keying in a closing command. **sleep like a log** to sleep very soundly. [from Middle English *logge*]

▣ *noun* **1** timber, trunk, branch, block, chunk. **2** record, account, diary, journal. **3** logbook, diary, journal, daybook. *verb* **1** record, register, note down, write up.

log² *noun colloq.* a logarithm.

loganberry *noun* (PL. **loganberries**) **1** a large dark red berry eaten as a fruit. **2** the plant which produces it, thought to be a cross between a raspberry and a blackberry. [from J H Logan (1841–1928), the American judge in whose garden it first grew]

logarithm *noun Maths.* the power to which a number *a* must be raised in order to give another number *b*. It is usually referred to as the logarithm to the base *a* of *b*, eg because $10^2 = 100$, the logarithm of 100 to the base 10 is 2 (written log100 = 2). [from Greek *logos*, ratio + *arithmos*, number]

logarithmic *adj.* in the nature of logarithms; relating to logarithms and their principles.

logarithmically *adv.* by or according to the principles of logarithms: *solved the problem logarithmically.*

logarithmic scale *Maths.* a scale of measurement that varies logarithmically with the quantity being measured, eg a scale in which an increase of one unit on the scale represents a tenfold increase in the quantity being measured.

logbook *noun* **1** a book containing an official record of the voyage of a ship, aircraft, etc including details of crew and any incidents which occur. **2** *Brit.* the registration documents of a motor vehicle.

loggerhead — **at loggerheads** arguing or disagreeing fiercely. [possibly from dialect *logger*, a block of wood for hobbling a horse + HEAD]

loggia /ˈlɒdʒə/ *noun* a roofed gallery or arcade on the side of a building, open to the garden. [from Italian *loggia*, lodge]

logging *noun* the work of cutting trees and preparing timber.

logic *noun* **1** the science of reasoning. **2** correct or incorrect use of reasoning; the ability to reason soundly. **3** an individual, personal, or particular way of reasoning: *feminine logic.* **4** the convincing and compelling force of a thing; the inevitability of a consequence of a thing: *the inescapable logic of events.* **5** *Electron., Comput.* the arrangement of circuit elements which allows specified arithmetical functions to be performed. [from Greek *logike techne*, logical art]

▣ **1** reasoning, rationale, deduction, argumentation. **2** reason, sense.

logical *adj.* **1** of or according to logic. **2** correctly reasoned or thought out. **3** able to reason correctly. **4** following reasonably or necessarily from facts or events.

▣ RATIONAL. **1** systematic, methodical. **2** reasoned, coherent, clear, consistent, valid, sound, well-founded. **3** sensible. **4** reasonable, necessary, deducible.

🔁 ILLOGICAL, IRRATIONAL.

-logical or **-logic** *combining form* forming adjectives corresponding to nouns in *-logy*: *archaeological/pathological.*

logicality *noun* the condition of being logical.

logically *adv.* according to the rules of logic; rationally.

logical positivism *Philos.* a philosophical movement, beginning with 'the Vienna Circle' in the 1920s, concerned with determining whether or not statements are meaningful.

logician *noun* a person who is skilled in or studies logic.

logistic or **logistical** *adj.* relating to or in terms of logistics.

logistically *adv.* in terms of logistics: *it is logistically impossible to arrive by ten o'clock.*

logistics *sing. or pl. noun* **1** the art of moving and supplying troops and military equipment. **2** the organizing of everything needed for any large-scale operation. [from French *logistique*, quartermaster's work, from *loger*, to lodge]

log jam **1** a jam caused by logs being floated down a river. **2** a complete stopping of movement or progress.

logo *noun* (PL. **logos**) a small design used as the symbol of an organization. [from *logotype*, from Greek *logos*, word]

logograph or **logogram** *noun* a symbol which represents a whole word or phrase (or, in some cases, parts of words), used in certain writing systems such as shorthand and scientific notation. [from Greek *logos*, word + *graphein*, to write]

-logy or **-ology** *combining form* forming words denoting: **1** a science or study: *geology*. **2** writing or speech: *trilogy*. [from Greek *logos*, word, reason]

loin *noun* **1** (**loins**) the waist and lower back area, between the ribs and the hips. **2** (**loins**) *poetic* the genitals, especially when thought of as the source of life: *fruit of one's loins*. **3** a cut from the lower back area of an animal. [from Old French *loigne*]

loincloth *noun* a piece of material worn round the hips, especially as the only garment of primitive peoples.

loiter *verb intrans.* (**loitered**, **loitering**) **1** to work slowly and idly. **2** to stand around or pass one's time doing nothing. [from Middle English *loteren*]

....
■ **1** dawdle, lag, *colloq.* dilly-dally. **2** hang about, linger, idle, dally, mooch.
....

loiterer *noun* a person who loiters or is loitering.

loll *verb intrans.* **1** (**loll about**) to lie or sit about lazily; to lounge or sprawl. **2** *said of the tongue* to hang down or out. [from Middle English *lollen*]

Lollard *noun* a derisive term applied to followers of the English theologian John Wycliffe in the 14c. The movement translated the Bible into the vernacular. [from Middle Dutch *lollaert*, mumbler]

lollipop *noun* a large round boiled sweet on a stick. [from dialect *lolly*, tongue + POP¹]

lollipop man or **lollipop lady** a man or woman whose job it is to see children safely across busy roads, recognized by carrying a pole with a circular sign on top.

lollop *verb intrans.* (**lolloped**, **lolloping**) *colloq.* to move about in a lively but ungainly manner. [possibly from LOLL]

lolly *noun* (PL. **lollies**) *colloq.* **1** a lollipop. **2** (*also* **ice lolly**) a frozen ice cream or flavoured water ice on a stick. **3** money. [from LOLLIPOP]

Lombard *noun* a member of a Germanic people settled in Hungary who invaded N Italy in AD 658 and in time controlled most of the peninsula. [from Latin *langobardus*, long beard]

London pride a plant of the saxifrage family with pink flowers.

lone *adj.* **1** *said of a person* alone; without a companion. **2** *said of a place* isolated and unfrequented.

....
■ **1** alone, solo, unaccompanied, solitary, sole, only, one, single, separate, unattached. **2** isolated, remote, cut off, separated, unfrequented, deserted.
☒ **1** accompanied.
....

loneliness *noun* being lonely or solitary.

....
■ aloneness, solitariness, solitude, seclusion, isolation, remoteness.

....

lonely *adj.* (**lonelier**, **loneliest**) **1** *said of a person* sad because without companions or friends. **2** solitary and without companionship: *a lonely existence*. **3** *said of a place* isolated and unfrequented.

....
■ **1** alone, friendless, *North Amer.* lonesome, abandoned, forsaken. **2** solitary, companionless, sequestered, secluded. **3** isolated, remote, out-of-the-way, uninhabited, unfrequented, abandoned, deserted, forsaken, desolate.
☒ **3** crowded, populous.
....

lonely heart a lonely person, especially one who is seeking a loving relationship.

loner *noun* a person who prefers to be alone and who avoids close relationships.

lonesome *adj. North Amer.* **1** sad and lonely. **2** causing feelings of loneliness.

lone wolf a person who prefers to live or act alone.

long¹ — *adj.* **1** measuring a great distance from one end to the other in space or time. **2** measuring a specified amount in space or time: *six centimetres long*. **3** having a large number of items: *a long list*. **4** measuring more in space or time than the average or more than is expected or wanted. **5** greater in value, amount, etc than is usual or expected. **6** lasting for an extended period of time. **7** *said of a dress, trousers, curtains, etc* reaching down to or close to the ground, floor, etc; full-length. **8** *said of a cold drink* large and thirst-quenching. **9** *said of stocks* bought in large amounts in expectation of a rise in prices. **10** *Phonetics, said of a vowel or syllable* having the greater of two recognized lengths, such as the *a* in *bake* and the *i* in *pile*, as distinct from the short *a* in *back* and the short *i* in *pill*. **11** *said of betting odds* showing a low level of probability. — *adv.* **1** for, during, or by a long period of time: *long ago/long-lasting*. **2** throughout the whole time: *all night long*. — *noun* anything that is long, especially a long period of time, or a long vowel or syllable. — **as long as** or **so long as 1** provided that. **2** while; during the time that. **before long** in the near future; soon. **in the long run** in the end. **long on something** *colloq.* having a lot of it: *not too long on brains*. **the long and the short of it** the most important facts in a few words. **no longer** not now as it was in the past. **so long** *colloq.* goodbye. [from Anglo-Saxon *lang*]

....
■ *adj.* **1** lengthy, extensive, great, large, big. **4** elongated, extended, prolonged, protracted. **6** slow, sustained, long-drawn-out, interminable.
☒ *adj.* **1** short, brief. **4** abbreviated. **6** fleeting.
....

long² *verb intrans.* (**long for something** or **someone**) to want them intensely. [from Anglo-Saxon *langian*, to yearn after]

....
■ want, wish for, desire, crave, hanker after, yearn for, pine for, ache for, hunger for, thirst for, itch for, lust after, covet, dream of.
....

longboat *noun* the largest small boat carried by a ship.

longbow *noun* a large bow drawn by hand.

long-distance *adj.* covering, travelling, operating, etc between or over long distances: *a long-distance runner/long-distance telephone calls*.

long division a division of numbers in which the working is shown in full.

long-drawn-out *adj.* taking a longer time than is normal or expected.

longevity *noun* great length of life. [from Latin *longus*, long + *aevum*, age]

long face a dismal or disappointed expression.

longhand *noun* ordinary writing as opposed to shorthand.

long haul 1 the carrying of cargo or passengers over a long distance. **2** any work requiring great effort or considerable time.

longing *noun* an intense desire or yearning: *a longing for freedom*. — *adj.* having this feeling.

....
■ *noun* wish, desire, craving, hankering, yearning, hunger, thirst, itch, yen, urge, aspiration, ambition.
....

longingly *adv.* with intense desire or yearning: *looked longingly out of the window*.

longitude *noun* any of a series of imaginary circles that pass around the Earth through both poles, crossing circles of latitude at right angles. All points on the *prime meridian*, which passes through Greenwich, UK, have a longitude of 0°, and the distance E or W of this is divided into 180° of longitude. Longitude is used together with latitude to specify any position on the Earth's surface. See also LATITUDE. [from Latin *longus*, long]

longitudinal *adj.* **1** relating to longitude; measured by longitude. **2** lengthways.

longitudinally *adv.* as regards longitude; in terms of longitude.

longitudinal wave *Physics* a wave in which particles are displaced in the same direction as that in which the wave is being propagated, eg sound waves.

long johns *colloq.* long underpants.

long jump an athletics contest in which competitors jump as far as possible along the ground from a running start.

long-lived *adj.* having a long life.

long-playing *adj.*, *said of a gramophone record* with each side playing for 20 to 30 minutes.

long-range *adj.* **1** *said of a missile or vehicle* able to reach to remote or far-off targets or destinations. **2** *said of a weather forecast* covering a period of several weeks or more.

longship *noun Hist.* a long narrow Viking warship propelled by rowers.

longshore *adj.* found on or employed along the shore. [from the phrase *along shore*]

longshoreman *noun North Amer.* a person who loads and unloads ships at a sea-port.

long shot *colloq.* a guess, attempt, etc which is unlikely to be successful. — **not by a long shot** not by any means.

long-sighted *adj.* **1** *said of a person* affected by hypermetropia, and only able to see distant objects clearly. **2** wise and prudent as to the future; far-sighted.

long-sightedness *noun* the condition of being long-sighted.

long-standing *adj.* having existed or continued for a long time.

. . . .

▤ well-established, time-honoured, traditional, longtime, long-lived, long-lasting, enduring, abiding.

. . . .

long-suffering *adj.* patiently tolerating difficulties and hardship.

. . . .

▤ patient, stoical, uncomplaining, forbearing, forgiving, tolerant.

. . . .

long-term *adj.*, *said of a plan, etc* occurring in or concerned with the future.

longtime *adj.* lasting for a long time; long-standing.

long wave a radio wave using wavelengths over 1000 metres.

longways *adv.*, *adj.* in the direction of a thing's length; lengthways.

long-winded *adj.*, *said of a speaker or speech* verbose and tedious.

. . . .

▤ lengthy, overlong, prolonged, protracted, long-drawn-out, verbose, wordy, diffuse, discursive, rambling, tedious.

▣ brief, terse.

. . . .

loo *noun Brit. colloq.* a lavatory. [of uncertain origin]

loofah or **loofa** *noun* the long thin dried inner part of a tropical gourd-like fruit, used as a sponge. [from Arabic *lufah*]

look — *verb*, *usually intrans.* **1** (**look at**) to turn the eyes in a certain direction so as to see; to use one's sight. **2** (**look at** or **to something**) to consider, examine, or give attention to. **3** to seem to be or appear. **4** to face or be turned towards: *a window looking south.* **5** (**look for something**) to search for it. **6** (**look to someone**) to rely on or turn or refer to them: *we look to you for support.* **7** (**look into something**) to investigate it: *please look into the matter for him.* **8**

trans. to direct one's sight towards in a particular way: *look her in the eyes.* **9** *trans.* to express by a look: *she was looking daggers at him.* **10** *trans.* to consider or realize: *just look where we are now!* — *noun* **1** an act of looking; a glance or view: *have a good look.* **2** the general appearance of a thing or person. **3** (**looks**) beauty; attractiveness. — *interj.* used to call for attention or to express protest. — **look after someone** or **something** to attend to or take care of them. **look ahead** to consider what will happen in the future. **look down on** or **look down one's nose at someone** to consider them as not good enough or not as good as oneself. **look forward to something** to wait for something or anticipate it with pleasure. **look here!** used to call for attention or to express protest. **look in on someone** to visit them briefly and often uninvited. **look on** to watch without taking part. **look on someone** or **something** to think of or consider them in a certain way: *you should look on me as a friend.* **look oneself** to appear one's normal healthy self: *he doesn't look quite himself yet, does he?* **look out** to keep watch and be careful. **look something out** to find it by searching: *looked out all her old clothes.* See also LOOKOUT. **look something over** to check it cursorily. **look sharp** *colloq.* to act quickly. **look up** to show signs of improving: *the weather's looking up at last.* **look someone up** *colloq.* to visit them. **look something up** to search for an item of information in a reference book. **look up to someone** to respect their behaviour, opinions, etc. **never look back** to continue to make progress or prosper. [from Anglo-Saxon *locian*]

. . . .

▤ *verb* **1** see, observe, watch, view, survey, scan, gaze at, stare at, *colloq.* gawp at, glance at, peep at. **2** consider, regard, contemplate, examine, study, inspect, scrutinize. **3** seem, appear. **7** investigate, examine, probe, research, study, go into, explore, check out, inspect, scrutinize. *noun* **1** gaze, stare, glance, glimpse, peek, *colloq.* once-over, sight, view, survey, inspection, examination. **2** appearance, semblance, aspect, manner, mien, bearing, expression, face. **look after** attend to, take care of, care for, tend, mind, keep an eye on, watch over, supervise, protect, guard. **look down on** despise, scorn, sneer at, deride, disdain, spurn **look forward to** await, wait for, anticipate, expect, hope for, long for, envisage, count on. **look out** keep watch, keep an eye out, be careful, pay attention, watch out, beware. **look over** inspect, examine, check, *colloq.* give a once-over, cast an eye over, look through, scan, skim. **look up** improve, get better, pick up, develop, advance, progress. **look someone up** visit, call on, drop in on, look in on. **look something up** search for, hunt for, research, find, track down. **look up to** respect, admire, esteem, revere.

▣ **look after** neglect, **look down on** look up to, admire. **look up to** look down on, despise.

. . . .

lookalike *noun* a person who looks very much like someone else; a double.

. . . .

▤ double, doppelgänger, twin, living image, *colloq.* spitting image, *colloq.* ringer, clone, replica.

. . . .

look and say a method of teaching reading through the recognition of whole words, rather than 'sounding' their constituent parts, as used in the phonics approach. See also PHONICS.

looker *noun colloq.* an attractive person.

looker-on a person who looks on.

look-in *noun* **1** a chance of joining in, being included, or doing something: *never get a look-in.* **2** a short visit.

looking-glass *noun old use* a mirror.

lookout *noun* **1** a careful watch. **2** a place from which such a watch can be kept. **3** a person set to watch, eg on board ship. **4** *colloq.* a personal concern or problem: *that's your lookout.* **5** prospect or outlook: *a dim lookout.*

■ **1** watch, vigil, guard. **2** watchtower, tower, post. **3** watch, watchman, guard, sentry, sentinel. **4** concern, responsibility, worry, problem, affair, business.

look-see *noun colloq.* a brief look around or inspection.

loom [1] *noun* a machine for weaving thread into fabric. [from Anglo-Saxon *loma*, tool]

loom [2] *verb intrans.* **1** (**loom up**) to appear indistinctly and usually in some enlarged or threatening form. **2** *said of an event* to be imminent, especially in some menacing or threatening way.

■ MENACE, THREATEN. **1** appear, emerge, take shape, rise, soar, tower, dominate, overshadow. **2** approach, impend, hang over.

loon *noun North Amer.* a diving bird with a slender body and sharp beak; a diver. [from Norse *lomr*]

loony *slang* — *noun* (PL. **loonies**) a mad person; a lunatic. — *adj.* (**loonier, looniest**) crazy; mad. [a shortening of LU-NATIC]

loony-bin *noun slang* a mental home or hospital.

loop — *noun* **1** an oval-shaped coil in a piece of rope, chain, etc, formed as it crosses over itself. **2** any similar oval-shaped or U-shaped bend, eg in a river. **3** a manoeuvre in which an aircraft describes a complete vertical circle in the sky. **4** a strip of magnetic tape or film forming a loop, allowing the sound or images on it to be continually repeated. **5** *Electron.* a closed circuit which a signal can pass round. **6** *Comput.* a sequence of instructions in a program that are repeated all the time a given condition exists. **7** a branch of a railway, telegraph line, etc that leaves the main line and then rejoins it. **8** a contraceptive coil. — *verb* **1** to fasten with or enclose in a loop. **2** *trans., intrans.* to form into a loop or loops. — **loop the loop** *said of an aircraft, etc* to make a loop in the sky. [from Middle English *loupe*, loop of cloth]

■ *noun* **1** coil, circle, ring, hoop, noose, spiral, whorl, curl, kink, twist, turn, bend, curve. **2** twist, turn, bend, curve. *verb* **1** fasten, connect, link, join, knot, encircle. **2** coil, roll, curve, bend, turn, twist.

loophole *noun* a means, usually based on a legal weakness or oversight, of avoiding obeying a rule or law or fulfilling a contract, without formally breaking it. [from Middle English *loop*, window + HOLE: it was originally a narrow slit in a wall for shooting arrows through and for letting in light, without undue risk from opponents' weapons]

■ let-out, escape, evasion, avoidance, excuse, pretext, plea.

loopy *adj.* (**loopier, loopiest**) *slang* mad; crazy.

loose — *adj.* **1** not or no longer tied or held in confinement; free. **2** not tight or close-fitting. **3** not held together; not fastened or firmly fixed in place; not packeted. **4** not tightly-packed or compact: *loose soil.* **5** vague or inexact: *a loose translation.* **6** immoral or promiscuous. **7** indiscreet: *loose talk.* **8** *Sport, said of a ball, etc* in play but not under a player's control. — *noun Rugby* the part of play where the players are not in scrums or close together round the ball. — *verb* **1** to release or set free. **2** to unfasten or untie. **3** to make loose tight, compact, or dense. **4** to relax: *loose one's hold.* **5** to discharge (a gun, bullet, arrow, etc). — **at a loose end** having nothing to do. **on the loose** free from confinement or control. [from Norse *lauss*]

■ *adj.* **1** free, unfastened, untied, undone. **2** slack, lax, baggy, roomy. **3** unattached, movable, insecure, wobbly. **5** vague, inexact, imprecise, ill-defined, indefinite, indistinct. *verb* **1** release, set free, let go, let out, free. **2** unfasten, untie, unbind, undo.

■ *adj.* **2** tight. **3** fixed, secure. **5** exact, precise.

loose box a part of a stable or horse-box where horses are kept untied.

loose cannon someone or something that is dangerously uncontrolled.

loose change coins kept in one's pocket or bag, for small expenses.

loose-leaf *adj., said of a folder, binder, etc* having clips or rings which open to allow pages to be removed and inserted.

loosely *adv.* **1** in a loose manner. **2** roughly; approximately; without precision.

loosen *verb trans., intrans.* (**loosened, loosening**) **1** to make or become loose or looser. **2** (**loosen up**) to make or become less tense, rigid, or stiff.

■ RELAX. **1** slacken, ease.
■ **1** tighten. **2** tense, stiffen up.

looseness *noun* being loose (often in the sense 'immoral'); freedom from restraint.

loot — *noun* **1** stolen goods, especially those stolen from an enemy in wartime. **2** *colloq.* money. — *verb* **1** to steal (money or goods) or to steal them from (someone, especially an enemy in wartime, or some place). **2** *intrans.* to rob and plunder. [from Hindi *lut*]

■ *noun* **1** spoils, booty, plunder, haul, *slang* swag. *verb* ROB. **1** steal, raid, ransack. **2** plunder, pillage, sack, maraud, ravage.

looter *noun* a person who loots or is looting.

looting *noun* the activity of people who loot; stealing from an enemy.

lop [1] *verb* (**lopped, lopping**) **1** (**lop off**) to cut off, especially the branches of a tree. **2** (**lop something off** or **away**) to cut away unnecessary or superfluous parts of something. [from Middle English *loppe*, parts cut off]

lop [2] *verb intrans.* (**lopped, lopping**) to hang down loosely.

lope — *verb intrans.* to run with long bounding steps. — *noun* a bounding leap. [from Norse *hlaupa*]

lop-eared *adj., said of animals* having ears that droop.

lopsided *adj.* **1** with one side smaller, lower, or lighter than the other. **2** leaning over to one side; unbalanced.

■ **1** asymmetrical, uneven. **2** unbalanced, off balance, askew.
■ **1** symmetrical. **2** balanced.

loquacious /lə'kweɪʃəs/ *adj. formal* highly talkative. [from Latin *loquax*, from *loqui*, to speak]

loquacity /lə'kwasɪtɪ/ or **loquaciousness** *noun formal* talkativeness.

lord — *noun* **1** a master or ruler. **2** *Hist.* a feudal superior. **3** *Brit.* a male member of the nobility. **4** (**Lord**) a title used to address some noblemen, eg earls, viscounts, the younger sons of dukes. **5** (**Lord** or **Our Lord**) God or Christ. — *interj.* (**Lord**) an expression of surprise or dismay. — **live like a lord** to live in luxury. **lord it over someone** *colloq.* to behave in a haughty and domineering manner. [from Anglo-Saxon *hlaford*, from *hlaf*, bread + *weard* guardian]

■ **1** master, ruler, leader, commander, governor, superior, overlord. **3** peer, noble, earl, baron, duke, count, viscount.

Lord Chamberlain in the UK, the chief official of the royal household, who oversees all aspects of its management, and bears responsibility for matters ranging from the care of works of art to the appointment of royal tradesmen.

Lord Chancellor or **Lord High Chancellor** in the UK, a high officer of state whose office combines the judicial, executive, and legislative functions of government. The Lord Chancellor is head of the judiciary, advises the Crown on senior appointments, appoints magistrates, and is also a government Minister and Speaker of the House of Lords.

Lord Chief Justice in England and Wales, and (separately) in Northern Ireland, the head of the Queen's Bench Division of the High Court; also the President of the Criminal Division of the Court of Appeal.

Lord High Chancellor see LORD CHANCELLOR.

lordliness *noun* being lordly or haughty.

lordly *adj.* (**lordlier**, **lordliest**) having the attributes popularly associated with lords, especially in being grand or haughty.

. . . .

▤ noble, aristocratic, grand, dignified, proud, arrogant, disdainful, haughty, imperious, condescending, high-handed, domineering, overbearing.
▤ lowly, humble.

. . . .

Lord Mayor the title of the mayor in the City of London and some other cities.

Lord Privy Seal a senior British cabinet minister without official duties.

Lord Provost the title of the mayor of certain Scottish cities.

lords-and-ladies *noun* a perennial plant (*Arum maculatum*), widespread in Europe, with large leaves shaped like arrow-heads and a pale green spathe partially surrounding a club-shaped reddish-purple *spadix* which develops into a spike of poisonous orange-red berries. Also called CUCKOO PINT.

Lord's Day (**the Lord's Day**) Sunday, regarded as a day of Christian worship.

Lordship *noun* (**His** or **Your Lordship**) a title used to address bishops, judges, and all peers except for dukes.

Lord's Prayer, also known as the **Pater Noster** (**Our Father**) a popular prayer of Christian worship, derived from Matthew 6.9–13 and (in different form) Luke 11.2–4, where Jesus taught his followers how to pray.

lords spiritual the archbishops and bishops in the House of Lords.

Lord's Supper (**the Lord's Supper**) *Christianity* the Eucharist.

lords temporal the members of the House of Lords who are not archbishops or bishops.

lore *noun* the whole body of knowledge, especially traditional knowledge, on a subject. [from Anglo-Saxon *lar*]

. . . .

▤ knowledge, wisdom, learning, erudition, scholarship, traditions, beliefs, sayings.

. . . .

lorgnette /lɔːnˈjet/ *noun* eyeglasses or opera-glasses held on a long handle. [from French *lorgnette*, from *lorgner*, to peer at]

loris /ˈlɔːrɪs/ *noun* a primitive primate, native to forests in S Asia, and having a pale face with dark rings around its large eyes, and no tail. [from French *loris*, possibly from Dutch]

lorry *noun* (PL. **lorries**) *Brit.* a large heavily built road vehicle for transporting heavy loads.

lose *verb* (PAST TENSE AND PAST PARTICIPLE **lost**) **1** to stop having; to fail to keep or obtain, especially in error or through carelessness. **2 a** to suffer the loss of or be bereaved of (especially a parent or spouse) through death. **b** to suffer the loss of (an unborn baby), usually through miscarriage. **3** to leave accidentally or be unable to find: *lose one's way.* **4** to fail to use or get; to miss: *lose a good opportunity.* **5** *trans., intrans.* to fail to win (a game, battle, etc). **6** to fail or cease to hear, see, or understand: *lost the thread of his argument.* **7** to waste (time, money, etc); to use to no purpose. **8** to escape or get away from. **9** to prevent the gaining or achieving of. **10** *trans., intrans., said of a clock or watch* to become slow (by a specified amount). **11** *intrans.* to be in a worse position or suffer as the result of

something. **12** to cause to disappear or die. — **lose oneself in something** to have all one's attention taken up by an activity. **lose out** *colloq.* **1** to suffer loss or be at a disadvantage. **2** to fail to get something one wants. **lose out on something** *colloq.* to be at a disadvantage in some way: *he really lost out on the bonus scheme.* [from Anglo-Saxon *losian*, to be lost]

. . . .

▤ **1** mislay, misplace. **4** miss, forfeit. **7** waste, squander, dissipate, use up, exhaust, drain. **8** elude, evade, throw off, shake off.
▤ **1, 10** gain. **5** win.

. . . .

loser *noun* **1** a person who loses. **2** *colloq.* a person who is habitually unsuccessful.

. . . .

▤ **1** runner-up, also-ran. **2** failure, no-hoper.
▤ WINNER.

. . . .

losing *adj.* failing; never likely to be successful: *a losing battle.*

loss *noun* **1** the act or fact of losing or being lost. **2** the thing, amount, etc lost. **3** the disadvantage or detriment resulting from losing: *be a great loss to the company.* — **at a loss 1** puzzled and uncertain. **2** *said of an article sold, etc* for less than was paid for it originally. **3** *said of a company, etc* losing more money than it is making. [from Anglo-Saxon *los*]

. . . .

▤ **1** disappearance, defeat, failure, death, bereavement, deprivation, depletion, destruction, ruin, waste. **2** deficit, deficiency. **3** disadvantage, detriment, damage.
▤ GAIN.

. . . .

loss-leader *noun* an item on sale at a lower price than normal, as a means of attracting custom for a wider range of goods.

lost past participle of LOSE. — *adj.* **1** missing; no longer to be found. **2** unable to find one's way. **3** confused, puzzled. **4** (**lost on someone**) not properly appreciated by them: *good music is lost on them.* **5** morally fallen: *lost women.* **6** damned: *lost souls.* **7** wasted: *lost time.* — **be lost in something** to have one's attention completely engrossed in something. **get lost** *slang* to go away and stay away. **lost to someone** to be no longer open or available to someone. **lost to something** to be no longer capable of feeling an emotion, etc.

. . . .

▤ **1** mislaid, misplaced, missing, astray, vanished, disappeared, ruined, destroyed. **2** astray, disoriented. **3** confused, bewildered, puzzled, baffled, perplexed. **7** wasted, squandered.
▤ **1** found.

. . . .

lost cause an aim, ideal, person, etc that has no chance of success.

lost generation a term applied by Gertrude Stein to a group of US expatriate writers living in Paris in the 1920s, including herself, whose work reflects the breakdown of order and values after World War I.

lot *noun* **1** *colloq.* (*often* **a lot of** or **lots of**) a great number or amount. **2** (**the lot**) the total; the whole number or amount. **3** any of a set of objects, eg a slip of paper, drawn from among a group, as a way of reaching a decision by chance: *draw lots/cast lots.* **4** this way of making a decision. **5** a person's fortune or destiny. **6** a separate part or portion. **7** a group, set, or batch. **8** an item or set of items for sale by auction. **9** *North Amer.* an area of land: *parking lot.* — **a bad lot** a person with a bad character or bad reputation. **cast** or **throw in one's lot with someone** to decide to share their fortunes. [Anglo-Saxon *hlot*, portion, choice]

. . . .

▤ **6** part, piece, portion, share, allowance, ration, quota. **7** group, set, batch, collection, assortment, number, quantity, amount.

. . . .

loth same as LOATH.

lotion *noun* a liquid for healing or cleaning the skin, as either a medicine or a cosmetic. [from Latin *lotio*, from *lavare*, to wash]

⊟ ointment, cream, balm, salve.

lottery *noun* (PL. **lotteries**) **1** a system of raising money by selling tickets and giving prizes for those tickets drawn at random. **2** anything which is thought of as being a matter of chance. [from Dutch *loterie*, related to LOT]

⊟ **1** draw, raffle, sweepstake. **2** risk, gamble, speculation, venture.

lotto *noun* a game like bingo, with numbers drawn instead of called. [from Italian *lotto*]

lotus *noun* **1** the jujube shrub (*Zizyphus lotus*), native to the Mediterranean region, whose fruit was used by the ancient Greeks to make bread and wine, thought to produce a state of blissful and dreamy forgetfulness. **2** a species of water lily (*Nymphaea lotus*) known as the sacred lotus of Egypt, often depicted in Egyptian art. **3** either of two species of water lily of the genus *Nelumbo*. **4** *Greek Mythol.* a fruit which causes the eater to enter a state of blissful and dreamy forgetfulness. **5** a representation of a water-lily in architecture or art, especially symbolically in ancient Egyptian or Hindu art. [from Greek *lotos*]

lotus-eater *noun* a person who lives a lazy and indulgent life.

lotus position *Yoga* a seated position with the legs crossed and each foot resting on the opposite thigh.

louche /luːʃ/ *adj.* shady, sinister, shifty or disreputable. [from French *louche*, squinting]

loud — *adj.* **1** making a great sound; noisy. **2** capable of making a great sound: *a loud horn*. **3** shrill and insistent: *loud complaints*. **4** *said of colours or a design* too bright; gaudy. **5** *said of behaviour* aggressively noisy and coarse. — *adv.* in a loud manner. — **out loud** aloud; loudly. [from Anglo-Saxon *hlud*]

⊟ *adj.* **1** noisy, deafening, blaring, booming, resounding, thundering, ear-piercing, ear-splitting. **3** shrill, clamorous, vociferous, insistent. **4** gaudy, garish, glaring, flashy, showy, ostentatious, brash, tasteless.
⊟ *adj.* **1, 2** quiet. **4** subdued.

loudhailer *noun* a portable electronic device which amplifies the voice.

loudly *adv.* in a loud way; with great sound.

loud-mouthed *adj. colloq.* noisily and aggressively boastful.

loudness *noun* being loud; much noise or sound.

loudspeaker *noun Electron.* an electronic device that converts electrical signals into audible sound waves, used in radio, television, telephone receivers, hi-fi systems, etc.

lough /lɒx/ *noun Irish* same as LOCH. [from Irish Gaelic *loch*, Middle English *lough*]

Louis period styles a range of Classical, Baroque, and Rococo stylistic variations used in the 17c and 18c, and particularly associated with the reign of Louis XIV of France.

lounge — *verb, usually intrans.* **1** to lie or recline comfortably. **2** (**lounge around**) to be idle or lazy. **3** *trans.* (**lounge away**) to pass (time) idly. — *noun* **1** a sitting-room in a private house. **2** a large room in a public building, eg in a hotel for sitting in, or in an airport for waiting in, often providing refreshment facilities. **3** (*also* **lounge bar**) *Brit.* a smarter and more expensive bar in a public house. **4** an act or spell of lounging. [thought to be from obsolete *lungis*, lout]

⊟ *verb* **1** recline, lie back, relax, take it easy, loll, slump, sprawl.

2 idle, laze, waste time, kill time, sit about, lie about. *noun* **1** sitting-room, living-room, drawing-room, parlour.

lounger *noun* **1** a person who lounges. **2** a comfortable chair for lounging on. **3** a woman's loose garment, worn when relaxing at home.

lounge suit *Brit.* a man's formal suit for ordinary everyday wear.

lour *or* **lower** /laʊə(r)/ *verb intrans.* (**loured, louring**) *said of the sky or elements* to become dark or threaten rain or storms. [from Middle English *louren*, to frown]

louring *or* **lowering** *adj.* menacing; threatening.

louse — *noun* **1** (PL. **lice**) a wingless insect with a flat body and short legs, which sucks the blood of the animal or person it is living on. **2** (PL. **louses**) *slang* a general term of abuse for a person. — *verb* to remove lice from. — **louse something up** *slang* to spoil or ruin it. [from Anglo-Saxon *lus*]

lousily *adv.* badly; disgustingly.

lousiness *noun* a lousy state; being unpleasant.

lousy *adj.* (**lousier, lousiest**) **1** having lice. **2** *slang* very bad, unpleasant, or disgusting. **3** (**lousy with something**) *slang* having a great deal of something unwelcome: *the place was lousy with police*.

lout *noun* an aggressively rough and coarse boy or man. [of uncertain origin]

loutish *adj.* characteristic of louts; aggressively rough and coarse.

louvre *or* **louver** /ˈluːvə(r)/ *noun* **1** any one of a set of horizontal, sloping, overlapping slats in a door, etc, which let air in but keep rain and light out. **2** a dome-like structure on a roof for letting smoke out and air in. [from Old French *lovier*]

louvred *or* **louvered** *adj.* having or equipped with louvres.

lovable *or* **loveable** *adj.* worthy of or inspiring love or affection.

⊟ adorable, endearing, winsome, sweet, cute, appealing, engaging, charming, attractive, fetching, lovely, pleasing, delightful.
⊟ detestable, hateful.

lovage *noun* a herb with small, greenish-yellow flowers, used for flavouring. [from Old French *luvesche*]

love — *noun* **1** a feeling of great affection for and devotion to another person. **2** strong sexual attraction. **3** a strong liking for something. **4** sexual passion; sexual relations. **5** *often used as a term of address* a person one loves. **6** *Brit. colloq.* a term of address used for anyone regardless of affection. **7** *Tennis, Squash* no score. — *verb* **1** to feel great affection for. **2** to enjoy very much; to like. — **fall in love with someone** to develop feelings of love and sexual attraction for someone. **in love with someone** feeling love and sexual attraction for them. **make love to** *or* **with someone 1** to have sexual intercourse with someone. **2** *old use* to woo. **not for love or money** under no circumstances. [from Anglo-Saxon *lufu*]

⊟ *noun* **1** adoration, affection, tenderness, warmth, fondness, attachment, devotion. **3** liking, taste, inclination, infatuation, passion, soft spot, weakness. **4** amorousness, ardour, passion, rapture, romance, love-making, sex. *verb* **1** adore, dote on, cherish, treasure, hold dear, idolize, worship. **2** like, enjoy, delight in, appreciate, desire, fancy.
⊟ *noun* **1** hate, hatred, loathing, detestation. *verb* HATE, DETEST.

love affair a romantic and sexual relationship, especially a transitory one.

⊟ affair, romance, amour, liaison, relationship, love, passion.

lovebird *noun* a small African parrot that shows strong attachment to its mate.

love-child *noun* an illegitimate child.

love-in-a-mist *noun* a garden plant with pale blue or white flowers and feathery leaves.

loveless *adj.* without love.

love-letter *noun* a letter expressing feelings of sexual love.

love-lies-bleeding *noun* a garden plant with drooping spikes of reddish-purple flowers.

love life a person's sexual activity.

loveliness *noun* being lovely or attractive; striking beauty.

lovelorn *adj.* left by or pining for the person one is in love with.

lovely — *adj.* (**lovelier, loveliest**) **1** strikingly attractive; beautiful. **2** *colloq.* delightful or pleasing. — *noun* (PL. **lovelies**) *colloq.* a pretty woman.

> ◨ *adj.* **1** beautiful, attractive, pretty, charming, enchanting, adorable, lovable, sweet, fine, exquisite. **2** delightful, pleasing, pleasant, agreeable, enjoyable.
> ◨ *adj.* **1** ugly, hideous.

love-making *noun* sexual activity between lovers.

love-match *noun* a marriage based on love.

lover *noun* **1** a person in love with another, especially a person having a romantic and sexual relationship. **2** (**lovers**) two people who are in love with one another or who are sharing a sexual relationship. **3** (*in combination*) a person who enjoys or is fond of something specified: *a dog-lover.*

> ◨ **1** beloved, sweetheart, boyfriend, girlfriend, admirer, suitor, mistress, *colloq.* toy boy.

lovesick *adj.* sad or pining because of love.

lovey-dovey *adj. colloq.* affectionate in a silly or sentimental way.

loving *adj.* feeling and showing affection or love.

> ◨ amorous, affectionate, tender, warm, fond, devoted, doting, ardent, passionate.

loving-cup *noun* a large two-handled drinking cup passed round at the end of a banquet.

lovingly *adv.* with love or affection.

low[1] — *adj.* **1** less than average in height; not reaching to a high level. **2** situated close to the ground, to sea-level, or to the horizon. **3** (**low in something**) containing less than average amount, etc: *low in fat.* **4** *said of numbers* small or reduced in amount. **5** with little value or quality. **6** (*often* **low on something**) not having much left of it: *running low on petrol.* **7** of humble rank or position; common. **8** *said of clothes* cut so as to expose the neck and part of the chest. **9** making little sound; soft: *a low voice.* **10** *said of sounds, notes, etc* produced by slow vibrations and having a deep pitch. **11** not physically or mentally strong; weak; with no energy or vitality: *be feeling low after the operation.* **12** unfavourable: *a low opinion.* **13** coarse, rude, and vulgar. **14** *said of latitudes* near the equator. **15** *said of a gear* giving a relatively slow engine speed. — *adv.* **1** in or to a low position, state, or manner. **2** in a small quantity or to a small degree. **3** with a low voice; quietly. **4** at or in a low pitch. — *noun* **1** the position, level, etc which is low or lowest: *the pound has reached a new low.* **2** *Meteorol.* an area of low atmospheric pressure. [from Norse *lagr*]

> ◨ *adj.* **1** short, small, little, squat, stunted, shallow, depressed, sunken. **6** inadequate, deficient, sparse, scant, meagre, paltry. **9** subdued, muted, soft, quiet. **10** deep, bass. **11** weak, down, depressed, downcast. **13** coarse, rude, vulgar, base, mean, contemptible.
> ◨ *adj.* **1** high, tall. **9** loud. **11** strong, cheerful.

low[2] — *verb intrans.*, *said of cattle* to make a low, gentle, mooing sound. — *noun* (*also* **lowing**) the low, gentle mooing sound made by cattle. [from Anglo-Saxon *hlowan*]

low-born *adj.* of humble birth.

lowbrow — *adj.* having or involving tastes that are relatively popular and unintellectual. — *noun* a lowbrow person.

Low Church a group within the Church of England which puts little value on ceremony and the authority of priests and which stresses evangelical theology.

low comedy comedy which borders on the farcical and absurd.

low-down *colloq.* — *adj.* mean and dishonourable. — *noun* information about someone or something, especially when disreputable or acquired surreptitiously: *I've got the low-down on your brother.*

lower[1] — *adj.* **1** not as high as something else in position, status, height, value, etc. **2** *said of an animal or plant* less highly developed than other species. — *adv.* in or to a lower position. — *verb* (**lowered, lowering**) **1** *trans., intrans.* to make or become lower in amount, value, status, sound, etc. **2** to close; to pull or let down: *we'd better lower the blinds.*

> ◨ *adj.* **1** inferior, lesser, minor, secondary, subordinate, junior.
> *verb* **1** reduce, decrease, lessen, diminish. **2** drop, let down, pull down, close.
> ◨ *adj.* HIGHER. *verb* **1** increase. **2** raise, open.

lower[2] (*low-* pronounced like *now*) same as LOUR.

lower case *Printing* small letters as opposed to capitals.

lower-case *adj.* consisting of small letters.

lower class the social class including manual workers and their families.

lower-class *adj.* belonging or relating to the lower class.

lower house or **lower chamber** the larger and normally elected part of a two-chamber (bicameral) parliament, such as the House of Commons in the United Kingdom.

lowest common denominator *Maths.* (ABBREV. **LCD**) in a group of fractions, the lowest common multiple of all the denominators, eg the LCD of $\frac{1}{3}$ and $\frac{1}{4}$ is 12. Fractions must be expressed in such a form if they are to be added or subtracted.

lowest common multiple *Maths.* (ABBREV. **LCM**) the smallest number into which every member of a group of numbers will divide exactly, eg the LCM of 2, 3, and 4 is 12.

low frequency a radio frequency between 30 and 300 kilohertz.

low-key *adj.* **1** restrained and subdued. **2** *said of a person* not easily excited.

lowland — *noun* **1** (*usually* **lowlands**) land which is low-lying in comparison with other areas. **2** (**Lowlands**) the less mountainous region of Scotland lying to the south and east of the Highlands. — *adj.* (*also* **Lowland**) of or relating to lowlands or the Scottish Lowlands.

Lowlander *noun* a person who lives in lowlands, especially the Scottish Lowlands.

low-level language *Comput.* a programming language in which each instruction represents a single machine-code operation. See also HIGH-LEVEL LANGUAGE.

lowliness *noun* a lowly or humble state or rank.

lowly *adj.* (**lowlier, lowliest**) **1** humble in rank, status, or behaviour. **2** simple, modest, and unpretentious.

> ◨ HUMBLE. **1** inferior, subordinate, low-born, obscure, plebeian, poor, mean, submissive, meek, mild. **2** plain, simple, modest, unpretentious, ordinary.
> ◨ **1** noble, lofty.

lowness *noun* a low state or condition.

low-pitched *adj.* **1** *said of a sound* low in pitch. **2** *said of a roof* having a gentle slope.

low-pressure *adj.*, *said of steam and steam-engines* using or creating little pressure.

low profile a deliberate avoidance of publicity and attention.

low-spirited *adj.* dejected or depressed.

. . . .

🔲 dejected, despondent, depressed, gloomy, heavy-hearted, low, down, sad, unhappy, miserable, *colloq.* fed up.

🔳 high-spirited, cheerful.
. . . .

low tech *colloq.* simple, unsophisticated technology used to make basic products. [a shortening of *low technology*]

low tide or **low water** the minimum level reached by a falling tide.

loyal *adj.* **1** faithful and true. **2** personally devoted to a sovereign, government, leader, friend, etc. **3** expressing or showing loyalty: *the loyal toast to the Queen.* [from Old French *loial*]

. . . .

🔲 **1** faithful, true, steadfast, staunch, trustworthy, sincere. **2** devoted, patriotic.

🔳 **1, 2** disloyal, treacherous.
. . . .

loyalist *noun* **1** a loyal supporter, especially of a sovereign or an established government. **2** (**Loyalist**) (in Northern Ireland) a supporter of the British Government.

loyalty *noun* (PL. **loyalties**) **1** the state or quality of being loyal. **2** (*often* **loyalties**) a feeling of loyalty or duty towards a person or institution.

. . . .

🔲 ALLEGIANCE. **1** faithfulness, fidelity, steadfastness, constancy, trustworthiness, reliability, devotion, patriotism.

🔳 **1** disloyalty, treachery.
. . . .

loyalty card a card issued by certain retailers allowing customers to gather credits to be redeemed for goods or cash.

lozenge *noun* **1** a small sweet or tablet which dissolves in the mouth. **2** a rhombus. [from Old French *losenge*]

LP *abbrev.* a long-playing gramophone record.

L-plate *noun* a small square sign with a red letter *L* on a white background, displayed by law at each end of cars being driven by learners.

Lr *symbol Chem.* lawrencium.

LRAM *abbrev.* Licentiate of the Royal Academy of Music.

LRCP *abbrev.* Licentiate of the Royal College of Physicians.

LRCS *abbrev.* Licentiate of the Royal College of Surgeons.

LSD *abbrev.* lysergic acid diethylamide, a drug which causes hallucinations.

L.S.D. or **l.s.d.** or **£.s.d.** *abbrev.* pounds, shillings, pence (with reference to pre-decimal coinage in the UK). [from Latin *librae, solidi, denarii*]

LSE *abbrev.* London School of Economics.

LSO *abbrev.* London Symphony Orchestra.

Lt or **Lt.** *abbrev.* Lieutenant.

Ltd or **Ltd.** *abbrev.* Limited, used in the names of limited liability companies.

Lu *symbol Chem.* lutetium.

lubber *noun* a big awkward and clumsy person. [from Middle English *lobre*]

lubberly *adj.*, *adv.* like a lubber; clumsy or clumsily.

lubricant — *noun* oil, grease, etc used to reduce friction. — *adj.* lubricating.

lubricate *verb* **1** to cover with oil, grease, or some other such substance, to reduce friction. **2** to make smooth, slippery, or greasy. [from Latin *lubricus*, slippery]

. . . .

🔲 **1** oil, grease. **2** wax, polish.

. . . .

lubrication *noun* the act or process of lubricating.

lubricator *noun* a person or thing that lubricates.

lubricious *adj. literary* lewd. [from Latin *lubricus*, slippery]

lubricity *noun literary* lewdness.

lucerne /lʊˈsɜːn/ *noun Brit.* same as ALFALFA. [from French *luzerne*]

lucid *adj.* **1** easily understood; expressed, or expressing something, clearly. **2** *said of a person's mind* sane and not confused, especially between periods of insanity. **3** bright, shining. [from Latin *lucidus*, full of light]

lucidity *noun* being lucid; clarity.

lucidly *adv.* with clear expression; so as to be understood easily.

Lucifer *noun* Satan. [from Latin *lucifer*, light-bringer]

luck *noun* **1** chance, especially when thought of as bringing good fortune. **2** good fortune. **3** events in life which cannot be controlled and seem to happen by chance: *bad luck.* — **down on one's luck** experiencing problems or suffering hardship. **push one's luck** *colloq.* to risk total failure by trying to gain too much when one has already been partly successful. **worse luck** *colloq.* unfortunately. [from Old Dutch *luc*]

. . . .

🔲 **1** chance, fortune, accident, fate, destiny, fortuity, *colloq.* fluke. **2** good fortune, luckiness.

🔳 **1** design. **2** misfortune, unluckiness.
. . . .

luckily *adv.* (applying to a whole sentence or phrase) as a piece of good fortune: *luckily, they were at home when we called.*

. . . .

🔲 fortunately, happily, providentially.

🔳 unfortunately.
. . . .

luckiness *noun* a lucky or fortunate state or situation.

luckless *adj.* unlucky, especially habitually; unfortunate.

lucky *adj.* (**luckier, luckiest**) **1** having good luck. **2** bringing good luck. **3** fortunate: *a lucky coincidence.*

. . . .

🔲 **1** fortunate, favoured, successful, prosperous. **2** favourable, auspicious. **3** fortunate, happy, providential, timely, opportune.

🔳 UNLUCKY.
. . . .

lucky dip a tub or container full of paper, bran, etc, from which prizes are drawn at random.

lucrative *adj.* affording financial gain; profitable. [from Latin *lucrativus*]

. . . .

🔲 profitable, well-paid, remunerative, advantageous.

🔳 unprofitable.
. . . .

lucratively *adv.* so as to provide financial gain; profitably.

lucre /ˈluːkə(r)/ *noun derog.* profit or financial gain. [from Latin *lucrum*, gain]

Luddite — *noun* **1** *Hist.* a member of a band of artisans who in 1811–12 destroyed newly-introduced textile machinery for fear that it would lead to many jobs being lost. **2** any person opposed to new technology or industrial change. — *adj.* relating to or characteristic of the Luddites. [from Ned Ludd, the leader of the 19c movement]

ludicrous *adj.* completely ridiculous; laughable. [from Latin *ludicrus*]

. . . .

🔲 absurd, ridiculous, preposterous, nonsensical, laughable, farcical, comical, funny, silly, crazy, outlandish.

🔳 serious.
. . . .

ludicrously *adv.* in a ludicrous way; to a ludicrous extent: *the price is ludicrously high.*

ludo *noun* a simple game in which counters are moved on a board according to the numbers shown on a dice. [from Latin *ludo*, I play]

luff *verb* **1** (*trans., intrans.*) to turn (a ship) towards the wind. **2** (*trans.*) to move (the jib of a crane or derrick) in and out or up and down, in order to move a load. [from Old French *lof*]

lug¹ *verb trans.* (**lugged, lugging**) to pull or drag (something bulky or heavy) with difficulty. [from Middle English *luggen*]

▣ pull, drag, haul, tow, heave, carry, *colloq.* hump.

lug² *noun* **1** *dialect or colloq.* an ear. **2** a projection on a thing, especially one by which it may be carried or turned.

luge /luːʒ/ *noun* a type of light toboggan on which the rider adopts a sitting rather than a prone position. The competition luge is approximately 1.5m (5ft) in length and is steered with the feet and a hand rope. — *verb intrans.* to travel across snow or ice on a luge. [from Swiss French *luge*]

luggage *noun* suitcases, bags, etc, used in travelling. [from LUG¹]

Types of luggage include: case, suitcase, vanity case, bag, holdall, portmanteau, valise, overnight bag, kitbag, flight bag, hand luggage, travel bag, Gladstone bag, grip, rucksack, knapsack, haversack, backpack, briefcase, attaché case, portfolio, satchel, basket, hamper, trunk, chest, box.

lugger *noun* a small vessel with square sails attached to yards hanging obliquely to the mast. [from Middle English *lugge*, pole]

lughole *noun colloq.* the ear.

lugubrious /lʊˈɡuːbrɪəs/ *adj.* sad and gloomy; mournful. [from Latin *lugere*, to mourn]

lugworm *noun* a worm which lives in the sand on a seashore, often used as bait.

lukewarm *adj.* **1** moderately warm. **2** *said of interest, support, etc* not enthusiastic; indifferent. [from Middle English *luke*, tepid + *warme*, warm]

▣ TEPID. **2** half-hearted, unenthusiastic, cool, indifferent, uninterested, unresponsive, apathetic.

lukewarmly *adv.* without enthusiasm; indifferently: *they responded lukewarmly to our suggestions.*

lull — *verb* **1** to make calm or quiet. **2** *intrans.* to become calm or quiet. **3** to deceive (someone) into feeling secure and not suspicious. — *noun* a period of calm and quiet. [from Middle English *lullen*, imitative]

▣ *verb* **1** soothe, calm, hush, quiet, quieten down, still, quell, subdue, pacify. *noun* calm, tranquillity, peace, quiet, hush, stillness, pause, *colloq.* let-up.
▣ *verb* **1** agitate. *noun* agitation.

lullaby *noun* (PL. **lullabies**) a soothing song to lull children to sleep.

lumbago /lʌmˈbeɪɡoʊ/ *noun Medicine* chronic pain in the lower (lumbar) region of the back, which is usually caused by a strained muscle or ligament, arthritis, a slipped disc, or a trapped nerve. [from Latin *lumbago*, from *lumbus*, loin]

lumbar *adj.* relating to the lower part of the back between the lowest ribs and the pelvis. [from Latin *lumbus*, loin]

lumbar puncture *Medicine* the insertion of a needle into the lower (lumbar) region of the spine, either to remove cerebrospinal fluid (eg to diagnose a disease or disorder of the nervous system), or to inject a drug (eg an anaesthetic).

lumber¹ — *noun* **1** useless and disused articles of furniture, etc which have been stored away. **2** *North Amer.* timber, especially when partly cut up ready for use. — *verb* **1** (**lumber someone with something**) *colloq.* to burden (someone) with an unwanted or difficult responsibility or task. **2** to fill with lumber or other useless items. **3** *intrans., esp. North Amer.* to fell trees and saw the wood into timber for transporting. [perhaps from LUMBER²]

▣ *noun* **1** clutter, jumble, rubbish, junk, bits and pieces, odds and ends.

lumber² *verb intrans.* (**lumbered, lumbering**) to move about heavily and clumsily. [from Middle English *lomeren*]

▣ clump, stump, plod, shamble, shuffle.

lumbering *adj.* moving about awkwardly and clumsily.
lumberjack *noun* a person employed to fell, saw up, and move trees.

lumen *noun* (PL. **lumina, lumens**) **1** *Physics* (SYMBOL lm) the SI unit of luminous flux, defined as the amount of light emitted by a point source of intensity one candela within a solid angle of one steradian. **2** *Biol.* in living organisms, the space enclosed by the walls of a vessel or tubular organ, eg within a blood vessel or intestine. [from Latin *lumen*, light]

luminaire *noun* **1** the British Standards Institution term for any sort of electric-light fitting. **2** a general term for any artificial light source (with its mountings and controls) used in photography and video production, such as flood lights, directional spot lights, etc. [from French]

luminance *Physics noun* **1** (SYMBOL L) the measure of brightness of a surface, measured in candela per square centimetre of the surface radiating normally. **2** the component controlling the brightness of a colour television picture; its point-to-point image brightness, as distinct from its colour. [from Latin *lumen, -inis*, light]

luminary — *noun* (PL. **luminaries**) **1** a famous or prominent member of a group. **2** a person considered as an expert or authority, and therefore able to enlighten or instruct others: *one of the luminaries of the British theatre.* **3** *literary* a source of light, such as the sun or moon. — *adj.* of or relating to light or enlightenment. [from Latin *luminaria*, lamp]

luminescence *noun Physics* the emission of light by a substance, usually a solid, in the absence of a rise in temperature. It is caused when electrons in the solid return to a lower energy state (ground state) after having been raised (excited) to a higher energy state, the surplus energy being emitted as light. The main types of luminescence are fluorescence and phosphorescence. [from Latin *lumen*, light]

luminescent *adj.* giving out light by luminescence.

luminosity *noun* **1** the property of emitting light. **2** *Astron.* the brightness of a celestial object, eg a star, which is influenced by its surface area and temperature, and is equal to the total energy radiated per unit time.

luminous *adj.* **1** full of or giving out light. **2** giving out light in the dark; phosphorescent. [from Latin *lumen*, light]

▣ **1** illuminated, lit, bright, radiant, shining, glowing, luminescent, fluorescent, brilliant.

luminous intensity *Physics* the amount of visible light capable of causing illumination that is emitted from a point source per unit solid angle. It is independent of the distance from the source. The SI unit of luminous intensity is the candela.

luminously *adv.* in a luminous way; so as to give out light.

lump¹ — *noun* **1** a small solid shapeless mass. **2** a swelling or tumour. **3** a feeling of tightening or swelling, especially in the throat. **4** the total number of things taken as a single whole. **5** a considerable quantity or heap. **6** a heavy dull or awkward person. **7** *Brit.* (**the lump**) self-employed casual workers especially in the building trade, paid in lump sums to evade tax. — *verb* **1** *trans., intrans.* to form or collect into a lump. **2** *trans.* (**lump something together**) to treat or consider as a single whole, especially without good reason. [from Middle English *lumpe*]

. . . .

⊟ *noun* **1** mass, cluster, clump, bunch, ball, piece, chunk, cake, nugget, hunk, wedge. **2** swelling, bulge, bump, protuberance, protrusion, growth, tumour. *verb* **1** collect, gather, cluster, combine, coalesce, consolidate.

. . . .

lump [2] *verb colloq.* to accept or put up with: *like it or lump it.*

lumpectomy *noun* (PL. **lumpectomies**) the surgical removal of a lump, especially a cancerous tumour, from the breast.

lumpfish or **lumpsucker** *noun* a heavy-bodied fish widespread in the N Atlantic and Arctic Oceans, up to 60cm in length, which has a rounded body bearing rows of spiny plates, and a large sucker on the underside of the body.

lumpily *adv.* in a lumpy way; with lumps.

lumpiness *noun* being lumpy; a lumpy quality.

lumpish *adj.*, *said of a person* heavy, dull, or awkward.

lump sugar sugar in small lumps or cubes.

lump sum a large single payment instead of several smaller ones spread out over a period of time.

lumpy *adj.* (**lumpier**, **lumpiest**) full of lumps.

lunacy *noun* (PL. **lunacies**) **1** insanity. **2** great foolishness or stupidity.

. . . .

⊟ MADNESS, CRAZINESS, INSANITY. **1** derangement, mania. **2** foolishness, folly, stupidity, absurdity, idiocy, imbecility. ⊟ **1** sanity.

. . . .

lunar *adj.* **1** resembling the moon. **2** relating to or caused by the moon. **3** for use on the surface of the moon or in connection with travel to the moon: *lunar vehicle*. [from Latin *luna*, moon]

lunate *adj.* crescent-shaped. [from Latin *luna*, moon]

lunatic — *adj.* **1** insane. **2** foolish, stupid, or wildly eccentric. — *noun* an insane or highly eccentric person; (more loosely) a foolish person. [from Latin *lunaticus*, moonstruck, from *luna*, moon, from the belief that intermittent insanity was caused by the phases of the moon]

. . . .

⊟ *adj.* MAD, CRAZY, INSANE. **1** deranged, psychotic, irrational. **2** foolish, stupid, senseless, absurd, idiotic, imbecilic. *noun* maniac, madman, psychopath, *colloq.* loony, nutcase, *colloq.* nutter, idiot, imbecile. ⊟ *adj.* **1** sane. **2** sensible.

. . . .

lunatic asylum *Hist.* a home or hospital for people regarded as insane.

lunatic fringe the most extreme, fanatical, or eccentric members of any group.

lunch — *noun* a meal eaten in the middle of the day. — *verb intrans.* to eat lunch. [a shortening of LUNCHEON]

luncheon *noun* a lunch, especially a formal one. [from Middle English *noneschench*, from *none*, noon + *schench*, drink]

luncheon meat a type of pre-cooked meat, processed and mixed with cereal, usually bought tinned and served cold.

luncheon voucher *Brit.* a voucher of a specified value given to employees by their employers and used to pay for lunches at restaurants and shops.

lunchtime *noun* the time set aside for lunch.

lung *noun* **1** in the chest cavity of air-breathing vertebrates, a large spongy respiratory organ, usually one of a pair, which removes carbon dioxide from the blood and replaces it with oxygen. **2** a simple respiratory organ found in some terrestrial molluscs, eg slugs and snails. [from Anglo-Saxon *lungen*]

lunge — *noun* **1** a sudden plunge forwards. **2** *Fencing* a sudden thrust with a sword. — *verb intrans.* to make a sud-

den strong or thrusting movement forwards, (*Fencing*) with a sword in one's hand. [from French *allonger*, to lengthen]

. . . .

⊟ *noun* **1** plunge, dive, charge, pounce, leap, spring. **2** thrust, stab, jab, pass. *verb* thrust, jab, stab, poke, plunge, dive, charge, pounce, leap, spring.

. . . .

lungfish *noun* a fish that has a lung as well as gills.

lupin *noun* a garden plant with long spikes of brightly coloured flowers. [from Latin *lupinus*, wolfish]

lupine *adj.* relating to or like a wolf. [from Latin *lupinus*, from *lupus*, wolf]

lupus *noun* a skin disease characterized by the formation of ulcers and lesions. [from Latin *lupus*, wolf; it is so called because it eats away the skin]

lurch [1] — *verb intrans.* to move or stagger unsteadily, especially rolling slightly to one side. — *noun* a sudden roll to one side.

. . . .

⊟ *verb* roll, rock, sway, pitch, list, stagger, reel.

. . . .

lurch [2] — **leave someone in the lurch** *colloq.* to leave them in a difficult situation and without help. [from Old French *lourche*, a game like backgammon]

lurcher *noun Brit.* a cross-bred dog, usually a cross between a sheepdog or a golden retriever and a greyhound, used for hunting. [from Middle English *lorchen*, to lurk]

lure — *verb trans.* (**lure someone away** or **into something**) to tempt, attract, or entice (someone), often by offering some reward. — *noun* **1** a person or thing which tempts, attracts, or entices. **2** (**the lure of something**) its attractive or tempting qualities: *the lure of the chase.* **3** *Angling* a metal or plastic bait with hooks attached. **4** a bunch of feathers to which meat may be attached, used by falconers to recall a hawk. [from Old French *luere*, bait]

. . . .

⊟ *verb* **1** tempt, entice, attract, draw, allure, seduce, lead on, ensnare. *noun* **1** temptation, enticement, attraction, bait, inducement, incentive.

. . . .

lurid *adj.* **1** glaringly bright: *lurid colours.* **2** horrifying or sensational: *lurid details.* **3** pale or wan. [from Latin *luridus*, pale yellow, wan]

. . . .

⊟ **1** garish, glaring, loud, vivid, bright. **2** sensational, shocking, horrifying, macabre, gruesome, grisly, gory, graphic.

. . . .

lurk *verb intrans.* **1** to lie in wait, especially in ambush, with some sinister purpose in mind. **2** to linger unseen or furtively; to be latent: *a lurking suspicion.* [from Middle English *lurken*]

. . . .

⊟ **1** skulk, prowl, lie in wait, crouch, lie low, hide.

. . . .

luscious *adj.* **1** richly sweet; delicious. **2** attractive in a voluptuous way. [from Middle English *lucius*, perhaps a variant of DELICIOUS]

. . . .

⊟ **1** delicious, appetizing, mouth-watering, tasty, sweet, savoury, juicy, succulent.

. . . .

lush [1] *adj.* **1** *said of grass or foliage, etc* green and growing abundantly. **2** luxurious. [from Middle English *lusch*, slack]

. . . .

⊟ RICH. **1** green, verdant, flourishing, luxuriant, abundant, prolific. **2** luxurious, sumptuous, opulent, ornate, plush.

. . . .

lush [2] *noun North Amer. slang* a drunkard or alcoholic. [perhaps from LUSH [1]]

lust — *noun* **1** strong sexual desire. **2** any strong desire; greed. **3** enthusiasm; relish: *a lust for life*. — *verb intrans.* **1** (**lust after** or **for someone**) to have a strong, especially sexual, desire for (someone). **2** (**lust after** or **for something**) to have a strong desire or need for (something). [from Anglo-Saxon *lust*, desire, appetite]

🔁 *noun* **1** libido, lechery, licentiousness, lewdness. **2** desire, craving, yearning, longing, appetite, hunger, thirst, greed, covetousness. *verb* DESIRE, WANT. **2** need, crave, yearn for, long for, hunger for, thirst for.

lustful *adj.* having or showing strong sexual desire; characterized by lust.

lustily *adv.* with a lusty or vigorously loud manner.

lustiness *noun* a lusty or loud state or quality.

lustre /ˈlʌstə(r)/ *noun* **1** the shiny appearance of a surface in reflected light. **2** shine, brightness, or gloss. **3** splendour and glory, on account of beauty or accomplishments, etc. **4** a thin metallic glaze for pottery. [from Latin *lustrare*, to light up]

🔁 **2** shine, sheen, gloss, gleam, glint, glitter, sparkle, brightness, radiance, brilliance, resplendence. **3** splendour, glory, honour, prestige, illustriousness.

lustrous *adj.* having a lustre; bright and shining.

lusty *adj.* (**lustier, lustiest**) **1** vigorous or loud: *a baby's lusty cries*. **2** strong and healthy.

🔁 VIGOROUS, ENERGETIC, STRONG, POWERFUL. **2** robust, sturdy, strapping, rugged, hale, hearty, healthy, fit.

lute *noun* a medieval and Renaissance stringed instrument with a pear-shaped body and a long neck. [from Arabic *al ud*]

luteinizing hormone *Physiol.* (ABBREV. **LH**) a hormone secreted by the pituitary gland in vertebrates, which stimulates ovulation and the formation of the corpus luteum in females, and the secretion of testosterone by the testes in males. [from Latin *luteum*, eggyolk]

lutenist *noun* a person who plays the lute.

lutetium /luːˈtiːʃəm/ *noun Chem.* (SYMBOL **Lu**, ATOMIC NUMBER **71**) a very rare soft silvery metal, belonging to the lanthanide series, that is usually obtained by the processing of other metals. It is used as a catalyst and in nuclear technology. [from Latin *Lutetia*, Paris, where it was discovered in 1907]

Lutheran — *noun* a follower of the German Protestant reformer Martin Luther, or a member of the Lutheran Church based on his teaching. — *adj.* relating to Martin Luther or his teaching.

luvvy *noun colloq.* (PL. **luvvies**) an actor or other member of the entertainment industry, especially when regarded as affectionate or camp. [respelling of LOVE]

lux *noun Physics* the SI unit of illumination, equal to one lumen per square metre. [from Latin *lux*, light]

luxe see DE LUXE.

luxuriance *noun* being luxuriant; lushness of vegetation.

luxuriant *adj.* **1** *said of plants, etc* growing abundantly; lush. **2** very elaborate; extravagant; flowery. [from Latin *luxuria*, luxury]

luxuriate *verb intrans.* **1** (**luxuriate in something**) to enjoy it greatly or revel in it. **2** to live in great comfort or luxury. **3** to grow richly or abundantly. [from Latin *luxuria*, luxury]

luxurious *adj.* **1** supplied or furnished with luxuries. **2** enjoying or providing luxury. [from Latin *luxuriosus*, from *luxus*, excess]

🔁 LUXURY, DE LUXE, PLUSH, EXPENSIVE, COSTLY. **2** sumptuous, opulent, magnificent, splendid, lavish, self-indulgent, pampered.

🔁 AUSTERE, SPARTAN.

luxuriously *adv.* in a luxurious way; with luxury.

luxury *noun* (PL. **luxuries**) **1** expensive, rich, extremely comfortable surroundings and possessions. **2** habitual indulgence in or enjoyment of luxurious surroundings. **3** something that is pleasant and enjoyable but not essential. **4** (*attributive*) relating to or providing luxury: *luxury hotels*. [from Latin *luxuria*, from *luxus*, excess]

🔁 **1** sumptuousness, opulence, affluence, richness, splendour, magnificence. **2** indulgence, gratification, comfort, pleasure, hedonism, extravagance. **3** comfort, extravagance.

🔁 **1, 2** austerity.

LV *abbrev.* luncheon voucher.

Lw *symbol Chem.* formerly used for lawrencium (now generally replaced by *Lr*).

-ly an element used: **1** to form adverbs: *cleverly/hopefully*. **2** to form adverbs and adjectives with the sense of 'at intervals of': *daily*. **3** to form adjectives with the sense 'in the manner of, like': *brotherly*. [from Anglo-Saxon forms]

lycanthropy *noun Relig.* in popular superstition, the power of changing from human shape into that of an animal, usually the most dangerous beast of the area. Also, a kind of madness, in which the patient has fantasies of being a wolf. [from Greek *lykos*, wolf + *anthropos*, man]

lyceum /laɪˈsɪəm/ *noun* **1** the garden in Athens where Aristotle taught. **2** a place or building devoted to teaching, especially literature and philosophy. [from Greek *Lykeion*, from *lykeios*, an epithet of Apollo. Apollo's temple stood near the Lyceum and gave it its name]

lychee /ˈlaɪˈtʃiː/ *noun* a small fruit with sweet, white, juicy flesh, originally from China. [from Chinese *lichi*]

lychgate same as LICHGATE.

Lycra /ˈlaɪkrə/ *noun trademark* fabric made from a lightweight synthetic elastomeric fibre, often used to make skintight clothing.

lye *noun* **1** a caustic solution made by passing water through wood ash. **2** a strong solution of sodium or potassium hydroxide. [from Anglo-Saxon *leag*]

lying see LIE[1], LIE[2].

lymph *noun* in animals, a colourless fluid, derived from blood, that bathes all the tissues, cleansing them of cellular debris and bacteria. It contains lymphocytes and antibodies which prevent the spread of infection, and it drains into the vessels of the lymphatic system. [from Latin *lympha*, water]

lymphatic *adj.* **1** relating to or carrying lymph. **2** *said of a person* slow and lethargic.

lymphatic system the network of vessels that carries lymph throughout the body.

lymph node or **lymph gland** *Anat.* one of a number of small rounded bodies found in the lymphatic system. It produces antibodies in immune responses, and filters bacteria and foreign bodies from the lymph before it rejoins the bloodstream, so preventing the spread of infection. There are large clusters of lymph nodes in the neck, armpit, and groin of the human body.

lymphocyte *noun Medicine* a type of white blood cell with a dense nucleus and clear cytoplasm, present in large numbers in lymphatic tissues such as the lymph nodes and spleen, and involved in immune responses in the body, such as the production of antibodies.

lymphoma *noun Medicine* a tumour of the lymph nodes, especially a malignant one.

lynch *verb*, *said of a body of people* to condemn and put to death, usually by hanging, without a legal trial. [named after William Lynch (1742–1820), who presided over self-instituted tribunals in Virginia, USA]

lynching *noun* the activity of people who lynch others; an occurrence of this.

lynx *noun* any of several bobtailed members of the cat family (Felidae), found in Europe, Asia, and N America, especially in pine forests, and having yellowish-grey or reddish fur, long legs with wide paws, a short stubby tail with a black tip, tufted ears, and a ruff of fur around the face. [from Greek *lynx*]

lynx-eyed *adj.* sharp-sighted.

lyophilic *adj. Chem.* denoting a substance that has an affinity for liquid solvents. [from Greek *lye*, separation + *phileein*, to love]

lyophobic *adj. Chem.* describing a substance that tends to repel liquid solvents.

lyre *noun* a U-shaped harp-like instrument plucked with a plectrum. It was used, especially in ancient Greece, to accompany poetry. [from Greek *lyra*]

lyre-bird *noun* either of two Australian pheasant-like birds, the male of which has lyre-shaped tail feathers displayed during courtship.

lyric — *adj.* **1** *said of poems or poets* expressing personal, private, or individual emotions. **2** having the form of a song; meant to be sung, originally to the lyre. — *noun* **1** a short lyric poem or a song. **2** (*usually* **lyrics**) the words of a song. [from Greek *lyrikos*, from *lyra*, lyre]

lyrical *adj.* **1** lyric; song-like. **2** full of enthusiastic praise.

lyrically *adv.* in a lyrical or song-like way.

lyricism *noun* **1** the state or quality of being lyrical. **2** a pouring out of emotions.

lyricist *noun* **1** a person who writes the words to songs. **2** a lyric poet.

lysergic acid diethylamide see LSD.

lysine /ˈlaɪsiːn/ *noun Biochem.* an essential amino acid that is found in proteins. [from Greek *lysis*, dissolution]

lysis *noun Biol.* any process that causes the destruction of a living cell by the disruption of the cell membrane and release of the cell contents. It may occur naturally in the case of damaged or worn out cells, or it may be caused by an antibody or bacterial toxin. [from Greek *lysis*]

lysosome /ˈlaɪsəsoʊm/ *noun Biol.* a specialized membrane-bound structure (organelle), found mainly in animal cells, that contains a range of digestive enzymes which can break down proteins and other biochemical compounds. Lysosomes play an important role in the destruction of foreign particles (eg bacteria), and the breakdown of damaged or worn out cells.

lysozyme /ˈlaɪsəzaɪm/ *noun Biochem.* an enzyme that breaks down bacterial cell walls and is present in many body fluids and secretions, including saliva, tears, and mucus, as well as egg white. [from Greek *lysis*, dissolution]

M

M¹ or **m** *noun* (PL. **Ms, M's, m's**) the thirteenth letter of the English alphabet.

M² *abbrev.* **1** Majesty. **2** mark (German currency). **3** Master. **4** (French) Monsieur. **5** Motorway.

M³ *symbol* the Roman numeral for 1000.

m *abbrev.* **1** male. **2** married. **3** masculine. **4** *meridiem* (Latin), noon. **5** metre. **6** mile. **7** million. **8** minute. **9** month.

'm *contr.* am: *I'm going.*

MA *abbrev.* **1** Massachusetts. **2** Master of Arts.

ma *noun colloq.* a mother.

ma'am /ma:m/ *noun* madam, used as a polite form of address, eg to female royalty.

MAC *abbrev.* Multiplex Analogue Components.

mac *noun colloq.* a mackintosh.

macabre /mə'kɑːbrə/ *adj.* **1** dealing with death. **2** ghastly or horrific. [from French *macabre*]
. . . .
▣ **2** gruesome, grisly, grim, ghastly, horrible, horrific, frightful, dreadful, ghostly, eerie.
. . . .

macadam *noun* **1** a road-making material consisting of layers of compacted broken stones, usually bound with tar. **2** a road surface made with this. See also TARMACADAM. [from John McAdam, Scottish engineer]

macadamize or **macadamise** *verb* to build or cover (a road) with macadam.

macaque /mə'kɑːk/ *noun* any of various short-tailed or tailless monkeys of Asia and Africa, with large cheek-pouches. [from French *macaque*, from Portuguese *macaco*, monkey]

macaroni *noun* (PL. **macaronis, macaronies**) **1** pasta in the form of short tubes. **2** in 18c Britain, a dandy. [from Italian *maccaroni*]

macaroon *noun* a sweet cake or biscuit made with sugar, eggs, and crushed almonds or coconut. [from French *macaron*]

macaw /mə'kɔː/ *noun* any of numerous large brilliantly coloured parrots with long tails and strong beaks, found mainly in the tropical forests of Central and S America. [from Portuguese *macao*]

mace¹ *noun* **1** a heavy club, usually with a spiked metal head, used as a weapon in medieval times. **2** a ceremonial rod carried as a symbol of authority. [from Old French *mace*]

mace² *noun* a spice ground from the dried fleshy covering around the nutmeg seed. [from Middle English *macis*]

macerate *verb technical* **1** *intrans., trans.* to break up or cause to break up or become soft by soaking. **2** *intrans.* to waste away as a result of fasting. [from Latin *macerare*, to soak]

maceration *noun* the act or process of macerating or being macerated.

Mach /mak/ *noun* (*also* **Mach number**) *Aeron.* the ratio of the speed of an object such as an aircraft to the speed of sound in the same medium, eg Mach 2 is twice the speed of sound. Speeds above Mach 1 are *supersonic*, and speeds above Mach 5 are *hypersonic*. [named after the 19c Austrian physicist and philosopher Ernst Mach]

machete /mə'ʃɛtɪ/ *noun* a long, heavy, broad-bladed knife used as a weapon or cutting tool, especially in S America and the W Indies. [from Spanish *machete*]

Machiavellian /makɪə'vɛlɪən/ *adj.* politically cunning and unscrupulous, seeking power or advantage at any price; amoral and opportunist. [from the Italian politician and political theorist Niccolò Machiavelli (1469–1527)]

Machiavellianism /makɪə'vɛlɪənɪzm/ *noun* **1** the principles described by Niccolò Machiavelli. **2** political cunning and unscrupulousness.

machinate *verb intrans.* to plot or scheme, usually for doing harm.

machination *noun* (*usually* **machinations**) *formal* a crafty scheme or plot, usually sinister. [from Latin *machinari*, from Greek *mechane*, contrivance]
. . . .
▣ scheme, intrigue, plot, device, manoeuvre, stratagem, tactic, wile, ruse.
. . . .

machine — *noun* **1** a device with moving parts, and usually powered, designed to perform a particular task. **2** a group of people or institutions, or a network of equipment, under a central control: *the party's political machine*. **3** *colloq.* a motor vehicle, especially a motorcycle. **4** *colloq.* a person with no initiative, capable only of following orders; a tireless or mechanically efficient worker. — *verb* **1** to make, shape, cut, etc with a machine. **2** to stitch with a sewing-machine. [from Latin *machina*, from Greek *mechane*, contrivance]
. . . .
▣ *noun* **1, 4** robot, automaton. **1** instrument, device, contrivance, tool, mechanism, engine, apparatus, appliance. **2** system, organization, agency, structure.
. . . .

machine code or **machine language** a numerical (eg binary) code used for writing instructions in a form which a computer can understand.

machine gun — *noun* any of various portable guns mounted on stands, that fire a continuous stream of bullets. — *verb* to shoot with a machine gun.

machinery *noun* **1** machines in general. **2** the working or moving parts of a machine. **3** the combination of processes, systems or people that keeps anything working.
. . . .
▣ **1** instruments, apparatus, equipment, tackle, gear, tools. **2** mechanism, *colloq.* works. **3** organization, channels, structure, system, procedure.
. . . .

machine tool any stationary power-driven machine that is used to shape or finish metal, wood, or plastic parts by cutting, planing, drilling, polishing, etc.

machinist *noun* **1** a person who operates a machine. **2** a person who makes or repairs machines.

machismo /mə'tʃɪzmoʊ/ *noun* exaggerated or aggressively asserted manliness. [from Spanish *machismo*, from *macho*, male]

macho /'matʃoʊ/ — *adj.* exaggeratedly or aggressively manly. — *noun* (PL. **machos**) **1** *colloq.* a man of this type. **2** machismo. [from Spanish *macho*, male]

macintosh same as MACINTOSH.

mack *noun colloq.* a mackintosh.

mackerel *noun* (PL. **mackerels, mackerel**) **1** a food fish belonging to the same family as the tuna and bonito, with a streamlined body that is blue-green above and silvery below. **2** the oily edible flesh of this fish. [from Old French *maquerel*]

mackerel sky *Geol.* a sky that is patterned with cirrocumulus (thin white ripples of cloud) or altocumulus (wavy rounded masses of cloud), so called because it resembles the markings on a mackerel.

mackintosh *noun* **1** a waterproof raincoat. **2** material waterproofed with rubber. [named after Charles Macintosh (1766–1843), a Scottish chemist who patented the waterproofing process]

macramé /məˈkrɑːmeɪ/ *noun* **1** the art of weaving and knotting string or coarse thread into patterns. **2** articles produced in this way. [from Turkish *maqrama*, towel]

macro *noun* (PL. **macros**) *Comput.* (*also* **macro-instruction**) a single instruction that brings a set of instructions into operation.

macro- or **macr-** *combining form* forming words meaning: **1** large, long, or large-scale: *macroeconomics*. **2** *Pathol.* abnormally large or overdeveloped: *macrocephaly*. [from Greek *makros*, long, great]

macrobiotic *adj.* **1** relating to macrobiotics. **2** relating to long life. **3** prolonging life. **4** long-lived.

macrobiotics *sing. noun* the science of devising diets using whole grains and organically-grown fruit and vegetables; the practice of following such a diet, thought to prolong life. [from MACRO- + Greek *biotos*, life]

macrocephaly /makroʊˈsefəlɪ/ *noun Pathol.* the condition of having a relatively large head. [from MACRO- + Greek *kephale*, head]

macrocosm *noun* **1** (**the macrocosm**) the universe as a whole. **2** any large or complex system or structure made up of similar smaller systems or structures. [from MACRO- + Greek *kosmos*, world]

macroeconomics *sing. noun* the study of economics on a large scale or of large economic units, especially the nation as a whole, and taking into account aspects such as trade, national income, output, and exchange rates.

macro-instruction see MACRO-.

macromolecule *noun Chem.* a very large molecule, usually consisting of a large number of relatively simple structural units, eg proteins, DNA, natural and synthetic polymers such as rubber and plastics.

macron *noun* a mark (‾) placed over a letter to show it is a long vowel. See also BREVE. [from Greek *makros*, long or great]

macrophotography *noun* also known as *photomacrography*: the photography of small objects or details in extreme close-up using normal camera lenses, resulting in an image size as large or larger than the actual subject.

macroscopic *adj.* **1** large enough to be seen by the naked eye. **2** considered in terms of large units or elements.

macula *noun* (PL. **maculae**) *technical* a spot or blemish, eg a freckle on the skin, a sunspot on the Sun. [from Latin *macula*]

mad *adj.* (**madder, maddest**) **1** mentally disturbed; insane. **2** foolish or senseless; extravagantly carefree. **3** *colloq.* (*often* **mad at** or **with someone**) very angry. **4** *colloq.* (**mad about something**) extremely enthusiastic; fanatical; infatuated. **5** marked by extreme confusion, haste, or excitement: *a mad dash for the door.* **6** *said of a dog* infected with rabies. — **like mad** *colloq.* frantically; very energetically. [from Anglo-Saxon *gemæded*, made insane]

▭ **1** crazy, insane, lunatic, unbalanced, psychotic, deranged, demented, out of one's mind, *slang* loony, *slang* bonkers. **2** foolish, senseless, *colloq.* nutty, irrational, illogical, unreasonable, absurd, preposterous, wild, hotheaded, extravagant, devil-may-care. **3** angry, furious, enraged, infuriated, incensed. **4** crazy about, wild about, fanatical

about, enthusiastic about, infatuated with. **5** frantic, hectic, chaotic, confused.

▣ **1** sane. **2** sensible. **3** calm. **4** apathetic.

madam *noun* (PL. **madams, mesdames** in sense I) **1** a polite form of address to a woman. **2** a form of address to a woman in authority, often prefixed to an official title: *Madam Chairman.* **3** *colloq.* an arrogant or spoiled girl or young woman. **4** a woman who manages a brothel. [see MADAME]

Madame /ˈmadəm, məˈdɑːm/ *noun* (PL. **Mesdames**) (ABBREV. **Mme**) a title equivalent to Mrs, used especially of a French or French-speaking (usually married) woman. [from French, originally *ma*, my + *dame*, lady]

madcap — *adj.* foolishly impulsive or reckless. — *noun* a foolishly impulsive person.

mad cow disease *colloq.* same as BSE.

madden *verb* (**maddened, maddening**) to make mad, especially to enrage.

▭ anger, enrage, infuriate, incense, exasperate, provoke, annoy, irritate.

▣ calm, pacify.

maddening *adj.* infuriating; extremely annoying.

madder *noun* **1** a Eurasian herbaceous plant with yellow flowers and a red root; any of various related plants. **2** a dark red dye, originally made from the root of this plant. [from Anglo-Saxon *mæddre* or *mædere*]

made past tense and past participle of MAKE. — *adj.* **1** artificially produced. **2** composed of various ingredients put together: *a made dish.* — **have it made** *colloq.* to enjoy or be assured of complete success or happiness. **made for someone** or **something** ideally suited to or for them.

-made *combining form* forming words meaning 'produced, constructed, or formed in the stated way': *handmade*.

Madeira /məˈdɪərə/ *noun* a strong white dessert wine made on the island of Madeira.

Madeira cake a kind of rich sponge cake.

made-up *adj.* **1** wearing make-up. **2** not true; invented. **3** *slang* extremely pleased.

▭ **2** false, untrue, fabricated, invented, fictitious, imaginary, fanciful, pretend, pretended, make-believe.

▣ **2** factual.

madhouse *noun* **1** *old use* a mental hospital. **2** *colloq.* a place of great confusion and noise.

madly *adv.* **1** in a mad way. **2** *colloq.* passionately: *I love you madly.*

▭ **1** insanely, dementedly, hysterically, wildly, excitedly, frantically, furiously, recklessly, violently, energetically, rapidly, hastily, hurriedly. **2** passionately, intensely, extremely, exceedingly, fervently, devotedly.

madman or **madwoman** *noun* an insane or foolish man or woman.

▭ lunatic, psychotic, psychopath, maniac, *colloq.* nutcase, *colloq.* nutter, *slang* loony.

madness *noun* **1** insanity. **2** extreme anger, excitement, or silliness.

▭ **1** insanity, lunacy, dementia, psychosis, mania, derangement. **2** fury, rage, raving, frenzy, hysteria, folly, craziness, absurdity, irrationality.

Madonna *noun* **1** (**the Madonna**) a title for the Virgin Mary, the mother of Christ. **2** a picture or statue of the Virgin Mary. [from Italian, originally *ma donna*, my lady]

madrigal *noun* a 16c or 17c unaccompanied song with different parts sung together, typically about love or nature. [from Italian *madrigale*]

maelstrom /'meɪlstrɒm/ *noun* **1** a violent whirlpool. **2** *literary* a place or state of uncontrollable confusion, especially one to which one is inevitably drawn. [from Dutch (now *maalstroom*), whirlpool]

maenad /'miːnad/ *noun* **1** *Mythol.* a female participant in orgies and rites in honour of Bacchus or Dionysus, the god of wine. **2** *literary* a woman who behaves in a frenzied or uncontrolled way. [from Greek *mainas*, raving]

maenadic *adj.* **1** relating to drinking or drunken revels. **2** furious.

maestro /'maɪstroʊ/ *noun* (PL. **maestros, maestri**) *often used as a title* a man regarded as the master of an art, especially a distinguished musical composer, performer, or teacher. [from Italian *maestro*, master]

Mae West /meɪ west/ an inflatable life-jacket worn by pilots. [named after Mae West, a US actress famous for her large bust]

MAFF *abbrev.* Ministry of Agriculture, Fisheries, and Food.

Mafia *noun* **1** (**the Mafia**) a secret organization controlling numerous illegal activities, especially in Italy, Sicily, and the USA. **2** any group exerting a secret and powerful influence, especially one operating unscrupulously. [from Sicilian Italian *mafia*, hostility to the law]

Mafioso *noun* (PL. **Mafiosi**) a member of the Mafia.

mag *noun colloq.* a magazine or periodical.

magazine *noun* **1** a paperback periodical publication containing articles, stories, etc by various writers, usually heavily illustrated. **2** a regular broadcast presenting reports on a variety of subjects. **3** a metal container for several cartridges, used in some automatic firearms. **4** a storeroom for ammunition, explosives, etc. **5** a container from which photographic slides are automatically fed through a projector. [from Italian *magazzino*, from Arabic *makhzan*, storehouse]

⊟ **1** journal, periodical, paper, weekly, monthly, quarterly. **4** arsenal, storehouse, ammunition dump, depot, ordnance.

magenta /mə'dʒɛntə/ — *adj.* having a dark purplish-red colour. — *noun* this colour. [from *Magenta*, an Italian town and scene of a bloody battle in 1859]

maggot *noun* the worm-like larva of various flies, especially the housefly. [from Middle English *maddok* or *mathek*]

maggoty *adj.* full of maggots.

magi see MAGUS.

magic — *noun* **1** the supposed art or practice of using the power of supernatural forces to affect people, objects, and events. **2** the art or practice of performing entertaining illusions and conjuring tricks. **3** the quality of being wonderful, charming, or delightful. — *adj.* **1** of, used in, or using sorcery or conjuring. **2** *colloq.* excellent. — *verb* (**magicked, magicking**) (**magic something away, up,** etc) to produce, transform, or otherwise affect it using, or as if using, sorcery or conjuring. — **like magic 1** mysteriously. **2** suddenly and unexpectedly. **3** excellently. [from Greek *magike*]

⊟ *noun* **1, 3** enchantment. **1** sorcery, occultism, black art, witchcraft, spell. **2** conjuring, illusion, sleight of hand, trickery. **3** charm, fascination, glamour, allure, wonder. *adj.* **1** supernatural, occult, mysterious, demonic. **2** great, super, terrific, tremendous.

magical *adj.* **1** relating to the art or practice of magic. **2** utterly delightful or fascinating.

⊟ **2** delightful, enchanting, bewitching, charming, fascinating, spellbinding.

magically *adv.* in a magical way; delightfully.

magic bullet a drug which is capable of destroying bacteria, cancer cells, etc without adversely affecting the host.

magic carpet a mythical carpet that can carry people through the air.

magic eye a light-sensitive electric switch; a photoelectric cell.

magician *noun* **1** a performer of illusions; a conjurer. **2** a person with supernatural powers.

⊟ **1** conjurer, illusionist. **2** sorcerer, enchanter, wizard, witch, warlock, miracle-worker, wonder-worker.

magic lantern an early form of slide projector.

magic square a square filled with rows of figures so arranged that the sums of all the rows (vertical, horizontal, diagonal) will be the same.

magisterial *adj.* **1** of, or administered by, a magistrate. **2** authoritative; commanding; dictatorial. **3** of, or suitable to, a teacher, instructor or master. [from Latin *magister*, master]

magistracy *noun* (PL. **magistracies**) **1** the rank or position of a magistrate. **2** magistrates as a whole. [from Latin *magister*, master]

magistrate *noun* **1** a judge in a lower court of law dealing with minor offences; a justice of the peace. **2** any public official administering the law. [from Latin *magister*, master]

maglev /'maglɛv/ *noun* a high-speed transport system in which magnetism is used to keep an electrically powered train gliding above a track. [a shortening of *magnetic levitation*]

magma *noun* (PL. **magmas, magmata**) **1** *Geol.* hot molten rock material generated deep within the Earth's crust or mantle, and consisting of a mixture of silicates, water, and dissolved gases. On cooling it solidifies to form igneous rock. **2** a pasty or doughy mass. [from Greek *magma*, thick ointment]

magnanimity *noun* generosity of spirit.

⊟ generosity, nobility, benevolence, selflessness, unselfishness, charity, forbearance.

magnanimous *adj.* having or showing generosity of spirit. [from Latin *magnus*, great + *animus*, mind]

⊟ generous, liberal, benevolent, selfless, charitable, bighearted, kind, noble, unselfish, ungrudging, forgiving.
⊟ mean.

magnate *noun* a person of high rank or great power, especially in industry. [from Latin *magnas*, from *magnus*, great]

⊟ tycoon, captain of industry, industrialist, mogul, entrepreneur, plutocrat, baron, personage, notable.

magnesia /mag'niːzɪə/ *noun* **1** *Chem.* the common name for magnesium oxide (MgO), a white powder obtained from the mineral magnesite, used to line furnaces, and as a component of semiconductors, insulators, cosmetics, antacids, laxatives, and reflective coatings for optical instruments. **2** (*also* **milk of magnesia**) a suspension of magnesium hydroxide in water, used as an antacid. [from the name *Magnesia* in Asia Minor (modern Turkey)]

magnesite *noun* *Geol.* the mineral form of magnesium carbonate ($MgCO_3$), which occurs as compact white or grey masses, and is produced as a result of the alteration of magnesium-rich rocks by fluids. It is an important ore of magnesium, and is also used as a refractory for lining furnaces.

magnesium *noun* *Chem.* (SYMBOL **Mg**, ATOMIC NUMBER **12**) a reactive silvery-grey metal found in seawater and several minerals, eg dolomite, talc, and asbestos, that burns with a brilliant white flame when ignited. It is used in lightweight alloys for aircraft components, and in fireworks, flares, and batteries.

magnesium sulphate *Chem.* (FORMULA MgSO₄) a white soluble compound used for fireproofing cotton and silk, and in ceramics, cosmetics, fertilizers, and explosives. One of the hydrated crystalline forms, known as Epsom salts, is used in mineral waters and as a laxative.

magnet *noun* **1** a piece of metal, especially iron, with the power to attract and repel iron, and the tendency to point in an approximate north-to-south direction when freely suspended. **2** a person or thing that attracts. [from Greek *magnetis lithos*, Magnesian stone, from *Magnesia*, in Asia Minor]

magnetic *adj.* **1** of, having the powers of, or operating by means of a magnet or magnetism. **2** able to be made into a magnet. **3** extremely charming or attractive.

- 3 attractive, alluring, fascinating, charming, mesmerizing, seductive, irresistible, entrancing, captivating, gripping, absorbing, charismatic.
- 3 repellent, repulsive.

magnetically *adv.* in a magnetic way; like a magnet.

magnetic disk *Comput.* a flat circular sheet of material coated with a magnetic oxide, used to store programs and data.

magnetic field *Physics* the region of physical space surrounding a permanent magnet, electromagnetic wave, or current-carrying conductor, within which magnetic forces may be detected.

magnetic flux *Physics* a measure of the size of the magnetic field from the north pole to the south pole of a magnet, or around a current-carrying wire. The SI unit of magnetic flux is the weber.

magnetic induction *Physics* the production of magnetic properties in a previously unmagnetized material, eg as a result of stroking it with another magnet, or placing it in the electromagnetic field of a current-carrying conductor.

magnetic mine a mine detonated when it detects a magnetic field created by the presence of a large metal object, eg a ship.

magnetic north the direction in which a magnetic needle of a compass points, slightly east or west of true north.

magnetic pole 1 *Physics* either of two regions, usually at opposite ends of a magnet and referred to as north and south, from which the lines of force of a magnetic field appear to radiate. Like poles of two magnets repel each other, and unlike poles attract each other. **2** *Geol.* either of two points on the Earth's surface where the magnetic field is vertical, and to or from which a magnetized compass needle points. The magnetic poles do not coincide with the geographic poles, and their exact positions vary with time.

magnetic storm a sudden, severe disturbance of the earth's magnetic field, caused by streams of particles from the sun.

magnetic tape *Electron.* a medium consisting of narrow plastic ribbon coated with a magnetizable material such as iron oxide powder, which is used to record and store data in audio and video tape recorders and computers.

magnetism *noun* **1** the properties of attraction possessed by magnets, or the scientific study of these. **2** strong personal charm.

- ATTRACTION. **2** allure, fascination, charm, lure, appeal, drawing power, draw, pull, hypnotism, mesmerism, charisma, grip, magic, power, spell.

magnetite /ˈmagnətaɪt/ *noun Geol.* a shiny black mineral form of iron oxide (Fe₂O₃) that is an important ore of iron. It is strongly magnetic, and some forms of magnetite,

known as lodestone, are natural magnets. See also LODE-STONE.

magnetize or **magnetise** *verb* **1** to make magnetic. **2** to attract strongly.

magneto /magˈniːtoʊ/ *noun* (PL. **magnetos**) *Electr.* a simple electric generator consisting of a rotating magnet that induces an alternating current in a coil surrounding it, and is used to provide the spark in the ignition system of petrol engines that have no batteries, eg in lawn mowers, outboard motors, and some motor cycles. [short for *magnetoelectric generator*]

magnetosphere *noun* **1** *Astron.* the region of space surrounding the Earth that contains charged particles held around the Earth by its magnetic field. It extends about 100,000km towards the Sun and about one million km away from it, and contains the Van Allen belts. **2** a similar region around any other planet that has a magnetic field.

magnetron /ˈmagnətron/ *noun Physics* a device for generating microwaves, developed during the 1940s for use in radar transmitters, and now widely used in microwave ovens.

magnificat /magˈnɪfɪkat/ *noun* **1** (**Magnificat**) *Relig.* the Virgin Mary's hymn of praise to God, sung in services in certain branches of the Christian Church. **2** any song of praise. [from the opening word of the hymn in the Latin New Testament (Luke 1.46–55)]

magnification *noun* **1** a measure of the extent to which an image of an object produced by a lens or optical instrument is enlarged or reduced. **2** an appearance enlarged by a stated amount. [from Latin *magnificare*, to magnify]

magnificence *noun* being magnificent.

- grandeur, majesty, sumptuousness, gorgeousness, elegance, richness, opulence, glory, brilliance, excellence.

magnificent *adj.* **1** splendidly impressive in size or extent. **2** *colloq.* excellent; admirable. [from Latin *magnificens*, doing great things]

- SPLENDID, GRAND, GLORIOUS, GORGEOUS, BRILLIANT. **1** imposing, impressive, majestic, sumptuous, noble, elegant, rich. **2** excellent, superb, fine.
- 1 modest, humble, poor.

magnifier *noun* **1** an instrument which magnifies. **2** a person who magnifies, or who praises highly.

magnify *verb* (**magnifies, magnified**) **1** to cause to appear larger, eg using a microscope or telescope. **2** to exaggerate. [from Latin *magnus*, great + *facere*, to make]

- ENLARGE, AMPLIFY. **1** increase, expand, intensify, boost, enhance, greaten, heighten, deepen. **2** exaggerate, dramatize, build up, overemphasize, overplay, overstate, overdo, *colloq.* blow up.
- 2 belittle, play down.

magnifying glass a convex (especially hand-held) lens through which objects appear larger.

magniloquence *noun* grandeur or pomposity of style.

magniloquent *adj.* speaking or spoken in a grand or pompous style. [from Latin *magnus*, great + *loqui*, to speak]

magnitude *noun* **1** size, largeness or extent. **2** importance. **3** *Astron.* the degree of brightness of a star. [from Latin *magnitudo*, from *magnus*, great]

- 1 size, bulk, largeness, extent, expanse, dimensions, proportions, measure, amount, mass, quantity, volume, space, strength, amplitude. **2** importance, consequence, significance, weight, greatness, moment, intensity.

magnolia — *noun* **1** a tree or shrub with large sweet-smelling white or pink flowers; one of its flowers. **2** a pale pinkish-white colour. — *adj.* of the colour magnolia. [from the French botanist Pierre Magnol (1638–1715)]

magnum *noun* a wine bottle holding twice the normal amount, approximately 15 litres. [from Latin *magnum*, big]

magnum opus *literary* a great work of art or literature, especially the greatest produced by a particular artist or writer. [from Latin *magnum opus*, great work]

magpie *noun* **1** a black-and-white bird of the crow family, known for its chattering call and its habit of collecting shiny objects. **2** a person who hoards things, especially useless trinkets. **3** a chattering person. [from *Mag*, a diminutive of *Margaret* + *pie*]

magus /'meɪgəs/ *noun* (PL. **magi** /'meɪdʒaɪ/) **1** an ancient Persian priest. **2** an ancient sorcerer or astrologer. **3** (**Magus**) each of the three wise men from the East who brought gifts to the infant Jesus. [from Old Persian *magus*, magician]

Magyar — *noun* **1** a member of the predominant race of people in Hungary, also found in NW Siberia. **2** the Hungarian language. — *adj.* of the Magyars or their language.

maharajah or **maharaja** /mɑːhəˈrɑːdʒə/ *noun, also used as a title* an Indian prince, especially any of the former rulers of the states of India. [from Hindi, from Sanskrit *mahat*, great + *rajan*, king]

maharani or **maharanee** /mɑːhəˈrɑːnɪ/ *noun, also used as a title* **1** the wife or widow of a maharajah. **2** a woman of the same rank as a maharajah in her own right. [from Hindi, from Sanskrit *mahat*, great + *rani*, queen]

mahatma /məˈhɑːtmə/ *noun* a wise and holy Hindu leader. [from Hindi, from Sanskrit *mahat*, great + *atman*, soul]

mahi-mahi *noun* the dolphin fish, especially its flesh prepared as food. [from Hawaiian *mahi*, strong]

mah-jong or **mah-jongg** /mɑːˈdʒɒŋ/ *noun* an originally Chinese game for four players, played with small patterned tiles of wood or bone, with rules similar to rummy. [from Chinese dialect *mah-jong*, sparrows]

mahlstick or **maulstick** /'mɔːlstɪk/ *noun* a stick or rod, with a pad on one end, used by painters to steady the painting hand while executing delicate brushwork in their pictures. [from Dutch *malen*, to paint]

mahogany — *noun* (PL. **mahoganies**) **1** any of various tall evergreen trees found in tropical Africa and America, especially species of the genus *Swietenia*, grown commercially for timber. **2** the hard reddish-brown wood of this tree, used in furniture-making, cabinetwork, and boatbuilding. **3** the colour of the wood, a reddish-brown. — *adj.* **1** made from this wood. **2** reddish-brown.

mahout /mɑːˈhaʊt/ *noun* a person who drives, trains, and looks after elephants, especially in India. [from Hindi *mahaut*]

maid *noun* **1** a female servant. **2** *old use, literary* an unmarried woman. [short form of MAIDEN]

⊟ **1** servant, domestic, housemaid, kitchenmaid, chambermaid, maid of all work, *colloq.* skivvy.

maiden — *noun* **1** *old use, literary* a young unmarried woman. **2** *old use, literary* a virgin. **3** a horse that has never won a race. **4** *Cricket* a maiden over. — *adj.* **1** first ever: *maiden voyage.* **2** *literary* unused; fresh. **3** *said of a horse race* open to maidens only. [from Anglo-Saxon *mægden*]

⊟ *noun* **1** girl, lass, lassie, *old use, literary* damsel, miss, spinster.

maidenhair *noun* any of various tropical ferns with delicate fan-shaped leaves.

maidenhair tree same as GINKGO.

maidenhead *noun old use, literary* **1** virginity. **2** the hymen.

maidenhood *noun* the state or time of being a maiden.

maiden name a married woman's surname before her marriage.

maiden over *Cricket* an over from which no runs are scored.

maid of honour (PL. **maids of honour**) **1** an unmarried female servant of a queen or princess. **2** the principal bridesmaid at a wedding, if unmarried. See also MATRON OF HONOUR.

maidservant *noun old use* a female servant.

mail[1] — *noun* **1** the postal system. **2** letters, parcels, etc sent by post. **3** a single collection or delivery of letters, etc. **4** a vehicle carrying letters, etc. **5** messages sent by electronic mail. — *verb* **1** to send by post. **2** to send a message by electronic mail. [from Old French *male*, bag or trunk]

⊟ *noun* **2** post, letters, correspondence, packages, parcels, delivery. *verb* **1** post, send, dispatch, forward.

mail[2] *noun* flexible armour for the body, made of small linked metal rings. [from Old French *maille*, mesh]

mailbag *noun* a large strong bag in which mail is carried.

mailed *adj.* covered in or protected by mail, armoured.

mailing list a list of the people to whom an organization regularly sends information.

mailmerge *noun Comput.* **1** the process of producing a series of letters addressed to individuals by merging a file of names and addresses with a file containing the text of the letter. **2** a computer program which carries out this process.

mail order a system of buying and selling goods by post.

mail-order *adj.* bought or sold by mail order, or dealing with mail order.

mailshot — *noun* an unrequested item of post, especially a piece of advertising material. — *verb* to send unsolicited advertising material to (a person or organization).

maim *verb* to wound seriously, especially to disable or cripple. [from Old French *mahaignier*, to wound]

⊟ mutilate, wound, incapacitate, injure, disable, hurt, impair, cripple, lame.

main — *adj.* **1** most important; chief. **2** *literary* extreme; utmost: *main force.* — *noun* **1** (**mains**) the chief pipe or cable in a branching system. **2** (**mains**) the network by which power, water, etc is distributed. **3** *old use* the open sea: *the Spanish main.* **4** *old use* great strength, now especially in the phrase *with might and main.* — **in the main** mostly; on the whole. [from Anglo-Saxon *mægen*, strength, and Norse *meginn*, strong]

⊟ *adj.* **1** principal, chief, leading, first, foremost, predominant, pre-eminent, primary, prime, supreme, paramount, central, cardinal, outstanding, essential, critical, crucial, necessary, vital. *noun* **1** pipe, duct, conduit, channel, cable, line. **in the main** mainly, mostly, for the most part, as a rule, on the whole, by and large.

⊟ *adj.* **1** minor, unimportant, insignificant.

mainbrace *noun Naut.* the rope controlling the movement of a ship's mainsail.

main clause *Grammar* a clause which can stand alone as a sentence.

mainframe *noun* a large computer, to which many smaller computers can be linked, that is capable of handling very large amounts of data at high speed, and can usually run several programs simultaneously.

mainland *noun* (**the mainland**) a country's principal mass of land, as distinct from a nearby island or islands forming part of the same country.

mainline *verb trans., intrans. slang* to inject (a drug) into a principal vein, so that it has the quickest possible effect.

main line the principal railway line between two places.

mainly *adv.* for the most part; largely.

▣ primarily, principally, chiefly, especially, above all, overall, in the main, mostly, on the whole, for the most part, as a rule, generally, in general, largely.

mainsail *noun* the largest and lowest sail on a sailing ship.

mainspring *noun* **1** the chief spring in a watch or clock. **2** a chief motive, reason or cause.

mainstay *noun* **1** *Naut.* a rope stretching forward and down from the top of the principal mast of a sailing ship. **2** the chief support.

▣ **2** support, buttress, bulwark, linchpin, prop, pillar, backbone, foundation.

mainstream *noun* **1** the principal current of a river. **2** the chief trend or direction of development in an activity.

maintain *verb* **1** to continue; to keep in existence. **2** to keep in good condition. **3** to pay the expenses of; to support financially. **4** to continue to argue; to assert. [from Old French *maintenir*, from Latin *manu tenere*, to hold in the hand]

▣ **1, 2** keep (up). **1** carry on, continue, sustain, retain. **2** care for, conserve, look after, take care of, preserve. **3** support, finance, supply. **4** assert, affirm, claim, contend, declare, hold, state, insist on, believe in, fight for.
▣ **2** neglect. **4** deny.

maintenance *noun* **1** the process of keeping something in good condition. **2** money paid by one person to support another, as ordered by a court of law, eg following a divorce. See also ALIMONY. **3** the process of continuing something or keeping something in existence. [from Old French *maintenir*, from Latin *manu tenere*, to hold in the hand]

▣ **1** care, conservation, preservation, support, repairs, protection, upkeep, running. **2** keep, subsistence, living, livelihood, allowance, alimony. **3** continuation, continuance, perpetuation.
▣ **1, 3** neglect.

maisonette or **maisonnette** *noun* an apartment within a larger house or block, especially on two floors, usually with its own separate entrance. [from French, diminutive of *maison*, house]

maître d'hôtel (PL. **maîtres d'hôtel**) **1** a head waiter. **2** the manager of a hotel or restaurant. [French, = master of the hotel]

maize *noun* a cereal (*Zea mays*) belonging to the grass family (Gramineae), and the only cereal native to the New World. It is now cultivated mainly in the tropics and subtropics, although some modern strains are suitable for temperate regions. Also called SWEETCORN, INDIAN CORN. [from Spanish *maîz*, from Taino (extinct S American Indian language) *mahiz*]

Maj. *abbrev.* Major.

majestic *adj.* having or exhibiting majesty; stately, grand.

▣ magnificent, grand, dignified, noble, royal, stately, splendid, imperial, impressive, exalted, imposing, regal, sublime, superb, lofty, monumental.
▣ lowly, unimpressive, unimposing.

majestically *adv.* in a majestic way.

majesty *noun* (PL. **majesties**) **1** great and impressive dignity. **2** splendour. **3** (**His** or **Her** or **Your Majesty**) a title used when speaking of or to a king or queen. [from Latin *majestas*]

▣ **1, 2** grandeur, glory, stateliness. **1** dignity, nobility, royalty,

exaltedness, loftiness. **2** magnificence, resplendence, splendour, pomp, impressiveness.

Majlis /mɑːdʒˈlɪs/ *noun* **1** the parliament of Iran. **2** (**majlis**) an assembly or council in various N African and Middle Eastern countries. [from Persian *majlis*]

majolica *noun* colourfully glazed or enamelled earthenware, especially popular in Italy from the 14c to the 16c. [from Italian, from Latin *Majorica*, Majorca, where it was originally made]

major — *adj.* **1** great, or greater, in number, size, importance, etc. **2** *said of a musical key or scale* having two full tones between the first and third notes. — *noun* **1** an army officer of the rank above captain and below lieutenant-colonel. **2** a major key, chord, or scale. **3** *North Amer., esp. US* a student's main subject of study; a student studying such a subject. **4** a person who has reached the age of full legal responsibility. — *verb intrans.* (**majored**, **majoring**) *North Amer., esp. US* to specialize in a particular subject of study. [from Latin, comparative of *magnus*, great]

▣ *adj.* **1** greater, larger, bigger, higher, chief, great, superior, pre-eminent, main, leading, supreme, uppermost, outstanding, notable, significant, crucial, important, key, vital, weighty, keynote.
▣ *adj.* **1** minor, unimportant, trivial.

major-domo *noun* (PL. **major-domos**) a chief servant in charge of the management of a household. [from Spanish *mayor-domo*]

majorette *noun* (*also* **drum majorette**) each of a group of girls who march in parades performing elaborate displays of baton-twirling.

major-general *noun* an army officer of the rank above brigadier and below lieutenant-general.

majority *noun* (PL. **majorities**) **1** the greater number; the largest group; the bulk. **2** the winning margin of votes in an election. **3** the age at which a person legally becomes an adult. — **in the majority** forming the larger group or greater part. [from Latin *majoritas*]

▣ **1** bulk, mass, preponderance, greater part. **3** adulthood, maturity, manhood, womanhood, years of discretion.
▣ **1, 3** minority.

majority rule *Politics* government by members, or by a body including members, of the largest racial, ethnic, or religious group(s) in a country, as opposed to a political system which excludes them.

make — *verb* (PAST TENSE AND PAST PARTICIPLE **made**) **1** to form, create, manufacture, or produce by mixing, combining, or shaping materials. **2** to cause to be or become. **3** to cause, bring about, or create by one's actions. **4** to force, induce, or cause. **5** to cause to change into something else: *make a man of him/made the barn into a cottage.* **6** to be suitable for; to have or develop the appropriate qualities for: *this material will make a nice dress/he'll never make a singer.* **7** to appoint. **8** to cause to appear; to represent as being: *long hair makes her look younger/the film makes him a hero.* **9** to gain, earn, or acquire: *make a fortune.* **10** to add up to or amount to; to constitute: *4 and 4 makes 8/ the book makes interesting reading.* **11** to calculate, judge, or estimate to be: *I make it three o'clock.* **12** to arrive at or reach; to succeed in achieving, reaching or gaining. **13** to score (points). **14** to ensure the success of: *made my day.* **15** to propose: *make an offer.* **16** to engage in; to perform, carry out, or produce: *make war/make a speech/make a decision.* **17** to tidy (a bed) after use. **18** (**make to do something**) to show an intention of doing it; to make an attempt or start to do it: *made to stand up, then sat down again.* **19** *slang* to succeed in having sexual intercourse with. — *noun* **1** a manufacturer's brand. **2** the way in which something is made. — **make away with someone** to kill them. **make away with something** to steal it. **make believe** to pretend. **make do with something** to make the best use of a second or inferior choice. **make do without something** to manage without it. **make for something** or **someone 1** to move rapidly or suddenly towards them. **2** to have a specific result: *fine weather made for an enjoyable holiday.* **make it** *colloq.* **1** to be successful. **2** to survive. **make like …** *colloq. North Amer., esp. US* to act or behave as if … **make of something** or **someone** to understand them to mean or signify: *what do you make of their comments?/ they did not know what to make of us.* **make off** to leave, especially hurriedly or secretly. **make off with something** or **someone** to run off with them; to steal or kidnap them. **make or break** to bring the success or failure of. **make out 1** to pretend: *made out that he was ill.* **2** *colloq.* to make progress: *how did they make out?* **3** *colloq. chiefly North Amer.* to manage, succeed, or survive: *we'll make out.* **make something out 1** to begin to discern it, especially to see or hear it: *could make out a vague figure in the distance.* **2** to write or fill in a document, etc: *make out a cheque for £20.* **make something** or **someone out to be something** to cause them to seem what they are not: *they made us out to be liars.* **make out a case for something** to support or justify it with argument. **make something over 1** to transfer ownership of it. **2** *North Amer., esp. US* to convert it. **make up** to resolve a disagreement with someone. **make someone up** to apply cosmetics to their face. **make something up 1** to fabricate or invent it. **2** to prepare or assemble it. **3** to constitute it; to be the parts of it: *the three villages together make up a district.* **4** to form the final element in something; to complete it: *another player to make up the team.* **5** to settle differences. **make up for something** to compensate or serve as an apology for it. **make up to someone** *colloq.* to seek their friendship or favour; to flirt with them. **on the make** *colloq.* seeking a large or illegal profit. [from Anglo-Saxon *macian*]

⊟ *verb* **1** create, manufacture, fabricate, construct, build, produce, put together, originate, compose, form, shape. **3** cause, bring about, effect, accomplish, occasion, give rise to, generate. **4** force, coerce, oblige, constrain, compel, prevail upon, pressurize, press, require. **5** turn, transform, convert, change. **7** appoint, elect, designate, nominate, ordain, install. **9** earn, gain, net, obtain, acquire. **10** constitute, compose, comprise, add up to, amount to. **12** reach, arrive at, attain, accomplish. **13** gain, score, chalk up, notch up. *noun* **1** brand, mark, sort, type, style, variety, model, kind. **2** form, structure, make-up, constitution, manufacture. **make believe** pretend, imagine, assume, suppose. **make off** run off, run away, depart, bolt, leave, fly, *colloq.* cut and run, beat a hasty retreat, *colloq.* clear off. **make off with** steal, *colloq.* pinch, *slang* nick, take, remove, run off with, elope with, kidnap. **make out 1** maintain, imply, claim, assert, pretend. **2**, **3** manage. **2** get on, progress, fare. **3** succeed, win through, get by, survive. **make something out 1** discern, perceive, decipher, distinguish, recognize, see, detect, discover, understand, work out, grasp, follow, fathom. **2** draw up, complete, fill in, write out. **make up** be reconciled, make peace, settle differences, *colloq.* bury the hatchet, *colloq.* forgive and forget, *colloq.* call it quits. **make something up 1** create, invent, devise, fabricate, construct, originate, formulate, dream up, compose. **3** comprise, constitute, compose, form. **4** complete, fill, supply, meet, supplement. **make up for** compensate for, make good, make amends for, redress, recompense, redeem, atone for. **make up to** ingratiate oneself with, *colloq.* get in with, curry favour with, cultivate, flatter, *colloq.* butter up, flirt with.

⊠ *verb* **1** dismantle. **9** spend.

make-believe — *noun* pretence, especially when playful or innocent. — *adj.* pretended; imaginary.

⊟ *noun* pretence, imagination, fantasy, unreality, play-acting, role-play, dream, charade. *adj.* imaginary, fanciful, pretend, pretended, made-up, invented.

⊠ *noun* reality. *adj.* real.

make-or-break *adj.* determining success or failure.

makeover *noun* a complete change made to the style of someone or something, in order to improve their image.

maker *noun* **1** *combining form* a person who makes. **2** (**Maker**) God.

⊟ **1** creator, manufacturer, constructor, builder, producer, director, architect, author.

makeshift *adj.* serving as a temporary and less adequate substitute.

⊟ temporary, improvised, rough and ready, provisional, substitute, stop-gap, expedient, make-do.
⊠ permanent.

make-up *noun* **1** cosmetics applied to the face, etc. **2** the combination of characteristics or ingredients that form something, eg a personality.

⊟ **1** cosmetics, paint, powder, maquillage, *colloq.* warpaint. **2** constitution, nature, composition, character, construction, form, format, formation, arrangement, organization, style, structure, assembly.

makeweight *noun* **1** a small quantity added to a scale to get the required weight. **2** a person or thing of little value or importance, included only to make up for a deficiency.

making *noun*, *combining form* the process of producing or forming something. — **be the making of someone** to ensure their success. **have the makings of …** to have the ability to become …; to show signs of becoming … **in the making** in the process of being made, formed, or developed. **of one's own making** caused by one's own actions.

mal- *combining form* forming words meaning: **1** bad or badly: *maladapted.* **2** incorrect or incorrectly: *malfunction.* [from Latin *male*, badly]

malabsorption *noun Medicine* the impaired absorption of one or more nutrients from digested food material in the small intestine, which can cause anaemia, weight loss, and symptoms of specific vitamin deficiencies.

malachite /ˈmaləkaɪt/ *noun Geol.* a bright green copper mineral that is used as a gemstone and as a minor ore of copper. [from Greek *malakhe*, mallow, whose leaves are a similar shade of green]

maladjusted *adj.* psychologically unable to deal with everyday situations and relationships, usually as a result of an emotionally disturbing experience.

⊟ disturbed, unstable, confused, alienated, neurotic, estranged.
⊠ well-adjusted.

maladjustment *noun* **1** poor or bad adjustment. **2** inability to cope with day-to-day life.

maladminister *verb* (**maladministered**, **maladministering**) to manage or administer badly.

maladministration *noun* incompetent or dishonest management, especially of public affairs.

maladroit /malə'drɔɪt/ *adj.* **1** characterized by clumsiness or a lack of finesse. **2** lacking in tact. [from French *maladroit*]

⊟ HEAVY-HANDED. **1** clumsy, awkward, inept, bumbling, *colloq.* ham-fisted, *colloq.* cack-handed, gauche. **2** tactless, insensitive, unsubtle.

malady *noun* (PL. **maladies**) *old use, formal* an illness or disease. [from French *maladie*, from Latin *male habitus*, in bad condition]

⊟ illness, disease, sickness, ailment, complaint.

malaise *noun* **1** a feeling of uneasiness or discontent. **2** a general feeling of ill health, not attributable to any particular disease. [from French *mal*, ill + *aise*, ease]

malapropism *noun* **1** the misuse of a word, usually with comic effect, through confusion with another which sounds similar but has a different meaning. **2** a word misused in this way. [from Mrs Malaprop in Sheridan's *The Rivals*; associated with French *mal à propos*, inappropriate]

malaria *noun* an infectious disease, mainly of tropical and subtropical regions, caused by a parasitic protozoan (of the genus *Plasmodium*) that is transmitted to humans by the bite of the *Anopheles* mosquito. Its main symptoms are anaemia and recurring bouts of fever. [from Italian *mal'aria*, bad air, formerly thought to be the cause of the disease]

malarial *adj.* **1** infected with malaria. **2** belonging to or of the nature of malaria.

malarkey *noun colloq.* nonsense; rubbish.

Malay — *noun* **1** a member of a people inhabiting Malaysia, Singapore, and Indonesia. **2** their language, the official language of Malaysia. — *adj.* relating to the Malays or their language. [from Malay *malayu*]

malcontent — *adj.*, *said of a person* dissatisfied and inclined to rebel. — *noun* a dissatisfied person. [from Old French *malcontent*]

male — *adj.* **1** denoting the sex that produces sperm and fertilizes the ovum (egg cell). **2** denoting the reproductive structure of a plant that produces the male gamete. **3** of or characteristic of men; masculine. **4** for or made up of men or boys. **5** *Engineering* denoting a piece of machinery that fits into another part (the female). — *noun* a male person, animal, or plant. [from Old French *masle*]

⊟ *adj.* **1** he-, masculine. **3** masculine, manly, virile, boyish.
⊟ FEMALE.

Male terms include: boy, lad, youth, man, gentleman, *colloq.* gent, bachelor, *colloq.* chap, *colloq.* bloke, *colloq.* guy, son, brother, boyfriend, beau, *slang* toy boy, fiancé, bridegroom, husband, father, uncle, nephew, grandfather, patriarch, godfather, widower, *slang* sugar daddy, *slang* hunk, gigolo, homosexual, gay, rent boy, *slang* male chauvinist pig (MCP); bull, dog, buck, tup, cock, cockerel, stallion, billy-goat, boar, dog fox, stag, ram, tom cat, drake, gander.

male bonding the establishment of empathy among men, especially through shared activities etc.

male chauvinism a self-interested prejudice shown by men against women.

male chauvinist or **male chauvinist pig** *derog.* a man who is prejudiced against women and is primarily concerned to promote the interests of men.

malediction *noun* a curse; an act of cursing. [from MAL- + Latin *dicere*, to speak]

maledictory *adj.* using or full of curses.

malefaction *noun* evil-doing, wrongdoing.

malefactor *noun old use, formal* a criminal; an evil-doer; a wrongdoer. [from MAL- + Latin *facere*, to do]

male fern a common woodland fern (*Dryopteris filix-mas*) with fronds up to 150cm long.

male menopause *colloq.* a crisis of confidence identified in middle-aged men, regarded as comparable with the menopause in women but caused by psychological factors such as fear of ageing.

maleness *noun* a male state or quality.

malevolence /mə'levələns/ *noun* being malevolent; ill will.

⊟ malice, malignancy, malignity, enmity, animosity, ill will, hatred, hate, spite, vindictiveness, bitterness.

malevolent /mə'levələnt/ *adj.* wishing to do evil to others; malicious. [from MAL- + Latin *velle*, to wish]

⊟ malicious, malign, spiteful, vindictive, ill-natured, hostile, vicious, venomous, evil-minded.
⊟ benevolent, kind.

malfeasance /mal'fiːzəns/ *noun Legal* an unlawful act, especially committed by a public official. [from French *malfaisance*]

malfeasant /mal'fiːzənt/ *adj.* that commits evil deeds.

malformation *noun* **1** the state or condition of being badly or wrongly formed or shaped. **2** a badly or wrongly formed part; a deformity.

⊟ irregularity, deformity, distortion, warp.

malformed *adj.* badly or wrongly formed.

⊟ misshapen, irregular, deformed, distorted, twisted, warped, crooked, bent.
⊟ perfect.

malfunction — *noun* the act or state of working imperfectly or not at all. — *verb intrans.* to work imperfectly; to fail to work.

⊟ *noun* fault, defect, failure, breakdown. *verb* break down, go wrong, fail.

malice *noun* **1** the desire or intention to harm or hurt others. **2** mischievousness. [from French, from Latin *malus*, bad]

⊟ **1** malevolence, enmity, animosity, ill-will, hatred, hate, spite, vindictiveness, bitterness.
⊟ **1** love.

malice aforethought *Legal* a firm intention to commit a crime, especially against a person.

malicious *adj.* feeling, or motivated by, hatred or a desire to cause harm.

⊟ malevolent, ill-natured, malign, spiteful, venomous, vicious, vengeful, evil-minded, bitter, resentful.
⊟ kind, friendly.

malign /mə'laɪn/ — *verb* to say or write unpleasant things about. — *adj.* **1** evil in nature or influence; displaying ill-will. **2** *said of a disease* harmful; malignant. [from Latin *malignus*, of evil disposition]

⊟ *verb* defame, slander, libel, disparage, abuse, *colloq.* run down, harm, injure. *adj.* MALIGNANT, HARMFUL. **1** malevolent, bad, evil, hurtful, injurious, destructive, hostile.
⊟ *verb* praise. *adj.* BENIGN.

malignancy /mə'lɪgnənsɪ/ *noun* (PL. **malignancies**) **1** being malignant. **2** a cancerous growth.

malignant /mə'lɪgnənt/ *adj.* **1** feeling or showing hatred or the desire to do harm; malicious or malevolent. **2** *Medicine* denoting any disorder that, if left untreated, may cause death, especially a cancerous tumour, ie one that invades and destroys the surrounding tissue, and may spread to more distant parts of the body via the bloodstream or lymphatic system. See also BENIGN. [from Latin *malignare*, to act maliciously]

⊟ **1** malevolent, malicious, spiteful, evil, hostile, vicious, venomous, destructive, harmful, hurtful, pernicious. **2** fatal, deadly, incurable, dangerous, cancerous, uncontrollable, virulent.

⊠ BENIGN. **1** kind.

malignity /mə'lɪgnɪtɪ/ noun **1** being malign, evil, or deadly. **2** a malicious act. **3** hatred.

malinger verb intrans. (**malingered, malingering**) to pretend to be ill, especially in order to avoid work. [from French malingre, sickly]

malingerer noun a person who malingers.

mall noun **1** a public promenade, especially tree-lined. **2** a shopping precinct closed to vehicles. [from The Mall, a street in London]

mallard noun (PL. **mallard, mallards**) a species of wild duck, native to most of Europe, Asia, and N America. The male has a dark green glossy head and neck with a white collar and dark brown breast, and the female is mottled brown. [from Old French mallart]

malleability noun a malleable state or condition.

malleable adj. **1** Chem. denoting certain metals and alloys that can be beaten into a different shape, hammered into thin sheets, and bent without fracture. **2** easily influenced. [from Latin malleabilis, from malleus, hammer]

⊟ PLIABLE, FLEXIBLE. **2** impressionable, receptive, susceptible, persuadable, pliant, compliant, yielding, tractable, biddable.

mallet noun **1** a hammer with a large wooden head. **2** a long-handled wooden hammer for playing croquet or polo. [from Old French maillet, wooden hammer]

malleus /'malɪəs/ noun Anat. a small hammer-shaped bone in the middle ear. Together with two other bones, the incus and stapes, it transmits sound waves from the eardrum to the inner ear. [from Latin malleus, hammer]

mallow noun any of various European plants with pink, purple, or white flowers and fine hairs on the leaves and stem. [from Anglo-Saxon mealwe]

malmsey /'mɑːmzɪ/ noun a strong sweet wine originally from Greece, but now usually from Madeira. [from Latin Malmasia, from Greek Monembasia, the Greek port from which it was shipped]

malnutrition noun any of various disorders resulting from inadequate food intake, an unbalanced diet (eg lack of protein or vitamins), or inability to absorb nutrients from food.

malodorous /mal'oʊdərəs/ adj. formal foul-smelling.

Malpighian body /mal'pɪgɪən/ Anat. in the mammalian kidney, the end of the kidney tubule, consisting of the glomerulus enclosed by a cup-shaped Bowman's capsule. Its function is to filter waste products from the blood. [named after the Italian anatomist Marcello Malpighi]

malpractice noun **1** improper, careless, or illegal professional conduct; an example of this. **2** any wrong or illegal act.

⊟ **1** misconduct, mismanagement, negligence, impropriety, formal dereliction of duty, abuse. **2** misdeed, malefaction.

malt — noun **1** a mixture prepared from barley or wheat grains that have been soaked in water, allowed to sprout, and then dried in a kiln. Malt is used in brewing and distilling to make beer and whisky. **2** malt whisky. — verb to make into malt; to treat or combine with malt. [from Anglo-Saxon mealt]

maltase /'mɔːlteɪz/ noun Biochem. an enzyme, found in animals and plants, that breaks down maltose (malt sugar) into glucose.

Maltese /mɔːl'tiːz/ — noun **1** (PL. **Maltese**) a native or citizen of Malta. **2** the language of Malta, a Semitic lan-guage with a strong Italian influence. **3** a small toy spaniel developed in Italy. — adj. relating to Malta or its people or language. [from Latin Melita]

Maltese cross a cross with four arms of equal length tapering towards the centre, each with a V cut into the end.

Malthusian — adj. relating to or supporting the theory of the English economist Thomas Malthus (1766–1834), that increases in populations tend to exceed the capacity to sustain them, and that there should therefore be restraint or control of sexual activity. — noun a supporter of this theory.

maltose /'mɔːltoʊz/ noun Biochem. a disaccharide sugar that occurs in starch and glycogen, and is composed of two glucose molecules linked together.

maltreat verb to treat roughly or cruelly.

⊟ ill-treat, mistreat, misuse, abuse, injure, harm, damage, hurt.

⊠ care for.

maltreatment noun bad, cruel, or rough treatment.

malt whisky whisky made entirely from malted barley.

malversation noun formal corruption in public affairs; the illegal use of public funds. [from French, from MAL- + Latin versari, to occupy oneself]

mama /mə'mɑː/ or **mamma** /'mɑːmə/ noun a child's word for mother. [from the reduplication of a baby's babbled syllable ma]

mamba noun a large poisonous black or green African snake. [from Zulu imamba]

mambo noun (PL. **mambos**) a Latin American rhythmic dance, or a piece of music for this. [from American Spanish mambo]

Mamluk noun one of the slave soldiers who constituted the army of the Ayyubid sultanate established in Egypt by Saladin in the 1170s.

mamma see MAMA.

mammal noun Zool. any warm-blooded vertebrate animal belonging to the class Mammalia, characterized by the possession in the female of mammary glands which secrete milk to feed the young, eg humans, monkeys, apes, whales, elephants, hoofed mammals, dogs and other carnivores, mice and other rodents, and bats. [from Latin mammalis, of the breast, from mamma, breast]

mammalian /ma'meɪlɪən/ adj. Biol. relating to or typical of mammals.

mammary adj. Biol., Medicine of the breasts or other milk-producing glands. [from Latin mamma, breast]

mammary gland the milk-producing gland of a mammal, eg woman's breast or cow's udder.

mammography noun Medicine X-ray photography of the breast, usually in order to detect any abnormal or malignant growths at an early stage.

mammon noun wealth when considered a source of evil and immorality, personified in the New Testament as a false god. [from Aramaic mamon, wealth]

mammoth — noun any of various prehistoric hairy elephants belonging to the same order (Proboscoidea) as present-day elephants. — adj. huge. [from Old Russian mammot]

⊟ adj. enormous, huge, vast, colossal, gigantic, giant, massive, immense, monumental, mighty.

⊠ adj. tiny, minute.

man — noun (PL. **men**) **1** an adult male human being. **2** human beings as a whole; the human race. **3** an adult male human being displaying typical masculine qualities: a real man. **4** colloq. a husband or boyfriend. **5** an ordinary employee, worker, or member of the armed forces, not a manager or officer. **6** one of the movable pieces in various board games. **7** a male member of a team. **8** old use any male servant, especially a valet. **9** colloq. used as a form of address in various contexts, eg indicating friendship or impatience: *damn it, man!* — *verb* (**manned, manning**) **1** to provide with sufficient (especially male) workers. **2** to operate: *man the pumps*. — *interj. colloq.* used to intensify a following statement: *man, is she gorgeous!* — **as one man** simultaneously; together. **man and boy** from childhood to manhood. **man to man** openly or frankly. **to a man** without exception. **men in grey suits** unseen establishment figures holding the ultimate power in an organization, political party, etc. [from Anglo-Saxon *mann*]

⊟ *noun* **1** male, gentleman, fellow, *colloq.* bloke, *colloq.* chap, *colloq.* guy. **2** humanity, humankind, mankind, human race, human beings, individuals, humans, people, mortals, Homo sapiens. **5** worker, employee, hand, soldier. **8** manservant, servant, valet, houseboy. *verb* **1** staff, crew, take charge of, occupy.

-man *combining form* forming words denoting: **1** a man associated with a specified activity: *postman*. **2** a man who is a native of a specified country or place: *Yorkshire-man*.

man-about-town *noun* (PL. **men-about-town**) a fashionable and sophisticated male socializer.

manacle — *noun* a handcuff. — *verb* to handcuff. [from Latin *manicula*, from *manus*, hand]

⊟ *noun* handcuff, shackle, fetter, chain, bond. *verb* handcuff, shackle, restrain, fetter, chain, put in chains, bind, curb, check, hamper, inhibit.
⊟ *verb* free, unshackle.

manage *verb* **1** to be in overall control or charge of: *manage my own affairs*. **2** to deal with or handle: *managed the situation rather well*. **3** to succeed in (doing something): *managed to persuade him to stop*. **4** (*intrans.*) to succeed or to survive despite difficulties: *manage on very little money*. **5** to have enough room, time, etc for. **6** to handle (a tool or weapon). **7** to control (an animal). [from Italian *maneggiare*, from Latin *manus*, hand]

⊟ **1** administer, direct, run, command, govern, preside over, rule, superintend, supervise, oversee, conduct, control, influence. **2** deal with, handle, cope with, tackle, treat. **4** cope, fare, survive, get by, get along, get on, make do. **5** fit in, accommodate. **6** handle, wield, operate, manipulate, guide.

manageable *adj.* **1** that can be handled without undue difficulty. **2** that can be easily controlled.

⊟ **1** reasonable, doable, feasible, practicable, acceptable, tolerable. **2** tractable, governable, controllable, amenable, submissive, docile.
⊟ UNMANAGEABLE.

management *noun* **1** the skill or practice of controlling something, especially a commercial enterprise. **2** the managers of a company, etc, as a group.

⊟ ADMINISTRATION. **1** direction, control, government, command, running, superintendence, supervision, charge, care, handling. **2** managers, directors, directorate, executive, executives, governors, board, *colloq.* bosses, supervisors.
⊟ **1** mismanagement. **2** workers.

management buyout *Commerce* the purchase of the majority of the shares in a company by members of its management, especially in order to forestall an outside takeover.

manager *noun* a person in overall charge, especially of a commercial enterprise.

⊟ director, executive, administrator, controller, superintendent, supervisor, overseer, governor, organizer, head, *colloq.* boss.

manageress *noun sometimes offensive* a female manager.

managerial *adj.* of a manager or management.

⊟ directorial, executive, administrative, controlling, supervisory, superintendent.

mañana /man'jɑːnə/ *noun, adv. colloq.* tomorrow; some later time. [from Spanish *mañana*, tomorrow]

man-at-arms *noun* (PL. **men-at-arms**) *Hist.* a soldier, especially heavily armed and mounted.

manatee /'manətiː/ *noun* a large plant-eating marine mammal of the tropical waters of America, Africa, and the West Indies. [from Spanish *manati*, from Carib (a West Indian language)]

Mancunian — *noun* a native or citizen of Manchester in NW England. — *adj.* relating to Manchester or its inhabitants. [from Latin *Mancunium*, Manchester]

mandala /'mʌndələ/ *noun Buddhism, Hinduism* a circular symbol representing the universe. [from Sanskrit *mandala*]

mandarin *noun* **1** (**Mandarin** or **Mandarin Chinese**) the official spoken language of China since 1917. **2** *Hist.* a senior official in the Chinese empire. **3** any high-ranking official, especially one thought to be outside political control. **4** a person of great influence, especially in the literary world. **5** a small citrus fruit similar to the tangerine; the tree that bears it. [from Portuguese *mandarim*, from Malay *mantri*, counsellor]

mandate — *noun* **1** a right given to a nation, person, or political party to act on behalf of others. **2** an order given by a superior. **3** *Hist.* (*also* **mandated territory**) a territory administered by a country on behalf of the League of Nations. — *verb* **1** to give authority or power to. **2** to assign (territory) to a nation under a mandate. [from Latin *mandare*, from *manus*, hand + *dare*, to give]

⊟ *noun* **1** authorization, authority, warrant, sanction. **2** order, command, decree, edict, injunction, charge, directive, instruction, commission. *verb* **1** authorize, empower, sanction, warrant, license.

mandatory /'mandətərɪ/ *adj.* **1** not allowing any choice; compulsory. **2** of the nature of, or containing, a mandate.

⊟ **1** obligatory, compulsory, binding, required, necessary, requisite, essential.
⊟ **1** optional.

mandible *noun Zool.* **1** the lower jaw of a vertebrate. **2** the upper or lower part of a bird's beak. **3** one of a pair of jaw-like mouthparts in insects, crustaceans, etc, used for cutting food. [from Latin *mandibula*, from *mandere*, to chew]

mandolin or **mandoline** *noun* a musical instrument like a small guitar, with four pairs of metal strings and a rounded body. [from Italian *mandolino*, diminutive of *mandora*, lute]

mandrake *noun* a Eurasian plant with purple flowers and a forked root, formerly thought to have magical powers; the root, formerly used to make sleep-inducing drugs. [from Latin *mandragora*]

mandrel or **mandril** *noun technical* **1** the rotating shaft on a lathe, to which the object being worked on is fixed. **2** the axle of a circular saw or grinding wheel. [from French *mandrin*, lathe]

mandrill *noun* a large W African baboon with a red and blue muzzle and hindquarters. [probably from MAN + DRILL[4]]

mane *noun* **1** the long hair growing from the neck of horses, lions, and other animals. **2** a long bushy or flowing head of human hair. [from Anglo-Saxon *manu*]

man-eater *noun* **1** a wild animal that attacks, kills, and eats people. **2** *colloq.* a woman who is domineering or aggressive in her relations with men.

manège or **manege** /ma'neɪʒ/ *noun technical* **1** the skill or practice of training or handling horses; the movements taught to a horse. **2** a riding-school. [from French, from Italian *maneggiare*, to manage]

Manes *pl. noun* in Roman religion, 'the dead'.

man Friday a junior male worker given various duties.

manful *adj.* brave and determined; manly.

manga *noun* a type of Japanese adult comic book, or animated film in the same style. [from Japanese]

manganese /'maŋɡəniːz/ *noun Chem.* (SYMBOL **Mn**, ATOMIC NUMBER 25) a hard brittle pinkish-grey metal obtained from the mineral pyrolusite, and widely used to make hard alloys, including manganese steels. [from Latin *magnesia*]

mange *noun* a skin disease of hairy animals, causing itching and loss of hair. [from Old French *mangeue*, itch]

mangel-wurzel *noun* a variety of beet with a large yellow root, used as cattle food. [from German *Mangold*, beet + *Wurzel*, root]

manger *noun old use* an open box or trough from which cattle or horses feed. [from Old French *mangeoire*, from *mangier*, to eat]

mangetout /mɒnʒ'tuː/ *noun* a variety of garden pea of which the whole pod is eaten. [from French *mange tout*, eat all]

mangily /'meɪndʒɪlɪ/ *adv.* in a mangy way.

manginess /'meɪndʒɪnɪs/ *noun* a mangy state or condition.

mangle[1] *verb* **1** to damage or destroy by cutting, crushing, or tearing. **2** to spoil, ruin, or bungle. [from Old French *mangler*, from *mahaigner*, to maim]

⊟ MUTILATE, WRECK. **1** disfigure, mar, maim, destroy, deform, twist, maul, distort, crush, cut, hack, tear, rend. **2** spoil, butcher, ruin, *colloq.* botch, bungle, make a mess of, *slang* screw up.

mangle[2] — *noun* a hand-operated device with two large rollers between which wet laundry is drawn to be squeezed dry. — *verb* to pass through a mangle. [from Dutch *mangel*]

mango *noun* (PL. **mangos**, **mangoes**) **1** a large evergreen tree (*Mangifera indica*) with glossy leaves and small fragrant yellow or red flowers, native to India but cultivated throughout the tropics for its edible fruit. **2** the heavy oblong fruit of this tree, containing a central stone surrounded by soft juicy orange flesh and a thick green, yellow, or red skin. [from Portuguese *manga*]

mangrove *noun* any of several unrelated tropical and subtropical evergreen trees, especially species of *Rhizophora*, that grow in salt marshes and on mudflats along tropical coasts and tidal estuaries, mainly in Asia, Africa, and the SW Pacific. [earlier *mangrow*, from Portuguese *mangue*]

mangy *adj.* (**mangier**, **mangiest**) **1** suffering from mange. **2** *derog.* shabby; seedy.

⊟ **2** seedy, shabby, scruffy, scabby, *colloq.* tatty, shoddy, moth-eaten, dirty, mean.

manhandle *verb* **1** to treat roughly. **2** to move or transport using manpower, not machinery.

⊟ **1** maul, mistreat, maltreat, misuse, abuse, knock about, *colloq.* rough up. **2** haul, heave, hump, pull, push, shove, tug.

manhole *noun* an opening large enough to allow a person through, especially in a road, usually leading to a sewer.

manhood *noun* **1** the state of being an adult male. **2** manly qualities. **3** men collectively.

⊟ **1** adulthood, maturity. **2** masculinity, virility, manliness, manfulness, machismo.

man-hour *noun* a unit of work equal to the work done by one person in one hour.

manhunt *noun* a concentrated and usually large-scale search for a person, especially a criminal.

mania *noun* **1** *Medicine* a mental disorder characterized by great excitement or euphoria, rapid and incoherent thought and speech, hyperactivity, grandiose delusions, and domineering behaviour which may become violent. It is usually treated with drugs, and severe cases require hospitalization. **2** a great desire or enthusiasm; a craze. [from Latin, from Greek *mainomai*, to be mad]

⊟ **1** madness, insanity, lunacy, psychosis, derangement, disorder, aberration, craziness, frenzy. **2** passion, craze, rage, obsession, compulsion, enthusiasm, *derog.* fad, infatuation, fixation, craving.

-mania *combining form* forming words denoting: **1** an abnormal or uncontrollable desire: *kleptomania*. **2** (often as ad hoc formations) great enthusiasm: *balletomania* (= great enthusiasm for ballet).

maniac *noun* **1** *colloq.* a person who behaves wildly. **2** an extremely keen enthusiast: *a video maniac*. **3** *old medical use* a person suffering from mania.

⊟ **2** enthusiast, fan, fanatic, *colloq.* fiend, freak. **3** lunatic, madman, madwoman.

-maniac *combining form* forming nouns denoting a person affected with a mania: *kleptomaniac*.

maniacal *adj.* **1** affected with or typical of mania. **2** typical of or like a maniac.

manic *adj.* **1** *Medicine* of, relating to, or suffering from mania. **2** *colloq.* very energetic or active.

⊟ **2** frantic, frenzied, hysterical, fretful, non-stop, energetic, active, lively.

manic-depressive — *adj.* affected by or suffering from an illness which produces alternating phases of extreme elation and severe depression. — *noun* a person suffering from this kind of depression.

manicure — *noun* a cosmetic treatment of the hands, especially the fingernails, usually carried out by a trained professional. — *verb* to carry out a manicure on (a person or hand). [from Latin *manus*, hand + *cura*, care]

manicurist *noun* a person who gives manicures.

manifest — *verb* **1** to show or display clearly. **2** to be evidence or proof of. **3** to reveal or declare (itself). — *adj.* easily seen; obvious. — *noun* **1** a customs document giving details of a ship or aircraft, its cargo and its destination. **2** a passenger list. [from Latin *manifestare*]

⊟ *verb* SHOW, REVEAL. **1** exhibit, display, demonstrate, set forth, expose. **2** prove, illustrate, establish, testify to, evince. *adj.* obvious, evident, clear, apparent, plain, open, patent, noticeable, conspicuous, unmistakable, visible, unconcealed.

✎ *verb* CONCEAL. *adj.* unclear.

manifestation *noun* **1** the act of disclosing or demonstrating. **2** display. **3** public demonstration.

⊟ DEMONSTRATION. **1**, **2** display, exhibition. **1** revelation, exposure, disclosure, expression. **2** show, appearance, sign, indication.

manifestly *adv.* obviously, undoubtedly.

manifesto *noun* (PL. **manifestos, manifestoes**) a written public declaration of policies or intentions, especially by a political party or candidate. [from Italian, from Latin *manifestare*, to manifest]

⊞ statement, declaration, policies, platform.

manifold — *adj.* **1** many and various; of many different kinds. **2** having many different features or functions. — *noun* **1** *formal* a thing with many different forms or functions. **2** *technical* a pipe with several inlets and outlets. [from MANY + -FOLD]

⊞ *adj.* **1** many, numerous, varied, various, diverse, multiple, kaleidoscopic, abundant, copious.

manikin or **mannikin** *noun* **1** *old use* an abnormally small person; a dwarf. **2** a model of the human body, used in teaching art and anatomy. [from Dutch *manneken*, double diminutive of *man*, man]

manila or **manilla** *noun* a type of thick strong brown paper, originally made from the fibre of a Philippine tree.

manipulate *verb* **1** to handle, especially skilfully. **2** to control or influence cleverly and unscrupulously, especially to one's own advantage. **3** to apply treatment with the hands to (a part of the body). [from Latin *manipulus*, handful]

⊞ **1, 2** use, control, manoeuvre, influence. **1** handle, wield, operate, engineer, guide, direct, steer, negotiate, work. **2, 3** massage. **2** exploit, take advantage of, impose on, abuse, falsify, rig, juggle with, doctor, fiddle, *colloq.* cook.

manipulation *noun* the act or process of manipulating.

⊞ use, control, handling, operation, exploitation, abuse, falsification, rigging, massage.

manipulative *adj.*, *said of a person* given to or skilled in manipulating or exploiting people or circumstances.

⊞ cunning, artful, wily, opportunistic, exploitative, self-seeking.

mankind *noun* the human race as a whole.

⊞ humanity, humankind, human race, man, Homo sapiens, people.

manky *adj.* (**mankier, mankiest**) *colloq.* **1** dirty. **2** of poor quality; shoddy. [from obsolete Scots *mank*, defective]

manliness *noun* a manly state or quality.

⊞ masculinity, virility, manhood, manfulness, machismo.

manly *adj.* (**manlier, manliest**) displaying qualities considered admirable in a man, usually strength, determination, courage, etc; suitable for a man.

⊞ masculine, male, virile, manful, macho, robust.

man-made *adj.* artificial or synthetic, not natural or naturally produced.

⊞ artificial, synthetic, manufactured, simulated, imitation.
⊟ natural.

manna *noun* **1** in the Old Testament, the food miraculously provided by God for the Israelites in the wilderness. **2** any unexpected gift or windfall: *manna from heaven.* [from Aramaic, possibly from Hebrew *man*, gift]

mannequin /'manəkɪn/ *noun* **1** a fashion model. **2** a life-size dummy of the human body, used in the making or displaying of clothes. [from French *mannequin*; see MANIKIN]

manner *noun* **1** way; fashion. **2** (*often* **manners**) behaviour towards others: *bad manners/don't like his manner.* **3** (**manners**) polite social behaviour: *have no manners.* **4** style: *dressed in the Chinese manner.* **5** kind or kinds: *all manner of things.* — **to the manner born** accustomed since birth (to a particular occupation, activity, etc). **by no manner of means** or **not by any manner of means** under no circumstances; certainly not. **in a manner of speaking** in a way; to some degree; so to speak. [from Old French *maniere*, from Latin *manuarius*, of the hand]

⊞ **1, 4** fashion, style, way. **1** method, means, procedure, process, form. **2** behaviour, conduct, bearing, demeanour, air, appearance, look, character. **3** politeness, courtesy, etiquette, conventions, formalities, social graces, *colloq.* ps and qs.

mannered *adj. formal usu. derog.* unnatural and artificial; affected.

-mannered *combining form* forming adjectives denoting a specified kind of social behaviour: *bad-mannered.*

mannerism *noun* **1** an individual characteristic, eg a gesture or facial expression. **2** *derog.* excessive use of an individual style in art or literature.

⊞ **1** idiosyncrasy, peculiarity, characteristic, quirk, trait, feature, foible, habit, tic.

mannerliness *noun old use* courtesy.

mannerly *adj. old use* polite.

mannikin SEE MANIKIN.

mannish *adj.*, *usually said of a woman* having an appearance or qualities regarded as more typical of a man.

manoeuvrability *noun* a manoeuvrable state or quality.

manoeuvrable *adj.* that can be easily or readily manoeuvred.

manoeuvre /mə'nu:və(r)/ — *noun* **1** a movement requiring, or performed with, considerable skill. **2** a clever handling of affairs, often involving deception. **3** (**manoeuvres**) military exercises, especially on a large scale. — *verb* **1** *trans., intrans.* to move (something) accurately and with skill: *manoeuvred the car into the garage.* **2** *trans., intrans.* to use ingenuity, and perhaps deceit, in handling (something or someone). **3** *intrans.* to carry out military exercises. [from French, from Latin *manu*, by hand + *opera*, work]

⊞ *noun* **1, 2** move. **1** movement, operation, action. **2** plan, ploy, plot, ruse, strategem, exercise, machination, gambit, tactic, trick, scheme, dodge. *verb* **1** move, handle, steer, drive. **2** contrive, manipulate, plot, scheme, wangle, manage, plan, devise, negotiate.

man of the world a man who is mature and widely experienced.

man-of-war or **man-o'-war** *noun* (PL. **men-of-war**) *Hist.* an armed sailing ship used as a warship.

manometer *noun Physics* an instrument for measuring the difference in pressure between two fluids (liquids or gases), especially by determining the difference in height between two columns of liquid, eg mercury, in a U-shaped glass tube. [from Greek *manos*, rare, thin + -METER]

manor *noun* **1** in medieval Europe, an area of land under the control of a lord. **2** (*also* **manor-house**) the principal residence on a country estate, often the former home of a medieval lord. **3** *slang* the area in which a particular person or group, especially a police unit or a criminal, operates. [from Old French *manoir*, from Latin *manere*, to stay]

manorial *adj.* relating to or associated with a manor.

manpower *noun* **1** number of employees. **2** human effort, as opposed to mechanical power.

manqué /ˈmɒŋkeɪ/ *adj. literary* (*used following a noun*) having once had the ambition or potential to be something, without achieving it: *an artist manqué*. [from French *manqué*, having missed]

mansard *noun* a four-sided roof, each side of which is in two parts, the lower part sloping more steeply. [from François Mansart (1598–1666), French architect]

manse *noun* the house of a religious minister, especially in Scotland. [from Latin *mansus*, dwelling]

manservant *noun* (PL. **menservants**) *old use* a male servant, especially a valet.

mansion *noun* **1** a large and usually luxurious house. **2** a manor-house. **3** (**mansions**) *Brit.* a large building divided into luxury apartments. [from Latin *mansio*, remaining]

manslaughter *noun* the crime of killing someone without intending to do so.

manta ray a giant ray with a broad mouth across the front of the head. [from Spanish *manta*]

mantel *noun old use* a mantelpiece or mantelshelf. [related to MANTLE]

mantelpiece *noun* the ornamental frame around a fireplace, especially the top part which forms a shelf.

mantelshelf *noun* the shelf part of a mantelpiece.

mantilla /manˈtilə/ *noun* **1** a scarf of lace or silk, worn by women over the hair and shoulders, especially in Spain and S America. **2** a short lightweight cape or cloak. [from Spanish *mantilla*, diminutive of *manta*, from *manto*, cloak]

mantis *noun* (PL. **mantises**, **mantes**) (*also* **praying mantis**) an insect-eating insect with a long body, large eyes, and a tendency to carry its two front legs raised as if in prayer. [from Greek *mantis*, prophet]

mantissa /manˈtisə/ *noun Maths.* the part of a logarithm comprising the decimal point and the figures following it. See also CHARACTERISTIC. [from Latin *mantissa*, something added]

mantle — *noun* **1** a fireproof mesh round a gas or oil lamp that glows when the lamp is lit. **2** a cloak or loose outer garment. **3** *literary* a position of responsibility: *given the leader's mantle*. **4** *literary* a covering: *a mantle of snow*. **5** *Geol.* the part of the Earth between the crust and the core. — *verb literary* to cover or conceal. [from Latin *mantellum*, diminutive of *mantum*, cloak]

◼ *noun* **2** cloak, cape, hood, shawl, veil, wrap. **4** cover, covering, blanket, shroud, screen.

man-to-man *adj.*, *said especially of personal discussion* open and frank.

mantra /ˈmantrə/ *noun* **1** a word or sound repeated as an aid to concentration when meditating. **2** any of the hymns of praise in the ancient sacred Hindu scriptures, the Vedas. [from Sanskrit *mantra*, instrument of thought]

mantrap *noun* **1** a trap or snare for catching trespassers, poachers, etc. **2** any source of potential danger.

manual — *adj.* **1** of the hand or hands. **2** using the body, rather than the mind; physical: *manual worker*. **3** worked, controlled or operated by hand; not automatic. — *noun* **1** a book of instructions, eg for repairing a car. **2** an organ keyboard. [from Latin *manualis*, from *manus*, hand]

◼ *adj.* **3** hand-operated, by hand. *noun* **1** handbook, guide, guidebook, instructions, Bible, vade mecum, directions.

manually *adv.* by manual means; by hand.

manufacture — *verb* **1** to make from raw materials, especially in large quantities using machinery. **2** to invent or fabricate: *manufacture evidence*. **3** *derog.* to produce in a mechanical fashion. — *noun* the practice or process of

manufacturing. [from Latin *manu*, by hand + *facere*, to make]

◼ *verb* **1** make, produce, construct, build, fabricate, create, assemble, mass-produce, turn out, process, forge, form. **2** invent, make up, concoct, fabricate, think up. *noun* production, making, construction, fabrication, mass-production, assembly, creation, formation.

manufacturer *noun* **1** a person or business that manufactures. **2** a person who makes or invents.

◼ **1** maker, producer, industrialist, constructor, factory-owner, builder, creator.

manufacturing — *adj.* relating to or engaged in manufacture. — *noun* the action, practice, or process of making or inventing.

manumission *noun* **1** the act of manumitting. **2** being manumitted.

manumit *verb* (**manumitted**, **manumitting**) *formal* to release from slavery; to set free. [from Latin *manu*, by hand + *mittere*, to send]

manure — *noun* any substance, especially animal dung, used on soil as a fertilizer. — *verb* to apply manure to. [from Old French *manouvrer*, to work by hand]

◼ *noun* fertilizer, compost, muck, dung.

manuscript (ABBREV. **MS**) *noun* **1** an author's handwritten or typed version of a book, etc, before it has been printed. **2** a book or document written by hand. [from Latin *manuscriptus*, written by hand]

◼ **1** typescript, MS.

Manx — *adj.* relating to the Isle of Man or its inhabitants. — *noun* an almost extinct Celtic language, formerly spoken widely on the Isle of Man. [from an earlier form *Maniske*, Man-ish]

Manx cat a breed of tailless cat, originally from the Isle of Man.

Manxman *noun* a man who is a native of the Isle of Man.

Manxwoman *noun* a woman who is a native of the Isle of Man.

many — *adj.* **1** great in number; numerous. **2** being one of numerous: *many a man*. — *pron.* a great number of people or things: *many of the victims were children*. — *noun* (**the many**) the majority; ordinary people, not nobility or royalty. — **in as many** in the same number of. [from Anglo-Saxon *manig*]

◼ *adj.* **1** numerous, countless, *colloq.* lots of, *colloq.* a lot of, manifold, various, varied, sundry, diverse, *colloq.* umpteen.
◼ *adj.* **1** few.

Maoism /ˈmaʊɪzm/ *noun* the policies and theories of Mao Zedong (or Mao Tse-tung) (1893–1976), the first leader of Communist China.

Maoist /ˈmaʊɪst/ — *noun* a follower of Chinese communism as expounded by Mao Zedong. — *adj.* relating to or characteristic of Maoism or a Maoist.

Maori /ˈmaʊəri/ — *noun* (PL. **Maori**, **Maoris**) **1** a member of the aboriginal Polynesian people of New Zealand. **2** the language of this people. — *adj.* of this people or their language. [from Maori]

map — *noun* **1** a diagram of any part of the earth's surface, showing geographical and other features, eg the position of towns and roads. **2** a similar diagram of the surface of the moon or a planet. **3** a diagram showing the position of the stars in the sky. **4** a diagram of the layout of anything. — *verb* (**mapped**, **mapping**) to make a map of. — **map something out** to plan a route, course of action, etc, in detail. **put something on the map** *colloq.* to cause it to become well-known or important. [from Latin *mappa*, napkin, painted cloth]

. . . .

⊟ *noun* **1** chart, plan, street plan, atlas, graph, plot, projection. *verb* chart, plot, draw, delineate. **map out** plan, chart, outline, draft, project, formulate, forecast.

. . . .

maple *noun* **1** (*also* **maple tree**) any of various broad-leaved deciduous trees of northern regions, whose seeds float by means of wing-like growths. **2** the hard light-coloured wood of these trees, used to make furniture, etc. [from Anglo-Saxon *mapul*]

maple syrup syrup made from the sap of the sugar maple tree.

maquette /ma'ket/ *noun* a model made by a sculptor as a preliminary study for a full-size work. A maquette is usually made in clay, wax, or plaster. [from French *maquette*]

Maquis /mɑːˈkiː/ *noun* **1** (**the Maquis**) the French resistance movement that fought against German occupying forces during World War II. **2** (**maquis**) a member of this movement. [from French *maquis*, from Italian *macchia*, thicket, referring to a type of thick shrubby vegetation found in coastal areas of the Mediterranean, which provided cover for those hiding in the hills]

Mar or **Mar.** *abbrev.* March.

mar *verb* (**marred, marring**) **1** to spoil. **2** to injure or damage. [from Anglo-Saxon *merran*]

. . . .

⊟ 1 spoil, impair, detract from, blemish, tarnish, taint. **2** harm, hurt, injure, damage, deface, disfigure, mutilate, maim, scar, mangle, ruin, wreck.

⊟ ENHANCE.

. . . .

marabou *noun* **1** a large black-and-white African stork. **2** its feathers, used to decorate clothes, trim hats, etc. [from Arabic *murabit*, hermit, holy man, the stork being considered holy in Islam]

maraca *noun* a musical instrument consisting of a hollow shell filled with beans, pebbles, etc, held by a handle and shaken, usually in pairs, originally used in Latin America. [from Portuguese *maraca*]

maraschino *noun* (PL. **maraschinos**) a liqueur made from cherries, with a taste like bitter almonds. [from Italian, from *amarasca*, sour cherry]

maraschino cherry a cherry preserved in maraschino or a similar liqueur, used for decorating cocktails, cakes, etc.

Marathi /məˈrɑːtɪ/ — *noun* an Indo-Aryan language spoken by c.30–50 million people in the state of Maharashtra, W India, and surrounding areas. — *adj.* relating to or spoken or written in Marathi.

marathon — *noun* **1** a long-distance race on foot, usually 42.195km (26mi 385yd). **2** any lengthy and difficult task. — *adj.* **1** relating to a marathon race. **2** requiring or displaying great powers of endurance: *a marathon effort.* [from *Marathon*, in Greece, from where a messenger is said to have run to Athens with news of victory over the Persians in 490BC; the length of the race is based on this distance, although in the more authentic accounts (eg Herodotus) the runner went to Sparta to appeal for help before the battle]

maraud *verb* to wander in search of people to attack and property to steal or destroy. [from French *marauder*, to prowl]

marauder *noun* a raider.

. . . .

⊟ bandit, brigand, robber, raider, plunderer, pillager, pirate, buccaneer, outlaw, ravager, predator.

. . . .

marauding *adj.* raiding, pillaging.

marble *noun* **1** *Geol.* a metamorphic rock, white when pure, but often mottled or streaked with red or grey, consisting of recrystallized limestone or dolomite. It can be cut and polished, and is widely used as an ornamental stone in the building industry. The pure white form is used by sculptors. **2** a general term for any rock that can be polished and used for decorative purposes. **3** a small hard ball originally of this rock, now of glass, used in children's games. [from Old French *marbre*]

marbled *adj.* having irregular streaks of different colours, like marble.

marbles *noun* **1** any of several children's games played with marbles. **2** *colloq.* mental faculties; wits: *have all one's marbles/lose one's marbles.*

marc *noun* the left-over skins and stems of grapes used in wine-making, or a kind of brandy made from these. [from French *marc*]

marcasite *noun* *Geol.* a pale yellow sulphide mineral formerly used to make jewellery, and now mined for use in the manufacture of sulphuric acid. [from Latin *marcasita*]

marcato /mɑːˈkɑːtoʊ/ *adj., adv. Mus.* stressed or accented; emphatic, distinct. A term used in musical scores to indicate the tempo and/or expression required for a particular passage or section. [from Italian *marcare*, to mark]

March *noun* the third month of the year. [from Latin *Martius*, of Mars]

march¹ — *verb* **1** *intrans.* to walk in a stiff upright formal manner, usually at a brisk pace and in step with others. **2** to force (especially soldiers) to walk in this way. **3** *intrans.* to walk in a purposeful and determined way. **4** *intrans.* to advance or continue steadily: *events marched on.* — *noun* **1** an act of marching; a distance travelled by marching. **2** a brisk walking pace. **3** a procession of people moving steadily forward. **4** a piece of music written in a marching rhythm. **5** unstoppable progress or movement: *the march of time.* — **steal a march on someone** to get an advantage over them, especially by trickery. [from French *marcher*, to walk]

. . . .

⊟ *verb* **1** walk, stride, parade, pace, file, tread, stalk. *noun* **1** walk, trek, hike, footslog. **3** procession, parade, demonstration, *colloq.* demo. **5** advance, development, progress, evolution, passage.

. . . .

march² *noun* **1** a boundary or border. **2** (**Marches**) a border district, especially those around the English–Welsh and English–Scottish borders, fought over continuously from the 13c to the 16c. [from French *marche*]

marcher *noun* **1** a person who marches. **2** a person who takes part in a march.

March hare **1** a hare during its breeding season in March, proverbially mad because of its excitable behaviour. **2** one of the mad characters encountered by Alice in Lewis Carroll's *Alice's Adventures in Wonderland*.

marching orders 1 orders to march in a certain way, given to soldiers, etc. **2** *colloq.* dismissal from a job, etc.

marchioness /ˈmɑːʃənəs, mɑːʃəˈnɛs/ *noun* **1** the wife or widow of a marquis. **2** a woman of the same rank in her own right. [from Latin *marchionissa*, from *marchio*, marquis]

Mardi Gras /ˈmɑːdɪ grɑː/ **1** Shrove Tuesday, celebrated with a festival in some places, especially in Rio de Janeiro, Brazil. **2** the festival. [from French *Mardi Gras*, fat Tuesday]

mare¹ *noun* an adult female horse or zebra. [from Anglo-Saxon *mere*]

mare² *noun* (PL. **maria**) any of numerous large flat areas on the surface of the Moon or Mars, seen from Earth as dark patches and originally thought to be seas. [from Latin *mare*, sea]

mare's nest a discovery that proves to be untrue or without value.

marg or **marge** *noun colloq.* margarine.

margarine *noun* a food product that is used as a substitute for butter. It is usually made from vegetable oils (although some margarines are made from animal fats), and also contains water, flavourings, and colourings. [from French, from Greek *margaron*, pearl]

margin *noun* **1** the blank space around a page of writing or print. **2** any edge or border. **3** something extra, beyond what should be needed; an amount by which one thing exceeds another: *allow a margin for error/win by a large margin*. **4** an upper or lower limit, especially beyond which it is impossible to exist or operate. [from Latin *margo*, border]

◻ **1**, **2** border, edge. **2** boundary, bound, periphery, perimeter, rim, brink, limit, confine, verge, side, skirt. **3** allowance, play, leeway, latitude, scope, room, space, surplus, extra. **4** ceiling, floor, threshold.

marginal — *adj.* **1** small and unimportant. **2** appearing in the margin of a page of text. **3** being on or close to a limit or boundary. **4** *said of a political constituency* whose current MP or other representative was elected by only a small majority of votes. — *noun* a marginal constituency.

◻ *adj.* **1** negligible, minimal, insignificant, minor, slight, low, small. **3** borderline, doubtful, peripheral.
◻ *adj.* **1** central, core.

marginal cost *Econ.* the cost of producing one extra unit, or the total cost saved if one less unit is produced.

marginally *adv.* to a marginal or small degree: *is only marginally longer*.

marguerite *noun* any of various garden plants whose large flowers have pale yellow or white petals round a yellow centre. [from French *marguerite*, daisy]

marigold *noun* any of various garden plants with bright orange or yellow flowers and strongly scented leaves. [from (the Virgin) *Mary* + *gold*, an obsolete name for the plant]

marijuana or **marihuana** /marɪˈwɑːnə/ *noun* **1** a narcotic drug prepared from the dried leaves and flowers of the hemp plant (*Cannabis sativa*). When swallowed, or smoked in the form of a cigarette (a 'joint'), it produces euphoria or mild hallucinations. Its use is illegal in many countries. Also called CANNABIS, HASHISH, POT². **2** the hemp plant from which this drug is obtained. [from Mexican Spanish]

marimba *noun* an originally African type of xylophone consisting of a set of hardwood strips which, when struck with soft hammers, vibrate metal plates underneath, producing musical sound. [from a W African language]

marina *noun* a harbour for private pleasure boats. [from Latin *marinus*; see MARINE]

marinade — *noun* any liquid mixture in which food, especially meat or fish, is soaked to add flavour before cooking. — *verb trans., intrans.* to marinate. [from French *marinade*, from Spanish *marinar*, to pickle in brine]

marinate *verb trans., intrans.* to soak in a marinade. [from Spanish *marinar*, to pickle in brine]

marine — *adj.* **1** of, concerned with, or found in the sea. **2** of ships, shipping trade, or the navy. — *noun* **1** a soldier trained to serve on land or at sea. **2** the merchant or naval ships of a nation collectively. [from Latin *marinus*, from *mare*, sea]

◻ *adj.* MARITIME. **1** sea, deep-sea, salt-water. **2** naval, nautical, seafaring, seagoing, ocean-going.

mariner *noun old use* a seaman.

◻ sailor, seaman, seafarer, deckhand, navigator, sea dog, salt, *old use, colloq.* tar.

marionette *noun* a puppet with jointed limbs moved by strings. [from French *marionette*, diminutive of *Marion*, woman's name]

marital *adj.* of or relating to marriage. [from Latin *maritus*, married]

◻ conjugal, matrimonial, married, wedded, nuptial, connubial.

maritally *adv.* as regards marriage.

maritime *adj.* **1** of the sea or ships. **2** living or growing near the sea. **3** *said of a climate* having relatively small temperature differences between summer and winter. [from Latin *maritimus*, of the sea]

◻ **1** marine, nautical, naval, seafaring, sea, oceanic. **2** coastal, seaside, littoral.

marjoram *noun* a purple-flowered Mediterranean plant whose sweet-smelling leaves are used to season food. [from Old French *marjorane*]

mark¹ — *noun* **1** a visible blemish, eg a scratch or stain. **2** a patch, stripe, spot, etc forming part of a larger pattern. **3** a grade of a student's, competitor's, etc proficiency, or a number or letter used to denote this. **4** a sign or symbol: *a question mark*. **5** an indication or representation: *a mark of respect*. **6** the position from which a competitor starts in a race: *on your marks*. **7** an object or thing aimed at; a target: *wide of the mark*. **8** a required standard: *up to the mark*. **9** influence: *your work bears his mark*. **10** a cross or other sign used instead of a signature. **11** (*often* Mark) a type of design, or model, especially of vehicles. — *verb* **1** (*trans., intrans.*) to make or become spoiled by a mark. **2** to award a grade to. **3** to show; to be a sign of: *X marks the spot/events marking a new era*. **4** to make a note of. **5** to pay close attention to: *mark my words*. **6** *Sport* to stay close to (an opposing player), limiting his or her influence on the game. **7** to characterize or label: *this incident marks him as a criminal*. — **leave** or **make one's mark** to make a strong or permanent impression. **mark something down** **1** to note it. **2** to reduce the price of it. **mark something off** or **out** to fix its boundaries or limits. **mark time 1** to move the feet up and down as if marching, but without going forward. **2** to merely keep things going while waiting to speed up or progress. **mark something up** to increase its price, to provide profit for the seller. [from Anglo-Saxon *merc*, boundary, limit]

◻ *noun* **1** spot, stain, blemish, blot, blotch, smudge, dent, impression, scar, scratch, bruise, line. **3** grade, percentage, *Brit.* tick, assessment, evaluation. **4, 5** sign, token. **4** symbol, emblem, brand, stamp. **5** indication, characteristic, feature, proof, evidence, badge. **7** target, goal, aim, objective, purpose. *verb* **1** stain, blemish, blot, smudge, dent, scar, scratch, bruise. **2** evaluate, assess, correct, grade. **3** brand, label, stamp, characterize, identify, distinguish. **4** note (down), write (down), enter. **5** heed, listen, mind, note, observe, regard, notice, take to heart.

mark² *noun* **1** the standard unit of currency in Germany. **2** a unit of weight for gold and silver. [from Anglo-Saxon *marc*]

mark-down *noun* a reduction in price, especially in determining level of profit.

marked *adj.* **1** obvious or noticeable. **2** watched with suspicion; selected as the target for an attack: *a marked man*.

◻ **1** noticeable, obvious, conspicuous, evident, pronounced, distinct, decided, emphatic, considerable, remarkable, apparent, glaring. **2** suspected, watched, doomed.
◻ **1** unnoticeable, slight.

markedly *adv.* to a marked or noticeable degree.

◻ noticeably, obviously, conspicuously, distinctly, decidedly, emphatically, considerably.

marker *noun* **1** a person who takes notes, eg of the score in a game. **2** anything used to mark the position of something. **3** (*also* **marker pen**) a pen with a thick point, for writing signs, etc.

market — *noun* **1** a periodic gathering of people to buy and sell various goods. **2** the building or other public place in which this takes place. **3** a particular region or section of the population considered as a potential customer: *the teenage market.* **4** a level of trading: *the market is slow.* **5** opportunity to trade; demand: *no market for these goods.* — *verb* (**marketed, marketing**) **1** to offer for sale; to promote. **2** *intrans.* to trade or deal. — **be in the market for something** to wish to buy it. **on the market** on sale; able to be bought. [from Anglo-Saxon, from Latin *mercatus*, trade, market]

⊟ *noun* **1, 2** mart, bazaar, fair. **2** market-place. **5** demand, call.
verb **1** sell, retail, hawk, peddle.
⊟ *verb* **1** buy.

marketable *adj.* saleable, suitable for sale.

market economy an economic system in which prices, wages, products, and services are determined by market forces of supply and demand, with no state interference.

market forces the willingness of customers to buy goods or services that suppliers offer at a particular price; supply and demand.

market-garden *noun* an area of land, usually near a large town or city, that is used to grow produce, especially vegetables, salad crops, soft fruit, and flowers, for immediate sale at a market.

market-gardener *noun* the owner of or person who tends a market-garden.

marketing *noun* the business techniques or processes by which anything may be sold.

market leader a company that sells more goods of a specific type than any other company; also, a brand of goods that sells more than any other of its kind.

market-place *noun* **1** the open space in a town in which a market is held. **2** (**the market-place**) the commercial world of buying and selling.

market price the price at which a thing is being sold at a particular time.

market research investigation of the habits, needs and preferences of customers.

market test to put a product on the market for a limited time so as to gauge consumer response.

market town a town, often at the centre of a farming area, where a market is regularly held.

marking *noun* (*often* **markings**) a distinctive pattern of colours on an animal or plant.

marksman *noun* a person able to shoot a gun or other weapon accurately, especially a trained soldier or policeman.

marksmanship *noun* the skill of a marksman.

mark-up *noun* an increase in price, especially in determining level of profit.

marl — *noun Geol.* a mixture of clay and limestone, formerly added to light sandy soil to improve its texture and fertility and to increase its water-holding capacity, this process being known as marling. — *verb* to apply marl to. [from Old French *marle*]

marlin *noun* (PL. **marlin, marlins**) a large fish of warm and tropical seas, with a long spear-like upper jaw. Also called SPEARFISH. [from MARLINSPIKE, because of its pointed snout]

marlinspike or **marlinespike** *noun Naut.* a pointed metal tool for separating the strands of rope to be spliced. [from Dutch *marlijn*, from *marren*, to tie + *lijn*, rope]

marly *adj.* **1** like marl. **2** containing marl.

marmalade *noun* jam made from any citrus fruit, especially oranges. [from Portuguese *marmelada*, from *marmelo*, quince, from which it was originally made]

marmoreal /mɑːˈmɔːrɪəl/ *adj. formal* of or like marble. [from Latin *marmor*, marble]

marmoset /ˈmɑːməzet/ *noun* any of various small S American monkeys with a long bushy tail and tufts of hair around the head and ears. [from Old French *marmouset*, grotesque figure]

marmot *noun* any of various stout, coarse-haired burrowing rodents of Europe, Asia, and N America. [from French *marmotte*]

maroon[1] — *adj.* having a dark brownish-red or purplish-red colour. — *noun* this colour. [from French *marron*, chestnut]

maroon[2] *verb* **1** to leave in isolation in a deserted place, especially on an island. **2** to leave helpless. [from Mexican Spanish *cimarrón*, wild]

⊟ ABANDON, DESERT, STRAND, LEAVE, ISOLATE. **1** cast away, put ashore.

marque *noun* a brand or make, especially of car. [from French *marque*]

marquee *noun* a very large tent used for circuses, parties, etc. [originally an army officer's tent, coined from MARQUISE, wrongly thought to be plural]

marquess /ˈmɑːkwɪs/ *noun* in the UK, a nobleman above an earl and below a duke in rank. [from Old French *marchis*, from Latin *marchensis*, prefect of the marches; see MARCH[2]]

marquetry *noun* the art or practice of making decorative arrangements of pieces of different woods, often set into the surface of wooden furniture. [from French *marqueterie*, from *marqueter*, to inlay]

marquis /ˈmɑːkwɪs/ *noun* in European countries, a nobleman next in rank above a count. [variant of MARQUESS]

marquise /mɑːˈkiːz/ *noun* in various countries, a marchioness. [from French *marquise*, related to MARQUESS]

marram *noun* a coarse grass that grows on sandy shores, often planted to stop sand erosion. [from Norse *marr*, sea + *halmr*, haulm or stem]

marriage *noun* **1** the state or relationship of being husband and wife. **2** the act of becoming husband and wife. **3** the ceremony within which this act is performed; a wedding. **4** a joining together; a union. [from Old French *mariage*]

⊟ **1** matrimony, wedlock. **2, 3** wedding, nuptials. **4** union, alliance, merger, coupling, amalgamation, link, association, confederation.
⊟ **1, 4** divorce, separation.

marriageability or **marriageableness** *noun* suitability for marriage.

marriageable *adj.* suitable, especially at a legal age, for marriage.

marriage certificate an official piece of paper showing that two people are legally married.

marriage guidance professional counselling given to couples with marital or personal problems.

marriage licence a paper giving official permission for a marriage to take place.

marriage of convenience a marriage entered into for the advantages it will bring, rather than for love.

married — *adj.* **1** having a husband or wife. **2** of or relating to marriage: *married life.* **3** fixed together; joined. — *noun* (**marrieds**) a married couple.

⊟ *adj.* WEDDED. **1** wed, *colloq.* hitched, *colloq.* spliced. **2** marital, matrimonial, conjugal, connubial.

marrow *noun* **1** (*in full* **bone marrow**) the soft tissue that fills the internal cavities of bones. **2** (*in full* **vegetable marrow**) an annual plant (*Cucurbita pepo*) with large prickly leaves, native to tropical America but cultivated worldwide for its large oblong edible fruit. **3** the fruit of this plant, which has a thick green or striped skin and soft white flesh, and is cooked as a vegetable. **4** the innermost, essential, or best part of anything. — **to the marrow** right through. [from Anglo-Saxon *mærg*]

⊟ **4** essence, heart, nub, kernel, core, soul, spirit, substance.

marrowbone *noun* a bone containing edible marrow.

marrowfat *noun* a variety of large edible pea; the plant that bears it.

marry *verb* (**marries, married**) **1** to take someone as one's husband or wife. **2** to perform the ceremony of marriage between. **3** to give (a son or daughter) in marriage. **4** *intrans.* to become husband and wife. **5** (*also* **marry something up**) to assemble it, join it up, or match it correctly. — **marry into something** to become involved in or associated with it by marriage: *married into money*. **marry someone off** to find a husband or wife for (someone, especially a son or daughter). [from Latin *maritare*]

⊟ WED. **2** join in matrimony. **4** *colloq.* tie the knot, *colloq.* get hitched, *colloq.* get spliced. **5** unite, ally, join, merge, match, link, knit.

⊟ **1, 4** divorce. **4** separate.

Mars *noun Astron.* the fourth planet from the Sun, and the nearest planet to the Earth. Its orbit lies between those of the Earth and Jupiter.

Marsala /maˈsɑːlə/ *noun* a dark sweet sherry-like wine made in *Marsala*, Sicily.

marsh *noun* **1** a poorly drained low-lying area of land, commonly found at the mouths of rivers and alongside ponds and lakes, that is frequently flooded. It is dominated by grasses, sedges, rushes, and reeds, and its soil consists of silts, clays, and other mineral deposits. **2** (*in full* **salt marsh**) such an area of land that lies in the intertidal zone and is periodically flooded by seawater. [from Anglo-Saxon *mersc* or *merisc*]

⊟ **1** marshland, bog, swamp, fen, morass, quagmire, slough.

marshal — *noun* **1** any of various high-ranking officers in the armed forces. **2** an official who organizes parades, etc, or controls crowds at large public events. **3** *North Amer., esp. US* a chief police or fire officer in some states. — *verb* (**marshalled, marshalling**) **1** to arrange (facts, etc) in order. **2** to direct, lead, or show the way to. [from Old French *mareschal*]

⊟ *verb* **1** arrange, dispose, order, line up, align, array, rank, organize, assemble, gather, muster, group, collect, draw up, deploy. **2** guide, lead, escort, conduct, usher.

marshalling-yard *noun* a place where railway wagons are arranged into trains.

marsh gas methane.

marsh harrier a harrier hawk, found in marshy regions of Europe, that has an owl-like head, long wings, and long legs, and flies low over the ground, swooping down to kill its prey.

marshmallow *noun* a spongy pink or white sweet, originally made from the root of the marsh mallow.

marsh mallow a pink-flowered plant that grows wild in coastal marshes.

marshy *adj.* (**marshier, marshiest**) **1** of the nature of a marsh. **2** covered with marshes.

⊟ **1** boggy, swampy, miry, muddy, waterlogged, wet, spongy, squelchy.

marsupial — *noun Zool.* any of a group of mammals in which the female lacks a placenta, and carries and suckles her young in a pouch (marsupium) that surrounds the mammary glands on her abdomen, eg kangaroo, wallaby, koala, wombat. — *adj.* of or like a marsupial. [from Latin *marsupium*, pouch]

mart *noun* a trading place; a market. [from Dutch *markt*]

martello *noun* (PL. **martellos**) (*also* **martello tower**) a small circular fortified tower used for coastal defence. [named after Cape *Mortella*, Corsica, where such a tower was captured with difficulty by a British fleet in 1794]

marten *noun* **1** any of various small tree-dwelling predatory mammals with a long thin body and a bushy tail. **2** their highly valued soft black or brown fur. [from Dutch *martren*, from Old French *martre*]

martial *adj.* of, relating to, or suitable for war or the military. [from Latin *martialis*, of Mars, Roman god of war]

⊟ warlike, military, belligerent, soldierly, militant, heroic, brave.

martial art any of various fighting sports or self-defence techniques of Far Eastern origin, eg karate or judo.

martial law law and order strictly enforced by the army when ordinary civil law has broken down, eg during a war or revolution.

Martian — *adj.* relating to or supposedly coming from the planet Mars. — *noun* a fictional inhabitant of Mars. [from Latin *Martius*]

martin *noun* any of various small birds of the swallow family, with a square or slightly forked tail. [from the name *Martin*]

martinet *noun derog.* a person who maintains strict discipline. [from Martinet, one of Louis XIV's generals]

Martini *noun trademark* **1** an Italian brand of vermouth. **2** a cocktail of gin and vermouth.

Martinmas *noun* St Martin's Day, 11 Nov.

martyr /ˈmɑːtə(r)/ — *noun* **1** a person who is put to death for refusing to abandon religious or other beliefs. **2** (**a martyr to something**) a person who suffers greatly for any cause or reason: *is a martyr to arthritis*. — *verb* (**martyred, martyring**) to put to death as a martyr. [from Latin, from Greek *martus*, witness]

martyrdom /ˈmɑːtədəm/ *noun* the death or suffering of a martyr.

marvel — *noun* an astonishing or wonderful person or thing. — *verb intrans.* (**marvelled, marvelling**) (**marvel at something**) to be filled with astonishment or wonder by it. [from French *merveille*]

⊟ *noun* wonder, miracle, phenomenon, prodigy, spectacle, sensation, genius. *verb* wonder, gape, gaze, be amazed at.

marvellous *adj.* **1** so wonderful or astonishing as to be almost beyond belief. **2** *colloq.* excellent.

⊟ WONDERFUL, UNBELIEVABLE, INCREDIBLE, AMAZING. **1** extraordinary, astonishing, astounding, miraculous, remarkable, surprising, glorious. **2** excellent, splendid, superb, magnificent, terrific, super, fantastic.

⊞ **1** ordinary, run-of-the-mill. **2** terrible, awful.

marvellously *adv.* in a marvellous way.

Marxism *noun* the theories of Karl Marx, German economist and political philosopher, stating that the struggle between different social classes is the main influence on political change, and that communism will eventually replace capitalism.

Marxist — *noun* a follower of Marxism. — *adj.* relating to or characteristic of Marxism or Marxists.

marzipan *noun* a sweet paste of crushed almonds and sugar, used to decorate cakes, make sweets, etc. [from Italian *marzapane*]

Masai or **Maasai** *noun* a people of the Rift Valley area of Kenya and Tanzania.

masala /məˈsɑːlə/ *noun* a mixture of ground spices used in Indian cookery. See also GARAM MASALA. [from Hindi, = mixture]

masc. *abbrev.* masculine.

mascara *noun* a cosmetic for darkening the eyelashes, applied with a brush. [from Italian *mascara*, mask]

mascarpone /maskəˈpəʊnɪ/ *noun* a soft Italian cream cheese. [from Italian *mascarpone*]

mascot *noun* a person, animal, or thing thought to bring good luck. [from French *mascotte*, from Provençal *mascotto*, charm]

masculine — *adj.* 1 of, typical of, or suitable for men. 2 *said of a woman* mannish; unfeminine. 3 *Grammar* of or referring to one of the (usually two or three) classes into which nouns are divided in many languages, the class including males. — *noun Grammar* the masculine gender. [from Latin *masculinus*, from *masculus*, male]

> ⊟ *adj.* 1 male, manlike, manly, virile, macho, vigorous, strong, strapping, robust, powerful, muscular, bold, brave, gallant, resolute, stout-hearted.
> ⊟ *adj.* 1 female, feminine.

masculinity *noun* 1 being masculine. 2 something that is masculine.

maser /ˈmeɪzə(r)/ *noun* a device for increasing the strength of microwaves, used in radar. [from the initial letters of *microwave amplification by stimulated emission of radiation*]

mash — *verb* 1 (*also* **mash something up**) to beat or crush it into a pulpy mass. 2 to mix (malt) with hot water. — *noun* 1 a boiled mixture of grain and water used to feed farm animals. 2 a mixture of crushed malt and hot water, used in brewing. 3 any soft mass. 4 *colloq.* mashed potatoes. [from Anglo-Saxon *masc*]

> ⊟ *verb* 1 crush, pulp, beat, pound, pulverize, pummel, grind, smash.

mashie or **mashy** *noun* an old-fashioned iron golf club for playing lofting shots; the modern equivalent is the number five iron. [perhaps from French *massue*, club]

mask — *noun* 1 any covering for the face, worn for amusement, for protection, or as a disguise. 2 *literary* anything that disguises the truth, eg false behaviour: *a mask of light-heartedness.* — *verb* 1 to put a mask on. 2 to disguise or conceal. [from Arabic *maskharah*, clown]

> ⊟ *noun* 1 disguise, visor. 2 façade, front, concealment, camouflage, cover-up, cover, guise, pretence, semblance, cloak, veil, blind, show, veneer. *verb* 2 disguise, camouflage, cover, conceal, cloak, veil, hide, obscure, screen, shield.
> ⊟ *verb* 2 expose, uncover.

masked *adj.* 1 wearing or as if wearing a mask. 2 disguised, concealed.

masking *noun Photog.* the process of using a screen (or mask) to cover part of a light-sensitive surface, usually so that a second image may be superimposed subsequently.

masking tape sticky paper tape used in painting to cover the edge of a surface to be left unpainted.

masochism /ˈmasəkɪzm/ *noun* 1 the practice of deriving sexual pleasure from pain or humiliation inflicted by another person. 2 *colloq.* a tendency to take pleasure in one's own suffering. [from Leopold von Sacher Masoch (1836–95), the Austrian novelist who described it]

masochist *noun* a person who derives sexual pleasure from pain.

masochistic *adj.* relating to or typical of masochism or a masochist.

mason *noun* 1 same as STONEMASON. 2 (*often* **Mason**) a freemason. [from Old French *masson*]

masonic /məˈsɒnɪk/ *adj.* (*often* **Masonic**) relating to freemasons.

masonry *noun* 1 the part of a building built by a mason; stonework and brickwork. 2 the craft of a mason. 3 (*often* **Masonry**) freemasonry.

masque /mɑːsk/ *noun* a kind of dramatic entertainment performed to music by masked actors in 16c–17c English royal courts. [from French *masque*, mask]

masquerade — *noun* 1 a pretence or show. 2 a formal dance at which the guests wear masks and costumes. — *verb intrans.* (*often* **masquerade as someone** or **something**) to disguise oneself; to pretend to be someone or something else: *was masquerading as a vicar/a squalid town masquerading as a city.* [from French *mascarade*]

> ⊟ *noun* 1 disguise, counterfeit, cover-up, cover, deception, front, pose, pretence, guise, cloak. 2 masque, masked ball, costume ball, fancy-dress party. *verb* disguise oneself as, impersonate, pose as, pass oneself off as, play, pretend to be, profess to be.

Mass. *abbrev.* Massachusetts.

mass¹ — *noun* 1 *Physics* the amount of matter that an object contains, which is a measure of its inertia, ie the extent to which it resists acceleration if acted on by a force. 2 a large (usually shapeless) quantity gathered together; a lump. 3 *colloq.* (*also* **masses**) a large quantity or number. 4 majority; bulk. 5 *technical* a measure of the quantity of matter in a body. 6 (**the masses**) ordinary people. 7 an area of uniform colour or shading in art. — *adj.* involving a large number of people: *a mass meeting.* — *verb intrans., trans.* to gather or cause to gather in large numbers. [from French *masse*, from Latin *massa*, lump]

> ⊟ *noun* 2 lump, piece, chunk, block, hunk, heap, pile, load, group, batch, bunch, throng, crowd, horde, mob, multitude, quantity, accumulation, collection, conglomeration. 3 *colloq.* lots, *colloq.* crowds, hordes, *colloq.* loads, *colloq.* heaps, *colloq.* piles. 4 majority, body, bulk, entirety, whole, totality, sum. 5 weight, bulk, size, dimension, magnitude. 6 the crowd, the herd, the mob, the lower classes, the working class(es), the proletariat, the commons, the rabble, the hoi polloi, the plebs, the riff-raff. *adj.* widespread, large-scale, extensive, comprehensive, general, indiscriminate, popular, across-the-board, sweeping, wholesale, blanket. *verb* collect, gather, assemble, congregate, crowd, rally, cluster, muster, swarm, throng.
> ⊟ *adj.* limited, small-scale. *verb* separate.

mass² *noun* (*also* **Mass**) 1 *in the Roman Catholic and Orthodox Churches* the Eucharist, a celebration of Christ's last supper; the ceremony in which this occurs. 2 a part of the text of this ceremony set to music and sung by a choir or congregation. [from Anglo-Saxon *mæsse*]

massacre — *noun* 1 a cruel killing of large numbers of people or animals. 2 *colloq.* an overwhelming defeat. — *verb* 1 to kill cruelly and in large numbers. 2 *colloq.* to defeat overwhelmingly. [from French *massacre*]

> ⊟ *noun* 1 slaughter, murder, extermination, carnage, butchery, holocaust, blood bath, annihilation, killing. *verb* SLAUGHTER. 1 butcher, murder, mow down, wipe out, exterminate, annihilate, kill, decimate. 2 rout, trounce, thrash, *colloq.* whop, *slang* wipe the floor with.

massage — *noun* a technique of easing pain or stiffness in the body, especially the muscles, by rubbing, kneading, and tapping with the hands; a body treatment using this technique. — *verb* 1 to perform massage on. 2 to alter (eg statistics) to produce a more favourable result. [from French *massage*, from Greek *massein*, to knead]

> ⊟ *noun* manipulation, kneading, rubbing, rub-down, physiotherapy, osteopathy. *verb* MANIPULATE. 1 knead, rub (down). 2 falsify, doctor, *colloq.* cook.

masseur /maˈsɜː(r)/ *noun* a person trained to carry out massage. [from French *masseur*]

masseuse /maˈsɜːz/ *noun* a woman trained to carry out massage. [from French *masseuse*]

massif /maˈsiːf/ *noun Geol.* a mountainous plateau that differs structurally and topographically from the surrounding lowland, the rocks of which is composed usually being older and harder. [from French *massif*; see MASSIVE]

massive *adj.* **1** very big, solid, and heavy. **2** *colloq.* very large: *a massive salary*. [from French *massif*, from *masse*, mass]

. . . .

HUGE, ENORMOUS, VAST, COLOSSAL, GIGANTIC, IMMENSE, MONUMENTAL, SUBSTANTIAL, BIG. **1** bulky, solid, heavy, weighty, large-scale, extensive.
TINY, SMALL.

. . . .

massively *adv.* in a massive way; to a massive degree.

mass market *Econ.* a market for goods that have been mass-produced.

mass media those forms of communication that reach large numbers of people, eg television and newspapers.

mass number *Chem.* the total number of protons and neutrons in the nucleus of an atom. It has different values for different isotopes of the same element. Also called NUCLEON NUMBER.

mass-produce *verb* to produce in a standard form in great quantities, especially using mechanization.

. . . .

manufacture, assemble, replicate, turn out, churn out.

. . . .

mass-produced *adj.* produced in a standardized form in large numbers.

mass-production *noun* the process or state of being mass-produced.

mass spectrograph *Chem.* an instrument used to measure the relative atomic masses of isotopes of chemical elements, by passing beams of ions (charged atoms) through electric and magnetic fields so that they can be separated according to the ratio of their charge to their mass. The ions strike a photographic plate, which is then developed in order to show their distribution.

mass spectrometer *Chem.* a mass spectrograph that is used to measure the relative atomic masses of isotopes of chemical elements, and that uses an electrical detector, as opposed to a photographic plate, to determine the distribution of ions (charged atoms).

mast[1] *noun* any upright wooden or metal supporting pole, especially one carrying the sails of a ship, or a radio or television aerial. — **before the mast** *Naut.* serving as an apprentice seaman. [from Anglo-Saxon *mæst*]

mast[2] *noun* the nuts of various forest trees, especially beech, oak, and chestnut, used as food for pigs. [from Anglo-Saxon *mæst*]

mastaba /ˈmastəbə/ *noun* an ancient Egyptian tomb built of brick or stone with sloping sides and a flat roof and a shaft which led to the underground burial chamber. [from Arabic *mastabah*, bench]

mastectomy *noun* (PL. **mastectomies**) the surgical removal of a woman's breast. [from Greek *mastos*, breast + -ECTOMY]

master — *noun* **1** a person, especially male, who commands or controls. **2** the owner, especially male, of a dog, slave, etc. **3** a person with outstanding skill in a particular activity. **4** the commanding officer on a merchant ship. **5** a fully qualified craftsman, allowed to train others. **6** *old use* a male teacher. **7** (**Master**) a title for the heads of certain university colleges. **8** (*also* **master copy**) an original from which copies are made. **9** (**Master**) a degree of the level above Bachelor, or a person who holds this degree: *Master of Arts*. **10** (**Master**) a title for a boy too young to be called Mr. — *adj.* **1** fully qualified; highly skilled; expert. **2** main; principal: *master bedroom*. **3** controlling: *master switch*.

— *verb* **1** to overcome or defeat (eg feelings or an opponent). **2** to become skilled in. [from Latin *magister*, from *magnus*, great]

. . . .

noun **1** ruler, chief, governor, head, lord, captain, *colloq.* boss, employer, commander, controller, director, manager, superintendent, overseer, principal, overlord, owner. **3** expert, genius, virtuoso, past master, maestro, dab hand, ace, *colloq.* pro. **6** teacher, tutor, instructor, schoolmaster, guide, guru. *adj.* **1** expert, masterly, skilled, skilful, proficient, virtuoso, *colloq.* ace. **2** chief, principal, main, leading, foremost, prime, great, grand. **3** predominant, controlling. *verb* **1** conquer, defeat, subdue, subjugate, vanquish, triumph over, overcome, quell, rule, control. **2** learn, grasp, acquire, *colloq.* get the hang of, manage.
noun **1** servant, underling. **3** amateur. **6** learner, pupil. *adj.* **1** inept. **2** subordinate.

. . . .

master-at-arms *noun* (PL. **masters-at-arms**) a ship's officer responsible for maintaining discipline.

masterful *adj.* showing the authority, skill, or power of a master.

. . . .

powerful, authoritative, dominant, strong, commanding, forceful, imperious, high-handed, domineering, arrogant, overbearing, despotic, dictatorial, tyrannical, autocratic, *colloq.* bossy.
humble, downtrodden, *colloq.* henpecked.

. . . .

master key a key which opens a number of locks, each of which has its own different key.

masterliness *noun* being masterly.

masterly *adj.* showing the skill of a master.

. . . .

expert, skilled, skilful, dexterous, adept, adroit, first-rate, *colloq.* ace, excellent, superb, superior, supreme.
inept, clumsy.

. . . .

mastermind — *noun* **1** a person of great intellectual ability. **2** the person responsible for devising a complex scheme or plan. — *verb* to be the mastermind of (a scheme, etc).

. . . .

noun **1** genius, prodigy, expert, brain, intellectual, *colloq.* egghead. **2** *colloq.* brains, ringleader. *verb* devise, think up, contrive, engineer, be behind, inspire.

. . . .

master of ceremonies an announcer, especially of speakers at a formal dinner, or of performers in a stage entertainment.

masterpiece or **masterwork** *noun* an extremely skilful piece of work, especially the greatest work of an artist or writer.

. . . .

magnum opus, pièce de résistance, chef d'oeuvre, tour de force, jewel.

. . . .

masterstroke *noun* a very clever or well-timed action.

mastery *noun* **1** (*often* **mastery of something**) great skill or knowledge in it. **2** (*often* **mastery over something** or **someone**) control over them.

. . . .

1 proficiency, skill, ability, command, expertise, virtuosity, knowledge, know-how, dexterity, familiarity, grasp. **2** control, command, domination, supremacy, upper hand, dominion, authority.
1 incompetence. **2** subjugation.

. . . .

masthead *noun* **1** the top of a ship's mast. **2** the title of a newspaper or periodical printed at the top of its front page.

mastic *noun* **1** a gum obtained from a Mediterranean evergreen tree, used in making varnish. **2** any of various waterproof putty-like pastes used as joint-sealers in the building trade. [from Greek *mastiche*]

masticate *verb trans., intrans. formal, technical* to chew (food). [from Latin *masticare*]

mastication *noun* the process of chewing.

mastiff *noun* a large powerful short-haired breed of dog, formerly used in hunting. [from Old French *mastin*, from Latin *mansuetus*, tame]

mastitis /maˈstaɪtɪs/ *noun* inflammation of a woman's breast or an animal's udder, usually caused by bacterial infection. [from Greek *mastos*, breast + -ITIS]

mastodon /ˈmastədɒn/ *noun* any of several extinct mammals that were widespread during the Tertiary Era, and from which elephants are thought to have evolved. [from Greek *mastos*, breast + *odontos*, tooth]

mastoid — *adj.* like a nipple or breast. — *noun* the raised area of bone behind the ear. [from Greek *mastoeides*, like a breast]

masturbate *verb intrans., trans.* to rub or stroke the genitals of (oneself or someone else) so as to produce sexual arousal, usually to the point of orgasm or ejaculation. [from Latin *masturbari*]

masturbation *noun* the act or practice of masturbating.

masturbatory *adj.* relating to or aiding masturbation.

mat¹ — *noun* **1** a flat piece of any of various materials in carpet-like form, used as a decorative or protective floor-covering, or for wiping shoes on to remove dirt. **2** a smaller piece of fabric, or a harder material, used under a plate, vase, etc to protect a surface from heat or scratches. **3** a carpet-like covering, eg of vegetation or hair. — *verb trans., intrans.* (**matted**, **matting**) to become or cause to become tangled into a dense untidy mass. [from Anglo-Saxon *matt* or *matte*]

mat² same as MATT.

matador *noun* the principal toreador in a bullfight, the man who kills the bull. [from Spanish *matador*, from *matar*, to kill]

match¹ *noun* **1** a short thin piece of wood or strip of card coated on the tip with a substance that ignites when rubbed against a rough surface, used to light fires, etc. **2** a slow-burning fuse used in cannons. [from Old French *mesche*]

match² — *noun* **1** a contest or game. **2** (**a match for someone** or **something**) a person or thing that is similar or identical to, or combines well with, another. **3** a person or thing able to equal, or surpass, another: *meet one's match*. **4** a partnership or pairing; a suitable partner, eg in marriage. — *verb* **1** *trans., intrans.* (*also* **match up** or **match something up**) to combine well; to be well suited or compatible; to put (matching people or things) together. **2** to set in competition; to hold up in comparison. **3** to be equal to; to make, produce, perform, etc an equivalent to: *cannot match let alone beat the offer*. [from Anglo-Saxon *gemæcca*, spouse]

⊟ *noun* **1** contest, competition, bout, game, test, trial. **2** equal to, rival to. **4** marriage, alliance, union, partnership, affiliation. *verb* **1** fit, accord, suit, correspond, harmonize, tally, co-ordinate, blend, adapt, relate, tone in with, join, marry, unite, mate, link, couple, combine, ally, pair, yoke, team. **2** pit against, oppose. **3** equal, compare, measure up to, rival, compete, contend, vie.

⊞ *verb* **1** clash.

matchbox *noun* a small cardboard box for holding matches.

matching *adj.* similar; compatible; part of the same set.

⊟ corresponding, comparable, equivalent, like, identical, co-ordinating, similar, duplicate, same, twin.

⊞ clashing.

matchless *adj. literary* having no equal; superior to all.

⊟ unequalled, peerless, incomparable, unmatched, unparalleled, unsurpassed, unrivalled, inimitable, unique.

matchmaker *noun* a person who tries to arrange romantic partnerships between people.

matchmaking *noun* the activity of a matchmaker.

match point the stage in a game at which only one more point is needed by a player to win; the winning point.

matchstick *noun* the stem of a wooden match.

matchwood *noun* **1** wood suitable for making matches. **2** splinters.

mate¹ — *noun* **1** an animal's breeding partner. **2** *colloq.* a person's sexual partner, especially a husband or wife. **3** *colloq.* a companion or friend, often used as a form of address, especially to a man. **4** (*in compounds*) a colleague; a person with whom one shares something: *workmate/flatmate*. **5** a tradesman's assistant. **6** one of a pair. **7** any officer below the rank of master on a merchant ship. — *verb* **1** *intrans., said of animals* to copulate. **2** to bring (animals) together for breeding. **3** *intrans., trans.* to marry. **4** to join as a pair. [related to Anglo-Saxon *gemetta*, guest at one's table]

⊟ *noun* **2** partner, spouse, husband, wife. **3** friend, companion, comrade, *colloq.* pal, *North Amer. colloq.* buddy, *colloq.* chum. **4** colleague, partner, fellow worker, co-worker, associate. **5** assistant, helper, subordinate. **6** match, fellow, twin. *verb* **1, 2** couple, pair. **1** breed, copulate. **3, 4** join, match, marry, wed.

mate² see CHECKMATE.

maté or **mate** /ˈmɑːteɪ/ *noun* **1** a S American species of holly tree. **2** a type of tea made from its dried leaves. [from Quechua *mati*, a gourd (in which the tea is made)]

mater /ˈmeɪtə(r)/ *noun humorous, old colloq. use* a mother, also used as a form of address. [from Latin *mater*]

material — *noun* **1** any substance out of which something is, or may be, made. **2** cloth; fabric. **3** (**materials**) instruments or tools needed for a particular activity. **4** information providing the substance from which a book, television programme, etc is prepared. — *adj.* **1** relating to, or consisting of, solid matter; not abstract or spiritual. **2** relating to physical, not emotional, well-being: *material comforts*. **3** *technical* important; significant; relevant: *facts not material to the discussion*. [from Latin *materia*, matter]

⊟ *noun* **1** stuff, substance, body, matter. **2** fabric, textile, cloth. **4** information, facts, data, evidence, constituents, work, notes. *adj.* **1** physical, concrete, tangible, substantial. **3** relevant, significant, important, meaningful, pertinent, essential, vital, indispensable, serious.

⊞ *adj.* **1** abstract. **2** irrelevant.

materialism *noun* **1** *often derog.* excessive interest in material possessions and financial success. **2** *Philos.* the theory stating that only material things exist, especially denying the existence of a soul or spirit.

materialist *noun* a follower of or believer in materialism.

materialistic *adj.* relating to or characteristic of materialism.

materialize or **materialise** *verb intrans.* **1** to become real, visible, or tangible; to appear. **2** to become fact; to happen.

⊟ **1** appear, arise, take shape, turn up, happen, occur.

⊞ **1** disappear.

materially *adv.* **1** *formal* to an important or significant extent. **2** with regard to physical well-being.

maternal *adj.* **1** of, typical of, or like a mother. **2** related on the mother's side of the family. [from Latin *maternus*, from *mater*, mother]

maternally *adv.* in a maternal way.

maternity — *noun* the state of being or becoming a mother. — *adj.* relating to pregnancy or giving birth. [from Latin *maternus*]

matey or **maty** *adj.* (**matier**, **matiest**) *colloq.* friendly or familiar, often in an insincere way.

mathematical *adj.* **1** of, relating to, or using mathematics. **2** very exact or accurate.

mathematically *adv.* by the use of mathematics.

mathematician *noun* a student of, or expert in, mathematics.

mathematics *sing. noun* the science dealing with measurements, numbers, quantities and shapes, usually expressed as symbols. [from Greek *mathematike*, relating to learning, from *manthanein*, to learn]

maths *sing. noun colloq.* mathematics.

matily *adv.* with a matey manner.

matinée or **matinee** /ˈmatɪneɪ/ *noun* an afternoon performance of a play or showing of a film. [from French *matinée*, morning]

matinée jacket or **matinée coat** a baby's short jacket or coat.

matins *sing. or pl. noun* **1** *RC Church* the first of the seven canonical hours, periods during the day set aside for formal prayer. See also COMPLINE, LAUDS, NONE[2], SEXT, TERCE, VESPERS. **2** *Church of E.* the service of morning prayer. [from Latin *matutinus*, of the morning]

matri- *combining form* of a woman or a mother: *matricide*. [from Latin *mater*, mother]

matriarch /ˈmeɪtrɪɑːk/ *noun* the female head of a family, community, or tribe. [from MATRI-, PATRIARCH]

matriarchal /meɪtrɪˈɑːkəl/ *adj.* of, ruled by, or resembling a matriarch.

matriarchy /ˈmeɪtrɪɑːkɪ/ *noun* (PL. **matriarchies**) a social system in which women are the heads of families or tribes, and property and power passes from mother to daughter.

matric /məˈtrɪk/ see MATRICULATION.

matrices /ˈmeɪtrɪsiːz/ see MATRIX.

matricidal /meɪtrɪˈsaɪdl/ *adj.* relating to or involving matricide.

matricide /ˈmeɪtrɪsaɪd/ *noun* **1** the killing of a mother by her own child. **2** a person who kills his or her own mother.

matriculate *verb trans., intrans.* to admit or become eligible to be admitted as a member, especially of a university or college. [from Latin *matriculare*, to register]

matriculation *noun* **1** the process of matriculating. **2** (*also colloq.* **matric**) formerly, a university or college entrance examination taken at school.

matrimonial *adj.* relating to marriage.

⊟ marital, nuptial, marriage, wedding, married, wedded, conjugal, connubial.

matrilineal *adj. Anthropol.* denoting descent or kinship reckoned through the mother or through females alone.

matrimony *noun* (PL. **matrimonies**) **1** the state of being married. **2** the wedding ceremony. [from Latin *matrimonium*, wedlock]

matrix /ˈmeɪtrɪks/ *noun* (PL. **matrices**, **matrixes**) **1** *Maths.* a square or rectangular arrangement of symbols or numbers, in rows or columns, usually enclosed by large parentheses, vertical lines, or square brackets. **2** *Biol.* in tissues such as bone and cartilage, the substance in which cells are embedded. **3** *Anat.* the tissue lying beneath the body and root of a fingernail or toenail, and from which it develops. **4** *Geol.* the rock in which a mineral or fossil is embedded. **5** *Printing* a mould, especially one from which printing type is produced. **6** *old use* the womb. [from Latin *matrix*, womb]

matron *noun* **1** the former title of the head of the nursing staff in a hospital (now usually called *senior nursing officer*). **2** a woman in charge of nursing and domestic arrangements in an institution, eg a school or old people's home. **3** any dignified or solemn middle-aged to elderly (especially married) woman. [from French *matrone*, from Latin *mater*, mother]

matronly *adj., said of a woman* **1** dignified; authoritative. **2** *euphemistic* plump because of middle-age.

matron of honour (PL. **matrons of honour**) a married woman who is a bride's chief attendant at a wedding. See also MAID OF HONOUR.

matt or **mat** *adj.* having a dull surface without gloss or shine. [from French *mat*, dull colour or unpolished surface]

matted *adj., often said of hair* tangled.

matter — *noun* **1** the substance from which all physical things are made; material. **2** material of a particular kind: *vegetable matter.* **3** a subject or topic; a concern, affair, or question: *if it's a matter of money/matters of principle.* **4** content as distinct from style or form. **5** (**a matter of ...**) an approximate amount: *in a matter of minutes.* **6** pus. — *verb intrans.* to be important or significant. — **as a matter of fact** in fact. **be the matter with someone** or **something** to be the trouble, difficulty, or thing that is wrong. **for that matter** as far as that is concerned. **no matter** it is not important. **no matter ...** regardless of: *no matter when she comes.* [from Latin *materia*, subject or substance]

⊟ *noun* **1, 2** material. **2** substance, stuff. **3** subject, issue, topic, question, affair, business, concern, event, episode, incident. *verb* count, be important, make a difference, mean something.

matter-of-fact *adj.* calm and straightforward, not excited or emotional.

⊟ unemotional, emotionless, straightforward, sober, unimaginative, flat, *colloq.* deadpan.

⊞ emotional.

matte shot /mat/ a motion picture scene in which a mask, or matte, restricts the image exposed so that a second image can be superimposed subsequently.

matting *noun* material of rough woven fibres for making mats.

mattock *noun* a kind of pickaxe whose blade is flattened horizontally at one end, used for breaking up soil, etc. [from Anglo-Saxon *mattuc*]

mattress *noun* a large flat fabric-covered pad, now usually of foam rubber or springs, used for sleeping on, by itself or on a supporting frame. [from Old French *materas*, from Arabic *almatrah*, place where anything is thrown]

maturate *verb trans., intrans.* **1** to make or become mature. **2** *Medicine* to discharge or cause to discharge pus. [from Latin *maturare*]

maturation *noun* bringing or coming to maturity.

mature — *adj.* **1** fully grown or developed. **2** having or showing adult good sense. **3** *said of cheese, wine, etc* having a fully developed flavour. **4** *said of bonds, insurance policies, etc* paying out, or beginning to pay out, money to the holder. **5** *formal* carefully or thoroughly thought out. — *verb* **1** *intrans.* to become fully developed, or adult in outlook. **2** to make mature; to ripen. **3** *intrans. said of a life insurance policy, etc* to begin to produce a return. [from Latin *maturus*, ripe]

⊟ *adj.* **1, 2** adult, grown-up. **1** grown, full-grown, fully fledged, complete, perfect, perfected. **2** sensible, wise, prudent, sound, judicious. **3** ripe, ripened, seasoned, mellow, ready. *verb* **1, 2** develop, mellow, ripen, age. **1** grow up, come of age, bloom. **2** perfect. **3** fall due.

⊞ *adj.* **2** childish, immature.

maturity *noun* ripeness, full development.

▣ ripeness, readiness, mellowness, perfection, adulthood, majority, womanhood, manhood, wisdom, experience. ▨ immaturity, childishness.

MATV *abbrev.* Master Antenna Television.

maty same as MATEY.

maudlin *adj.* foolishly sad or sentimental, especially when drunk. [from Anglo-Saxon *Maudelein*, Mary Magdalene, often portrayed weeping]

maul *verb* **1** to attack fiercely, usually tearing flesh. **2** to handle roughly or clumsily. **3** to subject to fierce criticism. — *noun Rugby* a quickly formed gathering of players from both teams around a player holding the ball. [from Latin *malleus*, hammer]

▣ *verb* **1** claw, lacerate, beat (up), knock about, *colloq.* rough up, batter, molest. **2** abuse, ill-treat, manhandle, maltreat.

maunder *verb intrans.* (**maundered, maundering**) **1** (*also* **maunder on**) to talk in a rambling way. **2** to wander about, or behave, in an aimless way. [perhaps from obsolete *maunder*, to beg]

Maundy money *Brit.* silver money that is specially minted for the sovereign to distribute on Maundy Thursday.

Maundy Thursday the day before Good Friday. [from Old French *mande*, from Latin *mandatum*, command (from Christ's command in John 23.34)]

mausoleum *noun* (PL. **mausoleums**) a grand or monumental tomb. [from Latin *mausoleum*, named after the Tomb of Mausolus]

mauve /məʊv/ — *adj.* having a pale purple colour. — *noun* this colour. [from French *mauve*, from Latin *malva*, mallow]

maverick *noun* **1** *North Amer., esp. US* an unbranded stray animal, especially a calf. **2** a determinedly independent person; a nonconformist. [from Samuel Maverick (1803–70), Texas cattle-raiser]

maw *noun* **1** the jaws, throat, or stomach of a voracious animal. **2** *facetious* a greedy person's stomach. **3** something that seems to swallow things up. [from Anglo-Saxon *maga*]

mawkish *adj.* weakly sentimental. [from Norse *mathkr*, maggot]

▣ sentimental, sickly, slushy, sloppy, *colloq.* schmaltzy, *colloq.* syrupy, cloying, maudlin.

max. *abbrev.* maximum.

maxi- *combining form* forming words meaning 'extra long' or 'extra large': *maxi-coat*. [a shortening of MAXIMUM]

maxilla *noun* (PL. **maxillae**) *Biol.* **1** the upper jaw or jawbone in animals. **2** the chewing organ or organs of an insect, just behind the mouth. [from Latin *maxilla*]

maxillary *adj.* relating to or in the region of the maxilla.

maxim *noun* **1** a saying expressing a general truth. **2** a general rule or principle. [from Latin *maxima propositio* or *sententia*, greatest axiom or opinion]

▣ **1** saying, proverb, adage, axiom, aphorism, epigram, motto, byword. **2** precept, rule, principle.

maximal *adj.* of a maximum; of the greatest possible size, value, etc.

▣ utmost, supreme, top, peak, optimal.

maximize or **maximise** *verb* to make as high, great, etc as possible.

maximum — *adj.* greatest possible. — *noun* **1** the greatest possible number, quantity, degree, etc. **2** *Geom.* in coordinate geometry, the point at which the slope of a curve changes from positive to negative. A tangent to a curve at its maximum has a gradient of zero. [from Latin *maximus*, greatest]

▣ *adj.* greatest, highest, largest, biggest, most, utmost, supreme, top, peak. *noun* **1** most, top (point), utmost, upper limit, peak, pinnacle, summit, height, ceiling, extremity, zenith. ▨ *adj.* minimum. *noun* **1** minimum.

May *noun* **1** the fifth month of the year. **2** (**may** or **may tree**) any variety of hawthorn tree, or its blossom. [from *Maia*, in ancient Greek and Roman mythology the mother of the god Mercury]

may *verb aux.* (PAST TENSE **might**) expressing: **1** permission: *you may go now.* **2** possibility: *I may well leave.* **3** ability or competence: *may I help you?* **4** *formal* a wish: *may you prosper!* **5** *formal, old use* purpose: *listen, so that you may learn.* **6** *old affected use, facetious* a question: *who may you be?* **7** used to introduce the first of a pair of statements, with the sense of 'although': *you may be rich, but you're not happy.* [from Anglo-Saxon *mæg*, present tense of *magan*, to be able]

maybe *adv.* it may be; it is possible; perhaps.

▣ perhaps, possibly. ▨ definitely.

May Day the first day of May, a national holiday in many countries, traditionally a day of festivities.

mayday *noun* (*often* **Mayday**) the international radio distress signal sent out by ships and aircraft. [from French *m'aider*, help me]

mayfly *noun* a short-lived insect with transparent wings, which appears briefly in spring.

mayhem *noun* **1** a state of great confusion and disorder; chaos. **2** *Legal* the crime of maiming someone. [from Old French *mahaignier*, to wound]

mayn't *contr.* may not.

mayonnaise *noun* a cold creamy sauce made of egg yolk, oil, vinegar or lemon juice, and seasoning. [from French]

mayor *noun* the head of the local council in a city, town, or borough in England, Wales, and N Ireland, or of any of various communities in other countries. [from Latin *major*, comparative of *magnus*, great]

mayoral *adj.* relating to a mayor or the office of a mayor.

mayoralty *noun* (PL. **mayoralties**) the position, or period of office, of a mayor.

mayoress *noun* **1** a mayor's wife. **2** *old use* a female mayor.

maypole *noun* a tall pole set up for dancing round on May Day.

May queen a young woman, crowned with flowers, chosen to preside over May Day festivities.

maze *noun* **1** a confusing network of paths, each bordered by high walls or hedges, designed to test orientation abilities. **2** any confusingly complicated system, procedure, etc. [related to AMAZE]

▣ LABYRINTH. **2** network, tangle, web, complex, confusion, puzzle, intricacy.

mazurka *noun* a lively Polish dance, or a piece of music for this. [from Polish *mazurka*, of Mazur, a Polish province]

MB *abbrev. Medicinae Baccalaureus* (Latin), Bachelor of Medicine.

MBA *abbrev.* Master of Business Administration.

MBE *abbrev.* Member of the Order of the British Empire.

MBO *abbrev.* management buyout.

MC *abbrev.* **1** master of ceremonies. **2** Military Cross.

MCC *abbrev.* Marylebone Cricket Club.

McCarthyism *noun* an anti-communist witchhunt which pervaded the USA at the height of the Cold War in the 1950s, named after Senator J R McCarthy of Wisconsin who made (unsubstantiated) claims that there were a large number of communists in the government, administration, and army.

McCoy *noun* — **the real McCoy** *colloq.* the genuine article, not an imitation.

McJob *noun facetious* a low-paid, menial job. [from the name of the international fast food company *McDonald's*, alluding to the idea that some of the work there is menial]

MCP *abbrev.* male chauvinist pig.

MD *abbrev.* **1** managing director. **2** Maryland. **3** *Medicinae Doctor* (Latin), Doctor of Medicine.

Md[1] *abbrev.* Maryland.

Md[2] *symbol Chem.* mendelevium.

ME *abbrev.* **1** Maine. **2** *Medicine* myalgic encephalomyelitis, severe muscle weakness and general fatigue, often the long-term effect of a viral infection.

Me *abbrev.* Maine.

me[1] *pron.* **1** the object form of I, used by a speaker or writer to refer to himself or herself. **2** used for *I* after the verb *be* or when standing alone: *it's only me.* — **be me** *colloq.* to be suited to me: *this dress isn't really me.* [from Anglo-Saxon *mē*]

me[2] same as MI.

mea culpa /ˈmeɪə ˈkʌlpə/ *literary, facetious* I am to blame. [from Latin *mea culpa*, my fault]

mead[1] *noun* an alcoholic drink made by fermenting honey and water, usually with spices added. [from Anglo-Saxon *meodu*]

mead[2] *noun old use, poetic* a meadow. [from Anglo-Saxon *mæd*]

meadow *noun* **1** a low-lying field of grass, used for grazing animals or making hay. **2** any moist grassy area near a river. [from Anglo-Saxon *mædwe*]

⊟ **1** field, grassland, pasture, lea.

meadow pipit a ground-dwelling songbird, about the size of a sparrow, with brown streaky plumage and a slender bill.

meadow saffron same as AUTUMN CROCUS.

meadowsweet *noun* a European and Asian wild plant of the rose family, with fragrant cream-coloured flowers.

meagre *adj.* **1** lacking in quality or quantity; inadequate; scanty. **2** *said of a person* thin, especially unhealthily so. [from Old French *maigre*, thin]

⊟ **1** scanty, sparse, inadequate, deficient, skimpy, paltry, negligible, poor. **2** thin, puny, insubstantial, bony, emaciated, scrawny, slight.
⊟ **1** ample. **2** fat.

meal[1] *noun* **1** an occasion on which food is eaten. **2** an amount of food eaten on one occasion. — **make a meal of something 1** to eat it as a meal. **2** *colloq.* to exaggerate the importance of, eg by taking unnecessary time or trouble. [from Anglo-Saxon *mæl*, measure, portion of time]

Meals include: breakfast, wedding breakfast, *colloq.* elevenses, brunch, lunch, luncheon, tea, tea break, tea party, tiffin, afternoon tea, cream tea, high tea, evening meal, dinner, TV dinner, supper, harvest supper, fork supper, banquet, feast, *slang* blow-out, barbecue, buffet, spread, picnic, snack, takeaway.

meal[2] *noun* (*often in compounds*) **1** the edible parts of any grain, usually excluding wheat, ground to a coarse powder: *oatmeal.* **2** any other food substance in ground form: *bone meal.* [from Anglo-Saxon *melu* or *melo*]

mealie *noun South Afr.* an ear of maize. [from Afrikaans *mielie*, maize]

mealie meal *South Afr.* maize ground to a fine flour.

meals-on-wheels *pl. noun* a welfare service delivering cooked meals by car to the homes of old or sick people.

meal ticket 1 *North Amer., esp. US* a luncheon voucher. **2** *colloq.* a person or situation providing a source of income or other means of living.

mealy *adj.* (**mealier, mealiest**) containing meal; dry and powdery, like meal.

mealy-mouthed *adj. derog.* afraid to speak plainly or openly.

mean[1] *verb* (PAST AND PAST PARTICIPLE **meant**) **1** to express or intend to express, show, or indicate. **2** to intend; to have as a purpose: *didn't mean any harm.* **3** to be serious or sincere about: *he means what he says.* **4** to be important to (the stated degree); to represent: *your approval means a lot to me.* **5** to entail necessarily; to result in; to involve: *war means hardship.* **6** (**be meant for something**) to be destined to it: *she was meant for stardom.* **7** to foretell or portend: *cold cloudless evenings mean overnight frost.* — **mean well** to have good intentions. [from Anglo-Saxon *mænan*]

⊟ **1** signify, represent, denote, stand for, symbolize, suggest, indicate, imply. **2** intend, aim, propose, design. **5** cause, give rise to, result in, involve, entail, necessitate. **7** portend, foretell, forebode, bode, augur, presage, foreshadow.

mean[2] *adj.* **1** not generous. **2** unkind; despicable. **3** poor; shabby; of inferior quality. **4** *colloq.* vicious; malicious. **5** *colloq.* good; skilful: *plays a mean guitar.* — **no mean ...** *colloq.* **1** an excellent: *no mean singer.* **2** not an easy...; a very difficult: *no mean feat.* [from Anglo-Saxon *gemæne*]

⊟ **1** miserly, niggardly, parsimonious, selfish, tight-fisted, stingy, *colloq.* tight, penny-pinching. **2** unkind, unpleasant, nasty, bad-tempered, cruel. **3** lowly, base, shabby, poor, humble, wretched.
⊟ **1** generous. **2** kind. **3** splendid.

mean[3] — *noun* **1** a midway position, course, etc between two extremes. **2** *Maths.* a mathematical average, in particular: **a** (*in full* **arithmetic mean**) the average value of a set of n numbers, equal to the sum of the numbers divided by n. **b** (*in full* **weighted mean**) the average value of a set of n numbers, also taking into account their frequency. Each number is multiplied by the number of times it occurs, and the resulting values are summed and divided by n. **c** (*in full* **geometric mean**) the nth root of the product of n quantities or numbers, eg the geometric mean of 2 and 3 is the second (square) root of 6, ie 6. — *adj.* **1** midway; intermediate. **2** average. [from Old French *meien*, from Latin *medius*, middle]

⊟ *noun* **1** middle, midpoint, median, compromise, middle course, middle way, happy medium, golden mean. **2** average, norm, standard. *adj.* **1** intermediate, middle, halfway, median. **2** average, normal, standard.
⊟ *noun* **1** extreme *adj.* **1** extreme.

meander /mɪˈandə(r)/ — *verb intrans.* (**meandered, meandering**) *formal* **1** *said of a river* to bend and curve. **2** (*also* **meander about**) to wander randomly or aimlessly. — *noun* (*often* **meanders**) a bend; a winding course. [from Latin *Maeander*, winding river in Turkey (now *Menderes*)]

⊟ *verb* **1** wind, zigzag, turn, twist, snake, curve. **2** wander, stray, amble, ramble, stroll.

meanie or **meany** *noun* (PL. **meanies**) *colloq.* a selfish or ungenerous person.

meaning — *noun* **1** the sense in which a statement, action, word, etc is intended to be understood. **2** significance, importance, or purpose, especially when hidden or special.

— *adj.* intended to express special significance: *a meaning look*.

▪ *noun* SIGNIFICANCE, POINT. **1** sense, import, purport, implication, gist, trend, explanation, interpretation. **2** aim, intention, idea, purpose, object, value, worth.

meaningful *adj.* **1** having meaning; significant. **2** conveying a meaning: *a meaningful look*. **3** *Logic* capable of interpretation.

▪ **1** important, significant, relevant, valid, useful, worthwhile, material, purposeful, serious. **2** expressive, speaking, suggestive, warning, pointed.
▫ **1** unimportant, worthless.

meaningfully *adv.* in a meaningful or significant way.
meaningless *adj.* **1** without meaning or reason. **2** of no importance. **3** having no purpose; pointless.

▪ **1, 3** senseless, pointless. **1** empty, hollow, vacuous, vain, nonsensical, absurd. **2** insignificant, unimportant, worthless, insubstantial, trifling, trivial. **3** purposeless, useless, aimless, futile.
▫ MEANINGFUL. **2** important. **3** worthwhile.

meanness *noun* a mean quality or disposition.

means *noun* **1** the instrument or method used to achieve some object. **2** wealth; resources. — **by all means** yes, of course. **by any means** using any available method. **by means of ...** using .... **by no means** or **not by any means** not at all; definitely not. **a means to an end** something treated merely as a way of achieving a desired result, considered unimportant in every other respect. [from MEAN[3]]

▪ **1** method, mode, way, medium, course, agency, process, instrument, mechanism, channel, vehicle. **2** resources, funds, money, income, wealth, riches, substance, wherewithal, fortune, affluence. **by all means** certainly, definitely, of course, with pleasure. **by means of** using, through, via, with the help of, as a result of. **by no means** certainly not, not at all, never, *slang* no way.

means test an official inquiry into a person's wealth or income to determine eligibility for financial benefit from the state.
means-test *verb* to carry out a means test on (someone).
meant see MEAN[1].
meantime — *noun* the time or period between. — *adv.* in the time between; meanwhile. [from MEAN[3] + TIME]
meanwhile *adv.* during the time in between; at the same time. [from MEAN[3] + WHILE]
meany *noun colloq.* see MEANIE.
measles *sing. noun* a highly infectious viral disease, common in children, characterized by fever, a sore throat, and a blotchy red rash. [from Middle English *maseles*]
measly *adj.* (**measlier**, **measliest**) **1** *derog. colloq.*, *said of an amount or value* very small; worth very little. **2** relating to, or suffering from, measles.

▪ **1** small, minute, miserable, paltry, derisory, trifling, insignificant, worthless, negligible.

measurable *adj.* **1** able to be measured; of sufficient quantity to be measured. **2** noticeable; significant.

▪ **1** quantifiable, determinable, countable, calculable, computable.

measure — *noun* **1** size, volume, etc determined by comparison with something of known size, etc, usually an in-

strument graded in standard units. **2** (*often in compounds*) such an instrument: *a tape-measure*. **3** a standard unit of size, etc; a system of such units; a standard amount: *metric measure/a measure of whisky*. **4** (*usually* **measures**) an action; a step: *drastic measures*. **5** a limited, or appropriate, amount or extent: *a measure of politeness/in some measure/had my measure of luck*. **6** *Mus.* time or rhythm; a bar. **7** *Poetry* rhythm. **8** (*usually* **measures**) a layer of rock containing a particular mineral, etc: *coal measures*. **9** *old use* a dance. — *verb* **1** *trans.*, *intrans.* to determine the size, volume, etc of, usually with a specially made instrument. **2** *intrans.* to be a (stated) size. **3** (*also* **measure something off** or **out**) to mark or divide into units of known size, etc. **4** to set in competition with: *measure his strength against mine*. — **beyond measure** *literary* exceptionally great; to an exceedingly great degree. **for good measure** as something extra, or above the minimum necessary. **get the measure of someone** to assess their character or abilities. **measure up** to reach the required standard. **measure up to** to be equal to; to be capable of fulfilling. [from Latin *mensura*, measure]

▪ *noun* **1** size, quantity, magnitude, amount, degree, extent, range, scope, proportion. **2** rule, gauge, scale, standard, criterion, norm, touchstone, yardstick, test, meter. **4** step, course, action, deed, procedure, method, act, bill, statute. **5** portion, share, allocation. *verb* **1** quantify, evaluate, assess, weigh, value, gauge, judge, calculate, estimate, survey, compute. **for good measure** as well, besides, in addition, furthermore, over and above. **measure up** be up to it, *colloq.* fit the bill, *colloq.* make it, *colloq.* make the grade. **measure up to** equal, meet, match, satisfy, fulfil, compare with, touch, rival, come up to.

measured *adj.* **1** slow and steady. **2** carefully chosen or considered: *a measured response*.

▪ DELIBERATE. **1** slow, unhurried, steady. **2** studied, well-thought-out, calculated, considered, planned, reasoned, precise, careful.

measurement *noun* **1** (*often* **measurements**) a size, amount, etc determined by measuring. **2** (*often* **measurements**) the size of a part of the body. **3** the act of measuring. **4** a standard system of measuring.

▪ **1** dimension, size, extent, amount, magnitude, area, capacity, height, depth, length, width, weight, volume. **3** assessment, evaluation, estimation, computation, calculation, calibration, gauging, judgement, appraisal, appreciation, survey.

meat *noun* **1** the flesh of any animal used as food. *Red meats* include beef and veal (from cattle), lamb and mutton (from sheep), and pork (from pigs). *White meat* is obtained from poultry, and *game* is the flesh of wild birds and animals, eg grouse, deer. Meat is a good source of protein, but it has a high cholesterol content. **2** the basic, most important part; the essence. **3** *old use* food in general; a meal. — **meat and drink 1** a source of enjoyment. **2** one's basic means of support. [from Anglo-Saxon *mete*]

▪ **1** flesh. **2** essence, substance, body, pith, core, marrow, kernel. **3** food, rations, provisions, nourishment, sustenance, subsistence, *colloq.* eats.

Kinds of meat include: beef, veal, lamb, mutton, ham, bacon, gammon, chicken, turkey, goose, duck, rabbit, hare, venison, pheasant, grouse, partridge, pigeon, quail; offal, liver, heart, tongue, kidney, brains, brawn, pig's knuckle, trotters, oxtail, sweetbread, tripe; steak, minced beef, sausage, rissole, faggot, beefburger, hamburger, black pudding, pâté.

Cuts of meat include: shoulder, collar, hand, loin, hock, leg, chop, shin, knuckle, rib, spare-rib, breast, brisket, chine, cutlet, fillet, rump, scrag, silverside, topside, sirloin, flank, escalope, neck, saddle.

meatball *noun* a small ball of minced meat mixed with breadcrumbs and herbs.

meatiness *noun* a meaty quality or condition.

meatus /mɪˈeɪtəs/ *noun* (PL. **meatuses**) *Anat.* a passage between body parts, or an opening, eg the passage that leads from the external surface of the ear to the eardrum. [from Latin *meatus*, from *meare*, to go]

meaty *adj.* (**meatier**, **meatiest**) **1** full of, or containing, animal flesh. **2** resembling or tasting like meat, especially cooked meat. **3** full of interesting information or ideas: *a meaty article.*

mecca or **Mecca** /ˈmɛkə/ *noun* any place of outstanding importance or significance, especially one much visited: *St Andrews, the mecca of golf.* [after the city of Mecca]

mechanic *noun* a skilled worker who repairs or maintains machinery. [from Greek *mechane*, contrivance]

mechanical *adj.* **1** of or concerning machines. **2** worked by, or performed with, machinery. **3** done without or not requiring much thought.

≣ **3** automatic, involuntary, instinctive, routine, habitual, impersonal, emotionless, cold, matter-of-fact, unfeeling, lifeless, dead, dull.

≣ **3** conscious.

mechanical advantage *Engineering* the ratio of the load (output force) to the effort (input force) for a simple machine.

mechanical engineering the branch of engineering concerned with the design, construction, and operation of machines of all types, and the design, operation, and testing of engines that produce power from steam, petrol, nuclear energy, etc.

mechanically *adv.* by means of or as regards mechanics.

mechanics *noun* **1** (*sing.*) the branch of physics that is concerned with the study of the motion of bodies and the forces that act on them. It includes dynamics (the study of forces that act on moving objects) and statics (the study of forces that do not produce motion). **2** (*sing.*) the art or science of machine construction. **3** (*pl.*) the system on which something works.

mechanism *noun* **1** a working part of a machine, or its system of working parts. **2** a means. **3** *Psychol.* an action serving some (often subconscious) purpose: *laughter is a common defence mechanism.*

≣ **1** machine, machinery, engine, appliance, instrument, tool, motor, works, workings, gadget, device, apparatus, contrivance, gears, components. **2** means, method, agency, process, procedure, system, technique, medium, structure, operation.

mechanistic *adj.* **1** relating to mechanics. **2** relating to a mechanism.

mechanization or **mechanisation** *noun* the act or process of mechanizing.

mechanize or **mechanise** *verb* **1** to cause to operate with, or be operated by, machines rather than people. **2** to supply (troops) with motor vehicles rather than horses.

MEd *abbrev.* Master of Education.

Med *noun* (**the Med**) *colloq.* the Mediterranean Sea.

med. *abbrev.* **1** medieval. **2** medical. **3** medicine. **4** medium.

medal *noun* a flat piece of metal decorated with a design or inscription and offered as an award for merit or bravery, or in celebration of a special occasion. [from French *médaille*, from Latin *metallum*, metal]

≣ insignia, award, badge, rosette.

medallion *noun* **1** a large medal-like piece of jewellery, usually worn on a chain. **2** an oval or circular decorative feature in architecture or on textiles. **3** a thin circular cut of meat. [from French *médaillon*; related to MEDAL]

medallist *noun* a person awarded a medal, especially for excellence in sport.

meddle *verb intrans.* **1** (**meddle in something**) to interfere in it. **2** (**meddle with something**) to tamper with it. [from Old French *medler*]

≣ **1** interfere in, intervene in, pry into, *colloq.* poke one's nose into, snoop into, intrude into, butt into. **2** interfere with, tamper with, fiddle with.

meddler *noun* a person who meddles.

meddlesome *adj. derog.* fond of meddling.

≣ interfering, meddling, prying, intrusive, intruding, mischievous.

Mede *noun* a member of an ancient people living in Media, SW of the Caspian Sea.

media see MEDIUM.

mediaeval see MEDIEVAL.

mediagenic /miːdɪəˈdʒɛnɪk/ *adj.*, *said of a person* able to communicate well or present a good image in the media, especially on television. [from MEDIA + PHOTOGENIC]

medial *adj.* of or situated in the middle; intermediate. [from Latin *medialis*, from *medius*, middle]

medially *adv.* **1** in a medial way. **2** so as to be medial.

median — *noun* **1** a middle point or part. **2** *Geom.* a straight line between any vertex (angle) of a triangle and the centre of the opposite side. The point at which the three medians of a triangle intersect is the *centroid*. **3** *Statistics* the middle value in a set of numbers or measurements arranged in order from smallest to largest, eg the median of 1, 5, 11 is 5. If there is an even number of measurements, the median is the average of the middle two measurements. — *adj.* situated in or passing through the middle. [from Latin *medianus*, from *medius*, middle]

mediate — *verb* **1** (*intrans.*) to act as the agent seeking to reconcile the two sides in a disagreement. **2** to intervene in or settle (a dispute) in this way. **3** to convey or transmit (views, etc) as an agent or intermediary. — *adj.* **1** resulting from mediation. **2** indirectly related or connected, eg through some other person. [from Latin *mediare*, to be in the middle]

≣ *verb* **1**, **2** arbitrate, adjudicate. **1** conciliate, negotiate, referee, umpire, moderate, intercede, step in. **2** intervene in, resolve, settle, reconcile.

mediation *noun* the act or process of mediating.

mediator *noun* a person who mediates.

≣ arbitrator, adjudicator, referee, umpire, intermediary, negotiator, go-between, interceder, judge, moderator, intercessor, conciliator, peacemaker, ombudsman.

medic *noun colloq.* a doctor or medical student.

Medicaid *noun* a scheme in the USA which provides assistance with medical expenses for people with low incomes.

medical — *adj.* **1** of doctors or the science or practice of medicine. **2** concerned with medicine rather than surgery. — *noun* a medical examination, to discover a person's physical health. [from Latin *medicus*, physician, from *mederi*, to heal]

medical certificate a certificate, provided by a doctor, outlining a person's state of health, especially for employment purposes.

medically *adv.* by medical means or as regards medical practice.

medicament *noun formal* a medicine. [from Latin *medicamentum*, from *medicare*, to cure]

Medicare *noun* **1** a scheme in the USA which provides medical insurance for people aged 65 and over, and for certain categories of disabled people. **2** a system providing universal medical insurance in Australia.

medicate *verb* **1** to treat with medicine. **2** to add a healing or health-giving substance to: *medicated shampoo*. [from Latin *medicare*, to cure]

medication *noun* medicine, or treatment by medicine.

Medici, *French* **Médicis** *noun* a banking family which virtually ruled Florence (1434–94), without formally holding office. They became hereditary Dukes of Florence (1537) and Grand Dukes of Tuscany (from 1569), and their dynastic power base moved first to Rome and then to France.

medicinal *adj.* **1** having healing qualities; used as a medicine. **2** of or relating to healing.

◨ THERAPEUTIC, HEALING, REMEDIAL, MEDICAL. **1** curative, restorative.

medicinally *adv.* by medicinal means.

medicine *noun* **1** any substance used to treat or prevent disease or illness, especially taken internally. **2** the science or practice of treating or preventing illness, especially using prepared substances rather than surgery. — **get a taste** or **dose of one's own medicine** to suffer the same unpleasant treatment one has used on others. **take one's medicine** to accept an unpleasant but deserved punishment. [from Latin *medicina*]

◨ **1** medication, drug, cure, remedy, medicament, prescription, pharmaceutical, panacea.

Types of medicine include: tablet, capsule, pill, painkiller, lozenge, pastille, gargle, linctus, tonic, laxative, suppository, antacid, ointment, arnica, eyedrops, ear drops, nasal spray, inhaler, *trademark* Ventolin, antibiotic, penicillin, emetic, gripe-water, paregoric. *See also* **drug**.

Forms of alternative medicine include: acupuncture, aromatherapy, chiropractic, herbal remedies, homeopathy, naturopathy, osteopathy, reflexology.

medicine ball a heavy, fabric-covered metal ball thrown from person to person as a form of exercise.

medicine man among certain peoples, a person believed to have magic powers, used for healing or sorcery.

medico *noun* (PL. **medicos**) *colloq.* a doctor or medical student.

medieval or **mediaeval** /mɛdɪ'iːvl/ *adj.* relating to or characteristic of the Middle Ages. [from Latin *medius*, middle + *aevum*, age]

medievalist or **mediaevalist** *noun* a student of, or expert in, any area or aspect of study of the medieval period.

mediocre /miːdɪ'oʊkə(r)/ *adj. derog.* only ordinary or average; rather inferior. [from Latin *mediocris*, from *medius*, middle]

◨ ordinary, average, middling, medium, indifferent, unexceptional, undistinguished, *colloq.* so-so, run-of-the-mill, commonplace, insignificant, second-rate, inferior, uninspired.

◳ exceptional, extraordinary, distinctive.

mediocrity /miːdɪ'ɒkrɪtɪ/ *noun* (PL. **mediocrities**) *derog.* **1** a mediocre quality or condition. **2** a mediocre person or thing.

◨ **1** ordinariness, unimportance, insignificance, poorness, inferiority, indifference. **2** nonentity, nobody.

meditate *verb* **1** *intrans.* to spend time in deep religious or spiritual thought, often with the mind in a practised state of emptiness. **2** (**meditate something** or **meditate on something**) to think deeply and carefully about it. [from Latin *meditari*, to reflect upon]

◨ **1** reflect, ponder, ruminate, contemplate, muse, brood, think. **2** think over, consider, deliberate, mull over, study, speculate on, scheme, plan, devise, intend.

meditation *noun* **1** the act of meditating. **2** deep thought, contemplation.

◨ CONTEMPLATION, RUMINATION, CONSIDERATION, DELIBERATION, COGITATION, STUDY. **2** reflection, musing, brooding, thought.

meditative *adj.* inclined to meditate.

Mediterranean — *noun* (**the Mediterranean**) a large land-locked sea lying between N Africa, SW Asia, and S Europe. — *adj.* **1** in or relating to the area of the Mediterranean. **2** characteristic of this area. [from Latin *mediterraneus*, from *medius*, middle + *terra*, earth]

medium — *noun* (PL. **mediums** except in sense 2, **media**) **1** something by or through which an effect is produced. **2** (*usually* **mass media**) means by which news, information, etc are communicated to the public, usually television, radio, and the press collectively. **3** a person through whom the spirits of dead people are said to communicate with the living. **4** *Biol.* a substance in which specimens are preserved, bacteria are grown, etc. **5** a middle position, condition, or course: *a happy medium*. **6** *Art* a particular category of materials seen as a means of expression, eg watercolours, photography, or clay. — *adj.* **1** intermediate; midway; average. **2** moderate. [from Latin *medius*, middle]

◨ *noun* **1** means, agency, channel, vehicle, instrument, way, mode, form, avenue, organ. **3** psychic, spiritualist, spiritist, clairvoyant. **5** average, middle, midpoint, middle ground, compromise, centre, happy medium, golden mean. *adj.* **1** average, middle, median, mean, medial, intermediate, midway, standard. **2** moderate, fair, middling.

medium wave a radio wave with a wavelength between 200 and 1000 metres.

medlar /'mɛdlə(r)/ *noun* **1** a small brown apple-like fruit eaten only when already decaying. **2** the small Eurasian tree that bears it. [from Old French *medler*]

medley *noun* (PL. **medleys**) **1** a piece of music made up of pieces from other songs, tunes, etc. **2** a mixture or miscellany. **3** a race in stages, each stage a different length or, in swimming, swum using a different stroke. [from Old French *medler*, to mix]

◨ **1, 2** potpourri. **2** assortment, mixture, miscellany, hotchpotch, *North Amer.* hodgepodge, collection, jumble.

medulla /mɛ'dʌlə/ *noun* (PL. **medullae**, **medullas**) **1** *Anat.* the central part of an organ or tissue, when this differs in structure or function from the outer layer, eg pith of plant stem, adrenal medulla in animals. **2** *Anat.* the medulla oblongata. [from Latin *medulla*, marrow]

medulla oblongata /mɛ'dʌlə ɒblɒŋ'gɑːtə/ *Anat.* in vertebrates, the part of the brain that arises from the spinal cord and forms the lower part of the brain stem. It contains centres that control breathing, heartbeat, and co-ordination of nerve impulses from special sense organs.

medusa /məˈdjuːsə/ *noun* (PL. **medusae**) *Zool.* in the life cycle of a coelenterate (eg jellyfish), a member of the sexually reproducing generation, which produces gametes. The medusa is free-swimming, and typically has a disc-shaped or bell-shaped body with marginal tentacles and a centrally located mouth on the underside. [from Latin *Medusa*, from Greek *Medousa*, the Gorgon]

meek *adj.* **1** having a mild and gentle temperament. **2** submissive. [from Norse *mjukr*]

. . . .

▤ **1** mild, gentle, peaceful, long-suffering, forbearing, patient, humble, modest, unassuming, unpretentious. **2** submissive, docile, resigned, tame, timid, spiritless.

▣ **1** arrogant. **2** assertive, rebellious.

. . . .

meerschaum /ˈmɪəʃəm/ *noun* **1** a fine whitish clay-like mineral. **2** a tobacco pipe with a bowl made of this. [from German *Meer*, sea + *Schaum*, foam]

meet[1] — *verb* (PAST TENSE AND PAST PARTICIPLE **met**) **1** to come together with by chance or arrangement. **2** *intrans.* to come together by chance or arrangement; to assemble in a group. **3** *trans., intrans.* to be introduced to (someone) for the first time. **4** to be present at the arrival of: *met the train.* **5** *trans., intrans.* to join; to come into contact with: *where the path meets the road.* **6** to satisfy: *meet your requirements.* **7** to pay: *meet costs.* **8** to come into the view, experience, or presence of: *the sight that met my eyes.* **9** *trans., intrans.* (**meet something** or **meet with something**) to come into opposition against it. **10** (*also* **meet with something**) to encounter or experience it: *met his death.* **11** (*also* **meet with something**) to receive it: *suggestions met with approval.* **12** to answer or oppose: *meet force with greater force.* — *noun* **1** a sporting event, especially a series of athletics competitions. **2** the assembly of hounds and huntsmen and women before a fox-hunt. — **more ... than meets the eye** more complicated, interesting, etc than it appears. [from Anglo-Saxon *metan*, to meet]

. . . .

▤ *verb* **1, 9, 10** encounter. **1** find, come across, run across, *colloq.* run into, chance on, *colloq.* bump into. **2** gather, collect, assemble, congregate, convene. **5** join, converge, come together (with), connect (with), cross, intersect, touch, abut. **6** fulfil, satisfy, match, answer, measure up to, equal, perform. **7** pay, settle, discharge. **9, 10** face. **10** experience, go through, undergo, endure.

▣ *verb* **2** scatter. **5** diverge.

. . . .

meet[2] *adj. old use* proper, correct, or suitable. [from Anglo-Saxon *gemæte*]

meeting *noun* **1** an act of coming together. **2** an assembly or gathering. **3** a sporting event, especially in athletics or horse-racing.

. . . .

▤ **1** encounter, confrontation, rendezvous, assignation, *old use* tryst, introduction, union, convergence, confluence, junction, intersection. **2** assembly, gathering, congregation, conference, convention, rally, *colloq.* get-together, forum, conclave, session. **3** event, tournament, competition, race(s).

. . . .

meetly *adv.* correctly, suitably.

mega *adj. slang* excellent. [from MEGA-]

mega- *combining form* forming words meaning: **1** a million: *megawatt.* **2** (*also* **megalo-**) large or great. **3** *colloq.* great: *megastar.* [from Greek *megas, megal-*, big]

megabit *noun Comput.* a unit of data equal to 1,048,576 bits.

megabyte *noun Comput.* a unit of storage capacity equal to 2^{20} or 1,048,576 bytes.

megalith *noun* a very large stone, especially one forming part of a prehistoric monument. [from MEGA- + Greek *lithos*, stone]

megalithic *adj.* **1** *said of a period of prehistory* characterized by the use of megaliths. **2** made of megaliths.

megalomania *noun* **1** *Medicine* a mental illness characterized by an exaggerated sense of power and self-importance. **2** *colloq.* greed for power. [from MEGA- + MANIA]

megalomaniac — *noun* a person affected by megalomania. — *adj.* relating to or affected by megalomania.

megaphone *noun* a funnel-shaped device which, when spoken through, amplifies the voice. [from MEGA- + Greek *phone*, sound]

megastructure *noun Archit.* a building or structure of gigantic proportions.

megaton *noun* **1** a unit of weight equal to one million tons. **2** a unit of explosive power equal to one million tons of TNT.

meiosis /maɪˈoʊsɪs/ *noun* (PL. **meioses** /maɪˈoʊsiːz/) **1** *Biol.* a type of cell division that results in the formation of male and female gametes (sperm and eggs). Also called REDUCTION, DIVISION. **2** *Grammar* understatement used for effect or as a figure of speech, as in *it's only a scratch* when referring to an injury. See also LITOTES. [from Greek *meion*, less]

melamine *noun Chem.* a white crystalline organic compound that is condensed with aldehydes to form artificial resins that are resistant to heat, water, and many chemicals, and are widely used as laminated coatings. [from German *Melamin*]

melancholia /mɛlənˈkoʊlɪə/ *noun old use* mental depression. [see MELANCHOLY]

melancholic /mɛlənˈkɒlɪk/ *adj.* relating to or suffering from melancholia or melancholy.

melancholy /ˈmɛlənkɒlɪ/ — *noun* **1** a tendency to be gloomy or depressed. **2** prolonged sadness. **3** a sad, pensive state of mind. — *adj.* sad; causing or expressing sadness. [from Greek *melas*, black + *chole*, bile]

. . . .

▤ *noun* **1, 2** depression, dejection, gloom, despondency. **1** low spirits, *colloq.* blues. **2** sadness, unhappiness, sorrow. *adj.* depressed, dejected, downcast, down, downhearted, gloomy, low, low-spirited, heavy-hearted, sad, unhappy, despondent, dispirited, miserable, mournful, dismal, sorrowful, moody.

▣ *noun* **2** elation, joy. *adj.* cheerful, elated, joyful.

. . . .

melange or **mélange** /meɪˈlɒnʒ/ *noun literary* a mixture, especially varied or confused. [from French *mélange*]

. . . .

▤ mixture, assortment, miscellany, potpourri, hotchpotch, *North Amer.* hodgepodge.

. . . .

melanin *noun* the black or dark brown pigment found to varying degrees in the skin, hair, and eyes of humans and animals. [from Greek *melas, melanos*, black]

melanoma *noun* (PL. **melanomas, melanomata**) *Medicine* a malignant (cancerous) tumour, usually of the skin, that is composed of melanocytes (cells that produce the dark pigment melanin), and may spread to other parts of the body, such as the lymph nodes. [from MELANIN + Greek *-oma*, suffix denoting the result of the action of a verb, used in English to denote a tumour]

melatonin *noun Physiol.* in vertebrates, a hormone secreted into the bloodstream by the pineal gland, higher levels being present in the blood during darkness than in the light. [from Greek *melas*, black]

Melba toast thin crisp toast. [named after the opera singer Dame Nellie Melba]

melee or **mêlée** /ˈmɛleɪ/ *noun literary* **1** a riotous brawl involving large numbers of people. **2** any confused or muddled collection. [from French *mêlée*, from *mêler*, to mix]

mellifluous /mɪˈlɪfluəs/ or **mellifluent** /mɪˈlɪfluənt/ *adj. literary, said of sounds, speech, etc* having a smooth sweet flowing quality. [from Latin *mel*, honey + *fluere*, to flow]

mellow — *adj.* **1** *said of a person or character* calm and relaxed with age or experience. **2** *said of sound, colour, light, etc* soft, rich, and pure. **3** *said of wine, cheese, etc* fully flavoured with age. **4** *said of fruit* sweet and ripe. **5** pleasantly relaxed or warm-hearted through being slightly drunk. — *verb trans., intrans.* to make or become mellow. [perhaps from Anglo-Saxon *mearu*, soft, tender]

. . . .

⊟ *adj.* **1** genial, cordial, affable, pleasant, relaxed, placid, serene, tranquil, cheerful, happy, jolly. **3** smooth, melodious, rich, rounded, soft. **3, 4** mature, ripe, juicy, full-flavoured. **4** sweet, tender, mild. *verb* mature, ripen, improve, sweeten, soften, season, perfect.

⊟ *adj.* **1** cold. **2** harsh.
. . . .

melodic *adj.* **1** relating to melody. **2** pleasant-sounding; tuneful; melodious.

melodically *adv.* in a melodic way.

melodious *adj.* **1** pleasant to listen to. **2** having a recognizable melody.

. . . .

⊟ **1** tuneful, musical, melodic, harmonious, dulcet, sweet-sounding, euphonious, silvery.

⊟ **1** discordant, grating, harsh.
. . . .

melodrama *noun* **1** drama featuring simplified characters, sensational events, and traditional justice, usually in the form of a happy ending. **2** a play or film of this kind. **3** *derog.* excessively dramatic behaviour. [from Greek *melos*, song + *drama*, action]

melodramatic *adj.* exaggerated or sensational in expressing emotion.

. . . .

⊟ histrionic, theatrical, overdramatic, exaggerated, overemotional, sensational, *colloq.* hammy.
. . . .

melodramatics *pl. noun* melodramatic behaviour.

melody *noun* (PL. **melodies**) **1** the sequence of single notes forming the core of a tune, as opposed to the harmony, the blend of other notes around it. **2** pleasantness of sound; tuneful music. **3** pleasant arrangement or combination of sounds, especially in poetry. [from Greek *melodia*, from *melos*, song + *aoidein*, to sing]

. . . .

⊟ **1** tune, music, song, refrain, theme, air, strain.
⊟ **1** harmony.
. . . .

melon *noun* the large rounded edible fruit of any of various climbing plants, with a thick skin, sweet juicy flesh, and many seeds. [from Greek *melon*, apple]

melt *verb* **1** *trans., intrans.* to make or become soft or liquid, especially through the action of heat; to dissolve. **2** *trans., intrans.* to combine or fuse, causing a loss of distinctness. **3** *intrans.* (*also* **melt away**) to disappear or disperse: *support for the scheme melted away.* **4** *trans., intrans., colloq.* to make or become emotionally or romantically tender or submissive. — **melt down** *technical, said of the core of a nuclear reactor* to overheat, causing radioactivity to escape. [from Anglo-Saxon *meltan*]

. . . .

⊟ **1, 3** dissolve, disperse. **1** liquefy, thaw. **2** combine, fuse, blend. **3** disappear, vanish, fade, evaporate.
⊟ **1** freeze, solidify.
. . . .

meltdown *noun* **1** *technical* the overheating of the core of a nuclear reactor, causing radioactivity to escape. **2** *colloq.* a major disaster or failure.

melting point (ABBREV. **m.p.**) the temperature at which a particular substance changes from a solid to a liquid. It is the same as the freezing point, but is usually used to refer to substances that are solid at room temperature, eg most metals.

melting-pot *noun* a place or situation in which varying beliefs, ideas, cultures, etc are mixed. — **in the melting-**

pot in the process of changing and forming something new.

member *noun* **1** a person belonging to a group or organization; a plant or animal belonging to a class or group. **2** (*often* **Member**) an elected representative of a governing body, eg Parliament or a local council. **3** a part of a whole, especially a limb or a petal. [from Latin *membrum*, limb, part]

. . . .

⊟ **1** adherent, associate, subscriber, representative, comrade, fellow.
. . . .

member of parliament (*also* **Member of Parliament**) a person elected to represent the people of a constituency in parliament.

membership *noun* **1** the state of being a member. **2** the members of an organization collectively; the number of members.

membrane *noun* **1** a thin sheet of tissue that lines a body cavity, surrounds a body part, or links adjacent structures, eg mucous membrane. **2** a thin layer of lipid and protein molecules that forms the boundary between a cell and its surroundings, and that usually allows only certain molecules to pass into or out of the cell. Also called CELL MEMBRANE, PLASMA MEMBRANE. **3** any thin flexible covering or lining, eg plastic film. [from Latin *membrana*, skin of the body]

membranous *adj.* of the nature of or like a membrane.

memento *noun* (PL. **mementos**, **mementoes**) a thing that serves as a reminder of the past; a souvenir. [from Latin *memento*, from *meminisse*, to remember]

. . . .

⊟ souvenir, keepsake, remembrance, reminder, token, memorial, record, relic.
. . . .

memento mori /məˈmɛntoʊ mɔriː/ an object intended as a reminder of the inevitability of death. [Latin, = remember you are to die]

memo *noun* (PL. **memos**) a memorandum.

memoir *noun* **1** a written record of events in the past, especially based on personal experience. **2** (**memoirs**) a person's written account of his or her own life; an autobiography. **3** a learned essay on any subject. [from French *mémoire*, memory]

. . . .

⊟ **1** record, history, chronicle, annals. **2** reminiscences, recollections, autobiography, life story, diary, journals, confessions, experiences. **3** essay, article, paper, monograph.
. . . .

memorabilia *pl. noun* souvenirs of people or events. [from Latin *memorabilis*, things for remembering]

memorable *adj.* worth remembering; easily remembered. [from Latin *memorare*, to remember]

. . . .

⊟ unforgettable, remarkable, significant, impressive, notable, noteworthy, extraordinary, important, outstanding, momentous.
⊟ forgettable, trivial, unimportant.
. . . .

memorably *adv.* in a memorable way.

memorandum *noun* (PL. **memorandums**, **memoranda**) **1** a note of something to be remembered. **2** a written statement or record, especially one circulated for the attention of colleagues. [from Latin *memorandum*, thing to be remembered]

. . . .

⊟ MEMO, NOTE. **1** jotting. **2** record, minute, circular, communication, message, round robin.
. . . .

memorial — *noun* a thing that honours or commemorates a person or an event, eg a statue. — *adj.* serving to preserve the memory of a person or an event. [from Latin *memoriale*, reminder]

. . . .

◱ *noun* remembrance, monument, record, stone, plaque, mausoleum. *adj.* commemorative, celebratory.

. . . .

Memorial Day a national holiday in the USA, held on the last Monday in May in honour of American war dead. It was first instituted in 1868 (when it was known as *Decoration Day*) in honour of the soldiers who died in the American Civil War.

memorize or **memorise** *verb* to learn thoroughly, so as to be able to reproduce exactly from memory.

. . . .

◱ learn, learn by heart, commit to memory, remember.
◲ forget.

. . . .

memory *noun* (PL. **memories**) **1** the ability of the mind to remember: *recite it from memory.* **2** the mind's store of remembered events, impressions, knowledge, and ideas. **3** the mental processes of memorizing information, retaining it, and recalling it on demand. **4** any such impression reproduced in the mind. **5** the limit in the past beyond which one's store of mental impressions does not extend: *not in living memory* (= the memory of any living person). **6** the act of remembering; commemoration: *in memory of.* **7** reputation after death. **8** the part of a computer that is used to store data and programs. [from Latin *memoria*]

. . . .

◱ **1, 3, 4, 5** recollection. **1, 3, 5** recall. **2, 4** remembrance. **3** retention. **4** reminiscence. **6** commemoration.
◲ **1, 3** forgetfulness.

. . . .

memsahib /ˈmɛmsɑːɪb/ *noun* formerly, in India, a European married woman; also used as a polite form of address. [from MA'AM + SAHIB]

men see MAN.

menace — *noun* **1** a source of threatening danger. **2** a threat; a show of hostility. **3** *colloq.* an annoying person or thing. — *verb* to threaten; to show an intention to cause damage or harm to. [from French *menace*, from Latin *minari*, to threaten]

. . . .

◱ *noun* **1** danger, peril, hazard, jeopardy, risk. **2** threat, warning, intimidation, terrorism. **3** nuisance, annoyance, pest, *colloq.* terror. *verb* threaten, frighten, alarm, intimidate, terrorize, loom over.

. . . .

menacing *adj.* causing a threat or danger.

. . . .

◱ threatening, intimidatory, warning, ominous, looming, impending, sinister, grim.

. . . .

ménage /meˈnɑːʒ/ *noun literary* a group of people living together; a household. [from French *ménage*]

ménage à trois /ˈmɛnɑːʒ ɑ trwɑː/ *literary* a household consisting of three people, especially a husband, a wife, and a lover of one of them. [French, = household of three]

menagerie /məˈnædʒərɪ/ *noun* **1** a collection of wild animals caged for exhibition; the place where they are kept. **2** a varied or confused mixture, especially of people. [from French *ménagerie*; related to MÉNAGE]

mend — *verb* **1** to repair. **2** *intrans.* to improve, especially in health; to heal. **3** to improve or correct: *mend one's ways.* — *noun* a repaired part or place. — **on the mend** getting better, especially in health. [shortened from AMEND]

. . . .

◱ *verb* **1** repair, renovate, restore, refit, fix, patch, cobble, darn, heal. **2** recover, get better, heal, improve. **3** remedy, correct, rectify, reform, revise.
◲ *verb* **1** break. **2** deteriorate. **3** destroy.

. . . .

mendacious *adj.* lying or likely to lie.

mendacity *noun* (PL. **mendacities**) *formal* **1** untruthfulness; the tendency to lie. **2** a lie. [from Latin *mendax*, untruthful]

mendelevium /mɛndəˈliːvɪəm/ *noun* (SYMBOL **Md**, ATOMIC NUMBER **101**) an artificially produced radioactive metallic element. [named after the Russian chemist D I Mendeleyev]

Mendelian /mɛnˈdiːlɪən/ *adj.* of or relating to the principles of heredity put forward by the Austrian monk and botanist Gregor Mendel.

mendicant — *noun* **1** *formal* a beggar. **2** a member of an order of monks that is not allowed to own property, and is therefore entirely dependent on charity. These include Dominicans, Franciscans, Augustinians, and Carmelites. — *adj.* **1** *formal* begging. **2** dependent on charity. [from Latin *mendicare*, to beg]

menfolk *pl. noun* men collectively, especially the male members of a family or group.

menhir /ˈmɛnhɪə(r)/ *noun* a prehistoric monument in the form of a single standing stone. [from Breton *men*, stone + *hir*, long]

menial — *adj.*, *said of work* unskilled, uninteresting, and of low status. — *noun derog.* a domestic servant. [from Old French *meinie*, household]

. . . .

◱ *adj.* unskilled, low-skilled, routine, dull, humdrum, low, lowly, humble, base, degrading, demeaning, ignominious, servile, slavish. *noun* servant, domestic, labourer, minion, attendant, drudge, slave, underling, *colloq.* skivvy, *colloq.* dogsbody.

. . . .

meningitis *noun* inflammation of the meninges (the three membranes that cover the brain and spinal cord), usually caused by bacterial or viral infections.

meninx *noun* (PL. **meninges**) any of the three membranes that envelop the brain and the spinal cord. [from Greek *meninx*, membrane]

meniscus /məˈnɪskəs/ *noun* (PL. **meniscuses**, **menisci**) **1** *Physics* the curved upper surface of a liquid in a partly filled narrow tube, caused by surface tension effects in which the liquid is either elevated or depressed in the tube. The meniscus may curve upward, as in mercury, or downward, as in water. **2** *Anat.* a crescent-shaped structure, such as the disc of cartilage that divides the cavity of the knee joint. **3** *Optics* a lens that is convex on one side and concave on the other. [from Greek *meniskos*, diminutive of *mene*, moon]

Mennonite *noun* one of the Dutch and Swiss Anabaptists who later called themselves Mennonites after one of their Dutch leaders, Menno Simons (1496–1559).

menopausal *adj.* **1** relating to or experiencing the menopause. **2** *colloq.* suffering from strange moods and behaviour in middle age.

menopause *noun* the period in a woman's life, typically between the ages of 45 and 55, when menstruation ceases and pregnancy is no longer possible. [from Greek *men*, month + *pausis*, cessation]

menorah /məˈnɔːrə/ *noun* a candlestick with seven branches used in Jewish worship and regarded as a symbol of Judaism. [from Hebrew *menorah*, candlestick]

menorrhagia /mɛnəˈreɪdʒɪə/ *noun Medicine* excessive and prolonged bleeding during menstruation. [from Greek *men*, month + *-rragia*, from *rhegnynai*, to break]

menses /ˈmɛnsiːz/ *pl. noun Medicine* the fluids discharged from the womb during menstruation. [from Latin *mensis*, month]

menstrual *adj.* relating to or involving menstruation.

menstrual cycle *Biol.* in some primates including humans, a repeating cycle of reproductive changes that is regulated by sex hormones, and during which ovulation (the release of an egg from the ovary) occurs, about once in every 28 days in humans. At the end of the cycle, if the egg has not been fertilized, the lining of the womb is shed from the vagina in the process of menstruation.

menstruate *verb intrans.* to discharge blood and other fluids from the womb through the vagina. [from Latin *menstruare*, from *mensis*, month]

menstruation *noun* **1** in women of childbearing age, the periodic discharge through the vagina of blood and fragments of mucous membrane that takes place at approximately monthly intervals if fertilization of an ovum (egg cell) has not occurred. It normally lasts from three to seven days. **2** the time or occurrence of menstruating.

mensuration *noun* **1** the application of geometric principles to the calculation of measurements such as length, volume, and area. **2** *formal* the process of measuring. [from Latin *mensurare*, to measure]

-ment *suffix* forming words denoting: **1** a process, action, or means: *repayment*/*treatment*. **2** a quality, state, or condition: *enjoyment*/*merriment*. [from Latin *-mentum*]

mental *adj.* **1** of, relating to, or done using the mind or intelligence: *a mental handicap*/*mental arithmetic*. **2** of, or suffering from, an illness or illnesses of the mind: *a mental patient*. **3** *colloq.* foolish; stupid. **4** *colloq.* ridiculous; unimaginable. [from Latin *mentalis*, from *mens*, the mind]

▪ **1** intellectual, abstract, conceptual, cognitive, cerebral, theoretical, rational. **3**, **4** mad, insane, lunatic, crazy, silly, stupid, *colloq.* nutty, *colloq.* daft, *slang* loony.
🔁 **1** physical. **3** sane.

mental age *Psychol.* the age in years, etc at which an average child would have reached the same stage of mental development as the individual under consideration.

mental cruelty conduct, not involving physical cruelty or violence, that wounds feelings and personal dignity, especially such conduct by one of the partners in a marriage; formerly one of the grounds for separation or divorce in the UK.

mental disorder *Psychol.* any of various disorders with psychological or behavioural symptoms.

mental handicap a condition in which a person has impaired intellectual abilities, characteristically having an intelligence quotient (IQ) of less than 70, and also suffers from some form of social malfunction, eg inability to live independently.

mentality *noun* (PL. **mentalities**) **1** an outlook; a certain way of thinking. **2** intellectual ability.

▪ **1** frame of mind, character, disposition, personality, psychology, outlook. **2** intellect, brains, understanding, faculty, rationality.

mentally *adv.* in the mind, relating to the mind.

menthol *noun* a sharp-smelling substance obtained from peppermint oil, used as a decongestant and a painkiller. [from Latin *mentha*, mint]

mentholated *adj.* containing menthol.

mention — *verb* (**mentioned**, **mentioning**) **1** to speak of or make reference to. **2** to remark on, usually briefly or indirectly. — *noun* **1** a remark, usually a brief reference: *made no mention of it*. **2** a reference made to an individual's merit in an official (especially military) report. — **don't mention it** *colloq.* no thanks are needed. **not to mention** ... without including (facts the speaker is nevertheless about to include, usually for emphasis). [from Latin *mentio*, a calling to mind]

▪ *verb* REFER TO, ALLUDE TO, CITE. **1** speak of, name, acknowledge, report, make known, impart, declare, communicate, divulge, disclose, broach, reveal, state, quote. **2** touch on, bring up, hint at, intimate, point out. *noun* CITATION, ACKNOWLEDGEMENT, RECOGNITION. **1** reference, allusion, observation, remark, announcement, notification, indication. **2** tribute.

mentor *noun* *literary* a trusted teacher or adviser. [from *Mentor*, adviser to Telemachus in the Homeric poems]

▪ teacher, tutor, adviser, counsellor, guru, guide.

menu *noun* **1** the range of dishes available in a restaurant, etc, or of the dishes to be served at a particular meal; also, a list of these: *the wedding menu*. **2** a list of optional computer functions displayed on a screen. [from French *menu*, small and detailed (list)]

MEP *abbrev.* Member of the European Parliament.

Mercalli scale /mɜːˈkalɪ/ *Geol.* a scale used to represent the intensity of an earthquake, ranging from 1 (not felt) to 12 (total devastation). [named after the Italian geologist Giuseppe Mercalli]

mercantile /ˈmɜːkəntaɪl/ *adj. formal* of trade or traders; commercial. [from Italian, from *mercante*, merchant]

mercantilism /ˈmɜːkəntɪlɪzm/ *noun* the business of merchants; trade, commerce; also, advocacy of the *mercantile system*, an old economic strategy that was based on the theory that a nation's interests were best served by development of overseas trade and restriction of imports: the impetus of much 17c and 18c colonization by European powers.

mercenary /ˈmɜːsənərɪ/ — *adj.* **1** *derog.* excessively concerned with the desire for personal gain, especially money. **2** paid, especially to fight as a soldier. — *noun* (PL. **mercenaries**) a soldier available for hire by a country or group. [from Latin *mercenarius*, from *merces*, reward, hire]

▪ *adj.* **1** greedy, avaricious, covetous, grasping, acquisitive, materialistic, venal. **2** hired, paid.

mercerize or **mercerise** *verb* to treat (especially cotton) with a substance which strengthens it and gives it a silky appearance. [from the English textile manufacturer John Mercer (1791–1866)]

mercerized or **mercerised** *adj.* strengthened by mercerizing.

merchandise — *noun* commercial goods. — *verb intrans., trans.* to trade; to buy and sell. [from French *marchandise*; related to MERCHANT]

▪ *noun* goods, commodities, stock, produce, products, wares, cargo, freight, shipment.

merchant — *noun* **1** a trader, especially wholesale. **2** *North Amer., esp. US, Scot.* a shopkeeper. **3** *slang* a person who indulges in a particular (especially undesirable) activity: *gossip merchant*. — *adj.* used for trade; commercial: *merchant ship*. [from Latin *mercari*, to trade]

▪ *noun* **1** trader, dealer, broker, trafficker, wholesaler, retailer, seller, shopkeeper, vendor.

merchant bank a bank whose main activity is lending money to industry.

merciful *adj.* showing mercy; forgiving.

▪ compassionate, forgiving, forbearing, humane, lenient, sparing, tender-hearted, pitying, gracious, humanitarian, kind, liberal, sympathetic, generous, mild.
🔁 hard-hearted, merciless.

mercifully *adv.* luckily; thankfully.

merciless *adj.* without mercy; cruel; pitiless.

▪ pitiless, relentless, unmerciful, ruthless, hard-hearted, hard, heartless, implacable, inhumane, unforgiving, remorseless, unpitying, unsparing, severe, cruel, callous, inhuman.

▣ compassionate, merciful.

mercilessly *adv.* in a merciless way.

mercurial *adj.* **1** of or containing mercury. **2** *said of a personality, mood, etc* lively or active; tending to change suddenly and unpredictably. [from the planet *Mercury*]

▣ **2** lively, vivacious, sparkling, ebullient, effervescent, volatile, unpredictable, changeable, temperamental, capricious, inconstant.

Mercury *noun Astron.* the closest planet to the Sun. Its orbit lies within that of Venus.

mercury *noun* (SYMBOL **Hg**, ATOMIC NUMBER **80**) a dense silvery-white metallic element, and the only metal that is liquid at room temperature. If inhaled or ingested in more than trace amounts it can cause skin disorders, kidney and brain damage, and birth defects. [from Latin *Mercurius*, the Roman god Mercury]

mercy *noun* (PL. **mercies**) **1** kindness or forgiveness shown when punishment is possible or justified. **2** an act or circumstance in which these qualities are displayed, especially by God. **3** a tendency to be forgiving. **4** a piece of good luck; a welcome happening: *grateful for small mercies.* — **at the mercy of someone** or **something** wholly in their power; liable to be harmed by them. [from Latin *merces*, reward, favour]

▣ **1, 2** grace. **1, 3** compassion, clemency, forbearance, leniency, kindness. **1** forgiveness, pity. **4** blessing, godsend, good luck, relief.

▣ **1** cruelty, harshness.

mercy flight   a flight by an aeroplane or helicopter, eg taking a seriously ill or injured person to hospital or transporting human organs for transplantation, when other means of transport are impracticable or unavailable.

mercy killing an act of killing painlessly to relieve suffering; euthanasia.

mere[1] *adj.* nothing more than; no better, more important, or useful than. [from Latin *merus*, unmixed]

▣ sheer, plain, simple, bare, utter, pure, absolute, complete, stark, unadulterated, common, paltry, petty.

mere[2] *noun old use poetic, often in English place names* a lake or pool. [from Anglo-Saxon]

merely *adv.* simply; only.

meretricious *adj.* **1** bright or attractive on the surface, but of no real value. **2** false and insincere. [from Latin *meretrix*, prostitute]

merganser /mɜːˈɡansə(r)/ *noun* any of various kinds of large diving duck of northern countries, with a long hooked serrated bill. [from Latin *mergus*, diving bird + *anser*, goose]

merge *verb* **1** *trans., intrans.* to blend, combine, or join with something else. **2** (**merge into something**) to become part of a larger whole, and therefore impossible to distinguish. [from Latin *mergere*, to plunge]

▣ **1** join, unite, combine, converge, amalgamate, integrate, blend, coalesce, fuse, mix, intermix, mingle, meld. **2** blend into, melt into, fuse with.

merger *noun* a joining together, especially of business firms.

▣ amalgamation, union, fusion, takeover, combination, integration, coalition, consolidation, confederation, incorporation.

meridian *noun* **1** *Geog.* an imaginary line on the Earth's surface passing through the poles at right angles to the equator; a line of longitude. **2** *literary* the peak, eg of success. **3** *Chinese Medicine* any of several lines or pathways through the body along which life energy flows. [from Latin *meridianus*, from *medius*, middle + *dies*, day]

meridional *adj.* **1** *technical* of, relating to, or along a meridian. **2** *literary* of the south, especially of Europe.

meringue /məˈraŋ/ *noun* a crisp cooked mixture of sugar and egg-whites, or a cake made from this. [from French]

merino *noun* (PL. **merinos**) **1** a type of sheep bred for its long fine wool. **2** fine yarn or fabric made from its wool. [from Spanish]

meristem /ˈmerɪstem/ *noun Bot.* in a plant, a region of actively dividing cells, mainly at the tips of shoots and roots. [from Greek *meristos*, divisible]

merit — *noun* **1** worth, excellence or praiseworthiness. **2** (*often* **merits**) a good point or quality. — *verb* (**merited**, **meriting**) to deserve; to be worthy of or entitled to. [from Latin *meritum*, reward]

▣ *noun* VIRTUE. **1** worth, excellence, value, quality, good, goodness. **2** asset, credit, advantage, strong point, talent, due, claim. *verb* deserve, be worthy of, earn, justify, warrant.

▣ *noun* **2** fault.

meritocracy *noun* (PL. **meritocracies**) a social system based on leadership by people of great talent or intelligence, rather than of wealth or noble birth.

meritorious *adj.* deserving reward or praise.

▣ praiseworthy, laudable, admirable, commendable, deserving, worthy.

merlin *noun* a species of small dark-coloured falcon with a black-striped tail. [from Old French *esmerillon*]

merlon *noun Fortification* the projecting part of the parapet between embrasures in a battlement. [from French *merlon*, from Italian *merlone*, battlements]

mermaid *noun* a mythical sea creature with a woman's head and upper body, and a fish's tail. [from Anglo-Saxon *mere*, lake, sea + MAID]

merman *noun* the male equivalent of a mermaid.

Merovingian /merəʊˈvɪndʒɪən/ — *noun* a member of a Frankish dynasty ruling in Gaul and Germany c.500–750. — *adj.* relating to the Merovingians.

merrily *adv.* happily; with a merry manner.

merriment *noun* gaiety with laughter and noise, hilarity.

▣ fun, jollity, mirth, hilarity, laughter, conviviality, festivity, amusement, revelry, frolic, liveliness, joviality.

▣ gloom, seriousness.

merry *adj.* (**merrier**, **merriest**) **1** cheerful and lively. **2** *colloq.* slightly drunk. — **make merry** *old use* to have fun; to celebrate. [from Anglo-Saxon *myrige*]

▣ **1** jolly, light-hearted, mirthful, joyful, happy, convivial, festive, cheerful, glad.

▣ **1** gloomy, melancholy, sober.

merry-go-round *noun* a fairground amusement consisting of a revolving platform fitted with rising and falling seats in the form of horses or other figures.

merrymaker *noun* a person who is having fun; a reveller.

merrymaking *noun* cheerful celebration or fun.

mesa /ˈmeɪsə/ *noun Geol.* an isolated flat-topped hill with at least one steep side or cliff, formed by the remnants of horizontal rocks resistant to erosion, which protect the softer rock lying underneath. [from Spanish *mesa*, from Latin *mensa*, table]

mésalliance /meɪˈzalɪɒns/ *noun literary* a marriage to someone of lower social status. [from French, = misalliance]

mescal or **peyote** *noun* a globe-shaped cactus of Mexico and the SW USA. Its sap is used to make the Mexican fermented drink, pulque, and the spirit, mescal. [from Aztec *mexcalli*]

mescalin or **mescaline** *noun* a hallucinogenic drug obtained from the button-like top of the mescal cactus. It is sometimes chewed, or can be made into tea or powder.

mesclun *noun* a mixed green salad of young leaves and shoots of rocket, chicory, fennel, etc. [from French, from Niçois *mesclumo*, mixture]

mesdames /meɪˈdam/ See MADAM, MADAME.

mesencephalon /mesenˈsɛfəlɒn/ *noun Anat.* the midbrain, which connects the forebrain to the hindbrain. [from Greek *mesos*, middle + *encephalon*, brain]

mesentery /ˈmezəntərɪ/ *noun Anat.* in animals, the double layer of membrane on the inner surface of the body wall that serves to hold the stomach, small intestine, spleen, and other abdominal organs in place. [from Greek *mesos*, middle + *enteron*, intestine]

mesh — *noun* 1 netting, or a piece of netting made of (especially fine) wire or thread. 2 each of the openings between the threads of a net. 3 (*usually* **meshes**) a network. — *verb intrans.* 1 *technical, said of the teeth on gear wheels* to engage. 2 to fit or work together. 3 to become entangled. [perhaps from Old Dutch *maesche*]

▪ *noun* 1 net, network, netting, lattice, web, tangle, entanglement, snare, trap. *verb* 1 engage, interlock, dovetail, fit, connect, combine, come together. 2 harmonize, coordinate.

mesmerism *noun* 1 a former term for HYPNOTISM. 2 a former method of hypnosis based on the ideas of the Austrian physician Franz Anton Mesmer (1734–1815), sometimes involving the use of magnets.

mesmerist *noun old use* a hypnotist.

mesmerize or **mesmerise** *verb* 1 *old use* to hypnotize. 2 to grip the attention of; to fascinate.

▪ HYPNOTIZE. 2 fascinate, grip, captivate, spellbind, enthral, rivet, absorb, engross.

mesmerizing or **mesmerising** *adj.* hypnotic.

Mesoamerican *adj.* relating to or originating from Central America, between N Mexico and Panama.

mesoderm *noun Zool.* in a multicellular animal that has two or more layers of body tissue, the layer of cells between the ectoderm and the endoderm, that develops into the circulatory system, muscles, and reproductive organs (and also the skeleton and excretory system in vertebrates). [from MESO- + Greek *derma*, skin]

mesolithic *adj.* (**also Mesolithic**) of the middle period of the Stone Age, from about 12,000 to 3,000BC in Europe. [from Greek *mesos*, middle + *lithos*, stone]

meson /ˈmiːzɒn/ *noun Physics* any of a group of unstable strongly interacting elementary particles, with a mass intermediate between that of an electron and a nucleon (a proton or neutron). [from Greek *mesos*, middle]

mesophyll *noun Bot.* the internal tissue that lies between the upper and lower epidermal surfaces of a plant leaf. [from Greek *mesos*, middle + *phyllon*, leaf]

mesosphere *noun* the layer of the atmosphere above the stratosphere and below the thermosphere, in which temperature rapidly decreases with height. [from Greek *mesos*, middle + SPHERE]

Mesozoic /mesoʊˈzoʊɪk/ *adj.* 1 *Geol.* relating to the era of geological time extending from about 250 million to 65 million years ago, and subdivided into the Triassic, Jurassic, and Cretaceous periods. During the Mesozoic era dinosaurs flourished, becoming extinct at the end of the era, and small mammals first appeared. 2 relating to the rocks formed during this era. [from Greek *mesos*, middle + Greek *zoion*, animal]

mess — *noun* 1 an untidy or dirty state. 2 a state of disorder or confusion. 3 a badly damaged state. 4 something in a damaged or disordered state. 5 a state of embarrassment or trouble: *a fine mess you've got me into.* 6 *colloq.* animal faeces. 7 a communal dining room, especially in the armed forces. 8 *old use* a portion of any pulpy food. — *verb* 1 *intrans. colloq.* (**mess with something**) to interfere or meddle in it. 2 (*also* **mess something up**) to put into an untidy, dirty, or damaged state. 3 *intrans., said of soldiers, etc* to eat, or live, together. 4 *intrans.* (**mess with someone**) *colloq.* to become involved in argument or conflict with them. — **mess about** or **around** *colloq.* to behave in an annoyingly foolish way; to potter or tinker. **mess about** or **around with someone** to treat them inconsiderately or unfairly. **mess about** or **around with something** to meddle or interfere in it. **mess something up** to cause it to fail or go wrong. **no messing** *colloq.* 1 without difficulty. 2 honestly; truthfully. [from Old French *mes*, dish]

▣ *noun* 1, 2 chaos, disorder, confusion, disarray, muddle. 1 untidiness, jumble, clutter, dirt, filth, squalor. 2 disorganization, mix-up. 4, 5 *colloq.* hole. 4 *colloq.* shambles, *colloq.* dog's breakfast, *colloq.* dump, *colloq.* tip. 5 difficulty, trouble, predicament, *colloq.* fix. *verb* 1 meddle with, interfere with, tamper with. 2 disarrange, jumble, muddle, tangle, dishevel, disrupt. **mess about** or **around** fool around, play, play around, play about, *colloq.* muck about. **mess about** or **around with** *someone* inconvenience, upset, bother, trouble, *Brit.* lead a (merry) dance, *colloq.* lead up the garden path, send on a wild-goose chase, *colloq.* muck about, *colloq.* make life hell for. *something* interfere with, tamper with, meddle with. **mess up** botch, bungle, spoil, *colloq.* muck up, *slang* cock up, *slang* screw up.

▣ *noun* 1 order, tidiness.

message *noun* 1 a spoken or written communication sent from one person to another. 2 the instructive principle contained within a story, religious teaching, etc. 3 (**messages**) *chiefly Scot.* an errand; household shopping. — **get the message** *colloq.* to understand. [from Latin *mittere*, to send]

▣ 1 communication, bulletin, dispatch, communiqué, report, letter, *literary* missive, memorandum, note, notice, cable. 2 meaning, idea, point, theme, moral.

messenger *noun* a person who carries communications between people.

▣ courier, emissary, envoy, go-between, herald, runner, carrier, bearer, harbinger, agent, ambassador.

messenger RNA (ABBREV. **mRNA**) *Biochem.* any of the single-stranded molecules of RNA that are responsible for transporting coded instructions for the manufacture of proteins from DNA in the nucleus to the ribosomes (which are the site of protein manufacture) in the cytoplasm.

Messiah /məˈsaɪə/ *noun* (**the Messiah**) 1 in Christianity, Jesus Christ. 2 in Judaism, the king of the Jews still to be sent by God to free them. 3 a person who sets free a country or a people. [from Hebrew *mashiah*, anointed]

Messianic /mesɪˈanɪk/ *adj.* 1 relating to or associated with a Messiah. 2 relating to any popular leader, especially a liberator.

Messianism /məˈsaɪənɪzm/ *noun Relig.* belief in a Messiah, specifically Jewish movements expressing the hope for a new and perfected age.

messily *adv.* so as to cause a mess; untidily.

Messrs see MR.

messy *adj.* (**messier, messiest**) 1 involving or causing dirt or mess. 2 confused, untidy.

. . . .

■ **1** dirty, grubby, filthy, sloppy, slovenly. **2** untidy, unkempt, dishevelled, disorganized, chaotic, confused, muddled, cluttered.

■ **2** neat, ordered, tidy.

. . . .

mestizo /mɛˈstiːzoʊ/ or **mestiza** /mɛˈstiːzə/ *noun* (PL. **mestizos, mestizas**) a male (**-zo**) or female (**-za**) person of mixed Spanish-American and American Indian parentage. [from Spanish]

Met *noun* (**the Met**) *colloq.* the London Metropolitan Police Force.

met see MEET.

meta- *combining form* forming words denoting: **1** a change: *metabolism*. **2** an area of study related to another subject of study, but going beyond it in some way: *metaphysics*. **3** a position behind or beyond: *metacarpal*. [from Greek *meta*, among, with, beside, after]

metabolic /mɛtəˈbɒlɪk/ *adj.* **1** relating to an organism's metabolism. **2** exhibiting metamorphosis.

metabolism /məˈtabəlɪzm/ *noun Biochem.* the sum of all the chemical reactions that occur within the cells of a living organism, including both formation (*anabolism*) and breakdown (*catabolism*) of complex organic compounds, eg proteins, fats, carbohydrates. The rates at which individual reactions occur are controlled by enzymes. [from Greek *metabole*, change]

metabolite *noun Biochem.* a molecule that participates in the biochemical reactions that take place in the cells of living organisms.

metabolize or **metabolise** /məˈtabəlaɪz/ *verb trans., intrans. Biochem.* within a living cell, to break down complex organic compounds into simpler molecules.

metacarpal *adj.* relating to or in the region of the metacarpus.

metacarpus *noun* (PL. **metacarpi**) the set of five bones in the hand between the wrist and the knuckles. [from META- + Greek *karpos*, wrist]

metal — *noun* **1** any of a class of chemical elements with certain characteristic properties. All metals except mercury are solid at room temperature, and most of them are shiny, malleable (able to be hammered into sheets and bent without fracture), and ductile (able to be drawn into thin wire). **2** road metal, small broken stones used to make and repair roads. **3** (**metals**) the rails of a railway. — *verb* (**metalled, metalling**) **1** to fit with metal. **2** to make or mend (a road) with small broken stones. [from Greek *metallon*, mine]

metallic *adj.* **1** made of metal. **2** characteristic of metal, eg in sound or appearance.

metallize or **metallise** *verb* **1** to give a metallic appearance to. **2** to apply a thin coating of metal to.

metalloid *noun Chem.* a chemical element that has both metallic and non-metallic properties, eg silicon, boron, germanium, arsenic. All metalloids are semiconductors, and are capable of combining with a metal to form an alloy.

metallurgist *noun* a person who studies or is expert in metallurgy.

metallurgy *noun* the scientific study of the nature and properties of metals and their extraction from the ground.

metalwork *noun* **1** the craft or practice of shaping metal. **2** articles made of metal.

metalworker *noun* a person who works with metal.

metamorphic *adj.* **1** relating to metamorphosis or metamorphism. **2** *Geol.* denoting any of a group of rocks that have been formed by the physical or chemical alteration of pre-existing rock as a result of the effects of intense heat or pressure, or both, beneath the Earth's surface, eg marble (formed from limestone). See also IGNEOUS, SEDIMENTARY.

metamorphism *noun Geol.* any changes in the structure or composition of a rock that take place in response to the effects of intense heat or pressure, or both, beneath the Earth's surface.

metamorphose *verb intrans., trans.* to undergo or cause to undergo metamorphosis.

metamorphosis *noun* (PL. **metamorphoses**) **1** a change of form, appearance, or character. **2** *Biol.* the change of physical form that occurs during the development into adulthood of some creatures, eg butterflies. [from META- + Greek *morphe*, form]

. . . .

■ **1** change, alteration, transformation, rebirth, regeneration, transfiguration, conversion, modification, change-over.

. . . .

metaphase *noun Genetics* the second phase of mitosis and meiosis, during which the membrane surrounding the nucleus breaks down, and the chromosomes are lined up along the equatorial region of the cell between the two poles of the spindle.

metaphor *noun* **1** an expression in which the person, action or thing referred to is described as if it really were what it merely resembles, as when a rejection is referred to as 'a slap in the face'. **2** such expressions in general, or their use. [from Greek *metaphora*]

. . . .

■ **1** figure of speech, allegory, analogy, symbol, picture, image.

. . . .

metaphorical *adj.* not actual or literal, only in a figure of speech.

. . . .

■ figurative, allegorical, symbolic.

. . . .

metaphorically *adv.* in a metaphorical way; in terms of metaphor.

metaphysical *adj.* **1** relating to metaphysics. **2** (*also* **Metaphysical**) denoting any of a group of 17c poets who used elaborate images to express intense feelings and complex ideas.

metaphysically *adv.* **1** in a metaphysical way. **2** in a metaphysical sense.

metaphysics *noun* **1** the branch of philosophy dealing with the nature of existence and the basic principles of truth and knowledge. **2** *colloq.* any type of abstract discussion, writing or thinking. [from Greek *ta meta ta physika*, the things after natural science, from the order of subjects dealt with in Aristotle's writings]

metastasis /mɛˈtastəsɪs/ *noun* (PL. **metastases**) **1** *Medicine* the spread of a disease, especially a malignant (cancerous) tumour, from one part of the body to another via the bloodstream or lymphatic system, or across a body cavity. **2** a secondary tumour that has developed as a result of the spread of a malignant disease in this way. [from Greek *metastasis*, change of place]

metatarsal /mɛtəˈtɑːsəl/ *adj.* relating to or in the region of the metatarsus.

metatarsus *noun* (PL. **metatarsi**) the set of five long bones in the foot, between the ankle and the toes. [from META- + Greek *tarsos*, instep]

metazoan — *noun Zool.* any animal that belongs to the subkingdom Metazoa, which includes all multicellular animals, ie those with bodies composed of many cells organized into distinct tissues, including a nervous system. — *adj.* of or relating to the Metazoa. [from META- + Greek *zoion*, animal]

mete — **mete something out** *verb* to give out or dispense (especially punishment). [from Anglo-Saxon *metan*, to measure]

. . . .

■ allot, apportion, deal out, dole out, hand out, measure out, share out, ration out, portion, distribute, dispense, divide out, assign, administer.

. . . .

meteor *noun* a dust particle that moves at high speed from space into the Earth's atmosphere, where it burns up as a result of friction, emitting a brief flash or streak of light.

Also called SHOOTING STAR. [from Greek *ta meteora*, things on high]

meteoric *adj.* 1 of or relating to meteors. 2 *said of success, etc* very rapid; very short-lived.
. . . .
🗉 2 rapid, speedy, swift, sudden, overnight, instantaneous, momentary, brief, spectacular, brilliant, dazzling.
. . . .

meteorically *adv.* like a meteor; very rapidly or brilliantly.

meteorite *noun Astron.* a lump of rock or metallic material from outer space that is large enough to fall to the Earth's surface without burning up as it passes through the atmosphere.

meteoroid *noun Astron.* a small moving solid object or dust particle in space; a meteor or meteorite.

meteorological *adj.* of or relating to meteorology.

Meteorological Office see MET OFFICE.

meteorologist *noun* a person who studies or is expert in meteorology.

meteorology *noun* the scientific study of weather and climate over a relatively short period, as opposed to climatology, in which long-term weather patterns are studied. [from Greek *ta meteora*, things on high + -LOGY]

meter — *noun* 1 an instrument for measuring and recording, especially quantities of electricity, gas, water, etc used. 2 a parking-meter. — *verb* (**metered**, **metering**) to measure and record using a meter. [from Anglo-Saxon *metan*, to measure]
. . . .
🗉 *noun* 1 dial, gauge, clock. *verb* measure, gauge, clock, record, plot.
. . . .

-meter *combining form* forming words denoting: 1 an instrument for measuring: *thermometer.* 2 a line of poetry with a specified number of units of stress, or feet: *pentameter.* [from Greek *metron*, measure]

methadone *noun* a drug similar to morphine, but less addictive, used as a painkiller and as a heroin substitute for drug-addicts. [from di*methyl*amino-*d*iphenyl-hept*anone*]

methanal *noun Chem.* same as FORMALDEHYDE.

methane *noun Chem.* (FORMULA CH_4) a colourless odourless flammable gas belonging to the alkane series of hydrocarbons. It is the main component of natural gas, and is used in the manufacture of organic chemicals and hydrogen, and as a cooking and heating fuel (in the form of natural gas). [from *methyl* as in METHYL ALCOHOL]

methanoic acid *Chem.* same as FORMIC ACID.

methanol *noun Chem.* (FORMULA CH_3OH) a colourless flammable toxic liquid, used as a solvent and antifreeze, and added to ethanol (absolute alcohol) to make methylated spirits. Also called METHYL ALCOHOL. [from METHANE + ALCOHOL]

methinks *verb* (PAST TENSE **methought**) *old use* it seems to me (that).

methionine *noun Biochem.* an essential amino acid found in proteins.

method *noun* 1 a way of doing something, especially an ordered set of procedures. 2 good planning; efficient organization. 3 (*often* **methods**) a technique used in a particular activity: *farming methods.* — **method in one's madness** reason or good sense underlying what seems an odd or chaotic situation or procedure. [from Greek *methodos*]
. . . .
🗉 1, 3 technique. 1 way, approach, means, course, manner, mode, fashion, process, procedure, route, style, plan, programme, scheme. 2 organization, planning, order, structure, system, pattern, form, regularity, routine.
. . . .

methodical *adj.* efficient and orderly; done in an orderly way.

. . . .
🗉 systematic, structured, organized, ordered, orderly, tidy, regular, planned, efficient, disciplined, businesslike, deliberate, neat, scrupulous, precise, meticulous, painstaking.
🗷 chaotic, irregular, confused.
. . . .

methodically *adv.* in a methodical way; systematically.

Methodism *noun* a Christian denomination founded (1739) by John Wesley as an evangelical movement within the Church of England. The movement became a separate body in 1795.

Methodist — *noun* a member of the Methodist Church, founded on the principles of Methodism. — *adj.* relating to Methodism.

methodological *adj.* relating to or according to methodology.

methodology *noun* (PL. **methodologies**) 1 the system of methods and principles used in a particular activity. 2 the study of method and procedure.

methought see METHINKS.

meths *sing. noun colloq.* methylated spirits.

methyl alcohol see METHANOL.

methylated spirits or **methylated spirit** ethanol (absolute alcohol) that has been mixed with small quantities of methanol and pyridine to make it undrinkable, so that it can be sold without excise duty for use as a fuel and solvent. It often contains a blue or purple dye.

methylene blue *Chem.* a blue dye used as a pH indicator, as a stain in the preparation of slides of tissue specimens for examination under an optical microscope, and as a dye for textiles.

methyl group *Chem.* in organic chemical compounds, the CH_3 group, eg methyl alcohol (CH_3OH).

meticulous *adj.* paying or showing careful attention to detail. [from Latin *meticulosus*, frightened]
. . . .
🗉 precise, scrupulous, exact, punctilious, fussy, detailed, accurate, thorough, fastidious, painstaking, strict.
🗷 careless, slapdash.
. . . .

meticulousness *noun* being meticulous.

Met Office *Brit. colloq.* the Meteorological Office, the government department that monitors national weather conditions and produces weather forecasts.

metonymy /mɪ'tɒnɪmɪ/ *noun* (PL. **metonymies**) the use of a word referring to an element or attribute of some related notion to mean the larger notion itself, eg *the bottle* for 'the drinking of alcohol' and *the Crown* for 'the sovereign'. [from META- + Greek *onoma*, name]

metope /'mɛtəpɪ/ *noun Archit.* a slab or tablet of plain or sculptured marble located between the triglyphs in the frieze of a Doric entablature. [from Greek *metope*, from *meta*, beside + *ope*, an opening for the end of a beam]

metre[1] *noun* the principal unit of length in the metric system, equal to 39.37 inches. [from Greek *metron*, measure]

metre[2] *noun* 1 *Poetry* the arrangement of words and syllables in a rhythmic pattern according to their length and stress; a particular pattern. 2 tempo in music. [from Greek *metron*, measure]

metric[1] *adj.* of or based on the metre or the metric system.

metric[2] or **metrical** *adj. technical* of or in verse as distinct from prose.

-metric *combining form* forming words denoting scientific measurement: *thermometric.*

metrically *adv.* 1 in or with the metric system of measurement. 2 in terms of metre; in metre.

metricate *verb trans., intrans.* to convert to units of the metric system.

metrication *noun* conversion to metric measurement.

metric system a standard system of measurement, based on decimal units, in which each successive multiple of a unit is 10 times larger than the one preceding it. Metric units have a prefix that denotes what multiples or fractions of the basic unit they represent, eg kilo- (k) denotes 10^3.

metro *noun* (PL. **metros**) an urban railway system, usually mostly underground, especially (**Metro**) the system in Paris. [from French *métro*, abbrev. of *chemin de fer métro-politain*, metropolitan railway]

metronome *noun* a device that indicates musical tempo by means of a ticking pendulum that can be set to move at different speeds. [from Greek *metron*, measure + *nomos*, law]

metroplex *noun* a large urban or metropolitan area, especially that formed by more than one city and the adjoining suburbs. [from METROPOLITAN + COMPLEX]

metropolis *noun* (PL. **metropolises**) a large city, especially the capital city of a nation or region. [from Greek *meter*, mother + *polis*, city]

. . . .

☐ capital, city, municipality, megalopolis.

. . . .

metropolitan — *adj.* **1** situated in or characteristic of a large city. **2** of or referring to a country's mainland, as opposed to its overseas territories. — *noun* **1** in the Catholic and Orthodox Churches, a bishop (usually an archbishop) with authority over all the bishops in a province. **2** an inhabitant of a metropolis.

-metry *combining form* forming words denoting a science involving measurement: *geometry*. [from Greek *metron*, measure]

mettle *noun literary* **1** courage, determination and endurance. **2** character; personal qualities: *show one's mettle*. — **on one's mettle** *literary* encouraged or forced to make one's best effort. [variant of METAL]

. . . .

☐ **1** spirit, courage, vigour, nerve, boldness, daring, indomitability, pluck, resolve, valour, bravery, fortitude. **2** character, temperament, disposition.

. . . .

mettlesome *adj. literary, said especially of horses* lively; high-spirited.

mew[1] — *verb intrans.* to make the cry of a cat; to miaow. — *noun* a cat's cry. [imitative]

mew[2] *noun* a seagull. [from Anglo-Saxon *mæw*]

mews *noun* (PL. **mews, mewses**) a set of stables around a yard or square, especially converted into garages or accommodation; also used in street-names. [from *mew*, cage for moulting hawks, originally the cages for royal hawks, later stables, at Charing Cross, London]

Mex. *abbrev.* **1** Mexican. **2** Mexico.

Mexican wave a rippling wave effect passing across the spectators in a stadium, as they stand up and raise their arms, then sit with lowered arms, in turn around the stadium. [so called because it was first publicized at the World Cup football competition in Mexico in 1986]

mezuzah /mə'zʊzə, mə'zuːzə/ *noun* (PL. **mezuzot**) a cylindrical box containing a parchment inscribed with religious texts from Deuteronomy, attached to the doorposts of Jewish houses as an act of faith. [Hebrew, = doorpost]

mezzanine /'mɛtsəniːn, 'mɛzəniːn/ *noun* a small floor built balcony-like between two other floors in a building, usually the ground and first floors. [from Italian *mezzanino*, from *mezzano*, middle]

mezzo /'mɛtsoʊ/ *adv. Mus.* moderately, quite, rather, as in **mezzo-forte**, rather loud. [from Italian *mezzo*, half]

mezzo-soprano /mɛtsoʊsə'prɑːnoʊ/ *noun* (PL. **mezzo-sopranos**) **1** a singing voice with a range between soprano and contralto. **2** a singer with this voice.

mezzotint /'mɛtsoʊtɪnt/ *noun* a method of engraving a metal plate by polishing and scraping to produce areas of light and shade; a print from a plate engraved in this way. [from Italian *mezzotinto*, from *mezzo*, half + *tinto*, shade]

Mg *symbol Chem.* magnesium.

mg *abbrev.* milligram.

Mgr *abbrev.* **1** manager. **2** Monsignor.

MHz *abbrev.* megahertz.

MI *abbrev.* **1** Michigan. **2** Military Intelligence.

mi *noun* in tonic sol-fa, the third note of the major scale. [from the first syllable of the word *Mira* in a medieval Latin hymn, certain syllables of which were used in naming the notes of the scale]

miaow /mɪ'aʊ/ — *verb intrans.* to make the cry of a cat. — *noun* a cat's cry. [imitative]

Miao-Yao — *adj.* denoting a family of languages used in S China and parts of SE Asia. The two principal languages are Miao and Yao, both written in the Roman alphabet. — *noun* the languages forming this family.

miasma *noun* (PL. **miasmata, miasmas**) *literary* **1** a thick foul-smelling vapour, especially as given off by swamps, marshes, etc. **2** an evil influence or atmosphere. [from Greek *miasma*, pollution]

miasmal *adj.* relating to or typical of miasma.

mica /'maɪkə/ *noun Geol.* any of a group of transparent, black, or coloured silicate minerals that have a layered structure and are readily split into thin flexible sheets. Micas are poor conductors of heat and electricity, and are used as electrical insulators, and as dielectrics in capacitors. [from Latin *mica*, crumb]

mice see MOUSE.

Mich. *abbrev.* **1** Michaelmas. **2** Michigan.

Michaelmas *noun* a Christian festival in honour of St Michael, held on 29 September. [from *Michael* + *mas*, from MASS[2]]

Michaelmas daisy any of various garden plants of the aster family, with purple, pink, or white flowers that bloom in autumn.

Michelangelo virus *Comput.* a virus set to destroy data on a computer's hard disk when the system date reads 6 Mar in any year. [named after the Italian sculptor, painter, and poet Michelangelo Buonarroti (1475–1564), whose birthday was 6 Mar]

mick *noun offensive slang* an Irishman. [from the name *Michael*]

mickey *noun* — **take the mickey out of someone** *colloq.* to tease or make fun of them. [origin uncertain]

Mickey Finn *slang* a drink, especially alcoholic, with a stupefying drug secretly added.

Mickey Mouse *derog. colloq.* **1** of the nature of a cheap imitation. **2** ridiculously simple or unprofessional. [from the Walt Disney cartoon film character]

micro *noun* (PL. **micros**) *colloq.* a microcomputer, microprocessor, or microwave oven.

micro- *combining form* forming words meaning: **1** very small: *microchip*. **2** one millionth part: *micrometre*. [from Greek *mikros*, little]

microbe *noun* imprecise term for any micro-organism, especially a bacterium that is capable of causing disease. [from Greek *mikros*, little + *bios*, life]

. . . .

☐ micro-organism, bacterium, bacillus, germ, virus, pathogen, *colloq.* bug.

. . . .

microbial or **microbic** *adj.* relating to or characteristic of microbes.

microbiological *adj.* relating to or involving microbiology.

microbiologist *noun* a person who studies or is expert in microbiology.

microbiology *noun* the branch of biology dealing with the study of micro-organisms.

microbrewery *noun* (PL. **microbreweries**) a small independent brewery, often located within a pub that sells the product. See also BREWPUB.

microchip *noun* see SILICON CHIP.

microcircuit *noun* an electronic circuit with components formed in one microchip.

microclimate *noun Biol.* the local uniform climate immediately surrounding a living organism (eg the climate surrounding the leaves of a tree) as opposed to the climate of the entire region in which the organism occurs (eg a forest).

microcomputer *noun* a small relatively inexpensive computer designed to be used by one person at a time, and containing an entire central processing unit on a single microchip. Also called PERSONAL COMPUTER.

microcosm *noun* **1** any structure or system which contains, in miniature, all the features of the larger structure or system that it is part of. **2** *Philos.* man regarded as a model or epitome of the universe. **— in microcosm** on a small scale; in miniature. [from MICRO- + Greek *kosmos*, world]

microcosmic *adj.* relating to or typical of a microcosm.

microdot *noun* a photograph, eg of secret documents, reduced to the size of a pinhead.

microeconomics *sing. noun* the branch of economics concerned with the financial circumstances of individual households, firms, industries, etc, and the way individual elements in an economy behave (such as specific products, commodities, or consumers).

microelectronic *adj.* relating to or involving microelectronics.

microelectronics *sing. noun* the branch of electronics dealing with the design and use of small-scale electrical circuits.

microfiche *noun Photog.* a flat sheet of film bearing printed text that has been photographically reduced, formerly widely used as a means of storing bulky items such as library catalogues, but now largely superseded by databases and compact discs that allow much more sophisticated searches to be conducted. [from MICRO- + French *fiche*, sheet of paper]

microfilm *noun* thin film on which printed material is stored in miniaturized form.

microlight *noun* a very lightweight small-engined aircraft, like a powered hang-glider.

micrometer *noun* an instrument for accurately measuring very small distances, thicknesses, or angles.

micron *noun* (SYMBOL μ) former name for the micrometre, a unit of length equal to 10^{-6}m, which has now replaced the micron as the SI unit. [from Greek *mikros*, small]

micro-organism *noun* a general term for any living organism that can only be observed with the aid of a microscope. Micro-organisms include bacteria, viruses, protozoans, and single-celled algae, and the term is often taken to include microscopic fungi, eg yeasts.

microphone *noun Electron.* an electronic device that converts sound waves into electrical signals that can be amplified, recorded, or transmitted over long distances, used in radio and television broadcasting, telephone receiver mouthpieces, etc. [from MICRO- + Greek *phone*, voice]

microphotography *noun* photography of normal-sized objects, especially documents, plans, and graphic material, as greatly reduced images of small area, which must be examined by magnification or enlarged projection.

microprocessor *noun Comput.* a single circuit performing most of the basic functions of a central processing unit.

micropyle *noun Bot.* **1** in flowering plants, a small opening or pore at the tip of the ovule, through which the pollen tube normally enters during pollination. It normally persists as an opening through which water is absorbed prior to germination of the developing seed. **2** *Zool.* a tiny opening or pore in the protective layer surrounding an insect's egg, through which sperm enters during the process of fertilization. [from MICRO- + Greek *pyle*, gate]

microscope *noun* any of a range of different instruments consisting of a system of lenses that produce a magnified image of objects that are too small to be seen with the naked eye, eg light microscope, electron microscope. See also LIGHT MICROSCOPE, ELECTRON MICROSCOPE.

microscopic *adj.* **1** too small to be seen without the aid of a microscope. **2** extremely small. **3** of, or by means of, a microscope.

· · · · · · · · · · · · · · · · · · ·

▣ **2** minute, tiny, minuscule, infinitesimal, indiscernible, imperceptible, negligible.

▣ **2** huge, enormous.

· · · · · · · · · · · · · · · · · · ·

microscopically *adv.* **1** in a microscopic way; to a microscopic degree. **2** with the aid of a microscope.

microsecond *noun* a unit of time equal to one millionth part of a second.

microsurgery *noun Medicine* any intricate surgical procedure that is performed on very small body structures. It requires the use of a powerful microscope and small specialized instruments; it is typically used in eye or brain surgery, or during the reconnection of the nerves and blood vessels when reattaching an amputated finger or limb.

microtome *noun Biol.* an instrument for cutting thin sections of objects for microscopic examination. [from MICRO- + Greek *tome*, a cut]

microtubule *noun Biol.* any of the microscopic hollow tubular filaments, composed of the protein tubulin, that are found in the cytoplasm of eukaryotic cells.

microwave **— noun 1** (*in full* **microwave radiation**) a form of electromagnetic radiation with wavelengths in the range 1mm to 0.3m, ie intermediate between those of infrared and radio waves, and overlapping with very high frequency radio waves. Microwaves are used in radar, communications, and cooking. **2** a microwave oven. **— verb** to cook in a microwave.

microwave oven an electrically operated oven that uses microwaves to cook food more rapidly than is possible in a conventional oven. Microwaves generate heat by causing water molecules within the food to vibrate.

micturate *verb intrans. formal* to urinate. [from Latin *micturire*]

micturition *noun* the act of urinating.

mid[1] *adj.* (*often in compounds*) being the part at or in the middle: *mid-March/in mid sentence.* [from Anglo-Saxon *midd*]

mid[2] *or* **'mid** *prep. poetic* amid.

mid-air *noun* any area or point above the ground.

midday *noun* the middle of the day; twelve o'clock.

midden *noun* **1** *old use, dialect* a rubbish heap; a pile of dung. **2** *dialect* an untidy mess. [from Middle English, of Scandinavian origin]

middle **— adj. 1** at, or being, a point or position between two others, usually two ends or extremes, and especially the same distance from each. **2** intermediate, not senior or chief: *middle management.* **3** moderate, not extreme; done, etc as a compromise: *a middle course.* **4** (**Middle**) *said especially of languages* belonging to a period coming after the Old period and before the Modern: *Middle English.* **— noun** the middle point, part, or position. **— verb 1** to place in the middle. **2** *Cricket* to hit (the ball) with the middle of the bat, therefore firmly and accurately. **— be in the middle of something** to be busy with it, and likely to remain so. **in the middle of ...** at a point during: *in the middle of the night.* [from Anglo-Saxon *middel* (adjective)]

· · · · · · · · · · · · · · · · · · ·

▣ *adj.* **1, 2, 3** intermediate. **1** central, halfway, mean, median, inner, inside, intervening. *noun* centre, halfway point, midpoint, mean, heart, core, midst, inside, bull's eye.

▣ *adj.* **1** extreme. *noun* **1** end, edge, beginning, border.

· · · · · · · · · · · · · · · · · · ·

middle age the years between youth and old age, usually reckoned as between ages 40 and 60.

middle-aged *adj.* of middle age, between youth and old age.

Middle Ages the period of European history between the fall of the Roman Empire in the West and the Renaissance (c.500–1500), or more narrowly between 1100 and 1500.

middle-age spread *or* **middle-aged spread** fat around the waist, often regarded as a consequence of reaching middle age.

middlebrow *derog.* — *adj.* intended for, or appealing to, people with conventional tastes and average intelligence. — *noun* a middlebrow person.

middle class the social class between the working class and the upper class, traditionally containing educated people with professional or business careers.

middle-class *adj.* relating to or characteristic of the middle class.

middle ear an air-filled cavity lying between the eardrum and the inner ear in vertebrates. It contains three small bones (the malleus, incus, and stapes) which transmit sound waves from the outer ear to the inner ear.

Middle East a loosely defined geographical region encompassing the largely Arab states to the E of the Mediterranean sea together with Cyprus and Turkey. It can also include the countries of N Africa.

Middle Eastern *adj.* relating to or characteristic of the Middle East.

Middle England the English middle classes outside London, regarded as politically and socially conservative.

middle lamella *Bot.* a thin layer, composed mainly of pectins, that cements together the walls of adjacent plant cells.

middleman *noun* **1** a dealer who buys goods from a producer or manufacturer and sells them to shopkeepers or to the public. **2** any intermediary.

⊟ BROKER, AGENT, CONTACT. **1** dealer, wholesaler. **2** intermediary, go-between, mediator.

middle management the junior managerial executives and senior supervisory personnel in a firm or institution.

middle name 1 a name which comes between a first name and a surname. **2** a quality or feature for which a person is well known.

middle-of-the-road *adj. often derog.* not extreme; of widespread appeal; boringly average or familiar.

⊟ moderate, mainstream, popular, middlebrow, average, ordinary, conventional, unadventurous, familiar, undemanding, run-of-the-mill, common-or-garden, mediocre, everyday, humdrum.

middle school a school for children between the ages of 8 or 9 and 12 or 13.

middleweight *noun* **1** a class for boxers, wrestlers, and weight-lifters of not more than a specified weight (73kg in professional boxing, 70kg for *light middleweight*, 77kg for *super-middleweight*; similar but different weights in the other sports). **2** a boxer, etc of this weight.

middling *colloq.* — *adj.* average; moderate; mediocre. — *adv.* fairly good; moderately: *middling good.* — **fair to middling** not bad; fairly good. [from Scots, from MID[1] + -LING]

⊟ *adj.* mediocre, medium, ordinary, moderate, average, unexceptional, unremarkable, run-of-the-mill, indifferent, modest, passable, tolerable, *colloq.* so-so, *colloq.* OK.

midge *noun* any of various kinds of small insect that gather near water, especially the kinds that bite people. [from Anglo-Saxon *mycge*]

midget — *noun* **1** an unusually small person whose limbs and features are of normal proportions. **2** any small thing of its kind. — *adj.* small of its kind. [related to MIDGE]

⊟ *noun* **1** person of restricted growth, pygmy, dwarf, Tom Thumb, gnome. **2** miniature, baby, *colloq.* mini. *adj* tiny, small, miniature, little, pocket, pocket-sized, baby, *colloq.* mini.
⊟ *noun* GIANT. *adj.* giant.

midi- *combining form* of medium size or length: *midi-skirt.* — *noun colloq.* a midi-skirt or coat. [from MID[1]]

Midianite, also called **Ishmaelite** *noun* a member of an ancient semi-nomadic people from the desert area of the Transjordan, who according to Genesis 25 were descended from the offspring (Midian) of one of Abraham's concubines (Keturah).

midiron /ˈmɪdaɪən/ *noun Golf* a heavy club used for long approach shots.

midi system a complete hi-fi system in the form of a single unit, compact but not portable.

midland *adj.* of the central inland part of a country.

midmost *adj., adv. literary* in the middle.

midnight — *noun* twelve o'clock at night. — *adj.* of or at midnight. — **burn the midnight oil** to work until very late into the night.

midnight sun *Astron.* a phenomenon that occurs during the summer in the Arctic and Antarctic regions, where the Sun remains visible for 24 hours a day (in winter there is a similar period during which the Sun never rises).

mid-on or **mid-off** *noun Cricket* a fielder in a rough horizontal line with, but at some distance from, the non-striking batsman, on the on or off side.

midpoint *noun* a point at or near the middle in distance or time.

⊟ middle, centre, midst, heart, hub, pivot, focus, mean, median.

midrib *noun Bot.* the rib that runs along the centre of a leaf and forms an extension of the leaf stalk or petiole.

midriff *noun* the part of the body between the chest and the waist. [from MID[1] + Anglo-Saxon *hrif*, belly]

midshipman *noun* (PL. **midshipmen**) a trainee naval officer, stationed on land. [so called because originally housed in quarters that were *amidships*]

midships see AMIDSHIPS.

midst *noun* — **in the midst of something 1** among, or in the centre of it. **2** at the same time as something; during it. **in someone's midst** among, or in the same place as them. [from Anglo-Saxon *in middes*, amidst]

midstream *noun* the area of water in the middle of a river or stream, away from its banks. — **in midstream** before a sentence, action, etc is finished.

midsummer *noun* the period of time near the summer solstice, around 21 June.

Midsummer Day or **Midsummer's Day** 24 June.

midterm *noun* **1** the middle of an academic term, term of office, etc. **2** a holiday, examination, etc, in the middle of term. — *adj.* relating to, or occurring at or around, the middle of a term.

midway *adj., adv.* halfway between two points in distance or time.

midweek *noun* the period of time in the middle of the week, especially Wednesday.

Midwestern *adj.* relating to or typical of the US Midwest.

mid-wicket *noun Cricket* the area between the stumps on the on side, roughly midway between the wicket and the boundary.

midwife *noun* (PL. **midwives**) a nurse, especially female, trained to supervise childbirth and provide care and advice before and after. [from Anglo-Saxon *mid*, with + *wif*, woman]

midwifery /ˈmɪdwɪfərɪ/ *noun* the skills or practice of a midwife, obstetrics.

midwife toad a European frog that lives away from water, may dig burrows, and mates on dry land. The male wraps the eggs around its legs and carries them until they hatch, and then transports the tadpoles to water.

midwinter *noun* the period of time in the middle of winter, around 22 December.

mien /miːn/ *noun literary* an appearance, expression, or manner, especially reflecting a mood. [perhaps from obsolete *demean*, appearance]

miff *colloq.* — *verb* **1** to offend. **2** (*intrans.*) to be offended. — *noun* **1** a quarrel. **2** a fit of sulking; a huff. [from German *muffen*, to sulk]

miffed *adj. colloq.* offended, upset, annoyed.

miffy *adj.* (**miffier**, **miffiest**) *colloq.* easily offended; touchy.

might [1] *verb, aux.* **1** past tense of **may**: *he asked if he might be of assistance.* **2** used to express possibility: *he might win if he tries hard.* **3** used to request permission: *might I speak to you a moment?* **4** used in suggesting that a person is not doing what he or she should: *you might carry these bags for me!* **5** *old affected use, facetious* used in asking a question: *and who might you be?* **6** used to introduce the first of a pair of statements, with the sense of 'although': *you might be the boss, but you're still an idiot!* [from Anglo-Saxon *miht*]

might [2] *noun* power or strength. — **with might and main** *literary* with great strength; with all one's strength. [from Anglo-Saxon *miht*]

mightily *adv.* **1** powerfully. **2** to a great extent.

mightiness *noun* a mighty state or condition; great strength.

mightn't *contr.* might not.

mighty — *adj.* (**mightier**, **mightiest**) **1** having great strength or power. **2** very large. — *adv. colloq. North Amer., esp. US* very: *mighty pretty.*

 ⊟ *adj.* **1** strong, powerful, potent, dominant, influential. **2** enormous, huge, *colloq.* terrific, tremendous, massive, gigantic.

migmatite *noun Geol.* a complex rock with a characteristic banded or veined appearance, consisting of a mixture of igneous and metamorphic rocks. Migmatites often occur near large masses of granite. [from Greek *migma*, mixture]

migraine *noun* a severe and recurring throbbing headache, more common in women than in men, that usually affects one side of the head, and is often accompanied by nausea or vomiting, and sometimes preceded by visual disturbances, eg blurring of vision. [from Greek *hemikrania*, half skull]

migrant — *noun* a person or animal that migrates. — *adj.* regularly moving from one place to another. [from Latin *migrare*, to migrate]

 ⊟ *noun* traveller, wanderer, itinerant, emigrant, immigrant, rover, nomad, *colloq.* globetrotter, drifter, Gypsy, tinker, vagrant.

migrate *verb intrans.* **1** *said of animals, esp. birds* to travel from one region to another at certain times of the year. **2** to leave one place and settle in another, especially another country, often regularly. [from Latin *migrare*]

 ⊟ **1** wander, roam, rove, journey, travel, voyage, trek, drift. **2** move, resettle, relocate, emigrate.

migration *noun Zool.* the movement of animals from one location to another, generally involving travel over very long distances by well-defined routes, in response to seasonal changes. It is usually associated with breeding or feeding.

migratory *adj.* **1** that migrate, or are accustomed to migrating. **2** wandering.

mihrab /mɪəˈrɑːb, ˈmiːxrɑːb/ *noun Relig.* a niche or slab in a mosque indicating the direction of Mecca. [from Arabic *mihrāb*]

mikado /mɪˈkɑːdoʊ/ *noun* (PL. **mikados**) (*often* **Mikado**) a title formerly given by foreigners to an emperor of Japan. [from Japanese *mikado*, exalted gate]

mike *noun colloq.* a microphone.

mil *noun* **1** a unit of length equal to one thousandth of an inch. **2** *colloq.* a millilitre or millimetre. [from Latin *mille*, a thousand]

milady /mɪˈleɪdɪ/ *noun* (PL. **miladies**) a term formerly used to address or refer to a rich, especially aristocratic, English woman. [from French, from *my lady*]

milch /mɪltʃ/ *adj., said of cattle* producing milk. [from Anglo-Saxon *milce*]

mild — *adj.* **1** gentle in temperament or behaviour. **2** not sharp or strong in flavour or effect. **3** not great or severe. **4** *said of climate, etc* not characterized by extremes; rather warm. — *noun* (*also* **mild ale**) dark beer less flavoured with hops than bitter beer. [from Anglo-Saxon *milde*]

 ⊟ *adj.* **1**, **3** kind, lenient, compassionate. **1** gentle, calm, peaceable, placid, tender, soft, good-natured, amiable. **2** bland, mellow, smooth, subtle, soothing. **3**, **4** temperate, clement, fair, pleasant. **4** calm, warm, balmy.
 ⊟ *adj.* **1** harsh, fierce. **2** strong. **4** stormy.

mildew — *noun* **1** any of various parasitic fungi that produce a fine white powdery coating on the surface of infected plants, or white or grey patches on the surface of products made from plant or animal material (eg paper, leather, fabrics) and subsequently exposed to moisture. A downy mildew (*Phytophthora infestans*) causes potato blight, the disease that was responsible for the Irish potato famine of the 1840s. **2** a white powdery coating that appears on the surface of a plant infected by certain parasitic fungi, or white or grey patches on the surface of products made from plant or animal material and subsequently exposed to moisture. — *verb trans., intrans.* to affect or become affected by mildew. [from Anglo-Saxon *mildeaw*]

mildewed *adj.* affected by mildew.

mild steel steel that contains little carbon and is easily worked.

mile *noun* **1** a unit of distance equal to 1760yd (1.61km). **2** a race over this distance, especially on foot. **3** *colloq.* a great distance; a large margin: *miss by a mile.* [from Anglo-Saxon *mil*, from Latin *mille passuum*, a thousand paces]

mileage *noun* **1** the number of miles travelled or to be travelled. **2** the number of miles a motor vehicle will travel on a fixed amount of fuel. **3** *colloq.* use; benefit; advantage.

mileometer or **milometer** *noun* an instrument in a motor vehicle for recording the total number of miles travelled.

miler *noun* an athlete or horse that runs races of one mile.

miles *adv.* **1** at a great distance: *miles away.* **2** *colloq.* very much: *miles better.*

milestone *noun* **1** a stone pillar at a roadside showing distances in miles to various places. **2** a very important event.

milieu /ˈmiːljɜː/ *noun* (PL. **milieux**, **milieus**) *literary* a social environment or set of surroundings. [from French *milieu*]

 ⊟ environment, surroundings, ambit, ambience, orbit, circle.

militancy *noun* being militant.

 ⊟ activism, zeal, partisanship, extremism, fanaticism, assertiveness, belligerence.

militant — *adj.* **1** taking, or ready to take, strong or violent action; aggressively active. **2** *formal* engaged in warfare. — *noun* a person with strong or extreme views who is prepared to take action to put them into effect. [from Latin *militare*, to serve as a soldier]

 ⊟ *adj.* **1** aggressive, belligerent, *literary* bellicose, vigorous, zealous, outspoken, doctrinaire. **2** fighting, warring, combatant. *noun* activist, partisan, zealot, fanatic, ideologue, doctrinaire, extremist, fighter, struggler.
 ⊟ *adj.* **1** moderate, lukewarm. **2** pacifist, peaceful.

militarily *adv.* in a military way; by military means.

militarism *noun often derog.* an aggressive readiness to engage in warfare; the vigorous pursuit of military aims and ideals.

militarist *noun* a supporter of militarism.

militaristic *adj.* relating to or characteristic of militarism.

militarize or **militarise** *verb* **1** to provide with a military force. **2** to make military in nature or character.

military — *adj.* **1** of, by, or for the armed forces. **2** characteristic of members of the armed forces: *military bearing.* — *noun* (**the military**) the armed forces. [from Latin *militaris*, from *miles*, soldier]

⊟ *adj.* **1** service, army. **2** martial, soldierly, warlike. *noun* the army, the armed forces, the forces, the services, soldiers.

military police a police force within an army, enforcing army rules.

military science the theoretical study of warfare and of the strategic, tactical, and logistic principles behind it.

militate *verb intrans.* **1** (**militate against something**) to act, or have a strong influence, against it. **2** (**militate for something**) to act, or have a strong influence, in its favour. [from Latin *militare*, to serve as a soldier]

⊟ **1** oppose, resist, contend against, counter, counteract, count against, tell against, weigh against.

militia *noun* a civilian fighting force used to supplement a regular army in emergencies. [from Latin *militia*, military force]

militiaman *noun* a member of a militia.

milk — *noun* **1** a white or yellowish liquid that is secreted by the mammary glands of female mammals for the nourishment of their young. **2** any preparation that resembles this, eg milk of magnesia. — *verb* **1** to take milk from (an animal). **2** *colloq.* to obtain money, information, or other benefit from, cleverly or relentlessly. — **cry over spilt milk** to waste time grieving over a mistake that cannot be undone. **milk and water** weak or weakly sentimental speech or writing. **milk and honey** comfort; luxury; plenty. [from Anglo-Saxon *milc*]

⊟ *verb* **1** drain, tap, extract, draw off, express, press. **2** exploit, use, *colloq.* bleed, squeeze, wring, pump.

milk chocolate chocolate containing milk.

milk float a vehicle, usually electrically-powered, used for delivering milk.

milkiness *noun* a milky state or condition.

milkmaid *noun* a woman who milks cows.

milkman *noun* a man who delivers milk to people's homes.

milk round **1** a milkman's regular route from house to house. **2** the periodic recruitment of undergraduates by large companies.

milkshake *noun* a drink consisting of a mixture of milk, flavouring, and sometimes ice-cream, whipped until creamy.

milksop *noun old derog. use* a weak or ineffectual man or youth.

milk sugar *Biochem.* lactose.

milk tooth any of a baby's first set of teeth.

milky *adj.* (**milkier, milkiest**) **1** like milk. **2** of or containing milk.

⊟ **1** white, milk-white, chalky, opaque, clouded, cloudy.

Milky Way (**the Milky Way**) **1** a band of diffuse light that circles the night sky as seen from Earth, and represents the combined light of billions of stars, too faint to be seen individually, in the plane of our Galaxy. **2** commonly used to refer to the Galaxy to which our Sun belongs.

mill — *noun* **1** a large machine that grinds grain into flour, or a building containing this. **2** any of various smaller machines or devices for grinding: *a pepper mill.* **3** a large machine that presses, rolls, or otherwise shapes; a factory containing one or more of these; any factory: *a woollen mill.* — *verb* **1** to grind (grain, etc). **2** to shape (eg metal) in a mill. **3** to cut grooves into the edge of (a coin). **4** *intrans., colloq.* (**mill about** or **around**) to move in an aimless or confused manner. — **go** or **put someone through the mill** to undergo or cause to undergo an unpleasant experience or difficult test. [from Anglo-Saxon *myln*, from Latin *molere*, to grind]

⊟ *noun* **1** grinder, crusher, roller, *Hist.* quern. **3** factory, plant, works, workshop, foundry. *verb* **1** grind, pulverize, powder, pound, crush, grate. **2** roll, press.

millenarian *noun* a person who believes that the coming of the millennium is a certainty.

millenarianism *noun* the beliefs of a millenarian.

millennial *adj.* of or relating to a or the millennium.

millennium *noun* (PL. **millennia**) **1** a period of a thousand years. **2** (**the millennium**) **a** a future period of a thousand years during which some Christians believe Christ will rule the world. **b** a future period of worldwide peace and happiness. [from Latin *mille*, a thousand + *annus*, year]

millennium bug a deficiency in some computer programs in which date codes had only the last two digits, not taking account of the change of century in the year 2000.

millepede same as MILLIPEDE.

miller *noun Hist.* a person who owns or operates a grain mill.

millesimal — *adj.* thousandth; consisting of thousandths. — *noun* a thousandth part. [from Latin *mille*, a thousand]

millet *noun* **1** the common name for several cereal grasses (especially *Panicum miliaceum* and *Sorghum bicolor*) that are tolerant of drought and poor soil, grow rapidly, and are cultivated as an important food crop in the dry regions. **2** the small edible seeds (grain) of this plant. [from Latin *milium*]

milli- *combining form* forming words denoting a thousandth part: *millisecond.* [from Latin *mille*, a thousand]

milliard *noun old use* a thousand million. [from French, from Latin *mille*, a thousand]

millibar *noun* (SYMBOL **mbar**) a unit of atmospheric pressure equal to 10^{-3} (one thousandth) of a bar, or 100Pa, commonly used in meteorology.

milligram or **milligramme** *noun* a unit of weight, equal to one thousandth of a gram.

millilitre *noun* a unit of volume, equal to one thousandth of a litre.

millimetre *noun* a unit of length, equal to one thousandth of a metre.

milliner *noun* a person who makes or sells women's hats. [originally from *Milaner*, a trader in the fancy goods for which *Milan* was once famous]

millinery *noun* the hats and trimmings made or sold by milliners; the craft of making them.

milling *noun* the grinding of cereal grain to produce flour for use in the making of bread and other foodstuffs.

million — *noun* (PL. **millions**, **million** after a number) **1** the number or quantity 10^6, a thousand thousands. **2** a numeral, figure or symbol representing this, eg 1,000,000. **3** *colloq.* a million pounds or dollars. **4** (*often* **millions**) *colloq.* a great number: *millions of books.* — *adj.* 1,000,000 in number. — **in a million** very rare of its kind, and therefore very valuable. [from Latin *millionis*, from *mille*, a thousand]

millionaire *noun* a person whose wealth amounts to a million pounds, dollars, etc or more.

millionairess *noun* a female millionaire.

millionth *noun, adj.* a thousand thousandth.

millipede *noun* a small worm-like creature with a many-jointed body and numerous pairs of legs. [from Latin *mille*, a thousand + *pedis*, foot]

millpond *noun* a pond containing water which is, or used to be, used for driving a grain mill.

millstone *noun* **1** either of the large heavy stones between which grain is ground in a mill. **2** any heavy burden, eg a duty or responsibility.

millwheel *noun* a wheel, especially a waterwheel, driving a grain mill.

milometer SEE MILEOMETER.

milord /mɪˈlɔːd/ *noun* a term formerly used on the continent to address or refer to a rich, especially aristocratic, English man. [from French, from *my lord*]

milt *noun* the testis or sperm of a fish. [from Anglo-Saxon *milte*, spleen]

mime — *noun* **1** the theatrical art of acting using movements and gestures alone. **2** a play or dramatic sequence performed in this way. **3** (*also* **mime artist**) an actor who practises this art. — *verb trans.*, *intrans.* **1** to act (feelings, etc) in this way. **2** to mouth the words to (a song) to match a recording, giving the illusion of singing. [from Greek *mimos*, imitator]

⊟ *noun* **1** dumb show, pantomime, gesture, mimicry. *verb* **1** gesture, signal, act, simulate, impersonate, mimic.

mimeograph — *noun* a machine that produces copies of printed or handwritten material from a stencil; a copy produced in this way. — *verb* to make a copy of in this way. [from *Mimeograph*, originally a trademark]

mimesis /mɪˈmiːsɪs/ *noun* in art or literature, imitative representation; mimicry. [from Greek *mimēsis*, imitation]

mimetic *adj.* **1** of or relating to imitation; imitative. **2** *Biol.* displaying mimicry. [from Greek *mimēsis*, imitation]

mimic — *verb* (**mimicked, mimicking**) **1** to imitate, especially for comic effect. **2** to copy. **3** to simulate. **4** *Biol.* to resemble closely. — *noun* **1** a person skilled in (especially comic) imitations of others. **2** *Biol.* a plant or animal displaying mimicry. [from Greek *mimikos*, from *mimos*, imitator]

⊟ *verb* **1** imitate, parody, caricature, take off, *Brit. colloq.* send up, ape, parrot, impersonate. **2** echo, mirror, copy. **3** simulate, look like. *noun* **1** imitator, impersonator, impressionist, caricaturist, copycat.

mimicry *noun* **1** the skill or practice of mimicking. **2** *Biol.* the close resemblance of one animal or plant species to another, or to a non-living feature of its natural environment, that serves to protect it from predators, or to deceive its prey.

⊟ **1** imitation, imitating, impersonation, copying, parody, impression, caricature, take-off, burlesque.

mimosa *noun* any of various tropical shrubs or trees with clusters of (especially yellow) flowers, and leaves that droop when touched. [from Greek *mimos*, imitator, from the leaf's imitation of a cowering animal]

Min. *abbrev.* **1** Minister. **2** Ministry.

min *noun colloq.* a minute.

min. *abbrev.* **1** minimum. **2** minute.

mina same as MYNA.

minaret *noun* a tower on a mosque, from which Muslims are called to prayer. [from Arabic *manarat*, lighthouse]

minatory *adj. formal* threatening. [from Latin *minari*, to threaten]

mince — *verb* **1** to cut or shred (especially meat) into very small pieces. **2** to soften the impact of (one's words). **3** *intrans.*, *derog.* to walk or speak with affected delicacy. — *noun* minced meat, especially beef. [from Old French *mincier*]

⊟ *verb* **1** chop, cut, hash, dice, grind, crumble. **2** diminish, suppress, play down, tone down, hold back, moderate, weaken, soften, spare.

mincemeat *noun* a spiced mixture of dried fruits, used as a filling for pies. — **make mincemeat of something** or **someone** *colloq.* to defeat or destroy them thoroughly.

mince pie a pie filled with mincemeat or with minced meat.

mincing *adj. derog.* over-delicate and affected.

mincingly *adv.* in a mincing way.

MIND *abbrev.* National Association of Mental Health.

mind — *noun* **1** the power of thinking and understanding; the place where thoughts and feelings exist; the intelligence. **2** memory; recollection: *call something to mind*. **3** opinion; judgement: *to my mind*. **4** attention: *his mind wanders*. **5** wish; inclination: *have a mind to go/change one's mind*. **6** a very intelligent person. **7** right senses; sanity: *lose one's mind*. — *verb* **1** to look after, care for, or keep safe. **2** *trans.*, *intrans.* to be upset, bothered or concerned (by). **3** to be careful or wary of: *mind the traffic*. **4** to take notice of, or pay attention to: *mind my advice/mind your own business*. **5** to take care to control: *mind one's language*. **6** *trans.*, *intrans.* to take care to protect: *mind your jacket near this wet grass!* **7** *dialect* to remember. — *interj.* be careful; watch out! — **bear something in mind** to remember it. **do you mind!** an exclamation expressing disagreement or objection. **in one's mind's eye** in one's imagination. **in two minds** undecided. **know one's own mind** to have firm opinions or intentions. **make up one's mind** to decide. **never mind** don't worry; it doesn't matter. **on one's mind** being thought about, considered, worried about, etc. **a piece of one's mind** a scolding or criticism. **put one in mind of something** to remind one of it. [from Anglo-Saxon *gemynd*, from *munan*, to think]

⊟ *noun* **1** intelligence, intellect, brains, reason, sense, understanding, wits, mentality, thinking, thoughts, *colloq.* grey matter, head, genius. **2** memory, remembrance, recollection. **3** opinion, view, point of view, judgement, belief, attitude, feeling, sentiment. **4** concentration, attention. **5** inclination, disposition, tendency, will, wish, intention, desire. *verb* **1** look after, take care of, watch over, guard, have charge of, keep an eye on, *colloq.* keep tabs on. **2** care (about), object (to), take offence (at), disapprove (of). **3** be careful of, watch, watch out for. **4** regard, heed, pay attention, pay heed to, note, obey, listen to, comply with, follow, observe. **bear in mind** consider, remember, note. **make up one's mind** decide, choose, determine, settle, resolve.

mind-blowing *adj. colloq.* very surprising, shocking, or exciting.

mind-boggling *adj. colloq.* too difficult, large, strange, etc to imagine or understand.

minded *adj.* **1** having an intention or desire: *not minded to reply to your letter*. **2** (*in compounds*) having a certain kind of mind or attitude: *open-minded*.

minder *noun* **1** (*in compounds*) a person who takes care of or supervises: *childminder*. **2** *colloq.* a bodyguard.

mindful *adj.* (**mindful of something**) keeping it in mind; attentive to it.

⊟ aware of, conscious of, alive to, alert to, attentive to, careful of, watchful of, wary of.

⊞ heedless of, inattentive to.

mindfulness *noun* being mindful, awareness.

mindless *adj.* **1** *derog.* senseless; done without a reason. **2** *derog.* needing no effort of mind. **3** (**mindless of something**) taking no account: *mindless of his responsibilities*.

▣ **1** thoughtless, senseless, illogical, irrational, stupid, foolish, gratuitous, negligent. **2** mechanical, automatic, routine, tedious.

▣ **1** thoughtful, intelligent.

mindlessly adv. in a mindless way.

mind-reader noun a person claiming to know other people's thoughts.

mind-reading noun the process of apparently discovering the thoughts of another.

mine[1] — pron. **1** something or someone belonging to, or connected with, me; those belonging to me. **2** my family or people. — adj. old use, poetic used for my, before a vowel sound or h: mine eye/mine host. — **of mine** belonging to, or connected with, me: a cousin of mine. [from Anglo-Saxon min]

mine[2] — noun **1** (often in compounds) an opening or excavation in the ground, used to remove minerals, metal ores, coal, etc, from the Earth's crust. **2** an explosive device that is placed in a fixed position just beneath the ground surface or in water, designed to destroy tanks, personnel, ships, etc, when detonated by contact. **3** a rich source: a mine of information. — verb **1** trans., intrans. to dig for (minerals, etc) in (an area). **2** to lay exploding mines in (land or water). **3** to destroy with exploding mines. [from French miner, to mine]

▣ noun **1** pit, colliery, coalfield, excavation, vein, seam, shaft, trench, deposit. **3** supply, source, stock, store, reserve, fund, hoard, treasury, wealth. verb **1** excavate, dig, quarry, extract, tunnel.

minefield noun **1** an area of land or water in which exploding mines have been laid. **2** a subject or situation presenting many (hidden) problems or dangers.

miner noun (often in compounds) a person who works in a mine, especially a coal mine.

mineral — noun **1** Geol. a naturally occurring substance that is inorganic (of non-biological origin), usually crystalline, and has characteristic physical and chemical properties by which it may be identified. Rocks consist of mixtures of minerals, eg quartz, mica, calcite, dolomite. **2** a loose term for any substance obtained by mining, including fossil fuels (eg coal, natural gas, petroleum), which strictly speaking are not minerals because they are of organic origin. **3** (usually **minerals**) mineral water. — adj. of the nature of a mineral; containing minerals. [from French minéral, from miner, to mine]

Minerals include: alabaster, albite, anhydrite, asbestos, aventurine, azurite, bentonite, blacklead, bloodstone, blue john, borax, cairngorm, calamine, calcite, calcspar, cassiterite, chalcedony, chlorite, chrysoberyl, cinnabar, corundum, dolomite, emery, feldspar, fluorite, fluorspar, fool's gold, French chalk, galena, graphite, gypsum, haematite, halite, haüyne, hornblende, hyacinth, idocrase, jacinth, jargoon, jet, kandite, kaolinite, lapis lazuli, lazurite, magnetite, malachite, meerschaum, mica, microcline, montmorillonite, orthoclase, plumbago, pyrites, quartz, rock salt, rutile, saltpetre, sanidine, silica, smithsonite, sodalite, spar, sphalerite, spinel, talc, uralite, uranite, vesuvianite, wurtzite, zircon.

mineralogical adj. relating to or involving mineralogy.

mineralogist noun a person who studies or is expert in mineralogy.

mineralogy noun the scientific study of minerals.

mineral oil any oil obtained from minerals, rather than from a plant or animal source.

mineral water **1** water containing small quantities of dissolved minerals, especially when occurring naturally in this state at a spring. **2** any fizzy non-alcoholic drink.

minestrone /mɪnɪ'strəʊnɪ/ noun thick soup containing vegetables and pasta. [from Italian minestrare, to serve]

minesweeper noun a ship equipped to clear mines from an area.

minginess noun meanness.

mingle verb (often **mingle with something** or **someone**) **1** intrans., trans. to become or cause to become blended or mixed; to associate or have dealings (with). **2** intrans. to move from person to person at a social engagement, briefly talking to each. [from Anglo-Saxon mengan, to mix]

▣ **1** mix, intermingle, intermix, combine, blend, merge, unite, alloy, coalesce, join, compound. **2** associate with, socialize with, circulate among, hobnob with, colloq. rub shoulders with.

mingy /'mɪndʒɪ/ adj. (**mingier**, **mingiest**) derog. colloq. ungenerous; mean; meagre. [perhaps a blend of MEAN[2] and STINGY]

mini colloq. — noun a small or short one of its kind, especially a miniskirt. — adj. small or short of its kind; miniature. [from MINI-]

mini- prefix forming words denoting something smaller or shorter than the standard: miniskirt/mini-submarine. [a shortening of MINIATURE or MINIMUM]

miniature — noun **1** a small copy or model of anything. **2** a very small painting, especially a portrait; the art of painting such pictures. — adj. of the nature of a miniature; small-scale. — **in miniature** on a small scale. [from Latin miniatura, from miniare, to paint red, to illustrate]

▣ adj. tiny, small, scaled-down, minute, diminutive, baby, pocket-size(d), pint-size(d), little, colloq. mini.

▣ adj. giant.

miniaturist noun an artist who paints miniatures.

miniaturize or **miniaturise** verb **1** to make very small. **2** to make something on a small scale.

minibar noun a small refrigerator in a hotel room, stocked with drinks and light snacks.

minibus noun a small bus, usually with between 12 and 15 seats.

minicab noun a taxi ordered by telephone from a private company, not stopped in the street.

minicom noun a device by which typed telephone messages can be sent, used by deaf people.

minicomputer noun a medium-sized computer, larger than a microcomputer but smaller than a mainframe computer.

MiniDisc noun trademark a small recordable compact disc.

minim noun **1** Mus. a note half the length of a semibreve. **2** a unit of liquid volume, equal to $^{-}$ of a fluid drachm (0.06ml). [from Latin minimus, smallest]

minimal adj. of the nature of a minimum; very small indeed; negligible. [from Latin minimus, smallest]

▣ least, smallest, minimum, slightest, littlest, negligible, minute, token.

minimalism noun the policy of using the minimum means to achieve the desired result, especially in art or music.

minimalist — noun a follower of minimalism. — adj. characteristic of minimalism.

minimally adv. in a minimal way; to a minimal extent.

minimize or **minimise** verb **1** to reduce to a minimum. **2** to treat as being of little importance or significance. [from Latin minimus, smallest]

▣ **1** reduce, decrease, diminish. **2** belittle, make light of, make

little of, disparage, deprecate, discount, play down, underestimate, underrate.
F3 1 maximize.

minimum — *noun* (PL. **minimums, minima**) the lowest possible number, value, quantity, or degree, or the lowest reached or allowed. — *adj.* of the nature of a minimum; lowest possible; lowest reached or allowed. [from Latin *minimus*, smallest]

E *noun* least, lowest point, slightest, bottom. *adj.* minimal, least, lowest, slightest, smallest, littlest, tiniest.
F3 *noun* maximum. *adj.* maximum.

minimum lending rate (ABBREV. **MLR**) *Econ.* formerly in the UK, the minimum rate of interest at which the Bank of England would lend to discount houses. It superseded the *bank rate* in 1973, and was itself replaced in 1981 by the *bank base rate*, on which all other interest rates are set.
minimum wage the lowest wage an employer is allowed to pay, by law or union agreement.
mining *noun* **1** the act or process of extracting minerals, etc from the ground. **2** the act or process of laying mines.
minion *noun derog.* **1** a subordinate. **2** an employee or follower, especially when fawning or subservient. [from French *mignon*, pretty, dainty]

E ATTENDANT, FOLLOWER. **1** underling, subordinate. **2** lackey, hireling, *colloq.* cohort, henchman, dependant, hanger-on, favourite, darling, sycophant, yes-man, *colloq.* bootlicker.

miniscule see MINUSCULE.
mini-series *noun* a short series of related television programmes, usually dramas, broadcast usually over consecutive days or weeks.
miniskirt *noun* a very short skirt, with a hemline well above the knee.
minister — *noun* **1** the political head of, or a senior politician with responsibilities in, a government department. **2** a member of the clergy in certain branches of the Christian church. **3** a high-ranking diplomat, especially the next in rank below an ambassador. **4** *formal* a person acting as agent for another, especially in business. — *verb intrans.* (**ministered, ministering**) **1** *formal* (**minister to someone**) to provide help or a service for them. **2** to perform the duties of a religious minister. [from Latin *minister*, servant]

E *noun* **1** cabinet minister, official, office-holder, politician, dignitary. **2** priest, pastor, vicar, clergyman, clergywoman, cleric, parson, preacher, churchman, churchwoman, divine. **3** diplomat, ambassador, delegate, envoy, consul, agent, aide, administrator, executive. *verb* **1** attend (on), serve, tend, take care of, wait on, cater to, accommodate, nurse.

ministerial *adj.* relating to or typical of a minister or a ministry.
Minister of State *Brit.* an assistant to a Minister of the Crown in a large government department, with no place in the Cabinet.
Minister of the Crown *Brit.* the political head of a government department, with a place in the Cabinet.
minister without portfolio in the UK, a government minister without responsibility for a department.
ministration *noun formal* **1** the act of ministering. **2** (*usually* **ministrations**) help or service given.
ministry *noun* (PL. **ministries**) **1** a government department, or its premises. **2** (**the ministry**) the profession, duties, or period of service of a religious minister; religious ministers collectively.

E 1 government, cabinet, department, office, bureau,

administration. **2** the church, holy orders, the priesthood.

mink *noun* (PL. **mink**) **1** a semi-aquatic nocturnal mammal related to the weasel, found near water in Europe and N America, with a slender body, thick brown fur except for a white patch on the chin, and webbed feet. **2** the highly valued fur of this animal. **3** a coat or other garment made of this. [perhaps from Swedish *mänk*]
Minn. *abbrev.* Minnesota.
minneola *noun* an orange-like citrus fruit, a cross between a grapefruit and a tangerine. [perhaps from *Mineola*, in Texas, USA]
minnow *noun* **1** any of several kinds of small freshwater fish of the carp family. **2** an insignificant person, group, etc. [probably from Anglo-Saxon *myne*]
Minoan /mɪˈnoʊən/ — *adj.* relating to the Bronze Age civilization of Crete and other Aegean islands, approximately 3000–1100BC. — *noun* an inhabitant of the Minoan world. [from *Minos*, mythological king of Crete]
minor — *adj.* **1** not as great in importance or size; fairly small or insignificant. **2** below the age of legal majority or adulthood. **3** *Mus.*, *said of a scale* having a semitone between the second and third, fifth and sixth, and seventh and eighth notes; based on such a scale. — *noun* **1** a person below the age of legal majority. **2** *Mus.* a minor key, chord, or scale. [from Latin *minor*, less]

E *adj.* **1** lesser, secondary, smaller, inferior, subordinate, subsidiary, junior, younger, insignificant, inconsiderable, negligible, petty, trivial, trifling, second-class, unclassified, slight, light.
F3 *adj.* **1** major, significant, important.

minority *noun* (PL. **minorities**) **1** a small number; the smaller of two groups. **2** a group of people who are different, especially in terms of race or religion, from most of the people in a country, region, etc. **3** the state of being the smaller of two groups: *in a minority.* **4** the state of being below the age of legal majority. [from Latin *minoritas*; related to MINOR]
minster *noun* a large church or cathedral, especially one originally attached to a monastery. [from Anglo-Saxon *mynster*, from Latin *monasterium*, monastery]
minstrel *noun* **1** a travelling singer in the Middle Ages. **2** any of a group of white-skinned entertainers made up to look black, performing song and dance superficially of Negro origin. [from Old French *menestrel*]
minstrelsy *noun* the art or occupation of a medieval minstrel.
mint[1] *noun* **1** any of various aromatic plants of the genus *Mentha*, having square stems, paired opposite leaves, and small white or purple flowers, widely grown as a garden herb. **2** the pungent-smelling leaves of this plant, used fresh or dried as a flavouring for food. **3** a sweet flavoured with an extract of these leaves, or a synthetic substitute. [from Anglo-Saxon *minte*, from Latin *mentha*]
mint[2] — *noun* **1** a place where coins are produced under government authority. **2** *colloq.* a large sum of money. — *verb* **1** to manufacture (coins). **2** to invent or coin (a new word, phrase, etc). — **in mint condition** brand new; never or hardly used. [from Anglo-Saxon *mynet*, money]

E *verb* COIN. **1** stamp, strike, cast, forge, punch, make, manufacture, produce, construct, devise, fashion. **2** invent, make up. **in mint condition** brand new, fresh, perfect, immaculate, unblemished, excellent, first-class.

minty *adj.* (**mintier, mintiest**) having the flavour of mint.
minuet *noun* a slow formal 17c–18c dance with short steps, or a piece of music for this. [from French *menuet*, from *menu*, small]
minus — *prep.* **1** made smaller by. **2** *colloq.* without. — *noun* (*also* **minus sign**) **1** a sign (–) indicating a negative

quantity, or indicating that a following quantity is to be subtracted. **2** *colloq.* a negative point; a disadvantage. — *adj.* **1** negative or less than zero. **2** *colloq.* of the nature of a disadvantage. **3** *said of a student's grade* indicating a level slightly below that indicated by the letter: *got a B minus for my essay.* [from Latin *minor*, less]

minuscule or **miniscule** / 'mɪnəskjuːl/ — *adj.* **1** *said of a letter* lower-case, not upper-case or capital. **2** extremely small. — *noun* a lower-case letter. [from Latin *littera minuscula*, small letter]

⬛ *adj.* tiny, infinitesimal, minute, microscopic, miniature, inconsiderable, negligible, small.

minute¹ / 'mɪnɪt/ — *noun* **1** a unit of time equal to — of an hour; (60 seconds). **2** *colloq.* a short while: *wait a minute.* **3** a particular point in time: *at that minute.* **4** the distance that can be travelled in a minute: *a house five minutes away.* **5** *Geom.* a unit of angular measurement equal to — of a degree; (60 seconds). **6** (*usually* **minutes**) the official written record of what is said at a formal meeting. **7** a written note or statement sent to a colleague; a memorandum. — *verb* **1** to make an official written record of. **2** to send a memorandum to. — **up to the minute** modern or recent. [related to MINUTE², often in the sense 'minute (very small) part']

⬛ *noun* **2, 3** moment, second, instant. **2** flash, *colloq.* jiffy, *colloq.* tick. **6** record(s), notes, proceedings, transactions, transcript, details, tapes. **7** memorandum, note.

minute² / maɪ'njuːt/ *adj.* **1** very small; tiny. **2** *formal* precise; detailed. **3** *formal* petty. [from Latin *minutus*, small]

⬛ **1** tiny, infinitesimal, minuscule, microscopic, miniature, inconsiderable, negligible, small. **2** detailed, precise, meticulous, painstaking, close, critical, exhaustive.
🅴 **1** gigantic, huge. **2** cursory, superficial.

minutely *adv.* in great detail.

minute steak / 'mɪnɪt/ a thin steak that can be cooked quickly.

minutiae / mɪ'njuːʃiɪ/ *pl. noun* small and often unimportant details. [from Latin *minutia*, smallness]

⬛ details, intricacies, complexities, small print.

minx *noun old use* a cheeky, sly, or flirtatious young woman.

Miocene / 'maɪəsiːn/ — *noun* the fourth epoch of the Tertiary period, lasting from about 25 million to 7 million years ago. During this time apes flourished in Africa, and herds of mammals grazed on the spreading grasslands. — *adj.* **1** relating to this epoch. **2** relating to rocks formed during this epoch. [from Greek *meion*, smaller + *kainos*, recent]

MIPS or **mips** *abbrev. Comput.* millions of instructions per second.

MIR *abbrev.* mortgage interest relief.

miracle *noun* **1** an act or event breaking the laws of nature, and therefore thought to be the result of direct intervention by a supernatural force, especially God. **2** *colloq.* a fortunate happening; an amazing event. **3** *colloq.* an amazing example or achievement of something: *a miracle of modern technology.* [from Latin *miraculum*, from *mirari*, to wonder at]

⬛ **2** wonder, marvel, prodigy, phenomenon.

miracle play see MYSTERY PLAY.
miraculous *adj.* **1** of the nature of a miracle. **2** *colloq.* wonderful; amazing; amazingly fortunate.

⬛ **1** supernatural, inexplicable, unaccountable, superhuman. **2** wonderful, marvellous, phenomenal, extraordinary, amazing, astounding, astonishing, unbelievable, incredible.
🅴 NATURAL, NORMAL.

mirage / 'mɪrɑːʒ/ *noun* **1** an optical illusion common in deserts and sometimes observed at sea, caused by the refraction (bending) of rays of light by a layer of hot air near the ground, or a layer of cold air near the surface of the sea. **2** anything illusory or imaginary. [from French *mirer*, to reflect]

⬛ **2** illusion, hallucination, fantasy, phantasm.

mire *literary* — *noun* **1** deep mud; a boggy area. **2** trouble; difficulty; anything unpleasant. — *verb* **1** (*trans., intrans.*) to sink or cause to sink in a mire. **2** to soil with mud. [from Norse *myrr*, bog]

⬛ *noun* **1** bog, swamp, slough, morass, quagmire.

mirin *noun* a sweet rice wine used in Japanese cookery. [from Japanese]

mirror — *noun* **1** any surface that reflects light. **2** a smooth highly polished surface, especially of glass coated with a thin layer of metal, that reflects images. **3** a faithful representation or reflection. — *verb* **1** to reflect as in a mirror. **2** to represent or depict faithfully. **3** to fit with a mirror or mirrors. [from Old French *mireor*, from Latin *mirari*, to wonder at]

⬛ *noun* **1** reflector. **2** glass, looking-glass. **3** reflection, likeness, image, double, copy. *verb* **1** reflect, echo. **2** represent, show, depict, mimic, imitate, copy.

mirror image 1 a reflected image as produced by a mirror, ie with right and left sides reversed. **2** an object that matches another as if it were its image as seen in a mirror, ie with features reversed.

mirth *noun* laughter; merriment. [from Anglo-Saxon *myrgth*, from *myrige*, merry]

⬛ merriment, hilarity, gaiety, fun, laughter, jollity, jocularity, amusement, revelry, glee, cheerfulness.
🅴 gloom, melancholy.

mirthful *adj.* **1** full of mirth. **2** causing mirth.
mirthless *adj.* without humour.

mis- *prefix* forming words meaning: **1** wrong or wrongly; bad or badly: *misconceive.* **2** a lack or absence of something: *mistrust.* [from Anglo-Saxon; related to MISS¹]

misadventure *noun* **1** *formal* an unfortunate happening; bad luck. **2** *Legal* an accident, with total absence of intent to commit crime: *death by misadventure.* [from Old French *mésaventure*, from *mésavenir*, to turn out badly]

misalliance *noun formal* a relationship or alliance, especially a marriage, in which the parties are not suited to each other. [from French *mésalliance*]

misanthrope / 'mɪsənθroʊp/ or **misanthropist** / mɪ'sanθrəpɪst/ *noun* a person who hates or distrusts all people. [from Greek *misanthropos*, from *miseein*, to hate + *anthropos*, man]

misanthropic / mɪsən'θrɒpɪk/ *adj.* hating or distrusting all people.
misanthropy / mɪ'sanθrəpɪ/ *noun* hatred or distrust of all people.
misapplication *noun* misapplying or being misapplied.
misapply *verb* (**misapplies, misapplied**) to use unwisely.
misapprehend *verb formal* to misunderstand.
misapprehension *noun* misunderstanding.

▤ misunderstanding, misconception, misinterpretation, misreading, error, mistake, fallacy, delusion.

misappropriate *verb formal Legal* to take (something, especially money) dishonestly for oneself; to put to a wrong use.

▤ steal, embezzle, *formal* peculate, *colloq.* pocket, swindle, misspend, misuse, misapply, *formal* misdirect, abuse, pervert.

misappropriation *noun* embezzlement, theft.

misbegotten *adj.* **1** *literary* illegally obtained. **2** *literary* foolishly planned or thought out. **3** *old use* illegitimate; bastard.

misbehave *verb intrans.* to behave badly.

▤ offend, transgress, trespass, get up to mischief, *colloq.* mess about, *colloq.* muck about, *colloq.* play up, *colloq.* act up.

misbehaviour *noun* bad behaviour.

▤ misconduct, misdemeanour, impropriety, disobedience, naughtiness, insubordination.

miscalculate *verb trans., intrans.* to calculate or estimate wrongly.

▤ misjudge, miscount, overestimate, underestimate, overrate, underrate, mistake, slip up (on), *colloq.* mess up, *colloq.* foul up, *slang* screw up.

miscalculation *noun* a mistake; a wrong estimate.

miscarriage *noun* **1** the expulsion of a fetus from the uterus (womb) before it is capable of independent survival, ie at any time up to about the 24th week of pregnancy. Also called SPONTANEOUS ABORTION. **2** a failure of a plan, etc to reach a desired objective. **3** (*in full* **miscarriage of justice**) a failure of a judicial system to serve the ends of justice in a particular case.

▤ **2** failure, breakdown, mishap, mismanagement, error, disappointment.
▨ **2** success.

miscarry *verb intrans.* (**miscarries, miscarried**) **1** *said of a woman* to have a miscarriage. **2** *formal* to fail.

▤ **2** fail, come to nothing, fall through, misfire, flounder, come to grief.
▨ **2** succeed.

miscast *verb* (PAST TENSE AND PAST PARTICIPLE **miscast**) to give an unsuitable part to (an actor) or put an unsuitable actor in (a part).

miscegenation /mɪsɪdʒəˈneɪʃən/ *noun formal* marriage or breeding between people of different races, especially of different skin colours. [from Latin *miscere*, to mix + *genus*, race]

miscellaneous *adj.* made up of various kinds; mixed. [from Latin *miscellaneus*, from *miscere*, to mix]

▤ mixed, varied, various, assorted, diverse, diversified, heterogeneous, sundry, motley, jumbled, indiscriminate.

miscellany /mɪˈsɛlənɪ, ˈmɪsələnɪ/ *noun* (PL. **miscellanies**) *formal* a mixture of various kinds, especially a collection of writings on different subjects, or by different authors. [from Latin *miscellanea*; as MISCELLANEOUS]

▤ mixture, variety, assortment, collection, anthology, medley, mixed bag, potpourri, hotchpotch, jumble, diversity.

mischance *noun* bad luck, or an instance of this. [from Old French *meschance*]

mischief *noun* **1** behaviour that annoys or irritates but causes no serious harm: *make mischief.* **2** the desire to behave in this way: *full of mischief.* **3** *old use* a person with a tendency to behave in this way. **4** damage or harm; an injury: *do oneself a mischief.* [from Old French *meschief*, disaster]

▤ **1, 2** impishness. **1** trouble, misbehaviour, naughtiness, pranks. **4** damage, harm, injury, disruption.

mischievous *adj.* **1** tending to make mischief; playfully troublesome. **2** *old use* causing damage or harm.

▤ **1** naughty, impish, rascally, roguish, playful, teasing. **2** malicious, evil, spiteful, vicious, wicked, pernicious, destructive, injurious.
▨ **1** well-behaved, good. **2** benign.

miscibility *noun* a miscible quality or condition.

miscible *adj. formal Chem.*, *said of a liquid or liquids* capable of dissolving in each other to form a single phase: *miscible with water.* [from Latin *miscere*, to mix]

misconceive *verb* **1** *trans., intrans.* (**misconceive something** or **misconceive of something**) to have the wrong idea or impression about it; to misunderstand it. **2** to plan or think out badly.

misconception *noun* a wrong or misguided attitude, opinion, or view.

▤ misapprehension, misunderstanding, misreading, error, fallacy, delusion, *colloq.* the wrong end of the stick.

misconduct *noun* **1** improper or unethical behaviour. **2** bad management.

▤ **1** misbehaviour, impropriety, misdemeanour, malpractice, misdealing, wrongdoing. **2** mismanagement, maladministration.

misconstruction *noun* an interpretation that is wrong.

misconstrue *verb* to interpret wrongly or mistakenly.

▤ misinterpret, misread, misunderstand, mistake, distort.

miscreant /ˈmɪskrɪənt/ *noun literary, old use* a malicious person; a rogue or scoundrel. [from Old French *mescreant*, unbelieving, heretical]

misdate — *verb* to date wrongly. — *noun* a wrong date.

misdeal — *noun* a wrong deal, as at cards. — *verb trans., intrans.* (PAST TENSE AND PAST PARTICIPLE **misdealt**) to deal or divide (especially playing cards) wrongly.

misdeed *noun literary* an example of bad or criminal behaviour; a wrongdoing. [from Anglo-Saxon *misdæd*]

misdemeanour *noun* **1** *formal* a wrongdoing; a misdeed. **2** *old use Legal* a crime less serious than a felony. [from obsolete *misdemean*, to misbehave]

misdirect *verb* **1** *formal* to give wrong directions to; to send to the wrong place. **2** *formal* to use (especially funds) for an unsuitable purpose. **3** *Legal, said of a judge* to provide incorrect legal information to (a jury).

misdirection *noun* **1** misdirecting or being misdirected. **2** the wrong directions or address.

mise-en-scène /miːzɒnˈsɛn/ *noun* **1** *Theatr.* the process of arranging, or the arrangement of, scenery and props. **2** *Cinema* the use of long scenes during which the position of the camera does not change. **3** *literary* the surroundings in which an event takes place. [French, = a putting-on-stage]

miser *noun* a person who lives in poor conditions in order to store up wealth; any ungenerous person. [from Latin *miser*, wretched]

▪ niggard, skinflint, *colloq.* penny-pincher, Scrooge, *North Amer. slang* tightwad.
▪ spendthrift.

miserable *adj.* **1** extremely or wretchedly unhappy. **2** marked by great unhappiness: *a miserable life.* **3** causing unhappiness or discomfort: *miserable weather.* **4** marked by poverty or squalor: *miserable living conditions.* **5** contemptible: *a miserable sinner.* **6** derisory; not worth having. **7** *dialect* ungenerous; mean. [from French *misérable*, from Latin *miser*, wretched]

▪ **1, 2** unhappy, sad, wretched. **1** dejected, despondent, downcast, heartbroken, distressed, crushed. **3** depressing, dreary, gloomy, dismal. **4** cheerless, impoverished, shabby, forlorn, joyless, squalid. **5** contemptible, despicable, ignominious, detestable, disgraceful, deplorable, shameful. **6** meagre, paltry, derisory, niggardly, worthless, pathetic, pitiful, measly.
▪ **1, 2** cheerful, happy. **2, 3, 4** pleasant.

miserably *adv.* in a miserable way.
misère /mɪˈzɛə(r)/ *noun Cards* an undertaking to take no tricks. [from French *misère*, misery]
misericord /mɪˈzɛrɪkɔːd/ *noun* a ledge on the underside of a seat in the choir stalls of a church, used, when the seat is folded up, as a support for the standing person. [from Latin *misericordia*, compassion]
miserliness *noun* being miserly.
miserly *adj.* of or like a miser.

▪ mean, niggardly, *colloq.* tight, tight-fisted, stingy, sparing, parsimonious, cheeseparing, beggarly, *colloq.* penny-pinching, *colloq.* mingy.
▪ generous, spendthrift.

misery *noun* (PL. **miseries**) **1** great unhappiness, or a cause of unhappiness. **2** poverty or squalor. **3** *colloq.* a habitually sad or bad-tempered person. [from Latin *miseria*]

▪ **1** unhappiness, sadness, suffering, distress, depression, despair, gloom, grief, wretchedness, affliction. **2** privation, hardship, deprivation, poverty, want, oppression, destitution. **3** spoilsport, pessimist, killjoy, *colloq.* wet blanket, *colloq.* party-pooper, prophet of doom, Jeremiah.
▪ **1** contentment. **2** comfort.

misfire — *verb intrans.* **1** *said of a gun* to fail to fire, or fail to fire properly. **2** *said of an engine* to fail to ignite the fuel at the right times. **3** to be unsuccessful; to produce the wrong effect. — *noun* an instance of misfiring.

▪ *verb* **3** miscarry, go wrong, abort, fail, fall through, *colloq.* flop, founder, fizzle out, *colloq.* come to grief.
▪ *verb* **3** succeed.

misfit *noun* **1** a person not suited to a particular situation or environment. **2** something that fits badly or not at all.

▪ **1** individualist, nonconformist, eccentric, maverick, dropout, loner, lone wolf.
▪ **1** conformist.

misfortune *noun* bad luck; an unfortunate incident.

▪ bad luck, mischance, mishap, ill-luck, trouble, hardship, setback, reverse, calamity, catastrophe,

disaster, blow, accident, tragedy, trial, tribulation.
▪ luck, success.

misgiving *noun* (*often* **misgivings**) a feeling of uneasiness, doubt, or suspicion.

▪ doubt, uncertainty, hesitation, qualm, reservation, apprehension, scruple, suspicion, second thoughts, niggle, anxiety, worry, fear.
▪ confidence.

misguided *adj.* acting from, or showing, mistaken ideas or bad judgement.

▪ misconceived, ill-considered, ill-advised, ill-judged, imprudent, rash, misplaced, deluded, foolish, erroneous.
▪ sensible, wise.

misguidedly *adv.* in a misguided way.
mishandle *verb* **1** to deal with carelessly or without skill. **2** to handle roughly; to mistreat.

▪ **1** mismanage, make a mess of, mess up, botch, bungle. **2** ill-treat, harm, mistreat, injure, misuse, abuse.

mishap *noun* an unfortunate (especially minor) accident; bad luck. [from MIS- + old *hap*, luck, happening]

▪ misfortune, misadventure, accident, setback, calamity, disaster, adversity.

mishear *verb* (PAST TENSE AND PAST PARTICIPLE **misheard**) to hear incorrectly.
mishit — *verb* (with stress on *-hit*) (**mishitting**; PAST TENSE AND PAST PARTICIPLE **mishit**) to fail to hit cleanly or accurately. — *noun* (with stress on *mis-*) an act of mishitting.
mishmash *noun colloq.* a disordered collection or mixture; a hotchpotch. [a reduplication of MASH]
misinform *verb* to give incorrect or misleading information to.

▪ mislead, misdirect, misguide, deceive, delude, lead astray, fool.

misinformation *noun* incorrect or misleading information.
misinterpret *verb* (**misinterpreted, misinterpreting**) to understand or explain incorrectly or misleadingly.

▪ misconstrue, misread, misunderstand, mistake, distort.

misinterpretation *noun* a wrong interpretation.
misjudge *verb* to judge wrongly; to have an unfairly low opinion of (someone).

▪ miscalculate, mistake, misinterpret, misconstrue, misunderstand, overestimate, underestimate, underrate, disparage.

misjudgement or **misjudgment** *noun* a wrong or unfair judgement.
miskey *verb* to key (data on a computer keyboard, etc) incorrectly.
mislay *verb* (PAST TENSE AND PAST PARTICIPLE **mislaid**) to lose (something), usually temporarily, especially by forgetting where it was put.

▪ lose, misplace, miss, lose sight of.

mislead *verb* (PAST TENSE AND PAST PARTICIPLE **misled**) to cause to take a wrong or undesirable course of action; to cause to have a false impression or belief.

⊟ misinform, misdirect, deceive, delude, lead astray, *colloq.* lead up the garden path, confuse, fool.

misleading *adj.* likely to mislead; deceptive.

⊟ deceptive, confusing, unreliable, ambiguous, biased, loaded, tendentious, evasive, tricky.
⊟ unequivocal, authoritative, informative.

mismanage *verb* to manage or handle badly or carelessly.

⊟ mishandle, botch, bungle, make a mess of, mess up, misjudge, *colloq.* foul up, mar, misspend, misapply, *formal* misdirect, waste.

mismanagement *noun* bad, wrong, or careless management or handling.
mismatch — *verb* (with stress on *-match*) to match unsuitably or incorrectly. — *noun* (with stress on *mis-*) an unsuitable or incorrect match.
misname *verb* **1** to give an unsuitable name to. **2** to call by the wrong name.
misnomer *noun* a wrong or unsuitable name; an act of using it. [from Old French *mesnommer*, to misname]
miso / 'mi:soʊ/ *noun* a soya bean paste that has been fermented in brine, used for flavouring. [from Japanese]
misogynist / mɪ'sɒdʒɪnɪst/ *noun* a person who hates women. [from Greek *miseein*, to hate + *gyne*, woman]
misogynous *adj.* hating women.
misogyny / mɪ'sɒdʒɪnɪ/ *noun* a hatred of women.
misplace *verb* **1** to lose (something), usually temporarily, especially by forgetting where it was put. **2** to give (trust, affection, etc) unwisely or inappropriately. **3** to put in the wrong place.
misprint — *noun* (with stress on *mis-*) a mistake in printing. — *verb* (with stress on *-print*) to print wrongly.

⊟ *noun* mistake, error, erratum, literal, typo.

misprision *noun Legal* a failure to inform the authorities of a serious crime; deliberate concealment of one's knowledge of a serious crime. [from Old French *mesprision*, error]
mispronounce *verb* to pronounce (words, etc) incorrectly.
mispronunciation *noun* a wrong or careless pronunciation.
misquotation *noun* an inaccurate quotation.
misquote *verb* to quote inaccurately, often with the intention of deceiving.
misread *verb* (PAST TENSE AND PAST PARTICIPLE **misread**) **1** to read incorrectly. **2** to misunderstand or misinterpret.
misrepresent *verb* to give a false or misleading account or impression of, often intentionally.

⊟ distort, falsify, slant, pervert, twist, garble, misquote, exaggerate, minimize, misconstrue, misinterpret.

misrepresentation *noun* **1** the act or process of misrepresenting. **2** an inaccurate or misleading representation.
misrule *formal* — *noun* **1** bad or unjust government. **2** civil disorder. — *verb* to govern in a disorderly or unjust way.
Miss. *abbrev.* Mississippi.
miss[1] — *verb* **1** *trans., intrans.* to fail to hit or catch (something). **2** to fail to arrive in time for. **3** to fail to take advantage of: *missed your chance.* **4** to regret the absence of. **5** to notice the absence of. **6** to fail to hear, see, or notice. **7** to

refrain from going to (a place or an event): *I'll have to miss the next class.* **8** to avoid or escape: *just missed being run over.* **9** *intrans., said of an engine* to fail to burn fuel at the right times. — *noun* a failure to hit, catch, etc something. — **give something a miss** *colloq.* to avoid or refrain from it. **miss something out** to fail to include it; to leave it out. **miss out on something** to fail to benefit from it or participate in it. [from Anglo-Saxon *missan*]

⊟ *verb* **3** lose, let slip, let go, omit, *colloq.* blow. **4** pine for, long for, yearn for, regret, grieve for, mourn, sorrow for, want, wish, need, lament. **6** overlook, pass over, leave out, let through, let pass, ignore, disregard. **7** forego, skip, bypass, circumvent. **8** avoid, escape, evade, dodge. *noun* failure, error, blunder, mistake, omission, oversight, fault. **miss out** omit, leave out, exclude, overlook, skip, drop, cut, ignore, disregard.

miss[2] *noun* **1** a girl or unmarried woman. **2** (**Miss**) a term used to address an unmarried woman. **3** (**Miss**) a term used to address a female school teacher, married or not. **4** (**Miss**) a title given to a beauty queen from a stated country, region, etc: *Miss France.* [an abbreviation of MISTRESS]
missal / 'mɪsl/ *noun RC Church* a book containing all the texts used in Mass in a year. [from Latin *missale*, from *missa*, mass]
missel-thrush same as MISTLE-THRUSH.
misshapen *adj.* badly shaped; deformed.

⊟ deformed, distorted, twisted, malformed, warped, contorted, crooked, crippled, grotesque, ugly, monstrous.
⊟ regular, shapely.

missile *noun* **1** a self-propelled flying bomb. **2** *formal* any weapon or object that is thrown or fired. [from Latin *missilis*, from *mittere*, to send]

⊟ **1** guided missile, rocket, flying bomb. **2** projectile, shot, arrow, shaft, dart, bomb, shell, grenade, torpedo, weapon.

missing *adj.* **1** absent; lost; not able to be found. **2** not able to be located, but not known to be dead or destroyed.

⊟ **1** absent, lost, lacking, gone, mislaid, unaccounted-for, wanting, disappeared, astray, strayed, misplaced.
⊟ **1** found, present.

missing link (**the missing link**) **1** any one thing needed to complete a series. **2** a hypothetical extinct creature at a supposed stage of evolutionary development between apes and humans.
mission *noun* **1** a purpose for which a person or group of people is sent. **2** a journey made for a scientific, military, or religious purpose; also, a group of people sent on such a journey. **3** a group of people sent to have (especially political) discussions. **4** one's supposed purpose or calling in life. **5** a group of missionaries, or the building occupied by them. [from Latin *missionis*, from *mittere*, to send]

⊟ **1** task, undertaking, assignment, operation, campaign, crusade, business. **2** commission, delegation, deputation, legation, embassy. **4** calling, duty, purpose, vocation, raison d'être, aim, charge, office, job, work, ministry.

missionary *noun* (PL. **missionaries**) a member of a religious organization seeking to carry out charitable works and religious teaching, often combined.

⊟ evangelist, campaigner, preacher, proselytizer, apostle, crusader, propagandist, champion, promoter, emissary, envoy, ambassador.

mission statement a statement by a business or other organization of its aims and principles.

missis same as MISSUS.

missive *noun literary Legal* a letter. [from Latin *missivus*, from *mittere*, to send]

misspell *verb* (PAST TENSE AND PAST PARTICIPLE **misspelt, misspelled**) to spell incorrectly.

misspend *verb* (PAST TENSE AND PAST PARTICIPLE **misspent**) to spend foolishly or wastefully.

∙∙∙∙∙∙∙∙∙∙∙∙∙∙∙∙∙∙∙

🔳 waste, squander, fritter away, dissipate, throw away, *colloq.* blow.

∙∙∙

missus *noun colloq.* **1** *humorous* a wife. **2** *old use* a term used to address an adult female stranger. [originally a spoken form of MISTRESS]

missy *noun old colloq. use usu. facetious, derog.* a term used to address a girl or young woman.

mist — *noun* **1** condensed water vapour in the air near the ground; thin fog or low cloud. **2** a mass of tiny droplets of liquid, eg forced under pressure from a container. **3** condensed water vapour on a surface. **4** *literary* a watery film: *a mist of tears.* **5** *literary* an obscuring influence: *the mists of time.* — *verb trans., intrans.* (*also* **mist up** or **over**) to cover or become covered with mist. [from Anglo-Saxon *mist*]

∙∙∙∙∙∙∙∙∙∙∙∙∙∙∙∙∙∙∙∙∙∙∙∙∙∙

🔳 *noun* **1** haze, fog, vapour, smog, cloud, drizzle. **2** spray, steam. **3** condensation, film, dew. **4** veil. *verb* cloud over, fog, dim, blur, steam up.

🔳 *verb* clear.

∙∙∙∙∙∙∙∙∙∙∙∙∙∙∙∙∙∙∙∙∙∙∙∙∙∙∙∙∙∙∙∙∙∙∙∙∙∙

mistake — *verb* (PAST TENSE **mistook**; PAST PARTICIPLE **mistaken**) **1** (**mistake one person** or **thing for another**) to identify them incorrectly as someone or something else; to wrongly assume or understand them to be what they are not: *they might mistake us for intruders/she mistook my silence for disapproval.* **2** to misinterpret. **3** to make the wrong choice of: *he mistook his road in the fog.* — *noun* **1** an error. **2** a regrettable action. **3** an act of understanding or interpreting something wrongly. [from Norse *mistaka*, to take wrongly]

∙∙∙∙∙∙∙∙∙∙∙∙∙∙∙∙∙∙∙∙∙∙∙∙∙∙

🔳 *verb* **1** confuse, mix up. **2** misjudge, miscalculate, misunderstand, misapprehend, misconstrue, misread. *noun* **1, 2** slip, *colloq.* slip-up, lapse, blunder, *colloq.* boob, gaffe, solecism. **1, 3** misunderstanding, misreading, mix-up. **1** error, inaccuracy, oversight, misjudgement, miscalculation, misprint, misspelling, mispronunciation, *colloq.* howler. **2** fault, faux pas, indiscretion, *colloq.* clanger.

∙∙∙

mistaken *adj.* **1** understood or identified wrongly. **2** guilty of, or displaying, a failure to understand or interpret correctly.

∙∙∙∙∙∙∙∙∙∙∙∙∙∙∙∙∙∙∙∙∙

🔳 WRONG, INCORRECT. **1** erroneous, inaccurate, inexact, untrue, inappropriate, ill-judged, inauthentic, false. **2** deceived, deluded, misinformed, misled, at fault.

🔳 CORRECT, RIGHT.

∙∙∙

mistakenly *adv.* in a mistaken way.

mister *noun* **1** (**Mister**) the full form of the abbreviation *Mr*. **2** *colloq.* a term used to address an adult male stranger. **3** a man not belonging to the nobility; an untitled man. [originally a spoken form of MASTER]

mistily *adv.* in or through a mist; in a misty way.

mistime *verb* **1** to do or say at a wrong or unsuitable time. **2** *Sport* to misjudge the timing of (a stroke) in relation to the speed of an approaching ball.

mistiness *noun* a misty condition or quality.

mistle-thrush *noun* a large European thrush fond of mistletoe berries. [from Anglo-Saxon *mistel*, mistletoe]

mistletoe /ˈmɪsltoʊ/ *noun* a Eurasian evergreen shrub that grows as a parasite on trees and produces clusters of white berries in winter; a similar American plant. [from Anglo-Saxon *misteltan*]

mistook see MISTAKE.

mistral /ˈmɪstrɑːl/ *noun* (**the mistral**) *Meteorol.* a cold gusty strong northerly wind that blows down the Rhône valley in S France. [from Provençal, from Latin *magistralis*, masterful]

mistreat *verb* to treat cruelly or without care.

∙∙∙∙∙∙∙∙∙∙∙∙∙∙∙∙∙∙∙∙∙∙∙∙

🔳 abuse, ill-treat, ill-use, maltreat, harm, hurt, batter, injure, knock about, molest.

∙∙∙

mistreatment *noun* bad or cruel treatment.

mistress *noun* **1** a woman in a commanding or controlling position; a female head or owner. **2** a female teacher. **3** the female lover of a man married to another woman. **4** *old use* a term used to address any woman, especially one in authority. [from Old French *maistresse*]

∙∙∙∙∙∙∙∙∙∙∙∙∙∙∙∙∙∙∙∙∙

🔳 **2** teacher, governess, tutor. **3** lover, live-in lover, kept woman, concubine, courtesan, girlfriend, paramour, woman, *colloq.* fancy woman, lady-love.

∙∙∙

mistrial *noun Legal* a trial not conducted properly according to the law, and declared invalid.

mistrust — *verb* to have no trust in; to be suspicious of. — *noun* lack of trust.

∙∙∙∙∙∙∙∙∙∙∙∙∙∙∙∙∙∙∙∙∙

🔳 *verb* distrust, doubt, suspect, be wary of, beware of, have reservations about. *noun* distrust, doubt, suspicion, wariness, misgiving, reservations, qualms, hesitancy, chariness, caution, uncertainty, scepticism, apprehension, fear.

🔳 *verb* trust. *noun* trust.

∙∙∙

mistrustful *adj.* without trust, suspicious.

∙∙∙∙∙∙∙∙∙∙∙∙∙∙∙∙∙∙∙∙∙

🔳 distrustful, doubtful, suspicious, wary, hesitant, chary, cautious, uncertain, sceptical, apprehensive.

∙∙∙

misty *adj.* (**mistier, mistiest**) **1** covered with, or obscured by, mist. **2** *literary* not clear; vague. **3** *said of the eyes* filled with tears.

∙∙∙∙∙∙∙∙∙∙∙∙∙∙∙∙∙∙∙∙∙∙∙∙∙∙

🔳 **1, 2** hazy, cloudy, unclear, indistinct, obscure, opaque, vague, blurred, fuzzy, veiled. **1** foggy, murky, smoky, dim.

🔳 **1, 2** clear.

∙∙∙

misunderstand *verb trans., intrans.* (PAST TENSE AND PAST PARTICIPLE **misunderstood**) to fail to understand properly.

∙∙∙∙∙∙∙∙∙∙∙∙∙∙∙∙∙∙∙∙∙

🔳 misapprehend, misconstrue, misinterpret, misjudge, mistake, get wrong, miss the point (of), mishear.

🔳 understand.

∙∙∙

misunderstanding *noun* **1** a failure to understand properly. **2** *euphemistic* a disagreement.

∙∙∙∙∙∙∙∙∙∙∙∙∙∙∙∙∙∙∙∙∙

🔳 **1** mistake, error, misapprehension, misconception, misjudgement, misinterpretation, misreading, mix-up. **2** disagreement, argument, dispute, conflict, clash, difference, breach, quarrel, discord, rift.

🔳 UNDERSTANDING. **2** agreement.

∙∙∙

misunderstood *adj., said of a person* not properly understood or appreciated as regards character, feelings, intentions, etc.

misuse /mɪsˈjuːs, mɪsˈjuːz/ — *noun* (pronounced -juːs) improper or inappropriate use: *the misuse of funds.* — *verb* (pronounced -juːz) **1** to put to improper or inappropriate use. **2** *formal* to treat badly.

• • • • • • • • • • • • • • • • • • • •

⊟ *noun* mistreatment, maltreatment, abuse, harm, ill-treatment, misapplication, misappropriation, waste, perversion, corruption, exploitation. *verb* ABUSE, ILL-USE. **1** misapply, misemploy, waste, squander, misappropriate, exploit, dissipate. **2** ill-treat, harm, mistreat, wrong, distort, injure, corrupt, pervert.

• •

MIT *abbrev.* the Massachusetts Institute of Technology, an institute of higher education renowned for its science facilities and research work, although it also offers courses in the arts and humanities.

mite[1] *noun* any of thousands of small, often microscopic, animals belonging to the same order (Acarina) as the ticks, with a simple rounded body and eight short legs. [from Anglo-Saxon]

mite[2] *noun* **1** any small person or animal, especially a child that is pitied. **2** a small amount of anything, especially money. — **a mite ...** *colloq.* rather ...; somewhat ...: *a mite jealous.* [from Old Dutch *mite*]

mitigate *verb* **1** *Legal* to partially excuse or make less serious: *mitigating circumstances.* **2** *formal* to make (pain, anger, etc) less severe. [from Latin *mitigare*, from *mitis*, mild + *agere*, to make]

• • • • • • • • • • • • • • • • • • • •

⊟ MODERATE, TEMPER. **1** extenuate, modify, qualify, justify, vindicate.

• •

mitosis /maɪˈtoʊsɪs/ *noun Biol.* a type of cell division that results in the production of two daughter cells with identical nuclei, each of which contains the same genes and the same number of chromosomes as the parent nucleus, and is said to be *diploid.* Mitosis occurs in all cells except sex cells. See also MEIOSIS. [from Greek *mitos*, fibre]

mitre[1] /ˈmaɪtə(r)/ *noun* the ceremonial headdress of a bishop or abbot, a tall pointed hat with front and back sections divided. [from French, from Greek *mitra*, fillet]

mitre[2] /ˈmaɪtə(r)/ — *noun* (*also* **mitre joint**) a corner joint between two lengths of wood, etc made by fitting together two 45 sloping surfaces cut into their ends. — *verb* to join with a mitre. [perhaps the same word as MITRE[1]]

mitt *noun* **1** a mitten. **2** *colloq.* a hand. **3** a padded leather glove worn in baseball. [a shortening of MITTEN]

mitten *noun* **1** a glove with one covering for the thumb and a large covering for all the other fingers together. **2** a glove covering the hand and wrist but not the whole length of the fingers. [from French *mitaine*]

mix — *verb* (*also in many senses* **mix up**) **1** (**mix one thing with another** or **things together**) to put them together or combine to form one mass. **2** to prepare or make by doing this: *mix a cake.* **3** *intrans.* to blend together to form one mass: *water and oil do not mix.* **4** *intrans.* to meet with people socially; to feel at ease in social situations. **5** to do at the same time; to combine: *mix business with pleasure.* **6** *technical* to adjust electronically (the sounds produced by individual musicians) to create an overall balance of sound. — *noun* **1** a collection of people or things mixed together. **2** a collection of (usually dried) ingredients from which something is prepared: *a cake mix.* — **be mixed up** *colloq.* to be upset or emotionally confused. **be mixed up in something** or **with something** or **someone** *colloq.* be involved in or with them, especially in something illicit or suspect. **mix it** *slang* to cause trouble, argument, a fight, etc. **mix something** or **someone up 1** to confuse them: *I always mix him up with his brother.* **2** *colloq.* to upset or put into a state of confusion. [from Latin *miscere*, to mix]

• • • • • • • • • • • • • • • • • • • •

⊟ *verb* **1, 3** combine, blend, merge, join, unite, fuse. **1** mingle, intermingle, intermix, amalgamate, incorporate, fold in. **2** compound, homogenize, synthesize. **3** coalesce. **4** associate, consort, fraternize, socialize, mingle, hobnob. *noun* MIXTURE. **1** blend, amalgam, assortment, combination,

conglomerate, compound, fusion, synthesis, medley, composite, *colloq.* mishmash. **mix up** CONFUSE, MUDDLE, CONFOUND. **1** mix, jumble, complicate, garble, snarl up. **2** bewilder, perplex, puzzle, disturb, upset.

⊞ *verb* **1** divide, separate.

• •

mixed *adj.* **1** made up of different things or kinds: *mixed bag.* **2** consisting of conflicting or opposing kinds: *mixed feelings.* **3** done, used, etc by people of both sexes.

• • • • • • • • • • • • • • • • • • • •

⊟ **1** assorted, varied, miscellaneous, diverse, diversified, motley, combined, blended, amalgamated, fused, composite, compound, mingled, hybrid, crossbred, mongrel. **2** ambivalent, equivocal, conflicting, contradictory, uncertain. **3** unisex, co-educational.

• •

mixed-ability *adj.* denoting the teaching of children of a wide range of ability in a single class or group.

mixed bag *colloq.* a collection of people or things of different kinds, standards, etc.

mixed blessing something which has both advantages and disadvantages.

mixed doubles a variety of tennis, table-tennis, or badminton played by two pairs, each consisting of a man and a woman.

mixed economy an economic system with some elements state-owned and others privately owned.

mixed farming farming of both crops and livestock.

mixed grill a dish of different kinds of grilled meat, and usually tomatoes and mushrooms.

mixed marriage a marriage between people of different races or religions.

mixed metaphor a combination of two or more metaphors which produces an inconsistent or incongruous mental image, and is often regarded as a stylistic flaw, as in *there are concrete steps in the pipeline.*

mixed-up *adj.* **1** mentally or emotionally confused. **2** socially badly adjusted.

• • • • • • • • • • • • • • • • • • • •

⊟ **1** confused, bewildered, perplexed, puzzled, disturbed, upset. **2** maladjusted, antisocial.

• •

mixer *noun* **1** a machine used for mixing. **2** a soft drink for mixing with alcoholic drinks. **3** *colloq.* a person considered in terms of his or her ability to mix socially: *a good mixer.*

mixture *noun* **1** a blend of ingredients prepared for a particular purpose: *cough mixture.* **2** a combination: *a mixture of sadness and relief.* **3** the act of mixing.

• • • • • • • • • • • • • • • • • • • •

⊟ **2, 3** combination, amalgamation, synthesis, union, fusion. **2** mix, blend, amalgam, compound, conglomeration, composite, assortment, variety, miscellany, medley, mélange, mixed bag, potpourri, jumble, hotchpotch, alloy, brew, concoction, cross, hybrid. **3** coalescence.

• •

mix-up *noun* a confusion or misunderstanding; mistaking one person or thing for another.

• • • • • • • • • • • • • • • • • • • •

⊟ confusion, misunderstanding, *colloq.* slip-up, lapse, blunder, *colloq.* boob, gaffe, solecism.

• •

mizzenmast *noun* on a ship with three or more masts, the third mast from the front of the ship. [from Italian *mezzano*, middle + MAST[1]]

Mk *abbrev.* mark (= a type of design, or model, especially of vehicles).

ml *abbrev.* **1** mile. **2** millilitre.

MLR *abbrev.* minimum lending rate.

MM *abbrev.* Military Medal.

mm *abbrev.* millimetre.

MMC *abbrev.* Monopolies and Mergers Commission.

Mme *abbrev.* (French) Madame.

MN *abbrev.* Minnesota.

Mn *symbol Chem.* manganese.

M'Naghten rules a set of legal principles which state that a defendant may not be convicted if insanity is proved. The rules were developed in England subsequent to the 19c murder trial of Daniel M'Naghten, a case in which insanity was proved.

mnemonic /nɪ'mɒnɪk/ — *noun* a device or form of words, often a short verse, used as an aid to memory. — *adj.* serving to help the memory. [from Greek *mneme*, memory]

MO *abbrev.* **1** Medical Officer, ie an army doctor. **2** Missouri. **3** modus operandi. **4** money order.

Mo[1] *abbrev.* Missouri.

Mo[2] *symbol Chem.* molybdenum.

mo *noun* (PL. **mos**) *colloq.* a short while; a moment. [a shortening of MOMENT]

moa /'moʊə/ *noun* an extinct flightless ostrich-like bird of New Zealand. [from Maori]

Moabite *noun* a member of an ancient Semitic people who in Old Testament times inhabited the area to the SE of the Dead Sea.

moan — *noun* **1** a low prolonged sound expressing sadness, grief, or pain. **2** any similar sound, eg made by the wind or an engine. **3** *colloq.* a complaint; a person who complains a lot. — *verb intrans.* **1** to utter or produce a moan. **2** *colloq.* to complain, especially without good reason. [from Anglo-Saxon *mænan*, to grieve over]

⸱⸱⸱⸱⸱⸱⸱⸱⸱⸱⸱

◼ *noun* **1** groan, sob, wail, howl, whimper, whine, lament, lamentation. **3** grumble, complaint, grievance, *colloq.* gripe, *colloq.* beef, *colloq.* whinge. *verb* **1** groan, lament, wail, sob, weep, howl, whimper, mourn, grieve. **2** complain, grumble, whine, *colloq.* whinge, *colloq.* gripe, carp, *colloq.* beef, *North Amer. slang* kvetch.

◲ *verb* **1** rejoice.

⸱⸱⸱⸱⸱⸱⸱⸱⸱⸱⸱⸱⸱⸱⸱⸱⸱⸱⸱⸱⸱⸱⸱⸱⸱

moaner *noun* a person who moans or constantly complains.

moat *noun* a deep trench, often filled with water, dug round a castle or other fortified position, to provide extra defence. [from Old French *mote*, mound]

mob — *noun* **1** a large disorderly crowd. **2** *colloq.* any group or gang. **3** *colloq.* (**the mob**) ordinary people; the masses. **4** (**the mob**) an organized gang of criminals, especially the Mafia. — *verb* (**mobbed**, **mobbing**) **1** to attack as a mob. **2** to crowd round curiously or admiringly. [a shortening of Latin *mobile vulgus*, fickle masses]

⸱⸱⸱⸱⸱⸱⸱⸱⸱⸱⸱⸱⸱⸱⸱⸱⸱⸱

◼ *noun* **1** crowd, mass, throng, multitude, horde, host, swarm, gathering, flock, herd. **2** pack, set, tribe, troop, company, crew, gang, group, collection. **3** the populace, the rabble, the masses, the hoi polloi, the plebs, the riff-raff, the crowd, the herd. *verb* **1** set upon, besiege, descend on, charge, jostle, overrun. **2** crowd, crowd round, surround, swarm round, throng, pack, pester.

⸱⸱⸱⸱⸱⸱⸱⸱⸱⸱⸱⸱⸱⸱⸱⸱⸱⸱⸱⸱⸱⸱

mobile — *adj.* **1** able to move or be moved easily; not fixed. **2** set up inside a vehicle travelling from place to place: *a mobile shop.* **3** *said of a face* frequently changing expression. **4** able, or willing, to move house or change jobs. **5** moving, or able to move, from one social class to another: *upwardly mobile.* **6** *colloq.* provided with transport and able to travel. — *noun* **1** a hanging decoration moved around by air currents. **2** short for MOBILE PHONE. [from Latin *mobilis*, from *movere*, to move]

⸱⸱⸱⸱⸱⸱⸱⸱⸱⸱⸱⸱⸱⸱⸱⸱⸱⸱

◼ *adj.* **1** moving, movable, portable, flexible, agile, active, energetic, nimble. **2** travelling, peripatetic, roaming, roving, itinerant, wandering, migrant. **3** changing, changeable, ever-changing, expressive, lively.

◲ *adj.* **1, 2** immobile.

⸱⸱⸱⸱⸱⸱⸱⸱⸱⸱⸱⸱⸱⸱⸱⸱⸱⸱⸱⸱⸱⸱⸱⸱

mobile phone a portable telephone operating by means of a cellular radio system.

mobility *noun* **1** the ability to move. **2** a tendency to move.

⸱⸱⸱⸱⸱⸱⸱⸱⸱⸱⸱⸱⸱⸱⸱⸱⸱⸱

◼ **1** movability, portability, flexibility, agility, nimbleness. **2** changeability, instability.

◲ FIXITY.

⸱⸱⸱⸱⸱⸱⸱⸱⸱⸱⸱⸱⸱⸱⸱⸱⸱⸱⸱⸱⸱⸱⸱⸱

mobility allowance money paid by the government to disabled people or the very ill to assist in meeting their travel costs.

mobilization or **mobilisation** *noun* the act or process of mobilizing or being mobilized.

mobilize or **mobilise** *verb* **1** to organize or prepare for use. **2** *trans., intrans.* to assemble and make or become ready for war. [from MOBILE]

⸱⸱⸱⸱⸱⸱⸱⸱⸱⸱⸱⸱⸱⸱⸱⸱⸱⸱

◼ MUSTER. **1** assemble, marshal, rally, conscript, activate, galvanize, animate, organize, prepare, ready, summon, call up, enlist.

⸱⸱⸱⸱⸱⸱⸱⸱⸱⸱⸱⸱⸱⸱⸱⸱⸱⸱⸱⸱⸱⸱⸱⸱

mobster *noun slang* a member of an organized group of criminals, especially the Mafia.

moccasin /'mɒkəsɪn/ *noun* **1** a deerskin shoe with a continuous sole and heel, as worn by Native Americans; any slipper or shoe resembling this. **2** (*also* **water moccasin**) a large poisonous snake of the swamps of the southern US. [from native American languages]

mocha /'mɒkə/ *noun* **1** dark brown coffee of fine quality. **2** a flavouring made from coffee and chocolate. [from *Mocha*, a port in the Yemen Arab Republic where the coffee was originally shipped from]

mock — *verb* **1** *trans., intrans.* to speak or behave disparagingly or contemptuously (towards). **2** to mimic. **3** *literary* to cause to seem impossible or useless; to seem to defy or frustrate: *violent winds mocked my attempt to pitch the tent.* — *adj.* **1** false; sham: *mock sincerity.* **2** serving as practice for something similar coming later: *a mock examination.* — *noun colloq.* a mock examination. [from Old French *mocquer*]

⸱⸱⸱⸱⸱⸱⸱⸱⸱⸱⸱⸱⸱⸱⸱⸱⸱⸱

◼ *verb* **1** jeer, scoff, sneer, taunt, scorn, tease, make fun (of), laugh (at), disparage, deride. **2** imitate, simulate, mimic, ape, caricature, satirize. *adj.* **1** imitation, counterfeit, artificial, sham, simulated, synthetic, false, fake, forged, fraudulent, bogus, phoney, *colloq.* pseudo, spurious, feigned, faked, pretended, dummy.

⸱⸱⸱⸱⸱⸱⸱⸱⸱⸱⸱⸱⸱⸱⸱⸱⸱⸱⸱⸱⸱⸱⸱⸱

mockers *pl. noun* — **put the mockers on someone** or **something** *colloq.* to end the chances of their success; to spoil them. [perhaps from MOCK]

mockery *noun* (PL. **mockeries**) **1** ridicule; contempt; the subject of ridicule or contempt: *make a mockery of.* **2** an imitation, especially contemptible or insulting. **3** any ridiculously inadequate person, action, or thing.

⸱⸱⸱⸱⸱⸱⸱⸱⸱⸱⸱⸱⸱⸱⸱⸱⸱⸱

◼ **1** ridicule, jeering, scoffing, scorn, derision, contempt, disdain, disrespect, sarcasm. **2** parody, satire, sham, travesty, caricature.

⸱⸱⸱⸱⸱⸱⸱⸱⸱⸱⸱⸱⸱⸱⸱⸱⸱⸱⸱⸱⸱⸱⸱⸱

mocking *adj.* that mocks.

⸱⸱⸱⸱⸱⸱⸱⸱⸱⸱⸱⸱⸱⸱⸱⸱⸱⸱

◼ scornful, derisive, contemptuous, sarcastic, satirical, taunting, scoffing, sardonic, snide, insulting, irreverent, impudent, disrespectful, disdainful, cynical.

⸱⸱⸱⸱⸱⸱⸱⸱⸱⸱⸱⸱⸱⸱⸱⸱⸱⸱⸱⸱⸱⸱⸱⸱

mockingbird *noun* a grey American bird that copies the calls of other birds.

mock orange *noun* the philadelphus.

mock turtle soup soup made in the style of turtle soup, but using a calf's head.

mock-up *noun* a full-size model or replica, built for experimental purposes.

. . . .
◫ model, replica, maquette, dummy, prototype.
. . . .

MOD or **MoD** *abbrev.* Ministry of Defence.

mod *colloq.* — *adj. old use* modern. — *noun* a follower of a British teenage culture originally of the 1960s, characterized by a liking for smart clothes and motor scooters. [a shortening of MODERN]

modal — *adj.* **1** relating to or concerning mode or a mode. **2** *said of music* using a particular mode. — *noun Grammar* (*also* **modal auxiliary** or **modal verb**) a verb used as the auxiliary of another verb to express grammatical mood such as condition, possibility, and obligation.

modality *noun* **1** *Mus.* the quality or characteristic of music as determined by its mode. **2** *Grammar* the modal property of a verb or construction.

mod cons *colloq.* modern household conveniences, eg central heating.

mode *noun* **1** a way of doing, living, operating, etc. **2** a fashion or style, eg in clothes or art. **3** *Mus.* any of several systems according to which notes are arranged. [from Latin *modus*, manner, measure]

. . . .
◫ **1**, **2** style. **1** manner, method, procedure, technique, modality. **2** fashion, vogue, trend.
. . . .

model — *noun* **1** a small-scale representation serving as a guide to construction. **2** a small-scale replica. **3** one of several types or designs of manufactured article. **4** a person who displays clothes to potential buyers by wearing them. **5** a (usually paid) human subject of the work of an artist, photographer, etc. **6** a thing from which something else is to be derived; a basis. **7** an excellent example; an example to be copied: *she's a model of loyalty.* — *adj.* exemplary; worthy of being copied: *a model boss.* — *verb* (**modelled**, **modelling**) **1** *trans., intrans.* to display (clothes) by wearing them. **2** *intrans.* to work as a model for an artist, photographer, etc. **3** *trans., intrans.* to make models of. **4** to shape into a particular form: *to model clay.* **5** (**model one thing on another**) to plan, build, or create it according to a model. [from French *modelle*, from Latin *modulus*]

. . . .
◫ *noun* **1** mock-up, maquette, lay figure, dummy, prototype, template, blueprint. **2** copy, replica, representation, facsimile, imitation. **3** design, style, type, version, mark. **4** mannequin. **5** sitter, subject, poser. **7** example, exemplar, pattern, standard, ideal. *adj.* exemplary, perfect, typical, ideal, excellent. *verb* **1** display, show off. **4** form, fashion, mould, sculpt, carve, cast, shape, work. **5** create, design, plan.
. . . .

modelling *noun* **1** the act or activity of making a model or models. **2** the activity or occupation of a person who models clothes.

modello *noun* (PL. **modelli**) a small but complete and detailed painting or drawing made to present the artist's ideas for a full-size work. It was often made to impress a patron and obtain a commission. Oil modelli by Peter Paul Rubens and Giovanni Battista Tiepolo still exist. [from Italian *modello*, model]

modem /ˈməʊdem/ *noun Comput.* an electronic device that transmits information from one computer to another along a telephone line, converting digital data into audio signals and back again. [from MODULATOR + DEMODULATOR]

moderate /ˈmɒdəreɪt, ˈmɒdərət/ — *adj.* (pronounced -rət) **1** not extreme; not strong or violent. **2** average; middle rate: *moderate intelligence.* — *noun* (pronounced -rət) a person holding moderate (especially political) views. —

verb (pronounced -reɪt) **1** to make or become less extreme or less violent. **2** *intrans.* to act as a moderator. [from Latin *moderatus*, from *modus*, measure]

. . . .
◫ *adj.* **1** reasonable, restrained, sensible, calm, controlled, cool, mild, well-regulated. **2** mediocre, medium, ordinary, fair, indifferent, average, middle-of-the-road. *verb* **1** control, regulate, decrease, lessen, soften, restrain, tone down, play down, diminish, ease, curb, calm, check, modulate, repress, subdue, soft-pedal, tame, subside, pacify, mitigate, allay, alleviate, abate.
◪ *adj.* **1** immoderate. **2** exceptional.
. . . .

moderately *adv.* in a moderate way; to a moderate degree.

. . . .
◫ somewhat, quite, rather, fairly, slightly, reasonably, passably, to some extent.
◪ extremely.
. . . .

moderation *noun* **1** the quality of being moderate. **2** an act of making or becoming less extreme. **3** lack of excess; self-control. — **in moderation** to a moderate degree; in moderate amounts.

. . . .
◫ **2**, **3** restraint, control. **2** decrease, reduction, abatement, mitigation. **3** self-control, caution, composure, sobriety, abstemiousness, temperance, reasonableness.
. . . .

moderato /mɒdəˈrɑːtəʊ/ *adv., adj. Mus.* to be played at a restrained and moderate tempo. [from Italian *moderato*]

moderator *noun* **1** a minister presiding over a court or assembly in any Presbyterian church. **2** a settler of disputes; a mediator. **3** a substance used for slowing down neutrons in nuclear reactors.

modern — *adj.* **1** belonging to the present or to recent times; not old or ancient. **2** *said of techniques, equipment, etc* involving, using, or being the very latest available: *modern transport.* **3** (*often* **Modern**) *said of a language* in the most recent stage of development; as used at present: *Modern English.* — *noun* a person living in modern times, especially a follower of the latest trends. [from Latin *modernus*]

. . . .
◫ *adj.* **1**, **2** current, contemporary, present, present-day, up-to-date, up-to-the-minute, advanced, latest, newfangled. **1** new, fresh, novel, recent, avant-garde, progressive, modernistic, innovative, inventive, go-ahead, fashionable, stylish, in vogue, in style, modish. **2** state-of-the-art.
◪ **1**, **2** old-fashioned, old, out-of-date, antiquated.
. . . .

modernism *noun* a generic term for various experimental methods in art in the early 20c, stimulated by a sharpened sense of the arbitrariness of existing artistic conventions, and doubts about human purpose in the world.

modernist *noun* a person who practises or advocates modernism.

modernistic *adj.* relating to or typical of modernism or modern ideas.

modernity /mɒˈdɜːnɪtɪ/ *noun* **1** being modern. **2** something modern.

modernization or **modernisation** *noun* **1** the act or process of modernizing. **2** being modernized.

modernize or **modernise** *verb* **1** to bring up to modern standards. **2** *intrans.* to switch to more modern methods or techniques.

. . . .
◫ UPDATE, REFORM. **1** renovate, refurbish, rejuvenate, regenerate, streamline, revamp, renew, improve, do up, redesign, remake, remodel, refresh, transform, modify. **2** progress.

◨ **2** regress.

. . . .

modest *adj.* **1** not having or showing pride; humble; not pretentious or showy. **2** not large; moderate: *a modest income.* **3** *old use, said especially of clothing* plain and restrained, not offending standards of decency: *a modest dress.* [from Latin *modestus*, from *modus*, a measure]

. . . .

◧ **1** unassuming, humble, self-effacing, self-deprecating, quiet, reserved, retiring, unpretentious, discreet, bashful, shy. **2** moderate, ordinary, unexceptional, fair, reasonable, limited, small.
◨ **1** immodest, conceited. **2** exceptional, excessive.

. . . .

modestly *adv.* in a modest way; to a modest extent.
modesty *noun* a modest or humble quality; lack of pride.

. . . .

◧ humility, humbleness, self-effacement, reticence, reserve, quietness, decency, propriety, demureness, shyness, bashfulness, coyness.
◨ immodesty, vanity, conceit.

. . . .

modicum *noun formal, facetious* a small amount: *a modicum of decency.* [from Latin *modicus*, moderate]
modification *noun* the process of changing or modifying.

. . . .

◧ change, alteration, redesign, revision, variation, adaptation, adjustment, transformation, reform, conversion, improvement, reorganization.

. . . .

modifier *noun Grammar* a word or phrase that modifies or identifies the meaning of another word, eg *in the green hat* in the phrase *the man in the green hat*, and *vaguely* in the phrase *he was vaguely embarrassed.*
modify *verb* (**modifies, modified**) **1** to change the form or quality of, usually slightly. **2** to make less extreme. **3** *Grammar* to act as a modifier of. [from Latin *modificare*]

. . . .

◧ **1** change, alter, redesign, revise, vary, adapt, adjust, transform, reform, convert, improve, tweak, reorganize. **2** moderate, reduce, temper, tone down, limit, soften, qualify.

. . . .

modish *adj.* conforming to the current mode or fashion; stylish, fashionable.
modiste /moʊˈdiːst/ *noun old formal use* a fashion designer. [from French; related to MODE]
modular *adj.* consisting of modules; constructed like a module.
modular construction *Electron.* a method of constructing a hardware or software system using standard compatible units (with differing functions) which are quickly interchangeable or which may be built up in combinations to provide a wide range of configurations.
modulate *verb* **1** *technical* to alter the tone or volume of (a sound or one's voice). **2** *formal* to change or alter. **3** *Radio* to cause modulation of a carrier wave (signal-carrying wave). [from Latin *modulari*]

. . . .

◧ **1, 2** vary. **1** harmonize, inflect, tune, soften, lower. **2** modify, adjust, balance, alter, regulate.

. . . .

modulation *noun Radio* in radio transmission, the process whereby the frequency, amplitude, or some other property of a carrier wave (signal-carrying wave) is made to increase or decrease instantaneously in response to variations in the characteristics of the signal being transmitted. See also AMPLITUDE MODULATION, FREQUENCY MODULATION.
modulator *noun* a person or device that modulates.
module *noun* **1** a separate unit that combines with others to form a larger unit, structure, or system. **2** a separate self-contained part of a space vehicle used for a particular

purpose: *lunar module.* [from Latin *modulus*, a small measure]
modulus *noun Maths.* the absolute value of a real number, regardless of whether it is positive or negative. [from Latin *modulus*, a diminutive of *modus*, measure]
modus operandi /ˈmoʊdəs ɒpeˈrandaɪ/ (PL. **modi operandi**) a way of working; the way something operates. [Latin, = way of working]
modus vivendi (PL. **modi vivendi**) **1** an arrangement by which people or groups in conflict can work or exist together; a compromise. **2** *affected* a way of living. [Latin, = way of living]
mog or **moggy** *noun* (PL. **moggies**) *slang* a cat.
mogul /ˈmoʊgəl/ — *noun* **1** an important, powerful, or influential person, especially in business or the film industry. **2** (**Mogul**) a Muslim ruler of India between the 16c and 19c. — *adj.* (**Mogul**) typical of or relating to the Moguls. [from Persian *Mughul*, Mongol]
MOH *abbrev.* Medical Officer of Health.
mohair *noun* the long soft hair of the angora goat; a yarn or fabric made of this, pure or mixed with wool. [from Arabic *mukhayyar*]
mohican *noun* a hairstyle with the head partially shaved, leaving a central front-to-back band of hair, usually coloured and formed into a spiky crest. [from *Mohicans*, Native American tribe on whose hairstyle this is based]
moiety /ˈmɔɪətɪ/ *noun* (PL. **moieties**) *literary Legal* a half; one of two parts or divisions. [from Old French *moité*]
moire /mwɑː(r)/ *noun* fabric, especially silk, with a pattern of glossy irregular waves. [from French]
moiré /ˈmwɑːreɪ/ — *adj., said of a fabric* having a pattern of glossy irregular waves. — *noun* this pattern.
moist *adj.* **1** damp; slightly wet. **2** *said of food, esp. cake* pleasantly soft and fresh, not dry. [from Old French *moiste*]

. . . .

◧ **1** damp, clammy, humid, wet, dewy, rainy, muggy, marshy, drizzly, watery, soggy.
◨ DRY. **1** arid.

. . . .

moisten *verb trans., intrans.* to make or become moist.

. . . .

◧ moisturize, dampen, damp, wet, water, lick, irrigate.
◨ dry.

. . . .

moisture *noun* liquid in vapour or spray form, or condensed as droplets; moistness.

. . . .

◧ water, liquid, wetness, wateriness, damp, dampness, dankness, humidity, vapour, dew, mugginess, condensation, steam, spray.
◨ dryness.

. . . .

moisturize or **moisturise** *verb* to make less dry, especially to add moisture to (the skin) by rubbing in a cream.
moisturizer or **moisturiser** *noun* something which moisturizes.
moke *noun slang* a donkey.
molar — *noun* any of the large back teeth in humans and other mammals, used for chewing and grinding. — *adj., said of a tooth* serving to grind. [from Latin *mola*, millstone]
molarity *noun Chem.* the concentration of a solution, expressed as the number of moles of a dissolved substance present in a litre of solution. See also MOLE[3].
molasses *sing. noun* the thickest kind of treacle, left over at the very end of the process of refining raw sugar. [from Portuguese *melaço*]
mole[1] *noun* a raised dark permanent spot on the skin, caused by a concentration of melanin. [from Anglo-Saxon *mal*]
mole[2] *noun* **1** any of about 20 species of small insectivorous burrowing mammals belonging to the family Tapidae,

which has velvety greyish-black fur, a naked muzzle, and very small eyes. **2** *colloq.* a spy working inside an organization and passing secret information to people outside it. [from Middle English *molle*]

mole³ *noun Chem.* (ABBREV. **mol**) the SI unit of amount of substance, equal to the amount of a substance (in grams) that contains as many atoms, molecules, etc, as there are atoms of carbon in 12 grams of the isotope carbon-12. One mole of a substance contains Avogadro's number (6.02×10^{23}) of atoms. [from German, from *Molekül*, molecule]

mole⁴ *noun* a pier, causeway, or breakwater made of stone; a harbour protected by any of these. [from Latin *moles*, mass]

molecular *adj.* of or relating to molecules.

molecular biology the study of the structure, properties, and functions of the large organic molecules that are found in the cells of living organisms, especially proteins and the nucleic acids DNA and RNA.

molecular weight *Chem.* relative molecular mass.

molecule *noun* the smallest particle of a chemical element or compound that can exist independently and participate in a chemical reaction. [from Latin *molecula*, from *moles*, mass]

molehill *noun* a little pile of earth thrown up by a burrowing mole.

moleskin *noun* **1** mole's fur. **2 a** a heavy twilled cotton fabric with a short nap. **b** (**moleskins**) trousers made of this.

molest *verb* **1** to attack or interfere with sexually. **2** *formal* to attack, causing physical harm. **3** *old use* to disturb or upset. [from Latin *molestare*]

⊟ **1, 2** assault. **2** attack, accost, assail, hurt, ill-treat, maltreat, mistreat, abuse, harm, injure. **3** annoy, disturb, bother, harass, irritate, persecute, pester, plague, tease, torment, hound, upset, worry, trouble, badger.

molestation *noun* **1** the act of molesting. **2** being molested.

moll *noun old slang use* **1** a gangster's girlfriend. **2** a prostitute. [from *Moll*, a woman's name]

mollification *noun* **1** the act of mollifying. **2** being mollified.

mollify *verb* (**mollifies, mollified**) **1** to make calmer or less angry. **2** to soothe or ease. [from Latin *mollis*, soft + *facere*, to make]

⊟ SOOTHE. **1** calm (down), placate, pacify, appease, assuage.

mollusc *noun Zool.* any invertebrate animal belonging to the phylum Mollusca and typically having a soft unsegmented body with a large flattened muscular foot on the underside, and a fold of skin (the mantle) covering the upper surface. Most molluscs are protected by a hard chalky shell secreted by the mantle. [from Latin *molluscus*]

mollycoddle *verb colloq.* to treat with fussy care and protection. [from *Molly*, a woman's name + CODDLE]

Molotov cocktail a small crude bomb for throwing, consisting of a bottle filled with petrol, usually with a burning cloth as a fuse. [named after the Russian politician V M Molotov (1890–1986)]

molten *adj.* in a melted state. [an old past participle of MELT]

molto *adv. Mus.* very. [from Italian *molto*]

molybdenum /məˈlɪbdənəm/ *noun Chem.* (SYMBOL **Mo**, ATOMIC NUMBER **42**) a hard silvery metal that is used as a hardening agent in various alloys, including alloy steels, and in resistors and X-ray tubes. Molybdenum disulphide is used as a lubricant. [from Greek *molybdaina*, lead-like substance]

mom or **mommy** *noun* (PL. **mommies**) *North Amer. colloq.* mother.

moment *noun* **1** a short while. **2** a particular point in time: *at that moment.* **3** *formal* importance; significance: *a lit-*

erary work of great moment. **4** *Physics* (*in full* **moment of force**) a measure of the turning effect or torque produced by a force which causes an object to rotate about an axis. It is equal to the force multiplied by the perpendicular distance of the axis from the line of action of the force. **— at the moment** at this particular time; now. **have one's** or **its** etc **moments** *colloq.* to experience or provide occasional but irregular times of happiness, success, etc. **of the moment** currently very popular, important, fashionable, etc. [from Latin *momentum*, movement]

⊟ **1, 2** second, instant, minute, split second. **1** trice, *colloq.* jiffy, *colloq.* tick. **3** significance, importance, import, weight, gravity, seriousness.

momentarily *adv.* **1** for a moment. **2** every moment.

momentary *adj.* lasting for only a moment.

⊟ brief, short, short-lived, temporary, transient, transitory, fleeting, ephemeral, hasty, quick, passing.
⊡ lasting, permanent.

moment of truth a very important or significant point in time, especially when a person or thing is put to the test.

momentous *adj.* of great importance or significance.

⊟ significant, important, critical, crucial, decisive, weighty, grave, serious, vital, fateful, historic, *colloq.* earth-shaking, epoch-making, eventful, major.
⊡ insignificant, unimportant, trivial.

momentum *noun* **1** *Physics* the product of the mass and the velocity of a moving object. See also ANGULAR MOMENTUM, LINEAR MOMENTUM. **2** continuous speed of progress; impetus: *the campaign gained momentum.* [from Latin *momentum*, movement]

⊟ **2** impetus, way, force, energy, impulse, drive, power, thrust, speed, velocity, strength, push.

MOMI *abbrev.* Museum of the Moving Image.

mommy see MOM.

Mon or **Mon.** *abbrev.* Monday.

mon- see MONO-.

monad /ˈmɒnad/ *noun* **1** *Philos.* any self-contained non-physical unit of being, eg a soul, God. **2** *Biol.* a single-celled organism. [from Greek *monas*, unit]

monandrous *adj.* **1** *Sociol.* having or allowing only one husband or male sexual partner at a time. **2** *Bot.* having only one stamen in each flower. See also POLYANDROUS. [from Greek *monos*, single + *andros*, man]

monandry *noun* being monandrous.

monarch /ˈmɒnək/ *noun* a king, queen, or other non-elected sovereign with a hereditary right to rule. [from Greek *monos*, single + *archein*, to rule]

⊟ sovereign, crowned head, ruler, king, queen, emperor, empress, prince, princess, tsar, potentate.

monarchic /məˈnɑːkɪk/ or **monarchical** /məˈnɑːkɪkəl/ *adj.* relating to or of the nature of a monarchy.

monarchism /ˈmɒnəkɪzm/ *noun* **1** the principles of monarchic government. **2** support for monarchy.

monarchist /ˈmɒnəkɪst/ *noun* a person in favour of rule by a monarch.

monarchy /ˈmɒnəkɪ/ *noun* (PL. **monarchies**) **1** a form of government in which the head of state is a monarch. **2** a country having this form of government.

⊟ **1** sovereignty, autocracy, monocracy, absolutism, despotism, tyranny. **2** kingdom, empire, principality, realm, domain, dominion.

....

monastery *noun* (PL. **monasteries**) the home of a community of monks, or sometimes nuns. [from Greek *monasterion*, from *monazein*, to live alone]

....

▣ friary, priory, abbey, cloister, charterhouse.

....

monastic *adj.* **1** of or relating to monasteries, monks, or nuns. **2** marked by simplicity and self-discipline, like life in a monastery. [from Greek *monastes*, monk]

....

▣ **2** reclusive, withdrawn, secluded, cloistered, austere, ascetic, celibate, contemplative.

▣ SECULAR. **2** worldly.

....

monastically *adv.* in a monastic manner.

monasticism *noun* the monastic system or way of life.

Monday *noun* the second day of the week. [from Anglo-Saxon *monandæg*, moon day]

monetarism *noun* the theory or practice of basing an economy on control of the supply of money in circulation. [from Latin *moneta*, money]

monetarist — *noun* a person who advocates policies based on monetarism. — *adj.* relating to or typical of monetarism.

monetary *adj.* of, or consisting of, money. [from Latin *moneta*, money]

....

▣ financial, fiscal, pecuniary, budgetary, economic, capital, cash.

....

money *noun* **1** coins or banknotes used as a means of buying things. **2** wealth in general. **3** *colloq.* a rich person; rich people: *marry money.* **4** (**moneys** or **monies**) *Commerce, Legal* sums of money. — **be in the money** *colloq.* to be wealthy. **for my, our,** etc, **money** *colloq.* in my, our, etc opinion. **get one's money's worth** to get full value for the money or other resources devoted to something. [from Latin *moneta*]

....

▣ **1, 2** cash. **1** currency, legal tender, banknotes, coin, *slang* dough, *slang* dosh. **2** riches, wealth, funds, capital.

....

moneybags *noun colloq.* a very rich person.

money-changer *noun* a person whose business is exchanging currencies.

moneyed *adj.* having much money; wealthy.

....

▣ rich, wealthy, affluent, well off, well-to-do, comfortable, prosperous.

....

money-grubber *noun derog. colloq.* a person who greedily acquires as much money as possible.

money-grubbing — *noun* greed for money. — *adj.* greedy for money.

moneylender *noun* a person whose business is lending money at (often relatively high) interest.

moneymaker *noun colloq.* **1** *often derog.* a person whose main interest in life is acquiring money. **2** a project, company, etc that makes a large profit.

money-making — *noun* the earning of profit. — *adj.* profitable.

money markets the finance companies, banks, etc of a country that borrow and lend money for short periods.

money order a written order for the transfer of money from one person to another, through a post office or bank.

money-spinner *noun colloq.* an idea or project that brings in large sums of money.

money supply the amount of money in circulation in an economy at a given time. Control of the money supply is the method favoured by monetarists for controlling inflation.

-monger *combining form* **1** a trader or dealer: *fishmonger.* **2** a person who spreads or promotes something undesirable or evil: *scandalmonger.* [from Latin *mango*, dealer]

Mongol *noun* a member of any of the tribes of central Asia and S Siberia who effected the collapse of the Abbasid Empire before converting to Islam. They now live in the Chinese autonomous region of Inner Mongolia, and the People's Republic of Mongolia.

mongol *noun old use, now offensive* a person affected by Down's Syndrome. [from the supposed physical likeness of Down's Syndrome sufferers to members of the Mongol people of Asia]

mongolism *noun old use, now offensive* Down's Syndrome.

mongoloid *adj. offensive* bearing symptoms of Down's Syndrome.

mongoose *noun* (PL. **mongooses**) a small mammal related to the civet, found in SE Asia, Africa, and Madagascar, with a long slender body, pointed muzzle, and a bushy tail. [from Marathi (a language of India) *mangus*]

mongrel — *noun* **1** an animal, especially a dog, of mixed breeding. **2** *derog.* a person or thing of mixed origin or nature. — *adj.* of mixed origin or nature. [perhaps from Anglo-Saxon *mengan*, to mix]

....

▣ *noun* **1** cross, cross-breed, hybrid. **2** half-breed. *adj.* cross-bred, hybrid, half-breed, bastard, mixed, ill-defined.

▣ *adj.* pure-bred, pedigree.

....

monied, monies see MONEY.

monism /ˈmɒnɪzm/ *noun Philos.* the theory that reality exists in one form only, especially that there is no difference in substance between body and soul. [from Greek *monos*, single]

monist /ˈmɒnɪst/ *noun* a follower of monism.

monistic *adj.* relating to or typical of monism.

monition *noun formal* a warning or telling-off. [from Latin *monere*, to warn or remind]

monitor — *noun* **1** any instrument or person that checks, records, or controls something on a regular basis. **2** a high-quality screen used in closed-circuit television systems. **3** the visual display unit of a computer, used to present information to the user. **4** a pupil who helps with specific tasks, or a senior pupil who helps to enforce discipline over other pupils. **5** (*in full* **monitor lizard**) any of various large carnivorous lizards of Africa, Asia, and Australia, so called because they are thought to give warnings of the presence of crocodiles. — *verb* to check, record, or control something on a regular basis; to observe. [from Latin *monere*, to warn or advise]

....

▣ *noun* **1** recorder, scanner, supervisor, watchdog, overseer, invigilator. **2, 3** screen. **3** display, VDU. **4** prefect. *verb* check, watch, keep track of, keep under surveillance, keep an eye on, supervise, observe, note, survey, detect, follow, track, trace, scan, record, plot.

....

monitory *adj. formal* serving as a warning or telling-off. [from Latin *monere*, to warn]

monk *noun* a member of a religious community of men living disciplined, austere lives devoted to worship. [from Greek *monachos*, from *monos*, alone]

....

▣ brother, friar, abbot, prior, monastic.

....

monkey — *noun* (PL. **monkeys**) **1** any member of the primates other than humans, apes, chimpanzees, gibbons, orang utans, and lemurs. **2** *colloq.* a mischievous child. **3** *slang* £500 or $500. — *verb intrans. colloq.* (**monkey about** or **around**) to play, fool, interfere, etc. — **make a monkey**

out of someone *colloq.* to make them seem ridiculous; to make a fool of them. **not give a monkey's** *slang* not to care at all. [perhaps from Old German dialect *moneke*]

▤ *noun* **1** primate, simian, ape. **2** scamp, imp, urchin, brat, rogue, *colloq.* scallywag, rascal. *verb* play, fool, tinker, tamper, fiddle, interfere, meddle.

monkey business *colloq.* mischief; illegal activities.
monkey nut a peanut.
monkey puzzle a S American conifer with close-set prickly leaves.
monkey wrench a spanner-like tool with movable jaws; an adjustable spanner.
monkfish *noun* a large cartilaginous fish, up to 1.8m in length, with a body shape intermediate between that of sharks and rays, a flattened head, lateral gill openings, broad pectoral fins, and a slender tail. It is a very popular food fish. Also called ANGEL SHARK.
monkish *adj.* **1** relating to or like a monk. **2** monastic.
monkshood see ACONITE.
mono *colloq.* — *adj.* short for **monophonic.** — *noun* monophonic sound reproduction.
mono- or **mon-** *combining form* forming words meaning 'one, single': *monocle.* [from Greek *monos*, single]
monochromatic *adj.* **1** *said of light* having only one wavelength. **2** monochrome.
monochrome *adj.* **1** *said of visual reproduction* done in one colour, or in black and white. **2** *said especially of painting* using shades of one colour only. [from MONO- + *chroma*, colour]
monocle *noun* a lens for correcting sight in one eye only, held in place between the bones of the cheek and brow. [from MONO- + Latin *oculus*, eye]
monocotyledon /mɒnoʊkɒtɪ'liːdən/ *noun Bot.* a flowering plant with an embryo that has one cotyledon (seed leaf), parallel leaf veins, vascular bundles scattered throughout the stem, and flower parts in multiples of three, eg lily, daffodil, cereals, and grasses, but only a few trees, eg palms. See also DICOTYLEDON.
monocular *adj.* having one eye only; for the use of one eye. [from MONO- + Latin *oculus*, eye]
monoculture *noun Agric.* the practice of growing the same crop each year on a given area of land, rather than growing different crops in rotation. It is a common practice among cereal growers in many parts of the world, but heavy use of chemical fertilizers may be necessary to maintain high yields.
monodic *adj.* relating to or typical of monody.
monody *noun* (PL. **monodies**) **1** a mournful song or speech performed by a single actor, especially in Greek tragedy. **2** a song in which the melody is sung by one voice only, with other voices accompanying. [from MONO- + Greek *oide*, song]
monoecious /mɒnoʊ'iːʃəs/ *adj. Biol.* **1** having male and female reproductive parts in separate flowers on the same plant. **2** *said of an animal* having both male and female sexual organs; hermaphrodite. See also DIOECIOUS. [from MONO- + Greek *oikos*, house]
monogamous *adj.* having only one spouse.
monogamy *noun* the state or practice of having only one husband or wife at any one time. See also POLYGAMY. [from MONO- + Greek *gamos*, marriage]
monogram — *noun* a design made up of interwoven letters, usually a person's initials. — *verb* (**monogrammed, monogramming**) to mark with a monogram. [from MONO- + Greek *gramma*, letter]
monograph *noun formal* a book or essay dealing with one particular subject or aspect of it. [from MONO- + Greek *graphein*, to write]
monolingual *adj.* able to speak one language only; expressed in, or dealing with, a single language: *a monolingual dictionary.* [from MONO- + Latin *lingua*, language]

monolith *noun* **1** a single tall block of stone, often shaped into a column or pillar. **2** anything resembling this in uniformity, immovability, or massiveness. [from MONO- + Greek *lithos*, stone]
monolithic *adj.* **1** relating to or like a monolith. **2** *said of an organization, etc* large and unchanging.

▤ **2** massive, monumental, giant, immovable, unmoving, unchanging, fossilized, hidebound.

monologue *noun* **1** a long speech by one actor in a film or play; a drama for one actor. **2** any long uninterrupted piece of speech preventing conversation. [from MONO- + Greek *logos*, speech]
monomania *noun* domination of the mind by a single subject or concern; an obsession. [from MONO- + Greek *mania*, madness]
monomaniac — *noun* a person affected by monomania. — *adj.* affected by monomania.
monomer /'mɒnəmə(r)/ *noun Chem.* a simple molecule that can be joined to many others to form a much larger molecule known as a *polymer*, eg amino acids are the monomers of which proteins are formed. [from MONO- + Greek *meros*, part]
mononucleosis *noun* glandular fever.
monophonic *adj.* recording or reproducing sound on one channel only, not splitting it into two, as with stereophonic systems. [from MONO- + Greek *phone*, sound]
monoplane *noun* an aeroplane with one set of wings.
monopolist *noun* a person who monopolizes, who has a monopoly, or who favours monopoly.
monopolistic *adj.* related to or connected with a monopoly or system of monopolies.
monopolization or **monopolisation** *noun* monopolizing; exercise of a monopoly.
monopolize or **monopolise** *verb* **1** to have a monopoly or exclusive control of trade in (a commodity or service). **2** to dominate (eg a conversation), excluding all others.

▤ DOMINATE. **1** control, *colloq.* corner. **2** take over, appropriate, *colloq.* hog, engross, occupy, preoccupy, take up, tie up.
▤ SHARE.

monopoly *noun* (PL. **monopolies**) (*often* **monopoly on** or **of something**) **1** the right to be, or the fact of being, the only supplier of a particular commodity or service. **2** a commodity or service controlled in this way. **3** exclusive possession or control of anything: *you don't have a monopoly on the truth!* [from MONO- + Greek *poleein*, to sell]
monopsony /mə'nɒpsənɪ/ *noun* a market structure where there is only one buyer of a product or service (a buyer's monopoly) or where there is only one major user of a factor of production. [from MONO- + Greek *opsonein*, to buy]
monorail *noun* a railway system in which the trains run on, or are suspended from, a single rail.
monosaccharide /mɒnoʊ'sakəraɪd/ *noun Biochem.* a simple sugar that cannot be broken down into smaller units, eg glucose, fructose.
monosodium glutamate a white crystalline chemical substance used to enhance the flavour of many processed savoury foods without imparting its own taste. It may cause allergic reactions such as headaches, dizziness, and nausea, in some people.
monosyllabic *adj.* **1** having one syllable. **2** using short words, especially 'yes' and 'no': *a monosyllabic reply.*
monosyllable *noun* a word consisting of only one syllable.
monotheism *noun* the belief that there is only one God. [from MONO- + Greek *theos*, God]
monotheist *noun* a person who believes in only one God.
monotheistic *adj.* relating to monotheism.
monotone — *noun* **1** a single unvarying tone in speech or sound. **2** a sequence of sounds of the same tone. **3** same-

ness, especially in colour. — *adj.* lacking in variety; unchanging. [from MONO- + Greek *tonos*, tone]

monotonous *adj.* lacking in variety; tediously unchanging.

· · · · · · · · · · · · · · · · · · · ·

■ boring, dull, tedious, uninteresting, tiresome, wearisome, unchanging, uneventful, unvaried, uniform, toneless, flat, colourless, repetitive, routine, plodding, humdrum, soul-destroying.

⊟ lively, exciting, varied, colourful.

· ·

monotonously *adv.* in a monotonous way.

monotony *noun* 1 dullness. 2 sameness.

· · · · · · · · · · · · · · · · · · · ·

■ 1 tedium, dullness, boredom, tiresomeness, uneventfulness, flatness, wearisomeness. 2 sameness, uniformity, routine, repetitiveness.

⊟ LIVELINESS, COLOUR.

· ·

monotreme *noun Zool.* an egg-laying mammal belonging to the order Monotremata (the most primitive group of mammals) that lays soft-shelled eggs, suckles its young, and has no teeth as an adult, eg duck-billed platypus. [from MONO- + Greek *trema*, hole]

monotype *noun Art* a one-off print made by painting oil paint or ink on a sheet of glass or a metal plate, and pressing a sheet of paper against the wet surface to create a reverse image of the original.

monoxide *noun* a chemical compound containing one oxygen atom in each molecule. [from MONO- + OXIDE]

Monsieur /mə'sjɜː(r)/ *noun* (ABBREV. **M**) a title equivalent to Mr, used especially of a French or French-speaking man. [from French, originally *mon*, my + *sieur*, lord]

Monsignor /mɒn'siːnjɔ(r)/ *noun* (PL. **Monsignors, Monsignori**) a title given to various high-ranking male members of the Roman Catholic church. [from Italian, from French *Monseigneur*, a title given to high-ranking clergy and nobility]

monsoon *noun* 1 in the area around the Indian Ocean and S Asia, and also around the coasts of W Africa and N Australia, a wind that blows from the north-east in winter and from the south-west in summer. 2 any strong relatively constant wind that blows in opposite directions at different times of year. 3 in India, the heavy rains accompanying the summer monsoon. 4 *colloq.* an extremely heavy fall of rain. [from Arabic *mawsim*, season]

monster — *noun* 1 any large and frightening imaginary creature. 2 a cruel or evil person. 3 any unusually large thing. 4 *old use* a deformed person, animal or plant. — *adj.* huge; gigantic: *monster portions*. [from Latin *monstrum*, evil omen]

· · · · · · · · · · · · · · · · · · · ·

■ *noun* 1 giant, ogre, ogress. 2 beast, fiend, brute, barbarian, savage, villain. 3 mammoth, jumbo. 4 freak, monstrosity, mutant. *adj.* huge, gigantic, giant, colossal, enormous, immense, massive, monstrous, jumbo, mammoth, vast, tremendous.

⊟ *adj.* tiny, minute.

· ·

monstera /mɒn'stɪərə/ *noun* a tall climbing plant (*Monstera deliciosa*), native to tropical America, which has stems with tough aerial roots, and large heart-shaped leaves that develop deep notches and sometimes holes as they mature. [a modern Latin form of *monster*]

monstrance *noun RC Church* a large gold or silver cup in which the host is displayed to the congregation during Mass. [from Latin *monstrare*, to show]

monstrosity *noun* (PL. **monstrosities**) 1 any ugly or outrageous thing. 2 the quality of being monstrous.

· · · · · · · · · · · · · · · · · ·

■ 1 eyesore, blot on the landscape, abortion, monster, freak, atrocity, obscenity, outrage.

· ·

monstrous *adj.* 1 like a monster; huge. 2 outrageous; absurd. 3 extremely cruel; evil. 4 *old use* deformed.

· · · · · · · · · · · · · · · · · · · ·

■ 1 huge, enormous, colossal, gigantic, vast, immense, massive, mammoth. 2 wicked, evil, vicious, cruel, criminal, heinous, outrageous, scandalous, disgraceful, atrocious, abhorrent, dreadful, frightful, horrible, horrifying, terrible. 3 unnatural, inhuman, freakish, grotesque, hideous, deformed, malformed, misshapen.

· ·

Mont. *abbrev.* Montana.

montage /mɒn'tɑːʒ/ *noun* 1 the process of creating a picture by piecing together elements from other pictures, photographs, etc; a picture made in this way. 2 the process of editing cinema film. 3 extensive use of changes in camera position to create an impression of movement or action in a filmed scene. See also MISE-EN-SCÈNE. 4 a film sequence made up of short clips, especially used to condense events taking place over a long period. [from French *montage*, from *monter*, to mount]

montbretia /mɒn'briːʃə/ *noun* a perennial plant (*Crocosmia x crocosmiiflora*) that produces corms and spreads by means of stolons. It has sword-shaped leaves and yellow or orange trumpet-shaped flowers borne in spikes. [named after the French botanist A F E Coquebert de Montbret (1780–1801)]

month *noun* 1 any of the 12 named divisions of the year, varying in length between 28 and 31 days. 2 a period of roughly four weeks or 30 days; the period between identical dates in consecutive months. [from Anglo-Saxon *monath*, from *mona*, moon]

monthly — *adj.* happening, published, etc once a month; lasting one month. — *adv.* once a month. — *noun* (PL. **monthlies**) 1 a monthly periodical. 2 *colloq.* a menstrual period.

montmorillonite /mɒntmə'rɪlənaɪt/ *noun Geol.* any of a group of soft opaque clay minerals, composed of aluminium silicates, that expand when they absorb liquids, and can take up or lose positively charged ions. Also called FULLER'S EARTH. [named after Montmorillon in France]

monty *noun colloq.* (*especially* **the full monty**) everything that there is or that one needs.

monument *noun* 1 something, eg a statue, built to preserve the memory of a person or event. 2 any ancient building or structure preserved for its historical value. 3 *formal* something serving as clear evidence; an excellent example: *the painting is a monument to her artistic skill*. 4 *formal* a tombstone. [from Latin *monumentum*, from *monere*, to remind]

· · · · · · · · · · · · · · · · · · · ·

■ 1 memorial, cenotaph, shrine, mausoleum, cairn, barrow, cross, marker, obelisk, pillar, statue, relic. 3 remembrance, commemoration, testament, reminder, record, memento, evidence, token. 4 headstone, gravestone, tombstone.

· ·

monumental *adj.* 1 of or being a monument. 2 like a monument, especially huge and impressive. 3 *colloq.* very great; extreme: *monumental arrogance*. 4 *formal* of tombstones: *monumental sculptor*.

· · · · · · · · · · · · · · · · · · · ·

■ 1 commemorative, memorial. 2, 3 immense, enormous, colossal, vast, tremendous. 2 huge, massive, great, impressive, imposing, awe-inspiring, awesome, overwhelming, significant, important, epoch-making, historic, magnificent, majestic, memorable, notable, outstanding, abiding, immortal, lasting, classic.

⊟ 2 insignificant, unimportant.

· ·

moo — *noun* the long low sound made by a cow. — *verb intrans.* to make this sound. [imitative]

mooch *verb colloq.* 1 *intrans.* (*usually* **mooch about** or **around**) to wander aimlessly. 2 *trans., intrans.* to get (things) for nothing by asking directly; to cadge. [perhaps from Old French *muchier*, to hide or lurk]

mood[1] *noun* **1** a state of mind at a particular time; a suitable or necessary state of mind: *not in the mood for dancing*. **2** a temporary grumpy state of mind. **3** an atmosphere: *the mood in the factory*. [from Anglo-Saxon *mod*, mind]

▣ **1** disposition, frame of mind, state of mind, temper, humour, caprice, whim. **2** bad temper, sulk, the sulks, pique, melancholy, depression, *colloq.* the blues, the doldrums, *colloq.* the dumps. **3** atmosphere, feeling, spirit, tenor, tone.

mood[2] *noun Grammar* each of several forms of a verb, indicating whether the verb is expressing a fact, a wish, possibility, or doubt, or a command: *the imperative mood*. [originally a variant of MODE]

moodily *adv.* in a moody way, sullenly.

moodiness *noun* a moody state.

moody *adj.* (**moodier**, **moodiest**) tending to change mood often; frequently bad-tempered.

▣ changeable, temperamental, unpredictable, capricious, irritable, short-tempered, *colloq.* crabby, *colloq.* crotchety, snappy, crusty, testy, *colloq.* touchy, morose, angry, broody, mopey, sulky, sullen, gloomy, miserable, downcast, glum, impulsive, fickle, flighty.
▣ equable, cheerful.

moon — *noun* **1** (**Moon**) the Earth's natural satellite, illuminated to varying degrees by the Sun depending on its position, and often visible in the sky, especially at night. **2** the appearance of this body to an observer on Earth, in respect of its degree of illumination, eg full moon, half moon. **3** a natural satellite of any planet. **4** something impossible to obtain: *promised me the moon*. — *verb intrans.* **1** (**moon about** or **around**) to wander aimlessly; to spend time idly. **2** *slang* to make a show of one's bare buttocks in public. — **over the moon** *colloq.* thrilled, delighted. [from Anglo-Saxon *mona*]

▣ *verb* **1** idle, loaf, *colloq.* mooch, languish, pine, mope, brood, daydream, dream, fantasize.

moonbeam *noun* a ray of sunlight reflected from the moon.

Moonie *noun* a member of the Unification Church, a religious movement founded (1954) in Korea by the Rev Sun Myung Moon.

moonlight — *noun* **1** sunlight reflected by the moon. **2** (*attributive*) illuminated by moonlight: *a moonlight swim*. — *verb intrans.* (PAST TENSE AND PAST PARTICIPLE **moonlighted**) *colloq.* to work at a second job outside the working hours of the main job, often evading income tax on the extra earnings.

moonlighter *noun* a person who moonlights.

moonlighting *noun* the practice of working as a moonlighter.

moonlit *adj.* illuminated by moonlight.

moonshine *noun colloq.* **1** foolish talk; nonsense. **2** smuggled or illegally distilled alcoholic spirit.

moonstone *noun Geol.* a transparent or opalescent silvery or bluish form of feldspar, used as a semi-precious stone in jewellery, and so called because it was once thought that its appearance changed with the waxing and waning of the moon.

moonstruck *adj. colloq.* behaving in an unusually wild or excited way, as if affected by the moon.

moony *adj.* (**moonier**, **mooniest**) *colloq.* in a dreamy mood.

Moor *noun* a member of a Muslim people from N Africa who conquered the Iberian Peninsula in the 8c.

moor[1] *noun* a large area of open uncultivated upland dominated by heather, and having an acid peaty soil. [from Anglo-Saxon *mor*]

▣ moorland, heath, fell, upland.

moor[2] *verb* **1** to fasten (a ship or boat) by a rope, cable, or anchor. **2** (*intrans.*) to be fastened in this way. [perhaps from Old Dutch *maren*]

▣ *verb* TIE UP, ANCHOR, BERTH, DOCK, MAKE FAST. **1** fasten, secure, fix, hitch, bind.
▣ **1** loose.

moorhen *noun* a small black water-bird with a red beak.

mooring *noun* **1** a place where a boat is moored. **2** (**moorings**) the ropes, anchors, etc used to moor a boat.

Moorish *adj.* relating to or characteristic of the Moors, an Arab people of NW Africa who conquered the Iberian peninsula in the 8c, or their civilization.

moorland *noun* a moor.

moose *noun* (PL. **moose**) a large N American deer with flat rounded antlers, also found in Europe and Asia, where it is called an elk. [from Algonkian (a Native American language) *moos*]

moot — *verb* to suggest; to bring up for discussion. — *adj.* open to argument; debatable: *a moot point*. — *noun* a court or administrative assembly in Anglo-Saxon England. [from Anglo-Saxon *mot*, assembly]

mop — *noun* **1** a tool for washing or wiping floors, consisting of a large sponge or a set of thick threads on a long handle. **2** a similar smaller tool for washing dishes. **3** *colloq.* a thick mass of hair. — *verb* (**mopped**, **mopping**) **1** to wash or wipe with a mop. **2** to wipe or clean (eg a sweaty brow). — **mop up** or **mop something up 1** to clean up with a mop. **2** *colloq.* to capture or kill (remaining enemy troops) after a victory; to deal with or get rid of (anything remaining). [perhaps from Latin *mappa*, napkin]

▣ *noun* **1** swab, sponge. **3** head of hair, shock, mane, tangle, thatch, mass. *verb* **1** swab, sponge, wipe, clean, wash.

mope — *verb intrans.* to behave in a depressed, sulky, or aimless way. — *noun* **1** a habitually sulky or depressed person. **2** (**the mopes**) low spirits; depression.

▣ *verb* brood, fret, sulk, pine, languish, droop, despair, grieve, idle.

moped *noun* a small-engined motorcycle, especially one started using pedals. [a shortening of *motor-assisted pedal-cycle*]

moppet *noun* a term of affection used to a small child. [from obsolete *mop*, rag doll]

moquette *noun* thick velvety material used to make carpets and upholstery. [from French]

moraine /məˈreɪn/ *noun Geol.* any jumbled accumulation of rock fragments of assorted sizes, ranging from sand to boulders, that has been carried from its place of origin and deposited by a glacier or ice sheet. [from French]

moral — *adj.* **1** of or relating to the principles of good and evil, or right and wrong. **2** conforming to what is considered by society to be good, right, or proper. **3** having a psychological effect: *moral support*. **4** considered in terms of psychological effect, rather than outward appearance: *a moral victory*. **5** capable of distinguishing between right and wrong. — *noun* **1** a principle to be learned from a story or event. **2** (**morals**) a sense of right and wrong, or a standard of behaviour based on this: *have no morals/loose morals*. [from Latin *moralis*, from *mores*, pl. of *mos*, custom]

▣ *adj.* **1, 2** ethical. **2** virtuous, good, right, principled, honourable, decent, upright, upstanding, straight,

righteous, high-minded, honest, incorruptible, proper, blameless, chaste, clean-living, pure, just, noble. *noun*
1 lesson, message, teaching, dictum, meaning, maxim, adage, precept, saying, proverb, aphorism, epigram.
2 morality, ethics, principles, standards, ideals, integrity, scruples, conduct, manners.
☒ *adj.* 2 immoral.

moral certainty something about which there is hardly any doubt.

morale *noun* level of confidence or optimism; spirits. [from French]

☐ confidence, spirits, esprit de corps, self-esteem, state of mind, heart, mood.

moralist *noun* 1 a person who lives according to strict moral principles. 2 a person who tends to lecture others on their low moral standards.

moralistic *adj.* 1 pertaining to or typical of a moralist. 2 given to moralizing. 3 characterized by moralism.

morality *noun* (PL. **moralities**) 1 the quality of being right or wrong; behaviour in relation to accepted moral standards. 2 a particular system of moral standards.

☐ ETHICS. 1 virtue, rectitude, righteousness, decency, goodness, honesty, integrity, justice, uprightness, propriety.
2 morals, ideals, principles, standards, conduct, manners.
☒ 1 immorality.

morality play *Hist.* an allegorical drama, originating in the Middle Ages, in which the characters act out a conflict between good and evil.

moralize or **moralise** *verb* 1 (*intrans.*) to write or speak (especially critically) about moral standards. 2 (*trans.*) to explain in terms of morals.

moral theology *Relig.* a theological discipline concerned with ethical questions considered from a specifically Christian perspective.

morass /məˈras/ *noun* 1 an area of marshy or swampy ground. 2 *literary* a dangerous or confused situation, especially one that entraps. [from Old French *maresc*]

☐ 1 quagmire, bog, marsh, swamp, slough, mire. 2 quandary, dilemma.

moratorium *noun* (PL. **moratoriums**, **moratoria**) 1 an agreed temporary break in an activity. 2 a legally authorized postponement of payment of a debt. [from Latin *mora*, delay]

☐ 1 break, adjournment, cooling-off period, truce, suspension, freeze.

moray /ˈmɔːreɪ/ *noun* a sharp-toothed eel of warm coastal waters. [from Portuguese *moreia*]

morbid *adj.* 1 displaying an unhealthy interest in unpleasant things, especially death. 2 *Medicine* relating to, or indicating the presence of, disease. [from Latin *morbus*, disease]

☐ 1 ghoulish, ghastly, gruesome, macabre, hideous, horrid, grim, gloomy, pessimistic, melancholy, sombre. 2 sick, unhealthy, unwholesome, insalubrious.

morbidity *noun* being morbid; a morbid state.

mordant — *adj.* sharply sarcastic or critical; biting. — *noun* 1 *Chem.* a chemical compound, usually a metallic oxide or salt, that is used to fix colour on textiles that cannot be dyed directly. 2 a corrosive substance. [from Latin *mordere*, to bite]

☐ *adj.* biting, acid, caustic, scathing, trenchant, cutting, incisive, sarcastic, derisive.

more — *adj.* a greater or additional number or quantity of. — *adv.* 1 used to form the comparative of many adjectives and adverbs, especially those of two or more syllables. 2 to a greater degree; with a greater frequency. 3 again: *once more.* — *pron.* a greater, or additional, number or quantity of people or things. — **more of ...** better described as ...; closer to being: *more of a painter than a writer.* **more or less** 1 almost: *more or less finished.* 2 roughly: *more or less two hours.* [from Anglo-Saxon *mara*, greater]

☐ *adj.* further, extra, additional, added, new, fresh, increased, other, supplementary, repeated, alternative, spare. *adv.* 2 further, longer, again, besides, moreover, better.
☒ *adj.* fewer, less. *adv.* less.

morel /məˈrɛl/ *noun Bot.* a highly prized edible fungus belonging to the genus *Morchella.* Its fruiting body consists of a pale stalk and a brownish egg-shaped head covered with a network of ridges. It appears in spring in woods and pastures and on bonfire sites. [from French *morille*]

morello *noun* (PL. **morellos**) a bitter-tasting dark-red cherry. [from Italian *morello*, blackish]

moreover *adv.* also; and what is more important.

☐ furthermore, further, besides, in addition, as well, also, additionally, what is more.

mores /ˈmɔːreɪz/ *pl. noun formal* social customs reflecting the basic moral and social values of a particular society. [from Latin *mos*, custom]

morganatic *adj. technical, said of marriage* between a person of high social rank and one of low rank, and allowing neither the lower-ranking person nor any child from the marriage to inherit the title or property of the higher-ranking person. [from Latin *matrimonium ad morganaticam*, marriage with a morning gift; the offering of the gift, after consummation, is the husband's only duty in such a marriage]

morgue *noun* 1 a building where corpses are kept until buried or cremated. 2 any gloomy or depressing place. 3 a store of miscellaneous information for reference. [from French *morgue*]

MORI *abbrev.* Market and Opinion Research Institute.

moribund *adj.* 1 dying; near the end of existence. 2 lacking strength or vitality. [from Latin *mori*, to die]

☐ 1 dying, expiring, failing, fading, on its last legs, on its way out, not long for this world. 2 feeble, weak, lifeless, declining.

Mormon *noun* a member of the Church of Jesus Christ of Latter-Day Saints, established in the US in 1830, accepting as scripture both the Bible and the Book of Mormon (a book regarded as a record of certain ancient American prophets).

Mormonism *noun* the beliefs and practices of the Mormons.

morn *noun poetic* morning. [from Anglo-Saxon *morgen*]

mornay *adj.* served in a cheese sauce: *cod mornay.* [perhaps from the French statesman Philippe de Mornay (1549–1623)]

morning — *noun* 1 the part of the day from sunrise to midday, or from midnight to midday. 2 sunrise; dawn. — *adj.* taken, or taking place, in the morning: *morning coffee.* — **the morning after** *colloq.* the morning after a celebration, as the time of a hangover. [from Middle English *morwening*]

☐ *noun* 1 a.m., *Scot.* forenoon. 2 daybreak, daylight, dawn, sunrise, break of day.

....

morning-after pill *Medicine* a contraceptive drug, consisting of a combination of oestrogen and progestogen, taken within 72 hours of unprotected sexual intercourse.

morning coat a man's tailed black or grey jacket worn as part of morning dress.

morning dress men's formal dress for the daytime, consisting of morning coat, grey trousers, and usually a top hat.

morning glory a tropical climbing plant with blue, pink, or white trumpet-shaped flowers that close in the afternoon.

morning sickness nausea and vomiting often experienced during the early stages of pregnancy, especially in the morning.

morning star a planet, usually Venus, seen in the eastern sky just before sunrise.

morocco *noun* soft fine goatskin leather, originally brought from Morocco.

moron *noun* **1** *derog. colloq.* a very stupid person. **2** a term formerly used to describe a person with a mild degree of mental handicap, but now considered obsolete and offensive. [from Greek *moros*, foolish]

....

▣ **1** *offensive* cretin, *colloq.* idiot, fool, dolt, *colloq.* dimwit, *colloq.* blockhead.

....

moronic *adj.* **1** like or characteristic of a moron. **2** *colloq.* stupid, foolish.

morose *adj.* silently gloomy or bad-tempered. [from Latin *morosus*, peevish]

....

▣ ill-tempered, bad-tempered, moody, sullen, sulky, surly, gloomy, grim, gruff, sour, taciturn, glum, grouchy, *colloq.* crabby, saturnine.

▣ cheerful, communicative.

....

morpheme *noun Grammar* any of the units of meaning contained in or forming a word, not divisible into smaller units, eg *out, go*, and *-ing*, contained in *outgoing*. See also MORPHOLOGY. [from Greek *morphe*, form]

morphine *noun* a sedative narcotic drug obtained from opium and used mainly as an analgesic to relieve severe and persistent pain, and as a sedative to induce sleep. [from *Morpheus*, Greek god of sleep]

morphing *noun* the use of computer graphics to blend one screen image into another in film-making, eg to transform or manipulate an actor's body. [from Greek *morphe*, form]

morphogenesis /mɔːfoʊˈdʒɛnəsɪs/ *noun Biol.* the development of form and structure in a living organism as a result of the growth and differentiation of its cells and tissues. [from Greek *morphe*, form + GENESIS]

morphological *adj.* relating to or involving morphology.

morphology *noun* **1** the study of morphemes and the rules by which they combine to form words. **2** the scientific study of the structure of plants and animals. **3** *formal* the structure of anything. [from Greek *morphe*, form + *logos*, discourse]

morris dance a ceremonial form of traditional English dance, in which performers dressed in white, some wearing bells, stamp and hop, waving a stick, handkerchief, or garland, accompanied by an accordion or concertina with bass drum. [from Middle English *moreys*, Moorish]

morris dancer a person who performs morris dances.

morris dancing the practice of performing morris dances.

morrow *noun old use, poetic* (**the morrow**) **1** the following day; the time after an event. **2** the morning. [from Anglo-Saxon *morgen*, morning]

Morse code a code used for sending messages, each letter of a word being represented as a series of short or long

radio signals or flashes of light. [from Samuel Morse (1791–1872), who invented it]

morsel *noun* a small piece, especially of food. [from Old French *mors*, bite]

....

▣ bit, scrap, piece, fragment, crumb, bite, mouthful, nibble, taste, soupçon, titbit, slice, fraction, modicum, grain, atom, part.

....

mortal — *adj.* **1** certain to die at some future time. **2** of or causing death. **3** extreme: *mortal fear*. **4** characterized by intense hostility: *mortal enemies*. **5** *used for emphasis* conceivable; single: *every mortal thing*. — *noun* a mortal (especially human) being. [from Latin *mortalis*, from *mori*, to die]

....

▣ *adj.* **1** worldly, earthly, bodily, human, perishable, temporal. **2** fatal, lethal, deadly. **3** extreme, great, severe, intense, grave, awful. *noun* human being, human, individual, person, being, body, creature.

▣ *adj.* **1** immortal. *noun* immortal, god.

....

mortality *noun* **1** the state of being mortal. **2** (*also* **mortality rate**) the number of deaths, eg in a war. **3** loss of life.

....

▣ **1** humanity, impermanence, perishability, transience.
2 fatalities, death rate.

▣ **1** immortality.

....

mortal sin *RC Church* a serious sin, affecting salvation of the soul. See also VENIAL SIN.

mortar — *noun* **1** a mixture of sand, water, and cement or lime, used in building to bond bricks or stones. **2** the small dish in which substances are ground with a pestle. **3** a type of short-barrelled artillery gun for firing shells over short distances. — *verb* (**mortared, mortaring**) **1** to fix (especially bricks) in place with mortar. **2** to bombard using a mortar. [from Latin *mortarium*]

mortarboard *noun* **1** a flat board used by bricklayers to carry mortar, held horizontally by a handle underneath. **2** a black cap with a hard square flat top, worn by academics at formal occasions.

mortgage /ˈmɔːɡɪdʒ/ — *noun* **1** a legal agreement by which a financial institution grants a client a loan for the purpose of buying property, ownership of the property being held by the institution until the loan is repaid. **2** the money borrowed, or the regular amounts repaid. **3** any loan for which property is used as security. — *verb* to give ownership of (property) as security for a loan. [from French *mort*, dead + *gage*, pledge]

mortice same as MORTISE.

mortician *noun North Amer., esp. US* an undertaker. [from Latin *mortis*, death]

mortification *noun* the act of mortifying or the state of being mortified.

mortify *verb* (**mortifies, mortified**) **1** to cause to feel humiliated or ashamed. **2** *Relig.* to control (physical desire) through self-discipline or self-inflicted hardship: *mortify the flesh*. **3** *intrans., said of a limb* to suffer from gangrene. [from Latin *mortificare*, to cause death to]

....

▣ **1** humiliate, shame, embarrass, abash, confound, humble, crush, deflate. **2** discipline, restrain, subjugate, subdue.

....

mortise /ˈmɔːtɪs/ — *noun* a hole cut in a piece of wood, into which a tenon, or shaped end of a second piece, fits to form a mortise and tenon joint. — *verb* to cut a mortise in; to join with a mortise and tenon joint. [from Old French *mortoise*]

mortise lock a lock fitted into a hole cut in the side edge of a door, rather than on to the door's surface.

mortuary *noun* (PL. **mortuaries**) a building or room where corpses are kept until buried or cremated. [from Latin *mortuarius*, of the dead]

Mosaic /moʊˈzeɪɪk/ adj. relating to Moses, or the laws attributed to him.

mosaic /moʊˈzeɪɪk/ noun a design formed by fitting together small pieces of coloured stone or glass. [from French mosaïque]

moselle /moʊˈzɛl/ noun (often **Moselle**) a dry German white wine from the regions around the river Mosel or Moselle.

Moses basket a portable cot for babies. [referring to the biblical story of Moses in the bulrushes]

mosey verb intrans. (**moseys, moseyed, moseying**) (usually **mosey along**) colloq. to walk in a leisurely way; to saunter or amble. [origin uncertain]

moshing noun a style of energetic and sinuous dancing done in a crowded space to heavy metal or thrash music. [perhaps a mixture of SQUASH and MASH]

Moslem see MUSLIM.

mosque noun a Muslim place of worship. [from Arabic masjid]

mosquito noun (PL. **mosquitos, mosquitoes**) any of about 2,500 species of small two-winged insects belonging to the family Culicidae, and having thin feathery antennae, long legs, and a slender body, distributed worldwide, although most species live in tropical regions. They transmit several serious diseases, including malaria and yellow fever. [from Spanish, a diminutive of mosca, fly]

mosquito net a fine net designed to keep away mosquitos, especially hung over a bed at night.

moss noun 1 the common name for any plant belonging to the class Musci, including many species of small spore-bearing bryophytes without a vascular system, closely related to liverworts, and typically found growing in dense spreading clusters in moist shady habitats. 2 any of various unrelated plants which superficially resemble true moss, eg clubmoss (a vascular plant), Irish moss (an alga). 3 dialect an area of boggy ground. [from Anglo-Saxon mos, bog]

mossy adj. (**mossier, mossiest**) 1 covered with moss. 2 like moss. 3 boggy.

most — adj. the greatest part, amount, or number (of): most children enjoy parties/who can count the most sheep? — adv. 1 (also **the most**) used to form the superlative of many adjectives and adverbs, especially those of more than two syllables. 2 (**the most**) to the greatest degree; with the greatest frequency. 3 extremely. — pron. the greatest number or quantity, or the majority of people or things: most of them are here/who has the most? — ... **at the most** certainly not more than: three at the most. **for the most part** mostly. **make the most of something** to take the greatest possible advantage of it. [from Anglo-Saxon mast or mæst]

-most combining form forming words meaning 'furthest in a particular direction': southernmost.

mostly adv. usually; mainly.

▣ mainly, on the whole, principally, chiefly, generally, usually, largely, for the most part, as a rule.

MOT noun Brit. an official annual test of roadworthiness, required by the Department (formerly Ministry) of Transport on all vehicles over three years old; the certificate supplied on successful completion of this.

mote noun a speck, especially of dust. [from Anglo-Saxon mot]

motel noun a hotel near a main road, intended for overnight stops by motorists, with extensive parking facilities. [from motor hotel]

motet noun a short piece of sacred music for several voices. [from Old French, diminutive of mot, word]

moth noun the common name for any of about 130000 species of winged insect belonging to the same order (Lepidoptera) as butterflies, and, apart from a few species in which the female is wingless, having four broad wings covered with tiny overlapping scales. [from Anglo-Saxon moththe]

mothball noun a small ball of camphor or naphthalene hung in wardrobes, etc to keep away clothes moths.

moth-eaten adj. 1 said of cloth damaged by clothes moths. 2 colloq. old and worn.

mother — noun 1 a female parent. 2 (**Mother** or **Mother Superior**) the head of a female religious (especially Christian) community. 3 the cause or origin: necessity is the mother of invention. — adj. like a mother in being protective, or being a source from which others spring: Mother Church. — verb 1 to give birth to; to give rise to. 2 to treat with (excessive) care and protection. —**the mother of all...** the most impressive or extreme example of: the mother of all battles. [from Anglo-Saxon modor]

▣ noun 1 colloq. mum, colloq. mummy, colloq. mama, slang old woman, matriarch, parent, progenitress, dam. 3 cause, origin, source. verb 1 bear, produce, nurture, raise, rear, nurse, care for, cherish. 2 pamper, spoil, baby, indulge, overprotect, fuss over, colloq. mollycoddle.

motherboard noun a printed circuit board that can be plugged into the back of a computer, and into which other boards can be slotted to allow the computer to operate various peripherals.

mother country 1 a person's native country. 2 the country that pilgrims leave to settle elsewhere.

motherese noun the speech used by adults to young children while they are learning to speak, typically consisting of shorter expressions than those normally used by adults, with clear pronunciation, often with exaggerated intonation patterns.

motherhood noun the position and responsibilities of a mother.

Mothering Sunday the fourth Sunday in Lent, traditionally a day on which children honour their mothers with gifts (see also MOTHER'S DAY).

mother-in-law noun (PL. **mothers-in-law**) the mother of one's husband or wife.

motherland noun a person's native country.

motherly adj. like or characteristic of a mother.

▣ maternal, caring, comforting, affectionate, kind, loving, protective, warm, tender, gentle, fond.

▣ neglectful, uncaring.

mother-of-pearl noun a hard shiny iridescent substance, consisting mainly of calcium carbonate, that forms the inner layer of the shell of certain bivalve molluscs, eg oysters. It is used to make buttons, beads, etc.

Mother's Day a day set apart in honour of mothers. In the USA, Canada, and Australia, it is the second Sunday in May; in the UK, it is Mothering Sunday.

mother tongue the language a person speaks from birth.

mothproof — adj., said of cloth treated with chemicals which resist attack by clothes moths. — verb to treat in this way.

motif noun 1 a shape repeated many times within a pattern; a single design or symbol, eg on clothing. 2 something often repeated throughout a work or works of art, eg a passage of music in a symphony, or a theme in a novel. [from French motif, motive]

▣ 1 pattern, design, figure, form, logo, shape, device, ornament, decoration. 2 theme, idea, topic, concept, leitmotif.

motile /ˈmoʊtaɪl/ adj. Biol. describing a living organism or a structure that is capable of spontaneous movement, eg spermatozoa. [from Latin motus, movement]

motion — noun 1 the act, state, or way of moving. 2 a single movement, especially of the body. 3 the ability to move a part of the body. **4** a proposal for formal discussion at a meeting. **5** *Medicine* an act of discharging faeces; (**motions**) faeces. — *verb trans., intrans.* (**motioned, motioning**) (**motion to someone**) to give them a signal or direction. — **go through the motions** to pretend; to perform a task mechanically or half-heartedly. **in motion** moving. [from Latin *motio*, from *movere*, to move]

▣ *noun* **1, 2, 3** movement. **1, 2** action. **1, 3** mobility. **1** moving, activity, locomotion, travel, transit, passage, passing, progress, change, flow. **2** gesture, gesticulation, signal, sign, wave, nod, inclination. **4** proposal, suggestion, recommendation, proposition. *verb* signal to, gesture to, gesticulate to, sign to, wave to, nod to, beckon to, direct, usher.

motionless *adj.* without moving, completely still.

▣ unmoving, still, stationary, static, immobile, at a standstill, fixed, halted, at rest, resting, standing, paralysed, inanimate, lifeless, frozen, rigid, stagnant.
▣ active, moving.

motion picture *North Amer., esp. US* a cinema film.
motivate *verb* **1** to be the motive of. **2** to cause or stimulate (a person) to act; to be the underlying cause of (action).

▣ PROMPT, INCITE, PROVOKE, STIMULATE, STIR, INSPIRE, ENCOURAGE, CAUSE, TRIGGER, INDUCE. **1** kindle, arouse. **2** impel, spur, drive, lead, urge, push, propel, persuade, move, bring, draw.
▣ DETER, DISCOURAGE.

motivation *noun* motivating force, incentive.

▣ incentive, impulse, motive, stimulus, inspiration, urge, grounds, object, rationale, intention.

motive — *noun* a reason for, or underlying cause of, action of a certain kind. — *adj.* **1** causing motion: *motive power.* **2** stimulating action: *motive force.* [from Latin *motivus*, from *movere*, to move]

▣ *noun* ground(s), cause, reason, purpose, rationale, motivation, object, intention, influence, rationale, thinking, incentive, impulse, stimulus, inspiration, incitement, urge, encouragement, design, desire, consideration.
▣ *noun* deterrent, disincentive.

motley — *adj.* **1** made up of many different kinds: *a motley crew.* **2** many-coloured. — *noun* a jester's multicoloured costume. [perhaps from Anglo-Saxon *mot*, speck]

▣ *adj.* **1** assorted, varied, mixed, miscellaneous, diverse, diversified, heterogeneous, multifarious. **2** multicoloured, variegated, particoloured, colourful, pied, piebald, tabby, dappled, brindled, mottled, spotted, striped, streaked.

motocross *noun* a form of motorcycle racing in which specially adapted motor cycles compete across rough terrain. Competitions are usually organized according to engine size. The first race was held at Camberley, Surrey in 1924.
motor — *noun* **1** *Electr.* a device that converts electrical energy into mechanical energy, using the forces that act on a current-carrying conductor, eg a coil, in the presence of a magnetic field. **2** an engine, especially the internal combustion engine of a vehicle or machine. **3** *colloq.* a car. — *adj.* **1** of or relating to cars or other road vehicles: *a motor show.* **2** driven by a motor: *a motor boat.* **3** *Anat.* denoting a nerve that transmits impulses from the central nervous system (the brain and spinal cord) to a muscle or gland. **4** *Anat.* denoting a neurone (nerve cell) that forms part of such a nerve. — *verb intrans.* (**motored, motoring**) **1** to travel by motor vehicle, especially by private car. **2** *colloq.* to move, work, etc fast and effectively. [from Latin *movere*, to move]

motorbike *noun colloq.* a motorcycle.
motorcade *noun* a procession of cars carrying important (especially political) figures.
motor car a motor vehicle, usually four-wheeled, for carrying a small number of people.
motorcycle *noun* any two-wheeled road vehicle powered by a petrol engine.
motorcyclist *noun* a person who drives a motorcycle.
motoring *noun* travelling by car, especially for pleasure.
motorist *noun* a person who drives a car.
motorize or **motorise** *verb* **1** to fit a motor to. **2** to supply (eg soldiers) with motor vehicles.
motor neurone *Anat.* a nerve cell that carries impulses from the spinal cord or the brain to an effector organ such as a muscle or gland.
motorway *noun* a major dual-carriageway road for fast-moving traffic, especially one with three lanes per carriageway.
Motown *noun* a style of music combining the styles of pop and rhythm and blues. [from *Motor Town*, a nickname for Detroit in the USA, where it originated in the early 1960s]
motte and bailey an earth and timber fortification commonly built by the Normans and consisting of an artificial mound (*motte*) surrounded by a ditch, with a walled outer court *(bailey)* adjoining it to one side. [from Old French *mote*; see BAILEY]
mottled *adj.* with a pattern of different coloured blotches or streaks. [probably from MOTLEY]

▣ speckled, dappled, blotchy, flecked, piebald, pied, stippled, streaked, tabby, spotted, freckled, variegated.
▣ monochrome, uniform.

motto *noun* (PL. **mottos, mottoes**) **1** a phrase adopted as a principle of behaviour. **2** a printed phrase or verse contained in a paper cracker. **3** a quotation at the beginning of a book or chapter, hinting at what is to follow. [from Italian, from Latin *muttum*, utterance]

▣ **1** slogan, maxim, watchword, catchword, byword, saying, precept, proverb, adage, formula, rule, golden rule, dictum.

mould¹ *noun* any of various fungi that produce an abundant woolly network (or *mycelium*) of thread-like strands (or *hyphae*), which may be white, grey-green, or black in colour. [from Middle English *mowle*]

▣ mildew, fungus, mouldiness, mustiness, blight.

mould² — *noun* **1** a hollow shaped container into which a liquid substance is poured to take on the container's shape when it cools and sets. **2** food, eg a pudding, shaped in such a container. **3** nature, character or personality. **4** a framework on which certain manufactured objects are built up. — *verb* **1** to shape using a mould. **2** to shape (a substance) with the hands; to form by shaping a substance with the hands. **3** *intrans., trans.* to fit or cause to fit tightly. **4** to exercise a controlling influence over the development of. [from Latin *modulus*, measure]

▣ *noun* **1** cast, form, die, template, pattern, matrix. **2, 3** shape. **3** character, nature, quality, form, format, pattern, structure, style, type, build, construction, cut, design, kind, model, sort, stamp, frame, line, make. *verb* **1, 2** shape, make, form, create. **1** forge, cast, stamp. **2** sculpt, model, work, throw. **4** influence, direct, control.

mould³ *noun* loose soft earth, especially rich in decayed matter: *leaf mould.* [from Anglo-Saxon *molde*]

moulder *verb intrans.* (*also* **moulder away**) to become gradually rotten with age; to decay.

〓 rot, decay, decompose, putrefy, crumble, corrupt.

moulding *noun* **1** a shaped decorative strip, especially of wood or plaster. **2** a technique used to convert molten plastics, clay, glass, brick, and other materials into specific three-dimensional shapes by using hollow moulds and applying heat or pressure. The moulding of metals is known as casting.

mouldy *adj.* (**mouldier, mouldiest**) **1** covered with mould; old and stale. **2** *derog. colloq.* a general term of dislike: *I don't want your mouldy advice.*

〓 **1** mildewed, blighted, musty, decaying, corrupt, rotten, fusty, putrid, bad, spoiled, stale.
🔲 **1** fresh, wholesome.

moult — *verb intrans.*, *said of an animal* to shed feathers, hair, or skin to make way for a new growth. — *noun* the process of moulting, or the time taken to moult. [from Anglo-Saxon *mutian*, to exchange]

mound *noun* **1** any small hill, or bank of earth or rock, natural or man-made. **2** a heap or pile.

〓 **1** hill, hillock, hummock, rise, knoll, bank, dune, elevation, ridge, embankment, earthwork. **2** heap, pile, stack.

mount[1] — *verb* **1** *trans.*, *intrans. formal* to go up: *mount stairs.* **2** *trans.*, *intrans.* to get up on to (eg a horse). **3** *intrans.* (*also* **mount up**) to increase in level or intensity. **4** to put in a frame or on a background for display; to hang or put up on a stand or support. **5** to organize or hold (a campaign, etc). **6** to carry out (eg an attack). — *noun* **1** a support or backing on which a thing is placed for display. **2** *formal* a horse that is ridden. [from Old French *monter*, to go up]

〓 *verb* **1** climb, ascend, go up, clamber up. **2** get on, jump on, get astride. **3** increase, grow, accumulate, multiply, rise, intensify, soar, swell. **4** frame, hang, display, show, exhibit. **5** produce, put on, set up, prepare, stage. **6** launch, carry out. *noun* **1** support, mounting, backing, frame, stand. **2** horse, steed.
🔲 *verb* **1**, **2**, **3** descend. **1** go down. **2** dismount. **3** decrease.

mount[2] *noun poetic* (*also* **Mount** *in place-names*) a mountain. [from Latin *montis*]

mountain *noun* **1** a very high steep hill, often of bare rock. **2** *colloq.* a great quantity; a heap or mass. **3** a huge surplus of some commodity. — **make a mountain out of a molehill** to exaggerate the seriousness or importance of a trivial matter. [from Latin *mons*]

〓 **1** height, elevation, mount, peak, mound, alp, tor, massif. **2** heap, pile, stack, mass, abundance, backlog.

mountain ash the rowan, a tree of the rose family, with feather-shaped leaves and red berries.

mountain bike a sturdy bicycle with thick deep-tread tyres and straight handlebars.

mountain dew whisky, especially when made illicitly.

mountaineer — *noun* a person skilled in climbing mountains. — *verb intrans.* to climb mountains.

mountaineering *noun* the sport of climbing mountains, usually aided by ropes and other accessories, such as crampons.

mountain lion a puma.

mountainous *adj.* **1** containing many mountains. **2** huge.

〓 **1** hilly, high, highland, upland, alpine, soaring, steep,

craggy, rocky. **2** huge, towering, enormous, immense.
🔲 **1** flat. **2** tiny.

mountain sickness feelings of nausea and light-headedness as a result of breathing low-oxygen mountain air.

mountebank /ˈmaʊntɪbaŋk/ *noun literary derog.* **1** originally, a person who sold quack medicines from a public platform. **2** any person who swindles or deceives. [from Italian *montimbanco*, a person who mounts a bench]

〓 **2** charlatan, swindler, cheat, fraud, *colloq.* con man, *slang* hustler.

mounted *adj.* **1** on horseback. **2** hung on a wall, or placed in a frame or on a background.

Mountie or **Mounty** *noun* (PL. **Mounties**) *colloq.* a member of the Royal Canadian Mounted Police.

mourn *verb trans.*, *intrans.* (**mourn for** or **over someone** or **something**) to feel or show deep sorrow at the death or loss of a person or thing. [from Anglo-Saxon *murnan*]

〓 grieve (for), lament, sorrow (for), regret, weep (for), wail.
🔲 rejoice (at).

mourner *noun* **1** a person who mourns. **2** a person attending a funeral.

mournful *adj.* **1** feeling or expressing grief. **2** suggesting sadness or gloom.

〓 SORROWFUL, SAD, UNHAPPY, MISERABLE, MELANCHOLY, GLOOMY, DISMAL. **1** desolate, grief-stricken, heavy-hearted, heartbroken, broken-hearted, cast-down, downcast, depressed, dejected. **2** tragic, woeful, sombre.
🔲 JOYFUL.

mourning *noun* **1** grief felt or shown over a death. **2** a symbol of grief, especially a black costume or armband; a period of time during which such symbols are worn.

〓 **1** bereavement, grief, grieving, lamentation, sadness, sorrow, desolation, weeping.
🔲 **1** rejoicing.

mouse — *noun* (PL. **mice**) **1** any of various small rodents, especially members of the genus *Mus*, found worldwide, and having a grey or brown coat, a pointed muzzle and bright eyes, sharp teeth, and a long naked tail. **2** *colloq.* a very shy quiet person. **3** *Comput.* a computer input device which can be moved around on a flat surface, causing a cursor to move around the computer screen in response. It usually has at least one selection button, and can be used to choose one of a number of specified options displayed. — *verb intrans.* **1** *said of an animal* to hunt mice. **2** *Comput.* to use a mouse to move a cursor around a computer screen. [from Anglo-Saxon *mus*]

mouse deer see CHEVROTAIN.

mouse mat a flat piece of hard material on which a computer mouse is moved.

mouse-milking *noun* the pursuit of a project requiring considerable time and money but yielding little profit. [referring to scientific efforts in the 1990s to produce human proteins in the milk of mice which had been injected with human genes]

mouser *noun* a cat used for catching mice.

mousetrap *noun* **1** a mechanical trap for catching and often killing mice. **2** *old colloq.* use poor quality cheese.

moussaka /muˈsɑːkə/ *noun* an oven-cooked dish of minced meat and vegetables covered with a cheese sauce, traditionally eaten in Greece. [from modern Greek *moussaka*]

mousse *noun* **1** a dessert made from a whipped mixture of cream, eggs, and flavouring, eaten cold. **2** a similar meat or fish dish. **3** (*also* **styling mousse**) a frothy chemical preparation applied to hair to make styling easier. [from French *mousse*, froth]

moustache *noun* a line of unshaved hair above a man's upper lip. [from French, from Italian *mostaccio*]

mousy or **mousey** *adj.* (mousier, mousiest) 1 of or like a mouse: *mousy smells.* 2 *said of hair* of a dull light brown colour. 3 shy or quiet, especially tiresomely so.

mouth — *noun* 1 in humans, animals, etc, an opening in the head through which food is taken in and speech or sounds emitted; in other creatures, an opening with similar functions. 2 the lips; the outer visible parts of the mouth. 3 an opening, eg of a bottle. 4 the part of a river that widens to meet the sea. 5 a person considered as a consumer of food: *five mouths to feed.* 6 *derog. colloq.* boastful talk. 7 backchat or cheek: *don't want any of your mouth.* 8 *derog. colloq.* a person who talks too much, especially indiscreetly. — *verb* 1 to form (words) without actually speaking. 2 *trans., intrans., derog.* to speak (words) pompously or without sincerity. — **down in the mouth** *colloq.* dejected; unhappy. [from Anglo-Saxon *muth*]

⊟ *noun* 1 jaws, *slang* trap, *coarse slang* gob, *slang* cakehole. 3 opening, aperture, orifice, cavity, entrance, gateway. 4 estuary, inlet, delta. *verb* 1 whisper, form.

-mouthed *combining form* forming words meaning: 1 using a certain kind of language: *foul-mouthed.* 2 having a certain kind of mouth: *wide-mouthed.*

mouthfeel *noun* the sensory perception of a particular food while being chewed or tasted in the mouth.

mouthful *noun* (PL. **mouthfuls**) 1 as much as fills the mouth. 2 a small quantity, especially of food. 3 *colloq.* a word or phrase difficult to pronounce. 4 *colloq.* an outburst of forceful, often abusive language.

mouth organ a harmonica.

mouthpiece *noun* 1 the part of a musical instrument, telephone receiver, tobacco pipe, etc held in or against the mouth. 2 a person or publication expressing the views of a group.

mouth-to-mouth *adj.* denoting a method of resuscitation in which air is breathed directly into the mouth of the person to be revived.

mouthwash *noun* an antiseptic liquid gargled to freshen the mouth.

mouth-watering *adj.* 1 *said of food* having a delicious appearance or smell. 2 *colloq.* highly desirable.

⊟ TOOTHSOME, *colloq.* SCRUMPTIOUS. 1 delicious, succulent, delectable, tasty.

movable or **moveable** *adj.* 1 not fixed in one place; portable. 2 *said of a religious festival* taking place on a different date each year: *Easter is a movable feast.*

⊟ 1 mobile, portable, transportable, changeable, alterable, adjustable, flexible, transferable.
⊟ FIXED, IMMOVABLE.

move — *verb* 1 *trans., intrans.* to change or cause to change position or go from one place to another. 2 *intrans.* to make progress of any kind: *move towards a political solution.* 3 (**move on, out, away**, etc, or **move house**) to change (one's place of living, working, operating, etc). 4 to affect the feelings or emotions of. 5 (**move someone to do something**) to affect them so as to do it: *what moved him to say that?* 6 *trans., intrans.* to change the position of (a piece in a board game). 7 *intrans., trans. formal* (**move for something**) to propose or request it formally. 8 *intrans.* to spend time; to associate with people: *move in fashionable circles.* 9 *intrans. colloq.* to progress speedily. 10 *trans., intrans. colloq.* to sell or be sold. 11 *trans., intrans. said of the bowels* to be evacuated or cause them to be evacuated. — *noun* 1 an act of moving the body. 2 an act of moving a piece in a board game, or the rules governing how the

pieces are moved; any of a series of actions taken as part of an overall strategy. 3 an act of changing homes. — **get a move on** or **get moving** *colloq.* to hurry up. **make a move** 1 to take a step; to begin to proceed. 2 *colloq.* to leave. **move heaven and earth** to make strenuous efforts to achieve something. **move in** to begin to occupy new premises. **move in on someone** 1 to advance towards them, especially threateningly. 2 to take steps towards controlling them or usurping their position, etc. **on the move** 1 moving from place to place. 2 advancing or making progress. [from Latin *movere*]

⊟ *verb* 1, 2, 3 change. 1 stir, budge, shift, switch, advance, retreat. 2 proceed, progress, make strides. 3 depart, go away, leave, decamp, migrate, remove, move house, relocate, transfer. 4 affect, touch, agitate, stir, impress, excite. 5 prompt, stimulate, urge, impel, drive, propel, motivate, incite, persuade, induce, inspire. 7 propose, request, suggest, advocate, recommend. 9 make progress, get on, press on. *noun* 1, 2 action, step, gesture. 1 movement, motion. 2 measure, act, manoeuvre, ploy, device, stratagem. 3 removal, relocation, migration, transfer.

movement *noun* 1 a process or act of changing position or going from one point to another. 2 an organization or association, especially one promoting a particular cause. 3 a general tendency. 4 the theatrical art of moving the body gracefully or with expression. 5 (**movements**) a person's actions during a particular time. 6 the moving parts of a watch or clock. 7 *Medicine* an act of evacuating the bowels; the waste matter evacuated. 8 a section of a large-scale piece of music, especially a symphony.

⊟ 1 repositioning, relocation, move, moving, change, activity, act, action, agitation, stirring, transfer, passage. 2 campaign, crusade, drive, group, organization, party, faction. 3 trend, tendency, development, progress, progression, advance, evolution, current, drift, flow, shift.

mover *noun* a person or thing that moves.

movie *noun* a cinema film. [a shortening of *moving picture*]

moving *adj.* 1 having an effect on the emotions; touching; stirring. 2 in motion; not static: *a moving staircase.*

⊟ 1 touching, affecting, poignant, impressive, emotive, arousing, stirring, inspiring, inspirational, exciting, thrilling, persuasive, stimulating. 2 mobile, active, in motion.
⊟ 1 uninspiring. 2 immobile.

mow *verb* (PAST TENSE **mowed**; PAST PARTICIPLE **mown**) to cut (grass or a crop) by hand or with a machine. — **mow someone** or **something down** *colloq.* to knock them down or kill them in large numbers. [from Anglo-Saxon *mawan*]

⊟ cut, trim, crop, clip, shear, scythe.

mower *noun* a machine for cutting grass.

MOX *noun* a nuclear fuel made from uranium and plutonium oxides, and used in breeder reactors. [from *m*ixed *ox*ides]

moxa *noun* a pithy material, eg wormwood down, sunflower pith, or cotton wool, formed into a cone or stick and burned as a counter-irritant or for cauterization in oriental medicine. [from Japanese *mogusa*]

moxibustion *noun* the burning of moxa as a counter-irritant or for cauterization in oriental medicine. [from MOXA + COMBUSTION]

mozzarella /mɒtsəˈrelə/ *noun* a soft white Italian cheese, especially used as a topping for pizza. [Italian]

MP *abbrev.* 1 Member of Parliament. 2 military police; military police officer. 3 mounted police.

MP3 *noun Comput.* a digital compression format used to compress audio files, which can then be stored on disk, posted on the Internet, etc. [short for MPEG-1 layer 3]

MPEG *noun Comput.* an standard for encoding digital video and audio. [from *Moving Picture Experts Group*, the international body who produce the standards]

mpg *abbrev.* miles per gallon.

mph *abbrev.* miles per hour.

MPhil *abbrev.* Master of Philosophy.

MPV *abbrev.* multipurpose vehicle.

Mr *noun* (PL. **Messrs**) the standard title given to a man, used before his surname; a title given to a man who holds an official position: *Mr Jones/Mr Chairman.* [an abbreviation of MISTER]

MRC *abbrev.* Medical Research Council.

MRCP *abbrev.* Member of the Royal College of Physicians.

Mrs *noun* the standard title given to a married woman, used before her family name. [an abbreviation of MISTRESS]

MS *abbrev.* **1** (PL. **MSS**) manuscript. **2** Mississippi. **3** multiple sclerosis.

Ms *noun* the standard title given to a woman, married or not, used before her family name: *Ms Brown.*

MSc *abbrev.* Master of Science.

MSDOS *abbrev. trademark Comput.* a widely used disk-operating system developed by the Microsoft Corporation. It is the standard operating system for all IBM-compatible computers. [from *Microsoft disk-operating system*]

MSG *abbrev.* monosodium glutamate.

Msgr *abbrev.* Monsignor.

MSS *abbrev.* manuscripts.

MT *abbrev.* Montana.

Mt *abbrev.* Mount.

much — *adj.* (**more, most**) a great amount or quantity (of something). — *adv.* **1** by a great deal: *much prettier.* **2** to a great degree: *don't like her much.* — *pron.* a great amount or quantity of something. — **a bit much** *colloq.* very unreasonable. **make much of something** to treat as very important. **as much as ...** although: *I cannot come, as much as I would like to.* **not much of ...** *colloq.* not very good as: *not much of a singer.* **not up to much** *colloq.* of a poor standard. [from Middle English *muche*, from Anglo-Saxon *mycel*]

⊟ *adj.* ample, abundant, considerable, *colloq.* a lot of, *colloq.* lots of, great, substantial, copious, plentiful. *adv.* **1** greatly, considerably, *colloq.* a lot, frequently, often. *pron.* plenty, *colloq.* a lot, *colloq.* lots.

⊟ LITTLE.

muchness *noun* — **much of a muchness** *colloq.* very similar; more or less the same.

mucilage /'mjuːsɪlɪdʒ/ *noun* **1** *Bot.* any of a group of gum-like substances that become viscous and slimy when added to water, present in the cell walls of many aquatic plants, the seed coats of certain terrestrial species, and also secreted by plant roots. **2** a sticky substance used as an adhesive. [from Latin *mucilago*, mouldy juice]

mucilaginous /mjuːsɪ'lædʒɪnəs/ *adj.* like or characteristic of mucilage.

muck — *noun* **1** *colloq.* dirt. **2** animal dung; manure. **3** *derog. colloq.* anything disgusting, or of very poor quality. — *verb* **1** *trans., intrans.* (*usually* **muck out** *or* **muck something out**) to clear dung from a farm building. **2** to treat (soil) with manure. — **make a muck of something** *colloq.* to do it badly; to ruin or spoil it. **muck about** *or* **around** *colloq.* to behave foolishly. **muck someone about** *or* **around** to treat them without consideration; to try their patience. **muck something about** *or* **around** to interfere with or disarrange it. **muck in** *colloq.* to take a share of work or responsibilities. **muck something up** *colloq.* **1** to make it dirty. **2** to do it badly or wrongly; to ruin or spoil it. [from Middle English *muk*]

⊟ *noun* **1, 2** dirt, sludge. **1** mire, filth, mud, slime, scum, *colloq.* gunge. **2** dung, manure, sewage, ordure. **muck about** *or* **around** fool around, play, play around, play about, *colloq.* mess about. **muck someone about** *or* **around** inconvenience, upset, bother, trouble, *Brit.* lead a (merry) dance, *colloq.* lead up the garden path, send on a wild-goose chase, *colloq.* mess about, *colloq.* make life hell for. **muck something about** *or* **around** interfere with, tamper with, meddle with, handle, *colloq.* mess about with, disarrange, disorder, untidy, dishevel, mess up. **muck up 2** ruin, wreck, spoil, mess up, make a mess of, botch, bungle, *slang* cock up, *slang* screw up.

muck-rake *verb intrans.* to seek out and expose scandal.

muck-raker *noun* a person who muck-rakes.

muck-raking *noun colloq.* the practice of searching for and exposing scandal, especially about famous people.

mucky *adj.* (**muckier, muckiest**) *colloq.* **1** very dirty; like muck. **2** featuring explicit sex; pornographic: *mucky films.*

⊟ DIRTY, FILTHY. **1** grimy, slimy, scummy, *colloq.* gungy, *colloq.* grotty, grungy.

mucous *adj.* of, like, or producing mucus.

mucous membrane *Zool.* in vertebrates, the moist mucus-secreting lining of various internal cavities of the body, eg nasal passages, gut.

mucus *noun* the thick slimy substance that serves to protect and lubricate the surface of mucous membranes (such as those lining the nasal and other body cavities) and to trap bacteria and dust particles. It contains water, the protein mucin, white blood cells, and various salts. [from Latin *mucus*, from *mungere*, to wipe away]

mud *noun* **1** soft wet earth. **2** any semi-solid mixture resembling this. **3** *colloq.* insults; slanderous attacks: *throw mud at.* — **my, his,** etc **name is mud** *colloq.* I am, he is, etc disgraced or out of favour. [probably from Old German *mudde*]

⊟ **1** clay, mire, ooze, dirt, sludge, silt.

mudbath *noun* **1** a medical treatment in which the body is covered in (especially hot) mud rich in minerals. **2** *colloq.* any outdoor event taking place in muddy conditions.

muddiness *noun* a muddy state or condition.

muddle — *verb* (*also* **muddle something up**) **1** to put into a disordered or confused state. **2** to confuse the mind of; to confuse (different things) in the mind. — *noun* a state of disorder or mental confusion. — **muddle along** *colloq.* to manage or make progress haphazardly. **muddle through** *colloq.* to succeed by persevering in spite of difficulties. [perhaps from Old Dutch *moddelen*, to make muddy]

⊟ *verb* CONFUSE, MIX UP, DISORGANIZE. **1** disorder, mess up, jumble, scramble, tangle. **2** bewilder, bemuse, perplex. *noun* chaos, confusion, disorder, mess, mix-up, jumble, clutter, tangle.

muddled *adj.* confused.

⊟ confused, disorganized, disordered, jumbled, mixed-up, bewildered, bemused, perplexed, in a tangle, in a mess, all at sea, at sixes and sevens.

muddle-headed *adj.* not capable of clear thinking; confused.

muddy — *adj.* (**muddier, muddiest**) **1** covered with or containing mud. **2** *said of a colour, a liquid, etc* dull or cloudy. **3** *said of thoughts, etc* not clear; vague. — *verb* (**muddies, muddied**) to make muddy, especially unclear or difficult to understand.

. . . .

▣ *adj.* **1** dirty, foul, miry, mucky, marshy, boggy, swampy, quaggy, grimy. **2, 3** cloudy, indistinct, obscure, opaque, murky, hazy, blurred, fuzzy. **2** dull, drab. **3** vague, ambiguous. *verb* dirty, mess, smear, smudge, begrime, bespatter, besmirch, dull, tarnish, blur, stir up.
▣ *adj.* **1** clean. **2, 3** clear.

. . . .

mudflat *noun* (*often* **mudflats**) a relatively flat area of land, especially near an estuary or sheltered bay, that consists of an accumulation of fine silt or mud that is brought in by the tide.

mudguard *noun* a curved metal guard over the upper half of the wheel of a bicycle or motorcycle to keep rain or mud from splashing up.

mudhopper or **mudskipper** *noun* a distinct fish widespread in the Indo-Pacific, locally common on mudflats of estuaries and mangrove swamps, and living for much of the time out of the water.

mudpack *noun* a thick paste applied to the face as a skin cleanser.

mudpuppy *noun* (PL. **mudpuppies**) a salamander from N America that spends its entire life in water, is brownish-grey with feathery gills, and has limbs with four toes, and a deep narrow tail. It feeds on invertebrates and fish.

mudskipper see MUDHOPPER.

mud-slinger *noun* a person who makes slanderous allegations to discredit another.

mud-slinging *noun colloq.* the making of slanderous personal attacks.

mudstone *noun Geol.* a fine-grained sedimentary rock that is a hardened consolidated form of mud, composed of approximately equal amounts of clay and silt. Mudstone is brittle, and disintegrates in water.

muesli /'mjuːzlɪ/ *noun* a mixture of crushed grain, nuts and dried fruit, eaten with milk, especially for breakfast. [from Swiss German]

muezzin /muˈɛzɪn/ *noun* the Muslim official who calls worshippers to prayer, usually from a minaret. [from Arabic *muˈadhdhin*]

muff[1] *noun* a wide fur tube, carried usually by women, inside which the hands are placed, one at each end, for warmth. [probably from Dutch *mof*]

muff[2] *colloq.* — *verb* **1** *Sport* to miss (a catch); to perform (a stroke) awkwardly or unsuccessfully. **2** to miss (an opportunity, etc). — *noun* a failure, especially to hold a catch.

muffin *noun* a small round flat bread-like cake, usually eaten hot with butter.

muffle *verb* **1** to make quieter; to suppress (sound). **2** to prevent from saying something. **3** (*also* **muffle up**) to wrap, especially the head, in warm clothing as a protection against the cold. [from Old French *moufle*, thick glove]

. . . .

▣ **1, 2** silence. **1** deaden, dull, quieten, stifle, dampen. **2** muzzle, suppress, gag. **3** wrap (up), envelop, cloak, swathe, cover.
▣ **1** amplify.

. . . .

muffler *noun* a thick scarf.

mufti /'mʌftɪ/ *noun old use* civilian clothes when worn by people who usually wear a uniform. [from Arabic]

mug[1] *noun* **1** a drinking-cup with a handle, used without a saucer. **2** the amount a mug will hold.

. . . .

▣ CUP, BEAKER, POT, TANKARD.

. . . .

mug[2] *verb* (**mugged, mugging**) to attack and rob violently or under threat of violence.

. . . .

▣ set upon, attack, assault, waylay, steal from, rob, beat up, jump (on).

. . . .

mug[3] *noun colloq.* a face or mouth.

mug[4] *noun colloq.* an easily fooled person. — **a mug's game** a worthless or foolish activity.

mug[5] *verb trans., intrans.* (**mugged, mugging**) — **mug something up** or **mug up on something** *colloq.* to study or revise a subject thoroughly, especially for an examination.

. . . .

▣ revise, *colloq.* swot, *colloq.* bone up on, brush up (on).

. . . .

mugful *noun* (PL. **mugfuls**) the amount a mug will hold (see MUG[1]).

mugger *noun* a person who attacks and robs another.

. . . .

▣ robber, thief, pickpocket, thug.

. . . .

mugginess *noun* a muggy state or condition.

mugging *noun* a beating up; assault and robbery.

muggins *noun colloq.* a foolish person, especially used of oneself when taken advantage of by others. [from MUG[4]]

muggy *adj.* (**muggier, muggiest**) *said of the weather* unpleasantly warm and damp; close. [perhaps from Norse *mugga*, mist]

. . . .

▣ humid, sticky, stuffy, sultry, close, clammy, oppressive, sweltering, moist, damp.
▣ dry.

. . . .

mugshot *noun colloq.* a photograph of a criminal's face, taken for police records.

mugwump *noun* **1** someone who is politically aloof. **2** a great man; a boss. [from Algonkian *mugquomp*, a great chief]

Muharram /muˈhʌrʌm/ *noun* **1** the first month of the Muslim year. **2** among Shiite Muslims, a period of mourning for Hasan and Husain, grandsons of Muhammad, during the first ten days of the month, with processions in which the faithful beat their breasts or whip themselves and a fast on the ninth day. [from Arabic *muharram*, sacred]

Mujahadeen or **Majahidin** /muːdʒəhəˈdiːn/ *pl. noun* Muslim guerrillas who resisted the Soviet occupation of Afghanistan after the invasion (Dec 1979). [from Arabic, = holy warriors]

mulatto /mʊˈlatoʊ/ *noun* (PL. **mulattos, mulattoes**) *old use, now usually offensive* a person of mixed race, especially with one black and one white parent. [from Spanish *mulato*, young mule]

mulberry *noun* (PL. **mulberries**) **1** a deciduous tree of temperate regions, producing small purple edible berries. **2** such a berry. **3** a dark purple colour. [from Old German *mulberi*]

mulch — *noun* straw, compost, or any of various manmade substances laid on the soil around plants to retain moisture and prevent the growth of weeds. — *verb* to cover with mulch. [from obsolete *mulch*, soft]

mulct — *noun* a fine or penalty. — *verb* **1** to fine. **2** (**mulct someone of something**) to deprive them of it. **3** to swindle. [from Latin *mulcta*, fine]

mule[1] *noun* **1** the offspring of a male donkey and a female horse, used as a working animal in many countries. **2** a stubborn person. [from Latin *mulus* or *mula*]

mule[2] *noun* a shoe or slipper with no back part covering the heel. [from French]

muleteer *noun* a person who drives mules.

mulish *adj.* stubborn; obstinate.

mull[1] *verb* — **mull something over** to consider it carefully; to ponder on it. [perhaps from obsolete *mull*, grind to powder]

. . . .

▣ reflect on, think about, think over, ponder, contemplate, meditate, ruminate, chew over, consider, weigh up, study, examine, deliberate.

. . . .

mull² *verb* to spice, sweeten, and warm (wine or beer).

mull³ *noun Scot.* a headland or promontory: *the Mull of Kintyre.* [from Gaelic *maol*]

mullah /ˈmʊlə/ *noun* a Muslim scholar and adviser in Islamic religion and sacred law. [from Arabic *maula*]

mulled *adj., said of ale, wine, etc* sweetened and spiced.

mullet *noun* any of a family of thick-bodied edible marine fish. [from Latin *mullus*]

mulligatawny /mʌlɪgəˈtɔːnɪ/ *noun* a thick curry-flavoured meat soup, originally made in E India. [from Tamil *milagu-tannir*, pepper-water]

mullion *noun Archit.* a vertical bar or post separating the panes or casements of a window. [from Old French *moinel*]

mullioned *adj.* having mullions.

multi- *combining form* forming words meaning 'many': *multicoloured.* [from Latin *multus*, much]

multicellular *adj. Biol.* having or made up of many cells.

multicoloured *adj.* having many colours.

. . . .

◼ variegated, particoloured, colourful, motley, pied, piebald, dappled, brindled, spotted, striped.

. . . .

multicultural *adj.* relating to or involving the cultures of several peoples within a single community.

multifarious /mʌltɪˈfɛərɪəs/ *adj. formal* of many different kinds; very varied. [from Latin *multifarius*, manifold]

. . . .

◼ assorted, varied, mixed, miscellaneous, diverse, diversified, heterogeneous, motley.

. . . .

multiform *adj. formal* having many different forms or shapes.

multilateral *adj.* **1** involving or affecting several people, groups or nations. **2** many-sided.

multilateralism *noun Econ.* support for an economic trading system in which many countries are encouraged to trade with each other.

multilingual *adj.* written or expressed in, or able to speak, several different languages.

. . . .

◼ bilingual, polyglot.

. . . .

multimedia *adj. Comput., said of a computer system* able to present and manipulate data in a variety of forms, eg text, graphics, and sound, often simultaneously.

multimillionaire *noun* a person whose wealth is valued at several million pounds, dollars, etc.

multinational — *adj.* operating in several different countries. — *noun* a multinational business or organization.

multiparous /mʌlˈtɪpərəs/ *adj. Biol.* producing several young at one birth. [from Latin *multiparus*]

multiparty *adj., said of a state, etc* having a political system with more than one organized party.

multiple — *adj.* having, involving, or affecting many parts, especially of the same kind; many, especially more than several. — *noun* a number or expression for which a given number or expression is a factor, eg 24 is a multiple of 12. [from Latin *multiplus*]

. . . .

◼ *adj.* many, numerous, manifold, various, several, sundry, collective.

. . . .

multiple-choice *adj., said of a test or exam* for which the correct answer must be chosen from several possible answers provided.

multiple sclerosis (ABBREV. **MS**) an incurable disease of the central nervous system caused by degeneration of the myelin sheath that encloses the neurones (nerve cells) in the brain and spinal cord.

multiplex — *adj. formal* having very many parts; complex. — *noun* a large cinema building divided into several smaller cinemas. [from Latin *plicare*, to fold]

multiplicand *noun Maths.* a number to be multiplied by a second number, the *multiplier.* [from Latin *multiplicare*, to multiply]

multiplication *noun* **1** a mathematical operation in which one number is added to itself as many times as is indicated by a second number; the process of performing this operation. **2** the process of increasing in number.

multiplication sign the symbol ×, used between two numbers to indicate that they are to be multiplied.

multiplication table a table listing the products of multiplying pairs of numbers, especially all pairs from 1 to 12 inclusive.

multiplicity *noun* (PL. **multiplicities**) *formal* **1** a great number and variety. **2** the state of being many and various. [from Latin *multiplex*, of many kinds]

. . . .

◼ VARIETY, DIVERSITY. **1** number, multitude, assortment, mixture, medley.

. . . .

multiplier *noun Maths.* a number indicating by how many times another number, the *multiplicand,* to which it is attached by a multiplication sign, is to be multiplied.

multiply *verb* (**multiplies, multiplied**) **1** (**multiply one number by another**) to add a number to itself a given number of times; to combine two numbers in multiplication. **2** *intrans.* to increase in number, especially by breeding. [from Latin *multiplicare*, from *multi*, much + *plicare*, to fold]

. . . .

◼ **2** increase, proliferate, mushroom, expand, spread, reproduce, propagate, breed, accumulate, intensify, extend, build up, augment, boost.

▣ **1** divide. **2** decrease, lessen.

. . . .

multiprogramming *noun Comput.* the execution of two or more programs by a single central processing unit, usually achieved by carrying out several instructions from one program, and then rapidly switching to the next one.

multipurpose *adj.* having many uses.

. . . .

◼ versatile, adaptable, flexible, all-round, variable.

. . . .

multiracial *adj.* of, for, or including people of many different races.

multistorey — *adj., said of a building* having many floors. — *noun* (PL. **multistoreys**) *colloq.* a multistorey car-park.

multitasking *noun Comput.* the action of running several processes or jobs simultaneously on a system.

multitude *noun* **1** a great number. **2** a huge crowd of people. **3** (**the multitude**) ordinary people. [from Latin *multitudo*]

. . . .

◼ **1, 2** crowd, mass, host, horde, swarm, legion. **1** lot, *colloq.* lots. **2** throng, mob, herd, congregation. **3** the public, the people, the populace, the crowd, the mob, the (common) herd.

▣ **2** few, scattering.

. . . .

multitudinous *adj.* very numerous.

multiuser *adj. Comput.* consisting of several terminals linked to a central computer, allowing access by several users at the same time.

multi-vision *noun Telecomm.* a technique of audio-visual presentation in which groups of slide projectors are programmed to show a complex sequence of images on a wide screen with accompanying sound from tape recordings.

mum¹ *noun* a mother; a term used to address one's own mother. [a child's word, derived from a baby's babbling]

mum[2] *adj. colloq.* silent; not speaking. — **mum's the word!** *colloq.* an exhortation to secrecy. [a sound produced with closed lips]

mumble — *verb trans., intrans.* to speak unclearly, especially with the mouth partly closed. — *noun* the sound of unclear or hushed speech. [from Middle English *momelen*, from MUM[2]]

⊟ *verb, noun* mutter, murmur, grumble, babble.

mumbo-jumbo *noun* (PL. **mumbo-jumbos**) *derog. colloq.* **1** foolish talk, especially of a religious or spiritual kind. **2** baffling jargon. **3** something, eg a statue, foolishly treated as an object of worship. [from Malinke (a W African language) *Mama Dyanbo*, a tribal god]

⊟ **1, 2** *colloq.* double Dutch. **1** gibberish, nonsense, *colloq.* hocus-pocus. **2** jargon, argot, *colloq.* psychobabble, *colloq.* computerspeak, gobbledygook.

mummer *noun* **1** *Hist.* an actor in a traditional mimed folk play, usually performed at Christmas. **2** a disguised child taking part in traditional merrymaking during religious festivals, especially Hallowe'en; a guiser. [from Old French *momer*, to mime]

mummery *noun* (PL. **mummeries**) **1** a performance of mumming. **2** *derog.* ridiculous or pretentious ceremony.

mummification *noun* **1** the process of mummifying. **2** being mummified.

mummify *verb* (**mummifies, mummified**) to preserve (a corpse) as a mummy.

mumming *noun* the activity of a mummer.

mummy[1] *noun* (PL. **mummies**) a child's word for mother. [a variant of MUM[1]]

mummy[2] *noun* (PL. **mummies**) a human or animal corpse preserved with spices and bandaged, especially in preparation for burial in ancient Egypt. [from Arabic and Persian *mumiya*, from Persian *mum*, wax]

mumps *noun* (*also* **the mumps**) an infectious viral disease, mainly affecting children, that causes fever, headache, and painful swelling of the salivary glands on one or both sides of the cheeks, and under the jaw. [from archaic *mump*, to grimace]

munch *verb trans., intrans.* to chew with a steady movement of the jaws, especially noisily. [probably imitative]

⊟ eat, chew, crunch, *formal* masticate.

munchies *pl. noun colloq.* **1** (**the munchies**) an alcohol- or drug-induced craving for food. **2** food to snack on; nibbles. [from MUNCH]

mundane *adj.* **1** ordinary; dull; everyday. **2** of this world, not some other spiritual world. [from Latin *mundus*, world]

⊟ **1** banal, ordinary, everyday, commonplace, prosaic, humdrum, workaday, routine. **2** secular, worldly.

⊟ **1** extraordinary. **2** spiritual.

mung bean 1 an E Asian plant producing an edible green or yellow bean, the source of beansprouts. **2** a bean from this plant. [from Hindi *mung*]

municipal *adj.* of, relating to, or controlled by the local government of a town or region. [from Latin *municipium*, free town]

⊟ civic, city, town, urban, borough, community, public.

municipality *noun* (PL. **municipalities**) a town or region having its own local government; the local government itself.

munificence *noun* magnificent generosity.

munificent *adj. formal* extremely generous. [from Latin *munus*, gift + *facere*, to make]

muniments /ˈmjuːnɪmənts/ *pl. noun Legal* official papers proving ownership, especially title deeds to property. [from Latin *munimentum*, title deed]

munitions *pl. noun* military equipment, especially ammunition and weapons. [from Latin *munire*, to defend or fortify]

muntin or **munting** *noun Archit.* a vertical framing piece separating the panels of a door. [from French *montant*, from *monter*, to rise]

muntjac or **muntjak** /ˈmʌntdʒak/ *noun* a true deer, native to India and SE Asia, and having a face with a V-shaped ridge, the arms of the 'V' being continued as freely projecting bony columns, the ends of the columns in the male bearing short antlers. [from a Malay name]

muon /ˈmjuːɒn/ *noun Physics* an elementary particle that behaves like a heavy electron, but decays to form an electron and neutrinos. [from Greek *mu*, the letter]

mural — *noun* a painting painted directly on to a wall. — *adj. formal* of or relating to a wall or walls. [from Latin *murus*, wall]

muralist *noun* a painter of murals.

murder — *noun* **1** the act of unlawfully and intentionally killing a person. **2** *colloq.* something, or a situation, which causes hardship or difficulty: *the traffic in town was murder.* — *verb* (**murdered, murdering**) **1** *trans., intrans.* to kill unlawfully and intentionally. **2** *colloq.* to spoil or ruin (eg a piece of music, by performing it very badly). **3** *colloq.* to defeat easily and by a huge margin. — **get away with murder** *colloq.* to behave very badly or dishonestly and not be caught or punished. **scream** or **shout** or **cry blue murder** *colloq.* to protest loudly or angrily. [from Anglo-Saxon *morthor*, from *morth*, death]

⊟ *noun* **1** killing, manslaughter, homicide, slaying, assassination, massacre, bloodshed. *verb* **1** kill, slay. **2, 3** massacre. **2** butcher. **3** *colloq.* slaughter, rout, trounce, thrash, *colloq.* whop, *slang* wipe the floor with, *North Amer. slang* cream.

murderer *noun* a person who has intentionally killed another unlawfully.

⊟ killer, homicide, slayer, slaughterer, assassin, butcher, cutthroat.

murderess *noun old use* a female murderer.

murderous *adj.* intending, intended for, or capable of murder.

⊟ homicidal, brutal, barbarous, bloodthirsty, bloody, cut-throat, killing, lethal, cruel, savage, ferocious, deadly.

murk *noun literary* darkness. [from Anglo-Saxon *mirce*]

murkiness *noun* a murky state or quality.

murky *adj.* (**murkier, murkiest**) **1** dark; gloomy. **2** *said of water* dark and dirty. **3** suspiciously vague or unknown; shady: *her murky past.*

⊟ DARK. **1** dismal, gloomy, dull, overcast, misty, foggy, dim, cloudy, obscure, veiled, grey. **3** mysterious, suspicious, shady.

⊟ **1, 2** bright, clear.

murmur — *noun* **1** a quiet continuous sound, eg of running water or low voices. **2** anything said in a low, indistinct voice. **3** a complaint. **4** *Medicine* an abnormal rustling sound made by the heart, usually indicating the presence of disease. — *verb* (**murmured, murmuring**) **1** *trans., intrans.* to speak (words) softly and indistinctly. **2** *intrans.* to complain or grumble. [from Latin *murmurare*]

🔳 *noun* **1, 2** mumble, whisper, grumble. **1** undertone, muttering, humming, rumble, drone. *verb* **1** mutter, mumble, whisper, buzz, hum, rumble, purr, burble.

murmurous *adj.* making murmurs.

Murphy's Law same as SOD'S LAW.

murrain /ˈmarɪn/ *noun* any infectious cattle disease, especially foot-and-mouth disease. [from Old French *morine*, pestilence]

mus. *abbrev.* music.

MusB or **MusBac** *abbrev. Musicae Baccalaureus* (Latin), Bachelor of Music.

Musca *noun Astron.* the Fly, a small constellation in the southern hemisphere.

Muscadet /ˈmʌskədeɪ/ *noun* a white wine from the Loire region of France; the grape variety from which it is produced.

muscat /ˈmʌskat/ *noun* **1** a variety of white grape with a musky smell. **2** muscatel. [from Provençal]

muscatel /ˈmʌskəˈtel/ or **muscat** or **muscadel** *noun* a sweet white wine made from muscat grapes.

muscle *noun* **1** an animal tissue composed of bundles of fibres that are capable of contracting (shortening) and so producing movement of different parts of the body. **2** a body structure composed of this tissue, eg biceps. **3** bodily strength. **4** power or influence of any kind: *financial muscle*. — **muscle in on something** *colloq.* to force one's way into it; to grab a share of it. [from Latin *musculus*]

muscle-bound *adj.* having over-enlarged muscles that are stiff and difficult to move.

muscleman *noun* a man with very big muscles, especially one employed to intimidate others.

Muscovite — *noun* a native or citizen of Moscow. — *adj.* relating to Moscow. [from *Muscovy*, an old name for Russia]

muscovite *noun Geol.* any of a group of colourless, silvery-grey, or pale brown mineral forms of potassium aluminosilicate, used principally as an insulator.

muscular *adj.* **1** of, relating to, or consisting of muscle. **2** having well-developed muscles; strong.

🔳 **2** brawny, *colloq.* beefy, sinewy, athletic, powerfully built, strapping, hefty, powerful, husky, robust, stalwart, vigorous, strong.
🔳 **2** puny, flabby, weak.

muscular dystrophy any of various forms of a hereditary disease in which there is progressive wasting of certain muscles, which are eventually replaced by fatty tissue.

muscularity *noun* a muscular state or condition.

musculature *noun* the arrangement, or degree of development, of muscles in a body or organ.

MusD or **MusDoc** *abbrev. Musicae Doctor* (Latin), Doctor of Music.

Muse *noun* any of the nine mythical Greek goddesses of the arts, said to be a source of creative inspiration to all artists, especially poets. [from Greek *Mousa*]

muse *verb* **1** *intrans.* to reflect or ponder on something. **2** *trans.* to say in a reflective way. [from Old French *muser*]

museum *noun* a place where objects of artistic, scientific or historic interest are displayed to the public. [from Greek *mouseion*, temple of the Muses]

museum-piece *noun* **1** any article displayed in a museum. **2** *humorous colloq.* any very old or old-fashioned person or thing.

mush[1] *noun* **1** a soft half-liquid mass of anything. **2** *derog. colloq.* sloppy sentimentality. [probably a variant of MASH]

mush[2] — *interj., used especially to a team of dogs* go on!; go faster! — *verb intrans. North Amer., esp. US* to travel on a sledge pulled by dogs. [probably from French *marcher*, to walk]

mushroom — *noun* **1** any of various fungi that produce a fruiting body consisting of a pale fleshy umbrella-shaped cap, on the underside of which are numerous brown or pinkish spore-bearing gills, supported by a short white stem. See also TOADSTOOL. **2** anything resembling this in shape or in speed of growth or development. — *verb intrans.* to develop or increase with alarming speed. [from Old French *mousseron*, perhaps from *mousse*, moss]

🔳 *verb* develop, increase, multiply, proliferate, expand, spread, reproduce, propagate, accumulate.

mushroom-cloud *noun* a huge mushroom-shaped cloud of radioactive dust produced by a nuclear explosion.

mushy *adj.* (**mushier, mushiest**) **1** in a soft half-liquid state. **2** sentimental in a sickly way.

music *noun* **1** the art of making sound in a rhythmically organized harmonious form, either sung or produced with instruments and usually communicating some idea or emotion. **2** such sound, especially produced by instruments rather than voices. **3** any written form in which such sound is expressed. — **face the music** *colloq.* to confront one's critics; to deal with the consequences of one's actions. — **music to one's ears** anything one is glad to hear. [from Greek *mousike*, of the Muses]

musical — *adj.* **1** of or producing music. **2** pleasant to hear; melodious. **3** having a talent for playing music. — *noun* a play or film featuring much singing and dancing.

🔳 *adj.* tuneful, melodious, melodic, harmonious, dulcet, sweet-sounding, lyrical.
🔳 *adj.* discordant, unmusical.

Musical instruments include: balalaika, banjo, cello, double-bass, guitar, harp, hurdy-gurdy, lute, lyre, mandolin, sitar, spinet, ukulele, viola, violin, *colloq.* fiddle, zither; accordion, concertina, *colloq.* squeeze-box, clavichord, harmonium, harpsichord, keyboard, melodeon, organ, *trademark* Wurlitzer, piano, grand piano, *trademark* Pianola, player-piano, synthesizer, virginals; bagpipes, bassoon, bugle, clarinet, cor anglais, cornet, didgeridoo, euphonium, fife, flugelhorn, flute, French horn, harmonica, horn, kazoo, mouth-organ, oboe, Pan-pipes, piccolo, recorder, saxophone, sousaphone, trombone, trumpet, tuba; castanets, cymbal, glockenspiel, maracas, marimba, tambourine, triangle, tubular bells, xylophone; bass-drum, bongo, kettle-drum, snare-drum, tenor-drum, timpani, tom-tom.

musical chairs a game in which players walk round a number of chairs while music is playing and rush to sit on the chairs when the music stops, those unable to find an empty chair being eliminated and the number of chairs available being reduced in each round until only one remains.

musical comedy a form of light entertainment derived from burlesque and light opera which became popular in the UK and the USA from the 1890s.

musicality *noun* a musical quality.

musically *adv.* in a musical way; as regards music.

music box or **musical box** a small box containing a device that plays music when the box is opened.

music centre a hi-fi unit incorporating an amplifier, radio, record-player, CD-player, and cassette recorder.

music hall **1** theatre entertainment including singers, dancers, and comedians. **2** a theatre in which such entertainment can be seen.

musician *noun* a person skilled in performing or composing music.

Musicians include: instrumentalist, accompanist, performer, player; bugler, busker, cellist, clarinettist, drummer, flautist, fiddler, guitarist, harpist, oboist, organist, pianist, piper, soloist, trombonist, trumpeter, violinist; singer, vocalist, balladeer, diva, prima donna; conductor, maestro; band, orchestra, group, backing group, ensemble, chamber orchestra, choir, duo, duet, trio, quartet, quintet, sextet, octet, nonet.

musicianship *noun* skill in music.

musicologist *noun* an academic expert in music.

musicology *noun* the academic study of music in all its aspects.

music therapy *Psychol.* the use of music in the treatment, education, etc, of people with physical or mental disabilities, also sometimes used as an aid to recovery from mental disorders.

musings *pl. noun literary* thoughts.

musique concrète /muːziːk kɒŋkret/ a type of mid-20c music made up of recorded sounds (not necessarily musical) from various sources, which were mixed, distorted, and manipulated on tape by the composer.

musk *noun* **1** a strong-smelling substance secreted by the glands of various animals, especially the male musk deer, much used in perfumes; any similar synthetic substance. **2** the smell of such substances. [from Latin *muscus*]

musk deer a small hornless central Asian mountain deer.

musket *noun* an early rifle-like gun loaded through the barrel and fired from the shoulder, used by soldiers between the 16th and 18th centuries. [from Old French *mousquet*]

musketeer *noun* a soldier armed with a musket.

musketry *noun* **1** muskets. **2** the use of or skill in using muskets etc. **3** a fusillade of muskets. **4** a body of troops armed with muskets.

muskiness *noun* a musky quality or condition.

musk ox a long-haired ox of Canada and Greenland, whose breath has a musky smell.

muskrat *noun* **1** a large N American water rodent. **2** its highly prized thick brown fur, used to make clothes.

musk rose a Mediterranean rambling rose whose flowers have a musky scent.

musky *adj.* (**muskier, muskiest**) of, or like the smell of, musk.

Muslim /ˈmʊzlɪm, ˈmʌzlɪm/ or **Moslem** /ˈmɒzləm, ˈmɒzləm/ — *noun* a follower of the religion of Islam. — *adj.* relating to Muslims or to Islam. [from Arabic *muslim*, one who submits]

muslin *noun* a fine cotton cloth with a gauze-like appearance. [from French *mousseline*]

musquash /ˈmʌskwɒʃ/ *noun* same as MUSKRAT. [from Algonkian (a Native American language group)]

muss *verb chiefly North Amer. colloq.* (*usually* **muss something up**) to make (something, especially clothes or hair) untidy; to ruffle.

mussel *noun* any of various species of bivalve mollusc, especially the common or edible mussel, often found in dense beds several miles long on temperate and subtropical coasts. Freshwater mussels are a source of mother-of-pearl. [from Latin *musculus*, diminutive of *mus*, mouse]

must[1] — *verb, aux.* expressing **1** need: *I must earn some extra money.* **2** duty or obligation: *you must help him.* **3** certainty: *you must be Charles.* **4** determination: *I must remember.* **5** probability: *she must be there by now.* **6** inevitability: *we must all die some time.* — *noun* something essential: *fitness is a must in professional sport.* [from Anglo-Saxon *moste*]

must[2] *noun* the juice of grapes or other fruit before it is fermented to become wine. [from Latin *mustum vinum*, new wine]

mustachio /mʊˈstɑːʃɪəʊ/ *noun* (PL. **mustachios**) an elaborately curly moustache. [from Italian *mostaccio*]

mustachioed /mʊˈstɑːʃɪəʊd/ *adj.* having a mustachio.

mustang *noun* a small wild horse native to the plains of the western US. [from Spanish *mestengo*]

mustard *noun* **1** any of several annual plants of the cabbage family, native to Europe and W Asia, that have bright yellow flowers, especially white mustard (*Sinapis alba*), which produces white seeds, and whose seedlings are eaten as a salad vegetable, and black mustard (*Sinapis nigra*), which produces black seeds. **2** a hot-tasting paste, used as a condiment or seasoning, prepared by grinding the seeds of black and/or white mustard to a powder, or crushing whole seeds, and mixing them with water or vinegar. **3** a light yellow or brown colour. — **as keen as mustard** *colloq.* extremely keen or enthusiastic. [from Old French *moustarde*]

mustard and cress a mixture of the seedlings of the mustard plant and cress, used as a salad vegetable.

mustard gas a highly poisonous gas that causes severe blistering of the skin, widely used as a chemical warfare agent in World War I.

muster — *verb* **1** *trans., intrans.* to gather (especially soldiers) together, for duty or inspection. **2** (*also* **muster something up**) to summon or gather (eg courage or energy). — *noun* any assembly or gathering, especially of troops for duty or inspection. — **pass muster** to be accepted as satisfactory. [from Latin *monstrare*, to show]

▪ *verb* **1** assemble, convene, gather, get together, mobilize, congregate, collect, group, rally, mass, enrol. **2** summon (up), call up (on), rouse, collect. *noun* assembly, gathering, round-up, convention, congregation, collection, group, parade, review, rally, march past.

mustiness *noun* a musty quality or condition.

mustn't *contr.* must not.

musty *adj.* (**mustier, mustiest**) **1** mouldy or damp. **2** smelling or tasting stale. [perhaps from obsolete *moisty*, moist]

▪ MOULDY, STALE, SMELLY. **1** mildewy, stuffy, fusty, dank, airless, decayed.

mutability *noun* the ability or tendency to change.

mutable *adj.* subject to change; variable. [see MUTATE]

▪ changeable, changing, variable, adaptable, unstable, inconstant, passing.

mutagen /ˈmjuːtədʒən/ *noun Biol.* a chemical or physical agent that induces or increases the frequency of mutations in living organisms, either by altering the DNA of the genes, or by damaging the chromosomes, eg X-rays, ultraviolet radiation, colchicine and other chemicals.

mutant — *noun* a living organism or cell that carries a specific mutation (alteration) of a gene which usually causes it to differ from previous generations with regard to a particular characteristic, especially a visible one. — *adj.* denoting an organism or cell carrying a mutation. [from Latin *mutare*, to change]

mutate *verb trans., intrans.* **1** *Biol.* to undergo or cause to undergo mutation. **2** *formal* to change.

mutation *noun* **1** *Genetics* in a living organism, a sudden change in the structure of a single gene, the arrangement of genes on a chromosome, or the number of chromosomes. It may result in a change in the appearance (phenotype) or behaviour of the organism. **2** *formal* a change of any kind. **3** *Linguistics* a change in a speech sound, especially a vowel, because of the nature of the sound next to it. [from Latin *mutatio*, from *mutare*, to change]

▪ **2** change, alteration, variation, modification, transformation, deviation, anomaly, evolution.

mutatis mutandis /mjuːˈteɪtɪs mjuːˈtandɪs/ allowing for respective differences of detail; with necessary adjustments made. [Latin, = having changed what needs to be changed]

mute — *adj.* **1** *said of a person* physically or psychologically unable to speak; dumb. **2** silent. **3** felt, but not expressed in words: *mute anger*. **4** *said of a letter in a word* not sounded. — *noun* **1** a person who is physically unable to speak, eg as a result of deafness since birth, or brain damage; also, a person who refuses to speak, eg as a result of psychological trauma. **2** any of various devices that soften or deaden the sound of a musical instrument. **3** an unsounded letter in a word. — *verb* to soften or deaden the sound of (a musical instrument). [from Latin *mutus*]

⊟ *adj.* **1**, **2** dumb. **2** silent, *colloq.* mum, speechless, noiseless, voiceless, wordless. **3** unspoken, unexpressed. **4** unvoiced, voiceless, unpronounced. *verb* tone down, subdue, muffle, lower, moderate, dampen, deaden, soften, soft-pedal, silence.
⊟ *adj.* **2** vocal, talkative.

muted *adj.* **1** *said of sound or colour* not loud or harsh; soft. **2** *said of feelings, etc* mildly expressed; not outspoken: *muted criticism.*

⊟ SUBDUED, GENTLE, MILD. **1** soft, muffled, subtle, pastel.

mute swan the commonest European swan.

mutilate *verb* **1** to cause severe injury to, especially by removing a limb or organ. **2** to severely damage, especially to alter (a text) beyond recognition. [from Latin *mutilare*, to cut off]

⊟ MANGLE, CUT TO PIECES, BUTCHER. **1** maim, injure, dismember, disable, disfigure, lame, cut up. **2** spoil, mar, damage, cut, censor.

mutilation *noun* **1** severe physical injury usually visible and permanent. **2** severe damage.

mutineer *noun* a person who mutinies.

⊟ rebel, insurgent, insurrectionist, revolutionary, rioter, subversive.

mutinous *adj.* **1** having mutinied; likely to mutiny. **2** of or relating to mutiny.

⊟ **1** rebellious, insurgent, insubordinate, disobedient, seditious, revolutionary, riotous, subversive, *slang* bolshie, unruly.
⊟ **1** obedient, compliant.

mutiny — *noun* (PL. **mutinies**) rebellion, or an act of rebellion, against established authority, especially in the armed services. — *verb intrans.* (**mutinies, mutinied**) to engage in mutiny. [from Old French *mutin*, rebellious]

⊟ *noun* rebellion, insurrection, revolt, revolution, rising, uprising, insubordination, disobedience, defiance, resistance, riot, strike. *verb* rebel, revolt, rise up, resist, protest, disobey, strike.

mutt *noun colloq.* **1** a dog, especially a mongrel. **2** a foolish person. [perhaps from MUTTONHEAD]

mutter — *verb* (**muttered, muttering**) **1** *trans., intrans.* to utter (words) in a quiet, barely audible voice. **2** *intrans.* to grumble or complain. — *noun* **1** a soft, barely audible tone of voice. **2** a complaint. [from Middle English *moteren*]

⊟ *verb* **1** mumble, murmur, rumble. **2** complain, grumble, *colloq.* grouse, *colloq.* beef.

mutton *noun* the flesh of an adult sheep, used as food. — **mutton dressed as lamb** *derog. colloq.* an older person, especially a woman, dressed (especially unbecomingly) in youthful clothes. [from Old French *moton*, sheep]

muttonhead *noun derog. colloq.* a stupid person.

mutual *adj.* **1** felt by each of two or more people about the other or others; reciprocal: *mutual admiration.* **2** of, to or towards each other: *mutual supporters.* **3** *colloq.* shared by each of two or more; common: *a mutual friend.* **4** *said of a building society or other financial institution* owned by its customers. [from Latin *mutuus*, borrowed or reciprocal]

⊟ **1** reciprocal, complementary, interchangeable, interchanged, exchanged. **3** shared, common, joint.

mutual fund an investment company that pools the funds of its shareholders, and invests in a diversified portfolio of stocks and shares. It grows continually by offering new shares for sale. A UK example is the unit trust company.

mutualism *noun Biol.* a relationship between two organisms of different species, that is beneficial to both of them.

mutuality *noun* a mutual state or condition.

mutually *adv.* **1** with mutual action or feeling, reciprocally. **2** jointly.

Muzak /ˈmjuːzak/ *noun trademark* light recorded music continuously played in restaurants, shops, lifts, etc; also, the system on which it is played.

muzzily *adv.* in a muzzy way.

muzziness *noun* a muzzy quality or condition.

muzzle — *noun* **1** the projecting jaws and nose of an animal, eg a dog. **2** an arrangement of straps fitted round an animal's jaws to prevent it biting. **3** the open end of a gun barrel. — *verb* **1** to put a muzzle on (eg a dog). **2** to prevent from speaking; to silence or gag. [from Old French *musel*]

⊟ *verb* **2** gag, silence, censor, restrain, stifle, suppress, choke, mute.

muzzy *adj.* (**muzzier, muzziest**) **1** not thinking clearly; confused. **2** blurred.

⊟ HAZY, VAGUE. **1** confused, fuddled, muddled, bewildered, at a loss, at sea. **2** blurred, fuzzy, cloudy, dim.

MW *abbrev.* **1** medium wave. **2** megawatt.

my — *adj.* **1** of or belonging to me. **2** used with nouns in various exclamations: *my goodness!/my foot!* — *interj.* expressing surprise: *my, how grown-up you look!* [from Anglo-Saxon *min*]

myalgia *noun Medicine* pain in the muscles. [from Greek *mys*, muscle + *algos*, pain]

myalgic encephalomyelitis /maɪˈaldʒɪk ɛnsɛfəloʊmaɪ-əˈlaɪtɪs/ (ABBREV. **ME**) a debilitating disorder characterized by extreme fatigue, muscular pain, lack of concentration, memory loss, and depression. Also called CHRONIC FATIGUE SYNDROME.

mycelium *noun* (PL. **mycelia**) *Biol.* in multicellular fungi, a mass or network of threadlike filaments (known as hyphae) that is formed as a result of the growth of the nonreproductive tissues. [from Greek *mykes*, mushroom]

Mycenaean /maɪsəˈnɪən/ — *adj.* relating to the ancient Bronze Age civilization in Greece (1500–1100BC), known from the Homeric poems and from remains at Mycenae and other sites in S Greece. — *noun* an inhabitant of the Mycenaean world.

mycology *noun Biol.* the study of fungi. [from Greek *mykes*, mushroom + -LOGY]

mycotoxin *noun Biol.* any poisonous substance produced by a fungus.

myelin /ˈmaɪɪlɪn/ *noun Zool.* a soft white substance that forms a thin insulating sheath around the axons (long threadlike outgrowths) of the nerve cells of vertebrates. [from Greek *mylos*, marrow]

myelitis /maɪəˈlaɪtɪs/ *noun* **1** inflammation of the spinal cord, most commonly associated with multiple sclerosis, which results in paralysis of the body below the affected region. **2** inflammation of the bone marrow, characterized by severe pain and swelling, which if untreated may result in bone deformity. Also called OSTEOMYELITIS. [from Greek *myelos*, marrow]

myeloma /maɪəˈloʊmə/ *noun Medicine* a tumour of the bone marrow, caused by the proliferation of malignant plasma cells. [from Greek *myelos*, marrow]

mylonite *noun Geol.* a dark fine-grained hard metamorphic rock, often banded or streaked and having a glassy appearance, formed as a result of recrystallization of mineral fragments after crushing and grinding. [from Greek *mylon*, mill]

myna or **mynah** /ˈmaɪnə/ *noun* any of various large SE Asian birds of the starling family, some of which can be taught to imitate human speech. [from Hindi *maina*]

myocardial or **myocardiac** *adj.* relating to or in the region of the myocardium.

myocarditis *noun Medicine* inflammation of the heart muscle (the myocardium).

myocardium *noun* (PL. **myocardia**) *Anat.* the muscular tissue of the heart. [from Greek *myos*, muscle + *kardia*, heart]

myofibril *noun Zool.* any of the minute filaments which together make up a single muscle fibre. [from Greek *myos*, muscle + FIBRIL]

myoglobin *noun Biochem.* a protein that stores oxygen in the muscles of vertebrates. [from Greek *mys myos*, muscle]

myopia *noun Medicine* short-sightedness, in which parallel rays of light entering the eye are brought to a focus in front of the retina, so that distant objects appear blurred. [from Greek *myops*, short-sighted]

myopic /maɪˈɒpɪk/ *adj.* short-sighted.

myriad *noun, adj.* denoting an exceedingly great number: *a myriad of stars*/*her myriad admirers.* [from Greek *myrias*, ten thousand]

Myrmidon *noun* in Greek legend, a member of a band of warriors from Thessaly who went to the Trojan War with Achilles.

myrmidon /ˈmɜːmɪdən/ *noun literary* **1** a hired thug; a henchman. **2** a follower. [named after the Myrmidons of Greek legend]

myrrh /mɜː(r)/ *noun* **1** any of various African and Asian trees and shrubs producing a brown aromatic resin, used medicinally and in perfumes. **2** the resin produced by these. [from Greek *myrra*]

myrtle *noun* a S European evergreen shrub with pink or white flowers and dark blue aromatic berries; any of various related shrubs. [from Greek *myrtos*]

myself *pron.* **1** the form of *me* used when the speaker or writer is the object of an action he or she performs: *I did myself a favour*/*I said to myself.* **2** used to emphasize *I* or *me*: *I myself prefer tea.* **3** my normal self: *am not myself today.* **4** (*also* **by myself**) alone; without help.

mysterious *adj.* **1** difficult or impossible to understand or explain; deeply curious. **2** creating or suggesting mystery.

▦ ENIGMATIC, CRYPTIC. **1** inexplicable, incomprehensible, unfathomable, unsearchable, puzzling, perplexing, mystifying, baffling, insoluble, curious. **2** obscure, strange, mystical, hidden, secret, weird, secretive, veiled, dark, furtive.

▣ STRAIGHTFORWARD. **1** comprehensible.

mystery *noun* (PL. **mysteries**) **1** an event or phenomenon that cannot be, or has not been, explained. **2** the quality of being difficult or impossible to explain or understand, or of being odd or obscure and arousing curiosity. **3** a person about whom very little is known. **4** a story about a crime that is difficult to solve. **5** a religious rite, especially the Eucharist. [from Greek *mysterion*]

▦ **1** enigma, puzzle, secret, riddle, conundrum, question. **2** obscurity, secrecy, ambiguity.

mystery play a medieval play based on the life of Christ, or of a saint.

mystery religion a cult of the Graeco-Roman world, admission to which was restricted to those who had undertaken secret initiation rites or mysteries.

mystery tour a round trip to a destination not revealed in advance.

mystic — *noun* a person whose life is devoted to meditation or prayer in an attempt to achieve direct communication with God, regarded as the ultimate reality. — *adj.* mystical. [from Greek *mystikos*, from *mystes*, an initiate]

mystical *adj.* **1** relating to or involving truths about the nature of God and reality revealed only to those people with a spiritually enlightened mind; esoteric. **2** mysterious. **3** wonderful or awe-inspiring.

▦ **1** esoteric, supernatural, paranormal, transcendental, metaphysical. **2** mysterious, hidden, mystic, arcane, occult.

mysticism *noun* the practice of gaining direct communication with God through prayer and meditation; the belief in the existence of such a state as a reality hidden from ordinary human understanding.

mystification *noun* **1** the act of mystifying. **2** being mystified.

mystify *verb* (**mystifies, mystified**) **1** to puzzle or bewilder. **2** to make mysterious. [from French *mystifier*]

▦ **1** puzzle, bewilder, baffle, perplex, confound, confuse.

mystifying *adj.* puzzling, bewildering.

mystique *noun* a mysterious quality possessed by a person or thing. [from French]

myth *noun* **1** an ancient story dealing with gods and heroes, especially one explaining some natural phenomenon; such stories in general. **2** a commonly held false notion. **3** a non-existent person or thing. [from Greek *mythos*]

▦ **1, 2** fable, fairy tale. **1** legend, allegory, parable, saga, story, tradition. **2, 3** fiction, fancy, fantasy, superstition.

mythical *adj.* **1** relating to myth. **2** imaginary.

▦ **1** mythological, legendary, fabled, fairytale. **2** fictitious, imaginary, made-up, invented, make-believe, non-existent, unreal, pretended, fanciful.

▣ **1** historical. **2** actual, real.

mythological *adj.* relating or belonging to mythology.

▦ legendary, mythic, fabled, fairytale, folk.

mythology *noun* (PL. **mythologies**) **1** myths in general. **2** a collection of myths.

▦ **1** legend, myths, lore, tradition(s), folklore, folk tales, tales.

myxomatosis *noun Biol.* an infectious viral disease of rabbits that is usually fatal and is transmitted by fleas. [Greek *myxa*, mucus]

N

N¹ or **n** *noun* (PL. **Ns, N's, n's**) the fourteenth letter of the English alphabet.

N² *abbrev.* **1** National or Nationalist. **2** newton. **3** New. **4** North or Northern.

N³ *symbol* **1** *Chem.* nitrogen. **2** *Chess* knight. **3** *as an international vehicle mark* Norway.

n¹ — *noun* **1** *Maths.* an indefinite number. **2** *colloq.* a large number. — *adj.* of an indefinite or large number.

n² *abbrev.* **1** noun. **2** neuter. **3** note. **4** nano-. **5** neutron.

'n' *colloq. abbrev.* and.

NA *abbrev.*, *as an international vehicle mark* Netherlands Antilles.

Na *symbol Chem.* sodium. [from Latin *natrium*]

NAACP *abbrev.* in the USA, the National Association for the Advancement of Colored People, a pressure group which aims to extend awareness among the country's black population of their political rights.

NAAFI — *abbrev.* Navy, Army and Air Force Institutes. — *noun* a canteen or shop run by the NAAFI.

nab *verb trans.* (**nabbed, nabbing**) *colloq.* **1** to catch in the act of doing wrong. **2** to arrest. **3** to grab or take.

⊟ CATCH. **1** catch out, trap. **2, 3** *colloq.* collar, *slang* nick. **2** arrest, capture. **3** bag, net.

nabob / 'neɪbɒb/ *noun* **1** *colloq.* a wealthy and influential person. **2** *old use* a European returned from India with a vast fortune. **3** *Hist.* a Muslim governor under the Mogul empire in India; a nawab. [from Urdu *nawwab*]

nacelle / nə'sel/ *noun Aeron.* **1** the streamlined outer casing of an aircraft engine. **2** the basket or gondola of a balloon or airship. [from French *nacelle*, from late Latin *navicella*, from Latin *navis*, ship]

nachos / 'natʃəʊz/ *pl. noun* a Mexican dish of tortilla chips topped with chillis and melted cheese. [from Mexican Spanish *nacho*]

nacre / 'neɪkə(r)/ *noun* mother-of-pearl obtained from the shell of certain molluscs. [from Arabic *naqqarah*, drum]

nacreous / 'neɪkrɪəs/ *adj.* like or made of nacre.

NACRO *abbrev.* National Association for the Care and Resettlement of Offenders.

nadir / 'neɪdɪə(r), 'nadɪə(r)/ *noun* **1** *Astron.* the point on the celestial sphere that is directly below an observer. It is diametrically opposite the zenith. See also ZENITH. **2** the absolute depth, eg of despair or degradation. [from Arabic *nazir-as-samt*, opposite the zenith]

⊟ **2** rock bottom, depths, abyss, pit, trough.

naevus / 'niːvəs/ *noun* (PL. **naevi**) a birthmark or mole on the skin. [from Latin *naevus*]

naff *adj. slang* **1** stupid; foolish. **2** tasteless; vulgar. **3** rubbishy; of poor quality.

NAFTA or **Nafta** *abbrev.* **1** North American Free Trade Association. **2** North American Free Trade Agreement, an agreement between the USA, Mexico, and Canada, allowing for the progressive lifting of tariffs and elimination of most import and export restrictions between the three countries.

nag¹ *noun* **1** *derog.* a broken-down old horse. **2** a small horse for riding. [from Middle English *nagge*]

nag² — *verb* (**nagged, nagging**) **1** *trans., intrans.* (*also* **nag at someone**) to scold them constantly; to keep finding fault. **2** *trans.* (**nag someone into something**) to keep urging them to do something. **3** *intrans.* (**nag at someone**) to cause them anxiety: *a nagging suspicion*. **4** *intrans.*, *said of pain* to persist. — *noun* a person who nags. [from Norse *nagga*, to rub, grumble, or quarrel]

⊟ *verb* **1** scold, berate, pester, badger, plague, torment, harass, *colloq.* henpeck, harry, vex, upbraid. **2** goad. **3** niggle, tease, worry, bother, trouble, irritate.

nagger *noun* a person or problem that nags or annoys.

nagging *adj.*, *said of a problem or anxiety* constantly worrying or causing concern.

⊟ niggling, worrying, troublesome, bothersome, persistent, continual, constant.

NAHT *abbrev.* National Association of Head Teachers.

Nahuatl / 'naːwaːtl/ see AZTEC.

naiad / 'naɪad/ *noun* (PL. **naiads, naiades**) **1** in Greek mythology, a nymph who inhabits springs, fountains, rivers, and lakes. **2** the aquatic larva of a dragonfly, mayfly, stone-fly, or damselfly. [from Greek *naias, naiados*, from *naein*, to flow]

nail — *noun* **1** a horny plate covering the upper surface of the tip of a finger or toe. **2** a metal spike hammered into something, eg to join two objects together or to serve as a hook. — *verb* **1** (*also* **nail something down** or **together**) to fasten it with, or as if with, a nail or nails. **2** *colloq.* to catch, trap, or corner. **3** to detect, identify, or expose (a lie, deception, etc). — **hit the nail on the head** to pinpoint a problem exactly; to describe something in terms that sum it up precisely. **nail someone down** *colloq.* to extract a definite decision or promise from them. **nail something down** to define or identify it clearly. **on the nail** *colloq.*, *said of payment* made immediately. [from Anglo-Saxon *nægl*]

⊟ *noun* **1** talon, claw. **2** fastener, pin, tack, brad, spike, screw. *verb* **1** fasten, attach, secure, pin, tack, fix, join. **2** catch (out), trap, seize, arrest, *colloq.* nab, corner, pin down.

naïve or **naive** / naɪ'iːv/ *adj.* **1** simple, innocent or unsophisticated. **2** *derog.* too trusting; credulous; not worldly enough. [from French *naïve*, feminine of *naïf*, from Latin *nativus*, native]

⊟ INGENUOUS, GUILELESS, SIMPLE. **1** unsophisticated, innocent, unaffected, artless, natural, childlike, open, wide-eyed. **2** trusting, unsuspecting, gullible, credulous.
⊟ **1** experienced, sophisticated. **2** shrewd, *colloq.* fly.

naïvely or **naively** *adv.* in a naïve or innocent way.

naïvety or **naivety** / naɪ'iːvətɪ/ *noun* excessive trust or innocence.

- - - - - - - - - - - - - - - - - - -
🔲 ingenuousness, innocence, inexperience, naturalness, simplicity, openness, frankness, gullibility, credulity.
🔳 experience, sophistication.
- -

naked adj. **1** wearing no clothes. **2** without fur, feathers, or foliage. **3** without covering, inscription, or contents. **4** undisguised: naked greed. **5** said of a light or flame uncovered; exposed. **6** said of the eye unaided by a telescope or microscope. **7** literary vulnerable; defenceless. [from Anglo-Saxon nacod]
- - - - - - - - - - - - - - - - - - -
🔲 **1, 2, 3** bare, uncovered. **1** nude, undressed, unclothed, stripped, stark-naked, disrobed, colloq. in the altogether. **2** denuded, exposed. **3** barren, blank, unadorned, plain, empty, void. **4** open, blatant, flagrant, overt, stark, undisguised, unqualified, unconcealed.
🔳 **1** clothed. **2, 3** covered. **4** concealed.
- -

nakedly adv. in a naked or undisguised way.

nakedness noun a naked state; being naked or undisguised.

naker /ˈneɪkə(r)/ noun a small high-pitched kettledrum of Arabic origin, played in pairs, and used throughout medieval Europe. [from Old French nacre, from Arabic naqara]

NALGO abbrev. National and Local Government Officers' Associaton.

namby-pamby adj. derog. **1** feebly sentimental; soppy. **2** prim; over-demure. [from the scornful nickname of the 17c poet Ambrose Phillips]

name — noun **1** a word or words by which an individual person, place, or thing is identified and referred to. **2** reputation: get a bad name/clear one's name. **3** a famous or important person, firm, etc: the big names in fashion. — verb trans. **1** to give a name to. **2** to mention or identify by name: name three French poets. **3** to specify or decide on. **4** (**name as**) to choose or appoint. — **call someone names** to insult or abuse them. **in all but name** in practice, though not officially: leader in all but name. **in the name of ... 1** by the authority of ... **2** for the sake of; using as justification: hundreds tortured in the name of religion. **in name only** officially, but not in practice: ruler in name only. **make a name for oneself** to become famous. **name someone after someone else** to call them by the same name as someone else, by way of commemoration, etc. **name someone for someone else** North Amer. to call them by the same name as someone else. **name the day** to announce the date of one's wedding. **name names** to identify, eg culprits, by name. **the name of the game** colloq. the predominant or essential aspect or aim of some activity. **to one's name** belonging to one. [from Anglo-Saxon nama]
- - - - - - - - - - - - - - - - - - -
🔲 noun **1** title, formal appellation, designation, label, term, epithet, slang handle, slang moniker. **2** reputation, character, repute, renown, esteem, eminence, fame, honour, distinction, note. verb **1** call, christen, baptize, term, title, entitle, dub, label, style. **2, 3, 4** designate, nominate. **2** cite, identify. **3** specify, decide on, choose, select. **4** appoint, commission.
- -

namecheck colloq. — verb to publicly mention (the name of someone or something), for instance on radio or television. — noun a public mention of a name.

name day the feast day of the saint after whom one is named.

name-drop verb intrans. (**name-dropped**, **name-dropping**) to indulge in name-dropping.

name-dropper noun a person who is given to name-dropping.

name-dropping noun derog. the practice of casually referring to well-known people as if they were friends, to impress one's hearers.

nameless adj. **1** having no name. **2** unidentified: the culprit shall remain nameless. **3** too awful to specify; unmentionable.
- - - - - - - - - - - - - - - - - - -
🔲 **2** unnamed, anonymous, unidentified, unknown, obscure. **3** inexpressible, indescribable, unutterable, unspeakable, unmentionable, unheard-of.
🔳 **2** named.
- -

namely adv. used to introduce an expansion or explanation of what has just been mentioned: her intention, namely to discredit the other candidates.
- - - - - - - - - - - - - - - - - - -
🔲 that is, that is to say, ie, specifically, viz, to wit.
- -

nameplate noun a plate on or beside a door, bearing the occupant's name, etc.

namesake noun a person with the same name as oneself.

nan noun a slightly leavened Indian bread, similar to pitta bread. [from Hindi nan]

nana see NANNY.

nancy noun (PL. **nancies**) (also **nancy boy**) derog. colloq. an effeminate young man.

nandrolone noun an anabolic steroid sometimes illegally taken by sportsmen and sportswomen to enhance performance.

nanny — noun (PL. **nannies**) **1** a children's nurse. **2** colloq. (also **nana**, **nanna**) a child's name for a grandmother. — verb trans. (**nannies**, **nannied**) to over-protect or oversupervise. [from Nanny, a form of Ann]

nanny goat an adult female goat.

nano- combining form forming words denoting: **1** a thousand millionth: nanometre/nanosecond. **2** microscopic size: nanoplankton. [from Greek nanos, dwarf]

nap[1] — noun a short sleep. — verb intrans. (**napped**, **napping**) to have a nap. — **catch someone napping** colloq. to find them unprepared or off guard. [from Anglo-Saxon hnappian, to sleep]
- - - - - - - - - - - - - - - - - - -
🔲 noun rest, sleep, siesta, catnap, colloq. forty winks, slang kip. verb doze, sleep, colloq. snooze, nod (off), drop off, rest, slang kip.
- -

nap[2] noun the raised surface on cloth such as velvet, corduroy, etc. [from Middle English noppe]

napalm /ˈneɪpɑːm/ Mil. — noun a highly flammable material consisting of a mixture of petrol and a thickening agent, used in incendiary bombs and flame-throwers. — verb to attack or destroy with a bomb made of this material. [from naphthenate palmitate]

nape noun the back of the neck. [from Middle English]

napery noun Scot. household linen, especially for the table. [from Old French naperie, from nape, tablecloth]

naphtha noun Chem. a highly flammable mixture of hydrocarbons obtained from coal and petroleum, used as an ingredient of petrol and dry-cleaning fluids, and as an industrial solvent. [from Greek naphtha]

naphthalene noun Chem. (FORMULA $C_{10}H_8$) a white solid aromatic hydrocarbon obtained from crude oil and responsible for the strong smell of mothballs. It is used as a starting material for the manufacture of dyes, resins, plasticizers, polyesters, and certain drugs, and is the main ingredient of moth repellents.

Napierian logarithm Maths. same as NATURAL LOGARITHM. [named after the Scottish mathematician John Napier]

napkin noun **1** (also **table napkin**) a piece of cloth or paper for wiping one's mouth and fingers at mealtimes. **2** a baby's nappy. [diminutive of Old French nappe, napkin, from Latin mappa]

nappe noun **1** Geol. a large-scale arch-shaped geological fold structure consisting of a sheet-like body of solid rock that has been overturned (so that it is lying on its side) and then often transported several kilometres or more over the underlying rocks by compressional stresses. **2** *Maths.* one of the two parts of a conical surface defined by the vertex. [from French *nappe*, tablecloth, from Latin *mappa*]

nappy *noun* (PL. **nappies**) a piece of towelling, or other soft cloth, or a pad of paper, secured round a baby's bottom to absorb its urine and faeces. [diminutive of NAPKIN]

narcissism / ˈnɑːsɪsɪzm/ *noun* **1** *Psychol.* a condition of self-infatuation arising from difficulties at an early stage of psychological development or, in psychoanalytic theory, sexual self-interest regarded as a normal characteristic of a child's psychosexual development. **2** excessive admiration for oneself or one's appearance. [from Narcissus who, in Greek mythology, fell in love with his own reflection in a pool]

narcissistic *adj.* inclined to admire oneself excessively; characterized by narcissism.

....

⊟ vain, conceited, exhibitionist, self-centred, egocentric, egoistic, egotistic.

....

narcissus /nɑːˈsɪsəs/ *noun* (PL. **narcissuses, narcissi**) a plant similar to the daffodil, which grows from a bulb and has white or yellow flowers. [from Greek *narkissos*, after Narcissus who was changed into this flower, later fancifully associated with *narke*, numbness, because of its narcotic properties]

narcolepsy *noun Medicine* a disorder characterized by an uncontrollable tendency to fall asleep for brief periods, the onset of sleep often being accompanied by hallucinations. [from Greek *narke*, numbness + *lepsis*, seizure]

narcosis *noun* (PL. **narcoses**) a state of unconsciousness or arrested activity. It is most commonly produced by a narcotic drug such as opium, but may also be caused by toxins formed within the body, as in uraemia. [from Greek *narkosis*, a numbing, from *narke*, numbness]

narcoterrorism *noun* terrorism by or on behalf of an organization involved in narcotics or drug dealing.

narcotic — *noun* **1** a drug which, in low doses, reduces the brain's awareness of sensory impulses, particularly pain, and can produce a temporary sense of well-being. In large doses, it induces sleep or unconsciousness, and may cause coma or convulsions. **2** in general use, any addictive drug. — *adj.* relating to narcotics or to narcosis. [from Greek *narkotikos*, numbing]

....

⊟ *noun* **1** drug, opiate, sedative, tranquillizer, painkiller. *adj.* soporific, hypnotic, sedative, opiate, analgesic, painkilling, numbing, dulling, calming, stupefying.

....

nard *noun* **1** an aromatic oil. Same as **spikenard**. **2** an Indian plant of the valerian family, from which this is obtained. [from Greek *nardos*]

nares *pl. noun Anat.* the paired openings of the nasal cavity. The external nares are the nostrils, and the internal nares open into the pharynx. [from Latin *nares*, nostrils]

nark — *noun slang* **1** a spy or informer working for the police. **2** a habitual grumbler. — *verb colloq.* **1** *trans.* to annoy. **2** *intrans.* to grumble. [perhaps from Romany *nak*, nose]

narky *adj.* (**narkier, narkiest**) *colloq.* irritable.

narrate *verb trans.* **1** to tell (a story); to relate. **2** to give a running commentary on (a film). [from Latin *narrare*, to relate]

....

⊟ **1** tell, relate, report, recount, describe, recite, state, detail.

....

narration *noun* **1** the act of narrating. **2** a continuous story or account.

....

⊟ **1** telling, recitation, unfolding. **2** story, tale, chronicle, account, history, report.

....

narrative — *noun* **1** an account of events. **2** those parts of a book, etc that recount events. — *adj.* **1** telling a story; recounting events: *narrative poetry.* **2** relating to the telling of stories: *narrative skills.* [from Latin *narrativus*, from *narrare*, to relate]

....

⊟ *noun* STORY. **1** tale, chronicle, account, history, report, detail, statement.

....

narrator *noun* a person who tells a story or narrative.

....

⊟ storyteller, chronicler, reporter, raconteur, commentator, writer.

....

narrow — *adj.* **1** of little breadth, especially in comparison with length. **2** *said of interests or experience* limited in extent or scope. **3** *said of attitudes or ideas* not liberal, enlightened or tolerant. **4** *said of the use of a word* restricted to its precise or original meaning; strict. **5** close; only just achieved, etc: *a narrow victory.* — *noun* (**narrows**) a narrow part of a channel, river, etc. — *verb intrans., trans.* **1** to make or become narrow. **2** (*also* **narrow down**) *said eg of a range of possibilities* to reduce or be reduced or limited. [from Anglo-Saxon *nearu*]

....

⊟ *adj.* **1, 2** slim, slender, confined, constricted. **1** tight, cramped, thin, fine, tapering, close. **2** limited, restricted, circumscribed. **3** narrow-minded, small-minded, intolerant, biased, bigoted, exclusive, dogmatic, illiberal, unenlightened. *verb* **1** constrict, contract, tighten. **2** reduce, diminish, simplify.
⊞ *adj.* **1, 2** wide, broad. **3** broad-minded, tolerant. *verb* BROADEN, WIDEN. **2** increase.

....

narrow boat a canal barge.

narrowcasting *noun* the broadcasting of material to a limited number of users, eg cable television users. Also, the production and distribution of material on video tapes, cassettes, etc to special interest groups.

narrow-gauge *adj., said of a railway* less than the standard gauge: in the UK less than 4ft 8-in (1.435m) in width.

narrowly *adv.* **1** only just; barely. **2** with close attention: *eyed him narrowly.* **3** in a narrow or restricted way.

....

⊟ **1** only just, barely, scarcely, by a hair's-breadth, by a whisker. **2** closely, sharply, attentively, intently.

....

narrow-minded *adj. derog.* having rigid and restricted views.

....

⊟ illiberal, biased, bigoted, prejudiced, reactionary, small-minded, conservative, intolerant, insular, petty.
⊞ broad-minded.

....

narrowness *noun* a narrow state; being narrow or restricted.

narthex *noun Archit.* **1** a transverse western portico or vestibule, inside or before the nave in an early Christian or Oriental church or basilica, to which women and catechumens were traditionally admitted. **2** any enclosed covered space before a main entrance. [from Greek *narthex*, casket]

narwhal / ˈnɑːwəl/ *noun* an arctic whale, the male of which has a long spiral tusk. [from Danish *narhval*, from *hval*, whale]

NASA *abbrev.* National Aeronautics and Space Administration, a US government agency responsible for conducting non-military space research in areas such as launch vehicle development, manned and robotic spaceflight, and aeronautics, and for developing operations that use such technology.

nasal *adj.* **1** relating to the nose. **2** *said of a sound, or letter such as m or n* pronounced through, or partly through, the nose. **3** *said of a voice, etc* abnormally or exceptionally full of nasal sounds. [from Latin *nasus*, nose]

nasalize or **nasalise** *verb trans., intrans.* to pronounce or speak nasally.

nasally *adv.*, *said of sounds* through the nose.

nascent /'neɪsənt/ *adj.* in the process of coming into being; in the early stages of development. [from Latin *nasci*, to be born]

NASDAQ *abbrev.* National Association of Securities Dealers Automated Quotation, a quotation system and market for American shares.

nastic movement *Bot.* the non-directional movement of a plant organ in response to an external stimulus, eg the opening or closing of some flowers in response to changes in temperature. [from Greek *nastos*, close-pressed, from *nasso*, to press]

nastily *adv.* in a nasty or unpleasant way.

nastiness *noun* being nasty or unpleasant.

nasturtium *noun* a climbing garden plant with flat round leaves and red, orange, or yellow trumpet-like flowers. [from Latin *nasturtium*, cress, said to be from *nasus*, nose + *torquere*, to twist, from its pungency]

nasty — *adj.* (**nastier, nastiest**) **1** unpleasant; disgusting. **2** malicious; ill-natured. **3** giving cause for concern: *a nasty wound/a nasty situation*. **4** *said of weather* wet or stormy. — *noun* (PL. **nasties**) something unpleasant or disgusting: *video nasties*.

🔲 *adj.* **1** unpleasant, repellent, repugnant, repulsive, objectionable, offensive, disgusting, sickening, horrible, filthy, foul, polluted, obscene. **2** malicious, mean, spiteful, vicious, malevolent. **3** serious, grave, worrying, disquieting, difficult, tricky.

🔁 *adj.* **1** agreeable, pleasant, decent. **2** benevolent, kind.

Nat. *abbrev.* **1** National. **2** Nationalist.

nation *noun* **1** the people living in, belonging to, and together forming, a single state. **2** a race of people of common descent, history, language, culture, etc. **3** a Native American tribe, or federation of tribes. [from Latin *natio*, tribe]

🔲 PEOPLE. **1** country, state, realm, population, community, society. **2** race.

national — *adj.* **1** belonging to a particular nation. **2** concerning or covering the whole nation. — *noun* a citizen of a particular nation. [from Latin *natio*, tribe]

🔲 *adj.* **1** civil, domestic, state, internal, governmental, public, social. **2** countrywide, nationwide, widespread, general. *noun* citizen, native, subject, inhabitant, resident.

national anthem a song or hymn adopted as a nation's official song and used to represent it on official occasions.

National Curriculum in the UK, the curriculum prescribed by the government for use in schools.

national debt the money borrowed by the government of a country and not yet repaid.

National Front (ABBREV. **NF**) in the UK, a strongly nationalist political party whose policy focuses on opposition to immigration, and calls for the repatriation of ethnic minorities, including those born in Britain.

national grid *Brit.* a national network of high-voltage electric power lines.

national insurance *Brit.* a system of state insurance contributed to by employers and employees, to provide for the sick, unemployed, and retired.

nationalism *noun* **1** extreme pride in the history, culture, successes, etc of one's nation; excessive patriotism. **2** a policy of, or movement aiming at, national unity or independence.

🔲 **1** patriotism, allegiance, loyalty, chauvinism, xenophobia, jingoism.

nationalist *noun* a person who supports nationalism.

nationalistic *adj.* characterized by nationalism or excessive patriotism.

nationalistically *adv.* in a way characterized by nationalism or excessive patriotism.

nationality *noun* (PL. **nationalities**) **1** the status of citizenship of a particular nation. **2** the racial or national group to which one belongs.

🔲 **2** race, nation, ethnic group, birth, tribe, clan.

nationalization or **nationalisation** *noun* the process of bringing an industry under state ownership. See also PRIVATIZATION, SOCIALISM.

nationalize or **nationalise** *verb* to bring (eg an industry) under state ownership.

National Lottery in Britain, a state-controlled lottery established in 1994.

nationally *adv.* in terms of nations or of an entire nation: *the statistics are valid nationally*.

national park an area of countryside, usually important for its natural beauty, wildlife, etc, under the ownership and care of the nation.

national service a period of compulsory service in the armed forces.

National Socialism *Politics* the political doctrines of nationalism and racial superiority adopted by the German Nazi Party (see NAZI PARTY).

national theatre a theatre endowed by the state, and usually situated in the national capital.

nationwide *adj.*, *adv.* (extending) throughout the whole nation.

native — *adj.* **1** being or belonging to the place of one's upbringing. **2** born a citizen of a particular place: *a native Italian*. **3** belonging naturally to one; inborn or innate: *native wit*. **4** having a particular language as one's first, or mother, tongue. **5** originating in a particular place: *native to China*. **6** belonging to the original inhabitants of a country: *native Balinese music*. — *noun* **1** a person born in a certain place. **2** a plant or animal originating in a particular place. **3** *often derog.* one of the original inhabitants of a place as distinct from later, especially European, settlers. — **go native** *colloq.*, *said of a visitor or immigrant* to adopt the customs, dress, routines, etc of the local people. [from Latin *nativus*, natural, from *nasci*, to be born]

🔲 *adj.* **1** local, indigenous, domestic, vernacular, home, aboriginal, mother, original. **3** inborn, inherent, innate, inbred, hereditary, inherited, congenital, instinctive, natural, intrinsic, natal. *noun* **1** inhabitant, resident, national, citizen, dweller, denizen. **3** aborigine, *formal* autochthon.

🔁 *noun* **3** foreigner, outsider, stranger.

Native American an indigenous inhabitant of North America; an American Indian.

nativity *noun* (PL. **nativities**) **1** birth, advent, or origin. **2** (**Nativity**) the birth of Christ. [from Latin *nativitas*, birth]

NATO *abbrev.* North Atlantic Treaty Organization, a permanent military alliance established to defend W Europe against Soviet aggression.

natron /'neɪtrən/ *noun Geol.* a mineral form of hydrated sodium carbonate found in dried lake beds. [from Arabic *natrun*, from Greek *nitron*]

natter — *verb intrans.* (**nattered, nattering**) *colloq.* to chat busily. — *noun* an intensive chat. [imitative]

🔲 *verb* chat, chatter, gossip, talk. *noun* chat, gossip, *colloq.*

chinwag, talk, conversation, heart-to-heart, tête-à-tête.

natterjack *noun* a European toad, and the rarer of the two UK species, with a greenish skin, a yellow stripe down its head and back, and very short legs.

nattily *adv.* in a neat and smart manner: *he was nattily dressed*.

natty *adj.* (**nattier, nattiest**) *colloq.* **1** *said of clothes* flashily smart. **2** clever; ingenious. [related to NEAT]

Natufian *Archaeol.* — *noun* a Mesolithic culture of SW Syria, Lebanon, and Palestine (c.10,000–8,000BC). — *adj.* relating to this culture. [named after the Palestinian site of Wadi en-*Natuf*]

natural — *adj.* **1** normal; unsurprising. **2** instinctive; not learnt. **3** born in one; innate: *a natural talent/kindness was natural to her.* **4** being such because of inborn qualities: *a natural communicator.* **5** *said of manner, etc* simple, easy, and direct; not artificial. **6** *said of looks* not, or apparently not, improved artificially. **7** relating to nature, or to parts of the physical world not made or altered by man: *natural sciences/areas of natural beauty.* **8** following the normal course of nature: *died a natural death.* **9** *said of materials* derived from plants and animals, as opposed to man-made: *natural fibres.* **10** wild; uncultivated or uncivilized. **11** related to one by blood: *one's natural parents.* **12** *euphemistic* born out of wedlock; illegitimate: *his natural son.* **13** *Mus.* not sharp or flat. — *noun* **1** *colloq.* a person with an inborn feel for something: *she's a natural when it comes to acting.* **2** *Mus.* (a sign (♮) indicating) a note that is not to be played sharp or flat. [from Latin *naturalis*, from *natura*, nature]

▣ *adj.* **1** ordinary, normal, common, regular, standard, usual, typical. **2** instinctive, intuitive, spontaneous. **3** innate, inborn, inherent, congenital, native, indigenous. **5** sincere, unaffected, genuine, artless, ingenuous, guileless, simple, unsophisticated, open, candid, spontaneous. **9** genuine, pure, authentic, unrefined, unprocessed, unmixed, real.
▣ *adj.* **1** unnatural, surprising. **3** acquired, learnt. **5** artificial, affected, disingenuous. **9** artificial.

natural abundance *Chem.* the ratio of the number of atoms of a particular isotope of a chemical element to the total number of atoms of all the isotopes present. It is usually expressed as a percentage, and refers to a natural source of the element.

Natural Environment Research Council (ABBREV. **NERC**) a UK organization established to undertake and fund research in the earth sciences, to advise on exploitation of natural resources and protection of the environment, and to support training of scientists in these fields.

natural frequency **1** *Physics* the frequency at which an object or system will vibrate freely, in the absence of external forces. For example, a pendulum moving with small swings under its own weight is displaying its natural frequency. **2** *Electr.* the lowest frequency at which resonance occurs in an electrical circuit.

natural gas *Geol.* a colourless highly flammable mixture of gaseous hydrocarbons, mainly methane, that occurs naturally in the Earth's crust, either alone or associated with petroleum (oil) deposits. It is an important fossil fuel, and is also used in the manufacture of some organic chemicals.

natural history the scientific study of plants, animals, and minerals. In technical use, it now denotes a purely descriptive treatment of the life sciences.

naturalism *noun* **1** (*also* **Naturalism**) extreme realism in art and literature. **2** the view that rejects supernatural explanations of phenomena, maintaining that all must be attributable to natural causes.

naturalist *noun* **1** a person who studies animal and plant life. **2** a follower of naturalism.

naturalistic *adj.* characterized by naturalism, or the realistic treatment of subjects in art and literature.

▣ natural, realistic, true-to-life, representational, lifelike, graphic, real-life, photographic.

naturalistically *adv.* in a naturalistic or realistic way.

naturalization or **naturalisation** *noun* the process of naturalizing, especially conferring citizenship.

naturalize or **naturalise** *verb trans.* **1** to confer citizenship on (a foreigner). **2** to admit (a word) into the language, or (a custom) among established traditions. **3** to cause (an introduced species of plant or animal) to adapt to the local environment.

natural logarithm *Maths.* a logarithm to the base *e* (where *e* is Euler's number, which may be represented to the sixth decimal place as 2.718 282), denoted by ln *x* or log_e*x*. It has useful applications in differential calculus, and serves as a natural base for logarithms. Also called NAPIERIAN LOGARITHM.

naturally *adv.* **1** of course; not surprisingly. **2** in accordance with the normal course of things. **3** by nature; as a natural characteristic: *sympathy came naturally to her.* **4** by means of a natural process, as opposed to being produced by an artificial man-made process: *gold, silver, and other naturally-occurring elements.* **5** in a relaxed or normal manner.

▣ **1, 2** of course, obviously. **1** certainly, absolutely. **2** as a matter of course, logically, typically. **3, 5** spontaneously. **3** by nature, instinctively, intuitively. **5** genuinely, sincerely, unaffectedly, openly.

naturalness *noun* a natural state or quality; being natural.

natural number *Maths.* any whole positive number, sometimes including zero.

natural philosophy physics.

natural resource any material that occurs naturally in the environment, and which can be exploited commercially by humans, eg water, coal, forests. See also NON-RENEWABLE RESOURCE.

natural selection the process whereby the survival and reproduction of certain members of a population of plants or animals that possess an advantageous hereditary characteristic is favoured, while other individuals lacking that characteristic do not survive and produce offspring. See also DARWINISM.

natural wastage non-replacement of employees who leave or retire, as a means of reducing staffing levels.

nature *noun* **1** (*often* **Nature**) all living and non-living matter and energy that forms part of the physical world and is not made by man, eg plants, animals, mountains, rivers. **2** what something is, or consists of. **3** a fundamental tendency; essential character; attitude or outlook: *human nature/a person modest by nature.* **4** a kind, type, etc. — **be second nature** to be instinctive. **one's better nature** one's kinder or nobler side. **call of nature** *euphemistic colloq.* a need to urinate. **in the nature of…** with the characteristics of …; like … [from Latin *natura*]

▣ **1** universe, world, creation, earth, environment, countryside, country, landscape, scenery, natural history. **2, 3** make-up, constitution, character, attributes. **2** essence, quality, substance. **3** character, features, disposition, personality, temperament, mood, outlook, temper. **4** kind, sort, type, description, category, variety, style, species.

nature reserve *Environ.* a protected area for the conservation and management of wildlife within a habitat which often provides a sanctuary for a rare species.

nature study the study of plants and animals.

nature trail a path through countryside, with signposts and markers pointing out interesting features for study.

naturism *noun* **1** nudism, regarded as a natural instinct. **2** the worship of natural objects.

naturist *noun* a nudist.

naturopathy /neɪtʃə'rɒpəθi/ *noun Medicine* therapy based on the belief that illness can be cured by the natural self-healing processes of the body. Natural foods, light, warmth, massage, regular exercise, and the avoidance of medication are prescribed in order to restore optimum health.

naught /nɔːt/ *noun* **1** *old use* nothing. **2** *North Amer., esp. US* nought. — **come to naught** to fail. **set at naught** *old use* to despise. [from Anglo-Saxon *nawiht*, from *na*, no + *wiht*, thing]

naughtily *adv.* in a naughty or mischievous way.

naughtiness *noun* **1** being naughty or mischievous. **2** mild indecency.

naughty *adj.* (**naughtier, naughtiest**) **1** mischievous; disobedient. **2** mildly shocking or indecent. [from NAUGHT, from its earlier meaning 'wickedness']
. . . .
▣ **1** bad, badly behaved, mischievous, disobedient, wayward, exasperating, playful, roguish. **2** indecent, obscene, bawdy, risqué, smutty.
▣ **1** good, well-behaved, obedient. **2** decent.
. . . .

nausea *noun* **1** an inclination to vomit. **2** disgust; revulsion. [from Latin *nausea*, from Greek *nausia*, seasickness, from *naus*, ship]
. . . .
▣ **1** vomiting, sickness, retching, queasiness, biliousness. **2** disgust, revulsion, loathing, repugnance.
. . . .

nauseate *verb trans.* **1** to cause to feel nausea. **2** to disgust. [from Latin *nauseare*, to be seasick]
. . . .
▣ SICKEN, TURN ONE'S STOMACH. **2** disgust, revolt, repel, offend.
. . . .

nauseating *adj.* **1** offensively unpleasant. **2** causing nausea.
. . . .
▣ **1** sickening, disgusting, revolting, repellent, repugnant, offensive, stomach-turning, bilious.
. . . .

nauseatingly *adv.* to a nauseating degree; repulsively.

nauseous *adj.* **1** sickening; disgusting. **2** affected by nausea. [from Latin *nauseosus*, from Greek *nausia*, seasickness]
. . . .
▣ **1** see NAUSEATING. **2** sick, ill, bilious, queasy.
. . . .

nautical *adj.* relating to ships or sailors. [from Greek *nautikos*, from *nautes*, sailor]
. . . .
▣ naval, marine, maritime, seagoing, seafaring, sailing, oceanic, boating.
. . . .

nautically *adv.* as regards ships or sailors.

nautical mile *Naut.* a measure of distance used at sea, equal to 1.852km.

nautilus *noun* (PL. **nautiluses, nautili**) a sea creature related to the squid and octopus. It has a spiral chambered shell with a pearly interior. [from Greek *nautilos*, sailor]

Navajo or **Navaho** *noun* an Athapascan-speaking Native American people.

naval *adj.* relating to a navy or to ships generally. [from Latin *navalis*, from *navis*, ship]

Navaratri /navə'rɑːtrɪ/ or **Navaratra** /navə'rɑːtrə/ *noun* a Hindu festival held in the autumn in honour of the goddess Durga, and also commemorating the victory of Rama over Ravana, the Demon King. [from Sanskrit *nava*, nine + *rātri* night]

nave¹ *noun* the main central part of a church, where the congregation sits. [from Latin *navis*, ship, from its similarity to an inverted hull]

nave² *noun* the hub of a wheel. [from Anglo-Saxon *nafu*]

navel *noun* **1** in mammals, a scar on the abdomen marking the point of attachment of the umbilical cord to the body of the fetus. **2** the central point of something. [from Anglo-Saxon *nafela*, a diminutive of *nafu*, hub]

navel orange a seedless orange with a navel-like pit on top.

navigability *noun* **1** suitability for use by a ship or boat. **2** seaworthiness.

navigable *adj.* **1** *said of a river, channel, etc* able to be sailed along, through, etc. **2** *said of a ship* seaworthy. **3** *said of a balloon or other craft* steerable. [from Latin *navigabilis*, from *navigare*, to sail]

navigate *verb* **1** *intrans.* to direct the course of a ship, aircraft, or other vehicle. **2** *intrans.* to find one's way and hold one's course. **3** *trans.* to steer (a ship or aircraft). **4** *trans.* to manage to sail along or through (a river, channel, etc); generally, to find one's way through, along, over, across, etc. **5** *intrans.* as a vehicle passenger, to give the driver directions on the correct route. [from Latin *navigare*, from *navis*, ship]
. . . .
▣ **3** steer, drive, direct, pilot, skipper, guide, handle, manoeuvre. **4** sail, cruise, voyage, journey, cross.
. . . .

navigation *noun* **1** the act, skill, or science of navigating. **2** the movement of ships and aircraft.
. . . .
▣ **1** sailing, steering, cruising, voyaging, seamanship, helmsmanship.
. . . .

navigational *adj.* concerning or relating to navigation.

navigation satellite an artificial object placed in orbit around the Earth, which acts as an aid to navigation for ships and aeroplanes.

navigator *noun* **1** a person who navigates, especially a ship or aircraft. **2** *old use* an explorer by sea.

navvy *noun* (PL. **navvies**) a labourer, especially one employed in road-building. [from NAVIGATION, from its earlier meaning 'canal']

navy *noun* (PL. **navies**) **1** the warships of a state, usually considered together with the officers and other personnel manning them; the organization to which they belong, one of the three armed services. **2** a body or fleet of ships with their crews: *the merchant navy.* **3** (*also* **navy blue**) a dark blue colour, typically used for naval uniforms. [from Old French *navie*, from Latin *navis*, ship]
. . . .
▣ **1, 2** fleet. **1** ships, warships. **2** flotilla, armada.
. . . .

nawab /nə'wɑːb/ *noun Hist.* a Muslim ruler or landowner in India. [from Urdu *nawwab*, from Arabic *nuwwab*, plural of *na'ib*, viceroy]

NAWSA *abbrev.* National American Woman Suffrage Association.

nay — *interj. old use* **1** no. **2** rather; to put it more strongly: *a misfortune, nay, a tragedy.* — *noun* the word 'no'. — **say someone nay** to contradict, or refuse something to, someone. [from Norse *nei*]

Nazarene — *adj.* belonging to Nazareth. — *noun* **1** a person of Nazareth. **2** (**the Nazarene**) *Hist.* Jesus Christ. **3** *Hist.* a Christian. [from Greek *Nazarenos*]

Nazi /'nɑːtsɪ/ *noun* a member of the German Nazi Party.

Nazi Party (ABBREV. **NSDAP**) a German political party, led by Adolf Hitler from 1921, whose ideology was extremely nationalist, imperialist, and racist.

Nazism /'nɑːtsɪzm/ *noun* the principles of the Nazis; the Nazi movement.

NB *abbrev.* **1** *nota bene* (Latin), note well. **2** Nebraska. **3** New Brunswick. **4** *Hist.* North Britain, ie Scotland.

Nb *symbol Chem.* niobium.

NBA *abbrev.* Net Book Agreement.

NBC *abbrev.* **1** National Broadcasting Company (in the USA). **2** *said of weapons* nuclear, biological, and chemical.

NBC suit a suit designed to protect the wearer against the physical effects of nuclear, biological, and chemical weapons.

NC or **N.C.** *abbrev.* North Carolina.

NCC *abbrev.* Nature Conservancy Council.

NCCL *abbrev.* National Council for Civil Liberties.

NCO *noun* (PL. **NCOs**, **NCO's**) non-commissioned officer.

ND or **N.D.** *abbrev.* North Dakota.

Nd *symbol Chem.* neodymium.

N. Dak. *abbrev.* North Dakota.

NE *abbrev.* **1** north-east; north-eastern. **2** Nebraska.

Ne *symbol Chem.* neon.

Neanderthal /nɪˈandətɑːl/ *adj.* denoting a primitive type of man of the early Stone Age in Europe, with a receding forehead and prominent brow ridges. [from *Neandertal*, a valley in Germany]

neap or **neaptide** *noun* a tidal pattern that occurs twice a month, when there is least difference in level between high and low tides. [from Anglo-Saxon *nepflod* (ie neap flood)]

near — *prep.* **1** at a short distance from. **2** close to (in amount, etc): *near tears/nearer 1000 than 500.* — *adv.* **1** (**near to**) close: *came near to hitting her.* **2** *old use* or *colloq.* almost; nearly: *near-disastrous results/she damn near died/nowhere near enough.* — *adj.* **1** being a short distance away; close. **2** being a short time away. **3** closer of two: *the near side.* **4** similar; comparable: *the nearest thing to a screwdriver.* **5** closely related to one: *a near relative.* **6** almost amounting to, or almost turning into: *a near tragedy.* **7** *old use* mean; miserly. — *verb trans., intrans.* to approach. — **near at hand** conveniently close. **not go near someone** or **something** to avoid them. [from Anglo-Saxon *near*, comparative of *neah*, nigh]

▄ *adj.* **1** nearby, close, bordering, adjacent, adjoining, alongside, neighbouring. **2** imminent, impending, forthcoming, coming, approaching, nigh. **4** close, similar, alike, comparable. **5** dear, familiar, close, related, intimate, akin.

▣ *adj.* **1**, **2**, **5** distant, remote. **1** far.

nearby *adj., adv.* a short distance away; close at hand.

▄ *adj.* near, neighbouring, adjoining, adjacent, accessible, convenient, handy. *adv.* near, within reach, at close quarters, close at hand, not far away.

▣ *adj.* faraway.

nearly *adv.* almost. — **not nearly** very far from; nothing like.

▄ almost, practically, virtually, closely, approximately, more or less, as good as, just about, roughly, well-nigh.

▣ completely, totally.

near miss something not quite achieved or only just avoided.

nearness *noun* being near; closeness; proximity.

nearside — *noun* the side of a vehicle or horse nearer the kerb: in the UK the left side, and in most other countries the right side. — *adj.* denoting this side: *the nearside front tyre is flat.*

near-sighted *adj.* short-sighted.

near thing a narrow escape; a success only just achieved.

neat *adj.* **1** tidy; clean; orderly. **2** pleasingly small or regular. **3** elegantly or cleverly simple: *a neat explanation.* **4** skilful or efficient: *neat work!* **5** *North Amer.* excellent. **6** *said of an alcoholic drink* undiluted. [from French *net*, clean, tidy]

▄ **1** tidy, orderly, smart, spruce, trim, clean, spick and span, shipshape. **2** compact, handy, convenient, well-designed, well-made, user-friendly. **3**, **4** deft, clever, adroit, skilful, expert. **6** undiluted, unmixed, unadulterated, straight, pure.

▣ **1** untidy. **2**, **3**, **4** clumsy. **6** diluted.

neaten *verb trans.* (**neatened**, **neatening**) to make neat.

▄ tidy, order, smarten (up), spruce up, trim, edge, round off, clean.

neatness *noun* being neat or tidy; a neat quality.

Neb or **Nebr.** *abbrev.* Nebraska.

nebula *noun* (PL. **nebulae**, **nebulas**) *Astron.* **1** a region or cloud of interstellar dust or gas, forming a fuzzy luminous or dark patch that can be seen in the night sky with the aid of a telescope. **2** formerly used to refer to galaxies too remote to be resolved into individual stars, and which therefore appeared as hazy smudges of light. [from Latin *nebula*, mist]

nebular *adj. Astron.* relating to a nebula or nebulae.

nebulous *adj.* lacking distinctness; indistinct in shape, form, or nature. [from Latin *nebulosus*, from *nebula*, mist]

▄ vague, hazy, imprecise, indefinite, indistinct, cloudy, misty, obscure, uncertain, unclear, dim, ambiguous, confused, fuzzy, shapeless, amorphous.

▣ clear, distinct.

nebulously *adv.* in a nebulous or vague way; hazily.

NEC *abbrev.* National Exhibition Centre.

necessarily *adv.* as a necessary or inevitable result.

necessary — *adj.* **1** that is needed or cannot be done without; that must be done. **2** that must be; that cannot be escaped: *a necessary evil.* **3** logically required or unavoidable. — *noun* (PL. **necessaries**) something that is necessary. — **the necessary** *humorous colloq.* **1** money needed for a purpose. **2** action that must be taken. [from Latin *necessarius*, from *necesse*, necessary]

▄ *adj.* **1** needed, required, needful, essential, indispensable, vital, imperative, compulsory, mandatory, obligatory. **2**, **3** unavoidable, inevitable, inescapable, inexorable, certain. *noun* requirement, prerequisite, necessity, essential, fundamental.

▣ *adj.* **1** unnecessary, inessential, unimportant.

necessitate *verb trans.* to make necessary or unavoidable. [from Latin *necessitare*, from *necessitas*, necessity]

▄ require, involve, entail, call for, demand, oblige, force, constrain, compel.

necessity *noun* (PL. **necessities**) **1** something necessary or essential: *food and other necessities.* **2** circumstances that make something necessary, obligatory, or unavoidable; the fact of being inevitable or indispensable: *from necessity rather than choice/must of necessity draw this conclusion.* **3** a pressing need: *no necessity to rush.* **4** poverty; want; need. [from Latin *necessitas*]

▄ NEED. **1** requirement, prerequisite, essential, fundamental, demand. **2**, **3** obligation, compulsion. **2** indispensability, inevitability, needfulness. **4** want, poverty, destitution, hardship.

neck — *noun* **1** the part of the body between the head and the shoulders. **2** the part of a garment at or covering the neck. **3** a narrow part; a narrow connecting part: *joined to the mainland by a neck of land.* **4** *Racing* a head-and-neck's length; a small margin: *won by a neck*. **5** the meat from the neck of an animal. — *verb intrans., trans. slang* to hug and kiss amorously. — **breathe down someone's neck** *colloq.* to supervise them so closely as to inhibit them. **get it in the neck** *colloq.* to be severely rebuked or punished. **neck and neck** *said of competitors in a race, etc* exactly level. **risk one's neck** to risk one's life or do something dangerous. **save one's neck** to escape from danger, etc without loss or harm. **stick one's neck out** to put oneself at risk of being attacked, contradicted, etc. **up to one's neck in something** *colloq.* deeply involved in it; busy; preoccupied. [from Anglo-Saxon *hnecca*]

neckband *noun* a band or strip of material sewn round the neck of a garment.

neckerchief *noun* (PL. **neckerchiefs, neckerchieves**) a cloth for wearing round the neck. [from NECK + KERCHIEF]

necklace *noun* a string of beads or jewels, etc, or a chain, worn round the neck as jewellery. [from NECK + LACE in the sense 'cord', 'tie']

. . . .

◼ string, chain, band, choker, pearls.

. . . .

necklacing *noun* the practice of placing a petrol-soaked tyre over someone's head and setting it alight, formerly used by some black South Africans as a punishment for those believed to be government sympathizers.

neckline *noun* the edge of a garment at the neck, or its shape.

neck of the woods *humorous* a neighbourhood or locality.

necktie *noun* a man's tie.

necromancer *noun* one who practises necromancy or divination; a magician.

necromancy *noun* divination or prophecy through communication with the dead; black magic; sorcery. [from Greek *nekros*, corpse + *mantis*, prophet]

necrophilia *noun* obsessive interest, especially of an erotic kind, in dead bodies. [from Greek *nekros*, corpse + -PHILIA]

necrophiliac *noun* a person with an obsessive interest in dead bodies.

necropolis *noun Archaeol.* a cemetery. [from Greek *nekros*, corpse + *polis*, city]

necrosis *noun* (PL. **necroses**) *Biol.* the death of cells in part of a tissue or organ as a result of disease, injury, or interruption of the blood supply. [from Greek *nekrosis*, from *nekros*, corpse]

necrotic *adj.* relating to or affected by necrosis.

nectar *noun* **1** *Bot.* the sticky concentrated sugar solution produced by the nectaries of flowers, which serves to attract insects and certain small birds which then pollinate the flowers as they retrieve the nectar. Bees use nectar to make honey. **2** *Greek Mythol.* the special drink of the gods. **3** any delicious drink. **4** anything delightfully welcome to the senses. [from Greek *nektar*]

nectarine *noun* a peach-like fruit with a shiny, downless skin. [from NECTAR]

nectary *noun* (PL. **nectaries**) *Bot.* in flowering plants, a specialized gland, usually situated at the base of the flower, that secretes nectar.

NEDC *abbrev.* National Economic Development Council.

née /neɪ/ *adj.* born, used in giving a woman's maiden name: *Jane Day, née Osborn*. [from French *née*, feminine of *né*, born]

need — *verb* **1** *trans.* to have want of; to require. **2** *intrans.* **a** to be required or obliged to do something: *we need to find a replacement.* **b** (*in negative and interrogative without to and with third person singular need*) to be required or obliged to be or do something: *they needn't stay/need we tell them?* — *noun* **1** something one requires. **2** (**need of** or **for something**) a condition of lacking or requiring it; an urge or desire. **3** (**need for something**) necessity or justification. — **if need** or **needs be** if necessary. **in need** needing

help or financial support. See also NEEDS. [from Anglo-Saxon *nead* or *nied*]

◼ *verb* **1** miss, lack, want, require, demand, call for, necessitate, have need of, crave. *noun* **1, 3** requirement, necessity. **1** essential, necessary, requi-site, prerequisite, desideratum, sine qua non. **2** want, lack, insufficiency, inadequacy, neediness, shortage, demand, craving. **3** call, obligation, justification.

. . . .

needful — *adj.* necessary. — *noun* (**the needful**) *humorous colloq.* **1** whatever action is necessary. **2** money needed for a purpose.

needle — *noun* **1** a slender pointed steel sewing instrument with a hole for the thread. **2** a longer, thicker implement of metal, wood, bone, plastic, etc without a hole, for knitting, crocheting, etc. **3** a hypodermic syringe, or its pointed end. **4** a gramophone stylus. **5** the moving pointer on a compass or other instrument. **6** the needle-shaped leaf of a tree such as the pine or fir. **7** *colloq.* provocation. — *verb trans. colloq.* to provoke or irritate, especially deliberately. [from Anglo-Saxon *nædl*]

needle bank a place where drug-users can exchange used hypodermic syringes for new ones free of charge, to help prevent the spread of disease or infection.

needlecord *noun* a finely ribbed corduroy.

needlepoint *noun* **1** embroidery on canvas. **2** lace made over a paper pattern, with needles rather than bobbins.

needless *adj.* unnecessary.

. . . .

◼ unnecessary, gratuitous, uncalled-for, unwanted, redundant, superfluous, useless, pointless, purposeless.
◼ necessary, essential.

. . . .

needlessly *adv.* without any need: *he needlessly locked the door.*

needlewoman *noun* a woman who sews; a seamstress.

needlework *noun* sewing and embroidery.

needn't *contr.* need not.

needs *adv. old use* of necessity; inevitably. [from Anglo-Saxon *niedes*, genitive of *nied*, need]

needy *adj.* (**needier, neediest**) in severe need; poverty-stricken; destitute.

. . . .

◼ poor, destitute, impoverished, penniless, disadvantaged, deprived, poverty-stricken, underprivileged.
◼ affluent, wealthy, well-off.

. . . .

nefarious /nɪˈfeərɪəs/ *adj.* wicked; evil. [from Latin *nefarius*, from *nefas*, wrong]

neg *abbrev.* negative.

negate *verb trans.* **1** to cancel or destroy the effect of. **2** to deny the existence of. [from Latin *negare*, to deny]

. . . .

◼ **1** nullify, annul, cancel, invalidate, undo, countermand, abrogate, neutralize, quash, retract, reverse, revoke, rescind, wipe out, void, repeal. **2** deny, contradict, oppose, disprove, refute, repudiate.
◼ **2** affirm.

. . . .

negation *noun* **1** the act of negating. **2** the absence or opposite of something. **3** the denial of the existence of something.

negative — *adj.* **1** meaning or saying 'no'; expressing denial, refusal, or prohibition. **2** *said of people, attitudes, etc* unenthusiastic, defeatist, or pessimistic. **3** *Maths.* less than zero. **4** contrary to, or cancelling the effect of, whatever is regarded as positive. **5** *Maths.* measured in the opposite direction to that chosen as positive. **6** *Electr.* having the kind of electric charge produced by an excess of electrons. **7** *Photog., said of film* having the light and shade of the actual image reversed, or complementary colours in place of actual ones. — *noun* **1** a word, statement, or grammatical form expressing denial: *replied in the negative.* **2** a photographic film with a negative image, from which prints are made. — *verb* **1** to reject; to veto. **2** to deny. **3** to neutralize or cancel out. **4** to disprove or prove the contrary of. [from Latin *negativus*, from *negare*, to deny]

▣ *adj.* **2** unco-operative, cynical, pessimistic, unenthusiastic, uninterested, unwilling. **4** contradictory, contrary, denying, opposing, invalidating, neutralizing, nullifying, annulling. *noun* **1** contradiction, denial, opposite, refusal.
◪ *adj.* **1** affirmative, positive. **2** constructive, positive.

negative equity a situation in which a property falls below the value of the mortgage held on it, usually caused by a drop in property values.

negative income tax a government payment to individuals whose income falls below a prescribed level, in order to bring them up to that level.

negatively *adv.* in a negative manner; so as to say 'no'.

neglect — *verb trans.* **1** not to give proper care and attention to. **2** to leave (duties, etc) undone. **3** to fail or omit (to do something). — *noun* **1** lack of proper care. **2** a state of disuse or decay: *fell into neglect.* [from Latin *negligere*, to neglect]

▣ *verb* **1** disregard, ignore, leave alone, abandon, pass by, rebuff, scorn, disdain, slight, spurn. **2, 3** forget, fail (in), omit. **2** overlook, let slide, shirk, skimp. *noun* **1** negligence, disregard, carelessness, failure, inattention, indifference, slackness, dereliction of duty, forgetfulness, heedlessness, oversight, slight, disrespect. **2** disrepair, decay, dilapidation, ruin.
◪ *verb* **1** cherish, appreciate. **2** remember. *noun* **1** care, attention, concern.

neglectful *adj.* inattentive or negligent; undutiful or unconscientious.

négligée or **negligee** /ˈnɛɡlɪʒeɪ/ *noun* a woman's thin light dressing-gown. [from French *négligé*, carelessness, undress, from *négliger*, to neglect]

negligence *noun* lack of proper attention or care; carelessness. [from Latin *negligentia*]

▣ inattentiveness, carelessness, laxity, neglect, slackness, thoughtlessness, forgetfulness, indifference, omission, oversight, disregard, failure, default.
◪ attentiveness, care, regard.

negligent *adj.* **1** not giving proper care and attention. **2** careless or offhand.

▣ NEGLECTFUL, INATTENTIVE, REMISS, THOUGHTLESS, CASUAL, LAX, CARELESS, SLACK, FORGETFUL. **2** indifferent, offhand, nonchalant, uncaring.
◪ ATTENTIVE, CAREFUL, SCRUPULOUS, METICULOUS.

negligible *adj.* small or unimportant enough to ignore. [from Latin *negligere*, to disregard]

▣ unimportant, insignificant, small, imperceptible, trifling, trivial, minor, minute.
◪ significant.

negligibly *adv.* so as to be negligible or insignificant: *a negligibly small amount.*

negotiable *adj.* **1** *said of a cash order or other asset* that can legally be negotiated, ie transferred to another person in exchange for its value in money. **2** open to discussion. **3** *said of a hazard or obstacle* able to be got past.

negotiate *verb* **1** (**negotiate with someone**) to confer with them to reach agreement on terms or arrangements affecting both parties. **2** to bring about (an agreement) or arrange (a treaty, price, etc) by conferring. **3** to pass safely

(a hazard on one's way, etc). [from Latin *negotiari*, to trade, from *negotium*, business]

▣ **1** confer with, deal with, consult, mediate between, arbitrate between, bargain with. **2** arrange, transact, work out, manage, settle. **3** get round, cross, surmount, traverse, pass.

negotiation *noun* the process of negotiating; a round of negotiating.

▣ mediation, arbitration, debate, discussion, diplomacy, bargaining, transaction.

negotiator *noun* a person who negotiates or is negotiating.

▣ arbitrator, go-between, mediator, intermediary, moderator, intercessor, adjudicator, broker, ambassador, diplomat.

Negress /ˈniːɡrɪs/ *noun often offensive* a female Negro.

Negro /ˈniːɡroʊ/ — *noun* (PL. **Negroes**) *often offensive* a person belonging to one of the black-skinned races originally from Africa. — *adj.* relating or belonging to these races. [from Spanish, from Latin *niger*, black]

Negroid — *adj.* having the physical characteristics of the Negro races, eg dark skin, a broad nose, and tightly curling hair. — *noun* a Negroid person.

neigh /neɪ/ — *noun* the characteristic cry of a horse. — *verb intrans.* to make this cry. [from Anglo-Saxon *hnægan*, to neigh]

neighbour *noun* **1** a person living near or next door to one. **2** an adjacent territory, person, etc. **3** *old use* any of one's fellow humans: *love your neighbour.* [from Anglo-Saxon *neah*, near + *gebur*, dweller]

neighbourhood *noun* **1** a district or locality. **2** the area near something or someone. — **in the neighbourhood of** roughly: *it cost in the neighbourhood of £500.*

▣ VICINITY. **1** district, region, locality, community, locale. **2** environs, confines, surroundings, proximity.

neighbourhood watch a scheme under which local residents agree to keep a general watch on each other's property and the surrounding streets to help prevent crime.

neighbouring *adj.* nearby.

▣ adjacent, bordering, near, nearby, adjoining, connecting, next, surrounding.
◪ distant, remote.

neighbourliness *noun* being neighbourly or friendly.

neighbourly *adj.* friendly, especially to the people around one.

▣ sociable, friendly, amiable, kind, helpful, genial, hospitable, obliging, considerate, companionable.

neither — *adj., pron.* not the one nor the other (thing or person): *neither proposal is acceptable/neither of the proposals is acceptable.* — *conj.* (*introducing the first of two or more alternatives; usually paired with nor*) not: *I neither know nor care.* — *adv.* nor; also not: *if you won't, neither will I.* — **neither here nor there** irrelevant; unimportant. [from Anglo-Saxon *nawther* or *nahwæther*]

nekton *noun Zool.* the actively swimming organisms (eg fishes, whales) that inhabit seas, lakes, etc, as opposed to the passively floating or drifting organisms that form the plankton. [from Greek *nekton* (neuter), swimming]

nelly — **not on your nelly** *old slang use* certainly not. [perhaps from the phrase 'not on your Nelly Duff', rhyming slang for 'puff', ie life]

nelson *noun* (*also* **full nelson**) a wrestling hold in which one passes one's arms under one's opponent's, from behind, and joins hands so that pressure can be applied against the back of the opponent's neck. [named after Horatio Nelson]

nematode *noun Zool.* any invertebrate animal belonging to the phylum Nematoda, which includes both free-living and parasitic worms with long slender unsegmented bodies that taper at both ends, and a smooth skin. [from Greek *nema*, thread + *eidos*, form]

nem. con. *abbrev. nemine contradicente* (Latin), with no one disagreeing; unanimously.

nemesis /ˈnɛməsɪs/ *noun* **1** retribution or just punishment. **2** something that brings this.

neo- *combining form* forming words meaning 'new, a new form, modern'. [from Greek *neos*, new]

neoclassical *adj., said of artistic or architectural style, especially in the late 18c and early 19c* imitating or adapting the styles of the ancient classical world.

Neoclassicism *noun* **1** a classical revival affecting all the visual arts, which flourished from c.1750 to the early 19c. See also CLASSICAL REVIVAL. **2** a 20c movement in music which sought to restore the ideals, and some of the style and vocabulary, of the 18c classical period.

neo-Darwinism *noun Biol.* a later development of Darwinism, laying greater stress on natural selection and denying the inheritance of acquired characteristics.

neodymium /niːoʊˈdɪmɪəm/ *noun Chem.* (SYMBOL **Nd**, ATOMIC NUMBER **60**) a soft silvery metal, belonging to the lanthanide series, that is used to make special glass for lasers and astronomical lenses, and to give glass a violet colour. [from NEO- + *didymium*, the name of a substance once thought to be an element]

Neo-fascism /niːoʊˈfaʃɪzm/ *noun Politics* a term used to describe various postwar fascist ideas and movements reminiscent of, or modelled on, the policies and ideology of the inter-war fascist dictatorships.

Neoimpressionism *noun Art* a movement reacting against the romanticism of Impressionism, lasting from c.1885 to c.1900.

neolithic *adj.* (*also* **Neolithic**) belonging or relating to the later Stone Age, in Europe lasting from about 40,000 to 2,400 BC, characterized by the manufacture of polished stone tools. [from NEO- + Greek *lithos*, stone]

neologism *noun* **1** a new word or expression. **2** a new meaning acquired by an existing word or expression. [from NEO- + Greek *logos*, word]

neon *noun Chem.* (SYMBOL **Ne**, ATOMIC NUMBER **10**) a colourless odourless inert gas that occurs in trace amounts in air. It is one of the rare or noble gases, and is used in fluorescent lighting, neon lamps (which give a red glow), and lasers. [from Greek *neon*, neuter form of *neos*, new]

neonatal *adj.* relating to newly born children. [from Latin *neonatus*, from Greek *neos*, new + Latin *natus*, born]

neonate *noun* a newly born child, especially one that is less than four weeks old.

neon lamp or **neon light 1** a neon-filled glass tube used for lighting. **2** *loosely* any similar tubular fluorescent light.

neophyte *noun* **1** a beginner. **2** a new convert to a religious faith. **3** a novice in a religious order. [from Greek *neophytos*, newly planted]

. . . .

▣ **1** beginner, learner, novice, apprentice, recruit, tyro.

. . . .

neoplasm *noun Medicine* a malignant or benign tumour consisting of a new and abnormal mass of tissue formed by the rapid and uncontrolled multiplication of cells.

nephew *noun* the son of one's brother or sister, or of one's brother- or sister-in-law. [from Old French *neveu*]

nephrectomy *noun Medicine* the surgical removal of a kidney. [from Greek *nephros*, kidney + -ECTOMY]

nephrite *noun Geol.* a hard glistening mineral, and one of the two minerals commonly known as jade (the other is jadeite). It occurs in a wide range of colours, including white and black. [from Greek *nephros*, kidney; so called because it was once thought to be effective in treating kidney disease]

nephritis *noun Medicine* inflammation of the kidneys. [from Greek *nephros*, kidney + -ITIS]

nephrology *noun Medicine* the branch of medicine concerned with the study of the structure, functions, and diseases of the kidney. [from Greek *nephros*, kidney + -LOGY]

nephron *noun Anat.* in the vertebrate kidney, one of over a million functional units responsible for the filtration of waste products from the blood to form urine. [from Greek *nephros*, kidney]

nepotism *noun* the practice of favouring one's relatives, especially in making official appointments. [from Latin *nepos*, grandson or nephew]

. . . .

▣ favouritism, preferential treatment, keeping it in the family, looking after one's own, jobs for the boys, bias, partiality.

. . . .

nepotistic *adj.* favouring one's relatives in giving favours or making appointments.

Neptune *noun Astron.* the eighth (or occasionally ninth) planet from the Sun.

neptunium *noun Chem.* (SYMBOL **Np**, ATOMIC NUMBER **93**) a silvery-white radioactive metal that occurs naturally in trace amounts, but is usually obtained as a by-product of plutonium production. [named after the planet Neptune]

NERC *abbrev.* Natural Environment Research Council.

nerd *noun derog. slang* **1** a foolish or annoying person. **2** a socially inept or unprepossessing person, although often (especially in computers) knowledgeable.

nereid *noun* in Greek mythology, a sea-nymph, a daughter of Nereus.

nerine /nəˈraɪnɪ/ *noun Bot.* any of various species of S African plant with attractive brightly coloured pink, orange, red, or white flowers, belonging to the lily family. [from Latin *nerine*]

nerve — *noun* **1** a bundle of nerve fibres, linked to individual nerve cells, that carries nerve impulses between the central nervous system (the brain and spinal cord) and the rest of the body. **2** the vein of a leaf, consisting of a strand of vascular tissue that conducts water and nutrients. **3** *colloq.* cheek; impudence. **4** (**nerves**) *colloq.* nervousness; tension or stress: *calm one's nerves.* **5** *colloq.* one's capacity to cope with stress or excitement. — *verb* (**nerve oneself for something**) to prepare oneself for a challenge or ordeal. — **get on someone's nerves** *colloq.* to annoy or irritate them. **lose one's nerve** to lose one's courage or resolve. **strain every nerve** to put every effort into an endeavour. [from Latin *nervus*, sinew, tendon, nerve]

. . . .

▣ *noun* **3** audacity, impudence, cheek, effrontery, brazenness, boldness, *colloq.* chutzpah, impertinence, insolence. **4** nervousness, tension, stress, anxiety, worry, strain, fretfulness. **5** courage, bravery, pluck, spirit, firmness, resolution, fortitude, steadfastness, will, determination, endurance, force. *verb* prepare oneself, steel oneself, pluck up courage. **get on someone's nerves** *colloq.* annoy, irritate, vex, bore, bother, plague, pester. **lose one's nerve** get cold feet, chicken out, *colloq.* cop out.

▣ *noun* **5** timidity.

. . . .

nerve cell a cell that transmits nerve impulses; a neurone.

nerve centre 1 a cluster of nerve cells responsible for a particular bodily function. **2** the centre of control within an organization, etc.

nerve gas a poisonous gas that acts on the nerves, especially those of respiration, used as a weapon.

nerveless *adj.* **1** lacking feeling or strength; inert. **2** fearless.

nervelessly *adv.* without feeling or strength.

nerve-racking *adj.* causing one to feel tense and anxious.

⊟ harrowing, distressing, trying, stressful, tense, maddening, worrying, difficult, frightening.

nervily *adv.* in a nervy or excitable manner.

nerviness *noun* a nervy or excitable manner.

nervous *adj.* **1** timid; easily agitated. **2** apprehensive; uneasy. **3** relating to the nerves: *nervous illnesses*. **4** consisting of nerves. [from Latin *nervosus*, sinewy, from *nervus*, sinew, nerve]

⊟ **1, 2** agitated, nervy, tense, on edge, edgy, jumpy, jittery. **1** highly-strung, excitable, fidgety, neurotic, shaky. **2** anxious, apprehensive, uneasy, worried, flustered, fearful.
⊟ **1, 2** calm, relaxed.

nervous breakdown a mental illness attributed loosely to stress, involving intense anxiety, low self-esteem, and loss of concentration.

nervous system in multicellular animals, the highly organized network of cells and tissues that control the vital functions of the body, and enable the animal to be aware of and respond to the surrounding environment.

nervy *adj.* (**nervier, nerviest**) excitable.

-ness *suffix* forming nouns indicating a state, condition, or degree: *slowness/darkness*.

nest — *noun* **1** a structure built by birds or other creatures, eg rats, wasps, etc, in which to lay eggs or give birth to and look after young. **2** a cosy habitation or retreat. **3** a den or haunt (eg of thieves) or secret centre (of vice, crime, etc). **4** a set of things that fit together or one inside the other. — *verb* **1** *intrans.* to build and occupy a nest. **2** *trans., intrans.* to fit together compactly. **3** *intrans.* to go in search of birds' nests. [from Anglo-Saxon *nest*]

⊟ *noun* **1** breeding-ground, roost, eyrie, lair. **2** retreat, refuge, den, haunt, hideaway.

nest egg **1** a real or artificial egg left in a nest to encourage laying. **2** *colloq.* a sum of money saved up for the future; one's savings.

nestle *verb intrans.* (**nestle down** or **together**) to lie or settle snugly. [from Anglo-Saxon *nestlian*, to make a nest]

⊟ snuggle (up), huddle together, cuddle up, curl up.

nestling *noun* a young bird still unable to fly. [from NEST + -LING]

Nestorian *noun* a member of a Christian sect that originated with the followers of Nestorius, Patriarch of Constantinople (AD 428–31), who taught that the divinity and humanity of Christ were not united in a single self-conscious personality.

net[1] — *noun* **1** an openwork material made of thread, cord, etc knotted, twisted, or woven so as to form regularly shaped meshes. **2** a piece of this in any of various shapes or qualities appropriate to such uses as catching fish or insects, protecting fruit bushes, confining hair, etc. **3** a strip of net dividing a tennis or badminton court, etc. **4** the net-backed goal in hockey, football, etc. **5** a snare or trap. **6** (**the Net**) short for the INTERNET. — *verb* (**netted, netting**) **1** *trans.* to catch in a net. **2** *trans.* to cover with a net. **3** *trans.* to hit, kick, etc (the ball) into the net or goal. **4** *intrans.* to construct net from thread, cord, etc. **5** *trans. Hist.* to make (a purse, etc) using a knotting and looping process. — **slip the net** to escape capture. [from Anglo-Saxon *nett*]

⊟ *noun* **1** mesh, web, network, netting, open work, lattice, lace. *verb* **1** catch, trap, capture, bag, ensnare, entangle, *colloq.* nab.

net[2] — *adj.* (*also* **nett**) **1** *said of profit* remaining after all expenses, etc have been paid. **2** *said of weight* not including packaging or container. — *verb trans.* (**netted, netting**) to produce, or earn, as clear profit. [from French *net*, clear, neat]

⊟ *adj.* **1** clear, after tax, final, lowest. *verb* bring in, clear, earn, make, realize, receive, gain, obtain, accumulate.

net- *prefix* denoting the Internet: *netsurf*.

netball *noun* a game played by women or girls on an outdoor court between teams of seven, the aim being to throw the ball through the opponents' net hanging from a ring at the top of a pole.

nether *adj. old use* lower or under. [from Anglo-Saxon *nither*, down]

nethermost *adj. old use* lowest.

nether world or **nether regions** the underworld; hell.

netiquette /ˈnɛtɪkɛt/ *noun colloq.* standards for polite on-line behaviour. [from NET- + ETIQUETTE]

nett see NET[2].

netting *noun* any material with meshes, made by knotting or twisting thread, cord, wire, etc.

nettle — *noun* a plant covered with hairs that sting if touched. — *verb trans.* to offend or irritate. — **grasp the nettle** to deal boldly with a difficult situation. [from Anglo-Saxon *netele*]

nettle rash an allergic skin reaction with raised red or white itchy patches.

network — *noun* **1** any arrangement resembling a mass of criss-crossing lines: *a network of streets*. **2** a system of interconnected telephone lines, electricity supply lines, etc, that allow information or resources to be passed from one location to another. **3** a group of radio or television stations that broadcast the same programmes at the same time. **4** *Comput.* a system of two or more computer terminals that are linked to each other, enabling users to share facilities such as printers, and to communicate and exchange data with other network users. **5** any group of people, businesses, organizations, etc that are interconnected or in close communication with one another. **6** netting. — *verb* **1** to broadcast on a network. **2** (*intrans.*) *Comput.*, *said of computer users* to communicate and exchange data with other network users.

⊟ *noun* **1, 2** grid, net. **1** maze, mesh, labyrinth, grille, web. **2** circuitry. **4** system. **5** organization, structure, grouping, set-up, complex, nexus, connections, channels, *colloq.* the grapevine, bush telegraph.

neur- see NEURO-.

neural *adj.* relating to the nerves or nervous system. [from Greek *neuron*, nerve]

neuralgia *noun* spasmodic pain along the course of a nerve. [from NEURO- + -ALGIA]

neuralgic *adj.* characterized or affected by neuralgia.

neural network *Comput.* an artificial network, consisting of many computer processing units connected in parallel, that attempts to imitate some of the structural and functional properties of the nerve cells (neurones) in the human nervous system.

neuritis *noun* inflammation of a nerve or nerves, in some cases with defective functioning of the affected part. [from NEURO- + -ITIS]

neuro- or **neur-** *combining form* forming words relating to the nerves: *neurosurgery*.

neurolinguistics *sing. noun* the study of the neurological basis of language development and use; in particular, the study of the areas of the brain thought to be involved in the processes of speech and comprehension.

neurology *noun Medicine* the branch of medicine concerned with the study of the structure, functions, and diseases and disorders of the central nervous system (the brain and spinal cord) and the peripheral nerves. [from NEURO- + -LOGY]

neurone or **neuron** *noun Anat.* any of a large number of specialized cells that transmit nerve impulses from one part of the body to another. Also called NERVE CELL. [from Greek *neuron*, nerve]

neuropsychology *noun Psychol.* the application of knowledge about the structure and functioning of the brain and the rest of the nervous system to the study of human behaviour and mental activity.

neurosis *noun* (PL. **neuroses**) **1** any of various relatively mild disorders or conditions, in which disturbances of mental function may cause exaggerated or inappropriate behaviour or thinking. Examples of neuroses include phobias, obsessions, anxiety, depression, hysteria and hypochondria. **2** a popular term for anxiety or obsession.

▪ **1** disorder, affliction, abnormality, disturbance, derangement, deviation, obsession, phobia, depression, angst.

neurotic — *adj.* **1** relating to, or suffering from, a neurosis. **2** *colloq.* over-anxious, over-sensitive or obsessive. — *noun* a person suffering from a neurosis.

▪ *adj.* COMPULSIVE, OBSESSIVE, DEPRESSIVE. **1** disturbed, maladjusted, deviant, abnormal, unhealthy. **2** anxious, nervous, overwrought, unstable.

neurotransmitter *noun Physiol.* a chemical substance (eg acetylcholine, noradrenaline) that is released from nerve-cell endings in response to the arrival of a nerve impulse. Its role is to mediate transfer of the impulse across the narrow gap (*synapse*) between adjacent nerve cells, or between a nerve cell and a muscle cell.

neuter — *adj.* **1** *Grammar* denoting a gender of nouns that are neither masculine nor feminine. **2** *said of plants* lacking pistils or stamens. **3** *said of animals* sexually undeveloped or castrated. **4** *said of insects* sexually undeveloped. — *noun* **1** the neuter gender. **2** a neuter word. **3** a neuter plant, animal, or insect, eg a worker bee or ant. — *verb trans.* (**neutered**, **neutering**) to castrate (an animal). [from Latin *neuter*, from *ne*, not + *uter*, either]

▪ *verb* castrate, emasculate, geld, spay, *colloq.* doctor.

neutral — *adj.* **1** not taking sides in a quarrel or war. **2** not belonging or relating to either side: *neutral ground.* **3** *said of colours, especially grey and fawn* indefinite enough to blend easily with brighter ones. **4** having no strong or noticeable qualities. **5** *Electr.* having no positive or negative electrical charge. **6** *Chem.* neither acidic nor alkaline. — *noun* **1** a person or nation taking no part in a war or quarrel. **2** the disengaged position of an engine's gears, with no power being transmitted to the moving parts. [from Latin *neutralis*, from *neuter*, neither]

▪ *adj.* **1** impartial, uncommitted, unbia(s)sed, non-aligned, disinterested, unprejudiced, undecided, non-partisan, non-committal, objective, indifferent, dispassionate, even-handed. **3** indefinite, quiet, pastel. **4** bland, inoffensive, unexceptionable, unassertive, indistinct, characterless, expressionless, colourless, nondescript, dull, drab.
▪ *adj.* **1** biased, partisan. **4** colourful.

neutrality *noun Politics* the fact or state of being neutral, especially in a war or dispute.

▪ non-alignment, non-belligerence, impartiality, objectivity, even-handedness, detachment.

neutralization or **neutralisation** *noun* the process of neutralizing or making ineffective or harmless.

neutralize or **neutralise** *verb* **1** to cancel out the effect of; to make useless or harmless. **2** to declare (a country, etc) neutral.

▪ **1** counteract, counterbalance, offset, negate, cancel (out), nullify, invalidate, undo, frustrate.

neutrino *noun* (PL. **neutrinos**) *Physics* a stable subatomic particle that has no electric charge, virtually no mass, and travels at or near the speed of light. Neutrinos are produced in vast quantities by the nuclear reactions that take place in the Sun and other stars.

neutron *noun Physics* any of the uncharged subatomic particles that are found inside the nucleus at the centre of an atom, together with positively charged particles known as protons (hydrogen is exceptional in that it does not have any neutrons). The mass of a neutron is 1.675×10^{-27} kg. [from Latin *neuter*, neither]

neutron bomb *Mil.* a type of nuclear bomb that releases large amounts of intense radiation in the form of neutrons, and is designed to cause widespread death and disability of human beings, but relatively little structural damage to buildings, etc.

neutron star *Astron.* a star that has collapsed to such an extent under gravity that it consists almost entirely of neutrons (particles that are found only in the nucleus of atoms).

Nev or **Nev.** *abbrev.* Nevada.

never *adv.* **1** not ever; at no time. **2** not: *I never realized that.* **3** emphatically not: *this will never do.* **4** surely not: *Those two are never twins!* — **never ever** absolutely never. **well I never!** an expression of astonishment. [from Anglo-Saxon *ne*, not + *æfre*, ever]

never-ending *adj.* continuing endlessly or incessantly.

▪ everlasting, eternal, non-stop, perpetual, unceasing, uninterrupted, unremitting, interminable, incessant, unbroken, permanent, persistent, unchanging, relentless.
▪ fleeting, transitory.

nevermore *adv.* never again.
nevertheless *adv.* in spite of that.

▪ nonetheless, notwithstanding, still, anyway, even so, yet, however, anyhow, but, regardless.

new — *adj.* **1** recently made, bought, built, opened, etc. **2** recently discovered: *a new planet.* **3** never having existed before; just invented, etc: *new techniques.* **4** fresh; additional; supplementary: *a new consignment.* **5** recently arrived, installed, etc: *under new management.* **6** (**new to something**) unfamiliar with it; experiencing it for the first time: *he's new to the work.* **7** (**new to someone** or **something**) previously unknown or unfamiliar to them: *a sensation new to me.* **8** changed physically, mentally, or morally for the better: *a new man since his operation.* **9** renewed: *gave us new hope.* **10** modern: *the new generation.* **11** used in naming a place just founded after an old-established one: *New York.* — *adv.* only just, or freshly: *a new-born babe/new-baked bread.* [from Anglo-Saxon *niwe*]

▪ *adj.* **1, 2, 3** brand-new. **1** mint, unused, virgin, newborn. **3** novel, original, different, innovative, ground-breaking, advanced, newfangled. **4** fresh, added, additional, extra, more, supplementary. **6** unfamiliar with, unacquainted with, inexperienced in, unversed in, unaccustomed to, ignorant of, a stranger to. **7** unfamiliar to, strange to, alien to, unknown to. **8** changed, altered, modernized, improved, redesigned. **9** renewed, restored. **10** modern, contemporary, current, latest, recent, up-to-date, up-to-the-minute, topical, *colloq.* trendy, ultra-modern.
▪ *adj.* **1, 2, 3, 10** old. **3** usual. **10** outdated, out-of-date.

New Age a modern cultural trend concerned with the union of mind, body, and spirit and expressing itself in an interest in a variety of beliefs and disciplines such as mysticism, meditation, astrology, and holistic medicine.

new blood new people with fresh ideas introduced into an organization, etc to revitalize it.

newborn *adj.*, *said of a child* newly or recently born.

new broom a new person in charge, bent on making sweeping improvements.

newcomer *noun* someone recently arrived.

. . . .

🔁 new arrival, incomer, immigrant, stranger, alien, foreigner, colonist, settler, outsider, novice, beginner.

. . . .

newel *noun* 1 the central spindle round which a spiral stair winds. 2 (*also* **newel post**) a post at the top or bottom of a flight of stairs, supporting the handrail. [from Old French *nouel*, nut kernel]

newfangled *adj.* modern, especially objectionably so. [from Middle English *newefangel*, eager for novelty]

Newfoundland *noun* a breed of dog developed in Newfoundland, which has a large thick-set body, an enormous heavy head, a broad deep muzzle, and small ears and eyes. It has a thick black double-layered water-resistant coat and webbed feet.

newly *adv.* 1 only just; recently: *newly-mown grass*. 2 again; anew: *newly awakened desire*.

newly-weds *pl. noun* a recently married couple.

New Man a man who is prepared to show his feelings and who has adopted modern ideas on health, the environment, and sharing of family responsibilities.

new maths an approach to teaching mathematics that is more concerned with creating an early understanding of basic concepts than with drilling in arithmetic.

newness *noun* being new; a new state or quality.

new potatoes the first-dug potatoes of the new crop.

news *sing. noun* 1 information about recent events, especially as reported in newspapers or on radio or television. 2 (**the news**) a radio or television broadcast report of news. 3 any fresh interesting information. 4 a currently celebrated person, thing, or event: *he's big news in America*. — **bad** or **good news** *slang* something or someone that is unwelcome (or welcome). **that's news to me** *colloq.* I have not heard that before.

. . . .

🔁 1 information, intelligence, report, account, dispatch, communiqué, bulletin, statement, release, exposé, disclosure, scandal, revelation. 2 bulletin, newscast, newsflash. 3 story, gossip, hearsay, rumour, word, tidings, latest, *colloq.* low-down, *colloq.* gen.

. . . .

news agency an agency that collects news stories and supplies them to newspapers, etc.

newsagent *noun* a person selling newspapers, confectionery, etc.

newscast *noun* a radio or television broadcast of news items.

newscaster *noun* a person who reads out radio or television news items; a newsreader.

news conference a press conference.

newsdealer *noun* a newsagent.

newsflash *noun* a brief announcement of important news interrupting a radio or television broadcast.

newsgroup *noun Comput.* a group of Internet users who exchange e-mail on a topic of mutual interest.

newshound *noun facetious* a newspaper reporter.

newsletter *noun* a sheet containing news issued to members of a society or other organization.

newsman *noun* a male reporter for a newspaper or a broadcast news programme.

newsmonger *noun* a gossip.

newspaper *noun* 1 a daily or weekly publication composed of folded sheets of paper, containing news, advertisements, topical articles, correspondence, etc. 2 the printed paper which makes up such a publication: *chips wrapped in newspaper.*

newspeak *noun ironic* the ambiguous language, full of the latest distortions and euphemisms, used by politicians and other persuaders. [from *Newspeak*, a deliberately impoverished English used as an official language, in George Orwell's novel *1984*]

newsprint *noun* 1 the paper on which newspapers are printed. 2 the ink used to print newspapers.

newsreader *noun* a person who reads out radio or television news items.

newsreel *noun* a film of news events, once a regular cinema feature.

newsroom *noun* an office in a newspaper office or broadcasting station where news stories are received and edited for publication or broadcasting.

news stand a stall or kiosk selling newspapers, magazines, etc.

New Style the present method of dating, using the Gregorian calendar. See also OLD STYLE.

news-vendor *noun* a person who sells newspapers.

newsworthy *adj.* interesting or important enough to be reported as news.

newsy *adj.* (**newsier, newsiest**) full of news.

newt *noun* any of various amphibians related to the salamanders, with long slender bodies and well-developed limbs, and differing from lizards in that the tail is flattened from side to side. [from Anglo-Saxon *efeta*; *an ewt* came to be understood as *a newt*]

New Testament the part of the Bible concerned with the teachings of Christ and his earliest followers. See also OLD TESTAMENT.

newton *noun* (SYMBOL N) the SI unit of force, equal to the force required to give a mass of one kilogram an acceleration of one metre per second per second. [named after the English scientist and mathematician Sir Isaac Newton]

Newtonian mechanics *Physics* a theory of mechanics, formulated by Sir Isaac Newton, which considers the relationships between force and motion for everyday objects, ie objects much larger than atoms and moving slowly relative to the speed of light.

Newton's laws of motion *Physics* the basic expression of Newtonian mechanics. The first law states that the velocity of an object does not change unless a force acts on it. The second law states that a force F applied to an object of mass m causes an acceleration a according to the equation $F=ma$. The third law states that every action has an equal and opposite reaction.

new town a town planned and built by the government as a unit, to relieve congestion in nearby cities, and encourage development.

new universities universities established to accommodate the expanding numbers entering higher education in Britain during the postwar period (see also REDBRICK).

New World (**the New World**) the American continent. See also OLD WORLD.

New Year the first day of the year or the days immediately following or preceding it.

New Year's Day 1 Jan, the first day of a new year.

New Year's Eve 31 December.

next — *adj.* 1 following in time or order: *next on the list / the next day.* 2 following this one: *next week.* 3 adjoining; neighbouring: *in the next compartment.* 4 first, counting from now: *the very next person I meet.* — *noun* someone or something that is next. — *adv.* 1 immediately after that or this: *what happened next?* 2 on the next occasion: *when I next saw her.* 3 following, in order of degree: *the next longest river after the Amazon.* — **next to someone** or **something** 1 beside or close by them. 2 after something in order of degree: *next to swimming I like dancing.* 3 almost: *wear-*

ing next to no clothes. [from Anglo-Saxon *nehst*, superlative of *neah*, near]

▣ *adj.* **1** following, subsequent, succeeding, ensuing, later. **3** adjacent, adjoining, neighbouring, nearest, closest. *adv.* **1** afterwards, subsequently, later, then.
▣ *adj.* **1** previous, preceding.

next door in or to the neighbouring house.
next-door *adj.* at or belonging to the neighbouring house.
next of kin one's closest relative.
nexus *noun* (PL. **nexus**, **nexuses**) **1** a connected series or group. **2** a bond or link. [from Latin *nectere*, to bind]
NF or **Nfd** or **Nld** *abbrev.* Newfoundland.
NFU *abbrev.* National Farmers' Union.
NFWI *abbrev.* National Federation of Women's Institutes.
NH or **N.H.** *abbrev.* New Hampshire.
NHBRC *abbrev.* National House-Builders' Registration Council (or Certificate).
NHS *abbrev.* the National Health Service.
NI *abbrev.* **1** National Insurance. **2** Northern Ireland.
Ni *symbol Chem.* nickel.
niacin *noun* same as NICOTINIC ACID.
nib *noun* **1** the writing-point of a pen, especially a metal one with a divided tip. **2** (**nibs**) crushed coffee or cocoa beans. [perhaps a variant of *neb*, nose]
nibble — *verb* **1** *trans.*, *intrans.* (*also* **nibble at something**) to take very small bites of it. **2** to bite gently. **3** *intrans. colloq.* to show cautious interest in a proposal, etc. — *noun* **1** an act of nibbling, or something nibbled. **2** *Comput.* a unit of storage capacity equal to half a byte, ie a series of four bits.

▣ *verb* **1**, **2**, bite. **1** eat, peck, pick (at), munch, gnaw. *noun* **1** bite, morsel, taste, titbit, bit, crumb, snack, piece.

nibbler *noun* a person or animal that nibbles.
niblick *noun Golf* an old-fashioned club with a heavy head and a wide face, used to make lofting shots; the modern equivalent is a number eight or nine iron. [origin uncertain]
nibs *noun* — **his** or **her nibs** *facetious* a derogatory mock title for an important or would-be important person.
nicad /ˈnaɪkad/ *noun* **1** nickel-cadmium, used to make batteries. **2** a battery made using nickel-cadmium.
NICAM or **nicam** /ˈnaɪkam/ *noun* a system by which digital stereo sound signals are transmitted along with the standard TV signal, to allow the viewer to receive sound of CD quality. [from *near-instantaneous companded audio multiplexing*]
nice *adj.* **1** pleasant. **2** *often ironic* good; satisfactory. **3** *ironic* nasty: *a nice mess*. **4** fine; subtle: *nice distinctions*. **5** exacting; particular: *nice in matters of etiquette*. — **nice and ...** *colloq.* satisfactorily; commendably: *nice and firm*. [originally 'foolish', 'coy', 'exotic', from Latin *nescius*, ignorant or unknown]

▣ **1** pleasant, agreeable, delightful, charming, likable, attractive, good, kind, friendly, well-mannered, polite, respectable. **4** subtle, delicate, fine. **5** fastidious, finicky, discriminating, scrupulous, precise, exact, accurate, careful, strict.
▣ **1** nasty, disagreeable, unpleasant. **5** careless.

nicely *adv.* **1** in a nice or satisfactory way. **2** precisely; carefully: *judged it nicely*. **3** suitably; effectively: *that will do nicely*.
niceness *noun* a nice or satisfactory quality; precision.
nicety *noun* (PL. **niceties**) **1** precision. **2** a subtle point of detail. — **to a nicety** exactly.

▣ REFINEMENT, SUBTLETY, DISTINCTION. **1** precision, accuracy, meticulousness, scrupulousness,

minuteness, finesse, delicacy. **2** detail, nuance.

niche /niːʃ/ *noun* **1** a shallow recess in a wall, suitable for a lamp, ornament, statue, etc. **2** a position in life in which one feels fulfilled and/or at ease. **3** *Biol.* the unique position of a particular living organism in its environment, defined by the physical space it inhabits, the food it consumes, its tolerance of physical and chemical factors, its interaction with other organisms, etc. [from French *niche*, from Latin *nidus*, nest]

▣ **1** recess, alcove, hollow, nook, cubbyhole, corner, opening. **2** position, place, vocation, calling, métier, slot.

niche marketing marketing of a product aimed at a relatively small and specialized group of consumers.
nick — *noun* **1** a small cut. **2** *colloq.* a prison or police station. — *verb trans.* **1** to make a small cut in; to cut slightly. **2** *slang* to arrest (a criminal). **3** *slang* to steal. — **in good nick** *colloq.* in good condition. **in the nick of time** at the last possible moment; just in time.

▣ *noun* **1** notch, indentation, chip, cut, groove, dent, scar, scratch, mark. **2** prison, jail, police station. *verb* **1** notch, cut, dent, indent, chip, score, scratch, scar, mark, damage, snick. **3** steal, pilfer, *colloq.* knock off, *colloq.* pinch.

nickel *noun* **1** *Chem.* (SYMBOL **Ni**, ATOMIC NUMBER **28**) a silvery-white metal that is very resistant to corrosion and tarnishing. It is used as a catalyst, and for electroplating, and is a component of various alloys (eg stainless steel, nickel silver). **2** in the USA and Canada, a coin worth five cents. [from German *Küpfernickel*, copper devil, so called by miners mistaking it for copper]
nickel silver *Chem.* an alloy of nickel, copper, and zinc, so called because it resembles silver in appearance. It is used to make coinage, cutlery, drawing instruments, cheap jewellery, etc.
nicker *noun* (PL. **nicker**) *old slang* use a pound sterling.
nick-nack *noun* same as KNICK-KNACK.
nickname — *noun* a name, usually additional to the real one, given to a person or place in fun, affection, or contempt. — *verb trans.* to give a nickname to. [from Middle English *eke*, addition, extra; *an ekename* came to be understood as *a nickname*]

▣ *noun* pet name, sobriquet, epithet.

nicotine *noun* a poisonous alkaloid compound, obtained from the tobacco plant, that is used as an insecticide. It is responsible for the addictive effects of cigarette smoke. [named after J Nicot (1530–1600), said to have introduced tobacco into France]
nicotinic acid *Biochem.* a member of the vitamin B complex, which is needed to make the coenzymes NAD and NADP, which act as hydrogen acceptors in many of the chemical reactions in living cells. Also called NIACIN, VITAMIN B$_7$.
nictitating membrane /ˈnɪktɪteɪtɪŋ/ *Zool.* in many reptiles, amphibians, and birds, and some mammals, eg seals, a transparent membrane that forms a third eyelid which can be drawn across the eye for protection. [from Latin *nictitare*, to wink]
niece *noun* the daughter of one's sister or brother, or of one's sister- or brother-in-law. [from Latin *neptis*, granddaughter or niece]
niello /nɪˈɛloʊ/ *noun* (PL. **nielli**) a small decorative silver or gold plate with the design engraved into the metal, which is then filled with a black composition called niello. [from Italian *niello*, from Late Latin *nigellum*, a black enamel]
nielsbohrium *noun Chem.* the name formerly suggested by Soviet scientists for the chemical element unnilpentium. [named after the Danish physicist Niels Bohr]

niff *slang* — *noun* a bad smell. — *verb intrans.* to smell bad.

niffy *adj.* (**niffier, niffiest**) smelly.

nifty *adj.* (**niftier, niftiest**) **1** clever; adroit; agile. **2** stylish.

Niger-Congo /ˈnaɪdʒə(r)/ — *adj.* denoting the largest family of African languages, containing c.1000 languages and several thousand varieties and dialects. — *noun* the languages forming this family.

niggard /ˈnɪɡəd/ *noun* a stingy person.

niggardliness *noun* being niggardly or stingy.

niggardly *adj.* **1** stingy; miserly. **2** meagre: *niggardly praise.*

nigger *noun offensive* a person of black African origin or race. [from French *nègre*, from Spanish *negro*]

niggle — *verb* **1** *intrans.* to complain about unimportant details. **2** *trans.* to bother, especially slightly but continually. — *noun* **1** a slight nagging worry. **2** a small complaint or criticism.

niggler *noun* a person who complains or criticizes trivially.

niggling *adj.* trivially troublesome or worrying.

nigh *adv. old use, poetic* near. — **nigh on** or **well nigh** nearly; almost. [from Anglo-Saxon *neah*]

night *noun* **1** the time of darkness between sunset and sunrise, during which most people sleep. **2** nightfall. **3** *poetic* darkness. **4** the evening: *stayed at home last night.* **5** an evening on which a particular activity or event takes place: *my aerobics night.* — **make a night of it** *colloq.* to celebrate late into the night. [from Anglo-Saxon *niht*]

🔲 **1** night-time, darkness, dark, dead of night.
🔳 **1** day, daytime.

. . . .

night blindness abnormally reduced vision in dim light or darkness.

nightcap *noun* **1** a cap formerly worn in bed at night. **2** a drink, especially alcoholic, taken before going to bed.

nightclub *noun* a club open at night for drinking, dancing, entertainment, etc.

nightdress *noun* a loose garment worn in bed by women.

nightfall *noun* the beginning of night; dusk.

. . . .

🔲 sunset, sundown, dusk, twilight, evening, gloaming.
🔳 dawn, sunrise.

. . . .

nightie *noun* (PL. **nighties**) *colloq.* a nightdress.

nightingale *noun* any of several species of small brown thrush, found in woodland undergrowth, scrub, and marshy areas of Europe and W Asia, although it overwinters in Africa. It is best known for the nocturnal song of the male common nightingale. [from Anglo-Saxon *nihtegale*]

nightjar *noun* a nocturnal bird of the swift family with a harsh discordant cry. [from NIGHT + JAR[2]]

nightlife *noun* entertainment available in a city, etc late into the night.

night light a dim-shining lamp or slow-burning candle that can be left alight all night.

nightlong *adj., adv.* throughout the night.

nightly *adj., adv.* every night.

nightmare *noun* **1** a frightening dream. **2** an intensely distressing or frightful experience or situation. [from NIGHT + Anglo-Saxon *mare*, an incubus, or nightmare-producing monster]

🔲 **1** bad dream, hallucination. **2** ordeal, horror, torment, trial.

. . . .

nightmarish *adj.* like a nightmare; intensely distressing or frightful.

. . . .

🔲 horrifying, terrifying, hair-raising, horrible, frightful, hideous, ghastly, grisly.

. . . .

night owl a person who likes to stay up late at night.

nights *adv.* at night; most nights or every night: *chooses to work nights.*

night safe a safe built into the outer wall of a bank, in which to deposit money when the bank is closed.

night school an institution providing educational evening classes for people who are at work during the day.

nightshade *noun* any of several wild plants, some with poisonous berries, including the belladonna or deadly nightshade. [from Anglo-Saxon *nihtscada*]

night shift 1 a session of work or duty during the night. **2** the staff working during this period. See also BACK SHIFT, DAY SHIFT.

nightshirt *noun* a long shirt-like garment, formerly usually for men, worn in bed.

night soil *old use* human excrement collected at night for use as a soil fertilizer.

night spot a nightclub.

night stick *North Amer.* a police truncheon.

night-time *noun* the time of darkness between sunset and sunrise.

nightwatchman *noun* **1** someone who looks after industrial, etc premises at night. **2** *Cricket* a batsman, not a high scorer, put in to defend a wicket till close of play.

nihilism /ˈnaɪɪlɪzm/ *noun* **1** the rejection of moral and religious principles. **2** a 19c Russian movement aimed at overturning all social institutions. **3** the view that nothing has real existence; extreme scepticism. [from Latin *nihil*, nothing]

nihilist *noun* a supporter of nihilism.

nihilistic *adj.* characterized by nihilism or extreme scepticism.

-nik *suffix sometimes derog.* forming nouns denoting someone concerned or associated with a certain cause, activity, etc: *peacenik/refusenik*. [from Yiddish, from Slavic]

nil *noun* in games, etc, a score of nothing; zero. [from Latin *nil* (*nihil*), nothing]

. . . .

🔲 nothing, zero, none, nought, naught, love, duck, *slang* zilch.

. . . .

Nilo-Saharan /naɪloʊsəˈhɑːrən/ — *adj.* denoting a family of more than 100 African languages spoken by the peoples of the Upper Nile in Sudan, Egypt, Uganda, and Kenya, in the Sahara, and in the area of the River Chari in central Africa. — *noun* the languages forming this group.

nimble *adj.* **1** quick and light in movement; agile. **2** *said of wits* sharp; alert. [from Anglo-Saxon *næmel*, receptive, and *numol*, quick to learn]

. . . .

🔲 QUICK. **1** agile, active, lively, sprightly, spry, smart, brisk, *colloq.* nippy, deft, alert, light-footed, prompt, ready, swift.
🔳 **1** clumsy, slow.

. . . .

nimbleness *noun* being nimble; sharpness; alertness.

nimbly *adv.* with a nimble or alert manner or movement.

nimbus *noun* (PL. **nimbuses, nimbi**) **1** *Meteorol.* a general term used to refer to any cloud, usually dark grey in colour, that produces precipitation, especially rainfall; a rain cloud. **2** a luminous mist or halo surrounding a god or goddess. [from Latin *nimbus*]

NIMBY *abbrev.* not in my back yard.

nincompoop *noun* a fool; an idiot.

nine — *noun* **1** the number or figure 9; any symbol for this number. **2** the age of 9. **3** something, eg a garment or a person, whose size is denoted by the number 9. **4** 9 o'clock. **5** a set of 9 people or things. **6** a playing-card with 9 pips. **7** a score of 9 points. — *adj.* **1** 9 in number. **2** aged 9. — **dressed up to the nines** *colloq.* wearing one's best clothes. [from Anglo-Saxon *nigon*]

ninefold — *adj.* **1** equal to nine times as much or many. **2** divided into, or consisting of, nine parts. — *adv.* by nine times as much or many.

ninepins *sing. noun* a game similar to skittles, using a wooden ball and nine skittles arranged in a triangle.

nineteen — *noun* **1** the number or figure 19; any symbol for this number. **2** the age of 19. **3** something, eg a garment or a person, denoted by the number 19. **4** a set of 19 people or things. — *adj.* **1** 19 in number. **2** aged 19. — **talk nineteen to the dozen** *colloq.* to chatter away animatedly. [from Anglo-Saxon *nigontiene*]

nineteenth *noun, adj.* the position in a series corresponding to 19 in a sequence of numbers.

nineties *pl. noun* **1** the period of time between one's 90th and 100th birthdays. **2** the range of temperatures between 90 and 100 degrees. **3** the period of time between the 90th and 100th years of a century.

ninetieth *noun, adj.* the position in a series corresponding to 90 in a sequence of numbers.

ninety — *noun* (PL. **nineties**) **1** the number or figure 90; any symbol for this number. **2** the age of 90. **3** a set of 90 people or things. — *adj.* **1** 90 in number. **2** aged 90. [from Anglo-Saxon *nigontig*]

ninety-five theses *Relig.* a series of points of academic debate with the pope, posted on the church door at Wittenburg in 1517 by Martin Luther, challenging many practices of the Church, and generally regarded as initiating the Protestant Reformation.

ninja /'nɪndʒə/ *noun* (PL. **ninja, ninjas**) *especially in medieval Japan* one of a body of professional assassins trained in martial arts and stealth. [from Japanese *nin*, endure + *-ja*, person]

ninjutsu or **ninjitsu** *noun* an armed Japanese martial art with a strong emphasis on stealth and camouflage. In the 1980s, it became a popular element in cinema, video games, and children's toys in the West. [from Japanese]

ninny *noun* (PL. **ninnies**) a foolish person.

Nintendo *noun trademark* a handheld device which allows video games to be viewed and played on a television screen.

ninth *noun, adj.* the position in a series corresponding to nine in a sequence of numbers.

ninthly *adv.* as ninth in a series.

niobium *noun Chem.* (SYMBOL **Nb**, ATOMIC NUMBER **41**) a relatively unreactive soft greyish-blue metal with a brilliant lustre. It is resistant to corrosion, and is used in stainless steels and other alloys with high melting points, superconductors, and nuclear reactors. Formerly known as *columbium*. [named after Niobe in Greek mythology, who was turned into a weeping rock]

Nip *noun offensive* a Japanese person. [short for *Nipponese*, 'Japanese']

nip[1] — *verb* **1** *trans.* to pinch or squeeze sharply. **2** *trans.* to give a sharp little bite to. **3** *trans., intrans.* to sting; to cause smarting. **4** *intrans. colloq.* (**nip off**, **nip away**) to go quickly: *nip round to the shop*. **5** *trans.* to halt the growth or development of: *nip it in the bud*. — *noun* **1** a pinch or squeeze. **2** a sharp little bite. **3** a sharp biting coldness, or stinging quality. [from Norse *hnippa*, to poke]

▤ *verb* **1** pinch, squeeze, tweak, catch, grip. **2** bite, nibble. **4** go, dash, *colloq.* pop. **5** snip, clip. *noun* **1** pinch, squeeze, tweak. **2** bite, nibble.

nip[2] *noun* a small quantity of alcoholic spirits: *a nip of brandy*. [from Dutch *nippen*, to sip]

▤ dram, draught, shot, swallow, mouthful, drop, sip, taste, portion.

nipper *noun* **1** the claw of a crab, lobster, etc. **2** (**nippers**) pincers, tweezers, forceps, or other gripping or severing tool. **3** *old colloq. use* a small child.

nippiness *noun* being nippy or quick-moving.

nipple *noun* **1** the deep-coloured pointed projection on a breast, in the female the outlet of the ducts from which the young suck milk. **2** *North Amer.* the teat on a baby's feeding-bottle. **3** *Mech.* any small projection with a hole through which a flow is regulated or machine parts lubricated.

nippy *adj.* (**nippier, nippiest**) *colloq.* **1** cold; chilly. **2** quick-moving; nimble.

▤ **1** cold, chilly, chill, fresh, cool, *Brit. colloq.* parky. **2** quick, smart, brisk, nimble, agile, lively, sprightly, spry.

nirvana /nɜ:'vɑːnə/ *noun* (*also* **Nirvana**) **1** *Buddhism, Hinduism* the ultimate state of spiritual tranquillity attained through release from everyday concerns and extinction of individual passions. **2** *colloq.* a place or state of perfect bliss. [from Sanskrit *nirvana*, extinction]

nisi /'naɪsaɪ/ *adj.*, *said of a court order* to take effect on the date stated, unless in the meantime a reason is given why it should not. See also DECREE NISI. [fom Latin *nisi*, unless]

Nissen hut a corrugated-iron hut in the shape of a semi-cylinder lying lengthwise. [from P N Nissen (1871–1930), its designer]

nit[1] *noun* the egg or young of a louse, found eg in hair. [from Anglo-Saxon *hnitu*]

nit[2] *noun slang* an idiot. [a shortening of NITWIT]

▤ fool, idiot, nitwit, *colloq.* dimwit, *colloq.* twit, *colloq.* clot.

nit-picker *noun* a person who indulges in nit-picking.

nit-picking *noun* petty criticism or fault-finding.

nitrate — *noun Chem.* a salt or ester of nitric acid, that contains the NO_3^- ion. Nitrates are essential for plant growth, and are used as artificial fertilizers. Nitrates are also used in explosives. — *verb* **1** to treat with nitric acid or a nitrate. **2** *trans., intrans.* to convert into a nitrate.

nitration *noun Chem.* a chemical reaction in which a nitro ($-NO_2$) group is incorporated into the structure of a molecule. It is usually achieved by treating an organic compound with a *nitrating mixture* of concentrated nitric and sulphuric acids.

nitre /'naɪtə(r)/ *noun Chem.* a former name for potassium nitrate; saltpetre. [from Greek *nitron*, sodium carbonate]

nitric *adj. Chem.* of or containing nitrogen.

nitric acid *Chem.* a colourless or yellowish toxic corrosive acid manufactured by the catalytic oxidation of ammonia. It is used in the manufacture of explosives, nitrate fertilizers, dyes, and plastics.

nitric oxide *Chem.* same as NITROGEN MONOXIDE.

nitride *noun* a compound of nitrogen with another, metallic, element.

nitrification *noun Biochem.* **1** treatment with nitric acid. **2** in the nitrogen cycle, the conversion of ammonia first to nitrites and then to nitrates, which can be taken up by the roots of plants. Nitrification is carried out by certain bacteria, known as *nitrifying bacteria*.

nitrify *verb trans., intrans.* (**nitrifies, nitrified**) *Chem.* to undergo or cause to undergo the process of nitrification.

nitrite *noun Chem.* a salt or ester of nitrous acid, containing the NO_2^- ion, eg potassium nitrite (KNO_2).

nitro- *combining form Chem.* forming words meaning: **1** of, made with, or containing nitrogen, nitric acid, or nitre. **2** containing the group $-NO_2$.

nitrogen *noun* (SYMBOL **N**, ATOMIC NUMBER **7**) a gas that is colourless, odourless, and tasteless and represents about 78% of the Earth's atmosphere by volume. [from NITRE + -GEN]

nitrogen cycle *Biol.* the continuous circulation of nitrogen and its compounds between the atmosphere and the biosphere as a result of the activity of living organisms.

nitrogen dioxide *Chem.* (FORMULA NO_2) a reddish-brown gas that is used in the production of nitric acid.

nitrogen fixation *Biochem.* the conversion of nitrogen in the atmosphere to nitrogen-containing compounds, especially nitrates, which can be utilized by plants. The process is carried out by nitrifying bacteria in the soil, and blue-green algae.

nitrogen monoxide *Chem.* (FORMULA NO) a colourless gas that reacts spontaneously with oxygen at room temperature to form nitrogen dioxide (NO_2). Nitrogen monoxide is an intermediate in the oxidation of ammonia to nitric acid. Also called NITRIC OXIDE.

nitrogenous *adj. Chem.* containing nitrogen.

nitroglycerine or **nitroglycerin** *noun Chem.* an explosive toxic oily yellow liquid that is an ester of nitric acid. It is used as a rocket fuel, an explosive (eg in dynamite), and as a vasodilatory drug in medicine.

nitrous *adj. Chem.* of or containing nitrogen in a low valency.

nitrous acid *Chem.* (FORMULA HNO_2) a weak unstable acid that decomposes in water, and is formed when a nitrite salt reacts with an acid. It is used as a source of nitric oxide, and in the synthesis of organic compounds.

nitrous oxide *Chem.* nitrogen monoxide.

nitty-gritty *noun colloq.* (**the nitty-gritty**) the fundamental issue or essential part of any matter, situation, activity, etc. [originally US; perhaps rhyming compound of *grit*]

▣ basics, fundamentals, brass tacks, the bottom line.

nitwit *noun* a stupid person. [from German dialect *nit*, variant of *nicht*, not + WIT[1]]

nix *North Amer.* — *noun slang* nothing. — *interj.* no. [from German, a form of *nichts*, nothing]

NJ or **N.J.** *abbrev.* New Jersey.

NM or **N.M.** or **N.Mex.** *abbrev.* New Mexico.

NNE *abbrev.* north-north-east.

NNEB *abbrev.* Nursery Nurses' Examination Board.

NNW *abbrev.* north-north-west.

No[1] see NOH.

No[2] *symbol Chem.* nobelium.

No. or **no.** *abbrev.* (usually followed by a numeral) number: *No.3.*

no[1] — *interj.* used as **1** a negative reply, expressing denial, refusal, or disagreement. **2** *colloq.* a question tag expecting agreement: *it's a deal, no?* **3** an astonished rejoinder: *No! You don't say!* — *adv.* **1** (*with comparative*) not any: *no bigger than one's thumb.* **2** (*used to indicate a negative alternative*) not: *whether he's willing or no.* — *noun* (PL. **noes**) a negative reply or vote. [from Anglo-Saxon *na*, from *ne*, not + *a*, ever]

no[2] *adj.* **1** not any. **2** certainly not a; far from a: *he's no fool/ no easy task.* **3** hardly any: *do it in no time.* **4** not allowed: *no smoking.* — **no go** *colloq.* impossible; no good. **no way** *colloq.* no; definitely not. [from Middle English, a variant of NONE]

no. see No.

nob *noun slang* a person of wealth or high social rank.

no-ball *noun Cricket, Baseball* a ball bowled in a manner disallowed by the rules.

nobble *verb trans. colloq.* **1** *Racing* to drug or otherwise interfere with (a horse) to stop it winning. **2** to persuade by bribes or threats. **3** to obtain dishonestly. **4** to catch (a criminal). **5** to swindle. [from *an hobbler*, a person who lames horses (later understood as *a nobbler*)]

▣ **1, 2** *colloq.* get at. **1** dope, drug, interfere with, disable, incapacitate, hamstring. **2** bribe, buy (off), *colloq.* fix, warn off, threaten, intimidate.

nobelium /nəʊˈbiːlɪəm/ *noun Chem.* (SYMBOL **No**, ATOMIC NUMBER 102) a synthetic radioactive metallic element produced by bombarding curium with carbon ions. [named after the Nobel Institute, Stockholm, where it was first produced]

Nobel prize any of the prizes, awarded annually for work in physics, chemistry, medicine, literature, and the promo-

tion of peace, instituted by Alfred Nobel, Swedish inventor of dynamite.

nobility *noun* **1** the quality of being noble, in character, conduct, or rank. **2** (**the nobility**) the class of people of noble birth. [from Latin *nobilitas*, from *nobilis*, noble]

▣ **1** nobleness, dignity, grandeur, illustriousness, stateliness, majesty, magnificence, eminence, excellence, superiority, uprightness, honour, virtue, worthiness. **2** aristocracy, peerage, nobles, gentry, elite, lords, high society.
▣ **1** baseness. **2** proletariat.

noble — *adj.* **1** honourable. **2** generous. **3** of high birth or rank. **4** grand, splendid, or imposing in appearance. — *noun* a person of noble rank. [from Latin *nobilis*, originally *gnobilis*, knowable, ie well-known]

▣ *adj.* **1** honourable, worthy, gentlemanly, chivalrous, principled, high-minded, virtuous. **2** generous, magnanimous, munificent. **3** aristocratic, high-born, titled, high-ranking, patrician, gentle, blue-blooded. **4** magnificent, splendid, stately, dignified, distinguished, eminent, grand, great, imposing, impressive, majestic, elevated, fine. *noun* aristocrat, peer, lord, lady, nobleman, noblewoman.
▣ *adj.* **1** ignoble, base, contemptible. **2** mean. **3** low-born. *noun* commoner.

noble gas *Chem.* any of the colourless odourless tasteless gases in group 0 of the periodic table of the elements, ie helium, neon, argon, krypton, xenon, and radon, in order of increasing atomic number. Also called INERT GAS.

nobleman *noun* a male member of the nobility.

noble metal *Chem.* any metal that is highly unreactive, such as gold or platinum, and is therefore resistant to oxidation, tarnishing, etc.

nobleness *noun* a noble state or quality.

noble rot *Bot.* on white grapes, a rot caused by the fungus *Botrytis cinerea*. Sweet white wines are made using the infected fruit.

noblesse oblige /nəʊˈblɛs əʊˈbliːʒ/ the maxim that it is the duty of those who are privileged to use their privilege to the benefit of the less fortunate. [French, = nobility obliges]

noblewoman *noun* a female member of the nobility.

nobly *adv.* with a noble or honourable manner: *behave nobly.*

nobody — *pron.* no person; no one. — *noun* (PL. **nobodies**) a person of no significance.

▣ *pron.* no one, none, nothing. *noun* nonentity, menial, cipher.
▣ *noun* somebody.

no-claims bonus a reduction in the fee one pays for insurance if one has made no claim for payment over a particular period.

nocturnal *adj.* **1** *said of animals, etc* active at night. **2** happening at night. **3** of, belonging to, or relating to the night. [from Latin *nocturnus*, from *nox*, night]

nocturnally *adv.* at night.

nocturne *noun* **1** a dreamy piece of music, usually for the piano. **2** *Art* a night or moonlight scene. [from French *nocturne*, from Latin *nocturnus*, from *nox*, night]

nod — *verb* (**nodded, nodding**) **1** *intrans., trans.* to make a brief bowing gesture with the head, in agreement, greeting, etc; to bow (the head) briefly. **2** *intrans.* to let the head droop with sleepiness; to become drowsy. **3** *intrans.* to make a mistake through momentary loss of concentration. **4** *trans.* to indicate or direct by nodding: *nodded her approval / was nodded through the Customs.* **5** *intrans.* said *of flowers, plumes, etc* to sway or bob about. — *noun* a brief bowing gesture with the head. — **have a nodding acquaintance with someone** to know them slightly. **the Land of**

Nod the imaginary country to which sleepers go. **nod off** *intrans.* to fall asleep in a chair, etc. **on the nod** *colloq.*, *said of the passing of a proposal, etc* by general agreement, without the formality of a vote.

. . . .

▣ *verb* **1** gesture, indicate, sign, signal, salute, acknowledge, agree, assent. **2** sleep, doze, drowse, nap. *noun* gesture, indication, sign, signal, salute, greeting, beck, acknowledgement. **nod off** fall asleep, doze off, *colloq.* drop off.

. . . .

nodal *adj.* relating to or consisting of a node or nodes.

noddle *noun colloq.* the head or brain.

noddy *noun* (PL. **noddies**) **1** a tropical bird of the tern family, so unafraid as to seem stupid. **2** a simpleton. [perhaps from an obsolete word *noddy*, silly]

noddy suit *Mil. slang* an NBC suit.

node *noun* **1** *Anat.* a small lump or mass of tissue, eg lymph node, or a junction of a system or network, eg of muscle fibres in the pacemaker of the heart. **2** *Bot.* the point on a plant stem from which leaves and axillary buds arise. **3** *Geom.* the point at which two or more branches of a curve meet. **4** *Astron.* the point at which one orbit crosses another, especially one of two points at which the orbit of a celestial body crosses a reference plane, such as the ecliptic (apparent path of the sun). **5** *Physics* in a system of standing waves, a point, line, or surface where there is zero amplitude (minimum disturbance), eg near the closed end of a resonating pipe. [from Latin *nodus*, knot]

nodular *adj.* relating to or consisting of a nodule or nodules.

nodule *noun* **1** a small round lump. **2** *Bot.* any of a number of small round swellings on the roots of leguminous plants, eg peas, beans, clover, containing bacteria capable of converting atmospheric nitrogen into nitrogen compounds that can be used by the plant. [from Latin *nodulus*, a diminutive of *nodus*, knot]

Noel *noun old use* Christmas. [from Old French *noel*, from Latin *natalis*, birthday]

no-fault principle *Legal* the principle that it should be possible to claim compensation for injury without proving fault against a defendant.

nog *noun* an alcoholic drink made with whipped eggs; an egg nog.

noggin *noun* **1** a small measure or quantity of alcoholic spirits. **2** a small mug or wooden cup. **3** *colloq.* one's head.

no-go area an area of a city to which access is controlled by one of the groups involved in an armed conflict or civil war, and is forbidden to others.

Noh or **No** *noun* classical Japanese theatre in which imitation, gesture, dance, mask-work, costume, song, and music are fused in a concise stage art. [from Japanese *no*, ability]

nohow *adv* dialect in no way.

noise — *noun* **1** a sound, especially a harsh or disagreeable sound. **2** a series of unpleasant or confused sounds, causing a continuous din. **3** unwanted and often random interference that makes it hard to detect the content of an electrical signal, such as a particular radio frequency band. Sources of noise include radio waves, electrical equipment, electric cables, computers, lightning, etc. **4** *facetious* something one utters by way of conventional response, vague indication of inclinations, etc: *make polite noises.* — *verb* (**noise something abroad**) to make it generally known; to spread a rumour, etc. [from Old French, from Latin *nausea*, seasickness]

. . . .

▣ *noun* **1** sound, bang, crash, clatter, blare, rustle, creak, squeak. **2** din, racket, row, clamour, commotion, outcry, hubbub, uproar, pandemonium, tumult, babble. *verb* report, rumour, publicize, announce, circulate, blaze abroad.

▣ *noun* **2** quiet, silence.

. . . .

noiseless *adj.* lacking noise; silent.

. . . .

▣ silent, inaudible, soundless, quiet, mute, still, hushed.

▣ loud, noisy.

. . . .

noise pollution an excessive or annoying degree of noise in a particular area, eg from traffic or aircraft.

noisily *adv.* with much noise; loudly.

noisiness *noun* much noise; loudness.

noisome *adj.* **1** disgusting; offensive; stinking. **2** harmful; poisonous: *noisome fumes.* [from earlier *noy*, a variant of ANNOY]

noisy *adj.* (**noisier, noisiest**) **1** making a lot of noise: *noisy children.* **2** full of noise: *noisy streets.*

. . . .

▣ **1** loud, deafening, ear-splitting, clamorous, piercing, vocal, vociferous, tumultuous, boisterous, obstreperous.

▣ QUIET, SILENT, PEACEFUL.

. . . .

nom. *abbrev. Grammar* nominative.

nomad *noun* **1** a member of a people without permanent home, who travel from place to place seeking food and pasture. **2** a wanderer. [from Greek *nomas*, from *nomos*, pasture]

. . . .

▣ MIGRANT. **2** traveller, wanderer, itinerant, rambler, roamer, rover.

. . . .

nomadic *adj.*, *said of a people* wandering from place to place; not settled.

. . . .

▣ migrant, migratory, travelling, wandering, itinerant, peripatetic, unsettled, rootless.

. . . .

nomadism *noun* the way of life of nomads, characterized by frequent movement from place to place.

no-man's-land *noun* **1** unclaimed land; waste land. **2** neutral territory between opposing armies or between two countries with a common border. **3** a state or situation that is neither one thing nor another.

nom-de-plume /ˈnɒm də pluːm/ *noun* (PL. **noms-de-plume**) a pseudonym used by a writer; a pen-name. [French, = pen-name]

nomenclature *noun* **1** a classified system of names, especially in scientific terminology, eg binomial nomenclature, in which each living organism is given a two-part scientific name, usually Latinized, denoting the genus and the species. **2** a list or set of names. [from Latin *nomenclatura*, from *nomen*, name + *calare*, to call]

nominal *adj.* **1** in name only; so called, but actually not: *a nominal head of state.* **2** very small in comparison to actual cost or value: *a nominal rent.* **3** *Grammar* of, being, or relating to a noun. [from Latin *nominalis*, from *nomen*, name]

. . . .

▣ **1** titular, supposed, purported, professed, ostensible, so-called, theoretical, self-styled, puppet, symbolic. **2** token, minimal, trifling, trivial, insignificant, small.

▣ **1** actual, genuine, real.

. . . .

nominalism *noun Philos.* the view that a general term such as 'book' is no more than a name, and does not refer to an actual entity.

nominally *adv.* in name only; theoretically rather than actually.

nominal value the stated or face value, on a bond, share certificate, etc.

nominate *verb* **1** (**nominate someone for something**) to propose them formally as a candidate for election, for a job, etc. **2** (**nominate someone to something**) to appoint them to a post or position. **3** to specify formally (eg a date). [from Latin *nominare*, to name]

⊟ **1** propose, submit, suggest, recommend, put up, present. **2, 3** designate. **2** appoint, name, choose, select, elect, assign, commission, elevate.

nomination *noun* **1** a formal proposal of a candidate for election or appointment. **2** appointing or being appointed.

⊟ **1** proposal, submission, suggestion, recommendation. **2** appointment, designation, election, choice, selection.

nominative *Grammar* — *adj.* denoting the case used, in inflected languages such as Latin, for the subject of the verb. — *noun* **1** the nominative case. **2** a word in this case. [from Latin *nominativus*, from *nominare*, to name]

nominee *noun* a person who is nominated as a candidate, or for or to a job, etc. [from Latin *nominare*, to name]

⊟ candidate, entrant, contestant, appointee, runner, assignee.

non- *prefix* forming words meaning: **1** not; the opposite: *non-essential / non-existent.* **2** *ironic* not deserving the name: *a non-event.* **3** not belonging to the specified category: *non-fiction / non-metals.* **4** not having the skill or desire: *non-swimmers/non-smokers.* **5** rejection, avoidance, or omission: *non-aggression/non-payment.* **6** not liable to: *non-shrink/non-drip.* **7** not requiring a certain treatment: *non-iron.* [from Latin *non*, not]

nonage /ˈnɒnɪdʒ/ *noun Legal* the condition of being under age; one's minority or period of immaturity. [from Old French, from *non*, non + *age*, age]

nonagenarian /nɒnədʒəˈnɛərɪən/ *adj.* between 90 and 99 years old. — *noun* a person of this age. [from Latin *nonagenarius*, containing or consisting of 90]

nonagon *noun Geom.* a nine-sided figure. [from Latin *nonus*, ninth + Greek *gonia*, angle]

non-aligned *adj.*, *said of a country* not allied to any of the major power blocs in world politics.

non-alignment *noun* being non-aligned; neutrality.

non-belligerent — *adj.* taking no part in a war. — *noun* a non-belligerent country.

nonce — **for the nonce** for the time being; for the present. [originally *for then ones*, for the once (*then once* coming to be understood as *the nonce*)]

nonce-word *noun* a word coined for one particular occasion.

nonchalance *noun* calm or indifferent lack of concern.

⊟ unconcern, detachment, insouciance, carelessness, casualness, calm, coolness, composure, sangfroid.

nonchalant *adj.* calmly or indifferently unconcerned. [from French *nonchaloir*, to lack warmth]

⊟ unconcerned, detached, dispassionate, offhand, blasé, indifferent, casual, carefree, careless, insouciant, cool, collected.
⊟ concerned, careful.

nonchalantly *adv.* with calm or indifferent lack of concern.

non-combatant *noun* a non-fighting member of the armed forces, eg a surgeon or chaplain.

non-commissioned officer an officer such as a corporal or sergeant, appointed from the lower ranks of the armed forces, not by being given a commission.

non-committal *adj.* avoiding expressing a definite opinion or decision.

⊟ guarded, cautious, wary, reserved, discreet, equivocal,

ambiguous, evasive, circumspect, careful, neutral, indefinite, politic, tactful, tentative, vague.

non-committally *adv.* without expressing a definite opinion or decision.

non compos mentis /ˈnɒn ˈkɒmpəs ˈmɛntɪs/ not of sound mind. [Latin, = not in command of the mind]

non-conductor *noun* a substance that does not conduct heat, electricity, or sound.

nonconformism *noun* refusal to conform to generally accepted practice.

nonconformist — *noun* **1** someone who refuses to conform to generally accepted practice. **2 (Nonconformist)** in England, a member of a Protestant church separated from the Church of England. — *adj.* of or relating to nonconformists.

⊟ *noun* **1** dissenter, rebel, dissident, radical, protester, heretic, individualist, eccentric, maverick, secessionist. *adj.* dissentient, rebel, dissident, unco-operative, radical, heretical, eccentric, individualistic.
⊟ *noun, adj.* conformist.

nonconformity *noun* **1** refusal to conform to established practice. **2** lack of correspondence or agreement between things.

⊟ **1** dissent, non-compliance, non-co-operation, rebellion, dissidence, individualism, eccentricity. **2** incongruence, incompatibility, inconsistency.

non-contributory *adj.*, *said of a pension scheme* paid for by the employer, without contributions from the employee.

non-custodial *adj.*, *said of a judicial sentence* not involving imprisonment.

non-denominational *adj.* not linked with any particular religious denomination; for the use or participation of members of all denominations.

nondescript *adj.* having no strongly noticeable characteristics or distinctive features. [from NON- + Latin *descriptus*, past participle of *describere*, to describe]

⊟ featureless, indeterminate, undistinctive, undistinguished, unexceptional, ordinary, commonplace, plain, dull, uninspiring, uninteresting, unclassified.
⊟ distinctive, remarkable.

none[1] *pron.* **1** not any. **2** no one: *none were as kind as she.* — **none but** only: *none but the finest ingredients.* **none of** ... I won't put up with: *none of your cheek.* **none other than** someone or something the very person or thing mentioned or thought of: *it was none other than Bill.* **none the** ... (*followed by a comparative*) not any: *none the worse for his adventure.* **none too** ... by no means: *none too clean.* [from Anglo-Saxon *nan*, not one, no]

⊟ **1** not any, not one, nil, zero. **2** no one, nobody.

none[2] or **nones** *noun* the fifth of the canonical hours, originally said at the ninth hour (ie 3pm). See also COMPLINE, LAUDS, MATINS, SEXT, TERCE, VESPERS. [from Latin *nona hora*, the ninth hour]

nonentity *noun* (PL. **nonentities**) a person of no significance, character, ability, etc.

nones[1] *pl. noun* in the Roman calendar, the seventh day of March, May, July, and October, the fifth day of other months. [from Latin *nonae*, from *nonus*, ninth: the nones were the ninth day before the Ides, counting inclusively]

nones[2] see NONE[2].

nonetheless *adv.* nevertheless, in spite of that.

⊟ nevertheless, still, anyway, even so, yet,

notwithstanding, however, anyhow, but, regardless.

....

non-Euclidean geometry any system of geometry that is not based on the theories of the Greek mathematician Euclid.

non-event *noun* an event one has been greatly looking forward to that turns out to be a disappointment.

non-ferrous *adj.*, *said of metals* not iron or steel.

non-fiction *noun* literature other than fiction, including biography, reference books, and textbooks.

non-flammable *adj.* not liable to catch fire or burn easily.

nonintervention *noun Politics* a policy of systematic abstention from interference in the affairs of other nations.

non-metal *noun Chem.* any chemical element that does not have the properties of a metal or a metalloid, and that does not form positive ions.

no-no *noun* (PL. **no-nos**) *colloq.* something which must not be done, said, etc.

non-observance *noun* failure to observe a rule, etc.

no-nonsense *adj.* sensible; practical.

nonpareil /nɒnpə'reɪl/ — *adj.* having no equal. — *noun* an unequalled person or thing. [from French *nonpareil*, from *non*, non- + *pareil*, equal]

non-person *noun* a person, once prominent, who has slipped into obscurity.

nonplus *verb trans.* (**nonplussed, nonplussing**) to puzzle; to disconcert. [from Latin *non plus*, no further]

nonplussed *adj.* puzzled; disconcerted.

....

▣ disconcerted, puzzled, confounded, taken aback, stunned, bewildered, astonished, astounded, dumbfounded, perplexed, stumped, flabbergasted, flummoxed, baffled, dismayed, embarrassed.

....

non-proliferation *noun* the policy of limiting the production and ownership of nuclear or chemical weapons.

non-renewable resource any naturally occurring substance that is economically valuable, but which forms over such a long time period (often millions of years) that for all practical purposes it cannot be replaced once it has been used, eg fossil fuels, mineral resources.

nonsense — *noun* **1** words or ideas that do not make sense. **2** foolishness; silly behaviour. — *interj.* you're quite wrong. — **make a nonsense of something** to destroy the effect of; to make pointless.

....

▣ *noun* **1** rubbish, trash, drivel, balderdash, gibberish, *colloq.* gobbledygook, *colloq.* rot, blather, *colloq.* twaddle, claptrap, *slang* cobblers. **2** stupidity, silliness, foolishness, folly, senselessness, ridiculousness.

▣ *noun* **1** sense, wisdom.

....

nonsense verse verse deliberately written to convey an absurd meaning, or with no obvious meaning at all.

nonsensical *adj.* making no sense; absurd.

....

▣ ridiculous, meaningless, senseless, foolish, inane, irrational, silly, incomprehensible, ludicrous, absurd, fatuous, crazy.

▣ reasonable, sensible, logical.

....

nonsensically *adv.* in a way that makes no sense.

non sequitur /nɒn 'sɛkwɪtə(r)/ an illogical step in an argument; a conclusion that does not follow from the premises. [from Latin *non sequitur*, it does not follow]

non-standard *adj.*, *said of use of language* not generally accepted as correct.

non-starter *noun* a person, thing, idea, etc that has no chance of success.

non-stick *adj.*, *said of a pan, etc* having a coating to which food does not stick during cooking.

non-stop *adj.*, *adv.* without a stop.

....

▣ *adj.* never-ending, uninterrupted, continuous, incessant, constant, endless, interminable, unending, unbroken, round-the-clock, on-going. *adv.* continuously, incessantly, constantly, endlessly, interminably, all the time, round the clock.

▣ *adj.* intermittent, occasional.

....

non-U *adj. Brit. colloq.*, *said especially of language* not acceptable among the upper classes. [from U^2, = upper class]

non-union *adj.* **1** not belonging to a trade union. **2** employing, or produced by, workers not belonging to a trade union.

nonverbal communication (ABBREV. **NVC**) forms of communication between people that supplement the spoken or written word, including gesture and posture (body language), and facial expression.

non-voting *adj.*, *said of shares* not giving the holder the right to vote on company decisions.

non-white — *adj.*, *said of a person* not belonging to one of the white-skinned races. — *noun* a non-white person.

noodle[1] *noun* (*usually* **noodles**) a thin strip of pasta, usually made with egg.

noodle[2] *noun colloq.* a simpleton.

nook *noun* **1** a secluded retreat. **2** a corner or recess. — **every nook and cranny** absolutely everywhere.

....

▣ CORNER. **1** hideaway, hideout, retreat, shelter. **2** recess, alcove, cranny, crevice, niche, cubbyhole, cavity.

....

noon *noun* midday; twelve o'clock. [from Latin *nona* (*hora*), the ninth hour, originally 3pm]

no one or **no-one** *noun* nobody; no person.

noose *noun* a loop made in the end of a rope, etc with a sliding knot, used eg for killing by hanging. — **put one's head in a noose** to walk into danger. [from Old French *nous*, from Latin *nodus*, knot]

NOP *abbrev.* National Opinion Poll.

nor — *conj.* **1** used to introduce alternatives after *neither*: *he neither knows nor cares/they eat neither fish nor meat nor eggs*. **2** and … not: *it didn't look appetizing, nor was it.* — *adv.* not either: *if you won't, nor shall I.* [a contraction of Anglo-Saxon *nother*, from *ne*, not + *other*, either]

nor' *combining form Naut.* north: *a nor'-wester/nor'-nor'-east.*

noradrenaline *noun Physiol.* a hormone, closely related to adrenaline, produced in small amounts by the adrenal glands.

Nordic *adj.* **1** of or belonging to Scandinavia or its inhabitants. **2** Germanic or Scandinavian in appearance, typically tall, blond, and blue-eyed. **3** (**nordic**) denoting a type of competitive skiing with cross-country racing and ski-jumping. [from French *nordique*, from *nord*, north]

Norf. *abbrev.* Norfolk.

norm *noun* **1** (**the norm**) a typical pattern or situation. **2** an accepted way of behaving, etc: *social norms*. **3** a standard, eg for achievement in industry: *production norms*. [from Latin *norma*, carpenter's square, rule]

....

▣ **1** the rule, the average, the mean, normality. **2, 3** standard. **3** criterion, pattern, model, yardstick, benchmark, point of reference.

....

normal — *adj.* **1** usual; typical; not extraordinary. **2** mentally or physically sound: *a normal baby*. **3** *Geom.* at right angles, perpendicular. **4** *Chem.* denoting a solution that contains 1 gram-equivalent of solute (dissolved substance) per litre of solution. — *noun* **1** what is average or usual. **2** *Geom.* a line that is drawn perpendicular to another line or surface. [from Latin *normalis*, regulated by a carpenter's square, from *norma*, carpenter's square]

▣ *adj.* **1** usual, standard, general, typical, common, ordinary, conventional, average, regular, routine, mainstream, natural, accustomed. **2** well-adjusted, straight, rational, reasonable.
▣ *adj.* **1, 2** abnormal. **1** extraordinary, irregular, peculiar.

normal distribution *Maths.* in statistics, a frequency distribution represented by a symmetrical bell-shaped curve.

normality or *North Amer.* **normalcy** *noun* being normal; a normal state or quality.

▣ usualness, commonness, ordinariness, regularity, routine, conventionality, balance, adjustment, typicality, naturalness, reason, rationality.
▣ abnormality, irregularity, peculiarity.

normalization or **normalisation** *noun* making or becoming normal or regular.

normalize or **normalise** *verb trans., intrans.* to make or become normal or regular.

normally *adv.* **1** in an ordinary or natural way. **2** usually.

▣ **2** ordinarily, usually, as a rule, typically, commonly, characteristically.
▣ **2** abnormally, exceptionally.

Norman — *noun* **1** a person from Normandy, especially one of the Scandinavian settlers of N France who conquered England in 1066. **2** Norman French. — *adj.* **1** relating to the Normans or their language or culture. **2** *Archit.* denoting a form of architecture prevalent in 11c and 12c England, corresponding to the European Romanesque (eg Durham Cathedral, 1093–1133). [from Old French *Normant*, from Norse *Northmathr*]

Norman French the dialect of Old French spoken by the Normans.

normative *adj.* establishing a guiding standard or rules: *normative grammar.* [from NORM]

Norn *noun Scandinavian Mythol.* any of three goddesses of destiny, the equivalent of the Fates, three sisters who sit under the tree Yggdrasil and spin the web of Destiny. [from Norse *Norn*]

Norse — *adj.* **1** of or belonging to ancient or medieval Scandinavia. **2** Norwegian. — *noun* **1** (*pl.*) esp. *Hist.* the Scandinavians, especially the Norwegians. **2 a** the Germanic language group of Scandinavia. **b** (*also* **Old Norse**) the language of this group used in medieval Norway and its colonies. [perhaps from Old Dutch *noorsch*]

north — *noun* (*also* **the north** or **the North**) the direction to one's left when one faces the rising sun, or any part of the earth, a country, town, etc lying in that direction. — *adj.* **1** in the north; on the side that is on or nearest the north. **2** coming from the direction of the north: *a north wind.* — *adv.* towards the north. [from Anglo-Saxon]

Northants. *abbrev.* Northamptonshire.

northbound *adj.* going or leading towards the north.

north-east — *noun* the direction midway between north and east or any part of the earth, a country, etc lying in that direction. — *adj.* **1** in the north-east. **2** from the direction of the north-east: *a north-east wind.*

northeaster *noun* a wind blowing from the north-east.

north-easterly *adj., adv.* from the north-east.

north-eastern *adj.* to the north-east.

northerly — *adj.* **1** *said of a wind, etc* coming from the north. **2** looking, lying, etc towards the north. — *adv.* to or towards the north. — *noun* (PL. **northerlies**) a northerly wind.

northern *adj.* **1** of or in the north. **2** facing or directed towards the north.

northerner *noun* a person who lives in or comes from the north, especially the northern part of England or of the USA.

northern lights (**the northern lights**) the aurora borealis.

northernmost *adj.* situated furthest north.

north-north-east a direction midway between north and north-east.

north-north-west a direction midway between north and north-west.

North Pole (**the North Pole**) the northernmost point of the Earth's axis of rotation, at 90°N, longitude 0°, lying beneath the Arctic Ocean.

Northumb. *abbrev.* Northumberland.

northward or **northwards** *adv., adj.* towards the north.

north-west — *noun* the direction midway between north and west or any part of the earth, a country, etc lying in that direction. — *adj.* **1** in the north-west. **2** from the direction of the north-west: *a north-west wind.*

northwester *noun* a wind blowing from the north-west.

north-westerly *adj., adv.* from the north-west.

north-western *adj.* to the north-west.

Norwegian — *adj.* of or belonging to Norway, its inhabitants, or their language. — *noun* **1** a native of Norway. **2** the language of Norway. [from Latin *Norvegia*, from Norse *northr*, north + *vegr*, way]

Nos. or **nos.** *abbrev.* numbers.

nose — *noun* **1** in humans and many other vertebrates, the organ above the mouth that acts as an air passage and is responsible for the sense of smell (olfaction). **2** the sense of smell. **3** (**a nose for something**) a faculty for detecting or recognizing something. **4** a scent or aroma, especially a wine's bouquet. **5** the front or projecting part of anything, eg a motor vehicle. **6** the nose as a symbol of inquisitiveness or interference: *poke one's nose into something/keep one's nose out of it.* — *verb trans., intrans. said of a vehicle or its driver* to move carefully and slowly forward: *nosed the car out of the drive/nosed slowly forward.* — **blow one's nose** to clear one's nose of mucus by breathing sharply through it. **by a nose** by a narrow margin. **cut off one's nose to spite one's face** to act from resentment in a way that can only cause injury to oneself. **follow one's nose** *colloq.* to go straight forward. **get up someone's nose** *colloq.* to annoy or irritate them. **keep one's nose clean** *colloq.* to avoid doing anything that might get one into trouble. **lead someone by the nose** to dominate them completely. **look down** or **turn up one's nose at someone** or **something** *colloq.* to show disdain for them. **nose about** or **around** *colloq.* to pry. **nose something out 1** to discover it by prying; to track it down. **2** to detect it by smell. **3** *said of an animal* to sniff at or nuzzle it. **nose to tail** *said of motor vehicles* moving slowly and close together in heavy traffic. **pay through the nose** *colloq.* to pay an exorbitant price. **powder one's nose** *euphemistic, said of a woman* to go to the lavatory. **put someone's nose out of joint** *colloq.* to affront them by neglecting or frustrating them. **rub someone's nose in it** *colloq.* to humiliate them by reminding them of a failure. **under one's very nose** *said of something sought* prominently in front of one.

▣ *noun* **1** nostrils, *Brit. colloq.* hooter, *slang* conk, *colloq.* beak, *facetious* proboscis. **3** sense, flair, feel. *verb* edge, inch, ease. **nose out 1** sniff out, smell out, track down, detect, uncover, unearth.

nosebag *noun* a food bag for a horse, hung over its head.

nose band the part of a bridle that goes over the horse's nose.

nosebleed *noun* a flow of blood from the nose.

nose cone the cone-shaped cap on the front of a rocket, etc.

nosedive — *noun* **1** a steep and rapid plunge by an aircraft, with the nose pointed down. **2** a sharp plunge or fall. **3** a sudden drop, eg in prices. — *verb intrans.* to plunge or fall suddenly.

nosegay *noun* a posy of flowers. [from NOSE + GAY in the obsolete sense 'ornament']

☐ bouquet, posy, spray, bunch.

nosey see NOSY.

nosh slang — noun food. — verb intrans. to eat. [from Yiddish]

nosh-up noun slang a hearty feed.

nostalgia noun 1 a yearning for the past. 2 homesickness. [from Greek nostos, homecoming + algos, pain]

☐ YEARNING, LONGING, REGRET, PINING. 1 remembrance, reminiscence. 2 homesickness.

nostalgic adj. yearning for the past.

☐ yearning, longing, wistful, emotional, regretful, sentimental, homesick.

nostalgically adv. with a yearning for the past.

nostril noun either of the two openings in the nose, through which one breathes, smells, etc. [from Anglo-Saxon nosthyrl, from nosu, nose + thyrel, hole]

nostrum noun 1 a patent medicine; a panacea or cure-all. 2 a pet solution or remedy, eg for political ills. [from Latin nostrum, our own (make, brand, etc)]

nosy or **nosey** adj. (**nosier, nosiest**) derog. inquisitive about the affairs, property etc of other people. [from NOSE]

☐ inquisitive, meddlesome, prying, interfering, snooping, curious, eavesdropping.

nosy parker derog. colloq. a nosy person; a busybody.

not adv. (with auxiliary and modal verbs, often shortened to -n't and joined to the verb) 1 used to make a negative statement, etc: that is not fair/those aren't right/why didn't they come? 2 used with verbs of opinion, intention, etc to make the clause or infinitive following the verb negative: I don't think he's right (= I think he is not right). 3 used in place of a negative clause or predicate: might be late, but I hope not. 4 (indicating surprise, an expectation of agreement, etc) surely it is the case that: haven't you heard?/lovely, isn't it? 5 used to contrast the untrue with the true: it's a cloud, not a mountain. 6 barely: with his face not two inches from mine. 7 (**not a**) absolutely no: not a sound. 8 by no means: not nearly enough/not everyone would agree. 9 used with only, just, etc to introduce what is usually the lesser of two points, etc: not just his family, but his wider public. — **not at all** don't mention it; it's a pleasure. **not that** ... though it is not the case that: not that I care. [a Middle English variant of NOUGHT]

notability noun (PL. **notabilities**) 1 being notable. 2 a notable person or thing.

☐ CELEBRITY, EMINENCE. 1 noteworthiness, significance, distinction. 2 dignitary, personage, somebody, worthy, colloq. bigwig.

notable — adj. 1 worth noting; significant. 2 distinguished. 3 (**notable for something**) famous on account of it: Dundee is notable for its cake. — noun a distinguished or important person. [from Latin notabilis, from notare, to note or observe]

☐ adj. 1 noteworthy, remarkable, noticeable, striking, extraordinary, impressive, outstanding, marked, unusual, rare. 2 celebrated, distinguished, famous, renowned, eminent, noted, well-known, notorious. 3 famous for, renowned for, noted for, well-known for, a byword for, notorious for. noun celebrity, notability, VIP, personage, somebody, dignitary, luminary, worthy.

☐ adj. 1 ordinary, commonplace, usual. noun nobody, nonentity.

notably adv. 1 in a notable way: notably absent during the debate. 2 as something or someone notable, especially in a list or group: several people, notably my father.

☐ 1 distinctly, conspicuously, markedly, noticeably, remarkably, strikingly, impressively, outstandingly, eminently. 2 in particular, particularly, especially, pre-eminently, above all.

notarial adj. 1 relating to notaries or their work. 2 said of a document drawn up by a notary.

notary noun (PL. **notaries**) (also **notary public**) a public officer with the legal power to draw up and witness official documents. [from Latin notarius, secretary, clerk]

notation noun 1 the representation of quantities, numbers, musical sounds, movements, etc by symbols. 2 any set of such symbols. [from Latin notatio, marking]

☐ 2 symbols, characters, code, signs, alphabet, system, script, shorthand.

notch — noun 1 a small V-shaped cut. 2 a mark, degree, or grade on a scale: move up a notch. — verb trans. to cut a notch in. — **notch something up** to record it as a score; to achieve it. [from Old French oche (an oche coming to be understood as a notch)]

☐ noun 1 cut, nick, indentation, incision, score, groove, cleft, snip. 2 mark, degree, grade, step. verb cut, nick, score, scratch, indent, mark. **notch up** score, register, chalk up, record, achieve, gain.

note — noun 1 (often **notes**) a brief record made for later reference: lecture notes/took a note of the number. 2 a short informal letter. 3 a brief comment explaining a textual point, etc: a footnote. 4 a short account or essay. 5 a banknote. 6 a formal, especially diplomatic, communication. 7 attention; notice: buildings worthy of note/take note of the warning. 8 distinction; eminence: women of note. 9 a written symbol indicating the pitch and length of a musical sound; the sound itself. 10 poetic the call or cry of a bird or animal. 11 an impression conveyed; feeling; mood: with a note of panic in his voice/end on an optimistic note. — verb 1 (also **note something down**) to write it down. 2 to notice; to be aware of: note this. — **compare notes** to exchange ideas and opinions. **strike the right note** to act or speak appropriately. [from Latin nota, mark, sign]

☐ noun 1 jotting, record, report, sketch, outline, synopsis, draft, impression. 2 communication, letter, message, memorandum, memo, reminder, line, jotting, record. 3 footnote, annotation, comment, gloss, remark. 7 heed, attention, regard, notice, observation. 8 eminence, distinction, consequence, fame, renown, reputation. verb 1 record, register, write down, enter. 2 notice, observe, perceive, heed, detect, mark, remark, mention, see, witness.

notebook noun 1 a small book in which to write notes. 2 Comput. a laptop computer small enough to fit into a briefcase.

notecase noun a case for banknotes; a wallet.

noted adj. well known: noted for their generosity.

☐ famous, well-known, renowned, notable, celebrated, eminent, prominent, great, acclaimed, illustrious, distinguished, respected, recognized.

☐ obscure, unknown.

notelet *noun* a folded piece of notepaper, often decorated, for short letters.

notepad *noun* a block of writing-paper for notes.

notepaper *noun* paper for writing letters.

noteworthiness *noun* a noteworthy or remarkable quality.

noteworthy *adj.* worthy of notice; remarkable.

⊟ remarkable, significant, important, notable, memorable, exceptional, extraordinary, unusual, outstanding.
⊞ commonplace, unexceptional, ordinary.

nothing — *noun* **1** no thing; not anything. **2** very little; something of no importance or not very impressive. **3** the number 0. **4** absence of anything: *a shriek and then nothing.* — *adv.* not at all: *nothing daunted.* — **be nothing to** ... to be much less than ...; to be trivial compared with ...: *that's nothing to what I saw.* **be nothing to do with someone** or **something 1** to be unconnected with them. **2** to be of no concern to them. **come to nothing** to fail. **for nothing 1** free; without payment or personal effort. **2** for no good reason; in vain: *all that work for nothing.* **have nothing on someone** or **something** *colloq.* to be not nearly as good, beautiful, etc as them. **have nothing to do with someone** or **something 1** to avoid them. **2** to be unconnected with them. **3** to be of no concern to them. **like nothing on earth** *colloq.* **1** grotesque. **2** frightful. **make nothing of someone** or **something** not to understand them. **mean nothing to someone 1** to be incomprehensible to them. **2** to be unimportant to them. **nothing but** ... *usually said of something unwelcome* only ...; merely ...: *nothing but trouble.* **nothing doing** *colloq.* **1** an expression of refusal. **2** no hope of success. **nothing for it but to** ... no alternative except to ...: *nothing for it but to own up.* **nothing if not** ... primarily ...; above all ...; very ...: *nothing if not keen.* **nothing like** ... by no means ...: *nothing like good enough.* **nothing like someone** or **something** not at all like them. **nothing much** very little. **nothing short of** or **less than** ... **1** downright ...; absolute ...: *they were nothing less than criminals.* **2** only ...: *will accept nothing less than an apology.* **nothing to it** or **in it** straightforward; easy. **think nothing of something** to regard it as normal or straightforward. **think nothing of it** it doesn't matter; there is no need for thanks. **to say nothing of** ... as well as ...; not to mention ...

⊟ *noun* **1, 2** *slang* zilch. **3** nought, zero. **4** nothingness, nullity, non-existence, emptiness, void.
⊞ *noun* something.

nothingness *noun* the state of being nothing or of not existing; emptiness.

notice — *noun* **1** an announcement displayed or delivered publicly. **2** one's attention: *something has come to my notice / it escaped their notice.* **3** a warning or notification given, eg before leaving, or dismissing someone from, a job: *give in one's notice/give notice of one's intentions/will continue until further notice.* **4** a review of a performance, book, etc. — *verb trans.* **1** to observe. **2** to remark on. — **at short notice** with little warning, time for preparation, etc. **take notice** to take interest in one's surroundings, etc. **take notice of someone** or **something** to pay attention to them; to heed them. [from Old French, from Latin *notitia*, from *notus*, known]

⊟ *noun* **1** advertisement, poster, sign, bill, announcement, declaration, news, information, instruction. **2** attention, observation, awareness, note, regard, consideration, heed. **3** notification, communication, warning. **4** review, comment, criticism, *colloq.* crit. *verb* **1** note, remark, perceive, observe, see, discern, distinguish, mark, detect, heed, spot. **2** remark on, comment on, point out, acknowledge.
⊞ *verb* IGNORE, OVERLOOK.

noticeable *adj.* easily seen; clearly apparent.

⊟ perceptible, observable, appreciable, unmistakable, conspicuous, evident, manifest, clear, distinct, significant, striking, plain, obvious, measurable.
⊞ inconspicuous, unnoticeable.

noticeably *adv.* in a noticeable way; to a noticeable degree: *it has grown noticeably.*

notice-board *noun* a board on which notices are displayed.

notifiable *adj.* denoting any disease that, if diagnosed or even suspected, is required by law to be reported to public health authorities so that appropriate action can be taken to prevent its spread.

notification *noun* **1** an announcement or warning. **2** the act of giving this.

⊟ ANNOUNCEMENT, DECLARATION, COMMUNICATION, STATEMENT, PUBLICATION. **1** information, notice, advice, warning, message.

notify *verb trans.* (**notifies, notified**) (**notify someone of something**) to inform or warn them about it. [from Latin *notus*, known + *facere*, to make]

⊟ inform, tell, advise, warn, acquaint, alert, announce, declare, publish, disclose.

notion *noun* **1** an impression, conception, or understanding. **2** a belief or principle. **3** an inclination, whim or fancy. **4** (**notions**) *North Amer., esp. US* pins, needles, and other small items used in sewing. [from Latin *notio*, idea, notion]

⊟ **1** idea, thought, concept, conception, impression, understanding. **2** belief, view, opinion, principle. **3** inclination, wish, whim, fancy, caprice, velleity.

notional *adj.* existing in imagination or theory only.

⊟ imaginary, theoretical, hypothetical, conjectural, supposed, assumed.

notochord *noun* *Zool.* a flexible rod-like structure, which strengthens and supports the body in the embryos and adults of more primitive animals belonging to the phylum Chordata, but in vertebrates is replaced by a spinal column before birth. [from Greek *notos*, back + *chorde*, string]

notoriety /nəʊtəˈraɪətɪ/ *noun* fame or reputation, usually for something disreputable.

⊟ infamy, disrepute, dishonour, disgrace, scandal.

notorious *adj.* famous, usually for something disreputable. [from Latin *notorius*, well known]

⊟ infamous, disreputable, scandalous, dishonourable, disgraceful, ignominious, flagrant, well-known.

notoriously *adv.* famously, usually for something disreputable.

Notts. *abbrev.* Nottinghamshire.

notwithstanding — *prep.* in spite of. — *adv.* in spite of that.

⊟ *prep.* in spite of, despite, regardless of. *adv.* nonetheless, nevertheless, still, anyway, even so, yet, however, anyhow, but, regardless.

nougat /'nu:gɑ:, 'nʌgət/ *noun* a chewy sweet containing nuts, etc. [from French *nougat*, from Latin *nux*, nut]

nought *noun* **1** the figure 0; zero. **2** *old use* nothing; naught. [from Anglo-Saxon *noht*, from *nowiht*, from *ne*, not + *owiht*, aught]

⊟ **1** zero, nil. **2** *slang* zilch, naught, nothing, nothingness.

noughts and crosses a game for two players with alternate turns, the aim being to complete a row of three noughts (for one player) or three crosses (for the other) within a square framework of nine squares.

noun *noun Grammar* a word used as the name of a person, animal, thing, place, or quality. [from Latin *nomen*, name]

nourish *verb trans.* **1** to supply with food needed for survival and growth. **2** to encourage the growth of; to foster (an idea, etc). [from Old French *norir*]

⊟ NURTURE, FOSTER, SUPPORT, MAINTAIN. **1** feed, care for, provide for, sustain, tend, nurse. **2** strengthen, encourage, promote, cherish, cultivate, stimulate.

nourishing *adj.*, *said of food* affording nourishment.

⊟ nutritious, wholesome, healthful, health-giving, good, beneficial, strengthening, substantial, invigorating.
⊟ bad, unwholesome.

nourishment *noun* something that nourishes; food.

⊟ nutrition, food, sustenance, diet.

nous /naʊs/ *noun* **1** *colloq.* common sense. **2** *Philos.* the intellect. [from Greek *nous*, mind]

nouveau riche /'nu:voʊ 'ri:ʃ/ (PL. **nouveaux riches**) *derog.* a person who has recently acquired wealth but lacks the upper-class breeding to go with it. [French, = new rich]

nouvelle cuisine /'nu:vɛl kwɪ'zi:n/ a simple style of cookery characterized by much use of fresh produce and elegant presentation. [French, = new cookery]

Nouvelle Vague, also known as **New Wave** a group of young French film directors of the late 1950s and 1960s, who wished to discard many of the conventional formulae of the cinema of their time.

Nov or **Nov.** *abbrev.* November.

nova *noun* (PL. **novae**) a faint star that suddenly becomes several thousand times brighter than normal, and remains so for a few days or weeks before fading again. [from Latin *nova stella*, new star]

novel[1] *noun* a book-length fictional story usually involving relationships between characters and events concerning them. [from Italian *novella*, short story, from Latin *novellus*, new]

⊟ fiction, story, tale, narrative, romance.

novel[2] *adj.* new; original; unheard-of previously. [from Latin *novellus*, new]

⊟ new, original, fresh, innovative, unfamiliar, unusual, uncommon, different, imaginative, unconventional, strange.
⊟ hackneyed, familiar, ordinary.

novelette *noun derog.* a short, especially trite or sentimental, novel.

novelist *noun* the writer of a novel.

novella *noun* a short story or short novel. [from Italian *novella*]

novelty *noun* (PL. **novelties**) **1** the quality of being new and intriguing. **2** something new and strange. **3** a small cheap toy or souvenir. [from Old French *novelete*, from Latin *novellitas*, newness]

⊟ **1** newness, originality, freshness, unfamiliarity, uniqueness, difference, strangeness. **2** innovation, departure, modification, gimmick, gadget. **3** trifle, memento, knick-knack, curiosity, souvenir, trinket, bauble, gimcrack.

November *noun* the eleventh month of the year. [from Latin, = the ninth month, from *novem*, nine]

novena *noun* (PL. **novenas**) *RC Church* a series of special prayers and services held over a period of nine days. [from Latin *noveni*, nine each, from *novem*, nine]

novice *noun* **1** a beginner. **2** a person who has recently joined a religious community but not yet taken vows; a probationary member. [from Latin *novicius*, from *novus*, new]

⊟ **1** beginner, tyro, learner, pupil, trainee, probationer, apprentice, neophyte, amateur, newcomer.
⊟ **1** expert.

noviciate or **novitiate** /nə'vɪʃɪət/ *noun* **1** the period of being a novice in a religious community. **2** the novices' quarters in such a community.

now — *adv.* **1** at the present time or moment. **2** immediately. **3** *in narrative* then: *he now turned from journalism to fiction.* **4** in these circumstances; as things are: *I planned to go, but now I can't.* **5** up to the present: *has now been teaching 13 years.* **6** used conversationally to accompany explanations, warnings, commands, rebukes, words of comfort, etc: *now, this is what happened/careful, now!* — *noun* the present time. — *conj.* (**now that**) because at last; because at this time: *now we're all here, we'll begin.* — **any day** or **moment** or **time now** at any time soon. **as of now** from this time onward. **for now** until later; for the time being. **just now 1** a moment ago. **2** at this very moment. **now and then** or **now and again** sometimes; occasionally. **now for** ... used in anticipation, or in turning from one thing to another: *now for some fun!/now for your second point.* **now** ... **now** ... one moment ... the next ...: *now crying, now laughing.* [from Anglo-Saxon *nu*]

⊟ *adv.* **1** at present, nowadays, these days. **2** immediately, at once, directly, instantly, straight away, promptly, next.

nowadays *adv.* in these present times. [from NOW + *a*, on + Anglo-Saxon *dæges*, of a day]

Nowell *noun* same as NOEL.

nowhere *adv.* in or to no place; not anywhere. — **from** or **out of nowhere** suddenly and inexplicably: *they appeared from nowhere.* **get nowhere** to make no progress. **in the middle of nowhere** *colloq.* isolated; remote from towns or cities, etc. **nowhere near** ... *colloq.* not nearly...; by no means ...: *nowhere near fast enough.*

no-win *adj. said of a situation* in which one is bound to lose or fail whatever one does.

nowt *noun colloq.*, *dialect* nothing. [Anglo-Saxon, as for NAUGHT]

noxious *adj.* harmful; poisonous. [from Latin *noxius*, harmful]

⊟ harmful, poisonous, pernicious, toxic, injurious, unhealthy, deadly, destructive, noisome, foul.
⊟ innocuous, wholesome.

nozzle *noun* a fitting attached as an outlet to the end of a hose, etc. [a diminutive of NOSE]

Np *symbol Chem.* neptunium.

NPL *abbrev.* National Physical Laboratory.

nr *abbrev.* near.

NRA *abbrev.* National Rifle Association.

NSPCC *abbrev.* National Society for the Prevention of Cruelty to Children.

NSW *abbrev.* New South Wales.

NT *abbrev.* National Trust.

-n't *contr.* forming negatives of auxiliary and modal verbs: *haven't/daren't*.

nth *adj.* **1** denoting an indefinite position in a sequence: *to the nth degree*. **2** denoting an item or occurrence that is at many removes from the first in a sequence: *I'm telling you for the nth time*.

NTP *abbrev. Physics* normal temperature and pressure, the former name for *standard temperature and pressure*.

NTS *abbrev.* National Trust for Scotland.

NTSC *abbrev.* National Television Systems Commission: a body responsible for the coding system of colour television introduced in the USA in 1954. See also PAL, SECAM.

NUAAW *abbrev.* National Union of Agricultural and Allied Workers.

nuance /'njuːɒns/ *noun* a subtle variation in colour, meaning, expression, etc. [from French *nuance*, shade, hue]

▣ subtlety, suggestion, shade, hint, suspicion, gradation, distinction, overtone, refinement, touch, trace, tinge, degree, nicety.

nub *noun* the central, most important issue; the crux. [from Old German *knubbe*, knob]

▣ centre, heart, core, nucleus, kernel, crux, gist, pith, point, essence.

nubile *adj.*, *said of a young woman* **1** physically mature and ready for marriage. **2** sexually attractive. [from Latin *nubilis*, from *nubere*, to veil oneself, marry]

▣ **1** mature, adult, marriageable. **2** attractive, good-looking, desirable, voluptuous, *colloq.* sexy.

nucellus /njuˈsɛləs/ *noun* (PL. **nucelli**) in seed-bearing plants, the tissue of which most of the ovule is composed, consisting of a mass of thin-walled cells. [a diminutive of Latin *nux*, nut]

nuclear *adj.* **1** having the nature of a nucleus: *the nuclear family*. **2** of or relating to atoms or their nuclei: *nuclear physics/nuclear fission*. **3** relating to or produced by the fission or fusion of atomic nuclei: *nuclear energy/nuclear weapons*.

nuclear accident an accident that occurs during the operation of a nuclear reactor or the production of nuclear weapons, or during the disposal of nuclear waste arising from either of these processes.

nuclear disarmament a country's act of giving up its nuclear weapons.

nuclear energy the energy that exists within the nuclei of atoms and is released during nuclear fission or nuclear fusion. It is used in nuclear reactors to generate electricity, and in nuclear weapons to cause widespread destruction. Also called ATOMIC ENERGY.

nuclear family the family consisting of mother, father, and children only. See also EXTENDED FAMILY.

nuclear fission a nuclear reaction in which a heavy nucleus of a radioactive element such as uranium or plutonium splits into two lighter nuclei (fission products), with the simultaneous release of large amounts of energy, and the emission of two or three neutrons that strike other nuclei and cause them to split in turn. The resulting chain reaction can be used as an energy source.

nuclear-free *adj.* where nuclear weapons and nuclear energy are banned: *nuclear-free zones*.

nuclear fuel a naturally occurring or artificially manufactured material, usually an isotope of uranium or plutonium, that is used as the main source of nuclear energy in a nuclear reactor.

nuclear fusion a nuclear reaction in which two light atomic nuclei combine to form a heavier nucleus, with the release of large amounts of energy. This process provides a continuous source of energy in the Sun and other stars, and in hydrogen bombs, but has not yet been successfully harnessed for commercial power production.

nuclear medicine *Medicine* the branch of medicine concerned with the use of radioactive isotopes to study, diagnose, and treat diseases.

nuclear power power, especially electricity, that is obtained from nuclear fission or nuclear fusion reactions, especially a controlled reaction that takes place within a nuclear reactor.

nuclear reaction any reaction involving a change in an atomic nucleus, such as its spontaneous radioactive decay, nuclear fusion, or artificial bombardment with high-energy particles, as in nuclear fission.

nuclear reactor a device that produces nuclear energy by allowing nuclear fission to take place in the form of a controlled chain reaction, using the radioactive isotopes uranium-235, uranium-233, or plutonium-239 as fuel.

nuclear waste the radioactive waste material that is produced during the operation of a nuclear reactor (eg at a nuclear power station), the manufacture of nuclear weapons, or the mining and extraction of nuclear fuels such as uranium.

nuclear weapon *Mil.* a bomb, missile, or other weapon that derives its destructive force from the energy released during nuclear fission or nuclear fusion.

nuclear winter *Environ.* the environmental conditions that some scientists have suggested might follow a nuclear war, in which the large quantities of smoke and dust particles produced would prevent sunlight from reaching the Earth for several years, resulting in global darkness and extremely low temperatures, with catastrophic effects on plant and animal life.

nuclease /'njuːklɪeɪz/ *noun Biochem.* any enzyme that catalyses the splitting of the chains of molecules of nucleic acids such as DNA.

nucleate — *verb trans., intrans.* to form, or form into, a nucleus. — *adj.* having a nucleus.

nucleic acid either of the acids DNA or RNA, found in all living cells. [from NUCLEUS]

nucleolus *noun Biol.* a small spherical body, composed mainly of protein, together with DNA and RNA, found within the nucleus of most plant and animal cells.

nucleon *noun Physics* a proton or neutron. [from NUCLEUS]

nucleonics *sing. noun* the study of the uses of radioactivity and nuclear energy.

nucleon number *Chem.* same as MASS NUMBER.

nucleotide /'njuːklɪətaɪd/ *noun Biochem.* an organic compound consisting of a purine or pyrimidine base, a sugar molecule, and a phosphate group bonded together. DNA and RNA are composed of long chains of nucleotides.

nucleus *noun* (PL. **nuclei**) **1** *Physics* the tiny central core of an atom, which is extremely dense and accounts for almost the entire mass of the atom. It contains protons (positively charged particles) and, except in the case of hydrogen, neutrons (uncharged particles). The nucleus is surrounded by negatively charged electrons. **2** *Biol.* a large spherical or oval structure, surrounded by a double membrane (known as the nuclear envelope), in the cytoplasm of virtually all animal and plant cells. It contains the genetic material of the cell in the form of DNA. **3** a core round which things accumulate. [from Latin *nucleus*, kernel]

▣ **3** centre, heart, nub, core, focus, kernel, pivot, basis, crux.

nuclide *noun Physics* one of two or more atoms that contain the same number of protons and the same number of neutrons in their nuclei, and so have the same atomic number and mass number.

NUCPS *abbrev.* National Union of Civil and Public Servants.

nude — *adj.* wearing no clothes; naked. — *noun* **1** a representation of a naked figure in painting, sculpture, etc. **2** someone naked. **3** the state of nakedness: *in the nude.* [from Latin *nudus*, naked]

◩ *adj.* naked, bare, undressed, unclothed, stripped, stark-naked, uncovered, *colloq.* starkers, *colloq.* in one's birthday suit.
▣ *adj.* clothed, dressed.

nudge — *verb trans.* **1** to poke or push gently, especially with the elbow, to get attention, etc. **2** to push slightly or little by little. — *noun* a gentle prod.

◩ *verb* PUSH, SHOVE. **1** poke, prod, dig, jog, prompt, elbow, bump. **2** edge, inch. *noun* push, poke, prod, shove, dig, jog, prompt, bump.

nudism *noun* the practice of not wearing clothes, as a matter of principle.
nudist *noun* someone who wears no clothes, as a matter of principle.
nudity *noun* the state or practice of being nude or naked.

◩ nakedness, bareness, undress, denudation, starkness, nudism, naturism.

nuée ardente /ˈnuːeɪ ɑːˈdɒnt/ *Geol.* a turbulent incandescent cloud of hot gas and volcanic ash erupted from a volcano and travelling at great speed down its sides. [French, = burning cloud]
nugatory /ˈnjuːɡətərɪ/ *adj. formal* **1** worthless; trifling; valueless. **2** ineffective; futile. **3** invalid. [from Latin *nugae*, trifles]
nugget *noun* **1** a lump, especially of gold. **2** a small piece of something precious: *nuggets of wisdom.*

◩ **1** lump, clump, chunk, hunk.

NUGMW *abbrev.* National Union of General and Municipal Workers.
nuisance *noun* **1** an annoying or troublesome person, thing, or circumstance. **2** *Legal* something obnoxious to the community or an individual, that is disallowed by law. — **make a nuisance of oneself** to behave annoyingly. [from Old French, from *nuire*, to injure]

◩ **1** annoyance, inconvenience, bother, irritation, pest, *colloq.* pain, *colloq.* drag, bore, problem, trial, trouble, drawback.

NUJ *abbrev.* National Union of Journalists.
nuke *slang* — *verb trans.* to attack with nuclear weapons. — *noun* a nuclear weapon.
null *adj.* **1** legally invalid: *declared null and void.* **2** *Maths.,* *said of a set* having no members; empty. [from Latin *nullus*, none]

◩ **1** void, invalid, ineffectual, useless, vain, worthless, powerless, inoperative.
▣ **1** valid.

null hypothesis *Maths.* a hypothesis consisting of a statement, which may be true or false, against which results can be tested, usually in order to disprove it.
nullification *noun* the act or process of nullifying or declaring invalid.
nullify *verb trans.* (**nullifies, nullified**) **1** to cause or declare to be legally invalid. **2** to make ineffective; to cancel out. [from Latin *nullus*, of no account + *facere*, to make]

◩ **1** annul, revoke, cancel, invalidate, abrogate, abolish, rescind, quash, repeal. **2** cancel out, counteract, offset, negate, negative.
▣ **1** validate.

nullity *noun* the status of being null and void.
NUM *abbrev.* in the UK, the National Union of Mineworkers.
numb — *adj.* **1** deprived completely, or to some degree, of sensation. **2** too stunned to feel emotion; stupefied: *numb with shock.* — *verb* to make numb. [from Middle English *nomen*, seized (ie with paralysis)]

◩ *adj.* FROZEN. **1** benumbed, insensible, unfeeling, deadened, insensitive, immobilized. **2** stunned, stupefied. *verb* deaden, anaesthetize, freeze, immobilize, paralyse, dull, stun.
▣ *adj.* **1** sensitive. *verb* sensitize.

number — *noun* **1** the means or system by which groups, sets, etc of individual things, etc are counted; a quantity calculated in units. **2** *Maths.* an arithmetical symbol, one or more of which can be used to represent a quantity or amount during such procedures as counting, measuring, and the performance of calculations. **3** a numeral or set of numerals identifying something or someone within a series: *telephone numbers.* **4** (*followed by a numeral*) the person, animal, vehicle, etc identified by the numeral: *number 21 is pulling ahead.* **5** a single issue of a magazine, etc. **6** a quantity of individuals. **7** an act or turn in a programme. **8** a piece of popular music or jazz. **9** *colloq.* an article or person considered appreciatively: *drives a white sports number.* **10** a group or set: *isn't one of our number.* **11** (**numbers**) numerical superiority: *by sheer weight of numbers.* **12** *Grammar* the property of expressing, or classification of word forms into, singular and plural. — *verb* (**numbered, numbering**) **1** to give a number to; to mark with a number. **2** to include: *I number her among my closest friends.* **3** to amount to: *a crowd numbering about 500.* **4** to count; to enumerate. — **any number of** ... many... **one's days are numbered** one is soon to suffer or die. **have someone's number** *colloq.* to have a grasp of their real character or intentions. **one's number is up** *colloq.* one is due for some unpleasant fate, especially death. **safety in numbers** security or comfort afforded in difficult circumstances by the support of others. **without number** more than can be counted; countless. [from French *nombre*, from Latin *numerus*]

◩ *noun* **2** figure, numeral, digit, integer, unit. **5** copy, issue, edition, impression, volume, printing. **6** total, sum, aggregate, collection, amount, quantity, several, many, company, crowd, multitude, throng, horde. *verb* **2, 4** count, reckon. **2** include. **4** calculate, enumerate, total, add, compute.

number-crunching *noun colloq.* the performing of vast and complex mathematical calculations on a computer.
numberless *adj.* too many to count.

◩ countless, innumerable, unnumbered, (a) myriad, *colloq.* umpteen.

number one — *noun colloq., ironic* oneself. — *adj.* first; of primary importance: *give it number-one priority.*
number plate one of the two plates at the front and rear of a motor vehicle, bearing its registration number.
Number Ten *Brit. colloq.* 10 Downing Street, the official home of the Prime Minister.
number theory *Maths.* the branch of mathematics that is concerned with the abstract study of the relationships between and properties of positive whole numbers.
numbskull see NUMSKULL.
numeracy *noun* being numerate; ability with numbers.

numeral *noun* an arithmetical symbol used to express a number; a figure. [from Latin *numerus*, number]

numerate *adj.* **1** able to perform arithmetical operations. **2** having some understanding of mathematics and science. [from Latin *numerus*, number, in imitation of LITERATE]

numeration *noun* **1** the process of counting or numbering. **2** a system of numbering. [from Latin *numerare*, to count]

numerator *noun* the number above the line in a fraction. See also DENOMINATOR. [from Latin *numerare*, to count]

numerical *adj.* relating to, using, or consisting of, numbers: *numerical superiority.* [from Latin *numerus*, number]

numerical control *Engineering* the automatic control of a machine tool by means of a computer (formerly by data stored on punched cards).

numerically *adv.* as regards number; by means of numbers.

numerology *noun* the study of numbers as an influence on human affairs. [from Latin *numerus*, number]

numerous *adj.* **1** many. **2** *said of an assembly, body, etc* containing a large number of people. [from Latin *numerosus*, from *numerus*, number]

· ·

■ **1** many, several, abundant, plentiful, copious, profuse, sundry.
🞂 **1** few.

· ·

numerously *adv.* to a numerous extent; in great numbers.

numinous *adj.* **1** mysterious; awe-inspiring. **2** characterized by the sense of a deity's presence. [from Latin *numen*, deity]

numismatic *adj.* relating to numismatics or the study of coins and medals.

numismatics *sing. noun* the study or collecting of coins and medals. [from Greek *nomisma*, coin]

numismatist *noun* a person who collects or studies coins and medals.

numskull or **numbskull** *noun colloq.* a stupid person. [from NUMB + SKULL]

nun *noun* a member of a female religious order living, in obedience to certain vows, in a community. [from Latin *nonna*]

nuncio /ˈnʌnʃɪoʊ/ *noun* (PL. **nuncios**) an ambassador from the pope. [from Latin *nuntius*, messenger]

nunnery *noun* (PL. **nunneries**) a house in which a group of nuns live.

NUPE *abbrev.* National Union of Public Employees.

nuptial — *adj.* relating to marriage, or *Zool.* to mating. — *noun* (*usually* **nuptials**) a marriage ceremony. [from Latin *nuptialis*, from *nuptiae*, marriage]

nuptiality *noun* the marriage rate in a society.

NUR *abbrev.* National Union of Railwaymen.

nurse — *noun* **1** a person who looks after sick or injured people, especially in hospital. **2** a person, especially a woman, who looks after small children in a household. — *verb* **1** *trans.* to look after (sick or injured people) especially in a hospital. **2** *intrans.* to follow the career of a nurse. **3** *trans., intrans.* to feed (a baby) at the breast, or (of a baby) to feed at the breast. **4** *trans.* to hold with care: *gave him the bag of meringues to nurse.* **5** *trans.* to tend with concern: *was at home nursing a cold.* **6** *trans.* to encourage (a feeling) in oneself. [from Old French *norrice*, from Latin *nutrire*, to nourish]

· ·

■ *noun* **1** sister, matron. **2** nursemaid, nanny. *verb* **1** tend, care for, look after, treat. **3** breastfeed, feed, suckle, nurture, nourish. **6** harbour, nurture, foster, promote, cherish, encourage, keep, preserve.

· ·

nursemaid *noun* a children's nurse in a household.

nursery *noun* (PL. **nurseries**) **1** a place where children are looked after while their parents are at work, etc. **2** *old use* a room in a house reserved for young children and their nurse. **3** a place where plants are grown for sale. [from NURSE]

nurseryman *noun* a person who grows plants for sale.

nursery rhyme a short simple traditional rhyme for children.

nursery school a school for children aged between three and five.

nursery slopes *Skiing* the lower gentle slopes used for practice by beginners.

nursing *noun* the branch of medicine which provides care for the sick and injured, the very young, and the very old, and assumes responsibility for the physical, social, and emotional needs of patients with the aim of restoring, maintaining, or promoting health.

nursing home a small private hospital or home, eg for old people.

nursing officer *Brit.* any of several grades of nurses having administrative duties.

nurture — *noun* care, nourishment, and encouragement given to a growing child, animal or plant. — *verb* **1** to nourish and tend (a growing child, animal, or plant). **2** to encourage the development of (a project, idea, feeling, etc). [from Old French *norriture*, from Latin *nutrire*, to nourish]

· ·

■ *noun* rearing, upbringing, training, care, cultivation, development, education, discipline. *verb* FOSTER, SUPPORT, SUSTAIN. **1** feed, nourish, nurse, tend, care for, bring up, rear, educate, instruct, train, school, discipline. **2** cultivate, develop, bring on.

· ·

NUS *abbrev.* **1** National Union of Seamen. **2** National Union of Students.

NUT *abbrev.* National Union of Teachers.

nut *noun* **1** *Bot.* a dry fruit containing a single seed enclosed by a hard woody shell (the *pericarp*) that does not split open on ripening to release the seed, but is shed intact from the plant, eg acorn, hazelnut. **2** a popular name for any hard fruit that resembles this structure, eg coconut, walnut, almond. **3** a small usually hexagonal piece of metal with a hole through it, for screwing on the end of a bolt. **4** *colloq.* a person's head. **5** *colloq.* a crazy person. **6** a small lump: *a nut of butter.* — **do one's nut** *colloq.* to be extremely angry or anxious. **for nuts** *colloq.* (*after a negative*) at all: *can't sing for nuts.* **a hard** or **tough nut to crack** *colloq.* a difficult problem to solve or an awkward person to deal with. **off one's nut** *colloq.* mad, crazy. [from Anglo-Saxon *hnutu*]

Varieties of nut include: almond, beech nut, brazilnut, cashew, chestnut, cobnut, coconut, filbert, hazelnut, macadamia, monkey nut, peanut, pecan, pistachio, walnut.

nutation /njʊˈteɪʃən/ *noun* **1** the act of nodding. **2** *Astron.* the irregular nodding or 'side-to-side' movement of the Earth's axis of rotation, caused by small changes in the gravitational pull of the Sun and Moon on the Earth. **3** *Bot.* the spiral growth pattern of the parts of some plants, eg climbing plants, especially the tips of the stems. **4** the periodic oscillation of a spinning top or gyroscope. [from Latin *nutare*, to nod]

nutcase *noun colloq.* a crazy person.

nutcracker *noun* **1** (*usually* **nutcrackers**) a utensil for cracking nuts. **2** a bird of the crow family that feeds on nuts and pine seeds.

nuthatch *noun* a small bird that inhabits rocks and woodland in the northern hemisphere, and has a short tail and a sharp straight bill. It feeds on insects, and sometimes nuts.

nuthouse *noun colloq., offensive* a mental hospital.

nutmeg *noun* the hard aromatic seed of the fruit of an E Indian tree, used ground or grated as a spice. [from Middle English *notemugge*]

nutrient — *noun* any substance taken in by a living organism that acts as a source of energy and materials for growth, maintenance, and repair of tissues. — *adj.* nourishing. [from Latin *nutrire*, to nourish]

nutriment *noun* nourishment; food. [from Latin *nutrimentum*, from *nutrire*, to nourish]

nutrition *noun* **1** the process of nourishment. **2** the study of the body's dietary needs. **3** food. [from Latin *nutrire*, to nourish]
. . . .
⊟ **3** food, nourishment, sustenance.
. . . .

nutritional *adj.* relating to nutrition or nourishment.

nutritious *adj.* nourishing; providing nutrition.
. . . .
⊟ nourishing, nutritive, wholesome, healthful, health-giving, good, beneficial, strengthening, substantial, invigorating.
⊟ bad, unwholesome.
. . . .

nutritive *adj.* **1** nourishing. **2** relating to nutrition.

nuts *adj. colloq.* **1** insane; crazy. **2** (**nuts about** or **on someone** or **something**) infatuated with or extremely fond of them.
. . . .
⊟ MAD, CRAZY, *colloq.* DAFT. **1** insane, *colloq.* nutty, *slang* loony, *slang* loopy.
. . . .

nuts and bolts essential or practical details.

nutshell *noun* the case containing the kernel of a nut. — **in a nutshell** concisely or very briefly expressed.

nutter *noun colloq.* a crazy person.

nuttiness *noun* **1** a taste of nuts. **2** *colloq.* a crazy state or quality.

nutty *adj.* (**nuttier, nuttiest**) **1** full of, or tasting of, nuts. **2** *colloq.* crazy.

nux vomica the seed of an E Indian tree, containing strychnine. [Latin, = vomiting nut]

nuzzle *verb trans., intrans.* (**nuzzle up to** or **against someone**) *usually said of animals* to push or rub them with the nose. [related to NOSE]

NV *abbrev.* Nevada.

NVQ *abbrev.* in the UK, the National Vocational Qualification, a certificate of attainment of up to five grades by which employees can prove their level of competence.

NW *abbrev.* north-west; north-western.

NWT *abbrev.* Northwest Territories.

NY or **N.Y.** *abbrev.* New York.

NYC *abbrev.* New York City.

nylon — *noun* **1** *Chem.* any of various strong elastic thermoplastics that are resistant to wear and chemicals, used to make textile fibres for durable fabrics, coatings, ropes, brushes, etc. **2** (**nylons**) *old use* a woman's nylon stockings. — *adj.* relating to such a material. [originally a trademark]

nymph *noun* **1** *Mythol.* a goddess inhabiting eg water or trees. **2** *poetic* a beautiful young woman. **3** *Zool.* the larval stage in the life cycle of certain insects, eg dragonfly, grasshopper, resembling a miniature version of the adult, but lacking wings and mature reproductive organs. The nymph develops directly into an adult without forming a pupa. [from Greek *nymphe*, nymph, bride]

nymphet *noun facetious* a sexually attractive and precocious girl in early adolescence. [from Old French *nymphette*, from Greek *nymphe*, nymph + feminine diminutive *-ette*]

nympho *noun* (PL. **nymphos**) *colloq.* a nymphomaniac.

nymphomania *noun* excessive sexual desire in women. [from Greek *nympho-* relating to brides]

nymphomaniac — *noun* a woman with excessive sexual desire. — *adj.* relating to or affected by nymphomania.

NYO *abbrev.* National Youth Orchestra.

nystatin /ˈnɪstətɪn/ *noun Medicine* an antibiotic, produced by the bacterium *Streptomyces noursei*, that is used to treat fungal infections. [from *New York State* (where it originated) + *-in*]

NZ *abbrev.* New Zealand.

Nzambi /nˈzambɪ/ *noun Relig.* a name for God in wide use throughout West Central Africa.

O¹ or **o** *noun* (PL. **Os**, **O's**, **o's**) **1** the fifteenth letter of the English alphabet. **2** zero; nought.

O² or **oh** *interj.* **1** (*usually* **oh**) used to express surprise, admiration, pleasure, anger, fear, etc. **2** used in addressing a person or thing, or in expressing a wish: *O God!*/*Oh for a bit of peace!*

O³ *abbrev.* **1** Ocean. **2** Old. **3** (*also* **o**) octavo.

O⁴ *symbol Chem.* oxygen.

O. *abbrev.* Ohio.

o' *prep.* **1** of. See also O'CLOCK. **2** on.

oaf *noun* a stupid or awkward person. [from Norse *alfr*, elf]

oafish *adj.* loutish, clumsy, idiotic.

oafishness *noun* being oafish, oafish behaviour.

oak *noun* **1** any tree or shrub of the genus *Quercus*, found mainly in north temperate regions, having acorns as fruits and including both deciduous species with lobed leaves, and evergreen species, usually with unlobed leaves. **2** the hard durable wood of this tree, which is attractively grained, and widely used in building construction, furniture, and flooring. **3** (**the Oaks**) a race for three-year-old fillies run annually at Epsom. [from Anglo-Saxon *ac*]

oak-apple *noun* (*also* **oak-gall**, **oak-nut**) a ball-like growth on an oak caused especially by the eggs of certain insects.

oaken *adj.* *old use* made of oak.

oakum *noun* pieces of old rope untwisted and pulled apart, used to fill small holes and cracks in wooden boats and ships. [from Anglo-Saxon *acumba*, from *a-*, away + *cemban*, to comb]

OAP *abbrev. Brit.* old age pensioner.

OAPEC *abbrev.* Organization of Arab Petroleum Exporting Countries.

oar *noun* **1** a long pole with a broad, flat blade used for rowing a boat. **2** a rower. — **put** or **stick one's oar in** *colloq.* to interfere or meddle, especially by offering one's own opinion when it is not wanted. [from Anglo-Saxon *ar*]

oarfish *noun* a long ribbon-shaped fish widespread in tropical and warm temperate seas, up to 7m in length, and having an extremely slender body, a dorsal fin that extends the full length of the body, and no tail fin.

oarsman or **oarswoman** *noun* a man or woman who rows.

oarsmanship *noun* skill in rowing.

OAS *abbrev.* **1** Organisation de l'Armée Secrète (in Algeria). **2** Organization of American States.

oasis *noun* (PL. **oases**) **1** a fertile area in a desert where water is found and plants grow. **2** any place of rest or pleasure in the middle of hard work, problems, or trouble. [from Greek *oasis*, from Egyptian]

▣ **1** spring, watering-hole. **2** refuge, haven, island, sanctuary, retreat.

oast *noun* a kiln for drying hops. [from Anglo-Saxon *ast*, kiln]

oast-house *noun* a building with a cone-shaped roof containing several kilns for drying hops.

oat *noun* **1** (*also* **oats**) a cereal (*Avena sativa*) belonging to the grass family (Gramineae), thought to be native to the

Mediterranean region, and now cultivated mainly in cool moist north temperate regions as a food crop. **2** (**oats**) the seeds of this plant, used as a foodstuff for animal livestock, and also as human food. — **off one's oats** *colloq.* having no appetite. **sow one's oats** or **one's wild oats** *colloq.* to indulge in adventures, excessive drinking, promiscuity, etc during youth. [from Anglo-Saxon *ate*]

oatcake *noun* a thin, hard, dry biscuit made from oatmeal.

oaten *adj.* made of oats.

oath *noun* **1** a solemn promise to tell the truth, be loyal, etc, usually naming God as a witness. **2** the form of words used to take an oath. **3** a swear-word, obscenity, or blasphemy. — **on** or **under oath** having sworn to tell the truth, eg in a court of law. [from Anglo-Saxon *ath*]

▣ **1** vow, promise, pledge, word, word of honour, affirmation, assurance. **2** vow, promise, pledge. **3** swear-word, obscenity, blasphemy, curse, imprecation, profanity, expletive.

oatmeal *noun* oats ground into meal.

OAU *abbrev.* Organization of African Unity.

ob. *abbrev. obiit* (Latin), he or she died.

Obad. or **Obad** *abbrev. Biblical* Obadiah.

obbligato /ɒblɪˈɡɑːtoʊ/ — *noun* (PL. **obbligatos**, **obbligati**) a musical accompaniment forming an essential part of a piece of music, especially that played by a single instrument accompanying a voice. — *adj.* to be played with an obbligato. [from Italian *obbligato*, obligatory]

obduracy /ˈɒbdjʊrəsɪ/ *noun* being obdurate, obstinacy.

obdurate /ˈɒbdjʊrət, ɒbˈdjʊərət/ *adj.* **1** hard-hearted. **2** hard to influence or change, especially morally. [from Latin *ob*, against + *durus*, hard]

obdurately *adv.* in a hard-hearted way.

OBE *abbrev. Brit.* Order of the British Empire, an award given to honour personal or professional excellence or services to the country.

obedience *noun* **1** the act or practice of obeying. **2** willingness to obey orders. [from Latin *obedientia*]

obedient *adj.* obeying, ready to obey.

▣ compliant, acquiescent, docile, submissive, tractable, yielding, dutiful, law-abiding, deferential, respectful, subservient, observant.

▣ disobedient, rebellious, wilful.

obeisance /oʊˈbeɪsəns/ *noun* a bow, act or other expression of obedience or respect. [from Old French *obeissance*]

obeli /ˈɒbəlaɪ/ see OBELUS.

obelisk *noun* **1** a tapering, needle-like, usually four-sided, stone pillar. **2** *Printing* a dagger-shaped mark used especially for referring to footnotes. [from Greek *obeliskos*, small spit]

obelus /ˈɒbələs/ *noun* (PL. **obeli**) **1** *Printing* a dagger-shaped mark used especially for referring to footnotes. **2** a sign used in ancient texts to mark passages which may not be by the original author of the text. [from Greek *obelos*, spit]

obese *adj.* very fat. [from Latin *obesus*, plump]

obesity *noun* the condition of someone who is overweight as a result of the accumulation of excess fat in the body.

. . . .

☰ fatness, overweight, corpulence, stoutness, grossness, plumpness, portliness, bulk.

☲ thinness, slenderness, skinniness.

. . . .

obey *verb* (**obeys, obeyed**) **1** to do what one is told to do by (someone). **2** to carry out (a command). **3** *intrans.* to do what one is told. **4** to be controlled by (a force, impulse, etc). [from Latin *obedire*, from *ob*, towards + *audire*, to hear]

. . . .

☰ **1** bow to, take orders from, defer (to), be ruled by. **2** carry out, discharge, execute, act upon, fulfil, perform, follow, observe, abide by, adhere to, comply with, heed, keep. **3** comply, conform, submit, give way, surrender, yield.

☲ DISOBEY.

. . . .

obfuscate *verb* to confuse or make difficult to understand; to bewilder. [from Latin *ob*, completely + *fuscus*, dark]

obfuscation *noun* **1** obfuscating. **2** being obfuscated. **3** something that obfuscates.

obfuscatory *adj.* tending to obscure or confuse.

obiter dictum /ˈɒbɪtə ˈdɪktəm/ (PL. **obiter dicta**) a remark that is in some way related to, but not essential to, the main argument. [Latin, = thing said by the way]

obituary *noun* (PL. **obituaries**) a notice or announcement of a person's death, often with a short account of his or her life. [from Latin *obitus*, death]

object[1] /ˈɒbdʒɛkt, ˈɒbdʒɪkt/ *noun* **1** a thing that can be seen or touched. **2** an aim or purpose. **3** the person or thing to which action, feelings, or thought are directed. **4** *Grammar* the noun, noun phrase, or pronoun affected by the action of the verb, or a preposition. See also SUBJECT, DIRECT OBJECT, INDIRECT OBJECT. **5** *Philos.* a thing which is outside of, and can be perceived by, the mind. — **be no object** not to be a difficulty or obstacle. [from Latin *objectus*, a throwing before]

. . . .

☰ **1** thing, entity, article, body. **2** aim, purpose, objective, goal, target, intention, motive, end, reason, point, design. **3** target, recipient, butt, victim.

. . . .

object[2] /ɒbˈdʒɛkt/ *verb* **1** *intrans.* (**object to** or **against something**) to feel or express dislike or disapproval for it. **2** *trans.* to state as a ground for disapproval or objection: *objected that they had not been consulted.* [from Latin *ob*, in the way of + *jacere*, to throw]

. . . .

☰ **1** dislike, disapprove of, oppose, take exception to. **2** protest, complain.

☲ **1** like, approve of, agree to, acquiesce to.

. . . .

object glass the lens in a camera, telescope, etc which is nearest to the object being viewed.

objection *noun* **1** an expression of disapproval. **2** (**objection against** or **to something**) a reason for disapproving.

. . . .

☰ **1** protest, disapproval, dissent, opposition, demur, complaint, challenge. **2** complaint against, opposition to.

☲ **1** agreement, assent.

. . . .

objectionable *adj.* unpleasant; likely to cause offence.

. . . .

☰ unpleasant, unacceptable, offensive, obnoxious, repugnant, disagreeable, abhorrent, detestable, deplorable, despicable.

☲ acceptable.

. . . .

objectival *adj.* relating to or of the nature of an objective.

objective — *adj.* **1** not depending on, or influenced by, personal opinions or prejudices. **2** *Philos.* having existence outside the mind; based on fact or reality. See also SUBJECTIVE. **3** *Grammar, said of a case or word* indicating the object; in the relation of object to a verb or preposition. — *noun* **1** a thing aimed at or wished for; a goal. **2** *Grammar* the object case. **3** an object glass. [from Latin *objectivus*, from *ob*, in the way of + *jacere*, to throw]

. . . .

☰ *adj.* **1** impartial, unbiased, detached, unprejudiced, open-minded, equitable, dispassionate, even-handed, neutral, disinterested, just, fair. *noun* **1** object, goal, aim, end, purpose, ambition, mark, target, intention, design.

☲ *adj.* **1** subjective, biased, prejudiced.

. . . .

objectivism *noun* a tendency to emphasize what is objective.

objectivity *noun* being objective.

objectless *adj.* without an object.

object lesson an experience, event, etc, which gives a practical example of especially a principle or ideal.

objector *noun* a person who objects.

objet d'art /ˈɒbʒeɪ ˈdɑː(r)/ (PL. **objets d'art**) a small object of artistic value. [French, = object of art]

oblast *noun* an administrative district in some republics of the former Soviet Union.

oblate *adj. Geom., said of something approximately spherical* flattened at the poles, like the Earth. [from Latin *oblatus*, lengthened]

oblation *noun* **1** a sacrifice or religious offering. **2** the offering of the bread and wine to God at a Eucharist. [from Latin *oblatio*]

obligate *verb* to bind by contract, duty, or moral obligation. [from Latin *ob*, down + *ligare*, to bind]

obligation *noun* **1** a moral or legal duty or tie. **2** the binding power of such a duty or tie. **3** a debt of gratitude for a service: *be under obligation to her.*

. . . .

☰ **1, 2** duty, responsibility, onus, charge, commitment, liability, requirement, bond, contract.

. . . .

obligatorily *adv.* in an obligatory way.

obligatoriness *noun* being obligatory.

obligatory *adj.* legally or morally binding; compulsory.

. . . .

☰ binding, compulsory, mandatory, statutory, required, essential, necessary, enforced.

☲ optional.

. . . .

oblige *verb* **1** to bind morally or legally; to compel. **2** to bind by a service or favour. **3** to please or do a favour for: *please oblige me by leaving at once.* **4** *intrans.* to do something stated as a favour or contribution: *obliged us with a song.* — **much obliged** an expression of gratitude. [from Latin *ob*, down + *ligare*, to bind]

. . . .

☰ **1** compel, constrain, coerce, require, make, necessitate, force. **3** please, do a favour for, help, assist, accommodate, serve, gratify.

. . . .

obliging *adj.* willing to help others; courteously helpful.

. . . .

☰ willing, helpful, accommodating, co-operative, considerate, agreeable, friendly, kind, civil.

☲ unhelpful.

. . . .

oblique /əˈbliːk/ — *adj.* **1** sloping; not vertical or horizontal. **2** not straight or direct; roundabout; underhand. **3** *Geom., said of lines, etc* not at a right angle. **4** *Grammar* being in, or in any case other than the nominative or vocative. — *noun* **1** an oblique line (/). **2** anything that is oblique. [from Latin *ob*, completely + *liquis*, slanting]

⊟ *adj.* **1** slanting, sloping, inclined, angled, tilted.

obliqueness or **obliquity** *noun* **1** being oblique. **2** a slanting direction. **3** crookedness.

obliterate *verb* **1** to destroy completely. **2** to cover and prevent from being seen. [from Latin *obliterare*, to blot out]

⊟ **1** destroy, eradicate, annihilate, delete, wipe out, erase. **2** blot out, obscure.

obliteration *noun* being obliterated, extinction.

oblivion *noun* **1** the state of having forgotten or being unconscious. **2** the state of being forgotten. [from Latin *oblivio*, forgetfulness]

⊟ **1** unconsciousness, void, limbo. **2** obscurity, nothingness.
⊟ **1** awareness.

oblivious *adj.* (**oblivious of** or **to something**) unaware or forgetful of it.

⊟ unaware of, forgetful of, unconscious of, careless of, heedless of, blind to, insensible to.
⊟ aware of, sensible of.

obliviously *adv.* in a state of oblivion, unconsciously.

oblong — *adj.*, *said of a figure* rectangular with adjacent sides unequal; having a greater breadth than height. — *noun* (not in technical use) a rectangular figure. [from Latin *ob*, over + *longus*, long]

obloquy /ˈɒblək wɪ/ *noun* (PL. **obloquies**) **1** abuse, blame or censure. **2** loss of honour, good name, or reputation. [from Latin *ob*, against + *loqui*, to speak]

obnoxious *adj.* offensive; objectionable. [from Latin *ob*, exposed to + *noxa*, harm]

⊟ offensive, objectionable, unpleasant, disagreeable, disgusting, loathsome, nasty, horrid, odious, repulsive, revolting, repugnant, sickening, nauseating.
⊟ pleasant.

obnoxiousness *noun* **1** being obnoxious. **2** obnoxious behaviour.

oboe /ˈəʊbəʊ/ *noun* a wind instrument with a double reed, treble pitch, and a penetrating tone. [from Italian *oboe*, from French *hautbois*, from *haut*, high + *bois*, wood]

oboist /ˈəʊbəʊɪst/ *noun* a person who plays an oboe.

obscene *adj.* **1** offensive to accepted standards of behaviour or morality, especially sexual morality. **2** *colloq.* indecent; disgusting. **3** *Brit. Legal, said of a publication* tending to deprave or corrupt. [from Latin *obscenus*, foul, indecent]

⊟ **1** indecent, improper, immoral, impure, filthy, dirty, bawdy, lewd, licentious, pornographic, X-rated, scurrilous, suggestive. **2** indecent, disgusting, foul, shocking, shameless, offensive.
⊟ **1** decent, wholesome, proper, moral.

obscenity *noun* (PL. **obscenities**) **1** the state or quality of being obscene. **2** an obscene act or word.

⊟ **1** indecency, immodesty, impurity, impropriety, lewdness, licentiousness, suggestiveness, pornography, dirtiness, filthiness, foulness, grossness, indelicacy, coarseness. **2** *act* atrocity, evil, outrage, offence, *word* profanity, expletive, swear-word, four-letter word.

obscurantism *noun* opposition to inquiry or the spreading or use of new knowledge, up-to-date scientific research, etc. [from Latin *obscurare*, to obscure]

obscurantist — *noun* a person who tries to prevent enlightenment or reform. — *adj.* relating to or characteristic of obscurantism.

obscure — *adj.* **1** dark; dim. **2** not clear; hidden; difficult to see. **3** not well known. **4** difficult to understand. — *verb* to hide; to make dark, or difficult to see or understand. [from Latin *obscurus*, dark]

⊟ *adj.* **1, 2** dark, dim, indistinct, unclear, indefinite, shadowy, murky, gloomy, dusky, blurred, cloudy, faint, hazy, misty, shady, vague. **3** unknown, little-known, unheard-of, unimportant, undistinguished, nameless, inconspicuous, humble, minor. **4** incomprehensible, enigmatic, cryptic, recondite, esoteric, mysterious, deep, abstruse, confusing. *verb* hide, conceal, cloud, obfuscate, cover, blur, disguise, mask, darken, overshadow, shadow, shade, cloak, veil, shroud, dim, eclipse, screen, block out.
⊟ *adj.* **1, 2** clear, definite. **3** famous, renowned. **4** intelligible, straightforward. *verb* clarify, illuminate.

obscurity *noun* (PL. **obscurities**) **1** the state of being obscure. **2** something that is obscure.

obsequies /ˈɒbsəkwɪz/ *pl. noun* funeral rites. [from Latin *obsequiae*]

obsequious /əbˈsiːkwɪəs/ *adj.* submissively obedient; fawning. [from Latin *obsequiosus*, compliant]

⊟ servile, fawning, submissive, subservient, slavish, ingratiating, grovelling, sycophantic, cringing, deferential, flattering, *colloq.* smarmy, unctuous, oily.

observable *adj.* **1** discernible, perceptible. **2** notable, worthy of note. **3** to be observed.

observance *noun* **1** the act of obeying rules, keeping customs, etc. **2** a custom or religious rite observed. [from Latin *observantia*, from *observare*, to observe]

⊟ **1** adherence, compliance, observation, performance, obedience, fulfilment, honouring. **2** custom, rite, ritual, ceremony, practice, celebration.

observant *adj.* **1** quick to notice. **2** carefully attentive.

⊟ **1** perceptive, eagle-eyed. **2** attentive, alert, vigilant, watchful, wide awake, heedful.
⊟ UNOBSERVANT.

observation *noun* **1** the act of noticing or watching; the state of being observed or watched. **2** the ability to observe; perception: *test her powers of observation.* **3** a remark or comment. **4** the noting of behaviour, symptoms, phenomena, etc as they occur, especially before analysis or diagnosis: *keep the patient under observation.* **5** the result of such observing. — **take an observation** to observe the position of the sun or stars in order to calculate one's geographical position. [from Latin *observatio*]

⊟ **1** attention, notice, watching, examination, inspection, scrutiny. **3** remark, comment, utterance, thought, statement, pronouncement, reflection, opinion, finding, note. **4** monitoring, study.

observational *adj.* **1** relating to or consisting of observing or noticing. **2** based on observation of behaviour, phenomena, etc as opposed to experiments.

observation car a railway carriage with large windows to allow passengers to view the scenery.

observatory *noun* (PL. **observatories**) a room, building, or site specially equipped for making systematic observations of natural phenomena, especially the stars and other celestial objects visible in the night sky. [from Latin *observatorium*]

observe *verb* **1** to notice or become conscious of. **2** to watch carefully. **3** *trans., intrans.* to examine and note (behaviour, symptoms, phenomena, etc). **4** to obey, follow, or keep (a law, custom, religious rite, etc). **5** *trans., intrans.* to make a remark or comment: *observed that he was late again.* [from Latin *ob*, towards + *servare*, to keep]
. . . .
▭ **1** notice, see, perceive. **2** watch, study, keep an eye on, contemplate. **3** monitor, study. **4** obey, follow, keep, abide by, comply with, honour, fulfil, celebrate, perform. **5** remark, comment, say, mention.
▣ **1** miss. **4** break, violate.
. . . .

observer *noun* **1** a person who observes. **2** a person who goes to meetings, etc to watch and listen but not take part.
. . . .
▭ **1** watcher, spectator, viewer, witness, looker-on, onlooker, eyewitness, commentator, bystander, beholder.
. . . .

obsess *verb* to occupy, grip, or haunt the mind of completely, persistently, or constantly: *be obsessed with winning.* [from Latin *obsidere*, to besiege]
. . . .
▭ preoccupy, haunt, plague, prey on, possess, dominate, rule, monopolize, grip.
. . . .

obsession *noun* **1** a persistent or dominating idea. **2** *Psychol.* a recurring thought, feeling, or impulse, generally of an unpleasant nature, that preoccupies a person and is a source of constant anxiety that cannot be suppressed, eg the desire to wash the hands repeatedly because of fear of contamination.
. . . .
▭ **1** preoccupation, fixation, idée fixe, ruling passion, compulsion, fetish, *colloq.* hang-up, infatuation, mania, enthusiasm.
. . . .

obsessional *adj.* in the nature of an obsession.
obsessive *adj.* **1** relating to or resulting from an obsession or obsessions. **2** *said of a person* affected by an obsession.
. . . .
▭ **1** consuming, compulsive, gripping, fixed, haunting, tormenting, maddening. **2** compulsive.
. . . .

obsessive-compulsive disorder *Psychol.* a form of neurosis in which a person becomes preoccupied with a recurring thought, feeling, or impulse, which is a source of constant anxiety. See also OBSESSION.
obsidian /ɒbˈsɪdɪən/ *noun Geol.* the commonest type of volcanic glass, usually black, but sometimes red or brown in colour, and formed by the rapid cooling and solidification of granite magma. [from Latin *obsidianus*]
obsolescence *noun* being obsolescent.
obsolescent *adj.* going out of use; becoming out of date. [from Latin *obsolescere*, to become obsolete]
obsolete *adj.* no longer in use; out of date. [from Latin *obsoletus*]
. . . .
▭ disused, out of date, outmoded, old-fashioned, passé, dated, outworn, old, antiquated, antique, dead, extinct.
▣ modern, current, up to date.
. . . .

obstacle *noun* a person or thing that stands in a person's way or prevents progress. [from Latin *obstaculum*, from *ob*, before + *stare*, to stand]
. . . .
▭ obstruction, impediment, hurdle, hindrance, barrier, bar, check, snag, stumbling-block, drawback, difficulty, hitch, catch, stop, interference, interruption.
▣ advantage, help.
. . . .

obstacle race a race in which runners have to climb over, crawl through, etc various obstacles.

obstetric *adj.* relating to obstetrics.
obstetrician *noun* a doctor specially qualified in obstetrics.
obstetrics *sing. noun* the branch of medicine and surgery which deals with pregnancy, childbirth and the care of the mother. [from Latin *obstetrix*, a midwife, from *ob*, before + *stare*, to stand]
obstinacy *noun* **1** being obstinate. **2** obstinate behaviour; an obstinate act.
obstinate *adj.* **1** refusing to change one's opinion or course of action; stubborn; inflexible. **2** difficult to defeat, remove, or treat; unyielding. [from Latin *obstinatus*, from *ob*, in the way of + *stare*, to stand]
. . . .
▭ **1** stubborn, inflexible, immovable, intractable, unyielding, intransigent, persistent, dogged, steadfast, firm, determined, headstrong, wilful, self-willed, pigheaded, bloody-minded, strong-minded. **2** unyielding, intractable, persistent, immovable, steadfast, firm, determined.
▣ FLEXIBLE, TRACTABLE.

obstreperous *adj.* noisy and hard to control; unruly. [from Latin *ob*, before + *strepere*, to make a noise]
obstruct *verb* **1** to block or close. **2** to prevent or hinder the movement or progress of. [from Latin *ob*, in the way of + *struere*, to pile up]
. . . .
▭ **1** block, shut off, cut off, obscure, clog, choke, barricade. **2** impede, hinder, prevent, check, frustrate, hamper, bar, stop, stall, retard, restrict, thwart, inhibit, hold up, curb, arrest, slow down, interrupt, interfere with.
▣ **2** assist, further.
. . . .

obstruction *noun* **1** a thing that obstructs or blocks. **2** the act of obstructing. **3** an act of hindering or unfairly getting in the way, eg in sport.
. . . .
▭ **1** barrier, blockage, bar, barricade, check, stop, difficulty, hindrance, impediment. **2** blockage, hindrance, stoppage.
▣ **1, 2** help.
. . . .

obstructionism *noun* the practice of obstructing parliamentary or legal action.
obstructionist *noun* a person, especially a politician, who practises obstruction.
obstructive *adj.* causing or designed to cause an obstruction.
. . . .
▭ hindering, delaying, blocking, stalling, unhelpful, awkward, difficult, restrictive, inhibiting.
▣ co-operative, helpful.
. . . .

obstructively *adv.* in an obstructive way; so as to obstruct.
obstructiveness *noun* **1** being obstructive. **2** obstructive behaviour.
obtain *verb* to get; to become the owner or come into possession of, often by effort or planning. **2** *intrans.* to be established, exist or hold good. [from Latin *obtinere*, to lay hold of]
. . . .
▭ **1** get, acquire, gain, come by, attain, procure, secure, earn, achieve. **2** prevail, exist, hold, be in force, be the case, stand, reign, rule, be prevalent.
. . . .

obtainable *adj.* capable of being obtained.
obtrude *verb* **1** *intrans.* to be or become unpleasantly noticeable or prominent. **2** (**obtrude something on** or **upon someone**) to push oneself, one's opinions, etc forward, especially when they are unwelcome. [from Latin *ob*, against + *trudere*, to thrust]
obtruder *noun* a person who obtrudes.

obtrusion *noun* **1** an act of obtruding. **2** that which obtrudes.

obtrusive *adj.* **1** unpleasantly noticeable or prominent: *an obtrusive new housing scheme on the edge of town.* **2** sticking out; protruding.

▣ **1** noticeable, prominent, obvious, blatant, intrusive. **2** protruding, prominent.
▢ UNOBTRUSIVE.

obtuse *adj.* **1** blunt; not pointed or sharp. **2** *colloq.* stupid and slow to understand. **3** *Geom.* denoting an angle that is greater than 90 and less than 180. [from Latin *obtusus*, dull]

▣ **1** blunt, dull, unsharpened. **2** slow, stupid, *colloq.* thick, dull, dense, crass, *colloq.* dumb, stolid, dull-witted, thick-skinned.
▢ **2** bright, quick, sharp.

obverse *noun* **1** the side of a coin with the head or main design on it. See also REVERSE. **2** the face, side, etc of anything which is normally on view. **3** an opposite or counterpart, eg of a fact or truth. [from Latin *obversus*, turned against]

obviate *verb* to prevent or remove (a potential difficulty, problem, etc) in advance. [from Latin *obviare*, to go to meet]

obvious *adj.* easily seen or understood; evident. [from Latin *obvius*, from *ob*, in the way of + *via*, way]

▣ evident, clear, self-evident, manifest, patent, plain, distinct, transparent, undeniable, unmistakable, conspicuous, glaring, apparent, open, unconcealed, visible, noticeable, perceptible, pronounced, recognizable, prominent.
▢ unclear, indistinct, obscure.

obviously *adv.* in an obvious way; as is obvious, clearly.

▣ plainly, clearly, evidently, manifestly, undeniably, unmistakably, without doubt, certainly, distinctly, of course.

ocarina *noun* a small simple wind instrument with an egg-shaped body and projecting mouthpiece. [from Italian *ocarina*, from *oca*, goose, so-called because of its shape]

occasion *noun* **1** a particular event or happening or the time at which it occurs. **2** a special event or celebration. **3** a suitable opportunity. **4** a reason; grounds: *have no occasion to be angry.* **5** an event which determines the time at which something happens, but which is not the actual cause of it. — *verb* to cause. — **on occasion** from time to time. **rise to the occasion** to produce the extra energy or ability needed by unusual circumstances. [from Latin *occasio*, from *ob*, in the way of + *cadere*, to fall]

▣ *noun* **1** event, happening, occurrence, incident, time, instance, case. **2** celebration, function, affair, party. **3** opportunity, chance. **4** reason, ground(s), cause, excuse, justification.

occasional *adj.* **1** happening irregularly and infrequently. **2** produced on or for a special occasion.

▣ **1** periodic, intermittent, irregular, infrequent, sporadic, uncommon, incidental, odd, rare, casual.
▢ **1** regular, frequent, constant.

occasionally *adv.* on occasions; now and then.

▣ sometimes, on occasion(s), now and then, now and again, from time to time, at times, at intervals, irregularly, periodically, every so often, once in a while, off and on, infrequently.

▢ frequently, often, always.

occasional table a small, usually decorated table with no regular use.

Occident *noun* **1** (**the Occident**) the countries in the west, especially those in Europe and America regarded as culturally distinct from eastern countries (the *Orient*). **2** that part of the sky where the sun sets. [from Latin *occidens*, from *occidere*, to go down]

occidental — *adj.* from or relating to the Occident; western. — *noun* (**Occidental**) a person born in the Occident; a westerner.

occipital *adj.* relating to or in the region of the back of the head.

occiput /ˈɒksɪpʌt/ *noun Anat.* the back of the head. [from Latin, from *ob*, over + *caput*, head]

occlude *verb* **1** to block up or cover (eg a pore or some other opening). **2** *Chem.*, *said of a solid* to absorb (a gas) so that atoms or molecules of the latter occupy the spaces within the lattice structure of the solid. **3** *Medicine* to close (an opening), eg to obstruct a blood vessel. **4** *Medicine* to close the surfaces of (the upper teeth) on those of the lower teeth. **5** to shut in or out. [from Latin *occludere*, to shut up]

occluded front *Meteorol.* the final stage in an atmospheric depression, when a cold front catches up with and overtakes a warm front, lifting the warm air mass off the ground.

occlusion *noun* **1** the closing of an orifice, etc. **2** the act of occluding or absorbing.

occult — *adj.* **1** involving, using, or dealing with that which is magical, mystical or supernatural. **2** beyond ordinary understanding. **3** secret, hidden, or esoteric. — *noun* (**the occult**) the knowledge and study of that which is magical, mystical, or supernatural. [from Latin *occultus*, hidden]

▣ *adj.* **1** magical, mystical, supernatural. **3** secret, hidden, veiled, esoteric, mysterious, concealed, arcane, recondite, obscure.

occultation *noun Astron.* a phenomenon that is observed when one celestial body (eg a planet or moon) passes directly in front of another (eg a star), so obscuring it. [from Latin *occulere*, to hide]

occultism *noun Relig.* the doctrine or study of the supernatural, and practices purporting to achieve communication with things hidden and mysterious, including magic, divination, certain types of spiritualism, and witchcraft.

occultist *noun* a person who believes in occult things.

occult sciences astrology, palmistry, tarot, etc.

occupancy *noun* (PL. **occupancies**) **1** the act of occupying (a house, etc). **2** a period of time during which a house, etc is occupied. [from Latin *occupare*, to seize]

occupant *noun* a person who occupies, has, or takes possession of something, not always the owner.

▣ occupier, holder, inhabitant, resident, householder, tenant, user, lessee, squatter, inmate.

occupation *noun* **1** a person's job or profession. **2** an activity that occupies a person's attention, free time, etc. **3** the act of occupying or state of being occupied. **4** the period of time during which a town, house, etc is occupied. **5** the act of taking and keeping control of a foreign country, using military power. [from Latin *occupatio*, seizing]

▣ **1** job, profession, work, vocation, employment, trade, craft, post, calling, business, line, walk of life. **2** activity, pursuit. **3** occupancy, possession, holding, habitation, use, tenancy, tenure, residence. **4** tenancy, tenure, residence. **5** invasion, seizure, conquest, control, takeover.

occupational *adj.* of, connected with, or caused by a person's job: *occupational disease.*

occupational hazard a risk or danger caused by the working conditions of a particular job.

occupationally *adv.* in an occupational way; as regards occupation.

occupational psychology *Psychol.* the branch of psychology that is concerned with the scientific study of human behaviour in the workplace, including the study of work skills and the working environment, vocational guidance, personnel selection, all forms of training, and principles of management.

occupational therapist a person who provides occupational therapy.

occupational therapy a form of rehabilitation in which patients with physical or mental illnesses are encouraged to participate in selected activities that will equip them to function independently in everyday life, such as household management, social skills, industrial work, educational programmes, woodwork, art and crafts, and gardening.

occupier *noun* a person who lives in a building, as either a tenant or owner.

occupy *verb* (**occupies**, **occupied**) 1 to have possession of or live in (a house, etc). 2 to be in or fill (time, space, etc). 3 to take possession of (a building, a foreign country, etc) by force. 4 to keep (oneself, a person, one's mind, etc) busy; to fill in (time). 5 to hold (a post or office). [from Latin *occupare*, to seize]

....

■ 1 inhabit, live in, possess, reside in, stay in, take possession of, own. 2 fill, take up, use. 3 invade, seize, capture, overrun, take over. 4 busy, interest, amuse, engross, preoccupy, absorb, engage, hold, involve.

....

occur *verb intrans.* (**occurred**, **occurring**) 1 to happen or take place. 2 (**occur to someone**) to come into their mind, especially unexpectedly or by chance: *it occurred to her that the train might be late*/*an idea has occurred to me*. 3 to be found or exist. [from Latin *occurrere*, to run towards]

....

■ 1 happen, come about, take place, transpire, chance, come to pass, materialize, befall, develop, crop up, arise, appear, turn up, obtain, result. 3 be found, exist, be present.

....

occurrence *noun* 1 anything that occurs; an event, especially an unexpected one. 2 the act of occurring.

....

■ 1 incident, event, happening, affair, circumstance, episode, instance, case, development, action. 2 incidence, existence, appearance, manifestation.

....

ocean *noun* 1 the continuous expanse of salt water that covers about 70% of the Earth's surface, and surrounds the continental land masses. 2 any one of its five main divisions, the Atlantic, Indian, Pacific, Arctic, and Southern. 3 the sea. 4 (*often* **oceans**) a very large number or expanse: *oceans of people*. [from Greek *Okeanos*, the stream supposed by the ancients to run round the earth]

oceanarium *noun* (PL. **oceanariums**) a large aquarium supplied with salt water, or an enclosed part of the sea, in which sea creatures are kept for research purposes or for display to the public. See also OCEAN, AQUARIUM.

ocean-going *adj.*, *said of a ship* built to sail in the sea rather than in rivers, etc.

oceanic /oʊʃɪˈanɪk/ *adj.* 1 relating to the ocean. 2 found or formed in the ocean.

oceanic ridge any undersea mountain range.

oceanographer *noun* an expert on oceanography.

oceanographic *adj.* relating to or involving oceanography.

oceanography *noun* the scientific study of the oceans, including the structure and origin of the ocean floor, the chemical properties of sea water, the physical processes that take place in the oceans, eg currents, waves, and tides, and the ecology of the marine organisms that inhabit the oceans.

ocelot /ˈɒsəlɒt/ *noun* a medium-sized wild cat, found in the forests of Central and S America, which has dark yellow fur marked with spots and stripes. [from Aztec *ocelotl*, jaguar]

och /ɒx/ *interj. Scot., Irish* an expression of surprise, impatience, disagreement, annoyance, regret, etc. [a Gaelic word]

ochone or **ohone** /oʊˈxoʊn/ *interj.* used in the Scottish Highlands and Ireland to express lamentation. [from Gaelic *ochoin*]

ochre /ˈoʊkə(r)/ *noun* 1 a kind of fine earth or clay, used as a yellow, red, or brown dye. 2 a pale brownish-yellow. [from Greek *ochros*, pale]

ochreous /ˈoʊkrɪəs/ *adj.* 1 of the nature of, containing, or full of ochre. 2 of the colour of ochre, yellowish.

o'clock *adv.* used after a number in specifying the time. [from the phrase *of the clock*]

OCR *abbrev. Comput.* optical character recognition, or reader.

Oct or **Oct.** *abbrev.* October.

oct- or **octa-** see OCTO-.

octad *noun* a group, series, set, etc of eight things. [from Greek *okto*, eight]

octagon *noun* a flat figure with eight straight sides and eight angles. [from Greek *okto*, eight + *gonia*, angle]

octagonal *adj.* having eight sides and angles.

octahedral *adj.* 1 shaped like an octahedron. 2 having eight plane surfaces.

octahedron *noun* (PL. **octahedra**, **octahedrons**) a solid figure with eight plane faces. [from Greek *okto*, eight + *hedra*, seat]

octane *noun Chem.* (FORMULA C_8H_8) a colourless liquid belonging to the alkane series of hydrocarbons, present in petroleum, and used in petrol, as a solvent, and in the manufacture of organic chemicals. [from Greek *okto*, eight +-*ane* as in METHANE]

octane number or **octane rating** a numerical system for classifying motor fuels according to their resistance to knocking. The higher the octane number, the better the quality of the petrol, and the lower the likelihood of knocking.

octant /ˈɒktənt/ *noun Maths.* 1 one eighth of the circumference of a circle. 2 a section, formed by drawing two straight lines from the centre to the circumference, of one eighth of a circle. [from Latin *octans*, an eighth]

octave /ˈɒktɪv, ˈɒkteɪv/ *noun* 1 *Mus.* the range of sound, or the series of notes, between the first note and the eighth note on a major or minor scale, eg from C to the C above. 2 a musical note that is an eighth above or below another. 3 *Poetry* a verse or stanza with eight lines. 4 the first eight lines of a sonnet. [from Latin *octavus*, eighth]

octavo /ɒkˈteɪvoʊ/ *noun* (PL. **octavos**) 1 a size of book or page produced by folding a standard-sized sheet of paper three times to give eight leaves. 2 a book of this size. [from Latin *octavus*, eighth]

octet *noun* 1 a group of eight, eg musicians, lines in a poem, etc. 2 a piece of music written for eight musicians or singers. 3 the first eight lines in a sonnet. [from Latin *octo*, eight + DUET]

octo- or **oct-** or **octa-** *combining form* forming words meaning eight. [from Greek *okto*, eight]

October *noun* the 10th month of the year. [from Latin, from *octo*, eight, so called because it was the eighth month in the Roman calendar]

Octobrist *noun* a member of a Russian political party which supported the political changes proposed by Tsar Nicholas II in October 1905.

octogenarian — *adj.* between 80 and 89 years old. — *noun* a person of this age. [from Latin *octogenarius*, of eighty]

octopus *noun* (PL. **octopuses**) any of about 150 species of marine mollusc, found mainly in tropical regions, with a soft rounded body, no external shell, and eight arms, each of which bears two rows of suckers. [from Greek *okto*, eight + *pous*, foot]

octopush *noun* an underwater game resembling hockey. It is played in a swimming pool by two teams of six players, who attempt to score goals by pushing a lead puck (a *squid*) along the bottom and hitting it against the opposing team's end of the pool. [from OCTOPUS + PUSH]

octoroon or **octaroon** *noun* a person having one black African or Caribbean great-grandparent. [from Latin *octo*, eight]

octosyllabic *adj.* consisting of eight syllables or composed of lines of eight syllables.

octosyllable *noun* 1 a word with eight syllables. 2 a line of verse containing eight syllables. [from Latin *octo*, eight + *syllaba*, syllable]

octuple *adj.* eight times as large; eightfold. [from Latin *octuplus*]

ocular *adj.* of or related to the eyes or vision. [from Latin *oculus*, eye]

oculist *noun* an optician or ophthalmologist. [from Latin *oculus*, eye]

oculus *noun* (PL. **oculi**) *Archit.* a round window. [from Latin *oculus*, eye]

OD /oʊˈdiː/ *slang* — *noun* (PL. **ODs**, **OD's**) an overdose of drugs. — *verb intrans.* (**OD'd**, **OD'ing**) to take a drug overdose. [abbreviation]

odalisque or **odalisk** *noun Hist.* a female slave or concubine in a harem, especially that belonging to the Turkish Sultan. [from Turkish *odalik*, from *oda*, room]

odd *adj.* 1 left over when others are put into groups or pairs. 2 not matching: *odd socks.* 3 not one of a complete set. 4 *Maths.* not exactly divisible by two. 5 unusual; strange. 6 occasional; not regular: *odd jobs.* 7 (*in compounds with a number*) a little more than the number stated: *twenty-odd replies.* 8 *said of pages, etc numbered consecutively* having an odd number: *put pictures on the odd pages.* 9 out of the way; standing apart. — **odd man out** 1 a person or thing that is different from, and often unwilling to be like, others. 2 a person or thing left over when teams, sets, etc have been formed. [from Norse *oddi*, odd number]

▪ 1 spare, surplus, left-over, remaining. 2 unmatched, unpaired. 3 sundry, various, miscellaneous, single. 5 unusual, strange, uncommon, peculiar, abnormal, exceptional, curious, atypical, different, queer, bizarre, eccentric, remarkable, unconventional, weird, irregular, extraordinary, outlandish, rare. 6 occasional, incidental, irregular, random, casual.
🔁 2 matching. 4 even. 5 normal, usual. 6 regular.

oddball *noun colloq.* a strange or eccentric person.

oddity *noun* (PL. **oddities**) 1 a strange person or thing. 2 the state of being strange or unusual.

▪ 1 curiosity, character, freak, misfit, phenomenon, quirk. 2 abnormality, peculiarity, rarity, eccentricity, idiosyncrasy.

oddly *adv.* in an odd way; as an odd circumstance: *oddly, he refused to stay.*

oddments *pl. noun* pieces left over from something much larger.

▪ bits, scraps, leftovers, fragments, offcuts, ends, remnants, shreds, snippets.

oddness *noun* 1 being odd. 2 an odd act. 3 odd behaviour.

odds *pl. noun* (*sometimes treated as sing.*) 1 the chance or probability, expressed as a ratio, that something will or will not happen: *the odds are 10–1 against.* 2 the difference between the amount placed as a bet and the money which might be won, expressed as a ratio: *offer odds of 2 to 1.* 3 an advantage that is thought to exist: *the odds are in her favour/it makes no odds how we go.* 4 likelihood: *the odds are he'll be late again.* — **against all the odds** in spite of

great difficulty or disadvantage. **at odds** in disagreement or dispute: *at odds with the management.* **odds and ends** *colloq.* small objects, of different kinds, and usually of little value or importance. **over the odds** more than is required or expected. **what's the odds?** *colloq.* what difference does it make?; what does it matter?

▪ 1, 4 likelihood, probability, chances. 3 advantage, edge, lead, superiority.

odds-on *adj.*, *said of a chance* better than even.

ode *noun* a usually long lyric poem, with lines of different lengths, addressed to a particular person or thing. [from Greek *oide*, from *aeidein*, to sing]

odious *adj.* hateful, extremely unpleasant or offensive. [from Latin *odiosus*, from *odi*, to hate]

▪ hateful, unpleasant, offensive, loathsome, obnoxious, disgusting, repulsive, revolting, repugnant, foul, execrable, detestable, abhorrent, horrible, horrid, abominable.
🔁 pleasant.

odium *noun* hatred, strong dislike, or disapproval of a person or thing, especially when widespread. [from Latin *odium*, hatred]

odometer *noun North Amer. Engineering* an instrument for measuring and displaying the distance travelled by a motor vehicle or a person, eg the milometer incorporated in the speedometer of a car. It consists of a wheel of known circumference, the number of revolutions made being used to calculate the distance travelled. [from Greek *hodos*, way + -METER]

odoriferous *adj.* having or giving off a sweet or pleasant smell. [from Latin *odorifer*, from *odor*, smell]

odorous *adj.* giving off an odour, especially a sweet or pleasant one.

odour *noun* 1 a distinctive smell. 2 reputation; standing; relationship: *in bad odour with someone.* 3 a characteristic or quality. [from Latin *odor*]

▪ 1 smell, scent, fragrance, aroma, perfume, redolence, stench, stink.

odourless *adj.* without odour.

odyssey *noun* (PL. **odysseys**) a long and adventurous journey. [after the Greek *Odysseia, The Odyssey*, an epic poem by Homer (c.8c BC) which tells the story of the 10-year journey of the Greek general Odysseus back to Ithaca after the fall of Troy]

OECD *abbrev.* Organization for Economic Co-operation and Development.

OED *abbrev.* Oxford English Dictionary.

oedema /ɪˈdiːmə/ *noun* (PL. **oedemata**, **oedemas**) an abnormal build-up of fluid in the tissues in the body, causing swelling. [from Greek *oidema*, swelling]

oedematous /ɪˈdiːmətəs/ *adj.* relating to or affected by oedema.

Oedipal /ˈiːdəpəl/ *adj.* relating to or characterized by the Oedipus complex.

Oedipus complex /ˈiːdɪpəs/ *Psychol.* 1 in psychoanalysis, the repressed sexual desire of a son for his mother, and the subsequent rivalry with his father. 2 the corresponding sexual desire of a daughter for her father, and the subsequent rivalry with her mother, also known as *Elektra complex.* [from Greek Oidipous, a king of Thebes, who unwittingly killed his father and married his mother]

OEEC *abbrev.* Organization for European Economic Co-operation.

o'er /oʊə(r)/ *prep.*, *adv. poetic, old use* over. [shortened form]

oesophageal /iːsɒfəˈdʒɪəl/ *adj.* relating to or in the region of the oesophagus.

oesophagus /iːˈsɒfəgəs/ *noun* (PL. **oesophagi**) the tube by which food passes from the mouth to the stomach. [from Greek *oisophagos*]

oestradiol or **estradiol** /iːstrəˈdaɪɒl/ *noun Physiol.* the most important female sex hormone, a steroid that is produced by the ovary and controls the development of the female secondary sexual characteristics and the functioning of the reproductive organs.

oestrogen /ˈiːstrədʒən/ *noun Biochem.* any of a group of steroid hormones, produced mainly by the ovaries, that control the growth and functioning of the female sex organs and the appearance of female secondary sexual characteristics, eg breast development, and that regulate the menstrual cycle. [from OESTRUS + Greek *genes*, born, produced]

oestrus /ˈiːstrəs/ *noun* a regularly recurring period of fertility and sexual preparedness in many female mammals, when pregnancy is possible; heat. [from Greek *oistros*, a gadfly noted for its frenzy]

of *prep.* **1** used to show origin, cause, or authorship: *people of Glasgow*/*die of hunger*/*poems of Keats*. **2** belonging to; connected with. **3** used to specify a component, ingredient, characteristic, etc: *built of bricks*/*an area of marsh*/*a heart of gold*. **4** at a given distance or amount of time from: *two miles out of the city*/*within a minute of arriving*. **5** about; concerning: *tales of Rome*/*think of the children*. **6** belonging to or forming a part: *most of the story*. **7** existing, happening, etc at, on, in, or during: *battle of Hastings*/*he works of a night*. **8** used with words denoting loss, removal, separation, etc: *cured of cancer / cheated of the money*. **9** used to show the connection between a verbal noun and the person who is performing, or who is the object of, the action stated: *the running of the deer*/*the eating of healthy food*. **10** *North Amer., esp. US* to; before a stated hour: *a quarter of one*. [from Anglo-Saxon]

off — *adv.* **1** away; at or to a distance. **2** in or into a position which is not attached; loose; separate: *the handle came off*/*take your coat off*. **3** ahead in time: *Easter is a week off*. **4** in or into a state of no longer working or operating: *turn the radio off*. **5** in or into a state of being stopped or cancelled: *the match was rained off*. **6** in or into a state of sleep: *doze off*. **7** to the end, so as to be completely finished: *finish the work off*. **8** away from work or one's duties: *take an hour off*. **9** away from a course; aside: *turn off into a side street*. **10** not available as a choice, especially on a menu: *peas are off*. **11** in or into a state of decay: *the milk has gone off*. **12** situated as regards money: *well off*. — *adj.* **1** most distant; furthest away. **2** *said of the side of a vehicle, etc* nearest the centre of the road, on the right in the UK. **3** not good; not up to standard: *an off day*. **4** *Cricket* on the side of the field towards which the batsman's feet are pointing, usually the bowler's left. See also ON 6. — *prep.* **1** from; away from. **2** removed from; no longer attached to. **3** opening out of; leading from: *a side street off the main road*. **4** not wanting; no longer attracted by: *go off him*/*off one's food*. **5** no longer using: *be off the tablets*. **6** not up to the usual standard: *off one's game*. **7** out to sea from: *off the coast of Spain*. — *noun* **1** the start, eg of a race or journey: *ready for the off*. **2** *Cricket* the side of a field towards which the batsman's feet are pointing, usually the bowler's left. See also ON. — **a bit off** *colloq.*, *said of behaviour* unacceptable or unfair. **off and on** now and then; occasionally. [from Anglo-Saxon *of*, away]

. . . .

▤ *adv.* **1** away, at a distance, elsewhere, out, apart, aside. **2** unattached, loose, separate, apart. **3** away. **5** cancelled, postponed. **11** bad, rotten, sour, rancid, mouldy, decomposed, turned. *adj.* **3** substandard, below par, disappointing, unsatisfactory, slack.

▧ *adj.* **2** near.

. . . .

offal *noun* **1** the heart, brains, liver, kidneys, etc of an animal, used as food. **2** rubbish, waste or refuse. [from Middle English, from *of*, off + *fal*, fall]

offbeat *adj. colloq.* unusual; not conventional; eccentric.

off-Broadway *adj.* a collective term used since the 1950s to designate theatres and plays operating outside the commercial US theatre centred on Broadway.

off chance see CHANCE.

off-colour *adj.* **1** *Brit.* unwell; not in good health. **2** *said of humour* rude; smutty.

. . . .

▤ **1** unwell, sick, ill, poorly, indisposed, off form, under the weather, out of sorts.

. . . .

offcut *noun* a small piece left over from a larger piece of eg wood, cloth, or meat.

offence *noun* **1** the breaking of a rule; a crime. **2** any cause of anger, annoyance, or displeasure. **3** displeasure, annoyance or resentment: *mean no offence*. **4** an attack or assault. — **give offence** to cause displeasure or annoyance. **take offence at something** to be offended by it. [from Latin *offendere*, to strike against]

. . . .

▤ **1** misdemeanour, transgression, crime, misdeed, sin, violation, wrong, wrongdoing, infringement, trespass. **3** displeasure, annoyance, resentment, indignation, pique, umbrage, outrage, hurt, hard feelings.

. . . .

offend *verb* **1** to cause (someone) to feel hurt or angry; to insult. **2** to be unpleasant or annoying to (someone). **3** *intrans.* (**offend against someone** or **something**) to commit a sin or crime; to act in a way that is not in accordance with custom, etc. [from Latin *offendere*, to strike against]

. . . .

▤ **1** hurt, insult, annoy, outrage, injure, upset, wound, affront, wrong, displease, snub. **2** disgust, repel, sicken. **3** transgress, violate, sin, err.

▧ **1, 2** please.

. . . .

offended *adj.* insulted, having taken offence.

offender *noun* a person who has committed an offence.

. . . .

▤ transgressor, wrongdoer, culprit, criminal, miscreant, guilty party, law-breaker, delinquent.

. . . .

offending *adj.* that offends, offensive.

offensive — *adj.* **1** giving or likely to give offence; insulting. **2** unpleasant, disgusting, repulsive, especially to the senses. **3** used for attacking. — *noun* **1** an aggressive action or attitude: *go on the offensive*. **2** an attack. **3** a great or aggressive effort to achieve something: *a peace offensive*. [from Latin *offendere*, to strike against]

. . . .

▤ *adj.* **1** insulting, insolent, abusive, rude, impertinent. **2** unpleasant, disagreeable, objectionable, displeasing, disgusting, repulsive, odious, obnoxious, repellent, repugnant, revolting, loathsome, vile, nauseating, nasty, detestable, abominable. *noun* **2** attack, assault, onslaught, invasion, raid, sortie.

▧ *adj.* **1** polite. **2** pleasant.

. . . .

offer — *verb* (**offered**, **offering**) **1** to put forward (a gift, payment, suggestion, etc) to be accepted, refused, or considered. **2** to provide: *a hill offering the best view*. **3** *intrans.* to state one's willingness (to do something). **4** to present for sale. **5** *said of a thing* to present for consideration, acceptance or refusal; to provide an opportunity for: *a job offering rapid promotion*. **6** *intrans.* to present itself; to occur: *if opportunity offers*. **7** *trans.*, *intrans.* to propose (a sum) as payment (to someone): *offer him £250 for the car*. **8** (*also* **offer something up**) to present (a prayer or sacrifice) to God. **9** to show (resistance, etc). — *noun* **1** an act of offering. **2** that which is offered, especially an amount of money offered to buy something. **3** a proposal, especially of marriage. — **on offer** for sale, especially at a reduced price. **under offer** *said of a house for sale* with a possible buyer who has made an offer, but still waiting for the contracts to be signed. [from Latin *offerre*, from *ob*, towards + *ferre*, to bring]

◼ *verb* **1** put forward, make available, present, advance, extend, submit, suggest, hold out. **2, 5** provide, afford, give. **3** volunteer, come forward, *colloq.* show willing. **4** sell. **7** proffer, propose, bid, tender. *noun* **2** bid, tender, submission. **3** proposal, suggestion, proposition, overture, approach, submission, bid, tender.

offering *noun* **1** anything offered, especially a gift. **2** a gift of money given to a church, usually during a religious service, used for charity, etc. **3** a sacrifice made to God.

◼ **1** present, gift. **2** donation, contribution, subscription.

offertory *noun* (PL. **offertories**) *Christianity* **1** the offering of bread and wine to God during a Eucharist. **2** an anthem or hymn sung while this is happening. **3** money collected during a church service. [from Latin *offerre*, to offer]

offhand or **offhanded** — *adj.* casual or careless, often with the result of being rude. — *adv.* from memory; without preparation, reference to documents, etc.

◼ *adj.* casual, careless, unconcerned, uninterested, brusque, abrupt, perfunctory, informal, cavalier. *adv. colloq.* off the cuff, *colloq.* off the top of one's head, extempore, impromptu, immediately.
◾ *adj.* calculated, planned.

offhandedly *adv.* in an offhand manner.
offhandedness *noun* being offhand.
office *noun* **1** the room, set of rooms or building in which the business of a firm is done. **2** a room or building used for a particular kind of business. **3** a local centre or department of a large business. **4** a position of authority, especially in the government or in public service: *run for office*. **5** *said of a political party* forming the government: *out of office*. **6** (**Office**) a government department: *the Home Office*. **7** the group of people working in an office. **8** a function or duty. **9** (*usually* **offices**) an act of kindness or service: *through her good offices*. **10** an authorized form of Christian worship or service, especially one for the dead (see also DIVINE OFFICE). [from Latin *officium*, favour, duty, service]

◼ **1, 2** workplace, workroom, bureau. **3** centre, department, branch, bureau, division. **4** post, appointment, occupation, situation, employment. **8** function, duty, responsibility, obligation, charge, commission, role.

office-bearer or **office-holder** *noun* a person with an official duty in a society, church organization, etc.
office-block *noun* a large, multistorey building divided into offices.
officer *noun* **1** a person in a position of authority and responsibility in the armed forces. **2** a person with an official position in an organization, society, or government department. **3** a policeman or policewoman. **4** a person in authority on a non-naval ship.

◼ **2** official, office-bearer, office-holder, public servant, functionary, dignitary, bureaucrat, administrator, representative, executive, agent, appointee.

official — *adj.* **1** of or relating to an office or position of authority. **2** given or authorized by a person in authority: *an official report*. **3** formal; suitable for or characteristic of a person holding office: *official dinners*. — *noun* a person who holds office or who is in a position of authority. [from Latin *officialis*]

◼ *adj.* **2** authorized, authoritative, legitimate, licensed, accredited, certified, approved, authenticated, authentic, bona fide, proper. *noun* office-bearer, office-holder, officer, functionary, bureaucrat, executive, representative, agent.
◾ *adj.* **1, 2** unofficial. **3** informal.

officialdom *noun* officials and bureaucrats as a group.
officialese *noun* the language of the government, civil service, etc, which is unclear, wordy and pompous.
officially *adv.* in an official way; in an official capacity.
official receiver a government officer appointed to deal with the affairs of a company, etc which has gone bankrupt.
officiate *verb intrans.* **1** to act in an official capacity; to perform official duties, especially at a particular function. **2** to conduct a religious service. [from Latin *officiare*, to serve]

◼ **1** preside.

officious *adj.* **1** offering help, advice, etc when this is not wanted; interfering. **2** *said of a diplomatic agreement* informal; unofficial. [from Latin *officiosus*, obliging]

◼ **1** intrusive, interfering, obtrusive, meddlesome, *colloq.* bossy, *colloq.* pushy, forward, bustling, importunate, dictatorial, over-zealous, self-important.

offing *noun* the more distant part of the sea that is visible from the shore. — **in the offing** not far off; likely to happen soon.
off-key *adj., adv.* **1** out of tune. **2** not quite suitable.
off-licence *noun* *Brit.* a shop licensed to sell alcohol to be drunk elsewhere.
off-limits *adj.* not to be entered.
off-line — *adj. Comput.* **1** *said of a peripheral device, eg a printer* not connected to a computer, and therefore not controlled by it. **2** *said of business, etc.* not conducted by means of computers. **3** *said of a person* not using a computer. — *adv.* not by means of or not while using a computer. See also ON-LINE.
offload *verb* to get rid of (especially something unpleasant) by giving it to someone else.

◼ get rid of, unburden, unload, jettison, dump, drop, deposit, discharge.

off-peak *adj., said of services* used at a time when there is little demand, and therefore usually cheaper.
offprint *noun* a copy of an article forming part of a larger magazine or periodical.
off-putting *adj. colloq.* disturbing; disconcerting; unpleasant.

◼ disturbing, disconcerting, unpleasant, intimidating, daunting, discouraging, disheartening, formidable, unnerving, unsettling, demoralizing.

off-road *adj.* **1** relating to paths, tracks etc, as opposed to roads. **2** relating to vehicles designed to operate away from roads.
off-season *noun* the less popular and less busy period.
offset — *noun* **1** a side-shoot on a plant, used for developing new plants. **2** a printing process in which an image is inked on to a rubber roller which then transfers it to paper, etc. **3** anything which compensates or is a counterbalance for something else. — *verb* (**offsetting**; PAST TENSE AND PAST PARTICIPLE **offset**) **1** to counterbalance or compensate for (something): *price rises offset by tax cuts*. **2** to print (something) using an offset process.

▣ *verb* **1** counterbalance, compensate for, cancel out, counteract, make up for, balance out, neutralize.

offset lithography or **offset litho** a method of printing, developed at the beginning of the 20c, by which an image created by photographic means on a printing plate is transferred to a rubber 'blanket' cylinder and then to the paper (or other material such as metal or plastic).

offshoot *noun* **1** a shoot growing from a plant's main stem. **2** anything which is a branch of, or has developed from, something else.

▣ **1** branch, limb, arm, outgrowth. **2** branch, development, spin-off, by-product, appendage.

offshore *adv., adj.* **1** situated in, at, or on the sea, not far from the coast: *offshore industries.* **2** *said of the wind* blowing away from the coast, out to sea.
offside — *adj., adv.* Football, Rugby in an illegal position between the ball and the opponents' goal. — *noun* the side of a vehicle or horse nearest the centre of the road, in the UK the right side.
offspring *noun* (PL. **offspring**) **1** a person's child. **2** the young of an animal. **3** a result or outcome.

▣ **1, 2** child, young, *formal* issue, progeny, brood. **1** heir(s), successor(s), descendant(s). **3** result, outcome, progeny, consequence, repercussion, upshot, issue.
▣ **1, 2** parent(s).

off-stage *adj., adv.* not on the stage, and so unable to be seen by the audience.
off-street *adj., said of parking* not on a road.
off-the-peg *adj., said of clothing* ready to wear; ready-made.
off-white — *adj.* yellowish or greyish white. — *noun* this colour, or anything which is this colour, eg paint.
OFT *abbrev.* Office of Fair Trading.
oft *adv. old use, poetic* often. [from Anglo-Saxon]
often *adv.* **1** many times; frequently. **2** in many cases. — **as often as not** quite often; in about half the cases. **every so often** sometimes; now and then. **more often than not** usually; in most of the cases. [from Middle English, from OFT]

▣ FREQUENTLY, REPEATEDLY, REGULARLY, GENERALLY, AGAIN AND AGAIN, TIME AFTER TIME, TIME AND TIME AGAIN.
▣ RARELY, SELDOM, NEVER.

Ogam or **Ogham** /ˈɒɡəm/ *noun* an ancient alphabet used from the 4cBC in Celtic and Pictish inscriptions, especially on stone monuments found in Ireland and Wales.
ogee /ˈoʊdʒiː/ *noun* an S-shaped curve, line or moulding. [from Old French *ogive*, a diagonal rib in a vault]
ogle *verb trans., intrans.* to look or stare at (a person) expressing sexual desire with the eyes. [perhaps from Dutch *oogen*, to make eyes at]
O-grade or **Ordinary grade** *noun formerly* in Scotland, an examination in a subject usually taken at the end of the fourth year in secondary schools; replaced by Standard Grade.
ogre /ˈoʊɡə(r)/ or **ogress** *noun* **1** in fairy stories, a frightening, cruel, ugly, man-eating male or female giant. **2** a cruel or frightening person. [from French *ogre*]

▣ **1** giant, demon, devil, troll. **2** monster, beast, brute, villain, fiend.

ogrish or **ogreish** *adj.* characteristic of or like an ogre.
OH *abbrev.* Ohio.

oh /oʊ/ see O[2].
ohm /oʊm/ *noun* (SYMBOL Ω) the SI unit of electrical resistance, equal to the resistance of a circuit in which a potential difference of one volt is required to maintain a current of one ampere. [named after the German physicist Georg Simon Ohm]
OHMS *abbrev. Brit.* On Her (or His) Majesty's Service, often written on mail from government departments.
Ohm's law *Physics* a law which states that the direct current flowing in an electrical circuit is directly proportional to the potential difference (voltage) applied to the circuit, and inversely proportional to the resistance of the circuit, ie $V = IR$, where V is voltage, I is current, and R is resistance. [named after the German physicist Georg Simon Ohm, who published it]
oho *interj. old use* an expression of surprise or triumphant satisfaction.
-oholic see -AHOLIC.
-oid *suffix* forming nouns and adjectives meaning 'having the form of': *humanoid* / *rhomboid*. [from Greek *eidos*, shape]
-oidal *suffix* forming adjectives corresponding to nouns in -oid.
oik *noun Brit.* a person thought of as inferior, especially because of being rude, ignorant, badly educated, or lower class.
oil — *noun* **1** any greasy, viscous, and usually flammable substance that is liquid at room temperature (20°C) and insoluble in water, used as a fuel, lubricant, or food. Oils may be derived from animals, plants, or mineral deposits, or may be manufactured artificially. **2** petroleum. **3** (*often* oils) oil-paint. **4** a picture painted with oil-paints. — *verb* to apply oil to, lubricate, or treat with oil. — **oil the wheels** to do something in order to make things go more smoothly or successfully. **pour oil on troubled waters** to soothe or calm a person or situation. [from Latin *oleum*, from Greek *elaia*, olive tree]

▣ *verb* grease, lubricate, anoint.

oil-cake *noun* a cattle-food made from linseed which has had its oil removed.
oilcloth *noun* canvas coated with oil to make it waterproof, used especially formerly as a covering for tables, etc.
oil colour an oil paint.
oiled *adj.* **1** smeared, treated, lubricated, or impregnated with oil. **2** preserved in oil. **3** *colloq.* drunk.
oilfield *noun* an area with reserves of mineral oil under the ground.
oil-fired *adj.* using oil as a fuel.
oilily *adv.* in an oily way, with an oily manner.
oiliness *noun* being oily.
oil paint a paint made by mixing ground pigment with oil.
oil painting **1** a picture painted with oil-paints. **2** the activity or art of painting in oils. — **no oil painting** *colloq.* not very beautiful.
oil rig a structure, plus all the equipment, machinery, etc that it supports, used for drilling oil.
oilseed rape an annual plant (*Brassica napus*) growing up to 1m high, and belonging to the cabbage family (Cruciferae). It has bluish-green leaves and yellow cross-shaped flowers, and tolerates a wide range of climatic conditions.
oil shale *Geol.* a fine-grained sedimentary rock containing high levels of organic matter, from which an oily substance can be distilled by heating the shale in the absence of air.
oilskin *noun* **1** a cloth treated with oil to make it waterproof. **2** (*often* oilskins) a garment made of this.
oil slick a patch of oil forming a film on the surface of water, eg as a result of damage to or discharge from an oil-tanker.

oil tanker a large ship for carrying oil in bulk.

oil well a well bored in the ground or sea-bed to obtain petroleum.

oily *adj.* (**oilier, oiliest**) **1** of, containing, or like oil. **2** covered with oil. **3** *derog., said of a person, behaviour, etc* unpleasantly friendly or polite; servile and flattering.

■ **1, 2** greasy, fatty. **3** servile, unctuous, smooth, obsequious, ingratiating, *colloq.* smarmy, glib, flattering.

oink — *noun* the characteristic noise of a pig. — *verb intrans.* to make this noise. [imitative]

ointment *noun* any greasy substance rubbed on the skin to heal injuries or as a cosmetic. — **a fly in the ointment** a minor nuisance or irritation which disturbs one's enjoyment. [from Latin *unguentum*, unguent]

■ salve, balm, cream, lotion, liniment, embrocation.

OK[1] *abbrev.* Oklahoma.

OK[2] or **okay** *colloq.* — *adj.* all right; satisfactory. — *adv.* well; satisfactorily. — *interj.* yes; I agree. — *noun* (PL. **OKs, OK's, okays**) approval, sanction, or agreement. — *verb* (**OK'ed, okayed, OK'ing, okaying**) to approve or pass as satisfactory. [from an abbreviation of American English *oll korrect*, a facetious spelling of *all correct*]

■ *adj.* all right, satisfactory, acceptable, fine, fair, reasonable, tolerable, passable, not bad, good, adequate, convenient, correct, accurate, in order. *interj.* yes, I agree, agreed, all right, fine, very well, right. *noun* approval, sanction, agreement, consent, authorization, endorsement, *colloq.* go- ahead, permission, *colloq.* green light. *verb* approve, authorize, pass, *colloq.* give the go-ahead to, *colloq.* give the green light to, rubber-stamp, agree to.

okapi /oʊˈkɑːpɪ/ *noun* (PL. **okapis, okapi**) an animal from Central Africa, related to the giraffe but with a shorter neck, and with a reddish-brown coat, white stripes on the legs, and small horns. [a Central African word]

okey-dokey *adv., adj., interj. slang* OK.

Okla. *abbrev.* Oklahoma.

okra *noun* a tropical plant which produces long, green, edible pods used as a vegetable. [a W African word]

Olbers' paradox a paradox expressed by the German astronomer Heinrich Olbers in 1826: why is the sky dark at night? In an infinitely large, unchanging universe uniformly populated with stars and galaxies, the sky would be dazzlingly bright. The paradox is resolved by modern cosmological theories of the expanding universe.

old — *adj.* **1** advanced in age; having existed for a long time. **2** having a stated age: *five years old.* **3** of or relating to the end period of a long life or existence: *old age.* **4** worn out or shabby through long use: *old shoes.* **5** no longer in use; out of date; old-fashioned. **6** belonging to the past. **7** former or earlier; earliest of two or more things: *their old house had no garden.* **8** of long standing or long existence: *an old member of the society.* **9** familiar, practised, or skilled through long experience: *an old hand/the same old excuses.* **10** having the characteristics (eg experience, maturity, or appearance) of age: *be old beyond one's years.* **11** *colloq.* used in expressions of affection or contempt: *good old Bill/silly old fool.* **12** *said of a language* being the earliest form known: *Old English.* **13** *colloq.* used for emphasis: *come round any old time.* — *noun* **1** an earlier time: *men of old.* **2** (**the old**) old people. — **as old as the hills** *colloq.* very old. **of old** formerly; a long time ago. [from Anglo-Saxon *eald*]

■ *adj.* **1** aged, elderly, advanced in years, ancient, antiquated, mature, grey, senile. **4** worn out, shabby, decayed, decrepit. **5** obsolete, old-fashioned, out of date. **6** former, past, earlier. **7** former, previous, earlier, one-time, ex-, original.

8 long-standing, long-established, time-honoured, traditional.

🔁 *adj.* **1, 3** young. **4, 8** new. **5** modern, up to date, fashionable, new. **6** modern, present. **7** current, present.

old age the later part of life.

old age pension a state pension paid to people who have retired from work.

old age pensioner a person in receipt of such a pension.

Old Believers *Relig.* Russian Orthodox traditionalists who rejected the reforms instituted in 1666. Although persecuted, they survived, established their own hierarchy in 1848, and were recognized by the state in 1881.

old boy 1 *Brit.* a former male pupil of a school. **2** *colloq.* an elderly man. **3** *colloq.* an affectionate or familiar form of address.

old boy network *Brit.* the system by which former members of the same public school secure advantages for each other in later life.

Old Church Slavonic see SLAVIC LANGUAGES.

old country the country of origin of immigrants.

old dear *slang, often derog.* **1** an old woman. **2** one's mother.

olden *adj. old use* former; past: *in olden days.*

Old English see ENGLISH.

Old English sheepdog a breed of dog developed in the UK in the 18c to protect cattle, having a large body, with the hindquarters higher than the shoulders, and a long untidy coat, often hiding the ears and eyes, and usually white with large dark patches.

old-fashioned *adj.* **1** belonging to, or in a style common, some time ago; out of date. **2** in favour of or living and acting according to the habits and moral views of the past.

■ **1** outmoded, out of date, outdated, dated, unfashionable, obsolete, behind the times, antiquated, archaic, passé, obsolescent.

🔁 **1** modern, up to date, fashionable.

old flame *colloq.* a person with whom one used to be in love.

old girl 1 *Brit.* a former female pupil of a school. **2** *colloq.* an elderly woman. **3** *colloq.* an affectionate or familiar form of address.

old guard the original or most conservative members of a society, group, or organization.

old hat *colloq.* something tediously familiar or well known.

Old High German the oldest form of official and literary German with written records dating from the 8c AD. See also GERMANIC LANGUAGES, HIGH GERMAN.

oldie *noun colloq.* an old person, song, story or thing.

old lady *slang* a person's wife or mother.

old lag *Brit. slang* a habitual criminal.

old maid *derog. colloq.* **1** a woman who is not married and is thought of as being unlikely ever to marry. **2** a woman or man who is prim and fussy.

old-maidish *adj.* characteristic of or like an old maid.

old man 1 *slang* a person's husband or father. **2** an affectionate form of address for a man or boy.

old man's beard a wild plant with fluffy white hairs around the seeds.

old master any great painter or painting from the period stretching from the Renaissance to about 1800.

old moon the moon in its last quarter, before the new moon.

Old Nick *colloq.* the devil.

Old Persian the old form of Persian spoken in the area of present-day Iran from around 1000 BC, and with surviving written records from c.6c BC. See also FARSI.

old school people with traditional or old-fashioned ways of thinking, ideas, beliefs, etc.

old school tie 1 a tie with a characteristic pattern or colour worn by former members of a public school. **2** *Brit.* the system by which former members of the same public school do favours for each other in later life. See also OLD BOY NETWORK.

oldster *noun colloq.* an old person.

old story something which one has heard before or which has happened before, especially frequently.

Old Style a method of dating using the Julian calendar. See also NEW STYLE.

Old Testament the first part of the Christian Bible, containing the Hebrew scriptures. See also NEW TESTAMENT.

old-time *adj.* belonging to or typical of the past.

old-timer *noun* **1** a person who has been in a job, position, profession, etc for a long time; a veteran. **2** *North Amer. colloq.*, *especially as a form of address* an old person.

old wives' tale an ancient belief or theory considered foolish and unscientific.

old woman *slang* **1** a person's wife or mother. **2** a person, especially a man, who is timid or fussy.

old-womanish *adj.* characteristic of or like an old woman.

Old World 1 the E hemisphere, comprising Europe, Asia, and Africa, which forms that part of the world known before the discovery of the Americas. **2** (*attributive*) **a** (**old-world**) belonging to earlier times, especially in being considered quaint or charming; not modern. **b** (**Old-World**) of the Old World.

oleaginous /oʊlɪˈædʒɪnəs/ *adj.* of, like, or producing oil. [from Latin *oleaginus*, from *oleum*, oil]

oleander /oʊlɪˈandə(r)/ *noun* a poisonous Mediterranean shrub with leathery evergreen leaves and clusters of white, pink, or purple flowers. [from Latin *oleander*]

olefin /ˈoʊlɪfɪn/ *noun Chem.* alkene. [from Latin *oleum*, oil]

oleograph *noun* a lithograph printed in oil-colours to imitate an oil-painting. [from Latin *oleum*, oil + Greek *graph-*, writing]

O-Level (*in full* **General Certificate of Education (GCE) Ordinary-level**) *formerly* in England, Wales, and Northern Ireland, an examination taken by (usually) secondary school pupils at around the age of 16. In 1988, it was replaced, along with the certificate of secondary education (CSE), by the General Certificate of Secondary Education (GCSE).

olfactory *adj.* relating to the sense of smell. [from Latin *olfacere*, to smell]

oligarch /ˈɒlɪɡɑːk/ *noun* a member of an oligarchy.

oligarchic or **oligarchical** *adj.* relating to or characteristic of an oligarchy.

oligarchy /ˈɒlɪɡɑːkɪ/ *noun* (PL. **oligarchies**) **1** government by a small group of people. **2** a state or organization governed by a small group of people. **3** a small group of people which forms a government. [from Greek *oligarchia*, from *oligos*, little, few + *archos*, leader]

oligo- *combining form* forming words denoting few in number. [from Greek *oligos*, little, few]

Oligocene /ˈɒlɪɡoʊsiːn/ *Geol.* — *noun* the third epoch of the Tertiary period, lasting from about 38 million to 25 million years ago. During this time the first apes appeared, many modern mammals began to evolve, and flowering plants became more abundant. — *adj.* **1** relating to this epoch. **2** relating to rocks formed during this epoch. [from Greek *oligos*, few + *kainos*, recent]

oligopoly *noun* (PL. **oligopolies**) an economic situation in which there are few sellers of a particular product or service, and a small number of competitive firms control the market. [from Greek *oligos*, little, few + *poleein*, to sell]

olive — *noun* **1** a small evergreen tree (*Olea europea*) with a twisted gnarled trunk and narrow leathery silvery-green leaves, cultivated mainly in the Mediterranean region for its edible fruit. **2** the small oval edible fruit of this tree, which has a hard stone and bitter oily flesh, and is harvested either when green and unripe or when purplish-black and ripe. **3** the wood of this tree, used to make furni-ture. **4** (*in full* **olive green**) the dull yellowish-green colour of unripe olives. — *adj.* **1** dull yellowish-green in colour. **2** *said of a complexion* sallow. [from Latin *oliva*]

olive branch a sign of a wish for peace or a gesture towards peace or reconciliation.

olive drab the dull grey-green colour of American army uniforms.

olive oil the pale yellow oil obtained by pressing ripe olives, used as a cooking and salad oil, and in soaps, ointments, and lubricants.

olivine /ˈɒlɪviːn/ *noun Geol.* any of a group of hard glassy rock-forming silicate minerals, typically olive green in colour, but sometimes yellowish or brown, commonly found in gabbros and basalts.

-ology see -LOGY.

Olympiad *noun* **1** a celebration of the modern Olympic Games. **2** a period of four years between Olympic Games, used by the ancient Greeks as a way of reckoning time. **3** an international contest in especially chess or bridge. [from Greek *Olympias*, of Olympus]

Olympian — *noun* **1** *Greek Mythol.* any of the twelve ancient Greek gods thought to live on Mount Olympus in N Greece. **2** a person who competes in the Olympic Games. — *adj.* **1** *Greek Mythol.* of or relating to Mount Olympus or the ancient Greek gods thought to live there. **2** godlike, especially in being superior or condescending in behaviour or manners. [from Greek *Olympios*, from Greek *Olympos*, Olympus]

Olympic — *adj.* **1** of the Olympic Games. **2** of ancient Olympia. — *noun* (**Olympics**) the Olympic Games. [from Greek *Olympikos*]

Olympic Games 1 *Hist.* games celebrated every four years in Olympia in ancient Greece, including athletic, musical, and literary competitions. **2** a modern international sports competition held every four years.

OM *abbrev. Brit.* Order of Merit.

Om *noun* in Hinduism, a mystical and sacred monosyllable. Believed to have a divine power, it is used at the beginning and end of prayers, and as a mantra for meditation.

ombudsman *noun* (PL. **ombudsmen**) an official appointed to investigate complaints against public authorities, government departments, or the people who work for them. [from Swedish *ombudsman*, legal representative]

omega /ˈoʊmɪɡə/ *noun* **1** the last letter of the Greek alphabet (Ω, ω). **2** the last of a series; a conclusion. [from Greek *o mega*, great O]

omelette or *North Amer., esp. US* **omelet** *noun* a dish of beaten eggs fried in a pan, often folded round a savoury or sweet filling such as cheese or jam. [from Old French *alemette*, from *lemelle*, knife-blade]

omen *noun* **1** a sign of a future event, either good or evil. **2** threatening or prophetic character: *bird of ill omen*. [from Latin *omen*]

   ⊟ **1** portent, sign, warning, premonition, foreboding, augury, indication.

ominous *adj.* threatening; containing a warning of something evil or bad that will happen. [from Latin *ominosus*, from *omen*, omen]

   ⊟ threatening, menacing, sinister, portentous, inauspicious, foreboding, fateful, unpromising.
   ⊞ auspicious, favourable.

ominously *adv.* in an ominous way; as an ominous circumstance.

omission *noun* **1** something that has been left out or neglected. **2** the act of leaving something out or neglecting it. [from Latin *omissio*, from *omittere*, to omit]

   ⊟ **1** oversight, gap, lack. **2** exclusion, neglect, failure, default, avoidance.

omit *verb* (**omitted, omitting**) **1** to leave out, either by mistake or on purpose. **2** to fail (to do something). [from Latin *omittere*, from *ob*, in front + *mittere*, to send]

. . . .

⊟ **1** leave out, exclude, miss out, overlook, pass over, drop, skip, eliminate, edit out. **2** fail, neglect, forget, leave undone.
⊟ **1** include.

. . . .

omni- *combining form* forming words meaning 'all, every'. [from Latin *omnis*, all]

omnibus — *noun* (PL. **omnibuses**) **1** *old use, formal* a bus. **2** a book containing a number of novels or stories by a single author. **3** a television or radio broadcast which brings together a number of programmes originally broadcast separately. — *adj.* **1** made up of or bringing together several different items or parts. **2** serving several different purposes at the same time. [from Latin *omnibus*, for all]

OMNIMAX or **Omnimax** *adj. trademark, said of a film* designed to be viewed on a special domed screen, producing a near-hemispherical image to the audience.

omnipotence /ɒmˈnɪpətəns/ *noun* unlimited power.

omnipotent /ɒmˈnɪpətənt/ *adj.* having very great or absolute power. [from Latin *omnis*, all + *potens*, powerful]

omnipresence *noun* being present everywhere at the same time.

omnipresent *adj., said especially of a god* present everywhere at the same time. [from Latin *omnis*, all + *praesens*, present]

omniscience /ɒmˈnɪsɪəns/ *noun* knowledge of all things.

omniscient /ɒmˈnɪsɪənt/ *adj.* knowing everything. [from Latin *omnis*, all + *scire*, to know]

omnivore *noun* an animal or plant that eats any type of food.

omnivorous *adj.* **1** eating any type of food, especially both meat and vegetable matter. **2** taking in, reading, using, etc everything. [from Latin *omnis*, all + *vorare*, to devour]

on — *prep.* **1** touching, supported by, attached to, covering, or enclosing: *a chair on the floor/a dog on a lead / a sheet on a bed.* **2** in or into (a vehicle, etc). **3** carried with: *I've got no money on me.* **4** very near to or along the side of: *a house on the shore.* **5** at or during (a certain day, time, etc). **6** immediately after, at, or before: *he found the letter on his return.* **7** within the (given) limits of: *a picture on page nine.* **8** about: *a book on Jane Austen.* **9** towards: *march on the town.* **10** through contact with; as a result of: *cut oneself on the broken bottle.* **11** in the state or process of: *on fire/on a journey.* **12** using as a means of transport. **13** using as a means or medium: *talk on the telephone / a tune on the piano.* **14** on the occasion of: *shoot on sight.* **15** having as a basis or source: *on good authority/arrested on suspicion.* **16** working for or being a member of: *on the committee/work on the case.* **17** at the expense of; to the disadvantage of: *treatment on the National Health/the joke's on him.* **18** supported by: *live on bread and cheese.* **19** regularly taking or using: *on tranquillizers.* **20** in a specified manner: *on the cheap.* **21** staked as a bet: *put money on a horse.* **22** following: *disappointment on disappointment.* — *adv.* **1** *said especially of clothes* covering; in contact with: *have no clothes on.* **2** ahead, forwards, or towards in space or time: *go on home/later on.* **3** continuously; without interruption: *keep on about something.* **4** in or into operation or activity: *put the radio on.* — *adj.* **1** working, broadcasting, or performing: *you're on in two minutes.* **2** taking place: *which films are on this week?* **3** *colloq.* possible, practicable, or acceptable: *that just isn't on.* **4** *colloq.* talking continuously, especially to complain or nag: *always on at him to try harder.* **5** in favour of a win: *odds of 3 to 4 on.* **6** Cricket on the side of the field towards which the bat is facing, usually the batsman's left and the bowler's right. See also OFF 4. — **be on to someone** or **something** *colloq.* **1** realize their importance or intentions. **2** be in touch with them: *we'll be on to you about the party on Saturday.* **get on to someone** *colloq.* get in touch with them. **just on** ... almost exactly...: *have collected just on £50.* **on and off** now and then; occasionally. **on and on** continually; at length. **on time** promptly;

at the right time. **on to** ... to a position on or in ... [from Anglo-Saxon]

onager /ˈɒnədʒə(r)/ *noun* a wild ass found in central Asia. [from Greek *onagros*]

onanism /ˈəʊnənɪzm/ *noun* **1** sexual intercourse in which the penis is withdrawn from the vagina before ejaculation. **2** masturbation. [from *Onan*, a character in the Bible (Gen 38.9)]

ONC *abbrev.* Ordinary National Certificate, a qualification in a technical subject, more or less equivalent to an A-level.

once — *adv.* **1** a single time; on one occasion. **2** at some time in the past. **3** ever; at any time: *if once you are late.* **4** by one degree of relationship: *a cousin once removed.* — *conj.* as soon as. — *noun* one time or occasion. — **all at once 1** suddenly. **2** all at the same time. **at once** immediately; without any delay. **just for once** on this one occasion only; as an exception. **once again** or **once more** one more time, as before. **once and for all** or **once for all** for the last time; now and never again. **once in a way** or **while** occasionally; rarely. **once or twice** a few times. **once upon a time** *used to begin fairy-tales* at a certain time in the past. [from Anglo-Saxon *ænes*]

. . . .

⊟ *adv.* **2** formerly, previously, in the past, at one time, long ago, in times past, once upon a time, in the old days. **all at once 1** suddenly, all of a sudden, in a flash, in a trice, without warning, unexpectedly. **2** simultaneously, together, all at the same time. **at once** immediately, without delay, instantly, directly, right away, straight away, now, promptly, forthwith.

. . . .

once-over *noun colloq.* a quick, often casual examination: *give the car the once-over.*

oncogene *noun Genetics* a gene that causes a normal cell to develop into a cancerous cell, or to multiply in an uncontrolled manner. [from Greek *onkos* bulk, mass, tumour]

oncologist *noun* a doctor who specializes in studying and treating tumours.

oncology *noun* the study of tumours, especially those which are cancerous. [from Greek *onkos*, mass, tumour + -LOGY]

oncoming — *adj.* approaching; advancing. — *noun* an approach.

. . . .

⊟ *adj.* approaching, advancing, upcoming, looming, gathering.

. . . .

oncovirus *noun Medicine* any virus that causes cancer.

OND *abbrev.* Ordinary National Diploma, a qualification in a technical subject reached after a two-year full-time or sandwich course, recognized by many professional institutions.

ondes Martenot or **ondes musicales** an electronic musical instrument patented in 1922 by Maurice Martenot. An early type of synthesizer, it consisted of a keyboard capable of producing a vibrato, with controls for timbre and dynamics, and loudspeakers.

one — *adj.* **1** being a single unit, number, or thing. **2** being a particular person or thing, especially as distinct from another or others of the same kind: *lift one leg and then the other.* **3** being a particular but unspecified instance or example: *visit him one day soon.* **4** being the only such: *the one woman who can beat her.* **5** same; identical: *of one mind.* **6** undivided; forming a single whole: *a choir singing with one voice.* **7** first: *page one.* **8** *colloq.* an exceptional example or instance of: *one hell of an argument.* **9** aged 1. — *noun* **1** the number or figure 1; any symbol for this number. **2** the age of 1. **3** a unity or unit. **4** something, especially a garment or a person whose size is denoted by the number 1. **5** 1 o'clock. **6** *colloq.* a story or joke: *heard the one about the singing policeman?* **7** *colloq.* (**one for**) an enthusiast: *she's quite a one for chess.* **8** *colloq.* a drink, especially an alcoholic one: *drop in for a quick one.* **9** *colloq.* a daring, remarkable, or cheeky person: *you are a one!* **10** a score of 1 point. — *pron.* **1** (often referring to a noun already mentioned or implied) an individual person, thing, or instance: *buy the blue one.* **2** anybody: *one can't do better than that.* **3** I; me: *one doesn't like to pry.* — **all one** just the same; of no consequence. **at one with someone** in complete agreement with them. **be one up on someone** *colloq.* to have an advantage over them. **for one** as one person: *I for one don't agree.* **all in one 1** together; combined; as one unit, object etc. **2** in one go or attempt. **just one of those things** an unfortunate event or situation that must be accepted. **one and all** everyone. **one and only** *used for emphasis* only. **one another** used as the object of a verb or preposition when an action takes place between two (or more than two) people, etc: *love one another / refuse to speak to one another.* See also EACH OTHER. **one by one** one after the other; individually. **one or two** *colloq.* a few. [from Anglo-Saxon *an*]

🔲 *adj.* **1** single, solitary, lone, individual. **3** some. **4** only, sole. **5** same, identical, alike, like-minded, equal. **6** united, undivided, whole, entire, complete, harmonious.

one-armed bandit a fruit machine with a long handle at the side which is pulled down hard to make the machine work.

one-horse *adj.* **1** using a single horse. **2** *colloq.* small, poor, and of little importance.

one-liner *noun colloq.* a short, amusing remark or joke made in a single sentence.

one-man or **one-woman** *adj.* done by one person.

oneness *noun* **1** the state or quality of being one; singleness. **2** agreement. **3** the state of being the same. **4** the state of being unique.

one-night stand 1 a performance given only once in any place, the next performance taking place elsewhere. **2** *colloq.* a brief or opportunistic sexual encounter.

one-off *colloq.* — *adj. chiefly Brit.* made or happening on one occasion only. — *noun* something that is one-off.

one-parent family a family consisting of a child or children and one parent, the other parent being dead or estranged.

one-piece *adj.* made in a single piece as opposed to separate parts.

onerous /'ounərəs/ *adj.* heavy; hard to bear or do; demanding a lot of effort. [from Latin *onerosus*, from *onus*, burden]

🔲 heavy, hard, taxing, difficult, troublesome, exacting, exhausting, oppressive, weighty, burdensome, demanding, laborious.
🔁 easy, light.

oneself *pron.* **1** the reflexive of *one*: *not able to help oneself.* **2** used for emphasis. **3** one's normal self: *one can hardly be feeling oneself after an operation.*

one-sided *adj.* **1** *said of a competition* with one person or side having a great advantage over the other. **2** seeing, accepting, representing, or favouring only one side of a subject; unfair; partial.

🔲 **1** unbalanced, unequal. **2** unfair, partial, unjust, prejudiced, biased, partisan.
🔁 **1** balanced. **2** impartial.

one-time *adj.* former.

one-to-one *adj.* **1** with one person or thing exactly corresponding to or matching another. **2** in which a person is involved with only one other person: *one-to-one teaching.*

one-track mind *colloq.* an obsession with one idea.

one-up *adj.* having a particular advantage.

one-upmanship *noun* the art of gaining pyschological, social, or professional advantages over other people.

one-way *adj.* **1** *said of a road or street* in which traffic can move in one direction only. **2** *said of a feeling or relationship* not returned or reciprocated. **3** *North Amer., esp. US,* *said of a ticket* valid for travel in one direction only, not back again.

one-woman see ONE-MAN.

ongoing *adj.* continuing; in progress.

🔲 continuing, in progress, developing, evolving, progressing, growing, unfinished, unfolding, continuous, unbroken, uninterrupted, constant.

onion *noun* **1** any of numerous varieties of a biennial plant (*Allium cepa*) belonging to the lily family, native to SW Asia but widely cultivated for its edible bulb, which consists of white fleshy scales rich in sugar and a pungent oil, surrounded by a brown papery outer layer. **2** the bulb of this plant, which may be eaten raw, cooked, or pickled. **3** the long tubular leaves of a young onion plant (spring onion), eaten as a salad vegetable. — **know one's onions** *colloq.* to know one's subject or one's job well. [from Latin *unio*, unity, large pearl, onion]

onion dome *Archit.* a bulb-shaped dome topped with a sharply tapering point, characteristic of Eastern Orthodox, especially Russian, church architecture.

oniony *adj.* containing or like onion.

on-line — *adj. Comput.* **1** *said of a peripheral device, eg a printer* connected to and controlled by a computer. **2** *said of business, etc.* conducted by means of computers. **3** *said of a person* using a computer. — *adv.* by means of or while using a computer. See also OFF-LINE.

onlooker *noun* a person who watches and does not take part; an observer.

🔲 bystander, observer, spectator, onlooker, looker-on, eyewitness, witness, watcher, viewer.

only — *adj.* **1** without any others of the same type. **2** *said of a child* having no brothers or sisters. **3** *colloq.* best: *flying is the only way to travel.* — *adv.* **1** not more than; just. **2** alone; solely. **3** not longer ago than; not until: *only a minute ago.* **4** merely; with no other result than: *I arrived only to find he had already left.* — *conj.* **1** but; however: *come if you want to, only don't complain if you're bored.* **2** if it were not for the fact that: *I'd come with you on the boat only I know I'll be sick if I do.* — **if only** ... I wish ...: *if only you could be on time for once.* **only too** ... very ...; extremely ...: *only too ready to help.* [from Anglo-Saxon *anlic*]

🔲 *adj.* **1** sole, single, solitary, lone, unique, exclusive, individual. *adv.* **1** just, at most, barely. **2** alone, solely, exclusively. **3** just. **4** merely, simply, purely.

o.n.o. *abbrev. Brit.* or near offer; or nearest offer.

on-off *adj.*, *said of a switch* able to be set to either the 'on' position or the 'off' position.

onomasticon *noun Linguistics* a dictionary or collection of proper names. [from Greek *onomastikos, -on,* from *onoma,* a name]

onomastics *sing. noun Linguistics* the study of the history, development, and geographical distribution of proper names. All categories of names are included: personal first names and surnames, place names, home names, and the names of boats, trains, and pets.

onomatopoeia /ɒnəmətə'pɪə/ *noun* the formation or use of a word which imitates the sound or action represented, such as *boo, hiss, squelch.* [from Greek *onoma,* name + *poieein,* to make]

onomatopoeic /ɒnəmətə'piːɪk/ *adj.* relating to or characterized by onomatopoeia.

onrush *noun* a sudden and strong movement forward.

onscreen *adj.*, *adv.* relating to information that is displayed on a television or computer screen.

onset *noun* **1** a beginning, especially of something unpleasant. **2** an attack.

⊟ **1** beginning, start, commencement, inception, outset, outbreak. **2** attack, assault, onslaught, onrush.
⊟ **1** end, finish.

onshore *adj.*, *adv.* **1** *said of the wind* blowing or moving towards the shore. **2** on, on to, or near the shore.

onside *adj.*, *adv. Football*, *Rugby* in a position where the ball may legally be played.

onslaught /'ɒnslɔːt/ *noun* a fierce attack. [from Old Dutch *aenslag*]

⊟ attack, assault, offensive, charge, bombardment, blitz.

on-stage *adj.*, *adv.* on the stage and able to be seen by the audience.

on-stream *adj.*, *adv.*, *said of an industrial plant, process, etc* in operation or ready to go into operation.

onto *prep.* on to.

ontogeny *noun Biol.* the history of the development of a living organism, from fertilization of the ovum (egg cell) to sexual maturity. [from Greek *on, ontos*, being]

ontological *adj.* relating to or involving ontology.

ontologically *adv.* as regards ontology.

ontology *noun Philos.* the science dealing with the nature of being. [from Greek *on*, being + -LOGY]

onus /'əʊnəs/ *noun* (PL. **onuses**) a responsibility or burden. [from Latin *onus*, burden]

⊟ responsibility, burden, load, obligation, duty, liability, task.

onward — *adj.* moving forward in place or time. — *adv.* (*also* **onwards**) **1** towards or at a place or time which is advanced or in front. **2** forward. **3** continuing to move forward or progress.

⊟ *adj.* forward. *adv.* FORWARD(S), ON, AHEAD. **1** in front, beyond. **2** forth.
⊟ *adj.* backward. *adv.* BACKWARD(S).

onyx /'ɒnɪks/ *noun Geol.* a very hard variety of agate with straight alternating bands of one or more colours, the form with black and white bands being widely used to make jewellery and ornaments. [from Greek *onyx*, nail]

oocyte /'əʊəsaɪt/ *noun Biol.* an early stage in the development of an ovum (egg cell). *Primary oocytes* are diploid, and undergo cell division by meiosis to give *secondary oocytes*, which are haploid. An ovum is produced by meiosis of a secondary oocyte. [from Greek *oion*, egg]

oodles *pl. noun colloq.* lots.

oogamy /əʊ'ɒgəmɪ/ *noun Biol.* a form of sexual reproduction in which a large non-motile female gamete (the ovum or egg cell) is fertilized by a small motile male gamete.

oogenesis /əʊə'dʒɛnəsɪs/ *noun Biol.* the production and development of an ovum (egg cell) in the ovary of an animal.

ooh *interj.* an expression of pleasure, surprise, excitement, or pain.

oölite or **oolite** /'əʊəlaɪt/ *noun Geol.* a sedimentary rock, usually a form of limestone, consisting of masses of small round particles of calcium carbonate (*oöliths*) that resemble fish eggs. [from Greek *oion*, egg + *lithos*, stone]

oompah *noun colloq.* a common way of representing the deep sound made by a large, brass musical instrument. [imitative]

oomph *noun colloq.* **1** energy; enthusiasm. **2** personal attractiveness, especially sex appeal.

oops *interj. colloq.* an exclamation of surprise or apology made when a person makes a mistake, drops something, etc.

oops-a-daisy *interj. colloq.* an expression used typically when helping up or encouraging a child who has had a slight accident, fallen over, etc.

oospore /'əʊəspɔː(r)/ *noun Biol.* **1** a fertilized ovum (egg cell). **2** in certain algae and fungi, the zygote that is produced as a result of fertilization of a large non-motile female gamete by a smaller motile male gamete.

ooze[1] — *verb* **1** *intrans.* to flow or leak out gently or slowly. **2** *intrans., said of a substance* to give out moisture. **3** to give out (a liquid, etc) slowly: *a wound oozing blood*. **4** to overflow with (a quality or feeling): *ooze charm.* — *noun* **1** anything which oozes. **2** a slow gentle leaking or oozing. **3** an infusion of bark and other vegetable matter used for tanning leather. [from Anglo-Saxon *wos*, sap, juice]

⊟ *verb* **1** seep, leak, percolate, escape, dribble, drip, drop, filter, drain. **2** bleed, leak. **3** discharge, exude, secrete, emit, overflow with.

ooze[2] *noun* **1** *Geol.* on the ocean floor, a deposit of fine organic sediments, shells of diatoms, etc, that accumulates very slowly over millions of years. **2** soft, boggy ground. [from Anglo-Saxon *wase*, marsh, mire]

oozy *adj.* (**oozier, ooziest**) like ooze; slimy, oozing.

op[1] *abbrev.* opus.

op[2] *noun colloq.* a surgical or military operation. [abbreviation]

opacity /əʊ'pasɪtɪ/ *noun* **1** opaqueness. **2** the state of having an obscure meaning and being difficult to understand. [from Latin *opacitas*, from *opacus*, opaque]

opal *noun Geol.* a milky white, black, or coloured form of silica, combined with variable amounts of water, usually with a characteristic internal 'play' of red, blue, green, or yellow flashes caused by light reflected from different layers within the stone. [probably Sanskrit *upala*, precious stone]

opalescence *noun* being opalescent.

opalescent *adj.* reflecting different colours as the surrounding light changes, like an opal.

opaque /əʊ'peɪk/ *adj.* **1** not allowing light to pass through, ie not transparent or translucent. **2** difficult to understand. See also OPACITY [from Latin *opacus*]

⊟ **1** cloudy, clouded, murky, dull, dim, hazy, muddied, muddy, turbid. **2** obscure, unclear, impenetrable, incomprehensible, unintelligible, enigmatic, difficult.
⊟ **1** transparent. **2** clear, obvious.

opaquely *adv.* without transmitting light; obscurely.

opaqueness *noun* being opaque, lack of transparency.

Op Art or **Optical Art** a modern art movement which exploits the illusions created by abstract compositions of spirals, grids, undulating lines, stripes, spots, etc to produce sensations of movement, space, and volume.

op. cit. *abbrev. opere citato* (Latin), in the work already quoted.

OPEC *abbrev.* Organization of Petroleum Exporting Countries.

Op-Ed *noun North Amer.* a page of a newspaper devoted to features and comment, usually situated opposite the editorial page.

open — *adj.* **1** allowing things or people to go in or out; not blocked, closed, or locked. **2** *said of a container* not sealed; with the inside visible. **3** not enclosed, confined, or restricted: *the open sea/an open view*. **4** not covered, guarded, or protected: *an open wound*. **5** spread out or unfolded: *an open book*. **6** *said of a shop, etc* receiving customers; ready for business. **7** generally known; public; undisguised: *an open secret*. **8** able to be attacked or questioned: *leave oneself open to abuse*. **9** not restricted, allowing anyone to compete or take part, especially both amateurs and professionals. **10** free from restraint or restrictions of any kind: *the open fishing season*. **11** not decided; still being discussed: *an open question*. **12** ready to consider new ideas; unprejudiced: *an open mind*. **13** ready and willing to talk honestly; candid. **14** *combining form* eagerly attentive, surprised, or alarmed: *open-mouthed disbelief/open-eyed*. **15** *said of cloth, etc* having a lot of small openings or gaps. **16** *Phonetics, said of a vowel* produced with the tongue low in the mouth. **17** *Phonetics, said of a syllable* ending in a vowel. **18** *Mus., said of a string* not stopped by a finger. **19** *Mus., said of a note* played on an open string, or without holes being covered by fingers. **20** *said of a cheque* to be paid in cash to the person named on it; not crossed. — *verb* (**opened, opening**) **1** *trans., intrans.* to make or become open or more open. **2** *trans., intrans.* to unfasten or become unfastened to allow access. **3** *trans., intrans.* (*also* **open out** or **open something out**) to spread out or be spread out or unfolded, especially so as to see or be seen. **4** *trans., intrans.* to start or begin working: *the shops open at nine.* **5** to declare open with an official ceremony: *open the new hospital.* **6** *trans., intrans.* to begin or start (speaking, writing, etc): *opened with a joke about the weather.* **7** *intrans.* (**open into** or **on to something**) to provide access to it: *a gate opening into a field.* **8** to arrange (a bank account), usually by making an initial deposit. **9** *trans., intrans. Cricket* to begin (the batting) for one's team. **10** *intrans., said of legal counsel* to make a preliminary statement about a case before beginning to call witnesses. — *noun* **1** (**the open**) an area of open country; an area not obstructed by buildings, etc. **2** (**the open**) public notice or attention: *bring the issue out into the open.* **3** (**Open**) a sports contest which both amateurs and professionals may enter. — **open and above board** thoroughly honest or legal. **open out** or **up** to begin to reveal one's feelings and thoughts or to behave with less restraint. **open up 1** to open the door. **2** to start firing. **3** *said of a game, etc* to become more interesting as it develops. **open something up 1** to make it more accessible or available: *roads opening up the more remote areas.* **2** to increase the speed of an engine, vehicle, etc. **3** (**open up one's thoughts, mind,** etc **to someone**) to reveal them. [from Anglo-Saxon]

....

■ *adj.* **1** unclosed, ajar, gaping, uncovered, unfastened, unlocked. **2** unsealed, lidless, uncovered. **3** unrestricted, unobstructed, clear, accessible, free, exposed, unprotected, unsheltered, wide. **4** uncovered, unguarded, unprotected, gaping, yawning, exposed. **7** widely known, well-known, public, undisguised, unconcealed, overt, obvious, plain, evident, manifest, noticeable, flagrant, conspicuous. **9** unrestricted, free, available, vacant. **11** undecided, unresolved, unsettled, debatable, problematic, moot. **13** frank, candid, honest, guileless, natural, ingenuous, unreserved. *verb* **1** uncover, unseal, unblock, uncork, clear, expose. **2** unfasten, undo, unlock, untie. **3** extend, spread (out), unfold, unfurl. **5** inaugurate, launch. **6** begin, start, commence, initiate, set in motion.

■ *adj.* **1** shut, blocked, closed, covered, locked, fastened. **2** sealed, shut, closed, covered. **3** restricted, sheltered, protected, narrow. **6** shut, closed. **7** closely guarded, hidden, secret, private, covert, disguised, underground. **9, 10** closed. **11** decided, settled. **13** reserved, guarded. **20** crossed. *verb* **1, 4, 5** close, shut. **2** fasten, shut. **3** close, shut, fold. **6** close, end, finish. **8** close.

....

open air unenclosed space outdoors.
open-air *adj.* in the open air; outside.

....

■ outdoor, outside, alfresco.
■ indoor, inside.

....

open-and-shut *adj.* easily proved, decided, or solved.
open book a person who keeps no secrets and is easily understood.
opencast *adj. Geol., said of mining* using a method in which the substance to be mined, eg coal or copper, is exposed by removing the overlying layers of material, without the need for shafts or tunnels.

open cluster *Astron.* a cluster of several hundred to several thousand relatively young stars that are usually loosely distributed, in contrast to the densely packed groups of stars that form globular clusters.
open day a day when members of the public are allowed to visit a place which is usually closed to them.
open-ended *adj.* with no limits or restrictions, eg of time, set in advance.
opener *noun* **1** *combining form* a device for opening something: *bottle-opener.* **2** the first item on a programme. **3** *Cricket* either of the two batsmen who begin the batting for their team. — **for openers** *colloq.* to start with.
open fire a fireplace in a house where coal, coke, or wood may be burnt.
open-handed *adj.* generous.
open-handedness *noun* being open-handed, generosity.
open-hearted *adj.* **1** honest, direct, and hiding nothing; candid. **2** kind; generous.
open-heartedness *noun* **1** honesty, frankness. **2** generosity.
open-hearth process *Chem.* a traditional steel-making process in which the molten pig iron from which the steel is to be made is not in direct contact with the fuel providing the heat, but only with the hot flames which play on a shallow open hearth containing pig iron, malleable scrap iron, and a flux, in a furnace with a low roof. The steel can be withdrawn continuously.
open-heart surgery surgery performed on a heart that has been stopped and opened up while the blood circulation is maintained by a heart-lung machine.
open house the state of being willing to welcome and entertain visitors at any time: *keep open house.*
opening — *noun* **1** a hole, gap. **2** the act of making or becoming open. **3** a beginning. **4** the first performance of a play, opera, etc. **5** *Chess* a recognized sequence of moves played at the beginning of a game. **6** an opportunity or chance. **7** a preliminary statement about a legal case made by counsel before witnesses are called. — *adj.* of, relating to, or forming an opening; first: *opening night at the opera.*

....

■ *noun* **1** hole, aperture, gap, breach, orifice, break, chink, crack, fissure, cleft, chasm, split, vent, rupture. **3** beginning, start, onset, inception, birth, dawn, inauguration, launch. **4** première, launch. **6** opportunity, chance, occasion, *colloq.* break, place, vacancy. *adj.* first, inaugural, initial, beginning, commencing, starting, introductory, early, primary.

■ *noun* **3** close, end. *adj.* closing.

....

opening time the time at which a public house, bar, hotel etc can begin to sell alcoholic drinks.
open letter a letter, especially one of protest, addressed to a person or organization, etc but intended also for publication in a newspaper or magazine.
openly *adv.* without trying to hide anything; in a direct and honest manner.

....

■ overtly, frankly, candidly, blatantly, flagrantly, plainly, unashamedly, unreservedly, glaringly, in public, in full view, shamelessly.
■ secretly, slyly.

....

open market a market in which buyers and sellers are allowed to compete without restriction.
open-minded *adj.* willing to consider or receive new ideas; unprejudiced.
openness *noun* being open, frankness.
open-plan *adj.* having few internal walls and large, undivided rooms.
open prison a prison which allows prisoners who are neither dangerous nor violent considerably more freedom of movement than in normal prisons.

open sandwich a sandwich without a top slice of bread.

open season a period of the year in which particular animals, birds, fish, etc may be legally killed for sport.

open sesame /'sesəmi/ a means of gaining access to something which is otherwise out of one's reach.

open shop a firm, business, etc which does not oblige its employees to belong to a trade union. See also CLOSED SHOP.

open stage a stage in a theatre building which is in the same space as the auditorium, with no separation between them. Usually it is a raised platform built against one wall of the auditorium, with the audience on three sides.

open verdict a verdict given by the coroner's jury at the end of an inquest that death has occurred, but without giving details of whether it was suicide, accidental, murder, etc.

open work work in cloth, metal, wood, etc, so constructed to have gaps or holes in it, used especially for decoration.

opera[1] *noun* 1 a dramatic work set to music, in which the singers are usually accompanied by an orchestra. 2 operas as an art-form. 3 a theatre where operas are performed. 4 a company which performs operas. [from Italian *opera*, from Latin, work]

opera[2] see OPUS.

operability *noun* being operable.

operable *adj.* 1 *said of a disease, injury, etc* that can be treated by surgery. 2 that can be operated. [from Latin *operabilis*, from *opus*, work]

opera buffa /'ɒpərə 'buːfə/ comic opera in the form that developed in Italy in the 18c. [Italian, = comic opera]

opéra comique /'ɒpərə kɒ'miːk/ a tradition of French opera with some spoken dialogue. In the 19c, the term was applied to any French opera with spoken dialogue alternating with songs, whether the subject matter was comic or tragic. [French, = comic opera]

opera-glass *noun* small binoculars used at the theatre or opera.

opera-hat *noun* a man's collapsible top hat.

opera house a theatre specially built for the performance of operas.

opera seria /'ɒpərə 'sɪərɪə/ 'serious' opera: the most common form of opera in the late 17c and throughout most of the 18c. It was characterized by its use of noble, often classical, subjects; the libretto was in Italian; and there was a rigid separation of the elaborate arias (and occasional ensemble) and recitative, with a general sense of formality. [Italian, = serious opera]

operate *verb* 1 *trans., intrans.* to function or cause to function or work. 2 *intrans.* to produce an effect or have an influence. 3 to manage, control, or direct (a business, etc). 4 *intrans.* (**operate on someone**) to treat them with surgery. 5 *intrans.* to perform military, naval, police, etc operations. [from Latin *operari*, to work]

⊟ 1 function, act, run, work, go, control, handle, manage, use, utilize, manoeuvre. 2 act, function. 3 manage, control, direct, run.

operatic *adj.* of or like an opera, especially in being dramatic.

operatically *adv.* in an operatic way.

operating system (ABBREV. **OS**) *Comput.* a group of programs that control all the main activities of a computer. It loads programs to be run, opens and closes files, recognizes input from the keyboard, sends output to the visual display unit or printer, controls the disk drive, keeps a record of files and directories on the disk, and controls the running of all other programs.

operating table a special table on which surgery is performed.

operating theatre or **operating room** the specially equipped room in a hospital where surgery is performed.

operation *noun* 1 an act, method, or process of working or operating. 2 the state of working or being active: *the factory is not yet in operation.* 3 an activity; something done. 4 an action or series of actions which have a particular effect. 5 any surgical procedure that is performed in order to treat a damaged or diseased part of the body. 6 (*often* **operations**) one of a series of military, naval, police, etc actions performed as part of a much larger plan. 7 *Maths.* a specific procedure, such as addition or multiplication, whereby one numerical value is derived from another value or values. 8 *Comput.* a series of actions that are specified by a single computer instruction. 9 a financial transaction. [from Latin *operatio*]

⊟ 1 control, handling, management, use, utilization, manipulation. 2 functioning, action, running, motion, movement, performance, working. 3, 4 undertaking, enterprise, affair, procedure, proceeding, process, business, effort. 6 campaign, action, task, manoeuvre, exercise. 9 transaction, deal.

operational *adj.* 1 of or relating to an operation. 2 able or ready to work.

⊟ 2 working, in working order, usable, functional, going, viable, workable, ready, prepared, in service.
⊟ 2 out of order.

operationally *adv.* in an operational way.

operational research or **operations research** the analysis of problems in business and industry in order to bring about more efficient work practices.

operative — *adj.* 1 working; in action; having an effect. 2 *said of a word* especially important or significant: *'must' is the operative word.* 3 of or relating to a surgical operation. — *noun* 1 a worker, especially one with special skills. 2 *North Amer., esp. US* a private detective. [from Latin *operativus*, from *opus*, work]

⊟ *adj.* 1 operational, working, in action, in operation, in force, functioning, active, effective, efficient, workable, viable, serviceable, functional. 2 key, crucial, important, relevant, significant.
⊟ *adj.* 1 inoperative, out of service.

operator *noun* 1 a person who operates a machine or apparatus. 2 a person who operates a telephone switchboard, connecting calls, etc. 3 a person who runs a business. 4 *Maths.* any symbol used to indicate that a particular mathematical operation is to be carried out, eg × which shows that two numbers are to be multiplied. 5 *colloq.* a calculating, shrewd, and manipulative person.

operculum /oʊ'pɜːkjʊləm/ *noun* (PL. **opercula**) 1 *Zool.* a plate that covers the opening of the shell in some gastropods. 2 in bony fishes, a flap that protects the gills. [from Latin *operculum*, from *operire*, to cover]

operetta *noun* a short light opera, with spoken dialogue and often dancing. [from Italian *operetta*, a diminutive of *opera*]

operon /'ɒpərɒn/ *noun Genetics* a group of closely linked genes that occur next to each other on a chromosome, and may be switched on and off as an integrated unit.

ophthalmia *noun* inflammation of the eye, especially of the conjunctiva. [from Greek *ophthalmos*, eye]

ophthalmic *adj.* of or relating to the eye. [from Greek *ophthalmos*, eye]

ophthalmic optician an optician qualified to test people's eyes and prescribe, make, and sell glasses and contact lenses.

ophthalmologist *noun* an expert in ophthalmology.

ophthalmology *noun* the scientific study of the eye. [from Greek *ophthalmos*, eye + -LOGY]

ophthalmoscope *noun* an instrument that is used to examine the interior of the eye, by directing a reflected beam of light through the pupil. [from Greek *ophthalmos*, eye + -SCOPE]

opiate /'oʊpɪət/ *noun* 1 any of a group of drugs containing or derived from opium, eg morphine, heroine, codeine. Opiates depress the central nervous system, and are mainly used medicinally to relieve severe pain. 2 anything that dulls physical or mental sensation.

opine /oʊ'paɪn/ *verb* to suppose or express as an opinion. [from Latin *opinari*, to think]

opinion *noun* 1 a belief or judgement which seems likely to be true, but which is not based on proof. 2 (**opinion on** or **about something**) what one thinks about something. 3 a professional judgement given by an expert: *medical opinion*. 4 estimation or appreciation: *have a low opinion of his abilities*. — **a matter of opinion** a matter about which people have different opinions. **be of the opinion that** ... to think or believe that ... [from Latin *opinio*, belief]

⊟ 1 belief, judgement, view, point of view, idea, perception, theory, impression, feeling, sentiment, mind, notion, way of thinking, persuasion, attitude. 2 stance on, feeling on or about, view on, theory about, attitude towards. 4 estimation, appreciation, assessment, conception.

opinionated *adj.* having very strong opinions which one refuses to change; stubborn.

⊟ dogmatic, doctrinaire, stubborn, inflexible, obstinate, uncompromising, single-minded, prejudiced, biased, bigoted, dictatorial, arrogant.
⊡ open-minded.

opinion poll *Politics* a test of public opinion made by questioning a representative sample of the population. It is used to determine the voting intentions of the electorate, their view of political leaders, and wider political attitudes.

opium *noun* 1 an addictive drug made from juice from the seeds of a variety of poppy, used in medicine to cause sleep and relieve pain. 2 anything which has a soothing, calming, or dulling effect on people's minds. [from Greek *opion*, poppy-juice]

opium poppy an annual plant (*Papaver somniferum*), native to Europe and Asia, and having oblong, shallowly lobed leaves, flowers with four petals, and a pepperpot-shaped capsule with a ring of pores around its rim. In the garden form (subspecies *hortense*) the flowers are mauve with a dark centre, and in the drug-producing form (subspecies *somniferum*) the flowers are white.

opossum /ə'pɒsəm/ *noun* any of several small, tree-dwelling, American or Australian marsupials with thick fur and a strong tail for gripping. [from an American Indian language]

opp. *abbrev.* opposite.

opponent *noun* a person who belongs to the opposing side in an argument, contest, or battle. [from Latin *opponere*, to set before or against]

⊟ adversary, enemy, antagonist, foe, competitor, contestant, challenger, opposer, opposition, rival, objector, dissident.
⊡ ally, friend.

opportune *adj.* 1 *said of an action* happening at a time which is suitable, proper, or correct. 2 *said of a time* suitable; proper. [from Latin *opportunus*, from *ob*, before + *portus*, harbour, used originally of a wind blowing towards a harbour]

opportunely *adv.* at an opportune time, in an opportune way.

opportuneness *noun* being opportune.

opportunism *noun* the practice of regulating actions by favourable opportunities rather than by consistent principles.

opportunist *noun* a person whose actions are governed by opportunism.

opportunistic *adj.* 1 characterized or determined by opportunism. 2 *Medicine*, *said of an infection* not affecting healthy people but attacking those whose immune system is weakened by drugs or disease.

opportunity *noun* (PL. **opportunities**) 1 an occasion offering a possibility; a chance. 2 favourable or advantageous conditions. [from Latin *opportunitas*, from *opportunus*, opportune]

⊟ CHANCE, OPENING, *colloq.* BREAK, POSSIBILITY, HOUR, MOMENT.

opportunity cost *Econ.* the real cost of acquiring any item, which is the alternative to be foregone in order to do so. For example, the opportunity cost of holding money is the amount of income that is sacrificed by holding assets in the form of money rather than investing them in interest-earning or dividend-paying securities.

oppose *verb* 1 to resist or fight against by force or argument. 2 *intrans.* to object. 3 *intrans.* to compete in a game, contest, etc against another person or team. 4 to place opposite or in contrast to so as to counterbalance. — **as opposed to** ... in contrast to ...; as distinct from ... [from Latin *opponere*, to set before or against, or French *poser*, to place]

⊟ 1 resist, withstand, counter, attack, combat, contest, stand up to, take a stand against, take issue with, confront, defy, face, fight, fly in the face of, hinder, obstruct, bar, check, prevent, thwart. 4 compare, contrast, counterbalance, offset, play off, match.
⊡ 1 support, defend.

opposer *noun* a person who opposes.

opposing *adj.* that opposes.

opposite — *adj.* 1 being on the other side of, or at the other end of, a real or imaginary line or space. 2 facing in a directly different direction: *opposite sides of the coin*. 3 completely or diametrically different. 4 being the other of a matching or contrasting pair: *the opposite sex*. 5 *Bot.*, *said of leaves or other organs* arranged in pairs on a stem, so that the two members of a pair are exactly opposite each other. — *noun* an opposite person or thing. — *adv.* in or into an opposite position: *live opposite*. — *prep.* 1 across from and facing: *a house opposite the station*. 2 *said of an actor* in a role which complements that taken by another actor; co-starring with: *played opposite Olivier*. [from Latin *oppositus*, from *ob*, against + *ponere*, to place]

⊟ *adj.* 1 facing, fronting. 3 different, contrasted, differing, unlike, contradictory, antithetical, irreconcilable, reverse, inconsistent, opposed. *noun* reverse, converse, contrary, antithesis, contradiction, inverse.
⊡ *adj.* 3 same.

opposite number a person with an equivalent position or job in another company, country, etc.

opposition *noun* 1 the act of resisting or fighting against (someone or something) by force or argument. 2 the state of being hostile or in conflict. 3 a person or group of people who are opposed to something. 4 (**Opposition**) a political party which opposes the party in power. 5 an act of opposing or being placed opposite. 6 *Astron.*, *Astrol.* the position of a planet or star when it is directly opposite another, especially the sun, as seen from the earth. [from Latin *oppositio*]

⊟ 1, 2 antagonism, hostility, resistance, obstructiveness, unfriendliness, disapproval. 3 opponent, antagonist, rival, foe, other side.
⊡ 1, 2 co-operation, support. 3 ally, supporter.

oppress *verb* 1 to govern with cruelty and injustice. 2 to worry, trouble, or make anxious; to weigh heavily upon.

[from Latin *oppressare*, from *ob*, against + *premere*, to press]

▣ **1** subjugate, suppress, subdue, overpower, overwhelm, crush, trample, tyrannize, persecute, maltreat, abuse. **2** worry, trouble, burden, afflict, weigh heavily upon, depress, sadden, torment, vex.

oppression *noun* **1** the state of suffering cruelty and injustice. **2** worry or mental distress.

▣ **1** tyranny, subjugation, subjection, repression, despotism, suppression, injustice, cruelty, brutality, abuse, persecution, maltreatment, harshness, hardship.

oppressive *adj.* **1** cruel, tyrannical, and unjust. **2** causing worry or mental distress; weighing heavily on the mind. **3** *said of the weather* hot and sultry.

▣ **1** cruel, tyrannical, unjust, despotic, overbearing, overwhelming, repressive, harsh, inhuman, brutal. **2** burdensome, onerous, intolerable. **3** sultry, muggy, heavy, close, stifling, suffocating, airless, stuffy. ▣ **1** just, gentle. **3** airy.

oppressor *noun* a person who oppresses.

▣ tyrant, bully, taskmaster, *colloq.* slave-driver, despot, dictator, persecutor, tormentor, autocrat.

opprobrious *adj.* insulting, abusive, or severely critical. [from Latin *opprobriosus*]

opprobrium *noun* public shame, disgrace, or loss of favour. [from Latin, from *ob*, against + *probrum*, reproach, disgrace]

oppugn /əˈpjuːn/ *verb* to call into question; to dispute. [from Latin *ob*, against + *pugnare*, to fight]

ops *pl. noun Mil.* operations.

opt *verb intrans.* (**opt for something**) to decide between several possibilities. — **opt out of something 1** to choose not to take part in something. **2** *said of a school or hospital* to leave local authority control. [from Latin *optare*, to choose]

optic *adj.* of or concerning the eye or vision. [from Greek *optikos*]

optical *adj.* **1** of or concerning sight or what one sees. **2** of or concerning light or optics. **3** *said of a lens* designed to help sight.

optical activity *Chem.* the ability of certain chemical compounds, when placed in the path of a beam of polarized light, to rotate the plane of polarization of the light to the left or to the right. Optical activity can be used to identify and measure the concentrations of transparent solutions such as sugar solution.

optical character recognition *Comput.* the scanning, identification, and recording of printed characters by a photoelectric device attached to a computer.

optical fibre *Telecomm.* a thin flexible strand of glass or plastic that transmits light with little leakage through the walls of the fibre, which are covered with a material of lower refractive index. This covering acts as a mirror, so that light is continually reflected back into the core of the fibre. Bundles of optical fibres are used in endoscopes, and for transmitting computer data, telephone messages, television signals, etc, over long distances in the form of modulated light signals.

optical illusion a thing which has an appearance which deceives the eye; misunderstanding caused by a deceptive appearance.

optically *adv.* as regards light or optics.

optical sensing the process of detecting light and converting it into electrical signals. In the human eye, the light stimulation from an image results in electrical impulses to the brain, which are then interpreted. Optical sensing by artificial means includes the use of photoelectric cells and photographic light meters.

optician *noun* **1** a person who fits and sells spectacles and contact lenses. Also called DISPENSING OPTICIAN. **2** a person qualified both to examine the eyes and vision and to prescribe and dispense spectacles and contact lenses for the improvement of vision. Also called OPHTHALMIC OPTICIAN, OPTOMETRIST. [from French *opticien*; as OPTIC]

optic nerve *Anat.* the second cranial nerve in vertebrates, responsible for the sense of vision. It transmits information from the retina of the eye to the visual cortex of the brain.

optics *sing. noun* the branch of physics that is concerned with the study of light (especially visible light, but also including ultraviolet and infra-red light), including the phenomena associated with its generation, propagation, and detection, and its practical applications in a range of devices and systems.

optimal *adj.* the best or most favourable. [from Latin *optimus*, best]

optimism *noun* **1** a tendency to take a bright, hopeful view of things and expect the best possible outcome. **2** *Philos.* the belief that we live in the best of all possible worlds. **3** the theory that good will ultimately triumph over evil. [from Latin *optimus*, best]

optimist *noun* **1** a person who has a hopeful, cheerful nature. **2** a person who follows the doctrine of optimism.

optimistic *adj.* relating to or characterized by optimism.

▣ confident, assured, sanguine, hopeful, positive, cheerful, buoyant, bright, idealistic, expectant. ▣ pessimistic.

optimistically *adv.* in an optimistic way.

optimize or **optimise** *verb* to make the most or best of; to make the most efficient use of. [from Latin *optimus*, best]

optimum — *noun* (PL. **optimums, optima**) the most favourable condition or situation. — *adj.* the best or most favourable. [from Latin *optimus*, best]

▣ *adj.* best, ideal, perfect, optimal, superlative. ▣ *adj.* worst.

option *noun* **1** an act of choosing. **2** that which is or which may be chosen. **3** the power or right to choose: *you have no option.* **4** the exclusive right to buy or sell something, eg stocks, at a fixed price and within a specified time-limit. — **keep** or **leave one's options open** to avoid making a choice or committing oneself to a particular course of action. [from Latin *optio*, from *optare*, to choose]

▣ **1** selection, choice. **2** choice, alternative, preference, possibility. **3** choice, alternative.

optional *adj.* a matter of choice; not compulsory.

▣ voluntary, discretionary, elective, free, unforced. ▣ compulsory, obligatory.

optionally *adv.* in an optional way, as an option.

optometrist *noun Optics* a person qualified both to examine the eyes and vision and to prescribe and dispense spectacles and contact lenses for the improvement of vision. [from Greek *optikos*, optic]

opulence *noun* conspicuous wealth, luxury.

opulent *adj.* **1** rich; wealthy. **2** luxurious. **3** abundant. [from Latin *opulentus*]

opus *noun* (PL. **opuses, opera**) an artistic work, especially a musical composition, often used with a number to show the order in which a composer's works were written or catalogued: *Beethoven, opus 18.* [from Latin *opus*, work]

OR *abbrev.* Oregon.

or[1] *conj.* used to introduce: **1** alternatives: *red or pink or blue.* **2** a synonym or explanation: *a puppy or young dog.* **3** an afterthought: *she's laughing or is she crying?* **4** the second part of an indirect question: *ask her whether she thinks he'll come or not.* **5** because if not; or else: *run or you'll be late.* **6** and not: *never joins in or helps.* — **or else 1** otherwise. **2** *colloq.* expressing a threat or warning: *give it to me or else!* **or rather** or to be more accurate: *he went too, or rather I heard he did.* **or so** about; roughly: *been there two hours or so.* [from Middle English *other*]

or[2] *noun Heraldry* a gold colour. [from French, from Latin *aurum,* gold]

-or *suffix* forming words denoting a person or thing that performs an action or function: *actor/elevator.* [from Middle English, from Old French]

Oracle /ˈɒrəkl/ *noun trademark* a former teletext service run by the Independent Broadcasting Authority.

oracle /ˈɒrəkl/ *noun* **1** a holy place in ancient Greece or Rome where a god was believed to give advice and prophecy. **2** a priest or priestess at an oracle, through whom the god was believed to speak. **3** the usually mysterious or ambiguous advice or prophecy given at an oracle. **4** a person who is believed to have great wisdom or be capable of prophesying the future. **5** a statement made by such a person. [from Latin *oraculum*]

oracular /ɒˈrakjʊlə(r)/ *adj.* **1** of or like an oracle. **2** difficult to interpret; mysterious and ambiguous. **3** prophetic.

oracy *noun* the ability to express oneself coherently and to communicate freely with others by word of mouth. The development of these skills is seen as an important goal of childhood education, together with literacy and numeracy. [from Latin *os, oris,* mouth]

oral — *adj.* **1** spoken or verbal; not written. **2** of or used in the mouth. **3** *said especially of a medicine* taken in through the mouth. **4** *Psychol.* of a supposed stage of infant development, when satisfaction is obtained through sucking. — *noun* a spoken test or examination. [from Latin *os,* mouth]

    ▣ *adj.* **1** verbal, spoken, unwritten, vocal.
    ▣ *adj.* **1** written.

orally *adv.* with the mouth; in words.

orange — *noun* **1** a round citrus fruit with a tough reddish-yellow outer rind or peel enclosing membranous segments filled with sweet or sharp-tasting juicy flesh that is rich in vitamin C. **2** the evergreen tree of the genus *Citrus* that bears this fruit, cultivated in most subtropical regions. **3** the reddish-yellow colour of the skin of this fruit. **4** an orange-flavoured drink. — *adj.* orange-coloured or orange-flavoured. [from Sanskrit *naranga*]

orangeade *noun* a usually fizzy orange-flavoured drink.

Orangeman *noun* (PL. **Orangemen**) a member of a society founded in 1795 to support Protestantism in Ireland. [from William of *Orange,* later William III of Great Britain and Ireland]

orangery *noun* (PL. **orangeries**) a greenhouse or building which allows orange trees to be grown in cool climates.

orangey *adj.* somewhat orange in colour or flavour, etc.

orang utan or **orang outang** the only tree-dwelling great ape, found in tropical forests in Borneo and Sumatra. Its arms are considerably longer than its legs, and it has a characteristic high forehead and coarse grey skin sparsely covered with long reddish hair. The male grows a moustache and beard, but the rest of the face is hairless. [from Malay *orang,* man + *hutan,* forest]

oration *noun* a formal or ceremonial public speech in dignified language. [from Latin *oratio*]

orator *noun* **1** a person who is skilled in persuading, moving, or exciting people through public speech. **2** a person who gives an oration. [from Latin, from *orare,* to pray]

oratorial *adj.* of an orator, an oratory, or an oratorio.

oratorical *adj.* **1** of an orator. **2** like oratory, especially in using rhetoric.

oratorio *noun* (PL. **oratorios**) a theme or story, usually on a Biblical or religious topic, set to music and sung by soloists and a chorus accompanied by an orchestra, but without scenery, costumes, or acting. [from Italian *oratorio,* from Latin *oratorium,* oratory, so called because it developed out of singing in religious services held in oratories]

oratory *noun* (PL. **oratories**) **1** the art of speaking well in public, especially using elegant rhetorical devices. **2** a small place or chapel for private prayer.

orb *noun* **1** a globe decorated with jewels and with a cross on top, carried by a monarch during important ceremonies. **2** anything in the shape of a globe. **3** *poetic* a star, the sun, or a planet. **4** *poetic* the eyeball. [from Latin *orbis,* circle]

orbit — *noun* **1** *Astron.* in space, the path of one celestial body around another, eg the Earth's orbit around the Sun, or the path of an artificial satellite around a celestial body. Most orbits are elliptical in shape. **2** *Physics* the path of an electron around the nucleus of an atom. **3** a sphere of influence or action. **4** *Anat.* in the skull of vertebrates, one of the two bony hollows in which the eyeball is situated. — *verb* (**orbited, orbiting**) **1** *intrans., trans.* to follow an orbital path around (an object). **2** to put (a spacecraft, etc) into orbit. [from Latin *orbitus,* from *orbis,* circle]

    ▤ *noun* **1, 2** circuit, cycle, circle, course, path, trajectory, track, revolution, rotation. **3** sphere of influence, range, scope, domain, influence, compass. *verb* **1** revolve, circle, encircle, circumnavigate.

orbital — *noun Chem.* any region of space outside the nucleus of an atom or molecule where there is a high probability of finding an electron. Up to two electrons are associated with each orbital. — *adj.* **1** of or going round in an orbit. **2** *said of a road* forming a complete circle or loop round a city.

Orcadian — *adj.* of the Orkney Islands. — *noun* a person who lives or was born in the Orkney Islands. [from Greek *Orkades,* Orkney]

orchard *noun* a garden or piece of land where fruit trees are grown. [from Anglo-Saxon *ortgeard*]

orchestra *noun* **1** a usually large group of musicians who play a variety of different instruments as an ensemble, led by a conductor. **2** (*also* **orchestra pit**) that part of a theatre or opera-house where the orchestra sits, usually in front of or under the stage. **3** in the ancient Greek theatre, a semicircular area in front of the stage where the chorus danced. [from Greek, from *orcheisthai,* to dance]

orchestral *adj.* of, for, or played by an orchestra.

orchestrate *verb* **1** to arrange or compose (a piece of music) for an orchestra. **2** to organize or arrange (something) so as to get the desired or best result.

orchestration *noun* **1** the process or technique of orchestrating music. **2** music which has been orchestrated.

orchestrator *noun* a person who orchestrates music.

orchid /ˈɔːkɪd/ *noun* a perennial plant belonging to the family Orchidaceae, one of the largest and most advanced families of flowering plants. Orchids are best known for their complex and exotic flowers, and for their highly sophisticated pollination mechanisms. [from Greek *orchis,* testicle, so called because of the shape of its root-tubers]

ordain *verb* **1** to make (someone) a priest or minister of the church. **2** to order or command formally. **3** to destine in mathematics, which shows that two numbers are to be multiplied. See also ORDINATION. [from Latin *ordinare,* from *ordo,* order]

ordained *adj.* appointed, consecrated, decreed, ordered.

ordainment *noun* ordaining.

ordeal *noun* **1** a difficult, painful, or testing experience. **2** *Hist.* a method of trial in which the accused person was subjected to physical danger from fire, water, etc, survival of which was taken as a sign from God of that person's innocence. [from Anglo-Saxon *ordal*]

. . . .

■ 1 trial, test, tribulation(s), affliction, trouble(s), suffering, anguish, agony, pain, persecution, torture, nightmare.

. . . .

order — *noun* **1** a state in which everything is in its proper place; tidiness. **2** an arrangement of objects according to importance, value, position, etc. **3** a command, instruction, or direction. **4** a state of peace and harmony in society, characterized by the absence of crime and the general obeying of laws. **5** the condition of being able to function properly: *out of order.* **6** a social class or rank making up a distinct social group: *the lower orders.* **7** a kind or sort. **8** an instruction to a manufacturer, supplier, waiter, etc to provide something. **9** the goods, food, etc supplied. **10** an established system of society: *a new world order.* **11** *Biol.* a category in the classification of animals and plants which is below a class and above a family. **12** *Commerce* a written instruction to pay money. **13** the usual procedure followed at especially official meetings and during debates: *a point of order.* **14** (**Order** or **Religious Order**) a religious community living according to a particular rule and bound by vows. **15** any of the different grades of the Christian ministry. **16** (**orders**) same as HOLY ORDERS. **17** the specified form of a religious service: *order of marriage.* **18** (**Order**) a group of people to which new members are admitted as a mark of honour or reward for services to the sovereign or country: *the Order of the Garter.* **19** any of the five classical styles of architecture characterized by the way a column and entablature are moulded and decorated. — *verb* (**ordered, ordering**) **1** to give a command to. **2** to command (someone) to go to a specified place: *order the regiment to Germany.* **3** to instruct a manufacturer, supplier, waiter to supply or provide (something). **4** to arrange or regulate: *order one's affairs.* **5** *intrans.* to give a command, request, or order, especially to a waiter for food. — *interj.* (**Order! Order!**) a call for quiet, calm, proper behaviour to be restored, especially during a debate. — **call to order 1** to request calm or attention. **2** to declare a formal meeting open. **in order 1** in accordance with the rules; properly arranged. **2** suitable or appropriate: *such behaviour just isn't in order.* **3** in the correct sequence. **in the order of** ... approximately (the number stated). **in order that** ... so that ... **in order to** ... so as to be able to ... **on order** *said of goods* having been ordered but not yet supplied. **order someone about** or **around** to give them orders continually and officiously. **order someone off** *Sport* to order a player to leave the field because of bad or illegal behaviour. **out of order 1** broken; not working. **2** not correct, proper, or suitable: *your behaviour is out of order.* **a tall order** *colloq.* a difficult or demanding job or task. **to order** according to a customer's particular or personal requirements. **under orders** having been commanded or instructed (to do something). [from Latin *ordo*]

. . . .

■ *noun* **1** orderliness, organization, tidiness, neatness, harmony. **2** arrangement, organization, grouping, disposition, sequence, categorization, classification, method, pattern, plan, system, array, layout, line-up, structure. **3** command, instruction, direction, directive, decree, injunction, edict, ordinance, mandate, regulation, rule, precept, law. **4** peace, harmony, law and order, discipline, quiet, calm, tranquillity. **7** kind, sort, type, class, rank, species, hierarchy, family. **8** requisition, request, booking, commission, reservation, application, demand. **14** community, fraternity, brotherhood, sisterhood. *verb* **1** command, instruct, direct, bid, decree, require, authorize. **3** request, reserve, book, apply for, requisition. **4** arrange, organize, dispose, classify, group, marshal, sort out, lay out, manage, control, catalogue.

■ *noun* **1** disorder, chaos, untidiness, confusion. **4** anarchy, disorder. **in order 1** arranged, organized, orderly. **2** fitting, proper, correct, suitable, seemly. **3** ordered, categorized. **out of order 1** broken, broken down, not working, inoperative. **2** improper, incorrect, unsuitable, uncalled-for, unseemly, wrong.

. . . .

ordered *adj.* **1** placed in order. **2** well-organized or arranged.

orderliness *noun* being orderly.

orderly — *adj.* **1** in good order; well-arranged. **2** well-behaved; quiet. — *noun* (PL. **orderlies**) **1** an attendant, usually without medical training, who does various jobs in a hospital, such as moving patients. **2** *Mil.* a soldier who carries an officer's orders and messages.

. . . .

■ *adj.* **1** ordered, systematic, neat, tidy, regular, methodical, in order, well-organized, well-regulated. **2** well-behaved, quiet, controlled, disciplined, law-abiding.

■ *adj.* **1** chaotic, disorderly, disorganized. **2** disorderly.

. . . .

order of battle the positions adopted by soldiers or ships before a battle.

Order of the British Empire see OBE.

order of the day 1 an agenda, eg for a meeting or for business in parliament. **2** that which is necessary, normal, or fashionable at a given time.

order paper a programme showing the order of business, especially in Parliament.

ordinal — *noun* **1** a Roman Catholic service book, or a service book containing the services for the ordination of ministers. **2** same as ORDINAL NUMBER. — *adj.* denoting an ordinal or to a position in a sequence. [from Latin *ordinalis*, from *ordo*, order]

ordinal number a number which shows a position in a sequence, eg *first, second, third,* etc. See also CARDINAL NUMBER.

ordinance *noun* **1** a law, order, or ruling. **2** an authorized religious ceremony. [from Latin *ordinare*, from *ordo*, order]

ordinand *noun* a person who is training to become a minister of the church. [from Latin *ordinare*, from *ordo*, order]

ordinarily *adv.* usually, normally.

ordinariness *noun* being ordinary.

ordinary — *adj.* usual; normal; unexceptional; familiar. — *noun* (PL. **ordinaries**) (**Ordinary**) those parts of the Mass which do not vary from day to day. — **in the ordinary way** if things are as normal; usually. **out of the ordinary** unusual; strange. [from Latin *ordinarius*, from *ordo*, order]

. . . .

■ *adj.* usual, normal, typical, customary, unexceptional, unremarkable, common, familiar, habitual, commonplace, regular, routine, standard, average, everyday, run-of-the-mill, common-or-garden, plain, simple, conventional, modest, mediocre, indifferent, pedestrian, prosaic, undistinguished.

■ *adj.* extraordinary, unusual.

. . . .

Ordinary grade See O-GRADE.

Ordinary level See O-LEVEL.

ordinary seaman a sailor of the lowest rank in the Royal Navy.

ordinate /ˈɔːdnət/ *noun Maths.* in coordinate geometry, the second of a pair of numbers (x, y), known as the y coordinate. It specifies the distance of a point from the horizontal or x-axis. See also ABSCISSA. [from Latin *ordinatus*, ordained, from *ordo*, order]

ordination *noun* the act or ceremony of ordaining a priest or minister of the church. [from Latin *ordinatio*, from *ordo*, order]

ordnance *noun* **1** heavy guns and military supplies. **2** the government department responsible for military supplies. [see ORDINANCE]

Ordovician /ˌɔːdəʊˈvɪʃən/ adj. Geol. denoting the second period of the Palaeozoic era, lasting from about 505 million to 440 million years ago. During this period the first vertebrates (jawless fishes) appeared, graptolites and trilobites were abundant, and echinoderms (eg starfish and sea urchins) became more widespread. [from Latin *Ordovices*, a British tribe]

ordure /ˈɔːdjʊə(r)/ noun waste matter from the bowels; excrement. [from Old French *ord*, foul]

Ore or **Oreg.** abbrev. Oregon.

ore noun Geol. a solid naturally occurring mineral deposit from which one or more economically valuable substances, especially metals, can be extracted, and for which it is mined. [from Anglo-Saxon *ora*, unwrought metal combined with Anglo-Saxon *ar*, brass]

oregano /ɒrɪˈɡɑːnəʊ/ noun a sweet-smelling Mediterranean herb used as a flavouring in cooking. [from Greek *origanon*]

organ noun 1 a part of a body or plant which has a special function, eg a kidney or leaf. 2 a usually large musical instrument with a keyboard and pedals, in which sound is produced by air being forced through pipes of different lengths. 3 any similar instrument without pipes, such as one producing sound electronically or with reeds. 4 a means of spreading information, such as a newspaper. 5 *euphemistic, humorous* the penis. [from Greek *organon*, tool]

⊞ **4** medium, newspaper, periodical, journal, publication, agency, forum, vehicle, voice, mouthpiece.

organdie /ˈɔːɡəndɪ/ noun a very fine, thin cotton fabric which has been stiffened. [from French *organdi*]

organelle noun Biol. in the cell of a living organism, any of various different types of membrane-bound structure, each of which has a specialized function, eg mitochondria (which produce energy by breaking down carbohydrate molecules), and chloroplasts (which are the site of photosynthesis in green plants).

organ-grinder noun a musician who plays a barrel organ in the streets for money.

organic adj. 1 *Medicine* relating to an organ of the body: *organic disease*. 2 *Biol.* relating to living organisms. 3 *Agric.* relating to farming practices that avoid the use of fertilizers, pesticides, etc, or to crops, especially fruit and vegetables, produced in this way. 4 being an inherent or natural part. 5 systematically organized. 6 *Chem.* relating to that branch of chemistry that is concerned with compounds that contain carbon atoms arranged in chains or rings, or relating to such compounds.

⊞ **2** biological, living, animate, natural.

organically adv. in an organic way.

organic architecture architecture which appears to grow out of, or be closely linked with, the surrounding landscape.

organic chemistry the branch of chemistry concerned with the study of compounds that contain chains or rings of carbon atoms, eg alcohols, aldehydes, plastics. See also INORGANIC CHEMISTRY.

organic compound Chem. a chemical compound that contains carbon atoms arranged in chains or rings, together with smaller amounts of other elements, mainly hydrogen and oxygen, but also often including nitrogen, sulphur, and halogens such as chlorine.

organic farming a system of farming that avoids the use of industrially manufactured chemical fertilizers and pesticides.

organic fertilizer a fertilizer that consists of natural animal or plant products, eg manure, compost, bonemeal. Organic fertilizers are much less harmful to the environment than inorganic ones.

organism noun 1 any living structure, such as a plant, animal, fungus, or bacterium, capable of growth and repro-

duction. 2 any establishment, system, or whole made up of parts that depend on each other. [from French *organisme*, from Latin *organizare*]

organist noun a person who plays the organ.

organization or **organisation** noun 1 a group of people formed into a society, union, or especially business. 2 the act of organizing. 3 the state of being organized.

⊞ **1** association, institution, society, federation, union, group, business, company, firm, corporation, confederation, consortium, league, club. 2, 3 arrangement, system, classification, methodology, order, formation, grouping, method, plan, structure, pattern, composition, configuration, design.

organizational or **organisational** adj. relating to organization or an organization.

organizationally or **organisationally** adv. as regards organization.

organize or **organise** verb 1 to give an orderly structure to: *organized the books into a neat pile*. 2 to arrange, provide, or prepare: *will organize a meal*. 3 to form or enrol (people or a person) into a society or organization, especially a trade union. 4 *intrans.* to form a society or organization, especially a trade union. [from Latin *organizare*]

⊞ **1** structure, co-ordinate, arrange, order, group, marshal, classify, systematize, tabulate, catalogue. 2 arrange, provide, prepare, make, develop, form, establish, frame, construct, shape, found, set up.
⊟ **1** disorganize.

organizer or **organiser** noun 1 someone or something that organizes. 2 a small bag or wallet which has (often removable) sections in which personal notes and information may be kept; a similar electronic device.

organza /ɔːˈɡanzə/ noun a very fine, thin dress material made of silk or synthetic fibres.

orgasm — noun 1 the highest point of sexual excitement. 2 violent excitement. — verb intrans. to experience an orgasm. [from Greek *orgasmos*, swelling]

orgasmic adj. relating to or associated with an orgasm.

orgiastic adj. relating to or characteristic of orgies.

orgy noun (PL. **orgies**) 1 a wild party or celebration involving excessive drinking and sexual activity. 2 any act of excessive or frenzied indulgence: *an orgy of shopping*. [from Greek *orgia*, secret rites]

⊞ **1** debauch, carousal, revelry, Bacchanalia. 2 spree, bout, indulgence, excess.

oriel-window noun (*also* **oriel**) a window which projects from the wall of a house, usually at an upper storey, and which is held in place by brackets. [from Old French *oriol*, gallery]

orient — noun 1 (**the Orient**) the countries in the east, especially those of E Asia regarded as culturally distinct from western countries (the *Occident*). 2 that part of the sky where the sun rises. — verb 1 to place in a definite position in relation to the points of the compass or some other fixed or known point. 2 to acquaint (oneself or someone) with the position relative to points known, or with details of a situation. 3 to position so as to face east. 4 to build (a church) so that it runs from east to west. [from Latin *oriens*, from *oriri*, to rise]

oriental — adj. from or relating to the Orient; eastern. — noun (**Oriental**) a person born in the Orient; an Asiatic.

Orientalist noun a person who studies, or is expert in, oriental culture, languages, etc.

orientate verb 1 to orient. 2 *intrans.* to face the east; to be oriented.

orientated adj. oriented.

orientation *noun* **1** the act or an instance of orienting or being oriented. **2** a position relative to a fixed point. **3** a person's position or attitude relative to his or her situation or circumstances. **4** a meeting giving information or training needed for a new situation; a briefing.

⊟ **1** acclimatization, familiarization, adaptation, adjustment, settling in, initiation, training. **2** position, situation, bearings, location, direction, alignment, placement.

oriented *adj.* **1** directed towards something. **2** interested in something.

orienteering *noun* a sport in which contestants race over an unfamiliar cross-country course, finding their way to official check points using a map and compass. [from Swedish *orientering*]

orifice /ˈɒrɪfɪs/ *noun* an opening or hole, especially in the body. [from Latin *os*, mouth + *facere*, to make]

origami /ɒrɪˈɡɑːmɪ/ *noun* the originally Japanese art of folding paper into shapes and figures. [from Japanese *ori* folding + *kami*, paper]

origin *noun* **1** a beginning or starting-point; a source. **2** (**origins**) a person's family background or ancestors. **3** *Anat.* the point of attachment of a muscle. **4** *Maths.* in co-ordinate geometry, the point where the horizontal *x*-axis and the vertical *y*-axis cross each other. It has a value of zero on both axes. [from Latin *origo*]

⊟ **1** *beginning* commencement, starting-point, start, inauguration, launch, dawning, creation, emergence. *source* derivation, provenance, roots, spring, fount, foundation, base, cause, wellspring. **2** ancestry, descent, extraction, background, heritage, family, lineage, parentage, pedigree, birth, paternity, stock.
⊟ **1** end, termination.

original — *adj.* **1** existing from the beginning; earliest; first. **2** *said of an idea* not thought of before; fresh or new. **3** *said of a person* creative or inventive. **4** being the first form from which copies, reproductions, or translations are made. — *noun* **1** the first example of something which is copied, reproduced, or translated to produce others. **2** a model from which a painting, etc is made. **3** an odd or eccentric person.

⊟ *adj.* **1** first, earliest, early, initial, primary, archetypal, rudimentary, embryonic, starting, opening, commencing, first-hand. **2** novel, new, fresh, innovative, unconventional, unusual, unique. **3** creative, imaginative, inventive, innovative. *noun* **1** prototype, master, paradigm, model, pattern, archetype, standard, type.
⊟ *adj.* **1** latest, last. **2** hackneyed, unoriginal.

originality *noun* **1** the quality of being original. **2** being creative or innovative. **3** an original act, idea, saying, etc.

originally *adv.* **1** in the first place, at the beginning. **2** in an original way.

original sin *Christianity* the supposed sinfulness of the human race as a result of Adam's disobedience to God.

originate *verb trans., intrans.* to bring or come into being; to start.

⊟ *bring into being* create, begin, commence, start, invent, inaugurate, introduce, give birth to, develop, discover, establish, set up, launch, pioneer, conceive, form, produce, generate. *come into being* begin, commence, start, rise, arise, spring, stem, issue, flow, proceed, derive, come, evolve, emerge, be born.
⊟ end, terminate.

origination *noun* **1** originating. **2** a source.

originator *noun* an author, inventor, or creator.

oriole /ˈɔːrɪəʊl/ *noun* any of several song-birds, the common European species of which has bright yellow and black plumage. [from Latin *aureolus*, from *aurum*, gold]

orlop *noun* the lowest deck in a ship with four or more decks, forming a covering for the hold. [from Dutch *overloop*, covering]

ormolu /ˈɔːməluː/ *noun* a gold-coloured alloy, eg copper, zinc, and sometimes tin, which is used to decorate furniture, make ornaments, etc. [from French *or*, gold + *moulu*, ground]

ornament — *noun* **1** anything that decorates or adds grace or beauty to a person or thing. **2** a small, usually decorative object. **3** a person whose talents add honour to the group, company, etc to which he or she belongs. **4** (*usually* **ornaments**) *Mus.* a note which embellishes or decorates the melody or harmony but does not belong to it. — *verb* to decorate or be an ornament to. [from Latin *ornare*, to adorn]

⊟ *noun* **1** decoration, adornment, embellishment, garnish, trimming, accessory, frill. **2** trinket, bauble, jewel. *verb* decorate, adorn, embellish, garnish, trim, beautify, brighten, dress up, deck, gild.

ornamental *adj.* used for decoration.

⊟ decorative, embellishing, adorning, attractive, showy.

ornamentally *adv.* in an ornamental way.
ornamentation *noun* ornamenting.
ornate *adj.* **1** highly or excessively decorated. **2** *said of language* not plain and simple; using many elaborate literary words or expressions. [from Latin *ornare*, to adorn]

⊟ **1** elaborate, decorated, ornamented, fancy, baroque, rococo, sumptuous, fussy. **2** florid, flowery, elaborate.
⊟ PLAIN.

ornithine *noun Biochem.* an amino acid that is found in proteins. [from Greek *ornis, ornith-*, bird]
ornithological *adj.* relating to or involving ornithology.
ornithologically *adv.* as regards ornithology.
ornithologist *noun* a person who studies ornithology.
ornithology *noun* the scientific study of birds and their behaviour. [from Greek *ornis*, bird + -LOGY]
orogeny or **orogenesis** *noun* **1** *Geol.* a period of mountain-building, often lasting for hundreds of millions of years, involving such processes as deformation and the subsequent uplift of rocks, folding, and usually the intrusion of igneous rocks. **2** the process of mountain-building. [from Greek *oros* mountain + GENESIS]
orographic or **oreographic** *adj. Geol.* denoting effects that are related to the presence of mountains or high ground, eg rainfall. [from Greek *oros, oreos* mountain + -GRAPHY]
orotund *adj.* **1** *said of the voice* full, loud, and grand. **2** *said of speaking* boastful or self-important; pompous. [from Latin *os*, mouth + *rotundus*, round]
orotundity *noun* being orotund.
orphan — *noun* a child who has lost both parents, or, more rarely, one parent. — *verb* (**orphaned, orphaning**) to cause to be an orphan. [from Greek *orphanos*]
orphanage *noun* a home for orphans.
Orphism *noun* **1** *Relig.* a set of unorthodox religious ideas that appeared in Greece in the 6c BC, taking its name from poems ascribed to the mythical singer Orpheus. The fate of the soul after death was the central concern, and the self was seen as a stranger in exile within the body. **2** *Art* a modern art movement that developed out of Cubism between 1910 and 1914.
orrery *noun* (PL. **orreries**) a clockwork model of the Sun and the planets which revolve around it. [from Charles

Boyle, Earl of Orrery (1676–1731), for whom one was made]

orris *noun* an iris, especially the Florentine iris. [a form of IRIS]

orris-root *noun* the dried, sweet-smelling root of this plant, used in perfumes and formerly in medicines.

ortho- *combining form* forming words meaning 'correct, straight, upright'. [from Greek *orthos*, straight]

orthodontic *adj.* relating to orthodontics.

orthodontics *sing. noun Dentistry* the branch of dentistry concerned with the correction of irregularities in the alignment of the teeth, eg by fitting dental braces, usually performed during childhood. [from ORTHO- + Greek *odous, odont-*, tooth]

orthodontist *noun* a dentist who specializes in preventing or correcting irregularities of teeth.

orthodox *adj.* **1** believing in, living according to, or conforming with established or generally accepted opinions, especially in religion or morals; conventional. **2** (**Orthodox**) of the Orthodox Church. **3** (**Orthodox**) of the branch of Judaism which keeps to strict, traditional interpretations of doctrine and scripture. [from Greek *orthos*, straight + *doxa*, opinion]

· · · · · · · · · · · · · · · · · · · ·

▣ **1** conformist, conventional, accepted, official, traditional, usual, well-established, established, received, customary, conservative, recognized, authoritative.

▣ **1** nonconformist, unorthodox.

· ·

orthodoxy *noun* (PL. **orthodoxies**) **1** the state of being orthodox or of having orthodox beliefs. **2** an orthodox belief or practice.

orthogonal *adj. Maths.* right-angled; perpendicular. [from ORTHO- + Greek *gonia*, angle]

orthographic or **orthographical** *adj.* relating to spelling.

orthographically *adv.* in an orthographic way, using spelling.

orthography *noun* (PL. **orthographies**) **1** correct or standard spelling. **2** the study of spelling.

orthopaedic /ɔːθəˈpiːdɪk/ *adj.* relating to orthopaedics.

orthopaedics /ɔːθəˈpiːdɪks/ *sing. noun Medicine* the branch of medicine concerned with the correction by surgery, manipulation, etc, of deformities arising from injury or disease of the bones and joints, eg broken bones, dislocated joints, arthritis. [from ORTHO- + Greek *pais*, child]

orthopaedist *noun* a specialist in orthopaedics.

orthoptics *sing. noun* the science or practice of correcting weak eyesight, especially through exercising the eye muscles. [from ORTHO- + Greek *optikos*, of sight]

ortolan /ˈɔːtələn/ *noun* a small European song-bird, eaten as a delicacy. [from Latin *hortulus*, small garden]

-ory[1] *suffix* forming nouns denoting a place for a specified activity: *dormitory/laboratory*. [from Latin *orium*]

-ory[2] *suffix* forming adjectives and occasionally nouns with the sense of relating to or involving the action of the verb: *depository/signatory*. [from Latin *orius*]

oryx *noun* a grazing antelope with very long slender horns and a pale coat, with striking white and dark markings on the face and underparts. [from Greek *oryx*]

OS *abbrev.* **1** *Comput.* operating system. **2** ordinary seaman. **3** Ordnance Survey. **4** outsize.

Os *symbol Chem.* osmium.

Oscar *noun* any of a number of statuettes awarded annually by the American Academy of Motion Picture Arts and Sciences for outstanding acting, directing, etc in films during the previous year. Also called ACADEMY AWARD. [from the name *Oscar*; of uncertain origin]

oscillate /ˈɒsɪleɪt/ *verb* **1** *trans., intrans.* to swing or cause to swing backwards and forwards like a pendulum. **2** *intrans.* to vary between opinions, choices, courses of action, etc. **3** *intrans., said of an electrical current* to vary

regularly in strength or direction between certain limits. [from Latin *oscillare*, to swing]

oscillation *noun* **1** oscillating. **2** a regular movement or change, such as the movement of a pendulum. **3** one such move from one position to another.

oscillator *noun* **1** an electronic device that produces an alternating current of a particular frequency. Oscillators are used to produce high-frequency radio waves for television and radio, and to make electronic musical instruments. **2** a person or thing that oscillates.

oscillograph *noun* an apparatus for recording (electrical) oscillations.

oscilloscope *noun* an apparatus with which electrical oscillations, appearing as waves, are shown on the screen of a cathode-ray tube.

osier /ˈoʊzɪə(r)/ *noun* **1** a willow tree whose branches and twigs are used for making baskets. **2** a flexible branch or twig from this tree. [from Old French]

-osis *suffix* (PL. **-oses**) forming nouns denoting: **1** a condition or process: *hypnosis/metamorphosis*. **2** a diseased or disordered state: *neurosis*. [from Greek *-osis*]

osmiridium *noun Chem.* a hard white naturally occurring alloy of osmium and iridium, in which the iridium content is less than 35 per cent. It is used to make the tips of pen nibs.

osmium *noun Chem.* (SYMBOL **Os**, ATOMIC NUMBER **76**) a very hard dense bluish-white metal used as a catalyst, and as a hardening agent in alloys with platinum and iridium, eg in pen nibs. [from Greek *osme*, smell, from the unpleasant smell of one of its forms]

osmoregulation *noun Biol.* the process whereby the water content and concentration of salts within a living organism are maintained at a constant level. In many animals the kidneys are responsible for osmoregulation. [from Greek *osmos*, impulse]

osmosis *noun* **1** *Chem.* the spontaneous movement of a solvent, eg water, across a semi-permeable membrane from a more dilute solution to a more concentrated one. Osmosis is largely responsible for the movement of water molecules into and out of cells of living organisms. **2** a gradual process of absorption. [from Greek *osmos*, impulse]

osmotic *adj.* relating to or caused by osmosis.

osmotically *adv.* by osmosis.

osmotic pressure 1 *Chem.* the minimum pressure that must be applied to prevent the spontaneous movement by osmosis of a solvent across a semi-permeable membrane from a more dilute solution to a more concentrated one. **2** the minimum pressure that must be applied to prevent the spontaneous movement by osmosis of a solvent across a semi-permeable membrane separating the pure solvent from a solution. See also OSMOSIS.

osprey *noun* (PL. **ospreys**) **1** a large bird of prey found near water in most parts of the world, with a dark brown body, white head and legs, and a characteristic dark line on the side of the head. **2** a feather used for trimming women's hats. [from Latin *ossifraga*, bone-breaker]

osseous *adj.* of, like, containing, or formed from bone. [from Latin *os*, bone]

ossification *noun Zool.* the process by which bone is formed, usually from cartilage. [from Latin *os, ossis*, bone]

ossified *adj.* **1** made into bone. **2** like bone, hardened.

ossify *verb* (**ossifies, ossified**) **1** *intrans., trans.* to turn into or cause to turn into bone. **2** *intrans. said of one's opinions, etc* to become rigid, fixed, or inflexible. [from Latin *os*, bone + *facere*, to make]

ostensibility *noun* being ostensible.

ostensible *adj., said of reasons, etc* stated or claimed, but not necessarily true; apparent. [from Latin *ostendere*, to show]

· · · · · · · · · · · · · · · · · · · ·

▣ alleged, apparent, presumed, seeming, supposed, so-called, professed, outward, pretended, superficial.

▣ real.

· ·

ostensibly *adv.* in an ostensible way; to outward appearance.

ostensive *adj.* directly showing.

ostentation *noun* pretentious display of wealth, knowledge, etc, especially to attract attention or admiration. [from Latin *ostendere*, to show]

ostentatious *adj.* characterized by ostentation; pretentious, showy.

....

⊟ pretentious, showy, flashy, vulgar, loud, garish, gaudy, flamboyant, conspicuous, extravagant.

⊟ restrained.

....

osteoarthritis *noun Medicine* the commonest form of arthritis, found mainly in the elderly, in which degeneration of the cartilage overlying the bones at a joint (especially the hip, knee, or thumb joint) leads to deformity of the bone surface, causing stiffness, swelling, and eventually deformity of the affected joint. [from Greek *osteon*, bone + ARTHRITIS]

osteomalacia /ɒstɪoʊməˈleɪʃɪə/ *noun Medicine* a disorder characterized by softening of the bones due to a reduction in the availability of calcium salts, caused by a deficiency of vitamin D, which is required for the uptake of calcium from food. [from Greek *osteon*, bone + *malakos*, soft]

osteopath *noun* a person who practises osteopathy.

osteopathic *adj.* relating to or involving osteopathy.

osteopathy *noun Medicine* a system of healing or treatment, mainly involving manipulation of the bones and joints and massage of the muscles, that provides relief for many bone and joint disorders. [from Greek *osteon*, bone + *patheia*, suffering]

osteoporosis /ɒstɪoʊpɔːˈroʊsɪs/ *noun Medicine* a disease in which the bones become porous, brittle, and liable to fracture, owing to the loss of calcium from the bone substance. It is a common feature of ageing. [from Greek *osteon* bone, + *poros*, passage]

ostler /ˈɒslə(r)/ *noun Hist.* a person who attends to horses at an inn. [from Old French *hostelier*]

Ostmark *noun Hist.* the standard unit of currency in the former German Democratic Republic (East Germany).

Ostpolitik *noun* the policy initiated in West Germany in the 1960s as part of the process of détente to normalize relations with communist countries which recognized the German Democratic Republic (GDR), and with the GDR itself.

ostracism *noun* **1** in ancient Athens, a process by which a citizen could be banished for up to ten years (without loss of property or citizenship) by popular vote. **2** social exclusion. [from Greek *ostrakismos*, from *ostrakon*, potsherd, used as a means of voting in ancient Greece]

ostracize or **ostracise** *verb* **1** to exclude (someone) from a group, society, etc; to refuse to associate with (someone). **2** in Athens and other ancient Greek cities, to banish (a person) for a fixed period by popular vote.

....

⊟ **1** *exclude* banish, exile, expel, excommunicate, reject, segregate. *refuse to associate with* send to Coventry, shun, snub, boycott, avoid, cold-shoulder, cut.

⊟ **1** accept, welcome.

....

ostrich *noun* **1** the largest living bird, up to 2.5m in height and incapable of flight, found on dry plains in E Africa, and having an extremely long neck and legs. **2** a person who refuses to face or accept unpleasant facts. [from Latin *avis*, bird + *struthio*, ostrich]

Ostrogoth *noun* a member of a Germanic tribe who by the beginning of the 4c had migrated from the Baltic to S Russia but were conquered by the Huns in AD375. They later conquered Italy and established a powerful and highly civilized kingdom.

OT *abbrev.* Old Testament.

OTC *abbrev. Brit.* Officers' Training Corps.

other — *adj.* **1** remaining from a group of two or more when one or some have been specified already: *close the other eye/the other children.* **2** different from the one or ones already mentioned, understood or implied: *other people.* **3** additional; further: *need to buy one other thing.* **4** far or opposite: *the other side of the garden.* — *pron.* another person or thing. — *adv. colloq.* otherwise; differently: *couldn't do other than hurry home.* — **every other** each alternate. **other than ... 1** except ...; apart from ... **2** different from ... **the other day, week**, etc a few days, weeks, etc, ago. [from Anglo-Saxon]

....

⊟ *adj.* **2** different, dissimilar, unlike, separate, distinct, contrasting. **3** more, further, extra, additional, supplementary, spare, alternative.

....

other ranks *chiefly Brit.* members of the armed services not having the rank of officer.

otherwise — *conj.* or else; if not. — *adv.* **1** in other respects: *he is good at languages but otherwise not very bright.* **2** in a different way: *couldn't act otherwise than as she did.* **3** under different circumstances: *might otherwise have been late.* — *adj.* different: *the truth is otherwise.* — **or otherwise** or the opposite; or not: *check all cars, fast or otherwise.*

otherworldliness *noun* being otherworldly.

otherworldly *adj.* concerned with spiritual or intellectual matters to the complete exclusion of practical matters.

otic /ˈoʊtɪk/ *adj.* of or relating to the ear. [from Greek *ous*, ear]

otiose /ˈoʊtɪoʊs/ *adj.* serving no purpose; unnecessary; useless. [from Latin *otiosus*, from *otium*, leisure]

otitis *noun Medicine* inflammation of the ear. [from Latin *ous, otos* ear + -ITIS]

OTT *abbrev. slang* over the top.

ottava rima /oʊˈtɑːvə ˈriːmə/ *Prosody* an Italian stanza of eight lines, rhyming *abababcc.* [Italian, = eighth rhyme]

otter *noun* any of about 20 species of solitary and rather elusive aquatic mammals belonging to the same family (Mustelidae) as badgers and weasels, found in all parts of the world except Australasia and Antarctica, and having a long body, a broad flat head, short legs, and a stout tail which is thick at the base and tapers towards the tip. [from Anglo-Saxon *otor*]

Ottoman /ˈɒtəmən/ — *adj.* relating to the Ottomans or the Ottoman Empire, which lasted from the 13c until the end of World War I. It was centred in what is now Turkey, and at different times reached into Europe and the Near East. — *noun* (PL. **Ottomans**) **1** an inhabitant of the Ottoman Empire; a Turk. **2** (**ottoman**) a long low seat, usually without a back or arms, and often in the form of a padded and upholstered box. [from Arabic *uthman*, Othman (1259–1326), the founder of the Ottoman Empire]

OU *abbrev.* **1** Open University. **2** Oxford University.

oubliette /uːblɪˈet/ *noun Hist.* a secret dungeon with a single often concealed opening at the top. [from French, from *oublier*, to forget]

ouch *interj.* an expression of sudden sharp pain. [imitative]

ought *verb aux.* used to express: **1** duty or obligation: *you ought to help if you can.* **2** advisability: *you ought to see a doctor.* **3** probability or expectation: *she ought to be here soon.* **4** shortcoming or failure: *he ought to have been here hours ago.* **5** enthusiastic desire on the part of the speaker: *you really ought to read this book.* **6** logical consequence: *the answer ought to be 'four'.* — **ought not to** ... used to express moral disapproval: *you ought not to speak to him like that.* [from Anglo-Saxon *ahte*]

Ouija /ˈwiːdʒə/ *noun* (*in full* **Ouija board**) *trademark* a board with the letters of the alphabet printed round the edge, used at séances with a glass, pointer, or other object to spell out messages supposed to be from spirits. [from French *oui*, yes + German *ja*, yes]

ounce[1] *noun* **1** a unit of weight equal to one sixteenth of a pound (28.35g). **2** a fluid ounce. **3** a small amount. [from Latin *uncia*, twelfth part]

ounce[2] *noun* a big cat native to Asia, with leopard-like markings on a thick, soft, cream-coloured coat. [from Old French *once*, from Greek *lynx*, lynx]

our *adj.* **1** of, belonging to, associated with, or done by us: *our children.* **2** *formal* used by a sovereign to mean 'my': *our royal will.* [from Anglo-Saxon *ure*]

Our Father same as LORD'S PRAYER.

Our Lady the Virgin Mary.

ours *pron.* the one or ones belonging to us. — **of ours** of or belonging to us.

ourselves *pron.* **1** used as the reflexive form of *we*: *we helped ourselves to cakes.* **2** used for emphasis: *we ourselves know nothing about that.* **3** our normal self: *we can relax and be ourselves.* **4** (*also* **by ourselves**) alone; without anyone else's help.

-ous *suffix* forming adjectives meaning: **1** having a particular character, quality, or nature: *marvellous/venomous.* **2** *Chem.* formed with an element in its lower valency. [from Latin *osus*]

ousel /'uːzl/ same as OUZEL.

oust *verb* to force (someone) out of a position and take their place. [from Old French *ouster*]

⊟ expel, eject, depose, displace, turn out, throw out, overthrow, evict, drive out, unseat, dispossess, disinherit, replace, topple.

⊞ install, settle.

out — *adv., adj.* **1** away from the inside; not in or at a place: *go out into the garden.* **2** not in one's home or place of work: *I called but you were out.* **3** to or at an end; to or into a state of being completely finished, exhausted, extinct, etc: *the milk has run out/before the day is out/put the candle out.* **4** aloud; openly. **5** with, or taking, care: *listen out for the baby/watch out.* **6** in all directions from a central point: *share out the sweets.* **7** to the fullest extent or amount: *spread the blanket out.* **8** to public attention or notice; revealed: *the secret is out.* **9** *Sport, said of a person batting* no longer able to bat, eg because of having the ball caught by an opponent: *bowled out.* **10** in or into a state of being removed, omitted or forgotten: *miss him out / rub out the mistake.* **11** not to be considered; rejected; not allowed: *that idea's out.* **12** removed; dislocated: *have a tooth out.* **13** not in authority; not having political power: *vote them out of office.* **14** into unconsciousness: *pass out in the heat.* **15** in error: *your total is out by three.* **16** *colloq.* existing: *the best car out.* **17** *said of a flower* in bloom. **18** *said of a book* published. **19** visible: *the moon's out.* **20** no longer in fashion. **21** *said of workers* on strike: *call the men out.* **22** *said of a jury* considering its verdict. **23** *old use, said of a young woman* introduced into fashionable society. **24** *said of a tide* at or to the lowest level of water. — *adj.* **1** external. **2** directing or showing direction outwards: *the out tray.* — *prep. North Amer., esp. US* out of. — *interj.* expressing: **1** *Sport* that the batsman is dismissed. **2** that a radio transmission has finished: *over and out.* — *noun* a way out, a way of escape; an excuse. — *verb* **1** *intrans.* to become publicly known: *murder will out.* **2** *trans.* to make public the homosexuality of (a famous person who has been attempting to keep his or her homosexuality secret). — **be out for something** *colloq.* be determined to achieve it: *out for revenge.* **out and about** active outside the house, especially after an illness. **out and away** by far; much. **out of something 1** from inside it: *drive out of the garage.* **2** not in or within it: *be out of the house.* **3** having exhausted a supply of it: *be out of butter.* **4** from among several: *two out of three cats.* **5** from a material: *made out of wood.* **6** because of it: *out of anger.* **7** beyond the range, scope, or bounds of it: *out of reach/out of the ordinary.* **8** excluded from it: *leave him out of the team.* **9** no longer in a stated condition: *out of practice.* **10** at a stated distance from a place: *a mile out of town.* **11** without or so as to be without something: *cheat him out of his money.* **out of date** old-fashioned and no longer of use; obsolete. **out of doors** in or into the open. **out of it 1** *colloq.* not part of, or wanted in, a group, activity, etc. **2** *slang* unable to behave normally or control oneself, usually because of drink or

drugs. **out of pocket** having spent more money than one can afford. **out of the way 1** difficult to reach or arrive at. **2** unusual; uncommon. **out to lunch** *slang, said of a person* slightly crazy; in a dream world. **out with it**! an exhortation to speak openly. [from Anglo-Saxon *ut*]

⊟ *adv., adj.* **1** outside, outdoors, away. **2** away, absent, elsewhere, not at home, gone, abroad. **3** ended, finished, over, exhausted, used up, extinct, gone, extinguished, expired, dead. **8** revealed, exposed, disclosed, public, evident, manifest. **11** unacceptable, impossible, rejected, disallowed, forbidden, excluded. **14** unconscious, knocked out, out cold, senseless, insensible, comatose. **15** wrong, inaccurate, short. **16** existing, available, on the market. **17** in bloom, in flower, blossoming. **18** published, available. **20** out of date, unfashionable, old-fashioned, dated, passé, antiquated.

⊞ *adv., adj.* **1** in, indoors, inside. **2** in, at home. **8** secret, concealed, hidden. **11** *colloq.* on, acceptable, allowed. **15** *colloq.* spot-on, right, correct, accurate. **20** up to date, in, fashionable. **out of the way** remote, isolated, far-flung, far-off, faraway, distant, inaccessible, little-known, obscure, unfrequented.

out- *combining form* forming words meaning; **1** external; separate; from outside: *outpatient/outhouse.* **2** away from the inside, especially as a result: *output/outpouring.* **3** going away or out of; outward: *outdoor/outboard.* **4** so as to excel or surpass: *outrun/outmanoeuvre.*

outage *noun* a period of time during which a power supply fails to operate.

out-and-out *adj.* complete; thorough: *an out-and-out liar.*

outback *noun* isolated, remote areas of a country, especially Australia.

outbalance *verb* to weigh more than or be more important than.

outbid *verb* (**outbidding**; PAST TENSE AND PAST PARTICIPLE **outbid**) to offer a higher price than (someone else), especially at an auction.

outboard — *adj.* **1** *said of a motor or engine* portable and designed to be attached to the outside of a boat's stern. **2** *said of a boat* having such a motor or engine. — *adv., adj.* of, nearer, or towards the outside of a ship or aircraft. — *noun* **1** an outboard motor or engine. **2** a boat with an outboard motor or engine. See also INBOARD.

outbound *adj., said of a vehicle or passenger* going away from home, a station, etc; departing.

outbreak *noun* a sudden, usually violent beginning or occurrence, usually of something unpleasant.

⊟ eruption, outburst, explosion, flare-up, upsurge, flash, rash, burst, epidemic.

outbreeding *noun Genetics* mating between distantly related or unrelated members of a species. It results in the production of greater genetic variation among the offspring than inbreeding.

outbuilding *noun* a building such as a barn, stable or garage, that is separate from the main house but within the grounds surrounding it.

outburst *noun* **1** a sudden, violent expression of strong emotion, especially anger. **2** a sudden period of great activity.

⊟ **1** fit of temper, explosion, eruption, flare-up, outpouring, fit, seizure. **2** outbreak, burst, surge.

outcast *noun* a person who has been rejected by his or her friends or society.

⊟ reject, pariah, persona non grata, exile, outsider,

untouchable, refugee, castaway.

outcaste *noun* **1** a Hindu who has lost his or her caste. **2** a person who has no caste.

outclass *verb* to be much better than.

outcome *noun* a result or consequence.

■ result, consequence, upshot, conclusion, effect, end result.

outcrop *noun* **1** a rock or group of rocks which sticks out above the surface of the ground. **2** an appearance or occurrence.

outcry *noun* (PL. **outcries**) a widespread and public show of anger or disapproval.

■ protest, protestation, objection, dissent, indignation, complaint, uproar, cry, exclamation, clamour, row, commotion, noise, hue and cry, *colloq.* hullaballoo, outburst.

outdated *adj.* no longer useful or in fashion.

■ out of date, old-fashioned, dated, unfashionable, outmoded, behind the times, obsolete, obsolescent, antiquated, archaic.
🔁 fashionable, modern.

outdistance *verb* to leave (a competitor) far behind.

outdo *verb* (**outdoes**; PAST TENSE **outdid**; PAST PARTICIPLE **outdone**) to do much better than.

■ surpass, exceed, beat, excel, outstrip, outshine, get the better of, overcome, outclass, outdistance.

outdoor *adj.* **1** done, taking place, situated, for use, etc in the open air. **2** preferring to be in the open air: *an outdoor person.*

■ OUT OF DOOR(S), OUTSIDE, OPEN-AIR.
🔁 **1** INDOOR.

outdoors — *adv.* in or into the open air; outside a building. — *sing. noun* the open air; the world outside buildings.

outer — *adj.* **1** external; belonging to or for the outside. **2** further from the centre or middle. — *noun Archery* **1** the outermost ring on a target. **2** a shot which hits this.

■ *adj.* **1** external, exterior, outside, outward, surface, peripheral. **2** outlying, distant, remote, further.
🔁 *adj.* **1** internal. **2** inner.

outer ear *Anat.* the part of the ear that transmits sound waves from outside the ear to the eardrum in vertebrates.

outermost *adj.* nearest the edge, furthest from the centre.

outer space space beyond the earth's atmosphere.

outface *verb* **1** to stare at (someone) until they look away. **2** to fight or deal with (someone) bravely.

outfall *noun* the mouth of a river, sewer, etc where it flows into the sea.

outfield *noun* **1** *Cricket* the area of the pitch far from the part where the stumps, etc are laid out. **2** *Baseball* the area of the field beyond the diamond-shaped pitch where the bases are laid out. **3** *Cricket, Baseball* the players who have positions in this area. See also INFIELD.

outfielder *noun Cricket, Baseball* a fielder in the outfield.

outfight *verb* (PAST TENSE AND PAST PARTICIPLE **outfought**) to fight better than; to defeat.

outfit — *noun* **1** a set of clothes worn together, especially for a particular occasion. **2** a set of articles, tools, equipment, etc for a particular task. **3** *colloq.* a group of people working as a single unit or team. — *verb* (**outfitted**, **outfitting**) to provide with an outfit, especially clothes.

■ *noun* **1** clothes, costume, ensemble, *colloq.* get-up, *colloq.* togs, *colloq.* gear, garb. **2** equipment, *colloq.* gear, kit, rig, trappings, paraphernalia. **3** group, team, unit, *colloq.* set-up, organization, firm, business, corporation, company, crew, gang, squad, set.

outfitter *noun* a person who provides outfits, especially one who sells men's clothes.

outflank *verb* **1** to go round the side or sides of an enemy's position and attack from behind. **2** to get the better of, especially by a surprise action.

outflow *noun* **1** a flowing out. **2** anything that flows out. **3** the amount that flows out.

outfox *verb* to get the better of (someone) by being more cunning; to outwit.

outgoing — *adj.* **1** friendly and sociable. **2** leaving: *the outgoing president/the outgoing flight.* — *noun* (**outgoings**) money spent.

■ *adj.* **1** sociable, friendly, unreserved, amiable, warm, approachable, expansive, open, extrovert, cordial, easygoing, communicative, demonstrative, sympathetic. **2** leaving, departing, retiring, former, last, past, ex-.
🔁 *adj.* **1** reserved. **2** incoming.

outgrow *verb* (PAST TENSE **outgrew**; PAST PARTICIPLE **outgrown**) **1** to grow too large for (one's clothes). **2** to become too old for (childish ailments, children's games, etc). **3** to grow larger or faster than.

outgrowth *noun* **1** a natural product. **2** anything which grows out of something else; a by-product.

outhouse *noun* a usually small building such as a shed, etc built close to a house.

outing *noun* a short pleasure trip.

■ pleasure trip, trip, excursion, expedition, jaunt, spin, picnic.

outlandish *adj., said of appearance, manner, habit, etc* very strange; odd; queer.

■ unconventional, strange, odd, unfamiliar, bizarre, queer, weird, eccentric, alien, exotic, barbarous, foreign, extraordinary.
🔁 familiar, ordinary.

outlast *verb* to last or live longer than.

outlaw — *noun* a criminal who is a fugitive from, or deprived of the protection of, the law. — *verb* **1** to make (someone) an outlaw. **2** to forbid officially. [from Anglo-Saxon *utlaga*]

■ *noun* bandit, brigand, robber, desperado, highwayman, criminal, marauder, pirate, fugitive. *verb* **1** condemn. **2** ban, disallow, forbid, prohibit, exclude, embargo, bar, debar, banish.
🔁 *verb* **2** allow, legalize.

outlawry *noun* the state of being or act of making someone an outlaw.

outlay *noun* money, or occasionally time, spent on something.

■ expenditure, expenses, outgoings, *formal* disbursement, cost, spending.
🔁 income.

outlet *noun* **1** a way or passage out, especially for water or steam. **2** a way of releasing or using energy, talents, strong feeling, etc: *an outlet for her frustrations.* **3** a market for, or a shop that sells, the goods produced by a particular manufacturer: *an outlet for free-range eggs.* **4** *North Amer.,* *esp. US* an electrical power point.

▣ **1** exit, way out, vent, egress, escape, opening, vent. **2** release, safety valve, channel. **3** retailer, shop, store, market. **4** power point, socket.
▣ **1** entry, inlet.

outline — *noun* **1** a line forming or marking the outer edge of an object. **2** a drawing with only the outer lines and no shading. **3** the main points, etc without the details. **4** (*usually* **outlines**) the most important features of something. **5** a line representing a word in shorthand. — *verb* **1** to draw the outline of. **2** to give a brief description of the main features of.

▣ *noun* **1, 2** profile, form, contour, silhouette, shape. **3** summary, synopsis, précis, bare facts, sketch, thumbnail sketch, abstract. *verb* **2** sketch, summarize, draft, trace, rough out.

outlive /aʊt'lɪv/ *verb* **1** to live or survive longer than. **2** to survive the effects of (a disease, etc).

outlook *noun* **1** a view from a particular place. **2** a person's mental attitude or point of view. **3** a prospect for the future.

▣ **1** view, prospect, aspect, panorama. **2** view, viewpoint, point of view, attitude, perspective, frame of mind, angle, slant, standpoint, opinion. **3** prospect(s), expectations, future, forecast, prognosis.

outlying *adj.* distant; away from (a city or central area).

▣ distant, remote, far-off, faraway, far-flung, outer, provincial.
▣ inner, central.

outmanoeuvre /aʊtmə'nu:və(r)/ *verb trans.* to gain an advantage over or defeat by more skilful manoeuvring.

outmoded *adj.* no longer in fashion; out of date.

outnumber *verb* (**outnumbered, outnumbering**) to be more in number than.

outpace *verb* to walk faster than; to outstrip.

outpatient *noun* a patient who visits a hospital for treatment but does not stay there overnight.

outplay *verb* to defeat or play better than in a game or contest.

outpost *noun* **1** a group of soldiers stationed at a distance from the main body, especially to protect it from a surprise attack. **2** a distant or remote settlement or branch.

outpouring *noun* **1** (*usually* **outpourings**) a powerful or violent show of emotion. **2** the amount that pours out.

output — *noun* **1** the quantity or amount produced. **2** *Comput.* the data that is transferred from the main memory of a computer to a disk, tape, or output device such as a visual display unit or printer. **3** the power or energy produced by an electrical component or apparatus. — *verb* (**outputting**; PAST TENSE AND PAST PARTICIPLE **output**) **1** to produce (information, power, etc) as output. **2** *Comput.* to transfer (data) from the main memory of a computer to a disk or tape, or to an output device such as a visual display unit or printer.

▣ *noun* **1** yield, production, productivity. *verb* **1** produce, generate, yield.

output device *Comput.* a device that displays computer-processed data to the user in an intelligible form, eg a visual display unit (VDU), printer, or plotter.

outrage — *noun* **1** an act of great cruelty or violence. **2** an act which breaks accepted standards of morality, honour and decency. **3** great anger or resentment. — *verb* **1** to insult, shock or anger greatly. **2** to do physical violence to,

especially *euphemistic* to rape. [from Old French *outrer,* to exceed]

▣ *noun* **1** atrocity, offence, injury, enormity, barbarism, crime, violation, evil. **2** offence, violation, scandal, abuse, affront, indignity. **3** anger, resentment, fury, rage, indignation, shock, affront, horror. *verb* **1** insult, shock, anger, infuriate, affront, incense, enrage, madden, disgust, injure, offend, scandalize. **2** assault, violate.

outrageous *adj.* **1** not moderate in behaviour; extravagant. **2** greatly offensive to accepted standards of morality, honour, and decency. **3** *colloq.* terrible; shocking.

▣ **1** extravagant, excessive, exorbitant, immoderate, unreasonable, extortionate, inordinate. **2, 3** atrocious, abominable, shocking, scandalous, offensive, disgraceful, monstrous, heinous, unspeakable, horrible.
▣ **1** moderate. **2** acceptable, reasonable.

outrageously *adv.* in an outrageous way; to an outrageous degree: *outrageously expensive.*

outrank *verb* to have a higher rank than.

outré /'u:treɪ/ *adj.* not conventional; eccentric; shocking. [from French, from *outrer,* to exceed]

outride *verb* (PAST TENSE **outrode**; PAST PARTICIPLE **outridden**) **1** to ride faster than. **2** *said especially of a ship* to come safely through (a storm).

outrider *noun* an attendant or guard who rides a horse or motorcycle at the side or ahead of a carriage or car conveying an important person.

outrigger *noun* **1** a beam or framework sticking out from the side of a boat to help balance the vessel and prevent it capsizing. **2** a boat that is fitted with this sort of structure.

outright — *adv.* **1** completely: *be proved outright.* **2** immediately; at once: *killed outright.* **3** openly; honestly: *ask outright.* — *adj.* **1** complete: *an outright fool.* **2** clear: *the outright winner.* **3** open; honest: *outright disapproval.*

▣ *adv.* **1** completely, totally, absolutely, utterly, thoroughly, positively. **2** immediately, at once, instantly, instantaneously, there and then. **3** openly, honestly, straightforwardly, directly, explicitly. *adj.* **1** complete, total, utter, absolute, downright, out-and-out, unqualified, unconditional, perfect, pure, thorough. **2** clear, undisputed, unquestionable, definite. **3** open, honest, direct, straightforward.
▣ *adj.* **2** disputed, ambiguous, indefinite.

outrun *verb* (**outrunning**; PAST TENSE **outran**; PAST PARTICIPLE **outrun**) **1** to run faster or further than. **2** to do better than or exceed.

outsell *verb* (PAST TENSE AND PAST PARTICIPLE **outsold**) to sell or be sold more quickly or in greater quantities than.

outset *noun* a beginning or start.

▣ start, beginning, opening, inception, commencement, inauguration, *colloq.* kick-off.
▣ end, conclusion.

outshine *verb* (PAST TENSE AND PAST PARTICIPLE **outshone**) **1** to shine brighter than. **2** to be very much better than.

outside — *noun* **1** the outer surface; the external parts. **2** everything that is not inside or within the bounds or scope of something: *view the problem from the outside.* **3** the farthest limit. **4** the side of a pavement next to the road. — *adj.* **1** of, on, or near the outside. **2** not forming part of a group, organization, one's regular job, etc: *outside interests.* **3** unlikely; remote. **4** *said of a guess, etc* stating the highest possible amount. — *adv.* **1** on or to the outside; outdoors. **2** *slang* not in prison. — *prep.* **1** on or to the outside of. **2** beyond the limits of. **3** except; apart from. — *at*

the outside at the most. **get outside of something** *slang* to eat or drink it. **outside in** inside out (see INSIDE).

- ▣ *noun* **1** surface, face, façade, exterior, front, appearance, cover. **2** exterior. *adj.* **1** external, exterior, outer, surface, superficial, outward, extraneous, outdoor, outermost, extreme. **2** external, extramural, extraneous, peripheral. **3** unlikely, remote, marginal, distant, faint, slight, slim, negligible.
- ▣ *noun* INSIDE. *adj.* **1** inside, central.

outside broadcast a radio or television programme that is recorded or filmed somewhere other than in a studio.

outside left *Brit. Football* the position at the extreme left of the middle of the field, or a player in this position.

outside line a connection by telephone from a building to another place.

outsider *noun* **1** a person who is not part of a group, etc or who refuses to accept the general values of society. **2** *in a race, contest, etc* a competitor who is not expected to win.

- ▣ **1** stranger, intruder, alien, non-member, non-resident, foreigner, newcomer, visitor, intruder, interloper, misfit, odd man out.

outside right *Brit. Football* the position at the extreme right of the middle of the field, or a player in this position.

outsize — *adj.* (*also* **outsized**) over normal or standard size. — *noun* anything which is larger than standard, especially a garment.

outskirts *pl. noun* the outer parts or area, especially of a town or city.

- ▣ suburbs, vicinity, periphery, fringes, borders, boundary, edge, margin.
- ▣ centre.

outsmart *verb colloq.* to get the better of by being more cunning or cleverer than; to outwit.

outsource *verb trans.* to obtain (goods or parts) from, or contract work with, an outside supplier.

outspoken *adj.* saying exactly what one thinks; frank.

- ▣ candid, frank, forthright, blunt, unreserved, plain-spoken, direct, explicit.
- ▣ diplomatic, reserved.

outspokenness *noun* being outspoken.

outspread *adj., said of the arms, etc* stretched or spread out widely or fully.

outstanding *adj.* **1** excellent; superior; remarkable. **2** not yet paid, done, etc: *outstanding debts.*

- ▣ **1** excellent, superior, remarkable, distinguished, eminent, pre-eminent, celebrated, exceptional, prominent, superb, great, notable, impressive, striking, superlative, important, noteworthy, memorable, special, extraordinary. **2** owing, unpaid, due, unsettled, unresolved, uncollected, pending, payable, remaining, ongoing, left-over.
- ▣ **1** ordinary, unexceptional. **2** paid, settled.

outstare *verb* to outdo in staring; to discomfort by staring.

outstation *noun* a position, post, or station in a remote or lonely area far from towns.

outstay *verb* **1** to stay longer than the length of (one's invitation, etc): *outstay one's welcome.* **2** to stay longer than (other people).

outstretch *verb* to stretch or spread out.

outstretched *adj.* extended, proffered.

outstrip *verb* (**outstripped, outstripping**) **1** to go faster than. **2** to leave behind; to surpass.

- ▣ **1** outrun, gain on. **2** leave behind, leave standing, overtake, pass, outdistance, outrun, surpass, exceed, better, outdo, beat, top, transcend, outshine, eclipse.

outtake *noun Cinema* a sequence of film removed from the final edited version of a motion picture or video. These include any takes which have had to be repeated during filming because of errors or technical problems, and any sequences that are discarded.

out-tray *noun* a shallow basket used in offices for letters, etc that are ready to be sent out.

outvote *verb* to defeat by a majority of votes.

outward — *adj.* **1** on or towards the outside. **2** *said of a journey* away from a place. **3** apparent or seeming: *outward appearances.* — *adv.* (*also* **outwards**) towards the outside; in an outward direction.

- ▣ *adj.* **1** external, exterior, outer, outside, surface, superficial. **3** apparent, seeming, supposed, professed, superficial, public, visible, observable, evident, ostensible.
- ▣ *adj.* **1** internal, interior, inner, inside. **2** return, homeward. **3** inner, private. *adv.* inward(s).

outwardly *adv.* in appearance; on the outside.

- ▣ apparently, externally, on the surface, at first sight, to all appearances, visibly, superficially, supposedly, seemingly.

outweigh *verb* to be greater than in weight, value or importance.

- ▣ *value, importance* override, prevail over, overcome, take precedence over, cancel out, make up for, compensate for, predominate.

outwit *verb* (**outwitted, outwitting**) to get the better of or defeat by being cleverer than.

- ▣ get the better of, outsmart, trick, better, beat, dupe.

outwith *prep. Scot.* outside; beyond.

outwork *noun* **1** (*usually* **outworks**) a defence work that is outside the main line of fortifications. **2** work done for a company, factory or shop by employees who work at home.

outworker *noun* a person who is commissioned to do outwork.

outworn *adj.* no longer useful or in fashion; out of date.

- ▣ rejected, obsolete, disused, outdated, out of date, outmoded, stale, discredited, defunct, old-fashioned, hackneyed, exhausted.
- ▣ fresh, new.

ouzel /'uːzl/ *noun* **1** (*also* **ring ouzel**) a thrush with a broad white band across its throat. **2** (*also* **water ouzel**) a small aquatic songbird; a dipper.

ouzo /'uːzoʊ/ *noun* (PL. **ouzos**) a Greek alcoholic drink, flavoured with aniseed and usually diluted with water. [from Modern Greek *ouzon*]

ova see OVUM.

oval — *adj.* shaped like an egg. — *noun* any egg-shaped figure or object. [from Latin *ovum*, egg]

- ▣ *adj.* egg-shaped, elliptical, ovoid.

oval window *Anat.* the upper of two membrane-covered openings between the middle ear and the inner ear in vertebrates. Also called FENESTRA OVALIS.

ovarian /oʊˈvɛərɪən/ *adj.* relating to or in the region of an ovary or ovaries.

ovarian follicle *Anat.* see GRAAFIAN FOLLICLE.

ovary *noun* (PL. **ovaries**) **1** in a female animal, the reproductive organ in which the ova (eggs) are produced. In vertebrates there are two ovaries, and they also produce the sex hormones. **2** in plants, the enlarged hollow base of the carpel of a flower, which contains one or more ovules. After fertilization the wall of the ovary develops into a fruit which contains one or more seeds. [from Latin *ovum*, egg]

ovation *noun* cheering or applause, etc to express approval, welcome, etc. [from Latin *ovare*, to exult]

. . . .

🄴 applause, acclaim, acclamation, praise, plaudits, tribute, clapping, cheering, bravos.
🄵 abuse, catcalls.

. . . .

oven *noun* an enclosed compartment which may be heated for baking or roasting food, or drying clay, etc. [from Anglo-Saxon *ofen*]

ovenproof *adj.*, *said of dishes, plates, etc* that will not crack at a high temperature.

oven-ready *adj.*, *said of food* prepared and only needing to be cooked.

ovenware *noun* heat-resistant dishes for use in ovens.

over — *adv.* **1** above and across. **2** outwards and downwards: *knock him over/the kettle boiled over.* **3** across a space; to or on the other side: *fly over from Australia.* **4** from one person, side, or condition to another: *win them over/turn the card over.* **5** through, from beginning to end, usually with concentration: *read the letter over/think it over thoroughly.* **6** again; in repetition: *do it twice over.* **7** at an end. **8** so as to cover completely: *paper the cracks over.* **9** beyond a limit; in excess. **10** remaining: *left over.* **11** until a later time: *hold payment over until February.* — *prep.* **1** in or to a position which is above or higher in place, importance, authority, value, number, etc. **2** above and from one side to another: *fly over the sea.* **3** so as to cover: *hair flopping over his eyes.* **4** out and down from: *fall over the edge.* **5** throughout the extent of: *read over that page again.* **6** during: *visit him sometime over the weekend.* **7** until after: *stay over Monday night.* **8** more than: *over a year ago.* **9** concerning; about: *argue over who would pay.* **10** while occupied with: *chat about it over coffee.* **11** occupying time with: *spend a day over the preparations.* **12** recovered from the effects of: *be over the accident.* **13** by means of: *hear about it over the radio.* **14** divided by. — *adj.* **1** upper; higher. **2** outer. **3** excessive. See also OVER-. — *interj.* used during two-way radio conversations to show that one has finished speaking and expects a reply. — *noun* Cricket **1** a series of six or eight balls bowled by the same bowler from the same end of the pitch. **2** play during such a series of balls. — **be all over someone** to make a great fuss of them, often ingratiatingly. **over again** once more. **over against something** opposite it; in contrast with it. **over and above something** in addition to it. **over and over again** repeatedly. **over head and ears** completely submerged. **over the top** *colloq.* excessive. [from Anglo-Saxon *ofer*]

. . . .

🄴 *adv.* **1** above, overhead, on high, beyond. **4** round. **7** finished, ended, done with, concluded, past, gone, completed, closed, in the past, settled, accomplished. **9** in excess, in addition, beyond. **10** remaining, extra, surplus, superfluous, left, unclaimed, unused, unwanted. *prep.* **1** above, on, on top of, upon, *authority* in charge of, in command of. **2** across. **5** through. **6** during, in the course of. **8** more than, exceeding, in excess of. **9** concerning, about, regarding, with regard to, with respect to. **10** during. **11**, **13** on.

. . . .

over- *combining form* forming words meaning: **1** excessively: *overconfident.* **2** above; in a higher position or authority: *overlord.* **3** across the surface; covering: *overcoat.* **4** down; away from an upright position: *overturn/ overhang.* **5** completely: *overwhelm.*

overact *verb intrans.*, *trans.* to act (a part) with too much expression or emotion.

. . . .

🄴 overplay, exaggerate, overdo, *colloq.* ham.
🄵 underact, underplay.

. . . .

over-age *adj.* **1** beyond a specified age limit. **2** too old.

overall — *noun* **1** *Brit.* a loose-fitting, coat-like garment worn over ordinary clothes to protect them. **2** (**overalls**) a one-piece garment with trousers to cover the legs and either a dungaree-type top, or top with sleeves, worn to protect clothes. — *adj.* **1** including everything: *the overall total.* **2** from end to end: *the overall length.* — *adv.* as a whole; in general.

. . . .

🄴 *adj.* TOTAL. **1** all-inclusive, all-embracing, comprehensive, inclusive, general, universal, global, broad, blanket, complete, all-over. *adv.* as a whole, in general, on the whole, by and large, broadly, generally speaking.

. . . .

over-anxious *adj.* excessively solicitous or eager (especially to please).

overarm *adj.*, *adv.* bowled or thrown with the hand and arm raised over and moving round the shoulder.

overawe *verb* to make silent by filling with awe, fear, or astonishment.

overbalance *verb intrans.*, *trans.* to lose or cause to lose one's balance and fall.

overbearing *adj.* **1** domineering; too powerful and proud. **2** of particularly great importance.

. . . .

🄴 **1** domineering, imperious, arrogant, dictatorial, tyrannical, high-handed, haughty, *colloq.* bossy, cavalier, autocratic, oppressive.
🄵 meek, unassertive.

. . . .

overblown *adj.* **1** self-important and pretentious. **2** *said of flowers* past their best; beginning to die.

overboard *adv.* over the side of a ship or boat into the water. — **go overboard** *colloq.* to be very or too enthusiastic. **throw something** or **someone overboard** to abandon or get rid of them.

overbook *verb trans.*, *intrans.* to make or allow more reservations for (an aircraft, restaurant, etc) than there are seats available.

overburden *verb* (**overburdened**, **overburdening**) to give (someone) too much to do, carry, or think about.

overburdened *adj.* having too great a burden; overworked.

overcast /oʊvəˈkɑːst, ˈoʊvəkɑːst/ *adj.*, *said of the sky* cloudy.

. . . .

🄴 cloudy, grey, dull, dark, sombre, sunless, hazy, lowering.
🄵 bright, clear.

. . . .

overcharge *verb* **1** *trans.*, *intrans.* to charge too much. **2** to fill or load with too much.

. . . .

🄴 **1** surcharge, short-change, cheat, extort, *colloq.* rip off, *slang* sting, *colloq.* do, *colloq.* diddle.
🄵 **1** undercharge.

. . . .

overcloud *verb* **1** *trans.*, *intrans.* to cover, or become covered, with clouds. **2** to make sad or worried.

overcoat *noun* a warm, heavy coat worn in winter.

overcome *verb* (PAST TENSE **overcame**; PAST PARTICIPLE **overcome**) **1** to defeat; to succeed in a struggle against; to deal successfully with. **2** *intrans.* to be victorious. **3** to affect strongly; to overwhelm: *overcome with sleep.* [from Anglo-Saxon *ofercuman*]

. . . .

🄴 **1** conquer, defeat, beat, surmount, triumph over, vanquish, rise above, master, overpower, overwhelm, overthrow,

subdue. **2** win, succeed, triumph.
. . . .

over-confident *adj.* excessively confident in one's abilities or personal attributes.

overcrowd *verb* to cause too many people or things to be in (a place).

overcrowded *adj.* too full of people or things.
. . . .

▣ congested, packed (out), *colloq.* jam-packed, crammed full, chock-full, overpopulated, overloaded, swarming.

▣ deserted, empty.
. . . .

overcrowding *noun* **1** being overcrowded. **2** filling with too many people, etc.

overdo *verb* (**overdoes**; PAST TENSE **overdid**; PAST PARTICIPLE **overdone**) **1** to do too much; to exaggerate. **2** to cook for too long. **3** to use too much of. — **overdo it** to work too hard.
. . . .

▣ **1** exaggerate, go too far, carry to excess, *colloq.* go overboard, *colloq.* lay it on thick, overindulge, overstate, overact, overplay, overwork. **3** *colloq.* go overboard with.
. . . .

overdose — *noun* an excessive dose of a drug, etc. — *verb intrans.* to take an overdose.

overdraft *noun* **1** a state in which one has taken more money out of one's bank account than was in it. **2** the excess of money taken from one's account over the sum that was in it.

overdraw *verb* (PAST TENSE **overdrew**; PAST PARTICIPLE **overdrawn**) **1** (*trans., intrans.*) to draw more money from (one's bank account) than one has in it. **2** to exaggerate in describing.

overdrawn *adj.* having an overdraft at a bank.

overdress *verb trans., intrans.* to dress or be dressed in clothes that are too formal, smart, or expensive for the occasion.

overdressed *adj.* wearing clothes that are too formal for the occasion.

overdrive *noun* an additional very high gear in a motor vehicle's gear box, which reduces wear on the engine and saves fuel when travelling at high speeds.

overdue /ouvə'dju:/ *adj., said of bills, work, etc* not yet paid, done, delivered, etc although the date for doing this has passed.
. . . .

▣ late, behindhand, behind schedule, delayed, owing, unpunctual, slow.

▣ early, punctual.
. . . .

over-emotional *adj.* given to displays of excessive or inappropriate emotion.

overestimate — *verb* (pronounced -meɪt) to estimate, judge, etc too highly. — *noun* (pronounced -mət) too high an estimate.

overestimation *noun* **1** overestimating. **2** an overestimate.

overexert *verb* to force (oneself) to work too hard.

overexertion *noun* excessive work or effort.

overexpose *verb* **1** to expose to too much publicity. **2** to expose (photographic film) to too much light.

overexposure *noun* excessive exposure, especially to publicity.

overfishing *noun* the removal of so many fish from a sea, river, etc that the numbers of fish can no longer be maintained by breeding, and populations of particular species become much reduced or even rare.

overflow — *verb* (with stress on *-flow*) (**overflowed**, **overflowing**) **1** to flow over (a brim) or go beyond (the limits or edge of). **2** *intrans.* to be filled so full that the contents spill over or out. **3** *intrans.* (**overflow with something**) to be full of it: *was overflowing with gratitude.* — *noun* (with stress on *over-*) **1** that which overflows. **2** the

act of flowing over. **3** a pipe or outlet for spare water. [from Anglo-Saxon *oferflowan*]
. . . .

▣ *verb* **1** spill, overrun, run over, pour over, well over, brim over, bubble over, surge, flood, inundate, deluge, shower, submerge, soak, swamp, teem. **2** flood, brim, teem. **3** brim with, teem with. *noun* **1** overspill, spill, inundation, flood, overabundance, surplus. **2** spilling, overspill, flooding. **3** overspill.
. . . .

overgrown /ouvə'groun/ *adj.* **1** *said of a garden, etc* dense with plants that have grown too large and thick. **2** grown too large.

overhand *adj., adv.* thrown, done, etc with the hand brought down from above the shoulder.

overhang — *verb* (with stress on *-hang*) (PAST TENSE AND PAST PARTICIPLE **overhung**) **1** *trans., intrans.* to project or hang out over. **2** to threaten. — *noun* (with stress on *over-*) **1** a piece of rock, part of a roof, etc that overhangs. **2** the amount by which something overhangs.
. . . .

▣ *verb* **1** jut, project, bulge, protrude, stick out, extend.
. . . .

overhaul — *verb* **1** to examine carefully and repair. **2** to catch up with and pass. — *noun* a thorough examination and repair.
. . . .

▣ *verb* **1** recondition, renovate, repair, service, mend, examine, inspect, check, survey, re-examine, fix. **2** overtake, pull ahead of, outpace, outstrip, gain on, pass. *noun* reconditioning, repair, renovation, check, service, examination, inspection, *colloq.* going-over.
. . . .

overhead — *adv., adj.* above; over one's head. — *noun* (**overheads**) the regular costs of a business, such as rent, wages and electricity.
. . . .

▣ *adv.* above, up above, on high, upward. *adj.* elevated, aerial, overhanging, raised.

▣ *adv.* below, underfoot.
. . . .

overhead projector a projector which sits on the speaker's desk and projects images on a screen behind it.

overhear *verb trans., intrans.* (PAST TENSE AND PAST PARTICIPLE **overheard**) to hear (someone or something) without the speaker knowing, either by accident or on purpose.

overheat *verb* to make or become too hot.

overheated *adj., said of an argument, discussion, etc* angry and excited; passionate.

overjoyed *adj.* very glad; elated.
. . . .

▣ elated, delighted, euphoric, ecstatic, in raptures, enraptured, thrilled, jubilant, *colloq.* over the moon.

▣ sad, disappointed, depressed.
. . . .

overkill *noun* **1** action, behaviour, treatment, etc which is far in excess of what is required. **2** the capability to destroy an enemy using a larger force than is actually needed to win a victory.

overladen *adj.* overloaded.

overland *adv., adj., said of a journey, etc* across land.

overlap — *verb* (with stress on *-lap*) (**overlapped**, **overlapping**) **1** *said of part of an object* to partly cover (another object). **2** *intrans., said of two parts* to have one part partly covering the other. **3** *intrans., said of two things* to have something in common; to partly coincide. — *noun* (with stress on *over-*) an overlapping part.

overlay — *verb* (PAST TENSE AND PAST PARTICIPLE **overlaid**) (**overlay one thing with another**) to cover it with a usually thin layer of something else, especially for decoration. — *noun* something that is laid over something else, especially for decoration.

overleaf *adv.* on the other side of the page.

overlie *verb* (**overlying**; PAST TENSE **overlay**; PAST PARTI-CIPLE **overlain**) **1** to lie on. **2** to smother and kill (a baby or small animal) by lying on it.

overload — *verb* (with stress on -*load*) **1** to load too heavily. **2** to put too great an electric current through (a circuit). — *noun* (with stress on *over-*) too great an electric current flowing through a circuit.

. . . .

◼ *verb* **1** burden, weigh down, overcharge, encumber, oppress, strain, tax.

. . . .

overlook *verb* **1** to give a view of by being opposite or above. **2** to fail to see or notice. **3** to allow (a mistake, crime, etc) to go unpunished. **4** to supervise.

. . . .

◼ **1** front on to, face, look on to, look over, command a view of. **2** miss, disregard, ignore. **3** excuse, forgive, pardon, condone, wink at, turn a blind eye to, pass over, let pass, let ride.
◻ **2** notice. **3** penalize, condemn.

. . . .

overlord *noun* a lord or ruler with supreme power.

overly *adv. formal* too much; excessively.

overmuch *adv.*, *adj.* too much.

overnice *adj.* fussy, critical, and hard to please.

overnight — *adv.* **1** during the night. **2** for the duration of the night. **3** suddenly. — *adj.* **1** done or occurring in the night. **2** sudden: *an overnight success*. **3** for use overnight: *an overnight case*.

overnight bag a small grip or case for carrying the clothes, toilet articles, etc needed for an overnight stay.

overpass *noun North Amer.*, *esp. US* same as FLYOVER.

overplay *verb* to exaggerate or overemphasize. — **overplay one's hand** to overestimate or overtax one's talents, assets, etc.

overpower *verb trans.* (**overpowered**, **overpowering**) **1** to defeat by greater strength. **2** to weaken or reduce to helplessness.

. . . .

◼ OVERCOME, OVERWHELM. **1** conquer, vanquish, defeat, beat, subdue, overthrow, quell, master. **2** crush, immobilize, *colloq.* floor.

. . . .

overpowering *adj.* very great; overwhelming.

. . . .

◼ overwhelming, powerful, strong, forceful, irresistible, uncontrollable, compelling, extreme, oppressive, suffocating, unbearable.

. . . .

overprint — *verb* to print over (something already printed, eg a stamp). — *noun* extra material printed on top of something printed, eg a stamp.

overrate *verb* to think too highly of.

. . . .

◼ overestimate, overvalue, overpraise, magnify, *colloq.* blow up, make too much of.
◻ underrate.

. . . .

overreach *verb* **1** to defeat (oneself) by trying to do too much, be too clever, etc. **2** *intrans.*, *said of a horse* to strike the hind foot against the forefoot.

overreact *verb intrans.* (**overreact to something**) to react too strongly to it.

overreaction *noun* a too strong reaction.

override — *verb* (with stress on -*ride*) (PAST TENSE **overrode**; PAST PARTICIPLE **overridden**) **1** to annul or set aside, especially to cancel the functioning of (eg an automatic control). **2** to be of more importance than. — *noun* (with stress on *over-*) the process or a means of overriding.

overriding *adj.* dominant; most important: *overriding considerations*.

overrule *verb* **1** to rule against or cancel (especially a previous decision or judgement) by higher authority. **2** to impose a decision on (a person) by higher authority.

. . . .

◼ **1** overturn, override, countermand, revoke, reject, rescind, reverse, invalidate, cancel, vote down, outvote. **2** vote down, outvote.

. . . .

overrun *verb* (**overrunning**; PAST TENSE **overran**; PAST PARTICIPLE **overrun**) **1** to spread over or through (something); to infest. **2** to invade and take possession of (another country) quickly and by force. **3** *trans.*, *intrans.* to go beyond (a fixed limit): *overrun the budget for the job.* [from Anglo-Saxon *oferyrnan*]

. . . .

◼ **1** invade, occupy, infest, overwhelm, inundate, run riot, spread over, swamp, swarm over, surge over, ravage, overgrow. **2** invade, occupy, conquer. **3** exceed, overshoot, overstep, overreach.

. . . .

overseas — *adv.* abroad. — *adj.* (*also* **oversea**) across or from beyond the sea; foreign.

oversee *verb* (PAST TENSE **oversaw**; PAST PARTICIPLE **overseen**) to supervise.

overseer *noun* a person who oversees workers, a supervisor.

. . . .

◼ supervisor, *colloq.* boss, chief, foreman, forewoman, manager, superintendent.

. . . .

oversell *verb* (PAST TENSE AND PAST PARTICIPLE **oversold**) **1** (*trans.*, *intrans.*) to sell at too high a price or in greater quantities than can be supplied. **2** to praise too highly.

oversew *verb* (PAST TENSE **oversewed**; PAST PARTICIPLE **oversewn**, **oversewed**) to sew (two edges) with close stitches that pass over both edges.

oversexed *adj.* having unusually strong sexual urges.

overshadow *verb* **1** to seem much more important than. **2** to cast a shadow over; to make seem more gloomy. [from Anglo-Saxon *ofersceadian*]

. . . .

◼ **1** surpass, eclipse, excel, dominate, outshine, dwarf, put in the shade, rise above, tower above. **2** obscure, cloud, darken, dim, spoil.

. . . .

overshoe *noun* a shoe, usually made of rubber or plastic, worn over a normal shoe to protect it in wet weather.

overshoot *verb* (PAST TENSE AND PAST PARTICIPLE **overshot**) to go farther than (a target aimed at). — **overshoot the mark** to make a mistake as a result of misjudging a situation.

oversight *noun* a mistake made through a failure to notice something.

. . . .

◼ lapse, omission, fault, error, *colloq.* slip-up, mistake, blunder, carelessness, neglect.

. . . .

oversimplification *noun* oversimplifying, or an instance of this.

oversimplify *verb trans.*, *intrans.* (**oversimplifies**, **oversimplified**) to simplify (something) so much as to cause a mistake or distortion.

oversleep *verb intrans.* (PAST TENSE AND PAST PARTICIPLE **overslept**) to sleep longer than one intended.

overspend — *verb intrans.* (with stress on -*spend*) (PAST TENSE AND PAST PARTICIPLE **overspent**) to spend too much money. — *noun* (with stress on *over-*) an amount overspent.

overspill *noun Brit.* the people leaving an overcrowded or derelict town area to live elsewhere.

overstate *verb* to state too strongly or with unnecessary emphasis.

overstatement *noun* exaggeration, or an instance of this.

overstay *verb* to stay longer than the length of (one's invitation, etc): *overstay one's welcome*.

oversteer *verb intrans., said of a vehicle* to turn more sharply than the driver intends.

overstep *verb* (**overstepped**, **overstepping**) — **overstep the mark** to go beyond what is prudent or reasonable.

overstretched *adj.* stretched too far; extended to the limit.

overstrung *adj.* too sensitive and nervous; tense.

oversubscribe *verb* to apply for or try to purchase in larger quantities than are available.

oversubscribed *adj.* having too few shares, places, etc to meet demand.

overt *adj.* not hidden or secret; open; public. [from Old French *ovrir*, to open]

. . . .
🔳 open, public, manifest, plain, evident, observable, obvious, apparent, professed, unconcealed.
🔳 covert, secret.
. . . .

overtake *verb* (PAST TENSE **overtook**; PAST PARTICIPLE **overtaken**) **1** *trans., intrans. chiefly Brit.* to catch up with and go past (a car, a person, etc) moving in the same direction. **2** to draw level with and begin to do better than. **3** to come upon (someone) suddenly or without warning: *overtaken by the bad weather*.

. . . .
🔳 **1, 2** pass, catch up with, outdistance, outstrip, draw level with, pull ahead of, overhaul. **3** come upon, happen to, strike, engulf, befall.
. . . .

overtax *verb* **1** to put too great a strain on (someone or oneself.) **2** to demand too much tax from.

overthrow — *verb* (with stress on *-throw*) (PAST TENSE **overthrew**; PAST PARTICIPLE **overthrown**) **1** to defeat completely. **2** to upset or overturn. — *noun* (with stress on *over-*) **1** a defeat or downfall. **2** *Cricket* an inaccurate return of the ball by a fielder which often allows the batsman to score extra runs.

. . . .
🔳 *verb* **1** defeat, conquer, vanquish, beat, crush, overcome, overpower, overturn, overwhelm, subdue, master, depose, oust, bring down, topple, unseat, displace, dethrone, abolish. **2** upset, overturn, topple, bring down. *noun* **1** defeat, downfall, fall, rout, undoing, suppression, end, ousting, unseating, deposition, dethronement, humiliation, destruction, ruin.
🔳 *verb* **1** install, protect, reinstate, restore.
. . . .

overtime — *noun* **1** time spent working at one's job beyond one's regular hours. **2** the money paid for this extra time. — *adv.* in addition to one's regular hours.

overtly *adv.* in an overt way.

overtone *noun* **1** (*usually* **overtones**) a subtle hint, quality, or meaning: *political overtones*. **2** *Mus.* a tone that contributes towards the musical sound and adds to its quality. [from German *Oberton*]

. . . .
🔳 **1** hint, suggestion, intimation, nuance, undercurrent, insinuation, connotation, association, feeling, implication, sense, flavour.
. . . .

overture *noun* **1** an orchestral introduction to an opera, oratorio or ballet. **2** (*usually* **overtures**) a proposal or offer intended to open a discussion. [from Old French, = opening]

. . . .
🔳 **1** prelude, opening, introduction. **2** opening move, (opening) gambit, proposal, offer, approach, advance, invitation, proposition, suggestion, signal, move, motion.
. . . .

overturn *verb* **1** *trans., intrans.* to turn or be turned over or upside down. **2** to bring down or destroy (a government). **3** to overrule or cancel (a previous legal decision).

. . . .
🔳 **1** capsize, upset, upturn, tip over, topple, overbalance, keel over, knock over, spill. **2** overthrow, bring down, topple, oust. **3** overrule, cancel, repeal, rescind, reverse, annul, abolish, destroy, quash, set aside.
. . . .

overview *noun* a brief general account or description.

overweening *adj.* **1** *said of a person* arrogant. **2** *said of pride* inflated and excessive.

overweight *adj.* above the desired, required, or usual weight.

overwhelm *verb* **1** to crush mentally; to overpower (a person's) emotions, thoughts, etc. **2** to defeat by superior force or numbers. **3** to supply or offer something in great amounts: *to be overwhelmed with offers of help*.

. . . .
🔳 **1** *colloq.* floor, *colloq.* bowl over, stagger, confuse. **2** defeat, overcome, overpower, destroy, crush, rout, devastate. **3** inundate, snow under, submerge, swamp, engulf, overrun.
. . . .

overwhelming *adj.* physically or mentally crushing; intensely powerful.

overwhelmingly *adv.* in an overwhelming way; so as to overwhelm.

overwork — *verb* **1** *intrans.* to work too hard. **2** to make (someone) work too hard. **3** to make too much use of. — *noun* the act of working too hard.

. . . .
🔳 *verb* **2** overload, overtax, exploit, exhaust, oppress, burden, weary. **3** overuse, overload, overtax, overstrain, strain, wear out.
. . . .

overworked *adj.* having too much work to do.

overwrite *verb* (PAST TENSE **overwrote**; PAST PARTICIPLE **overwritten**) **1** *Comput.* to write new information over (existing data), thereby destroying it. **2** to write excessively.

overwrought /oʊvəˈrɔːt/ *adj.* very nervous or excited; over-emotional.

. . . .
🔳 tense, excited, agitated, keyed up, on edge, worked up, wound up, frantic, overcharged, overexcited, beside oneself, *colloq.* uptight.
🔳 calm.
. . . .

oviduct *noun* the tube which carries the egg from the ovary. [from Latin *ovum*, egg + *ducere*, to lead]

oviform *adj.* egg-shaped. [from Latin *ovum*, egg + -FORM]

ovine *adj.* of or like sheep. [from Latin *ovis*, sheep]

oviparity *noun* *Zool.* the laying of fertilized eggs which hatch outside the body of a female animal. [from Latin *ovum*, egg + *parere*, to bring forth]

oviparous /oʊˈvɪpərəs/ *adj., said of birds, fish, etc* producing eggs which hatch outside the mother's body. See also VIVIPAROUS. [from Latin *ovum*, egg + *parere*, to produce]

ovipositor *noun* *Zool.* in female insects, the egg-laying organ, which is often long and tube-like, at the rear end of the abdomen. [from Latin *ovum*, egg + *positor*, from *ponere*, to place]

ovoid — *adj.* egg-shaped. — *noun* an egg-shaped form or object. [from Latin *ovum*, egg + -OID]

ovoviviparous *adj.* *Zool.* describing certain fish and reptiles, and many insects, in which the fertilized eggs hatch within the body of the female. The developing embryo is retained within the body of the mother, and derives nutrients from a yolk store instead of a placenta. [from Latin *ovum*, egg + VIVIPAROUS]

ovulate *verb intrans.* to produce eggs from the ovary. [from Latin *ovulum*, diminutive of *ovum*, egg]

ovulation noun **1** the production and release of eggs in an ovary. **2** an instance of this.

ovule noun Bot. in flowering and cone-bearing plants, the structure that develops into a seed after fertilization. It consists of a mass of tissue (the *nucellus*) containing the embryo sac, surrounded by one or two protective layers (*integuments*), which develop into the seed coat. [from Latin *ovulum*, diminutive of *ovum*, egg]

ovum noun (PL. **ova**) Biol. an unfertilized egg or egg cell produced by the ovary of an animal; a female gamete. [from Latin *ovum*, egg]

ow interj. used to express sudden, usually mild, pain.

owe verb **1** trans., intrans. to be under an obligation to pay (money) to (someone). **2** to feel required by duty or gratitude to do or give: *owe you an explanation.* **3** to have or enjoy as a result of: *owe her promotion to her hard work.* [from Anglo-Saxon *agan*, to own]

owing adj. still to be paid; due. — **owing to something** because of it; on account of it: *trains will be delayed owing to bad weather.*

▣ unpaid, due, owed, in arrears, outstanding, payable, unsettled, overdue. **owing to** because of, on account of, as a result of.

owl noun any nocturnal bird of prey belonging to the order Strigiformes, found in all parts of the world except Antarctica, and having a large broad head, a flat face, large forward-facing eyes, and a short hooked beak. It is noted for its hooting call. [from Anglo-Saxon *ule*]

owlet noun a young owl.

owlish adj. **1** like an owl. **2** solemn or wise.

own — adj., often used for emphasis belonging to or for oneself or itself: *my own sister.* — pron. one or something belonging to oneself or itself: *have a room of one's own.* — verb **1** to have as a possession or property. **2** (**own something** or **own to something**) to admit or confess it: *one should own one's faults/owned to many weaknesses.* — **get one's own back on someone** colloq. to get even with them; to have one's revenge. **on one's own 1** alone. **2** without help. **own up to something** to admit a wrongdoing, etc. [from Anglo-Saxon *agen*]

▣ adj. personal, individual, private, particular, idiosyncratic. verb **1** possess, have, hold, retain, keep, enjoy. **2** admit, confess, acknowledge. **own up to** admit, confess, colloq. come clean, tell the truth, acknowledge.

owner noun a person who owns something.

▣ possessor, holder, landlord, landlady, proprietor, proprietress, master, mistress, freeholder.

owner-occupier noun a person who owns the property he or she is living in.

ownership noun **1** the status of owner. **2** legal right or possession.

own goal 1 a goal scored by mistake for the opposing side. **2** colloq. a move that turns out to be to the disadvantage of the person who took it.

ox noun (PL. **oxen**) **1** any common domestic cattle, both bulls and cows, used for pulling loads, or supplying meat and milk. **2** a castrated bull. [from Anglo-Saxon *oxa*]

oxalic acid Chem. (FORMULA (COOH)$_2$) a highly poisonous white crystalline solid that occurs in the leaves of rhubarb, wood sorrel, and certain other plants, and is also excreted in the form of crystals by many fungi. It is used as a rust and stain remover, and in tanning and bleaching. Also called ETHANEDIOIC ACID. [from Greek *oxalis*, wood sorrel]

oxbow lake Geol. a shallow curved lake found on a flat floodplain alongside a meandering river, and formed when one of the meanders has been cut off from the river as a result of the formation of a stream across the neck of the bend, which shortens the course of the river.

Oxbridge noun Brit. the universities of Oxford and Cambridge considered together and usually in contrast to other universities.

oxen see OX.

oxeye daisy a daisy with long white petals and a dark yellow centre.

OXFAM in the UK, a charity based in Oxford, founded as the Oxford Committee for Famine Relief (1942). It is dedicated to alleviating poverty and distress throughout the world, mainly through long-term development aid in Third World countries.

oxidant noun **1** Chem. an oxidizing agent. **2** Engineering a chemical compound, usually containing oxygen, that is mixed with fuel and burned in the combustion chamber of a rocket.

oxidase /'ɒksɪdeɪz/ noun Biochem. any of a group of enzymes that catalyse oxidation in plant and animal cells.

oxidation noun Chem. a chemical reaction that involves the addition of oxygen to or the removal of hydrogen from a substance, which loses electrons. It is always accompanied by *reduction*. Both combustion and corrosion, such as rusting, are examples of processes involving oxidation. See also REDUCTION.

oxide noun Chem. a compound of oxygen and another element. [from French, from *oxygène*, oxygen]

oxidization or **oxidisation** noun the process of oxidizing.

oxidize or **oxidise** verb trans., intrans. Chem. **1** to combine with oxygen. **2** to make or become rusty.

oxidizing agent Chem. any substance that oxidizes another substance in a chemical reaction, and is itself reduced in the process, by accepting electrons.

oxlip noun **1** a naturally occurring hybrid of the common primrose (*Primula vulgaris*) and the cowslip (*Primula veris*), with deep yellow flowers that are not borne in a one-sided cluster. Also called FALSE OXLIP. **2** the true oxlip (*Primula elatior*), which is a separate species from the primrose and cowslip, and has pale yellow flowers borne in a one-sided cluster.

Oxon abbrev. **1** Oxfordshire. **2** especially in degree titles Oxford University. [from Latin *Oxoniensis*, of Oxford]

Oxonian — noun **1** an inhabitant of Oxford. **2** a student or graduate of Oxford University. — adj. of Oxford or Oxford University. [from Latin *Oxonia*, Oxford]

oxtail noun the tail of an ox, used especially in soups and stews.

oxyacetylene /ɒksɪə'setɪliːn/ noun a mixture of oxygen and acetylene, which burns at a very high temperature, and is used for cutting and welding metals. [from OXYGEN + ACETYLENE]

oxygen noun (SYMBOL O, ATOMIC NUMBER 8) a colourless odourless tasteless gas, produced by photosynthesis, and an essential requirement of most forms of plant and animal life. It is the most abundant element in the Earth's crust, and constitutes about 21% (by volume) of the Earth's atmosphere. [from Greek *oxys*, sharp + *gennaein*, to generate, from the old belief that all acids contained oxygen]

oxygenate verb **1** to supply (eg the blood) with oxygen. **2** to treat with oxygen.

oxygenation noun **1** Physiol. the recharging of the blood with oxygen from air inhaled into the lungs. **2** Chem. treatment with or combination with oxygen.

oxygenator noun an apparatus that oxygenates the blood, especially while a patient is being operated on.

oxygen debt a temporary loss of oxygen from the body during very active exercise.

oxygen mask a mask through which oxygen is supplied from a tank.

oxygen tent a tent-like apparatus erected over a patient's bed, into which oxygen can be pumped to help his or her breathing.

oxyhaemoglobin /ɒksɪˈhiːməɡloʊbɪn/ *noun Biochem.* the red compound formed in blood by the combination of oxygen and the pigment haemoglobin as a result of respiration.

oxymoron /ɒksɪˈmɔːrɒn/ *noun* a figure of speech in which contradictory terms are used together: *holy cruel.* [from Greek *oxymoros*, from *oxys*, sharp + *moros*, foolish]

oxytocin /ɒksɪˈtoʊsɪn/ *noun Medicine* a hormone, released by the pituitary gland, that induces contractions of the smooth muscle of the uterus during labour, and stimulates the flow of milk from the breasts during suckling. A synthetic form of the hormone is used to accelerate labour by inducing uterine contractions. [from Greek *oxys*, sharp + *tokos*, birth]

oyez or **oyes** /oʊˈjeɪ/ *interj. Hist.* a cry for silence and attention, usually shouted three times by an official before a public announcement or in a court of law. [from Old French *oir*, to hear]

oyster *noun* 1 the common name for a marine bivalve mollusc belonging to the family Ostreidae, and having a soft fleshy body enclosed by a hinged shell. The fleshy part is a popular sea food. 2 the pale greyish beige or pink colour of an oyster. — **the world is one's oyster** one has everything one needs or wants within one's grasp. [from Greek *ostreon*]

oyster bed a place where oysters breed or are bred.

oystercatcher *noun* a black and white wading bird with a long orange-red beak, that feeds on mussels and limpets (but not oysters).

Oz *noun slang* Australia.

oz *abbrev.* ounce. [from Italian *onza*, ounce]

ozone *noun* 1 *Chem.* (FORMULA O$_3$) a pungent unstable bluish gas that is an allotrope of oxygen, and contains three oxygen atoms in its molecule. 2 *colloq.* fresh, bracing sea air. [from Greek *ozein*, to smell]

ozone-friendly *adj.* denoting a product that does not contain chemicals that deplete the ozone layer, eg chlorofluorocarbons.

ozone layer a layer of the upper atmosphere, between 15 and 30km above the Earth's surface, where ozone is formed. It filters harmful ultraviolet radiation from the Sun and prevents it from reaching the Earth.

P

P¹ or **p** *noun* (PL. **Ps, P's, p's**) the sixteenth letter of the English alphabet. — **mind one's ps and qs** *colloq.* to behave well and carefully.

P² *abbrev.* **1** *as a street sign* parking. **2** *Chess* pawn. **3** *Knitting* purl.

P³ *symbol Chem.* phosphorus.

p or **p.** *abbrev.* **1** page. **2** penny or pence.

PA *abbrev.* **1** (*also* **Pa**) Pennsylvania. **2** personal assistant. **3** public-address (system).

Pa *symbol Chem.* protactinium.

p.a. *abbrev. per annum* (Latin), yearly; per year.

pace¹ — *noun* **1** a single step. **2** the distance covered by one step. **3** rate of movement or progress: *can't stand the pace/at one's own pace*. **4** a manner of walking or running. **5** any of the gaits used by a horse. — *verb* **1** *intrans., trans.* (*often* **pace about** or **around**) to keep walking about: *was pacing about all morning/began to pace the floor.* **2** *intrans.* to walk steadily. **3** *trans.* to set the pace for (others) in a race, etc. **4** (**pace something out**) to measure out a distance in paces. — **go through** or **show one's paces** to demonstrate one's skills at something. **keep pace with someone** to go as fast as them. **put someone through their paces** to test them in some activity. **set the pace** to be ahead of, and so set the rate for, others. [from French *pas*, step]

■ *noun* **1, 2** step, stride. **3** movement, motion, progress, rate, speed, velocity, celerity, quickness, rapidity, tempo, measure. **4** walk, gait, tread. *verb* **1, 2** stride, walk, step, march, tramp, pound, patrol. **4** mark out, measure.

pace² *prep.* with the permission of; with due respect to (someone with whom one is disagreeing). [from Latin *pace*, ablative of *pax*, peace, pardon]

pacemaker *noun* **1** *Physiol.* the sinoatrial node, a small mass of specialized muscle cells in the heart which control the rate and the rhythm of the heartbeat. **2** *Medicine* an electronic device that stimulates the heart muscle to contract at a specific and regular rate, used to correct weak or irregular heart rhythms. **3** a pacesetter.

pacesetter *noun* a person who sets the pace; a leader.

pachisi /pɑːˈtʃiːsɪ/ *noun* an Indian board game resembling backgammon or ludo. [from Hindi *pacisi*, of 25, referring to the highest throw in the game]

pachyderm /ˈpakɪdɜːm/ *noun* a large thick-skinned animal, especially a rhinoceros, elephant, or hippopotamus. [from Greek *pachys*, thick + *derma*, skin]

Pacific /pəˈsɪfɪk/ — *noun* (**the Pacific (Ocean)**) the largest ocean on Earth, extending from the Arctic to the Antarctic with N and S America on its E side and Asia and Oceania on its W side. — *adj.* in or relating to the area of the Pacific. [from PACIFIC, because the ocean was notably calm when discovered by Ferdinand Magellan]

pacific /pəˈsɪfɪk/ *adj.* tending to make peace or keep the peace; peaceful; peaceable. [from Latin *pacificus*]

pacification /pasɪfɪˈkeɪʃən/ *noun* the policy or process of pacifying.

pacifier *noun North Amer.* a baby's dummy.

pacifism /ˈpasɪfɪzm/ *noun Politics* the beliefs and practices of pacifists.

pacifist /ˈpasɪfɪst/ *noun* someone who believes violence is unjustified and who refuses to take part in war.

■ pacificist, conscientious objector, peace-lover, peacemaker, peace-monger, dove.
🗷 warmonger, hawk.

pacify /ˈpasɪfaɪ/ *verb* (**pacifies, pacified**) **1** to calm, soothe, or appease. **2** to restore to a peaceful condition. **3** *euphemistic* to subdue. [from Latin *pax*, peace + *facere*, to make]

■ **1, 2** calm, soothe, appease, conciliate, placate, mollify, compose, assuage, allay, moderate, soften, lull, still, quiet, silence. **3** subdue, quell, crush, put down, tame.
🗷 **1** anger.

pack¹ — *noun* **1** things tied into a bundle for carrying. **2** a rucksack; a backpack. **3** a complete set of playing-cards. **4** a troop of animals hunting together, eg dogs or wolves. **5** a compact package, eg of equipment for a purpose: *a first-aid pack*. **6** *derog.* a collection or bunch: *a pack of idiots/a pack of lies*. **7** a troop of Brownie Guides or Cub Scouts. **8** *Rugby* the forwards in a team. **9** a medicinal or cosmetic skin preparation: *a face pack*. **10** pack ice. — *verb* **1** to stow (goods, clothes, etc) compactly in cases, boxes, etc for transport or travel. **2** *intrans.* to put one's belongings into a travelling-bag, etc, ready for a journey. **3 a** (*also* **pack something out**) to fill it tightly. **b** (*also* **pack something in**) to cram it in. **4** to be capable of giving (a punch) of some force. **5** *North Amer. colloq.* to make a habit of carrying (a gun). **6** *intrans., said of animals* to form a pack. — **pack it in** *colloq.* to give up or stop what one is doing. **pack someone off** to send them off hastily or abruptly: *packed the children off to their friend's house*. **pack up 1** to stop work, etc. **2** *colloq., said of machinery, etc* to break down. **pack something up** to put it in containers and store it. **send someone packing** *colloq.* to dismiss them unceremoniously. [origin unknown]

■ *noun* **1** package, packet, parcel, bundle, box, carton, burden, load. **2** backpack, rucksack, haversack, knapsack, kitbag. **4** troop, group, herd, flock, company, band. **5** package, kit, box. **6** collection, bunch, bundle, batch, group, crowd, gang, mob, band. *verb* **1** wrap (up), parcel (up), package (up), bundle (up), stow, store. **3** fill, load, charge, cram, stuff, crowd, throng, press, ram, wedge, compact, compress.

pack² *verb* to fill (a jury, meeting, etc) illicitly with people one can rely on to support one.

package — *noun* **1** something wrapped and secured with string, adhesive tape, etc; a parcel. **2** a package deal. **3** *Comput.* a group of related computer programs designed to perform a particular function and therefore meeting the requirements of a large number of users, eg Microsoft's Wordstar. — *verb* to wrap up in a parcel.

■ *noun* **1** parcel, pack, packet, box, carton, bale, consignment.

verb parcel (up), wrap (up), pack (up), box, batch.

....

package deal a deal covering a number of related proposals that must be accepted as a whole or not at all.

package holiday or **package tour** a holiday or tour for which one pays a fixed price that includes travel, accommodation, meals, etc.

packaging *noun* the wrappers or containers in which goods are packed.

packet *noun* **1** a paper, cardboard, or plastic bag, wrapper, or container, with its contents. **2** a small pack or package. **3** (*also* **packet boat**) a mail boat also carrying cargo and passengers, plying a fixed route. **4** *colloq.* a large sum of money: *cost a packet*. **5** *Comput.* a block of coded data. [from Old French *pacquet*]

....

▤ **1, 2** pack, carton, box, bag, package, parcel, case, container.

....

packet switching *Telecomm.* a method of directing digitally-encoded data communications over a network from source to receiver. The message is broken down into small 'packets' comprising address, control, and data signals, and these are sent over the network to be reconstituted into the full message at the destination.

packhorse *noun Hist.* a horse used to carry luggage or goods for sale.

pack ice pieces of floating ice driven together into a mass by wind and currents.

packing *noun* materials used for padding or wrapping goods for transport, etc.

packing-case *noun* a wooden crate in which to pack goods for transport or storage.

pact *noun* an agreement reached between two or more especially opposing parties, states, etc. [from Latin *pactum*]

....

▤ treaty, agreement, convention, covenant, deal, bargain, compact, contract, arrangement, understanding, bond, alliance, cartel.

▣ disagreement, quarrel.

....

pad¹ — *noun* **1** a wad of material used to cushion, protect, shape, or clean. **2** a leg-guard for a cricketer, etc. **3** a quantity of sheets of paper fixed together into a block. **4** a rocket-launching platform. **5** the fleshy underside of an animal's paw. **6** a compactly laid out set of keys pressed to dial a telephone number, operate a television set, etc: *a key pad*. **7** *North Amer., esp. US* a large water-lily leaf. **8** *slang* one's living quarters. — *verb* (**padded, padding**) **1** to cover, fill, stuff, cushion, or shape with layers of soft material. **2** (*also* **pad something out**) to include unnecessary or irrelevant material in a piece of writing, speech, etc for the sake of length.

....

▤ *noun* **1** cushion, pillow, wad, buffer, padding, protection. **3** writing-pad, notepad, jotter, block. *verb* **1** fill, stuff, wad, pack, wrap, line, cushion, protect. **2** fill out, lengthen, stretch, protract, spin out, expand, inflate, augment, amplify, elaborate, flesh out.

....

pad² *verb* (**padded, padding**) **1** *intrans.* to walk softly or with a muffled tread. **2** *trans., intrans.* to tramp along (a road); to travel on foot. [from Old Dutch *pad*, path]

padding *noun* **1** material for cushioning, shaping, or filling. **2** irrelevant or unnecessary matter in a speech or piece of writing.

....

▤ **1** filling, stuffing, wadding, packing, protection. **2** verbiage, verbosity, wordiness, *colloq.* waffle, bombast, *colloq.* hot air.

....

paddle¹ — *verb* **1** *intrans.* to walk about barefoot in shallow water. **2** *trans.* to trail or dabble (fingers, etc) in water. — *noun* a spell of paddling.

....

▤ *verb* **1** wade. **2** dabble, dibble, splash, slop.

....

paddle² — *noun* **1** a short light oar with a blade at one or both ends, used to propel and steer a canoe, etc. **2** one of the slats fitted round the edge of a paddle wheel or mill wheel. — *verb* **1** *trans., intrans.* to propel (a canoe, etc) with paddles. **2** *intrans.* (*also* **paddle along**) to move through water using, or as if using, a paddle or paddles.

....

▤ *noun* **1** oar, scull. *verb* ROW, SCULL. **1** propel, steer.

....

paddle steamer a steamer driven by paddle wheels.

paddle wheel a large engine-driven wheel at the side or back of a ship which propels the ship through the water as it turns.

paddock *noun* **1** a small enclosed field for keeping a horse in. **2** *Racing* an enclosure beside a race track where horses are saddled and walked round before a race. [from Anglo-Saxon *pearroc*, fence, enclosure]

paddy¹ *noun* (PL. **paddies**) **1** (*also* **paddy field**) a field filled with water in which rice is grown. **2** rice as a growing crop; harvested rice grains that have not been processed in any way. [from Malay *padi*]

paddy² *noun* (PL. **paddies**) *colloq.* a fit of rage. [from *Paddy*, colloquial name for an Irishman]

padlock — *noun* a detachable lock with a U-shaped bar that pivots at one side so that it can be passed through a ring or chain and locked in position. — *verb* to fasten with a padlock.

padre /ˈpɑːdreɪ/ *noun* a chaplain in any of the armed services. [from Portuguese, Spanish, and Italian *padre*, father (as a form of address to a priest)]

padsaw *noun* a small saw-blade with a detachable handle, used for cutting curves and awkward angles. [from PAD¹]

paean /ˈpɪən/ *noun* a song of triumph, praise, or thanksgiving. [from Greek *Paian*, healer, used in hymns as a title of Apollo]

paed- see PAEDO-.

paederast or **paederasty** see PEDERAST.

paediatric /piːdɪˈatrɪk/ *adj.* relating to or involving paediatrics.

paediatrician /piːdɪəˈtrɪʃən/ *noun* a doctor specializing in studying and treating children's illnesses.

paediatrics /piːdɪˈatrɪks/ *sing. noun Medicine* the branch of medicine concerned with the care of children, and with the diagnosis and treatment of children's diseases. [from Greek *pais*, child + *iatrikos*, medical]

paedo- or **paed-** *combining form* forming words associated with a child or children: *paedophile/paediatrics*. [from Greek *pais*, child]

paedophile /ˈpiːdoʊfaɪl/ *noun* an adult who is sexually attracted to or engages in sexual activity with children.

paedophilia /piːdoʊˈfɪlɪə/ *noun* sexual attraction to children.

paella /paɪˈɛlə/ *noun* a Spanish dish of rice, fish, or chicken, vegetables, and saffron. [from Catalan *paella*, from Latin *patella*, pan]

pagan /ˈpeɪgən/ — *adj.* **1** not a Christian, Jew, or Muslim; of or following a religion in which a number of gods are worshipped. **2** without religious belief. — *noun* a pagan person. [from Latin *paganus*, rustic, peasant, civilian (ie not a soldier of Christ)]

....

▤ *adj.* **1** heathen, infidel, idolatrous. **2** irreligious, infidel, atheistic, godless. *noun* heathen, infidel, idolater, atheist, unbeliever.

▣ *noun* believer.

....

paganism *noun* pagan beliefs and practices.

page[1] — *noun* **1** one side of a leaf in a book, etc. **2** a leaf of a book, etc. **3** *literary* an episode or incident in history, one's life, etc. **4** short for WEB PAGE. — *verb* to paginate (a text). [from French *page*, from Latin *pagina*]

. . . .

☐ *noun* **1** side, folio. **2** leaf, sheet, folio.

. . . .

page[2] — *noun* **1** a boy who carries messages or luggage, etc. **2** *Hist.* a boy attendant serving a knight, and training for knighthood. **3** a boy attending the bride at a wedding. — *verb* to summon through a public-address system or pager. [from Old French *page*, from Old Italian *paggio*]

. . . .

☐ *noun* PAGEBOY. **1** messenger, bell-boy, footman. *verb* call, send for, summon, bid.

. . . .

pageant /'padʒənt/ *noun* **1** a series of tableaux or dramatic scenes, usually depicting historical events. **2** any colourful and varied spectacle. [from Latin *pagina*, page, scene, stage]

. . . .

☐ **1** procession, parade, show, display, tableau, scene, play. **2** spectacle, extravaganza.

. . . .

pageantry /'padʒəntrɪ/ *noun* splendid display, pomp.

. . . .

☐ pomp, ceremony, splendour, grandeur, magnificence, glamour, glitter, spectacle, parade, display, show, extravagance, theatricality, drama.

. . . .

pageboy — *noun* a page. — *adj.* denoting a smooth jaw-length hairstyle with the ends curling under.

page description language (ABBREV. **PDL**) *Comput.* a programming language used to describe the composition of a printed page, which can be interpreted by a compatible printer.

pager *noun Radio* a small individually worn radio receiver and transmitter that enables its user to receive a signal, typically a 'beep', or to send a signal to alert another person.

paginate /'padʒɪneɪt/ *verb* to give numbers to the pages of (a text) as part of the printing process. [from Latin *pagina*, page]

pagination *noun* **1** a system or process of paginating. **2** the figures and symbols used to mark pages.

pagoda /pə'goudə/ *noun* an oriental temple, especially in the form of a tall tower, each storey having its own projecting roof with upturned eaves. [from Portuguese *pagode*, from Persian *butkada*, from *but*, idol + *kada*, temple]

paid see PAY.

paid-up *adj.*, *said of a society member, etc* having paid a membership fee.

pail *noun* **1** a bucket. **2** the amount contained in a bucket. [from Anglo-Saxon *pægel*, gill (liquid measure), associated with Old French *paielle*, pan]

pailful *noun* (PL. **pailfuls**) the amount a pail will hold.

pain — *noun* **1** an uncomfortable, distressing, or agonizing sensation that is usually relatively localized, and is caused by the stimulation of specialized nerve endings by a strong stimulus, eg heat, cold, pressure, or tissue damage. **2** emotional suffering. **3** (*also* **pain in the neck**) *derog. colloq.* an irritating or troublesome person or thing. **4** (**pains**) trouble taken or efforts made in doing something. — *verb* to cause distress to. — **be at pains to do something** to be anxious to do it with due care and thoroughly. **for one's pains** *ironic* as a (usually poor) reward for the trouble one has taken. **on pain of something** at the risk of incurring it as a punishment. **take pains** to be careful to do something properly; to be thorough over a task, etc. [from Latin *poena*, punishment]

. . . .

☐ *noun* **1** hurt, ache, soreness, tenderness, discomfort, agony, throb, cramp, spasm, twinge, pang, stab, sting. **2** suffering,

distress, hurt, affliction, trouble, anguish, agony, torment, torture, ache, pang. **3** nuisance, *colloq.* bore, burden, *colloq.* headache. **4** trouble, effort(s), bother, care, diligence. *verb* distress, upset, hurt, afflict, sadden, grieve, torment, torture, agonize.

☒ *verb* please, delight, gratify.

. . . .

pained *adj.* expressing distress or disapproval: *a pained look*.

. . . .

☐ distressed, upset, hurt, injured, wounded, stung, offended, aggrieved, reproachful, saddened, grieved.

☒ pleased, gratified.

. . . .

painful *adj.* **1** causing pain: *a painful injury*. **2** affected by something which causes pain: *a painful finger*. **3** causing distress: *a painful duty*. **4** laborious: *painful progress*.

. . . .

☐ **1, 2** sore, tender, aching, throbbing, smarting, agonizing, excruciating. **3** distressing, unpleasant, disagreeable, upsetting, saddening, harrowing, traumatic. **4** laborious, tedious, hard, difficult.

☒ **1** painless, soothing. **3** pleasant, agreeable. **4** easy.

. . . .

painfully *adv.* in a painful way; so as to cause pain.

painkiller *noun* a drug that reduces or gets rid of pain.

. . . .

☐ analgesic, anodyne, anaesthetic, palliative, sedative, drug, remedy.

. . . .

painless *adj.* without pain.

. . . .

☐ pain-free, trouble-free, effortless, easy, simple, undemanding.

☒ painful, difficult.

. . . .

painstaking *adj.* conscientious and thorough.

. . . .

☐ conscientious, thorough, careful, meticulous, scrupulous, diligent, assiduous, industrious, hardworking, dedicated, devoted, persevering.

☒ careless, negligent.

. . . .

paint — *noun* **1** colouring matter in the form of a liquid, for applying to a surface; a dried coating of this. **2** a tube or tablet of colouring matter for creating pictures. **3** *old use* face make-up; cosmetics. — *verb* **1** to apply a coat of paint to (walls, woodwork, etc). **2** to turn (something) a certain colour by this means: *paint the door yellow*. **3** *trans., intrans.* to make (pictures) using paint. **4** to depict (a person, place, or thing) in paint. **5** *trans., intrans., old use* to put make-up on (one's face). [from Old French *peint*, past participle of *peindre*, to paint]

. . . .

☐ *noun* **1** colour, colouring, pigment, dye, tint, stain. *verb* **1** colour, dye, tint, stain, daub, coat, cover, decorate. **2** colour, dye, tint, stain. **4** depict, portray, picture, represent.

. . . .

Paints include: acrylic paint, colourwash, distemper, eggshell, emulsion, enamel, glaze, gloss paint, gouache, lacquer, masonry paint, matt paint, oilpaint, oils, pastel, poster paint, primer, undercoat, varnish, watercolour, whitewash.

paintball *noun* a game in which participants stalk each other and fight battles with paint fired from compressed-air guns.

paintbox *noun* a case of paints in a variety of colours, for painting pictures.

paintbrush *noun* a brush used for applying paint.

painter[1] *noun* **1** a person who decorates houses internally or externally with paint. **2** an artist who paints pictures.

painter² *noun Naut.* a rope for fastening a boat. [perhaps related to Old French *pentoir*, rope]

painting *noun* **1** the art or process of applying paint to walls, etc. **2** the art of creating pictures in paint. **3** a painted picture.

▣ **2** art. **3** picture, oil-painting, oil, watercolour, portrait, landscape, still life, miniature, illustration, fresco, mural.

pair — *noun* **1** a set of two identical or corresponding things, eg shoes, gloves, etc, intended for use together. **2** something consisting of two joined and corresponding parts: *a pair of pants/a pair of scissors.* **3** one of a matching pair: *where's its pair?* **4** two people associated in a relationship. **5** two mating animals, birds, fishes, etc. **6** two horses harnessed together: *a coach and pair.* — *verb* **1** *trans., intrans.* (*also* **pair off**) to divide into pairs. **2** *intrans.* (**pair up with someone**) to join with them for some purpose. — **in pairs** in twos. [from Old French *paire*]

▣ *noun* **1** duo, brace, twins, two of a kind. **3** partner. **4** couple, twosome, duo. *verb* **1** match (up), team up, put together, bracket. **2** join, team up with, couple with, link with, twin with, mate, marry, wed.
▣ *verb* SEPARATE, PART.

pair-royal *noun Cards* a set of three cards of the same denomination. Also called PRIAL.

pajamas see PYJAMAS.

pakora /pə'kɔːrə/ *noun* an Indian dish of chopped spiced vegetables formed into balls, coated in batter, and deep-fried. [from Hindi]

PAL *abbrev.* Phase Alternating Line: the coding system for colour television developed in Germany and the UK from 1965 and widely adopted in Europe and many other parts of the world for 625 line/50Hz transmission (see also NTSC, SECAM).

pal *colloq.* — *noun* a friend. — *verb intrans.* (**palled, palling**) (*usually* **pal up with someone**) to make friends with them. [from Romany *pal*, brother]

palace /'paləs/ *noun* **1** the official residence of a sovereign, bishop, archbishop, or president. **2** a spacious and magnificent residence or other building. [from Old French *paleis*, from Latin *Palatium*, the Roman emperors' residence on the Palatine Hill]

▣ **2** castle, château, mansion, stately home.

pala d'altare /'paːla: dal'taːreɪ/ the type of altarpiece that first appeared in Florence c.1430, consisting of a single large picture or panel (instead of several small ones). [from Italian *pala d'altare*, altarpiece]

paladin /'palədɪn/ *noun Hist.* **1** any of the 12 peers of Charlemagne's court. **2** a knight errant; a champion of a sovereign. [from Italian *paladino*, from Latin *palatinus*, belonging to the palace]

palaeo- or **palae-** *combining form* forming words meaning 'old, ancient, former'. [from Greek *palaios*, old]

palaeobotany or **paleobotany** *noun Geol.* the scientific study of fossil plants.

Palaeocene /'paliousiːn/ *adj. Geol.* the earliest epoch of the Tertiary period, lasting from about 65 to 54 million years ago. [from PALAEO- + Greek *kainos*, new]

palaeoecology or **paleoecology** *noun Geol.* the scientific study of the ecology of fossil animals and plants.

palaeographer or **paleographer** /palɪ'ɒgrəfə(r)/ *noun* a person who studies ancient manuscripts.

palaeography *noun* the study of ancient writing and manuscripts.

palaeolithic or **Palaeolithic** /palɪoʊ'lɪθɪk/ *adj.* relating to or belonging to the early part of the Stone Age, during which chipped stones served as primitive tools. [from PALAEO- + Greek *lithos*, stone]

palaeontologist *noun* an expert in palaeontology.

palaeontology *noun Geol.* the scientific study of the structure, distribution, environment, and evolution of extinct life forms by interpretation of the fossil remains of animals and plants. [from PALAEO- + Greek *onta*, neuter pl. present participle of *einai*, to be + -LOGY]

Palaeosiberian — *adj.* denoting a family of languages used in NE Siberia, using the Cyrillic alphabet. — *noun* the languages forming this family.

Palaeozoic /palioʊ'zoʊɪk/ *adj. Geol.* relating to the era of geological time extending from about 580 million to 250 million years ago, and subdivided into the Cambrian, Ordovician, Silurian, Devonian, Carboniferous, and Permian periods. [from PALAEO- + Greek *zoion*, animal]

palanquin or **palankeen** /palən'kiːn/ *noun Hist.* a light portable bed used in the Orient, suspended from poles carried on the shoulders of four bearers. [from Portuguese *palanquim*]

palatable /'palətəbl/ *adj.* **1** having a pleasant taste; appetizing. **2** acceptable; agreeable. [from PALATE]

▣ **1** tasty, appetizing, eatable, edible. **2** acceptable, satisfactory, pleasant, agreeable, enjoyable, attractive.
▣ UNPALATABLE. **2** unacceptable, unpleasant, disagreeable.

palate /'palət/ *noun* **1** the roof of the mouth. **2** the sense of taste; an ability to discriminate between wines, etc. [from Latin *palatum*]

palatial /pə'leɪʃl/ *adj.* like a palace in magnificence, spaciousness, etc. [from Latin *palatium*, palace]

▣ magnificent, splendid, majestic, regal, stately, grand, grandiose, imposing, luxurious, de luxe, sumptuous, opulent, *colloq.* plush, spacious.

palaver /pə'laːvə(r)/ *noun* **1** *colloq.* unnecessary fuss. **2** *Hist.* an act of conferring between European traders, settlers, etc and native inhabitants. [from Portuguese *palavra*, from Latin *parabola*, speech]

pale¹ — *adj.* **1** *said of a person, face, etc* having less colour than normal, eg from illness, fear, shock, etc. **2** *said of a colour* closer to white than black; light: *pale green.* **3** lacking brightness or vividness; subdued: *pale sunlight.* — *verb intrans.* **1** to become pale. **2** to fade by comparison: *pale into insignificance.* [from Old French *palle*, from Latin *pallidus*]

▣ *adj.* **1** pallid, ashen, ashy, white, chalky, pasty, pasty-faced, waxen, waxy, wan, sallow, anaemic, livid. **2** light, pastel, faded, washed-out, bleached, colourless. **3** subdued, weak, feeble, faint, dim, insipid, vapid. *verb* **1** whiten, blanch, bleach, fade. **2** fade, dim.
▣ *adj.* **1** ruddy, flushed. **2** dark. **3** vivid, bright. *verb* **1** colour, blush.

pale² *noun* **1** a post used for making fences. **2** a fence made of these; a boundary fence. — **beyond the pale** outside the limits of acceptable behaviour. [from Latin *palus*, stake]

paleface *noun* the term supposed to have been used by Native Americans for the white settlers.

palely *adv.* in a pale way, faintly.

paleness *noun* a pale quality or colour.

paleo- same as PALAEO-.

Palestinian /palə'stɪnɪən/ — *noun* **1** a native of ancient or modern Palestine. **2** an Arab who is a native or a descendant of a native of the area formerly called Palestine. — *adj.* relating to ancient or modern Palestine.

palette /'palət/ *noun* **1** a hand-held board with a thumb hole, on which an artist mixes colours. **2** the assortment or range of colours used by a particular artist, in a particular picture, etc. [from French, from Italian *paletta*, diminutive of *pala*, spade]

palette knife 1 an artist's knife for mixing and applying paint. **2** a flexible-bladed, round-ended knife used for spreading butter, mixing ingredients, etc.

palimpsest /'palɪmpsest/ *noun* **1** a parchment or other writing surface re-used after the original content has been erased. **2** a monumental brass that has been turned over and inscribed on the reverse. [from Greek *palin*, again + *psaein*, to rub]

palindrome /'palɪndroʊm/ *noun* a word or phrase that reads the same backwards and forwards, eg *eye*, *radar*, and *sums are not set as a test on Erasmus*. [from Greek *palin*, back + *dromein*, run]

palindromic /palɪn'drɒmɪk/ *adj.* in the nature of a palindrome; having the same spelling backwards and forwards.

paling *noun* any of a row of wooden posts fixed edge to edge to form a solid fence; a fence of this kind. [from Latin *palus*, stake]

palisade /palɪ'seɪd/ *noun* a tall fence of pointed wooden stakes fixed edge to edge, for defence or protection. [from Provençal *palissada*, from Latin *palus*, stake]

pall[1] /pɔːl/ *noun* **1** the cloth that covers a coffin at a funeral; the coffin itself. **2** anything spreading or hanging over: *a pall of smoke*. [from Anglo-Saxon *pæll*, robe, covering]
·······················
◨ **2** shroud, veil, mantle, cloak, cloud, shadow.
·······················

pall[2] /pɔːl/ *verb intrans.* to begin to bore or seem tedious. [a variant of APPAL]
·······················
◨ tire, weary, jade.
·······················

palladium /pə'leɪdɪəm/ *noun Chem.* (SYMBOL **Pd**, ATOMIC NUMBER **46**) a soft silvery-white metal used as a catalyst, and in gold dental alloys, jewellery, electrical components, and catalytic converters for car exhausts. It is also combined with gold to form the alloy white gold. [named after the asteroid *Pallas*, discovered in 1802]

pall-bearer *noun* one of those carrying the coffin or walking beside it at a funeral.

pallet[1] *noun* **1** a small wooden platform on which goods can be stacked for lifting and transporting by fork-lift truck. **2** a flat-bladed wooden tool used for shaping pottery. [see PALETTE]

pallet[2] *noun* **1** a straw mattress. **2** a small makeshift bed. [from Old French *paillette*, from *paille*, straw]

palliasse /palɪ'as/ *noun* a straw mattress. [from French *paillasse*, from *paille*, straw]

palliate *verb* **1** to ease the symptoms of (a disease) without curing it. **2** to serve to lessen the gravity of (an offence, etc); to excuse to some extent. **3** to reduce the effect of (anything disagreeable). [from Latin *pallium*, cloak]

palliative /'palɪətɪv/ — *noun* anything used to reduce pain or anxiety. — *adj.* having the effect of palliating or reducing pain.

pallid *adj.* **1** pale, especially unhealthily so. **2** lacking vigour or conviction. [from Latin *pallidus*, pale]

palliness *noun* chumminess, friendliness.

pallium /'palɪəm/ or **pall** *noun Relig.* a white woollen vestment shaped like a double Y embroidered with six purple crosses signifying episcopal power, and union with the Holy See (of Rome). It is worn by the pope, and conferred by him on archbishops. [from Latin *pallium*, a cloak]

pallor *noun* paleness, especially of complexion. [from Latin *pallor*]

pally *adj.* (**pallier, palliest**) *colloq.* friendly.

palm[1] — *noun* **1** the inner surface of the hand between the wrist and the fingers. **2** the part of a glove covering this. — *verb* to conceal in the palm of the hand. — **palm something off on someone** or **someone off with something** *colloq.* to give them something unwanted or unwelcome, especially by trickery. [from Latin *palma*]
·······················
◨ **palm off** *something on someone* foist, fob off, impose,

offload, unload, pass off. *someone with something* fob off, inflict.
·······················

palm[2] *noun* **1** a large tropical plant belonging to the family *Palmae*, found in tropical and subtropical regions worldwide, with a few species reaching warm temperate regions (and even cool temperate regions in special situations, eg areas influenced by the Gulf Stream). **2** a leaf of this carried as a symbol of triumph or victory; the supreme prize. [from Latin *palma*, originally palm of the hand]

palmate /'palmeɪt/ *adj.* **1** *Bot.*, *said of a leaf* divided into lobes that radiate from a central point, resembling an open hand. **2** *Zool.*, *said of an animal* having webbed toes, as in many aquatic birds. [from Latin *palmatus*, from *palma*, palm of the hand]

palmetto /pal'metoʊ/ *noun* (PL. **palmettos**) a small palm tree with fan-like leaves. [from Spanish *palmito*, diminutive of *palma*, palm]

palmistry /'pɑːmɪstrɪ/ *noun* the art or practice of telling a person's fortune by the lines on their palm.

palmitic acid /pal'mɪtɪk/ *Chem.* (FORMULA C_5H_3COOH) a fatty acid, obtained from many animal and plant oils and fats, including palm oil and spermaceti, that is insoluble in water, and is used in the manufacture of soaps, lubricating oils, and waterproofing agents.

palm oil the red oil obtained from the outer pulp of the fruit of the oil palm, used in cooking fats and margarines.

Palm Sunday in the Christian Church, the Sunday before Easter, commemorating Christ's triumphal entry into Jerusalem, when the crowd spread palm branches before him.

palmtop *noun* a portable computer small enough to be held in the hand.

palmy *adj.* (**palmier, palmiest**) *humorous colloq.* characterized by effortless success and prosperity: *one's palmy days*. [from PALM[2], as a symbol of triumph]

palomino /palə'miːnoʊ/ *noun* (PL. **palominos**) a golden or cream horse with a white tail and mane. [from Spanish *palomino*, dove-like]

palpable /'palpəbl/ *adj.* **1** easily detected; obvious. **2** *Medicine* able to be felt. [from Latin *palpare*, to touch]
·······················
◨ **1** obvious, evident, manifest, conspicuous, blatant, unmistakable, clear, plain, apparent, visible, touchable, tangible, real, solid, substantial, material.
◪ IMPALPABLE. **1** imperceptible, intangible, elusive.
·······················

palpably *adv.* in a palpable way, obviously.

palpate /'palpeɪt/ *verb Medicine* to examine (the body or a part of it) by touching or pressing, especially in order to diagnose medical disorders or diseases. [from Latin *palpare*, to touch]

palpitate /'palpɪteɪt/ *verb intrans.* **1** *Medicine*, *said of the heart* to beat abnormally rapidly, eg as a result of physical exertion, fear, emotion, or heart disease. **2** to tremble or throb. [from Latin *palpitare*, to throb]
·······················
◨ **1** pound, thump. **2** tremble, throb, quiver, shiver, flutter, vibrate, beat, pulsate.
·······················

palpitation *noun* (*often* **palpitations**) **1** palpitating. **2** a trembling.

palsy /'pɔːlzɪ/ — *noun* paralysis, or loss of control or feeling in a part of the body. — *verb* (**palsies, palsied**) to affect with palsy; to paralyse. [from Old French *paralisie*, from Latin and Greek *paralysis*]

paltriness *noun* inadequacy, insignificance.

paltry /'pɔːltrɪ/ *adj.* (**paltrier, paltriest**) worthless; trivial; meagre; insignificant; insultingly inadequate. [from German dialect *paltrig*, ragged]
·······················
◨ worthless, trivial, meagre, insignificant, derisory, contemptible, mean, low, miserable, wretched, poor,

sorry, small, slight, trifling, inconsiderable, negligible, minor, petty, unimportant.

🇫🇷 substantial, significant, valuable.

palynology /palɪˈnɒlədʒɪ/ *noun* the analysis of spores and pollen grains, principally those preserved in ancient sediments and soils, in order to reconstruct variations in vegetation over time. [from Greek *palynein*, to sprinkle + -LOGY]

pampas grass /ˈpampəs/ a large perennial grass (*Cortaderia selloana*), native to S America, that forms dense tufts of arching bluish leaves and has tall erect stems, 3m high, bearing silvery-white, sometimes pink, plume-like panicles.

pamper *verb* (**pampered, pampering**) to treat over-indulgently and over-protectively; to cosset or spoil. [from Middle English, originally Germanic]

🇪 cosset, spoil, coddle, mollycoddle, humour, gratify, indulge, overindulge, pet.

🇫🇷 neglect, ill-treat.

pamphlet /ˈpamflət/ *noun* a booklet or leaflet providing information or dealing with a current topic. [from Old French *pamphilet*, from the title of the medieval Latin love poem, *Pamphilus, seu de Amore*]

🇪 leaflet, booklet, brochure, folder, circular, handout, notice.

pan[1] — *noun* 1 a usually metal pot used for cooking. 2 (*often in compounds*) any of various usually shallow vessels, with domestic, industrial or other uses: *a dustpan/bedpan* etc. 3 the bowl of a lavatory. 4 either dish on a pair of scales. 5 a shallow hollow in the ground: *a salt pan*. 6 *Hist.* the hollow part of an old gun lock, holding the priming. — *verb* (**panned, panning**) 1 *intrans., trans.* to wash (river gravel) in a shallow metal vessel in search of gold. 2 *colloq.* to criticize or review harshly.

🇪 *noun* 1 saucepan, frying-pan, pot, container, vessel.

pan[2] — *verb trans., intrans.* (**panned, panning**) *said of a film camera, etc* to swing round so as to follow a moving object or show a panoramic view. — *noun* a panning movement or shot. [a shortening of PANORAMA]

pan- *combining form* forming words meaning 'all, entire': *Pan-African*. [from Greek *pas, pantos*, all]

panacea /panəˈsɪə/ *noun* a universal remedy; a cure-all for any ill, problem, etc. [from PAN- + Greek *akos*, remedy]

panache /pəˈnaʃ/ *noun* flamboyant self-assurance. [from French *panache*, plume]

🇪 flamboyance, self-assurance, style, flair, élan, dash, flourish, ostentation, spirit.

panama /ˈpanəmɑː/ *noun* (*also* **panama hat**) a lightweight brimmed hat for men made from the plaited leaves of a palm-like Central American tree. [from *Panama* in Central America]

panatella /panəˈtɛlə/ *noun* a long slim cigar. [from American Spanish *panatella*, long thin biscuit]

pancake *noun* a round of thin batter cooked on both sides in a frying-pan or on a griddle.

Pancake Day Shrove Tuesday, when pancakes are traditionally eaten.

pancake landing an aircraft landing made in an emergency, with the wheels up and landing flat on the belly of the aircraft.

pancetta /panˈtʃɛtə/ *noun* a highly cured type of Italian bacon. [from Italian, diminutive of *pancio*, belly]

Panchen Lama a spiritual leader and teacher in Tibetan Buddhism, second in importance to the Dalai Lama, and said to be the reincarnation of the Buddha Amitabha.

panchromatic /pankrəʊˈmatɪk/ *adj. Photog.*, *said of a film* sensitive to all colours.

pancreas /ˈpaŋkrɪəs/ *noun* in vertebrates, a large carrot-shaped gland lying between the duodenum and the spleen, that has hormonal and digestive functions. [from PAN- + Greek *kreas*, flesh]

panda *noun* 1 See GIANT PANDA. 2 (*also* **red panda**) a tree-dwelling mammal (*Ailurus fulgens*) related to the giant panda, found in mountain forests of Nepal, Sikkim, Bhutan, and China. [from Nepalese]

panda car in the UK, a small police patrol car, formerly white with black markings.

pandemic /panˈdɛmɪk/ *adj. Medicine* describing a widespread epidemic of a disease, eg one that affects a whole country or the whole world. [from Greek *pandemios*, from *demos*, people]

pandemonium /pandəˈmoʊnɪəm/ *noun* noise, chaos, and confusion. [from John Milton's name for the capital of Hell in *Paradise Lost*, from PAN- + Greek *daimon*, demon]

🇪 chaos, disorder, confusion, commotion, rumpus, turmoil, turbulence, tumult, uproar, noise, din, bedlam, hubbub, *colloq.* hullaballoo, hue and cry, *colloq.* to-do.

🇫🇷 order, calm, peace.

pander — *verb intrans.* (**pandered, pandering**) (**pander to someone**) to indulge or gratify them or their wishes or tastes. — *noun* a person who obtains a sexual partner for another. [from *Pandarus* in Chaucer and Shakespeare, the go-between who procures Cressida for Troilus]

🇪 *verb* humour, indulge, pamper, please, gratify, satisfy, fulfil.

Pandora's box /panˈdɔːrəz/ a potential source of unlimited evils.

pane *noun* a sheet of glass, especially one fitted into a window or door. [from Old French *pan*, strip of cloth]

panegyric /panəˈdʒɪrɪk/ *noun* a speech or piece of writing in praise of someone or something; a eulogy. [from Greek *panegyrikos*, fit for a national festival]

panel /ˈpanl/ — *noun* 1 a rectangular wooden board forming a section, especially ornamentally sunken or raised, of a wall or door. 2 one of several strips of fabric making up a garment. 3 any of the metal sections forming the bodywork of a vehicle. 4 a board bearing the instruments and dials for controlling an aircraft, etc. 5 a team of people selected to judge a contest, or participate in a discussion, quiz, or other game before an audience. 6 a list of jurors; the people serving on a jury. — *verb* (**panelled, panelling**) to fit (a wall or door) with wooden panels. [from Old French, diminutive of *pan*, a strip of cloth, etc]

🇪 *noun* 5 team, board, committee, jury.

panel-beater *noun* a person whose job is panel-beating.

panel-beating *noun* the removal of dents from metal, especially from the bodywork of a vehicle, using a soft-headed hammer.

panel game one played by a panel of people.

panelling *noun* panels in walls or doors, or material for making these.

panellist *noun* a member of a panel or team of people, especially in broadcasting.

panel pin a small slender nail with a very small head.

pang *noun* a painfully acute feeling of hunger, remorse, etc.

🇪 twinge, stab, sting, prick, stitch, gripe, spasm, throe, pain, ache, agony, anguish, discomfort, distress.

Pangaea *or* **Pangea** /panˈdʒɪə/ *noun Geol.* the name given to the hypothetical 'supercontinent' that is thought to have represented the entire land mass of the Earth about 200 million years ago, before it drifted apart to form Laurasia and Gondwanaland. [from PAN- + Greek *ge*, earth]

pangolin /ˈpaŋɡoʊlɪn/ *noun* a mammal native to Africa and S and SE Asia, which has a pointed head with small eyes, a long broad tail, a long tongue, and no teeth. It is covered with large overlapping horny plates, and can curl into an armoured ball when threatened by a predator. [from Malay *peng-goling*, roller]

pangram /ˈpangram/ *noun* a sentence containing all the letters of the alphabet, such as *the quick brown fox jumps over the lazy dog*. [from PAN- + Greek *gramma*, letter]

panic — *noun* a sudden overpowering fear, especially one that grips a crowd or population. — *verb trans., intrans.* (**panicked, panicking**) to feel or cause to feel panic. [from Greek *panikon*, baseless terror, caused by *Pan*, god of flocks and pastures]

▪ *noun* agitation, *colloq.* flap, alarm, dismay, consternation, fright, fear, horror, terror, frenzy, hysteria. *verb* lose one's nerve, lose one's head, *colloq.* go to pieces, *colloq.* flap, overreact.

▫ *noun* calm, calmness, self-control, confidence.

panic attack *Psychol.* an attack of intense terror and anxiety, lasting from several minutes to several hours.

panic-buy *verb* to buy (a commodity) in large quantities, in expectation of a shortage.

panicky *adj.* panicking or likely to panic.

panicle /ˈpanɪkl/ *noun Bot.* a branched inflorescence (flower-head), common in grasses, in which the youngest flowers are at the tip of the flower stalk, and the oldest ones are near its base. [from Latin *panicula*, tuft]

panic-stricken *adj.* terrified.

▪ terrified, petrified, scared stiff, in a cold sweat, panicky, frantic, frenzied, hysterical, alarmed, frightened, horrified.

▫ relaxed, confident.

Panjabi same as PUNJABI.

panjandrum /panˈdʒandrəm/ *noun humorous* a pompous official. [from a string of nonsense composed by Samuel Foote (1720–77)]

pannier /ˈpanɪə(r)/ *noun* 1 one of a pair of baskets carried over the back of a donkey or other beast of burden; one of a pair of bags carried on either side of the rear wheel of a bicycle, etc. 2 *Hist.* a tucked-up arrangement of fabric on either side of a woman's skirt. [from French *panier*, from Latin *panarium*, bread basket]

panoply /ˈpanəplɪ/ *noun* (PL. **panoplies**) 1 the full splendid assemblage got together for a ceremony, etc: *the full panoply of a society wedding.* 2 *Hist.* a full set of armour and weapons. [from Greek *panoplia*, from *pan-*, all + *hopla*, weapons]

panorama /panəˈrɑːmə/ *noun* 1 an open and extensive or all-round view, eg of a landscape. 2 a view of something in all its range and variety: *the panorama of history.* [from PAN- + Greek *horama*, view]

▪ 1 view, vista, prospect, scenery, landscape, scene, spectacle. 2 view, vista, perspective, overview, survey.

panoramic *adj., said of a view or prospect* like a panorama; open and extensive.

▪ scenic, wide, sweeping, extensive, far-reaching, widespread, overall, general, universal.

▫ narrow, restricted, limited.

panoramically *adv.* in a panoramic way.

panpipes *pl. noun* a musical instrument consisting of pipes of graded lengths bound together, played by blowing along their open ends. [from *Pan*, Greek god of forests and pastures]

pansy /ˈpanzɪ/ *noun* (PL. **pansies**) 1 a small garden plant of the violet family with multi-coloured broad-petalled flowers. 2 *offensive slang* an effeminate man or boy; a male homosexual. [from Old French *pensée*, thought]

pant — *verb* 1 *intrans.* to breathe in gasps as a result of exertion. 2 *trans.* to say breathlessly. 3 (**be panting for something**) to be longing for it: *panting for a drink.* — *noun* a gasping breath. [from Old French *pantaisier*, from Greek *phantasioun*, to hallucinate]

▪ *verb* 1 puff, blow, gasp, heave. 2 breathe, sigh, wheeze, gasp.

pantaloons *pl. noun* 1 baggy trousers gathered at the ankle. 2 tight-fitting trousers for men worn at the turn of the 19c. [from *Pantalone*, a figure from Italian comedy, a skinny old man in tight hose]

pantechnicon /panˈtɛknɪkɒn/ *noun* a large furniture-removal van. [from the name of the premises of a London art-dealer (later a furniture warehouse), from PAN- + Greek *techne*, art]

pantheism /ˈpanθiːɪzm/ *noun* 1 the belief that equates all the matter and forces in the universe with God. 2 readiness to believe in any god. [from PAN- + Greek *theos*, god]

pantheist /ˈpanθiːɪst/ *noun* a person who upholds the doctrine of pantheism.

pantheistic *adj.* relating to pantheism or pantheists.

pantheon /ˈpanθɪən/ *noun* 1 all the gods of a particular people: *the ancient Greek pantheon.* 2 a temple sacred to all the gods. 3 a building in which the glorious dead of a nation have memorials or are buried. [from Greek *pantheios*, of all the gods]

panther *noun* 1 common name for a black leopard. 2 *North Amer.* a puma. [from Greek *panther*, leopard]

panties *pl. noun* thin light knickers for women.

pantihose see PANTY HOSE.

pantile *noun* a roofing-tile with an S-shaped cross-section, laid so that the upward curve of one tile fits under the downward curve of the next. [from PAN¹ + TILE]

panto *noun* (PL. **pantos**) *colloq.* pantomime.

panto- or **pant-** *combining form* forming words meaning 'all, entire'. [from Greek *pas, pantos*, all]

pantograph *noun* 1 a device consisting of jointed rods forming an adjustable parallelogram, for copying maps, plans, etc to any scale. 2 a similarly shaped metal framework on the roof of an electric train, transmitting current from an overhead wire.

pantomime *noun* 1 a Christmas entertainment usually based on a popular fairy tale, with songs, dancing, comedy acts, etc. 2 communication by gesture and facial expression; dumbshow. [from Greek *pantomimos*, mime actor, literally 'imitator of all']

pantothenic acid /pantəˈθɛnɪk/ *Biochem.* a member of the vitamin B complex that is found in many foods, especially cereal grains, egg yolk, liver, yeast, and peas, and is required for the oxidation (breakdown) of fats and carbohydrates. [from Greek *pantothen*, from every side, of its wide occurrence]

pantry *noun* (PL. **pantries**) a room or cupboard for storing food. [from Old French *paneterie*, from Latin *panis*, bread]

pants — *pl. noun* 1 *Brit.* an undergarment worn over the buttocks and genital area. 2 *North Amer.* trousers. — *adj. slang* very poor in quality or taste. — **caught with one's pants down** *colloq.* caught embarrassingly unprepared. **wear the pants** *colloq.* to be the member of a household who makes the decisions. [a shortening of PANTALOONS]

▪ 1 underpants, drawers, panties, briefs, knickers, Y-fronts, boxer shorts, trunks, shorts. 2 trousers, slacks, jeans.

pant suit or **pants suit** *North Amer.* a trouser suit.

panty hose or **pantihose** *North Amer.* women's tights.

pap[1] *noun* **1** soft semi-liquid food for babies and invalids. **2** *derog.* trivial or worthless reading matter or entertainment.

pap[2] *noun* **1** *old use* a nipple or teat. **2** *Scot.* in place-names, a rounded hill.

papa /pə'pɑː, 'pɑːpə/ *noun old use* a child's word for father. [from French *papa* and Greek *pappas*, father]

papacy /'peɪpəsɪ/ *noun* (PL. **papacies**) **1** the position, power, or period of office of a pope. **2** government by popes. [from Latin *papatia*, from *papa*, pope]

papal /'peɪpl/ *adj.* of, or relating to, the pope or the papacy. [from Latin *papalis*, from *papa*, pope]

paparazzo /papə'ratsəʊ/ *noun* (PL. **paparazzi**) a newspaper photographer who follows famous people about in the hope of photographing them in unguarded moments. [from the name of the photographer in the film *La Dolce Vita* (1959)]

papaya /pə'paɪə/ *noun* **1** a small evergreen tree with a crown of large segmented leaves and yellow flowers, widely cultivated in the tropics for its edible fruit. **2** the large yellow or orange fruit of this tree, which has sweet orange flesh and may be eaten raw, squeezed for its juice, or canned. Also called PAWPAW. [from Spanish *papaya*]

paper *noun* **1** a material manufactured in thin sheets from wood, rags, etc, used for writing and printing on, wrapping things, etc. **2** a loose piece of paper, eg a wrapper or printed sheet. **3** wallpaper. **4** a newspaper. **5** a set of questions on a certain subject for a written examination. **6** a written article dealing with a certain subject, especially for reading to an audience. **7** (**papers**) personal documents establishing one's identity, nationality, etc. **8** (**papers**) a person's accumulated correspondence, diaries, etc. — *verb* (**papered, papering**) to decorate with wallpaper: *paper the hall*. — **on paper 1** in theory as distinct from practice: *plans that look good on paper*. **2** captured in written form: *get one's ideas down on paper*. **paper over something** to conceal or avoid an awkward fact, mistake, etc. [from Old French *papier*, from Greek *papyros*, papyrus]

. . . .

▤ *noun* **4** newspaper, daily, broadsheet, tabloid, *colloq.* rag, journal, organ. **6** essay, composition, dissertation, thesis, treatise, lecture, article, report. **7** documents, credentials, authorization, identification, certificates.

. . . .

Types of paper include: art paper, bank, blotting paper, bond, carbon paper, cartridge paper, crêpe paper, graph paper, greaseproof paper, manila, notepaper, parchment, rice paper, silver paper, sugar paper, tissue paper, toilet paper, tracing paper, vellum, wallpaper, wrapping paper, writing-paper; card, cardboard, pasteboard; A4, foolscap, quarto, atlas, crown.

paperback *noun* a book with a paper binding.

paperboy or **papergirl** *noun* a boy or girl who delivers or sells newspapers.

paper chase a cross-country race in which runners follow a trail of dropped shreds of paper.

paper chromatography *Chem.* a form of chromatography used to analyse complex mixtures of chemical compounds that are applied to one end of a sheet of a special grade of filter paper, which is then suspended vertically in a solvent. The distance moved by the various compounds within a certain time can be used to identify them.

paper clip 1 a metal clip formed from bent wire, for holding papers together. **2** a round-headed brass device with two flexible legs that can be pushed through papers, then separated and folded back to secure them.

paper fastener same as PAPER CLIP 2.

paper hanger a person who puts up wallpaper.

paperknife *noun* a knife for slitting open envelopes, etc.

paper mâché same as PAPIER-MÂCHÉ.

paper money bank notes.

paper tiger something or someone more apparently threatening than actually dangerous.

paperweight *noun* a heavy usually ornamental object for holding papers down.

paperwork *noun* routine written work, eg keeping files, writing letters and reports, etc.

papery *adj.* like paper in texture.

papier-mâché /papjeɪ'maʃeɪ/ *noun* a light material consisting of pulped paper mixed with glue and sometimes other substances, moulded into shape while wet. [from French *papier mâché*, chewed paper]

papilla /pə'pɪlə/ *noun Anat.* (PL. **papillae**) *Biol.* a small nipple-like projection from the surface of a structure, eg any of the protuberances on the tongue that are associated with the taste buds.

papilloma /papɪ'ləʊmə/ *noun Medicine* a benign tumour on the surface of the skin or an organ lined with mucous membrane (eg the vagina), such as a wart. [from Latin *papilloma*]

papillon /'papɪlɒn/ *noun* a breed of toy dog developed in France, which has a small body and a long fine coat that is thickest on the neck, chest, and upper legs. The ears have fringes of hair resembling a butterfly's wings. [from French *papillon*, butterfly]

papist /'peɪpɪst/ *noun offensive* a Roman Catholic. [from Latin *papa*, pope]

papoose /pə'puːs/ *noun* a Native American baby or young child. [from Narragansett (native American language) *papoos*]

paprika /'paprɪkə, pə'priːkə/ *noun* a powdered seasoning for food, made from red peppers. [from Hungarian *paprika*]

papyrus /pə'paɪərəs/ *noun* (PL. **papyri, papyruses**) **1** a tall plant (*Cyperus papyrus*) of the sedge family, common in ancient Egypt. The pith from the flowering stems was used to form a writing material similar to paper. **2** the writing material prepared from this plant, used by the ancient Egyptians, Greeks, and Romans. **3** an ancient manuscript written on this material. [from Greek *papyros*]

par *noun* **1** a normal level or standard. **2** *Golf* the standard number of strokes that a good golfer would take for a certain course or hole. **3** *Commerce* (*also* **par of exchange**) the established value of the unit of one national currency against that of another. — **below** or **not up to par** *colloq.* **1** not up to the usual or required standard. **2** unwell. **on a par with something** or **someone** equal to them; the equivalent of them. **par for the course** *colloq.* only to be expected; predictable; typical. [from Latin *par*, equal]

par- see PARA-[1].

par. or **para.** *abbrev.* paragraph.

para *noun colloq.* a paratrooper.

para-[1] or **par-** *combining form* forming words meaning: **1** alongside: *parathyroid.* **2** beyond: *parapsychology.* **3** resembling: *paramilitary.* **4** auxiliary: *paramedical.* **5** abnormal: *paraesthesia.* [from Greek *para*]

para-[2] *combining form* forming words denoting protection: *paratrooper.* [from Latin *parare*, defend]

parable /'parəbl/ *noun* a story whose purpose is to convey a moral or religious lesson; an allegorical tale. [from Greek *parabole*, analogy]

. . . .

▤ fable, allegory, lesson, moral tale, story.

. . . .

parabola /pə'rabələ/ *noun Geom.* a conic section produced when a plane intersects a cone parallel to its sloping side. [from Greek *parabole*, placing alongside]

parabolic /parə'bɒlɪk/ *adj.* **1** like or expressed in a parable. **2** like or in the form of a parabola.

paracetamol /parə'siːtəmɒl, parə'setəmɒl/ *noun* a mild pain-relieving and fever-reducing drug. [from the medical name *para-acetylaminophenol*]

parachute — *noun* an apparatus consisting of a loose umbrella of light fabric, with a harness for attaching to, and slowing the fall of, a person or package dropped from an aircraft. — *verb intrans., trans.* to drop by parachute. [from PARA-[2] + French *chute*, fall]

parachuting *noun* the act of jumping out of an aircraft and eventually landing with the aid of a parachute.

parachutist *noun* a person who parachutes.

parade — *noun* **1** a ceremonial procession of people, vehicles, etc. **2** *said of soldiers, etc* the state of being drawn up in rank for formal marching or inspection; a body of soldiers, etc drawn up in this way: *be on parade.* **3** a self-advertising display: *make a parade of one's generosity.* **4** used as a name for a promenade, shopping street, etc. — *verb* **1** *intrans., trans.* to walk or cause to walk or march in procession. **2** to display ostentatiously; to flaunt. [from French, from Spanish *parada*, halt, stopping-place]

. . . .

◧ *noun* **1** procession, cavalcade, motorcade, march, column, file, train. **2** review. **3** spectacle, show, display, exhibition. *verb* **1** march, process, file past. **2** display, flaunt, show off, vaunt, brandish, exhibit, show.

. . . .

parade ground the square or yard where soldiers assemble for inspection, marching practice, etc.

paradigm /'parədaɪm/ *noun* **1** an example, model, or pattern. **2** *Grammar* a table of the inflected forms of a word serving as a pattern for words of the same declension or conjugation; the words showing a particular pattern. [from Greek *paradeigma*, pattern]

paradigmatic /parədɪg'matɪk/ *adj.* serving as a paradigm or example.

paradise *noun* **1** heaven. **2** a place of utter bliss or delight. **3** the Garden of Eden. [from Greek *paradeisos*, park]

. . . .

◧ **2** heaven, utopia, Shangri-La, Elysium.
◪ **1, 2** hell, Hades.

. . . .

paradox *noun* **1** a statement that seems to contradict itself, as *more haste, less speed.* **2** a situation involving apparently contradictory elements. **3** *Logic* a proposition that is essentially absurd or leads to an absurd conclusion. [from Greek *paradoxos*, incredible, from *para*, against + *doxa*, opinion]

. . . .

◧ **1** contradiction. **2** contradiction, inconsistency, anomaly, absurdity, incongruity, oddity, mystery, enigma, riddle, puzzle.

. . . .

paradoxical /parə'dɒksɪkl/ *adj.* **1** of the nature of a paradox. **2** showing or using paradox. **3** showing contradictions.

. . . .

◧ SELF-CONTRADICTORY, CONTRADICTORY, CONFLICTING, INCONSISTENT, INCONGRUOUS, ABSURD, ILLOGICAL, IMPROBABLE, IMPOSSIBLE, MYSTERIOUS, ENIGMATIC, PUZZLING.

. . . .

paradoxically *adv.* in a paradoxical way.

paradoxical sleep a phase of sleep in which there is increased electrical activity in the brain, and, in humans, dreaming and rapid eye movement.

paraesthesia /parɛs'θiːzɪə/ *noun Medicine* an abnormal tingling sensation, sometimes described as 'pins and needles', and often caused by pressure on a nerve. [from PARA-[1] + Greek *aisthesis*, sensation]

paraffin *noun* **1** a fuel oil obtained from petroleum or coal and used in aircraft, domestic heaters, etc. **2** any of a range of unreactive, saturated hydrocarbons. [from Latin *parum*, little + *affinis*, having an affinity, with reference to its unreactiveness]

paraffin oil 1 *Chem.* a viscous yellow oil made from petroleum and used as a lubricant and a laxative. **2** kerosene.

paraffin wax *Chem.* a white tasteless odourless translucent solid, insoluble in water, consisting of a mixture of solid hydrocarbons obtained from petroleum, and used to make candles, polishes, and cosmetics, and for coating paper. Also called PETROLEUM WAX.

paraglider *noun Aeron.* a glider with inflatable wings.

paragliding *noun* a sport in which the participant is towed through the air by a light aircraft while wearing a modified type of parachute, then released to drift to the ground.

paragon /'parəgən/ *noun* someone who is a model of excellence or perfection. [from Old Italian *paragone*, comparison]

. . . .

◧ ideal, exemplar, epitome, quintessence, model, pattern, archetype, prototype, standard.

. . . .

paragraph — *noun* **1** a section of a piece of writing, starting on a fresh, often indented, line, and dealing with a distinct point or idea. **2** a short report in a newspaper. **3** (*also* **paragraph mark**) *Printing* a sign (¶), indicating the start of a new paragraph. — *verb* to divide (text) into paragraphs. [from Greek *paragraphe*, marked passage, from *para*, beside + *graphein*, to write]

. . . .

◧ *noun* **1** passage, section, part, portion, subsection, subdivision, clause, item. **2** report, article, passage.

. . . .

parakeet /'parəkiːt/ *noun* any of various small, long-tailed parrots. [from Old French *paroquet*, parrot]

paralanguage *noun* those elements of communication other than words, ie tone of voice, gesture, or body language, facial expression, etc.

paraldehyde /pə'raldɪhaɪd/ *noun Chem.* (FORMULA $C_6H_{12}O_3$) a colourless flammable toxic liquid that is a polymer of acetaldehyde, and is used as a solvent and sleep-inducing drug.

parallax *noun* **1** *Physics* the apparent change in the position of an object, relative to a distant background, when it is viewed from two different positions. **2** *Astron.* the angle between two straight lines joining two different observation points to a celestial body. Parallax is used to measure the distance of stars from the Earth. [from Greek *parallaxis*, change]

parallel — *adj.* (*often* **parallel to something**) **1** *said of lines or planes* being at every point the same distance apart. **2** similar; exactly equivalent; corresponding. — *adv.* (*often* **parallel to something**) alongside and at an unvarying distance from. — *noun* **1** *Geom.* a line or plane parallel to another. **2** a corresponding or equivalent instance. **3** (*also* **parallel of latitude**) any of the lines of latitude circling the earth parallel to the equator and representing the angular degrees of distance from it. **4** (**parallels**) *Printing* the sign (‖) used as a reference mark. — *verb* (**paralleled, paralleling**) **1** to equal. **2** to correspond to or be equivalent to. — **in parallel** *said of electrical appliances* so co-ordinated that terminals of the same polarity are connected. **on a parallel with something** corresponding to it. **without parallel** unequalled; unprecedented. [from Greek *parallelos*, side by side]

. . . .

◧ *adj.* **1** aligned, equidistant. **2** similar, equivalent, corresponding, analogous, matching, like, resembling. *noun* **2** correspondence, correlation, equivalence, equivalent, analogy, comparison, coun-terpart, similarity, resemblance, likeness, match, equal, twin, duplicate, analogue. *verb* **1** match. **2** correspond, correlate, compare, liken, echo, conform, agree.
◪ *adj.* DIVERGENT. **2** different. *verb* DIVERGE, DIFFER.

. . . .

parallel bars two parallel shoulder-height rails fixed to upright posts, used by men for gymnastic exercises.

parallel circuit *Physics* an electrical circuit in which only a fraction of the total current flows through each of the circuit components, because they are arranged in such a way that the current is split between two or more parallel paths.

parallelism *noun* **1** being parallel. **2** resemblance in corresponding details.

parallelogram /parə'lɛləgram/ *noun Geom.* a four-sided plane (two-dimensional) figure in which opposite sides are parallel and equal in length, and opposite angles are equal. A parallelogram in which all four sides are of equal length is known as a *rhombus*.

parallelogram of vectors *Maths.* a figure that is constructed in order to add two vectors, by drawing them to scale so that they form two adjacent sides of the parallelogram, and then completing the remaining two sides of the figure. The diagonal of the parallelogram, from the angle between the two added vectors, is equal to their sum.

parallel port *Comput.* a socket or plug for connecting a peripheral device such as a printer to a computer.

paralympics /parə'lɪmpɪks/ *noun* an Olympic competition for people with physical disabilities, held at the same time as the traditional Olympic games. [from PARALLEL + OLYMPICS]

paralyse *verb* 1 to affect (a person or bodily part) with paralysis. 2 *said of fear, etc* to have an immobilizing effect on. 3 to disrupt or bring to a standstill. [from Greek *paralyein*, to enfeeble]

∷ · · · · · · · · · · · · · · · · · ·
⊟ **1** cripple, lame, disable, immobilize, incapacitate, deaden, numb. **2** immobilize, freeze, transfix. **3** disrupt, halt, stop.
· ·

paralysis /pə'ralɪsɪs/ *noun* 1 a temporary or permanent loss of muscular function or sensation in any part of the body, the most commonly affected muscles being those that are normally under voluntary control. 2 a state of immobility; a standstill.

· ·
⊟ **1** paraplegia, quadriplegia, palsy, numbness, deadness, immobility. **2** halt, standstill, immobility, stoppage, shutdown.
· ·

paralytic /parə'lɪtɪk/ — *adj.* 1 relating to, caused by, or suffering from paralysis. 2 *colloq.* helplessly drunk. — *noun* a person affected by paralysis.

paralytically *adv.* so as to be paralytic.

Paramecium /parə'mi:sɪəm/ *noun* a single-celled protozoan, common in aquatic habitats, ovoid in shape, and up to 0.33mm in length. [from Greek *paramekes*, long-shaped]

paramedic *noun* a person, such as a technician or member of an ambulance crew, who helps medical staff or whose work supplements medical work.

paramedical *adj. Medicine* denoting personnel or services that are supplementary to and support the work of the medical profession, eg nursing staff, physiotherapists, and ambulance crews.

parameter /pə'ramɪtə(r)/ *noun* 1 *Maths.* a constant or variable that, when altered, affects the form of a mathematical expression in which it appears. 2 *Physics* a quantity which under a particular set of conditions remains constant, but may be altered if the conditions change. 3 (*often* **parameters**) a limiting factor that serves to define the scope of a task, project, discussion, etc. [from modern Latin *parametrum*, from PARA-¹ + Greek *metron*, measure]

· · · · · · · · · · · · · · · · · · · ·
⊟ **3** limitation, restriction, criterion, specification, limit, boundary, guideline, indication.
· ·

paramilitary *adj.* organized on the same basis as a military force, and usually reinforcing it.

paramount *adj.* foremost; supreme; of supreme importance. [from Old French *par*, by + *amont*, above, upwards]

· · · · · · · · · · · · · · · · · · · ·
⊟ foremost, supreme, highest, topmost, predominant, pre-eminent, prime, principal, main, chief, cardinal, primary, first.
⊟ lowest, last.
· ·

paranoia /parə'nɔɪə/ *noun* 1 *Psychol.* a rare mental disorder, characterized by delusions of persecution by others,

especially if this is attributed to one's own importance or unique gifts. 2 a strong feeling that one is being persecuted by others, resulting in a tendency to be suspicious and distrustful, and to become increasingly isolated. [from Greek *paranoia*, from *para*, beside, beyond + *nous*, mind]

paranoiac or **paranoid** — *adj.* relating to or affected by paranoia. — *noun* a person affected by paranoia.

paranoiacally *adv.* in a paranoiac way.

paranormal — *adj.*, *said of occurrences* beyond the normal scope of scientific explanation. — *noun* (**the paranormal**) paranormal occurrences.

parapet /'parəpɪt/ *noun* 1 a low wall along the edge of a bridge, balcony, etc. 2 an embankment of earth or sandbags protecting the soldiers in a military trench. [from Italian *parapetto*, from *parare*, to defend + *petto*, chest]

paraphernalia /parəfə'neɪlɪə/ *pl. noun* 1 the equipment and accessories associated with an activity, etc. 2 personal belongings. [from Greek *parapherna*, a bride's personal effects, ie not part of her dowry, from *para*, beside + *pherne*, dowry]

· · · · · · · · · · · · · · · · · · · ·
⊟ **1** equipment, *colloq.* gear, tackle, apparatus, accessories, trappings. **2** belongings, bits and pieces, odds and ends, effects, stuff, *colloq.* gear, things, baggage.
· ·

paraphrase — *noun* a restatement of something giving its meaning in other words; a rewording or rephrasing. — *verb* to express in other words. [from PARA-¹ + Greek *phrazein*, to speak]

· · · · · · · · · · · · · · · · · · · ·
⊟ *noun* rewording, rephrasing, restatement, version, interpretation, rendering, translation. *verb* reword, rephrase, restate, interpret, render, translate.
· ·

paraplegia /parə'pli:dʒɪə/ *noun Medicine* paralysis of the lower half of the body, including both legs, usually caused by injury or disease of the spinal cord. [from Greek *paraplegia*, a one-sided stroke, from *para*, beside + *plege*, blow]

paraplegic /parə'pli:dʒɪk/ — *adj.* 1 affected with paraplegia. 2 marked by or typical of paraplegia. — *noun* a person affected with paraplegia.

parapsychological *adj.* relating to or involving parapsychology.

parapsychologist *noun* a person who studies parapsychology.

parapsychology *noun* the study of those mental phenomena, eg telepathy and clairvoyance, that imply an acquisition of knowledge other than through the known senses.

Paraquat /'parəkwɒt/ *noun trademark* a weedkiller highly poisonous to humans. [from part of the technical description of the chemical]

parasailing *noun* a sport similar to paragliding in which the participant is towed into the air by a motorboat, wearing water-skis and a modified type of parachute. [from PARA-² + SAIL]

parasite /'parəsaɪt/ *noun* 1 a plant or animal that for all or part of its life obtains food and physical protection from a living organism of another species (the *host*), which is usually damaged by the presence of the parasite, and never benefits from the association. 2 *derog.* a person who lives at the expense of others. [from PARA-¹ + Greek *sitos*, food]

· · · · · · · · · · · · · · · · · · · ·
⊟ **2** *colloq.* sponger, scrounger, cadger, hanger-on, leech, *colloq.* bloodsucker.
· ·

parasitic /parə'sɪtɪk/ or **parasitical** *adj.* 1 *said of an animal or plant* living on another. 2 *said of a person* depending on others.

parasitically *adv.* in a parasitic way; as a parasite.

parasitism /'parəsaɪtɪzm/ *noun* a close association between two living organisms in which one (the parasite) obtains food and physical protection from the other (the host).

parasitology /parəsaɪ'tɒlədʒɪ/ *noun Zool.* the scientific study of parasites, especially protozoans, worms, and arthropods (eg mosquitoes, lice) that cause or transmit diseases to humans and animals.

parasol /'parəsɒl/ *noun* a light umbrella used as a protection against the sun; a sunshade. [from French, from Italian *parasole*, from *parare*, to ward off + *sole*, sun]

parasympathetic nervous system *Zool.* in vertebrates, a subdivision of the autonomic nervous system. The activity of the parasympathetic nervous system tends to slow down the heart rate, promote digestion, dilate blood vessels, and generally conserve energy by decreasing the activity of the glands and smooth muscles. See also SYMPATHETIC NERVOUS SYSTEM.

parathormone /parə'θɔːmoʊn/ *noun Physiol.* parathyroid hormone.

parathyroid *noun Physiol.* in mammals, any of four small glands near or within the thyroid, producing parathyroid hormone.

parathyroid hormone *Medicine* a hormone, released by the parathyroid glands in response to low blood calcium levels, that raises blood calcium levels by stimulating the removal of calcium from bone, and inhibiting its excretion by the kidneys. Also called PARATHORMONE.

paratrooper *noun* a member of the paratroops.

paratroops *pl. noun* troops trained to parachute into enemy territory or a battle zone.

paratyphoid *noun Medicine* an infectious disease, similar to but milder than typhoid fever, caused by the bacterium *Salmonella paratyphi*, and characterized by a pink rash, fever, abdominal pain, and diarrhoea.

parboil /'pɑːbɔɪl/ *verb* to boil until partially cooked. [from Old French *parboillir*, from Latin *perbullire*, to boil thoroughly; meaning altered by confusion of *par* with PART]

parcel — *noun* **1** something wrapped in paper, etc and secured with string or sticky tape. **2** a portion, eg of land. **3** a group of people, etc. **4** a lot or portion of goods for sale; a deal or transaction. — *verb* (**parcelled, parcelling**) **1** (*also* **parcel something up**) to wrap it up in a parcel. **2** (*also* **parcel something out**) to divide it into portions and share it out. [from Old French *parcelle*, from Latin *particula*, diminutive of *pars*, part]

> ■ *noun* **1** package, packet, pack, box, carton, bundle. **2** portion, piece, plot. **4** lot, deal, transaction, package. *verb* **1** package, pack, wrap, bundle, tie up. **2** divide, carve up, apportion, allocate, allot, share out, distribute, dispense, dole out, deal out, mete out.

parch *verb* **1** to dry up; to deprive (soil, plants, etc) of water. **2** to make thirsty. **3** to roast (peas) slightly. [from Middle English *perchen*]

> ■ **1** dry (up), desiccate, dehydrate, bake, burn, scorch, sear, blister, wither, shrivel.

parchment *noun* **1** a material formerly used for bookbinding and for writing on, made from goatskin, calfskin, or sheepskin; a piece of this, or a manuscript written on it. **2** stiff off-white writing-paper resembling this. [from Old French *parchemin* from Latin *Pergamena charta*, paper of Pergamum, influenced by Old French *parche*, leather]

pardon — *verb* (**pardoned, pardoning**) **1** to forgive or excuse (someone) for (a fault or offence). **2** to cancel the punishment of. — *noun* **1** forgiveness. **2** the cancellation of a punishment. — **I beg your pardon** or **pardon me** a formula of apology, or (*often shortened to* **pardon**) a request to someone to repeat something said. [from French *pardonner*, from Latin *perdonare*, to overlook]

> ■ *verb* **1** forgive, condone, overlook, excuse, vindicate, acquit,

absolve. **2** let off, reprieve, free, liberate, release. *noun* **1** forgiveness, amnesty, acquittal, absolution. **2** reprieve, release, discharge, indulgence, mercy, clemency.
> ⊟ *verb* PUNISH, DISCIPLINE. *noun* PUNISHMENT, CONDEMNATION.

pardonable *adj.* that may be pardoned; excusable.

> ■ forgivable, excusable, justifiable, warrantable, understandable, allowable, permissible, minor, venial.
> ⊟ unpardonable, inexcusable.

pardoner *noun* in the Middle Ages, a person licensed to sell pardons from the pope, freeing people from punishment for their sins.

pare *verb* **1** (*also* **pare something away**) to trim off (skin, etc) in layers. **2** to cut (fingernails or toenails). **3** to peel (fruit). **4** (*also* **pare something down**) to reduce expenses, funding, etc gradually, in order to economize. [from French *parer*, from Latin *parare*, to prepare]

> ■ **1, 3** peel, skin. **2** cut, clip, trim. **4** cut, cut back, reduce, decrease, prune, crop, dock, lop.

parenchyma /pə'reŋkɪmə/ *noun* **1** *Bot.* in plants, a tissue composed of thin-walled relatively unspecialized cells, that serves mainly as a packing tissue. **2** *Zool.* the loosely packed cells that form much of the body tissue of simple animals such as flatworms. [from PARA-[1] + Greek *enchyma*, infusion]

parent — *noun* **1** a father or mother. **2** the adopter or guardian of a child. **3** an animal that has produced offspring. **4** a plant that has produced offspring. **5** that from which anything is derived; a source or origin. — *verb intrans., trans.* to be or act as a parent; to care for as a parent. [from Latin *parens*, from *parere*, to bring forth]

> ■ *noun* **1** father, mother, progenitor, begetter, procreator. **3** dam, sire. **5** source, origin, progenitor, begetter.

parentage *noun* family or ancestry.

parental /pə'rentl/ *adj.* related to or concerning parents.

parentally *adv.* in a parental way; by parents.

parent company a business company owning other, usually smaller companies.

parenthesis /pə'renθəsɪs/ *noun* (PL. **parentheses**) **1** a word or phrase inserted into a sentence as a comment, usually marked off by brackets or dashes. **2** (**parentheses**) a pair of round brackets () used to enclose such a comment. [from PARA-[1] + Greek *en*, in + *thesis*, placing]

parenthetic /parən'θetɪk/ or **parenthetical** *adj.* **1** of the nature of a parenthesis. **2** using parenthesis.

parenthetically *adv.* in a parenthetic way; in parenthesis.

parenthood *noun* **1** being a parent. **2** the responsibilities of a parent.

parenting *noun* the activities and duties of a parent.

par excellence /pɑː 'reksəlɒ̃s/ in the highest degree; in the truest sense of the word; beyond compare. [French, = as an example of excellence]

pariah /pə'raɪə/ *noun* **1** someone scorned and avoided by others; a social outcast. **2** in S India and Burma, a person of no, or low, caste. [from Tamil *paraiyan*, drummer]

parietal /pə'raɪɪtl/ *adj.* relating to, or forming, the wall of a bodily cavity, eg the skull: *the parietal bones*. [from Latin *paries*, wall]

parish *noun* **1** a district or area served by its own church and priest or minister. **2** (*also* **civil parish**) especially in England, the smallest unit of local government. **3** the inhabitants of a parish. [from Old French *paroisse*, from Greek *paroikia*, from *paroikos*, neighbour]

> ■ **3** parishioners, church, churchgoers, congregation,

flock, fold, community.

. . . .

parish clerk an official performing various duties connected with a parish church.

parish council the administrative body of a civil parish.

parish councillor a member of a parish council.

parishioner *noun* a member or inhabitant of a parish.

parish register a book in which the christenings, marriages, and deaths in a parish are recorded.

parity /'parɪtɪ/ *noun* (PL. **parities**) **1** equality, eg in pay. **2** precise equivalence; exact correspondence. **3** *Commerce* an established equivalence between a unit of national currency and an amount in another national currency. [from Latin *paritas*, from *par*, equal]

park — *noun* **1** an area in a town with grass and trees, reserved for public recreation. **2** an area of land kept as a nature reserve, etc: *a wildlife park.* **3** the woodland and pasture forming the estate of a large country house. **4** (**Park**) used in street names. **5** *chiefly North Amer.* a sports field or stadium. **6** (**the park**) *colloq.* the pitch in use in a football game. **7** a place where vehicles can be left temporarily. — *verb* **1** *trans., intrans.* to leave (a vehicle) temporarily at the side of the road or in a car park; to manoeuvre (a vehicle) into this position. **2** *colloq.* to lay, place, or leave (something) somewhere temporarily. **3** *colloq.* to install or sit (oneself). [from Old French *parc*]

. . . .

◨ *noun* **1** garden(s). **2** reserve, sanctuary. **3** grounds, estate, parkland, gardens, woodland. *verb* **2** put, lay, place, leave, deposit.

. . . .

parka *noun* **1** a hooded jacket made of skins, worn by the Inuit and Aleut people of the Arctic. **2** a windproof jacket, especially quilted with a fur-trimmed hood; an anorak. [from Aleut *parka*, skin, coat, from Russian *parka*, pelt, skin jacket]

park-and-ride *noun* a system of travel to an urban centre by means of bus and train links from large car parks on the outskirts.

parkin *noun* a moist ginger-flavoured oatmeal cake made with treacle.

parking-lot *noun North Amer.* a car park.

parking meter a coin-operated meter in the street beside which a car may be parked for a limited period.

parking ticket an official notice of a fine served on a motorist for illegal parking.

parkinsonism /'pɑːkɪnsənɪzm/ *noun Medicine* the symptoms of Parkinson's disease, which have developed as a complication of another disease, such as encephalitis, or as a side-effect of certain drugs. [named after the English physician James Parkinson, who first described Parkinson's disease]

Parkinson's disease *Medicine* a slowly progressive disorder of the central nervous system that usually occurs later in life. Symptoms include trembling of the muscles of the hands and limbs, slowing of voluntary movements, muscular weakness, and a slow shuffling gait and stooping posture. [named after James Parkinson, who first described it]

Parkinson's law the maxim that work expands to fill the time available for its completion. [from the English writer, historian, and political scientist C Northcote Parkinson, who wrote about it]

parkland *noun* pasture and woodland forming part of a country estate.

parkway *noun* a broad thoroughfare incorporating grassy areas and lined with trees, often connecting the parks of a town.

parky *adj.* (**parkier, parkiest**) *Brit. colloq., said of the weather* somewhat cold; chilly.

parlance /'pɑːləns/ *noun* a particular style of using words: *in legal parlance.* [from Old French, from *parler*, to talk]

parley /'pɑːlɪ/ — *verb intrans.* (**parleys, parleyed**) to discuss peace terms, etc with an enemy. — *noun* (PL. **parleys**) a meeting with an enemy to discuss peace terms, etc. [from Old French *parler*, to talk]

parliament /'pɑːləmənt/ *noun* the highest law-making assembly of a nation; (**Parliament**) in Britain, the House of Commons and House of Lords. [from Old French *parlement*, from *parler*, to talk]

. . . .

◨ legislature, senate, congress, house, assembly, convocation, council, diet.

. . . .

Names of parliaments and political assemblies include: House of Representatives, Senate (*Australia*); Nationalrat, Bundesrat (*Austria*); Narodno Sobraniye (*Bulgaria*); House of Commons, Senate (*Canada*); National People's Congress (*China*); Folketing (*Denmark*); People's Assembly (*Egypt*); Eduskunta (*Finland*); National Assembly, Senate (*France*); Bundesrat, Bundestag, Landtag (*Germany*); Althing (*Iceland*); Lok Sabha, Rajya Sabha (*India*); Majlis (*Iran*); Dáil, Seanad (*Ireland*); Knesset (*Israel*); Camera dei Deputati, Senato (*Italy*); Diet (*Japan*); Staten-Generaal (*Netherlands*); House of Representatives (*New Zealand*); Storting (*Norway*); Sejm (*Poland*); Cortes (*Portugal*); Congress of People's Deputies, Supreme Soviet (*Russia*); House of Assembly (*South Africa*); Cortes (*Spain*); Riksdag (*Sweden*); Nationalrat, Ständerat, Bundesrat (*Switzerland*); Porte (*Turkey*); House of Commons, House of Lords (*UK*); House of Representatives, Senate (*US*); National Assembly (*Vietnam*).

parliamentarian /pɑːləmən'teərɪən/ *noun* **1** an expert in parliamentary procedure. **2** an experienced parliamentary debater. **3** *Hist.* a supporter of the Parliamentary party in the 17c English Civil War.

parliamentary /pɑːlə'mentərɪ/ *adj.* **1** relating to, or issued by, a parliament. **2** *said of conduct or procedure* in keeping with the rules of parliament. **3** *said of language* admissible in parliament.

. . . .

◨ **1** governmental, senatorial, congressional, legislative, law-making.

. . . .

parlour *noun* **1** a sitting-room for receiving visitors. **2** a shop or commercial premises providing particular goods or services: *an ice-cream parlour/beauty parlour/funeral parlour* etc. [from Old French *parlur*, from *parler*, to talk]

parlour game a game such as charades, suitable for playing in the sitting-room.

parlous /'pɑːləs/ *adj.* precarious; perilous; dire. [a variant of PERILOUS]

Parmesan /pɑːmə'zan/ *noun* a hard dry Italian cheese, especially served grated with pasta dishes. [from Italian *Parmegiano*, from Parma]

parochial /pə'rəʊkɪəl/ *adj.* **1** *derog.* concerned only with local affairs; narrow, limited, or provincial in outlook. **2** of, or relating to, a parish. [from Latin *parochialis*, from *parochia*, parish]

. . . .

◨ **1** insular, provincial, petty, small-minded, narrow-minded, inward-looking, blinkered, limited, restricted, confined.

. . . .

parochialism *noun* **1** narrowness of view, provincialism. **2** a system of local government based on the parish as a unit.

parodist *noun* the author of a parody.

parody /'parədɪ/ — *noun* (PL. **parodies**) **1** a comic or satirical imitation of a work, or the style, of a particular writer, composer, etc. **2** a poor attempt at something; a mockery or travesty. — *verb* (**parodies, parodied**) to ridicule through parody; to mimic satirically. [from PARA-[1] and Greek *oide*, song]

⊟ *noun* **1** caricature, satire, lampoon, burlesque, *Brit. colloq.* send-up, *colloq.* spoof, take-off, skit, mimicry, imitation. **2** travesty, mockery, distortion. *verb* ridicule, mimic, caricature, lampoon, burlesque, satirize, send up, *colloq.* spoof, imitate, ape, take off.

parole /pə'roʊl/ — *noun* **1** the release of a prisoner before the end of his or her sentence, on promise of good behaviour: *released on parole.* **2** the promise of a prisoner so released to behave well. — *verb* to release or place (a prisoner) on parole. [from French *parole d'honneur*, word of honour]

parousia /pə'ruːzɪə/ *noun Relig.* the second coming of Christ. In Christian thought, it will be marked by a heavenly appearance, God's judgement of all humanity, and the resurrection of the dead. [from Greek *parousia*, presence, arrival]

paroxysm /'parəksɪzm/ *noun* **1** a sudden emotional outburst, eg of rage or laughter. **2** a spasm, convulsion, or seizure, eg of coughing or acute pain. **3** a sudden reappearance of or increase in the severity of the symptoms of a disease or disorder. [from Greek *paroxysmos*, a fit]

⊟ **1** outburst, explosion. **2** spasm, convulsion, seizure, fit, attack. **3** outbreak.

paroxysmal *adj.* relating to or of the nature of a paroxysm; marked by paroxysms.

parquet /'pɑːkeɪ/ *noun* flooring composed of small inlaid blocks of wood arranged in a geometric pattern. [from Old French, diminutive of *parc*, enclosure]

parquetry /'pɑːkətrɪ/ *noun* inlaid work in wood used for flooring.

parr *noun* (PL. **parr, parrs**) a young salmon aged up to two years.

parricidal *adj.* relating to or involving parricide.

parricide /'parɪsaɪd/ *noun* the killing of, or a person who kills, a parent or near relative. [from Latin *parricidium* (the killing), *parricida* (the killer), probably from *pater*, father + *caedere*, to kill]

parrot — *noun* **1** any of about 317 species of bird, including the cockatoos, lories, macaws, parakeets, budgerigars, and lovebirds, found in forests in most of the warmer regions of the world. **2** a person who merely imitates or mimics others. — *verb* (**parroted, parroting**) to repeat or mimic (another's words, etc) unthinkingly. [from Old French *paroquet*, perhaps diminutive of *Pierre*]

parrot-fashion *adv.* by mindless repetition.

parrotfish *noun* a colourful fish, so called because the jaw teeth are fused into a parrot-like beak that is used for scraping algal and coral growth from reefs.

parry — *verb* (**parries, parried**) **1** to fend off (a blow). **2** to sidestep (a question) adroitly. — *noun* (PL. **parries**) an act of parrying. [from French *parer*, to ward off]

⊟ *verb* **1** fend off, ward off, repel, deflect, block. **2** sidestep, evade, avoid, *colloq.* duck, dodge, shun, field.

parse /pɑːz/ *verb trans., intrans.* **1** *Grammar* to analyse (a sentence) grammatically; to give the part of speech and explain the grammatical role of (a word). **2** *Comput.* to analyse (a string of input symbols) in terms of the computing language being used. [from Latin *pars orationis*, part of speech]

parsec /'pɑːsɛk/ *noun Astron.* a unit of distance in space equal to 3.26 light years or 3.09×10^{13} km, used for distances that extend beyond the Solar System. [from PARALLAX + SECOND]

Parsee /'pɑːsiː, pɑːsiː/ *noun* one of the descendants of the ancient Zoroastrians, who fled from Persia to settle in the Bombay area of India in the 8CAD. [from Persian *Parsee*, Persian]

Parseeism *noun* the religion of the Parsees, based on a rule of life that conforms to the purity of Ahura Mazda.

parser *noun Comput.* a program which analyses and structures text or other input data.

parsimonious /pɑːsɪ'moʊnɪəs/ *adj.* too careful in spending money; stingy. [from Latin *parsimonia*, thrift]

parsimony /'pɑːsɪmənɪ/ *noun* **1** reluctance or extreme care in spending money. **2** praiseworthy economy. **3** avoiding excess. **4** meanness.

parsley *noun* a plant with curled feathery leaves used as a garnish and flavouring. [from Greek *petroselinon*, from *petra*, rock + *selinon*, parsley]

parsnip *noun* a pungent-tasting root vegetable that looks like a thick white carrot. [from Latin *pastinacum* (from *pastinum*, dibble) + Middle English *nepe*, turnip]

parson *noun* **1** a parish priest in the Church of England. **2** any clergyman. [from Latin *persona*, parish priest, person, personage, mask]

⊟ **2** vicar, rector, priest, minister, pastor, preacher, clergyman, clergywoman, reverend, cleric, churchman, churchwoman.

parsonage *noun* the residence of a parson.

parson's nose *colloq.* a piece of fatty flesh at the rump of a plucked fowl, especially a turkey or chicken.

part — *noun* **1** a portion, piece, or bit; some but not all. **2** one of a set of equal divisions or amounts that compose a whole: *in the proportion of five parts cement to two of sand.* **3** an essential piece; a component: *vehicle spare parts.* **4** a section of a book; any of the episodes of a story, etc issued or broadcast as a serial. **5** a performer's role in a play, opera, etc; the words, actions, etc belonging to the role. **6** the melody, etc given to a particular instrument or voice in a musical work. **7** one's share, responsibility, or duty in something: *do one's part/want no part in/of it.* **8** (*usually* **parts**) a region: *foreign parts.* **9** (**parts**) talents; abilities: *a woman of parts.* — *verb* **1** to separate (eg curtains, combatants, etc). **2** *intrans.* (**part from** or **with someone**) to leave them or separate from them. **3** *intrans., said of more than one person* to leave one another; to separate or diverge. **4** *intrans., trans.* (**part with something** or **be parted from it**) to give it up or hand it over: *they were reluctant to part with/be parted from their money.* **5** to put a parting in (hair). — **the better** or **best** or **greater part of something** most of it. **for the most part 1** usually. **2** mostly or mainly. **for my part** as far as I am concerned. **in great** or **large part** mostly. **in part** partly. **on the part of someone 1** as done by them. **2** so far as they are concerned. **part and parcel of something** an essential part of it. **part company with someone** to separate from them. **play a part** to be involved. **take something in good part** to take no offence at a criticism, joke, etc. **take part in something** to participate in it; to share in it. **take someone's part** to support someone; to take someone's side. [from Latin *pars*, part]

⊟ *noun* **1** portion, piece, bit, particle, fragment, scrap, division, segment, fraction, portion, section, department, component, constituent, element, factor. **4** *section* chapter, passage, scene, *episode* episode, instalment. **5** role, character. **7** share, duty, responsibility, task, office, function, capacity. **8** region, district, territory, sector. *verb* **1** separate, detach, disconnect, sever, split, tear, break, break up, take apart, dismantle, come apart, split up, divide. **2** part company from or with, split up from, separate from, leave, withdraw from, go away from, depart from. **3** disperse, separate, diverge, disband, scatter, split up, break up. **4** give up, hand over, relinquish, let go of, yield, surrender, renounce, forego, abandon, discard, jettison.

⊞ *noun* **1** whole, totality.

partake *verb intrans.* (PAST TENSE **partook**; PAST PARTICIPLE **partaken**) (*usually* **partake in** or **of something**) **1** to participate in something. **2** to eat or drink. **3** *literary* to have a certain quality, etc to a degree. [formed from *partaking*, from Middle English *part-taking*]

parterre /pɑːˈtɛə(r)/ *noun* **1** a formal, ornamental flower-garden laid out with lawns and paths. **2** the pit of a theatre. [from French *par terre*, on the ground]

part exchange a purchase or sale made by exchanging used goods for part of the value of new goods.

parthenogenesis /pɑːθənoʊˈdʒɛnəsɪs/ *noun Biol.* in some insects and plants, reproduction without fertilization by the male. [from Greek *parthenos*, maiden + GENESIS]

Parthian /ˈpɑːθɪən/ — *noun* a member of an ancient people who, from the 3c BC, ruled an empire that stretched from the Euphrates to the Indus but were finally conquered in AD 224. — *adj.* relating to the Parthians.

Parthian shot a final hostile remark made on departing. See also PARTING SHOT. [from the practice of the horsemen of ancient Parthia of turning to shoot arrows at following enemies as they rode off]

partial /ˈpɑːʃəl/ *adj.* **1** incomplete; in part only. **2** (**partial to something**) having a liking for it. **3** favouring one side or person unfairly; biased. [from Latin *partialis*, from *pars*, part]

....

🔲 **1** incomplete, limited, restricted, imperfect, fragmentary, unfinished. **2** fond of, keen on, *colloq.* crazy about, *colloq.* mad about. **3** biased, prejudiced, partisan, one-sided, discriminatory, unfair, unjust, predisposed, coloured, affected.

🔀 **1** complete, total. **3** impartial, disinterested, unbiased, fair.

....

partial fraction *Maths.* one of a number of fractions into which another fraction can be separated, eg – and – are partial fractions of –.

partiality *noun* **1** being partial. **2** favourable bias or prejudice. **3** fondness.

....

🔲 **3** liking, fondness, predilection, inclination, preference, proclivity.

....

partially *adv.* not completely or wholly; not yet to the point of completion.

participant /pɑːˈtɪsɪpənt/ or **participator** *noun* a person or group that takes part.

....

🔲 contributor, entrant, member, party, co-operator, helper, worker.

....

participate /pɑːˈtɪsɪpeɪt/ *verb intrans.* (**participate in something**) to take part or be involved in it. [from Latin *pars*, part + *capere*, to take]

....

🔲 take part in, join in, contribute to, engage in, be involved in, enter, share in, partake of, help with, assist with.

....

participation *noun* participating; involvement.

....

🔲 participating, involvement, sharing, partnership, co-operation, contribution, assistance.

....

participatory /pɑːtɪsɪˈpeɪtərɪ/ *adj.* capable of being participated in or shared.

participial /pɑːtɪˈsɪpɪəl/ *adj. Grammar* having the role of a participle.

participially *adv.* as a participle.

participle /ˈpɑːtɪsɪpl/ *noun* a word formed from a verb and used as an adjective or to form tenses. In English, the present participle is formed with *-ing* (as in *going* and *hitting*), and the *past participle* generally with *-ed, -t, -en,* or *-n* (as in *asked, burned* or *burnt, taken,* and *shown*). [from Latin *participium*, a sharing, participle, from *pars*, part + *capere*, to take (from its sharing features of both a verb and an adjective)]

particle /ˈpɑːtɪkl/ *noun* **1** *Physics* a tiny unit of matter such as a molecule, atom, or electron. **2** a tiny piece. **3** the least bit: *not a particle of sympathy.* **4** *Grammar* an uninflected word, eg a preposition, conjunction, or interjection. **5** *Grammar* an affix, such as *un-* and *-ly*. [from Latin *particula*, diminutive of *pars*, part]

....

🔲 **2, 3** bit, fragment, scrap, shred, sliver, speck, morsel, crumb, iota, whit, jot, tittle, atom, grain, drop.

....

particle accelerator *Physics* a device that is used to accelerate charged subatomic particles, especially electrons or protons, to a high velocity.

particle beam weapons weapons in which high-energy sub-atomic particles, generated in nuclear accelerators, are turned into a directable beam.

particle physics the branch of physics concerned with the study of the elementary particles that are the fundamental components of matter, and the forces between them.

particoloured *adj.* partly one colour, partly another; variegated. [from Old French *parti*, variegated]

particular — *adj.* **1** specific; single; individually known or referred to. **2** especial: *took particular care.* **3** difficult to satisfy; fastidious; exacting. **4** exact; detailed. — *noun* **1** a detail. **2** (**particulars**) personal details: *took down her particulars.* — **in particular** especially; specifically. [from Latin *particularis*, from *particula*, diminutive of *pars*, part]

....

🔲 *adj.* **1** specific, single, distinct, peculiar, special. **2** especial, special, exceptional, notable, marked, unusual, uncommon. **3** fussy, fastidious, exacting, *colloq.* choosy, finicky, discriminating. **4** exact, detailed, thorough, precise. *noun* **1** detail, specific, point, feature, item, fact, circumstance.

🔀 *adj.* **1** general. **3** easy-going.

....

particularization or **particularisation** *noun* particularizing, detailing.

particularize or **particularise** *verb* **1** to specify individually. **2** to give specific examples of. **3** *intrans.* to go into detail.

particularly *adv.* **1** more than usually: *particularly good.* **2** specifically; especially: *particularly hates board games.*

....

🔲 **1** exceptionally, remarkably, notably, especially, extraordinarily, unusually, uncommonly, surprisingly, in particular. **2** specifically, especially, explicitly.

....

parting *noun* **1** the act of taking leave. **2** a divergence or separation: *a parting of the ways.* **3** a line of exposed scalp dividing hair brushed in opposite directions.

....

🔲 **1** departure, going, leave-taking, farewell, goodbye, adieu. **2** divergence, separation, division, partition, rift, split, rupture, breaking.

🔀 **1** meeting. **2** convergence.

....

parting shot a last hostile remark made on leaving. See also PARTHIAN SHOT.

partisan /pɑːtɪˈzan, ˈpɑːtɪzan/ — *noun* **1** an enthusiastic supporter of a party, person, cause, etc. **2** a member of a resistance group in a country occupied by an enemy. — *adj.* strongly loyal to one side, especially blindly so; biased. [from French *partisan*]

....

🔲 *noun* **1** supporter, follower, devotee, adherent, disciple, backer, champion, stalwart. **2** guerrilla, resistance fighter, freedom fighter, irregular. *adj.* biased, prejudiced, partial, predisposed, discriminatory, one-sided, factional, sectarian.

🔀 *adj.* impartial.

....

partisanship *noun* the quality of being partisan.

partita /pɑːˈtiːtə/ *noun Mus.* **1** (PL. **partite**) in the 17c, one of a set of instrumental variations. **2** (PL. **partitas**) especially in the 18c, a suite of instrumental dances. [from Italian *partita*, division]

partition — *noun* **1** a screen or thin wall dividing a room. **2** the dividing of a country into two or more independent states. — *verb* (**partitioned**, **partitioning**) **1** to divide (a country) into independent states. **2** (*also* **partition something off**) to separate it off with a partition. [from Latin *partitio*, division]

> ■ *noun* **1** screen, wall, room-divider, divider, barrier, panel. **2** division, break-up, splitting, separation, parting, severance. *verb* **1** divide, split up, parcel out. **2** separate (off), divide (off), screen (off), wall off, fence off.

partitive /ˈpɑːtɪtɪv/ *Grammar* — *adj.*, *said of a word, form, etc* denoting a part of a whole. — *noun* a partitive word or form, eg *some*, *any*, *most*. [from Latin *partire*, to divide]

partly *adv.* in part, or in some parts; to a certain extent; not wholly.

> ■ in part, somewhat, to a certain extent, to some extent, up to a point, slightly, fractionally, moderately, relatively, incompletely.
> ▣ completely, wholly, totally.

partner — *noun* **1** one of two or more people jointly owning or running a business or other enterprise on an equal footing. **2** a person one dances with. **3** a person who is on the same side as oneself in a game of eg bridge, tennis, etc. **4** a person with whom one has an especially long-term sexual relationship, eg one's husband or wife. — *verb* (**partnered**, **partnering**) to act as a partner to. [from Middle English *partener*, from *parcener*, joint inheritor, influenced by PART]

> ■ *noun* **1** associate, colleague, collaborator, accomplice, confederate, helper, *colloq.* sidekick, ally. **3** team-mate. **4** spouse, husband, wife, lover, mate, consort, companion.

partnership *noun* **1** a relationship in which two or more people or groups operate together as partners. **2** the status of a partner: *offered her a partnership.* **3** a business or other enterprise jointly owned or run by two or more people, etc.

> ■ **1** alliance, confederation, affiliation, combination, fellowship, fraternity, brotherhood, collaboration, co-operation, participation, sharing, union. **3** syndicate, co-operative, association, society, corporation, company, firm, union.

part of speech *Grammar* any of the grammatical classes of words, eg noun, adjective, verb, preposition, etc.

partook See PARTAKE.

partridge *noun* a plump-bodied, grey-and-brown game bird. [from Old French *perdriz*, from Latin and Greek *perdix*]

part song a song for singing in harmonized parts.

part-time *adj.*, *adv.* during only part of the full working day.

part-timer *noun* a person who works, serves, etc on a part-time basis.

parturient /pɑːˈtjʊərɪənt/ *adj. Medicine* giving birth. [from Latin *parturire*, to give birth]

parturition /pɑːtjʊˈrɪʃən/ *noun Medicine* the process of giving birth; childbirth.

party *noun* (PL. **parties**) **1** a social gathering, especially of invited guests, for enjoyment or celebration. **2** a group of people involved in a certain activity together. **3** an especially national organization of people united by a common, especially political, aim. **4** *Legal* each of the

individuals or groups concerned in a contract, agreement, lawsuit, etc: *third-party insurance.* **5** *old facetious use* a person: *an elderly party.* — **be a party to something** to be involved in or partly responsible for an agreement, decision, action, etc. [from Old French *partie*, past participle of *partir*, to divide]

> ■ **1** celebration, festivity, social, *colloq.* do, *colloq.* knees-up, *colloq.* rave-up, get-together, gathering, reunion, function, reception, at-home, house-warming. **2** team, squad, crew, gang, band, group, company, detachment. **3** faction, side, league, cabal, alliance, association, grouping, combination. **4** individual, person, group, litigant, plaintiff, defendant.

party line 1 a telephone line shared by two or more people. **2** the official opinion of a political party on any particular issue.

party piece an act or turn that one can be called on to perform to entertain others, eg at a party.

party wall a wall that divides two houses, etc, being the joint responsibility of both owners.

par value the value shown on a share certificate at time of issue; face value.

parvenu or **parvenue** /ˈpɑːvənjuː/ *noun derog.* respectively a man or woman who has recently acquired substantial wealth but lacks the social refinement to go with it. [from French, past participle of *parvenir*, to arrive]

pas /pɑː/ *noun* (PL. **pas**) *Ballet* a step. [from French *pas*]

PASCAL /ˈpasˈkal/ *noun Comput.* a high-level computer programming language, designed in the 1960s as an aid to the teaching of structured programming, and still widely used for general programming purposes, especially in universities. [named after the French mathematician, physicist, and theologian Blaise Pascal (1623–62)]

pascal /ˈpaskal/ *noun* (ABBREV. **Pa**) the SI unit of pressure, equal to a force of one newton per square metre.

Pascal's triangle *Maths.* a triangular pattern of numbers in which, except for the number 1, each digit is the sum of the two digits above it. [named after the French mathematician, physicist, and theologian Blaise Pascal (1623–62)]

paschal /ˈpaskəl/ *adj.* **1** relating to the Jewish festival of Passover. **2** relating to Easter. [from Latin *paschalis*, from Greek *pascha*, from Hebrew *pesah*, Passover]

pas de deux /pɑː də ˈdɜː/ (PL. **pas de deux**) a dance for two performers.

pasha *noun Hist.* a high-ranking Turkish official; placed after the name in titles. [from Turkish *pasha*]

pashmina /paʃˈmiːnə/ *noun* **1** fine material made from the underfleece of goats of Northern India. **2** a pashmina shawl. [from Persian *pašm*, wool]

Pashtun a group of Pashto-speaking agricultural and herding people of NW Pakistan and SE Afghanistan.

pasqueflower /ˈpɑːskflaʊə(r)/ *noun* a purple-flowered anemone that blooms at Easter. [from Old French *passe-fleur* (from *passer*, to surpass + *fleur*, flower), influenced by *pasques*, Easter]

pass *verb* **1** *trans.*, *intrans.* to come alongside and progress beyond: *passed her on the stairs.* **2** *intrans.* to run, flow, progress, etc: *the blood passing through our veins.* **3** *trans.*, *intrans.* (*also* **pass** or **pass something through, into**, *etc*) to go or cause it to go, penetrate, etc: *pass through a filter.* **4** *trans.*, *intrans.* to move lightly across, over, etc: *pass a duster over the furniture.* **5** *intrans.* to move from one state or stage to another: *pass from the larva to the pupal stage.* **6** to exceed or surpass: *pass the target.* **7** *trans.*, *intrans.*, *said of a vehicle* to overtake. **8** *trans.*, *intrans.* to achieve the required standard in (a test, etc); to award (a student, etc) the marks required for success in a test, etc. **9** *intrans.* to take place: *what passed between them.* **10** *intrans.*, *trans.*, *said of time* to go by; to use up (time) in some activity, etc. **11** *trans.*, *intrans.* (**pass** or **be passed round, on**, *etc*) to hand or transfer; to be transferred; to circulate. **12** *trans.*, *intrans.* (**pass down** or **pass something down**) to be inherited; to hand it down. **13** *trans.*, *intrans.*, *Sport* to throw or kick (the ball, etc) to another player in one's team. **14** *trans., intrans.* to agree to (a proposal or resolution) or be agreed to; to vote (a law) into effect. **15** *said of a judge or lawcourt* to pronounce (judgement). **16** *intrans.* to go away after a while: *her nausea passed.* **17** *intrans.* to be accepted, tolerated, or ignored: *let it pass.* **18** (**pass as** or **for something** or **someone**) to be accepted as or mistaken for something or someone: *insults that pass as wit/a child that would pass for an adult.* **19** *intrans.* to choose not to answer in a quiz, etc or bid in a card game. **20** to make (a comment, etc). **21** to discharge (urine or faeces). — *noun* **1** a route through a gap in a mountain range. **2** an official card or document permitting one to enter somewhere, be absent from duty, etc. **3** a successful result in an examination, but usually without distinction or honours. **4** *Sport* a throw, kick, hit, etc to another player in one's team. **5** a state of affairs: *reach a sorry/pretty pass.* **6** a decision not to answer in a quiz, etc, or not to bid in a card game. — **come** or **be brought to pass** to happen. **in passing** while dealing with something else; casually; by allusion rather than directly. **make a pass at someone** make a casual sexual advance towards them: *made a pass at the girl in the flower shop.* **pass away** or **on** *euphemistic* to die. **pass by** to go past. **pass by something** or **someone** to go past them. **pass something** or **someone by** to overlook or ignore them. **pass off 1** *said of a sickness or feeling, etc* to go away; to diminish. **2** *said of an arranged event* to take place with the result specified: *the party passed off very well.* **pass oneself off as someone** or **something** to represent oneself in that way: *tried to pass themselves off as students.* **pass out 1** to faint. **2** to leave a military or police college having successfully completed one's training. **pass over something** to overlook it; to ignore it. **pass something up** *colloq.* to neglect or sacrifice an opportunity. [from Latin *passus*, step, pace]

. . . .

▣ *verb* **1** overtake, cross. **2** flow, run, progress, proceed, move, go, roll. **3** run through, flow through, percolate through, permeate, pervade, suffuse. **4** run, flick, flutter. **5** change, go, move, transfer, mutate. **6** exceed, surpass, go beyond, outdo, outstrip, overtake, leave behind. **8** get through, succeed, qualify, graduate. **9** take place, happen, occur, come about, transpire. **10** go by, go past, elapse, spend, use up, while away, fill, occupy. **11** give, hand, transfer, transmit, circulate. **12** leave, will, bequeath. **14** approve, authorize, sanction, ratify, validate, adopt, enact. **15** pronounce, declare, hand down. **16** go (away), disappear, vanish. **17** go. *noun* **1** gap, passage, col, defile, gorge, ravine, canyon. **2** permit, passport, identification, ticket, licence, authorization, warrant, permission. **5** state, condition, situation. **pass away** or **on** die, expire, decease, *colloq.* give up the ghost. **pass off 2** go (off), take place, happen, occur. **pass out 1** faint, lose consciousness, black out, collapse, *colloq.* flake out, *colloq.* keel over, drop. **pass over** overlook, ignore, disregard, omit, leave, miss, neglect.

. . . .

passable *adj.* **1** barely adequate or *colloq.* fairly good. **2** *said of a road, etc* able to be travelled along, crossed, etc.

. . . .

▣ **1** satisfactory, acceptable, allowable, tolerable, average, ordinary, unexceptional, moderate, fair, adequate, all right, *colloq.* OK, mediocre. **2** clear, unobstructed, unblocked, open, navigable.
▣ **1** unacceptable, excellent. **2** obstructed, blocked, impassable.

. . . .

passably *adv.* in a passable way, reasonably well.

passacaglia /pasəˈkɑːljə/ *noun Mus.* a slow stately old Spanish dance in triple time; also, the music for it. See also CHACONNE. [Italian, probably from Spanish *passacalle*, street song]

passage *noun* **1** a route through; a corridor, narrow street, or channel. **2** a tubular vessel in the body. **3** a piece of a text or musical composition. **4** the process of passing: *the pas-*

sage of time. **5** a journey by boat; also, the cost of a journey. **6** permission or freedom to pass through a territory, etc. **7** the voting of a law, etc into effect. [from Old French, from *passer*, to pass]

. . . .

▣ **1** passageway, aisle, corridor, hall, doorway, opening, entrance, exit, thoroughfare, way, route, alley, lane, path, road, avenue. **3** extract, excerpt, quotation, text, paragraph, section, piece, clause, verse. **5** journey, voyage, trip, crossing.

. . . .

passage grave *Archaeol.* an underground burial chamber connected to the surface by a passage.

passage rites *Anthropol.* rituals that involve the public declaration of a change of status of an individual. The principal passage rites include birth, baptism, confirmation or initiation, marriage, and death.

passageway *noun* a narrow passage or way, usually with walls on each side.

passata /paˈsɑːtə/ *noun* an Italian sauce of puréed and sieved tomatoes. [from Italian *passata*, passed (ie through a sieve)]

passbook *noun* a book in which the amounts of money put into and taken out of a bank account, etc are recorded.

passé /ˈpɑːseɪ/ *adj.* outmoded; old-fashioned; having faded out of popularity. [French, = passed]

passenger *noun* **1** a traveller in a vehicle, boat, aeroplane, etc driven, sailed, or piloted by someone else. **2** *derog.* someone not doing his or her share of the work in a joint project, etc. [from Old French *passagier*, from *passage*, with inserted *n* as in *messenger*]

. . . .

▣ **1** traveller, voyager, commuter, rider, fare.

. . . .

passer-by *noun* (PL. **passers-by**) a person walking past.

. . . .

▣ bystander, witness, looker-on, onlooker, spectator.

. . . .

passerine /ˈpasəraɪn/ *Zool.* — *adj.*, *said of a bird* belonging to the order of perching birds, including all British songbirds. — *noun* a passerine bird. [from Latin *passer*, sparrow]

passim /ˈpasɪm/ *adv.*, *said of a word, etc* occurring frequently throughout the literary or academic work in question. [Latin, = here and there]

passing *adj.* **1** lasting only briefly. **2** casual: *a passing glance, reference etc.*

. . . .

▣ **1** ephemeral, transient, short-lived, temporary, momentary, fleeting, brief, short, hasty, quick, slight, cursory. **2** casual, superficial, shallow, incidental.
▣ **1** lasting, permanent.

. . . .

passion *noun* **1** a violent emotion, eg hate, anger, or envy. **2** a fit of anger. **3** sexual love or desire. **4** an enthusiasm; something for which one has great enthusiasm. **5** (**the Passion**) the suffering and death of Christ; an account of this from one of the Gospels; a musical setting of one of these accounts. [from Old French, from Latin *passio*, from *pati*, to suffer]

. . . .

▣ **1** feeling, emotion, ardour, fervour, warmth, heat, spirit, intensity, vehemence. **2** outburst, explosion, anger, indignation, wrath, rage. **3** love, desire, ardour, lust, adoration, infatuation, fondness, affection, craving. **4** enthusiasm, obsession, mania, craze, eagerness, keenness, avidity, zest, fanaticism, zeal.
▣ **1** coolness, indifference.

. . . .

passionate /ˈpaʃənət/ *adj.* **1** easily moved to passion; strongly emotional. **2** having strong feelings of sexual love or desire. **3** keen; enthusiastic.

◪ 1 emotional, excitable, hotheaded, impetuous, impulsive, warm, hot, fiery, inflamed, aroused, excited, impassioned, intense, strong, fierce, vehement, violent, stormy, tempestuous, wild, frenzied. **2** loving, affectionate, lustful, erotic, sexy, sensual. **3** keen, eager, avid, enthusiastic, fanatical, zealous, ardent, fervent.
◨ 1 cool, phlegmatic, *colloq.* laid back, cold. **2** frigid.

passionately *adv.* in a passionate way, with passion.

passion flower any of several tropical climbing plants of the genus *Passiflora*, so called because the different parts of the large distinctive flowers were once thought to resemble the crown of thorns, nails, and other emblems of Christ's Passion.

passion fruit the edible fruit of the passion flower, egg-shaped, with a yellow or purple hard skin. Also called GRANADILLA.

passion play a religious drama representing the suffering and death of Christ.

passive *adj.* **1** lacking positive or assertive qualities; submissive. **2** lethargic; inert. **3** *Grammar* denoting the form of the verb used when the subject undergoes, rather than performs, the action of the verb. See also ACTIVE.

◪ 1 unassertive, submissive, docile, unresisting, receptive, non-violent, patient, resigned, long-suffering. **2** lethargic, lifeless, inert, inactive, indifferent, apathetic, non-participating.
◨ 1, 3 active. **2** lively, responsive.

passiveness or **passivity** *noun* being passive.

passive resistance the use of non-violent means, eg fasting, to resist authority.

passive smoking the involuntary breathing in of others' tobacco smoke.

passkey *noun* a key designed to open a varied set of locks; a master key.

pass law formerly in South Africa, a law restricting the movement of non-whites, requiring them to carry identification at all times.

Passover *noun* an annual Jewish festival held in March or April. It commemorates the deliverance of the Israelites from bondage in Egypt, and is so called because the angel of death passed over the houses of the Israelites when he killed the first-born of the Egyptians (Exodus 13).

passport *noun* **1** an official document issued by the government, giving proof of the holder's identity and nationality, and permission to travel abroad with its protection. **2** an asset that guarantees one something: *a degree is your passport to a good job.*

password *noun* **1** a secret word allowing entry to a high-security area or past a checkpoint, etc. **2** *Comput.* a set of characters which a user inputs to gain access to a computer or network.

past — *adj.* **1** of an earlier time; of long ago; bygone. **2** recently ended; just gone by: *the past year.* **3** over; finished. **4** former: *past presidents.* **5** *Grammar, said of the tense of a verb* indicating a past action or condition. — *prep.* **1** up to and beyond: *went past me.* **2** after in time or age. **3** beyond; farther away than. **4** having advanced too far for: *she's past playing with dolls.* **5** beyond the reach of: *past help/past belief.* — *adv.* **1** so as to pass by: *go past.* **2** ago: *two months past.* — *noun* **1** the time before the present; events, etc belonging to this. **2** one's earlier life or career. **3** a disreputable episode earlier in one's life: *who hasn't a past?* **4** *Grammar* the past tense. — **not put it past someone** *colloq.* to believe them quite liable or disposed to do a certain thing. **past it** *colloq.* having lost the vigour of one's youth or prime. [an obsolete past participle of PASS]

◪ *adj.* **1** ancient, bygone, olden, early, gone, no more, extinct, defunct, forgotten. **2** recent. **3** over, ended, finished, completed, done, over and done with. **4** former, previous,

preceding, foregoing, late, recent. *noun* **1** history, former times, olden days, antiquity. **2** life, background, experience, track record.
◨ *adj.* **1, 2, 4, 5** future. *noun* **1, 2, 4** future.

pasta *noun* **1** a dough made with flour, water, and eggs shaped in a variety of forms such as spaghetti, macaroni, lasagne, etc. **2** a cooked dish of this, usually with a sauce. [from Italian, from Latin *pasta*, paste, dough, from Greek *pasta*, barley porridge]

paste — *noun* **1** a stiff moist mixture usually of powder and water, eg a mixture of flour and water used as an adhesive. **2** a spread for sandwiches, etc made from ground meat or fish. **3** any fine dough-like mixture: *almond paste.* **4** a hard brilliant glass used in making imitation gems. — *verb* **1** to stick with paste. **2** *colloq.* to thrash or beat soundly. **3** (*also* **paste something up**) *Printing* to mount (text, illustrations, etc) on a backing for photographing, etc. [from Old French, from Latin *pasta*, paste, dough, from Greek *pasta*, barley porridge]

◪ *noun* **1** adhesive, glue, gum, mastic, putty, cement. *verb* **1** stick, glue, gum, cement, fix.

pasteboard *noun* stiff board built up from thin sheets of paper pasted together.

pastel /ˈpastəl/ — *noun* **1** a chalk-like crayon made from ground pigment. **2** a picture drawn with pastels. — *adj.*, *said of colours* delicately pale. [from French, from Italian *pastello*, from Latin *pastillus*, a ball or cake of something]

◪ *adj.* pale, light, delicate, soft, soft-hued, subdued, faint.

pastern /ˈpastən/ *noun* part of a horse's foot between the hoof and the fetlock. [from Old French *pasturon*, from *pasture*, pasture, tether]

paste-up *noun* a set of text, illustrations, etc, mounted on a board, prepared for copying or photographing.

pasteurization or **pasteurisation** *noun* the partial sterilization of a food, especially milk, by heating it to a specific temperature for a short period before rapidly cooling it. This kills or inactivates harmful bacteria, and delays the development of others. [named after the French chemist Louis Pasteur (1822–95), who introduced the technique]

pasteurize or **pasteurise** /ˈpastjʊraɪz/ *verb* to submit (food, especially milk) to the process of pasteurization.

pastiche /paˈstiːʃ/ *noun* a musical, artistic, or literary work in someone else's style, or in a mixture of styles. [from French, from Italian *pasticcio*, pie, bungle, pastiche]

pastille /ˈpastɪl/ *noun* **1** a small fruit-flavoured, especially medicinal, sweet. **2** a cone of fragrant paste for scenting a room. [from French, from Latin *pastillus*, a ball or cake of something]

pastime *noun* a spare-time pursuit; a hobby. [from PASS + TIME]

◪ hobby, activity, recreation, game, sport, play, fun, amusement, entertainment, diversion, distraction, relaxation.
◨ work, employment.

pastiness *noun* being pasty.

pasting /ˈpeɪstɪŋ/ *noun colloq.* a thrashing.

past master an expert.

pastor /ˈpɑːstə(r)/ *noun* a member of the clergy, especially in Churches other than Anglican and Catholic, with responsibility for a congregation. [from Latin *pastor*, shepherd]

pastoral /ˈpɑːstərəl/ — *adj.* **1** relating to, or (of a poem, painting, musical work, etc) depicting, the countryside or country life. **2** relating to a member of the clergy and his or her work. **3** relating to a shepherd and his or her work. **4**

said of land used for pasture. — *noun* **1** a pastoral poem or painting. **2** *Mus.* same as PASTORALE. **3** a letter from a bishop to the clergy and people of the diocese. [from Latin *pastor,* shepherd]

▤ *adj.* **1** rural, country, rustic, bucolic, agricultural, agrarian, idyllic. **2** ecclesiastical, clerical, priestly, ministerial.

▣ *adj.* **1** urban.

pastoral care help, advice, and moral guidance offered by a clergyman or other spiritual advisor to a group, such as the children in a school, members of the armed forces, a church congregation, etc.

pastorale /pastəˈraːl/ *noun* (PL. **pastorales**) a musical work evoking the countryside. [from Italian *pastorale,* pastoral]

pastoralism *noun* a way of life characterized by keeping herds of animals, such as cattle, sheep, camels, reindeer, goats, and llamas. It is common in dry, mountainous, or severely cold climates not suitable for agriculture.

pastorate *noun* **1** the office, authority, or residence of a pastor. **2** a body of pastors.

past participle see PARTICIPLE.

pastrami /pəˈstraːmɪ/ *noun* strongly spiced smoked beef. [from Yiddish *pastrami*]

pastry /ˈpeɪstrɪ/ *noun* (PL. **pastries**) **1** dough made with flour, fat, and water, used for piecrusts. **2** a sweet baked article made with this; a pie, tart, etc. [from PASTE]

pasturage *noun* an area of land where livestock is allowed to graze.

pasture — *noun* **1** (*also* **pasture-land**) an area of grassland suitable or used for the grazing of livestock, in contrast to a meadow which is cut to produce hay or silage. — *verb* **1** to put (animals) in pasture to graze. **2** *intrans.,* *said of animals* to graze. [from Old French, from Latin *pastura,* from *pascere,* to feed]

▤ *noun* grass, grassland, meadow, field, paddock, pasturage, grazing.

pasty[1] /ˈpeɪstɪ/ *adj.* (**pastier, pastiest**) *said of the complexion* unhealthily pale. [from PASTE]

▤ pale, pallid, wan, anaemic, pasty-faced, sickly, unhealthy.

▣ ruddy, healthy.

pasty[2] /ˈpastɪ/ *noun* (PL. **pasties**) a pie consisting of pastry folded round a savoury or sweet filling. [from Old French *pastée*]

Pat. *abbrev.* patent.

pat — *verb* (**patted, patting**) **1** to strike lightly or affectionately with the palm of one's hand. **2** to shape by striking lightly with the palm or a flat instrument: *pat it into shape.* — *noun* **1** a light, especially affectionate, blow with the palm of the hand. **2** a round flat mass. — *adv.,* *especially of things said* immediately and fluently, as if memorized: *their answers came too pat.* — *adj., said of answers, etc* quickly and easily supplied. — **have** or **know something off pat** to have memorized and know it perfectly. **a pat on the back** an approving word or gesture. **pat someone on the back** to congratulate them approvingly. **stand pat** *North Amer.* to stand firmly by one's opinion, decision, etc. [imitative]

▤ *verb* **1** tap, dab, slap, touch. *noun* **1** tap, dab, slap, touch. **2** cake. *adv.* readily, smoothly, easily, fluently, glibly. *adj.* ready, easy, smooth, fluent, glib, slick, facile, simplistic. **off pat** perfectly, precisely, exactly, flawlessly, faultlessly.

patch — *noun* **1** a piece of material sewn on or applied so as to cover a hole or reinforce a worn area. **2** a plot of earth: *a vegetable patch.* **3** a pad or cover worn as protection over an injured eye. **4** a small expanse contrasting with its surroundings: *patches of ice.* **5** *Hist.* a tiny piece of

black silk worn on the face in imitation of a mole or beauty spot, to enhance the whiteness of the complexion. **6** a scrap or shred. **7** *colloq.* a phase or period: *go through a bad patch.* **8** *slang* the area patrolled by a policeman or covered by a particular police station. **9** *Comput.* a set of instructions added to a program to correct an error. — *verb* **1** to mend (a hole or garment) by sewing patches on. **2** (*also* **patch something up**) to repair it hastily and temporarily. **3** (*also* **patch something together**) to assemble it hastily. **4** *Comput.* to make a temporary correction in (a program). — **not a patch on someone** or **something** *colloq.* not nearly as good as them. **patch something up** *colloq.* to settle a quarrel, etc, especially hurriedly or temporarily. [from Middle English *pacche*]

▤ *noun* **2** bed, plot, lot, parcel, tract. **4** spot, area. **6** scrap, shred, piece, bit. **7** phase, period, stretch, time. **8** area, beat. *verb* **1** mend, repair, fix, cover, reinforce. **2** mend, repair, fix.

patchily *adv.* in a patchy way.

patchiness *noun* being patchy.

patchouli /ˈpatʃʊlɪ, pəˈtʃuːlɪ/ *noun* a shrubby aromatic perennial plant (*Pogostemon cablin*) that grows to a height of 1m or more, native to the tropics and subtropics of SE Asia. [from Tamil *pacculi*]

patch pocket a pocket made by sewing a piece of fabric on the outside of a garment.

patch test an allergy test in which substances are applied to areas of skin which are later examined for signs of irritation.

patchwork *noun* **1** needlework done by sewing together pieces of contrasting patterned fabric. **2** a variegated expanse: *a patchwork of fields.*

patchy *adj.* (**patchier, patchiest**) **1** forming, or occurring in, patches. **2** uneven or variable in quality.

▤ UNEVEN, IRREGULAR, INCONSISTENT, VARIABLE, RANDOM, FITFUL, ERRATIC, SKETCHY, BITTY, SPOTTY, BLOTCHY.

▣ EVEN, UNIFORM, REGULAR, CONSISTENT.

pate /peɪt/ *noun old use, facetious* the head or skull.

pâté /ˈpateɪ/ *noun* a spread made from ground or chopped meat or fish blended with herbs, spices, etc. [from French *pâté,* pasty]

pâté de foie gras /ˈpateɪ də fwaː ˈgraː/ pâté made from the livers of specially fattened geese.

patella /pəˈtelə/ *noun* (PL. **patellae, patellas**) the triangular plate of bone covering the front of the knee joint; the knee-cap. [from Latin, diminutive of *patina,* dish]

paten /ˈpatən/ *noun Relig.* a circular metal plate, often of silver or gold, on which the bread is placed at the celebration of the Eucharist. [from Latin *patena, patina,* a plate]

patent /ˈpeɪtənt, ˈpatənt/ — *noun* **1** an official licence from the government granting a person or business the sole right, for a certain period, to make and sell a particular article. **2** the right so granted. **3** the invention so protected. — *verb* to obtain a patent for (an invention, design, etc). — *adj.* **1** very evident. **2** concerned with the granting of, or protection by, patents. **3** *said of a product* made or protected under patent. **4** *colloq.* ingenious; infallible; original. **5** open for inspection: *letters patent.* [from Latin *patere,* to lie open]

▤ *adj.* **1** evident, obvious, conspicuous, manifest, clear, transparent, apparent, visible, palpable, unequivocal, open, overt, blatant, flagrant, glaring.

▣ *adj.* **1** hidden, opaque.

patentee *noun* the person obtaining or holding a patent.

patent leather leather made glossy by varnishing.

patently *adv.* obviously; clearly.

patent medicine 1 *technical* a patented medicine which is available without prescription. **2** *colloq.* any proprietary medicine, especially one claimed as an infallible cure.

Patent Office the government department that issues patents.

pater /ˈpeɪtə(r)/ *noun old slang use* father. [from Latin *pater*]

paterfamilias /patəfəˈmɪlɪas/ *noun* (PL. **patresfamilias** /patreɪsfəˈmɪlɪas/) the father as head of the household. [from Latin *pater*, father + *familias*, a form of *familia*, family]

paternal /pəˈtɜːnl/ *adj.* **1** of, relating to, or appropriate to, a father. **2** *said of a relation or ancestor* related on one's father's side. [from Latin *paternalis*, from *pater*, father]

paternalism *noun* governmental or managerial benevolence taken to the extreme of over-protectiveness and authoritarianism.

paternalistic *adj.* characterized by or involving paternalism.

paternity /pəˈtɜːnətɪ/ *noun* **1** fatherhood. **2** the identity of a child's father. **3** the authorship, source, or origin of something. [from Latin *paternitas*, from *pater*, father]

paternity leave leave of absence from work granted to a man so that he can be with his wife or partner and assist her during and after childbirth.

paternity suit a lawsuit brought by the mother of a child to establish that a certain man is the father of her child and therefore liable for its financial support.

paternoster /patəˈnɒstə(r)/ *noun* the Lord's Prayer, especially in Latin. [from Latin *Pater noster*, Our Father]

path *noun* **1** a track trodden by, or specially surfaced for, walking. **2** the line along which something is travelling: *the path of Jupiter*. **3** a course of action: *the path to ruin*. **4** *Comput.* the location of a file in terms of a computer's disk drives and directory structure. **— beat a path to someone's door** *colloq.* to compete for their services or attention. **cross someone's path** to encounter them, especially by chance. [from Anglo-Saxon *pæth*]

⬛ **1** footpath, bridle way, trail, track, walk. **2, 3** route, course, direction, way, road.

path- see PATHO-.

-path *combining form* forming words denoting: **1** a sufferer from a disorder: *psychopath*. **2** a practitioner of a therapy: *homoeopath/osteopath*.

Pathan see PASHTUN.

pathetic /pəˈθɛtɪk/ *adj.* **1** moving one to pity; touching, heart-rending, poignant, or pitiful. **2** *derog. colloq.* hopelessly inadequate.

⬛ **1** pitiable, moving, touching, poignant, plaintive, heart-rending, heartbreaking, poor, sorry, lamentable, miserable, sad, distressing. **2** useless, inadequate, feeble, contemptible, derisory, deplorable, worthless, meagre.
Ⓕ **1** cheerful. **2** admirable, excellent, valuable.

pathetically *adv.* in a pathetic way.

pathetic fallacy especially in literature, the transference of human qualities to inanimate things, as in *a frowning landscape*.

pathfinder *noun* **1** an explorer who finds routes through unexplored territory. **2** someone who devises new methods of doing things.

-pathic *combining form* forming adjectives corresponding to nouns in *-pathy*.

patho- or **path-** *combining form* forming words denoting disease: *pathology*. [from Greek *pathos*, experience, suffering]

pathogen /ˈpaθədʒɛn/ *noun Pathol.* any micro-organism, eg a bacterium or virus, that causes disease in a living organism.

pathogenic /paθəˈdʒɛnɪk/ *adj.* producing disease.

pathogenicity /paθədʒəˈnɪsɪtɪ/ *noun* the capacity to produce disease.

pathological /paθəˈlɒdʒɪkl/ *adj.* **1** relating to pathology. **2** caused by, or relating to, illness: *a pathological fear of dirt*. **3** *colloq.* compulsive; habitual: *a pathological liar*.

pathologist *noun* a person skilled in pathology.

pathology /pəˈθɒlədʒɪ/ *noun* the branch of medicine concerned with the study of the nature and causes of diseases.

pathos /ˈpeɪθɒs/ *noun* a quality in a situation, etc that moves one to pity. [from Greek *pathos*, feeling, suffering]

-pathy *combining form* forming words denoting: **1** feeling: *telepathy*. **2** disease or disorder: *psychopathy*. **3** a method of treating disease: *homoeopathy*. [from Greek *pathos*, suffering]

patience *noun* **1** the ability to endure delay, trouble, pain, or hardship calmly. **2** tolerance and forbearance. **3** perseverance. **4** *Cards* a solo game in which the player, in turning each card over, has to fit it into a certain scheme. [from Latin *patientia*]

⬛ **1** calmness, composure, self-control, restraint. **2** tolerance, forbearance, endurance, fortitude, long-suffering, submission, resignation, stoicism. **3** persistence, perseverance, diligence.
Ⓕ **1** impatience. **2** intolerance.

patient **—** *adj.* having or showing patience. **—** *noun* a person who is being treated by, or is registered with, a doctor, dentist, etc.

⬛ *adj.* calm, composed, self-possessed, self-controlled, restrained, even-tempered, mild, lenient, indulgent, understanding, forgiving, tolerant, accommodating, forbearing, long-suffering, uncomplaining, submissive, resigned, philosophical, stoical, persistent, persevering. *noun* client, case, invalid, sufferer.
Ⓕ *adj.* impatient, restless, intolerant.

patiently *adv.* in a patient way; with patience.

patina /ˈpatɪnə/ *noun* **1** a coating formed on a metal surface through oxidation, especially the greenish coating of verdigris on bronze or copper. **2** a mature shine on wood resulting from continual polishing and handling. **3** any fine finish acquired with age. **4** *Archaeol.* a surface appearance that develops with prolonged exposure or burial. [from Italian *patina*, coating, from Latin *patina*, dish]

patio /ˈpatɪəʊ/ *noun* (PL. **patios**) **1** an open paved area beside a house. **2** an inner courtyard in a Spanish or Spanish-American house. [from Spanish *patio*]

patisserie /pəˈtiːsərɪ/ *noun* a shop selling fancy cakes, sweet pastries, etc. [from French *pâtisserie*, from Latin *pasta*, dough]

patois /ˈpatwɑː/ *noun* (PL. **patois** /ˈpatwɑːz/) **1** the local dialect of a region, used usually in informal everyday situations, as opposed to the language used in literature, education, etc. **2** jargon. [from French *patois*]

patrial /ˈpeɪtrɪəl/ *noun formerly* a person who, being a citizen of the UK, a British colony, or the British Commonwealth, or the child or grandchild of someone born in the UK, has a legal right to live in the UK. [from Latin *patria*, fatherland]

patriality *noun* the condition of being a patrial.

patriarch /ˈpeɪtrɪɑːk/ *noun* **1** the male head of a family or tribe. **2** in the Eastern Orthodox Church, a high-ranking bishop. **3** in the Roman Catholic Church, the pope. **4** in the Old Testament, any of the ancestors of the human race or of the tribes of Israel, eg Adam, Abraham, or Jacob. **5** a venerable old man, especially the senior member of a community or group. [from Greek *patriarches*, senior bishop, father of a family]

patriarchal *adj.* **1** of the nature of a patriarch. **2** like a patriarch. **3** belonging to or subject to a patriarch.

patriarchal society a society governed by a patriarch or patriarchs. Many tribal societies, eg in Africa, are ruled by elders, who are venerated for their wisdom.

patriarchate *noun* the office, authority, or residence of a church patriarch.

patriarchy *noun* (PL. **patriarchies**) a social system in which a male is head of the family and descent is traced through the male line; also, a society based on this system.

patrician — *noun* 1 a member of the ancient Roman nobility; a descendant of one of the founding families of Rome. 2 an aristocrat. 3 a person of taste, culture, and refinement. — *adj.* 1 relating to the ancient Roman nobility. 2 aristocratic; noble; of refined tastes. [from Latin *patricius*, patrician, noble]

patricidal *adj.* relating to or involving patricide.

patricide *noun* 1 the act of killing one's father. 2 a person who commits this act. [variant of earlier PARRICIDE, influenced by Latin *pater*, father]

patrilineal /patrɪˈlɪnɪəl/ *adj. Anthropol.* denoting descent or kinship reckoned through the father, or through males alone.

patrimonial *adj.* being or involving patrimony.

patrimony /ˈpatrɪmənɪ/ *noun* (PL. **patrimonies**) 1 property inherited from one's father or ancestors. 2 something inherited; a heritage. 3 a church estate or revenue. [from Latin *patrimonium*, from *pater*, father]

patriot /ˈpeɪtrɪət, ˈpatrɪət/ *noun* someone who loves and serves his or her fatherland devotedly. [from Greek *patriotes*, fellow-countryman]

patriotic /patrɪˈɒtɪk, peɪtrɪˈɒtɪk/ *adj.* 1 loyal or devoted to one's country. 2 like a patriot.

⊟ NATIONALISTIC, CHAUVINISTIC, JINGOISTIC, LOYAL, FLAG-WAVING.

patriotically *adv.* in a patriotic way.

patriotism *noun* loyalty to and devotion to one's country.

patrol /pəˈtroʊl/ — *verb* (**patrolled, patrolling**) to make a regular systematic tour of (an area) to maintain security or surveillance. — *noun* 1 a person or group of people performing this duty. 2 the act of patrolling: *on patrol.* 3 any of the units of six or so into which a troop of Scouts or Guides is divided. [from French *patrouiller*]

⊟ *verb* police, guard, protect, defend, go the rounds, tour, inspect. *noun* 1 guard, sentry, sentinel, watch. 2 policing, protection, surveillance, watch, defence.

patrol car a police car equipped with a radio telephone, used to patrol streets and motorways.

patrolman *noun* 1 *North Amer.* the lowest-ranking police officer; a police officer on the beat. 2 a person employed by a motoring organization to patrol a certain area and help motorists in difficulty.

patron /ˈpeɪtrən/ *noun* 1 a person who gives financial support and encouragement eg to an artist, the arts, a movement, or charity. 2 a regular customer of a shop, attender at a theatre, etc. [from Latin *patronus*, protector]

⊟ 1 benefactor, philanthropist, sponsor, backer, supporter, sympathizer, advocate, champion, defender, protector, guardian, helper. 2 customer, client, frequenter, regular, shopper, buyer, purchaser, subscriber.

patronage *noun* 1 the support given by a patron. 2 regular custom given to a shop, theatre, etc. 3 the power of bestowing, or recommending people for, offices.

⊟ 1 support, backing, sponsorship. 2 custom, business, trade.

patronize or **patronise** /ˈpatrənaɪz/ *verb* 1 to treat condescendingly, or with benevolent superiority, especially inappropriately. 2 to give especially regular custom to (a shop, theatre, restaurant, etc).

⊟ 2 frequent, shop at, buy from, deal with.

patronizing or **patronising** *adj.* treating condescendingly.

⊟ condescending, stooping, overbearing, high-handed, haughty, superior, snobbish, supercilious, disdainful.
🔺 humble, lowly.

patronizingly or **patronisingly** *adv.* in a patronizing way.

patron saint the guardian saint of a country, profession, craft, etc.

patronymic /patrəˈnɪmɪk/ *noun* a name derived from one's father's or other male ancestor's name, usually with a suffix or prefix, as in *Donaldson* or *Macdonald*. [from Greek *pater*, father + *onyma*, name]

patten *noun Hist.* an overshoe with a wooden or metal mount, for raising the wearer above mud or water. [from Old French *patin*, clog]

patter[1] — *verb intrans.* (**pattered, pattering**) 1 *said of rain, footsteps, etc* to make a light rapid tapping noise. 2 to move with light rapid footsteps. — *noun* the light rapid tapping of footsteps or rain. [from PAT]

⊟ *verb* 1 tap, pat, beat. 2 scuttle, scurry. *noun* pattering, tapping, pitter-patter, beating.

patter[2] — *noun* 1 the fast persuasive talk of a salesman, or the quick speech of a comedian. 2 the jargon or speech of a particular group or area: *Glasgow patter.* — *verb intrans., trans.* (**pattered, pattering**) to say or speak rapidly or glibly. [from Latin *pater noster*, Our Father, from the fast mumbling of the prayer]

⊟ *noun* 1 chatter, gabble, jabber, line, pitch, *colloq.* spiel. 2 jargon, *colloq.* lingo.

pattern /ˈpatn/ — *noun* 1 a model, guide, or set of instructions for making something. 2 a decorative design eg on wallpaper or fabric. 3 a piece, eg of fabric, as a sample. 4 any excellent example suitable for imitation. 5 a coherent series of occurrences or set of features: *a pattern of events.* — *verb* (**pattern one thing on another**) to model it on another type, design, etc. [from Old French, from Latin *patronus*, example, defender]

⊟ *noun* 1 model, guide, template, stencil, original, prototype, system, method, order, plan. 2 design, decoration, ornamentation, ornament, figure, motif, style. 3 sample, swatch. 4 example, standard, norm. 5 sequence, series.

patterned *adj., said of a fabric, etc* having a decorative design; not plain.

⊟ decorated, ornamented, figured, printed.
🔺 plain.

patty *noun* (PL. **patties**) 1 *North Amer.* a flat round cake of minced meat, vegetables, etc. 2 a small meat pie. [from French *pâté*, from Latin *pasta*, dough, paste]

paucity /ˈpɔːsɪtɪ/ *noun* smallness of quantity; fewness; scarcity or lack. [from Latin *pauci*, few]

paunch *noun* a protruding belly, especially in a man.

⊟ *colloq.* pot-belly, *colloq.* beer-belly, *facetious* corporation, abdomen, belly.

paunchiness *noun* having a paunch.

paunchy *adj.* (**paunchier, paunchiest**) having a large paunch.

pauper /'pɔːpə(r)/ *noun* **1** a poverty-stricken person. **2** *Hist.* someone living on public charity. [from Latin *pauper*, poor]

pauperism *noun* **1** poverty. **2** being a pauper.

pause — *noun* **1** a relatively short break in some activity, etc. **2** *Mus.* the prolonging of a note or rest beyond its normal duration, or a sign indicating this. — *verb intrans.* **1** to have a break; to stop briefly. **2** to hesitate. — **give someone pause** to cause them to hesitate before acting. [from Latin *pausa*]

🔲 *noun* **1** break, rest, halt, stoppage, interruption, *colloq.* breather, lull, *colloq.* let-up, respite, gap, interval, interlude, intermission, wait, delay, hesitation. *verb* **1** break off, take a break, rest, wait, delay, stop, halt, cease, discontinue, interrupt.

pavan /'pavən/ *or* **pavane** /pə'vɑːn/ *noun* a stately 16c and 17c dance, or a piece of music for this. [from Spanish *pavana*, from Spanish *pavo*, peacock, or Italian *Padovana*, (dance) of Padua]

pave *verb* to surface (a street, path, etc) with stone slabs, cobbles, etc. — **pave the way for something** or **someone** to prepare for the introduction or development of something, or for the arrival of someone. [from Latin *pavire*, to ram or tread down]

🔲 flag, tile, floor, surface, cover, asphalt, concrete.

pavement *noun* **1** a raised paved footpath edging a road, etc. **2** a paved road or expanse: *a mosaic pavement.* **3** a road surface; road-surfacing material. [from Latin *pavimentum*, hard floor]

pavement artist 1 an artist who draws sketches and coloured pictures on a pavement, especially in order to receive money from passers-by. **2** an artist who sells pictures displayed on a pavement.

pavilion /pə'vɪlɪən/ *noun* **1** a building in a sports ground in which players change their clothes and store equipment. **2** a light temporary building in which to display exhibits at a trade fair, etc. **3** a summerhouse or ornamental shelter. **4** a large ornamental building for public pleasure and entertainment. **5** a large and elaborate tent. [from French *pavillon*, from Latin *papilio*, butterfly, tent]

paving *noun* **1** stones or slabs used to pave a surface. **2** a paved surface.

paving-stone *noun* a large flat regular-shaped stone used for paving.

pavlova /pav'loʊvə/ *noun* a dessert consisting of meringue topped with fruit and whipped cream. [named after the Russian ballerina Anna Pavlova]

paw — *noun* **1** the foot of a four-legged mammal. **2** *colloq.* a hand. — *verb* **1** (**paw something** or **paw at something**) *said of an animal* to scrape or strike it with a paw. **2** to finger or handle clumsily; to touch or caress (someone) with unwelcome familiarity. [from Old French *poue*]

🔲 *noun* **1** foot, pad, forefoot. **2** hand, *colloq.* mitt. *verb* **2** maul, manhandle, mishandle, molest.

pawkily *adv.* in a pawky way.

pawkiness *noun* being pawky.

pawky *adj.* (**pawkier, pawkiest**) drily witty. [from Scot. *pawk*, a trick]

pawl *noun* a catch that engages with the teeth of a ratchet wheel to limit its movement to one direction only.

pawn¹ — *verb* **1** to deposit (an article of value) with a pawnbroker as a pledge for a sum of money borrowed. **2** to pledge or stake. — *noun* **1** the condition of being deposited as a pledge: *in pawn.* **2** an article so pledged. [from Old French *pan*, pledge, surety]

🔲 *verb* **1** deposit, *colloq.* hock, *slang* pop.

pawn² *noun* **1** a chess piece of lowest value. **2** a person used and manipulated by others. [from Old French *poun*, from Latin *pedones*, infantry]

🔲 **2** dupe, puppet, tool, instrument, toy, plaything.

pawnbroker *noun* a person who lends money in exchange for pawned articles.

pawnbroking *noun* the business of a pawnbroker.

pawnshop *noun* a pawnbroker's place of business.

pawpaw see PAPAYA.

pay — *verb* (PAST TENSE AND PAST PARTICIPLE **paid**) **1** *trans., intrans.* to give (money) to (someone) in exchange for goods, services, etc: *I paid him £10 for the books.* **2** *trans., intrans.* to settle (a bill, debt, etc). **3** *trans., intrans.* to give (wages or salary) to an employee. **4** *trans., intrans.* to make a profit, or make as profit: *businesses that don't pay/an investment that pays £500 per annum.* **5** *intrans., trans.* to benefit; to be worthwhile: *it pays one to be polite/dishonesty doesn't pay.* **6** *trans., intrans.* (also **pay for something**) to suffer a penalty on account of it; to be punished for it: *pay dearly for one's crimes/paid with his life.* **7** to do (someone) the honour of (a visit or call); to offer (someone) (a compliment or one's respects). **8** to give (heed or attention). — *noun* money given or received for work, etc; wages; salary. — **in the pay of someone** employed by them, especially for a secret or dishonest purpose. **pay someone back** to revenge oneself on them. **pay something back** to return money owed. **pay something in** to put money, etc into a bank account. **pay off** to have profitable results. **pay someone off** to make them redundant with a final payment. **pay something off** to finish paying a debt, etc. **pay something out 1** to spend or give (money), eg to pay bills, debts, etc. **2** to release or slacken (a rope, etc) especially by passing it little by little through one's hands. **pay up** *colloq.* to pay what is due, especially reluctantly. **pay one's way** to pay one's own debts and living expenses. **put paid to something** or **someone** *colloq.* to put an end to them; to deal effectively or finally with them. [from Latin *pacare*, to pacify, settle (a debt)]

🔲 *verb* **1** reward, remunerate, recompense, reimburse, repay, refund, pay out, remit. **2** settle, discharge, clear. **3** remunerate. **4** bring in, yield, return. **5** benefit, be worthwhile, profit, pay off. **6** suffer, atone, make amends, compensate, answer. *noun* remuneration, wages, salary, earnings, income, fee, stipend, honorarium, emoluments, payment, reward, recompense, compensation, reimbursement. **pay back** *someone* take revenge, get one's own back, get even with, retaliate, reciprocate, counter-attack. **pay off** succeed, work. *someone* dismiss, *colloq.* fire, *colloq.* sack, lay off. *something* discharge, settle, square, clear. **pay out 1** spend, disburse, hand over, *colloq.* fork out, *colloq.* shell out, *colloq.* lay out.

payable *adj.* that can or must be paid: *make cheques payable to me/payable by 1 July.*

🔲 owed, owing, unpaid, outstanding, in arrears, due, mature.

pay-as-you-earn *noun* a method of collecting income tax from employees by deducting it from the wages or salary due to be paid to them.

pay-bed *noun* a bed in a National Health Service hospital reserved for patients paying for their own treatment.

pay day the day when wages or salaries are paid.

PAYE *abbrev.* pay-as-you-earn.

payee *noun* a person to whom money is paid or a cheque made out.

payer *noun* a person who pays.

paying guest a lodger.

payload *noun* **1** the revenue-earning part of a vehicle's load. **2** the operating equipment carried by a spaceship or satellite. **3** the quantity and strength of the explosive carried by a missile. **4** the quantity of goods, passengers, etc carried by an aircraft.

paymaster *noun* an official in charge of the payment of wages and salaries.

payment *noun* **1** a sum of money paid. **2** the act of paying or process of being paid. **3** a reward or punishment.

⊟ **1** premium, outlay, advance, deposit, instalment, contribution, donation, remittance, allowance, reward, remuneration, pay, fee, hire, fare, toll. **2** remittance, settlement, discharge, remuneration, donation.

pay-off *noun colloq.* **1** a fruitful result. **2** a bribe. **3** a final settling of accounts. **4** a climax, outcome, or final resolution.

payola /peɪ'oʊlə/ *noun* **1** a bribe for promoting a product, given to someone, eg a disc jockey, in a position to do this. **2** the practice of giving or receiving such bribes. [from PAY + suffix *-ola*, of no precise meaning]

pay packet *said of the container or its contents* an envelope or packet containing an employee's weekly wages.

pay-per-view *noun* a form of pay TV in which viewers subscribe to watch a particular programme or event.

payphone *noun* a telephone operated by coins or a phonecard.

payroll *noun* **1** a register of employees listing the wage or salary due to each. **2** the total amount of money required for employees' wages or salaries.

pay slip a note of pay, showing deductions for tax and national insurance, supplied weekly or monthly to employees.

pay TV *colloq.* non-broadcast video entertainment distributed to an audience of subscribers who pay for the programmes viewed. Programmes are received either through a cable network or by a scrambled microwave or satellite transmission requiring a rented decoder.

Pb *symbol Chem.* lead.

PC *abbrev.* **1** personal computer. **2** Police Constable. **3 a** political correctness. **b** politically correct. **4** Privy Councillor.

pc *abbrev.* **1** per cent. **2** *colloq.* postcard.

PCB *abbrev. Comput.* printed circuit board.

pcm *abbrev.* per calendar month.

PCV *abbrev.* passenger carrying vehicle.

Pd *symbol Chem.* palladium.

pd *abbrev.* paid.

pd or **PD** *abbrev. Physics* potential difference.

Pde *abbrev.* Parade, as a street name.

PDL *abbrev. Comput.* page description language.

PDSA *abbrev.* People's Dispensary for Sick Animals.

PE *abbrev.* physical education.

pea *noun* **1** an annual climbing plant (*Pisum sativum*) of the pulse family (Leguminosae), cultivated in cool temperate regions for its edible seeds. Also called GARDEN PEA. **2** the round seed of this plant, which has a very high protein content. [a singular form of *pease*, which was mistaken for a plural; see PEASE PUDDING]

peace *noun* **1** freedom from war. **2** a treaty or agreement ending a war. **3** freedom from noise, disturbance, or disorder; quietness or calm. **4** freedom from mental agitation; serenity: *peace of mind*. — **at peace 1** not at war; not fighting. **2** in harmony or friendship. **3** in a calm or serene state. **4** freed from earthly worries; dead. **hold one's peace** to remain silent. **keep the peace 1** *Legal* to preserve law and order. **2** to prevent, or refrain from, fighting or quarrelling. **make peace** to end a war, quarrel, etc. **make one's peace with someone** to be reconciled with them. [from Old French *pais*, from Latin *pax*]

⊟ **1** harmony, concord, armistice, truce, cease-fire, conciliation. **2** agreement, treaty, concord. **3** silence, quiet, quietness, hush, stillness, rest, relaxation, tranquillity, calm, calmness. **4** serenity, composure, contentment, tranquillity, calm, calmness.
⊞ **1** war, conflict, disagreement. **3** noise, disturbance. **4** agitation, anxiety, worry, stress, tension.

peaceable *adj.* peace-loving; mild; placid.

⊟ peace-loving, mild, placid, gentle, friendly, amicable, easy-going, conciliatory, pacific, unwarlike, non-violent, inoffensive.
⊞ belligerent, aggressive.

peace dividend money left over from a government's defence budget as a result of negotiated arms reduction policies, available for non-military use.

peaceful *adj.* **1** calm and quiet. **2** unworried; serene. **3** free from war, violence, disturbance, or disorder.

⊟ **1** calm, quiet, still, restful, relaxing, tranquil. **2** serene, calm, placid, unruffled, undisturbed, untroubled. **3** amicable, friendly, peaceable, pacific.
⊞ **1** noisy. **2** worried, disturbed, troubled. **3** violent.

peacemaker *noun* a person who makes or brings about peace.

peace offering something offered to end a quarrel or as an apology.

peace pipe (*also* **pipe of peace**) a long ornate pipe smoked by Native Americans as a token of peace.

peace studies educational courses designed to explore the role of the military in society, international strategic relationships, and those conditions that most promote peace and human welfare in society.

peacetime *noun* periods that are free of war.

peach¹ *noun* **1** any of numerous varieties of a small deciduous tree (*Prunus persica*) of the rose family, widely cultivated in warm temperate regions for its edible fruit. **2** the large round fruit of this tree, which contains a hard stone surrounded by sweet juicy yellow flesh and a yellowish-pink velvety skin. **3** the yellowish-pink colour of this fruit. **4** *colloq.* something delightful: *a peach of a day.* **5** *colloq.* a lovely young woman. [from Old French *peche*, from Latin *persicum malum*, Persian apple]

peach² *verb intrans.* (**peach on someone**) *colloq.* to betray or inform on someone, especially an accomplice. [from Middle English *peche* from *apeche*, to hinder]

peach Melba a dessert consisting of peaches, ice-cream and raspberry sauce.

peachy *adj.* (**peachier, peachiest**) **1** coloured like or tasting like a peach. **2** *colloq.* very good.

peacock *noun* (PL. **peacock, peacocks**) **1** (*also* **peafowl**) any of three species of large bird belonging to the pheasant family. The male of the common peacock is best known for its train of green and gold eye-spot feathers. **2** the male peafowl, the female being known as the peahen. **3** *derog.* a vain person. [from Anglo-Saxon *pea*, from Latin *pavo*, peacock + COCK]

peacock blue the rich greenish blue in a peacock's plumage.

peacock butterfly a medium-sized butterfly with a prominent eyespot on each reddish-brown wing.

pea green bright green or yellowish green.

pea-green *adj.* having a colour of pea green.

peahen *noun* a female peacock.

peak — *noun* **1** a pointed summit; a pointed mountain or hill. **2** a maximum, eg in consumer use: *electricity consumed at peak periods.* **3** a time of maximum achievement, etc. **4** the front projecting part of a cap. — *verb intrans.* **1** to reach a maximum. **2** to reach the height of one's powers or popularity. [perhaps related to PICK]

....

🖃 *noun* **1** top, summit, pinnacle, crest, tip, apex, point. **3** crown, zenith, climax, culmination, apex, height. *verb* **2** climax, culminate, come to a head.

🖃 *noun* **3** nadir, trough.

....

peakiness *noun* being peaky.

peaky *adj.* (**peakier, peakiest**) ill-looking; pallid.

peal — *noun* **1** the ringing of a bell or set of bells. **2** a set of bells, each with a different note. **3** a burst of noise: *peals of laughter/thunder.* — *verb* **1** *intrans.* to ring or resound. **2** *trans.* to sound or signal (eg a welcome) by ringing. [from Middle English *pele*]

....

🖃 *noun* **1** chime, carillon, toll, knell, ring, clang, ringing. **3** rumble, roar, crash, clap, reverberation. *verb* **1** chime, toll, ring, clang, resonate, reverberate, resound, rumble, roll, roar, crash. **2** ring, toll, chime.

....

peanut *noun* **1** a low-growing annual plant (*Arachis hypogaea*) of the pulse family (Leguminosae). It is native to S America, but widely cultivated as an important food crop for its edible seeds, which are produced in wrinkled yellowish underground pods. **2** the seed of this plant, consisting of white flesh rich in protein, surrounded by a reddish-brown papery skin. Also called GROUNDNUT, MONKEY NUT.

peanut butter a spread made from ground roasted peanuts.

pear *noun* **1** a deciduous tree belonging to the genus *Pyrus* of the rose family, especially varieties of *P. communis*, widely cultivated in temperate regions for its edible fruit and its ornamental flowers. **2** the cone-shaped fruit of this tree, which consists of a core of small seeds surrounded by sweet juicy white pulp and a yellowish-green skin. [from Anglo-Saxon *peru*, from Latin *pirum*]

pearl — *noun* **1** a bead of smooth hard lustrous material found inside the shell of certain molluscs, eg oysters. It is formed by the deposition of layers of nacre (mother-of-pearl) around a minute grain of sand or other foreign particle that has entered the shell. **2** an artificial imitation of this. **3** (**pearls**) a necklace of pearls. **4** mother-of-pearl. **5** something resembling a pearl. **6** something valued or precious: *pearls of wisdom.* — *adj.* **1** like a pearl in colour or shape. **2** made of or set with pearls or mother-of-pearl. — *verb* **1** to set with, or as if with, pearls. **2** to grind down (barley) into small pearl-like grains. **3** *intrans.* to form pearl-like beads or drops. [from Middle English *perle*, from a diminutive of Latin *perna*, sea mussel]

pearl barley seeds of barley ground into round polished grains, used in soups and stews.

pearlies *pl. noun* the traditional costume of costermongers, sewn with pearl buttons.

pearl spar *Geol.* a crystalline carbonate mineral that has a pearly lustre.

pearly *adj.* (**pearlier, pearliest**) **1** like pearl. **2** covered in pearl.

pearly gates *colloq.* the gates of Heaven.

pearly king and queen the London costermonger couple whose pearl-button-covered costumes are judged the most splendid.

pear-shaped *adj.* — **go pear-shaped** *colloq.* to go wrong or out of kilter.

peasant *noun* **1** in poor agricultural societies, a farm worker or small farmer. **2** *derog.* a rough, unmannerly or culturally ignorant person. [from Old French *pasant*, from Latin *pagus*, country district]

....

🖃 **1** rustic, provincial, yokel, bumpkin. **2** oaf, lout, boor.

....

peasantry *noun* the peasant class.

pease pudding a purée made from split peas soaked and then boiled. [from Anglo-Saxon *pise*, pea, from Latin *pisa*]

pea-shooter *noun* a short tube through which to fire dried peas by blowing.

pea soup thick soup made from dried peas.

pea-souper *noun colloq.* a thick yellowish fog.

peat *noun* **1** a mass of dark brown or black fibrous plant material produced by the compression of partially decomposed vegetation in a waterlogged environment where the temperatures are relatively low. It is an early stage in the development of coal, used in compost and manure to improve the quality of soil, and in dried form as a fuel in parts of N Europe. **2** a cut block of this material.

peaty *adj.* (**peatier, peatiest**) **1** like or consisting of peat. **2** having a smoky taste or smell reminiscent of peat.

pebble *noun* **1** a small fragment of rock, with a diameter of 4 to 64mm, often worn round and smooth by water or wind action. **2** a colourless rock crystal; also, a lens made from this. [from Anglo-Saxon *papol*]

pebbledash *noun* cement or plaster with small stones embedded in it, used as a coating for exterior walls.

pebbly *adj.* (**pebblier, pebbliest**) full of or covered with pebbles.

pecan /ˈpiːkən/ *noun* **1** an oval brown smooth-shelled oily nut. **2** the hickory tree of the southern USA, which bears this nut. [from Illinois (Native American language) *pakani*]

peccadillo /pɛkəˈdɪloʊ/ *noun* (PL. **peccadillos, peccadilloes**) a minor misdeed. [from Spanish *pecadillo*, diminutive of *pecado*, sin]

peccary *noun* (PL. **peccaries**) a small wild pig of tropical America. [from Carib (S American Indian language) *pakira*]

peck¹ — *verb* **1** (**peck something** or **peck at something**) *said of a bird* to strike, nip, or pick it with the beak. **2** to poke (a hole) with the beak. **3** (**peck at something**) to eat food desultorily and without relish. **4** to kiss perfunctorily: *pecked her on the cheek.* — *noun* **1** a tap or nip with the beak. **2** a perfunctory kiss. [related to PICK¹]

peck² *noun* an old measure of capacity of dry goods, especially grain, equal to two gallons (9.1 litres) or a quarter of a bushel. [from Old French *pek*]

pecker *noun* **1** that which pecks; a beak. **2** *colloq.* spirits: *keep one's pecker up.* **3** *North Amer. coarse slang* the penis.

pecking order a scale of ascendancy noticeably operating in a flock of poultry, such that any bird may peck one of lesser importance but must submit to being pecked by those of greater importance; any social hierarchy in animals or humans or system of ranks and associated privileges.

peckish *adj. colloq.* somewhat hungry.

pectic acid *Biochem.* an acid that is obtained from the pectin found within ripening fruits.

pectin *noun Biochem.* a complex polysaccharide carbohydrate that functions as a cement-like material within plant cell walls and also between adjacent cell walls, and is particularly abundant in ripening fruit, eg apples. Pectin forms a gel at low temperatures, and for this reason is widely used in jam-making. [from Greek *pektos*, congealed]

pectoral /ˈpɛktərəl/ — *adj.* **1** of or relating to the breast or chest. **2** worn on the breast. — *noun* **1** a pectoral muscle or pectoral fin. **2** a neck ornament worn covering the chest. [from Latin *pectoralis*, from *pectus*, chest]

pectoral fin in fishes, one of a pair of fins situated just behind the gills and corresponding to the forelimbs of terrestrial vertebrates. The pectoral fins are used to control the angle of ascent or descent in the water, and for braking.

peculiar *adj.* **1** strange; odd. **2** (**peculiar to someone** or **something**) exclusively or typically belonging to or associated with them: *habits peculiar to cats.* **3** special; individual: *their own peculiar methods.* **4** especial; particular: *of peculiar interest.* [from Latin *peculium*, private property]

....

🖃 **1** strange, odd, curious, funny, weird, bizarre, extraordinary, unusual, abnormal, exceptional, unconventional, *colloq.*

offbeat, eccentric, *slang* way-out, outlandish, exotic. **2** characteristic of, typical of. **3** special, individual, personal, idiosyncratic, characteristic, distinctive, specific, particular, unique, singular.

E3 1 ordinary, normal. **3** general.

....

peculiarity *noun* (PL. **peculiarities**) **1** the quality of being strange or odd. **2** a distinctive feature, characteristic or trait. **3** an eccentricity or idiosyncrasy.

....

E3 1 oddity, bizarreness, abnormality, distinctiveness, eccentricity. **2** mannerism, characteristic, feature, trait, mark, quality, attribute. **3** eccentricity, idiosyncrasy, quirk, peculiarity, oddity.

....

pecuniary *adj.* of, concerning or consisting of money. [from Latin *pecunia*, money, from *pecus*, flock]

ped- see PEDI-.

-ped or **-pede** *combining form* forming words meaning 'foot': *quadruped/millipede*. [from Latin *pes*, foot]

pedagogic /pɛdəˈgɒdʒɪk, pɛdəˈgɒgɪk/ or **pedagogical** *adj.* relating to or characteristic of a pedagogue.

pedagogically *adv.* in a pedagogic way.

pedagogue /ˈpɛdəgɒg/ *noun old derog. use* a teacher, especially a strict or pedantic one. [from Greek *paidagogos*, a child's tutor]

pedagogy /ˈpɛdəgɒdʒɪ, ˈpɛdəgɒgɪ/ *noun* the science, principles, or work of teaching. [from Greek *paidagogia*, tutorship, from *pais*, child + *agein*, to lead]

pedal — *noun* a lever operated by the foot, eg on a machine, vehicle, or musical instrument. — *verb trans.*, *intrans.* (**pedalled**, **pedalling**) to move or operate by means of a pedal or pedals. [from Latin *pedalis*, of the foot]

pedalo /ˈpɛdəloʊ/ *noun* (PL. **pedalos**) a small pedal-operated pleasure boat.

pedant /ˈpɛdnt/ *noun derog.* someone over-concerned with correctness of detail, especially in academic matters. [from Italian *pedante*, teacher]

pedantic *adj.* over-concerned with correctness.

....

E3 fussy, particular, precise, exact, punctilious, hair-splitting, nit-picking, finicky, academic, bookish, erudite.

E3 casual, informal, imprecise.

....

pedantically *adv.* in a pedantic way.

pedantry *noun* **1** excessive concern with correctness. **2** a pedantic expression. **3** unnecessary formality.

peddle *verb* **1** *trans.*, *intrans.* to go from place to place selling (small goods); to be a pedlar. **2** *colloq.* to deal illegally in (narcotic drugs). **3** *colloq.* to publicize and try to win acceptance for (ideas, theories, etc). [from PEDLAR]

....

E3 1 hawk, sell, vend, *colloq.* flog, tout, trade. **2** push, traffic. **3** push, *colloq.* plug, market.

....

peddler *noun* **1** *North Amer.*, *esp. US* a pedlar. **2** someone dealing illegally in narcotics: *a dope peddler*.

-pede see -PED.

pederast or **paederast** *noun* a man who is sexually attracted to or has sexual relations with boys. [from Greek *pais*, child + *erastes*, lover]

pederasty or **paederasty** *noun* sexual relations between a man and a boy.

pedestal *noun* the base on which a statue or column is mounted. — **put someone on a pedestal** to admire or revere them extremely; to idolize them. [from Italian *piedistallo*, foot of stall]

....

E3 plinth, stand, base, support, mounting, foot, foundation, platform, podium.

....

pedestrian — *noun* a person travelling on foot, especially in a street; a walker. — *adj.* **1** of or for pedestrians. **2** dull; unimaginative: *a pedestrian rendering by the orchestra*. [from Latin *pedester*, on foot]

....

E3 *noun* walker, foot-traveller. *adj.* **2** dull, unimaginative, boring, flat, uninspired, banal, mundane, run-of-the-mill, commonplace, ordinary, mediocre, indifferent, prosaic, stodgy, plodding.

E3 *adj.* **2** exciting, imaginative.

....

pedestrian crossing a specially marked crossing-place for pedestrians, where they have priority over traffic.

pedestrianization or **pedestrianisation** *noun* pedestrianizing or being pedestrianized.

pedestrianize or **pedestrianise** *verb* to convert (a street, etc) into an area for pedestrians only.

pedestrian precinct a shopping street or area from which traffic is excluded.

pedi- or **ped-** *combining form* forming words meaning 'foot': *pedicure*. [from Latin *pes*, foot]

pediatrics another spelling of **paediatrics**.

pedicure *noun* a medical or cosmetic treatment of the feet and toenails. [from PEDI- + Latin *curare*, to look after]

pedigree — *noun* **1** a person's or animal's line of descent, especially if long and distinguished, or proof of pure breeding. **2** a genealogical table showing this; a family tree. — *adj.*, *said of an animal* pure-bred; descended from a long line of known ancestors of the same breed. [from Old French *pie de grue*, crane's foot, from its similarity to a branching family tree]

....

E3 *noun* **1** genealogy, lineage, ancestry, descent, line, family, parentage, family tree, derivation, extraction, race, breed, stock, blood. **2** genealogy, family tree.

....

pediment *noun* **1** *Archit.* a wide triangular gable set over a classical portico or the face of a building. **2** *Geol.* a gently sloping surface, usually consisting of bare rock covered by a thin layer of sediment, formed by the erosion of cliffs or steep slopes. [earlier *periment*, thought to be a corruption of PYRAMID]

pedlar *noun* a person who goes from place to place peddling small articles. [from Middle English *ped*, basket]

pedo- same as PAEDO-.

pedology *noun* **1** *Geol.* the scientific study of the origin, properties, and uses of soil. **2** *Medicine* the scientific study of physiological and psychological aspects of childhood. [from Greek *pedon*, ground + *logos*, discourse]

pedometer *noun* a device that measures distance walked by recording the number of steps taken.

peduncle /pɪˈdʌŋkl/ *noun* **1** *Bot.* a short stalk, eg one carrying a single flower head. **2** *Anat.*, *Pathol.* any stalk-like structure. [from Latin *pedunculus*, diminutive of *pes*, foot]

pee *colloq.* — *verb intrans.* to urinate. — *noun* **1** an act of urinating. **2** urine. [from the first letter of PISS]

peek — *verb intrans.* to glance briefly and surreptitiously; to peep. — *noun* a brief furtive glance. [from Middle English *piken*, to peek]

peel — *verb* **1** to strip the skin or rind off (a fruit or vegetable). **2** *intrans.* to be able to be peeled: *peel easily*. **3** (*also* **peel something away** or **off**) to strip off (an outer layer). **4** *intrans.*, *said of a wall or other surface* to shed its outer coating in flaky shapes. **5** *intrans.*, *said of skin, paint, or other coverings* to flake off in patches. **6** *intrans.*, *said of a person or part of the body* to shed skin in flaky layers after sunburn. — *noun* the skin or rind of vegetables or fruit, especially citrus fruit. — **peel off 1** *said of an aircraft or vehicle* to veer away from the main group. **2** *colloq.* to undress. [from Anglo-Saxon, from Latin *pilare*, to deprive of hair]

....

E3 *verb* **1** pare, skin. **3** strip (off), flake off, scale. **4** flake.

5 flake (off), scale. *noun* skin, rind, zest, peeling.

. . . .

peeler *noun* a small knife or device for peeling fruit and vegetables.

peelings *pl. noun* strips of peel removed from a fruit or vegetable.

peep[1] — *verb intrans.* **1** to look quickly or covertly, eg through a narrow opening or from a place of concealment; to peek. **2** to emerge briefly or partially. — *noun* **1** a quick covert look. **2** a first faint glimmering: *at peep of day*. [a variant of PEEK]

. . . .

■ *verb* **1** look, peek, glimpse, spy, squint, peer. **2** emerge, appear. *noun* **1** look, peek, glimpse, glance, squint.

. . . .

peep[2] — *noun* **1** the faint high-pitched cry of a baby bird, etc; a cheep. **2** the least utterance: *not another peep out of you!* — *verb intrans.* **1** *said of a young bird, etc* to utter a high-pitched cry; to cheep. **2** *colloq.* to sound or cause to sound: *peep the horn*. [imitative]

peepers *pl. noun old colloq. use* eyes.

peephole *noun* **1** a hole, crack, etc through which to peep. **2** a tiny aperture in a front door, fitted with a convex lens, through which one can check on callers before opening the door.

. . . .

■ **1** spyhole, keyhole, pinhole, hole, opening, aperture, slit, chink, crack, fissure, cleft, crevice. **2** spyhole.

. . . .

peeping Tom a voyeur.

peepshow *noun* a box with a peephole through which a series of moving pictures can be watched.

peer[1] *noun* **1** a member of the nobility, ie, in Britain, a duke, marquess, earl, viscount, or baron. **2** someone who is one's equal in age, rank, etc; a contemporary, companion, or fellow. [from Old French *per*, from Latin *par*, equal]

. . . .

■ **1** aristocrat, noble, nobleman, noblewoman, lord, duke, marquess, marquis, earl, count, viscount, baron. **2** equal, counterpart, equivalent, match, contemporary, companion, fellow.

. . . .

peer[2] *verb intrans.* **1** (**peer at something** or **someone**) to look hard at them, especially through narrowed eyes, as if having difficulty in seeing. **2** to peep out or emerge briefly or partially.

. . . .

■ **1** look at, squint at, gaze at, scan, scrutinize, examine, inspect, peep at. **2** peep, emerge, appear.

. . . .

peerage *noun* **1** the title or rank of a peer: *granted a peerage/raised to the peerage*. **2** (*sing., pl.*) the members of the nobility as a group. **3** a book containing a list of peers with details of their families and descent.

. . . .

■ **2** aristocracy, nobility, upper crust.

. . . .

peeress *noun* **1** the wife or widow of a peer. **2** a female peer in her own right.

. . . .

■ ARISTOCRAT, NOBLE, NOBLEWOMAN, LADY, DAME, DUCHESS, MARCHIONESS, COUNTESS, VISCOUNTESS, BARONESS.

. . . .

peer group one's peers or companions as a group, especially as an influence on one's attitude and aspirations.

peerless *adj.* without equal; excelling all; matchless.

peerlessly *adv.* without equal.

peerlessness *noun* being without equal.

peer of the realm a member of the nobility with the right to sit in the House of Lords.

peeve — *verb colloq.* to irritate, annoy, or offend. — *noun* a cause of vexation or irritation. [a back-formation from PEEVISH]

peeved *adj.* annoyed, irritated, offended.

peevish *adj.* irritable; cantankerous; inclined to whine or complain.

. . . .

■ irritable, cantankerous, whining, complaining, grumpy, *colloq.* ratty, *colloq.* crotchety, bad-tempered, ill-tempered, short-tempered, crabbed, crusty, snappy, cross, surly, sullen, sulky, touchy, petulant, querulous, fractious, fretful.

✦ good-tempered.

. . . .

peewit *noun* a lapwing. [imitative of its cry]

peg — *noun* **1** a little shaft of wood, metal, or plastic shaped for any of various fixing, fastening, or marking uses. **2** a coat hook fixed to a wall, etc. **3** a wooden or plastic clip for fastening washed clothes to a line to dry; a clothes peg. **4** any of several wooden pins on a stringed instrument, turned to tune it. **5** a point of reference on which to base an argument, etc. **6** *old colloq. use* a drink of spirits. — *verb* (**pegged, pegging**) **1** to insert a peg into. **2** to fasten with a peg or pegs. **3** to freeze (prices, incomes, etc) at a certain level. — **off the peg** *said of clothes* ready to wear; ready-made. **peg away at something** *colloq.* to work steadily at it. **peg out** *colloq.* to die. **peg something out** to mark out (ground) with pegs. **a square peg in a round hole** a person who does not fit in well in his or her environment, job, etc. **take someone down a peg or two** *colloq.* to humble them. [from Old Dutch *pegge*]

. . . .

■ *noun* **1** pin, dowel, marker, post, stake. **2** hook, knob. **5** hook. *verb* **2** fasten, secure, fix, attach, join, mark. **3** freeze, fix, set, control, stabilize, limit.

. . . .

peg board a board with holes for receiving pegs that are used for scoring in games, or for attaching matter for display.

peg leg *colloq.* an artificial leg, or a person with an artificial leg.

pegmatite *noun Geol.* any of various very coarse-grained igneous rocks, many of which are important sources of economically important minerals such as mica, feldspar, tourmaline, topaz, beryl, and garnet. The commonest type is granite pegmatite. [from Greek *pegma*, bond, framework]

PEI *abbrev.* Prince Edward Island.

peignoir /'peɪnwɑ:(r)/ *noun* a woman's light dressing-gown. [from French *peignoir*, from *peigner*, to comb]

pejorative — *adj., said of a word or expression* disapproving, derogatory, disparaging, or uncomplimentary. — *noun* a word or affix with derogatory force. [from Latin *peiorare*, to make worse]

. . . .

■ *adj.* disapproving, derogatory, disparaging, uncomplimentary, belittling, slighting, unflattering, unpleasant, bad, negative.

✦ *adj.* complimentary.

. . . .

peke *noun colloq.* a Pekinese.

Pekinese or **Pekingese** /pi:kɪ'ni:z/ *noun* (PL. **Pekinese**) a small dog with a flat face and a silky coat, originally a Chinese breed. [from *Peking* (Beijing) in China]

pekoe /'pi:kəʊ/ *noun* a high-quality black China tea. [from Chinese dialect *pek-ho*]

pelagic /pɪ'lædʒɪk/ *adj.* **1** *technical* relating to, or carried out on, the deep open sea. **2** denoting plankton that float and fish and other organisms that swim freely (nekton) in the surface waters, as opposed to *benthic* organisms that live on the bottom of a sea or lake. [from Greek *pelagos*, sea]

pelargonium /pɛlə'goʊnɪəm/ *noun* any of a genus of plants of the geranium family, with red, pink, or white flowers and strong-smelling leaves, often grown as house and garden plants under the name of geranium. [from Greek *pelargos*, stork]

Pelasgians *pl. noun* the name given by the ancient Greeks to the indigenous peoples who inhabited Greece before the 12c BC.

pelican *noun* (PL. **pelican**, **pelicans**) an aquatic bird related to the cormorants, found on coasts and inland waters in most warm regions of the world. It has an enormous beak with a pouch below that is used to scoop up fish. [from Greek *pelekan*]

pelican crossing a pedestrian crossing with pedestrian-controlled traffic lights. [from *pedestrian light-controlled crossing*]

pellagra /pə'lagrə/ *noun Medicine* a disease caused by a dietary deficiency of nicotinic acid or the amino acid tryptophan, from which it is made, and characterized by scaly discoloration of the skin, diarrhoea, vomiting, and psychological disturbances such as depression. [from Italian *pellagra*, from Latin *pellis*, skin + Greek *agra*, seizure]

pellet *noun* 1 a small rounded mass of compressed material, eg paper. 2 a piece of small shot for an airgun, etc. 3 a ball of undigested material regurgitated by an owl or hawk. [from Old French *pelote*, from Latin *pila*, ball]

pell-mell *adv.* headlong; in confused haste; helter-skelter. [from Old French *pesle-mesle*, rhyming compound from *mesler*, to mix]

pellucid /pɛ'ljuːsɪd/ *adj.* 1 transparent. 2 absolutely clear in expression and meaning. [from Latin *per*, utterly + *lucidus*, clear]

pelmet *noun* a strip of fabric or a narrow board fitted along the top of a window to conceal the curtain rail.

pelota /pɛ'loʊtə/ *noun* a Spanish and Latin American court game, in which the players use a basket strapped to their wrists to hit a ball against a specially marked wall. [from Spanish *pelota*, ball]

peloton /'pɛlɒtɒn/ *noun* the leading group of cyclists in a race. [from French *peloton*, small ball, cluster]

pelt¹ — *verb* 1 to bombard with missiles: *was pelted with stones.* 2 (*also* **pelt down**) *said of rain, hail, etc* to fall fast and heavily. 3 *intrans.* to rush along at top speed. — *noun* an act or spell of pelting. — **at full pelt** as fast as possible.

⊟ *verb* 1 bombard, shower, assail, batter, beat, hit, strike. 2 pour (down), teem (down), *colloq.* bucket (down), *colloq.* rain cats and dogs. 3 rush, hurry, charge, *colloq.* belt, tear, dash, hurtle, speed, career.

pelt² *noun* 1 the skin of a dead animal, especially with the fur still on it. 2 the coat of a living animal. 3 a hide stripped of hair for tanning. [from Old French *pelleterie*, animal skins, from Latin *pellis*, skin]

pelvic *adj.* relating to or in the region of the pelvis.

pelvic inflammatory disease *Medicine* any pelvic infection of the upper reproductive tract in women, usually affecting the uterus, Fallopian tubes, and ovaries, and generally caused by the spread of infection from an infected organ nearby, eg the vagina or the appendix. It can cause blockage of the Fallopian tubes.

pelvis *noun Anat.* 1 the basin-shaped cavity formed by the bones of the pelvic girdle. 2 the pelvic girdle itself, which articulates with the spine and the bones of the legs or hindlimbs. 3 in the mammalian kidney, the expanded upper end of the ureter, into which the urine drains. [from Latin *pelvis*, basin]

pemmican *noun* 1 a Native American food of dried meat beaten to a paste and mixed with fat. 2 a similarly condensed and nutritious mixture of dried ingredients used as emergency rations. [from Cree (Native American language) *pimekan*]

PEN *abbrev.* Poets, Playwrights, Editors, Essayists, and Novelists, an international association of writers which promotes friendship and understanding between writers, and defends freedom of expression within and between all nations.

pen¹ — *noun* 1 a small enclosure for animals. 2 (*often in compounds*) any small enclosure or area of confinement: *a playpen.* 3 a bomb-proof dock for submarines. — *verb* (**penned**, **penning**) (**pen someone** or **something in** or **up**) to enclose or confine them in a pen, or as if in a pen. [from Anglo-Saxon *penn*]

⊟ *noun* 1 enclosure, fold, stall, sty, coop, cage, hutch. *verb* enclose, fence in, hedge in, hem in, confine, cage, coop up, shut up.

pen² — *noun* 1 a writing instrument that uses ink, formerly a quill, now any of various implements fitted with a nib, rotating ball, or felt or nylon point. 2 this as a symbol of the writing profession. — *verb* (**penned**, **penning**) to compose and write (a letter, poem, etc) with a pen. [from Latin *penna*, feather]

⊟ *noun* 1 fountain pen, ballpoint, *trademark* Biro, felt-tip pen. *verb* write, compose, draft, scribble, jot down.

pen³ *noun North Amer. colloq.* a penitentiary.

pen⁴ *noun* a female swan.

penal *adj.* relating to punishment, especially by law. [from Latin *poenalis*, from *poena*, penalty]

penal code a system of laws concerning the punishment of crime.

penalization or **penalisation** *noun* penalizing or being penalized.

penalize or **penalise** *verb* 1 to impose a penalty on, for wrongdoing, cheating, breaking a rule, committing a foul, etc. 2 to disadvantage: *income groups that are penalized by the new tax laws.*

⊟ 1 punish, discipline, correct, fine. 2 disadvantage, handicap. ⊠ 1 reward.

penally *adv.* as punishment.

penal servitude *Hist.* imprisonment with hard labour.

penalty *noun* (PL. **penalties**) 1 a punishment for wrongdoing, breaking a contract or rule, etc. 2 a punishment that one brings on oneself through ill-advised action: *pay the penalty for my error.* 3 *Sport* a handicap imposed on a competitor or team for a foul or other infringement of the rules, in team games taking the form of an advantage awarded to the opposing side. [from Latin *poenalitas*, from *poena*, punishment]

⊟ 1 punishment, retribution, fine, forfeit. 2 price, forfeit, sacrifice, consequence(s). 3 handicap, disadvantage. ⊠ 1, 2 reward. 3 advantage.

penalty area or **penalty box** *Football* an area in front of either goal within which a foul by any player in the defending team is punished by a penalty awarded to the attacking team.

penalty kick 1 *Rugby* a free kick. 2 *Football* a free kick at goal from a distance of 11m (12yd), awarded to the attacking team for a foul committed in the penalty area by the defending team.

penance *noun* 1 repentance or atonement for an offence or wrongdoing, or an act of repentance: *do penance.* 2 *RC Church* a sacrament involving confession, repentance, forgiveness, and the performance of a penance suggested by one's confessor. [from Old French *peneance*, from Latin *paenitentia*, penitence]

⊟ 1 atonement, reparation, punishment, penalty.

Penates /pə'nɑːtiːz/ *pl. noun* in Roman religion, the guardians of the storeroom.

pence see PENNY.

-pence *combining form* denoting a number of pennies (as a value): *threepence*.

penchant /'pɒnʃɒŋ/ *noun* a taste, liking, inclination, or tendency: *a penchant for childish pranks*. [from French *penchant*, present participle of *pencher*, to lean]

pencil — *noun* 1 a writing and drawing instrument consisting of a wooden shaft containing a stick of graphite or other material, sharpened for use and making more or less erasable marks. 2 such material, especially with regard to the alterability of marks made with it: *written in pencil*. 3 something with a similar function or shape: *an eyebrow pencil/a pencil of light*. — *verb* (**pencilled**, **pencilling**) to write, draw, or mark with a pencil. — **pencil something in** to note down a provisional commitment in one's diary, for later confirmation. [from Latin *penicillus*, painter's brush, diminutive of *peniculus*, little tail]

🔲 1 medallion, locket, necklace.

pendant *noun* 1 an ornament suspended from a neck chain, necklace, bracelet, etc; a necklace with a pendant hanging from it. 2 any of several hanging articles, eg an earring, ceiling light, etc. 3 a companion piece, eg a painting or poem. [from Latin *pendere*, to hang]

🔲 1 medallion, locket, necklace.

pendent *adj.* 1 hanging; suspended; dangling. 2 projecting; jutting; overhanging. 3 undetermined or undecided; pending. [from Latin *pendere*, to hang]

pending — *adj.* 1 waiting to be decided or dealt with. 2 *said of a patent* about to come into effect. — *prep.* until; awaiting; during: *held in prison pending trial*. [from Latin *pendere*, to hang]

🔲 *adj.* 1 impending, in the offing, forthcoming, imminent, undecided, in the balance.

🔲 *adj.* 1 finished, settled.

pendulous *adj.* hanging down loosely; drooping; swinging freely. [from Latin *pendulus*, hanging]

pendulum *noun* 1 *Physics* a weight that is suspended from a fixed point and swings back and forth through a small angle with *simple harmonic motion*. 2 a swinging lever used to regulate the movement of a clock. [from Latin *pendulum*, neuter of *pendulus*, hanging]

penetrability *noun* the quality of being penetrable.

penetrable *adj.* capable of being penetrated.

penetrate *verb* 1 (**penetrate something** or **into something**) to find a way in; to enter, especially with difficulty. 2 to infiltrate (an organization, etc). 3 to find a way through; to pierce or permeate: *penetrate enemy lines/ penetrated the silence*. 4 *intrans.* to be understood: *the news didn't penetrate at first*. 5 to see through (a disguise). 6 to fathom, solve, or understand (a mystery). 7 *said of a man* to insert his penis into the vagina of (a woman). [from Latin *penetrare*, to penetrate]

🔲 1, 3 pierce, stab, prick, puncture, probe, sink, bore, enter, infiltrate, permeate, seep in, pervade, suffuse. 4 be understood, *colloq.* sink in.

penetrating *adj.* 1 *said of a voice, etc* all too loud and clear; strident; carrying. 2 *said of a person's mind* acute; discerning. 3 *said of the eyes or a look* piercing; probing.

🔲 1 piercing, strident, carrying, shrill. 2 acute, discerning, incisive, sharp, keen, shrewd, perceptive, observant, profound, deep. 3 piercing, probing, searching, sharp, keen.

penetration *noun* 1 the process of penetrating or being penetrated. 2 mental acuteness; perspicacity; insight.

penfriend or **penpal** *noun* a person, especially foreign and otherwise unknown to one, with whom one regularly corresponds.

penguin *noun* any of 17 species of a flightless sea bird belonging to the family Spheniscidae, found in the S hemisphere, especially the Antarctic region, and having a stout body, small almost featherless wings modified to form powerful flippers, short legs, bluish-grey or black waterproof plumage, with a white belly.

penicillin *noun* any of a group of antibiotics derived from the mould *Penicillium notatum*, or produced synthetically, that prevent the growth of a wide range of bacteria by inhibiting manufacture of the bacterial cell wall. [from Latin *penicillus*, hairy tuft, from the appearance of the mould]

penile *adj.* relating to or resembling the penis.

peninsula *noun* a piece of land almost surrounded by water or projecting into water from a larger land mass. [from Latin *paene*, almost + *insula*, island]

peninsular *adj.* relating to or of the nature of a peninsula.

penis *noun* in higher vertebrates, the male organ of copulation, which is used to transfer sperm to the female reproductive tract. In mammals it is made erect by the swelling of vessels that fill with blood. It also contains the urethra through which urine is passed. [from Latin *penis*, originally = tail]

penitence *noun* being penitent and wishing to improve.

🔲 repentance, contrition, remorse, regret, shame, self-reproach.

penitent — *adj.* regretful for wrong one has done; repentant. — *noun* a repentant person, especially one doing penance on the instruction of a confessor. [from Latin *paenitens*, repentant]

🔲 *adj.* regretful, repentant, contrite, sorry, apologetic, remorseful, conscience-stricken, shamefaced, humble.

🔲 *adj.* unrepentant, hard-hearted, callous.

penitential *adj.* relating to penitence or penance.

penitential psalms *Relig.* a set of seven Old Testament psalms which have been used in Christian liturgy since at least the early Middle Ages, when they were regularly recited on Fridays during Lent.

penitentiary — *noun* (PL. **penitentiaries**) *North Amer.* a federal or state prison. — *adj.* of or relating to punishment or penance. [from Latin *paenitens*, repentant]

penknife *noun* a pocket knife with blades that fold into the handle. [originally used for cutting quills]

penmanship *noun* skill with the pen, whether calligraphic or literary.

Penn. *abbrev.* Pennsylvania.

pen name a pseudonym used by a writer.

pennant *noun* a small narrow triangular flag, used on vessels for identification or for signalling. [probably from PENNON + PENDANT]

penniless *adj.* poverty-stricken.

🔲 poverty-stricken, poor, impoverished, destitute, bankrupt, ruined, *colloq.* bust, *colloq.* broke, *colloq.* stony-broke.

🔲 rich, wealthy, affluent, well off.

pennon *noun* 1 *Hist.* a long narrow flag with a tapering divided tip, eg borne on his lance by a knight. 2 a pennant. [from Latin *penna*, feather]

penny *noun* (PL. **pence**, **pennies**) 1 in the UK, a hundredth part of £1, or a bronze coin having this value. 2 in the UK before decimalization in 1971, — of a shilling or — of £1, or a bronze coin having this value. 3 the least quantity of money: *won't cost a penny*. 4 *North Amer.* one cent, or a coin having this value. 5 a coin of low value in certain other countries. — **in for a penny, in for a pound** (*often shortened to* **in for a penny**) once involved, one may as well be totally committed. **in penny numbers** *colloq.* in small quantities. **the penny dropped** *colloq.* understanding came. **a pretty penny** *ironic* a huge sum. **spend a penny** *euphemistic colloq.* to urinate. **turn an honest penny** *colloq.* to earn one's living honestly. **two** or **ten a penny** very common. [from Anglo-Saxon *pening*]

-penny *combining form* denoting a number of pennies (as a value): *a five-penny piece.*

penny dreadful *colloq.* a cheap trivial novel or thriller.

penny farthing *Brit.* an early type of bicycle with a large front wheel and small back wheel.

penny-halfpenny *noun* formerly in the UK, one and a half pre-decimal pence.

penny-in-the-slot *adj.*, *said of a machine* coin-operated.

penny-pincher *noun* a person who is too careful with money, a miser.

penny-pinching *adj. derog.* too careful with one's money; miserly; stingy.

pennyworth *noun old use* an amount that can be bought for one penny.

penological *adj.* relating to or involving penology.

penologist *noun* a person who studies and is expert in penology.

penology /piːˈnɒlədʒɪ/ *noun* the study of crime and punishment.

pen-pusher *noun* a clerk or minor official whose job includes much tedious paperwork.

pen-pushing *noun* doing tedious paperwork.

pension — *noun* a government allowance to a retired, disabled, or widowed person; a regular payment by an employer to a retired employee. — *verb* (**pensioned, pensioning**) to grant a pension to. — **pension someone off** to put them into retirement on a pension. [from Old French, from Latin *pensio*, payment]

▣ *noun* annuity, superannuation, allowance, benefit.

pensionable *adj.* entitling one to a pension.

pensioner *noun* a person in receipt of a pension.

pensive *adj.* preoccupied with one's thoughts; thoughtful. [from Old French *pensif*, from *penser*, to think]

▣ preoccupied, thoughtful, reflective, contemplative, meditative, ruminative, absorbed, absent-minded, wistful.

pent — **pent up** *said of feelings, energy, etc* repressed or stifled; bursting to be released. [an old past participle of PEN[1]]

▣ **pent up** repressed, inhibited, restrained, bottled-up, suppressed, stifled.

penta- or **pent-** *combining form* forming words meaning 'five': *pentatonic.* [from Greek *pente*, five]

pentagon *noun* a two-dimensional figure with five sides and five angles. [from Greek *pente*, five + *gonia*, angle]

pentagonal *adj.* having five sides and angles.

pentagram *noun* a five-pointed star, especially used as a magic symbol. [from Greek *pente*, five + *gramma*, character, letter]

pentameter /penˈtæmɪtə(r)/ *noun* a line of verse with five metrical feet. [from Greek *pente*, five + *metron*, measure]

Pentateuch /ˈpentəˈtjuːkəl/ *adj.* of the Pentateuch, the five books of Moses in the Hebrew Bible and Old Testament: Genesis, Exodus, Leviticus, Numbers, and Deuteronomy.

pentathlon *noun* any of several athletic competitions composed of five events in all of which contestants must compete, the **modern pentathlon** comprising swimming, cross-country riding and running, fencing, and pistol-shooting. [from Greek *pente*, five + *athlon*, contest]

pentatonic *adj. Mus.*, *said of a musical scale* having five notes to the octave, most commonly equivalent to the first, second, third, fifth, and sixth degrees of the major scale. [from Greek *pente*, five + *tonos*, tone]

pentavalent /pentəˈveɪlənt/ *adj. Chem.* having a valency of five.

Pentecost /ˈpentɪkɒst/ *noun* **1** *Christianity* a festival on Whit Sunday, the seventh Sunday after Easter, commemorating the descent of the Holy Spirit on the Apostles. **2** *Judaism* Shabuoth or the Feast of Weeks. [from Greek *pentecoste hemera*, fiftieth day]

Pentecostal *adj.* **1** denoting any of several fundamentalist Christian groups that put emphasis on God's gifts through the Holy Spirit. **2** relating to Pentecost.

Pentecostalism *noun Relig.* a modern Christian renewal movement begun in 1901 at Topeka, Kansas, USA, and becoming organized in 1905 at Los Angeles, which was inspired by the descent of the Holy Spirit experienced by the Apostles at the first Christian Pentecost.

penthouse *noun* an apartment, especially luxuriously appointed, built on to the roof of a tall building. [earlier *pentice*, from Old French *appentis*, from Latin *appendicium*, appendage]

pent up see PENT.

penultimate *adj.* the last but one. [from Latin *paene*, almost + *ultimus*, last]

penumbra *noun* (PL. **penumbrae**, **penumbras**) **1** a rim of lighter shadow round the shadow proper of a body, eg the sun or moon during an eclipse; an area where dark and light blend. **2** a lighter border round the edge of a sunspot. [from Latin *paene*, almost + *umbra*, shadow]

penumbral *adj.* relating to or characterized by a penumbra.

penurious *adj.* **1** mean with money; miserly. **2** poor; impoverished.

penury /ˈpenjʊrɪ/ *noun* **1** extreme poverty. **2** lack; scarcity. [from Latin *penuria*]

Penutian languages /peˈnjuːʃən/ a group of about 20 Native American languages spoken by small numbers in SW Canada and W USA. In some classifications, a further 40 languages of Mexico and Central and S America are included in the group.

peon *noun* **1** in India and Ceylon, an office messenger; an attendant. **2** in Latin America, a farm labourer. [from Spanish *peón*, from Latin *pedo*, foot soldier]

peony *noun* (PL. **peonies**) a garden plant or small shrub with large globular red, pink, yellow, or white flowers. [from Greek *paionia*, from *Paion*, the healer of the gods, from the plant's medicinal use]

people — *noun* (*usually pl.*) **1** persons. **2** men and women in general. **3** (**the people**) ordinary citizens without special rank; the populace. **4** (**the people**) the voters as a body. **5** subjects or supporters of a monarch, etc. **6** (*sing.*) a nation or race: *a warlike people.* **7** *colloq.* one's parents, or the wider circle of one's relations. — *verb* **1** to fill or supply (a region) with people; to populate. **2** to inhabit. — **of all people** especially; more than anyone else. [from Old French *poeple*]

▣ *noun* **1, 2** persons, individuals, human beings, humans, humanity, mankind, folk. **3** citizens, public, general public, populace, rank and file, population, inhabitants, community, society. **7** parents, relations, folks, family. *verb* **1** populate, colonize. **2** inhabit, occupy, settle, colonize.

people carrier a vehicle with seating capacity for a number of people, for example a large family.

PEP *abbrev.* personal equity plan.

pep — *noun colloq.* energy; vitality; go. — *verb* (**pepped, pepping**) (*often* **pep someone** or **something up**) to enliven or invigorate them. [a shortening of PEPPER]

▣ *noun* energy, vitality, vigour, verve, spirit, liveliness, *colloq.* go, *colloq.* get-up-and-go, exuberance, high spirits. *verb* enliven, invigorate, vitalize, liven up, quicken, stimulate, excite, exhilarate, inspire.

. . . .

peplum *noun* a short skirt-like section attached to the waistline of a dress, blouse, or jacket. [from Greek *peplos*, an outer robe or overskirt worn by women in ancient Greece]

pepper — *noun* **1** a perennial climbing shrub (*Piper nigrum*), widely cultivated for its pea-sized red berries which are dried to form peppercorns. **2** a pungent seasoning prepared from the dried berries of this plant. **3** any of various tropical shrubs of the genus *Capsicum*, unrelated to true pepper, cultivated for their large red, green, or yellow edible fruits. It includes varieties with a hot spicy flavour such as chilli pepper. **4** the fruit of this plant, which has a hollow seedy interior and is eaten raw in salads or cooked as a vegetable. Also called CAPSICUM. — *verb* (**peppered**, **peppering**) **1** to bombard (with missiles). **2** to sprinkle liberally: *a text peppered with errors*. **3** to season with pepper. [from Anglo-Saxon *pipor*, from Latin *piper*]

peppercorn *noun* the dried berry of the pepper plant.

peppermill *noun* a device for grinding peppercorns.

peppermint *noun* **1** a species of mint (*Mentha piperita*) with dark green leaves and spikes of small purple flowers, widely cultivated in Europe, America, and N Africa for its aromatic oil, which is used in confectionery, as a food flavouring, and as a treatment for indigestion. **2** this flavouring. **3** a sweet flavoured with peppermint.

peppery *adj.* **1** well seasoned with pepper; tasting of pepper; hot-tasting or pungent. **2** short-tempered; irascible.

pep pill a pill containing a stimulant drug.

pepsin *noun Biochem.* a digestive enzyme produced by the gastric glands in the stomach of vertebrates, which under acid conditions brings about the partial breakdown of dietary protein to polypeptides (chains of amino acids). [from Greek *pepsis*, digestion]

pep talk a brief talk intended to raise morale.

peptic *adj.* **1** relating to, or promoting, digestion. **2** relating to pepsin or the digestive juices. [from Greek *peptikos*]

peptic ulcer *Medicine* an ulcer, usually of the stomach or duodenum, that is caused by digestion of part of the lining of the digestive tract by gastric juices containing pepsin and acid.

peptide *noun Biochem.* a molecule that consists of a relatively short chain of amino acids, and is obtained by the partial hydrolysis of proteins. [from Greek *pepsis*, digestion]

per *prep.* **1** out of every: *two per thousand*. **2** for every: *£5 per head*. **3** in every: *60 miles per hour/100 accidents per week*. **4** through; by means of: *per post*. — **as per** ... according to: *proceed as per instructions*. **as per usual** *colloq.* as always. [from Latin *per-*, for, each, by]

per- *prefix* forming words denoting: **1** *Chem.* the highest degree of combination with oxygen or other element or radical. **2** *in words derived from Latin* through, beyond, thoroughly, utterly. [from Latin]

peradventure *adv.* perhaps; by chance. [from Old French *par aventure*, by chance]

perambulate *verb formal* **1** to walk about (a place). **2** *intrans.* to stroll around. [from Latin *per*, through or *ambulare*, to walk]

perambulation *noun* perambulating.

perambulator *noun* a pram.

per annum for each year; by the year. [Latin]

per capita for each person: *income per capita*. [from Latin *per capita*, by heads]

perceivable *adj.* capable of being perceived.

perceive *verb* **1** to observe, notice, or discern: *perceived a change*. **2** to understand, interpret, or view: *how one perceives one's role*. [from Old French *percever*, from Latin *percipere*]

. . . .

☒ **1** observe, notice, see, discern, make out, detect, discover,

spot, catch sight of, observe, view, remark, note, distinguish, recognize. **2** understand, interpret, view, sense, feel, apprehend, learn, realize, appreciate, be aware of, know, grasp, gather, deduce, conclude.

. . . .

per cent (SYMBOL **%**) — *adv.* **1** in or for every 100. **2** on a scale of 1 to 100: *90 per cent certain*. — *noun* (*usually* **per cent**) **1** a percentage or proportion. **2** (*usually* **percents**) a security yielding a certain rate of interest: *invest in four-percents*. **3** one part in every 100: *half a percent*. [from Latin *per centum*, for every 100]

percentage *noun* **1** an amount, number, or rate stated as a proportion of one hundred. **2** a proportion: *a large percentage of students fail*.

percentile *noun Statistics* one of the points or values that divide a range of statistical data, such as numerical scores or measurements, arranged in order, into 100 equal parts, eg the 90th percentile is the value below which 90 per cent of the scores lie. The *median* is the 50th percentile.

perceptibility *noun* being perceptible.

perceptible *adj.* able to be perceived; noticeable; detectable.

. . . .

☒ perceivable, noticeable, detectable, discernible, appreciable, distinguishable, observable, apparent, visible.
☒ imperceptible, inconspicuous.

. . . .

perception *noun* **1** *Psychol.* the process whereby information about one's environment, received by the senses, is organized and interpreted so that it becomes meaningful. **2** one's powers of observation; discernment; insight. **3** one's view or interpretation of something. [from Latin *percipere*, to perceive]

. . . .

☒ **1** awareness, consciousness, observation, recognition. **2** insight, discernment, understanding, grasp. **3** view, interpretation, understanding, sense, feeling, impression, idea, conception, apprehension.

. . . .

perceptive *adj.* quick to notice or discern; astute.

. . . .

☒ discerning, astute, observant, sensitive, responsive, aware, alert, quick, sharp, shrewd.
☒ unobservant.

. . . .

perceptively *adv.* with perception.

perch[1] — *noun* **1** a branch or other narrow support above ground for a bird to rest on. **2** any place selected, especially temporarily, as a seat. **3** a high position or vantage point. **4** an old measure of length equal to 5.03m or 5.5yd (also called ROD, POLE). — *verb* **1** *intrans.*, *said of a bird* to alight and rest on a perch. **2** *intrans.* to sit, especially insecurely or temporarily. **3** *intrans.*, *trans.* to sit or place high up. [from Old French *perche*, from Latin *pertica*, rod]

. . . .

☒ *verb* **1** land, alight, settle, sit, roost, balance, rest.

. . . .

perch[2] *noun* (PL. **perch**, **perches**) any of several edible, spiny-finned fish. [from Greek *perke*]

perchance *adv. old use* **1** by chance. **2** perhaps. [from Old French *par chance*, by chance]

percipient *adj.* perceptive; acutely observant; discerning. [from Latin *percipere*, to perceive]

percolate *verb* **1** *intrans.*, *trans.* to pass through a porous material; to ooze, trickle, or filter. **2** *intrans.*, *colloq.*, *said of news or information* to trickle or spread slowly. **3** *trans.*, *intrans.*, *said of coffee* to make it or be made in a percolator. [from Latin *percolare*, to filter through]

. . . .

☒ **1** ooze, filter, trickle, strain, seep, leak, drip, penetrate, permeate, pervade.

. . . .

percolation *noun* percolating.

percolator *noun* a pot for making coffee, in which boiling water is kept circulating up through a tube and down through ground coffee beans.

percussion *noun* **1** the striking of one hard object against another. **2** musical instruments played by striking, eg drums, cymbals, xylophone, etc; these as a section of an orchestra. **3** *Medicine* a technique whereby part of the body is examined by tapping it with the fingers and using the sound or vibrations produced to determine the size, location, and condition of internal structures, or to detect the presence of fluid. [from Latin *percussio*, striking]

percussion cap a metal case containing a material that explodes when struck, formerly used for firing rifles.

percussionist *noun* a person who plays percussion instruments.

percussive *adj.* relating to or involving percussion.

perdition *noun* everlasting punishment after death; damnation; hell. [from Latin *perditio*, from *perdere*, to lose utterly]

peregrinate *verb intrans.* to travel, voyage, or roam; to wander abroad. [from Latin *peregrinari*, to roam, from *per*, through + *ager*, field]

peregrination *noun* (*usually* **peregrinations**) a journey or travel.

peregrine /'perəgrɪn/ *noun* (*also* **peregrine falcon**) a small falcon with a dark back and streaked underparts, notable for its acrobatic flight. [from Latin *peregrinus*, wandering abroad, the birds being captured during flight]

peremptorily *adv.* in a peremptory way.

peremptory *adj.* **1** *said of an order* made in expectation of immediate compliance: *a peremptory summons.* **2** *said of a tone or manner* arrogantly impatient. **3** *said of a statement, conclusion, etc* allowing no denial or discussion; dogmatic. [from Latin *peremptorius*, deadly]

⊟ IMPERIOUS. **1** authoritative, dictatorial. **2** high-handed, overbearing, domineering, *colloq.* bossy, abrupt, curt, summary. **3** dogmatic, dictatorial, autocratic, assertive, commanding, curt.

perennial — *adj.* **1** *Bot. said of a plant* living for several to many years, either growing continuously, as in the case of woody trees and shrubs, or having stems that die back each autumn and are replaced by new growth the following spring, as in the case of herbaceous perennials. See also ANNUAL, BIENNIAL. **2** lasting throughout the year. **3** constant; continual. — *noun* a perennial plant. [from Latin *perennis*, from *per*, through + *annus*, year]

⊟ *adj.* **3** constant, continual, uninterrupted, unceasing, incessant, never-ending, persistent, perpetual, unfailing, lasting, enduring, everlasting, eternal, immortal, undying, imperishable.

perennially *adv.* every year; year by year; everlastingly.

perestroika /perə'strɔɪkə/ *noun* a restructuring or reorganization, specifically that of the economic and political system of the former USSR begun in the 1980s. [from Russian, = reconstruction]

perfect — *adj.* (with stress on *per-*) **1** complete in all essential elements. **2** faultless; flawless. **3** excellent; absolutely, or quite, satisfactory. **4** exact: *a perfect circle.* **5** *colloq.* absolute; utter: *perfect nonsense.* **6** *Grammar, said of the tense of a verb* denoting completed action. — *noun* (with stress on *per-*) *Grammar* the perfect tense, in English formed with the auxiliary verb *have* and the past participle. — *verb* (with stress on *-fect*) **1** to improve to one's satisfaction: *perfect one's German.* **2** to finalize or complete. **3** to develop (a technique, etc) to a reliable standard. [from Latin *perficere*, to complete]

⊟ *adj.* **2** faultless, flawless, impeccable, immaculate, spotless, blameless, pure. **3** excellent, superb, matchless, incom-

parable, ideal, model, exemplary, ultimate. **4** exact, precise, accurate, true. **5** absolute, utter, sheer, total, complete, entire, pure, consummate. *verb* **1, 3** polish, refine. **2** finalize, complete, finish, fulfil, consummate.

⊟ *adj.* **1** imperfect. **2** imperfect, flawed, blemished.

perfectibility *noun* capability of becoming perfect.

perfectible *adj.* capable of becoming perfect.

perfection *noun* **1** the state of being perfect. **2** the process of making or being made perfect, complete, etc. **3** flawlessness. **4** *colloq.* an instance of absolute excellence: *the meal was perfection.* — **to perfection** perfectly.

⊟ **1, 3** excellence, faultlessness, flawlessness, superiority. **2** improvement, betterment, completion, consummation, realization. **4** ideal, model, paragon, crown, pinnacle, acme.

⊟ **1, 3** imperfection.

perfectionism *noun* **1** the doctrine that perfection is attainable. **2** an expectation of the very highest standard.

perfectionist *noun* a person inclined to be dissatisfied with standards of achievement, especially his or her own, if they are not absolutely perfect.

⊟ idealist, purist, pedant, stickler.

perfectly *adv.* **1** in a perfect way. **2** completely; quite: *a perfectly reasonable reaction.*

⊟ **1** faultlessly, flawlessly, impeccably, ideally, exactly, correctly. **2** completely, quite, utterly, totally, absolutely, thoroughly, wholly, entirely, fully.

⊟ **1** imperfectly, badly. **2** partially.

perfect number *Maths.* a number that is equal to the sum of all its factors (except itself), eg the number 6, because the sum of its factors $(1+2+3)$ is equal to 6.

perfect pitch or **absolute pitch** the ability to recognize a note from its pitch, or spontaneously sing any note with correct pitch.

perfidious *adj.* treacherous, double-dealing, or disloyal. [from Latin *perfidus*]

perfidy /'pɑːfɪdɪ/ *noun* (PL. **perfidies**) perfidious behaviour, or an instance of this.

perforate *verb* **1** to make a hole or holes in; to pierce. **2** to make a row of holes in, for ease of tearing. **3** *intrans., said of an ulcer, diseased appendix, etc* to develop a hole; to burst. [from Latin *perforare*, to pierce]

⊟ **1** pierce, hole, punch, drill, bore, prick, stab, puncture, penetrate. **3** burst, puncture, rupture, tear, split.

perforation *noun* **1** a hole made in something. **2** a row of small holes made in paper, a sheet of stamps, etc for ease of tearing. **3** the process of perforating or being perforated.

⊟ **1** hole, bore, prick, puncture. **2** dotted line.

perforce *adv.* necessarily; inevitably or unavoidably. [from Old French *par force*]

perform *verb* **1** to carry out (a task, job, action, etc); to do or accomplish. **2** to fulfil (a function) or provide (a service, etc). **3** *trans., intrans.* to act, sing, play, dance, etc to entertain an audience. **4** *intrans., said eg of an engine* to function. **5** *intrans.* to conduct oneself, especially when presenting oneself for assessment: *performs well in interviews.* **6** *intrans., said of commercial products, shares, currencies, etc* to fare in competition. [from Old French *parfournir*]

⊟ **1, 2** do, carry out, execute, discharge, fulfil, achieve, accomplish, bring off, pull off, effect, bring about, complete, satisfy. **3** act, play, appear as, represent, stage, put on, present, enact. **4** function, work, operate, run. **5** behave, conduct oneself, acquit oneself, function, operate. **6** fare, do.

performance *noun* **1** the performing of a play, part, dance, piece of music, etc before an audience; a dramatic or artistic presentation or entertainment. **2** the act or process of performing a task, etc. **3** a level of achievement, success, or, in commerce, profitability. **4** manner or efficiency of functioning. **5** *derog.* an instance of outrageous behaviour, especially in public.

■ **1** *performing* acting, portrayal, rendition, representation, interpretation, appearance, *show* show, play, *slang* gig, presentation, production. **2** act, action, doing, carrying out, execution, implementation, discharge, fulfilment, completion, achievement, accomplishment, functioning, operation, behaviour, conduct. **3** achievement, attainment, success, profitability, productivity, return, value, effectiveness. **4** operation, conduct, efficiency, effectiveness, productivity.

performance art a theatrical presentation in which several art forms, such as acting, music and photography, are combined.

performance poetry poetry written primarily for public performance by the poet.

performer *noun* **1** a person who performs, especially music. **2** a person who accomplishes what is expected of him or her. **3** an entertainer.

■ **1, 3** artiste, player, actor, actress, entertainer. **2** achiever.

performing arts (**the performing arts**) the forms of art that require performance to be appreciated, especially music, drama, and dance.

perfume — *noun* **1** a sweet smell; a scent or fragrance. **2** a fragrant liquid prepared from the extracts of flowers, etc, for applying to the skin or clothes; scent. — *verb* to give a sweet smell to; to apply perfume to. [from Old French *parfum*, from Latin *per* through + *fumare*, to impregnate with smoke]

■ *noun* **1** scent, fragrance, smell, odour, aroma, bouquet, sweetness. **2** scent, cologne, toilet water, essence, essential oil, incense, balm. *verb* scent.

perfumer *noun* a maker of or dealer in perfumes.

perfumery *noun* (PL. **perfumeries**) **1** perfumes. **2** making perfumes. **3** a place where perfumes are made or sold.

perfunctorily *adv.* in a perfunctory way.

perfunctory /pəˈfʌŋktərɪ/ *adj.* done merely as a duty or routine, without genuine care or feeling. [from Latin *perfunctorius*, slapdash]

perfusion *noun* **1** *Biol.* the movement of a fluid through a tissue or organ. **2** the deliberate introduction of a fluid into a tissue or organ, usually by injection into a nearby blood vessel. [from Latin *perfusus* poured over]

pergola /ˈpɜːgələ/ *noun* a framework constructed from slender branches, for plants to climb up; a trellis. [from Italian, from Latin *pergula*, shed]

perhaps *adv.* possibly; maybe. [earlier *perhappes*, from Old French *par*, by + Norse *happ*, fortune]

■ possibly, maybe, conceivably, feasibly.

peri- *prefix* forming words meaning: **1** around: *periscope/pericardium*. **2** near: *perinatal/perigee*. [from Greek *peri*, round]

perianth /ˈpɛrɪanθ/ *noun Bot.* the outer part of a flower, usually consisting of a circle of petals (the *corolla*) within a circle of sepals (the *calyx*), that surrounds the stamens and carpels. [from PERI- + Greek *anthos*, flower]

pericardium *noun* (PL. **pericardia**) the sac enclosing the heart. [from PERI- + Greek *kardia*, heart]

pericarp *noun Bot.* in plants, the wall of a fruit, which develops from the ovary wall after fertilization. [from PERI- + Greek *karpos*, fruit]

peridotite /pɛrɪˈdoʊtaɪt/ *noun Geol.* a coarse-grained igneous rock, composed mainly of olivine, with smaller amounts of pyroxene or other minerals. It is thought to be a constituent of the Earth's upper mantle. [from French *péridot*]

perigee /ˈpɛrɪdʒiː/ *noun Astron.* the point in the orbit of the Moon or an artificial satellite around the Earth when it is closest to the Earth. See also APOGEE. [from French *perigée*, from Greek *perigeion*, from *peri*, near + *ge*, earth]

perihelion *noun* (PL. **perihelia**) the point in a planet's orbit round the Sun when it is closest to the Sun. See also APHELION. [from PERI- + Greek *helios*, sun]

peril *noun* **1** grave danger. **2** a hazard. — **at one's peril** at the risk of one's life. [from Old French, from Latin *periculum*, danger]

■ *noun* **1** danger, jeopardy, threat, menace. **2** hazard, risk, threat, menace.
✷ **1** safety.

perilous *adj.* dangerous.

■ dangerous, unsafe, hazardous, risky, chancy, precarious, insecure, unsure, vulnerable, exposed, menacing, threatening, dire.
✷ safe, secure.

perilously *adv.* dangerously.

perimeter *noun* **1** the boundary of an enclosed area. **2** *Geom.* the enclosing line or circumference of a two-dimensional figure; its length. [from Greek *perimetros*, from *peri*, round + *metros*, measure]

■ **1** boundary, edge, border, circumference, frontier, limit, bounds, confines, fringe, margin, periphery.
✷ **1** middle, centre, heart.

perinatal *adj. Medicine* denoting the period extending from the 28th week of pregnancy to about one month after childbirth.

period — *noun* **1** a portion of time. **2** a phase or stage in history, development, etc. **3** *Geol.* **a** a unit of geological time that is a subdivision of an era, and is itself divided into epochs. It represents the time interval during which a particular system of rocks was formed, eg the Cretaceous period. **b** any long interval of geological time, eg glacial period. **4** any of the sessions of equal length into which the school day is divided, and to which particular subjects or activities are assigned. **5** a punctuation mark (.), used at the end of a sentence and to mark an abbreviation; a full stop. **6** *colloq.* added to a statement to emphasize its finality: *you may not go, period*. **7** the periodic discharge of blood during a woman's menstrual cycle. **8** *Chem.* in the periodic table, any of the seven horizontal rows of chemical elements, which show a steady progression from alkali metals on the left-hand side to non-metals on the right-hand side, each period ending with a noble gas. **9** *Physics* the time interval after which a cyclical phenomenon, eg a wave motion, or the orbit of a planet around the Sun, repeats itself. — *adj.* dating from, or designed in the style of, the historical period in question: *period costume/period furniture*. [from Greek *periodos*, from *peri*, round + *hodos*, way]

■ *noun* **1** time, season, stretch, space, span, spell, term, turn, session, interval, cycle. **2** stage, phase, era, epoch, age, generation, date, years. **7** menstruation, *colloq.* the curse.

periodic *adj.* happening at especially regular intervals; occasional.

▣ occasional, infrequent, sporadic, intermittent, recurrent, repeated, regular, periodical, seasonal.

periodical — *adj.* periodic. — *noun* a magazine published weekly, monthly, quarterly, etc.

▣ *noun* magazine, journal, publication, weekly, monthly, quarterly.

periodically *adv.* from time to time, occasionally.

periodic function *Maths.* one whose values recur in a cycle as the variable increases.

periodicity *noun* the fact of recurring, or tendency to recur, at intervals.

periodic law *Chem.* the law that the properties of elements are periodic functions of their atomic numbers.

periodic table *Chem.* a table of all the chemical elements arranged in order of increasing atomic number.

periodontitis /perɪoʊdɒnˈtaɪtɪs/ *noun Medicine* inflammation of the tissues surrounding a tooth. [from PERI- + *odous, odontos* tooth]

period piece 1 a piece of furniture, etc dating from, and in the distinctive style of, a certain historical period. **2** *facetious* something quaintly old-fashioned.

peripatetic /perɪpəˈtetɪk/ — *adj.* **1** travelling about from place to place. **2** *said of a teacher* employed by several schools and so obliged to travel between them. **3** (*also* **Peripatetic**) denoting the school of philosophers founded by Aristotle, given to promenading while lecturing. — *noun* a peripatetic teacher or philosopher. [from Greek *peri*, round + *pateein*, to tread]

peripatetically *adv.* in a peripatetic way.

peripheral — *adj.* **1** relating to, or belonging to, the outer edge or outer surface: *peripheral nerves.* **2** (**peripheral to something**) not central to the issue in hand; marginal. **3** *Comput.* supplementary; auxiliary. **4** relating to the outer edge of the field of vision. — *noun Comput.* (*also* **peripheral device**) a device concerned with the input, output, or backing storage of data, eg a printer, mouse, or disk drive. Peripheral devices are connected to a computer system and controlled by it, but are not part of the central processing unit or main memory.

▣ *adj.* **1** outer, outermost, outlying. **2** marginal, minor, secondary, incidental, borderline, surface, superficial, unimportant, irrelevant, unnecessary.
▣ *adj.* **1** central. **2** major, crucial.

periphery *noun* (PL. **peripheries**) **1** the edge or boundary of something. **2** the external surface of something. [from Greek *periphereia*, circumference, surface]

periphrasis /pəˈrɪfrəsɪs/ *noun* (PL. **periphrases**) a roundabout way of saying something; a circumlocution. [from Greek *peri*, round + *phrasis*, speech]

periphrastic *adj.* using periphrasis.

periphrastically *adv.* in a periphrastic way.

periscope *noun Optics* a system of reflecting prisms or angled mirrors that enables the user to view objects that are above eye level, or which are positioned so that they are obscured by a closer object. Periscopes are used in submerged submarines (often in conjunction with telescopes) for scanning the horizon, and in military tanks. [from Greek *periskopeein*, to look around]

periscopic *adj.*, *said of a lens* giving a wide field of vision.

perish *verb* **1** *intrans.* to die; to be destroyed or ruined. **2** *trans.*, *intrans.*, *said of materials* to decay or cause to decay or rot. [from Old French *perir*]

▣ **1** die, expire, pass away, decay, crumble, collapse, fall, disintegrate. **2** decay, rot, decompose.

perishability *noun* being perishable.

perishable *adj.*, *said of commodities, especially food* liable to rot or go bad quickly.

▣ short-lived, destructible, biodegradable, decomposable.
▣ imperishable, durable.

perished *adj. colloq.* feeling the cold severely.

perisher *noun old colloq. use* a mischievous child or other troublesome person.

perishing *adj.* **1** *colloq.* very cold. **2** *old colloq. use* damned, infernal, or confounded.

perishingly *adv.* so as to perish; intensely: *is perishingly cold.*

peristalsis *noun Physiol.* in hollow tubular organs, especially the intestines and oesophagus, the involuntary muscle contractions that force the contents of the tube, eg food, further forward. [from Greek *peristellein*, to contract round]

peristaltic *adj.*, *said of the alimentary canal* forcing onwards by waves of contraction.

peristyle *noun Archit.* a colonnade round a courtyard or building. [from Greek *peri*, round + *stylos*, column]

peritoneal /perɪtəˈnɪəl/ *adj.* relating to or in the region of the peritoneum.

peritoneum /perɪtəˈnɪəm/ *noun* (PL. **peritonea**, **peritoneums**) the membrane that lines the abdominal cavity. [from Greek *peritonaion*, from *periteinein*, to stretch all round]

peritonitis /perɪtəˈnaɪtɪs/ *noun* inflammation of the peritoneum.

periwig *noun* a man's wig of the 17c and 18c. [a variant of PERUKE]

periwinkle[1] *noun* any of several evergreen plants with trailing stems and blue or white flowers. [from Anglo-Saxon *perwince*, from Latin *pervinca*]

periwinkle[2] *noun* any one of several edible marine snails; its shell. [from Anglo-Saxon *pinewincle*]

perjure /ˈpɜːdʒə(r)/ *verb* to forswear (oneself) in a court of law, ie lie while under oath to tell the truth. [from Latin *perjurare*]

perjurer *noun* a person who commits perjury.

perjury /ˈpɜːdʒərɪ/ *noun* (PL. **perjuries**) the crime of lying while under oath in a court of law.

perk[1] *verb intrans.*, *trans.* (*also* **perk up** or **perk someone up**) **1** to become or make more lively and cheerful. **2** *said of an animal's ears* to prick up. [from Middle English *perken*]

▣ **1** cheer up, brighten, liven up, *colloq.* buck up, revive, *colloq.* pep up, rally, recover, improve, look up.

perk[2] *noun colloq.* a benefit, additional to income, derived from employment, such as the use of a company car. [a shortening of PERQUISITE]

▣ perquisite, fringe benefit, benefit, bonus, dividend, gratuity, tip, extra, *colloq.* plus.

perk[3] *verb intrans.*, *trans. colloq.* to percolate.

perkily *adv.* in a perky way.

perkiness *noun* being perky.

perky *adj.* (**perkier**, **perkiest**) lively and cheerful.

Perl *noun Comput. trademark* a programming language.

perm[1] — *noun* a hair treatment using chemicals that give a long-lasting wave or curl. — *verb* to curl or wave (hair) with a perm. [a shortening of PERMANENT WAVE]

perm[2] *colloq.* — *noun* a permutation (see PERMUTATION 2). — *verb* to make a permutation of.

permafrost *noun Geol.* an area of subsoil or rock that has remained below freezing point (0°C) for at least a year, although it does not necessarily contain ice. [from *permanent frost*]

permanence or **permanency** *noun* being permanent.

⊟ fixedness, stability, imperishability, constancy, endurance, durability.
⊡ impermanence, transience.

permanent *adj.* **1** lasting, or intended to last, indefinitely; not temporary. **2** *said of a condition, etc* unlikely to alter. [from Latin *permanere*, to remain]

⊟ **1** everlasting, eternal, lasting, long-lasting, enduring, lifelong, perpetual, constant, steadfast, perennial, durable, imperishable, indestructible, unfading. **2** stable, unchanging, fixed.
⊡ TEMPORARY. **1** temporary, ephemeral, fleeting.

permanently *adv.* so as to be permanent; everlastingly.

permanent magnet *Physics* a magnet that retains its magnetic properties after the force which magnetized it has been removed.

permanent tooth *Anat.* each of the set of teeth that develops in most mammals for use in adult life, after the milk or deciduous teeth have been shed.

permanent wave a perm.

permanent way a railway track, including the rails, sleepers, and stones.

permanganate /pəˈmaŋɡəneɪt/ *noun* any of the salts of *permanganic acid*, especially *potassium permanganate*, used as an oxidizing and bleaching agent and disinfectant. [from PER + MANGANESE]

permeability *noun* being permeable.

permeable *adj.* able to be permeated by liquids, gases, etc. [from Latin *permeabilis*]

⊟ porous, absorbent, absorptive, penetrable.
⊡ impermeable, watertight.

permeate *verb* **1** (**permeate something** or **through something**) *said of a liquid* to pass or seep through a fine or porous material, a membrane, etc. **2** *trans., intrans., said of a smell, gas, etc* to spread through a room or other space; to fill or impregnate. [from Latin *permeare*, to penetrate]

⊟ FILTER THROUGH, SEEP THROUGH, PASS THROUGH, PENETRATE, INFILTRATE, PERVADE, IMBUE, SATURATE, IMPREGNATE, FILL.

permeation *noun* permeating or being permeating.

Permian *adj. Geol.* **1** relating to the last period of the Palaeozoic era, lasting from about 290 million to 250 million years ago. **2** relating to the rocks formed during this period. [from *Perm* in Russia]

permissibility *noun* being permissible.

permissible *adj.* allowable; permitted.

⊟ allowable, permitted, allowed, admissible, all right, acceptable, proper, authorized, sanctioned, lawful, legal, legitimate.
⊡ forbidden, prohibited, banned.

permission *noun* consent, agreement, or authorization. [from Latin *permissio*]

⊟ consent, agreement, authorization, assent, approval, *colloq.* go-ahead, *colloq.* green light, sanction, leave, warrant, permit, licence, dispensation, freedom, liberty.

⊡ prohibition.

permissive *adj.* allowing usually excessive freedom, especially in sexual matters; tolerant; liberal.

⊟ liberal, tolerant, broad-minded, forbearing, lenient, easy-going, lax, free, indulgent, overindulgent.
⊡ strict, rigid.

permit — *verb* (with stress on -*mit*) (**permitted, permitting**) **1** to consent to or give permission for. **2** to give (someone) leave or authorization. **3** to allow (someone something): *permitted him access to his children.* **4** (**permit something** or **permit of something**) to enable it to happen or take effect; to give scope or opportunity for it: *an outrage that permits of no excuses.* — *noun* (with stress on *per-*) a document authorizing something. [from Latin *permittere*, to allow]

⊟ *verb* **1** allow, let, consent to, agree to, grant, authorize, sanction, license. **2** allow, authorize, grant, let, license. **3** allow, grant. **4** allow, admit of. *noun* authorization, pass, passport, visa, licence, warrant, sanction, permission.
⊡ *verb* **1, 2, 3** forbid, prohibit. *noun* prohibition.

permittivity *noun* (*in full* **absolute permittivity**) *Physics* (SYMBOL ε) the ratio of the electric displacement (the electric charge per unit area that would be displaced across a layer of conductor placed across an electric field) in a medium to the intensity of the electric field that is producing it. It is measured in farads per metre.

permutability *noun* being permutable.

permutable /pəˈmjuːtəbl/ *adj.* interchangeable.

permutation *noun* **1** *Maths.* **a** any of a number of different ways in which a set of objects or numbers can be arranged. **b** any of the resulting combinations. **2** a fixed combination in football pools for selecting the results of matches. [from Latin *permutare*, to change completely]

permute or **permutate** *verb* to rearrange (a set of things) in different orders, especially in every possible order in succession. [from Latin *permutare*, to interchange]

pernicious *adj.* harmful; destructive; deadly. [from Latin *perniciosus*, from *pernicies*, ruin, bane]

pernicious anaemia *Medicine* a form of anaemia caused by a dietary deficiency of vitamin B_2, or by failure of the body to absorb the vitamin, leading to a reduction in red blood cells, sometimes accompanied by degeneration of the spinal cord.

pernickety *adj.* **1** over-particular about small details; fussy. **2** *said of a task* tricky; intricate.

peroration *noun* **1** the concluding section of a speech, in which the points made are summed up. **2** *colloq.* a long formal speech. [from Latin *peroratio*]

peroxide — *noun* **1** *Chem.* any chemical compound that contains the O_2^{2-} ion, and releases hydrogen peroxide when treated with acid. Peroxides are strong oxidizing agents, and are used in rocket fuels, antiseptics, disinfectants, and bleaches. **2** a solution of hydrogen peroxide (H_2O_2), used as a bleach for hair and textiles. — *verb* to bleach (hair) with hydrogen peroxide. [from PER- 1 + OXIDE]

perpendicular — *adj.* **1** vertical; upright. **2** at right angles. **3** *said of a cliff, etc* precipitous; steep. **4** (*usually* **Perpendicular**) *Archit.* See PERPENDICULAR STYLE. — *noun* a perpendicular line, position, or direction. [from Latin *perpendicularis*, from *perpendiculum*, a plumbline]

⊟ *adj.* **1** vertical, upright, erect, plumb. **3** precipitous, steep, sheer.
⊡ *adj.* **1** horizontal.

perpendicularity *noun* being perpendicular; a perpendicular direction or position.

perpendicularly *adv.* so as to be perpendicular; vertically.

Perpendicular style the form of English Gothic architecture from the late 14c to the 16c, developed from the Decorated style, and characterized by the use of slender vertical lines, vaulting (especially fan-vaulting), and large areas of windows decorated with simple tracery and stained glass.

perpetrate *verb* to commit, or be guilty of (a crime, misdeed, error, etc). [from Latin *perpetrare*, to bring about, commit]

■ commit, be guilty of, carry out, execute, do, perform, inflict, wreak.

perpetration *noun* **1** perpetrating. **2** something that is perpetrated.

perpetrator *noun* a person who perpetrates; the one who is guilty.

perpetual *adj.* **1** everlasting; eternal; continuous; permanent: *in perpetual bliss.* **2** continual: *perpetual quarrels.* [from Latin *perpetualis*, from *perpetuus*, uninterrupted]

■ **1** everlasting, eternal, continuous, permanent, infinite, endless, unending, never-ending, interminable, ceaseless, unceasing, incessant, uninterrupted, lasting, enduring, abiding, unchanging. **2** continual, constant, persistent, repeated, recurrent, perennial.
🡒 **1** temporary, intermittent, ephemeral, transient.

perpetual calendar 1 a calendar for ascertaining on which day of the week any date falls. **2** a calendar that is usable for any year or for several years.

perpetual motion the motion of a hypothetical machine that keeps going indefinitely without any external source of energy.

perpetuate *verb* **1** to cause to last or continue: *perpetuate a feud/perpetuate a species.* **2** to preserve the memory of (a name, etc). **3** to repeat and pass on (an error, etc). [from Latin *perpetuare*, to make perpetual]

■ **1** continue, keep up, maintain, preserve, keep alive. **2** preserve, keep alive, immortalize, commemorate, keep up, maintain.

perpetuation *noun* perpetuating, continuation.

perpetuity /pɜːpəˈtjuːɪtɪ/ *noun* (PL. **perpetuities**) **1** the state of being perpetual. **2** eternity. **3** duration for an indefinite period. **4** something perpetual, eg an allowance to be paid indefinitely. — **in perpetuity** for ever. [from Latin *perpetuitas*, from *perpetuus*, perpetual]

perplex *verb* **1** to puzzle, confuse, or baffle. **2** to complicate. [from Latin *per-*, thoroughly + *plexus*, entangled]

■ **1** puzzle, confuse, baffle, mystify, stump, muddle, confound, bewilder, dumbfound.

perplexedly *adv.* in a perplexed way.

perplexing *adj.* that perplexes; puzzling.

perplexity *noun* (PL. **perplexities**) **1** the state of being perplexed. **2** something baffling or confusing.

per pro. *abbrev. per procurationem* (Latin), by the agency of.

perquisite /ˈpɜːkwɪzɪt/ *noun* **1** a benefit, additional to income, derived from employment, such as the use of a company car. **2** a tip expected on some occasions. **3** something regarded as due to one by right. [from Latin *perquisitum*, something acquired]

perry *noun* (PL. **perries**) an alcoholic drink made from fermented pear juice. [from Old French *peré*, from Latin *pirum*, pear]

pers. *abbrev.* person or personal.

per se /pə ˈseɪ/ in itself; intrinsically: *not valuable per se.* [Latin, = through itself]

persecute *verb* **1** to ill-treat, oppress, or torment, especially on the grounds of religious or political beliefs. **2** to harass, pester, or bother continually. [from Latin *persequi*, to pursue, ill-treat]

■ **1** ill-treat, maltreat, oppress, torment, tyrannize, victimize, martyr, molest, abuse, torture, crucify. **2** harass, pester, bother, distress, afflict, hound, pursue, hunt, worry, annoy.
🡒 **1** pamper, spoil.

persecution *noun* persecuting or being persecuted.

■ maltreatment, oppression, harassment, subjugation, suppression, discrimination, tyranny, punishment, torture, martyrdom, molestation, abuse.

persecutor *noun* a person who persecutes.

perseverance *noun* persevering; continued effort despite setbacks.

■ persistence, determination, resolution, doggedness, tenacity, diligence, assiduity, dedication, commitment, constancy, steadfastness, stamina, endurance, indefatigability.

persevere *verb intrans.* (**persevere in** or **with something**) to keep on striving for it; to persist steadily with an endeavour. [from Old French *perseverer*]

■ continue with, carry on with, *colloq.* stick at, soldier on with, persist with, *colloq.* plug away at, keep going, stand firm, stand fast.
🡒 give up, stop, discontinue.

Persian — *adj.* relating to Persia (modern Iran), or its people or language. — *noun* **1** a native or citizen of Persia. **2** the language of Persia or Iran.

Persian carpet a distinctively patterned hand-woven woollen or silk carpet made in Persia or elsewhere in the Near East.

Persian cat a breed of cat with long silky fur.

Persian lamb the black curly fur of the karakul lamb, used for coats and trimmings.

persiflage /ˈpɜːsɪflɑːʒ/ *noun* banter, teasing, flippancy, or frivolous talk. [from French *persiflage*]

persimmon /pɜːˈsɪmən/ *noun* a tropical plum-like fruit of America and Asia, or the tree that bears it. [from an Algonkian (Native American) language]

persist *verb* **1** *intrans.* (**persist in** or **with something**) to continue it in spite of resistance, discouragement, etc. **2** *said of rain, etc* to continue steadily. **3** *said eg of a mistaken idea* to remain current. [from Latin *persistere*, to stand firm]

■ **1** continue with, carry on with, keep at, persevere with. **3** remain, linger, last, endure, abide.
🡒 **1, 2** desist, stop.

persistence *noun* **1** persisting. **2** being persistent.

persistence of vision *Physiol.* the persistence of a visual image on the retina for a short period after removal of the visual stimulus. This phenomenon plays an important role in the viewing of films or television.

persistent *adj.* **1** continuing with determination in spite of discouragement; dogged. **2** constant; unrelenting: *persistent questions.*

■ **1** determined, dogged, persevering, resolute, tenacious, steadfast, tireless, unflagging, indefatigable, stubborn, obstinate, zealous. **2** constant, unrelenting, incessant, continuous, relentless, unremitting, steady, continual, repeated, perpetual, interminable, endless, never-ending, lasting, enduring.

....

persistent vegetative state (ABBREV. **PVS**) *Medicine* an irreversible condition induced by lack of oxygen, in which the organism is still alive but incapable of any thought processes or voluntary action.

person *noun* **1** (PL. **persons, people**) an individual human being. **2** (PL. **persons**) one's body: *drugs concealed on his person.* **3** (PL. **persons**) *Grammar* each of the three classes into which pronouns and verb forms fall, *first person* denoting the speaker (or the speaker and others), *second person* the person addressed (with or without others) and *third person* the person(s) or thing(s) spoken of. **4** (**Person**) *Relig.* in Christian doctrine, any of the three forms or manifestations of God (Father, Son, and Holy Spirit) that together form the Trinity. — **be no respecter of persons** to make no allowances for rank or status. **in person 1** actually present oneself: *was there in person.* **2** doing something oneself, not asking or allowing others to do it for one. [from Latin *persona*, actor's mask]

🔲 **1** individual, being, human being, human, man, woman, body, soul, character.

....

-person *combining form* used instead of *man, woman, lady*, etc, to denote a specified activity or office: *chairperson.*

persona /pə'soʊnə/ *noun* (PL. **personae, personas**) one's character as one presents it to other people. See also PERSONA NON GRATA. [from Latin *persona*, actor's mask]

personable *adj.* good-looking or likeable.

personage *noun* a well-known, important, or distinguished person. [from Latin *personagium*, from *persona*, person]

personal *adj.* **1** coming from someone as an individual, not from a group or organization: *my personal opinion.* **2** done, attended to, etc by the individual person in question, not by a substitute: *give it my personal attention.* **3** relating to oneself in particular: *a personal triumph.* **4** relating to one's private concerns: *details of her personal life.* **5** *said of remarks* referring, often disparagingly, to an individual's physical or other characteristics. **6** relating to the body: *personal hygiene.* [from Latin *personalis*, from *persona*, person]

🔲 **1** own. **2** individual, special, particular, exclusive. **3** individual, idiosyncratic, distinctive. **4** private, confidential, intimate. **6** bodily.
🔁 **1, 3** general, universal. **4** public.

....

personal assistant a secretary, especially of a senior executive, manager, etc.

personal column a newspaper column or section in which members of the public may place advertisements, enquiries, etc.

personal computer a microcomputer that is designed for use by one person, especially for applications involving word-processing, or database or spreadsheet programs.

personal effects a person's belongings, especially those regularly carried about.

personality *noun* (PL. **personalities**) **1** a person's nature or disposition; the qualities that give one's character individuality. **2** strength or distinctiveness of character: *lots of personality.* **3** a well-known person; a celebrity. **4** (**personalities**) offensive personal remarks. [from Latin *personalitas*, from *persona*, person]

🔲 **1** nature, disposition, character, temperament, individuality, psyche, traits, make-up. **2** charm, charisma, magnetism, character. **3** celebrity, *colloq.* VIP, star, public figure, notable, personage.

....

personalize or **personalise** *verb* **1** to mark distinctively as the property of a particular person. **2** to focus (a discussion, etc) on personalities instead of the matter in hand. **3** to personify.

personally *adv.* **1** as far as one is concerned: *personally, I disapprove.* **2** in person. **3** as a person. **4** as directed against one: *take a remark personally.*

personal pronoun *Grammar* any of the pronouns representing a person or thing, eg *I, you, he, him, she, it, they, us.*

personal property everything one owns other than land or buildings. See also REAL[1] *noun* 5.

personal stereo a small audio cassette player with earphones, that can be worn on one's person.

persona non grata /pə'soʊnə nɒn 'grɑːtə/ (PL. **personae non gratae**) a person who is not wanted or welcome within a particular group. [Latin, = person not welcome]

personification *noun* **1** giving human qualities to things or ideas. **2** in art or literature, representing an idea or quality as a person. **3** a person or thing which personifies. **4** a person or thing that is seen as embodying a quality: *the personification of patience.*

personify *verb* (**personifies, personified**) **1** in literature, etc, to represent (an abstract quality, etc) as a human or as having human qualities. **2** *said of a figure in art, etc* to represent or symbolize (a quality, etc). **3** to embody in human form; to be the perfect example of: *she's patience personified.*

🔲 **2** represent, symbolize, mirror. **3** embody, epitomize, typify, exemplify.

....

personnel /pɜːsə'nɛl/ *noun* **1** (*pl.*) the people employed in a business company, an armed service, or other organization. **2** a department within such an organization dealing with matters concerning employees. [from French, = personal]

🔲 **1** staff, workforce, workers, employees, manpower, people, crew, members, human resources.

....

perspective *noun* **1** the observer's view of objects in relation to one another, especially with regard to the way they seem smaller the more distant they are. **2** the representation of this phenomenon in drawing and painting. **3** the balanced or objective view of a situation, in which its elements assume their due importance: *get things into/out of perspective.* **4** an individual way of regarding a situation, eg one influenced by personal experience or considerations. [from Latin *ars perspectiva*, optical science]

🔲 **3** proportion, relation, balance. **4** attitude, standpoint, viewpoint, point of view, view, aspect, angle, slant, prospect, outlook.

....

Perspex *noun* *trademark* the trade name for polymethylmethacrylate, a tough transparent lightweight plastic used to make windshields, visors, domestic baths, advertising signs, etc.

perspicacious *adj.* shrewd, astute, perceptive, or discerning. [from Latin *perspicax*]

perspicacity *noun* being perspicacious.

perspicuity *noun* clarity of expression.

perspicuous *adj.*, *said of speech or writing* clearly expressed and easily understood. [from Latin *perspicuus*, transparent, manifest]

perspiration *noun* the salty moisture produced by the sweat glands of the skin.

🔲 sweat, secretion, moisture, wetness.

....

perspire *verb intrans.* to sweat. [from Latin *perspirare*, to breathe through, sweat]

. . . .
☐ sweat, swelter, drip.
. . . .

persuadable or **persuasible** *adj.* capable of being persuaded.
persuade *verb* **1** to urge successfully; to prevail on or induce. **2** (**persuade someone of something** or **to do something**) to convince them that it is true, valid, advisable, etc. [from Latin *persuadere*]
. . . .
☐ **1** prevail (up)on, induce, coax, urge, talk into, incite, prompt, lean on, cajole, wheedle. **2** bring round, win over, convince, convert, sway, influence.
Ea DISSUADE. **1** deter, discourage .
. . . .

persuader *noun* a person or thing that persuades.
persuasion *noun* **1** the act of urging, coaxing, or persuading. **2** a creed, conviction, or set of beliefs, especially that of a political group or religious sect.
. . . .
☐ **1** coaxing, cajolery, wheedling, inducement, enticement, conviction, conversion. **2** creed, conviction, faith, belief, opinion, school (of thought), party, faction, side, denomination, sect.
. . . .

persuasive *adj.* having the power to persuade; convincing or plausible.
. . . .
☐ convincing, plausible, influential, cogent, sound, valid, forceful, weighty, effective, telling, potent, compelling, moving, touching.
Ea unconvincing, implausible.
. . . .

pert *adj.* **1** impudent; cheeky. **2** *said of clothing or style* jaunty; saucy. [from Old French *apert*, open]
pertain *verb intrans.* (*often* **pertain to someone** or **something**) **1** to concern or relate to; to have to do with. **2** to belong to: *skills pertaining to the job.* **3** to be appropriate; to apply. [from Old French *partenir*]
pertinacious *adj.* determined in one's purpose; dogged; tenacious. [from Latin *pertinax*]
pertinacity *noun* being pertinacious or resolute; obstinacy.
pertinence or **pertinency** *noun* being pertinent; relevance.
pertinent *adj.* (**pertinent to someone** or **something**) relating to or concerned with them; relevant. [from Latin *pertinere*, to relate]
. . . .
☐ relevant, apposite, suitable, fitting, appropriate, apt, to the point, material, applicable.
Ea inappropriate, unsuitable, irrelevant.
. . . .

pertness *noun* being pert; impudence.
perturb *verb* to make anxious or agitated. [from Latin *perturbare*, to throw into confusion]
. . . .
☐ worry, trouble, disturb, agitate, bother, alarm, disconcert, unsettle, discompose, upset, ruffle, fluster, vex.
Ea reassure, compose.
. . . .

perturbation *noun* perturbing or being perturbed.
perturbed *adj.* disturbed, worried.
pertussis /pə'tʌsɪs/ *noun Medicine* whooping cough. [from PER- 2 + Latin *tussis*, cough]
peruke /pə'ruːk/ *noun* a 17c to 18c style of wig, with side curls and a tail at the back. [from Old French *perruque*, head of hair]
perusal /pə'ruːzəl/ *noun* perusing; careful study, reading.
peruse /pə'ruːz/ *verb* **1** to read through carefully. **2** to browse through casually. **3** to examine or study attentively. [from PER- 2 + USE¹]

. . . .
☐ **1** read, study, examine. **2** browse through, look through, scan. **3** examine, study, scrutinize, pore over, inspect, check.
. . . .

pervade *verb* to spread or extend throughout; to affect throughout. [from Latin *pervadere*]
. . . .
☐ affect, permeate, imbue, infuse, suffuse, saturate, impregnate, percolate, penetrate, charge, fill.
. . . .

pervasive *adj.* tending to spread everywhere.
. . . .
☐ extensive, widespread, prevalent, common, general, universal, inescapable, omnipresent, ubiquitous.
. . . .

perverse *adj.* deliberately departing from what is normal and reasonable; unreasonable, awkward, stubborn, or wilful. [from Latin *perversus*, from *pervertere*, to overturn]
. . . .
☐ contrary, wayward, unreasonable, awkward, stubborn, wilful, headstrong, rebellious, troublesome, unmanageable, obstinate, unyielding, intransigent, cantankerous, incorrect, improper.
Ea obliging, co-operative, reasonable.
. . . .

perversely *adv.* in a perverse way.
perversion *noun* **1** the process of perverting or condition of being perverted. **2** a distortion. **3** an abnormal sexual activity. [from Latin *pervertere*, to corrupt]
. . . .
☐ **1** corruption, depravity, debauchery, immorality, vice, wickedness, deviance, abnormality. **2** distortion, twisting, misrepresentation, travesty, mis-interpretation, aberration, deviation, misuse, misapplication.
. . . .

perversity *noun* (PL. **perversities**) being perverse.
pervert — *verb* (with stress on *-vert*) **1** to divert illicitly from what is normal or right. **2** to lead into evil or unnatural behaviour; to corrupt. **3** to distort or misinterpret (words, etc). — *noun* (with stress on *per-*) someone who is morally or sexually perverted. [from Latin *pervertere*, to corrupt]
. . . .
☐ *verb* **1** misapply, misdirect, misuse, abuse, lead astray. **2** corrupt, lead astray, deprave, debauch, debase, degrade. **3** distort, misinterpret, misrepresent, twist, warp, falsify, garble. *noun* deviant, debauchee, degenerate, *colloq.* weirdo.
. . . .

Pesach or **Pesah** /'peɪsax/ *noun* the Hebrew name for the Jewish festival of Passover.
peseta /pə'seɪtə/ *noun* the standard unit of currency in Spain. [from Spanish *peseta*, diminutive of *pesa*, weight]
peskily *adv.* so as to be annoying; infuriating.
pesky *adj.* (**peskier, peskiest**) *North Amer. colloq.* troublesome or infuriating. [probably from PEST]
peso /'peɪsoʊ/ *noun* (PL. **pesos**) the standard unit of currency in many Central and S American countries and the Philippines. [from Spanish *peso*, weight]
pessary *noun* (PL. **pessaries**) **1** a medicated dissolving tablet inserted into the vagina to treat an infection, etc; a vaginal suppository. **2** a device worn in the vagina as a contraceptive, or as a support for the womb. [from Latin *pessarium*, from Greek *pessos*, pebble, plug]
pessimism *noun* **1** the tendency to emphasize the gloomiest aspects of anything, and to expect the worst to happen. **2** the belief that this is the worst of all possible worlds, and that evil is triumphing over good. [from *pessimus*, worst]
pessimist *noun* **1** a person who has a sombre, gloomy nature. **2** a person who follows the doctrine of pessimism.

pessimistic *adj.* relating to or characterized by pessimism.

▣ negative, cynical, fatalistic, defeatist, resigned, hopeless, despairing, despondent, dejected, downhearted, glum, morose, melancholy, depressed, dismal, gloomy, bleak. **▣** optimistic.

pessimistically *adv.* in a pessimistic way.

pest *noun* **1** a living organism, such as an insect, fungus, or weed, that has a damaging effect on animal livestock, crop plants, or stored foodstuffs. **2** a person or thing that is a constant nuisance. [from Latin *pestis*, plague]

▣ **1** bug, blight, scourge. **2** nuisance, bother, annoyance, irritation, vexation, trial, bane, curse.

pester *verb* (**pestered, pestering**) **1** to annoy constantly. **2** to harass or hound with requests. [from Old French *empestrer*, to entangle, influenced by PEST]

▣ **1** plague, torment, annoy, worry, bother, disturb, irritate. **2** nag, badger, hound, *colloq.* hassle, harass, *colloq.* get at.

pesticide *noun* any chemical compound that is used to kill pests, ie living organisms that are considered to be harmful to plants, animals, humans, or stored foodstuffs.

pestilence *noun* a deadly epidemic disease such as bubonic plague. [from Latin *pestilentia*, from *pestis*, plague]

pestilent *adj.* **1** deadly, harmful, or destructive. **2** infuriating; troublesome. [from Latin *pestilens*, from *pestis*, plague]

pestilential *adj.* infuriating; troublesome.

pestle /'pesl, 'pestl/ *noun* a club-like utensil for pounding substances in a mortar. [from Old French *pestel*]

pesto /'pestoʊ/ *noun* an Italian sauce originating in Liguria and made from fresh basil leaves, pine kernels, olive oil, garlic, and Parmesan cheese. [from Italian *pesto*, from *pestare*, to crush, pound]

pet[1] — *noun* **1** a tame animal or bird kept as a companion. **2** someone's favourite. **3** a darling or love. — *adj.* **1** kept as a pet. **2** of or for pets. **3** favourite; own special. — *verb* (**petted, petting**) **1** to pat or stroke (an animal, etc). **2** to treat indulgently; to make a fuss of. **3** *trans., intrans.* to fondle and caress for erotic pleasure.

▣ *noun* **2, 3** favourite, darling, idol, treasure, jewel. *adj.* **3** favourite, favoured, preferred, dearest, cherished, special, particular, personal. *verb* **1** stroke, caress, fondle. **2** pamper, indulge, cosset, spoil. **3** fondle, caress, cuddle, *colloq.* canoodle, *slang* neck, *slang* snog, kiss.

pet[2] *noun* a fit of bad temper or sulks.

petal *noun Bot.* in a flower, one of the modified leaves, often scented and brightly coloured, that together form the *corolla*, and in insect-pollinated plants serve to attract passing insects. [from Greek *petalon*, leaf]

petard *noun Hist.* a small bomb for blasting a hole in a wall, door, etc. — **hoist with one's own petard** blown up by one's own bomb, ie the victim of one's own trick or cunning. [from Old French, from *peter*, to crack or explode, from Latin *pedere*, to break wind]

peter *verb intrans.* (**petered, petering**) (**peter out**) to dwindle away to nothing. [originally US mining slang]

▣ dwindle, taper off, fade, wane, ebb, fail, cease, stop.

petersham *noun* a stiff ribbed silk ribbon used for reinforcing waistbands, etc. [from Lord Petersham, 19c English army officer]

pethidine /'peθɪdiːn/ *noun* a synthetic pain-relieving drug widely used in childbirth.

petiole /'petɪoʊl/ *noun Bot.* the stalk that attaches a leaf to the stem of a plant. [from Latin *petiolus*, little foot]

petit bourgeois /'petɪ bʊə'ʒwɑː/ (PL. petits bourgeois) a member of the lower middle class. [French]

petite /pə'tiːt/ *adj., said of a woman or girl* having a small and dainty build. [from French *petite*, feminine of *petit*, small]

petite bourgeoisie /pə'tiːt bʊəʒwɑː'ziː/ the lower middle class. [French]

petit four /petɪ 'fʊə(r)/ (PL. petits fours) a small sweet biscuit, usually decorated with icing. [from French, = little oven]

petition — *noun* **1** a formal written request to an authority to take some action, signed by a large number of people. **2** any appeal to a higher authority. **3** *Legal* an application to a court for some procedure to be set in motion. — *verb trans., intrans.* (**petitioned, petitioning**) (**petition** or **petition someone for** or **against something**) to address a petition to them for some cause; to make an appeal or request. [from Latin *petitio*, from *petere*, to seek]

▣ *noun* **1** round robin. **2** appeal, application, request, solicitation, plea, entreaty, prayer, supplication, invocation. *verb* appeal to, call upon, ask, crave, solicit, bid, urge, press, implore, beg, plead, entreat, beseech, supplicate, pray.

petitioner *noun* **1** a person who petitions. **2** a person who applies for a divorce.

petition of right in the UK, before the Crown Proceedings Act of 1947, a personal petition by which someone could take certain proceedings against the Crown, such as in cases of breach of contract. The 1947 Act permitted action in tort against servants of the Crown, though the monarch remains personally immune from civil or criminal liability.

petit mal /petɪ 'mal/ *Medicine* a mild form of epilepsy without convulsions, characterized by short periods of loss of consciousness or 'absences'.

petit point /petɪ 'pɔɪnt/ **1** a small diagonal stitch used for fine work in needlepoint. **2** needlework using this stitch. [from French *petit point*, small point]

pet name a special name used as an endearment.

petrel /'petrəl/ *noun* any of several seabirds that live far from land, especially the storm petrel. [altered from earlier *pitteral*, perhaps by association with St Peter's walking on the water, as some species of storm petrel walk across the surface of the sea while feeding]

Petri-dish /'piːtrɪ/ *noun Biol.* a shallow circular glass or plastic plate with a flat base and a loosely fitting lid, used mainly for culturing bacteria and other micro-organisms. [named after the German bacteriologist Julius R Petri (1852–1921)]

petrifaction or **petrification** *noun Geol.* the process whereby the hard parts of an organism (eg wood, shell, bone) are turned into stone as the original tissue is gradually replaced by minerals, the shape and minute structural detail being preserved.

petrify *verb* (**petrifies, petrified**) **1** to terrify; to paralyse with fright. **2** *trans., intrans., said of organic material* to turn into stone by the process of petrifaction. **3** *trans., intrans.* to fix or become fixed in an inflexible mould. [from Greek *petra*, stone]

▣ **1** terrify, horrify, appal, paralyse, numb, stun, dumbfound.

petro- *combining form* forming words meaning: **1** relating to petroleum and its products: *petrochemical*. **2** relating to stone or rocks: *petrology*.

petrochemical *noun* any chemical, eg ethyl alcohol or acetone, obtained from petroleum or natural gas.

petrochemically *adv.* using petrochemicals.

petrochemistry *noun* **1** the chemistry of petroleum and its derivatives. **2** the chemistry of rocks.

petrocurrency *noun* currency, usually in the form of US dollars (*petrodollars*), pounds sterling, or Deutschmarks, available in oil-producing countries on their balance of payments, and which is surplus to their own requirements. The currency is available for investment elsewhere, mainly in the USA and W Europe.

petrodollar *noun* the US dollar as representative of the foreign currency earned on a vast scale by oil-exporting countries.

petrol *noun* a volatile flammable liquid fuel, used in most internal combustion engines, consisting of a mixture of hydrocarbons obtained by purification of petroleum. Also called GASOLINE. [from Old French *petrole*, from Latin *petroleum*]

petrolatum /pɛtrəˈleɪtəm/ *noun* petroleum jelly. [from modern Latin *petrolatum*]

petrol bomb a crude bomb consisting of a petrol-filled bottle stopped with rags that are set alight just as the bottle is thrown.

petrol engine a type of internal combustion engine in which a mixture of petrol and air is burned inside a cylinder fitted with a piston. It is the type of engine most widely used in motor vehicles.

petroleum *noun* a naturally occurring oil consisting of a thick black, brown, or greenish liquid mixture of hydrocarbons. [from Latin *petroleum*, from Greek *petra*, rock + Latin *oleum*, oil]

petroleum jelly a greasy jelly-like substance obtained from petroleum, used in ointments and as a lubricant.

petrological *adj.* relating to or involving petrology.

petrologist *noun* a person who studies and is expert in petrology.

petrology *noun Geol.* the scientific study of the structure, origin, distribution, and history of rocks.

petrol station a filling-station.

petticoat — *noun* 1 a woman's underskirt. 2 (**petticoats**) *Hist.* skirts in general, those worn by boys in early childhood in particular. 3 (*attributive*) *said eg of organization, tactics, etc* of or by women; feminine or female. [from PETTY + COAT]

pettifog *verb intrans.* (**pettifogged, pettifogging**) to act as a pettifogger.

pettifogger *noun* 1 a lawyer dealing with unimportant cases, especially somewhat deceitfully or quibblingly. 2 *derog.* someone who argues over trivial details; a quibbler. [from PETTY + German dialect *voger*, arranger]

pettifogging — *noun* trivial or petty behaviour. — *adj.* trivial or petty.

pettish *adj.* peevish, sulky.

pettishly *adv.* with a bad-tempered manner; sulkily.

petty *adj.* (**pettier, pettiest**) 1 of minor importance; trivial. 2 small-minded or childishly spiteful. 3 of low or subordinate rank. [from Old French *petit*, small]

· · · · · · · · · · · · · · · · · · · ·

⊟ 1 minor, trivial, unimportant, insignificant, secondary, lesser, small, little, slight, trifling, paltry, inconsiderable, negligible. 2 small-minded, mean, ungenerous, grudging, spiteful.

⊟ 1 important, significant. 2 generous.

· · · · · · · · · · · · · · · · · · · ·

petty cash money kept for small everyday expenses in an office, etc.

petty officer a non-commissioned officer in the navy.

petulance *noun* being petulant or peevish.

petulant *adj.* ill-tempered; peevish. [from Latin *petulans*, from *petere*, to seek]

· · · · · · · · · · · · · · · · · · · ·

⊟ ill-tempered, bad-tempered, ill-humoured, peevish, cross, irritable, snappish, fretful, moody, sullen, sulky, sour, ungracious.

· · · · · · · · · · · · · · · · · · · ·

petunia /pəˈtjuːnɪə/ *noun* a plant native to tropical America, with white, pink, or purple funnel-shaped flowers.

[from French *petun*, tobacco plant (from its similarity), from Guarani (S American Indian language) *pety*]

pew *noun* 1 one of the long benches with backs used as seating in a church. 2 *humorous colloq.* a seat: *take a pew.* [from Old French *puie*, from Latin *podium*, part of a choir stall]

pewter *noun* 1 a silvery alloy with a bluish tinge, consisting of tin and small amounts of lead, used to make tableware (eg tankards), jewellery, and other decorative objects. 2 articles made of pewter. [from Old French *peutre*]

peyote /peɪˈoʊtɪ/ *noun* the Mexican cactus mescal, or the intoxicant got from it. [from Aztec *peyotl*]

pfennig /ˈfenɪg/ *noun* a German unit of currency worth a hundredth of a mark. [from German *Pfennig*, related to PENNY]

PFI *abbrev.* Private Finance Initiative.

PG *abbrev.* 1 *colloq.* paying guest. 2 *as a film classification* parental guidance, ie containing scenes possibly unsuitable for children.

PGA *abbrev.* Professional Golfers' Association.

pH *noun* (*also* **pH value**) *Chem.* a measure of the relative acidity or alkalinity of a solution.

phagocyte /ˈfagoʊsaɪt/ *noun* a cell, especially a white blood cell, that engulfs and absorbs micro-organisms such as bacteria. [from Greek *phagein*, to eat + -CYTE]

phagocytosis *noun Biol.* the process whereby specialized cells, such as phagocytes and macrophages, engulf and digest bacteria, cell debris, or other solid material that is outside the cell. Various single-celled organisms, especially protozoans, engulf food particles by phagocytosis.

phalanger /fəˈlandʒə(r)/ *noun* a tree-dwelling thick-furred Australasian marsupial with webbed hind toes and a long prehensile tail. [from Greek *phalangion*, spider's web, from its webbed toes]

phalanges /faˈlandʒiːz/ *noun pl.* (SING. **phalanx**) *Anat.* the bones of the digits (fingers and toes) in vertebrates. [from Greek *phalanx, -angos*, roller]

phalanx /ˈfalaŋks/ *noun* 1 *Hist.* in ancient Greece, a body of infantry in close-packed formation. 2 a solid body of people, especially representing united support or opposition. 3 any of the bones of the finger or toe. [from Greek *phalanx*, line of soldiers drawn up for battle]

phalarope *noun* a wading bird of the sandpiper family, native to northern parts but wintering in the southern tropics. [from Greek *phalaris*, coot + *pous*, foot]

phallic *adj.* relating to or resembling a phallus.

phallus /ˈfaləs/ *noun* (PL. **phalluses, phalli**) a representation or image of an erect penis, especially as a symbol of male reproductive power. [from Greek *phallos*]

Phanerozoic /fanərəˈzoʊɪk/ *adj. Geol.* relating to the eon that consists of the Palaeozoic, Mesozoic, and Cenozoic eras, extending from about 570 million years ago until the present time. [from Greek *phaneros*, visible + *zoion*, animal]

phantasm *noun* 1 an illusion or fantasy. 2 a ghost or phantom. [from Greek *phantasma*, apparition]

phantasmagoria /fantazməˈɡɔːrɪə/ *noun* a fantastic succession of real or illusory images seen as if in a dream. [from Greek *phantasma*, apparition + (perhaps) *agora*, assembly]

phantasmagoric /fantazməˈɡɒrɪk/ or **phantasmagorical** *adj.* relating to or like a phantasmagoria.

phantasmal *adj.* of the nature of a phantasm; spectral, unreal.

phantasy *noun* (PL. **phantasies**) an old spelling of **fantasy**.

phantom — *noun* 1 a ghost or spectre. 2 an illusory image or vision. — *adj.* of the nature of a phantom; spectral, imaginary; fancied; not real. [from Old French *fantosme*, from Greek *phantasma*, apparition]

· · · · · · · · · · · · · · · · · · · ·

⊟ *noun* 1 ghost, spectre, spirit, apparition. 2 illusion, vision, hallucination, apparition, figment.

· · · · · · · · · · · · · · · · · · · ·

pharaoh /'fɛərəʊ/ noun the title of the kings of ancient Eygpt. [from Greek *pharao*, from Hebrew *par'oh*, from Egyptian *pr-'o*, great house]

Pharisaic /farɪ'seɪik/ adj. **1** relating to or characteristic of the Pharisees or their faith. **2** (often **pharisaic**) self-righteous, hypocritical.

Pharisee /'farɪsiː/ noun **1** a member of the Pharisees, an influential minority group within Palestinian Judaism before AD 70. **2** a self-righteous or hypocritical person. [from Greek *pharisaios*, from Hebrew *parush*, separated]

pharmaceutical adj. of or relating to the preparation of drugs and medicines. [from Greek *pharmakeutikos*, from *pharmakon*, drug]

pharmaceutics sing. noun the preparation and dispensing of drugs and medicine.

pharmacist noun a person trained to prepare and dispense drugs and medicines.

pharmacological adj. relating to or involving pharmacology.

pharmacologist noun an expert in pharmacology.

pharmacology noun the scientific study of medicines and drugs and their effects and uses. [from Greek *pharmakon*, drug + -LOGY]

pharmacopoeia /fɑːməkə'pɪə/ noun Medicine an authoritative book containing a list of drugs, together with details of their properties, uses, side-effects, methods of preparation, and recommended dosages. [from Greek *pharmakopoiia*, preparation of drugs]

pharmacy noun (PL. **pharmacies**) **1** the mixing and dispensing of drugs and medicines. **2** a dispensary in a hospital, etc. **3** a pharmacist's or chemist's shop. [from Greek *pharmakeia*, use of drugs]

pharyngeal /fə'rɪndʒɪəl/ adj. relating to or in the region of the pharynx.

pharyngitis noun Medicine inflammation of the mucous membrane of the pharynx, characterized by a sore throat, fever, and difficulty in swallowing, and often associated with tonsillitis.

pharynx noun (PL. **pharynxes**, **pharynges**) **1** Anat. in mammals, the part of the alimentary canal that links the mouth and nasal passages with the oesophagus (gullet) and trachea (windpipe). **2** the throat. [from Greek *pharynx*, throat]

phase — noun **1** a stage or period in growth or development. **2** Astron. any of the different shapes assumed by the illuminated surface of a celestial body, eg the Moon, resulting from changes in its position relative to the Sun and the Earth. **3** Physics the stage that a periodically varying waveform has reached at any particular moment, usually in relation to another waveform of the same frequency. **4** Chem. a homogeneous part of a chemical system that is separated from other such parts of the system by distinct boundaries, eg ice and water form a two-phase mixture. — verb to organize or carry out in stages. — **in** or **out of phase** coinciding, or failing to coincide, phase by phase throughout a series of changes. **phase something in** or **out** to introduce it, or get rid of it, in stages. [from Greek *phasis*, appearance]

· · · · · · · · · · · · · · · · · · · ·

▣ noun **1** stage, period, time, spell, season, chapter, position, point, step, aspect, state, condition. **phase in** introduce, ease in, bring in, initiate. **phase out** wind down, run down, ease off, taper off, eliminate, dispose of, get rid of, remove, withdraw.

· ·

phase difference Physics the amount by which one wave is behind or ahead of another wave of the same frequency (see WAVE 2).

phatic communion Linguistics spoken language used for social reasons rather than to communicate ideas or facts. It includes many conventional greetings such as *hello*, and statements or observations about the weather such as *isn't it a nice day*. [from Greek *phasis*, utterance]

PhD abbrev. *philosophiae doctor* (Latin), Doctor of Philosophy. See also DPHIL.

pheasant noun (PL. **pheasant**, **pheasants**) **1** any of various species of ground-dwelling bird, mainly of E Asia, including the junglefowl, partridge, peafowl, and true pheasant. **2** the common or ringed pheasant, introduced to many parts of the world as a gamebird. [from Old French *fesan*, from Greek *phasianos ornis*, bird of the Phasis river in Asia Minor]

phenobarbitone /fiːnəʊ'bɑːbɪtəʊn/ or *chiefly North Amer.* **phenobarbital** /-təl/ noun a hypnotic and sedative drug used to treat epilepsy and insomnia.

phenocryst /'fiːnəʊkrɪst/ noun Geol. in an igneous rock, a conspicuous crystal that is larger than the others. Rocks characterized by the presence of such crystals are described as *porphyritic*. [from Greek *phainein*, to show + CRYSTAL]

phenol /'fiːnɒl/ noun Chem. **1** (FORMULA C_6H_5OH) a colourless crystalline toxic solid, soluble in water and alcohol, that turns pink on exposure to air and light. It is used in the manufacture of phenolic and epoxy resins, nylon, explosives, drugs, and perfumes. Also called CARBOLIC ACID. **2** any member of a group of organic chemical compounds that contain one or more hydroxyl groups attached to a benzene ring, and are weakly acidic. [from *phene*, an old name for benzene]

phenolphthalein /fiːnɒl'fθaliːn/ noun Chem. a dye, consisting of pale yellow crystals soluble in alcohol, that is used as a pH indicator, as it is colourless in acidic solutions and turns carmine red in alkaline solutions. It is also used as a laxative.

phenomenal adj. **1** remarkable; extraordinary; abnormal. **2** of the nature of a phenomenon. **3** relating to phenomena.

· · · · · · · · · · · · · · · · · · · ·

▣ **1** remarkable, extraordinary, abnormal, marvellous, sensational, stupendous, amazing, exceptional, unusual, unbelievable, incredible.

▣ **1** ordinary, usual.

· ·

phenomenalism noun Philos. a theory that human knowledge is confined to collections of sense-data (phenomena) and that we know nothing that is not given to us by sense experience.

phenomenally adv. in a remarkable way or to a remarkable degree: *phenomenally rich*.

phenomenon noun (PL. **phenomena**) **1** a happening perceived through the senses, especially if something unusual or not scientifically explainable. **2** an extraordinary or abnormal person or thing; a prodigy. **3** a feature of life, social existence, etc: *stress as a work-related phenomenon*. [from Greek *phainomenon*, neuter present participle of *phainesthai*, to appear]

· · · · · · · · · · · · · · · · · · · ·

▣ **1** occurrence, happening, event, incident, episode, fact, appearance, sight. **2** wonder, marvel, miracle, prodigy, rarity, curiosity, spectacle, sensation. **3** factor, feature, circumstance.

· ·

phenotype /'fiːnəʊtaɪp/ noun Genetics the observable characteristics of an organism, determined by the interaction between its genetic make-up (*genotype*) and environmental factors.

phenylalanine or **phenylalanin** /fiːnaɪl'aləniːn/ noun Biochem. an essential amino acid present in most proteins.

phenylketonuria /fiːnaɪlkiːtəʊ'njʊərɪə/ noun Medicine in infants, an inherited metabolic disorder in which the amino acid phenylalanine accumulates in the body, damages the nervous system, and may cause mental retardation.

pheromone /'fɛrəməʊn/ noun Zool. any chemical substance secreted in minute amounts by an animal, especially an insect or mammal, which has a specific effect on the behaviour of other members of the same species. Pheromones play a role in the attraction of mates, trail marking, and other forms of social behaviour. [from Greek *pherein*, to bear + HORMONE]

phew *interj.* used to express relief, astonishment, or exhaustion. [imitative of a whistle]

phial /faɪəl/ *noun* a little medicine bottle. [from Greek *phiale*, shallow dish]

Phil. *abbrev.* **1** Philadelphia. **2** philosophy or (Latin) *philosophiae*, of philosophy.

phil- or **philo-** *combining form* forming words denoting fondness or liking. [from Greek *philos*, loving]

-phil see -PHILE.

philadelphus *noun* any of a genus of tall deciduous shrubs with highly perfumed showy flowers, especially the mock orange. [from Greek *philadelphon*, loving one's brother]

philander *verb intrans.* (**philandered**, **philandering**) to flirt, or have casual love affairs, with women. [from Greek *philandros*, loving men, used in Greek literature as a proper name for a lover]

philanderer *noun* a womanizer.

philanthropic *adj.* benevolent.

⊟ benevolent, charitable, public-spirited, altruistic, humanitarian, unselfish, kind, generous, liberal, open-handed.
⊟ misanthropic.

philanthropist *noun* a philanthropic or benevolent person.

⊟ benefactor, patron, sponsor, humanitarian, altruist.
⊟ misanthrope.

philanthropy *noun* a charitable regard for one's fellow human beings, especially in the form of benevolence to those in need. [from Greek *philanthropia*, from *phil-*, loving + *anthropos*, man]

⊟ benevolence, humanitarianism, public-spiritedness, altruism, patronage, generosity, open-handedness, charity, unselfishness, kind-heartedness, liberality.
⊟ misanthropy.

philatelic /fɪlə'telɪk/ *adj.* relating to or concerned with philately.

philatelist /fɪ'lætəlɪst/ *noun* a stamp-collector.

philately /fɪ'lætəlɪ/ *noun* the study and collecting of postage stamps. [from PHIL- + Greek *ateles*, untaxed (mail being delivered 'free' if prepaid by a stamp)]

-phile or **-phil** *combining form* forming words denoting fondness or attraction: *bibliophile/paedophile*. [from Greek *philos*, loving]

philharmonic *adj., used in names of choirs and orchestras* dedicated to music. [from PHIL- + Greek *harmonia*, harmony]

-philia *combining form* forming words denoting: **1** a tendency: *haemophilia*. **2** an unnatural liking: *necrophilia*.

-philiac *combining form* forming nouns and adjectives corresponding to nouns in *-philia*: *haemophiliac*.

philippic *noun* a speech making a bitter attack on someone or something. [from the orations of the Athenian Demosthenes against Philip of Macedon]

Philistine *noun* a member of an ancient Aegean warlike people who inhabited the SE coast of Palestine in the 12c BC.

philistine — *adj.* having no interest in or appreciation of art, literature, music, etc, and tending rather towards materialism. — *noun* a philistine person. [named after the Philistines]

philistinism *noun* being a philistine; the beliefs and practices of a philistine.

philo- see PHIL-.

philological *adj.* relating to or involving philology.

philologically *adv.* as regards philology.

philologist *noun* a person who studies or is expert in philology.

philology *noun* **1** the study of language, its history and development; the comparative study of related languages; linguistics. **2** the study of especially older literary and non-literary texts. [from Greek *philologia*, love of argument, literature or learning, from *philo-*, loving + *logos*, reason, word]

philosopher *noun* a person who studies philosophy, especially one who develops a particular set of doctrines or theories.

philosopher's stone *Hist.* a hypothetical substance able to turn any metal into gold, long sought by alchemists.

philosophical *adj.* **1** of or relating to philosophy or philosophers. **2** calm and dispassionate in the face of adversity; resigned, stoical, or patient.

⊟ **1** metaphysical, abstract, theoretical, analytical, rational, logical, erudite, learned, wise, thoughtful. **2** dispassionate, calm, resigned, stoical, patient, unruffled, composed.

philosophize or **philosophise** *verb intrans.* to form philosophical theories; to reason or speculate in the manner of a philosopher.

philosophizer or **philosophiser** *noun* a person who philosophizes.

philosophy *noun* (PL. **philosophies**) **1** the search for truth and knowledge concerning the universe, human existence, perception, and behaviour, pursued by means of reflection, reasoning, and argument. **2** any particular system or set of beliefs established as a result of this. **3** a set of principles serving as a basis for making judgements and decisions: *one's philosophy of life*. [from Greek *philosophia*, love of wisdom, from *philo-*, loving + *sophia*, wisdom]

⊟ **1** metaphysics, rationalism, reason, logic, thought, thinking, wisdom, knowledge. **3** ideology, doctrine, beliefs, convictions, values, principles, attitude, viewpoint, world-view.

philtre /'fɪltə(r)/ *noun* a magic potion for arousing sexual desire. [from Greek *philtron*, love charm]

phlebitis /flɪ'baɪtɪs/ *noun Medicine* inflammation of the wall of a vein, often resulting in the formation of a thrombus (blood clot) at the affected site. It most often occurs as a complication of varicose veins in the legs. [from Greek *phleps phlebos*, vein + -ITIS]

phlebotomy *noun Medicine* the removal of blood by puncturing or making a surgical incision in a vein. [from Greek *phleps phlebos*, a vein]

phlegm /flem/ *noun* **1** a thick, yellowish substance produced by the mucous membrane lining the nose, throat, and lungs, brought up by coughing. **2** calmness or impassiveness; stolidity or sluggishness of temperament. [from Greek *phlegma*, flame, heat, phlegm (thought to be the result of heat), inflammation]

phlegmatic /fleg'mætɪk/ *adj.* **1** *said of a person* calm, not easily excited. **2** producing or having phlegm.

⊟ **1** calm, placid, stolid, impassive, unemotional, unconcerned, indifferent, matter-of-fact, stoical.
⊟ emotional, passionate.

phlegmatically *adv.* in a phlegmatic way.

phloem /'floʊəm/ *noun Bot.* the plant tissue that is responsible for transport of sugars (mainly sucrose) and other nutrients from the leaves, where they are manufactured by photosynthesis, to all other parts of the plant. See also XYLEM. [from Greek *phloios*, bark]

phlogiston /flɒ'dʒɪstɒn/ *noun* a substance believed in the 18c to separate from a material during combustion; the theory was discredited as it was clear that the products of combustion weigh more than the material before burning.

phlox /flɒks/ *noun* a plant with clusters of variegated flowers in purple, red, and white. [from Greek *phlox*, flame, wallflower]

-phobe *combining form* denoting a person affected by a particular form of phobia.

phobia *noun* an obsessive and persistent fear of a specific object or situation (eg spiders, open spaces, flying), known as a *simple phobia*, or of one's behaviour in front of others, known as a *social phobia*. [an absolute use of the element -PHOBIA]

    . . . .

▤ fear, terror, dread, anxiety, neurosis, obsession, *colloq.* hang-up, *colloq.* thing, aversion, dislike, hatred, horror, loathing, revulsion, repulsion.

▣ love, liking.

  . . . .

Phobias (by name of fear) include: zoophobia (*animals*), apiphobia (*bees*), ailurophobia (*cats*), necrophobia (*corpses*), scotophobia (*darkness*), cynophobia (*dogs*), claustrophobia (*enclosed places*), panphobia (*everything*), pyrophobia (*fire*), xenophobia (*foreigners*), phasmophobia (*ghosts*), acrophobia (*high places*), hippophobia (*horses*), entomophobia (*insects*), astraphobia (*lightning*), autophobia (*loneliness*), agoraphobia (*open spaces*), toxiphobia (*poison*), herpetophobia (*reptiles*), tachophobia (*speed*), ophiophobia (*snakes*), arachnophobia (*spiders*), triskaidekaphobia (*thirteen*), brontophobia (*thunder*), hydrophobia (*water*).

-phobia *combining form* forming nouns denoting obsessive and persistent fears: *claustrophobia*. [from Greek *phobos*, fear]

phobic *adj.* 1 relating to or involving a phobia. 2 affected by a phobia.

-phobic *combining form* forming adjectives corresponding to nouns in *-phobia*: *claustrophobic*.

Phoenician /fə'niːʃən/ — *adj.* relating to ancient Phoenicia (a narrow strip in the E Mediterranean between the mountains of Lebanon and the sea, where the ancient cities of Arad, Byblos, Sidon, and Tyre were located) or its people or culture. — *noun* 1 a member of the Phoenician people. 2 their Semitic language.

phoenix /'fiːnɪks/ *noun* in Arabian legend, a bird which every 500 years sets itself on fire and is reborn from its ashes to live a further 500 years. [from Greek *phoinix*]

phone — *noun* a telephone. — *verb trans., intrans.* to telephone. — **phone in** to take part in a broadcast phone-in. [a shortening of TELEPHONE]

    . . . .

▤ *verb* telephone, ring (up), call (up), dial, contact, get in touch (with), *colloq.* give a buzz (to), *colloq.* give a bell (to), *colloq.* give a tinkle (to).

  . . . .

-phone *combining form* forming nouns and adjectives denoting: 1 an instrument transmitting or reproducing sound: *telephone/microphone*. 2 a musical instrument: *saxophone*. 3 a speech sound: *homophone*. 4 speaking, or a speaker of, a language: *Francophone*. [from Greek *phone*, sound, voice]

phonecard *noun* a card obtainable from post offices, etc and usable in place of cash to pay for calls from cardphones.

phone-in *noun* a radio or television programme in which telephoned contributions from listeners or viewers are invited and discussed live by an expert or panel in the studio.

phoneme *noun* the smallest unit of sound in a language that has significance in distinguishing one word from another. [from Greek *phonema*, a sound uttered]

phonemic *adj.* relating to a phoneme or phonemics.

phonemically *adv.* by means of phonemes.

phonemics *sing. noun* 1 the study and analysis of phonemes. 2 the system or pattern of phonemes in a language.

phonetic *adj.* 1 of or relating to the sounds of a spoken language. 2 *said eg of a spelling* intended to represent the pronunciation. 3 denoting a pronunciation scheme using symbols that each represent one sound only. [from Greek *phonetikos*, from *phoneein*, to speak]

phonetically *adv.* as regards phonetics; by means of phonetic characters.

phonetics *sing. noun* the branch of linguistics dealing with speech sounds, how they are produced and perceived.

phoney — *adj.* (**phonier, phoniest**) not genuine; fake, sham, bogus, or insincere. — *noun* (PL. **phoneys**) someone or something bogus; a fake or humbug.

    . . . .

▤ *adj.* fake, sham, bogus, insincere, counterfeit, forged, trick, false, *colloq.* pseudo, imitation, spurious, assumed, affected, put-on.

▣ *adj.* real, genuine.

  . . . .

phoneyness *noun* being phoney.

phonic /'fɒnɪk/ *adj.* 1 relating to especially vocal sound. 2 denoting a method of learning to read by pronouncing each word letter by letter. [from Greek *phonikos*, from *phone*, sound, voice]

-phonic *combining form* forming adjectives corresponding to nouns ending in *-phone*.

phonically *adv.* in terms of or by means of sound.

phonics or **phonic method** a method used in the teaching of reading, based on recognition of the relationships between individual letters and sounds. See also LOOK AND SAY.

phoniness *noun chiefly North Amer.* same as PHONEYNESS.

phono- or **phon-** *combining form* forming words denoting sound or voice: *phonology/phonograph*. [from Greek *phone*, sound, voice]

phonograph *noun North Amer. old use* a record-player.

phonological *adj.* relating to or involving phonology.

phonologically *adv.* in terms of phonology.

phonologist *noun* a person who studies and is expert in phonology.

phonology *noun* (PL. **phonologies**) 1 the study of speech sounds, or of those in any particular language. 2 any particular system of speech sounds.

phony (PL. **phonies**) *chiefly North Amer.* same as PHONEY.

phooey *interj. colloq.* an exclamation of scorn, contempt, disbelief, etc.

phosphate *noun Chem.* a salt or ester of phosphoric acid (H_3PO_4) that contains the PO_4^{3-} ion. [see PHOSPHORUS]

phosphor /'fɒsfə(r)/ *noun Chem.* any substance that is capable of phosphorescence. Phosphors are used to coat the inner surface of television screens and fluorescent light tubes, and as brighteners in detergents. [from Greek *phosphoros*; see PHOSPHORUS]

phosphoresce /fɒsfə'res/ *verb intrans.* to be phosphorescent; to shine in the dark.

phosphorescence /fɒsfə'resəns/ *noun* 1 the emission of light from a substance after it has absorbed energy from a source such as ultraviolet radiation, X-rays, etc. It differs from fluorescence in that light is emitted for a considerable time after the energy source has been removed. 2 a general term for the emission of light by a substance in the absence of a significant rise in temperature, eg the glow of white phosphorus in the dark.

phosphorescent /fɒsfə'resənt/ *adj.* 1 phosphorescing. 2 having the property of phosphorescing.

phosphoric acid *Chem.* (FORMULA H_3PO_4) a transparent crystalline compound that is soluble in water. It is used in soft drinks, rust removers, and for forming a corrosion-resistant layer on iron and steel. Also called ORTHO-PHOSPHORIC ACID.

phosphorus *noun Chem.* (SYMBOL **P**, ATOMIC NUMBER 15) a non-metallic element that exists as several different

photo 922 Photostat

allotropes, and is mainly obtained from the mineral apatite. [from Greek *phosphoros*, bringer of light]

photo *noun* (PL. **photos**) *colloq.* a photograph.

photo- *combining form* forming words meaning: **1** relating to photography: *photomontage*. **2** (*also* **phot-**) relating to light: *photoelectric*. [from Greek *phos*, light]

photocell *noun* same as PHOTOELECTRIC CELL.

photochemistry *noun Chem.* the branch of chemistry concerned with the study of chemical reactions that will only take place in the presence of visible light or ultraviolet radiation, as well as chemical reactions in which light is produced.

photocopier *noun* a machine that makes copies of printed documents or illustrations by any of various photographic techniques, especially xerography.

photocopy — *noun* (PL. **photocopies**) a photographic copy of a document, drawing, etc. — *verb trans.* (**photocopies, photocopied**) to make a photographic copy of.

⬛ *noun* copy, *trademark* Photostat, *trademark* Xerox, duplicate. *verb* copy, duplicate, *trademark* photostat, *trademark* xerox, print, run off.

photodegradable *adj.* able to be broken down by the action of light, and so decay naturally. See also BIODEGRADABLE. [from PHOTO- 2 + DEGRADE]

photoelectric *adj.* relating to electrical or electronic activity triggered by light or other electromagnetic radiation.

photoelectric cell a device activated by photoelectricity, used eg in burglar alarms.

photoelectric effect *Physics* the emission of electrons from the surface of some semi-metallic materials as a result of irradiation with light. It is exploited in photoelectric cells, which convert light energy into an electric current and are used in light meters (eg in photography), light detectors (eg in burglar alarms), etc.

photoelectricity *noun* electrical or electronic activity triggered by light or other electromagnetic radiation.

photoengraving *noun* techniques for producing metal printing plates on cylinders carrying the image of continuous-tone and half-tone text and illustrations, for both letterpress and gravure printing. The image is photographed and the film exposed on the metal plate which is first coated with light-sensitive emulsion. The resulting image will be in relief (on a letterpress plate) or etched into the surface (on a gravure cylinder).

photo finish a race finish in which the runners are so close that the result must be decided by photograph.

Photofit *noun trademark* **1** a system used by the police for building up a likeness of someone to fit a witness's description, similar to Identikit but using photographs rather than drawings of individual features. It has been largely replaced by E-FIT. **2** a likeness so produced.

photogenic *adj.* **1** having the quality of photographing well; looking attractive in photographs. **2** producing, or produced by, light.

photogrammetry *noun* the use of photographic records for precise measurements of distances or dimensions, for example aerial photographs used in surveying and mapmaking. The technique is also used for medical, forensic, and architectural purposes.

photograph — *noun* a permanent record of an image that has been produced on photosensitive film or paper by the process of photography. — *verb trans., intrans.* to take a photograph of (a person, thing, etc).

⬛ *noun* photo, snap, snapshot, print, shot, slide, transparency, picture, image, likeness. *verb* snap, take, film, shoot, video, record.

photographer /fə'tɒgrəfə(r)/ *noun* a person who takes photographs, especially professionally.

photographic /foʊtə'græf ɪk/ *adj.* **1** relating to or similar to

photographs or photography. **2** *said of memory* retaining images in exact detail.

photographically *adv.* **1** in a photographic way. **2** by means of photography or photographs.

photography /fə'tɒgrəf ɪ/ *noun* the process of making a permanent record of an image on light-sensitive film or some other sensitized material using visible light, X-rays, or some other form of radiant energy.

photogravure /foʊtoʊgrə'vjʊə(r)/ *noun* **1** a method of engraving in which the design is photographed on to a metal plate, and then etched in. **2** a picture so produced. [from PHOTO- + French *gravure*, engraving]

photolithography *noun* a process of lithographic printing from a photographically produced plate.

photolysis /foʊ'tɒl ɪs ɪs/ *noun Chem.* a chemical reaction in which the breaking of a chemical bond within a molecule of a substance is brought about by exposure to light or ultraviolet radiation.

photometry /foʊ'tɒmɪtrɪ/ *noun Physics* the measurement of visible light and its rate of flow. Photometry takes account of the varying sensitivity of the eye to light of different frequencies, and has important applications in photography and lighting design.

photomicrograph /foʊtoʊ'maɪkrəgrɑːf/ *noun Physics* a photograph of an object observed through a microscope.

photomicrography /foʊtoʊmaɪ'krɒgrəf ɪ/ *noun* photography of objects or details through the lens of a microscope.

photomontage /foʊtoʊmɒn'tɑːʒ/ *noun* the assembling of selected photographic images, either by mounting cut-out portions of prints on a backing, or by combining several separate negatives in succession during printing. See also MONTAGE. [from PHOTO- + French *montage*, mounting]

photomultiplier *noun Physics* a device for the electronic detection of very low intensities of light. It consists of a photoelectric cell, and incoming light causes the emission of electrons via the photoelectric effect. The number of electrons emitted is multiplied by a series of electrodes until a detectable current is obtained.

photon *noun Physics* a particle of electromagnetic radiation that travels at the speed of light. It can be regarded as a unit of energy equal to hv, where h is Planck's constant (a fundamental constant) and v is the frequency of the electromagnetic radiation. This means that the energy of the photon is proportional to the frequency of the radiation. Photons are used to explain phenomena that require light to behave as particles rather than waves. [from Greek *phos photon*, light]

photo opportunity an event organized or attended by a public figure intended to draw press photographers or television cameras to record it.

photoperiodism *noun Biol.* the physiological and behavioural responses of living organisms to changes in daylength, eg flowering of plants or migration of animals.

photophobia *noun Medicine* **1** a fear of or aversion to light. **2** an abnormal intolerance of and avoidance of light, which may be a symptom of various disorders, eg migraine, measles, meningitis. [from Greek *phos photos*, light + -PHOBIA]

photoreceptor *noun Zool.* a cell or group of cells that is sensitive to and responds to light stimuli.

photosensitive *adj.* reacting to light or other electromagnetic radiation.

photosensitivity *noun* being photosensitive.

photosphere *noun* **1** *Astron.* the visible surface of the Sun, consisting of a layer of gas about 500km thick, and having an average temperature of about 6000C. It is the zone where the Sun's layers progress from being completely opaque to radiation to being transparent, and hence it is the zone from which the light is emitted. **2** the visible surface of any other star.

Photostat — *noun trademark* **1** a photographic apparatus for copying documents, drawings, etc. **2** a copy made by this. — *verb* (**photostat**) (**photostatted, photostatting**) to make a Photostat of.

photosynthesis *noun* **1** *Bot.* the process whereby green plants manufacture carbohydrates from carbon dioxide and water, using the light energy from sunlight trapped by the pigment chlorophyll. Photosynthesis takes place in chloroplasts, specialized structures that are present in the cells of green plants, especially in the leaves. **2** a similar process that occurs in certain bacteria, whereby carbohydrates are manufactured using a hydrogen source other than water, and by-products other than oxygen are produced.

photosynthesize or **photosynthesise** *verb intrans., trans.* to practise photosynthesis on, or undergo photosynthesis.

photosynthetic *adj.* relating to or affected by photosynthesis.

phototaxis *noun Biol.* the movement of a cell (eg a gamete) or a motile organism in response to a directional light stimulus.

phototropism /fo͞otoͦo'troͦupɪzm/ *noun Bot.* the growth of the roots or shoots of plants in response to light. Shoots show positive phototropism, ie they grow in the direction of light, whereas roots show negative phototropism, ie they grow away from light.

phototypesetter *noun* a machine for composing type (and certain illustrations) and creating an image of the composed type on film or on paper, ready for exposure to a plate for printing.

phrasal *adj.* relating to phrases; consisting of, or of the nature of, a phrase.

phrasally *adv.* by means of phrases.

phrasal verb a phrase consisting of a verb plus adverb or preposition, or a combination of these, frequently, as with *let on* and *come up with*, with a meaning or meanings that cannot be determined from the meanings of the individual words.

phrase — *noun* **1** a set of words expressing a single idea, forming part of a sentence though not constituting a clause. **2** an idiomatic expression. **3** *Mus.* a run of notes making up an individually distinct part of a melody. — *verb* **1** to express; to word: *a carefully phrased reply.* **2** *Mus.* to bring out the phrases in (music) as one plays. [from Greek *phrasis*, expression, from *phrazein*, to tell]

. . . .

▤ *noun* **1** expression, construction. **2** idiom, expression, saying, utterance, remark. *verb* **1** express, word, formulate, couch, present, put, frame, say, utter, pronounce.

. . . .

phrase book a book listing words and phrases in a foreign language, especially for the use of visitors.

phraseological *adj.* relating to or involving phraseology.

phraseology /freɪzɪ'ɒlədʒɪ/ *noun* **1** one's choice of words and way of combining them, in expressing oneself. **2** the language belonging to a particular subject, group, etc: *legal phraseology.*

phreaking or **phone phreaking** /'friːkɪŋ/ *colloq.* the practice of tampering electronically with a telephone to enable the user to make free calls. [a variant of FREAK]

phrenological /frenə'lɒdʒɪkəl/ *adj.* relating to or involving phrenology.

phrenologist *noun* a person skilled in phrenology.

phrenology /fre'nɒlədʒɪ/ *noun* the practice, popular in the 19c but now discredited, of assessing a person's character and aptitudes by examining the shape of the skull. [from Greek *phren*, mind + -LOGY]

phthisis /'θaɪsɪs, 'fθaɪsɪs, 'taɪsɪs/ *noun* (PL. **phthises**) any wasting disease, especially tuberculosis. [from Greek *phthisis*, emaciation; consumption]

phut /fʌt/ *colloq. noun* the noise of a small explosion. — **go phut 1** to break down or cease to function. **2** to go wrong. [imitative, or connected with Hindi and Urdu *phatna*, to burst]

phycology /faɪ'kɒlədʒɪ/ *noun Bot.* the scientific study of algae. [from Greek *phykos* seaweed + -LOGY]

phylactery /fɪ'læktərɪ/ *noun* (PL. **phylacteries**) **1** either of two small boxes containing religious texts worn on the arm and forehead by Jewish men during prayers. **2** a charm or amulet. [from Greek *phylakterion*, from *phylassein*, to guard]

phyllite /'fɪlaɪt/ *noun Geol.* any of various fine-grained metamorphic rocks intermediate between slate and schist. Phyllites have a silky sheen, with light and dark minerals arranged in bands, and they are derived from sedimentary rocks. [from Greek *phyllon*, a leaf]

phyllotaxis /fɪloʊ'tæksɪs/ or **phyllotaxy** /fɪloʊ'tæksɪ/ *noun Bot.* the arrangement of leaves on a plant stem. [from Greek *phyllon*, a leaf + *taxis*, arrangement]

phylogeny /faɪ'lɒdʒənɪ/ *noun Biol.* the sequence of changes that has occurred during the evolution of a particular species of living organism, or a group of related organisms. [from Greek *phylon*, race + GENESIS]

phylum /'faɪləm/ *noun* (PL. **phyla**) *Biol.* each of the major groups into which the animal kingdom is divided, eg *Arthropoda* (insects, crustaceans, and spiders), *Mollusca* (molluscs). Each phylum is in turn subdivided into one or more classes. [from Greek *phylon*, race]

physic *old use* — *noun* **1** the skill or art of healing. **2** a medicine. **3** anything with a curative or reinvigorating effect. — *verb* (**physicked**, **physicking**) to dose with medicine. [from Greek *physike episteme*, knowledge of nature]

physical *adj.* **1** of the body rather than the mind; bodily: *physical strength.* **2** relating to objects that can be seen or felt; material: *the physical world.* **3** relating to nature or to the laws of nature: *physical features/a physical impossibility.* **4** relating to physics. **5** involving bodily contact: *physical force.* [from Greek *physikos*, of nature, from *physis*, nature]

. . . .

▤ **1** bodily, corporeal, fleshy, incarnate, mortal, earthly. **2** material, concrete, solid, substantial, tangible, visible, real, actual.
▣ **1** mental, spiritual. **2** intangible, spiritual.

. . . .

physical anthropology the study of local biological adaptations in man and man's evolutionary history.

physical chemistry the branch of chemistry concerned with the relationship between the chemical structure of compounds and their physical properties.

physical education or **physical training** instruction in sport and gymnastics as part of a school or college curriculum.

physical geography the study of the earth's natural features, eg mountain ranges, ocean currents, etc.

physicality *noun* **1** a physical quality. **2** preoccupation with bodily matters.

physical jerks *colloq.* bodily exercises, especially done regularly to keep fit.

physically *adv.* in terms of the material world.

physical science any of the sciences dealing with non-living matter, eg astronomy, physics, chemistry, and geology.

physician *noun* **1** in the UK, a registered medical practitioner who specializes in medical as opposed to surgical treatment of diseases and disorders. **2** in other parts of the world, any person who is legally qualified to practise medicine.

. . . .

▤ DOCTOR, MEDICAL PRACTITIONER, *colloq.* MEDIC, GENERAL PRACTITIONER, GP, HEALER, HOUSEMAN, INTERN, REGISTRAR, CONSULTANT, SPECIALIST.

. . . .

physicist *noun* a student of or expert in physics.

physics *sing. noun* the scientific study of the properties and interrelationships of matter and energy. Classical physics includes mechanics, thermodynamics, electricity, magnetism, optics, and acoustics, and important recent developments include quantum mechanics and relativity theory. [from Greek *ta physika*, natural things]

physio *noun* (PL. **physios**) *colloq.* a physiotherapist.

physio- or **physi-** *combining form* forming words meaning 'physical or physiological'. [from Greek *physis*, nature, make-up]

physiognomy /fɪzɪ'ɒnəmɪ/ *noun* (PL. **physiognomies**) **1** the face or features, especially as a key to personality. **2** the general appearance of something, eg the countryside. [from Greek *physis*, nature + *gnomon*, interpreter]

physiological *adj.* relating to or involving physiology.

physiologist *noun* a person skilled in physiology.

physiology *noun Biol.* the branch of biology that is concerned with the internal processes and functions of living organisms, such as respiration, nutrition, and reproduction, as opposed to anatomy, which is concerned with their structure. [from Greek *physis*, nature + -LOGY]

physiotherapist *noun* a person skilled in treatment by physiotherapy.

physiotherapy *noun Medicine* the treatment of injury and disease by external physical methods, such as remedial exercises, manipulation, heat, or massage, as opposed to drugs or surgery.

physique /fɪ'ziːk/ *noun* the structure of the body with regard to size, shape, proportions, and muscular development. [from French *physique*, originally = physical, from Greek *physikos*, of nature]

▪ body, figure, build, shape, form, frame, structure, constitution, make-up.

phytopathology /faɪtoʊpə'θɒlədʒɪ/ *noun Bot.* the scientific study of plant diseases. [from Greek *phyton*, plant]

phytoplankton /faɪtoʊ'plaŋktən/ *noun Bot.* the part of the plankton that is composed of microscopic plants.

pi /paɪ/ *noun* **1** the sixteenth letter of the Greek alphabet (π). **2** *Maths.* this as a symbol representing the ratio of the circumference of a circle to its diameter, in numerical terms 3.14159.

pia mater /paɪə 'meɪtə(r)/ *noun* (PL. **piae matres**) *Anat.* the delicate innermost membrane enclosing the brain and spinal cord. [from Latin *pia mater*, tender mother]

pianissimo /pɪə'nɪsɪmoʊ/ *adj., adv. Mus.* played very softly. [from Italian *pianissimo*, superlative of *piano*, quiet]

pianist *noun* a person who plays the piano.

piano [1] *noun* (PL. **pianos**) a large musical instrument with a keyboard, the keys being pressed down to operate a set of hammers that strike tautened wires to produce the sound. [from PIANOFORTE]

piano [2] *adj., adv. Mus.* played softly. [from Italian *piano*]

piano accordion an accordion with a keyboard like that of a piano.

pianoforte /pɪænoʊ'fɔːtɪ/ *noun* the full formal term for a piano. [from Italian *piano e forte*, soft and loud]

Pianola /pɪə'noʊlə/ *noun trademark* a mechanical piano operated by means of interchangeable paper rolls bearing coded music in the form of perforations.

piazza /pɪ'atsə/ *noun* a public square in an Italian town. [from Italian *piazza*, from Latin *platea* and Greek *plateia*, street]

pibroch /'piːbrɒx/ *noun* a series of variations on a martial theme or lament, played on the Scottish bagpipes. [from Gaelic *piobaireachd*]

pic *noun* (PL. **pics, pix**) *colloq.* a photograph or picture.

pica /'paɪkə/ *noun Printing* an old type size, giving about six lines to the inch. [from Latin *pica*, magpie]

picador /'pɪkədɔː(r)/ *noun Bullfighting* a horseman who weakens the bull by wounding it with a lance. [from Spanish *picador*, from *pica*, lance]

picaresque /pɪkə'rɛsk/ *adj., said of a novel, etc* telling of the adventures of a usually likeable rogue in separate, only loosely connected, episodes. [from Spanish *picaro*, rogue]

piccalilli /pɪkə'lɪlɪ/ *noun* a pickle consisting of mixed vegetables in a mustard sauce.

piccaninny or *North Amer., esp. US* **pickaninny** *noun* (PL. **piccaninnies**) *now offensive* an African-American or Australian Aboriginal child. [perhaps from Portuguese *pequenino*, diminutive of *pequeno*, little]

piccolo /'pɪkəloʊ/ *noun* (PL. **piccolos**) a small transverse flute pitched one octave higher than the standard instrument, and with a range of about three octaves. [a shortening of Italian *flauto piccolo*, little flute]

pick [1] — *verb* **1** *trans., intrans.* to choose or select. **2** to detach and gather (flowers from a plant, fruit from a tree, etc). **3** (**pick something up, off, out**, etc) to lift, remove, detach, or extract it: *picked a crumb off the carpet.* **4** to open (a lock) with a device other than a key. **5** to get, take, or extract whatever is of use or value from: *pick a bone clean / pick someone's brains.* **6** to steal money or valuables from (someone's pocket). **7** to undo; to unpick: *pick a dress to pieces.* **8** to make (a hole) by unpicking. **9** to remove pieces of matter from (one's nose, teeth, a scab, etc) with one's fingernails, etc. **10** to provoke (a fight, quarrel, etc) with someone. — *noun* **1** the best of a group: *the pick of the bunch.* **2** one's own preferred selection. — **have** or **take one's pick** to keep selecting and rejecting until one is satisfied. **pick and choose** be over-fussy in one's choice. **pick at something 1** to eat only small quantities of one's food. **2** to keep pulling at a scab, etc with one's fingernails. **pick holes in something** to find fault with it. **pick people** or **things off 1** to shoot them. **2** to deal with opposition bit by bit. **pick on someone 1** to blame them unfairly. **2** to bully them. **3** to choose them for an unpleasant job. **pick on something** to choose it; to light on it. **pick someone** or **something out 1** to select them from a group. **2** to recognize or distinguish them among a group or crowd. **pick something out 1** to play a tune uncertainly, especially by ear. **2** to mark it so as to distinguish it from its surroundings: *beige walls with the picture rail picked out in brown.* **pick something over** to examine one by one and reject whatever is unwanted. **pick someone** or **something to pieces** to criticize them severely. **pick up** *said of a person, a person's health, or a situation* to recover or improve: *she picked up after seeing me/ sales have picked up now.* **pick up** or **pick something up** to resume: *pick up where one left off/pick up the threads of a relationship/pick up the trail.* **pick someone up 1** to arrest or seize them: *was picked up by the police.* **2** *colloq.* to approach them, especially with a view to sexual relations. **pick oneself up** to restore oneself to an upright position after a fall. **pick something up 1** to lift or raise it from a surface, from the ground, etc. **2** to learn or acquire a habit, skill, language, etc over a time. **3** to notice or become aware of something: *picked up a faint odour.* **4** to obtain or acquire something casually, by chance, etc: *pick up a bargain/pick up an infection.* **5** *Telecomm.* to receive a signal, programme, etc. **6** to refer back in conversation or discourse to a point previously made, in order to deal with it further. **7** *colloq.* to agree to pay a bill. **pick someone** or **something up 1** to stop one's vehicle for, and give a lift to or take someone or something where required. **2** to go and fetch someone or something waiting to be collected. **pick someone up on something** to point out their error. **pick up the pieces** to have to restore things to normality or make things better after some trouble or disaster. **pick up speed** to increase speed gradually. **pick one's way** to go carefully so as to avoid hazards. [from Middle English *piken*]

▪ *verb* **1** select, choose, opt for, decide on, settle on, single out. **2** gather, collect, pluck, harvest, cull. *noun* **1** best, cream, flower, elite, elect. **2** choice, selection, option, decision, preference. **pick on** *someone* **1** blame, find fault with, criticize. **2** bully, torment, persecute, nag, *colloq.* get at, *colloq.* needle, bait. *something* choose, select, light on, single out. **pick someone** or **something out 1** select, choose, single out, hand-pick. **2** distinguish, tell apart, spot, notice, perceive, recognize, separate. **pick up** *of a person, a person's health, or a situation* recover, improve, rally, *colloq.* perk up. *something* **1** lift, raise, hoist. **2** learn, acquire, master, grasp. **3** notice, become aware of, detect, perceive, discern, spot. **4** buy, purchase, obtain, acquire, gain, catch, contract, get. **5** call for, fetch, collect.

. . . .

pick [2] *noun* **1** a tool with a long metal head pointed at one or both ends, for breaking ground, rock, ice, etc. **2** a poking or cleaning tool: *a toothpick*. **3** a plectrum. [from Middle English *pikke*]

pickaback see PIGGYBACK.

pickaxe *noun* a large pick, especially with a point at one end of its head and a cutting edge at the other. [from Old French *picois*]

picker *noun* **1** a person who picks or gathers. **2** a tool or machine for picking.

picket — *noun* **1** a person or group stationed outside a place of work to persuade other employees not to go in during a strike. **2** a body of soldiers on patrol or sentry duty. **3** a stake fixed in the ground, eg as part of a fence. — *verb* (**picketed, picketing**) **1** to station pickets, or act as a picket, at (a factory, etc). **2** to guard or patrol with, or as, a military picket. [from French *piquet*, diminutive of *pic*, pick]

. . . .

▣ *noun* **1** picketer, protester, demonstrator, striker. *verb* **1** protest, demonstrate, boycott, blockade.

. . . .

picket line a line of people acting as pickets in an industrial dispute.

pickings *pl. noun colloq.* profits made easily or casually from something.

pickle — *noun* **1** a preserve of vegetables, eg onions, cucumber, or cauliflower, in vinegar, salt water, or a tart sauce. **2** a vegetable so preserved. **3** the liquid used for this preserve. **4** *colloq.* a mess; a quandary: *get oneself in a pickle.* — *verb* to preserve in vinegar, salt water, etc. [from Old German *pekel*]

. . . .

▣ *noun* **4** mess, quandary, predicament, *colloq.* fix, muddle. *verb* preserve, conserve, souse, marinade, steep, cure, salt.

. . . .

pickled *adj.* **1** preserved in pickle. **2** *colloq.* drunk.

pick-me-up *noun* **1** a stimulating drink. **2** anything that revives and invigorates.

pickpocket *noun* a thief who steals from people's pockets.

pick-up *noun* **1** the stylus on a record-player. **2** a small lorry, truck, or van. **3** *colloq.* an acquaintance made casually, especially with a view to sexual relations; the making of such an acquaintance. **4** a halt to load goods or passengers; the goods or passengers so loaded.

picky *adj.* (**pickier, pickiest**) *colloq.* choosy; difficult to please.

picnic — *noun* **1** an outing on which one takes food for eating in the open; the food so taken or eaten. **2** (*usually* **no picnic**) *colloq.* an agreeable job or situation: *minding young children is no picnic.* — *verb intrans.* (**picnicked, picnicking**) to have a picnic. [from French *pique-nique*]

picnicker *noun* a person having a picnic.

pico- *combining form* denoting a millionth of a millionth part, or 10^{-12}. [from Spanish *pico*, a small quantity]

Pict *noun* a general term coined by the Romans in the 3c for their Barbarian enemies in Britain north of the Antonine Wall, and then used for the subjects of kings who ruled north and south of the E Grampians. [from Latin *picti*, painted men]

Pictish *adj.* belonging or relating to the Picts.

pictograph or **pictogram** *noun* **1** a picture or symbol representing a word, as in Chinese writing. **2** a pictorial or diagrammatic representation of values, statistics, etc. [from Latin *pictus*, painted + -GRAPH, -GRAM]

pictorial — *adj.* relating to, or consisting of, pictures. — *noun* a periodical with a high proportion of pictures. [from Latin *pictor*, painter]

. . . .

▣ *adj.* graphic, diagrammatic, schematic, representational, illustrated.

. . . .

pictorially *adv.* by means of pictures.

picture — *noun* **1** a representation of someone or something on a flat surface; a drawing, painting, or photograph. **2** someone's portrait. **3** a view; a mental image; a description intended to produce a mental image: *a clear picture of the battle.* **4** a situation or outlook: *a gloomy financial picture.* **5** a person or thing strikingly like another: *she is the picture of her mother.* **6** a visible embodiment: *was the picture of happiness.* **7** an image of beauty: *looks a picture.* **8** the image received on a television screen. **9** a film; a motion picture. **10** *colloq.* (**the pictures**) the cinema. — *verb* **1** to imagine or visualize. **2** to describe vividly; to depict. **3** to represent or show in a picture or photograph. — **in the picture** informed of all the relevant facts. [from Latin *pictura*]

. . . .

▣ *noun* **1** drawing, painting, photograph, illustration, sketch, print, engraving, portrait, likeness, landscape, representation, image. **2** portrait, likeness. **3** impression, view, representation, image, description, depiction, portrayal, account, report. **4** situation, outlook, perspective, prospect, future. **5** spitting image, double. **6** embodiment, personification, epitome, archetype, essence. **9** film, *colloq.* movie, motion picture. **10** cinema, films, *old colloq. use* flicks, *colloq.* movies, big screen. *verb* **1** imagine, visualize, envisage, envision, conceive, see. **2** depict, describe, portray, illustrate. **3** represent, show, portray, draw, sketch, paint, photograph, illustrate.

. . . .

picture postcard a postcard with a picture on the front.

picture rail a narrow moulding running round the walls of a room just below the ceiling, from which to hang pictures.

picturesque /ˌpɪktʃəˈrɛsk/ *adj.* **1** *said of places or buildings* charming to look at, especially if rather quaint. **2** *said of language* colourful, expressive, or graphic; *facetious* vivid or strong to the point of offensiveness. [from French *pittoresque*, influenced by PICTURE]

. . . .

▣ **1** charming, attractive, quaint, pretty, idyllic, scenic, beautiful. **2** colourful, graphic, expressive, descriptive, vivid, striking.

▣ **1** unattractive. **2** dull, prosaic.

. . . .

picture window a large window with a plate-glass pane, usually affording an extensive view.

piddle *colloq.* — *verb intrans.* **1** to urinate. **2** (**piddle about** or **around**) to mess about or waste time. — *noun* urine or the act of urinating.

piddling *adj.* trivial; trifling.

pidgin /ˈpɪdʒɪn/ *noun* **1** a type of simplified language used especially for trading purposes between speakers of different languages, consisting of a combination and often simplification of the vocabulary, grammar, and pronunciation systems of the languages concerned. See also CREOLE. **2** *colloq.* (*also* **pigeon**) one's own affair, business, or concern. [said to be a Chinese pronunciation of *business*]

pidgin English a pidgin in which one element is English, especially that formerly spoken between the Chinese and Europeans.

pie *noun* a savoury or sweet dish, usually cooked in a container, consisting of a quantity of food with a covering and/or base of pastry. — **easy as pie** very easy. **pie in the sky** some hoped-for but unguaranteed future prospect.

piebald — *adj.* having contrasting patches of colour, especially black and white. — *noun* a piebald horse. [from *pie*, magpie + BALD]

piece — *noun* **1** a portion of some material; a bit. **2** any of the sections into which something (eg a cake) is divided; a portion taken from a whole. **3** a component part: *a jigsaw piece.* **4** an item in a set: *an 18-piece teaset.* **5** an individual member of a class of things represented by a collective noun: *a piece of fruit/a piece of clothing.* **6** a specimen: *a* *fine piece of Chippendale.* **7** an instance: *a piece of nonsense.* **8** a musical, artistic, literary, or dramatic work. **9** an article in a newspaper, etc. **10** a coin: *a 50-pence piece.* **11** *Chess* one of the tokens or men used in a board game. **12** a cannon or firearm. **13** *offensive colloq.* a woman. — *verb* **1** (**piece something** or **things together**) to join them together to form a whole. **2** (**piece something up**) to patch or insert pieces into a garment. — **all of a piece** forming an indivisible whole. **go to pieces** *colloq.* to lose emotional control; to panic. **all in one piece** undamaged, unhurt, intact. **in pieces 1** separated into a number of component parts. **2** broken; shattered. **of a piece with something** consistent or uniform with it. **say one's piece** to make one's contribution to a discussion. **to pieces 1** into its component parts: *take to pieces.* **2** into fragments, shreds, tatters, etc. [from Old French *piece*]

....

◨ *noun* **1** portion, bit, fragment, scrap, morsel, mouthful, bite, lump, chunk, slice, sliver, snippet, shred, offcut, sample. **2** segment, section, division, portion, share, fraction, quantity. **3** component, part, constituent, element. **5** item. **6** specimen, example. **8** work, composition, creation, study, item. **9** article, item, story. **10** coin, bit.

....

pièce de résistance /pɪ'ɛs də reɪ'zɪstɒns/ (PL. **pièces de résistance**) the best or most impressive item. [French]
piecemeal *adv.* a bit at a time.
piece of eight (PL. **pieces of eight**) an old Spanish gold coin worth eight reals.
piece rate a fixed rate of pay for a particular amount of work done.
piecework *noun* work paid for according to the amount done, not the time taken to do it.
pie chart a diagram consisting of a circle divided into sectors, used to display statistical data. Each sector contains one category of information, and its size is calculated as a percentage of the total.
pied /paɪd/ *adj., said of a bird* having variegated plumage, especially of black and white. [from *pie*, magpie]
pied-à-terre /pjeɪdɑ'teə(r)/ *noun* (PL. **pieds-à-terre**) a house or apartment, eg in a city, that one keeps as a lodging for one's occasional visits there. [from French *pied-à-terre*, literally 'foot on the ground']
pie-eyed *adj. colloq.* drunk.
pier /pɪə(r)/ *noun* **1** a structure built of stone, wood, or iron, projecting into water for use as a landing-stage or breakwater. **2** a pillar supporting a bridge or arch. **3** the masonry between two openings in the wall of a building. [from Middle English *per*, from Latin *pera*]

....

◨ **1** jetty, landing-stage, breakwater, quay, wharf. **2** pillar, support, upright, post.

....

pierce *verb* (**pierce something** or **pierce through something**) **1** *said of a sharp object, or a person using one* to make a hole in or through; to puncture; to make (a hole) with something sharp. **2** to penetrate or force a way through or into: *the wind pierced through her thin clothing.* **3** *said of light or sound* to burst through (darkness or silence). **4** to affect or touch (someone's heart, soul, etc) keenly or painfully. [from Old French *percer*]

....

◨ **1** penetrate, puncture, enter, stick into, perforate, punch, prick, stab, lance, bayonet, run through, spear, skewer, spike, drill, bore, probe, impale. **4** stab, sting, cut, disturb.

....

piercing *adj.* that pierces; penetrating, acute, keen, shrill.

....

◨ *penetrating* probing, searching. *acute* acute, painful, agonizing, excruciating, stabbing, lacerating. *keen* raw, biting, cold, bitter, fierce, severe, wintry, frosty, freezing. *shrill* high-pitched, loud, ear-splitting, sharp.

....

Pierrot /'pɪəroʊ/ *noun* a traditional male character from French pantomime, with a whitened face, white frilled outfit, and pointed hat. [from French name *Pierrot*, diminutive of *Pierre*, Peter]
pietà /pjeɪ'tɑ:/ *noun* in painting and sculpture, the representation of the dead Christ mourned by angels, apostles, or holy women. [Italian, from Latin *pieta*, pity]
pietism /'paɪətɪzm/ *noun* pious feeling, or an exaggerated show of piety.
pietist /'paɪətɪst/ *noun* a person marked by strong devotional feeling.
pietistic *adj.* relating to pietists.
piety /'paɪətɪ/ *noun* the quality of being pious, dutiful, or religiously devout. [from Latin *pietas*]

....

◨ piousness, devoutness, devotion, godliness, saintliness, holiness, sanctity, religion, faith, reverence.
◨ impiety, irreligion.

....

piezoelectric /pi:zoʊə'lɛktrɪk/ *adj.* relating to or using piezoelectricity.
piezoelectric effect 1 *Physics* the generation of an electrical potential across certain crystals, eg quartz, when they are stretched or compressed. This effect is exploited in the crystal pick-ups of record-players, and in certain types of microphone. **2** the reverse effect, in which an electrical potential can produce slight physical distortion in such crystals. For example, in a quartz watch or clock the piezoelectric effect causes the crystal to vibrate at a particular frequency by expanding and contracting rhythmically, so that the instrument keeps almost perfect time.
piezoelectricity *noun* electricity produced by the piezoelectric effect. [from Greek *piezo*, to press + ELECTRICITY]
piffle *noun* nonsense; rubbish.
piffling *adj.* trivial, trifling, or petty.
pig — *noun* **1** an ungulate (hoofed mammal) belonging to the family Suidae, kept worldwide for its meat. It has a stout heavy body covered with coarse bristly hairs, relatively short legs, and a protruding flattened snout. **2** an abusive term for a person, especially someone greedy, dirty, selfish, or brutal. **3** *slang* an unpleasant job or situation. **4** *offensive slang* a policeman. **5** a quantity of metal cast into an oblong mass. — *verb* (**pigged, pigging**) **1** *intrans., said of a pig* to produce young. **2** *said of a person* to eat greedily. — **make a pig of oneself** *colloq.* to eat greedily. **make a pig's ear of something** *colloq.* to make a mess of it; to botch it. **a pig in a poke** *colloq.* a purchase made without preliminary investigation as to suitability. **pig it** *colloq.* **1** to eat greedily. **2** to live squalidly. **pigs might fly** *colloq.* an expression of scepticism. [from Middle English *pigge*]

....

◨ *noun* **1** swine, hog, sow, boar. **2** brute, animal, beast, glutton, gourmand.

....

pigeon[1] *noun* **1** any of many species of medium-sized bird belonging to the same family (Columbidae) as doves, and having a plump body, rounded tail, and dense soft grey, brown, or pink plumage. **2** *slang* a dupe or simpleton. [from Old French *pijon*, from Latin *pipio*, from *pipare*, to cheep]
pigeon[2] same as PIDGIN 2.
pigeonhole — *noun* **1** any of a set of compartments, eg in a desk, for filing letters or papers. **2** a compartment of the mind or memory. — *verb* **1** to put into a pigeonhole. **2** to put mentally into a category, especially too readily. **3** to set aside for future consideration.

....

◨ *noun* **1** compartment, cubbyhole, cubicle, box, locker. **2** compartment, place, niche, slot, section, class, category, classification. *verb* **2** compartmentalize, classify, label, sort, file, catalogue. **3** shelve, defer.

....

pigeon-toed *adj.*, *said of a person* standing and walking with the toes turned in.

piggery *noun* (PL. **piggeries**) **1** a place where pigs are bred. **2** *colloq.* greediness or otherwise disgusting behaviour.

piggish *adj. derog.* greedy, dirty, selfish, mean, or ill-mannered.

piggishness *noun* **1** being piggish. **2** piggish behaviour.

piggy — *noun* (PL. **piggies**) a child's diminutive for a pig; a little pig. — *adj.* (**piggier, piggiest**) **1** pig-like. **2** *said of the eyes* small and mean-looking.

piggyback or **pickaback** — *noun* a ride on someone's back, with the legs supported by the bearer's arms. — *adv.* on the back of someone else.

piggy bank a child's pig-shaped china container for saving money.

pigheaded *adj.* stupidly obstinate.

pig-in-the-middle *noun* **1** a game in which one person stands between two others and tries to intercept the ball they are throwing to each other. **2** any person helplessly caught between two contending parties.

pig iron *Metall.* an impure form of iron containing about 4% carbon, produced by smelting iron in a blast furnace, and so called because it is cast into blocks called *pigs*. Most pig iron is processed to make steel.

piglet *noun* a young pig.

pigment — *noun* **1** any insoluble colouring matter that is used in suspension in water, oil, or other liquids to give colour to paint, paper, etc. **2** a coloured substance that occurs naturally in plant and animal tissues, eg the red blood pigment haemoglobin, chlorophyll in the leaves of green plants. — *verb* to colour with pigment; to dye or stain. [from Latin *pigmentum*]

⊞ *noun* **1** colour, hue, tint, dye, stain, paint, colouring, tincture.

pigmentation *noun* coloration or discoloration caused by pigments in the tissues.

pigmy another spelling of **pygmy**.

pigskin *noun* **1** leather made from the skin of a pig. **2** *North Amer. colloq.* a football.

pigsty *noun* (PL. **pigsties**) **1** a pen on a farm, etc for pigs; a sty. **2** a place of filth and disorder.

pigswill *noun* kitchen or brewery waste fed to pigs.

pigtail *noun* a plaited length of hair, especially one of a pair, worn hanging at the sides or back of the head.

pika /ˈpaɪkə/ *noun* a mammal, native to Asia and N America, that resembles a small rabbit and has short legs, short rounded ears, and a minute tail. Also called CONY. [from a N American name]

pike[1] *noun* (PL. **pike, pikes**) a fierce freshwater fish with a long pointed snout. [from Anglo-Saxon *pic*, point, pick]

pike[2] *noun Hist.* a weapon like a spear, consisting of a metal point mounted on a long shaft. [from Anglo-Saxon *pic*, point]

pikestaff *noun* the shaft of a pike. — **plain as a pikestaff** all too obvious.

pilaff or **pilaf** /ˈpɪlaf/ or **pilau** /pɪˈlaʊ/ *noun* an oriental dish of spiced rice with chicken, fish, etc. [from Turkish *pilaw*]

pilaster /pɪˈlastə(r)/ *noun* a rectangular column standing out in relief from the façade of a building, as a decorative feature. [from French *pilastre*, from Latin *pila*, pillar]

Pilates /pɪˈlɑtiːz/ *noun* gentle exercises to stretch the muscles, performed lying down. [after Joseph Pilates, who invented the system]

pilau see PILAFF.

pilchard /ˈpɪltʃəd/ *noun* an edible sea fish of the herring family, but smaller, thicker, and rounder.

pile[1] — *noun* **1** a number of things lying on top of each other; a quantity of something in a heap or mound. **2** (**a pile** or **piles**) *colloq.* a large quantity. **3** a fortune: *made a/ her pile on the horses.* **4** a massive or imposing building. **5** (*also* **funeral pile**) a pyre. **6** (*also* **atomic pile**) a nuclear re-

actor. **7** *Electr.* a vertical series of plates of two different metals arranged alternately to produce an electric current. — *verb* **1** (*usually* **pile up** or **pile something up**) to accumulate into a pile. **2** (**pile in, into something, off, out**, etc) to move in a crowd or confused bunch. — **pile it on** *colloq.* to exaggerate. [from Latin *pila*, stone pier]

⊞ *noun* **1** heap, mound, stack, mountain, mass, accumulation, collection, assortment, hoard, stockpile. **2** ton(s), heap(s). *verb* **1** stack, heap, mass, amass, accumulate, build up, gather, assemble, collect, hoard, stockpile, store. **2** pack, crowd, flock, flood, stream, rush, charge.

pile[2] *noun* the raised cropped threads that give a soft thick surface to carpeting, velvet, etc; nap. [from Latin *pilus*, hair]

⊞ nap, shag, plush.

pile[3] *noun* a heavy wooden shaft, stone, or concrete pillar, etc driven into the ground as a support for a building, bridge, etc. [from Latin *pilum*, javelin]

⊞ shaft, post, column, upright, support, foundation.

pile[4] *noun* (*usually* **piles**) a haemorrhoid. [from Latin *pila*, ball]

pile-driver *noun* a machine for driving piles into the ground.

pile-up *noun* a multi-vehicle collision.

pilfer *verb trans., intrans.* (**pilfered, pilfering**) to steal in small quantities. [from Old French *pelfre*, booty]

⊞ steal, *colloq.* pinch, *slang* nick, *colloq.* knock off, filch, lift, shoplift, rob, thieve.

pilferer *noun* a person who pilfers.

pilgrim *noun* **1** a person who makes a journey to a holy place as an act of reverence and religious faith. **2** a traveller. [from Latin *peregrinus*, foreigner, stranger]

⊞ **2** traveller, wanderer.

pilgrimage *noun* a journey to a shrine or other holy place, or to a place celebrated or made special by its associations.

⊞ expedition, journey, trip, tour.

Pilipino /pɪlɪˈpiːnəʊ/ — *noun* the national language of the Philippines, a standardized version of Tagalog. — *adj.* relating to or spoken or written in Pilipino.

pill *noun* **1** a small ball or tablet of medicine, for swallowing. **2** something unpleasant that one must accept. **3** (**the pill**) any of various oral contraceptives. — **sugar** or **sweeten the pill** to make something unpleasant easier to accept or cope with. [from Latin *pila*, ball]

⊞ **1** tablet, capsule, pellet.

pillage — *verb trans., intrans.* to plunder or loot. — *noun* **1** the act of pillaging. **2** loot, plunder, or booty. [from Old French *piller*, to pillage]

pillager *noun* a person who pillages.

pillar *noun* **1** a vertical post of wood, stone, metal, or concrete serving as a support; a column. **2** any slender vertical mass, eg of smoke, rock, etc. **3** a strong and reliable supporter of a cause or organization. — **from pillar to post** from one place to another, especially in desperation, frustration, etc. [from Old French *piler*, from Latin *pila*, pillar]

⊞ **1** column, shaft, post, mast, pier, upright, pile, support. **2** column, tower, shaft. **3** prop, mainstay, bastion, tower of strength.

· ·

pillar box a free-standing cylindrical public letter box.

pillbox *noun* **1** a small round container for pills. **2** *Mil.* a small usually circular concrete shelter for use as a lookout post and gun emplacement. **3** a small round flat-topped hat.

pillion — *noun* a seat for a passenger on a motorcycle or horse, behind the rider. — *adv.* on a pillion. [from Gaelic *pillinn* or Irish *pillin*, diminutive of *peall*, skin or blanket]

pillory — *noun* (PL. **pillories**) *Hist.* a wooden frame with holes for the hands and head into which wrongdoers were locked as a punishment, and publicly ridiculed. — *verb* (**pillories, pilloried**) **1** to hold up to public ridicule. **2** to put in a pillory. [from Old French *pilori*]

pillow — *noun* a cushion for the head, especially a large rectangular one on a bed. — *verb* **1** to rest (one's head) as though on a pillow: *pillowed her head on her arms.* **2** to serve as pillow for. [from Anglo-Saxon *pylwe*, from Latin *pulvinus*, cushion]

pillowcase or **pillowslip** *noun* a washable cover for a pillow.

pillow lace lace worked over a cushion-like support, using bobbins.

pilot — *noun* **1** a person who flies an aircraft. **2** a person employed to conduct or steer ships into and out of harbour. **3** a guide. **4** *Mech.* a device that guides a tool or machine part. **5** (*attributive*) *said of a scheme* serving as a preliminary test; experimental. — *verb* (**piloted, piloting**) **1** to act as pilot to. **2** to direct, guide, or steer (a project, etc). [from Old French *pillote*, from Old Italian *pilota*, earlier *pedota*, from Greek *pedon*, oar]

· · · · · · · · · · · · · · · · · ·

▣ *noun* **1** aviator, flyer, airman, airwoman. **2** navigator, steersman, helmsman. **3** guide, leader, navigator, steersman, helmsman, director. **5** experimental, trial, test, model. *verb* **1** fly, drive, steer, navigate. **2** direct, guide, steer, navigate, control, handle, manage, conduct, lead, operate, run.

· ·

pilot light 1 a small permanent gas flame, eg on a gas cooker, that ignites the main burners when they are turned on. **2** an indicator light on an electrical apparatus, showing when it is switched on.

pilot officer the lowest-ranking officer in the Royal Air Force.

pimento /pɪˈmentəʊ/ *noun* (PL. **pimentos**) **1** the dried unripe fruit of a West Indian tree of the myrtle family; allspice. **2** the pimiento. [altered from Spanish *pimiento*; see PIMIENTO]

pimiento /pɪˈmjentəʊ/ *noun* (PL. **pimientos**) **1** the red mild-tasting fruit of the sweet pepper, used as a relish, a stuffing for olives, etc. **2** the pimento or allspice. [from Spanish *pimiento*, from Latin *pigmenta*, spiced drink, spice, pepper]

pimp — *noun* a man who finds customers for a prostitute or a brothel, and lives off the earnings. — *verb intrans.* to act as a pimp.

pimpernel *noun* a sprawling plant with small five-petalled flowers on long slender stems. [from Old French *pimprenelle*]

pimple *noun* a small raised pus-containing swelling on the skin; a spot. [from Anglo-Saxon *pyplian*, to break out in pimples]

· · · · · · · · · · · · · · · · · · ·

▣ spot, *slang* zit, blackhead, boil, swelling.

· ·

pimply *adj.* (**pimplier, pimpliest**) having pimples.

PIN *noun, abbrev.* personal identification number, a multi-digit number used to authorize electronic transactions, such as cash withdrawal from a dispenser at a bank, etc.

pin — *noun* **1** a short slender usually stainless steel implement with a sharp point and small round head, for fastening, attaching, etc, used especially in dressmaking. **2** (*in compounds*) any of several fastening devices consisting of or incorporating a slender metal or wire shaft: *hatpin/ safety pin.* **3** a narrow brooch. **4** (*in compounds*) any of several cylindrical wooden or metal objects with various functions: *a rolling-pin.* **5** a peg of any of various kinds. **6** any or either of the cylindrical or square-sectioned legs on an electric plug. **7** *Bowling* a club-shaped object set upright for toppling with a ball. **8** the clip on a grenade, removed before throwing. **9** *Golf* the metal shaft of the flag marking a hole. **10** (**pins**) *colloq.* one's legs. **11** *old use* the least bit: *doesn't care a pin.* — *verb* (**pinned, pinning**) **1** (**pin something together, back, up**, etc) to secure it with a pin. **2** (**pin something on someone**) *colloq.* to put the blame for a crime or offence on them. — **for two pins** *colloq.*, *said of a wish, inclination, etc* expressed as likely to be realized with minimum persuasion (although not normally realized): *for two pins, I'd come with you.* **pin one's hopes on something** or **someone** to rely on them entirely. **pin someone down** to force a commitment or definite expression of opinion from them. **pin something down** to identify or define it precisely. (**pin something** or **someone down**) to hold them fast or trap them: *was pinned to the ground by a fallen tree.* [from Anglo-Saxon *pinn*, from Latin *pinna*, point]

· · · · · · · · · · · · · · · · · ·

▣ *noun* **1** tack, nail. **5** peg, fastener, clip, staple, spike, rivet, bolt. *verb* **1** tack, nail, fix, affix, attach, join, staple, clip, fasten, secure. **pin down** *someone* press, pressurize, force, make. *something* pinpoint, identify, define, determine, specify. *something or someone* hold down, restrain, immobilize, trap.

· ·

pinafore *noun* **1** an apron, especially one with a bib. **2** (*also* **pinafore dress**) a sleeveless dress for wearing over a blouse, sweater, etc. [from PIN + AFORE because it was formerly 'pinned afore', ie pinned to the front of a dress]

pinball *noun* a game played on a slot machine in which a small metal ball is propelled round a course, the score depending on what hazards it avoids and targets it hits; a form of bagatelle.

pince-nez /ˈpansneɪ/ *pl. noun* spectacles that are held in position by gripping the nose instead of being supported over the ears. [from French *pince-nez*, pinch-nose]

pincer movement *Mil.* an advance that closes in on a target from both sides simultaneously.

pincers *pl. noun* **1** a hinged tool with claw-like jaws for gripping things. **2** the hinged end of a crab's or lobster's claw, adapted for gripping. [from Old French *pincer*, to pinch]

pinch — *verb* **1** to squeeze or nip the flesh of, between thumb and finger. **2** to compress or squeeze painfully. **3** *trans., intrans., said of tight shoes* to hurt or chafe. **4** *trans., intrans., colloq.* to steal. **5** *intrans., said of controls, restrictions, shortages, etc* to cause hardship. **6** (**pinch something off, out, back,** etc) to prune a plant by removing the tips of shoots. **7** *intrans.* to economize: *pinch and scrape.* **8** *colloq.* to arrest. — *noun* **1** an act of pinching; a nip or squeeze. **2** a quantity of eg salt that can be held between thumb and finger; a small amount. — **at a pinch** if absolutely necessary. [from Old French *pincier*, to pinch]

· · · · · · · · · · · · · · · · · · ·

▣ *verb* **1** squeeze, nip, tweak. **2** compress, squeeze, press, crush, hurt, grip, grasp. **4** steal, *slang* nick, pilfer, filch. **5** hurt. *noun* **1** squeeze, tweak, nip. **2** dash, soupçon, taste, bit, speck, jot, mite. **at a pinch** in an emergency.

· ·

pinchbeck — *noun* a copper alloy with the appearance of gold, used in cheap jewellery. — *adj.* cheap, artificial, sham, counterfeit, or imitation.

pinched *adj. said of a person's appearance* pale and haggard from tiredness, cold, or other discomfort.

pincushion *noun* a pad into which to stick dressmaking pins for convenient storage.

pine[1] *noun* **1** any of about 200 species of evergreen coniferous tree belonging to the genus *Pinus* of the family Pinaceae, and having narrow needle-like leaves, widespread in cool north temperate regions. **2** the pale durable wood of this tree, which is used to make furniture, telegraph poles, etc, and paper pulp, and is widely used in construction work. [from Latin *pinus*]

pine[2] *verb intrans.* **1** to long or yearn. **2** (*also* **pine away**) to waste away from grief or longing. [from Anglo-Saxon *pinian*, to torment]

. . . .

▣ **1** long, yearn, ache, sigh, grieve, mourn, wish, desire, crave, hanker, hunger, thirst.

. . . .

pineal gland *or* **pineal body** /'pɪnɪəl/ *Physiol.* in vertebrates, a small outgrowth from the roof of the forebrain. It produces the hormone melatonin, and may be involved in the control of biological rhythms related to seasonal changes in daylength, eg breeding. Also called EPIPHYSIS. [from Latin *pinea*, pine cone, from its shape]

pineapple *noun* **1** a tropical plant (*Ananas comosus*) with spiky sword-shaped leaves, native to S America but widely cultivated in tropical regions for its large edible fruit. **2** the fruit of this plant, which has sweet juicy yellow flesh covered by a yellowish-brown spiny skin, and is crowned by a rosette of pointed green leaves. [from Middle English *pinappel*, pine cone, the name passing in the 17c to the tropical fruit]

pine cone *Bot.* the fruit of the pine.

pine marten an animal found especially in coniferous forests, which is related to the weasel and has dark brown fur with yellowish underparts.

ping — *noun* a sharp ringing sound like that made by plucking a taut wire, lightly striking glass or metal, etc. — *verb intrans., trans.* to make or cause to make this sound. [imitative]

ping-pong *noun* table tennis. [imitative of the sound of the ball]

pinhead *noun* the little rounded or flattened head of a pin, proverbial for smallness.

pinion[1] — *verb* (**pinioned**, **pinioning**) **1** to immobilize by holding or binding the arms of; to hold or bind (someone's arms). **2** to hold fast or bind: *pinioned against a wall.* — *noun* **1** the extreme tip of a bird's wing. **2** a bird's flight feather. [from Old French *pignon*, wing]

pinion[2] *noun* a small cogwheel that engages with a larger wheel or rack. [from Old French *pignon*, cogwheel]

pink[1] — *noun* **1** a colour between red and white. **2** a genus of plants with fragrant red, pink, or variegated flowers, including the carnation and sweet william. **3** a scarlet hunting-coat or its colour. **4** the highest point; the acme: *in the pink of condition.* **5** a person of mildly left-wing views. — *adj.* **1** of the colour pink. **2** slightly left-wing or communist. **3** relating to homosexuals. — **in the pink** *colloq.* in the best of health.

pink[2] *verb* to cut (cloth) with a notched or serrated edge that frays less readily than a straight edge. [from Anglo-Saxon *pyngan*, to prick]

pink[3] *verb intrans., said of a vehicle engine* to make a metallic knocking noise due to faulty combustion timing. [imitative]

pink eye an inflamed condition of the membrane covering the eye; conjunctivitis.

pink gin gin flavoured with and stained pink by angostura bitters.

pinkie *or* **pinky** *noun* (PL. **pinkies**) *Scot., North Amer., esp. US* the little finger. [from Dutch *pinkje*]

pinking shears scissors for cutting a notched or serrated edge in cloth (see PINK[2]).

pinkish *adj.* somewhat pink.

pinko *noun* (PL. **pinkos**) *colloq.* a mild or half-hearted socialist.

pink pound the combined purchasing power of homosexuals considered as a consumer group.

pinky *adj.* (**pinkier, pinkiest**) slightly pink.

pin money extra cash earned for spending on oneself, on luxury items, etc.

pinna *noun* (PL. **pinnae**) **1** *Anat.* in mammals, the part of the outer ear that projects from the head, and that in certain mammals (eg dogs) can be moved independently in order to detect the direction of sounds. It consists of a thin layer of cartilage covered with skin. **2** in a compound leaf, one of the leaflets on either side of the midrib. **3** in birds, a feather or wing. **4** in fish, a fin. [from Latin *pinna*, feather]

pinnace /'pɪnəs/ *noun* a small boat carried on a larger ship; a ship's boat. [from Old French *pinace*, from Old Spanish *pinaza*, something of pine]

pinnacle *noun* **1** a slender spire crowning a buttress, gable, roof, or tower. **2** a rocky peak. **3** a high point of achievement. [from Latin *pinnaculum*, diminutive of *pinna*, feather]

. . . .

▣ **1** spire, steeple, turret, pyramid, cone, obelisk, needle.
2 peak, summit, top, cap, crown, crest, apex, vertex.
3 height, zenith, acme, eminence, apex, vertex.

. . . .

pinnate /'pɪneɪt/ *adj. Bot.* denoting a compound leaf that consists of pairs of leaflets, the members of each pair being arranged opposite each other on either side of a central axis or midrib. [from Latin *pinnatus*, feathered]

pinny *noun* (PL. **pinnies**) *colloq.* a pinafore.

pinochle /'pi:nʌkl/ *noun* a card game derived from bézique, especially popular in the USA. [origin unknown]

pinole /pi:'noʊleɪ/ *noun* a fine flour made from parched Indian corn or other seeds, sweetened with sugar and eaten with milk in Mexico and SW states of the USA. [from Spanish *pinole*, from Nahuatl *pinolli*]

pinpoint *verb* to place, define, or identify precisely.

. . . .

▣ place, define, identify, locate, distinguish, spot, home in on, *colloq.* zero in on, pin down, specify, determine.

. . . .

pinprick *noun* **1** a tiny hole made by, or as if by, a pin. **2** a slight irritation or annoyance.

pins and needles a prickling sensation in a limb, etc, felt as the flow of blood returns to it after being temporarily obstructed.

pinstripe *noun* a narrow stripe in cloth.

pint *noun* **1** a unit of liquid measure, ⅛ of a gallon. **2** *colloq.* a drink of beer of this quantity. [from Old French *pinte*]

pinta /'paɪntə/ *noun colloq.* a pint of milk. [a contraction of *pint of*]

pintail *noun* a type of duck with a pointed tail.

pint-size *or* **pint-sized** *adj. humorous, said of a person* small.

pin tuck a narrow decorative tuck in a garment.

pin-up *noun* **1** a picture of a glamorous or otherwise admirable person that one pins on one's wall. **2** the person in such a picture.

pinwheel *noun* **1** a whirling firework; Catherine wheel. **2** *North Amer., esp. US* a toy windmill.

Pinyin *noun* a system for writing Chinese with letters of the Roman alphabet. [from Chinese *Pinyin*, phonetic spelling]

pioneer — *noun* **1** an explorer of, or settler in, hitherto unknown or wild country. **2** someone who breaks new ground in anything; an innovator or initiator. — *verb* **1** *intrans.* to be a pioneer; to be innovative. **2** to explore and open up (a route, etc). **3** to try out, originate, or develop (a new technique, etc). [from Old French *peonier*, from Latin *pedo*, foot soldier]

. . . .

▣ *noun* **1** explorer, colonist, settler, frontiersman, frontierswoman, developer, pathfinder, trailblazer. **2** innovator, initiator, inventor, trailblazer, pathfinder, leader, discoverer, founder. *verb* **2** explore, open up, develop. **3** invent, discover, originate, develop, create, initiate, instigate, begin, start, launch, institute, found, establish, set up.

pious /ˈpaɪəs/ *adj.* **1** religiously devout. **2** dutiful. **3** *derog.* ostentatiously virtuous; sanctimonious. [from Latin *pius*, dutiful]

▣ **1** devout, godly, saintly, holy, spiritual, religious, reverent. **2** dutiful, good, righteous, virtuous. **3** sanctimonious, holier-than-thou, self-righteous, *colloq.* goody-goody, virtuous, hypocritical.
▣ **1** impious, irreligious, irreverent.

pip[1] *noun* the small seed of a fruit such as an apple, pear, orange, or grape. [shortening of PIPPIN]

pip[2] *noun* (*usually* **pips**) one of a series of short high-pitched signals on the radio, telephone, etc. [imitative]

pip[3] *verb* (**pipped, pipping**) to defeat narrowly. — **pipped at the post** *colloq.* overtaken narrowly in the closing stages of a contest, etc.

pip[4] *noun* **1** one of the emblems or spots on playing-cards, dice, or dominoes. **2** *Mil.* in the British army, a star on a uniform indicating rank.

pip[5] *noun* a disease of poultry and other fowl. — **give someone the pip** *colloq.* to irritate them. [from Middle English *pippe*]

pipe — *noun* **1** a tubular conveyance for water, gas, oil, etc. **2** a little bowl with a hollow stem for smoking tobacco, etc; a quantity of tobacco so smoked. **3** a wind instrument consisting of a simple wooden or metal tube. **4** (**pipes**) the bagpipes. **5** any of the vertical metal tubes through which sound is produced on an organ. **6** *old use esp. combining form* any of the air passages in an animal body: *the windpipe.* — *verb* **1** to convey (gas, water, oil, etc) through pipes. **2** *trans., intrans.* to play on a pipe or the pipes. **3** to welcome or convoy with music from the bagpipes. **4** *intrans., trans., said of a child* to speak or say in a small shrill voice. **5** using a bag with a nozzle, to force (icing or cream) into long strings for decorating a cake or dessert; to make (designs, etc) on a cake, etc by this means. **6** *Comput.* to direct (the output of one program) into (another program) as its input. — **pipe down** *colloq.* to stop talking; to be quiet. **pipe up** to speak unexpectedly, breaking a silence, etc. **put that in your pipe and smoke it** *colloq.* a dismissive conclusion to a frank censure, disagreement, instruction, etc. [from Anglo-Saxon *pipe*, from Latin *pipare*, to chirp or play a pipe]

▣ *noun* **1** tube, hose, piping, tubing, pipeline, line, main, flue, duct, conduit, channel, passage, conveyor. *verb* **1** channel, funnel, siphon, carry, convey, conduct, transmit, supply, deliver. **2** chirp, trill, cry.

pipeclay *noun* fine white clay for making tobacco pipes and delicate crockery.

pipe-cleaner *noun* a piece of wire with a woolly tufted covering, for cleaning a tobacco pipe.

piped music recorded music played through loudspeakers, especially in public places.

pipe dream a delightful fantasy of the kind indulged in while smoking a pipe, originally one filled with opium.

pipeline *noun* a series of connected pipes laid underground to carry oil, natural gas, water, etc, across large distances in cases where alternative forms of transport would be more costly. — **in the pipeline** *colloq.* under consideration; forthcoming or in preparation.

pipe of peace SEE PEACE PIPE.

piper *noun* a player of a pipe or the bagpipes.

pipette /pɪˈpɛt/ *noun* a narrow glass tube into which liquid can be sucked for transferring or measuring. [from French *pipette*, diminutive of *pipe*, pipe]

piping — *noun* **1** the art of playing a pipe or the bagpipes. **2** a length of pipe, or system, or series of pipes conveying water, oil, etc. **3** covered cord forming a decorative edging on upholstery or clothing. **4** strings and knots of icing or cream decorating a cake or dessert. — *adj.*, *said of a child's voice* small and shrill. — **piping hot** *said of food* satisfyingly hot.

pipistrelle /pɪpɪˈstrɛl/ *noun* a reddish-brown bat, the smallest in Britain. [from French *pipistrelle*, from Italian *pipistrello*, from Latin *vespertilio*, bat, from *vesper*, evening]

pipit *noun* any of several lark-like songbirds related to the wagtail. [imitative of its call]

pippin *noun* any of several sweet apples, usually rosy-skinned. [from Old French *pepin*]

pipsqueak *noun derog. colloq.* someone or something insignificant or contemptible. [perhaps from PEEP[2]]

piquancy /ˈpiːkənsɪ/ *noun* being piquant.

piquant /ˈpiːkənt/ *adj.* **1** having a pleasantly spicy taste or tang. **2** amusing, intriguing, provocative, or stimulating. [from French *piquer*, to prick]

▣ **1** spicy, tangy, sharp, pungent, savoury, peppery. **2** amusing, intriguing, provocative, stimulating, lively, spirited, sparkling, interesting.
▣ BLAND, INSIPID. **2** dull, banal.

pique /piːk/ — *noun* resentment; hurt pride. — *verb* **1** to hurt the pride of; to offend or nettle. **2** to arouse (curiosity or interest). **3** to pride (oneself) on: *piqued himself on his good taste.* [from French *piquer*, to prick]

▣ *noun* resentment, irritation, offence, annoyance, vexation, displeasure, huff, grudge. *verb* **1** offend, put out, nettle, annoy, irritate, vex, rile, anger, displease.

piqué /ˈpiːkeɪ/ *noun* a stiff corded fabric, especially of cotton. [from French *piquer*, to prick]

piquet /pɪˈkɛt, pɪˈkeɪ/ *noun* a card game for two, played with 32 cards. [from French *piquet*, from *pic*, the score of 30 points in this game, literally 'prick']

piracy /ˈpaɪərəsɪ/ *noun* **1** the activity of pirates. **2** unauthorized publication or reproduction of copyright material.

piranha /pɪˈrɑːnə/ *noun* a small fierce carnivorous S American freshwater fish. [from Portuguese *piranha*, from Tupí (S American Indian language) *piranya*]

pirate — *noun* **1** someone who attacks and robs ships at sea. **2** a ship used by pirates. **3** someone who publishes material without permission from the copyright-holder, or otherwise uses someone else's work illegally. **4** someone who runs a radio station without a licence. — *verb* to publish, reproduce, or use (someone else's literary or artistic work, or ideas) without legal permission. [from Greek *peirates*, from *peiraein*, to try one's fortune]

piratical *adj.* **1** relating to pirates. **2** practising piracy.

pirouette /pɪrʊˈɛt/ — *noun* a spin or twirl executed on tiptoe in dancing. — *verb intrans.* to execute a pirouette or a series of them. [from French *pirouette*, originally a spinning top]

piscatorial *adj. formal* relating to fish or fishing. [from Latin *piscatorius*, fisherman]

Pisces /ˈpaɪsiːz/ *noun* **1** *Astron.* the Fishes, a large but faint northern constellation of the zodiac, most clearly seen in the autumn, and lying between Aquarius and Aries. **2** the twelfth sign of the zodiac, the Fishes. **3** a person born between 20 Feb and 20 Mar, under this sign. **4** *Zool.* in the animal kingdom, the superclass of fishes, consisting of the classes Agnatha (jawless fish, ie hagfish and lampreys), Elasmobranchii (cartilaginous fish, ie sharks, rays), and Osteichthyes (bony fish). [from Latin *pisces*, fishes]

pisciculture /ˈpɪsɪkʌltʃə(r)/ *noun* the rearing of fish by artificial methods or under controlled conditions. [from Latin *piscis*, fish + CULTURE]

piscina /pɪ'siːnə/ *noun* a basin with a drain, found in older churches, in which to empty water used for rinsing the sacred vessels. [from Latin *piscina*, basin, originally fish pond]

piss *coarse slang* — *verb* **1** *intrans.* to urinate. **2** to discharge (eg blood) in the urine. **3** to wet with one's urine: *piss the bed*. **4** *intrans.* (*also* **piss down**) to rain hard. — *noun* **1** urine. **2** an act of urinating. — **piss about** or **around** to mess about; to waste time. **piss off** to go away. **piss someone off** to irritate or bore them. **take the piss out of someone** or **something** to ridicule them. [from French *pisser*, from a colloquial Latin word; imitative]

pissed *adj. coarse slang* drunk.

pistachio /pɪ'staːʃɪoʊ/ *noun* (PL. **pistachios**) the edible nut of a Eurasian tree, of the cashew family, with a green kernel. [from Italian *pistacchio*]

piste /piːst/ *noun* a ski slope or track of smooth compacted snow. [from French *piste*, race track]

pistil *noun Bot.* the female reproductive structure in a flowering plant, which may be a single carpel consisting of a stigma, style, and ovary, or a group of carpels that are fused to form a single structure. [from Latin *pistillum*, pestle]

pistol *noun* a small gun held in one hand when fired. [from Old French *pistole*, from Czech]

piston *noun* **1** *Engineering* a cylindrical device, usually closed at one end, that moves up and down in the cylinder of a petrol, diesel, or steam engine, and is driven by the pressure of hot gases or the expansion of steam. The motion of the piston is converted into the rotating motion of the driving wheels by the crankshaft. **2** a sliding valve on a brass wind instrument. [from French, from Italian *pistone*, from *pestare*, to pound]

piston ring a split metal ring fitting into a groove round a piston and forming an airtight seal between it and its containing cylinder.

piston rod in a vehicle engine, a rod attached to the piston, that transfers its motion by means of a crankshaft to the wheels.

pit[1] — *noun* **1** a big deep hole in the ground. **2** a coalmine. **3** a cavity sunk into the ground from which to inspect vehicle engines, etc. **4** *Motor Racing* any of a set of compartments beside a racetrack, where vehicles can refuel, etc. **5** an enclosure in which fighting animals or birds are put. **6** the floor of the auditorium in a theatre, or the people sitting there. **7** (*also* **orchestra pit**) a sunken area in front of a stage, in which an orchestra is positioned. **8** *Anat.* a hollow, indentation, or depression, eg (**pit of the stomach**) the small hollow below the breastbone. **9** a scar left by a smallpox or acne pustule. **10** *old use* (**the pit**) hell. **11** (**the pits**) *slang* an awful or intolerable situation. — *verb* (**pitted, pitting**) **1** to set or match in competition or opposition. **2** to mark by scars and holes: *pitted with craters*. **3** to put in a pit. [from Anglo-Saxon *pytt*, from Latin *puteus*, well]

- - - - - - - - - - - - - - - - - - - -

▣ *noun* **1** hole, cavity, crater, pothole, gulf, chasm, abyss, excavation, trench, ditch, hollow, depression, indentation. **2** mine, coalmine, dent. *verb* **2** pockmark, blemish, scar, dent, pothole.

- - - - - - - - - - - - - - - - - - - -

pit[2] — *noun North Amer., esp. US* the stone in a peach, apricot, plum, etc. — *verb* (**pitted, pitting**) to remove the stone from. [from Dutch *pit*, kernel]

pit-a-pat — *noun* a noise of pattering. — *adv.* with this noise. [imitative]

pit bull terrier a large breed of bull terrier originally developed for dogfighting.

pitch[1] — *verb* **1** to set up (a tent or camp). **2** to throw or fling. **3** *intrans.* to fall heavily forward. **4** *intrans.*, *said of a ship* to plunge and lift alternately at bow and stern. **5** *trans.*, *intrans.*, *said of a roof* to slope: *pitched at a steep angle*. **6** to give a particular musical pitch to (a note) in singing or playing, or to set (a song, etc) at a higher or lower level within a possible range: *pitched too high for me*. **7** to

choose a level, eg of difficulty, sophistication, etc at which to present (a talk, etc). **8a** *Cricket* to bowl (the ball) so that it lands where the batsman can hit it. **b** *Golf* to hit (the ball) high and gently, so that it stays where it is on landing. **c** *trans.*, *intrans.*, *Baseball*, *said of the pitcher* to throw to the batter overarm or underarm. — *noun* **1** the field or area of play in any of several sports. **2** an act or style of pitching or throwing. **3** a degree of intensity; a level: *reached such a pitch.* **4** the angle of steepness of a slope. **5** *Mus.* the degree of highness or lowness of a note that results from the frequency of the vibrations producing it. **6** a street trader's station. **7** a line in sales talk, especially one often made use of. **8** the distance between points on a saw, or between threads on a screw. **9** the plunging and rising motion of a ship. — **pitch in** *colloq.* **1** to begin enthusiastically. **2** to join in; to make a contribution. **pitch into someone** *colloq.* to rebuke or blame them angrily. [from Middle English *picchen*, to throw, put up]

- - - - - - - - - - - - - - - - - - - -

▣ *verb* **1** set up, put up, erect, station. **2** throw, fling, toss, *colloq.* chuck, lob, bowl, hurl, heave, *colloq.* sling, fire, launch. **3** fall headlong, plunge, dive, tumble. **4** lurch, roll, wallow. **7** aim, direct. *noun* **1** ground, field, playing-field, arena, stadium. **4** gradient, incline, slope, tilt, angle, degree, steepness. **5** sound, tone, level, timbre, modulation, frequency.

- - - - - - - - - - - - - - - - - - - -

pitch[2] — *noun* **1** a thick black sticky substance obtained from tar, used for filling ships' seams, etc. **2** any of various bituminous or resinous substances. **3** resin from certain pine trees. — *verb* to coat or treat with pitch. [from Anglo-Saxon *pic*]

pitch-black or **pitch-dark** *adj.* utterly, intensely, or unrelievedly black or dark.

pitchblende /'pɪtʃblend/ *noun Geol.* a radioactive glossy brown or black form of uraninite, a mineral variety of uranium(IV) oxide. It is the main ore of uranium and radium. [from German *Pechblende*]

pitched battle 1 a battle between armies that are prepared and drawn up in readiness. **2** a fierce dispute.

pitched roof a sloping roof as distinct from a flat one.

pitcher[1] *noun* a large earthenware jug with one or two handles. [from Old French *pichier*, from Latin *bicarium*, beaker]

pitcher[2] *noun Baseball* the player who throws the ball to the batter to hit.

pitcher plant any of various insectivorous plants belonging to the genera *Nepenthes* or *Sarracenia*, so called because it has modified leaves resembling pitchers that collect rainwater, in which insects attracted to the plant by its colouring and nectar are trapped and drowned.

pitchfork *noun* a long-handled fork with two or three sharp prongs, for tossing hay.

piteous *adj.* rousing one's pity; moving, poignant, heart-rending or pathetic.

- - - - - - - - - - - - - - - - - - - -

▣ moving, poignant, heart-rending, pathetic, pitiful, pitiable, touching, distressing, plaintive, mournful, sad, sorrowful, woeful, wretched.

- - - - - - - - - - - - - - - - - - - -

pitfall *noun* a hidden danger, unsuspected hazard, or unforeseen difficulty.

- - - - - - - - - - - - - - - - - - - -

▣ danger, hazard, peril, trap, snare, stumbling-block, catch, snag, drawback, difficulty.

- - - - - - - - - - - - - - - - - - - -

pith *noun* **1** *Bot.* the soft white tissue lying beneath the rind of many citrus fruits, eg orange. **2** *Bot.* in the stem of many plants, a central cylinder of generally soft tissue, composed of parenchyma cells, that is surrounded by vascular (conducting) tissue in dicotyledonous species. **3** the most important part of an argument, etc. **4** substance, forcefulness, or vigour as a quality in writing, etc. [from Anglo-Saxon *pitha*]

3 gist, meat, essence, crux, nub, heart, core, kernel, matter, marrow, importance, significance. **4** consequence, substance, forcefulness, vigour, moment, weight, value.

pithead *noun* the entrance to a mineshaft and the machinery round it.

pith helmet a large light rigid hat made from the pith of the sola plant, worn especially formerly in the tropics to protect the head from the sun.

pithy *adj.* (**pithier, pithiest**) *said of a saying, comment, etc* brief, forceful, and to the point.

brief, forceful, succinct, concise, compact, cogent, trenchant, telling, terse, short, pointed.

wordy, verbose.

pitiable *adj.* **1** arousing pity. **2** miserably inadequate; contemptible.

pitiful *adj.* **1** arousing pity; wretched or pathetic. **2** sadly inadequate or ineffective.

1 piteous, distressing, heart-rending, pathetic, pitiable, sad, miserable, doleful, mournful, wretched, poor, sorry. **2** inadequate, ineffective, woeful, inadequate, hopeless, *colloq.* pathetic, insignificant, poor, sorry, miserable, wretched, paltry, worthless, deplorable, lamentable.

pitiless *adj.* showing no pity; merciless, cruel or relentless.

merciless, cruel, relentless, cold-hearted, unsympathetic, unfeeling, uncaring, hard-hearted, callous, inhuman, brutal, cold-blooded, ruthless, unremitting, inexorable, harsh.

merciful, compassionate, kind, gentle.

piton /ˈpiːtɒn/ *noun Mountaineering* a metal peg or spike with an eye for passing a rope through, hammered into a rockface as an aid to climbers. [from French *piton*, ring-bolt]

pitstop *noun* a pause made at a refuelling pit by a racing driver.

pitta /ˈpɪtə/ *noun* **1** a Middle-Eastern slightly leavened bread, usually baked in hollow ovals that can be filled with other foods. **2** one such oval. [from Modern Greek *pitta*, cake, pie]

pittance *noun* a meagre allowance or wage. [from Old French *pietance*, ration]

colloq. chickenfeed, *slang* peanuts, trifle, modicum, crumb, drop (in the ocean).

pitter-patter — *noun* the sound of pattering. — *adv.* with this sound. [imitative]

pituitary /pɪˈtjuːɪtərɪ/ — *noun* (PL. **pituitaries**) (*in full pituitary gland*) *Physiol.* in vertebrates, a gland at the base of the brain that is responsible for the production of a number of important hormones, many of which control the activity of other glands. It therefore has a central role in the control of growth, sexual development, reproduction, water balance, adrenaline production, and general metabolism. — *adj.* relating to this gland. [from Latin *pituita*, phlegm, rheum]

pit viper a viper of the subfamily Crotalinae, sometimes treated as a separate family (Crotalidae), the remaining vipers being called true vipers.

pity — *noun* **1** a feeling of sorrow for the troubles and sufferings of others; compassion. **2** a cause of sorrow or regret. — *verb* (**pities, pitied**) to feel or show pity for. — **for pity's sake** an expression of earnest entreaty or of exasperation. **have** or **take pity on someone** to feel or show pity for them, especially in some practical way. **more's the pity** *colloq.* a formula of regret: unfortunately; I'm sor-

ry to say. [from Old French *pite*, from Latin *pietas*, piety, dutifulness]

noun **1** sympathy, compassion, commiseration, understanding, sorrow, regret, fellow feeling, kindness, tenderness, mercy, forbearance. **2** shame, misfortune, bad luck. *verb* feel sorry for, feel for, sympathize with, commiserate with, grieve for, weep for.

noun **1** hard-heartedness, scorn, cruelty.

pitying *adj.* compassionate.

pityingly *adv.* with pity, compassionately.

pivot /ˈpɪvət/ — *noun* **1** a central pin, spindle, or shaft round which something turns, swivels, or revolves. **2** someone or something crucial, on which everyone or everything else depends. — *verb intrans.* (**pivoted, pivoting**) (*often* **pivot on something**) **1** to turn, swivel, or revolve: *pivot on one's heel.* **2** to depend. [from French *pivot*]

noun **1** axis, hinge, axle, spindle, kingpin, linchpin, swivel. **2** hub, kingpin, linchpin, focal point, centre, heart. *verb* **1** swivel, turn, revolve, spin, rotate, swing. **2** depend, hinge, hang, lie, rely.

pivotal *adj.* **1** constructed as or acting like a pivot. **2** crucially important; critical.

pix see PIC.

pixel *noun Electron.* the smallest element of the image displayed on a computer or television screen, consisting of a single dot which may be illuminated (on) or dark (off). The resolution of the screen is determined by the number of pixels available. [a contraction of *picture element*]

pixie or **pixy** *noun* (PL. **pixies**) a kind of fairy, traditionally with mischievous tendencies. [originally dialect]

pizza /ˈpiːtsə/ *noun* a circle of dough spread with cheese, tomatoes, etc and baked, made originally in Italy. [Italian]

pizzazz or **pizazz** or **pzazz** /pəˈzaz/ *noun colloq.* a quality that is a combination of boldness, vigour, dash and flamboyance. [thought to have been coined in the 1930s by Diana Vreeland, US fashion editor]

pizzeria /piːtsəˈriːə/ *noun* a restaurant specializing in pizzas. [from Italian *pizzeria*, from *pizza*]

pizzicato /pɪtsɪˈkɑːtoʊ/ *adj., adv., said of music for stringed instruments* played using the fingers to pluck the strings. [from Italian *pizzicato*, twitched]

Pk *abbrev., used in street names* Park.

Pl *abbrev., used in street names* Place.

pl or **pl.** *abbrev.* plural.

placard /ˈplakɑːd/ — *noun* a board or stiff card bearing a notice, advertisement, slogan, message of protest, etc, carried or displayed in public. — *verb* **1** to put placards on (a wall, etc). **2** to announce (a forthcoming event, etc) by placard. [from Old French *placard*]

noun poster, bill, notice, sign, advertisement.

placate *verb* to pacify or appease (an angry person, etc). [from Latin *placere*, to appease]

pacify, appease, mollify, conciliate, calm, assuage, soothe, lull, quiet.

anger, enrage, incense, infuriate.

placation *noun* placating.

placatory *adj.* that placates.

place — *noun* **1** an area, region, district, locality, etc; a country, city, town, village, building, room, etc. **2** *colloq.* one's home or lodging. **3** (*often in compounds*) somewhere with a certain association or function: *one's birthplace/a hiding-place.* **4** a seat or space, eg at table: *lay three places.* **5** an area on the surface of something, eg the body: *point to the sore place.* **6** something's or someone's customary position: *put it back in its place*. **7** a point reached, eg in a conversation, narrative, series of developments, etc: *a good place to stop*. **8** a point in a book, etc, especially where one stopped reading: *made me lose my place*. **9** a position within an order, eg of competitors in a contest, a set of priorities, etc: *finished in third place/lost his place in the queue/lets her family take second place*. **10** social or political rank: *know/keep one's place/corruption in high places*. **11** a vacancy at an institution, on a committee, in a firm, etc: *gain a university place*. **12** one's role, function, duty, etc: *not my place to tell him*. **13** a useful role: *there's a place for judicious lying*. **14** *often used in street names* an open square, or row of houses: *the market place*. **15** *Maths*. the position of a number in a series, especially of decimals after the point. — *verb* **1** to put. **2** to submit: *place an order/place an advertisement*. **3** to find a place, home, job, publisher, etc for. **4** to assign final positions to (contestants, etc): *was placed fourth*. **5** to identify or categorize: *a familiar voice that I couldn't quite place*. — **all over the place** in disorder or confusion. **be placed 1** *Racing, Athletics* to finish as one of the first three. **2** to be in a position to do something: *was well placed to influence the decision*. **fall into place** to become clear; to make sense. **give place to someone** or **something** to make way for them or yield to them. **go places** *colloq*. **1** to travel. **2** to be successful. **in the first place** in any event; anyway: *I never liked it in the first place*. **in the first, second,** etc **place** used to introduce successive points. **in place** in the correct position. **in place of ...** instead of ... **in places** here and there. **in your,** etc **place** if I were you, etc. **out of place 1** not in the correct position. **2** inappropriate. **put someone in his** or **her place** to humble them as they deserve. **take place** to happen, occur, be held, etc. **take the place of someone** or **something** to replace or supersede them. [from Anglo-Saxon *plæce* and Old French *place*, open place or street]

⊟ *noun* **1** area, region, district, locality, neighbourhood, country, city, town, village, building, property. **2** home, house, flat, apartment, lodging, dwelling, residence, *slang* pad. **3** site, locale, venue, location, situation, position. **5** spot, area, region, point. **6** home, position. **10** rank, situation, status. **11** position, post. *verb* **1** put, set, plant, fix, position, locate, situate, rest, settle, lay, stand, deposit, leave. **2** submit, tender, put in. **in place of** instead of, in lieu of, as a replacement for, as a substitute for, as an alternative to. **out of place 2** inappropriate, unsuitable, unfitting, unbecoming, unseemly. **take place** happen, occur, come about, be held.

placebo /plə'si:boʊ/ *noun* (PL. **placebos**) *Medicine* a substance that is administered as a drug but has no medicinal content, either given to a patient for its reassuring and therefore beneficial effect (the *placebo effect*), or used in a clinical trial of a real drug, in which participants who have been given a placebo (without their knowledge) serve as untreated control subjects for comparison with those given the drug. [from Latin *placebo*, I shall please]

place card a small card at someone's place at table, bearing his or her name.

place kick *Rugby* a kick made with the ball placed ready on the ground.

placeman *noun colloq*. someone appointed by a government, etc to a committee or organization, and expected to represent the appointer's opinion.

place mat a table mat for use in a place setting.

placement *noun* **1** the act or process of placing or positioning. **2** the finding of a job or home for someone. **3** a temporary job providing work experience, especially for someone on a training course.

place-name *noun* the name of a town, village, hill, lake, etc.

placenta /plə'sentə/ *noun* (PL. **placentae, placentas**) **1** *Anat*. in mammals, a disc-shaped organ attached to the lining of the uterus (womb) during pregnancy, and to which the fetus is linked by the umbilical cord. It provides

the embryo with nutrients and oxygen, secretes hormones that maintain the pregnancy, and removes waste products. **2** *Bot*. in seed-bearing plants, that part of the ovary to which the ovules are attached. [from Latin *placenta*, flat cake]

place of work same as WORKPLACE.

place setting see SETTING.

placid *adj*. calm; tranquil. [from Latin *placidus*, from *placere*, to please]

⊟ calm, tranquil, composed, unruffled, untroubled, serene, still, quiet, peaceful, restful, cool, self-possessed, level-headed, imperturbable, mild, gentle, equable, even-tempered.
🔄 excitable, agitated, disturbed.

placidity *noun* being placid.

plagiarism /'pleɪdʒərɪzm/ *noun* plagiarizing.

plagiarist /'pleɪdʒərɪst/ *noun* a person who plagiarizes.

plagiarize or **plagiarise** /'pleɪdʒəraɪz/ *verb trans*. to copy (ideas, passages of text, etc) from someone else's work, and use them as if they were one's own. [from Latin *plagiarius*, kidnapper]

⊟ crib, lift, pirate, infringe copyright, poach, steal, appropriate, borrow, copy, reproduce, counterfeit.

plague — *noun* **1** *Medicine* any of several epidemic diseases with a high mortality rate; specifically, an infectious epidemic disease of rats and other rodents, caused by the bacterium *Yersinia pestis*, and transmitted to humans by flea bites. **2** an overwhelming intrusion by something unwelcome: *a plague of tourists*. **3** *colloq*. a nuisance. — *verb* **1** to afflict: *plagued by headaches*. **2** to pester; to annoy continually. [from Middle English *plage*, from Latin *plaga*, blow, disaster, pestilence]

⊟ *noun* **1** pestilence, epidemic, disease, infection, contagion. **2** infestation, influx. **3** nuisance, annoyance, trial, affliction, curse, scourge. *verb* **1** afflict, torment, torture, persecute, haunt, bedevil. **2** annoy, vex, bother, disturb, trouble, distress, upset, pester, harass, hound.

plaice *noun* (PL. **plaice**) a flatfish related to the dab, flounder, and sole, found in shallow coastal waters of the northern oceans, and one of the most important food fish. [from Old French *plais*, from Latin *platessa*, flatfish]

plaid *noun* **1** tartan cloth. **2** *Hist*. a long piece of this worn over the shoulder with a kilt. [from Gaelic *plaide*, blanket]

plain — *adj*. **1** all of one colour; unpatterned; undecorated. **2** simple; unsophisticated; without improvement: *plain food/not Dr or Professor, just plain Mr*. **3** obvious; clear. **4** straightforward; direct: *plain language/plain dealing*. **5** frank; open. **6** *said of a person* lacking beauty. **7** sheer: *plain selfishness*. — *noun* **1** a large area of relatively smooth flat land without significant hills or valleys. **2** *Knitting* the simpler of two basic stitches, with the wool passed round the front of the needle. See also PURL. — *adv*. utterly; quite: *plain ridiculous*. [from Old French, from Latin *planus*, level]

⊟ *adj*. **1** unpatterned, undecorated, unvariegated, uncoloured, self-coloured. **2** simple, ordinary, basic, unsophisticated, unpretentious, modest, unadorned, unelaborate, restrained. **3** obvious, clear, evident, patent, understandable, apparent, visible, unmistakable. **4** straightforward, direct, blunt, outspoken, forthright, unambiguous, plain-spoken. **5** frank, candid, open, honest, truthful. **6** unattractive, ugly, unprepossessing, unlovely. *noun* **1** grassland, prairie, steppe, lowland, flat, plateau, tableland.
🔄 *adj*. **1** patterned. **2** fancy, elaborate. **3** unclear, obscure. **4, 5** devious, deceitful. **6** attractive, good-looking, beautiful.

plain chocolate dark chocolate made without milk.

plain clothes ordinary clothes worn by police detectives on duty, as distinct from a uniform.

plain-clothes or **plain-clothed** *adj.* wearing ordinary clothes, not uniformed.

plain flour flour containing no raising agent.

plainly *adv.* **1** in a plain way. **2** clearly.

plainness *noun* being plain.

plain sailing 1 easy, unimpeded progress. **2** *Naut.* sailing in unobstructed waters.

plainsong or **plainchant** *noun* in the medieval Church, music for unaccompanied voices, sung in unison.

plain-spoken *adj.* frank to the point of bluntness.

plaint *noun* **1** *poetic* an expression of woe; a lamentation. **2** *Legal* a written statement of grievance against someone, submitted to a court of law. [from Old French, from Latin *planctus*, a blow]

plaintiff *noun* a person who brings a case against someone else in a court of law. See also DEFENDANT. [from Old French *plaintif*, complaining]

plaintive *adj.* mournful-sounding; sad; wistful. [from Old French *plaintif*]

. . . .

▤ doleful, mournful, sad, wistful, sorrowful, melancholy, grief-stricken, piteous, heart-rending.

. . . .

plait /plat/ — *verb* to arrange (especially hair) by interweaving three or more lengths. — *noun* a length of hair or other material so interwoven. [from Old French *pleit*, from Latin *plicare*, to fold]

plan — *noun* **1** a thought-out arrangement or method for doing something. **2** (*usually* **plans**) intentions. **3** a sketch, outline, scheme, or set of guidelines. **4** a drawing or diagram of a floor of a house, the streets of a town, etc done as though from above. — *verb* (**planned, planning**) **1** to devise a scheme for. **2** *intrans.* to prepare; to make plans: *plan ahead.* **3** (**plan something** or **plan for something**) to make preparations or arrangements for it. **4** (**plan something** or **plan on something**) to intend it. **5** (**not plan on** or **for something**) not to reckon on or allow for it; to be surprised or embarrassed by it: *had not planned on all of them coming.* **6** to draw up plans for; to design. [from French *plan*, ground plan, from Latin *planus*, flat]

. . . .

▤ *noun* **1** proposal, proposition, idea, suggestion, project, scheme, plot. **3** outline, system, method, scheme, procedure, strategy, programme, schedule, scenario. **4** blueprint, diagram, drawing, chart, map, layout, sketch, representation, design. *verb* **1**, **6** devise, design, invent, contrive, formulate, frame, draft, outline. **2** prepare, scheme, plot. **3** prepare, organize, arrange. **4** intend, propose, contemplate, envisage.

. . . .

Planck's constant *Physics* (SYMBOL **h**) a fundamental constant, equal to 6.626×10^{-34} joule seconds, that relates the energy E of a quantum of light to its frequency v by the equation $E = hv$. [named after the German physicist Max Planck]

plane[1] *noun* an aeroplane. [a shortening of AEROPLANE]

plane[2] — *noun* **1** *Maths.* a flat surface, either real or imaginary, such that a straight line joining any two points lies entirely on it. **2** a level surface. **3** a level or standard: *on a higher intellectual plane.* — *adj.* **1** flat; level. **2** *Maths.* lying in one plane: *a plane figure/plane geometry.* — *verb intrans.* **1** *said of a boat* to skim over the surface of the water. **2** *said of a bird* to wheel or soar with wings motionless. [from Latin *planum*, level surface]

plane[3] — *noun* a carpenter's tool for smoothing wood by shaving away unevennesses. — *verb* **1** (*also* **plane something down**) to smooth a surface, especially wood, with a plane. **2** (**plane something off** or **away**) to remove it from a surface with a plane. [from French *plane*, from Latin *planare*, to smooth]

plane[4] *noun* **1** a tree with large lobed leaves and flaking bark. **2** *Scot.* the sycamore tree. [from French *plane*, from Greek *platanos*]

plane angle *Geom.* the two-dimensional angle formed by two lines in a plane figure, such as a polygon.

planet /ˈplanɪt/ *noun* **1** a celestial body, in orbit around the Sun or another star, which has too small a mass to become a star itself, and is not luminous but shines by reflecting light from the star around which it revolves. **2** one of nine such bodies (Mercury, Venus, Earth, Mars, Jupiter, Saturn, Uranus, Neptune, and Pluto) that revolve around the Sun in the Solar System. [from French *planète*, from Greek *planetes*, wanderer]

Planets within the Earth's solar system (nearest the Sun shown first) are: Mercury, Venus, Earth, Mars, Jupiter, Saturn, Uranus, Neptune, Pluto.

planetarium /planəˈtɛərɪəm/ *noun* (PL. **planetaria, planetariums**) **1** a special projector by means of which the positions and movements of stars and planets can be projected on to a hemispherical domed ceiling in order to simulate the appearance of the night sky to an audience seated below. **2** the building that houses such a projector. [from Latin *planetarius*, planetary]

planetary /ˈplanɪtərɪ/ *adj.* **1** relating to planets. **2** consisting of or produced by planets. **3** *Astrol.* under the influence of a planet. **4** erratic. **5** revolving in an orbit.

planetology *noun* *Geol.* the scientific study of the planets, their natural satellites, and the interplanetary material of the solar system, including the asteroids and meteors.

plangency /ˈplandʒənsɪ/ *noun* being plangent.

plangent /ˈplandʒənt/ *adj.*, *said of a sound* deep, ringing, and mournful. [from Latin *plangere*, to beat]

planimeter /pləˈnɪmɪtə(r)/ *noun* a mathematical instrument for measuring the area of a plane figure, eg an indicator diagram. A tracing point on an arm is moved round the closed curve, whose area is then given to scale by the revolutions of a small wheel supporting the arm. [from Latin *planus*, level]

plank — *noun* **1** a long flat piece of timber. **2** any of the policies forming the platform or programme of a political party. — *verb* **1** to fit or cover with planks. **2** (**plank something down**) *colloq.* to put it down roughly or noisily. — **walk the plank** to be made to walk blindfold along a plank projecting over a ship's side until one falls into the sea and drowns. [from Latin *planca*, board]

planking *noun* planks, or a surface, etc constructed of them.

plankton *pl. noun* (SING. **plankter**) *Biol.* microscopic animals (*zooplankton*) and plants (*phytoplankton*) that float or drift with the current in the surface waters of seas and lakes and form the basis of all marine food chains. [from Greek *planktos*, wandering]

planner *noun* **1** someone who draws up plans or designs: *a town planner.* **2** a wall calendar showing the whole year, on which holidays, etc can be marked.

planning *noun* control exercised by a local authority over the erection and alteration of buildings and use of land.

planning permission *Brit.* permission required from a local authority to erect or convert a building or to change the use to which a building or piece of land is put.

planographic printing 'flat surface' printing using lithography. The image is drawn on a litho-stone or flexible metal plate of zinc or aluminium, from which a positive image is reproduced.

plant — *noun* **1** any living organism (extant or extinct) belonging to the kingdom Plantae, and characterized by its ability to manufacture carbohydrates by the process of photosynthesis. **2** a relatively small organism of this type, eg a herb or shrub as opposed to a tree. **3** the buildings, equipment, and machinery used in manufacturing or production industries, eg a factory or nuclear power station. **4** *colloq.* something deliberately placed for others to find and be misled by. — *verb* **1** to put (seeds or plants) into the ground to grow. **2** to put plants or seeds into (ground, a garden, bed, etc). **3** to introduce (an idea, doubt, etc) into someone's mind. **4** to place firmly. **5 (plant something on someone)** to give them a kiss or blow. **6** to post (someone) as a spy, in an office, factory, etc. **7** *colloq.* to place (something) deliberately so as to mislead the finder, eg as a means of incriminating an innocent person. **8** to establish (a colony, etc). [from Latin *planta*, shoot, sprig]

◼ *noun* **3** building(s) factory, works, foundry, mill, shop, yard, workshop. *equipment* machinery, apparatus, gear. *verb* **1** sow, bury, transplant. **2** sow, seed. **3** introduce, put, lodge, root. **4** place, put, set, fix, insert, lodge, root. **8** settle, found, establish.

Plants include: annual, biennial, perennial, herbaceous plant, evergreen, succulent, cultivar, hybrid, house plant, pot plant; flower, herb, shrub, bush, tree, vegetable, grass, vine, weed, cereal, wild flower, airplant, water-plant, cactus, fern, moss, algae, lichen, fungus; bulb, corm, seedling, sapling, bush, climber. *See also* **flower; shrub**.

Plantagenet *noun* the name given by historians to the royal dynasty in England from Henry II to Richard II (1154–1399), then continued until 1485 by the two rival houses of Lancaster and York. The dynasty was allegedly named after the sprig of broom (Old French, *plante genêt*) that Henry II's father Geoffrey, Count of Anjou, sported in his cap.

plantain[1] *noun* a tropical green-skinned fruit like a large banana. [from Spanish *plátano*]

plantain[2] *noun* a plant that presses its leaves close to the ground, having a flower on a tall slender stem. [from Latin *plantago*, from *planta*, sole of the foot]

plantation *noun* **1** an estate, especially in the tropics, that specializes in the large-scale production of a single cash crop, eg tea, coffee, cotton, or rubber. **2** an area of land planted with a certain kind of tree for commercial purposes, eg conifer plantation. **3** *Hist.* a colony. [from Latin *plantatio*, a planting]

planter *noun* **1** the owner or manager of a plantation. **2** a device for planting bulbs, etc. **3** a container for house plants.

plantigrade *adj. Zool.* denoting animals that walk with the entire lower surface of the foot in contact with the ground, including humans, bears, and many other mammals. [from Latin *planta*, sole + *gradi*, to walk]

plant pot a pot for growing a plant.

plaque /plɑːk, plak/ *noun* **1** a commemorative inscribed tablet fixed to or set into a wall. **2** a wall ornament made of pottery, etc. **3** *Dentistry* a thin layer of food debris, bacteria, and calcium salts that forms on the surface of teeth. **4** *Medicine* a raised area of scar tissue on a body part or surface. [from French *plaque*]

plasma *noun* **1** the colourless liquid component of blood or lymph, in which the blood cells are suspended. **2** *Physics* a gas that has been heated to a very high temperature so that most of its atoms or molecules are broken down into approximately equal numbers of free electrons and positive ions. [from Greek *plasma*, something moulded]

plasma membrane *Biol.* a thin membrane, composed mainly of lipid and protein, that surrounds the cytoplasm of all living cells, as well as the organelles (eg the nucleus) within cells. It acts as a filter, only allowing certain substances to pass across it in either direction. Also called CELL MEMBRANE.

plasmid *noun Biol.* a small circular loop of DNA that moves from one bacterium to another, transferring genetic information and often endowing its host with useful characteristics, eg resistance to antibiotics.

Plasmodium /plaz'moʊdɪəm/ *noun* any of various species of parasitic protozoan that carry the micro-organisms which cause malaria in humans. [related to PLASMA]

plaster — *noun* **1** a material consisting of lime, sand, and water, that is applied to walls when soft and dries to form a hard smooth surface. **2** plaster of Paris. **3** (*also* **sticking-plaster**) a piece of sticky tape, usually with a dressing attached, for protecting a wound. — *verb* (**plastered, plastering**) **1** to apply plaster to (walls). **2** *colloq.* to coat or spread thickly: *plaster gel on one's hair/plaster one's hair with gel*. **3** to fix with some wet or sticky substance: *hair plastered to his skull*. **4** to cover liberally: *walls plastered with photos*. [from Latin *plastrum*, from Greek *emplastron*, salve]

◼ *noun* **1** stucco. *verb* **2** coat, spread, smear, cover, daub.

plasterboard *noun* board consisting of a layer of plaster between two layers of fibreboard, used for making partitions, ceilings, etc.

plastered *adj. colloq.* drunk.

plasterer *noun* a person who applies plaster to walls, ceilings, etc.

plaster of Paris powdered gypsum, mixed with water to make a material that dries hard, used for sculpting and for making casts for broken limbs.

plastic — *noun* **1** any of a large number of synthetic materials that can be moulded by heat and/or pressure into a rigid or semi-rigid shape that is retained when the heat and pressure are removed. **2** *colloq.* a credit card, or credit cards collectively: *do you have any plastic?* — *adj.* **1** made of plastic. **2** easily moulded or shaped; pliant. **3** easily influenced. **4** *derog.* artificial; lacking genuine substance. **5** *said of money* in the form of, or funded by, a credit card. **6** relating to sculpture and modelling. [from Greek *plastikos*, moulded, from *plassein*, to mould]

◼ *adj.* **1** pliant, pliable, flexible, supple, malleable, mouldable, ductile, soft. **3** impressionable, malleable, receptive.

◼ *adj.* **2** rigid, inflexible.

plastic arts (**the plastic arts**) the sculptural arts.

plastic bomb a bomb made with plastic explosive.

plastic bullet a small solid plastic cylinder fired by the police to disperse riots.

plastic explosive an explosive substance resembling putty that can be moulded by hand, eg Semtex.

Plasticine /ˈplastɪsiːn/ *noun trademark* a non-hardening modelling material, used especially by children.

plasticity /plaˈstɪsɪtɪ/ *noun* being plastic.

plasticizer or **plasticiser** *noun Chem.* any substance that is added to a rigid synthetic resin or plastic in order to make it flexible and so more easily workable.

plastic surgeon a surgeon who specializes in plastic surgery.

plastic surgery *Medicine* the branch of surgery concerned with the repair, restoration, or reconstruction of deformed or damaged tissue or body parts, or the replacement of missing parts. It mainly involves the treatment of burns and other injuries, and the correction of congenital deformities, eg cleft palate, but also includes cosmetic surgery, eg facelifts.

plastid *noun Bot.* any of various highly specialized membrane-bound structures found within the cytoplasm of plant cells, eg chloroplasts (which are the site of photosynthesis), and amyloplasts (which store starch). [from Greek *plastis, -idos*]

plate — *noun* **1** a shallow dish, especially of earthenware or porcelain, for serving food on. **2** the amount held by this; a plateful. **3** a shallow vessel in which to take the collection in church. **4** a sheet of metal, glass or other rigid material. **5** a flat piece of metal, plastic, etc inscribed with a name, etc. **6** gold and silver vessels or cutlery; a gold or silver cup as the prize in a horse race, etc. **7** a thin coating of gold, silver, or tin applied to a base metal. **8** an illustration on glossy paper in a book. **9** *Photog.* a sheet of glass prepared with a light-sensitive coating for receiving an image. **10** a sheet of metal with an image engraved on it, or a print taken from it. **11** any of various surfaces set up with type ready for printing. **12** a moulded plastic fitting for the mouth with false teeth attached; a denture. **13** any of the rigid sections that make up the earth's crust. **14** *Anat.* a thin flat piece of bone or horn. — *verb* **1** to coat (a base metal) with a thin layer of a precious one. **2** to cover with metal plates. — **have a lot on one's plate** *colloq.* have a great deal of work, commitments, etc. **on a plate** *colloq.* presented to one without one's having to make the least effort. [from Old French *plate*, something flat]

. . . .

◼ *noun* **1** dish, platter, salver. **2** plateful, helping, serving, portion. **4** sheet, pane, panel. **5** plaque. **8** illustration, picture, print, lithograph. *verb* **1** coat, cover, overlay, veneer, laminate, electroplate, anodize, galvanize, platinize, gild, silver, tin.

. . . .

plateau / ˈplatoʊ, plaˈtoʊ/ *noun* (PL. **plateaux, plateaus**) **1** an extensive area of relatively flat high land, usually bounded by steep sides, common in limestone areas. **2** a stable, unvarying condition of prices, etc after a rise. [from French, from Old French *platel*, something flat]

plateful *noun* (PL. **platefuls**) **1** the amount a plate will hold. **2** (*usually* **platefuls**) *colloq.* a great deal; a lot.

plate glass glass made in tough sheets for shop windows, mirrors, etc.

platelayer *noun* a person who lays and repairs railway lines.

platelet *noun Anat.* in mammalian blood, any of the small disc-shaped cell fragments, without nuclei, that are responsible for starting the formation of a blood clot when bleeding occurs. [a diminutive of PLATE]

platen / ˈplatn/ *noun* **1** a plate in some printing-presses that pushes the paper against the type. **2** the roller of a typewriter. [from Old French *platine*]

plate tectonics *Geol.* a geological theory, developed in the late 1960s, according to which the Earth's crust is composed of a small number of large plates of solid rock, whose movements in relation to each other are responsible for continental drift.

platform *noun* **1** a raised floor for speakers, performers, etc. **2** the raised walkway alongside the track at a railway station, giving access to trains. **3** a floating installation moored to the sea bed, for oil-drilling, marine research, etc. **4** an open step at the back of some, especially older, buses, for passengers getting on or off. **5** a thick rigid sole for a shoe. **6** the publicly declared principles and intentions of a political party, forming the basis of its policies. **7** any situation giving one access to an audience, that one can exploit to promote one's views. **8** *Comput.* the hardware for a system, which determines the kind of software it can run. [from Old French *platte forme*, flat figure]

. . . .

◼ **1** stage, podium, dais, rostrum, stand. **6** policy, party line, principles, tenets, manifesto, programme, objectives.

. . . .

plating *noun* same as PLATE *noun* 7.

platinum / ˈplatɪnəm/ *noun Chem.* (SYMBOL **Pt**, ATOMIC NUMBER **78**) a silvery-white precious metal that does not tarnish or corrode, used as the free metal and in alloys to make jewellery, coins, electrical contacts and resistance wires, electrodes, thermocouples, and surgical instruments.

platinum-blond *adj.*, *said of hair* of a silvery fairness.

platinum blonde a woman with silvery fair hair.

platitude / ˈplatɪtjuːd/ *noun* an empty, unoriginal, or redundant comment, especially made as though it were important. [from French *platitude*, flatness]

. . . .

◼ banality, commonplace, truism, cliché, chestnut.

. . . .

platitudinous / platɪˈtjuːdɪnəs/ *adj.* **1** characterized by or of the nature of a platitude. **2** using platitudes. **3** full of platitudes.

Platonic / pləˈtɒnɪk/ *adj.* **1** relating to the Greek philosopher Plato. **2** (*usually* **platonic**) *said of human love* not in-

volving sexual relations. **3** restricted to theorizing; not involving action.

platonically *adv.* in a platonic way.

Platonic solid *Maths.* any solid whose faces are congruent regular polygons. There are five such solids: the tetrahedron (four faces, each an equilateral triangle); the cube (six faces, each a square); the octahedron (eight faces, each a pentagon); the dodecahedron (12 faces, each a hexagon); and the icosahedron (20 faces, each an equilateral triangle). All five were described by the Greek philosopher Plato, who showed how to construct models of the solids.

platoon / pləˈtuːn/ *noun* **1** *Mil.* a subdivision of a company. **2** a squad of people acting in co-operation. [from French *peloton*, diminutive of *pelote*, ball]

platter *noun* **1** a large flat dish. **2** *North Amer. colloq.* a gramophone record. [from Old French *plater*, from *plat*, plate]

platypus / ˈplatɪpəs/ *noun* (PL. **platypuses**) (*in full* **duck-billed platypus**) an egg-laying amphibious mammal with dense brown fur, a long flattened toothless snout, webbed feet, and a broad flat tail, found in Tasmania and E Australia. [from Greek *platys*, wide + *pous*, foot]

plaudit / ˈplɔːdɪt/ *noun* (*usually* **plaudits**) a commendation; an expression of praise. [from Latin *plaudite*, imperative of *plaudere*, to praise]

plausibility *noun* a plausible quality.

plausible / ˈplɔːzɪbl/ *adj.* **1** *said of an explanation, etc* credible, reasonable, or likely. **2** *said of a person* having a pleasant and persuasive manner; smooth-tongued or glib. [from Latin *plausibilis*, deserving applause]

. . . .

◼ **1** credible, believable, reasonable, likely, logical, possible, probable, convincing, persuasive. **2** smooth-tongued, smooth-talking, glib, convincing, persuasive, credible.
◼ **1** implausible, unlikely, improbable.

. . . .

play — *verb* **1** *intrans.*, *said especially of children* to spend time in recreation. **2** (**play about** or **around with something** or **someone**) to fiddle or meddle with them; to behave irresponsibly towards someone, someone's affections, etc. **3** (**play something** or **play at something**) to take part in a recreative pursuit, game, sport, match, round, etc. **4** (**play someone** or **play against someone**) to compete against them in a game or sport. **5** *intrans.*, *colloq.* to co-operate: *he refuses to play.* **6** to include as a team member: *playing McGuire in goal.* **7** to hit or kick (the ball), deliver (a shot), etc in a sport. **8** *Cards* to use (a card) in the course of a game. **9** to speculate or gamble on (the Stock Exchange, etc). **10** (**play something on someone**) to perpetrate a trick or joke against them. **11** *trans.*, *intrans.* to act or behave in a certain way: *play it cool/not playing fair.* **12** to act (a role) in a play, etc. **13** *trans.*, *intrans.* to perform a role in a play. **14** *trans.*, *intrans.* to perform in (a place). **15** *said of a film, play, etc* being shown or performed publicly: *playing all next week.* **16** *trans.*, *intrans.* to pretend to be: *play the dumb blonde.* **17** to act as: *play host to the delegates.* **18** to perform (music) on an instrument; to perform on (an instrument). **19** to turn on (a radio, tape-recording, etc). **20** *intrans.* **a** *said of recorded music, etc* to be heard from a radio, etc. **b** *said of a radio, etc* to produce sound. **21** (**play over** or **across something**) *said eg of light, facial expression, etc* to flicker over, across, etc. **22** *intrans.*, *said of a fountain* to be in operation. **23** to direct (a hose, etc). **24** to allow (a fish) to tire itself by its struggles to get away. — *noun* **1** recreation; playing games: *children at play.* **2** the playing of a game, performance in a sport, etc: *rain stopped play.* **3** *colloq.* behaviour; conduct: *fair/foul play.* **4** a dramatic piece for the stage, or a performance of it. **5** fun; jest: *said in play.* **6** range; scope: *give full play to the imagination.* **7** freedom of movement; looseness: *too much play in the brake.* **8** action or interaction: *play of sunlight on water/play of emotions.* **9** use: *bring all one's cunning into play.* — **in** or **out of play** *Sport*, *said of a ball* in (or not in) a position where it may be played. **make great play of something** to emphasize it or stress its importance. **make a play for something** to try to get (eg someone's attention). **make play with something** to make effective or over-obvious use of it. **play about** or **around with something** to behave ineffectively or irresponsibly. **play along with someone** to co-operate for the time being; to humour them. **play at something 1** to make a pretence of it, especially in play: *play at being cowboys.* **2** to indulge in it trivially or flippantly: *play at politics.* **3** *ironic* to try to achieve: *what are they playing at?* **play something back** to play a film or sound recording through immediately after making it. **play something down** to represent it as unimportant; to minimize, make light of, or discount it. **play off** to replay a match, etc after a draw. **play one person against another** to set them in rivalry, especially for one's own advantage. **play on something 1** to exploit someone's fears, feelings, sympathies, etc for one's own benefit. **2** to make a pun on it: *played on the two meanings of 'batter'.* **play something out 1** to act out in real life a part, scene, etc that is so predictable that it could have come from a play. **2** (*usually* **be played out**) *colloq.* to be exhausted or over-used. **play up 1** *colloq.* to behave unco-operatively. **2** *colloq.* to cause one pain or discomfort. **3** *colloq.* to function faultily. **4** to try one's hardest in a game, match, etc. **play something up** to highlight it or give prominence to it. **play up to someone** to flatter them; to ingratiate oneself with them. **play with something** to contemplate it: *played with the idea of becoming a writer.* [from Anglo-Saxon *plegan*]

> ▣ *verb* **1** amuse oneself, have fun, enjoy oneself, revel, sport, romp, frolic, caper. **2** *fiddle with* tinker with, toy with, fidget with. *meddle with* meddle with, tamper with, interfere with. *behave irresponsibly towards* trifle with, dally with. **3** participate in, take part in, join in with, compete at. **4** compete against, oppose, vie with, challenge, take on. **12, 13** act, portray, represent, impersonate, perform. **16** act. *noun* **1** recreation, fun, amusement, entertainment, diversion, sport, game, hobby, pastime. **4** drama, tragedy, comedy, farce, show, performance. **7** movement, action, flexibility, give, leeway, latitude, margin, room, space. **play down** minimize, make light of, gloss over, underplay, understate, undervalue, discount, underestimate. **play on 1** exploit, take advantage of, turn to account, profit by, trade on, capitalize on. **play up 1** misbehave. **2** trouble, bother, hurt. **3** malfunction. **play something up 1** exaggerate, highlight, spotlight, accentuate, emphasize, stress.
> ▣ *verb* **1** work. *noun* **1** work. **play down** exaggerate

playable *adj.* **1** *said of a pitch, ground, etc* fit to be played on. **2** *said of a ball* lying where it can be played.

play-act *verb intrans.* to behave in an insincere fashion, disguising one's true feelings or intentions.

play-acting *noun* insincere or misleading behaviour.

playback *noun* a playing back of a sound recording or film.

playbill *noun* a poster advertising a play or show.

playboy *noun* a man of wealth, leisure, and frivolous lifestyle.

> ▣ rake, libertine, philanderer, womanizer, ladies' man.

played out exhausted; lacking energy.

player *noun* **1** a participant in a game or sport. **2** a performer on a musical instrument. **3** *old use* an actor.

> ▣ **1** contestant, competitor, participant, sportsman, sportswoman. **2** musician, instrumentalist, performer, artiste.

player piano a piano fitted with a machinery enabling it to be played automatically.

playfellow *noun* a playmate.

playful *adj.* **1** full of fun; frisky. **2** *said of a remark, etc* humorous.

> ▣ **1** frisky, sportive, ludic, frolicsome, lively, spirited, mischievous, roguish, impish, puckish, kittenish. **2** humorous, tongue in cheek, jesting, teasing.
> ▣ SERIOUS.

playground *noun* **1** an area for children's recreation, especially as part of a school's grounds. **2** a resort for people who take frivolous recreation seriously.

playgroup *noun* a number of children organized into a group for regular supervised play together.

playhouse *noun old use* a theatre.

playing card each of a pack of usually 52 cards used in card games.

playing field a grassy expanse prepared and marked out for playing games.

playmate *noun* one's companion in play.

play-off *noun* a match or game played to resolve a draw or other undecided contest.

play on words a pun or punning.

playpen *noun* a collapsible frame that when erected forms an enclosure inside which a baby may safely play.

playschool *noun* a playgroup, or a school for children between two and five.

plaything *noun* a toy.

playtime *noun* a period for recreation, especially as part of a school timetable.

playwright *noun* an author of plays.

> ▣ dramatist, scriptwriter, screenwriter.

plaza *noun* **1** a large public square or market place especially in a Spanish town. **2** *North Amer.* a shopping centre or complex. [from Spanish *plaza*, a square or market place]

PLC or **plc** *abbrev.* public limited company.

plea *noun* **1** an earnest appeal. **2** a statement made in a court of law by or on behalf of the defendant. **3** an excuse: *refused the invitation on the plea of a headache.* [from Old French *plaid*]

> ▣ **1** appeal, petition, request, entreaty, supplication, prayer, invocation. **3** excuse, explanation, justification, defence, claim.

plead *verb* (PAST TENSE AND PAST PARTICIPLE **pleaded**, *Scot., North Amer., esp. US* **pled**) **1** (*usually* **plead with someone for something**) to appeal earnestly. **2** *intrans.*, *said of an accused person* to state in a court of law that one is guilty or not guilty. **3** (**plead something** or **plead for something**) to argue in defence of it: *plead someone's case.* **4** to give as an excuse: *plead ignorance.* [from Old French *plaidier*]

> ▣ **1** appeal, beg, implore, beseech, entreat, petition, ask, request. **4** assert, maintain, claim, allege.

pleading *adj.* appealing earnestly.

pleadingly *adv.* in a pleading way, with pleading.

pleadings *pl. noun* the formal statements submitted by defendant and plaintiff in a lawsuit.

pleasant *adj.* **1** giving pleasure; enjoyable; agreeable. **2** *said of a person* friendly; affable. [from Old French *plaisant*, from *plaisir*, to please]

> ▣ **1** agreeable, enjoyable, nice, fine, lovely, delightful, charming, congenial, amusing, pleasing, gratifying, satisfying, acceptable, welcome, refreshing. **2** friendly, affable, likable, amiable, good-humoured, cheerful, congenial.

◫ UNPLEASANT, NASTY. **2** unfriendly.

pleasantry /ˈplɛzəntrɪ/ noun (PL. **pleasantries**) **1** (usually **pleasantries**) a remark made for the sake of politeness or friendliness. **2** humour; teasing.

please — verb **1** trans., intrans. to give satisfaction, pleasure, or enjoyment; to be agreeable to. **2** (with it as subject) to be the inclination of: if it should please you to join us. **3** trans., intrans. to choose; to like: do what/as you please. — adv. used politely to accompany a request, order, acceptance of an offer, protest, a call for attention, etc. — **if you please 1** old use please. **2** ironic of all things: is engaged to a baronet, if you please. **please oneself** to do as one likes. [from Old French plaisir]

◫ verb **1** delight, charm, captivate, entertain, amuse, cheer, gladden, humour, indulge, gratify, satisfy, content. **2** suit. **3** choose, like, want, will, wish, desire, prefer, think fit.
◫ verb **1** displease, annoy, anger, sadden.

pleased adj. **1** (**pleased about** or **with someone** or **something**) happy; satisfied. **2** glad; delighted. — **pleased with oneself** derog. self-satisfied; conceited.

◫ **1** happy, satisfied, contented, gratified, glad. **2** glad, delighted, thrilled, euphoric.
◫ DISPLEASED, ANNOYED.

pleasing adj. causing pleasure or satisfaction.

◫ satisfying, gratifying, acceptable, good, pleasant, agreeable, nice, delightful, charming, attractive, engaging, winning.
◫ unpleasant, disagreeable.

pleasurable adj. enjoyable; pleasant.

pleasure — noun **1** a feeling of enjoyment or satisfaction: take pleasure in one's surroundings. **2** a source of such a feeling: have the pleasure of your company. **3** one's will, desire, wish, preference, or inclination. **4** recreation: combine business with pleasure. **5** gratification of a sensual kind: pleasure and pain. — verb old use to give (especially sexual) pleasure to. — adj. used for or done for pleasure: a pleasure boat/a pleasure trip. — **a** or **my pleasure** a formula of courtesy: not at all; it's no trouble. **at pleasure** when or as one likes. **with pleasure** a formula of courtesy: gladly; willingly; of course. [from Old French plaisir, originally infinitive]

◫ noun **1** enjoyment, satisfaction, gratification, contentment, happiness, joy, delight. **2** joy, delight. **4** recreation, amusement, entertainment, fun.
◫ noun **1** sorrow, pain, trouble, displeasure.

pleat — noun a fold sewn or pressed into cloth, etc. — verb to make pleats in. [a variant of PLAIT]

◫ noun tuck, fold. verb tuck, fold, crease, flute, crimp, gather, pucker.

pleated adj. having pleats.

pleb noun derog. a person of coarse or vulgar tastes, manners, or habits. [a shortening of PLEBEIAN]

plebeian /plɪˈbiːən/ — noun **1** a member of the common people, especially of ancient Rome. **2** derog. a person lacking refinement or culture. — adj. **1** of or belonging to the common people. **2** derog. coarse; vulgar; unrefined. [from Latin plebeius, from plebs, the people]

plebiscite /ˈplɛbɪsɪt/ noun a vote of all the electors, taken to decide a matter of public importance; a referendum. [from Latin plebiscitum, decree of the plebs]

plectrum noun a small flat implement of metal, plastic, horn, etc, used for plucking the strings of a guitar. [from Latin, from Greek plectron, from plessein, to strike]

pled see PLEAD.

pledge — noun **1** a solemn promise. **2** something left as security with someone to whom one owes money, etc. **3** something put into pawn. **4** a token or symbol: a ring as a pledge of love. **5** a toast drunk as proof of friendship, etc. — verb **1** to promise (money, loyalty, etc) to someone. **2** to bind or commit (oneself, etc). **3** to offer or give as a pledge or guarantee. **4** old use to drink the health of. — **take** or **sign the pledge** old facetious use to undertake to drink no alcohol. [from Old French plege]

◫ noun **1** promise, vow, word of honour, oath, bond, covenant, guarantee, warrant, assurance, undertaking. **2** deposit, security, surety, bail. verb **1** promise, vow, swear, contract, engage, undertake. **3** vouch, guarantee, secure.

Pleiades pl. noun in Greek mythology, the seven daughters of Atlas and Pleione who were changed into the star-cluster of the same name after being pursued by Orion.

plein air /plɛn ˈɛə(r)/ a term used in art history, and applied to pictures, especially landscapes, which give a vivid sense of the light and atmosphere of the open air. Also applied to pictures painted out of doors, instead of in the studio. [from French plein air, open air]

Pleiocene same as **Pliocene**.

Pleistocene /ˈplaɪstəʊsiːn/ adj. Geol. denoting the first of the two epochs of the Quaternary period, lasting from about two million to 10000 years ago. [from Greek pleisto, most + kainos, recent]

plenary /ˈpliːnərɪ/ adj. **1** full; complete: plenary powers. **2** said of a meeting attended by all members. [from Latin plenarius, from plenus, full]

plenipotentiary /plɛnɪpəˈtɛnʃərɪ/ — adj. entrusted with, or conveying, full authority to act on behalf of one's government or other organization. — noun (PL. **plenipotentiaries**) someone, eg an ambassador, invested with such authority. [from Latin plenus, full + potentia, power]

plenitude /ˈplɛnɪtjuːd/ noun **1** abundance; profusion. **2** completeness; fullness. [from Latin plenitudo, from plenus, full]

plenteous adj. plentiful; abundant. [from Middle English plentivous, from Old French plentif, from plente, plenty]

plenteously adv. plentifully; abundantly.

plentiful adj. in good supply; abundant. [from PLENTY]

◫ ample, abundant, profuse, copious, overflowing, lavish, generous, liberal, bountiful, fruitful, productive.
◫ scarce, scanty, rare.

plenty — pron. **1** enough, or more than enough. **2** a lot: plenty of folk would agree. — noun wealth or sufficiency: in times of plenty. — adv. colloq. fully: plenty wide enough. — **in plenty** in abundant quantities. [from Old French plente, from Latin plenitas, abundance]

◫ pron. **2** colloq. lots, colloq. loads, colloq. masses, colloq. heaps, colloq. piles, colloq. stacks. noun abundance, profusion, plethora, sufficiency, mass, volume, fund, mine, store.
◫ noun scarcity, lack, want, need.

pleonasm /ˈpliːənazm/ noun **1** the use of more words than are needed to express something. **2** a superfluous word or words. [from Greek pleonasmos, superfluity]

pleonastic adj. characterized by pleonasm; using more words than are needed.

pleonastically adv. by means of pleonasm.

plethora /ˈplɛθərə/ noun a large or excessive amount. [from Greek plethora, fullness]

pleura /ˈplʊərə/ noun Anat. in mammals, the double membrane that covers the lungs and lines the chest cavity. [from Greek pleura, side, rib]

pleurisy /ˈplʊərɪsɪ/ noun inflammation of the pleura. [from Old French pleurisie]

plexus *noun Anat.* a network of nerves or blood vessels, such as the *solar plexus* behind the stomach. [from Latin *plexus*, a weaving]

pliability *noun* being pliable.

pliable *adj.* **1** easily bent; flexible. **2** adaptable or alterable. **3** easily persuaded or influenced. [from French *plier*, to fold]

■ **1** pliant, flexible, bendable, *colloq.* bendy, supple, lithe, malleable, plastic, yielding. **2** adaptable, alterable, accommodating. **3** impressionable, susceptible, compliant, yielding, biddable, persuadable, responsive, receptive, docile, flexible, manageable, tractable.

☒ **1** rigid, inflexible. **3** headstrong.

pliancy /'plaɪənsɪ/ *noun* being pliant.

pliant /'plaɪənt/ *adj.* **1** bending easily; pliable, flexible, or supple. **2** easily influenced. [from Old French, from *plier*, to fold]

pliers *pl. noun* a hinged tool with jaws for gripping, bending, or cutting wire, etc. [from *ply*, to bend or fold]

plight[1] *noun* a danger, difficulty, or situation of hardship that one finds oneself in; a predicament. [from Middle English *plit*, fold, condition, influenced by the spelling of PLIGHT[2]]

■ predicament, quandary, dilemma, trouble, difficulty, straits, state, extremity.

plight[2] *verb old use* to promise solemnly; to pledge. — **plight one's troth** to pledge oneself in marriage. [from Anglo-Saxon *pliht*, peril, risk]

plimsoll /'plɪmsəl/ *noun old use* a light rubber-soled canvas shoe worn for gymnastics, etc; a gymshoe. [from the resemblance of the line of the sole to the Plimsoll line]

Plimsoll line /'plɪmsəl/ a line painted round a ship's hull showing how far down into the water it may safely sit when loaded. [named after Samuel Plimsoll (1824–98), who put forward the Merchant Shipping Act of 1876]

plinth *noun* **1** *Archit.* a square block serving as the base of a column, pillar, etc. **2** a base or pedestal for a statue or other sculpture, or a vase. [from Greek *plinthos*, brick, stone block]

Pliocene /'plaɪəʊsiːn/ *adj. Geol.* the last epoch of the Tertiary period, lasting from about seven million to two million years ago. [from Greek *pleion*, more + *kainos*, recent]

PLO *abbrev.* the Palestine Liberation Organization, an organization that consists of several of the Palestinian groups opposed to Israel.

plod *verb intrans.* (**plodded, plodding**) **1** to walk slowly with a heavy tread. **2** to work slowly, methodically, and thoroughly, if without inspiration. [imitative]

■ **1** trudge, tramp, stump, lumber, plough through. **2** drudge, labour, toil, grind, slog, persevere, soldier on.

plodder *noun* **1** a person who plods on. **2** a dull uninteresting person. **3** a person who progresses by toil rather than by inspiration.

ploidy *noun Biol.* the number of chromosome sets that are present in the nucleus of a cell.

plonk[1] *colloq.* — *noun* the resounding thud made by a heavy object falling. — *verb* **1** to put or place with a thud or with finality: *plonked himself in the best chair.* **2** *intrans.* to place oneself, fall, etc with a plonk. — *adv.* with a thud: *landed plonk beside her.* [imitative]

plonk[2] *noun colloq.* cheap, undistinguished wine. [said to be from French *vin blanc*, white wine]

plop — *noun* the sound of a small object dropping into water. — *verb intrans., trans.* (**plopped, plopping**) to fall or drop with this sound. — *adv.* with a plop. [imitative]

plosive — *adj., said of a sound* made by the sudden release of breath after stoppage. — *noun* a plosive consonant or sound. [a shortening of EXPLOSIVE]

plot[1] — *noun* **1** a secret plan, especially laid jointly with others, for contriving something illegal or evil; a conspiracy. **2** the story of a play, film, novel, etc. — *verb* (**plotted, plotting**) **1** *trans., intrans.* to plan (something, especially illegal or evil), usually with others. **2** to make a plan of; to mark the course or progress of. **3** *Maths.* to mark a series of individual points on a graph, or to draw a curve through them. — **lose the plot** *colloq.* to become disorganized, confused or agitated. [from PLOT[2], influenced by French *complot*, conspiracy]

■ *noun* **1** conspiracy, intrigue, machination, scheme, plan, stratagem. **2** story, narrative, subject, theme, storyline, thread, outline, scenario. *verb* **1** conspire, intrigue, machinate, scheme, plan, hatch, lay, cook up, devise, contrive, design, draft. **2** chart, map, mark, locate, draw, calculate.

plot[2] *noun* a piece of ground for any of various uses. [from Anglo-Saxon *plot*]

■ patch, tract, area, allotment, lot, parcel.

plotter *noun Comput.* in a computer system, an output device which draws graphs, diagrams, contour maps, plans, overhead slides, etc on paper or film using an automatically controlled pen.

plough /plaʊ/ — *noun* **1** a bladed farm implement used to turn over the surface of the soil, forming ridges and furrows, and burying stubble, weeds, or other surface vegetation in preparation for the cultivation of a crop. **2** any similar implement, especially one for shovelling snow off roads. **3** *Astron.* (**the Plough**) the seven brightest stars in the constellation Ursa Major, whose configuration resembles the shape of a plough. Also called BIG DIPPER. — *verb* **1** (*also* **plough something up**) to till or turn over soil, land, etc with a plough. **2** to make a furrow or to turn over the surface of the soil with a plough. **3** (*usually* **plough through something**) to move through it with a ploughing action. **4** *intrans.* (*usually* **plough through** or **on**) *colloq.* to make steady but laborious progress. **5** (*usually* **plough into something**) *colloq., said of a vehicle or its driver* to crash into something at speed. **6** *Brit. old colloq. use* **a** to fail (a candidate in an examination). **b** *intrans., said of a candidate* to fail an examination. — **plough something back** to re-invest profits in a business. **plough something in** to mix the remains of a crop with the soil by means of a plough after harvesting. [from Anglo-Saxon *plog, ploh*]

ploughman *noun* a person who steers a plough.

ploughman's lunch a cold meal of bread, cheese, pickle, and (sometimes) meat, often served in pubs.

Plough Monday the Monday following the Epiphany, so called because it was the day when traditionally ploughmen and others resumed their daily work after the Christmas holidays.

ploughshare *noun* a blade of a plough.

plover /'plʌvə(r)/ *noun* any of various, especially seashore, birds, most with long wings and a short straight beak. [from Old French *plovier*, rain bird]

plow *noun* the US spelling of **plough**.

ploy *noun* a stratagem, dodge, or manoeuvre to gain an advantage. [possibly from Latin *plicare*, to bend]

■ stratagem, dodge, manoeuvre, tactic, move, device, contrivance, scheme, game, trick, artifice, wile, ruse, subterfuge.

PLP *abbrev.* Parliamentary Labour Party.

PLR *abbrev.* public lending right.

pluck — *verb* **1** to pull the feathers off (a bird) before cooking. **2** to pick (flowers or fruit) from a plant or tree. **3** (*also* **pluck something out**) to remove it by pulling: *plucked out his grey hairs.* **4** to shape by removing hairs from (eyebrows). **5** (**pluck** or **pluck at something**) to pull or tug it. **6**

to sound (the strings of a violin, etc) using the fingers or a plectrum. **7** to grab or save at the last minute: *plucked from the jaws of death.* — *noun* **1** courage; guts. **2** a little tug. **3** the heart, liver, and lungs of an animal. — **pluck up courage** to strengthen one's resolve for a difficult undertaking, etc. [from Anglo-Saxon *pluccian*, to pluck or tear]

■ *verb* **2** pick, collect, gather, harvest. **3** pull out, draw, tug out, pull off, remove. **5** pull (at), tug (at), snatch (at). **6** pick, twang, strum. **7** snatch, rescue, pull. *noun* **1** courage, *colloq.* guts, bravery, spirit, mettle, *colloq.* nerve, *colloq.* grit, backbone, fortitude, resolution, determination.
⊟ *noun* **1** cowardice.

pluckily *adv.* in a plucky way.
pluckiness *noun* being plucky.
plucky *adj.* (**pluckier, pluckiest**) *colloq.* courageous; spirited.

■ courageous, spirited, brave, bold, daring, intrepid, heroic, valiant.
⊟ cowardly, weak, feeble.

plug — *noun* **1** a piece of rubber, plastic, etc shaped to fit a hole as a stopper, eg in a bath or sink. **2** (*often in compounds*) any device or piece of material for a similar purpose: *earplugs*. **3** the plastic or rubber device with metal pins, fitted to the end of the flex of an electrical apparatus, that is pushed into a socket to connect with the power supply; also *colloq.* the socket. **4** *colloq.* a piece of favourable publicity given to a product, programme, etc, eg on television. **5** a spark plug. **6** a lump of tobacco for chewing. — *verb* (**plugged, plugging**) **1** (*also* **plug something up**) to stop or block up a hole, etc with something. **2** *colloq.* to give favourable publicity to (a product, programme, etc), especially repeatedly. **3** *slang* to shoot with a gun. **4** (**plug away** or **along**) *colloq.* to work or progress steadily. — **plug something in** to connect an electrical appliance to the power supply by means of an electrical plug. [from Dutch *plug*, bung, peg]

■ *noun* **1** stopper, bung, cork, spigot. **4** advertisement, publicity, mention, puff. *verb* **1** stop (up), block (up), bung (up), cork, choke, close, seal, fill, pack, stuff. **2** advertise, publicize, promote, push, mention.

plughole *noun* the hole in a bath or sink through which water flows into the waste pipe.
plum *noun* **1** any of a number of varieties of shrub or small tree belonging to the genus *Prunus*, cultivated in temperate regions for its edible fruit, or for its ornamental pink or white flowers and deep red or purple foliage. **2** the smooth-skinned red, purple, green, or yellow fruit of this tree, which has a hard central stone surrounded by sweet juicy flesh, eg damson, greengage. **3** a raisin used in cakes, etc: *plum pudding.* **4** (*also attributive*) *colloq.* something especially valued or sought: *a plum job.* [from Anglo-Saxon *plume*, from Greek *proumnon*]
plumage /ˈpluːmɪdʒ/ *noun* a bird's feathers, especially with regard to colour. [from Old French, from *plume*, feather]
plumb¹ /plʌm/ — *noun* a lead weight hanging on the end of a line, used for measuring water depth or for testing a wall, etc for perpendicularity. — *adj., adv.* straight, vertical, or perpendicular. — *adv.* **1** *colloq.* exactly: *plumb in the middle.* **2** *North Amer., esp. US colloq.* utterly: *plumb crazy.* — *verb* **1** to measure the depth of (water), test (a structure) for verticality, or adjust to the vertical, using a plumb. **2** to penetrate, probe, or understand (a mystery, etc). — **out of plumb** not vertical. **plumb the depths of something** to experience the worst extreme of a bad feeling, etc: *plumb the depths of misery.* [from Latin *plumbum*, lead]

■ *adv.* **1** exactly, precisely, dead, *colloq.* slap, *colloq.* bang, *colloq.* slap-bang. *verb* **1** sound, fathom, measure, gauge.

2 penetrate, probe, understand, fathom.

plumb² *verb* (**plumb something in**) to connect a water-using appliance to the water supply or waste pipe. [from Latin *plumbum*, lead, used for making pipes]
plumbago /plʌmˈbeɪɡoʊ/ *noun Chem.* graphite. [from Latin *plumbago*, Pliny's translation of the Greek name *molybdaina*, lead, lead ore]
plumber *noun* a person who fits and repairs water pipes, and water- or gas-using appliances.
plumbing *noun* **1** the system of water and gas pipes in a building, etc. **2** the work of a plumber. **3** *facetious* the lavatory.
plumb line a line with a plumb on it for measuring depth or testing for verticality.
plume — *noun* **1** an imposing feather. **2** such a feather, or a tuft or bunch of feathers, worn as an ornament or crest, represented in a coat of arms, etc. **3** a curling column (of smoke etc). — *verb* **1** *said of a bird* to clean or preen (itself or its feathers). **2** to decorate with plumes. **3** (**plume oneself on something**) to pride or congratulate oneself on something, usually trivial. [from Old French, from Latin *pluma*, soft feather]
plummet /ˈplʌmɪt/ — *verb intrans.* (**plummeted, plummeting**) to fall or drop rapidly; to plunge or hurtle downwards. — *noun* the weight on a plumbline or fishing-line. [from Old French *plommet*, diminutive of *plomb*, lead]

■ *verb* plunge, dive, nosedive, descend, drop, fall, tumble.
⊟ *verb* soar.

plummy *adj.* (**plummier, plummiest**) **1** *colloq.,* said of a job, etc desirable; worth having; choice. **2** *derog.,* said of a voice affectedly or excessively rich and deep.
plump¹ — *adj.* full, rounded, fleshy, chubby, or not unattractively fat. — *verb* (*also* **plump something up**) to shake cushions or pillows to give them their full soft bulk. [from Old Dutch *plomp*, blunt]

■ *adj.* full, fleshy, rounded, round, chubby, stout, rotund, portly, ample, buxom, tubby, fat, obese, dumpy, podgy.
⊟ *adj.* thin, skinny.

plump² — *verb trans., intrans.* (*also* **plump down** or **plump something down**) to put down, drop, fall, or sit heavily. — *noun* a sudden heavy fall, or the sound of it. — *adv.* with a plump. — **plump for something** or **someone** to decide on or choose them. [imitative]

■ **plump for** decide on, choose, opt for, select, favour, back, support.

plumule /ˈpluːmjuːl/ *noun* **1** *Bot.* the embryonic shoot of a germinating seedling. **2** *Zool.* one of the down feathers of a bird. [from Latin *plumula*, diminutive of *pluma*, feather]
plumy *adj.* (**plumier, plumiest**) **1** covered or adorned with down or plumes. **2** like a plume.
plunder — *verb trans., intrans.* (**plundered, plundering**) to steal (valuable goods), or loot (a place), especially with open force during a war; to rob or ransack. — *noun* the goods plundered; loot; booty. [from Dutch *plunderen*]

■ *verb* steal, loot, pillage, rob, ransack, raid, rifle, ravage, sack, strip. *noun* loot, pillage, booty, *slang* swag, spoils, pickings, ill-gotten gains, prize.

plunderer *noun* a person who plunders.
plunge — *verb* (*usually* **plunge in** or **into something**) **1** *intrans.* to dive, throw oneself, fall or rush headlong. **2** *intrans.* to involve oneself rapidly and enthusiastically. **3** to thrust or push. **4** to put into a particular state or condition. **5** to dip briefly into water or other liquid. **6** *intrans.* to steeply: *plunging necklines/the ship plunged and rose.* —

noun 1 an act of plunging; a dive. **2** *colloq.* a dip or swim. — **take the plunge** *colloq.* to commit oneself finally after hesitation; to take an irreversible decision. [from Old French *plungier*, from Latin *plumbum*, lead]

. . . .

◼ *verb* **1** dive, jump, nosedive, swoop, dive-bomb, plummet, descend, go down, sink, drop, fall, pitch, tumble, hurtle, career, charge, dash, rush, tear. **2** immerse oneself, throw oneself. **3** thrust, push, stick, stab, shove, ram. **4** throw. **5** dip, submerge. *noun* **1** dive, jump, swoop, descent, drop, fall, tumble.

. . . .

plunger *noun* **1** a rubber cup at the end of a long handle, used with thrusting action to clear blocked drains, etc. **2** a part of a mechanism that moves up and down like a piston.

pluperfect /pluː'pɜːfɪkt/ *Grammar* — *adj.* denoting a tense, formed in English by *had* and a past participle, referring to action already accomplished at the time of the past action being related, as in *they had often gone there before, but this time they lost their way.* — *noun* the pluperfect tense, or a word in the pluperfect tense. [from Latin *plus quam perfectum tempus*, more than perfect time]

plural /'plʊərəl/ — *noun Grammar* the form of a noun, pronoun, adjective or verb used for two or more people, things, etc. See also SINGULAR. — *adj.* **1** *Grammar* denoting or in the plural. **2** consisting of more than one, or of different kinds. [from Latin *plus*, more]

pluralism *noun* **1** the existence within a society of a variety of ethnic, cultural and religious groups. **2** the holding of more than one post, especially in the Church.

pluralist *noun* **1** a person who holds more than one office at once. **2** a believer in pluralism.

pluralistic *adj.* relating to or characterized by pluralism.

plurality *noun* (PL. **pluralities**) **1** the fact of being plural or more than one. **2** a large number or variety. **3** a majority that is not absolute, ie a winning number of votes that represents less than half of the votes cast; any majority.

plural society a society in which pluralism is found, ie one in which everyone has a say in the ruling of the society.

plus — *prep.* **1** *Maths.* with the addition of: *2 plus 5.* **2** in combination with; with the added factor of: *bad luck, plus his own obstinacy.* **3** *(after an amount)* with something more besides: *earns £20,000 plus.* — *adj.* **1** denoting the symbol +: *the plus sign.* **2** mathematically positive; above zero: *plus 3.* **3** advantageous: *a plus factor.* **4** *in grades* denoting a slightly higher mark than the letter alone: *B plus.* **5** *Physics, Electr.* electrically positive. — *noun* (PL. **pluses**) **1** *(also* **plus sign**) the symbol +, denoting addition or positive value. **2** *colloq.* something positive or good; a bonus, advantage, surplus, or extra. — *conj. colloq.* in addition to the fact that. [from Latin *plus*, more]

plus fours loose breeches gathered below the knee, once popular as golfing wear. [from *plus 4* inches of fabric extending below the knee]

plush — *noun* cotton, silk, etc fabric with a long velvety pile. — *adj.* **1** made of plush. **2** *colloq.* plushy. [from French *pluche*, earlier *peluche*, from Latin *pilus*, hair]

plushy *adj.* (**plushier, plushiest**) *colloq.* luxurious, opulent, stylish, or costly.

plutocracy /pluː'tɒkrəsɪ/ *noun* (PL. **plutocracies**) **1** government or domination by the wealthy. **2** a state governed by the wealthy. **3** an influential group whose power is backed by their wealth. [from Greek *ploutos*, wealth + -CRACY]

plutocrat /'pluːtoʊkrat/ *noun* **1** a member of a plutocracy. **2** *colloq.* a wealthy person.

plutocratic *adj.* relating to or characteristic of a plutocracy.

plutonic /pluˈtɒnɪk/ *adj. Geol.* relating to coarse-grained igneous rocks that are formed by the slow crystallization of magma deep within the Earth's crust, eg granites, gabbros.

plutonium /pluˈtoʊnɪəm/ *noun Chem.* (SYMBOL **Pu**, ATOMIC NUMBER **94**) a dense highly poisonous silvery-grey radioactive metal that is prepared in quantity from uranium-238 in breeder reactors. The isotope plutonium-239 is used as an energy source for nuclear weapons and some nuclear reactors. [named after the planet *Pluto*]

ply[1] *noun* (PL. **plies**) **1** thickness of yarn, rope, or wood, measured by the number of strands or layers that compose it: *three-ply wool.* **2** a strand or layer. [from Old French *pli*, fold]

. . . .

◼ **2** strand, layer, sheet, leaf.

. . . .

ply[2] *verb* (**plies, plied**) **1** (**ply someone with something**) to keep supplying or importuning them: *plied them with drinks/plied them with questions.* **2** *trans., intrans.* (**ply between one place and another**) to travel (a route) regularly; to go regularly to and fro between destinations. **3** *old use* to work at (a trade). **4** *old use* to use (a tool, etc): *ply one's needle.* [from APPLY]

plywood *noun* wood made up of thin layers glued together.

PM *abbrev.* **1** Paymaster. **2** Postmaster. **3** post mortem. **4** Prime Minister.

Pm *symbol Chem.* promethium.

p.m. or **pm** *abbrev. post meridiem* (Latin), after midday; in the afternoon.

PMG *abbrev.* Paymaster-General.

PMS *abbrev.* premenstrual syndrome.

PMT *abbrev.* premenstrual tension.

pneumatic /njʊˈmatɪk/ *adj.* **1** relating to air or gases. **2** containing or inflated with air, eg pneumatic tyres, which are inflated by increasing the air pressure within them by means of a pump. **3** denoting a tool or piece of machinery that is operated or driven by compressed air, eg a pneumatic drill. [from Greek *pneuma*, wind, breath]

pneumatically *adv.* by pneumatic means.

pneumonia /njuˈmoʊnɪə/ *noun* inflammation of one or more lobes of the lungs, usually as a result of infection by bacteria or viruses. The *alveoli* (clustered air sacs) at the ends of the air passages become congested with fluid so that oxygen and carbon dioxide can no longer be exchanged, and the affected areas of the lung become solid. [from Greek *pneumon*, lung]

PNG *abbrev.* Papua New Guinea.

PO *abbrev.* **1** Petty Officer. **2** Pilot Officer. **3** Post Office.

Po *symbol Chem.* polonium.

po[1] *noun* (PL. **pos**) *colloq.* a chamberpot.

po[2] *abbrev.* postal order.

poa /ˈpoʊə/ *noun Bot.* any of various species of grass belonging to the genus *Poa.* [from Greek *poa*, grass]

poach[1] *verb* **1** to cook (an egg without its shell) in or over boiling water. **2** to simmer (fish) in milk or other liquid. [from Old French *pocher*, to pocket (the egg yolk inside the white), from *poche*, pocket]

poach[2] *verb* **1** *trans., intrans.* to catch (game or fish) illegally on someone else's property. **2** *intrans.* (**poach on something**) to intrude on another's territory or area of responsibility. **3** to steal (ideas, etc). **4** to lure away (personnel at a rival business, etc) to work for one's own business. [from Old French *pocher*, to gouge]

. . . .

◼ **1** steal, pilfer. **2** trespass on, encroach on, infringe. **3** appropriate, pirate, plagiarize.

. . . .

poacher *noun* **1** a container in which to poach eggs. **2** a person who poaches game, work, customers, etc.

poaching *noun* **1** cooking by gentle simmering. **2** the activity of a poacher, stealing.

PO box a numbered box, pigeonhole, etc at a post office, to which mail may be sent for collection by a recipient without a permanent address.

pochade /pɒˈʃɑːd/ *noun Art* a quick sketch in colour, usually oils, made in the open air. Many landscape painters make studies of this type as a preliminary stage in the planning of a full-size picture. [from French *pochade*]

pochard /'pɒtʃəd/ *noun* any of various diving ducks found in Europe and N America.

pock *noun* 1 a small inflamed area on the skin, containing pus, especially one caused by smallpox. 2 a pockmark. [from Anglo-Saxon *poc*]

pocket — *noun* 1 an extra piece sewn into or on to a garment to form an enclosed section for carrying things in. 2 any container similarly fitted or attached. 3 one's financial resources: *well beyond my pocket*. 4 a rock cavity filled with ore. 5 in conditions of air turbulence, a place in the atmosphere where the air pressure drops or rises abruptly. 6 an isolated patch or area of something: *pockets of unemployment*. 7 *Billiards, etc* any of the nets or pouches hanging from the side of the table, into which balls are played. — *adj.* designed, or small enough, to be carried in a pocket; smaller than standard. — *verb* (**pocketed, pocketing**) 1 to put in one's pocket. 2 *colloq.* to take dishonestly; to steal. 3 *Billiards, etc* to drive (a ball) into a pocket. 4 to swallow or suppress (one's pride), eg to make a humble request. — **in one another's pocket** *said of two people* in close intimacy with, or dependence on, one another. **in one's pocket** in one's power. **in** or **out of pocket** having gained (or lost) money on a transaction. **out-of-pocket expenses** those incurred on behalf of an employer. **line one's pocket** to make money, especially dishonestly or immorally, from something. **put one's hand in one's pocket** to be willing to contribute money. [from Old French *poquet*, diminutive of *poque*, from Old Dutch *poke*, pocket]

⊞ *noun* 2 pouch, bag, envelope, receptacle, compartment, hollow, cavity. 3 resources, funds, means, money, wherewithal. *adj* small, little, *colloq.* mini, concise, compact, portable, miniature. *verb* 2 take, steal, *slang* nick, *colloq.* pinch, appropriate, help oneself to, lift, pilfer, filch.

pocketbook *noun* 1 *North Amer., esp. US* a wallet for money and papers. 2 *North Amer., esp. US* a woman's strapless handbag or purse. 3 a notebook.

pocket borough *Hist.* in the UK before the 1832 Reform Act, an electoral constituency under the control of one person or family.

pocketful *noun* (PL. **pocketfuls**) the amount a pocket will hold.

pocket knife a knife with folding blades; a penknife.

pockmark *noun* a small pit or hollow in the skin left by a pock, especially in chickenpox or smallpox.

pockmarked *adj.* pitted, scarred.

pod — *noun* 1 *Bot.* the long dry fruit produced by plants belonging to the Leguminosae family, eg peas and beans, which splits down both sides to release its seeds. 2 *Aeron.* in an aeroplane or space vehicle, a detachable container or housing, eg for an engine. — *verb* (**podded, podding**) 1 to extract (peas, beans, etc) from their pods. 2 *intrans. said of a plant* to produce pods.

⊞ *noun* 1 shell, husk, case, hull. *verb* 1 shell, hull.

podgy *adj.* (**podgier, podgiest**) *derog.* plump or chubby; short and squat. [from *podge*, a short fat person]

podiatrist /pɒ'daɪətrɪst/ *noun North Amer.* a chiropodist.

podiatry /pɒ'daɪətrɪ/ *noun North Amer.* chiropody. [from Greek *pod* foot + *iatros*, doctor]

podium /'pəʊdɪəm/ *noun* (PL. **podiums, podia**) 1 a small platform for a public speaker, orchestra conductor, etc. 2 *Archit.* a projecting base for a colonnade, wall, etc. [from Latin *podium*, platform, from Greek *pous*, foot]

podsol or **podzol** /'pɒdzɒl/ *noun Geol.* any of a group of soils characterized by a bleached upper layer, from which aluminium and iron compounds have leached, and a lower layer where they have accumulated to from a hardpan or iron band. [from Russian, from *pod*, under + *zola*, ash]

poem /'pəʊɪm/ *noun* 1 a composition in verse, often of elevated and imaginatively expressed content. 2 an object,

scene, or creation of inspiring beauty. [from Greek *poiema*, creation, poem, from *poieein*, to make]

Types of poem include: ballad, elegy, epic, haiku, idyll, lay, limerick, lyric, madrigal, nursery-rhyme, ode, pastoral, roundelay, sonnet, tanka.

poesy /'pəʊɪzɪ/ *noun old use* poetry. [from Greek *poiesis*, from *poieein*, to make]

poet /'pəʊɪt/ *noun* a writer of poems. [from Greek *poietes*, from *poieein*, to make]

⊞ versifier, lyricist, bard, minstrel.

poetess *noun* a female poet.

poetic /pəʊ'etɪk/ *adj.* 1 of, relating, or suitable to poets or poetry. 2 having grace, beauty, or inspiration suggestive of poetry.

⊞ POETICAL. 1 metrical, rhythmical, rhyming. 2 lyrical, moving, artistic, graceful, flowing.
⊟ 2 prosaic.

poetical *adj.* 1 poetic. 2 written in verse: *the complete poetical works*.

poetically *adv.* 1 in a poetic way. 2 in or by means of poetry.

poetic justice a situation in which evil is punished or good rewarded in a strikingly fitting way.

poetic licence a poet's or writer's departure from strict fact or correct grammar, for the sake of effect.

poet laureate (PL. **poets laureate, poet laureates**) in the UK, an officially appointed court poet, commissioned to produce poems for state occasions.

poetry *noun* 1 the art of composing poems. 2 poems collectively. 3 poetic quality, feeling, beauty, or grace. [from Latin *poetria*, from *poeta*, poet]

po-faced *adj. derog. colloq.* wearing a disapproving expression.

pogo stick a spring-mounted pole with a handlebar and foot rests, on which to bounce, or progress by bounces.

pogrom /'pɒgrəm/ *noun* an organized massacre, originally of Jews in 19c Russia. [from Russian *pogrom*, destruction]

poignancy /'pɔɪnjənsɪ/ *noun* a poignant quality.

poignant /'pɔɪnjənt/ *adj.* 1 painful to the feelings: *a poignant reminder*. 2 deeply moving; full of pathos. [from Old French, present participle of *poindre*, to sting]

⊞ 1 painful, agonizing, distressing, upsetting, heartbreaking, heart-rending. 2 moving, touching, affecting, tender, piteous, pathetic, sad.

poikilothermic /pɔɪkɪləʊ'θɜːmɪk/ *adj. Zool.* describing an animal that has no mechanism for maintaining its internal body temperature at a constant level, as a result of which its body temperature fluctuates with changes in environmental temperature. Also called COLD-BLOODED. [from Greek *poikilos*, variegated]

poinsettia /pɔɪn'setɪə/ *noun* a Central American shrub, popular because of its scarlet leaves. [from J R Poinsett (1779–1851), American Minister to Mexico]

point — *noun* 1 a sharp or tapering end or tip. 2 a dot, eg that inserted before a decimal fraction, as in *2.1* or *2·1* = *two point one*. 3 a punctuation mark, especially a full stop. 4 *Geom.* a position found by means of coordinates. 5 a position, place or location: *a look-out point*. 6 a moment: *lost his temper at that point*. 7 a stage in a process, etc. 8 a stage, temperature, etc: *boiling-point*. 9 the right moment for doing something: *lost courage when it came to the point*. 10 a feature or characteristic: *her good points*. 11 a detail or particular. 12 aim or intention: *the point of this procedure*. 13 use or value: *no point in trying*. 14 the significance (of a remark, story, joke, etc). **15** a unit or mark in scoring. **16** any of the 32 directions marked on, or indicated by, a compass. **17** (*usually* **points**) an adjustable tapering rail by means of which a train changes lines. **18** *Electr.* a socket or power point. **19** (*usually* **points**) in an internal combustion engine, either of the two electrical contacts completing the circuit in the distributor. **20** *Printing* a unit of type measurement, equal to — of a pica. **21** *Cricket* an off-side fielding position at right angles to the batsman. **22** (*usually* **points**) *Ballet* the tip of the toe, or a block inserted into the toe of a ballet shoe. **23** a headland or promontory. **24** (*usually* **points**) any of an animal's extremities, eg ears, tail, and feet. **25** the tip of a deer's horn or antler. — *verb* **1** to aim: *pointed a gun at her.* **2** *trans., intrans.* **a** to extend (one's finger or a pointed object) towards someone or something, so as to direct attention there. **b** *said of a sign, etc* to indicate a certain direction. **3** *intrans.* to extend or face in a certain direction: *lay with toes pointing upward.* **4** *intrans., said of a gun dog* to stand with the nose turned to where the dead game lies. **5** *often facetious* to direct (someone): *point me towards a pub.* **6** (**point to something** or **someone**) to indicate or suggest them: *it points to one solution.* **7** to extend (the toes) to form a point, as in dancing. **8** to fill gaps or cracks in (stonework or brickwork) with cement or mortar. — **beside the point** irrelevant. **carry** or **gain one's point** to persuade others of the validity of one's opinion. **come** or **get to the point** to cut out the irrelevancies and say what one wants to say. **in point of fact** actually; in truth. **make a point of doing something** to be sure of doing it or take care to do it. **make one's point** to state one's opinion forcefully. **on the point of doing something** about to do it. **point something out** to indicate or draw attention to it. **point something up** to highlight or emphasize it. **score points off someone** to argue cleverly and successfully against them, usually on trivial or detailed grounds. **to the point** relevant. **to the point of ...** to a degree that could be fairly described as ...: *brave to the point of recklessness.* **up to a point** to a limited degree. [from Old French, from Latin *pungere*, to pierce]

■ *noun* **2** dot, spot. **3** full stop, period. **5** position, place, location, situation, site, spot. **6** moment, instant, juncture. **7** stage, juncture, time, period. **9** *colloq.* crunch. **10** feature, characteristic, attribute, aspect, facet. **11** detail, particular, item, subject, topic. **12** aim, intention, object, end, goal, objective, motive, reason, purpose. **14** significance, essence, crux, core, pith, gist, thrust, meaning, drift, burden. *verb* **1** aim, direct, train, level. **2** *of a sign* indicate, signal, show, signify, denote, designate. **point out** indicate, draw attention to, show, point to, reveal, identify, specify, mention, bring up, allude to, remind.

point-blank — *adj.* **1** *said of a shot* fired at very close range. **2** *said of a question, refusal, etc* bluntly worded and direct. — *adv.* **1** at close range. **2** in a blunt, direct manner. [from POINT *verb* + BLANK, the white centre of a target, from French *blanc*, white]

■ *adj.* **2** blunt, direct, forthright, frank, candid, straightforward, forthright, plain, explicit, open, unreserved. *adv.* **2** bluntly, directly, frankly, candidly, straightforwardly, forthrightly, plainly, explicitly, openly.

point duty the task or station of a policeman or -woman who is directing traffic.

pointed *adj.* **1** having, or ending in, a point. **2** *said of a remark, etc* intended for, though not directly addressed to, a particular person; intended to convey a particular meaning or message although not directly expressing it. **3** *said of a remark, etc* cutting, sharply critical.

■ **1** sharp, keen. **3** cutting, incisive, trenchant, biting, penetrating, edged, barbed, telling.

pointer *noun* **1** a rod used by a speaker for indicating positions on a wall map, chart, etc. **2** the indicating finger or needle on a measuring instrument. **3** *colloq.* a suggestion or hint. **4** a breed of gun dog trained to point its muzzle in the direction where the dead game lies.

■ **2** arrow, indicator, needle, hand. **3** suggestion, hint, tip, recommendation, guide, indication, advice, warning, caution.

Pointillism / ˈpwantɪlɪzm, ˈpɔɪntɪlɪzm/ *noun Art* a method of painting by which shapes and colour tones are suggested by means of small dabs of pure colour painted side by side. See also DIVISIONISM. [from French *pointillisme*, from *pointillé*, stippled]

Pointillist *noun* a painter using Pointillism.

pointing *noun* the cement or mortar filling the gaps between the bricks or stones of a wall.

pointless *adj.* lacking purpose or meaning.

■ meaningless, useless, futile, vain, fruitless, unproductive, unprofitable, worthless, senseless, absurd, aimless. ⊟ meaningful, useful, profitable.

pointlessly *adv.* to no purpose; without a point or objective.

point of no return a stage reached in a process, etc after which there is no possibility of stopping or going back.

point of order (PL. **points of order**) a question raised in an assembly as to whether the business is being done according to the rules.

point of sale (PL. **points of sale**) the place in a shop, etc where goods are paid for; a pay desk or checkout.

point-of-sale *adj., said of a payment or computer terminal, etc* made or installed at the point of sale.

point of view (PL. **points of view**) one's own way of seeing something, influenced by personal considerations and experience; one's standpoint or viewpoint.

■ standpoint, viewpoint, opinion, view, belief, judgement, attitude, position, outlook, perspective, approach, angle, slant.

point-to-point *noun* (PL. **point-to-points**) a horse race across open country, from landmark to landmark.

poise — *noun* **1** self-confidence, calm, or composure. **2** grace of posture or carriage. **3** a state of equilibrium, balance, or stability eg between extremes. — *verb* **1** to balance or suspend. **2** (*often* **be poised for something** or **to do something**) to hold in a state of readiness. [from Old French *pois*, weight]

■ *noun* **1** self-confidence, calm, calmness, composure, equanimity, aplomb, coolness, self-possession, presence of mind, assurance, dignity. **2** grace, elegance. *verb* **2** be prepared for, be ready for, be set for.

poised *adj., said of behaviour, etc* calm and dignified.

■ calm, dignified, composed, unruffled, collected, self-possessed, cool, self-confident, assured.

poison — *noun* **1** any substance that damages tissues or causes death when absorbed or swallowed by living organisms, especially a substance that is harmful in relatively small amounts, eg arsenic, cyanide. **2** any destructive or corrupting influence: *a poison spreading through society.* — *verb* (**poisoned, poisoning**) **1** to harm or kill with poison. **2** to put poison into (food, etc). **3** to contaminate or pollute: *rivers poisoned by effluents.* **4** to corrupt or pervert (someone's mind). **5** (**poison one person against another**) to influence them to be hostile. **6** to harm or spoil in an unpleasant or malicious way: *poison a relationship.* **7** *colloq.* to infect: *a poisoned toe.* [from Old French *puisun,* from Latin *potio,* drink, potion]

    . . . .

■ *noun* **1** toxin, venom. **2** bane, blight, cancer, malignancy, contagion, contamination, corruption. *verb* **3** contaminate, pollute, taint, adulterate, infect, corrupt, deprave, pervert.

. . . .

poison-arrow frog see ARROW-POISON FROG.

poisoner *noun* a person who poisons.

poison gas any of several gases used in chemical warfare, that cause injury or death through contact or inhalation.

poison ivy an American climbing plant whose leaves produce a juice that causes intense skin irritation.

poisonous *adj.* **1** liable to cause injury or death if swallowed or absorbed. **2** producing, or able to inject, a poison: *poisonous snakes.* **3** *colloq., said of a person, remark, etc* malicious.

    . . . .

■ **1** toxic, lethal, deadly, noxious, pernicious, fatal, mortal. **2** venomous. **3** malicious, pernicious, venomous, spiteful.

. . . .

poison-pen letter a malicious anonymous letter.

poke[1] — *verb* **1** to thrust (something pointed): *poke a stick into the hole.* **2** to prod or jab: *poke the fire/poked her in the ribs with his elbow.* **3** to make (a hole) by prodding. **4** *trans., intrans.* to project or cause to project: *poked his head out of the door/her big toe poked a hole in her sock.* **5** to make (a fire) burn more brightly by stirring it with a poker. — *noun* a prod or jab. — **poke about** or **around** to search; to pry or snoop. **poke one's nose into something** *colloq.* to pry into or interfere in it. [from Middle English *poke,* from a Germanic source]

    . . . .

■ *verb* **1** thrust, stick, stab, jab, push, shove. **2** prod, stab, jab, nudge, elbow, dig. **4** stick, shove. *noun* prod, jab, thrust, shove, nudge, dig, butt, punch.

. . . .

poke[2] *noun Scot.* a paper bag. [from Middle English *poke,* from Old Dutch]

poker[1] *noun* a metal rod for stirring a fire to make it burn better.

poker[2] *noun* a card game in which players bet on the hands they hold, relying on bluff to outwit their opponents.

poker face the expressionless countenance of an experienced poker-player, or of anyone who gives nothing away.

poker-faced *adj.* having a poker face.

pokeweed or **pokeberry** *noun Bot.* a hardy American plant of the genus *Phytolacca,* with pale yellow flowers and purple berries.

pokiness *noun* being poky; a cramped condition.

poky *adj.* (**pokier, pokiest**) *colloq., said of a room, house, etc* small and confined or cramped. [from POKE[1]]

polar *adj.* **1** relating to the earth's North or South Pole or the regions round them. **2** relating to, or having, electric or magnetic poles. **3** as different as possible: *polar opposites.* [from Latin *polaris,* from *polus,* from Greek *polos,* pivot, axis, pole]

polar bear a large white bear (*Thalarctos maritimus*) belonging to the same family (Ursidae) as the brown bear, but found only in the Arctic region, and having thick creamy-white fur, and a smaller more pointed head and longer neck than most other bears.

polarimetry /pəʊləˈrɪmətrɪ/ *noun Physics* the measurement of the optical activity of any of various chemical compounds which, when placed in the path of a beam of polarized light, rotate the plane of polarization of light to the left or to the right. The optical activity can be used to identify and measure concentrations of transparent solutions such as sugar solutions.

Polaris /pəʊˈlɑːrɪs/ *noun* **1** *Astron.* the Pole Star, the brightest star in the constellation Ursa Minor. It was formerly

much used for navigation. **2** a guide or director. [from Greek *polos,* pivot, axis, firmament]

polarity /pəʊˈlarɪtɪ/ *noun* (PL. **polarities**) **1** the state of having two opposite poles: *magnetic polarity.* **2** the status, i.e. whether positive or negative, of an electrode, etc: *negative polarity.* **3** the tendency to develop, or be drawn, in opposite directions; oppositeness or an opposite: *the political polarities of left and right.*

polarization or **polarisation** /pəʊlərʌɪˈzeɪʃən/ *noun* **1** *Chem.* the separation of the positive and negative charges of an atom or molecule, especially by an electric field. **2** *Physics* the process whereby waves of electromagnetic radiation, eg light, which would normally vibrate in all directions, are restricted to vibration in one direction only.

polarize or **polarise** /ˈpəʊləraɪz/ *verb* **1** to give magnetic or electrical polarity to. **2** to restrict the vibrations of electromagnetic waves, eg light, to one direction only by the process of polarization. **3** *trans., intrans., said of people or opinions* to split according to opposing views.

polarizing filter *Telecomm.* a filter which allows the passage of light which is polarized in one direction only. It is used in general photography for the control of surface reflections, eg from glass or water, and to darken blue skies. Other applications include definition of mineral structures in photomicrography.

Polaroid /ˈpəʊlərɔɪd/ *noun trademark* a plastic material able to polarize light, used in sunglasses, etc to reduce glare.

Polaroid camera a camera with an internal developing and printing process, which produces a print within seconds of exposure.

polder /ˈpəʊldə(r)/ *noun* an area of land lying below sea level, from which the sea has been drained; a piece of reclaimed land. [from Old Dutch *polre*]

Pole *noun* a native or citizen of Poland.

pole[1] *noun* **1** either of two points representing the north and south ends of the axis about which the Earth rotates, and known as the North Pole and South Pole, respectively. **2** *Astron.* either of two corresponding points on the celestial sphere, towards which the north and south ends of the Earth's axis point, and about which the stars appear to rotate daily. **3** same as MAGNETIC POLE. **4** either of the two terminals of a battery. **5** either of two opposite positions in argument, opinion, etc. — **poles apart** *colloq.* widely different or apart. [from Latin *polus,* from Greek *polos,* axis, pivot]

    . . . .

■ **5** extremity, extreme, limit. **poles apart** irreconcilable, worlds apart, incompatible, like chalk and cheese.

. . . .

pole[2] *noun* **1** a rod, especially cylindrical in section and fixed in the ground as a support. **2** an old measure of length equal to 5-yd or 5.30m (also called PERCH, ROD). — **up the pole** *colloq.* mad; crazy. [from Anglo-Saxon *pal,* from Latin *palus,* stake]

    . . . .

■ **1** post, stake, bar, rod, stick, shaft, spar, upright, mast, staff.

. . . .

poleaxe — *noun* **1** a short-handled axe with a spike or hammer opposite the blade, used, especially formerly, for slaughtering cattle. **2** *Hist.* a long-handled battleaxe. — *verb* to strike, fell, or floor with or as if with a poleaxe. [from Middle English *pollax,* head axe, from POLL, head]

polecat *noun* **1** a dark-brown animal of the weasel family, that emits a foul smell. **2** *North Amer., esp. US* a skunk. [from Middle English *polcat*]

polemic /pəˈlɛmɪk/ — *noun* a piece of writing or a speech fiercely attacking or defending an idea, opinion, etc; writing or oratory of this sort. — *adj.* (*also* **polemical**) relating to or involving polemic or polemics. [from Greek *polemikos,* from *polemos,* war]

polemically *adv.* in a polemic way, controversially.

polemicist *noun* someone who writes polemics or engages in controversy.

polemics *sing. or pl. noun* the art of verbal wrangling; the cut and thrust of fierce disputation.

polenta /pɒ'lentə/ *noun* an Italian dish of cooked ground maize. [from Italian, from Latin *polenta*, hulled and crushed grain]

pole position the position at the inside of the front row of cars at the start of a race; an advantageous position at the start of any contest.

Pole Star a popular name for the star *Polaris*.

pole vault an athletic event consisting of a jump over a high horizontal bar with the help of a long flexible pole to haul one's body into the air.

pole-vaulter *noun* an athlete who takes part in a pole vault.

police /pə'liːs/ — *pl. noun* **1** the body of men and women employed by the government of a country to keep order, enforce the law, prevent crime, etc. **2** members of this body: *over 200 police were on duty.* — *verb* **1** to keep law and order in (an area) using the police, army, etc. **2** to supervise (an operation, etc) to ensure that it is fairly or properly run. [from French *police*, from Greek *politeia*, political constitution]

> ⊟ *noun* **1** police force, constabulary, *colloq.* the law, *slang* the Bill, *slang* the fuzz. **2** officers, constables, PCs, *slang* cops, *slang* coppers, *colloq.* bobbies. *verb* **1** patrol, guard, protect, defend, keep the peace. **2** supervise, oversee, monitor, regulate, control, watch, observe, check.

police constable a police officer of the lowest rank.

police dog a dog trained to work with policemen.

policeman *noun* a male police officer.

police officer a member of a police force.

police state a state with a repressive government that operates through secret police to eliminate opposition to it.

police station the office of a local police force.

policewoman *noun* a female police officer.

policy[1] /'pɒlɪsɪ/ *noun* (PL. **policies**) **1** a plan of action, usually based on certain principles, decided on by a body or individual. **2** a principle or set of principles on which to base decisions: *it is not our policy to charge for service.* **3** a course of conduct for following: *your best policy is to keep quiet.* [from Old French *policie*, from Greek *politeia*, political constitution]

> ⊟ **1** plan, programme, scheme, code of practice, rules, guidelines, protocol. **2** principle, practice, custom. **3** course, course of action or conduct, stance, position, line, procedure, method.

policy[2] *noun* (PL. **policies**) (*also* **insurance policy**) an insurance agreement, or the document confirming it. [from Old French *police*, from Latin *apodixis*, receipt, from Greek *apodeixis*, proof]

policy-holder *noun* a person who holds a contract of insurance.

policy unit *Politics* a group of officials in a government department or other public agency, whose role is to supply information, advice, and analysis to policy makers.

polio *noun colloq.* poliomyelitis.

poliomyelitis /pəʊlɪəʊmaɪə'laɪtɪs/ *noun* a viral disease of the brain and spinal cord, in some cases resulting in permanent paralysis. [from Greek *polios*, grey + *myelos*, marrow + -ITIS]

Polish /'pəʊlɪʃ/ — *adj.* of or relating to Poland, its language, culture, or people. — *noun* the language of Poland.

polish /'pɒlɪʃ/ — *verb* **1** *trans., intrans.* to make or become smooth and glossy by rubbing. **2** to improve or perfect. **3** to make cultivated, refined, or elegant: *polished manners.* — *noun* **1** a substance used for polishing surfaces. **2** a smooth shiny finish; a gloss. **3** an act of polishing. **4** refinement or elegance. — **polish something off** *colloq.* to complete work, etc or consume food, especially speedily.

polish something up 1 to work up a shine on it by polishing. **2** to improve a skill, etc by working at it. [from Old French *polir*, from Latin *polire*]

> ⊟ *verb* **1** buff, burnish, wax, shine, brighten, smooth, rub, clean. **2** improve, perfect, refine, enhance, brush up, touch up. **3** cultivate, refine, finish. *noun* **1** wax. **2** shine, gloss, sheen, lustre, brightness, brilliance, sparkle, smoothness, finish, glaze, veneer. **3** shine. **4** refinement, elegance, cultivation, sophistication, finesse, style, grace, poise, class, breeding.
> ⊟ *verb* **1** tarnish, dull. *noun* **2** dullness. **4** clumsiness.

polisher *noun* a person, device, or machine that polishes.

politburo /'pɒlɪtbjʊərəʊ/ *noun* (PL. **politburos**) (*also* **Politburo**) the policy-forming committee of a Communist state. [from Russian *politburo*]

polite *adj.* **1** well-mannered; considerate towards others; courteous. **2** well-bred, cultivated, or refined: *polite society.* [from Latin *politus*, from *polire*, to polish]

> ⊟ **1** well-mannered, considerate, courteous, respectful, civil, obliging, thoughtful, tactful, diplomatic. **2** well-bred, cultivated, refined, cultured, gentlemanly, ladylike, gracious.
> ⊟ **1** impolite, discourteous, rude.

politely *adv.* in a polite way.

politeness *noun* being polite, courtesy.

politic /'pɒlɪtɪk/ — *adj.* **1** *said of a course of action* prudent; wise; shrewd. **2** *said of a person* cunning; crafty. **3** *old use* political: *the body politic* (= the people of a state considered as a political group). — *verb intrans.* (**politicked, politicking**) *derog.* to indulge in politics. [from Old French *politique*, from Greek *politikos*, civic]

political *adj.* **1** of or relating to government or public affairs. **2** relating to politics. **3** interested or involved in politics. **4** *said of a course of action* made in the interests of gaining or keeping power. **5** *said of a map* showing political and social structure rather than physical features.

political asylum protection given by a country to political refugees from a foreign country.

political correctness the avoidance of expressions or actions that may be understood to exclude or denigrate people on the grounds of race, gender, or sexual orientation.

politically *adv.* in a political way; in terms of politics.

political prisoner a person imprisoned for dissenting from the government.

political science the study of politics and government.

politician *noun* **1** someone engaged in politics, especially as a member of parliament. **2** *derog.* someone who goes in for power-seeking manoeuvres. [from Greek *politikos*, civic]

> ⊟ **1** Member of Parliament, MP, minister, statesman, stateswoman, legislator.

politicization or **politicisation** *noun* politicizing or being politicized.

politicize or **politicise** /pə'lɪtɪsaɪz/ *verb* **1** *intrans.* to go in for political activities or discussion. **2** to give a political nature to: *the politicizing of sport.* **3** to make (someone) aware of or informed about politics.

politico /pə'lɪtɪkəʊ/ *noun* (PL. **politicos, politicoes**) *derog.* a politician or someone keen on politics. [from Italian or Spanish *politico*]

politico- *combining form* forming words meaning 'political': *politico-philosophical writings*.

politics *noun* (*usually sing.*) **1** the science or business of government. **2** political science. **3** a political life as a career. **4** (*sing., pl.*) political activities, wrangling, etc. **5** (*pl.*) moves and manoeuvres concerned with the acquisition of power or getting one's way, eg in business. **6** (*pl.*) one's political sympathies or principles: *what are your politics?*

. . . .

■ **1** government, affairs of state, statecraft, public affairs, diplomacy, statesmanship. **2** political science, civics.

. . . .

polity /'pɒlɪtɪ/ *noun* (PL. **polities**) **1** a politically organized body such as a state, church, or association. **2** any form of political institution or government. [from Greek *politeia*, political constitution]

polka /'pɒlkə/ — *noun* a lively dance performed usually with a partner, with a pattern of three steps followed by a hop; also, a piece of music for this. — *verb intrans.* (**polkaed, polkaing**) to dance a polka. [from Czech *pulka*, half-step, or *Polka*, Polish woman]

polka dot any of numerous regularly spaced dots forming a pattern on fabric, etc.

poll /pəʊl/ — *noun* **1** (**polls**) a political election: *victory at the polls.* **2** the voting, or votes cast, at an election: *a heavy poll.* **3** (*also* **opinion poll**) a survey of public opinion carried out by directly questioning a representative sample of the populace. **4** *old use* the head; this as a unit in numbering. — *verb* **1** to win (a number of votes) in an election. **2** to register the votes of (a population). **3** *trans., intrans.* to cast (one's vote). **4** to conduct an opinion poll among. **5** to cut off the horns of (cattle). **6** to cut the top off (a tree); to make a pollard of. [from Middle English *polle*, (the hair of) the head]

. . . .

■ *noun* **1** ballot, ballot-box, vote. **2** voting, vote, count, tally. **3** opinion poll, survey, census, straw poll.

. . . .

pollack /'pɒlək/ *noun* (PL. **pollack, pollacks**) an edible fish of northern waters, related to the cod.

pollard /'pɒləd/ — *noun* **1** *Bot.* a tree whose branches have been cut back, usually to a height of about 2m above the ground, in order to produce a crown of shoots at the top of the trunk, out of reach of farm livestock and deer. Wood is then periodically harvested for firewood, fencing, etc. **2** *Zool.* an animal whose horns have been removed. — *verb* to make a pollard of (a tree or animal). [from POLL + suffix *-ard* denoting a person, animal, etc of a certain type]

pollen /'pɒlən/ *noun* the fine dust-like powder, usually yellow in colour, that is produced by the anthers of the stamens of angiosperms (flowering plants), and by the male cones of gymnosperms (cone-bearing plants). See also POLLINATION.

pollen count a measure of the amount of pollen in the air at any particular time, published for the benefit of those who have a pollen allergy.

pollen sac *Bot.* in flowering plants, one of the four cavities in the anther of a stamen in which the pollen is produced and stored.

pollen tube *Bot.* a slender tube that grows out from the wall of a pollen grain after pollination. In flowering plants it grows down through the stigma and style, and into the ovule, and carries within it two male gametes, one of which fertilizes the egg cell after the pollen tube has entered the ovule.

pollinate *verb Bot.* in flowering and cone-bearing plants, to transfer pollen by the process of pollination in order to achieve fertilization and subsequent development of seed. [from Latin *pollen*, flour]

pollination *noun Bot.* in flowering plants, the transfer of pollen from the anther of a stamen to the stigma of the same flower (*self-pollination*) or another flower of the same species (*cross-pollination*). In cone-bearing plants it involves the transfer of pollen from the male cone to the female cone. Pollination can be achieved by any of a number of different agents, eg insects, wind, water, birds, or humans.

polling-booth *noun* an enclosed compartment at a polling-station in which to mark one's ballot paper in private.

polling-station *noun* the centre one attends to cast one's vote.

pollster /'pəʊlstə(r)/ *noun* a person who organizes opinion polls.

poll tax 1 *Hist.* a fixed tax levied on each member of a population. **2** the community charge.

pollutant /pə'luːtənt/ — *noun* something that pollutes. — *adj.* polluting.

pollute /pə'luːt/ *verb* **1** to contaminate with harmful substances; to make impure. **2** to corrupt (someone's mind, etc). [from Latin *polluere*, to soil, defile]

. . . .

■ CONTAMINATE, INFECT, POISON, TAINT, ADULTERATE. **1** dirty, foul, soil. **2** corrupt, debase, defile, sully, stain, mar, spoil.

. . . .

pollution *noun* the adverse effect on the natural environment, including human, animal, and plant life, of a harmful substance that does not occur naturally (eg industrial and radioactive waste, pesticides), or the concentration to harmful levels of a naturally occurring substance (eg nitrates). It also includes the damaging effects of noise and changes in temperature.

. . . .

■ contamination, infection, tainting, adulteration, dirtiness, foulness, defilement, impurity.
☒ purification, purity, cleanness.

. . . .

polo *noun* a stick-and-ball game played on horseback by teams of four using long-handled hammers to propel the ball along the ground. [from Tibetan dialect *polo*, ball]

polonaise /pɒlə'neɪz/ *noun* a stately Polish promenading dance, or a piece of music for this. [from French *polonaise*, feminine of *polonais*, Polish]

polo neck 1 a high close-fitting neck band on a sweater or shirt, worn folded over. **2** a sweater or shirt with such a neck.

polo-neck *adj.* having a polo neck.

polonium /pə'ləʊnɪəm/ *noun Chem.* (SYMBOL **Po**, ATOMIC NUMBER **84**) a rare radioactive metal that emits alpha particles, occurs naturally in uranium ores, and is prepared artificially by bombarding bismuth with neutrons. It is used in portable radiation sources, as an energy source in satellites, and for dissipating static electricity. [from Latin *Polonia*, Poland, the discoverer's native country]

polony /pə'ləʊnɪ/ *noun* (PL. **polonies**) a dry sausage made of partly cooked meat. [probably from *Bologna*, Italy]

poltergeist /'pɒltəgaɪst/ *noun* a type of household ghost responsible for otherwise unaccountable noises, given also to shifting objects about. [from German *poltern*, to make a racket + *Geist*, spirit, ghost]

poltroon /pɒl'truːn/ *noun* a despicable coward. [from Italian *poltrone*, lazybones]

poly /'pɒlɪ/ *noun* (PL. **polys**) *colloq.* a polytechnic.

poly- *combining form* forming words meaning: **1** many or much. **2** *Chem.* polymerized. [from Greek *poly*, many, much]

polyamide /pɒlɪ'amaɪd/ *noun Chem.* a polymer formed by the linking of the amino group of one molecule with the carboxyl group of the next, eg nylon.

polyandrous /pɒlɪ'andrəs/ *adj.* **1** having more than one husband at the same time. **2** *Bot.* having many stamens. See also MONANDROUS. [from POLY- + Greek *aner*, man, husband]

polyandry /'pɒlɪandrɪ/ *noun* the custom or practice of having more than one husband at the same time.

polyanthus /pɒlɪ'anθəs/ *noun* (PL. **polyanthuses**) a cultivated hybrid plant related to the primrose, with several brightly coloured flowers to each stem. [from POLY- + Greek *anthos*, flower]

polyarchy /'pɒlɪɑːkɪ/ *noun Politics* government by the many: a characteristic of modern, Western, liberal democracies. The main features are opposition, and the absence of strictly hierarchical organizations (these tend to be segmented with people participating in political processes of direct interest to them).

polycarbonate *noun Chem.* a strong rigid thermoplastic material, formed by the polymerization of monomers that are linked to each other by means of carbonate groups, and used to make safety helmets, protective windows, soft drink bottles, and electrical terminals.

polycentrism *noun Politics* the condition of having, or the tendency to have, many centres. In politics, the term has been applied to the growing independence of European communist parties from the Soviet Union after the Stalinist era. This trend was begun by the Yugoslavian Communist Party under Tito, and was adopted to varying degrees by other national parties as a means of taking account of local conditions.

polychromatic *adj.* 1 multicoloured. 2 *said of radiation* having more than one wavelength. [from POLY- + Greek *chroma*, colour]

polychromy /'pɒlɪkroʊmɪ/ *noun* 1 *Art* the practice of colouring sculpture, especially common in ancient Egypt and Greece, and in medieval times, but largely abandoned from c.1500 in favour of monochrome sculpture. It has been revived in the 20c. 2 *Archit.* the use of coloured marbles, bricks, flint, stone, etc on buildings for decorative effect.

polyester /pɒlɪˈestə(r)/ *noun* a synthetic resin made from certain alcohols and acids, and used to form artificial fibres, eg Terylene, that are strong, durable, resistant to creasing, and quick drying. These are widely used in textiles to make clothing, often in blends with natural fibres. [from POLY- + ESTER]

polyethylene /pɒlɪˈɛθɪliːn/ *noun* polythene.

polygamist /pəˈlɪɡəmɪst/ *noun* a person who has more than one husband or wife at the same time.

polygamous /pəˈlɪɡəməs/ *adj.* having more than one husband or wife at the same time.

polygamously *adv.* in a polygamous way.

polygamy /pəˈlɪɡəmɪ/ *noun* the custom or practice of having more than one husband or wife at the same time. [from POLY- + Greek *gamos*, marriage]

polyglot /'pɒlɪɡlɒt/ — *adj.* speaking, using, or written in, many languages. — *noun* a person who speaks many languages. [from POLY- + Greek *glotta*, tongue, language]

polygon /'pɒlɪɡɒn/ *noun Geom.* a plane (two-dimensional) figure with a number of straight sides, usually more than three, eg pentagon, hexagon, octagon. In a *regular polygon* all the sides are of the same length, and all the internal angles are equal. The greater the number of sides, the larger the sum of the internal angles, and the more closely the polygon resembles a circle. [from POLY- + Greek *gonia*, angle]

polygonal /pəˈlɪɡənəl/ *adj.* having the form of a polygon, many-sided.

polygraph /'pɒlɪɡrɑːf/ *noun Medicine* a device that monitors several body functions simultaneously, eg pulse, blood pressure, and conductivity of the skin (to detect perspiration). Such devices have sometimes been used as lie-detectors, although the scientific accuracy of the data obtained is debatable, and cannot generally be used as legal evidence. [from POLY- + Greek *graphein*, to write]

polygyny /pəˈlɪdʒɪnɪ/ *noun* the condition or custom of having more than one wife at the same time. [from POLY + Greek *gyne*, woman, wife]

polyhedral /pɒlɪˈhiːdrəl/ *adj.* having the form of a polyhedron, many-sided.

polyhedron /pɒlɪˈhiːdrən/ *noun* (PL. **polyhedrons, polyhedra**) *Geom.* a solid (three-dimensional) figure with four or more faces, all of which are polygons, eg tetrahedron (four triangular faces). In a *regular polyhedron* all the faces are regular polygons, eg cube (six square faces), and the greater the number of faces, the more closely the polyhedron resembles a sphere. [from POLY- + Greek *hedra*, seat, base, face]

polymath /'pɒlɪmæθ/ *noun* a person who is learned in a large variety of subjects. [from POLY- + Greek *manthanein*, to learn]

polymer /'pɒlɪmə(r)/ *noun Chem.* a very large molecule consisting of a long chain of much smaller molecules

(*monomers*) linked end to end to form a series of repeating units. [from POLY- + Greek *meros*, part]

polymeric /pɒlɪˈmɛrɪk/ *adj.* related to or of the nature of a polymer.

polymerization or **polymerisation** /pɒlɪməraɪˈzeɪʃən/ *noun Chem.* a chemical reaction in which two or more small molecules or *monomers* are joined together in a chain to form a large molecule or polymer.

polymerize or **polymerise** *verb trans., intrans. Chem.* to undergo or cause to undergo polymerization.

polymorphism *noun* 1 *Biol.* the occurrence of a living organism in two or more different structural forms at different stages of its life cycle. 2 *Genetics* the occurrence of several genetically determined and distinct forms within a single population, eg the different blood groups in humans. 3 *Chem.* the occurrence of a chemical substance in two or more different crystalline forms, eg diamond and graphite are different crystalline forms of carbon.

polymorphous or **polymorphic** *adj. Biol.* 1 denoting a living organism that occurs in different structural forms at different stages of its life cycle. 2 denoting a species or population in which several distinct forms exist, eg worker, drone, and queen bees. [from POLY- + Greek *morphe*, shape]

polyp /'pɒlɪp/ *noun* 1 *Zool.* a tiny tube-shaped sea creature with a ring of tentacles round its mouth. 2 *Pathol.* a small growth with a stalk-like base, projecting from the mucous membrane, eg inside the nose. [from Greek *polypous*, many-footed, from Greek *poly*, many + *pous*, foot]

polyphonic /pɒlɪˈfɒnɪk/ *adj.* 1 having many voices. 2 relating to polyphony.

polyphony /pəˈlɪfənɪ/ *noun* a style of musical composition in which each part or voice has an independent melodic value (as distinct from *homophony*, in which only one part or voice carries the melody, with simple choral accompaniment). True polyphony first appeared in the 11c, and its most important forms are the motet, the rota or round, the canon, polyphonic masses, madrigals, and (in the 18c) the fugue. The term generally denotes contrapuntal music. [from POLY- + Greek *phone*, voice, sound]

polyploidy *noun Genetics* the condition in which three or more sets of chromosomes are present within a cell nucleus. It arises spontaneously and is common in many crop plants, including wheat, but rarely occurs in animals (and would result in sterility).

polypous /'pɒlɪpəs/ *adj.* of the nature of a polyp.

polypropene *noun Chem.* a white translucent thermoplastic, formed by the polymerization of propene (propylene), that is tough, and resistant to water, solvents, oil, and high temperatures. It is used to make fibres, film, rope, and moulded articles, eg toys.

polypropylene *noun* same as POLYPROPENE.

polyptych /'pɒlɪptɪk/ *noun* an altarpiece consisting of several panels with a separate picture in each, surrounded by an elaborate, usually gilded, frame. Common in the Middle Ages, the form was partly superseded in the Renaissance by the unified *pala d'altare*. [from POLY- + Greek *ptychos*, a fold]

polysaccharide *noun Biochem.* a large carbohydrate molecule consisting of a large number of monosaccharides (simple sugars) linked together to form long chains which may or may not be branched, eg starch, cellulose.

polystyrene /pɒlɪˈstaɪriːn/ *noun Chem.* a tough transparent thermoplastic, formed by the polymerization of styrene (phenylethene), that is a good thermal and electrical insulator, with a high resistance to impact. It is widely used in packaging, insulation, ceiling tiles, etc, and can also be expanded to form polystyrene foam.

polysyllabic /pɒlɪsɪˈlæbɪk/ *adj.*, *said of a word* having three or more syllables.

polysyllable *noun* a word of three or more syllables.

polysynthetic language a language type using long and complex words made up of many smaller words, parts of words, and inflected forms. Examples include certain

Native American languages such as Mohawk and Eskimo, and the Australian aboriginal languages.

polytechnic /pɒlɪˈtɛknɪk/ — *noun* a college of higher education in which courses in a large range of subjects, especially of a technical or vocational kind, are available. — *adj.* relating to technical training. [from POLY- + Greek *techne*, art]

polytheism /pɒlɪˈθiːɪzm/ *noun* belief in, or worship of, more than one god. [from POLY- + Greek *theos*, god]

polytheist *noun* a believer in the doctrine of polytheism.

polytheistic *adj.* relating to or characterized by polytheism.

polythene /ˈpɒlɪθiːn/ *noun* a waxy translucent thermoplastic, formed by the polymerization of ethene (ethylene), that is a good insulator, easily moulded, and resistant to chemicals such as acids. It is used in the form of film or sheeting to package food products, clothing, etc, and to make pipes, moulded articles, and electrical insulators. Also called POLYETHYLENE.

polyunsaturated *adj. Chem.* denoting a compound, especially a fat or oil, that contains two or more double bonds per molecule, eg polyunsaturated margarine. It has been suggested that such compounds are less likely to cause cardiovascular disease, but it has not yet been established whether they also have adverse effects.

polyurethane /pɒlɪˈjʊərəθeɪn/ *noun Chem.* any of various polymers that contain the urethane group, and are used in protective coatings, adhesives, paints, varnishes, plastics, rubbers, and foams. [from POLY- + *urethane*, an ester]

polyvinyl chloride /pɒlɪˈvaɪnɪl ˈklɔːraɪd/ *Chem.* (ABBREV. PVC) a tough white thermoplastic, formed by the polymerization of vinyl chloride, that is resistant to fire, chemicals, moisture, and weathering, is easily dyed, and can be softened by mixing with a plasticizer. It is used in pipes and other moulded products, gramophone records, food packaging, waterproof clothing, and insulation for electric wires and cables.

pom *noun colloq. Austral., New Zealand* a pommy.

pomace /ˈpʌmɪs/ *noun* **1** crushed apples for cider-making; the residue of these or of any similar fruit after pressing. **2** anything crushed or ground to a pulp. [from Latin *pomum*, fruit, apple]

pomade /pɒˈmɑːd/ *noun Hist.* a perfumed ointment for the hair and scalp. [from French *pomade*, from Italian *pomata*, from Latin *pomum*, apple, a one-time ingredient]

pomander /pɒˈmændə(r)/ *noun* **1** a perfumed ball composed of various substances, used to scent wardrobes, originally carried to ward off infection. **2** a perforated container for this or, now more commonly, a mixture of scented flower-petals, etc. [from Old French *pomme d'ambre*, apple of amber]

pome *noun Bot.* a type of fruit in which a fleshy outer layer, which develops from the receptacle of the flower, surrounds a central core that develops from the fused carpels, and contains a number of seeds, eg apple, pear. [from Latin *pomum*, apple]

pomegranate /ˈpɒmɪɡranət/ *noun* **1** a small deciduous tree or shrub of the genus *Punica*, native to Asia but widely cultivated in warm temperate regions both for its edible fruit and for its attractive white, orange, or red flowers. **2** the fruit of this plant, similar in size to an apple, which has tough red or brown skin surrounding a mass of seeds, each of which is enclosed by red juicy edible flesh. It is eaten raw, squeezed for its juice, or used to make grenadine syrup. [from Latin *pomum granatum*, seedy apple]

pomelo /ˈpɒmələʊ/ *noun* (PL. **pomelos**) a yellow citrus fruit similar to a grapefruit, native to SE Asia. [from Dutch *pompelmoes*, shaddock, grapefruit]

Pomeranian /pɒməˈreɪnɪən/ *noun* a small breed of dog with a sharp-pointed face and thick long silky coat.

pomfret /ˈpʌmfrɪt/ *noun* (*also* **pomfret cake**) a disc-shaped liquorice sweet traditionally made in *Pontefract*, Yorkshire. [from Old French *Pontfret*, Pontefract, from Latin *pons*, bridge + *fractus*, broken]

pommel /ˈpʌml/ — *noun* **1** the raised forepart of a saddle. **2** a rounded knob forming the end of a sword hilt. — *verb* (**pommelled**, **pommelling**) to pummel. [from Old French *pomel*, knob]

pommy *noun* (PL. **pommies**) *Austral., New Zealand derog. colloq.* a British, or especially English, person.

pomp *noun* **1** ceremonial grandeur. **2** vain ostentation. [from Latin *pompa*, procession]

⊞ **1** grandeur, splendour, magnificence, pageantry, ceremony, ceremonial, ritual, solemnity, formality, ceremoniousness. **2** ostentation, flourish, show, display, parade.
⊟ AUSTERITY, SIMPLICITY.

pompom or **pompon** *noun* a ball of cut wool or other yarn, used as a trimming on clothes. [from French *pompon*]

pom-pom *noun* an automatic quick-firing gun; a machine gun; a multi-barrelled anti-aircraft gun. [imitative]

pomposity /pɒmˈpɒsɪtɪ/ *noun* a pompous quality or manner.

pompous *adj.* **1** solemnly self-important. **2** *said of language* inappropriately grand and flowery; pretentious. [from Latin *pomposus*, from *pompa*, procession]

⊞ **1** self-important, arrogant, grandiose, supercilious, overbearing, imperious, magisterial. **2** bombastic, pretentious, ostentatious, high-flown, flowery, over-blown, windy, affected.
⊟ **1** unassuming, modest. **2** simple, unaffected.

pompously *adv.* in a pompous way.

ponce /pɒns/ — *noun offensive slang* **1** an effeminate man. **2** a pimp. — *verb intrans.* (**ponce about or around**) **1** to mince about in an effeminate manner. **2** to mess around.

poncho /ˈpɒntʃoʊ/ *noun* (PL. **ponchos**) an originally S American outer garment made of, or like, a blanket with a hole for the head to go through. [from Spanish *poncho*]

pond *noun* a small body of water, whether natural or artificial. [from Middle English *ponde*, enclosure]

ponder *verb trans., intrans.* (**pondered**, **pondering**) (**ponder something** or **on something**) to consider or contemplate it. [from Latin *ponderare*, to weigh]

ponderous *adj.* **1** *said of speech, humour, etc* heavy-handed, laborious, over-solemn, or pompous. **2** heavy or cumbersome; lumbering in movement. **3** weighty; important. [from Latin *ponderosus*, from *ponderare*, to weigh]

ponderously *adv.* in a ponderous way.

ponderousness *noun* being ponderous.

pong *colloq.* — *noun* a stink; a bad smell. — *verb intrans.* to smell badly.

pongy *adj.* (**pongier, pongiest**) *colloq.* stinking, smelly.

poniard /ˈpɒnjəd/ *noun* a slim-bladed dagger. [from French *poignard*, from *poing*, fist]

pons /pɒnz/ *noun* (PL. **pontes**) *Anat.* in the brain of mammals, the mass of nerve fibres that connects the medulla oblongata to the thalamus, and is responsible for relaying nerve impulses between different parts of the brain. [from Latin *pons*, bridge]

pontiff *noun* a title for the Pope, formerly applied to any Roman Catholic bishop. [from Latin *pontifex*, high priest]

pontifical /pɒnˈtɪfɪkəl/ *adj.* **1** belonging or relating to a pontiff. **2** *derog.* pompously opinionated; dogmatic. [from Latin *pontificalis*, from *pontifex*, high priest]

pontificals *pl. noun* the ceremonial dress of a bishop or pope.

pontificate — *verb intrans.* (pronounced -keɪt) to pronounce one's opinion pompously and arrogantly. — *noun* (pronounced -kət) the office of a pope. [from Latin *pontificatus*, high priesthood, from *pontifex*, priest]

pontoon[1] *noun* any of a number of flat-bottomed craft, punts, barges, etc, anchored side by side across a river, to support a temporary bridge. [from French *ponton*, from Latin *ponto*, punt]

pontoon[2] *noun Cards* a game in which the object is to collect sets of cards that add up to 21 and no more. [alteration of French *vingt-et-un*, twenty-one]

pontoon bridge a bridge supported on pontoons.

pony *noun* (PL. **ponies**) any of several small breeds of horse, usually less than 14.2 hands (1.5m) in height when fully grown, and noted for their intelligence, hardiness, and endurance. [from Scot. *powney*, from French *poulenet*, diminutive of *poulain*, colt]

ponytail *noun* a person's hair drawn back and tied at the back of the head, so that it hangs free like a pony's tail.

pony-trekking *noun* the recreational activity of cross-country pony-riding in groups.

poodle *noun* a breed of dog whose curly coat is traditionally clipped in an elaborate style. [from German *Pudel*, from *pudeln*, to splash]

poof *noun offensive slang* a male homosexual. [from French *pouffe*, puff]

pooh *interj. colloq.* an exclamation of scorn or of disgust, eg at a smell. [imitative]

pooh-pooh *verb colloq.* to express scorn for (a suggestion, etc).

pool[1] *noun* **1** a small area of still water: *a rock pool.* **2** a puddle; a patch of spilt liquid: *pools of blood.* **3** a swimming-pool. **4** a deep part of a stream or river. [from Anglo-Saxon *pol*]

▣ **1** pond, lake, mere, tarn, watering-hole. **3** swimming-pool, paddling-pool.

pool[2] — *noun* **1** a reserve of money, personnel, vehicles, etc used as a communal resource: *a typing pool.* **2** the combined stakes of those betting on something; a jackpot. **3** *Commerce* a group of businesses with a common arrangement to maintain high prices, so eliminating competition and preserving profits. **4** a game like billiards played with a white cue ball and usually 15 numbered coloured balls, the aim being to shoot specified balls into specified pockets using the cue ball. **5** (*also* **football pool** or **pools**) a competition involving betting by post on the results of a number of football matches. — *verb* to put (money or other resources) into a common supply for general use. [from French *poule*, hen, stakes]

▣ *noun* **1** fund, reserve, accumulation, bank, kitty. **2** jackpot, pot, purse. **3** syndicate, cartel, ring, combine, consortium, collective, group, team. *verb* contribute, *colloq.* chip in, *colloq.* muck in, combine, amalgamate, merge, share.

poop[1] *noun* the raised, enclosed part at the stern of old sailing ships. [from Latin *puppis*]

poop[2] *colloq. verb* **1** (*usually* **be pooped**) to exhaust. **2** (*intrans.*) to become exhausted. — **poop out** to give up from exhaustion.

poop deck a ship's deck surmounting the poop.

poop scoop or **pooper scooper** *colloq.* a small scoop used to lift and remove dog faeces from pavements, etc.

poor *adj.* **1** not having sufficient money or means to live comfortably. **2** (**poor in something**) not well supplied with it: *a country poor in minerals.* **3** not good; weak; unsatisfactory. **4** unsatisfactorily small or sparse: *a poor attendance.* **5** used in expressing pity or sympathy: *poor fellow!* — **poor man's** *derog.* denoting a substitute of lower quality or price: *a flower called 'poor man's orchid'.* [from Old French *povre*, from Latin *pauper*, poor]

▣ **1** impoverished, poverty-stricken, badly off, *colloq.* hard up, *colloq.* broke, *colloq.* stony-broke, *slang* skint, bankrupt, penniless, destitute, straitened, needy. **2** lacking in, deficient in. **3** unsatisfactory, weak, substandard, inferior, mediocre, below par, low-grade, second-rate, third-rate, *colloq.* low-

rent, shoddy, bad, imperfect, faulty, feeble, *colloq.* pathetic, sorry, miserable, wretched, worthless, fruitless. **4** insufficient, sparse, scanty, skimpy, meagre, depleted, exhausted. **5** unfortunate, unhappy, pitiable, pitiful, unlucky, luckless, ill-fated, miserable, pathetic.

🗷 **1** rich, wealthy, affluent. **3** excellent, superior, impressive. **4** good, strong, large. **5** fortunate, lucky.

poorhouse *noun Hist.* an institution maintained at public expense, for sheltering the poor; a workhouse.

poor law *Hist.* a law or set of laws concerned with the public support of the poor.

poorly — *adv.* not well; badly. — *adj.* old *colloq. use, dialect* ill.

▣ *adj.* ill, sick, unwell, indisposed, ailing, sickly, *Brit.* off-colour, below par, *colloq.* out of sorts, *colloq.* under the weather, *colloq.* seedy, *colloq.* groggy, *colloq.* rotten.

🗷 *adj.* well, healthy.

poorness *noun* being poor.

poor white *derog.* a member of an impoverished and deprived class of white people living amongst blacks in the southern USA or South Africa.

pop[1] — *noun* **1** a sharp explosive noise, like that of a cork coming out of a bottle. **2** *colloq.* sweet non-alcoholic fizzy drinks. — *verb* (**popped, popping**) **1** *trans., intrans.* to make or cause to make a pop. **2** *trans., intrans.* to burst with a pop. **3** (*also* **pop out**) to spring out; to protrude. **4** *intrans., colloq.* to go quickly in a direction specified: *pop next door.* **5** *colloq.* to put quickly or briefly: *just pop it in the oven.* — *adv.* with a pop. — **pop off** *colloq.* to die. **pop the question** *humorous colloq.* to propose marriage. **pop up** (*intrans.*) to appear or occur, especially unexpectedly. [imitative]

▣ *noun* **1** bang, crack, snap, burst, explosion. *verb* **1** burst, explode, go off, bang, crack, snap. **2** burst, explode. **4** *colloq.* nip.

pop[2] — *noun* (*also* **pop music**) modern music popular especially among young people, usually with a strong beat, often played with electronic equipment (guitars, keyboards, etc). — *adj.* **1** performing or featuring pop music. **2** popular: *pop culture.* [a shortening of POPULAR]

pop[3] *noun North Amer. colloq., often as a form of address* one's father or an elderly man. [see PAPA]

pop. *abbrev.* population.

popcorn *noun* maize grains heated till they puff up and burst open.

pope *noun* **1** (*often* **Pope**) the Bishop of Rome, the head of the Roman Catholic Church. **2** a priest in the Eastern Orthodox Church. [from Greek *pappas*, papa, in the early Church used respectfully to bishops]

popery *noun offensive* Roman Catholicism.

pop-eyed *adj. colloq.* with eyes protruding, especially in amazement.

popgun *noun* a toy gun that fires a cork or pellet with a pop.

popinjay /ˈpɒpɪndʒeɪ/ *noun old derog. use* someone vain or conceited; a dandy or fop. [from Old French *papegai*, parrot]

popish *adj. offensive* Roman Catholic; of Roman Catholicism.

poplar *noun* **1** a tall slender deciduous tree of the genus *Populus*, found in north temperate regions, with broad simple leaves, which often tremble in a slight breeze, and flowers produced in catkins. Poplars grow fast and are often planted as ornamental trees or to give shelter. **2** the soft fine-grained yellowish wood of this tree, which is used to make plywood, matches, boxes, and paper pulp. [from Latin *populus*]

poplin *noun* a strong cotton cloth with a finely ribbed finish. [from French *popeline*, from Italian *papalina*, papal cloth, because it was made in the *papal* city of Avignon]

poppadum or **poppadom** /ˈpɒpədəm/ *noun* a paper-thin pancake grilled till crisp for serving with Indian dishes. [from Tamil *poppadum*]

popper *noun* a press stud.

poppet *noun* **1** a term of endearment for someone lovable. **2** in vehicle engines, a valve that rises and falls in its housing. [an earlier form of PUPPET]

popping-crease *noun Cricket* the line behind which the batsman must stand, parallel to, and four feet in front of, the wicket.

pop poetry a term used from the 1970s for a type of verse which is written primarily for public performance rather than private reading. It is often topical, satirical, and may be accompanied by music.

poppy *noun* (PL. **poppies**) **1** a cornfield plant with large scarlet flowers and a hairy, wiry stem; any of several related plants, eg one from which opium is obtained. **2** an artificial red poppy, worn for Poppy Day, symbolizing the poppies that grew on the battlefields of Flanders after World War I. [from Anglo-Saxon *popig*]

poppycock *noun colloq.* nonsense. [from Dutch dialect *pappekak*, soft dung]

Poppy Day another name for REMEMBRANCE DAY.

popsy *noun* (PL. **popsies**) *old use, derog. colloq.* a girlfriend.

populace /ˈpɒpjʊləs/ *noun* the body of ordinary citizens; the common people. [from French *populace*, from Italian *popolaccio*, from Latin *populus*, people]

popular *adj.* **1** liked or enjoyed by most people: *a pastime still popular with the young*. **2** *said of beliefs, etc* accepted by many people. **3** catering for the tastes and abilities of ordinary people as distinct from specialists, etc: *a popular history of science*. **4** *said of a person* generally liked and admired. **5** involving the will or preferences of the public in general: *by popular demand*. [from Latin *popularis*, from *populus*, people]

∎ **1** well-liked, favourite, liked, favoured, approved, in demand, sought-after, fashionable, modish, *colloq.* trendy. **2** prevailing, current, accepted, conventional, standard, stock, common, prevalent, widespread, universal, general, household. **4** well-liked, liked, admired, in demand. **5** general, universal, common.
⊠ **1, 4** unpopular.

popular front a left-wing group or faction, eg any of those set up from the 1930s onwards to oppose fascism.

popularity *noun* being popular.

popularization or **popularisation** *noun* popularizing or being popularized.

popularize or **popularise** *verb* **1** to make popular: *popularize a fashion*. **2** to present in a simple, easily understood way, so as to have general appeal.

∎ **1** spread, propagate, universalize. **2** simplify.

popularly *adv.* in a popular way; in terms of most people: *is popularly believed to be a hero*.

∎ commonly, widely, universally, generally, usually, customarily, conventionally, traditionally.

populate *verb* **1** *said of people, animals, or plants* to inhabit or live in (a certain area). **2** to supply (uninhabited places) with inhabitants; to people. [from Latin *populare*, from *populus*, people]

∎ **1** inhabit, live in, occupy, people, colonize. **2** people, colonize, settle.

population *noun* **1** all the people living in a particular country, area, etc. **2** the number of people living in a particular area, etc: *a population of two million*. **3** a group of animals or plants of the same species living in a certain area; the total number of these: *the declining elephant population*. **4** the process of populating an area. **5** *Statistics* a group consisting of all the possible quantities or values relevant to a statistical study, from which representative samples are taken in order to determine the characteristics of the entire population.

∎ **1** inhabitants, residents, occupants, citizens, natives, community, society, people, folk.

populism /ˈpɒpjʊlɪzm/ *noun* political activity or notions that are thought to reflect the opinions and interests of ordinary people. [from Latin *populus*, people]

populist /ˈpɒpjʊlɪst/ *noun* **1** a person who believes in the right and ability of the common people to play a major part in government. **2** a person who studies, supports, or attracts the support of the common people.

populous *adj.* thickly populated. [from Latin *populosus*, from *populus*, people]

∎ crowded, packed, swarming, teeming, crawling, overpopulated.
⊠ deserted.

pop-up *adj.*, *said of a picture book* having cut-out parts designed to stand upright as the page is opened.

porbeagle /ˈpɔːbiːgl/ *noun* a mackerel shark. [a Cornish dialect word]

porcelain /ˈpɔːslɪn/ *noun* **1** a fine white translucent earthenware, originally made in China. **2** objects made of this. [from Old French *porcelaine*, from Italian *porcellana*, cowrie shell]

porch *noun* **1** a structure forming a covered entrance to the doorway of a building. **2** *North Amer.* a verandah. [from Old French *porche*]

porcine /ˈpɔːsaɪn/ *adj.* of or like a pig. [from Latin *porcus*, pig]

porcupine /ˈpɔːkjʊpaɪn/ *noun* any of various large nocturnal rodents belonging to either of two families, namely Hystricidae (Old World species) and Erethizontidae (New World species), and noted for the long sharp black and white spikes, known as quills, borne on the back and sides of the body. These serve as defence and are also rattled to warn off predators. [from Old French *porc d'espine*, literally 'spiny pig']

pore¹ *noun* **1** a small usually round opening in the surface of a living organism, eg in the skin, or the undersurface of plant leaves, through which fluids, gases, and other substances can pass, eg during sweating in mammals. **2** any tiny cavity or gap, eg in soil or rock. [from Latin *porus*, from Greek *poros*, passage, duct]

pore² *verb intrans.* (**pore over something**) to study books, etc with intense concentration. [from Middle English *pouren*]

pork *noun* the flesh of a pig used as food. [from Old French *porc*, from Latin *porcus*, pig]

porker *noun* a pig that shows fast growth and reaches maturity at a relatively light weight, reared for fresh meat as opposed to processed meats such as bacon.

porky *adj.* (**porkier, porkiest**) **1** of or like pork. **2** *colloq.* plump.

porn *noun colloq.* pornography.

porno *colloq.* — *noun* pornography. — *adj.* pornographic.

pornographer /pɔːˈnɒɡrəfə(r)/ *noun* a person who makes or sells pornography.

pornographic /pɔːnəˈɡræfɪk/ *adj.* relating to or of the nature of pornography.

∎ obscene, indecent, dirty, filthy, blue, risqué, bawdy, coarse, gross, lewd, erotic, titillating.

. . . .

pornographically *adv.* in a pornographic way.

pornography /pɔː'nɒɡrəfɪ/ *noun* books, pictures, films, etc designed to be sexually arousing, often offensive owing to their explicit nature. [from Greek *pornographos*, writing about prostitutes, from *porne*, prostitute + *graphein*, to write]

porosity /pɔː'rɒsɪtɪ/ *noun* **1** being porous. **2** *Geol.* the ratio of the volume of pores to the total volume of a rock, etc.

porous /'pɔːrəs/ *adj.* **1** having pores or cavities. **2** that liquids can pass through. [from Latin *porosus*, from *porus*, pore]

. . . .

▣ **2** permeable, pervious, penetrable, absorbent, spongy, honeycombed, pitted.

▣ **2** impermeable, impervious.

. . . .

porphyritic /pɔːfɪ'rɪtɪk/ *adj.* **1** like or of the nature of porphyry. **2** having large crystals scattered among small.

porphyry /'pɔːfɪrɪ/ *noun* **1** *Geol.* a loose term for any igneous rock that contains large crystals surrounded by much smaller crystals. **2** a very hard purple and white rock used in sculpture. [from Greek *porphyrites*, purplish]

porpoise /'pɔːpəs/ *noun* **1** a small beakless whale, smaller than a dolphin and with a blunt snout, found in northern coastal waters and around the coasts of S America and SE Asia. Porpoises feed on fish, and often swim in the bow waves of fast-moving ships. **2** a loose term for a dolphin. [from Latin *porcus*, pig + *piscis*, fish]

porridge /'pɒrɪdʒ/ *noun* **1** a dish of oatmeal boiled in water, or of some other cereal boiled in water or milk. **2** *slang* time served by a criminal in prison. [a variant of POTTAGE]

porringer /'pɒrɪndʒə(r)/ *noun* a bowl for soup or porridge, with a handle. [from Middle English *potinger*, variation of *potager*, soup bowl]

port[1] *noun* **1** harbour. **2** a town with a harbour. [from Latin *portus*]

port[2] *noun* the left side of a ship or aircraft.

port[3] *noun* **1** an opening in a ship's side for loading, etc. **2** a porthole. **3** *Comput.* a socket on a computer through which electronic information can pass to and from peripheral units. **4** *old Scot. use* a town gate. [from Latin *porta*, gate]

port[4] *noun* a dark-red or tawny fortified wine of Portugal. [from *Oporto*, originally the place from which it was exported]

port[5] *verb Mil.* to hold (a rifle, etc) across the body with both hands, the barrel close to the left shoulder. [from French *porter*, to carry]

portability *noun* the quality of being portable.

portable — *adj.* **1** easily carried or moved, and usually designed to be. **2** *Comput.*, *said of a program* adaptable for use in a variety of systems. — *noun* a portable radio, television, typewriter, etc. [see PORT[5]]

. . . .

▣ *adj.* **1** movable, transportable, compact, lightweight, manageable, handy, convenient.

▣ *adj.* **1** fixed, immovable.

. . . .

portage — *noun* **1** the carrying of ships, equipment, etc overland from one waterway to another. **2** the route used for this. — *verb* to transport (ships, etc) overland. [from French *portage*, from *porter*, to carry]

portal /'pɔːtl/ *noun* an entrance, gateway, or doorway, especially an imposing or awesome one. [from Old French, from Latin *portale*, from *porta*, gate]

portal vein *Anat.* any vein that connects two networks of capillaries, eg the hepatic portal vein which connects the capillaries of the intestine to those of the liver.

portcullis /pɔːt'kʌlɪs/ *noun Hist.* a vertical iron or wooden grating fitted into a town gateway or castle entrance,

lowered to bar intruders. [from Old French *porte coleïce*, sliding gate]

portend /pɔː'tɛnd/ *verb* to warn of; to signify or foreshadow; to be an omen of. [from Latin *portendere*]

portent /'pɔːtɛnt/ *noun* **1** a prophetic sign; an omen. **2** fateful significance: *an event of grim portent*. **3** a marvel or prodigy. [from Latin *portentum*]

portentous /pɔː'tɛntəs/ *adj.* **1** ominous or fateful; of or relating to portents. **2** weighty, solemn, or pompous.

porter[1] *noun* a doorman, caretaker, or janitor at a college, office, or factory. [from Latin *portarius*, gatekeeper]

. . . .

▣ doorman, caretaker, janitor, concierge, commissionaire.

. . . .

porter[2] *noun* **1** a person employed to carry luggage or parcels, eg at a railway station. **2** a heavy, dark-brown beer formerly reputed to be popular with porters. **3** *North Amer.* a sleeping-car attendant. [from Old French *porteour*, from Latin *portator*, from *portare*, to carry]

. . . .

▣ **1** baggage-attendant, baggage-handler, bearer, carrier.

. . . .

porterhouse *noun* a choice cut of beefsteak from the back of the sirloin. [originally a public house or chophouse]

portfolio /pɔːt'fəʊlɪəʊ/ *noun* (PL. **portfolios**) **1** a case for carrying papers, drawings, photographs, etc; the contents of such a case. **2** the post of a government minister with responsibility for a specific department. **3** a list of one's investments. [from Italian *portafoglio*, from *portare*, to carry + *foglio*, leaf]

porthole *noun* a usually round opening in a ship's side to admit light and air. [from PORT[3] + HOLE]

portico /'pɔːtɪkəʊ/ *noun* (PL. **porticos**, **porticoes**) *Archit.* a colonnade forming a porch or covered way alongside a building. [from Italian *portico*, from Latin *porticus*, porch]

portion — *noun* **1** a piece or part of a whole: *divide into 12 equal portions*. **2** a share; a part allotted to one. **3** an individual helping of food. **4** one's destiny or fate. **5** *Legal* a woman's dowry. — *verb* (**portioned**, **portioning**) (*also* **portion something out**) to distribute it portion by portion. [from Latin *portio*]

. . . .

▣ *noun* **1** part, piece, bit, fragment, morsel, section, division, fraction, percentage, segment, slice. **2** share, allocation, allotment, parcel, allowance, ration, quota, measure. **3** helping, serving.

. . . .

portly *adj.* (**portlier**, **portliest**) *said especially of a man* somewhat stout. [from Old French *port*, deportment]

. . . .

▣ stout, corpulent, rotund, round, fat, plump, obese, overweight, heavy, large.

▣ slim, thin, slight.

. . . .

portmanteau /pɔːt'mantəʊ/ *noun* (PL. **portmanteaus**, **portmanteaux**) a leather travelling-bag that opens flat in two halves. [from French *portemanteau*, from *porter*, to carry + *manteau*, coat, cloak]

portmanteau word an invented word composed of parts of two words and conveying the sense of both, eg *motel* from *motor* and *hotel*.

port of call (PL. **ports of call**) a place called at during a journey.

portrait /'pɔːtrət/ *noun* **1** a drawing, painting, or photograph of a person, especially of the face only. **2** a written description, film depiction, etc of someone or something: *a portrait of country life*. [from Old French *portrait*, past participle of *portraire*, to portray]

. . . .

▣ **1** picture, painting, drawing, sketch, caricature, miniature, icon, photograph, likeness, image, representation. **2** picture, description, depiction, portrayal, characterization, representation, vignette, profile, image.

portraiture /ˈpɔːtrətʃʊə(r)/ *noun* the art of making portraits, or of depiction in writing, film, etc.
portray *verb* **1** to make a portrait of. **2** to describe or depict. **3** to act the part of (a character) in a play, film, etc. [from Old French *portraire*, to portray]

■ **1** draw, sketch, paint, illustrate, picture, depict, represent. **2** depict, describe, picture, represent, illustrate, evoke. **3** play, act, impersonate, characterize, personify.

portrayal *noun* **1** representation in a picture or pictures. **2** portraying.

■ **1** representation, interpretation, depiction. **2** characterization, depiction, description, evocation, presentation, performance, interpretation, rendering.

Portuguese /pɔːtjʊˈɡiːz/ — *noun* **1** a native or citizen of Portugal. **2** (**the Portuguese**) the people of Portugal. **3** the language of Portugal. — *adj.* relating to Portugal, or its inhabitants or language.
Portuguese man-of-war a jellyfish with an inflated sail-like crest, whose sting is highly poisonous.
POS *abbrev.* point of sale.
pose — *noun* **1** a position or attitude of the body: *adopt a relaxed pose.* **2** an artificial way of behaving, adopted for effect: *his punk style is just a pose.* — *verb* **1** *intrans., trans.* to take up a position oneself, or position (someone else), for a photograph, portrait, etc. **2** *intrans., derog.* to behave in an exaggerated or artificial way so as to draw attention to oneself. **3** *intrans.* (**pose as someone** or **something**) to pretend to be someone or something. **4** to ask or put forward (a question). **5** to cause (a problem, etc) or present (a threat, etc). — **strike a pose** to adopt a position or attitude, especially a commanding or impressive one. [from Old French *poser*, to place, from Latin *pausare*, to cease, pause, but influenced by Latin *ponere*, to place]

■ *noun* **1** bearing, posture, position, attitude, stance, air. **2** pretence, sham, affectation, façade, front, masquerade, act. *verb* **1** model, sit, position. **2** pretend to be, masquerade as, pass oneself off as, impersonate, feign, affect, put on an act. **4** ask, put forward, submit, present, set.

poser *noun* **1** *derog.* someone who tries to impress others by putting on an act; a poseur. **2** *colloq.* a difficult problem; a puzzle.

■ **1** poseur, posturer, attitudinizer, exhibitionist, *colloq.* show-off, *colloq.* pseud, *colloq.* phoney. **2** puzzle, problem, riddle, conundrum, brainteaser, mystery, enigma, vexed question.

poseur /poʊˈzɜː(r)/ *noun derog.* a person who behaves affectedly or insincerely. [from French *poseur*]
posh *colloq.* — *adj.* **1** high-quality, expensive, smart or stylish. **2** upper-class. — *adv.* in a posh manner: *talk posh.* — *verb* (*also* **posh something up**) to smarten it. [perhaps related to *posh*, a dandy]

■ *adj.* **1** high-quality, high-class, expensive, smart, stylish, *colloq.* swanky, luxurious, luxury, de luxe, up-market, exclusive, select, *colloq.* classy, *colloq.* swish, grand, lavish. **2** upper-class, *colloq.* la-di-da.
🔁 *adj.* **1** inferior, cheap.

posit /ˈpɒzɪt/ *verb* (**posited, positing**) to lay down, or assume, as a basis for discussion; to postulate. [from Latin *ponere*, to place]
position — *noun* **1** a place where something or someone is: *a fine position overlooking the bay.* **2** the right or proper

place: *in/out of position.* **3** the relationship of things to one another in space; arrangement. **4** a way of sitting, standing, lying, facing, being held or placed, etc: *an upright position.* **5** *Mil.* a place occupied for strategic purposes. **6** one's opinion or viewpoint. **7** a job or post: *a senior position at the bank.* **8** rank; status; importance in society: *wealth and position.* **9** the place of a competitor in the finishing order, or at an earlier stage in a contest: *lying in fourth position.* **10** *Games* one's allotted place on the pitch, as a team member: *the centre-forward position.* **11** the set of circumstances in which one is placed: *not in a position to help.* — *verb* (**positioned, positioning**) to place; to put in position. — **be in no position to do something** to have no right to complain, criticize, etc. [from Latin *positio*, from *ponere*, to place]

■ *noun* **1** place, situation, location, site, spot, point. **3** arrangement, disposition. **4** posture, stance, pose. **6** opinion, viewpoint, point of view, belief, view, outlook, standpoint, stand. **7** job, post, office, duty, function, role, occupation, employment. **8** rank, status, grade, level, standing. *verb* put, place, set, fix, stand, deploy, station, locate, situate, site, arrange, dispose, lay out.

positional *adj.* relating to or determined by position.
positive /ˈpɒzɪtɪv/ — *adj.* **1** sure; certain; convinced. **2** definite; allowing no doubt: *positive proof of her guilt.* **3** expressing agreement or approval: *a positive response.* **4** optimistic: *feeling more positive.* **5** forceful or determined; not tentative. **6** constructive; contributing to progress or improvement; helpful. **7** clear and explicit: *positive directions.* **8** *colloq.* downright: *a positive scandal.* **9** denoting a chemical test result that confirms the existence of the suspected condition. **10** *Maths.* denoting a number or quantity greater than zero. **11** *Physics, Electr.* having a deficiency of electrons, and so being able to attract them, ie attracted by a negative charge; describing one of two terminals having the higher electrical potential. **12** *Photog.* having light and shade, or colours, as in the actual image, not reversed, etc. **13** *Grammar* expressing quality in the simple form, as distinct from the comparative or superlative forms. — *noun* **1** *Photog.* a print in which light, shade, and colour correspond to those of the actual image. **2** *Grammar* a positive adjective or adverb; the positive form or degree in comparison. **3** a positive thing, especially a positive quantity or a positive electrical terminal. [from Latin *positivus*, from *ponere*, to place]

■ *adj.* **1** sure, certain, convinced, confident, assured. **2** definite, decisive, conclusive, undeniable, irrefutable, indisputable, incontrovertible, unequivocal, express, firm, emphatic, categorical. **4** optimistic, hopeful, promising. **6** helpful, constructive, practical, useful. **7** clear, explicit, unmistakable. **8** absolute, utter, sheer, complete, perfect.
🔁 *adj.* **1** uncertain. **2** indefinite, vague. **3, 4 6, 10, 11, 12** negative.

positive discrimination the creation of special employment opportunities, etc for those previously disadvantaged or discriminated against.
positive feedback *Engineering, Biol.* a form of feedback in which the output of a system is used to increase the input.
positively *adv.* **1** in a positive way. **2** definitely.
positiveness *noun* being positive.
positive vetting investigation of the connections and sympathies of a person being considered for a position of trust, eg in the senior civil service.
positivism *noun* **1** a school of philosophy maintaining that knowledge can come only from observable phenomena and positive facts. **2** (*also* **logical positivism**) a 20c development of this, concerned with the significance and verifiability of statements.
positivist — *noun* a believer in positivism. *adj.* characteristic of positivism.

positron /ˈpɒzɪtrɒn/ *noun Physics* a particle that has the same mass as an electron, and an equal but opposite charge. [a contraction of *positive electron*]

poss — *adj. colloq.* possible. — *abbrev.* (*usually* **poss.**) **1** possible or possibly. **2** *Grammar* possessive.

posse /ˈpɒsɪ/ *noun North Amer. Hist.* a mounted troop of men at the service of a local sheriff. [from Latin *posse*, to be able]

possess *verb* **1** to own. **2** to have as a feature or quality: *possesses a quick mind.* **3** *said of an emotion, evil spirit, etc* to take hold of (someone): *what possessed you to behave like that?* [from Old French *possesser*, from Latin *possessio*, possession]

◨ **1** own, have, hold. **2** have, enjoy, be endowed with. **3** seize, take, take over, occupy, control, dominate, bewitch, haunt.

possessed *adj.* **1** *formal* (**possessed of something**) owning it; having it: *possessed of great wealth.* **2** controlled or driven by demons, etc.

possession *noun* **1** the condition of possessing something; ownership: *take possession of/come into one's possession.* **2** the crime of possessing something illegally: *charged with possession of firearms.* **3** occupancy of property: *take possession of the house.* **4** *Football* control of the ball by one or other team in a match. **5** something owned. **6** (**possessions**) one's property or belongings. **7** (**possessions**) a country's dominions abroad: *foreign possessions.* — **be in possession of something** to hold or possess it.

◨ **1** ownership, title, tenure, custody, control. **3** occupancy, occupation, tenancy. **6** property, belongings, things, paraphernalia, effects, goods, chattels, movables, assets, estate, wealth, riches.

possessive — *adj.* **1** relating to possession. **2** unwilling to share, or allow others use of, things one owns: *possessive about my car.* **3** inclined to dominate, monopolize, and allow no independence to, eg one's wife, husband, child, etc: *a possessive husband.* **4** *Grammar* denoting the form of a noun, pronoun, or adjective that shows possession, eg *Jack's, its, her.* — *noun Grammar* **1** the possessive form of a word. **2** a word in the possessive.

◨ *adj.* **2** selfish, acquisitive, grasping. **3** domineering, dominating, overprotective, clinging, jealous, covetous.
◪ *adj.* **2** unselfish, sharing.

possessively *adv.* in a possessive way.
possessiveness *noun* being possessive.
possessor *noun* a person who possesses something.
possibility *noun* (PL. **possibilities**) **1** something that is possible. **2** the state of being possible. **3** a candidate for selection, etc. **4** (**possibilities**) promise or potential: *an idea with possibilities.*

◨ **1** likelihood, probability, prospect, hope, risk, danger. **2** potentiality, conceivability, likelihood, probability, practicability, feasibility, odds, chance.
◪ **1, 2** impossibility, impracticability.

possible — *adj.* **1** achievable; able to be done. **2** that may happen: *the possible outcome.* **3** imaginable; conceivable: *a possible explanation/it's possible that he's dead.* — *noun* a person or thing potentially selectable; a possibility. [from Latin *possibilis*, from *posse*, to be able]

◨ *adj.* **1** achievable, attainable, accomplishable, realizable, practicable, feasible, viable, tenable, workable. **2** potential, promising, likely, probable. **3** imaginable, conceivable, feasible.

◪ *adj.* IMPOSSIBLE. **1** impracticable, unattainable. **3** unthinkable.

possibly *adv.* **1** perhaps; maybe. **2** within the limits of possibility: *doing all we possibly can.* **3** used for emphasis: *how could you possibly think that?*

◨ **1** perhaps, maybe, *colloq.* hopefully. **2** by any means, by any chance. **3** conceivably, at all.

possum /ˈpɒsəm/ *noun colloq.* an opossum. — **play possum** to pretend to be unconscious, asleep, or unaware of what is happening.

post[1] — *noun* **1** a shaft or rod fixed upright in the ground, as a support, marker, etc. **2** (*often in compounds*) a vertical timber supporting a horizontal one: *a doorpost.* **3** an upright pole marking the beginning or end of a race track. — *verb* **1** (*also* **post something up**) to put up (a notice, etc) for public viewing. **2** to announce the name of (someone) among others in a published list: *posted missing.* **3** *Comput.* to put (information) on the Internet. [from Latin *postis*]

◨ *noun* **1** pole, shaft, rod, stake, picket, pale, pillar, column, support, baluster, upright, stanchion, strut, leg. *verb* **1** display, stick up, pin up. **2** announce, make known, report, publish, advertise, publicize.

post[2] — *noun* **1** a job: *a teaching post.* **2** a position to which one is assigned for military duty: *never left his post.* **3** a settlement or establishment, especially in a remote area: *trading-post/military post.* **4** *Mil.* a bugle call summoning soldiers to their quarters at night, or (**last post**) sounded at funerals. — *verb* to station (someone) somewhere on duty; to transfer (personnel) to a new location: *posted abroad.* [from Italian *posto*, from Latin *positum*, from *ponere*, to place]

◨ *noun* **1** job, position, situation, place, office, employment, vacancy, appointment, assignment. **2** station, beat. *verb* station, transfer, move, send, locate, situate, position, place, put, appoint, assign, second.

post[3] — *noun* **1** the official system for the delivery of mail. **2** letters and parcels delivered by this system; mail. **3** a collection of mail, eg from a postbox: *catch the next post.* **4** a delivery of mail: *came by the second post.* **5** a place for mail collection; a postbox or post office: *took it to the post.* **6** used as a newspaper title: *the Washington Post.* — *verb* **1** to put (mail) into a postbox; to send by post. **2** *Commerce* **a** to enter (an item) in a ledger. **b** (*usually* **post up**) to update (a ledger). **3** to supply with the latest news: *keep us posted.* [from Italian *posta*, from Latin *posita*, from *ponere*, to place]

◨ *noun* **1** mail. **2** mail, letters, parcels. **3** collection. **4** delivery. *verb* **1** mail, send, dispatch, transmit. **3** inform.

post- *combining form* forming words meaning 'after': *postwar.* [from Latin *post*, after, behind]

postage *noun* the charge for sending a letter, etc through the post.

postage stamp a small printed label stuck on a letter, etc showing that the appropriate postage has been paid.

postal *adj.* **1** of or relating to the post office or delivery of mail. **2** sent by post: *a postal vote.*

postal code same as POSTCODE.

postal order a money order available from, and payable by, a post office.

postbag *noun* **1** a mailbag. **2** the letters received by eg a radio or television programme, magazine, or celebrated person.

postbox *noun* a public box in which to post letters; a letter box.

postcard *noun* a card for writing messages on, often with a picture on one side, designed for sending through the post without an envelope.

post chaise a fast usually four-wheeled coach carrying up to four passengers, and mail, drawn by horses. [see POST³]

postcode *noun* a code used to identify a postal address, usually a combination of letters and numerals.

post-consumer waste newspapers and other household waste, as opposed to industrial; waste used for recycling.

postdate *verb* **1** to put a future date on (a cheque, etc). **2** to assign a later date than that previously accepted to (an event, etc). **3** to occur at a later date than.

poster *noun* **1** a large notice or advertisement for public display. **2** a large printed picture. [from POST¹]

. . . .
▤ **1** notice, advertisement, bill, sign, placard, sticker, announcement.
. . . .

poster art posters as an art form from the late 19c, when there were improvements in printing techniques, especially in colour lithography. Many major artists worked in the field: Toulouse-Lautrec is especially renowned for his striking commercial posters; Aubrey Beardsley's illustrations were influenced by his study of Japanese prints; and posters by the Czech artist Alphonse Mucha have enjoyed a wide revival.

poste restante / poʊst reˈstɒnt/ a facility at a post office for holding mail until collected by the recipient, eg when a private address is not available. [from French *poste restante*, post remaining]

posterior — *noun facetious* one's buttocks. — *adj. Anat., Archit.* placed behind or after. [from Latin *posterior*, comparative of *posterus*, coming after]

posterity *noun* **1** future generations. **2** one's descendants. [from Latin *posteritas*, from *posterus*, coming after]

. . . .
▤ **2** descendants, successors, progeny, issue, offspring, children.
. . . .

postern *noun Hist.* a back door, back gate, or private entrance. [from Old French *posterne*]

poster paint or **poster colour** a water-based paint in a bright opaque colour.

post-free *adj.* **1** with postage prepaid. **2** without charge for postage.

postgraduate — *noun* a person studying for an advanced degree or qualification after obtaining a first degree. — *adj.* relating to such a person or degree.

posthaste *adv.* with all speed. [from *post*, a courier + HASTE]

posthouse *noun Hist.* an inn where horses were kept for conveying the mail and for the use of travellers wishing to change horses, etc.

posthumous / ˈpɒstjʊməs/ *adj.* **1** published after the death of the author, composer, etc. **2** *said of a child* born after its father's death. **3** awarded or coming after death: *posthumous decoration/acclaim*. [from Latin *postumus*, superlative of *posterus*, coming after; *h* inserted by mistaken association with *humus*, earth, ie burial]

posthumously *adv.* after death.

postilion or **postillion** *noun Hist.* a rider on the nearside horse of one of the pairs of horses drawing a carriage, who, in the absence of a coachman, guides the team. [from Italian *postiglione*, from *posta*, POST³]

Postimpressionism *noun* an imprecise term associated with the art critic Roger Fry, used to describe the more progressive forms of French painting since c.1880.

post-industrial society a term coined in 1973 by the US sociologist Daniel Bell (1919) to describe an economically and technologically advanced society no longer dependent for its productivity on large-scale, labour intensive industrial manufacture.

postman or **postwoman** *noun* a man or woman whose job is to deliver mail.

postmark *noun* a mark stamped on mail by the post office, cancelling the stamp and showing the date and place of posting.

postmaster *noun* **1** a man in charge of a local post office. **2** *Comput.* a person who manages the electronic mail at a site.

Postmaster General (PL. **Postmasters General**) a government minister in charge of the country's postal services.

postmeridian *adj.* **1** occurring after noon. **2** relating to the afternoon.

post meridiem after noon. [from Latin *post meridiem*]

postmistress *noun* a woman in charge of a local post office.

post-mortem *noun* **1** a medical examination of a dead person to establish the cause of death. **2** *facetious* an after-the-event discussion. [from Latin *post mortem*, after death]

postnatal *adj.* belonging to, or occurring in, the period immediately after birth, or after giving birth.

postnatal depression *Psychol.* a relatively common form of depression that occurs shortly after giving birth.

post office **1** a local office handling postal business, issuing various types of licence, etc. **2** (**Post Office**) the government department in charge of postal services.

post-operative *adj.* belonging to, or occurring in, the period immediately following a surgical operation: *post-operative discomfort*.

post-paid *adj.* with postage prepaid.

postpartum *adj. Medicine* after childbirth.

postpone / poʊsˈpoʊn/ *verb* to defer or put off till later. [from Latin *postponere*, to place after]

. . . .
▤ defer, put off, put back, hold over, delay, adjourn, suspend, shelve, pigeonhole, freeze, *colloq.* put on ice, *colloq.* put on the back burner.
▣ advance, bring forward.
. . . .

postponement *noun* postponing.

postprandial *adj. facetious* following a meal: *a postprandial doze*. [from POST- + Latin *prandium*, breakfast, lunch]

post-production *noun* the stages in the making of a film or video after shooting and before the first public showing. Processes include recording and adding music and sound track, and final editing.

postscript *noun* **1** a message added to a letter as an afterthought, after one's signature. **2** anything serving as an addition or follow-up to something. [from Latin *postscribere*, to write after]

. . . .
▤ **1** PS. **2** addition, supplement, afterthought, addendum, codicil, appendix, afterword, epilogue.
▣ **2** introduction, prologue.
. . . .

post-traumatic stress disorder or **post-traumatic stress syndrome** *Psychol.* a psychological disorder associated with an extremely traumatic event, such as military combat, rape, torture, natural disasters (eg earthquake), or serious physical injury.

postulacy *noun* the state or time of being a postulant.

postulant *noun* a candidate for holy orders or for admission to a religious community. [from Latin *postulare*, to ask]

postulate — *verb* to assume or suggest as the basis for discussion; to take for granted. — *noun* something postulated. [from Latin *postulare*, to demand]

. . . .
▤ *verb* assume, suppose, suggest, theorize, hypothesize, propose, advance, lay down, stipulate.
. . . .

postulation *noun* **1** postulating. **2** a request, claim, or assumption.

postural *adj.* relating to posture.

posture — *noun* **1** the way one holds one's body in standing, sitting, or walking. **2** a particular position or attitude of the body. **3** an attitude adopted towards a particular issue, etc. **4** a pose adopted for effect. — *verb intrans.*, *derog.* to pose, strike attitudes, etc so as to draw attention to oneself. [from Latin *positura*, from *ponere*, to place]
. . . .

☲ *noun* **1** bearing, carriage, deportment. **2** pose, position, stance, attitude. **3** attitude, disposition.
. . . .

posturer *noun* a person who poses or assumes attitudes for effect.

postviral syndrome (ABBREV. **PVS**) a condition following viral infection, characterized by fatigue, poor concentration, depression and dizziness.

postwar *adj.* relating or belonging to the period following a war.

posy *noun* (PL. **posies**) a small bunch of flowers. [a variant of POESY]
. . . .

☲ bouquet, spray, buttonhole, corsage.
. . . .

pot[1] — *noun* **1** any of various usually deep and round domestic containers used as cooking or serving utensils or for storage. **2** the amount held by such a container: *a pot of tea.* **3** *Pottery* any handmade vessel. **4** the pool of accumulated bets in any gambling game. **5** *Billiards* a shot that pockets a ball. **6** a casual shot: *take a pot at something.* **7** a chamberpot. **8** a flowerpot or plant pot. **9** (**pots**) *colloq.* a great deal, especially of money. **10** *colloq.* a trophy, especially a cup. **11** a pot-belly. — *verb* (**potted, potting**) **1** to plant in a plant pot. **2** to preserve (a type of food) in a pot. **3** to summarize, especially in a popular style: *a potted history.* **4** *Billiards* to shoot (a ball) into a pocket. **5** (**pot** or **pot at someone** or **something**) *colloq.* to shoot at them, especially indiscriminately or wildly. — **go to pot** *colloq.* to degenerate badly. **keep the pot boiling** *colloq.* to sustain public interest in something. [from Anglo-Saxon *pott*]
. . . .

☲ *noun* **1** receptacle, vessel, teapot, coffee pot, urn, jar, vase, bowl, basin, pan, cauldron, crucible. **4** kitty, purse.
. . . .

pot[2] *noun colloq.* marijuana. [from Mexican Spanish *potiguaya*]

potable *adj.* fit for drinking; drinkable. [from Latin *potabilis*]

potash *noun* any of various compounds of potassium, especially the fertilizer potassium carbonate or (*also* **caustic potash**) potassium hydroxide.

potassium *noun Chem.* (SYMBOL **K**, ATOMIC NUMBER **19**) a soft silvery-white metal that occurs as various compounds in the Earth's crust and in seawater. The pure metal reacts violently with water and is generally stored under paraffin. Its compounds are used in fertilizers, explosives, laboratory reagents, soaps, and some types of glass. It is an essential element for plants and animals, and plays a central role in the transmission of nerve impulses. [from POTASH]

potassium bicarbonate *Chem.* same as POTASSIUM HYDROGENCARBONATE.

potassium hydrogencarbonate *Chem.* (FORMULA $KHCO_3$) a white crystalline powder, soluble in water, that is used in baking powder, some detergents, carbonated soft drinks, carbon-dioxide fire extinguishers, and as an antacid to treat indigestion.

potassium hydrogentartrate *Chem.* (FORMULA $KHC_4H_4O_6$) a white crystalline powder, soluble in water, found in vegetables and fruit juices, and used in baking powders and carbonated drinks. Also called CREAM OF TARTAR.

potassium hydroxide *Chem.* (FORMULA **KOH**) a highly corrosive white crystalline solid that readily absorbs moisture from the atmosphere, and dissolves in water to form a strong alkaline solution. It is used in the manufacture of soft soap, and as an electrolyte in batteries and an intermediate in the manufacture of other chemicals. Also called CAUSTIC POTASH.

potassium nitrate *Chem.* (FORMULA KNO_3) a white or transparent crystalline solid, soluble in water, that is highly explosive and a very strong oxidizing agent. It is used in the manufacture of fireworks, matches, gunpowder, fertilizers, and some types of glass, and as a food preservative, especially for curing meats. Also called NITRE, SALTPETRE.

potassium permanganate *Chem.* (FORMULA $KMnO_4$) a dark purple crystalline solid that is soluble in water, and an extremely powerful oxidizing agent. It is used in disinfectants, fungicides, dyes, and bleaches, and in chemical analysis. Also called *permanganate of potash, potassium manganate(vii).*

potation *noun facetious* **1** the act of drinking. **2** a drink, especially an alcoholic one. [from Latin *potatio*]

potato *noun* (PL. **potatoes**) **1** any of thousands of varieties of a perennial plant (*Solanum tuberosum*) that produces edible tubers (swollen underground stems) and is a staple crop of temperate regions worldwide. **2** the tuber of this plant, which is rich in starch, vitamin C, and protein, and can be cooked and eaten as a vegetable, or processed to form crisps or chips. [from Spanish *batata*, from a S American language]

potato blight *Bot.* a widespread disease of potato and related plants, in which the entire plant is affected and rapidly dies, caused by the fungus *Phytophthora infestans*, especially in wet weather.

potato crisp same as CRISP *noun.*

pot-bellied *adj.* having a pot-belly.

pot-belly *noun* (PL. **pot-bellies**) *derog. colloq.* a large overhanging belly.

potboiler *noun derog.* an inferior work of literature or art produced by a writer or artist capable of better work, simply to make money and stay in the public view.

potbound *adj.*, *said of a plant* with its roots cramped by too small a pot.

poteen /pɒ'tʃiːn/ *noun Irish* illicitly distilled Irish whiskey. [from Irish *poitín*]

potency *noun* (PL. **potencies**) **1** being potent, power. **2** the capacity for development.

potent *adj.* **1** strong; effective; powerful. **2** *said of an argument, etc* persuasive; convincing. **3** *said of a drug or poison* powerful and swift in effect. **4** *said of a male* capable of sexual intercourse. [from Latin *potens*, present participle of *posse*, to be able]
. . . .

☲ **1** strong, effective, powerful, pungent, overpowering, dynamic, vigorous, mighty, authoritative, commanding, dominant, influential. **2** persuasive, convincing, cogent, compelling, forceful, impressive. **3** powerful, strong, intoxicating.
☳ **1** impotent, weak. **2** weak, unconvincing. **4** impotent.
. . . .

potentate *noun literary* a powerful ruler; a monarch. [from Latin *potentatus*, from *potens*, powerful]

potential — *adj.* possible or likely, though as yet not tested or actual. — *noun* **1** the range of capabilities that a person or thing has; powers or resources not yet developed or made use of: *fulfil one's potential.* **2** *Physics* the energy required to move a unit of mass, electric charge, etc, from an infinite distance to the point in a gravitational or electric field where it is to be measured. **3** potential difference. [from Latin *potentialis*, from *potentia*, power]
. . . .

☲ *adj.* possible, likely, probable, prospective, future, aspiring, would-be, promising, budding, embryonic, undeveloped, dormant, latent, hidden, concealed, unrealized. *noun* **1** capability, capacity, ability, aptitude, talent, powers, resources.

. . . .

potential difference (ABBREV. **pd**) *Physics* the difference in electric potential between two points in an electric field or circuit, usually expressed in volts.

potential energy *Physics* the energy stored by an object by virtue of its position. For example, if an object is raised above the Earth's surface, then it acquires potential energy equal to the work done against the force of gravity in lifting it. Work done in compressing a spring is stored as elastic potential energy in the spring.

potentially *adv.* in terms of potential; possibly: *a potentially difficult problem.*

potentilla *noun Bot.* any plant of the genus *Potentilla* of the rose family.

potentiometer *noun Physics* an instrument that is used to measure electric potential. Potentiometers are used in electronic circuits, especially as volume controls in transistor radios.

potherb *noun* a plant whose leaves or stems are used in cooking to season or garnish food.

pothole *noun* **1** a roughly circular hole worn in the bedrock of a river as pebbles are swirled around by water eddies. **2** a vertical cave system or deep hole eroded in limestone. **3** a hole worn in a road surface. [from POT[1]]

potholer *noun* a person who takes part in potholing.

potholing *noun* the sport of exploring deep caves and potholes.

pothook *noun* **1** a hook on which to hang a pot over a fire. **2** a hooked stroke in handwriting.

potion *noun* a draught of medicine, poison, or some magic elixir. [from Latin *potio*, from *potare*, to drink]

. . . .

▤ draught, medicine, tonic, elixir, mixture, concoction, brew, beverage, drink, dose.

. . . .

pot luck whatever is available.

potpourri /pou'puərı, poupə'ri:/ *noun* **1** a fragrant mixture of dried flowers, leaves, etc placed in containers and used to scent rooms. **2** a medley or mixture: *a potpourri of old tunes.* [from French *potpourri*, literally 'rotten pot']

. . . .

▤ **1** medley, mixture, jumble, hotchpotch, miscellany, collection.

. . . .

pot roast a cut of meat braised with a little water in a covered pot.

potsherd /'pɒtʃɜ:d/ *noun* a fragment of pottery.

pot-shot *noun* **1** an easy shot at close range. **2** a shot made without taking careful aim.

potter[1] *noun* a person who makes pottery.

potter[2] *verb intrans.* (**pottered, pottering**) **1** (*usually* **potter about**) to busy oneself in a mild way with trifling tasks. **2** (*usually* **potter about** or **along**) to progress in an unhurried manner; to dawdle. [from Anglo-Saxon *potian*, to thrust]

. . . .

▤ **1** *colloq.* mess about, tinker around, fiddle about, dabble. **2** dawdle, *colloq.* toddle along, amble along.

. . . .

potter's wheel an apparatus with a heavy rotating stone platter, on which clay pots can be shaped by hand before firing.

pottery *noun* (PL. **potteries**) **1** vessels or other objects of baked clay. **2** the art of making such objects. **3** a factory where such objects are produced commercially.

. . . .

▤ **1** earthenware, stoneware, terracotta, ceramics, crockery, china, porcelain. **2** ceramics.

. . . .

pottiness *noun* being potty.

potting-shed *noun* a shed in which to keep garden tools, put plants into pots, etc.

potty[1] *adj.* (**pottier, pottiest**) *colloq.* **1** mad; crazy. **2** (**potty about someone** or **something**) intensely interested in or keen on them.

potty[2] *noun* (PL. **potties**) *colloq.* a child's chamberpot. [a diminutive of POT[1]]

pouch *noun* **1** *old use* a purse or small bag. **2** in marsupials such as the kangaroo, a pocket of skin on the belly, in which the young are carried till weaned. **3** a fleshy fold in the cheek of hamsters and other rodents, for storing undigested food. **4** a puffy bulge under the eyes. [from Old French *poche*, pocket]

pouffe /pu:f/ *noun* a firmly stuffed drum-shaped or cube-shaped cushion for use as a low seat. [from French *pouffe*]

poulterer *noun* a dealer in poultry and game. [from *poult*, a chicken]

poultice *noun* a hot semi-liquid mixture spread on a bandage and applied to the skin to reduce inflammation, formerly used as a treatment for boils. [from Latin *pultes*, plural of *puls*, porridge]

poultry *noun* **1** a collective term for domesticated birds that are kept for their eggs or meat, or both, eg chickens, which are the most common poultry birds. Ducks, geese, and turkeys are also classified as poultry, and are farmed mainly for their meat. **2** the meat of such birds. [from *poult*, chicken, from Old French *poulet*, chicken]

pounce — *verb intrans.* (*often* **pounce on something** or **someone**) **1** to leap on a victim or prey. **2** to seize on; to grab eagerly. — *noun* an act of pouncing.

. . . .

▤ *verb* **1** spring, leap, jump, strike, swoop.

. . . .

pound[1] *noun* **1** (*in full* **pound sterling**) (SYMBOL **£**) the principal currency unit of the United Kingdom, divided into 100 pence. **2** the English name for the principal currency unit in several other countries, eg Malta, Cyprus, and Egypt. **3** (ABBREV. **lb**) a measure of weight equal to 16 ounces (453 grams) avoirdupois, or 12 ounces (373 grams) troy. [from Anglo-Saxon *pund*]

pound[2] *noun* an enclosure where stray animals or illegally parked cars that have been taken into police charge are kept for collection. [from Anglo-Saxon *pund*, enclosure]

. . . .

▤ enclosure, compound, *North Amer.* corral, yard, pen, fold.

. . . .

pound[3] *verb* **1** *trans., intrans.* (**pound something** or **on** or **at something**) to beat or bang it vigorously. **2** (*also* **pound something out**) to produce it by pounding: *pounding out articles on her typewriter.* **3** *intrans., said of the heart, etc.* to beat very fast; to throb or thud. **4** *intrans.* to walk or run with heavy thudding steps. **5** to crush or grind to a powder. [from Anglo-Saxon *punian*]

. . . .

▤ **1** beat, bang, hammer, batter, drum, thump, strike, pelt, bash, smash. **3** thump, thud, pulsate, palpitate, throb. **5** crush, grind, pulverize, powder, mash.

. . . .

poundage *noun* a fee or commission charged per pound in weight or money.

-pounder *combining form* forming words meaning: **1** something weighing a certain number of pounds: *a three-pounder trout.* **2** a field gun designed to fire shot weighing a certain number of pounds: *a twenty-four-pounder.*

pound force *Physics* a unit of force equal to the gravitational force experienced by a pound mass when the acceleration due to gravity has a value of 9.8m s^{-2}.

pound of flesh the strict exacting of one's due in the fulfilment of a bargain, to the extent of causing unreasonable suffering to the other party. [used in allusion to Shakespeare, *The Merchant of Venice* IV.i, in which a pound of flesh is stipulated as a penalty in a bargain]

pour verb 1 trans., intrans. to flow or cause to flow in a downward stream. 2 intrans., trans., said of a jug, etc to discharge (liquid) in a certain way: doesn't pour very well. 3 (also **pour something out**) to serve a drink, etc by pouring. 4 intrans., to rain heavily. 5 intrans. (**pour in** or **out**) to come or go in large numbers: people were pouring out of the cinema. 6 intrans. (**pour in** or **out**, etc) to flow or issue plentifully: donations poured in/words poured from her pen. 7 (**pour something out**) to reveal it without inhibition: pour out one's feelings. 8 to invest (money, energy, etc) liberally in something: poured all his savings into the company. — **pour cold water on something** to be discouraging or depreciatory about an idea, scheme, etc. **pour scorn on something** to be contemptuous about it. [origin unknown]

⊟ **1** flow, stream, gush, cascade, rush, spout, spew, spill, run. **3** serve, decant, tip. **4** teem (down), colloq. bucket (down). **5** rush, throng, swarm, crowd.

pourboire /pʊəˈbwɑː(r)/ noun a tip or gratuity. [from French pourboire]

pourer noun a person or thing that pours: the jug is not a good pourer.

pout — verb **1** intrans., trans. to push the lower lip or both lips forward as an indication of sulkiness or seductiveness. **2** intrans., said of the lips to stick out in this way. — noun an act of pouting or a pouting expression.

⊟ verb **1** scowl, glower, grimace, pull a face, sulk, mope. noun scowl, long face, glower, grimace.
⊟ verb **1** smile, grin. noun smile, grin.

pouter noun a variety of pigeon that can puff out its crop.

poverty noun **1** the condition of being poor; want. **2** poor quality: poverty of the soil. **3** inadequacy; deficiency: poverty of imagination. [from Old French poverte]

⊟ **1** poorness, impoverishment, want, pennilessness, penury, destitution, privation, need, necessity, distress, hardship, insolvency, bankruptcy. **2** poorness, impoverishment, deficiency, depletion. **3** lack, deficiency, shortage, inadequacy, poorness, insufficiency, depletion, scarcity, meagreness, paucity, dearth.
⊟ **1** wealth, richness, affluence, plenty.

poverty line the minimum income needed to purchase the basic needs of life.

poverty-stricken adj. suffering from poverty.

poverty trap the inescapable poverty of someone who, in achieving an improvement in income, has his or her state benefits cut.

POW abbrev. prisoner of war.

powder — noun **1** any substance in the form of fine dust-like particles. **2** (also **face powder**) a cosmetic patted on to the skin to give it a soft smooth appearance. **3** gunpowder. **4** a dose of medicine in powder form. — verb (**powdered**, **powdering**) **1** to apply powder to; to sprinkle or cover with powder. **2** to reduce to a powder by crushing; to pulverize. [from Old French poudre]

powder metallurgy Chem. a method of shaping heat-resistant metals or alloys, by reducing them to powder form, pressing them into moulds and heating them to very high temperatures. First used to make tungsten lamp filaments, the process is now used to make tungsten carbide cutting tools, self-lubricating bearings, etc.

powder puff a pad of velvety or fluffy material for patting powder on to the skin.

powder room a women's toilet in a restaurant, hotel, etc.

powdery adj. **1** of the consistency or nature of powder. **2** covered with or full of powder. **3** dusty. **4** friable.

⊟ **1** powdered, pulverized, ground, grainy, granular,

fine, dusty, sandy, chalky, loose, dry. **4** friable, crumbly.

power — noun **1** control and influence exercised over others. **2** strength, vigour, force, or effectiveness. **3** military strength: sea power. **4** the physical ability, skill, opportunity, or authority, to do something: if it is within my power. **5** an individual faculty or skill: the power of speech/at the height of one's powers. **6** a right, privilege, or responsibility: the power of arrest/power of attorney. **7** political control: assume power. **8** a state that has an influential role in international affairs. **9** a person or group exercising control or influence: the real power behind the prime minister. **10** colloq. a great deal: did her a power of good. **11** any form of energy, especially when used as the driving force for a machine, eg nuclear power. **12** Maths. an exponent or index, denoted by a small numeral placed above and to the right of a numerical quantity, which indicates the number of times that quantity is multiplied by itself, eg 12 to the power of 4, or 12^4, is equal to 12 x 12 x 12 x 12. A quantity raised to the power of 2 is said to be squared, and a quantity raised to the power of 3 is said to be cubed. **13** Physics the rate of doing work or converting energy from one form into another. The SI unit of power is the watt (W), which is equivalent to one joule per second. **14** mechanical or electrical energy, as distinct from manual effort: power-assisted steering. **15** Optics a measure of the extent to which a lens, optical instrument, or curved mirror can deviate light rays and so magnify an image of an object. For a simple lens the unit of power is the dioptre. — adj. **1** using mechanical or electrical power; motor-driven: power tools. **2** denoting the practices of people who convey authority in business or politics: power dressing / a power breakfast. — verb (**powered**, **powering**) to supply with power: nuclear-powered warships. — **the powers that be** those in authority. [from Old French poer, originally an infinitive, related to Latin posse, to be able]

⊟ noun **1** control, influence, rule, dominion, command, authority, sovereignty. **2** strength, vigour, force, effectiveness, potency, intensity, energy. **4** ability, capability, skill, capacity, opportunity, potential, faculty, competence. **6** right, privilege, responsibility, prerogative, authorization, warrant.
⊟ noun **1** subjection. **2** weakness. **4** inability.

power cut a break in an electricity supply.

power dressing the wearing by businesswomen of tailored suits and dresses, intended to convey professionalism and assertiveness.

powerful adj. having great power, strength, vigour, authority, influence, force, or effectiveness.

⊟ dominant, prevailing, strong, authoritative, influential, high-powered, commanding, leading, potent, effective, mighty, robust, muscular, energetic, forceful, telling, impressive, convincing, persuasive, compelling, winning, overwhelming.
⊟ impotent, ineffective, weak.

powerfully adv. in a powerful way.

powerhouse noun **1** a power station. **2** colloq. a forceful or vigorous person.

powerless adj. deprived of power or authority.

⊟ impotent, incapable, ineffective, weak, feeble, frail, infirm, incapacitated, disabled, paralysed, helpless, vulnerable, defenceless, unarmed.
⊟ powerful, potent, able.

power lunch a high-level business discussion held over lunch.

power pack a device for adjusting an electric current to the voltages required by a piece of electronic equipment.

power plant 1 a power station. **2** the engine and parts making up the unit that supplies the propelling power in a vehicle.

power point a socket for connecting an electrical device to the mains.

power station a building where electricity is generated on a large scale from another form of energy, eg coal, nuclear fuel, moving water. The main power stations in the UK are connected by the *national grid*, a network that allows the exchange of power between areas with differing demands for electricity.

power steering or **power-assisted steering** in a motor vehicle, a system in which a hydraulic ram connects to the steering linkage and assists the steering effort. The ram is powered by a hydraulic pump driven off the engine and is controlled by a valve which responds to movements of the steering wheel.

power tool a powerful electric working tool.

powwow — *noun* **1** *colloq.* a meeting for discussion. **2** *Hist.* a meeting of N American Indians. — *verb intrans.* to hold a powwow. [from Narragansett (N American Indian language) *powwaw*, priest]

pox *noun* **1** *combining form Medicine* any of various infectious viral diseases that cause a skin rash consisting of pimples that contain pus, eg chickenpox, smallpox. **2** former name for syphilis. [a variant of *pocks*]

pp *abbrev.* **1** pages. **2** *per procurationem* (Latin), by the agency of. **3** *Mus.* pianissimo.

PPARC *abbrev.* Particle Physics and Astronomy Research Council.

PPE *abbrev.* Philosophy, Politics, and Economics.

ppm *abbrev.* parts per million.

PPS *abbrev.* **1** Parliamentary Private Secretary. **2** *post postscriptum* (Latin), after the postscript, ie an additional postscript.

PR *abbrev.* **1** proportional representation. **2** public relations.

Pr *symbol Chem.* praseodymium.

practicability *noun* being practicable.

practicable *adj.* **1** capable of being done, used, or successfully carried out; feasible. **2** *said eg of a road* fit for use. [from Latin *practicare*, to practise]

⊟ **1** possible, feasible, achievable, attainable, viable, workable, practical, realistic, performable.
⊟ **1** impracticable.

practicably *adv.* in a practicable way.

practical — *adj.* **1** concerned with action with some purpose or result in contrast to theory: *put one's knowledge to practical use.* **2** effective, or capable of being effective, in actual use: *practical ideas/a practical knowledge of German.* **3** *said eg of clothes* designed for tough or everyday use; sensibly plain. **4** *said of a person* sensible and efficient in deciding and acting; good at doing manual jobs. **5** in effect; virtual: *a practical walkover.* — *noun* a practical lesson or examination, eg in a scientific subject. [from obsolete *practic*, practical, from Greek *praktikos*]

⊟ *adj.* **1** applied, hands on. **2** realistic, workable, feasible, sensible, commonsense, practicable. **3** utilitarian, functional, working, everyday, ordinary, serviceable, useful, handy. **4** down-to-earth, matter-of-fact, pragmatic, *colloq.* hard-nosed, hard-headed, businesslike, experienced, trained, qualified, skilled, accomplished, proficient. **5** virtual, effective, essential.
⊟ *adj.* **1** theoretical. **2, 3** impractical. **4** impractical, unskilled.

practicality *noun* (PL. **practicalities**) **1** being practical. **2** a practical matter. **3** a practical aspect or feature.

practical joke a trick played on someone, as distinct from a joke told.

practically *adv.* **1** almost. **2** in a practical manner.

⊟ **1** almost, nearly, well-nigh, virtually, pretty well, all but, just about, in principle, in effect, essentially, fundamentally, to all intents and purposes. **2** realistically, sensibly, reasonably, rationally, pragmatically.

practice *noun* **1** the process of carrying something out: *easier in theory than in practice/put one's ideas into practice.* **2** a habit, activity, procedure, or custom: *don't make a practice of it.* **3** repeated exercise to improve one's technique in an art, sport, etc. **4** a doctor's or lawyer's business or clientele. — **be in** or **out of practice** to have maintained, or failed to maintain, one's skill in an art, sport, etc. [from PRACTISE]

⊟ **1** effect, reality, actuality, action, operation, performance, use, application. **2** habit, custom, tradition, convention, routine, activity, procedure, way, method, system, policy, usage. **3** training, drill, exercise, workout, rehearsal, run-through, dry run, dummy run, *colloq.* try-out.
⊟ **1** theory, principle.

practise *verb* **1** *trans., intrans.* to do exercises repeatedly in (an art, sport, etc) so as to improve one's performance. **2** to make a habit of: *practise self-control.* **3** to go in for as a custom: *tribes that practise bigamy.* **4** to work at, or follow (an art or profession, especially medicine or law). **5** to perform (a wrongful act) against someone: *had practised a cruel deception on them.* [from Latin *practicare*, from Greek *praktikos*, practical]

⊟ **1** train, rehearse, exercise, run through, repeat, drill, study, perfect. **2, 3** engage in, perform, carry out, put into practice, apply, implement. **4** work at, follow, pursue, engage in, do, perform, carry out, undertake. **5** do, carry out, perform, execute.

practised *adj.* skilled; experienced; expert.

⊟ skilled, experienced, expert, accomplished, knowledgeable, able, proficient, masterly, seasoned, veteran, trained, qualified, versed, consummate, finished.
⊟ unpractised, inexperienced, inexpert.

practitioner *noun* someone practising an art or profession, especially medicine. [altered from earlier *practician*]

praetor /ˈpriːtə, ˈpriːtɔː(r)/ *noun* in ancient Rome, one of the chief law officers of the state, elected annually, second to the consul in importance. The office could not be held before the age of 33.

pragmatic *adj.* concerned with what is practicable, expedient, and convenient, rather than with theories and ideals; matter-of-fact; realistic. [from Greek *pragma*, deed]

⊟ practical, realistic, sensible, matter-of-fact, businesslike, efficient, hard-headed, *colloq.* hard-nosed, unsentimental.
⊟ unrealistic, idealistic, romantic.

pragmatism *noun* **1** a practical, matter-of-fact approach to dealing with problems, etc. **2** *Philos.* a school of thought that assesses concepts' truth in terms of their practical implications.

pragmatist *noun* a pragmatic person.

Prague Spring the period of political liberalization and reform in Czechoslovakia in early 1968, ended by Soviet intervention in the summer of the same year.

prairie *noun* in N America, a treeless, grass-covered plain. [from French *prairie*, meadow]

prairie dog a N American rodent similar to a marmot, that lives in labyrinthine burrows and barks like a dog.

prairie schooner a type of long covered wagon used by emigrants making the journey west across the USA in the 19c. Also called *Conestoga wagon*, from the place in Pennsylvania where they were originally manufactured.

praise — *verb* 1 to express admiration or approval of. 2 to worship or glorify (God) with hymns, thanksgiving, etc. — *noun* 1 the expression of admiration or approval; commendation. 2 worship of God. — **sing the praises of someone** to commend them enthusiastically. [from Old French *preisier*, from Latin *pretiare*, to value]

. . . .

▣ *verb* 1 admire, compliment, flatter, eulogize, commend, congratulate, wax lyrical over, *colloq.* rave over, extol, promote, applaud, cheer, acclaim, hail, recognize, acknowledge, pay tribute to, honour, laud. 2 worship, glorify, magnify, exalt, honour, adore, bless. *noun* 1 approval, admiration, commendation, congratulation, flattery, adulation, acclaim, recognition, testimonial, compliment, tribute, eulogy, accolade, applause, ovation, cheering. 2 worship, glory, adoration, devotion, thanksgiving, homage, honour.
▣ *verb* 1 criticize, revile. *noun* 1 criticism, revilement.

. . . .

praiseworthily *adv.* in a praiseworthy way.
praiseworthiness *noun* being praiseworthy.
praiseworthy *adj.* deserving praise; commendable.

. . . .

▣ commendable, fine, excellent, admirable, worthy, deserving, honourable, reputable, estimable, sterling.
▣ blameworthy, dishonourable, ignoble.

. . . .

praline / 'prɑːliːn/ *noun* a sweet consisting of nuts in caramelized sugar. [from Marshal Duplessis-Praslin (1598–1675), French soldier whose cook invented it]
pram *noun* a wheeled carriage for a baby, pushed by someone on foot. [a shortening of PERAMBULATOR]
prance *verb intrans.* 1 *said especially of a horse* to walk with lively springing steps. 2 to frisk or skip about. 3 to parade about in a swaggering manner. [from Middle English *praunce*]
prang *colloq.* — *verb* to crash (a vehicle). — *noun* a vehicle crash. [imitative]
prank *noun* a trick; a practical joke.

. . . .

▣ trick, practical joke, joke, stunt, caper, frolic, lark, antic, escapade.

. . . .

prankster *noun* a person who plays pranks, a practical joker.
praseodymium *noun Chem.* (SYMBOL **Pr**, ATOMIC NUMBER **59**) a soft silvery metallic element that is used in the alloy mischmetal, eg to make lighter flints. [from Greek *prasios*, leek-green]
prat *noun slang* 1 *offensive* someone stupid. 2 the buttocks.
prate *verb intrans.*, *trans.* to talk or utter foolishly. [from Old Dutch *praeten*]
prattle — *verb intrans.*, *trans.* to chatter or utter childishly or foolishly. — *noun* childish or foolish chatter. [from Old German *pratelen*, to chatter]
prattler *noun* a person who prattles.
prawn *noun* an edible shellfish like a large shrimp. [from Middle English *prane*]
pray — *verb* 1 *intrans.* to address one's god, making earnest requests or giving thanks. 2 *old use* to entreat or implore. 3 to hope desperately. — *interj.* meaning 'please', or 'may I ask', uttered with quaint politeness or cold irony: *pray come in/who asked you, pray?* [from Old French *preier*, from Latin *precari*, to pray]

. . . .

▣ *verb* 1 supplicate. 2 entreat, implore, beseech, beg, supplicate, invoke, call on, petition, ask, solicit, request, crave, plead.

. . . .

prayer *noun* 1 an address to one's god, making a request or giving thanks: *say one's prayers*. 2 the activity of praying. 3 an earnest hope, desire, or entreaty.

. . . .

▣ 1 collect, litany, devotions. 2 invocation, supplication, devotions, communion. 3 hope, desire, entreaty, plea, appeal, petition, request.

. . . .

prayer book a book of set prayers appropriate for various occasions and types of church service.
prayer rug or **prayer mat** a small carpet on which a Muslim kneels when praying.
prayer wheel *Buddhism* a drum that turns on a spindle, inscribed with prayers that are regarded as uttered as the drum is rotated.
praying mantis any of about 1800 species of predatory insect, usually green or brown in colour, found mainly in tropical regions, and so called because the spiky front legs are held up in front of the head as if in an attitude of prayer while the insect is waiting for its prey, which includes grasshoppers, flies, moths, and butterflies. Also called MANTIS, MANTID.
pre- *prefix* forming words meaning 'before': 1 in time: *prewar*. 2 in position: *premolar*. 3 in importance: *preeminent*. [from Latin *prae*]
preach *verb* 1 *intrans.*, *trans.* to deliver (a sermon) as part of a religious service. 2 (**preach at someone**) to give them advice in a tedious or obtrusive manner. 3 to advise; to advocate: *preach caution*. [from Latin *praedicare*, to give advice, command]

. . . .

▣ 2 lecture, harangue, evangelize. 3 advise, advocate, urge, exhort.

. . . .

preamble *noun* an introduction or preface, eg to a speech or document; an opening statement. [from Latin *praeambulare*, to walk before]
prearrange *verb* to arrange in advance: *a prearranged signal*.
prearrangement *noun* an arrangement made previously.
prebend / 'prebənd/ *noun* an allowance paid out of the revenues of a cathedral or collegiate church to its canons or chapter members. [from Latin *praebenda*, allowance]
prebendal / prɪ'bendl/ *adj.* relating to a prebend or prebendary.
prebendary / 'prebəndərɪ/ *noun* (PL. **prebendaries**) a clergyman in receipt of a prebend.
Precambrian *adj.* 1 *Geol.* relating to the earliest geological era, extending from the formation of the Earth about 4550 million years ago, to the beginning of the Palaeozoic era, about 580 million years ago. 2 relating to the rocks formed during this period.
precancerous *adj.* denoting a condition that could become cancerous if untreated.
precarious *adj.* 1 unsafe; insecure; dangerous. 2 uncertain; chancy. [from Latin *precarius*, obtained by prayer, uncertain, from *prex*, prayer]

. . . .

▣ 1 unsafe, insecure, dangerous, treacherous, risky, hazardous, vulnerable, unsteady, unstable, shaky, wobbly. 2 chancy, uncertain, unsure, dubious, doubtful, unpredictable, unreliable.
▣ 1 safe, secure, stable. 2 certain.

. . . .

precariously *adv.* in a precarious state or way.
precariousness *noun* being precarious.
precast *adj.*, *said of concrete, etc* made into blocks, etc ready for use in building.
precaution *noun* a measure taken to ensure a satisfactory outcome, or to avoid a risk or danger. [from Latin *praecautio*]

. . . .

▣ safeguard, security, protection, provision, insurance,

providence, forethought, caution, prudence, foresight, anticipation, preparation.

....

precautionary adj. **1** suggesting precaution. **2** of the nature of precaution.

....

▤ PROTECTIVE, PREVENTIVE, PROVIDENT, CAUTIOUS, PRUDENT, JUDICIOUS, PREPARATORY, PRELIMINARY, SAFETY.

....

precede verb trans., intrans. **1** to go or be before, in time, order, position, rank, or importance. **2** to preface or introduce: preceded her lecture with a word of explanation. [from Latin praecedere, to go before]

....

▤ **1** come before, lead, come first, go before, take precedence. **2** introduce, herald, usher in.
▣ **1** follow, succeed.

....

precedence noun **1** priority: safety takes precedence over all else. **2** the fact of preceding, in order, rank, importance, etc; the right to precede others: were introduced in order of precedence.

....

▤ **1** priority, preference, pride of place, superiority, supremacy, pre-eminence. **2** seniority, rank.

....

precedent noun a previous incident, legal case, etc that is parallel to one under consideration; the measures taken or judgement given in that case, serving as a basis for a decision in the present one.

....

▤ model, standard, criterion, pattern, example.

....

precentor noun a person who leads the singing of a church congregation, or leads the prayers in a synagogue. [from Latin praecentor, from prae, before + canere, to sing]

precept noun a rule or principle, especially of a moral kind, that guides one's behaviour. [from Latin praeceptum]

precession noun **1** Physics the gradual change in direction of the axis of rotation of a spinning body. For example, the axis of a spinning top gradually moves in a circle because of precession. As the top slows down, the circle of precession gets larger and larger until the top wobbles and finally falls over. The Earth's axis undergoes precession caused by the gravitational pull of the Moon, Sun, and planets. **2** Astron. (in full precession of the equinoxes) the progressively earlier occurrence of the equinoxes, resulting from the gradual change in direction of the Earth's axis of rotation, which over thousands of years produces an apparent change in the position of the stars as seen from Earth. **3** the act of preceding. [from Latin praecessio, from praecedere, to precede]

precessional adj. relating to or involving precession.

precinct noun **1** (also **precincts**) the enclosed grounds of a large building, etc: the cathedral precinct/within the university precincts. **2** (also **precincts**) the neighbourhood or environs of a place. **3** a traffic-free zone in a town, etc: a pedestrian precinct. **4** North Amer., esp. US any of the districts into which a city is divided for administrative or policing purposes. [from Latin praecinctum, from praecingere, to surround]

....

▤ **4** zone, area, district, quarter, sector, division, section.

....

preciosity /preʃɪˈɒsɪtɪ/ noun affectedness or exaggerated refinement in speech or manner. [from Latin pretiositas, from pretiosus, valuable]

precious adj. **1** valuable. **2** dear; beloved; treasured: memories still precious to her. **3** derog., said of speech or manner affected or over-precise. **4** ironic confounded: him and his

precious goldfish! — **precious few** or **little** almost none. [from Latin pretiosus, valuable]

....

▤ **1** valuable, expensive, costly, dear, priceless, inestimable, rare, choice, fine. **2** dear, beloved, treasured, prized, valued, cherished, dearest, darling, favourite, loved, adored, idolized.

....

preciously adv. in a precious way.
precious metal gold, silver, or platinum.
preciousness noun being precious.
precious stone a mineral valued for its beauty and rarity; a gem.
precipice noun a sheer cliff. [from Latin praecipitium, from praecipitare, to fall headlong]
precipitate — verb (pronounced -teɪt) **1** to cause, or hasten the advent of: precipitate a war. **2** to throw or plunge: precipitated himself into the controversy. **3** Chem. to (cause to) form a suspension of small solid particles in a solution as a result of certain chemical reactions. — adj. (pronounced -tət) said of actions or decisions recklessly hasty or ill-considered. — noun (pronounced -tət) **1** Chem. a suspension of small solid particles that are formed in a solution as a result of certain chemical reactions. **2** moisture deposited as rain, snow, etc. [from Latin praecipitare, to fall or throw headlong]

....

▤ verb **1** cause, hasten, bring on, induce, trigger, occasion, hurry, speed, accelerate, quicken, expedite, advance, further. adj. hasty, ill-considered, impetuous, impulsive, rash, reckless, heedless, hurried, headlong, breakneck, frantic, impatient, hotheaded, indiscreet, sudden, unexpected, abrupt, quick, swift, rapid, brief, violent.
▣ adj. cautious, careful.

....

precipitately adv. in a precipitate way.
precipitation noun **1** rash haste. **2** frozen or liquid water that falls from clouds in the atmosphere to the Earth's surface in the form of rain, snow, sleet, hail, etc. **3** the act of precipitating or process of being precipitated. **4** Chem. the formation of a precipitate.
precipitous adj. **1** dangerously steep. **2** said of actions or decisions precipitate. [from French précipiteux]

....

▤ **1** steep, sheer, perpendicular, vertical, high.
▣ **1** gradual, gentle.

....

précis /ˈpreɪsiː/ — noun (PL. **précis**) a summary of a piece of writing. — verb (**précised**, **précising**) to make a précis of. [from French précis, cut short]
precise adj. **1** exact; very: at this precise moment. **2** clear; detailed: precise instructions. **3** accurate: precise timing. **4** said of a person careful over details. [from Latin praecisus, shortened]

....

▤ **1** exact, very, particular, specific. **2** clear, detailed, explicit, unequivocal, unambiguous, clear-cut, distinct, express, definite, blow-by-blow. **3** accurate, right, correct, factual, faithful, authentic. **4** punctilious, scrupulous, fastidious, careful, strict.
▣ **2** ambiguous. **3** imprecise, inexact. **4** careless.

....

precisely adv. **1** exactly. **2** in a precise manner. **3** said as a rejoinder you are quite right.

....

▤ **1** exactly, accurately, correctly. **2** strictly, minutely, clearly, distinctly, literally, verbatim. **3** exactly, absolutely, just so.

....

preciseness noun being precise.
precision — noun accuracy. — adj., said of tools, etc designed to operate with minute accuracy.

∎ *noun* accuracy, exactness, correctness, faithfulness, particularity, rigour, meticulousness, scrupulousness.
∎ *noun* imprecision, inaccuracy.

precision-approach radar (ABBREV. **PAR**) *Aeron.* a radar system that shows the exact position of an approaching aircraft, and allows an air traffic controller to issue detailed landing instructions to the pilot.

preclude *verb* **1** to rule out, eliminate, or make impossible. **2 (preclude someone from something)** to prevent their involvement in it: *precluded from attending the meeting.* [from Latin *praecludere*, to impede]

preclusion *noun* **1** precluding. **2** prevention.

precocious *adj.* **1** *said eg of a child* unusually advanced in mental development, speech, behaviour, etc. **2** *said of behaviour, achievements, etc* indicating advanced development. [from Latin *praecox*, ripening early, precocious]

∎ **1** mature, developed, gifted, clever, bright, smart, quick, fast. **2** forward, ahead, advanced, early, premature.
∎ **1** backward.

precociously *adv.* with a precocious manner.
precocity *noun* being precocious.
precognition *noun* the supposed ability to foresee events; foreknowledge. [from Latin *praecognitio*]
precognitive *adj.* characterized by precognition.
precolumbian *adj.* denoting the period of American history before the discovery of America by Christopher Columbus.
preconceive *verb* (*usually* **preconceived**) to form (an idea) of something before having direct experience of it.

∎ imagine, conceive, envisage, expect, visualize, picture, presuppose, presume, assume, anticipate, project.

preconception *noun* an assumption about something not yet experienced; a preconceived idea.

∎ presupposition, presumption, assumption, conjecture, anticipation, expectation, prejudgement, bias, prejudice.

precondition *noun* a condition to be satisfied in advance.

∎ condition, stipulation, requirement, prerequisite, essential, necessity, must.

precursor *noun* **1** something that precedes, and is a sign of, an approaching event. **2** *Chem.* any chemical compound from which another compound, such as a hormone or enzyme, is directly produced by some form of chemical modification. [from Latin *praecursor*, forerunner, advance guard]

∎ **1** antecedent, forerunner, sign, indication, herald, harbinger, messenger, usher.
∎ **1** follower, successor.

predacious *adj.* predatory. [altered from PREDATORY]
pre-date *verb* **1** to write a bygone date on (a document, etc). **2** to occur at an earlier date than.
predator /ˈprɛdətə(r)/ *noun* **1** any living organism that obtains food by catching, usually killing, and eating other organisms (the *prey*). **2** *derog.* a predatory person. [from Latin *praedator*, plunderer, hunter]
predatoriness /ˈprɛdətərɪnəs/ *noun* being predatory.
predatory /ˈprɛdətərɪ/ *adj.* **1** *said of an animal* killing and feeding on others. **2** *said of people* cruelly exploiting the weakness or good will of others for personal gain.
predecease *verb* to die before (someone).

predecessor *noun* **1** the person who preceded one in one's job or position. **2** the previous version, model, etc of a particular thing or product. **3** an ancestor. [from Latin *praedecessor*, from *prae*, before + *decedere*, to withdraw, give place]

∎ **3** ancestor, forefather, forebear, antecedent, forerunner, precursor.
∎ SUCCESSOR. **3** descendant.

predella /prɪˈdɛlə/ *noun* **1** a small painting or panel enclosed in a compartment attached to the lower edge of an altarpiece. An altarpiece often has several such panels illustrating scenes from the life of the saint represented in the main panel. **2** the platform or uppermost step on which an altar stands. **3** a retable. [from Italian *predella*, altar-step]
predestination *noun* **1** the act of predestining or fact of being predestined. **2** *Relig.* the doctrine that whatever is to happen has been unalterably fixed by God from the beginning of time, especially with regard to which souls are to be saved and which damned.

∎ PREDETERMINATION, FOREORDINATION. **1** destiny, fate, lot, doom.

predestine *verb* (*usually* **be predestined**) **1** to destine or doom: *were predestined to meet.* **2** to ordain or decree by fate: *it happened as if predestined.* [from Latin *praedestinare*, to determine in advance]
predetermination *noun* predetermining or being predetermined.
predetermine *verb* **1** to decide, settle, or fix in advance. **2** to influence, shape, or cause to tend a certain way.

∎ **1** prearrange, arrange, agree, fix, set. **2** influence, shape, predestine, destine, fate, doom, ordain, foreordain.

predicament *noun* a difficulty that one finds oneself in; a plight or dilemma. [from Latin *praedicamentum*, something asserted]

∎ plight, dilemma, mess, *colloq.* fix, *colloq.* spot, quandary, impasse, crisis, emergency.

predicate — *noun* (pronounced -kət) **1** *Grammar* the word or words in a sentence that make a statement about the subject. It usually consists of a verb and its complement, eg *knew what to do* in *the people in charge knew what to do.* **2** *Logic* what is stated as a property of the subject of a proposition. — *verb* (pronounced -keɪt) **1** to assert. **2** to imply; to entail the existence of. **3** *Logic* to state as a property of the subject of a proposition. **4 (predicate one thing on another)** to make the viability of an idea, etc depend on something else being true. [from Latin *praedicare*, to assert]
predication *noun* **1** predicating or asserting, or an instance of this. **2** *Logic* an assertion made of or about a subject.
predicative /prɪˈdɪkətɪv/ *adj.* **1** *Grammar, said of an adjective* forming part of a predicate, as *asleep* in *they were asleep.* See also ATTRIBUTIVE. **2** relating to predicates.
predicatively *adv. Grammar* with a predicative function.
predict *verb* to prophesy, foretell, or forecast. [from Latin *praedicare*, to foretell]

∎ prophesy, foretell, forecast, foresee, prognosticate, project.

predictability *noun* being predictable.
predictable *adj.* **1** able to be predicted; easily foreseen. **2** *derog.* boringly consistent in one's behaviour or reactions, etc; unoriginal.

1 foreseeable, expected, anticipated, likely, probable, imaginable, foreseen, foregone, certain, sure. **2** reliable, dependable.

UNPREDICTABLE. **1** uncertain.

predictably *adv.* in a predictable way.
prediction *noun* **1** the act or art of predicting. **2** something foretold.

1 divination, fortune-telling, soothsaying, augury. **2** prophecy, forecast, prognosis, augury.

predilection *noun* a special liking or preference for something. [from Latin *praediligere*, to prefer]
predispose *verb* **1** to incline (someone) to react in a particular way: *clear handwriting will predispose the examiners in your favour*. **2** to make susceptible to (especially illness).

DISPOSE, INCLINE **1** prompt, induce, make, sway, influence, affect, bias, prejudice.

predisposition *noun* **1** the condition of being predisposed. **2** *Medicine* a likelihood of being affected by certain diseases or conditions.
predominance *noun* being predominant.
predominant *adj.* more numerous, prominent, or powerful.

dominant, prevailing, prominent, powerful, preponderant, chief, main, principal, primary, prime, important, influential, capital, paramount, supreme, sovereign, ruling, controlling, leading, potent, forceful, strong.

minor, lesser, weak.

predominantly *adv.* in a predominant way.
predominate *verb intrans.* **1** to be more numerous: *girls predominate over boys in this class*. **2** to be more noticeable or prominent. **3** to have more influence: *the 'green' lobby is beginning to predominate*. [from Latin *prae*, above others + *dominari*, to have mastery]
pre-eminence *noun* a pre-eminent quality.
pre-eminent *adj.* outstanding; excelling all others. [from Latin *praeeminere*, to be prominent]

outstanding, supreme, unsurpassed, unrivalled, unequalled, unmatched, matchless, incomparable, inimitable, chief, foremost, leading, eminent, distinguished, renowned, famous, prominent, exceptional, excellent, superlative, transcendent, superior.

inferior, unknown.

pre-eminently *adv.* in a pre-eminent way.
pre-empt *verb* **1** to forestall and so make pointless (an action planned by someone else). **2** to obtain in advance for oneself.
pre-emption *noun* **1** the buying of, or right to buy, property, before others get the chance. **2** the act of pre-empting. [from Latin *praeemere*, to buy before]
pre-emptive *adj.* **1** having the effect of pre-empting. **2** *Mil.*, *said of an attack or strike* effectively destroying the enemy's weapons before they can be used.
pre-emptive strike *Mil.* an attack which has the effect of destroying the enemy's weapons before they can be used.
preen *verb* **1** *trans.*, *intrans.*, *said of a bird* to clean and smooth (its feathers) with its beak. **2** to groom (oneself), especially in a vain manner. **3** (**preen oneself on something**) to pride or congratulate oneself on account of it. [from Middle English *prene*]
prefab *noun* a prefabricated building, especially a dwelling.

prefabricate *verb* to manufacture standard sections of (a building) for later quick assembly.
prefabrication *noun* prefabricating or being prefabricated.
preface /ˈprɛfəs/ — *noun* **1** an explanatory statement at the beginning of a book. **2** anything of an introductory or preliminary character. — *verb* **1** to provide (a book, etc) with a preface. **2** to introduce or precede with some preliminary matter. [from Latin *praefatio*, from *praefari*, to say beforehand]

noun FOREWORD, INTRODUCTION, PREAMBLE, PROLOGUE, PRELUDE, PRELIMINARIES. *verb* **2** introduce, precede, prefix, lead up to, launch, open, begin, start.

noun EPILOGUE, POSTSCRIPT. *verb* **2** end, finish, complete.

prefatory /ˈprɛfətərɪ/ *adj.* **1** relating to a preface. **2** serving as a preface or introduction. **3** introductory.
prefect *noun* **1** a senior pupil with minor disciplinary powers in a school. **2** in some countries, the senior official of an administrative district. [from Latin *praefectus*, an official in charge, overseer, director, etc]
prefecture /ˈpriːfɛktʃə(r)/ *noun* the office of, or the district presided over by, a prefect.
prefer *verb* (**preferred**, **preferring**) **1** (**prefer one thing to another**) to like it better: *prefer tea to coffee*. **2** *Legal* to submit (a charge, accusation, etc) to a court of law for consideration. **3** to promote (a person) over his or her colleagues. [from Latin *praeferre*, to place before, especially in esteem]

1 favour, like better, desire, choose, select, pick, opt for, go for, plump for, single out, advocate, recommend, back, support, fancy, elect, adopt, would rather, would sooner, want, wish. **3** favour.

1 reject.

preferable *adj.* more desirable, suitable, or advisable; better. [from French *préférable*]

better, desirable, advisable, superior, nicer, preferred, favoured, chosen, advantageous, recommended.

inferior, undesirable.

preferably *adv.* **1** by preference; from choice. **2** as is better or more desirable.
preference *noun* **1** the preferring of one thing, etc to another: *chose pink in preference to purple*. **2** one's choice of, or liking for, someone or something particular: *have no special preferences*. **3** favourable consideration: *give preference to experienced applicants*.

1 inclination, predilection, liking, fancy. **2** favourite, first choice, choice, pick, selection, option, wish, desire. **3** partiality, favouritism, preferential treatment.

preference shares shares on which the dividend must be paid before that on ordinary shares.
preferential *adj.* bestowing special favours or advantages: *preferential treatment*.

favourable, advantageous, favoured, privileged, special, better, superior.

equal.

preferment *noun* promotion to a more responsible position.
prefiguration *noun* prefiguring or representation beforehand, or an instance of this.
prefigure *verb* to be an advance sign or representation of (something that is to come); to foreshadow. [from Latin *praefigurare*]
prefix — *noun* **1** *Grammar* an element such as *un-*, *re-*, *non-*, and *de-* added to the beginning of a word to create a

new word. **2** a title such as *Mr, Dr*, and *Ms*, used before a person's name. — *verb* **1** to add as an introduction. **2** to attach as a prefix to a word. **3** to add a prefix to. [from Latin *praefixum*]

prefrontal lobotomy *Medicine* a surgical procedure, formerly used in the treatment of some severe mental disorders, in which the nerve fibres connecting the frontal lobes to the rest of the brain are severed. The operation had serious side-effects and often caused marked personality changes.

pregnancy (PL. **pregnancies**) *noun* in female mammals, including humans, the period during which a developing embryo is carried in the womb. In humans it usually lasts for up to 40 weeks (280 days), from conception until birth. Also called GESTATION.

pregnant *adj*. **1** carrying an unborn child or young in the womb. **2** *said of a remark, pause, etc* loaded with a significance only too obvious to those present. [from Latin *praegnans*]

....

■ **1** expectant, expecting, *old use* with child. **2** significant, meaningful, suggestive, charged, loaded, full, eloquent, expressive.

....

preheat *verb* to heat (an oven, furnace, etc) before use.

prehensile /prɪˈhɛnsaɪl/ *adj*. denoting a part of an animal that is adapted for grasping, eg the tail of certain vertebrates which enables them to hang from tree branches. [from Latin *prehendere*, to grasp]

prehistoric *adj*. belonging or relating to the period before historical records.

prehistorically *adv*. in prehistoric times.

prehistory *noun* the period before historical records. Prehistory is classified (according to the types of tools and weapons used by early humans) as part of the Stone Age, Bronze Age, and Iron Age.

prejudge *verb* **1** to form an opinion on (an issue, etc) without having all the relevant facts. **2** to condemn (someone) unheard.

prejudgement *noun* prejudging; a conclusion reached before examining the facts.

prejudice — *noun* **1** a biased opinion, based on insufficient knowledge. **2** unthinking hostility, eg towards a particular racial or religious group. **3** *Legal* harm; detriment: *without prejudice to your parental rights*. — *verb* **1** (*often* **be prejudiced**) to cause (someone) to feel prejudice; to bias. **2** to harm or endanger: *a poor interview will prejudice your chances of success*. [from Latin *praejudicium*, harm]

....

■ *noun* **1** bias, partiality, partisanship, unfairness, injustice. **2** discrimination, narrow-mindedness, bigotry, chauvinism, racism, sexism, intolerance. **3** harm, detriment, damage, disadvantage, impairment, hurt, injury, loss, ruin. *verb* **1** bias, predispose, incline, sway, influence, condition, colour, slant, distort, load, weight. **2** harm, endanger, damage, impair, hinder, undermine, hurt, injure, mar, spoil, ruin, wreck.

Fa *noun* **1** fairness. **2** tolerance. **3** benefit, advantage. *verb* **2** benefit, help, advance.

....

prejudicial *adj*. **1** causing prejudice. **2** harmful.

....

■ **2** harmful, damaging, hurtful, injurious, detrimental, disadvantageous, unfavourable, inimical.

Fa **2** beneficial, advantageous.

....

prelacy /ˈprɛləsɪ/ *noun* (PL. **prelacies**) **1** the office of a prelate. **2** the entire body of prelates. **3** administration of the church by prelates.

prelate /ˈprɛlət/ *noun* a bishop, abbot, or other high-ranking ecclesiastic. [from Latin *praelatus*, from *praeferre*, to prefer]

preliminary — *adj*. occurring at the beginning; introductory or preparatory. — *noun* (PL. **preliminaries**) **1**

(*usually* **preliminaries**) something done or said by way of introduction or preparation. **2** a preliminary round in a competition. [from Latin *prae-*, before + *limen*, threshold]

....

■ *adj*. opening, introductory, preparatory, initial, primary, first, early, earliest, advance, prior, inaugural, qualifying, exploratory, experimental, trial, test, pilot. *noun* **1** preparation, groundwork, introduction, preface, prelude, opening, beginning, start, foundations, basics, rudiments, formalities.

Fa *adj*. final, closing.

....

prelims /ˈpriːlɪmz/ *pl. noun colloq*. **1** a set of preliminary examinations; the first public examinations in certain universities. **2** *Printing* the title page, contents page, and other matter preceding the main text of a book.

prelude *noun* **1** *Mus*. an introductory passage or first movement, eg of a fugue or suite. **2** a name sometimes given to a short musical piece, a poetical composition, etc. **3** some event that precedes, and prepares the ground for, one of greater significance: *talks that are being seen as a prelude to peace*. [from Latin *praeludium*, from *prae-*, before + *ludere*, to play]

....

■ **3** overture, introduction, preliminary, preface, foreword, preamble, prologue, precursor, curtain-raiser, opening, opener, preparation, beginning, start, commencement.

Fa **3** finale, epilogue.

....

premarital *adj*. belonging to, or occurring in, the period before marriage.

premature *adj*. **1** *Medicine, said of human birth* occurring before the expected time, ie less than 37 weeks after conception, or involving a birth weight of less than 2500g (5.5lb). **2** occurring before the usual or expected time: *premature senility*. **3** *said of a decision, etc* over-hasty. [from Latin *praematurus*]

....

■ **1** early. **2** early, untimely, inopportune, ill-timed. **3** hasty, rash, ill-considered.

Fa **1** late. **2** late, tardy.

....

prematurely *adv*. so as to be premature, too early.

premed /ˈpriːmɛd/ *noun colloq*. premedication.

premedication *noun* the drugs given to a surgical patient in preparation for a general anaesthetic.

premeditate *verb* to plan; to think out beforehand: *premeditated murder*. [from Latin *praemeditari*]

....

■ plan, intend, calculate, consider, contrive, preplan, prearrange, predetermine.

....

premenstrual *adj*. belonging to the time just before a menstrual period.

premenstrual tension or **premenstrual syndrome** (ABBREV. **PMT, PMS**) *Medicine* a group of symptoms associated with hormonal changes and experienced by some women for up to 10 days before the onset of menstruation.

premier — *adj*. first in rank; most important; leading. — *noun* a prime minister. [from Old French *premier*, first, of first rank]

première /ˈprɛmɪɛə(r)/ — *noun* the first public performance of a play or showing of a film. — *verb* (**premièred, premièring**) to present a première of. [from French *première*, feminine of *premier*, first]

....

■ *noun* opening, opening night, first night, début.

....

premiership *noun* the office of prime minister.

premise /ˈprɛmɪs/ *noun* **1** something assumed to be true as a basis for stating something further, especially in logic either of the propositions introducing a syllogism. **2** (**premises**) *Legal* the preliminary matter in a document, etc; matters explained, or property referred to, earlier in the document. **3 (premises)** a building and its grounds. [from Latin *praemissa*, things preceding, premise]

. . . .

▣ **1** presupposition, assumption, supposition, hypothesis, postulate, thesis, argument, basis, proposition, statement, assertion. **3** building, property, establishment, office, grounds, estate, site, place.

. . . .

premiss *noun* same as PREMISE 1.

premium *noun* **1** an amount paid usually annually on an insurance agreement. **2** an extra sum added to wages or to interest. — **be at a premium** to be scarce and greatly in demand. **put a premium on something** to attach special importance to it: *put a premium on punctuality.* [from Latin *praemium*, prize]

Premium Bond or **Premium Savings Bond** in the UK, a government bond yielding no interest, but eligible for a draw for cash prizes.

premolar /priːˈmoʊlə(r)/ *noun* any of the four teeth between the canines and first molars.

premonition *noun* a feeling that something is about to happen, before it actually does; an intuition or presentiment. [from Latin *praemonitio*, forewarning]

. . . .

▣ intuition, presentiment, suspicion, foreboding, misgiving, feeling, hunch, idea, fear, omen, sign, warning.

. . . .

Premonstratensian *noun* a member of a religious order, also known as the Norbertines or White Canons, noted for parish education and mission work.

prenatal *adj.* belonging to the period before childbirth.

prenup *noun North Amer. colloq* a prenuptial agreement.

prenuptial agreement a contract made between a man and a woman in advance of their marriage, agreeing the ownership of their assets in the event of the marriage failing.

preoccupation *noun* **1** being preoccupied. **2** something that preoccupies.

. . . .

▣ **1** distraction, absent-mindedness, reverie, obliviousness, oblivion. **2** obsession, fixation, *colloq.* hang-up, concern, interest, enthusiasm, hobby-horse.

. . . .

preoccupied *adj.* (**preoccupied by** or **with something**) **1** lost in thought. **2** having one's attention completely taken up, engrossed. **3** already occupied.

. . . .

▣ **1** distracted, abstracted, absent-minded, daydreaming, absorbed, faraway, heedless, oblivious, pensive. **2** obsessed with, intent on, immersed in, engrossed in, engaged in, taken up by, wrapped up in, involved in.

. . . .

preoccupy *verb* (**preoccupies, preoccupied**) to occupy the attention of wholly; to engross or obsess. [from Latin *praeoccupare*, to occupy beforehand]

preordain *verb* to decree or determine in advance. [from Latin *praeordinare*, to ordain in advance]

prep *noun colloq.* homework; preparation.

prep. *abbrev. Grammar* preposition.

prepack *verb* to pack (eg food) before offering it for sale.

preparation *noun* **1** the process of preparing or being prepared. **2** (*usually* **preparations**) something done by way of preparing or getting ready. **3** preparatory work done by students; homework. **4** a medicine, cosmetic, or other such prepared substance.

. . . .

▣ **1** readiness, provision. **2** preliminaries, plans, arrangements, basics, rudiments, precautions, safeguards, foundations, groundwork, spadework. **4** medicine, cosmetic, mixture, compound, concoction, potion, lotion, application.

. . . .

preparatory /prɪˈparətərɪ/ *adj.* **1** serving to prepare for something; introductory; preliminary. **2** (**preparatory to something**) before it; in preparation for it: *checked the windows preparatory to leaving.*

. . . .

▣ **1** preliminary, introductory, opening, initial, primary, basic, fundamental, rudimentary, elementary.

. . . .

preparatory school 1 in Britain, a private school for children aged between seven and thirteen, usually preparing them for public school. **2** in the US, a private secondary school, preparing pupils for college.

prepare *verb* **1** *trans., intrans.* to make or get ready. **2** to make (a meal). **3** to clean or chop (vegetables or fruit). **4** to get (someone or oneself) into a fit state to receive a shock, etc: *we must be prepared for bad news.* **5** *intrans.* to brace oneself (to do something): *prepare to jump.* [from Latin *praeparare*, to prepare]

. . . .

▣ **1** get ready, make ready, plan, organize, arrange, pave the way, warm up, train, coach, study, adapt, adjust, provide, supply, equip, fit out, rig out, construct, assemble, concoct, contrive, devise, draft, draw up, compose. **2** make, produce, *North Amer.* fix, concoct. **4, 5** brace oneself, steel oneself, gird oneself, fortify oneself.

. . . .

prepared *adj.* willing: *not prepared to lend any more.*

. . . .

▣ willing, ready, inclined, disposed.

. . . .

prepay *verb* (PAST TENSE AND PAST PARTICIPLE **prepaid**) **1** to pay for in advance. **2** to pay the postage on in advance.

prepayment *noun* payment in advance.

preponderance *noun* **1** the circumstance of being more numerous. **2** a superior number; a majority. [from Latin *praeponderare*, to outweigh]

preponderant *adj.* greater in force, influence, or weight, etc.

. . . .

▣ greater, larger, superior, predominant, prevailing, overriding, overruling, controlling, foremost, important, significant.

. . . .

preponderate *verb intrans.* to be more numerous; to predominate.

preposition *noun Grammar* a word such as *to, from, into, against,* that deals with the position, movement, etc of things or people in relation to one another, and is followed by an object. [from Latin *praepositio*, from *praeponere*, to put before]

prepositional *adj. Grammar* having the role of a preposition.

prepossess *verb* **1** to charm: *I was not prepossessed by his manners.* **2** to win over; to incline or bias: *was prepossessed in her favour.*

prepossessing *adj.* attractive; winning.

preposterous *adj.* ridiculous, absurd, or outrageous. [from Latin *praeposterus*, literally 'back to front']

. . . .

▣ ridiculous, absurd, incredible, outrageous, unbelievable, ludicrous, foolish, crazy, nonsensical, unreasonable, monstrous, shocking, intolerable, unthinkable, impossible.

▣ sensible, reasonable, acceptable.

. . . .

preposterously *adv.* in a preposterous way; to a preposterous degree.

prep school a preparatory school.

prepuce /ˈpriːpjuːs/ *noun Anat.* the loose skin that covers the top of the penis. Also called FORESKIN. [from Latin *praeputium*]

prequel /ˈpriːkwəl/ *noun* a book or film produced after one that has been a popular success, based on the same leading characters but with the story beginning prior to the start of the original story. [from PRE- + SEQUEL]

Pre-Raphaelite — *noun* a member of the Pre-Raphaelite Brotherhood. — *adj.* relating to or characteristic of the Pre-Raphaelites.

prerecord *verb* to record (a programme for radio or television) in advance of its scheduled broadcasting time.

prerequisite — *noun* a preliminary requirement that must be satisfied. — *adj.*, *said of a condition, etc* that must be satisfied beforehand.

....

🔲 *noun* precondition, requirement, proviso, condition, qualification, requisite, imperative, necessity, essential, must.

....

prerogative *noun* an exclusive right or privilege arising from one's rank or position. [from Latin *praerogativa*, privilege]

Pres. *abbrev.* President.

presage /'prɛsɪdʒ / — *verb* to be a warning sign of; to foreshadow, forebode, or portend. — *noun* a portent, warning, or omen. [from Latin *praesagire*, to forebode]

presbyopia *noun* difficulty in focusing the eye, a defect common in old age. [from Greek *presbys*, old + *opia*, condition of the eyes]

presbyter /'prɛzbɪtə(r)/ *noun* 1 in the early church, an administrative official with some teaching and priestly duties. 2 in episcopal churches, another word for a priest. 3 in presbyterian churches, an elder. [from Greek *presbyteros*, elder]

presbyterian /prɛzbɪ'tɪərɪən/ — *adj.* 1 denoting Church administration by presbyters or elders. 2 (**Presbyterian**) designating a church governed by elders. — *noun* (**Presbyterian**) a member of a Presbyterian church.

presbytery /'prɛzbɪtərɪ/ *noun* (PL. **presbyteries**) 1 in a presbyterian church, an area of local administration. 2 a body of elders or presbyters, especially one sitting as a local church court. 3 the eastern section of a church, beyond the choir. 4 the residence of a Roman Catholic priest.

preschool *adj.* denoting or relating to children before they are old enough to attend school: *preschool playgroups.*

preschool education the education of children who have not yet reached the statutory school age. This may be provided in nursery or kindergarten, where there are usually trained personnel; or in playgroups, where parent volunteers work with playgroup leaders.

prescience /'prɛsɪəns, 'prɛʃəns/ *noun* foreknowledge, foresight.

prescient /'prɛsɪənt, 'prɛʃənt/ *adj.* having or showing an understanding of what the future will bring. [from Latin *praescientia*, from *praescire*, to know beforehand]

prescribe *verb* 1 *said especially of a doctor* to advise (a medicine) as a remedy, especially by completing a prescription for it. 2 to recommend officially (eg a text for academic study). 3 to lay down or establish officially (a duty, penalty, etc). [from Latin *praescribere*, to write down beforehand]

....

🔲 **2** set, specify, stipulate. **3** lay down, ordain, decree, dictate, rule, command, order, require, direct, assign, appoint, impose, fix, define, limit.

....

prescript *noun* a law, rule, principle, etc that has been laid down. [from Latin *praescriptum*, from *praescribere*, to write down beforehand]

prescription *noun* 1 a set of instructions from a doctor for preparing and taking a medicine, etc. 2 the medicine, etc so prescribed by a doctor. 3 the act of prescribing. — **on prescription** *said of medicines* available only on the presentation to the pharmacist of a prescription from a doctor. [from Latin *praescriptio*, order]

....

🔲 **1** instruction, direction, formula. **2** medicine, drug, preparation, mixture, remedy, treatment.

....

prescriptive *adj.* 1 having an authoritative role or purpose; laying down rules. 2 *said of a right, etc* established by custom. [from Latin *praescribere*, to write down beforehand]

prescriptivism *noun* the practice of laying down rules, especially on the correct or incorrect use of language. Examples of these rules as applied to the English language include: the use of '*I shall*', not '*I will*', to express future time; and the rule that a sentence should never end with a preposition (eg *to whom do I owe the money?* and not *who do I owe the money to?*). Many of these rules bear little correspondence to everyday usages in English speech, and nowadays are often considered to be unnecessarily formal.

presence *noun* 1 the state, or circumstance, of being present. 2 one's attendance at an event, etc: *your presence is requested.* 3 someone's company or nearness: *said so in my presence.* 4 one's physical bearing, especially if commanding or authoritative: *people with presence.* 5 a being felt to be present, especially in a supernatural way. 6 a situation or activity demonstrating influence or power in a place: *maintain a military presence in the area.* [from Latin *praesentia*, from *praesens*, present]

....

🔲 **1** attendance, occupancy, residence, existence, company. **3** company, nearness, closeness, proximity, vicinity. **4** aura, air, demeanour, personality, charisma, bearing, carriage, appearance, poise, self-assurance.

🔳 **1** absence.

....

presence of mind calmness and the ability to act sensibly, especially in an emergency.

present[1] (with stress on *pres-*) — *adj.* 1 being at the place or occasion in question. 2 existing, detectable, or able to be found: *gases present in the atmosphere.* 3 existing now: *the present situation.* 4 now being considered: *the present subject.* 5 *Grammar, said of the tense of a verb* denoting action now, or action that is continuing or habitual. — *noun* 1 the present time. 2 *Grammar* the present tense, or a verb in the present tense. 3 (**presents**) *old use Legal* the present document; this statement, these words, etc. — **at present** now. **for the present** for the time being. [from Latin *praesens*]

....

🔲 *adj.* **1** attending, here, there, near, at hand, to hand, available, ready. **3** existing, existent, current, contemporary, present-day. **4** immediate.

🔳 *adj.* **1, 2** absent. **3** past, out of date.

....

present[2] *verb* (with stress on *-sent*) 1 (**present someone with something**) to give it to them, especially formally or ceremonially: *presented them with gold medals.* 2 (**present one person to another**) to introduce them, especially formally. 3 to introduce or compère (a television or radio show). 4 to stage (a play), show (a film), etc. 5 to offer for consideration: *presented proposals.* 6 to pose; to set: *shouldn't present any problem/presented us with a few problems.* 7 *said of an idea* to suggest (itself). 8 to hand over (a cheque) for acceptance or (a bill) for payment. 9 to set out: *presents her work neatly.* 10 to depict; to represent: *her biographer presents her in an over-sympathetic light.* 11 to put on (eg a cheerful face) in public. 12 to offer (one's compliments) formally. 13 to hold (a weapon) in aiming position. 14 *intrans. Medicine* to report to a doctor with certain symptoms or signs. 15 *intrans. Medicine, said of a baby's head or buttocks in childbirth* to be in a position to emerge first. — **present arms** to hold a rifle or other weapon vertically in front of one as a salute. **present oneself** to appear in person. [from Latin *praesentare*, to present]

....

🔲 **1** award, grant, give, donate, hand over, confer, bestow, entrust, extend, hold out. **3** introduce, compère, host, announce. **4** stage, put on, show, display, exhibit, mount, demonstrate. **5** offer, tender, submit. **10** depict, represent, portray.

....

present³ *noun* (with stress on *pres-*) something given; a gift. [related to PRESENT²]

⊟ gift, *colloq.* prezzie, offering, donation, grant, endowment, benefaction, bounty, largesse, gratuity, tip, favour.

presentability *noun* a presentable quality.

presentable *adj.* **1** fit to be seen, appear in company, etc. **2** passable; satisfactory.

⊟ **1** neat, tidy, clean, respectable, decent, proper, suitable. **2** passable, acceptable, satisfactory, tolerable.
⊞ **1** unpresentable, untidy, shabby. **2** unsatisfactory.

presentably *adv.* in a presentable way; so as to be presentable.

presentation *noun* **1** the act of presenting. **2** the manner in which something is presented, laid out, explained, or advertised. **3** something performed for an audience; a play, show, or other entertainment. **4** *Medicine* the position of a baby in the womb just before birth, i.e. whether head or buttocks downward.

⊟ **1** award, conferral, bestowal, investiture. **2** layout, appearance, arrangement, form, format. **3** show, performance, production, staging, representation, display, exhibition, demonstration, talk, delivery.

present-day *adj.* modern; of nowadays.

⊟ modern, current, present, contemporary, existing, living, up to date, fashionable.
⊞ past, future.

presenter *noun Broadcasting* a person who introduces a programme and provides a linking commentary between items.

presentiment *noun* a feeling that something, especially bad, is about to happen, just before it does. [from French *presentiment*, earlier spelling of *pressentiment*, foreboding]

presently *adv.* **1** soon; shortly. **2** *North Amer., esp. US* at the present time; now.

⊟ **1** soon, shortly, in a minute, before long, by and by. **2** currently, at present, now.

preservation *noun* preserving or being preserved.

preservative — *adj.* having the effect of preserving. — *noun* a chemical substance that when added to food or other perishable material slows down or prevents its decay by bacteria and fungi, eg salt, sugar, sulphur dioxide, essential oils.

preserve — *verb* **1** to save from loss, damage, decay, or deterioration. **2** to treat (food), eg by freezing, smoking, drying, pickling, or boiling in sugar, so that it will last. **3** to maintain (eg peace, the status quo, standards, etc). **4** to keep safe from danger or death. — *noun* **1** an area of work or activity restricted to certain people: *politics was once a male preserve*. **2** an area of land or water where creatures are protected for private hunting, shooting, or fishing: *a game preserve*. **3** a jam, pickle, or other form in which fruit or vegetables are preserved by cooking in sugar, salt, vinegar, etc. [from Latin *praeservare*, to guard]

⊟ *verb* **1, 4** protect, safeguard, guard, defend, shield, shelter, care for. **2** conserve, bottle, tin, can, pickle, salt, cure, dry. **3** maintain, uphold, sustain, continue, perpetuate, keep, retain, conserve. *noun* **1** domain, realm, sphere, area, field, speciality. **2** reservation, reserve. **3** conserve, jam, marmalade, jelly, pickle.
⊞ *verb* **1, 4** destroy, ruin.

preserver *noun* a person or thing that preserves or keeps safe.

preset — *verb* (with stress on *-set*) (**presetting**; PAST TENSE AND PAST PARTICIPLE **preset**) to adjust (a piece of electronic equipment, etc) so that it will operate at the required time. — *noun* (with stress on *pre-*) a device or facility for presetting.

preside *verb intrans.* **1** (**preside at** or **over something**) to take the lead at an event, the chair at a meeting, etc; to be in charge. **2** to dominate; to be a dominating presence: *his statue presided over the park*. [from Latin *praesidere*, to command, preside]

⊟ **1** chair at, officiate at, conduct, direct, manage, administer, control, run, head, lead, govern, rule.

presidency *noun* (PL. **presidencies**) the rank or office of a president.

president *noun* **1** (*often* **President**) the elected head of state in a republic. **2** the chief office-bearer in a society or club. **3** the head of a business organization. **4** the head of a college or other higher-education institution. [from Latin *praesidens*, present participle of *praesidere*, to preside]

presidential *adj.* **1** relating to a president or the office of president. **2** of the nature of a president.

presidium *noun* (PL. **presidiums, presidia**) a standing executive committee in a Communist state. [from Latin *presidium*, guard, garrison]

Presocratic /priːsɒˈkratɪk/ *noun* any of the earliest Western philosophers who preceded Socrates, and were active in Greece, Asia Minor, and Italy in the 5c BC and 6c BC.

press¹ — *verb* **1** to push steadily, especially with the finger: *press the bell*. **2** to hold firmly against something; to flatten: *press one's nose against the glass*. **3** (**press against** or **on** or **down on something**) to push it; to apply pressure to it: *press down on the accelerator*. **4** to compress or squash. **5** to squeeze (eg someone's hand) affectionately. **6** to preserve (plants) by flattening and drying, eg between the pages of a book. **7** to squeeze (fruit) to extract juice; to extract (juice) from fruit by squeezing. **8** to iron (clothes, etc). **9** to urge or compel; to ask insistently. **10** to insist on; to urge recognition or discussion of: *press one's claim/ press the point*. **11** (**press for something**) to demand it: *press for a pay rise*. **12** (**press something on someone**) to insist on giving it to them. **13** *Legal* to bring (charges) officially against someone. **14** (**press round something**) to crowd round it. **15** (**press on** or **ahead** or **forward**) to hurry on. **16** to produce (eg a gramophone record) from a mould by a compressing process. — *noun* **1** an act of pressing. **2** any apparatus for pressing, flattening, squeezing, etc. **3** a printing-press. **4** the process or art of printing. **5** a printing-house. **6** newspapers or journalists in general. **7** newspaper publicity or reviews received by a show, book, etc: *got a poor press*. **8** a crowd: *the press of onlookers*. **9** *old use Scot.* a cupboard. — **go to press** to be sent for printing. [from Old French *presser*]

⊟ *verb* **1, 3** push, depress. **2** push, flatten, squash. **4** compress, crush, squash, squeeze, stuff, cram, crowd. **5** squeeze, crush, clasp, hug, embrace. **7** squeeze, crush. **8** iron, smooth, flatten. **9** urge, compel, constrain, pressure, pressurize, petition, harass, demand, plead. **10** insist on, push, plead, force. **11** demand, campaign for. *noun* **1** push, squeeze. **2** squeezer, crusher, squasher. **6** the media, journalists, reporters, correspondents, newspapers, papers, Fleet Street, fourth estate. **8** crowd, throng, multitude, mob, horde, swarm, pack, crush, push.

press² *verb* **1** to force (men) into the army or navy. **2** to put to especially emergency use: *press something or someone into service*. [from older *prest*, to recruit, originally 'enlistment money']

press agent a person who arranges newspaper advertising or publicity for a performer or other celebrity, etc.

press conference an interview granted to reporters by a politician or other person in the news, for the purpose of announcing something, answering questions, etc.

press cutting a paragraph or article cut from a newspaper, etc.

pressed *adj.* under pressure; in a hurry. — **be hard pressed** to be in difficulties: *will be hard pressed to find a replacement.* **be pressed for something** *colloq.* to be short of it, especially time or money.

press gallery in the UK, the gallery reserved for journalists in parliament or the law courts.

pressgang — *noun* a gang employed to seize men and force them into the army or navy. — *verb* **1** to force into the army or navy. **2** *facetious* to force into service: *pressganged into helping with the party.*

pressing — *adj.* urgent: *pressing engagements.* — *noun* a number of gramophone records produced from a single mould.

     . . . .

   ◨ *adj.* urgent, high-priority, burning, crucial, vital, essential, imperative, serious, important.
   ◨ *adj.* unimportant, trivial.

. . . .

pressman or **presswoman** *noun* a journalist or reporter.

press officer a person employed by an organization to give information about it to journalists.

press release an official statement given to the press by an organization, etc.

press stud a type of button-like fastener, one part of which is pressed into the other.

press-up *noun* an exercise performed face down, raising and lowering the body on the arms while keeping the trunk and legs rigid.

pressure — *noun* **1** the force exerted on a surface divided by the area of the surface to which it is applied. The SI unit of pressure is the pascal (Pa), which is equal to a force of one newton per square metre of surface. Other units of pressure include bars and millibars (used in meteorology), millimetres of mercury (used in barometers), and atmospheres. **2** the act of pressing or process of being pressed. **3** force or coercion; forceful persuasion: *bring pressure to bear.* **4** the need to perform a great deal at speed: *work under pressure.* **5** tension or stress: *the pressures of family life.* — *verb* to try to persuade; to coerce, force, or pressurize. [from Latin *pressura*]

     . . . .

   ◨ *noun* **1** force, power, load, burden, weight, heaviness, compression, stress, strain. **2** pushing, squeezing, compression. **5** tension, stress, difficulties, problems, demands, constraints, obligations. *verb* push, force, pressurize, persuade, coerce.

. . . .

pressure cooker a thick-walled pan with an airtight lid, in which food is cooked at speed by steam under high pressure.

pressure gauge *Physics* a gauge which measures the pressure of fluids (liquids or gases) in enclosed vessels and containers, such as boilers and pipes.

pressure group a number of people who join together to influence public opinion and government policy on some issue.

pressurize or **pressurise** *verb* **1** to adjust the pressure within (an enclosed compartment such as an aircraft cabin) so that nearly normal atmospheric pressure is constantly maintained. **2** to put pressure on; to force or coerce: *was pressurized into resigning.*

     . . . .

   ◨ **2** force, coerce, pressure, compel, constrain, oblige, drive, bulldoze, press, *colloq.* lean on, browbeat, bully.

. . . .

pressurized water reactor a nuclear reactor in which the coolant is water under such pressure that it reaches a

high temperature without evaporation and can be used to heat boiler water through a heat exchanger.

prestidigitation *noun* sleight of hand.

prestidigitator /prestɪˈdɪdʒɪteɪtə(r)/ *noun* someone expert at sleight of hand; a conjurer. [from French *prestidigitateur*, conjurer, a 19c coinage from *preste*, adroit + Latin *digitus*, finger]

prestige /preˈstiːʒ/ *noun* **1** fame, distinction, or reputation due to rank or success. **2** standing and influence: *a job with prestige.* **3** (*attributive*) said of a job, etc considered to give prestige. [from Latin *praestigiae*, sleight of hand, magic]

     . . . .

   ◨ **1, 2** distinction, reputation, standing, stature, status, eminence, esteem, regard, importance, authority, influence, fame, renown, kudos, credit, honour.

. . . .

prestigious *adj.* having prestige; esteemed, influential, impressive.

     . . . .

   ◨ esteemed, influential, impressive, respected, reputable, important, great, eminent, prominent, illustrious, renowned, celebrated, exalted, imposing, up-market.
   ◨ humble, modest.

. . . .

presto *Mus.* — *adj.*, *adv.* very fast. — *noun* (PL. **prestos**) a passage to be played very fast. [from Italian *presto*]

pre-stressed *adj.*, *said of concrete* having stretched wires or rods embedded in it in order to increase its tensile strength.

presumably *adv.* I suppose.

presume *verb* **1** to suppose (something to be the case) though one has no proof; to take for granted: *presumed he was dead.* **2** to be so bold as (to do something) without the proper right or knowledge; to venture: *wouldn't presume to advise the experts.* **3** (**presume on** or **upon something**) to count on someone's goodwill, especially without justification; to take unfair advantage of someone's good nature, etc. [from Latin *praesumere*, to take in advance, suppose]

     . . . .

   ◨ **1** suppose, assume, take it, take for granted, think, believe, surmise, infer, presuppose, trust. **2** dare, make so bold, go so far, venture, undertake. **3** count on, rely on, depend on, bank on, take for granted.

. . . .

presumption *noun* **1** the act of presuming. **2** something presumed: *she remarried on the presumption that her first husband was dead.* **3** grounds or justification for presuming something. **4** *derog.* unsuitable boldness in one's behaviour towards others; insolence or arrogance. [from Latin *praesumptio*]

     . . . .

   ◨ **1** assumption, presupposition, supposition, conjecture. **2, 3** assumption, presupposition, supposition, belief, opinion, hypothesis, conjecture, surmise, guess, likelihood, probability. **4** presumptuousness, boldness, insolence, impudence, audacity, impertinence, *colloq.* cheek, *colloq.* nerve, forwardness, assurance.

. . . .

presumptive *adj.* presumed rather than absolutely certain. See also under HEIR.

presumptuous *adj. derog.* over-bold in one's behaviour towards others; insolent or arrogant. [from Latin *praesumptuosus*]

     . . . .

   ◨ bold, audacious, impertinent, impudent, insolent, over-familiar, forward, pushy, arrogant, over-confident, conceited.
   ◨ humble, modest.

. . . .

presumptuously *adv.* in a presumptuous way.

presuppose *verb* **1** to take for granted; to assume as true. **2** to require as a necessary condition; to imply the existence of: *forgiveness presupposes offence.*

presupposition *noun* **1** assuming or presupposing. **2** something taken for granted. **3** an assumption.

pretence *noun* **1** the act of pretending. **2** make-believe. **3** an act one puts on deliberately to mislead: *his anger was mere pretence.* **4** a claim, especially an unjustified one: *make no pretence to expert knowledge.* **5** show, affectation or ostentation; pretentiousness. **6** (*usually* **pretences**) a misleading declaration of intention: *won their support under false pretences.* **7** show or semblance: *abandoned all pretence of fair play.* [from Old French *pretensse*, from Latin *praetendere*, to pretend]

■ **1** feigning, faking, simulation, deception, trickery, sham. **3** sham, fake, simulation, deception, wile, ruse, cover, front, façade, veneer, cloak, veil, mask, guise, display, appearance. **5** show, affectation, ostentation, pretentiousness, posing. **6** pretext, bluff, falsehood, fabrication, invention, excuse, deceit, wile, ruse. **7** charade, acting, play-acting, posturing.
■ **1** honesty, openness.

pretend — *verb* **1** *trans., intrans.* to make believe; to act as if, or give the impression that, something is the case when it is not: *pretend it's winter/pretend to be asleep.* **2** *trans., intrans.* to imply or claim falsely: *pretended not to know.* **3** (**pretend to something**) to claim to have a skill, etc, especially a doubtful claim (eg to the throne). **4** to claim to feel; to profess falsely: *pretend friendship towards someone.* — *adj. colloq., especially used by or to children* imaginary: *a pretend cave.* [from Latin *praetendere*, to give as an excuse, pretend]

■ *verb* **1** imagine, make believe, suppose, affect, put on, assume, feign, counterfeit, fake, simulate, sham, act, play-act, mime, bluff, impersonate, pass oneself off, go through the motions. **2** claim, allege, profess, purport. **4** affect, put on, assume, feign, counterfeit, fake, simulate.

pretender *noun* someone who lays especially dubious claim to something, especially the throne.

■ claimant, aspirant, candidate.

pretension *noun* **1** foolish vanity, self-importance or affectation; pretentiousness. **2** a claim or aspiration: *a house with no pretensions to elegance.* [from Latin *praetensio*]

■ **1** pretentiousness, affectation, pretence, pomposity, self-importance, airs, conceit, vanity, snobbishness, show, showiness, ostentation. **2** claim, aspiration, ambition, profession, demand.
■ **1** modesty, humility, simplicity.

pretentious *adj.* **1** pompous, self-important, or foolishly grandiose. **2** phoney or affected. **3** showy; ostentatious. [formerly *pretensious*, from Latin *praetensio*, pretension]

■ **1** pompous, self-important, grandiose, conceited, immodest, snobbish, inflated, magniloquent, high-sounding, ambitious, overambitious. **2** affected, *colloq.* phoney, mannered. **3** showy, ostentatious, extravagant, over-the-top, exaggerated.
■ **1** modest, humble. **3** simple, straightforward.

preterite /'prɛtərɪt/ *Grammar* — *noun* **1** a verb tense that expresses past action, eg *hit, moved, ran.* **2** a verb in this tense. — *adj.* denoting this tense. [from Latin *praeteritum tempus*, past time]

preternatural *adj.* **1** exceeding the normal; uncanny; ex-

traordinary. **2** supernatural. [from Latin *praeternaturalis*, from *praeter naturam*, beyond nature]

preternaturally *adv.* in a preternatural way.

pretext *noun* a false reason given for doing something, to disguise the real one; an excuse. [from Latin *praetextum*, from *praetexere*, to fringe, adorn, give as an excuse]

■ excuse, ploy, ruse, cover, cloak, mask, guise, semblance, appearance, pretence, show.

prettification /ˌprɪtɪfɪ'keɪʃən/ *noun* prettifying or being prettified.

prettify /'prɪtɪfaɪ/ *verb* (**prettifies, prettified**) to attempt to make prettier by superficial ornamentation.

prettily *adv.* in a pretty way, pleasingly.

prettiness *noun* being pretty.

pretty — *adj.* (**prettier, prettiest**) **1** *usually said of a woman or girl* facially attractive, especially in a feminine way. **2** charming to look at; decorative. **3** *said of music, sound, etc* delicately melodious. **4** neat, elegant, or skilful: *a pretty solution.* **5** *ironic* grand; fine: *a pretty mess.* — *adv.* fairly; satisfactorily; rather; decidedly. — **pretty much** *colloq.* more or less. **pretty nearly** almost. **pretty well** *colloq.* almost; more or less. **sitting pretty** *colloq.* happily unaffected by problems besetting others; in an advantageous position. [from Anglo-Saxon *prættig*, astute]

■ *adj.* **1** attractive, good-looking, beautiful, fair, lovely, bonny, cute, winsome, appealing. **2** charming, decorative, attractive, dainty, graceful, elegant, fine, delicate, nice, lovely, bonny, cute, winsome, appealing. **3** tuneful, catchy. *adv.* fairly, satisfactorily, rather, somewhat, decidedly, quite, reasonably, moderately, tolerably.
■ *adj.* **1, 2** plain, unattractive, ugly.

pretty pass *colloq.* a deplorable state of affairs.

pretty-pretty *adj. derog. colloq.* pretty in an over-sweet way.

pretzel *noun* a salted and glazed biscuit in the shape of a knot. [from German *Pretzel*]

prevail *verb intrans.* **1** (**prevail over** or **against someone** or **something**) to be victorious; to win through. **2** to be common, usual, or generally accepted: *the prevailing opinion/custom.* etc. **3** to be predominant: *the prevailing mood.* **4** (**prevail on** or **upon someone**) to persuade them: *prevailed on us to stay.* [from Latin *praevalere*, to prove superior]

■ **1** win (through), triumph over, overcome, overrule, rule (over), beat. **2** common, customary, conventional, normal, accepted, general. **3** predominate, preponderate, abound. **4** persuade, talk into, prompt, induce, incline, sway, influence, convince, win over.
■ **1** lose.

prevailing wind the wind most commonly blowing in a region: *the prevailing south-west wind.*

prevalence *noun* being prevalent; common practice or acceptance.

prevalent *adj.* common; widespread. [from Latin *praevalere*, to prevail]

■ common, widespread, general, customary, usual, universal, ubiquitous, everyday, popular, current, prevailing, extensive, rampant, rife, frequent.
■ uncommon, rare.

prevalently *adv.* in a prevalent way.

prevaricate *verb intrans.* to avoid stating the truth or coming directly to the point; to behave or speak evasively. [from Latin *praevaricari*, to walk with splayed legs, behave dishonestly]

⊟ hedge, equivocate, quibble, cavil, dodge, evade, shift, shuffle, lie, deceive.

prevarication *noun* prevaricating.

prevaricator *noun* a person who prevaricates.

prevent *verb* 1 to stop (someone from doing something, or something from happening); to hinder. 2 to stop the occurrence of; to make impossible; to avert. [from Latin *praevenire*, to anticipate, prevent]

⊟ STOP. 1 hinder, stop, hamper, frustrate, thwart, impede, check, restrain, inhibit, obstruct, block, bar. 2 avert, avoid, head off, ward off, stave off, intercept, forestall, anticipate.
◨ CAUSE, HELP, FOSTER, ENCOURAGE, ALLOW.

preventable or **preventible** *adj.* capable of being prevented.

prevention *noun* preventing.

⊟ avoidance, frustration, check, hindrance, impediment, obstruction, obstacle, bar, elimination, precaution, safeguard, deterrence.
◨ cause, help.

preventive or **preventative** — *adj.* tending, or intended, to prevent something, eg illness. — *noun* 1 a preventive drug. 2 a precautionary measure taken against something.

⊟ *adj.* anticipatory, pre-emptive, inhibitory, obstructive, precautionary, protective, counteractive, deterrent.
◨ causative.

preventive detention a term of imprisonment for a habitual or dangerous criminal.

preventive medicine the branch of medicine concerned with the prevention of disease, as opposed to its treatment and cure.

preview — *noun* an advance showing of a film, play, exhibition, etc, before presentation to the general public. — *verb* to show in advance to a select audience.

previous *adj.* 1 earlier: *a previous occasion.* 2 former: *the previous chairman.* 3 prior: *a previous engagement.* 4 *facetious* premature; over-prompt or over-hasty. 5 (**previous to something**) before an event, etc. [from Latin *praevius*, leading the way]

⊟ 1 preceding, foregoing, earlier, prior, past. 2 former, ex-, one-time, sometime, erstwhile.
◨ 1 following, subsequent, later.

previously *adv.* before, earlier.

⊟ earlier, before, formerly, once, beforehand.
◨ later.

pre-war *adj.* belonging to the period before a war, especially World War II.

prey — *noun* 1 a creature, or the creatures, that a predatory beast hunts and kills as food: *in search of prey.* 2 a victim or victims: *easy prey for muggers.* 3 (**a prey to something**) liable to suffer from an illness, a bad feeling, etc. — *verb intrans.* 1 (**prey on something**) *said of an animal* to attack it as prey. 2 (**prey on someone**) **a** to bully, exploit, or terrorize them as victims. **b** to afflict them: *preyed on by anxieties.* [from Old French *preie*, from Latin *praeda*, booty]

⊟ *noun* 1 quarry, kill, game. *verb* 1 hunt, kill, devour, feed on, live off. 2 *bully* exploit, terrorize, persecute, torment, tyrannize, *afflict* haunt, trouble, distress,

worry, burden, weigh down, oppress.

prial /praɪəl/ *noun Cards* a set of three cards of the same denomination. [a contraction of PAIR-ROYAL]

priapism /ˈpraɪəpɪzm/ *noun Medicine* persistent abnormal erection of the penis, which may be a symptom of spinal injury, or of various diseases and disorders. [from Greek *Priapos*, a phallic deity]

price — *noun* 1 the amount, usually in money, for which a thing is sold or offered. 2 what one must give up or suffer in gaining something: *loss of freedom is the price of celebrity.* 3 the sum by which one may be bribed. 4 *Betting* odds. — *verb* 1 to fix a price for, or mark a price on. 2 to find out the price of. — **a price on someone's head** a reward offered for capturing or killing them. **at a price** at great expense. **beyond** or **without price** priceless; invaluable. [from Old French *pris*, from Latin *pretium*]

⊟ *noun* 1 cost, fee, charge, levy, toll, value, worth, figure, amount, sum, expense, outlay, expenditure, payment, assessment, valuation, estimate, quotation, rate, bill. 2 cost, payment, penalty, forfeit, sacrifice, consequences, reward. *verb* 1 value, rate, cost. 2 evaluate, assess, estimate, cost, value.

price control a maximum or, rarely, minimum limit set on prices by the government.

price-fixing *noun* the fixing of a price by agreement between suppliers.

priceless *adj.* 1 too valuable to have a price; inestimably precious. 2 *colloq.* hilariously funny.

⊟ 1 invaluable, precious, valuable, prized, treasured, irreplaceable, inestimable, incalculable, expensive, costly, dear. 2 hilarious, funny, riotous, side-splitting, *colloq.* killing, amusing, comic, *colloq.* rich .

price tag 1 a label showing a price. 2 the cost of something, eg a proposed building, etc.

pricey or **pricy** *adj.* (**pricier, priciest**) *colloq.* expensive.

prick — *verb* 1 to pierce slightly with a fine point. 2 to make (a hole) by this means. 3 *trans., intrans.* to hurt by this means. 4 *intrans., trans.* to smart or cause to smart: *feel one's eyes pricking.* 5 *trans., intrans.* (also **prick up**) *said of a dog or its ears* to stick them upright in response to sound. 6 to mark out (a pattern) in punctured holes. — *noun* 1 an act of pricking or feeling of being pricked; the pain of this. 2 a puncture made by pricking. 3 *coarse slang* a penis. 4 *coarse slang* an abusive term for a man, especially a self-important fool. — **kick against the pricks** to react against discipline or authority. **prick up one's ears** *colloq.* to start listening attentively. [from Anglo-Saxon *prica*, point]

⊟ *verb* 1 pierce, puncture, perforate, punch, jab, stab. 2 pierce, punch, jab, stab. 4 smart, sting, prickle, tingle, itch. *noun* 1 *act of pricking* puncture, perforation, stab, *pain* sting, pang, twinge. 2 puncture, pinprick, pinhole, hole.

prickle — *noun* 1 a sharp point or thorn-like growth on a plant or creature, eg a hedgehog. 2 a pricking sensation: *a prickle of fear.* — *verb intrans., trans.* to cause, affect with, or be affected with, a pricking sensation. [from Anglo-Saxon *pricel*]

⊟ *noun* 1 thorn, spine, barb, spur, point, spike, needle. 2 tingle. *verb* tingle, itch, smart, sting, prick.

prickliness *noun* being prickly.

prickly *adj.* (**pricklier, prickliest**) 1 having prickles. 2 causing prickling. 3 *colloq.*, *said of a person* irritable; oversensitive. 4 *said of a topic* liable to cause controversy.

▣ **1** thorny, brambly, spiny, barbed, spiky, bristly. **2** rough, scratchy. **3** irritable, over-sensitive, edgy, touchy, grumpy, short-tempered. **4** controversial, contentious, delicate.
▣ **1, 2** smooth. **3** relaxed, easy-going.

prickly heat an itchy skin condition, with inflammation around the sweat glands, occurring in intensely hot weather.

prickly pear a prickly reddish pear-shaped fruit; the cactus on which it grows.

pride — *noun* **1** a feeling of pleasure and satisfaction at one's own or another's accomplishments, one's possessions, etc. **2** whatever inspires this feeling: *it's my pride and joy.* **3** self-respect; personal dignity. **4** an unjustified assumption of superiority; arrogance. **5** *poetic* the finest state; prime or bloom. **6** the finest item: *the pride of the collection.* **7** a number of lions keeping together as a group. — *verb* (**pride oneself on something**) to congratulate oneself on account of it: *prided himself on his youthful figure.* — **swallow one's pride** to be forced to humble oneself. **take a pride in something** or **someone 1** to be proud of them. **2** to be conscientious about maintaining high standards in one's work, etc. [from Anglo-Saxon *pryde*]

▣ **1** pleasure, satisfaction, gratification, delight. **3** dignity, self-respect, self-esteem, honour. **4** arrogance, self-importance, conceit, vanity, egotism, big-headedness, boastfulness, smugness, presumption, haughtiness, superciliousness, snobbery, pretentiousness.
▣ **1** shame. **4** humility, modesty.

pride of place special prominence; the position of chief importance.

priest *noun* **1** in the Roman Catholic and Orthodox churches, an ordained minister; in the Anglican church, a minister ranking between deacon and bishop. **2** in non-Christian religions, an official who performs sacrifices and other religious rites. [from Anglo-Saxon *preost*, from Latin *presbyter*, elder]

▣ **1** minister, vicar, padre, father, man of God, man of the cloth, clergyman, clergywoman, churchman, churchwoman.

priestess *noun* in non-Christian religions, a female priest.

priesthood *noun* **1** the office of a priest. **2** the role or character of a priest. **3** priests collectively: *members of the priesthood.*

priestly *adj.* relating to or characteristic of a priest or priests.

prig *noun* a person who is self-righteously moralistic. [originally a coxcomb]

priggish *adj.* self-righteously moralistic.

▣ self-righteous, *colloq.* goody-goody, sanctimonious, holier-than-thou, puritanical, smug, prim, prudish, narrow-minded.
▣ broad-minded.

priggishly *adv.* in a priggish or self-righteous way.

priggishness *noun* being priggish.

prim *adj.* **1** stiffly formal, over-modest, or over-proper. **2** prudishly disapproving. [from 17c slang]

▣ **1** formal, demure, proper, priggish, prissy, fussy, particular, precise, fastidious. **2** prudish, strait-laced.
▣ **1** informal, relaxed, easy-going.

prima ballerina /ˈpriːmə/ the leading female dancer in a ballet company. [from Italian *prima ballerina*, first ballerina]

primacy *noun* (PL. **primacies**) **1** the condition of being first in rank, importance, or order. **2** the rank, office, or area of jurisdiction of a primate of the Church. [from Latin *primatia*, from *primus*, first]

prima donna /ˈpriːmə/ **1** a leading female opera singer. **2** someone difficult to please, especially if given to melodramatic tantrums when displeased. [from Italian *prima donna*, first lady]

primaeval See PRIMEVAL.

prima facie /ˈpraɪmə ˈfeɪʃɪ/ — *adv.* at first sight; on the evidence available; on the face of it. — *adj.* apparent; based on first impressions: *prima facie evidence.* [from Latin *prima facie*]

primal *adj.* **1** relating to the beginnings of life; original: *man's primal innocence.* **2** basic; fundamental. [from Latin *primus*, first]

primarily *adv.* **1** chiefly; mainly. **2** in the first place; initially.

▣ **1** chiefly, principally, mainly, mostly, basically, fundamentally, especially, particularly, essentially.

primary — *adj.* **1** first or most important; principal: *our primary concern.* **2** earliest in order or development: *the primary stage.* **3** (**Primary**) *Geol.* Palaeozoic. **4** basic; fundamental: *primary causes.* **5** of the elementary stage or level. **6** *said of education* for children aged between 5 and 11: *primary schools.* See also SECONDARY, TERTIARY. **7** *said of a bird's wing feather* outermost and longest. **8** firsthand; direct: *primary sources of information.* **9** *said of a product or industry* being or concerned with produce in its raw natural state. **10** *Electr.* **a** *said of a battery or cell* producing electricity by an irreversible chemical reaction. **b** *said of a circuit or current* inducing a current in a neighbouring circuit. — *noun* (PL. **primaries**) **1** something that is first in order, importance, etc. **2** a primary school. **3** (*also* **primary election**) in the US, a preliminary election at state level in which voters choose candidates for political office. **4** a bird's primary feather. [from Latin *primarius*, principal]

▣ *adj.* **1** first, chief, principal, main, dominant, leading, foremost, supreme, cardinal, capital, paramount, greatest, highest, ultimate. **2** earliest, first, initial, original, introductory, beginning. **4** basic, fundamental, essential. **5** elementary, rudimentary, simple.
▣ *adj.* **1** secondary, subsidiary, minor.

primary cell or **primary battery** *Physics* a cell or battery that produces an electric current by chemical reactions that are not readily reversible, so that the cell cannot be recharged by applying an electric current.

primary colour 1 when mixing lights, any of the three colours red, green, and blue-violet, which together give white light. They can also be combined in various proportions to give all the other colours of the spectrum. **2** when mixing pigments, any of the three colours red, yellow, and blue, which together give black. They can also be combined in various proportions to give all the other colours of the spectrum.

primary sexual characteristics *Zool.* sexual features that are present from birth, ie the testes in males and the ovaries in females, as opposed to the secondary sexual characteristics that develop after the onset of puberty.

primary stress *Linguistics* the main stress on a word in which there is more than one stress, as in *fundamentalism*, in which the primary stress is on the syllable *-ment-*.

primate /ˈpraɪmeɪt/ *noun* **1** an archbishop. **2** *Zool.* any mammalian vertebrate belonging to the order Primates, which includes humans, apes, gibbons, monkeys, lemurs, bushbabies, lorises, tarsiers, and tree shrews. [from Latin *primas*, from *primus*, first]

prime — *adj.* **1** chief; fundamental. **2** of best quality: *prime beef.* **3** excellent: *in prime condition.* **4** supremely typical: *a prime example.* **5** having the greatest potential for attracting interest or custom: *prime viewing time/prime sites on the high street.* — *noun* the best, most productive or active stage in the life of a person or thing: *vehicles past their* *prime/cut off in her prime/in the prime of life.* — *verb* **1** to prepare (something), eg (wood for painting) by applying a sealing coat of size, etc, (a gun or explosive device for firing or detonating) by inserting the igniting material, or (a pump for use) by filling it with water, etc. **2** to supply (someone) with the necessary facts in advance; to brief. **3** *facetious* to supply (someone) with drink or food by way of relaxing, emboldening, or bribing them. [from Latin *primus*, first]

▪ *adj.* **1** chief, fundamental, principal, main, predominant, primary, senior, leading, ruling. **2, 3** best, choice, select, quality, first-class, first-rate, excellent, top, supreme, pre-eminent, superior. *noun* height, peak, zenith, heyday, maturity, perfection, flower, bloom.

▪ *adj.* **1** secondary. **2, 3** second-rate.

prime lending rate the lowest rate of interest charged by a bank at any time to creditworthy customers.

prime meridian the 0° line of longitude, passing through Greenwich.

prime minister the chief minister of a government.

prime mover the force that is most effective in setting something in motion.

prime number a whole number that can only be divided by itself and 1, eg 3, 5, 7, 11.

primer[1] *noun* a first or introductory book of instruction. [from Latin *primarium*, from *primarius*, primary]

primer[2] *noun* **1** a substance for sealing wood, before painting. **2** an igniting or detonating device for firing the main charge in a gun or mine.

prime rate the US bank base lending rate, at which the bank will lend to its best ('prime') customers. The rate applies to only 50 or so large US corporations, all others paying higher rates. An increase in the prime rate triggers increases in all other interest rates.

primeval or **primaeval** /praɪˈmiːvl/ *adj.* **1** belonging to earth's beginnings. **2** primitive. **3** instinctive. [from Latin *primaevus*, young, from *primus*, first + *aevum*, age]

▪ **1** earliest, first, original, primordial, early, old, ancient, prehistoric.

▪ **1** modern.

primigravida /praɪmɪˈɡrævɪdə/ *noun Medicine* a woman who is pregnant for the first time. [from *primus*, first + *gravida*, pregnant]

primitive — *adj.* **1** belonging to earliest times, or the earliest stages of development: *primitive stone tools.* **2** simple, rough, crude, or rudimentary: *living in primitive conditions.* — *noun Art* a work by an artist in naïve style; also, the artist. [from Latin *primitivus*]

▪ *adj.* **1** early, primary, first, original, earliest, elementary, rudimentary. **2** simple, crude, rough, rudimentary, unsophisticated, uncivilized, barbarian, savage.

▪ *adj.* **2** advanced, sophisticated, civilized.

primitively *adv.* in a primitive way.
primitiveness *noun* being primitive.
primitivism *noun Art* the deliberate rejection of Western techniques and skills in pursuit of stronger effects found, for example, in African tribal or Oceanic art. In this sense, it has been applied to Gauguin, and to Picasso's work from c.1906. The term is also synonymous with naïve art, ie works by contemporary untrained artists whose appeal is in their freshness of vision.

primogeniture *noun* **1** the circumstance of being the first-born child. **2** the right or principle of succession or inheritance of an eldest son. [from Latin *primogenitura*, first birth]

primordial *adj.* existing from the beginning, especially of the world; formed earliest: *primordial matter.* [from Latin *primordialis*, from *primus*, first + *ordiri*, to begin]

primordially *adv.* in a primordial way.

primp *verb trans., intrans.* to groom, preen, or titivate (oneself). [perhaps related to PRIM]

primrose *noun* **1** a small, low-growing wild plant with pale yellow flowers that appear in spring. **2** the pale yellow colour of these flowers. [from Latin *prima rosa*, first rose]

primrose path an untroubled pleasurable way of life.

primula *noun* (PL. **primulae, primulas**) any of a genus of plants that includes the primrose and cowslip, especially a low-growing cultivated variety with white, pink, or purple five-petalled flowers. [from Latin *primula veris*, first little one of the spring]

Primus *noun* (PL. **Primuses**) (*also* **Primus stove**) *trademark* a portable camping stove fuelled by vaporized oil.

prince *noun* **1** the son of a sovereign. **2** a non-reigning male member of a royal or imperial family. **3** a sovereign of a small territory. **4** a ruler or sovereign generally. **5** a nobleman in certain countries. **6** someone or something celebrated or outstanding within a type or class: *the prince of highwaymen*. See also PRINCIPALITY. [from Latin *princeps*, leader, ruler]

Prince Charming the prince in the tale of Cinderella, as representing the ideal handsome husband.

prince consort the title given to a reigning queen's husband, who is himself a prince.

princedom *noun* a principality; the estate, jurisdiction, sovereignty, or rank of a prince.

princely *adj.* **1** of, or suitable to, a prince. **2** *often ironic* lavish; generous: *the princely sum of five pence.*

▪ **1** royal, regal, majestic, sovereign, imperial, stately, grand, noble. **2** lavish, generous, magnificent, handsome, liberal, sumptuous.

prince regent a prince ruling on behalf of a sovereign who is too ill, young, etc to rule.

princess *noun* **1** the wife or daughter of a prince. **2** the daughter of a sovereign, or a non-reigning female member of a royal or imperial family.

principal — *adj.* **1** first in rank or importance. **2** chief; main. — *noun* **1** the head of an educational institution. **2** a leading actor, singer or dancer in a theatrical production. **3** *Legal* the person on behalf of whom an agent is acting. **4** *Legal* a person ultimately responsible for fulfilling an obligation. **5** a person who commits or participates in a crime. **6** *Commerce* the sum of money on which interest is paid. [from Latin *principalis*, chief, principal]

▪ *adj.* MAIN, CHIEF, KEY, ESSENTIAL, CARDINAL, PRIMARY, FIRST, FOREMOST, LEADING, DOMINANT, PRIME, PARAMOUNT, PRE-EMINENT, SUPREME, HIGHEST. *noun* **1** head, head teacher, headmaster, headmistress, chief, boss, director, manager, superintendent. **2** prima donna.

▪ *adj.* MINOR, SUBSIDIARY, LESSER, LEAST.

principal boy the part of the young male hero in a pantomime, usually played by a woman.

principal clause a main clause.

principality *noun* (PL. **principalities**) **1** a territory ruled by a prince, or one that he derives his title from. **2** (**the Principality**) Wales. [from Latin *principalitas*]

principally *adv.* mainly, mostly.

▪ mainly, mostly, chiefly, primarily, predominantly, above all, particularly, especially.

principal parts *Grammar* the main forms of a verb from which all other forms can be deduced, eg in English the infinitive, the past tense, and the past participle.

principle *noun* **1** a general truth or assumption from which to argue. **2** a scientific law, especially as explaining a natural phenomenon or the way a machine works. **3** a general rule of morality that guides one's conduct; the having of or holding to such rules: *a woman of principle*. **4** a norm of procedure: *the principle of primogeniture*. **5** a fundamental element or source: *the vital principle*. **6** *Chem.* a constituent of a substance that gives it its distinctive characteristics. — **in principle** *said of a decision or action* as far as a principle or rule is concerned, although not necessarily in a particular case: *they have agreed to make a donation in principle*. **on principle** on the grounds of a particular principle of morality or wisdom. [from Latin *principium*, beginning, source]

. . . .

▣ **1** rule, truth, tenet, formula, law, canon, axiom, dictum, precept, maxim, doctrine, creed, dogma, code, standard, criterion, proposition, fundamental, essential. **3** honour, integrity, rectitude, uprightness, virtue, decency, morality, morals, ethics, standards, scruples, conscience.

. . . .

principled *adj.* having, or proceeding from, especially high moral principles.

prink *verb trans., intrans.* to dress (oneself) up; to smarten (oneself) up. [perhaps related to older *prank*, to dress up]

print — *verb* **1** to reproduce (text or pictures) on paper with ink, using a printing-press or other mechanical means. **2** to publish (a book, article, etc). **3** *trans., intrans.* to write in separate, as opposed to joined-up, letters, in the style of mechanically printed text. **4** to make (a positive photograph) from a negative. **5** to mark designs on (fabric). **6** to fix (a scene) indelibly (on the memory, etc). — *noun* **1** (*often in compounds*) a mark made on a surface by the pressure of something in contact with it: *footprints/ fingerprints*. **2** a fingerprint. **3** hand-done lettering with each letter written separately. **4** mechanically printed text, especially produced on a printing-press: *small print*. **5** a printed publication. **6** a design printed from an engraved wood block or metal plate. **7** a positive photograph made from a negative. **8** a fabric with a printed or stamped design. — **be in** or **out of print** *said of a publication* to be currently available, or no longer available, from a publisher. **print something out** to produce a printed version of it, eg computer data. [from Middle English *prenten*, from Old French *priente*, a print]

. . . .

▣ *verb* **1** reproduce, run off, copy, mark, stamp, imprint, impress, engrave. **2** publish, issue. *noun* **1** mark, impression, imprint, fingerprint, footprint. **2** *slang* dab. **4** letters, characters, lettering, type, typescript, typeface, fount. **6** picture, engraving, lithograph, reproduction.

. . . .

printable *adj.* **1** capable of being printed. **2** fit to be published.

printed circuit 1 *Electron.* an electronic circuit that contains no loose wiring, but is formed by printing or etching thin strips of a conductor such as copper on to the surface of a thin board of insulating material, allowing automatic assembly of large numbers of circuits without wiring errors. Circuit components are then attached to the board by inserting their connecting wires into pre-drilled holes. **2** the board of such a circuit.

printed circuit board (ABBREV. **PCB**) *Electron.* a piece of insulating material mounted with interconnected chips, which is added to a computer to enhance its memory or provide new features.

printer *noun* **1** a person or business engaged in printing books, newspapers, etc. **2** a machine that prints, eg photographs. **3** *Comput.* a computer output device that produces printed copies of text or graphics. There are many different types, and the optimum choice depends on the acceptable cost, print quality, and printing speed.

printing *noun* **1** the art or business of producing books, etc in print. **2** the run of books, etc printed all at one time; an impression. **3** the form of handwriting in which the letters are separately written.

printing-press *noun* a machine for printing books, newspapers, etc, operating in any of various ways.

printout *noun Comput.* output in printed form.

print run the number of copies of a book, newspaper, etc printed at a time.

prior[1] *adj.* **1** *said of an engagement* already arranged for the time in question; previous. **2** more urgent or pressing: *a prior claim*. — **prior to something** before an event: *prior to departure*. [from Latin *prior*, previous]

. . . .

▣ **1** earlier, preceding, foregoing, previous, former. **prior to** before, preceding, earlier than.

▣ **prior to** after, following.

. . . .

prior[2] *noun* **1** the head of a community of certain orders of monks and friars. **2** in an abbey, the deputy of the abbot. [from Latin *prior*, head]

prioress *noun* a female prior.

prioritize or **prioritise** *verb* to schedule for immediate, or earliest, attention.

priority *noun* (PL. **priorities**) **1** the right to be or go first; precedence or preference. **2** something that must be attended to before anything else. **3** the fact or condition of being earlier. [from Latin *prioritas*, from *prior*, previous]

. . . .

▣ **1** right of way, precedence, seniority, rank, superiority, pre-eminence, supremacy, the lead, first place.

▣ **1** inferiority.

. . . .

priory *noun* (PL. **priories**) a religious house under the supervision of a prior or prioress.

prise *verb* to lever (something) open, off, out, etc: *prised open the lid/prised the shell off the rock*. [from Old French *prise*, something captured]

prism *noun* **1** *Geom.* a solid figure in which the two ends are matching parallel polygons (eg triangles, squares) and all other surfaces are rectangles or parallelograms. A cross-section at any point along the length of a prism remains the same. **2** *Optics* a transparent block, usually of glass and with triangular ends and rectangular sides, that disperses (separates) a beam of white light into the colours of the visible spectrum. [from Greek *prisma*, something sawn]

prismatic *adj.* **1** of, like, or using a prism: *a prismatic compass*. **2** *said of colour or light* produced or separated by, or as if by, a prism; bright and clear.

prison *noun* **1** a public building for the confinement of convicted criminals and accused persons waiting to be tried. **2** any place of confinement or situation of intolerable restriction. **3** custody; imprisonment: *no alternative to prison*. [from Old French *prisun*, from Latin *prehensio*, right of arrest]

. . . .

▣ **1** jail, *colloq.* nick, *slang* clink, *slang* cooler, penitentiary, cell, lockup. **2** cage, dungeon. **3** imprisonment, confinement, detention, custody.

. . . .

prison camp an enclosed guarded camp where prisoners of war or political prisoners are kept.

prisoner *noun* **1** a person who is under arrest or confined in prison. **2** a captive, especially in war. — **take someone prisoner** to capture and hold them as a prisoner.

. . . .

▣ **1** convict, *colloq.* jailbird, inmate, internee, detainee. **2** captive, hostage.

. . . .

prisoner of conscience a person imprisoned for his or her political beliefs.

prisoner of war (PL. **prisoners of war**) (ABBREV. **POW**) someone taken prisoner during a war, especially a member of the armed forces.

prissily *adv.* in a prissy way.

prissiness *noun* being prissy.

prissy *adj.* (**prissier, prissiest**) insipidly prim and prudish. [probably from PRIM + SISSY]

pristine /ˈprɪstiːn/ adj. **1** former: *restore to its pristine glory.* **2** original; unchanged or unspoilt: *still in its pristine state.* **3** fresh, clean, unused, or untouched. [from Latin *pristinus*, former, early]

privacy noun **1** freedom from intrusion by the public, especially as a right: *respect her privacy.* **2** seclusion: *in the privacy of one's own home.*

· · · · · · · · · · · · · · · · · ·

■ **1** secrecy, confidentiality, independence. **2** seclusion, isolation, solitude, concealment, retirement, retreat.

· ·

private — adj. **1** not open to, or available for the use of, the general public: *a private bathroom.* **2** not holding public office: *private individuals.* **3** kept secret from others; confidential: *private discussions.* **4** relating to one's personal, as distinct from one's professional, life: *a private engagement.* **5** said of thoughts or opinions personal and usually kept to oneself. **6** quiet and reserved by nature. **7** said of a place secluded. **8** not coming under the state system of education, health care, social welfare, etc.; paid for, or paying, individually by fee, etc. **9** said of an industry, etc owned and run by private individuals, not by the state. **10** said of a soldier not an officer or NCO. **11** said of a member of parliament not holding government office. — noun **1** a private soldier. **2** (**privates**) colloq. the private parts. — **in private** not in public; in secret; confidentially. [from Latin *privare*, to withdraw or separate from public life]

· ·

■ adj. **1** exclusive, particular, own, special. **3** secret, confidential, classified, colloq. hush-hush, off the record, unofficial. **4, 5** personal, confidential, intimate, individual. **6** quiet, reserved, withdrawn, independent, solitary, separate. **7** secluded, isolated, hidden, concealed. **in private** privately, in confidence, confidentially, secretly, in secret, behind closed doors, in camera, publicly, openly.

🔁 adj. **1, 3** public, open. **4** public, professional, business.

· ·

private detective or **private investigator** someone who is not a member of the police force, engaged by a private individual to do detective work.

private enterprise the management and financing of industry, etc by private individuals or companies, not the state.

privateer noun Hist. **1** a privately owned ship engaged by a government to seize and plunder an enemy's ships in wartime. **2** the commander, or a crew member, of such a ship.

Private Finance Initiative (ABBREV. **PFI**) a British government scheme giving incentives for private investment in public projects.

privately adv. in a private way.

private means or **private income** income from investments, etc, not from one's employment.

private parts euphemistic the external genitals and excretory organs.

private sector that part of a country's economy consisting of privately owned and operated businesses, etc.

privation /praɪˈveɪʃən/ noun the condition of not having, or being deprived of, life's comforts or necessities; a lack of something particular. [from Latin *privatio*, deprivation]

privatization noun the sale of state-owned industries into private ownership.

privatize or **privatise** verb to transfer (a nationally owned business) to private ownership.

privet /ˈprɪvɪt/ noun a type of bush of which hedges are commonly composed.

privilege noun **1** a right granted to an individual or a select few, bestowing an advantage not enjoyed by others. **2** advantages and power enjoyed by people of wealth and high social class. **3** an opportunity to do something that brings one delight; a pleasure or honour: *have the privilege of meeting you.* [from Latin *privilegium*, prerogative]

· · · · · · · · · · · · · · · · · · · ·

■ **1** right, advantage, benefit, concession, due, prerogative, entitlement, freedom, liberty, franchise, licence, sanction, authority, immunity, exemption. **2** birthright, title.

🔁 **1** disadvantage.

· ·

privileged adj. **1** enjoying the advantages of wealth and class. **2** favoured with the opportunity to do something.

· · · · · · · · · · · · · · · · · · · ·

■ **1** elite, ruling, powerful, honoured, advantaged, favoured. **2** advantaged, favoured, special, sanctioned, authorized, immune, exempt.

🔁 **1** disadvantaged, under-privileged.

· ·

privily adv. old use secretly.

privy — adj. **1** (**privy to something**) allowed to share in secret discussions, etc or be in the know about secret plans, happenings, etc. **2** old use secret; hidden. — noun (PL. **privies**) old use a lavatory. [from Old French *privé*, private, a private place or close friend]

Privy Council a private advisory council appointed by the sovereign, consisting chiefly of current and former members of the Cabinet, whose functions are mainly formal.

Privy Councillor a member of the Privy Council.

Privy Purse an allowance granted to the sovereign by Parliament, for his or her private expenses.

prize¹ — noun **1** something won in a competition, lottery, etc. **2** a reward given in recognition of excellence. **3** something striven for, or worth striving for. **4** something captured or taken by force, especially a ship in war; a trophy. **5** (attributive) **a** deserving, or having won, a prize: *a prize bull.* **b** valued highly by a person: *her prize possession.* **c** ironic perfect; great: *a prize fool.* — verb to value highly.

· · · · · · · · · · · · · · · · · · · ·

■ noun **1, 2** reward, trophy, medal, award, winnings, jackpot, purse, honour, accolade. **5** deserving a prize best, top, first-rate, excellent, outstanding, champion, winning, prize-winning, award-winning. verb treasure, value, appreciate, esteem, revere, cherish, hold dear.

🔁 verb despise.

· ·

prize² same as PRISE.

prize fight a boxing-match fought for a money prize. [partly Old French *pris*, price, partly Old French *prise*, something captured]

prize-fighter noun a professional boxer.

prize-fighting noun professional boxing.

PRO abbrev. Public Relations Officer.

pro¹ — adv. in favour. — prep. in favour of. — noun (PL. **pros**) a reason, argument, or choice in favour of something.

pro² noun (PL. **pros**) colloq. **1** a professional. **2** a prostitute.

pro- prefix forming words meaning: **1** in favour of; admiring or supporting: *pro-French.* **2** serving in place of; acting for: *procathedral/proconsul.* [from Latin *pro*]

proa /ˈprəʊə/ or **prahu** /ˈprɑːhuː, ˈprɑːuː/ or **prau** /ˈprɑːuː, praʊ/ noun a Malay sailing-boat or rowing-boat, especially a fast sailing-vessel with a large triangular, usually lateen, sail, an outrigger kept to leeward, and both ends (ie prow and stern) alike. [from Malay *prāu*]

proactive adj. **1** actively instigating changes in anticipation of future developments, as opposed to merely reacting to events as they occur. **2** ready to take the initiative; acting without being prompted by others. **3** Psychol., said of a prior mental experience tending to affect, interfere with, or inhibit a subsequent process, especially a learning process.

pro-am adj. Golf denoting a competition involving both professionals and amateurs.

probability noun (PL. **probabilities**) **1** the state of being probable; likelihood. **2** something that is probable. **3** Statistics a mathematical expression of the likelihood or chance of a particular event occurring, usually expressed as a fraction or numeral: *a probability of one in four.* — **in all probability** most probably.

⊟ **1** likelihood, odds, chances, chance, prospect, expectation, possibility. **2** possibility, likelihood.

⊡ IMPROBABILITY.

probability theory *Maths.* see PROBABILITY.

probable — *adj.* **1** likely to happen: *the probable outcome.* **2** likely to be the case; likely to have happened: *probable that she's left.* **3** *said of an explanation, etc* likely to be correct. — *noun* a person or thing likely to be selected. [from Latin *probabilis*, from *probare*, to prove]

⊟ *adj.* likely, odds-on. **1** expected. **2** credible, believable, plausible, feasible, possible. **3** apparent, seeming.

⊡ *adj.* IMPROBABLE, UNLIKELY.

probably *adv.* almost certainly; in all likelihood.

proband /ˈprəʊband/ *noun Genetics* a person who is regarded as the starting point for an investigation of the inheritance of a particular disease or disorder within a family. [from Latin *probandus*, gerundive of *probare*, to test]

probate /ˈprəʊbeɪt, ˈprəʊbət/ *noun* **1** *Legal* the process of establishing that a will is valid. **2** an official copy of a will, with the document certifying its validity. [from Latin *probare*, to prove]

probation *noun* **1** the system whereby (especially young or first) offenders are allowed their freedom under supervision, on condition of good behaviour: *was put on probation for six months.* **2** in certain types of employment, a period during which a new employee is observed on the job, to confirm whether or not he or she can do it satisfactorily. [from Latin *probatio*, trial, test]

⊟ **2** trial period, trial, test.

probationary *adj.* **1** relating to or serving as probation. **2** on probation. **3** that is a probationer or is made up of probationers.

probationer *noun* a person on probation.

probation officer a person with responsibility as supervisor for an offender on probation.

probe — *noun* **1** a long slender usually metal instrument used by doctors to examine a wound, locate a bullet, etc. **2** an investigation: *a police probe into drug-dealing.* **3** (*also* **space probe**) an unmanned spacecraft that records and transmits back to earth data about the environment it is passing through. **4** an act of probing; a poke or prod. — *verb trans., intrans.* (**probe** or **probe into something**) **1** to investigate it closely. **2** to examine it with a probe. **3** to poke or prod it. [from Latin *probare*, to test, prove]

⊟ *noun* **2** investigation, inquiry, inquest, exploration, examination, test, scrutiny, study, research. *verb* **1** investigate, go into, look into, search, sift, test, examine, scrutinize, explore. **2** examine, scrutinize, explore. **3** prod, poke, pierce, penetrate.

probiotic — *noun* a culture of bacteria that grows in the gut and helps to prevent disease-forming bacteria from attaching and multiplying. — *adj. said of a substance* containing probiotic bacteria.

probity /ˈprəʊbɪtɪ/ *noun* integrity; honesty. [from Latin *probitas*]

problem *noun* **1** a situation or matter that is difficult to understand or deal with. **2** a person or thing that is difficult to deal with. **3** a puzzle or mathematical question set for solving. **4** (*attributive*) **a** *said of a child, etc* difficult to deal with, especially in being disruptive or anti-social. **b** *said of a play, etc* dealing with a moral or social problem. — **no problem** *colloq.* **1** *said in response to a request, or to thanks* it's a pleasure, no trouble, etc. **2** easily: *found our*

way, no problem. [from Greek *problema*, question for solving]

⊟ **1** trouble, worry, predicament, quandary, dilemma, difficulty, complication, snag. **3** question, poser, puzzle, brainteaser, conundrum, riddle, enigma. **4** *difficult to deal with* difficult, unmanageable, uncontrollable, unruly, delinquent.

⊡ **4** well-behaved, manageable.

problematic or **problematical** *adj.* **1** causing problems. **2** uncertain.

problematically *adv.* in a problematic way.

proboscis /prəʊˈbɒsɪs/ *noun* **1** a flexible, elongated nose or snout, eg the trunk of an elephant. **2** the elongated mouth part of certain insects. **3** *facetious* the human nose. [from Greek *proboskis*, from *pro*, in front + *boskein*, to nourish]

proboscis monkey an Old World monkey native to Borneo, and having a pale coat with a darker 'cap' on its head, and a dark back. It has a long tail and a protruding nose, which in adult males becomes bulbous and pendulous. It is an excellent swimmer, inhabits forest near fresh water, and feeds on leaves.

procedural *adj.* relating to or concerning (correct) procedure.

procedurally *adv.* as regards (correct) procedure.

procedure *noun* **1** the method and order followed in doing something. **2** an established routine for conducting business at a meeting or in a law case. **3** a course of action; a step or measure taken. [from French *procédure*, from Latin *procedere*, to advance, proceed]

⊟ **1** routine, process, method, system, technique, scheme, operation, performance. **2** routine, custom, practice, policy, formula. **3** course, strategy, plan of action, policy, move, step, action.

proceed *verb intrans.* **1** to make one's way: *proceeding along the road.* **2** (**proceed with something**) to go on with it; to continue after stopping: *proceed with one's work/ please proceed.* **3** to set about a task, etc: *instructions on how to proceed.* **4** *colloq.* to begin: *proceeded to question her.* **5** (**proceed from something**) to arise from it: *fear proceeds from ignorance.* **6** (**proceed against someone**) *Legal* to take legal action against them. [from Latin *procedere*, to advance, proceed]

⊟ **1** make one's way, move along, advance, go ahead, move on, progress. **2** continue, carry on, press on (with). **3** behave, act, operate, conduct oneself. **4** start, begin, set about. **5** arise from, start from, stem from, spring from, come from, derive from, flow from, originate from, result from, issue from.

⊡ **1** stop, retreat. **2, 3, 4** stop.

proceeding *noun* **1** an action; a piece of behaviour. **2** (**proceedings**) a published record of the business done or papers read at a meeting of a society, etc. **3** (**proceedings**) legal action: *begin divorce proceedings.*

⊟ **1** action, course of action, deed, move, step, measure, event, happening. **2** minutes, records, transactions, matters, affairs, business, dealings, archives, annals. **3** action, litigation, lawsuit, prosecution.

proceeds *pl. noun* money made by an event, sale, etc.

⊟ income, returns, receipts, takings, earnings, revenue, gain, profit, yield, produce.

⊡ expenditure, outlay.

process — *noun* **1** a series of operations performed on something during manufacture, etc. **2** a series of stages passed through, resulting in development or transformation. **3** an operation or procedure: *a slow process.* **4** *Anat.* a projection or prominence, eg on a bone: *the mastoid process.* — *verb* **1** to put through the required process; to deal with appropriately: *process a film/process an application.* **2** to prepare (agricultural produce) for marketing, eg by canning, bottling, or treating chemically. **3** to analyse (data) by computer. — **in the process of ...** in the course of ... [from Latin *processus*, progression]

▣ *noun* **1** procedure, operation, practice, technique, stage, step, method, system. **2** course, progression, advance, progress, development, evolution, formation, growth, movement, action, proceeding. **3** procedure, operation, business. *verb* **1** deal with, handle. **2** treat, prepare, refine, transform, convert, change, alter.

procession *noun* **1** a file of people or vehicles proceeding ceremonially in orderly formation. **2** this kind of succession or sequence: *moving in procession.* [from Latin *processio*, an advance]

▣ **1** file, column, train, march, parade, cavalcade, motorcade, cortège. **2** succession, series, sequence, course, run.

processor *noun* **1** a machine or person that processes something: *a word processor.* **2** *Comput.* a central processing unit.
pro-choice *adj.* supporting the right of a woman to have an abortion.
proclaim *verb* **1** to announce publicly. **2** to declare (someone) to be (something): *proclaimed a traitor.* **3** to attest or prove all too clearly: *cigarette smoke proclaimed his presence.* [from Latin *proclamare*, to cry out]

▣ **1** announce, declare, pronounce, affirm, give out, publish, advertise, make known, profess. **2** declare, pronounce. **3** attest, prove, testify to, show, indicate.

proclamation *noun* **1** an official public announcement of something nationally important. **2** the act of proclaiming. [from Latin *proclamatio*]

▣ ANNOUNCEMENT, DECLARATION, PRONOUNCEMENT, AFFIRMATION, NOTIFICATION. **1** notice, manifesto, decree, edict. **2** publication, promulgation.

proclivity *noun* (PL. **proclivities**) a tendency or liking: *has a proclivity for gourmet meals.* [from Latin *proclivitas*, from *proclivis*, sloping]
procrastinate *verb intrans.* to keep putting off doing something that should be done straight away. [from Latin *procrastinare*, to delay or defer, from *cras*, tomorrow]

▣ delay, stall, temporize, play for time, dally, *colloq.* dilly-dally, drag one's feet.
▣ advance, proceed.

procrastination *noun* procrastinating, dilatoriness.
procrastinator *noun* a person who procrastinates.
procreate *verb trans., intrans.* to produce (offspring); to reproduce. [from Latin *procreare*, to beget]
procreation *noun* **1** procreating. **2** being generated or begotten.
proctor *noun* an official in some English universities whose functions include enforcement of discipline. [a contraction of PROCURATOR]
procurator *noun* **1** in the Roman empire, a financial agent or administrator in a province. **2** an agent with power of attorney in a law court. [from Latin *procurator*, agent, manager]
procurator fiscal in Scotland, a district official who combines the roles of coroner and public prosecutor.

procuratorship or **procuracy** *noun* (PL. **procuracies**) the office of a procurator.
procure *verb* **1** to manage to obtain or bring about. **2** *trans., intrans.* to provide (prostitutes) for clients. [from Latin *procurare*, from *pro*, on behalf of + *curare*, to attend to]

▣ **1** acquire, buy, purchase, get, obtain, find, come by, pick up, lay hands on, earn, gain, win, secure, appropriate, requisition. **2** provide, acquire, get, obtain.

procurement *noun* procuring.
procurer or **procuress** *noun* a man or woman who provides prostitutes for clients.
prod — *verb* (**prodded, prodding**) **1** (**prod** or **prod at something**) to poke or jab it. **2** to nudge, prompt, or spur into action. — *noun* **1** a poke, jab, or nudge. **2** a reminder. **3** a goad or similar pointed instrument.

▣ *verb* **1** poke, jab, dig, elbow, nudge. **2** nudge, prompt, spur, urge, *colloq.* egg on, stimulate, motivate, push, goad. *noun* **1** poke, jab, dig, elbow, nudge. **2** prompt, reminder, stimulus, motivation.

prodigal — *adj.* **1** heedlessly extravagant or wasteful. **2** (**prodigal of something**) lavish in bestowing it; generous: *be prodigal of praise.* — *noun* **1** a squanderer, wastrel, or spendthrift. **2** (*also* **prodigal son**) a repentant ne'er-do-well or a returned wanderer. [from Latin *prodigus*, wasteful]
prodigality *noun* **1** being prodigal or extravagant. **2** profusion. **3** great liberality.
prodigally *adv.* in a prodigal way; to a prodigal degree.
prodigious *adj.* **1** extraordinary or marvellous. **2** enormous; vast: *prodigious wealth.* [from Latin *prodigiosus*, from *prodigium*, wonder]
prodigiously *adv.* in a prodigious way.
prodigy *noun* (PL. **prodigies**) **1** something that causes astonishment; a wonder; an extraordinary phenomenon. **2** a person, especially a child, of extraordinary brilliance or talent. [from Latin *prodigium*, portent, wonder]

▣ **1** wonder, marvel, miracle, phenomenon, sensation, freak, curiosity, rarity. **2** genius, virtuoso, child genius, wonder child, *colloq.* whizz kid.

produce — *verb* (with stress on *-duce*) **1** to bring out or present to view. **2** to bear (children, young, leaves, etc). **3** to yield (crops, fruit, etc). **4** to secrete (a substance), give off (a smell), etc. **5** to make or manufacture. **6** to give rise to or prompt (a reaction) from people: *produced a subdued response.* **7** to direct (a play), arrange (a radio or television programme) for presentation, or finance and schedule the making of (a film). **8** *Geom.* to extend (a line). — *noun* (with stress on *prod-*) foodstuffs derived from crops or animal livestock, eg fruit, vegetables, eggs, and dairy products: *farm produce.* [from Latin *producere*, to bring forth]

▣ *verb* **1** bring out, bring forth, show, exhibit, demonstrate, put forward, present, offer, advance. **2** bear, bring forth, put forth, have. **3** yield, give, supply, provide, furnish, deliver. **4** secrete, give off, generate. **5** make, manufacture, fabricate, construct, compose, invent. **6** give rise to, prompt, cause, generate, occasion, provoke, bring about, result in, effect, create, originate. **7** direct, stage, mount, put on. *noun* crop, harvest, yield, output, product(s).

producer *noun* a person, organization, or thing that produces.
producible *adj.* capable of being produced.
product *noun* **1** something produced, eg through manufacture or agriculture. **2** a result: *the product of hours of*

thought. **3** *Maths.* the value obtained by multiplying two or more numbers: *the product of 2 and 4 is 8.* **4** *Chem.* a substance formed during a chemical reaction. [from Latin *producere*, to produce]

⊟ **1** commodity, merchandise, goods, end-product, artefact, work, creation, invention, production, output, yield, produce, fruit, return. **2** result, consequence, outcome, issue, upshot, offshoot, spin-off, by-product, legacy.

production *noun* **1** the act of producing; the process of producing or being produced: *goes into production next year.* **2** the quantity produced or rate of producing it. **3** something created; a literary or artistic work. **4** a particular presentation of a play, opera, ballet, etc. [from Latin *productio*, from *producere*, to produce]

⊟ **1** making, manufacture, fabrication, construction, assembly, creation, origination, preparation, formation. **2** productivity. **4** presentation, staging.
⊞ **1** consumption.

productive *adj.* **1** yielding a lot; fertile; fruitful. **2** useful; profitable: *a productive meeting.* **3** (**productive of something**) giving rise to it; resulting in it: *productive of ideas.*

⊟ **1** fruitful, fertile, rich, efficient, effective, energetic, vigorous. **2** useful, profitable, worthwhile, constructive, fruitful, valuable, rewarding. **3** creative, inventive.
⊞ UNPRODUCTIVE. **1** fruitless, barren. **2** fruitless, useless.

productively *adv.* in a productive way.
productivity *noun* rate and efficiency of work in industrial production, etc.

⊟ productiveness, yield, output, work rate, efficiency.

proem /ˈprəʊɛm/ *noun* an introduction, prelude, or preface. [from Greek *prooimion*, from *pro*, before + *oime*, song]
prof *noun colloq.* a professor.
profanation *noun* profaning, violation, pollution.
profane — *adj.* **1** showing disrespect for sacred things; irreverent. **2** not sacred or spiritual; temporal or worldly. — *verb* **1** to treat (something sacred) irreverently. **2** to violate or defile (what should be respected). [from Latin *profanus*, not holy]

⊟ *adj.* **1** irreverent, disrespectful, sacrilegious, blasphemous, ungodly, abusive, crude, coarse, foul, filthy. **2** secular, temporal, worldly, lay, unconsecrated, unhallowed, unsanctified, unholy, irreligious, impious. *verb* DEFILE, VIOLATE. **1** desecrate. **2** abuse, misuse, debase, pervert, contaminate, pollute.
⊞ *adj.* **1** respectful, reverent. **2** holy, sacred, religious. *verb* REVERE, HONOUR.

profanely *adv.* in a profane way.
profanity *noun* (PL. **profanities**) **1** lack of respect for sacred things. **2** blasphemous language; a blasphemy; swear word, oath, etc.
profess *verb* **1** to make an open declaration of (beliefs, etc). **2** to declare one's adherence to: *profess Christianity.* **3** to claim or pretend: *profess ignorance/profess to be an expert.* [from Latin *profiteri*, to declare]

⊟ **1** declare, announce, proclaim, state, assert, affirm, admit, confess, acknowledge, own, confirm, certify. **3** claim, allege, pretend, make out, maintain.

professed *adj.* **1** self-acknowledged; self-confessed: *a*

professed agnostic. **2** claimed by oneself; pretended: *a professed indifference to money.*
professedly *adv.* avowedly, ostensibly.
profession *noun* **1** an occupation, especially one that requires specialist academic and practical training, eg medicine, law, teaching, engineering. **2** the body of people engaged in a particular one of these: *the medical profession.* **3** an act of professing; a declaration: *a profession of loyalty.*

⊟ **1** occupation, job, career, employment, business, line (of work), trade, vocation, calling, métier, craft, office, position. **2** community, people. **3** declaration, announcement, statement, testimony, assertion, affirmation, claim, acknowledgement, admission, confession.

professional — *adj.* **1** earning one's living in the performance, practice, or teaching of something that is a pastime for others. **2** belonging to a trained profession: *professional skills.* **3** having the competence, expertise, or conscientiousness of someone with professional training: *a professional performance, attitude,* etc. — *noun* someone who is professional.

⊟ *adj.* **3** skilled, expert, masterly, proficient, competent, businesslike, efficient, experienced, practised, qualified, licensed, trained. *noun* expert, authority, specialist, *colloq.* pro, master, virtuoso, dab hand.
⊞ *adj.* AMATEUR. **3** unprofessional. *noun* amateur.

professionalism *noun* **1** a professional status. **2** professional expertise or competence.
professionally *adv.* in a professional way; in terms of one's profession: *professionally qualified.*
professor *noun* **1** a teacher of the highest rank in a university; the head of a university department. **2** *North Amer., esp. US* a university teacher. [from Latin *professor*, public teacher]
professorial *adj.* relating to or having the status of a professor.
professorship *noun* the office of a professor.
proffer *verb* (**proffered, proffering**) to offer. [from Old French *proffrir*]
proficiency *noun* **1** being proficient. **2** degree of expertise.

⊟ **1** skill, skilfulness, expertise, mastery, talent, dexterity, finesse. **2** aptitude, ability, competence.
⊞ **1** incompetence.

proficient *adj.* fully trained and competent; expert. [from Latin *proficere*, to make progress]

⊟ competent, efficient, expert, skilled, qualified, trained, able, capable, experienced, accomplished, masterly, gifted, talented, clever, skilful.
⊞ unskilled, incompetent.

proficiently *adv.* in a proficient way.
profile *noun* **1** a side view of something, especially a face or head; a side face. **2** a brief outline, sketch, or assessment, especially of a person. **3** the extent to which one advertises one's presence or involvement: *keep a low profile.* [from Italian *profilo*, from *profilare*, to outline]

⊟ **1** side view, outline, contour, silhouette, shape, form, figure, sketch, drawing, diagram, chart, graph. **2** biography, thumbnail sketch, vignette, portrait, outline, sketch, assessment, study, analysis, examination, survey, review, curriculum vitae.

profit — *noun* **1** money gained from selling something for more than one paid for it. **2** an excess of income over expenses. **3** advantage or benefit. — *verb intrans.* (**profited, profiting**) (**profit from** or **by something**) to benefit from it.

• • • • • • • • • • • • • • • • • • •

☐ *noun* **1, 2** gain, revenue, return, yield, proceeds, receipts, takings, earnings, winnings, interest, surplus, excess, bottom line. **3** advantage, benefit, use, avail, value, worth. *verb* benefit from, make money from, take advantage of, exploit, use, utilize, turn to advantage, capitalize on, cash in on, reap the benefit of, gain from.
☒ *noun* LOSS. *verb* lose.

• • • • • • • • • • • • • • • • • • •

profitability *noun* the capacity for being profitable.
profitable *adj.* **1** *said of a business, etc* making a profit. **2** useful; fruitful.

• • • • • • • • • • • • • • • • • • •

☐ **1** cost-effective, economic, commercial, money-making, lucrative, remunerative, paying, rewarding, successful. **2** useful, fruitful, beneficial, productive, advantageous, valuable, worthwhile.
☒ unprofitable. **1** loss-making, non-profit-making.

• • • • • • • • • • • • • • • • • • •

profitably *adv.* in a profitable way.
profiteer — *noun* a person who takes advantage of a shortage or other emergency to make exorbitant profits. — *verb intrans.* to make excessive profits in such a way.
profiterole *noun* a small sweet or savoury confection of choux pastry. [from French, said to be a diminutive from *profiter*, to profit]
profit margin the difference between the buying or production price and the selling price.
profit-sharing *noun* an agreement whereby employees receive a proportion, fixed in advance, of a company's profits.
profligacy *noun* being profligate.
profligate — *adj.* **1** immoral and irresponsible; licentious or dissolute. **2** scandalously extravagant. — *noun* a profligate person. [from Latin *profligare*, to strike down]
pro forma (*also* **pro-forma invoice**) an invoice sent in advance of the goods ordered. [from Latin *pro forma*, for the sake of form]
profound *adj.* **1** radical, extensive, far-reaching: *profound changes.* **2** *said of a feeling* deeply felt or rooted. **3** *said of comments, etc* showing understanding or penetration. **4** intense; impenetrable: *profound deafness/profound silence.* **5** *said of sleep* deep; sound. [from Latin *profundus*, deep, profound]

• • • • • • • • • • • • • • • • • • •

☐ **1** radical, far-reaching, extensive, exhaustive, extreme, great, marked. **2** deep, intense, heartfelt, extreme, great. **3** serious, weighty, penetrating, thoughtful, philosophical, wise, learned, erudite, abstruse. **4** intense, impenetrable, deep, severe, extreme. **5** deep, sound, heavy.
☒ **1** slight, mild, insignificant, superficial. **2** mild, gentle, superficial. **3** shallow, superficial, inane. **5** light, shallow.

• • • • • • • • • • • • • • • • • • •

profoundly *adv.* in a profound way; deeply, intensely: *profoundly sorry.*
profundity *noun* (PL. **profundities**) **1** being profound. **2** depth. **3** something which is profound.
profuse *adj.* **1** overflowing; exaggerated; excessive: *offered profuse apologies.* **2** copious: *profuse bleeding.* [from Latin *profusus*, lavish]

• • • • • • • • • • • • • • • • • • •

☐ AMPLE, ABUNDANT, PLENTIFUL, COPIOUS, GENEROUS, LIBERAL, LAVISH, RICH, LUXURIANT, EXCESSIVE, IMMODERATE, EXTRAVAGANT, OVERABUNDANT, SUPERABUNDANT, OVERFLOWING.
☒ INADEQUATE, SPARSE.

• • • • • • • • • • • • • • • • • • •

profusely *adv.* in a profuse way; to a profuse or copious degree.

profusion *noun* **1** being profuse. **2** extravagance.

• • • • • • • • • • • • • • • • • • •

☐ ABUNDANCE, PLENTY, WEALTH, MULTITUDE, PLETHORA, GLUT, EXCESS, SURPLUS, SUPERFLUITY, EXTRAVAGANCE.
☒ INADEQUACY, SCARCITY.

• • • • • • • • • • • • • • • • • • •

progenitor *noun* **1** an ancestor, forebear, or forefather. **2** the begetter or originator of a movement, etc. [from Latin, from *progignere*, to beget]
progeny /'prɒdʒənɪ/ *pl. noun* **1** children; offspring; descendants. **2** what results from or is generated by something; derivatives and offshoots. [from Latin *progenies*, offspring]
progesterone /proʊ'dʒɛstəroʊn/ *noun Biochem.* a steroid sex hormone that is produced mainly by the corpus luteum of the ovary. It prepares the lining of the uterus (womb) for implantation of a fertilized egg, and if pregnancy occurs progesterone is secreted in large amounts by the placenta to maintain the pregnancy, stimulate growth of the mammary glands, and prevent the release of further eggs from the ovary. [from PRO- + GESTATION + STEROL]
prognosis *noun* (PL. **prognoses**) **1** an informed forecast of developments in any situation. **2** a doctor's prediction on the course of a patient's illness and his or her chances of recovery. [from Greek *prognosis*, knowing before]
prognosticate *verb* to foretell, to indicate in advance; to be a sign of. [from Latin *prognosticare*, to foretell, from Greek *prognostikon*, sign of the future]
prognostication *noun* **1** prognosticating. **2** a prophecy. **3** a foreboding.
prognosticator *noun* a person or thing that prognosticates.
programmable *adj.* capable of being programmed to perform a task automatically.
programme or *North Amer.* **program** — *noun* **1** the schedule of proceedings for, and list of participants in, a theatre performance, entertainment, ceremony, etc; also, a leaflet or booklet describing these. **2** an agenda, plan, or schedule. **3** a series of planned projects to be undertaken: *the building programme for 2005.* **4** a scheduled radio or television presentation. **5** (*usually* **program**) a set of coded instructions to a computer for the performance of a series of operations. — *verb* (**programmed, programming**) **1** to include in a programme; to schedule. **2** to draw up a programme for. **3** to set (a computer) by program to perform a set of operations. **4** to set so as to operate at the required time: *heating programmed to come on at 7.00pm.* [from Greek *programma*, the order of the day, schedule]

• • • • • • • • • • • • • • • • • • •

☐ *noun* **1** order of events, listing, line-up. **2** agenda, plan, schedule, timetable, calendar, scheme, syllabus, curriculum. **3** scheme, project, schedule, plan. **4** broadcast, transmission, show, performance, production, presentation.

• • • • • • • • • • • • • • • • • • •

programmed learning a form of learning developed in the 1960s, and based on the behaviourist learning theories of US psychologist B F Skinner. The learner is given short frames of information which he or she must follow with some active response, and correct answers are immediately reinforced.
programme music instrumental music which aims to depict a story or scene.
programmer *noun* a person who writes computer programs.
progress — *noun* (with stress on *pro*-) **1** movement while travelling in any direction. **2** course: *watched her erratic progress/followed the progress of the trial.* **3** movement towards a destination, goal, or state of completion: *make slow progress.* **4** advances or development: *make progress in the treatment of cancer.* **5** *old use* a journey made in state by a sovereign, etc. — *verb* (with stress on *-gress*) **1** *intrans.* to move forwards or onwards; to proceed towards a goal. **2** *intrans.* to advance or develop. **3** *intrans.* to improve. **4** to

put (something planned) into operation; to expedite. — **in progress** taking place; in the course of being done. [from Latin *progressus*, from *progredi*, to move forward]

....

◨ *noun* **1** movement, progression, advance, headway. **2** course, path, passage, journey, way. **3**, **4** development, step(s) forward, breakthrough, evolution, growth, increase, improvement, betterment, promotion. *verb* **1** proceed, advance, go forward, forge ahead, make progress, make headway. **2** advance, develop, come on, proceed, go forward, forge ahead, make progress, make headway, grow, mature, increase. **3** improve, blossom, better, prosper, advance, make progress, make headway, come on, develop, go forward, forge ahead.

◱ *noun* **3**, **4** recession, deterioration, decline. *verb* **2**, **3** deteriorate, decline.

....

progression *noun* **1** the process of moving forwards or advancing in stages. **2** *Mus.* a succession of chords, the advance from one to the next being determined on a fixed pattern. **3** *Maths.* a sequence of numbers, each of which bears a specific relationship to the preceding term. The numbers in an *arithmetic progression* increase or decrease by a constant amount, eg 2, 4, 6, 8, 10 ... In a *geometric progression* the ratio of each number to its predecessor is constant, eg 1, 2, 4, 8, 16, ...

....

◨ **1** advance, headway, progress, development, course, succession, series, sequence, order, cycle, chain, string.

....

progressive — *adj.* **1** advanced in outlook; using, or favouring, new methods. **2** moving forward or advancing continuously or by stages: *progressive loss of memory*. **3** *said of a disease* continuously increasing in severity or complication. **4** *said of a dance or game* involving changes of partner at intervals. **5** *said of taxation* increasing as the sum taxed increases. **6** *Grammar* denoting the forms of a verb that express continuing action, in English formed with the present participle, as in *I am doing it* and *they will be going*. — *noun* **1** a person with progressive ideas. **2** *Grammar* a verb in a progressive form.

....

◨ *adj.* **1** advanced, modern, avant-garde, forward-looking, enlightened, liberal, radical, revolutionary, reformist, dynamic, enterprising, *colloq.* go-ahead, up-and-coming. **2** advancing, continuing, developing, growing, increasing, intensifying.

◱ *adj.* **1**, **2** regressive.

....

progressive education a term used for an educational system which places greater emphasis on the needs and capacities of the individual child than traditional forms of teaching. It usually involves greater freedom of choice, activity, and movement, and stresses social as well as academic development.

progressively *adv.* in a progressive way; gradually and steadily.

prohibit *verb* (**prohibited**, **prohibiting**) **1** to forbid, especially by law; to ban. **2** to prevent or hinder. [from Latin *prohibere*, to hinder, forbid]

....

◨ **1** forbid, ban, bar, veto, proscribe, outlaw, rule out. **2** prevent, stop, hinder, hamper, impede, obstruct, restrict, rule out, preclude.

◱ PERMIT, ALLOW. **1** authorize.

....

Prohibition *noun* an attempt (1920–33) to forbid the manufacture and sale of all alcoholic drinks in the USA.

prohibition *noun* **1** the act of prohibiting or state of being prohibited. **2** a law or decree prohibiting something. **3** a ban by law on the manufacture and sale of alcoholic drinks.

prohibitionist *noun* a person who supports prohibition.

prohibitive *adj.* **1** banning; prohibiting. **2** tending to prevent or discourage. **3** *said of prices, etc* unaffordably high.

prohibitory *adj.* prohibiting; restraining.

project — *noun* (with stress on *proj-*) **1** a plan, scheme, or proposal. **2** a research or study assignment. — *verb* (with stress on *-ject*) **1** *intrans.* to jut out; to protrude. **2** to throw forwards; to propel. **3** to throw (a shadow or image) on to a surface. **4** to propose or plan. **5** to forecast from present trends and other known data; to extrapolate. **6** to imagine (oneself) in another situation, especially a future one. **7** to ascribe (feelings of one's own) to other people. **8** to cause (one's voice) to be heard clearly at some distance. **9** *intrans.*, *colloq.* to make good contact with an audience through the strength of one's personality. [from Latin *projicere*, to throw forward]

....

◨ *noun* **1** plan, scheme, proposal, idea, programme, design, enterprise, undertaking, venture, task, job, conception. *verb* **1** jut out, protrude, stick out, bulge, overhang. **2** throw, fling, hurl, launch, propel. **3** cast. **5** forecast, extrapolate, estimate, reckon, calculate, predict.

....

projectile — *noun* an object designed to be propelled with force, especially a missile such as a bullet or rocket. — *adj.* hurling, or (designed to be) hurled, forwards. [from Modern Latin *projectilis*, from Latin *projicere*, to throw forward]

projection *noun* **1** the act of projecting or process of being projected. **2** something that protrudes from a surface. **3** the showing of a film or transparencies on a screen. **4** a forecast based on present trends and other known data. **5** *Maths.* maps the representation of a solid object, especially part of the Earth's sphere, on a flat surface. **6** *Psychol.* a mental process by which a subjective mental image is perceived as belonging to the external world.

....

◨ **2** protuberance, bulge, overhang, ledge, sill, shelf, ridge. **4** forecast, extrapolation, estimate, prediction, reckoning, calculation, computation.

....

projectionist *noun* a person who operates a projector, especially in a cinema.

projector *noun* an instrument containing a system of lenses that projects an enlarged version of an illuminated image on to a screen. The image may be still (as in a slide projector) or moving (as in a film projector).

prokaryote or **procaryote** /proʊˈkarɪəʊt/ *noun Biol.* an organism in which the cells lack a distinct nucleus containing chromosomes, and the genetic material consists of a single double-stranded DNA molecule coiled in a loop. See also EUKARYOTE. [from PRO- + Greek *karyon*, kernel]

prolactin *noun Physiol.* a hormone, secreted by the pituitary gland, which initiates lactation (secretion of milk) in mammals, and stimulates the production of another hormone, progesterone, by the corpus luteum.

prolapse *noun Medicine* the slipping out of place or falling down of an organ or other body part, especially the slipping of the uterus (womb) into the vagina. [from Latin *prolabi*, *prolapsus* to slip forward]

prole *noun*, *adj. derog. colloq.* proletarian.

proletarian /proʊləˈtɛərɪən/ — *adj.* relating to the proletariat. — *noun* a member of the proletariat. [from Latin *proletarius*, a citizen who has nothing to offer society but his offspring, from *proles*, offspring]

proletariat /proʊləˈtɛərɪət/ *noun* the working class, especially unskilled labourers and industrial workers.

pro-life *adj.* opposing abortion, euthanasia, and experimentation on human embryos.

proliferate *verb* **1** *intrans.*, *said of a plant or animal species* to reproduce rapidly. **2** *intrans.* to increase in numbers; to multiply. **3** to reproduce (cells, etc) rapidly. [from Latin *prolifer*, bearing offspring]

⊟ MULTIPLY. **1** reproduce, breed, flourish, thrive. **2** increase, build up, intensify, escalate, mushroom, snowball, spread, expand, flourish, thrive. **3** reproduce, breed, increase.
⊞ **1, 2** dwindle.

proliferation *noun* **1** a great and rapid increase in numbers. **2** *Biol.* in living organisms, the multiplication of cells, tissues, or structures. **3** the spread of nuclear weapons to countries not already possessing them.

prolific *adj.* **1** abundant in growth; producing plentiful fruit or offspring. **2** *said of a writer, artist, etc* constantly productive of new work. **3** (**prolific of** or **in something**) productive of it; abounding in it. [from Latin *prolificus*, fertile]

⊟ **1** productive, fruitful, fertile, profuse, abundant.
⊞ **1, 2** unproductive.

prolifically *adv.* in a prolific way; to a prolific degree.
proline /ˈprəʊliːn/ *noun Biochem.* an amino acid that is found in proteins. [from German *Prolin*]
prolix /ˈprəʊlɪks/ *adj.*, *said of speech or writing* tediously long-winded; wordy; verbose. [from Latin *prolixus*, stretched out]
prolixity *noun* (PL. **prolixities**) being prolix.
PROLOG /ˈprəʊlɒg/ *noun Comput.* a high-level programming language, often used in artificial intelligence research. [contraction of *programming in logic*]
prologue /ˈprəʊlɒg/ *noun* **1** a speech addressed to the audience at the beginning of a play; the actor delivering it. **2** a preface to a literary work. **3** an event serving as an introduction or prelude. [from Greek *prologos*, from *pro*, before + *logos*, discourse]
prolong *verb* to make longer; to extend or protract. [from Latin *prolongare*]

⊟ lengthen, extend, stretch, protract, draw out, spin out, drag out, delay, continue, perpetuate.
⊞ shorten.

prolongation *noun* a continuation or lengthening; a piece added in continuation.
PROM *abbrev. Comput.* programmable read-only memory, a type of read-only memory which can be programmed, usually only once, after manufacture, and thereafter is fixed.
prom *noun colloq.* **1** a walk or promenade. **2** a promenade concert.
promenade /prɒməˈnɑːd/ — *noun* **1** a broad paved walk, especially along a sea front. **2** *facetious* a stately stroll. — *verb* **1** *intrans.* to stroll in a stately fashion. **2** to walk (the streets, etc). **3** to take for an airing; to parade: *promenaded her children through the park*. [from French, from *promener*, to lead about]
promenade concert a concert at which part of the audience is accommodated in a standing area and can move about.
promenade deck an upper deck on board a ship, along which passengers can promenade.
promenader *noun* an especially regular attender at promenade concerts.
promethium /prəˈmiːθɪəm/ *noun Chem.* (SYMBOL **Pm**, ATOMIC NUMBER 61) a radioactive metallic element, produced by the fission of uranium, thorium, or plutonium, that occurs naturally in minute amounts as a result of the fission of uranium in pitchblende and other uranium ores, and is also found in nuclear waste material. It is manufactured artificially by bombarding neodymium with neutrons, and is used as an X-ray source, and in phosphorescent paints. [named after the Greek Titan Prometheus]
prominence *noun* **1** being prominent. **2** a prominent point or thing. **3** a projection.

⊟ **1** fame, celebrity, renown, eminence, distinction, greatness, importance, reputation, name, standing, rank, prestige. **2** celebrity. **3** bulge, protuberance, bump, hump, lump, mound, rise, elevation, projection, process, headland, promontory, cliff, crag.
⊞ **1** unimportance, insignificance.

prominent *adj.* **1** jutting out; projecting; protruding; bulging: *a prominent chin/prominent eyes*. **2** noticeable; conspicuous: *a prominent landmark*. **3** leading; notable: *a prominent politician, role*, etc. [from Latin *prominere*, to jut out]

⊟ **1** projecting, protruding, protuberant, bulging, jutting, obtrusive. **2** noticeable, conspicuous, obvious, unmistakable, striking, eye-catching, obtrusive. **3** leading, notable, noted, famous, well-known, celebrated, renowned, eminent, distinguished, respected, foremost, important, outstanding.
⊞ **2** inconspicuous. **3** unknown, unimportant, insignificant.

prominently *adv.* in a prominent way.
promiscuity *noun* **1** being promiscuous. **2** mixture without order or distinction. **3** promiscuous sexual activity.

⊟ **1, 3** looseness, laxity, permissiveness, wantonness, immorality, licentiousness, debauchery, depravity.
⊞ **1, 3** chastity, morality.

promiscuous *adj.* **1** *derog.* indulging in casual or indiscriminate sexual relations. **2** haphazardly mixed. [from Latin *promiscuus*, mixed up]

⊟ **1** loose, immoral, licentious, dissolute. **2** haphazard, random, casual, indiscriminate.
⊞ **1** chaste, moral.

promise — *verb* **1** to give an undertaking (to do or not do something). **2** to undertake to give (someone something). **3** to show signs of bringing: *clouds that promise rain*. **4** to look likely (to do something): *promises to have a great future*. **5** to assure or warn: *will be heavy going, I promise you*. — *noun* **1** an undertaking to give, do, or not do, something. **2** a sign: *a promise of spring in the air*. **3** signs of future excellence: *shows promise*. — **promise well** or **badly** to give grounds for hope, or despondency. [from Latin *promissum*, from *promittere*, to send forth, promise]

⊟ *verb* **1** vow, pledge, swear, take an oath, contract, undertake, give one's word, warrant, guarantee, vouch. **3, 4** indicate, suggest, hint at, augur, presage. **5** assure, warrant, guarantee, vouch. *noun* **1** undertaking, pledge, guarantee, vow, oath, word of honour, bond, compact, covenant, assurance, engagement, commitment. **2** sign, hint, suggestion, indication, evidence. **3** potential, ability, capability, aptitude, talent.

promised land 1 *Biblical* the fertile land promised by God to the Israelites. **2** any longed-for place of contentment and prosperity.
promising *adj.* **1** showing promise; talented; apt. **2** seeming to bode well for the future.

⊟ **1** talented, apt, gifted, budding, up-and-coming. **2** auspicious, propitious, favourable, rosy, bright, encouraging, hopeful.
⊞ **2** unpromising, inauspicious, discouraging.

promisingly *adv.* in a promising way.
promissory /ˈprɒmɪsərɪ/ *adj.* expressing a promise, especially in **promissory note**, a signed promise to pay a stated

sum of money. [from Latin *promissorius*, from *promissum*, promise]

promontory /'prɒməntərɪ/ *noun* (PL. **promontories**) a usually hilly part of a coastline that projects into the sea; a headland. [from Latin *promontorium*, mountain ridge, promontory]

promote *verb* **1** to raise to a more senior position: *was promoted to lieutenant.* **2** to contribute to: *exercise promotes health.* **3** to work for the cause of: *promote peace.* **4** to publicize; to try to boost the sales of (a product) by advertising. **5** to be the organizer or financer of (an undertaking). [from Latin *promovere*, to cause to advance]

- **1** elevate, raise, move up, exalt, honour, upgrade, advance. **2** contribute to, help, aid, assist, foster, nurture, further, forward, encourage, boost, stimulate. **3** work for, campaign for, champion, sponsor, support, back, urge, foster, nurture, further, forward, advocate, endorse. **4** publicize, advertise, *colloq.* plug, *colloq.* hype, popularize, market, sell, push, recommend. **5** sponsor, finance, support, back.
- **1** demote. **2** hinder. **4** disparage.

promoter *noun* the organizer or financer of a sporting event or other undertaking.

promotion *noun* **1** promoting. **2** advancement in rank or honour. **3** encouragement. **4** preferment. **5** a venture or undertaking, especially in show business. **6** advertising, or an effort to publicize and increase sales of a particular brand.

- **1** support, backing, furtherance, development, boosting. **2, 4** advancement, upgrading, rise, preferment, elevation. **6** advertising, *colloq.* plugging, publicity, *colloq.* hype, campaign, propaganda, marketing, pushing.
- **1** obstruction. **2, 4** demotion. **3** disparagement.

promotional *adj.* relating to or involving promotion.

prompt — *adj.* **1** immediate; quick; punctual. **2** instantly willing; ready; unhesitating: *prompt with offers of help.* — *adv.* punctually: *at 2.15 prompt.* — *noun* **1** something serving as a reminder. **2** words supplied by a prompter to an actor. **3** a prompter. — *verb* **1** to cause, lead, or remind (someone to do something). **2** to produce or elicit (a reaction or response): *what prompted that remark?* **3** *trans., intrans.* to help (an actor) to remember his or her next words by supplying the first few. [from Latin *promptus*, ready, quick, and *promptare*, to incite]

- *adj.* **1** immediate, quick, punctual, on time, instantaneous, instant, direct, swift, rapid, speedy. **2** ready, unhesitating, willing, alert, responsive, timely, early. *adv.* promptly, punctually, exactly, on the dot, to the minute, sharp. *noun* **1** reminder, hint, help, jolt, prod, spur, stimulus, cue. *verb* **1** cause, lead, remind, move, stimulate, motivate, spur, prod, urge, encourage, incite, provoke. **2** produce, elicit, give rise to, result in, occasion, instigate, call forth, provoke, inspire.
- *adj.* SLOW. **1** late. **2** hesitant. *verb* **1** deter, dissuade.

prompter *noun* a person positioned offstage to prompt actors when they forget their lines.

promptitude *noun* being prompt.

promptly *adv.* **1** without delay. **2** punctually.

promptness *noun* being prompt.

promulgate *verb* **1** to make (a decree, etc) effective by means of an official public announcment. **2** to publicize or promote (an idea, theory, etc) widely. [from Latin *promulgare*, to make known]

promulgation *noun* promulgating or being promulgated.

promulgator *noun* a person who promulgates.

pron. *abbrev.* pronoun.

prone *adj.* **1** lying flat, especially face downwards. **2 (prone to something)** predisposed to it, or liable to suffer from it:

is prone to bronchitis/accident-prone. **3** inclined or liable to do something: *prone to make mistakes.* [from Latin *pronus*, bent forwards]

- **1** face down, prostrate, flat, horizontal, full-length, stretched, recumbent. **2, 3** predisposed to, inclined to, disposed to, liable to, subject to, susceptible to, vulnerable to, apt to, likely to.
- **1** upright. **2, 3** unlikely to.

proneness *noun* being prone.

prong *noun* a point or spike, especially one of those making up the head of a fork. [from Middle English *pronge*, pang]

pronged *adj.* having a certain number of prongs or directions: *a three-pronged attack* (ie one made by forces attacking from three directions).

pronghorn or **prongbuck** *noun* a N American mammal, often referred to as the pronghorn antelope, but not in fact a true antelope. It has a pale brown coat and prominent eyes. The female has short horns, and the male has horns with a frontal 'prong' and backward curving tips. The animal will approach moving objects (including predators), and it inhabits grasslands.

pronking *noun* Zool. behaviour exhibited by the springbok and several other ungulates, in which the back is arched and the legs held stiffly downwards as the animal leaps off the ground and then lands on all four legs simultaneously, repeating the action several times as if on springs. [from Afrikaans *pronk*, to show off, strut, prance]

pronominal *adj.* of, or being, a pronoun; relating to pronouns. [from Latin *pronominalis*, from *pronomen*, pronoun]

pronominally *adv.* Grammar as a pronoun.

pronoun *noun* a word such as *she*, *him*, *they*, and *it* used in place of, and to refer to, a noun or noun phrase. [from Latin *pronomen*, from *pro*, on behalf of + *nomen*, noun]

pronounce *verb* **1** to say or utter (words, sounds, letters, etc); to articulate or enunciate. **2** to declare officially, formally, or authoritatively: *pronounced her innocent.* **3** to pass or deliver (judgement). **4 (pronounce on something)** to give one's opinion or verdict on it. See also PRONUNCIATION. [from Latin *pronuntiare*, to declaim, pronounce]

- **1** say, utter, speak, enunciate, articulate, express, voice, vocalize, sound, stress. **2** declare, announce, proclaim, decree, judge, affirm, assert. **3** pass, deliver, hand down.

pronounceable *adj.* capable of being pronounced.

pronounced *adj.* noticeable; distinct: *a pronounced limp.*

- noticeable, distinct, clear, definite, positive, decided, marked, conspicuous, evident, obvious, striking, unmistakable, strong, broad.
- faint, vague.

pronouncedly *adv.* in a pronounced way.

pronouncement *noun* **1** a formal announcement. **2** a declaration of opinion; a verdict.

pronto *adv.* colloq. immediately. [from Spanish *pronto*, quick]

pronunciation *noun* the act, or a manner, or the usual way, of pronouncing words, sounds, letters, etc. [from Latin *pronuntiatio*, expression, delivery]

- speech, diction, elocution, enunciation, articulation, delivery, accent, stress, inflection, intonation.

proof — *noun* **1** evidence, especially conclusive, that something is true or a fact. **2** *Legal* the accumulated evidence on which a verdict is based. **3** the activity or process of testing or proving: *capable of proof.* **4** a test, trial, or demonstration: *as a proof of her love.* **5** *Maths.* a step-by-step verification of a proposed mathematical statement. **6** *Printing* a trial copy of a sheet of printed text for examination or correction. **7** a trial print from a photographic negative. **8** a trial impression from an engraved plate. **9** a measure of the alcohol content of a distilled liquid, especially an alcoholic beverage. It is expressed in degrees of proof as the percentage of proof spirit (which contains about 57% alcohol by volume) present. — *adj.* (*often in compounds*) able or designed to withstand, deter, or be free from: *proof against storms/leakproof*. — *verb* **1** (*also in compounds*) to make resistant to, or proof against, something; to waterproof. **2** to take a proof of (printed material). [from French *preuve*, from Latin *proba*, test, proof]

◼ *noun* **1** evidence, documentation, confirmation, corroboration, substantiation, verification, demonstration. **3** demonstration, verification, confirmation, corroboration, substantiation.

proof-read *verb trans., intrans.* to read and mark for correction the proofs of (a text, etc).

proof-reader *noun* a person who reads and corrects proofs.

proof spirit a mixture of alcohol and water in which the alcohol content is 49·28% of the weight or 57·1% of the volume.

prop[1] — *noun* **1** a rigid, especially vertical, support of any of various kinds. **2** a person or thing that one depends on for help or emotional support. **3** *Rugby* (*also* **prop forward**) a forward at either end of the front row of the scrum. — *verb* (**propped, propping**) **1** (*also* **prop something up**) to support or hold it upright with, or as if with, a prop. **2** (**prop one thing against another**) to lean or put it against something: *propped her bike against the wall*. **3** to serve as a prop to. [from Middle English *proppe*]

◼ *noun* **1** support, strut, buttress, brace, truss. **2** support, stay, mainstay. *verb* **1, 3** support, sustain, uphold, maintain, shore, stay, buttress, bolster, underpin. **2** lean, rest, stand.

prop[2] *noun colloq.* **1** a propeller. **2** *Theatr.* a stage property.

propaganda *noun* the organized circulation by a political group, etc of information, misinformation, rumour or opinion, presented so as to influence public feeling; also, the material circulated in this way. [from the Roman Catholic *Congregatio de propaganda fide* 'congregation for propagating the faith', responsible for foreign missions and training missionaries]

◼ indoctrination, brainwashing, disinformation.

propagandist *noun* a person who prepares or circulates propaganda.

propagandize or **propagandise** *verb* **1** to subject to propaganda. **2** *intrans.* to circulate propaganda.

propagate *verb* **1** *intrans., trans. Bot., said of a plant* to multiply. **2** *Bot.* to grow (new plants), either by natural means or artificially. **3** to spread or popularize (ideas, etc). **4** *Physics* to transmit energy, eg sound, electromagnetism, over a distance in wave form. [from Latin *propagare*, to grow plants by grafting, etc]

◼ **1** increase, multiply, proliferate, generate, produce, breed, beget, spawn, procreate, reproduce. **2** grow, reproduce, produce, generate, breed. **3** spread, popularize, promulgate, publicize, promote, disseminate, circulate, publish, transmit, broadcast, diffuse.

propagation *noun* **1** *Bot.* the multiplication of plants, especially in horticulture, either by natural means, eg from seed, or by artificial methods which allow the mass production of plants with desirable traits that might be lost if they were bred from seed, eg grafting, taking cuttings, growing new plants from stolons, tubers, or runners, tissue culture. **2** *Physics* the transmission of energy (eg sound, electromagnetism) from one point to another in the form of waves in a direction perpendicular to the wavefront.

propagator *noun* **1** a person or thing that propagates. **2** a heated box with a cover in which plants may be grown from cuttings or seeds.

propane *noun Chem.* (FORMULA C_3H_8) a colourless odourless flammable gas obtained from petroleum and belonging to the alkane series of hydrocarbons. It readily liquefies under pressure, and is used as a fuel supply for portable stoves, etc, and as a solvent and refrigerant. [from *propionic acid*, a fatty acid]

propel *verb* (**propelled, propelling**) **1** to drive or push forward. **2** to steer or send in a certain direction. [from Latin *propellere*, to drive forward]

◼ MOVE, DRIVE, IMPEL, FORCE, THRUST, PUSH, SHOVE, LAUNCH, SHOOT, SEND.
◼ STOP.

propellant *noun* **1** something that propels. **2** *Chem.* a compressed inert gas in an aerosol that is used to release the liquid contents as a fine spray when the pressure is released. **3** *Engineering* the fuel and oxidizer that are burned in a rocket in order to provide thrust. **4** an explosive charge that is used to propel a projectile, eg a bullet or shell.

propellent *adj.* driving; propelling.

propeller *noun* a device consisting of a shaft with radiating blades that rotate to propel a ship or an aircraft.

propelling-pencil *noun* a type of pencil in which the lead is held in a casing and can be propelled forward as it is worn down.

propensity *noun* (PL. **propensities**) a tendency or inclination. [from Latin *propendere*, to be inclined]

proper *adj.* **1** real; genuine; that can rightly be described as: *have a proper holiday*. **2** right; correct: *learn the proper grip*. **3** appropriate: *at the proper time*. **4** own particular; correct: *everything in its proper place*. **5** socially accepted; respectable: *the proper way to behave*. **6** *derog.* morally strict; prim: *is a bit proper*. **7** (**proper to something**) belonging or appropriate to it; suitable: *the form of address proper to her rank*. **8** (*used after a noun*) strictly so called; itself: *we are now entering the city proper*. **9** *colloq.* utter: *felt a proper fool*. [from Old French *propre*, own]

◼ **1** real, true, genuine, actual. **2** right, correct, accurate, exact, precise. **3, 7** suitable, appropriate, fitting, correct. **5** respectable, decent, polite, accepted, acceptable, correct. **6** prim, prudish, formal. **9** utter, *colloq.* right, real, complete, absolute.
◼ **2, 3, 4** wrong. **5** improper, indecent, wrong.

proper fraction *Maths.* a fraction such as - and - in which the number above the line is smaller than the one below.

properly *adv.* **1** suitably; appropriately; correctly. **2** with strict accuracy: *spiders can't properly be called insects*. **3** fully; thoroughly; completely. **4** *colloq.* utterly.

proper noun or **proper name** *Grammar* the name of a particular person, place, or thing. See also COMMON NOUN.

propertied *adj.* owning property, especially land.

property *noun* (PL. **properties**) **1** something one owns: *that book is my property*. **2** one's possessions collectively. **3** the concept of ownership. **4** land or real estate, or an item of this. **5** a quality or attribute: *the properties of copper sulphate*. **6** *Theatr.* an object or piece of furniture used on stage during a performance. [from Middle English *proprete*, from Latin *proprietas*, attribute, ownership]

◼ **2** belongings, possessions, effects, goods, chattels, capital, assets, holding(s), resources, means, wealth, riches. **4** land, real estate, estate, acres, premises, buildings, house(s). **5** quality, attribute, characteristic, feature, trait, idiosyncrasy, peculiarity, mark.

....

property man or **property mistress** *Theatr.* a person in charge of stage properties.

propfan *noun* a propeller fan: an aircraft propeller consisting of a rotor carrying several blades working in a cylindrical casing, sometimes provided with fixed blades, and usually driven by a direct-coupled motor.

prophase *noun Biol.* the first stage of cell division in mitosis and meiosis, during which the chromosomes coil and thicken, and divide longitudinally to form chromatids, and the membrane surrounding the nucleus disintegrates.

prophecy *noun* (**PL. prophecies**) **1** the interpretation of divine will or the foretelling of the future; a gift or aptitude for this. **2** a prophetic utterance; something foretold; a prediction. [from Old French *prophecie*, from Greek *propheteia*]

....

⊟ PREDICTION, AUGURY. **2** forecast, prognosis.

....

prophesy *verb* (**prophesies, prophesied**) **1** *trans., intrans.* to foretell (future happenings); to predict. **2** *intrans.* to utter prophecies; to interpret divine will. [a variant of PRO-PHECY]

....

⊟ **1** predict, foresee, foretell, forewarn, forecast, augur.

....

prophet *noun* **1** a person inspired to express the divine will or reveal the future. **2** *Biblical* any of the writers of prophecy in the Old Testament, or the books attributed to them. **3** (**the Prophet**) Muhammad. **4** someone claiming to be able to tell what will happen in the future: *prophets of mass destruction.* **5** a leading advocate of, or spokesperson for, a movement or cause: *a prophet of the green revolution.* [from Greek *prophetes*, an expounder of divine will]

....

⊟ **1, 4** seer, soothsayer, foreteller, forecaster, oracle, clairvoyant.

....

prophetess *noun* a female prophet.
prophetic *adj.* **1** foretelling the future: *prophetic remarks.* **2** of or relating to prophets or prophecy.
prophetically *adv.* in a prophetic way.
prophylactic /prɒfɪ'laktɪk/ — *adj.* guarding against, or preventing, disease or other mishap. — *noun* a prophylactic drug or device; a precautionary measure. [from Greek *prophylassein*, to take precautions against]
prophylaxis *noun* action or treatment to prevent something unwanted; precautionary measures.
propinquity /prə'pɪŋkwɪtɪ/ *noun* **1** nearness in place or time; proximity. **2** closeness of kinship. [from Latin *propinquitas*, from *propinquus*, near]
propitiable /prə'pɪʃɪəbl/ *adj.* capable of being propitiated or made propitious.
propitiate /prə'pɪʃɪeɪt/ *verb* to appease or placate (an angry person or god). [from Latin *propitiare*, to appease]
propitiation *noun* propitiating, atonement.
propitiator *noun* a person who propitiates.
propitiatory *adj.* propitiating, making up for a wrong.
propitious /prə'pɪʃəs/ *adj.* **1** favourable; auspicious; advantageous: *a propitious moment to sell.* **2** (**propitious for** or **to something**) likely to favour or encourage it: *circumstances propitious to development.* [from Latin *propitius*, favourable]
propitiously *adv.* in a propitious way; so as to be propitious.
proponent *noun* a supporter or advocate: *a proponent of recycling.* [from Latin *proponere*, to propose]
proportion — *noun* **1** a part of a total: *a large proportion of the population.* **2** the size of one element or group in re-

lation to the whole or total: *only a small proportion of lawyers are women.* **3** the size of one group or component in relation to another: *mixed in a proportion of two parts to one.* **4** the correct balance between parts or elements: *the hands are out of proportion with the head/get things into proportion.* **5** (**proportions**) size; dimensions: *a task of huge proportions.* **6** *Maths.* correspondence between the ratios of two pairs of quantities, as expressed in *2 is to 8 as 3 is to 12.* — *verb* (**proportioned, proportioning**) **1** to adjust the proportions, or balance the parts, of: *a well-proportioned room.* **2** (**proportion one thing to another**) to adjust their proportions. — **in proportion to something 1** in relation to it; in comparison with it. **2** in parallel with it; in correspondence with it; at the same rate. [from Latin *proportio*, proportion, symmetry]

....

⊟ *noun* **1, 2** percentage, fraction, part, division, share, quota, amount. **3** ratio, distribution. **4** balance, correspondence, symmetry, relationship. **5** size, dimensions, measurements, magnitude, volume, capacity.
⊟ **4** disproportion, imbalance.

....

proportional *adj.* (**proportional to something**) **1** corresponding or matching in size, rate, etc. **2** in correct proportion; proportionate.

....

⊟ **1** corresponding, analogous, comparable, relative, commensurate, consistent. **2** proportionate, relative, commensurate, consistent, equitable, even.
⊟ DISPROPORTIONATE.

....

proportionally *adv.* in a proportional way; in proportion.
proportional representation an electoral system in which each political party is represented in parliament in proportion to the votes it receives.
proportionate *adj.* (**proportionate to something**) being in correct proportion: *a reward proportionate to the work done.*
proportionately *adv.* in a proportionate way.
proposal *noun* **1** the act of proposing something. **2** something proposed or suggested; a plan. **3** an offer of marriage.

....

⊟ **1** proposition, suggestion, recommendation. **2** proposition, suggestion, recommendation, motion, plan, scheme, project, design, programme, manifesto, bid, offer, tender, terms.

....

propose *verb* **1** to offer (a plan, etc) for consideration; to suggest. **2** to suggest or nominate (someone for a position, task, etc). **3** *trans., intrans.* to be the proposer of (the motion in a debate). **4** to intend: *don't propose to sell.* **5** to announce the drinking of (a toast) or of (someone's health). **6** *intrans.* (**propose to someone**) to make them an offer of marriage. [from Latin *proponere*, to propose]

....

⊟ **1** suggest, recommend, move, advance, put forward, introduce, bring up, submit, present, offer, tender. **2** suggest, nominate, put up, recommend, put forward. **3** table, submit, present. **4** intend, mean, aim, plan, purpose.
⊟ **1** withdraw.

....

proposer *noun* **1** someone who proposes or advocates something. **2** the leading speaker in favour of the motion in a debate.
proposition — *noun* **1** a proposal or suggestion. **2** something to be dealt with or undertaken: *an awkward proposition.* **3** *euphemistic colloq.* an invitation to have sexual intercourse. **4** *Logic* a form of statement affirming or denying something, that can be true or false; a premise. **5** *Maths.* a statement of a problem or theorem, especially incorporating its solution or proof. — *verb* (**propositioned, propositioning**) *euphemistic colloq.* to propose sexual in-

tercourse to. [from Latin *propositio*, a setting forth, premise, proposition]

propound *verb* to put forward (an idea, theory, etc) for consideration or discussion. [from Latin *proponere*, to propose]

propranolol /prɒˈpranəlɒl/ *noun Medicine* a beta-blocker drug used especially in the treatment of abnormal heart rhythms, angina, and high blood pressure. It can also prevent migraine attacks and relieve symptoms of anxiety. [from PROPYL + PROPANOL]

proprietary *adj.* **1** *said eg of rights* belonging to an owner or proprietor. **2** suggestive or indicative of ownership: *had a proprietary attitude towards his wife.* **3** *said of medicines, etc* marketed under a tradename. **4** privately owned and managed. [from Latin *proprietarius*, from *proprietas*, ownership]

proprietary name a tradename.

proprietor *noun* an owner, especially of a shop, hotel, business, etc. [from Latin *proprietarius*, from *proprietas*, ownership]

▤ owner, landlord, landlady, title-holder, freeholder, leaseholder, landowner, possessor.

proprietorial /prəpraɪəˈtɔːrɪəl/ *adj.* **1** having the position of proprietor. **2** characteristic of a proprietor.

proprietress *noun* a female proprietor.

propriety /prəˈpraɪətɪ/ *noun* (PL. **proprieties**) **1** socially acceptable behaviour, especially between the sexes; modesty or decorum. **2** rightness; moral acceptability: *the dubious propriety of getting children to report on their teachers.* **3** (**proprieties**) the details of correct behaviour; accepted standards of conduct: *observe the proprieties.* [from Middle English *propriete*, one's own nature, from Old French, from Latin *proprietas*, ownership]

proprioceptor *noun Zool.* a cell or group of cells that is sensitive to movement, pressure, or stretching within the body. Proprioceptors play an important role in the maintenance of balance and posture, and the coordination of muscular activity. [from Latin *proprius*, own]

props *noun Theatr.* a property man or property mistress.

propulsion *noun* the process of driving, or of being driven, forward; a force that propels: *jet propulsion.* [from Latin *propulsio*]

propulsive *adj.* having a tendency to propel or the quality of propelling; driving forward.

propylaeum /prɒpɪˈliːəm/ or **propylon** /ˈprɒpɪlɒn/ *noun* (PL. **propylaea, propyla**) *Archit.* in classical architecture, a monumental entrance gateway or vestibule, usually in front of a temple. A famous example is the Propylaea at the W of the Acropolis, Athens, built 437–432 BC. [from Greek *propylaion*, and *propylon*, from *pro*, before + *pyle*, a gate]

pro rata /proʊ ˈrɑːtə/ in proportion; in accordance with a certain rate. [from Latin *pro rata*]

prorogation *noun* proroguing.

prorogue /prəˈroʊg/ *verb* **1** to discontinue the meetings of (a legislative assembly) for a time, without dissolving it. **2** *intrans.*, *said of a legislative assembly* to suspend a session. [from Latin *prorogare*, to propose, continue, defer]

prosaic /proʊˈzeɪɪk/ *adj.* **1** unpoetic; unimaginative. **2** dull, ordinary and uninteresting. [from Latin *prosaicus*, from *prosa*, prose]

prosaically *adv.* in a prosaic way.

pros and cons advantages and disadvantages. [from Latin *pro*, in favour of, and *contra*, against]

proscenium /proʊˈsiːnɪəm/ *noun* (PL. **prosceniums, proscenia**) *Theatr.* **1** the part of a stage in front of the curtain. **2** (*also* **proscenium arch**) the arch framing the stage and separating it from the auditorium. [from Greek *proskenion*, from *pro*, in front + *skene*, stage]

prosciutto /proʊˈʃuːtoʊ/ *noun* finely cured uncooked ham, often smoked. [Italian, = pre-dried]

proscribe *verb* **1** to prohibit or condemn (something, eg a practice). **2** *Hist.* to outlaw or exile (someone). [from Latin *proscribere*, to outlaw]

proscription *noun* proscribing or being proscribed.

proscriptive *adj.* characterized by proscribing; tending to proscribe.

prose *noun* **1** ordinary written or spoken language as distinct from verse or poetry. **2** a passage of prose set for translation into a foreign language. [from Latin *prosa oratio*, straightforward speech]

prosecute *verb* **1** *trans., intrans.* to bring a criminal action against (someone). **2** *formal* to carry on or carry out: *prosecuting her enquiries.* [from Latin *prosequi*, to pursue]

▤ **1** prefer charges, take to court, indict, sue, litigate, summon, put on trial, try, accuse.
▣ **1** defend.

prosecution *noun* **1** the act of prosecuting or process of being prosecuted. **2** the bringing of a criminal action against someone. **3** (*sing., pl.*) the prosecuting party in a criminal case, or the lawyers involved in this. **4** *formal* the process of carrying something out: *in the prosecution of my duties.*

prosecutor *noun* a person who brings or conducts a criminal action against someone.

proselyte /ˈprɒsəlaɪt/ *noun* a convert, especially to Judaism. [from Greek *proselytos*, new arrival, convert to Judaism]

proselytism /ˈprɒsəlɪtɪzm/ *noun* **1** the process of becoming a convert; conversion. **2** the practice of making converts.

proselytize or **proselytise** /ˈprɒsəlɪtaɪz/ *verb trans., intrans.* to try to convert; to make converts.

prose poem a work or passage printed continuously as prose but having many of the elements found in poetry (eg striking imagery, rhythm, internal rhyme).

prosodic /prəˈsɒdɪk/ *adj.* relating to or characterized by prosody.

prosodics /prəˈsɒdɪks/ *sing. noun* same as PROSODY 2.

prosodist /ˈprɒsədɪst/ *noun* a person skilled in prosody.

prosody /ˈprɒsədɪ/ *noun* **1** the study of verse composition, especially poetic metre. **2** the study of rhythm, stress, and intonation in speech. [from Greek *prosoidia*, from *pros*, to + *oide*, song]

prospect — *noun* (with stress on *pros*-) **1** a visualization of something due or likely to happen: *the prospect of losing her job.* **2** an outlook for the future. **3** (**prospects**) chances of success, improvement, recovery, etc. **4** (**prospects**) opportunities for advancement: *a job with prospects.* **5** a potentially selectable candidate, team member, etc: *is a doubtful prospect for Saturday's match.* **6** a potential client or customer. **7** a broad view: *a prospect of the bay.* **8** Gold-mining an area with potential as a mine. — *verb* (with stress on *-spect*) *intrans.* (**prospect for**) **1** to search for (gold, etc). **2** to hunt for or look out for (eg a job). — **in prospect** expected soon. [from Latin *prospectus*, view]

▤ *noun* **1** probability, likelihood, possibility, expectation, anticipation. **2** outlook, forecast, prognosis. **3** chance(s), odds, prognosis. **4** future, opportunities. **5** possibility, candidate.

prospective *adj.* likely or expected; future: *a prospective buyer.*

▤ likely, expected, future, possible, probable, potential, aspiring, would-be, -to-be, intended, designate, destined, forthcoming, approaching, coming, imminent, awaited, anticipated.
▣ current.

prospector *noun* a person prospecting for oil, gold, etc.

prospectus noun (**prospectuses**) 1 a booklet giving information about a school or other institution; a brochure. 2 a document outlining a proposal for something, eg a literary work, or an issue of shares. [from Latin prospectus, prospect]

■ 1 brochure, pamphlet, leaflet, catalogue, list. 2 outline, synopsis, plan, scheme, syllabus, programme, manifesto.

prosper verb intrans. (**prospered, prospering**) to do well, especially financially; to thrive or flourish. [from Latin prosperari, to prosper]

■ thrive, flourish, flower, bloom, boom, succeed, get on, advance, progress, grow rich.
Ea fail.

prosperity noun the state of being prosperous; success; wealth.

■ success, good fortune, wealth, affluence, riches, fortune, wellbeing, luxury, the good life, boom, plenty.
Ea adversity, poverty.

prosperous adj. wealthy and successful.

■ wealthy, successful, rich, affluent, well off, well-to-do, thriving, flourishing, blooming, booming, fortunate, lucky.
Ea unfortunate, poor.

prosperously adv. in a prosperous way.

prostaglandin noun Physiol. any of a group of hormones that are secreted by many of the body tissues and have a wide range of specific effects (eg the regulation of kidney function and the contraction or relaxation of smooth muscle). Prostaglandins are sometimes used therapeutically to induce contractions of the uterus, either to accelerate labour or to induce abortion.

prostate noun (in full **prostate gland**) Anat. in male mammals, a muscular gland around the base of the bladder, controlled by sex hormones, which produces an alkaline fluid that activates sperm during ejaculation. [from Greek prostates, literally 'one that stands in front']

prosthesis noun (PL. **prostheses**) 1 Medicine an artificial substitute for a part of the body that is missing (as a result of surgery or injury) or non-functional, eg an artificial eye, hand, limb, breast, or pacemaker. 2 the fitting of such a part to the body. [from Greek, from pros, to + tithenai, to put]

prostitute — noun a person, especially a woman or homosexual man, who accepts money in return for sexual intercourse or sexual acts. — verb 1 to put (eg one's talents) to an unworthy use. 2 to offer (oneself or someone else) as a prostitute. [from Latin prostituere, to offer for sale]

prostitution noun the act or practice of prostituting.

prostrate — adj. (with stress on pros-) 1 lying face downwards in an attitude of abject submission, humility or adoration. 2 lying flat. 3 exhausted by illness, grief, etc. — verb (with stress on -strate) 1 to throw (oneself) face down in submission or adoration. 2 to exhaust physically or emotionally. [from Latin prosternere, to throw forwards]

■ adj. 1 prone. 2 prone, flat, horizontal, supine. 3 exhausted, overcome, overwhelmed, crushed, paralysed, powerless, helpless, defenceless, fallen. verb 1 abase oneself, bow down, kneel, kowtow, submit. 2 exhaust, overcome, overwhelm, crush, lay low, drain, tire, wear out, fatigue, overthrow, ruin.

prostration noun the act of prostrating.

prosy adj. (**prosier, prosiest**) said of speech or writing dull and tedious.

prot- see PROTO-.

protactinium noun (SYMBOL **Pa,** ATOMIC NUMBER **91**) a radioactive metallic element that occurs in all uranium ores. [from PROTO- + ACTINIUM]

protagonist noun 1 the main character in a play or story. 2 the person, or any of the people, at the centre of a story or event. 3 a leader or champion of a movement, cause, etc. [from Greek protagonistes, from protos, first + agonistes, combatant]

■ 1 hero, heroine, lead. 2 principal. 3 leader, prime mover, champion, advocate, supporter, proponent, exponent.

protea /ˈprəʊtɪə/ noun Bot. any plant of the S African genus Protea of shrubs and small trees.

protean /prəʊˈtɪən/ adj. 1 readily able to change shape or appearance; variable; changeable. 2 versatile; diverse. [from Proteus, a Greek sea god able to assume different shapes]

protease /ˈprəʊtɪeɪs/ noun Biochem. any enzyme that breaks down proteins. [from Greek proteios primary]

protect verb 1 to shield from danger; to guard against injury, destruction, etc; to keep safe. 2 to cover against loss, etc by insurance. 3 to shield (home industries) from foreign competition by taxing imports. [from Latin protegere, to cover in front, protect]

■ 1 safeguard, defend, guard, escort, screen, shield, secure, watch over, look after, care for, support, shelter, harbour, keep, conserve, preserve, save. 2 cover, insure, indemnify.
Ea 1 attack, neglect.

protection noun 1 the action of protecting or condition of being protected; shelter, refuge, cover, safety, or care. 2 something that protects: grow a hedge as a protection against the wind. 3 the system of protecting home industries against foreign competition by taxing imports. 4 the criminal practice of extorting money from shop-owners, etc in return for leaving their premises unharmed; (also **protection money**) the money so extorted. 5 insurance cover.

■ 1 care, custody, charge, guardianship, safekeeping, conservation, preservation, safety, safeguard. 2 barrier, buffer, bulwark, defence, guard, shield, armour, screen, cover, shelter, refuge, security, insurance, safeguard. 5 insurance, assurance, cover, indemnity.
Ea 1 neglect, attack.

protectionism noun the policy of protecting home industry from foreign competition.

protectionist noun a person who favours protectionism.

protective adj. 1 giving, or designed to give, protection. 2 inclined or tending to protect: feel protective towards one's children.

■ 1 waterproof, fireproof, insulating. 2 possessive, defensive, motherly, maternal, fatherly, paternal, watchful, vigilant, careful.

protective custody the detention of someone in prison, officially for his or her own safety.

protectively adv. in a protective way.

protectiveness noun being protective.

protector noun 1 a person or thing that protects. 2 a patron or benefactor. 3 a person ruling a country during the childhood of the sovereign, or in the absence of a sovereign; a regent.

protectorate /prəˈtektərət/ noun 1 the office, or period of rule, of a protector. 2 protectorship of a weak or backward country assumed by a more powerful one; the status of a territory that is so protected without actual annexation.

protectress noun a female protector.

protégé or **protégée** /'prəʊtəʒeɪ/ noun a man or woman under the guidance, protection, and patronage of a more important or wiser person. [from French protéger, to protect]

protein noun Biochem. any of a group of thousands of different organic compounds that are present in all living organisms and have large molecules consisting of long chains of amino acids. [from Greek proteios, primary]

pro tem colloq. short for pro tempore (Latin), for the time being.

Proterozoic /prəʊtərəʊ'zəʊɪk/ adj. Geol. denoting the eon of geological time between the Archaean and Phanerozoic eons, lasting from about 2500 million years ago until the beginning of the Cambrian period about 580 million years ago. It is usually regarded as representing the second of the two major subdivisions of the Precambrian, but is sometimes used to refer to the entire Precambrian. [from Greek proteros, earlier + zoe, life]

protest — verb 1 intrans. to express an objection, disapproval, opposition or disagreement. 2 North Amer., esp. US to challenge or object to (eg a decision or measure). 3 to declare solemnly, eg in response to an accusation: protest one's innocence. 4 Legal to obtain or write a protest with reference to (a bill). — noun 1 a declaration of disapproval or dissent; an objection. 2 an organized public demonstration of disapproval. 3 Legal a written statement that a bill has been presented and payment refused. — under protest reluctantly; unwillingly. [from Latin protestari, to declare, testify]

. . . .
■ verb 1 object, disapprove, disagree, argue, take exception, complain, appeal, demonstrate. 3 assert, maintain, contend, insist, profess. noun 1 objection, disapproval, opposition, dissent, complaint, protestation, outcry, appeal.
◪ verb 1 accept. noun 1 acceptance.
. . . .

Protestant — noun a member of any of the Christian Churches which in the 16c embraced the principles of the Reformation and, rejecting the authority of the pope, separated from the Roman Catholic Church; a member of any body descended from these. — adj. relating to or belonging to Protestants. [originally applied to those princes and others who in 1529 protested against an edict denouncing the Reformation]

Protestantism noun the beliefs and practices of Protestants.

protestation noun 1 a protest or objection. 2 a solemn declaration or avowal.

protester or **protestor** noun a person who protests.
. . . .
■ rebel, dissident, dissenter, demonstrator, agitator.
. . . .

prothrombin /prəʊ'θrɒmbɪn/ noun Biochem. one of the clotting factors in blood, which is manufactured in the liver and converted to the enzyme thrombin, which catalyses the conversion of the soluble protein fibrinogen to the insoluble protein fibrin.

Protista /prəʊ'tɪstə/ pl. noun Biol. in the classification of animals and plants, the kingdom that includes algae, bacteria, fungi, and protozoans. [from Greek protistos very first, from protos first]

proto- or **prot-** combining form forming words meaning 'first, earliest': prototype. [from Greek protos, first]

protocol noun 1 correct formal or diplomatic etiquette or procedure. 2 a first draft of a diplomatic document, eg setting out the terms of a treaty. 3 North Amer., esp. US a plan of a scientific experiment or other procedure. [from Greek protokollon, a note of the contents of a document, glued to the front sheet, from protos, first + kolla, glue]
. . . .
■ 1 procedure, formalities, convention, custom, etiquette, manners, good form, propriety.
. . . .

Proto-Indo-European — noun the parent language from which all Indo-European languages are descended, thought to have been spoken throughout Europe and S Asia before 3000 BC. — adj. relating to this parent language.

proton noun Physics any of the positively charged subatomic particles that are found inside the nucleus at the centre of an atom, together with uncharged particles known as neutrons. Protons are slightly lighter than neutrons but about 1850 times heavier than electrons. The number of protons in the nucleus is known as the atomic number. The mass of a proton is 1.672×10^{-27} kg, and it carries a charge of 1.602×10^{-19} coulombs. [from Greek protos, first]

protoplasm noun the translucent, colourless, semi-liquid substance of which living cells are chiefly composed. [from PROTO- + Greek plasma, form]

prototype noun 1 an original model from which later forms are copied, developed or derived. 2 a first working version, eg of a vehicle, aircraft, etc. 3 a person or thing that exemplifies a type. 4 a primitive or ancestral form of something. [from Greek prototypos, primitive, original]

protozoan — noun a single-celled organism belonging to the phylum Protozoa, a subkingdom of single-celled organisms that include both plant-like and animal-like forms, eg amoeba, Paramecium. Many protozoans are parasitic, and some cause important diseases, eg Plasmodium, the malaria parasite. — adj. relating to the Protozoa. [from PROTO- + Greek zoion, animal]

protozoon noun same as PROTOZOAN.

protract verb to prolong; to cause to last a long time. [from Latin protrahere, to drag forth, prolong]

protracted adj. lasting longer than usual or longer than expected.
. . . .
■ long, lengthy, prolonged, extended, drawn-out, long-drawn-out, overlong, interminable.
◪ brief, shortened.
. . . .

protractor noun Geom. an instrument, usually a transparent plastic semicircle marked in degrees, for drawing and measuring angles. [from Latin, from protrahere, to draw forth]

protrude verb 1 intrans. to project; to stick out. 2 trans. to push out or forward. [from Latin protrudere, to thrust forward]
. . . .
■ 1 stick out, poke out, come through, bulge, jut out, project, extend, stand out, obtrude. 2 stick out, poke out, project, extend.
. . . .

protrusion noun 1 protruding. 2 something which protrudes.

protrusive adj. thrusting forward, protruding.

protuberance noun a bulging out, a swelling.

protuberant adj. projecting; bulging; swelling out. [from Latin protuberare, to swell out]

proud adj. 1 (often **proud of someone** or **something**) feeling pride at one's own or another's accomplishments, one's possessions, etc. 2 being a cause or occasion for pride: a proud day/her proudest possession. 3 arrogant; conceited: too proud to talk to us. 4 concerned for one's dignity and self-respect: too proud to accept help. 5 honoured; gratified; delighted: proud to be invited. 6 splendid; imposing: a proud sight. 7 poetic lofty; high: trees waving their proud tops. 8 projecting slightly from the surrounding surface. 9 said of flesh forming a protuberant mass round a healing wound. — **do someone proud** to entertain or treat them grandly. **do oneself proud** to succeed gloriously. [from Anglo-Saxon prud]
. . . .
■ 1 gratified, pleased, delighted, satisfied, contented. 2 noble, honourable, worthy. 3 conceited, arrogant, self-important, cocky, presumptuous, haughty, high and mighty, vain, egotistical, big-headed, boastful, smug, complacent,

overbearing, supercilious, *colloq.* snooty, snobbish, *colloq.* toffee-nosed, *colloq.* stuck-up. **4** self-respecting, dignified. **5** gratified, pleased, delighted, honoured. **6** splendid, grand, imposing, glorious, magnificent, outstanding, noble, honourable, worthy.

⊟ 1 ashamed. **2** ignoble. **3** humble, modest, unassuming, deferential.

proudly *adv.* in a proud way.
provable or **proveable** *adj.* capable of being proved.
prove *verb* (PAST PARTICIPLE **proved, proven**) **1** to show to be true, correct or a fact. **2** to show to be: *was proved innocent/drugs of proven effectiveness.* **3** *intrans.* to be found to be, when tried; to turn out to be: *her advice proved sound.* **4** to show (oneself) to be: *has proved himself reliable.* **5** to show (oneself) capable or daring. **6** *Legal* to establish the validity of (a will). **7** *said of dough* to rise or cause it to rise. — **not proven** *Scot. Legal* a verdict resorted to where there is insufficient evidence to prove guilt. [from Latin *probare*, to test, prove]

⊟ 1 show, demonstrate, verify, confirm, corroborate, substantiate, bear out, authenticate, validate, establish. **2** show, demonstrate, verify, confirm, authenticate, validate, establish, bear out, justify, attest, determine, ascertain, document, certify. **4, 5** show, demonstrate.
⊟ 1, 2 disprove, discredit, falsify.

provenance *noun* the place of origin, or source, of eg a work of art, archaeological find, etc. [from French *provenance,* from Latin *provenire,* to come forth]
Provençal /prɒvɒnˈsɑːl/ — *adj.* of or relating to Provence in the south of France, its inhabitants, culture, or language. — *noun* **1** a language spoken in Provence, related to French and Spanish. **2** a native of Provence.
provender /ˈprɒvɪndə(r)/ *noun* **1** dry food for livestock, eg corn and hay. **2** *facetious* food. [from Old French *provendre,* from Latin *praebenda,* payment]
proverb *noun* any of a body of well-known, neatly expressed sayings that give advice or express a supposed truth. [from Latin *proverbium*]

⊟ saying, adage, aphorism, maxim, byword, dictum, precept.

proverbial *adj.* **1** of, like or being a proverb. **2** referred to in a proverb; traditionally quoted; well known: *a cat's proverbial nine lives.*

⊟ 1 axiomatic. **2** conventional, traditional, customary, time-honoured, famous, well known, legendary, notorious, typical, archetypal.

proverbially *adv.* in a proverbial way; by tradition or reputation.
provide *verb* **1** to supply. **2** *said eg of a circumstance, situation, etc* to offer: *provide enjoyment/provide an opportunity.* **3** *intrans.* (**provide for** or **against something**) to be prepared for an unexpected contingency, an emergency, etc. **4** *intrans.* (**provide for someone**) to support or keep a dependant. **5** *chiefly Legal* to stipulate or require (that something should be done, etc). **6** *intrans.* (**provide for something**) *chiefly Legal* to specify it as a requirement, or enable it to be done. [from Latin *providere,* to see ahead, provide for]

⊟ 1 supply, furnish, stock, equip, outfit, prepare for, cater, serve, contribute. **2** offer, present, give, extend, hold out, furnish, yield, lend, add, bring. **3** plan for, prepare for, allow for, make provision for, accommodate, arrange for, take precautions against. **4** support, keep, maintain. **5, 6** stipulate, specify, lay down, require, state.
⊟ 1 take, remove.

provided or **providing (that)** *conj.* **1** on the condition or understanding that. **2** if and only if.

⊟ WITH THE PROVISO THAT, GIVEN THAT, AS LONG AS, ON CONDITION THAT, ON THE UNDERSTANDING THAT.

providence *noun* **1** a mysterious power or force that operates to keep one from harm, etc; the benevolent foresight of God. **2** (**Providence**) God or Nature regarded as an all-seeing protector of the world. **3** the quality of being provident; prudent foresight or thrifty planning. [from Latin *providentia,* foresight]

⊟ 1 fate, destiny, divine intervention, God's will, fortune, luck. **3** prudence, foresight, far-sightedness, thrift, caution, care.
⊟ 3 improvidence.

provident *adj.* careful and thrifty in planning ahead.

⊟ careful, thrifty, prudent, far-sighted, judicious, cautious, economical, frugal.
⊟ improvident.

providential *adj.* due to providence; fortunate; lucky; opportune.

⊟ fortunate, lucky, timely, opportune, convenient, happy, welcome, heaven-sent.
⊟ untimely.

providentially *adv.* in a providential way.
providently *adv.* in a provident way.
provider *noun* a person who provides, a supplier.
province *noun* **1** an administrative division of a country. **2** *Roman Hist.* a territory outside Italy, governed by Rome as part of its empire. **3** one's allotted range of duties, or one's field of knowledge or experience: *a task outside my province.* **4** (**the provinces**) the parts of a country away from the capital, typically thought of as culturally backward. [from Latin *provincia,* official charge, province]

⊟ 1 region, area, district, zone, county, shire, department, territory, colony, dependency. **3** responsibility, concern, duty, office, role, function, field, sphere, domain, department, line. **4** *colloq.* the sticks, the backwaters, the backwoods.

provincial *adj.* **1** of, belonging to, or relating to a province. **2** relating to the parts of a country away from the capital: *a provincial accent.* **3** supposedly typical of provinces in being culturally backward, unsophisticated, or narrow in outlook. [from Latin *provincialis,* from *provincia,* province]

⊟ 2 regional, local, rural, rustic, country. **3** home-grown, small-town, parish-pump, parochial, insular, inward-looking, limited, narrow, narrow-minded, small-minded.
⊟ NATIONAL, COSMOPOLITAN. **3** sophisticated.

provincialism *noun* **1** being provincial. **2** the attitude, behaviour, or speech peculiar to a province or country district. **3** a local expression. **4** ignorance and narrowness of interests.
provincially *adv.* in a provincial way or capacity.
proving-ground *noun* a place used for scientific testing; a place where something is tried out for the first time.
provision — *noun* **1** the act of providing. **2** something provided or made available; facilities: *provision for disabled pupils.* **3** preparations; measures taken in advance: *make provision for the future.* **4** (**provisions**) food and other necessaries. **5** *Legal* a condition or requirement; a clause stipulating or enabling something. — *verb* (**provisioned,**

provisioning) to supply with food. [from Latin *provisio*, forethought, precaution]

- *noun* **1** supply. **2** facilities, amenities, services, resources. **3** plans, arrangements, preparations, measures, precautions. **4** food, foodstuff, groceries, *colloq.* eatables, sustenance, rations, supplies, stocks, stores. **5** condition, requirement, proviso, stipulation, specification, term.

provisional *adj.* temporary; conditional; for the time being, or immediate purposes, only; liable to be altered.

- temporary, conditional, interim, transitional, stopgap, makeshift, tentative.
- permanent, fixed, definite.

provisionally *adv.* for the time being, temporarily.

proviso *noun* (PL. **provisos**) **1** a condition: *agreed, with one proviso.* **2** *Legal* a clause stating a condition. [from Latin *proviso quod*, it being provided that]

- CONDITION, REQUIREMENT, STIPULATION, QUALIFICATION, RESERVATION, RESTRICTION, LIMITATION, PROVISION, RIDER.

provisory *adj.* **1** containing a proviso or condition, conditional. **2** making provision for the time being, temporary.

provocateur see AGENT PROVOCATEUR.

provocation *noun* **1** the act of provoking or state of being provoked; incitement. **2** a cause of anger, irritation, or indignation. [from Latin *provocatio*, calling forth, challenge]

- **1** incitement, instigation, annoyance, *colloq.* aggravation, vexation, taunt, challenge, dare. **2** cause, grounds, justification, reason, motive, stimulus, motivation, grievance, offence, insult, affront, injury.

provocative *adj.* **1** tending, or intended, to cause anger; deliberately infuriating. **2** sexually arousing or stimulating, especially by design: *provocative clothes/provocative behaviour.*

- **1** annoying, *colloq.* aggravating, galling, outrageous, offensive, insulting, abusive. **2** erotic, titillating, arousing, sexy, seductive, alluring, tempting, inviting, tantalizing, teasing, suggestive.
- **1** conciliatory.

provocatively *adv.* in a provocative way.

provoke *verb* **1** to annoy or infuriate, especially deliberately. **2** to incite or goad. **3** to rouse (someone's anger, etc). **4** to cause, stir up or bring about: *provoked a storm of protest.* [from Latin *provocare*, to call forth, challenge, stimulate]

- **1** annoy, irritate, rile, *colloq.* aggravate, offend, insult, anger, enrage, infuriate, incense, madden, exasperate. **2** incite, goad, tease, taunt. **3, 4** cause, occasion, bring about, give rise to, rouse, produce, generate, induce, elicit, evoke, excite, inspire, move, stir up, prompt, stimulate, motivate, incite, instigate.
- **1** please, pacify.

provoking *adj.* annoying.

provost *noun* **1** the head of some university colleges. **2** in Scotland, the chief magistrate of a burgh. [from Old French, from Latin *propositus*, placed at the head]

provost marshal an officer in charge of military police.

prow *noun* the projecting front part of a ship; the bow. [from French *proue*]

prowess *noun* **1** skill; ability; expertise. **2** valour; dauntlessness. [from Old French *proesse*]

- **1** skill, ability, expertise, accomplishment, attainment, aptitude, mastery, command, talent, genius.

prowl — *verb intrans.* **1** to go about stealthily, eg in search of prey. **2** to pace restlessly. — *noun* an act of prowling. — **on the prowl** prowling about menacingly. [from Middle English *prollen*]

prowler *noun* a person who prowls.

proxemics /prɒkˈsiːmɪks/ *sing. noun* the study of how people use physical space as an aspect of non-verbal communication. It is concerned with the intimate, personal, social, and public distances that individuals, classes, and cultures maintain in their interactions with each other. [from PROXIMITY]

Proxima Centauri /ˈprɒksɪmə senˈtɔːraɪ/ *Astron.* the closest star to the Sun, and a faint companion to the double star Alpha Centauri in the constellation Centaurus.

proximal *adj. Biol.* pertaining to or situated at the inner end, nearest to the point of attachment. [from Latin *proximus*, next]

proximate *adj.* nearest; immediately before or after in time, place, or order of occurrence. [from Latin *proximare*, to approach]

proximity *noun* nearness; closeness in space or time: *lives in close proximity to the station.* [from Latin *proximitas*, from *proximus*, next]

- closeness, nearness, vicinity, neighbourhood, adjacency, juxtaposition.
- remoteness.

proxy *noun* (PL. **proxies**) **1** a person authorized to act or vote on another's behalf; the agency of such a person. **2** the authority to act or vote for someone else, or a document granting this. [a contraction of PROCURACY]

- **1** agent, factor, deputy, stand-in, substitute, representative, delegate, attorney. **2** power of attorney.

Prozac *noun trademark* an anti-depressant drug that increases the levels of serotonin in the central nervous system.

PRP *abbrev.* **1** profit related pay. **2** performance related pay.

PRS *abbrev.* Performing Rights Society.

prude *noun* a person who is or affects to be shocked by improper behaviour, mention of sexual matters, etc; a prim or priggish person. [from French *prude femme*, respectable woman]

prudence *noun* **1** being prudent. **2** caution, descretion. **3** taking care of one's resources or one's own interests.

prudent *adj.* **1** wise or careful in conduct. **2** shrewd or thrifty in planning ahead. **3** wary; discreet: *a prudent withdrawal.* [from Latin *prudens*, contracted from *providens*, from *providere*, to see ahead]

- WISE, SENSIBLE, POLITIC, JUDICIOUS, SHREWD, DISCERNING, CAREFUL, CAUTIOUS, WARY, VIGILANT, CIRCUMSPECT, DISCREET, PROVIDENT, FAR-SIGHTED, THRIFTY.
- IMPRUDENT, UNWISE, CARELESS, RASH.

prudential *adj. old use* characterized by, or exercising, careful forethought. [from Latin *prudentialis*, from *prudentia*, prudence]

prudently *adv.* in a prudent way.

prudery *noun* **1** being prudish. **2** prudish opinions or behaviour.

prudish *adj.* having the character of or being like a prude.

prudishly *adv.* in a prudish way.

prudishness *noun* being prudish, prudish behaviour.

prune[1] — *verb* **1** to cut off (unneeded branches, etc) from (a tree or shrub) to improve its growth. **2** to cut out (superfluous matter) from (a piece of writing, etc); to trim or edit. — *noun* an act of pruning. [from Old French *proognier*, to prune (vines)]

prune² *noun* a dried plum. [from Latin *prunum*, plum]

pruning-hook *noun* a garden tool with a curved blade, for pruning.

prurience *noun* marked or excessive interest in sexual matters.

prurient *adj.* 1 unhealthily or excessively interested in sexual matters. 2 tending to arouse such unhealthy interest. [from Latin *prurire*, to itch, lust after]

pruriently *adv.* in a prurient way.

pruritis /prʊəˈraɪtəs/ *noun Medicine* itching. [from Latin *prurire*, to itch]

Prussian — *adj.* relating to Prussia. — *noun* a native or inhabitant of Prussia.

Prussian blue a deep blue pigment first made in Berlin; its colour.

prussic acid a deadly poison first obtained from Prussian blue; a solution of hydrogen cyanide in water.

pry¹ *verb intrans.* (**pries**, **pried**) 1 (*also* **pry into something**) to investigate matters that do not concern one, especially the personal affairs of others; to nose or snoop. 2 to peer or peep inquisitively. [from Middle English *prien*]

          ⊟ 1 meddle, interfere, intrude, *colloq.* poke one's nose in, nose, snoop, ferret, dig, delve. 2 peep, peer, snoop.
          ⊟ 1 mind one's own business.

pry² *verb* (**pries**, **pried**) *North Amer., esp. US* to prise. [from PRISE, regarded as *pries*, which suggested a notional form *pry*]

PS *abbrev.* postscript.

PSA *abbrev.* Property Services Agency.

psalm /sɑːm/ *noun* a sacred song, especially one from the Book of Psalms in the Old Testament, traditionally attributed to King David. [from Greek *psalmos*, song sung to a harp]

psalmist /ˈsɑːmɪst/ *noun* a composer of psalms.

psalmody /ˈsalmədɪ, ˈsɑːmədɪ/ *noun* 1 the art of singing psalms. 2 a collected body of psalms. [from Greek *psalmos*, psalm + *oide*, song]

psalter /ˈsɔːltə(r)/ *noun* 1 (**Psalter**) the Book of Psalms. 2 a book containing the Biblical psalms. [from Greek *psalterion*, stringed instrument]

psaltery /ˈsɔːltərɪ/ *noun* (PL. **psalteries**) *Hist.* a zither-like stringed instrument played by plucking. [from Greek *psalterion*, stringed instrument, harp]

PSBR *abbrev.* public-sector borrowing requirement, the money needed by the public sector to finance services, etc not covered by revenue.

psephological /sefəˈlɒdʒɪkəl/ *adj.* relating to or involving psephology.

psephologist /seˈfɒlədʒɪst/ *noun* a person who studies or is expert in psephology.

psephology /seˈfɒlədʒɪ/ *noun* the study of elections and voting patterns. [from Greek *psephos*, pebble, vote + -LOGY]

pseud /sjuːd/ *colloq.* — *noun* a pretentious person; a bogus intellectual; a phoney. — *adj.* bogus, sham or phoney. [see PSEUDO]

pseudo /ˈsjuːdəʊ/ *adj. colloq.* false; sham; phoney.

pseudo- /ˈsjuːdəʊ/ or **pseud-** /sjuːd/ *combining form* forming words meaning: 1 false. 2 pretending to be: *pseudo-intellectuals.* 3 deceptively resembling: *pseudo-scientific jargon.* [from Greek *pseudes*, false]

pseudocarp /ˈsjuːdəʊkɑːp/ *noun Bot.* false fruit.

pseudonym /ˈsjuːdənɪm/ *noun* a false name used by an author; a pen name or nom-de-plume. [from Greek *pseudes*, false + *onyma*, name]

          ⊟ false name, assumed name, alias, incognito, pen

name, nom-de-plume, stage name.

pseudonymous /sjuːˈdɒnɪməs/ *adj.* 1 assuming a false name, especially as an author. 2 written under a pseudonym.

pseudopodium /sjuːdəʊˈpəʊdɪəm/ *noun* (PL. **pseudopodia**) *Zool.* any of a number of temporary lobe-like protrusions from the cell of a protozoan (eg amoeba), produced by the streaming of cytoplasm into a projection that gradually increases in length, and is used as a means of locomotion, as well as for engulfing food particles. [from PSEUDO- + Greek *pous, podos*, foot]

psi *abbrev.* pounds per square inch, a unit of pressure measurement.

psittacosis /sɪtəˈkəʊsɪs/ *noun* a disease of parrots that can be transmitted to human beings. [from Greek *psittakos*, parrot + -OSIS]

psoriasis /səˈraɪəsɪs/ *noun Medicine* a common non-contagious skin disease characterized by red patches covered with white scales, mainly on the elbows, knees, scalp, and trunk. The cause of the disease is unknown, although attacks may be triggered by stress, injury, or drugs. It is usually hereditary. [from Greek, from *psora*, itch]

PSV *abbrev.* public service vehicle.

psych /saɪk/ *verb colloq.* 1 (**be psyched up**) to prepare or steel oneself for a challenge, etc. 2 (**psych someone out**) to undermine the confidence of an opponent, etc; to intimidate or demoralize them. 3 to psychoanalyse. [a shortening of PSYCHOLOGICAL and related words]

psych- see PSYCHO-.

psyche /ˈsaɪkɪ/ *noun* one's mind, especially with regard to the deep feelings and attitudes that account for one's opinions and behaviour. [from Greek *psyche*]

psychedelic /saɪkəˈdɛlɪk/ *adj.* 1 denoting a state of mind with heightened perceptions and increased mental powers. 2 *said of a drug* inducing such a state. 3 *said of perceived phenomena, eg colour* startlingly clear and vivid. [from PSYCHE + Greek *delos*, clear]

psychedelic art an art style of the late 1960s, influenced by the prevalence of hallucinatory drugs, especially LSD. Typical designs feature abstract swirls of intense colour with curvilinear calligraphy reminiscent of Art Nouveau.

psychiatric /saɪkɪˈatrɪk/ *adj.* relating to or involving psychiatry.

psychiatrist /saɪˈkaɪətrɪst/ *noun* an expert in or practitioner of psychiatry.

psychiatry /saɪˈkaɪətrɪ/ *noun* the branch of medicine concerned with the study, diagnosis, treatment, and prevention of mental and emotional disorders, including psychoses, neuroses, depression, eating disorders, childhood behavioural problems, drug and alcohol dependence, schizophrenia, and mental handicap. The main forms of psychiatric treatment are psychotherapy, and the use of certain drugs to relieve symptoms. There is a considerable overlap between psychiatry and clinical psychology. [from PSYCHO- + Greek *iatros*, doctor]

psychic /ˈsaɪkɪk/ *adj.* 1 (*also* **psychical**) relating to mental processes or experiences that are not scientifically explainable, eg telepathy. 2 *said of a person* sensitive to influences producing such experiences; having mental powers that are not scientifically explainable. [from Greek *psychikos*, relating to the psyche]

          ⊟ 1 spiritual, supernatural, telepathic, occult, mystic(al), extrasensory, mental, psychological, intellectual, cognitive. 2 clairvoyant, telepathic.

psycho /ˈsaɪkəʊ/ *colloq.* — *noun* (PL. **psychos**) a psychopath. — *adj.* psychopathic.

psycho- /ˈsaɪkəʊ/ or **psych-** /saɪk/ *combining form* forming words denoting the mind and its workings: *psychodrama/psychology.*

psychoanalyse or *North Amer.* **psychoanalyze** /saɪkəʊˈanəlaɪz/ *verb* to examine or treat by psychoanalysis.

psychoanalysis /saɪkəʊə'nalɪsɪs/ *noun Psychol.* a theory and method of treatment for mental disorders, pioneered by Sigmund Freud, which emphasizes the effects of unconscious motivation and conflict on a person's behaviour.

psychoanalyst /saɪkəʊ'anəlɪst/ *noun* a person who practises psychoanalysis.

psychoanalytic /saɪkəʊənə'lɪtɪk/ or **psychoanalytical** /saɪkəʊənə'lɪtɪkəl/ *adj.* relating to or involving psychoanalysis.

psychoanalytic criticism an approach to literary criticism using the analytic techniques and insights of psychoanalysis as described by Sigmund Freud, and applied by Freud himself to his reading of *Hamlet*, in terms of the Oedipus complex. It makes the assumption that the writer's unconscious desires may shape the text or that it is possible to analyse the characters by exposing their repressed emotions.

psychobabble *noun colloq.* language made impenetrable by the overuse of popular psychological jargon.

psychodrama *noun Psychol.* a technique involving a combination of behavioural and psychoanalytic psychotherapy in which, by acting out real-life situations, a patient learns new ways of dealing with both emotional and interpersonal problems.

psychological /saɪkə'lɒdʒɪkəl/ *adj.* relating to the mind or to psychology.

■ mental, cerebral, intellectual, cognitive, subconscious, unconscious, emotional, subjective, psychosomatic, irrational, unreal.

◼ physical, real.

psychologically *adv.* in a psychological way; as regards psychology.

psychological moment the moment at which one is most likely to succeed in influencing someone to react as one wants.

psychological warfare propaganda and other methods used in wartime to influence enemy opinion and sap enemy morale.

psychologist /saɪ'kɒlədʒɪst/ *noun* an expert in psychology.

psychology /saɪ'kɒlədʒɪ/ *noun* **1** the scientific study of the mind and behaviour of humans and animals. **2** the mental attitudes and associated behaviour characteristic of a certain individual or group: *mob psychology.* **3** the ability to understand how people's minds work, useful when trying to influence them: *good/bad psychology.*

psychometrics *sing. noun Psychol.* the branch of psychology concerned with the measurement of psychological characteristics, especially intelligence, personality, and mood states.

psychopath /'saɪkəpaθ/ *noun* **1** *technical* a person with a personality disorder characterized by extreme callousness, who is liable to behave antisocially or violently in getting his or her own way. **2** *colloq.* a person who is dangerously unstable mentally or emotionally. [from PSYCHO- + -PATH]

psychopathic *adj.* relating to or characteristic of a psychopath.

psychopathically *adv.* in a psychopathic way.

psychopathology *noun Medicine* **1** the scientific study of mental disorders, as opposed to the treatment of such disorders. **2** the symptoms of a mental disorder.

psychopathy /saɪ'kɒpəθɪ/ *noun Psychol.* a personality disorder characterized by an inability to form close relationships with other people, lack of social responsibility, and rejection of authority and discipline, with little or no guilt for antisocial behaviour such as violence and vandalism.

psychosis /saɪ'kəʊsɪs/ *noun* (PL. **psychoses**) *Psychol.* any of various severe mental disorders in which there is a loss of contact with reality, in the form of delusions (false beliefs) or hallucinations. [from Greek *psykhosis*, animation; in modern use, condition of the psyche]

psychosomatic /saɪkəʊsə'matɪk/ *adj. Medicine, said of physical symptoms or disorders* strongly associated with psychological factors, especially mental stress. Common psychosomatic disorders include peptic ulcers, eczema, and asthma. [from PSYCHO- + Greek *soma*, body]

psychosomatically *adv.* in a psychosomatic way.

psychosurgery *noun Psychol.* brain surgery that is performed with the aim of treating a mental disorder.

psychotherapist *noun* an expert in psychotherapy.

psychotherapy *noun Psychol.* the treatment of mental disorders and emotional and behavioural problems by psychological means, rather than by drugs or surgery.

psychotic /saɪ'kɒtɪk/ — *adj.* relating to or involving a psychosis. — *noun* a person suffering from a psychosis.

psychotically *adv.* in a psychotic way.

PT *abbrev.* physical training.

Pt[1] *abbrev.* Port.

Pt[2] *symbol Chem.* platinum.

pt *abbrev.* **1** part. **2** pint. **3** point.

PTA *abbrev.* Parent-Teacher Association.

ptarmigan /'tɑːmɪɡən/ *noun* a mountain-dwelling grouse with white winter plumage. [from Gaelic *tàrmachan*; the *p* wrongly added under the influence of Greek words beginning with *pt*]

Pte *abbrev. Mil.* Private, the title for an ordinary soldier.

pteridophyte /'terɪdəʊfaɪt/ *noun Bot.* any plant belonging to the division Pteridophyta (according to some classifications of the plant kingdom), which includes the ferns, clubmosses, and horsetails. [from Greek *pteris*, fern + *phyton*, plant]

pterodactyl *noun* same as PTEROSAUR. [from Greek *pteron*, wing + *daktylos*, finger]

pterosaur /'terəsɔː(r)/ *noun* an extinct flying reptile that lived during the Jurassic and Cretaceous periods (at the same time as the dinosaurs), and was similar in size to a present-day bird, with a fur-covered body and leathery wings. Formerly called PTERODACTYL. [from Greek *pteron*, wing, after DINOSAUR]

PTO *abbrev.* please turn over.

ptomaine /'təʊmeɪn/ *noun Biochem.* any of a group of organic compounds containing nitrogen, some of which are poisonous, produced during the bacterial decomposition of dead animal and plant matter, eg putrescine, cadaverine. [from Italian *ptomaina*, from Greek *ptoma*, corpse]

pty *abbrev.* proprietary.

ptyalin /'taɪəlɪn/ *noun Biochem.* in mammals, an enzyme present in the saliva that is responsible for the initial stages of breakdown of starch. [from Greek *ptyalon*, spittle]

Pu *symbol Chem.* plutonium.

pub *noun* a public house, a place where alcoholic drinks may be bought for consumption on the premises.

puberty *noun* the onset of sexual maturity in humans and other primates, when the secondary sexual characteristics appear and the reproductive organs become functional. It includes breast development and the start of menstruation in females, and deepening of the voice and sperm production in males. [from Latin *pubertas*]

■ pubescence, adolescence, teens, youth, growing up, maturity.

◼ childhood, immaturity, old age.

pubes *noun* (PL. **pubes**) **1** *Anat.* the pubic region of the lower abdomen; the groin. **2** the hair that grows on this part from puberty onward. [from Latin *pubes*]

pubescence *noun* **1** the onset of puberty. **2** a soft downy covering on plants. [from Latin *pubescere*, to reach puberty, become downy]

pubescent *adj.* reaching or having reached puberty.

pubic *adj.* relating to the pubis or pubes.

pubis *noun* (PL. **pubes**) *Anat.* in most vertebrates, one of the two bones forming the lower front part of each side of the pelvis. They meet at the *pubic symphysis*. [from Latin *os pubis*, bone of the pubes]

public — *adj.* **1** of, or concerning, all the people of a country or community: *public health/public opinion.* **2** relating to the organization and administration of a community: *the public prosecutor.* **3** provided for the use of the community: *public parks.* **4** well known through exposure in the media: *public figures.* **5** made, done, held, etc openly, for all to see, hear or participate in: *a public announcement/a public inquiry.* **6** known to all: *when the facts became public/is public knowledge/make one's views public.* **7** watched or attended by an audience, spectators, etc: *her last public appearance.* **8** open to view; not private or secluded: *it's too public here.* — *sing. or pl. noun* **1** the people or community. **2** a particular class of people: *the concert-going public.* **3** an author's, performer's, etc audience or group of devotees: *mustn't disappoint my public.* — **go public** to become a public company. **in public** in the presence of other people. **in the public eye** *said of a person, etc* well known through media exposure. [from Latin *publicus*, from *populus*, people]

⬛ *adj.* **1** common, general, universal, national, civil. **2** civil, community, social. **3** community, social, collective, communal, civil, state, national. **4, 6** known, well known, recognized, acknowledged, published, exposed. **5** open, unrestricted, overt, published. **8** exposed. *noun* **1** people, nation, country, population, populace, masses, citizens, society, community. **2** people, citizens, population, community. **3** audience, followers, supporters, fans, voters, electorate, patrons, clientèle, customers, buyers, consumers.

▨ *adj.* **1, 3** private, personal, individual. **5** private, secret, closed. **6** secret.

public-address system (ABBREV. **PA**) a system of microphones, amplifiers, and loudspeakers, by means of which public announcements, etc can be communicated over a large area.

publican *noun* **1** *Brit.* the keeper of a public house. **2** *Biblical* a tax-collector. [from Latin *publicanus*, tax-farmer]

publication *noun* **1** the act of publishing a printed work; the process of publishing or of being published. **2** a book, magazine, newspaper, or other printed and published work. **3** the act of making something known to the public.

⬛ **1** publishing, printing, release. **2** book, newspaper, magazine, periodical, booklet, leaflet, pamphlet, handbill. **3** announcement, declaration, notification, disclosure, publishing, printing, release, issue.

public bar a bar less well furnished and serving drinks more cheaply than a lounge bar.

public company a company whose shares are available for purchase by the public.

public convenience a public toilet.

public enemy someone whose behaviour threatens the community, especially a criminal.

public holiday a day kept as an official holiday, on which businesses, etc are closed.

public house an establishment where alcoholic drinks are sold for consumption on the premises; a pub.

⬛ *colloq.* pub, *colloq.* local, bar, inn, tavern, saloon.

publicity *noun* **1** advertising or other activity designed to rouse public interest in something. **2** public interest so attracted. **3** the condition of being the object of public attention.

⬛ **1** advertising, *colloq.* hype, promotion, build-up, boost, *colloq.* plug. **2** interest, attention, limelight.

publicize or **publicise** *verb* **1** to make generally or widely known. **2** to advertise.

⬛ BROADCAST, ADVERTISE, MAKE KNOWN, BLAZE, PROMOTE, SPOTLIGHT, PUSH, *colloq.* PLUG, *colloq.* HYPE.

public nuisance an illegal act causing trouble or danger to the general public.

public prosecutor a public official whose function is to prosecute those charged with criminal offences.

public relations (ABBREV. **PR**) **1** (*pl., sing.*) the relationship of an organization, etc with the public, especially with regard to its reputation and its communication of information about itself. **2** (*sing.*) the department of an organization responsible for this.

public school 1 in the UK, a secondary school run independently of the state, financed by endowments and by pupils' fees. **2** in the US, a school run by a public authority.

public sector that part of a country's economy consisting of nationalized industries and of institutions and services run by the state or local authorities.

public servant an elected or appointed holder of public office; a government employee.

public spending spending by a government or local authority, financed either by tax revenues or by borrowing. In the UK, public spending levels by various government departments (and by local government) are broadly determined by negotiation between the departments and the Treasury.

public-spirited *adj.* acting from, or showing, concern for the general good of all.

public utility a supply eg of gas, water or electricity, or other service, provided for a community.

public works buildings, roads, etc built by the state for public use.

publish *verb trans., intrans.* **1** to prepare, produce, and distribute (printed material, computer software, etc) for sale to the public. **2** *intrans., trans., said of an author* to have (one's work) published. **3** to publish the work of (an author). **4** to announce publicly: *published their engagement.* **5** *Legal* to circulate (a libel). [from Old French *publier*, from Latin *publicare*, to make public]

⬛ **1** produce, print, issue, bring out, distribute, circulate. **4** announce, declare, communicate, make known, divulge, disclose, reveal, release, publicize, advertise, spread, diffuse.

publisher *noun* **1** a person or company engaged in the business of publishing books, newspapers, music, software, etc. **2** *North Amer.* a newspaper proprietor.

publishing *noun* the activity or trade of a publisher, or of publishers collectively. It includes the selection or commissioning of material for publication; production of books, magazines, newspapers, audio-visual material, and computer-based information; and marketing.

puce *noun* a colour anywhere in the range between deep purplish pink and purplish brown. [from French *couleur de puce*, flea colour]

puck *noun* a thick disc of hard rubber used in ice-hockey in place of a ball. [perhaps connected with POKE[1]]

pucker — *verb trans., intrans.* (**puckered**, **puckering**) to gather into creases, folds or wrinkles; to wrinkle. — *noun* a wrinkle, fold or crease. [perhaps connected with POKE[2]]

⬛ *verb* gather, ruffle, wrinkle, crinkle, crumple, crease, furrow, purse, screw up, contract, shrivel, compress.

puckish *adj.* mischievous; impish. [from Anglo-Saxon *puca*, from Old Norse *puki*, a mischievous demon]

pudding *noun* **1** any of several sweet or savoury foods usually made with flour and eggs and cooked by steaming, boiling, or baking. **2** any sweet food served as dessert; the dessert course. **3** a type of sausage made with minced meat, spices, blood, oatmeal, etc: *black pudding.* [from Middle English *poding*]

puddle — *noun* **1** a small pool, especially of rainwater on the road. **2** (*in full* **puddle clay**) a non-porous watertight material consisting of thoroughly mixed wet clay, sand, and water. — *verb* **1** to make watertight by means of puddle. **2** to knead (clay, sand, and water) to make puddle. **3** *Metall.* to produce (wrought iron) from molten pig iron by the now obsolete process of puddling. [probably a diminutive of Anglo-Saxon *pudd*, ditch]

puddling *noun* the original process for converting pig iron into wrought iron by melting it in a furnace in the presence of iron oxide.

pudenda /pjuː'dɛndə/ *noun* the external sexual organs, especially of a woman. [plural of Latin *pudendum*, something to be ashamed of; the singular is also occasionally used]

pudgy *adj.* (**pudgier, pudgiest**) same as PODGY.

pueblo /'pwebloʊ/ *noun* (PL. **pueblos**) a town or settlement in Spanish-speaking countries. [from Spanish *pueblo*, town, from Latin *populus*, a people]

puerile /'pjʊəraɪl/ *adj.* childish; silly; immature. [from Latin *puerilis*, from *puer*, boy]

⊟ childish, babyish, infantile, silly, juvenile, immature, irresponsible, foolish, inane, trivial.
⊞ mature.

puerility /pjʊə'rɪlɪti/ *noun* a puerile state or quality.

puerperal /pjuː'ɜːpərəl/ *adj.* connected with childbirth. [from Latin *puerpera*, woman in labour]

puerperal fever fever accompanying blood poisoning caused by infection of the uterus during childbirth.

puerperium /pjʊə'pɪəriəm/ *noun Medicine* the period between childbirth and the return of the uterus to its normal state, usually about six weeks. [from Latin *puerpera*, a woman in labour]

puff — *noun* **1** a small rush, gust or blast of air, wind, etc; the sound made by it. **2** a small cloud of smoke, dust, or steam emitted from something. **3** *colloq.* breath: *quite out of puff.* **4** an act of inhaling and exhaling smoke from a pipe or cigarette; a drag or draw. **5** a light pastry: *jam puffs.* **6** a powder puff. **7** an item of publicity intended, or serving, as an advertisement. — *verb trans., intrans.* **1** to blow or breathe in small blasts. **2** *intrans.*, *said of smoke, steam, etc* to emerge in small gusts or blasts. **3** to inhale and exhale smoke from, or draw at (a cigarette, etc). **4** *intrans.* (**puff along**) *said of a train, boat, etc* to go along emitting puffs of steam. **5** *intrans.* to pant, or go along panting: *puffing up the hill.* **6** (**be puffed** or **puffed out**) to be breathless after exertion. **7** *trans., intrans.* (*also* **puff out** or **up**) to swell or cause to swell: *puffed out its feathers/a puffed-up eye.* **8** to praise extravagantly by way of advertisement. — **be puffed up** to show great self-importance. [from Anglo-Saxon *pyffan*; imitative]

⊟ *noun* **1** breath, waft, whiff, draught, flurry, gust, blast. **4** pull, *colloq.* drag, draw. *verb* **1** pant, blow, breathe, gasp, gulp, wheeze. **2** blow, waft. **3** smoke, pull, *colloq.* drag, draw, suck. **4** chug along. **5** pant, wheeze, gasp. **7** swell, inflate, expand.

puff adder a large African viper that inflates the upper part of its body when startled.

puffball *noun* the fruiting body (spore-bearing structure) of fungi of the genus *Lycoperdon*, consisting of a hollow ball of white or beige fleshy tissue. When it is mature, a hole develops at the top, through which clouds of spores are released as puffs of fine dust.

puffer *noun Scot. Hist.* a small steamboat used to carry cargo around the west coast and western isles of Scotland.

puffer fish *Zool.* any of several fish, found mainly near tropical reefs, that are able to inflate their spine-covered bodies to become almost spherical, in response to attacks by predators.

puffin *noun* a short stout black and white seabird of the auk family, found on the N Atlantic, N Pacific, and Arctic

coasts, and best known for its large triangular bill with red, yellow, and blue stripes.

puffiness *noun* a puffy quality or condition.

puff pastry light flaky pastry made with a high proportion of fat.

puffy *adj.* (**puffier, puffiest**) swollen as a result of injury or ill health.

⊟ puffed up, swollen, bloated, distended, enlarged, inflated.

pug *noun* a small dog with a flattened snout and curly tail.

pugilism /'pjuːdʒɪlɪzm/ *noun old use* the sport of boxing or prize-fighting. [from Latin *pugil*, boxer]

pugilist *noun* a boxer.

pugnacious *adj.* given to fighting; quarrelsome, belligerent, or combative. [from Latin *pugnax*, from *pugnare*, to fight]

⊟ quarrelsome, belligerent, aggressive, combative, hostile, argumentative, hot-tempered.
⊞ peaceable.

pugnacity *noun* a tendency or inclination to quarrel or fight.

pug nose a short upturned nose.

pug-nosed *adj.* having a pug nose.

puissance /'pwiːsɒns/ *noun Showjumping* a competition testing the horse's ability to jump high fences. [from Old French *puissance*, power]

puissant /'pjuːɪsənt, 'pwiːsənt/ *adj. old use, poetic* strong, mighty or powerful. [from Old French, from Latin *posse*, to be able]

puke *colloq.* — *verb trans., intrans.* to vomit. — *noun* **1** vomit. **2** an act of vomiting. [possibly imitative]

pukka /'pʌkə/ *adj. colloq.* **1** superior; high-quality. **2** upper-class; well-bred. **3** genuine. [from Hindi *pakka*, cooked, firm, ripe]

pulchritude /'pʌlkrɪtjuːd/ *noun literary* beauty of face and form. [from Latin *pulchritudo*, beauty]

pull — *verb* **1** *trans., intrans.* (**pull** or **pull at something**) to grip it strongly and draw or force it towards oneself; to tug or drag it. **2** to remove or extract (a cork, tooth, weeds, etc) with this action. **3** to operate (a trigger, lever, or switch) with this action. **4** to draw (a trailer, etc). **5** to open or close (curtains or a blind). **6** to tear or take apart with a tugging action: *pulled it to pieces.* **7** (**pull something on someone**) to produce a weapon as a threat to them: *pulled a gun on us.* **8 a** to row (a boat). **b** (*often* **pull away, off, etc**) *said of a boat* to be rowed or caused to move in a particular direction. **c** *intrans.* (**pull at an oar**) to execute strokes with it. **9** to draw (beer, etc) from a cask by operating a lever. **10** *intrans., said of a driver or vehicle* to steer or move in a particular direction: *pulled right.* **11** *Golf, Cricket* to hit (a ball) so that it veers off its intended course, especially to the left or the leg side. **12** *intrans., said of an engine or vehicle* to produce the required propelling power. **13** *intrans.* (**pull at something**) to inhale and exhale smoke from a cigarette, etc; to draw or suck at it. **14** to attract (a crowd, votes, etc). **15** to strain (a muscle or tendon). **16** to practise or execute (especially a trick) successfully: *pull a fast one.* **17** *Printing* to print (a proof). — *noun* **1** an act of pulling. **2** attraction; attracting force: *magnetic pull/the pull of one's homeland.* **3** useful influence: *has some pull with the education department.* **4** a drag at a pipe; a swallow of liquor, etc. **5** a tab, etc for pulling. **6** a stroke made with an oar. **7** *Printing* a proof. — **pull ahead of** or **away from someone** or **something** to get in front of them; to gain a lead. **pull something apart 1** to rip or tear it; to reduce it to pieces. **2** to criticize it severely. **pull back** or **pull something back** to withdraw or cause it to withdraw or retreat. **pull something down** to demolish a building, etc. **pull in 1** *said of a train* to arrive and halt at a station. **2** *said of a vehicle* to move off, or to the side of, the road. **pull someone in** *colloq.* to arrest them. **pull something in** *slang* to make money, especially a large amount. **pull something off** *col-*

loq. to arrange or accomplish it sucessfully: *pull off a deal.* **pull something on** to put on clothes hastily. **pull out** or **pull someone out** to withdraw from combat, from a competition, project, etc. **pull something out 1** to extract or remove it. **2** *intrans., said of a driver or vehicle* to move away from the kerb, or into the centre of the road to overtake. **pull over** to move off, or to the side of, the road and stop. **pull round** or **pull someone round** to recover or help them to recover from an illness. **pull through** or **pull someone through** to recover or help them to recover from an illness. **pull together** to work together towards a common aim; to co-operate. **pull oneself together** to regain self-control. **pull up** *said of a driver or vehicle* to stop. **pull someone up** to reprimand them: *was pulled up for being late.* **pull something up** to uproot a plant. **pull up on** or **with someone** or **something** to catch up with them. **pull someone up short 1** to check someone, often oneself. **2** to take them aback. [from Anglo-Saxon *pullian*, to pluck, draw, pull]

. . . .

▣ *verb* **1** tug, drag, haul, draw, jerk, *colloq.* yank . **2** remove, take out, extract, pull out, pluck, uproot, pull up, rip up or out, tear out. **3** operate, throw. **4** tow, draw. **5** draw, open, close. **6** tear, rip. **13** draw at, *colloq.* drag at, suck at, puff. **14** attract, draw, lure, allure, entice, tempt, magnetize. **15** strain, sprain, wrench, twist. *noun* **1** tow, drag, tug, jerk, *colloq.* yank. **2** attraction, lure, allurement, drawing power, magnetism. **3** influence, weight. **pull apart 1** rip apart, tear up, dismember, dismantle, take to pieces, separate, part. **pull down** demolish, knock down, bulldoze, destroy, build, erect, put up. **pull off** arrange, accomplish, achieve, bring off, succeed, manage, carry out. **pull out** *withdraw from combat, etc.* retreat, withdraw, leave, depart, quit, move out, evacuate, desert, abandon. **pull through** recover, rally, recuperate, survive, weather. **pull together** co-operate, work together, collaborate, team up. **pull up** *said of a driver* stop, halt, park, draw up, pull in, pull over, brake, *someone* reprimand, *colloq.* tell off, *colloq.* tick off, take to task, rebuke, criticize.

▣ *verb* **1** push. **3** push, press. **14** repel, deter, discourage. **pull apart 1** join. **pull off** fail. **pull out** join, arrive. **pull together** fight.

. . . .

pullet /ˈpʊlɪt/ *noun* a young female hen in its first laying year. [from Old French *poulet*, chicken]

pulley *noun* (PL. **pulleys**) **1** a device for lifting and lowering weights, consisting of a wheel with a grooved rim over which a rope or belt runs. **2** a clothes-drying frame suspended by ropes from the ceiling, raised and lowered by means of such a device. [from Old French *polie*]

pull-out *noun* **1** a self-contained detachable section of a magazine designed to be kept for reference. **2** a withdrawal from combat, etc.

pullover *noun* a knitted garment pulled on over one's head; a sweater or jumper.

pullulate *verb intrans.* **1** *literary* to teem or abound. **2** *Biol.* to reproduce by pullulation. [from Latin *pullulare*, from *pullulus*, chick]

pullulation *noun Biol.* **1** reproduction by vegetative budding, as in yeast cells. **2** germination of a seed.

pulmonary /ˈpʌlmənərɪ/ *adj.* **1** of, relating to, or affecting the lungs. **2** having the function of a lung. [from Latin *pulmonarius*, from *pulmo*, lung]

pulp — *noun* **1** the flesh of a fruit or vegetable. **2** a soft wet mass of mashed food or other material: *wood pulp.* **3** *derog.* worthless literature, novels, magazines, etc, printed on poor paper. — *verb trans., intrans.* to reduce, or be reduced, to a pulp. [from Latin *pulpa*, flesh, pulp]

. . . .

▣ *noun* **2** mash, mush, pap, paste, purée. **3** *pap. verb* crush, squash, pulverize, mash, purée, liquidize.

. . . .

pulpit *noun* **1** a small enclosed platform in a church, from which the preacher delivers the sermon. **2** church preachers in general: *the message from the pulpit.* [from Latin *pulpitum*, platform]

pulpy *adj.* (**pulpier, pulpiest**) consisting of or like pulp.

pulsar /ˈpʌlsɑː(r)/ *noun Astron.* in space, a source of electromagnetic radiation emitted in brief regular pulses, mainly at radio frequency. Pulsars are believed to be rapidly revolving neutron stars that emit a pulse of radiation each time they rotate. [from *pulsating star*]

pulsate *verb intrans.* **1** to beat or throb. **2** to contract and expand rhythmically. **3** to vibrate. **4** *Physics* to vary in force or intensity in a regularly recurring pattern. [from Latin *pulsare*, to beat]

. . . .

▣ **1** beat, throb, pound, hammer, drum, thud, thump. **2** pulse. **3** vibrate, oscillate, quiver.

. . . .

pulsating star *Astron.* a variable star whose brightness changes in a regular manner as it alternately expands and contracts.

pulsation *noun* **1** a beating or throbbing. **2** a motion of a heart or pulse.

pulse[1] — *noun* **1** the rhythmic beat that can be detected in an artery, eg the radial artery, corresponding to the regular contraction of the left ventricle of the heart as it pumps blood around the body and so generates a series of pressure waves. **2** the rate of this beat, often measured as an indicator of a person's state of health. The average resting pulse rate is 60 to 80 beats per minute, but it is increased by physical exertion, illness, injury, fear, and other emotions: *feel/take someone's pulse.* **3** a regular throbbing beat in music. **4** *Physics* a signal, eg of light or electric current, of very short duration. **5** the hum or bustle of a busy place. **6** a thrill of excitement, etc. **7** the attitude or feelings of a group or community at any one time: *check the pulse of the electorate.* — *verb intrans.* to throb or pulsate. [from Latin *pulsus*, a beating]

. . . .

▣ *noun* **3** beat, throb, rhythm, pulsation, beating, pounding, drumming. **7** attitude, feeling, mood, state of mind, tenor.

. . . .

pulse[2] *noun* **1** the dried seed of a legume (a plant belonging to the pea family), used as food, eg pea, bean, lentil. **2** any plant that bears this seed. [from Latin *puls*, meal porridge or bean pottage]

pulverization or **pulverisation** *noun* pulverizing; reducing to powder or dust.

pulverize or **pulverise** *verb* **1** *trans., intrans.* to crush or crumble to dust or powder. **2** *facetious* to defeat utterly; to annihilate. [from Latin *pulverizare*, from *pulvis*, dust]

. . . .

▣ **1** crush, pound, grind, mill, powder. **2** defeat, destroy, demolish, annihilate.

. . . .

puma /ˈpjuːmə/ *noun* one of the large cats of America, with short yellowish-brown or reddish fur, found in mountain regions, forests, plains, and deserts. Pumas feed mainly on deer and other small mammals, and in the USA, where they are regarded as pests, they have been hunted almost to extinction. Also called COUGAR, MOUNTAIN LION, PANTHER. [from Spanish, from Quechua (a S American Indian language)]

pumice /ˈpʌmɪs/ *noun* (*in full* **pumice stone**) *Geol.* a very light porous white or grey form of solidified lava, full of cavities formed by the sudden release of dissolved gases at the time when the lava solidified. It is used as an abrasive and polishing agent. [from Latin *pumex*]

pummel *verb* (**pummelled, pummelling**) to beat repeatedly with the fists. [a variant of POMMEL]

pump[1] — *noun* **1** any of various piston-operated or other devices for forcing or driving liquids or gases into or out of something, etc. **2** a standing device with a handle that is worked up and down for raising water from beneath the ground, especially one serving as the water supply to a community. **3** a device for forcing air into a tyre. **4** (*also* **petrol pump**) a device for raising petrol from an underground storage tank to fill a vehicle's petrol tank. — *verb* **1** *trans., intrans.* to raise, force or drive (liquids or gases) out of or into something with a pump. **2** (*also* **pump something up**) to inflate a tyre, etc with a pump. **3** to force in large gushes or flowing amounts: *pumping waste into the sea.* **4** to pour (money or other resources) into a project, etc. **5** to force out the contents of (someone's stomach) to rid it of a poison, etc. **6** to try to extract information from (someone) by persistent questioning. **7** to work (something) vigorously up and down, as though operating a pump handle: *pumped my hand in greeting.* **8** to fire (bullets); to fire bullets into: *pumped bullets into her/pumped her full of bullets.* — **pump iron** *colloq.* to exercise with weights; to go in for weight-training. [from Old Dutch *pumpe*, pipe]

▪ *verb* **1** push, drive, force, inject, siphon, draw, drain. **2** inflate, blow up, puff up, fill. **3** pour, discharge, spew.

pump[2] *noun* **1** a rubber-soled canvas sports shoe; a gym-shoe or plimsoll. **2** a light dancing shoe. **3** a plain low-cut shoe for women; a court shoe.

pumpernickel *noun* a dark heavy coarse rye bread, eaten especially in Germany. [from German *Pumpernickel*, lout, perhaps literally 'stink-devil' or 'fart-devil']

pumpkin *noun* **1** a perennial trailing or climbing plant (*Cucurbita maxima* or *C. pepo*) which produces yellow flowers and large round orange fruits at ground level. **2** the fruit of this plant, which contains pulpy flesh and many seeds, enclosed by a hard leathery orange rind. It is used to make pumpkin pie (traditionally eaten on Thanksgiving Day in the USA), and whole fruits are carved into lanterns at Hallowe'en. [from Old French *pompon*, from Greek *pepon*, melon]

pun — *noun* a form of joke consisting of a play on words, especially one where an association is created between words of similar sound but different meaning, eg *A pun is a punishable offence.* — *verb intrans.* (**punned, punning**) to make a pun.

▪ *noun* play on words, double entendre, witticism, quip.

Punch *noun* a humpbacked puppet character in the traditional show called *Punch and Judy.* — **pleased as Punch** highly gratified. [from Italian *Pulcinella*, a commedia dell'arte character]

punch[1] — *verb trans., intrans.* to hit with one's fist. — *noun* **1** a blow with the fist. **2** vigour and effectiveness in speech or writing: *lacks punch.* — **pack a punch** *colloq.* to be capable of delivering a powerful blow; to be forceful or effective. **pull one's punches** to be deliberately less hard-hitting than one might be. [from Middle English *punchen*, variant of POUNCE]

▪ *verb* hit, strike, bash, clout, cuff, box, thump, *slang* sock, *colloq.* slug, *colloq.* wallop, pummel, jab. *noun* **1** blow, bash, clout, thump, *colloq.* wallop, jab. **2** vigour, impact, effectiveness, force, drive, verve, panache.

punch[2] — *noun* **1** a tool for cutting holes or notches, or stamping designs, in leather, paper, metal, etc. **2** a tool for driving nail heads well down into a surface. — *verb* **1** to pierce, notch or stamp with a punch: *punched our tickets/punch a hole.* **2** *Comput.* to use a key punch to record (data) on (a card or tape). — **punch in** or **out** *North Amer.* to clock in or out. [from Middle English *puncheon*, piercing tool]

▪ *verb* **1** perforate, puncture, prick, pierce, bore, drill, stamp, cut.

punch[3] *noun* a drink made originally from five ingredi-

ents (spirits, water, lemon juice, sugar, and spice) but now also from a variety of others. [said to be from Hindi *panch*, five]

punch-bag *noun* a heavy stuffed leather bag hanging from the ceiling on a rope, used for boxing practice.

punch-ball *noun* a leather ball mounted on a flexible stand, used for boxing practice.

punch bowl 1 a large bowl for mixing and serving punch. **2** a bowl-shaped hollow in the mountains.

punch-drunk *adj.* **1** *said of a boxer* brain-damaged from repeated blows to the head, with resultant unsteadiness and confusion. **2** dazed from over-intensive work or other shattering experience.

punched card or **punch card** *Comput.* a card bearing coded data or instructions in the form of punched holes.

punchline *noun* the words that conclude a funny story and contain its point.

punch-up *noun colloq.* a fight.

punchy *adj.* (**punchier, punchiest**) *said of speech or writing* vigorous and effective; forcefully expressed.

punctilio *noun* (PL. **punctilios**) **1** strictness in observing the finer details of etiquette, ceremony, or correct formal behaviour. **2** a fine detail of this kind. [from Italian *puntiglio*, from Spanish diminutive of *punto*, point]

punctilious *adj.* carefully attentive to details of correct, polite or considerate behaviour; making a point of observing a rule or custom: *always punctilious about remembering birthdays.*

▪ scrupulous, conscientious, meticulous, careful, particular, finicky, fussy, exact, precise, strict, formal, proper.
▪ lax, informal.

punctiliously *adv.* in a punctilious way.

punctual *adj.* **1** arriving or happening at the arranged time; not late. **2** *said of a person* making a habit of arriving on time. [from Latin *punctualis*, from *punctus*, point]

▪ **1** prompt, on time, on the dot, exact, precise, early, in good time.
▪ UNPUNCTUAL. **1** late.

punctuality *noun* being punctual.

punctually *adv.* on time.

punctuate *verb* **1** *trans., intrans.* to put punctuation marks into (a piece of writing). **2** to interrupt repeatedly: *a speech punctuated by bursts of applause.* **3** to give emphasis to: *punctuating her comments with taps on the desk.* [from Latin *punctuare*, to prick, point, from *punctus*, point]

punctuation *noun* **1** a system of marks used in a text to clarify its meaning for the reader. **2** the use of such marks, or the process of inserting them.

punctuation mark any of the set of marks such as the full stop, comma, question mark, colon, etc that in written matter indicate the pauses and intonations that would be used in speech, and make the meaning clear to the reader.

Punctuation marks include: comma, full stop or period, colon, semicolon, brackets, parentheses, square brackets, inverted commas or speech marks or quotation marks (*colloq.* quotes), exclamation mark, question mark, apostrophe, asterisk, star, hyphen, dash, oblique stroke or solidus or backslash.

puncture — *noun* **1** a small hole pierced in something with a sharp point. **2** a perforation in an inflated object, especially a pneumatic tyre; the resulting flat tyre. — *verb* **1** *trans., intrans.* to make a puncture in, or be punctured. **2** to deflate (someone's pride, self-importance, etc). [from Latin *punctura*, pricking]

▪ *noun* **1** hole, perforation, cut, nick. **2** perforation, leak, flat tyre, *colloq.* flat, *colloq.* blow-out. *verb* **1** prick, pierce, penetrate, perforate, hole, cut, nick, burst, rupture, flatten, deflate. **2** prick, flatten, deflate.

....

pundit *noun* **1** an authority or supposed authority on a particular subject, especially one regularly consulted. **2** a Hindu learned in Hindu culture, philosophy, and law. [from Hindi *pandit*]

pungency *noun* **1** having a pungent flavour or smell. **2** such a flavour or smell.

pungent *adj.* **1** *said of a taste or smell* sharp and strong. **2** *said of remarks, wit, etc* cleverly caustic or biting. [from Latin *pungere*, to prick]

....

⊟ **1** strong, hot, peppery, spicy, aromatic, tangy, piquant, sharp, keen, acute, sour, bitter, acrid. **2** caustic, biting, stinging, cutting, incisive, pointed, piercing, penetrating, sarcastic, scathing.
🗦 **1** mild, bland, tasteless.

....

pungently *adv.* in a pungent way.

punish *verb* **1** to cause (an offender) to suffer for an offence. **2** to impose a penalty for (an offence). **3** *colloq.* to treat roughly: *really punishes that car of hers.* **4** to beat or defeat (an opponent, etc) soundly. [from French *punir*, from Latin *punire*]

....

⊟ **1** penalize, discipline, correct, chastise, castigate, scold, beat, flog, lash, cane, spank, fine, imprison. **3** *colloq.* hammer. **4** beat, defeat, thrash, *colloq.* hammer.
🗦 **1, 2** reward.

....

punishable *adj.*, *said of an offence* liable to be punished, especially by law.

punishing *adj.* harsh; severe: *punishing conditions.*

punishment *noun* **1** the act of punishing or process of being punished. **2** any method of punishing; a type of penalty. **3** *colloq.* rough treatment, suffering, or hardship.

....

⊟ **1** discipline, correction, chastisement, beating, flogging, imprisonment, retribution, revenge. **2** penalty, discipline, fine, imprisonment, sentence, chastisement, beating, flogging, deserts.
🗦 **1, 2** reward.

....

punitive *adj.* **1** relating to, inflicting, or intended to inflict, punishment: *punitive measures.* **2** severe; inflicting hardship: *punitive taxation.* [from Latin *punitivus*, from *punire*, to punish]

....

⊟ **1** penal, disciplinary, retributive, retaliatory, vindictive. **2** severe, harsh, punishing.

....

punitively *adv.* in a punitive way.

Punjabi /pʊnˈdʒɑːbɪ/ or **Panjabi** /pʌnˈdʒɑːbɪ/ — *noun* an Indo-Aryan language spoken by c.15 million people in the state of Punjab, India, and in Pakistan. See also INDO-ARYAN LANGUAGES, INDO-IRANIAN LANGUAGES. — *adj.* relating to or spoken or written in Punjabi.

punk — *noun* **1** an anti-establishment movement among the youth of the 1970s and 1980s, manifesting itself in aggressive music and weirdness of dress and hairstyle, and the wearing of cheap utility articles, eg safety pins, as ornament. **2** a follower of punk styles or punk rock. **3** punk rock. **4** *North Amer.* a worthless or stupid person. — *adj.* **1** relating to, or characteristic of, punk as a movement. **2** *North Amer.* worthless; inferior. [perhaps a combination of older *punk*, prostitute or *punk*, fire-lighting tinder]

punk rock a type of loud, aggressive rock music popular in the late 1970s and early 1980s, with violent and often crude lyrics.

punnet *noun* a small basket or container, usually of cardboard or plastic, for soft fruit.

punster *noun* a person who makes puns, especially habitually.

punt[1] — *noun* a long flat-bottomed open boat with square ends, propelled by a pole pushed against the bed of the river, etc. — *verb* **1** *intrans.* to travel by, or operate, a punt. **2** to propel (a punt, etc) with a pole. **3** to convey (passengers) in a punt. [from Latin *ponto*, punt, pontoon]

punt[2] — *noun Rugby* a kick given with the toe of the boot to a ball dropped directly from the hands. — *verb trans., intrans.* to kick in this way.

punt[3] *verb intrans.* **1** *colloq.* to bet on horses. **2** *Cards* to bet against the bank. [from French *ponter*, to bet]

punt[4] *noun* the chief currency unit of the Republic of Ireland. [from Irish Gaelic *punt*, pound]

punter *noun colloq.* **1** someone who bets on horses; a gambler. **2** the average consumer, customer, or member of the public.

puny *adj.* (**punier, puniest**) **1** small, weak, or undersized. **2** feeble or ineffective. [from Old French *puisne*, born later]

....

⊟ **1** small, weak, undersized, undeveloped, underdeveloped, stunted, diminutive, little, tiny, feeble, frail, sickly. **2** feeble, ineffective, inadequate, lame, poor, insignificant.
🗦 **1** strong, sturdy, large.

....

pup — *noun* **1** a young dog. **2** the young of other animals, eg the seal, wolf, and rat. — *verb intrans.* (**pupped, pupping**) to give birth to pups. — **be sold a pup** *colloq.* to be swindled. **in pup** *said of a bitch* pregnant. [a shortening of PUPPY]

pupa /ˈpjuːpə/ *noun* (PL. **pupae, pupas**) in the life cycle of insects that undergo metamorphosis, eg butterflies and moths, the inactive stage during which a larva is transformed into a sexually mature adult, by undergoing extensive changes in body structure while enclosed in a protective case. [from Latin *pupa*, doll]

pupal /ˈpjuːpəl/ *adj.* relating to or having the form of a pupa.

pupil[1] *noun* **1** someone who is being taught; a schoolchild or student. **2** someone studying under a particular master, etc: *a pupil of Beethoven's.* **3** *Legal* a ward. [from Old French *pupille*, from Latin *pupillus, pupilla*, diminutives of *pupus*, boy, *pupa*, girl]

....

⊟ **1** student, scholar, schoolboy, schoolgirl, learner, apprentice, beginner, novice. **2** student, disciple, protégé(e).
🗦 **1, 2** teacher.

....

pupil[2] *noun Anat.* in the eye of vertebrates, the circular opening in the centre of the iris through which light passes to the retina. Its size can be altered, according to the amount of light available, by tiny muscles in the iris. [from Latin *pupilla*, diminutive of *pupa*, girl, doll]

puppet *noun* **1** a doll that can be made to move in a lifelike way, of any of several types, eg operated by strings or sticks attached to its limbs, or designed to fit over the hand and operated by the fingers and thumb. **2** a person who is being controlled or manipulated by someone else. [a variant of POPPET, from Latin *pupa*, doll]

puppeteer *noun* a person skilled in manipulating puppets and giving puppet shows.

puppetry *noun* the art of making and manipulating puppets.

puppet show an entertainment with puppets as performers.

puppet state an apparently independent country actually under the control of another.

puppy *noun* (PL. **puppies**) **1** a young dog. **2** a conceited young man. [related to French *poupée*, doll]

puppy fat a temporary plumpness in children, usually at the pre-adolescent stage.

puppy love the romantic love of an adolescent for an older person of the opposite sex; calf love.

purblind /'pɜːblaɪnd/ adj. **1** nearly blind; dim-sighted. **2** dull-witted; obtuse. [originally = completely blind, from PURE + BLIND]

purchase — verb **1** to obtain in return for payment; to buy. **2** to get or achieve through labour, effort, sacrifice, or risk. — noun **1** something that has been bought. **2** the act of buying. **3** firmness in holding or gripping; a sure grasp or foothold. **4** Mech. the advantage given by a device such as a pulley or lever. [from Old French pourchacier, to seek to obtain]

⊟ verb **1** buy, pay for, colloq. invest in. **2** obtain, get, gain, earn, win, secure, procure, acquire. noun **1** acquisition, colloq. buy, investment, asset, possession, property. **2** acquisition, investment.

⊠ verb **1** sell. noun **2** sale.

purchaser noun a buyer.

⊟ buyer, consumer, shopper, customer, client.

⊠ seller, vendor.

purchase tax a tax levied on goods, at a higher rate on those considered non-essential.

purdah /'pɜːdə/ noun the seclusion or veiling of women from public view in some Muslim and Hindu societies. [from Hindi and Urdu pardah, curtain]

pure adj. **1** consisting of itself only; unmixed with anything else: pure gold/pure white. **2** unpolluted; uncontaminated; wholesome: pure water/pure air. **3** virtuous; chaste; free from sin or guilt: pure thoughts. **4** utter; nothing but: pure lunacy/pure coincidence. **5** said of mathematics or science dealing with theory and abstractions rather than practical applications. **6** of unmixed blood or descent: of pure Manx stock. **7** said of sound, eg a sung note clear, unwavering and exactly in tune. **8** absolutely true to type or style: pure Art Deco. **9** said of speech or language free of imported, intrusive or debased elements. **10** said of a vowel simple in sound quality, like the o in box, as distinct from a diphthong like the oy in boy. — **pure and simple** and nothing else: jealousy pure and simple. [from Latin purus]

⊟ **1** unadulterated, unalloyed, unmixed, undiluted, neat, solid, simple, natural, real, authentic, genuine, true. **2** uncontaminated, unpolluted, clean, wholesome, clear, germ-free, aseptic, sterile, antiseptic, disinfected, sterilized, hygienic, sanitary, immaculate, spotless. **3** virtuous, chaste, virginal, innocent, undefiled, unsullied, moral, upright, blameless. **4** sheer, utter, complete, total, thorough, absolute, perfect, unqualified. **5** theoretical, abstract, conjectural, speculative, academic.

⊠ **1** impure, adulterated. **2** impure, contaminated, polluted. **3** immoral, sinful. **5** applied.

pure-bred adj. denoting an animal or plant that is the offspring of parents of the same breed or variety.

purée /'pjʊəreɪ/ — noun a quantity of fruit or vegetables reduced to a pulp by liquidizing or rubbing through a sieve. — verb (**purées, puréed**) to reduce to a purée. [from French purer, to strain]

purely adv. **1** in a pure way. **2** wholly; entirely: won purely on her merits. **3** merely: purely a formality.

⊟ **2** wholly, entirely, utterly, completely, totally, thoroughly, absolutely. **3** merely, only, just, simply, solely.

pure mathematics Maths. the branch of mathematics concerned with the study of abstract mathematical theory without application to observed phenomena in everyday life.

pureness noun a pure state or quality.

purgative — noun a medicine that causes the bowels to empty. — adj., said of a medicine, etc having this effect. [from Latin purgativus, from purgare, to clean out]

purgatory /'pɜːɡətərɪ/ noun **1** (**Purgatory**) chiefly RC Church a place or state into which the soul passes after death to be cleansed of pardonable sins before going to heaven. **2** humorous colloq. any state of discomfort or suffering; an excruciating experience. [from Latin purgatorium, from purgare, to cleanse]

purge — verb **1** to rid (eg the soul or body) of unwholesome thoughts or substances; to get rid of (impure elements) from (anything). **2** to rid (a political party, community, etc) of (undesirable members). **3** trans., intrans., old use to take or give a purgative to empty (the bowels), or the bowels of (a person). **4** Legal to rid (oneself) of guilt by atoning for one's offence. **5** Legal to clear (oneself or someone else) of an accusation. — noun **1** an act of purging. **2** the process of purging a party or community of undesirable members. **3** the process of purging the bowels. **4** a medicine to empty the bowels. [from Latin purgare, to cleanse, purify]

⊟ verb **1** purify, cleanse, clean out, scour, clear, absolve. **2** oust, remove, get rid of, eject, expel, root out, eradicate, exterminate, wipe out. noun **1**, **2** removal, ejection, expulsion, witch hunt, eradication, extermination.

puri /'pʊərɪ/ noun a small cake of unleavened Indian bread, deep-fried and served hot. [from Hindi puri]

purification noun purifying, cleansing.

purifier noun a person, apparatus, or thing that purifies.

purify verb (**purifies, purified**) **1** to make pure. **2** to cleanse of contaminating or harmful substances. **3** to rid of intrusive elements. **4** Relig. to free from sin or guilt. [from Latin purus, pure + facere, to make]

⊟ **1**, **2** refine, filter, clarify, clean, cleanse, decontaminate, sanitize, disinfect, sterilize, fumigate, deodorize.

⊠ **1**, **2** contaminate, pollute, defile.

Purim /pʊə'riːm/ noun the Jewish Festival of Lots held about 1 March, commemorating the deliverance of the Jews from the plot of Haman to have them massacred, as related in the Book of Esther. [from Hebrew pūrim (singular pūr), lots]

purine /'pjʊəriːn/ or **purin** /'pjʊərɪn/ noun Biochem. a nitrogenous base with a double ring structure. The most important derivatives of purine are adenine and guanine, which are major constituents of nucleotides and the nucleic acids DNA and RNA. [contracted from Latin purum uricum acidum, pure uric acid]

purism noun insistence on purity, especially of language.

purist noun a person who insists on correctness of word usage, grammar, etc or authenticity of detail in design, etc.

⊟ pedant, stickler, quibbler, nit-picker, literalist, formalist.

puritan noun **1** (**Puritan**) Hist. a supporter of the 16c to 17c Protestant movement in England and America that sought to rid church worship of ritual. **2** a person of strict, especially over-strict, moral principles; someone who disapproves generally of luxuries and amusements. [from Latin puritas, purity]

puritanical adj. realting to or characteristic of puritans; having the qualities or characteristics of a puritan or puritans.

⊟ puritan, moralistic, disciplinarian, ascetic, abstemious, austere, severe, stern, strict, strait-laced, prim, proper, prudish, disapproving, stuffy, stiff, rigid, narrow-minded, bigoted, fanatical, zealous.

⊠ hedonistic, liberal, indulgent, broad-minded.

Puritanism noun a movement based on the belief that further reformation was required in the Church of England under Elizabeth I and the Stuarts, which arose in the 1560s out of disapproval of the 'popery' (eg surplices) retained by the Elizabethan religious settlement.

purity *noun* 1 the state of being pure or unmixed. 2 freedom from contamination, pollution or unwholesome or intrusive elements. 3 chasteness or innocence. [from Latin *puritas*, from *purus*, pure]

▪ 1, 2 clearness, clarity, cleanness, cleanliness, untaintedness, wholesomeness. 3 chastity, decency, morality, integrity, rectitude, uprightness, virtue, innocence, blamelessness.
◪ 1, 2 impurity. 3 immorality.

purl¹ — *noun* 1 *Knitting* the more complex of two basic stitches, with the wool passed behind the needle. See also PLAIN. 2 cord made from gold or silver wire. 3 a decorative looped edging on lace, braid, etc. — *verb* to knit in purl. [from Middle English *pirl*, to twist, *purl*, to embroider]

purl² *verb intrans.* 1 to flow with a murmuring sound. 2 to eddy or swirl. [related to Norwegian *purla*, to babble]

purlieus /ˈpɜːljuːz/ *pl. noun* the surroundings, or immediate neighbourhood, of a place. [from Old French *puralé*, a going through]

purlin /ˈpɜːlɪn/ or **purline** /ˈpɜːliːn/ *noun* a roof timber stretching across the principal rafters or between the tops of walls, and supporting the common or subsidiary rafters or the sheets of roof-covering material. [origin unknown]

purloin /pɜːˈlɔɪn/ *verb* to steal, filch, or pilfer. [from Old French *purloigner*, to remove to a distance]

purple — *noun* 1 a colour that is a mixture of blue and red. 2 *Hist.* a crimson dye got from various shellfish. 3 crimson cloth, or a robe made from it worn by eg emperors and cardinals, symbolic of their authority. — *adj.* 1 of either of these colours. 2 *said of writing* self-consciously fine in style; over-elaborate; flowery. — **born in the purple** born into a royal or noble family. [from Greek *porphyra*, dye-yielding shellfish]

purple heart *colloq.* a heart-shaped violet pill containing a stimulant drug.

purple patch a passage of purple prose.

purport — *noun* (with stress on *pur-*) meaning, significance, point, or gist. — *verb intrans.* (with stress on *-port*) to present itself so as to seem or claim: *a work purporting to have been written by Charles I.* [from Old French *purporter*, to convey]

purpose — *noun* 1 one's object or aim in doing something. 2 the function for which something is intended: *a multi-purpose gadget.* 3 one's intentions, aspirations, aim, or goal: *one's purpose in life/a sense of purpose.* 4 determination; resolve: *a woman of purpose.* — *verb* to intend (to do something). — **on purpose** intentionally; deliberately. **to little or no purpose** with few (or no) useful results. **to the purpose** relevant; to the point. [from Old French *pourpos*, from Latin *proponere*, to intend]

▪ *noun* 1, 3 intention, aim, objective, end, goal, target, plan, design, vision, idea, point, object, reason, motive, rationale, principle, result, outcome. 2 function, use, application, good, advantage, benefit, value. 4 determination, resolve, resolution, drive, single-mindedness, dedication, devotion, constancy, steadfastness, persistence, tenacity, zeal. **on purpose** purposely, deliberately, intentionally, consciously, knowingly, wittingly, wilfully.
◪ **on purpose** accidentally, impulsively, spontaneously.

purpose-built *adj.* designed to meet specific requirements: *a purpose-built medical centre.*

purposeful *adj.* determined; intent; resolute; showing a sense of purpose.

▪ determined, intent, resolute, decided, resolved, persistent, persevering, tenacious, strong-willed, single-minded, constant, steadfast, positive, firm, deliberate.
◪ purposeless, aimless.

purposefully *adv.* in a purposeful way.

purposeless *adj.* without purpose, aimless.

purposely *adv.* intentionally; on purpose.

purposive *adj.* 1 having a clear purpose. 2 purposeful.

purr — *verb* 1 *intrans.*, *said of a cat* to make a soft, low, vibrating sound associated with contentment. 2 *intrans.*, *said of a vehicle or machine* to make a sound similar to this, suggestive of good running order. 3 *intrans.*, *trans.* to express pleasure, or say, in a tone vibrating with satisfaction. — *noun* a purring sound. [imitative]

purse — *noun* 1 a small container carried in the pocket or handbag, for keeping one's cash, etc in. 2 *North Amer.* a woman's handbag. 3 the funds available to one for spending: *beyond my purse.* — *verb* to draw (the lips) together in disapproval or deep thought. — **hold the purse strings** to be the person in control of spending, eg in a family or organization. [from Anglo-Saxon *purs*]

▪ *noun* 1 moneybag, wallet, pouch. 3 funds, means, resources, finances, money, coffers, treasury, exchequer. *verb* draw together, tighten, compress, pucker, wrinkle, contract, close.

purser *noun* the ship's officer responsible for keeping the accounts and, on a passenger ship, seeing to the welfare of passengers.

pursuance *noun* the process of pursuing: *in pursuance of his duties.*

pursue *verb* 1 *trans.*, *intrans.* to follow in order to overtake, capture, attack, etc; to chase. 2 to proceed along (a course or route). 3 to put one's efforts into achieving (a goal or aim). 4 to occupy oneself with (one's career, etc). 5 to continue with, or follow up (investigations, enquiries, etc). [from Old French *pursuer*]

▪ 1 chase, go after, follow, track, trail, shadow, tail, dog, harass, harry, hound, hunt, seek, search for. 2 follow. 3 aspire to, aim for, strive for, try for, persevere in, persist in, hold to. 4 perform, engage in, practise, conduct. 5 investigate, inquire into, carry on, continue with, keep on with, keep up, maintain.

pursuer *noun* 1 someone pursuing one: *escaped their pursuers.* 2 *Scot. Legal* a plaintiff or prosecutor.

pursuit *noun* 1 the act of pursuing or chasing: *the pursuit of happiness/followed in hot pursuit.* 2 an occupation or hobby. [from Old French *purseute*]

▪ 1 chase, hue and cry, tracking, stalking, trail, hunt, quest, search, investigation. 2 activity, occupation, hobby, pastime, interest, trade, craft, line, speciality, vocation.

pursuivant /ˈpɜːsɪvənt/ *noun Heraldry* an officer of the College of Arms ranking below a herald. [from French *poursuivre*, to follow]

purulence /ˈpjʊərjʊləns/ *noun* 1 being purulent. 2 the formation or secretion of pus. 3 pus.

purulent /ˈpjʊərjʊlənt/ *adj.* full of, or discharging, pus. [from Latin *purulentus*, from *pus*, pus]

purvey *verb trans.*, *intrans.* (**purveys**, **purveyed**) *technical*, *said of a trader* to supply (food, provisions, etc). [from Old French *purveier*, from Latin *providere*, to provide for]

purveyance *noun* purveying.

purveyor *noun* a person whose business is to provide food or meals.

purview *noun* 1 scope of responsibility or concern, eg of a court of law. 2 the range of one's knowledge, experience, or activities. [from Old French *purveu*, provided]

pus *noun* the thick, yellowish liquid that forms in abscesses or infected wounds, composed of dead white blood cells, serum, bacteria and tissue debris. [from Latin *pus*]

push — *verb* 1 (**push something** or **push against**, **at**, or **against something**) to exert pressure to force it away from one; to press, thrust, or shove it. **2** to touch or grasp and move forward in front of one: *push a wheelchair*. **3** *intrans.*, *trans*. (**push** or **push one's way through, in, past**, *etc*) to force one's way, thrusting aside people or obstacles. **4** *intrans*. to progress especially laboriously: *pushing forward through the unknown*. **5** (*often* **push something down, up**, *etc*) to force in a particular direction: *push up prices*. **6** (**push someone into something**) to coax, urge, persuade, or goad them to do it: *pushed them into agreeing*. **7** to pressurize them into working harder, achieving more, *etc*: *pushes himself too hard*. **8** (**push something** or **push for something**) to recommend it strongly; to campaign or press for it. **9** to promote (products) or urge acceptance of (ideas). **10** to sell (drugs) illegally. — *noun* **1** an act of pushing; a thrust or shove. **2** a burst of effort towards achieving something. **3** determination, aggression, or drive. — **at a push** if forced; at a pinch. **be pushed for something** *colloq*. to be short of (eg time or money). **be pushing** *colloq*. to be nearly (a specified age). **get the push** *colloq*. to be dismissed from a job, *etc*; to be rejected by someone. **give someone the push** to dismiss or reject them. **push along** *colloq*. to leave; to make one's departure. **push someone around** or **about** *colloq*. **1** to bully them; to treat them roughly. **2** to dictate to them; to order them about. **push off** *colloq*. to make one's departure; to go away. **push on** to continue on one's way, *etc*. **push someone** or **something over** to knock them down. **push something through** to force acceptance of a proposal, bill, *etc* by a legislative body, *etc*. [from Old French *pousser*]

⊟ *verb* **1** press, thrust, shove, propel, prod, poke, ram, depress, squeeze, squash. **2** propel, wheel, drive, move. **3** shove, jostle, elbow one's way. **5** force, drive. **6, 7** coax, urge, *colloq*. egg on, encourage, incite, spur, drive, constrain, influence, persuade, pressurize, bully. **8** recommend, promote, campaign for, press for. **9** promote, advertise, publicize, boost. **10** *colloq*. peddle. *noun* **1** shove, thrust, prod, poke, nudge, jolt, knock. **2** drive, effort. **3** determination, aggression, drive, ambition, dynamism, enterprise, initiative, energy, vigour, vitality, *colloq*. go.

⊟ *verb* **1, 2** pull. **6** discourage, dissuade.

pushbike *noun colloq*. a bicycle propelled by pedals alone.

push button a button pressed to operate a machine, *etc*.

push-button *adj*. operated by pushing a button.

pushchair *noun* a small folding perambulator for a toddler.

pusher *noun colloq*. a person who sells illegal drugs.

pushover *noun colloq*. **1** someone who is easily defeated or outwitted. **2** a task easily accomplished.

pushy *adj*. (**pushier, pushiest**) *colloq*. aggressively self-assertive or ambitious.

⊟ assertive, self-assertive, ambitious, forceful, aggressive, over-confident, forward, bold, brash, *colloq*. in-your-face, arrogant, presumptuous, assuming, *colloq*. bossy.

⊟ unassertive, unassuming.

pusillanimity /pjuːsɪləˈnɪmɪtɪ/ *noun* being pusillanimous; cowardliness, timidity.

pusillanimous /pjuːsɪˈlanɪməs/ *adj*. timid, cowardly, weak-spirited or faint-hearted. [from Latin *pusillus*, diffident + *animus*, spirit]

pusillanimously *adv*. in a pusillanimous way.

puss[1] *noun colloq*. a cat. [related to Dutch *poes*]

puss[2] *noun slang* the face. [from Irish *pus*, mouth]

pussy *noun* (PL. **pussies**) **1** *colloq*. a cat. **2** *coarse slang* the female genitals; the vulva.

pussyfoot *verb intrans*. **1** to behave indecisively; to avoid committing oneself. **2** to pad about stealthily.

pussy willow a willow tree with silky grey catkins.

pustular *adj*. **1** relating to or of the nature of pustules. **2** characterized by pustules.

pustule *noun* a small inflammation on the skin, containing pus; a pimple. [from Latin *pustula*]

put *verb* (**putting**; PAST TENSE AND PAST PARTICIPLE **put**) **1** to place in, or convey to, a position or situation that is specified. **2** to fit: *put a new lock on the door*. **3** to cause to be: *put someone in a good mood*. **4** to apply: *put pressure on them/put paint on the brush*. **5** to set or impose: *put a tax on luxuries/put an end to free lunches*. **6** to lay (blame, reliance, emphasis, *etc*) on something. **7** to set (someone) to work, *etc* or apply (something) to a good purpose, *etc*. **8** to translate: *put this into French*. **9** to invest or pour (energy, money or other resources) into something. **10** to classify, categorize or put in order: *would put accuracy before speed*. **11** to estimate: *put the costs at £10,000*. **12** to submit (questions for answering, ideas for considering) to someone; to suggest: *put it to her that she was lying*. **13** to express: *don't know how to put it/a disaster, to put it mildly*. **14** to write: *don't know what to put*. **15** *intrans*. *Naut*. to sail in a certain direction: *put out to sea*. **16** *Athletics* to throw (the shot). — **put about** *Naut*. to turn round; to change course. **put something about** to spread reports or rumours. **put something across** to communicate ideas, *etc* to others. **put something aside 1** to save money, especially regularly, for future use. **2** to discount or deliberately disregard problems, differences of opinion, *etc* for the sake of convenience, peace, *etc*. **put someone away** *colloq*. to imprison them, or confine them in a mental institution. **put something away 1** to replace it tidily. **2** to save it for future use. **3** *colloq*. to consume food or drink, especially in large amounts. **4** *old use* to reject, discard, or renounce it. **put something back 1** to replace it. **2** to postpone it: *put the meeting back a month*. **3** to adjust a clock, *etc* to an earlier time. **put something by** to save it for the future. **put down** *said of an aircraft* to land. **put someone down** to humiliate or snub them. **put something down 1** to put it on a surface after holding it, *etc*. **2** to crush a revolt, *etc*. **3** to kill an animal painlessly, especially one near death. **4** to write it down: *put down suggestions*. **5** to pay money as a deposit on an intended purchase. **put someone down for something 1** to sum them up or dismiss them as specified: *had put him down for a playboy*. **2** to include them in a list of participants, subscribers, *etc*: *put me down for the trip/put them down for ten pounds*. **put something down to something else** to regard it as caused by something specified: *the errors were put down to inexperience*. **put someone forward** to propose someone's name for a post, *etc*; to nominate them. **put something forward 1** to offer a proposal or suggestion. **2** to advance the time or date of an event or occasion: *will have to put the wedding forward a month*. **3** to adjust a clock, *etc* to a later time. **put in** *Naut*. to enter a port or harbour. **put something in 1** to fit or install it. **2** to spend time working at something: *puts in four hours' violin practice daily*. **3** to submit a claim, *etc*. **4** to interrupt with a comment, *etc*. **put in for something** to apply for it. **put someone off 1** to cancel or postpone an engagement with them: *have to put the Smiths off*. **2** to cause to lose concentration; to distract. **3** to cause them to lose enthusiasm, or to feel disgust, for something: *her accident put me off climbing/he was put off the cheese by its smell*. **put something off 1** to switch off a light, *etc*. **2** to postpone an event or arrangement. **put something on 1** to switch on an electrical device, *etc*. **2** to dress oneself in it. **3** to gain weight or speed. **4** to present a play, show, *etc*. **5** to provide transport, *etc*. **6** to assume an accent, manner, *etc* for effect or to deceive. **7** to bet money on a horse, *etc*. **put someone on to something** or **someone 1** to recommend them to try it: *a friend put me on to these biscuits*. **2** to give them an indication of someone's whereabouts or involvement: *what put the police on to her?* **put one over on someone** *colloq*. to trick or fool them. **put someone out 1** to inconvenience them. **2** to offend or annoy them. **3** *Cricket* to dismiss a player or team from the batting. **put something out 1** to extinguish a light or fire. **2** to issue eg a distress call. **3** to publish eg a leaflet. **4** to strain or dislocate a part of the body. **put something over** to communicate ideas, *etc* to someone else. **put something right** to mend or make it better. **put someone through** to connect them by telephone: *was put through to the manager*. **put something**

through 1 to arrange a deal, agreement, etc. **2** to make a telephone call: *will you put through a call to Zurich?* **put something together** to join up the parts of it; to assemble it. **put up** to stay for the night: *we'd better put up at the local hotel.* **put someone up** to give them a bed for the night. **put something up 1** to build it; to erect it. **2** to raise prices. **3** to present a plan, etc. **4** to offer one's house, etc for sale. **5** to provide funds for a project, etc. **6** to show resistance; to offer a fight. **put up** or **put someone up for something** to offer oneself, or nominate someone, as a candidate: *we are putting you up for chairman.* **put someone up to something** *colloq.* to coerce or manipulate them into doing something devious or illicit: *someone put them up to forging lottery tickets.* **put up with someone** or **something** to bear or tolerate them. **put upon someone** to presume on their good will; to take unfair advantage of them. [from Anglo-Saxon *putian*]

. . . .

◳ **1** place, lay, deposit, *colloq.* plonk, stand, position, set, situate, station, post, settle, establish, dispose. **2** fit, fix. **4** apply, impose, inflict, lay, subject. **5** set, impose, apply, levy, assign, inflict. **6** lay, attribute, assign, ascribe. **8** translate, transcribe. **12** submit, present, offer, suggest, propose. **13** express, word, phrase, formulate, frame, couch, voice, utter, state. **put across** put over, communicate, convey, express, explain, spell out, bring home to, get through to. **put aside 1** put by, put away, save, set aside, keep, retain, reserve, store, stow, stockpile, *colloq.* stash, hoard, salt away. **2** discount, set aside, disregard, ignore, gloss over. **put away** *someone* imprison, jail, lock up, commit, certify, *something* **2** put aside, put by, save, set aside, keep, retain, reserve, store, stow, stockpile, *colloq.* stash, hoard, salt away. **3** consume, devour, eat, drink, *colloq.* knock back. **put back 1** replace, return. **2** postpone, delay, defer, reschedule. **3** retard. **put by** save, put away, put aside, set aside, keep, retain, reserve, store, stow, stockpile, *colloq.* stash, hoard, salt away. **put down** *someone* humiliate, snub, slight, squash, deflate, humble, *colloq.* take down a peg, shame, mortify, *something* **1** replace. **2** crush, quash, suppress, defeat, quell, silence. **3** kill, put to sleep. **4** write down, transcribe, enter, log, register, record, note. **put something down to something else** ascribe, attribute, blame, charge. **put someone forward** nominate, suggest, recommend. **put something forward 1** offer, submit, suggest, propose, advance, move, table, introduce, present, tender. **2** advance, bring forward. **3** advance. **put in** *something* **3** submit, tender, present. **put off** *someone* **2** confuse, distract. **3** deter, dissuade, discourage, dishearten, demoralize, daunt, dismay, intimidate, disconcert, disgust, *something* **2** delay, defer, postpone, reschedule. **put on 1** turn on, start, activate, illuminate. **2** wear. **4** present, stage, mount, produce, do, perform. **5** provide, supply. **6** assume, affect, pretend, feign, fake, sham, simulate. **7** bet, stake. **put out** *someone* **1** inconvenience, trouble, impose on. **2** offend, annoy, bother, irritate, upset, hurt, *something* **1** extinguish, quench, douse, smother, switch off, turn off. **2, 3** publish, announce, broadcast, circulate. **put through** *something* **1** arrange, accomplish, achieve, bring off, complete, conclude, finalize, execute, manage. **put up** *someone* accommodate, house, lodge, shelter, *something* **1** build, erect, construct, assemble. **2** raise, increase. **3** present, submit. **5** pay, invest, give, advance, float, provide, supply, pledge. **put up to** encourage, prompt, incite, coerce, *colloq.* egg on, urge, goad. **put up with** bear, tolerate, stand, abide, stomach, endure, suffer, allow, accept, stand for, take, take lying down.

◱ **put back 2, 3** bring forward, advance. **put forward 3, 4** put back. **put off** *someone* **3** encourage. **put up to** discourage, dissuade. **put up with** object to, reject.

. . . .

putative *adj.* supposed; assumed: *the putative father of the child.* [from Latin *putativus*, from *putare*, to think]

put-down *noun colloq.* a snub or humiliation.

put-on — *adj.*, *said of an accent, manner, etc* assumed; pretended. — *noun colloq.* a trick or deception.

putrefaction *noun* becoming bad or putrid; festering.

putrefy *verb intrans.* (**putrefies**, **putrefied**) to go bad, rot, or decay, especially with a foul smell. [from Latin *putrefacere*, to rot]

putrescent *adj.* decaying; rotting; putrefying. [from Latin *putrescere*, to rot]

putrid *adj.* **1** decayed; rotten. **2** stinking; foul; disgusting. **3** *colloq.* repellent; worthless. [from Latin *putridus*, rotten]

. . . .

◳ **1** rotten, decayed, decomposed, mouldy, off, bad, rancid, addled, corrupt, contaminated, tainted, polluted. **2** stinking, foul, disgusting, rank, fetid.

◱ **1** fresh. **2** fresh, wholesome.

. . . .

putsch /pʊtʃ/ *noun* a secretly planned, sudden attempt to remove a government from power. [from Swiss German *Putsch*]

putt — *verb trans., intrans. Golf, Putting* to send (the ball) gently forward along the ground towards the hole. — *noun* a putting stroke. [originally a form of PUT]

putter *noun* **1** a golf club used for putting. **2** a person who putts.

putting *noun* **1** the act of putting a ball towards a hole. **2** a game somewhat similar to golf, played on a putting-green using only putting strokes.

putting green 1 on a golf course, a smoothly mown patch of grass surrounding a hole. **2** an area of mown turf laid out like a tiny golf course, on which to play putting.

putty *noun* (PL. **putties**) a paste of ground chalk and linseed oil, used for fixing glass in window frames, filling holes in wood, etc. [from French *potée*, potful]

put-up job something dishonestly prearranged to give a false impression.

put-upon *adj.*, *said of a person* taken advantage of, especially unfairly.

. . . .

◳ imposed on, taken advantage of, exploited, used, abused, maltreated, persecuted.

. . . .

puzzle — *verb* **1** to perplex, mystify, bewilder or baffle. **2** *intrans.* (**puzzle about** or **over something**) to brood, ponder, wonder, or worry about it. **3** (*usually* **puzzle something out**) to solve it after prolonged thought. — *noun* **1** a baffling problem. **2** a game or toy taking the form of something for solving, designed to test one's knowledge, memory, powers of reasoning or observation, manipulative skill, etc. — **puzzle one's brains** or **head** to think hard about a problem.

. . . .

◳ *verb* **1** perplex, baffle, mystify, bewilder, confound, *colloq.* stump, *colloq.* floor, confuse, *colloq.* flummox, nonplus. **2** think about, ponder (on), meditate on, consider, mull over, deliberate, rack one's brains. **3** solve, work out, figure out, sort out, resolve, clear up, decipher, decode, crack, unravel, untangle. *noun* **1** poser, brainteaser, mind-bender, question, conundrum, mystery, enigma, paradox, riddle.

. . . .

puzzlement *noun* a puzzled state.

puzzler *noun* **1** a challenging problem or question; a poser. **2** a person who enjoys solving puzzles.

puzzling *adj.* that puzzles.

PVC *abbrev.* polyvinyl chloride.

PVS *abbrev.* **1** persistent vegetative state. **2** postviral syndrome.

PW *abbrev.* policewoman.

pyaemia or **pyemia** /paɪˈiːmɪə/ *noun Medicine* a form of blood poisoning caused by the release of pus-forming micro-organisms, especially bacteria, into the bloodstream from an abscess or wound, and resulting in the formation of multiple abscesses in different parts of the body. [from Greek *pyon*, pus + *haima*, blood]

pye-dog or **pie-dog** *noun* a stray mongrel in Oriental regions; a pariah dog. [from Hindi *pahi*, outsider]

pygmy or **pigmy** — *noun* (PL. **pygmies**) **1** (Pygmy) a member of one of the unusually short peoples of equatorial Africa. **2** an undersized person; a dwarf. **3** *derog.* someone of no significance: *an intellectual pygmy*. — *adj.* of a small-sized breed: *pygmy hippopotamuses*. [from Greek *pygmaios*, literally 'measuring a *pygme* (= the distance from knuckle to elbow)']

pygmy shrew a small shrew, the most widespread in Europe, 3.9 to 6.4cm long (not including the tail) with a brown coat and pale underparts. It is rarely visible, although its shrill squeaking can often be heard in hedge bottoms.

pyjamas or *North Amer.* **pajamas** *pl. noun* a sleeping-suit consisting of a loose jacket or top, and trousers. [from Persian and Hindi *payjamah*, leg-clothing]

pylon *noun* **1** a tall steel structure for supporting electric power cables. **2** a post or tower to guide a pilot at an airfield. **3** an external structure on an aircraft for supporting an engine, etc. **4** *Archaeol.* a gate tower or ornamental gateway. [from Greek *pylon*, from *pyle*, gate]

pyorrhoea or *North Amer.* **pyorrhea** /paɪəˈrɪə/ *noun* a discharge of pus, especially from the gums or tooth sockets. [from Greek *pyon*, pus + *rheein*, to flow]

pyramid *noun* **1** any of the huge ancient Egyptian royal tombs built on a square base, with four sloping triangular sides meeting in a common apex. **2** *Geom.* a solid of this shape, with a square or triangular base. **3** any structure, pile, etc of similar shape. [from Greek *pyramis*]

pyramidal *adj.* having the form of a pyramid.

pyramid selling the sale of goods in bulk to a distributor who divides them and sells them to sub-distributors at a profit, and so on.

pyre *noun* a pile of wood on which a dead body is ceremonially cremated. [from Greek *pyra*, from *pyr*, fire]

Pyrenean mountain dog a breed of dog developed in the Pyrenees several centuries ago to protect sheep. It has a large powerful body with a heavy head, and a thick coat, usually pale in colour.

pyrethrum /paɪˈriːθrəm/ *noun* **1** a flower of the chrysanthemum family. **2** an insecticide prepared from its flower-heads. [from Greek *pyrethron*, a plant of the nettle family]

pyretic *adj. Medicine* relating to, or accompanied by, fever. [from Greek *pyretos*, fever]

Pyrex *noun trademark* a type of heat-resistant glass used especially for ovenware.

pyrexia *noun Medicine* fever. [from Greek *pyrexis*, from *pyressein*, to be feverish]

pyridine /ˈpɪrɪdiːn/ *noun Chem.* (SYMBOL C_5H_5N) a carcinogenic flammable colourless liquid with a strong unpleasant smell, present in coal tar, that is used in the manufacture of other organic chemicals, in paints and textile dyes, and as a solvent. [from Greek *pyr*, fire]

pyridoxine /pɪrɪˈdɒksiːn/ *noun* vitamin B_6. [from *pyridine* + OXYGEN]

pyrimidine /paɪˈrɪmɪdiːn/ *noun Biochem.* a nitrogenous base with a single ring structure. The most important derivatives of pyrimidine are cytosine, thymine, and uracil, which are major components of nucleotides and the nucleic acids DNA (which contains cytosine and thymine) and RNA (which contains cytosine and uracil).

pyrite /ˈpaɪraɪt/ *noun Geol.* the commonest sulphide mineral, used as a source of sulphur, and in the production of sulphuric acid. It is often called fool's gold because of its yellowish-gold colour and metallic lustre, although it is harder and more brittle than gold. Also called IRON PYRITES.

pyro- *combining form* forming words denoting fire: *pyromania*/*pyrotechnics*. [from Greek *pyr*, fire]

pyroclast *noun Geol.* an individual fragment of lava, of any size, that has been ejected into the atmosphere during a volcanic eruption. [from Greek *pyr*, fire + *klastos*, broken]

pyrolusite *noun Geol.* (SYMBOL MnO_2) a soft black mineral that is the most important ore of manganese.

pyrolysis /paɪˈrɒlɪsɪs/ *noun Chem.* the chemical decomposition of a substance (eg heavy oil, rubber) that occurs when it is heated to a high temperature in the absence of air.

pyromania *noun Psychol.* an obsessive urge to set fire to things. [from PYRO- + -MANIA]

pyromaniac *noun Psychol.* a person who has an obsessive urge to set fire to things.

. . . .

▣ arsonist, incendiary, fire-raiser, *colloq.* firebug.

. . . .

pyrometer *noun Physics* a type of thermometer that is used to measure high temperatures.

pyrotechnics *noun* **1** (*sing.*) the art of making fireworks. **2** (*pl.*) a fireworks display. **3** (*pl.*) a display of fiery brilliance in speech, music, etc.

pyroxene *noun Geol.* any of a group of important rock-forming silicate minerals that are found both in igneous and in metamorphic rocks, and may be white, yellow, green, greenish-black, or brown in colour. They include jadeite (the most highly prized form of jade). [from PYRO- + Greek *xenos*, stranger, because it was thought that pyroxene crystals in lava had been caught up accidentally]

Pyrrhic victory /ˈpɪrɪk/ a victory won at so great a cost in lives, etc that it can hardly be regarded as a triumph at all. [named after Pyrrhus, king of Epirus in Greece, who won such victories against the Romans in the 3c BC]

pyruvic acid *Biochem.* an organic acid that is the end-product of the breakdown of carbohydrates by glycolysis, and if oxygen is available is then oxidized to carbon dioxide and water by the Krebs cycle, a sequence of reactions that release large amounts of energy. [from Greek *pyr*, fire + Latin *uva*, grape]

Pythagoras's theorem /paɪˈθagərəsɪz/ *Maths.* a theorem which states that, in a right-angled triangle, the square of the length of the hypotenuse (the longest side) is equal to the sum of the squares of the other two sides. It can be used to calculate the length of any side of such a triangle if the lengths of the other sides are known. [named after the Greek philosopher and mathematician Pythagoras]

python *noun* any non-venomous constricting egg-laying snake of the boa family, found in most tropical regions except for N and S America and Madagascar. It coils its body around its prey, which includes hares, rats, and antelopes, and squeezes it until it suffocates. [named after Python, a monster killed by the Greek god Apollo]

pyx /pɪks/ *noun* **1** *Christianity* a container in which the consecrated Communion bread is kept. **2** a box at the Royal Mint in which sample coins for testing are kept. [from Greek *pyxis*, a box of boxwood]

pzazz see PIZZAZZ.

Q

Q¹ or **q** *noun* (PL. **Qs, Q's, q's**) the seventeenth letter of the English alphabet.

Q² *abbrev.* **1** Queen or Queen's. **2** *Chess* queen. **3** question.

QC *abbrev.* Queen's Counsel.

QC *abbrev.* quality control.

QED *abbrev. quod erat demonstrandum* (Latin), which was what had to be proved.

qi or **chi** /tʃiː/ *noun Chinese Medicine* an individual person's life force, the free flow of which within the body is believed to ensure physical and spiritual health. [from Chinese *qi*, breath, energy]

qi gong /tʃiː ˈgʊŋ/ a system of meditational exercises combined with deep breathing designed to promote physical and spiritual health. [from Chinese *qi*, breath, energy]

QM *abbrev.* quartermaster.

qq.v. or **qqv.** *abbrev. quae vide* (Latin), which see; see these words (used when referring to more than one item).

qr *abbrev.* quarter.

qt *abbrev.* quart.

q.t. — **on the q.t.** *colloq.* on the quiet; secretly.

qua /kweɪ, kwaː/ *prep.* considered as; as being: *the cartoonist's art qua art.* [from Latin *qua*, feminine ablative singular of *qui*, who]

quack¹ — *noun* the cry of a duck. — *verb intrans.* **1** *said of a duck* to make this cry. **2** to talk in a loud silly voice. [imitative]

quack² *noun* **1** a medically unqualified person who claims a doctor's knowledge and skill. **2** *colloq., often derog.* a doctor. [from Old Dutch *quacksalver*]

quackery *noun* the activities or methods of a quack.

quad¹ /kwɒd/ *noun colloq.* a quadruplet.

quad² /kwɒd/ *noun colloq.* a quadrangle.

quad³ /kwɒd/ *colloq.* — *adj.* quadraphonic. — *noun* quadraphonics.

quad bike /kwɒd/ a small, powerful, four-wheel drive vehicle, used in military, agricultural, and sporting activities. [from QUADRUPLE]

quadr- or **quadri-** *combining form* forming words meaning 'four'. [from Latin, from *quattuor*, four]

Quadragesima /kwɒdrəˈdʒɛsɪmə/ *noun* in the Christian calendar, the first Sunday in Lent. [from Latin *quadragesima dies*, fortieth day]

quadrangle *noun* **1** *Geom.* a square, rectangle, or other four-sided two-dimensional figure. **2** an open rectangular court within the buildings of a college, school, etc. [from Latin *quadrangulum*, from *quadr-*, four + *angulus*, angle]

quadrant *noun* **1** *Geom.* a quarter of the circumference of a circle. **2** *Geom.* a quarter of a circle, ie an area bounded by two radii meeting at right angles. **3** *Geom.* a quarter of a sphere, ie a section cut by two planes intersecting at right angles at the centre. **4** any device or mechanical part in the shape of a 90° arc. **5** *Naut., Astron.* an instrument incorporating a graduated 90° arc, used for measuring altitude, eg of the stars.

quadraphonic *adj.*, *said of sound reproduction* using four loudspeakers fed by four separate channels. [from QUADR- + STEREOPHONIC]

quadraphonics *sing. noun* a sound system employing at least four loudspeakers fed by four separate amplified signals.

quadraphony /kwɒˈdrɒfənɪ/ *noun* a quadraphonic sound system.

quadrat /ˈkwɒdrat/ *noun Biol.* a random sample area of ground enclosed within a frame, often one metre square, which is studied in order to determine the plant and animal species it supports. Permanent quadrats can be examined at intervals in order to assess changes in species composition over time. [from Latin *quadratus*, squared]

quadrate /ˈkwɒdreɪt, ˈkwɒdrət/ — *noun Anat.* in the upper jaw of bony fish, amphibians, birds, and reptiles, one of a pair of bones that articulates with the lower jaw. In mammals it is represented by the *incus*, a small bone in the middle ear. — *adj. Bot.* square or almost square in cross-section or face view. [from Latin *quadrare*, to make square]

quadratic equation *Maths.* an algebraic equation that involves the square, but no higher power, of an unknown quantity or variable. It has the general formula $ax^2 + bx + c = 0$, where x is the unknown variable. In coordinate geometry, a quadratic equation represents a parabola.

quadrennial *adj.* **1** lasting four years. **2** occurring every four years. [from Latin *quadriennium*, four-year period, from *quadri-*, four + *annus*, year]

quadrennially *adv.* every four years.

quadrilateral — *noun Geom.* a four-sided two-dimensional figure. — *adj.* four-sided. [from Latin quadrilaterus, from *quadri-*, four + *latus*, side]

quadrille¹ /kwɒˈdrɪl, kwəˈdrɪl/ *noun* a square dance for four couples, in five or six movements; music for this. [from Spanish *cuadrilla*, troop]

quadrille² /kwɒˈdrɪl, kwəˈdrɪl/ *noun Cards* a game for four players using 40 cards. [from Spanish *cuartillo*]

quadriplegia /kwɒdrɪˈpliːdʒɪə/ *noun* paralysis affecting the arms and legs. [from QUADR- + Greek *plege*, blow, stroke]

quadriplegic *adj.* paralysed in all four limbs.

quadruped /ˈkwɒdrʊped/ *noun* a four-footed animal, especially a mammal. [from Latin *quadrupes*, from *quadru-*, a variant of QUADRI- + *pes*, foot]

quadruple /ˈkwɒdrʊpl, kwɒˈdruːpl/ — *verb trans., intrans.* to multiply by four or increase fourfold. — *adj.* **1** four times as many or much. **2** composed of four parts. **3** *Mus.*, *said of time* having four beats to the bar. — *noun* a quadruple number or amount. [from Latin *quadruplus*, fourfold]

quadruplet /ˈkwɒdrʊplət, kwɒˈdruːplət/ *noun* each of four children or animals born at one birth.

quadruplicate — *verb* (pronounced -keɪt) to make quadruple or fourfold. — *adj.* (pronounced -kət) fourfold; copied four times.— **in quadruplicate** copied four times. [from Latin *quadruplicare*, to multiply by four]

quadruply *adv.* in a fourfold way.

quaff /kwɒf/ *verb trans., intrans. literary, facetious* to drink eagerly or deeply.

quagga *noun* an extinct Southern African wild ass, related to the zebra but striped on head and shoulders only. [perhaps from Hottentot *quacha*]

quagmire /'kwagmaɪə(r)/ *noun* an area of soft marshy ground; a bog. [from *quag*, bog + MIRE]
. . . .
▣ bog, marsh, fen, swamp, morass, mire, quicksand.
. . . .

quaich /kweɪx/ *noun Scot.* a two-handled drinking-cup usually of silver or pewter. [from Gaelic *cuach*, cup]

quail[1] *verb intrans.* to lose courage or feel fear; to flinch.
. . . .
▣ flinch, cringe, cower, tremble, quake, shudder, falter, recoil, shrink, back away, shy away.
. . . .

quail[2] *noun* a small bird of the partridge family. [from French *quaille*]

quaint *adj.* charmingly or pleasingly odd or old-fashioned. [from Old French *cointe*, from Latin *cognitus*, known]
. . . .
▣ charming, *colloq.* twee, old-fashioned, antiquated, old-world, *colloq.* olde-worlde, picturesque, unusual, strange, odd, curious, whimsical, bizarre, fanciful.
▣ modern.
. . . .

quake[1] — *verb intrans.* **1** *said of people* to shake or tremble with fear, etc. **2** *said of a building, etc* to rock or shudder. — *noun* a shudder or tremor, of fear, etc. [from Anglo-Saxon *cwacian*]
. . . .
▣ *verb* SHAKE, TREMBLE, SHUDDER, QUIVER, SHIVER. **1** quail. **2** vibrate, wobble, rock, sway, move, convulse, heave.
. . . .

quake[2] *noun colloq.* an earthquake.

Quaker *noun* a member of a Christian movement, the Society of Friends, founded by George Fox in the 17c.

qualification *noun* **1** an official record that one has completed a training, performed satisfactorily in an examination, etc. **2** a skill or ability that fits one for some job, etc. **3** the act, process, or fact of qualifying. **4** an addition to a statement, etc that narrows or restricts it; a condition, limitation, or modification.
. . . .
▣ **1** certificate, diploma. **2** skill, ability, competence, capability, capacity, aptitude, suitability, fitness, eligibility. **3** training. **4** condition, restriction, limitation, modification, caveat, provision, proviso, rider, stipulation, reservation, exception, exemption.
. . . .

qualifier *noun* a person or thing that qualifies.

qualify *verb* (**qualifies, qualified**) **1** *intrans.* to complete a training, pass an examination, etc, that gives one professional status: *has qualified as a nurse.* **2** to make suitable for a task, job, etc: *is hardly qualified to judge.* **3** *intrans.* (**qualify for something**) to fulfil requirements that give one a right to an award, privilege, etc: *doesn't qualify for a grant.* **4** *intrans.* to be seen as having the right characteristics to be: *what qualifies as news these days?* **5** to add something to (a statement, etc) that restricts or limits it. **6** to modify, tone down, or restrict: *qualified approval.* **7** *Grammar, said of an adjective* to define or describe (a noun). **8** *intrans. Sport* to reach a standard in a preliminary round that entitles one to participate in subsequent rounds. [from Latin *qualis*, of what kind + *facere*, to make]
. . . .
▣ **1** pass, graduate, train, prepare. **2** equip, fit, entitle, authorize, sanction, permit, empower. **4** count, pass. **5** limit, restrict, delimit. **6** modify, moderate, tone down, reduce, lessen, diminish, temper, soften, weaken, mitigate, ease, adjust, restrain, restrict.
. . . .

qualitative /'kwɒlɪtətɪv, 'kwɒlɪteɪtɪv/ *adj.* relating to, investigating, or affecting the qualities or standard of something.

quality *noun* (PL. **qualities**) **1** standard of goodness. **2** excellence; high standard: *novels of quality.* **3** (*attributive*) of a high quality or standard: *quality newspapers.* **4** a characteristic or attribute: *has a silky quality.* **5** the character given to a voice or other sound by attributes other than pitch or loudness. **6** *old use* high social status. [from Latin *qualitas*, from *qualis*, of what kind]
. . . .
▣ **1** standard, grade, class, calibre, status, rank, value, worth, merit, condition, kind, sort. **2** excellence, superiority, pre-eminence, distinction, refinement. **4** characteristic, attribute, property, aspect, feature, character, nature, trait, mark.
. . . .

quality control the regular sampling of the output of an industrial process in order to detect any variations in quality.

quality time a concentrated amount of time spent with a companion or child without interruptions or distractions.

qualm /kwɑːm/ *noun* **1** a sudden feeling of nervousness or apprehension. **2** a feeling of uneasiness about whether what one is doing is right; a scruple, misgiving, or pang of conscience. **3** a feeling of faintness or nausea. [from Anglo-Saxon *cwealm*, death, murder, slaughter, plague]
. . . .
▣ **1** misgiving, apprehension, fear, anxiety, worry, disquiet, uneasiness. **2** misgiving, scruple, hesitation, reluctance, uncertainty, doubt.
. . . .

quandary /'kwɒndərɪ/ *noun* (PL. **quandaries**) a situation in which one is at a loss what to do; a dilemma or predicament.
. . . .
▣ dilemma, predicament, impasse, mess, fix, *colloq.* hole, problem, difficulty.
. . . .

quango *noun* (PL. **quangos**) a government-funded body responsible for some area of public concern. Its senior appointments are made by the government. [from quasi-autonomous non-governmental organization]

quantify *verb* (**quantifies, quantified**) to find out the quantity of; to express as a quantity. [from Latin *quantus*, how much + *facere*, to make]

quantitative /'kwɒntɪtətɪv, 'kwɒntɪteɪtɪv/ *adj.* **1** relating to quantity. **2** estimated, or measurable, in terms of quantity.

quantity *noun* (PL. **quantities**) **1** the property things have that makes them measurable or countable; size or amount. **2** an amount that can be counted or measured; a specified amount: *a tiny quantity.* **3** largeness of amount; bulk: *buy in quantity/quality, not quantity, is what counts.* **4** (**quantities**) a large amount: *quantities of food.* **5** *Maths.* a value that may be expressed as a number, or the symbol or figure representing it. **6** *Prosody* the length or duration of a vowel sound or syllable. — **an unknown quantity** a person or thing whose importance or influence cannot be foreseen. [from Latin *quantitas*, from *quantus*, how much]
. . . .
▣ **1** amount, number, size, magnitude, capacity, volume, weight, mass, bulk, expanse, extent, length, breadth. **2** sum, total, aggregate, measure, dose, proportion, part, lot, share, portion, quota, allotment, content. **4** *colloq.* masses, *colloq.* lots, *colloq.* tons, *colloq.* loads, *colloq.* heaps, *colloq.* stacks.
. . . .

quantity surveyor a person who estimates the quantities of materials needed to build something, and their probable cost.

quantize or **quantise** *verb Physics* to form into quanta (see QUANTUM).

quantum /'kwɒntəm/ *noun* (PL. **quanta**) **1** an amount or quantity. **2** *Physics* a tiny indivisible packet of energy, representing the form in which atoms give off electromagnetic radiation, eg light, according to quantum theory (a quantum of electromagnetic radiation is known as a *photon*). [from Latin *quantus*, how much]

quantum leap or **quantum jump** a sudden transition; a spectacular advance.

quantum theory *Physics* a theory which states that electromagnetic radiation, such as light, is emitted in separate packets of energy called *quanta* or *photons*. Electrons move in fixed orbits around the nucleus of an atom, and when that atom absorbs energy (eg as a result of being heated), one of its electrons may be raised to a higher energy level or orbit. When the electron returns to its original orbit, it emits the same 'packet' of energy as a photon of radiation.

quarantine /'kwɒrəntiːn/ — *noun* the isolation of people or animals to prevent the spread of any infectious disease that they could be developing; the duration of such isolation. — *verb* to impose such isolation on; to put into quarantine. [from Italian *quarantina*, period of 40 days]

quark /kwɑːk, kwɔːk/ *noun Physics* any of a group of subatomic particles of which all hadrons (subatomic particles such as protons and neutrons) are composed. It is thought that there are six types or 'flavours' of quark (up, down, top, bottom, strange, and charm), and each type of quark is believed to have an antiparticle known as an antiquark. [coined by the writer James Joyce in *Finnegans Wake*; adopted for scientific use by the American physicist Murray Gell-Mann]

quarrel — *noun* 1 an angry disagreement or argument. 2 a cause of such disagreement; a complaint: *I've no quarrel with the management*. 3 a break in a friendship; a breach or rupture. — *verb intrans.* (**quarrelled**, **quarrelling**) 1 to argue or dispute angrily. 2 to disagree and remain on bad terms: *I think they must have quarrelled.* 3 to find fault: *I can't quarrel with her reasoning.* [from Latin *querela*, complaint]

· · · · · · · · · · · · · · · · · · · ·

▣ *noun* **1** row, argument, *colloq.* slanging match, wrangle, squabble, tiff, misunderstanding, disagreement, dispute, dissension, controversy, difference, conflict, clash, contention, strife, fight, *colloq.* scrap, brawl, feud, vendetta. **2** complaint, quibble, grievance. **3** breach, rupture, difference, rift, split, division, feud, vendetta, schism. *verb* **1** row, argue, bicker, squabble, wrangle, disagree, dispute, dissent, differ, be at variance, clash, contend, fight, *colloq.* scrap. **2** fall out, be at loggerheads, feud. **3** fault, criticize, dispute.

▣ *noun* **1, 3** agreement, harmony. *verb* **1** agree.

· ·

quarrelsome *adj.* inclined to quarrel or dispute.

· · · · · · · · · · · · · · · · · · · ·

▣ argumentative, disputatious, contentious, belligerent, ill-tempered, irritable.

▣ peaceable, placid.

· ·

quarry[1] — *noun* (PL. **quarries**) 1 an open excavation for the purpose of extracting stone or slate for building. 2 any source from which a supply of information or other material is obtained. — *verb* (**quarries**, **quarried**) 1 to extract (stone, etc) from a quarry. 2 to excavate a quarry in (land). 3 to get a supply of (material or information) from a source. [from Latin *quadrare*, to square]

quarry[2] *noun* (PL. **quarries**) 1 a hunted animal or bird; a prey. 2 someone or something that is the object of pursuit. [from Old French *cuiree*, from *cuir*, hide]

· · · · · · · · · · · · · · · · · · · ·

▣ **1** prey, victim, game, kill. **2** object, goal, target, prize.

· ·

quarry tile an unglazed floor tile.

quart /kwɔːt/ *noun* a liquid measure equivalent to a quarter of a gallon or two pints (1.136 litres). [from Latin *quartus*, fourth]

quarter — *noun* 1 one of four equal parts into which an object or quantity may be divided; the fraction -, one divided by four. 2 any of the three-month divisions of the year, especially beginning or ending on a quarter day. 3 a unit of weight equal to a quarter of a hundredweight or 28lbs. 4 *colloq.* 4ozs, or a quarter of a pound. 5 a unit of measure for grain, equal to eight bushels. 6 *North Amer.* 25 cents, or a coin of this value. 7 a period of 15 minutes; a point of time 15 minutes after or before any hour. 8 a fourth part of the moon's cycle; either of the visible shapes (phases) of the moon when half its surface is lit, at the point between the first and second, and the third and fourth, quarters of its cycle. 9 any of the four compass directions; any direction. 10 a district of a city, etc, eg identified by the predominant nationality of its population: *living in the Spanish quarter*. 11 (*often* **quarters**) a section of the public; certain people or a certain person: *disapproval in certain quarters/no sympathy from that quarter*. 12 (**quarters**) lodgings or accommodation, eg for soldiers and their families: *married quarters*. 13 *old use* mercy shown to someone in one's power, eg a defeated enemy: *give no quarter*. 14 *Heraldry* any of the four parts into which a shield is divided by intersecting horizontal and vertical lines. 15 any limb of a four-limbed animal: *hindquarters*. 16 *Sport* any of four equal parts into which a match in some sports is divided. — *verb* (**quartered**, **quartering**) 1 to divide into quarters. 2 to accommodate or billet in lodgings. 3 *Hist.* to divide (the body of a hanged traitor, etc) into four parts. 4 *Heraldry* to fill each quarter of (a shield) with bearings. 5 *said of hounds* to cross and recross (an area) searching for game. — *adj.* being one of four equal parts: *a quarter hour*. [from Old French *quartier*, from Latin *quartarius*, fourth part]

· · · · · · · · · · · · · · · · · · · ·

▣ *noun* **9** direction, side, point. **10** district, sector, zone, neighbourhood, locality, vicinity, area, region, province, territory, division, section, part, place, spot. **12** accommodation, lodgings, billet, *colloq.* digs, rooms, barracks, residence, dwelling, habitation, domicile, station. *verb* **2** billet, accommodate, put up, lodge, board, house, shelter, station, post.

· ·

quarterback *noun Amer. Football* a player between the forwards and halfbacks, who directs his team's attacking play.

quarter day any of the four days beginning or ending one of the year's quarters, on which rent or interest is paid.

quarterdeck *noun* the stern part of a ship's upper deck, usually reserved for officers.

quarter final (*also* **quarter finals**) the round of a competition involving four games or matches, preceding the semi-final.

quarter-finalist *noun* a person who qualifies to take part in a quarter final.

quartering *noun Heraldry* (*usually* **quarterings**) the coats of arms displayed on a shield to indicate family alliances.

quarterlight *noun* a small window in either front door of a car, that pivots open for ventilation.

quarterly — *adj.* done, occurring, or published once every quarter of a year. — *adv.* once every quarter. — *noun* (PL. **quarterlies**) a quarterly publication.

quartermaster *noun* 1 an army officer responsible for soldiers' accommodation, food, and clothing. 2 *Naut.* a petty officer responsible for navigation and signals.

quarter note *North Amer.* a crotchet.

quarter sessions *Hist.* a local court of law presided over by a justice of the peace, formerly held quarterly.

quarterstaff *noun Hist.* a 6ft (1.83m) pole used as a weapon.

quartet or **quartette** *noun* 1 an ensemble of four singers or instrumental players. 2 a piece of music for four such performers. 3 any group or set of four. [from Italian *quartetto*, from Latin *quartus*, fourth]

quarto /'kwɔːtoʊ/ *noun* (PL. **quartos**) *Printing* a size of paper produced by folding a sheet into four leaves or eight pages. [from Latin *in quarto*, in one fourth]

quartz /kwɔːts/ *noun Geol.* one of the commonest minerals, consisting of pure silica. [from German *Quarz*]

quartz clock a clock whose moving mechanism is controlled by the vibrations of a quartz crystal. Such a system is also used in quartz watches.

quartz crystal 1 a transparent colourless form of quartz, either naturally occurring or manufactured synthetically, used in optics and electronics. **2** a piezoelectric crystal of quartz that vibrates at a fixed frequency when a suitable electrical signal is applied to it, used to control the moving mechanism of quartz clocks and watches.

quartzite *noun* **1** *Geol.* any of various pale or white highly durable metamorphic rocks, composed largely or entirely of quartz, and formed by the recrystallization of sandstone under increasing temperature and pressure. Quartzites are used as a construction material in the building industry. **2** a non-metamorphic sandstone consisting of grains of quartz cemented together by silica.

quasar /'kweɪzɑː(r), 'kweɪsɑː(r)/ *noun* a highly luminous star-like point source of radiation (including radio waves) outside our galaxy. Quasars are thought to be the most distant and luminous bodies so far discovered in the universe. [from *quasi-stellar object*]

quash /kwɒʃ/ *verb* **1** to reject (a verdict, etc) as invalid. **2** to annul (a law, etc). **3** to subdue, crush, or suppress (a rebellion, etc). [from Latin *quassare*, to shake]

⊟ **1** invalidate, squash, overrule, annul, revoke, rescind, reverse, set aside, cancel, nullify, void. **2** annul, revoke, rescind, cancel, nullify, reverse, set aside, void. **3** subdue, crush, quell, suppress, defeat, overthrow.

⊟ **1** confirm, vindicate. **2** reinstate.

quasi- /'kweɪsaɪ, 'kwɑːziː/ *prefix* forming words meaning: **1** to some extent; virtually: *a quasi-official role*. **2** in many respects similar to; virtual: *a quasi-deity*. **3** seeming or seemingly, but not actually so: *quasi-technical jargon* / *quasi-experts*. [from Latin *quasi*, as if]

quassia /'kwɒʃə/ *noun* **1** a S American tree whose bitter wood and bark are used as a tonic. **2** a West Indian tree of the same family. [from Graman Quassi, an 18c Negro slave in Surinam who discovered its medicinal properties]

quaternary /kwɒ'tɜːnərɪ/ — *adj.* **1** having four parts. **2** (**Quaternary**) *Geol.* belonging or relating to the second period of the Cenozoic era, which began about two million years ago at the end of the Tertiary. It is the most recent period of geological time, and includes the Pleistocene and Holocene epochs. Modern man (*Homo sapiens*) evolved during this period. — *noun* (**Quaternary**) *Geol.* this period. [from Latin *quaterni*, four each]

quatrain /'kwɒtreɪn/ *noun Poetry* a verse or poem of four lines, usually rhyming alternately. [from French, from *quatre*, four]

quatrefoil /'katrəfɔɪl/ *noun* **1** *Bot.* **a** a flower with four petals. **b** a leaf composed of four lobes or leaflets. **2** *Archit.* a four-lobed design used especially in open stonework. [from Old French *quatre*, four + *foil*, leaf]

quattrocento /'kwatrou'tʃentou/ *noun* the 15c, usually with reference to Italian Renaissance art. [from Italian *quattrocento*, four (for fourteen) hundred]

quaver — *verb* (**quavered, quavering**) **1** *intrans.*, *said of someone's voice* to be unsteady; to shake or tremble. **2** *trans.* to say or sing in a trembling voice. — *noun* **1** *Mus.* a note that lasts half as long as a crotchet. **2** a tremble in the voice. [perhaps imitative]

⊟ *verb* **1** shake, tremble, quake, shudder, quiver, vibrate, pulsate, oscillate, flutter, flicker, trill, warble. **2** trill, warble.

quavery *adj.* likely to quaver, quavering.

quay /kiː/ *noun* a wharf for the loading and unloading of ships. [from Old French *kay*]

⊟ wharf, pier, jetty, dock, harbour.

queasily *adv.* in a queasy way.

queasiness *noun* a queasy state or feeling.

queasy *adj.* (**queasier, queasiest**) **1** feeling slightly sick. **2** *said of the stomach or digestion* easily upset. **3** *said of food* causing feelings of nausea. **4** *said of the conscience* readily made uneasy.

⊟ **1** sick, ill, unwell, queer, groggy, green, nauseated, sickened, bilious, faint, dizzy, giddy.

Quechua /'ketʃwə/ — *noun* a S American language of the Andean-Equatorial group. It is the official language of the Incas, and has a written history dating from the 7c AD. — *adj.* relating to or spoken or written in Quechua.

queen — *noun* **1** a woman who rules a country, having inherited her position by birth. **2** the wife of a king. **3** a woman supreme in her field; a place or thing considered supreme in some way. **4** a large female ant, bee, or wasp that lays eggs. **5** the most powerful chess piece, able to move forwards, backwards, sideways, or diagonally. **6** a playing-card bearing the picture of a queen. **7** *offensive slang* an effeminate male homosexual. — *verb trans.*, *intrans. Chess* to make (a pawn) into a queen; (of a pawn) to be converted into a queen. — **queen it** *colloq.*, *said of a woman* to behave overbearingly.

⊟ *noun* **1** monarch, sovereign, ruler, majesty, empress. **2** consort.

Queen Anne's lace cow parsley.

queen consort the wife of a reigning king.

queenly *adj.* characteristic of or suitable for a queen.

queen mother the widow of a king who is also the mother of a reigning king or queen.

queen post *Archit.* one of two upright posts in a trussed roof, supporting the principal rafter.

Queen's Bench or **King's Bench** in the UK, a division of the High Court of Justice.

Queensberry Rules the code of rules used in boxing, drawn up in 1867 for the Marquess of Queensberry.

Queen's English or **King's English** standard written or spoken English, generally regarded as the most correct or acceptable form.

Queen's evidence or **King's evidence** evidence for the prosecution given by a participant in a crime. — **turn Queen's** or **King's evidence** *said of a criminal* to give such evidence.

Queen's Guide or **King's Guide** a Guide who has reached the highest level of proficiency.

Queen's highway or **King's highway** a public road, regarded as being under royal control.

Queen's Scout or **King's Scout** a Scout who has reached the highest level of proficiency.

queer /kwɪə(r)/ *adj.* **1** odd, strange, or unusual. **2** *colloq.* slightly mad. **3** faint or ill: *feeling queer*. **4** *colloq.* suspicious; shady: *queer doings*. **5** *offensive slang*, *said of a man* homosexual. — **in queer street** *colloq.* in debt or financial difficulties. **queer someone's pitch** *colloq.* to spoil their plans; to thwart them.

⊟ **1** odd, strange, unusual, mysterious, uncommon, weird, unnatural, bizarre, eccentric, peculiar, funny, puzzling, curious, remarkable. **2** crazy, *colloq.* barmy, daft, *colloq.* dotty. **3** faint, unwell, ill, sick, queasy, light-headed, giddy, dizzy. **4** suspicious, suspect, shifty, dubious, *colloq.* shady. **5** homosexual, gay.

⊟ **1** ordinary, usual, common. **3** well.

queerly *adv.* in a queer way; oddly.

queerness *noun* a queer state or feeling.

quell *verb* **1** to crush or subdue (riots, disturbances, opposition, etc). **2** to suppress or overcome (unwanted feelings, etc). [from Anglo-Saxon *cwellan*, to kill]

■ **1** crush, subdue, quash, squash, suppress, put down, defeat, overpower, overcome, conquer. **2** suppress, overcome, conquer, allay, alleviate, soothe, calm, pacify, silence, hush, quiet, stifle, extinguish, moderate, mitigate.

quench *verb* **1** to get rid of (one's thirst) by drinking. **2** to extinguish (a fire). **3** to damp or crush (ardour, enthusiasm, desire, etc). **4** to cool a metal rapidly by plunging it in a liquid or gas, eg water, oil, or air, in order to alter its properties, especially to harden steel or to soften copper. [from Anglo-Saxon *acwencan*]

■ **1** satisfy, slake, sate, cool. **2** extinguish, douse, put out, snuff out. **3** damp, crush, quash, suppress, overcome, conquer, allay, alleviate, soothe, calm, pacify, silence, hush, quiet, stifle, extinguish, moderate, mitigate.

quenelle /kəˈnɛl/ *noun* a dumpling of fish, chicken, veal, etc. [from French *quenelle*]

quern /kwɜːn/ *noun Hist., Archaeol.* a stone implement of any of several kinds for grinding grain by hand. [from Anglo-Saxon *cweorn*]

querulous /ˈkwɛrjʊləs, ˈkwɛrʊləs/ *adj.* **1** inclined to complain. **2** *said of a voice, tone, etc* complaining, grumbling, or whining. [from Latin *querulus*, from *queri*, to complain]

■ **1** peevish, fretful, fractious, cantankerous, cross, irritable, complaining, grumbling, discontented, dissatisfied, critical, carping, captious, fault-finding, fussy. **2** complaining, grumbling, whining, peevish, cross, irritable, discontented. ✇ CHEERFUL. **1** placid, uncomplaining, contented.

query — *noun* (PL. **queries**) **1** a question, especially one that raises a doubt. **2** a request for information; an inquiry. **3** a question mark. — *verb* (**queries, queried**) **1** to raise a doubt about: *query a bill.* **2** to ask: *'How much?' she queried.* [from Latin *quaere*, imperative of *quaerere*, to ask]

■ *noun* **1** question, problem, uncertainty, doubt, suspicion, scepticism, reservation, hesitation. **2** request, inquiry. *verb* **1** question, challenge, dispute, quarrel with, doubt, suspect, distrust, mistrust, disbelieve. **2** ask, inquire. ✇ *verb* **1** accept.

quest /kwɛst/ — *noun* **1** a search or hunt. **2** the object of one's search; one's goal. — *verb intrans.* (*often* **quest about** or **quest for something**) **1** to search about; to roam around in search of something. **2** *said of a dog* to search for game. — **in quest of something** looking for it. [from Latin *quaerere*, to seek]

■ *noun* **1** search, hunt, pursuit, investigation, inquiry, mission, crusade, enterprise, undertaking, venture, journey, voyage, expedition, exploration, adventure.

question — *noun* **1** an utterance which requests information or other answer; the interrogative sentence or other form of words in which this is expressed. **2** a doubt or query: *raises questions about their loyalty.* **3** an uncertainty: *no question about the cause.* **4** a problem or difficulty: *the Northern Ireland question.* **5** a problem set for discussion or solution in an examination paper, etc. **6** an investigation or search for information: *still pursuing the question.* **7** a matter or issue: *when it's a question of safety.* **8** an issue on which something is dependent: *a question of time rather than money.* — *verb* (**questioned, questioning**) **1** to ask (someone) questions; to interrogate. **2** to raise doubts about; to query: *would question her motives/question whether it's possible.* — **beyond question** not in doubt; beyond doubt. **bring something into question** to focus attention on it. **call something in** or **into question** to suggest reasons for doubting. **in question 1** presently under discussion or being referred to: *has an alibi for the time in question.* **2** in doubt: *her ability is not in question.* **no question of** ... no possibility or intention of ... **out of the question** impossible and so not worth considering. **without question** unhesitatingly. [from Latin *quaestio*, from *quaerere*, to ask]

■ *noun* **1** query, inquiry. **2** doubt, query, debate, dispute, controversy. **3** uncertainty, doubt. **4** problem, difficulty, dilemma, issue, dispute, controversy. **7** issue, matter, subject, topic, point. **8** matter, issue, point. *verb* **1** interrogate, quiz, *colloq.* grill, pump, interview, examine, cross-examine, debrief, ask, inquire, investigate, probe. **2** query, challenge, dispute, doubt, disbelieve.

questionable *adj.* **1** doubtful; dubious; suspect: *questionable motives.* **2** of dubious value or benefit: *questionable schemes.*

■ **1** doubtful, dubious, suspicious, suspect, *colloq.* shady, *colloq.* fishy, *colloq.* iffy. **2** unproven, controversial, arguable, debatable, disputable, vexed, uncertain, unsettled, undetermined. ✇ **2** unquestionable, indisputable, certain.

questioner *noun* a person who questions.

question mark 1 the punctuation mark (?) placed after a question. **2** a doubt: *still a question mark over funds.*

question master the person who asks the questions in a quiz, etc.

questionnaire *noun* a set of questions, usually in the form of a printed leaflet, for distribution to a number of people, as a means of collecting information, surveying opinions, etc. [from French *questionnaire*]

■ survey, opinion poll, test.

question time in parliament, a daily period set aside for members' questions to government ministers.

queue /kjuː/ — *noun* **1** a line or file of people or vehicles waiting for something. **2** *Comput.* a list of items, eg programs or data, held in a computer system in the order in which they are to be processed. The items that arrive earliest are processed first, and subsequent ones are placed at the end of the list. — *verb intrans.* **1** (*also* **queue up**) to form a queue or wait in a queue. **2** *Comput.* to line up tasks for a computer to process. [from French *queue*, tail]

■ *noun* **1** line, file, tailback, crocodile, procession, train, string, succession, series, sequence, order.

quibble — *verb intrans.* to argue over trifles; to make petty objections. — *noun* **1** a trifling objection. **2** *old use* a pun.

■ *verb* carp, cavil, split hairs, nit-pick, equivocate, prevaricate. *noun* **1** complaint, objection, criticism, query.

quiche /kiːʃ/ *noun* a tart with a savoury filling usually made with eggs. [from French *quiche*, from German *Kuchen*, cake]

quick — *adj.* **1** taking little time; speedy. **2** lasting briefly: *a quick glance.* **3** not delayed; immediate: *a quick response.* **4** intelligent; alert; sharp: *quick-witted.* **5** (of the temper) easily roused: *quick-tempered.* **6** nimble, deft, or brisk. **7** not reluctant or slow (to do something); apt or ready: *quick to take offence.* — *adv.* rapidly: *came as quick as we could / a quick-acting drug.* — *noun* **1** an area of sensitive flesh, especially at the base of the finger or toenail. **2** (**the quick**) *old use* those who are alive: *the quick and the dead.* [from Anglo-Saxon *cwic*, living]

■ *adj.* **1** fast, rapid, swift, speedy, express. **2** brief, fleeting, cursory, swift, hurried, hasty. **3** immediate, prompt, ready, instant, instantaneous, sudden, brisk. **4** intelligent, clever, alert, sharp, quick-witted, smart, keen, shrewd, astute, discerning, perceptive, responsive, receptive. **6** nimble, deft, brisk, sprightly, agile.

◪ *adj.* **1, 3** slow, sluggish, lethargic. **4** slow, unintelligent, dull.

quicken *verb* (**quickened, quickening**) **1** *intrans., trans.* to make or become quicker. **2** to stimulate or stir (someone's interest, imagination, etc). **3** *intrans.* **a** *said of a baby in the womb* to begin to move perceptibly. **b** *said of a pregnant woman* to begin to feel her baby's movements.

■ **1** accelerate, speed, hurry, hasten, precipitate, expedite, dispatch, advance. **2** stimulate, excite, inspire, galvanize, animate, enliven, invigorate, energize, activate, rouse, arouse, revive, refresh, reinvigorate, reactivate.

◪ **1** slow, retard. **2** dull.

quick-freeze *verb* (PAST TENSE **quick-froze**; PAST PARTICIPLE **quick-frozen**) to freeze (food) rapidly by exposing it to moving air at a very low temperature, so that only small ice crystals form, and the internal structure of the food, eg soft fruit such as strawberries, is not damaged.

quickie *noun colloq.* something quickly dealt with or done, eg an easy question.

quicklime *noun* calcium oxide.

quickly *adv.* rapidly, speedily.

quickness *noun* **1** a quick understanding. **2** speed.

quick one *colloq.* a quickly consumed alcoholic drink.

quicksand *noun* loose, wet sand that sucks down people or heavy objects standing on it.

quickset — *adj., said of cuttings, etc* planted so as to grow into a hedge. — *noun* a hedge so formed.

quicksilver *noun old use* mercury.

quickstep *noun* a ballroom dance with fast steps; a piece of music for this.

quid [1] *noun* (PL. **quid**) *slang* a pound (sterling).— **quids in** in a profitable or advantageous position.

quid [2] *noun* a bit of tobacco for chewing. [from dialect *quid*, cud]

quiddity *noun* **1** the essence of anything. **2** a quibble; a trifling detail or point. [from Latin *quidditas*, essence]

quid pro quo /kwɪd proʊ kwoʊ/ (PL. **quid pro quos**) something given or taken in recompense or retaliation for something. [Latin, = something for something]

quiescence /kwɪˈɛsəns/ *noun* a quiescent state.

quiescent /kwɪˈɛsənt/ *adj.* **1** quiet; silent; at rest; in an inactive state, especially one unlikely to last. **2** *Biol.* denoting an organism or structure which, because of unfavourable environmental conditions, eg low temperature, has temporarily stopped growing or functioning. [from Latin *quiescere*, to rest]

quiet — *adj.* **1** making little or no noise; soft. **2** *said of a place, etc* peaceful; tranquil; without noise or bustle. **3** silent; saying nothing: *kept quiet about it*. **4** *said of a person* reserved; unassertive. **5** *said of the weather* calm. **6** not disturbed by trouble or excitement: *a quiet life*. **7** without fuss or publicity: *a quiet wedding*. **8** *said of business or trade* poor; not flourishing. **9** secret; private: *had a quiet word with her*. **10** undeclared: *quiet satisfaction*. **11** *said of humour* subtle; not overdone. **12** enjoyed in peace: *a quiet read*. **13** *said of the mind or conscience* untroubled by anxiety, guilt, etc. — *noun* absence of, or freedom from, noise, commotion, etc; calm, tranquillity, or repose: *longing for peace and quiet*. — *verb trans., intrans.* (**quieted, quieting**) to make or become quiet or calm. — **on the quiet** secretly; discreetly. [from Latin *quietus*, quiet]

■ *adj.* **1** hushed, soft, low, silent, noiseless, inaudible. **2, 6** peaceful, tranquil, still, serene, calm, composed, undisturbed, untroubled, placid. **3** silent, taciturn, uncommunicative, unforthcoming, thoughtful, subdued. **4** reserved, unassertive, shy, reticent, retiring, withdrawn, meek. **5** calm, still, tranquil. **13** serene, calm, composed, undisturbed, untroubled. *noun* quietness, silence, hush, calm, tranquillity, peace, serenity, repose, rest, lull, stillness.

◪ *adj.* **1** noisy, loud. **4** excitable, extrovert. **5** rough, stormy. *noun* noise, loudness, disturbance, bustle.

quieten *verb* (**quietened, quietening**) **1** *trans., intrans.* to make or become quiet. **2** to calm (doubts, fears, etc).

■ **1** silence, hush, mute, soften, lower, diminish, reduce, stifle, muffle, deaden, dull. **2** calm, soothe, subdue, pacify, quell, still, quiet, smooth, compose, sober.

◪ **2** disturb, agitate.

quietism *noun* calm, passive acceptance of events.

quietist *noun* a person characterized by quietism.

quietly *adv.* in a quiet way; with little or no sound.

quietness *noun* being quiet.

quietude *noun* quietness; tranquillity.

quietus /kwaɪˈiːtəs, kwɪˈɛːtʊs/ *noun* **1** release from life; death. **2** release or discharge from debts or duties. [from Latin *quietus est*, he is at peace]

quiff *noun* a lock of hair brushed up into a point over the forehead.

quill *noun* **1** a large stiff feather from a bird's wing or tail; the hollow base part of this. **2** a pen made from a bird's feather. **3** one of the long spines on a porcupine. [related to German dialect *quiele*]

quilt — *noun* **1** a bedcover containing padding or a filling of feathers, etc, kept in place by intersecting seams. **2** a duvet; a continental quilt. — *verb trans., intrans.* to sew (material, garments, etc) in two layers with a filling, especially with decorative seaming. [from Old French *cuilte*, from Latin *culcita*, mattress, cushion]

■ *noun* **1** bedcover, coverlet, bedspread, counterpane, eiderdown.

quilted *adj.* padded.

quin *noun colloq.* a quintuplet.

quince *noun* the round or pear-shaped acid fruit of an Asian tree, used to make jams, jellies, etc. [originally pl. of Middle English *quyne*, quince, from Greek *melon Kydonion*, apple of Cydonia, in Crete]

quincentenary /kwɪnsɛnˈtiːnərɪ/ *noun* (PL. **quincentenaries**) a 500th anniversary. [from Latin *quinque*, five + CENTENARY]

quincunx /ˈkwɪŋkʌŋks/ *noun* **1** an arrangement of five things at the corners and centre of a square. **2** a repeating pattern based on this arrangement, eg in tree-planting. [from Latin *quincunx*, five twelfths]

quinine /ˈkwɪniːn/ *noun Medicine* a bitter-tasting alkaloid drug, obtained from cinchona bark, that has antipyretic (fever-reducing) and analgesic properties, and was formerly widely used to treat malaria. It has now been largely superseded by less toxic drugs. [from Spanish *quina*, cinchona bark]

quinoa /ˈkiːnoʊə/ *noun* **1** a S American plant with edible seeds and leaves. **2** a rice-like grain consisting of the seeds of this plant. [from Spanish *quinoa*, from Quechua *kinua*]

quinoline /ˈkwɪnəliːn/ *noun Chem.* an aromatic nitrogen compound, formerly obtained from quinine, consisting of an oily colourless liquid that is soluble in water and used in the manufacture of dyes and drugs.

Quinquagesima /kwɪŋkwəˈdʒɛsɪmə/ *noun* in the Christian calendar, the Sunday before Lent. [from Latin *quinquagesima*, fiftieth (day before Easter Day)]

quinquennial *adj.* **1** lasting five years. **2** occurring every five years. [from Latin *quinque*, five + *annus*, year]

quinquennially *adv.* every five years.

quinquereme /'kwɪnkwɪriːm/ *noun colloq.* a galley of the ancient world with five oarsmen to each oar, or five banks of oars. [from Latin *quinque*, five + *remus*, oar]

quinsy /'kwɪnzɪ/ *noun* inflammation of the throat with an abscess on the tonsils. [from Latin *quinancia*, from Greek *kynanche*, 'throttle-dog', from *kyon*, dog + *anchein*, to strangle]

quintal *noun* **1** a metric unit of weight equal to 100kg. **2** *formerly* a hundredweight, 112lbs. [from Arabic *qintar*, from Latin *centum*, 100]

quintessence *noun* **1** the central, essential nature of something. **2** a perfect example or embodiment of something. **3** *old use* the purest, most concentrated extract of a substance. [from Latin *quinta essentia*, fifth essence]

quintessential *adj.* central, essential.

quintessentially *adv.* centrally, essentially.

quintet or **quintette** *noun* **1** an ensemble of five singers or instrumental players. **2** a piece of music for five such performers. **3** any group or set of five. [from Italian *quintetto*, from Latin *quintus*, five]

quintuple — *verb trans., intrans.* to multiply by five or increase fivefold. — *adj.* **1** five times as many or much. **2** composed of five parts. — *noun* a quintuple number or amount. [from Latin *quintuplus*, fivefold]

quintuplet /'kwɪntjʊplət, kwɪn'tjuːplət/ *noun* one of five children born to a mother at one birth.

quip — *noun* a witty remark. — *verb* (**quipped**, **quipping**) **1** *intrans.* to make a quip or quips. **2** *trans.* to say in jest. [perhaps from Latin *quippe*, to be sure]

⊟ *noun* joke, jest, *colloq.* crack, *colloq.* gag, witticism, riposte, retort, gibe. *verb* JOKE, JEST.

quipu /'kiːpuː/ *noun* a device consisting of a complex system of knotted cords of various lengths, shapes, and colours, used by the Peruvian Incas as an accounting system for keeping detailed records, such as census information, and for sending messages. [from Quechua *quipu*, knot]

quire *noun* **1** a paper measure, 25 (formerly 24) sheets. **2** *old use* a set of folded sheets fitting inside one another for binding into book form. [from Old French *quaier*, from Latin *quattuor*, four]

quirk *noun* **1** an odd habit, mannerism, or aspect of personality that someone has. **2** an odd twist in affairs or turn of events; a strange coincidence: *quirks of fate*.

⊟ **1** habit, mannerism, idiosyncrasy, peculiarity, eccentricity, curiosity, oddity, trait, foible. **2** turn, twist, whim, caprice, freak.

quirky *adj.* (**quirkier**, **quirkiest**) odd, tricky.

quisling *noun* a traitor or collaborator. [named after the Norwegian diplomat and fascist leader Vidkun Quisling]

quit — *verb* (**quitting**; PAST TENSE AND PAST PARTICIPLE **quitted**, **quit**) **1** to leave (a place, etc). **2** *trans., intrans.* to leave, give up or resign (a job). **3** *colloq. esp. North Amer., esp. US* to cease (something, or doing something): *quit that racket*. **4** *trans., intrans., said of a tenant* to move out of (rented premises). — *adj.* (**quit of something**) free of it; rid of it. [from Old French *quiter*, from Latin *quietare*, to pay]

⊟ *verb* **1** leave, depart, go, exit, decamp, desert, forsake, abandon. **2** surrender, give up, renounce, relinquish, desert, forsake, abandon, resign, retire, withdraw. **3** stop, cease, end, discontinue, drop, give up, *colloq.* pack in.

quitch *noun* couch grass. [from Anglo-Saxon *cwice*]

quite *adv.* **1** completely; entirely: *don't quite understand / not quite clear*. **2** to a high degree: *quite exceptional*. **3** rather; fairly; to some, or a limited, degree: *quite promis-* *ing/quite a nice day/quite enjoyed it*. **4** *used in reply* I agree, see your point, etc. — **quite a** .. or **some** ... a striking, impressive, daunting, challenging: *that's quite a task/ quite some task you have there*. **quite so** I agree; you're right. **quite something** something impressive. [variant of QUIT]

⊟ **1** completely, entirely, wholly, fully, totally. **2** utterly, absolutely, totally, completely, entirely, wholly, fully, perfectly. **3** rather, fairly, somewhat, moderately, relatively, comparatively. **4** absolutely, exactly, precisely.

quits *adj. colloq.* even with one another; on an equal footing. — **call it quits** to agree to stop a quarrel or dispute, acknowledging that the outcome is even.

quittance *noun* a person's release from debt or other obligation, or a document acknowledging this.

quitter *noun colloq.* **1** someone who gives up too easily. **2** a shirker.

quiver[1] — *verb intrans.* (**quivered**, **quivering**) to shake or tremble slightly; to shiver. — *noun* a tremble or shiver. [perhaps from older meaning *quiver*, nimble]

⊟ *verb* shake, tremble, shudder, shiver, quake, quaver, vibrate, palpitate, flutter, flicker, oscillate, wobble. *noun* tremble, shiver, shake, shudder, tremor, vibration, palpitation, flutter, flicker, oscillation, wobble.

quiver[2] *noun* a long narrow case for carrying arrows in. [from Old French *cuivre*]

quixotic *adj.* **1** absurdly generous or chivalrous. **2** unrealistically romantic or idealistic. [from Don Quixote, hero of a romance by the Spanish writer Cervantes]

quiz — *noun* (PL. **quizzes**) **1** an entertainment, eg on radio or television, in which the knowledge of a panel of contestants is tested. **2** any series of questions as a test of general or specialized knowledge. **3** an interrogation. — *verb* (**quizzed**, **quizzing**) to question; to interrogate.

⊟ *noun* **1** panel game, game show. **2** test, examination, competition, questionnaire. *verb* question, interrogate, grill, pump, examine, cross-examine.

quizmaster *noun* the question master in a television quiz, etc.

quizzical *adj., said of a look, expression, etc* mocking; questioning; amused.

⊟ mocking, questioning, inquiring, curious, amused, humorous, teasing, satirical, sardonic, sceptical.

quod *noun slang* jail; prison.

quoin /kɔɪn, kwɔɪn/ *noun* **1** the angle of a building. **2** a cornerstone. **3** a wedge, eg *Printing* for locking type into a frame. [variant of *coin*]

quoit /kɔɪt, kwɔɪt/ *noun* **1** a ring of metal, rubber, or rope used in the game of quoits. **2** (**quoits**) a game in which such rings are thrown at pegs, with the aim of encircling them.

quondam /'kwɒndam/ *adj.* former: *his quondam secretary.* [from Latin *quondam*, formerly]

quorate /'kwɔːreɪt/ *adj.* said of a meeting, etc attended by enough people to amount to a quorum.

Quorn /kwɔːn/ *noun trademark* a fibrous vegetable protein made from microscopic plant filaments, used as a low-calorie and cholesterol-free meat substitute in cooking.

quorum /'kwɔːrəm/ *noun* (PL. **quorums**) the minimum number of members who must be present at a meeting for its business to be valid. [from Latin *quorum*, of whom]

quota *noun* **1** a total number or quantity that is permitted or required. **2** someone's allocated share, eg of work. [from Latin *quotus*, of what number]

▣ **1** ration, allowance, allocation, assignment. **2** share, portion, ration, allocation, part, *colloq.* slice, *colloq.* cut, percentage, proportion.

....

quotable *adj.* worth quoting.

quotation *noun* **1** something quoted. **2** the act of quoting. **3** an estimated price for a job submitted by a contractor to a client.

....

▣ **1** citation, quote, extract, excerpt, passage, piece, cutting, reference. **2** citation. **3** estimate, quote, tender, figure, price, cost, charge, rate.

....

quotation mark each of a pair of punctuation marks (" " or ' ') used to show the beginning and end of a quotation, or on either side of a word or phrase on which attention is focused for some reason.

quote — *verb* **1** *trans., intrans.* to repeat the exact words of: *quote Milton/quote a poem/quote from a speech, etc.* **2** to refer to (a law, etc) as authority or support. **3** *trans., intrans.* (**quote for something**) *said of a contractor* to submit (a price) for a particular job. — *noun* **1** a quotation. **2** a price quoted. **3** (**quotes**) quotation marks. — *interj. col-*

loq. used in speech to indicate that one is quoting: *her quote 'reluctance' unquote.* [from Latin *quotare*, to mark passages with numbers]

....

▣ *verb* **1** cite, echo, repeat, recite, reproduce, recall, recollect. **2** refer to, cite, mention, name.

....

quoth /kwoʊθ/ *verb old use* said: *quoth she, he, I.* [from Anglo-Saxon *cwæth*]

quotidian /kwoʊˈtɪdɪən/ *adj.* everyday; commonplace. **1** daily. **2** *said of a fever* recurring daily. [from Latin *quotidianus*, daily]

quotient /ˈkwoʊʃənt/ *noun* the number of times one number is contained in another, found by dividing the latter by the former. [from Latin *quotiens*, how often?]

Qur'an or **Quran** /kɔːˈrɑːn/ same as KORAN.

q.v. or **qv.** *abbrev. quod vide* (Latin), which see, see this word (used to refer a reader from a word used in a dictionary or encyclopedia text, etc to the entry dealing with it).

qwerty *noun* the standard arrangement of keys on a typewriter or keyboard designed for English-language users, with the letters *q w e r t y*, in that order, at the top left of the letters section of the keyboard.

R

R¹ or **r** *noun* (PL. **Rs, R's, r's**) the eighteenth letter of the English alphabet. **the three Rs** reading, writing, and arithmetic, regarded as the three most important skills to be taught in primary school.

R² *abbrev.* **1** Regina (Latin), Queen. **2** Rex (Latin), King. **3** River. **4** *Chess* rook.

r *abbrev.* **1** radius. **2** recto. **3** right.

RA *abbrev.* **1** *Brit.* Royal Academy or Academician. **2** Rear Admiral.

Ra *symbol Chem.* radium.

RAAF *abbrev.* Royal Australian Air Force.

rabbet /'rabɪt/ — *noun* a groove cut along the edge of a piece of wood, etc, usually to join with a tongue or projection in a matching piece. — *verb* (**rabbeted, rabbeting**) **1** to cut a rabbet in. **2** to join by a rabbet. [from Old French *rabattre*, to beat down]

rabbi /'rabaɪ/ *noun* **1** a Jewish religious leader. **2** a Jewish scholar or teacher of the law. [from Hebrew *rabbi*, my master]

rabbinical *adj.* relating to the rabbis, or their teachings and writings.

rabbit — *noun* **1** any of various herbivorous mammals belonging to the same family (Leporidae) as the hare, native to SW Europe and NW Africa, but now distributed worldwide. Rabbits are smaller than hares, and have greyish-brown fur, long ears, prominent eyes, and a very short tail, upturned at the tip and white below. **2** *Brit. colloq.* a poor performer in any sport or game. — *verb intrans.* (**rabbited, rabbiting**) **1** to hunt rabbits. **2** (**rabbit on, away,** *etc*) *colloq.* to talk at great length; to chatter idly. [from Middle English *rabet*]

rabbit punch a sharp blow on the back of the neck.

rabbit warren a system of burrows in which wild rabbits live.

rabble *noun* **1** a noisy disorderly crowd. **2** (**the rabble**) the lowest class of people. [from Middle English]

⊞ **1** crowd, throng, horde, herd, mob. **2** the herd, the mob, the masses, the populace, the riff-raff.

rabble-rouser *noun* a person who makes speeches, especially calling for social or political change, which are meant to arouse feelings of anger and violence in those listening.

⊞ agitator, troublemaker, incendiary, demagogue, ringleader.

rabble-rousing — *adj.* characteristic of a rabble-rouser. — *noun* the language and tactics of a rabble-rouser.

⊞ *adj.* incendiary, inflammatory, demagogic, troublemaking, crowd-pleasing.

Rabelaisian /rabə'leɪzɪən/ *adj.* relating to or characteristic of the works of the French satirist François Rabelais (c.1494–c.1553), especially in being satirical and coarsely humorous.

rabid /'rabɪd, 'reɪbɪd/ *adj.* **1** *said of dogs, etc* suffering from rabies. **2** holding or expressing views with extreme ferocity. [from Latin *rabidus*]

⊞ **2** ferocious, fanatical, extreme, burning, ardent, fervent, unreasoning, obsessive, intransigent, bigoted.

rabidity *noun* being rabid.

rabidly *adv.* as if rabid, madly.

rabidness *noun* being rabid.

rabies /'reɪbiːz/ *noun* a disease of the nervous system that causes madness and usually death, and which is transmitted by the bite of an infected animal. [from Latin *rabere*, to rave]

RAC *abbrev. Brit.* Royal Automobile Club, a British organization which helps drivers with breakdowns or technical problems, gives travel information, etc. See also AA.

raccoon or **racoon** *noun* any of seven species of solitary nocturnal mammal, about the size of a cat, found in N and Central America, with dense greyish fur, characteristic black patches around the eyes, and black rings on the tail. [a Native American name]

race¹ — *noun* **1** a contest of speed between runners, horses, cars, etc. **2** (**races**) a series of such contests over a fixed course, especially for horses or dogs. **3** any contest or rivalry, especially to be the first to do or get something. **4** a strong or rapid current of water in the sea or a river. **5** a channel conveying water to and from a mill wheel. **6** a groove in which something, eg a ball-bearing, moves or slides. — *verb* **1** *intrans.* to take part in a race. **2** to have a race with (someone). **3** to enter (a horse, car, etc) in a race. **4** (**race about** or **along** or **around**) to run or move quickly and energetically. **5** *trans., intrans.* to move or cause to move more quickly than usual. **6** *intrans.* to own racehorses, or watch horse-racing as a hobby. [from Norse *ras*]

⊞ *noun* **1** sprint, steeplechase, marathon, scramble, regatta. **3** competition, contest, contention, rivalry, chase, pursuit, quest. *verb* **1, 4** run. **4** sprint, dash, tear, fly, gallop, speed, career, dart, zoom, rush, hurry, hasten.

race² *noun* **1** a major division of mankind having a particular set of physical characteristics, such as size, hair type, or skin colour. **2** a tribe, nation, or other group of people thought of as distinct from others. **3** human beings as a group: *the human race*. **4** a group of animals or plants within a species, which have characteristics which make them distinct from other members of that species. See also RACIAL. [from Italian *razza*]

⊞ **2, 3** species. **2** nation, people, tribe, clan, house, dynasty, family, kindred, ancestry, line.

racecard *noun* a list of all the competitors and races at a race meeting.

racecourse or **racetrack** *noun* a course or track used for racing horses, cars, bicycles, runners, etc.

⊞ course, track, circuit, lap, turf, speedway.

racehorse *noun* a horse bred and used for racing.

raceme /rə'siːm/ *noun Bot.* a flower-head consisting of individual flowers attached to a long stem by means of short
stalks, the youngest flowers being at the tip of the stem and
the oldest ones near its base, eg bluebell, lupin. [from Latin
racemus, bunch of grapes]

race meeting a series of horse races taking place over the
same course and on the same day.

racer *noun colloq.* a bicycle or horse used for racing.

race relations social relations between people of different races in the same community or country.

race riot a riot caused by hostility between people of different races or alleged discrimination against people of a
particular race.

rachis or **rhachis** /'reɪkɪs/ *noun* **1** *Bot.* the main axis of a
compound leaf or a flower-head. **2** *Zool.* the main axis or
shaft of a feather. [from Greek *rhachis*, spine]

racial *adj.* **1** relating to a particular race. **2** based on race.

> ▣ **1** national, tribal, ethnic, folk, genealogical, ancestral,
> inherited, genetic.

racialism or **racism** *noun* **1** a belief that a particular race
is inherently superior to others. **2** abusive, oppressive behaviour, discrimination, and prejudice caused by such a
belief.

> ▣ **1** chauvinism, jingoism, xenophobia. **2** discrimination,
> prejudice, bias.

racially *adv.* in a racial way.

racily *adv.* in a racy way.

raciness *noun* being racy.

racing *noun* the sport or practice of using animals (such as
horses or dogs) or vehicles in contests of speed.

racist or **racialist** *noun* a person who practises or supports racism. — *adj.* relating to or characteristic of racism.

rack[1] — *noun* **1** a framework with rails, shelves, hooks, etc
for holding or storing things. **2** a framework for holding
hay, etc from which livestock can feed. **3** a bar with teeth
which connect with teeth on a cogwheel or pinion to change
the position of something, or to convert linear motion into
rotary motion or vice versa. **4** *Hist.* an instrument for tor-
turing people by stretching their bodies. — *verb* **1** to cause
pain or suffering to: *be racked with guilt*. **2** to put in a rack.
3 *Hist.* to torture on a rack. — **rack one's brains** to think as
hard as one can. [from Middle English *rakke*]

> ▣ *noun* **1, 2** structure, frame, framework. **1** shelf, stand,
> support. *verb* **1** torment, oppress, afflict, beset, distress.

rack[2] — **go to rack and ruin** to get into a state of neglect
and decay. [from Anglo-Saxon *wræc*, misery]

rack[3] *verb* to draw off (wine or beer) from its sediment.
[from Provençal *raca*, dregs]

rack[4] *noun* a joint of meat, especially of lamb, including
the neck and front ribs.

racket[1] or **racquet** *noun* a wooden or metal oval frame
with catgut or nylon strings stretched across it, used for
playing tennis, badminton, squash, etc. [from French *ra-
quette*]

racket[2] *noun* **1** a loud confused noise or disturbance; din.
2 a fraudulent or illegal means of making money. **3** *slang* a
job or occupation.

> ▣ **1** noise, din, uproar, row, fuss, outcry, clamour, commotion,
> disturbance, pandemonium, hurly-burly, hubbub. **2** swindle,
> *colloq.* con, fraud, *colloq.* fiddle, deception, trick, dodge,
> scheme, business, game, *slang* scam.

racketeer — *noun* a person who makes money in some illegal way, often by threats of violence. — *verb intrans.* to
make money as a racketeer.

racketeering *noun* operating a racket.

rackets *sing. noun* a ball game for two or four players
played using rackets in a court with four walls.

rack railway a mountain railway with a toothed rack
which engages with the cogged wheels of the locomotive.

rack rent an excessive or unreasonably high rent.

raconteur /rakɒn'tɜː(r)/ *noun* a person who tells anecdotes
in an amusing or entertaining way. [from French *raconteur*]

racoon see RACCOON.

racquet /'rakɪt/ see RACKET[1].

racy *adj.* (**racier, raciest**) **1** lively or spirited. **2** slightly indecent; risqué.

> ▣ **1** lively, animated, spirited, energetic, dynamic, buoyant,
> boisterous. **2** ribald, bawdy, risqué, naughty, indecent,
> indelicate, suggestive.

rad *noun Physics* the unit formerly used to measure the
amount of ionizing radiation absorbed, equal to 0.01
joules per kilogram of absorbing material. It has now been
replaced by the gray in SI units.

RADA *abbrev.* Royal Academy of Dramatic Art.

radar /'reɪdɑː(r)/ *noun* **1** *Radio* a system for detecting the
presence, position, speed, and direction of movement of
distant objects by transmitting short pulses of high-
frequency radio waves from a rotating aerial, and detecting the signals reflected back from the surface of any object in their path, which produce 'blips' of light on a screen.
Radar is widely used in air and sea navigation, and in warfare to detect enemy aircraft. **2** the equipment for sending
out and receiving such radio waves. [from *radio detection
and ranging*]

radar astronomy *Astron.* the use of pulsed radio signals
to measure the distances and map the surfaces of objects
in the solar system, and to determine their speed of rotation.

radar trap a device using radar which allows the
police to detect vehicles travelling faster than the speed
limit.

raddled *adj.* worn out and haggard-looking through debauchery. [from *raddle*, red ochre]

radial — *adj.* **1** *said of lines* spreading out from the centre of
a circle, like rays. **2** of or relating to rays, a radius, or radii.
3 along or in the direction of a radius or radii. **4** *Anat.* of
the radius. — *noun* **1** (*in full* **radial-ply tyre**) a tyre which
has fabric cords laid at a right angle to the centre of the
tread, allowing the walls to be flexible. See also CROSS-
PLY. **2** *Anat.* a radial artery or nerve. [from Latin *radius*,
spoke, ray]

radially *adv.* in the manner of radii or rays; outward from
the centre.

radial symmetry the arrangement of parts in an object
or living organism such that a line drawn through its centre in any direction produces two halves that are mirror
images of each other, eg the arrangement of parts in a jellyfish, or the stems and roots of plants.

radian *noun Maths.* (ABBREV. **rad**) the SI unit of plane angular measurement, defined as the angle that is made at
the centre of a circle by an arc (a segment of the circumference) whose length is equal to the radius of the circle. One
radian is approximately 57° being radiant. **2** a measure of
the amount of electromagnetic radiation being transmitted from or to a point on a surface.

> ▣ **1** light, luminosity, incandescence, radiation, brightness,
> brilliance, shine, lustre, gleam, glow, glitter, resplendence,
> splendour, happiness, joy, pleasure, delight, rapture.

radiant — *adj.* **1** emitting electromagnetic radiation, eg
rays of light or heat. **2** glowing or shining. **3** beaming with
abundant joy, love, hope, or health. **4** transmitted by or as
radiation. — *noun* **1** a point or object which emits electromagnetic radiation, eg light or heat. **2** *Astron.* the point in

the sky from which meteors appear to radiate outward during a meteor shower. [from Latin *radiare*, to radiate]

◻ *adj.* **2, 3** glowing, beaming. **2** bright, luminous, shining, gleaming, glittering, sparkling, brilliant, resplendent, splendid, glorious. **3** happy, joyful, delighted, ecstatic.
◻ *adj.* **2** dull. **3** miserable.

radiant energy energy given out as electromagnetic radiation.

radiant heat heat transmitted by electromagnetic radiation.

radiantly *adv.* in a radiant way.

radiate — *verb* **1** *trans., intrans.* to send out rays of (light, heat, electromagnetic radiation, etc). **2** *intrans. said of light, heat, radiation, etc* to be emitted in rays. **3** to show a lot of (happiness, good health, etc) clearly: *radiate vitality.* **4** *trans., intrans.* to spread or cause to spread out from a central point as radii. — *adj.* having rays, radii, or a radial structure. [from Latin *radiare*, to shine]

◻ *verb* **1, 2** emanate, diffuse. **1** emit. **2** pour, issue, shine, gleam. **3** glow with, shine with, beam with, shed, give off, disseminate. **4** spread (out), diverge, branch, scatter.

radiation *noun* **1** energy that is emitted from a source and travels in the form of waves or particles (photons) through a medium, eg air or a vacuum. The term usually refers to electromagnetic radiation, eg radio waves, microwaves, infrared, visible light, ultraviolet, X-rays, etc. **2** a stream of particles, eg alpha particles, beta particles, electrons, neutrons, etc, emitted by a radioactive substance. **3** the act of radiating.

radiation sickness an illness caused by exposure to high levels of radiation, eg nuclear fallout, or to relatively low levels over a long period.

radiator *noun* **1** an apparatus for heating, consisting of a series of pipes through which hot water (or hot oil) is circulated. **2** an apparatus for heating in which wires are made hot by electricity. **3** an apparatus for cooling an internal combustion engine, eg in a car, consisting of a series of tubes which water passes through, and a fan.

radical — *adj.* **1** concerning or relating to the basic nature of something; fundamental. **2** far-reaching; thoroughgoing: *radical changes.* **3** in favour of or tending to produce thoroughgoing or extreme political and social reforms. **4** of a political group or party in favour of extreme reforms. **5** *Bot.* of or relating to the root of a plant. **6** *Maths.* relating to the root of a number. **7** *Linguistics* relating to the roots of words. — *noun* **1** a person who is a member of a radical political group, or who holds radical political views. **2** *Chem.* within a molecule, a group of atoms which remains unchanged during a series of chemical reactions, but is normally incapable of independent existence. **3** *Maths.* the root of a number, usually denoted by the radical sign $\sqrt{}$. **4** *Linguistics* the root of a word. [from Latin *radix*, root]

◻ *adj.* **1** basic, fundamental, primary, essential, natural, native, innate, intrinsic, deep-seated, profound. **2** far-reaching, thoroughgoing, drastic, comprehensive, thorough, sweeping, complete, total, entire. **3, 4** fanatical, militant, extreme, extremist, revolutionary. *noun* **1** fanatic, militant, extremist, revolutionary, reformer, reformist, fundamentalist.
◻ *adj.* **1** superficial. **3, 4** moderate.

radicalism *noun* **1** the beliefs and opinions of radicals, especially a set of ideas which advocates more substantial social and political change than is supported by the political mainstream. **2** extreme thoroughness.

radically *adv.* in a radical way.

radicalness *noun* being radical.

radical sign the sign $\sqrt{}$, showing a square root.

radicchio /ra'diːkɪʊʊ/ *noun* (PL. **radicchios**) a purple-leaved variety of chicory, used raw in salads. [from Italian *radicchio*]

radicle *noun* **1** *Bot.* the part of a plant embryo which develops into the root. **2** *Anat.* the root-like origin of a vein or nerve. [from Latin *radicula*, small root]

radii /'reɪdɪaɪ, 'radiː/ see RADIUS.

radio — *noun* (PL. **radios**) **1** the use of radio waves (a form of electromagnetic radiation) to transmit and receive information such as television or radio programmes, telecommunications, and computer data, without connecting wires. **2** a wireless device that receives, and may also transmit, information in this manner. **3** a message or broadcast that is transmitted in this manner. — *adj.* **1** of or for transmitting or transmitted by radio. **2** controlled by radio. — *verb* (**radios, radioed**) **1** to send (a message) to (someone) by radio. **2** *intrans.* to broadcast or communicate by radio. [from Latin *radius*, spoke, ray]

radio- *combining form* forming words denoting: **1** radio or broadcasting. **2** radioactivity. **3** rays or radiation.

radioactive *adj.* relating to or affected by radioactivity.

radioactive decay *Physics* the spontaneous decay of the nucleus of an atom, which results in the emission of alpha particles, beta particles, or gamma rays.

radioactive tracer *Biochem.* a radioactive isotope of a chemical element that is deliberately substituted for one of the atoms in a chemical compound in order to 'tag' it. In this way the path of a particular atom through a whole series of reactions can be followed. Radioactive tracers are widely used in scientific and medical research.

radioactive waste see NUCLEAR WASTE.

radioactivity *noun* **1** the spontaneous disintegration of the nuclei of certain atoms, accompanied by the emission of alpha particles, beta particles, or gamma rays. Radioactivity is measured in units called becquerels. **2** the subatomic particles or radiation emitted during this process.

radio astronomy the exploration of the Universe by studying the radio waves emitted or reflected by stars (especially the Sun), planets (especially Jupiter), pulsars, quasars, interstellar gas, radio galaxies, etc, as well as the cosmic background radiation of the Universe itself.

radiobiology *noun Biol.* the branch of biology concerned with the study of the effect of radiation and radioactive materials on living matter.

radiocarbon *noun* a radioactive isotope of carbon, especially carbon-14.

radiocarbon dating same as CARBON DATING.

radiochemistry *noun Chem.* the branch of chemistry concerned with the study of radioactive elements and their compounds, including their preparation, properties, and practical uses.

radio frequency a frequency of electromagnetic waves used for radio and television broadcasting.

radio galaxy *Astron.* a galaxy that is an intense source of cosmic radio waves, about one galaxy in a million. Investigation of radio galaxies led directly to the discovery of quasars.

radiogram *noun* **1** same as RADIOGRAPH. **2** *old use* an apparatus consisting of a radio and record-player.

radiograph *noun* a photograph taken using a form of radiation other than light, such as X-rays or gamma rays, especially of the inside of the body.

radiographer *noun* a technician involved in radiology, eg in taking radiographs or giving radiotherapy.

radiography *noun Medicine* the technique of examining the interior of the body by means of recorded images, known as *radiographs*, produced by X-rays on photographic film.

radioisotope *noun Physics* a naturally occurring or synthetic radioactive isotope of a chemical element, eg tritium. Radioisotopes are used in radiotherapy to treat cancer, as radioactive tracers in scientific research, and as long-term power sources in spacecraft and satellites.

radiological *adj.* 1 relating to or involving radiology. 2 involving radioactive materials.

radiologist *noun* a specialist in the use of X-rays and in methods of imaging the internal structure of the body for diagnosis and treatment of disease.

radiology *noun* the branch of medicine concerned with the use of radiation (eg X-rays) and radioactive isotopes to diagnose and treat diseases.

radio-pager *noun* a very small radio receiver which emits a bleeping sound in response to a signal, used for paging people.

radio-paging *noun* paging by means of a radio-pager.

radiophonic *adj.* relating to sound produced electronically. [from RADIO- + Greek *phone*, sound]

radioscopic *adj.* relating to or involving radioscopy.

radioscopy *noun* the examination of the inside of the body, or of opaque objects, using X-rays.

radio telephone a telephone which works by radio waves, used especially in cars and other vehicles.

radio telescope a large usually dish-shaped aerial, together with amplifiers and recording equipment, that is used to study distant stars, galaxies, etc, by detecting the radio waves they emit. Many celestial bodies are so faint or distant that they can only be detected by radio telescope.

radiotherapy *noun* the treatment of disease, especially cancer, by X-rays and other forms of radiation.

radio wave *Physics* an electromagnetic wave that has a low frequency and a long wavelength (in the range of about 1mm to 10^4m), widely used for communication.

radish *noun* a plant of the mustard family, with pungent-tasting, red-skinned white roots, which are eaten raw in salads. [from Anglo-Saxon *rædic*, from Latin *radix*, root]

radium *noun Chem.* (SYMBOL **Ra**, ATOMIC NUMBER **88**) a silvery-white highly toxic radioactive metal obtained from uranium ores, especially pitchblende. The radioactive isotope radium-226 is used in radiotherapy to treat cancer, and as a neutron source. Radium compounds are used in luminous paints. [from Latin *radius*, ray]

radius *noun* (PL. **radii**, **radiuses**) 1 a straight line running from the centre of a circle to a point on its circumference. 2 the length of such a line. 3 a usually specified distance from a central point, thought of as limiting an area: *all the houses within a radius of 10km*. 4 *Anat.* the shorter of the two bones in the human forearm, on the thumb side. 5 anything placed like a radius, such as a spoke in a wheel. [from Latin *radius*, spoke, ray]

radon /'reɪdɒn/ *noun Chem.* (SYMBOL **Rn**, ATOMIC NUMBER **86**) a highly toxic colourless radioactive gas that emits alpha particles and is formed by the decay of radium. It is one of the rare or noble gases, forms very few compounds, and is used in radiotherapy to treat cancer, and as a tracer to detect leakages of radioactivity. It occurs naturally in certain areas of granite rock, which are a recognized health hazard. [from RADIUM]

RAEC *abbrev.* Royal Army Educational Corps.

RAF *abbrev.* Royal Air Force.

raffia *noun* ribbon-like fibre obtained from the leaves of certain palm trees, used for weaving mats, baskets, etc. [a native word from Madagascar]

raffish *adj.* slightly shady or disreputable; rakish. [related to RIFF-RAFF]

raffle — *noun* a lottery, often to raise money for charity, in which certain numbered tickets win prizes. — *verb* to offer as a prize in a raffle. [from Middle English *rafle*, dice game]

⊟ *noun* draw, lottery, sweepstake, sweep, tombola.

raft — *noun* 1 a flat structure of logs, timber, etc fastened together so as to float on water, used for transport or as a platform. 2 a flat, floating mass of ice, vegetation, etc. — *verb* 1 to transport by raft. 2 *intrans.* to travel by raft. [from Norse *raptr*, rafter]

rafter *noun* any of several sloping beams supporting a roof. [from Anglo-Saxon *ræfter*]

rag[1] *noun* 1 a scrap of cloth, especially a piece which has been worn, or torn off old clothes. 2 (*usually* **rags**) a piece of clothing, especially when old and tattered. 3 *derog. colloq.* a newspaper. — **lose one's rag** *slang* to lose one's temper. [from Anglo-Saxon *raggig*, shaggy]

rag[2] — *verb* (**ragged**, **ragging**) 1 *trans., intrans. esp. Brit.* to tease; to play rough tricks on (someone). 2 to scold. — *noun Brit.* a series of stunts and events put on by university or college students to raise money for charity: *rag week*.

rag[3] *noun* a piece of ragtime music.

raga /'rɑːgɑ/ *noun* 1 a traditional pattern of notes in Hindu classical music, around which melodies can be improvised. 2 a piece of music composed around such a pattern. [from Sanskrit *raga*, colour, musical tone]

ragamuffin /'ragəmʌfɪn/ *noun* a ragged, disreputable child. [from Middle English *Ragamoffyn*, the name of a demon in the poem *Piers Plowman* by William Langland]

rag-and-bone man a person who collects and deals in old clothes and furniture, etc.

rag-bag *noun* 1 *colloq.* a scruffy, untidy person. 2 a bag for storing rags and scraps of material.

rage — *noun* 1 violent anger, or a fit of anger. 2 violent, stormy action, eg of the wind, sea, or a battle. 3 an intense desire or passion for something. 4 a widespread, usually temporary fashion or craze. — *verb intrans.* 1 to be violently angry. 2 to speak wildly with anger or passion; to rave. 3 *said of the wind, sea, a battle, etc* to be stormy and unchecked. — **all the rage** *colloq.* very much in fashion. [from Latin *rabies*, madness]

⊟ *noun* 1, 2 anger, wrath, fury, frenzy. 1 tantrum, temper. 4 craze, fad, thing, fashion, vogue, style, passion, enthusiasm, obsession. *verb* 1 fume, seethe, explode, rampage. 2 rant, rave, storm, thunder.

ragga *noun* a style of rap music influenced by dance rhythms. [from RAGAMUFFIN]

ragged *adj.* 1 *said of clothes* old, worn, and tattered. 2 dressed in old, worn, tattered clothing. 3 with a rough and irregular edge; jagged. 4 untidy; straggly.

⊟ 1, 2 shabby, scruffy. 1 frayed, torn, ripped, tattered, worn-out, threadbare, tatty. 2 unkempt, down-at-heel. 3 jagged, serrated, indented, notched, rough, uneven, irregular. 4 untidy, disorderly, straggling, straggly, erratic, disorganized, fragmented.

ragged Robin a wild flower with pink, ragged-edged petals.

raging *adj.* 1 that rages. 2 very angry.

⊟ 1, 2 furious, wild, angry. 1 violent, stormy. 2 enraged, infuriated, incensed, fuming, *colloq.* boiling.

raglan *adj.* 1 *said of a sleeve* attached to a garment by two seams running diagonally from the neck to the armpit. 2 *said of a garment* having such sleeves. [named after Lord Raglan]

ragout /ra'guː/ *noun* a highly seasoned stew of meat and vegetables. [from French *ragoût*]

ragtime *noun* a type of jazz piano music with a highly syncopated rhythm, originated by black American musicians in the 1890s. [a contraction of *ragged time*]

rag trade the business of designing, making, and selling clothes.

ragwort /'ragwɜːt/ *noun* a common plant with yellow flowers with ragged petals.

rai /raɪ/ *noun* a style of popular music from Algeria, blending traditional Arabic, Spanish flamenco, and Western disco rhythms. [from Arabic *ra'y*, opinion, view]

raid — *noun* **1** a sudden unexpected attack. **2** a sudden unexpected visit by the police searching for suspected criminals or illicit goods. **3** a robbery or break-in. **4** the selling of shares by a group of speculators in an attempt to lower share prices. — *verb* **1** to make a raid on. **2** *intrans.* to go on a raid. [from Anglo-Saxon *rad*, road]

⊟ *noun* **1** attack, onset, onslaught, invasion, inroad, incursion, foray, sortie, strike, blitz. **2** swoop, *slang* bust. **3** robbery, break-in, hold-up. *verb* **1** loot, pillage, plunder, ransack, rifle, attack, descend on, invade, storm.

raider *noun* a person that raids.

⊟ attacker, invader, looter, plunderer, ransacker, marauder, robber, thief, brigand, pirate.

rail¹ — *noun* **1** a usually horizontal bar supported by vertical posts, forming a fence or barrier. **2** a horizontal bar used to hang things on. **3** either of a pair of lengths of steel forming a track for the wheels of a train. **4** the railway. — *verb* (**rail something off**) to enclose a space within a rail or rails. — **off the rails** not functioning or behaving normally or properly. [from Old French *reille*]

rail² *verb intrans.* (**rail at** or **against something** or **someone**) to complain or criticize abusively or bitterly. [from Old French *railler*, to deride]

rail³ *noun* any of various species of birds, usually living near water, with a short neck and wings and long legs, such as the corncrake and coot. [from Old French *rasle*]

railcar *noun North Amer.* **1** a railway carriage. **2** a self-propelled railway carriage.

railcard *noun* a special card, eg for students, the elderly, etc, giving the holder the right to reduced train fares.

railhead *noun* **1** a railway terminal. **2** the furthest point reached by a railway under construction.

railing *noun* **1** (*usually* **railings**) a fence or barrier. **2** material for building fences.

⊟ **1** fence, paling, barrier, parapet, rail, balustrade.

raillery *noun* good-humoured teasing, or an instance of this. [related to RAIL²]

railroad — *noun North Amer., esp. US* a railway. — *verb colloq.* (**railroad someone into something**) to rush them unfairly into doing something.

railway *noun* **1** a track or set of tracks formed by two parallel steel rails fixed to sleepers, for trains to run on. **2** a system of such tracks, plus all the trains, buildings, and people required for it to function. **3** a company responsible for operating such a system. **4** a similar set of tracks for a different type of vehicle: *funicular railway.*

⊟ **1**, **2** line. **1** track, rails.

raiment *noun old use, poetic* clothing. [from Old French *areer*, to array]

rain — *noun* **1** a form of precipitation consisting of water droplets that fall from the clouds. **2** (*also* **rains**) the season of heavy rainfall in tropical countries. **3** a heavy fall of something. — *verb* **1** *intrans. said of rain* to fall. **2** *intrans., trans.* to fall or cause to fall like rain: *bullets raining down on them/rain down compliments on her head.* — **be rained off** *Brit., said of a sporting or other event* to be cancelled because of rain. **come rain or shine** whatever the weather or circumstances. **rain cats and dogs** *colloq.* to rain very hard. **right as rain** *colloq.* perfectly all right or in order. [from Anglo-Saxon *regn*]

⊟ *noun* **1** rainfall, precipitation, raindrops, drizzle, shower, cloudburst, downpour, deluge, torrent, storm,

thunderstorm, squall. *verb* **1** spit, drizzle, shower, pour, teem, pelt, *colloq.* bucket (down), deluge.

rainbow *noun* **1** an arch of all the colours of the spectrum, ie red, orange, yellow, green, blue, indigo, and violet, that can be seen in the sky when falling raindrops reflect and refract sunlight that is shining from behind the observer. **2** a collection or array of bright colours.

rainbow coalition a political alliance between minority groups or parties of varying opinions.

rainbow trout a freshwater N American and European trout.

raincoat *noun* a light waterproof coat worn to keep out the rain.

rainfall *noun* **1** the amount of rain, hail, and snow that falls in a certain place over a certain period. **2** a shower of rain.

rainforest *noun* a type of dense forest, generally dominated by tall broad-leaved evergreen trees, that usually occurs in hot humid equatorial regions (tropical rainforest), but is also found in some temperate regions with high rainfall (temperate rainforest).

rain shadow *Meteorol.* a region on the lee side of mountains or hills that receives significantly less rainfall than land on the windward side, because prevailing winds are forced to rise, cool, and thereby lose most of their moisture by precipitation while moving across the high ground.

rainy *adj.* (**rainier, rainiest**) **1** *said of the weather, etc* having many rain showers. **2** *said of clouds, etc* threatening rain.

⊟ **1** wet, damp, showery, drizzly.

⊞ **1** dry.

rainy day a notional time of particular need in the future: *saving it for a rainy day.*

raise — *verb* **1** to move up or lift to a high position or level. **2** to put in an upright or standing position. **3** to build. **4** to increase the value, amount, or strength of: *raise prices/raise one's voice.* **5** to put forward for consideration or discussion: *raise an objection.* **6** to collect, levy, or gather together. **7** to stir up or incite: *raise a protest.* **8** to bring into being; to provoke: *raise a laugh/raise the alarm.* **9** to promote to a higher rank. **10** to awaken or arouse from sleep or death. **11** to grow (vegetables, a crop, etc). **12** to bring up or rear: *raise a family.* **13** to bring to an end or remove: *raise the siege.* **14** to cause (bread or dough) to rise with yeast. **15** to establish radio contact with. **16** *Maths.* to increase (a quantity) to a given power: *3 raised to the power of 4 is 81.* **17** *Cards* to bet more than (another player). **18** *Naut.* to cause (land) to come into sight by approaching. **19** to produce a nap on (cloth) by brushing. **20** to cause (a lump, blister, etc) to form or swell. — *noun* **1** an act of raising or lifting. **2** *colloq. esp. North Amer.* an increase in salary. — **raise hell** or **the devil** *colloq.* to make a lot of trouble. **raise someone's hopes** to give them reason to be hopeful. **raise someone's spirits** to make them more cheerful or optimistic. [from Norse *reisa*]

⊟ *verb* **1** lift, elevate, hoist, jack up. **3** build, construct, erect. **4** increase, augment, escalate, magnify, heighten, strengthen, intensify, amplify, boost, enhance. **5** bring up, broach, introduce, present, put forward, moot, suggest. **6** obtain, collect, gather, assemble, rally, muster, recruit. **11** propagate, grow, cultivate. **12** bring up, rear, breed, develop.

⊞ *verb* **1** lower. **4** decrease, reduce. **5** suppress.

raisin *noun* a dried grape. [from Old French *raisin*, grape]

raison d'être /rezon'detr(ə)/ (PL. **raisons d'être**) a purpose or reason that justifies a thing's or person's existence. [French, = reason for being]

raita /raɪ'iːtə/ *noun* an Indian dish of chopped vegetables, especially cucumber, in yoghurt. [from Hindi]

Raj /rɑːdʒ/ *noun Hist.* the British rule in India, 1858–1947. [from Sanskrit *rajan*, king]

rajah or **raja** /rɑːdʒə/ *noun Hist.* an Indian king or prince.

rake[1] — *noun* **1** a long-handled tool with a comb-like part at one end, used for smoothing or breaking up earth, gathering leaves together, etc. **2** any tool with a similar shape or use, eg a croupier's tool for gathering money together. — *verb* **1** (**rake things up** or **together**) to collect, gather, or remove with, or as if with, a rake. **2** (**rake something over**) to make it smooth with a rake. **3** *intrans.* to work with a rake. **4** *trans., intrans.* (**rake through** or **among something**) to search it carefully. **5** to sweep gradually along the length of, especially with gunfire or one's eyes. **6** to scratch or scrape. — **rake something in** *colloq.* to earn or acquire it in large amounts. **rake something up** *colloq.* **1** to revive or uncover (something forgotten or lost): *rake up old memories.* **2** to find it, especially with difficulty. [from Anglo-Saxon *raca*]

⊟ *verb* **1** gather, collect, amass, accumulate. **4** comb, scour, search, hunt. **6** scratch, scrape, graze. **rake up** UNCOVER. **1** bring up, drag up, revive, resurrect, rekindle. **2** unearth, dig up, track down.

rake[2] *noun old use* a fashionable man who lives a dissolute and immoral life. [a shortening of obsolete *rakehell*]

rake[3] — *noun* **1** a sloping position, especially of a ship's funnel or mast backwards towards the stern, of a ship's bow or stern in relation to the keel, or a theatre stage. **2** the amount by which something slopes. — *verb* **1** *trans., intrans.* to set or be set at a sloping angle. **2** *intrans.* *said of a ship's mast or funnel* to slope backwards towards the stern. **3** *intrans. said of a ship's bow or stern* to project out beyond the keel.

rake-off *noun slang* a share of the profits, especially when dishonest or illegal.

rakish *adj.* **1** *said of a ship* having a smart sleek appearance. **2** having a jaunty, rather provocative and unconventional air.

⊟ **2** jaunty, dashing, careless, carefree, perky, breezy, cheeky, debonair, casual, nonchalant, daring, adventurous, raffish.

rakishly *adv.* with a rakish manner.

rakishness *noun* a rakish style or manner.

raku /'raːkuː/ *noun* a type of coarse-grained, lead-glazed pottery fired at low temperature, traditionally used in Japan to make tea bowls. [from Japanese, = pleasure, enjoyment]

rallentando /raləntandoʊ/ — *adj., adv. Mus.* becoming gradually slower. — *noun* (PL. **rallentandos, rallentandi**) a passage to be played in this way. [from Italian *rallentando*]

rally — *verb* (**rallies, rallied**) **1** *trans., intrans.* to come or bring together again after being dispersed. **2** *trans., intrans.* to come or bring together for some common cause or action. **3** to revive (one's spirits, strength, abilities, etc) by making an effort. **4** *intrans.* to recover one's lost health, fitness, strength, etc, especially after an illness. **5** *intrans. said of share prices* to increase again after a fall. — *noun* (PL. **rallies**) **1** a reassembling of forces to make a new effort. **2** a mass meeting of people with a common cause or interest. **3** a recovering of lost health, fitness, strength, especially after an illness. **4** *Tennis* a usually long series of strokes between players before one of them finally wins the point. **5** a competition to test skill in driving, usually held on public roads. — **rally round someone** to come together to support or help them. [from Old French *rallier*, to rejoin]

⊟ *verb* **1** reassemble, regroup, reorganize. **2** gather, collect, assemble, congregate, convene, muster, unite, organize, mobilize. **4, 5** improve, pick up. **4** recover, recuperate, revive. *noun* **2** gathering, assembly, convention, convocation, conference, meeting, jamboree, reunion, march, demonstration. **3** recovery, recuperation, revival, comeback, improvement, resurgence, renewal.

rallycross *noun* motor racing over a course made up of both proper roads and rough ground.

RAM *abbrev.* **1** *Comput.* random access memory, a temporary memory available to the user which allows programs to be loaded and run, and data to be changed. **2** Royal Academy of Music.

ram — *noun* **1** an uncastrated male sheep or goat. **2** (**the Ram**) the constellation Aries. **3** a battering-ram. **4** a pointed device on a warship's prow, for making holes in enemy ships. **5** the falling weight of a pile-driver. **6** a piston or plunger operated by hydraulic or other power. — *verb* (**rammed, ramming**) **1** to force down or into position by pushing hard. **2** *trans., intrans.* to strike or crash against violently: *ram the car into the wall.* — **ram something down someone's throat** *colloq.* to force them to believe, accept, or listen to (a statement, idea, etc) by talking about it or repeating it constantly. **ram something home** to emphasize it forcefully. [from Anglo-Saxon *ramm*]

⊟ *verb* **1** force, drive, thrust, cram, stuff, pack, crowd, jam, wedge, hammer, pound. **2** crash, smash, slam, bang.

Ramadan or **Ramadhan** /'raməda:n, 'ramədan/ *noun* **1** the ninth month of the Muslim year, during which Muslims fast between sunrise and sunset. **2** the fast itself. [from Arabic]

ramble — *verb intrans.* **1** to go for a long walk or walks, especially in the countryside, for pleasure. **2** (*also* **ramble on**) to speak or write in an aimless or confused way. **3** to grow or extend in a straggling, trailing way. — *noun* a walk, especially in the countryside, for pleasure.

⊟ *verb* **1** wander, roam, walk, hike, trek, tramp, traipse, stroll, amble, saunter, rove. **2** chatter, babble, *colloq.* rabbit (on), *formal* expatiate, digress, drift. **3** meander, wind, zigzag, straggle. *noun* walk, hike, trek, tramp, stroll, saunter, tour, trip, excursion.

rambler *noun* **1** a climbing plant, especially a rose. **2** a person who goes walking in the country for pleasure.

⊟ **2** hiker, walker, stroller, rover, roamer, wanderer, wayfarer.

rambling — *noun* walking for pleasure, usually in the countryside. — *adj.* that rambles; wandering, straggling. *said of speech* disconnected.

⊟ *adj.* **1** spreading, sprawling, wandering, straggling, trailing. **2** circuitous, roundabout, digressive, wordy, long-winded, long-drawn-out, disconnected, incoherent.
⊟ *adj.* **2** direct.

rambutan /ram'buːtən/ *noun* **1** a tree (*Nephelium lappaceum*) of the same family as the lychee, found throughout SE Asia. **2** the fruit of this tree, which has edible translucent flesh and a thick red shell covered with hooked hairs. [from Malay, from *rambut*, hair]

RAMC *abbrev. Brit.* Royal Army Medical Corps.

ramekin /'raməkɪn/ *noun* **1** a small baking dish for a single serving of food. **2** an individual serving, especially of a savoury dish containing cheese and eggs, served in a ramekin. [from French *ramequin*]

ramification *noun* **1** an arrangement of branches; a branched structure. **2** a single part or section of a complex subject, plot, etc. **3** a consequence, especially a serious or complicated one. [from Latin *ramus*, branch]

⊟ **2** branch, offshoot, development. **3** result, consequence, upshot, implication, complication.

ramify *verb trans., intrans.* (**ramifies, ramified**) to separate or cause to separate into branches or sections.

ramjet *noun Aeron.* **1** a type of jet engine that consists of a tube with two open ends. Air enters at one end and is compressed by the forward movement of the vehicle. Fuel is then injected into the compressed air, and the mixture is continuously burned. The hot gases produced during combustion are ejected backwards in the form of a jet, which produces the forward thrust. **2** an aircraft or missile that is propelled by such an engine.

ramp — *noun* **1** a sloping surface between two different levels, especially one which can be used instead of steps. **2** a set of movable stairs for entering and leaving an aircraft. **3** *Brit.* a low hump lying across a road, designed to slow traffic down. **4** *Brit.* a place where the level of the road surface changes or is uneven due to roadworks. — *verb* **1** to provide with a ramp. **2** *intrans.* to slope from one level to another. **3** *intrans.* to dash about in a wild, violent, and threatening way. [from Old French *ramper*, to creep]

. . . .

☰ *noun* **1** slope, incline, gradient, rise.

. . . .

rampage *verb intrans.* to rush about wildly, angrily, violently, or excitedly. — **on the rampage** rampaging, often destructively. [related to RAMP]

. . . .

☰ run wild, run amok, run riot, rush, tear, storm, rage, rant, rave. **on the rampage** wild, amok, berserk, violent, out of control.

. . . .

rampant *adj.* **1** uncontrolled; unrestrained: *rampant violence.* **2** *Heraldry* in profile and standing erect on the left hind leg with the other legs raised. [related to RAMP]

. . . .

☰ **1** unrestrained, uncontrolled, unbridled, unchecked, wanton, excessive, fierce, violent, raging, wild, riotous, rank, profuse, rife, widespread, prevalent.

. . . .

rampart *noun* a broad mound or wall for defence, usually with a wall or parapet on top. [from Old French *remparer*, to defend]

. . . .

☰ mound, wall, bastion, bulwark, earthwork, defence, stockade, redoubt.

. . . .

ramping *noun* the practice of causing large false increases in the prices of shares, etc by dishonest means.

ram-raid *noun* a robbery done by ram-raiding.

ram-raiding *noun* the practice of smashing through the front window of a shop or store with a heavy vehicle and looting the goods inside.

ramrod *noun* **1** a rod for ramming charge down into, or for cleaning, the barrel of a gun. **2** a person who is strict, stern, and inflexible, both physically and morally.

ramshackle *adj.*, *said especially of buildings* badly made and likely to fall down; rickety. [from obsolete *ranshackle*, to ransack]

. . . .

☰ dilapidated, tumbledown, broken-down, crumbling, ruined, derelict, jerry-built, unsafe, rickety, shaky, unsteady, tottering, decrepit.

☲ solid, stable.

. . . .

ramsons /ˈramzənz/ *noun* a perennial plant (*Allium ursinum*), native to woodland of Europe and Asia, that forms large carpets of long-stalked, spear-shaped shiny leaves which smell strongly of garlic. Its slender upright stems bear flat-topped clusters of white star-shaped flowers. [from Anglo-Saxon *hramsa*]

ran see RUN.

ranch — *noun* **1** an extensive grassland farm, especially in N America, S America, or Australia, where sheep, cattle, or horses are raised. **2** in N America, a farm that specializes in the production of a particular crop or animal. — *verb intrans.* to raise large numbers of sheep, cattle, or horses on a ranch. [from Spanish *rancho*, mess-room]

rancher *noun* a person who ranches.

rancid /ˈransɪd/ *adj.*, *said of butter, oil, etc* tasting or smelling sour. [from Latin *rancidus*, stinking]

. . . .

☰ sour, off, bad, musty, stale, rank, foul, fetid, putrid, rotten.

☲ sweet.

. . . .

rancidity or **rancidness** *noun* a rancid state or quality.

rancorous *adj.* feeling or expressing bitter resentment or dislike.

. . . .

☰ resentful, bitter, acrimonious, acerbic, hostile, spiteful, malicious, vindictive.

. . . .

rancour /ˈraŋkə(r)/ *noun* a long-lasting feeling of bitterness, dislike, or hatred. [from Latin *rancor*, from *rancere*, to be rancid]

rand *noun* (PL. **rand**, **rands**) the standard monetary unit used in South Africa and some neighbouring countries. [from Witwatersrand, a large gold-mining area near Johannesburg]

R & B *abbrev.* rhythm and blues.

R & D *abbrev.* research and development.

randily *adv.* in a randy way.

randiness *noun* being randy.

random *adj.* lacking a definite plan, system, or order; irregular; haphazard. — **at random** without any particular plan, system or purpose. [from Old French *randon*, gallop]

. . . .

☰ arbitrary, chance, fortuitous, casual, incidental, haphazard, irregular, unsystematic, unplanned, accidental, aimless, purposeless, indiscriminate, stray.

☲ systematic, deliberate.

. . . .

random access a method of access that enables a particular item of data stored on a disk or in the memory of a computer to be located without the need to read any other data stored on the same device, ie it can be read out of sequence.

random access memory see RAM.

randomly *adv.* in a random way.

randomness *noun* being random.

randy *adj.* (**randier**, **randiest**) *colloq.* sexually excited; lustful. [perhaps related to RANT]

ranee /ˈrɑːniː/ see RANI.

rang see RING[2].

range — *noun* **1** an area between limits within which things may move, function, etc; the limits forming this area. **2** a number of items, products, etc forming a distinct series. **3** the distance between the lowest and highest notes which may be produced by a musical instrument or a singing voice. **4** the distance to which a gun may be fired or an object thrown. **5** the distance between a weapon and its target. **6** the distance that can be covered by a vehicle without it needing to refuel. **7** an area where shooting may be practised and rockets tested. **8** a group of mountains forming a distinct series or row. **9** *North Amer.* a large area of open land for grazing livestock. **10** the region over which a plant or animal is distributed. **11** *Maths.* the set of values that a function or dependent variable may take. **12** an enclosed kitchen fireplace fitted with a large cooking stove with one or more ovens and a flat top surface for heating pans. — *verb* **1** to put in a row or rows. **2** to put (someone, oneself, etc) into a specified category or group: *he ranged himself among her enemies.* **3** *intrans.* to vary or change between specified limits. **4** (**range over** or **through something**) to roam freely in it. **5** *intrans.* to stretch or extend in a specified direction or over a specified area. [from Old French *range*, row, rank]

. . . .

☰ *noun* **1** scope, compass, scale, gamut, spectrum, sweep, spread, extent, distance, reach, span, limits, bounds, parameters, area, field, domain, province, sphere, orbit. **2** variety, diversity, assortment, selection, sort, kind, class, order, series, string, chain. *verb* **1** align, arrange, order, rank, classify, catalogue. **3** vary, fluctuate, change. **4** roam, wander through, explore. **5** extend, stretch, reach, spread.

rangefinder *noun* an instrument which can estimate the distance of an object, especially a target to be shot or photographed.

ranger *noun* **1** a person who looks after a royal or national forest or park. **2** *North Amer., esp. US* a soldier who has been specially trained for raiding and combat; a commando. **3** *North Amer., esp. US* a member of a group of armed men who patrol and police a region. **4** (**Ranger** or **Ranger Guide**) *Brit.* a member of the senior branch of the Guide Association.

rangy /ˈreɪndʒɪ/ *adj.* (**rangier, rangiest**) *said of a person* having long thin limbs and a slender body.

rani or **ranee** /ˈrɑːnɪ/ *noun Hist.* the wife or widow of a rajah. [from Sanskrit *rajni*, queen]

rank[1] — *noun* **1** a line or row of people or things. **2** a line of soldiers standing side by side. **3** a position of seniority within an organization, society, the armed forces, etc. **4** a distinct class or group, eg according to ability. **5** high social position or status. **6** (**the ranks**) ordinary soldiers (eg privates and corporals) as opposed to officers. **7** *Brit.* a place where taxis wait for passengers. **8** a row of squares along the player's side of a chessboard. — *verb* **1** to arrange (people or things) in a row or line. **2** to grade or classify in relation to others. **3** *intrans.* to have a particular grade, position, or status in relation to others. **4** to have a higher position, status, etc than (someone); to outrank (someone). — **close ranks** *said of a group of people* to keep their solidarity. **pull rank** to use one's higher rank or status to get what one wants. **the rank and file 1** the ordinary members of an organization or society as opposed to the leaders or principal members. **2** the ordinary soldiers as opposed to the officers. [from Old French *renc*]

 noun **1, 2** row, line, column, file, formation. **3** grade, degree, title, status, standing, position, station, condition, estate, caste. **4** class, classification, sort, type, group, division, echelon, level, stratum, tier. *verb* **1** align, order, arrange, organize, marshal. **2, 3** rate. **2** grade, class, place, position, range, sort, classify, categorize.

Ranks in the armed services include: air force: aircraftman, aircraftwoman, corporal, sergeant, warrant officer, pilot officer, flying officer, flight lieutenant, squadron-leader, wing commander, group-captain, air-commodore, air-vice-marshal, air-marshal, air-chief-marshal, marshal of the Royal Air Force; army: private, lance-corporal, corporal, sergeant, warrant officer, lieutenant, captain, major, lieutenant-colonel, colonel, brigadier, major general, lieutenant-general, general, field marshal; navy: able seaman, rating, petty officer, chief petty officer, sublieutenant, lieutenant, lieutenant-commander, commander, captain, commodore, rear admiral, vice-admiral, admiral, admiral of the fleet. See also **soldier***.*

rank[2] *adj.* **1** coarsely overgrown and untidy. **2** offensively strong in smell or taste. **3** bold, open, and shocking: *rank disobedience.* **4** complete: *a rank beginner.* [from Anglo-Saxon *ranc*, proud, overbearing]

 1 overgrown, lush, abundant, dense, profuse. **2** foul, repulsive, disgusting, revolting, stinking, putrid, rancid, stale. **3, 4** utter, total, complete, absolute, thorough. **3** sheer, downright, out-and-out, arrant, gross, flagrant, glaring, unmitigated, outrageous.

ranker *noun* a soldier who serves or has served in the ranks, especially an officer who has been promoted up through the ranks.

rankle *verb intrans.* to continue to cause feelings of annoyance or bitterness: *his refusal still rankles.* [from Old French *draoncle*, festering sore]

 hurt, irritate, offend.

rankly *adv.* in a rank way.

rankness *noun* being rank.

ransack *verb* **1** to search thoroughly and often roughly. **2** to rob or plunder. [from Norse *rannsaka* from *rann*, house + *skja*, to seek]

 1 search, scour, comb, rummage through. **2** rifle, raid, sack, strip, despoil, ravage, loot, plunder, pillage.

ransom — *noun* **1** money paid in return for the release of a kidnapped person. **2** the releasing of a kidnapped person in return for this. — *verb* (**ransomed, ransoming**) **1** to pay a ransom for (someone's) release. **2** to demand a ransom before releasing (someone). — **hold someone to ransom 1** to keep them prisoner until a ransom is paid. **2** to blackmail them into agreeing to one's demands. **a king's ransom** a vast amount of money. [from Latin *redemptio*, redemption]

 noun **1** price, money, payment, pay-off. **2** redemption, deliverance, rescue, liberation, release. *verb* **1** buy off, redeem, deliver, rescue, liberate, free, release.

ransomer *noun* a person who ransoms.

rant — *verb* **1** *intrans.* to talk in a loud, angry, pompous way. **2** *trans.* to declaim in a loud, pompous, self-important way. — *noun* loud, pompous, empty speech. [from Dutch *ranten*, to rave]

 verb **1** shout, cry, yell, roar, bellow, bluster, rave. **2** declaim. *noun* bluster, bombast, declamation, pomposity, grandiloquence.

ranter *noun* a person who rants.

ranting — *noun* **1** a rant. **2** raving, scolding. — *adj.* that rants.

RAOC *abbrev. Brit.* Royal Army Ordnance Corps.

rap[1] — *noun* **1** a quick sharp tap or blow, or the sound made by this. **2** *slang* blame or punishment: *take the rap.* **3** a fast rhythmic monologue recited over a musical backing with a pronounced beat. **4** (*in full* **rap music**) a style of rock music based on rhythmic monologues. **5** *colloq.* a conversation. — *verb* (**rapped, rapping**) **1** to strike sharply. **2** *intrans.* to make a sharp tapping sound. **3** (*usually* **rap something out**) to utter (eg a command) sharply and quickly. **4** to criticize sharply. **5** to communicate (a message) by raps or knocks. **6** *intrans. colloq.* to talk or have a discussion. **7** *intrans. colloq.* to perform a fast rhythmic monologue to music with a pronounced beat. — **beat the rap** *North Amer. slang* to escape punishment for a crime (whether guilty or not). [from Middle English *rappen*]

 noun **1** knock, blow, tap, thump. **2** rebuke, reprimand, censure, blame, punishment. *verb* **1, 2** knock, tap, beat, thump. **1** hit, strike. **2** drum. **4** reprove, reprimand, criticize, censure, *colloq.* slam.

rap[2] *noun* the least bit: *not care a rap.* [a former Irish counterfeit halfpenny]

rapacious /rəˈpeɪʃəs/ *adj.* **1** greedy and grasping, especially for money. **2** *said of an animal or bird* living by catching prey. [from Latin *rapere*, to seize and carry off]

 1 greedy, covetous, acquisitive, avid, grasping, avaricious.

rapaciously *adv.* in a rapacious way.

rapaciousness or **rapacity** *noun* **1** being rapacious. **2** rapacious behaviour.

rape¹ — *noun* **1** the crime of forcing a woman to have sexual intercourse against her will. **2** the crime of sodomizing a person against his or her will. **3** violation, despoiling, or abuse. — *verb* to commit rape on. [from Latin *rapere*, to seize and carry off]

■ *noun* VIOLATION, ASSAULT, ABUSE, MALTREATMENT.
verb violate, assault, abuse, maltreat.

rape² *noun* same as OILSEED RAPE. [from Latin *rapum*, turnip]

rapid — *adj.* moving, acting, or happening quickly; fast. — *noun* (**rapids**) a part of a river where the water flows quickly, usually over dangerous, sharply descending rocks. [from Latin *rapidus*]

■ *adj.* fast, express, lightning, prompt, brisk, hurried, hasty, precipitate, headlong.
◼ *adj.* slow, leisurely, sluggish.

rapid eye movement (ABBREV. REM) *Physiol.* a stage of relatively shallow sleep during which the eyes move rapidly from side to side behind the closed eyelids, generally accompanying a period of dreaming.

rapidity or **rapidness** *noun* being rapid, speed.

■ speed, swiftness, quickness, promptness, immediacy, briskness, alacrity, dispatch, *formal* celerity.

rapidly *adv.* quickly.

rapier /ˈreɪpɪə(r)/ *noun* a long, thin, two-edged sword for thrusting. [from French *rapière*]

rapine /ˈrapaɪn, ˈrapɪn/ *noun* plundering; robbery. [from Latin *rapere*, to seize and carry off]

rapist *noun* a person who commits rape.

rapper *noun* **1** a person that raps something, eg a knocker. **2** a performer of rap music.

rapport /raˈpɔː(r)/ *noun* a feeling of sympathy and understanding; a close emotional bond. [from French *rapport*]

■ bond, link, affinity, relationship, empathy, sympathy, understanding, harmony.

rapprochement /raˈprɒʃmɒn/ *noun* the establishment or renewal of a close, friendly relationship, especially between states. [from French *rapprochement*]

rapscallion *noun old use* a rascal or scamp. [perhaps related to RASCAL]

rapt *adj.* **1** enraptured; enchanted. **2** completely absorbed. [from Latin *rapere*, to seize and carry off]

■ SPELLBOUND, ENTHRALLED, CAPTIVATED, FASCINATED. **1** entranced, charmed, enchanted, delighted, ravished, enraptured, transported. **2** engrossed, absorbed, preoccupied, intent, gripped.

raptor *noun* any bird of prey, eg an owl or falcon. [from Latin *raptor*, plunderer]

raptorial *adj.* **1** predatory. **2** adapted to predatory life.

rapture *noun* **1** great delight; ecstasy. **2** (**raptures**) great enthusiasm for or pleasure in something. [related to RAPT]

■ **1** delight, happiness, joy, bliss, ecstasy, euphoria, exaltation.

rapturous *adj.* experiencing or demonstrating rapture.

■ delighted, happy, joyful, overjoyed, blissful, ecstatic, euphoric, enthusiastic.

rare¹ *adj.* **1** not done, found, or occurring very often. **2** *said of the atmosphere at high altitudes* thin; rarefied. **3** excellent; unusually good: *rare abilities*. **4** *colloq.* extreme; severe: *a rare old fright*. [from Latin *rarus*, sparse]

■ **1, 3** uncommon, unusual. **1** scarce, sparse, sporadic, infrequent. **3** exquisite, superb, excellent, superlative, incomparable, exceptional, remarkable, precious.
◼ **1** common, abundant, frequent.

rare² *adj.*, *said of meat* cooked on the outside but still raw on the inside. [from Anglo-Saxon *hrere*, lightly boiled]

rarebit see WELSH RABBIT.

rare earth *Chem.* an oxide of a *rare earth element*, an element of the lanthanide series.

rarefied /ˈreərɪfaɪd/ *adj.* **1** *said of the air, atmosphere, etc* thin; with a very low oxygen content. **2** select; exclusive: *move in rarefied circles*. **3** esoteric, mysterious, spiritual.

■ **2** exclusive, select, private, esoteric, refined, high, noble, sublime.

rarefy /ˈreərɪfaɪ/ *verb* (**rarefies**, **rarefied**) **1** *trans., intrans.* to make or become less dense or solid. **2** to refine or purify. [from Latin *rarus*, rare + *facere*, to make]

rare gas same as NOBLE GAS.

rarely *adv.* **1** not often. **2** extremely well.

■ **1** seldom, hardly ever, infrequently, little.
◼ **1** often, frequently.

raring *adj.* keen and enthusiastic: *raring to go*. [related to REAR²]

■ eager, keen, enthusiastic, ready, willing, impatient, longing, itching, desperate.

rarity *noun* (PL. **rarities**) **1** the state of being rare. **2** something valued because it is rare.

■ **1** uncommonness, unusualness, strangeness, scarcity, shortage, sparseness, infrequency. **2** curiosity, curio, gem, pearl, treasure, find.
◼ **1** commonness, frequency.

rascal *noun* **1** a dishonest person; a rogue. **2** *humorous* a cheeky or mischievous child. [from Old French *rascaille*, rabble]

■ ROGUE, DEVIL. **1** scoundrel, villain, good-for-nothing, wastrel. **2** scamp, scallywag, imp.

rascally *adj.* dishonest.

rase same as RAZE.

rash¹ *adj.* acting, or done, with little caution or thought; hasty. [from Middle English]

■ hasty, reckless, ill-considered, foolhardy, ill-advised, madcap, hare-brained, hot-headed, headstrong, impulsive, impetuous, headlong, unguarded, unwary, indiscreet, imprudent, careless, heedless, unthinking.
◼ cautious, wary, careful.

rash² *noun* **1** a temporary outbreak of red spots or patches on the skin, often accompanied by itching, and usually either a symptom of an infectious disease such as measles or chickenpox, or of a skin allergy. **2** a large number of instances of a thing happening at the same time: *a rash of burglaries*. [from Latin *radere*, to scratch]

⊟ ERUPTION. **2** outbreak, epidemic, plague.

rasher *noun* a thin slice of bacon or ham.
rashly *adv.* in a rash way.
rashness *noun* **1** being rash. **2** rash behaviour.

⊟ RECKLESSNESS, INDISCRETION, IMPRUDENCE,
CARELESSNESS, HEEDLESSNESS, IMPULSIVENESS.

rasp — *noun* **1** a coarse, rough file. **2** a harsh, rough, grating sound. — *verb* **1** to scrape roughly, especially with a rasp. **2** to grate upon or irritate (eg someone's nerves). **3** *intrans., trans.* to speak or utter in a harsh, grating voice. [from Old French *raspe*]

⊟ *noun* **2** grating, scrape, grinding, scratch, harshness, hoarseness, croak. *verb* **1, 2** grate (on). **1** scrape, grind, file, sand, scour, abrade, rub.

raspberry /ˈrɑːzbəri/ *noun* (PL. **raspberries**) **1** a deciduous shrub of the genus *Rubus* that produces upright thorny canes, and is cultivated in Europe and N America for its edible fruit. **2** the cone-shaped fruit of this plant, consisting of red, black, or pale yellow drupelets (small spherical structures) each of which contains a single seed. It may be eaten raw, preserved by canning or freezing, or used to make jam. **3** *slang* a sound made by sticking the tongue out and blowing through the lips, usually to express disapproval. [from earlier *raspis*, of unknown origin]

rasper *noun* a person or thing that rasps.
rasping *adj.* grating, harsh.
raspingly *adv.* with a grating sound.
raspy *adj.* (**raspier, raspiest**) rough.
Rasta *noun, adj. colloq.* Rastafarian.
Rastafarian /rɑstəˈfɛərɪən/ — *noun* a follower of an originally West Indian sect, which regards blacks as the chosen people and reveres Haile Selassie, the former Emperor of Ethiopia, as God. — *adj.* relating to or characteristic of Rastafarians. [from *Ras Tafari*, the name and title of Haile Selassie]

rat — *noun* **1** any of various small rodents belonging to the family Muridae, found worldwide in huge numbers, usually blackish-brown in colour with a long scaly tail. They are notorious pests and transmitters of disease. **2** any of various unrelated rodents that resemble this animal, eg kangaroo rat. **3** *colloq.* a person who is disloyal towards his or her friends, party, etc. **4** *colloq.* a strike-breaker; a blackleg. — *verb intrans.* (**ratted, ratting**) **1** to hunt rats. **2** (**rat on someone**) *colloq.* to betray or desert them. **3** *colloq.* to work as a blackleg. — **smell a rat** *colloq.* to sense that something is not as it should be. [from Anglo-Saxon *ræt*]

ratable /ˈreɪtəbl/ same as RATEABLE.

ratafia /rætəˈfiə/ *noun* **1** a flavouring essence made with the essential oil of almonds. **2** a cordial or liqueur flavoured with fruit kernels and almonds. **3** an almond-flavoured biscuit or small cake. [from French *ratafia*, probably from Creole, or *tafia*, a type of rum]

ratan /raˈtan/ same as RATTAN.

rat-a-tat-tat *noun* a sound of knocking on a door. [imitative]

ratatouille /ratəˈtuːɪ/ *noun* a southern French stew made with tomatoes, peppers, courgettes, aubergines, onions, and garlic. [from French *ratatouille*]

ratbag *noun slang* a mean, despicable person.

ratchet *noun* **1** a bar which fits into the notches of a toothed wheel so as to cause the wheel to turn in one direction only. **2** (*also* **ratchet-wheel**) a wheel with a toothed rim. **3** the mechanism including the bar and toothed wheel together. [from French *rochet*]

rate¹ — *noun* **1** the number of times something happens,

etc within a given period of time; the amount of something considered in relation to, or measured according to, another amount: *a high yearly suicide rate/at the rate of 40kph.* **2** a price or charge, often measured per unit: *the rate of pay for the job.* **3** a price or charge fixed according to a standard scale: *rate of exchange.* **4** class or rank: *second-rate.* **5** the speed of movement or change: *rate of progress.* **6** (**rates**) in the UK until 1990, a tax collected by a local authority, the amount of each person's contribution being based on the value of their property, used to pay for public services, such as libraries, rubbish collection, etc. See also COMMUNITY CHARGE. — *verb* **1** to give a value to: *be rated an excellent teacher/rate him number two in the world.* **2** to be worthy of; to deserve: *an answer not rating full marks.* **3** *intrans.* to be placed in a certain class or rank: *rates as the best book on the subject for years.* **4** *colloq.* to think highly of; to admire. **5** in the UK until 1990, to determine the value of (property) for the purposes of assessing the rates payable on it. — **at any rate** in any case; anyway. **at this** or **that rate** if this or that is or continues to be the case. [from Latin *rata*, from *reri*, to reckon]

⊟ *noun* **1, 2** amount, figure, scale. **1** frequency, incidence, occurrence, recurrence, ratio, proportion, relation, basis, measure, percentage. **2** charge, fee, hire, toll, tariff, price, cost, value, worth, tax, duty. **4** degree, grade, rank, rating, standard. **5** speed, velocity, tempo. *verb* **1** judge, regard, consider, deem, count, reckon, estimate, evaluate, assess, weigh, measure, grade, rank, class, classify. **2** deserve, merit. **3** rank, stand. **4** admire, respect, esteem, value, prize.

rate² *verb* to scold severely. [from Middle English *raten*]

rateable *adj.* **1** able to have its value estimated for the purposes of rates. **2** in the UK until 1990, having to pay rates.

rateable value in the UK until 1990, the fixed value of a piece of property used to calculate the rates to be paid on it.

rate-cap *verb* (**rate-capped, rate-capping**) *said of a government* to impose rate-capping on (a local authority).

rate-capping *noun* the setting by central government of an upper limit on the rate that can be levied by a local authority.

rate of reaction *Chem.* the speed of a chemical reaction, usually expressed as the rate at which the products are formed or the rate at which the reactants disappear, and influenced by temperature, the concentration of the reactants, and the presence of a catalyst. In living cells the rates of chemical reactions depend on the activity of enzymes.

ratepayer *noun Brit. Hist.* a person or institution that pays local rates.

rather — *adv.* **1** more readily; from preference. **2** more truly or properly: *my parents, or rather my mother and step-father.* **3** to a certain extent; somewhat. **4** on the contrary: *she said she'd help me; rather, she just sat around watching.* — *interj.* yes indeed; very much. [from Anglo-Saxon *hrathor*]

⊟ *adv.* **1** by preference, preferably, sooner, instead. **3** somewhat, fairly, quite, moderately, relatively, slightly, a bit, pretty, noticeably, significantly, very.

ratification *noun* **1** ratifying or being ratified. **2** confirmation, sanction.

ratify *verb* (**ratifies, ratified**) to give formal consent to (eg a treaty, agreement, etc), especially by signature. [from Latin *ratificare*]

⊟ approve, uphold, endorse, sign, legalize, sanction, authorize, establish, affirm, confirm, certify, validate, authenticate.

⊟ repudiate, reject.

rating *noun* **1** a classification according to order, rank or value. **2** *Brit.* an ordinary seaman. **3** an estimated value of a person's position, especially as regards credit. **4** the proportion of viewers or listeners forming the estimated audience of a television or radio programme, used as a measure of that programme's popularity.

⊟ **1** classification, category, rank, degree, status, standing, position, placing, order, grade, mark, class. **3** evaluation, assessment.

ratio /'reɪʃɪoʊ/ *noun* (PL. **ratios**) **1** the number or degree of one class of things in relation to another, or between one thing and another, expressed as a proportion: *the ratio of dogs to cats is 5 to 3.* **2** the number of times one mathematical quantity can be divided by another. [from Latin *ratio*, reckoning]

⊟ **1** percentage, fraction, proportion, relation, relationship, correspondence, correlation.

ration — *noun* **1** a fixed allowance of food, clothing, petrol, etc during a time of shortage. **2** (**rations**) one's daily allowance of food, especially in the army. — *verb* (**rationed, rationing**) **1** (**ration something out**) to distribute or share out something (especially in short supply), usually in fixed amounts. **2** to restrict the supply of provisions to (someone). [from Latin *ratio*, reckoning]

⊟ *noun* **1** quota, allowance, allocation, allotment, share, portion, helping, part, measure, amount, supply, provisions. *verb* **1** apportion, allot, allocate, share, deal out, distribute, dole out, dispense, supply, issue. **2** restrict, limit, control, conserve, save.

rational *adj.* **1** of or based on reason or logic. **2** able to think, form opinions, make judgements, etc. **3** sensible; reasonable. **4** sane. [from Latin *rationalis*]

⊟ **1, 2, 3** reasonable. **1** logical. **2** reasoning, thinking, intelligent, enlightened. **3** sound, well-founded, realistic, sensible, clear-headed, judicious, wise. **4** sane, normal, balanced, lucid.
⊟ IRRATIONAL. **1** illogical. **4** insane, crazy.

rationale /raʃə'nɑːl/ *noun* the underlying principles or reasons on which a decision, belief, action, etc is based. [from Latin *rationalis*]

⊟ logic, reasoning, philosophy, principle, basis, grounds, explanation, reason, motive, motivation, theory.

rationalism *noun* the theory that an individual's actions and beliefs should be based on reason rather than on intuition or the teachings of others.

rationalist *noun* a person who forms opinions by reasoning.

rationalistic *adj.* **1** characterized by rationalism. **2** inclined to rationalism.

rationality *noun* **1** being rational. **2** the possession or due exercise of reason. **3** reasonableness.

rationalization or **rationalisation** *noun* rationalizing or being rationalized.

rationalize or **rationalise** *verb* **1** to attribute (one's behaviour or attitude) to sensible, well-thought-out reasons or motives, especially after the event. **2** *intrans.* to explain one's behaviour, etc in this way. **3** to make logical or rational. **4** to make (an industry or organization) more efficient and profitable by reorganizing it to get rid of unnecessary costs and labour.

⊟ **1** justify, excuse, vindicate, explain, account for.
4 reorganize, restructure, slim down, streamline.

rationally *adv.* in a rational way.

rational number *Maths.* a number which can be expressed in the form of a fraction, eg ⁴⁄₅, where *a* and *b* are whole numbers, and *b* is not zero, eg -.

ration book or **ration card** a book or card containing coupons which can be exchanged for rationed goods.

rationing *noun* supplying rations; dividing into rations.

ratpack *noun* *slang* **1** a rowdy gang of young people. **2** a group of photographers, especially from tabloid newspapers, who follow and photograph famous people.

rat race *colloq.* the fierce, unending competition for success, wealth, etc in business, society, etc.

rattan /rə'tan/ *noun* a climbing palm with very long, thin, tough stems which are used to make walking sticks and wickerwork. [from Malay *rotan*]

ratter *noun* a dog or other animal that catches and kills rats.

rattle — *verb* **1** *intrans.* to make a series of short, sharp, hard sounds in quick succession. **2** to cause (eg crockery) to make such a noise. **3** *intrans.* to move along rapidly, often with a rattling noise. **4** *intrans.* (*usually* **rattle on**) to chatter thoughtlessly or idly. **5** (**rattle something off** or **rattle through something**) to say or recite it rapidly and unthinkingly. **6** *colloq.* to make anxious or nervous; to upset. — *noun* **1** a series of short sharp sounds made in quick succession, having the effect of a continuous sound. **2** a baby's toy consisting of a container filled with small pellets which rattle when the container is shaken. **3** a device for making a whirring sound, used especially at football matches. **4** the loose horny structures at the end of a rattlesnake's tail, which produce a rattling sound when vibrated. **5** lively, empty chatter. **6** the rough harsh breathing sound caused by air passing through mucus in the back of the throat. [from Middle English *ratelen*]

⊟ *verb* **1, 2** clatter, jingle, jangle, clank, shake, vibrate, jolt, jar, bounce, bump. **5** reel off, list, run through, recite, repeat. **6** shake (up), scare, frighten, upset, worry, agitate, disturb, ruffle, fluster, disconcert.

rattler *noun* *colloq.* a rattlesnake.

rattlesnake *noun* any of 29 species of poisonous American snake of the pit viper family, that prey on small mammals and give birth to live young. If threatened, the snake vibrates a series of dry horny structures at the end of its tail, producing a loud rattling sound.

rattletrap *noun* *colloq.* a broken-down, rickety old vehicle, especially a car.

rattling *adj., adv. old use* **1** smart or smartly. **2** brisk or briskly. **3** *as a general intensifying word* good or well; very: *told us a rattling good yarn.*

rattly *adj.* (**rattlier, rattliest**) making a rattling noise; often rattling.

ratty *adj.* (**rattier, rattiest**) **1** of or like a rat. **2** *colloq.* irritable.

raucous *adj.* hoarse, harsh. [from Latin *raucus*]

⊟ harsh, rough, hoarse, husky, rasping, grating, jarring, strident, noisy, loud.

raucously *adv.* in a raucous way.

raucousness *noun* being raucous.

raunchily *adv.* in a raunchy way.

raunchy *adj.* (**raunchier, raunchiest**) *slang* coarsely or openly sexual.

ravage /'ravɪdʒ/ — *verb trans., intrans.* to cause extensive damage to a place; to destroy. — *noun* (*usually* **ravages**) damage or destruction: *the ravages of time.* [from Old French *ravir*, to ravish]

⊟ *verb* destroy, devastate, lay waste, demolish, raze, wreck, ruin, spoil, damage, loot, pillage, plunder, sack, despoil.

noun destruction, devastation, havoc, damage, ruin, desolation, wreckage, pillage, plunder.

rave — *verb* **1** *intrans.* to talk wildly as if mad or delirious. **2** *intrans.* (**rave about** or **over something**) to talk enthusiastically or passionately about it. — *noun colloq.* **1** extravagant praise. **2** a rave-up. **3** an acid-house party. — *adj. colloq.* extremely enthusiastic: *rave reviews.* [from Middle English *raven*]

▣ *verb* **1** rage, storm, thunder, roar, rant, ramble, babble, splutter. **2** enthuse about, sing the praises of, *colloq.* be mad about, wax lyrical about, extol, acclaim, hail. *adj.* enthusiastic, rapturous, favourable, excellent, wonderful.

ravel — *verb* (**ravelled, ravelling**) **1** *trans., intrans.* to tangle or become tangled up. **2** (**ravel something out**) to untangle, unravel, or untwist it. **3** *intrans.* to fray. — *noun* **1** a tangle or knot. **2** a complication. **3** a loose or broken thread. [from Dutch *rafelen*]

raven — *noun* a large blue-black bird of the crow family. — *adj.* glossy blue-black in colour: *raven-haired.* [from Anglo-Saxon *hræfn*]

ravening *adj., said especially of meat-eating animals* hungrily seeking food. [from *raven*, to devour, hunt for food]

ravenous *adj.* **1** extremely hungry or greedy. **2** *said of hunger, a desire, etc* intensely strong. **3** *said of an animal, etc* living on prey; predatory.

▣ **1** hungry, starving, starved, famished, greedy, voracious, insatiable.

ravenously *adv.* in a ravenous way.
ravenousness *noun* being ravenous.
raver *noun colloq.* a person who leads a full, lively, uninhibited social life.
rave-up *noun colloq.* a lively party or celebration.
ravine /rəˈviːn/ *noun* a deep, narrow, steep-sided gorge. [from Old French *ravine*, violent rushing]

▣ canyon, gorge, gully, pass.

raving — *adj., adv.* **1** frenzied; delirious. **2** *colloq.* great; extreme: *a raving beauty.* — *noun* (*usually* **ravings**) wild, frenzied, or delirious talk.

▣ *adj.* **1** mad, insane, crazy, hysterical, delirious, wild, frenzied, furious, berserk.

ravioli /ravɪˈoʊlɪ/ *sing. or pl. noun* small, square pasta cases with a savoury filling of meat, cheese, etc. [from Italian *ravioli*]

ravish *verb* **1** to cause to be overcome with joy, delight, etc; to enrapture. **2** to rape. [from Latin *rapere*, to seize and carry off]

▣ **1** enrapture, delight, overjoy, enchant, charm, captivate, entrance, fascinate, spellbind.

ravishing *adj.* delightful; lovely.

▣ delightful, enchanting, charming, lovely, beautiful, gorgeous, stunning, radiant, dazzling, alluring, seductive.

ravishingly *adv.* in a ravishing way.

raw — *adj.* **1** not cooked. **2** not processed, purified or refined. **3** *said of alcoholic spirit* undiluted. **4** *said of statistics, data, etc* not analysed. **5** *said of a person* not trained or experienced. **6** *said of a wound, etc* with a sore, inflamed surface. **7** *said of the weather* cold and damp. — *noun* a sore, inflamed, or sensitive place. — **in the raw**

1 in a natural or crude state. **2** naked. [from Anglo-Saxon *hreaw*]

▣ *adj.* **1** uncooked, fresh. **2** unprocessed, unrefined, untreated, crude, natural. **5** new, green, immature, callow, inexperienced, untrained, unskilled. **6** scratched, grazed, scraped, open, bloody, sore, tender, sensitive. **7** cold, chilly, bitter, biting, piercing, freezing, bleak.

▣ *adj.* **1** cooked, done. **2** processed, refined. **5** experienced, skilled, trained. **7** warm, hot.

rawboned *adj.* lean and gaunt.
raw deal *colloq.* harsh, unfair treatment.
rawhide *noun* **1** untanned leather. **2** a whip made from this.
raw material **1** any material, in its natural unprocessed state, that serves as the starting point for a production or manufacturing process. **2** material out of which something is or can be made, or may develop.
rawness *noun* being raw.
raw umber untanned umber.
ray[1] *noun* **1** a narrow beam of light or radioactive particles. **2** any of a set of lines fanning out from a central point. **3** a small amount of or the beginnings of (especially hope or understanding). **4** any of the set of spines which support a fish's fin. [from Latin *radius*, rod]

▣ **1** beam, shaft, flash. **3** gleam, flicker, glimmer, glint, spark, trace, hint, indication.

ray[2] *noun* any of numerous cartilaginous fish, related to the sharks, with a flattened body, large pectoral fins extending from the head to the base of the tail, and both eyes on the upper surface, eg stingray, manta ray, sawfish. Most of the marine species live on the sea bed, where they feed on shellfish. [from Latin *raia*]

ray[3] same as RE[1].

Ray-Bans *pl. noun trademark* a type of sunglasses with dark green lenses and gold frames.
ray-gun *noun* especially in science fiction, a gun that fires destructive rays, used as a weapon.
Raynaud's disease /ˈreɪnoʊz/ *Medicine* a disorder in which the fingers, toes, ears, and nose turn white or develop a bluish tinge as a result of spasm of the arteries supplying the affected parts. It usually occurs in response to exposure to cold or emotional stress. [named after the French physician Maurice Raynaud (1834–81)]
rayon *noun* a strong durable easily dyed artificial fibre consisting of regenerated cellulose that has been spun into filaments, used to make textiles for clothing, conveyer belts, hoses, etc. [probably from RAY[1]]
raze *verb* to destroy or demolish (buildings, a town, etc) completely. [from Latin *radere*, to scrape]

▣ demolish, pull down, tear down, bulldoze, flatten, level, destroy.

razor *noun* a sharp-edged instrument used for shaving. [from Old French *rasour*]
razorbill *noun* a type of seabird with a sharp-edged bill.
razor edge **1** a very fine, sharp edge. **2** a critical, delicately balanced situation.
razor shell a burrowing marine bivalve with two similar elongated shell valves, the two halves of the shell being closed by two muscles. It burrows actively in the sand using a muscular foot.
razor wire thick wire with sharp pieces of metal attached, used like barbed wire for fences, etc.
razzle *noun slang* a lively spree, outing or party, especially involving a lot of drinking: *on the razzle.* [related to DAZZLE]
razzle-dazzle *noun slang* **1** excitement, confusion, dazzling show, etc. **2** a lively spree.

razzmatazz *noun* **1** razzle-dazzle. **2** humbug.

Rb *symbol Chem.* rubidium.

RC *abbrev.* **1** Red Cross. **2** Roman Catholic.

RCA *abbrev.* Radio Corporation of America.

RCAF *abbrev.* Royal Canadian Air Force.

RCM *abbrev.* Royal College of Music.

RCMP *abbrev.* Royal Canadian Mounted Police.

RCN *abbrev.* Royal Canadian Navy.

Rd *abbrev.* road.

RDA *abbrev.* recommended daily (or dietary) allowance: the amount of essential nutrient (vitamins, protein, etc) needed to meet a normal healthy person's nutritional requirements. Judged by a national or international committee, RDAs have several uses, including dietary planning, the assessment of food aid, and food labelling.

Re *symbol Chem.* rhenium.

RE *abbrev.* religious education.

re[1] /reɪ/ *noun Mus.* the second note in the sol-fa scale. [from the first syllable of the word *resonare* in a medieval Latin hymn, certain syllables of which were used to name the notes]

re[2] /riː/ *prep.* with regard to; concerning. [from Latin *res*, thing]

🔲 about, concerning, regarding, with regard to, with reference to.

re- *prefix* forming words denoting a repetition or reversal of the action of the root word: *reread/rewrite/replacement.* [from Latin *re-*]

reach — *verb* **1** to arrive at; to get as far as. **2** *trans., intrans.* to be able to touch or get hold of. **3** *trans., intrans.* to project or extend to a point. **4** *intrans.* (**reach across, out, up,** *etc*) to stretch out one's arm to try to touch or get hold of something. **5** *colloq.* to hand or pass. **6** to make contact or communicate with, especially by telephone. — *noun* **1** the distance one can stretch one's arm, hand, etc: *out of reach/within reach.* **2** the distance that can be travelled easily: *within reach of London.* **3** an act of reaching out. **4** range of influence, power, understanding, or abilities. **5** (*usually* **reaches**) a section within clear limits, eg part of a river or canal between two bends or locks. **6** (*usually* **reaches**) level or rank: *the upper reaches of government.* [from Anglo-Saxon *ræcan*]

🔲 *verb* **1** arrive at, get to, attain, achieve, make, amount to, touch. **3** stretch (to), extend (to), spread (to). **6** contact, get through to. *noun* **1** grasp. **4** range, scope, compass, distance, spread, extent, stretch, jurisdiction, command, power, influence.

reachable *adj.* **1** capable of being reached; accessible. **2** capable of being achieved.

🔲 **1** accessible, *colloq.* get-at-able, handy, nearby, within reach, within range. **2** achievable, attainable, feasible, realizable.

reach-me-down *noun* a second-hand or ready-made item of clothing.

react *verb* **1** (**react to something** or **someone**) to respond to in a certain way to something said or done. **2** (**react against something**) to respond to it in a way which shows dislike or disapproval. **3** *intrans., trans.* to undergo or cause to undergo a chemical reaction. [from Latin *reagere*]

🔲 **1** respond to, retaliate, reciprocate, reply to, answer, acknowledge, act towards, behave towards.

reactance *noun Electr.* in an electric circuit carrying alternating current, the property of an inductor or capacitor that causes it to oppose the flow of current. Like resistance, it is measured in ohms, and together with resistance it represents the *impedance* of the circuit.

reaction *noun* **1** a reacting or response to something. **2** opposition to change, especially political change, and a desire to return to a former system. **3** a complete change of opinions, feelings, etc to the opposite of what they were: *the idea was popular at first but then a reaction set in.* **4** a bodily response (eg to a drug). **5** *Chem.* a chemical reaction in which one or more elements or compounds (reactants) react to form one or more new compounds (products). Only the electrons surrounding the nucleus are involved in such reactions. **6** *Physics* a nuclear reaction involving a change in an atomic nucleus, eg radioactive decay, nuclear fission, nuclear fusion. **7** *Physics* the force offered by a body that is equal in magnitude but opposite in direction to a force applied to that body.

🔲 **1** response, effect, reply, answer, acknowledgement, feedback, counteraction, reflex, recoil, reciprocation, retaliation. **2** conservatism, traditionalism.

reactionary — *adj.*, *said of a person or policies* opposed to change or progress and in favour of a return to a former system. — *noun* (PL. **reactionaries**) a reactionary person.

🔲 *adj.* conservative, right-wing, rightist, diehard, counter-revolutionary. *noun* conservative, right-winger, rightist, diehard, counter-revolutionary.

🔲 *adj.* progressive, revolutionary. *noun* progressive, revolutionary.

reactivate *verb* to make active again.

🔲 revive, reanimate, revitalize, restore, reawaken, rekindle.

reactivation *noun* reactivating or being reactivated.

reactive *adj.* showing a reaction; liable to react; sensitive to stimuli.

reactor same as NUCLEAR REACTOR.

read /riːd/ — *verb* (PAST TENSE AND PAST PARTICIPLE **read**/red/) **1** *trans., intrans.* to look at and understand (printed or written words). **2** *trans., intrans.* to speak (words which are printed or written). **3** *trans., intrans.* to learn or gain knowledge of by reading: *read the election results in the newspaper.* **4** *trans., intrans.* to pass one's leisure time reading (books): *I have little time for reading.* **5** to look at or be able to see (something) and get information from it: *cannot read the clock without my glasses.* **6** to interpret or understand the meaning of: *read a map.* **7** to interpret or understand (signs, marks, etc) without using one's eyes: *read Braille.* **8** to know (a language) well enough to be able to understand something written in it: *speaks Chinese but cannot read it.* **9** *intrans.* to have a certain wording: *the letter reads as follows.* **10** *trans., intrans.* to think that (a statement, etc) has a particular meaning: *read it as criticism.* **11** *intrans.* *said of writing* to be, or not to be, coherent, fluent, and logical: *an essay which reads well.* **12** *said of a dial, instrument, etc* to show a particular measurement: *the barometer reads 'fair'.* **13** to replace (a word, phrase, etc) to be replaced by another: *for 'three' read 'four'.* **14** to put into a specified condition by reading: *she read the child to sleep.* **15** to study (a subject) at university. **16** to hear and understand, especially when using two-way radio. **17** (**read something in** or **out**) *Comput.* to transfer data from a disk or other storage device into the main memory of a computer. — *noun* **1** a period or act of reading. **2** a book, etc thought of as being interesting, etc: *a good read.* — **read between the lines** to understand a meaning which is implied but not stated. **read into something** to find (in a person's writing, words, etc) a meaning which is not stated clearly and which may not have been intended. **read something out** to read it aloud. **read something up** to learn a subject by reading books about it. **take something as read** to accept or assume it. **well** or **widely**

read educated, especially in literature, through reading. [from Anglo-Saxon *rædan*]

....

▣ *verb* **2** recite, deliver, speak. **3** learn, find out. **5** study, peruse, scan, skim. **6**, **7** understand, comprehend, interpret, decipher, decode. **10** construe. **12** indicate, show, display, register, record.

....

readability or **readableness** *noun* the capacity to be readable.

readable *adj.* **1** legible; able to be read. **2** pleasant or quite interesting to read.

....

▣ **1** legible, decipherable, intelligible, clear, understandable, comprehensible. **2** interesting, enjoyable, entertaining, gripping, *colloq.* unputdownable.

▣ UNREADABLE. **1** illegible.

....

reader *noun* **1** a person who reads. **2** *Brit.* a university lecturer ranking between professor and senior lecturer. **3** a person who reads prayers in a church. **4** a book containing usually short texts, especially one used for learning a foreign language. **5** a person who reads and reports on manuscripts for a publisher. **6** a person who reads and corrects proofs. **7** a machine which produces a magnified image from a microfilm so that it can be read.

readership *noun* **1** the total number of people who read a newspaper, the novels of a particular author, etc. **2** *Brit.* the post of reader in a university.

readily *adv.* **1** promptly, willingly. **2** quickly.

....

▣ **1** willingly, unhesitatingly, gladly, eagerly, promptly. **2** quickly, freely, smoothly, easily, effortlessly.

▣ **1** unwillingly, reluctantly.

....

readiness *noun* **1** promptness, willingness. **2** quickness.

reading — *noun* **1** the action of a person who reads. **2** the ability to read: *his reading is poor.* **3** books, material, etc for reading. **4** an event at which a play, poetry, etc is read to an audience. **5** a passage from a text which is read out, eg a passage from the Bible. **6** any one of three stages in the passage of a bill through parliament. **7** the actual word or words that can be read in a text, especially where more than one version is possible: *one of many disputed readings in the Bible.* **8** information, figures, etc shown by an instrument or meter. **9** an understanding or interpretation: *one's reading of the situation.* — *adj.* of, for, or fond of reading.

....

▣ *noun* **1**, **4** rendering, rendition, recital, recitation, performance. **1** study, perusal, scrutiny, examination, inspection. **6** passage, lesson. **9** interpretation, take, understanding, assessment, appraisal, sense, opinion.

....

read-only memory see ROM.

read-out *noun Comput.* **1** the act of copying data from the main memory of a computer into an external storage device, eg a disk or tape, or a display device, eg a visual display unit or plotter. **2** data that has been copied in this way.

read-write head *Comput.* a head in a disk drive which allows data to be written on to, or retrieved from, the disk.

read-write memory a computer memory which allows data to be both read and changed.

ready — *adj.* (**readier**, **readiest**) **1** prepared and complete. **2** available for action or use. **3** willing: *always ready to help.* **4** prompt; quick: *be too ready to find fault.* **5** likely or about to do: *a plant just ready to flower.* — *noun* (PL. **readies**) *colloq.* (also **ready money**) cash, especially bank notes, for immediate use. — *adv.* prepared or made beforehand: *ready cooked meals.* — *verb* to make ready. — **at the ready 1** *said of a gun* aimed and ready to be fired. **2** ready for immediate action. [from Anglo-Saxon *ræde*]

....

▣ *adj.* **1** prepared, waiting, set, fit, arranged, organized, completed, finished. **2** available, to hand, present, near, accessible, convenient, handy. **3** willing, inclined, disposed, happy, *colloq.* game, eager, keen. **4** prompt, immediate, quick, sharp, astute, perceptive, alert. *verb* get ready, make ready, prepare, organize, arrange, warm up.

▣ *adj.* **1** unprepared, unavailable, inaccessible. **3** unwilling, reluctant, disinclined. **4** slow.

....

ready-made *adj.* **1** *said of clothes* made to a standard size, not made-to-measure. **2** convenient; useful: *a ready-made excuse.*

ready money *colloq.* money available for immediate use.

ready reckoner a book listing standard or useful calculations.

ready-to-wear *adj.*, *said of clothes* same as READY-MADE.

reafforest *verb Bot.* to replant trees in a cleared area of land that was formerly forested.

reafforestation *noun Bot.* replanting or being replanted with trees.

Reaganomics /reigəˈnɒmiks/ *sing. noun* the economic practice of cutting taxes to stimulate production, as advocated by Ronald Reagan, the 40th US President.

reagent /riːˈeɪdʒənt/ *noun Chem.* **1** any chemical compound that participates in a chemical reaction. **2** a common laboratory chemical that is used in chemical analysis and experiments, eg hydrochloric acid, sodium hydroxide. [from Latin *reagere*, to react]

real[1] — *adj.* **1** which actually exists; not imaginary. **2** not imitation; genuine. **3** actual; true: *the real reason.* **4** great, important, or serious: *a real problem.* **5** *Legal* consisting of or relating to property which cannot be moved, such as land and houses. **6** *said of income, etc* measured in terms of what it will buy rather than its nominal value. **7** *Maths.* involving or containing real numbers. — *adv. North Amer.*, *Scot.* really; very: *real nice.* — **for real** *slang* in reality; seriously. [from Latin *realis*, from *res*, thing]

....

▣ *adj.* **1**, **2**, **3** actual. **1** existing, physical, material, substantial, tangible. **2**, **3** genuine, true, authentic, bona fide. **3** valid, factual, official, certain, sure, positive, veritable, honest, sincere, heartfelt, unfeigned, unaffected.

▣ *adj.* **1** unreal, imaginary. **2**, **3** false. **2** imitation, fake.

....

real[2] /reɪˈɑːl/ *noun* **1** the standard unit of currency in Brazil. **2** *Hist.* a small silver Spanish or Spanish-American coin. [from Spanish, from Latin *regalis*, royal]

real estate *North Amer.* property in the form of houses or land.

realign *verb* **1** to group in a new or different way. **2** to bring back into line or alignment.

....

▣ REARRANGE. **1** reorganize, reorder, regroup, redeploy. **2** straighten, even (up), adjust, readjust.

....

realignment *noun* realigning or being realigned.

realism *noun* **1** an acceptance of things or a willingness to deal with things as they really are. **2** realistic or lifelike representation in writing and the arts. **3** *Philos.* the theory that physical objects exist even when they are not perceived by the mind (see also IDEALISM).

....

▣ **1** practicality, common sense, level-headedness, pragmatism, objectivity, rationality, reasonableness, matter-of-factness, straightforwardness.

....

realist *noun* **1** a person who is aware of and accepts reality. **2** a writer or artist who represents matters in a realistic way.

realistic *adj.* **1** representing things as they really are; lifelike. **2** accepting and dealing with things as they really are; practical. **3** relating to realism or realists.

▤ **1** lifelike, faithful, truthful, true, genuine, authentic, natural, real, real-life, graphic, representational. **2** practical, down-to-earth, commonsense, sensible, level-headed, clear-sighted, businesslike, hard-headed, pragmatic, matter-of-fact, rational, logical, objective, detached, unsentimental, unromantic.

▣ **1**, **2** unrealistic. **2** impractical, irrational, idealistic.

realistically *adv.* in a realistic way.

reality *noun* (PL. **realities**) **1** the state or fact of being real. **2** the real nature of something; the truth. **3** that which is real and not imaginary. — **in reality** as a fact, often as distinct from a thought or idea.

▤ **1** actuality, existence, materiality, tangibility, realism. **2** truth, genuineness, authenticity, validity. **3** fact, real life. **in reality** in fact, as a matter of fact, actually, really, in truth.

realizable or **realisable** *adj.* capable of being realized.

▤ possible, achievable, attainable, feasible, practicable, reachable.

realization or **realisation** *noun* realizing or being realized.

realize or **realise** *verb* **1** *trans., intrans.* to begin to know or understand. **2** to make real; to make come true. **3** to cause to seem real; to act out: *realize the story on film.* **4** to convert (property or goods) into actual money: *realize one's assets.* **5** to gain (money): *realized £45,000 on the sale of the house.* [from Old French *realiser*]

▤ **1** understand, comprehend, grasp, *colloq.* catch on (to), *colloq.* cotton on (to), recognize, accept, appreciate. **2** achieve, accomplish, fulfil, complete, implement, perform. **5** sell for, fetch, make, earn, produce, net, clear.

really — *adv.* **1** actually; in fact. **2** very; genuinely: *a really lovely day.* — *interj.* an expression of surprise, doubt, or mild protest.

▤ *adv.* TRULY, GENUINELY. **1** actually, honestly, sincerely, positively, certainly, absolutely, categorically, indeed. **2** very.

realm /rɛlm/ *noun* **1** a kingdom. **2** a field of interest, study, or activity. [from Old French *realme*]

▤ AREA, PROVINCE, DOMAIN. **1** kingdom, monarchy, principality, empire, country, state, land, territory, region. **2** sphere, orbit, field, department.

real number *Maths.* any rational or irrational number.

realpolitik /reɪˈɑːlpɒlɪtiːk/ *noun* politics based on the practical needs of life rather than on moral or ethical ideas. [German, = politics of realism]

real tennis an early form of tennis played on a walled, indoor court. See also LAWN TENNIS.

real-time *adj. Comput.* of or relating to a system in which data is processed as it is generated.

realtor /ˈrɪəltə(r)/ *noun North Amer.* (*also* **Realtor**) an estate agent, especially one who is a member of the National Association of Realtors.

realty same as REAL ESTATE.

ream *noun* **1** a number of sheets of paper equivalent to 20 quires, formerly 480, now usually 500 or 516. **2** (**reams**) *colloq.* a large amount, especially of paper or writing: *wrote reams.* [from Old French *reame*, from Arabic *rizmah*, bale]

reap *verb trans., intrans.* **1** to cut or gather (grain, etc). **2** to clear (a field) by cutting a crop. **3** to receive as a consequence of one's actions. [from Anglo-Saxon *ripan*]

reaper *noun* **1** a person or machine that reaps. **2** (**the reaper** or **grim reaper**) death.

reapply *verb trans., intrans.* to apply again or afresh.

rear [1] — *noun* **1** the back part; the area at the back. **2** that part of an army which is farthest away from the enemy. **3** *euphemistic colloq.* the buttocks. — *adj.* at the back: *rear window.*

▤ *noun* **1** back, stern, end, tail. **3** rump, buttocks, posterior, behind, bottom, *colloq.* backside. *adj.* back, hind, hindmost, rearmost, last.

▣ *noun* FRONT. *adj.* front.

rear [2] *verb* **1** to feed, care for, and educate: *rear three children.* **2** to breed (animals) or grow (crops). **3** (*also* **rear up**) *said especially of a horse* to rise up on the hind legs. **4** to raise (the head, etc) upright. **5** *intrans.* to reach a great height, especially in relation to surroundings. [from Anglo-Saxon *ræran*]

▤ **1**, **2** raise, breed. **1** bring up, foster, nurse, nurture, train, educate. **2** grow, cultivate. **4** raise, lift. **5** rise, tower, soar.

rear admiral a naval officer with the rank below vice-admiral.

rearguard *noun* a group of soldiers who protect the rear of an army, especially in retreats.

rearguard action 1 military action undertaken by the rearguard. **2** an effort to prevent or delay defeat, eg in an argument.

rearm /riːˈɑːm/ *verb trans., intrans.* to arm or become armed again with new or improved weapons.

rearmament /riːˈɑːməmənt/ *noun* the process of rearming.

rearmost *adj.* last of all.

rear-view mirror a mirror fixed to a car's windscreen, or attached to a motorbicycle's handles, which allows the driver to see vehicles, etc behind.

rearward — *adj.* at or to the rear. — *adv.* (*also* **rearwards**) towards the rear.

reason — *noun* **1** a justification or motive for an action, belief, etc. **2** an underlying explanation or cause. **3** the power of the mind to think, form opinions and judgements, reach conclusions, etc. **4** sanity. — *verb* (**reasoned**, **reasoning**) **1** *intrans.* to use one's mind and reason to form opinions and judgements, reach conclusions, etc. **2** (**reason with someone**) to try to persuade them by means of argument. **3** (**reason someone into** or **out of something**) to persuade or influence them with argument. **4** (*also* **reason something out**) to think it or set it out logically. — **by reason of ...** because of ...; as a consequence of .... **it stands to reason** it is obvious or logical. **within reason** within the bounds of what is sensible or possible. [from Old French *reison*]

▤ *noun* **1**, **2** cause, explanation, motive, incentive. **1** rationale, excuse, justification, defence, warrant, ground, basis, case, argument. **2** aim, intention, purpose. **3** sense, logic, reasoning, rationality, mind, wit, brain, intellect, understanding, wisdom, judgement, common sense, gumption. *verb* **1** think. **2** urge, persuade, remonstrate with, argue with, debate with, discuss with. **4** work out, solve, resolve, conclude, deduce, infer.

reasonable *adj.* **1** sensible; showing reason or good judgement. **2** willing to listen to reason or argument. **3** in accordance with reason; fair; not extreme or excessive. **4** satisfactory or equal to what one might expect.

▣ **1, 2** sensible. **1** wise, well-advised, sane, intelligent, rational, logical, practical, sound, reasoned, well-thought-out, plausible, credible, possible, viable. **2** tractable, amenable. **3, 4** moderate, acceptable, tolerable, average. **4** satisfactory, fair, equitable, just, modest, inexpensive.
▣ **1** irrational, illogical. **3** extreme, excessive.

reasonableness *noun* being reasonable.
reasonably *adv.* in a reasonable way.
reasoning *noun* **1** the forming of judgements or opinions using reason or careful argument. **2** the opinions or judgements formed in this way.

▣ **1, 2** thought, analysis, interpretation, deduction, supposition. **1** logic, thinking. **2** hypothesis, argument, case, proof.

reassurance *noun* reassuring.

▣ comfort, cheer, encouragement, consolation, relief.

reassure *verb* to relieve (someone) of anxiety and so give confidence to (them).

▣ comfort, cheer, encourage, hearten, inspirit, brace, bolster.
▣ alarm.

reassuring *adj.* that reassures.

▣ comforting, cheering, encouraging, heartening, consoling, hopeful, promising.

reassuringly *adv.* in a reassuring way.
rebate *noun* **1** a return of part of a sum of money paid. **2** a discount. [from Old French *rabattre*, to beat back]

▣ **1** refund, repayment. **2** reduction, discount, deduction, allowance.

rebel / 'rɛbl, rɪ'bɛl/ — *noun* (with stress on *reb-*) **1** a person who opposes or fights against people in authority or oppressive conditions. **2** a person who does not accept the rules of normal behaviour, dress, etc. — *adj.* rebelling. — *verb intrans.* (with stress on *-bel*) (**rebelled**, **rebelling**) **1** to resist authority or oppressive conditions openly and with force. **2** to reject the accepted rules of behaviour, dress, etc. **3** to feel aversion or dislike. [from Latin *rebellis*, from *bellum*, war]

▣ *noun* **1** revolutionary, insurrectionist, mutineer, dissenter, nonconformist, schismatic, heretic. *verb* **1** revolt, mutiny, rise up, run riot, dissent, disobey, resist. **3** recoil, shrink.
▣ *noun* CONFORMIST. *verb* **1, 2** conform.

rebellion *noun* an act of rebelling; a revolt.

▣ revolt, revolution, rising, uprising, insurrection, insurgence, mutiny, resistance, opposition, defiance, disobedience, insubordination, dissent, heresy.
▣ conformism, obedience, submission.

rebellious *adj.* rebelling or likely to rebel.

▣ revolutionary, insurgent, seditious, mutinous, resistant, defiant, disobedient, insubordinate, unruly, disorderly, ungovernable, unmanageable, intractable, obstinate.
▣ obedient, submissive.

rebirth *noun* a revival, renaissance, or renewal, often a spiritual one.

▣ reincarnation, resurrection, renaissance, regeneration, renewal, restoration, revival, revitalization, rejuvenation.

rebirthing *noun* a type of psychotherapy involving reliving the experience of being born in order to release anxieties believed to result from the original experience.
reboot *Comput. verb trans., intrans.* to restart (a computer), either by switching off and switching on again at the power source or pressing a reset button, etc.
rebore — *verb* (with stress on *-bore*) to renew or widen the bore of (a cylinder) in an internal combustion engine. — *noun* (with stress on *re-*) the process or result of this.
reborn *adj.* born again, especially in the sense of having received new spiritual life.
rebound /rɪ'baʊnd, 'riːbaʊnd/ — *verb intrans.* (with stress on *-bound*) **1** to bounce or spring back. **2** (**rebound on** or **upon someone**) *said of an action* to have a bad effect on the person performing the action. — *noun* (with stress on *re-*) an instance of rebounding; a recoil. — **on the rebound 1** while still recovering from an emotional shock, especially the ending of a love affair or attachment. **2** while bouncing. [from Old French *rebonder*]

▣ *verb* **1** return, bounce, ricochet, boomerang. **2** recoil on.

rebuff /rɪ'bʌf/ — *noun* an unkind or unfriendly refusal to help someone or a rejection of help, advice, etc from someone. — *verb* to reject or refuse (an offer of or plea for help, a request, etc) unkindly. [from Old French *rebuffe*]

▣ *noun* rejection, refusal, repulse, check, discouragement, snub, *colloq.* brush-off, slight, *colloq.* put-down, cold shoulder. *verb* spurn, reject, refuse, decline, turn down, repulse, discourage, snub, slight, cut, cold-shoulder.

rebuild *verb* (PAST TENSE AND PAST PARTICIPLE **rebuilt**) to build again or anew.

▣ reconstruct, remake, re-erect, reassemble, recreate, restore, renovate, renew, reorganize, regenerate.

rebuke — *verb* to speak severely to (someone) because he or she has done wrong. — *noun* the act of speaking severely to someone, or being spoken severely to. [from Old French *rebuker*]

▣ *verb* reprove, castigate, chide, scold, tell off, admonish, *colloq.* tick off, *colloq.* dress down, reprimand, upbraid, rate, censure, blame, reproach. *noun* reproach, reproof, reprimand, lecture, *colloq.* dressing-down, telling-off, *colloq.* ticking-off, admonition, censure, blame.
▣ *verb* praise, compliment. *noun* praise, commendation.

rebus / 'riːbəs/ *noun* (PL. **rebuses**) a puzzle in which pictures and symbols are used to represent words and parts of words to form a message or phrase. [from Latin *rebus*, by things]
rebut /rɪ'bʌt/ *verb* (**rebutted**, **rebutting**) **1** to disprove (a charge or claim) especially by offering opposing evidence. **2** to force to turn back. [from Old French *rebouter*]
rebuttal *noun* a rejection or contradiction.
recalcitrance *noun* **1** being recalcitrant. **2** recalcitrant behaviour.
recalcitrant *adj.* not willing to accept authority or discipline. [from Latin *recalcitare*, to kick back]

▣ rebellious, refractory, difficult, defiant, disobedient, insubordinate, obstinate, intractable, reluctant.

recall — *verb* (with stress on -*call*) **1** to order to return. **2** to remember. **3** to cancel or revoke. — *noun* (with stress on *re-*) **1** an act of recalling. **2** the ability to remember accurately and in detail: *total recall*. — **beyond recall** unable to be stopped or cancelled.

· ·

▤ *verb* **2** remember, recollect, cast one's mind back to, evoke, bring back, call back.

· ·

recant *verb* **1** *intrans.* to reject one's (usually religious or political) beliefs, especially publicly. **2** *trans., intrans.* to withdraw (a statement). [from Latin *recantare*, to revoke]

recantation *noun* recanting.

recap /'riːkap, riː'kap/ *colloq.* — *verb trans., intrans.* (**re-capped, recapping**) to recapitulate. —*noun* recapitulation.

recapitulate *verb trans., intrans.* to go over the chief points of (an argument, statement, etc) again. [from Latin *recapitulare*]

· · · · · · · · · · · · · · · · · · ·

▤ recap, summarize, repeat, reiterate, restate, sum up.

· ·

recapitulation *noun* **1** an act or instance of recapitulating or summing up. **2** *Mus.* the final repetition of themes, after development, in a movement written in sonata form.

recapture — *verb* **1** to capture again. **2** to convey, produce, or experience (images or feelings from the past): *recapture the atmosphere of Victorian London.* — *noun* the act of recapturing or being recaptured.

· · · · · · · · · · · · · · · · · · ·

▤ *verb* **2** convey, communicate, evoke, call up, summon up, conjure up, reawaken, rekindle.

· ·

recce /'rɛki/ *colloq.* — *noun* a reconnaissance. — *verb trans., intrans.* (**recced** or **recceed, recceing**) to reconnoi- tre.

recede *verb intrans.* **1** to go or move back or backwards. **2** to become more distant. **3** to grow less. **4** to bend or slope backwards. [from Latin *recedere*]

· · · · · · · · · · · · · · · · · · ·

▤ **1** go back, return, retire, withdraw, retreat. **3** diminish, dwindle, decrease, lessen, decline, ebb, wane, sink, shrink, slacken, subside, abate.

▤ **1** advance.

· ·

receding *adj.* that recedes.

receipt /rɪ'siːt/ *noun* **1** a written note saying that money or goods have been received. **2** the act of receiving or being received: *acknowledge receipt of the money*. **3** (*usually* re- ceipts) money received during a given period of time, especially by a shop or business. [from Latin *recipere*, to receive]

· · · · · · · · · · · · · · · · · · ·

▤ **1** voucher, ticket, slip, counterfoil, stub, acknowledgement, chit. **2** receiving, reception, acceptance, delivery. **3** takings, proceeds, profits, income, gains, return.

· ·

receive *verb* **1** to get, be given, or accept. **2** to experience or suffer: *receive injuries*. **3** to give attention to or consider: *receive a petition*. **4** to react in a specified way in response to: *receive the news well*. **5** to be awarded (an honour). **6** *trans., intrans.* to welcome or greet (guests), especially for- mally. **7** to permit to become part of: *be received into the priesthood*. **8** *trans., intrans. Tennis* to be the player who re- turns (the opposing player's service). **9** *trans., intrans. Brit.* to accept and often sell (goods one knows are stolen). **10** *trans., intrans.* to change (radio or television signals) into sounds or pictures. [from Latin *recipere*]

· · · · · · · · · · · · · · · · · · ·

▤ **1** take, accept, get, obtain, derive, acquire, pick up, collect, inherit. **2** experience, undergo, suffer, sustain, meet with, encounter. **3** hear, consider, give attention to. **4** react to, respond to. **6** entertain, be at home (to).

▤ **1** give, donate.

· ·

received *adj.* generally accepted.

Received Pronunciation the particular pronunciation of British English which is regarded by many as being least regionally limited, most socially acceptable, and most 'standard'.

receiver *noun* **1** a person or thing that receives. **2** (*in full* **official receiver**) a person who is appointed by a court to take control of the business of someone who has gone bankrupt or who is certified as insane. **3** the part of a tele- phone which is held to the ear. **4** the equipment in a tele- phone, radio, or television that changes signals into sounds or pictures. **5** a person who receives stolen goods.

receivership *noun* the status of a business that is under the control of an official receiver; the office of receiver.

recent *adj.* happening, done, having appeared, etc not long ago. [from Latin *recens*, fresh]

· · · · · · · · · · · · · · · · · · ·

▤ late, latest, current, present-day, contemporary, modern, up-to-date, new, novel, fresh, young.

▤ old, out-of-date, long ago.

· ·

recently *adv.* a short time ago.

· · · · · · · · · · · · · · · · · · ·

▤ lately, just now, not long ago, newly, freshly, latterly.

· ·

receptacle *noun* **1** a container. **2** *Bot.* the top of a flower stalk, from which the different flower parts (sepals, petals, stamens, and carpels) arise. **3** *Bot.* in certain algae, any of a number of swollen regions that contain the reproductive structures. [from Latin *receptaculum*, reservoir]

· · · · · · · · · · · · · · · · · · ·

▤ **1** container, vessel, holder.

· ·

reception *noun* **1** the act of receiving or being received. **2** a response, reaction, or welcome: *a hostile reception*. **3** a for- mal party or social gathering to welcome guests, espe- cially after a wedding. **4** the quality of radio or television signals received: *poor reception because of the weather*. **5** an office or desk where visitors or clients are welcomed on arrival, eg in a hotel or factory. [from Latin *receptio*]

· · · · · · · · · · · · · · · · · · ·

▤ **1** acceptance, admission, greeting, recognition, acknow- ledgement, receipt. **2** response, reaction, welcome, treat- ment. **3** party, function, *colloq.* do, entertainment.

· ·

receptionist *noun* a person employed in a hotel, office, surgery, etc to deal with visitors and guests, accept tele- phone bookings, etc.

receptive *adj.* able, willing, and quick to understand and accept new ideas.

· · · · · · · · · · · · · · · · · · ·

▤ open-minded, amenable, accommodating, suggestible, susceptible, sensitive, responsive, open, accessible, approachable, friendly, hospitable, welcoming, sympathetic, favourable, interested.

▤ narrow-minded, resistant, unresponsive.

· ·

receptively *adv.* in a receptive way.

receptiveness or **receptivity** *noun* being able or willing to receive or take in.

receptor *noun Biol.* **1** an element of the nervous system adapted for reception of stimuli, eg a sense organ or sen- sory nerve-ending. **2** an area on the surface of a cell to which a specific antigen may attach itself. **3** a site in or on a cell to which a drug or hormone can become attached, stimulating a reaction inside the cell. [from Latin *recipere*, *receptum* to receive]

recess /rɪ'sɛs, 'riːsɛs/ — *noun* **1** an open space or alcove set in a wall. **2** (*often* **recesses**) a hidden, inner, or secret place: *the dark recesses of her mind*. **3** a temporary break from work, especially of a lawcourt, or of Parliament dur- ing a vacation. **4** *North Amer.* a short break between school classes. — *verb* **1** to put in a recess. **2** to make a recess in. **3**

intrans. to take a break or adjourn. [from Latin *recessus*, retreat]

. . . .
1, 2 nook, corner. **1** alcove, niche, bay, cavity, hollow, depression, indentation. **3** break, interval, intermission, rest, respite, holiday, vacation.
. . . .

recession *noun* **1** a temporary decline in economic activity, trade, and prosperity. **2** the act of receding or state of being set back.

. . . .
1 slump, depression, downturn, decline.
▪ boom, upturn.
. . . .

recessional *noun* a hymn sung during the departure of the clergy and choir after a service.

recessive *adj.* **1** tending to recede. **2** *Biol.* denoting a gene, or the characteristic determined by it, whose phenotype is only expressed in an individual if its allele is also recessive, ie two recessive genes must be present if their effect is to be apparent. If a dominant gene is present it will mask the effect of the recessive gene. **3** describing a characteristic determined by such a gene. See also DOMINANT.

recheck — *verb trans., intrans.* to check again. — *noun* a second or further check.

recherché /rə'ʃeəʃeɪ/ *adj.* **1** rare, exotic, or particularly choice. **2** obscure and affected. [from French *recherché*]

rechipping *noun* the practice of changing the electronic identity of stolen mobile telephones in order to resell them.

recidivism /rɪ'sɪdɪvɪzm/ *noun* the habit of relapsing into crime. [from Latin *recidivus*, falling back]

recidivist /rɪ'sɪdɪvɪst/ *noun* a person who relapses, especially one who habitually returns to a life of crime.

recipe /'resɪpɪ/ *noun* **1** a list of ingredients for and set of instructions on how to prepare and cook a particular kind of meal, cake, etc. **2** (**a recipe for something**) a way of achieving something (usually desired): *a recipe for success*. [from Latin *recipere*, to take]

. . . .
INGREDIENTS. 1 list, instructions, directions. **2** formula, prescription, method, system, procedure, technique.
. . . .

recipient *noun* a person or thing that receives. [from Latin *recipere*, to receive]

. . . .
▪ receiver, addressee, payee, beneficiary.
. . . .

reciprocal /rɪ'sɪprəkəl/ — *adj.* **1** given to and received from in return; mutual. **2** *Grammar, said of a pronoun* expressing a relationship between two people or things, or mutual action, eg *one another* in *John and Mary love one another*. — *noun Maths.* the value obtained when 1 is divided by the number concerned, eg the reciprocal of 4 is –. There is no reciprocal of zero.

. . . .
▪ *adj.* **1** mutual, joint, shared, give-and-take, complementary, alternating, corresponding, equivalent, interchangeable.
. . . .

reciprocally *adv.* in a reciprocal way.
reciprocate /rɪ'sɪprəkeɪt/ *verb* **1** to return (affection, love, etc). **2** (**reciprocate with something**) to give it in return: *reciprocate with an offer of money.* **3** *intrans., said of part of a machine* to move backwards and forwards. [from Latin *reciprocus*]

. . . .
1 return, requite, respond to, match, equal, correspond to, exchange, interchange, trade, alternate. **2** respond with, reply with, come back with.
. . . .

reciprocation *noun* reciprocating.

reciprocity /resɪ'prɒsɪtɪ/ *noun* **1** reciprocal action. **2** a mutual exchange of privileges or advantages between countries, trade organizations, businesses, etc.

recital /rɪ'saɪtəl/ *noun* **1** a public performance of music or songs usually by one person or a small number of people. **2** a detailed statement about or list of: *a recital of his grievances.* **3** an act of reciting.

. . . .
1 performance, concert, rendition. **2** list, listing, catalogue, enumeration, itemization. **3** recitation, reading, narration, account.
. . . .

recitalist *noun* a person who gives recitals.

recitation /resɪ'teɪʃən/ *noun* **1** something which is recited from memory. **2** an act of reciting.

. . . .
1 passage, piece, party piece, poem, monologue, narration, story, tale. **2** recital, telling.
. . . .

recitative /resɪtə'tiːv/ *noun* **1** a style of singing akin to speech, used for narrative sequences in opera or oratorio. It may be accompanied or unaccompanied, and its main purpose is to progress the action. **2** a passage sung in this way. [from Italian *recitativo*]

recite *verb trans., intrans.* **1** to repeat aloud from memory. **2** to make a detailed statement about or list: *recite one's grievances.* [from Latin *recitare*]

. . . .
1 repeat, narrate, relate, recount, speak, deliver, articulate, perform, reel off. **2** itemize, enumerate.
. . . .

reckless *adj.* very careless; acting or done without any thought of the consequences. [from Anglo-Saxon *receleas*]

. . . .
▪ heedless, thoughtless, mindless, careless, negligent, irresponsible, imprudent, ill-advised, indiscreet, rash, hasty, foolhardy, daredevil, wild.
▪ cautious, wary, careful, prudent.
. . . .

recklessly *adv.* in a reckless way.

recklessness *noun* **1** being reckless. **2** reckless behaviour or an instance of this.

reckon *verb* (**reckoned, reckoning**) **1** to calculate, compute, or estimate. **2** to think of as part of or belonging to: *reckon him among my friends.* **3** to consider or think of in a specified way: *be reckoned a world authority.* **4** *intrans. colloq.* to think or suppose. **5** *intrans.* (**reckon on someone** or **something**) to rely on or expect them: *we reckoned on their support.* **6** *slang* to esteem or admire highly. — **reckon something up** to count or calculate it: *reckon up the cost.* **reckon with** or **without something** to expect, or not expect, trouble or difficulties. **someone** or **something to be reckoned with** a person or thing that is not to be ignored. [from Anglo-Saxon *recenian*, to explain]

. . . .
1, 2 count, number. **1** calculate, compute, figure out, work out, add up, total, tally, enumerate. **3** deem, regard, consider, esteem, value, rate, judge, evaluate, assess, estimate, gauge. **4** think, suppose, believe, imagine, fancy, surmise, assume, guess, conjecture. **5** rely on, depend on, bank on, count on, trust in, hope for, expect, anticipate, foresee, plan for, bargain for, figure on, take into account, face. **reckon something up** count (up), calculate, compute, figure out, work out, add up, total. **reckon with** expect, anticipate, foresee, plan for, bargain for, figure on, take into account.
. . . .

reckoning *noun* **1** calculation; counting: *by my reckoning, we must be about eight miles from the town.* **2** a settling of accounts, debts, grievances, etc. — **day of reckoning** a time when one has to account for one's actions; a time of judgement.

▣ **1** calculation, computation, estimate. **2** bill, account, charge, due, score, settlement.

reclaim verb **1** to seek to regain possession of; to claim back. **2** to make available for agricultural or commercial purposes marshland (especially by draining), land that has never been cultivated, or land that is derelict or has already been developed. **3** to recover useful materials from industrial or domestic waste. **4** old use to reform (someone). [from Latin reclamare, to cry out against]

▣ **1, 2, 3** recover, retrieve, salvage. **1** regain, recapture, restore, reinstate, rescue. **2** regenerate.

reclaimable adj. capable of being reclaimed.
reclamation noun reclaiming or being reclaimed.
recline verb **1** intrans. to lean or lie on one's back or side. **2** trans. to lean or lay (eg one's head) in a resting position. [from Latin reclinare]

▣ REST, REPOSE. **1** lean back, lie, lounge, sprawl, stretch out.

recliner noun someone or something that reclines, especially a comfortable chair with a back which can slope at different angles.
recluse /rɪˈkluːs/ noun a person who lives alone and in seclusion; a hermit. [from Latin reclusus, from claudere, to shut]

▣ hermit, solitary, monk, anchorite.

recognition /rekəgˈnɪʃən/ noun **1** the act of identifying a person or thing known or known about before. **2** the act of admitting or becoming aware of. **3** appreciation of talent, merit, loyal service, etc; gratitude. **4** acknowledgement of the legality or validity of something.

▣ **1** identification, detection, discovery, recollection, recall, remembrance. **2** awareness, perception, realization, understanding, admission, confession, acceptance. **3** acknowledgement, gratitude, appreciation, honour, respect, greeting.

recognizable or **recognisable** adj. capable of being recognized.
recognizably or **recognisably** adv. in a recognizable way.
recognizance /rɪˈkɒɡnɪzəns, rɪˈkɒnɪzəns/ or **recognisance** noun **1** a legally binding promise made to a magistrate or court to do or not do something specified. **2** money pledged as a guarantee of such a promise being kept.
recognize or **recognise** verb **1** to identify (a person or thing known or experienced before). **2** to admit or be aware of: recognize one's mistakes. **3** to show approval of and gratitude for: recognize her courage by giving her a medal. **4** to acknowledge the status or legality of (especially a government or state). **5** to accept as valid: recognize the authority of the court. [from Latin recognoscere]

▣ **1** identify, know, remember, recollect, recall, place, see, notice, spot, perceive. **2, 3** acknowledge, appreciate. **2** admit, confess, own, own up to, accept, grant, concede, allow, understand, realize. **3** honour, pay tribute to, acclaim, hail, praise.

recoil — verb intrans. (with variable stress) **1** (**recoil at** or **from something**) to move or jump back or away quickly or suddenly, usually in horror or fear. **2** to spring back or re-

bound. **3** said of a gun to spring powerfully backwards under the force of being fired. — noun (with stress on re-) the act of recoiling, especially the backwards movement of a gun when fired. [from Old French reculer]
recollect verb to remember, especially with an effort. [from Latin recolligere, to gather up]

▣ recall, remember, cast one's mind back to, recognize, reminisce.

recollection noun **1** the act or power of recollecting. **2** a memory or reminiscence. **3** something remembered.

▣ MEMORY, REMEMBRANCE. **1** recall. **2** souvenir, reminiscence, impression.

recombinant DNA Biol. genetic material produced by the combining of DNA molecules from different organisms.
recombination noun Genetics the process whereby the genetic material is rearranged or 'shuffled' during the formation of gametes (specialized reproductive cells), so that the offspring possess different combinations of characteristics to either of the parents.
recommend verb **1** to advise. **2** to suggest as being suitable to be accepted, chosen, etc; to commend. **3** to make acceptable, desirable or pleasing: an applicant with very little to recommend him. [from Latin commendare, to commend]

▣ **1** advocate, urge, exhort, advise, counsel, suggest, propose, put forward, advance. **2** praise, commend, colloq. plug, endorse, approve, vouch for.
▣ **2** disapprove of.

recommendable adj. capable of being recommended.
recommendation noun **1** recommending. **2** something that recommends; a testimonial. **3** something that is recommended.

▣ **1** advice, counsel, suggestion, proposal, advocacy, endorsement, approval, sanction, blessing, praise, commendation, colloq. plug. **2** reference, testimonial.
▣ **1** disapproval.

recompense /ˈrekɒmpens/ — verb to pay or give (someone) compensation for injury or hardship suffered or reward for services, work done, etc. — noun money, etc given in compensation for injury or hardship suffered or as a reward for work done, etc. [from Latin compensare]

▣ verb compensate, indemnify, make amends to, repay, pay, reward, remunerate. noun compensation, indemnification, damages, reparation, restitution, amends, requital, repayment, reward, payment, remuneration, pay, wages.

reconcile verb **1 a** (**reconcile one person with another**) to put them on friendly terms again, especially after a quarrel. **b** (**be reconciled**) said of two or more people to be on friendly terms again. **2** (**reconcile one thing with another**) to bring two or more different aims, points of view, etc into agreement; to harmonize them. **3** (**be reconciled to** or **reconcile oneself to something**) to agree to accept an unwelcome fact or situation patiently. [from Latin reconciliare]

▣ **1** reunite, conciliate, pacify, appease, placate, propitiate. **2** accord, harmonize, accommodate, adjust, resolve, settle, square. **3** resign oneself to, face up to, accept.
▣ **1** estrange, alienate.

reconciliation noun the act of reconciling or being reconciled.

■ reunion, conciliation, pacification, appeasement, propitiation, rapprochement, détente, settlement, agreement, harmony, accommodation, adjustment, compromise.
🔁 estrangement, separation.

reconciliatory /rɛkən'sɪlɪətərɪ/ *adj.* that reconciles.
recondite *adj.* 1 *said of a subject or knowledge* little known. 2 dealing with profound, abstruse, or obscure knowledge. [from Latin *reconditus*, hidden]

■ 1 abstruse, esoteric, profound, obscure, recherché.

recondition *verb* (**reconditioned, reconditioning**) to repair or restore to original or good working condition, eg by cleaning or replacing broken parts.
reconditioned *adj.* repaired, restored.
reconnaissance /rɪ'kɒnɪsəns/ *noun* 1 a survey of land, enemy troops, etc to obtain information about the enemy. 2 a preliminary survey. [from French *reconnaissance*]

■ 1 exploration, survey, *colloq.* recce, expedition, inspection, examination, investigation, search, patrol.

reconnoitre /rɛkə'nɔɪtə(r)/ *verb trans., intrans.* to make a reconnaissance of (land, enemy troops, etc). [from Old French *reconnoître*, to examine, recognize]

■ explore, survey, scan, spy out, *colloq.* recce, inspect, examine, scrutinize, investigate, patrol.

reconsider *verb trans., intrans.* (**reconsidered, reconsidering**) to consider (something) again and possibly change one's opinion or decision.

■ rethink, reassess, reflect (on), change one's mind (about).

reconsideration *noun* reconsidering or being reconsidered.
reconstitute *verb* 1 to put or change back to the original form, eg by adding water. 2 to form or make up in a different way.
reconstitution *noun* 1 reconstituting. 2 restoration to an original condition.
reconstruct *verb* 1 to create a description or idea (of eg a crime) from the evidence available. 2 to rebuild.

■ 2 remake, rebuild, reassemble, re-establish, refashion, remodel, reform, reorganize, recreate, restore, renovate, regenerate.

reconstruction *noun* 1 a period or process of reconstructing or being reconstructed. 2 something that is reconstructed.
record /'rɛkɔːd, rɪ'kɔːd/ *noun* (with stress on *rec*-) 1 a formal written report or statement of facts, events, or information. 2 (*often* **records**) information, facts, etc, collected over a usually long period of time. 3 the state or fact of being recorded. 4 a thin plastic disc used as a recording medium for reproducing music or other sound. 5 *especially in sports* a performance which is officially recorded as the best of a particular kind or in a particular class. 6 a description of the history and achievements of a person, institution, company, etc. 7 a list of the crimes of which a person has been convicted. 8 *Comput.* in database systems, a subdivision of a file, consisting of a collection of fields, each of which contains a particular item of information, eg a name or address. A record can be treated as a single unit of stored information. 9 anything that recalls or commemorates past events. — *verb* (with stress on -*cord*) 1 to set down in writing or some other permanent

form, especially for use in the future. 2 *trans., intrans.* to register (sound, music, speech, etc) on a record or tape so that it can be listened to in the future. 3 *said of a dial, instrument, person's face, etc* to show or register (a particular figure, feeling, etc). — **go on record** to make a public statement. **off the record** *said of information, statements, etc* not intended to be repeated or made public. **on record** officially recorded; publicly known. **set the record straight** to correct a mistake or false impression. [from Latin *recordari*, to remember]

■ *noun* 1 register, log, report, account, minutes, memorandum, note, entry, document, documentation, file, dossier, diary, journal, memoir. 2 annals, archives, history. 3 evidence, testimony, trace. 4 recording, disc, single, CD, compact disc, album, release, LP. 5 fastest time, best performance, personal best, world record. 6 background, track record, curriculum vitae, career. *verb* 1 note, enter, inscribe, write down, transcribe, register, log, put down, enrol, report, minute, chronicle, document, keep, preserve. 2 tape-record, tape, videotape, video. 3 show, register, indicate, display, express.

recorded delivery a Post Office service in which the sending and receiving of a letter or parcel are recorded.
recorder *noun* 1 a wooden or plastic wind instrument with a tapering mouthpiece and holes which are covered by the player's fingers. 2 a solicitor or barrister who sits as a part-time judge in a court. 3 a person who records something. 4 a tape-recorder.
recording *noun* 1 the process of registering sounds or images on a record, tape, etc. 2 sound or images which have been recorded.

■ 2 release, performance, record, disc, CD, cassette, tape, video.

record-player *noun* an apparatus which reproduces the sounds recorded on records.
recount /rɪ'kaʊnt/ *verb* (with stress on -*count*) to tell (a story, etc) in detail. [from Old French *reconter*, from *conter*, to tell]

■ tell, relate, impart, communicate, report, narrate, describe, depict, portray, detail, repeat, rehearse, recite.

re-count /riː'kaʊnt, 'riːkaʊnt/ *verb* (with stress on -*count*) to count again. — *noun* (with stress on *re*-) a process of re-counting, especially of votes in an election.
recoup /rɪ'kuːp/ *verb* 1 to recover or get back (something lost, eg money). 2 to compensate (eg for something lost). [from French *recouper*, to cut back]

■ 1 recover, retrieve, regain, get back. 2 compensate, make good, repay, refund, reimburse.

recoupment *noun* recouping or being recouped.
recourse /rɪ'kɔːs/ *noun* 1 a source of help or protection. 2 the right to demand payment. — **have recourse to someone** or **something** to turn to them for help, especially in an emergency or in a case of extreme need. [from Latin *recursus*, return]

■ 1 resort, refuge, course (of action), alternative, option, chance, possibility. **have recourse to** resort to, turn to, apply to, employ, make use of, exercise.

recover *verb* (**recovered, recovering**) 1 to get or find again. 2 *intrans.* to regain one's good health, spirits, or composure. 3 *intrans.* to regain a former and usually better condition. 4 to regain control of (one's emotions, actions, etc): *recover one's senses.* 5 to gain (compensation or damages) by legal action. **6** to get money to make up for (expenses, loss, etc) **7** to obtain (a valuable or usable substance) from a waste product or by-product. [from Latin *recuperare*]

⬛ **1** regain, get back, retrieve, retake, recapture, repossess, reclaim, restore. **2, 3** get better, improve, pick up, rally, revive. **2** pull through, get over, recuperate, convalesce, come round. **6** recoup. **7** reclaim, salvage.

⬛ **1** lose, forfeit. **2, 3** worsen.

recoverability *noun* being recoverable.

recoverable *adj.* capable of being recovered.

recovered memory *Psychol.* memory of repressed childhood experiences, especially of sexual abuse, apparently recovered by psychoanalysis.

recovery *noun* (PL. **recoveries**) an act, instance, or process of recovering, or state of having recovered.

⬛ retrieval, salvage, reclamation, repossession, recapture, recuperation, rehabilitation, mending, healing, convalescence, improvement, upturn, rally, revival, restoration.

⬛ loss, forfeit, worsening.

recreant /ˈrɛkrɪənt/ — *noun* a cowardly or disloyal person. — *adj.* cowardly or disloyal. [from Middle English]

recreate /riːkrɪˈeɪt/ *verb* to create again; to reproduce.

recreation /rɛkrɪˈeɪʃən/ *noun* a pleasant, enjoyable, and often refreshing activity done in one's spare time.

⬛ fun, enjoyment, pleasure, amusement, diversion, distraction, entertainment, hobby, pastime, game, sport, play, leisure, relaxation, refreshment.

recreational /rɛkrɪˈeɪʃənəl/ *adj.* relating to or of the nature of recreation.

recreational drug a drug taken for its intoxicating effects, not for medical reasons.

recreation ground an area of land for playing sports, games, etc on.

recrimination *noun* an accusation made by an accused person against his or her accuser. [from Latin *criminari*, to accuse]

⬛ counter-charge, accusation, counter-attack, retaliation, reprisal, retort, quarrel, bickering.

recriminatory /rɪˈkrɪmɪnətərɪ/ *adj.* of the nature of or involving recrimination.

recrudesce /riːkruːˈdɛs/ *verb intrans. technical, said especially of a disease* to become active again, especially after a dormant period. [from Latin *recrudescere*]

recrudescence *noun* the act of breaking out again.

recrudescent *adj.* breaking out again.

recruit /rɪˈkruːt/ — *noun* **1** a newly enlisted member of the army, air force, navy, etc. **2** a new member of a society, group, organization, etc. — *verb trans., intrans.* to enlist (people) as recruits. [from French *recrue*, new growth]

⬛ *noun* **1** conscript. **2** beginner, novice, initiate, learner, trainee, apprentice, convert. *verb* enlist, draft, conscript, enrol, sign up, engage, take on, mobilize, raise, gather, obtain, procure.

recruitment *noun* recruiting.

recrystallization or **recrystallisation** /riːkrɪstəlaɪˈzeɪʃən/ *noun* **1** *Chem.* the purification of a substance by repeated crystallization from fresh solvent. **2** a change in crystalline structure that is not accompanied by a chemical change.

recta see RECTUM.

rectal *adj.* of the rectum.

rectangle *noun* a four-sided figure with opposite sides which are equal and four right angles. [from Latin *rectus*, straight + *angulus*, angle]

rectangular *adj.* **1** of or like a rectangle. **2** placed at right angles.

rectifiable /ˈrɛktɪfaɪəbl/ *adj.* capable of being rectified.

rectification *noun* rectifying or being rectified.

rectifier *noun Electr.* an electrical device, usually a semiconductor diode, that is used to convert an alternating current into a direct current. Rectifiers are used in power supplies, and to detect radio and television signals.

rectify *verb* (**rectifies, rectified**) **1** to put right or correct (a mistake, etc). **2** to purify (eg alcohol) by repeated distillation. **3** to change (an alternating current) into a direct current. **4** to determine the length of (a curve). [from Latin *rectus*, straight + *facere*, to make]

⬛ **1** correct, put right, right, remedy, cure, repair, fix, mend, improve, amend, adjust, reform.

rectilinear *adj.* **1** in or forming a straight line. **2** bounded by straight lines. [from Latin *rectus*, straight + *linea*, line]

rectitude *noun* honesty; correctness of behaviour or judgement; moral integrity. [from Latin *rectus*, straight]

recto *noun* (PL. **rectos**) the right-hand page of an open book. See also VERSO. [from Latin *recto*, on the right]

rector *noun* **1** in the Church of England, a clergyman in charge of a parish where the tithes would formerly all have gone to him. **2** in the Roman Catholic Church, a priest in charge of a congregation or a religious house, especially a Jesuit seminary. **3** the headmaster of some schools and colleges, especially in Scotland. **4** *Scot.* a senior university official elected by and representing the students; occasionally in other countries, the head of a university or college. [from Latin *rector*, from *regere*, to rule]

rectorial *adj.* of a rector.

rectorship *noun* the office of a rector.

rectory *noun* (PL. **rectories**) the house of a rector.

rectum *noun* (PL. **recta, rectums**) the lower part of the alimentary canal, ending at the anus. [from Latin *rectus*, straight]

recumbent *adj.* lying down; reclining. [from Latin *recumbere*, to recline]

recuperable *adj.* recoverable.

recuperate *verb* **1** *intrans.* to recover, especially from illness. **2** *trans.* to recover (something lost, one's health, etc). [from Latin *recuperare*]

⬛ RECOVER. **1** get better, improve, pick up, rally, revive, mend, convalesce. **2** regain, get back, recoup.

⬛ **1** worsen.

recuperation *noun* recovery.

recuperative /rɪˈkuːpərətɪv/ *adj.* **1** capable of restoring to health. **2** relating to or involving a recovery.

recur /rɪˈkɜː(r)/ *verb intrans.* (**recurred, recurring**) **1** to happen or come round again or at intervals. **2** *said of a thought, etc* to come back into one's mind. [from Latin *recurrere*, to run back]

⬛ **1** repeat, persist, return, reappear.

recurrence *noun* **1** the process of recurring. **2** something that recurs.

recurrent *adj.* **1** happening often or regularly. **2** *said of a nerve, vein, etc* turning back to run in the opposite direction.

⬛ **1** recurring, chronic, persistent, repeated, repetitive, regular, periodic, frequent, intermittent.

recurrently *adv.* in a recurrent way.

recurring decimal a decimal fraction in which a figure or group of figures is repeated to infinity, eg 1 divided by 3 gives the recurring decimal 0.3333...

recusancy /ˈrekjʊzənsɪ/ *noun* **1** *Hist.* refusal of Roman Catholics to attend services of the Church of England. **2** refusal to obey a command or authority.

recusant /ˈrekjʊzənt/ — *noun* **1** *Hist.* a person (especially a Roman Catholic) who refused to attend Church of England services when these were obligatory (between c.1570 and c.1790). **2** a person who refuses to submit to authority. — *adj.* of or like recusants. [from Latin *recusare*, to object]

recyclable *adj.* capable of being recycled.

recycle *verb* to pass through a series of changes so as to return to a former state, especially to process waste material so that it can be used again.

∎ reuse, reprocess, reclaim, recover, salvage, save.

recycling the processing of industrial and domestic waste material (eg paper, glass, scrap metal, some plastics) so that it can be used again, so minimizing wastage and reducing the problems of environmental pollution associated with the disposal of large amounts of non-biodegradable refuse (eg many plastics).

red — *adj.* (**redder, reddest**) **1** of the colour of blood. **2** *said of hair or fur* of a colour which varies between a golden brown and a deep reddish-brown. **3** *said of the eyes* bloodshot or with red rims. **4** having a red or flushed face, especially from shame or anger. **5** *said of wine* made with black grapes whose skins colour the wine. **6** *derog. colloq.* communist. **7** (**Red**) relating to the former USSR; Soviet: *the Red Army.* — *noun* **1** the colour of blood, or a similar shade. **2** red dye or paint. **3** red material or clothes. **4** the red traffic light, a sign that cars should stop. **5** anything that is red. **6** the debit side of an account; the state of being in debt eg to a bank. **7** *derog. colloq.* (*often* **Red**) a communist or socialist. — **paint the town red** *colloq.* to go out to enjoy oneself in a lively, noisy, and often drunken way. **see red** *colloq.* to become angry. [from Anglo-Saxon *read*]

∎ *adj* **1** scarlet, vermilion, cherry, ruby, crimson, maroon, pink, reddish. **2** ginger, carroty, auburn, chestnut, Titian. **3** bloodshot, inflamed. **4** ruddy, florid, glowing, rosy, flushed, blushing, embarrassed, shamefaced. **6** communist, socialist, Bolshevik, revolutionary.

red admiral a common N American and European butterfly which has broad red bands on its wings.

red alga *Bot.* any alga belonging to the class Rhodophyceae, typically having a pink or reddish colour due to the presence of the pigment phycoerythrin, which masks the green colour of chlorophyll.

red blood cell or **red corpuscle** a doughnut-shaped blood cell, produced in the bone marrow, that contains the pigment haemoglobin, which gives the cell its red colour. Red blood cells take up oxygen in the lungs and release it in the body tissues. Also called ERYTHROCYTE.

red-blooded *adj.* active; manly; virile.

red-bloodedness *noun* being red-blooded.

redbreast *noun* a robin.

redbrick *adj.*, *said of a British university* founded in the late 19c or early 20c.

red card *Football* a piece of red card or plastic shown by the referee to a player who is being sent off. See also YELLOW CARD.

red carpet a strip of carpet put out for an important person to walk on; special treatment given to an important person or guest.

redcoat *noun* **1** *Hist.* a British soldier. **2** an attendant at a Butlin's holiday camp.

red corpuscle see RED BLOOD CELL.

Red Crescent an organization equivalent to the Red Cross in Muslim countries.

redcurrant *noun* a small edible red berry which grows on a widely cultivated European shrub.

red deer a species of deer, similar to but smaller than the elk, with a reddish-brown summer coat and brownish-grey winter coat, found in dense forest and on moorland in Europe, W Asia, and NW Africa, and introduced to various other parts of the world.

redden *verb* (**reddened, reddening**) **1** *trans.*, *intrans.* to make or become red or redder. **2** *intrans.* to blush.

∎ **2** blush, flush, colour, go red.

reddish *adj.* somewhat red.

red dwarf *Astron.* a cool faint star of about one-tenth the mass and diameter of the Sun, eg Proxima Centauri, Barnard's Star.

redeem *verb* **1** to buy back. **2** to recover (eg something that has been pawned or mortgaged) by payment or service. **3** to fulfil (a promise). **4** to set (a person) free or save (a person's life) by paying a ransom. **5** to free (someone, oneself) from blame or debt. **6** *Christianity, said of Christ* to free (humanity) from sin by his death on the cross. **7** to make up or compensate for (something bad or wrong). **8** to exchange (tokens, vouchers, etc) for goods. **9** to exchange (bonds, shares, etc) for cash. [from Latin *redimere*, to buy back]

∎ **1** buy back, repurchase. **2** regain, repossess, recoup, recover, recuperate, retrieve, salvage. **4** ransom, reclaim, release, liberate, emancipate, free, deliver, rescue, save. **5** absolve, acquit, discharge. **7** compensate for, make up for, offset, outweigh, atone for, expiate. **8, 9** exchange, change, trade. **9** cash (in).

redeemable *adj.* capable of being redeemed.

redeemer *noun* **1** a person who redeems. **2** (**the Redeemer**) a name for Jesus Christ.

redeeming *adj.* that redeems.

redemption *noun* **1** the act of redeeming or state of being redeemed, especially the freeing of humanity from sin by Christ. **2** anything which redeems. — **beyond** or **past redemption** too bad to be redeemed, improved, or saved. [from Latin *redemptio*, buying back]

redemptive *adj.* redeeming, tending to redeem.

Red Ensign see ENSIGN.

redeploy /riːdɪˈplɔɪ/ *verb trans.*, *intrans.* to move (soldiers, workers, etc) to another place or job.

redeployment *noun* redeploying or being redeployed.

redevelop *verb* (**redeveloped, redeveloping**) to build new buildings, etc in a run-down urban area.

redeveloper *noun* a person or organization that redevelops, especially land.

redevelopment *noun* redeveloping, especially of land.

red flag 1 a red banner used as a symbol of socialism or of revolution. **2** a flag used to warn of danger.

red fox a fox native to Europe, temperate Asia, N Africa, and N America, which has a reddish-brown coat with white underparts.

red giant *Astron.* a large cool red star, 10 to 100 times the diameter of the Sun but of similar mass. It appears very bright because of its size, eg Betelgeuse, a red supergiant in the constellation Orion. Red giants represent a late stage in stellar evolution, when a star has exhausted the nuclear fuel in its central core, and its outer layers have expanded greatly in size.

red-handed *adj.* in the act of committing a crime or immediately after having committed it: *caught red-handed.*

red hat a cardinal's hat; a symbol of a cardinal's office.

redhead *noun* a person, especially a woman, with red hair.

redheaded *adj.* **1** *said of a person* having red hair. **2** *said of an animal, etc* having a red head.

red herring 1 a herring which has been cured and smoked to a dark reddish colour. **2** a subject, idea, clue, etc introduced into a discussion, investigation, etc to divert attention from the real issue or to mislead someone (from the fact that a red herring drawn across a track can put a dog off the scent).

red-hot *adj.* **1** *said of metal, etc* heated until it glows red. **2** feeling or showing passionate or intense emotion or excitement: *red-hot anger*. **3** *colloq.* feeling or showing great enthusiasm: *a red-hot favourite*. **4** *said of news, information, etc* completely new and up to date.

red-hot poker a garden plant with long spikes of usually red or orange flowers.

redial *verb trans., intrans.* to dial (a telephone number) again.

Red Indian *often offensive* — *noun* a Native American. — *adj.* of a Native American.

red lead a bright red poisonous oxide of lead, used in making paints.

red-letter day a day which will always be remembered because something particularly pleasant or important happened on it (from the custom of marking saints' days in red on ecclesiastical calendars).

red light 1 a red warning light, especially one which warns vehicles to stop. **2** a refusal or rejection.

red-light district *colloq.* a district where prostitutes work.

red-lining *noun* the practice of refusing credit to those living in an area with a bad record of repayment.

red mist *colloq.* the onset of rage.

redness *noun* a red quality.

redo /riːˈduː/ *verb* (**redoes**; PAST TENSE **redid**; PAST PARTICIPLE **redone**) **1** to do again or differently. **2** to redecorate.

□ **1** repeat, reproduce, copy, remake, rebuild, reconstruct, reattempt, try again. **2** redecorate, repaint, repaper, renovate, refurbish, *colloq.* do up.

redolence *noun* sweet smell, perfume.

redolent *adj.* (**redolent of** or **with something**) **1** smelling strongly of it. **2** suggesting it strongly: *a street redolent of Victorian England*. [from Latin *redolere*, to give off a smell]

□ **2** reminiscent of, evocative of, suggestive of, steeped in, imbued with.

redolently *adv.* so as to be redolent.

redouble *verb trans., intrans.* **1** to make or become greater or more intense. **2** *Bridge* to double (a bid that an opponent has already doubled).

redoubt /rɪˈdaʊt/ *noun* **1** a fortification, especially a temporary one defending a pass or hilltop. **2** a stronghold. [from Latin *reductus*, refuge]

redoubtable *adj.* **1** causing fear or respect. **2** brave; valiant. [from Old French *redouter*, to fear greatly]

□ **1** formidable, fearsome, frightening, daunting, challenging, intimidating, strict, stern. **2** brave, courageous, valiant, stalwart, dauntless, fearless, indomitable.

redoubtably *adv.* in a redoubtable way.

redound /rɪˈdaʊnd/ *verb intrans.* **1** (**redound to someone**) to have a direct, usually advantageous effect on them. **2** (**redound on someone**) to come back to them as a consequence. [from Latin *redundare*, to surge]

redox reaction *Chem.* a chemical reaction in which one of the reacting substances (reactants) is reduced, while the other is simultaneously oxidized. [from REDUCTION + OXIDATION]

red panda see PANDA.

red pepper 1 cayenne pepper. **2** a red capsicum or sweet pepper, eaten as a vegetable. See also GREEN PEPPER.

red rag anything which is likely to provoke someone or make him or her very angry.

redress /rɪˈdrɛs/ — *verb* **1** to set right or compensate for (something wrong). **2** to make even or equal again: *redress the balance*. — *noun* **1** the act of redressing or being redressed. **2** money, etc paid as compensation for loss or wrong done. [from Old French *redrecier*, to straighten]

□ *verb* **1** right, put right, remedy, avenge, requite, compensate for, make amends for, atone for. **2** adjust, correct, amend.

redshank *noun* a wading bird with a scarlet bill and legs, a white rump, and a broad white wing bar that can be clearly seen during flight. It is commonly found on coasts in winter.

redshift *noun Astron.* an increase in the wavelength of light or other electromagnetic radiation emitted by certain galaxies or quasars, so called because an increase in wavelength moves light towards the *red* end of the visible spectrum. It is generally interpreted as a *Doppler effect* resulting from the movement of the source of radiation away from the Earth, and is regarded as evidence that the Universe is expanding.

redskin *noun derog. colloq.* a Native American.

red spider mite a pest that infests the underside of the leaves of garden and houseplants, and weaves sheet webs between the leaves and the main stem.

Red Spot *Astron.* a large oval feature, varying in colour from pale pink to orange-red, in the atmosphere of the planet Jupiter, S of the equator.

red squirrel a native British squirrel with reddish-brown fur.

redstart *noun* **1** a European bird having a conspicuous chestnut-coloured tail. **2** an American warbler that is superficially similar.

red tape *derog.* unnecessary rules and regulations which result in delay.

reduce *verb* **1** *trans., intrans.* to make or become less, smaller, etc. **2** to change into a usually worse or undesirable state or form: *reduced her to tears*. **3** to lower the rank, status, or grade of. **4** to bring into a state of obedience; to subdue. **5** to make weaker or poorer: *reduced circumstances*. **6** to lower the price of. **7** *intrans.* to lose weight by dieting. **8** to convert (a substance) into a simpler form: *reduce chalk to a powder*. **9** to simplify or make more easily understood by considering only the essential elements: *reduce the plan to four main points*. **10** to thicken (a sauce) by boiling off excess liquid. **11** *Chem.* to cause a substance to undergo a chemical reaction whereby it gains hydrogen or loses oxygen. **12** *Maths.* to convert (a fraction) to a form with numerator and denominator as low in value as possible, eg - to -. **13** to convert (ore, etc) into metal. [from Latin *reducere*, to lead back]

□ **1** decrease, lower, lessen, contract, shrink, slim, shorten, moderate, weaken, diminish, impair, abate. **2** drive, force. **3** degrade, downgrade, demote, humble, humiliate. **4** subdue, overpower, master, vanquish. **5** impoverish, straiten. **6** cut, slash, discount, rebate. **7** slim. **9** boil down, simplify, clarify, summarize.

■ **1, 6** increase, raise.

reducer *noun* **1** a person who reduces. **2** a means of reducing.

reducibility *noun* being reducible.

reducible *adj.* capable of being reduced.

reducing agent *Chem.* any substance that brings about chemical reduction of an atom, molecule, or ion of another substance, by donating electrons, usually by adding hydrogen or removing oxygen, eg hydrogen, carbon monoxide.

reductase noun Biochem. an enzyme which brings about the reduction of organic compounds.

reductio ad absurdum /re'dʌktɪʊ ad ab'sʊrdʊm/ noun **1** a way of proving that a premise is wrong by showing that its logical consequence is absurd. **2** the applying of a principle or rule so strictly that it is carried to absurd lengths. [Latin, = reduction to the absurd]

reduction noun **1** an act or instance of reducing; the state of being reduced. **2** the amount by which something is reduced. **3** a reduced copy of a picture, document, etc. **4** Chem. a chemical reaction that involves the addition of hydrogen to or the removal of oxygen from a substance, which in both cases gains electrons. It is always accompanied by oxidation. See also OXIDATION. [from Latin reductio]

> ⊟ **1, 2** decrease, diminution, depreciation, deduction, loss. **1** lessening, moderation, weakening, contraction, compression, narrowing, shortening, curtailment, restriction, limitation, devaluation, subtraction. **2** drop, fall, decline, shrinkage, cutback, cut, discount, rebate.
> ⊠ **1, 2** increase. **1** enlargement. **2** rise.

redundancy noun (PL. **redundancies**) **1** being redundant, or an instance of this. **2** a dismissal or a person dismissed because of redundancy.

> ⊟ **1** unemployment, superfluity, surplus, excess, extra, repetition, verbosity, wordiness, tautology.

redundant adj. **1** said of an employee no longer needed and therefore dismissed. **2** not needed; superfluous. **3** said of a word or phrase expressing an idea which is already conveyed by another word or phrase, eg little in little midget is redundant because midget already conveys the sense of smallness. [from Latin redundare, to overflow]

> ⊟ **1** unemployed, out of work, laid off, dismissed. **2** superfluous, surplus, excess, extra, supernumerary, unneeded, unnecessary, unwanted. **3** wordy, verbose, repetitious, tautological.
> ⊠ **2** necessary, essential, indispensable. **3** concise.

reduplicate verb **1** to repeat, copy, or double. **2** Grammar to repeat (a word or syllable), often with some minor change, to form a new word, as in hubble-bubble, riff-raff. [from Latin reduplicare]

reduplication noun a folding or doubling.

redwood noun **1** either of two extremely tall coniferous trees, native to California. Both species, the giant sequoia (Sequoiadendron giganteum) and the coast redwood (Sequoia sempervirens), are very long-lived, and the coast redwood is probably the world's tallest tree, reaching heights of 120m. **2** the soft fine-grained reddish-brown wood of these trees.

reed noun **1** Bot. any of a group of grasses, most of which are species of the genus Phragmites, that grow in shallow water by the margins of streams, lakes, and ponds. The common reed is used to make thatched roofs, furniture, and fencing. **2** a thin piece of cane or metal in certain musical instruments which vibrates and makes a sound when air passes over it. **3** a wind instrument or organ pipe with reeds. **4** a comb-like device on a loom for spacing the threads of the warp evenly and putting the weft into position. [from Anglo-Saxon hreod]

readily adv. in a reedy way, with a reedy sound.

reediness noun being reedy.

reedmace noun Bot. a reed-like plant of the genus Typha.

reed warbler a warbler that frequents marshy places and builds its nest on reeds.

reedy adj. (**reedier, reediest**) **1** full of reeds. **2** having a tone like a reed instrument, especially in being thin and piping. **3** thin and weak.

reef[1] noun **1** in shallow coastal water, a mass of rock that either projects above the surface at low tide, or is

permanently covered by a shallow layer of water. **2** a coral reef. [from Dutch rif]

reef[2] — noun a part of a sail which may be folded in in rough weather or let out in calm weather, so as to alter the area exposed to the wind. — verb to reduce the area of (a sail) exposed to the wind. [from Middle English refe]

reefer noun **1** (also **reefer-jacket**) a thick woollen double-breasted jacket. **2** slang a cigarette containing marijuana.

reefing-jacket noun same as REEFER 1.

reef knot a knot made by passing one end of the rope over and under the other end, and then back over and under it again.

reek — noun **1** a strong, unpleasant, and often offensive smell. **2** Scot., dialect smoke. — verb intrans. **1** to give off a strong, usually unpleasant smell. **2** (**reek of something**) to suggest or hint at something unpleasant: this scheme reeks of racism. **3** Scot. dialect to give off smoke. [from Anglo-Saxon reocan]

> ⊟ noun **1** smell, stink, stench, whiff, colloq. pong. verb **1** smell, stink, whiff, colloq. pong. **2** be redolent of, suggest.

reel — noun **1** a round wheel-shaped or cylindrical object of plastic, metal, etc on which thread, film, fishing-lines, etc can be wound. **2** the quantity of film, thread, etc wound on one of these. **3** a device for winding and unwinding a fishing-line. **4** a lively Scottish or Irish dance, or the music for it. — verb **1** to wind on a reel. **2** (usually **reel something in** or **up**) to pull it in or up using a reel: reel in a fish. **3** intrans. to stagger or sway; to move unsteadily. **4** intrans. to whirl or appear to move: the room began to reel and then she fainted. **5** intrans. (also **reel back**) to be shaken physically or mentally: reel back in horror. **6** intrans. to dance a reel. — **reel something off** to say, repeat, or write it rapidly and often unthinkingly. [from Anglo-Saxon hreol]

> ⊟ verb **3, 4** spin, wheel, twirl, whirl, swirl, revolve, gyrate, rock, sway. **3** stagger, totter, wobble, waver, falter, stumble, lurch, pitch, roll.

re-entry noun (PL. **re-entries**) Astron. the return of a spacecraft to the Earth's atmosphere.

reeve[1] noun Hist. **1** the chief magistrate of a town or district. **2** an official who supervises a lord's manor or estate. [from Anglo-Saxon refa]

reeve[2] verb (PAST TENSE **rove, reeved**) to pass (a rope, etc) through a hole, opening, or ring. [from Dutch reven, to reef]

reeve[3] noun a female ruff. See RUFF[3].

ref noun colloq. a referee in a game.

refectory noun (PL. **refectories**) a dining-hall in a monastery or college. [from Latin reficere, to refresh]

refer verb (**referred, referring**) (usually **refer to something** or **someone**) **1** intrans. to talk or write about them; to mention them. **2** intrans. to relate, concern, or apply to them: does this refer to me? **3** intrans to look for information in a specified place: I must refer to my notes. **4** to direct (a person, etc) to some authority for discussion, information, a decision, treatment, etc. **5** to explain something as being caused by. **6** to consider as belonging to a specified place, time or category.

> ⊟ **1** allude to, mention, touch on, speak of, bring up, cite, quote, recommend. **2** apply to, concern, relate to, belong to, pertain to, appertain to. **3** consult, look up, turn to, resort to. **4** send, direct, point, pass on, transfer, commit.

referable or **referrable** adj. capable of being referred or assigned.

referee /refə'riː/ — noun **1** an umpire or judge, eg of a game or in a dispute. **2** a person who is willing to testify to a person's character, talents, and abilities. — verb trans., intrans. to act as a referee in a game or dispute.

■ *noun* **1** umpire, judge, adjudicator, arbitrator, mediator, *colloq.* ref. *verb* umpire, judge, adjudicate, arbitrate.

reference *noun* **1** (*usually* **reference to something**) a mention of it; an allusion to it. **2** a direction in a book to another passage or book where information can be found. **3** a book or passage referred to. **4** the act of referring to a book or passage for information. **5** a written report on a person's character, talents, and abilities, especially of his or her aptitude for a particular job or position. **6** a person referred to for such a report. **7** the providing of facts and information: *a reference library.* **8** the directing of a person, question, etc to some authority for information, a decision, etc. **9** a relation, correspondence, or connection: *with reference to your last letter.* **10** a standard for measuring or judging: *a point of reference.*

■ **1** allusion, remark, mention, citation, quotation, illustration, instance, note. **5** testimonial, recommendation, endorsement, character. **9** relation, regard, respect, connection, bearing.

reference book any book, such as an encyclopedia or dictionary, that is consulted occasionally for information and which is not usually read through as, for example, a novel or biography is.

referendum *noun* (PL. **referendums, referenda**) the act or principle of giving the people of a country the chance to state their opinion on a matter by voting for or against it. [from Latin *referre*, to carry back]

referential *adj.* **1** containing a reference. **2** having reference to something. **3** used for reference.

referral /rɪˈfɜːrəl/ *noun* the act of referring someone to an expert, especially the sending of a patient by a GP to a specialist for treatment.

referred *adj. Medicine, said of pain* felt in a part of the body other than its actual source.

refill — *noun* (with stress on *re-*) a new filling for something which becomes empty through use, or a container for this. — *verb* (with stress on *-fill*) to fill again.

refillable *adj.* capable of being refilled.

refine *verb* **1** to make pure by removing dirt, waste substances, etc. **2** *trans., intrans.* to make or become more elegant, polished, or subtle.

■ **1** process, treat, purify, clarify, filter, distil. **2** polish, hone, improve, perfect, elevate, exalt.

refined *adj.* **1** very polite; well-mannered; elegant. **2** having had all the dirt, waste substances, etc removed. **3** improved; polished.

■ **1** civilized, cultured, cultivated, polished, sophisticated, urbane, genteel, gentlemanly, ladylike, well-bred, well-mannered, polite, civil, elegant, fine, delicate, subtle, precise, exact, sensitive, discriminating.
■ **1, 3** coarse. **1** vulgar, rude.

refinement *noun* **1** the act or process of refining. **2** good manners or good taste; polite speech; elegance. **3** an improvement or perfection. **4** a subtle distinction.

■ **1, 2** cultivation, sophistication. **1, 3** modification, alteration, amendment, improvement. **2** urbanity, gentility, breeding, style, elegance, taste, discrimination, subtlety, finesse.
■ **2** coarseness, vulgarity. **3** deterioration.

refinery *noun* (PL. **refineries**) a factory where raw materials such as sugar and oil are refined.

refining *noun* any process whereby a substance is purified by the removal of impurities, eg the separation of petroleum (crude oil) into its various components, such as hydrocarbon fuels, or the removal of impurities from a metal after it has been extracted from its ore.

refit — *verb* (with stress on *-fit*) (**refitted, refitting**) **1** to repair or fit new parts to (especially a ship). **2** *intrans. said of a ship* to be repaired or have new parts fitted. — *noun* (with stress on *re-*) the process of refitting or being refitted.

reflag *verb* (**reflagged, reflagging**) to change the country of registration of (a merchant ship) usually for some commercial advantage; also, to replace the national flag of (a ship) with that of a more powerful nation, so that it sails under that nation's protection.

reflate *verb* to cause reflation of (an economy).

reflation *noun* an increase in the amount of money and credit available and, in economic activity, designed to increase industrial production after a period of deflation. See also DEFLATION, INFLATION.

reflationary *adj.* characterized by or involving inflation.

reflect *verb* **1** *trans., intrans. said of a surface* to send back (light, heat, sound, etc). **2** *trans., intrans. said of a mirror, etc* to give an image of. **3** *intrans. said of a sound, image, etc* to be reflected back. **4** to have as a cause or be a consequence of: *price increases reflect greater demand for the goods.* **5** to show or give an idea of: *a poem which reflects one's mood.* **6** (**reflect on** or **upon something**) to consider it carefully. **7** (**reflect on** or **upon someone**) *said of an action, etc* to bring praise, or blame, to them: *her behaviour reflects on her mother* (= reflects badly on)/*your behaviour reflects well on you.* [from Latin *reflectere*, to bend back]

■ **2** mirror, echo, imitate, reproduce. **5** portray, depict, show, reveal, display, exhibit, manifest, demonstrate, indicate, express, communicate. **6** think about, ponder, consider, mull (over), deliberate (on), contemplate, meditate (on), muse on.

reflectance *noun Physics* the ratio of the intensity of the radiation that is reflected by a surface to the intensity of radiation that is incident (falling) on that surface.

reflecting telescope a telescope in which light rays are collected and focused by means of a concave mirror. The largest astronomical telescopes are of this type.

reflection or **reflexion** *noun* **1** the change in direction of a particle or wave, eg the turning back of a ray of light, either when it strikes a smooth surface that it does not penetrate, such as a mirror or polished metal, or when it reaches the boundary between two media. See also REFRACTION. **2** the act of reflecting. **3** a reflected image; an indication. **4** careful and thoughtful consideration; contemplation. **5** a thought or opinion. **6** blame, discredit or censure.

■ **3** image, likeness, echo, impression, indication, manifestation. **4, 5** thought, meditation, musing. **4** thinking, study, consideration, deliberation, contemplation. **5** observation, view, opinion.

reflective *adj.* **1** thoughtful; meditative. **2** *said of a surface* able to reflect images, light, sound, etc. **3** reflected: *reflective glare of the sun on the water.*

reflectively *adv.* in a reflective way.

reflector *noun* **1** a polished surface which reflects light, heat, etc, especially a piece of red plastic or glass on the back of a bicycle which glows when light shines on it. **2** a reflecting telescope.

reflex — *noun* **1** a series of nerve impulses that produce a rapid involuntary response to an external stimulus, eg withdrawal of the finger from a pin-prick, or an internal stimulus, eg control of blood pressure or walking movements. The rapidity of a reflex response is due to the fact that the brain is not directly involved. **2** the ability to respond rapidly to a stimulus. **3** reflected light, sound, heat, etc, or a reflected image. **4** a sign or expression of something. **5** a word formed or element of speech which has developed from a corresponding earlier form. — *adj.* **1** occurring as an automatic response without being thought about. **2** bent or turned backwards. **3** directed back on the source; reflected. **4** *said of a thought* introspective. **5** *Maths.* denoting an angle that is greater than 180° but less than 360°. [from Latin *reflexus*, bent back]

reflex action a rapid involuntary movement produced by a reflex.

reflex camera a camera in which the image transmitted through the lens is directed by a mirror to the viewfinder for more accurate composition and focusing.

reflexion SEE REFLECTION.

reflexive *adj. Grammar* **1** *said of a pronoun* showing that the object of a verb is the same as the subject, eg in *he cut himself*, *himself* is a reflexive pronoun. **2** *said of a verb* used with a reflexive pronoun as object.

reflexively *adv.* in a reflexive way.

reflexologist *noun* a therapist who specializes in reflexology.

reflexology *noun* therapy for particular health problems and illnesses in which the soles of the feet are massaged, based on the belief that different parts of the soles relate to different parts of the body and different organs.

reflux /ˈriːflʌks/ *noun Chem.* the boiling of a liquid for long periods in a vessel attached to a condenser (known as a *reflux condenser*), so that the vapour produced condenses and continuously flows back into the vessel. It is widely used in the synthesis of organic chemical compounds. [from RE- + Latin *fluxus*, flow]

reform — *verb* **1** to improve or remove faults from (a person, behaviour, etc). **2** *intrans.* to give up bad habits, improve one's behaviour, etc. **3** to stop or abolish (misconduct, an abuse, etc). — *noun* **1** a correction or improvement, especially in some social or political system. **2** improvement in one's behaviour or morals. [from Latin *reformare*]

⊟ *verb* **1, 2** change, amend, improve, ameliorate, mend. **1** better, rectify, correct, repair, rehabilitate, rebuild, reconstruct, remodel, revamp, renovate, restore, regenerate, reconstitute, reorganize, *colloq.* shake up, revolutionize. **3** abolish, eliminate, eradicate, stamp out, purge. *noun* CHANGE, AMENDMENT, IMPROVEMENT, REHABILITATION. **1** rectification, correction, renovation, reorganization, *colloq.* shake-up, purge.

reformable *adj.* capable of reform.

Reformation the Protestant reform movements in the Christian Church, inspired by and derived from Martin Luther, John Calvin, and others in 16c Europe.

reformation /refəˈmeɪʃən/ *noun* the act or process of reforming or being reformed; improvement.

reformative *adj.* reforming.

reformatory *noun* (PL. **reformatories**) *old use esp. North Amer.*, *esp.* US a school for reforming the behaviour of young people who break the law.

reformer *noun* a person who reforms or who advocates reform.

reformism *noun Politics* any doctrine or movement that advocates social and political change in a gradual manner within a democratic framework, rather than revolutionary change.

refract *verb*, *said of a medium, eg water, glass* to cause the direction of (a wave of light, sound, etc) to change when it crosses the boundary between one medium and another through which it travels at a different speed, eg air and glass. [from Latin *refringere*, to break up]

refracting telescope or **refractor** a telescope in which light rays are collected by means of a lens of long focal length (the *objective*) and magnified by means of a lens of short focal length (the *eyepiece*).

refraction *noun Physics* a change in the direction of a wave when it passes from one medium to another in which

its speed is different, eg a light wave passing from air to glass. Mirages, and the distortion of all partially submerged objects, are caused by the refraction of light.

refractive *adj.* **1** relating to or involving refraction. **2** capable of causing refraction.

refractive index *Physics* (SYMBOL *n*) the ratio of the speed of light (or other electromagnetic radiation) in air or a vacuum to its speed in another medium. For example, the refractive index between air and glass is approximately 1.6, ie light travels 1.6 times faster through air than through glass.

refractoriness *noun* being refractory.

refractory — *adj.* **1** *said of a material* having a high melting point and therefore able to withstand high temperatures without crumbling or softening, eg silica, fireclay, and metal oxides, which are used to line furnaces, etc. **2** difficult to control; stubborn; unmanageable. **3** *said of a disease* not responding to treatment. — *noun* (PL. **refractories**) *Chem.* a refractory material. [from Latin *refractarius*, stubborn]

⊟ *adj.* **2** stubborn, obstinate, intractable, unmanageable, difficult, defiant, disobedient, insubordinate.

refrain¹ *noun* a phrase or group of lines, or the music for them, repeated at the end of each stanza or verse in a poem or song. [from Old French *refrain*, from Latin *frangere*, to break]

refrain² *verb intrans.* (**refrain from something**) to keep oneself from acting in some way; to avoid it. [from Latin *refrenare*, from *frenum*, bridle]

⊟ stop, cease, quit, leave off, renounce, desist from, abstain from, forbear to, avoid.

refrangibility *noun* being refrangible.

refrangible *adj.* able to be refracted. [from Latin *refringere*, from *frangere*, to break]

refresh *verb* **1** *said of food, rest, etc* to give renewed strength, energy, and enthusiasm to. **2** to revive (someone, oneself, etc) with food, rest, etc. **3** to provide a new supply of; to replenish. **4** to make cool. **5** to make (one's memory) clearer and stronger by reading or listening to the source of information again. [from Old French *refreschir*]

⊟ **1, 2** revive, restore, renew, enliven, invigorate, fortify, rejuvenate, revitalize, reinvigorate. **3** replenish, refill. **4** cool, freshen. **5** jog, stimulate, prompt, prod.
⊟ **1** tire, exhaust.

refresher *noun* **1** anything, eg a cold drink, that refreshes. **2** *Legal* an extra fee paid to counsel during a long case or an adjournment.

refresher course a course of study or training intended to increase or update a person's previous knowledge or skill.

refreshing *adj.* **1** giving new strength, energy, and enthusiasm; cooling. **2** particularly pleasing because different, unexpected, or new.

⊟ **1** cool, thirst-quenching, bracing, invigorating, energizing, stimulating, inspiring. **2** fresh, new, novel, original.

refreshingly *adv.* in a refreshing way.

refreshment *noun* **1** the act of refreshing or state of being refreshed. **2** anything which refreshes. **3** (**refreshments**) food and drink.

⊟ **1** revival, restoration, renewal, reanimation, reinvigoration, revitalization. **3** sustenance, food, drink.

refrigerant — *noun* a liquid used in the cooling mechanism of a refrigerator. — *adj.* cooling.

refrigerate *verb* to make or keep (food) cold or frozen to prevent it from going bad. [from Latin *refrigerare*, from *frigus*, cold]

....

⊟ cool, freeze, deep-freeze, freeze-dry.

....

refrigeration *noun* the process whereby a cabinet or room and its contents are kept at a temperature significantly lower than that of the surrounding environment, especially in order to slow down the rate of decay of food or other perishable materials. It occurs as a result of a continuous cycle in which a volatile liquid *refrigerant* evaporates, absorbing heat as it does so, and is then compressed back to a liquid by means of a compressor pump outside the cabinet or room.

refrigerator *noun* an insulated cabinet or room maintained at a temperature above 0°C and below 5°C in order to slow down the rate of decay of food or other perishable materials stored within it.

refuel *verb* (**refuelled, refuelling**) **1** to supply (an aircraft, etc) with more fuel. **2** *intrans.* *said of an aircraft, etc* to take on more fuel.

refuge /'rɛfjuːdʒ/ *noun* **1** shelter or protection from danger or trouble. **2** any place, person, or thing offering such shelter. [from Latin *refugium*]

....

⊟ SANCTUARY, ASYLUM, SHELTER. **1** protection, security. **2** retreat, hideout, hideaway, resort, harbour, haven.

....

refugee *noun* a person who seeks refuge, especially from religious or political persecution, in another country.

....

⊟ exile, émigré, displaced person, fugitive, runaway, escapee.

....

refulgence *noun* **1** being refulgent. **2** brightness.

refulgent *adj. literary* shining brightly; radiant; beaming. [from Latin *refulgere*, to shine brightly]

refund — *verb* (with stress on *-fund*) to pay (money, etc) back to (someone). — *noun* (with stress on *re-*) **1** the paying back of money, etc. **2** the money, etc paid back. [from Latin *refundere*, to pour back]

....

⊟ *verb* repay, reimburse, rebate, return, restore. *noun* REPAYMENT. **1** reimbursement, return. **2** rebate.

....

refundable *adj.*, *said of a deposit, etc* that may be refunded.

refurbish *verb* to renovate and redecorate.

....

⊟ renovate, decorate, redecorate, rebuild, *colloq.* do up.

....

refurbishment *noun* refurbishing or being refurbished.

refusal *noun* an act of refusing. — **first refusal** the opportunity to buy, accept or refuse something before it is offered, given, sold, etc to anyone else.

....

⊟ rejection, no, rebuff, repudiation, denial, negation.
⊟ acceptance.

....

refuse[1] /rɪ'fjuːz/ *verb* **1** *trans., intrans.* to declare oneself unwilling to do what one has been asked or told to do, etc; to say 'no'. **2** not to accept (something): *refuse the offer of help.* **3** not to allow (access, etc) or give (permission). **4** *trans., intrans.* to show or express unwillingness: *the car refused to start.* **5** *trans., intrans. said of a horse* to stop at (a fence), and not jump over it. [from Old French *refuser*, to pour back]

....

⊟ **2** reject, turn down, decline, spurn, repudiate, rebuff, repel. **3** deny, withhold.
⊟ **1, 2** accept. **3** allow, permit.

....

refuse[2] /'rɛfjuːs/ *noun* rubbish; anything thrown away; waste. [from Old French *refus*, rejection]

....

⊟ rubbish, waste, trash, garbage, junk, litter.

....

refuse-derived fuel **1** refuse which has had any metal or mineral content removed so that it can be fed into a suitably-designed furnace. **2** the product of small-scale fermentation of domestic and animal waste to produce gas (methane) for domestic use. The process has been promoted in certain Third World countries as a cheaper alternative to the burning of wood or fossil fuels.

refusenik /rɪ'fjuːznɪk/ *noun* a person, especially a Jew, living in the former Soviet Union who was refused permission to emigrate (usually to Israel).

refutable /rɪ'fjuːtəbl, 'rɛfjuːtəbl/ *adj.* capable of being refuted.

refutation *noun* **1** refuting. **2** an argument, etc that refutes.

refute *verb* **1** to prove that (a person, statement, theory, etc) is wrong. **2** *colloq.* to deny. [from Latin *refutare*, to drive back]

....

⊟ **1** disprove, rebut, confute, give the lie to, discredit, counter, negate.

....

regain *verb* **1** to get back again or recover. **2** to get back to (a place).

....

⊟ **1** recover, get back, recoup, reclaim, repossess, retake, recapture, retrieve. **2** get back to, return to.

....

regal *adj.* of, like, or suitable for a king or queen. [from Latin *regalis*, royal]

....

⊟ majestic, kingly, queenly, princely, imperial, royal, sovereign, stately, magnificent, noble, lordly.

....

regale *verb* **1** (**regale someone with something**) to amuse them with stories or other entertainment. **2** to entertain (someone) lavishly. [from French *régaler*]

regalia /rɪ'geɪlɪə/ *pl. noun* **1** objects such as the crown and sceptre which are a sign of royalty, used at coronations, etc. **2** any ornaments, ceremonial clothes, etc worn as a sign of a person's importance or authority, eg by a mayor. [from Latin *regalia*, things worthy of a king]

regality *noun* **1** being regal. **2** royalty. **3** sovereignty.

regally *adv.* in a regal way.

regard *verb* **1** to consider (someone or something) in a specified way: *regarded him as a friend.* **2** to pay attention to; to take notice of. **3** to look at attentively or steadily. **4** to have a connection with or relate to. — *noun* **1** thought or attention. **2** care or consideration; sympathy. **3** respect and affection: *be held in high regard.* **4** a gaze or look. **5** (**regards**) greetings; good wishes. — **as regards** ... concerning ...; **as far as** ... is concerned. **with regard to** ... about ...; concerning ... [from Middle English]

....

⊟ *verb* **1** consider, deem, judge, rate, value, think, believe, suppose, imagine, look upon. **3** view, observe, watch. **4** concern, relate to, involve. *noun* **1, 2** concern, consideration. **1** attention, notice, heed. **2** care, sympathy. **3** respect, deference, honour, esteem, admiration, affection, love. **as regards** with regard to, regarding, concerning, with reference to, re, about, as to.
⊟ *noun* **1, 2, 3** disregard. **3** contempt.

....

regardful *adj.* (**regardful of something**) paying attention to it; taking notice of it.

regarding *prep.* about; concerning.

▤ with regard to, as regards, concerning, with reference to, re, about, as to.

regardless — *adv.* not thinking or caring about costs, problems, dangers, etc; in spite of everything: *carry on regardless.* — *adj.* (**regardless of something**) taking no notice of it: *regardless of the consequences.*

▤ *adv.* anyway, nevertheless, nonetheless, despite everything, come what may. *adj* disregarding, heedless of, unmindful of, inattentive to, unconcerned about, indifferent to.
▣ *adj.* heedful of, mindful of, attentive to.

regardlessly *adv.* heedlessly, inconsiderately.

regatta *noun* a meeting for yacht or boat races. [from Italian *regata*]

regency — *noun* (PL. **regencies**) **1** the position of a regent. **2** government, or the period of government, by a regent. [from Latin *regens*, from *regere*, to rule]

regenerate — *verb* **1** *trans., intrans.* to make or become morally or spiritually improved. **2** *trans., intrans.* to develop or give new life or energy; to be brought back or bring back to life or original strength again. **3** to grow new tissue to replace (a damaged part of the body). **4** *intrans. said of a damaged part of the body* to be replaced by new tissue. — *adj.* having been regenerated, especially in having improved morally, spiritually, or physically. [from Latin *regenerare*, to bring forth again]

▤ *verb* **1** reform, amend, improve. **2** revive, reinvigorate, reawaken, rekindle, renew, restore.
▣ *verb* **1**, **2** degenerate.

regeneration *noun* **1** regenerating or being regenerated. **2** the regrowth of parts that have been destroyed.

regenerative *adj.* characterized by regeneration, likely to regenerate.

regenerator *noun* a person or thing that regenerates.

regent — *noun* a person who governs a country during a monarch's childhood or illness. — *adj.* acting as regent; ruling.

reggae /'rɛgeɪ/ *noun* popular West Indian music which has a strong syncopated beat. [from Jamaican English]

regicide /'rɛdʒɪsaɪd/ *noun* **1** the killing of a king. **2** a person who kills a king. [from Latin *rex*, king + -CIDE]

regime /reɪ'ʒiːm/ or **régime** *noun* **1** a system of government or a particular government. **2** a regimen. [from French *régime*]

▤ **1** government, rule, administration, management, leadership, command, control, establishment, system.

regimen /'rɛdʒɪmɛn/ *noun* a course of treatment, especially of diet and exercise, which is necessary for one's good health. [from Latin *regimen*, from *regere*, to rule]

regiment /'rɛdʒɪmənt, 'rɛdʒɪmɛnt, rɛdʒɪ'mɛnt/ — *noun* pronounced -ənt) **1** a permanent army unit consisting of several companies, etc and commanded by a colonel. **2** a large number. — *verb* (pronounced -ent, with variable stress) **1** to organize or control strictly, usually too strictly. **2** to form into a regiment or regiments. [from Latin *regimentum*, from *regere*, to rule]

regimental — *adj.* of a regiment. — *noun* (**regimentals**) a military uniform, especially of a particular regiment.

regimentation *noun* regimenting.

regimented *adj.* **1** strictly organized. **2** formed into a regiment or regiments.

▤ **1** strict, disciplined, controlled, regulated, standardized, ordered, methodical, systematic, organized.
▣ **1** free, lax, disorganized.

Regina /rɪ'dʒaɪnə/ *noun* the reigning queen, now used mainly on coins and in official documents. [from Latin *regina*, queen]

region *noun* **1** an area of the world or a country with particular geographical, social, etc characteristics. **2** an administrative area. **3** an area of the body round or near a specific part, organ, etc: *the abdominal region.* **4** any of the different layers which the atmosphere and sea are divided into according to height or depth. **5** an area of activity or interest. — **in the region of** ... approximately...; nearly: *it cost in the region of a hundred pounds.* [from Latin *regio*, from *regere*, to rule]

▤ **1**, **3** area, zone. **1** land, terrain, territory, country, province, district, sector, neighbourhood. **5** domain, realm, sphere, field. **in the region of** about, around, approximately, almost, nearly, of the order of, more or less.

regional *adj.* **1** of a region. **2** *said of pain* affecting a particular area of the body.

▤ LOCAL. **1** district, provincial, neighbourhood.

regionally *adv.* in a regional way; by regions.

register — *noun* **1** a written list or record of names, events, etc, or a book containing this. **2** a machine or device which records and lists information, especially (**cash register**) one in a shop which lists sales and in which money is kept. **3** the range of tones produced by the human voice or a musical instrument. **4** the set of pipes controlled by an organ stop. **5** a style of speech or language suitable for and used in a particular situation. — *verb* (**registered, registering**) **1** to enter (an event, name, etc) in an official register. **2** *intrans.* to enter one's name and address in a hotel register on arrival. **3** *trans., intrans.* (**register for something**) to enrol formally for it. **4** to insure (a letter or parcel) against getting lost in the post. **5** *said of a device* to record and usually show (speed, information, etc) automatically. **6** *said of a person's face, etc* to show (a particular feeling). **7** *intrans.* to make an impression on someone, eg being understood, remembered, etc: *the name didn't register.* **8** to obtain, achieve, or win: *register one's first success.* [from Latin *regesta*, things recorded]

▤ *noun* **1** roll, roster, list, index, catalogue, directory, log, record, chronicle, annals, archives, file, ledger, schedule, diary, almanac. *verb* **1** record, note, log, enter, inscribe, mark, list, catalogue, chronicle, enrol. **2** check in. **3** enrol for, enlist in, sign on for, sign up for. **5**, **6** show, display, indicate. **5** record, read. **6** reveal, betray, exhibit, manifest, express.

registered *adj.* recorded, entered (in a list, etc), enrolled.

Registered General Nurse a nurse who has passed the examination of the General Nursing Council for Scotland. See also STATE REGISTERED NURSE.

register office *Brit.* an office where records of births, deaths, and marriages are kept and where marriages may be performed.

registrar *noun* **1** a person who keeps an official register, especially of births, deaths, and marriages. **2** a senior administrator in a university responsible for student records, enrolment, etc. **3** *Brit.* a middle-ranking hospital doctor who is training to become a specialist, and who works under a consultant. [related to REGISTER]

registration *noun* **1** registering. **2** something registered. **3** the art or act of combining stops in organ-playing.

registration number the sequence of letters and

numbers by which a vehicle is registered, displayed on its number plate.

registry noun (PL. **registries**) 1 an office or place where registers are kept. 2 registration.

registry office same as REGISTER OFFICE.

Regius professor /ˈriːdʒɪəs/ *Brit.* a professor holding a chair which was founded by a king or queen. [from Latin *regius*, royal]

regrade *verb* to assign or award a different grade to (something).

regress /ˈriːgres, rɪˈgres/ — *verb intrans.* (with stress on *-gress*) to return to a former less perfect, less desirable, less advanced, etc state or condition. — *noun* (with stress on *re-*) a return to a former less perfect, less advanced, etc state or condition. [from Latin *regressus*, return]

▣ *verb* relapse, backslide, revert, degenerate, deteriorate. *noun* relapse, backsliding, reversion, degeneration, deterioration.

regression *noun* 1 an act of regressing. 2 *Psychol.* a return to an earlier level of functioning, eg a return to infantile or adolescent behaviour by an adult. It may accompany mental illness such as schizophrenia. 3 *Medicine* the stage of a disease in which symptoms disappear. 4 *Statistics* a measure of the relationship between the value of a particular variable and the values of one or more possibly related variables.

regressive *adj.* going back, reverting, returning.

regressively *adv.* in a regressive way.

regret — *verb* (**regretted, regretting**) to feel sorry, repentant, distressed, disappointed, etc about. — *noun* 1 a feeling of sorrow, repentance, distress, disappointment, etc. 2 (**regrets**) a polite expression of disappointment, etc used especially when declining an invitation. [from Old French *regreter*]

▣ *verb* rue, repent, lament, mourn, grieve, deplore. *noun* 1 remorse, contrition, compunction, self-reproach, shame, sorrow, grief, disappointment, bitterness.

regretful *adj.* feeling or showing regret.

▣ remorseful, rueful, repentant, contrite, penitent, conscience-stricken, ashamed, sorry, apologetic, sad, sorrowful, disappointed.
▣ impenitent, unashamed.

regretfully *adv.* with regret.

regrettable *adj.* that should be regretted; unwelcome; unfortunate.

▣ unfortunate, unwelcome, unlucky, unhappy, sad, disappointing, upsetting, distressing, lamentable, deplorable, shameful, wrong, ill-advised.
▣ fortunate, happy.

regrettably *adv.* in a regrettable way.

regroup *verb trans., intrans.* 1 to form into a new or different group. 2 *Mil.* to organize (soldiers) into a new fighting formation.

▣ REDEPLOY. 1 reorganize, re-form, reassemble.

regt *abbrev.* regiment.

regular — *adj.* 1 usual; normal; customary. 2 arranged, occurring, acting, etc in a fixed pattern of predictable or equal intervals of space or time: *visit one's parents at regular intervals.* 3 agreeing with some rule, custom, or normal practice, etc and accepted as correct. 4 symmetrical or even; having all the faces, sides, or angles, etc the same. 5 having bowel movements or menstrual periods with nor-

mal frequency. 6 of ordinary size: *a regular portion of chips.* 7 *colloq.* complete; absolute: *that child is a regular little monster.* 8 *Grammar,* said of a noun, verb, etc following one of the usual patterns of formation. 9 *said of troops, the army, etc* of or forming a permanent professional body. 10 officially qualified or recognized; professional. 11 belonging to a religious order and subject to the rule of that order. 12 *North Amer. colloq.* behaving in an acceptable, likeable way: *a regular guy.* — *noun* 1 a soldier in a professional regular army. 2 *colloq.* a frequent customer. 3 a member of a religious order. [from Latin *regula*, rule]

▣ *adj.* 1, 3 usual, customary, normal. 1 ordinary, common, commonplace, everyday, routine, habitual, typical, time-honoured. 2 periodic, rhythmic, steady, constant, fixed, set, unvarying, uniform, orderly, systematic, methodical. 3 conventional, orthodox, correct, official, standard. 4 even, level, smooth, balanced, symmetrical.
▣ *adj.* 1, 3 unusual, unconventional. 2, 3 irregular.

regularity *noun* being regular.

▣ steadiness, constancy, rhythm, repetition, uniformity, invariability, evenness, balance, symmetry.

regularization or **regularisation** *noun* regularizing.

regularize or **regularise** *verb* to make regular.

regularly *adv.* 1 in a regular way. 2 at a regular time.

regulate *verb* 1 to control or adjust (a piece of machinery, the heat or sound available, etc) as required. 2 to control or direct (a person, thing, etc) according to rules. [from Latin *regula*, rule]

▣ 1 set, adjust, tune. 2 control, direct, guide, govern, rule, administer, manage, handle, conduct, run, organize, order, arrange, settle, square, monitor, moderate.

regulation — *noun* 1 a rule or instruction. 2 the act of regulating or state of being regulated. — *adj.* conforming to or governed by rules or by stated standards.

▣ *noun* 1 rule, statute, law, ordinance, edict, decree, order, commandment, precept, dictate, requirement, prodecure. 2 adjustment, tuning, setting, monitoring, control, direction, government, conduct, ordering, organization, arrangement. *adj.* standard, official, statutory, prescribed, required, orthodox, accepted, customary, usual, normal.

regulator *noun* a thing that regulates eg a piece of machinery.

regulo *noun* each of several numbers in a series which indicate the temperature of a gas oven: *bake at regulo five.* [from *Regulo,* originally a trademark for a thermostatic control system for gas ovens]

regurgitate *verb* 1 to bring back (food) into the mouth after it has been swallowed. 2 *derog.* to repeat exactly (something already said). 3 *intrans.* to gush back up again. [from Latin *regurgitare*]

regurgitation *noun* regurgitating.

rehabilitate *verb* 1 to help (usually a prisoner or someone who has been ill) re-adapt to normal life, especially by providing vocational training. 2 to restore to a former state or rank, or to restore former rights or privileges. [from Latin *rehabilitare*]

rehabilitation *noun* rehabilitating or being rehabilitated.

rehash *colloq.* — *verb* (with stress on *-hash*) to use or present (subject matter which has been used before) in a slightly different form but with no improvements. — *noun* (with stress on *re-*) a speech, book, etc which re-uses existing subject matter with little or no change.

rehearsal *noun* 1 the act of practising or preparing. 2 a performance of a play, etc for practice.

▣ **1** practice, drill, exercise, preparation. **2** reading, run-through, dry run.

rehearse *verb* **1** *trans., intrans.* to practise (a play, piece of music, etc) before performing it in front of an audience. **2** to train (a person) for performing in front of an audience. **3** to give a list of or describe: *rehearse one's grievances.* **4** to repeat or say over again. [from Old French *rehercier*, to harrow again]

▣ **1, 2** drill, train. **1** practise, prepare, try out. **3** recite, recount, relate, describe, go over, list, enumerate, itemize. **4** repeat.

reheat — *verb* (with stress on *-heat*) to heat again. — *noun* (with stress on *re-*) a device for injecting fuel into the hot exhaust gases of a turbojet in order to obtain increased thrust; also the use of such a device.

rehouse *verb* to provide with new and usually better quality accommodation.

reign /reɪn/ — *noun* **1** the time during which a king or queen rules. **2** the time during which something rules or is in control: *reign of terror.* — *verb intrans.* **1** to be a monarch. **2** to be present, exist, or dominate: *silence reigns.* [from Latin *regnum*]

▣ *noun* **1** rule, supremacy. *verb* **1** rule, govern, command, hold sway. **2** prevail, predominate.

reigning *adj., said of a winner, champion, etc* holding the title of champion, etc.

reiki /ˈreɪki/ *noun* a Japanese natural therapy, developed in the 19c, using the laying on of hands to channel healing energy into the body and so activate natural healing processes. [from Japanese, = universal energy]

reimburse *verb* to pay (a person) money to cover (expenses, losses, etc). [from RE- + Latin *imbursare*, from *bursa*, purse]

▣ refund, repay, return, restore, recompense, compensate, indemnify, remunerate.

reimbursement *noun* **1** reimbursing. **2** repayment.

rein — *noun* **1** (*usually* **reins**) each of two straps attached to a bridle for guiding a horse. **2** (**reins**) a set of similar straps for guiding a young child. **3** a means of control or government: *take the reins.* — *verb* (*usually* **rein someone** or **something in**) to stop or restrain them with or as if with reins. — **give a free rein to someone** to allow them freedom to act as they think fit. **keep a tight rein on something** or **someone** to keep strict control of them. [from Old French *resne*]

reincarnate — *verb* to cause (a person or soul) to be born again after death in a different body. — *adj.* reborn. [from Latin *incarnare*, to make flesh]

reincarnation *noun* **1** in some beliefs, the rebirth of the soul in another body after death. **2** a person who has been reincarnated. **3** an idea or principle presented in a different form.

reindeer *noun* (PL. **reindeer, reindeers**) a species of deer found in arctic and subarctic regions of Europe and Asia, closely related to the N American caribou. It is the only deer in which the female bears antlers, and it has been domesticated in Scandinavia and S Siberia for centuries for its meat, milk, hide, and hair, and for pulling sledges, etc. The Chernobyl accident in 1986 caused serious pollution of reindeer herds that had eaten contaminated plants. [from Norse *hreindýri*]

reinforce *verb* **1** to make stronger or give additional support to. **2** to make (an army, force, etc) stronger by providing more soldiers and weapons, etc. [from earlier *renforce*, from French *renforcer*]

▣ **1** strengthen, fortify, toughen, harden, stiffen, steel, brace, support, buttress, shore, prop, stay, supplement, augment, increase, emphasize, stress, underline.

▣ **1** weaken, undermine.

reinforced concrete *Engineering* concrete in which steel bars or wires have been embedded in order to increase its tensile strength.

reinforcement *noun* **1** the act of reinforcing. **2** anything which reinforces. **3** (**reinforcements**) soldiers, etc added to an army, force, etc to make it stronger.

▣ **1, 2** strengthening, support, stiffening, fortification. **1** augmentation, supplementation, increase, underlining, stressing, emphasizing. **2, 3** backup. **2** brace, strut, prop, buttress. **3** reserves, auxiliaries.

reinstate *verb* to restore to a former, more powerful, position, status, or rank. [from RE- + *instate*, to install]

▣ restore, return, replace, recall, reappoint, reinstall, re-establish.

reinstatement *noun* **1** reinstating. **2** re-establishment.

reissue /riːˈɪʃuː, riːˈɪsjuː/ *verb* to issue again. — *noun* a magazine, etc that is issued again.

reiterate *verb* to repeat, especially several times. [from Latin *reiterare*]

reiteration *noun* reiterating.

reject /rɪˈdʒɛkt, ˈriːdʒɛkt/ — *verb* (with stress on *-ject*) **1** to refuse to accept, agree to, admit, believe, etc. **2** to throw away or discard. **3** *said of the body* to fail to accept (new tissue or an organ from another body). — *noun* (with stress on *re-*) a person or thing which is rejected. [from Latin *rejicere*, from *jacere*, to throw]

▣ *verb* **1** refuse, deny, decline, turn down, veto, disallow, condemn, despise, spurn, rebuff, jilt, exclude, repudiate, repel, renounce. **2** scrap, discard, jettison, cast off. *noun* failure, second, discard, cast-off.

▣ *verb* **1** accept, choose, select.

rejection *noun* **1** rejecting or being rejected. **2** something that is rejected.

▣ **1** refusal, denial, veto, dismissal, rebuff, *colloq.* brush-off, exclusion, repudiation, renunciation, elimination.

▣ **1** acceptance, choice, selection.

rejig *verb* (**rejigged, rejigging**) **1** to re-equip. **2** to rearrange, often in a way which is considered dishonest or unethical.

rejoice *verb* **1** *intrans.* to feel or show great happiness. **2** *trans.* to give joy to; to make glad. [from Old French *rejouir*]

▣ DELIGHT. **1** celebrate, revel, glory, exult, triumph.

rejoicer *noun* **1** a person who rejoices. **2** a person or thing that causes rejoicing.

rejoicing *noun* **1** being joyful. **2** an expression, subject, or experience of joy. **3** festivities, celebrations, merrymaking.

▣ **1** happiness, gladness, joy, delight, elation, jubilation, exultation, triumph. **3** celebration, revelry, merrymaking, festivity.

rejoin[1] *verb* **1** to say in reply, especially abruptly or wittily. **2** *intrans. Legal* to reply to a charge or pleading. [from Old French *rejoindre*]

rejoin[2] *verb intrans., trans.* to join again.

rejoinder *noun* **1** an answer or remark, especially one made abruptly or wittily in reply. **2** *Legal* a defendant's answer to a plaintiff.

rejuvenate *verb trans.* to make (a person) feel, look, etc young again. [from Latin *juvenis*, young]

∎ revitalize, reinvigorate, reanimate, revive, renew, freshen up.

rejuvenation *noun* rejuvenating.

relapse — *verb intrans.* to return to a former bad or undesirable state or condition such as ill health or bad habits. — *noun* the act or process of relapsing, especially a return to ill health after a partial recovery. [from Latin *relabi*, from *labi*, to slide]

∎ *verb* lapse, revert, regress, backslide, worsen, deteriorate, degenerate, weaken, sink, fail. *noun* worsening, deterioration, setback, recurrence, weakening, lapse, reversion, regression, backsliding.

relate *verb* **1** to tell or narrate (a story). **2 (relate one thing to or with another)** to show or form a connection or relationship between facts, events, etc: *related his unhappiness to a deprived childhood*. **3** *intrans.* **(relate to or with something)** to have or form a connection or relationship: *crime relates to poverty*. **4** *intrans.* **(relate to something)** to be about or concerned with: *I have information relating to/ that relates to their activities*. **5** *intrans.* **(relate to someone)** *colloq.* to get on well with them; to react favourably to them. [from Latin *relatus*, brought back]

∎ **1** tell, recount, narrate, report, describe, recite. **2, 3** link to, connect to. **2** associate with, correlate with. **4** refer to, apply to, concern, pertain to, appertain to. **5** identify with, sympathize with, empathize with, understand, feel for.

related *adj.* **1** belonging to the same family. **2** connected.

∎ **2** associated, connected, linked, akin, interrelated, interconnected, affiliated, allied, accompanying, concomitant, joint, mutual.
Ⅎ **2** unrelated, unconnected.

relation *noun* **1** a connection or relationship between one person or thing and another. **2** a person who belongs to the same family through birth or marriage; a relative. **3** kinship. **4** reference; respect: *in relation to*. **5** a telling or narrating. **6 (relations)** social, political, or personal contact between people, countries, etc. **7 (relations)** sexual intercourse.

∎ **1** link, connection, bond, relationship, correlation, comparison, similarity, affiliation, interrelation, interconnection, interdependence. **2, 3** kindred. **2** relative, family, kin, kinsman, kinswoman, sibling, *colloq.* in-law. **3** kinship, consanguinity. **4** regard, reference, respect. **5** telling, recounting, narration, recital, description, statement. **6** contact, associations, connections, links, ties, dealings, affairs, communications, intercourse, interaction, rapport, liaison, terms. **7** (sexual) intercourse, sex, coitus, intimacy, affair, liaison.

relationship *noun* **1** the state of being related. **2** the state of being related by birth or marriage. **3** the friendship, contact, communications, etc which exist between people, countries, etc. **4** an emotional or sexual affair.

∎ **1, 3** bond, connection, association. **1, 3** link, rapport. **1** affinity, closeness, similarity, parallel, correlation, ratio, proportion. **2** kindred, kinship, consanguinity. **3** contact, relations, ties, dealings, affairs, communications.

4 affair, love affair, romance, intimacy, liaison, friendship.

relative — *noun* a person who is related to someone else by birth or marriage. — *adj.* **1** compared with something else; comparative: *the relative speeds of a car and train*. **2** existing only in relation to something else: *'hot' and 'cold' are relative terms*. **3 (relative to something)** in proportion to it: *salary relative to experience*. **4** which relates to; relevant: *information relative to the problem*. **5** *Grammar* a said *of a pronoun* referring to something real or implied which has already been stated and attaching a subordinate clause to it, as *who* in *the children who are leaving*. b *said of a clause* attached to a preceding word, phrase, etc by a relative word such as *which* and *who*. **6** *Mus.*, *said of major and minor keys* having the same key signature. [from Latin *relativus*]

∎ *noun* relation, family, kin, kindred, kinsman, kinswoman, sibling. *adj.* **1** comparative, respective. **3** proportional to, proportionate to, commensurate with, corresponding to. **4** appropriate, relevant, applicable, related, connected, interrelated, dependent.

relative atomic mass *Chem.* the average mass of one atom of all the naturally occurring isotopes of a particular chemical element, expressed in atomic mass units. Also called ATOMIC WEIGHT.

relative density *Physics* the ratio of the density of a particular substance to that of some standard, usually water at 20°C; formerly known as specific gravity.

relative humidity *Physics* the ratio of the amount of water vapour present in the air to the amount that would be present if the air was saturated (at the same temperature and pressure). It is usually expressed as a percentage.

relatively *adv.* **1** in a relative way. **2** comparatively.

∎ **2** comparatively, fairly, moderately, reasonably, rather, quite, somewhat.

relativism *noun* a philosophical position that maintains that there are truths and values, but denies that they are absolute. It asserts that what may be true or rational in one situation may not be true or rational in another.

relativity *noun* **1** the condition of being relative to and therefore affected by something else. **2** (*in full* **general theory of relativity**, **special theory of relativity**) two theories of motion developed by Albert Einstein, which recognize the dependence of space, time, and other physical measurements on the position and motion of the observer who is making the measurements.

relax *verb* **1** *trans., intrans.* to make or become less tense, nervous, or worried. **2** *intrans.* to rest completely from work or effort. **3** *trans., intrans.* to make or become less strict or severe: *relax the rules*. **4** to lessen the force, strength, or intensity of: *relax one's vigilance*. **5** *intrans.* to become weak or loose. [from Latin *relaxare*]

∎ **1** calm. **2** rest, unwind, wind down, *slang* chill out, let up. **3** soften, moderate, abate, remit, ease. **4** lessen, reduce, diminish, weaken, lower. **5** slacken, loosen.
Ⅎ **4, 5** tighten (up). **4** intensify.

relaxant *noun Medicine* a drug that can make a person feel less tense and help him or her relax.

relaxation *noun* **1** the act of relaxing or state of being relaxed. **2** rest after work or effort. **3** a relaxing activity.

∎ **1** slackening, lessening, reduction, moderation, abatement, *colloq.* let-up, détente, easing. **2, 3** recreation, amusement, entertainment. **2** rest, repose, refreshment, fun, leisure, enjoyment, pleasure.
Ⅎ **1** tension, intensification.

relaxation therapy *Medicine* a form of therapy that involves learning to relax certain muscle groups, with the aim of eventually being able to relax the entire body, especially in stressful situations.

relaxed *adj.* **1** loosened, not tense, at ease. **2** *informal*, tolerant, not strict.

. . . .

☰ **1** at ease, unhurried, leisurely, cool, calm, composed, collected. **2** *informal*, casual, *colloq.* laid back, easy-going, carefree, happy-go-lucky.
☷ **1** tense, nervous. **2** formal.

. . . .

relaxing *adj.* that relaxes.

relay /ˈriːleɪ, rɪˈleɪ/ — *noun* (with stress on *re-*) **1** a set of people, supply of materials, etc that replace others doing or being used for some task, etc. **2** *old use* a supply of horses which relieve others on a journey. **3** a relay race. **4** *Electr.* an electrical switching device that, in response to a change in an electric circuit, eg a small change in current, opens or closes one or more contacts in the same or another circuit. Relays have been largely superseded by transistors and other solid-state devices. **5** *Telecomm.* a device fitted at regular intervals along TV broadcasting networks, underwater telecommunications cables, etc to amplify weak signals and pass them on from one communication link to the next. **6** something, especially a signal or broadcast, which is relayed. — *verb* (with variable stress) (**relayed**) **1** to receive and pass on (news, a message, a television programme, etc). **2** *Radio* to rebroadcast (a programme received from another station or source). [from Old French *relaier*, to leave behind]

. . . .

☰ *noun* **1** shift, turn, relief. **6** broadcast, transmission, programme, communication, message, dispatch. *verb* **1** broadcast, transmit, communicate, send, spread, carry, supply.

. . . .

relay race a race between teams of runners, swimmers, etc in which each member of the team runs, swims, etc part of the total distance to be covered.

release — *verb* **1** to free (a prisoner, etc) from captivity. **2** to relieve (someone) suffering from something unpleasant, a duty, burden, etc. **3** to loosen one's grip and stop holding. **4** to make (news, information, etc) known publicly. **5** to offer (a film, record, book, etc) for sale, performance, etc. **6** to move (a catch, brake, etc) so that it no longer prevents something from moving, operating, etc. **7** to give off or emit (heat, gas, etc). — *noun* **1** the act of releasing or state of being released, from captivity, duty, oppression, etc. **2** the act of making available for sale, performance, publication, etc. **3** something made available for sale, performance, etc, especially a new record or film. **4** an item of news which is made public, or a document containing this. **5** an order or document allowing a prisoner, etc to be released. **6** a handle or catch which holds and releases part of a mechanism. [from Old French *relaissier*]

. . . .

☰ *verb* **1** free, liberate, deliver, emancipate, acquit, absolve, exonerate. **2** excuse, exempt, discharge. **3** loose, unloose, unleash. **4** issue, publish, circulate, distribute. **5** present, launch, unveil. **6** unfasten, unlock. *noun* **1** freedom, liberty, liberation, deliverance, emancipation, acquittal, absolution, exoneration, exemption, discharge. **2** issue, publication, announcement, proclamation.
☷ *verb* **1** imprison, detain. *noun* **1** imprisonment, detention.

. . . .

relegate *verb* **1** to move (someone, a sports team, etc) down to a lower grade, position, status, division, etc. **2** to refer (a decision, etc) to (someone or something) for action to be taken. [from Latin *relegare*, to send away]

. . . .

☰ **1** demote, downgrade, degrade, reduce. **2** refer, delegate.

. . . .

relegation *noun* relegating or being relegated.

relent *verb intrans.* **1** to become less severe or unkind. **2** to give way and agree to something one initially would not accept. [from Latin *re-*, back + *lentus*, flexible]

. . . .

☰ **WEAKEN. 1** unbend, relax, slacken, soften. **2** give in, give way, yield, capitulate.

. . . .

relentless *adj.* **1** without pity; harsh. **2** never stopping; unrelenting: *a relentless fight against crime.*

. . . .

☰ **REMORSELESS, UNRELENTING. 1** ruthless, implacable, merciless, pitiless, unforgiving, cruel, harsh, fierce, grim, hard, punishing, uncompromising, inflexible, unyielding, inexorable. **2** unremitting, incessant, persistent, unflagging.
☷ **1** merciful, yielding.

. . . .

relet *verb* to let (property, land, etc) again.

relevance or **relevancy** *noun* being relevant.

. . . .

☰ applicability, appositeness, aptness, appropriateness, suitability, pertinence, materiality, significance, germaneness, admissibility.
☷ irrelevance, inapplicability, inappropriateness, unsuitability.

. . . .

relevant *adj.* directly connected with the matter in hand, being discussed, etc. [from Latin *relevare*, to raise up, relieve]

. . . .

☰ pertinent, material, significant, germane, related, applicable, apposite, apt, appropriate, suitable, fitting, proper, admissible.
☷ irrelevant, inapplicable, inappropriate, unsuitable.

. . . .

reliability *noun* being reliable.

. . . .

☰ certainty, sureness, dependability, responsibility, trustworthiness, honesty, faithfulness, constancy, regularity, stability.
☷ unreliabilty, untrustworthiness, doubtfulness.

. . . .

reliable *adj.* able to be trusted or relied on.

. . . .

☰ unfailing, certain, sure, dependable, responsible, trusty, trustworthy, honest, true, faithful, constant, staunch, solid, safe, sound, stable, predictable, regular.
☷ unreliable, doubtful, untrustworthy.

. . . .

reliably *adv.* in a reliable way.

reliance *noun* the act or state of relying or depending upon, or trusting in, a person or thing.

. . . .

☰ dependence, trust, faith, belief, confidence, assurance.

. . . .

reliant *adj.* relying on or having confidence in, trusting.

relic *noun* **1** (*often* **relics**) a part or fragment of an object left after the rest has decayed. **2** any object valued as being a memorial or souvenir of the past. **3** something left from a past time, especially a custom, belief or practice, etc. **4** part of the body of a saint or martyr or of some object connected with him or her, preserved as holy. **5** (**relics**) the remains of a dead person; a corpse. [from Latin *reliquiae*, remains]

. . . .

☰ **1** remains, remnant, scrap, fragment, vestige, trace.
2 memento, souvenir, keepsake, token.

. . . .

relict /ˈrelɪkt, rɪˈlɪkt/ *noun Biol.* a species occurring in circumstances different from those in which it originated. [from Latin *relictus*, left]

relief *noun* **1** the lessening or removal of pain, worry, oppression, or distress. **2** the calmness, relaxation, happiness, etc which follows the lessening or removal of pain, worry, etc. **3** anything which lessens pain, worry, boredom or monotony. **4** help, often in the form of money, food, clothing, and medicine, given to people in need. **5** a person who takes over a job or task from another person, usually after a given period of time. **6** a bus, train, etc which supplements public transport at particularly busy times. **7** the freeing of a besieged or endangered town, fortress, or military post. **8** a method of sculpture in which figures project from a flat surface. **9** a clear, sharp outline caused by contrast. **10** the variations in height above sea level of an area of land. [from Old French *relief*, from Latin *relevare*, to reduce the load]

⊟ **1** alleviation, cure, remedy, easing, abatement, remission, release, deliverance. **2, 3** reassurance, consolation, comfort. **3** refreshment, diversion, relaxation, rest, respite, break, *colloq.* breather, *colloq.* let-up. **4** help, aid, assistance, support, sustenance.

relief map a map which shows the variations in the height of the land, either by shading, or by being a three-dimensional model.

relieve *verb* **1** to lessen or stop (a person's pain, worry, boredom, etc). **2 (relieve someone of something)** to take a physical or mental burden from them: *relieved her of many responsibilities.* **3 (relieve someone of something)** *facetious* to take or steal it from them: *the thief relieved him of his wallet.* **4** to give help or assistance to (someone in need). **5** to make less monotonous or tedious, especially by providing a contrast. **6** to free or dismiss from a duty or restriction. **7** to take over a job or task from (someone). **8** to come to the help of (a besieged town, fortress, military post, etc). — **relieve oneself** to urinate or defecate. [from Latin *relevare*, to reduce the load]

⊟ **1** alleviate, mitigate, cure, remedy, reassure, console, comfort, ease, soothe, lighten, soften, slacken, relax, calm. **2, 6** release, free. **2** deliver, unburden, liberate. **4** help, aid, assist, support, sustain, succour. **6** exempt, excuse, discharge.
⊡ **1** aggravate, intensify.

relieved *adj.* freed from anxiety or concern, usually about a particular matter.

religion *noun* **1** a belief in, or the worship of, a god or gods. **2** a particular system of belief or worship, such as Christianity or Judaism. **3** anything to which one is totally devoted and which rules one's life: *mountaineering is his religion.* **4** the monastic way of life. [from Latin *religio*]

Religions include: Christianity, Church of England (C of E), Church of Scotland, Baptists, Catholicism, Methodism, Protestantism, Presbyterianism, Anglicanism, Congregationalism, Calvinism, evangelicalism, Free Church, Jehovah's Witnesses, Mormonism, Quakerism, Amish; Baha'ism, Buddhism, Confucianism, Hinduism, Islam, Jainism, Judaism, Sikhism, Taoism, Shintoism, Zen, Zoroastrianism, voodoo, druidism.

religious — *adj.* **1** of or relating to religion. **2** following the rules or forms of worship of a particular religion very closely; pious; devout. **3** taking great care to do something properly; conscientious. **4** of or relating to the monastic way of life. — *noun* (PL. **religious**) a person bound by monastic vows, eg a monk or nun.

⊟ *adj.* **1** sacred, holy, divine, spiritual, devotional, scriptural, theological, doctrinal. **2** devout, godly, pious, God-fearing, church-going, reverent, righteous. **3** conscientious, careful, attentive, meticulous, painstaking, scrupulous, punctilious.
⊡ *adj.* **1** secular. **2** irreligious, ungodly.

Religious officers include: abbess, abbot, archbishop, archdeacon, bishop, canon, cardinal, chancellor, chaplain, clergy, clergyman, clergywoman, curate, deacon, deaconess, dean, elder, father, friar, minister, monk, Monsignor, mother superior, nun, padre, parson, pastor, pope, prelate, priest, prior, proctor, rector, vicar; ayatollah, Dalai Lama, guru, imam, rabbi.

religiously *adv.* **1** in a religious way. **2** conscientiously.
religious order see ORDER.
relinquish *verb* **1** to give up or abandon. **2** to release one's hold of. **3** to renounce possession or control of (a claim, right, etc). [from Latin *relinquere*, to leave behind]

⊟ **1, 3** hand over, surrender, yield, cede, give up, resign, renounce, repudiate, waive, forgo, abandon. **1** desert, forsake, drop, discard. **2** let go, release, drop.
⊡ KEEP, RETAIN.

relinquishment *noun* relinquishing.
reliquary /ˈrɛlɪkwərɪ/ *noun* (PL. **reliquaries**) a container for holy relics. [from Latin *reliquiae*, remains]
relish — *verb* **1** to enjoy greatly or with discrimination. **2** to look forward to with great pleasure. — *noun* **1** pleasure; enjoyment. **2** a spicy appetizing flavour, or a sauce or pickle which adds this to food. **3** zest, charm, liveliness, or gusto. [from Old French *reles*, remainder]

⊟ *verb* **1** like, enjoy, savour, appreciate, revel in. *noun* **1** enjoyment, pleasure, delight. **2** seasoning, condiment, sauce, pickle, spice, piquancy, tang. **3** gusto, zest, liveliness, vivacity, vigour, charm.

relive /riːˈlɪv/ *verb* to experience again, especially in the imagination.
reload *verb trans., intrans.* **1** to load (a gun, etc) with fresh ammunition, etc. **2** to load (data) into a computer again.
relocate *verb trans., intrans.* to move (a business, one's home, etc) from one place, town, etc to another.
relocation *noun* relocating or being relocated.
reluctance *noun* **1** unwillingness; lack of enthusiasm. **2** *Physics* (SYMBOL **R**) a measure of the opposition to magnetic flux in a magnetic circuit, analogous to resistance in an electric circuit. [from Latin *reluctari*, to resist]

⊟ **1** unwillingness, hesitancy, slowness, backwardness, loathness, unenthusiasm, disinclination, grudgingness.
⊡ willingness, readiness, eagerness.

reluctant *adj.* unwilling; not wanting.

⊟ unwilling, disinclined, indisposed, hesitant, slow, backward, loth, averse, unenthusiastic, grudging.
⊡ willing, ready, eager.

reluctantly *adv.* with reluctance, in a reluctant way.
rely *verb* (**relies**, **relied**) (**rely on** or **upon someone** or **something**) **1** to depend on or need them. **2** to trust someone to do something; to be certain of something happening. [from Old French *relier*, to bind together]

⊟ **1** depend on, lean on, need. **2** count on, bank on, reckon on, trust, swear by.

REM *abbrev.* rapid eye movement.
remain *verb intrans.* **1** to be left when something else, another part, etc has been lost, taken away, used up, etc. **2** to stay in the same place; to not leave. **3** to be still (the same); to continue to be. **4** to still need (to be done, shown, dealt with, etc): *that remains to be decided.* [from Latin *remanere*, to stay behind]

🔲 **2** stay, rest, linger, wait, dwell. **3** stand, abide, last, endure, survive, prevail, persist, continue.
🔳 **2** go, leave, depart. **3** disappear.

remainder — *noun* **1** the number or part that is left after the rest has gone, been taken away, used up, etc. **2** *Maths.* the amount left over when one number cannot be divided exactly by another number: *7 divided by 2 gives 3 with a remainder of 1.* **3** *Maths.* the amount left when one number is subtracted from another. **4** a copy of a book which is sold at a reduced price when demand for that book comes to an end. **5** *Legal* an interest in an estate which comes into effect only if another interest established at the same time comes to an end. — *verb* (**remaindered, remaindering**) to sell (a book) at a reduced price because demand for it has come to an end.

🔲 *noun* **1** rest, balance, surplus, excess, remnant, remains, residue.

remaining *adj.* left after the rest has been taken away, used up, has come to an end, etc.

🔲 left, unused, unspent, unfinished, residual, left-over, outstanding, surviving, persisting, lingering, lasting, abiding.

remains *pl. noun* **1** what is left after part has been taken away, eaten, destroyed, etc. **2** a dead body.

🔲 **1** rest, remainder, residue, dregs, leavings, leftovers, scraps, crumbs, fragments, remnants, oddments, traces, vestiges, relics. **2** body, corpse, carcase, ashes, debris.

remake — *verb* (with stress on *-make*) (PAST TENSE AND PAST PARTICIPLE **remade**) to make again, especially in a new way. — *noun* (with stress on *re-*) something which is made again, especially a new version of a cinema film.

remand — *verb* to send (a person accused of a crime) back into custody until more evidence can be collected and the case can be tried. — *noun* the act of remanding.— **on remand** having been remanded in prison or on bail. [from Latin *remandare*, to send back word, to repeat a command]

remand centre *Brit.* a place of detention for those on remand or awaiting trial.

remand home *Brit. old use* a place to which a judge may send a child or young person who has broken the law, either on remand or as punishment.

remark — *verb* **1** *trans., intrans.* (**remark something** or **remark on something**) to notice and comment on it. **2** to make a comment. — *noun* a comment; an observation. [from Old French *remarque*]

🔲 *verb* OBSERVE, NOTE. **1** notice, comment on. **2** comment, mention, say, state, declare. *noun* comment, observation, opinion, reflection, mention, utterance, statement, assertion, declaration.

remarkable *adj.* worth mentioning or commenting on; unusual; extraordinary.

🔲 striking, impressive, noteworthy, surprising, amazing, strange, odd, unusual, uncommon, extraordinary, phenomenal, exceptional, outstanding, notable, conspicuous, prominent, distinguished.
🔳 average, ordinary, commonplace, usual.

remarkably *adv.* in a remarkable way.

remarry *verb trans., intrans.* (**remarries, remarried**) to marry again, especially after a separation.

REME *abbrev.* Royal Electrical and Mechanical Engineers.

remediable *adj.* capable of being remedied.

remedial *adj.* **1** serving as a remedy; able to or intended to correct or put right. **2** *said of teaching* intended to help those pupils with learning difficulties.

remedially *adv.* as a remedy.

remedy — *noun* (PL. **remedies**) **1** any drug or treatment which cures or controls a disease. **2** anything which solves a problem or gets rid of something undesirable: *a remedy for the country's economic problems.* — *verb* (**remedies, remedied**) to put right or correct; to be a remedy for. [from Latin *remedium*]

🔲 *noun* CURE, ANTIDOTE. **1** medicine, treatment, therapy, restorative. **2** countermeasure, corrective, relief, solution, answer, panacea. *verb* correct, rectify, put right, redress, counteract, cure, heal, restore, treat, help, relieve, soothe, ease, mitigate, mend, repair, fix, solve.

remember *verb* (**remembered, remembering**) **1** *trans., intrans.* to bring to mind (something or someone that had been forgotten). **2** to keep (a fact, idea, etc) in one's mind. **3** to reward or make a present to, eg in one's will. **4** to pass (a person's) good wishes and greetings to: *remember me to your parents.* **5** to commemorate. [from Latin *rememorari*]

🔲 **1** recall, recollect, think back (to), reminisce (about). **2** memorize, learn, retain.
🔳 **1, 2** forget.

remembrance *noun* **1** the act of remembering or being remembered. **2** something which reminds a person of something or someone; a souvenir. **3** a memory or recollection: *a dim remembrance of the night's events.*

🔲 **1, 3** memory, recollection, reminiscence. **1** recall, recognition. **2** souvenir, keepsake, token.

Remembrance Day or **Remembrance Sunday** in the UK, the Sunday nearest to 11 Nov, on which services are held to commemorate servicemen and servicewomen who have died in war.

remind *verb* (**remind someone of something**) **1** to cause them to remember it. **2** to make them think about someone or something else, especially because of a similarity: *she reminds me of her sister.*

🔲 *verb* **1** prompt, nudge, hint to, jog someone's memory, refresh someone's memory. **2** bring to mind, call to mind, call up.

reminder *noun* something that makes a person remember something or someone.

🔲 *noun* prompt, nudge, hint, suggestion, memorandum, memo, souvenir, memento.

reminisce /rɛmɪˈnɪs/ *verb intrans.* to think, talk, or write about things remembered from the past. [from Latin *reminisci*, to remember]

reminiscence /rɛmɪˈnɪsəns/ *noun* **1** the act of thinking, talking, or writing about the past. **2** an experience remembered from the past.

🔲 MEMORY, REMEMBRANCE, RECOLLECTION. **1** recall, retrospection, review, reflection, nostalgia. **2** memoir, anecdote.

reminiscent /rɛmɪˈnɪsənt/ *adj.* **1** (**reminiscent of something**) reminding one of them: *a painting reminiscent of Turner.* **2** *said of a person* thinking often about the past; given to reminiscing.

▣ **1** suggestive of, evocative of, redolent of. **2** nostalgic.

remiss *adj.* failing to pay attention or to use sufficient care. [from Latin *remittere*, to loosen]

▣ careless, negligent, neglectful, inattentive, lax, slack, thoughtless, casual, wayward.

remission *noun* **1** a lessening in force or effect, especially in the symptoms of a disease. **2** a reduction of a prison sentence. **3** pardon; forgiveness from sin. **4** an act of remitting. [from Latin *remissio*, from *remittere*, to loosen]

remissly *adj.* carelessly, negligently.

remissness *noun* being remiss.

remit — *verb* (with stress on -*mit*) (**remitted, remitting**) **1** to cancel or refrain from demanding (a debt, punishment, etc). **2** *trans.*, *intrans.* to make or become loose, slack, or relaxed. **3** to send (money) in payment. **4** to refer (a matter for decision, etc) to some other authority. **5** to refer (a case) to a lower court. **6** *intrans. said of a disease, pain, rain, etc* to become less severe for a period of time. **7** to send or put back into a previous state. **8** *said of God* to forgive (sins). — *noun* (usually with stress on *re-*) the authority or terms of reference given to an official, committee, etc in dealing with a matter. [from Latin *remittere*, to loosen]

▣ *verb* **1** cancel, set aside, hold over, suspend. **3** send, transmit, dispatch, post, mail, forward, pay, settle. *noun* brief, orders, instructions, guidelines, terms of reference, parameters, scope, authorization, responsibility, jurisdiction.

remittance *noun* **1** the sending of money in payment. **2** the money sent.

▣ PAYMENT. **1** sending, dispatch. **2** fee, allowance, consideration, retainer.

remittent *adj., said of a disease* becoming less severe at times.

remix — *verb* (with stress on -*mix*) to mix again in a different way, especially to mix (a record) again, changing the balance of the different parts, etc. — *noun* (with stress on *re-*) a remixed recording.

remnant *noun* **1** a small piece or amount of something larger, or a small number of a large quantity of things left unsold, especially a piece of material from the end of a roll. **2** a surviving trace or vestige. [from Old French *remenoir*, to remain]

▣ LEFTOVER. **1** scrap, piece, bit, fragment, end, off cut, shred. **2** trace, vestige, remainder, balance, residue.

remonstrance /rɪ'mɒnstrəns/ *noun* **1** an act of remonstrating. **2** a strong, usually formal, protest. [from Latin *remonstrare*, to demonstrate]

remonstrate /'remənstreɪt, rɪ'mɒnstreɪt/ *verb trans., intrans.* **1** (**remonstrate with someone**) to protest to them. **2** to protest forcefully: *remonstrated that they knew nothing about it.* [from Latin *remonstrare*, to demonstrate]

▣ **1** protest to, complain to, appeal to, plead with, argue with, quarrel with, join issue with, reproach, reprove, rebuke, reprimand, scold.

remonstration *noun* **1** remonstrating. **2** an instance of this.

remorse *noun* a deep feeling of guilt, regret, and bitterness for something wrong or bad which one has done. [from Latin *remorsus*]

▣ regret, repentance, penitence, contrition, self-reproach, shame, guilt, bad conscience, compunction, ruefulness, sorrow, grief.

remorseful *adj.* full of remorse, sorrowful.

▣ regretful, repentant, penitent, contrite, ashamed, guilty, rueful, sorrowful.

remorsefully *adv.* in a remorseful way, sorrowfully.

remorseless *adj.* cruel; without pity.

▣ relentless, unrelenting, ruthless, implacable, merciless, pitiless, unforgiving, cruel, harsh, fierce, grim, hard, punishing, uncompromising, inflexible, unyielding, inexorable, unremitting, incessant.

remorselessly *adv.* in a remorseless way.

remote *adj.* **1** far away or distant in time or place. **2** out of the way; away from civilization. **3** operated or controlled from a distance. **4** distantly related. **5** very small or slight: *a remote chance.* **6** *said of a person's manner* not friendly or interested; aloof. [from Latin *remotus*, removed]

▣ **1, 2** outlying, out-of-the-way, inaccessible, isolated, secluded. **1** distant, far, faraway, far-off. **2** God-forsaken, lonely. **5** slight, small, slim, slender, faint, negligible, unlikely, improbable. **6** detached, aloof, standoffish, uninvolved, reserved, withdrawn.

F⃥ **1, 2** close, nearby, accessible. **6** friendly, approachable.

remote control *Electron.* the control of machinery or electrical devices from a distance, by the making or breaking of an electric circuit, or by means of radio waves, eg remote control television.

remote-controlled *adj.* operated by remote control.

remotely *adv.* in a remote way or degree: *not remotely the same.*

remoteness *noun* being remote.

remould /ri:'məʊld, 'ri:məʊld/ — *verb* (with stress on -*mould*) to bond new tread on to (an old or worn tyre). — *noun* (with stress on *re-*) a worn tyre which has had new tread bonded on to it.

remount — *verb trans., intrans.* (with stress on -*mount*) to mount again, especially on a fresh horse. — *noun* (with stress on *re-*) a fresh horse.

removable *adj.* capable of being removed.

removal *noun* **1** the act of removing or state of being removed. **2** the moving of furniture, etc to a new home.

▣ **1** move, moving, transfer, shift, shifting, transporting, displacement, relocation, detachment, amputation, extraction, withdrawal, elimination, abolition, discharge, dismissal, ejection.

remove — *verb* **1** to move (a person, thing, etc) to a different place. **2** to take off or detach. **3** to get rid of. **4** to dismiss (from a job, position, etc). **5** *intrans.* to change one's position, place, location, etc, especially to move to a new house. — *noun* **1** a removal. **2** the degree of difference separating two things: *a form of government which is at only one remove from tyranny.* **3** *Brit.* an intermediate form or class in some schools. [from Latin *removere*]

▣ *verb* **1, 5** move, transfer, relocate. **1** shift, transport, carry, convey. **2** take away, take off, detach, pull off, amputate, cut off, extract, pull out, withdraw, strip, shed, doff. **3** get rid of, eliminate, expunge, efface, erase, delete, strike out, abolish, purge. **4** dismiss, discharge, eject, throw out, oust.

removed *adj.* **1** separated or distant. **2** *said of cousins* separated by a usually specified number of generations.

remover *noun* a person or thing that removes, especially who moves furniture, etc from one house to another.

remunerate *verb* **1** to pay for services done. **2** to recompense. [from Latin *remunerari*, from *munus*, gift]

remuneration *noun* **1** remunerating or being remunerated. **2** recompense, reward, pay.

◫ PAYMENT, REPAYMENT, REIMBURSEMENT, COMPENSATION. **2** pay, wages, salary, emolument, stipend, fee, retainer, remittance, earnings, income, profit, reward, recompense, indemnity.

remunerative *adj.* bringing a good profit or having a good salary.

Renaissance /rɪˈneɪsəns, rɪˈneɪsɒns/ the revival of arts, literature, and classical scholarship, and the beginnings of modern science, in Europe in the 14c to 16c.

renaissance /rɪˈneɪsəns, rɪˈneɪsɒns/ *noun* a rebirth or revival, especially of learning, culture, and the arts. [from Latin *renasci*, to be born again]

renal /ˈriːnl/ *adj.* of, relating to, or in the area of the kidneys. [from Latin *renes*, kidneys]

rename *verb* to give a new name to.

renascence /rɪˈnasəns/ *noun* being born again.

renascent /rɪˈnasənt, rɪˈneɪsənt/ *adj.* becoming active or lively again. [from Latin *renasci*, to be born again]

rend *verb* (PAST TENSE AND PAST PARTICIPLE **rent**) *old use* **1** to tear, especially using force or violence. **2** *intrans.* to become torn, especially violently. [from Anglo-Saxon *rendan*]

render *verb* (**rendered, rendering**) **1** to cause to become. **2** to give or provide (help, a service, etc). **3** to pay (money) or perform (a duty), especially in return for something: *render thanks to God.* **4** (also **render something up**) to give up, release, or yield: *the grave will never render up its dead.* **5** to translate. **6** to perform (the role of a character in a play, a piece of music, etc). **7** to portray or reproduce, especially in painting or music. **8** to present or submit for payment, approval, consideration, etc. **9** to cover (brick or stone) with a coat of plaster. **10** (**render something down**) to melt down fat, especially to clarify it; to remove fat by melting. [from Old French *rendre*]

◫ **1** make, cause to be, leave. **2, 3** give, tender, present. **2** provide, supply, submit, hand over, deliver. **5** translate, interpret, transcribe, explain, clarify, represent. **6** perform, play, sing.

rendering *noun* **1** a coat of plaster. **2** a performance.

rendezvous /ˈrɒndeɪvuː/ — *noun* **1** an appointment to meet, or the meeting itself, at a specified time and in a specified place. **2** the place where such a meeting is to be; a place where people meet. — *verb intrans.* to meet at an appointed place. [from French *rendezvous*, present yourselves]

◫ *noun* meeting, appointment, *colloq.* date, assignation, *old use* tryst, encounter.

rendition *noun* **1** a performance or interpretation (of a piece of music or a dramatic role, etc). **2** an act of rendering, especially of translating. [from Old French]

◫ **1** rendering, performance, presentation, recital, interpetation.

rendzina /rendˈziːnə/ *noun Geol.* any of a group of dark fertile soils, rich in humus and calcium carbonate, that have developed over limestone bedrock. Large areas of such soils are found in humid or semi-arid grassland and limestone regions. [from Russian *rendzina*, from Polish *redzina*]

renegade *noun* a person who deserts the religious, political, etc group to which he or she belongs to join an enemy or rival group. [from Spanish *renegado*]

renege /rɪˈniːg, rɪˈneɪg/ *verb* **1** *intrans.* (**renege on something**) to go back on a promise, agreement, one's word, etc. **2** to renounce (a promise, etc) or desert (a person, faith, etc). **3** *Cards* to revoke. [from Latin *renegare*, from *negare*, to deny]

reneger *noun* a person who reneges.

renew *verb* **1** to make fresh or like new again; to restore to the original condition. **2** to begin or begin to do again; to repeat. **3** to begin (some activity) again after a break. **4** *trans., intrans.* to make (a licence, lease, loan, etc) valid for a further period of time. **5** to replenish or replace: *renew the water in the vases.* **6** to recover (youth, strength, etc).

◫ **1** renovate, modernize, refurbish, refit, recondition, mend, repair, overhaul, remodel, reform, transform, recreate, reconstitute, re-establish, regenerate, revive, resuscitate, refresh, restore, rejuvenate, rein-vigorate, revitalize. **2, 3** recommence. **2** repeat, restate, reaffirm, extend, prolong, continue. **3** restart, resume. **5** replace, replenish, restock.

renewable *adj.* capable of renewal.

renewable resource any energy source that is naturally occurring and that cannot in theory be exhausted, eg solar energy, hydroelectric power, tidal, wind, or wave power, geothermal energy. See also NON-RENEWABLE RESOURCE.

renewal *noun* **1** renewing or being renewed. **2** something that is renewed.

renewer *noun* a person who renews something.

renin /ˈriːnɪn/ *noun Physiol.* a hormone, produced by the kidneys, that is secreted into the bloodstream, where it constricts the arteries and thereby raises the blood pressure. [from Latin *renes*, the kidneys]

rennet *noun* an extract obtained from the stomachs of calves that contains the enzyme rennin, which curdles milk. It is used to make junket and certain cheeses. [from Middle English]

rennin /ˈrenɪn/ *noun Biochem.* an enzyme, found in gastric juice, that causes milk to curdle. [from RENNET]

renounce *verb* **1** to give up (a claim, title, right, etc), especially formally and publicly. **2** to renounce or associate with. **3** to give up (a bad habit). **4** *intrans. Cards* to fail to follow suit. [from Latin *renuntiare*]

◫ **1, 2, 3** abandon, forsake, give up, repudiate. **1** resign, relinquish, surrender. **2** reject, spurn, disown, disclaim, deny.

renouncement *noun* **1** renouncing. **2** a renunciation.

renouncer *noun* a person who renounces.

renovate *verb* to restore (especially a building) to a former and better condition. [from Latin *renovare*, from *novus*, new]

◫ restore, renew, recondition, repair, overhaul, modernize, refurbish, refit, redecorate, *colloq.* do up, remodel, reform, revamp, improve.

renovation *noun* **1** renovating or being renovated. **2** a renewal.

renovator *noun* a person who renovates.

renown *noun* fame. [from Old French *renom*]

◫ fame, celebrity, stardom, acclaim, glory, eminence, illustriousness, distinction, note, mark, esteem, reputation, honour.
◪ obscurity, anonymity.

renowned *adj.* famous; celebrated.
. . . .
▣ famous, well-known, celebrated, acclaimed, famed, noted, eminent, distinguished, illustrious, notable.
▣ unknown, obscure.
. . . .

rent¹ — *noun* money paid to the owner of a property by a tenant in return for the use or occupation of that property. — *verb* **1** to pay rent for (a building, etc). **2** (**rent something** or **rent something out**) to allow the use of (one's property) in return for payment of rent. **3** *intrans.* to be hired out for rent. [from Old French *rente*]
. . . .
▣ *noun* rental, lease, hire, payment, fee. *verb* **1, 2** lease. **1** hire, charter. **2** *Brit.* let, sublet.
. . . .

rent² *noun old use* an opening or split made by tearing, often violently. [a form of REND]
rental *noun* **1** money paid as rent. **2** the act of renting.
rent boy a young male homosexual prostitute.
renunciation *noun* **1** an act of renouncing. **2** a formal declaration of renouncing something. **3** self-denial. [from Latin *renuntiatio*]
. . . .
▣ **1** repudiation, resignation, relinquishment, surrender, rejection, denial. **2** disclaimer. **3** self-denial, self-sacrifice, asceticism, abstemiousness, selflessness, altruism.
. . . .

reopen *verb* (**reopened, reopening**) **1** *trans., intrans.* to open again. **2** to begin to discuss (a subject which has already been discussed) again.
reorder *verb* **1** to order again; to place a repeat order for (a product, etc). **2** to place or arrange in a diffrent order.
rep *noun* **1** a representative. **2** a repertory company or theatre.
repaint /riːˈpeɪnt, ˈriːpeɪnt/ — *verb* (with stress on *-paint*) to paint over or again. — *noun* (with stress on *re-*) a repainted golf ball.
repair¹ — *verb* **1** to restore (something damaged or broken) to good, working condition. **2** to put right, heal, or make up for (something wrong that has been done). — *noun* **1** an act of repairing. **2** a condition or state: *in good repair.* **3** a part or place that has been mended or repaired. [from Latin *reparare*]
. . . .
▣ *verb* MEND, PATCH UP, RECTIFY. **1** fix, overhaul, service, restore, renovate, renew. **2** redress. *noun* **1** overhaul, service, maintenance, restoration, adjustment, improvement. **3** mend, patch, darn.
. . . .

repair² *verb intrans.* (**repair to a place**) *old use* to go there; to take oneself off to it. [from Latin *repatriare*, to return to one's homeland]
repairable *adj.* capable of being repaired.
reparable /ˈrepərəbl/ *adj.* able to be put right. [from Latin *reparabilis*, able to be repaired]
reparation *noun* **1** the act of making up for (something wrong that has been done). **2** money paid or something done for this purpose. **3** (*usually* **reparations**) compensation paid after a war by a defeated nation for the damage caused. [from Latin *reparatio*]
. . . .
▣ **1, 2** compensation. **1** amends, atonement, expiation, redress. **2** indemnity, damages.
. . . .

repartee /repɑːˈtiː/ *noun* **1** the practice or skill of making spontaneous witty replies. **2** conversation having many such replies. [from French *repartie*]
. . . .
▣ WIT. **2** banter, badinage, jesting, riposte, retort.
. . . .

repast /rɪˈpɑːst/ *noun formal, old use* a meal. [from Old French *repaistre*, to eat a meal]
repatriate *verb* to send (someone) back to their country of origin. [from Latin *repatriare*]
repatriation *noun* repatriating or being repatriated.
repay *verb* (PAST TENSE AND PAST PARTICIPLE **repaid**) **1** to pay back (money). **2** to do or give something to (someone) in return for (something done or given to oneself): *repay his kindness.*
. . . .
▣ PAY BACK. **1** refund, reimburse. **2** compensate, recompense, reward, remunerate, settle with, square, get even with, retaliate against, reciprocate, avenge, revenge.
. . . .

repayable *adj.* that may or must be repaid.
repayment *noun* repaying.
repeal — *verb* to make (a law, etc) no longer valid. — *noun* the act of repealing (a law, etc). [from Old French *repeler*]
. . . .
▣ *verb* revoke, rescind, abrogate, quash, annul, nullify, void, invalidate, cancel, countermand, reverse, abolish.
▣ *verb* enact.
. . . .

repealable *adj.* capable of being repealed.
repeat — *verb* **1** to say, do, etc again. **2** to tell (something one has heard) to someone else, especially when one ought not to. **3** to say (something) from memory. **4** *intrans. said of food* to be tasted again after being swallowed. **5** *intrans.* to occur again; to recur. **6** *intrans. said of a gun* to fire several times without being reloaded. **7** *intrans. said of a clock or watch* to strike the last hour or quarter hour when a spring is pressed. — *noun* **1** an act of repeating. **2** something which is repeated, especially a television programme which has been broadcast before. **3** *Mus.* a musical passage which is to be repeated, or a sign which marks this. — *adj.* repeated: *a repeat showing.* — **repeat itself** to happen in exactly the same way more than once. **repeat oneself** to say the same thing more than once. [from Latin *repetere*, to attack again]
. . . .
▣ *verb* **1** restate, reiterate, recapitulate, echo, relate, retell, reproduce, duplicate, renew, rebroadcast, reshow, replay, rerun, redo. **3** quote, recite. *noun* **1** repetition, reproduction. **2** echo, duplicate, rebroadcast, reshowing, replay, rerun.
. . . .

repeatable *adj.* **1** fit to be told to others. **2** able to be repeated.
repeated *adj.* **1** done again. **2** reiterated.
repeatedly *adv.* again and again, frequently.
. . . .
▣ time after time, time and (time) again, again and again, over and over, frequently, often.
. . . .

repeater *noun* **1** a clock or watch which strikes the last hour or quarter hour if a spring is pressed. **2** a gun which can be fired several times without having to be reloaded. **3** *Maths.* a figure or sequence of figures in a decimal fraction which would recur infinitely.
repel *verb* (**repelled, repelling**) **1** to force or drive back or away. **2** to cause a feeling of disgust or loathing. **3** *trans., intrans.* to fail to mix with, absorb, or be attracted by (something else): *oil repels water.* **4** to reject: *repel his advances.* [from Latin *repellere*, to drive back]
. . . .
▣ **1** drive back, repulse, check, hold off, ward off, parry, resist, oppose, fight. **2** disgust, revolt, nauseate, sicken, offend. **4** reject, rebuff, refuse, decline.
▣ **1** attract. **2** delight.
. . . .

repellent — *noun* something that repels, especially insects. — *adj.* repelling, esp causing a feeling of disgust or loathing.

repellently *adv.* in a repellent way.

repent *verb* **1** *trans., intrans.* (**repent something** or **repent of something**) to feel great sorrow or regret for something one has done; to wish an action, etc undone. **2** *intrans.* to be sorry for all the evil or bad things one has done and decide to live a better life. [from Old French *repentir*]

☒ **1** regret, rue, sorrow (over), lament, deplore, atone. **2** reform, see the light.

repentance *noun* **1** repenting. **2** being penitent.

☒ PENITENCE, CONTRITION. **2** remorse, regret, sorrow, grief, guilt, shame, compunction.

repentant *adj.* experiencing or expressing repentance.

☒ penitent, contrite, sorry, apologetic, remorseful, regretful, rueful, chastened, ashamed.
☒ unrepentant.

repercussion *noun* **1** (*often* **repercussions**) a usually bad unforeseen or indirect result or consequence of some action or event. **2** an echo or reverberation. [from Latin *repercussio*]

☒ **1** result, consequence, aftermath, after-effect, backlash, rebound, recoil. **2** reverberation, echo.

repercussive *adj.* reverberating, echoing, repeated.

repertoire /'repǝtwɑ:(r)/ *noun* **1** the list of songs, plays, operas, etc that a performer, singer, group of actors, etc is able or ready to perform. **2** a range or stock of skills, techniques, talents, etc that someone or something has, eg the total list of commands and codes that a computer can execute. [from French *repertoire*]

repertory /'repǝtǝrɪ/ *noun* (PL. **repertories**) **1** the complete list of plays that a theatre company is able and ready to perform. **2** (*also* **repertory company**) a group of actors who perform a series of plays from their repertoire in the course of a season at one theatre. **3** (*also* **repertory theatre**) a theatre where a repertory company performs its plays. **4** repertory theatres in general: *worked in repertory for a few years.* [from Latin *repertorium*, inventory]

repetition *noun* **1** the act of repeating or being repeated. **2** a thing that is repeated. **3** a copy or replica. **4** something, eg a piece of music, which is played or recited from memory. [from Latin *repetere*, to attack again]

☒ **1, 2** restatement, reiteration, recapitulation, echo, recurrence, tautology. **1** return, reappearance, duplication. **3** copy, replica, duplicate, reproduction.

repetitious /repǝ'tɪʃǝs/ or **repetitive** *adj.* having too much repetition.

☒ boring, monotonous, dull, mechanical, unvarying, unchanging.

repetitiously or **repetitively** *adv.* in a repetitious way.
repetitiousness or **repetitiveness** *noun* being repetitious.
repetitive strain injury (ABBREV. **RSI**) inflammation of the tendons and joints of the hands and lower arms, caused by repeated performance of identical manual operations.
repine /rɪ'paɪn/ *verb intrans.* to fret or feel discontented. [from PINE[2]]
replace *verb* **1** to put (something) back in a previous or proper position. **2** to take the place of or be a substitute for. **3** (**replace one person** or **thing by** or **with another**) to use or substitute another person or thing in place of an

existing one: *was replaced by a man twenty years younger/ we want to replace it with a new one.*

☒ **1** put back, return, restore, make good, reinstate, reinstall, re-establish. **2** supersede, succeed, follow, supplant, oust, deputize for, substitute for.

replaceable *adj.* capable of being replaced.
replacement *noun* **1** the act of replacing something. **2** a person or thing that replaces another.

☒ **1** return, restoration, reinstatement, reinstallation, re-establishment, ousting, substitution. **2** substitute, stand-in, understudy, fill-in, supply, proxy, surrogate, successor.

replant *verb trans., intrans.* to plant again or anew, to replace surgically (a severed limb, digit, etc).
replay /ri:'pleɪ, 'ri:pleɪ/ — *noun* (with stress on *re-*) **1** the playing of a tape or recording again. **2** the playing of a football, etc match again, usually because neither team won the previous match. — *verb* (with stress on *-play*) to play (a tape, recording, football match, etc) again.
replenish *verb* to fill up again or stock, especially a supply of something which has been used up. [from Old French *replenir*, from Latin *plenus*, full]

☒ refill, restock, reload, recharge, replace, restore, renew, supply, provide, furnish, stock, fill, top up.

replenishment *noun* **1** replenishing. **2** that which replenishes. **3** a fresh supply.
replete /rɪ'pli:t/ *adj.* **1** (**replete with something**) completely or well supplied with it. **2** *formal* having eaten enough or more than enough. [from Latin *replere*, to refill]
repleteness or **repletion** *noun* being replete.
replica *noun* **1** an exact copy, especially of a work of art, sometimes by the original artist, and often on a smaller scale. **2** a facsimile. [from Latin *replicare*, to repeat]

☒ **1** model, imitation, reproduction. **2** facsimile, copy, duplicate, *colloq.* clone.

replicable *adj.* capable of being replicated.
replicate *verb* **1** to make a replica of. **2** to repeat (an experiment). **3** *intrans. said of a molecule, virus, etc* to make a replica of itself. [from Latin *replicare*, to fold back]
reply — *verb* (**replies, replied**) **1** *intrans.* to respond in words, writing, or action. **2** to say or do (something) in response. **3** *intrans.* to make a speech of thanks in answer to a speech of welcome. **4** *intrans. Legal* to answer a defendant's plea. — *noun* (PL. **replies**) something said, written, or done in answer or response. [from Latin *replicare*, to fold back]

☒ *verb* **1, 2** answer, respond, retort, rejoin, acknowledge, reciprocate. **1** react, echo, counter, retaliate. *noun* answer, response, retort, rejoinder, riposte, repartee, reaction, comeback, acknowledgement, return, echo, retaliation.

repoint *verb* to repair (stone or brickwork) by renewing the mortar between the joints.
report — *noun* **1** a detailed statement, description, or account, especially after investigation. **2** a detailed and usually formal account of the discussions and decisions of a committee, inquiry, or other group of people. **3** *Brit.* a statement of a pupil's work and behaviour at school given to the parents, usually at the end of each school year or each term. **4** rumour; general talk. **5** character or reputation. **6** a loud, explosive noise, eg of a gun firing. — *verb* **1** to bring back as an answer, news, or account. **2** *trans., intrans.* to give a formal or official account or description of, especially after an investigation. **3** to make a complaint

about (someone), especially to a person in authority. **4** to make (something) known to a person in authority. **5** *intrans.* (**report for something** or **to someone**) to present oneself at an appointed place or time, for a particular purpose: *please report to reception on arrival.* **6** (**report to someone**) to be responsible to them or under their authority. **7** *intrans.* to account for oneself in a particular way: *report sick.* **8** *intrans.* to act as a news reporter. [from Latin *reportare*, to carry back]

■ *noun* **1** account, relation, narrative, description, statement, communiqué, declaration, announcement, communication, information, news, article, piece, write-up, story, message, note. **2** record, minutes. **4** gossip, hearsay, rumour, talk. **6** explosion, shot, bang, crack. *verb* **1** state, announce, declare, proclaim, air, broadcast, relay, publish, circulate, communicate, recount, tell, relate, narrate, describe, detail, cover, document, record, note.

reportedly *adv.* according to report.

■ it is said, so they say, by all accounts, allegedly, apparently.

reported speech *Grammar* indirect speech.

reporter *noun* a person who writes articles and reports for a newspaper, or for broadcast on television or radio.

■ journalist, correspondent, columnist, newspaperman, newspaperwoman, hack, newscaster, commentator, announcer.

repose[1] — *noun* a state of rest, calm, or peacefulness. — *verb* **1** *intrans.* to lie resting. **2** to lay (oneself, one's head, etc) to rest. **3** *intrans.* to lie dead. [from Latin *repausare*]

■ *verb* REST. **1, 3** lie. **1** loll, lounge, relax. **2** lay, lean.

repose[2] *verb* **1** to place (confidence, trust, etc) in a person or thing. **2** *intrans.* to be placed (in a person or thing). [from Latin *reponere*, to replace]

repository /rɪˈpɒzɪtərɪ/ *noun* (PL. **repositories**) **1** a place or container where things may be stored, especially a museum or warehouse. **2** a person or thing thought of as a store of information, knowledge, etc. **3** a trusted person to whom one can confide secrets. [from Latin *reponere*, to replace]

repossess *verb, said of a creditor* to regain possession of (property or goods), especially because the debtor has defaulted on payment.

repossession *noun* repossessing or being repossessed.

reprehend *verb* to find fault with; to blame or reprove. [from Latin *reprehendere*, to seize, blame]

reprehensible *adj.* deserving blame or criticism. [from Latin *reprehensibilis*]

■ wrong, blameworthy, wicked, evil, bad, immoral, sinful, remiss.

reprehensibly *adv.* in a reprehensible way.

represent *verb* **1** to serve as a symbol or sign for; to stand for or correspond to: *letters represent sounds/a thesis represents years of hard work.* **2** to speak or act on behalf of. **3** to be a good example of; to typify: *what he said represents the feelings of many people.* **4** to present an image of or portray, especially through painting or sculpture. **5** to bring clearly to mind: *a film representing all the horrors of war.* **6** to describe in a specified way; to attribute a specified character or quality to: *represented themselves as experts.* **7** to show, state, or explain: *represent the difficulties forcibly to the committee.* **8** to be an elected member of Parliament for. **9** to act out or play the part of on stage. [from Latin *repraesentare*]

■ **1, 3** express. **1** stand for, symbolize, designate, denote, mean, be, constitute. **2** act for. **3** exemplify, typify, epitomize, embody, personify, show. **4** depict, portray, describe, picture, draw, sketch, illustrate, evoke. **9** act as, enact, perform, appear as.

representation *noun* **1** the act of representing or state of being represented. **2** a person or thing (especially a painting) which represents someone or something else. **3** a body of representatives. **4** (*often* **representations**) a strong statement made to present facts, opinions, complaints, or demands.

■ **1, 2** expression, depiction, portrayal, description. **2** likeness, image, icon, picture, portrait, illustration, sketch, model, statue, bust, account, explanation, performance, production.

representational *adj.*, *said especially of art* depicting objects in a realistic rather than an abstract form.

representative — *adj.* **1** representing. **2** being a good example (of something); typical. **3** standing or acting as a deputy for someone. **4** *said of government* carried on by elected people. — *noun* **1** a person who represents someone or something else, especially a person who represents, or sells the goods of, a business or company, or a person who represents a constituency in Parliament. **2** a typical example.

■ *adj.* **1, 2** typical, illustrative. **1** symbolic. **2** exemplary, archetypal, characteristic, usual, normal. *noun* **1** delegate, deputy, proxy, stand-in, spokesperson, spokesman, spokeswoman, ambassador, commissioner, agent, salesman, saleswoman, *colloq.* rep, traveller.
E3 *adj.* **2** unrepresentative, atypical.

repress *verb* **1** to keep (an impulse, a desire to do something, etc) under control. **2** to put down, especially using force: *repress the insurrection.* **3** to exclude (an unpleasant thought) from one's conscious mind. [from Latin *reprimere*, to keep back]

■ **1** inhibit, check, control, curb, restrain, suppress, bottle up, hold back, stifle, smother, muffle, silence, quell. **2** crush, quash, subdue, overpower, overcome, master, subjugate, oppress.

repression *noun* **1** the act of repressing or the state of being repressed. **2** *Psychol.* in psychoanalysis, the defence mechanism whereby an unpleasant or unacceptable thought, memory, or wish is deliberately excluded from conscious thought. Such repressed material still controls behaviour, and may later give rise to symptoms of neurosis.

■ **1** inhibition, restraint, suppression, suffocation, gagging, censorship, authoritarianism, despotism, tyranny, oppression, domination, control, constraint, coercion.

repressive *adj.* exercising harsh control.

■ oppressive, authoritarian, despotic, tyrannical, dictatorial, autocratic, totalitarian, absolute, harsh, severe, tough, coercive.

repressiveness *noun* being repressive.

repressor *noun* a person or thing that represses.

reprieve — *verb* **1** to delay or cancel the punishment of (a prisoner condemned to death). **2** to give temporary relief from trouble, difficulty, pain, etc. — *noun* **1** the act of delaying or cancelling a death sentence. **2** temporary relief from trouble, difficulty, pain, etc. [from Old French *repris*, taken back]

▣ *verb* SPARE. **1** pardon, let off, rescue, redeem. **2** relieve, respite. *noun* **1** pardon, amnesty, remission. **2** suspension, abeyance, postponement, deferment, respite, relief, *colloq.* let-up, abatement.

reprimand — *verb* to criticize or rebuke angrily or severely, especially formally. — *noun* angry or severe and usually formal criticism or rebuke. [from Latin *reprimere*, to keep back]

▣ *verb* rebuke, reprove, reproach, admonish, scold, chide, *colloq.* tell off, *colloq.* tick off, lecture, criticize, *colloq.* slate, censure, blame. *noun* rebuke, reproof, reproach, admonition, *colloq.* telling-off, *colloq.* ticking-off, lecture, *colloq.* talking-to, *colloq.* dressing-down, censure, blame.

reprint — *noun* (with stress on *re*-) **1** a copy of a book made by reprinting the original without any changes. **2** an occasion of reprinting. **3** the number of copies of a book which is reprinted. — *verb* (with stress on *-print*) **1** to print more copies of (a book). **2** *intrans.*, *said of a book* to have more copies printed.

reprisal /rɪˈpraɪzəl/ *noun* **1** an act of taking revenge or retaliating. **2** the usually forcible taking of foreign land in retaliation. [from Old French *reprisaille*]

▣ **1** retaliation, counter-attack, retribution, requital, revenge, vengeance.

reprise /rɪˈpraɪz, rɪˈpriːz/ — *noun* a repeated passage or theme in music. — *verb* to repeat (an earlier passage or theme) in music. [from Old French *reprise*, a taking back]

reproach — *verb* to express disapproval of or disappointment with (a person) for a fault or some wrong done. — *noun* **1** an act of reproaching. **2** (*often* **reproaches**) a rebuke or expression of disapproval. **3** a cause of disgrace or shame. — **above** or **beyond reproach** too good to be criticized; excellent; perfect. [from Old French *reprochier*]

▣ *verb* rebuke, reprove, reprimand, upbraid, scold, chide, reprehend, blame, censure, condemn, criticize, disparage, defame. *noun* **2** rebuke, reproof, reprimand, scolding, blame, censure, condemnation, criticism, disapproval, scorn, contempt. **3** shame, disgrace.

reproachful *adj.* expressing or full of reproach.

▣ reproving, upbraiding, scolding, censorious, critical, fault-finding, disapproving, scornful.
▣ complimentary.

reprobate — *noun* a person of immoral habits with no principles. — *adj.* immoral and unprincipled. [from Latin *reprobatus*, disapproved of]

reproduce *verb* **1** to make or produce a copy or imitation of; to duplicate. **2** to make or produce again or anew. **3** *intrans.* to turn out (well, badly, etc) when copied. **4** *intrans.*, *trans.* to produce (new individuals) either sexually or asexually, so perpetuating a species.

▣ **1** copy, transcribe, print, duplicate, mirror, echo, repeat, imitate, emulate, match, simulate, recreate, reconstruct. **4** breed, spawn, procreate, generate, propagate, multiply.

reproducible *adj.* capable of being reproduced.

reproduction — *noun* **1** the act or process of reproducing offspring. **2** a copy or imitation, especially of a work of art. — *adj.*, *said of furniture, etc* made in imitation of an earlier style.

▣ *noun* **1** breeding, procreation, generation, propagation, multiplication. **2** copy, print, picture, duplicate, facsimile, replica, *colloq.* clone, imitation.
▣ *noun* **2** original.

reproductive *adj.* of or for reproduction.

▣ procreative, generative, sexual, sex, genital.

reproductively *adv.* in a reproductive way.
reproof *noun* blame or criticism; a rebuke. [related to RE-PROVE]

▣ rebuke, reproach, reprimand, admonition, upbraiding, *colloq.* dressing-down, scolding, *colloq.* telling-off, *colloq.* ticking-off, censure, condemnation, criticism.
▣ praise.

reprove *verb* to blame or condemn (someone) for a fault or some wrong done. [from Old French *reprover*, from Latin *reprobare*, to disapprove of]

▣ rebuke, reproach, reprimand, upbraid, scold, chide, *colloq.* tell off, *colloq.* dress down, reprehend, admonish, censure, condemn, criticize.
▣ praise.

reproving *adj.* disapproving, condemnatory.
reptile *noun* **1** *Zool.* any cold-blooded vertebrate animal belonging to the class Reptilia, eg lizards, snakes, tortoises, turtles, crocodiles, alligators, and many extinct species, including dinosaurs and pterodactyls. **2** a mean or despicable person. [from Latin *reptilis*, creeping]

Reptiles include: adder, puff adder, grass snake, tree snake, asp, viper, rattlesnake, sidewinder, anaconda, boa constrictor, cobra, king cobra, mamba, python; lizard, frilled lizard, chameleon, gecko, iguana, skink, slow-worm; turtle, green turtle, hawksbill turtle, terrapin, tortoise, giant tortoise; alligator, crocodile.

reptilian *adj.* of or like reptiles.
republic *noun* **1** a form of government in which there is no monarch, and in which supreme power is held by the people or their elected representatives, especially one in which the head of state is an elected or nominated president. **2** a country, state, or unit within a state (eg in the former Soviet Union) having such a form of government. [from Latin *respublica*, from *res*, concern, affair + *publicus*, public]

republican — *adj.* **1** of or like a republic. **2** in favour of or supporting a republican system of government. **3** (**Republican**) of the Republican Party in the US. — *noun* **1** a person who favours a republican system of government. **2** (**Republican**) a member or supporter of the US Republican Party.

republicanism *noun* **1** the principles and theory of a republican system of government. **2** support for republican government, or a particular example of this.

repudiate *verb* **1** to deny or reject: *repudiate the suggestion*. **2** to refuse to recognize or have anything to do with; to disown. **3** to refuse to acknowledge or pay (a debt, obligation, etc). [from Latin *repudiare*]

▣ **1, 2** reject, spurn, disclaim, deny, renounce. **2** disown.

repudiation *noun* repudiating.

repugnance *noun* aversion.

⊟ aversion, hatred, loathing, abhorrence, horror, repulsion, revulsion, disgust, distaste, dislike, reluctance.
⊡ liking, pleasure, delight.

repugnant *adj.* **1** causing a feeling of disgust or loathing. **2** (**repugnant with something**) inconsistent or incompatible with it. [from Latin *repugnare*, to fight against]

⊟ **1** distasteful, repellent, repulsive, revolting, nauseating, offensive, obnoxious, hateful, loathsome, foul, vile.

repulse — *verb* **1** to drive or force back (an enemy). **2** to reject (a person's offer of help, kindness, etc) with coldness and discourtesy. **3** to cause a feeling of disgust, horror, or loathing in. — *noun* **1** an act of repulsing or state of being repulsed. **2** a cold, discourteous rejection. [from Latin *repulsus*, driven back]

⊟ *verb* REPEL. **1** drive back, drive off, beat off, ward off, check, defeat. **2** reject, rebuff. **3** disgust, horrify, sicken, revolt. *noun* **1** defeat, rout, check, reverse. **2** rejection, rebuff.

repulsion *noun* **1** a feeling of disgust, horror, or loathing. **2** a forcing back or being forced back. **3** *Physics* a force that tends to push two objects further apart, such as that between like electric charges or like magnetic poles. See also ATTRACTION. [from Latin *repulsus*, driven back]

repulsive *adj.* causing a feeling of disgust, horror, or loathing.

⊟ repellent, repugnant, revolting, disgusting, nauseating, sickening, offensive, distasteful, objectionable, obnoxious, foul, vile, loathsome, abominable, abhorrent, hateful, horrid, unpleasant, disagreeable, ugly, hideous, forbidding.
⊡ attractive, pleasant, delightful.

reputable /ˈrɛpjʊtəbl/ *adj.* respectable; well thought of; trustworthy. [from Latin *reputabilis*]

⊟ respectable, reliable, dependable, trustworthy, upright, honourable, creditable, worthy, good, excellent, irreproachable.
⊡ disreputable, infamous.

reputably /ˈrɛpjʊtəblɪ/ *adv.* in a reputable way.

reputation *noun* **1** a generally held opinion about a person with regard to his or her abilities, moral character, etc. **2** a high opinion generally held about a person or thing; a good name. [from Latin *reputatio*]

⊟ **1** opinion, credit, repute, name, character, standing, stature, infamy, notoriety. **2** esteem, fame, renown, celebrity, distinction, good name, honour.

repute — *verb* (**be reputed**) to be generally considered: *she is reputed to be a fine tennis player.* — *noun* reputation. — **by repute** reputedly. **a person of repute** a person who is generally well thought of and respected. [from Latin *reputare*, to reckon]

⊟ *verb* be said, be considered, be supposed, be rumoured, be believed, be thought, be reckoned, be held, be alleged, seem, appear.

reputedly *adv.* as is generally believed; by reputation.

request — *noun* **1** the act of asking for something. **2** something asked for. **3** the state of being asked for or sought after: *be in request.* — *verb* to ask (someone) for (something), especially politely or as a favour. — **on request** if or when requested. [from Latin *requirere*, to seek for]

⊟ *noun* **1, 2, 3** demand. **1, 2** desire. **1** appeal, call, requisition, application, solicitation, petition, entreaty, supplication, prayer. *verb* ask for, solicit, demand, require, seek, desire, beg, entreat, supplicate, petition, appeal.

request stop a bus stop that a bus will only stop at if signalled to do so.

requiem /ˈrɛkwɪɛm, ˈrɛkwɪəm/ *noun* **1** (*also* **Requiem**) in the Roman Catholic Church, a mass for the souls of the dead. **2** a piece of music written to accompany this service. [from Latin *requiem*, rest, the first word of the Latin version of this mass]

require *verb* **1** to need; to wish to have. **2** to have as a necessary or essential condition for success, fulfilment, etc. **3** to demand, exact or command by authority. [from Latin *requirere*, to search for]

⊟ **1** need, want, wish, desire, lack, miss. **2** demand, necessitate, take, involve. **3** command, oblige, force, compel, exact, constrain, make, ask, request, instruct, direct, order.

requirement *noun* something that is needed, asked for, essential, ordered, etc.

⊟ need, necessity, essential, must, requisite, prerequisite, demand, stipulation, condition, term, specification, proviso, qualification, provision.

requisite /ˈrɛkwɪzɪt/ — *adj.* required; necessary; indispensable. — *noun* something which is required, necessary, or indispensable for some purpose: *toilet requisites.* [from Latin *requisitus*, sought for]

⊟ *adj.* required, needed, necessary, essential, obligatory, compulsory, set, prescribed. *noun* requirement, necessary, essential, condition, sine qua non.

requisition — *noun* **1** a (usually written) formal and authoritative demand or request, especially for supplies or the use of something, and especially by the army. **2** the act of formally demanding, requesting or taking something. — *verb* (**requisitioned, requisitioning**) to demand, take or order (supplies, the use of something, etc) by official requisition. [from Latin *requisitio*, a searching for]

⊟ *verb* request, put in for, demand, commandeer, appropriate, take, confiscate, seize, occupy.

requital /rɪˈkwaɪtl/ *noun* **1** requiting. **2** recompense, reward.

requite *verb formal* **1** to make a suitable return to or repay (a person) for some act. **2** (**requite one thing for** or **with another**) to repay (eg good with good or evil with evil). [from Middle English *quitten*, to pay]

reredos /ˈrɪədɒs/ *noun* a usually ornamental stone or wooden screen or partition wall behind an altar. [from Old French *areredos*, from *arere*, behind + *dos*, back]

reroute *verb* (**rerouteing**) to direct (traffic, aircraft, etc) along an alternative route.

rerun /rɪːˈrʌn, ˈriːrʌn/ — *verb* (with stress on *-run*) (**rerunning**; PAST TENSE **reran**; PAST PARTICIPLE **rerun**) **1** to run (a race) again. **2** to broadcast (a series of television or radio programmes) for a second or further time. — *noun* (with stress on *re-*) **1** a race that is run again. **2** a series of television or radio programmes which are broadcast for a second or further time.

resale price maintenance a device, now illegal in the UK, used by sellers acting together to prevent price-cutting by retailers. All agree to maintain their prices at a certain level, in effect forming a cartel.

rescind /rɪˈsɪnd/ *verb* to cancel, annul or revoke (an order, law, custom, etc). [from Latin *rescindere*, to cut off]

rescindment or **rescission** *noun* rescinding.

rescue — *verb* to free (a person or thing) from danger, evil, trouble, captivity, etc. — *noun* the act of rescuing or being rescued. [from Old French *rescourre*]

■ *verb* save, recover, salvage, deliver, free, liberate, release, redeem, ransom. *noun* saving, recovery, salvage, deliverance, liberation, release, redemption, salvation.
F3 *verb* capture, imprison. *noun* capture.

rescuer *noun* a person who rescues.

research — *noun* (with stress on -*search*, or on *re*-) a detailed and careful investigation into some area of study to (try to) discover and apply (new) facts or information. — *verb trans., intrans.* (with stress on -*search*) (**research into something**) to carry out such an investigation. [from Old French *recercher*, to seek]

■ *noun* investigation, inquiry, fact-finding, groundwork, examination, analysis, scrutiny, study, search, probe, exploration, experimentation. *verb* investigate, examine, analyse, scrutinize, study, search, probe, explore, experiment (on).

researcher *noun* a person who carries out research.

resemblance *noun* 1 likeness. 2 appearance. 3 an image.

■ 1 likeness, similarity, sameness, parity, conformity, closeness, affinity, parallel, comparison, analogy, correspondence. 3 image, facsimile.
F3 1 dissimilarity.

resemble *verb* to be or look like or similar to. [from Old French *resembler*]

■ be like, look like, take after, favour, mirror, echo, duplicate, parallel, approach.
F3 differ from.

resent *verb* to feel anger, bitterness, or ill-will towards. [from Old French *ressentir*]

■ grudge, begrudge, envy, take offence at, take umbrage at, take amiss, object to, grumble at, take exception to, dislike.
F3 accept, like.

resentful *adj.* full of or caused by resentment.

■ grudging, envious, jealous, bitter, embittered, hurt, wounded, offended, aggrieved, put out, *colloq.* miffed, *colloq.* peeved, indignant, angry, vindictive.
F3 satisfied, contented.

resentfully *adv.* in a resentful way, with resentment.

resentfulness or **resentment** *noun* being resentful.

■ grudge, envy, jealousy, bitterness, rancour, spite, malice, vindictiveness, ill-feeling, ill-will, animosity, umbrage, pique, displeasure, irritation, anger.
F3 contentment, happiness.

reservation *noun* 1 the act of reserving something for future use. 2 a booking; something (eg a hotel room, a table in a restaurant) which has been reserved. 3 (*usually* **reservations**) a doubt or objection which prevents one being able to accept or approve something wholeheartedly. 4 a limiting condition or proviso. 5 an area of land set aside for a particular purpose, especially in the US and Canada for the original inhabitants. 6 *Brit.* a strip of land between the two carriageways of a dual carriageway or motorway. 7 in some Christian churches, the practice of keeping back part of the consecrated bread and wine for some particular purpose after the service, eg for taking to the sick. 8 the right of the pope to nominate someone to a vacant benefice.

■ 2 booking, engagement, appointment. 3 doubt, scepticism, misgiving, qualm, scruple, hesitation, second thought(s). 4 proviso, stipulation, qualification. 5 reserve, preserve, park, sanctuary, homeland, enclave.

reserve — *verb* 1 to obtain or order in advance. 2 to keep back or set aside for the use of a particular person or for a particular purpose. 3 to delay or postpone (a legal judgement, taking a decision, etc). — *noun* 1 something which is kept back or set aside for later use or possible need. 2 the state or condition of being reserved or an act of reserving. 3 an area of land set aside for a particular purpose, especially for the protection of animals, for hunting or fishing, or (especially in Australia) for the original native inhabitants. 4 shy, cool, cautious, and distant manner. 5 (*also* **reserves**) one of those members of a nation's armed forces who are not part of the regular services, but who are called up when needed. 6 an extra player or participant who can take the place of another if needed. 7 (*also* **reserves**) a company's money or assets, or a country's gold and foreign currency, held at a bank to meet liabilities. [from Latin *reservare*, to keep back]

■ *verb* 1 book, engage, order, secure. 2 set apart, earmark, keep, retain, hold back, save, store, stockpile. *noun* 1 store, stock, supply, fund, stockpile, cache, hoard, savings. 3 reservation, preserve, park, sanctuary. 4 shyness, reticence, secretiveness, coolness, aloofness, modesty, restraint. 6 replacement, substitute, stand-in.
F3 *verb* 2 use up. *noun* 4 friendliness, openness.

reserved *adj.* 1 booked. 2 *said of a person* showing reserve; not open and friendly.

■ 1 booked, engaged, taken, spoken for, set aside, earmarked, meant, intended, designated, destined, saved, held, kept, retained. 2 shy, retiring, reticent, unforthcoming, uncommunicative, secretive, silent, taciturn, unsociable, cool, aloof, distant, remote, standoffish, unapproachable, modest, restrained, cautious.
F3 1 unreserved, free, available. 2 friendly, open.

reserve price the lowest price that the owner of something which is being sold by auction is prepared to accept.

reservist *noun* a member of a nation's reserve forces.

reservoir /ˈrezəvwɑːr/ *noun* 1 a place, usually a man-made lake, where water is collected and stored for use by the community. 2 a part of a machine, etc where liquid is stored. 3 a large store or supply of something. [from French]

■ 2 tank, cistern, vat, container. 3 pool, reserve, supply, store, fund, bank.

reshuffle — *verb* (with stress on -*shuffle*) 1 to shuffle (cards) again or differently. 2 to reorganize or redistribute (eg government posts). — *noun* (with stress on *re*-) an act of reshuffling.

reside *verb intrans.* 1 *formal* to live or have one's home (in), especially permanently. 2 (**reside in someone** or **something**) *said of power, authority, a quality, etc* to be present in or attributable to them. [from Latin *residere*, to settle down]

■ 1 live, inhabit, dwell, lodge, stay, sojourn, settle, remain. 2 be present in, exist in, inhere in, belong to.

residence *noun* 1 a house or dwelling, especially a large, impressive and imposing one. 2 the act of living in a place. 3 the period of time one lives in a place.— **in residence** 1 living in a particular place, especially officially. 2 *said especially of a creative artist* working in a particular place for a period of time: *the university has an artist in residence*. [from Latin *residere*, to settle down]

■ 1 dwelling, habitation, *formal* domicile, *formal* abode, seat, place, home, house, lodgings, quarters, hall, manor, mansion, palace, villa, country house, country seat.

residency *noun* (PL. **residencies**) 1 a residence, especially the official dwelling of a governor, etc in a colony, etc. 2 a period of advanced, specialized medical training in hospitals for doctors.

resident — *noun* 1 a person who lives in a place. 2 a bird or animal that does not migrate. 3 a guest staying in a hotel. 4 a doctor undergoing advanced or specialized training in a hospital. — *adj.* 1 living or dwelling (in). 2 living or required to live in the place where one works. 3 *said of birds and animals* not migrating.

■ *noun* 1 inhabitant, citizen, local, householder, occupier, tenant, lodger. 3 guest.
E3 *noun* 1, 3 non-resident.

residential *adj.* 1 containing houses rather than factories and businesses, etc. 2 requiring residence in the same place as one works or studies: *a residential course*. 3 used as a residence: *a residential home for the elderly*. 4 relating to or connected with residence or residences: *residential qualifications*.

residual — *adj.* remaining; left over. — *noun* something which remains or is left over.

■ *adj.* remaining, left-over, unused, unconsumed, net.

residue / 'rezɪdjuː/ *noun* 1 what remains or is left over when a part has been taken away. 2 *Legal* what is left of a dead person's estate after all of the debts and legacies have been paid. 3 *Chem.* a substance which remains after evaporation, combustion, or distillation. [from Latin *residuus*, remaining]

■ 1 remainder, rest, balance, surplus, excess, remnant, remains, leftovers, dregs, lees, grounds. 3 sediment, deposit.

resign /rɪˈzaɪn/ *verb* 1 *intrans.* to give up one's employment or official position. 2 to give up or relinquish (a right, claim, etc). 3 (**resign oneself to something**) to come to accept something (especially unwelcome) with patience. [from Latin *resignare*, to unseal]

■ 1 stand down, leave, quit, abdicate, vacate. 2 renounce, relinquish, forego, waive, surrender, yield, abandon, forsake. 3 reconcile oneself to, accept, bow to, submit to, yield to, comply with, acquiesce in.
E3 1 join. 3 resist.

resignation /rezɪgˈneɪʃən/ *noun* 1 the act of resigning. 2 a formal letter or notice of one's intention to resign. 3 the state or quality of having or showing patient and calm acceptance.

■ 1 standing-down, abdication, retirement, departure, notice, renunciation, relinquishment, surrender. 3 acceptance, acquiescence, submission, non-resistance, passivity, patience, stoicism, defeatism.
E3 3 resistance.

resigned /rɪˈzaɪnd/ *adj.* having or showing patient and calm acceptance of something thought of as inevitable.

■ philosophical, stoical, patient, unprotesting, unresisting, submissive, defeatist.
E3 resistant.

resignedly /rɪˈzaɪnɪdlɪ/ *adv.* with resignation.
resilience or **resiliency** *noun* being resilient.
resilient *adj.* 1 *said of a person* able to deal readily with or recover quickly from differing circumstances, unexpected difficulties, etc. 2 *said of an object* quickly returning to its original shape after being bent, twisted, stretched, etc. [from Latin *resilire*, to leap back]

■ STRONG, TOUGH. 1 hardy, adaptable, buoyant. 2 flexible, pliable, supple, plastic, elastic, springy, bouncy.
E3 2 rigid, brittle.

resin / 'rezɪn/ *noun Chem.* any of several natural or synthetic organic compounds, mostly polymers, usually in the form of a brittle translucent solid or viscous liquid. Natural resins are produced by various trees, especially conifers, and synthetic resins are used to make plastics, and as components of paints, varnishes, textiles, etc. [from Latin *resina*]

resinous *adj.* like or containing resin.
resist *verb* 1 to fight against (someone or something). 2 *intrans.* to remain undamaged by or withstand: *a metal which resists corrosion*. 4 to be unaffected by in spite of temptation or attraction: *he just can't resist chocolate*. [from Latin *resistere*, to oppose, resist]

■ 1 oppose, defy, confront, fight, combat, weather, withstand, repel, counteract, check, avoid, refuse.
E3 1 submit, accept.

resistance *noun* 1 the act of resisting. 2 a measure of the extent to which a living organism can limit the effects of an infection. 3 *Physics* in damped harmonic motion, the ratio of the frictional forces to the speed. 4 *Electr.* a measure of the extent to which a material or an electrical device opposes the flow of an electric current through it. It is equal to the ratio of the voltage across the device to the current passing through it. The SI unit of resistance is the ohm. 5 a measure of the extent to which a material opposes the flow of heat through it. 6 a resistor. 7 (*often* **Resistance**) an underground organization which fights for the freedom of a country which has been conquered by a foreign power.

■ 1 opposition, defiance, fight, confrontation, unwillingness, reluctance, refusal.

resistant — *adj.* 1 showing resistance. 2 able to remain unaffected or undamaged by something. — *noun* a person or thing that resists.

■ *adj.* 1 opposed, antagonistic, defiant, unyielding, intransigent, unwilling. 2 proof, impervious, immune, invulnerable, tough, strong.
E3 *adj.* 1 compliant, yielding.

resistible *adj.* capable of being resisted.
resistivity /rezɪˈstɪvɪtɪ/ *noun Physics* (SYMBOL ρ) a measure of the ability of a cubic metre of material to oppose the flow of an electric current. It is measured in ohm metres, and the reciprocal of resistivity is conductivity.
resistor *noun* a device which introduces a known value of resistance into a circuit, etc.
reskill *verb trans.* to retrain (employees) to do new work.
resocialization *noun* the process of altering the behaviour of criminals and other deviants so that they learn to conform to the norms in a society. Resocialization may

take place within the penal system, in institutions, or in the community.

resoluble /rɪˈzɒljʊbl/ *adj.* able to be resolved or analysed. [from Latin *resolvere*, to loose]

resolute /ˈrezəluːt, ˈrezəljuːt/ *adj.* having a fixed purpose or belief, and determined and firm in pursuing it. [from Latin *resolutus*]

- ▣ determined, resolved, set, fixed, unwavering, staunch, firm, steadfast, relentless, single-minded, persevering, dogged, tenacious, stubborn, obstinate, strong-willed, undaunted, unflinching, bold.
- ▣ irresolute, weak-willed, half-hearted.

resolutely *adv.* in a resolute way.

resoluteness *noun* being resolute.

resolution /rezəˈluːʃən, rezəˈljuːʃən/ *noun* 1 the act of making a firm decision. 2 a firm decision. 3 a formal expression of opinion, will, etc by a group of people, eg at a public meeting. 4 determination or resoluteness. 5 the act of solving or finding the answer to (a problem, question, etc). 6 the ability of a television screen, photographic film, etc to reproduce an image in very fine detail. 7 *Mus.* the passing of a chord from discord to concord. 8 the ability of a microscope, telescope, etc to distinguish between objects which are very close together. 9 the act of separating something (eg a chemical compound) into its constituent parts. [from Latin *resolutio*]

- ▣ 2 decision, judgement, finding. 3 declaration, proposition, motion. 4 determination, resolve, willpower, commitment, dedication, devotion, firmness, steadfastness, persistence, perseverance, doggedness, tenacity, zeal, courage, boldness. 5 solution, settlement, conclusion, determination, arrangement.
- ▣ 4 half-heartedness, uncertainty, indecision.

resolve — *verb* 1 (**resolve on something** or **to do something**) to take a firm decision about it. 2 to pass (a resolution), especially formally by vote. 3 to find an answer to (a problem, question, etc). 4 to take away or bring an end to (a doubt, fear, etc). 5 *trans., intrans.* to break up or cause to break up into separate or constituent parts. 6 *said of a television screen, photographic film, etc* to produce an image of in fine detail. 7 *Mus.* to make (a chord) pass from discord into concord. 8 *said of a microscope, telescope, etc* to distinguish clearly between (objects which are very close together). — *noun* 1 determination or firm intention. 2 a firm decision; a resolution. [from Latin *resolvere*, to loose]

- ▣ *verb* 1, 3 decide, determine. 1 make up one's mind. 3 fix, settle, conclude, sort out, work out, solve. *noun* RESOLUTION, DETERMINATION. 1 willpower, commitment, dedication, devotion, firmness, steadfastness, persistence, perseverance, doggedness, tenacity.

resolved *adj.* determined; fixed in purpose.

- ▣ determined, set, fixed, intent, staunch, firm, steadfast, single-minded, dogged, tenacious, resolute.

resolving power same as RESOLUTION 8.

resonance /ˈrezənəns/ *noun* 1 the quality or state of being resonant. 2 *Physics* a phenomenon that occurs when an object or system is made to vibrate at its natural frequency. A large vibration can be set up if a force is applied that vibrates at the same natural frequency. 3 *Chem.* the movement of electrons from one atom of a molecule to another atom of the same molecule to form a stable structure called a *resonance hybrid*. Resonance occurs in aromatic compounds such as benzene. 4 the ringing quality of the human voice when produced in such a way that the vibration of the vocal cords is accompanied by sympathetic vibration of air in areas in the head, chest and throat. [from Latin *resonare*, to resound]

resonant *adj.* 1 *said of sounds* echoing; continuing to sound; resounding. 2 producing echoing sounds: *resonant walls.* 3 full of or made stronger by a ringing quality: *a resonant voice.*

- ▣ 1, 3 ringing. 1 echoing, resounding, resonating, reverberating. 3 bell-like, sonorous, booming, thunderous, full, rich, vibrant, thrilling.

resonantly *adv.* in a resonant way.

resonate *verb trans., intrans.* to resound or cause to resound or echo.

- ▣ reverberate, echo, re-echo.

resonator /ˈrezəneɪtə(r)/ *noun* a resonating body or device.

resort — *verb intrans.* (**resort to something**) 1 to turn to it as a means of solving a problem, etc. 2 to go to a place, especially frequently or in great numbers. — *noun* 1 a place visited by many people, especially one providing accommodation and recreation for holidaymakers. 2 someone or something looked to for help.— **in the last resort** when all other methods, etc have failed. [from Old French *resortir*, to rebound]

- ▣ *verb* 1 have recourse to, turn to, employ, make use of, exercise. 2 go to, visit, frequent, patronize, haunt. *noun* 2 recourse, refuge, course (of action), alternative, option, chance, possibility.

resound /rɪˈzaʊnd/ *verb* 1 *intrans. said of sounds* to ring or echo. 2 *intrans.* (**resound with** or **to something**) to be filled with echoing or ringing sounds: *the hall resounded to their cheers.* 3 *intrans.* to be widely known: *her fame resounded throughout the country.* 4 *said of a place* to cause (a sound) to echo or ring. 5 to repeat or spread (the praises of a person or thing). [from Latin *resonare*]

- ▣ 1, 2 reverberate, echo, re-echo, ring, thunder. 1 resonate, boom.

resounding *adj.* 1 echoing and ringing; reverberating. 2 thorough, clear and decisive: *a resounding victory.*

- ▣ 1 resonant, reverberating, ringing, sonorous, booming, thunderous, full, rich, vibrant. 2 decisive, conclusive, crushing, thorough.
- ▣ 1 faint.

resoundingly *adv.* in a resounding way.

resource /rɪˈzɔːs, rɪˈsɔːs/ *noun* 1 a person or thing which gives help, support, etc when needed. 2 a means of solving difficulties, problems, etc. 3 skill at finding ways of solving difficulties, problems, etc. 4 a supply of energy, natural materials, or minerals, which may or may not be renewable. 5 (*usually* **resources**) a means of support, eg money and property. 6 (*usually* **resources**) the principal source of wealth or income of a country or institution: *natural resources.* 7 a means of occupying one's spare time or amusing oneself. [from Latin *resurgere*, to rise again]

- ▣ 2 expedient, contrivance, device, stratagem. 3 resourcefulness, initiative, ingenuity, inventiveness, talent, ability, capability. 4 supply, reserve, stockpile, source. 5, 6 reserves. 5 means, assets, capital, money, funds, holdings, property, wealth, riches. 6 materials, supplies.

resourceful *adj.* good at finding ways of solving difficulties, problems, etc.

▤ ingenious, imaginative, creative, inventive, innovative, original, clever, bright, sharp, quick-witted, able, capable, talented.

resourcefully *adv.* in a resourceful way.

resourcefulness *noun* being resourceful.

respect — *noun* **1** admiration; good opinion: *be held in great respect.* **2** the state of being admired or well thought of. **3** (**respect for something** or **someone**) consideration of or attention to them: *show no respect for the law.* **4** (**respects**) a greeting or expression of admiration, esteem, and honour. **5** a particular detail, feature, or characteristic. **6** reference or connection: *in what respect are they different?* — *verb* **1** to show or feel admiration or high regard for. **2** to show consideration, attention or thoughtfulness to: *respect other people's feelings.* — **in respect of** ... or **with respect to** ... with reference to ...; in connection with ... **pay one's respects to someone** to visit them as a sign of respect or out of politeness. [from Latin *respicere*, to look back]

▤ *noun* **1** admiration, esteem, appreciation, recognition, regard, honour, veneration. **3** regard for, consideration for, attention to, deference to, reverence for, veneration for, politeness to, courtesy to. **5** point, aspect, facet, feature, characteristic, particular, detail. **6** regard, reference, relation, connection, sense, way. *verb* **1** admire, esteem, regard, appreciate, value. **2** obey, observe, heed, follow, honour, fulfil.
▣ *noun* **1** disrespect. *verb* **1** despise, scorn. **2** ignore, disobey.

respectability *noun* being respectable.

respectable *adj.* **1** deserving respect. **2** having a good reputation or character, especially as regards morals. **3** *said of behaviour* correct, acceptable. **4** fit to be seen, heard, etc in decent society. **5** fairly or relatively good or large.

▤ **2** honourable, worthy, respected, dignified, upright, honest, decent, clean-living. **3, 4** suitable, proper. **3** acceptable, correct, in order. **4** presentable, neat, tidy, clean, decent. **5** passable, adequate, fair, reasonable, appreciable, considerable.
▣ **1** dishonourable, disreputable. **2** inadequate, paltry.

respectably *adv.* in a respectable way.

respectful *adj.* having or showing respect.

▤ deferential, reverential, humble, polite, well-mannered, courteous, civil.
▣ disrespectful.

respectfully *adv.* in a respectful way.

respectfulness *noun* being respectful.

respecting *prep.* about; concerning.

respective *adj.* belonging to or relating to each person or thing mentioned; particular; separate: *our respective homes.*

▤ corresponding, relevant, various, several, separate, individual, personal, own, particular, special.

respectively *adv.* referring to each person or thing separately and in turn.

respell *verb* to spell anew or in a different way.

respiration *noun* **1** the act of breathing. **2** *Physiol.* the exchange of gases between an organism and its environment, consisting of the uptake of oxygen from and the release of carbon dioxide to the environment. It takes place in the lungs of terrestrial vertebrates, and in the gills of fishes and many other aquatic animals. In plants it occurs via specialized pores called stomata, which are found mainly on the lower surface of leaves. **3** (*in full* **tissue respiration**) *Biochem.* a biochemical process that takes place in the cells of all living organisms, and involves the release of energy as a result of the breakdown of carbohydrates or other foodstuffs.

respirator *noun* **1** a mask worn over the mouth and nose to prevent poisonous gas, dust, etc being breathed in. **2** apparatus used to help very ill or injured people breathe when they are unable to do so naturally.

respiratory /ˈrɛspɪrətərɪ/ *adj.* relating to breathing or respiration.

respire *verb* **1** *intrans., trans.* to breathe. **2** *intrans.* to release energy as a result of the breakdown of organic compounds such as fats or carbohydrates. [from Latin *respirare*]

respite /ˈrɛspaɪt, ˈrɛspɪt/ — *noun* **1** a pause; a period of rest or relief from, or a temporary stopping of, something unpleasant, difficult, etc. **2** a temporary delay; a reprieve. — *verb* **1** to grant a respite to. **2** to delay (eg the execution of a sentence). [from Old French *respit*]

▤ *noun* **1** pause, rest, relief, break, *colloq.* breather, *colloq.* let-up, stoppage, cessation. **2** delay, postponement, deferment, remission, reprieve, abatement.

resplendence *noun* brilliance.

resplendent *adj.* brilliant or splendid in appearance. [from Latin *resplendere*, to shine brightly]

▤ brilliant, splendid, magnificent, gorgeous, glorious, glittering, gleaming, radiant.

resplendently *adv.* in a resplendent way.

respond *verb* **1** *intrans., trans.* to answer or reply; to say in reply. **2** *intrans.* to act or behave in reply or response: *I smiled at her, but she didn't respond.* **3** *intrans.* to react favourably or well: *respond to treatment.* [from Latin *respondere*, to return like for like]

▤ **1** answer, reply, retort. **2** react, reciprocate, acknowledge.

respondent — *noun* **1** a person who answers or makes replies. **2** *Legal* a defendant, especially in a divorce suit. — *adj.* answering; making a reply or response.

response *noun* **1** an act of responding, replying, or reacting. **2** a reply or answer. **3** a reaction: *meet with little response.* **4** an answer or reply, especially in the form of a short verse which is either sung or spoken, made by the congregation or the choir to something said by the priest or minister during a service. [from Old French *respons*]

▤ **1** answer, reply, retort. **2** reaction, comeback, acknowledgement, feedback.
▣ **1** question, query.

responsibility *noun* (PL. **responsibilities**) **1** something or someone for which one is responsible. **2** the state of being responsible or having important duties for which one is responsible.

▤ **3** the fact of being the cause of or to blame for something. **1** duty, obligation, burden, onus, charge, care. **2** authority, power, trust. **3** fault, blame, guilt, culpability, answerability, accountability.

responsible *adj.* **1** (**responsible for someone** or **something**) having charge or control over them and being accountable for them: *was responsible for a class of 20 children/is responsible for ordering the stationery.* **2** (**responsible to someone**) having to account for one's actions to them. **3** *said of a job, position, etc* having many important duties, especially the taking of important decisions;

involving much responsibility. **4 (responsible for something)** being the cause of it: *who is responsible for this?* **5** *said of a person* **a** able to be trusted. **b** able to answer for one's own conduct; capable of rational and socially acceptable behaviour. [from Latin *respondere*, to respond]

▣ **1** in charge of, in control of. **2** answerable to, accountable to. **3** important, authoritative, executive, decision-making. **4** guilty, culpable, at fault, to blame, liable, answerable, accountable. **5** dependable, reliable, conscientious, trustworthy, honest, sound, steady, sober, mature, sensible, rational.

▣ **5** irresponsible, unreliable, untrustworthy.

responsibly *adv.* in a responsible way.
responsive *adj.* **1** *said of a person* quick to react or respond. **2** reacting well or favourably: *a disease responsive to drugs.* **3** made as or forming a response: *a responsive smile.* [from Latin *responsivus*]

▣ **1** alert, aware, *colloq.* on the ball, *colloq.* with it, prompt, receptive.

responsively *adv.* in a responsive way.
responsiveness *noun* being responsive.
respray — *verb* (with stress on *-spray*) to spray (especially the bodywork of a vehicle) with new paint. — *noun* (with stress on *re-*) the act or an instance of respraying.
rest[1] — *noun* **1** a period of relaxation or freedom from work, activity, worry, etc. **2** sleep; repose. **3** calm; tranquillity. **4** a state of not moving or working. **5** death thought of as repose: *lay someone to rest* (= to bury a corpse). **6** (*often in compounds*) something which holds or supports (something): *a headrest on a car seat.* **7** a pause in reading, speaking, etc. **8** an interval of silence in a piece of music, or a mark showing this. **9** a place for resting, especially a lodging for sailors. — *verb* **1** *trans., intrans.* to stop or cause to stop working or moving. **2** *intrans.* to relax, especially by sleeping. **3** *intrans.* to be calm and free from worry. **4** *trans., intrans.* to set, place, or lie on or against something for support: *rested her arm on the chair.* **5** *trans., intrans.* to depend or cause to depend or be based on or in: *will rest my argument on practicalities.* **6** *trans., intrans., said of the eyes* to remain or cause them to remain looking in a certain direction. **7** *intrans.* to be left without further attention, discussion, or action: *let the matter rest there.* **8** *intrans.* to lie dead or buried. **9** *intrans., said of farmland* to lie without a crop in order to regain its fertility. — **at rest 1** not moving. **2** free from pain, worry, etc: *set his mind at rest.* **3** dead. **rest one's case** to conclude the calling of witnesses and presentation of arguments in a law case. [from Anglo-Saxon]

▣ *noun* **1** break, pause, breathing-space, *colloq.* breather, intermission, interlude, interval, recess, holiday, vacation, halt, cessation, lull, respite, lie-down, snooze, nap, siesta. **2** sleep, repose, leisure, relaxation. **3** tranquillity, calm, stillness, peace. **4** idleness, inactivity, motionlessness, standstill. **6** support, prop, stand, base. *verb* **1** pause, halt, stop. **2, 4** relax. **2** repose, *colloq.* take it easy, sit, recline, lounge, laze, lie down, sleep, snooze, doze. **3** lean, stand. **at rest 1** still, stationary, motionless, unmoving, inert. **2** at ease, easy, calm, peaceful, relaxed, serene, untroubled, unworried, unruffled.

▣ *noun* **1, 4** work. **4** action, activity. *verb* **1** continue. **2** work. **at rest 1** moving, in motion. **2** uneasy.

rest[2] — **the rest 1** what is left when part of something is taken away, finished, etc, the remainder. **2** the others. — *verb intrans.* to continue to be: *rest assured.* [from Latin *restare*, to remain]

▣ **the rest 1** the remainder, the balance, the surplus, the excess, the residue, the remains, the leftovers, the remnants. **2** the others.

restaurant *noun* a place where meals may be bought and eaten. [from French]

▣ eating-house, bistro, steakhouse, grill room, dining-room, snack bar, buffet, cafeteria, café, *colloq.* eatery, *North Amer.* diner.

restaurant car a carriage on a train in which meals are served to travellers.
restaurateur /rɛstərəˈtɜː(r)/ *noun* the owner or manager of a restaurant. [from French]
restful *adj.* **1** bringing rest or causing a person to feel calm, peaceful, and rested. **2** relaxed; at rest.

▣ CALM, TRANQUIL, SERENE, PEACEFUL, QUIET. **1** relaxing, soothing, leisurely, unhurried. **2** relaxed, comfortable, undisturbed.

▣ **1** tiring. **2** restless.

restfully *adv.* in a restful way.
restfulness *noun* being restful.
resting potential *Physiol.* the potential difference between the inner and outer surfaces of a nerve that is not conducting a nerve impulse. It has a negative value, in contrast to the positive value of the *action potential* which occurs during the passage of a nerve impulse. See also ACTION POTENTIAL.
restitution *noun* **1** the act of giving back to the rightful owner something lost or stolen. **2** the paying of compensation for loss or injury. [from Latin *restituere*, to put up again]

▣ **1** return, restoration, replacement. **2** reimbursement, compensation, indemnification, reparation.

restive *adj.* **1** unwilling to accept control or authority. **2** restless; nervous. **3** *said of a horse* unwilling to move forwards. [from Old French *restif*, inert]

▣ **1** impatient, unruly, wayward, wilful, turbulent, undisciplined. **2** restless, agitated, fidgety, unsettled, nervous, anxious, fretful, edgy.

restively *adv.* in a restive way, nervously.
restiveness *noun* being restive.
restless *adj.* **1** constantly moving or fidgeting; unable to stay still or quiet. **2** giving no rest: *a restless night.* **3** worried, nervous and uneasy.

▣ **1** fidgety, restive, unruly, turbulent, impatient. **2** sleepless. **3** agitated, nervous, anxious, worried, uneasy, unsettled, disturbed, troubled, fretful, edgy, jumpy.

▣ **1, 3** calm, relaxed.

restorable *adj.* capable of being restored.
Restoration the return of Charles II to England (May 1660) at the request of the Convention Parliament following the collapse of the Protectorate regime.
restoration *noun* **1** the act or process of restoring. **2** the act of giving back something lost or stolen. **3** something restored or given back. **4** a model or reconstruction (eg of a ruin, extinct animal, etc). **5** the act of returning to a former and higher status, rank, etc. [from Latin *restauratio*, from *restaurare*, to restore]

▣ **1** renovation, renewal, rebuilding, reconstruction, refurbishment. **2** return, restitution, replacement, reimbursement. **5** reinstatement, reinstallation, recall.

restorative /rɪˈstɒrətɪv, rɪˈstɔːrətɪv/ — *adj.* tending or helping to restore or improve health, strength, spirits, etc. — *noun* a restorative food or medicine.

▣ *adj.* tonic, bracing, fortifying, invigorating, refreshing. *noun* tonic, cordial, pick-me-up.

restore *verb* **1** to return (a building, painting, etc) to a former condition by repairing or cleaning it, etc. **2** to bring (someone or something) back to a normal or proper state: *be restored to health.* **3** to bring back (a normal or proper state): *restore discipline.* **4** to return (something) lost or stolen to the rightful owner. **5** to bring or put back to a former and higher status, rank, etc. **6** to reconstruct or make a model or representation of (a ruin, extinct animal, etc). [from Latin *restaurare*]

▣ **1** renovate, renew, rebuild, reconstruct, refurbish, retouch, recondition, repair, mend, fix. **2** revive, refresh, rejuvenate, revitalize, strengthen. **3** re-establish, reintroduce. **4** replace, return. **5** reinstate, rehabilitate.
▣ **1** damage. **2** weaken. **4** remove.

restorer *noun* a person who restores.

restrain *verb* **1** to prevent (someone, oneself, etc) from doing something. **2** to keep (one's temper, ambition, etc) under control. **3** to take away (a person's) freedom, especially by arresting them. [from Latin *restringere*, to draw back tightly]

▣ **1** stop, prevent. **2** restrict, regulate, control, govern, hold back, keep back, suppress, subdue, repress, inhibit, check, curb, bridle, moderate. **3** arrest, bind, tie, chain, fetter, manacle, imprison, jail, confine,
▣ encourage, liberate.

restrained *adj.* **1** controlling, or able to control, one's emotions. **2** showing restraint; without excess.

▣ MODERATE, TEMPERATE, MILD, CALM. **1** controlled, steady, self-controlled. **2** subdued, muted, quiet, soft, low-key, unobtrusive, discreet, tasteful.
▣ UNRESTRAINED.

restraint *noun* **1** the act of restraining or state of being restrained. **2** something that restrains; a limit or restriction. **3** the avoidance of exaggeration or excess; the ability to remain calm and reasonable.

▣ **1, 2** restriction, control, constraint, limitation. **1** hindrance, prevention, suppression, bondage, captivity, confinement, imprisonment. **2** limit, tie, hold, grip, check, curb, rein, bridle, bonds, chains, fetters, straitjacket. **3** moderation, inhibition, self-control, self-discipline.
▣ **1** liberty.

restrict *verb* **1** to keep (someone or something) within certain limits. **2** to limit or regulate the use of, especially to withhold from general use. [from Latin *restrictus*, drawn back]

▣ LIMIT, CONFINE. **1** bound, demarcate, contain, cramp, constrain, impede, hinder, hamper, handicap, tie, restrain, curtail. **2** control, regulate.
▣ **1** broaden. **2** free.

restricted *adj.* **1** limited in space. **2** not for general use, circulation, etc. **3** *said of an area, place, etc* which only certain people, especially military personnel, may enter.

▣ **1, 2** limited. **1** narrow, cramped, confined, tight, restrictive. **2** closed, private, exclusive.

restricted area an area in which a special speed limit is in force, or to which access is limited.

restriction *noun* **1** an act or instance of restricting. **2** something that restricts. **3** a regulation or rule that restricts or limits.

▣ **1, 2** limitation, constraint, restraint. **2** limit, bound, confine, handicap, check, curb. **3** ban, embargo, control, regulation, rule, stipulation, condition, proviso.
▣ **1** freedom.

restriction enzyme *Biochem.* any of a large group of enzymes that can be used to break molecules of DNA at specific points. Restriction enzymes are used extensively in genetic engineering to analyse the structure of chromosomes.

restrictive *adj.* restricting or intended to restrict, especially excessively.

restrictive covenant *Legal* a deed, most commonly found in title deeds for land or property, which restricts the purchaser's use of it in some way.

restrictively *adv.* in a restrictive way.

restrictive practice (*often* **restrictive practices**) **1** an agreement between manufacturers, companies, etc to keep production of goods down or limit the supply of goods on the market to keep prices high. **2** a practice by a trade union which limits and restricts the activities of members of other trade unions.

rest room *North Amer.* a room with lavatories, wash basins, and sometimes a seating area, in a shop, theatre, factory, etc, for the use of the staff or public.

result — *noun* **1** an outcome or consequence of something. **2** (*often* **results**) a positive or favourable outcome or consequence. **3** a number or quantity obtained by calculation, etc. **4** (**results**) a list of final scores (in a series of football matches, etc). **5** *colloq.* a win in a game. **6** (**results**) a list of marks a student has obtained in an examination or series of examinations. — *verb intrans.* **1** (**result from something**) to be a consequence or outcome of some action, event, etc. **2** (**result in something**) to end in a specified way: *carelessness results in mistakes.* [from Latin *resultare*, to leap back]

▣ *noun* **1** outcome, consequence, effect, sequel, repercussion, reaction, upshot, issue, end-product, fruit, score, answer, verdict, judgement, decision, conclusion. *verb* **1** follow, ensue from, issue from, emerge from, arise from, spring from, derive from, stem from, flow from, proceed from, develop from. **2** end in, finish in, terminate in, culminate in.
▣ *noun* **1** cause. *verb* CAUSE.

resultant — *adj.* resulting. — *noun Maths., Physics* a single force which is the equivalent of two or more forces acting on an object.

resume *verb* **1** *trans., intrans.* to return to or begin again after an interruption. **2** to take back or go to (a former position, etc): *resume one's seat.* [from Latin *resumere*]

▣ **1** restart, recommence, reopen, reconvene, continue, carry on. **2** return to, go back to, take back, reoccupy.
▣ **1** cease.

résumé /ˈrezjʊmeɪ/ *noun* **1** a summary. **2** *North Amer.* a curriculum vitae. [from French]

▣ **1** summary, précis, synopsis, outline, sketch, abstract, breakdown, round-up, run-down.

resumption *noun* the act of resuming. [from Latin *resumptio*]

▣ restart, recommencement, reopening, renewal, resurgence, continuation.
▣ cessation.

resurgence *noun* the act of returning to life, to a state of activity, importance, influence, etc after a period of decline. [from Latin *resurgere*, to rise again]

. . . .

▤ revival, renaissance, restoration, resurrection, revitalization, revivification, upsurge, upturn, renewal, reintroduction.

. . . .

resurgent *adj.* capable of rising again; that rises again.
resurrect /rɛzəˈrɛkt/ *verb* **1** to bring back to life from the dead. **2** to bring back into general use, view, activity, etc.

. . . .

▤ RESTORE, REVIVE, RESUSCITATE. **2** reactivate, bring back, reintroduce, renew.

🄴 **1** kill, bury.

. . . .

resurrection *noun* **1** the act of resurrecting or bringing (something) back into use. **2** the act of coming back to life after death. **3** (**Resurrection**) *Christianity* **a** Christ's coming back to life three days after his death on the cross. **b** the coming back to life of all the dead at the Last Judgement. [from Latin *resurgere*, to rise again]

. . . .

▤ **2** restoration, revival, resuscitation, renaissance, rebirth, renewal, resurgence, reappearance, return, comeback.

. . . .

resuscitate /rɪˈsʌsɪteɪt/ *verb trans., intrans.* to bring or come back to consciousness; to revive. [from Latin *resuscitare*, to raise again]

. . . .

▤ revive, resurrect, save, rescue, reanimate, quicken, reinvigorate, revitalize, restore, renew.

. . . .

resuscitation *noun* resuscitating or being resuscitated.
retail /ˈriːteɪl, riːˈteɪl/ — *noun* the sale of goods either individually or in small quantities to customers who will not resell them. — *adj.* relating to or concerned with such sale of goods. — *adv.* by retail; at a retail price. — *verb* **1** *trans., intrans.* to sell (goods) in small quantities to customers; (of goods) to be sold in this way. **2** to tell or recount (a story, gossip, etc) in great detail. [from Old French *retailler*, to cut off]

retailer *noun* a retail outlet.
retail price index a monthly index of the retail prices of certain household goods, taken as indicative of the cost of living for that month, and as a way of monitoring changes in the cost of living over a period of time.
retain *verb* **1** to continue to have, contain, hold, use, etc. **2** *said of a person* to be able to remember. **3** to hold back or keep in place. **4** to secure the services of (a person, especially a lawyer) by paying a preliminary fee, often before the actual work begins. [from Latin *retinere*, to hold back]

. . . .

▤ **1, 3** hold, hold back. **1** keep, reserve, save, preserve.
2 remember, memorize. **3** keep in place, secure, fix.
4 employ, engage, hire, commission.

🄴 **1** release. **2** forget. **4** dismiss.

. . . .

retainer *noun* **1** a fee paid to secure a person's professional services, especially those of a lawyer or barrister. **2** a domestic servant who has been with a family for a long time. **3** a reduced rent paid for property while it is not occupied.

. . . .

▤ **2** servant, maid, domestic, attendant, footman, valet, vassal.

. . . .

retaining wall a wall built to support and hold back a mass of earth, rock, or water.
retake /riːˈteɪk, ˈriːteɪk/ — *verb* (with stress on *-take*) (PAST TENSE **retook**; PAST PARTICIPLE **retaken**) **1** to capture again. **2** to take (eg an examination) again. **3** to photograph (eg a scene in a film) again. — *noun* (with stress on *re-*) a second taking of a photograph, filming of a scene, or sitting of an exam.

retaliate *verb intrans.* to repay an injury, wrong, etc in kind; to get revenge. [from Latin *retaliare*]

. . . .

▤ reciprocate, counter-attack, hit back, strike back, fight back, get one's own back, get even with, take revenge.

. . . .

retaliation *noun* an act of retaliating; revenge.

. . . .

▤ reprisal, counter-attack, revenge, vengeance, retribution.

. . . .

retaliatory /rɪˈtalɪətərɪ, rɪˈtalɪeɪtərɪ/ *adj.* relating to or involving retaliation.
retard /rɪˈtɑːd/ *verb* **1** to make slow or delay. **2** to keep back the progress, development, etc of (eg a person's mental abilities). [from Latin *retardare*, from *tardus*, slow]
retardant *adj.* making something slower or delayed.
retardation *noun* retarding or being retarded.
retarded *adj.* not having made the expected physical or especially mental development.
retch — *verb intrans.* to strain to vomit or almost vomit, but not actually do so. — *noun* an act of retching. [from Anglo-Saxon *hræcan*]
retention *noun* **1** the act of retaining or state of being retained. **2** the ability to remember experiences and things learnt. **3** the failure to get rid of fluid from the body. [from Latin *retentio*]
retentive *adj.* able to retain or keep, especially fluid, memories, or information.
retentively *adv.* in a retentive way.
retentiveness *noun* being retentive.
retexture *verb* to treat (a blanket, garment, etc) with chemicals which restore the original texture of the material.
rethink — *verb* (with stress on *-think*) (PAST TENSE AND PAST PARTICIPLE **rethought**) to think about or consider (a plan, etc) again, usually with a view to changing one's mind. — *noun* (with stress on *re-*) an act of rethinking.

. . . .

▤ *verb* reconsider, reassess, reflect (on), change one's mind (about).

. . . .

reticence *noun* being reticent.

. . . .

▤ reserve, shyness, uncommunicativeness, restraint, silence, taciturnity, secretiveness, low profile.

. . . .

reticent *adj.* not saying very much; not willing to communicate; not communicating everything that one knows. [from Latin *reticere*, to be silent]

. . . .

▤ reserved, shy, uncommunicative, unforthcoming, tight-lipped, secretive, taciturn, silent, quiet.

🄴 communicative, forward, frank.

. . . .

reticulate — *adj.* (pronounced -lət) like a net, especially in having lines, veins, etc crossing. — *verb trans., intrans.* (pronounced -leɪt) to form or be formed into a network; to mark or be marked with a network of lines, etc. [from Latin *reticulatus*, like a net]
reticule *noun Hist.* a woman's small, often netted or beaded pouch-like bag which fastens with a drawstring. [from Latin *reticulum*, little net]
retina /ˈrɛtɪnə/ *noun* (PL. **retinas**) *Anat.* the light-sensitive tissue that lines the back of the vertebrate eye. In humans it consists of an outer pigmented layer, and an inner layer containing two types of light-sensitive cell, the rods and cones. Nerve impulses generated in these cells are relayed to the brain, where they are interpreted as vision. [from Latin, from *rete*, net]
retinal *adj.* relating to or in the region of the retina.
retinue /ˈrɛtɪnjuː/ *noun* the servants, officials, aides, etc who travel with and attend to an important person. [from Old French *retenue*]

▤ suite, entourage, train, attendants, court, household, followers.

retiral *noun* an act of retiring (eg from work) or going away from (a place).

retire *verb* **1** *trans., intrans.* to stop or cause to stop working permanently, usually on reaching an age at which a pension can be received. **2** *intrans.* to go away to rest, especially to go to bed. **3** *intrans.* to go away from or to; to leave: *retire to the drawing room.* **4** *trans., intrans.* to withdraw or cause to withdraw from a sporting contest, especially because of injury. **5** *trans., intrans. said of a military force, etc* to move or be moved back away from a dangerous position. [from French *retirer*]

▤ **3** leave, depart, withdraw, retreat, recede. **4** scratch. **5** retreat.
▣ **1** join. **3** enter, advance.

retired *adj.* **1** having permanently stopped working because of age. **2** secluded.

retirement *noun* **1** the act of retiring or state of being retired from work. **2** seclusion and privacy.

▤ **2** seclusion, privacy, obscurity, withdrawal, retreat, solitude, loneliness.

retirement pension *Brit.* a weekly payment by the state to people who have retired from work.
retirement pregnancy artificially induced pregnancy in an elderly or postmenopausal woman.
retiring *adj.* shy and reserved; not liking to be noticed.

▤ shy, bashful, timid, shrinking, quiet, reticent, reserved, self-effacing, unassertive, modest, unassuming, humble.
▣ bold, forward, assertive.

retort — *verb* **1** *intrans.* to make a quick and clever or angry reply. **2** to turn (an argument, criticism, blame, etc) back on the person who first used that argument, criticism, blame, etc. **3** to heat and purify (metal). — *noun* **1** a quick and clever or angry reply. **2** an argument, criticism, blame, etc which is turned back upon the originator. **3** a glass vessel with a long neck which curves downwards, used in distilling. **4** a vessel for heating metals such as iron and carbon to make steel, or for heating coal to produce gas. [from Latin *retorquere*, to twist back]

▤ *verb* **1** answer, reply, respond, rejoin, return, counter, retaliate. *noun* **1** answer, reply, response, rejoinder, riposte, repartee, quip.

retouch *verb* to improve or repair (a photograph, negative, painting, etc) by adding extra touches.
retrace *verb* **1** to go back over (one's route, path, etc). **2** to go over (recent events, etc) again in one's memory. **3** to trace back: *retrace one's roots.*
retract *verb trans., intrans.* **1** to withdraw (a statement, claim, charge, etc) as wrong, offensive, or unjustified. **2** to refuse to acknowledge (a promise, agreement, etc that one has made). **3** to draw in or back or be drawn in or back. [from Latin *retrahere*, to draw back]

▤ **1, 3** take back, withdraw. **1** recant, reverse, revoke, rescind, cancel, repeal. **2** repudiate, disown, disclaim, deny.
▣ **1** assert, maintain.

retractable *adj.* able to be drawn up, in, or back.
retractile *adj. technical, said eg of a cat's claws* able to be drawn up, in, or back.

retraction *noun* a retracting, especially of something one has said, agreed or promised.

▤ withdrawal, apology, recantation, revocation, rescindment, cancellation, repeal.

retrain *verb* **1** to teach (someone) new skills, eg those necessary to qualify for alternative employment. **2** *intrans.* to learn new skills.
retread /riːˈtrɛd, ˈriːtrɛd/ — *verb* (with stress on *-tread*) (PAST TENSE **retrod**; PAST PARTICIPLE **retrodden**, **retreaded**) to bond new tread on to (an old or worn tyre). — *noun* (with stress on *re*-) an old or worn tyre which has had new tread bonded on to it.
retreat — *verb* **1** *intrans., trans. said of a military force* to move back or away from, or be caused to move back or away from, a position or battle. **2** *intrans.* to move backwards or away. **3** *intrans.* to slope backwards; to recede. — *noun* **1** the act of retreating, especially from battle, a military position, danger, etc. **2** a signal, especially one given on a bugle, to retreat. **3** a place of privacy, safety and seclusion. **4** a period of retirement from the world, especially for prayer, meditation and study. [from Latin *retrahere*, to draw back]

▤ *verb* **1, 2** draw back, withdraw, retire. **2** leave, depart, quit, recoil, shrink, turn tail. *noun* **1** withdrawal, departure, evacuation, flight. **3** seclusion, privacy, hideaway, den, refuge, asylum, sanctuary, shelter, haven.
▣ *verb* **1, 2** advance. *noun* **1** advance, charge.

retrench *verb trans., intrans.* to reduce or cut down (expenses, money spent, etc); to economize. [from Old French *retrenchier*, to cut off or back]

▤ cut down, cut back, economize.

retrenchment *noun* **1** cutting down, limitation, reduction. **2** economizing.
retrial /riːˈtraɪəl, ˈriːtraɪəl/ *noun* a further judicial trial.
retribution *noun* deserved punishment, especially for sin or wrongdoing. [from Latin *retribuere*, to give back]
retributive *adj.* being or forming a punishment which is deserved or suitable.
retrievable *adj.* capable of being retrieved.
retrieval *noun* the act or possibility of retrieving or getting back.
retrieve *verb* **1** to get or bring back again; to recover. **2** to rescue or save: *retrieve the situation.* **3** to recover (information) from storage in a computer memory. **4** to remember or recall to mind. **5** *trans., intrans. said of a dog* to search for and bring back (game which has been shot by a hunter, or a ball, stick, etc which has been thrown). [from Old French *retrouver*, to find again]

▤ **1** recover, fetch, bring back, regain, get back, recapture, repossess, recoup. **2** save, salvage, rescue, redeem, restore.
▣ **1** lose.

retriever *noun* a breed of dog with a short golden or black water-resistant coat, trained to retrieve game.
retro *colloq* — *adj.* reminiscent of or reverting to the past, especially for effect. — *noun* design or style that deliberately recreates the past.
retro- *prefix* forming words meaning: **1** back or backwards in time or space. **2** behind. [from Latin *retro*, backwards]
retroactive *adj.* applying to or affecting things from a date in the past: *retroactive legislation.* [from Latin *retro-agere*, to drive back]
retroactivity *noun* being retroactive.
retrograde — *adj.* **1** being, tending towards or causing a worse, less advanced or less desirable state. **2** moving or

bending backwards. **3** in a reversed or opposite order. **4** *Astron.*, *said of a planet, etc* seeming to move in the opposite or contrary direction to other planets, etc. **5** *Astron.*, *said of a planet, etc* seeming to move from east to west. — *verb intrans.* **1** to move backwards. **2** to deteriorate or decline. **3** *Astron.*, *said of a planet* to show retrograde movement. [from Latin *retrogradus*, going backwards]

. . . .

■ *adj.* **1** retrogressive, regressive, backward, reverse, negative, downward, declining, deteriorating.

◨ *adj.* **1** progressive.

. . . .

retrogress *verb intrans.* to go back to an earlier, worse, or less advanced condition or state; to deteriorate. [from Latin *retrogressus*, a movement backwards]

retrogression *noun* **1** a going backward or reversion. **2** a decline in quality or merit. **3** *Astron.* retrograde movement.

retrogressive *adj.* involving retrogression.

. . . .

■ retrograde, regressive, backward, reverse, negative, downward, declining, deteriorating.

. . . .

retro-rocket *noun Astron.* a small rocket motor that is fired in the opposite direction to that in which a spacecraft, artificial satellite, etc is moving, in order to slow it down.

retrospect — **in retrospect** when considering or looking back on what has happened in the past. [from Latin *retrospicere*, to look back]

. . . .

■ **in retrospect** looking back on it, retrospectively, with hindsight, on re-examination, on review, on reconsideration, on recollection.

. . . .

retrospection *noun* **1** an act of looking back at the past. **2** a tendency to look back on one's past life.

retrospective — *adj.* **1** *said of a law, etc* applying to the past as well as to the present and to the future. **2** looking back on past events. — *noun* an exhibition which shows how an artist's work has developed over the years.

retroussé /rə'truːseɪ/ *adj.*, *said especially of the nose* turned up at the end. [from French *retroussé*, tucked up]

retrovirus /'rɛtroʊvaɪərəs/ *noun* any of a group of viruses with genetic material consisting of RNA rather than DNA, including many carcinogenic (cancer-causing) viruses, as well as the HIV virus which causes AIDS. [from *reverse transcriptase* (the active enzyme in these viruses) + VIRUS]

retry *verb* (**retries, retried**) **1** to submit to a further judicial trial. **2** to make a further attempt.

retsina /rɛt'siːnə/ *noun* a Greek white resin-flavoured wine. [from modern Greek]

return — *verb* **1** *intrans.* to come or go back again to a former place, state, or owner. **2** to give, send, put back, etc in a former position. **3** *intrans.* to come back to in thought or speech: *return to the topic later.* **4** to repay with something of the same value: *return the compliment.* **5** *trans., intrans.* to answer or reply. **6** to report or state officially or formally. **7** to earn or produce (profit, interest, etc). **8** to elect as a Member of Parliament. **9** *said of a jury* to give (a verdict). **10** *Tennis, Badminton* to hit (a ball, etc) served by one's opponent. — *noun* **1** an act of coming back from a place, state, etc. **2** an act of returning something, especially to a former place, state, ownership, etc. **3** something returned, especially unsold newspapers and magazines returned to the publisher or a theatre ticket returned to the theatre for resale. **4** profit from work, a business, or investment. **5** (*often* **returns**) a statement of a person's income and allowances, used for calculating the tax which must be paid. **6** (*usually* **returns**) a statement of the votes polled in an election. **7** *Brit.* a return ticket. **8** an answer or reply. **9** a ball, etc hit back after one's opponent's service in tennis, etc. — *adj.* forming, causing, or relating to a return. — **by return**

of post by the next post in the return direction. **in return** in exchange; in reply; as compensation. **many happy returns of the day** an expression of good wishes on a person's birthday. [from Old French *retorner*]

. . . .

■ *verb* **1** come back, reappear, recur, go back, backtrack, regress, revert. **2** give back, hand back, send back, deliver, put back, replace, restore. **4** reciprocate, requite, repay, refund, reimburse, recompense. **5** answer, reply, retort, riposte, counter. *noun* **1** reappearance, recurrence, comeback, home-coming. **2** replacement, restoration, reinstatement, reciprocation. **4** revenue, income, proceeds, takings, yield, gain, profit, reward, advantage, benefit.

◨ *verb* **1** leave, depart. **2** take. *noun* **1** departure, disappearance. **2** removal. **4** payment, expense, loss.

. . . .

returnable *adj.* that may or must be returned.

returning officer *Brit.* an official in charge of running an election in a constituency, counting the votes, and declaring the result.

return match a second match played between the same players or teams, usually at the home ground of the side previously playing away.

return ticket a ticket which allows a person to travel to a place and back again.

reunion *noun* **1** a meeting of people (eg relatives or friends) who have not met for some time. **2** the act of reuniting or state of being reunited.

reunite *verb trans., intrans.* to bring or come together after being separated.

Rev. or **Revd** *abbrev.* Reverend.

rev *colloq.* — *noun* (*usually* **revs**) a revolution in an internal combustion engine, the number of revolutions often being used as an indication of engine speed. — *verb* (**revved**, **revving**) *colloq.* (*also* **rev up**) **1** to increase the speed of a car engine, etc. **2** *intrans.* *said of an engine or vehicle* to run faster. [a shortening of REVOLUTION]

revalue or **re-evaluate** *verb* **1** to make a new valuation of. **2** to adjust the exchange rate of (a currency).

revamp *verb* to revise, renovate, or patch up, usually with the aim of improving.

Revd see REV.

reveal *verb* **1** to make known (a secret, etc). **2** to show; to allow to be seen. **3** *said of a deity* to make known through divine inspiration or supernatural means. [from Latin *revelare*, to unveil]

. . . .

■ **1, 2** expose, uncover, disclose. **1** divulge, betray, leak, tell, impart, communicate, broadcast, publish, announce, proclaim. **2** show, display, exhibit, manifest, unveil, unmask.

◨ **1, 2** conceal. **2** hide, mask.

. . . .

revealing *adj.* **1** that reveals much about a person's character, intentions, etc. **2** *said of a dress, neckline, etc* that leaves much of the wearer's body visible.

. . . .

■ **1** indicative, significant, revelatory, give-away. **2** low-cut, plunging, daring, see-through, diaphanous, sheer.

. . . .

reveille /rɪ'valɪ, rɪ'vɛlɪ/ *noun* a bugle or drum call at daybreak to waken soldiers, etc. [from French *réveillez!*, wake up!]

revel — *verb intrans.* (**revelled, revelling**) **1** (**revel in something**) to take great delight in it. **2** to enjoy oneself in a noisy, lively way. — *noun* (*usually* **revels**) noisy, lively enjoyment, festivities or merrymaking. [from Old French *reveler*, to riot]

. . . .

■ *verb* **1** enjoy, delight in, relish, savour, like, love, thrive on, bask in, glory in, lap up, indulge in, wallow in, luxuriate in.

. . . .

revelation *noun* **1** the act of revealing (secrets, information, etc). **2** that which is made known or seen. **3** something revealed to man by God through divine inspiration or supernatural means. **4** (**Revelation** or **Revelations**) the last book of the New Testament, which contains prophecies of the end of the world. [from Latin *revelatio*, from *revelare*, to unveil]

☐ **1, 2** disclosure, confession, admission, betrayal, show, display, exhibition, manifestation, communication, publication, announcement, proclamation. **1** uncovering, unveiling, exposure, unmasking, broadcasting. **2** news, information, *colloq.* give-away, leak.

revelatory /ˈrevələtərɪ, revəlˈeɪtərɪ/ *adj.* revealing.
reveller *noun* a merrymaker, a partygoer.
revelry *noun* (PL. **revelries**) noisy lively enjoyment, festivities, or merrymaking.

☐ celebration, festivity, party, merrymaking, jollity, fun, carousal, debauchery,
☒ sobriety.

revenge — *noun* **1** malicious injury, harm, or wrong done in return for injury, harm, or wrong received. **2** something done as a means of returning injury, harm, etc for injury, harm, etc received. **3** the desire to do such injury, harm, etc. — *verb* **1** to do injury, harm, etc in return for (injury, harm, etc) received. **2** to take revenge on someone on behalf of (oneself or someone else). [from Old French *revenger*]

☐ *noun* **1, 2** vengeance. **2** satisfaction, reprisal, retaliation, requital, retribution. *verb* AVENGE. **1** repay, retaliate for, get one's own back for.

revengeful *adj.* ready to seek revenge.
revenue *noun* **1** money which comes to a person, etc from any source (eg property, shares), especially the money raised by the government from taxes, etc. **2** (*often* **Revenue**) a government department responsible for collecting this money. [from Old French, from *revenir*, to return]

☐ **1** income, return, yield, interest, profit, gain, proceeds, receipts, takings.
☒ **1** expenditure.

reverberate *verb* **1** *intrans. said of a sound, light, heat, etc* to be echoed, repeated or reflected repeatedly. **2** to echo, repeat or reflect (a sound, light, etc) repeatedly. **3** *intrans. said of a story, scandal, etc* to be repeated continually. [from Latin *reverberare*, to beat back]

☐ **1, 2** echo, re-echo, resonate. **1** resound, ring, boom, vibrate.

reverberation *noun* reverberating.
reverberatory furnace a furnace in which the material (eg steel, ceramics, or glass) is not heated directly by the burning fuel, but by flame directed at a low roof which radiates heat downwards on to the material.
revere *verb* to feel or show great affection and respect for. [from Latin *revereri*, to stand in awe of]

☐ respect, esteem, honour, pay homage to, venerate, worship, adore, exalt.
☒ despise, scorn.

reverence *noun* **1** great respect, especially that shown to something sacred or holy. **2** (**His** or **Your Reverence**) a title used to address or refer to some members of the clergy.

☐ **1** respect, awe, deference, honour, homage, admiration, veneration, worship, adoration, devotion.
☒ **1** contempt, scorn.

reverend — *adj.* **1** worthy of being revered or respected. **2** (**Reverend**) used before proper names as a title for members of the clergy. — *noun colloq.* a member of the clergy.
reverent *adj.* showing or feeling great respect.

☐ respectful, deferential, reverential, humble, dutiful, awed, solemn, pious, devout, adoring, loving.
☒ irreverent, disrespectful.

reverential *adj.* showing great respect or reverence.

☐ respectful, deferential, reverent, humble, dutiful.

reverentially *adv.* in a reverential way.
reverently *adv.* with reverence.
reverie *noun* **1** a state of pleasantly dreamy and absent-minded thought. **2** a day-dream or absent-minded idea or thought. [from Old French *reverie*, from *rever*, to speak wildly]
revers /rəˈveə(r)/ *noun* (PL. **revers**) any part of a garment that is turned back, especially a lapel. [from French *revers*, reverse]
reversal *noun* **1** the act of reversing or state of being reversed. **2** a change in fortune, especially for the worse.

☐ REVERSE. **1** negation, cancellation, annulment, nullification, countermanding, revocation, rescinding, repeal, turnabout, turnaround, U-turn, volte-face. **2** upset, misfortune, mishap, setback, disappointment, defeat.
☒ **1** advancement, progress.

reverse — *verb* **1** *trans., intrans.* to move or cause to move in an opposite or backwards direction. **2** to put into an opposite or contrary position, state, order, etc. **3** to change (a policy, decision, etc) to the exact opposite or contrary. **4** to set aside or overthrow (a legal decision or judgement). — *noun* **1** the opposite or contrary of something. **2** an act of changing to an opposite or contrary position, direction, etc or of being changed in this way. **3** the back or rear side of something, especially the back cover of a book. **4** the side of a coin, medal, note, etc with a secondary design on. See also OBVERSE. **5** a piece of bad luck; a defeat; a reversal. **6** a mechanism, eg a car gear, which makes a machine, vehicle, etc move in a backwards direction. — *adj.* opposite, contrary or turned round in order, position, direction, etc. — **in reverse** in an opposite or backwards direction. **reverse the charges** to make a telephone call to be paid for by the person called instead of by the caller. [from Latin *reversare*, to turn round]

☐ *verb* **1** back, retreat, backtrack. **2, 3** turn round, transpose, overturn, upset, change, alter. **2** invert, up-end, undo, negate. **4** cancel, annul, invalidate, countermand, overrule, revoke, rescind, repeal, retract, quash, overthrow. *noun* **1** inverse, converse, contrary, opposite, antithesis. **2** reversal, turnabout, turnaround, U-turn. **3** underside, back, rear. **5** misfortune, mishap, misadventure, adversity, affliction, hardship, trial, blow, disappointment, setback, check, delay, problem, difficulty, failure, defeat. *adj.* opposite, contrary, converse, inverse, inverted, backward, back, rear.
☒ *verb* **1** advance. **4** enforce.

reversed *adj.* **1** turned the other way about, backwards, or upside down. **2** overturned, annulled.
reversible *adj.* **1** able to be reversed. **2** *said of clothes* able to be worn with either side out.

reversible reaction 1 *Chem.* a chemical reaction that occurs in both directions simultaneously, so that products are being converted back to reactants at the same time that reactants are being converted to products. **2** a chemical reaction that can be made to proceed in one direction or the other by changing the conditions.

reversing light a usually white light on the rear of a vehicle which warns the drivers and pedestrians behind that the vehicle is going to move, or is moving, backwards.

reversion *noun* **1** a return to an earlier state, belief, etc. **2** the legal right (eg of an original owner or that owner's heirs) to possess a property when the present owner dies. **3** property to which a person has such a right. **4** insurance which is paid on a person's death. **5** *Biol.* a return to an earlier, ancestral, and usually less advanced, type. [from Latin *reversio*]

revert *verb usually intrans.* **1** to return to a topic in thought or conversation. **2** to return to a former and usually worse state, practice, etc. **3** *Biol.* to return to an earlier, ancestral, and usually simpler type. **4** *said especially of property* to return to an original owner or his or her heirs after belonging temporarily to someone else. **5** *trans.* to turn (something) back. [from Latin *revertere*, to turn back]

◼ **1** return to, go back to, resume. **2** lapse, relapse, regress.

review — *noun* **1** an act of examining, reviewing, or revising, or the state of being examined, reviewed, or revised. **2** a general survey. **3** a survey of the past and past events: *the newspaper's annual review of the year.* **4** a critical report on a book, play, film, etc. **5** a magazine or newspaper, or a section of one, which contains mainly reviews of books, etc and other feature articles. **6** a second or additional study or consideration of facts, events, etc. **7** a formal or official inspection of troops, ships, etc. **8** *Legal* a re-examination of a case. — *verb* **1** to examine or go over, especially critically or formally. **2** to look back on and examine (events in the past). **3** to inspect (troops, ships, etc), especially formally or officially. **4** to write a critical report on (a book, play, film, etc). **5** *intrans.* to write reviews. **6** *Legal* to re-examine (a case). [from Old French *revue*, from *revoir*, to see again]

◼ *noun* **1, 4** criticism, critique, assessment, evaluation. **1** judgement, report, commentary, examination, scrutiny, analysis, study, revision. **2** survey, reassessment, re-evaluation, re-examination. **5** magazine, periodical, journal. *verb* **1** criticize, assess, evaluate, judge, weigh, discuss, examine, inspect, scrutinize, study, survey, recapitulate. **2** reassess, re-evaluate, re-examine, reconsider, rethink, revise.

reviewer *noun* a person who writes critical reviews of books, plays, etc.

revile *verb* **1** to abuse or criticize (someone or something) bitterly or scornfully. **2** *intrans.* to speak scornfully or use abusive langauge. [from Old French *reviler*, from Latin *vilis*, worthless]

◼ **1** abuse, vilify, denigrate, disparage, malign, criticize, censure, condemn, scorn.

revilement *noun* **1** reviling. **2** a speech that reviles.
reviler *noun* a person who reviles.
revise *verb* **1** to examine again in order to identify and correct faults, take new circumstances into account, or otherwise improve. **2** to correct faults in, make improvements in and bring up to date (a previously printed book) usually to prepare a new edition. **3** *trans., intrans.* to study (a subject or one's notes on it) again, to prepare for an examination. **4** to change or amend (an opinion, etc). [from Latin *revisere*, to look back]

◼ **1, 4** change, alter, modify, amend, reconsider, re-examine, review. **2** correct, update, edit, rewrite, reword, recast, revamp. **3** study, learn, cram, *colloq.* swot.

reviser *noun* a person who revises.
revision *noun* **1** the act of revising or process of being revised. **2** a revised book, edition, article, etc.

◼ **1** change, alteration, modification, amendment, reconsideration, re-examination, review, correction, updating, editing, rewriting.

revisionism *noun* **1** a policy of revising a doctrine. **2** a form of Communism which favours evolution rather than revolution as a way of achieving socialism.
revisionist *noun* an advocate of revisionism.
revitalize or **revitalise** *verb* to give new life and energy to.

◼ reanimate, reinvigorate, revive, revivify, restore, renew, refresh, quicken, rouse, galvanize.

revival *noun* **1** the act of reviving or state of being revived. **2** a renewed interest, especially in old customs and fashions. **3** a new production or performance, eg of an old and almost forgotten play. **4** a period of renewed religious faith and spirituality. **5** a series of evangelistic and often emotional meetings to encourage renewed religious faith.

◼ **1** resuscitation, revitalization, restoration, renewal, renaissance, rebirth, reawakening, resurgence, upsurge.

revivalism *noun* the promotion of renewed religious faith and spirituality through evangelistic meetings.
revivalist *noun* a person who promotes revival or revivalism.
revive *verb trans., intrans.* **1** to come or bring back to consciousness, strength, health, vitality, etc. **2** to come or bring back to use, to an active state, to notice, etc: *revive an old play.* [from Latin *revivere*, to live again]

◼ REVITALIZE, RESUSCITATE, RESTORE, RENEW. **1** reanimate, refresh, animate, invigorate, quicken, rouse, awaken, recover, rally, reawaken, rekindle. **2** reactivate, reintroduce.

revivification *noun* revival.
revivify *verb* (**revivifies, revivified**) to put new life into.

◼ reanimate, reinvigorate, revive, revitalize, restore, renew, refresh, quicken, rouse, galvanize.

revocable /ˈrevəkəbl/ *adj.* capable of being revoked or recalled.
revocation *noun* revoking.
revoke — *verb* **1** to cancel or make (a will, agreement, etc) no longer valid. **2** *intrans.* to fail to follow suit in cards when able to do so. — *noun* an act of revoking at cards. [from Latin *revocare*, to call back]

◼ *verb* **1** repeal, rescind, quash, abrogate, annul, nullify, invalidate, negate, cancel, countermand, reverse, retract, withdraw.
◼ *verb* **1** enforce.

revolt — *verb* **1** *intrans.* to rebel against a government, authority, etc. **2** *intrans.* to feel disgust, loathing, or revulsion. **3** to cause feelings of disgust or loathing. — *noun* an act of rebelling; a rebellion against authority. [from Latin *revolvere*, to roll back]

revolted *adj.* disgusted, horrified.

revolting *adj.* causing a feeling of disgust, loathing, etc; nauseating.

▣ verb 1 rebel, mutiny, rise, riot, resist, dissent, defect. 3 disgust, sicken, nauseate, repel, offend, shock, outrage, scandalize. *noun* revolution, rebellion, mutiny, rising, uprising, insurrection, putsch, coup (d'état), secession, defection.

▣ verb 1 submit. 3 please, delight.

▣ disgusting, sickening, nauseating, repulsive, repellent, obnoxious, nasty, horrible, foul, loathsome, abhorrent, distasteful, offensive, shocking, appalling.

▣ pleasant, delightful, attractive, palatable.

revolution *noun* 1 the usually violent overthrow of a government or political system by the governed. 2 in Marxism, the class struggle which will end in the working class becoming the ruling class and the establishment of Communism. 3 a complete, drastic and usually far-reaching change in ideas, ways of doing things, etc: *the Industrial Revolution*. 4 a complete circle or turn round an axis. 5 an act of turning or moving round an axis. 6 a planet's orbit, or the time taken to go round it once. 7 a cycle of events, or the time taken to go through all of them and return to the beginning. [from Latin *revolutio*]

▣ 1 revolt, rebellion, mutiny, rising, uprising, insurrection, putsch, coup (d'état). 3 reformation, change, transformation, innovation, upheaval, cataclysm. 4 rotation, turn, spin, circuit, round, circle, orbit, gyration. 7 cycle.

revolutionary — *adj.* 1 of or like a revolution. 2 in favour of and supporting revolution. 3 completely new or different; involving radical change. — *noun* (PL. **revolutionaries**) a person who takes part in or is in favour of revolution in general or a particular revolution.

▣ *adj.* 2, 3 radical. 2 rebel, rebellious, mutinous, insurgent, subversive, seditious, anarchistic. 3 new, innovative, avant-garde, different, drastic, thoroughgoing. *noun* rebel, mutineer, insurgent, anarchist, revolutionist.

▣ *adj.* 2 conservative.

revolutionize or **revolutionise** *verb* to cause great, radical or fundamental changes in.

▣ transform, reform, restructure, reorganize, transfigure, turn upside down.

revolvable *adj.* capable of being revolved.

revolve *verb* 1 *trans., intrans.* to move or turn, or cause to move or turn in a circle around a central point; to rotate. 2 *intrans.* (**revolve around** or **about something**) to have it as a centre, focus, or main point. 3 *intrans.* to occur in cycles or regularly. 4 *trans., intrans.* to consider or be considered in turn; to ponder: *revolve the ideas in her head.* [from Latin *revolvere*, to roll back]

▣ 1 rotate, turn, pivot, swivel, spin, wheel, whirl, gyrate, circle, orbit. 2 centre on, focus on, turn on, hinge on, hang on. 4 ponder, reflect on, consider, mull over.

revolver *noun* a pistol with a revolving cylinder which holds several bullets, and which can be fired several times without needing to be reloaded.

revolving — *noun* turning, rotation. — *adj.* that revolves.

revue /rɪˈvjuː/ *noun* an amusing and varied show, with songs, sketches, etc which are often satirical, and which usually feature popular performers. [from French *revue*, review]

revulsion *noun* 1 a feeling of complete disgust, distaste, or repugnance. 2 a sudden and often violent change of feeling, especially from love to hate. [from Latin *revulsio*]

▣ 1 repugnance, disgust, distaste, dislike, aversion, hatred, loathing, abhorrence, abomination. 2 turnabout, recoil, reversal, volte-face, transformation.

▣ 1 delight, pleasure, approval.

reward — *noun* 1 something given or received in return for work done, a service rendered, good behaviour, etc. 2 something given or received in return for good or evil. 3 a sum of money offered usually for finding or helping to find a criminal, stolen or lost property, etc. — *verb* to give a reward of some form to (someone) for work done, services rendered, help, good behaviour, etc. [from Old French *reguarder*]

▣ *noun* 1 prize, honour, medal, decoration, bounty, pay-off, bonus, premium, payment, remuneration, recompense, compensation, gain, profit, return, benefit. 2 repayment, requital, desert, retribution. *verb* pay, remunerate, recompense, repay, requite, compensate, honour, decorate.

▣ *noun* 1 punishment. *verb* punish.

rewarding *adj.* giving personal pleasure or satisfaction.

▣ worthwhile, satisfying, gratifying, pleasing, fulfilling, enriching, valuable, advantageous, beneficial, profitable, remunerative, lucrative, productive, fruitful.

▣ unrewarding.

rewind *verb* to wind (tape, film, etc) back to the beginning.

rewire *verb* to fit (a house, etc) with a new system of electrical wiring.

reword *verb* to express in different words.

▣ rephrase, recast, restate, rewrite, paraphrase.

rewrite — *verb* (with stress on *-write*) 1 to write again or anew. 2 *Comput.* to retain (data) in an area of store by recording it in the location from which it has been read. — *noun* (with stress on *re-*) the process or result of rewriting.

▣ *verb* 1 recast, rephrase, reword, paraphrase.

Rex *noun* the reigning king, now used mainly on coins and in official documents. [from Latin *rex*, king]

RFC *abbrev.* 1 Royal Flying Corps. 2 *Hist.* Rugby Football Club.

RGN *abbrev.* Registered General Nurse.

RGV *abbrev.* Remote Guidance Vehicle.

Rh *symbol* 1 rhesus. 2 *Chem.* rhodium.

Rhaetian /ˈriːʃən/ — *noun* a generic name for the various Romance dialects spoken in Switzerland and N Italy. They are: Romansch, spoken in Switzerland (Grisons) and N Italy; Ladin, spoken in Italy (S Tyrol); and Friulian, spoken in N Italy. — *adj.* relating to these dialects. [from *Rhaetia*, a province of the Roman Empire]

rhapsodic /rapˈsɒdɪk/ or **rhapsodical** *adj.* relating to or characteristic of rhapsodies.

rhapsodically *adv.* in a rhapsodic way.

rhapsodize or **rhapsodise** *verb trans., intrans.* to speak or write with great enthusiasm or emotion.

rhapsody *noun* (PL. **rhapsodies**) 1 an enthusiastic and highly emotional speech, piece of writing, etc. 2 an emotional piece of music usually written to suggest a free form or improvisation. [from Greek *rhapsoidia*, an epic]

☒ 1 effusion, outpouring, poem, lyric, prose poem, purple passage, purple patch.

rhea /ˈriːə/ noun a S American flightless bird resembling, but smaller than, the ostrich. [from Greek *Rhea*, the mother of Zeus in Greek mythology]

rhenium /ˈriːnɪəm/ noun Chem. (SYMBOL **Re**, ATOMIC NUMBER **75**) a rare silvery-white metal with a very high melting point, used to make alloys that act as superconductors or that are resistant to high temperatures, eg for use in thermocouples, electrical components and filaments, and photographic flash lamps. [from Latin *Rhenus*, the Rhine]

rheology noun Physics the scientific study of the deformation and flow of materials subjected to force. It includes the viscosity of fluids (liquids and gases) strain and shear due to stresses in solids, and plastic deformation in metals. [from Greek *rheos*, flow + -LOGY]

rheostat noun a variable resistor that enables the resistance of an electric circuit to be increased or decreased, thereby varying the current without interrupting the current flow. [from Greek *rheos*, flow + *statos*, stationary]

rhesus /ˈriːsəs/ noun (also **rhesus monkey**) a small N Indian monkey. [from Greek *Rhesos*, a mythical king of Thrace]

rhesus factor or **Rh factor** Medicine an antigen that is present in the red blood cells of about 84% of the human population, who are said to be rhesus-positive, and absent in the remaining 16%, who are said to be rhesus-negative.

rhetoric /ˈretərɪk/ noun **1** the art of speaking and writing well, elegantly and effectively, especially when used to persuade or influence others. **2** language which is full of unnecessarily long, formal or literary words and phrases, and which is also often insincere or meaningless. [from Greek *rhetorike techne*, rhetorical art]

☒ 1 eloquence, oratory. **2** grandiloquence, magniloquence, bombast, pomposity, hyperbole, verbosity, wordiness.

rhetorical adj. **1** relating to or using rhetoric. **2** overelaborate or insincere in style.

☒ 2 oratorical, grandiloquent, magniloquent, bombastic, declamatory, pompous, high-sounding, grand, high-flown, flowery, florid, flamboyant, showy, pretentious, artificial, insincere.
☒ 2 simple.

rhetorical question a question which is asked to produce an effect and not because the speaker wants an answer.

rheum /ruːm/ noun a watery discharge from the nose or eyes. [from Greek *rheuma*, flow]

rheumatic /rʊˈmatɪk, ˈruːmətɪk/ — noun **1** a person suffering from rheumatism. **2** (**rheumatics**) colloq. rheumatism, or pain caused by it. — adj. relating to or caused by rheumatism.

rheumatic fever Medicine a disease caused by infection with streptococci (a type of bacterium), mainly affecting children and young adults, and characterized by fever, arthritis that spreads from one joint to another, skin disorders, and inflammation of the heart which may cause permanent damage or lead to heart failure.

rheumatism /ˈruːmətɪzm/ noun a disease marked by painful swelling of the joints (eg one's hips, knees, fingers, etc) and which causes stiffness and pain when moving them. [from Greek *rheumatismos*, from *rheuma*, flow]

rheumatoid adj. of or like rheumatism or rheumatoid arthritis.

rheumatoid arthritis Medicine a form of arthritis, particularly common in women, that causes pain, swelling,

stiffness, and deformity of the joints, especially of the fingers, wrists, ankles, feet, or hips.

rhinestone noun an imitation diamond usually made from glass or plastic. [from *Rhine*, a river in Germany + STONE]

rhinitis /raɪˈnaɪtɪs/ noun Medicine inflammation of the mucous membrane of the nasal passages, accompanied by the discharge of mucus, eg as a symptom of the common cold, or of certain allergies. [from Greek *rhis, rhinos*, nose + -ITIS]

rhino noun (PL. **rhinos**) a rhinoceros.

rhinoceros /raɪˈnɒsərəs/ noun (PL. **rhinoceroses**, **rhinoceros**) any of five species of a large herbivorous mammal, including three Asian species (genus *Rhinoceros*) and two African species (genus *Diceros*), with a huge body, very thick skin that is usually almost hairless, and either one or two horns on its snout. [from Greek *rhinokeros*, from *rhis*, nose + *keros*, horn]

rhinovirus /ˈraɪnoʊvaɪərəs/ noun Biol. a virus belonging to a subgroup thought to be responsible for the common cold and other respiratory diseases. [from Greek *rhis, rhinos*, nose]

rhizoid /ˈraɪzɔɪd/ noun Bot. a small often colourless hairlike outgrowth that functions as a root in certain algae, and in mosses, liverworts, and some ferns, absorbing water and mineral salts, and providing anchorage.

rhizome /ˈraɪzoʊm/ noun a thick horizontal underground stem which produces roots and leafy shoots. [from Greek *rhiza*, root]

rhodium /ˈroʊdɪəm/ noun Chem. (SYMBOL **Rh**, ATOMIC NUMBER **45**) a silvery-white metal, resistant to tarnishing and chemicals, that is used to make temperature-resistant platinum alloys for thermocouples and electrical components, to plate jewellery, and to coat reflectors on optical instruments. It is also used as a catalyst to control car exhaust emissions. [from Greek *rhodon*, rose, from its rose-coloured salts]

rhododendron /roʊdəˈdendrən/ noun a flowering shrub with thick evergreen leaves and large showy colourful flowers. [from Greek *rhodon*, rose + *dendron*, tree]

rhodopsin /roʊˈdɒpsɪn/ noun Biochem. the light-sensitive pigment found in rod cells in the retina of the vertebrate eye. On exposure to light, rhodopsin is chemically converted to its components, opsin and retinal, and this stimulates the production of a nerve impulse. Also called VISUAL PURPLE. [from Greek *rhodos*, rose, red + *opsis*, sight]

rhomboid — noun a four-sided shape with opposite sides and angles equal, two angles being greater and two smaller than a right angle, and two sides being longer than the other two. — adj. (also **rhomboidal**) shaped like a rhomboid or a rhombus. [from Greek *rhomboeides*, from *rhombos*, rhombus]

rhombus noun (PL. **rhombuses**, **rhombi**) a four-sided shape with all four sides equal, two opposite angles being greater than a right angle and two smaller; a diamond shape. [from Greek *rhombos*, anything which may be spun round]

rhubarb /ˈruːbɑːb/ noun **1** a perennial plant of the genus *Rheum*, cultivated in north temperate regions, that has very large leaves with long fleshy edible stalks. The leaves are poisonous. **2** the reddish fleshy leafstalks of this plant which can be sweetened with sugar, cooked, and eaten. **3** the roots of a type of rhubarb found in China and Tibet, dried and taken as a laxative. **4** colloq. the sound of continuous murmured background conversation made by a group of actors, especially by repeating the word *rhubarb*. **5** colloq. nonsense; rubbish. [from Old French *reubarbe*, from Greek *rheon barbaron*, foreign rhubarb]

rhyme — noun **1** a pattern of words which have the same final sounds at the ends of lines in a poem. **2** the use of such patterns in poetry, etc. **3** a word which has the same sound as another: *'beef' is a rhyme for 'leaf'*. **4** a short poem, verse, or jingle written in rhyme. — verb **1** intrans. said of words to have the same final sounds and so form rhymes. **2** to use (a word) as a rhyme for another. **3** intrans.

to write using rhymes. **4** to put (a story, etc) into rhyme.— **without rhyme or reason** without sense, reason, or any discernible system. [from Greek *rhythmos*, rhythm]

◨ **4** poem, ode, limerick, jingle, song, ditty.

rhyming slang slang in which the word meant is replaced by a phrase in which the last word rhymes with the word meant, the phrase then often being shortened to the first word, eg '*butcher's hook*' is rhyming slang for '*look*', normally shortened to '*butcher's*', as in '*have a butcher's*'.

rhyolite /ˈraɪəlaɪt/ *noun Geol.* any of a group of light-coloured igneous rocks that often contain larger crystals (phenocrysts) of potassium feldspar embedded within a fine-grained glassy matrix. Rhyolite is the volcanic equivalent of granite. [from Greek *rhyax*, lava stream + *lithos*, stone]

rhythm /ˈrɪðm/ *noun* **1** a regular repeated pattern, movement, beat, or sequence of events. **2** the regular arrangement of stress, notes of different lengths and pauses in a piece of music. **3** a particular pattern of stress, notes, etc in music: *tango rhythm*. **4** a regular arrangement of sounds and stressed and unstressed syllables in poetry or other writing, suggesting movement; metre. **5** an ability to sing, speak, move, etc rhythmically. **6** (*in full* **rhythm section**) a group of instruments (eg drums, guitar and bass) in a dance or jazz band which supply the rhythm for the music. **7** *in painting, sculpture, architecture, etc* a regular and harmonious pattern of shapes, colours, areas of shade and light, empty spaces, etc. [from Greek *rhythmos*, from *rheein*, to flow]

◨ **1, 2, 3, 4** beat. **1** pulse, movement, flow, lilt, swing, accent, cadence, pattern. **2, 3** time, tempo. **4** metre, measure.

rhythm and blues (**R & B**) a style of popular music of the 1950s and 1960s, almost exclusively played by US black artists. It combined certain features of the blues with lively rhythms which came to be more widely associated with rock music, played on guitars, drums, and keyboard.

rhythmic or **rhythmical** *adj.* of or with rhythm.

rhythmically *adv.* in a rhythmic way; as regards rhythm.

RI *abbrev.* **1** religious instruction. **2** Rhode Island.

ria /ˈriːə/ *noun Geol.* a long narrow coastal inlet, differing from a fjord in that it gradually decreases in depth and width from its mouth inland. Most rias are surrounded by hills, and they are formed by the flooding of river valleys. [from Spanish *ria*, rivermouth]

rib[1] — *noun* **1** any one of the slightly flexible bones which curve round and forward from the spine, forming the chest wall and protecting the heart and lungs. **2** a cut of meat including one or more ribs. **3** a rod-like bar which supports and strengthens a layer of fabric, membrane, etc, eg in an umbrella, insect's wing or aircraft wing. **4** one of the pieces of wood which curve round and upward from a ship's keel to form the framework of the hull. **5** a raised ridge in knitted or woven material. — *verb* (**ribbed, ribbing**) **1** to provide or enclose with ribs. **2** to knit ribs in by alternating plain and purl stitches. [from Anglo-Saxon *ribbe*]

rib[2] *verb* (**ribbed, ribbing**) *colloq.* to tease. [perhaps from the phrase *rib tickle*, to make someone laugh]

RIBA *abbrev.* Royal Institute of British Architects.

ribald /ˈrɪbəld, ˈraɪbəld/ *adj., said of language, a speaker, humour, etc* humorous in a rude, vulgar, indecent and disrespectful way. [from Old French *ribauld*]

◨ rude, bawdy, earthy, coarse, vulgar, lewd, indecent, disrespectful, irreverent, satirical.

ribaldry /ˈrɪbəldrɪ/ *noun* ribald talk or behaviour.

riband /ˈrɪbənd/ or **ribband** *noun* a ribbon, especially one awarded as a prize. [from Old French *reubon*]

ribbed *adj.* having ribs; ridged.

ribbing *noun* a pattern or arrangement of ribs, especially in knitting.

ribbon *noun* **1** a long narrow strip of usually coloured material used for decorating clothes, tying hair and parcels, etc. **2** any ribbon-like strip. **3** a small piece of coloured cloth worn to show membership of a team, or as a sign of having won an award. **4** a narrow strip of inked cloth used to produce print in a typewriter. **5** (**ribbons**) strips or tatters of torn material: *hanging in ribbons*. [from Old French *reubon*]

ribbon development the extensive building of houses, etc along the side of a main road leading out of a town.

rib cage the chest wall formed by the ribs which protects the heart and lungs.

riboflavin /raɪbəʊˈfleɪvɪn/ *noun Biochem.* a member of the vitamin B complex that is found in yeast, liver, milk, and green vegetables. It is required for the metabolism of all major nutrients, and deficiency of the vitamin causes retarded growth, mouth sores, and inflammation of the tongue and lips. Also called VITAMIN B$_2$. [from *ribose* (a sugar) + Latin *flavus*, yellow]

ribonucleic acid /raɪbəʊnjuːˈkliːɪk ˈasɪd/ *Biochem.* (ABBREV. **RNA**) the nucleic acid, containing the sugar ribose, that participates in the copying of the genetic code from DNA (another nucleic acid) and the manufacture of proteins from a long chain of amino acids, the order of which is specified by the genetic code. [from *ribose* (a sugar) + NUCLEIC ACID]

ribose /ˈraɪbəʊs/ *noun Biochem.* (FORMULA C$_5$H$_{10}$O$_5$) a monosaccharide sugar that is an important component of RNA (ribonucleic acid). One of its derivatives, deoxyribose, is an important component of DNA (deoxyribonucleic acid).

ribosome /ˈraɪbəʊsəʊm/ *Biol.* in the cytoplasm of a living cell, any of many small particles that are the site of protein manufacture. Each consists of two subunits of different sizes, and is composed of RNA (ribonucleic acid) and protein.

rice *noun* **1** an important cereal plant (*Oryza sativa*) of the grass family (Gramineae), native to SE Asia, and having branched flower-heads bearing numerous starchy grain-like seeds. **2** the edible starchy seeds, resembling grains, produced by this plant. [from Greek *oryza*]

rice paper very thin paper made from the bark of an oriental tree, used in cookery and for painting on.

rich *adj.* **1** having a lot of money, property, or possessions. **2** costly and elaborate: *rich clothes*. **3** high in value or quality: *a rich harvest*. **4** (**rich in something**) well supplied with it; having it in great abundance. **5** *said of soil, a region, etc* productive, fertile. **6** *said of colours* vivid and deep. **7** *said of a drink, especially alcoholic* with a full, mellow, well-matured flavour. **8** *said of food* heavily seasoned, or containing much fat, oil, or dried fruit. **9** *said of an odour* pungent and spicy. **10** *said of a voice* full, mellow, and deep. **11** *said of a remark or suggestion* unacceptable; outrageous; ridiculous: *that's a bit rich!* **12** *said of the mixture in an internal combustion engine* having a high proportion of fuel to air. [from Anglo-Saxon *rice*, strong, powerful]

◨ **1** wealthy, affluent, moneyed, prosperous, well-to-do, well-off, *colloq.* loaded, *colloq.* rolling (in it). **2** costly, precious, valuable, lavish, sumptuous, opulent, luxurious, splendid, gorgeous, fine, elaborate, ornate. **3** plentiful, abundant, copious, profuse, prolific, ample, full. **4** high in, full of, packed with, steeped in. **5** fertile, fruitful, productive, lush. **6** deep, intense, vivid, bright, vibrant, warm. **8** creamy, fatty, full-bodied, heavy, full-flavoured, strong, spicy, savoury, tasty, delicious, luscious, juicy, sweet. **10** deep, mellow, full, sonorous.

◨ **1, 3, 5** poor. **1** impoverished. **2** plain. **4** low in. **5** barren. **6** dull, soft. **8** plain, bland.

riches *pl. noun* wealth. [from Old French *richesse*]

◨ wealth, affluence, money, gold, treasure, fortune, assets, property, substance, resources, means.
◧ poverty.

richly *adv.* **1** in a rich or elaborate way. **2** fully and suitably: *richly deserved.*

richness *noun* the state of being rich; wealth, abundance.

Richter scale /ˈrɪxtə/ *Meteorol.* a logarithmic scale, ranging from 0 to 10, used to measure the magnitude of an earthquake. [named after the US seismologist Charles Richter (1900–85)]

rick[1] *noun* a stack or heap, especially of hay or corn and usually thatched. [from Anglo-Saxon *hreac*]

rick[2] — *verb* to sprain or wrench (one's neck, ankle, etc). — *noun* a sprain or wrench. [a form of WRICK]

rickets *sing. or pl. noun Medicine* a disease of children in which the bones fail to harden and so become deformed. It is caused by deficiency of vitamin D, which is needed for the deposition of calcium salts within the bones to make them rigid, and may be due either to a dietary deficiency or lack of sunlight. [origin uncertain; perhaps from Greek *rachitis*]

rickety *adj.* **1** having or affected by rickets. **2** unsteady and likely to collapse.

◨ unsteady, wobbly, shaky, unstable, insecure, flimsy, jerry-built, decrepit, ramshackle, broken-down, dilapidated, derelict.
◧ stable, strong.

rick-rack *noun* a zigzag braid for decorating or trimming clothes, soft furnishings, etc. [related to RACK[1]]

rickshaw or **ricksha** *noun* a small, two-wheeled, hooded carriage drawn either by a person on foot, or attached to a bicycle or motorcycle. [from Japanese *jinrikisha*, from *jin*, man + *riki*, power + *sha*, carriage]

ricochet /ˈrɪkəʃeɪ/ — *noun* the action, especially of a bullet or other missile, of hitting a surface and then rebounding. — *verb intrans.* (**ricocheted**, **ricocheting** or **ricochetted**, **ricochetting**) *said of a bullet, etc* to hit a surface and rebound. [from French]

RICS *abbrev.* Royal Institute of Chartered Surveyors.

rid *verb* (**ridding**; PAST TENSE AND PAST PARTICIPLE **rid**) (**rid someone of something**) to free or clear them from something undesirable or unwanted. — **get rid of something** or **someone** to free or relieve oneself of something or someone unwanted. [from Norse *rythja*, to clear]

◨ clear, purge, free, deliver, relieve, unburden. **get rid of** throw away, throw out, dispose of, discard, dump, scrap, jettison, *colloq.* chuck (out), *slang* ditch, abolish, put an end to, eliminate, do away with, kill, murder, *slang* bump off.

riddance *noun* the act of freeing oneself from something undesirable or unwanted. — **good riddance** a welcome relief from an undesirable or unwanted person or thing.

ridden see RIDE.

riddle[1] — *noun* **1** a short usually humorous puzzle, often in the form of a question, which describes an object, person, etc in a mysterious or misleading way, and which can only be solved using ingenuity. **2** a person, thing or fact which is puzzling or difficult to understand. — *verb* **1** *intrans.* to speak in riddles. **2** *trans.* to solve (a riddle). [from Anglo-Saxon *rædels*]

◨ *noun* PUZZLE, CONUNDRUM, PROBLEM. **1** brain-teaser, poser. **2** enigma, mystery.

riddle[2] — *noun* a large coarse sieve used eg for sifting gravel or grain. — *verb* **1** to pass (gravel, grain, etc) through a riddle. **2** to fill with holes, especially with gunshot: *riddled with bullets.* **3** to spread through; to fill: *a govern-*

ment department riddled with corruption. [from Anglo-Saxon *hriddel*]

◨ *verb* **1** sift, sieve, strain, filter, mar, winnow. **2** perforate, pierce, puncture, pepper. **3** fill, permeate, pervade, infest.

ride — *verb* (PAST TENSE **rode**; PAST PARTICIPLE **ridden**) **1** to sit on and control (a bicycle, horse, etc). **2** *intrans.* to travel or be carried in a car, train, etc or on a bicycle, horse, etc. **3** *chiefly North Amer.* to travel on (a vehicle). **4** *intrans.* to go out on horseback, especially regularly. **5** to take part on horseback in (a race). **6** to move or float on: *a ship riding the waves.* **7** *intrans. said of a ship* to float at anchor. **8** *intrans. said especially of the moon* to appear to float. **9** to travel over or across by car, horse, etc. **10** *intrans.* to rest on or be supported while moving: *a kite riding on the wind.* **11** (**be ridden**) to be dominated or oppressed by a feeling: *ridden with guilt.* **12** *intrans.* to remain undisturbed or unchanged: *let matters ride.* **13** (**ride on something**) to depend on it. **14** to bend before (a blow, punch, etc) to reduce its impact. **15** *coarse slang* to have sexual intercourse with. — *noun* **1** a journey on horseback or by vehicle. **2** a lift: *gave him a ride to the shop.* **3** the type of movement felt in a vehicle: *a smooth ride.* **4** a path, especially one through a wood, for horseback riding. **5** a fairground entertainment, such as a roller-coaster or big wheel. — **ride something out** to survive or get through it safely: *ride out the storm.* **ride up** *said of an item of clothing* to move gradually up the body out of position. **riding high** successful, confident, and elated. **take someone for a ride** *colloq.* to trick, cheat, or deceive them. [from Anglo-Saxon *ridan*]

◨ *verb* **1** sit, pedal, drive, steer, control, handle, manage. **2**, **9** travel, journey. **2** move, progress. **9** range, roam. *noun* **1** journey, trip, outing, jaunt, spin, drive.

rider *noun* **1** a person who rides, especially a horse. **2** an addition to what has already been said or written, especially an extra clause added to a document; a qualification or amendment.

ridge — *noun* **1** a strip of ground raised either side of a ploughed furrow. **2** any long, narrow raised area on an otherwise flat surface. **3** the top edge of something where two upward sloping surfaces meet, eg on a roof. **4** a long narrow strip of relatively high ground with steep slopes on either side. Ridges are often found between valleys. **5** *Meteorol.* a long narrow area of high atmospheric pressure, often associated with fine weather and strong breezes. — *verb trans., intrans.* to form or make into ridges. [from Anglo-Saxon *hrycg*]

ridged *adj.* having ridges.

ridgepole *noun* **1** (*also* **ridgepiece**) the beam along the ridge of a roof to which the upper ends of the rafters are attached. **2** the horizontal pole at the top of a tent.

ridicule — *noun* language, laughter, behaviour, etc which makes someone or something appear foolish or humiliated; derision; mockery: *held him up to ridicule.* — *verb* to laugh at, make fun of, or mock. [from Latin *ridere*, to laugh]

◨ *noun* scorn, derision, mockery, laughter, satire, irony, sarcasm, jeering, taunting, teasing, chaff, banter. *verb* mock, make fun of, satirize, send up, caricature, lampoon, burlesque, parody, jeer at, scoff at, deride, sneer at, *colloq.* rib, humiliate, taunt.
◧ praise.

ridiculous *adj.* very silly or absurd; deserving to be laughed at.

◨ ludicrous, absurd, nonsensical, silly, foolish, stupid, contemptible, derisory, laughable, farcical, comical, funny, hilarious, outrageous, preposterous, incredible, unbelievable.
◧ sensible.

ridiculously *adv.* in a ridiculous way; to a ridiculous degree.

riding[1] *noun* the art and practice of riding horses.

riding[2] *noun* (*often* **Riding**) any of the three former administrative divisions of Yorkshire, the *East Riding*, the *North Riding*, and the *West Riding*. [from Norse *thridjungr*, third part]

riding the marches the traditional ceremony of riding round the boundaries of a town, or a border district (especially in S Scotland).

Riesling /ˈriːzlɪŋ/ *noun* a dry white wine produced in Germany and Austria from a grape of the same name.

rife *adj.* 1 *usually said of something unfavourable* very common; extensive. 2 (**rife with something**) having a large amount or number of something bad or undesirable. [from Anglo-Saxon *ryfe*]

. . . .

🖪 1 rampant, raging, epidemic, prevalent, widespread, abundant, general, common, frequent. 2 teeming with, swarming with, overrun with.

🖪 1 scarce.
. . . .

riff *noun Jazz* a short passage of music played repeatedly. [perhaps a shortening of REFRAIN[1]]

riffle — *verb* 1 *trans., intrans.* (**riffle something** or **riffle through something**) to flick or leaf through (the pages of a book, a pile of papers, etc) rapidly, especially in a casual search for something. 2 to shuffle (playing cards) by dividing the pack into two equal piles, bending the cards back slightly, and controlling the fall of the corners of the cards with the thumbs, so that cards from each pile fall alternately. — *noun* 1 the action of riffling (eg cards), or the sound made by this. 2 *North Amer.* a section of a stream or river where shallow water flows swiftly over a rough rocky surface. 3 *North Amer.* a ripple or patch of ripples on the surface of water. [a combination of RIPPLE and RUFFLE]

riff-raff *noun* worthless, disreputable or undesirable people. [from Old French *rif et raf*]

rifle[1] — *noun* 1 a large gun fired from the shoulder, with a long barrel with a spiral groove on the inside which gives the gun greater accuracy over a long distance. 2 (*usually* **rifles**) a body of soldiers armed with rifles. — *verb* to cut spiral grooves in (a gun or its barrel). [from Old German *rifeln*, to groove]

rifle[2] *verb* 1 *trans., intrans.* to search through (a house, safe, etc) thoroughly in order to steal something from it. 2 to steal (something). [from Old French *rifler*, to plunder]

rift — *noun* 1 a split or crack, especially one in the ground. 2 a breaking of friendly relations between previously friendly people. — *verb* to tear apart or split. [from Norse *ript*, breaking of an agreement]

. . . .

🖪 *noun* SPLIT, BREACH. 1 break, fracture, crack, fault, chink, cleft, cranny, crevice, gap, space, opening. 2 disagreement, difference, separation, division, schism, alienation.

🖪 *noun* 2 unity.
. . . .

rift valley *Geol.* a long steep-sided valley with a flat floor, formed when part of the Earth's crust subsided between two faults.

rig — *verb* (**rigged, rigging**) 1 to fit (a ship) with ropes, sails, and rigging. 2 to control or manipulate for dishonest purposes, for personal profit or advantage. — *noun* 1 the arrangement of sails, ropes, and masts on a ship. 2 an oil-rig. 3 gear or equipment, especially that used for a specific task. 4 clothing or a uniform worn for a particular occasion or task. — **rig someone out** 1 to dress them in clothes of a stated or special kind. 2 to provide them with special equipment. **rig something up** to build or prepare it, especially quickly and with whatever material is available. [probably Scandinavian]

. . . .

🖪 *noun* 3, 4 gear, kit, outfit. 3 equipment, tackle, apparatus, machinery, fittings, fixtures. **rig out** KIT OUT, OUTFIT,

FIT (OUT). 1 clothe, dress (up). 2 equip, supply, furnish.
. . . .

rigging *noun* 1 the system of ropes, wires, etc which support and control a ship's masts and sails. 2 the ropes and wires, etc which support the structure of an airship or the wings of a biplane.

right — *adj.* 1 of or on the side of someone or something which is towards the east when the front is facing north. 2 on or close to a spectator's right side: *stage right*. 3 *said of a river bank* on the right hand of a person going downstream. 4 correct; true. 5 morally or legally correct or good. 6 suitable; appropriate. 7 in a correct, proper, satisfactory, or healthy condition: *not in one's right mind / put things right*. 8 of or on the side of fabric, a garment, etc which is intended to be seen: *turn the right side of the dress out*. 9 with an axis perpendicular to the base: *a right angle*. 10 relating to the political right. 11 socially acceptable: *know all the right people*. 12 *Brit. colloq.* complete; utter; real: *a right mess*. — *adv.* 1 exactly or precisely. 2 immediately; without delay: *he'll be right over*. 3 completely; all the way: *right round the field*. 4 straight; directly: *right to the top*. 5 to or on the right side. 6 correctly; properly; satisfactorily. 7 *old use, dialect* very; to the full: *be right glad to see her*. — *noun* 1 (*often* **rights**) a power, privilege, etc that a person may claim legally or morally. 2 (*often* **rights**) a just or legal claim to something: *mineral rights*. 3 that which is correct, good, or just: *the rights and wrongs of the case*. 4 fairness, truth, and justice. 5 the right side, part, or direction. 6 the members of any political party holding the most conservative views. 7 (**the Right**) the political party, group of people within a party, etc which has the most conservative views (from the practice of European parliaments in which members holding the most conservative views sat on the president's right). 8 *Boxing* the right hand, or a punch with this. 9 (**rights**) *Commerce* the privilege given to a company's existing shareholders to buy new shares, usually for less than the market value. 10 (**rights**) the legal permission to print, publish, film, etc a book, usually sold to a company by the author or by another company. — *verb* 1 *trans., intrans.* to return or come back to the correct, especially upright, position. 2 to avenge or compensate for (something wrong done). 3 to correct; to put in order. — *interj.* an expression of agreement, assent or readiness. — **by rights** rightfully. **in one's own right** because of one's own qualifications, abilities, work, possessions, etc. **in the right** right; with justice on one's side. **keep on the right side of someone** to maintain their goodwill. **put** or **set something** or **someone to rights** to put them in a proper order, place, or state. **right away** or **right now** immediately; at once. **serve someone right** to be what they deserve, especially as a consequence of ill-advised or malicious action. [from Anglo-Saxon *riht*]

. . . .

🖪 *adj.* 4 correct, accurate, exact, precise, true, factual, actual, real. 5, 6 proper, fitting, seemly, becoming. 5 fair, just, equitable, lawful, honest, upright, good, virtuous, righteous, moral, ethical, honourable. 6 appropriate, suitable, fit, admissible, satisfactory, reasonable, desirable, favourable, advantageous. 10 right-wing, conservative, Tory. *adv.* 1 exactly, precisely. 2, 4 straight, directly. 2 immediately, at once. 3 completely, utterly, all the way. 6 correctly, accurately, factually, properly, satisfactorily, well, fairly. *noun* 1 privilege, prerogative, due, claim, business, authority, power. 4 justice, legality, equity, fairness, good, virtue, righteousness, morality, honour, integrity, uprightness, truth. *verb* 1 straighten, stand up. 2 redress, vindicate, avenge, settle. 3 rectify, correct, put right, fix, repair. **right away** straight away, immediately, at once, now, instantly, directly, forthwith, without delay, promptly.

🖪 *adj.* 4 wrong, incorrect. 5 unfair, wrong. 6 improper, unsuitable. 10 left-wing. *adv.* 6 wrongly, incorrectly, unfairly. *noun* 4 wrong. **right away** later, eventually.
. . . .

right angle an angle of 90°, formed by two lines which are perpendicular to each other. — **at right angles** perpendicular.

right-angled *adj.* having a right angle.

right ascension *Astron.* a coordinate on the celestial sphere that is analogous to longitude on Earth. It is measured in hours, minutes, and seconds eastward along the celestial equator from the vernal equinox.

righteous /ˈraɪtjəs/ *adj.* **1** *said of a person* virtuous, free from sin or guilt. **2** *said of an action* morally good. **3** caused by justifiable anger: *righteous indignation.* [from Anglo-Saxon *rihtwis*, from *riht*, right + *wise*, manner]

   ◨ **1, 2** just, good, virtuous, moral. **1** worthy, upright, honourable, irreproachable, blameless.

rightful *adj.* **1** having a legally just claim. **2** *said of property, a privilege, etc* held by just right. **3** fair; just; equitable.

   ◨ **1** legitimate, legal, true. **2, 3** lawful. **2** bona fide, real, genuine, valid. **3** fair, just, equitable, correct, proper, due.
   ◪ **2, 3** wrongful, unlawful.

rightfully *adv.* fairly, justly, legally.

right-hand *adj.* **1** at, on or towards the right. **2** done with the right hand.

right-handed *adj.* **1** using the right hand more easily than the left. **2** *said of a tool, etc* designed to be used by the right hand. **3** *said of a blow, etc* done with the right hand. **4** *said of a screw* needing to be turned clockwise to be screwed in.

right-handedness *noun* being right-handed.

right-hander *noun* **1** a right-handed person. **2** a blow with the right hand.

right-hand man or **right-hand woman** a valuable, indispensable, and trusted assistant.

right-hand rule 1 *Physics* a rule that is used to demonstrate the relative directions of the induced current, magnetic field, and movement in an electric generator. The right hand is held with the thumb (representing the direction of movement), the first finger (representing the direction of the magnetic field), and the second finger (representing the direction of the induced current) at right angles to each other. **2** a rule that is used to demonstrate the direction of a concentric magnetic field around a current-carrying conductor. The right hand is held with the thumb (representing the direction of the current) pointing upwards, and the fingers (representing the direction of the magnetic field) curled around the base of the thumb joint.

Right Honourable a title given to British peers below the rank of marquis, privy councillors, present and past cabinet ministers, and to some Lord Mayors and Lord Provosts.

rightism *noun* the political opinions of conservatives or the right; also, support for and promotion of this.

rightist — *noun* a supporter of the political right, a conservative. — *adj.* relating to or characteristic of the political right.

rightly *adv.* **1** correctly. **2** justly. **3** fairly; properly. **4** with good reason; justifiably. **5** with certainty.

right-minded *adj.* thinking, judging, and acting according to principles which are just, honest, and sensible.

right of way (PL. **rights of way**) **1** the right of the public to use a path that crosses private property. **2** a path used by this right. **3** the right of one vehicle to proceed before other vehicles coming from different directions at junctions, roundabouts, etc.

Right Reverend a title of a bishop.

rightward or rightwards *adj.*, *adv.* on or towards the right.

right whale a baleen whale with a large head that represents up to 40 per cent of the total body length.

right wing 1 the more conservative members of a political party. **2** the right-hand side of a football pitch, etc, or the player in this position.

right-wing *adj.* politically conservative.

right-winger *noun* a member of a political right wing.

rigid *adj.* **1** completely stiff and inflexible. **2** not able to be moved. **3** *said of a person* strictly and inflexibly adhering to one's ideas, opinions and rules. **4** *said of rules, etc* strictly maintained and not relaxed. [from Latin *rigidus*]

   ◨ **1, 3, 4** inflexible, unbending, firm. **1** stiff, hard. **2** set, fixed. **3, 4** austere, harsh, severe, unrelenting, strict, rigorous, stringent, stern, uncompromising, unyielding. **4** cast-iron, unalterable, invariable.
   ◪ **1, 3, 4** flexible.

rigidity or **rigidness** *noun* a rigid state or quality.

rigidly *adv.* in a rigid state; stiffly, without yielding.

   ◨ inflexibly, strictly, rigorously, sternly, uncompromisingly, unalterably.

rigmarole /ˈrɪgmərəʊl/ *noun* **1** an unnecessarily or absurdly long complicated series of actions, instructions or procedures. **2** a long rambling or confused statement or speech. [from *ragman rolls*, a series of documents in which the Scottish nobles promised allegiance to Edward I of England in 1291–2 and 1296] .

rigor mortis /ˈrɪgə ˈmɔːtɪs/ the temporary stiffening of the body after death. [from Latin *rigor mortis*, stiffness of death]

rigorous *adj.* **1** showing or having rigour; strict; harsh; severe. **2** *said of the weather or climate* cold, harsh, and unpleasant. **3** strictly accurate.

   ◨ **1, 2** harsh. **1** strict, stringent, rigid, firm, severe, stern, austere. **3** exact, precise, accurate, meticulous, painstaking, scrupulous, conscientious, thorough.
   ◪ **1, 3** lax, superficial.

rigorously *adv.* in a rigorous way.

rigorousness *noun* being rigorous.

rigour /ˈrɪgə(r)/ *noun* **1** stiffness; hardness. **2** strictness or severity of temper, behaviour, or judgement. **3** strict enforcement of rules or the law. **4** (*usually* **rigours**) a harsh or severe condition, especially of weather or climate. **5** harshness or severity of life; austerity. **6** strict precision or exactitude, eg of thought. [from Latin *rigor*, stiffness]

   ◨ **1, 2, 3** rigidity, firmness. **2, 3** strictness, stringency, severity, sternness. **2, 3, 4, 5** harshness. **5** austerity, abstemiousness, self-denial, puritanism. **6** exactitude, precision, accuracy, meticulousness, thoroughness.
   ◪ **3, 5, 6** laxity.

rig-out *noun colloq.* a person's full set of clothes.

rile *verb* to anger or annoy. [a variant of *roil*, to make (water) muddy or turbid]

   ◨ annoy, irritate, nettle, pique, *colloq.* peeve, put out, upset, irk, vex, anger, exasperate.
   ◪ calm, soothe.

rill *noun* a small stream or brook. [from German *Rille*, channel]

rille or **rill** *noun* a long broad winding valley on the surface of the Moon. [from German *Rille*, channel]

rim — *noun* **1** a raised or often curved edge or border. **2** the outer circular edge of a wheel to which the tyre is attached. — *verb* (**rimmed**, **rimming**) to form or provide an edge or rim to. [from Anglo-Saxon *rima*]

   ◨ *noun* EDGE. **1** lip, brim, brink, verge, margin, border, circumference.
   ◪ *noun* **1** centre, middle.

rime[1] — *noun* thick white frost formed especially from frozen water droplets from cloud or fog. — *verb* to cover with rime. [from Anglo-Saxon *hrim*]

rime[2] same as RHYME.

rimless *adj.* without a rim.

rimmed *adj.* having a rim.

rimy *adj.* (**rimier, rimiest**) frosty, covered with rime.

rind /raɪnd/ — *noun* **1** a thick, hard outer layer or covering as on cheese or bacon, or the peel of fruit. **2** the bark of a tree or plant. — *verb* to strip bark from. [from Anglo-Saxon *rinde*]

⊟ *noun* **1** peel, skin, husk, crust.

ring[1] — *noun* **1** a small circle of gold, silver, or some other metal or material, worn on the finger. **2** a circle of metal, wood, plastic, etc for holding, keeping in place, connecting, hanging, etc. **3** any object, mark, or figure which is circular in shape. **4** a circular course. **5** a group of people or things arranged in a circle. **6** an enclosed and usually circular area for competitions or exhibitions, especially at a circus. **7** a square area marked off by ropes on a platform, where boxers or wrestlers fight. **8** (**the ring**) boxing as a profession. **9** a group of people who act together to control an antiques or drugs market, betting, etc for their own profit. **10** a circular electric element or gas burner on top of a cooker. **11** *Chem.* a closed chain of atoms in a molecule. **12** a thin band of particles orbiting some planets, such as Saturn and Uranus. — *verb* **1** to make, form, draw, etc a ring round. **2** to put a ring on the leg of (a bird) as a means of identifying it. **3** to fit a ring in the nose of (a bull) to make it easy to lead.— **run rings round someone** *colloq.* to beat them or be much better than them. **throw one's hat into the ring** *colloq.* to offer oneself as a candidate or contestant. [from Anglo-Saxon *hring*]

⊟ *noun* **1, 2, 3, 4, 5** circle. **2, 3** loop, hoop. **2** band, girdle, collar. **3** round, halo. **4** circuit, orbit. **6** arena, enclosure. **9** cartel, syndicate, association, organization, gang, crew, mob, band, cell, clique, coterie. *verb* **1** surround, encircle, gird, circumscribe, encompass, enclose.

ring[2] — *verb* (PAST TENSE **rang**; PAST PARTICIPLE **rung**) **1** *trans., intrans.* to make or cause to make a sound, especially a ringing, bell-like sound. **2** *trans., intrans.* (**ring someone up**) *Brit.* to call them by telephone. **3** (**ring for someone**) to ring a bell as a summons to them. **4** *intrans.* *said of a place or building* to be filled with sound: *the office rang with the news.* **5** *intrans.* to sound repeatedly; to resound: *criticisms rang in his ears.* **6** *intrans.* *said of the ears* to be filled with a buzzing, humming or ringing sensation or sound. **7** *intrans.* *said of words, etc* to give a stated impression: *his promises ring false.* — *noun* **1** the act or sound of ringing. **2** the act of ringing a bell. **3** the clear, resonant sound of a bell, or a similarly resonant sound. **4** *Brit.* a telephone call. **5** a suggestion or impression of a particular feeling or quality: *a story with a ring of truth about it.* **6** a set of bells, especially in a church. — **ring someone back 1** to telephone someone again. **2** to telephone someone who telephoned earlier. **ring the changes 1** to vary the way something is done, used, said, etc. **2** to go through all the various orders possible when ringing a peel of church bells. **ring down** or **up the curtain 1** to give the signal for lowering, or raising, the curtain in a theatre. **2** to put an end to, or begin, a project or undertaking. **ring someone in** or **out** to announce their arrival or departure with, or as if with, bell-ringing: *ring out the old year.* **ring off** to end a telephone call. **ring out** to make a sudden clear loud sound: *shots rang out.* **ring someone up** to call them by telephone. **ring something up** to record the price of an item sold on a cash register. [from Anglo-Saxon *hringan*]

⊟ *verb* **1** chime, peal, toll, tinkle, clink, jingle, clang. **2** telephone, phone, call, *colloq.* give a buzz. **4** be buzzing with, resound with. **5** sound, resound, resonate, reverberate, echo. *noun* **1, 2, 3** chime, peal, toll. **3** tinkle, clink, jingle, clang. **4** phone call, call, *colloq.* buzz, *colloq.* tinkle.

ring binder a loose-leaf binder with metal rings which can be opened to add more pages or take them out.

ringbolt *noun* a bolt with a ring attached.

ring dove a wood pigeon.

ringed *adj.* **1** surrounded by, marked with, bearing, or wearing a ring or rings. **2** ring-shaped. **3** made up of rings.

ringer *noun* **1** a person or thing that rings. **2** (*also* **dead ringer**) *colloq.* a person or thing that is almost identical to some other person or thing. **3** *North Amer., esp. US* a horse or athlete entered into a race or competition under a false name or other false pretences. **4** *North Amer., esp. US* an impostor or fake.

ring-fence — *noun* **1** a fence encircling an estate. **2** the compulsory reservation of funds for use within a specific, limited sector of government, a company etc. — *verb* **1** to surround (land) with a ring-fence. **2** to apply a ring-fence to (funds).

ring finger the third finger, especially on the left hand, on which a wedding ring is worn.

ringleader *noun* the leader of a group of people who are doing something wrong or making trouble.

ringlet *noun* a long spiral curl of hair.

ring main a domestic electrical supply system in which power points are connected to the mains in a closed circuit.

ringmaster *noun* a person who is in charge of performances in a circus ring.

ring ouzel see OUZEL.

ring-pull *noun* a tongue of metal with a ring attached to it, which when pulled breaks a seal and opens a can or similar container.

ring road *Brit.* a road that goes round a town or through its suburbs to keep its centre relatively free of traffic.

ringside *noun* **1** the seating area immediately by a boxing, circus, etc ring. **2** any place that gives a good clear view.

ringway *noun* same as RING ROAD.

ringworm *noun* *Medicine* a highly contagious fungal infection characterized by the formation of small red itchy circular patches on soft areas of skin such as the scalp or groin. One of the commonest forms is *athlete's foot*, which affects the skin between the toes. Also called TINEA.

rink *noun* **1** an area of ice prepared for skating, curling, or ice-hockey, or a building containing this. **2** an area of smooth floor for roller skating, or a building containing this. **3** a strip of grass or ice allotted to a team or set of players in bowling and curling. [from Old French *renc*, rank, row]

rinse — *verb* **1** to wash (soap, detergent, etc) out of (clothes, hair, dishes, etc) with clean water. **2** to remove traces of dirt by washing lightly in clean water, usually without soap. **3** (*also* **rinse something out**) to clean (a cup, one's mouth, etc) by filling it with water, swirling the water round and throwing or spitting it out. **4** (*also* **rinse something away**) to remove (soap, detergent, dirt, etc) from a place using clean water. — *noun* **1** an act of rinsing. **2** liquid used for rinsing. **3** a solution used in hairdressing to give a temporary tint to the hair. [from Old French *recincier*]

⊟ *verb* **2** wash, clean, cleanse, bathe, wet, dip. **3** flush out, swill out. **4** flush away.

rinser *noun* a board or rack for rinsing washed dishes.

riot — *noun* **1** a noisy public disturbance or disorder by a usually large group of people, or *Legal* by three or more people. **2** uncontrolled or wild revelry and feasting. **3** a striking display (especially of colour). **4** a very amusing person or thing. — *verb intrans.* (**rioted, rioting**) to take part in a riot. — **read the riot act** to give an angry warning that bad behaviour must stop. **run riot** to act, speak, grow, etc in a wild and uncontrolled way. [from Old French *riote*, debate, quarrel]

. . . .

■ *noun* **1** insurrection, rising, uprising, revolt, rebellion, anarchy, lawlessness, affray, disturbance, turbulence, disorder, confusion, commotion, tumult, turmoil, uproar, strife. **2** revelry, merrymaking, feasting, indulgence, debauchery, orgy. **4** *colloq.* laugh, *colloq.* scream, *colloq.* hoot. *verb* revolt, rebel, rise up, run riot, run wild, rampage.
■ *noun* **1** order, calm.

. . . .

rioter *noun* a person who takes part in a riot or uprising.

riotous /ˈraɪətəs/ *adj.* **1** participating in, likely to start, or like, a riot. **2** very active, noisy, cheerful, and wild. **3** filled with wild revelry, parties, etc: *riotous living*.

riotously *adv.* in a riotous way.

riotousness *noun* being riotous.

RIP *abbrev. requiescat in pace* (Latin), may he or she rest in peace.

rip — *verb* (**ripped, ripping**) **1** *trans., intrans.* to tear or come apart violently or roughly. **2** (**rip something off, out, etc**) to remove it quickly and violently. **3** *intrans. colloq.* to rush along or move quickly without restraint. **4** to saw (wood or timber) along the grain. — *noun* **1** a violent or rough tear or split. **2** an act of ripping.— **rip someone off** *colloq.* **1** to cheat or steal from them. **2** to overcharge them.

. . . .

■ *verb* **1, 2** tear, rend, split, slit, separate. **1** rupture, burst. **2** cut, slash, hack. *noun* **1** tear, rent, split, cleavage, rupture, cut, slit, slash, gash, hole. **rip off** *slang* STING. **1** swindle, defraud, cheat, *colloq.* diddle, *colloq.* do, *colloq.* con, trick, dupe. **2** overcharge, exploit, *slang* fleece.

. . . .

riparian /raɪˈpɛərɪən/ *adj. formal* of, occurring on, or living on a riverbank. [from Latin *ripa*, riverbank]

ripcord *noun* a cord which releases a parachute from its pack when pulled.

ripe *adj.* **1** *said of fruit, grain, etc* fully matured and ready to be picked and eaten. **2** *said of cheese* having been allowed to age to develop its full flavour. **3** resembling ripe fruit, especially in being plump and pink. **4** mature in mind and body; fully developed. **5** suitable or appropriate: *time is ripe/ripe for expansion*. **6** (**ripe for something**) eager or ready for it. **7** *said of language, etc* slightly indecent; smutty. — **ripe old age** a very old age. [from Anglo-Saxon *ripe*]

. . . .

■ **1, 2** ripened, mature, mellow. **1** seasoned, grown, developed, complete, finished, perfect. **5** ready, suitable, appropriate, right, favourable, auspicious, propitious, timely, opportune.
■ **5** untimely, inopportune.

. . . .

ripen *verb trans., intrans.* (**ripened, ripening**) to make or become ripe or riper.

. . . .

■ develop, mature, mellow, season, age.

. . . .

ripeness *noun* being ripe.

ripieno /rɪˈpjeɪnoʊ/ *Mus.* — *noun* (PL. **ripieni, ripienos**) **1** the full body (or full section) of the orchestra. The term is most often applied in the concerto grosso of the Baroque period to distinguish those passages to be played by the full orchestra from those to be played by the soloist or solo group. **2** a supplementary instrument or performer. — *adj.* supplementary, full. [from Italian *ripieno*, full]

rip-off *noun colloq.* **1** an act or instance of stealing from, cheating, or defrauding someone. **2** an item which is outrageously overpriced.

. . . .

■ **1** swindle, fraud, cheat, trick, *colloq.* diddle, *colloq.* con, *slang* sting.

. . . .

riposte /rɪˈpɒst, rɪˈpoʊst/ — *noun* **1** a quick, sharp reply; a retort. **2** a fencer's quick return thrust. — *verb intrans.* to answer with a riposte. [from French, from Italian *risposta*, reply]

. . . .

■ *noun* **1** retort, rejoinder, answer, reply, comeback.

. . . .

ripper *noun* **1** a person who rips. **2** a tool for ripping.

ripple — *noun* **1** a slight wave or series of slight waves on the surface of water. **2** a sound that rises and falls quickly and gently like that of rippling water, especially of laughter or applause. **3** a wavy appearance, eg of material. — *verb* **1** *intrans., trans.* to form or cause to form or flow with ripples or a rippling motion. **2** *intrans.* to make a rippling sound.

. . . .

■ *verb* **1** ruffle, wrinkle, undulate, crease, pucker, crumple.

. . . .

ripple tank *Physics* a shallow tank of water, used to demonstrate the behaviour of waves, especially properties such as reflection, refraction, diffraction, and interference.

rippling or **ripply** *adj.* (**ripplier, rippliest**) having ripples.

rip-roaring *adj.* wild, noisy, and exciting.

ripsaw *noun* a saw for cutting along the grain of timber.

RISC *abbrev. Comput.* reduced instruction set computer, a computer with a central processor which has a very small instruction set to enable faster processing.

rise — *verb intrans.* (PAST TENSE **rose**; PAST PARTICIPLE **risen**) **1** to get or stand up, especially from a sitting, kneeling, or lying position. **2** to get up from bed, especially after a night's sleep. **3** to move upwards; to ascend. **4** to increase in size, amount, volume, strength, degree, intensity, etc. **5** *said of the sun, moon, planets, etc* to appear above the horizon. **6** to stretch or slope upwards: *ground which rises gently*. **7** (**rise up** or **rise against someone**) to rebel. **8** to move from a lower position, rank, level, etc to a higher one. **9** to begin or originate: *a river that rises in the mountains*. **10** *said especially of a person's spirits* to become more cheerful. **11** *said especially of an animal's fur, a person's hair, etc* to become straight and stiff, eg because of fear or anger. **12** *said of a committee, court, parliament, etc* to finish a session; to adjourn. **13** to come back to life. **14** to come to the surface of water: *wait for the fish to rise*. **15** *said of dough* to swell up. **16** to be built: *new office blocks rising all over town*. **17** (**rise to something**) to respond to something (eg provocation or criticism). — *noun* **1** an act of rising. **2** an increase in size, amount, volume, strength, status, rank, etc. **3** *Brit.* an increase in salary. **4** a piece of rising ground; a slope or hill. **5** a beginning or origin. **6** the vertical height of a step or flight of stairs. — **get** or **take a rise out of someone** *colloq.* to make them angry or upset, especially through teasing or provocation. **give rise to something** to cause it. **rise above something** to remain unaffected by teasing, provocation, criticism, etc. **rise to the bait** to do what someone else suggests by means of suggestions, hints, etc that one should do. [from Anglo-Saxon *risan*]

. . . .

■ *verb* **1, 2** get up. **1** stand up, arise, jump up, spring up. **3, 6** go up, ascend, climb, mount. **4** grow, increase, escalate, intensify. **6** slope (up), soar, tower. **7** rebel, revolt, mutiny. **8** advance, progress, improve, prosper. **9** originate, spring, flow, issue, emerge. *noun* **2** increase, increment, upsurge, upturn, advance, progress, improvement, advancement, promotion. **4** ascent, climb, slope, incline, hill, elevation.
■ *verb* **1** sit down. **3, 4, 6** fall. **3, 6** descend. **4** decrease. *noun* **2** fall. **4** descent, valley.

. . . .

riser *noun* **1** a person who gets out of bed: *an early riser*. **2** any of the vertical parts between the horizontal steps of a set of stairs.

risibility *noun* **1** laughter. **2** inclination to laugh.

risible /ˈrɪzɪbl/ *adj.* **1** causing laughter; ludicrous; ridiculous. **2** inclined to laughter. [from Latin *risibilis*]

rising — *noun* **1** the act of rising. **2** a rebellion. — *adj.* **1** moving or sloping upwards; getting higher. **2** approaching greater age, maturity, status, reputation, or importance. **3** approaching a stated age: *the rising sevens.*

rising damp wetness which rises up through the bricks of a wall.

risk — *noun* **1** the chance or possibility of suffering loss, injury, damage, or failure. **2** a person or thing likely to cause loss, injury, damage, etc. **3** a person or thing thought of as likely (a *bad risk*) or unlikely (a *good risk*) to suffer loss, injury, damage, etc. — *verb* **1** to expose to danger or risk. **2** to take the chance of (a problem, failure, danger, etc occurring): *not risk being late.* — **at one's own risk** accepting personal responsibility for any loss, injury, etc which might occur. **at risk** in danger; in a position which might lead to loss, injury, etc. **at the risk of something** with the possibility of loss, injury, or some other unfortunate consequence. **run the risk of something** to risk it: *run the risk of being late.* **run** or **take a risk** to act in a certain way despite the risk involved. [from French *risque*]

⬛ *noun* **1, 2** danger. **1** peril, jeopardy, hazard, chance, possibility, uncertainty. **2** gamble, speculation, venture, adventure. *verb* **1** endanger, imperil, jeopardize, hazard, chance, gamble, venture, dare.

🔳 *noun* **1** safety, certainty.

risk analysis a methodical investigation undertaken to assess the financial and physical risks which may affect a business venture. In insurance, risk is calculated by actuaries for the purpose of determining premium levels.

riskily *adv.* in a risky way.

risky *adj.* (**riskier, riskiest**) dangerous, liable to accident or mishap.

⬛ dangerous, unsafe, perilous, hazardous, chancy, uncertain, touch and go, *colloq.* dicey, tricky, precarious.

🔳 safe.

Risorgimento the 19c movement by which Italy achieved unity and nationhood. [from Italian *risorgimento*, resurgence]

risotto /rɪ'zɒtoʊ/ *noun* (PL. **risottos**) an Italian dish of rice cooked in a meat or seafood stock with onions, tomatoes, cheese, etc. [from Italian *riso*, rice]

risqué /'rɪskeɪ/ *adj.* said of a story, joke, etc bordering on the rude or indecent. [from French *risqué*, risky]

⬛ indecent, indelicate, improper, suggestive, coarse, crude, earthy, bawdy, racy, naughty, blue.

🔳 decent, proper.

rissole /'rɪsoʊl/ *noun* a small fried cake or ball of chopped meat coated in breadcrumbs. [from Old French *roissole*]

ritardando /riːtaː'dandoʊ/ *adj., adv., noun* (PL. **ritardandos, ritardandi**) *Mus.* same as RALLENTANDO. [from Italian]

rite *noun* **1** a religious ceremony or observance. **2** the required words or actions for such a ceremony. **3** a body of such acts or ceremonies which are characteristic of a particular church: *the Latin rite of the Roman Catholic church.* [from Latin *ritus*]

ritual /'rɪtʃʊəl/ — *noun* **1** the set order or words used in a religious ceremony. **2** a body of such rituals, especially of a particular church. **3** the use of rituals in a religious ceremony. **4** an often repeated series of actions or procedure. — *adj.* relating to or like rites or ritual. [from Latin *ritualis*]

⬛ *noun* **1** liturgy. **2** use, rite, service, sacrament. **3** ceremony, ceremonial, solemnity. **4** custom, tradition, convention, usage, practice, habit, wont, routine, procedure, ordinance, prescription, form, formality, act. *adj.*

customary, traditional, conventional, habitual, routine, procedural, prescribed, set, formal, ceremonial.

🔳 *adj.* informal.

ritualism *noun* excessive belief in the importance of, or excessive practice of, ritual.

ritualist *noun* a person skilled in or devoted to a ritual.

ritualistic *adj.* **1** relating to or characteristic of ritualism. **2** fond of or devoted to ritual.

ritualistically *adv.* in a ritualistic way.

ritually *adv.* according to ritual.

ritzy *adj.* (**ritzier, ritziest**) *colloq.* very smart and elegant. [from *Ritz*, a name often used for luxury hotels]

rival — *noun* **1** a person or group of people that tries to compete with another for the same goal or in the same field. **2** a person or thing which equals another in quality, ability, etc: *be without a rival.* — *adj.* being a rival; in competition for the same goal or in the same field. — *verb* (**rivalled, rivalling**) **1** to try to gain the same goal as (someone else); to be in competition with. **2** to try to equal or be better than. **3** to be able to be compared with as being equal or nearly so. [from Latin *rivalis*, one who uses the same stream as another]

⬛ *noun* **1** competitor, contestant, contender, challenger, opponent, adversary, antagonist. **2** match, equal, peer. *adj.* competitive, competing, opposed, opposing, conflicting. *verb* COMPETE WITH. **1, 2** vie with. **1** contend with, oppose. **2, 3** match, equal. **2** emulate.

🔳 *noun* **1** colleague, associate. *verb* **1** co-operate.

rivalry /'raɪvlrɪ/ *noun* (PL. **rivalries**) **1** the state of being a rival or rivals. **2** an act of rivalling.

⬛ **1** competition, competitiveness, contest, contention, conflict, struggle, strife, opposition, antagonism.

🔳 **1** co-operation.

riven /'rɪvn/ *adj.* having been violently torn or split apart. [from Norse *rifa*]

river *noun* **1** *Geol.* a permanent natural flow of water, larger than a stream, along a fixed course. **2** an abundant or plentiful stream or flow. [from Old French *riviere*, from Latin *ripa*, riverbank]

⬛ **1** waterway, watercourse, tributary, stream, brook, beck, creek, estuary.

river basin *Geol.* the area of land drained by a river and its tributaries. Also called DRAINAGE BASIN.

river dolphin any of various species of a small toothed whale with a long narrow beak, found in rivers and brackish water in S Asia and S America.

riverine /'rɪvəraɪn, 'rɪvəriːn/ *adj.* of, on, or near a river.

rivet — *noun* *Engineering* a metal pin or bolt, with a head at one end, that is passed through a hole in each of two or more pieces of metal that are to be joined. The protruding end is then hammered flat. — *verb* (**riveted, riveting**) **1** to fasten two or more pieces of metal with such a device. **2** to flatten or beat down (the head of a nail, etc). **3** to fix securely. **4** to attract and hold firmly, to engross (eg a person's attention). **5** to cause (a person) to be fixed, especially with horror or fear: *be riveted to the spot.* [from Old French *river*, to attach]

riveter *noun* a person or tool that rivets.

riveting *adj.* **1** the joining of two or more pieces of metal by passing a metal rivet through a hole in each piece and then hammering the protruding end of the rivet flat. Formerly widely used in the building of ships, bridges, etc, riveting has now been largely superseded by welding. **2** fascinating; enthralling.

riviera /rɪvɪ'ɛərə/ *noun* **1** a coastal area with a warm climate. **2** (**Riviera**) the Mediterranean coast between Toulon,

France, and La Spezia, Italy. It is a narrow coastal strip bordered by the Alps to the N, and includes many holiday resorts. [from Italian *riviera*, coast]

rivulet /'rɪvjʊlət/ *noun* a small stream or river. [from Latin *rivulus*]

RM *abbrev.* **1** Resident Magistrate. **2** Royal Mail. **3** Royal Marines.

rm *abbrev.* room.

RMA *abbrev.* Royal Military Academy, Sandhurst.

RN *abbrev.* Royal Navy.

Rn *symbol Chem.* radon.

RNA *abbrev.* ribonucleic acid.

RNAS *abbrev.* Royal Navy Air Service(s).

RNIB *abbrev.* Royal National Institute for the Blind.

RNID *abbrev.* Royal National Institute for the Deaf.

RNLI *abbrev.* Royal National Lifeboat Institution.

RNR *abbrev.* Royal Naval Reserve.

RNVR *abbrev.* Royal Naval Volunteer Reserve.

RNZAF *abbrev.* Royal New Zealand Air Force.

RNZN *abbrev.* Royal New Zealand Navy.

roach¹ /rəʊtʃ/ *noun* a silvery freshwater fish of the carp family. [from Old French *roche*]

roach² /rəʊtʃ/ *noun North Amer.* **1** a cockroach. **2** *slang* the butt of a marijuana cigarette.

road *noun* **1** an open, usually specially surfaced or paved way, for people, vehicles, or animals to travel on from one place to another. **2** a route or way: *the road to ruin.* **3** (*usually* **roads**) a relatively sheltered area of water near the shore where ships may be anchored. — **get out of someone's road** *colloq. chiefly Scot.* to get out of their way. **one for the road** a final, usually alcoholic, drink before leaving. **on the road** travelling from place to place, especially as a commercial traveller or tramp. [from Anglo-Saxon *rad*]

⊞ **1** roadway, *Brit.* motorway, bypass, highway, thoroughfare, street, avenue, boulevard, crescent, drive, lane, track. **2** route, course, way, direction, path.

roadbed *noun* **1** the foundation of a railway track on which the sleepers are laid. **2** the material laid down to form a road, and which forms a foundation for the road surface.

roadblock *noun* a barrier put across a road (eg by the police or army) to stop and check vehicles and drivers.

road-hog *noun colloq.* an aggressive and selfish driver, especially one who tries to intimidate other drivers.

roadholding *noun* the extent to which a vehicle remains stable when turning corners at high speed, in wet conditions, etc.

roadhouse *noun* a public house or inn on the side of a major road.

roadie *noun colloq.* a person who helps move the instruments and equipment which belong to especially a rock or pop group.

road metal broken stone or rock used for building or mending roads.

road rage uncontrolled anger or aggression between road users.

roadside *noun* a strip of ground or land beside or along a road.

road sign a sign beside or over a road, motorway, etc, giving information on routes, speed limits, hazards, traffic systems, etc.

roadstead same as ROAD 3.

roadster *noun* **1** an open sports car for two people. **2** a strong bicycle. **3** a horse for riding or pulling carriages on roads.

roadway *noun* the part of a road or street used by cars.

roadwork *noun* **1** (**roadworks**) the building or repairing of a road. **2** training, eg for marathons, boxing matches, etc in the form of long runs on roads.

roadworthiness *noun* a roadworthy state.

roadworthy *adj.* in a suitable condition and safe to be used on the road.

roam — *verb trans., intrans.* to ramble or wander about. — *noun* the act of roaming; a ramble. [from Middle English *romen*]

⊞ *verb* wander, rove, range, travel, walk, ramble, stroll, amble, prowl, drift, stray.
⊟ *verb* stay.

roamer *noun* a person who roams, a wanderer.

roan /rəʊn/ — *adj., usually said of horses or cattle* having a reddish-brown or bay coat thickly flecked with grey or white hairs. — *noun* an animal, especially a horse, with a coat of this type. [from Old Spanish *roano*]

roar — *verb* **1** *intrans.* to give a loud growling cry. **2** *intrans.* to laugh loudly, deeply, and wildly. **3** *intrans.* to make a deep loud reverberating sound, as of cannons, busy traffic, wind, and waves in a storm, or a fiercely burning fire. **4** to say (something) with a deep, loud cry, especially as in anger. **5** (**roar about, away, past,**) to go fast and noisily, usually in a motor vehicle. **6** (**roar someone on**) to shout encouragement to them. **7** *intrans. said of a horse* to breathe with a loud noise as a sign of disease. — *noun* **1** a loud, deep, prolonged cry, as of lions, a cheering crowd, a person in pain or anger, etc. **2** a loud, deep, prolonged sound, as of cannons, busy traffic, an engine made to roar, the wind or waves in a storm, or a fiercely burning fire. — **do a roaring trade** to do very brisk and profitable business. [from Anglo-Saxon *rarian*]

⊞ *verb* **1, 2** howl. **1, 4** bellow. **2** hoot, guffaw. **3** thunder, crash, blare, rumble. **4** yell, shout, cry, bawl. *noun* **1** bellow, howl, yell, shout, cry, bawl. **2** thunder, crash, blare, rumble.
⊟ *verb* **4** whisper.

roaring *adj.* **1** uttering or emitting roars. **2** riotous. **3** proceeding with great activity or success.

roaring drunk *colloq.* very drunk.

roaring forties *Meteorol.* a belt of strong westerly winds, lying between 40° and 50° S of the Equator, that are not interrupted by landmasses and often blow at gale force.

roast — *verb* **1** *trans., intrans.* to cook (meat or other food) by exposure to dry heat, especially in an oven. **2** to dry and make brown (coffee beans, nuts, etc) by exposure to dry heat. **3** *intrans. said of meat, coffee beans, nuts, etc* to be cooked or dried and made brown by being exposed to dry heat. **4** *trans., intrans. colloq.* to make or become extremely or excessively hot. **5** *colloq.* to criticize severely. — *noun* **1** a piece of meat which has been roasted or is suitable for roasting. **2** *North Amer.* a party in the open air at which food is roasted and eaten. — *adj.* roasted: *roast potatoes.* [from Old French *rostir*]

roaster *noun* **1** an oven or dish for roasting food. **2** a vegetable, fowl, etc suitable for roasting.

roasting *colloq.* — *adj.* very hot. — *noun* a dose of severe criticism.

rob *verb* (**robbed, robbing**) **1** to steal something from (a person or place), especially by force or threats. **2** to deprive (someone) of something expected as a right or due. **3** *intrans.* to commit robbery. [from Old French *robber*]

⊞ **1, 2** cheat, defraud. **1, 3** burgle, loot, pillage, plunder. **1** steal from, hold up, mug, raid, sack, rifle, ransack, swindle, *colloq.* rip off, *colloq.* do. **2** deprive, disappoint.

robber *noun* a person who robs; a thief.

⊞ thief, burglar, mugger, *colloq.* crook, swindler, embezzler, *colloq.* con man.

robbery *noun* (PL. **robberies**) the act of robbing, especially theft with threats, force, or violence.

▣ theft, stealing, larceny, mugging, hold-up, *slang* stick-up, *slang* heist, raid, burglary, pillage, plunder, fraud, embezzlement, swindle, *colloq.* rip-off.

robe — *noun* **1** (*often* **robes**) a long, loose, flowing garment, especially one worn for special ceremonies by peers, judges, mayors, academics, etc. **2** *North Amer.* a dressing-gown or bathrobe. — *verb trans., intrans.* to clothe (oneself or someone) in a robe or robes. [from Old French *robe*, booty]

robin *noun* **1** (*also* **robin redbreast**) a small brown European thrush with a red breast. **2** a N American thrush with an orange-red breast, larger than the European robin. [a diminutive of *Robert*]

robot *noun* **1** especially in science fiction stories, etc, a machine which looks and functions like a human. **2** an automatic machine that can be programmed to perform specific tasks. **3** a person who works efficiently but who lacks human warmth or sensitivity. [from Czech *robota*, work]

▣ AUTOMATON. **1** android. **2, 3** machine. **3** zombie.

robotics *sing. noun* **1** the branch of engineering concerned with the design, construction, operation, and use of industrial robots. It incorporates many of the concepts that are used in artificial intelligence. **2** a form of dancing in which dancers imitate the stiff, jerky, and sharp movements of robots.

robust *adj.* **1** strong and healthy; with a strong constitution. **2** strongly built or constructed. **3** *said of exercise, etc* requiring strength and energy. **4** rough, earthy, and slightly rude. **5** *said of wine* with a full, rich quality. [from Latin *robustus*, from *robur*, oak, strength]

▣ **1, 2** strong, sturdy, tough. **1** hardy, vigorous, powerful, muscular, athletic, fit, healthy, well. **4** coarse, earthy, rude, ribald, risqué.

▣ **1, 2** weak, feeble, unhealthy.

robustly *adv.* in a robust way.
robustness *noun* being robust.
ROC *abbrev.* Royal Observer Corps.
roc /rɒk/ *noun* an enormous bird in Arabian legends, strong enough to carry off an elephant. [from Persian *rukh*]
rochet /ˈrɒtʃɪt/ *noun Relig.* a full-length white linen robe worn by bishops, especially of the Anglican Communion, on ceremonial occasions. [from Old French; of Germanic origin]
rock[1] *noun* **1** *Geol.* a loose or consolidated mass of one or more minerals that forms part of the Earth's crust, eg granite, limestone. Rocks are classified as igneous, metamorphic, or sedimentary, according to the way in which they were formed, and may be hard or soft. **2** a large natural mass of this material forming a reef, tor, etc. **3** a large stone or boulder. **4** *North Amer.* a stone or pebble. **5** someone or something which provides a firm foundation or support and can be depended upon. **6** (*usually* **rocks**) a cause or source of difficulty, danger or disaster. **7** *Brit.* a hard sweet usually made in the form of long, cylindrical sticks, which is brightly coloured and flavoured with peppermint, etc. **8** *slang* a precious stone, especially a diamond. — **on the rocks** *colloq.* **1** *said of a marriage* broken down; failed. **2** *said of an alcoholic drink* served with ice cubes. **3** *said of a business firm* in a state of great financial difficulty. [from Old French *rocque*]

▣ **2** crag, outcrop. **3** boulder, stone.

Rocks include: basalt, breccia, chalk, coal, conglomerate, flint, gabbro, gneiss, granite, gravel, lava, limestone, marble, marl, obsidian, ore, porphyry, pumice stone, sandstone, schist, serpentine, shale, slate.

rock[2] — *verb* **1** *trans., intrans.* to sway or cause to sway gently backwards and forwards or from side to side: *rock the baby to sleep.* **2** *trans., intrans.* to move or cause to move or shake violently. **3** to disturb, upset, or shock. **4** *intrans.* to dance to or play rock music. — *noun* **1** a rocking movement. **2** (*also* **rock music**) a form of popular music with a very strong beat, usually played on electronic instruments and derived from rock and roll. **3** rock and roll. — *adj.* relating to rock music. [from Anglo-Saxon *roccian*]

▣ *verb* **1** sway, swing, tilt, tip. **2** shake, wobble, roll, pitch, toss. **3** shock, stun, daze, dumbfound, astound, astonish, surprise, startle, stagger.

rockabilly *noun* a style of music which combines elements from both rock and roll and hillbilly.
rock and roll or **rock 'n' roll** *noun* a form of popular music with a lively jive beat and simple melodies. — *verb intrans.* to dance to or play rock and roll music.
rock bottom the lowest level possible.
rock-bottom *adj.*, *said of prices, etc* having reached the lowest possible level.
rock cake a small round cake with a rough surface, made with fruit and spices.
rock crystal a transparent colourless quartz.
rocker *noun* **1** one of usually two curved supports on which a chair, cradle, etc rocks. **2** something that rocks on such supports, especially a rocking chair. **3** a person or thing that rocks. **4** a device which is operated with a movement from side to side, backwards and forwards, or up and down, especially a switch between the 'on' and 'off' positions. **5** *Brit.* (**Rocker**) in the 1960s, a member of a sometimes violent teenage gang, typically wearing leather jackets and riding motorcycles. See also MOD. **6** an object with a part which is curved like a rocker, especially a skate with a curved blade. — **off one's rocker** *colloq.* mad; crazy.
rockery *noun* (PL. **rockeries**) a garden made with both rocks and earth, and where rock plants are grown.
rocket — *noun* **1** a cylinder containing inflammable material, which when ignited is projected through the air for signalling, carrying a line to a ship in distress, or as part of a firework display. **2** a projectile or vehicle, especially a space vehicle, that obtains its thrust from a backward jet of hot gases produced by the burning of a mixture of fuel and oxygen that is carried within the projectile or vehicle. **3** *Brit. colloq.* a severe reprimand. — *verb* (**rocketed**, **rocketing**) **1** *intrans.* to move (especially upwards) extremely quickly, as if with the speed of a rocket. **2** to attack with rockets. [from Italian *rochetta*]
rock garden a rockery, or a garden containing rockeries.
rockily *adv.* in a rocky way.
rockiness *noun* being ocky.
rocking chair a chair which rocks backwards and forwards on two curved supports.
rocking horse a toy horse mounted on two curved supports on which a child can sit and rock backwards and forwards.
rock plant any small alpine plant which grows among rocks and needs very little soil.
rockrose *noun* a small evergreen shrub of the genus *Helianthemum*, native to the Mediterranean region and parts of Asia. It has lance-shaped or oblong leaves, and white, yellow, or red flowers with five petals. Some species are grown as ornamentals in gardens.
rock salmon the dogfish or other fish, especially when sold as food.
rock salt common salt occurring as a mass of solid mineral.
rocky[1] *adj.* (**rockier**, **rockiest**) **1** full of rocks; made of or like rock. **2** full of problems and obstacles.

▣ ROUGH, HARD. **1** stony, pebbly, craggy, rugged, flinty.
▣ SMOOTH. **1** soft.

rocky[2] *adj.* (**rockier, rockiest**) shaky; unsteady.

. . . .

▣ unsteady, shaky, wobbly, staggering, tottering, unstable, unreliable, uncertain, weak.

▣ steady, stable, dependable, strong.

. . . .

rococo /rə'koʊkoʊ/ — *noun* an elaborate 18c ornamental style, characterized by shells, scrolls, and asymmetric patterns. — *adj.* **1** of or in this style. **2** florid and elaborate. [from French *rocaille*, rock-work]

rod *noun* **1** a long slender stick or bar of wood, metal, etc. **2** a stick or bundle of twigs used to beat people as a punishment. **3** a stick, wand, or sceptre carried as a symbol of office or authority. **4** a fishing-rod. **5** in surveying, a unit of length equivalent to 5.5yd (5.03m). **6** *Anat.* in the retina of the vertebrate eye, one of over 100 million rod-shaped cells containing the light-sensitive pigment rhodopsin, and concerned with the perception of light intensity. Rods are essential for vision in dim light. **7** *coarse slang* a penis. **8** *North Amer. slang* a pistol. [from Anglo-Saxon *rodd*]

. . . .

▣ **1, 2** stick, cane. **1** bar, shaft, strut, pole. **2** switch. **3** baton, wand, staff, mace, sceptre.

. . . .

rode see RIDE.

rodent *noun* an animal belonging to the order Rodentia, a large group of mostly nocturnal mammals with chisel-like incisor teeth that grow continuously and are adapted for gnawing, eg rats, mice, squirrels, beavers. [from Latin *rodere*, to gnaw]

rodeo /'roʊdɪoʊ, roʊ'deɪoʊ/ *noun* (PL. **rodeos**) a show or contest of cowboy skills, including riding, lassoing, and animal-handling. [from Spanish, from *rodear*, to go round]

rodomontade /rɒdəmɒn'teɪd, rɒdəmɒn'tɑːd/ — *noun* **1** boastful or bragging words or behaviour. **2** a boastful or bragging speech. — *verb intrans.* to talk boastfully; to brag. [from Italian *Rodomonte*, the boastful king of Algiers in Ariosto's *Orlando Furioso* (1516)]

roe[1] *noun* **1** (*in full* **hard roe**) the mass of eggs in the body cavity of a female fish. **2** (*in full* **soft roe**) the sperm of a male fish. [from Middle English *rowe*]

roe[2] *noun* (*also* **roe deer**) a small deer found in Europe and Asia. [from Anglo-Saxon *ra*]

roentgen /'rɜːntgən, 'rentgən/ same as RÖNTGEN.

Rogation Day any of the three days before Ascension Day. [from Latin *rogatio*, from *rogare*, to ask]

roger /'rɒdʒə/ — *interj.*, *in radio communications and signalling* message received and understood. — *verb* (**rogered, rogering**) *coarse slang, said of a man* to have sexual intercourse with. [from the name ROGER]

rogue /roʊg/ — *noun* **1** a dishonest person. **2** a person, especially a child, who is playfully mischievous. **3** someone or something, especially a plant, which is not true to its type and is inferior. **4** a vicious wild animal which lives apart from or has been driven from its herd. — *adj.* of or like a rogue. [a cant word]

. . . .

▣ *noun* **1, 2** rascal, scamp. **1** scoundrel, villain, miscreant, *colloq.* crook, swindler, fraud, cheat, *colloq.* con man, reprobate, wastrel.

. . . .

roguery /'roʊgərɪ/ *noun* (PL. **rogueries**) the behaviour or an action which is typical of a rogue.

rogues gallery a police collection of photographs of known criminals, used to identify suspects.

roguish /'roʊgɪʃ/ *adj.* characteristic of a rogue; mischievous, dishonest.

roguishly *adv.* in a roguish way.

roguishness *noun* being roguish.

roister *verb intrans.* (**roistered, roistering**) to enjoy oneself noisily. [from Old French *rustre*, ruffian]

roisterer *noun* a noisy reveller, a swaggering fellow.

role or **rôle** *noun* **1** an actor's part in a play, film, etc. **2** a part played in life, business, etc; the function of a person or thing. [from French *rôle*]

. . . .

▣ PART. **1** character, lines. **2** function, capacity, task, duty, job, post, position.

. . . .

role model a person whose life and behaviour is taken as an example to follow by someone else.

Rolfing *noun* a therapeutic technique for correcting postural faults and improving physical wellbeing through manipulation of the muscles and joints, so that the body is realigned symmetrically and the best use of gravity made in maintaining balance. [named after the originator of the technique, Ida Rolf]

roll — *noun* **1** anything flat (such as paper, fabric, etc) which is rolled up to form a cylinder or tube. **2** a small portion of bread for one person, often with a specified filling. **3** a folded piece of pastry or cake with a specified filling: *a sausage roll.* **4** a rolled mass of something: *rolls of fat.* **5** an official list of names, eg of school pupils, members of a club, or people eligible to vote. **6** an act of rolling. **7** a swaying or rolling movement, eg in walking or dancing, or of a ship. **8** a long, low, prolonged sound. **9** a series of quick beats on a drum. **10** a complete rotation around its longitudinal axis by an aircraft. **11** a roller or cylinder used to press, shape, or apply something. — *verb* **1** *trans., intrans.* to move or cause to move by turning over and over, as if on an axis, and often in a specified direction. **2** *trans., intrans.* to move or cause to move on wheels, rollers, etc, or in a vehicle with wheels. **3** (*also* **roll over**) *said of a person or animal, etc. lying down* to turn with a rolling movement to face in another direction. **4** *trans., intrans.* to move or cause to move or flow gently and steadily. **5** *intrans.* to seem to move like or in waves: *a garden rolling down to the river.* **6** *intrans. said eg of a ship* to sway or rock gently from side to side. **7** *intrans.* to walk with a swaying movement. **8** *intrans., trans.* to begin to operate or work: *the cameras rolled.* **9** *trans., intrans.* to move or cause (one's eyes) to move in a circle, especially in disbelief, despair, or amazement. **10** *trans., intrans.* to form or cause to form a tube or cylinder by winding or being wound round and round. **11** (*also* **roll up** or **roll something up**) to wrap it or be wrapped by rolling. **12** (*also* **roll out** or **roll something out**) to spread it out or make it flat or flatter, especially by pressing and smoothing with something heavy. **13** to make a series of long low rumbling sounds. **14** to pronounce (especially an 'r' sound) with a trill. **15** *intrans.* to move in the same direction as something so as to reduce its strength or impact: *roll with the punches.* — **on a roll** *colloq.* having continuing luck or success. **be rolling in something** *colloq.* to have large amounts of something (especially money). **roll by** or **on** *said especially of time* to pass or follow steadily: *the weeks rolled by.* **roll in** to come or arrive in large quantities. **roll on** *interj.* may a particular or specified time come soon. **roll up 1** *colloq.* to arrive. **2** to come in large numbers. **roll up** or **roll something up** to form or cause it to form into a roll. [from Old French *rolle*]

. . . .

▣ *noun* **1, 11** cylinder. **1** reel, spool, bobbin, scroll. **5** register, roster, census, list, inventory, index, catalogue, directory, schedule, record, chronicle, annals. **6** rotation, revolution, cycle, turn, spin, wheel, twirl, whirl, gyration. **8** rumble, roar, thunder, boom, resonance, reverberation. **11** roller, drum. *verb* **1** rotate, revolve, turn, spin, twirl, whirl, gyrate, wheel. **4** move, run, pass. **6** rock, sway, swing, pitch, toss, lurch, reel, wallow. **10** wind, coil, furl, twist, curl. **11** wrap, envelop, enfold, bind. **12** press, flatten, smooth, level. **13** rumble, roar, thunder, boom, resound, reverberate. **roll up 1** arrive, turn up, *colloq.* show up, appear. **2** assemble, gather, congregate, convene.

▣ **roll up 1** leave.

. . . .

roll-call *noun* the calling out of names from a list at an assembly, meeting, etc to check who is present.

rolled gold metal covered with a thin coating of gold.

roller *noun* 1 any of a number of cylindrical objects or machines used for flattening, crushing, spreading, printing, applying paint, etc. 2 a rod for rolling cloth, etc round. 3 a small cylinder on which hair is rolled for curling. 4 a solid wheel or cylinder attached to heavy machinery, etc, which makes it easier to move. 5 a long heavy sea wave. 6 a bird of a family related to the kingfishers, with a rolling manner of flight.

Rollerblades *pl. noun trademark* a set of roller skates with wheels set in a line along the centre of the shoe.

rollercoaster *noun* a raised railway with sharp curves and steep inclines, ridden on for pleasure and excitement, and usually found at funfairs.

roller skate a series of wheels attached to a framework which can be fitted over one's shoe, or a shoe with wheels attached to the sole.

roller-skate *verb intrans.* to move, dance, etc on roller skates.

roller-skater *noun* a person who roller-skates.

roller-skating *noun* the practice or skill of using roller skates.

roller towel a usually long towel with the ends sewn together, hung on a roller.

rollicking *adj.* boisterous, noisy, and carefree. [perhaps from ROMP + FROLIC]

rolling *adj.* 1 *said of land, countryside, etc* with low, gentle hills and valleys, and without steep slopes and crags. 2 *said of a contract* subject to review at regular intervals.

rolling mill 1 a machine for rolling metal ingots (slabs) into sheets, bars, or other shapes between pairs of rollers revolving in opposite directions. It is often used to improve the mechanical properties of a metal, or to give it a bright finish. 2 a factory containing such machines.

rolling-pin *noun* a wooden, pottery, etc cylinder for flattening out pastry.

rolling stock the engines, wagons, coaches, etc used on a railway.

rolling stone a person who leads a restless or unsettled life.

rollmop *noun* a fillet of herring rolled up usually round a slice of onion, and pickled in spiced vinegar. [from German *Rollmops*, from *rollen*, to roll + *Mops*, pug-dog]

rollneck *adj., said of a piece of clothing* having a high neck which is turned down over itself.

roll-on *noun* 1 a woman's light elastic corset. 2 a liquid deodorant or antiperspirant in a small container with a rotating ball at the top.

roll-on roll-off *adj., said of a passenger ferry, etc* with entrances at both the front and back of the ship, so that vehicles can be driven on through one entrance and off through the other.

roll-top desk a desk with a flexible cover of slats that may be rolled down when the desk is not being used.

roll-up *noun Brit. colloq.* a cigarette which one makes oneself by rolling paper round loose tobacco.

roly-poly — *adj.* round and podgy. — *noun* (PL. **roly-polies**) a strip of suet pastry filled with jam and rolled up, then baked or steamed. [probably from ROLL]

ROM /rɒm/ *abbrev. Comput.* read-only memory, a memory which holds data permanently and allows it to be read and used but not changed.

Roman — *adj.* 1 of or related to modern or ancient Rome and the Roman Empire, its history, culture, or inhabitants. 2 of the Roman Catholic Church. 3 (**roman**) (of printing type) written in ordinary upright letters (as opposed to italics). — *noun* 1 an inhabitant of modern or ancient Rome. 2 a Roman Catholic. 3 (**roman**) roman letters or type. [from Latin *Romanus*, from *Roma*, Rome]

roman-à-clef /rɒʊˈmɒn a kleɪ/ *noun* a novel with characters based on real people under disguised names. [French, = novel with a key]

Roman alphabet the alphabet developed by the ancient Romans for writing Latin, and now used for most writing in W European languages including English.

Roman Catholic — *adj.* of the Christian church which recognizes the pope as its head. — *noun* a member of this church.

romance — *noun* 1 a love affair. 2 sentimentalized or idealized love, valued especially for its beauty, purity, and the mutual devotion of the lovers. 3 an atmosphere, the feelings or behaviour associated with romantic love. 4 a sentimental account, especially in writing or on film, of a love affair. 5 such writing, films, etc as a group or genre. 6 a fictitious story which deals with imaginary, adventurous, and mysterious events, characters, places, etc. 7 an atmosphere or quality associated with adventurous, mysterious, or glamorous places, events, etc. 8 a medieval verse narrative dealing with chivalry, highly idealized love, and fantastic adventures. 9 an exaggeration or absurd account or lie. 10 (**Romance**) the group of languages, including French, Spanish, and Italian, which have developed from Latin. 11 a short, informal, ballad-like piece of music. — *adj.* (**Romance**) of or relating to the languages which have developed from Latin, such as French, Spanish, and Italian. — *verb* 1 to try to win the love of. 2 *intrans.* to talk or write extravagantly, romantically, or fantastically. 3 *intrans.* to lie. [from Old French *romanz*]

⊞ *noun* 1 love affair, affair, relationship, liaison, intrigue, passion, *colloq.* fling. 4 love story, novel, novelette. 6 story, tale, fairytale, legend, idyll, fiction, fantasy. 7 adventure, excitement, melodrama, mystery, charm, fascination, glamour, sentiment. *verb* 2 fantasize, exaggerate, overstate.

Romanesque /rəʊməˈnɛsk/ — *noun* the style of architecture found in W and S Europe from the 9c to the 12c, characterized by the use of a round arch, clear plans and elevations and, typically, a two-tower façade. — *adj.* in or relating to this style of architecture. [from French]

roman fleuve /rɒʊˈmɒn flɜːv/ a series of novels, each of which exists as a separate novel in its own right, but which are linked, usually because some or all of the characters appear in each successive work. Examples include Emile Zola's 20-volume series *Les Rougon-Macquart* (1871–93), the seven parts of Proust's *A la recherche du temps perdu* (1913–27), John Galsworthy's *Forsyte Saga* (1906–28), C P Snow's *Strangers and Brothers* (1940–70), and Anthony Powell's 12-volume *Dance to the Music of Time* (1951–76). [French, literally = river novel]

Romanian /rɒʊˈmeɪnɪən/ — *noun* 1 the official language of Romania. 2 an inhabitant of or person from Romania. — *adj.* of or relating to the Romanian people, their country, language, history, or culture.

romanization or **romanisation** *noun* the adoption of the Roman alphabet to transcribe a language that uses a different writing system, for example Arabic, Chinese, Greek, Hindi, and Russian. Since there are variations in the principles of romanization, romanized names from these languages can have several variants.

Roman nose a nose with a high bridge.

Roman numeral any of the figures used to represent numbers in the system developed by the ancient Romans, eg I (= 1), V (= 5), X (= 10), etc. See also ARABIC NUMERAL.

romantic — *adj.* 1 characterized by or inclined towards sentimental and idealized love. 2 dealing with or suggesting adventure, mystery, and sentimentalized love: *romantic fiction*. 3 highly impractical or imaginative, and often also foolish. 4 (*often* **Romantic**) *said of literature, art, music, etc* relating to or in the style of Romanticism. — *noun* 1 a person with a romantic, idealized, and sentimental idea of love, life, etc. 2 a person who writes, paints, etc in the style of Romanticism. [from Old French *romanz*, romance]

⊞ *adj.* 1 sentimental, loving, amorous, passionate, tender, fond, *colloq.* lovey-dovey, *colloq.* soppy, mushy, mawkish, maudlin. 2 exciting, fascinating, thrilling, adventurous, mysterious, fantastic, legendary, fairy-tale, idyllic, imaginary, fictitious. 3 utopian, idealistic, quixotic, visionary, starry-eyed, dreamy, fanciful, unrealistic, impractical, improbable, wild, extravagant. *noun* **1** sentimentalist, dreamer, visionary, idealist, utopian.

🖃 *adj.* **1** unromantic, unsentimental. **3** real, practical. *noun* **1** realist.

- -

romantically *adv.* in a romantic way; with romantic feeling.

Romanticism *noun* a late 18c and early 19c movement in art, literature, and music, characterized by an emphasis on feelings and emotions, often using imagery taken from nature, and creating forms which are relatively free from rules and set orders.

Romanticist *noun* a person whose art or writing, etc is characterized by Romanticism.

romanticize or **romanticise** *verb* **1** to make seem romantic. **2** *trans., intrans.* to describe or think of in a romantic, idealized, unrealistic, and sometimes misleading way. **3** *intrans.* to hold romantic ideas or act in a romantic way.

- - - - - - - - - - - - - - - - - - - -

🖃 **2** glamorize, sentimentalize. **3** fantasize.

- -

Romany /ˈroʊmənɪ/ — *noun* (PL. **Romanies**) **1** a Gypsy. **2** the language spoken by Gypsies, belonging to the Indic branch of Indo-European. — *adj.* of the Romanies, their language, and culture. [from Romany *rom*, man]

Romeo /ˈroʊmɪoʊ/ **1** the love-struck hero of Shakespeare's *Romeo and Juliet*. **2** (PL. **Romeos**) an ardent young male lover.

Romish /ˈroʊmɪʃ/ *adj. derog.* Roman Catholic.

romp — *verb intrans.* **1** to play in a lively, boisterous way. **2** (**romp in, home, through,**) to succeed in a race, competition, task, etc quickly and easily. — *noun* **1** an act of romping; boisterous play. **2** a swift pace. **3** a young person, especially a girl, who romps. [perhaps a variant of RAMP]

rompers *pl. noun* (*also* **romper suit**) a suit for a baby, with short-legged trousers and either a short-sleeved top or a bib top.

rondeau /ˈrɒndoʊ/ *noun* (PL. **rondeaux**) a poem of 10 or 13 lines with only two rhymes, and with the first line used as a refrain after the eighth, and thirteenth lines. [from Old French *rondel*, from *rond*, round]

rondo /ˈrɒndoʊ/ *noun* (PL. **rondos**) a piece of music, especially one forming the last movement of a sonata or a concerto, with a principal theme which recurs or is repeated as a refrain. [from Italian]

röntgen /ˈrɜːntgən, ˈrɛntgən/ *noun* a unit used for measuring the dose of X-rays. [named after the German physicist Wilhelm Konrad von Röntgen (1845–1923), who discovered X-rays]

rood *noun* **1** a cross or crucifix, especially a large one at the entrance to a church. **2** *literary* the cross on which Christ was crucified. [from Anglo-Saxon *rod*]

rood screen an ornamental wooden or stone screen separating the choir from the nave.

roof — *noun* (PL. **roofs**) **1** the top, usually rigid covering of a building or vehicle. **2** the top inner surface of an oven, refrigerator, the mouth, etc. **3** a dwelling or home: *two families sharing a single roof*. **4** a high, or the highest, level: *the roof of the world*. — *verb* **1** to cover with a roof. **2** to serve as a roof or shelter for. — **go through** or **hit the roof** *colloq.* **1** to become very angry. **2** *said of prices* to become extremely high. **raise the roof** *colloq.* to be very noisy. [from Anglo-Saxon *hrof*]

roof garden a garden on a building's flat roof.

roofing *noun* materials for building a roof.

roof rack a frame for attaching to the roof of a car to carry luggage.

rooftop *noun* the outside of a roof of a building.

rook[1] /rʊk/ — *noun* a large crow-like bird which nests in colonies in the tops of trees, found in Europe and Asia. — *verb colloq.* to cheat or defraud, especially at cards. [from Anglo-Saxon *hroc*]

rook[2] /rʊk/ *Chess* see CASTLE. [from Persian *rukh*]

rookery /ˈrʊkərɪ/ *noun* (PL. **rookeries**) **1** a colony of rooks. **2** a colony of penguins, other sea birds, or seals.

rookie /ˈrʊkɪ/ *noun colloq.* a new or raw recruit. [a corruption of RECRUIT]

room — *noun* **1** a part of a building which is separated from the rest of the building by having a ceiling, floor, and walls. **2** a space or area which is occupied by or is available to someone or something. **3** all of the people present in a room: *the room suddenly became silent*. **4** opportunity, scope, or possibility: *room for improvement*. **5** (**rooms**) rented lodgings. — *verb intrans. chiefly North Amer.* to lodge or share a room. [from Anglo-Saxon *rum*]

- - - - - - - - - - - - - - - - - - - -

🖃 *noun* **2, 4** scope. **2** space, volume, capacity, headroom, legroom, elbow-room, range, extent, leeway, latitude, margin, allowance. **4** chance, opportunity.

- -

Types of room include: attic, loft, boxroom, bedroom, boudoir, spare room, dressing-room, guest room, nursery, playroom, sitting-room, lounge, front room, living-room, drawing-room, salon, reception room, chamber, lounge-diner, dining room, study, *colloq.* den, library, kitchen, kitchen-diner, kitchenette, breakfast room, larder, pantry, scullery, bathroom, en suite bathroom, toilet, lavatory, WC, *colloq.* loo, cloakroom, laundry, utility room, porch, hall, landing, conservatory, sun lounge, cellar, basement; classroom, music room, laboratory, office, sickroom, dormitory, workroom, studio, workshop, storeroom, waiting-room, anteroom, foyer, mezzanine, family room, games room.

roomful *noun* (PL. **roomfuls**) as many or as much as a room will hold.

roominess *noun* being roomy.

roommate *noun* a person who shares a room with another person, especially in a students' hostel.

room service the serving of food, drinks, etc to a hotel guest in his or her bedroom or suite.

roomy *adj.* (**roomier, roomiest**) having plenty of room; spacious.

- - - - - - - - - - - - - - - - - - - -

🖃 spacious, capacious, large, sizeable, broad, wide, extensive, ample, generous.

🖃 cramped, small, tiny.

- -

roost — *noun* **1** a branch, perch, etc on which birds, especially domestic fowl, rest at night. **2** a group of birds, especially domestic fowl, resting together on the same branch or perch. **3** a place offering temporary sleeping accommodation. — *verb intrans., said especially of birds* to settle on a roost, especially for sleep. — **come home to roost** *said of a scheme, etc* to have unpleasant consequences for or a bad effect on the originator. **rule the roost** to be dominant. [from Anglo-Saxon *hrost*]

rooster *noun North Amer.* a farmyard cock.

root[1] — *noun* **1** *Bot.* in vascular plants, the descending structure, lacking leaves and chlorophyll, that usually grows beneath the soil surface, and whose function is to anchor the plant in the soil, and to absorb water and mineral nutrients. **2** the part by which anything is attached to or embedded in something larger. **3** *Anat.* the embedded part of a tooth, hair, nail, or similar structure. **4** the basic cause, source, or origin of something. **5** (**roots**) one's ancestry or family origins. **6** (**roots**) one's feeling of belonging to a community or in a place. **7** the basic element in a word which remains after all the affixes have been removed, and which may form the basis of a number of related words, eg *love* is the root of *lovable, lovely, lover,* and *unloved*. **8** *Maths.* a factor of a quantity that when multiplied by itself a specified number of times produces that quantity again, eg 2 is the square root of 4 and the cube root of 8. **9** *Maths.* in an algebraic equation, the value or values of an unknown quantity or variable that represent the solution to that equation. **10** *Mus.* the fundamental note on which a chord is built. — *verb* **1** *intrans.* to grow roots; to become firmly established. **2** to fix with or as if with roots. **3** to provide with roots. — **root something out** to remove or destroy it completely. **root something up** to dig it up by the roots. **take root 1** to grow roots. **2** to become firmly established. [from Anglo-Saxon *rot*]

. . . .

🔳 *noun* **1** tuber, rhizome, stem. **4** origin, source, derivation, cause, starting point, fount, fountainhead, seed, germ, nucleus, heart, core, nub, essence, seat, base, bottom, basis, foundation. **5** beginnings, origins, family, heritage, background, birthplace, home. *verb* **2** fasten, fix, set, stick, implant, embed, entrench, establish, ground, base, anchor, moor. **root out** uproot, eradicate, *formal* extirpate, eliminate, exterminate, destroy, abolish, clear away, remove. **root up** uproot, clear (away), remove.

. . . .

root[2] *verb* **1** *intrans. said especially of pigs* to dig up the ground with the snout in search of food. **2** *intrans.* (*usually* **root around** or **about**) to poke about in looking for something; to rummage. **3** (*usually* **root something out** or **up**) to find or extract it by rummaging, etc. [from Anglo-Saxon *wrotan*, from *wrot*, snout]

. . . .

🔳 **1, 2** dig, delve, burrow, forage. **2** hunt, rummage, ferret, poke, pry, nose. **3** unearth, dig out, uncover, discover.

. . . .

root[3] *verb intrans.* (**root for someone**) *chiefly North Amer. colloq.* to support them with loud cheering and encouragement.

root beer *North Amer., esp. US* a fizzy drink made from the roots of certain plants, eg dandelions, and flavoured with herbs.

root crop any plant that is grown mainly for its edible root, tuber, or corm, eg carrot, swede, turnip, potato, sugar beet, yam. The foliage of many root crops serves as valuable fodder for animal livestock.

rooted *adj.* fixed by or as if by roots; firmly established.

root hair *Bot.* any of many fine tubular outgrowths from the surface cells of plant roots. The root hairs greatly increase the surface area of the root that is available to absorb water from the soil.

rootless *adj.* **1** having no roots. **2** having no home; wandering.

roots music popular music of a style showing the influence of folk music and having a certain ethnic identity.

rootstock *noun Bot.* an underground plant stem that bears buds; a rhizome.

ropable or **ropeable** *adj. Austral. colloq.* **1**, *said of cattle or horses* wild and unmanageable. **2** *said of a person* extremely or uncontrollably angry.

rope — *noun* **1** strong thick cord made by twisting fibres together; also, a length of this. **2** a number of objects, especially pearls or onions, strung together. **3** a hangman's noose. **4** a long thin sticky strand. — *verb* **1** to tie, fasten, or bind with a rope. **2** (**rope something off**) to enclose, separate, or divide it with a rope. **3** (*also* **rope up** or **rope someone up**) to attach climbers or be attached to a rope for safety. **4** *chiefly North Amer.* to catch with a rope; to lasso. — **know the ropes** to have a thorough knowledge and experience of what needs to be done in a particular circumstance or for a particular job. **rope someone in** to persuade them to take part. [from Anglo-Saxon *rap*]

. . . .

🔳 *noun* **1** line, cable, cord, string, strand. *verb* **1** tie, bind, lash, fasten, hitch, moor, tether. **rope in** enlist, engage, involve, persuade.

. . . .

rope walk a long narrow shed or covered alley where ropes are made.

ropeway *noun* a means of transmission by ropes.

ropy or **ropey** *adj.* (**ropier, ropiest**) **1** *colloq.* poor in quality. **2** forming sticky strands.

Roquefort /ˈrɒkfɔː(r)/ *noun* a strong, soft, blue-veined cheese made from ewes' milk. [from the village in S France where it was originally made]

ro-ro *adj., said of a passenger ferry, etc* same as ROLL-ON ROLL-OFF.

rorqual /ˈrɔːkwəl/ (*in full* **common rorqual**) a baleen whale, found worldwide, having a throat with 10 to a hundred longitudinal furrows, allowing it to expand when feeding. There is a small dorsal fin near the tail. Also called FIN WHALE. [from Norwegian *riyrkval*]

Rorschach test /ˈrɔːʃɑk test, ˈrɔːʃɑːk test/ *Psychol.* a test designed to show intelligence, type of personality, mental state, etc in which the subject is asked to describe the pictures formed by a number of inkblots. [named after the Swiss psychiatrist and neurologist Hermann Rorschach (1884–1922), who devised it]

rosaceous /rəʊˈzeɪʃəs/ *adj.* **1** *Bot.* denoting a plant that belongs to the family Rosaceae, eg rose, apple, strawberry, cherry, almond. **2** *Bot.* resembling a rose. [from Latin *rosa*, rose]

rosary /ˈrəʊzərɪ/ *noun* (PL. **rosaries**) *RC Church* **1** a string of beads used to count prayers as they are recited. **2** a series of prayers with a set form and order counted on a string of beads. [from Latin *rosarium*, rose garden]

rose[1] — *noun* **1** an erect or climbing thorny shrub of the genus *Rosa*, that produces large and often fragrant flowers which may be red, pink, yellow, orange, white, or some combination of these colours, followed by brightly coloured fleshy fruits known as hips. The rose is cultivated worldwide as an ornamental garden plant, and it is a very popular cut flower. Its petals are used in perfumery, and rose-hip syrup is a rich source of vitamin C. **2** the flower produced by this plant. **3** this flower as the national emblem of England. **4** any flowering plant that superficially resembles a rose, eg Christmas rose. **5** a darkish pink colour. **6** (**roses**) a light pink, glowing complexion: *put the roses back in one's cheeks*. **7** a nozzle with holes, usually attached to the end of a hose, watering can, shower, etc to make the water come out in a spray. **8** a circular fitting in a ceiling through which an electric light flex hangs. **9** a rose-like design, eg round the sound hole of a guitar or lute, or on a compass card. **10** a cut diamond with a flat base and many small triangular facets forming a rounded shape which rises to a point. **11** a rose window. **12** a rosette. — *adj.* of or like roses, especially in colour or scent. [from Anglo-Saxon, from Latin *rosa*]

rose[2] see RISE.

rosé /ˈrəʊzeɪ/ *noun* a light pink wine made by removing the skins of red grapes after fermentation has begun. [from French *rosé*, pink]

roseate /ˈrəʊzɪət, ˈrəʊzɪeɪt/ *adj.* **1** like a rose, especially in colour. **2** unrealistically hopeful or cheerful.

rosebay willowherb a common wild plant that has spikes of dark pink flowers and produces many fluffy seeds.

rose-coloured or **rose-tinted** *adj.* pink. — **see through rose-coloured glasses** to have an unrealistically hopeful or cheerful view of circumstances.

rosehip *noun* the red, berry-like fruit of the rose.

rosemary *noun* an evergreen fragrant shrub with stiff needle-like leaves used in cookery and perfumery. [from Latin *rosmarinus*, from *ros*, dew + *marinus*, sea]

rosette /rəʊˈzet/ *noun* **1** a badge or decoration made in coloured ribbon to resemble the shape and form of a rose, often awarded as a prize or worn as a sign of affiliation. **2** *Bot.* a circular cluster of leaves arising from a central point. [from French *rosette*, little rose]

rose window a circular window with ornamental tracery coming out in a symmetrical pattern from the centre.

rosewood *noun* a valuable dark red or purplish wood used in making furniture of the highest quality.

Rosh Hashanah /rɒʃ həˈʃɑːnə/ *noun* the Jewish festival of New Year, which falls in September or October. During the New Year's service, a ram's horn is blown as a call to repentance and spiritual renewal. [from Hebrew, literally head of the year]

Rosicrucianism *noun* an esoteric movement which spread across Europe in the early 17c.

rosily *adv.* like a rose, in a rosy way.

rosin /ˈrozɪn/ — *noun* a clear hard resin produced by distilling turpentine prepared from dead pine wood, rubbed on the bows of stringed musical instruments. — *verb* (**rosined, rosining**) to rub rosin on (a violin bow, etc). [a variant of RESIN]

rosiness *noun* being rosy.

roster — *noun* a list of people showing the order in which they are to do various duties, go on leave, etc. — *verb* (**rostered, rostering**) to put (a name) on a roster. [from Dutch *rooster*, list]

🞂 *noun* rota, schedule, register, roll, list.

rostral *adj.* of or like a rostrum.

rostrum *noun* (PL. **rostrums, rostra**) **1** a platform on which a public speaker stands. **2** a raised platform, eg that on which a conductor stands before the orchestra, or for carrying a camera. **3** *Zool.* the beak of a bird, or a structure similar to a beak in other animals. [from Latin *rostrum*, beak]

🞂 **1, 2** platform. **2** stage, dais, podium.

rosy *adj.* (**rosier, rosiest**) **1** rose-coloured; pink. **2** hopeful; optimistic; cheerful.

rot — *verb* (**rotted, rotting**) **1** *trans., intrans.* (*also* **rot down**) to decay or cause to decay or become putrefied as a result of the activity of bacteria and/or fungi. **2** *intrans.* to become corrupt. **3** *intrans.* to become physically weak. — *noun* **1** decay; something which has rotted or decomposed. **2** *colloq.* nonsense; rubbish. **3** (*in compounds*) any of several plant or animal diseases caused by fungi or bacteria, eg foot rot, the name given to a bacterial disease of sheep and a fungal disease of peas. See also ROTTEN. [from Anglo-Saxon *rotian*]

🞂 *verb* **1, 2** degenerate, deteriorate. **1** decay, decompose, putrefy, fester, perish, corrode, spoil, go bad, go off, crumble, disintegrate. **2** taint, corrupt. *noun* **1** decay, decomposition, putrefaction, corrosion, rust, mould. **2** nonsense, rubbish, *colloq.* poppycock, drivel, claptrap.

rota *noun Brit.* a list of duties that are to be done and the names and order of the people who are to take turns in doing them. [from Latin *rota*, wheel]

🞂 list, roster, schedule.

Rotarian /roʊˈtɛərɪən/ *noun* a member of Rotary International. See ROTARY CLUB.

rotary — *adj.* turning on an axis like a wheel. — *noun* (PL. **rotaries**) **1** a rotary machine. **2** *North Amer.* a traffic roundabout. [from Latin *rota*, wheel]

🞂 *adj.* rotating, revolving, turning, spinning, whirling, gyrating.
🞂 *adj.* fixed.

Rotary Club a local branch of Rotary International, the first service club, formed in 1905 in Chicago, for men and (since 1987) women to perform volunteer community service.

rotate *verb* **1** *trans., intrans.* to turn or cause to turn on an axis like a wheel. **2** to arrange in an ordered sequence. **3** *intrans.* to take turns according to an ordered sequence. [from Latin *rota*, wheel]

🞂 **1** revolve, turn, spin, gyrate, pivot, swivel, roll. **2, 3** alternate.

rotation *noun* **1** an act of rotating or state of being rotated. **2** one complete turn around an axis. **3** a regular and recurring sequence. **4** (*also* **crop rotation**) the growing of different crops on a field, usually in an ordered sequence, to help keep the land fertile.

🞂 **1** turning, spinning. **2** revolution, turn, spin, gyration, orbit. **3** cycle, sequence, succession.

rote *noun* the mechanical use of the memory without necessarily understanding what is memorized. — **by rote** by memory; by heart. [from Middle English]

rotgut *noun slang* cheap, poor-quality alcoholic drink, especially spirits.

roti /ˈroʊti/ *noun* (PL. **rotis**) **1** a cake of unleavened bread, traditionally made in parts of India and the Caribbean. **2** a kind of sandwich made of this wrapped around curried vegetables, seafood, or chicken. [from Hindi, = bread]

rotifer /ˈroʊtɪfə(r)/ *noun Zool.* a microscopic aquatic invertebrate animal, belonging to the phylum Rotifera, that has an unsegmented body. Rotifers swim by means of a ring of beating hair-like structures (cilia) that resembles a spinning wheel. [from Latin *rota*, wheel + *ferre*, to carry]

rotisserie /roʊˈtɪsəri/ *noun* **1** a cooking apparatus with a spit on which meat, poultry, etc may be cooked by direct heat. **2** a shop or restaurant which sells or serves meat cooked in this way. [from French *rôtisserie*, from *rôtir*, to roast]

rotor /ˈroʊtə(r)/ *noun* **1** a rotating part of a machine, especially in an internal combustion engine. **2** a system of blades projecting from a cylinder which rotate at high speed to provide the force to lift and propel a helicopter.

Rotovator or **Rotavator** /ˈroʊtəveɪtə(r)/ *noun trademark* a machine with a rotating blade for breaking up the soil. [a contraction of *rotary cultivator*]

rotten *adj.* **1** having gone bad, decayed, rotted, or fallen to pieces. **2** morally corrupt. **3** *colloq.* miserably unwell. **4** *colloq.* unsatisfactory: *a rotten plan.* **5** *colloq.* unpleasant; disagreeable: *rotten weather.* [from Norse *rotinn*]

🞂 BAD. **1** decayed, decomposed, putrid, addled, off, mouldy, fetid, stinking, rank, foul, rotting, decaying, disintegrating. **2** mean, nasty, beastly, dirty, despicable, contemptible, dishonourable, wicked. **3, 4, 5** lousy, *colloq.* ropy, *colloq.* grotty. **3** ill, sick, unwell, poorly, *colloq.* rough. **4** inferior, poor, inadequate, low-grade, *colloq.* crummy.
🞀 **1** fresh. **2, 4, 5** good. **3** well.

rotten borough *Hist.* before 1832, a borough that could elect an MP even though it had few or no inhabitants.

rottenness *noun* being rotten.

rotter *noun old slang use* a worthless, despicable, or depraved person.

Rottweiler /ˈrɒtvaɪlə(r), ˈrɒtwaɪlə(r)/ *noun* a large powerfully built black and tan dog, originally from Germany. [from *Rottweil* in SW Germany]

rotund *adj.* **1** round. **2** plump. **3** impressive or grandiloquent. [from Latin *rotundus*, from *rota*, wheel]

🞂 plump, chubby, tubby, portly, fat, obese.

rotunda *noun* a round, usually domed, building or hall. [from Italian *rotonda camera*, round room]

rotundity or **rotundness** *noun* **1** roundness. **2** a round mass.

rotundly *adv.* in a rotund way.

rouble or **ruble** /ˈruːbəl/ *noun* the standard unit of currency in the countries of the former Soviet Union, equal to 100 kopecks. [from Russian *rubl*]

roué /ˈruːeɪ/ *noun old use* a disreputable man; a rake. [from French *roué*, a man deserving to be broken on a wheel. This was a former method of torture or capital punishment in which victims were stretched out on a wheel and their arms and legs were broken with an iron bar]

rouge /ruːʒ/ — *noun* a pink or red powder or cream used to colour the cheeks. — *verb* **1** *intrans.* to use rouge. **2** to apply rouge to. [from French *rouge*, red]

rough /rʌf/ — *adj.* **1** *said of a surface* not smooth, even, or regular. **2** *said of ground* covered with stones, tall grass, bushes and/or scrub. **3** covered with shaggy or coarse hair. **4** harsh or grating: *a rough voice*. **5** *said of a person's character, behaviour, etc* noisy, coarse, or violent. **6** stormy. **7** requiring hard work or considerable physical effort, or involving great difficulty, tension, etc: *a rough day at work*. **8** (**rough on**) unpleasant and hard to bear: *a decision which is rough on the employees*. **9** *said of a guess, calculation, etc* approximate. **10** not polished or refined: *a rough draft*. **11** *colloq.* slightly unwell and tired, especially because of heavy drinking or lack of sleep. — *noun* **1** rough ground, especially the uncut grass at the side of a golf fairway. **2** the unpleasant or disagreeable side of something: *take the rough with the smooth*. **3** a rough or crude state. **4** a crude preliminary sketch. **5** a thug or hooligan. — **rough it** *colloq.* to live primitively, without the usual comforts of life. **rough something out** to do a preliminary sketch of it or give a preliminary explanation of it. **rough someone up** *colloq.* to beat them up. **sleep rough** to sleep in the open without proper shelter. [from Anglo-Saxon *ruh*]

▣ *adj.* **1** uneven, bumpy, lumpy, rugged, craggy, jagged, irregular, coarse, bristly, scratchy. **4, 5, 7** harsh. **5, 7** severe, tough, hard. **5** violent, brutal, cruel, noisy, crude, vulgar, brusque, curt, sharp. **6** choppy, agitated, turbulent, stormy, tempestuous, violent, wild. **7** drastic, extreme. **8** hard on, tough on, difficult for. **9** approximate, estimated, imprecise, inexact, vague, general. **10** cursory, hasty, incomplete, unfinished, crude, rudimentary. **11** ill, sick, unwell, poorly, off colour, *colloq.* rotten.

▣ *adj.* **1** smooth. **5, 6** mild. **6** calm. **9** accurate. **11** well.

roughage /ˈrʌfɪdʒ/ *noun* dietary fibre.

rough-and-ready *adj.* **1** quickly prepared and not polished or perfect but good enough. **2** *said or a person* friendly and pleasant but not polite or refined.

▣ **1** makeshift, temporary, improvised, provisional, stopgap, make-do.

rough-and-tumble *noun* a bout of disorderly but usually friendly fighting or scuffling.

roughcast — *noun* a mixture of plaster and small stones used to cover outside walls. — *verb* (PAST TENSE AND PAST PARTICIPLE **roughcast**) to cover with roughcast.

rough diamond 1 an uncut and unpolished diamond. **2** a good-natured person with rough, unrefined manners.

roughen /ˈrʌfən/ *verb trans., intrans.* (**roughened**, **roughening**) to make or become rough.

rough-hew *verb* to shape crudely and without refining.

rough-hewn *adj.* crude, unpolished, unrefined.

roughhouse *noun colloq.* a disturbance or brawl.

roughly *adv.* **1** in a rough way. **2** approximately.

▣ **2** approximately, about, around, circa, more or less, or so, or thereabouts, give or take a little.

roughneck *noun* **1** a worker on an oil rig. **2** a rough and rowdy person.

roughness *noun* a rough quality.

roughshod *adj.*, *said of a horse* having horse-shoes with projecting nails which prevent the horse from slipping in wet weather. — **ride roughshod over someone** to treat them arrogantly and without regard for their feelings.

roulette /ruːˈlet/ *noun* **1** a gambling game in which a ball is dropped into a spinning wheel divided up into many small, numbered compartments coloured black and red alternately, with the players betting on which compartment the ball will come to rest in. **2** a small tool with a

toothed wheel, used for making a line of dots and perforating paper. [from French]

round — *adj.* **1** shaped like, or approximately, a circle or a ball. **2** not angular; curved and plump. **3** moving in or forming a circle. **4** *said of numbers* complete and exact: *a round dozen*. **5** *said of a number* without a fraction. **6** *said of a number* approximate, without taking minor amounts into account. **7** *said of a sum of money* considerable; substantial. **8** plain-spoken; candid. — *adv.* **1** in or to the opposite direction, position or opinion: *win someone round*. **2** in a circular direction or with a circular or revolving movement. **3** in, by, or along a circuitous or indirect route. **4** on all sides so as to surround: *gather round*. **5** from one person to another: *pass it round*. **6** in rotation, so as to return to the starting point: *wait until spring comes round*. **7** from place to place: *drive round for a while*. **8** in circumference: *measures six feet round*. **9** to a particular place, especially a person's home: *come round for supper*. — *prep.* **1** on all sides of so as to surround or enclose. **2** so as to move or revolve around a centre or axis and return to the starting point: *run round the field*. **3** *colloq.* having as a central point or basis: *a story built round her experiences*. **4** from place to place in: *we went round the town shopping*. **5** in all or various directions from; close to (a place). **6** so as to pass, or having passed, in a curved course: *drive round the corner*. — *noun* **1** something round (and often flat) in shape. **2** a complete revolution round a circuit or path. **3** a single complete slice of bread. **4** a sandwich, or set of sandwiches, made from two complete slices of bread. **5** the playing of all 18 holes on a golf course in a single session. **6** one of a recurring series of events, actions, etc: *a round of talks*. **7** a series of regular activities: *one's daily round*. **8** a regular route followed, especially for the delivery of something: *a milk round*. **9** (*usually* **rounds**) a sequence of visits made by a doctor to patients, in a hospital or in their homes. **10** a stage in a competition. **11** a single period of play, competition, etc in a group of several, eg in boxing. **12** a burst of applause or cheering. **13** a single bullet or charge of ammunition. **14** a set of drinks bought at the same time for all the members of a group. **15** an unaccompanied song in which different people all sing the same part continuously but start (and therefore end) at different times. — *verb* **1** *trans., intrans.* to make or become round. **2** to go round: *the car rounded the corner.*— **go the rounds** *said of news, information, etc* to be passed round from person to person. **in the round 1** with all details shown or considered. **2** *Theatr.* with the audience seated on at least three, and often four, sides of the stage. **round about 1** on all sides; in a ring surrounding. **2** approximately. **round the clock** all day and all night; for twenty-four hours. **round on someone** to turn on them in anger, usually in speech. **round something down** to lower a number so that it can be expressed as a round number: *round 15.47 down to 15*. **round something off 1** to make corners, angles, etc smooth. **2** to complete something successfully and pleasantly: *round off the meal with a glass of brandy*. **round something up 1** to raise a number so that it can be expressed as a round number: *round 15.89 up to 16*. **2** to collect (people, or things such as livestock or facts) together. [from Latin *rotundus*]

▣ *adj.* **1** circular, ring-shaped, disc-shaped, spherical, globular, ball-shaped, cylindrical. **2** rounded, curved, rotund, plump, stout, portly. *noun* **1** circle, ring, band, disc, sphere, ball, orb. **2** circuit, lap, course, orbit. **6** cycle, series, sequence, succession, period, bout, session. **7** routine. **8** beat, circuit, route, path. *verb* **2** circle, skirt, flank, bypass. **round off 2** finish (off), complete, end, close, conclude, cap, crown. **round on** turn on, attack, lay into, abuse. **round up 2** herd, marshal, assemble, gather, rally, collect, group.

▣ **round off 2** begin. **round up 2** disperse, scatter.

roundabout — *noun* **1** *Brit.* a revolving platform, usually with seats, on which one can ride for pleasure; a merry-go-round. **2** *Brit.* a circular road junction, usually with an island in the middle, where several roads meet, and round which traffic must travel in the same direction. — *adj.* not direct; circuitous.

- *adj.* circuitous, tortuous, twisting, winding, indirect, oblique, devious, evasive.
- *adj.* straight, direct.

rounded *adj.* curved.

roundel *noun* **1** a small circular window or design. **2** a coloured round identification disc on the wing of a military aircraft. [from Old French *rondel*, little circle]

roundelay /ˈrɒndəleɪ/ *noun* a simple song with a refrain. [from Old French *rondelet*, from *rondel*, little circle]

rounders *noun* a team game similar to baseball, in which each team sends players in to bat in turn while the other team bowls and fields, with the batter scoring a run if he or she successfully runs round a square course in one go.

Roundhead *noun Hist.* a supporter of the parliamentary party against Charles I in the English Civil War (1642–9).

roundly *adv.* plainly and often rudely; bluntly; thoroughly.

roundness *noun* a round quality.

round robin 1 a petition or protest, especially one in which the names are written in a circle to conceal the ringleader. **2** a tournament in which each competitor plays each of the others in turn.

round-shouldered *adj.* with stooping shoulders and a back which bends forward slightly at the top.

round table 1 (**Round Table**) the table at which King Arthur and his knights sat, round in shape so that no individual knight should have precedence. **2** a meeting or conference at which the participants meet on equal terms.

round trip a trip to a place and back again, usually by a different route.

round-up *noun* **1** a rounding up of people or things. **2** a summary.

- **2** summary, résumé, précis, synopsis, outline, sketch, abstract, breakdown, run-down.

round window *Anat.* the lower of the two membrane-covered openings between the middle ear and the inner ear in vertebrates. Also called FENESTRA ROTUNDA.

roundworm *noun Zool.* an invertebrate animal with a long slender unsegmented body, belonging to the phylum Nematoda. Some species live as parasites within the bodies (usually the intestines) of humans and animals. Roundworms include hookworms and threadworms, and can cause various diseases.

rouse *verb trans., intrans.* **1** to arouse (someone or oneself) or become aroused from sleep, listlessness or lethargy. **2** to excite or provoke, or be excited or provoked.

- **1** wake (up), awaken, arouse, call, stir. **2** excite, provoke, stimulate, move, start, instigate, incite, inflame, galvanize, whip up, disturb, agitate, anger.
- **2** calm.

rousing *adj.* stirring; exciting.

- stirring, exciting, stimulating, exhilarating, spirited, lively, vigorous.

roustabout /ˈraʊstəbaʊt/ *noun* an unskilled labourer, eg on an oil-rig or a farm.

rout¹ — *verb* to defeat completely and cause to flee in confusion. — *noun* **1** a complete and overwhelming defeat. **2** a confused and disorderly retreat. **3** *Legal* a group of three or more people gathered together to commit a crime or some unlawful act. **4** a disorderly and noisy group of people. [from Old French *route*, from Latin *rumpere*, to break]

- *verb* defeat, conquer, overthrow, crush, beat, *colloq.* hammer, thrash, *colloq.* lick, put to flight, chase, dispel,

scatter. *noun* **1** defeat, conquest, overthrow, beating, thrashing, flight, stampede.

- *noun* victory.

rout² *verb* **1** *trans., intrans.* to dig up, especially with the snout. **2** (**rout someone out** or **up**) to find or fetch them by searching. [a variant of ROOT²]

route — *noun* **1** the way travelled on a regular journey. **2** a particular group of roads followed to get to a place. **3** a sequence of actions or events that lead to a particular result: *route to success.* — *verb* (**routed**, **routeing**) to arrange a route for; to send by a selected route. [from Latin *rupta via*, broken road]

- *noun* WAY. **1, 2** run. **1** circuit, round, beat. **2** course, itinerary, journey. **3** path, road.

route march a long and tiring march, especially one for soldiers in training.

router *noun Comput.* a device on a network that directs items of data to their destination.

routine — *noun* **1** a regular or fixed way of doing things. **2** a set series of movements, actions, jokes, etc in a dance, performance, etc. **3** a part of a computer program which performs a specific function. — *adj.* unvarying; regular; ordinary; done as part of a routine. [related to ROUTE]

- *noun* **1** procedure, way, method, system, order, pattern, formula, practice, usage, custom, habit. **2** sequence, set, act, piece, programme, performance. *adj.* customary, habitual, usual, typical, ordinary, run-of-the-mill, normal, standard, conventional, unoriginal, predictable, familiar, everyday, banal, humdrum, dull, boring, monotonous, tedious.
- *adj.* unusual, different, exciting.

routinely *adv.* at routine intervals; in a routine way.

roux /ruː/ *noun* (PL. **roux**) a cooked mixture of flour and fat, used to thicken sauces. [from French *beurre roux*, brown butter]

rove *verb* **1** *trans., intrans.* to wander or roam over aimlessly. **2** *intrans. said of the eyes* to keep looking in different directions.

- **1** roam, stray, wander, range, travel, drift, ramble.

rover *noun* a wanderer, especially a wandering pirate or robber.

roving *adj.* wandering; likely to ramble or stray.

row¹ *noun* /rəʊ/ **1** a number of people or things, such as theatre seats, numbers, vegetables, etc arranged in a line. **2** a street with a line of houses on one or both sides. — **a hard row to hoe** a difficult job or destiny. **in a row** in an unbroken sequence; in succession. [from Anglo-Saxon *raw*]

- **1** line, tier, bank, rank, range, column, file, queue, string, series, sequence. **in a row** in succession, successive, in sequence, one after the other.

row² /rəʊ/ — *verb* **1** *trans., intrans.* to move (a boat) through the water using oars. **2** to carry (people, goods, etc) in a rowing boat. **3** *intrans.* to race in rowing boats for sport. **4** to compete in (a race) in a rowing boat. — *noun* **1** an act of rowing a boat. **2** a trip in a rowing boat. [from Anglo-Saxon *rowan*]

row³ /raʊ/ — *noun* **1** a noisy quarrel. **2** a loud unpleasant noise or disturbance. **3** a severe reprimand. — *verb intrans.* to quarrel noisily.

- *noun* **1** argument, quarrel, dispute, controversy, squabble, tiff, *colloq.* slanging match, *colloq.* spat, fight, brawl.

2 noise, racket, din, uproar, commotion, disturbance, rumpus, fracas. *verb* argue, quarrel, wrangle, bicker, squabble, fight, scrap, *colloq.* spat.

🔁 *noun* **2** calm.

....

rowan /'rouən, rauən/ *noun* **1** a European tree with clusters of white flowers and bright red berries. Also called MOUNTAIN ASH. **2** a small red berry from this tree. [from Scandinavian]

rowboat *noun North Amer.* a rowing boat.

rowdily *adv.* in a rowdy way.

rowdiness *noun* **1** being rowdy. **2** rowdy behaviour.

rowdy /'raudɪ/ — *adj.* (**rowdier, rowdiest**) noisy and rough. — *noun colloq.* a noisy, rough person. [perhaps from ROW³]

....

🔁 *adj.* noisy, loud, rough, boisterous, disorderly, unruly, riotous, wild.

🔁 *adj.* quiet, peaceful.

....

rowdyism *noun* rowdy behaviour.

rowel /'rauəl/ *noun* a small spiked wheel on a spur. [from Old French *roel*, small wheel]

rower *noun* a person who rows.

rowing boat *Brit.* a small boat which is moved by oars.

rowlock /'rɒlək/ *noun* a device for holding an oar in place and serving as a pivot for it to turn on. [a variant of *oarlock*, from Anglo-Saxon *arloc*]

royal — *adj.* **1** of or suitable for a king or queen. **2** under the patronage or in the service of the king or queen: *Royal Geographical Society.* **3** belonging to the king or queen. **4** being a member of the king's or queen's family. **5** regal; magnificent. **6** larger and more splendid than usual. — *noun* **1** *colloq.* a member of the royal family. **2** a sail immediately above the topgallant sail. **3** a stag with antlers of 12 or more points. **4** a size of paper, either 19 by 24in (483 by 610mm) of writing paper or 20 by 25in (508 by 635mm) of printing paper. [from Old French *roial*, from Latin *regalis*]

....

🔁 *adj.* **5** regal, majestic, kingly, queenly, princely, imperial, monarchical, sovereign, august, grand, stately, magnificent, splendid, superb.

....

royal assent in the UK, formal permission given by the sovereign for a parliamentary act to become law.

royal blue a rich, bright, deep-coloured blue.

royal commission in the UK, a group of people appointed by the crown at the request of the government to inquire into and report on some matter.

Royal Greenwich Observatory In the UK, an observatory founded by Charles II at Greenwich in 1675. The prime meridian of longitude runs through this site. The observatory moved to Herstmonceux in 1948 and to Cambridge in 1990. Since 1994 it has been part of the Royal Observatories.

royalism *noun* belief in or support of the institution of monarchy.

royalist — *noun* **1** a supporter of the monarchy. **2** (**Royalist**) *Hist.* a supporter of Charles I during the English Civil War (1642–9). — *adj.* relating to royalists.

royal jelly a rich protein substance secreted by worker bees and fed by them to certain female larvae that are destined to develop into queen bees instead of sterile workers. Royal jelly is used in face creams and as a health food supplement.

royally *adv.* in a royal way, with a royal manner.

royal prerogative the rights of the monarch, in theory not restricted in any way, but in practice laid down by custom.

Royal Society for the Protection of Birds (ABBREV. RSPB) a UK organization founded in 1889 to promote the conservation of birds and their habitats by maintaining nature reserves, to prevent the loss of rare species and to popularize bird-watching.

royalty *noun* (PL. **royalties**) **1** the character, state, office or power of a king or queen. **2** members of the royal family, either individually or collectively. **3** a percentage of the profits from each copy of a book, piece of music, invention, etc sold, performed or used, which is paid to the author, composer, inventor, etc. **4** a payment made by companies who mine minerals, oil or gas to the person who owns the land or owns the mineral rights to the land that the company is mining. **5** a right (especially to minerals) granted by a king or queen to an individual or company.

royal warrant an official authorization to a tradesman to supply goods to a royal household.

rozzer *noun Brit. old slang use* a policeman.

RP *abbrev.* Received Pronunciation.

RPI *abbrev. Brit.* retail price index, a list of the prices of selected consumer goods which is compiled regularly to show how prices are changing and how the cost of living is rising.

RPM *abbrev.* retail price maintenance.

rpm *abbrev.* revolutions per minute.

RR *abbrev.* Right Reverend.

RS *abbrev.* Royal Society.

RSA *abbrev.* **1** Republic of South Africa. **2** *Brit.* Royal Scottish Academy, or Academician. **3** *Brit.* Royal Society of Arts.

RSC *abbrev.* Royal Shakespeare Company.

RSI *Medicine abbrev.* repetitive strain injury.

RSM *abbrev.* regimental sergeant-major.

RSNO *abbrev.* Royal Scottish National Orchestra.

RSPB *abbrev.* the Royal Society for the Protection of Birds.

RSPCA *abbrev.* in the UK, the Royal Society for the Prevention of Cruelty to Animals, the main animal welfare society, funded by voluntary contributions.

RSSPCC *abbrev.* Royal Scottish Society for the Prevention of Cruelty to Children.

RSV *abbrev.* Revised Standard Version (of the Bible).

RSVP *abbrev. répondez s'il vous plaît* (French), please reply.

RTE *abbrev. Radio Telefís Éireann* (Ir Gaelic) Irish Radio and Television.

Rt Hon *abbrev.* Right Honourable.

Rt Rev *abbrev.* Right Reverend.

Ru *symbol Chem.* ruthenium.

rub — *verb* (**rubbed, rubbing**) **1** to move one's hand, an object, etc back and forwards over the surface of (something) with pressure and friction. **2** to move (one's hand, an object, etc) backwards and forwards over a surface with pressure and friction. **3** (**rub against** or **on something**) to move backwards and forwards over a surface with pressure and friction. **4** (**rub something in** or **on**) to apply ointment, lotion, polish, etc. **5** to clean, polish, dry, smooth, etc. **6** *trans., intrans.* (**rub** or **rub something away, off, out,** etc) to remove or be removed by pressure and friction. **7** *trans., intrans.* to make (something) sore by pressure and friction. **8** *trans., intrans.* to fray by pressure and friction. — *noun* **1** an act of rubbing. **2** an obstacle or difficulty.— **rub along** *colloq.* to manage to get along, make progress, etc without any particular difficulties. **rub along with someone** to be on more or less friendly terms with them. **rub something down 1** to rub one's body, a horse, etc briskly from head to foot, eg to dry it. **2** to prepare a surface to receive new paint or varnish by rubbing the old paint or varnish off. **rub something in 1** to apply ointment, etc by rubbing. **2** *colloq.* to insist on talking about or emphasizing an embarrassing fact or circumstance. **rub off on someone** to have an effect on or be passed to someone else by close association: *some of his bad habits have rubbed off on you.* **rub someone out** *North Amer. slang* to murder them. **rub something out** to remove it by rubbing. **rub something up 1** to polish it. **2** to refresh one's memory or knowledge of it. **rub someone up the wrong way** to annoy or irritate them. [from Middle English *rubben*]

....

🔁 *verb* **1** stroke, caress, massage, knead. **3** chafe, grate, scrape. **4** apply, spread, smear. **5** clean, smooth, polish, buff, shine. **6** abrade, scour, scrub, wipe. **7** chafe, pinch. **rub in 2** emphasize, make much of, highlight, insist on, harp on. **rub off on** influence, affect, have an effect on, change, alter, transform. **rub out** erase, efface, obliterate, delete, cancel.

rubato /ru'bɑːtəʊ/ *Mus.* — *noun* (PL. **rubati**, **rubatos**) a modified or distorted tempo in which notes may be deprived of part of their length (with a slight quickening of tempo) or may have their length increased (by a slight slowing of tempo) without the overall flow of the music being impaired. — *adj.*, *adv.* with such freedom of tempo. [from Italian *rubato*, robbed]

rubber[1] — *noun* **1** a strong elastic substance obtained from the latex of various trees or plants or produced synthetically. **2** *Brit.* a small piece of rubber or plastic used for rubbing out pencil or ink marks on paper; an eraser. **3** *North Amer. slang* a condom. **4** (*usually* **rubbers**) *North Amer.* waterproof rubber overshoes; galoshes. **5** any person, device or machine part that rubs. — *adj.* of or producing rubber.

rubber[2] *noun* a match, especially in bridge or whist, consisting of either three or five games.

rubber band same as ELASTIC BAND.

rubberize or **rubberise** *verb* to coat or impregnate (a substance, especially a textile) with rubber. Rubberized fabric is used to make conveyor belts, pneumatic tyres, inflatable dinghies, etc.

rubberneck — *noun North Amer. slang* a person who stares or gapes inquisitively or stupidly, especially a tourist on a guided tour. — *verb intrans.* to behave in this way.

rubber plant 1 a house plant with large, shiny, dark green leaves. **2** same as RUBBER TREE.

rubber stamp 1 an instrument made of rubber with figures, letters, names, etc on it, used to stamp a name, date, etc on books or papers. **2** an automatic, unthinking or routine agreement or authorization. **3** a person or group of people required to approve or authorize another person's or group's decisions and actions without having the power, courage, etc to withhold this approval or authorization.

rubber-stamp *verb* to give automatic, unthinking, or routine approval of or authorization for.

rubber tree any of various trees which produce a milky white liquid (latex) that is used to make rubber, especially *Hevea brasiliensis*, a large tree native to S America, and extensively cultivated in plantations in SE Asia, especially Malaya. It is the source of about 90 per cent of the natural rubber produced worldwide.

rubbery *adj.* like rubber; flexible.

rubbing *noun* an impression or copy made by placing paper over a raised surface and rubbing the paper with crayon, wax, chalk, etc.

rubbish — *noun* **1** waste material; things that have been or are to be thrown away. **2** worthless or useless material or objects. **3** nonsense. — *verb colloq.* to criticize or dismiss as worthless. [from Middle English *rubbes*]

⊟ *noun* **1, 2** garbage, trash, junk. **1** refuse, litter, waste, dross, debris, flotsam and jetsam. **3** nonsense, drivel, claptrap, twaddle, gibberish, *colloq.* gobbledygook, *colloq.* poppycock, *colloq.* rot, *Brit. slang* cobblers, *old use* balderdash. *verb* criticize, denigrate, dismiss, *colloq.* slate, *colloq.* slam, *colloq.* pooh-pooh, trash.
⊟ *noun* **3** sense.

rubbishy *adj.* worthless, trashy.

rubble *noun* **1** broken stones, bricks, plaster, etc from ruined or demolished buildings. **2** small, rough stones used in building, especially as a filling between walls. [from Middle English *rubel*]

⊟ **1** debris, wreckage, ruins, fragments.

rub-down *noun* an act of rubbing down, especially to clean or prepare a surface.

rubella /ru'belə/ *noun Medicine* a highly contagious viral disease characterized by a reddish-pink rash, similar to measles but milder, and swelling of the lymph glands. If the disease is contracted during the early stages of pregnancy it can cause abnormalities of the fetus, and most girls are now immunized against rubella before puberty. Also called GERMAN MEASLES. [from Latin *rubeus*, red]

Rubicon /'ruːbɪkɒn/ *noun* a boundary which, once crossed, commits the person crossing it to an irrevocable course of action. — **cross the Rubicon** to take an irrevocable decision. [from Latin *Rubico*, a stream in N Italy separating Italy and the province of Cisalpine Gaul where Caesar was serving. Caesar's crossing of the stream with his army in 49BC was tantamount to a declaration of war on the Roman republic, and began a civil war]

rubicund /'ruːbɪkənd/ *adj.*, *said especially of the face or complexion* red or rosy; ruddy. [from Latin *rubicundus*]

rubidium /rʊ'bɪdɪəm/ *noun Chem.* (SYMBOL **Rb**, ATOMIC NUMBER **37**) a silvery-white highly reactive metal, used in photoelectric cells. The naturally occurring radioactive isotope rubidium-87 is used to determine the age of rocks more than 10m years old. [from Latin *rubidus*, red, so called because of the two red lines in its spectrum]

Rubik's cube a cube-shaped puzzle consisting of 26 small cubes with faces coloured in any of six colours, fixed to a central spindle that allows them to be rotated on three axes, the solved puzzle presenting a uniform colour on each face. Millions of incorrect combinations are possible. [named after the Hungarian designer Ernö Rubik (1940–)]

ruble /'ruːbəl/ see ROUBLE.

rubric /'ruːbrɪk/ *noun* **1** a heading in a book or manuscript, especially one written or underlined in red. **2** an authoritative rule, especially one for the conduct of divine service added in red to the liturgy. [from Latin *rubrica*, red ochre]

ruby — *noun* (PL. **rubies**) **1** *Geol.* a transparent red impure variety of the mineral corundum, containing traces of chromium. It is a valuable gemstone, and synthetic rubies are used in lasers, and as bearings in watches and other precision intruments. **2** the rich, deep red colour characteristic of this stone. — *adj.* of this colour. [from Latin *rubinus lapis*, red stone]

ruby wedding a fortieth wedding anniversary.

RUC *abbrev.* Royal Ulster Constabulary.

ruche /ruːʃ/ *noun* a pleated or gathered frill of lace, ribbon, etc used as a trimming. [from French *ruche*, beehive]

ruched /ruːʃt/ *adj.* trimmed with ruches.

ruck[1] *noun* **1** a heap or mass of indistinguishable people or things. **2** *Rugby* a loose scrum that forms around a ball on the ground. [from Middle English *ruke*]

ruck[2] — *noun* a wrinkle or crease. — *verb trans., intrans.* (*also* **ruck up**) to wrinkle or crease. [from Norse *hrukka*]

rucksack *noun* a bag carried on the back by means of straps over the shoulders, used especially by climbers and walkers. [from German *Rücken*, back + *Sack*, bag]

ruction *noun* **1** a noisy disturbance; uproar. **2** (**ructions**) a noisy and usually unpleasant or violent argument.

rudd *noun* a freshwater fish, widespread in European rivers and lakes, greenish-brown in colour on the back, with yellow sides and reddish fins. It feeds on invertebrates and some plant material, and is a popular fish with anglers. [probably from Anglo-Saxon *rudu*, redness]

rudder *noun* **1** a flat piece of wood, metal, etc fixed vertically to a ship's stern for steering. **2** a movable aerofoil attached to the fin of an aircraft which helps control its movement along a horizontal plane. [from Anglo-Saxon *rothor*]

rudderless *adj.* **1** without a rudder. **2** aimless.

ruddy *adj.* (**ruddier**, **ruddiest**) **1** *said of the face, complexion, etc* having a healthy, glowing, rosy or pink colour. **2** red; reddish. [from Anglo-Saxon *rudig*]

⊟ RED. **1** blushing, flushed, rosy, glowing, healthy, blooming, florid, sunburnt. **2** scarlet, crimson.
⊟ **1** pale.

rude *adj.* **1** impolite; showing bad manners; discourteous. **2** roughly made; lacking refinement or polish: *build a rude shelter.* **3** ignorant, uneducated or primitive: *rude chaos.* **4** sudden and unpleasant: *a rude awakening.* **5** vigorous; robust: *rude health.* **6** vulgar; indecent. [from Latin *rudis*, unwrought, rough]

▣ **1, 2, 6** crude. **1** impolite, discourteous, disrespectful, impertinent, impudent, cheeky, insolent, offensive, insulting, abusive, ill-mannered, ill-bred, uncouth, uncivil, curt, brusque, abrupt, sharp, short. **2, 3** rough, rough-and-ready. **3** uncivilized, unrefined, unpolished, uneducated, untutored. **6** obscene, vulgar, coarse, dirty, naughty, gross.
▣ **1** polite, courteous, civil. **2** clean, decent.

rudely *adv.* in a rude way.
rudeness *noun* **1** being rude. **2** rude language or behaviour.
rudiment /ˈruːdɪmənt/ *noun* **1** (*usually* **rudiments**) a first or fundamental fact, rule or skill: *the rudiments of cooking.* **2** (*usually* **rudiments**) anything in an early and incomplete stage of development. **3** *Biol.* an organ or part which does not develop fully, usually because it no longer has a function, such as the breast in male mammals. [from Latin *rudimentum*]

▣ **1, 2** elements, foundations. **1** basics, fundamentals, essentials, principles, ABC. **2** beginnings, first stage(s).

rudimentary *adj.* **1** basic; fundamental. **2** primitive or undeveloped; only partially developed because now useless.

▣ **1** primary, initial, introductory, elementary, basic, fundamental. **2** primitive, undeveloped, embryonic.
▣ **1** advanced. **2** developed.

rue[1] *verb* (**rued, ruing, rueing**) to regret; to wish that (something) had not happened. [from Anglo-Saxon *hreowan*]
rue[2] *noun* a strongly scented evergreen plant with bitter leaves which were formerly used in medicine, taken as a symbol of repentance. [from Greek *rhyte*; the symbol of repentance is in allusion to RUE[1]]
rueful *adj.* regretful or sorrowful, either genuinely so or not.
ruefully *adv.* with a rueful manner.
ruefulness *noun* being rueful.
ruff[1] *noun* **1** a circular pleated or frilled linen collar worn round the neck in the late 16c and early 17c, or in modern times by some choirs. **2** a fringe or frill of feathers or hair growing on a bird's or animal's neck. [perhaps from RUFFLE]
ruff[2] — *verb trans., intrans.* to trump at cards. — *noun* an act of trumping at cards. [from the name of a card game, French *rouffle*]
ruff[3] *noun* **1** a bird of the sandpiper family, the male of which grows a large ruff of feathers during the breeding season. **2** the male of this species; the female is called a *reeve*. [perhaps from RUFF[1]]
ruffian *noun* a violent, brutal and lawless person. [from Old French *ruffian*]

▣ thug, lout, tough, rowdy, mugger, delinquent, *slang* heavy.

ruffianly *adj.* **1** having the appearance, character, or manner of a ruffian. **2** characteristic or typical of a ruffian.
ruffle — *verb* **1** to make wrinkled or uneven; to spoil the smoothness of. **2** *trans., intrans.* to make or become irritated, annoyed or discomposed. **3** *said of a bird* to erect (its feathers), usually in anger or display. **4** to gather lace, linen, etc into a ruff or ruffle. — *noun* **1** a frill of lace, linen, etc worn either round one's neck or round one's wrists. **2**

any ruffling or disturbance of the evenness and smoothness of a surface or of the peace, a person's temper, etc. **3** the feathers round a bird's neck which are ruffled in anger or display. [from Middle English *ruffelen*]

▣ *verb* **1** wrinkle, crease, pucker, rumple, crumple, ripple. **2** annoy, upset, irritate, anger, put out, perturb, discompose, fluster, confuse.

rufous /ˈruːfəs/ *adj.*, *said especially of a bird or animal* reddish or brownish-red in colour. [from Latin *rufus*, red, reddish]
rug *noun* **1** a thick heavy mat or small carpet for covering a floor. **2** a thick blanket or wrap, especially used when travelling or for horses. **3** *North Amer. slang* a toupee or hairpiece. — **pull the rug from under someone** to leave them without defence, support, etc, especially by some sudden discovery, action, or argument. [from Norse *rogg*, wool]
Rugby *noun* (*also* **rugby**; *in full* **Rugby** *or* **rugby football**) a form of football played with an oval ball which players may pick up and run with and may pass from hand to hand. [from *Rugby*, the public school in Warwickshire where the game was first played]
Rugby League (*also* **rugby league**) a partly professional form of Rugby, played with teams of 13 players.
Rugby Union (*also* **rugby union**) an amateur form of Rugby, played with teams of 15 players.
rugged /ˈrʌɡɪd/ *adj.* **1** *said of hills, ground, etc* having a rough, uneven surface; steep and rocky. **2** *said of the face* having features that are strongly marked, irregular and furrowed and which suggest physical strength. **3** *said of a person's physique* strong and muscular. **4** *said especially of a person's character* stern, austere, and unbending. **5** involving physical hardships: *a rugged life.* **6** *said of machinery, equipment, etc* strongly or sturdily built to withstand vigorous use. [from Middle English]

▣ **1, 2** craggy, irregular. **1** rough, bumpy, uneven, jagged, rocky, stark. **2** weather-beaten. **3, 6** strong, sturdy, robust, hardy, tough. **3** muscular, sinewy. **4, 5** hard, tough.
▣ **1** smooth.

ruggedly *adv.* in a rugged way.
ruggedness *noun* being rugged.
rugger *noun Brit. colloq.* Rugby (Union).
ruin — *noun* **1** a broken, destroyed, decayed, or collapsed state. **2** something which has been broken, destroyed, or caused to decay or collapse, especially (**ruins**) a building. **3** a complete loss of wealth, social position, power, etc. **4** a person, company, etc that has lost all of his, her, or its wealth, social position, power, etc. **5** a cause of a complete loss of wealth, social position, etc, or of physical destruction, decay, etc. — *verb* (**ruined, ruining**) **1** to cause ruin to; to destroy. **2** to spoil (eg a child by treating him or her too indulgently). — **in ruins** *said of buildings, or schemes, plans, etc* in a ruined state; completely wrecked or destroyed. [from Latin *ruina*, from *ruere*, to tumble down]

▣ *noun* **1** destruction, devastation, wreckage, havoc, damage, disrepair, decay, disintegration, breakdown, collapse. **2** remains, debris, rubble, fragments, traces. **3, 5** downfall. **3** fall, failure, defeat, overthrow, ruination, insolvency, bankruptcy. **5** undoing. *verb* spoil, mar, botch, mess up, damage, break, smash, shatter, wreck, destroy, demolish, raze, devastate, overwhelm, overthrow, defeat, crush, impoverish, bankrupt. **in ruins** ruined, ruinous, damaged, spoiled, beyond repair, dilapidated, brokendown, destroyed, devastated, wrecked, shattered.
▣ *noun* **1** development, reconstruction. *verb* **1** develop, restore.

ruination *noun* the act of ruining or state of being ruined.
ruinous *adj.* **1** likely to cause ruin: *ruinous prices.* **2** in ruins.

▣ **1** exorbitant, extortionate, excessive, unreasonable. **2** in ruins, ruined, damaged, dilapidated, broken-down, destroyed, devastated, wrecked, shattered.

ruinously *adv.* in a ruinous way; to a ruinous degree.

rule — *noun* **1** a principle, regulation, order or direction which governs or controls some action, function, form, use, etc. **2** government or control, or the period during which government or control is exercised. **3** a general principle, standard, guideline or custom: *make it a rule always to be punctual.* **4** the laws and customs which form the basis of a monastic or religious order and are followed by all members of that order: *the Benedictine rule.* **5** a strip of wood, metal or plastic with a straight edge marked off in units, used for measuring. **6** *Printing* a thin straight line or dash. **7** an order made by a court and judge which applies to a particular case only. — *verb* **1** *trans., intrans.* to govern; to exercise authority (over). **2** to keep control of or restrain. **3** to make an authoritative and usually official or judicial decision. **4** *intrans.* to be common or prevalent: *anarchy ruled after the war.* **5** to draw (a straight line). **6** to draw a straight line or a series of parallel lines on (eg paper).— **as a rule** usually. **rule something off** to draw a line in order to separate. **rule something out 1** to leave it out or not consider it. **2** to make it no longer possible; to preclude it. [from Latin *regula*, straight stick]

▣ *noun* **1** regulation, law, statute, ordinance, decree, order, direction. **2** reign, sovereignty, supremacy, dominion, mastery, power, authority, command, control, influence, regime, government, leadership. **3** principle, formula, guideline, guide, precept, tenet, canon, maxim, axiom, standard, criterion, custom, convention, practice, routine, habit, wont. *verb* **1, 2** control, regulate. **1** reign over, govern, command, lead, administer, manage, direct, guide. **2** restrain, keep in check, subdue. **3** judge, adjudicate, decide, find, determine, resolve, establish, decree, pronounce. **4** prevail, predominate. **as a rule** usually, normally, ordinarily, generally. **rule out 1** exclude, eliminate, reject, dismiss, ban, prohibit, forbid, disallow. **2** preclude, prevent.

rule of thumb a method of doing something, based on experience rather than theory or careful calculation.

ruler *noun* **1** a person, eg a sovereign, who rules or governs. **2** a strip of wood, metal or plastic with straight edges which is marked off in units (usually inches or centimetres), and is used for drawing straight lines and measuring.

Titles of rulers include: Aga, begum, caesar, caliph, consul, duce, emir, emperor, empress, Führer, governor, governor-general, head of state, kaiser, khan, king, maharajah, maharani, mikado, monarch, nawab, nizam, pharoah, president, prince, princess, queen, rajah, rani, regent, shah, sheikh, shogun, sovereign, sultan, sultana, suzerain, tsar, viceroy.

ruling — *noun* an official or authoritative decision. — *adj.* **1** governing; controlling. **2** most important or strongest; predominant.

▣ *noun* judgement, adjudication, verdict, decision, finding, resolution, decree, pronouncement. *adj* **1** reigning, sovereign, supreme, governing, commanding. **2** main, chief, leading, principal, dominant, predominant, controlling.

rum¹ *noun* a spirit distilled from sugar cane.

rum² *adj.* (**rummer**, **rummest**) *Brit. colloq.* strange; odd; queer; bizarre.

Rumanian /rʊˈmeɪnɪən/ same as ROMANIAN.

rumba /ˈrʌmbə/ *noun* **1** an originally Cuban dance, popular as a ballroom dance, with pronounced hip movements produced by transferring the weight from one foot to the other. **2** music for the dance, with a stressed second beat. [from American Spanish *rumba*]

rum baba see BABA.

rumble — *verb* **1** *intrans.* to make a deep, low, grumbling sound. **2** *intrans.* (*usually* **rumble along, by, past**, etc) to move making a rumbling noise. **3** to say or utter with a rumbling voice or sound. **4** *Brit. slang* to find out about (someone or something). — *noun* **1** a deep low grumbling sound. **2** *North Amer. slang* a street fight, especially one between gangs. [from Middle English *romblen*]

rumbling *noun* making a rumble.

rumbustious *adj. Brit. colloq.* noisy and cheerful; boisterous. [probably from ROBUST]

rumen /ˈruːmen/ *noun* (PL. **rumina**) *Zool.* the first chamber of the complex stomach of a ruminant animal, such as a cow or sheep, in which food is temporarily stored before being regurgitated. See also RUMINANT. [from Latin *rumen*, gullet]

ruminant — *noun* a herbivorous mammal that chews the cud and has a complex stomach with four chambers, eg cattle, sheep, goats. The first chamber is the *rumen*, where food is temporarily stored while bacteria break down the cellulose in plant material. The partially digested food is then regurgitated and chewed in the mouth before finally being swallowed and digested. — *adj.* **1** of or belonging to this group of mammals. **2** meditating or contemplating. [from Latin *ruminari*, to chew the cud]

ruminate *verb intrans.* **1** *said of a ruminant* to chew the cud. **2** to think deeply about something. [from Latin *ruminari*, to chew the cud]

▣ **2** ponder, reflect, muse, think, meditate, cogitate, deliberate.

rumination *noun* in ruminant animals, the act of regurgitating partially digested food from the rumen (first stomach chamber) to the mouth, where it is chewed to a pulp and then swallowed.

ruminative *adj.* meditative, contemplative.

rummage /ˈrʌmɪdʒ/ — *verb* **1** *intrans.* to search for something by turning things out or over untidily. **2** to search thoroughly or turn things over untidily in: *rummage one's drawers.* — *noun* **1** a thorough search. **2** things found by rummaging, especially *North Amer.* jumble. [from Old French *arrumage*, stowing of cargo on a ship]

▣ *verb* **1** search, ferret, forage, hunt, delve, dig. *noun* **2** jumble, junk, *Brit.* tat, bric-á-brac, odds and ends.

rummy *noun* a card game in which each player tries to collect sets or sequences of three or more cards.

rumour — *noun* **1** an item of news or information which is passed from person to person and which may or may not be true. **2** general talk or gossip; hearsay. — *verb* (*usually* **be rumoured**) to report or spread by rumour: *it is rumoured that she is going to have a baby.* [from Latin *rumor*, noise]

▣ *noun* **1** word, news, report, story, whisper. **2** hearsay, gossip, talk, grapevine, bush telegraph.

rump *noun* **1** the rear part of an animal's or bird's body; a person's buttocks. **2** (*in full* **rump steak**) a cut of beef from the rump. **3** *usually derog.* a small or inferior remnant. [from Middle English *rumpe*]

rumple — *verb trans., intrans.* to make or become untidy, creased or wrinkled. — *noun* a wrinkle or crease. [from Dutch *rompel*, wrinkle]

▣ *verb* wrinkle, crease, pucker, crumple, ruffle.

rumpled *adj.* **1** crumpled. **2** dishevelled.

rumpus *noun* a noisy disturbance, brawl or uproar.

rumpy-pumpy *noun slang* sexual intercourse.

run — *verb* (**running**; PAST TENSE **ran**; PAST PARTICIPLE **run**) **1** *intrans. said of a person or animal* to move on foot in such a way that both or all feet are off the ground together for an instant during each step. **2** to cover or perform by, or as if by, running: *run a mile / run errands.* **3** *intrans.* to move quickly and easily on, or as if on, wheels. **4** *intrans.* to flee. **5** *trans., intrans.* to move or cause to move in a specified way or direction or with a specified result: *run the car up the ramp / let the dog run free/run him out of town.* **6** *intrans. said of water, etc* to flow: *rivers running to the sea.* **7** to cause or allow (liquid) to flow: *run cold water into the bath.* **8** *trans., intrans. said of a tap, container, etc* to give out or cause it to give out liquid: *run the tap/ leave the tap running.* **9** to fill (a bath) with water: *run a hot bath.* **10** *intrans.* to come into a specified condition by, or as if by, flowing or running: *run dry/run short of time/ her blood ran cold.* **11** to be full of or flow with. **12** *trans., intrans.* to operate or work. **13** to organize or manage. **14** *intrans.* (**run over, round, up**, etc) to make a brief or casual visit: *run up to town for the afternoon.* **15** *intrans., trans.* to travel or cause to travel on a regular route: *a train running between Paris and Nice/run an extra train.* **16** *intrans., trans.* to continue or cause to continue or extend in a specified direction, for a specified time or distance, or over a specified range: *a road running south/colours running from pink to deep red/the play ran for ten years.* **17** *intrans.* to continue to have legal force: *a lease with a year still to run.* **18** to drive (someone) in a vehicle, usually to a specified place. **19** (**run** or **run something along, over, through,** etc) to move or cause it to move or pass quickly, lightly, or freely: *run your eyes over the report/excitement ran through the audience.* **20** *intrans.* to race or finish a race in a specified position. **21** *intrans. chiefly North Amer.* to stand as a candidate: *is running for governor.* **22** to enter (a contestant) in a race or as a candidate for office. **23** *intrans.* to spread, dissolve, or circulate quickly: *the colour in his shirt ran/the rumour ran through the office.* **24** *intrans.* to be worded: *the report runs as follows.* **25** to be affected by or subjected to, or likely to be affected by: *run a high temperature/run risks.* **26** *intrans.* to develop relatively quickly in a specified direction; to tend (towards): *run to fat.* **27** *intrans.* to have as or be an inherent or recurring part of: *blue eyes run in the family.* **28** to own, drive, and maintain (a car). **29** to publish: *run the story in the magazine.* **30** *trans., intrans.* to accumulate or allow to accumulate: *run up debts at the bank.* **31** *intrans. said of stitches* to become undone or (of a garment, eg hosiery) to have stitches come undone and form a ladder. **32** to graze (cattle): *run cattle in the valley.* **33** to hunt or track down. **34** to get past or through: *run a blockade.* **35** to smuggle: *run guns.* **36** *intrans. said of fish* to migrate upstream, especially to spawn. **37** to score (a run) by, or as if by, running. — *noun* **1** an act of running. **2** the distance covered or time taken up by an act of running. **3** a rapid running movement: *break into a run.* **4** a trip in a vehicle, especially one taken for pleasure. **5** a continuous and unbroken period or series of something: *a run of bad luck/the play had a run of six weeks.* **6** freedom to move about or come and go as one pleases: *have the run of the house.* **7** a high or urgent demand (for a currency, money, etc). **8** a route which is regularly travelled: *a coach on the London to Glasgow run.* **9** a row of unravelled stitches, especially in hosiery; a ladder. **10** the average type or class: *the usual run of new students.* **11** (**the runs**) *colloq.* diarrhoea. **12** a number produced in a single period of production: *a print run.* **13** three or more playing cards forming a series or sequence. **14** an inclined course, especially one covered with snow used for skiing. **15** a point scored in cricket either by a batter running from one wicket to the other or in any of certain other ways. **16** a unit of scoring in baseball made by the batter successfully completing a circuit of four bases. **17** (*often in compounds*) an enclosure or pen for domestic fowls or animals: *a chicken-run.* **18** a shoal of migrating fish. **19** a track used regularly by wild animals. — **on the run** fleeing, especially from the police. **run across someone** to meet them

unexpectedly. **run after someone** or **something** to chase them. **run along** *colloq.* (*usually as an exclamation*) to go away. **run away** to escape or flee. **run away with someone 1** to elope with them. **2** *said of a horse* to gallop off uncontrollably with someone on its back. **run away with something 1** to steal it. **2** *said of a person* to be over-enthusiastic about or carried away by an idea, etc. **3** to win a competition, etc comfortably. **4** to use it up rapidly. **run down** *said of a clock, battery, etc* to cease to work because of a gradual loss of power. **run someone down** *said of a vehicle or its driver* to knock someone to the ground. **run something down** to allow something (eg an operation or business) to be gradually reduced or closed. **run someone** or **something down 1** to speak badly of them, usually without good reason. **2** to chase or search for them until they are found or captured. **be run down** *said of a person* to be weak and exhausted, usually through overwork or a lack of proper food. **run for it** *colloq.* to try to escape. **run high** *said of feelings* to be very strong. **run something in** to run a new car or engine gently to prevent damage to the engine. **run someone in** *colloq.* **1** to arrest them. **2** to give them a lift in a car, etc for a short distance, especially to a regular destination. **run into someone** *colloq.* to meet them unexpectedly. **run into someone** or **something** to collide with them. **run into something 1** to suffer from or be beset by a problem, difficulty, etc: *our plans quickly ran into problems.* **2** to reach as far as; to extend into: *his debts run into hundreds.* **run off 1** to leave quickly; to run away. **2** *said of a liquid* to be drained. **run something off 1** to produce it (especially printed material) quickly or promptly. **2** to drain a liquid. **3** to decide a tied contest with a further round. **run off with something 1** to steal it. **2** to win a competition, etc comfortably. **run off with someone** to elope with them. **run on 1** to talk at length or incessantly. **2** *Printing* to continue or be continued in the same line without starting a new paragraph. **run out** *said of a supply* to come to an end; to be used up. **run out of something** to use up a supply of it: *run out of money.* **run someone out 1** *Cricket* to put out a batter running towards a wicket by hitting that wicket with the ball. **2** *chiefly North Amer. colloq.* to force them to leave: *run them out of town.* **run out on someone** *colloq.* to abandon or desert them. **run over 1** to overflow; to go beyond a limit. **2** to make a quick brief visit. **run over** or **through something 1** to repeat or glance over quickly, especially for practice. **2** to read or perform it quickly, especially for practice or as a rehearsal. **run someone over** *said of a vehicle or driver* to knock them down and injure or kill them. **run through something** to use up money, resources, etc quickly and recklessly. **run someone through** to pierce them with a sword or similar weapon. **run to something 1** to have enough money for it: *we can't run to a holiday this year.* **2** *said of money, resources, etc* to be sufficient for particular needs. **run something up 1** to make a piece of clothing quickly or promptly. **2** to amass or accumulate bills, debts, etc. **3** to hoist a flag. **run up against someone** or **something** to be faced with a challenging opponent or difficulty. [from Anglo-Saxon *rinnan*]

. . . .

▣ *verb* **1** sprint, jog, race, career, tear, dash, hurry, rush, speed, bolt, dart, scoot, scuttle. **3** move, glide, slide, skim. **4** see RUN AWAY. **6** flow, stream, pour, gush. **12** work, operate, function. **13** head, lead, administer, direct, manage, superintend, supervise, oversee, control, regulate. **16, 17** continue, extend. **16** project, stretch, spread. **17** last. **18** drive, take, convey, transport. **21** compete, contend, stand, challenge. *noun* **1** jog, gallop, race, sprint, spurt, dash, rush. **4** drive, ride, spin, jaunt, excursion, outing, trip, journey. **5** sequence, series, string, chain, course. **run across** see RUN INTO (SOMEONE). **run after** chase, pursue, follow, tail. **run away** escape, flee, abscond, bolt, *colloq.* scarper, *slang* beat it, run off, make off, *colloq.* clear off. **run down** *someone* run over, knock over, hit, strike. *something* reduce, decrease, drop, cut, trim, curtail. *someone or something* criticize, belittle, disparage, denigrate, defame. **run into** *someone colloq.* bump into, meet, encounter, run across.

someone or something hit, strike, collide with. **run out** expire, terminate, end, cease, close, finish, dry up, fail.

⊟ run after flee. **run away** stay. **run down** something increase. someone or something praise. **run into** someone or something miss.

runabout noun a small light car, boat, or aircraft.

runaway — noun a person or animal that has run away or fled. — adj. **1** that is running away or out of control. **2** said of a race, victory, etc easily and convincingly won. **3** done or managed as a result of running away.

⊟ noun escaper, escapee, fugitive, absconder, deserter, refugee. adj. **1** escaped, fugitive, loose, uncontrolled.

run-down — adj. **1** said of a person tired or exhausted; in weakened health. **2** said of a building in a bad state of repair. — noun **1** a gradual reduction in numbers, size, etc. **2** a brief statement of the main points or items; a summary.

⊟ adj. **1** weak, tired, weary, exhausted, worn out, debilitated. **2** neglected, uncared-for, dilapidated, decaying, shabby, dingy, worn-out. noun **1** reduction, decrease, decline, drop, cut. **2** summary, résumé, synopsis, outline, review, recap, run-through.

rune noun **1** any of the letters of an early alphabet used by the Germanic peoples between about AD 200 and AD 600, used especially in carvings. **2** a mystical symbol or inscription. [from Norse run, secret]

rung[1] noun **1** a step on a ladder. **2** a crosspiece on a chair. [from Anglo-Saxon hrung]

rung[2] see RING[2].

runic adj. **1** written in or inscribed with runes. **2** in the style of ancient interlaced ornamentation.

run-in noun colloq. a quarrel or argument.

runnel noun a small stream. [from Anglo-Saxon rynel]

runner noun **1** a person or thing that runs. **2** a messenger. **3** a groove or strip along which a drawer, sliding door, etc slides. **4** either of the strips of metal or wood running the length of a sledge, on which it moves. **5** a blade on an ice skate. **6** Bot. in certain plants, eg strawberry, creeping buttercup, a long stem that grows horizontally along the surface of the ground, putting down roots from nodes along its length, or from a terminal bud at the end of the stem. At each of these sites a new plant develops and eventually becomes detached from the parent plant. **7** a long narrow strip of cloth or carpet used to decorate or cover a table, dresser, floor, etc. **8** a runner bean. **9** a smuggler. — **do a runner** slang to leave a place hastily; to escape.

⊟ **1** jogger, sprinter, athlete, competitor, participant. **2** courier, messenger.

runner bean a climbing plant which produces bright red flowers and long, green, edible beans.

runner-up noun (PL. **runners-up**) a competitor who finishes in second place.

running — noun **1** the act of moving quickly. **2** the act of managing, organizing or operating. — adj. **1** of or for running. **2** done or performed while running, working, etc: running repairs / a running jump. **3** continuous. **4** consecutive: two days running. **5** flowing. **6** giving out pus. — **in** or **out of the running** having, or not having, a chance of success.

⊟ noun **2** administration, direction, management, organization, co-ordination, superintendency, supervision, leadership, charge, control, regulation, functioning, working, operation, performance, conduct. adj. **3** unbroken,

uninterrupted, continuous, constant, perpetual, incessant, unceasing. **4** successive, consecutive. **5** moving, flowing.

⊟ adj. **3** broken, occasional.

running-board noun a footboard along the side of a vehicle.

running head a title occurring at the top of every page in a book.

running knot a knot that changes the size of a noose as it is pulled.

running mate North Amer. a candidate standing for election to a post of secondary importance when considered as the partner of the candidate for a more important post; especially the candidate for the post of vice-president of the USA.

runny adj. (**runnier, runniest**) **1** tending to run or flow with liquid. **2** liquid; watery.

⊟ **2** flowing, fluid, liquid, liquefied, melted, molten, watery, diluted.

⊟ **2** solid.

run-off noun **1** rainwater that moves over the ground and flows into surface streams and rivers under conditions of heavy rainfall, when the ground is saturated with water. **2** an extra race, contest, etc, between two people or teams who have tied, to decide the winner.

run-of-the-mill adj. ordinary; not special.

⊟ ordinary, common, everyday, average, unexceptional, unremarkable, undistinguished, unimpressive, mediocre.

⊟ exceptional, extraordinary.

runt noun **1** the smallest animal in a litter. **2** an undersized and weak person.

run-through noun **1** a practice or rehearsal. **2** a summary.

run time the time needed to run a computer program completely.

run-up noun an approach or period of preparation (eg for some event).

runway noun a wide, hard surface from which aircraft take off and on which they land.

rupee /ruːˈpiː/ noun the standard unit of currency in India, Pakistan, Bhutan, Nepal, Sri Lanka, Mauritius, and the Seychelles. [from Sanskrit rupya, wrought silver]

rupture — noun **1** the act of breaking or bursting or state of being broken or burst. **2** a breach of harmony or friendly relations. **3** a hernia. — verb trans., intrans. **1** to break, tear, or burst. **2** to suffer or cause to suffer a breach of harmony or friendly relations. **3** to cause (someone or oneself) to suffer, or to be affected by, a hernia. [from Latin rumpere, to break]

⊟ noun **1, 2** split, breach. **1** tear, burst, puncture, break, fracture, crack, separation. **2** division, estrangement, schism, rift, disagreement, quarrel, falling-out, colloq. bust-up. verb **1, 2** split, separate, sever, divide. **1** tear, burst, puncture, break, fracture, crack.

rural adj. of the countryside; pastoral or agricultural. [from Latin ruralis, from rus, country]

⊟ country, rustic, pastoral, agricultural, agrarian.

⊟ urban.

rural dean in the Church of England, a clergyman with responsibility over a group of parishes.

ruse noun a clever trick or plan intended to deceive or trick. [from Old French ruser, to retreat]

⊟ plan, trick, stratagem, tactic, manoeuvre, ploy, plot, scheme, dodge, wile, subterfuge.

rush [1] *verb* — **1** *trans., intrans.* to hurry or cause to hurry or go quickly. **2** to perform or deal with too quickly or hurriedly. **3** to attack suddenly. **4** (**rush something** or **rush at something**) to approach it or carry it out hastily and impetuously: *rush at one's work.* **5** to force (someone) to act more quickly than he or she wants to. — *noun* **1** a sudden quick movement, especially forwards. **2** a sudden general movement, usually towards a single goal: *a gold rush.* **3** haste; hurry: *be in a dreadful rush.* **4** a period of great activity. **5** a sudden demand (for something). **6** *slang* a feeling of euphoria after taking a drug. — *adj.* done, or needing to be done, quickly. — **rush one's fences** to act too hastily. [from Old French *ruser*, from Latin *recusare*, to push back]

■ *verb* **1** hurry, hasten, quicken, accelerate, speed (up), dispatch, bolt, dart, shoot, fly, tear, career, dash, race, run, sprint, scramble, stampede, charge. *noun* **1** dash, race, scramble, stampede, charge, flow, surge. **3** hurry, haste, urgency, speed, swiftness.

rush [2] *noun Bot.* a densely tufted annual or evergreen perennial plant belonging to the genus *Luzula* or the genus *Juncus*, typically found in cold wet regions of the northern hemisphere, usually on moors or marshy ground. Its leaves may be flat and narrow or cylindrical and pointed, and it bears dense heads of brownish flowers, which are sometimes below the tip of the stem. Rushes are used in mats, chair seats, and basketwork. [from Anglo-Saxon *risc*]

rush candle or **rush light** a candle or night-light with a wick of rush.

rush hour a period at the beginning or end of the day when traffic is at its busiest because people are travelling to or from work.

rushy *adj.* full of rushes.

rusk *noun* a slice of bread which has been rebaked, or a hard dry biscuit resembling this, given as a food to babies. [from Spanish or Portuguese *rosca*, twist of bread]

russet — *noun* **1** a reddish-brown colour. **2** a variety of apple with a reddish-brown skin. — *adj.* reddish-brown in colour. [from Latin *russus*, red]

Russian /ˈrʌʃən/ — *noun* **1** a person born in or living in Russia or *loosely* the other former Soviet republics. **2** the Slavonic language spoken in Russia and the main official language of the former Soviet Union. — *adj.* of Russia or *loosely* the other former Soviet republics, their people, culture, or language.

Russian roulette an act of daring, especially that in which one spins the cylinder of a revolver which is loaded with one bullet only, points the revolver at one's own head, and pulls the trigger.

Russian tea tea served with lemon instead of milk.

Russo- *combining form* of Russia or *loosely* the former Soviet republics. : *a Russo-American treaty.*

rust — *noun* **1** a reddish-brown coating that forms on the surface of iron or steel that has been exposed to air and moisture. It is caused by the oxidation of the metal by oxygen from the air to form hydrated iron oxides, and is a form of corrosion. **2** a similar coating which forms on other metals. **3** the colour of rust, usually a reddish-brown. **4** a parasitic fungus that causes a serious disease of cereals and other crops, characterized by the appearance of reddish-brown patches on the leaves and other surfaces of infected plants. It commonly refers to *Puccinia graminis*, which attacks wheat. **5** the disease caused by such a fungus, which may incur serious economic losses as it affects important cereal crops, such as wheat. **6** a weakening or injurious influence or consequence, especially mental or physical laziness or inactivity. — *verb* **1** *trans., intrans.* to become or cause to become coated with rust. **2** *intrans.* to become weaker and inefficient, usually through lack of use. [from Anglo-Saxon]

■ *noun* **1** corrosion, oxidation. *verb* **1** corrode, oxidize, tarnish. **2** deteriorate, decline, decay, rot.

rust belt an area with a concentration of declining heavy industries, such as steel production, especially that in the Midwestern and NE USA.

rustic — *adj.* **1** of or living in the country. **2** having the characteristics of country life or country people, especially in being simple and unsophisticated, or awkward and uncouth. **3** made of rough, untrimmed branches: *rustic furniture.* — *noun* a person from or living in the country, especially one who is thought of as being simple and unsophisticated. [from Latin *rusticus*, from *rus*, country]

■ *adj.* **1** pastoral, sylvan, bucolic, countrified, country, rural. **2** plain, simple, rough, crude, coarse, rude, clumsy, awkward, artless, unsophisticated, unrefined, uncultured, provincial, uncouth, boorish, oafish.
🔁 *adj.* **1** urban. **2** urbane, sophisticated, cultivated, polished.

rustically *adv.* in a rustic way.

rusticate *verb* **1** *trans., intrans.* to live, go to live or send to live in the country. **2** to suspend (a student) from college or university temporarily because of some wrongdoing. **3** to make rustic or rural. [from Latin *rusticari*, to live in the country]

rusticity *noun* being rustic.

rustily *adv.* in a rusty way or state.

rustiness *noun* a rusty state.

rustle — *verb* **1** *trans., intrans.* to make or cause to make a soft whispering sound as of dry leaves. **2** *intrans.* to move with such a sound. **3** *trans., intrans. esp. North Amer.* to steal (cattle or horses). — *noun* a quick succession of soft, dry, crisp, whisper-like sounds. — **rustle something up** to arrange, gather together, or prepare quickly. [from Middle English *rustlen*]

■ *verb* **1** crackle. **2** whoosh, swish. *noun* crackle, whoosh, swish, whisper. **rustle up** arrange, cook up, concoct, *colloq.* knock up, throw together, improvise.

rustproof *adj.* that will not rust or will prevent rust from forming.

rusty *adj.* (**rustier, rustiest**) **1** covered with or affected by rust. **2** *said of a skill, knowledge of a subject, etc* not as good as it used to be through lack of practice. **3** rust-coloured. **4** *said especially of black clothes* discoloured, often with a brownish sheen, through age.

■ **1** corroded, rusted, rust-covered, oxidized, tarnished, discoloured, dull. **2** unpractised, weak, poor, deficient, dated, old-fashioned, outmoded, antiquated, stale, stiff, creaking.

rut [1] *noun* **1** a deep track or furrow in soft ground made by wheels. **2** an established and usually boring or dreary routine.

rut [2] — *noun* **1** in many male mammals, eg deer, a period of sexual excitement that occurs one or more times a year when they fight competitively for females and defend their territory prior to mating. **2** (*also* **rutting season**) the time of year when this occurs. — *verb intrans.* (**rutted, rutting**) *said of male animals* to be in a period of sexual excitement. [from Old French *rut*, roar]

ruthenium *noun Chem.* (SYMBOL **Ru**, ATOMIC NUMBER **44**) a silvery-white brittle metallic element that occurs in small amounts in some platinum ores. It has a high melting point, and is used to increase the hardness of platinum alloys. [from Latin *Ruthenia*, Russia, so called because it was discovered in ore from the Urals]

rutherfordium /rʌðəˈfɔːdɪəm/ *noun Chem.* (SYMBOL **Rf**, ATOMIC NUMBER **104**) the name proposed in the USA for an unstable radioactive metal that is manufactured artificially by bombarding an actinide with carbon, oxygen, or neon atoms. [named after the New Zealand-born British physicist Ernest Rutherford (1871–1937)]

ruthless /'ruːθlɪs/ *adj.* without pity. [from Middle English *ruthe*, pity + -LESS]

. . . .

🗦 merciless, pitiless, hard-hearted, hard, heartless, unfeeling, callous, cruel, inhuman, brutal, savage, cut-throat, fierce, ferocious, relentless, unrelenting, inexorable, implacable, harsh, severe.

🗧 merciful, compassionate.

. . . .

rutile /'ruːtaɪl/ *noun Geol.* a reddish-brown or black lustrous mineral form of titanium oxide (TiO_2), commonly found in igneous and metamorphic rocks, and in beach sand. It is an important ore of titanium, and is also used as a brilliant white pigment in paper, paint, and plastics. [from Latin *rutilus*, reddish]

rutted *adj.* marked with ruts.

RV *abbrev.* Revised Version (of the Bible).

rye *noun* **1** a cereal (*Secale cereale*), belonging to the grass family (Gramineae), that resembles barley but has longer narrower ears. **2** (*in full* **rye whisky**) whisky distilled from fermented rye.

S

S¹ or **s** *noun* (PL. **Ss, S's, s's**) **1** the nineteenth letter of the English alphabet. **2** something shaped like an S.

S² *abbrev.* **1** Society. **2** soprano. **3** South.

S³ *symbol Chem.* sulphur.

s *abbrev.* **1** second(s) of time. **2** *formerly* in the UK, shilling(s). [from Latin *solidus*]

's¹ *suffix* **1** used to form the possessive, as in *John's/the children's*. **2** used to form the plural of numbers and symbols, as in *3's/X's*.

's² **1** the shortened form of **is**, as in *he's not here*. **2** the shortened form of **has**, as in *she's taken it*. **3** the shortened form of **us**, as in *let's go*.

-s¹ or **-es** *suffix* forming the plural of nouns: *dogs/churches*.

-s² or **-es** *suffix* forming the third person singular of the present tense of verbs: *walks/misses*.

SA *abbrev.* **1** Salvation Army. **2** South Africa. **3** South America. **4** South Australia.

Sabbath /'sabəθ/ *noun* (*usually* **the Sabbath**) a day of the week set aside for religious worship and rest, Saturday among Jews and Sunday among most Christians. [from Hebrew *shabbath*, rest]

sabbatical — *adj.* **1** of or being a period of leave given especially to teachers in higher education, especially for study. **2** relating to or typical of the Sabbath. — *noun* a period of sabbatical leave. [see SABBATH]

Sabine /'sabaın/ *noun* a member of a people of ancient Italy, who inhabited the mountainous country NE of Rome and were often at war with the Romans.

sable¹ *noun* **1** a small flesh-eating mammal of N Europe and Asia, related to the marten. **2** its shiny dark-brown fur. **3** an artist's paintbrush made of this. [from Old French *sable*]

sable² *adj.* **1** *poetic* dark. **2** *Heraldry* black.

sable antelope a large southern African antelope, the male of which is mostly black.

sabot /'sabəʊ/ *noun* a wooden clog, or a shoe with a wooden sole. [from French *sabot*]

sabotage /'sabətɑːʒ/ — *noun* **1** deliberate damage or destruction, especially carried out for military or political reasons. **2** action designed to disrupt any plan or scheme. — *verb* to destroy, damage, or disrupt deliberately. [from French *saboter*, to ruin through carelessness]

▬ *noun* **1** vandalism, damage, impairment. **2** disruption, destruction, wrecking. *verb* damage, spoil, mar, vandalize, destroy, wreck, disrupt, thwart, scupper, cripple, incapacitate, disable, undermine, weaken.

saboteur /sabə'tɜː(r)/ *noun* a person carrying out sabotage.

sabre /'seıbə(r)/ *noun* **1** a curved single-edged cavalry sword. **2** a lightweight fencing sword with a tapering blade. [from French *sabre*]

sabre-rattling *noun* aggressive talk or action, especially from politicians or military leaders, intended as a show of power.

sabretooth *noun Zool.* an extinct member of the cat family that lived during the late Tertiary era. It is often re-

ferred to as *sabre-toothed tiger*, but is not in fact closely related to the tiger. Its extremely long upper canine teeth were adapted for stabbing prey.

sac *noun Biol.* any bag-like part in a plant or animal, especially filled with fluid. [from Latin *saccus*, bag]

saccade /sa'kɑːd/ *noun* the sharp lateral movement of the eye as it switches from one point to another, in contrast with its slow drifting movement. [from French *saccade*, a jerk]

saccharide /'sakəraıd/ *noun Chem.* any of a group of water-soluble carbohydrates composed of one or more simple sugars (monosaccharides), and typically having a sweet taste, eg glucose, fructose, sucrose. [from Latin *saccharum*, sugar]

saccharin or **saccharine** /'sakərın/ — *noun* a white crystalline substance, about 550 times sweeter than sugar and with no energy value (calorie content), used as an artificial sweetener by diabetics and dieters. — *adj.* oversentimental or over-sweet; cloying. [from Greek *sakcharon*, sugar]

Saccharomyces /sakərəʊ'maısız/ *noun Biol.* the yeast genus of ascomycete fungi.

sacerdotal /sasə'dəʊtl/ *adj.* **1** of or relating to priests. **2** resembling a priest; priestly. [from Latin *sacerdos*, priest]

sachet /'saʃeı/ *noun* **1** a small sealed packet containing a liquid or powder. **2** a small bag containing a scented substance, used to perfume wardrobes, drawers, etc. [from French, diminutive of *sac*, bag]

sack¹ — *noun* **1** a large bag, especially of coarse cloth or paper. **2** the amount a sack will hold. **3** *colloq.* (**the sack**) dismissal from employment: *give someone the sack/get the sack*. **4** (**the sack**) *slang* bed. — *verb* **1** *colloq.* to dismiss from employment. **2** to put into a sack or sacks. — **hit the sack** *slang* to go to bed. [from Latin *saccus*, bag]

▬ *noun* **3** dismissal, discharge, one's cards, one's notice, *colloq.* the boot, *colloq.* the push, *colloq.* the elbow, *colloq.* the axe, *colloq.* the chop. *verb* **1** dismiss, *colloq.* fire, discharge, *colloq.* axe, lay off, make redundant.

sack² — *verb* to plunder and destroy (a town). — *noun* the act of sacking a town. [from French *mettre sac*, to put (plunder) into a bag]

sack³ *noun Hist.* a dry white wine from Spain, Portugal, and the Canary Islands. [from French *sec*, dry]

sackbut *noun* an early trombone-like wind instrument. [from French *saquebute*]

sackcloth *noun* **1** coarse cloth used to make sacks; sacking. **2** a garment made from this, formerly worn in mourning or as a self-punishment for sin. — **sackcloth and ashes** a display of sorrow or remorse.

sackful *noun* (PL. **sackfuls**) the amount a sack will hold.

sacking *noun* **1** coarse cloth used to make sacks. **2** *colloq.* dismissal from, or the act of dismissing from, employment.

sacra see SACRUM.

sacral¹ /'seıkrəl/ *adj.* relating to sacred rites.

sacral² /'seıkrəl/ *adj.* relating to or in the region of the sacrum.

sacrament *noun* **1** *Christianity* any of various symbolic ceremonies, eg marriage or baptism. **2 (Sacrament)** *Christianity* the service of the Eucharist or Holy Communion; the consecrated bread and wine consumed. **3** a sign, token, or pledge. [from Latin *sacrare*, to consecrate]

sacramental *adj.* relating to or having the nature of a sacrament.

sacred /'seɪkrɪd/ *adj.* **1** devoted to a deity and therefore regarded with deep and solemn respect. **2** connected with religion or worship: *sacred music.* **3 a** traditional and greatly respected. **b** *said of rules, etc* not to be challenged or broken in any circumstances. **4** dedicated or appropriate to a saint, deity, etc: *a church sacred to the Trinity.* [from Latin *sacer*, holy]

⊟ **1** holy, divine, heavenly, blessed, hallowed, sanctified. **2** religious, holy, godly, devotional, ecclesiastical, priestly, saintly. **3** traditional, respected, revered, venerable, sacrosanct, inviolable. **4** consecrated, dedicated, holy.
⊟ **2** temporal, profane.

Sacred writings include: Holy Bible, the Gospel, Old Testament, New Testament, Epistle, Torah, Pentateuch, Talmud, Koran, Bhagavad-Gita, Veda, Granth, Zend-Avesta.

sacred baboon see HAMADRYAS BABOON.

sacred cow a thing, especially a custom or institution, regarded as above criticism.

sacred ibis an ibis native to Africa south of the Sahara, S Arabia, and Aldabra (formerly also Egypt). It has white plumage with a dark head and neck, and soft dark plumes on its tail.

sacrifice — *noun* **1** the slaughter of a person or animal as an offering to God or a god; the person or animal slaughtered. **2** any offering made to a deity. **3 a** a thing of value given up or given away for the sake of another thing or person. **b** the act of giving up or giving away such a thing. — *verb* **1** to offer as a sacrifice to a deity. **2** to give up or give away for the sake of some other person or thing. [from Latin *sacer*, sacred + *facere*, to make]

⊟ *noun* **1** offering, immolation, slaughter, destruction. **2** offering. **3** surrender, forfeit, renunciation, loss. *verb* **1** offer, immolate, slaughter. **2** surrender, forfeit, relinquish, let go, abandon, renounce, give up, forego.

----

sacrificial *adj.* relating to or having the nature of a sacrifice.

sacrilege /'sakrɪlɪdʒ/ *noun* wilful damage to or disrespect for something holy or something regarded with great respect by others. [from Latin *sacrilegus*, stealer of sacred things]

⊟ desecration, profanation, violation, blasphemy, profanity, heresy, outrage, irreverence, disrespect, mockery.
⊟ piety, reverence, respect.

----

sacrilegious *adj.* committing or involving sacrilege.

sacristan /'sakrɪstən/ or **sacrist** /'sakrɪst, 'seɪkrɪst/ *noun* **1** a person responsible for the safety of the contents of a church. **2** a person who looks after the church buildings and churchyard; a sexton. [from Latin *sacer*, holy]

sacristy /'sakrɪstɪ/ *noun* (PL. **sacristies**) a room in a church where sacred utensils and garments are kept. [from Latin *sacristia*, vestry]

sacrosanct /'sakrousaŋkt/ *adj.* supremely holy or sacred; not to be violated. [from Latin *sacer*, holy + *sanctus*, hallowed]

⊟ holy, sacred, hallowed, untouchable, inviolable, impregnable, protected, secure.

----

sacrosanctity *noun* sacredness.

sacrum /'seɪkrəm, 'sakrəm/ *noun* (PL. **sacra**) a large triangular bone in the lower back, forming part of the pelvis. [from Latin *os sacrum*, holy bone, from its use in sacrifices]

SAD *abbrev. Psychol.* seasonal affective disorder.

sad *adj.* (**sadder, saddest**) **1** feeling unhappy. **2** causing unhappiness: *sad news.* **3** expressing or suggesting unhappiness: *sad music* **4** very bad; deplorable: *a sad state.* **5** *colloq., said of a person* dull or unsociable. [from Anglo-Saxon *sæd*, weary]

⊟ **1** unhappy, sorrowful, tearful, grief-stricken, heavy-hearted, upset, distressed, miserable, downcast, glum, crestfallen, dejected, downhearted, despondent, melancholy, depressed. **2** upsetting, distressing, painful, depressing, touching, moving, poignant, heart-rending, tragic, serious, grave, disastrous. **3** poignant, heart-rending, touching, moving, melancholy, gloomy, dismal. **4** grievous, lamentable, regrettable, deplorable, sorry, unfortunate.
⊟ **1, 2** happy, cheerful.

----

sadden *verb* (**saddened, saddening**) **1** to make (someone) sad. **2** *intrans.* to become sad.

⊟ GRIEVE. **1** upset, distress, depress, dismay, discourage, dishearten.
⊟ CHEER. **1** please, gratify, delight.

----

saddle — *noun* **1** a horse-rider's leather seat, which fits on the horse's back and is secured under its belly. **2** a fixed seat on a bicycle or motorcycle. **3** a cut of meat consisting of the two loins with a section of the backbone. **4** a mountain ridge connecting two peaks. — *verb* **1** to put a saddle on (a horse). **2** to burden (someone) with a problem, duty, etc: *did not wish to be saddled with the responsibility.* — **in the saddle 1** on horseback. **2** in a position of power or control. [from Anglo-Saxon *sadol*]

⊟ *verb* **2** burden, encumber, lumber, impose, tax, charge, load.

----

saddleback *noun* **1** an animal or bird with a saddle-shaped marking on its back. **2** a roof or mountain peak that dips in the middle.

saddlebacked *adj.* having a saddleback.

saddler *noun* a maker of saddles and harness for horses.

saddlery /'sadlərɪ/ *noun* (PL. **saddleries**) **1** the occupation of a saddler. **2** a saddler's shop or stock-in-trade. **3** a saddle-room at a stables, etc.

saddle soap soft soap for cleaning and preserving leather.

Sadducee /'sadjuːsiː/ *noun* a member of a major party within Judaism (c.2c BC–AD 70), probably named from the priest Zadok, whose descendants held priestly office from the time of Solomon. Mainly aristocrats, they were associated with the Jerusalem priesthood and influential in Israel's political and economic life.

sadhu /'saːduː/ *noun* a wandering Hindu holy man, living on charity. [from Sanskrit *sadhu*, pious]

sadism /'seɪdɪzm/ *noun* **1** the practice of gaining sexual pleasure from inflicting pain on others. **2** *loosely* the inflicting of suffering on others for one's own satisfaction. [named after Comte (called Marquis) de Sade, the French novelist]

sadist *noun* a person who indulges in sadism, or enjoys inflicting pain on another.

sadistic *adj.* relating to or involving sadism.

⊟ cruel, inhuman, brutal, savage, vicious, merciless, pitiless, barbarous, bestial, unnatural, perverted.

----

sadly *adv.* with sadness, in a sad way.

sadness *noun* being sad, unhappiness.

sado-masochism *noun* the practice of deriving sexual pleasure from inflicting pain on oneself and others.

sado-masochist *noun* a person who enjoys sado-masochism.

sado-masochistic *adj.* relating to or involving sado-masochism.

SAE or **sae** *abbrev.* stamped addressed envelope.

safari *noun* an expedition or tour to hunt or observe wild animals, especially in Africa: *on safari.* [from Swahili *safari,* journey]

safari jacket a long, square-cut jacket with four pleated pockets.

safari park a large enclosed area in which wild animals roam freely and can be observed by the public from vehicles driven through.

Safavids a dynasty, possibly of Kurdish origin, which provided the shahs of Persia (1501–1722) and laid the foundations of the modern Iranian state.

safe — *adj.* **1** free from danger. **2** not hurt or injured; not damaged or broken. **3** giving protection from harm; secure: *a safe place.* **4** not dangerous: *is it safe to go out?* **5** involving no risk of loss; assured: *a safe bet.* **6** cautious: *better safe than sorry.* — *noun* a sturdily constructed metal cabinet in which valuables can be locked away. — **be** or **err on the safe side** to be doubly cautious; to choose the safer alternative. [from Latin *salvus*]

....
⊟ *adj.* **1** immune, invulnerable. **2** unharmed, unscathed, uninjured, unhurt, undamaged, intact. **3** secure, protected, guarded, impregnable. **4** harmless, innocuous, non-toxic, non-poisonous, uncontaminated. **5** sure, certain, proven, tried, tested, sound, dependable, reliable, trustworthy. **6** cautious, unadventurous, prudent, conservative.
⊞ *adj.* **1** vulnerable, exposed. **2** hurt, injured, damaged, broken. **4** unsafe, dangerous, harmful. **5** risky. **6** rash.
....

safe-conduct *noun* official permission to pass or travel without arrest or interference, especially in wartime; also, a document authorizing this.

safe-deposit or **safety-deposit** *noun* a vault, eg in a bank, in which valuables can be locked away.

safeguard — *noun* a device or arrangement giving protection against danger or harm. — *verb* to protect; to ensure the safety of.

....
⊟ *noun* protection, defence, shield, security, guarantee, assurance, insurance, cover, precaution. *verb* protect, preserve, defend, guard, shield, screen, shelter, secure.
⊞ *verb* endanger, jeopardize.
....

safe haven part of a country officially designated for the protection of an ethnic minority.

safekeeping *noun* care and protection.

....
⊟ care, protection, custody, keeping, charge, trust, guardianship, surveillance, supervision.
....

safe light a light used in a photographic darkroom, etc, which emits light of an intensity and colour which will not damage the materials being processed.

safe sex sexual activity in which the transmission of disease, especially Aids, is guarded against, eg by the use of a condom or the avoidance of penetration.

safety *noun* **1** the quality or condition of being safe. **2** a safe place: *led them to safety.*

....
⊟ **1** protection, security, safeguard, immunity, invulnerability, impregnability, harmlessness, reliability, dependability. **2** sanctuary, refuge, shelter, cover.
⊞ **1** danger, jeopardy, risk.
....

safety belt any strap for securing a person and preventing accidents, especially a seat belt in a vehicle.

safety curtain a fireproof curtain above a theatre stage, lowered to control the spread of fire.

safety-deposit see SAFE-DEPOSIT.

safety lamp a miner's oil lamp designed not to ignite any flammable gases encountered in the mine.

safety match a match that ignites only when struck on a specially prepared surface.

safety net 1 a large net positioned to catch a trapeze artist, etc, accidentally falling. **2** any measure protecting against loss or failure.

safety pin a U-shaped pin with an attached guard fitting over the point.

safety razor a shaving razor with a guard over the blade to prevent deep cuts.

safety valve 1 a device in a boiler or pipe system that opens when the pressure exceeds a certain preset level, and closes again when the pressure falls. **2** a way of harmlessly releasing emotion, eg anger or frustration.

safflower *noun* a Eurasian plant with large orange-yellow flowers, yielding a dye and an oil used in cooking. [from Old French *saffleur*]

saffron *noun* **1** a species of crocus with purple or white flowers whose pollen-receiving parts, or stigmas, are bright orange. **2** the dried stigmas, used to colour and flavour food. **3** a bright orange-yellow colour. [from Arabic *zafaran*]

sag — *verb intrans.* (**sagged**, **sagging**) **1** to sink or bend, especially in the middle, under or as if under weight. **2** to hang loosely or bulge downwards through lack of firmness. **3** to decline or fail. — *noun* a sagging state or position. [from Norse *sag*]

....
⊟ *verb* **1** bend, give, droop, sink, dip. **2** bag, droop, hang, fall, drop, flop. **3** decline, slump, fail, flag, weaken, wilt.
⊞ *verb* **1**, **3** rise. **2** bulge.
....

saga /ˈsɑːgə/ *noun* **1** a medieval Scandinavian tale of legendary heroes and events. **2** any long and detailed artistic work, especially a piece of modern fiction, often serialized, depicting successive generations of the same family. **3** *colloq.* a long series of events. [from Norse *saga*]

sagacious /səˈgeɪʃəs/ *adj. formal* having or showing intelligence and good judgement; wise. [from Latin *sagax*]

sagacity /səˈgasɪtɪ/ *noun* discernment, good judgement.

sage[1] *noun* a Mediterranean plant with aromatic grey-green leaves; the leaves used as a flavouring in cooking. [from Latin *salvia*, healing plant]

sage[2] — *noun* a man of great wisdom, especially an ancient philosopher. — *adj.* wise; prudent. [from Latin *sapere*, to be wise]

sagebrush *noun* a white-flowered aromatic shrub growing in clumps in the deserts of the USA.

saggar or **sagger** /ˈsagə(r)/ *noun* a large clay box in which pottery is packed for firing in a kiln.

saggy *adj.* (**saggier**, **saggiest**) tending to sag.

Sagittarian /sadʒɪˈteərɪən/ — *noun* a person born under the sign Sagittarius. — *adj.* relating to this sign.

Sagittarius /sadʒɪˈteərɪəs/ *noun* **1** *Astron.* the Archer, a large southern zodiacal constellation with many bright stars, lying partly in the Milky Way, and containing star clusters and gaseous nebulae. **2** the ninth sign of the zodiac, the Archer. **3** a person born between 22 Nov and 20 Dec, under this sign. [from Latin, from *sagitta*, arrow]

sago *noun* **1** a starchy grain or powder obtained from the soft pith inside the trunk of the sago palm, marketed in Europe for use in desserts. **2** any of various species of palm that yield this substance. [from Malay *sagu*]

sago palm a small tree of the genus *Metroxylon*, native to SE Asia and the Pacific region, characterized by large feathery leaves. Sago is obtained from the pith of trunks cut when the first flowers appear.

sahib /ˈsɑːɪb/ *noun* in India, a term equivalent to 'Mr' or 'Sir', used after a man's surname, or (especially formerly) on its own to address or refer to a European man. [from Arabic *sahib*, lord or friend]

said past tense and past participle of SAY. — *adj.* (**the said ...**) *often formal* the previously mentioned or named ...

sail — *noun* **1** a sheet of canvas spread to catch the wind as a means of propelling a ship. **2** a trip in a boat or ship (with or without sails); also, a voyage of a specified distance travelled by boat or ship. **3** (PL. **sail** *usually especially after a number*) *Naut.* a ship with sails: *thirty sail.* **4** any of a windmill's revolving arms. — *verb* **1** *trans., intrans.* to travel by boat or ship: *sail the Pacific.* **2** to control (a boat or ship). **3** *intrans.* to depart by boat or ship: *we sail at two-thirty.* **4** (*usually* **sail along** or **past**) to move smoothly and swiftly. — **sail close to the wind 1** *Naut.* to arrange a ship's sails to catch as much wind as is safely possible. **2** to come dangerously close to overstepping a limit, eg of good taste or decency. **sail through something** *colloq.* to succeed in it effortlessly: *she sailed through all her exams.* **set sail** to begin a journey by boat or ship.[from Anglo-Saxon *segel*]

....

⊟ *verb* **1** cruise, voyage. **2** captain, skipper, pilot, navigate, steer. **3** embark, set sail, weigh anchor, put to sea. **4** glide, plane, sweep, float, skim, scud, fly.

....

sailboard *noun* a windsurfing board, like a surfboard with a sail attached.

sailboarding *noun* windsurfing.

sailcloth *noun* **1** strong cloth, eg canvas, used to make sails. **2** heavy cotton cloth used for garments.

sailfish *noun* a large agile fish widely distributed in open ocean surface waters, up to 3.5m in length, bluish-grey in colour above and silver underneath, and easily recognized by its tall dorsal fin.

sailing *noun* a sport or pastime which involves travelling over water in a suitable craft.

sailor *noun* **1** any member of a ship's crew, especially one who is not an officer. **2** a person considered in terms of ability to travel on water without becoming seasick: *a good sailor.*

....

⊟ **1** seafarer, mariner, seaman, marine, rating.

....

sainfoin /ˈseɪnfɔɪn/ *noun* a flowering Eurasian plant of the pea family, grown as animal fodder. [from French *sain foin*, healthy hay]

saint *noun* **1** a person whose profound holiness is formally recognized after death by a Christian Church, and who is declared worthy of everlasting praise. **2** *colloq.* a very good and kind person. [from Latin *sanctus*, holy]

Saint Bernard a very large dog with a thick brown and white coat, originally kept by monks to rescue snowbound travellers in the St Bernard Passes in the Alps.

sainted *adj.* **1** formally declared a saint. **2** greatly respected; hallowed.

St Elmo's fire a blue-green coloured electrical discharge which occurs during thunderstorm weather around the masts of ships, weather vanes, and aircraft wing tips.

sainthood *noun* the position or status of a saint.

St John's wort a plant of the *Hypericum* genus with distinctive yellow flowers, used in herbal medicine as an antidepressant. [so named because it blooms near the feast day of St John the Baptist, 24 June]

saintliness *noun* a saintly state.

saintly *adj.* **1** of or relating to a saint. **2** very good or holy.

....

⊟ HOLY. **1** blessed. **2** godly, pious, devout, God-fearing, religious, pure, innocent, blameless, sinless, virtuous, upright, worthy, righteous.

....

⊟ **2** godless, unholy, wicked.

....

saint's day a date in the Church calendar on which a particular saint is honoured.

St Swithin's Day 15 Jul, the feast day of Saint Swithin, a 9c bishop of Winchester. According to a traditional rhyme, if it rains on this day, it will rain for 40 days; if it is dry on this day, it will remain dry for 40 days.

St Valentine's Day 14 Feb, the feast day of two Christian martyrs of that name, on which special greetings cards are sent to sweethearts or people to whom one is attracted (see also VALENTINE).

Saint Vitus's dance chorea.

saith /seɪθ/ *old use* says.

sake[1] *noun* benefit; behalf; account: *for my sake.* — **for God's** or **heaven's sake** expressions used in annoyance or when begging, eg for forgiveness. **for the sake of ...** for the purpose of ...; in order to ... [from Anglo-Saxon *sacu*, lawsuit]

....

⊟ benefit, advantage, good, welfare, wellbeing, gain, profit, behalf, interest, account, regard, respect, cause, reason.

....

sake[2] or **saki** /ˈsɑːkɪ/ *noun* a Japanese alcoholic drink made from rice. [from Japanese *sake*]

salaam /səˈlɑːm/ — *noun* **1** a word used as a greeting in Eastern countries, especially by Muslims. **2** a low bow with the palm of the right hand on the forehead, a Muslim greeting or show of respect. **3** (**salaams**) greetings; compliments. — *verb trans., intrans.* to perform a salaam to someone. [from Arabic *salam*, peace]

salable same as SALEABLE.

salacious *adj.* **1** seeking to arouse sexual desire, especially crudely or obscenely. **2** unnaturally preoccupied with sex; lecherous. [from Latin *salax*, fond of leaping]

salad *noun* a cold dish of usually raw vegetables, usually served with a dressing, often accompanying other foods.

salad days *literary* years of youthful inexperience and carefree innocence.

salad dressing any sauce served with a salad, eg mayonnaise or a mixture of oil and vinegar.

salamander *noun* **1** any of about 300 species of small amphibian belonging to the order Caudata, found in damp regions or in water, with a long body and tail similar to those of a lizard, but having a rounded head, moist skin without scales, and toes without claws. **2** a mythical reptile or spirit living in fire. [from Greek *salamandra*]

salami /səˈlɑːmɪ/ *noun* (PL. **salamis**) a highly seasoned type of sausage, usually served sliced. [from Italian *salami*]

salami tactics the business practice of cutting staff or parts of an organization one by one.

sal ammoniac *Chem.* former name for ammonium chloride (NH_4Cl), a white or colourless crystalline mineral.

salaried *adj.* **1** having or receiving a salary. **2** *said of employment* paid by a salary.

salary *noun* (PL. **salaries**) a fixed regular payment for (especially non-manual) work, usually made monthly. [from Latin *salarium*, soldier's allowance to buy salt]

....

⊟ pay, remuneration, emolument, stipend, wages, earnings, income.

....

sale — *noun* **1** the act or practice of selling. **2** the selling of an item. **3** an item sold. **4** (*usually* **sales**) the value of the items sold. **5** a period during which goods are offered at reduced prices. **6** any event at which goods can be bought: *a book sale.* **7** (**sales**) the operations associated with, or the staff responsible for, selling. — *adj.* intended for selling, especially at reduced prices or by auction. — **for** or **on sale** available for buying. [from Anglo-Saxon *sala*]

....

⊟ *noun* **1** selling, marketing, vending, disposal, trade, commerce, traffic. **2** transaction, deal. **6** auction.

....

saleable or **salable** *adj.* **1** fit to be sold. **2** for which there is a demand.

sale of work a sale of items made in the community, to raise money for a charity or other organization.

saleroom *noun* a room in which public auctions are held, or goods to be auctioned displayed.

salesman or **saleswoman** or **salesperson** *noun* a person who sells goods to customers, especially in a shop.

....

☐ sales assistant, shop assistant, shopkeeper, representative, *colloq.* rep.

....

salesmanship *noun* the techniques involved in persuading people to buy things.

sales talk persuasive talk used by salespeople.

Salic Law in normal usage, a rule of succession to the throne that bars all women and men whose royal descent is only through females. [from Latin *Lex Salica*, the code of the Salian Franks]

salicylic acid /salɪˈsɪlɪk/ *Chem.* a white crystalline solid that occurs naturally in certain plants, eg in willow bark and oil of wintergreen, and is used in the manufacture of aspirin, antiseptic ointments, dyes, food preservatives, and perfumes. [from Latin *salyx*, willow, from the bark of which it was originally prepared]

salient /ˈseɪlɪənt/ — *adj.* **1** striking; outstanding; significant. **2** *Archit.* jutting out or up. — *noun* a projecting part or section, eg of a fortification or a defensive line of troops. [from Latin *salire*, to leap]

....

☐ *adj.* **1** striking, conspicuous, noticeable, obvious, prominent, outstanding, remarkable, important, significant, chief, main, principal.

....

saline /ˈseɪlaɪn/ — *adj., said of a substance* containing sodium chloride; salty. — *noun* (*also* **saline solution**) a solution of sodium chloride (common salt) in water, having the same pH and concentration as body fluids, which is used to dilute drugs, and in intravenous drips. [from Latin *sal*, salt]

salinity *noun* being saline.

saliva *noun* the clear alkaline liquid produced by the salivary glands and mucous membranes of the mouth, that softens and moistens food and begins the process of digestion. [from Latin *saliva*]

salivary *adj.* relating to, secreting, or conveying saliva.

salivate *verb intrans.* **1** to have (especially excessive amounts of) saliva in the mouth, as at the thought or sight of food. **2** to drool.

salivation *noun* the flow of saliva, especially in excess, and in the expectation of food.

sallow — *adj., said of a person's complexion* yellowish-brown, often through poor health. — *verb trans., intrans.* to make or become sallow. [from Anglo-Saxon *salo* or *salu*]

....

☐ *adj.* yellowish, pale, pallid, wan, pasty, sickly, unhealthy, anaemic, colourless.

☐ *adj.* rosy, healthy.

....

sally — *noun* (PL. **sallies**) **1** a sudden attack by troops rushing forward. **2** an excursion. — *verb intrans.* (**sallies**, **sallied**) **1** *said of troops* to carry out a sally. **2** *humorous* (*also* **sally forth**) to rush out or surge forward; to set off. [from Latin *salire*, to leap]

salmon /ˈsamən/ *noun* (PL. **salmon**, **salmons**) **1** any of various medium-sized to large fish, belonging to the family Salmonidae, that are native to the N Atlantic and N Pacific Oceans, but migrate to freshwater rivers and streams of Europe and N America in order to spawn. **2** the edible reddish-orange flesh of this fish, highly prized

as a food. **3** (*also* **salmon pink**) an orange-pink colour. [from Latin *salmo*, from *salire*, to leap]

salmonella /salməˈnɛlə/ *noun* (PL. **salmonellae**) **1** (**Salmonella**) any member of a large genus of rod-shaped bacteria that are found in the intestines of humans and animals, and include many bacteria associated with food poisoning, gastroenteritis, and diseases such as typhoid and paratyphoid fever. **2** food poisoning caused by such bacteria. [named after the US veterinary surgeon Daniel E Salmon (1850–1914)]

salmon ladder a series of steps built in a river to help salmon swim upstream to lay eggs.

salon *noun* **1** a shop or other establishment where clients are beautified in some way: *a hairdressing salon.* **2** a drawing-room, especially in a large continental house. **3** a gathering of arts celebrities in a fashionable (especially 17c or 18c Parisian) household. **4** an art exhibition. [from French *salon*]

saloon *noun* **1** a large public room, eg for functions or some other specified purpose: *a billiard saloon.* **2** a large public room on a passenger ship. **3** *old use* a lounge bar. **4** *North Amer., esp. US* any bar where alcohol is sold. **5** *colloq.* (*in full* **saloon car**) any motor car not an estate, coupé, convertible, or sports model. [see SALON]

Salop /ˈsaləp/ *noun* a form used as an abbreviation of Shropshire. [from Old French *Salopescira*, Shropshire]

salopettes /saləˈpɛts/ *pl. noun* skiing trousers reaching to the chest, held up by shoulder-straps. [from French *salopettes*]

salpingectomy /salpɪnˈdʒɛktəmɪ/ *noun Medicine* the surgical removal of a Fallopian tube. [from Greek *salpinx -ingos*, trumpet + -ECTOMY]

salsa /ˈsalsə/ *noun* **1** rhythmic dance music of S American origin, mixing jazz with rock. **2** a dance performed to such music. **3** a spicy sauce of Mexican origin, made with tomatoes, onions, chillies, and oil. [from Spanish *salsa*, sauce]

salsify /ˈsalsɪfɪ/ *noun* (PL. **salsifies**) a purple-flowered Mediterranean plant with a long cylindrical edible root; the root. [from Italian *sassefrica*]

salt — *noun* **1** (**common salt**) sodium chloride, a white crystalline compound that occurs as a mineral and in solution in seawater, used since ancient times to season and preserve food. **2** a chemical compound that is formed when an acid reacts with a base, so that one or more hydrogen atoms of the acid are replaced by metal ions or other positive ions, eg the ammonium ion. **3** (**salts**) any substance resembling salt in appearance or taste, especially a medicine: *Epsom salts.* **4** liveliness; interest; wit. **5** (*also* **old salt**) an experienced sailor. — *verb* **1** to season or preserve (food) with salt. **2** to cover (an icy road) with a scattering of salt to melt the ice. — *adj.* **1** preserved with salt: *salt pork.* **2** containing salt: *salt water.* **3** tasting of salt; not bitter, sweet or sour. — **rub salt in someone's wounds** to add to their discomfort. **salt something away** to store it up for future use; to hoard it. **the salt of the earth** a consistently reliable or dependable person. **take something with a pinch of salt** to treat a statement or proposition sceptically or with suspicion. **worth one's salt** competent; worthy of respect. [from Anglo-Saxon *salt*]

salt cellar a container holding salt for use at the dinner table.

salted *adj.* **1** cured or preserved in salt. **2** containing salt.

saltiness *noun* a salty quality.

saltpetre /sɔːltˈpiːtə(r)/ *noun* potassium nitrate. [from Latin *salpetra*, salt of rock]

salty *adj.* (**saltier**, **saltiest**) **1** containing salt. **2** tasting strongly or excessively of salt. **3** *said of humour* sharp.

....

☐ **1** salt, salted, saline, briny, brackish.

☐ **1** fresh.

....

salubrious *adj.* **1** *formal* health-giving; promoting wellbeing: *a salubrious climate.* **2** respectable; pleasant: *not a very salubrious neighbourhood.* [from Latin *salus*, health]

....

■ **1** sanitary, hygienic, health-giving, healthy, wholesome. **2** respectable, decent, pleasant.

....

saluki /sə'luːkɪ/ *noun* (PL. **salukis**) a tall slender silky-haired dog of Arabian origin, with a tufty tail and ears. [from Arabic *seluqi*]

salutarily *adv.* in a salutary way.

salutary *adj.* **1** beneficial, or intended to be beneficial: *a salutary warning*. **2** healthy; wholesome. [from Latin *salus*, health]

....

■ GOOD. **1** beneficial, advantageous, profitable, valuable, helpful, useful, practical, timely. **2** healthy, wholesome.

....

salutation *noun* an act, gesture, or phrase of greeting.

salutatory *adj.* relating to or of the nature of a salutation.

salute — *verb* **1** *trans., intrans. Mil.* to pay formal respect to (someone) with a set gesture, especially with the right arm or a weapon. **2** to pay tribute to: *we salute your bravery.* **3** to greet with a show of friendship or respect. — *noun* **1** a military gesture of respect. **2** a greeting. [from Latin *salutare*, to greet]

....

■ *verb* **2** acknowledge, recognize, honour. **3** greet, wave to, hail, address. *noun* **2** greeting, acknowledgement, recognition, wave, gesture, address, handshake, nod, bow.

....

salvage — *verb* **1** to rescue (eg property or a vessel) from potential damage or loss, eg in a fire or shipwreck, or from disposal as waste. **2** to recover (a sunken ship). **3** to manage to retain (eg one's pride) in adverse circumstances. — *noun* **1** the act of salvaging property, a vessel, etc. **2** property salvaged. **3** payment made as a reward for saving a ship from destruction or loss. [from Latin *salvare*, to save]

....

■ *verb* **1** save, preserve, conserve, rescue, recover, retrieve, reclaim, redeem, repair, restore. **2** recover, retrieve, reclaim. **3** retain, keep, preserve, conserve.

▨ *verb* **1** waste. **2, 3** abandon.

....

salvageable *adj.* capable of being salvaged.

salvation *noun* **1** the act of saving a person or thing from harm. **2** a person or thing that saves another from harm. **3** *Relig.* liberation from the influence of sin, or its consequences for the human soul. [from Latin *salvare*, to save]

....

■ **1** rescue, saving, preservation, reclamation. **3** deliverance, redemption, liberation.

▨ **1** loss. **3** damnation.

....

Salvation Army a Christian organization, with a semi-military structure of ranks, aiming to help the poor and spread Christianity.

salve — *noun* **1** ointment to heal or soothe. **2** anything that comforts or consoles. — *verb* to ease or comfort: *salve one's conscience.* [from Anglo-Saxon *sealf*]

....

■ *noun* **1** ointment, lotion, cream, balm, liniment, embrocation, medication, preparation, application.

....

salver *noun* a small ornamented tray, usually of silver. [from French *salve*, tray for presenting the king's food for tasting]

salvia *noun Bot.* any plant of the genus *Salvia*, including sage. [from Latin *salvia*, sage]

salvo *noun* (PL. **salvos**, **salvoes**) **1** a burst of gunfire from several guns firing at the same time. **2** a sudden round of applause. **3** a ferocious outburst of criticism or insults. [from Italian *salva*, salute]

sal volatile /sal vɒ'latɪlɪ/ an old name for ammonium carbonate, especially in a solution that slowly gives off ammonia gas, and is used as smelling salts. [from Latin *sal volatile*, volatile salt]

Samaritan — *noun* **1** (*also* **good Samaritan**) a kind or helpful person. **2** a worker with the Samaritans, a group named after the Good Samaritan in Christ's parable, operated by volunteers, and providing a 24-hour telephone counselling service in many cities in the UK to support those who are in emotional distress. **3** *Biblical* an inhabitant of ancient Samaria. — *adj.* relating to Samaria or the Samaritans.

samarium /sə'mɛərɪəm/ *noun Chem.* (SYMBOL **Sm**, ATOMIC NUMBER 62) a soft silvery metal that is used in magnetic alloys with cobalt to make very strong permanent magnets. It is also a neutron absorber, and some of its alloys are used in components of nuclear reactors. [named after Col Samarski, a 19c Russian mines inspector]

samba /'sambə/ *noun* **1** a lively Brazilian dance, or a short-stepping ballroom dance developed from it. **2** a piece of music for either. [from Portuguese *samba*]

same — *adj.* **1** exactly alike or very similar. **2** not different. **3** unchanged or unchanging. **4** previously mentioned; the actual one in question: *this same man.* — *pron.* (**the same**) the same person or thing, or the one previously mentioned: *she drank whisky, and I drank the same.* — *adv.* (**the same**) **1** similarly; likewise: *I feel the same.* **2** *colloq.* equally: *we love each of you the same.* — **all** or **just the same** nevertheless. **at the same time** however; on the other hand. **be all the same to someone** to make no difference to them. **same here!** *colloq.* an exclamation of agreement or involvement. [from Norse *samr*]

....

■ *adj.* **1** identical, twin, duplicate, indistinguishable, alike, like, similar, comparable, equivalent, mutual, reciprocal, interchangeable, substitutable. **2** equal. **3** unchanged, unchanging, changeless, unvarying, consistent, uniform. **4** selfsame, very.

▨ *adj.* DIFFERENT. **3** variable, changeable.

....

sameness *noun* **1** being the same. **2** tedious monotony.

samey *adj. colloq.* boringly similar or unchanging.

samizdat /'samɪzdat/ *noun* in the former Soviet Union, the secret printing and distribution of writings banned by the government; the writings themselves. [from Russian *samizdat*, self-published]

samosa /sə'mousə, sə'mouzə/ *noun* a small deep-fried triangular spicy meat or vegetable pasty of Indian origin. [from Hindi *samosa*]

samovar /'saməvɑː(r), samə'vɑː(r)/ *noun* a Russian urn for boiling water for tea, often elaborately decorated, traditionally heated by a central charcoal-filled pipe. [from Russian *samovar*]

Samoyed /'saməɪɛd/ *noun* a sturdy dog of Siberian origin, with a thick cream or white coat and an upward-curling tail. [from Russian *Samoed*]

sampan /'sampan/ *noun* any small flat-bottomed oriental boat propelled by oars rather than sails. [from Chinese *san*, three + *pan*, plank]

samphire *noun* a flowering cliff plant whose fleshy leaves are used in pickles. [from French *herbe de Saint Pierre*, herb of St Peter]

sample — *noun* a unit or part taken, displayed, or considered as representative of others or of a whole. — *verb* **1** to take or try as a sample. **2** to get experience of: *sampled life abroad.* [from Old French *essample*, from Latin *exemplum*, example]

....

■ *noun* specimen, example, cross section, model, pattern, swatch, piece, demonstration, illustration, instance, sign, indication, foretaste. *verb* **1** try, test, taste, sip, inspect. **2** experience.

....

sampler *noun* a piece of embroidery produced as a show or test of skill.

sampling *noun* the mixing of short extracts from previous sound recordings into a new backing track.

samurai /ˈsamʊraɪ/ *noun* (PL. **samurai**) **1** a member of an aristocratic class of Japanese warriors between the 11c and 19c; also, this class collectively. **2** *loosely* a samurai's sword, a two-handed sword with a curved blade. [from Japanese *samurai*]

sanatorium *noun* (PL. **sanatoriums, sanatoria**) **1** a hospital for the chronically ill, or for patients recovering from illnesses treated elsewhere. **2** a sickroom in a school, etc. [from Latin, from *sanare*, to heal]

sanctification *noun* sanctifying, consecrating.

sanctify *verb* (**sanctifies, sanctified**) **1** to make sacred. **2** to free from sin. **3** to declare legitimate or binding in the eyes of the Church: *sanctify a marriage*. [from Latin *sanctus*, holy + *facere*, to make]

◼ **1** hallow, consecrate, dedicate, bless, anoint, canonize. **2** cleanse, purify.
◻ **1** desecrate. **2** defile.

sanctimonious *adj.* displaying exaggerated holiness or virtuousness, especially hypocritically. [from Latin *sanctimonia*, sanctity]

◼ self-righteous, holier-than-thou, pious, moralizing, smug, superior, hypocritical, pharisaic.
◻ humble.

sanction — *noun* **1** official permission or authority. **2** an economic or military measure taken by one nation to persuade another to adopt a particular policy, eg restricting trade. **3** a means of encouraging adherence to a social custom, eg a penalty or reward. **4** any penalty attached to an offence. — *verb* (**sanctioned, sanctioning**) **1** to authorize or confirm formally. **2** to allow or agree to. **3** to encourage. [from Latin *sancire*, to decree]

◼ *noun* **1** authorization, permission, approval, agreement, *colloq.* OK, *colloq.* go-ahead, authority, licence, ratification, confirmation, support, backing, endorsement. **2** restriction, boycott, embargo, ban, prohibition. **3** penalty, deterrent, reward, incentive. *verb* **1** authorize, ratify, confirm, accredit, license, warrant. **2** allow, permit, approve, agree to. **3** encourage, support, back, endorse, underwrite.
◻ *noun* **1** veto, disapproval. *verb* **1** veto. **2** forbid, disapprove.

sanctity *noun* **1** the quality of being holy or sacred. **2** the quality of deserving to be respected, and not violated or flouted. [from Latin *sanctitas*]

◼ **1** holiness, sacredness, piety, godliness, religiousness, devotion, grace, spirituality, purity, goodness, righteousness. **2** inviolability.
◻ **1** unholiness, secularity, worldliness, godlessness, impurity.

sanctuary *noun* (PL. **sanctuaries**) **1** a holy or sacred place, eg a church or temple. **2** the most sacred area within such a place, eg around an altar. **3** a place, historically a church, giving immunity from arrest or other interference. **4** freedom from disturbance: *the sanctuary of the garden*. **5** a nature reserve in which the animals or plants are protected by law. [from Latin *sanctuarium*, from *sanctus*, holy]

◼ **1** church, temple, tabernacle, shrine. **2** altar. **3** asylum, refuge, haven, retreat. **4** protection, shelter.

sanctum *noun* (PL. **sanctums, sancta**) **1** a sacred place. **2** a place providing total privacy. [from Latin *sanctum*, holy]

sand — *noun* **1** *Geol.* particles of rock, especially quartz, with diameters ranging from 0.06 to 2mm, produced as a result of weathering and erosion by wind, water, and ice. **2** (**sands**) an area covered with this substance, especially a seashore or desert. — *verb* to smooth or polish with sandpaper or a sander. [from Anglo-Saxon *sand*]

◼ *noun* **1** grit. **2** beach, shore, strand.

sandal *noun* a light shoe with little or no upper and straps attached for holding it on the foot. [from Greek *sandalon*]

sandalwood *noun* **1** a light-coloured fragrant wood from the heart of a SE Asian tree. It is used for carving, and yields an oil used in perfumes. **2** the tree. [from Sanskrit *candana*]

sandbag — *noun* a sand-filled sack used with others to form a barrier against gunfire or flood, or as ballast. — *verb* to barricade or weigh down with sandbags.

sandbank *noun* a bank of sand in a river or sea, formed by currents, often exposed at low tides.

sandblast — *noun* a jet of sand forced from a tube by air or steam pressure. — *verb* to clean (eg stonework) with a sandblast.

sandboy — **as happy as a sandboy** extremely happy.

sandcastle *noun* a pile of sand moulded for fun into a (perhaps only approximate) castle shape.

sander *noun* a power-driven tool to which sandpaper or an abrasive disc can be fitted for speedy sanding of wood, etc.

sandhopper *noun* a semiterrestrial crustacean, with a flattened body, capable of vigorous jumping, often abundant along the seashore.

sand lizard a lizard native to Europe and W Asia, brown or green in colour with small dark rings and two pale lines along its back.

sandman *noun* (**the sandman**) a man in folklore who supposedly sprinkles sand on children's eyes to make them sleepy.

sand martin a small European bird of the martin family that nests in tunnels hollowed out of sandy banks.

sandpaper — *noun* abrasive paper with a coating originally of sand, now usually of crushed glass, for smoothing and polishing wood. — *verb* to smooth or polish with sandpaper.

sandpiper *noun* any of various wading birds of northern shores, with a high-pitched piping call.

sandpit *noun* a shallow pit filled with sand for children to play in.

sandstone *noun Geol.* a sedimentary rock consisting of compacted sand cemented together with clay, calcium carbonate, iron oxide, or silica, widely used in the construction of buildings.

sandstorm *noun* a strong wind sweeping along clouds of sand.

sandwich — *noun* a snack consisting of two slices of bread or a roll with a filling of cheese, meat, etc. — *verb* to place, especially with little or no gaps, between two other things. [named after its inventor, the 4th Earl of Sandwich (1718–92)]

sandwich board either of two boards carried against a person's chest and back by means of shoulder straps, for the purpose of displaying advertisements.

sandwich course an educational course involving alternate periods of study and work experience.

sandy *adj.* (**sandier, sandiest**) **1** containing sand. **2** of the colour of sand, a pale yellowish-brown, or (of hair) reddish-brown.

sane *adj.* **1** sound in mind; not mad. **2** sensible. See also SANITY. [from Latin *sanus*, healthy]

◼ **1** normal, rational, right-minded, *colloq.* all there, balanced, stable, sound. **2** sensible, judicious, reasonable, moderate, sober, level-headed.
◻ INSANE, CRAZY. **1** mad. **2** foolish.

sang see SING.

sangfroid /ˌsɒŋˈfrwɑː/ *noun* cool-headedness; calmness; composure. [from French *sang froid*, cold blood]

sangria /saŋˈɡriːə/ *noun* a Spanish drink of red wine, fruit juice, and sugar. [from Spanish *sangria*, bleeding]

sanguinary *adj.* 1 bloody; involving much bloodshed. 2 bloodthirsty. [see SANGUINE]

sanguine /ˈsaŋɡwɪn/ *adj.* 1 cheerful and full of hope. 2 *said of a complexion* ruddy. [from Latin *sanguis*, blood]

Sanhedrin /sanˈhiːdrɪn/ a Jewish council of elders that met in Jerusalem (until AD 70), and during the Graeco-Roman period acquired internal administrative and judicial functions over Palestinian Jews, despite foreign domination. [from Greek *synedrion*, council]

sanitary *adj.* 1 promoting good health and the prevention of disease; hygienic. 2 relating to health, especially waste and sewage disposal. [from Latin *sanitas*, health]

. . . .

▣ 1 hygienic, salubrious, healthy, wholesome, clean, pure, uncontaminated, unpolluted, aseptic, germ-free, disinfected.
▣ 1 insanitary, unwholesome.

. . . .

sanitary towel an absorbent pad worn next to the vagina to catch menstrual fluids.

sanitation *noun* 1 standards of public hygiene. 2 measures taken to preserve public health, especially waste and sewage disposal. [see SANITARY]

sanitization or **sanitisation** *noun* sanitizing or being sanitized.

sanitize or **sanitise** *verb* 1 to make hygienic. 2 to make less controversial by removing potentially offensive elements. [see SANITARY]

sanity *noun* 1 soundness of mind. 2 good sense. [from Latin *sanitas*, health]

. . . .

▣ 1 normality, rationality, reason, balance of mind, stability, soundness. 2 sense, common sense, judiciousness, level-headedness.
▣ 1 insanity, madness.

. . . .

sank see SINK.

sanpro *noun colloq.* sanitary towels and tampons, etc collectively. [from SANITARY + PROTECTION]

sans-culotte /sãzkjʊˈlɒt/ the French name for a member of the working populace in French towns at the time of the Revolution. [French, without knee-breeches]

sanserif /sanˈsɛrɪf/ *noun* (*also* **sans serif**) a style of printing in which the letters have no serifs. [from French *sans*, without + SERIF]

Sanskrit — *noun* a language of ancient India, the religious language of Hinduism since ancient times. — *adj.* relating to or expressed in this language. [from Sanskrit *samskrta*, perfected]

Santa Claus a jolly old man dressed in red who, in folklore, brings children presents on Christmas Eve or St Nicholas' Day. Also called FATHER CHRISTMAS. [from Dutch dialect *Sante Klaas*, St Nicholas]

sap[1] — *noun* 1 *Bot.* a liquid containing sugars and other nutrients that circulates within the phloem tissue of plants, and exudes from wounded tissue. 2 vitality. 3 *slang* a weak or easily fooled person. — *verb* (**sapped, sapping**) 1 to drain sap from. 2 to weaken or exhaust; to drain (eg a person's energy). [from Anglo-Saxon *sæp*]

. . . .

▣ *verb* DRAIN. 1 bleed. 2 exhaust, weaken, undermine, deplete, reduce, diminish, impair.
▣ *verb* 2 strengthen, build up, increase.

. . . .

sap[2] — *noun* a hidden trench by means of which an attack is made on an enemy position. — *verb* (**sapped, sapping**) 1 to attack by means of a sap. 2 to undermine or weaken. [from Italian *zappa*, spadework]

sapience /ˈseɪpɪəns/ *noun* 1 discernment, judgement. 2 *often ironic* wisdom.

sapient /ˈseɪpɪənt/ *adj. formal, often ironic* having or showing good judgement; wise. [from Latin *sapere*, to be wise]

sapling *noun* a young tree.

saponification *noun Chem.* the hydrolysis of an ester by an alkali, resulting in the production of the alcohol from which the ester was derived, together with a salt of the acid. The process is used to convert fats into soap. [from Latin *sapo*, *-onis*, soap]

sapper *noun Brit.* a soldier, especially a private, in the Royal Engineers.

sapphic /ˈsafɪk/ *adj.* 1 *literary* lesbian. 2 *Poetry* written in verses of four lines, with a short fourth line. [from Sappho, poetess of ancient Greece, and reputed lesbian]

sapphire *noun* 1 *Geol.* any gem variety of the mineral corundum other than ruby, especially the transparent blue variety, although green, yellow, pink, orange, and purple sapphires also occur. 2 the deep blue colour of this stone. [from Greek *sappheiros*]

sappiness *noun* being full of sap.

sappy *adj.* (**sappier, sappiest**) 1 *said of plants* full of sap. 2 full of energy.

saprolite /ˈsaprəʊlɪt/ *noun Geol.* a soft earthy red or brown chemically decomposed rock that is rich in clay. It is formed by chemical weathering of igneous or metamorphic rock, especially in humid climates. [from Greek *sapros*, rotten + *lithos*, stone]

saprophyte /ˈsaprəʊfaɪt/ *noun Biol.* a plant, fungus, or micro-organism that feeds on dead and decaying organic matter. [from Greek *sapros*, rotten + *phyton*, plant]

saraband *noun* 1 a slow formal dance of 17c Spain. 2 a piece of music for, or in the rhythm of, this dance. [from Spanish *zarabanda*]

Saracen /ˈsarəsən/ *noun* 1 a member of a wandering Syrian people of Roman times. 2 a Muslim defending the Holy Land from medieval Christian crusaders. [from Greek *Sarakenos*]

sarcasm *noun* 1 an ironical expression of scorn or contempt. 2 the use of such remarks. 3 their bitter, contemptuous quality. [from Greek *sarkazein*, to tear the flesh]

. . . .

▣ 1, 2 irony, satire, mockery, sneering, derision, scorn, contempt. 3 bitterness, cynicism.

. . . .

sarcastic *adj.* 1 containing sarcasm. 2 tending to use sarcasm.

. . . .

▣ 1 ironical, satirical, mocking, sneering, derisive, scathing, disparaging, incisive, cutting, biting, caustic. 2 scornful, contemptuous, bitter, cynical.

. . . .

sarcastically *adv.* in a sarcastic way.

sarcoma /sɑːˈkəʊmə/ *noun* (PL. **sarcomas, sarcomata**) *Medicine* a cancerous tumour developing in connective tissue. [from Greek *sarkoma*, fleshy growth]

sarcophagus /sɑːˈkɒfəɡəs/ *noun* (PL. **sarcophagi, sarcophaguses**) a stone coffin or tomb, especially one decorated with carvings. [from Greek *sarkophagos*, flesh-eating, a supposed quality of the limestone often used]

sardine *noun* a young pilchard, closely related to the herring. — **like sardines** crowded closely together. [from Greek *sardinos*]

Sardinian — *noun* 1 a native or inhabitant of Sardinia. 2 an Indo-European Romance language spoken by between half and one million people in Sardinia. — *adj.* relating to Sardinia or its people or language.

sardonic *adj.* mocking or scornful. [from Greek *sardonion*, bitter-tasting Mediterranean plant]

. . . .

▣ mocking, jeering, sneering, derisive, scornful, contemptuous, sarcastic, biting, cruel, malicious, cynical, bitter.

. . . .

sardonyx /ˈsɑːdənɪks/ *noun Geol.* a variety of onyx containing alternating straight parallel bands of white and yellow or orange. [from Greek *sardonyx*]

sargasso /sɑːˈɡasəʊ/ *noun* (PL. **sargassos**, **sargassoes**) a brown ribbon-like seaweed that floats in huge masses. [from Portuguese *sargaço*]

sarge *noun colloq.* sergeant.

sari or **saree** /ˈsɑːrɪ/ *noun* (PL. **saris**, **sarees**) a traditional garment of Hindu women, a single long piece of fabric wound round the body and draped over one shoulder and sometimes the head. [from Hindi *sari*]

sarky *adj.* (**sarkier**, **sarkiest**) *colloq.* sarcastic.

sarnie *noun slang* a sandwich.

sarong /səˈrɒŋ/ *noun* a Malaysian garment worn by both sexes, a single piece of fabric wrapped around the body to cover it from the waist or chest down. [from Malay *sarung*]

sarsaparilla /sɑːspəˈrɪlə/ *noun* **1** a tropical American climbing plant with heart-shaped leaves. **2** its dried root, used medicinally. **3** a soft drink flavoured with the root. **4** a liquid medicine prepared from the root. [from Spanish *zarzaparilla*]

sartorial *adj.* relating to tailoring, or to clothes in general: *sartorial elegance.* [from Latin *sartor*, patcher]

SAS *abbrev.* Special Air Service.

sash[1] *noun* a broad band of cloth worn round the waist or over one shoulder, originally as part of a uniform. [from Arabic *shash*]

....

⊟ belt, girdle, cummerbund.

....

sash[2] *noun* either of two glazed frames forming a sash window. [from French *châssis*, frame]

sash cord a cord connecting the system of weights and pulleys by which a sash window is opened and held open.

sash window a window consisting of two sashes, one or either of which can slide vertically past the other.

Sask. *abbrev.* Saskatchewan.

sassafras /ˈsasəfras/ *noun* **1** a N American deciduous tree of the laurel family. **2** its aromatic bark, used as a flavouring and in perfumes and medicine. [from Spanish *sasafrás*]

Sassenach /ˈsasənax/ — *noun Scot. usually derog.* an English person, a Lowlander. — *adj.* English. [from Gaelic *Sassunach*, from Latin *Saxones*, Saxons]

SAT *abbrev.* **1** in England and Wales, standard assessment task, taken by primary and secondary school pupils at the ages of 7, 11, 14, and 16. **2** in the USA, Scholastic Aptitude Test, a general examination of verbal and mathematical skills not related to specific course work, taken by high-school pupils wishing to attend university.

Sat *abbrev.* (*also* **Sat.**) Saturday.

sat see SIT.

Satan /ˈseɪtn/ *noun* **1** in some beliefs, the Devil, the primary evil spirit and the enemy of God. **2** the fallen angel and wicked tempter of Adam and Eve in John Milton's poem *Paradise Lost.* [from Hebrew *satan*, enemy]

satanic /səˈtanɪk/ *adj.* **1** of or relating to Satan. **2** evil; abominable.

....

⊟ **1** satanical, diabolical, devilish, demonic, fiendish, hellish, infernal, black. **2** evil, wicked, malevolent, abominable, inhuman.

⊟ **1** holy, divine, godly, saintly. **2** benevolent.

....

Satanism *noun* the worship of Satan.

Satanist *noun* a person who practices Satanism.

SATB *abbrev.* soprano, alto, tenor, bass (in choral music).

satchel *noun* a small briefcase-like bag for schoolbooks, usually with a shoulder strap. [from Old French *sachel*, little bag]

sate *verb* to satisfy (a desire or appetite) to the full or to excess. [from Anglo-Saxon *sadian*]

satellite *noun* **1** (*in full* **natural satellite**) a celestial body that orbits around a much larger celestial body, eg the Moon (which is a satellite of the Earth), or the Earth (which is a satellite of the Sun). **2** (*in full* **artificial satellite**) a man-made device, especially a spacecraft, that is launched by a rocket into space and placed in orbit around a planet, especially the Earth, used for communication, etc. **3** a nation or state dependent, especially economically or politically, on a larger neighbour. **4** a follower or hanger-on. [from Latin *satelles*, attendant]

satellite broadcasting or **satellite television** *Telecomm.* television transmission using super-high-frequency beam linkage via an artificial satellite.

satellite dish *Radio* a dish-shaped aerial for receiving television signals for programmes broadcast via artificial satellite.

satellite town a small town near a larger city, especially one originally developed to prevent the city becoming undesirably large.

sati same as SUTTEE.

satiability *noun* being satiable.

satiable *adj.* capable of being satisfied.

satiate /ˈseɪʃɪeɪt/ *verb* to satisfy fully or to excess. [from Latin *satiare*, from *satis*, enough]

satiation *noun* satisfaction.

satiety /səˈtaɪətɪ/ *noun* the state of being satiated.

satin *noun* silk or rayon closely woven to produce a shiny finish. [from *Zaitun*, Arabic form of the Chinese name of the town where it was originally produced]

satinwood *noun* **1** a shiny light-coloured hardwood used for fine furniture. **2** the E Indian tree that produces it.

satiny *adj.* of or like satin.

satire *noun* **1** a variety of humour aiming at mockery or ridicule, often using sarcasm and irony. **2** any work, eg a play or film, using this kind of humour. [from Latin *satira*, mixture]

....

⊟ BURLESQUE, PARODY, CARICATURE. **1** mockery, ridicule, irony, sarcasm, wit. **2** skit, *colloq.* send-up, *colloq.* spoof, take-off, travesty.

....

satirical *adj.* **1** relating to or of the nature of satire. **2** characterized by satire.

....

⊟ IRONICAL, SARCASTIC, MOCKING, IRREVERENT, DERISIVE, SARDONIC, INCISIVE, CUTTING, BITING, CAUSTIC, CYNICAL, BITTER.

....

satirist *noun* **1** a writer or performer of satires. **2** a person who frequently uses satire.

satirization or **satirisation** *noun* satirizing or being satirized.

satirize or **satirise** *verb* to mock or ridicule using satire.

....

⊟ mock, ridicule, make fun of, burlesque, lampoon, *colloq.* send up, take off, parody, caricature, deride.

⊟ acclaim, honour.

....

satisfaction *noun* **1** the act of satisfying, or the state or feeling of being satisfied. **2** compensation for mistreatment.

....

⊟ **1** gratification, contentment, happiness, pleasure, enjoyment, comfort, ease, wellbeing, fulfilment, self-satisfaction, pride. **2** compensation, reimbursement, indemnification, damages, reparation, amends, redress, recompense, requital, settlement.

⊟ **1** dissatisfaction, displeasure.

....

satisfactorily *adv.* in a satisfactory way.

satisfactory *adj.* giving satisfaction; adequate; acceptable.

🔲 acceptable, passable, up to the mark, all right, *colloq*. OK, fair, average, adequate, sufficient, suitable, proper.
🔳 unsatisfactory, unacceptable, inadequate.

satisfied *adj*. pleased, contented.

satisfy *verb* (**satisfies, satisfied**) **1** to fulfil the needs, desires, or expectations of; to fulfil (eg a desire). **2** to meet the requirements of; to meet (a requirement). **3** to remove the doubts of; to convince. **4** *intrans*. to please; to remove all desire for others: *the taste that satisfies*. **5** to compensate for; to give compensation to. [from Latin *satis*, enough + *facere*, to make]

🔲 **1** gratify, indulge, content, please, delight, fulfil, quench, slake, sate, satiate, surfeit. **2** meet, fulfil, discharge, settle, answer, fill, suffice, serve, qualify. **3** assure, convince, persuade.
🔳 **1** dissatisfy. **2** fail.

satisfying *adj*. that satisfies; pleasing.

satrap /'satrəp/ *noun* a viceroy or governor of a province of the Achaemenid (ancient Persian) Empire. [from Greek *satrapēs*, from Old Persian *khshathrapāvan-*, protector of the kingdom]

satsuma *noun* a thin-skinned seedless type of mandarin orange. [from *Satsuma*, former Japanese province]

saturate *verb* **1** to make soaking wet. **2** to fill or cover with a large amount of something. **3** to add a solid, liquid, or gas to a solution until no more of that substance can be dissolved at a given temperature. **4** to treat an organic chemical compound in such a way that it no longer contains any double or triple bonds. [from Latin *satur*, full]

🔲 **1** soak, steep, souse, drench, waterlog. **2** fill, impregnate, permeate, imbue, suffuse.

saturated vapour pressure *Physics* the pressure that is exerted by a vapour which is in equilibrium with the liquid form of the same substance. It is dependent on temperature.

saturation *noun* **1** saturating or being saturated. **2** *Chem*. the point at which a solution contains the maximum possible amount of dissolved solid, liquid, or gas at a given temperature.

saturation point 1 a limit beyond which no more can be added or accepted. **2** *Chem*. same as SATURATION 2.

Saturday *noun* the seventh day of the week. [from Anglo-Saxon *Sæterndæg*, Saturn's day]

Saturn *Astron*. the sixth planet from the Sun, and the second-largest planet in the solar system. Its orbit lies between those of Jupiter and Uranus.

saturnalia /satə'neɪlɪə/ *noun* **1** (**Saturnalia**) the ancient Roman festival of the god Saturn in mid-December, a time of merry-making and gift-giving. **2** *literary* a scene of rowdy celebration; a wild party.

saturnine /'satənaɪn/ *adj*. *literary* **1** grim-faced; unsmiling. **2** melancholy in character. [from the supposed gloomy influence of the planet in astrology]

satyr /'satə(r)/ *noun* **1** a mythological woodland god, part man, part goat, noted for lechery. **2** a lustful man. [from Greek *satyros*]

satyr play *Greek Theatr*. a burlesque performed as comic relief after a series of three classical Greek tragedies. The hero, often Herakles, was presented in a farcical situation, with a chorus of Sileni, or satyrs.

sauce — *noun* **1** any seasoned liquid that food is cooked or served in or flavoured with after serving. **2** added interest or excitement. **3** *colloq*. impertinence; cheek. — *verb colloq*. to be cheeky to. [from Latin *salsa*, from *sal*, salt]

sauce boat a long shallow jug for serving sauce.

saucepan *noun* a deep cooking pot with a long handle and usually with a lid.

saucer *noun* **1** a small shallow round dish for placing under a tea or coffee cup. **2** something shaped like this. [from Old French *saussiere*]

sauciness *noun* a saucy quality; impertinence.

saucy *adj*. (**saucier, sauciest**) *colloq*. **1** impertinent or cheeky; attractively bold or forward. **2** dealing with sex, especially in an amusing way: *saucy postcards*. **3** *said of clothes* smart.

🔲 **1** impertinent, *colloq*. cheeky, impudent, insolent, disrespectful, pert, bold, forward, presumptuous, flippant.
🔳 **1** polite, respectful.

sauerkraut /'saʊəkraʊt/ *noun* shredded cabbage pickled in salt water, a popular German dish. [from German *sauerkraut*, sour cabbage]

sauna /'sɔːnə/ *noun* **1** a Finnish-style steam bath, the steam created by pouring water on hot coals. **2** a building or room equipped for this. [from Finnish *sauna*]

saunter — *verb intrans*. (**sauntered, sauntering**) (**saunter along, past**, etc) to walk at a leisurely pace, often aimlessly; to stroll. — *noun* **1** a lazy walking pace. **2** a leisurely walk; an amble.

🔲 *verb* stroll, amble, *colloq*. mosey, *colloq*. mooch, wander, ramble, meander. *noun* **2** stroll, walk, constitutional, ramble.

saurian *Biol*. — *adj*. of or relating to lizards; lizard-like. — *noun* a lizard. [from Greek *sauros*, lizard]

sausage *noun* **1** a mass of minced and seasoned meat enclosed in a thin tube-shaped casing, usually served hot and whole when small, and cold and in slices when large. **2** any vaguely cylindrical object, especially with rounded ends. — **not a sausage** *colloq*. nothing at all. [from Old French *saussiche*]

sausage meat minced meat of the kind used for making sausages.

sausage roll a small pastry case filled with sausage meat and baked.

sauté — *verb* (**sautés, sautéd** or **sautéed, sautéing** or **sautéeing**) to fry gently for a short time. — *adj*. fried in this way: *sauté potatoes*. [from French *sauté*, tossed]

savage — *adj*. **1** untamed; uncivilized. **2** ferocious: *savage temper*. **3** cruel; barbaric. **4** uncultivated; rugged. — *noun* **1** *old use, now offensive* a member of a primitive people. **2** an uncultured, brutish, or cruel person. — *verb* to attack with ferocity, causing severe injury. [from Old French *sauvage*, wild, from Latin *silvaticus*, of the woods]

🔲 *adj*. **1** wild, untamed, undomesticated, uncivilized, primitive, barbarous. **2** fierce, ferocious, vicious, beastly. **3** cruel, inhuman, barbaric, brutal, sadistic, bloodthirsty, bloody, murderous, pitiless, merciless, ruthless. **4** harsh, rugged, wild, uncultivated. *noun* **2** brute, beast. *verb* attack, bite, claw, maul.
🔳 *adj*. **1** tame, civilized. **2** mild. **3** humane.

savagery *noun* (PL. **savageries**) **1** cruelty or barbarousness; an act of cruelty. **2** the state of being wild or uncivilized.

savannah or **savanna** *noun* dry grassland of the tropics and subtropics, located between areas of tropical rainforest and desert.

savant /'savənt/ *noun* a male learned person. [from French, from *savoir*, to know]

savante /'savənt/ *noun* a female learned person.

save — *verb* **1** to rescue from danger, harm, loss, or failure. **2** (*also* **save something up**) to set it aside for future use. **3** (*also* **save up**) to set money aside for future use. **4** to use economically so as to avoid waste. **5** to cause or allow to escape potential unpleasantness or inconvenience; to spare: *that will save you the trouble of making the trip*. **6** *Sport* to prevent (a ball or shot) from reaching the goal; to prevent (a goal) from being scored. **7** *Relig.* to free from the influence or consequences of sin. **8** *Comput.* to transfer the contents of a computer file from the main memory on to disk or tape for storage, so that data are not lost in the event of an interruption to the power supply. — *noun* an act of saving a ball or shot, or preventing a goal. — *prep.* (*also* **save for**) except: *lost all the books save one.* — *conj.* *old use* (**save that ...**) were it not that: *I would have gone with her, save that she had already left.* [from Latin *salvare*]

- *verb* **1** rescue, deliver, liberate, free, salvage, recover, reclaim. **2, 3** set aside, put by, reserve, store, lay up, hoard, *colloq.* stash, collect, gather, keep, retain, hold. **4** economize on, cut back on, conserve, preserve. **5** spare, protect, guard, screen, shield, safeguard. **6** prevent, hinder.
- *verb* **2** discard. **3** spend. **4** spend, squander, waste.

saveloy /ˈsavələɪ/ *noun* a spicy smoked pork sausage. [from French *cervelat*]

saving *noun* **1** a thing saved, especially an economy made. **2** (**savings**) money saved up. — *prep. formal* except; save.

- *noun* **1** economy, bargain, discount, reduction, cut. **2** capital, investments, *colloq.* nest egg, fund, store, reserves, resources.
- *noun* **1** expense, waste, loss.

saving grace a desirable feature that compensates for undesirable ones.

saviour *noun* **1** a person who saves someone or something from danger or destruction. **2** a person who frees others from sin or evil. **3** (**Saviour**) *Christianity* a name for Christ. [from Middle English *sauveur*]

- **1** rescuer, redeemer, deliverer, liberator, guardian, protector, defender. **2** redeemer, deliverer, liberator, emancipator.
- **1** destroyer.

savoir-faire /savwaːˈfɛə(r)/ *noun* **1** expertise. **2** tact. [French, = know what to do]

savory *noun* (PL. **savories**) any of various aromatic plants of the mint family whose leaves are widely used as a flavouring in cooking. [from Latin *satureia*]

savour — *verb* **1** to taste or smell with relish. **2** to take pleasure in. **3** to flavour or season (food). **4** (**savour of something**) to show signs of it; to smack of it. — *noun* **1** taste or smell as possessed by something. **2** a faint but unmistakable quality. **3** a hint or trace. [from Latin *sapere*, to taste]

- *verb* **1** taste, smell, relish. **2** relish, enjoy, delight in, revel in, like, appreciate. **3** flavour, season, salt, spice. *noun* **1** taste, flavour, tang, smell, smack, piquancy, relish, zest. **3** hint, trace, dash, drop, smack.
- *verb* **2** dislike, shrink from.

savouriness *noun* being savoury.

savoury *adj.* **1** having a salty or sharp taste or smell; not sweet. **2** pleasant, especially morally pleasing or acceptable: *not a very savoury character.* **3** appetizing. — *noun* (PL. **savouries**) a savoury food, especially served as an hors d'oeuvre.

- *adj.* **1** salty, spicy, aromatic, piquant, tangy. **2** pleasant, nice, acceptable, decent, respectable. **3** appetizing, palatable, tasty, delicious, mouthwatering, luscious, succulent.
- *adj.* **1** sweet. **2** unsavoury, unpleasant. **3** unappetizing, tasteless, insipid.

savoy *noun* a winter variety of cabbage with wrinkled leaves. [from *Savoie*, the region of France where it was originally grown]

savvy *slang* — *verb trans., intrans.* (**savvies, savvied**) to know or understand. — *noun* **1** common sense; shrewdness. **2** know-how. [from Spanish *saber*, to know]

saw[1] see SEE[1].

saw[2] — *noun* any of various tools with a toothed metal blade for cutting, hand-operated or power-driven. — *verb* (PAST TENSE **sawed**; PAST PARTICIPLE **sawn**) **1** to cut with, or as if with, a saw. **2** *intrans.* to move to and fro, like a hand-operated saw. [from Anglo-Saxon *sagu*]

sawdust *noun* dust in the form of tiny fragments of wood, made by sawing.

sawfish *noun* a large ray that has a long snout edged with tooth-like spikes.

sawfly *noun* (PL. **sawflies**) a wasp-like insect which lacks a constricted waist, and uses its large egg-laying tube to deposit eggs deep within plant tissues. The larvae feed on or bore into plant stems, leaves, or wood.

sawmill *noun* a factory in which timber is cut.

sawn-off shotgun a shotgun with the end of the barrel cut off, making it easier to carry concealed.

sawyer *noun* a person who saws timber in a sawmill.

sax *noun colloq.* a saxophone.

saxhorn *noun* a musical instrument made of brass tubing, resembling a small tuba, with the mouthpiece set at right angles, and an upright bell. It was patented in the 1840s by the Belgian instrument-maker Adolphe Sax (1814–94).

saxifrage /ˈsaksɪfreɪdʒ/ *noun* any of a family of rock plants with tufted or mossy leaves and small white, yellow, or red flowers. [from Latin *saxifraga*, rock-breaker]

Saxon — *noun* **1** a member of a Germanic people who, with the Angles, formed the bulk of the invaders who in the two centuries following the Roman withdrawal from Britain (409) conquered and colonized most of what became England. **2** any of various Germanic dialects spoken by them. **3** a native or inhabitant of the region of Saxony in modern Germany. — *adj.* relating to the (especially ancient) Saxons. [from Latin *Saxones*, Saxons]

saxophone *noun* a wind instrument with a long S-shaped metal body. [named after Adolphe Sax (1814–94), Belgian instrument-maker]

saxophonist *noun* a person who plays the saxophone.

say — *verb* (PAST TENSE AND PAST PARTICIPLE **said**) **1** to utter or pronounce. **2** to express in words: *say what you mean.* **3** to state as an opinion: *I say we should refuse.* **4** to suppose: *say he doesn't come, what do we do then?* **5** to recite or repeat: *say a blessing.* **6** to judge or decide: *difficult to say which is best.* **7** (**say for** or **against something**) to argue in favour of it or against it: *a lot to be said for it.* **8** to communicate: *she talked for ages but didn't actually say much / what is the poem trying to say?* **9** to indicate: *the clock says 10 o'clock.* **10** to report or claim: *said to be still alive.* **11** *intrans., trans.* to make a statement (about); to tell: *I'd rather not say.* — *noun* **1** a chance to express an opinion: *you've had your say.* **2** the right to an opinion; the power to influence a decision: *have no say in the matter.* — *interj., North Amer., esp. US* an expression of surprise, protest, or sudden joy. — **it goes without saying** it is obvious. **not to say** indeed; even: *expensive, not to say extortionate.* **that is to say** in other words. **there's no saying** it is impossible to guess or judge. [from Anglo-Saxon *secgan*]

- *verb* **1** utter, voice, articulate, pronounce, enunciate, deliver, speak, comment, remark, observe, mention, answer, reply, exclaim, ejaculate. **2** express, phrase, put. **3** state, declare, assert, affirm, maintain, claim. **4** suppose, assume, presume, surmise, imagine. **5** recite, repeat. **6** judge, decide, reckon, guess, estimate. **8** communicate, convey, impart, intimate. **9** indicate, read. **10** report, announce, claim, allege, rumour, suggest, imply, reveal, disclose, divulge. **11** comment, remark, answer, reply.

SAYE *abbrev.* Save As You Earn.

saying *noun* **1** a proverb or maxim. **2** an expression. **3** something said.

⊟ **1** proverb, maxim, adage, dictum, precept, axiom, aphorism, motto, slogan. **2** phrase, expression. **3** quotation, statement, remark.

say-so *noun* **1** the right to make the final decision. **2** an unsupported claim or assertion.

Sb *symbol Chem.* antimony. [from Latin *stibium*]

SBN *abbrev.* Standard Book Number (see ISBN).

SC or **S.C.** *abbrev.* South Carolina.

Sc *symbol Chem.* scandium.

scab — *noun* **1** a crust of dried blood formed over a healing wound. **2** a contagious skin disease of sheep. **3** a plant disease caused by a fungus, producing crusty spots. **4** *derog. slang* a worker who defies a union's instruction to strike. — *verb intrans.* (**scabbed, scabbing**) **1** (*also* **scab over**) to become covered by a scab. **2** *slang* to work as a scab. [from Anglo-Saxon *sceabb*]

scabbard /ˈskabəd/ *noun* a sheath for a sword or dagger. [from Middle English *scauberc*]

scabbiness *noun* being scabby.

scabby *adj.* (**scabbier, scabbiest**) **1** covered with scabs. **2** *derog. colloq.* contemptible; worthless.

scabies *noun Medicine* a contagious skin disease that causes severe itching of the skin, caused by the secretion of the itch mite (*Sarcoptes scabiei*), which bores under the skin to lay its eggs. [from Latin, from *scabere*, to scratch]

scabious *noun* any of a family of Mediterranean flowering plants with long stalks and dome-shaped flower heads. [from Latin *scabiosa herba*, scabies plant, from its use in curing scabies]

scabrous /ˈskeɪbrəs/ *adj.* **1** *said of skin, etc* rough and flaky or scaly. **2** bawdy; smutty. [from Latin *scaber*, rough]

scaffold *noun* **1** a framework of metal poles and planks used as a temporary platform from which building repair or construction is carried out. **2** a makeshift platform from which a person is hanged. **3** any temporary platform. [from Old French *escadafault*]

scaffolding *noun* **1** a building scaffold or arrangement of scaffolds. **2** materials used for building scaffolds.

scalar /ˈskeɪlə(r)/ *Maths.* — *adj.* denoting a quantity that has magnitude but no direction, eg distance, speed, and mass. — *noun* a scalar quantity. See also VECTOR [from Latin *scala*, ladder]

scald — *verb* **1** to injure with hot liquid or steam. **2** to treat with hot water so as to sterilize. **3** to heat to just short of boiling point. — *noun* an injury caused by scalding. [from Latin *excaldare*, to bathe in warm water]

scale¹ — *noun* **1** a series of markings or divisions at regular known intervals, for use in measuring; a system of such markings or divisions. **2** a measuring instrument with such markings. **3** the relationship between actual size and size as represented on a model or drawing. **4** a complete sequence of notes in music, especially of those between two octaves. **5** any graded system, eg of employees' salaries. **6** extent or level relative to others: *on a grand scale*. — *verb* **1** to climb. **2** to change the size of (something), making it larger (*scale up*) or smaller (*scale down*) while keeping to the same proportions. — **to scale** with all sizes and distances in correct proportion to the real thing. [from Latin *scala*, ladder]

⊟ *noun* **1** graduation, calibration, register. **3** ratio, proportion. **4** sequence, series, gamut, progression. **5** hierarchy, ranking, order, ladder. **6** extent, level, degree, measure, spread, reach, range, scope, compass, spectrum, gamut. *verb* **1** climb, ascend, mount, clamber up, scramble up, shin up, conquer, surmount.

scale² — *noun* **1** any of the small thin plates that cover the skin of fish and reptiles. **2** a flaky piece of anything, especially skin. **3** tartar on the teeth. **4** a crusty white deposit formed when hard water is heated, eg in kettles.

— *verb* **1** to remove the scales from (eg a fish), or scale from (eg a kettle). **2** to remove in thin layers. **3** *intrans.* to come off in thin layers or flakes. [from Old French *escale*, husk]

⊟ *noun* **1** plate, flake. **2** flake, scurf. **4** deposit, fur, crust, encrustation, layer, film.

scale³ *noun* **1** (**scales**) an instrument for weighing. **2** either of the pans of a balance. **3** (**the Scales**) the constellation and sign of the zodiac Libra. — **tip** or **turn the scales 1** to have one's weight measured at a specified amount: *tip the scales at 80kg.* **2** to prompt a firm decision; to be the decisive factor. [from Norse *skal*, pan of a balance]

scale insect a small bug that feeds on the sap of plants and is wingless, often lacking legs as well, so called because many of the females are covered with a waxy or horny scale.

scalene *adj.*, *said of a triangle* having each side a different length. [from Greek *skalenos*, uneven]

scallawag same as SCALLYWAG.

scallion *noun* any vegetable of the onion family that has a small bulb and long edible leaves, eg the leek and the spring onion. [from Old French *escalogne*]

scallop /ˈskɒləp/ — *noun* **1** an edible shellfish that has a pair of hinged, fan-shaped shells. **2** one of these shells, especially when served filled with food. **3** any of a series of curves that together form a wavy edge, eg on fabric. — *verb* (**scalloped, scalloping**) **1** to shape (an edge) in scallops. **2** to bake in a scallop shell or small shallow dish. [from Old French *escalope*]

scallywag or **scallawag** *noun colloq.* a naughty child; a rascal.

scalp — *noun* **1** the part of the head covered, or usually covered, by hair; the skin at this part. **2** a piece of this skin with its hair, formerly taken from slain enemies as a trophy, especially by some tribes of Native Americans. — *verb* **1** to remove the scalp of. **2** *colloq.* to buy up (eg theatre tickets) for resale at inflated prices. [from Middle English *scalp*]

scalpel *noun* a small surgical knife with a thin blade. [from Latin *scalpellum*, small knife]

scaly *adj.* (**scalier, scaliest**) **1** covered with scales. **2** like scales. **3** peeling off in scales.

scam *noun slang* a trick or swindle.

scamp *noun* a mischievous person, especially a child. [from Old French *escamper*, to decamp]

⊟ rogue, rascal, scallywag, monkey, imp, devil.

scamper — *verb intrans.* (**scampered, scampering**) to run quickly taking short steps, especially in play. — *noun* **1** an act of scampering. **2** a scampering movement or pace. [see SCAMP]

⊟ *verb* scuttle, scurry, scoot, dart, dash, run, sprint, rush, hurry, romp, frolic, gambol.

scampi /ˈskampɪ/ *noun* **1** *pl.* large prawns. **2** a dish of these, usually deep-fried in breadcrumbs. [from plural of Italian *scampo*, shrimp]

scan — *verb* (**scanned, scanning**) **1** to read through or examine carefully. **2** to look over quickly. **3** *Medicine* to examine (the body, especially an internal part of it) without physical penetration, by any of various techniques, eg by ultrasound or by computerized axial tomography (CAT). **4** *Engineering* to search (an area) by means of radar or by sweeping a beam of light over it. **5** *Comput.* to examine (data) on a magnetic disk. **6** to examine the rhythm of (a piece of poetry). **7** *intrans.*, *said of verse* to conform to a pattern of rhythm. — *noun* **1** an act of scanning. **2** *Medicine* an image obtained by examining the body, especially an internal part of it, using ultrasound, computerized axial tomography, etc. [from Latin *scandere*, to climb]

....

■ *verb* **1** examine, scrutinize, study. **2** skim, glance at, flick through, thumb through. **4** search, survey, sweep. *noun* **1** examination, scrutiny, search, probe, survey, review. **2** screening, examination, check, investigation.

....

scandal *noun* **1** widespread public outrage and loss of reputation; an event or fact causing this. **2** any extremely objectionable fact or situation. **3** malicious gossip. [from Greek *skandalon*, stumbling-block]

....

■ **1** outrage, offence, outcry, uproar, furore, discredit, dishonour, disgrace, shame, embarrassment, ignominy. **3** gossip, rumours, smear, dirt.

....

scandalize or **scandalise** *verb* to shock or outrage.

....

■ shock, outrage, horrify, appal, dismay, disgust, repel, revolt, offend, affront.

....

scandalmonger *noun* a person who spreads malicious gossip.

scandalous *adj.* disgraceful; outrageous.

....

■ disgraceful, shameful, outrageous, shocking, appalling, atrocious, abominable, monstrous, unspeakable, infamous, improper, unseemly.

....

scandalously *adv.* in a scandalous way; to a scandalous extent.

Scandinavian — *noun* **1** a native or inhabitant of Scandinavia. **2** a group of northern Germanic languages spoken in Scandinavia. — *adj.* relating to Scandinavia or its people or languages.

scandium *noun Chem.* (SYMBOL **Sc**, ATOMIC NUMBER **21**) a soft silvery-white metal with a pinkish tinge (a member of the lanthanide series), which has no major uses, although its oxide is used in ceramics and as a catalyst. [from the name *Scandinavia*, where it was discovered]

scanner *noun* a person or device that scans.

scanning electron microscope *Biol.* (ABBREV. **SEM**) an electron microscope that produces a three-dimensional image of an object, allowing the surface structure of a relatively thick specimen, eg a tissue sample, to be examined.

scansion *noun* **1** the act or practice of scanning poetry. **2** a poem's particular pattern of rhythm. [from Latin *scansio*]

scant *adj.* **1** in short supply. **2** meagre; inadequate. [from Norse *skamt*]

scantily *adv.* in a scanty way; hardly, barely.

scantiness *noun* being scant.

scanty *adj.* (**scantier, scantiest**) small in size or amount; barely enough: *scanty clothing/a scanty meal*.

....

■ deficient, short, inadequate, insufficient, scant, little, limited, restricted, narrow, small, poor, meagre, insubstantial, thin, skimpy, sparse, bare.
☒ adequate, sufficient, ample, plentiful, substantial.

....

scapegoat *noun* a person made to take the blame or punishment for the mistakes of others. [from ESCAPE + GOAT, from the biblical Jewish practice of symbolically loading the sins of the people on to a goat which was then released into the wilderness]

scapula /'skapjʊlə/ *noun* (PL. **scapulae, scapulas**) *Medicine* the shoulder-blade. [from Latin *scapula*]

scapular /'skapjʊlə(r)/ — *adj. Medicine* of the scapula. — *noun* a monk's garment consisting of a broad cloth strip with a hole for the head, hanging loosely over a habit in front and behind.

scar[1] — *noun* **1** a mark left on the skin after a wound has healed. **2** a permanent damaging emotional effect. **3** a blemish. **4** a mark on a plant where a leaf was formerly attached. — *verb trans., intrans.* (**scarred, scarring**) to mark or become marked with a scar. [from Greek *eschara*]

....

■ *noun* **1** mark, lesion, wound, injury. **3** blemish, stigma. *verb* mark, disfigure, spoil, damage, brand, stigmatize.

....

scar[2] *noun* a steep rocky outcrop on the side of a hill or mountain. [from Norse *sker*, low reef]

scarab /'skarəb/ *noun* **1** any of various dung-beetles, especially the black dung-beetle, regarded as sacred by the ancient Egyptians. **2** an image or carving of the sacred beetle, or a gemstone carved in its shape. [from Latin *scarabaeus*]

scarce — *adj.* **1** not often found; rare. **2** in short supply. — *adv.* scarcely: *could scarce see it through the mist.* — **make oneself scarce** *colloq.* to leave or stay away. [from Old French *eschars*]

....

■ *adj.* **1** rare, infrequent, uncommon, unusual. **2** few, sparse, scanty, insufficient, deficient, lacking. *adv.* scarcely, hardly, barely, only just.
☒ *adj.* **1** common. **2** plentiful.

....

scarcely *adv.* **1** only just. **2** hardly ever. **3** not really; not at all: *it is scarcely a reason to hit him.*

....

■ **1** only just, barely. **3** hardly.

....

scarcity *noun* (PL. **scarcities**) a scarce state; a lack.

....

■ lack, shortage, dearth, deficiency, insufficiency, paucity, rareness, uncommonness, sparseness, scantiness.
☒ glut, plenty, abundance, sufficiency, enough.

....

scare — *verb* **1 a** to make afraid. **b** *intrans.* to become afraid: *he scares easily.* **2** to startle. **3** (*also* **scare someone** or **something away** or **off**) to drive them away by frightening them. — *noun* **1** a fright. **2** a sudden and widespread (often unwarranted) feeling of alarm provoked by foreboding news: *a bomb scare.* [from Norse *skirra*, to avoid]

....

■ *verb* **1** frighten, alarm, dismay, daunt, intimidate, unnerve, threaten, menace, terrorize. **2** startle, shock. *noun* **1** fright, start, shock. **2** alarm, panic, hysteria.
☒ *verb* **1** reassure, calm.

....

scarecrow *noun* **1** a rough model of a human figure set up in a field, etc to scare birds off crops. **2** *colloq.* a raggedly dressed person. **3** *colloq.* a very thin person.

scared *adj.* afraid; frightened.

....

■ afraid, frightened, fearful, nervous, anxious, worried, startled, panic-stricken, terrified.
☒ confident, reassured.

....

scaremonger *noun* a person who causes alarm by spreading rumours of (especially imminent) disaster.

scaremongering *noun* causing unnecessary alarm.

scarf[1] *noun* (PL. **scarves, scarfs**) a strip or square of fabric worn around the neck, shoulders, or head for warmth or decoration. [perhaps from Old French *escarpe*, sash or sling]

scarf[2] — *noun* a glued or bolted joint made between two ends, especially of timber, cut so as to overlap and produce a continuous flush surface. — *verb* to join by means of such a joint.

scarification *noun* scarifying or being scarified.

scarify *verb* (**scarifies, scarified**) **1** to make scratches or shallow cuts on the surface of. **2** to break up the surface of soil with a tool such as a wire rake, without turning the soil over. **3** to hurt with severe criticism. [from Greek *skari-phos*, etching tool]

scarlatina /skɑːləˈtiːnə/ *noun Medicine* scarlet fever. [from Italian *scarlattina*]

scarlet *noun* a bright red colour. [from Persian *saqalat*, scarlet cloth]

scarlet fever an infectious disease causing fever, inflammation of the nose, throat, and mouth, and a rash on the body.

scarlet woman *old use or humorous* a sexually promiscuous woman, especially a prostitute.

scarp *noun* **1** an escarpment. **2** the inner side of a defensive ditch, nearest to or flush with the wall of a castle, etc. [from Italian *scarpa*]

scarp and dip *Geol.* the two slopes formed by the outcropping of a bed of sedimentary rock. The scarp and dip are usually steep and relatively gentle slopes, respectively.

scarper *verb intrans.* (**scarpered**, **scarpering**) *colloq.* to run away; to leave quickly and unnoticed. [from Italian *scappare*, to escape]

SCART *noun* a connector with 21 or 24 pins used to link parts of an audio or video system. [from *Syndicat des Constructeurs des Appareils Radiocépteurs et Téléviseurs*, the European syndicate that developed it]

scarves see SCARF[1].

scary *adj.* (**scarier**, **scariest**) *colloq.* causing fear or alarm.

⊞ frightening, alarming, daunting, intimidating, disturbing, shocking, horrifying, terrifying, hair-raising, bloodcurdling, spine-chilling, creepy, eerie, *colloq.* spooky.

scat[1] *verb intrans.* (**scatted**, **scatting**) *colloq. especially as a command* to go away; to run off. [perhaps from SCATTER]

scat[2] — *noun* jazz singing consisting of improvised sounds, not words. — *verb intrans.* (**scatted**, **scatting**) to sing jazz in this way. [perhaps imitative]

scathing *adj.* scornfully critical. [from Norse *skathe*, injury]

⊞ scornful, critical, sarcastic, trenchant, cutting, biting, caustic, acid, vitriolic, bitter, harsh, brutal, savage, unsparing.
⊟ complimentary.

scatological *adj.* **1** relating to or involving scatology. **2** characterized or preoccupied with obscenity.

scatology *noun* **1** preoccupation with the obscene, especially with excrement and related bodily functions. **2** *Medicine* the study of excrement for the purpose of diagnosis. [from Greek *skor*, dung + -LOGY]

scatter — *verb* (**scattered**, **scattering**) **1** to lay or throw haphazardly. **2** *trans., intrans.* to depart or send off in different directions. — *noun* **1** an act of scattering. **2** a quantity of scattered things. **3** *Statistics* a measure of the extent to which the measurements of two random variables, plotted as paired values on a graph, are grouped close together or scattered apart. It indicates whether the mean value is likely to be representative of all the measurements. [from Middle English *scatter*]

⊞ *verb* SPREAD. **1** sprinkle, sow, strew, shower. **2** disperse, dissipate, disband, disunite, separate, divide, break up, diffuse.
⊟ *verb* GATHER, COLLECT.

scatterbrain *noun colloq.* a scatterbrained person.

scatterbrained *adj.* incapable of organized thought; having a tendency to forget things.

⊞ muddle-headed, absent-minded, forgetful, *colloq.* scatty, *slang* dizzy, careless, inattentive, unreliable, irresponsible, frivolous, feather-brained, *North Amer. slang* ditsy.

⊟ sensible, careful, attentive.

scatter diagram *Maths.* a graph which shows the extent to which two random variables, plotted as paired values, are grouped close together or scattered apart.

scattering *noun* **1** dispersion. **2** something that is scattered. **3** a small amount.

⊞ **3** sprinkling, few, handful, smattering.
⊟ **3** mass, abundance.

scatty *adj.* (**scattier**, **scattiest**) *colloq.* **1** mentally disorganized. **2** crazy; daft. [a shortening of SCATTERBRAINED]

scavenge *verb* **1** *intrans.* to search among waste for usable things. **2** *trans. Chem.* to remove impurities from. [from Old French *scawage*, inspection]

⊞ **1** forage, rummage, rake, search.

scavenger *noun* **1** an animal that feeds on refuse or decaying flesh. **2** a person who searches among rubbish for usable things.

ScD *abbrev. Scientiae Doctor* (Latin), Doctor of Science.

SCE *abbrev.* Scottish Certificate of Education.

scenario /sɪˈnɑːrɪəʊ/ *noun* (PL. **scenarios**) **1** a rough written outline of a dramatic work, eg a film; a synopsis. **2** a detailed script. **3** a hypothetical situation or sequence of events. [from Italian *scenario*]

⊞ **1** outline, synopsis, summary, résumé, storyline, plot, scheme, plan, programme, projection. **2** script, screenplay. **3** situation, scene.

scene *noun* **1** the setting in which a real or imaginary event takes place. **2** a unit of action in a play or film. See also ACT. **3** any of the pieces making up a stage or film set, or the set as a whole. **4** a landscape, situation, etc as seen by someone: *a delightful scene met their eyes.* **5** an embarrassing display of emotion in public: *make a scene.* **6** *colloq.* a state of affairs with regard to a particular activity: *the current music scene.* **7** *colloq.* a liked or preferred area of interest or activity: *not my scene.* — **behind the scenes 1** out of sight of the audience. **2** unknown to, or out of sight of, the public. **come on the scene** to arrive; to become part of the current situation. **set the scene** to describe the situation in which an event takes place. [from Greek *skene*, tent, stage]

⊞ **1** place, area, spot, site, location, locality, environment, milieu, setting, context, background. **2** part, division, shot, clip, episode, incident. **4** landscape, scenery, panorama, view, vista, prospect, sight, spectacle, picture. **5** fuss, commotion, *colloq.* to-do, exhibition, display, show, performance, drama.

scenery *noun* **1** landscape, especially when attractively rural. **2** the items making up a stage or film set.

⊞ BACKGROUND, SETTING, SCENE. **1** landscape, panorama, view, vista, outlook, surroundings. **2** set, backdrop, flats, *colloq.* props.

scenic *adj.* **1** of, being, or including attractive natural landscapes: *a scenic trip.* **2** of or relating to scenery on stage or in film.

⊞ **1** panoramic, picturesque, attractive, pretty, beautiful, grand, striking, impressive, spectacular, breathtaking.
⊟ **1** dull, dreary.

scent — *noun* **1** the distinctive smell of a person, animal, or plant. **2** a trail of this left behind: *dogs on the scent.* **3** a series of findings leading to a major discovery: *police on* *the scent of the drug baron.* **4** a sweet-smelling liquid; perfume. — *verb* **1** to smell; to discover by the sense of smell. **2** to sense; to be aware of by instinct or intuition. **3** to impart a smell, especially a pleasant one. [from Latin *sentire*, to perceive]

▣ *noun* **1** smell, odour, spoor, perfume, fragrance. **2, 3** track, trail. **4** perfume, fragrance. *verb* **1** smell, sniff (out), nose (out). **2** sense, perceive, detect, discern. **3** perfume.

sceptic /ˈskɛptɪk/ *noun* **1** a person who believes that nothing can be known with absolute certainty. **2** a person who questions widely accepted (especially religious) beliefs. [from Greek *skeptikos*, thoughtful]

▣ DOUBTER, UNBELIEVER, DISBELIEVER. **2** questioner, agnostic, atheist.
▣ BELIEVER.

sceptical /ˈskɛptɪkəl/ *adj.* doubtful, tending to be incredulous.

▣ doubting, doubtful, unconvinced, unbelieving, disbelieving, incredulous, questioning, distrustful, mistrustful, dubious, suspicious, cynical, pessimistic.
▣ convinced, confident, credulous, trusting.

scepticism /ˈskɛptɪsɪzm/ *noun* **1** doubt, or the disposition to doubt. **2** a philosophical tradition that doubts the possibility of human knowledge. **3** agnosticism.

▣ **1** doubt, unbelief, disbelief, distrust, suspicion, cynicism, pessimism. **3** agnosticism, atheism.
▣ **1, 3** belief, faith.

sceptre /ˈsɛptə(r)/ *noun* a ceremonial rod carried by a monarch as a symbol of sovereignty. [from Greek *skeptron*, staff]

Sch *abbrev.* schilling.

schedule /ˈʃɛdjuːl, ˈskɛdjuːl/ — *noun* **1** a list of activities or events planned to take place at specific times. **2** the state of happening on time according to plan: *behind schedule.* **3** any list or inventory. **4** a timetable. **5** a supplement to a document. — *verb* **1** to plan (something) to happen at a specific time. **2** to put on a schedule. [from Latin *schedula*, from *scheda*, strip of papyrus]

▣ *noun* **1** programme, agenda, timetable, diary, calendar, itinerary, plan, scheme. **3** list, inventory, catalogue. *verb* **1** plan, organize, arrange, appoint, assign, book, timetable, time, programme. **2** list.

schema /ˈskiːmə/ *noun* (PL. **schemata**) **1** a diagram or plan. **2** an outline or synopsis. [from Greek *schema*, form]

schematic *adj.* **1** following a particular plan or arrangement. **2** in the form of a diagram or plan.

▣ **2** diagrammatic, representational, symbolic, illustrative, graphic.

schematization or **schematisation** *noun* schematizing.

schematize or **schematise** *verb* to represent by means of a diagram or plan.

scheme — *noun* **1** a plan of action. **2** a system or programme: *a pension scheme.* **3** a careful arrangement of different parts: *a colour scheme.* **4** a secret plan to cause harm or damage. **5** a diagram or table. — *verb intrans.* to plan or act secretly and usually maliciously. [see SCHEMA]

▣ *noun* **1** plan, project, idea, proposal, proposition, suggestion, strategy, tactic(s). **2** system, method,

procedure, programme, schedule. **3** arrangement, layout, pattern, design, shape, configuration. **4** intrigue, plot, conspiracy, machination, manoeuvre, stratagem, ruse, ploy. **5** diagram, schema, chart, table. *verb* plan, plot, conspire, connive, collude, intrigue, machinate, manoeuvre.

schemer /ˈskiːmə(r)/ *noun* a person who schemes.

scherzo /ˈskɛətsoʊ/ *noun* (PL. **scherzos, scherzi**) a lively piece of music, especially a vigorous or light-hearted movement in a symphony or sonata. [from Italian *scherzo*, joke]

schilling /ˈʃɪlɪŋ/ *noun* the standard unit of currency in Austria, divided into 100 groschen. [from German *schilling*]

schism /ˈskɪzm/ *noun* **1** *Relig.* separation from the main group, or into opposing groups. **2** the act of encouraging such separation. **3** a breakaway group formed. [from Greek *schisma*, split]

▣ **1** separation, division, split, rift, rupture, break, severance, estrangement, disunion, discord. **3** splinter group, faction, sect.

schismatic /skɪzˈmatɪk/ *adj.* relating to or involving schism.

schist /ʃɪst/ *noun Geol.* any of a group of common coarse-grained metamorphic rocks that characteristically contain broad wavy bands corresponding to zones of minerals, eg mica, hornblende, talc, and graphite, that readily split into layers. [from Greek *schistos*, split]

schistosomiasis /ˌʃɪstəsoʊˈmaɪəsɪs/ *noun Medicine* a tropical disease caused by infestation with parasitic flukes belonging to the genus *Schistosoma* and transmitted by drinking water contaminated with human sewage. [from Greek *schistos*, split]

schizo /ˈskɪtsoʊ/ *colloq.* — *noun* (PL. **schizos**) a schizophrenic. — *adj.* schizophrenic.

schizoid /ˈskɪtsɔɪd/ — *adj.* showing some of the qualities of schizophrenia, eg extreme shyness and indulgence in fantasy, but without definite mental disorder. — *noun* a schizoid person. [from Greek *schizein*, to split + -OID]

schizophrenia /ˌskɪtsəˈfriːnɪə/ *noun* any of various forms of a severe mental disorder characterized by loss of contact with reality, impairment of thought processes, a marked personality change, loss of emotional responsiveness, and social withdrawal. [from Greek *schizein*, to split + *phren*, mind]

schizophrenic /ˌskɪtsəˈfrɛnɪk/ — *noun* a person suffering from schizophrenia. — *adj.* relating to or suffering from schizophrenia.

schlep or **schlepp** /ʃlɛp/ *slang* — *verb* to carry, pull, or drag with difficulty. — *noun* **1** a clumsy, stupid, or incompetent person. **2** a journey or procedure requiring great effort or involving great difficulty. [from Yiddish *schlep*]

schlock /ʃlɒk/ *noun* **1** inferior quality; shoddy production. **2** a shoddy or defective article. [from Yiddish *schlock*, from German *Schlag*, a blow]

schmaltz /ʃmɔːlts/ *noun colloq.* excessive sentimentality, especially in music or other art. [from Yiddish *schmaltz*, from German *Schmalz*, cooking fat]

schmaltzy /ˈʃmɔːltsɪ/ *adj.* (**schmaltzier, schmaltziest**) characterized by schmaltz.

schmooze or **shmooze** /ʃmuːz/ *verb intrans.* to chat or gossip, especially at a social gathering. [Yiddish]

schnapps /ʃnaps/ *noun* in N Europe, any strong dry alcoholic spirit, especially Dutch gin distilled from potatoes. [from German *Schnapps*, dram of liquor]

Schnauzer /ˈʃnaʊtsə(r)/ *noun* a German breed of dog, terrier-like with a thick wiry coat, marked eyebrows, moustache, and beard. The top of the head is flat, and it has short pendulous ears. [from German *Schnauze*, snout]

schnitzel /ˈʃnɪtsl/ *noun* a veal cutlet. [from German *Schnitzel*]

scholar / 'skɒlə(r)/ *noun* **1** a learned person, especially an academic. **2** a person who studies; a pupil or student. **3** a person receiving a scholarship. [from Latin *scholaris*; see SCHOOL]

⊟ **1** academic, intellectual, *colloq.* egghead, authority, expert. **2** pupil, student.
🔁 **1** dunce, ignoramus.

scholarly *adj.* **1** showing evidence of extensive study. **2** typical of work produced by scholars: *a book too scholarly to be popular.*

⊟ **1** learned, erudite, knowledgeable, well-read. **2** academic, intellectual, highbrow.
🔁 **1** uneducated, illiterate.

scholarship *noun* **1** a sum of money awarded for the purposes of further study, usually to an outstanding student. **2** the achievements or methods of a scholar.

⊟ **1** grant, award, bursary, endowment, fellowship, exhibition. **2** erudition, learning, knowledge, wisdom, education, schooling.

scholastic *adj.* **1** of or relating to learning; academic; educational. **2** of or relating to scholasticism. [from Greek *scholastikos*]

scholasticism *noun* **1** the system of (especially religious and moral) teaching, based on the writings of the Greek philosopher Aristotle, that dominated W Europe in the Middle Ages. **2** stubborn adherence to traditional teaching methods and values.

school[1] — *noun* **1** a place where a formal general education is received especially as a child or teenager. **2** a place offering formal instruction in a particular subject, often part of a university: *art school.* **3** the body of students and teachers that occupy any such place. **4** the period of the day or year during which such a place is open to students: *stay behind after school.* **5** a group of painters, writers, or other artists sharing the same style or master. **6** any activity or set of surroundings as a provider of experience: *factories are the schools of life.* **7** *colloq.* a group of people meeting regularly for some purpose, eg gambling: *a card school.* — *verb* **1** to educate in a school. **2** to give training of a particular kind to. **3** to discipline. [from Greek *schole*, leisure, lecture-place]

⊟ *noun* **2** college, academy, institute, faculty, department. **3** pupils, students, teachers, staff. *verb* **1** educate, teach, instruct, tutor, coach. **2** train, drill, verse, prime, prepare.

school[2] — *noun* a group of fish, whales, or other marine animals swimming together. — *verb intrans.* to form, or move about in, a school. [from Dutch *school*]

schoolchild *noun* a child who attends a school.

schoolhouse *noun* **1** a building used as a school, especially in a rural area. **2** a house for a teacher within the grounds of a school.

schooling *noun* education or instruction, especially received at school.

⊟ education, learning, teaching, instruction, tuition, coaching, training, drill, preparation, grounding.

school-leaver *noun* a young person recently completing a course of education and no longer attending a school.

schoolmarm *noun colloq.* **1** *North Amer., esp. US* a schoolmistress. **2** a woman with old-fashioned manners or attitudes, especially regarding sex.

schoolmarmish *adj.* like or typical of a schoolmarm.

schoolmaster *noun* a male schoolteacher or head of a school.

schoolmistress *noun* a female schoolteacher or head of a school.

schoolteacher *noun* a person who teaches in a school.

schooner / 'skuːnə(r)/ *noun* **1** a fast sailing-ship with two or more masts. **2** a large sherry glass. **3** *North Amer., esp. US* a large beer glass. [in 18c English *skooner* or *scooner*, possibly from dialect *scoon*, to skim]

schottische / ʃɒˈtiːʃ/ *noun* **1** a folk dance, originally from Germany, with short steps and hops, like a slow polka. **2** a piece of music for such a dance. [from German *der schottische Tanz*, the Scottish dance]

schwa / ʃwɑː/ *noun* **1** the indistinct English vowel sound that occurs in unstressed syllables, as in the first and last syllables of *together* in normal speech, and in other words such as *to* and *the* in rapid speech. **2** the phonetic symbol (ə) used to represent this sound. [from Hebrew *schewa*]

sciatic / saɪˈatɪk/ *adj.* **1** relating to the hip or the region round the hip. **2** affected by sciatica. [from Latin *sciaticus*, from Greek *ischion*, hip-joint]

sciatica / saɪˈatɪkə/ *noun* intense and intermittent pain in the lower back, buttocks, and backs of the thighs caused by pressure on the sciatic nerve that runs from the pelvis to the thigh.

SCID *abbrev. Medicine* severe combined immunodeficiency.

science *noun* **1** the systematic observation and classification of natural phenomena in order to learn about them and formulate laws which can then be verified by further investigation. **2** the body of knowledge obtained in this way, or any specific subdivison of it, eg astronomy, chemistry, genetics. **3** any area of knowledge obtained using, or arranged according to, formal principles: *political science.* **4** acquired skill or technique, as opposed to natural ability. [from Latin *scientia*, knowledge]

⊟ **3** discipline, specialization, knowledge. **4** skill, proficiency, technique.

science fiction fiction presenting a view of life in the future, especially incorporating space travel and other technological developments the writer imagines will be current at the future time portrayed.

science park a group of establishments combining scientific research with commerce, often attached to a university.

scientific *adj.* **1** of, relating to, or used in science. **2** displaying the kind of principled approach characteristic of science: *not very scientific but it works.*

⊟ **2** methodical, systematic, controlled, regulated, analytical, exact, precise, accurate, thorough.

scientifically *adv.* in a scientific way; by scientific means.

scientist *noun* a student of or expert in science.

sci-fi / 'saɪfaɪ/ *noun colloq.* science fiction.

scilicet / 'saɪlɪsɛt/ *adv. formal, only in writing* namely; that is to say. [from Latin *scire licet*, it is permitted to know]

scimitar / 'sɪmɪtə(r)/ *noun* a Middle-Eastern sword with a curved single-edged blade, usually broadening towards the tip. [perhaps from Persian *shimshir*]

scintilla / sɪnˈtɪlə/ *noun literary* a hint or trace; an iota. [from Latin *scintilla*, spark]

scintillate *verb intrans.* **1** *Physics, said of an atom* to emit a flash of light after having been struck by a photon or a particle of ionizing radiation. **2** to sparkle or send out sparks. **3** to capture attention with one's vitality or wit. [from Latin *scintilla*, spark]

scintillating *adj.* **1** that sparkles or flashes. **2** that excites or stimulates.

⊟ BRILLIANT, DAZZLING. **1** sparkling, glittering, flashing, bright, shining. **2** exciting, stimulating, lively, animated, vivacious, ebullient, witty.
🔁 DULL.

scintillation *noun* **1** *Physics* the emission of a flash of light by an atom as it returns to its normal energy state after having been raised to a higher energy state by collision with a photon or a particle of ionizing radiation. **2** *Astron.* the twinkling of stars due to rapid changes in their brightness caused by variations in the density of the atmosphere through which the light rays pass.

scintillation counter *Physics* a device for detecting very low levels of radiation. It contains a medium, usually a solid or liquid, which scintillates (emits light) when charged particles or radiation fall on it. The scintillation medium is connected to a photomultiplier, which produces detectable pulses of current (corresponding to each scintillation) that are either counted or added together to give a numerical value.

scion /ˈsaɪən/ *noun* **1** *Bot.* a piece of plant tissue, usually a shoot, that is inserted into a cut in the outer stem of another plant (the *stock*) when making a graft. **2** a descendant or offspring. [from Old French *cion*]

scissors *pl. noun* a one-handed cutting tool with two long blades joined in the middle so as to pivot with cutting edges coming together. [from Latin *cisorium*, cutting tool]

sclera /ˈsklɪərə/ see SCLEROTIC.

sclerosis *noun* abnormal hardening or thickening of body tissue, organs, or blood vessels. [from Greek *skleros*, hard]

sclerotic — *noun Anat.* in vertebrates, the white fibrous outer layer of the eyeball, which is modified at the front of the eye to form the transparent cornea. Also called SCLERA — *adj.* **1** hard, firm. **2** relating to or affected with sclerosis. [from Greek *skleros*, hard]

scoff[1] — *verb intrans.* **1** to express scorn or contempt. **2** (**scoff at someone** or **something**) to jeer at; to mock or deride. — *noun* an expression of scorn; a jeer.

⬛ *verb* **1** jeer, sneer, laugh, poke fun. **2** jeer at, mock, ridicule, deride, scorn, belittle, disparage, *colloq.* knock. *noun* jeer, sneer, gibe, taunt.

🇫🇦 *verb* **1** praise, compliment, flatter.

scoff[2] — *verb trans. intrans.*, *colloq.* to eat (food) rapidly and greedily. — *noun slang* food. [from Scots *scaff*, food]

⬛ *verb* eat, devour, gobble, guzzle, *colloq.* wolf, gulp.

scoffing *adj.* scornful.

scold — *verb* to reprimand angrily. — *noun*, *old use* a nagging or quarrelsome person, especially a woman. [from Norse *skald*]

⬛ *verb* reprimand, reprove, chide, *colloq.* tell off, *colloq.* tick off, rebuke, take to task, admonish, upbraid, reproach, blame, censure, lecture, nag.

🇫🇦 *verb* praise, commend.

scolding *noun* a bout of fault-finding, a telling-off.

⬛ reprimand, castigation, *colloq.* telling-off, *colloq.* ticking-off, *colloq.* dressing-down, reproof, rebuke, lecture, talking-to, *colloq.* earful.

🇫🇦 praise, commendation.

scollop same as SCALLOP.

sconce *noun* a candlestick with a handle, or one fixed by bracket to a wall. [from Latin *absconsa*, dark lantern]

scone /skɒn, skəʊn/ *noun* a small round flattish plain cake, usually halved and spread with butter and jam. [from Scots *scone*]

scoop — *verb* **1** (*also* **scoop something up**) to lift or dig it with a sweeping circular movement. **2** (*also* **scoop something out**) to empty or hollow it with such movements. **3** to do better than (rival newspapers) in being the first to publish a story. — *noun* **1** any of various spoon-like implements for handling or serving food. **2** a hollow shovel-like part of a mechanical digger. **3** a scooping movement. **4** a quantity scooped. **5** a news story printed by one newspaper in advance of all others. [from Old Dutch *schoppe*, shovel]

⬛ *verb* **1**, **2** dig. **1** shovel, ladle, spoon, bail. **2** gouge, hollow, empty, excavate. *noun* **1** ladle, spoon, dipper. **5** exclusive, coup, inside story, revelation, exposé, sensation.

scoot *verb intrans.*, *colloq.* to go away quickly.

scooter *noun* **1** a child's toy vehicle consisting of a board on a two-wheeled frame with tall handlebars, propelled by pushing against the ground with one foot while standing on the board with the other. **2** (*also* **motor-scooter**) a small-engined motorcycle with a protective front shield curving back at the bottom to form a supporting board for the feet which joins the casing containing the engine at the back of the vehicle.

scope *noun* **1** the size (of a subject or topic). **2** the range of topics dealt with. **3** the limits within which there is the freedom or opportunity to act. **4** range of understanding: *beyond his scope*. [from Greek *skopos*, point watched]

⬛ **1** size, extent, reach, span, breadth. **2** range, compass, field, area, sphere, ambit, coverage. **3** latitude, leeway, freedom, liberty, opportunity, room, elbow-room, space, capacity, terms of reference, confines.

-scope *combining form* forming words denoting an instrument for viewing, examining, or detecting: *telescope*. [from Greek *skopeein*, to view]

-scopic *combining form* forming words: **1** relating to instruments with names ending in -*scope*: *telescopic*. **2** relating to observation or observed size: *microscopic*.

-scopy *combining form* forming words denoting observation or examination, usually with the use of instruments ending in -*scope*: *microscopy*.

scorbutic /skɔːˈbjuːtɪk/ *adj. Medicine* relating to or suffering from scurvy. [from Latin *scorbuticus*]

scorch — *verb* **1** *trans.*, *intrans.* to burn or be burned slightly on the surface. **2** to dry up or wither. **3** to injure with severe criticism or scorn. — *noun* **1** a scorched area. **2** a mark made by scorching. [from Middle English *skorken*]

⬛ *verb* **1**, **2** sear. **1** burn, singe, char, blacken. **2** parch, shrivel, wither.

scorcher *noun colloq.* an extremely hot day.

scorching *adj.* that scorches; burning; extremely hot.

⬛ searing, red-hot, burning, boiling, baking, roasting, sizzling, blistering, sweltering, torrid, tropical.

score — *verb* **1** *trans.*, *intrans.* to achieve (a point, etc) in games. **2** *trans.*, *intrans.* to keep a record of points gained during (a game). **3** to make cuts or scratches in the surface of; to mark (eg a line) by a shallow cut. **4** (*also* **score something out**) to cancel it with a line drawn through it. **5** to be equivalent to (a number of points): *black king scores three*. **6 a** to break down (music) into parts for individual instruments or voices. **b** to adapt (music) for instruments or voices other than those originally intended. **7** to compose music for (a film or play). **8** *intrans.* to achieve a rating; to be judged or regarded: *always score low in written tests/this film scores high for entertainment value*. **9** *intrans.*, *slang* to obtain drugs for illegal use. **10** (**score with someone**) *slang, often offensive* to succeed in having sexual intercourse with them. — *noun* **1** a number of points, etc scored. **2** an act of scoring a point, etc. **3** a scratch or shallow cut, especially made as a mark. **4** a set of twenty: *three score* **5** (**scores**) very many; lots: *have scores of letters to write*. **6** *colloq.* (**the score**) the current situation; the essential facts: *what's the score?* **7** a written copy of music scored. **8**

the music from a film or play. **9 (the score)** a reason; grounds: *accepted on the score of suitability.* **10** matter; concern; aspect: *no worries on that score.* **11** a grievance or grudge: *settle old scores.* **12** a record of amounts owed. **13** *slang* a successful attempt to obtain drugs for illegal use. **14** *slang, often offensive* an act of sexual intercourse, regarded as a conquest or achievement. **— over the score** *colloq.* beyond reasonable limits; unfair. **score off someone** to humiliate them for personal advantage. [from Anglo-Saxon *scoru*]

⊟ *verb* **1** win, gain. **2** count, record. **3** cut, scratch, scrape, graze, mark, groove, gouge, incise, engrave, indent, nick, slash. **4** cancel, delete, cross out. *noun* **1** result, total, sum, tally, points, marks. **3** scratch, line, groove, mark, nick, notch. **10** matter, subject, question, issue, concern, aspect. **11** grievance, grudge, complaint, dispute, quarrel, argument, bone of contention.

scoreboard *noun* a board on which the score in a game is displayed, altered as the score changes.

scorer *noun* **1** a person who scores a point, etc. **2** a person who keeps a written record of the score during a game.

scorn — *noun* mocking or disparaging contempt. — *verb* **1** to treat with scorn. **2** to reject with scorn. [from Old French *escarn*, mockery]

⊟ *noun* contempt, scornfulness, disdain, sneering, derision, mockery, ridicule, sarcasm, disparagement, disgust. *verb* **1** despise, look down on, disdain, sneer at, scoff at, deride, mock, laugh at. **2** reject, refuse, spurn, dismiss.
⊞ *noun* admiration, respect. *verb* **1** admire, respect.

scornful *adj.* contemptuous; mocking; disparaging.

⊟ contemptuous, disdainful, supercilious, haughty, arrogant, sneering, scoffing, derisive, mocking, jeering, sarcastic, scathing, disparaging, insulting, slighting, dismissive.
⊞ admiring, respectful.

Scorpio *noun* (PL. **Scorpios**) **1** *Astron.* (*also* **Scorpius**) the Scorpion, a large bright zodiacal constellation of the S hemisphere. **2** the eighth sign of the zodiac, the Scorpion. **3** a person born under the sign, between 23 Oct and 21 Nov.

scorpion *noun* any of about 650 species of an invertebrate animal belonging to the order Scorpiones, and related to the spider, found in hot regions, especially deserts, worldwide, having eight legs, powerful pincers resembling the claws of a lobster, and a long thin segmented abdomen or 'tail' that is carried arched over its back, and bears a sharp poisonous sting at the tip. [from Greek *skorpios*]

Scot *noun* a native of Scotland. [from Latin *Scottus*]

Scot. *abbrev.* **1** Scotland. **2** Scottish.

Scotch — *adj.*, *said of things, especially products; not now usually said of people* Scottish. — *noun* Scotch whisky. [from SCOTTISH]

scotch — *verb* **1** to ruin or hinder (eg plans). **2** to reveal (especially rumours) to be untrue. — *noun* any of the lines marked on the ground for hopscotch.

Scotch broth a thick soup made with barley and chopped vegetables.

Scotch egg a hard-boiled egg in a sausage meat case, fried in breadcrumbs.

Scotch mist very fine rain, common in the Scottish Highlands.

Scotch terrier see SCOTTISH TERRIER.

Scotch whisky whisky distilled in Scotland from barley or other grain.

scot-free *adj.* unpunished or unharmed. [from obsolete *scot*, payment, tax]

Scots — *adj.*, *said especially of law and language* Scottish. — *noun* any of the dialects related to English used in (especially Lowland) Scotland. [from Scots *Scottis*, Scottish]

Scotsman or **Scotswoman** *noun* a native of Scotland.

Scots pine a coniferous tree of Europe and Asia, the only native British pine.

Scottie see SCOTTISH TERRIER.

Scottish *adj.* of Scotland or its people. [from Anglo-Saxon *Scottisc*]

Scottish terrier a breed of dog with a long body, short legs, and a short erect tail. It has a long head, with eyebrows, moustache, and beard, short erect ears, and a thick wiry coat, almost reaching the ground. Also called SCOTTIE, SCOTCH TERRIER.

scoundrel *noun* a person without principles or morals; a rogue or villain.

scour [1] — *verb* **1** to clean by hard rubbing. **2** to flush clean with a jet or current of water. **3** to wash sheep wool in order to remove grease and impurities. — *noun* **1** an act of scouring. **2** (**scours**) diarrhoea in animal livestock. [from Latin *excurare*, to cleanse]

⊟ *verb* **1** scrub, clean, scrape, abrade, rub, polish, burnish. **2** flush, purge, cleanse, wash.

scour [2] *verb* to make an exhaustive search of (eg an area). [from Norse *skur*, storm, shower]

⊟ search, hunt, comb, drag, ransack, rummage, forage, rake.

scourer *noun* **1** a person who scours. **2** a device or container for scouring.

scourge /skɜːdʒ/ — *noun* **1** a cause of great suffering to many people: *cancer is the scourge of Western society.* **2** a whip used for punishing. — *verb* **1** to cause suffering to; to afflict. **2** to whip. [from Latin *excoriare*, to flay]

⊟ *noun* **1** affliction, misfortune, torment, terror, bane, evil, curse, plague. **2** whip, lash. *verb* **1** afflict, torment, curse, plague, devastate. **2** whip, flog, beat, lash, flail, thrash, punish, chastise, discipline.
⊞ *noun* **1** blessing, godsend, boon.

Scouse /skaʊs/ *colloq.* — *noun* **1** the dialect of English spoken in Liverpool. **2** a Scouser. — *adj.* of Liverpool, its people, or their dialect. [a short form of *lobscouse*, a sailor's stew]

Scouser /ˈskaʊsə(r)/ *noun colloq.* a native of Liverpool.

scout — *noun* **1** *Mil.* a person or group sent out to observe the enemy and bring back information. **2** (**talent scout**) a person whose job is to discover and recruit talented people, especially in the fields of sport and entertainment. **3** (*often* **Scout**; *formerly* **Boy Scout**) a member of the Scout Association, a worldwide youth organization promoting outdoor skills and community spirit. **4** *colloq.* a search: *have a scout around for it in my bag.* — *verb intrans.* **1** to act as a scout. **2** (*often* **scout about** or **around**) *colloq.* to make a search: *scouting about for new premises.* [from Old French *escouter*]

⊟ *noun* **1** spy, vanguard, outrider, lookout. **2** recruiter, spotter. **4** search, hunt, look. *verb* **1** reconnoitre, explore, survey, watch, observe, spy, snoop. **2** search, hunt, look.

Scouter *noun* an adult leader in the Scout Association.

scow /skaʊ/ *noun* a large flat-bottomed barge for freight. [from Dutch *schouw*]

scowl — *verb intrans.* **1** to wrinkle the brow in displeasure or anger. **2** to look disapprovingly, angrily, or threateningly. — *noun* a scowling expression. [from Middle English *scowl*]

⊟ *verb* FROWN. **2** glower, glare, pout, grimace. *noun* frown, glare, pout, grimace.
⊞ *verb* SMILE, GRIN, BEAM. *noun* smile, grin, beam.

SCR *abbrev.* senior common room.

scrabble — *verb intrans.* to scratch, grope, or struggle frantically. — *noun* an act of scrabbling. [from Dutch *schrabben*, to scratch]

scrag — *noun* 1 (*also* **scrag-end**) the thin part of a neck of mutton or veal, providing poor-quality meat. 2 an unhealthily thin person or animal. — *verb* (**scragged**, **scragging**) *colloq.* 1 to wring the neck of; to throttle. 2 to attack angrily; to beat up. [perhaps from CRAG]

scragginess *noun* being scraggy.

scraggy *adj.* (**scraggier**, **scraggiest**) unhealthily thin; scrawny.

- ▣ scrawny, skinny, thin, lean, lanky, bony, angular, gaunt, undernourished, emaciated, wasted.
- ▣ plump, sleek.

scram *verb intrans.* (**scrammed**, **scramming**) *colloq. often as a command* to go away at once. [perhaps from SCRAMBLE]

scramble — *verb* 1 to crawl or climb using hands and feet, especially frantically. 2 *intrans.* to struggle violently against others: *starving people scrambling to grab food.* 3 to cook (eggs) whisked up with milk. 4 to throw together haphazardly; to jumble. 5 to rewrite (a message) in code form, for secret transmission; to transmit (a message) in a distorted form via an electronic scrambler. 6 *intrans.*, *said of aircraft or air crew* to take off immediately in response to an emergency. — *noun* 1 an act of scrambling. 2 a violent struggle to beat others in getting something. 3 a walk or half-climb over rough ground. 4 an immediate take-off in an emergency. 5 a cross-country motorcycle race. [perhaps from SCRABBLE]

- ▣ *verb* 1 climb, scale, clamber, crawl, shuffle, scrabble, grope. 2 push, jostle, struggle, strive, vie, contend, race, rush, hurry, hasten, run. *noun* 2 struggle, free-for-all, melee, race, dash, rush, hurry, hustle, bustle, commotion, confusion, muddle.

scrambler *noun Electron.* an electronic device that modifies signals transmitted by radio or telephone so that they can only be made intelligible by means of a special decoding device. Scramblers are used to transmit secret communications, to protect television broadcasting rights, etc.

scrambling circuit a circuit used to protect the security of sound, data, or video signals in communication systems. The original signal is coded by a scrambler before transmission and interpreted by a decoder at the receiver. The technique prevents unauthorized personnel gaining access to the signals during transmission.

scramjet *noun* a jet engine in which compressed air is drawn into the engine by means of turbo fans and mixed with fuel to improve combustion at a supersonic speed. [from *supersonic combustion ramjet*]

scrap¹ — *noun* 1 a small piece; a fragment. 2 the smallest piece or amount: *not a scrap of advice.* 3 waste material; waste metal for recycling or re-using. 4 (**scraps**) leftover pieces of food. — *verb* (**scrapped**, **scrapping**) to discard as useless or abandon as unworkable. [from Norse *skrap*]

- ▣ *noun* 1 bit, piece, fragment, part, fraction, crumb, morsel, bite, mouthful, sliver, shred, snippet. 2 atom, iota, grain, particle, mite, trace, vestige. 3 waste, rubbish, junk. 4 leftovers, remnants. *verb* discard, throw away, jettison, shed, drop, dump, *slang* ditch, abandon, cancel, *colloq.* axe, demolish, break up, write off.
- ▣ *verb* recover, restore.

scrap² *colloq.* — *noun* a fight or quarrel. — *verb intrans.* (**scrapped**, **scrapping**) to fight or quarrel.

- ▣ *noun* fight, scuffle, brawl, *colloq.* dust-up, quarrel, row, argument, squabble, wrangle, dispute, disagreement. *verb*

fight, brawl, quarrel, argue, squabble, bicker, wrangle, disagree.

- ▣ *noun* agreement. *verb* agree.

scrapbook *noun* a book with blank pages on which newspaper cuttings, etc can be mounted.

scrape — *verb* 1 to push or drag (something, especially a sharp object) along (a hard or rough surface). 2 *intrans.* to move along a surface with a grazing action. 3 (*also* **scrape something off**) to remove it from a surface with such an action. 4 to damage by such contact: *scraped his elbow.* 5 *intrans.* to make savings through hardship: *scrimp and scrape.* 6 *intrans.* to slide the foot backwards when bowing: *bow and scrape.* — *noun* 1 an instance, or the action, of dragging or grazing. 2 a part damaged or cleaned by scraping. 3 *colloq.* a difficult or embarrassing situation; a predicament. 4 *colloq.* a fight or quarrel. — **scrape through** or **by** to manage or succeed (in doing something) narrowly or with difficulty: *just scraped through the interview.* **scrape something together** or **up** to collect it little by little, usually with difficulty. [from Anglo-Saxon *scrapian*]

- ▣ *verb* 1 scratch, grate, grind, rasp, file, abrade, scour, rub. 3 remove, erase. 4 scratch, graze, skin, bark, scuff.

scraper *noun* 1 a person who scrapes. 2 a scraping tool, instrument, or machine.

scraperboard or **scratchboard** *noun* a technique used mainly by commercial illustrators for producing sharply defined designs similar in appearance to linocuts. The board is coated with two layers, black over white or vice versa, and the artist scrapes or scratches away the top surface using a set of special blades. See also SGRAFFITO.

scrap heap 1 a place where unwanted objects, eg old furniture, are collected. 2 the state of being discarded or abandoned: *consign the idea to the scrap heap.*

scrapie /ˈskreɪpɪ/ *noun Agric.* an often fatal disease of sheep, in which there is progressive degeneration of the central nervous system. In one form of the disease there is uncontrollable itching, which the animal attempts to relieve by rubbing itself against trees and other objects, resulting in wool loss. [from Old English *scrapian* or Old Norse *skrapa*]

scrappily *adv.* in a scrappy way.

scrappiness *noun* a scrappy state.

scrappy *adj.* (**scrappier**, **scrappiest**) not uniform, continuous, or flowing; disjointed; fragmented; bitty.

- ▣ disjointed, fragmented, bitty, piecemeal, fragmentary, incomplete, sketchy, superficial, slapdash, slipshod.
- ▣ complete, finished.

scratch — *verb* 1 to rub or drag (a sharp or pointed object) across (a surface), causing damage or making marks. 2 to make (eg a mark) by such action. 3 *trans., intrans.* to rub (the skin) lightly with the fingernails, eg to relieve itching. 4 (*usually* **scratch something out** or **off**) to cross it out or cancel it. 5 *intrans.* to make a grating noise. 6 *intrans.* to withdraw from a contest. — *noun* 1 a mark made by scratching. 2 an act of scratching. 3 a superficial wound or minor injury. — *adj.* 1 hastily got together; improvised: *a scratch meal.* 2 *said of a competitor* not given a handicap. — **from scratch** from the beginning; without the benefit of preparation or previous experience. **scratch the surface** to deal only superficially with an issue or problem. **up to scratch** *colloq.* meeting the required or expected standard. [from Middle English *scratch*]

- ▣ *verb* 1 mark, gouge, score, cut, incise, etch, engrave, scrape, scuff, graze, claw, gash, lacerate. *noun* 1 mark, line, scrape, scuff. 3 graze, abrasion, laceration.

scratch card a form of lottery card with a thin opaque film, which is scratched off to reveal the allocated numbers printed beneath.

scratchily *adv.* in a scratchy way.

scratchiness *noun* being scratchy.

scratch video a video film produced by piecing together images from other films.

scratchy *adj.* (**scratchier, scratchiest**) **1** making the marks or noises of scratching. **2** causing or likely to cause itching.

scrawl — *verb trans., intrans.* to write or draw untidily or hurriedly. — *noun* untidy or illegible handwriting.

scrawly *adj.* (**scrawlier, scrawliest**) *said of writing* careless, untidy.

scrawniness *noun* a scrawny state.

scrawny *adj.* (**scrawnier, scrawniest**) very thin and bony.
. . . .

▣ scraggy, skinny, thin, lean, lanky, angular, bony, underfed, undernourished, emaciated.

▣ fat, plump.
. . . .

scream — *verb* **1** *trans., intrans.* to utter or cry out in a loud high-pitched voice, eg in fear, pain, or anger. **2** *intrans.* to laugh uproariously. **3** *intrans.* (**scream past, through,** etc) to go at great speed, especially making a shrill noise: *the train screamed through the tunnel.* **4** (**scream at someone**) *usually said of something unpleasant or unwelcome* to be patently obvious or apparent: *the orange curtains scream at you / his incompetence screamed at them.* — *noun* **1** a loud piercing cry or other sound. **2** *colloq.* an extremely amusing person, thing, or event. [from Anglo-Saxon *scræmen*]
. . . .

▣ *verb* **1** shriek, screech, cry, shout, yell, bawl, roar, howl, wail, squeal. *noun* **1** shriek, screech, cry, shout, yell, roar, howl, wail, squeal.
. . . .

scree *noun Geol.* **1** loose fragments of rock debris that cover a mountain slope, or pile up below bare rock faces or summits. **2** a slope covered with such material. [from Norse *skritha,* landslip]

screech — *noun* a harsh shrill cry, voice, or noise. — *verb* **1** *trans., intrans.* to utter a screech or as a screech. **2** *intrans.* to make a screech: *screeching brakes.* [from Middle English *scrichen*]

screech owl the barn owl, whose call is more of a screech than a hoot.

screechy *adj.* (**screechier, screechiest**) like a screech, shrill and harsh.

screed *noun* a long, often tedious, speech or piece of writing. [from Anglo-Saxon *screade,* shred]

screen — *noun* **1** a movable set of hinged panels, used to partition part of a room off for privacy. **2** a panel or something similar used for concealment or protection, especially against strong heat or light. **3** the part of a television set on which the images are formed. **4** a white (usually cloth) surface on to which films or slides are projected. **5** (*often* **the screen**) the medium of cinema or television: *a star of stage and screen.* **6** *Cricket* a sight-screen. **7** a windscreen. — *verb* **1** to protect, cover, or conceal with a screen. **2** (*usually* **screen something off**) to separate or partition it with a screen. **3** to show at the cinema or on television. **4** to subject to an examination, eg to test (someone) for reliability or check for the presence of disease. [from Old French *escran*]
. . . .

▣ *noun* **1** partition, divider. **2** shield, guard, cover, mask, veil, shelter, shade, awning, canopy. *verb* **1** shield, protect, guard, cover, mask, veil, cloak, shroud, hide, conceal, shelter, shade. **2** separate, partition, divide. **3** show, present, broadcast. **4** test, examine, scan, vet, sort, grade, sift, sieve, filter, process.

▣ *verb* **1** uncover, expose.
. . . .

screen dump *Comput.* the action of sending the contents of a screen display to a printer or file, eg by pressing a specified function key.

screenplay *noun* the text of a film, comprising dialogue, stage directions, and details for sets.

screen printing or **screen process** a printing technique in which ink is forced through a fine silk or nylon mesh, with areas to be left blank blocked chemically.

screensaver *noun Comput.* a program which temporarily blanks out a screen display, or displays a preset pattern, when a computer is switched on but is not in active use.

screen test a filmed audition to test an actor's suitability for a film role.

screen writer a writer of screenplays for film, television, etc.

screw — *noun* **1** a type of nail with a spiral ridge down its shaft and a slot in its head, driven firmly into place using a twisting action with a special tool. **2** any object similar in shape or function. **3** *Snooker, Billiards* a shot in which sidespin or backspin is put on the ball. **4** *slang* a prison officer. **5** *coarse slang* an act of sexual intercourse. **6** *coarse slang* a person judged by sexual prowess or suitability as a sexual partner. **7** *slang* wages. — *verb* **1** to twist (a screw) into place. **2 a** (**screw something up** or **together**) to attach or assemble it by means of screws. **b** (**screw up** or **together**) to be attached or assembled by means of screws. **3** to push or pull with a twisting action. **4** (**screw something from** or **out of someone**) *colloq.* to obtain it by intense persuasion or threats: *tried to screw more money out of them.* **5** *colloq.* to swindle. **6** *Snooker, Billiards* to put sidespin or backspin on (the cue ball). **7** *trans., intrans., coarse slang* to have sexual intercourse with (someone). — **have one's head screwed on the right way** *colloq.* to be a sensible person. **have a screw loose** *colloq.* to be slightly mad or crazy. **put the screws on someone** *colloq.* to use pressure on them, especially in the form of threats of violence. **screw someone up** *North Amer. slang* to cause them to become extremely anxious, nervous, or psychologically disturbed. **screw something up** *slang* to ruin or bungle it. **screw up one's courage** to prepare oneself for an ordeal or difficulty. [from Old French *escroue*]
. . . .

▣ *verb* **2** attach, fasten, adjust, tighten. **3** turn, wind, twist, wring, distort, wrinkle. **4** extort from, extract from, squeeze out of.
. . . .

screwball *noun North Amer., esp. US slang* a crazy person; an eccentric.

screwdriver *noun* a hand-held tool with a metal shaft whose shaped end fits into the slot on a screw's head, turned repeatedly to twist a screw into position.

screwed-up *adj. slang, said of a person* extremely anxious, nervous, or psychologically disturbed.

screw top 1 a round lid that is screwed off and on to open and re-seal a bottle or other container. **2** a container with such a top.

screw-top *adj.* having a screw top.

screwy *adj.* (**screwier, screwiest**) *colloq.* crazy; eccentric.

scribble — *verb* **1** *trans., intrans.* to write quickly or untidily. **2** *intrans.* to draw meaningless lines or shapes absentmindedly. — *noun* **1** untidy or illegible handwriting. **2** meaningless written lines or shapes. [from Latin *scribere,* to write]
. . . .

▣ *verb* SCRAWL. **1** write, jot. **2** doodle.
. . . .

scribbler *noun, derog.* a worthless writer.

scribbly *adj.* (**scribblier, scribbliest**) like a scribble; scribbled.

scribe *noun* **1** a person employed to make handwritten copies of documents before printing was invented. **2** a Jewish lawyer or teacher of law in biblical times. **3** a tool with a pointed blade for scoring lines on wood or metal. [from Latin *scriba,* from *scribere,* to write]

目 1 writer, copyist, amanuensis, secretary, clerk.

scrim *noun* heavy cotton fabric used as lining in upholstery, and in bookbinding.

scrimmage — *noun* a fist-fight or brawl. — *verb intrans.* to take part in a scrimmage. [a variant of SKIRMISH]

scrimp *verb intrans.* to live economically; to be frugal or sparing: *scrimp and save.* [from Scot. *scrimp*]

scrimpy *adj.* (**scrimpier, scrimpiest**) scanty.

scrimshank *verb intrans., colloq.* to evade work or duties.

scrimshanker *noun* a person who evades work or duties, a skiver.

scrip *noun* 1 a scrap of writing paper. 2 *colloq.* a doctor's prescription. 3 *Commerce* a provisional certificate issued before a formal share certificate is drawn up. [a shortened form of PRESCRIPTION and SUBSCRIPTION]

script — *noun* 1 the printed text, or the spoken dialogue, of a play, film, or broadcast. 2 a system of characters used for writing; an alphabet: *Chinese script.* 3 handwriting. 4 an examination candidate's answer paper. — *verb* to write the script of (a play, film, or broadcast). [from Latin *scriptum*, from *scribere*, to write]

目 *noun* 1 text, lines, words, dialogue, screenplay, libretto, book. 2 alphabet, characters, letters. 3 writing, handwriting, hand, longhand, calligraphy.

scriptural *adj.* relating to or derived from scripture.

scripture *noun* 1 the sacred writings of a religion. 2 (**Scriptures**) the Christian Bible. [from Latin *scriptura*, from *scribere*, to write]

scriptwriter *noun* a person who writes scripts.

scrivener *noun Hist.* a person who drafts, or makes handwritten copies of, legal or other official documents. [related to SCRIBE]

scrofula /ˈskrɒfjʊlə/ *noun Medicine old use* former name for tuberculosis of the lymph nodes, especially of the neck. [from Latin *scrofulae*, from *scrofa*, a sow, apparently prone to it]

scrofulous *adj.* affected by scrofula.

scroll — *noun* 1 a roll of paper or parchment written on, now only a ceremonial format, eg for academic degrees. 2 an ancient text in this format: *the Dead Sea Scrolls.* 3 a decorative spiral shape, eg in stonework or handwriting. — *verb trans., intrans.* (*often* **scroll up** *or* **down**) to move the displayed text on a computer screen up or down to bring into view data that cannot all be seen at the same time. [from Middle English *scrowle*]

Scrooge *noun* a miserly person. [from the miserly character in Charles Dickens's *A Christmas Carol*]

scrotal /ˈskrəʊtəl/ *adj.* relating to or in the region of the scrotum.

scrotum /ˈskrəʊtəm/ *noun* (PL. **scrota, scrotums**) the bag of skin enclosing the testicles in mammals. [from Latin *scrotum*]

scrounge *verb trans., intrans. colloq.* to get (something) by shamelessly asking or begging; to cadge or sponge: *scrounged a fiver off his old granny.* [from dialect *scrunge*, to steal]

目 beg, cadge, sponge.

scrounger *noun* a person who scrounges.

目 cadger, sponger, parasite.

scrub[1] — *verb* (**scrubbed, scrubbing**) 1 *trans., intrans.* to rub hard, especially with a brush, to remove dirt. 2 to clean by hard rubbing. 3 (*also* **scrub up**) *said of a surgeon, etc* to wash the hands and arms thoroughly before taking part in an operation. 4 *colloq.* to cancel or abandon (eg

plans). — *noun* an act of scrubbing. [from Old German *schrubben*]

目 *verb* 1 rub, brush. 2 clean, wash, cleanse, scour. 4 cancel, abandon, give up, drop, discontinue, abolish.

scrub[2] *noun* 1 an area of land with a poor soil or low rainfall, covered with vegetation consisting mainly of dwarf or stunted trees and evergreen shrubs. 2 an inferior domestic animal of mixed or unknown parentage. 3 a small or insignificant person. [a variant of SHRUB]

scrubber *noun offensive slang* 1 an unattractive woman. 2 a woman who regularly indulges in casual sex.

scrubby *adj.* (**scrubbier, scrubbiest**) 1 covered with scrub. 2 stunted. 3 insignificant.

scrubland *noun* an area covered with scrub.

scruff[1] *noun* the back of the neck; the nape.

scruff[2] *noun colloq.* a scruffy person.

scruffily *adv.* in a scruffy way.

scruffiness *noun* a scruffy state.

scruffy *adj.* (**scruffier, scruffiest**) shabbily dressed and untidy-looking.

目 untidy, messy, unkempt, dishevelled, bedraggled, shabby, worn-out, ragged, tattered, slovenly, disreputable, seedy.
目 tidy, well-dressed, respectable.

scrum — *noun* 1 *Rugby* a formation of players from both teams, hunched and with arms and heads tightly interlocked; a re-starting of play in which the ball is thrown into such a formation and struggled for with the feet. 2 *colloq.* a riotous struggle. — *verb intrans.* (**scrummed, scrumming**) (*usually* **scrum down**) to form a scrum. [a shortening of SCRUMMAGE]

scrum half *Rugby* the player from each side who puts the ball into scrums.

scrummage *Rugby* — *noun* a scrum. — *verb intrans.* to form a scrum. [a variant of SCRIMMAGE]

scrummy *adj.* (**scrummier, scrummiest**) *colloq.* scrumptious.

scrumptious *adj. colloq.* 1 delicious. 2 delightful.

scrumpy *noun* (PL. **scrumpies**) strong dry cider with a harsh taste, especially as brewed in SW England. [from dialect *scrump*, withered apples]

scrunch — *verb* 1 *trans., intrans.* to crunch or crumple, or become crunched or crumpled. 2 *intrans.* to make a crunching sound. — *noun* an act, or the sound, of scrunching.

scrunch-dry *verb* to squeeze (hair) into bunches during blow-drying to give it more body.

scruple — *noun* 1 (*usually* **scruples**) a sense of moral responsibility that makes one reluctant or unwilling to do wrong: *has no scruples.* 2 a unit of weight equal to 20 grains. — *verb intrans.* to be hesitant or unwilling because of scruples: *wouldn't scruple to steal if we were starving.* [from Latin *scrupulus*, pebble, anxiety]

目 *noun* 1 reluctance, hesitation, qualms, misgivings, standards, morals, principles, ethics. *verb* hesitate, think twice, hold back, shrink.

scrupulous *adj.* 1 taking great care to do nothing morally wrong. 2 paying careful attention to even the smallest details.

目 1 principled, moral, ethical, honourable, upright. 2 painstaking, meticulous, conscientious, careful, rigorous, strict, exact, precise, minute, nice.
目 1 unscrupulous, unprincipled. 2 superficial, careless.

scrupulously *adv.* 1 in a scrupulous way. 2 with great attention to detail.

scrutineer *noun* a person who scrutinises something, especially the collecting and counting of votes.

scrutinize or **scrutinise** *verb* to subject to scrutiny; to look at carefully.

▣ examine, inspect, study, scan, analyse, sift, investigate, probe, search, explore.

scrutiny *noun* (PL. **scrutinies**) **1** a close and thorough examination or inspection. **2** a penetrating or critical look. [from Latin *scrutari*, to search]

▣ **1** examination, inspection, study, analysis, investigation, inquiry, search, exploration.

SCSI /'skʌzɪ/ *abbrev. Comput.* Small Computer Systems Interface, a control system that allows communication between a computer and a device such as a hard disk.

scuba /'sku:bə/ *noun* a portable breathing device for underwater divers, consisting of one or two cylinders of compressed air connected to a mouthpiece via a breathing tube. [from *self-contained underwater breathing apparatus*]

Scud *noun* a surface-to-surface missile of a kind made in the former Soviet Union.

scud — *verb intrans.* (**scudded**, **scudding**) **1** *said especially of clouds* to sweep quickly across the sky. **2** *Naut.* to sail swiftly under the force of a strong wind. — *noun* cloud, rain, or spray driven by the wind.

scuff — *verb trans., intrans.* **1** to graze or scrape, or become grazed or scraped, through wear. **2** to drag (the feet) when walking. — *noun* an area worn away by scuffing. [imitative]

▣ *verb* **1** graze, scrape, scratch, abrade, rub, brush.

scuffle — *noun* a confused fight or struggle. — *verb intrans.* to take part in a scuffle.

▣ *noun* fight, scrap, tussle, brawl, fray, set-to, rumpus, commotion, disturbance, affray. *verb* fight, scrap, tussle, brawl, grapple, struggle, contend, clash.

scull — *noun* **1** either of a pair of short light oars used by a lone rower. **2** a racing boat propelled by a solitary rower using a pair of such oars. **3** a large single oar at the stern, moved from side to side to propel a boat. — *verb* to propel with a scull or sculls.

sculler *noun* a person who sculls or rows.

scullery *noun* (PL. **sculleries**) a room, attached to the kitchen in a large house, where basic kitchen work, eg washing up and chopping vegetables, is done. [from Old French *escuelerie*]

sculpt *verb* **1** *trans., intrans.* to carve or model (clay, etc). **2** to create (a solid model of something) in clay, etc. **3** to create a solid model of (someone or something) in clay, etc. [from Latin *sculpere*, to carve]

▣ SCULPTURE, CARVE, MODEL. **2** cut, chisel, hew, mould, cast, form, shape, fashion.

sculptor *noun* a person who practises sculpture.

sculptural /'skʌlptʃərəl/ *adj.* **1** relating to sculpture. **2** having the qualities of sculpture.

sculpture — *noun* **1** the art of carving or modelling with clay, wood, stone, plaster, etc. **2** a work or works of art produced in this way. — *verb trans., intrans.* to sculpt.

sculptured *adj., said of physical features* fine and regular, like those of figures in classical sculpture.

scum — *noun* **1** dirt or waste matter floating on the surface of a liquid. **2** *colloq., derog.* a contemptible person or people. — *verb* (**scummed**, **scumming**) to remove the scum from (a liquid). [from Old Dutch *schum*, foam]

▣ *noun* **1** froth, foam, film, impurities, dross. **2** dregs, rubbish, trash.

scumbag *noun derog. slang* a contemptible person.

scumbling *noun Art* a technique in painting, developed by the Venetian school, in which colour is applied using a dragging, stippling, or dabbing motion to produce a textured effect. [perhaps related to SCUM]

scummy *adj.* (**scummier**, **scummiest**) **1** covered with a layer of scum. **2** *slang* contemptible; despicable.

scupper[1] *verb* (**scuppered**, **scuppering**) **1** *colloq.* to ruin or put an end to (eg plans). **2** to deliberately sink (a ship).

scupper[2] *noun Naut.* a hole or pipe in a ship's side through which water is drained off the deck.

scurf *noun* **1** dandruff. **2** any flaking or peeling substance. [from Anglo-Saxon *scurf*]

scurfy *adj.* (**scurfier**, **scurfiest**) covered or affected with scurf.

scurrility *noun* **1** being scurrilous. **2** a scurrilous comment or remark.

scurrilous *adj.* insulting or abusive, and unjustly damaging to the reputation: *scurrilous remarks*. [from Latin *scurrilis*, from *scurra*, buffoon]

▣ rude, offensive, abusive, insulting, disparaging, defamatory, slanderous, libellous, scandalous, salacious.
▣ polite, courteous, complimentary.

scurry — *verb intrans.* (**scurries**, **scurried**) (**scurry along**, **away**, etc) to move hurriedly, especially with short quick steps. — *noun* (PL. **scurries**) **1** an act, or sound, of scurrying. **2** a sudden brief gust or fall, eg of wind or snow; a flurry. [from *hurry-scurry*, a reduplication of HURRY]

▣ *verb* scamper, scuttle, dash, rush, hurry, hasten, bustle, scramble, scoot, dart, run, sprint, race, fly.

scurvy — *noun Medicine* a disease caused by deficiency of vitamin C due to lack of fresh fruit and vegetables in the diet. It is characterized by swollen bleeding gums, subcutaneous bleeding, anaemia, bruising, and pain in the joints. — *adj.* (**scurvier**, **scurviest**) vile; contemptible. [from Anglo-Saxon *scurf*]

scut *noun* a short tail, especially of a rabbit, hare, or deer. [from Middle English *scut*]

scutellum /skjʊ'teləm/ *noun Bot.* a structure, supposed to be the cotyledon, by which a grass embryo absorbs the endosperm. [from Latin *scutella*, tray]

scuttle[1] *noun* a container for a small amount of coal, usually kept near a fire. [from Anglo-Saxon *scutel*]

scuttle[2] — *verb intrans.* to move quickly with short steps; to scurry. — *noun* a scuttling pace or movement. [related to SCUD]

scuttle[3] — *verb* **1** to deliberately sink (a ship) by making holes in it. **2** to ruin (eg plans). — *noun* a lidded opening in a ship's side or deck. [from Old French *escoutille*, hatchway]

scuzzy *adj. North Amer. slang* filthy, scummy; sleazy. [perhaps a mixture of SCUM and FUZZY]

Scylla and Charybdis /'sɪlə ənd kə'rɪbdɪs/ *Greek Mythol.* a sea monster and a whirlpool on each side of the Straits of Messina between Italy and Sicily, so situated that the avoidance of one forced a ship closer to the other. — **between Scylla and Charybdis** faced with danger on both sides, so that avoidance of one involves exposure to the other.

scythe /saɪð/ — *noun* a tool with a handle and a long curved blade, for cutting tall crops or grass by hand with a sweeping action. — *verb* to cut with a scythe. [from Anglo-Saxon *sithe*]

Scythian /'sɪðɪən/ *noun* in Greco-Roman times, a member of a nomadic people of the Russian steppes who migrated to the area N of the Black Sea in the 8c BC. Their empire survived until the 2c AD.

SD *abbrev.* **1** (*also* **S. Dak.**) South Dakota. **2** *Maths.* standard deviation.

SDA *abbrev.* Scottish Development Agency.

SDI *abbrev.* Strategic Defence Initiative.

SDLP *abbrev.* Social and Democratic Labour Party.

SDP *abbrev.* Social Democratic Party.

SE *abbrev.* **1** south-east or south-eastern. **2** *Maths.* standard error.

Se *symbol Chem.* selenium.

sea *noun* **1** (*usually* **the sea**) the continuous expanse of salt water that covers about 70 per cent of the Earth's surface, and surrounds the continental land masses. **2** any geographical division of this, usually smaller than an ocean, eg the Mediterranean Sea. **3** an area of this with reference to its calmness or turbulence: *choppy seas.* **4** a large inland saltwater lake, eg the Dead Sea. **5** a vast expanse or crowd: *a sea of worshippers.* — **all at sea** completely disorganized or at a loss. **at sea** in a ship on the sea. **go to sea** to become a sailor. **put** or **put out to sea** to start a journey by sea. [from Anglo-Saxon *sæ*]

🔲 **1** ocean, main, deep, *colloq.* the briny. **5** crowd, multitude, abundance, profusion, mass. **all at sea** confused, bewildered, baffled, puzzled, perplexed, mystified.

sea anchor a device, especially a canvas funnel, dragged by a moving ship to slow it or prevent it drifting off course.

sea anemone any of various solitary marine invertebrates, closely related to corals and found in all the oceans, attached by their bases to submerged weeds and rocks. They are usually brightly coloured, with a cylindrical body and numerous stinging tentacles surrounding the mouth, giving the animal a flower-like appearance.

sea bed the bottom or floor of the sea.

seaboard *noun* a coast.

seaborgium *noun Chem.* (SYMBOL **Sg**, ATOMIC NUMBER **106**) an artificially manufactured chemical element with a half-life of less than a second. [named after the US atomic scientist Glen Theodore Seaborg]

sea breeze a breeze blowing inland from the sea.

sea change a complete change or transformation.

sea cow a dugong or manatee.

sea cucumber a typically sausage-shaped soft-bodied marine invertebrate, with a mouth at one end surrounded by up to 30 tentacles. It has a leathery skin containing minute bony structures (ossicles), and is found on or near the sea bed.

sea dog an old or experienced sailor.

sea eagle any of several fish-eating eagles that live near the sea.

seafarer *noun* a person who travels by sea, a sailor.

seafaring *adj.* travelling by or working at sea.

🔲 seagoing, ocean-going, nautical, naval, marine, maritime.

sea-floor spreading *Geol.* the hypothesis that the oceanic crust is expanding outwards (sideways) away from the oceanic ridges at the rate of 1cm to 10cm per year, as a result of the welling up of magma. Together with the theory of continental drift, it has been incorporated into the theory of plate tectonics.

seafood *noun* shellfish and other edible marine fish.

seagoing *adj.*, *said of a ship* designed for sea travel.

seagull same as GULL[1].

sea horse any of various small fish found among weeds in warm coastal waters. It is covered with bony plates and swims in an upright position, with its elongated head bent at right angles to its body, so that it resembles a chessboard knight.

sea kale a plant of European coastal waters, with edible spiky green leaves.

seal [1] — *noun* **1** a device, eg a strip of plastic or metal, serving to keep something closed, damage to which is proof of interference. **2** a piece of rubber or other material serving to keep a joint airtight or watertight. **3** a piece of wax or other material attached to a document and stamped with an official mark to show authenticity. **4** such a mark: *the royal seal.* **5** an engraved metal stamp or ring for making such a mark. **6** an object given, or a gesture made, as a pledge or guarantee. **7** a decorative adhesive label or stamp. — *verb* **1** (*also* **seal something up**) to make it securely closed, airtight, or watertight with a seal. **2** to fix a seal to, or stamp with a seal. **3** to decide or settle: *seal someone's fate/seal a business agreement.* **4** to paint (eg wood) with a substance that protects against damage, eg by weather. — **seal something off** to isolate an area, preventing entry by unauthorized persons. **set one's seal to something** to authorize, approve, or formally endorse it. [from Latin *sigillum*, from *signum*, mark]

🔲 *noun* **4** stamp, signet, insignia, imprimatur, authentication. **6** guarantee, assurance, attestation, confirmation, ratification. *verb* **1** close, shut, stop, plug, cork, stopper, waterproof. **3** decide, settle, conclude, finalize. **seal off** block up, close off, shut off, fence off, cut off, isolate, quarantine.

seal [2] — *noun* **1** any of various marine mammals belonging to the family Phocidae which have streamlined bodies which may be smooth-skinned or furry, limbs modified to form webbed flippers, and are found mainly in cool coastal waters, especially near the poles. **2** sealskin. — *verb intrans.* to hunt seals. [from Anglo-Saxon *seolh*]

sealant *noun* any material used for sealing, especially one painted on to protect against weathering or wear.

sea legs ability to resist seasickness and walk steadily on the deck of a rolling ship.

sea level the mean level of the surface of the sea between high and low tides; the point from which land height is measured.

sealing-wax *noun* a waxy mixture of shellac and turpentine used for seals on documents.

sea lion any of a number of species of marine mammal with small ears (unlike true seals), long whiskers, paddle-like forelimbs, and large hind flippers, found in coastal waters of the N Pacific, and close to the S American and Australasian coasts.

seal of approval *often facetious* official approval.

sealskin *noun* **1** the skin of a furry seal, or an imitation of it. **2** a garment made from this.

Sealyham terrier /ˈsiːlɪəm/ a breed of dog, developed during the 19c on the Sealyham estate, Haverfordwest, Wales, which has a long body with short legs, a short erect tail, a long head with eyebrows, moustache, and beard, short pendulous ears, and a thick wiry coat of pale hair.

seam — *noun* **1** a join between edges, especially one sewn or welded. **2** a layer of coal or ore in the earth. **3** a wrinkle or scar. — *verb* **1** to join edge to edge. **2** to scar or wrinkle. [from Anglo-Saxon *seam*]

🔲 *noun* **1** join, joint, weld, closure. **2** layer, stratum, vein, lode. **3** wrinkle, line, scar.

seaman *noun* a sailor below the rank of officer.

seamanship *noun* sailing skills, including navigation.

seamer *noun Cricket* a ball delivered by seam bowling, in which the seam of the ball is used by the bowler to make the ball swerve in flight, or first to swerve and then to break in the opposite direction in pitching.

seaminess *noun* being seamy.

seamless *adj.* **1** having no seams; made from a single piece. **2** seeming to be a unified whole; showing no signs of having been pieced together.

seamstress *noun* a woman who sews, especially professionally.

seamy *adj.* (**seamier**, **seamiest**) sordid; disreputable. [from SEAM]

◻ sordid, squalid, disreputable, sleazy, unsavoury, rough, dark, low, nasty, unpleasant.
◻ respectable, wholesome, pleasant.

séance or **seance** /ˈseɪɑːns/ *noun* a meeting at which a person attempts to contact the spirits of dead people on behalf of other people present. [from French *séance*, sitting]

sea otter a mammal native to N Pacific coasts, that lives mostly in the water, and has thick insulating fur, small front feet that are not webbed, and a broader body than freshwater otters.

sea pink same as THRIFT 2.

seaplane *noun* an aeroplane designed to take off from and land on water.

seaport *noun* a coastal town with a port for seagoing ships.

SEAQ *abbrev.* Stock Exchange Automated Quotation.

sear — *verb* 1 to scorch. 2 to wither. — *noun* a mark made by scorching. [from Anglo-Saxon *searian*, to dry up]

◻ *verb* 1 scorch, burn, brown, fry, sizzle, seal, cauterize, brand. 2 parch, shrivel, wither.

search — *verb* 1 a *intrans.* to carry out a thorough exploration to try to find something. **b** to carry out such an exploration in (a place). 2 to check the clothing or body of (a person) for concealed objects. 3 to examine closely: *search one's conscience.* 4 (*also* **search something out**) to uncover it after a thorough check or exploration. — *noun* an act of searching. — **in search of something** searching for it. **search me** *colloq.* an expression of ignorance about something. [from Old French *cerchier*, from Latin *circare*, to go around]

◻ *verb* 1 seek, look, hunt, rummage, rifle, ransack, scour, comb, sift, probe. 2 inspect, check, *slang* frisk. 3 examine, scrutinize, scan. *noun* hunt, quest, pursuit, rummage, probe, exploration, examination, scrutiny, inspection, investigation, inquiry, survey.

search engine *Comput.* software that retrieves information, especially on the Internet.

searching *adj.* that seeks to discover the truth by intensive examination or observation: *a searching inquiry.*

◻ penetrating, piercing, keen, sharp, probing, thorough, intensive, minute.
◻ vague, superficial.

searchlight *noun* 1 a pivoting exterior light with a powerful beam, used to monitor an area in darkness. 2 its beam.

search party a group of people taking part in an organized search for a missing person or thing.

search warrant a document, issued by a justice of the peace, giving a police officer the legal right to search premises.

searing *adj.* burning; intense.

seascape *noun* a picture of a scene at sea.

Sea Scout a member of a division of the Scout Association that provides training in seamanship.

seashell *noun* the empty shell of an oyster, mussel, or other mollusc.

seashore *noun* the land immediately adjacent to the sea.

seasick *adj.* suffering from seasickness.

seasickness *noun* nausea brought on by the rolling or dipping motion of a ship.

seaside *noun* (*usually* **the seaside**) a coastal area, especially a holiday resort.

◻ coast, shore, seashore, beach, sands.

season — *noun* 1 any of the four major periods (spring, summer, autumn, and winter), into which the year is divided according to differences in weather patterns and other natural phenomena. 2 a period of the year during which a particular sport is played or some other activity carried out: *fishing season/holiday season.* 3 any period having particular characteristics: *rainy season/our busy season.* 4 a period during which a particular fruit or vegetable is in plentiful supply. — *verb* (**seasoned**, **seasoning**) 1 to flavour (food) by adding salt, pepper, or other herbs and spices. 2 to prepare (eg timber) for use. 3 to make mature or experienced: *seasoned travellers.* 4 to tone down or temper. 5 to add interest or liveliness to. — **in season** 1 *said of food* available, as determined by its growing season. 2 *said of game animals* for which the legal right to hunt exists, according to the time of year. 3 *said of a female animal* ready to mate; on heat. **out of season** 1 *said of food* not yet available. 2 *said of game animals* not yet to be hunted. [from Old French *seson*]

◻ *noun* PERIOD, TIME. 2 term. 3 spell, phase, span, interval. *verb* 1 flavour, spice, salt. 2 prepare, treat, age, mature, ripen, harden, toughen. 3 mature, harden, toughen, condition, train, prepare. 4 temper, moderate, tone down.

seasonable *adj.* 1 *said of weather* appropriate to the season. 2 coming at the right time; opportune.

◻ 2 timely, well-timed, opportune, convenient, suitable, appropriate, fitting.
◻ UNSEASONABLE. 2 inopportune.

seasonal *adj.* available, happening, or taking place only at certain times of the year.

seasonal affective disorder *Psychol.* (ABBREV. **SAD**) a recurrent change in mood occurring at a particular time of year, especially a pattern of repeated depression during the winter months.

seasoned *adj.* 1 flavoured. 2 matured, conditioned.

◻ 2 matured, hardened, toughened, conditioned, acclimatized, weathered, mature, experienced, practised, well-versed, veteran, old.
◻ 2 inexperienced, novice.

seasoning *noun* any substance used to season food.

◻ flavouring, herb, spice, salt, pepper, condiment, relish, sauce, dressing.

season ticket a ticket giving the right to a specified or unlimited number of visits or journeys during a fixed period.

Seaspeak *noun* the common name for *Essential English for International Maritime Use*, developed in the 1980s to facilitate international communication at sea.

seat — *noun* 1 a thing designed for sitting on, eg a chair or bench. 2 the part of it on which one sits. 3 a place for sitting, eg in a cinema or theatre, often reserved; a reservation for such a place. 4 the buttocks. 5 the part of a garment covering the buttocks. 6 the base of an object, or any part on which it rests or fits. 7 a position in Parliament or local government; a position on a committee or other administrative body. 8 an established centre: *seats of learning.* 9 a large country house. — *verb* 1 to assign a seat to, eg at a dinner table. 2 to provide seats for: *the car seats five.* 3 to place in any situation or location. 4 to fit firmly and accurately. — **be seated** to sit down. **take a** or **one's seat** to sit down. [from Norse *sæti*]

◻ *noun* 1 chair, bench, pew, stool, throne. 3 place,

reservation, booking. **6** bottom, base. **7** position, place. **8** centre, headquarters, heart, site, situation, location. **9** house, mansion, residence, *formal* abode. *verb* **1** sit, place. **2** accommodate, hold, contain, take. **3** place, set, locate, install, settle. **4** fit, fix.

seat belt a safety belt that prevents a passenger in a vehicle from being thrown violently forward in the event of a crash.

-seater *combining form* forming words meaning 'having seats for a specified number of people': *a three-seater sofa.*

seating *noun* the number or arrangement of seats, eg in a dining-room.

☱ seats, chairs, places.

sea urchin the common name for any of 800 species of echinoderm, related to the starfish and brittle stars, but having a spherical or heart-shaped shell formed by fusion of the five arms.

seaward — *adj.* facing or moving toward the sea. — *adv.* (*also* **seawards**) towards the sea.

seaweed *noun* **1** *Bot.* common name for any of a number of large marine algae. **2** such plants collectively.

seaworthiness *noun* a seaworthy state.

seaworthy *adj., said of a ship* fit for a voyage at sea.

sebaceous /sɪˈbeɪʃəs/ *adj.* of, like, or secreting sebum. [from Latin *sebaceous*]

sebaceous gland *Anat.* any of the tiny glands, found in the skin of mammals, which open into hair follicles just beneath the skin surface, and secrete *sebum.*

sebum /ˈsiːbəm/ *noun Zool.* an oily substance, produced by the sebaceous glands, that lubricates the skin and hair. It protects the skin from excessive dryness by reducing water loss, and has an antibacterial effect. [from Latin *sebum*, grease]

SEC *abbrev.* Securities and Exchange Commission.

Sec. *abbrev.* Secretary.

sec[1] /sek/ *noun colloq.* a second: *wait a sec.*

sec[2] *adj.* **1** *said of wine* dry. **2** *said of champagne* medium sweet. [from French *sec*, dry]

sec[3] *abbrev.* secant.

sec. *abbrev.* second.

SECAM *abbrev. Séquential Couleur à Mémoire* (French): a coding system for colour television developed in France in the 1960s, and later adopted in the USSR, Eastern Europe, and certain Middle East countries. See also NTSC, PAL.

secant /ˈsiːkənt/ *noun* (ABBREV. **sec**) **1** *Geom.* a straight line that cuts a curve in two or more places. **2** *Maths.* for a given angle in a right-angled triangle, the ratio of the length of the hypotenuse to the length of the side adjacent to the angle under consideration; the reciprocal of the cosine of an angle. [from Latin *secans*, from *secare*, to cut]

secateurs /ˈsekətəːz/ *pl. noun* small sharp shears for pruning bushes. [from French *secateurs*]

secede /sɪˈsiːd/ *verb intrans.* to withdraw formally, eg from a political or religious body or alliance. [from Latin *secedere*, to go apart]

secession /sɪˈseʃən/ *noun* **1** seceding. **2** a group of seceders.

seclude *verb* **1** to keep away from others; to isolate. **2** to keep out of view. [from Latin *secludere*]

secluded *adj.* **1** away from people and noise; private and quiet. **2** hidden from view.

☱ **1** private, quiet, cloistered, sequestered, shut away, cut off, isolated, lonely, solitary, remote, out-of-the-way. **2** hidden, concealed.
☲ **1** public, accessible.

seclusion *noun* the state of being secluded; peacefulness and privacy.

☱ privacy, peace, retirement, retreat, isolation, solitude, remoteness, hiding, concealment.

second[1] — *adj.* **1** next after the first, in order of sequence or importance. **2** alternate: *every second week.* **3** additional; supplementary: *have a second go.* **4** subordinate; inferior: *second to none.* **5** so similarly talented as to be worthy of the same name: *a writer described as a second Shakespeare.* **6** *Mus.* indicating an instrument or voice with a subordinate role to, or a slightly lower pitch than, another: *second soprano.* — *noun* **1** a person or thing next in sequence after the first. **2** the second gear in an engine. **3** a second-class honours degree. **4** an assistant to a boxer or duellist. **5** (**seconds**) flawed goods sold at reduced prices. **6** (**seconds**) *colloq.* a second helping of food. **7** (**seconds**) *colloq.* the second course of a meal. **8** a Cub Scout or Brownie Guide next in rank to a sixer. — *verb* **1** to declare formal support for (a proposal, or the person making it). **2** to give support or encouragement of any kind to. **3** to act as second to (a boxer or duellist). — *adv.* in second place: *came second in the race.* [from Latin *secundus*]

☱ *adj.* **1** next, following, subsequent, succeeding. **2** alternate, other. **3** additional, further, extra, supplementary, repeated, double, duplicate. **4** secondary, subordinate, lower, inferior, lesser, supporting. *noun* **4** assistant, helper, supporter, backer. *verb* **2** approve, agree with, support, endorse, back, help, assist, aid, encourage, further, advance, promote.

second[2] *noun* **1** (ABBREV. **sec, s**) an SI unit of time, equal to — of a minute, and defined as the duration of 9,192,631,770 periods of the radiation corresponding to the transition between two hyperfine levels of the ground state of the caesium-133 atom. **2** a unit of angular measurement equal to — of a degree or — of a minute. **3** a moment: *wait a second.* [from Latin *secunda minuta*, secondary minute]

☱ **3** moment, minute, *colloq.* tick, instant, flash, *colloq.* jiffy.

second[3] *verb* (with stress on *-cond*) to transfer temporarily to a different post, place, or duty. [from French *en second*, in the second rank]

secondary *adj.* **1** of lesser importance than the principal or primary concern; subordinate. **2** developed from something earlier or original: *a secondary infection.* **3** *said of education* between primary and higher or further; for pupils between ages 11 and 18. See also PRIMARY, TERTIARY. [from Latin *secundarius*]

☱ **1** subsidiary, subordinate, lower, inferior, lesser, minor, unimportant, ancillary, auxiliary, supporting, reserve, spare, extra, second, alternative. **2** indirect, derived, resulting.
☲ **1, 2** primary. **1** main, major.

secondary cell *Physics* an electrolytic cell that must be charged before use by passing an electric current through it, and can then be recharged when necessary.

secondary colour a colour obtained by mixing two primary colours, eg orange.

secondary growth or **secondary thickening** *Bot.* **1** the increase in girth of a stem or root that results from the activity of cambium after elongation has ceased. **2** the formation by a cell of a secondary wall.

secondary picketing picketing of firms that have business connections with the employer against whom action is being taken.

secondary sexual characteristics *Zool.* features other than the reproductive organs that distinguish males from females after the onset of puberty, eg beard growth in human males, breast development in human females.

secondary stress *Linguistics* the second-strongest stress in a word, etc. See also PRIMARY STRESS.

second best the next after the best. — **come off second best** *colloq.* to lose.

second-best *adj.* **1** next after the best. **2** somewhat inferior.

second childhood senility; dotage.

second class the class or category below the first in quality or value.

second-class — *adj.* **1** relating to the class below the first. **2** of a poor standard; inferior. **3** not having as many rights or privileges as others: *a second-class citizen.* — *adv.* by second-class mail or transport.

second cousin a child of one's parent's first cousin.

second-degree *adj. Medicine* denoting the second most serious of the three degrees of burning, with blistering but not permanent damage to the skin.

seconder *noun* a person who seconds a proposal or seconds the person making it.

second hand the pointer on a watch or clock that measures the time in seconds.

second-hand — *adj.* **1** previously owned or used by someone else. **2** not directly received or obtained, but coming via an intermediary: *second-hand information.* — *adv.* **1** in a second-hand state: *buy furniture second-hand.* **2** not directly, but from someone else: *heard it second-hand.*

    ☐ *adj.* **1** used, pre-owned, old, worn, hand-me-down, borrowed, derivative. **2** indirect, secondary, vicarious.
    ☒ *adj.* **1** new. **2** first-hand.

second lieutenant an army or navy officer of the lowest commissioned rank, the rank below lieutenant.

secondly *adv.* in the second place; as a second consideration.

secondment *noun* a temporary transfer to another position.

second nature a habit so firmly fixed as to seem an innate part of a person's nature.

second person see PERSON.

second-rate *adj.* inferior; substandard.

    ☐ inferior, substandard, second-class, second-best, poor, shoddy, cheap, tawdry, mediocre, undistinguished.
    ☒ first-rate, excellent.

second sight the supposed power to see into the future or to see things happening elsewhere.

second-strike capability *Mil.* in nuclear warfare, the capability of a state to launch a counter-attack following a first strike by an enemy.

second thoughts **1** doubts: *having second thoughts.* **2** a process of reconsidering and reaching a different decision: *on second thoughts.*

second wind **1** the recovery of normal breathing after exertion. **2** a burst of renewed energy or enthusiasm.

secrecy *noun* **1** the state or fact of being secret. **2** the ability or tendency to keep information secret. [from Middle English *secretie*, from *secre*, secret]

    ☐ **1** confidentiality, confidence, privacy, seclusion, concealment, furtiveness, surreptitiousness, stealth, mystery. **2** secretiveness, reticence, reserve.
    ☒ OPENNESS.

secret — *adj.* **1** hidden from or undisclosed to others, or to all but a few. **2** whose activities are unknown to or unobserved by others: *a secret army.* **3** tending to conceal things from others; secretive. — *noun* **1** a piece of information not revealed, or not to be revealed, to others. **2** an unknown or unrevealed method of achievement: *the secret of eternal youth.* **3** a fact or purpose that remains unexplained; a mystery. — **in secret** secretly; unknown to others. [from Latin *secretus*, set apart]

    ☐ *adj.* **1** classified, restricted, confidential, *colloq.* hush-hush, unpublished, undisclosed, unrevealed, unknown, cryptic, mysterious, occult, arcane, recondite, private, secluded, out-of-the-way, discreet, covert, hidden, concealed, unseen. **2** undercover, disguised, camouflaged, underground, back-door, under-the-counter, hole-and-corner, cloak-and-dagger, clandestine. **3** secretive, close, deep, furtive, surreptitious, stealthy, sly. *noun* **1** confidence. **2** formula, recipe, key, code. **3** mystery, enigma.
    ☒ *adj.* **1** public, open, well-known.

secret agent a member of the secret service; a spy.

secretaire /ˈsɛkrəteə(r)/ *noun* same as ESCRITOIRE. [from French *secretaire*, secretary]

secretarial /sɛkrəˈteərɪəl/ *adj.* relating to secretaries or their work.

secretariat /sɛkrəˈteərɪət/ *noun* **1** the administrative department of any large organization, especially a legislative body. **2** its staff or premises. [from French *secrtariat*]

secretary *noun* (PL. **secretaries**) **1** a person employed to perform administrative or clerical tasks. **2** the member of a club or society responsible for its correspondence and business records. **3** a senior civil servant assisting a government minister or ambassador. [from Latin *secretarius*, person spoken to in confidence]

    ☐ **1** personal assistant, PA, typist, stenographer, clerk.

secretary bird a long-legged, long-tailed, snake-eating African bird of prey.

secretary-general *noun* the principal administrative official in a large (especially political) organization.

Secretary of State 1 in the UK, a minister at the head of a major government department. **2** in the US, the head of the department dealing with foreign affairs.

secrete[1] /sɪˈkriːt/ *verb, said of a gland or similar organ* to form and release (a substance) for use in the body, or as an excretion. [related to SECRET]

    ☐ exude, discharge, release, emit, emanate, produce.

secrete[2] /sɪˈkriːt/ *verb* to hide away or conceal. [related to SECRET]

    ☐ hide, conceal, bury, cover, screen, shroud, veil, disguise.
    ☒ uncover, reveal, disclose.

secretion *noun* **1** a substance secreted. **2** the process of secreting.

    ☐ DISCHARGE, EMISSION. **2** exudation, release.

secretive *adj.* inclined not to reveal things to others; fond of secrecy.

    ☐ tight-lipped, close, *colloq.* cagey, uncommunicative, unforthcoming, reticent, reserved, withdrawn, quiet, deep, mysterious, enigmatic.
    ☒ open, communicative, forthcoming.

secretly *adv.* **1** in secret. **2** in concealment.

secretory /sɪˈkriːtərɪ/ *adj.* that secretes.

secret police a police force operating in secret to stamp out opposition to the government.

secret service a government department responsible for espionage and matters of national security.

secret society an association or group whose activites are kept secret from the world at large and whose members usually take an oath of secrecy.

sect *noun* a religious or other group whose views and practices differ from those of an established body or from those of a body from which it has separated. [from Latin *secta*, a following]

◻ denomination, cult, division, subdivision, group, splinter group, faction, camp, wing, party, school.

sectarian /sɛkˈtɛərɪən/ — *adj.* **1** of, relating to, or belonging to a sect. **2** having, showing, or caused by hostility towards those outside one's own group or belonging to a particular group: *sectarian violence.* — *noun* a member of a sect, especially a bigoted person.

◻ *adj.* **1** factional, partisan, cliquish, exclusive. **2** narrow, limited, parochial, insular, narrow-minded, bigoted, fanatical, doctrinaire, dogmatic.
◼ *adj.* NON-SECTARIAN. **1** cosmopolitan. **2** broad-minded.

sectarianism *noun* loyalty or excessive attachment to a particular sect or party.

section — *noun* **1** any of the parts into which a thing is or can be divided, or from which it is constructed. **2** a subdivision of an army platoon. **3** *Geom.* the surface formed when a plane cuts through a solid geometric figure. **4** the act of cutting through a solid figure. **5** a plan or diagram showing a view of an object as if it had been cut through. **6** *Biol.* a thin slice of a specimen of tissue that is prepared for examination under a microscope. **7** *Medicine* in surgery, the act or process of cutting, or the cut or division made. — *verb* (**sectioned**, **sectioning**) *Medicine* to issue an order for the compulsory admission of (a person suffering from mental illness) to a psychiatric hospital under the relevant section of mental health legislation. [from Latin *secare*, to cut]

◻ *noun* **1** division, subdivision, chapter, paragraph, passage, instalment, part, component, piece, slice, portion, segment, sector, zone, district, area, region, department, branch, wing.
◼ *noun* **1** whole.

sectional *adj.* **1** made in sections. **2** relating, or restricted, to a particular group or area.

sector *noun* **1** a part of an area divided up for military purposes. **2** a separate part into which any sphere of activity, eg a nation's economy, can be divided: *the public and private sectors.* **3** a portion of a circle formed by two radii and the part of the circumference lying between them. [from Latin *sector*, cutter]

◻ **1** zone, district, quarter, area, region. **2** section, division, subdivision, part.

secular *adj.* **1** not religious or ecclesiastical; civil or lay. **2** relating to this world; not heavenly or spiritual. **3** *said of members of the clergy* not bound by vows to a particular religious order. **4** occurring only once in a lifetime, century, or age. [from Latin *saecularis*, from *saeculum*, generation, century]

◻ **1** lay, temporal, civil, state. **2** worldly, earthly, temporal.
◼ **1** religious, ecclesiastical. **2** heavenly, spiritual.

secularism *noun* the view that society's values and standards should not be influenced or controlled by religion or the Church.

secularist *noun* a person who favours secularism.

secularize or **secularise** *verb* to make secular.

secure — *adj.* **1** free from danger; providing freedom from danger. **2** free from trouble or worry. **3** firmly fixed or attached. **4** not likely to be lost or taken away; assured: *a secure job.* — *verb* **1** to fasten or attach firmly. **2** to get or get possession of. **3** to make free from danger or risk. **4** to

guarantee. [from Latin *securus*, from *se-*, without + *cura*, care]

◻ *adj.* **1** safe, unharmed, undamaged, protected, sheltered, immune, impregnable, fortified, fast, tight, fastened, locked. **2** confident, assured, reassured, carefree. **3** fixed, immovable, stable, steady, solid, firm. **4** certain, sure, guaranteed, assured, reliable, dependable. *verb* **1** fasten, attach, fix, make fast, tie, chain, lock (up), padlock, bolt, batten down, nail, rivet. **2** get, obtain, acquire, gain. **3** protect, fortify. **4** guarantee, assure.
◼ *adj.* INSECURE. **1** vulnerable. **2** uneasy, ill at ease. *verb* **1** unfasten. **2** lose.

security *noun* (PL. **securities**) **1** the state of being secure. **2** freedom from the possibility of future financial difficulty. **3** protection from physical harm, especially assassination. **4** freedom from vulnerability to political or military takeover: *national security.* **5** something given as a guarantee, eg of repayment of a loan. **6** (*usually* **securities**) a certificate stating ownership of stocks or shares; the monetary value represented by such certificates.

◻ **1** safety, immunity, sanctuary, refuge. **3** protection, defence, safekeeping, care, custody, surveillance. **5** collateral, surety, pledge, guarantee, warranty, assurance.
◼ **1** insecurity.

security blanket 1 a blanket or other familiar piece of cloth carried around by a toddler for comfort. **2** any familiar object whose presence provides a sense of security or comfort.

security risk a person or activity considered to be a threat to a nation's security, eg because of a likelihood of giving away military secrets.

SED *abbrev.* Scottish Education Department.

sedan /sɪˈdan/ *noun* **1** *Hist.* (*also* **sedan chair**) a large enclosed chair which can be lifted and carried on horizontal poles. **2** *North Amer.* a saloon car.

sedate[1] *adj.* **1** calm and dignified in manner. **2** slow and unexciting. [from Latin *sedare*, to still]

◻ **1** staid, dignified, solemn, serious, sober, decorous, seemly, demure, calm, composed, unruffled, serene, imperturbable, *colloq.* unflappable. **2** slow, deliberate.
◼ **1** undignified, agitated. **2** lively.

sedate[2] *verb* to make calm by means of a sedative. [from Latin *sedare*, to still]

sedation *noun* *Medicine* the act of calming, or state of being calmed, especially by means of sedative drugs.

sedative /ˈsɛdətɪv/ — *noun* *Medicine* any agent, especially a drug, that has a calming effect and is used to treat insomnia, pain, delirium, etc. — *adj.*, *said of a drug, etc* having a calming effect.

◻ *noun* tranquillizer, sleeping pill, narcotic, barbiturate. *adj.* calming, soothing, anodyne, lenitive, tranquillizing, relaxing, soporific, depressant.

sedentary /ˈsɛdəntərɪ/ *adj.* **1** *said of work* involving much sitting. **2** *said of a person* spending much time sitting; taking little exercise. [from Latin *sedere*, to sit]

◻ **1** desk-bound, sitting, seated. **2** inactive, idle, still, stationary, immobile.
◼ **2** active.

sedge *noun* any plant resembling a grass or rush and belonging to the family Cyperaceae, especially *Cladium mariscus*, or any of about 200 species of the genus *Carex*. [from Anglo-Saxon *secg*]

sediment *noun* **1** insoluble solid particles that have settled at the bottom of a liquid in which they were previously suspended. **2** *Geol.* solid material such as rock fragments, or plant or animal debris, that has been deposited by the action of gravity, wind, water, or ice, especially such material that has settled at the bottom of a sea, lake, or river. [from Latin *sedimentum*, from *sedere*, to sit]

☐ **1** deposit, residue, grounds, lees, dregs.

sedimentary *adj.* **1** relating to or of the nature of sediment. **2** *Geol.* denoting any of a group of rocks, eg clay, limestone, coal, sandstone, that have formed as a result of the accumulation and compaction of layers of sediment, itself consisting of small particles of pre-existing rock that have been transported from their place of origin by water, wind, ice, or gravity.

sedimentation *noun* **1** *Geol.* the process of accumulating or depositing sediment in layers, eg during the formation of sedimentary rock. **2** *Chem.* the settling of solid particles from a suspension, either naturally as a result of gravity, or as a result of centrifugation.

sedition *noun* speech, writing, or action encouraging public disorder, especially rebellion against the government. [from Latin *seditio*, a going apart]

☐ agitation, rabble-rousing, subversion, disloyalty, treachery, treason, insubordination, mutiny, rebellion, revolt.
☒ pacification, loyalty.

seditious *adj.* **1** relating to or involving sedition. **2** encouraging or taking part in sedition.

seduce *verb* **1** to entice into having sexual relations. **2** to tempt, especially into wrongdoing. [from Latin *seducere*, to lead aside]

☐ **1** entice, lure, allure, attract, charm, beguile. **2** tempt, lead astray, corrupt.
☒ **1** repel.

seduction *noun* seducing or being seduced.

☐ enticement, lure, attraction, temptation, corruption.

seductive *adj.* **1** sexually very attractive and charming. **2** creating, or designed to create, the mood for sex: *seductive lighting.* **3** tempting; enticing.

☐ **1** sexy, provocative, flirtatious, attractive, charming, beguiling, captivating, bewitching. **3** tempting, tantalizing, inviting, enticing, alluring, attractive, irresistible.
☒ **1** unattractive, repulsive.

sedulity *noun* being sedulous, diligence.

sedulous *adj. formal* **1** steadily hardworking and conscientious; diligent. **2** painstakingly carried out. [from Latin *sedulus*]

sedum /ˈsiːdəm/ *noun* any of a family of rock plants with fleshy leaves and white, yellow, or pink flowers. [from Latin *sedum*]

see[1] *verb* (PAST TENSE **saw**; PAST PARTICIPLE **seen**) **1** to perceive with the eyes. **2** *intrans.* to have the power of vision. **3** to watch: *see a play.* **4** *trans., intrans.* to understand: *I don't see what you mean.* **5** to be aware of or know, especially by looking: *I see from your letter that you're married.* **6** *trans., intrans.* to find out: *wait and see.* **7** to meet up with; to be in the company of: *not seen her for ages.* **8** to spend time with, especially romantically: *seeing a married woman.* **9** to speak to or consult: *asking to see the manager.* **10** to receive as a visitor: *the manager refused to see me.* **11** to make sure of something: *see that you lock the door.* **12** (**see to something**) attend to it; take care of it: *will you see to it?* **13** to imagine, especially to regard as likely; to

picture in the mind: *can't see him agreeing/can still see her as a little girl.* **14** to consider: *see her more as a writer than a politician.* **15** *intrans.* (**see something in someone**) to find an attractive feature in them: *it is hard to know what he sees in her.* **16** to be witness to as a sight or event: *do not wish to see her hurt/now seeing huge increases in unemployment.* **17** to escort: *see you home.* **18** to refer to for information: *see page 5.* **19** *Cards* to match the bet of by staking the same sum: *see you and raise you five.* — **see about something** to attend to a matter or concern. **see fit to do something** to think it appropriate or proper to do it. **see into something** to investigate it; to look into it. **see the light 1** to discover religious feelings within oneself. **2** to recognize the merits of, and adopt, some widely held point of view. **see someone off 1** to accompany them to a place of departure. **2** *colloq.* to get rid of them by force. **see someone out 1** to escort them out of a building, etc. **2** to outlive them. **see something out** to stay until the end of it. **see over something** to inspect it; to look over it. **see things** to have hallucinations. **see through something 1** to discern what is implied by an idea or scheme, etc. **2** to recognize an essential truth underlying a lie, trick, etc. **see something through** to participate in it to the end. **see you later** *colloq.* an expression of temporary farewell.

☐ **1** perceive, glimpse, discern, spot, make out, distinguish, identify, sight, notice, observe. **3** watch, view, look at. **4** understand, comprehend, follow. **5** know, realize, recognize, appreciate. **6** find out, discover, learn. **8** go out with, date. **9** visit, consult, speak to. **10** receive, interview. **12** attend to, deal with, take care of, look after, arrange, organize, sort out, do. **13** imagine, picture, visualize, envisage, foresee, anticipate. **14** consider, regard, deem. **17** escort, accompany, usher, lead.

see[2] *noun* **1** the post of bishop. **2** the area under the religious authority of a bishop or archbishop. [from Latin *sedes*, seat]

seed — *noun* (PL. **seeds**, **seed**) **1** *Bot.* in flowering and cone-bearing plants, the highly resistant structure that develops from the ovule after fertilization, and is capable of developing into a new plant. It contains the developing embryo and a food store, surrounded by a protective coat or *testa.* **2** a source or origin: *the seeds of the idea.* **3** *literary* offspring; descendants. **4** *literary* semen. **5** *Sport* a seeded player. — *verb* **1** *intrans.* *said of a plant* to produce seeds. **2** to plant (seeds). **3** to remove seeds from (eg a fruit). **4** *Chem.* to use a single crystal to induce the formation of more from a concentrated solution. **5** *Microbiol.* to add bacteria, viruses, etc to (a culture medium). **6** *Sport* to rank (a player in a tournament) according to his or her likelihood of winning; to arrange (a tournament) so that high-ranking players only meet each other in the latter stages of the contest. — **go to seed 1** (*also* **run to seed**) *Bot.*, *said of a plant* to stop flowering prior to the development of seed. **2** *colloq.* to allow oneself to become unkempt or unhealthy through lack of care. [from Anglo-Saxon *sæd*]

☐ *noun* **1** pip, stone, kernel, nucleus, grain, germ. **2** source, origin, start, beginning.

seedbed *noun* **1** a piece of ground prepared for the planting of seeds. **2** an environment in which something (especially undesirable) develops.

seed drill *Agric.* a farm implement that is used to sow seeds in rows by making a series of furrows, dropping the seeds into them, and covering them with soil.

seeded *adj.* **1** with the seeds removed. **2** bearing or having seeds. **3** sown. **4** *Sport*, *said of a tournament player* who has been seeded.

seedhead *noun* a compact mass or cluster of seeds on a plant.

seedless *adj.* bearing no or few seeds.

seedling *noun* a young plant grown from seed.

seed pearl a tiny pearl.

seed potato a potato kept for planting, from which a new potato plant grows.

seedy *adj.* (**seedier, seediest**) **1** *said of a fruit, etc* full of seeds. **2** *said of a plant* at the stage of producing seeds. **3** *colloq.* mildly ill. **4** *colloq.* shabby or run-down; dirty or disreputable: *seedy areas of town.*

▤ **3** unwell, ill, sick, poorly, ailing, off-colour. **4** shabby, scruffy, tatty, disreputable, sleazy, run-down, dilapidated, dirty, squalid, *colloq.* grotty, *colloq.* crummy.
▣ **3** well. **4** respectable.

seeing — *noun* the ability to see; the power of vision. — *conj.* (*also* **seeing that**) given (that); since: *seeing you are opposed to the plan, I shall not pursue it.*

seek *verb* (PAST TENSE AND PAST PARTICIPLE **sought**) **1** to look for. **2** to try to get or achieve. **3** to try or endeavour: *seeking to please.* **4** to take oneself off to; to go to get: *seek shelter in a cave.* **5** to ask for: *sought his advice.* — **seek something** or **someone out** to search intensively for and find them. [from Anglo-Saxon *secan*]

▤ **1** look for, search for, hunt, pursue, follow. **2** aim for, aspire to, want, desire. **3** try, attempt, endeavour, strive. **5** ask for, invite, request, solicit, petition.

seem *verb intrans.* **1** to appear to the eye; to give the impression of (being). **2** to be apparent; to appear to the mind: *there seems to be no good reason for refusing.* **3** to think or believe oneself (to be, do, etc): *I seem to know you from somewhere.* [from Norse *soemr*, fitting]

▤ **1** appear, look, feel, sound.

seeming *adj.* apparent: *her seeming indifference.*

▤ apparent, ostensible, outward, superficial, quasi-, pseudo-.

seemingly *adv.* apparently.

seemly *adj.* (**seemlier, seemliest**) *old use* fitting; suitable.

seen see SEE[1].

seep *verb intrans., said of a liquid* to escape slowly, through or as if through a narrow opening. [perhaps from Anglo-Saxon *sipian*, to soak]

▤ leak, ooze, exude, trickle, dribble, percolate, permeate, soak.

seepage *noun* **1** seeping. **2** liquid that has seeped.

seer *noun* **1** a person who predicts future events; a clairvoyant. **2** a person of great wisdom and insight; a prophet. [literally 'a person who sees', from SEE[1]]

seersucker *noun* lightweight cotton or linen cloth with a crinkly appearance. [from Persian *shir o shakkar*, milk and sugar]

seesaw — *noun* **1** a plaything consisting of a plank balanced in the middle, allowing people, especially children, seated on its ends to propel each other up and down by pushing off the ground with the feet. **2** an alternate up-and-down or back-and-forth movement. — *verb intrans.* (**seesawed, seesawing**) to move alternately up-and-down or back-and-forth. [a reduplication of SAW[2], from the sawing action]

seethe *verb intrans.* **1** *said of a liquid* to churn and foam because of or as if boiling. **2** to be extremely agitated, especially with anger. [from Anglo-Saxon *seothan*]

▤ **1** boil, simmer, bubble, effervesce, fizz, foam, froth, ferment, rise, swell. **2** rage, fume, smoulder, storm.

seething *adj.* **1** that seethes; boiling. **2** furious.

see-through *adj.* said especially of a fabric or clothing, able to be seen through; translucent.

▤ transparent, translucent, sheer, filmy, gauzy, flimsy.
▣ opaque.

segment — *noun* (with stress on *seg-*) **1** a part, section, or portion. **2** *Geom.* in a circle or ellipse, the region enclosed by an arc (a segment of the circumference) and its chord (a straight line drawn from one end of the arc to the other). **3** *Zool.* each of a number of repeating units in the body of certain animals, eg some worms. — *verb* (with stress on *-ment*) to divide into segments. [from Latin *segmentum*, from *secare*, to cut]

▤ *noun* **1** section, division, part, portion, bit, piece, slice, wedge.
▣ *noun* **1** whole.

segmentation *noun* **1** division into segments, or an instance of this. **2** repeated cell division in a fertilized ovum.

segregate *verb* to separate (a group or groups) from others or from each other. [from Latin *se-*, apart + *grex*, flock]

▤ separate, keep apart, cut off, isolate, quarantine, set apart, exclude.
▣ unite, join.

segregated *adj.* separated out, isolated.

segregation *noun* **1** enforced separation into groups. **2** systematic isolation of one group, especially a racial or ethnic minority, from the rest of society.

▤ **1** separation, isolation. **2** apartheid, discrimination.
▣ UNIFICATION.

segregational *adj.* involving or characterized by segregation.

seigneur /sɛˈnjɑː(r)/ *noun* a feudal lord, especially in France. [from French *seigneur*]

seine /seɪn/ — *noun* a large fishing net kept hanging vertically underwater by means of floats and weights. — *verb trans., intrans.* to catch (fish) with a seine. [from Anglo-Saxon *segne*]

seismic /ˈsaɪzmɪk/ *adj.* **1** of or relating to earthquakes. **2** *colloq.* gigantic: *an increase of seismic proportions.* [from Greek *seismos*, a shaking]

seismograph *noun* an instrument that measures and records the force of earthquakes. [from Greek *seismos*, a shaking + -GRAPH]

seismography *noun* the scientific study of earthquakes.

seismological *adj.* relating to or involving seismology.

seismologist *noun* a scientist skilled in seismology.

seismology *noun Geol.* the branch of geology concerned with the scientific study of earthquakes, including their origin and effects, and possible methods by which they may be predicted. [from Greek *seismos*, a shaking + -LOGY]

seize *verb* **1** to take or grab suddenly. **2** to affect suddenly and deeply; to overcome: *seized by panic.* **3** to take by force; to capture. **4** to take legal possession of. **5** (**seize on** or **upon something**) to use or exploit it eagerly: *they seized every chance to embarrass us.* — **seize up** *said of a machine or engine* to become stiff or jammed, eg through overuse or lack of lubrication. [from Old French *saisir*]

▤ **1** take, grab, snatch, grasp, clutch, grip, hold, catch, arrest. **2** overcome, overwhelm. **3** capture, hijack, annex, abduct. **4** take, confiscate, impound, appropriate, commandeer.
▣ **1, 3** let go, release.

seizure /ˈsiːʒə(r)/ *noun* **1** the act of seizing. **2** a sudden attack of an illness, especially producing spasms or loss of movement.

- **1** taking, confiscation, appropriation, capture, hijack, annexation, abduction. **2** attack, fit, convulsion, paroxysm, spasm.
- **1** release, liberation.

seldom *adv.* rarely. [from Anglo-Saxon *seldum*]

- rarely, infrequently, occasionally, hardly ever.
- often, usually.

select — *verb* to choose from among several. — *adj.* **1** picked out in preference to others. **2** to which entrance or membership is restricted; exclusive. [from Latin *seligere*]

- *verb* choose, pick, single out, decide on, opt for, appoint, elect. *adj.* **1** selected, choice, top, prime, first-class, first-rate, hand-picked, elite. **2** exclusive, limited, restricted, special.
- *adj.* **1** second-rate, ordinary. **2** general.

select committee *Politics* a committee made up of members of a legislature, whose task is to examine a specific subject, such as education or defence.

selection *noun* **1** the act or process of selecting or being selected. **2** a thing or set of things selected. **3** a range from which to choose. **4** natural selection. **5** artificial selection.

- **1** choice, pick. **2** choice, option, preference, assortment, variety, miscellany, medley, potpourri, collection, anthology. **3** range, choice, assortment, variety.

selective *adj.* **1** exercising the right to reject some in favour of others. **2** able or tending to select; discriminating. **3** involving only certain people or things; exclusive.

- **2** particular, *colloq.* choosy, discriminating, discerning. **3** exclusive, select.
- **3** indiscriminate.

selectivity *noun* the ability to discriminate.
selectness *noun* being select.
selector *noun* a person who selects.
selenite *noun* Geol. a variety of gypsum that occurs as clear colourless crystals. [from Greek *selene*, moon]
selenium /səˈliːnɪəm/ *noun* Chem. (SYMBOL **Se**, ATOMIC NUMBER **34**) a metalloid element that exists as several different allotropes, one of which conducts electricity in the presence of light, and is used in photoelectric cells, photographic exposure meters, and xerography (photocopying). [from Greek *selene*, moon]
self — *noun* (PL. **selves**) **1** personality, or a particular aspect of it. **2** a person as a whole, a combination of characteristics of appearance and behaviour: *his usual happy self.* **3** personal interest or advantage. — *pron. colloq.* myself, yourself, himself, or herself. [from Anglo-Saxon *seolf*]

- *noun* **1** personality, identity, ego.

self- *combining form* forming words meaning: **1** by or for oneself; in relation to oneself: *self-doubt/self-inflicted.* **2** acting automatically: *self-closing.*
self-abuse *noun* masturbation.
self-addressed *adj.* addressed by the sender for return to him or herself.
self-appointed *adj.* acting on one's own authority, without being asked or chosen by others.
self-assertion *noun* self-asserting, being self-assertive.

self-assertive *adj.* always ready to make others aware of one's presence or opinions, especially arrogantly or aggressively.
self-assurance *noun* self-confidence.
self-assured *adj.* self-confident.
self-catering *adj.*, *said of accommodation* in which guests or residents have facilities for preparing their own meals.
self-centred *adj.* interested only in oneself and one's own affairs.

- selfish, self-seeking, self-serving, self-interested, egotistic, narcissistic, self-absorbed, egocentric.
- altruistic.

self-coloured *adj.* **1** of the same colour all over. **2** in its natural colour; undyed.
self-confessed *adj.* as openly admitted by oneself: *a self-confessed cheat.*
self-confidence *noun* total absence of shyness; confidence in one's own abilities.
self-confident *adj.* confident of one's own powers, sometimes arrogantly so.

- confident, self-reliant, self-assured, assured, self-possessed, cool, fearless.
- unsure, self-conscious.

self-conscious *adj.* ill at ease in company as a result of feeling oneself to be observed by others.

- uncomfortable, ill at ease, awkward, embarrassed, shy, bashful, coy, retiring, shrinking, self-effacing, nervous, insecure.
- natural, confident.

self-contained *adj.* **1** *said of accommodation* of which no part is shared with others. **2** content to be on one's own; independent. **3** needing nothing added; complete.
self-control *noun* the ability to control one's emotions and impulses.

- calmness, composure, *colloq.* cool, patience, self-restraint, self-denial, temperance, self-discipline, self-mastery, willpower.

self-controlled *adj.* characterized by or showing self-control.
self-defence *noun* **1** the act or techniques of defending oneself from physical attack. **2** the act of defending one's own rights or principles.
self-denial *noun* the act or practice of denying one's own needs or wishes.

- moderation, temperance, abstemiousness, asceticism, self-sacrifice, unselfishness, selflessness.
- self-indulgence.

self-deprecating *adj.* modest or dismissive about oneself or one's achievements.
self-determination *noun* **1** the freedom to make one's own decisions without interference from others. **2** a nation's freedom to govern itself, without outside control.
self-drive *adj.*, *said of a hired vehicle* to be driven by the hirer.
self-effacement *noun* being self-effacing.
self-effacing *adj.* tending to avoid making others aware of one's presence or one's achievements, because of shyness or modesty.
self-employed *adj.* working on one's own behalf and under one's own control, rather than as an employee.
self-esteem *noun* one's opinion, especially good opinion, of oneself; self-respect.

self-evident *adj.* clear enough to need no explanation or proof.

. . . .

☰ obvious, manifest, clear, undeniable, axiomatic, unquestionable, incontrovertible.

. . . .

self-explanatory *adj.* easily understood; needing no further explanation.

self-fulfilling *adj.*, *said of a forecast, etc* which, by virtue of its being made, has the effect of bringing about the results it predicts: *a self-fulfilling prophecy.*

self-governing *adj.* controlling itself, not controlled from outside by others.

self-government *noun* being self-governing.

. . . .

☰ autonomy, independence, home rule, democracy.
☲ subjection.

. . . .

self-harming *noun* the habitual practice of inflicting physical damage on oneself.

self-heal *noun* a perennial plant (*Prunella vulgaris*), widespread in Europe, with creeping rooting stems that carpet the ground and dense heads of violet-blue flowers. Its name derives from the fact that it was formerly used as a medicinal herb.

self-help *noun* the practice of solving one's own problems using abilities developed in oneself, rather than relying on assistance from others.

self-importance *noun* being self-important; arrogance.

self-important *adj.* having an exaggerated sense of one's own importance; arrogant; pompous.

. . . .

☰ arrogant, pompous, big-headed, conceited, vain, proud.
☲ humble.

. . . .

self-imposed *adj.* forced on oneself by oneself, not imposed by others.

self-indulgence *noun* being self-indulgent, or an instance of this.

self-indulgent *adj.* giving in, or tending to give in, to one's own wishes or whims.

. . . .

☰ hedonistic, dissolute, dissipated, profligate, extravagant, intemperate, immoderate.
☲ abstemious.

. . . .

self-inflicted *adj.* inflicted by oneself on oneself.

selfing *noun Biol.* self-fertilization, self-pollination.

self-interest *noun* one's own personal welfare or advantage.

self-interested *adj.* characterized by self-interest.

selfish *adj.* **1** tending to be concerned only with personal welfare, not the welfare of others. **2** *said of an act* revealing such a tendency.

. . . .

☰ SELF-SERVING, MEAN. **1** self-interested, self-seeking, greedy, covetous, self-centred, egocentric, egotistic.
☲ UNSELFISH, SELFLESS, ALTRUISTIC, GENEROUS.

. . . .

selfishness *noun* being selfish, or an instance of this.

selfless *adj.* **1** tending to consider the welfare of others before one's own. **2** *said of an act* revealing such a tendency.

. . . .

☰ UNSELFISH, ALTRUISTIC, GENEROUS, PHILANTHROPIC. **1** self-denying, self-sacrificing.
☲ SELFISH. **1** self-centred.

. . . .

selflessness *noun* being selfless, or an instance of this.

self-made *adj.* having acquired wealth or achieved success through one's own efforts, rather than through advantages given by birth.

self-opinionated *adj.* tending to insist that one's own opinions, forcefully stated, are superior to all others.

self-pity *noun* excessive grumbling or moaning about one's own misfortunes.

self-pollination *noun Bot.* in flowering plants, the transfer of pollen from the anther of the stamen to the stigma of the same flower.

self-possessed *adj.* calm and controlled, especially in an emergency.

. . . .

☰ calm, controlled, composed, self-assured.

. . . .

self-possession *noun* calmness.

self-preservation *noun* the protection of one's own life; the instinct underlying this.

self-raising *adj.*, *said of flour* containing an ingredient to make dough or pastry rise.

self-reliance *noun* reliance on one's own abilities and resources, etc.

self-reliant *adj.* never needing or seeking help from others; independent.

self-respect *noun* respect for oneself and concern for one's dignity and reputation.

. . . .

☰ pride, dignity, self-esteem, self-assurance, self-confidence.

. . . .

self-respecting *adj.* having self-respect.

self-restraint *noun* the act of controlling, or the capacity to control, one's own desires or feelings.

self-righteous *adj.* having too high an opinion of one's own goodness, and intolerant of other people's faults.

. . . .

☰ smug, complacent, superior, *colloq.* goody-goody, pious, sanctimonious, holier-than-thou, pietistic, hypocritical, pharisaic.

. . . .

self-sacrifice *noun* the sacrifice of one's own wishes or interests for the sake of other people's.

. . . .

☰ self-denial, self-renunciation, selflessness, altruism, unselfishness, generosity.
☲ selfishness.

. . . .

self-sacrificing *adj.* characterized by self-sacrifice.

selfsame *adj.* very same; identical.

self-satisfaction *noun* self-satisfying, being self-satisfied.

self-satisfied *adj.* feeling or showing complacent or arrogant satisfaction with oneself or one's achievements; smug.

. . . .

☰ smug, complacent, self-congratulatory, self-righteous.
☲ humble.

. . . .

self-sealing *adj.* **1** *said of an envelope* whose flap is coated with an adhesive which sticks without being moistened. **2** *said eg of a tyre* capable of automatically sealing small punctures.

self-seeker *noun* someone who looks mainly to their own interests or advantage.

self-seeking — *adj.* preoccupied with one's own interests and the opportunities for personal advantage. — *noun* behaviour of this kind.

self-service — *noun* a system, especially in catering, in which customers serve themselves and pay at a checkout. — *adj.*, *said of a restaurant, etc* operating such a system.

self-serving *adj.* benefiting or seeking to benefit oneself, often to the disadvantage of others.

self-starter *noun* **1** an electric starting device in a vehicle's engine. **2** *colloq.* a person who requires little supervision in a job, being able to motivate himself or herself and use his or her own initiative.

self-styled *adj.* called or considered so only by oneself: *a self-styled superstar.*

. . . .

▣ self-appointed, professed, so-called, would-be.

. . . .

self-sufficiency *noun* being self-sufficient.

self-sufficient *adj.*, *said of a person or thing* able to provide oneself or itself with everything needed to live on or survive.

self-supporting *adj.* 1 earning enough money to meet all one's own expenses. 2 self-sufficient. 3 needing no additional supports or attachments to stay firmly fixed or upright.

. . . .

▣ 2 self-sufficient, independent, self-reliant.
▣ 1, 2 dependent.

. . . .

self-willed *adj.* strongly or stubbornly determined to do or have what one wants.

sell — *verb* (PAST TENSE AND PAST PARTICIPLE **sold**) 1 to give to someone in exchange for money: *she sold it to her brother/can I sell you a crate of whisky?* 2 to have available for buying. 3 (**sell at** or **for something**) to be available for buying at a specified price. 4 *intrans.* to be bought by customers; to be in demand. 5 to cause to be bought; to promote the sale of: *the author's name sells the book.* 6 to persuade (someone) to acquire or agree to something, especially by emphasizing its merits or advantages: *it was difficult to sell them the idea.* 7 (**sell one thing for another**) to lose or betray (eg one's principles) in the process of getting something (especially dishonourable). — *noun* 1 the style of persuasion used in selling: *the hard sell.* 2 *colloq.* a trick or deception. — **sell someone down the river** *colloq.* to betray them. **sell something off** to sell remaining goods quickly and cheaply. **sell out of something** to sell one's entire stock of it. **sell out to someone** to betray one's principles or associates to another party: *he sold out to the opposition.* **sell someone** or **something short** *colloq.* to understate their good qualities. **sell up** to sell one's house or business. [from Anglo-Saxon *sellan*, to hand over]

. . . .

▣ *verb* 1 exchange, trade, barter, auction, vend, retail, hawk, peddle. 2 stock, handle, deal in, trade in, traffic in. 5 promote, advertise, market.
▣ *verb* 1 buy.

. . . .

sell-by date a date on a manufacturer's or distributor's label indicating when goods, especially foods, are considered no longer fit to be sold.

seller *noun* a person who sells or is selling something.

. . . .

▣ vendor, merchant, trader, dealer, supplier, stockist, retailer, shopkeeper, salesman, saleswoman, agent, representative, *colloq.* rep.
▣ buyer, purchaser.

. . . .

seller's market *Commerce* a situation where demand exceeds supply and sellers may control the price of a commodity, product, etc.

Sellotape — *noun trademark* a type of transparent adhesive tape, especially for use on paper. — *verb* to stick with Sellotape.

sell-out *noun* an event for which all the tickets have been sold.

sell-through *noun* retail sale, especially of video cassettes.

selvage or **selvedge** *noun* an edge of a length of fabric woven so as to prevent fraying. [from SELF + EDGE]

selves see SELF.

SEM *abbrev. Maths.* standard error of the mean.

semantic *adj.* of or relating to meaning. [from Greek *semantikos*, significant]

semantically *adv.* in a semantic way; in terms of semantics.

semantics *sing. noun* the branch of linguistics that deals with meaning.

semaphore — *noun* 1 a system of signalling in which flags, or simply the arms, are held in positions that represent individual letters and numbers. 2 a signalling device, especially a pole with arms that can be set in different positions. — *verb trans., intrans.* to signal using semaphore or a semaphore. [from Greek *sema*, sign + *-phoros*, bearer]

semblance *noun* 1 appearance, especially superficial or deceiving. 2 a hint or trace. [from Old French *sembler*, to seem]

. . . .

▣ 1 appearance, air, show, pretence, guise, mask, front, façade, veneer, apparition, image.

. . . .

semen /ˈsiːmən/ *noun* a thick whitish liquid containing sperm, ejaculated by the penis. See also SEMINAL. [from Latin *semen*, seed]

semester *noun* an academic term lasting half an academic year. [from Latin *semestris*, six-monthly]

semi *noun* (PL. **semis**) *colloq.* a semi-detached house.

semi- *prefix* forming words meaning: 1 half: *semiquaver.* 2 partly: *semiconscious.* 3 occurring twice in the stated period: *semiannual.* [from Latin *semi*, half]

semi-automatic *adj.* 1 partially automatic. 2 *said of a firearm* continuously reloading bullets, but only firing one at a time.

semibreve /ˈsemibriːv/ *noun* the longest musical note in common use, equal to half a breve, two minims, or four crotchets.

semicircle *noun* 1 one half of a circle. 2 an arrangement in this form.

semicircular *adj.* having the form of a semicircle.

semicircular canal *Anat.* in the inner ear of mammals, one of the three fluid-filled semicircular tubes that are involved in the maintenance of balance.

semicolon /ˈsemikəʊlən/ *noun* a punctuation mark (;) indicating a pause stronger than that marked by a comma and weaker than that marked by a full stop. Its principal use is to separate clauses, as in *We will bring the drink; you can provide the food.*

semiconductor *noun Electron.* a crystalline material that behaves either as an electrical conductor or as an insulator, depending on the temperature and the purity of the material, eg silicon, germanium. Semiconductors are used to make diodes, transistors, photoelectric devices, etc.

semi-detached — *adj.*, *said of a house* forming part of the same building with another house on one side. — *noun* a semi-detached house.

semi-final *noun* in competitions, either of two matches, the winners of which play each other in the final.

semi-finalist *noun* a competitor who qualifies for a semi-final.

seminal *adj.* 1 highly original and at the root of a trend or movement: *seminal writings.* 2 of or relating to seed, semen, or reproduction in general. [from Latin *semen semin*, seed]

seminar *noun* 1 a small class for the discussion of a particular topic between students and a tutor. 2 any meeting set up for the purpose of discussion. [from Latin *seminarium*, seed-plot]

seminarian /semiˈneəriən/ *noun* 1 a student in a seminary or in a seminar. 2 a Roman Catholic priest educated in a foreign seminary. 3 a teacher in a seminary.

seminary *noun* (PL. **seminaries**) 1 a college for the training of members of the clergy. 2 *old use* a school, especially for girls. [see SEMINAR]

seminiferous tubule *Anat.* in mammals, any of many long tightly coiled tubules that form the bulk of the testes, and in which the sperm are produced. [from Latin *semen semin-*, seed]

semiology *noun* same as SEMIOTICS.

semiotic *adj.* 1 relating to signs and symbols. 2 relating to semiotics. 3 relating to or resembling symptoms of disease.

semiotics *sing. noun* the study of human communication, especially the relationship between words and the objects or concepts they refer to. [from Greek *semeiotikos*, of signs; *semeion*, sign + -LOGY]

semi-permeable *adj.* 1 only partly permeable. 2 *Biol.* denoting a membrane through which only certain molecules can pass, eg it may be permeable to water but impermeable to sugars and salts.

semi-precious *adj.*, *said of a gem* considered less valuable than a precious stone.

semi-professional — *adj.* 1 engaging only part-time in a professional activity. 2 *said of an activity* engaged in only as a part-time profession. — *noun* a semi-professional person.

semiquaver *noun* a musical note equal to half a quaver or one-sixteenth of a semibreve.

semi-skilled *adj.* having or requiring a degree of training less advanced than that needed for specialised work.

semi-skimmed milk milk from which half of the cream has been removed.

Semite a member of a group of peoples found in SW Asia. The most prominent modern Semitic peoples include the Jews and the Arabs.

Semitic /sə'mɪtɪk/ — *noun* any of a group of Afro-Asiatic languages that includes Hebrew, Arabic, and Aramaic. — *adj.* 1 relating to or speaking any such language. 2 relating to Semites. 3 relating to the Jews; Jewish.

semitone *noun* half a tone in the musical scale, the interval between adjacent notes on a keyboard instrument.

semi-tropical *adj.* subtropical.

semivowel *noun* 1 a speech sound having the qualities of both a vowel and a consonant, such as the sounds represented by the letters *y* and *w*. 2 a letter representing such a sound.

semolina /sɛmə'liːnə/ *noun* hard particles of wheat not ground into flour during milling, used to thicken soups and make puddings. [from Italian *semolino*, diminutive of *semola*, bran]

Semtex *noun trademark* a powerful type of plastic explosive.

SEN *abbrev.* State Enrolled Nurse.

Sen. *abbrev.* 1 senate. 2 senator. 3 senior.

senate /'sɛnət/ *noun* (*often* **Senate**) 1 the chief legislative and administrative body in ancient Rome. 2 a law-making body, especially the upper chamber of the national assembly in the USA, Australia, and other countries. 3 the governing council in some British universities. [from Latin *senatus*, from *senex*, old man]

senator /'sɛnətə(r)/ *noun* (*often* **Senator**) a member of a senate.

senatorial *adj.* 1 relating to or characteristic of a senator. 2 made up of senators.

send *verb* (PAST TENSE AND PAST PARTICIPLE **sent**) 1 to cause or order to go or be conveyed or transmitted. 2 to force or propel: *sent me flying.* 3 to cause to become or pass into a specified state: *sent him into fits of laughter/ sent me mad.* 4 to bring about, especially by divine providence: *a plague sent by God.* 5 *old slang* use to put into a state of ecstasy; to thrill. — **send away for something** to order goods by post. **send someone down** 1 *colloq.* to send them to prison. 2 to expel them from university. **send for someone** to ask or order them to come; to summon them. **send for something** to order it to be brought or delivered. **send something in** to offer or submit it by post. **send someone off** to dismiss them, especially from the field of play in sport. **send something off** to dispatch it, especially by post. **send off for something** to order goods by post. **send something on** 1 to re-address and re-post a letter, etc; to forward it. 2 to post or send it, so as to arrive in advance of oneself. **send something out** 1 to distribute it by post. 2 to dispatch it. **send someone out for something** to send them to fetch it. **send someone** or **something up** *Brit. colloq.* to ridicule or parody them. [from Anglo-Saxon *sendan*]

⊟ 1 post, mail, dispatch, consign, remit, forward, convey, transmit, broadcast, communicate. 2 force, propel, drive, throw, fling, hurl, launch, fire, shoot, discharge, emit, direct. **send for** *someone* summon, call. *something* request, call for, order. **send up** satirize, mock, ridicule, parody, take off.

⊟ 1 receive.

sender *noun* 1 a person who sends something, especially by post. 2 a transmitting device.

send-off *noun* a display of good wishes from an assembled crowd to a departing person or group.

⊟ farewell, goodbye, leave-taking, departure, start.

⊟ arrival.

send-up *noun Brit. colloq.* a parody or satire.

senescence /sɪ'nɛsəns/ *noun Biol.* the changes that take place in a living organism during the process of ageing, eg the production of flowers and fruit in plants.

senescent /sɪ'nɛsənt/ *adj. formal* growing old; ageing. [from Latin *senescere*, to grow old]

seneschal /'sɛnɪʃəl/ *noun* a steward in charge of the household or estate of a medieval lord or prince. [from Old French, = old servant]

senile /'siːnaɪl/ *adj.* 1 displaying the feebleness of mind or body brought on by old age. 2 of or caused by old age. [from Latin *senilis*, from *senex*, old]

⊟ 1 old, aged, doddering, decrepit, failing, confused.

senile dementia mental deterioration brought on by old age.

senility *noun* 1 old age. 2 mental deterioration in old age.

senior — *adj.* 1 (*often* **senior to someone**) a older than someone. b higher in rank or authority than someone. 2 of or for schoolchildren over the age of 11. 3 *North Amer.* of final-year college or university students. 4 older than a person of the same name, especially distinguishing parent from child: *James Smith, Senior.* — *noun* 1 a person who is older or of a higher rank. 2 a pupil in a senior school, or in the senior part of a school. 3 *North Amer.* a final-year student. [from Latin *senior*, older]

⊟ *adj.* 1 older, elder, higher, superior, high-ranking, major, chief. *noun* 1 elder, superior.

⊟ *adj.* JUNIOR. *noun* JUNIOR.

senior citizen an elderly person, especially one retired.

seniority *noun* 1 the state of being senior. 2 a privileged position earned through long service in a profession or with a company.

⊟ 1 priority, precedence, rank, standing, status, age, superiority, importance.

senior service (*usually* **the senior service**) the Royal Navy.

senna *noun* 1 any of a family of tropical trees and shrubs that produce long seed pods. 2 a laxative prepared from the dried pods. [from Arabic *sana*]

sensation *noun* 1 awareness of an external or internal stimulus, eg heat, pain, or emotions, as a result of its perception by sensory receptors or sense organs of the nervous system, and subsequent interpretation by the brain. 2 a physical feeling: *a burning sensation in my mouth.* 3 an emotion or general feeling. 4 a sudden widespread feeling of excitement or shock; also, the cause of this. [from Latin *sensatio*, from *sentire*, to feel]

⊟ 2, 3 feeling, sense, impression, perception, awareness,

consciousness. **4** excitement, thrill, commotion, stir, agitation, shock, outrage, furore, scandal.

....

sensational *adj.* **1** causing, or intended to cause, widespread excitement, intense interest, or shock. **2** *colloq.* excellent; marvellous. **3** of the senses.

....

🔳 **1** exciting, thrilling, electrifying, breathtaking, startling, amazing, astounding, staggering, shocking, horrifying, scandalous, melodramatic, lurid, dramatic, spectacular, impressive. **2** excellent, wonderful, marvellous, exceptional, *colloq.* smashing, *colloq.* fantastic.
🔳 **2** ordinary, run-of-the-mill.

....

sensationalism *noun* the practice of, or methods used in, deliberately setting out to cause widespread excitement, intense interest, or shock.

sensationalist *noun* **1** a person who aims to cause a sensation. **2** a person who believes that the senses are the ultimate source of all knowledge.

sense — *noun* **1** any of the faculties used by an animal to obtain information about its external or internal environment. The five main senses are sight, hearing, smell, taste, and touch. **2** an awareness or appreciation of, or an ability to make judgements regarding, some specified thing: *sense of direction/bad business sense*. **3** (*often* **senses**) soundness of mind; reasonableness: *lost his senses*. **4** wisdom; practical worth: *no sense in doing it now*. **5** a general feeling, not perceived using any of the five natural powers: *a sense of guilt*. **6** overall meaning: *understood the sense of the passage, if not all the words.* **7** specific meaning. **8** general opinion; consensus: *the sense of the meeting.* — *verb* **1** to detect a stimulus by means of any of the five main senses. **2** to be aware of something by means other than the five main senses: *sensed that someone was following me.* **3** to realize or comprehend. — **come to one's senses 1** to act sensibly after a period of foolishness. **2** to regain consciousness. **in a sense** in one respect; in a way. **make sense 1** to be able to be understood. **2** to be wise or reasonable. [from Latin *sensus*, from *sentire*, to feel]

....

🔳 *noun* **1** faculty. **2** awareness, consciousness, appreciation, discernment, judgement. **3** mind, brain(s), wit(s), wisdom, intelligence, understanding, reason, logic, intuition. **4** wisdom, point, purpose, value, worth. **5** feeling, sensation, impression, perception. **6** meaning, significance, gist, substance, implication. **7** meaning, definition, interpretation. *verb* **1** detect, perceive, notice, observe. **2** feel, suspect, intuit. **3** realize, appreciate, understand, comprehend, grasp.

....

sense-datum *noun* (PL. **sense-data**) that which is received immediately through the stimulation of a sense organ, unaffected by inference or other knowledge. It is how a thing appears to be to one person, not how it really is, nor how it appears to someone else.

senseless *adj.* **1** unconscious. **2** unwise; foolish.

....

🔳 **1** unconscious, out, stunned, anaesthetized, deadened, numb. **2** unwise, foolish, stupid, silly, idiotic, mad, crazy, daft, ridiculous, absurd, meaningless, nonsensical, irrational, illogical, pointless, purposeless, futile.
🔳 **1** conscious. **2** sensible, meaningful.

....

sense organ *Physiol.* in animals, any organ consisting of specialized receptor cells that are capable of responding to a particular stimulus, eg light, sound, smell. In mammals the main sense organs are the eyes, ears, nose, skin, and taste buds of the tongue.

sensibility *noun* (PL. **sensibilities**) **1** the ability to feel or have sensations. **2** the capacity to be affected emotionally; sensitivity: *sensibility to his grief.* **3** (**sensibilities**) feelings, when easily offended or hurt. [see SENSIBLE]

sensible *adj.* **1** wise; having or showing reasonableness or good judgement. **2** perceptible by the senses. **3** able to feel; sensitive: *sensible to pain.* [from Latin *sensibilis*]

....

🔳 **1** wise, prudent, judicious, well-advised, shrewd, far-sighted, intelligent, level-headed, down-to-earth, common-sense, sane, rational, logical, reasonable, realistic, practical, functional. **3** sensitive, responsive, aware, perceptive, discerning, susceptible, vulnerable.
🔳 **1** senseless, unwise, foolish. **3** insensible, unaware.

....

sensitive *adj.* **1** responding readily, strongly, or painfully: *sensitive to our feelings.* **2** able to feel or respond. **3** easily upset or offended. **4** about which there is much strong feeling or difference of opinion: *sensitive issues.* **5** *said of documents, etc* not for public discussion or scrutiny, eg because involving matters of national security or embarrassing to the government. **6** *said of scientific instruments* reacting to or recording very small changes. **7** *Photog.* responding to the action of light. **8** *Physics* responding to the action of some force or stimulus: *pressure-sensitive.* [from Latin *sensitivus*, from *sentire*, to feel]

....

🔳 **1** perceptive, discerning, appreciative, impressionable, susceptible, vulnerable, tender, emotional. **2** sensitized, sensible, responsive, aware. **3** thin-skinned, temperamental, touchy, irritable. **6** exact, precise, delicate, fine.
🔳 **1** insensitive. **3** thick-skinned. **6** imprecise, approximate.

....

sensitive plant a perennial plant (*Mimosa pudica*), native to S America, with a prickly stem, and leaves divided into narrow leaflets. The leaves close up at night, and this response can also be triggered by touching the plant.

sensitivity *noun* **1** a sensitive quality or inclination. **2** being sensitive or reacting to an allergen, drug, or other external stimulus. **3** the readiness and delicacy of an instrument in recording changes.

sensitization or **sensitisation** *noun* sensitizing or being sensitized.

sensitize or **sensitise** *verb* to make sensitive.

sensor /ˈsɛnsə(r)/ *noun Electr.* any device that detects or measures a change in a physical quantity, eg temperature, light, or sound, usually by converting it into an electrical signal. Examples of sensors include burglar alarms, smoke detectors, and photocells.

sensory *adj.* of the senses or sensation. [from Latin *sensorium*, brain, seat of the senses]

sensory nerve *Anat.* a nerve that relays nerve impulses from sensory receptor cells and sense organs to the central nervous system (the brain and spinal cord). [from Latin *sensorius*, from Latin *sentire* to feel]

sensual /ˈsɛnʃʊəl/ *adj.* **1** of the senses and the body rather than the mind or the spirit. **2** suggesting, enjoying, or providing physical (especially sexual) pleasure. **3** pursuing physical pleasures, especially those derived from sex or food and drink. [from Latin *sensus*, sense]

....

🔳 **1** physical, bodily, animal, sexual, carnal, fleshly, worldly. **2** erotic, sexy, voluptuous. **3** self-indulgent, lustful, lecherous, lewd, licentious.
🔳 **1** spiritual. **3** ascetic.

....

sensuality *noun* **1** the quality of being sensual. **2** indulgence in physical pleasures.

sensuous *adj.* **1** appealing to or designed to stimulate the senses aesthetically, with no suggestion of sexual pleasure. **2** pleasing to the senses. **3** very aware of what is perceived by the senses. [from Latin *sensus*, sense]

....

🔳 **2** pleasurable, gratifying, rich, lush, luxurious, sumptuous.
🔳 **2** plain, simple.

....

sent see SEND.

sentence — *noun* **1** a sequence of words forming a meaningful and more or less complete grammatical structure, usually with a subject and verb and making a statement, asking a question, or making an exclamation. **2** a punishment determined by a court or judge; its announcement in court. — *verb* **1** to announce the punishment to be given to (someone). **2** to condemn to a punishment: *sentenced him to five years' imprisonment.* — **pass sentence on someone** to announce the punishment to be given to someone. [from Latin *sententia*, opinion]

⊟ *noun* **2** judgement, decision, verdict, pronouncement, ruling, condemnation, punishment. *verb* **1** judge, pass judgement on. **2** condemn, doom, punish, penalize.

sententious *adj.* **1** tending to lecture others on morals. **2** full of, or fond of using, sayings or proverbs. [from Latin *sententiosus*, full of meaning]

sentience *noun* being sentient.

sentient /'sɛnʃənt/ *adj.* able to feel; capable of sensation: *sentient beings.* [from Latin *sentire*, to feel]

sentiment *noun* **1** an emotion, especially when expressed. **2** emotion or emotional behaviour in general, especially when considered excessive, self-indulgent, or insincere. **3** (*often* **sentiments**) an opinion or view. [from Latin *sentimentum*, from *sentire*, to feel]

⊟ **1** emotion, feeling. **2** emotion, sensibility, tenderness, softheartedness, romanticism, sentimentality, mawkishness. **3** opinion, view, judgement, belief, thought, idea, feeling, attitude.

sentimental *adj.* **1** easily feeling and expressing tender emotions, especially love, friendship, and pity. **2** provoking or designed to provoke such emotions, especially in large measure and without subtlety. **3** closely associated with, or moved (to tears) by, fond memories of the past: *objects of sentimental value.*

⊟ **1** tender, soft-hearted, loving, caring, emotional, gushing. **2** touching, pathetic, tear-jerking, romantic, *colloq.* lovey-dovey, slushy, mushy, *colloq.* soppy, *colloq.* corny. **3** nostalgic, maudlin, mawkish.
🗝 **1** unsentimental, cynical.

sentimentalism *noun* sentimentality.

sentimentalist *noun* a person who indulges in sentimentalism.

sentimentality *noun* **1** a sentimental quality or inclination. **2** a tendency to indulge in sentiment or to affect fine feelings.

sentimentalize or **sentimentalise** *verb* **1** *intrans.* to behave sentimentally. **2** *trans.* to react to emotionally, rather than taking a frank and practical approach.

sentimental novel a type of fiction, popular in the 18c, concerned with the idea that honourable and moral behaviour (especially of a virtuous heroine) would be justly rewarded.

sentinel *noun* a sentry. [from French *sentinelle*]

sentry *noun* (PL. **sentries**) a soldier or other person on guard to control entry or passage.

⊟ sentinel, guard, picket, watchman, watch, lookout.

sentry box a small open-fronted shelter for a sentry.
Sep or **Sep.** *abbrev.* September.

sepal /'sɛpəl/ *noun Bot.* in a flower, one of the modified leaves, usually green but sometimes brightly coloured, that together form the *calyx* which surrounds the petals and protects the developing flower bud. [from French *sépale*]

separability *noun* being separable.

separable *adj.* able to be separated. [from Latin *separabilis*]

⊟ divisible, detachable, removable, distinguishable, distinct.
🗝 inseparable.

separate — *verb* (pronounced -reit) **1** to set, take, keep, or force apart (from others or each other). **2** *intrans.* to move apart; to become detached; to cease to be or live together. **3** (*also* **separate up**) to divide or become divided into parts. — *adj.* (pronounced -rət) **1** distinctly different or individual; unrelated: *a separate issue.* **2** physically unattached; isolated. — *noun* (pronounced -rət) (*usually* **separates**) a piece of clothing intended for wear with a variety of others, not forming part of a suit. [from Latin *separare*]

⊟ *verb* **1** divide, sever, disconnect, uncouple, disunite, segregate, isolate, cut off, remove, detach. **2** part, split up, divorce, part company, diverge, withdraw, secede. **3** divide, split. *adj.* **1** different, disparate, unrelated, unconnected, distinct, discrete, several, sundry, single, individual, particular, independent. **2** unattached, detached, disunited, disconnected, alone, solitary, isolated, apart, divorced, divided.
🗝 *verb* **1** join, unite. **2** converge. **3** combine. *adj.* CONNECTED. **1** related. **2** attached.

separation *noun* **1** the act of separating or the state or process of being separated. **2** a place or line where there is a division. **3** a gap or interval that separates. **4** an arrangement, approved mutually or by a court, under which a husband and wife live apart while remaining married, usually prior to divorce.

⊟ **1** division, severance, parting, leave-taking, divergence, disconnection, dissociation, segregation, isolation, detachment. **3** gap, rift, split. **4** split-up, break-up, divorce, estrangement.
🗝 **1** unification.

separation of powers a political doctrine which argues that, to avoid tyranny, the three branches of government (legislature, executive, and judiciary) should be separated as far as possible, with their relationships governed by checks and balances.

separatism *noun* **1** a tendency to separate or to be separate. **2** support for separation. **3** the practices and principles of separatists.

separatist *noun* a person who encourages, or takes action to achieve, independence from a country or an established institution, eg a Church.

separator *noun* a person, thing, or machine that separates.

sepek takraw a court game popular in SE Asia, played on a badminton court by two teams of three players with a rattan palm ball. The ball is propelled over a central net using any part of the body other than the arms and hands. [from Malay *sepek*, kick + Thai *takraw*, rattan ball]

Sephardim /sɪ'fɑːdɪm/ *pl. noun* the descendants of the Jews who lived in Spain and Portugal before 1492, when they were expelled for not accepting Christianity. [Hebrew, = Spaniards]

sepia /'siːpɪə/ *noun* **1** a yellowish-brown tint used in photography. **2** a dark reddish-brown colour. **3** a pigment of this colour, obtained from a fluid secreted by the cuttlefish. [from Greek *sepia*, cuttlefish]

sepoy /'siːpɔɪ/ *noun Hist.* an Indian soldier in service with a European (especially British) army. [from Urdu and Persian *sipahi*, horseman]

sepsis *noun* (PL. **sepses**) *Medicine* the presence of disease-causing micro-organisms, especially viruses or bacteria, and their toxins in the body tissues, which can result in infection, inflammation, and eventual destruction of the affected areas. [from Greek *sepsis*, putrefaction]

Sept or **Sept.** *abbrev.* **1** September. **2** Septuagint.

sept *noun* a clan, especially in Ireland. [an alteration of SECT]

septa see SEPTUM.

September *noun* the ninth month of the year. [from Latin *September*, seventh, ie the seventh month in the original Roman calendar]

septennial *adj.* **1** occurring once every seven years. **2** lasting seven years. [from Latin *septem*, seven + *annus*, year]

septet *noun* **1** a group of seven musicians. **2** a piece of music for seven performers. **3** any group or set of seven. [from Latin *septem*, seven]

septic *adj.* **1** *Medicine, said of a wound* contaminated with disease-causing bacteria. **2** putrefying. [from Greek *septikos*; related to SEPSIS]
. . . .
◼ **1** infected, poisoned, contaminated. **2** festering, putrefying, putrid.
. . . .

septicaemia /sɛptɪˈsiːmɪə/ *noun* blood-poisoning. [from Greek *septikos*, putrefied + *haima*, blood]

septic tank a tank, usually underground, in which sewage is broken down by the action of bacteria.

septuagenarian /sɛptjʊədʒəˈnɛərɪən/ — *adj.* between 70 and 79 years old. — *noun* a septuagenarian person. [from Latin *septuaginta*, seventy]

Septuagesima /sɛptjʊəˈdʒɛsɪmə/ *noun* the third Sunday before Lent, apparently so called by analogy with Quadragesima and Quinquagesima; the 70th day (in fact, the 64th day) before Easter. [from Latin *septuagesimus*, seventieth]

Septuagint /ˈsɛptjʊədʒɪnt/ *noun* a translation into Greek of the Hebrew Bible, named from a legend in the *Letter of Aristeas* (2c BC) which described it as the work of 72 scholars, six from each of the 12 tribes of Israel. [from Latin *septuaginta*, 70]

septum *noun* (PL. **septa**) *Anat.* any partition between cavities, eg nostrils, or areas of soft tissue. [from Latin *saeptum*, fence]

septuple /sɛpˈtjuːpl/ — *adj.* being seven times as much or as many; sevenfold. — *verb trans., intrans.* to multiply or increase sevenfold. [from Latin *septuplus*]

septuplet /ˈsɛptjʊplət, sɛpˈtjuːplət/ *noun* any of seven children born at the same time to the same mother.

sepulchral /sɪˈpʌlkrəl/ *adj.* **1** of a tomb; of burial. **2** suggestive of death or burial; gloomy; funereal.

sepulchre /ˈsɛpəlkə(r)/ — *noun* a grave or burial vault. — *verb* to bury in a sepulchre; to entomb. [from Latin *sepulcrum*]

sequel /ˈsiːkwəl/ *noun* **1** a book, film, or play that continues an earlier story. **2** a result or consequence. [from Latin *sequi*, to follow]
. . . .
◼ **1** follow-up, continuation, development. **2** result, consequence, outcome, issue, upshot.
. . . .

sequence *noun* **1** a series of things following each other in a particular order; the order they follow. **2** a succession of short pieces of action making up a scene in a film. **3** *Maths.* a set of values in which each is a fixed amount greater or smaller than its predecessor, as determined by a given rule. [from Latin *sequi*, to follow]
. . . .
◼ **1** series, succession, run, progression, chain, string, train, line, procession, order, arrangement, course, cycle, set.
. . . .

sequencing *noun* the process of determining the order of amino acids in a protein or of nucleotides in DNA or RNA.

sequential *adj.* **1** following a particular order. **2** consequent; of which each element is a direct consequence of its predecessor.

sequester /sɪˈkwɛstə(r)/ *verb* (**sequestered, sequestering**) **1** to set apart or isolate. **2** to seclude: *a sequestered garden.* **3** *Legal* to sequestrate. [from Latin *sequester*, depository]

sequestrate /ˈsiːkwəstreɪt/ *verb Legal* to remove from someone's possession until a dispute or debt has been settled. [from Latin *sequestrare*, from *sequester*, depository]

sequestration /siːkwəˈstreɪʃən/ *noun* sequestrating or being sequestrated.

sequestrator /ˈsiːkwəstreɪtə(r)/ *noun* a person who sequestrates.

sequin /ˈsiːkwɪn/ *noun* a tiny round shiny disc of foil or plastic, sewn on a garment for decoration. [from Italian *zecchino*]

sequined *adj.* covered or decorated with sequins.

sequoia /sɪˈkwɔɪə/ *noun* either of two types of gigantic Californian coniferous tree, the big tree or giant sequoia, or the redwood. [named after the Cherokee scholar Sequoiah]

seraglio /səˈrɑːlɪoʊ/ *noun* (PL. **seraglios**) **1** a harem. **2** *Hist.* a Turkish palace, especially that of the sultans at Constantinople. [from Italian *serraglio*, from Persian *saray*, palace]

seraph /ˈsɛrəf/ *noun* (PL. **seraphs, seraphim**) an angel of the highest of the nine celestial orders. [from Hebrew *seraph*]

seraphic /səˈrafɪk/ *adj.* of or like a seraph.

Serbo-Croat /sɑːboʊˈkroʊat/ *noun* a Slavonic language spoken in Serbia, Croatia, etc; the main language of the former Yugoslavia.

SERC *abbrev.* Science and Engineering Research Council.

serenade — *noun* **1** a song or tune performed at night under a woman's window by her suitor. **2** any musical piece with a gentle tempo suggestive of romance. **3** a piece of classical music of symphony length but lighter in tone and for a smaller orchestra. — *verb* to entertain (a person) with a serenade. [from Latin *serenus*, bright clear sky]

serendipitous /sɛrənˈdɪpɪtəs/ *adj.* discovered by luck or chance.

serendipity /sɛrənˈdɪpɪtɪ/ *noun* the state of frequently making lucky finds. [from the folk tale 'The Three Princes of *Serendip*' (= Sri Lanka)]

serene *adj.* **1** *said of a person* calm; at peace. **2** *said of a sky* cloudless. **3** (**Serene**) a word incorporated in the titles of members of some European royal families: *Her Serene Highness.* [from Latin *serenus*, clear]
. . . .
◼ **1** calm, tranquil, cool, composed, placid, untroubled, undisturbed, still, quiet, peaceful.
◼ **1** troubled, disturbed.
. . . .

serenity *noun* a serene quality.

serf *noun* in medieval Europe, a worker of near-slave status, bought and sold with the land on which he or she worked. [from Latin *servus*, slave]

serfdom *noun* the condition of a serf; bondage.

serge *noun* a hard-wearing twilled fabric, especially of wool. [from Old French *serge*]

sergeant /ˈsɑːdʒənt/ *noun* **1** a non-commissioned officer of the rank next above corporal in the armed forces. **2** a police officer of the rank between constable and inspector. [from Old French *sergent*, from Latin *serviens*, servant]

sergeant-at-arms *noun* (*also* **serjeant-at-arms**) an officer of a court or parliament, responsible for keeping order.

sergeant-major *noun* a non-commissioned officer of the highest rank in the armed forces.

serial — *noun* **1** a story published or broadcast in regular instalments. **2** a periodical. — *adj.* **1** appearing in instalments. **2** forming a series or part of a series.

serialism *noun Mus.* the technique of using a series (or succession) of related notes as the basis for a musical composition. Once the series has been established it can be treated in various ways, eg presented vertically as chords or horizontally as melodic lines, played backwards, or turned upside down, etc.

serialization or **serialisation** *noun* production in instalments.

serialize or **serialise** *verb* to publish or broadcast (a story, etc) in instalments.

serial killer a person committing a succession of murders.

serial number any of a set of consecutive numbers printed on identical products to identify them as a batch.

series *noun* (PL. **series**) **1** a number of similar, related, or identical things arranged or produced one after the other. **2** a television or radio programme in which the same characters appear, or a similar subject is addressed, in regularly broadcast shows. **3** *Maths.* in a sequence of numbers, the sum obtained when each term is added to the previous ones. **4** *Physics* an electric circuit whose components are arranged so that the same current passes through each of them in turn. **5** *Geol.* a group of rocks, fossils, or minerals that can be arranged in a natural sequence on the basis of certain properties, eg composition. [from Latin *series*, chain, row]

. . . .

▣ **1** set, cycle, succession, sequence, run, progression, chain, string, line, train, order.

. . . .

series circuit *Physics* an electric circuit in which the circuit components are connected end to end, so that the same amount of current flows through all the components one after the other.

serif /ˈsɛrɪf/ *noun* a short decorative line or stroke on the end of a printed letter, as in E as opposed to the sanserif (= without serifs).

serigraph *noun* a print made by silk-screen process. [from Latin *sericum*, silk + Greek *graphe*, writing]

serine /ˈsɛriːn/ *noun Biochem.* an amino acid that is found in proteins. [from Greek *serikos*, silken]

seriocomic *adj.* having both serious and comic elements or qualities.

serious *adj.* **1** solemn; not light-hearted or flippant. **2** dealing with important issues: *a serious newspaper.* **3** severe: *a serious accident.* **4** important; significant: *serious differences of opinion.* **5** earnest; sincere; not joking: *I am serious about doing it.* [from Latin *serius*]

. . . .

▣ **1** solemn, sober, stern, unsmiling, humourless, thoughtful, pensive. **2** profound, deep, far-reaching. **3** severe, acute, grave, dangerous. **4** important, significant, weighty, momentous, crucial, critical, urgent, pressing. **5** earnest, sincere.

▣ **1** light-hearted, frivolous, flippant, facetious. **3** slight. **4** trivial.

. . . .

seriously *adv.* in a serious way.

seriousness *noun* being serious.

serjeant see SERGEANT.

sermon *noun* **1** a public speech about morals, religious duties, or some aspect of religious doctrine, especially one forming part of a church service. **2** a lengthy moral or advisory speech. [from Latin *sermo*, discourse]

. . . .

▣ **1** address, discourse. **2** lecture, harangue, homily.

. . . .

sermonize or **sermonise** *verb intrans.* to moralize.

serology *noun Biol.* the branch of biology that is concerned with the study of blood serum and its constituents, especially antibodies and antigens.

seropositive *adj.*, *said of a person* having blood that is shown by tests to be infected by the specific disease tested for, usually Aids.

serotonin /sɪərəˈtoʊnɪn/ *noun Physiol.* a hormone that is found mainly in the brain, blood platelets, and intestinal tissues, but also occurs in many other body tissues. It acts

as a neurotransmitter in the central nervous system, and is also a vasoconstrictor, ie it causes narrowing of blood vessels by stimulating their contraction. [from SERUM + TONIC]

serous /ˈsɪərəs/ *adj.* **1** of or relating to serum. **2** *said of a liquid* resembling serum; watery.

serpent *noun* **1** a snake. **2** a sneaky or malicious person. [from Latin *serpens*, creeping thing]

serpentine — *adj.* **1** snake-like. **2** winding; full of twists and bends. — *noun Geol.* a soft green or white rock-forming mineral derived from magnesium silicates, so called because it is often mottled like a snake's skin.

SERPS *abbrev.* state earnings-related pension scheme.

serrated *adj.* having notches or teeth like the blade of a saw. [from Latin *serra*, saw]

. . . .

▣ toothed, notched, indented, jagged.

▣ smooth.

. . . .

serration *noun* **1** a saw-edged condition. **2** a sawlike tooth.

serried *adj.* closely packed or grouped together: *soldiers in serried ranks.* [from French *serrer*, to put close together]

serum /ˈsɪərəm/ *noun* (PL. **sera**) (*in full* **blood serum**) the straw-coloured fluid component of blood that remains after removal of the blood cells and clotting factors. It contains specific antibodies, and can therefore be used as a vaccine to confer protection against specific diseases. [from Latin *serum*, whey]

servant *noun* **1** a person employed by another to do household work. **2** a person who acts for the good of others in any capacity: *public servant.*

. . . .

▣ **1** domestic, maid, valet, steward, attendant, retainer, hireling, lackey, menial, *colloq.* skivvy, help, helper, assistant.

▣ **1** master, mistress.

. . . .

serve — *verb* **1** to work for the benefit of: *served the community well.* **2** *intrans.* to carry out duties as a member of some body: *serve on a committee.* **3** *intrans.* to act as a member of the armed forces: *served in the marines/served in France.* **4** *trans., intrans.* to give assistance to (customers); to provide to customers. **5** *trans., intrans.* to respond to the needs or demands of (someone): *shoes have served me well/if my memory serves me.* **6** *trans., intrans.* to bring, distribute, or present (food or drink) to (someone). **7** to provide specified facilities to: *trams serving the entire city.* **8** *intrans.* to be of use; to fulfil a need; to suffice: *there's no chair, but this box will serve.* **9** to satisfy (a requirement, etc): *it will serve our purpose.* **10** *intrans.* to have a specified effect or result: *his long speech served to delay proceedings.* **11** to undergo as a requirement: *serve an apprenticeship.* **12** *trans., intrans.* to put (the ball) into play in racket sports. **13** to work for as a domestic servant. **14** to deliver or present a legal document: *served him with a writ/served a summons on her.* — *noun Sport* an act of serving. — **serve someone right** *colloq.* to be the misfortune or punishment that they deserve. [from Latin *servire*, to serve]

. . . .

▣ *verb* **4** help, assist, attend. **6** supply, provide, distribute. **8** function, act, perform, suffice. **9** satisfy, answer, fulfil, discharge, further, benefit. **13** work for, attend, minister to, wait on, help, assist. **14** deliver, present.

. . . .

server *noun* **1** a person who serves. **2** *RC Church* a person who assists a priest during mass. **3** a fork, spoon, or other instrument for distributing food. **4** *Comput.* a dedicated computer in a network that stores communal files, processes electronic mail, etc.

service — *noun* **1** work performed for or on behalf of others; use or usefulness; a favour, or any act with beneficial results: *do someone a service/your services are no longer required/the car has given me good service/can I be of* *service?* **2** employment or engagement as a member of an organization working to serve or benefit others in some way; such an organization: *a public service/the civil service.* **3** assistance given to customers. **4** a facility provided: *the bus company runs a great service.* **5** an occasion of worship or other religious ceremony; the words, etc used on such an occasion: *the marriage service.* **6** a complete set of crockery: *a dinner service.* **7** a periodic check of the workings of a vehicle or other machine. **8** an act of putting the ball into play in racket sports; the game in which it is a particular player's turn to do so; the stroke used: *lose one's service/a poor service.* **9** a service charge: *service not included.* **10** (*often* **services**) any of the armed forces. **11** employment as a domestic servant. **12** *attributive* for use by domestic servants: *service entrance.* **13** *attributive* of the army, navy, or air force. — *verb* **1** to subject to a periodic (especially mechanical) check. **2** *said of a male animal* to mate with (a female). — **at someone's service** ready to serve or give assistance to someone. **be of service to someone** to help them; to be useful to them. **in service 1** in use; operating. **2** working as a domestic servant. [from Latin *servitium*, from *servire*, to serve]

. . . .

🔳 *noun* **1** work, labour, use, usefulness, utility, advantage, benefit, favour, help, assistance. **2** employment, work, business, duty, function, performance. **3** help, assistance. **5** worship, observance, ceremony, rite. **7** servicing, maintenance, overhaul, check. *verb* **1** maintain, overhaul, check, repair.

. . . .

serviceability *noun* being serviceable.

serviceable *adj.* **1** capable of being used. **2** giving long-term use; durable.

. . . .

🔳 **1** usable, useful, helpful, profitable, advantageous, beneficial, utilitarian, functional, practical. **2** strong, tough, durable, hard-wearing, reliable, dependable.

🔳 **1** unserviceable, unusable.

. . . .

service area a group of establishments near a motorway or major road, providing refuelling, restaurant, and toilet facilities.

service charge a percentage of a restaurant or hotel bill added on to cover (at least nominally) the cost of service.

service flat a rented flat with the cost of certain services, eg domestic cleaning, included in the rent.

service industry an industry whose business is providing services, eg dry-cleaning, rather than manufacturing goods.

serviceman *noun* a male member of any of the armed forces.

service station a petrol station providing additional facilities for motorists, eg car-washing.

servicewoman *noun* a female member of any of the armed forces.

serviette *noun* a table napkin. [from Old French *serviette*]

servile *adj.* **1** slavishly respectful, obedient, or attentive; fawning. **2** of, relating to, or suitable for slaves: *servile tasks.* [from Latin *servilis*]

. . . .

🔳 **1** obsequious, sycophantic, toadying, fawning, cringing, grovelling, slavish, subservient, supplicant, submissive, humble. **2** menial, low, mean, base, abject.

🔳 **1** assertive, aggressive.

. . . .

servility *noun* being servile.

serving *noun* a portion of food served at one time; a helping.

servitude *noun* **1** slavery. **2** dependence: *servitude to drugs.* [from Latin *servitudo*, from *servus*, slave]

servo or **servomechanism** *noun* (PL. **servos**) an automatic device used to control machinery. An error in the operation of the machine produces an electrical signal which is amplified and used to power a *servomotor*, which corrects the error until the error signal falls to zero. Servos are used in satellite tracking systems, and to control robots and keep ships on course. [from Latin *servus*, servant]

sesame /ˈsesəmɪ/ *noun* a SE Asian plant cultivated for its edible seeds, used in cooking and cooking-oil production. [from Greek *sesamon*]

sessile /ˈsesaɪl/ *adj.* **1** *said of a flower or leaf* attached directly to the plant, rather than by a short stalk. **2** *said of a part of the body* attached directly to the body. **3** *said of an animal* stationary; immobile. [from Latin *sessilis*, low, squat]

session *noun* **1** a meeting of a court, council, or parliament; a period during which such meetings are regularly held. **2** a period of time spent engaged in one particular activity. **3** an academic term or year. — **in session** *said of a committee, etc* conducting or engaged in a meeting. [from Latin *sessio*, a sitting]

. . . .

🔳 **1** meeting, assembly, sitting, hearing, conference, discussion. **2** period, time, spell, bout. **3** term, semester, year.

. . . .

sessional *adj.* relating to a session or sessions.

sestet *noun* **1** a poem or verse of six lines. **2** the last six lines of a sonnet. **3** a group of six people or things; a sextet. [from Italian *sestetto*, from Latin *sextus*, sixth]

set[1] — *verb* (**setting**; PAST TENSE AND PAST PARTICIPLE **set**) **1** to put into a certain position or condition: *set high up/set free/set fire to.* **2** *trans., intrans.* to make or become solid, rigid, firm, or motionless: *the cement has not set/set someone's jaw.* **3** to fix, establish, or settle: *set a date.* **4** to put into a state of readiness: *set the table.* **5** to adjust (an instrument) to the correct reading: *set a clock.* **6** to adjust (a device) so that its controls are activated at a fixed time. **7** to fix (a broken bone) in its normal position, for healing. **8** to impose or assign as an exercise or duty: *set a test.* **9** to present or fix as a lead to be followed: *set an example/set the tone.* **10** to place on or against a background, or in surroundings: *diamonds set in a gold bracelet/a poem set to music.* **11** to stir, provoke, or force into activity: *set me thinking/set her to work.* **12** to treat (hair) so as to stay firm in the required style. **13** to place as a value or consideration of worth: *set a high price on honesty/set great store by.* **14** *intrans., said of the sun or moon* to disappear below the horizon. **15** to arrange (type) for printing. **16** *said of a plant* to produce (seed). **17** to decorate: *a bracelet set with diamonds.* — *noun* **1** form; shape: *the set of his jaw.* **2** posture or bearing. **3** the area within which filmed action takes place; the scenery and props used to create a particular location in filming. **4** the process of setting hair; a hairstyle produced by setting: *a shampoo and set.* — *adj.* **1** fixed; allowing no alterations or variations: *a set menu.* **2** never changing: *set in his ways.* **3** predetermined or conventional: *set phrases.* **4** ready, prepared. **5** about to receive or experience; due: *set for a pay rise.* **6** (**set on something**) determined to do it: *dead set on resigning.* **7** assigned; prescribed: *set texts for study.* — **set about someone** to attack them. **set about something** to start or begin it: *set about digging the garden.* **set one thing against another 1** to compare or contrast them. **2** to deduct one from the other: *set expenses against tax.* **set one person against another** to make them mutually hostile: *set him against his own family.* **set something** or **someone apart** to reveal them to be different, especially superior. **set something aside 1** to disregard or reject it. **2** to put it away for later use. **set something back 1** to delay or hinder its progress. **2** to cause it to return to an earlier and less advanced stage: *changes that will set the health service back decades.* **3** *slang* to cost: *set me back a fiver.* **set something down 1** to record it in writing. **2** to judge or view: *set the scheme down as a failure.* **set someone down** to allow them to leave a vehicle at their destination. **set forth** to begin a journey. **set something forth** to propose or explain it: *set forth her views.* **set in** to become firmly established: *winter has set in.* **set off** to start out on a journey. **set someone off** to provoke them into action or behaviour of a particular kind: *set them off laughing.* **set something off 1** to cause or start it: *set off a terrible argument* **2** to detonate an explosive. **3** to show it off to good advantage; to enhance its appearance. **4** to deduct it from another source; to offset it. **set on someone** to attack them. **set someone** or **something on someone** to order them to attack: *set the dogs on him.* **set out** to begin a journey. **set something out 1** to present or explain it: *set out her proposals* **2** to lay it out for display. **set out to do something** to resolve or intend to do it: *set out to make me look foolish.* **set to 1** to begin working; to apply oneself to a task. **2** to start fighting or arguing. **set someone up 1** to put them into a position of guaranteed security: *the inheritance has set him up for life.* **2** to improve or restore their health. **3** *slang* to trick them into becoming a target for blame or accusations. **set something up 1** to bring it into being or operation; to establish it. **2** to arrange a meeting, etc. **3** to erect something: *set the tents up over here.* [from Anglo-Saxon *settan*]

⊟ *verb* **1** put, place, locate, situate, position, arrange, lodge, fix, stick, park, deposit. **2** congeal, thicken, gel, stiffen, solidify, harden. **3** fix, establish, determine, decide, conclude, settle, resolve, schedule, appoint, designate, specify, name. **4** prepare, arrange, lay. **5** adjust, regulate. **6** adjust, synchronize. **8** impose, assign, prescribe, ordain. **14** go down, sink, dip, disappear, vanish. *adj.* **1** fixed, established, scheduled, appointed, arranged, pre-arranged, decided, agreed, settled, firm, strict, rigid, inflexible. **2** routine, regular, usual, customary, traditional. **3** standard, stock, stereotyped, conventional. **4** ready, prepared. **7** prescribed, ordained, assigned, specified. **set about** *someone* attack, fall on, lay into. *something* begin, start, embark on, undertake, tackle. **set aside 1** reject, discard, disregard, overrule, annul, cancel, revoke, reverse. **2** put aside, lay aside, keep, save, reserve. **set back 1** delay, hold up, slow, retard, hinder, impede. **set off** leave, depart, set out, set forth, start (out), begin. **set something off 2** trigger off, detonate, light, ignite, explode. **3** display, show off, enhance, contrast. **set on** set upon, attack, turn on, go for, fall on, lay into, *colloq.* beat up. **set out** leave, depart, set off, set forth, start (out), begin. **set something out 1** present, describe, explain, lay out, arrange, display, exhibit. **set something up 1** create, establish, institute, found, inaugurate, initiate, begin, start, introduce. **2** organize, arrange. **3** erect, build, construct, assemble, raise, elevate.

⊞ *verb* **14** rise. *adj.* **1** movable. **3** spontaneous. **4** unprepared. **set off** arrive. **set out** arrive.

set² *noun* **1** a group of related or similar things regarded as a complete unit. **2** *Maths.* a group of objects (known as *elements*) that have at least one characteristic in common, so that it is possible to decide exactly whether a given element does or does not belong to that group, eg the set of even numbers. **3** a complete collection of pieces needed for a particular activity: *a chess set/a train set.* **4** one of the major divisions of a match in some sports, eg tennis, subdivided into games. **5** a group of people with common characteristics or interests. **6** an instrument for receiving television or radio broadcasts. **7** the songs or tunes performed at a concert. [from Old French *sette*]

⊟ **1** batch, series, sequence, class, category, group. **3** kit, outfit, compendium, assortment, collection. **5** group, band, gang, crowd, circle, clique, faction. **6** receiver, television, radio.

set³ or **sett** *noun* **1** a badger's burrow. **2** a block of stone or wood used in paving. [see SET¹]

set-aside *noun* the policy of taking agricultural land out of production, used to reduce surpluses of specific commodities.

setback *noun* **1** a check or reversal to progress. **2** a disappointment or misfortune.

⊟ **1** delay, hold-up, problem, snag, hitch, *colloq.* hiccup. **2** misfortune, disappointment, upset, *colloq.* whammy, reverse.

⊞ **1** boost, advance, help, advantage.

set piece 1 a carefully prepared performance or sequence of movements. **2** an arrangement of fireworks on a scaffold, etc.

set square a triangular (usually plastic) plate used as an aid to drawing lines and angles.

settee *noun* a sofa. [from SETTLE²]

setter *noun* any of various breeds of dog originally trained to stand rigid to signal that a hunted animal has been scented.

setting *noun* **1** a position in which an instrument's controls are set. **2 a** a situation or background within or against which action takes place. **b** the scenery and props used in filming a scene. **3** (*also* **place setting**) a set of cutlery, crockery, and glassware laid out for use by one diner. **4** a mounting for a jewel.

⊟ **2** background, frame, surroundings, environment, milieu, context, period, position, location, scene, scenery.

settle¹ *verb* **1** *trans., intrans.* to make or become firmly, comfortably, or satisfactorily positioned or established. **2** *trans., intrans.* (**settle something** or **settle on something**) to come to an agreement about it; to fix or choose it: *settle on a date.* **3** to resolve or conclude (an argument, business, etc). **4** *intrans.* to come lightly to rest. **5** *trans., intrans.* (*also* **settle down** or **settle someone down**) to make or become calm, stable, or disciplined after a period of noisy excitement or upheaval. **6** *trans., intrans.* to establish a permanent home or colony (in). **7** *trans., intrans.* (*also* **settle up**) to pay off or clear (a debt): *I will settle the bill/you settle up with them.* **8** *intrans.* to sink to the bottom of something; to sink lower. **9** to transfer ownership of legally: *settled her estate on her son.* — **settle for something** to accept it as a compromise or in place of something more suitable. [from Anglo-Saxon *setlan*, to place]

⊟ **2** agree (on), fix, establish, determine, decide (on), choose, appoint, arrange. **3** decide, resolve, reconcile, complete, conclude. **4** land, alight, descend, fall, drop. **8** sink, subside, fall, drop.

settle² *noun* a wooden bench with arms and a solid high back, often with a storage chest fitted below the seat. [from Anglo-Saxon *setl*]

settlement *noun* **1** the act of settling or the state of being settled. **2** a community or colony of recently settled people. **3** an agreement, especially ending an official dispute. **4** subsidence. **5** an act of legally transferring ownership of property; a document enforcing this. **6** the payment of a debt.

⊟ **2** community, colony, outpost, camp, encampment. **3** agreement, arrangement, resolution, decision, conclusion, termination, satisfaction. **6** payment, clearance, clearing, discharge.

settler *noun* a person who settles in a country that is being newly populated.

⊟ colonist, colonizer, pioneer, frontiersman, frontierswoman, planter, immigrant, incomer.

⊞ native.

set-to *noun* **1** a fight or argument. **2** a fierce contest.

set-top box a device that converts digital television signals into images on a television set.

set-up *noun* **1** *colloq.* an arrangement or set of arrangements. **2** *slang* a trick to get a person unjustly blamed or accused.

⊟ **1** arrangement, organization, system, structure, conditions, circumstances.

seven — *noun* **1** the number or figure 7; any symbol for this number. **2** the age of 7. **3** something, eg a garment or a person, whose size is denoted by the number 7. **4** a playing-card with 7 pips. **5** a set of 7 people or things. **6** 7 o'clock. **7** a score of 7 points. — *adj.* **1** 7 in number. **2** aged 7. [from Anglo-Saxon *seofon*]

sevenfold — *adj.* **1** equal to 7 times as much or as many. **2** divided into, or consisting of, 7 parts. — *adv.* by 7 times as much.

seven seas (*usually* **the seven seas**) the oceans of the world: the Arctic, Antarctic, N Atlantic, Southern Atlantic, Indian, N Pacific, and S Pacific Oceans.

seventeen — *noun* **1** the number or figure 17; any symbol for this number. **2** the age of 17. **3** something, eg a garment or a person, whose size is denoted by the number 17. **4** a set of 17 people or things. — *adj.* **1** 17 in number. **2** aged 17. [from Anglo-Saxon *seofon*, seven + *tien*, ten]

seventeenth *noun, adj.* **1** the position in a series corresponding to 17 in a sequence of numbers. **2** one of 17 equal parts.

seventh *noun, adj.* **1** the position in a series corresponding to 7 in a sequence of numbers. **2** one of 7 equal parts. **3** *Mus.* a tone or semitone less than an octave; a note at that interval from another, or a combination of two tones separated by that interval.

seventh heaven a state of intense happiness or joy.

seventhly *adv.* as seventh in a series.

seventies *pl. noun* **1** the period of time between one's seventieth and eightieth birthdays. **2** the range of temperatures between seventy and eighty degrees. **3** the period of time between the seventieth and eightieth years of a century.

seventieth *noun, adj.* **1** the position in a series corresponding to 70 in a sequence of numbers. **2** one of 70 equal parts.

seventy — *noun* (PL. **seventies**) **1** the number or figure 70; any symbol for this number. **2** the age of 70. **3** a set of 70 people or things. — *adj.* **1** 70 in number. **2** aged 70. [from Anglo-Saxon *seofontig*]

sever / ˈsɛvə(r)/ *verb* (**severed**, **severing**) **1** to cut off physically: *severed limbs*. **2** to break off or end: *severed relations with them*. [from Latin *separare*, to separate]

⊟ **1** cut off, amputate, detach, disconnect, split, part, separate, divide. **2** break off, dissolve, end, terminate, disunite, dissociate.
⊟ **1** attach, join. **2** unite.

several — *adj.* **1** more than a few, but not a great number. **2** different and distinct; respective: *went their several ways*. — *pron.* quite a few people or things. [from Old French *several*, separate]

⊟ *adj.* DIVERSE. **1** some, various, assorted, sundry. **2** different, distinct, separate, particular, individual, respective.

severally *adv. formal* separately or singly: *travelling severally.*

severance *noun* **1** severing or being severed. **2** separation.

severance pay compensation paid by an employer to an employee dismissed through no fault of his or her own.

severe *adj.* **1** extreme and difficult to endure; marked by extreme conditions. **2** very strict towards others. **3** suggesting seriousness and a lack of informality; austere. **4** having serious consequences; grave. **5** rigorous; demanding. [from Latin *severus*]

⊟ **1** extreme, acute, intense, fierce, violent, cruel, pitiless, merciless, relentless, inexorable, harsh, tough, hard, difficult, grim, forbidding. **2** strict, rigid, unbending, stern, disapproving, sober, strait-laced. **3** austere, ascetic, plain, simple, unadorned. **4** serious, grave, critical, dangerous. **5** hard, difficult, demanding, rigorous, arduous, punishing.
⊟ **1** mild. **2** lenient. **3** ornate. **4** minor. **5** easy.

severe combined immunodeficiency *Medicine* (ABBREV. **SCID**) a severe form of congenital immunological deficiency.

severely *adv.* in a severe way; to a severe degree.

severity *noun* being severe; strictness, harshness, gravity.

sew /səʊ/ *verb* (PAST PARTICIPLE **sewn**, **sewed**) **1** to stitch, attach, or repair (especially fabric) with thread, by hand with a needle or by machine. **2** to make (garments) by stitching pieces of fabric together. **3** *intrans.* to perform such tasks: *can you sew?* — **sew something up 1** to mend or join it by sewing. **2** *slang* to arrange or complete it successfully. [from Anglo-Saxon *siwian*]

⊟ **1** stitch, tack, baste, hem, darn, embroider.

sewage *noun* waste matter, especially excrement, carried away in drains. [from SEWER]

sewage farm a place where sewage is treated so as to be usable as manure.

sewer *noun* a large underground pipe or channel for carrying away sewage from drains and water from road surfaces; a main drain. [from Old French *essever*, to drain off]

sewerage *noun* **1** a network of sewers. **2** drainage of sewage and surface water using sewers.

sewing *noun* **1** the act of sewing. **2** something that is being sewn.

sewing machine a machine for sewing, especially an electric machine for sewing clothes, etc.

sex — *noun* **1** either of the two classes male and female into which animals and plants (or certain parts of plants) are divided according to their role in reproduction. **2** membership of one of these classes, or the attributes that determine this. **3** sexual intercourse, often including other lovemaking activities. — *adj.* **1** of or relating to sexual matters in general: *sex education*. **2** of or based on the fact of being male or female: *sex discrimination*. — *verb* to identify the sex of (an animal). [from Latin *sexus*]

⊟ *noun* **1** gender, sexuality. **3** sexual intercourse, sexual relations, copulation, coitus, reproduction, love-making, intimacy.

sexagenarian — *adj.*, *said of a person* aged between 60 and 69. — *noun* a person of this age. [from Latin *sexaginta*, sixty]

Sexagesima /ˌsɛksəˈdʒɛsɪmə/ *noun* the second Sunday before Lent, apparently so called by analogy with Quadragesima and Quinquagesima; the 60th day (in round numbers) before Easter. [from Latin *sexagesimus*, sixtieth]

sex appeal sexual attractiveness.

sex chromosome *Genetics* any chromosome that carries the genes which determine the sex of an organism. In mammals, including humans, females have two identical sex chromosomes, known as X-chromosomes, and males have an X-chromosome together with a smaller chromosome known as a Y-chromosome.

sexed *adj.* having a desire as specified to engage in sexual activity: *highly sexed*.

sexily *adv.* in a sexy way.

sexiness *noun* being sexy.

sexism *noun* contempt shown for a particular sex, usually by men of women, based on prejudice or stereotype.

sexist — *noun* a person whose beliefs and actions are characterized by sexism. — *adj.* relating to or characteristic of sexism.

sexless *adj.* **1** neither male nor female. **2** having no desire to engage in sexual activity. **3** *derog.* sexually unattractive.

sex linkage *Genetics* the tendency for certain inherited characteristics to occur predominantly or exclusively in one of the sexes because the genes for those characteristics are carried on the sex chromosomes (usually the X chromosome), eg the hereditary disorder haemophilia occurs predominantly in human males.

sexologist *noun* a person who studies human sexual behaviour.

sexology *noun* the study of sexual behaviour, especially in humans.

sexploitation *noun* the commercial exploitation of sex in films and other media.

sext *noun* the fourth of the canonical hours. [from Latin *sexta hora*, the sixth hour]

sextant *noun* an instrument like a small telescope mounted on a graded metal arc, used in navigation and surveying for measuring distance by means of angles. [from Latin *sextans*, sixth, the arc being one sixth of a full circle]

sextet *noun* **1** a group of six singers or musicians, or a piece of music for these. **2** any set of six. [a variant of SESTET]

sex therapy *Medicine* a form of therapy that deals with physical and psychological problems relating to sexual intercourse.

sexton *noun* a person who looks after church property, often also having bell-ringing, grave-digging and other duties. [from SACRISTAN]

sex tourism tourism organized to take advantage of more liberal sexual laws or practices than exist in one's own country.

sextuple /ˈsɛkstjʊpəl, sɛkˈstjuːpəl/ — *noun* a value or quantity six times as much. — *adj.* **1** sixfold. **2** made up of six parts. — *verb trans., intrans.* to multiply or increase sixfold. [from Latin *sextuplus*]

sextuplet *noun* any of six children born at the same time to the same mother.

sexual *adj.* **1** concerned with or suggestive of sex or love-making. **2** relating to sexual reproduction involving the fusion of two gametes to form a zygote. **3** of, relating to, or according to membership of, the male or female sex.

. . . .

⊞ **1** sex, venereal, carnal, sensual, erotic. **2** reproductive, genital, procreative, coital.

. . . .

sexual abuse subjection to sexual activity likely to cause physical or psychological harm.

sexual harassment harassment in the form of unwelcome, often offensive, sexual advances or remarks, usually made by men towards women, especially in the workplace.

sexual intercourse the insertion of a man's penis into a woman's vagina, usually with the release of semen into the vagina.

sexuality *noun* a sexual state or condition.

sexually transmitted disease (ABBREV. STD) any disease that is characteristically transmitted by sexual intercourse, formerly known as venereal disease, eg AIDS, gonorrhoea, syphilis.

sexual reproduction a form of reproduction in which new individuals are produced by the fusion of two unlike gametes (specialized reproductive cells). The gametes are typically male (a sperm) and female (an ovum or egg).

sexy *adj.* (**sexier, sexiest**) *colloq.* **1** sexually attractive; arousing sexual desire. **2** currently popular or interesting: *sexy products.*

. . . .

⊞ **1** sensual, voluptuous, nubile, *slang* beddable, seductive, inviting, flirtatious, arousing, provocative,

titillating, pornographic, erotic, salacious.

⊞ **1** sexless.

. . . .

SF or **sf** *abbrev.* science fiction.

sf or **sfz** *abbrev.* sforzando.

SFA *abbrev.* Scottish Football Association.

sforzando /sfɔːtˈsandoʊ/ *adv., adj. Mus.* to be played with sudden emphasis. [from Italian *sforzando*]

sfumato /sfuˈmɑːtoʊ/ *noun* a term used in art history for the smooth imperceptible transitions from one colour to the other achieved by such artists as Leonardo da Vinci and Correggio. [from Italian, from *fumo*, smoke]

SGML *abbrev. Comput.* Standard Generalized Mark-up Language, a form of coding of electronic data.

sgraffito /zgrəˈfiːtoʊ/ or **graffito** *noun* (PL. **sgraffiti**) a technique in art in which one colour is laid over another and the top layer scratched away to form a design, by revealing the colour beneath. It is used in pottery decoration, and on plasterwork in medieval and Renaissance buildings. [from Italian *sgraffito*, from Latin *ex-*, + Greek *graphein*, to write]

Sgt *abbrev.* Sergeant.

sh *interj.* hush; be quiet. [imitative]

shabbily *adv.* in a shabby way.

shabbiness *noun* being shabby.

shabby *adj.* (**shabbier, shabbiest**) **1** *said especially of clothes or furnishings* old and worn; threadbare; dingy. **2** *said of a person* wearing such clothes. **3** nasty; mean: *shabby conduct.* [from Anglo-Saxon *sceabb*]

. . . .

⊞ **1** worn, worn-out, mangy, moth-eaten, ragged, tattered, frayed, scruffy, tatty, disreputable, dilapidated, run-down, seedy, dirty, dingy, poky. **3** nasty, rotten, mean, low, cheap, shoddy, shameful, dishonourable, contemptible, despicable.

⊞ **1** smart. **3** fair, honourable.

. . . .

Shabuoth or **Shavuoth** or **Shavuot** /ʃaˈvjuːɒθ/ *noun* the Jewish 'Feast of Weeks', celebrated seven weeks after the first day of Passover to commemorate the giving of the Law to Moses. [from Hebrew *Shabuoth*]

shack — *noun* a roughly built hut. — *verb* (*usually* **shack up with someone**) *slang* to live with them, usually without being married.

. . . .

⊞ *noun* hut, cabin, shanty, hovel, shed, lean-to.

. . . .

shackle — *noun* **1** either of a pair of metal bands, joined by a chain, locked round a prisoner's wrists or ankles to limit movement. **2** anything that restricts freedom. **3** a U-shaped metal loop closed over by a bolt, used for fastening ropes or chains together. — *verb* to restrain with, or as if with, shackles. [from Anglo-Saxon *sceacul*]

shad *noun* (PL. **shad, shads**) any of a family of edible herring-like fish. [from Anglo-Saxon *sceadd*]

shade — *noun* **1** the blocking or partial blocking out of sunlight, or the dimness caused by this. **2** an area from which sunlight has been wholly or partially blocked. **3** such an area represented in a drawing or painting. **4** the state of appearing comparatively unimpressive: *lived in the shade of his brother's achievements/her singing puts mine in the shade.* **5** any device used as a shield from direct light; a lampshade. **6** a colour, especially one similar to but slightly different from a principal colour. **7** a small amount; a touch. — *verb* **1** to block or partially block out sunlight from. **2** to draw or paint so as to give the impression of shade. **3** (*usually* **shade off** or **away**) to change gradually or unnoticeably. [from Anglo-Saxon *sceadu*]

. . . .

⊞ *noun* **1** shadiness, shadow, darkness, obscurity, semi-darkness, dimness, gloom. **5** screen, blind, curtain, shield, visor, awning, canopy, parasol. **6** colour, hue, tint, tone, tinge. **7** touch, trace, dash, hint, suggestion, suspicion, nuance, degree. *verb* **1** screen, shield, protect, shroud, veil, obscure, cloud, dim, darken, shadow.

shadiness *noun* being shady.

shading *noun* the representation of areas of shade, eg by close parallel lines in a drawing.

shadoof or **shaduf** /ʃaːˈduːf/ *noun* an apparatus for lifting water from rivers and watercourses and transferring it to the land or into a trough. It consists of a bucket suspended from a counterpoised pivoted rod, and is chiefly used for irrigation in the flood plain of the Nile. [from Egyptian Arabic *shaduf*]

shadow — *noun* 1 a dark shape on a surface, produced when an object stands between the surface and a source of light. 2 an area darkened by the blocking out of light. 3 a slight amount; a hint or trace. 4 a sense of gloom or foreboding: *cast a shadow over the proceedings*. 5 a greatly weakened or otherwise reduced version: *a shadow of her former self*. 6 a constant companion. 7 a person following another closely and secretively. — *verb* 1 to follow closely and secretively. 2 to put into darkness by blocking out light. — *adj.* denoting a spokesperson or persons with the main opposition political party, who would become minister if the party were elected to power: *shadow Foreign Secretary*. [from Anglo-Saxon *sceadwe*, accusative case of *sceadu*. See SHADE]

▣ *noun* 1 silhouette, shape, image, representation. 2 shade, darkness, obscurity, semi-darkness, dimness, gloom. 3 trace, hint, suggestion, suspicion. 4 cloud. 5 vestige, remnant. *verb* 1 follow, tail, dog, stalk, trail, watch, observe. 2 shade, shield, screen, obscure, darken, overshadow.

shadow-box *verb intrans.* to practise shadow-boxing.

shadow-boxing *noun* boxing against an imaginary opponent as training.

shadow cabinet *Politics* a body made up of leading members of an opposition party ready to take office should their party assume power.

shadow-mask tube a type of cathode-ray tube for colour television, in which electron beams from three separate guns, modulated by the red, green, and blue signals, are deflected by the scanning system through holes on the shadow-mask plate to fall on minute phosphor dots of the appropriate colour making up the screen. The dots glow according to the intensity of the beam reaching them.

shadow puppets puppets which are manipulated to cast a shadow on a screen.

shadowy *adj.* 1 dark and not clearly visible. 2 darkened by shadows.

▣ 1 dark, gloomy, murky, obscure, dim, faint, indistinct, ill-defined, vague, hazy, intangible, unsubstantial, ghostly, spectral. 2 shadowed, shaded, shady, dark.

shady *adj.* (**shadier, shadiest**) 1 sheltered, or giving shelter, from sunlight. 2 *colloq.* disreputable; probably dishonest or illegal.

▣ 1 shaded, shadowy, dim, dark, cool. 2 disreputable, dubious, questionable, suspect, suspicious, *colloq.* fishy, dishonest, *colloq.* crooked, unreliable, untrustworthy, unscrupulous, unethical.
▣ 1 sunny, sunlit, bright. 2 honest, trustworthy, honourable.

SHAEF *abbrev.* Supreme Headquarters of the Allied Expeditionary Force.

shaft *noun* 1 the long straight handle of a tool or weapon. 2 any long straight part, eg a revolving rod that transmits motion in vehicle engines. 3 a vertical passageway, especially one through which a lift moves. 4 either of the projecting parts of a cart, etc to which a horse or other animal is fastened. 5 a thing moving or aimed with the directness or violent force of an arrow or missile: *shaft of*

light/shafts of sarcasm. 6 *Archit.* the long middle part of a column, between the base and the capital. [from Anglo-Saxon *sceaft*]

▣ 1 handle, shank, stem. 2 rod, bar, stick, pole. 3 duct, passage. 5 beam, ray, dart, arrow. 6 upright, pillar.

shaft grave *Archaeol.* a deep burial, especially a group of six tombs behind the Lion's Gate at the W end of the citadel of Mycenae in Greece.

shag¹ *noun* 1 a ragged mass of hair. 2 a long coarse pile or nap on fabric. 3 tobacco coarsely cut into shreds. [from Anglo-Saxon *sceacga*]

shag² *noun* a species of cormorant which has a shaggy tuft on its head. [see SHAG¹]

shag³ *coarse slang* — *verb* (**shagged, shagging**) 1 to have sexual intercourse with. 2 to tire. — *noun* an act of sexual intercourse.

shagginess *noun* a shaggy state.

shaggy *adj.* (**shaggier, shaggiest**) 1 *said of hair or fur* rough and untidy in appearance. 2 *said of a person or animal* having shaggy hair or fur.

▣ 1 untidy, uncombed, long, bushy. 2 hairy, long-haired, hirsute, woolly, dishevelled, unkempt.
▣ 1 close-cropped. 2 bald.

shaggy dog story a rambling story or joke amusing only because of its ridiculous length and pointlessness.

shagreen /ʃəˈɡriːn/ *noun* 1 coarse grainy leather, especially made from the skin of a horse or donkey. 2 the rough skin of a shark or ray, used as an abrasive. [from Turkish *sagri*, horse's rump]

shah /ʃɑː/ *noun Hist.* a title of the former rulers of Iran. [from Persian *shah*]

shahtoosh /ʃɑːˈtuːʃ/ *noun* wool from the neck hair of the ibex, used especially for high-quality shawls. [from Punjabi 'material fit for a king', from Persian SHAH + Kashmiri *tośa*, fine material]

shake — *verb* (PAST TENSE **shook**; PAST PARTICIPLE **shaken**) 1 to move with quick, often violent to-and-fro or up-and-down movements. 2 (*also* **shake something up**) to mix it in this way. 3 to wave, especially in a violent and threatening manner. 4 *intrans.* to tremble, totter, or shiver. 5 to cause to tremble or rock. 6 to cause intense shock or agitation within: *revelations that shook the nation.* 7 (*also* **shake someone up**) to disturb or upset them greatly. 8 to cause to waver; to weaken: *shook my confidence.* 9 *intrans.* to shake hands. — *noun* 1 an act or the action of shaking. 2 *colloq.* a very short while; a moment. 3 (**the shakes**) *colloq.* a fit of uncontrollable trembling. 4 a milk shake. — **no great shakes** *colloq.* of no great importance, ability, or worth. **shake a leg** *colloq.* to hurry up or get moving. **shake down** to go to bed, especially in a makeshift bed. **shake someone down** *slang* to extort money from them. **shake something down** *slang* to search it thoroughly. **shake hands with someone** to greet someone by clasping hands. **shake one's head** to move one's head from side to side as a sign of rejection or disagreement. **shake something or someone off** 1 to get rid of them; to free oneself from them. 2 to escape from them. **shake someone up** *colloq.* to stimulate them into action, from a state of lethargy or apathy. **shake something up** *colloq.* to reorganize it thoroughly. [from Anglo-Saxon *sceacan*]

▣ *verb* 1 wag, agitate, rattle, jolt, jerk, twitch, convulse, heave, throb, vibrate, oscillate. 3 wave, flourish, brandish. 4 tremble, quiver, quake, wobble, totter, sway, rock, shiver, shudder. 5 wobble, sway, rock. 6 shock, stir, rouse, agitate. 7 upset, distress, disturb, discompose, unsettle, frighten, unnerve, intimidate. 8 weaken, undermine. **shake off** 1 get rid of, lose. 2 escape from, elude, give the slip, leave behind, outdistance, outstrip.

shakedown *noun colloq.* **1** a makeshift bed, originally made by shaking down straw. **2** an act of extortion. **3** *chiefly North Amer.* a trial run or operation to familiarize personnel with equipment and procedures.

shake-out *noun colloq.* same as SHAKE-UP.

Shaker the popular name for a member of the United Society for Believers in Christ's Second Appearing, a millenarian sect. Their popular name arose from their ecstatic dancing.

shaker *noun* a container from which something, eg salt, is dispensed by shaking, or in which something, eg a cocktail, is mixed by shaking.

Shakespearean or **Shakespearian** /ʃeɪkˈspɪərɪən/ *adj.* relating to or characteristic of the literary works or style of William Shakespeare.

shake-up *noun colloq.* a fundamental change or reorganization.

⊟ change, reform, reorganization, reshuffle, disturbance, upheaval.

shakily *adv.* in a shaky way, unsteadily.

shakiness *noun* being shaky.

shako /ˈʃakoʊ/ *noun* (PL. **shakos**, **shakoes**) a tall nearly cylindrical military cap with a plume. [from Hungarian *csákó*]

shaky *adj.* (**shakier**, **shakiest**) **1** trembling, as with weakness or illness. **2** *colloq.* not solid, sound, or secure.

⊟ **1** trembling, quivering, weak, faltering, tentative. **2** insecure, precarious, unstable, unsteady, wobbly, rickety, unsound, unreliable, dubious, questionable, uncertain, unsure.
⊟ **2** firm, steady, sound.

shale *noun Geol.* a fine-grained black, grey, brown, or red sedimentary rock formed by the compression of clay, silt, or sand under the weight of overlying rocks. [from Anglo-Saxon *scealu*]

shall *verb, aux.* expressing: **1** the future tense of other verbs, especially when the subject is *I* or *we*. **2** determination, intention, certainty, and obligation, especially when the subject is *you, he, she, it,* or *they*: *they shall succeed/you shall have what you want/he shall become king/you shall not kill.* **3** a question implying future action, often with the sense of an offer or suggestion, especially when the subject is *I* or *we*: *what shall we do?/shall I give you a hand?* [from Anglo-Saxon *sceal*]

shallot /ʃəˈlɒt/ *noun* a plant of the onion family, with a smallish oval bulb growing in clusters. [from Old French *eschalote*]

shallow — *adj.* **1** having little depth. **2** not profound or sincere; superficial. — *noun* (*often* **shallows**) a shallow place or part, especially in water. [from Middle English *schalowe*]

⊟ *adj.* SUPERFICIAL. **1** surface, skin-deep. **2** simple, slight, flimsy, trivial, frivolous, idle, empty, insincere.
⊟ *adj.* DEEP. **2** profound, sincere.

shalom /ʃaˈlɒm/ *noun, interj.* a Jewish greeting or farewell. [from Hebrew *shalom*, peace (be with you)]

shalt the form of the verb **shall** used after *thou*.

shaly *adj.* consisting of or like shale.

sham — *adj.* false; pretended; insincere. — *verb trans., intrans.* (**shammed**, **shamming**) to pretend or fake. — *noun* **1** anything not genuine. **2** a person who shams, especially an impostor.

⊟ *adj.* false, fake, counterfeit, spurious, bogus, *colloq.* phoney, pretended, feigned, put-on, insincere, artificial, mock, imitation, simulated, synthetic. *verb* pretend, feign, affect, put on, simulate, fake, counterfeit. *noun* **1** pretence, fraud, counterfeit, forgery, fake,

imitation, simulation, hoax. **2** fraud, fake, impostor.
⊟ *adj.* genuine, authentic, real.

shaman /ˈʃamən, ˈʃeɪmən/ *noun* (PL. **shamans**) a priest who uses magic, especially his ability to make his spirit leave his body, to cure illness, commune with gods and spirits, prophesy, influence the weather and food supply, etc. [from Russian *shaman*]

shamanism *noun* a religion, especially of N Asia, dominated by shamans and belief in their powers.

shamanistic *adj.* relating to shamanism.

shamble — *verb intrans.* (**shamble along, past,** etc) to walk with slow, awkward, tottering steps. — *noun* such a walk or pace. [from SHAMBLES, suggesting trestle-like legs]

shambles *sing. noun* **1** *colloq.* a confused mess; a state of total disorder. **2** a meat market. **3** a slaughterhouse. **4** a scene of slaughter or carnage. [from Anglo-Saxon *scamel*, stool]

shambling — *noun* awkward or unsteady progress. — *adj.* that shambles; awkward and unsteady.

shambolic *adj. colloq.* totally disorganized; chaotic.

shame — *noun* **1** an embarrassing or degrading sense of guilt, foolishness, or failure as a result of one's own actions or those of another person associated with one. **2** the capacity to feel this. **3** disgrace or loss of reputation; a person or thing bringing this. **4** a regrettable or disappointing event or situation. — *verb* **1** to cause to feel shame. **2** (**shame someone into something**) to provoke them into taking action by inspiring feelings of shame: *shamed him into telling the truth.* **3** to bring disgrace on. — **put someone to shame** to make them seem inadequate by comparison. [from Anglo-Saxon *sceamu*]

⊟ *noun* **1** remorse, guilt, embarrassment, mortification, humiliation, degradation. **3** disgrace, dishonour, discredit, disrepute, stain, stigma, infamy, scandal, ignominy. **4** pity. *verb* **1** embarrass, mortify, abash, humiliate, ridicule, humble, put to shame, show up. **3** disgrace, dishonour, discredit, debase, degrade, sully, taint, stain.
⊟ *noun* **1** pride. **3** honour, credit.

shamefaced *adj.* **1** showing shame or embarrassment. **2** modest or bashful. [originally *shamefast*, held by shame]

⊟ **1** ashamed, conscience-stricken, remorseful, contrite, apologetic, sorry, sheepish, red-faced, blushing, embarrassed, mortified, abashed. **2** modest, bashful, shy, coy.
⊟ **1** unashamed, proud.

shameful *adj.* bringing or deserving shame; disgraceful.

⊟ disgraceful, outrageous, scandalous, indecent, atrocious, wicked, reprehensible, contemptible, unworthy, ignoble, embarrassing, mortifying, humiliating, ignominious.
⊟ honourable, creditable, worthy.

shameless *adj.* **1** showing no shame; not capable of feeling shame. **2** done entirely without shame; blatant.

⊟ **1** unashamed, unabashed, unrepentant, impenitent, hardened, incorrigible, immodest, indecent, improper, unprincipled, wanton, dissolute, corrupt, depraved. **2** blatant, flagrant, barefaced, brazen, brash, audacious, wanton, indecent, improper.
⊟ **1** ashamed, shamefaced, contrite, modest.

shammy *noun* (PL. **shammies**) *colloq.* a chamois leather.

shampoo — *noun* (PL. **shampoos**) **1** a soapy liquid for washing the hair and scalp. **2** a similar liquid for cleaning carpets or upholstery. **3** a treatment with either liquid. — *verb* (**shampoos**, **shampooed**) to wash or clean with shampoo. [from Hindi *champo*, squeeze]

shamrock *noun* any of various plants whose green leaves have three rounded leaflets, eg clover, used as the national emblem of Ireland. [from Irish Gaelic *seamrog*]

shandy *noun* (PL. **shandies**) a mixture of beer and lemonade or ginger beer.

shanghai /ʃaŋˈhaɪ/ *verb* (**shanghais, shanghaied, shanghaiing**) *colloq.* **1** to kidnap and send to sea as a sailor. **2** to trick into any unpleasant situation. [named after Shanghai in China, from the former use of this method in recruiting sailors for trips to the East]

shank *noun* **1** the lower leg of an animal, especially a horse, between the knee and the foot. **2** a cut of meat from the (especially upper) leg of an animal. **3** a shaft or other long straight part. [from Anglo-Saxon *sceanca*, leg]

shanks's pony *colloq.* one's own legs as a means of travelling.

shan't shall not.

shantung /ʃanˈtʌŋ/ *noun* a plain and usually undyed silk fabric with a rugged, slightly coarse finish. [from *Shantung*, province in China where it was originally made]

shanty[1] *noun* (PL. **shanties**) a roughly built hut; a shack. [from Canadian French *chantier*, woodcutter's cabin]

shanty[2] *noun* (PL. **shanties**) a rhythmical song of a kind formerly sung by sailors working in unison. [from French *chanter*, to sing]

shanty town an area in which poor people live in makeshift or ramshackle housing.

SHAPE *abbrev.* Supreme Headquarters Allied Powers Europe.

shape — *noun* **1** the outline or form of anything. **2** a person's body or figure. **3** form, person, etc: *an assistant in the shape of my brother.* **4** a desired form or (especially physical) condition: *get the contract into shape/keep in shape.* **5** condition generally: *in bad shape.* **6** an unidentifiable figure: *shapes lurking in the dark.* **7** a mould or pattern. **8** a figure, especially geometric. — *verb* **1** to give a particular form to; to fashion. **2** to influence to an important extent: *shaped history.* **3** to devise or develop to suit a particular purpose. — **shape up** *colloq.* **1** to appear to be developing in a particular way: *is shaping up well.* **2** to be promising; to progress or develop well. **take shape 1** to take on a definite form. **2** to become recognizable as the desired result of plans or theories. [from Anglo-Saxon *scieppan*]

▣ *noun* **1** form, outline, silhouette, profile, lines, contours. **2** figure, physique, build, frame. **4** condition, state, form, health, trim, fettle. **7** mould, model, pattern, format, configuration. *verb* **1** form, fashion, model, mould, cast, forge, sculpt, carve, adapt, accommodate, modify, remodel. **3** create, devise, frame, plan, prepare, develop.

Geometrical shapes include: polygon, circle, semicircle, quadrant, oval, ellipse, crescent, triangle, equilateral triangle, isosceles triangle, scalene triangle, quadrilateral, square, rectangle, oblong, rhombus, diamond, kite, trapezium, parallelogram, pentagon, hexagon, heptagon, octagon, nonagon, decagon, polyhedron, cube, cuboid, prism, pyramid, tetrahedron, pentahedron, octahedron, cylinder, cone, sphere, hemisphere.

shapeless *adj.* **1** not having a regular describable shape. **2** unattractively shaped.

▣ **1** formless, amorphous, unformed, unstructured, irregular. **2** misshapen, deformed, dumpy.
▣ **2** shapely.

shapeliness *noun* being shapely.

shapely *adj.*, *said especially of the human body* well proportioned; attractively shaped.

shard or **sherd** *noun* a fragment of something brittle, usually pottery, especially when found on an archaeological site. [from Anglo-Saxon *sceard*]

share[1] — *noun* **1** a portion given to or contributed by each of several people or groups. **2** any of the units into which the total wealth of a business company is divided, ownership of which gives the right to a portion of the company's profits. — *verb* **1** (**share something** or **share in something**) to have joint possession or use of it, or joint responsibility for it, with another or others. **2** (*also* **share something out**) to divide it into portions, distributed to each of several people or groups. [from Anglo-Saxon *scearu*]

▣ *noun* **1** portion, ration, quota, allowance, lot, part, proportion, percentage, *slang* cut, dividend, due, contribution, *colloq.* whack. *verb* **2** divide, split, distribute, dole out, deal out, apportion, allot, allocate, assign.

share[2] *noun* a ploughshare. [from Anglo-Saxon *scear*]

shareholder *noun* a person who owns shares in a company.

share-out *noun* a division into shares; a distribution.

shareware *noun* *Comput.* software readily available for a nominal fee.

Shari'ah /ʃəˈrɪə/ the sacred law of Islam, which embraces all aspects of a Muslim's life.

shark *noun* **1** any of various large fishes belonging to the class Elasmobranchii, found in seas worldwide, but most common in tropical waters, having a skeleton made of cartilage, skin covered with tooth-like scales, and a tail fin with a long upper lobe and a shorter lower lobe. **2** *colloq.* a ruthless or dishonest person, especially one who swindles or exploits. [perhaps from German *Schurke*, scoundrel; the second sense may be a different word]

sharkskin *noun* **1** leather made from a shark's skin. **2** smooth rayon fabric with a dull sheen.

sharp — *adj.* **1** having a thin edge that can cut or a point that can pierce. **2** having a bitter pungent taste. **3** severely felt: *sharp pain.* **4** sudden and acute: *sharp increases/a sharp bend.* **5** quick to perceive, act, or react; keenly intelligent: *sharp-witted.* **6** abrupt or harsh in speech. **7** easily perceived; clear-cut: *in sharp contrast.* **8** sarcastic: *sharp-tongued.* **9** *colloq.* stylish. **10** *Mus.* higher in pitch by a semitone: *C sharp.* **11** *Mus.* out of tune by being slightly too high in pitch. — *noun* **1** *Mus.* a sharp note; a sign indicating this. **2** *colloq.* a practised cheat: *a card sharp.* — *adv.* **1** punctually; on the dot. **2** suddenly: *pulled up sharp.* **3** *Mus.* untunefully high in pitch. — **look sharp** *colloq.* to hurry up. [from Anglo-Saxon *scearp*]

▣ *adj.* **1** pointed, keen, edged, cutting, serrated, jagged, barbed, spiky. **2** pungent, piquant, sour, tart, vinegary, bitter, acerbic, acid. **3** severe, intense, extreme, acute, piercing, stabbing. **4** sudden, abrupt, violent, acute, severe. **5** quick-witted, alert, shrewd, astute, perceptive, observant, discerning, penetrating, clever, crafty, cunning, artful, sly. **6** abrupt, brusque, curt, gruff, harsh. **7** clear, clear-cut, well-defined, distinct, marked, crisp. **8** sarcastic, sardonic, trenchant, incisive, cutting, biting, caustic, scathing, vitriolic, acrimonious. *adv.* **1** punctually, promptly, on the dot, exactly, precisely. **2** abruptly, suddenly, unexpectedly.
▣ *adj.* **1** blunt. **2** bland. **3** mild. **4** gentle. **5** slow, stupid. **7** blurred. *adv.* **1** approximately, roughly.

sharpen *verb trans., intrans.* (**sharpened, sharpening**) to make or become sharp.

▣ edge, whet, hone, grind, file.
▣ blunt.

sharpener *noun* a person or tool that sharpens.

sharper *noun* *colloq.* a practised cheat; a sharp.

sharply *adv.* in a sharp way; harshly.

sharpness *noun* a sharp quality.

sharp practice dishonesty; cheating.

sharpshooter *noun* a good marksman.

sharpshooting *noun* accurate shooting.

shatter *verb* (**shattered, shattering**) **1** *trans., intrans.* to break into tiny pieces, usually suddenly or forcefully. **2** to destroy completely, or cause to break down: *shattered hopes.* **3** to upset greatly. **4** *colloq.* to tire out; to exhaust.

⊞ **1** break, smash, splinter, shiver, crack, split, burst. **2** destroy, demolish, crush, devastate, wreck, ruin. **3** upset, overwhelm, devastate.

shattered *adj. colloq.* exhausted, extremely upset.

shattering *adj.* that shatters; devastating.

shave — *verb* **1** to cut off (hair) from (the face or other part of the body) with a razor or shaver. **2** *intrans.* to remove one's growth of beard in this way. **3** to remove thin slivers from the surface of (especially wood) with a bladed tool. **4** to graze the surface of, or narrowly miss, in passing. — *noun* **1** an act or the process of shaving one's growth of beard. **2** a narrow miss or escape: *a close shave.* **3** a tool for shaving wood. [from Anglo-Saxon *sceafan*]

shaven *adj.* shaved.

shaver *noun* **1** an electrical device with a moving blade or set of blades for shaving hair. **2** *old colloq. use* a young boy.

shaving *noun* **1** the removal of hair with a razor. **2** a thin sliver, especially of wood, taken off with a sharp tool.

shawl *noun* a large single piece of fabric used as a loose covering for the head or shoulders, or for wrapping a baby in. [from Persian *shal*]

she *pron.* the female person or animal, or thing thought of as female (eg a ship), named before or understood from the context. [from Anglo-Saxon *seo*]

sheaf — *noun* (PL. **sheaves**) a bundle, especially of reaped corn, tied together. — *verb* (*also* **sheave**) to tie up in a bundle. [from Anglo-Saxon *sceaf*]

shear — *verb* (PAST TENSE **sheared**; PAST PARTICIPLE **shorn**) **1** to clip or cut off with a large pair of clippers. **2** to cut the fleece off (a sheep). **3** (*usually* **be shorn of something**) to be stripped or deprived of it: *was shorn of all authority.* **4** *trans., intrans.* (*also* **shear off**) *said of metal* to twist or break under strain. — *noun* **1** (**shears**) a two-bladed cutting tool like a large pair of scissors; clippers. **2** a twisting or breaking of metal under strain. [from Anglo-Saxon *sceran*]

shearer *noun* a person who shears sheep.

shearwater *noun* **1** a petrel with a long slender bill, dark plumage on the upper part of the body, and pale plumage beneath. **2** a skimmer.

sheath *noun* **1** a covering for the blade of a sword or knife. **2** a long close-fitting covering. **3** *old use* a condom. **4** a straight tight-fitting dress. [from Anglo-Saxon *sceath*]

⊞ **1** scabbard, case. **2** sleeve, envelope, shell, casing, covering. **3** condom, *slang* rubber, *slang* French letter.

sheathe *verb* to put into, or protect or cover with, a sheath.

sheave and **sheaves** see SHEAF.

shebang /ʃɪ'baŋ/ *noun slang* affair; matter: *the whole shebang.*

shed[1] *noun* a wooden or metal outbuilding of any size, for working in or for storage or shelter. [from SHADE]

⊞ outbuilding, outhouse, lean-to, hut, shack.

shed[2] *verb* (**shedding**; PAST TENSE AND PAST PARTICIPLE **shed**) **1** to release or cause to flow: *shed tears.* **2** to cast off or get rid of: *shed a skin/shed jobs.* **3** to cast: *shed light on.* **4** to allow to flow off: *this fabric sheds water.* [from Anglo-Saxon *sceadan*]

⊞ **1** release, spill. **2** cast (off), moult, slough, discard, get

rid of, drop. **3** cast, throw, pour, scatter, diffuse, emit, radiate, shine.

she'd *contr.* **1** she had. **2** she would.

sheen *noun* shine; glossiness; lustre. [from Anglo-Saxon *scene*]

⊞ lustre, gloss, shine, shimmer, brightness, brilliance, shininess, glossiness, polish, burnish.
⊟ dullness, tarnish.

sheep *noun* (PL. **sheep**) **1** any of various wild or domesticated species of a herbivorous mammal, belonging to the family Bovidae, and having a stocky body covered with a thick woolly fleece. **2** a meek person, especially one who follows or obeys unquestioningly. **3** a member of a congregation (thought of as being looked after by the pastor). [from Anglo-Saxon *sceap*]

sheep dip an approved chemical used to disinfect sheep in a dipping bath, in order to control parasitic diseases such as sheep scab.

sheepdog *noun* **1** a dog trained to herd sheep. **2** any of various breeds of dog originally trained to herd sheep.

sheepish *adj.* embarrassed because of having done something wrong or foolish.

⊞ ashamed, shamefaced, embarrassed, mortified, chastened, abashed, uncomfortable, self-conscious, silly, foolish.
⊟ unabashed, brazen, bold.

sheepshank *noun* a knot used for shortening a rope.

sheepskin *noun* **1** a sheep's skin with the wool left on it, or a rug or piece of clothing made from it. **2** leather made from sheep's skin.

sheer[1] — *adj.* **1** complete; absolute; nothing but: *sheer madness.* **2** *said of a cliff, etc* vertical or nearly vertical. **3** so fine as to be almost transparent. — *adv.* **1** completely. **2** vertically or nearly vertically: *rock face rising sheer.* [from Middle English *schere*]

⊞ *adj.* **1** utter, complete, total, absolute, thorough, pure, unadulterated, downright, thoroughgoing, unqualified, unmitigated. **2** vertical, perpendicular, precipitous, abrupt, steep. **3** thin, fine, flimsy, gauzy, translucent, transparent, see-through.
⊟ *adj.* **2** gentle, gradual. **3** thick, heavy.

sheer[2] *verb intrans.* (**sheer off, away,** etc) **1** to change course suddenly; to swerve. **2** to move (away), especially from a person or thing disliked or feared.

sheet[1] — *noun* **1** a large broad piece of fabric, especially for covering the mattress of a bed. **2** any large broad piece or expanse. **3** a piece (of paper), especially of a size for writing on. **4** a pamphlet or newspaper. — *verb* **1** to provide or cover with sheets. **2** *intrans., said of rain, ice, etc* to form, or fall in, a sheet-like mass. [from Anglo-Saxon *scete*]

⊞ *noun* **1** cover, blanket. **2** panel, slab, pane, plate, lamina, veneer, layer, stratum, covering, coating, expanse. **3** leaf, page, folio, piece.

sheet[2] *noun Naut.* a controlling rope attached to the lower corner of a sail. [from Anglo-Saxon *sceata*, corner]

sheet anchor **1** an extra anchor for use in an emergency. **2** a person or thing relied on for support, especially in a crisis; a last hope. [originally *shoot-anchor*]

sheeting *noun* fabric used for making sheets.

sheet music music printed on loose sheets of paper.

sheikh or **sheik** /ʃeɪk/ *noun* **1** the head of an Arab tribe, village or family. **2** a Muslim leader. [from Arabic *shaikh*, old man]

sheikhdom or **sheikdom** /ˈʃeɪkdəm/ *noun* the territory of a sheikh.

sheila /ˈʃiːlə/ *noun Austral., New Zealand colloq.* a woman or girl. [from the name SHEILA]

shekel /ˈʃɛkəl/ *noun* **1** the standard unit of currency in Israel, divided into 100 agorot. **2** an ancient Jewish coin and weight. **3** (**shekels**) *slang* money. [from Hebrew *sheqel*]

sheldrake *noun* a male shelduck.

shelduck *noun* a large brightly coloured duck of Europe, Africa and Asia. [from dialect *sheld*, pied + DUCK]

shelf *noun* (PL. **shelves**) **1** a (usually narrow) horizontal board for laying things on, fixed to a wall or as part of a cupboard, etc. **2** a sandbank or rocky ledge, especially partially submerged. — **on the shelf 1** *said of a person or thing* no longer used, employed, or active. **2** *said of a person* no longer likely to have the opportunity to marry, especially because of being too old. [from Anglo-Saxon *scylf*]

⊟ LEDGE. **1** mantelpiece, sill, bench, counter, bar. **2** bank, sandbank, reef, terrace.

shelf-life *noun* the length of time that a stored product remains usable.

shell — *noun* **1** *Bot.* the hard protective layer that surrounds the seed, nut, or fruit of some plants. **2** *Zool.* the tough protective structure that covers the body of certain animals, eg molluscs (snails and shellfish), crabs, lobsters, turtles, and tortoises. It is usually made of calcium carbonate, chitin, or a horny or bony material. **3** the protective outer covering of an egg, eg the hard chalky covering of a bird's egg, or the leathery covering of a reptile's egg. **4** the empty covering of a mollusc, found on the seashore. **5** any hard outer case. **6** a round of ammunition for a large-bore gun, eg a mortar; a shotgun cartridge. **7** an empty framework or outer case, the early stage of construction or the undestroyed remains of something, eg a building. **8** *Comput.* a program that acts as a user-friendly interface between an operating system and the user. **9** *Chem.* one of a series of concentric spheres representing the possible orbits of electrons as they revolve around the nucleus of an atom. Also called ORBITAL. **10** a person very much weaker than before in body or personality. **11** a narrow light rowing-boat for racing. — *verb* **1** to remove the shell from. **2** to bombard with (eg mortar) shells. — **come out of one's shell** to become more friendly or sociable. **shell something out** *colloq.* to pay it out or spend it. [from Anglo-Saxon *scell*]

⊟ *noun* **1** hull, husk, pod, rind. **5** case, casing. **7** framework, structure, skeleton, body, chassis, frame. *verb* **1** hull, husk, pod. **2** bomb, bombard, barrage, blitz, attack.

she'll *contr.* she will; she shall.

shellac /ˈʃɛlak/ — *noun* **1** a yellow or orange resin produced by the lac insect and others. **2** a solution of this in alcohol, used as a varnish. — *verb* (**shellacked, shellacking**) to coat with shellac. [from SHELL + LAC]

shellfish *noun* **1** common name for an edible aquatic invertebrate that has a hard shell or exoskeleton, especially a mollusc or crustacean, eg prawn, crab, lobster, shrimp. **2** a collective term for such animals.

shelling *noun* **1** removing the shell or shells. **2** bombarding with ammunition, bombing.

shell-shock *noun* nervous breakdown caused by prolonged exposure to combat conditions.

shell-shocked *adj.* affected with shell-shock.

shell suit a tracksuit of very lightweight multi-coloured fabric, commonly used as everyday casual wear.

shelter — *noun* **1** protection against weather or danger. **2** a place or structure giving this. — *verb* (**sheltered, sheltering**) **1** to protect from danger or the effects of weather. **2** *intrans.* to take cover.

⊟ *noun* COVER, SANCTUARY. **1** protection, defence, safety, security, asylum. **2** haven, refuge, retreat, accommodation, lodging, roof, shade. *verb* HIDE. **1** cover, screen, shade, protect, defend, guard, shield, harbour, accommodate, put up.

⊞ *noun* **1** exposure. *verb* **1** expose.

sheltered *adj.* **1** protected from the effects of weather. **2** kept ignorant of the world's unpleasantnesses: *a sheltered upbringing.*

⊟ **1** covered, shaded, shielded, protected, cosy, snug, warm, quiet. **2** cloistered, retired, withdrawn, isolated, reclusive, unworldly.

⊞ **1** exposed.

sheltered housing flats or bungalows specially designed for the elderly or disabled, especially in a safe enclosed complex, with a resident warden.

shelve *verb* **1** to store on a shelf. **2** to fit with shelves. **3** to postpone the use or implementation of; to abandon. **4** to remove from active service. **5** *intrans., said of ground* to slope gently.

⊟ **3** postpone, defer, put off, suspend, halt, pigeonhole, mothball.

⊞ **3** expedite, implement.

shelves see SHELF.

shelving *noun* **1** material for use as shelves. **2** shelves collectively.

shenanigans *pl. noun colloq.* **1** boisterous misbehaviour. **2** foolish behaviour; nonsense. **3** underhand dealings; trickery.

shepherd — *noun* **1** a person who looks after sheep. **2** *literary* a religious minister. — *verb* to guide or herd (a group or crowd). [from Anglo-Saxon *sceaphirde*, sheep herd]

shepherdess *noun old use* a female shepherd.

shepherd's pie a baked dish of minced meat with mashed potatoes on the top.

shepherd's purse a small annual weed (*Capsella bursa-pastoris*), found almost everywhere, and having a rosette of oblong lobed leaves and white cross-shaped flowers. The seed capsules are heart-shaped, reminiscent of an old-style peasant's purse.

sherbet *noun* **1** a fruit-flavoured powder, or a fizzy drink made from it. **2** a drink of sweetened fruit juices in Middle Eastern countries. [from Turkish and Persian *serbet*]

sherd see SHARD.

sheriff *noun* **1** the chief police officer in a US county. **2** the chief judge of a sheriff court. **3** the chief representative of the monarch in an English county, whose duties are now mainly ceremonial. [from Anglo-Saxon *scir*, shire + *gerefa*, reeve]

sheriff court a court in a Scottish town or region dealing with civil actions and trying all but the most serious crimes.

Sherpa *noun* a member of an Eastern Tibetan people living high on the south side of the Himalayas. [from Tibetan *shar*, east + *pa*, inhabitant]

sherry *noun* (PL. **sherries**) a fortified wine ranging in colour from pale gold to dark brown, strictly speaking one produced in or near the S Spanish town of *Jerez*.

she's *contr.* **1** she is. **2** she has.

Shetland pony (PL. **Shetland ponies**) a breed of small sturdy pony with a long thick coat, originally bred in the Shetland Isles.

SHF *Radio* super high frequency.

Shia or **Shiah** /ˈʃiːə/ *noun* one of the two main branches of Islam, the branch which regards Mohammed's son-in-law, Ali, as his true successor as leader of Islam. See also SUNNI. [from Arabic *shia*, sect]

shiatsu or **shiatzu** /ʃiˈatsuː/ *noun Medicine* a Japanese massage technique that aims to heal disorders and promote health by the application of pressure, especially with the fingers and palms of the hands, to parts of the body that are distant from the affected region. Also called ACU-PRESSURE [from Japanese, = finger pressure]

shibboleth /'ʃɪbələθ/ *noun* 1 a common saying. 2 a slogan, custom, or belief, especially if considered outdated. 3 a use of a word, phrase, or pronunciation that characterizes members of a particular group. [a Hebrew word of uncertain meaning (probably either 'ear of corn', or 'flooded stream'), used in Judges 12.5–6 as an oral test by which Jephthah and his Gileadites detected the enemy Ephraimites, who could not pronounce *sh*]

shield — *noun* 1 a piece of armour carried to block an attack with a weapon. 2 a representation of this, usually a vertical rectangle with a rounded bottom, used as an emblem. 3 a medal or trophy shaped (perhaps only vaguely) like this. 4 a protective plate or screen. 5 a person or thing that protects from danger or harm. — *verb* to protect from danger or harm. [from Anglo-Saxon *sceld*]

. . . .

⊟ *noun* 1 buckler, escutcheon. 4 screen, guard, cover, shelter. 5 defence, bulwark, rampart, protection, safeguard. *verb* defend, guard, protect, safeguard, screen, shade, cover, shelter.

⊟ *verb* expose.
. . . .

shift — *verb* 1 *trans., intrans.* to change the position or direction of; to change position or direction. 2 to transfer, switch, or re-direct: *shift the blame on to someone else.* 3 to change (gear in a vehicle). 4 to remove or dislodge. 5 *intrans. colloq.* to move quickly. — *noun* 1 a change, or change of position. 2 one of a set of consecutive periods into which a 24-hour working day is divided. 3 the group of workers on duty during any one of these periods. 4 a handy method of proceeding or dealing with something; an expedient. 5 a trick or other underhand scheme. — **shift one's ground** to adopt a new opinion, position in an argument, etc. [from Anglo-Saxon *sciftan*, to divide]

. . . .

⊟ *verb* 1 change, vary, alter, move, budge, relocate, reposition. 2 transfer, switch, re-direct. 4 remove, dislodge, displace. *noun* 1 change, alteration, modification, move, rearrangement, transposition, transfer, switch.

. . . .

shiftily *adv.* in a shifty way.

shiftiness *noun* being shifty.

shiftless *adj.* 1 having no motivation or initiative. 2 inefficient.

shifty *adj.* (**shiftier, shiftiest**) *said of a person or behaviour* sly, untrustworthy, or dishonest.

. . . .

⊟ untrustworthy, dishonest, deceitful, scheming, tricky, wily, crafty, cunning, sly, devious, evasive, slippery, furtive, *colloq.* shady.

⊟ honest, open.
. . . .

shiitake /ʃiːˈtɑːkeɪ, ʃiːˈtɑːkeɪ/ *noun* (PL. **shiitake**) a large dark-brown mushroom cultivated on tree logs, widely used in Oriental cookery. [from Japanese *shii* a type of tree + *take* mushroom]

Shiite /'ʃiːaɪt/ — *noun* a Muslim who is an adherent of Shia. — *adj.* of or relating to Shia.

shilling *noun* 1 in the UK before the introduction of decimal currency, a monetary unit and coin worth one twentieth of £1 or 12 old pence (12d). 2 the standard unit of currency in several E African countries. [from Anglo-Saxon *scilling*]

shilly-shally *verb intrans.* (**shilly-shallies, shilly-shallied**) to be slow to make up one's mind; to be indecisive. [reduplication of *shall I?*]

shim — *noun* a thin washer, or a metal or plastic strip, used to fill a gap between machine parts, especially gears. — *verb* (**shimmed, shimming**) to fill or adjust with a shim.

shimmer — *verb intrans.* (**shimmered, shimmering**) to shine quiveringly with reflected light. — *noun* a quivering gleam of reflected light. [from Anglo-Saxon *scimerian*]

. . . .

⊟ *verb* glisten, gleam, glimmer, glitter, scintillate, twinkle. *noun* lustre, gleam, glimmer, glitter, glow.
. . . .

shimmery *adj.* that shimmers.

shin — *noun* 1 the bony front part of the leg below the knee. 2 the lower part of a leg of beef. — *verb trans., intrans.* (**shinned, shinning**) (*usually* **shin up**) to climb by gripping with the hands and legs. [from Anglo-Saxon *scinu*]

shinbone *noun* the tibia.

shindig *noun colloq.* 1 a lively party or celebration. 2 a noisy disturbance; a commotion. [perhaps from SHINTY]

shine — *verb* (PAST TENSE AND PAST PARTICIPLE **shone**, **shined** sense 3) 1 *intrans.* to give out or reflect light. 2 to direct the light from: *shone the torch in my face.* 3 to make bright and gleaming by polishing. 4 *intrans.* to command attention or be outstandingly impressive: *she shines at maths.* — *noun* 1 shining quality; brightness; lustre. 2 sunny weather: *rain or shine.* — **take a shine to someone** *colloq.* to like them on first acquaintance. [from Anglo-Saxon *scinan*]

. . . .

⊟ *verb* 1 beam, radiate, glow, flash, glare, gleam, glint, glitter, sparkle, twinkle, shimmer, glisten, glimmer. 3 polish, burnish, buff, rub. 4 excel, stand out. *noun* 1 light, radiance, glow, brightness, glare, gleam, sparkle, shimmer, lustre, sheen, gloss, polish.

. . . .

shiner *noun colloq.* a black eye.

shingle [1] *noun Geol.* a mass of small rounded pebbles that have been worn smooth by the action of water, often found in a series of parallel ridges on seashores.

shingle [2] — *noun* 1 a thin rectangular (especially wooden) roof-tile. 2 a woman's short hairstyle, cropped at the back. — *verb* 1 to tile with shingles. 2 to cut in a shingle. [from Latin *scindula*, wooden tile]

shingles *sing. noun Medicine* herpes zoster, a painful viral infection in which acute inflammation of the nerve ganglia produces a series of blisters on one side of the body along the path of the affected nerves. It is caused by the same virus that is responsible for chickenpox in children. [from Latin *cingulum*, belt]

shingly *adj.* 1 covered with or consisting of shingle. 2 of the nature of shingle.

Shinto *noun* the indigenous religion of Japan, so named in the 8c to distinguish it from Buddhism, although it subsequently incorporated many Buddhist features. [from Japanese *Shinto*, from Chinese *shen*, god + *tao*, way]

Shintoism /'ʃɪntoʊɪzm/ *noun* the beliefs and practices of Shinto.

Shintoist /'ʃɪntoʊɪst/ — *noun* an adherent of Shinto. — *adj.* of or relating to Shinto.

shinty *noun* (PL. **shinties**) 1 a stick-and-ball game played by two teams of 12. 2 the stick or ball used for this game.

shiny *adj.* (**shinier, shiniest**) 1 reflecting light; polished to brightness. 2 *said of part of a piece of clothing* at which the fabric has been badly worn, leaving a glossy surface.

. . . .

⊟ 1 polished, burnished, lustrous, glossy, sleek, bright, brilliant, gleaming, glistening, glittering, sparkling, twinkling.

⊟ 1 dull, matt.
. . . .

ship — *noun* 1 any large boat intended for sea travel. 2 *colloq.* a spaceship or airship. — *verb* (**shipped, shipping**) 1 to send or transport by ship, or any other means. 2 (**ship someone off**) *colloq.* to send them away: *shipped the children off to their grandparents.* 3 *Naut.*, *said of a boat* to have (water, eg waves) coming on board over the side. 4 *Naut.* to bring on board a boat or ship: *ship oars.* — **when one's**

ship comes in or **comes home** when one becomes rich. [from Anglo-Saxon *scip*]

● *noun* CRAFT. **1** vessel, liner, steamer, tanker, trawler, ferry, boat, yacht.

-ship *suffix* forming words denoting: **1** rank, position, or status: *lordship*. **2** a period of office or rule: *during his chairmanship*. **3** a state or condition: *friendship*. **4** a type of skill: *craftsmanship*. **5** a group of individuals: *membership*. [from Anglo-Saxon *scipe*]

shipboard *adj.* taking place, or situated, on board a ship.

shipmate *noun* a fellow sailor.

shipment *noun* **1** a cargo or consignment (not necessarily one sent by ship). **2** the act or practice of shipping cargo.

shipping *noun* **1** ships as traffic. **2** the commercial transporting of freight, especially by ship.

shipshape *adj.* in good order; neat and tidy.

shipwreck — *noun* **1** the accidental sinking or destruction of a ship. **2** the remains of a sunken or destroyed ship. **3** ruin; disaster. — *verb* **1** *trans., intrans.* to be or cause to be the victim of accidental sinking or destruction. **2** to ruin (eg plans).

shipwright *noun* a person who builds or repairs (especially wooden) ships.

shipyard *noun* a place where ships are built and repaired.

shire *noun* a county. [from Anglo-Saxon *scir*, authority]

shire horse a large strong horse bred for pulling carts, etc, originally in the Midlands.

Shires *pl. noun* (**the Shires**) the rural areas of England as opposed to the towns, specifically the Midland counties or the fox-hunting counties of Leicestershire and Northamptonshire.

shirk *verb trans., intrans.* to avoid doing (work) or carrying out (a duty). [perhaps from German *Schurke*, scoundrel]

● slack, idle, *colloq.* skive.

shirker *noun* a person who avoids work or responsibilities.

shirt *noun* a piece of clothing of cotton, silk, etc for the upper body, usually with a collar and buttons down the front, especially worn by men under a jacket. — **keep one's shirt on** *colloq.* to control one's temper. **put one's shirt on something** *colloq.* to bet all one has on it. [from Anglo-Saxon *scyrte*]

shirt dress or **shirtwaister** a woman's dress with a shirt-like bodice.

shirtsleeve *noun* a sleeve of a shirt. — **in one's shirt-sleeves** not wearing a jacket or coat.

shirt-tail *noun* the flap hanging down at the back of a shirt.

shirty *adj.* (**shirtier, shirtiest**) *colloq.* bad-tempered; annoyed.

shish kebab see KEBAB.

shit or **shite** *coarse slang* — *noun* **1** faeces. **2** an act of defecating. **3** *derog.* rubbish; nonsense. **4** *derog.* a despicable person. — *verb* (**shitting;** PAST TENSE AND PAST PARTICIPLE **shit, shitted**) *intrans.* to defecate. — *interj.* an expression of annoyance or disappointment. [from Anglo-Saxon *scitan*, to defecate]

shitty *adj.* (**shittier, shittiest**) *coarse slang* **1** filthy; soiled with, or as if with, shit. **2** *derog.* mean; despicable.

shiver¹ — *verb intrans.* (**shivered, shivering**) to quiver or tremble, eg with fear, or as a result of involuntary movement of the muscles in response to low temperatures. — *noun* an act of shivering; a shivering movement or sensation. — **the shivers** *colloq.* a fit of shivering. [from Middle English *chivere*]

● *verb* shudder, tremble, quiver, quake, shake, vibrate, palpitate, flutter. *noun* shudder, quiver, shake, tremor, twitch, start.

shiver² — *noun* a splinter or other small fragment. — *verb trans., intrans.* (**shivered, shivering**) to shatter. [from Middle English *scifre*]

shivery *adj.* inclined to shiver or to cause shivers.

shoal¹ — *noun* **1** a large number of fish swimming together. **2** a huge crowd; a multitude or swarm. — *verb intrans.* to gather or move in a shoal. [from Anglo-Saxon *scolu*, a troop]

shoal² — *noun* **1** an area of shallow water in a river, lake, or sea where sediment has accumulated, often hazardous to shipping. **2** such an accumulation of sediment. — *verb trans., intrans.* to make or become shallow. [from Anglo-Saxon *sceald*, shallow]

shock¹ — *noun* **1** a strong emotional disturbance, especially a feeling of extreme surprise, outrage, or disgust; also, a cause of this. **2** a convulsion caused by the passage of an electric current through the body. **3** a heavy jarring blow or impact. **4** *Medicine* **a** a state of extreme physical collapse that occurs when the blood pressure within the arteries becomes too low to maintain an adequate blood supply to the tissues, eg as a result of haemorrhage, coronary thrombosis, or a sudden extreme emotional disturbance. **b** *Scot. or dialect* a stroke. — *verb* **1** to cause to feel extreme surprise, outrage, or disgust. **2** to shake or jar suddenly and forcefully. [from French *choc*]

● *noun* **1** fright, start, jolt, surprise, bombshell, thunderbolt, blow, trauma, upset, distress, dismay, consternation, disgust, outrage, horror. **3** blow, impact, collision. *verb* **1** disgust, revolt, sicken, offend, appal, outrage, scandalize, horrify, astound, stagger, stun, stupefy, traumatize, unnerve, dismay. **2** jolt, jar, shake, agitate.

● *noun* **1** delight, pleasure, reassurance. *verb* **1** delight, please, reassure.

shock² *noun* a bushy mass of hair.

shock³ — *noun* a number of sheaves of corn propped up against each other to dry. — *verb* to set up to dry in this way. [from Middle English *schokke*]

shock absorber a device, such as a coiled spring, in the suspension system of a vehicle, that damps vibrations caused by the wheels passing over bumps in the road, absorbing the shock waves that would otherwise jar the body of the vehicle, and so ensuring a smoother ride for passengers.

shocking *adj.* **1** extremely surprising, outrageous, or disgusting. **2** *colloq.* very bad.

● APPALLING, ATROCIOUS. **1** outrageous, scandalous, horrifying, disgraceful, deplorable, abominable, monstrous, unspeakable, disgusting, sickening, nauseating, distressing. **2** dreadful, awful, terrible, frightful, ghastly.

● **1** acceptable, satisfactory, pleasant, delightful.

shock tactics any course of action that seeks to achieve its object by means of suddenness and force.

shock therapy see ELECTRO-CONVULSIVE THERAPY.

shock wave *Physics* an exceptionally intense sound wave, caused by a violent explosion or the movement of an object at a speed greater than that of sound.

shod see SHOE.

shoddily *adv.* in a shoddy way.

shoddiness *noun* being shoddy.

shoddy *adj.* (**shoddier, shoddiest**) **1** of poor quality; carelessly done or made. **2** of the nature of a cheap imitation.

● **1** inferior, second-rate, poor, careless, slipshod, slapdash. **2** cheap, tawdry, trashy, rubbishy.

● **1** superior, well-made.

shoe — *noun* **1** either of a pair of shaped outer coverings for the feet, especially made of leather or other stiff material, usually finishing below the ankle. **2** anything like this in shape or function. **3** a horseshoe. — *verb* (**shoeing**; PAST TENSE AND PAST PARTICIPLE **shod**) to fit (usually a horse) with shoes. — **in someone's shoes** in the same situation as them; in their place. [from Anglo-Saxon *scoh*]

shoehorn *noun* a curved shaped piece of metal, plastic or (originally) horn, used for gently levering a foot into a shoe.

shoelace *noun* a string or cord for fastening a shoe.

shoestring *noun North Amer.* a shoelace. — **on a shoestring** *colloq.* with or using a very small amount of money.

shoe tree a support put inside a shoe to preserve its shape when not being worn.

shogi /ˈʃoːgɪ/ *noun* a Japanese form of chess, played on a squared board, each player having 20 pieces. [from Japanese *shogi*]

shone see SHINE.

shoo — *interj.* an expression used to chase away a person or animal. — *verb* (**shooed, shooing**) (**shoo someone** or **something away or off**) to chase them away by, or as if by, shouting 'Shoo!'. [imitative]

shook see SHAKE.

shoot — *verb* (PAST TENSE AND PAST PARTICIPLE **shot**) **1** *trans., intrans.* to fire (a gun or other weapon, or bullets, arrows or other missiles). **2** to hit, wound, or kill with a weapon or missile. **3** to direct forcefully and rapidly: *shot questions at them.* **4** *intrans.* to move or progress extremely fast. **5** to cause to move or progress in this way: *that last victory shot them to the top of the table.* **6** *trans., intrans. Sport* to strike (the ball, etc) at goal. **7** *trans., intrans.* to film, or take photographs (of). **8** *intrans., said of pain* to dart with a stabbing sensation. **9** *intrans., said of a plant* to produce new growth; (especially of a vegetable) to produce unwanted flowers and seeds. **10** *colloq.* to pass through (a set of traffic lights at red) without stopping. **11** *colloq.* to pass quickly through: *shoot rapids.* **12** *slang* to play a game of (eg pool or golf); to have as a score at golf. **13** *slang* to inject (especially oneself) with (drugs) illegally. — *noun* **1** an act of shooting. **2** a new or young plant growth. **3** an outing to hunt animals with firearms; an area of land within which animals are hunted in this way. — **shoot someone** or **something down 1** to fire guns at an aircraft so as to make it crash. **2** to kill with gunfire. **3** to dismiss mercilessly with criticism or ridicule. **shoot one's mouth off** *colloq.* to speak indiscreetly or boastfully. **shoot up** to grow or increase extremely quickly. [from Anglo-Saxon *sceotan*]

·······················

⊟ *verb* **1** fire, discharge. **2** hit, wound, injure, kill, blast, bombard, gun down, snipe at, pick off. **3** fire, direct, aim, throw, hurl, fling. **4** dart, bolt, dash, tear, rush, race, sprint, speed, charge, hurtle. **5** launch, propel, project. **7** film, photograph. *noun* **2** sprout, bud, offshoot, branch, twig, sprig, slip, scion.

·······················

shooter *noun* **1** a person or thing that shoots. **2** *colloq.* a gun.

shooting brake *old use* an estate car.

shooting star a meteor.

shooting-stick *noun* a sturdy pointed walking-stick whose two-part handle folds out to form a small seat.

shop — *noun* **1** a place where goods (or services) are sold. **2** a place in which (especially manual) work of a particular kind is carried out: *machine shop.* — *verb* (PAST TENSE AND PAST PARTICIPLE **shopped, shopping**) **1** *intrans.* to visit a shop or shops in order to buy goods. **2** *trans. slang* to inform on (someone), eg to the police. — **all over the shop** *colloq.* scattered everywhere; in numerous places. **shop around 1** to compare the price and quality of goods in various shops before deciding to buy. **2** *colloq.* to explore the full range of options available before committing oneself to any. **shut up shop** *colloq.* to stop trading, whether at the end of the working day or permanently. **talk shop** *colloq.* to talk about one's work, especially in a tedious way. [from Anglo-Saxon *sceoppa*, treasury]

Types of shop include: bazaar, market, indoor market, mini-market, corner shop, shopping mall, department store, supermarket, superstore, hypermarket, cash-and-carry; butcher, baker, grocer, greengrocer, fishmonger, dairy, delicatessen, health food shop, farmshop, fish and chip shop, take-away, off-licence, tobacconist, sweet shop, confectioner, tuck shop; bookshop, newsagent, stationer, chemist, pharmacy, tailor, outfitter, dress shop, boutique, milliner, shoe shop, haberdasher, draper, florist, jeweller, toy shop, hardware shop, ironmonger, saddler, radio and TV shop, video shop; launderette, hairdresser, barber, betting shop, bookmaker, *colloq.* bookie, pawnbroker, post office.

shop assistant a person serving customers in a shop.

shop floor 1 the part of a factory where the manual work is carried out. **2** the workers in a factory, as opposed to the management.

shopkeeper *noun* a person who owns and manages a shop.

shoplift *verb* to steal goods from shops.

shoplifter *noun* a person who shoplifts.

shoplifting *noun* stealing goods from shops.

shopper *noun* **1** a person who shops. **2** a shopping bag or basket.

shopping *noun* **1** the activity of visiting shops to buy goods. **2** goods bought in shops.

shopping centre 1 an area containing a large number of shops of different kinds. **2** a collection of different shops under one roof, often providing other facilities, eg restaurants and toilets.

shop-soiled *adj.* slightly dirty or spoiled from being used as a display in a shop.

shop steward a worker elected by others to be an official trade union representative in negotiations with the management.

shopwalker *noun* a person who supervises shop assistants in a large department store.

shore[1] *noun* **1** land bordering on the sea or any area of water. **2** (**shores**) *literary* lands; countries: *foreign shores.* [from Middle English *schore*]

·······················

⊟ **1** seashore, beach, sand(s), shingle, strand, waterfront, coast, seaboard, lakeside, bank.

·······················

shore[2] — *noun* a prop. — *verb* (*usually* **shore something up**) **1** to support it with props. **2** to give support to it; to sustain or strengthen it. [from Old Dutch *schore*]

·······················

⊟ *verb* SUPPORT, UNDERPIN, BUTTRESS. **1** prop, stay. **2** strengthen, reinforce, brace.

·······················

shoreline *noun* the line formed where land meets water.

shorn see SHEAR.

short — *adj.* **1** of little physical length; not long. **2** of little height. **3** brief; concise. **4** *said of a temper* easily lost. **5** rudely or angrily abrupt; curt. **6** (**short of** or **on something**) lacking in it; not having enough of it; deficient. **7** *said of the memory* tending not to retain things for long. **8** *said of pastry* crisp and crumbling easily. **9** *said of betting odds* providing the winner with only a small profit; near even. **10** *said of a vowel sound* being the briefer of two possible lengths of vowel. **11** *Cricket, said of fielding positions* relatively close to the batsman. — *adv.* **1** abruptly: *stopped short.* **2** (**short of ...**) without going as far as ...; except: *tried every kind of persuasion short of threats.* — *noun* **1** a drink of an alcoholic spirit. **2** a short cinema film shown before the main feature. **3** a short circuit. — *verb trans., intrans.* to short-circuit. — **be caught** or **taken short** *colloq.* to have an urgent need to urinate or defecate. **fall short** to be less than a required, expected, or stated amount. **for short** as an abbreviated form. **go** or **run short of** some-

thing not to have enough of it. **in short** concisely stated. **short and sweet** *colloq.* agreeably brief. **short for something** an abbreviated form of it. [from Anglo-Saxon *sceort*]

....

⬛ *adj.* **1** small, little. **2** small, little, low, petite, diminutive, squat, dumpy. **3** brief, cursory, fleeting, momentary, transitory, ephemeral, concise, succinct, terse, pithy, compact, compressed, shortened, curtailed, abbreviated, abridged, summarized. **5** brusque, curt, gruff, snappy, sharp, abrupt, rude, impolite, discourteous, uncivil. **6** deficient in, lacking in, wanting.
⬛ *adj.* **1** long. **2** tall, high. **3** long, lasting. **5** polite.

....

shortage *noun* a lack or deficiency.

....

⬛ lack, want, need, deficiency, shortfall, deficit, inadequacy, insufficiency, scarcity, paucity, dearth, absence.
⬛ sufficiency, abundance, surplus.

....

shortbread *noun* a rich sweet crumbly biscuit made with flour, butter, and sugar.

shortcake *noun* **1** shortbread. **2** a dessert cake consisting of a biscuit base topped with fruit, served with cream.

short-change *verb* **1** to give (a customer) less than the correct amount of change, whether by accident or intentionally. **2** *colloq.* to treat dishonestly; to cheat.

short circuit a connection across an electric circuit with a very low resistance, usually caused accidentally, eg by an insulation failure. Short circuits can pass a very high current which may damage electrical equipment or be a fire hazard.

short-circuit *verb* to cause a short circuit in (an electrical circuit).

shortcoming *noun* a fault or defect.

....

⬛ fault, flaw, defect, imperfection, drawback, failing, weakness, foible.

....

short cut 1 a quicker route between two places. **2** a method that saves time or effort.

shorten *verb* (**shortened, shortening**) **1** to make shorter. **2** *intrans.* to become shorter.

....

⬛ REDUCE, LESSEN, DECREASE. **1** cut, trim, prune, crop, dock, curtail, truncate, abbreviate, abridge, take up.
⬛ LENGTHEN, INCREASE.

....

shortening *noun* butter, lard or other fat used for making pastry more crumbly.

shortfall *noun* **1** a failure to reach a desired or expected level. **2** the amount or margin by which something is deficient: *a shortfall of 100.*

shorthand — *noun* **1** any of various systems of strokes and dots representing speech sounds and groups of sounds, used as a fast way of recording speech in writing. **2** any method of abbreviated writing. — *adv.* using any such system.

short-handed *adj.* understaffed.

shorthorn *noun* a breed of cattle with short horns.

shortie same as SHORTY.

shortlist — *noun* a selection of the best candidates from the total number submitted or nominated, from which the successful candidate will be chosen. — *verb* to place on a shortlist.

short-lived *adj.* lasting only for a short time.

shortly *adv.* **1** soon. **2** in a curt or abrupt manner.

....

⬛ **1** soon, before long, presently, by and by. **2** brusquely, curtly, sharply, abruptly.

....

shortness *noun* **1** being short. **2** deficiency.

shorts *pl. noun* trousers extending from the waist to anywhere between the upper thigh and the knee.

short shrift discourteously brief or disdainful consideration: *their suggestions were given short shrift.*

short-sighted *adj.* **1** *said of a person* affected by myopia, and able to see clearly only those objects that are relatively near. **2** *said of a person, plan, etc* lacking foresight; showing a lack of foresight.

....

⬛ **1** myopic, near-sighted. **2** improvident, imprudent, injudicious, unwise, impolitic, ill-advised, ill-considered, hasty.
⬛ **1** long-sighted, far-sighted.

....

short story a work of prose narrative shorter than a novel (usually of not more than around 10,000 words), often concentrating on a single episode or experience and its effect.

short-tempered *adj.* easily made angry.

short-term *adj.* **1** concerned only with the near future. **2** lasting only a short time.

short wave a radio wave with a wavelength of between 10 and 100 metres.

short-winded *adj.* easily running out of breath.

shorty *noun* (PL. **shorties**) *colloq.* a shorter-than-average person or thing.

shot[1] *noun* **1** an act of firing a gun; the sound of a gun being fired. **2** small metal pellets fired in clusters from a shotgun. **3** a person considered in terms of ability to fire a gun accurately: *a good shot.* **4** *Sport* an act of shooting or playing a stroke. **5** a photograph. **6** a single piece of filmed action recorded without a break by one camera. **7** a heavy metal ball thrown as a field event in athletics. **8** *colloq.* an attempt: *have a shot at.* **9** *colloq.* a turn or go: *it's my shot now.* **10** *colloq.* an injection. **11** *North Amer., esp. US colloq.* a drink of alcoholic spirit. **12** *old use* the launch of a spacecraft, especially a rocket: *moon shot.* — **call the shots** *colloq.* to give the orders; to be in charge. **like a shot** extremely quickly; without hesitating. **a shot in the arm** an uplifting or reviving influence; a boost. **a shot in the dark** a wild guess. [from Anglo-Saxon *sceot*]

....

⬛ **1** discharge, blast. **2** bullet, missile, projectile, ball, pellet, *colloq.* slug. **8** attempt, try, effort, endeavour, *colloq.* go, *colloq.* bash, *colloq.* crack, *colloq.* stab.

....

shot[2] past tense and past participle of SHOOT. — *adj.* **1** *said of a fabric* woven with different-coloured threads and in such a way that movement produces the effect of changing colours. **2** streaked with a different colour. — **be** or **get shot of someone** or **something** *colloq.* be or get rid of them.

shotgun *noun* a gun with a long wide smooth barrel for firing clusters of pellets.

shotgun wedding or **shotgun marriage** a marriage into which the couple has been forced, especially because of the woman's pregnancy.

shot put an athletics event in which a heavy metal ball is thrown from the shoulder as far as possible.

shot-putter *noun* an athlete who puts the shot.

should *verb, aux.* expressing: **1** obligation, duty, or recommendation; ought to: *you should brush your teeth regularly.* **2** likelihood or probability: *he should have left by now.* **3** condition: *if I should die before you.* **4** *with first person pronouns* a past tense of *shall* in reported speech: *I told them I should be back soon.* **5** statements in clauses with *that*, following expressions of feeling or mood: *it seems odd that we should both have had the same idea.* **6** *with first person pronouns* doubt or polite indirectness in statements: *I should imagine he's left/I should think I'll get the job.* **7** *literary* purpose: *in order that we should not have to leave.* [from Anglo-Saxon *sceolde*]

shoulder — *noun* **1** the part of the body between the neck and upper arm. **2** the part of a garment covering this. **3** the part of an animal's or bird's body where the foreleg or wing joins the trunk. **4** a cut of meat consisting of the animal's upper foreleg. **5** (**shoulders**) the person as a bearer of burdens; capacity to bear burdens: *a lot of responsibility on his shoulders/have broad shoulders*. **6** any object or part resembling a human shoulder. **7** either edge of a road. — *verb* (**shouldered, shouldering**) **1** to bear (eg a responsibility). **2** to carry on one's shoulders. **3** to thrust with the shoulder. — **straight from the shoulder** *colloq*. frankly and forcefully. **put one's shoulder to the wheel** to get down to some hard work; to begin making a great effort. **rub shoulders with someone** *colloq*. to meet or associate with them. **shoulder arms** to bring one's rifle to a vertical position tight in to the right side with the barrel against the shoulder. **a shoulder to cry on** a person to tell one's troubles to. **shoulder to shoulder** together in friendship or agreement; side by side. [from Anglo-Saxon *sculdor*]

◾ *verb* **1** bear, carry, accept, assume, take on. **3** thrust, push, shove, jostle, press.

shoulder blade the broad flat triangular bone behind either shoulder; the scapula.

shoulder strap a strap worn over the shoulder to support a garment or bag.

shouldn't *contr*. should not.

shout — *noun* **1** a loud cry or call. **2** *colloq*. a turn to buy a round of drinks. — *verb trans., intrans. (also* **shout out**) to utter (with) a loud cry or call. — **shout someone down** to force them to give up speaking, or make it impossible to hear them, by means of persistent shouting.

◾ *noun* **1** call, cry, scream, shriek, yell, roar, bellow, howl, cheer. *verb* call, cry, scream, shriek, yell, roar, bellow, bawl.

shove — *verb* **1** *trans., intrans.* to push or thrust with force. **2** *colloq*. to place or put, especially roughly: *shove it in the bag*. — *noun* a forceful push. — **shove off 1** to start a boat moving by pushing against the shore or jetty. **2** *colloq*. to go away. [from Anglo-Saxon *scufan*]

◾ *verb* **1** push, thrust, jostle. *noun* push, thrust.

shovel — *noun* **1** a tool with a deep-sided spade-like blade and a handle, for lifting and carrying loose material. **2** a machine or device with a scooping action. — *verb* (**shovelled, shovelling**) **1** to lift or carry with, or as if with, a shovel. **2** to take crudely, rapidly and in huge quantities: *shovelling food into her mouth*. [from Anglo-Saxon *scofl*, from *scufan*, to shove]

◾ *noun* **1** spade. **2** scoop, bucket. *verb* **1** dig, scoop, dredge, clear.

shoveller *noun Zool*. a duck that frequents marshes and muddy shallows, having a long rounded spade-like bill.

show — *verb* (PAST PARTICIPLE **shown, showed**) **1** to make visible or noticeable. **2** *intrans*. to become visible or noticeable. **3** to present or give to be viewed. **4** to display or exhibit. **5** to prove, indicate, or reveal. **6** to teach by demonstrating: *showed me how to draw*. **7** to lead, guide, or escort: *show you to your room*. **8** to give: *show him some respect*. **9** to represent or manifest: *exam results show a marked improvement*. **10** *intrans., said of a cinema film* to be part of a current programme: *now showing at the local Odeon*. **11** *intrans. slang* to appear or arrive: *what time did he show?* — *noun* **1** an entertainment or spectacle of any kind. **2** an exhibition. **3** a pretence: *a show of friendship between sworn enemies*. **4** a display of true feeling: *no show of emotion*. **5** outward appearance: *all done for show*. **6** *colloq*. proceedings; affair: *who's running the show?* **7** *old colloq. use* effort; attempt: *jolly good show*. — **have something** or **nothing to show** have, or not have, a reward or benefit for one's efforts. **on show** on display; available to be seen. **show off** to display oneself or one's talents precociously,

inviting attention or admiration. **show off something** to display it to good effect: *the cream rug shows off the red carpet nicely*. **show something off** to display it proudly, inviting admiration. **show up 1** *colloq*. to arrive; to turn up. **2** to be clearly visible. **show someone up** to embarrass or humiliate them in public. **show something up** to make it seem inadequate or inferior by comparison. [from Anglo-Saxon *sceawian*, to look]

◾ *verb* **1** reveal, expose, uncover, disclose. **2** appear. **3** present, offer. **4** display, exhibit. **5** prove, demonstrate, illustrate, exemplify, indicate, register, reveal, disclose, divulge. **6** teach, instruct. **7** lead, guide, conduct, usher, escort, accompany, attend. **9** represent, manifest, display, reveal. *noun* **1** entertainment, performance, production, staging, showing, spectacle, extravaganza. **2** exhibition, exposition, fair, display, parade, presentation, demonstration. **3** pretence, illusion, semblance. **4** display, manifestation, representation, demonstration. **5** appearance, air, impression, façade, front, ostentation, parade, display, flamboyance, panache, showiness, exhibitionism, pose, affectation. **show off** parade, strut, swagger, brag, boast, *colloq*. swank. **show off something** set off, enhance. **show something off** flaunt, brandish, display, exhibit. **show up 1** arrive, come, turn up, appear, *colloq*. materialize, *slang* show. **show someone up** humiliate, embarrass, mortify, shame, disgrace, let down.

◲ *verb* **1** hide, cover.

showbiz *noun colloq*. show business.

show business the entertainment industry.

showcase *noun* **1** a glass case for displaying objects, eg in a museum or shop. **2** any setting in which a person or thing is displayed to good advantage.

showdown *noun colloq*. a fight or other contest settling a long-term dispute.

◾ confrontation, clash, crisis, climax, culmination.

shower — *noun* **1** a sudden but brief fall of rain, snow, or hail. **2** a device producing a stream of water for bathing under, usually while standing. **3** a room or cubicle fitted with such a device or devices. **4** an act of bathing under such a device. **5** a sudden (especially heavy) burst or fall: *a shower of bullets/a shower of abuse*. **6** *colloq*. a bunch of worthless people. — *verb* (**showered, showering**) **1** to cover or bestow abundantly: *showered them with gifts*. **2** *intrans*. to fall or come abundantly: *arrows showering down from the battlements*. **3** *intrans*. to bathe under a shower. **4** *intrans*. to rain in showers. [from Anglo-Saxon *scur*]

◾ *noun* **5** stream, torrent, deluge, hail, volley, barrage. *verb* **1** spray, sprinkle, deluge, inundate, load, heap. **2** rain, pour.

showery *adj*. (**showerier, showeriest**) raining in showers.

showiness *noun* being showy.

showing *noun* **1** an act of exhibiting or displaying. **2** a screening of a cinema film. **3** a performance. **4** a display of behaviour as evidence of a fact: *on this showing, he certainly won't get the job*.

showjumper *noun* a horse or rider that takes part in showjumping.

showjumping *noun* a competitive sport in which riders on horseback take turns to jump a variety of obstacles, often against time.

showman *noun* **1** a person who owns or manages a circus, a stall at a fairground, or other entertainment. **2** a person skilled in displaying things, especially personal abilities, so as to attract maximum attention.

showmanship *noun* skilful display or a talent for it.

shown see SHOW.

show-off *noun colloq.* a person who shows off to attract attention; an exhibitionist.

...

◨ swaggerer, braggart, boaster, *colloq.* swanker, exhibitionist, poser, poseur.

...

showpiece *noun* 1 an item in an exhibition. 2 a thing presented as an excellent example of its type, to be copied or admired.

showroom *noun* a room where examples of goods for sale, especially relatively expensive items, are displayed.

showy *adj.* (**showier**, **showiest**) 1 attractively and impressively bright. 2 ostentatious; gaudy; flashy.

...

◨ 2 flashy, flamboyant, ostentatious, pretentious, *colloq.* flash, gaudy, garish, loud, tawdry, fancy, ornate.

◨ 2 quiet, restrained.

...

shoyu /ˈʃɔɪjuː/ *noun* a rich Japanese sauce made from soy beans naturally fermented with wheat or barley. [from Japanese]

shrank see SHRINK.

shrapnel *noun* 1 flying fragments of the casing of any exploding shell. 2 an explosive shell, filled with pellets or metal fragments, detonated shortly before impact. [from H *Shrapnel* (1761–1842), British inventor of the pellet-filled shell]

shred — *noun* 1 a thin strip cut or ripped off. 2 the smallest piece or amount: *not a shred of evidence.* — *verb* (**shredded**, **shredding**) to reduce to shreds by cutting or ripping. [from Anglo-Saxon *screade*]

...

◨ *noun* SCRAP, BIT. 1 ribbon, tatter, rag, snippet, sliver, fragment. 2 jot, iota, atom, grain, mite, whit, trace.

...

shredder *noun* a device or machine for shredding documents.

shrew *noun* 1 a small nocturnal mammal, resembling a mouse, found in Europe, Asia, N and S America, and Africa, and having velvety fur, small eyes, and a pointed snout. 2 a quarrelsome or scolding woman. [from Anglo-Saxon *screawa*]

shrewd *adj.* having or showing good judgement gained from practical experience.

...

◨ astute, judicious, well-advised, far-sighted, smart, clever, intelligent, sharp, keen, acute, alert, perceptive, observant, discerning, discriminating, knowing, cunning, crafty.

◨ unwise, obtuse, naïve, unsophisticated.

...

shrewish *adj.* 1 like a shrew. 2 scolding.

shriek — *verb trans., intrans.* to cry out with a piercing scream. — *noun* such a cry.

...

◨ *verb* scream, screech, squawk, squeal, cry, shout, yell, wail, howl. *noun* scream, screech, squawk, squeal, cry, shout, yell, wail, howl.

...

shrift see SHORT SHRIFT.

shrike *noun* any of various hook-billed songbirds that feed on insects or small birds and animals, some species being noted for impaling their prey on thorns, etc. [from Anglo-Saxon *scric*]

shrill *adj.*, *said of a sound, voice, etc* high-pitched and piercing. — *verb* to utter in such a voice.

...

◨ *adj.* high, high-pitched, piercing, penetrating, screaming, screeching, ear-splitting.

◨ *adj.* deep, low, soft, gentle.

...

shrimp — *noun* 1 a small edible long-tailed shellfish, smaller than a prawn. 2 *colloq.* a very small slight person. — *verb intrans.* to fish for shrimps.

shrimping *noun slang* the practice of sucking a partner's toes for sexual stimulation.

shrimp plant a bushy perennial plant (*Beloperone guttata*), native to Mexico, and so called because its flower spikes superficially resemble a shrimp.

shrine *noun* 1 a sacred place of worship. 2 the tomb of a saint or other holy person, or a monument erected near it. 3 any place or thing greatly respected because of its associations. [from Anglo-Saxon *scrin*]

shrink — *verb* (PAST TENSE **shrank**; PAST PARTICIPLE **shrunk**, **shrunken** as adj.) 1 *trans., intrans.* to make or become smaller, especially through exposure to heat, cold or moisture. 2 (**shrink from something**) to move away in horror or disgust. 3 (**shrink from something**) to be reluctant to do it. — *noun slang* a psychiatrist. [from Anglo-Saxon *scrincan*]

...

◨ *verb* 1 contract, shorten, narrow, decrease, lessen, shrivel, wrinkle, wither. 2 recoil from, back away from, shy away from, withdraw from, retire from, flinch from. 3 balk at, shun.

◨ *verb* 1 expand, stretch.

...

shrinkage *noun* the act or amount of shrinking.

shrinking violet *colloq.* a shy hesitant person.

shrink-wrap *verb* to wrap in clear plastic film that is then shrunk, eg by heating, so as to fit tightly.

shrivel *verb trans., intrans.* (**shrivelled**, **shrivelling**) (*also* **shrivel up**) to make or become shrunken and wrinkled, especially through drying out.

...

◨ wrinkle, pucker, wither, shrink, dry, dehydrate, scorch, sear.

...

shroud — *noun* 1 a cloth in which a dead body is wrapped. 2 anything that obscures, masks or hides: *shrouds of fog.* — *verb* 1 to wrap in a shroud. 2 to obscure, mask, or hide: *proceedings shrouded in secrecy.* [from Anglo-Saxon *scrud*, garment]

...

◨ *noun* 1 winding-sheet. 2 pall, mantle, cloak, veil, screen, blanket, covering. *verb* 1 wrap, envelop, swathe, blanket, cover. 2 cloak, veil, mask, screen, hide, conceal.

◨ *verb* 1 uncover, expose.

...

Shrove Tuesday the day in the Christian calendar before Ash Wednesday, on which it was customary to confess one's sins; Pancake Day. [from Anglo-Saxon *scrifan*, to confess sins]

shrub *noun Bot.* a woody plant, without a main trunk, which branches into several main stems at or just below ground level. [from Anglo-Saxon *scrybb*, scrub]

Shrubs include: azalea, berberis, broom, buddleia, camellia, clematis, cotoneaster, daphne, dogwood, euonymus, firethorn, flowering currant, forsythia, fuchsia, heather, hebe, holly, honeysuckle, hydrangea, ivy, japonica, jasmine, laburnum, laurel, lavender, lilac, magnolia, mallow, mimosa, mock orange, peony, privet, musk rose, rhododendron, rose, spiraea, viburnum, weigela, witch hazel, wistaria. *See also* **flower**; **plant**.

shrubbery *noun* (PL. **shrubberies**) a place, especially a part of a garden, where shrubs are grown.

shrubby *adj.* (**shrubbier**, **shrubbiest**) 1 like or having the character of a shrub. 2 covered with shrubs.

shrug — *verb trans., intrans.* (**shrugged**, **shrugging**) to raise (the shoulders) briefly as an indication of doubt or indifference. — *noun* an act of shrugging. — **shrug something off** 1 to get rid of it with ease. 2 to dismiss (especially criticism) lightly.

shrunk, **shrunken** see SHRINK.

shudder — *verb intrans.* (**shuddered**, **shuddering**) to tremble, especially with fear or disgust. — *noun* 1 such a trembling movement or feeling. **2** a heavy vibration or shaking. — **shudder to think** to be inwardly embarrassed or appalled when imagining some consequence, etc.

■ *verb* shiver, shake, tremble, quiver, quake, heave, convulse. *noun* **1** shiver, quiver, tremor, spasm, convulsion.

shuffle — *verb* **1** to move (one's feet) with short quick sliding movements. **2** *intrans.* to walk in this way. **3** to rearrange or mix up roughly or carelessly. **4** to jumble up (playing cards) into a random order. — *noun* **1** an act or sound of shuffling. **2** a short quick sliding of the feet in dancing.

■ *verb* **1** drag, scuff, scrape. **2** shamble, limp, hobble. **3** mix (up), jumble (up), confuse, rearrange, reorganize, shift, switch.

shuffleboard or **shovelboard** *noun* a popular deck game played aboard ship. A larger version of shovehalfpenny, it is played by pushing wooden discs with long-handled drivers into a scoring area.

shufti /ˈʃʊftɪ/ *noun colloq.* a look or glance: *have a shufti at this.* [from Arabic *shufti*, literally 'have you seen?']

shun *verb* (**shunned**, **shunning**) to avoid or keep away from. [from Anglo-Saxon *scunian*]

■ avoid, evade, elude, steer clear of, keep away from, spurn, ignore, cold-shoulder, ostracize.

shunt — *verb* **1** to move (a train or carriage) from one track to another. **2** to move around; to change the place or places of. **3** to transfer (eg a task) on to someone else, as an evasion. — *noun* **1** an act of shunting or being shunted. **2** a conductor diverting part of an electric current. **3** a railway siding. **4** *colloq.* a minor collision between vehicles.

shush — *interj.* be quiet! — *verb* to command to be quiet by, or as if by, saying 'Shush!'. [imitative]

shut — *verb trans., intrans.* (**shutting**; PAST TENSE AND PAST PARTICIPLE **shut**) **1** to place or move so as to close an opening: *shut a door/the door shut.* **2** to close or cause to close over, denying open access to the contents: *shut the cupboard/the book shut.* **3** not to allow access (to): *shut the shop/the office shuts at weekends.* — *adj.* not open; closed. — **shut down** or **shut something down** to stop or cause it to stop working or operating, for a time or permanently. **shut someone** or **something in** to enclose or confine them. **shut something off** to switch it off; to stop the flow of it. **shut someone** or **something out 1** to prevent them coming into a room, building, etc. **2** to exclude them. **3** to block out (eg light). **shut up** *colloq.* to stop speaking. **shut someone up 1** *colloq.* to make them stop speaking. **2** to confine them. **shut something up** to close and lock premises, for a time or permanently: *shut up shop.* [from Anglo-Saxon *scyttan*, to bar]

■ *verb* CLOSE. **1** slam, fasten, lock, bolt. **shut down** close (down), stop, cease, terminate, halt, discontinue, suspend, switch off, inactivate. **shut in** enclose, box in, hem in, fence in, confine, imprison, cage. **shut off** switch off, cut off, isolate. **shut out 1** lock out, bar. **2** exclude, bar, debar, ostracize. **shut up** hold one's tongue, *colloq.* pipe down, *colloq.* clam up. **shut someone up 1** silence, gag. **2** confine, coop up, imprison, incarcerate, jail, intern.

◪ *verb* OPEN.

shutdown *noun* **1** a temporary closing of a factory or business. **2** a reduction of power in a nuclear reactor, especially as a safety measure.

shuteye *noun slang* sleep.

shutter — *noun* **1** a movable exterior cover for a window, especially either of a pair of hinged wooden panels. **2** a de-

vice in a camera that opens and closes at a variable speed, exposing the film to light. — *verb* (**shuttered, shuttering**) to fit or cover (a window) with a shutter or shutters. — **put up the shutters** *colloq.* to stop trading, for the day or permanently.

shuttle — *noun* **1** in weaving, the device carrying the horizontal thread (the *weft*) backwards and forwards between the vertical threads (the *warp*). **2** the device carrying the lower thread through the loop formed by the upper in a sewing machine. **3** an aircraft, train, or bus running a frequent service between two places, usually at a relatively short distance from one another. — *verb trans., intrans.* to move or cause to move or travel back and forth. [from Anglo-Saxon *scytel*, dart]

shuttlecock *noun* a cone of feathers or of feathered plastic, with a rounded cork fixed on its narrow end, hit back and forth in badminton.

shy¹ — *adj.* (**shyer, shyest** or **shier, shiest**) **1** *said of a person* embarrassed or unnerved by the company or attention of others. **2** easily scared; timid. **3** (**shy of something**) wary or distrustful of it. **4** *colloq.* short in payment by a specified amount: *10p shy.* — *verb intrans.* (**shies, shied**) **1** to jump suddenly aside or back, startled. **2** (*usually* **shy away**) to move away mentally, showing reluctance: *shied away from arguing with them.* — *noun* (PL. **shies**) an act of shying. [from Anglo-Saxon *sceoh*, timid]

■ *adj.* **1** bashful, reticent, reserved, retiring, diffident, coy, self-conscious, inhibited, modest, self-effacing. **2** timid, nervous. **3** wary of, chary of, suspicious of, distrustful of.
◪ *adj.* **1** assertive, confident. **2** bold.

shy² — *verb* (**shies, shied**) to throw (eg a stone). — *noun* (PL. **shies**) **1** a throw. **2** a fairground stall where balls are thrown to knock over objects, especially coconuts.

shyly *adv.* with a shy manner.

shyness *noun* being shy.

shyster /ˈʃaɪstə(r)/ *noun North Amer., esp. US slang* an unscrupulous or disreputable person, especially in business. [probably from *Scheuster*, a disreputable 19c US lawyer]

SI *abbrev.* Système International d'Unités. An international system of scientific units in which the fundamental quantities are length, time, mass, electric current, temperature, luminous intensity, and amount of substance, and the corresponding units are the metre, second, kilogram, ampere, kelvin, candela, and mole. [from French *Système International*]

Si *symbol Chem.* silicon.

si same as TI.

sial /ˈsaɪal/ *noun Geol.* the granite rocks rich in silica and aluminium that form the upper layer of the Earth's crust. It is equivalent to the upper part of the continental crust, above the sima. See also SIMA. [from *silica* and *alumina*]

Siamese /saɪəˈmiːz/ — *adj.* relating to Siam (now Thailand) in SE Asia, or its people or language. — *noun* **1** a native of Siam. **2** the language of Siam. **3** a Siamese cat.

Siamese cat a fawn-coloured smooth-haired domestic cat with blue eyes and a small head.

Siamese twins 1 same as CONJOINED TWINS. **2** any two people always together.

SIB *abbrev.* Security and Investments Board.

sibilance or **sibilancy** *noun* hissing.

sibilant — *adj.* of, like, or pronounced with a hissing sound. — *noun* a consonant with such a sound, eg *s* and *z*. [from Latin *sibilare*, to hiss]

sibling *noun* a brother or sister. [from Anglo-Saxon *sibb*, relationship + -LING]

Sibylline Books /ˈsɪbɪlaɪn/ *Roman Hist.* prophetic books offered to Tarquinus Superbus by the Cumaean Sibyl, of which he ultimately bought three for the price he had refused to give for nine, these three being held in the Capitol and referred to by the ancient Roman senate in times of emergency and disaster; also, a later set made after the first collection was destroyed by fire in 83 BC.

sic /sɪk/ *adv.* a term used in brackets after a word or phrase in a quotation that appears to be a mistake, to indicate that it is in fact quoted accurately. [from Latin *sic*, thus, so]

sick — *adj.* **1** vomiting; feeling the desire to vomit. **2** ill; unwell. **3** relating to ill health: *sick pay*. **4** extremely annoyed; disgusted. **5** mentally deranged. **6** (**sick of someone** or **something**) thoroughly weary or fed up with them. **7** *said of humour* exploiting subjects like death and disease in an unpleasant way. **8** *colloq.* very inadequate in comparison: *makes my effort look a bit sick.* — *noun colloq.* vomit. — *verb trans., intrans.* (usually **sick something up**) to vomit. [from Anglo-Saxon *seoc*]

⊟ *adj.* **1** vomiting, queasy, bilious, seasick, airsick. **2** ill, unwell, indisposed, laid up, poorly, ailing, sickly, *colloq.* under the weather, weak, feeble. **4** disgusted, annoyed, angry, enraged. **6** *colloq.* fed up with, tired of, weary of, bored with.

⊟ *adj.* **2** well, healthy.

sick bay a room where ill or injured people are treated, eg in a place of work.

sick building syndrome *Medicine* a disorder first diagnosed among office workers in the 1980s, typical symptoms including headache, fatigue, and sore throat. It is thought to be caused by inadequate ventilation or air-conditioning.

sicken *verb* (**sickened**, **sickening**) **1** to cause to feel like vomiting. **2** to annoy greatly or disgust. **3** *intrans.* (**sicken for something**) to show symptoms of an illness: *sickening for the flu.*

⊟ **1** nauseate, revolt. **2** disgust, repel, annoy, anger, enrage.
⊟ **2** delight, attract.

sickening *adj.* that sickens.

⊟ nauseating, revolting, disgusting, offensive, distasteful, annoying, infuriating.
⊟ delightful, pleasing, attractive.

sickle *noun* a tool with a short handle and a curved blade for cutting grain crops with a sweeping action. [from Anglo-Saxon *sicol*]

sick leave time taken off because of sickness.

sickle-cell anaemia *Medicine* an incurable hereditary blood disorder, common in African peoples, in which the red blood cells contain an abnormal type of haemoglobin. As a result, the cells become sickle-shaped and very fragile, and their rapid removal from the circulation leads to anaemia.

sickly — *adj.* (**sicklier**, **sickliest**) **1** susceptible to illness; often ill. **2** of or suggesting illness. **3** inducing the desire to vomit: *a sickly smell.* **4** unhealthy-looking: *a sickly plant.* **5** weakly and contemptibly sentimental. — *adv.* to an extent that suggests illness: *sickly pale.*

⊟ *adj.* **1** unhealthy, ailing, infirm, delicate, weak, feeble, frail. **3** nauseating, revolting. **4** wan, pallid. **5** cloying, mawkish.
⊟ *adj.* **1** healthy, robust, sturdy, strong.

sickness *noun* **1** an illness; ill-health. **2** vomiting. **3** nausea.

⊟ **1** illness, disease, ailment, complaint, ill-health, indisposition, infirmity. **3** nausea, queasiness, biliousness.
⊟ **1** health.

sick verse a modern term used to describe a type of poetry (from any period) that is macabre, satirical, or unsettlingly humorous and whose themes are misfortune, death, disease, decay, cruelty, mental illness, etc.

side — *noun* **1** any of the usually flat or flattish surfaces that form the outer extent of something; any of these surfaces other than the top and bottom, or other than the front, back, top, and bottom. **2** an edge or border, or the area adjoining this: *at the side of the road.* **3** either of the parts or areas produced when the whole is divided up the middle: *the right side of your body.* **4** either of the broad surfaces of a flat or flattish object: *two sides of a coin.* **5** any of the lines forming a geometric figure. **6** any of the groups or teams, or opposing positions, in a conflict or competition. **7** an aspect: *saw a different side to him.* **8** the slope of a hill. **9** the part of the body between armpit and hip. **10** a part of an area of land; district: *the north side of the town.* **11** father's or mother's family or ancestors: *related to him on her mother's side.* **12** *Brit. colloq.* television channel: *on the other side.* **13** *slang* a pretentious or superior air: *to put on side.* — *adj.* **1** located at the side: *side entrance.* **2** subsidiary or subordinate: *side road.* — *verb intrans.* (**side with someone**) to adopt their position or point of view; to join forces with them. — **let the side down** to disappoint one's own group, or frustrate its efforts, by falling below the standards set by its other members. **on** or **to one side** in or to a position removed from the main concern; aside. **on the side** as a secondary job or source of income, often dishonestly or illegally. **on the ... side** *colloq.* rather ...; of a ... nature: *found his comments a bit on the offensive side.* **side by side 1** close together. **2** with sides touching. **take sides** to support one particular side in a conflict or argument. [from Anglo-Saxon *side*]

⊟ *noun* **1** face, facet, surface. **2** edge, margin, fringe, border, boundary, limit, verge, brink, bank, shore, flank, wing, hand. **6** team, party, faction, camp, cause, interest. **7** aspect, angle, slant, standpoint, viewpoint, view. **10** district, quarter, area, region. *adj.* **1** lateral, flanking. **2** secondary, subsidiary, subordinate, lesser, minor, incidental, indirect. *verb* agree with, join forces with, team up with, support, favour.

sideboard *noun* **1** a large piece of furniture consisting of shelves or cabinets mounted above drawers or cupboards. **2** a sideburn.

sideburn *noun* the line of short hair growing down in front of each of a man's ears.

sidecar *noun* a small carriage for one or two passengers, fixed to the side of a motorcycle.

side effect an additional unexpected (usually undesirable) effect, especially of a drug.

sidekick *noun colloq.* a close friend, partner, or deputy.

sidelight *noun* **1** a small light fitted on each outside edge of the front and rear of a motor vehicle, used in fading daylight. **2** a light on each side of a moving boat or ship, one red, one green. **3** light coming from the side.

sideline *noun* **1** a line marking either side boundary of a sports pitch. **2** (**sidelines**) the areas just outside these boundaries; the area to which non-participants in any activity are confined. **3** a business, etc carried on in addition to regular work.

sidelong *adj., adv.* from or to one side; not direct or directly: *a sidelong glance.*

sidereal /saɪˈdɪərɪəl/ *adj. formal* of, relating to, or determined by the stars: *sidereal year.* [from Latin *sidus*, star]

siderite /ˈsɪdəraɪt/ *noun Geol.* a brown, grey, greenish, or yellowish mineral form of ferrous carbonate ($FeCO_3$) that occurs in sedimentary deposits, hydrothermal veins (veins formed from magma containing a high proportion of hot water), and some metamorphic rocks. It is an important ore of iron. [from Greek *sideros*, iron]

side-saddle — *noun* a horse's saddle enabling a woman in a skirt to sit with both legs on the same side. — *adv.* sitting in this way.

sideshow *noun* a stall with some form of amusement or game at a fair, beside a circus, etc.

sidespin *noun* a spinning motion imparted to a struck ball that causes it to rotate about its vertical axis while going forward. See also BACKSPIN, TOPSPIN.

side-splitting *adj.* provoking uproarious laughter.

side-step — *verb* to avoid by, or as if by, stepping aside. — *noun* a step taken to one side.

■ *verb* avoid, dodge, duck, evade, elude, skirt, bypass.
🗷 *verb* tackle, deal with.

sideswipe *noun* **1** a blow coming from the side, not head-on. **2** a criticism or rebuke made in passing, incidentally to the main discussion.

sidetrack *verb* to divert the attention of away from the matter in hand.

■ divert, distract, deflect, head off.

sidewalk *noun North Amer., esp. US* a pavement.

sideways — *adv.* **1** from, to, or towards one side. **2** with one side foremost: *slid sideways into the wall.* — *adj.* from, to, or towards one side.

■ *adv.* **1** laterally, obliquely. **2** sidewards, edgeways. *adj.* lateral, oblique, indirect, sidelong, sideward.

side whiskers sideburns.

sidewinder *noun* **1** a snake which moves by pushing its head forward on to the ground, then winding the body forwards and sideways until it lies stretched out to one side; meanwhile the head is moved forward again. By repeating this action, it is able to move rapidly over soft sand. **2** the N American horned rattlesnake, which usually moves by this method.

siding *noun* a short dead-end railway line on to which wagons, etc can be moved temporarily from the main line.

sidle *verb intrans.* to go or move slowly and cautiously or secretively, avoiding notice. [a back-formation from obsolete *sideling*, sideways]

■ slink, edge, inch, creep, sneak.

SIDS *abbrev.* sudden infant death syndrome.

siege *noun* **1** an attempt to capture a fort or town by surrounding it with troops and forcing surrender. **2** a police operation using similar tactics, eg to force a criminal out of a building. — **lay siege to a place** to subject it to a siege. [from Old French *sege*, seat]

siemens /'siːmənz/ *noun* the standard unit of electrical conductance. [named after the German electrical engineer Werner von *Siemens* (1816–92)]

sienna /sɪ'enə/ *noun* **1** a pigment obtained from a type of earth with a high clay and iron content. **2** its colour, browny-yellow in its original state (*raw sienna*), reddish-brown when roasted (*burnt sienna*). [named after Siena in Italy]

sierra /sɪ'eərə/ *noun* a mountain range in Spanish-speaking countries and the US, especially when jagged. [from Spanish *sierra*, a saw]

siesta /sɪ'estə/ *noun* a sleep or rest after the midday meal in hot countries. [from Spanish *siesta*]

sieve /sɪv/ — *noun* a utensil with a meshed or perforated bottom, used to separate solids from liquids or large particles from smaller ones. — *verb* to strain or separate with a sieve. — **have a head** or **memory like a sieve** to be habitually forgetful. [from Anglo-Saxon *sife*]

■ *noun* colander, strainer, sifter, riddle, screen. *verb* sift, strain, filter, separate, remove.

sievert /'siːvət/ *noun Physics* (ABBREV. **Sv**) the SI unit of radiation dose equivalent, equal to the absorbed dose multiplied by its relative biological effectiveness. It therefore takes account of the fact that different types of radiation cause differing amounts of biological damage, and it is used in radiation safety measurements. [named after the Swedish physicist R M *Sievert*]

sieve tube *Bot.* in the phloem tissue of a flowering plant, any of the tubular structures, each consisting of a column of long cells joined end to end, through which organic compounds manufactured in the leaves by photosynthesis are transported to the rest of the plant.

sift *verb* **1** to pass through a sieve in order to separate out lumps or larger particles. **2** to separate out by, or as if by, passing through a sieve. **3** to examine closely and discriminatingly. [from Anglo-Saxon *siftan*, from *sife*, sieve]

■ **1** sieve, strain, filter, riddle, screen, winnow. **2** separate, sort, winnow, screen. **3** examine, scrutinize, investigate, analyse, probe.

sigh — *verb* **1** *intrans.* to release a long deep breath, especially indicating sadness, longing, or relief. **2** *intrans.* to make a similar sound, especially suggesting breakdown or failure: *heard the engine sigh.* **3** to express with such a sound. — *noun* an act or the sound of sighing. — **sigh for** someone or something *literary* to regret, grieve over, or yearn for them. [from Anglo-Saxon *sican*]

sight — *noun* **1** the power of seeing; vision. **2** a thing seen. **3** one's field of vision, or the opportunity to see things that this provides: *catch sight of/within/out of sight.* **4** (*usually* **sights**) a place, building, etc that is particularly interesting to see: *seeing the sights of the town.* **5** a device on a firearm through or along which one looks to take aim. **6** opinion or judgement: *just a failure in his sight.* **7** *colloq.* a person or thing unpleasant to look at: *looked a sight without his teeth in.* — *verb* **1** to get a look at or glimpse of. **2** to adjust the sight of (a firearm). **3** to aim (a firearm) using the sight. — **at** or **on sight 1** as soon as seen. **2** without previous view or study. **lose sight of something** or **someone 1** to no longer be able to see them. **2** to fail to keep them in mind; to no longer be familiar with them. **a sight more** *colloq.* a great deal or great many more: *a sight more people than expected.* **a sight for sore eyes** a very welcome sight. **set one's sights on something** to decide on it as an ambition or aim. **sight unseen** without seeing or having seen the thing in question beforehand: *buy a house sight unseen.* [from Anglo-Saxon *sihth*]

■ *noun* **1** vision, eyesight, seeing, observation, perception. **2** view, scene, appearance, spectacle, show, display, exhibition. **3** field of vision, range, visibility, look, glance, glimpse. **7** eyesore, *colloq.* fright. *verb* **1** see, spot, glimpse, discern, distinguish, make out.

sighted *adj.* having the power of sight; not blind.

sightless *adj.* blind.

sight-read *verb trans., intrans.* to play or sing from music not previously seen.

sight-reading *noun* playing or singing from printed music that one has not seen before.

sight-screen *noun* any of a set of large white movable screens at either end of a cricket ground, providing a background against which the batsman can see the ball clearly.

sightsee *verb intrans.* to go sightseeing.

sightseeing *noun* visiting places of interest.

sightseer *noun* a person who goes sightseeing.

■ tourist, visitor, holidaymaker, tripper, excursionist.

sigillography *noun* the study of seals used on documents, etc as a sign of authenticity. [from Latin *sigillum*, diminutive of *signum*, sign + Greek *graphe*, writing]

sign — *noun* **1** a printed mark with a meaning; a symbol: *a multiplication sign.* **2** an indication: *signs of improvement.* **3** a board or panel displaying information for public view. **4** a signal: *gave me the sign to enter by waving his hat.* **5** a sign of the zodiac. — *verb* **1** to write a signature on; to confirm one's assent to with a signature. **2** to write (one's name) as a signature. **3** *trans., intrans.* to employ or become employed with the signing of a contract: *they have* *signed a new player/he has signed for another team.* **4** *trans.,* *intrans.* to give a signal or indication. **5** *trans., intrans.* to communicate using sign language. — **sign something away** to give it away or transfer it by signing a legally binding document. **sign in** to record one's arrival, eg at work, by writing one's name. **sign someone in** to give someone (eg a non-member) official permission to enter a club, etc by signing one's name. **sign off 1** to bring a broadcast to an end. **2** to remove oneself from the register of unemployed people. **sign someone off** to dismiss them from employment. **sign on** *colloq.* to register oneself as unemployed; to sign one's name as a formal declaration that one is (still) unemployed, as part of a regular report to an unemployment office. **sign someone on** to engage them, eg for work. **sign up** to engage oneself, eg with an organization (especially the army) or for a task, by signing a contract. **sign someone up** to engage them for work by signing a contract. [from Latin *signum*]

⊞ *noun* **1** symbol, token, character, figure, emblem, badge, insignia, logo. **2** indication, mark, evidence, manifestation, clue, hint, suggestion, portent, omen. **3** board, notice, poster, placard, pointer. **4** signal, gesture. *verb* **1** autograph, initial, endorse. **sign up** enlist, enrol, join (up), volunteer, register, sign on. *someone* recruit, take on, hire, engage, employ.

signal — *noun* **1** a message in the form of a gesture, light, sound, etc, conveying information or indicating the time for action. **2** (*often* **signals**) the apparatus used to send such a message, eg coloured lights or movable arms or metal poles on a railway network. **3** an event that marks the moment for action to be taken: *their arrival was a signal for the party to begin.* **4** any set of transmitted electrical impulses received as a sound or image, in television, or the message conveyed by them. — *verb* (**signalled, signalling**) **1** to transmit (a message) using signals, gestures, etc. **2** *intrans.* to communicate using signals, gestures, etc; to give a signal. **3** to indicate: *a fall in interest rates signalled increased trading in sterling.* — *adj.* notable: *a signal triumph.* [from Latin *signum*]

⊞ *noun* **1** sign, indicator, mark, gesture, cue, *colloq.* go-ahead. **2** light, beacon, flare, rocket, alarm, alert. *verb* **1** communicate, sign, gesture, beckon, motion. **2** communicate, sign, wave, gesticulate, gesture, beckon, nod. **3** indicate, mark, show, reveal.

signal-box *noun* the building from which signals on a railway line are controlled.

signalize or **signalise** *verb* to distinguish; to make notable.

signally *adv.* notably.

signalman *noun* a controller of railway signals.

signal-to-noise ratio *Electron.* the ratio of the power of a desired electrical signal to the power of the unwanted background signal or noise. It is usually expressed in decibels.

signatory — *noun* (PL. **signatories**) a person, organization, or state that is a party to a contract, treaty, or other document. — *adj.* being a party to a contract, etc: *signatory nations.*

signature *noun* **1** one's name written by oneself as a formal mark of authorization, acceptance, etc. **2** an indication of key (*key signature*) or time (*time signature*) at the beginning of a line of music. **3** a large sheet of paper with a number of printed pages on it, folded to form a section of a book; a letter or number at the foot of such a sheet, indicating the sequence in which such sheets are to be put together. [from Latin *signare*, to sign]

⊞ **1** autograph, name, initials, mark, endorsement.

signature tune a tune used to identify or introduce a particular radio or television programme or performer.

signet *noun* a small seal used for stamping documents, etc. [from Latin *signum*, sign]

signet ring a finger ring carrying a signet.

significance *noun* meaning or importance. [see SIGNIFY]

⊞ meaning, implication, sense, importance, relevance, consequence, matter, interest, weight, force.
⊟ insignificance, unimportance.

significance test *Maths.* a test which is used to demonstrate the probability that observed patterns cannot be explained by chance.

significant *adj.* **1** important; worth noting. **2** having some meaning; indicating or implying something.

⊞ **1** important, relevant, consequential, momentous, weighty, serious, critical, vital, noteworthy, marked, considerable, appreciable. **2** meaningful, symbolic, expressive, suggestive, indicative, symptomatic.
⊟ **1** insignificant, unimportant, trivial. **2** meaningless.

significant figure or **significant digits** *Maths.* the number of digits that contribute to a number and so denote its value to a specified degree of accuracy, eg the value 5068.35 is accurate to six significant figures. If written as 5068, it is accurate to four significant figures.

significantly *adv.* in a significant way; to a significant degree.

signify *verb* (**signifies, signified**) **1** to be a sign of; to suggest or mean. **2** to denote; to be a symbol of. **3** *intrans.* to be important or significant. [from Latin *signum*, sign + *facere*, to make]

⊞ **1** mean, indicate, show, express, convey, transmit, communicate, intimate, imply, suggest. **2** denote, symbolize, represent, stand for. **3** matter, count.

sign language any form of communication using bodily gestures to represent words and ideas, especially a formal system of hand gestures used by deaf people.

sign of the cross a Christian sign made in representation of the cross, by moving the hand from the forehead to the chest and then across to each shoulder, or by making a similar movement in front of oneself.

sign of the zodiac see ZODIAC.

signpost — *noun* a post carrying a sign giving information to motorists or pedestrians. — *verb* to mark (a route) with signposts.

Sikh /siːk/ — *noun* a follower of Sikhism. — *adj.* relating to the Sikhs or their beliefs or customs. [from Hindi *Sikh*, disciple]

Sikhism /ˈsiːkɪzm/ a religion which combines elements from Hinduism and Islam.

silage /ˈsaɪlɪdʒ/ *noun* animal fodder made from forage crops such as grass, maize, kale, etc, which are compressed and then preserved in a succulent condition by controlled fermentation in an airtight tower or *silo*. [from SILO]

silence — *noun* **1** absence of sound or speech, or a period marked by this. **2** failure or unwillingness to disclose information or give away secrets. — *verb* to cause to stop speaking, stop making a noise, or stop giving away information. — *interj.* be quiet. — **in silence** without speaking. [from Latin *silere*, to be quiet]

⊞ *noun* **1** quiet, quietness, hush, peace, stillness, calm, noiselessness, soundlessness, muteness, dumbness, speechlessness, taciturnity. **2** reticence, reserve. *verb* quiet, quieten, hush, mute, deaden, muffle, gag, muzzle, suppress, quell, still, dumbfound.
⊟ *noun* **1** noise, sound, din, uproar.

silencer *noun* a device fitted to a gun barrel or engine exhaust to muffle noise.

silent — *adj.* **1** free from noise; making no noise. **2** not speaking; not mentioning or divulging something. **3** unspoken but expressed: *silent joy.* **4** not pronounced: *the silent p in pneumonia.* **5** *said of a cinema film* that has no soundtrack. — *noun* a silent film.

■ *adj.* **1** inaudible, noiseless, soundless, quiet, peaceful, still, hushed, muted. **2** mute, dumb, speechless, wordless, tongue-tied, taciturn, mum, reticent, reserved. **3** tacit, unspoken, unexpressed, understood.
🗷 *adj.* **1** noisy, loud. **2** talkative.

silently *adv.* without making any sound; in silence.
silent partner same as SLEEPING PARTNER.
silhouette /sɪluːˈɛt/ — *noun* **1** a dark shape seen against a light background. **2** an outline drawing of a person, esp a portrait in profile, usually filled in with black. — *verb* to represent, or cause to appear, as a silhouette. [named after E de *Silhouette* (1709–67), French finance minister]

■ *noun* **1** shape, form, configuration, shadow. **2** outline, contour, delineation, profile.

silica /ˈsɪlɪkə/ *noun Geol.* a hard white or colourless vitreous (glassy) solid that is the commonest constituent of the Earth's crust. Also called SILICON DIOXIDE.
silica gel *Chem.* a highly absorbent form of silica that is used as a drying and dehumidifying agent, and as a catalyst in many chemical processes.
silicate *noun Chem.* **1** any of a group of chemical compounds containing silicon, oxygen, and one or more metals. Natural silicates are the main components of most rocks and many minerals, eg clay, mica, feldspar, garnet, beryl. **2** any salt of silicic acid.
silicon /ˈsɪlɪkən/ *noun* (SYMBOL **Si**, ATOMIC NUMBER **14**) a non-metallic element that occurs naturally as silicate minerals in clays and rocks, and as silica in sand and quartz. It is the second most abundant element in the Earth's crust (after oxygen). [from Latin *silex*, flint]
silicon carbide *Chem.* (FORMULA **SiC**) a hard iridescent bluish-black crystalline compound, widely used as an abrasive, in cutting, grinding, and polishing instruments, and in light-emitting diodes to produce green or yellow light. Also called CARBORUNDUM.
silicon chip 1 *Electron.* a very thin piece of silicon or other semiconductor material, only a few millimetres square, on which all the components of an integrated circuit are arranged. Also called CHIP, MICROCHIP. **2** popular term for an integrated circuit.
silicone *noun Chem.* any of a large group of synthetic polymers consisting of chains of alternating silicon and oxygen atoms, with various organic groups linked to the silicon atoms. Silicone materials usually occur in the form of oily liquids, waxes, plastics, or rubbers, are resistant to heat and water, and do not conduct electricity. They are used in lubricants, electrical insulators, paints, and adhesives.
silicosis /sɪlɪˈkəʊsɪs/ *noun* a lung disease caused by prolonged inhaling of dust containing silica.
silk *noun* **1** a fine soft fibre produced by the silkworm. **2** thread or fabric made from such fibres. **3** (*usually* **silks**) a garment made from such fabric. **4** the silk gown worn by a Queen's or King's Counsel; the rank conferred by this. — **take silk** *said of a barrister* to be appointed a Queen's or King's Counsel. [from Anglo-Saxon *seolc*, from Latin *sericum*]
silken *adj. literary* **1** made of silk. **2** as soft or smooth as silk.
silkiness *noun* a silky quality.
silk-screen see SCREEN PRINTING.
silkworm *noun* the caterpillar of the silk moth, domesticated for centuries in India, China, and Japan to provide silk on a commercial basis.
silky *adj.* (**silkier**, **silkiest**) **1** soft and shiny like silk. **2** *said of a person's manner or voice* suave.

■ SMOOTH. **1** silken, fine, soft, velvety, sleek, shiny, lustrous, glossy, satiny.

sill *noun* the bottom part of a framework around an opening such as a window or door; also, a ledge of wood, stone, or metal forming this. [from Anglo-Saxon *syll*]
sillabub see SYLLABUB.
sillily *adv.* in a silly way.
silliness *noun* **1** being silly. **2** silly behaviour.
silly — *adj.* (**sillier**, **silliest**) **1** not sensible; foolish; frivolous. **2** dazed; senseless. **3** *Cricket* in a position very near the batsman: *silly mid-on.* **4** senseless: *knocked him silly.* — *noun* (PL. **sillies**) *colloq.* a foolish person. [from Anglo-Saxon *sælig*, happy]

■ *adj.* **1** foolish, stupid, imprudent, senseless, pointless, idiotic, daft, ridiculous, ludicrous, preposterous, absurd, irrational, illogical, childish, puerile, immature, irresponsible. **2** dazed, stunned, senseless, unconscious.
🗷 *adj.* **1** sensible, wise, mature, clever, intelligent.

silo /ˈsaɪləʊ/ *noun* (PL. **silos**) **1** an airtight pit or tall round tower for storing grain or silage. **2** an underground chamber housing a missile ready for firing. [from Spanish *silo*, from Greek *siros*, pit]
silt — *noun* fine sand and mud deposited by flowing water. — *verb trans., intrans.* (*usually* **silt up**) to become or cause to become blocked by silt. [from Middle English *sylt*]

■ *noun* sediment, deposit, alluvium, sludge, mud. *verb* block, clog, choke.

Silurian /sɪˈlʊərɪən/ *adj. Geol.* denoting the period of geological time between the Ordovician and Devonian periods, lasting from about 440 to 395 million years ago. [from Latin *Silures*, an ancient people of Wales]
silvan same as SYLVAN.
silver — *noun* **1** (SYMBOL **Ag**, ATOMIC NUMBER **47**) a soft white lustrous precious metal that is malleable, ductile, and an excellent conductor of heat and electricity. **2** coins made of this metal. **3** articles made of (or coated with) this metal, especially cutlery and other tableware. **4** a silver medal. — *adj.* **1** of a whitish-grey colour: *silver-haired.* **2** denoting a 25th wedding or other anniversary. — *verb* **1** to apply a thin coating of silver to. **2** to give a whitish metallic sheen to. [from Anglo-Saxon *seolfor*]
silver birch a species of birch tree with silvery-white peeling bark.
silverfish *noun* a small wingless silver-coloured insect common in houses.
silver lining a positive aspect of an otherwise unpleasant or unfortunate situation.
silver medal a medal of silver awarded especially in sporting competitions, usually to the person in second place.
silver nitrate *Chem.* (FORMULA **AgNO₃**) a colourless crystalline compound, soluble in water and sensitive to light, used in photographic film, silver plating, and in the form of a cream or lotion for removing warts and treating skin injuries.
silver plate 1 a thin coating of silver on metal objects, eg cutlery. **2** such objects coated with silver.
silver-plated *adj.* plated with silver.
silver screen (**the silver screen**) *colloq.* the film industry or films in general.
silverside *noun* a fine cut of beef from just below the rump.
silversmith *noun* a person who makes or repairs articles made of silver.
silvery *adj.* **1** having the colour or shiny quality of silver. **2** having a pleasantly light ringing sound: *silvery bells.*

silviculture *noun technical Bot.* the cultivation of forest trees, or the management of woodland to produce timber, etc. [from Latin *silva*, wood + CULTURE]

sima /ˈsaɪmə/ *noun Geol.* the basaltic rocks rich in silica and magnesium that form the lower layer of the Earth's crust. It is equivalent to the oceanic crust and the lower part of the continental crust, beneath the sial. See also SIAL [from SILICON and MAGNESIUM]

simian /ˈsɪmɪən/ — *noun* a monkey or ape. — *adj.* relating to or resembling monkeys or apes. [from Latin *simia*, ape]

similar *adj.* having a close resemblance to something; of the same kind, but not identical; alike. [from Latin *similis*, like]

∙∙∙∙∙∙∙∙∙∙∙∙∙∙∙∙∙∙∙∙∙∙

■ like, alike, close, related, akin, corresponding, equivalent, analogous, comparable.
❋ dissimilar, different.

∙∙

similarity *noun* (PL. **similarities**) being similar; likeness; resemblance.

∙∙∙∙∙∙∙∙∙∙∙∙∙∙∙∙∙∙∙∙∙∙∙

■ likeness, resemblance, similitude, closeness, relation, correspondence, congruence, equivalence, analogy, comparability, compatibility, affinity.
❋ dissimilarity, difference.

∙∙∙∙∙∙∙∙∙∙∙∙∙∙∙∙∙∙∙∙∙∙∙∙∙∙∙∙∙∙∙∙

similarly *adv.* in a similar way.

simile /ˈsɪmɪlɪ/ *noun* a figure of speech in which a thing is described by being likened to something, usually using *as* or *like*, as in *eyes sparkling like diamonds*, and in set phrases such as *bold as brass*.

similitude *noun formal* similarity; resemblance. [see SIMILAR]

SIMM *abbrev. Comput.* single in-line memory module, a small circuit board containing random-access memory chips.

simmer — *verb* (**simmered, simmering**) **1** *trans., intrans.* to cook or cause to cook gently at or just below boiling point. **2** *intrans.* to be near to an outburst of emotion, usually anger. — *noun* a simmering state. — **simmer down** to calm down after a commotion, especially an angry outburst. [from Middle English *simperen*]

∙∙∙∙∙∙∙∙∙∙∙∙∙∙∙∙∙∙∙∙∙∙∙

■ *verb* **1** boil, stew. **2** smoulder, fume, rage. **simmer down** calm down, cool down, control oneself, collect oneself.

∙∙

simnel *noun* a sweet marzipan-covered fruit cake, traditionally baked at Easter or Mid-Lent. [from Latin *simila*, fine flour]

simony /ˈsaɪmənɪ/ *noun* the practice of buying or selling a religious post or other privilege. [from *Simon* Magus, biblical sorcerer who offered money for the power to convey the gift of the Holy Spirit]

simper — *verb* (**simpered, simpering**) **1** *intrans.* to smile in a foolishly weak manner. **2** to express by or while smiling in this way. — *noun* a simpering smile.

simple *adj.* **1** easy; not difficult. **2** straightforward; not complex or complicated. **3** plain or basic; not elaborate or luxurious. **4** down-to-earth; unpretentious. **5** *often ironic* foolish; gullible; lacking intelligence. **6** plain; mere; not altered or adulterated: *the simple facts*. **7** *Grammar*, *said of a sentence* consisting of only one clause. See also COMPOUND, COMPLEX. [from Latin *simplus, simplex*]

∙∙∙∙∙∙∙∙∙∙∙∙∙∙∙∙∙∙∙∙∙∙∙

■ **1** easy, elementary. **2** straightforward, uncomplicated, uninvolved, clear, plain, understandable, comprehensible. **3** plain, unadorned, basic, ordinary. **4** natural, unaffected, unpretentious, unsophisticated, artless, guileless, ingenuous. **5** foolish, stupid, silly, idiotic, simple-minded, feeble-minded, backward.
❋ **1** difficult, hard. **2** complex, complicated. **3** elaborate, fancy. **4** pretentious, sophisticated, worldly. **5** clever.

∙∙

simple fracture a fracture of the bone only, with no breaking of the skin.

simple harmonic motion *Physics* (ABBREV. **SHM**) a periodic motion in which the restoring influence acting towards the rest position is proportional to the displacement from rest, as in a pendulum undergoing small swings.

simple interest interest paid only on the basic sum initially borrowed, rather than on an ever-increasing amount which is this basic sum with interest progressively added. See also COMPOUND INTEREST.

simple-minded *adj.* **1** lacking intelligence; foolish. **2** over-simple; unsophisticated.

simple sentence a sentence consisting of one clause. See also COMPOUND SENTENCE, COMPLEX SENTENCE.

simpleton *noun* a foolish or unintelligent person.

simplicity *noun* a simple state or quality.

∙∙∙∙∙∙∙∙∙∙∙∙∙∙∙∙∙∙∙∙∙∙∙

■ simpleness, ease, straightforwardness, uncomplicatedness, clarity, plainness, naturalness, artlessness, directness.
❋ difficulty, complexity, intricacy, sophistication.

∙∙

simplification *noun* **1** simplifying or being simplified. **2** something that is simplified.

simplify *verb* (**simplifies, simplified**) to make less complicated or easier to understand. [from Latin *simplus, simplex*, simple + *facere*, to make]

∙∙∙∙∙∙∙∙∙∙∙∙∙∙∙∙∙∙∙∙∙∙∙

■ clarify, explain, disentangle, untangle, decipher, paraphrase, abridge, reduce, streamline.
❋ complicate, elaborate.

∙∙

simplistic *adj.* unrealistically straightforward or uncomplicated. [see SIMPLE]

∙∙∙∙∙∙∙∙∙∙∙∙∙∙∙∙∙∙∙∙∙∙∙

■ oversimplified, superficial, shallow, sweeping, facile, simple, naïve.
❋ analytical, detailed.

∙∙

simplistically *adv.* in a simplistic way.

simply *adv.* **1** in a straightforward, uncomplicated way. **2** just: *simply not true*. **3** absolutely: *simply marvellous*. **4** merely: *simply wanted to help*.

∙∙∙∙∙∙∙∙∙∙∙∙∙∙∙∙∙∙∙∙∙∙∙

■ **1** easily, straightforwardly, clearly, plainly, directly. **3** utterly, completely, totally, absolutely, quite, really. **4** merely, just, only, solely, purely.

∙∙

simulate *verb* **1** to produce a convincing re-creation of (a real-life event or set of conditions). **2** to pretend to have, do, or feel. [from Latin *simulare*]

∙∙∙∙∙∙∙∙∙∙∙∙∙∙∙∙∙∙∙∙∙∙∙

■ **1** recreate, reproduce, duplicate, copy, imitate, mimic, echo, reflect. **2** pretend, affect, assume, put on, feign, sham, fake, counterfeit.

∙∙

simulated *adj.* imitation: *simulated leather*.

simulation *noun* simulating; something that is simulated.

simulator *noun* a device that simulates required conditions, eg for training purposes: *flight simulator*.

simulcast *noun* **1** a programme broadcast simultaneously on radio and television. **2** the transmission of a programme in this way. [a shortening of *simultaneous broadcast*]

simultaneous *adj.* happening, or done, at exactly the same time. [from Latin *simul*, at the same time]

∙∙∙∙∙∙∙∙∙∙∙∙∙∙∙∙∙∙∙∙∙∙∙

■ synchronous, concurrent, contemporaneous, coinciding, parallel.
❋ asynchronous.

∙∙

simultaneous equations *Maths.* two or more equations whose variables have the same values in both or all the equations.

simultaneously *adv.* at the same time.

sin[1] — *noun* **1** an act that breaks a moral and especially a religious law or teaching. **2** the condition of offending a deity by committing a moral offence. **3** an act that offends common standards of morality or decency; an outrage. **4** *old colloq. use* a great shame. — *verb intrans.* (**sinned, sinning**) to commit a sin. — **live in sin** *colloq.* to live together as husband and wife without being married. [from Anglo-Saxon *synn*]

⊟ *noun* **1** wrong, transgression, trespass, misdeed, lapse, fault, error. **2** sinfulness, wickedness, iniquity, evil, impiety, ungodliness, unrighteousness, wrongdoing, guilt. **3** wrong, offence, outrage, crime, iniquity. *verb* offend, transgress, trespass, lapse, err, stray, go astray, fall, fall from grace.

sin[2] *abbrev.* sine.

since — *conj.* **1** during or throughout the period between now and some earlier stated time. **2** as; because. — *prep.* during or throughout the period between now and some earlier stated time. — *adv.* **1** from that time onwards. **2** ago: *five years since.* [from Middle English *sithens*]

sincere *adj.* genuine; not pretended or affected. [from Latin *sincerus*, clean]

⊟ real, true, genuine, serious, earnest, heartfelt, wholehearted, honest, truthful, candid, frank, open, direct, natural, unaffected, simple.
⊟ insincere, hypocritical, affected.

sincerely *adv.* in a sincere way.
sincerity *noun* being sincere.

⊟ honour, integrity, probity, honesty, truthfulness, candour, frankness, openness, directness, seriousness, earnestness, wholeheartedness, genuineness.
⊟ insincerity.

sine /saɪn/ *noun Maths.* (**ABBREV. sin**) in trigonometry, a function of an angle in a right-angled triangle, defined as the length of the side opposite the angle divided by the length of the hypotenuse (the longest side). [from Latin *sinus*, curve, bay]

sinecure /'saɪnɪkjʊə(r)/ *noun* a paid job involving little or no work. [from Latin *sine*, without + *cura*, care]

sine die /sɪne 'daɪɪ/ indefinitely; with no future time fixed. [Latin, = without a day]

sine qua non /sɪne kwa: 'nɒn/ an essential condition or requirement. [Latin, = without which not]

sinew /'sɪnjuː/ *noun* **1** a strong piece of fibrous tissue joining a muscle to a bone; a tendon. **2** (**sinews**) physical strength; muscle. **3** (*often* **sinews**) strength or power of any kind, or a source of this. [from Anglo-Saxon *sinu*]

sine wave *Maths.* a waveform whose shape resembles that obtained by plotting a graph of the size of an angle against the value of its sine. Simple harmonic motion can be represented by a sine wave.

sinewy *adj.* **1** lean and muscular. **2** strong; tough; vigorous.

⊟ **1** muscular, brawny, athletic, wiry, stringy. **2** strong, tough, sturdy, robust, vigorous.

sinfonietta /sɪnfoʊ'njɛtə/ *noun* **1** an orchestral piece, usually in several movements but shorter and on a smaller scale than a symphony. **2** a small symphony or chamber orchestra. [from Italian, a diminutive of *sinfonia*]

sinful *adj.* wicked; involving sin, morally wrong.

⊟ wrong, bad, wicked, iniquitous, criminal, erring, fallen, immoral, corrupt, depraved, impious, ungodly, unholy, guilty.
⊟ sinless, good, pure, righteous, godly, innocent.

sing *verb* (PAST TENSE **sang**; PAST PARTICIPLE **sung**) **1** *trans., intrans.* to speak (words) in a musical, rhythmic fashion, especially to the accompaniment of music. **2** to cause to pass into a particular state with such sound: *sang him to sleep.* **3** *intrans.* to make a sound like a musical voice; to hum, ring, or whistle: *birds singing in the trees/ the kettle singing on the stove/bullets singing past his ears.* **4** *intrans.* to suffer a ringing sound: *my ears were singing.* **5** *intrans. slang* to inform or confess. — **sing out** to shout or call out. **sing someone's praises** to praise them enthusiastically. [from Anglo-Saxon *singan*]

⊟ **1** chant, croon, trill, warble. **3** chirp, warble, pipe, whistle, hum.

sing. *abbrev.* singular.

singe — *verb trans., intrans.* (**singed, singeing**) to burn lightly on the surface; to scorch or become scorched. — *noun* a light surface burn. [from Anglo-Saxon *sengan*]

⊟ *verb* scorch, char, blacken, burn, sear.

singer *noun* **1** a person or bird that sings. **2** a person who sings professionally.

Singers include: balladeer, minstrel, troubadour, opera singer, diva, prima donna, soloist, precentor, choirboy, choirgirl, chorister, chorus, folk singer, popstar, crooner, carol singer; soprano, coloratura soprano, castrato, tenor, treble, contralto, alto, baritone, bass; songster, vocalist.

singing *noun* **1** the performing of songs. **2** the sound of singing or a sound like it; ringing.

single — *adj.* **1** of which there is only one; solitary. **2** unmarried, especially never having been married. **3** for use by one person only: *a single room.* **4** valid for an outward journey only; not return. **5** *used for emphasis* even one: *not a single person.* **6** *said of a flower* having only one set of petals. — *noun* **1** a single room. **2** a ticket for an outward journey only. **3** a record with only one track on each side. **4** a pound coin or note. **5** *Cricket* one run. — *verb* (**single someone** or **something out**) to pick them from among others. [from Latin *singuli*, one by one]

⊟ *adj.* **1** one, unique, singular, individual, sole, only, lone, solitary, separate, distinct. **2** unmarried, celibate, unattached, free. **3** unshared, individual, particular, exclusive. *verb* choose, select, pick, hand-pick, distinguish, identify, separate, set apart, isolate, highlight, pinpoint.
⊟ *adj.* **1** multiple. **2** married. **3** double. **4** return.

single-breasted *adj., said of a coat or jacket* having only one row of buttons and a slight overlap at the front.

single combat fighting between two individuals.

single-figure *adj.* denoting a number from 1 to 9.

single figures the numbers from 1 to 9.

single file a line of people standing or moving one behind the other.

single-handed *adj., adv.* done, etc by oneself, without help from others.

⊟ solo, alone, unaccompanied, unaided, unassisted.

single-handedly *adv.* without any help.

single-minded *adj.* determinedly pursuing a single aim or object.

⊟ determined, resolute, dogged, persevering, tireless, unwavering, fixed, unswerving, undeviating, steadfast, dedicated, devoted.

single parent a mother or father bringing up a child alone.

singles *noun* a sports match with one player on each side.

singles bar a bar intended as a meeting place for unmarried or unattached people.

singlet *noun* a man's vest or other vest-like garment. [see SINGLE]

singleton *noun* **1** a solitary person or thing, especially the only playing-card of a particular suit in a hand. **2** a single person who is not involved in a romantic relationship.

singly *adv.* one at a time; individually.

singsong — *noun* an informal bout of singing for pleasure. — *adj.*, *said of a speaking voice, etc* having a fluctuating or monotonous rhythm.

Singspiel *noun* a type of German comic opera with spoken dialogue, popular in the 18c and early 19c. The term was later applied in Germany to musical comedy. [German, = singing play]

singular — *adj.* **1** single; unique. **2** extraordinary; exceptional. **3** strange; odd. **4** *Grammar* denoting or referring to one person, thing, etc as opposed to two or more than two. See also PLURAL. — *noun Grammar* a word or form of a word expressing the idea of one person, thing, etc as opposed to two or more than two. [from Latin *singularis*]

singularity *noun* **1** being singular. **2** peculiarity, individuality.

singularly *adv.* **1** extraordinarily. **2** strangely. **3** singly. **4** very.

Sinhalese /sinhə'li:z/ — *noun* **1** (PL. **Sinhalese**) a member of a people living in Sri Lanka. **2** the Indo-European language spoken by this people, derived from Sanskrit. — *adj.* relating to this people or their language. [from Sanskrit *Simhala*, Sri Lanka]

sinister *adj.* **1** suggesting or threatening evil or danger. **2** *Heraldry* on the left side of the shield, from the bearer's point of view, not the observer's. See also DEXTER. [from Latin *sinister*, left, thought by the Romans to be the unlucky side]

     ▣ **1** ominous, menacing, threatening, disturbing, inauspicious, malevolent, evil.
     ▣ **1** auspicious, harmless, innocent.

Sinitic /sɪ'nɪtɪk/ — *adj.* denoting a group of languages belonging to the Sino-Tibetan family, used mainly in China and Taiwan. — *noun* the languages forming this group.

sink — *verb* (PAST TENSE **sank**; PAST PARTICIPLE **sunk**, as *adj.* **sunken**) **1** *intrans.* to fall and usually remain below the surface of water. **2** to cause to fall below the surface of water. **3** *intrans.* to collapse downwardly or inwardly; to fall because of a collapsing base or foundation. **4** *intrans.* to produce the sensation of a downward collapse within the body: *my heart sank at the news.* **5** to embed: *sank the pole into the ground.* **6** *intrans.* to pass steadily (and often dangerously) into a worse state. **7** *intrans.* (*also* **sink in**) to penetrate or be absorbed. **8** to invest (money) heavily. **9** *colloq.* to ruin the plans of; to ruin (plans): *we are sunk.* **10** *intrans.*, *said of the sun* to disappear slowly below the horizon. **11** *colloq.* to send (a ball) into a pocket in snooker, billiards, etc and into the hole in golf. — *noun* a wall-mounted basin with built-in water supply and drainage. — *adj. said of a housing estate, school, etc* run-down and disreputable. — **sink in** *colloq.* to be fully understood or realized. [from Anglo-Saxon *sincan*]

     ▣ *verb* **1** founder, dive, plunge, plummet, submerge, drown. **2** plunge, submerge, immerse, engulf, drown. **3** descend, slip, collapse, fall, drop, slump, droop, sag, dip. **6** decline, deteriorate, worsen, degenerate, decay, weaken, fail, decrease, lessen, dwindle, diminish, fade. **10** set, disappear, vanish.
     ▣ *verb* **1** rise, float. **2** raise, float. **3, 10** rise. **6** improve, increase.

sinker *noun* a weight used to make something, eg a fishing-line, sink.

sink unit a piece of kitchen furniture consisting of a sink and draining-board with cupboards underneath.

sinner *noun* a person who sins or has sinned.

     ▣ wrongdoer, miscreant, offender, transgressor, trespasser, backslider, reprobate, evildoer, malefactor.

Sinn Féin /ʃɪn 'feɪn/ *noun* an Irish political party supporting Irish independence from Britain and having close contacts with the Irish Republican Army (IRA). [from Gaelic, = ourselves alone]

Sino- /saɪnoʊ/ *combining form* forming words meaning 'Chinese': *Sino-Soviet.* [from Greek *Sinai*, Chinese]

Sinologist /saɪ'nɒlədʒɪst, sɪ'nɒlədʒɪst/ *noun* an expert in Sinology.

Sinology /saɪ'nɒlədʒɪ, sɪ'nɒlədʒɪ/ *noun* the study of China in all its aspects, eg cultural and political.

Sino-Tibetan — *adj.* denoting the family of languages spoken in China, Tibet, and Burma (Myanmar). It consists of some 300 languages, including the eight Chinese (or Sinitic) languages, Tibetan, and Burmese. — *noun* the languages forming this group.

sinuosity or **sinuousness** *noun* being sinuous.

sinuous *adj.* **1** having many curves or bends; meandering. **2** having a twisting and turning motion. [see SINUS]

     ▣ TWISTING, SERPENTINE. **1** meandering, winding, tortuous, curved, wavy, undulating. **2** slinky.
     ▣ **1** straight.

sinus /'saɪnəs/ *noun Anat.* a cavity or depression filled with air, especially in the bones of the face in mammals, or blood, especially in the brain and certain blood vessels. [from Latin *sinus*, curve]

sinusitis *noun* inflammation of the lining of the sinuses.

Sioux /su:/ (also called **Dakota**) a group of Native American peoples belonging to the Plains people culture.

sip — *verb trans.*, *intrans.* (**sipped**, **sipping**) to drink in very small mouthfuls. — *noun* **1** an act of sipping. **2** an amount sipped at one time. [perhaps a variation of SUP]

     ▣ *verb* taste, drink. *noun* TASTE. **1** drink. **2** drop, mouthful.

siphon or **syphon** /'saɪfən/ — *noun* **1** an inverted U-tube that can be used to transfer liquid from one container at a higher level into another at a lower level, provided that the tube is filled with liquid initially. **2** a bottle from which a liquid, especially soda water, is forced by pressure of gas. **3** *Zool.* in certain animals, eg bivalve molluscs, an organ resembling a tube through which water flows in and out. — *verb* (**siphoned**, **siphoning**) (*usually* **siphon something off**) **1** to transfer liquid from one container to another using such a device. **2** to take something slowly and continuously from a store or fund. [from Greek *siphon*, pipe]

sir *noun* **1** (**Sir**) a title used before the Christian name of a knight or baronet. **2** a term of politeness or respect used in addressing a man. [see SIRE]

sire — *noun* **1** the father of a horse or other animal. **2** *old use* a term of respect used in addressing a king. — *verb*, *said of an animal* to father (young). [from Old French, from Latin *senior*, elder]

siren *noun* **1** a device that gives out a loud wailing noise, usually as a warning signal. **2** an irresistible woman thought capable of ruining men's lives.

Sirius /'sɪrɪəs/ *Astron.* the Dog Star, the brightest star in the night sky, in the constellation Canis Major.

sirloin *noun* a fine cut of beef from the upper side of the part of the back just in front of the rump. [from French *surlonge*, from *sur*, above + *longe*, loin]

sirocco /sɪ'rɒkoʊ/ noun (PL. **siroccos**) a dry hot dust-carrying wind blowing into S Europe from N Africa. [from Italian *sirocco*, from Arabic *sharq*, east wind]

sis noun colloq. sister.

sisal /'saɪsəl, 'saɪzəl/ noun a strong fibre from the leaves of the agave plant of central America, used to make rope. [from *Sisal*, the Mexican port from where it was first exported]

siskin noun a yellowish-green Eurasian songbird of the finch family. [from Old Dutch *siseken*]

sissy or **cissy** noun (PL. **sissies**) derog. a weak, cowardly person. [see SISTER]

sister — noun 1 a female child of the same parents as another. 2 a nun. 3 a senior female nurse, especially one in charge of a ward. 4 a close female associate; a fellow female member of a profession, class or racial group. — adj. of the same origin or design: *a sister ship*. [from Anglo-Saxon *sweostor* or Norse *systir*]

sisterhood noun 1 the state of being a sister or sisters. 2 a religious community of women; a body of nuns. 3 a group of women with common interests or beliefs.

sister-in-law noun (PL. **sisters-in-law**) 1 the sister of one's husband or wife. 2 the wife of one's brother.

sisterliness noun being sisterly.

sisterly adj., *said of a woman or her behaviour* like a sister, especially in being kind and affectionate.

sit verb (**sitting**; PAST TENSE AND PAST PARTICIPLE **sat**) 1 intrans. to rest the body on the buttocks or hindquarters. 2 intrans. *said of a bird* to perch or lie. 3 intrans., *said of an object* to lie, rest, or hang: *a cup sitting on the shelf/the dress sits nicely around her waist*. 4 intrans. to lie unused: *tools sitting in the shed*. 5 intrans. to hold a meeting or other session: *court sits tomorrow*. 6 intrans. to be a member, taking regular part in meetings: *sit on a committee*. 7 to take (an examination); to be a candidate for (a degree or other award). 8 to conduct to a seat; to assign a seat to: *sat me next to him*. 9 intrans. to be or exist in a specified comparison or relation: *his smoking sits awkwardly with his being a doctor*. 10 intrans. to serve as an artist's or photographer's model. — **be sitting pretty** colloq. to be in a very advantageous position. **sit back 1** to sit comfortably, especially with the back rested. **2** to merely observe, taking no action, especially when action is needed. **sit down** or **sit someone down** to adopt or cause them to adopt a sitting position. **sit down under something** to submit meekly to an insult, etc. **sit in on something** to be present at, especially without taking part. **sit in for someone** to act as a substitute or deputy for them. **sit on someone** colloq. to force them to say or do nothing. **sit on something** colloq. 1 to delay taking action about a matter in one's care. 2 to keep it secret; to suppress it. **sit something out 1** to stay until the end of it. 2 to take no part in a dance or game. **sit tight 1** to maintain one's position determinedly. 2 to wait patiently. **sit up 1** to bring oneself from a slouching or lying position into an upright sitting position. 2 to remain out of bed longer than usual. 3 to take notice suddenly or show a sudden interest. [from Anglo-Saxon *sittan*]

▤ **1** settle, rest. **2** perch, roost. **3** rest, lie, stand, hang. **5** meet, assemble, gather, convene, deliberate. **8** seat. **10** pose.

sitar /'sɪtɑ:(r)/ noun a guitar-like instrument of Indian origin, with a long neck, rounded body and two sets of strings. [from Hindi *sitar*]

sitcom noun colloq. a situation comedy.

sit-down — noun colloq. a short rest in a seated position. — adj. 1 *said of a meal* for which the diners are seated. 2 *said of a strike* in which the workers occupy the workplace until an agreement is reached.

site noun 1 the place where something was, is, or is to be situated. 2 an area set aside for a specific activity: *camping site*. 3 short for WEBSITE. [from Latin *situs*, position]

▤ **1** location, place, spot, position, situation, setting, scene.

2 plot, lot, ground, area.

sit-in noun an occupation of a building, etc as a protest.

Sitka spruce Bot. a spruce tree (*Picea sitchensis*), with sharp blue-green needles, grown for its timber.

sitter noun 1 a person who poses for an artist or photographer. 2 a baby-sitter.

sitting noun 1 a period of continuous action: *wrote it at one sitting*. 2 a turn to eat for any of two or more groups too numerous to eat at the same time in the same place. 3 a period of posing for an artist or photographer. 4 a session or meeting of an official body.

▤ **1** session, period, spell. **4** session, meeting, assembly, hearing, consultation.

sitting duck or **sitting target** a person or thing in a defenceless position, easily attacked, criticized, etc.

sitting-room noun a room, especially in a private house, for relaxing in; a living-room.

sitting tenant a tenant occupying a property when it changes ownership.

situate verb to put in a certain position or set of circumstances. [from Latin *situare*, to position]

situation noun 1 a set of circumstances; a state of affairs. 2 a position or location. 3 a job: *situations vacant*.

▤ **1** state of affairs, case, circumstances, state, condition. **2** site, location, position, place, spot, seat, locale, setting, scenario. **3** job, employment, post, office, status, rank, station.

situation comedy a comedy in series form in which the same characters are featured in a more or less fixed set of surroundings.

sit-up noun a physical exercise in which, from a lying position, the torso is raised up and over the thighs, often with the hands behind the head.

six — noun 1 the number or figure 6; any symbol for this number. 2 the age of 6. 3 something, eg a garment or a person, whose size is denoted by the number 6. 4 a group of 6 people or things. 5 a playing card with 6 pips. 6 6 o'clock. 7 a score of 6 points. 8 *Cricket* a hit scoring 6 runs. 9 a team of (more or less) 6 Cub Scouts or Brownie Guides. — adj. 1 6 in number. 2 aged 6. — **at sixes and sevens** in a state of total disorder or confusion. **knock someone for six** colloq. 1 to defeat or ruin them completely. 2 to shock or surprise them greatly. **six of one and half a dozen of the other** equal; equally acceptable or unacceptable; the same on both sides. [from Anglo-Saxon *siex*]

sixer noun the Cub Scout or Brownie Guide leader of a six.

sixfold — adj. 1 equal to six times as much or as many. 2 divided into, or consisting of, six parts. — adv. by six times as much.

six-pack noun 1 a pack containing six items sold as one unit, especially a pack of six cans of beer. 2 a set of well-developed stomach muscles in a man.

sixpence noun a former small British silver coin worth six old pennies (6d), equivalent in value to 2½p.

sixpenny adj. worth or costing six old pennies.

sixteen — noun 1 the number or figure 16; any symbol for this number. 2 the age of 16. 3 something, eg a garment or a person, whose size is denoted by the number 16. 4 a set of 16 people or things. — adj. 1 16 in number. 2 aged 16. [from Anglo-Saxon *siextene*]

sixteenth noun, adj. 1 the position in a series corresponding to 16 in a sequence of numbers. 2 one of 16 equal parts.

sixth noun, adj. 1 the position in a series corresponding to 6 in a sequence of numbers. 2 one of six equal parts. 3 *Mus.* an interval of five diatonic degrees; a tone at that interval from another, or a combination of two tones separated by that interval.

sixth form the stage in secondary education in which school subjects are taught to a level that prepares for higher education.

sixth-former *noun* a member of a sixth form.

sixthly *adv.* as sixth in a series.

sixth sense an unexplained power of intuition by which one is aware of things not seen, heard, touched, smelled, or tasted.

sixties *pl. noun* **1** the period of time between one's sixtieth and seventieth birthdays. **2** the range of temperatures between sixty and seventy degrees. **3** the period of time between the sixtieth and seventieth years of a century, especially this period of the 20c.

sixtieth *noun, adj.* **1** the position in a series corresponding to 60 in a sequence of numbers. **2** one of sixty equal parts.

sixty — *noun* (PL. **sixties**) **1** the number or figure 60; any symbol for this number. **2** the age of 60. **3** a set of 60 people or things. — *adj.* **1** 60 in number. **2** aged 60. [from Anglo-Saxon *siextig*]

size [1] — *noun* **1** length, breadth, height or volume, or a combination of all or any of these. **2** largeness: *astonished by its size.* **3** any of a range of graded measurements, eg of garments. — *verb* **1** to measure in order to determine size. **2** to sort or arrange according to size. **3** (**size something** or **someone up**) to judge their nature, quality, or worth. [from Old French *sise*]

. . . .

◼ *noun* **1** magnitude, measurement, dimensions, proportions, volume, mass, height, length, width, breadth, extent, range, scale, amount. **2** largeness, bigness, greatness, vastness, immensity. *verb* **1** measure. **2** grade. **3** gauge, assess, evaluate, weigh up.

. . . .

size [2] — *noun* a weak kind of glue used to stiffen paper and fabric, and to prepare walls for plastering and wallpapering. — *verb* to treat with size.

sizeable or **sizable** *adj.* fairly large.

. . . .

◼ large, substantial, considerable, respectable, decent, generous.
◪ small, tiny.

. . . .

sizzle — *verb intrans.* **1** to make a hissing sound when, or as if when, frying in hot fat. **2** *colloq.* to be in a state of intense emotion, especially anger or excitement. — *noun* a sizzling sound. [imitative]

. . . .

◼ *verb* **1** hiss, crackle, spit, sputter, fry, frizzle. *noun* hiss, crackle.

. . . .

ska /skɑː/ *noun* a style of Jamaican popular music, developed in the 1960s, played on trumpet, saxophone, etc, in an unpolished style with loud, blaring rhythms. [perhaps in imitation of the characteristic sound of the music]

skate [1] — *noun* **1** a boot with a device fitted to the sole for gliding smoothly over surfaces, either a steel blade for use on ice (*ice-skate*) or a set of small wheels for use on wooden and other surfaces (*roller-skate*). **2** the blade of an ice-skate. — *verb intrans.* to move around on skates. — **get one's skates on** *colloq.* to hurry up. **skate on thin ice** to risk danger or harm, especially through lack of care or good judgement. **skate over** or **round something** to avoid dealing with or considering a difficulty. [from Old French *eschasse*, stilt]

skate [2] *noun* (**skate**, **skates**) a large flat edible fish of the ray family. [from Norse *skata*]

skateboard *noun* a narrow shaped board mounted on sets of small wheels, for riding on in a standing or crouching position.

skater *noun* a person who skates.

skating *noun* moving on skates.

skedaddle /skɪˈdadəl/ *verb intrans. colloq.* to run away quickly.

skein /skeɪn/ *noun* a loose coil of wool or thread. [from Old French *escaigne*]

skeletal *adj.* **1** like a skeleton. **2** existing in outline only.

skeleton *noun* **1** the framework of bones that supports and often protects the body of an animal, and to which the muscles are usually attached. **2** an initial basic structure or idea upon or around which anything is built. **3** *colloq.* an unhealthily thin person. [from Greek *skeleton soma*, dried body]

. . . .

◼ **1** bones, frame, structure, framework. **2** structure, framework, bare bones, outline, draft, sketch.

. . . .

skeleton in the cupboard or **skeleton in the closet** a shameful fact concerning oneself or one's family that one tries to keep secret.

skeleton key a key filed in such a way that it can open many different locks.

skeleton staff a set of staff reduced to a bare minimum.

sketch — *noun* **1** a rough drawing quickly done. **2** a rough plan or outline. **3** any of several short pieces of comedy presented as a programme. — *verb* **1** *trans., intrans.* to do a rough drawing or drawings (of). **2** to give a rough outline of. [from Greek *schedios*, offhand]

. . . .

◼ *noun* **1** drawing, vignette. **2** draft, outline, delineation, skeleton, plan, diagram. *verb* **1** draw. **2** outline, delineate, draft, rough out, block out.

. . . .

sketchily *adv.* in a sketchy way.

sketchiness *noun* being sketchy.

sketchy *adj.* (**sketchier**, **sketchiest**) lacking detail; not complete or substantial.

. . . .

◼ rough, vague, incomplete, unfinished, scrappy, bitty, imperfect, inadequate, insufficient, slight, superficial, cursory, hasty.
◪ full, complete.

. . . .

skew — *adj.* slanted; oblique; askew. — *verb* **1** *trans., intrans.* to slant or cause to slant. **2** to distort. — *noun* a slanting position: *on the skew.* [from Old French *eschuer*]

skewbald — *adj., said of an animal, especially a horse* with patches of white and another colour (other than black). — *noun* a skewbald horse.

skewer — *noun* a long wooden or metal pin pushed through chunks of meat, etc which are to be roasted. — *verb* (**skewered**, **skewering**) to fasten or pierce with, or as if with, a skewer. [from dialect *skiver*]

skewness *noun Maths.* a measure of the degree of asymmetry about the central value of a distribution.

skew-whiff *adj., adv. colloq.* lying in a slanted position; awry.

ski — *noun* (PL. **skis**) **1** a long narrow strip of wood, metal or plastic, upturned at the front, for gliding over snow, attached to each of a pair of boots or to a vehicle. **2** (*also* **water-ski**) a similar object worn on each foot for gliding over water. — *verb* (**skis**, **skied** or **ski'd**, **skiing**) *intrans.* to move on skis, especially as a sport or leisure activity. [from Norse *skith*, piece of split wood]

skid — *verb intrans.* (**skidded**, **skidding**) **1** *said of a wheel, etc* to slide along without revolving. **2** *said of a vehicle* to slide at an angle, especially out of control. — *noun* an instance of skidding. — **put the skids under someone** *colloq.* **1** to cause them to hurry. **2** to bring about their downfall.

skid pan a special slippery track on which drivers learn to control skidding vehicles.

skid row the poorest or most squalid part of a town.

skier /ˈskiːə(r)/ *noun* a person who skis.

skiff *noun* a small light boat. [from French *esquif*]

skiing *noun* the art of propelling oneself along snow while standing on skis, and with the aid of poles.

skilful *adj.* having or showing skill.

⊟ able, capable, adept, competent, proficient, deft, adroit, expert, masterly, accomplished, skilled, practised, experienced, professional, clever, tactical, cunning.
⊟ inept, clumsy, awkward.

ski lift a device for carrying skiers to the top of a slope so that they can ski down.

skill *noun* **1** expertness; dexterity. **2** a talent or accomplishment, naturally acquired or developed through training. [from Norse *skil*, distinction]

⊟ **1** skilfulness, expertness, expertise, mastery, proficiency, competence, dexterity, deftness. **2** talent, gift, knack, art, technique, ability, aptitude, facility, accomplishment.

skilled *adj.* **1** *said of people* possessing skill; trained, experienced. **2** *said of work* requiring skill or showing the use of skill.

⊟ **1** trained, qualified, professional, experienced, practised, accomplished, expert, masterly, proficient, able, skilful.
⊟ UNSKILLED. **1** inexperienced.

skillet *noun* a small long-handled frying-pan or saucepan. [perhaps from Norse *skjola*, bucket]

skim *verb* (**skimmed, skimming**) **1** to remove (floating matter) from the surface of (a liquid). **2** to brush or cause to brush against or glide lightly over (a surface): *skimming stones on the sea/the plane skimmed the trees.* **3** *intrans.* to glide lightly: *skimming over the water.* **4** *trans., intrans.* (**skim through something**) to read it superficially. [from Old French *escume*, scum]

⊟ **1** cream. **2** brush, touch. **3** skate, plane, float, sail, glide, fly. **4** scan, look over, look through.

skimmed milk or **skim milk** milk from which the cream has been removed.

skimmer *noun* a bird that inhabits tropical freshwater and coasts in America, Africa, India, and SE Asia, related to the tern, and having a lower bill longer and narrower than the upper one. It catches fish by flying low with its lower bill cutting the water surface. Also called SHEARWATER.

skimp *verb intrans.* (**skimp on something**) to spend, use, or give too little or only just enough of it. [perhaps from SCANT + SCRIMP]

⊟ economize on, stint, withhold.
⊟ squander, waste.

skimpily *adv.* in a skimpy way.

skimpiness *noun* being skimpy.

skimpy *adj.* (**skimpier, skimpiest**) **1** inadequate; barely enough. **2** *said of clothes* leaving much of the body uncovered.

skin — *noun* **1** the tough flexible waterproof covering of the human or animal body. **2** the outer covering of certain fruits and vegetables. **3** complexion: *greasy skin.* **4** an animal hide, with or without fur or hair attached. **5** a semisolid coating on the surface of a liquid. **6** a container for liquids made from an animal hide. — *verb* (**skinned, skinning**) **1** to strip the skin from. **2** to injure by scraping the skin from. **3** *slang* to cheat or swindle. — **by the skin of one's teeth** very narrowly; only just. **get under someone's skin** *colloq.* **1** to greatly annoy and upset them. **2** to become their consuming passion. **no skin off one's nose** *colloq.* not a cause of even slight concern or nuisance to one. **save one's skin** to save oneself from death or other harm. [from Norse *skinn*]

⊟ *noun* **2** peel, rind, husk, casing. **4** hide, pelt, fleece.

5 coating, film, membrane, crust. *verb* **1** flay, fleece, strip, peel. **2** scrape, graze.

skin-deep *adj.* superficial.

skin-diver *noun* a person who practises skin-diving.

skin-diving *noun* underwater swimming with no wet suit and only simple breathing and other equipment.

skin flick *slang* a pornographic film.

skinflint *noun colloq.* a very ungenerous person.

skinful *noun* (PL. **skinfuls**) *slang* a large amount of alcohol, enough to make one thoroughly drunk.

skinhead *noun* a person with closely cropped hair, especially a white youth with tight jeans, heavy boots and anti-establishment attitudes.

skink *noun* a lizard found in tropical and temperate regions worldwide, and usually having a long thin body and short legs (some species are without legs). Its head often bears large flat scales, and it has a broad rounded tongue. [from Greek *skinkos*]

skinny *adj.* (**skinnier, skinniest**) *said of a person* very thin.

⊟ thin, lean, scrawny, scraggy, skeletal, skin-and-bone, emaciated, underfed, undernourished.
⊟ fat, plump.

skinny-dip *verb intrans. colloq.* to go swimming naked.

skinny-dipping *noun colloq.* naked swimming.

skint *adj. slang* without money; hard up. [from *skinned*]

skin-tight *adj.*, *said of a piece of clothing* very tight-fitting.

skip¹ — *verb* (**skipped, skipping**) **1** to go along with light springing or hopping steps on alternate feet. **2** *intrans.* to make jumps over a skipping-rope. **3** to omit, leave out or pass over. **4** *colloq.* not to attend (eg a class in school). — *noun* a skipping movement. — **skip it!** *colloq.* forget it; ignore it; it is not important. [from Middle English *skippen*]

⊟ *verb* **1** hop, jump, leap, dance, gambol, frisk, frolic, caper, prance. **3** miss, pass over, omit, leave out, cut. **4** miss, cut. *noun* hop, jump, leap, caper.

skip² *noun* **1** a large metal container for rubbish for eg building work. **2** a large (especially wicker) chest, eg for storing theatrical costumes. **3** a lift in a coal mine. [a variant of *skep*, beehive]

skipper — *noun* the captain of a ship, aeroplane or team. — *verb* (**skippered, skippering**) to act as skipper of. [from Old Dutch *schipper*, shipper]

skipping-rope *noun* a rope swung backwards and forwards or twirled in a circular motion by the person skipping or by two other people each holding an end, jumping over as exercise or as a children's game.

skirl — *noun* the high-pitched screaming sound of bagpipes. — *verb intrans.* to make this sound.

skirmish — *noun* **1** a brief battle during a war, especially away from the main fighting. **2** any minor fight or dispute. — *verb intrans.* to engage in a skirmish. [from Old French *escarmouche*]

⊟ *noun* FIGHT. **1** battle, engagement, encounter, conflict, clash. **2** scrap, tussle, scuffle, set-to, dispute, wrangle. *verb* fight, battle, scrap, tussle, dispute, wrangle.

skirt — *noun* **1** a woman's garment that hangs from the waist. **2** the part of a woman's dress from the waist down. **3** any part or attachment resembling a skirt, eg the flap around the base of a hovercraft. **4** a cut of beef from the rear part of the belly; the flank. **5** (*also* **a bit of skirt**) *offensive slang* a woman regarded as an object of sexual desire. — *verb* **1** to border. **2** to pass along or around the edge of. **3** to avoid confronting (eg a problem). [from Norse *skyrta*, shirt]

◨ *verb* **1** border, edge, flank. **2** circle. **3** avoid, evade, circumvent, bypass.

skit *noun* a short satirical piece of writing or drama.

◨ satire, parody, caricature, spoof, take-off, *Brit. colloq.* send-up, sketch.

skittish *adj.* **1** lively and playful. **2** frequently changing mood or opinion; capricious. **3** *said of a horse* easily frightened.

skittle *noun* **1** each of the upright targets used in a game of skittles. **2** (**skittles**) a game in which balls are rolled towards a set of (usually nine or ten) free-standing bottle-shaped wooden or plastic targets, the object being to knock over as many of these as possible.

skive *verb intrans. colloq.* (**skive off**) to evade work or a duty, especially through laziness.

skiver *noun* a person who avoids work.

skivvy *colloq.* — *noun derog.* (PL. **skivvies**) a servant, especially a woman, who does unpleasant household jobs. — *verb intrans.* (**skivvies, skivvied**) to work as, or as if, a skivvy.

skua /skjoʊə/ *noun* any of various large predatory gull-like birds. [from Norse *skufr*]

skulduggery *noun* unscrupulous or dishonest behaviour; trickery. [from Scots *sculduddery*, unchastity]

skulk *verb intrans.* **1** to sneak off. **2** to hide or lurk, planning mischief. [from Norse *skulk*]

◨ **1** sneak, creep, slink. **2** hide, lurk, prowl.

skull *noun* **1** in vertebrates, the hard cartilaginous or bony framework of the head, including the cranium (which encloses the brain), face and jaws. **2** *colloq.* the head or brain. [from Norse]

skull and crossbones a representation of a human skull with two bones arranged in an X underneath, used formerly as a pirate's symbol, now as a symbol of death or danger.

skullcap *noun* a small brimless cap fitting closely on the head.

skunk *noun* **1** any of several small American mammals related to the weasel, and best known for the foul-smelling liquid which it squirts from musk glands at the base of its tail in order to deter predators, and the bold black and white warning coloration of its fur. **2** *derog.* a despised person. [from Algonkian (Native American) language *segonku*]

sky — *noun* (PL. **skies**) **1** the apparent dome of space in which the Sun, Moon and stars can be seen; the heavens. **2** the appearance of this area as a reflection of weather: *dismal skies.* — *verb* (**skies, skied**) to mishit (a ball) high into the air. — **the sky's the limit** there is no upper limit, eg to the amount of money that may be spent. **to the skies** in a lavish or extremely enthusiastic manner: *praise him to the skies.* [from Norse, = cloud]

◨ *noun* **1** space, atmosphere, air, heavens.

sky-blue *noun* bright light blue, the colour of a cloudless sky.

skydiver *noun* a person who practises skydiving.

skydiving *noun* free-falling from an aircraft, often involving performing manoeuvres in mid-air, with a long delay before the parachute is opened.

Skye terrier a small long-haired terrier originally bred on the island of Skye.

sky-high *adv. adj.*, *said especially of prices* very high.

skyjack *verb slang* to hijack (an aircraft).

skylark — *noun* the common lark, which sings when fly-

ing vertically and hovering. — *verb intrans. old use* to lark about.

skylight *noun* a (usually small) window in a roof or ceiling.

skyline *noun* the outline of buildings, hills and trees seen against the sky.

skyscraper *noun* an extremely tall building.

skyward — *adj.* towards the sky. — *adv.* (*also* **skywards**) towards the sky.

skyway *noun* a route used by aircraft.

slab — *noun* a thick flat rectangular piece, slice or object. — *verb* (**slabbed, slabbing**) to pave with concrete slabs.

◨ *noun* piece, block, lump, chunk, hunk, wedge, slice, portion.

slack¹ — *adj.* **1** loose; not pulled or stretched tight. **2** not careful or diligent; remiss. **3** not busy. **4** *said of the tide, etc* still; neither ebbing nor flowing. — *noun* **1** a loosely hanging part. **2** a period of little trade or other activity. — *verb* (*often* **slack off**) **1** *intrans.* (*also* **slack off** or **up**) to become slower; to slow one's working pace through tiredness or laziness. **2** *trans., intrans.* to make or become looser. **3** *intrans.* to become less busy. **4** *trans., intrans.* to make or become less rigid and more easy or relaxed. [from Anglo-Saxon *slæc*]

◨ *adj.* **1** loose, limp, sagging, baggy. **2** neglectful, negligent, careless, inattentive, remiss, lax. **3** sluggish, slow, quiet, idle, inactive. *verb* **1** slow down, idle, shirk, *colloq.* skive. **2** slacken, loosen. **4** relax, ease, moderate.
◧ *adj.* **1** tight, taut, stiff, rigid. **2** careful, diligent. **3** busy.

slack² *noun* coal dust or tiny fragments of coal. [from Old German *slecke*]

slacken *verb* same as SLACK *verb.*

slacker *noun* a person who does not work hard enough; a shirker.

◨ idler, shirker, *colloq.* skiver, good-for-nothing, layabout.

slacks *pl. noun old use* a type of loose casual trousers.

slag¹ — *noun* **1** waste material formed on the surface of molten metal ore. **2** waste left over from coal mining. — *verb intrans.* (**slagged, slagging**) *said of molten metal ore* to throw up a surface layer of slag. [from Old German *slagge*]

slag² *verb* (**slagged, slagging**) *slang* (**slag someone off**) to criticize them harshly or speak disparagingly about them.

slag³ *noun derog. slang* a person, especially a woman, who regularly has casual sex with different people.

slag heap a hill or mound formed from coal-mining waste.

slain see SLAY.

slake *verb* **1** *literary* to satisfy or quench (thirst, desire, or anger). **2** to cause (lime) to crumble by adding water. [from Anglo-Saxon *slacian*]

slaked lime *Chem.* calcium hydroxide prepared by adding water to quicklime (calcium oxide) in a process that evolves much heat, known as slaking.

slalom /ˈslɑːləm/ *noun* a race, on skis or in canoes, in and out of obstacles on a winding course. [from Norwegian *slalom*]

slam¹ — *verb* (**slammed, slamming**) **1** *trans., intrans.* to shut loudly and with violence. **2** *trans., intrans.* (*usually* **slam against, into**, etc) *colloq.* to make or cause to make loud heavy contact. **3** *slang* to criticize severely. — *noun* the act or sound of slamming.

◨ *verb* **1** bang. **2** dash, smash. **3** criticize, *colloq.* slate, *colloq.* pan. *noun* bang, crash.

slam² see GRAND SLAM, LITTLE SLAM.

slammer *noun* (**the slammer**) *slang* prison.

slander /'slɑːndə(r)/ — *noun* **1** a false and damaging spoken statement about a person. **2** the making of such statements. — *verb* (**slandered, slandering**) to speak about in such a way. See also LIBEL. [from Old French *esclandre*, from Greek *skandalon*, snare, scandal]

⊟ *noun* **1** smear, slur, aspersion. **2** defamation, calumny, misrepresentation, *verb* defame, vilify, malign, denigrate, disparage, smear, slur.
⊠ *verb* praise, compliment.

slanderous *adj.* **1** *said of words, reports, etc* characterized by slander. **2** *said of a person* given to the use of slander, using slander.

⊟ MALICIOUS. **1** defamatory, false, untrue, damaging.

slang — *noun* words and phrases used only very informally, not usually in writing or polite speech, and often only by members of a particular social group or profession. — *verb* to speak abusively to (someone) using coarse language.

slanging match *colloq.* an angry exchange of abuse.

slangy *adj.* (**slangier, slangiest**) **1** of the nature of slang. **2** using slang.

slant — *verb* **1** *intrans.* to be at an angle, not horizontal or vertical; to slope. **2** to present (information, etc) in a biased way, or for a particular audience or readership. — *noun* **1** a sloping position, surface, or line. **2** an attitude or viewpoint, sometimes one that shows a lack of objectivity: *a different slant on the issue.* — *adj.* sloping; lying at an angle. [from Middle English *slent*]

⊟ *verb* **1** tilt, slope, incline, lean, list. **2** distort, twist, warp, bend, skew, angle, bias, colour. *noun* **1** slope, incline, gradient, ramp, camber, pitch, tilt, angle, diagonal. **2** attitude, viewpoint, angle, emphasis, bias.

slanting *adj.* that slants.

⊟ sloping, tilted, oblique, diagonal.

slap — *noun* **1** a blow with the palm of the hand or anything flat. **2** the sound made by such a blow, or by the impact of one flat surface with another. — *verb* (**slapped, slapping**) **1** to strike with the open hand or anything flat. **2** to bring or send with a slapping sound: *slapped the newspaper down on the table.* **3** *colloq.* to apply thickly and carelessly: *slapped make-up on her face.* — *adv. colloq.* **1** exactly or precisely: *slap in the middle.* **2** heavily; with a slap: *fell slap on his face.* — **slap someone down** *colloq.* to reject or contradict them abruptly. **a slap in the face** *colloq.* an insult or rebuff. **a slap on the back** *colloq.* congratulations. **a slap on the wrist** *colloq., often facetious* a mild reprimand. [from German dialect *slapp*; originally imitative]

⊟ *noun* SMACK. **1** blow, cuff. **2** bang, clap. *verb* **1** smack, spank, hit, strike, cuff, clout. **2** bang, slam. **3** daub, plaster, spread.

slap and tickle *humorous colloq.* kissing and cuddling; sexual activity of any kind.

slap-bang *adv. colloq.* **1** exactly or precisely: *slap-bang in the middle.* **2** directly and with force: *drove slap-bang into the wall.*

slapdash *adj.* careless and hurried.

slap-happy *adj. colloq.* **1** cheerfully carefree or careless. **2** punch-drunk.

slaphead *noun slang* a person with a bald head.

slapper *noun offensive slang* a promiscuous woman.

slapstick *noun* comedy in which the humour is derived from boisterous antics of all kinds. [from a mechanical sound-effects device, used to punctuate (comic) stage fights with loud reports]

slap-up *adj. colloq., said of a meal* lavish; extravagant.

slash¹ — *verb* **1** *trans., intrans.* to make sweeping cuts or cutting strokes, especially repeatedly. **2** *colloq.* to reduce suddenly and drastically. — *noun* **1** a long (especially deep) cut. **2** a sweeping cutting stroke. **3** (*also* **slash mark**) an oblique line in writing or printing; a solidus.

⊟ *verb* CUT. **1** slit, gash, lacerate, rip, tear. *noun* **1** cut, incision, slit, gash, laceration, rip, tear.

slash² *coarse slang* — *verb intrans.* to urinate. — *noun* an act of urinating. [perhaps from Scot. dialect, large splash]

slash and burn *Agric.* a system of agriculture, common in tropical regions, in which trees and natural undergrowth are cut down and burned, and crops are then grown on the bare soil for a few years until it loses its fertility. The process is then repeated in a new area.

slat *noun* a thin strip, especially of wood or metal. [from Old French *esclat*]

slate¹ — *noun* **1** *Geol.* a shiny dark grey metamorphic rock, formed by the compression of clays and shales, that is easily split into thin flat layers, and is used for roofing and flooring. **2** a roofing tile made of this. **3** *formerly* a piece of this for writing on. **4** a record of credit given to a customer: *put it on my slate.* **5** a dull grey colour. — *verb* to cover (a roof) with slates. — **a clean slate** a fresh start, released from all previous obligations, faults, or commitments. [from Old French *esclate*]

slate² *verb colloq.* to criticize harshly. [from Norse *slate*]

⊟ criticize, *slang* slam, censure, blame, scold, rebuke, reprimand, berate.
⊠ praise.

slating *adj.* **1** covering with slates. **2** a covering of slates. **3** materials for covering with slates.

slatted *adj.* having or composed of slats.

slattern /'slatən/ *noun old use* a woman of dirty or untidy appearance or habits. [from dialect *slatter*, to slop]

slatternliness *noun* being slatternly.

slatternly *adj.* slovenly.

slaughter /'slɔːtə(r)/ — *noun* **1** the killing of animals for food. **2** cruel and violent murder. **3** the large-scale indiscriminate killing of people or animals. — *verb* (**slaughtered, slaughtering**) **1** to subject to slaughter. **2** *colloq.* to defeat resoundingly; to trounce. [from Norse *slatr*, butchers' meat]

⊟ *noun* KILLING. **2** murder. **3** massacre, extermination, butchery, carnage. *verb* **1** kill, slay, murder, massacre, exterminate, butcher. **2** defeat, trounce, thrash, *colloq.* hammer.

slaughterhouse *noun* a place where animals are killed to be sold for food; an abattoir.

Slav /slɑːv/ *noun* a member of any of various central and E European peoples speaking Slavonic languages such as Russian, Bulgarian, and Polish. [from Latin *Sclavus*]

slave — *noun* **1** *Hist.* a person owned by and acting as servant to another, with no personal freedom. **2** a person who works extremely hard for another; a drudge. **3** a person submissively devoted to another. **4** (**a slave to something**) a person whose life is dominated by some activity or thing: *a slave to her work.* — *verb intrans.* to work hard and ceaselessly. [from Old French *esclave*, originally 'Slav', the Slavs being much-conquered peoples in the Middle Ages]

⊟ *noun* **1** servant, vassal, serf, villein. **2** drudge. *verb* toil, labour, drudge, sweat, slog.

....

slave-driver *noun* **1** *Hist.* a person employed to ensure that slaves work hard. **2** *colloq.* a person who demands very hard work from others.

slaver[1] /ˈsleɪvə(r)/ *noun Hist.* **1** a person engaging in the buying and selling of slaves. **2** a ship for transporting slaves.

slaver[2] /ˈslavə(r)/ — *noun* spittle running from the mouth. — *verb intrans.* (**slavered, slavering**) **1** to let spittle run from the mouth; to dribble. **2** *colloq.* to talk nonsense.

....

■ *verb* **1** dribble, slobber, drool, salivate.

....

slavery *noun* **1** the state of being a slave. **2** the practice of owning slaves. **3** extremely hard work; toil.

....

■ **1** servitude, bondage, captivity, enslavement, serfdom, thraldom, subjugation. **3** toil, labour, drudgery.
☒ **1** freedom, liberty.

....

Slavic *adj.* relating to the Slavs.

Slavic languages or **Slavonic languages** the NE branch of the Indo-European languages, often grouped with the Baltic languages. Slavic languages are divided into South Slavic (eg Bulgarian), West Slavic (eg Polish), and East Slavic (eg Russian).

slavish /ˈsleɪvɪʃ/ *adj.* **1** rigid or unwavering in following rules or instructions. **2** very closely copied or imitated; unoriginal. **3** of or like a slave.

....

■ **1** strict, rigid, inflexible, unwavering. **2** unoriginal, imitative, unimaginative, uninspired. **3** servile, abject, submissive, sycophantic, grovelling, cringing, fawning, menial, low.
☒ **2** original, imaginative. **3** free, liberated, independent.

....

Slavonic /sləˈvɒnɪk/ — *noun* a group of Central and Eastern European languages that includes Russian, Polish, Czech, Slovak, Serb, and Slovenian. — *adj.* of these languages, the peoples speaking them, or their cultures.[see SLAV]

slay *verb* (PAST TENSE **slew**; PAST PARTICIPLE **slain**) *old use, literary* to kill. [from Anglo-Saxon *slean*]

slayer *noun* a person who kills.

sleaze *noun colloq.* corrupt or illicit practices, especially in public life.

sleaziness *noun* a sleazy quality.

sleazy *adj.* (**sleazier, sleaziest**) *colloq.* **1** dirty and neglected-looking. **2** cheaply suggestive of sex or crime; disreputable.

sled — *noun* a sledge. — *verb intrans.* (**sledded, sledding**) to sledge. [from Old German *sledde*]

sledge — *noun* **1** a vehicle with ski-like runners for travelling over snow, drawn by horses or dogs. **2** a child's toy vehicle of similar design, propelled by the hands or feet; a toboggan. — *verb intrans.* **1** to travel by sledge. **2** to play on a sledge. [from Old Dutch *sleedse*]

sledgehammer *noun* a large heavy hammer swung with both arms. [from Anglo-Saxon *slecg*, from *slean*, to strike]

sleek — *adj.* **1** *said of hair, fur, etc* smooth, soft and glossy. **2** having a well-fed and prosperous appearance. **3** insincerely polite or flattering. — *verb* to smooth (especially hair). [a form of SLICK]

....

■ *adj.* **1** shiny, glossy, lustrous, smooth, silky, well-groomed.
☒ *adj.* **1** rough, unkempt.

....

sleep — *noun* **1** in humans and many animals, a readily reversible state of natural unconsciousness during which the body's functional powers are restored, and physical movements are minimal. **2** a period of such rest. **3** *colloq.* mucus that collects in the corners of the eyes during such rest. **4** *poetic* death. — *verb usually intrans.* (PAST TENSE

AND PAST PARTICIPLE **slept**) **1** to rest in a state of sleep. **2** to be motionless, inactive or dormant. **3** *trans.* to provide or contain sleeping accommodation for: *the caravan sleeps four.* **4** *colloq.* to be in a dreamy state, not paying attention. **5** *poetic* to be dead. — **go to sleep 1** to pass into a state of sleep. **2** *colloq., said of a limb* to be temporarily numb through lack of blood circulation. **lose sleep over something** *colloq.* to be worried or preoccupied by it. **put someone or something to sleep 1** to anaesthetize them. **2** *euphemistic* to kill an animal painlessly with an injected drug. **sleep around** to engage in casual sexual relations. **sleep in 1** to sleep later than usual in the morning. **2** to sleep at one's place of work; to live in. **sleep something off** to recover from it by sleeping. **sleep on something** to delay taking a decision about it until the following morning. **sleep out 1** to sleep out of doors. **2** to sleep away from one's place of work; to live out. **sleep with someone** to have sexual relations with them. [from Anglo-Saxon *slæp*]

....

■ *noun* **1** slumber, *slang* kip, *slang* shuteye, rest, repose, hibernation. **2** doze, snooze, nap, *colloq.* forty winks, *slang* kip, siesta. *verb* **1** doze, snooze, slumber, *slang* kip, drop off, nod off, rest, repose, hibernate.

....

sleeper *noun* **1** a person who sleeps, especially in a specified way: *a light sleeper.* **2** any of the horizontal wooden or concrete beams supporting the rails on a railway track. **3** a railway carriage providing sleeping accommodation for passengers; a train with such carriages. **4** *colloq.* a record, film, book, etc, which suddenly becomes popular after an initial period of uninterest.

sleepily *adv.* in a sleepy way.

sleepiness *noun* being sleepy.

sleeping-bag *noun* a large quilted sack for sleeping in when camping, etc.

sleeping partner a partner who invests money in a business without taking part in its running.

sleeping pill a pill which contains a sedative drug that induces sleep.

sleeping policeman each of a series of low transverse humps built into the surface of a road, intended to slow down motor traffic in residential areas, parks, etc.

sleeping sickness a disease, often fatal, causing violent fever and extreme drowsiness, transmitted by the tsetse fly of Africa.

sleepless *adj.* **1** during which one is or was unable to sleep. **2** unable to sleep.

....

■ RESTLESS. **1** disturbed. **2** unsleeping, awake, wakeful, watchful, vigilant.

....

sleepwalk *verb intrans.* to indulge in sleepwalking; to walk while asleep.

sleepwalker *noun* a person who sleepwalks.

sleepwalking *noun* a condition in which the affected person walks about while asleep, with the eyes either open or closed, but on waking has no memory of the event. Also called SOMNAMBULISM.

sleepy *adj.* (**sleepier, sleepiest**) **1** feeling the desire to sleep; drowsy. **2** suggesting sleep or drowsiness: *sleepy music.* **3** characterized by quietness and a lack of activity: *a sleepy village.*

....

■ **1** drowsy, somnolent, tired, weary, heavy, slow, sluggish, torpid, lethargic, inactive. **2** soporific. **3** quiet, dull.
☒ **1** awake, alert, wakeful, restless.

....

sleepyhead *noun colloq.* **1** a person who often feels sleepy, or who needs a lot of sleep. **2** a person who tends to daydream a lot.

sleet — *noun* rain mixed with snow or hail. — *verb intrans.* to rain simultaneously with snow or hail.

sleety *adj.* (**sleetier, sleetiest**) characterized by sleet, carrying sleet.

sleeve *noun* **1** the part of a garment that covers the arm. **2** any tube-like cover. **3** the cardboard or paper envelope in which a record is stored. — **up one's sleeve** held secretly in reserve, for possible later use. [from Anglo-Saxon *slefe*]

sleeveless *adj.* having no sleeves.

sleigh /sleɪ/ — *noun* a large horse-drawn sledge. — *verb intrans.* to travel by sleigh. [from Dutch *slee*]

sleight of hand /slaɪt/ skill in moving the hands quickly and deceptively, in the performing of magic tricks. [from Norse *slægth*, cunning]

slender *adj.* **1** attractively slim. **2** narrow; slight: *by a slender margin.* **3** meagre: *slender means.*

⬛ **1** slim, thin, lean, slight, svelte, graceful. **2** slight, narrow, inconsiderable, tenuous, flimsy, faint, remote. **3** meagre, scanty, inadequate, insufficient.
🔺 **1** fat. **2** appreciable, considerable. **3** ample.

slept see SLEEP.

sleuth /sluːθ/ — *noun* a detective. — *verb intrans.* to work as a detective. [from Norse *sloth*, trail]

slew¹ /sluː/ see SLAY.

slew² — *verb trans., intrans.* to twist or cause to twist or swing round, especially suddenly and uncontrollably. — *noun* an instance of slewing.

slewed *adj. slang* extremely drunk.

slice — *noun* **1** a thin broad piece, or a wedge, cut off. **2** *colloq.* a share or portion: *a slice of the business.* **3** a kitchen tool with a broad flat blade for sliding under and lifting solid food. **4** *Sport* a stroke causing a ball to spin sideways and curve away in a particular direction; the spin imparted. — *verb* **1** to cut up into slices. **2** (*also* **slice something off**) to cut it off as or like a slice: *sliced a piece off the end.* **3** *intrans.* to cut deeply and easily; to move easily and forcefully, as if cutting with a knife: *a boat slicing through the water.* **4** to strike (a ball) with a slice. [from Old German *slizan*, to split]

⬛ *noun* **1** piece, sliver, wafer, rasher, slab, wedge, segment, section, portion, helping. **2** share, portion, *slang* cut, *colloq.* whack. *verb* **1** carve, cut.

slicer *noun* a person or machine that slices.

slick — *adj.* **1** dishonestly or slyly clever. **2** impressively and only superficially smart or efficient: *slick organization.* **3** smooth and glossy; sleek. — *verb* to smooth (especially hair). — *noun* (*also* **oil slick**) a wide layer of spilled oil floating on the surface of water. [from Anglo-Saxon *slician*, to smooth]

⬛ *adj.* **1** glib, plausible, smart, clever. **3** smooth, sleek, glossy, shiny, polished.

slickenside *noun Geol.* a smooth rock surface that has become polished and striated as a result of grinding or sliding against an adjacent rock mass during slippage along a fault plane. [from SLICK]

slicker *noun* **1** a sophisticated city-dweller. **2** a shifty or swindling person.

slide — *verb* (PAST TENSE AND PAST PARTICIPLE **slid**) **1** *intrans.* to move or run smoothly along a surface, down a slope, etc. **2** to cause to move in this way. **3** *trans., intrans.* to move or place softly and unobtrusively: *slid the letter into his pocket.* **4** *intrans.* to lose one's footing; to slip. **5** *intrans.* to pass gradually, especially through neglect or laziness: *slid back into his old habits.* — *noun* **1** an act or instance of sliding. **2** any part that glides smoothly, eg the moving part of a trombone. **3** an apparatus for children to play on, usually with a ladder to climb up and a narrow sloping part to slide down. **4** a small glass plate on which specimens are placed to be viewed through a microscope. **5** a small transparent photograph viewed in magnified size by means of a projector. **6** a large decorative hair-clip.

— **let something slide** to allow a situation to deteriorate. [from Anglo-Saxon *slidan*]

⬛ *verb* SLIP. **1** skate, ski, toboggan, glide, plane, coast, skim. **4** slither, skid.

slide-rule *noun* a hand-held mechanical device, now largely superseded by the pocket calculator, used to perform quick numerical calculations, especially multiplication or division. It consists of a ruler bearing several logarithmic scales that can be moved in relation to each other.

sliding scale a scale, eg of fees charged, that varies according to changes in conditions, eg unforeseen difficulties in performing the service requested.

slight — *adj.* **1** small in extent, significance or seriousness. **2** slender. **3** lacking solidity; flimsy. **4** lacking substance or value: *slight works of literature.* — *verb* to insult by ignoring or dismissing abruptly; to snub. — *noun* an insult or snub. — **not in the slightest** not at all; not even to the smallest degree. [from the root seen in Anglo-Saxon *eorthslihtes*, close to the ground]

⬛ *adj.* **1** *extent* small, little, inconsiderable, insubstantial, modest. *significance* minor, unimportant, insignificant, negligible, trivial, paltry. **2** slender, slim, diminutive, petite. **3** flimsy, delicate. *verb* insult, affront, offend, snub, cold-shoulder, ignore, disregard, neglect, scorn, despise, disdain, disparage. *noun* insult, affront, slur, snub, rebuff.
🔺 *adj.* **1** *extent* large, considerable. *significance* major, significant. **2** well-built. *verb* praise, compliment, flatter, respect.

slightly *adv.* to a small extent, in a small way.

slily see SLYLY.

slim — *adj.* (**slimmer, slimmest**) **1** attractively thin; slender. **2** of little thickness or width. **3** not great; slight: *a slim chance.* — *verb intrans.* (**slimmed, slimming**) to make oneself slim, especially by diet and exercise. [from Dutch *slim*, crafty]

⬛ *adj.* **1** slender, thin, lean, svelte, trim. **2** thin, narrow. **3** slight, remote, faint, poor. *verb* lose weight, diet, reduce.
🔺 *adj.* **1** fat, chubby. **2** thick, wide. **3** strong, considerable.

slime *noun* **1** any thin unpleasantly slippery or gluey mudlike substance. **2** any mucus-like substance secreted, eg by snails. [from Anglo-Saxon *slim*]

slime mould *Biol.* a small simple organism, resembling a fungus and usually consisting of a naked mass of protoplasm, that lives in damp habitats and feeds on dead or decaying plant material. Slime moulds reproduce by means of spores, and for convenience are usually classified as fungi.

slimily *adv.* in a slimy way.

sliminess *noun* a slimy quality.

slimmer *noun* a person who is trying to lose weight.

slimming *noun* losing weight.

slimy *adj.* (**slimier, slimiest**) **1** like, covered with or consisting of slime. **2** *colloq.* exaggeratedly and unpleasantly obedient or attentive; obsequious.

⬛ *adj.* **1** muddy, miry, mucous, viscous, oily, greasy, slippery. **2** servile, obsequious, sycophantic, toadying, *colloq.* smarmy, oily, unctuous.

sling¹ — *noun* **1** a cloth hoop supporting an injured arm, one end hanging round the neck and the arm passed through the other end. **2** a primitive weapon for launching stones, consisting of a strap or pouch in which the stone is placed and swung round fast. **3** a strap or loop for hoisting, lowering or carrying a weight. — *verb* (PAST TENSE AND PAST PARTICIPLE **slung**) **1** *colloq.* to throw, especially with force; to fling. **2** to hang loosely: *a jacket slung over his shoulder.* **3** to launch from a sling. — **sling one's hook** *slang* to go away.

■ *verb* **1** throw, hurl, fling, pitch, toss, *colloq.* chuck. **2** hang, suspend, dangle, swing. **3** launch, catapult.

sling² *noun* a drink of alcoholic spirit (especially gin) and water, sweetened and flavoured.

slingback *noun* a shoe with no cover for the heel, just a strap passing round it to hold the shoe on.

slingshot *noun North Amer., esp. US* a catapult.

slink *verb intrans.* (PAST TENSE AND PAST PARTICIPLE **slunk**) to go or move sneakingly or ashamedly. [from Anglo-Saxon *slincan*]

■ sneak, steal, creep, sidle, slip, prowl, skulk.

slinkily *adv.* in a slinky way.
slinkiness *noun* being slinky.
slinky *adj.* (**slinkier, slinkiest**) *colloq.* **1** *said of clothing* attractively close-fitting. **2** slender. **3** *said of a person* walking with slow rolling movements that emphasize the body's curves.

■ **1** close-fitting, figure-hugging, clinging, skin-tight. **2** slender, slim. **3** sinuous.

slip¹ — *verb* (**slipped, slipping**) **1** *intrans.* to lose one's footing and slide accidentally. **2** *intrans.* to slide, move, or drop accidentally. **3** to place smoothly, quietly, or secretively: *slipped the envelope into her pocket.* **4** (**slip in, out,** etc) to move quietly and unnoticed. **5** *trans., intrans.* to move or cause to move smoothly with a sliding motion. **6** to pull free from smoothly and swiftly; to suddenly escape from: *the dog slipped its lead/the name has slipped my mind.* **7** (*also* **slip up**) to make a slight mistake inadvertently. **8** *colloq.* to give or pass secretly: *slipped him a fiver.* **9** *intrans. colloq.* to lose one's former skill or expertise, or control of a situation. **10** to dislocate (especially a spinal disc). — *noun* **1** an instance of losing one's footing and sliding accidentally. **2** a minor and usually inadvertent mistake: *a slip of the tongue*/pen. **3** a woman's loose undergarment worn under a dress or skirt. **4** a loose covering for a pillow. **5** a slipway. **6** *Cricket* a fielder standing near to and roughly in line with the wicket-keeper on the on side; (*also* **slips**) this fielding position. — **give someone the slip** *colloq.* to escape from them adroitly. **let something slip 1** to reveal it in speech accidentally. **2** to fail to take advantage of something (eg an opportunity). [from Old German dialect *slippen*]

■ *verb* **1** slide, slither, skid, stumble, trip, fall. **4** slink, sneak, steal, creep. *noun* **2** mistake, error, *colloq.* slip-up, blunder, indiscretion, omission, oversight. **3** underskirt, petticoat.

slip² *noun* **1** a small strip or piece of paper. **2** a small pre-printed form. **3** a mere youngster; an exceptionally slender person: *just a slip of a girl.* [from Middle English *slippe*]

■ **1** piece, strip. **2** form, chit, voucher, coupon, certificate.

slip³ *noun* a creamy mixture of clay and water used for decorating and casting pottery. [from Anglo-Saxon *slipa*, paste]

slip-knot *noun* **1** a knot undone simply by pulling one end of the cord. **2** a knot finishing off a noose, and slipping along the cord to adjust the noose's size.

slip-on *noun* a shoe or other item of clothing that is easily put on, without laces, buttons, or other fastenings.

slipped disc a dislocation of the layer of cartilage between any of the vertebrae, causing painful pressure on a spinal nerve.

slipper *noun* a soft loose laceless indoor shoe.
slippered *adj.* wearing a slipper or slippers.
slipperiness *noun* being slippery.
slippery *adj.* **1** so smooth as to cause slipping. **2** difficult to catch or keep hold of. **3** unpredictable or untrustworthy.

■ **1** smooth, glassy, *colloq.* slippy, icy, greasy, dangerous, treacherous. **3** unpredictable, unreliable, untrustworthy, dishonest, crafty, cunning, devious, smooth, smarmy.
3 **1** rough. **3** reliable, trustworthy.

slippy *adj.* (**slippier, slippiest**) *colloq., said of a thing* liable to slip; slippery.

slip road a road for joining or leaving a motorway.

slipshod *adj.* untidy and careless or carelessly done.

■ untidy, slapdash, sloppy, slovenly, careless, negligent, lax.
3 tidy, neat, careful.

slipstream *noun* **1** an area of decreased wind resistance immediately behind a moving vehicle or other object. **2** a stream of air driven back by a moving vehicle, especially an aircraft.

slip-up *noun colloq.* a minor and usually inadvertent mistake.

slipway *noun* a ramp that slopes into water, for launching boats.

slit — *noun* a long narrow cut or opening. — *verb* (**slitted, slitting**) **1** to cut a slit in. **2** to cut into strips. [from Middle English *slitten*]

■ *noun* cut, incision, gash, slash, split, tear, opening, aperture, vent. *verb* CUT. **1** gash, slash, rip, tear. **2** slice, split.

slither — *verb intrans.* (**slithered, slithering**) **1** to slide or slip unsteadily while walking, eg on ice. **2** to move slidingly, like a snake. — *noun* a slithering movement. [from Anglo-Saxon *slidrian*]

■ *verb* **1** slide, slip. **2** slink, creep, snake, worm.

slithery *adj.* slippery.

sliver — *noun* a long thin piece cut or broken off. — *verb intrans.* (**slivered, slivering**) to become broken or cut into slivers. [from Anglo-Saxon *slifan*, to cleave]

■ *noun* chip, splinter, shiver, shard, flake, shaving, paring, slice, wafer, shred, fragment.

slivovitz /ˈslɪvəvɪts/ *noun* a dry colourless plum brandy from E Europe. [from Serbo-Croat *sljivovica*, from *sljiva*, plum]

slob *colloq.* — *noun* a lazy, untidy or coarse person. — *verb intrans.* (**slobbed, slobbing**) (*usually* **slob about** or **around**) to move or behave in a lazy, untidy or slovenly way. [from Irish Gaelic *slab*, mud]

slobber — *verb intrans.* (**slobbered, slobbering**) **1** to let saliva run from the mouth; to dribble or slaver. **2** (**slobber over something**) *colloq.* to express extreme or excessive enthusiasm or admiration for it. — *noun* dribbled saliva. [from Middle English *slobber*]

■ *verb* DROOL. **1** dribble, slaver, salivate.

slobbish or **slobby** *adj.* (**slobbier, slobbiest**) like a slob; lazy, untidy.

sloe *noun* the blackthorn fruit or bush. [from Anglo-Saxon *sla*]

sloe gin gin flavoured by having sloes soaked in it.

slog *colloq.* — *verb* (**slogged, slogging**) **1** to hit hard and wildly. **2** to labour or toil. — *noun* **1** a hard wild blow or stroke. **2** extremely tiring work.

slogan *noun* a phrase used to identify a group or organization, or to advertise a product. [from Gaelic *sluagh*, army + *gairm*, cry]

- jingle, motto, catchphrase, catchword, watchword, battle-cry, rallying-cry.

sloop *noun* a single-masted sailing boat with fore-and-aft sails. [from Dutch *sloep*]

slop — *verb* (**slopped, slopping**) (*often* **slop about** or **around**) **1** *trans., intrans.* to splash or cause to splash or spill violently. **2** *intrans. colloq.* to move or behave in an untidy or slovenly way. — *noun* **1** spilled liquid. **2** (*often* **slops**) unappetizing watery food. **3** (**slops**) waste food. **4** (**slops**) liquid food fed to pigs. **5** (**slops**) urine and excrement. **6** gushy sentiment. — **slop out** *intrans, said of prisoners* to empty slops (sense 5). [from Anglo-Saxon *cusloppe*, cow dung]

- *verb* **1** spill, slosh, splash, splatter.

slope — *noun* **1** a position or direction that is neither level nor upright; an upward or downward slant. **2** a slanting surface; an incline; the side of a hill or mountain. **3** a specially prepared track for skiing, on the side of a snow-covered hill or mountain. — *verb intrans.* **1** to rise or fall at an angle. **2** to be slanted or inclined. — **slope off** *colloq.* to leave furtively. [from Anglo-Saxon *aslupan*, to slip away]

- *noun* **1** slant, tilt, pitch, inclination. **2** incline, gradient, ramp, hill, ascent, descent. *verb* **1** rise, fall. **2** slant, incline, lean, tilt, tip.

sloppily *adv.* in a sloppy way.
sloppiness *noun* being sloppy.
sloppy *adj.* (**sloppier, sloppiest**) **1** wet or muddy. **2** watery. **3** *said of language, work, etc* inaccurate, careless.

- **1** wet, muddy, slushy. **2** watery, liquid, runny, mushy. **3** careless, inaccurate, hit-or-miss, slapdash, slipshod, slovenly, untidy, messy.
- **1** dry. **2** solid. **3** careful, exact, precise.

slosh — *verb* **1** *trans., intrans.* (*often* **slosh about** or **around**) to splash or cause to splash or spill noisily. **2** *slang* to strike with a heavy blow. — *noun* **1** the sound of splashing or spilling. **2** slush; a watery mess. **3** *slang* a heavy blow. [a form of SLUSH]

sloshed *adj. colloq.* drunk.

slot — *noun* **1** a small narrow rectangular opening into which something is fitted or inserted. **2** a time, place, or position in a schedule, eg of broadcasts or airport take-offs and landings. — *verb* (**slotted, slotting**) **1** (*also* **slot something in**) to fit or insert it, or place it in a slot. **2** to make a slot in. [from Old French *esclot*]

- *noun* **1** hole, opening, aperture, slit, vent, groove, channel. **2** gap, space, time, window, vacancy, place, spot, position, niche. *verb* **1** insert, fit, place, position.

sloth /sloʊθ/ *noun* **1** a herbivorous tree-dwelling mammal, belonging to the same order (Edentata) as armadillos and anteaters, and found in tropical forests of America. It has long slender limbs, and is noted for its very slow movements. **2** the desire to avoid all activity or exertion; laziness; indolence. [from Anglo-Saxon *slæwth*, from *slaw*, slow]

slothful *adj.* inactive, lazy.

slot machine a machine operated by inserting a coin in a slot, eg a vending machine or fruit machine.

slouch — *verb intrans.* to sit, stand, or walk with a tired or lazy drooping posture. — *noun* **1** such a posture. **2** *colloq.* (**no slouch at something**) a person who is able or competent in some respect: *she's no slouch at dancing.*

- *verb* stoop, hunch, droop, slump, lounge, loll, shuffle, shamble.

slough[1] /slaʊ/ *noun* **1** a mud-filled hollow. **2** an area of boggy land; a mire. **3** *literary* a state of deep and gloomy emotion: *in a slough of depression.* [from Anglo-Saxon *sloh*]

slough[2] /slʌf/ — *noun* any part of an animal cast off or moulted, especially a snake's dead skin. — *verb* **1** to shed (eg a dead skin). **2** to cast off or dismiss (eg worries). [from Middle English *sloh*]

sloven /ˈslʌən/ *noun* a slovenly person.

slovenliness *noun* being slovenly.

slovenly — *adj.* careless, untidy or dirty in appearance, habits or methods of working. — *adv.* in a slovenly manner.

- *adj.* careless, sloppy, slipshod, untidy, scruffy, dirty, slatternly, sluttish.
- *adj.* neat, smart.

slow — *adj.* **1** having little speed or pace; not moving fast or quickly. **2** taking a long time, or longer than usual or expected. **3** *said of a watch or clock* showing a time earlier than the correct time. **4** not quickly or easily learning, understanding or appreciating. **5** progressing at a boringly gentle pace: *a slow film.* **6** not allowing fast progress or movement: *traffic was slow/a golf course with slow greens.* **7** needing much provocation in order to do something: *slow to get angry.* **8** *said of business* slack. **9** *said of photographic film* needing a relatively long exposure time. — *adv.* in a slow manner. — *verb* (*also* **slow down** or **up**) **1** *intrans.* to reduce speed, pace, or rate of progress. **2** to cause to reduce speed, pace, or rate of progress. [from Anglo-Saxon *slaw*]

- *adj.* **1** leisurely, unhurried, lingering, loitering, dawdling, sluggish, slow-moving, gradual, deliberate, measured, plodding. **2** prolonged, protracted, long-drawn-out. **4** slow-witted, stupid, dim, *colloq.* thick. **5** boring, tedious, dull, uninteresting, uneventful. **8** slack, sluggish. *verb* **1** brake, decelerate. **2** delay, hold up, retard, handicap, check, curb.
- *adj.* **1** quick, fast, swift, rapid, speedy, brisk. **4** quick-witted, clever, intelligent. **5** lively, exciting. *verb* SPEED, ACCELERATE.

slowcoach *noun colloq.* a person who moves or works at a slow pace.

slowly *adv.* at a slow rate, in a slow way.

slow motion 1 a speed of movement in film or television that is much slower than real-life movement, created by increasing the speed at which the camera records the action. **2** an imitation of this in real-life movement.

slow-motion *adj.* having or using slow motion.

slow neutron *Physics* a neutron with a relatively low energy content, which can be captured by the nucleus of an atom, and is used to initiate various nuclear reactions, especially nuclear fission.

slow-worm *noun* a small legless Eurasian lizard with a snake-like body. [from Anglo-Saxon *slawyrm*; the first part is not related to SLOW but has been assimilated to it]

SLR *abbrev.* single-lens reflex.

sludge *noun* **1** soft slimy mud. **2** muddy sediment. **3** sewage. **4** half-melted snow; slush. [probably from SLUSH]

sludgy *adj.* (**sludgier, sludgiest**) like or consisting of sludge.

slug[1] *noun* any of various terrestrial molluscs belonging to the same class (Gastropoda) as snails, but having a long fleshy body and little or no shell.

slug[2] *noun* 1 *colloq.* a bullet. 2 *Printing* a solid line or section of metal type produced by a composing machine.

slug[3] *colloq.* — *noun* a heavy blow. — *verb* (**slugged, slugging**) to strike with a heavy blow.

slug[4] *noun colloq.* a large gulped mouthful of liquid, especially alcohol spirit.

sluggard *noun old use* a lazy, inactive person.

sluggish *adj.* 1 unenergetic; lazy; inactive. 2 less lively, active or responsive than usual: *the engine is a bit sluggish.*

▣ 1 lethargic, listless, torpid, heavy, dull, slow, slow-moving, lazy, slothful, idle, inactive. 2 unresponsive.

🔁 LIVELY. 1 energetic, vigorous, brisk.

sluice /sluːs/ — *noun* 1 a channel or drain for water. 2 (*also* **sluice-gate**) a valve or sliding gate for controlling the flow of water in such a channel. 3 a trough for washing gold or other minerals out of sand, etc. 4 an act of washing down or rinsing. — *verb* 1 to drain by means of a sluice. 2 to wash down or rinse by throwing water on. [from Old French *escluse*, from Latin *excludere*, to shut out]

slum — *noun* 1 a run-down, dirty, usually overcrowded house. 2 (*often* **slums**) an area of such housing. — *verb intrans.* (**slummed, slumming**) 1 to visit a socially deprived area, especially out of curiosity or for amusement. 2 to adopt the tastes or behaviour of members of a lower social class, out of pretentiousness. — **slum it** *colloq., often facetious* to experience circumstances that are less affluent or more squalid than one is used to.

slumber *poetic* — *noun* sleep. — *verb intrans.* (**slumbered, slumbering**) to sleep. [from Middle English *slumeren*]

slumbering *adj.* sleeping.

slumberous *adj.* 1 inviting or causing sleep. 2 sleepy.

slummy *adj.* (**slummier, slummiest**) *colloq.* like a slum; run-down or squalid.

slump — *verb intrans.* 1 to drop or sink suddenly and heavily, eg with tiredness: *slumped into an armchair.* 2 *said of trade, etc* to decline suddenly and sharply. — *noun* a serious and usually long-term decline, eg in a nation's economy.

▣ *verb* 1 collapse, flop, fall, drop, sink. 2 decline, deteriorate, worsen, crash, fail, collapse, plunge, plummet. *noun* recession, depression, low, trough, decline, deterioration, worsening, downturn, fall, drop, crash, failure, collapse.

🔁 *noun* boom.

slung see SLING.

slunk see SLINK.

slur — *verb* (**slurred, slurring**) 1 *trans., intrans.* to pronounce (words) unclearly, eg through drunkenness. 2 to speak or write about very disparagingly. 3 to mention only briefly or deal with only superficially. 4 *Mus.* to sing or play as a flowing sequence without pauses. — *noun* 1 a disparaging remark intended to damage a reputation. 2 a slurred word or slurring way of speaking. 3 *Mus.* a flowing pauseless style of singing or playing.

▣ *noun* 1 insult, slight, smear, stain.

slurp — *verb* to eat or drink noisily with a sucking action. — *noun* a slurping sound. [from Dutch *slurpen*, to sip audibly]

slurry *noun* (PL. **slurries**) 1 a runny mixture of solid particles and water, especially watery concrete. 2 liquid manure that is either treated to form fertilizer, or stored in a lagoon or tank from which it can be piped on to fields or distributed by tanker.

slush *noun* 1 half-melted snow. 2 any watery half-liquid substance. 3 sickly sentimentality.

slush fund a fund of money used for dishonest purposes, eg bribery, especially by a political party.

slushy *adj.* (**slushier, slushiest**) like or consisting of slush.

slut *noun derog.* 1 a woman who regularly engages in casual sex. 2 a prostitute. 3 an untidy or dirty woman.

sluttish *adj.* characteristic of a slut; dirty and untidy.

sly *adj.* (**slyer, slyest** or **slier, sliest**) 1 clever; cunning. 2 secretive; secretively deceitful or dishonest. 3 playfully mischievous: *a sly smile.* — **on the sly** *colloq.* secretly or furtively. [from Norse *slægr*]

▣ 1 clever, canny, shrewd, astute, crafty, cunning, wily, foxy, artful, guileful, knowing, subtle, devious, tricky. 2 secretive, covert, furtive, stealthy, surreptitious, underhand, shifty, scheming, conniving. 3 mischievous, roguish.

🔁 2 open, frank, candid.

slyly or **slily** *adv.* in a sly way.

SM *abbrev.* 1 sado-masochism. 2 sado-masochistic.

Sm *symbol Chem.* samarium.

smack[1] — *verb* 1 *trans.* to slap, especially with the hand. 2 *trans., intrans. colloq.* to hit loudly and heavily: *her head smacked against the wall.* 3 to part (the lips) loudly, with relish or in pleasant anticipation. — *noun* 1 an act, or the sound, of smacking. 2 a loud enthusiastic kiss. — *adv. colloq.* 1 directly and with force: *drove smack into the tree.* 2 precisely: *smack in the middle.* [from Old Dutch *smacken*]

▣ *verb* 1 hit, strike, slap, spank, *colloq.* whack, box, cuff, pat, tap. 2 hit, strike, bang, crash. *noun* 1 blow, slap, spank, *colloq.* whack, box, cuff, pat, tap. *adv.* 1 bang, slap-bang, right, plumb, straight, directly. 2 exactly, precisely.

smack[2] — *verb intrans.* (**smack of something**) 1 to have the flavour of it. 2 to have a suggestion or trace of it. — *noun* 1 taste; distinctive flavour. 2 a hint or trace. [from Anglo-Saxon *smæc*]

smack[3] /smak/ *noun* a small single-masted fishing boat. [from Dutch *smak*]

smack[4] *noun slang* heroin.

smacker *noun* 1 *colloq.* a loud enthusiastic kiss. 2 *slang* a pound sterling or a dollar.

small — *adj.* 1 little in size or quantity. 2 little in extent, importance or worth; not great. 3 humble: *small beginnings.* 4 petty: *small-minded.* 5 young: *a small child.* 6 *said of a printed or written letter* lower-case; not capital. 7 humiliated: *feel small.* — *noun* 1 the narrow part, especially of the back. 2 (**smalls**) *colloq.* underclothes. — *adv.* 1 on a small scale. 2 into small pieces. [from Anglo-Saxon *smæl*]

▣ *adj.* 1 *size* little, tiny, minute, minuscule, short, slight, petite, diminutive, miniature, mini, pocket, pocket-sized. *quantity* inadequate, insufficient, scanty, meagre, paltry, limited. 2 minor, unimportant, insignificant, inconsiderable, negligible, trivial, trifling, petty.

🔁 *adj.* 1 *size* large, big, huge. *quantity* ample. 2 great, considerable.

small ads *colloq.* short advertisements in a newspaper, advertising items for sale, etc.

small arms hand-held firearms.

small beer something unimportant.

small change coins of little value.

small fry *colloq.* 1 *sing., pl.* a person or thing, or people or things, of little importance or influence. 2 *pl.* young children.

smallholder *noun* a person who farms a smallholding.

smallholding *noun* a small area of cultivated land, in the UK under 20 hectares in area, usually devoted to one aspect of farming, eg market gardening or raising goats; also, a general term for a small farm.

small hours (**the small hours**) the hours immediately after midnight.

small-minded adj. narrow-minded; petty-minded.

▨ petty, mean, ungenerous, illiberal, narrow-minded, parochial, insular, rigid, hidebound.
▣ liberal, broad-minded.

smallpox noun Medicine a highly contagious viral disease, characterized by fever, vomiting, backache, and a rash that usually leaves permanent pitted scars (pocks) on the skin.

small print the details of a contract or other undertaking, often printed very small, especially when considered likely to contain unattractive conditions that the writer of the contract does not want to be noticed.

small screen (**the small screen**) television, as opposed to cinema.

small talk polite conversation about trivial matters.

small-time adj. operating on a small scale.

smarm — verb **1** to smooth or flatten (the hair) with an oily substance. **2** intrans. colloq. to be exaggeratedly and insincerely flattering or respectful. — noun colloq. exaggerated or insincere flattery.

smarmily adv. in a smarmy way.

smarminess noun being smarmy.

smarmy adj. (**smarmier, smarmiest**) colloq. **1** ingratiatingly flattering or respectful. **2** self-consciously suave or charming.

▨ **1** ingratiating, crawling, fawning, servile, obsequious, sycophantic. **2** suave, smooth, oily, unctuous.

smart — adj. **1 a** said of clothes, etc elegant and stylish. **b** said of a person neat and well-dressed. **2** clever; astute; shrewd. **3** expensive and sophisticated: a smart hotel. **4** said of pain, etc sharp and stinging. **5** brisk: at a smart pace. **6** computer-guided or electronically controlled: a smart bomb. **7** colloq. impressive; excellent. — verb intrans. **1** to feel or be the cause of a sharp stinging pain. **2** to feel or be the cause of acute irritation or distress. **3** intrans. to suffer harsh consequences or punishment. — noun a sharp stinging pain. — adv. in a smart manner. — **look smart** to hurry up. [from Anglo-Saxon smeortan]

▨ adj. **1** elegant, stylish, chic, fashionable, neat, tidy, spruce, trim, well-dressed, well-groomed. **2** clever, intelligent, bright, sharp, acute, shrewd, astute. **3** colloq. posh, luxury, fashionable, expensive, sophisticated, upmarket. **5** brisk, rapid, quick, fast. verb **1** sting, hurt, prick, burn, tingle, twinge, throb.
▣ adj. **1** dowdy, unfashionable, untidy, scruffy. **2** stupid, slow.

smart alec or **smart aleck** colloq. a person who thinks himself or herself cleverer than others; a know-all.

smart-alecky adj. characteristic of a smart-alec.

smart card a plastic card like a bank card, fitted with a microprocessor (including a memory) instead of a magnetic strip, used in commercial transactions, telecommunications, etc.

smart drug a drug designed to enhance mental powers or perception.

smarten verb trans., intrans. (**smartened, smartening**) (also **smarten up**) to make or become smarter; to brighten up.

▨ neaten, tidy, spruce up, groom, clean, brighten up.

smartly adv. in a smart way; promptly, quickly.

smash — verb **1** trans., intrans. to break violently into pieces; to destroy or be destroyed in this way. **2** to strike with violence, often causing damage: smashed his fist down on the table. **3** intrans. to burst with great force:

smashed through the door. **4** colloq. to break up or ruin completely: smash an international drugs ring. **5** to hit (a ball) with a smash. — noun **1** an act, or the sound, of smashing. **2** a powerful overhead stroke in racket sports. **3** colloq. a road traffic accident. **4** colloq. a smash hit. — adv. with a smashing sound. [imitative]

▨ verb **1** break, shatter, shiver. **2** strike, bang, bash, thump. **3** burst, crash. **4** ruin, wreck, demolish, destroy, defeat, crush. noun **3** accident, crash, collision, pile-up.

smash-and-grab adj. colloq., said of a robbery carried out by smashing a shop window and snatching the items on display.

smashed adj. colloq. extremely drunk.

smasher noun colloq. a person or thing very much liked or admired.

smash hit colloq. an overwhelming success, especially a song, film, play, etc.

smashing adj. colloq. excellent; splendid.

smash-up noun colloq. a violent road traffic accident.

smattering noun **1** a few scraps of knowledge. **2** a small amount scattered around. [from Middle English smateren, to rattle]

▨ **1** basics, rudiments, elements. **2** bit, modicum, dash, sprinkling.

smear — verb **1** to spread (something sticky or oily) thickly over (a surface). **2** trans., intrans. to make or become blurred; to smudge. **3** to say or write abusively damaging things about (someone). — noun **1** a greasy mark or patch. **2** a damaging criticism or accusation; a slur. **3** an amount of a substance, especially of cervical tissue, placed on a slide for examination under a microscope. **4** colloq. a smear test. [from Anglo-Saxon smeru, fat, grease]

▨ verb **1** daub, plaster, spread, cover, coat, rub. **2** smudge, streak. **3** defame, slander, libel, malign, vilify, blacken, sully, stain. noun **1** streak, smudge, blot, blotch, splodge, daub. **2** slur, slander, libel.

smear campaign a series of verbal or written attacks intended to defame and discredit an individual, group, or institution.

smear test an examination, under a microscope, of a small amount of tissue from a woman's cervix, to test for the presence of cervical cancer.

smeary adj. sticky, greasy; showing smears.

smegma noun a thick white secretion produced by the glands of the foreskin of the penis. [from Greek smegma, soap]

smell — noun **1** the sense by which one becomes aware of the odour of things, located in the nose. **2** the quality perceived by this sense; (an) odour or scent. **3** an unpleasant odour. **4** an act of using this sense: have a smell of this. — verb (PAST TENSE AND PAST PARTICIPLE **smelled, smelt**) **1** to be aware of, or take in, the odour of. **2** (**smell of something**) to give off an odour of it. **3** intrans. to give off an unpleasant odour. **4** to be aware of by intuition; to recognize signs or traces of: I smell a government cover-up. **5** (**smell of something**) to show signs or traces of it: an organization smelling of corruption. — **smell someone** or **something out** to track them down by smell, or as if by smell. [from Middle English smel]

▨ noun **2** odour, whiff, scent, perfume, fragrance, bouquet, aroma. **3** stench, stink, colloq. pong. verb **1** sniff, nose, scent. **3** stink, reek, colloq. pong.

smelliness noun being smelly.

smelling-salts pl. noun crystals of ammonium carbonate, whose strong sharp odour stimulates consciousness after fainting.

smelly *adj.* (**smellier**, **smelliest**) *colloq.* unpleasant-smelling.

▣ malodorous, *colloq.* pongy, stinking, reeking, foul, fetid, putrid, high.

smelt[1] *verb* to melt (ore) in order to separate out the metal it contains. [from Old German *smelten*]

smelt[2] see SMELL.

smelt[3] *noun* (PL. **smelts**, **smelt**) any of various small silvery edible fish of the salmon family. [from Anglo-Saxon *smylt*]

smelter *noun* 1 a person whose work is smelting metal. 2 an industrial plant where smelting is done.

smidgen or **smidgeon** or **smidgin** /ˈsmɪdʒən/ *noun colloq.* a very small amount: *add a smidgen of paprika.* [origin uncertain]

smile — *verb* 1 *intrans.* to turn up the corners of the mouth, often showing the teeth, usually as an expression of pleasure, favour or amusement. 2 (**smile at someone** or **something**) to react to them with such an expression. 3 to show with such an expression: *smiled his agreement* 4 (**smile on someone** or **something**) to show favour towards them. — *noun* an act or way of smiling. [from Middle English *smilen*]

▣ *verb* 1 grin, beam, simper, smirk, leer. *noun* grin, beam, simper, smirk, leer.

smiley *noun colloq.* same as EMOTICON.

smirch — *verb* 1 to make dirty; to soil or stain. 2 to damage or sully (a reputation, etc); to besmirch. — *noun* 1 a stain. 2 a smear on a reputation. [from Old French *esmorcher*, to hurt]

smirk — *verb intrans.* to smile in a self-satisfied or foolish manner. — *noun* such a smile. [from Anglo-Saxon *smercian*]

smite *verb* (PAST TENSE **smote**; PAST PARTICIPLE **smitten**) *usually literary* 1 to strike or beat with a heavy blow or blows. 2 to kill. 3 to afflict. 4 to cause to fall immediately and overpoweringly in love: *not fail to be smitten by such beauty.* 5 *intrans.* to come suddenly and forcefully: *the king's authority smote down on him.* [from Anglo-Saxon *smitan*, to smear]

smith *noun, combining form* 1 a person who makes articles in (a particular) metal: *silversmith.* 2 a blacksmith. 3 a person who makes skilful use of something: *wordsmith.* [from Anglo-Saxon *smith*]

smithereens *pl. noun colloq.* tiny fragments: *smashed it to smithereens.* [from Irish Gaelic *smidirín*, diminutive of *smiodar*, fragment]

smithy /ˈsmɪðɪ/ *noun* (PL. **smithies**) a blacksmith's workshop.

smitten past participle of SMITE. — *adj.* in love; obsessed.

SMMT *abbrev.* Society of Motor Manufacturers and Traders.

smock *noun* 1 any loose shirt-like garment worn, eg by artists, over other clothes for protection, especially one slipped over the head. 2 a woman's long loose-fitting blouse. 3 *Hist.* a loose-fitting overall of coarse linen worn by farm-workers. [from Anglo-Saxon *smoc*]

smocking *noun* decorative stitching used on gathered or tucked material.

smog *noun* fog mixed with smoke and fumes. [from SMOKE + FOG]

smoggy *adj.* (**smoggier**, **smoggiest**) like or full of smog.

smoke — *noun* 1 a visible cloud given off by a burning substance, and consisting of tiny particles of carbon dispersed in a gas or a mixture of gases, eg air. 2 visible fumes or vapours. 3 *colloq.* the act of or time spent smoking tobacco. 4 *colloq.* a cigarette or cigar. — *verb* 1 *intrans.*

to give off smoke or visible fumes or vapours. 2 *trans., intrans.* to inhale and then exhale the smoke from burning tobacco or other substances in a cigarette, cigar, or pipe, especially as a habit. 3 to preserve or flavour food by exposing it to smoke. — **go up in smoke** 1 to be completely destroyed by fire. 2 *said of plans, etc* to be ruined completely; to come to nothing. **the smoke** or **big smoke** *colloq.* the nearby big city; a country's capital city. **smoke someone** or **something out** 1 to drive an animal into the open by filling its burrow with smoke. 2 to uncover someone or something by persistent searching or investigation. [from Anglo-Saxon *smoca*]

▣ *noun* 2 fumes, exhaust, gas, vapour(s), mist, fog, smog. *verb* 1 fume, smoulder. 3 cure, dry.

smoked *adj.* 1 cured or treated with smoke. 2 darkened by smoke.

smokeless *adj.* 1 *said of a fuel* giving off little or no smoke when burned, eg coke. 2 *said of an area* **a** in which the use of smoke-producing fuel is prohibited. **b** in which tobacco-smoking is prohibited.

smoker *noun* 1 a person who smokes tobacco products. 2 a railway carriage in which tobacco-smoking is permitted.

smokescreen *noun* 1 a cloud of smoke used to conceal the movements of troops, etc. 2 anything said or done to hide or deceive.

smokestack *noun* 1 a tall industrial chimney. 2 a funnel on a ship or steam train.

smokiness *noun* being smoky.

smoking — *noun* 1 the practice of inhaling the fumes from burning cigarettes or other forms of tobacco. 2 a process used to preserve and improve the flavour of some foods (eg ham, some cheeses), which are exposed to wood smoke (usually from oak or ash) for long periods. — *adj.* in which tobacco-smoking is allowed.

smoky *adj.* (**smokier**, **smokiest**) 1 giving out much or excessive smoke. 2 filled with (especially tobacco) smoke. 3 having a smoked flavour. 4 hazy, especially in colour: *smoky blue.* 5 made dirty by smoke.

▣ 4 hazy, foggy, cloudy, murky. 5 sooty, black, grey, grimy.

smolt *noun* a young salmon migrating from fresh water to the sea. [from Scot. *smolt*]

smooch *colloq.* — *verb intrans.* 1 to kiss and cuddle. 2 to dance slowly in an embrace. — *noun* a period of smooching.

smoochy *adj.* (**smoochier**, **smoochiest**) *said of music* sentimental, romantic.

smooth — *adj.* 1 having an even regular surface; not rough, coarse, bumpy or wavy. 2 having few or no lumps; of even texture. 3 free from problems or difficulties: *a smooth journey.* 4 characterized by steady movement and a lack of jolts: *a smooth ferry crossing.* 5 not sharp or bitter: *a smooth sherry.* 6 very elegant or charming, especially self-consciously or insincerely so. — *verb* 1 (*also* **smooth something down** or **out**) to make it smooth. 2 (*usually* **smooth over something**) to cause a difficulty, etc to seem less serious or important. 3 to make easier: *smooth the way to promotion.* — *adv.* smoothly: *a smooth-running system.* — *noun* the easy, pleasurable, or trouble-free part or aspect: *take the rough with the smooth.* [from Anglo-Saxon *smoth*]

▣ *adj.* 1 level, plane, flat, even, uniform, regular, shiny, polished, glassy, glossy, silky, sleek. 3 easy, effortless. 4 steady, flowing, unbroken, undisturbed, calm, tranquil, peaceful. 6 suave, agreeable, smooth-talking, glib, plausible, persuasive, slick, *colloq.* smarmy, unctuous, ingratiating. *verb* 1 iron, press, roll, flatten, level, plane, file, sand, polish. 3 ease.

⊟ *adj.* ROUGH. **1**, **2** coarse, lumpy. **4** unsteady, bumpy, choppy. *verb* **1** roughen, wrinkle, crease.

smoothie or **smoothy** *noun* (PL. **smoothies**) *colloq.* a very elegant or charming person, especially one self-consciously or insincerely so.

smooth muscle *Anat.* see INVOLUNTARY MUSCLE.

smooth snake a harmless European snake having smooth scales and a dark horizontal line on the side of the head.

smooth-talking or **smooth-tongued** *adj.* **1** exaggeratedly and insincerely flattering. **2** charmingly persuasive.

smorgasbord /'smɔːgəsbɔːd/ *noun* an assortment of hot and cold savoury dishes served as a buffet. [from Swedish *smörgåsbord*, from *smörgås*, open sandwich + *bord*, table]

smote see SMITE.

smother *verb* (**smothered, smothering**) **1** to cause to die from lack of air, especially with an obstruction over the mouth and nose; to suffocate. **2** to extinguish (a fire) by cutting off the air supply, eg by throwing a blanket over it. **3** to cover with a thick layer: *bread smothered with jam.* **4** to give an oppressive or stifling amount to: *smothered the children with love.* **5** to suppress or contain (eg laughter). [from Middle English *smorther*, from Anglo-Saxon *smorian*]

⊟ **1** suffocate, asphyxiate, strangle, throttle, choke, stifle. **2** extinguish, snuff. **3** cover, envelop, wrap. **5** muffle, suppress, contain, repress, hide, conceal.

smoulder — *verb intrans.* (**smouldered, smouldering**) **1** to burn slowly or without flame. **2** to linger on in a suppressed state: *smouldering anger.* — *noun* a smouldering fire or emotion. [from Middle English *smolder*]

⊟ *verb* **1** burn, smoke, fume. **2** seethe, simmer.

smudge — *noun* **1** a mark or blot spread by rubbing. **2** a faint or blurred shape, eg an object seen from afar. — *verb* **1** to make a smudge on or of. **2** *intrans.* to become a smudge.

⊟ *noun* **1** blot, stain, smear, streak. **2** blur. *verb* **1** blur, smear, mark, spot, stain, soil.

smudgy *adj.* (**smudgier, smudgiest**) smudged.

smug *adj.* (**smugger, smuggest**) arrogantly pleased with oneself; self-satisfied. [from German dialect *smuck*, neat]

⊟ complacent, self-satisfied, arrogant, conceited, superior, holier-than-thou, self-righteous, priggish.

⊟ modest, humble.

smuggle *verb* **1** to take (goods) into or out of a country secretly and illegally, eg to avoid paying duty. **2** to bring or take secretly, usually breaking a rule or restriction. [from German dialect *smuggeln*]

smuggler *noun* a person who smuggles.

smuggling *noun* illegal import or export; conveying illegally.

smut — *noun* **1** soot. **2** a speck of dirt or soot. **3** mildly obscene language, pictures or images. **4** any of a group of parasitic fungi, some of which cause a serious disease of cereal crops such as wheat, maize, and oats, characterized by the appearance of masses of black spores, resembling soot, on the leaves and other plant surfaces. **5** the disease caused by such a fungus. — *verb* (**smutted, smutting**) to dirty or affect with smut. [from Middle English *smotten*, to stain]

smuttiness *noun* being smutty.

smutty *adj.* (**smuttier, smuttiest**) **1** dirtied by smut. **2** mildly obscene.

Sn *symbol Chem.* tin.

snack *noun* a light meal quickly taken, or a bite to eat between meals. [perhaps from Old Dutch *snacken*, to snap]

⊟ refreshment(s), bite, nibble, titbit.

snack bar a café, kiosk, or counter serving snacks.

snaffle — *noun* a simple bridle-bit for a horse. — *verb* **1** to fit (a horse) with a snaffle. **2** *colloq.* to take sneakily or without permission.

snag — *noun* **1** a problem or drawback. **2** a sharp or jagged edge on which clothes, etc could get caught. **3** a hole or tear in clothes, etc caused by such catching. **4** a part of a tree submerged in water, hazardous to navigation. — *verb* (**snagged, snagging**) to catch or tear on a snag. [from perhaps Norse *snagi*, peg]

⊟ *noun* **1** disadvantage, inconvenience, drawback, catch, problem, difficulty, complication, setback, hitch, obstacle, stumbling-block. *verb* catch, rip, tear, hole, ladder.

snail *noun* any of over 80,000 species of mollusc belonging to the same class (Gastropoda) as slugs, but carrying a coiled or conical shell on its back, into which the whole body can be withdrawn for safety. — **at a snail's pace** extremely slowly. [from Anglo-Saxon *snæl*]

snail mail *facetious* normal, as opposed to electronic, mail.

snake — *noun* **1** any of about 2300 species of a carnivorous reptile having a long narrow body covered with scaly skin, and belonging to the same order (Squamata) as lizards, but differing from lizards in that it lacks limbs, moveable eyelids, or visible ears. **2** any long and flexible or winding thing or shape. **3** *colloq.* (**snake in the grass**) a treacherous person; a friend revealed to be an enemy. — *verb intrans.* to move windingly or follow a winding course. [from Anglo-Saxon *snaca*]

snakebite *noun* **1** the wound or poisoned condition caused by the bite of a venomous snake. **2** *colloq.* a drink of cider and beer or lager in equal measures.

snake-charmer *noun* a street entertainer who seemingly induces snakes to perform rhythmical movements, especially by playing music.

snakes and ladders a game played with counters and dice on a board marked with an ascending path on which ladders allow short cuts to the goal and snakes force one to go back towards the beginning.

snakily *adv.* in a snaky way, like a snake.

snaky *adj.* (**snakier, snakiest**) **1** like a snake, especially long, thin, and flexible or winding. **2** treacherous or cruelly deceitful.

snap — *verb* (**snapped, snapping**) **1** *trans.*, *intrans.* to break suddenly and cleanly with a sharp cracking noise: *snapped the stick over his knee.* **2** *trans.*, *intrans.* to move quickly and forcefully with a sharp sound: *the lid snapped shut.* **3** *intrans.* (**snap at something**) to make a biting or grasping movement towards it. **4** (**snap at someone**) to speak abruptly with anger or impatience. **5** *colloq.* to take a photograph of, especially spontaneously and with simple equipment. **6** *intrans. colloq.* to lose one's senses or self-control suddenly. — *noun* **1** the act or sound of snapping. **2** *colloq.* a photograph, especially taken spontaneously and with simple equipment. **3** a catch or other fastening that closes with a snapping sound. **4** a crisp biscuit or savoury. **5** (*also* **cold snap**) a sudden brief period of cold weather. **6** a card game in which all the cards played are collected by the first player to shout 'snap' whenever matching cards are laid down by consecutive players. — *interj.* **1** the word shouted in the card game. **2** the word used to highlight any matching pair. — *adj.* taken or made spontaneously, without long consideration: *a snap decision.* — *adv.* with a snapping sound. — **snap one's fingers 1** to make a short loud snapping sound by flicking one's fingers sharply, usually to attract attention. **2** to show contempt or defiance. **snap out of it** *colloq.* to bring oneself out of a state or condition, eg of sulking or depression. **snap something up** to acquire or seize it eagerly: *snapped up the opportunity.* [probably from Dutch *snappen*]

. . . .

⊟ *verb* **1** break, crack, split, separate. **3** bite, nip, snatch, seize, grasp. **4** growl at, snarl at. *noun* **1** break, crack, bite, nip. **2** snapshot, photograph, photo. *adj.* immediate, instant, on-the-spot, abrupt, sudden.

. . . .

snapdragon *noun* an antirrhinum, a garden plant whose flower, when pinched, opens and closes like a mouth.

snapper *noun* a deep-bodied fish that is widespread and locally common in tropical seas, so called because it has long conical front teeth and highly mobile jaws.

snappily *adv.* in a snappy way, curtly.

snappiness *noun* being snappy.

snappy *adj.* (**snappier, snappiest**) **1** irritable; inclined to snap. **2** smart and fashionable: *a snappy dresser.* **3** lively: *at a snappy tempo.* — **make it snappy!** *colloq.* hurry up!; be quick about it!

. . . .

⊟ **1** cross, irritable, edgy, touchy, brusque, quick-tempered, crabbed, testy. **2** smart, stylish, chic, fashionable, *colloq.* trendy. **3** lively, energetic, brisk, quick, hasty.
⊞ **1** good-natured. **2** dowdy. **3** slow.

. . . .

snapshot *noun* a photograph, especially taken spontaneously and with simple equipment.

snare — *noun* **1** an animal trap, especially one with a string or wire noose to catch the animal's foot. **2** anything that traps or entangles. **3** the set of wires fitted to a snare drum. — *verb* to trap or entangle in, or as if in, a snare. [from Anglo-Saxon *sneare*]

. . . .

⊟ *noun* **1** trap, wire, net, noose. **2** trap, catch, pitfall. *verb* trap, ensnare, entrap, catch, net, entangle, enmesh.

. . . .

snare drum a medium-sized drum sitting horizontally, with a set of wires fitted to its underside that rattle sharply when the drum is struck.

snarl[1] — *verb* **1** *intrans., said of an animal* to growl angrily, showing the teeth. **2** *trans., intrans.* to speak or say aggressively in anger or irritation. — *noun* **1** an act of snarling. **2** a snarling sound or facial expression.

snarl[2] — *noun* **1** a knotted or tangled mass. **2** a confused or congested situation or state. — *verb* (*also* **snarl up**) **1** to make knotted, tangled, confused, or congested. **2** *intrans.* to become knotted, tangled, confused, or congested. [related to SNARE]

. . . .

⊟ *noun* **1** tangle, knot. *verb* TANGLE, KNOT. **1** entangle, enmesh, embroil, confuse, muddle, complicate, congest.

. . . .

snarl-up *noun colloq.* any muddled or congested situation, especially a traffic jam.

snatch — *verb* **1** to seize or grab suddenly. **2** *intrans.* to make a sudden grabbing movement. **3** to pull suddenly and forcefully: *snatched her hand away.* **4** *colloq.* to take or have as soon as the opportunity arises: *snatch a bite to eat.* — *noun* **1** an act of snatching. **2** a fragment overheard or remembered: *a few snatches of the old song.* **3** a brief period: *snatches of rest between long shifts.* **4** *colloq.* a robbery. [from Middle English *snacchen*]

. . . .

⊟ *verb* **1** grab, seize, take, *colloq.* nab, clutch, grasp, grip. **3** pull, wrench, wrest.

. . . .

snazzily *adv.* in a snazzy way.

snazzy *adj.* (**snazzier, snazziest**) *colloq.* fashionably smart or elegant.

SNCF *abbrev. Société Nationale des Chemins de Fer Français* (French), French national railways.

sneak — *verb* **1** *intrans.* to move or go quietly and avoiding notice. **2** to bring or take secretly, especially breaking a rule or prohibition: *sneaked a girl into his room/sneak a look at the letter.* **3** *intrans. colloq.* to inform about someone. — *noun colloq.* a person who sneaks; a tell-tale. [perhaps from Anglo-Saxon *snican*, to creep]

. . . .

⊟ *verb* **1** creep, steal, slip, slink, sidle, skulk, lurk, prowl. **2** smuggle. **3** tell tales, *slang* split, inform, *slang* grass. *noun* tell-tale, informer, *slang* grass.

. . . .

sneakers *pl. noun esp. North Amer., esp. US* sports shoes; training shoes.

sneakily *adv.* in a sneaky way.

sneaking *adj., said of a feeling, etc* slight but not easy to suppress.

. . . .

⊟ private, secret, hidden, lurking, suppressed, nagging, niggling, persistent.

. . . .

sneak thief a thief who enters premises through unlocked doors or windows, without breaking in.

sneaky *adj.* (**sneakier, sneakiest**) done or operating with secretive unfairness or dishonesty; underhand.

sneer — *verb* **1** *intrans.* to show scorn or contempt, especially by drawing the top lip up at one side. **2** *trans.* to say scornfully or contemptuously. — *noun* an expression of scorn or contempt made with a raised lip, or otherwise.

. . . .

⊟ *verb* **1** deride, scoff, jeer, mock, snigger. *noun* jeer, snigger.

. . . .

sneering *adj.* contemptuous, scornful.

sneeze — *verb intrans.* to blow air out through the nose suddenly, violently, and involuntarily, especially because of irritation in the nostrils. — *noun* an act or the sound of sneezing. — **not to be sneezed at** *colloq.* not to be disregarded or overlooked. [from Anglo-Saxon *fnesan*]

snick — *noun* **1** a small cut; a nick. **2** *Cricket* a glancing contact with the edge of the bat. — *verb* **1** to make a small cut in. **2** *Cricket* to hit with a snick.

snicker same as SNIGGER.

snide *adj.* expressing criticism or disapproval in an indirect way intended to offend.

. . . .

⊟ derogatory, disparaging, sarcastic, scornful, sneering, hurtful, offensive, unkind, nasty, spiteful, malicious.
⊞ complimentary.

. . . .

sniff — *verb* **1** *intrans.* to draw in air through the nose in short sharp bursts, eg when crying. **2** *trans., intrans.* (**sniff something** or **sniff at something**) to smell it in this way. **3** to inhale the fumes from (a dangerous or addictive substance). — *noun* an act or the sound of sniffing. — **not to be sniffed at** *colloq.* not to be disregarded or overlooked: *an offer not to be sniffed at.* **sniff someone** or **something out** to discover or detect them by, or as if by, the sense of smell. [imitative]

. . . .

⊟ *verb* **1** breathe, inhale, sniffle, snuffle. **2** smell, nose, scent.

. . . .

sniffer dog a dog specially trained to seek out or locate illicit or dangerous substances (eg illegal drugs, explosives, etc) by smell.

sniffily *adv.* in a sniffy way.

sniffle — *verb intrans.* to sniff repeatedly, eg because of having a cold. — *noun* **1** an act or the sound of sniffling. **2** (*also* **sniffles**) *colloq.* a slight cold.

sniffy *adj.* (**sniffier, sniffiest**) *colloq.* **1** contemptuous or disdainful. **2** sniffing repeatedly, or feeling that one wants to, because of having a cold.

snifter *noun slang* a drink of alcohol, especially alcoholic spirit; a tipple or dram. [from dialect *snift*, to sniff]

snigger — *verb intrans.* (**sniggered, sniggering**) to laugh quietly in a foolish or mocking way. — *noun* such a laugh. [imitative]

⊟ *verb, noun* laugh, giggle, titter, chuckle, sneer.

snip — *verb* (**snipped, snipping**) to cut, especially with a single quick action or actions with scissors. — *noun* **1** an act or the action of snipping. **2** a small piece snipped off. **3** a small cut or notch. **4** *colloq.* a bargain. **5** *colloq.* a certainty; a thing easily done. [from Dutch *snippen*]

⊟ *verb* cut, clip, trim, crop, dock, slit, nick, notch. *noun* **2** snippet, scrap, piece, cutting, clipping. **3** cut, nick, notch.

snipe — *noun* **1** a marshland wading bird with a long straight bill. **2** a quick verbal attack or criticism. — *verb intrans.* (**snipe at someone**) **1** to shoot at them from a hidden position. **2** to criticize them bad-temperedly. [from Middle English *snipe*]

sniper *noun* a person who shoots from a concealed position.

snippet *noun* a scrap, eg of information. [see SNIP]

⊟ piece, scrap, snip, cutting, clipping, shred, fragment, part, portion, segment, section.

snitch *slang* — *noun* **1** the nose. **2** an informer. — *verb* **1** *intrans.* to betray others; to inform. **2** *trans.* to steal; to pilfer.

snitcher *noun slang* an informer.

snivel — *verb intrans.* (**snivelled, snivelling**) **1** to whine or complain tearfully. **2** to have a runny nose. — *noun* an act of snivelling. [from Anglo-Saxon *snofl*, mucus]

SNO *abbrev.* **1** Scottish National Orchestra (now RSNO). **2** Scottish National Opera.

snob *noun* **1** a person who places too high a value on social status, admiring those higher up the social ladder and despising those lower down. **2** a person who judges a thing solely according to the values of those people regarded as socially or intellectually superior: *a wine snob*.

snobbery *noun* **1** snobbishness. **2** snobbish behaviour.

⊟ **1** snobbishness, superciliousness, *colloq.* snootiness, loftiness, condescension, arrogance, pride.

snobbish *adj.* characteristic of a snob.

⊟ snobby, supercilious, disdainful, *colloq.* snooty, *colloq.* stuck-up, *colloq.* toffee-nosed, superior, lofty, high and mighty, arrogant, pretentious, affected, condescending, patronizing.

snobbishness *noun* being snobbish.

snobby *adj.* (**snobbier, snobbiest**) snobbish.

snog *slang* — *verb intrans.* (**snogged, snogging**) to kiss and cuddle. — *noun* a kiss and cuddle.

snood *noun* **1** a pouch of netting or fabric worn by women on the back of the head, to keep hair in a bundle. **2** a hood formed from a piece of woollen material, worn as a fashion garment. [from Anglo-Saxon *snod*]

snook — **cock a snook at someone** *colloq.* **1** to put the thumb to the nose and wave the fingers at them, as a gesture of contempt or defiance. **2** to express open contempt for them.

snooker — *noun* **1** a game in which long leather-tipped sticks are used to force a white ball to knock coloured balls into holes on the corners and sides of a large cloth-covered table. **2** in this game, a position in which the path between the white ball and the target ball is obstructed by another ball. — *verb* (**snookered, snookering**) **1** in snooker, to force (an opponent) to attempt to hit an obstructed target ball. **2** *colloq.* to thwart (a person or plan).

snoop — *verb intrans.* to go about inquisitively; to pry. — *noun* **1** an act of snooping. **2** a person who snoops. [from Dutch *snoepen*, to eat or steal]

⊟ *verb* spy, sneak, pry, nose, interfere, meddle.

snooper *noun* a person who snoops.

snootily *adv.* in a snooty way.

snootiness *noun* being snooty.

snooty *adj.* (**snootier, snootiest**) *colloq.* haughty; snobbish.

snooze — *verb intrans.* to sleep lightly; to doze. — *noun* a period of light sleeping, especially when brief; a nap.

⊟ *verb* nap, doze, sleep, *slang* kip. *noun* nap, catnap, *colloq.* forty winks, doze, siesta, sleep, *slang* kip.

snore — *verb intrans.* to breathe heavily and with a snorting sound while sleeping. — *noun* an act or the sound of snoring. [imitative]

snorkel — *noun* **1** a rigid tube through which air from above the surface of water can be drawn into the mouth while one is swimming just below the surface. **2** a set of tubes on a submarine extended above the surface of the sea to take in air and release exhaust gases. — *verb intrans.* (**snorkelled, snorkelling**) to swim with a snorkel. [from German *Schnorchel*]

snort — *verb* **1** *intrans.*, *said especially of animals* to force air violently and noisily out through the nostrils; to make a similar noise while taking air in. **2** *trans.*, *intrans.* to speak or say in this way, especially expressing contempt or anger. **3** *slang* to inhale (a powdered drug, especially cocaine) through the nose. — *noun* **1** an act or the sound of snorting. **2** *colloq.* a small drink of alcoholic spirit. **3** *slang* an amount of a powdered drug inhaled in one breath. [from Middle English *snorten*]

snot *noun* **1** *coarse slang* mucus of the nose. **2** *derog.* a contemptible person. [from Anglo-Saxon *gesnot*]

snottily *adv. colloq.* in a snotty way.

snottiness *noun colloq.* being snotty.

snotty *adj.* (**snottier, snottiest**) *colloq.* **1** *coarse slang* covered or dripping with nasal mucus: *snotty-nosed kids.* **2** haughty; having or showing contempt. **3** *derog.* contemptible; worthless: *I don't want your snotty advice.*

snout *noun* **1** the projecting nose and mouth parts of certain animals, eg the pig. **2** *colloq.* the human nose. **3** any projecting part. [from Old German *snut*]

snow — *noun* **1** frozen water vapour falling to the ground in soft white flakes, or lying on the ground as a soft white mass. **2** a fall of this: *heavy snows.* **3** *colloq.* flickering white speckles on a television screen caused by interference or a poor signal. **4** *slang* cocaine. — *verb intrans.*, *said of snow* to fall. — **be snowed under** be overwhelmed with work, etc. **snow someone in** or **up** to bury or block them with snow. [from Anglo-Saxon *snaw*]

snowball — *noun* a small mass of snow pressed hard together, used by children as a missile. — *verb* **1** *trans.*, *intrans.* to throw snowballs (at). **2** *intrans.* to develop or increase rapidly and uncontrollably.

snowberry *noun* (PL. **snowberries**) *Bot.* **1** a N American shrub (*Symphoricarpos albus*) of the honeysuckle family. **2** a white berry of this shrub.

snow-blind *adj.* affected by snow blindness.

snow blindness severely (but temporarily) impaired eyesight caused by prolonged exposure of the eyes to bright sunlight reflected by snow.

snowboard — *noun* a board resembling a wheel-less skateboard, used on snow. — *verb intrans.* to ski on a snowboard.

snowboarding *noun* the sport of skiing on a snowboard.

snowbound *adj.* shut in or prevented from travelling because of heavy falls of snow.

snow bunting a black-and-white (in summer, partly tawny) bunting of Arctic regions, a winter visitor in Britain.

snowcap *noun* a cap of snow, as on the polar regions or a mountain-top.

snow-capped *adj.*, *said especially of mountains* with a covering of snow on the top.

snowdrift *noun* a bank of snow blown together by the wind.

snowdrop *noun* a European plant of the daffodil family producing small white drooping flowers in early spring.

snowfall *noun* 1 a fall of snow. 2 an amount of fallen snow.

snowflake *noun* any of the single small feathery clumps of crystals of frozen water vapour that snow is made up of.

snow goose a white Arctic American goose with black-tipped wings.

snow leopard a large wild cat with long soft creamy or pale-grey fur patterned with black rosette spots, found in the mountains of central Asia. Also called OUNCE.

snowline *noun* the level or height on a mountain or other upland area above which there is a permanent covering of snow, or where snow accumulates seasonally.

snowman *noun* a crude human figure made of packed snow.

snowmobile *noun* a motorized vehicle, on skis or tracks, for travelling on snow.

snowplough *noun* 1 a large shovel-like device for clearing snow from roads or tracks. 2 a vehicle or train fitted with this.

snowshoe *noun* either of a pair of racket-like frameworks strapped to the feet for walking over deep snow.

snowy *adj.* (**snowier, snowiest**) 1 abounding or covered with snow. 2 white like snow. 3 pure.

snowy owl *Zool.* an owl native to northern regions of the N hemisphere, that inhabits tundra, marshes, and Arctic islands, and is so called because it has mainly white plumage.

SNP *abbrev.* Scottish National Party.

Snr or **snr** *abbrev.* senior.

snub — *verb* (**snubbed, snubbing**) to insult by openly ignoring, rejecting, or otherwise showing contempt. — *noun* an act of snubbing. — *adj.*, *said of a nose* short and flat. [from Norse *snubba*, to scold]

⊟ *verb* rebuff, brush off, cut, cold-shoulder, ignore, *slang* blank, reject, slight, rebuke, *colloq.* put down, squash, humble, shame, humiliate, mortify. *noun* rebuff, brush-off, slight, affront, insult, rebuke, *colloq.* put-down, humiliation.

snuff¹ — *noun* powdered tobacco for inhaling through the nose. — *verb intrans.* to take snuff. [from Old Dutch *snuffen*, to snuffle]

snuff² — *verb* 1 (*also* **snuff something out**) to extinguish a candle. 2 to snip off the burnt part of the wick of (a candle or lamp). 3 (*also* **snuff something out**) to put an end to it: *tried to snuff out all opposition.* — *noun* the burnt part of the wick of a lamp or candle. — **snuff it** *slang* to die. [from Middle English *snoffe*]

snuffbox *noun* a small lidded (especially metal) container for snuff.

snuffle — *verb* 1 *intrans.* to breathe, especially breathe in, through a partially blocked nose. 2 *trans., intrans.* to say or speak in a nasal tone. 3 *intrans.* to snivel. — *noun* 1 the sound of breathing through a partially blocked nose. 2 (**the snuffles**) *colloq.* a slight cold. [see SNUFF¹]

snuff movie or **snuff film** *slang* a pornographic film in which the climax is the real-life murder of one of the participants.

snug *adj.* (**snugger, snuggest**) 1 enjoying or providing warmth, comfort, and shelter; cosy. 2 comfortably close-fitting. *noun* a small comfortable room or compartment in a pub.

⊟ *adj.* 1 cosy, warm, comfortable, homely, friendly, intimate, sheltered, secure. 2 close-fitting, figure-hugging, tight.

snuggery *noun* (PL. **snuggeries**) *Brit.* a small comfortable room or compartment in a pub.

snuggle *verb intrans.* (*usually* **snuggle down** or **in**) to settle oneself into a position of warmth and comfort.

SO *abbrev.* standing order.

so¹ — *adv.* 1 to such an extent: *so expensive that nobody buys it.* 2 to this, that, or the same extent; as: *this one is lovely, but that one is not so nice.* 3 extremely: *she is so talented!* 4 in that state or condition: *promised to be faithful, and has remained so.* 5 also; likewise: *she's my friend and so are you.* 6 used to avoid repeating a previous statement: *you've to take your medicine because I said so.* — *conj.* 1 therefore; thereafter: *he insulted me, so I hit him.* 2 (*also* **so that ...**) in order that: *lend me the book, so that I can read it.* — *adj.* the case; true: *you think I'm mad, but it's not so.* — *interj.* used to express discovery: *so, that's what you've been doing!* — **and so on** or **and so forth** or **and so on and so forth** and more of the same; continuing in the same way. **just so** neatly, precisely, or perfectly: *with her hair arranged just so.* ... **or so** approximately: *five or so days ago.* **so as to ...** in order to ...; in such a way as to ... **so be it** used to express acceptance or defiant resignation. **so much** or **many** 1 such a lot: *so much work to do!* 2 just; mere: *politicians squabbling like so many children.* **so much for ...** nothing has come of ...; that has disposed of or ruined: *so much for all our plans!* **so to speak** or **to say** used as an apology for an unfamiliar or slightly inappropriate expression. **so what?** *colloq.* that is of no importance or consequence at all. [from Anglo-Saxon *swa*]

so² same as SOH.

soak — *verb* 1 *trans.* to stand or leave to stand in a liquid for some time. 2 to make thoroughly wet; to drench. 3 (*also* **soak in** or **through**) to penetrate or pass. 4 (*also* **soak something up**) to absorb it. — *noun* 1 an act of soaking. 2 *colloq.* a long period of lying in a bath. 3 *colloq.* a person who habitually drinks a lot of alcohol. [from Anglo-Saxon *socian*]

⊟ *verb* 1 steep, marinate, souse. 2 wet, drench, saturate. 3 penetrate, permeate, infuse. 4 absorb, imbibe.

soaked *adj.* 1 drenched, saturated, steeped. 2 *colloq.* drunk.

soaking *adj.* wet, drenched.

⊟ soaked, drenched, sodden, waterlogged, saturated, sopping, wringing, dripping, streaming.
⊟ dry.

so-and-so *noun colloq.* 1 a person whose name one does not know or cannot remember. 2 used in place of a vulgar word: *you crafty little so-and-so!*

soap — *noun* 1 a sodium or potassium salt of a fatty acid (an acid derived from a fat) that is soluble in water and has detergent properties, ie it dissolves grease and acts as a wetting agent. 2 such a substance used as a cleaning agent in the form of a solid block, liquid, or powder. 3 *colloq.* a soap opera. — *verb* to apply soap to. — **soap someone up** *colloq.* to charm or persuade them with flattery. [from Anglo-Saxon *sape*]

soapbox *noun* an improvised platform for public speech-making, originally an upturned crate for carrying soap.

soap opera a radio or television series dealing with the daily life and troubles of a regular group of characters, originally applied to those sponsored in the USA by soap manufacturing companies.

soapstone *noun* a soft (usually grey or brown) variety of the talc mineral, widely used for ornamental carvings.

soapy *adj.* (**soapier, soapiest**) 1 like soap. 2 containing soap. 3 smeared with soap. 4 covered with soapsuds.

soar *verb intrans.* 1 to fly high into the air. 2 to glide through the air at a high altitude. 3 to rise sharply to a great height or level: *temperatures soaring* [from Old French *essorer*, to expose to air by raising up]

☐ **1** fly, wing, climb, ascend, rise. **2** fly, glide, plane. **3** climb, ascend, rise, mount, escalate, rocket.
☒ FALL, PLUMMET.

sob — *verb* (**sobbed, sobbing**) **1** *intrans.* to cry uncontrollably with intermittent gulps for breath. **2** *trans.* to say while crying in this way. — *noun* a gulp for breath between bouts of crying. [imitative]

☐ *verb* **1** cry, weep, bawl, howl, blubber, snivel.

sober — *adj.* **1** not at all drunk. **2** serious or solemn; not frivolous. **3** suggesting sedateness or seriousness rather than exuberance or frivolity: *sober clothes.* **4** plain; unembellished: *the sober truth.* — *verb trans., intrans.* (**sobered, sobering**) **1** (**sober down** or **sober someone down**) to become or make someone quieter, less excited, etc. **2** (**sober up** or **sober someone up**) to become or make someone free from the effects of alcohol. [from Latin *sobrius*, from *se-*, not + *ebrius*, drunk]

☐ *adj.* **1** teetotal, temperate, moderate, abstinent, abstemious. **2** solemn, dignified, serious, staid, sedate, quiet, serene, calm, composed, dispassionate, level-headed, reasonable, rational, clear-headed. **3** sombre, drab, dull, plain, subdued, restrained.
☒ *adj.* **1** drunk, intemperate. **2** frivolous, excited. **3** flashy, garish.

sobering *adj.* provoking serious reflection: *a sobering thought.*

sobriety /sə'braɪətɪ/ *noun* the state of being sober, especially not drunk. [from Latin *sobrietas*]

sobriquet or **soubriquet** /'soʊbrɪkeɪ/ *noun literary* a nickname. [from French *sobriquet*]

sob-story *noun colloq.* a story of personal misfortune told in order to gain sympathy.

Soc. *abbrev.* **1** Socialist. **2** Society.

soca /'soʊkə/ *noun* a type of Caribbean calypso incorporating elements of American soul music. [from SOUL + CALYPSO]

so-called *adj.* known or presented as such (with the implication that the term is wrongly or inappropriately used): *a panel of so-called experts.*

☐ alleged, supposed, purported, ostensible, nominal, self-styled, professed, would-be, pretended.

soccer *noun* Association Football. [formed from the abbreviation *assoc.* = association]

sociability or **sociableness** *noun* being sociable.

sociable *adj.* **1** fond of the company of others; friendly. **2** characterized by friendliness: *a sociable meeting.* [from Latin *sociabilis*; see SOCIAL]

☐ FRIENDLY, WARM. **1** outgoing, gregarious, affable, companionable, genial, cordial, hospitable, neighbourly, approachable, accessible, familiar. **2** convivial, informal.
☒ UNFRIENDLY, HOSTILE. **1** unsociable, withdrawn.

social — *adj.* **1** of or for people or society as a whole: *social policies.* **2** relating to the organization and behaviour of people in societies or communities: *social studies.* **3** tending or needing to live with others; not solitary: *social creatures.* **4** intended for or promoting friendly gatherings of people: *a social club.* — *noun* **1** a social gathering, especially one organized by a club or other group. **2** (**the social**) *colloq.* social security. [from Latin *socius*, companion]

☐ *adj.* **1** communal, public, community, common, general, collective, group. *noun* **1** party, *colloq.* do, get-together, gathering.

social action *Politics* action taken by a group or movement to achieve some reform or to promote a particular cause, outside the normal or formal channels of a government or political system, and aimed at gaining support from the wider public.

social anthropology the study of living societies with a view to establishing, by comparison, the range of variation in social organization, institutions, etc, and the reasons for these differences.

social behaviourism a school of thought in social psychology which holds that all observable social action is in response to the hidden needs, desires, and beliefs of the deeper 'self'.

Social Chapter a social charter agreed by members of the European Community in 1991, dealing especially with employment rights.

social cleansing the killing or forced removal of those considered socially undesirable from a particular area.

social climber *often derog.* a person who seeks to gain higher social status, often by despicable methods.

social contract an agreement between individuals within a society to work together for the benefit of all, often involving the sacrifice of some personal freedoms.

social democracy a branch of socialism which supports gradual social change through reform within a framework of democratic politics rather than by revolutionary means.

social democrat **1** a supporter of social democracy. **2** a member of a social democratic party.

Social Democratic Party (ABBREV. **SDP**) a UK political party which merged with the Liberal Party to become the Social and Liberal Democratic Party.

social engineering a term used (often critically) to describe the techniques dominant social groups may use to manipulate the subordinate population. It is applied in particular to the policies of government that lack democratic accountability.

social exclusion lack of access to, and opportunities in, areas of society such as employment and housing.

socialism *noun* a political doctrine or system which aims to create a classless society by removing the nation's wealth (land, industries, transport systems, etc) out of private and into public hands.

socialist — *noun* a supporter of socialism. — *adj.* relating to or characteristic of socialism.

socialite *noun* a person who mixes with people of high social status.

socialization or **socialisation** *noun* **1** the act or process of socializing. **2** the process by which infants and young children become aware of society and their relationships with others.

socialize or **socialise** *verb* **1** *intrans.* to meet with people on an informal, friendly basis. **2** *intrans.* to circulate among guests at a party; to mingle. **3** to organize into societies or communities.

☐ **1** mix, fraternize, get together, go out, entertain. **2** circulate, mingle.

social mobility the way individuals or groups move (upwards or downwards) from one status or class position to another within the social hierarchy.

social realism *Art* a term current in art criticism since World War II, referring to pictures which treat 'real-life' subjects in a way that challenges the values of 'bourgeois' society.

social sciences those subjects that deal with the organization and behaviour of people in societies and communities, including sociology, anthropology, economics, and history.

social scientist an expert in social science.

social security **1** a system by which members of a society pay money into a common fund, from which payments are made to individuals in times of unemployment, illness, and old age. **2** a payment or scheme of payments from such a fund.

social services services provided by local or national government for the general welfare of people in society, eg housing, education, and health.

social work work in any of the services provided by local government for the care of underprivileged people.

social worker an official who carries out social work.

society *noun* (PL. **societies**) **1** mankind as a whole, or a part of it such as one nation, considered as a single community. **2** a division of mankind with common characteristics, eg of nationality, race, or religion. **3** an organized group or association. **4** the rich and fashionable section of the upper class: *a society wedding*. **5** *formal* company: *prefers the society of women*. [from Latin *societas*]

         · · · · · · · · · · · · · · · · · · ·

▣ **1** mankind, humanity, civilization, culture. **2** community, population, nation, people. **3** club, circle, group, association, organization, league, union, guild, fellowship, fraternity, brotherhood, sisterhood, sorority. **4** upper class, aristocracy, gentry, nobility, elite. **5** company, companionship, fellowship, camaraderie, friendship.

· ·

socio- *combining form* forming words meaning 'social, of society or sociology': *socioeconomic*.

sociobiology *noun Psychol.* the integrated study of the biological basis of social behaviour, based on the assumption that all behaviour is adaptive.

sociogram *noun* a graphic representation of a network of social relationships.

sociolinguistics *sing. noun* the study of the relationships between language and the society which uses it.

sociological *adj.* **1** relating to or involving sociology. **2** dealing or concerned with social questions and problems of human society.

sociologist *noun* an expert in sociology.

sociology *noun* the scientific study of the nature, structure, and workings of human society. [from Latin *socius*, companion + -LOGY]

sociometry *noun* a technique for mapping social networks. The networks are based on respondents ranking those people they find more or less desirable. The technique can be used by psychologists to build up a theory of association between people.

sock¹ *noun* a fabric covering for the foot and ankle, sometimes reaching to the knee, worn inside a shoe or boot. — **pull one's socks up** *colloq.* to make an effort to do better. **put a sock in it** *slang* to become silent; to be quiet. [from Anglo-Saxon *socc*, light shoe]

sock² *slang* — *verb* to hit with a powerful blow. — *noun* a powerful blow. — **sock it to someone** *slang* to make a powerful impression on them.

socket *noun* **1** a specially-shaped hole or set of holes into which something is fitted: *an electrical socket*. **2** a hollow structure in the body into which another part fits: *a ball-and-socket joint*. [from Old French *soket*]

socle /ˈsoʊkl/ *noun Archit.* a plain projecting block or plinth at the base of a wall, column, or pier. [from French, from Latin *socculus*, diminutive of *soccus*, a shoe]

Socratic /səˈkratɪk/ *adj.* relating to the Greek philosopher Socrates (469–399 BC), his philosophy, or his method of teaching or inquiry by a series of questions and answers.

sod¹ *noun* **1** a slab of earth with grass growing on it; a turf. **2** *poetic* the ground. [from Old German *sode*]

sod² *coarse slang* — *noun* **1** a term of abuse for a person. **2** a person in general: *lucky sod*. — *verb* used as an exclamation of annoyance or contempt: *sod the lot of them*. — **sod all** *coarse slang* nothing at all. **sod off** *coarse slang* go away. [a shortening of SODOMITE]

soda *noun* **1** a common name given to any of various compounds of sodium in everyday use, eg sodium carbonate (*washing soda*) or sodium bicarbonate (*baking soda*). **2** soda water. **3** *North Amer., esp. US* a fizzy soft drink of any kind. [from Latin *soda*]

soda ash *Chem.* the common name for the commercial grade of anhydrous sodium carbonate (Na_2CO_3), a

greyish-white powder that is soluble in water, and used in soaps, detergents, paper and glass manufacture, and petroleum refining.

soda bread bread in which the raising ingredient is baking soda, not yeast.

soda fountain *North Amer., esp. US* a counter in a shop from which fizzy drinks, ice-cream, and snacks are served.

soda lime *Chem.* a solid mixture of sodium or potassium hydroxide and calcium oxide, consisting of greyish-white granules that are used as a drying agent, and to absorb carbon dioxide gas.

soda water water made fizzy by the addition of carbon dioxide, widely used as a mixer with alcoholic spirits.

sodden *adj.* **1** heavy with moisture; thoroughly soaked. **2** made lifeless or sluggish, especially through excessive consumption of alcohol: *drink-sodden brain*.

sodding *adj. coarse slang* a general term of disparagement.

sodium *noun Chem.* (SYMBOL **Na**, ATOMIC NUMBER **11**) a soft silvery-white metal that occurs mainly as sodium chloride (common salt) in seawater and underground deposits. [from SODA]

sodium bicarbonate *Chem.* same as SODIUM HYDRO-GENCARBONATE.

sodium carbonate *Chem.* (FORMULA Na_2CO_3) a white powder or crystalline solid, that dissolves in water to form an alkaline solution, and readily forms hydrates on exposure to air. It is used as a water softener and food additive, and in glass making, photography, and the manufacture of various sodium compounds. Also called WASHING SODA, SODA ASH.

sodium chloride *Chem.* (FORMULA **NaCl**) a white crystalline salt, soluble in water, obtained from underground deposits of the mineral halite, and from seawater. It has been used since ancient times for seasoning and preserving food, and is also used as a de-icing and water-softening agent, and in the manufacture of chlorine, and many other chemicals. Also called COMMON SALT, SALT, TABLE SALT.

sodium hydrogencarbonate *Chem.* (FORMULA **NaHCO₃**) a white crystalline or powdery solid, soluble in water, used in antacids to treat indigestion, and in baking powder, carbonated beverages, and ceramics. Also called SODIUM BICARBONATE, BICARBONATE OF SODA, BAKING SODA.

sodium hydroxide *Chem.* (FORMULA **NaOH**) a white crystalline solid that dissolves in water to form a strongly alkaline solution. It absorbs carbon dioxide and water from the air, and is prepared by the electrolysis of brine. Sodium hydroxide is used in the manufacture of soap, pharmaceuticals, and paper, in petroleum refining, and as an intermediate in the manufacture of chemical compounds. Also called CAUSTIC SODA, SODA.

sodium nitrate *Chem.* (FORMULA **NaNO₃**) a toxic colourless crystalline solid with a bitter taste, soluble in water, that decomposes when heated and explodes at high temperatures. It is used in the manufacture of explosives, fireworks, matches, and glass, and is also used as a food preservative, especially for cured meats.

sodomite *noun* a person who engages in sodomy.

sodomize or **sodomise** *verb* to practise sodomy on.

sodomy *noun* **1** a form of intercourse in which the penis is inserted into the anus of a man or woman; buggery. **2** sexual intercourse between a man and an animal. [from *Sodom*, a biblical city renowned for vice]

Sod's law *slang* a facetious maxim stating that if something can go wrong, it will go wrong, or that the most inconvenient thing that could happen is what is most likely to happen.

sofa *noun* an upholstered seat with a back and arms, for two or more people. [from Arabic *suffah*]

sofa bed a piece of furniture designed to be converted from a sofa to a bed and vice versa.

soffit *noun Archit.* a term variously applied to the under surface (or intrados) of an arch; to a ceiling on the underside of a stair; and to the underside of the top of a door or window opening. [from Italian *soffito*, ultimately from Latin *suffigere*, to fasten beneath]

soft — *adj.* **1** easily yielding or changing shape when pressed; pliable. **2** *said of fabric, etc* having a smooth surface producing little or no friction. **3** quiet: *a soft voice*. **4** of little brightness: *soft colours*. **5** kind or sympathetic, especially excessively so. **6** not able to endure rough treatment or hardship. **7** lacking strength of character; easily influenced. **8** weak in the mind; simple: *soft in the head*. **9** weakly sentimental. **10** *said of water* low in or free from mineral salts and so lathering easily. **11** tender; loving: *soft words*. **12** *colloq.* requiring little effort; easy: *a soft job*. **13** *said of drugs* not severely addictive. **14** with moderate rather than hardline or extreme policies: *the soft left*. **15** *said of the consonants c and g* pronounced as in *dance* and *age* respectively. — *adv.* softly: *speaks soft*. — **soft on someone** *colloq.* **1** lenient towards them. **2** infatuated with them. [from Anglo-Saxon *softe*]

▣ *adj.* **1** yielding, pliable, flexible, elastic, plastic, malleable, spongy, squashy, pulpy. **2** smooth, silky, velvety, downy, furry. **3** quiet, low, muted, subdued, faint. **4** pale, light, pastel, delicate, subdued, muted, dim, faint, diffuse. **5** kind, sympathetic, soft-hearted, lenient, lax, permissive, indulgent, tolerant, easy-going, generous, gentle, merciful. **6** sensitive, tender. **7** weak, spineless. **8** simple, stupid, foolish, silly. **11** tender, loving, kind, gentle.
▣ *adj.* **1** hard. **2** rough. **3** loud. **4** harsh. **5** strict, severe. **6** tough.

softball *noun* a game similar to baseball, played with a larger, softer ball.

soft-boiled *adj.*, *said of eggs* boiled for a short while only, leaving the yolk soft.

soft drink a non-alcoholic drink.

soften *verb* (**softened, softening**) **1** *trans., intrans.* to make or become less hard, firm, or solid. **2** *trans., intrans.* to make or become less harsh, severe, etc. **3** to make less loud, bright, etc. — **soften someone up** to prepare them for an unwelcome or difficult request.

▣ **1** moderate, lower, lessen, diminish, abate, ease, lighten. **2** melt, thaw, liquefy, dissolve. **3** muffle, mute, subdue.
▣ **1** harden, solidify.

softener *noun* a substance added to another to increase its softness, pliability, etc, especially a substance used to soften water.

soft furnishings rugs, curtains, and other articles made of fabric.

soft-hearted *adj.* kind-hearted and generous; compassionate.

▣ kind-hearted, warm-hearted, tender, compassionate, sympathetic, kind, benevolent, charitable, generous.
▣ hard-hearted, callous.

soft iron *Chem.* a form of iron that has a low carbon content, and is unable to retain magnetism. It is used to make the cores of electromagnets, motors, generators, and transformers.

soft option the easier or easiest of several alternative courses of action.

soft palate *Anat.* the fleshy muscular back part of the palate.

soft pedal a pedal on a piano pressed to make the sound from the strings less lingering or ringing.

soft-pedal *verb* (**soft-pedalled, soft-pedalling**) *colloq.* to tone down, or avoid emphasizing or mentioning: *the government were soft-pedalling the scheme's disadvantages*.

soft porn *colloq.* pornography in which sexual acts are not shown or described explicitly.

soft sell the use of gentle persuasion as a selling technique, rather than heavy-handed pressure.

soft-soap *verb colloq.* to speak flatteringly to, especially in order to persuade or deceive.

soft-spoken *adj.* having a soft voice, and usually a mild manner.

soft spot a fondness: *have a soft spot for.*

soft touch *slang* a person easily taken advantage of, especially one giving money willingly.

software *noun Comput.* the programs that are used in a computer system (eg operating systems, and applications programs such as word-processing or database programs), and the magnetic disks, tapes, etc, on which they are recorded, as opposed to the computer's electronic, electrical, magnetic, and mechanical components, which form the hardware. See also HARDWARE.

soft water *Chem.* water that naturally contains very low levels of calcium and magnesium salts, or from which these salts have been removed artificially. It lathers easily with soap, and does not cause scaling of kettles, boilers, etc.

softwood *noun* **1** *Bot.* the wood of a coniferous tree, eg pine. The name is misleading, as some softwoods are in fact very hard and durable. **2** *Bot.* any tree which produces such wood. See also HARDWOOD.

softy or **softie** *noun* (PL. **softies**) *colloq.* **1** a person easily upset. **2** a weakly sentimental person. **3** a person not able to endure rough treatment or hardship.

SOGAT *abbrev.* Society of Graphical and Allied Trades.

soggily *adv.* in a soggy way.

sogginess *noun* being soggy.

soggy *adj.* (**soggier, soggiest**) **1** thoroughly wet; saturated. **2** *said of ground* waterlogged; boggy. [from dialect *sog*, bog]

▣ **1** saturated, soaked, drenched, sodden, sopping, dripping, wet, damp, moist. **2** waterlogged, boggy, spongy, pulpy.

soh /sou/ *noun Mus.* in tonic sol-fa, the fifth note of the major scale. [from the first syllable of the word *solve* in a medieval Latin hymn, certain syllables of which were used to name the notes of the scale]

soil[1] *noun* **1** the mixture of fragmented rock and plant and animal debris that lies on the surface of the Earth, above the bedrock. It contains water and air, as well as living organisms such as bacteria, fungi, and invertebrate animals. **2** *literary* country; land: *on foreign soil*. [from Latin *solum*, ground]

▣ **1** earth, clay, loam, humus, dirt, dust, ground. **2** land, region, country.

soil[2] — *verb* **1** to stain or make dirty. **2** to bring discredit on; to sully: *soiled reputation*. — *noun* **1** a stain. **2** dirt. **3** dung; sewage. [from Old French *souil*, wallowing-place]

▣ *verb* **1** dirty, begrime, stain, spot, smudge, smear, foul, muddy, pollute, defile. **2** sully, tarnish, besmirch.

soil horizon SEE SOIL PROFILE.

soil profile a vertical section through the soil revealing a series of basic soil levels: the surface layer or topsoil containing humus; the upper subsoil containing little organic matter but rich in soil mineral washed down from the topsoil; the lower subsoil of partially weathered mineral material; and the bedrock from which the upper layers may be derived. Each level may be further classified according to its composition.

soil science the scientific study of soil and its management as a medium for plant growth. It includes the cultivation, drainage, and irrigation of soil, and the control of its nutrient content, acidity, and salinity.

soirée or **soiree** /'swɑːreɪ/ *noun* **1** a formal party held in the evening. **2** an evening of entertainment of any kind. [French, = evening]

sojourn /ˈsɒdʒən, ˈsʌdʒən/ *formal* — *noun* a short stay. — *verb intrans.* to stay for a short while. [from Old French *sojorner*]

sol[1] same as SOH.

sol[2] *noun Chem.* a type of colloid that consists of small solid particles dispersed in a liquid.

solace /ˈsɒləs/ — *noun* comfort in time of disappointment or sorrow; also, a source of comfort. — *verb* 1 to provide with such comfort. 2 to bring relief from. [from Latin *solari*, to comfort in distress]

....

▣ *noun* comfort, consolation, relief, alleviation, support, cheer. *verb* 1 comfort, console, support, cheer. 2 relieve, alleviate.

....

solacement *noun* solace, consolation.

solar /ˈsoʊlə(r)/ *adj.* 1 of or relating to the sun. 2 of, by, or using energy from the sun's rays: *solar-powered.* [from Latin *sol*, sun]

solar battery *Electr.* a battery consisting of a number of solar cells.

solar cell *Electr.* an electric cell that converts solar energy (from sunlight) directly into electricity. Solar cells are an expensive and relatively inefficient source of large-scale power, but are used in pocket calculators, light meters, etc. Also called PHOTOVOLTAIC CELL.

solar energy energy that is radiated from the Sun, mainly in the form of heat and light, and only a minute proportion of which falls on the Earth. It is required for photosynthesis, which is essential for the survival of living organisms.

solar flare *Astron.* a sudden release of energy in the vicinity of an active region on the Sun's surface, generally associated with a sunspot.

solarium /səˈleərɪəm/ *noun* (PL. **solariums, solaria**) 1 a room or establishment equipped with sun-beds. 2 a conservatory or other room designed to allow exposure to sunlight.

solar plexus an area in the abdomen in which there is a concentration of nerves radiating from a central point.

solar system the Sun, and the system of nine major planets (Mercury, Venus, Earth, Mars, Jupiter, Saturn, Uranus, Neptune, and Pluto), together with their natural satellites, and the asteroids (minor planets), comets, and meteors that revolve around it, held in their orbits by the Sun's gravitational pull.

solar wind *Astron.* a stream of charged particles that flows outward from the Sun in all directions at speeds of over one million kph. It passes the Earth and the other planets as it moves through the solar system.

sold past tense and past participle of SELL. — **sold on** *something colloq.* convinced or enthusiastic about it.

solder — *noun Engineering* any of several alloys with a low melting point, often containing tin and lead, applied when molten to the joint between two metals to form an airtight seal. — *verb* (**soldered, soldering**) to join two pieces of metal, without melting them, by applying a layer of molten alloy to the joint between them and allowing it to cool and solidify. [from Latin *solidare*, to strengthen]

soldering iron *noun* a tool with a probe-like part, usually electrically heated, used to melt and apply solder.

soldier — *noun* 1 a member of a fighting force, especially a national army. 2 a member of an army below officer rank. — *verb intrans.* (**soldiered, soldiering**) to serve as a soldier. — **soldier on** to continue determinedly in spite of difficulties. [from Old French *soudier*, from *soude*, pay]

Types of soldier include: cadet, private, sapper, NCO, orderly, officer, gunner, infantryman, trooper, fusilier, rifleman, paratrooper, sentry, guardsman, marine, commando, tommy, dragoon, cavalryman, lancer, hussar, conscript, recruit, regular, Territorial, *US* GI, warrior, mercenary, legionnaire, guerrilla, partisan, centurion; troops; serviceman, servicewoman, fighter. *See also* **rank**.

soldierly *adj.* like a soldier.

soldier of fortune a person willing to serve in any army that pays him or her.

sole[1] — *noun* 1 the underside of the foot. 2 the underside of a shoe or boot, especially the part not including the heel. 3 the flattish underside of anything. — *verb* to fit (a shoe or boot) with a sole. [from Latin *solum*, bottom]

sole[2] *noun* (PL. **sole, soles**) a flatfish found in shallow waters in tropical and temperate regions, with a slender brown body and both eyes on the left side of the head. It is an important food fish, the Dover sole being especially highly prized. [from Latin *solea*]

sole[3] *adj.* 1 only. 2 exclusive: *has sole rights to the story.* [from Latin *solus*, alone]

....

▣ 1 only, unique, singular, individual, single, one, lone, solitary, alone. 2 exclusive, undivided, unshared, total.

▣ 1 multiple. 2 shared.

....

solecism /ˈsɒlɪsɪzm/ *noun* 1 a mistake in the use of language. 2 an instance of bad or incorrect behaviour. [from Greek *soloikismos*]

solecistic *adj.* of the nature of or involving solecism.

solely *adv.* 1 alone; without others: *solely to blame.* 2 only; excluding all else: *done solely for profit.*

solemn /ˈsɒləm/ *adj.* 1 done, made, etc in earnest: *a solemn vow.* 2 of a very serious and formal nature; suggesting seriousness: *a solemn occasion/solemn music.* 3 glum or sombre in appearance. [from Latin *sollemnis*, annual, customary, appointed]

....

▣ SERIOUS. 1 grave, earnest, wholehearted, formal. 2 grand, stately, ceremonial, ritual, formal, dignified, awe-inspiring, impressive, imposing. 3 glum, sombre, sober, sedate, thoughtful.

▣ 1 light-hearted, frivolous.

....

solemnity /səˈlemnɪtɪ/ *noun* (PL. **solemnities**) 1 being solemn. 2 a solemn ceremony.

solemnization or **solemnisation** *noun* solemnizing or being solemnized.

solemnize or **solemnise** *verb* 1 to perform (especially a marriage) with a formal or religious ceremony. 2 to make solemn.

solenoid /ˈsoʊlənɔɪd, ˈsɒlənɔɪd/ *noun* a cylindrical coil of wire that produces a magnetic field when an electric current is passed through it. Solenoids often contain a movable iron or steel core that can be used to operate a switch, relay, circuit breaker, etc. [from Greek *solen*, tube]

sol-fa /ˈsɒlfɑ/ *noun* a system of musical notation in which the notes of a scale are represented by syllables, especially by *doh, re, me, fah, soh, la, ti,* written down or sung. [from *sol* (a form of SOH) + FAH]

solicit *verb* (**solicited, soliciting**) 1 *formal* to ask for, or for something from: *solicit aid from other countries/solicited me for advice.* 2 *intrans., said of a prostitute* to approach people with open offers of sex for money. 3 *formal* to require or call for. [from Latin *solicitare*]

....

▣ 1 ask for, request, seek, crave, beg, beseech. 2 importune. 3 require, call for, petition for, canvass for.

....

solicitation *noun* 1 an act of soliciting, an earnest request. 2 an invitation.

solicitor *noun* a lawyer who prepares legal documents, gives legal advice, and (in the lower courts only) speaks on behalf of clients.

....

▣ lawyer, advocate, attorney.

....

solicitor-advocate *noun Scot. Legal* a solicitor with the right to represent clients in the High Court or Court of Session.

Solicitor-General in the UK, one of the government's law officers, who is a member of the House of Commons and junior to the Attorney-General. The Solicitor-General for Scotland holds a similar position.

solicitous *adj.* **1** (**solicitous about** or **for someone** or **something**) anxious or concerned about them. **2** (**solicitous to do something**) willing or eager to do it.

⊟ **1** anxious about, worried about, concerned about, attentive to. **2** willing to, ready to, eager to.

solicitously *adv.* in a solicitous way.

solicitude *noun* **1** anxiety or uneasiness of mind. **2** the state of being solicitous.

solid — *adj.* **1** in a form other than a liquid or a gas, and resisting changes in shape. **2** of the same nature or material throughout; pure: *a solid oak table*. **3** firmly constructed or attached; not easily breaking or loosening. **4** difficult to undermine or destroy; sound: *solid support for the scheme*. **5** not hollow. **6** without breaks; continuous: *waited for four solid hours*. **7** competent, rather than outstanding: *a solid piece of work*. — *noun* **1** *Chem.* a state of matter in which the constituent molecules or ions can only vibrate about fixed positions, and are unable to move freely. It has a definite shape, and at a specific temperature (the melting point) becomes a liquid. **2** a three-dimensional geometric figure. **3** (**solids**) non-liquid food. **4** (**solids**) particles of solid matter in a liquid. [from Latin *solidus*]

⊟ *adj.* **1** hard, firm, dense, compact. **2** real, genuine, pure. **3** firm, strong, sturdy, substantial, sound, stable, secure. **4** sound, unshakable, reliable, dependable. **6** unbroken, continuous, uninterrupted.
⊞ *adj.* **1** liquid, gaseous. **3** unstable. **4** unreliable. **5** hollow. **6** broken, dotted.

solid angle *Geom.* a three-dimensional cone-shaped angle representing the region subtended at a point by a *surface*, as opposed to a line in the case of a two-dimensional (plane) angle. The unit of measurement of solid angles is the steradian.

solidarity *noun* mutual support and unity of interests and actions among members of a group.

⊟ unity, agreement, accord, unanimity, consensus, like-mindedness, camaraderie, team spirit.
⊞ discord, division, schism.

solidification *noun* solidifying or being solidified.

solidify *verb trans., intrans.* (**solidifies, solidified**) to make or become solid.

⊟ harden, set, gel, congeal, coagulate, clot, crystallize.
⊞ soften, liquefy, dissolve.

solidity *noun* being solid.

solidly *adv.* in a solid way.

solid-state *adj.* **1** *Electron.* denoting an electronic device or component, eg a semiconductor or transistor, that functions by the movement of electrons through solids, and contains no heated filaments or vacuums. **2** *Physics* denoting the branch of physics concerned with the study of matter in the solid state, especially the electrical properties of semiconductors at the atomic level.

solidus *noun* a printed line sloping from right to left, eg separating alternatives, as in *and* / *or*; a stroke or slash mark. [from Latin *solidus*]

soliloquize or **soliloquise** *verb intrans.* to speak a soliloquy.

soliloquy /səˈlɪləkwɪ/ *noun* (PL. **soliloquies**) **1** an act of talking to oneself, especially a speech in a play, etc in which a character reveals thoughts or intentions to the audience by talking aloud. **2** the use of such speeches as a

device in drama. [from Latin *solus*, alone + *loqui*, to speak]

solipsism /ˈsɒlɪpsɪzm/ *noun Philos.* the theory that one's own self is the only thing whose existence one can be sure of. [from Latin *solus*, alone + *ipse*, self]

solipsist *noun* a believer in solipsism.

solitaire *noun* **1** any of several games for one player only, especially one whose object is to eliminate pegs or marbles from a board and leave only one. **2** a single gem in a setting on its own. **3** *North Amer., esp. US* the card game patience. [from French; related to SOLITARY]

solitariness *noun* a solitary state.

solitary — *adj.* **1** single; lone. **2** preferring to be alone; not social. **3** without companions; lonely. **4** remote; secluded. — *noun* **1** a person who lives alone, especially a hermit. **2** *colloq.* solitary confinement. [from Latin *solitarius*, from *solus*, alone]

⊟ *adj.* **1** sole, single, lone. **2** unsociable, reclusive, withdrawn, retired, sequestered, cloistered. **3** alone, lonely, lonesome, friendless. **4** secluded, separate, isolated, remote, out-of-the-way, inaccessible, God-forsaken.
⊞ *adj.* **2** gregarious. **3** accompanied.

solitary confinement imprisonment in a cell by one-self.

solitude *noun* the state of being (especially pleasantly) alone or secluded. [from Latin *solitudo*, from *solus*, alone]

⊟ privacy, seclusion, isolation, remoteness, solitariness, aloneness, loneliness.
⊞ companionship.

solmization or **solmisation** /sɒlmɪˈzeɪʃən/ *noun Mus.* in musical reference and training, a system in which syllables are used to designate the notes of the hexachord. The system used in Western music from medieval times is attributed to the French music theorist and teacher Guido d'Arezzo (d.c.1050), who fitted the first syllables of each of the first six lines of a plainsong Latin hymn to the notes of the hexachord to make: *ut* (later changed to *do*), *re, mi, fa, sol*, and *la* (*si* or *ti* was added later). The modern sight-singing and ear-training systems of *tonic sol-fa, solfeggio* (in Italy), and *solfège* (in France) are based on these syllables. [from French *solmisation*, related to the terms SOL[1] + MI]

solo — *noun* (PL. **solos**) a piece of music, or a passage within it, for a single voice or instrument, with or without accompaniment. — *adj.* performed alone, without assistance or accompaniment. — *adv.* alone: *fly solo*. [from Italian *solo*, from Latin *solus*, alone]

soloist *noun* a person who performs a solo or solos.

Solomon's seal a perennial plant (*Polygonatum multiflorum*), native to Europe and Asia, which has arching stems, oval leaves borne in two rows on the stem, and white bell-shaped flowers that hang in clusters beneath the stem.

solstice *noun* either of the times when the sun is furthest from the equator: the longest day (*summer solstice*) around Jun 21 in the N hemisphere and the shortest day (*winter solstice*) around Dec 21 in the N hemisphere. [from Latin *solstitium*, the standing still of the sun]

solubility *noun* a soluble state.

soluble *adj.* **1** denoting a substance (a *solute*) that is capable of being dissolved in a liquid (a *solvent*). **2** capable of being solved or resolved. [from Latin *solubilis*]

solute /ˈsɒljuːt/ *noun Chem.* any substance that is dissolved in a solvent (eg water) to form a solution. [from Latin *solutus*, from *solvere*, to loosen]

solution *noun* **1** the process of finding an answer to a problem or puzzle; also, the answer sought or found. **2** *Chem.* a homogeneous mixture consisting of a solid or gas (the *solute*) and the liquid (the *solvent*) in which it is completely dissolved. **3** the act of dissolving or the state of being dissolved: *in solution*. **4** *Maths*. in a mathematical equation, the value that one or more of the variables must have for that equation to be valid. [from Latin *solutio*]

. . . .

◼ **1** answer, result, explanation, resolution, key, remedy. **2** mixture, blend, compound.

. . . .

solvable *adj*. capable of being solved.

solvation /sɒlˈveɪʃən/ *noun Chem*. the interaction between the ions of a solute and the molecules of a solvent, which enables an ionic solid to dissolve in a solvent to form a solution, or to swell or form a gel in the presence of a solvent. If the solvent is water, the process is referred to as hydration. [from Latin *solvere*, to loosen]

solve *verb* to discover the answer to (a puzzle) or a way out of (a problem). [from Latin *solvere*, to loosen]

. . . .

◼ work out, figure out, puzzle out, decipher, crack, disentangle, unravel, answer, resolve, settle, clear up, clarify, explain, interpret.

. . . .

solvency *noun* ability to pay all debts.

solvent — *adj*. **1** able to pay all one's debts. **2** in a solution, the liquid in which a solid or gas (the *solute*) is dissolved, eg water and organic chemicals such as ethanol (alcohol), ether, and acetone. — *noun* a solvent substance.

solvent abuse inhalation of the intoxicating fumes given off by various solvents, eg adhesives, petrol, or fuel gases such as butane in cigarette-lighter refills, in order to induce euphoria. Solvent abuse is an increasingly common practice among children, especially teenagers. It is highly addictive, and damages the brain and lungs, as well as the mucous membranes that line the nasal cavity. Also called GLUE-SNIFFING.

Som. *abbrev*. Somerset.

Somali a Cushitic-speaking people of Somalia and parts of Kenya, Ethiopia, and Djibouti.

somatic *adj. Medicine, Biol*. **1** of the body, rather than the mind. **2** of the body, as opposed to reproduction: *somatic cells*. [from Greek *soma*, body]

somatotrophin /soʊmətoʊˈtroʊfɪn/ *noun Physiol*. growth hormone. [from Greek *soma*, body]

sombre /ˈsɒmbə(r)/ *adj*. **1** sad and serious; grave. **2** dark and gloomy. **3** suggesting seriousness, rather than lightheartedness. [from French *sombre*, perhaps from Latin *sub*, under + *umbra*, shade]

. . . .

◼ **1** sad, joyless, dismal, melancholy, mournful, serious, grave. **2** dark, funereal, gloomy, drab, dull, dim, obscure, shady, shadowy. **3** serious, grave, sober.
◻ **1** cheerful, happy. **2** bright. **3** light-hearted.

. . . .

sombrely *adv*. in a sombre way.

sombrero /sɒmˈbreərəʊ/ *noun* (PL. **sombreros**) a man's straw or felt hat with a very wide brim, popular in Mexico. [from Spanish *sombrero*, from *sombra*, shade]

some — *adj*. **1** denoting an unknown or unspecified amount or number of. **2** of unknown or unspecified nature or identity: *some problem with the engine*. **3** quite a lot of: *have been waiting for some time*. **4** at least a little: *try to feel some excitement*. **5** a poor example of: *some friend you are!* **6** *colloq*. an excellent or impressive example of: *that was some shot!* — *pron*. **1** certain unspecified things or people: *some say he should resign*. **2** an unspecified amount or number: *give him some, too*. — *adv*. **1** to an unspecified extent: *play some more*. **2** approximately: *some twenty feet deep*. [from Anglo-Saxon *sum*]

-some *suffix* forming words meaning: **1** causing or producing: *troublesome*. **2** inviting: *cuddlesome*. **3** tending to: *quarrelsome*. **4** a group of the specified number of people or things: *a foursome*. [from Anglo-Saxon *sum*]

somebody *pron*. **1** an unknown or unspecified person; someone. **2** a person of importance: *tried to be somebody*.

someday *adv*. at an unknown or unspecified time in the future.

. . . .

◼ sometime, one day, eventually, ultimately.
◻ never.

. . . .

somehow *adv*. **1** in some way not yet known. **2** for a reason not easy to explain.

someone *pron*. somebody.

somersault /ˈsʌməsɔːlt, ˈsʌməsɒlt/ — *noun* a leap or roll in which the whole body turns a complete circle forwards or backwards, leading with the head. — *verb intrans*. to perform such a leap or roll. [from Latin *supra*, over + *saltus*, leap]

something — *pron*. **1** a thing not known or not stated: *take something to eat*. **2** an amount or number not known or not stated: *something short of 1000 people/aged about 40 something*. **3** a person or thing of importance: *make something of oneself/make something out of a casual remark*. **4** a certain truth or value: *there is something in what you say*. **5** *colloq*. an impressive person or thing: *that meal was really something*. — *adv*. to some degree; rather: *the garden looks something like a scrapyard*. — **something of a** ... a ... to some extent: *she's something of a local celebrity*.

sometime *adv*. at an unknown or unspecified time in the future or the past.

sometimes *adv*. occasionally.

. . . .

◼ occasionally, now and again, now and then, once in a while, from time to time.
◻ always, never.

. . . .

somewhat *adv*. rather; a little. — **somewhat of** ... ... to some extent: *has lost somewhat of his strength*.

somewhere *adv*. in or to some place or degree, or at some point, not known or not specified.

somnambulism /sɒmˈnambjʊlɪzm/ *noun formal* sleepwalking. [from Latin *somnus*, sleep + *ambulare*, to walk]

somnambulist *noun* a sleepwalker.

somnolence *noun* sleepiness, drowsiness.

somnolent *adj. formal* sleepy or drowsy; causing sleepiness or drowsiness. [from Latin *somnus*, sleep]

son¹ *noun* **1** a male child. **2** a male person closely associated with, or seen as developing from, a particular activity or set of circumstances: *a son of the Russian revolution*. **3** a familiar and often patronizing term of address used to a boy or man. **4** (**the Son**) *Christianity* Christ considered as the second person of the Trinity. [from Anglo-Saxon *sunu*]

son² /sʌn/ *noun* a style of Cuban music played with claves, bongo drums, and guitar. [from Spanish *son*, sound]

sonar *noun* a system that is used to determine the location of underwater objects, eg submarines, shipwrecks, shoals of fish, by transmitting ultrasound signals from the bottom of a ship and measuring the time taken for their echoes to return when they strike an obstacle (*active sonar*). Passive sonar uses a listening device to locate sources of underwater sounds. [from *sound navigation and ranging*]

sonata *noun* a piece of classical music, in three or more movements, for a solo instrument, especially the piano. [from Italian *sonata*, from *sonare*, to sound]

sonata form the plan or form most often used since c.1750 in the design of the first movement (and occasionally the slow movement and finale) of a sonata or symphony. It is divided into three basic sections: exposition, development, and recapitulation.

sonatina /sɒnəˈtiːnə/ *noun* a short sonata, usually one which is relatively straightforward technically. [from Italian, a diminutive of *sonata*]

son et lumière a dramatic night-time outdoor spectacle with lights, music, and narration on a particular theme, often staged at and presenting the history of a famous building. [French, = sound and light]

song *noun* 1 a set of words to be sung, usually with accompanying music. 2 the musical call of certain birds. 3 singing: *poetry and song.* 4 a bargain price: *going for a song.* — **make a song and dance about something** *colloq.* to make an unnecessary fuss about it. [from Anglo-Saxon *sang*]

☰ 1 ballad, madrigal, lullaby, shanty, anthem, hymn, carol, chant, chorus, air, tune, melody, lyric, number, ditty.

songbird *noun* any of various kinds of bird with a musical call.

song cycle a set of songs, often to words by a single poet and connected by some common theme or narrative thread: usually intended to be performed complete. Beethoven's *An die ferne Geliebte* ('To the distant Beloved') is one of the earliest examples.

songster *noun, old use* a talented (especially male) singer.

songstress *noun, old use* a talented female singer.

song thrush a common European thrush, well known for its tuneful call.

sonic *adj.* 1 relating to or using sound or sound waves. 2 travelling at (approximately) the speed of sound. [from Latin *sonus*]

sonic boom a loud boom that is heard when an aircraft flying through the Earth's atmosphere reaches supersonic speed, ie passes through the sound barrier. It is heard at the point where a high-pressure shock wave reaches the Earth's surface.

son-in-law *noun* (PL. **sons-in-law**) the husband of one's daughter.

sonnet *noun* a poem with 14 lines of 10 or 11 syllables each and a regular rhyming pattern. [from Italian *sonetto*]

sonny *noun* a familiar (often condescending) term of address used to a boy or man.

sonority or **sonorousness** *noun* a sonorous quality or character.

sonorous *adj.* 1 sounding impressively loud and deep. 2 giving out a deep clear sound when struck: *a sonorous bell.* 3 *said of language* impressively eloquent. [from Latin *sonare*, to sound]

soon *adv.* 1 in a short time from now or from a stated time. 2 quickly; with little delay. 3 willingly: *would sooner pay the fine than go to prison.* — **as soon as** ... at or not before the moment when: *will pay you as soon as I receive the goods.* **as soon ... as** ... used to state that the first alternative is slightly preferable to the second: *would just as soon die as marry him.* **no sooner ... than** ... immediately after ... then: *no sooner had I mentioned his name than he appeared.* **no sooner said than done** *said of a request, promise, etc* immediately fulfilled. **sooner or later** eventually. [from Anglo-Saxon *sona*]

☰ 1 shortly, presently, in a minute, before long, in the near future.

soot *noun* a black powdery substance produced when coal or wood is burned; smut. [from Anglo-Saxon *sot*]

soothe *verb* 1 to bring relief from (a pain, etc). 2 to comfort or calm (someone). [from Anglo-Saxon *gesothian*, to confirm as true]

☰ 1 relieve, ease, alleviate, allay, salve. 2 comfort, calm, compose, tranquillize, settle, still, quiet, lull, pacify, appease.
☷ 1 aggravate, irritate. 2 worry, vex.

soothing *adj.* that soothes.

soothsay *verb intrans.* to foretell or divine.

soothsayer *noun* a person who predicts the future; a seer. [from archaic *sooth*, truth + SAY]

sooty *adj.* (**sootier, sootiest**) 1 covered with soot. 2 like or consisting of soot.

sop — *noun* 1 (*often* **sops**) a piece of food, especially bread, dipped in a liquid, eg soup. 2 something given or done as a bribe or in order to pacify someone. — *verb* (**sopped, sopping**) (*usually* **sop something up**) to mop or soak it up. [from Anglo-Saxon *sopp*]

sophism *noun* a convincing but false argument or explanation, especially one intended to deceive. [from Greek *sophisma*, clever device, from *sophia*, wisdom]

Sophist a 5c BC Greek itinerant teacher of rhetoric, statecraft, and philosophy.

sophist *noun* a person who employs sophism.

sophisticate — *verb* to make sophisticated. — *noun* a sophisticated person. [from Latin *sophisticare*, to adulterate]

sophisticated *adj.* 1 having or displaying a broad knowledge and experience of the world, especially of artistic and intellectual things; appealing to or frequented by people with such knowledge and experience. 2 complex and subtle: *sophisticated weaponry/sophisticated arguments.*

☰ 1 urbane, cosmopolitan, worldly, worldly-wise, cultured, cultivated, refined, polished. 2 advanced, highly-developed, complicated, complex, intricate, elaborate, subtle, delicate.
☷ 1 unsophisticated, naïve. 2 primitive, simple.

sophistication *noun* being sophisticated.

sophistry *noun* (PL. **sophistries**) 1 plausibly deceptive or fallacious reasoning, or an instance of this. 2 the art of reasoning speciously.

sophomore /'sɒfəmɔː(r)/ *noun North Amer., esp. US* a second-year student at a school or university. [from Greek *sophos*, wise + *moros*, foolish]

soporific — *adj.* 1 causing sleep. 2 extremely slow and boring: *a soporific speech.* — *noun* a sleep-inducing drug. [from Latin *sopor*, deep sleep + *facere*, to make]

☰ *adj.* sleep-inducing, hypnotic, sedative, tranquillizing.
noun sleeping pill, sedative, tranquillizer.
☷ *adj.* STIMULATING.

soppily *adv.* in a soppy way.

soppiness *noun* 1 being soppy. 2 soppy behaviour.

sopping *adj., adv.* (*also* **sopping wet**) thoroughly wet; soaking.

soppy *adj.* (**soppier, soppiest**) *colloq.* weakly sentimental. [from SOP]

☰ sentimental, sloppy, slushy, mushy, *colloq.* corny, mawkish, cloying, soft, silly.

soprano *noun* (PL. **sopranos**) 1 a singing voice of the highest pitch for a woman or a boy; also, a person having this voice. 2 a musical part for such a voice. 3 a musical instrument high or highest in pitch in relation to others in its family. [from Italian *soprano*, from Latin *supra*, above]

sorbet /'sɔːbeɪ/ *noun* a dish of sweetened fruit juice, frozen and served as a kind of ice-cream; a water ice. [from French *sorbet*, from Arabic *sharbah*, drink]

sorbitol /'sɔːbɪtɒl/ *noun Chem.* (FORMULA $C_6H_8(OH)_6$) a white crystalline carbohydrate, soluble in water, that is used in cosmetics, toothpastes, resins, and pharmaceuticals, and as a food additive and sweetening agent. It is used by diabetics as a substitute for sugar.

sorcerer *noun* a person who practises sorcery.

sorceress *noun* a woman who practises sorcery.

sorcery *noun* the performing of magic using the power of supernatural forces, especially of black magic using the power of evil spirits. [from Old French *sorcerie*]

☰ magic, black magic, witchcraft, wizardry, necromancy, voodoo.

sordid *adj.* 1 repulsively filthy; squalid. 2 morally revolting; ignoble. [from Latin *sordidus*, dirty]

▣ 1 dirty, filthy, foul, vile, squalid, sleazy, seamy, seedy, disreputable, shabby. **2** corrupt, degraded, degenerate, debauched, low, base, ignoble, despicable, shameful, wretched, mean, mercenary.

▣ 1 clean, pure. **2** honourable, upright.

sordino /sɔːˈdiːnoʊ/ *noun* (PL. **sordini**) *Mus.* a mute (or damper) used to soften or deaden the sound of a musical instrument. The indication on musical scores that a part or passage is to be played *con sordino* means 'with the mute'; the term *senza sordino* means 'without the mute'. [from Italian, from Latin *surdus*, deaf, noiseless]

sore — *adj.* **1** painful when touched; tender. **2** *North Amer., esp. US* angry or resentful. — *noun* a diseased spot or area, especially an ulcer or boil. — **stick out like a sore thumb** *colloq.* to be awkwardly obvious or noticeable, especially by being different or out of place. [from Anglo-Saxon *sar*]

▣ *adj.* **1** painful, hurting, aching, smarting, stinging, tender, sensitive, inflamed, red, raw. **2** annoyed, irritated, vexed, angry, upset, hurt, wounded, resentful, aggrieved. *noun* swelling, inflammation, ulcer, boil, abscess, wound, lesion.
▣ *adj.* **2** pleased, happy.

sorely *adv.* acutely; very much.

sore point a subject causing much anger or resentment when raised.

sorghum /ˈsɔːgəm/ *noun* **1** a cereal of the genus *Sorghum* belonging to the grass family (Gramineae), and having broad leaves and a tall pithy stem bearing dense terminal clusters of small grains. It is resistant to drought, and can be grown in semi-arid tropical regions such as Mexico and the Sudan. The juice extracted from the cane of sweet varieties of sorghum is used as a source of molasses. **2** syrup obtained from this plant. [from Italian *sorgo*]

sorority /səˈrɒrɪtɪ/ *noun* (PL. **sororities**) a women's club or society, especially any of several such societies in a US university. [from Latin *soror*, sister]

sorrel[1] *noun* any of various sour-tasting herbs of the dock family, used medicinally and in salads. [from Old French *sorele*, from *sur*, sour]

sorrel[2] — *adj.* of a reddish-brown or light chestnut colour. — *noun* a horse of this colour. [from Old French *sorel*]

sorrow — *noun* **1** grief or deep sadness arising from loss or disappointment. **2** a cause of this. — *verb intrans.* to have or express such feelings. [from Anglo-Saxon *sorg*]

▣ *noun* AFFLICTION, TROUBLE. **1** sadness, unhappiness, grief, mourning, misery, woe, anguish, heartache, heartbreak, distress, regret, remorse. **2** misfortune, hardship, worry, trial, tribulation. *verb* grieve, mourn, lament.
▣ *noun* **1** happiness, joy. *verb* rejoice.

sorrowful *adj.* **1** full of sorrow; sad, dejected. **2** causing, showing, or expressing sorrow.

sorrowfully *adv.* in a sorrowful way.

sorry — *adj.* (**sorrier**, **sorriest**) **1** (*often* **sorry for something**) feeling regret or shame about something one has done or for which one is responsible. **2** (*often* **sorry for someone**) feeling pity or sympathy towards someone; feeling sad about something. **3** pitifully bad: *in a sorry state*. **4** contemptibly bad; extremely poor: *a sorry excuse*. — *interj.* **1** used as an apology. **2** *said as a question* asking for something just said to be repeated. [from Anglo-Saxon *sarig*, wounded, influenced in meaning by SORROW]

▣ *adj.* **1** apologetic, regretful, remorseful, contrite, penitent, repentant, conscience-stricken, ashamed. **2** sad, concerned, moved, sympathetic, compassionate, understanding, pitying. **3** pathetic, pitiful, poor, wretched, miserable, sad, unhappy, dismal.

▣ *adj.* **1** impenitent, unashamed. **2** unconcerned, unsympathetic.

sort — *noun* **1** a kind, type, or class. **2** *colloq.* a person: *not a bad sort*. — *verb* **1** to arrange into different groups according to type or kind. **2** *colloq.* to put right. **3** *colloq.* to deal with, especially to punish. — **a sort of ...** something like a: *a sort of bottle with a tube attached*. **of a sort** or **of sorts** of an inferior or untypical kind: *an author of a sort/a container of sorts*. **out of sorts** *colloq.* **1** slightly unwell. **2** peevish; bad-tempered. **sort of ...** *colloq.* rather ...; ... in a way; ... to a certain extent: *feeling sort of embarrassed*. **sort someone out** *colloq.* to deal with them firmly and decisively. **sort something out 1** to separate it out from a mixed collection into a group or groups according to kind. **2** to put it into order; to arrange it methodically. **3** to resolve the difficulties relating to it; to put it right. [from Latin *sortis*, a lot, from *sortiri*, to draw lots]

▣ *noun* **1** kind, type, genre, ilk, family, species, variety, order, class, category, group, style, brand, quality, nature, character, description. *verb* **1** class, group, categorize, classify, divide, separate, segregate, sift, screen, grade, rank, order, catalogue, arrange, organize, systematize.
sort something out choose, select, organize, arrange, resolve, clear up, clarify.

sorted *adj. slang* supplied with something, especially recreational drugs.

sortie /ˈsɔːtɪ/ — *noun* **1** a sudden attack by besieged troops. **2** an operational flight by a single military aircraft. **3** *colloq.* a short trip to an unpleasant or unfamiliar place. — *verb intrans.* (**sortied**, **sortieing**) to make a sortie. [from French *sortie*, from *sortir*, to go out]

sorus /ˈsɔːrəs/ *noun* (PL. **sori**) *Bot.* a cluster of sporangia or soredia. [from Greek *soros*, heap]

SOS *noun* **1** a ship's or aircraft's call for help, consisting of these letters repeated in Morse code. **2** *colloq.* any call for help. [letters chosen for ease of transmission and recognition in Morse code]

so-so *adj., adv. colloq.* neither very good nor very bad; passable; middling.

sostenuto /sɒstəˈnuːtoʊ/ *adv., adj. Mus.* in a steady flowing way, without cutting short any notes. [from Italian *sostenuto*, sustained]

sot *noun, old use* a person who is continually drunk. [from Old French *sot*]

sottish *adj.* **1** like a sot. **2** befuddled with drink.

sotto voce /sɒtoʊ ˈvoʊtʃeɪ/ **1** in a quiet voice, so as not to be overheard. **2** *Mus.* very softly. [from Italian *sotto voce*, below the voice]

sou /suː/ *noun* **1** a former French coin of low value. **2** *colloq.* the smallest amount of money: *haven't a sou*. [from French *sou*]

sou' *combining form Naut.* south: *a sou'wester*.

soubrette /suːˈbrɛt/ *noun* a minor female part in a play, especially that of an impudent, flirtatious, or intriguing maid. [from French *soubrette*, from Provençal *soubreto*, coy]

soubriquet see SOBRIQUET.

soufflé /ˈsuːfleɪ/ *noun* a light sweet or savoury baked dish, a frothy mass of whipped egg-whites with other ingredients mixed in. [from French *soufflé*, from *souffler*, to puff up]

sough /saʊ/ — *noun* a sighing sound made by the wind blowing through trees. — *verb intrans.* to make this sound. [from Anglo-Saxon *swogan*, to rustle]

sought past tense and past participle of SEEK.

sought-after *adj.* desired; in demand.

souk /suːk/ *noun* a market-place in Muslim countries. [from Arabic *suq*]

soukous /ˈsuːkuːs/ a central African style of dance music, originating in Zaire, combining guitar, drumming, and vocal melodies. [from French *secouer*, to shake]

soul — *noun* **1** the non-physical part of a person, with personality, emotions, and intellect, widely believed to survive in some form after the death of the body. **2** emotional sensitivity; ordinary human feelings of sympathy: *a singer with no soul/cruelty committed by brutes with no soul.* **3** essential nature: *recognize the soul of the political movement.* **4** motivating force; leader: *the soul of the revolution.* **5** (**the soul of ...**) a perfect example of ...; a personification of: *she is the soul of discretion.* **6** *colloq.* a person: *a kind soul.* **7** soul music. — *adj.* relating to Black American culture: *soul food.*

. . . .

◼ *noun* **1** spirit, psyche, mind, reason, intellect, character, inner being, life, vital force. **2** sensitivity, sympathy, compassion, humanity. **3** nature, essence. **6** individual, person, man, woman.

. . . .

soul-destroying *adj.* **1** extremely dull, boring, or repetitive. **2** extremely difficult to tolerate or accept emotionally.

soulful *adj.* having or expressing deep feelings, especially of sadness.

soulfully *adv.* in a soulful way.

soulless *adj.* **1** having no emotional sensitivity or ordinary human sympathy. **2** *said of a task, etc* for which no human qualities are required; extremely monotonous or mechanical. **3** *said of a place* bleak; lifeless.

soul mate a person with whom one shares the same feelings, thoughts, and ideas.

soul music a jazzier, more mainstream type of blues music, typically earthy and emotional in tone, usually dealing with love.

soul-searching *noun* critical examination of one's own conscience, motives, actions, etc.

sound[1] — *noun* **1** *Physics* periodic vibrations that are propagated through a medium, eg air, as pressure waves, so that the medium is displaced from its equilibrium state. Unlike electromagnetic radiation, such as light, sound cannot travel through a vacuum. **2** the noise that is heard as a result of such periodic vibrations. **3** audible quality: *the guitar has a nice sound.* **4** the mental impression created by something heard: *don't like the sound of that.* **5** aural material, eg spoken commentary and music, accompanying a film or broadcast: *sound editor.* **6** *colloq.* volume or volume control, especially on a television set. **7** (*often* **sounds**) *slang* music, especially pop music: *the sounds of the 60s.* — *verb* **1** *intrans.* to produce a sound. **2** to cause to produce a sound. **3** *intrans.* to create an impression in the mind when heard: *sounds like fun.* **4** to pronounce: *does not sound his h's.* **5** to announce or signal with a sound: *sound the alarm.* **6** *Medicine* to examine by tapping or listening. See also SOUND[3] *verb* 2. — **sound off** *intrans. colloq.* to state one's opinions forcefully, especially one's complaints angrily. [from Latin *sonus*]

. . . .

◼ *noun* **2** noise, din, resonance, reverberation. **3** tone, timbre. *verb* **1** ring, toll, chime, peal, resound, resonate, reverberate, echo. **2** ring, toll, play, blow, beat. **4** pronounce, enunciate, articulate, voice.

. . . .

sound[2] — *adj.* **1** not damaged or injured; in good condition; healthy. **2** sensible; well-founded; reliable: *sound advice.* **3** acceptable or approved of. **4** *said especially of punishment, etc* severe, hard, thorough: *a sound spanking.* **5** *said of sleep* deep and undisturbed. — *adv.* deeply: *sound asleep.* [from Anglo-Saxon *gesund*]

. . . .

◼ *adj.* **1** fit, well, healthy, robust, sturdy, firm, solid, whole, complete, intact, perfect, unbroken, undamaged, unimpaired, unhurt, uninjured. **2** valid, well-founded, sensible, reasonable, rational, logical, right, true, proven, reliable, trustworthy. **4** thorough, good.

◪ *adj.* **1** unfit, ill, damaged, injured. **2** unsound, shaky, unreliable.

. . . .

sound[3] — *verb* **1** to measure the depth of (especially the sea). **2** *Medicine* to examine (a hollow organ, etc) with a probe (see also SOUND[1] *verb* 5). — *noun* a probe for examining hollow organs. — **sound someone out** to try to discover their opinions or intentions. [from Old French *sonder*]

. . . .

◼ *verb* **1** measure, plumb, fathom. **2** probe, examine, test, inspect.

. . . .

sound[4] *noun* a narrow passage of water connecting two seas or separating an island and the mainland; a strait. [from Anglo-Saxon *sund*]

sound barrier the resistance an aircraft meets when it reaches speeds close to the speed of sound. At this point the power required to increase speed rises steeply because of the formation of shock waves.

soundbite *noun* a short and succinct statement delivered on television or radio by a public figure, usually in a form inviting quotation.

soundboard *noun Comput.* a printed circuit board added to a computer to provide or enhance sound effects.

sound-box *noun* the hollow body of a violin, guitar, etc.

sound effects artificially produced sounds matching actions in film, broadcasting or theatre.

sounding *noun* **1** the act of measuring depth, especially of the sea. **2** a depth measured. **3** (*often* **soundings**) a sampling of opinions or (eg voting) intentions.

sounding-board *noun* **1** a board over a stage or pulpit directing the speaker's voice towards the audience. **2** a means of testing the acceptability or popularity of ideas or opinions.

soundly *adv.* in a sound way; sensibly, correctly.

soundtrack *noun* **1** a band of magnetic tape along the edge of a cinematographic film, on which the sound is recorded. **2** a recording of the music from a film or broadcast.

soup *noun* a liquid food made by stewing meat, vegetables, or grains. — **in the soup** *slang* in trouble or difficulty. **soup something up** *colloq.* to make changes to a vehicle or its engine to increase its speed or power. [from Old French *soupe*]

soupçon /ˈsuːpsɒn/ *noun literary, facetious* the slightest amount; a hint or dash. [from French *soupçon*, suspicion]

soup kitchen a place where volunteer workers supply free food to people in need.

soupy *adj.* (**soupier**, **soupiest**) having the appearance or consistency of soup.

sour — *adj.* **1** having an acid taste or smell, similar to that of lemon juice or vinegar. **2** rancid or stale because of fermentation: *sour milk.* **3** sullen; miserable: *sour-faced old man.* **4** bad, unsuccessful, or inharmonious: *the marriage turned sour.* — *verb trans., intrans.* to make or become sour, especially bad, unsuccessful, or inharmonious. [from Anglo-Saxon *sur*]

. . . .

◼ *adj.* **1** tart, acid, sharp, pungent, vinegary, bitter. **2** rancid, off. **3** sullen, ill-tempered, peevish, crabbed, crusty, disagreeable, miserable, embittered, acrimonious.

◪ *adj.* **1** sweet, sugary. **2** fresh. **3** good-natured.

. . . .

source *noun* **1** the place, thing, person, or circumstance from which anything begins or develops; origin. **2** the point where a river or stream begins. **3** a thing, place, etc, from which something may be obtained: *a source of dietary fibre.* **4** a person, or a book or other document, providing information or evidence. [from Latin *surgere*, to rise]

. . . .

◼ **1** origin, derivation, beginning, start, commencement, cause, root. **2** spring, fountainhead, wellhead. **3** supply, mine. **4** authority, informant.

. . . .

sour cream cream deliberately made sour by the action of bacteria, for use in savoury dishes.

sour grapes envy and resentment in the form of pretended dislike or disapproval of the thing or person envied.

sourly *adv.* in a sour way, with a sour expression.

sourpuss *noun colloq.* a habitually sullen or miserable person.

souse /saʊs/ — *verb* **1** to steep or cook in vinegar or white wine. **2** to pickle. **3** to plunge in a liquid. **4** to make thoroughly wet; to drench. — *noun* **1** an act of sousing. **2** the liquid in which food is soused. **3** *North Amer., esp. US* pickle; any pickled food. [from Old German *sulza*]

soused *adj. slang* drunk.

soutane /suːˈtɑːn/ *noun* the robe or cassock worn by a Roman Catholic priest. [from French *soutane*, from Latin *subtus*, beneath]

south — *noun* (*also* **the south** or **the South**) the direction to the right of a person facing the rising sun in the N hemisphere; directly opposite north; any part of the earth, a country, a town, etc lying in this direction. — *adv.* towards the south. — *adj.* **1** of, facing, or lying in the south; on the side or in the part nearest the south. **2** *said of the wind* blowing from the south. [from Anglo-Saxon *suth*]

southbound *adj.* going or leading towards the south.

south-east — *noun* **1** the direction midway between south and east. **2** (**the south-east** or **South-East**) an area lying in this direction. — *adv.* in this direction. — *adj.* of, facing, or lying in the south-east.

southeaster *noun* a wind blowing form the south-east.

south-easterly — *adj., adv.* **1** south-east. **2** *said of the wind* blowing from the south-east. — *noun* (PL. **south-easterlies**) a wind blowing from the south-east.

south-eastern *adj.* to the south-east.

southerly — *adj.* **1** *said of a wind, etc* coming from the south. **2** looking, lying, etc towards the south. — *adv.* to or towards the south. — *noun* (PL. **southerlies**) a southerly wind.

southern *adj.* **1** of or in the south. **2** facing or directed towards the south.

southerner *noun* a person who lives in or comes from the south, especially the southern part of England or of the USA.

southern lights (**the southern lights**) the aurora australis.

southernmost *adj.* situated furthest south.

southpaw *colloq.* — *noun* a left-handed person, especially a left-handed boxer (ie one who leads with the right hand). — *adj.* left-handed.

South Pole (**the South Pole**) the southernmost point of the Earth's axis of rotation, at 90°S, longitude 0°, in central Antarctica.

South Sea (**the South Sea**) the southern part of the Pacific Ocean.

southward or **southwards** *adv., adj.* towards the south.

south-west — *noun* **1** the direction midway between south and west. **2** (**the south-west** or **South-West**) an area lying in this direction. — *adv.* in this direction. — *adj.* of, facing, or lying in the south-west.

southwester *noun* a wind blowing form the south-west.

south-westerly — *adj., adv.* **1** south-west. **2** *said of the wind* blowing from the south-west. — *noun* (PL. **south-westerlies**) a wind blowing from the south-west.

south-western *adj.* to the south-west.

souvenir /suːvəˈnɪə(r)/ *noun* a thing bought, kept, or given as a reminder of a place, person, or occasion; a memento. [from French *souvenir*]

     ⊟ memento, reminder, remembrance, keepsake, relic, token.

sou'wester *noun* a seaman's waterproof hat with a large flap-like brim at the back. [a contraction of SOUTH-WESTER]

sovereign /ˈsɒvrɪn/ — *noun* **1** a supreme ruler or head, especially a monarch. **2** a former British gold coin worth £1. — *adj.* **1** having supreme power or authority: *a sovereign ruler*. **2** politically independent: *a sovereign state*. **3** outstanding; unrivalled; utmost: *sovereign intelligence*. [from Old French *sovrain*]

     ⊟ *noun* **1** ruler, monarch, king, queen, emperor, empress, potentate, chief. *adj.* **1** ruling, royal, imperial, absolute, unlimited, supreme, paramount. **2** independent, autonomous. **3** extreme, utmost, outstanding, unrivalled, unequalled.

sovereignty *noun* (PL. **sovereignties**) **1** supreme and independent political power or authority. **2** a politically independent state.

soviet /ˈsəʊvɪət, ˈsɒvɪət/ — *noun* **1** any of the councils that made up the local and national governments in the former Soviet Union. **2** (**Soviet**) a native or inhabitant of the former Soviet Union. — *adj.* (**Soviet**) of the former Soviet Union. [from Russian *sovet*, council]

sow[1] *verb* (pronounced like *so*) (PAST TENSE **sowed**; PAST PARTICIPLE **sown, sowed**) **1** to plant (seed); to plant (land) with (crops of a particular kind). **2** to introduce or arouse: *sowed the seeds of doubt in his mind*. [from Anglo-Saxon *sawan*]

     ⊟ **1** plant, seed, scatter, strew. **2** lodge, implant, spread, disseminate.

sow[2] *noun* (pronounced like *now*) an adult female pig. [from Anglo-Saxon *sugu*]

soya bean or **soy bean 1** any of numerous varieties of an annual plant (*Glycine max*) of the pulse family native to SW Asia but widely cultivated for its edible seeds (beans). **2** the edible seed of this plant, which is rich in protein and oil. Soya-bean oil is used as a cooking oil and in the manufacture of margarine, soap, enamels, paints, and varnishes. The residue left after oil extraction is used as a protein concentrate for human diets, and as a feed for animal livestock. Soya beans are also ground into flour, fermented to make soy sauce, and used to make soya milk and bean curd (used as a meat substitute). [from Japanese *sho-yu*]

soy sauce a salty brown sauce made from soya beans, widely used in Eastern (especially Chinese) cooking. [from Chinese *shi-yu*, salt bean oil]

sozzled *adj. colloq.* drunk.

spa *noun* **1** a mineral water spring. **2** a town where such a spring is or was once located. [from *Spa*, a Belgian town]

space — *noun* **1** the three-dimensional medium in which all matter exists. **2** a portion of this; room: *enough space in the garden for a pool*. **3** an interval of distance; a gap. **4** an empty place: *a space at our table*. **5** a period of time: *within the space of ten minutes*. **6** (*also* **outer space**) all those regions of the Universe that lie beyond the Earth's atmosphere: *space technology/intergalactic space*. — *verb* (*usually* **space something out**) to arrange things with intervals, or greater intervals, of distance or time between each. — **spaced out** *slang* in a dazed or stupefied state from, or as if from, the effects of drugs. [from Latin *spatium*]

     ⊟ *noun* **2** room, scope, range, elbow-room, leeway, margin, capacity, volume. **3** gap, opening, interval, blank, omission, lacuna. **4** place, seat, accommodation.

space age — *noun* (*usually* **the space age**) the present period in history, in which travel in space has become possible. — *adj.* (**space-age**) **1** technologically very advanced. **2** having a futuristic appearance.

spacecraft *noun* a manned or unmanned vehicle for travel in space or for orbiting the Earth.

Space Invaders *trademark* any of various video games in which players use buttons or levers to fire at invading creatures descending the screen.

space law a branch of international law which is concerned with rights in air space and outer space. Foreign aircraft have no right to fly over the territory or territorial waters of another state. In practice, states enter into bilateral agreements to permit use of each other's air space. The Outer Space Treaty of 1967 provides that outer space may be used by all states.

spaceman or **spacewoman** *noun* a male or female traveller in space.

space platform a space station.

space probe an unmanned spacecraft that is designed to study conditions in space, especially on or around one or more planets or their natural satellites, and to transmit scientific data back to Earth.

space shuttle a reusable crewed US launch vehicle, used to put a payload such as a satellite, space probe, scientific equipment, or the Spacelab module, into space. First launched in 1981, it was developed by NASA to make repeated journeys into space, taking off like a rocket but landing on a runway like an aircraft.

space sickness a collection of symptoms, similar to those of travel sickness, experienced by astronauts during their first few days in space, until their bodies have adapted to conditions of weightlessness.

space station a large orbiting spacecraft that is designed to provide accommodation and scientific and technological research facilities in space for crews of astronauts over periods of weeks or months, eg Skylab, Salyut, Mir. Space stations enable detailed astronomical observations to be made, and long-term experiments on the effects of weightlessness to be conducted. All space stations to date have been large Earth-orbiting satellites.

space suit a suit specially designed for use in space travel.

spacetime continuum reality regarded as having four dimensions: length, breadth, height, and time.

space walk an excursion by one or more astronauts, wearing pressurized space suits, outside their spacecraft while in space.

spacious *adj.* having ample room or space; extending over a large area.

. . . .

■ roomy, capacious, ample, big, large, broad, wide, huge, vast, extensive, open, uncrowded.

🖪 small, narrow, cramped, confined.

. . . .

spaciousness *noun* being spacious.

spade¹ *noun* 1 a long-handled digging tool with a broad metal blade which is pushed into the ground with the foot. 2 a child's toy version of this, usually of plastic: *bucket and spade.* — **call a spade a spade** to speak plainly and frankly. [from Anglo-Saxon *spadu*]

spade² *noun* 1 any of the suit of playing-cards that carries an emblem like a black inverted heart. 2 (**spades**) this suit. 3 *offensive slang* a black person. [from Greek *spathe*, broad blade]

spadework *noun* hard or boring preparatory work.

spadix /ˈspeɪdɪks/ *noun* (PL. **spadices**) *Bot.* a fleshy spike of flowers. [from Greek *spadix-ikos*, a torn-off branch]

spaghetti /spəˈgɛtɪ/ *noun* pasta in the form of long thin string-like strands. [from Italian *spaghetti*, from *spago*, cord]

Spaghetti Junction *Brit.* a popular name for the complex system of intersecting motorways at Gravelly Hill, Birmingham, with many underpasses and overpasses designed to carry large volumes of traffic from and to the M6, A38, and A5127. Hence, any complex interchange which resembles the intertwined strands of cooked spaghetti.

spaghetti western a western film shot in Europe with an international cast, typically by an Italian director, and typically violent and melodramatic.

spake *old use.* past tense of SPEAK.

Spam *noun trademark* tinned processed meat made mainly from pork. [from *spiced ham*]

spam — *noun* electronic junk mail. — *verb trans., intrans.* to send out electronic junk mail. [from the repetition of

the word SPAM on a sketch from the British television show 'Monty Python's Flying Circus']

span — *noun* 1 the length between the supports of a bridge or arch. 2 a measure of length equal to the distance between the tips of thumb and little finger on an extended hand, conventionally taken as 9in (23cm). 3 *often in compounds* length from end to end in distance or time: *the wingspan of an aircraft/the timespan of the war.* — *verb* (**spanned, spanning**) to extend across or over. [from Anglo-Saxon *spann*]

. . . .

🖿 *noun* 3 spread, stretch, reach, range, length, distance, duration, period, spell. *verb* arch, vault, bridge, link, cross, extend across *or* over, traverse, cover.

. . . .

Spandex or **spandex** *noun trademark* 1 a synthetic elastic fibre made chiefly from polyurethane. 2 a fabric made from this. [an inversion of EXPAND]

spandrel or **spandril** /ˈspandrəl/ *noun* the triangular space between the curve of an arch and the enclosing mouldings, string-course, etc. It also refers, particularly in 20c architecture, to an infill panel below a window.

spangle — *noun* a small piece of glittering material, especially a sequin. — *verb* 1 to decorate (eg a piece of clothing) with spangles. 2 *intrans.* to glitter. [from Anglo-Saxon *spang*, clasp]

Spanglish *noun* a language consisting of a mixture of English and Spanish words and phrases, especially that used in Hispanic communities in the USA.

Spaniard /ˈspanjəd/ *noun* a native or citizen of Spain. [from Old French *Espaignart*]

spaniel — *noun* any of several breeds of dog with long drooping ears and a silky coat. — *adj.* expressing unwavering devotion or subservience: *his spaniel eyes.* [from Old French *espaigneul*, Spanish dog]

Spanish — *noun* 1 (**the Spanish**) the people of Spain. 2 their language, also spoken in the southern USA and Central and S America. — *adj.* relating to Spain, its people, or their language. [from *Spain* + -ISH]

Spanish guitar a six-stringed acoustic guitar of the kind normally used for playing classical and folk music.

spank — *verb* to smack on the buttocks with the flat of the hand, usually several times as a punishment. — *noun* such a smack. [imitative]

. . . .

🖿 *verb* smack, slap, *colloq.* wallop, thrash.

. . . .

spanker *noun* a fore-and-aft sail on the aftermost mast (mizzenmast) of a sailing ship, used to take advantage of a following wind.

spanking — *noun* a series of spanks, especially as a punishment. — *adv. colloq.* absolutely; strikingly: *a spanking new watch.* — *adj. colloq.* 1 brisk: *a spanking pace.* 2 impressively fine; striking.

spanner *noun* a tool for turning a nut or bolt, a lever with a shaped end. — **throw a spanner in the works** to frustrate or upset a plan or system. [from German, from *spannen*, to stretch]

spar¹ *noun* a strong thick pole of wood or metal, especially one used as a mast or beam on a ship. [from Norse *sperra*]

spar² *verb intrans.* (**sparred, sparring**) (*often* **spar with someone**) 1 to engage in boxing practice with a partner; to box against an imaginary opponent, for practice. 2 to engage in lively and light-hearted argument. [perhaps from Old French *esparer*, to kick out]

spar³ *noun combining form* any of various translucent non-metallic minerals splitting easily into layers: *feldspar/fluorspar.* [from Old German *spar*]

spare — *adj.* 1 held in reserve as a replacement. 2 available for use; unoccupied: *a spare seat next to me.* 3 lean; thin. 4 frugal; scanty. — *verb* 1 to afford to give or give away. 2 to refrain from harming, punishing, killing, or destroying: *spare his life/spare their feelings.* 3 to avoid causing or bringing on: *will spare your blushes*. **4** to avoid incurring: *no expense spared*. — *noun* a duplicate kept in reserve for use as a replacement. — **go spare** *slang* to become extremely angry or distressed. **to spare** left over; surplus to what is required. [from Anglo-Saxon *sparian*]

⊟ *adj.* **1** reserve, emergency, extra, additional, unused, over, surplus. **2** free, unoccupied. **3** thin, lean, skinny, bony, gaunt. *verb* **1** grant, allow, afford. **2** pardon, let off, reprieve, release, free.

spare part a part, for a machine, etc, held in reserve to replace an existing identical part that becomes faulty.
spare ribs ribs of pork with only a small amount of meat on them.
spare tyre 1 an extra tyre carried to replace a punctured tyre. **2** *colloq.* a band of fat just above a person's waist.
sparing *adj.* economical or frugal, often to the point of inadequacy or meanness.

⊟ economical, thrifty, careful, frugal, meagre, miserly, mean.
⊠ unsparing, liberal, lavish.

sparingly *adv.* economically, frugally.
spark — *noun* **1** a tiny red-hot glowing particle thrown off by burning material, or by the friction between two hard (especially metal or stone) surfaces. **2** an electrical charge flashing across a gap between two conductors. **3** a trace, hint, or glimmer: *not a spark of intelligence*. **4** a lively, witty, or intelligent person: *a bright spark*. — *verb intrans.* to throw off sparks. — **spark something off** to stimulate or provoke it, especially as the final cause of several. [from Anglo-Saxon *spærca*]

⊟ *noun* **1, 2** flash, flare. **3** flicker, glimmer, hint, trace, vestige, scrap, atom, jot. **spark off** kindle, ignite, set off, trigger, start, cause, prompt, provoke, stimulate, excite, inspire.

spark gap *Engineering* the space between two electrodes across which a high-voltage spark passes.
sparkle — *verb intrans.* **1** to give off sparks. **2** to shine with tiny points of bright light. **3** *said of wine, etc* to give off bubbles of carbon dioxide; to effervesce. **4** to be impressively lively or witty. — *noun* **1** an act of sparkling; sparkling appearance. **2** liveliness; vivacity; wit. [a diminutive of SPARK]

⊟ *verb* **2** twinkle, glitter, flash, gleam, glint, glisten, shimmer, coruscate, shine, beam. **3** effervesce, fizz, bubble. **4** scintillate. *noun* **1** twinkle, glitter, flash, gleam, glint, flicker, spark, radiance, brilliance. **2** liveliness, vivacity, life, animation, vitality, spirit, wit.

sparkler *noun* **1** a hand-held firework that gives off sparks. **2** *colloq.* a diamond or other impressive jewel.
sparkling *adj.* that sparkles.
spark plug or **sparking plug** in a petrol engine, an insulated plug supporting two electrodes between which a high-voltage spark passes, igniting the explosive mixture of fuel and air in the cylinder.
sparring partner 1 a person with whom a boxer practises. **2** a person with whom one enjoys a lively argument.
sparrow *noun* **1** any of various small grey or brown perching birds with a short conical bill adapted for cracking seeds, found in many parts of the world. The continual cheeping and chirruping of house sparrows serves to keep together large flocks, which feed, dust-bathe, and roost together. **2** (*in compounds*) applied to some similar small birds: *hedge sparrow* [from Anglo-Saxon *spearwa*]
sparrow-hawk *noun* a short-winged bird of prey of the falcon family.
sparse *adj.* thinly scattered or dotted about; scanty. [from Latin *spargere*, to scatter]

⊟ scarce, scanty, meagre, scattered, infrequent, sporadic, ⊠ plentiful, thick, dense.

sparsely *adv.* in a sparse way.
sparseness or **sparsity** *noun* being sparse.
spartan — *adj.* **1** *said eg of living conditions* austere; frugal; harshly basic. **2** militaristic. — *noun* a spartan person. [from *Sparta*, an ancient Greek city noted for its austerity]

⊟ *adj.* **1** austere, harsh, severe, rigorous, ascetic, abstemious, frugal, plain, simple, bleak.
⊠ *adj.* **1** luxurious, self-indulgent.

spasm *noun* **1** a sudden uncontrollable jerk caused by a contraction of the muscles. **2** a short period of activity; a spell. **3** a sudden burst of emotion: *spasm of anger*. [from Greek *spasma*, contraction]

⊟ **1** contraction, jerk, twitch, tic, fit, convulsion, seizure, attack. **2** spell, burst, bout. **3** eruption, outburst, frenzy.

spasmodic *adj.* occurring in or consisting of short periods; not constant or regular; intermittent.

⊟ sporadic, occasional, intermittent, erratic, irregular, fitful, jerky.
⊠ continuous, uninterrupted.

spasmodically *adv.* in a spasmodic way.
spastic — *noun* **1** a person suffering from spastic paralysis. **2** *derog. slang* a clumsy or useless person. — *adj.* affected with spastic paralysis. [from Greek *spastikos*; see SPASM]
spastic paralysis permanent uncontrollable jerky muscle movement caused by injury to the muscle-controlling part of the brain.
spat[1] see SPIT[1].
spat[2] *colloq.* — *noun* a trivial or petty fight or quarrel. — *verb intrans.* (**spatted, spatting**) to engage in a spat. [probably imitative]
spat[3] *noun* either of a pair of cloth coverings fitting round the ankles and over the tops of the shoes. [an abbreviation of obsolete *spatterdash*, a long gaiter protecting the trousers from mud splashes]
spate *noun* a sudden rush or increased quantity; a burst: *received a spate of complaints*. — **in spate** *said of a river* fast-flowing due to flooding.

⊟ flood, deluge, torrent, rush, burst.

spathe /speɪð/ *noun Bot.* a large petal-like bract that surrounds and protects a certain type of flower-head, known as a *spadix* (a large cylindrical fleshy axis), eg in lords-and-ladies. [from Greek *spathe*, a broad blade]
spatial /ˈspeɪʃəl/ *adj.* of or relating to space. [from Latin *spatium*, space]
spatter — *verb trans., intrans.* (**spattered, spattering**) to splash in scattered drops or patches. — *noun* **1** a quantity spattered. **2** the act of spattering.
spatula *noun* a mixing or spreading tool with a broad blunt (often flexible) blade. [from Latin *spatula*, broad blade]
spawn — *noun* the eggs of frogs, fish, and molluscs, laid in water in a soft transparent jelly-like mass. — *verb* **1** *intrans., said of frogs, fish, etc* to lay eggs. **2** *trans.* to give rise to; to lead to: *the film's success spawned several sequels*. [from Old French *espandre*, to shed]
spay *verb* to remove the ovaries from (a female animal). [from Old French *espeier*, to cut with a sword]
SPCK *abbrev.* Society for Promoting Christian Knowledge.
speak *verb* (PAST TENSE **spoke**; PAST PARTICIPLE **spoken**) **1** *intrans.* to utter words; to talk. **2** to say; to utter. **3** (*also*

speak to or **with someone** *said of one person or several to* talk to someone, or to each other: *they haven't spoken for years/may I speak with you for a moment?* **4** *intrans.* to make a speech. **5** to communicate, or be able to communicate, in (a particular language): *he speaks French well and German fluently.* **6** *intrans.* (**speak of something**) to make mention of it; to refer to it. **7** *intrans.* to convey meaning: *actions speak louder than words.* — **be on speaking terms** to be sufficiently friendly or familiar to hold a conversation. **speak for someone** to give an opinion on their behalf: *I will be there, but I can't speak for the others.* **speak for itself** to have an obvious meaning; to need no further explanation or comment. **speak one's mind** to say boldly what one thinks. **speak out** *intrans.* **1** to speak openly; to state one's views forcefully. **2** to speak more loudly. **speak up** *intrans.* to speak more loudly. **no ... to speak of** no ... worth mentioning: *received no education to speak of.* [from Anglo-Saxon *specan*]

⊞ **1** talk, communicate. **2** say, state, declare, express, utter, voice, articulate, enunciate, pronounce. **3** talk, converse. **4** lecture, hold forth, declaim. **6** mention, refer to, talk about, discuss.

speakeasy *noun* (PL. **speakeasies**) *slang* in the US, a bar or other place selling alcohol illicitly during Prohibition.

speaker *noun* **1** a person who speaks, especially one making a formal speech. **2** a loudspeaker. **3** (*also* **Speaker**) the person presiding over debate in a law-making assembly, eg the House of Commons.

⊞ **1** orator, lecturer, spokesperson.

speaking clock *Brit.* a telephone service in which the exact time is given by means of a recorded message.

spear — *noun* **1** a weapon consisting of a long pole with a sharp (especially metal) point, for throwing from the shoulder. **2** a spiky plant shoot, eg a blade of grass. — *verb* to pierce with, or as if with, a spear. [from Anglo-Saxon *spere*]

spearhead — *noun* the leading part of an attacking force. — *verb* to lead (a movement, campaign, or attack).

spearmint *noun* **1** a common variety of mint plant, from which a flavouring is made for use in sweets, toothpaste, etc. **2** the flavouring.

spec[1] — **on spec** *colloq.* as a speculation or gamble, in the hope of success: *wrote to them on spec, asking for a job.* [a shortening of SPECULATION]

spec[2] *noun colloq.* specification.

special — *adj.* **1** distinct from, especially better than, others of the same kind; exceptional. **2** designed for a particular purpose. **3** not ordinary or common: *special circumstances.* **4** particular; great: *make a special effort.* — *noun* a special thing or person, eg an extra edition of a newspaper or a train running a particular service. [from Latin *specialis*]

⊞ *adj.* **1** exceptional, different, distinctive, characteristic, peculiar, select, choice, important, significant, major, noteworthy, remarkable, extraordinary. **2** particular, specific, individual, unique, exclusive. **3** unusual, uncommon, exceptional.

⊟ *adj.* **2** general. **3** ordinary, common, usual, normal.

Special Branch a British police department dealing with matters of political security.

special constable a member of a reserve police force, called upon eg in times of national emergency.

special delivery a delivery of post outside normal delivery times.

special education the education of children with special needs, especially those physically or mentally handicapped.

specialism *noun* **1** a subject of study one specialises in. **2** the act of specialising in some subject.

specialist *noun* **1** a person whose work, interest, or expertise is concentrated on a particular subject. **2** an organism with a narrow range of food and habitat preferences.

⊞ **1** consultant, authority, expert, master, professional, connoisseur.

speciality or *North Amer.* **specialty** *noun* (PL. **specialities, specialties**) **1** a thing specialized in: *seafood is the restaurant's speciality.* **2** a special feature, service, or product.

⊞ strength, forte, field, pièce de résistance.

specialization or **specialisation** *noun* specializing.

specialize or **specialise** *verb* **1** (*often* **specialize in something**) to devote all one's efforts to, or reserve one's best efforts for, one particular activity, field of study, etc. **2** to adapt to be used for a specific purpose.

specialized or **specialised** *adj.* adapted, developed, or modified for a particular purpose.

special licence a licence allowing a marriage to take place at short notice, without the usual legal formalities.

specially *adv.* **1** in a special way. **2** for a special purpose.

special school a school designed for the teaching of children with particular needs, especially arising from physical or mental handicaps.

speciation *noun Biol.* the process whereby one or more new species are formed from an existing species, eg as a result of geographical separation of different populations of the parent species.

specie /ˈspiːʃiː/ *noun technical* money in coin form, as distinct from notes. [from Latin *in specie*, in kind]

species /ˈspiːʃiːz/ *noun* (PL. **species**) **1** the fundamental unit in plant and animal classification, consisting of a group of organisms that are able to interbreed among themselves and produce fertile offspring. Related species are grouped into genera, and some species may be divided into subspecies, varieties, breeds, etc. **2** *Chem.* a particular type of atom, molecule, or ion. **3** a kind or type. [from Latin *species*, kind, appearance]

speciesism /ˈspiːʃiːzɪzm, ˈspiːsiːzɪzm/ *noun* the assumption that humans are superior to all other species of animals and are therefore justified in exploiting them for their own use.

specific — *adj.* **1** of a particular nature; precisely identified. **2** precise in meaning; not vague. — *noun* **1** (*usually* **specifics**) a specific detail, eg of a plan or scheme. **2** a drug used to treat a specific disease. [from Latin *species*, kind + *facere*, to make]

⊞ *adj.* **1** particular, special, fixed, definite. **2** precise, exact, clear-cut, explicit, express, unambiguous, unequivocal.

⊟ *adj.* **1** general. **2** vague, approximate.

specifically *adv.* **1** in a specific way. **2** as a specific instance.

specification *noun* **1** (*often* **specifications**) a detailed description of a thing built or constructed. **2** the nature and quality of the parts that it is made up of: *a car with a hi-tech specification.* **3** the act of specifying. **4** something specified.

⊞ **1** description, listing. **4** requirement, condition, particular, detail.

specific gravity relative density.

specific heat capacity see HEAT CAPACITY.

specify *verb* (**specifies, specified**) **1** to refer to or identify precisely. **2** to state as a condition or requirement. [see SPECIFIC]

⊞ **1** define, spell out, designate, name, cite, mention, describe, delineate. **2** stipulate, particularize, detail, itemize, enumerate, list.

specimen *noun* **1** a sample or example of something, especially an object studied or put in a collection. **2** a sample of blood, urine, or tissue on which medical tests are carried out. **3** *colloq.* a person of a particular kind: *an ugly specimen*. [from Latin, from *specere*, to see]

☐ **1** sample, example, instance, illustration, model, exemplar, representative, copy, exhibit.

specious /'spiːʃəs/ *adj.* seeming to be good, sound, or just, but really false or flawed: *specious arguments*. [from Latin *species*, appearance]

speciousness or **speciosity** *noun* being specious.

speck *noun* a small spot, stain, or particle. [from Anglo-Saxon *specca*]

speckle — *noun* a little spot, especially one of several on a different-coloured background. — *verb* to mark with speckles. [a diminutive of SPECK]

speckled *adj.* covered or marked with specks or speckles.

specs *pl. noun colloq.* spectacles.

spectacle *noun* **1** a thing seen; a sight, especially impressive, wonderful, or ridiculous. **2** a public display or exhibition. **3** (**spectacles**) a pair of lenses held in a frame over the eyes, used to correct faulty eyesight. — **make a spectacle of oneself** to behave in a way that attracts ridicule or scorn. [from Latin *spectaculum*, from *specere*, to look at]

☐ **1** scene, sight, curiosity, wonder, marvel, phenomenon. **2** show, performance, display, exhibition, parade, pageant, extravaganza.

spectacled bear the only bear native to the S hemisphere, found in forests in the W foothills of the Andes. It has a small body with dark fur, and is so called because there are pale rings around its eyes.

spectacular — *adj.* **1** impressively striking to see or watch. **2** remarkable; dramatic. — *noun* a spectacular show or display. [see SPECTACLE]

☐ *adj.* IMPRESSIVE, STRIKING. **1** grand, splendid, magnificent, daring, breathtaking, dazzling, eye-catching, colourful. **2** remarkable, dramatic, stunning, staggering, amazing.
☒ *adj.* UNIMPRESSIVE.

spectacularly *adv.* in a spectacular way.

spectate *verb intrans.* to be a spectator; to look on.

spectator *noun* a person who watches an event or incident. [from Latin, from *spectare*, to look]

☐ watcher, viewer, onlooker, looker-on, bystander, witness, eyewitness, observer.
☒ player, participant.

spectral *adj.* relating to or like a spectre.

spectre /'spɛktə(r)/ *noun* **1** a visible ghost; an apparition. **2** a haunting fear; the threat of something unpleasant. [from French *spectre*, from Latin *specere*, to look at]

☐ **1** ghost, phantom, spirit, apparition, vision. **2** fear, dread, threat, menace.

spectrometer *noun* an instrument for measuring spectra in terms of wavelength and energy.

spectroscope *noun Chem.* an optical instrument that is used to produce a spectrum for a particular chemical compound, which can then be observed and analysed in order to identify the compound, determine its structure, etc.

spectrum *noun* (PL. **spectra, spectrums**) **1** *Physics* (*in full* **visible spectrum**) the band of colours (red, orange, yellow, green, blue, indigo, and violet) produced when white light is split into its constituent wavelengths by passing it through a prism. **2** a continuous band or a series of lines representing the wavelengths or frequencies of electromagnetic radiation (eg visible light, X-rays, radio waves) emitted or absorbed by a particular substance. **3** any full range: *the whole spectrum of human emotions*. [from Latin *spectrum*, appearance]

speculate *verb intrans.* **1** (*often* **speculate on** or **about something**) to consider the circumstances or possibilities regarding it, usually without any factual basis and without coming to a definite conclusion. **2** to engage in risky financial transactions, usually in the hope of making a quick profit. [from Latin *speculari*, to look out]

☐ **1** wonder, contemplate, muse, reflect, consider, theorize, hypothesize, suppose, guess, conjecture, surmise. **2** gamble, risk, hazard, venture.

speculation *noun* **1** speculating or a result of speculating. **2** a risky investment of money for the sake of large profit.
speculative /'spɛkjʊlətɪv/ *adj.* involving speculation.

☐ conjectural, hypothetical, theoretical, notional, abstract, academic, risky, hazardous, uncertain, unpredictable.

speculator *noun* a person who speculates, especially financially.

speculum *noun* (PL. **specula**) **1** *Optics* a mirror with a reflective surface, usually of polished metal. **2** *Medicine* an instrument that is used to enlarge the opening of a body cavity so that the interior may be inspected. [from Latin *speculum*, mirror, from *specere*, to look at]

sped see SPEED.

speech *noun* **1** the ability to speak. **2** a way of speaking: *slurred speech*. **3** that which is spoken; spoken language. **4** a talk addressed to other people. [from Anglo-Saxon *spec*]

☐ **2** diction, articulation, enunciation, elocution, delivery. **3** utterance, language, tongue, parlance, dialect, jargon. **4** oration, address, discourse, talk, lecture, harangue, *colloq.* spiel, monologue, soliloquy.

speechify *verb intrans.* (**speechifies, speechified**) *colloq.* to make (especially long and tedious) speeches.

speechless *adj.* temporarily unable to speak, because of surprise, shock, emotion, etc.

☐ dumbfounded, dumbstruck, thunderstruck, amazed, aghast, tongue-tied, inarticulate, mute, dumb, silent.
☒ talkative.

speech recognition *Comput.* the understanding of an individual's speech patterns, or of continuous speech, by a computer.

speech therapist a person who provides speech therapy.
speech therapy the treatment of speech and language disorders.

speed — *noun* **1** rate of movement or action. **2** quickness; rapidity: *with speed*. **3** a gear setting on a vehicle: *five-speed gearbox*. **4** a photographic film's sensitivity to light. **5** *slang* amphetamines. — *verb intrans.* (PAST TENSE AND PAST PARTICIPLE **sped**) **1** to move quickly. **2** to drive at a speed higher than the legal limit. — **at speed** quickly. **speed up** or **speed something up** to increase speed or cause it to increase in speed. [from Anglo-Saxon *sped*]

☐ *noun* **1** velocity, rate, pace, tempo. **2** quickness, swiftness, rapidity, alacrity, haste, acceleration. *verb* **1** race, tear, *colloq.* belt, zoom, career, bowl along, sprint, gallop, hasten, hurry, rush. **speed up** accelerate, quicken.
☒ *noun* **2** slowness, delay. **speed up** slow down.

speedboat *noun* a motor boat capable of high speeds.

speed bump a low hump across a road intended to slow down traffic.

speedily *adv.* in a speedy way, with haste.

speed limit the maximum speed a vehicle may legally travel at on a given stretch of road.

speedo *noun* (PL. **speedos**) *colloq.* a speedometer.

speed of light *Physics* (SYMBOL **C**) the speed at which electromagnetic waves, including visible light, travel through empty space, ie a vacuum. The speed of light is about 3 x 10⁸ metres per second, the highest speed possible in the universe.

speedometer *noun* an instrument that indicates the speed at which a motor vehicle is travelling. It often incorporates an odometer that displays the total mileage.

speed trap a stretch of road over which police monitor the speed of vehicles, often with electronic equipment.

speedway *noun* **1** racing on lightweight motorcycles round a cinder track. **2** the track used.

speedwell *noun* a plant of the foxglove family, with small blue or pink flowers.

speedy *adj.* (**speedier, speediest**) fast; prompt; without delay.

▪ fast, quick, swift, rapid, nimble, express, prompt, immediate, hurried, hasty, cursory.
▪ slow, leisurely.

spelaeology or **speleology** /spiːliˈɒlədʒɪ/ *noun* **1** the scientific study of caves. **2** cave exploring. [from Greek *spelaion*, cave + -LOGY]

spell¹ *verb* (PAST TENSE AND PAST PARTICIPLE **spelt, spelled**) **1** *trans., intrans.* to write or name the letters making up (a word or words) in their correct order. **2** to form (a word) when written in sequence: *B, A, D spells 'bad'.* **3** to indicate clearly: *his angry expression spelt trouble.* — **spell something out 1** to read, write, or speak the letters of (a word) one by one. **2** to explain something clearly and in detail. [from Old French *espeller*]

spell² *noun* **1** a set of words which, especially when spoken, is believed to have magical power. **2** the influence of such power: *cast a spell on someone.* **3** a strong attracting influence; a fascination. [from Anglo-Saxon *spell*, narrative, from *spellian*, to speak or announce]

▪ **1** charm, incantation. **2** magic, sorcery, bewitchment, enchantment. **3** fascination, glamour.

spell³ *noun* a period, eg of illness, work, or weather of a particular kind. [from Anglo-Saxon *spelian*, to act for another]

▪ period, time, bout, session, term, season, interval, stretch, patch, turn, stint.

spellbinding *adj.* causing one to be spellbound.

spellbound *adj.* completely charmed or fascinated, as if held by magical power.

▪ bewitched, enchanted, charmed, fascinated, enthralled, captivated, entranced, transfixed, hypnotized, mesmerized.

spellcheck or **spellchecker** *noun* a program in a word processor that checks the accuracy of the user's spelling.

spelling *noun* **1** ability to spell. **2** a way a word is spelt.

spelling reform a movement that aims to make English spelling more regular in relation to speech. Many schemes have been suggested, both in Britain and the USA, with the aim of standardizing and simplifying spelling. Examples include: standardizing systems, such as *Regularized English*, which make use of the existing alphabet; and,

augmenting or supplementing systems, such as *i.t.a.*, which add new symbols to the regular alphabet.

spelt see SPELL¹.

spelunking /spəˈlʌŋkɪŋ/ *noun North Amer.* the sport or activity of exploring caves; potholing. [from Latin *spelunca*, from Greek *spelynx*, a cave]

spend *verb* (PAST TENSE AND PAST PARTICIPLE **spent**) **1** *trans., intrans.* to use up or pay out (money). **2** to use or devote (eg time or energy): *needed to spend a few hours on the cleaning.* **3** to use up completely; to exhaust: *their passion was spent.* — **spend a penny** *colloq.* to urinate. [from Latin *expendere*]

▪ **1** pay out, *colloq.* fork out, *colloq.* shell out, invest, *colloq.* splash out. **2** use, employ, apply, devote, expend, pass, fill, occupy. **3** use up, exhaust, consume.
▪ **1** save, hoard.

spendthrift *noun* a person who spends money freely and carelessly.

▪ squanderer, prodigal, profligate, wastrel.
▪ miser.

spent past tense and past participle of SPEND. — *adj.* used up; exhausted.

sperm *noun* **1** in animals, the small motile male gamete (reproductive cell) that locates, penetrates, and fertilizes the female gamete (the egg or ovum). In mammals it is produced in the testes, and consists of a head containing a nucleus but very little cytoplasm, and a long flagellum or 'tail' that lashes to move the sperm forward. **2** semen, a fluid containing millions of such gametes, together with nutrients, produced in the reproductive organs of male mammals, and introduced into the reproductive tract of the female during copulation. [from Greek *sperma*, seed]

spermaceti /spɜːməˈsetɪ/ *noun* a white translucent waxy solid present in the tissue behind the forehead of the sperm whale, and thought to be involved in echolocation. It is used to make candles, soap, cosmetics, and ointments.

spermatogenesis /spɜːmətəʊˈdʒɛnəsɪs/ *noun Zool.* the formation of sperm in the testes.

spermatophyte /ˈspɜːmətəʊfɪt/ *noun Bot.* any plant belonging to the division *Spermatophyta*, which includes all seed-bearing plants. [from Greek *sperma, -atos*, seed, semen, from *speirein*, to sow]

spermatozoon /spɜːmətəʊˈzəʊɒn/ *noun* (PL. **spermatozoa**) *Biol.* in male animals, a mature sperm cell.

sperm bank a refrigerated store of semen for use in artificial insemination.

spermicide *noun* a substance that kills sperm, used in conjunction with various methods of barrier contraception, eg the condom and the diaphragm.

sperm whale the largest of the toothed whales, with an enormous head (representing a third of the total body length) and a square snout. It is now an endangered species, having been widely hunted for spermaceti, a clear oil found in a large cavity in the head, and for ambergris, produced in the intestines; both substances are used in the cosmetics and perfume industry.

spew — *verb trans., intrans.* **1** to vomit. **2** to pour or cause to pour or stream out. — *noun* vomit. [from Anglo-Saxon *spiowan*, to spit]

SPF *abbrev.* sun protection factor.

sphagnum *noun* (PL. **sphagna**) any moss of the genus *Sphagnum*, the main constituent of peat bogs in temperate regions. It has a spongy structure that retains water, and is used as a packing material, eg for potting plants. [from Greek *sphagnos*]

sphalerite /ˈsfalərʌɪt/ *noun Geol.* a yellowish-brown to brownish-black mineral form of zinc sulphide (ZnS), usually with a resinous lustre, commonly found in coarse or fine granular masses in association with galena. It is the principal ore of zinc, and is also a source of cadmium.

Also called ZINC BLENDE. [from Greek *sphaleros*, deceptive, from its resemblance to galena]

sphere *noun* **1** a round solid figure with a surface on which all points are an equal distance from the centre; a globe or ball. **2** a field of activity. **3** range or extent: *extend one's sphere of influence.* **4** a class or circle within society: *moves in a different sphere.* [from Greek *sphaira*]

· ·

▣ **1** ball, globe, orb, round. **2** field, territory, domain, realm, province, department. **3** range, scope, compass. **4** class, group, circle, set.

· ·

spherical *adj.* sphere-shaped.

· · · · · · · · · · · · · · · · · · · ·

▣ round, sphere-shaped, ball-shaped, globe-shaped.

· ·

spheroid /'sfɪərɔɪd/ *noun* a solid figure that is obtained by rotating an ellipse about its major axis (producing an elongated sphere) or its minor axis (producing a flattened sphere).

sphincter *noun* a ring of muscle that expands and contracts to open and close the entrance to a cavity in the body: *anal sphincter.* [from Greek *sphingein*, to bind tight]

sphinx *noun* **1** (**Sphinx**) *Greek Mythol.* a monster with the head of a woman and the body of a lion, which killed travellers who could not solve the riddles it set. **2** (*also* **Sphinx**) a stone carving or other representation of a sphinx, especially the huge monument near the Egyptian pyramids at Giza. **3** a mysterious or enigmatic person. [from Greek *sphigx*, probably from *sphiggo*, to squeeze]

sphygmomanometer or **sphygmometer** /sfɪg-moʊmə'nɒmɪtə(r)/ *noun Medicine* an instrument for measuring blood pressure in the arteries, consisting of an inflatable cuff for the arm connected to a column of mercury with a graduated scale which indicates blood pressure in millimetres of mercury. [from Greek *sphygmos*, pulse]

spice — *noun* **1** any of numerous strong-smelling vegetable substances used to flavour food, eg pepper, ginger, and nutmeg. **2** such substances collectively. **3** something that adds interest or enjoyment: *variety is the spice of life.* — *verb* **1** to flavour with spice. **2** (*also* **spice something up**) to add interest or enjoyment to it. [from Old French *espice*]

spick and span neat, clean, and tidy. [from obsolete *spick and span new*, extension of Middle English *span new*, brand new]

spicy *adj.* (**spicier**, **spiciest**) **1** tasting or smelling of spices; pungent; piquant. **2** *colloq.* dealing with (especially sexual) scandal.

· · · · · · · · · · · · · · · · · · · ·

▣ **1** hot, piquant, pungent, tangy, seasoned, aromatic, fragrant. **2** scandalous, sensational, racy, risqué, ribald, suggestive, indelicate, improper, indecorous, unseemly.

▣ **1** bland, insipid.

· ·

spider *noun* **1** any of at least 32,000 species of invertebrate animal having eight legs and two main body parts, belonging to the order Araneae, and found in virtually all habitats, including Antarctica. **2** a thing resembling this creature, eg a multi-pointed rest used in snooker. [from Anglo-Saxon *spithra*, from *spinnan*, to spin]

spider monkey an American tree-dwelling monkey with long thin limbs and a long tail.

spider plant a perennial plant (*Chlorophytum comosum*) that has fleshy roots, long narrow curved leaves, and a branched flower stalk bearing white flowers and tufts of small leaves that root on contact with the soil, and develop into new plants. A variety with cream-striped leaves is widely grown as a house plant.

spidery *adj.* **1** thin and untidy: *spidery handwriting.* **2** full of spiders.

spiel /ʃpiːl/ *noun colloq.* **1** a long rambling story, especially given as an excuse: *gave me this whole spiel about missing*

the train. **2** plausible talk, especially sales patter. [from German *spiel*, play]

spiffing *adj. old colloq. use* excellent; splendid.

spigot /'spɪgət/ *noun* **1** a plug used to stop up the vent hole in a cask. **2** a tap fitted to a cask. [from Provençal *espigot*]

spike¹ — *noun* **1** a thin sharp point. **2** a pointed piece of metal, eg one of several on railings or the soles of running-shoes. **3** (**spikes**) running-shoes with such soles. **4** a large metal nail. — *verb* **1** to strike, pierce, or impale with a pointed object. **2** *colloq.* to make (a drink) stronger by adding alcohol or extra alcohol. — **spike someone's guns** *colloq.* to spoil their plans. [from Anglo-Saxon *spicing*]

· · · · · · · · · · · · · · · · · · · ·

▣ *noun* **1** point, spine, barb. **2** prong, tine, nail, stake. *verb* **1** impale, stick, spear, skewer, spit.

· ·

spike² *noun Bot.* a long pointed inflorescence (flower-head) bearing small stalkless flowers along its length, eg plantain, or bearing small secondary spikes or *spikelets* which branch from it, eg grasses and sedges. The youngest flowers are at the tip of the stem and the oldest ones near its base. [from Latin *spica*, ear of corn]

spikelet *noun Bot.* a structure peculiar to the flower heads of grasses, and consisting of one to several reduced flowers enclosed in a series of small bracts. The inflorescence (flower head) of the grass consists of a large number of spikelets arranged in many different ways, according to the species.

spikenard /'spaɪknɑːd/ *noun* **1** a sweet-smelling Indian plant with purple flowers. **2** an oil or ointment made from it. [from Latin *spica nardi*]

spikily *adv.* in a spiky way.

spikiness *noun* being spiky.

spiky *adj.* (**spikier**, **spikiest**) **1** having spikes or pointed ends. **2** *colloq.* bad-tempered.

spill¹ — *verb* (PAST TENSE AND PAST PARTICIPLE **spilt**, **spilled**) **1** *intrans.* to run or flow out from a container, especially accidentally. **2** to cause to run or flow out from a container, especially accidentally. **3** *intrans.* to come or go in large crowds, especially quickly: *spectators spilling out of the stadium.* **4** to shed (blood, especially of other people). **5** *colloq.* to throw from a vehicle or saddle. — *noun* **1** an act of spilling. **2** *colloq.* a fall, especially from a vehicle or horse. — **spill the beans** *colloq.* to reveal confidential information, usually inadvertently. [from Anglo-Saxon *spillan*]

· · · · · · · · · · · · · · · · · · · ·

▣ *verb* **1** overflow, slop, pour, tip. **2** overturn, upset, slop, pour, tip. **3** disgorge, pour.

· ·

spill² *noun* a thin strip of wood or twisted paper for lighting a fire, candle, etc.

spillage *noun* **1** the act of spilling. **2** an amount spilt.

spilt see SPILL¹.

spin — *verb* (**spinning**; PAST TENSE AND PAST PARTICIPLE **spun**) **1** *trans.*, *intrans.* to rotate or cause to rotate repeatedly, especially quickly. **2** to draw out and twist (fibres, etc) into thread. **3** to construct from thread. **4** to throw or strike (a ball) so that it rotates while moving forward, causing deviation through the air or on impact with the ground or a second ball. **5** *intrans.* to have a revolving sensation that disorientates: *my head was spinning.* **6** to dry in a spin-drier. — *noun* **1** an act of spinning or a spinning motion. **2** rotation in a ball thrown or struck. **3** a nose-first spiral descent in an aircraft, especially uncontrolled. **4** *colloq.* a short trip in a vehicle, for pleasure. **5** a way of presenting something, especially a political event, that is intended to influence public opinion. — **spin something out 1** to prolong an activity. **2** to cause it to last longer by economical use. **spin a yarn** to tell a story, especially a long improbable one. [from Anglo-Saxon *spinnan*]

· · · · · · · · · · · · · · · · · · · ·

▣ *verb* **1** turn, revolve, rotate, twist, twirl, whirl, swirl. *noun*

1 turn, revolution, rotation, gyration, pirouette, twirl, whirl, swirl. **4** drive, ride, run. **spin out 1** prolong, protract, extend, lengthen, amplify, pad out.

. . . .

spina bifida / spaɪnə 'bɪfɪdə/ *Medicine* a congenital defect in which one or more vertebrae fail to unite during the development of the embryo, resulting in protrusion of part of the spinal cord through the backbone. It may cause permanent paralysis of the legs, and mental retardation. [from Latin *spina bifida*, split spine]

spinach / 'spɪnɪʃ, 'spɪnɪdʒ/ *noun* **1** a plant of the beet family. **2** its dark green succulent leaves eaten as a vegetable. [from Old French *espinache*, from Arabic *isfanakh*]

spinal *adj.* of or relating to the spine.

spinal column the spine.

spinal cord a cord-like mass of nerve tissue running along the spine and connecting the brain to nerves in all other parts of the body.

spinal nerve *Anat.* in humans, any of 31 pairs of nerves that arise from the spinal cord and extend to all parts of the body, forming many branches as they do so. Each spinal nerve contains a bundle of sensory nerve fibres, which relay information to the brain, and a bundle of motor nerve fibres, which relay information from the brain.

spin bowler *Cricket* a slow bowler who spins the ball sharply with his fingers as he releases it.

spindle *noun* **1** a rod with a notched or tapered end, for twisting the thread in spinning. **2** a pin or axis on which anything turns. **3** *Biol.* in the cytoplasm of a cell, a structure consisting of protein fibres to which chromosomes become attached during cell division. [from Anglo-Saxon *spinel*, from *spinnan*, to spin]

. . . .

▣ **2** axis, pivot, pin, rod, axle.

. . . .

spindly *adj.* (**spindlier, spindliest**) *colloq.* long, thin, and frail-looking.

spin doctor *colloq.* a person, such as a senior public relations advisor to a politician or political party, who is employed to influence public opinion by putting a favourable bias or 'spin' on information when it is presented to the public or to the media. The term originated in the USA in the 1980s.

spin-drier or **spin-dryer** *noun* a machine that forces the water out of wet laundry by spinning it at high speed in a revolving drum.

spindrift *noun* spray blown from the crests of waves. [a Scot. variation of obsolete *spoondrift*, from *spoon*, to be blown by the wind + DRIFT]

spin-dry *verb* to partly dry (wet laundry) by using a spin-dryer.

spine *noun* **1** in vertebrates, the flexible bony column consisting of a row of vertebrae connected by cartilage discs. It surrounds and protects the spinal cord, and articulates with the skull, ribs, and pelvic girdle. **2** the narrow middle section of a book's cover, covering the part where the pages are fastened in. **3** in certain plants and animals, eg cacti, hedgehogs, one of many sharply pointed structures that provide protection against predators. **4** *colloq.* courage; strength of character: *he has little spine.* [from Latin *spina*, thorn]

. . . .

▣ **1** backbone, spinal column, vertebral column, vertebrae. **3** thorn, barb, prickle, bristle, quill.

. . . .

spine-chiller *noun* a frightening story, thought, or happening.

spine-chilling *adj. colloq.* frightening; scary.

spineless *adj.* **1** having no spine; invertebrate. **2** *colloq.* lacking courage or strength of character.

. . . .

▣ **2** weak, feeble, irresolute, ineffective, cowardly, faint-hearted, lily-livered, *colloq.* yellow, soft, wet,

submissive, weak-kneed.

F3 2 strong, brave.

. . . .

spinet / 'spɪnɪt, spɪ'nɛt/ *noun* a musical instrument like a small harpsichord. [from Italian *spinetta*]

spinnaker / 'spɪnəkə(r)/ *noun* a large triangular sail set at the front of a yacht.

spinner *noun* **1** a spin-drier. **2** an angler's lure shaped so as to spin in the water when the line is pulled. **3** *Cricket* a spin bowler, or a ball bowled by one.

spinneret *noun Zool.* in spiders and some insects, a small tubular organ from which silk is produced.

spinney *noun* (PL. **spinneys**) *Bot.* a small wood containing undergrowth, especially one that consists of thorn-bearing trees and shrubs. [from Latin *spinetum*, thorn-hedge]

spinning-jenny *noun* an early type of spinning machine, with several spindles.

spinning-wheel *noun* a machine for spinning thread, consisting of a spindle driven by a hand or foot-operated wheel.

spin-off *noun* **1** a side-effect or by-product, especially valuable. **2** a thing developed from an earlier product or idea, eg a television series derived from a successful film.

spinster *noun* a woman who has never been married, especially when elderly. [from Middle English *spinnestere*, woman who spins thread]

spinsterhood *noun* the status of a spinster.

spiny *adj.* (**spinier, spiniest**) **1** *said of plants or animals* covered with spines. **2** troublesome; difficult to deal with: *a spiny problem.*

spiracle / 'spaɪərakl/ *noun Zool.* in insects, any of various openings (arranged in 10 pairs) along the side of the body that are used for breathing. Each spiracle represents the external opening of a trachea (a flexible air tube that penetrates the body tissues). [from Latin *spiraculum*, from *spirare*, to breath]

spiraea or **spirea** *noun* a deciduous shrub of the genus *Spiraea*, native to north temperate regions. It has narrow to broadly oval leaves, and dense clusters of white or pink flowers. It is a popular ornamental plant. [from Greek *speiraia*, privet, from *speira*, coil]

spiral — *noun* **1** the pattern made by a line winding outwards from a central point in near-circles of ever-increasing size. **2** the pattern made by a line winding downwards from a point in near-circles of the same or ever-increasing size, as if round a cylinder or cone. **3** a curve or course following such a pattern. **4** a gradual but continuous rise or fall, eg of prices. — *adj.* of the shape or nature of a spiral. — *verb intrans.* (**spiralled, spiralling**) to follow a spiral course or pattern. [from Greek *speira*, coil]

. . . .

▣ *noun* **1** coil, whorl. **2** helix, corkscrew. *adj.* winding, coiled, whorled, helical, corkscrew.

. . . .

spirally *adv.* in a spiral way.

spire *noun* a tall thin structure tapering upwards to a point, especially a tower on a church roof. [from Anglo-Saxon *spir*, shoot, sprout]

. . . .

▣ steeple, pinnacle, peak, tip, point, spike.

. . . .

spirit — *noun* **1** the force within a person that is or provides the will to live: *sad news broke his spirit.* **2** this force as an independent part of a person, widely believed to survive the body after death, and sometimes visible as a ghost. **3** a supernatural being without a body: *evil spirits.* **4** one's thoughts, concerns, etc (as opposed to one's actual presence): *be with you in spirit, though not in person.* **5** (usually **spirits**) emotional state; mood: *in high spirits.* **6** overall atmosphere or feeling generated by several people together: *enter into the spirit of the party/team spirit.* **7** courage; liveliness or vivacity. **8** the underlying essential meaning or intention as distinct from literal interpretation: *in accordance with the spirit, not the letter, of the law.* **9** a distilled alcoholic liquid for drinking, eg whisky, brandy, or gin. **10** *Chem.* a volatile liquid obtained by distillation. — *verb* (**spirited**, **spiriting**) (*usually* **spirit something** or **someone away** or **off**) to carry or convey mysteriously or magically. [from Latin *spiritus*, breath]

▤ *noun* **1** soul, psyche, mind, life. **2** ghost, spectre, phantom, apparition. **3** angel, demon, fairy, sprite. **5** mood, humour, temper, disposition, temperament, feeling, morale, attitude, outlook. **7** courage, mettle, liveliness, vivacity, animation, vigour, energy, zest, ardour, motivation, enthusiasm, zeal, enterprise, resolution, willpower. **8** meaning, sense, substance, essence, gist, tenor, character, quality.

spirited *adj.* **1** full of courage or liveliness. **2** *in compounds* showing a particular kind of spirit, mood, or attitude: *high-spirited/public-spirited*.

▤ **1** bold, courageous, mettlesome, plucky, feisty, lively, vivacious, animated, sparkling, high-spirited, vigorous, energetic, active, ardent, zealous.
▣ **1** spiritless, cowardly, lethargic.

spirit-lamp *noun* a lamp fuelled by methylated or other spirit as opposed to oil.
spirit level a flat-edged bar with a short liquid-filled glass tube set inside it, showing the perfect levelness of a surface on which it is placed when a large bubble in the liquid lies between two markings on the tube.
spiritual — *adj.* **1** of or relating to the spirit or soul, rather than to the body or to physical things. **2** religious: *a spiritual leader.* — *noun* (*also* **Negro spiritual**) a religious song developed from the communal singing traditions of black people in the southern USA. [from Latin *spiritualis*; see SPIRIT]

▤ *adj.* **1** unworldly, incorporeal, immaterial, metaphysical, abstract. **2** religious, ecclesiastical, divine, holy, sacred.
▣ *adj.* **1** physical, material.

spiritualism *noun* belief in, or the practice of, communication with the spirits of dead people through a medium, a specially sensitive person.
spiritualist *noun* a person who believes in or practises spiritualism.
spirituality *noun* **1** a spiritual state. **2** something that is spiritual.
spiritually *adv.* in a spiritual way.
spirituous *adj.* containing alcohol obtained by distillation.
spirochaete /ˈspaɪrəʊkiːt/ *noun Biol.* any of a group of non-rigid spiral-shaped Gram-negative bacteria, many of which feed on dead organic matter, although some are parasitic and live in the intestines and genital regions of animals, causing various diseases, including syphilis in humans. [from Greek *speira*, a coil + *chaite*, hair, mane]
spirogyra /spaɪrəˈdʒaɪərə/ *noun* a filament-like green alga of the genus *Spirogyra*, found in ponds and streams, either floating or fixed to stones. It consists of filaments or chains of cells containing green chloroplasts which form a spiral within each cell. Division of the cells leads to an increase in length of the filament, and broken fragments can form new filaments.
spit¹ — *verb* (**spitting**; PAST TENSE AND PAST PARTICIPLE **spat**) **1** *intrans.* to expel saliva from the mouth, often as a gesture of contempt. **2** (*also* **spit something out**) to force (eg food) out of the mouth. **3** to emit in a short explosive burst: *the frying pan spat hot oil on me.* **4** to speak or utter with hate or violence. **5** *intrans.*, *said of rain* to fall in light intermittent drops. — *noun* **1** saliva spat from the mouth; spittle. **2** (**the spit** or **very spit of someone or something**) *colloq.* an exact likeness of them; a spitting image: *he's the very spit of his father.* — **spit it out** *colloq.* usually as a com-

mand to speak out what one is hesitating to say. [from Anglo-Saxon *spittan*]

▤ *verb* **1** expectorate. **2** eject, discharge. *noun* **1** spittle, saliva, slaver, drool, dribble, sputum, phlegm, expectoration.

spit² *noun* **1** a long thin metal rod on which meat is skewered and held over a fire for roasting. **2** a long narrow strip of land jutting out into the sea. [from Anglo-Saxon *spitu*]
spit and polish *colloq.* rigorous attention to cleanliness and tidiness, especially in the armed forces.
spit-and-sawdust *adj.* lacking luxury or refinement, like the sawdust-covered floors of many pubs in former times.
spite — *noun* the desire to hurt or offend; ill-will. — *verb* to annoy or offend intentionally. — **in spite of someone** or **something** regardless of them; in opposition to their efforts. [see DESPITE]

▤ *noun* spitefulness, malice, venom, gall, bitterness, rancour, animosity, ill-feeling, ill-will, malevolence, hate, hatred. *verb* annoy, irritate, vex, provoke, gall, hurt, injure, offend, put out.
▣ *noun* goodwill, compassion, affection.

spiteful *adj.* motivated by spite; vengeful, malicious.

▤ malicious, venomous, catty, bitchy, snide, barbed, cruel, vindictive, vengeful, malevolent, malignant, nasty.
▣ charitable, affectionate.

spitefully *adv.* in a spiteful way.
spitefulness *noun* **1** being spiteful. **2** a spiteful act or remark.
spitfire *noun* a hot-tempered person, especially a woman or girl.
spitting image *colloq.* an exact likeness; a double.
spittle *noun* saliva, especially when spat from the mouth; spit. [from Anglo-Saxon *spætl*]
spittoon *noun* a container for spitting into, especially a bucket on the floor of a pub in former times.
spiv *noun colloq.* a man, typically flashily dressed, engaging in small-time trade in illicit or stolen goods.
spivvy *adj.* (**spivvier**, **spivviest**) characteristic of a spiv.
splash — *verb* **1** *trans.*, *intrans.* to cause large drops of (a liquid or semi-liquid substance) to be thrown about. **2** *intrans.*, *said of such a substance* to fly around or land in large drops. **3** to make wet or dirty with such drops. **4** to print or display boldly: *photograph splashed across the front page.* — *noun* **1** a sound of splashing. **2** an amount splashed. **3** a stain made by splashing. **4** an irregular spot or patch: *splashes of colour.* **5** *colloq.* a small amount of liquid; a dash. — **make a splash** to attract much attention, especially deliberately. **splash down** *said of the crew or crew capsule of a space rocket* to land at sea. **splash out on something** or **someone** *colloq.* to spend a lot of money on them. [originally *plash*, probably imitative]

▤ *verb* **1** slop, slosh, splosh. **3** wet, shower, spray, squirt, sprinkle, spatter, splatter, splodge, daub, plaster. *noun* **4** spot, patch, splodge. **5** touch, dash, drop, spot.

splashdown *noun* a landing at sea of the crew or crew capsule of a space rocket.
splat — *noun* the sound made by a soft wet object striking a surface. — *adv.* with this sound: *fell splat on the floor.* [imitative]
splatter — *verb trans.*, *intrans.* (**splattered**, **splattering**) to splash with or in small scattered drops. — *noun* a splashing sound, especially when repeated or continuous.
splay *verb* to spread (eg the fingers). [related to DISPLAY]
spleen *noun* **1** a small delicate organ, situated on the left side of the abdomen, beside the liver and beneath the dia-

phragm in man. It produces phagocytes, which remove bacteria and other foreign bodies from the bloodstream, and it destroys red blood cells that are no longer functional. The spleen acts as a reservoir for blood, and if ruptured must be surgically removed. **2** bad temper; spitefulness. [from Greek *splen*]

splendid *adj.* **1** magnificent; impressively grand or sumptuous. **2** very good; excellent. [from Latin *splendidus*, shining, brilliant]

◨ **1** magnificent, glorious, resplendent, brilliant, dazzling, glittering, bright, sumptuous, luxurious, lavish, rich, fine, grand, stately, imposing, impressive. **2** great, outstanding, remarkable, exceptional, sublime, supreme, excellent, first-class, wonderful, marvellous, admirable.
◪ **1** drab, dull. **2** ordinary, run-of-the-mill.

splendidly *adv.* in a splendid way.

splendiferous *adj. colloq.* splendid. [from SPLENDOUR + *ferous* from other words with this ending (from Latin *ferre*, to carry)]

splendour *noun* the state or quality of being splendid. [from Latin *splendor*]

◨ magnificence, resplendence, brightness, brilliance, dazzle, lustre, richness, grandeur, majesty, solemnity, pomp, ceremony, display, show, spectacle.
◪ drabness, squalor.

splenetic *adj.* **1** (*also* **splenic**) relating to the spleen. **2** bad-tempered; spiteful; full of spleen.

splice — *verb* **1** to join (two pieces of rope) by weaving the strands of one into the other. **2** to join (two pieces of film, magnetic tape, etc) end to end with an adhesive. — *noun* a join made in either of these ways. — **get spliced** *colloq.* to get married. [from Dutch *splissen*]

◨ *verb* JOIN, UNITE. **1** interweave, interlace, intertwine, entwine, plait, braid, knit. **2** graft.

splint *noun* a piece of wood strapped to a broken limb to fix it in position while the bone heals. [from Old Dutch *splinte*]

splinter — *noun* a small thin sharp piece broken off a hard substance, eg wood or glass. — *verb trans., intrans.* (**splintered, splintering**) to break into splinters. [see SPLINT]

◨ *noun* sliver, shiver, chip, shard, fragment, flake, shaving, paring. *verb* split, smash, shatter, shiver, fragment.

splinter group a small (especially political) group formed by individuals breaking away from a larger one.

split — *verb* (**splitting**; PAST TENSE AND PAST PARTICIPLE **split**) **1** *trans., intrans.* to break or cause to break apart or into pieces, especially lengthways. **2** (*also* **split up** or **split something up**) to separate or cause it to separate into smaller amounts or groups. **3** (*also* **split up** or **split someone up**) to break or cause them to break away from each other or from a group through disagreement. **4** *intrans., slang* to go away or leave. **5** (**split on someone**) *slang* to inform on them. — *noun* **1** a lengthways break or crack. **2** a separation or division through disagreement. **3** a dessert of fruit, especially a banana, sliced open and topped with cream or ice-cream. **4** (**the splits**) an acrobatic leap or drop to the floor with the legs splayed in a straight line, each leg at right angles to the torso. — **split the difference 1** *said of two people or parties* to compromise by each making an equal concession. **2** to divide a remaining amount equally. **split hairs** to make or argue about fine and trivial distinctions. **split one's sides** *colloq.* to laugh uncontrollably. [from Dutch *splitten*]

◨ *verb* **1** break, splinter, shiver, crack, burst, rupture, tear, rip,

cleave, open. **2** divide, separate, partition, halve, bisect, share. **3** part, disunite, disband, break up, divide, separate, divorce. *noun* **1** break, breach, gap, rift, cleft, crevice, crack, fissure, rupture, tear, rip, slit, slash. **2** division, separation, rift, schism, disunion, dissension, discord, difference, divergence, break-up, divorce.

split infinitive an infinitive with an adverb or other word between the particle *to* and the verb, as in *to really believe*.

split-level *adj.* consisting of, or existing on, more than one level.

split pea a dried pea split in half, used in soups and stews.

split personality the displaying of two or more distinct types of behaviour by a single person, a feature of various mental disorders, especially schizophrenia.

split second a fraction of a second.

split-second *adj.* made or occurring in a fraction of a second: *a split-second decision*.

splitting *adj., said of a headache* intense, severe.

splodge — *noun* a large splash, stain, or patch. — *verb* to mark with splodges.

splurge — *noun* a spending spree or extravagance. — *verb intrans.* to spend extravagantly.

splutter — *verb* (**spluttered, spluttering**) **1** *intrans.* to make spitting sounds and throw out drops of liquid, sparks, etc. **2** *trans., intrans.* to speak or say haltingly or incoherently, eg through embarrassment. — *noun* the act or noise of spluttering. [originally SPUTTER, from Dutch *sputteren*, influenced by SPLASH]

spoil — *verb* (PAST TENSE AND PAST PARTICIPLE **spoilt**, **spoiled**) **1** to impair, ruin, or make useless or valueless. **2** to make selfish and unable to accept hardship or disappointment by consistently indulging all demands or wishes: *a spoilt child*. **3** *intrans., said of food* to become unfit to eat. — *noun* (**spoils**) **1** possessions taken by force; plunder: *the spoils of war*. **2** any benefits or rewards. — **be spoiling for something** to seek out a fight or argument eagerly. [from Latin *spolium*, plunder]

◨ *verb* **1** mar, upset, wreck, ruin, destroy, damage, impair, harm, hurt, injure, deface, disfigure, blemish. **2** indulge, pamper, cosset, coddle, mollycoddle, baby, spoon-feed. **3** deteriorate, go bad, go off, sour, turn, curdle, decay, decompose. *noun* **1** plunder, loot, booty, haul, *slang* swag, pickings. **2** benefits, rewards, prizes, winnings.

spoiler *noun* **1** a flap on an aircraft wing that reduces lift and so assists descent. **2** a fixed horizontal fin on a car that increases its roadholding at high speeds.

spoilsport *noun colloq.* a person who spoils, or refuses to join in, the fun of others.

spoke[1] see SPEAK.

spoke[2] *noun* any of the radiating rods or bars attaching the rim of a wheel to its centre. — **put a spoke in someone's wheel** to upset their plans, especially maliciously. [from Anglo-Saxon *spaca*]

spoken past participle of SPEAK. — *adj.* **1** uttered or expressed in speech. **2** *in compounds* speaking in a particular way: *soft-spoken*. — **be spoken for 1** to be reserved or taken. **2** *said of a person* to be married, engaged, or in a steady relationship.

spokesman *noun* (PL. **spokesmen**) a person appointed to speak on behalf of others or of a government, business, etc.

spokesperson *noun* a spokesman or spokeswoman (without regard to gender).

spokeswoman *noun* (PL. **spokeswomen**) a woman appointed to speak on behalf of others or of a government, business, etc.

spoliation /spəʊlɪ'eɪʃən/ *noun* robbing; plundering. [from Latin *spoliare*]

spondaic /spɒn'deɪɪk/ *adj.* consisting of or written in spondees.

spondee /'spɒndiː/ *noun* a foot (= unit of poetical rhythm) consisting of two long syllables. [from Greek *spondeios*]

sponge — *noun* **1** the common name for any of about 3,000 species of an aquatic invertebrate animal belonging to the phylum Porifera. Almost all species are marine, although a few are found in fresh water. Sponges are the most primitive multicellular animals, and consist of a large cluster of cells, resembling a plant, always fixed to a solid object such as a rock. **2** the soft porous skeleton of this animal, from which the jelly-like flesh has been removed by allowing it to dry and then beating the sponge to dislodge the dried debris. It can hold a large amount of water and remains soft when wet, and is widely used in baths. **3** a piece of this material, or a similar absorbent synthetic material, used for cleansing surfaces. **4** a sponge cake or pudding. **5** an act of cleaning with a sponge. **6** *colloq.* a person who is regularly drunk. — *verb* **1** to wash or clean with a sponge and water. **2** (**sponge off** or **on someone**) to live by taking advantage of others' generosity. [from Greek *spongia*]

⊟ *verb* **1** wipe, mop, clean, wash. **2** cadge from, scrounge from.

sponge bag a small waterproof bag for carrying toiletries in when travelling.

sponge cake or **sponge pudding** a very light cake or steamed cake-like pudding.

sponger *noun colloq.* a person who sponges off others.

⊟ cadger, scrounger, parasite, hanger-on.

spongy *adj.* (**spongier**, **spongiest**) soft and springy, and perhaps absorbent, like a sponge.

⊟ soft, yielding, elastic, springy, porous, absorbent.

sponsor — *noun* **1** a person or organization that finances an event or broadcast, usually in return for advertising. **2** a person who promises a sum of money to a participant in a forthcoming fund-raising event. **3** a person who offers to be responsible for another, especially a godparent. **4** a person who submits a proposal, eg for new legislation. — *verb* (**sponsored**, **sponsoring**) to act as a sponsor for. [from Latin *spondere*, to promise]

⊟ *noun* **1** patron, backer, *colloq.* angel, promoter, underwriter. *verb* finance, fund, *colloq.* bankroll, subsidize, patronize, back, promote, underwrite.

sponsored *adj.* **1** having a sponsor or sponsors. **2** *said of an activity or event* financially supported by sponsors.

sponsorship *noun* sponsoring.

spontaneity *noun* being spontaneous.

spontaneous *adj.* **1** unplanned and voluntary or instinctive, not provoked or invited by others. **2** occurring naturally or by itself, not caused or influenced from outside. **3** *said of a manner or style* natural; not affected or studied. [from Latin *sponte*, of one's own accord]

⊟ **1** instinctive, impulsive, unplanned, unpremeditated, voluntary, unprompted, free, willing, unhesitating, impromptu, extempore. **3** natural, unaffected.
⊡ **1** planned, deliberate. **3** affected, studied.

spontaneous combustion the catching fire of a substance as a result of heat generated within it, not applied from outside.

spontaneous generation *Biol.* the theory, now discredited, that living organisms, eg bacteria, can arise spontaneously from non-living matter.

spoof *colloq.* — *noun* **1** a satirical imitation; a parody. **2** a light-hearted hoax or trick. — *verb* to subject to a spoof. [originally the name of a hoaxing game]

spook *colloq.* — *noun* a ghost. — *verb* to frighten or startle. [from Old German *spok*]

spooky *adj.* (**spookier**, **spookiest**) *colloq.* suggestive of ghosts or the supernatural; eerie.

spool *noun* a small cylinder on which thread, photographic film, tape, etc is wound; a reel. [from Old German *spole*]

spoon — *noun* **1** a kitchen utensil with a handle and a round or oval shallow bowl-like part, for eating, serving, or stirring food. **2** the amount a spoon will hold. — *verb* **1** to lift (food) with a spoon. **2** *intrans.*, *old use* to kiss and cuddle. [from Anglo-Saxon *spon*]

spoonbill *noun* any bird of a family similar to the ibises, with a long flat broad bill that is spoon-shaped at the tip.

spoonerism *noun* an accidental and often comic slip in speech which reverses the positions of the first sounds of a pair of words, as in *shoving leopard* for *loving shepherd*. [named after Rev. W A Spooner]

spoon-feed *verb* **1** to feed (eg a baby) with a spoon. **2** to supply (someone) with everything needed or required, making any personal effort unnecessary.

spoonful *noun* (PL. **spoonfuls**) the amount a spoon will hold.

spoor /spʊə(r), spɔː(r)/ *noun* the track or scent left by an animal. [from Dutch *spoor*, track]

sporadic *adj.* occurring from time to time, at irregular intervals; intermittent. [from Greek *sporados*, scattered]

⊟ occasional, intermittent, infrequent, isolated, spasmodic, erratic, irregular, uneven, random, scattered.
⊡ frequent, regular.

sporadically *adv.* in a sporadic way; from time to time.

sporangium *noun* (PL. **sporangia**) *Bot.* in fungi and some plants, the hollow structure within which the spores are produced. [from Greek *spora*, seed]

spore *noun* an asexual reproductive structure, usually consisting of one cell, from which a new organism or stage in the life cycle develops either immediately or after a resting period, without the need for fusion with another cell. Spores are produced in large numbers by fungi, bacteria, some protozoans, and certain plants, eg ferns, mosses. [from Greek *spora*, seed]

sporophyll or **sporophyl** *noun Bot.* in certain plants, a leaf (often highly modified) that bears sporangia. [from Greek *spora*, seed + *phyllon*, leaf]

sporophyte *noun Bot.* in plants whose life cycle shows alternation of generations, a plant of the generation that produces spores and reproduces asexually. [from Greek *spora*, seed]

sporran *noun* a leather pouch worn hanging in front of the kilt in Scottish Highland dress. [from Gaelic *sporan*]

sport — *noun* **1** an activity or competition designed to test physical skills. **2** such activities collectively. **3** the pleasure or amusement gained from such an activity: *hunting for sport.* **4** good-humoured fun: *did it in sport.* **5** *colloq.* a person who cheerfully accepts defeat, inconvenience, or being the butt of jokes: *a good sport.* **6** *literary* a person or thing manipulated or controlled by outside influences; a plaything. **7** *Biol.* an animal or especially a plant that possesses abnormal characteristics as a result of a mutation. — *verb* to wear or display, especially proudly. — **make sport of someone** or **something** *old use* to make fun of them. [a shortening of DISPORT]

⊟ *noun* **1** game, exercise, activity, pastime. **2** games, recreation, play. **3** pleasure, fun, amusement, entertainment, diversion. **4** fun, mirth, humour, joking, jesting, banter, play. *verb* wear, display, exhibit, show off.

Sports include: badminton, fives, lacrosse, squash, table-tennis, *colloq.* ping-pong, tennis; American football, baseball, basketball, billiards, boules, bowls, cricket, croquet, football, golf, handball, hockey, netball, pétanque, pitch and putt, polo, pool, putting, rounders, Rugby, snooker, soccer, tenpin bowling, volleyball; athletics, cross-country, decathlon, discus, high jump, hurdling, javelin, long jump, marathon, pentathlon, pole vault, running, shotput, triple jump; angling, canoeing, diving, fishing, rowing, sailing, skin-diving, surfing, swimming, synchronized swimming, water polo, water-skiing, windsurfing, yachting; bobsleigh, curling, ice hockey, ice-skating, skiing, speed skating, tobogganing (luging); aerobics, fencing, gymnastics, jogging, keep-fit, roller-skating, trampolining; archery, darts, quoits; boxing, judo, jujitsu, karate, tae kwon do, weightlifting, wrestling; climbing, mountaineering, rock climbing, walking, orienteering, pot-holing; cycle racing, drag racing, go-karting, motor racing, speedway racing, stock car racing, greyhound racing, horse racing, showjumping, trotting, hunting, shooting, clay pigeon shooting; gliding, skydiving.

sporting *adj.* **1** of or relating to sport: *sporting achievements.* **2** having or displaying fairness or generosity of character. — **a sporting chance** a reasonable chance of success.

▤ **2** sportsmanlike, gentlemanly, decent, fair.
Ⓕ **2** unsporting, ungentlemanly, unfair.

sportingly *adv.* in a sporting way.
sportive *adj.* playful.
sports car a small fast car, especially a two-seater, whose body sits close to the ground.
sports jacket a man's jacket for casual wear.
sportsman or **sportswoman** *noun* **1** a person who takes part in sport. **2** a person who plays fair and accepts defeat cheerfully.
sportsmanlike *adj.* characteristic of a sportsman, fair, sporting.
sportsmanship *noun* being sportsmanlike.
sportswoman *noun* a woman taking part in sport.
sporty *adj.* (**sportier, sportiest**) **1** fond of, and often taking part in, sport. **2** *said of a car* that looks like or handles like a sports car.

▤ **1** athletic, fit, energetic, outdoor.

spot — *noun* **1** a small mark or stain. **2** a drop of liquid. **3** a small amount, especially of liquid. **4** an eruption on the skin; a pimple. **5** a place. **6** *colloq.* a small amount of work: *did a spot of ironing.* **7** a place or period within a schedule or programme: *a five-minute comedy spot.* **8** *colloq.* a spotlight. — *verb* (**spotted, spotting**) **1** to mark with spots. **2** to see; to catch sight of. **3** to watch for and record the sighting of (eg trains). **4** to search for (new talent). **5** *intrans. said of rain* to fall lightly. — **in a tight spot** *colloq.* in trouble or difficulty. **knock spots off someone** or **something** *colloq.* to be overwhelmingly better than them. **on the spot 1** immediately and often without warning: *motorists caught speeding are fined on the spot.* **2** at the scene of some notable event. **3** in an awkward situation, especially one requiring immediate action or response: *put someone on the spot.* [from Norse *spotti*, small bit]

▤ *noun* **1** dot, speckle, fleck, mark, speck, blotch, blot, smudge, stain, blemish, flaw. **3** drop, dash, touch, splash. **5** place, point, position, situation, location, site, scene, locality. *verb* **1** dot, speckle, fleck, mark. **2** see, notice, observe, detect, discern, glimpse, catch sight of. **3** identify, recognize.

spot check an inspection made at random and without warning.
spotless *adj.* absolutely clean; unblemished.

▤ immaculate, clean, spick and span, unmarked, unstained, unblemished, unsullied, pure, chaste, virgin, untouched, faultless, irreproachable.

Ⓕ dirty, impure.

spotlessly *adv.* so as to be spotless.
spotlessness *noun* being spotless.
spotlight — *noun* **1** a concentrated circle of light on a small area, especially of a theatre stage; also, a lamp casting this light. **2** (**the spotlight**) the attention or gaze of others: *put him in the spotlight.* — *verb* (PAST TENSE AND PAST PARTICIPLE **spotlit, spotlighted**) **1** to illuminate with a spotlight. **2** to direct attention to; to highlight.
spot-on *adj. colloq.* **1** exactly right; perfectly accurate. **2** precisely what was required; excellent.
spotted *adj.* **1** having spots, covered with spots. **2** stained, marked.

▤ **1** dotted, speckled, flecked, mottled, dappled, pied.

spotted dick suet pudding containing dried fruit.
spotter *noun* a person who spots (eg trains).
spottiness *noun* being spotty.
spotty *adj.* (**spottier, spottiest**) **1** marked with a pattern of spots. **2** whose skin, especially of the face, has many spots on it.

▤ **1** spotted, dotted. **2** pimply, pimpled, blotchy.

spouse *noun* a husband or wife. [from Latin *sponsus*, from *spondere*, to promise]

▤ husband, wife, partner, mate, *colloq.* better half.

spout — *noun* **1** a projecting tube or lip through which liquid flows or is poured. **2** a jet or stream of liquid, eg from a fountain or the blowhole of a whale. — *verb* **1** *intrans.* to flow out in a jet or stream. **2** to cause to flow out in a jet or stream. **3** *trans., intrans.* to speak or say, especially at length and boringly. — **up the spout** *slang* **1** ruined or damaged beyond repair. **2** pregnant. [from Middle English *spouten*]

▤ *noun* **1** outlet, nozzle, rose, spray, gargoyle. **2** jet, stream, fountain. *verb* **1** jet, spurt, squirt, spray, shoot, gush, stream, surge, erupt. **2** squirt, spray, emit, discharge.

sprain — *verb* to injure (a ligament) by sudden overstretching or tearing. — *noun* such an injury, which causes painful swelling, and may take several months to heal.
sprang see SPRING.
sprat *noun* a small edible fish of the herring family. [from Anglo-Saxon *sprot*]
sprawl — *verb intrans.* **1** to sit, lie, or fall lazily with the arms and legs spread out wide. **2** to spread or extend in an irregular, straggling, untidy way: *sprawling towns.* — *noun* a sprawling position. [from Anglo-Saxon *spreawlian*, to move convulsively]

▤ *verb* **1** flop, slump, slouch, loll, lounge, recline. **2** spread, straggle.

spray[1] — *noun* **1** a fine mist of small flying drops of liquid. **2** a liquid designed to be applied as a mist: *hairspray.* **3** a device for dispensing a liquid as a mist; an atomiser or aerosol. — *verb* **1** to apply or dispense (a liquid) in spray form. **2** to apply a spray to. **3** to subject to a heavy and widespread stream: *sprayed the car with bullets.* [from Old Dutch *sprayen*]

▤ *noun* **1** moisture, drizzle, mist, foam, froth. **3** aerosol, atomizer, sprinkler. *verb* **1** squirt, atomize, diffuse, scatter. **2** sprinkle, wet, drench.

spray[2] *noun* a small branch of a tree or plant with leaves and flowers attached, used for decoration. [perhaps from Anglo-Saxon *spræc*, twig]

⊟ sprig, branch, corsage, posy, bouquet, garland, wreath.

....

spray-gun *noun* a container with a trigger-operated aerosol attached, for dispensing liquid, eg paint, in spray form.

spread — *verb* (PAST TENSE AND PAST PARTICIPLE **spread**) **1** *trans.*, *intrans.* to apply, or be capable of being applied, in a smooth coating over a surface. **2** (*also* **spread out** or **spread something out**) to extend or cause it to extend or scatter, often more widely or more thinly. **3** (*also* **spread something out**) to open it out or unfold it. **4** to transmit, disseminate, or distribute: *flies spread disease.* **5** *intrans.* to be transmitted, disseminated, or distributed: *rumours began to spread.* — *noun* **1** the act or extent of spreading. **2** a food in paste form, for spreading on bread, etc. **3** a pair of facing pages in a newspaper or magazine. **4** *colloq.* a lavish meal. **5** *colloq.* increased fatness around the waist and hips: *middle-aged spread.* [from Anglo-Saxon *sprædan*]

....

⊟ *verb* **2** stretch, extend, broaden, widen, expand, swell, scatter, strew, diffuse, radiate. **3** open, unroll, unfurl, unfold, lay out, arrange. **4** transmit, communicate, promulgate, propagate, disseminate, broadcast, publicize, advertise, circulate, distribute. *noun* **1** development, expansion, increase, escalation, proliferation, diffusion, dissemination, dispersion, stretch, reach, span, extent.
⊟ *verb* **3** close, fold.

....

spread betting a system of betting in which the sum of money won depends on how different the result of a sporting event is from that specified by the gambler.

spread-eagled *adj.* with arms and legs stretched wide.

spreadsheet *noun* a computer program that enables numerical data to be entered and displayed in a table of rows and columns. The user can then instruct the program to perform mathematical operations on the data. Spreadsheets are widely used for business and financial planning, bookkeeping, and analysis of experimental data.

spree *noun* a period of extravagance or excess, especially in spending money or drinking alcohol. [perhaps from Scots *spreath*, cattle raid]

....

⊟ bout, fling, binge, splurge, orgy, revel.

....

sprig *noun* a small shoot or twig: *sprig of heather.*

sprightliness *noun* being sprightly, liveliness.

sprightly *adj.* **1** lively and quick-moving. **2** performed at a brisk pace. [related to SPRITE]

....

⊟ **1** lively, spirited, energetic, active, agile, nimble, spry. **2** brisk, jaunty.
⊟ **1** doddering, inactive. **2** slow.

....

spring — *verb* (PAST TENSE **sprang**; PAST PARTICIPLE **sprung**) **1** *intrans.* to leap with a sudden quick launching action. **2** *intrans.* to move suddenly and swiftly by elastic force. **3** (*also* **spring up**) to appear or come into being suddenly. **4** *intrans.* to develop or originate. **5** (**spring something on someone**) to present or reveal it suddenly and unexpectedly. **6** to fit (eg a mattress) with springs. **7** *slang* to secure the escape of (a prisoner) from jail. — *noun* **1** a metal coil that can be stretched or compressed, and returns to its original shape when released. Springs store energy when distorted, and slowly unwinding springs can be used to release energy at a controlled rate, eg to turn the mechanism of some clocks and watches. **2** any place where water emerges from underground and flows on to the Earth's surface or into a body of water such as a lake. Springs may be permanent or intermittent, and they often occur at points where the water table reaches the ground surface. Spring water may contain large amounts of dis-

solved minerals, and is highly valued as drinking water. **3** the season between winter and summer, when most plants begin to grow. **4** a sudden vigorous leap. **5** the ability of a material to return rapidly to its original shape after a distorting force, eg stretching, bending, compression, has been removed: *the mattress has lost its spring.* **6** a lively bouncing or jaunty quality: *a spring in his step.* [from Anglo-Saxon *springan*]

....

⊟ *verb* **1** jump, leap, vault, bound, hop. **2** bounce, rebound, recoil. **4** originate, derive, come, stem, arise, start, proceed, issue, emanate, develop, grow. *noun* **2** wellspring, wellhead, fountainhead, well, geyser, spa. **4** jump, leap, vault, bound, bounce. **5** springiness, resilience, give, flexibility, elasticity.

....

spring balance a device that measures weight by the downward pull on a large spring to which the weighed object is attached.

springboard *noun* **1** a board that springs up after being jumped on, used by divers and gymnasts as a launching device. **2** anything that serves to get things moving.

springbok *noun* a South African antelope renowned for its high springing leap when running.

spring chicken 1 a very young chicken valued for its tender edible flesh. **2** *colloq.* a young person.

spring-clean *verb trans.*, *intrans.* to carry out spring-cleaning; to clean out thoroughly.

spring cleaning a thorough cleaning of a house, traditionally carried out in spring.

springer *noun* a large spaniel with a domed head.

springiness *noun* a springy quality.

spring onion an onion picked when young, while just a tiny white bulb with long thin shoots, usually eaten raw in salads.

springtail *noun* a blind primitively wingless insect that is often extremely abundant in soils or leaf litter, and leaps by means of a forked spring organ folded up on the underside of the abdomen.

spring tide a tidal pattern that occurs twice a month, when the difference in level between high and low tides is greatest. It occurs at full and new moon, when the Earth, Moon, and Sun are aligned so that the combined gravitational pull of the Moon and Sun makes high tides higher and low tides lower.

springtime *noun* the season of spring.

springy *adj.* (**springier**, **springiest**) readily springing back into its original shape when released; elastic; resilient.

....

⊟ bouncy, resilient, flexible, elastic, stretchy, rubbery, spongy.
⊟ hard, stiff.

....

sprinkle *verb* **1** to scatter in, or cover with a scattering of, tiny drops or particles. **2** to arrange or distribute in a thin scattering: *houses sprinkled across the valley.* [from Anglo-Saxon *springan*, to spring]

....

⊟ SCATTER, STREW, DOT, PEPPER. **1** shower, spray, spatter, dust, powder.

....

sprinkler *noun* a device that sprinkles, especially one sprinkling water over plants or on a fire to extinguish it.

sprinkling *noun* a small amount thinly scattered.

sprint — *noun* **1** a race at high speed over a short distance. **2** a burst of speed eg at the end of a long race. — *verb trans.*, *intrans.* to run at full speed. [from Norse *sprinta*]

....

⊟ *verb* run, race, dash, tear, *colloq.* belt, dart, shoot.

....

sprinter *noun* an athlete who sprints.

sprit *noun* a small diagonal spar used to spread a sail. [from Anglo-Saxon *spreot*, pole]

sprite *noun* **1** *Folklore* a playful fairy; an elf or imp. **2** a number of pixels that can be moved in a group around a screen, eg those representing a figure in a computer game. [from Old French *esprit*, spirit]

spritsail /ˈsprɪtsl/ *noun* a sail spread wide by a sprit.

spritzer *noun* a drink of white wine and soda water. [from German *spritzen*, to spray]

sprocket *noun* **1** any of a set of teeth on the rim of a driving wheel, eg fitting into the links of a chain or the holes on a strip of film. **2** a wheel with sprockets.

sprout — *verb* **1** to develop (a new growth, eg of leaves or hair). **2** *intrans.* to develop new shoots, leaves, buds, etc. **3** (*also* **sprout up**) to grow or develop; to spring up. — *noun* **1** a new growth; a shoot or bud. **2** a Brussels sprout. [from Anglo-Saxon *sprutan*]

■ *verb* GROW, DEVELOP. **2** shoot, bud, germinate. **3** come up, spring up.

spruce¹ *noun* **1** an evergreen cone-bearing tree with a thick pyramid-shaped growth of needle-like leaves. **2** the wood of this tree. [from obsolete *Pruce*, Prussia]

spruce² *adj.* neat and smart, especially in appearance and dress. — **spruce up** or **spruce someone up** to smarten up or make them smart. [from smart 16c clothing made of *spruce leather* from *Pruce*, Prussia]

■ smart, elegant, neat, trim, dapper, well-dressed, well-groomed, sleek. **spruce up** smarten up, neaten, tidy, groom.
🔄 scruffy, untidy.

sprung see SPRING.

sprung rhythm *Poetry* a term invented by the poet Gerard Manley Hopkins to describe his own metrical system which related back to techniques used in Old and Middle English alliterative verse. It is close to the rhythm of natural speech, with mixed feet and frequent single stressed syllables.

spry *adj.* (**spryer, spryest**) **1** lively; active. **2** light on one's feet; nimble.

spryly *adv.* nimbly.

spryness *noun* being spry.

spud *noun colloq.* a potato. [from Middle English *spudde*, short knife]

spume — *noun* foam or froth. — *verb intrans.* to make spume. [from Latin *spuma*, from *spuere*, to spew]

spumy *adj.* (**spumier, spumiest**) foaming.

spun see SPIN.

spunk *noun* **1** *colloq.* courage; mettle. **2** *coarse slang* semen. [from Irish Gaelic *sponc*, tinder]

spunky *adj.* (**spunkier, spunkiest**) *colloq.* courageous; spirited.

spur — *noun* **1** a device with a spiky metal wheel, fitted to the heel of a horse-rider's boot, dug into the horse's side to make it go faster. **2** anything that urges or encourages greater effort or progress. **3** a spike or pointed part, eg on a cock's leg. **4** a ridge of high land that projects out into a valley. — *verb* (**spurred, spurring**) (*usually* **spur someone on**) to urge them on. — **on the spur of the moment** suddenly; on an impulse. [from Anglo-Saxon *spura*]

■ *noun* **2** incentive, encouragement, inducement, stimulus, incitement, impetus, motive. *verb* goad, prod, urge, impel, drive, incite, prompt, stimulate, motivate, encourage.
🔄 *noun* **2** curb, disincentive. *verb* curb, discourage.

spurge *noun* any of various plants producing a bitter, often poisonous, milky juice formerly used as a laxative. [from Old French *espurge*, from Latin *expurgare*, to purge]

spurious *adj.* **1** not what it seems or claims to be; false. **2** based on false or mistaken reasoning. [from Latin *spurius*, false]

■ **1** false, fake, counterfeit, forged, bogus, *colloq.* phoney, mock, simulated, artificial. **2** fallacious, flawed, illogical, wrong.
🔄 **1** genuine, authentic, real.

spurn *verb* to reject (eg a person's love) scornfully. [from Anglo-Saxon *spurnan*]

■ reject, turn down, scorn, despise, rebuff, repulse, slight, snub, cold-shoulder.
🔄 accept, embrace.

spurt — *verb* **1** *intrans.* to flow out in a sudden sharp jet. **2** to cause to flow out in a sudden sharp jet. — *noun* **1** a jet of liquid suddenly flowing out. **2** a short spell of intensified activity or increased speed.

■ *verb* GUSH, SQUIRT. **1** jet, shoot, burst, erupt, surge. *noun* **1** jet, gush, squirt. **2** burst, rush, surge.

Sputnik *noun* the name given to the series of 10 Earth-orbiting artificial satellites launched by the former Soviet Union in 1957 and 1958. Sputnik 1 was the world's first artificial satellite. [named after the first Soviet satellite, literally = 'travelling companion']

sputter same as SPLUTTER. [imitative]

sputum *noun* (PL. **sputa**) saliva mixed with mucus that is coughed up from the bronchial passages. Also called PHLEGM [from Latin *sputum*, from *spuere*, to spit]

spy — *noun* (PL. **spies**) **1** a person employed by a government or organization to gather information about political enemies or competitors. **2** a person observing others in secret. — *verb* (**spies, spied**) **1** (*also* **spy on someone**) to act as a spy; to keep a secret watch on someone. **2** to catch sight of; to spot. — **spy someone** or **something out** to discover or uncover them by spying. [from Old French *espier*]

■ *noun* **1** secret agent, undercover agent, double agent, *colloq.* mole, fifth columnist. **2** scout, snooper. *verb* OBSERVE. **1** watch. **2** spot, glimpse, notice, discover.

spyglass *noun* a small telescope.

spyhole *noun* a peephole.

spy ship a ship specially equipped to collect and relay information on the position and movements of enemy ships, submarines, etc. In the past, spy ships were frequently disguised as commercial, especially fishing, vessels; with the development of advanced satellite technology their importance has diminished.

spy story a form of fiction based on the theme of espionage. Important landmarks in the development of the genre were the stories by Willian Le Queux (1864–1927), Erskine Childers' *The Riddle of the Sands* (1903), Joseph Conrad's *The Secret Agent* (1907), and John Buchan's *The Thirty-Nine Steps* (1915). Between the wars Somerset Maugham, Eric Ambler, and Graham Greene presented spies in a realistic and unsensational way; Ian Fleming glamorized the role of spy in his James Bond stories of the 1950s; and in the 1960s there was a return to a more realistic form by writers such as John Le Carré and Len Deighton.

sq. *abbrev.* square.

SQL *abbrev. Comput.* structured query language, a standard programming language used to access information from databases.

squab /skwɒb/ *noun* **1** a young unfledged bird, especially a pigeon. **2** a short fat person.

squabble — *verb intrans.* to quarrel noisily, especially about something trivial. — *noun* a noisy (especially petty) quarrel.

■ *verb* bicker, wrangle, quarrel, row, argue, brawl, scrap, fight. *noun* quarrel, row, argument, dispute.

squabby *adj.* (**squabbier**, **squabbiest**) short and fat; stumpy.

squad *noun* **1** a small group of soldiers, often twelve, drilling or working together. **2** any group of people working together. **3** a set of players from which a sporting team is selected. [from Italian *squadra*, square]

■ **2** crew, team, gang, band, group, company, brigade, troop, force, outfit.

squaddy or **squaddie** *noun* (PL. **squaddies**) *slang* an ordinary soldier; a private.

squadron *noun* **1** a group of between 10 and 18 military aircraft, the principal unit of an air force. **2** a group of warships sent on a particular mission. **3** a division of an armoured regiment of soldiers. [from Italian *squadrone*; related to SQUAD]

squadron leader an air force officer of the rank below wing commander, in charge of a squadron.

squalid *adj.* **1** disgustingly filthy and neglected. **2** morally repulsive; sordid. See also SQUALOR. [from Latin *squalidus*, dirty]

■ **1** dirty, filthy, foul, disgusting, repulsive, neglected, uncared-for, run-down, seedy, dingy, untidy. **2** sordid, low, mean, nasty.
E3 1 clean, pleasant, attractive.

squall / skwɔːl/ — *noun* **1** *Meteorol.* a storm consisting of sudden and short-lived violent gusts of wind. **2** a loud cry; a yell. — *verb* **1** *trans., intrans.* to yell. **2** *said of a wind* to blow in a squall.

squally *adj.* characterized by squalls.

squalor *noun* the state of being squalid. [from Latin *squalor*, roughness]

squander *verb* (**squandered**, **squandering**) to use up wastefully.

■ waste, misspend, misuse, lavish, *colloq.* blow, fritter away, throw away, dissipate, scatter, spend, expend, consume.
E3 save.

square — *noun* **1** a two-dimensional figure with four sides of equal length and four right angles. **2** anything shaped like this. **3** an open space in a town, usually roughly square in shape, and including the surrounding buildings. **4** an L-shaped or T-shaped instrument with which angles can be measured or straight lines drawn. **5** the figure produced when a number is multiplied by itself. **6** *colloq.* a person with traditional or old-fashioned values or tastes. — *adj.* **1** square-shaped. **2** measured in length and breadth; *of an area equal to a square whose sides are the stated length*: *an area of three square metres/one room is three metres square*. **3** less rounded than normal: *a square jaw*. **4** measuring almost the same in breadth as in length or height: *a squat, square-framed man*. **5** fair; honest: *a square deal*. **6** (**all square**) equal; with each side owing nothing. **7** complete; outright: *a square denial*. **8** *colloq.* having traditional or old-fashioned values or tastes. — *verb* **1** to make square in shape, especially to make right-angled. **2** to multiply (a number) by itself. **3** (*also* **square up** or **square something up**) to pay off or settle a debt. **4** to make the scores in (a match) level. **5** (**square something with someone**) to get their approval or permission for it. **6** (**square with something**) to agree or correspond with it. **7** to mark with a pattern of squares. — *adv.* **1** solidly and directly: *hit me square on the jaw*. **2** fairly; honestly. — **back to square one** *colloq.* back to the beginning, with no progress made. **square the circle** to do the impossible. **square up to something** to face up

to a task, difficulty, etc and prepare to tackle it. [from Old French *esquarre*, from Latin *quadra*]

■ *noun* **1** quadrilateral, rectangle. *adj.* **1** quadrilateral, rectangular, right-angled. **5** fair, equitable, just, ethical, honourable, honest, genuine, above-board, *colloq.* on the level. *verb* **3** settle, pay off. **6** agree with, accord with, tally with, correspond with, match.

square-bashing *noun slang* military drill on a barracks square.

square bracket each of a pair of printed brackets ([ ]), chiefly used to contain special information such as comment by an editor of a text.

square cloth a fabric in which the number of warp and weft threads per centimetre is approximately equal. It is more expensive to make than most fabrics and is mainly used where a woven design has a square repeat sequence.

square dance a folk dance performed by couples in a square formation.

square leg *Cricket* a fielding position level with the batsman, at some distance from him, and facing his back; also, a fielder in this position.

squarely *adv.* **1** square. **2** at right angles.

square meal a good nourishing meal.

square root *Maths.* a number or quantity that when multiplied by itself gives a particular number, eg the square root of 9 (written as $\sqrt{9}$ or $9^{\frac{1}{2}}$) is 3, because 3 x 3 = 9.

squaring the circle *Geom.* an attempt by the ancient Greeks to construct a square of exactly the same area as a circle, using only a ruler and compass. It puzzled mathematicians for centuries, and was proved to be impossible by Ferdinand von Lindemann in 1882.

squash¹ — *verb* **1** to crush or flatten by pressing or squeezing. **2** *intrans.* to force one's body into a confined space. **3** to suppress or put down (eg a rebellion). **4** to force into silence with a cutting reply. — *noun* **1** a concentrated fruit syrup, or a drink made by diluting this. **2** a crushed or crowded state. **3** (*also* **squash rackets**) a game for two players on a walled indoor court, played with rackets and a small hard rubber ball. [from Old French *esquacer*, to crush]

■ *verb* **1** crush, flatten, press, squeeze, compress, trample, stamp, pound, pulp. **3** suppress, quell, quash, put down. **4** silence, snub, put down, humiliate.
E3 *verb* **1** stretch, expand.

squash² *noun North Amer., esp. US* **1** any marrow-like vegetable of the cucumber family. **2** any of the plants bearing them. [from Narragansett (Native American language) *askutasquash*]

squashy *adj.* (**squashier**, **squashiest**) *colloq.* soft and easily squashed.

squat — *verb intrans.* (**squatted**, **squatting**) **1** to take up, or be sitting in, a low position with the knees fully bent and the weight on the soles of the feet. **2** to occupy an empty building without legal right. — *noun* **1** a squatting position. **2** an empty building unlawfully occupied. **3** *colloq.* a squat thrust. — *adj.* short and broad or fat. [from Old French *esquatir*, to crush]

■ *verb* **1** crouch, stoop, bend, sit. *adj.* short, stocky, thickset, dumpy, chunky, stubby.
E3 *adj.* slim, lanky.

squatter *noun* a person unlawfully occupying an empty building.

squat thrust a fitness exercise in which, from an all-fours position, the feet are made to jump forwards so that the knees touch the elbows, then back again.

squaw *noun offensive* a Native American woman or wife. [from Massachusett (Native American language) *squa*]

squawk

squawk — *noun* **1** a high-pitched croaking cry, like that of a parrot. **2** a loud protest or complaint. — *verb intrans.* **1** to make a high-pitched croaking cry. **2** to complain loudly. [imitative]

- *noun* **1** screech, shriek, croak, cackle, crow, hoot. *verb* **1** screech, shriek, croak, cackle, crow, hoot.

squawky *adj.* (**squawkier, squawkiest**) **1** characterized by or like squawks. **2** tending to squawk.

squeak — *noun* **1** a short high-pitched cry or sound, like that of a mouse or a rusty gate. **2** (*also* **narrow squeak**) a narrow escape; a victory or success achieved by the slimmest of margins. — *verb trans., intrans.* to utter a squeak or with a squeak. — **squeak through something** to succeed in it by a narrow margin. [imitative]

- *noun* **1** squeal, whine, creak, peep, cheep. *verb* squeal, whine, creak, peep, cheep.

squeakiness *noun* being squeaky.
squeaky *adj.* (**squeakier, squeakiest**) **1** characterized by squeaks. **2** tending to squeak.
squeaky clean *colloq.* **1** spotlessly clean. **2** virtuous, impeccable; above reproach or criticism. [originally used of wet hair, which squeaks when pulled]
squeal — *noun* a long high-pitched cry or yelp, like that of a pig or a child in pain. — *verb* **1** *trans., intrans.* to utter a squeal or with a squeal. **2** *intrans. colloq.* to inform or tell tales. **3** *intrans.* to complain or protest loudly. [imitative]

- *noun* cry, shout, yell, yelp, wail, scream, screech, shriek, squawk. *verb* **1** cry, shout, yell, yelp, wail, scream, screech, shriek, squawk. **2** inform, *slang* grass, *slang* split, tell tales, sneak.

squealer *noun* **1** a person or thing that squeals. **2** a bird or animal that squeals, especially a piglet. **3** *colloq.* an informer.
squeamish *adj.* **1** slightly nauseous. **2** easily made nauseous. [from Old French *escoymous*]

- **1** queasy, nauseated, sick. **2** delicate, fastidious, particular, prudish.

squeegee /ˈskwiːdʒiː/ *noun* a device with a rubber blade for scraping water off a surface, eg a window. [a fanciful variation of SQUEEZE]
squeegie *noun* someone who washes the windscreens of cars stopped at traffic lights, in the hope of being tipped by drivers. [a variant of SQUEEGEE]
squeeze — *verb* **1** to grasp or embrace tightly. **2** to press forcefully, especially from at least two sides. **3** to press or crush so as to extract (eg juice); to extract (eg toothpaste) by pressing or crushing. **4** to force (someone or something) into a confined space. **5** *intrans.* to force one's body into or through a confined space. **6** (**squeeze something out of someone**) to obtain it from them by hard persuasion or extortion. — *noun* **1** an act of squeezing. **2** a crowded or crushed state: *it's a bit of a squeeze with four on the sofa.* **3** an amount of fruit juice, etc got by squeezing. **4** a restriction, especially on spending or borrowing money. — **put the squeeze on someone** *colloq.* to pressurize them into giving something. [from Anglo-Saxon *cwysan*, to press]

- *verb* **1** grasp, grip, clasp, clutch, hug, embrace, enfold, cuddle. **2** press, squash, crush, pinch, nip, compress. **4** force, ram, push, cram, stuff, pack, crowd, wedge, jam. *noun* **1** press, grasp, clasp, hug, embrace. **2** press, squash, crush, crowd, congestion, jam.

squeeze-box *noun colloq.* an accordion or concertina.
squeezer *noun* a person, device, or machine, etc that squeezes (especially fruit).
squelch — *noun* a loud gurgling or sucking sound made by contact with a thick sticky substance, eg wet mud. — *verb intrans.* to make this sound. [imitative]
squelchy *adj.* (**squelchier, squelchiest**) having a squelching feeling.
squib *noun* **1** a small firework that jumps around on the ground before exploding. **2** a satirical criticism or attack; a lampoon. [perhaps imitative]
squid *noun* (PL. **squid, squids**) any of about 350 species of marine mollusc, related to the octopus and cuttlefish, with a torpedo-shaped body supported by an internal horny plate, two well-developed eyes, eight sucker-bearing arms surrounding the mouth, and two longer tentacles. Squid feed on fish, which they seize with their arms and tentacles, and they are capable of changing colour to match their surroundings, and emitting a cloud of dark ink when threatened by predators. Squid is a popular food item in some parts of the world.
squiffy *adj.* (**squiffier, squiffiest**) *colloq.* slightly drunk; tipsy.
squiggle *noun* a wavy scribbled line. [perhaps from SQUIRM and WRIGGLE]
squiggly *adj.* (**squigglier, squiggliest**) characterized by squiggles.
squinch *noun Archit.* a small arch running diagonally across each corner of a square building or room, creating an octagonal base on which a tower or circular dome may be supported.
squint — *noun* **1** the condition of having one or both eyes set slightly off-centre, preventing parallel vision. **2** *colloq.* a quick look; a peep. — *verb intrans.* **1** to be affected by a squint. **2** to look with eyes half-closed; to peer. — *adj.* **1** squinting. **2** *colloq.* not properly straight or centred. [perhaps from Dutch *schuinte*, slant]
squire *noun* **1** an owner of a large area of rural land, especially the chief landowner in a district. **2** *colloq.* a term of address used between men. [see ESQUIRE]
squirm — *verb intrans.* **1** to wriggle. **2** to feel or show embarrassment, shame, or nervousness, often with slight wriggling movements of the body. — *noun* a squirming movement. [perhaps connected with WORM]
squirrel *noun* any of various medium-sized rodents belonging to the family Sciuridae, found almost worldwide, and having a large soft bushy tail and long strong hind legs. Squirrels are noted for grasping their food, mainly seeds and nuts, in their front paws as they feed. [from Greek *skiouros*, from *skia*, shade + *oura*, tail]
squirt — *verb trans., intrans.* to shoot out or cause (a liquid) to shoot out in a narrow jet. — *noun* **1** an act of squirting or an amount of liquid squirted. **2** *colloq.* a small or insignificant person, especially when arrogant. [imitative]

- *verb* spray, spurt, shoot, spout, gush, ejaculate, discharge. *noun* **1** spray, spurt, jet.

squish — *noun* a gentle splashing or squelching sound. — *verb intrans.* to make, or move with, this sound. [imitative]
Sr [1] *abbrev. used after a name* Senior: *John Smith, Sr.*
Sr [2] *symbol, Chem.* strontium.
SRN *abbrev.* State Registered Nurse.
SS [1] *abbrev.* **1** Saints. **2** steamship.
SS [2] *abbrev.* Schutzstaffel ('protective squad') a Nazi organization founded as Hitler's small personal bodyguard and later expanded into an élite force which within the Third Reich controlled a dominant repressive apparatus, responsible for concentration camps and racial extermination policy.
SSP *abbrev.* statutory sick pay.
St *abbrev.* **1** Saint. **2** Street.

st. *abbrev.* stone (the unit of weight).

stab — *verb* (**stabbed, stabbing**) **1** to wound or pierce with a pointed instrument or weapon. **2** (**stab at something**) to make a quick thrusting movement towards it with something sharp. **3** *intrans.* to produce a sharp piercing sensation: *stabbing pain.* — *noun* **1** an act of stabbing. **2** a stabbing sensation. **3** *colloq.* a try: *have a stab at.* — **stab someone in the back** to slander or betray them, especially in a cowardly way. [from Middle English *stab*]

■ *verb* **1** pierce, puncture, cut, wound, injure, gore, knife, spear, stick, jab. *noun* **1** puncture, cut, incision, gash, wound, jab, prick. **2** ache, pang, twinge. **3** try, attempt, endeavour, *colloq.* bash, *colloq.* go.

stability *noun* the state or quality of being stable. [from Latin *stabilitas*]

■ steadiness, firmness, soundness, constancy, steadfastness, strength, sturdiness, solidity, durability, permanence.

🡢 instability, unsteadiness, insecurity, weakness.

stabilization or **stabilisation** *noun* stabilizing or being stabilized.

stabilize or **stabilise** *verb trans., intrans.* to make or become stable or more stable.

stabilizer or **stabiliser** *noun* **1** one or more aerofoils used to give stability to an aircraft. **2** a device used to reduce rolling and pitching of a ship. **3** each of two small wheels fitted to the back wheel of a child's bicycle to give it added stability. **4** any substance that prevents deterioration or breakdown of another substance when added to it. **5** a chemical substance that allows food ingredients that would not otherwise mix well to remain together in a homogeneous state. For example, stabilizers prevent the coagulation of oil droplets in salad cream. **6** *Econ.* any of various factors in a modern economic system which help to keep the economy stable, avoiding the worst effects of trade cycle fluctuations. They mainly relate to fiscal policy, in that tax receipts will change with rises and falls in income; and may also include direct intervention by government, as in a programme of public works.

stable¹ *adj.* **1** firmly balanced or fixed; not likely to wobble or fall. **2** firmly established; not likely to be abolished, overthrown, or destroyed: *a stable government.* **3** regular or constant; not erratic or changing: *the patient's condition is stable.* [from Latin *stabilis*]

■ **1** balanced, fixed, static, steady, firm, secure, fast, sound, strong, sturdy, sure, reliable. **2** established, well-founded, deep-rooted, lasting, enduring, abiding, permanent, unchangeable, invariable. **3** regular, uniform, steady, constant, unchanging.

🡢 UNSTABLE. **1** wobbly, shaky, weak. **3** irregular, erratic.

stable² *noun* **1** a building in which horses are kept. **2** a place where horses are bred and trained. **3** *colloq.* a number of people or things with a common background or origin, eg a number of athletes trained by the same coach. [from Latin *stabulum*]

staccato /stə'kɑːtoʊ/ *adj., adv.* **1** *Mus.* with notes played as a series of short, abrupt, audibly separate units rather than as a flowing sequence. **2** with, or consisting of, a series of short distinct sounds. [from Italian *staccato*, from *distaccare*, to separate]

stack — *noun* **1** a large neat pile of hay or straw. **2** any large neat pile. **3** (*usually* **a stack of** or **stacks of something**) *colloq.* a large amount. **4** a large industrial chimney: *smokestack* — *verb* **1** to arrange in a stack or stacks. **2** to prearrange (playing cards) in a pack so as to allow cheating. **3** to arrange (circumstances, etc) to favour or disadvantage a particular person. **4** to arrange (aircraft waiting to land) into a queue in which each circles the airport at a different altitude. [from Norse *stakkr*, haystack]

■ *noun* **2** heap, pile, mound. **3** mass, load, hoard, stockpile.
verb **1** heap, pile, amass, accumulate, save, hoard, stockpile.

stadium *noun* (PL. **stadiums, stadia**) a large sports arena with spectators' seats on different tiers. [from Greek *stadion*]

staff — *noun, usually treated as pl.* **1** the total number of employees working in an establishment or organization. **2** the employees working for or assisting a manager. **3** *Mil.* the officers assisting a senior commander. **4** (PL. **staffs, staves**) any stick or rod carried in the hand. **5** *Mus.* a set of lines and spaces on which music is written. — *verb* to provide (an establishment) with staff.

■ *noun* **1** personnel, workforce, employees, workers, crew.
4 stick, cane, rod, baton, wand.

staff nurse a qualified nurse next below a sister in rank.

Staffs. *abbrev.* Staffordshire.

staff sergeant the senior sergeant in an army company.

stag — *noun* **1** an adult male deer, especially a red deer. **2** *slang* a person who buys shares in the hope of selling them immediately for a profit. — *adj.* male; of or for men only. [from Anglo-Saxon *stagga*]

stag beetle a beetle with large antler-like jaw parts.

stage — *noun* **1** a platform on which a performance takes place. **2** any of several distinct and successive periods. **3** a part of a journey or route. **4** (**the stage**) the theatre as a profession or art form. **5** *colloq.* a stagecoach. — *verb* **1** to present as a performance; to present a performance of (a play). **2** to pre-arrange to happen in a particular way. **3** to organize or hold as an event. [from Old French *estage*, storey, tier]

■ *noun* **2** phase, period, step, level. **3** division, leg, length, lap.
verb **1** mount, put on, present, produce, give, do, perform. **2** stage-manage, orchestrate, engineer. **3** arrange, organize.

stagecoach *noun* a large horse-drawn coach formerly carrying passengers and mail on a regular fixed route.

stage directions instructions relating to actors' movements, and often sound and lighting effects, written as part of the script of a play.

stage diving the practice of jumping from the stage on to the crowd at a rock concert.

stage fright nervousness felt by an actor or other performer or speaker when about to appear in front of an audience, especially for the first time.

stagehand *noun* a person responsible for moving scenery and props in a theatre.

stage-manage *verb* **1** to be the stage manager of (a play). **2** to pre-arrange to happen in a certain way, in order to create a particular effect.

stage manager a person supervising the arrangement of scenery and props for a play.

stage-struck *adj.* having an overwhelming desire to be an actor.

stage whisper 1 an actor's loud whisper intended to be heard by the audience. **2** any loud whisper intended to be heard by people other than the person addressed.

stagflation *noun* inflation in an economy without the expected growth in employment or demand for goods. [from STAGNATION + INFLATION]

stagger — *verb* (**staggered, staggering**) **1** *intrans.* to walk or move unsteadily. **2** to cause extreme shock or surprise to. **3** to arrange so as to take place or begin at different times: *we need to stagger working hours.* — *noun* **1** an act of staggering. **2** (**staggers**) a disease of the brain in horses and cattle, causing staggering. **3** (**the staggers**) giddiness. [from Norse *staka*, to push]

▣ *verb* **1** lurch, totter, teeter, wobble, sway, rock, reel.
2 surprise, amaze, astound, astonish, stun, stupefy,
dumbfound, *colloq.* flabbergast, shake, shock, confound,
overwhelm.

staggering *adj.* that staggers; shockingly surprising.

staginess *noun* being stagy, artificiality.

staging *noun* **1** scaffolding, or the planks used for walking
on; any temporary platform. **2** the putting on of a play or
other spectacle.

stagnant *adj.* **1** *said of water* not flowing; dirty and foul-
smelling because of not flowing. **2** not moving or developing; dull and inactive. [from Latin *stagnum*, pond]

▣ **1** still, motionless, standing, brackish, stale. **2** inactive,
slow, sluggish, torpid, lethargic.
▣ **1** fresh. **2** moving.

stagnate *verb intrans.* to be or become stagnant.

▣ vegetate, idle, languish, decline, deteriorate, decay, rot,
rust.

stagnation *noun* **1** stagnating. **2** being stagnant.

stag party or **stag night** a party for men only, especially
in honour of a man about to be married.

stagy *adj.* (**stagier, stagiest**) theatrical; artificial or affected.

staid *adj.* serious or sober in character or manner, especially to the point of being dull. [an obsolete past participle of STAY]

▣ solemn, serious, grave, sober, demure, sedate, calm,
composed, quiet, steady.
▣ jaunty, debonair, frivolous, adventurous.

stain — *verb* **1** *trans., intrans.* to make or become marked
or discoloured, often permanently. **2** to change the colour
of (eg wood) by applying a liquid chemical. — *noun* **1** a
mark or discoloration. **2** a liquid chemical applied (eg to
wood) to bring about a change of colour. **3** a cause of
shame or dishonour: *a stain on his reputation.* [from Middle English *steynen*, to paint]

▣ *verb* **1** mark, spot, blot, smudge, discolour, soil, tarnish. **2**
dye, tint, colour, paint, varnish. *noun* **1** mark, spot, blemish,
blot, smudge, smear, discoloration. **2** dye, tint, colour,
paint, varnish. **3** smear, slur, disgrace, shame, dishonour.

stained glass decorative glass coloured by a chemical
process, especially used in church windows.

stainless steel any of a group of iron alloys containing
chromium and nickel that are highly resistant to corrosion
(rusting) and abrasion, and have a high tensile strength.
Stainless steel can be polished to a bright shine, and is
used to make cutlery, surgical instruments, ball bearings,
turbine blades, exhaust pipes, etc.

stair *noun* **1** any of a set of indoor steps connecting the
floors of a building. **2** (*also* **stairs**) a set of these. [from
Anglo-Saxon *stæger*]

staircase or **stairway** *noun* a set of stairs, often including
the stairwell.

stairwell *noun* the vertical shaft containing a staircase.

stake[1] — *noun* **1** a stick or post, usually with one end
pointed, knocked into the ground as a support, eg for a
young tree or a fence. **2** (**the stake**) *formerly* a post to
which a person is tied to be burned alive as a punishment;
the punishment. — *verb* to support or fasten to the ground
with a stake. — **stake a claim** to assert or establish a right
or ownership. **stake something out 1** to mark the boundary of (a piece of land) with stakes. **2** *colloq.* to place (a per-

son or a building) under surveillance. [from Anglo-Saxon
staca]

▣ **1** post, pole, picket, paling, spike, stick.

stake[2] — *noun* **1** a sum of money risked in betting. **2** an
interest, especially financial: *have a stake in the project's
success.* **3** (**stakes**) a prize, especially in horse-racing. —
verb **1** to risk as a bet. **2** to give (especially financial) support to. — **at stake 1** to be won or lost; wagered. **2** at risk;
in danger. [perhaps from Old Dutch *staken*, to place]

▣ *noun* **1** bet, wager. **2** interest, concern, involvement,
investment, share, claim. *verb* **1** gamble, bet, wager, risk,
chance, hazard, venture.

stakeholder economy or **society** an economy or society in which all individuals are regarded as having an interest.

stake-out *noun colloq.* surveillance of a person or building.

stalactite *noun* an icicle-like mass of limestone attached
to the roof of a cave, etc, formed by the dripping of water
containing limestone. [from Greek *stalaktos*, a dripping]

stalagmite *noun* a spiky mass of limestone sticking up
from the floor of a cave, etc, formed by the dripping of
water from a stalactite. [from Greek *stalagma*, a drop]

stale *adj.* **1** *said of food* not fresh, and therefore dry and unpalatable. **2** *said of air* not fresh; musty. **3** overused and no
longer interesting or original. **4** out of condition because
of over-training or overstudy. [from Old French *estaler*, to
halt]

▣ **1** dry, hard, old, flat, insipid, tasteless. **2** musty, fusty. **3**
overused, hackneyed, clichéd, stereotyped, unoriginal,
trite, banal, commonplace.
▣ FRESH, CRISP. **3** new, original.

stalemate *noun* **1** *Chess* a position from which a player
cannot move without leaving his or her king in check, resulting in a draw. **2** a position, in any contest or dispute,
from which no progress can be made nor winner emerge;
a deadlock. [from Middle English *stale*, stalemate +
MATE[2]]

▣ **1** draw, tie. **2** deadlock, impasse, standstill, halt.
▣ **2** progress.

staleness *noun* a stale quality.

Stalinism /'stɑːlɪnɪzm/ *noun Politics* the rigorous rule of
Stalin in the period 1929–53, characterized by socialism,
centralization of power, the total subservience of society
and culture to political ends, and the suppression of political opponents.

stalk[1] /stɔːk/ *noun* **1** *Bot.* the main stem of a plant, or the
stem that attaches a leaf, flower, or fruit to the plant. **2**
any slender connecting part. [from Anglo-Saxon *stalu*]

▣ **1** stem, twig, branch, trunk.

stalk[2] /stɔːk/ *verb* **1** to hunt, follow, or approach stealthily.
2 *intrans.* to walk or stride stiffly or proudly. [from Anglo-
Saxon *stealcian*]

▣ **1** track, trail, hunt, follow, pursue, shadow, tail, haunt. **2**
stride, march.

stalker *noun* a person who stalks.

stalking-horse *noun* **1** a horse behind which a hunter
hides while approaching the hunted animal. **2** a person or
thing used to conceal real plans or intentions, especially a
planned attack.

stall[1] — *noun* **1** a compartment for housing a single animal in a cowshed, stable, etc. **2** a platform or stand on

which goods or services for sale are displayed or advertised. **3** a church seat with arms, especially one in the choir or chancel. **4** (**stalls**) the seats on the ground floor of a theatre or cinema. **5** an act of stalling a vehicle or its engine. — *verb* **1** *trans., intrans. said of a motor vehicle or its engine* to cut out or cause it to cut out unintentionally. **2** to put (an animal) into a stall. [from Anglo-Saxon *stall*]

stall² — *verb* **1** to delay. **2** *intrans.* to do something in order to delay something else; to be evasive. — *noun* an act of stalling; a delaying tactic. [from obsolete *stale*, decoy]

⊟ *verb* DELAY. **1** hold up, put off, defer, postpone. **2** temporize, play for time, hedge, equivocate, stonewall.

stallion *noun* an uncastrated adult male horse, especially one kept for breeding. [from Old French *estalon*]

stalwart /'stɔːlwət/ — *adj.* **1** strong and sturdy. **2** unwavering in commitment and support; reliable. — *noun* a stalwart supporter. [from Anglo-Saxon *stælwierthe*, serviceable]

⊟ *adj.* STOUT. **1** strong, sturdy, robust, rugged, strapping, muscular, athletic, valiant, daring, intrepid, indomitable. **2** staunch, steadfast, reliable, dependable.
⊟ *adj.* **1** weak, feeble, timid. **2** unreliable.

stamen /'steɪmən/ *noun Bot.* in a flowering plant, the male reproductive structure, consisting of a stalk-like *filament* bearing a specialized chamber (the *anther*), within which pollen grains are produced. The number and arrangement of the stamens are often used as an aid to identification of a flower. [from Latin *stamen*, warp thread]

stamina *noun* energy needed to withstand prolonged physical or mental exertion. [an old plural of STAMEN]

⊟ energy, vigour, strength, power, force, resilience, resistance, endurance, indefatigability, staying power.
⊟ weakness.

stammer — *noun* an inability to utter, without hesitation, certain speech sounds at the beginning of words, resulting in a repetition of the sound; the resulting repetition. — *verb trans., intrans.* (**stammered, stammering**) to speak or say with a stammer. [from Anglo-Saxon *stamerian*]

⊟ *noun* stutter. *verb* stutter, falter, splutter.

stamp — *verb* **1** *trans., intrans.* to bring (the foot) down with force. **2** *intrans.* to walk with a heavy tread. **3** to imprint or impress (a mark or design); to imprint or impress (something) with a mark or design. **4** to fix or mark deeply: *the number was stamped on his memory.* **5** to prove to be; to characterize: *his lies stamp him as untrustworthy* **6** to fix a postage or other stamp on. — *noun* **1** a small piece of gummed paper bearing an official mark and indicating that a tax or fee has been paid, especially a postage stamp. **2** an instrument for stamping a mark or design; the mark or design stamped. **3** a characteristic mark or sign: *the crime bears the stamp of a professional.* **4** an act of stamping the foot. — **stamp something out 1** to put out a fire by stamping on it. **2** to put an end to an activity or practice, especially an illicit one. [from Anglo-Saxon *stampian*]

⊟ *verb* **2** stomp, stump. **3** imprint, impress, print, emboss, mark. **4** inscribe, engrave. **5** characterize, identify, brand, label. *noun* **2** print, imprint, impression, seal, brand. **3** mark, hallmark, signature.

stamp duty a tax on the drawing up of certain legal documents, eg those transferring ownership of property.

stampede — *noun* **1** a sudden wild rush of animals, especially when alarmed. **2** an excited or hysterical rush by a crowd of people. — *verb intrans.* to rush in a herd or crowd. [from Spanish *estampar*, to stamp]

⊟ *noun* CHARGE, RUSH. **2** dash, sprint, flight, rout. *verb* charge, rush, dash, run, gallop, fly, flee.

stamping-ground *noun* a person's usual haunt or place of action. [originally used of wild animals]

stance *noun* **1** position or manner of standing, eg when preparing to play a stroke in sport. **2** point of view. [from Latin *stare*, to stand]

⊟ POSITION. **1** posture, deportment, carriage, bearing. **2** standpoint, viewpoint, angle, point of view, attitude.

stanch /stɑːntʃ/ same as STAUNCH².

stanchion /'stɑːnʃən, 'stanʃən/ *noun* an upright beam or pole serving as a support. [from Old French *estançon*]

stand — *verb* (PAST TENSE AND PAST PARTICIPLE **stood**) **1** *intrans.* (*also* **stand up**) to be in, or move into, an upright position supported by the legs or a base. **2** (*also* **stand up**) to place (something) in an upright position, usually resting on its base. **3** to place or situate. **4** *intrans.* to be placed or situated. **5** *intrans.* to be a particular height: *the tower stands 300 feet tall.* **6** to tolerate or put up with: *could not stand them/how can you stand it?* **7** *intrans.* to be in a particular state or condition: *I stand corrected / the score stands at 3–1.* **8** *intrans.* to be in a position to do something: *we stand to make a lot of money.* **9** *intrans.* to continue to apply or be valid: *the decision stands.* **10** (**stand for something**) *said of a symbol or device* to represent or signify it. **11** *intrans.* to be a candidate, especially in an election. **12** to withstand or survive: *stood the test.* **13** *colloq.* to buy (something) for (someone): *stood me lunch.* — *noun* **1** a base on which something is supported: *a cake-stand.* **2** a stall displaying or advertising goods or services for sale. **3** a structure with sitting or standing accommodation for spectators. **4** a rack or other device on which coats, hats, umbrellas, etc may be hung. **5** an attitude or course of action resolutely adopted: *take a stand against further building.* **6** an act of resisting attack: *make a stand.* **7** *Cricket* a partnership between batsmen, expressed in terms of the time it lasts or the runs scored. — **stand by 1** to be in a state of readiness to act. **2** to look on without taking the required or expected action: *stood by and watched them go.* **stand by someone** to give them loyalty or support, especially in time of difficulty. **stand down** to resign, especially in favour of someone else. **stand for something** to tolerate or allow it: *will not stand for it.* **stand in for someone** to act as a substitute for them. **stand off** to stay some distance away. **stand one's ground** to maintain one's position resolutely; to refuse to give in. **stand out** to be noticeable or prominent. **stand out for something** to persist in demanding or seeking a concession, etc; to hold out. **stand out for** or **against something** to remain resolutely in favour of or opposed to it. **stand up 1** to assume a standing position; to stand. **2** to prove to be valid on examination: *an argument that will stand up in court.* **stand someone up** *colloq.* to fail to keep an appointment with them. **stand up for someone** or **something** to be outspoken in one's support for or defence of them. **stand up to someone** or **something** to face or resist someone (eg an opponent); to withstand something (eg hard wear or criticism). [from Anglo-Saxon *standan*]

⊟ *verb* **1** rise, get up. **2** erect. **3** put, place, set, locate, situate, position, station. **6** tolerate, put up with, bear, abide, endure, suffer. **10** represent, symbolize, signify, mean, denote, indicate. **12** withstand, weather, survive, endure. *noun* **1** base, pedestal, support, frame, rack. **3** stall, booth. **stand by** support, back, champion, defend, stick by, stick up for. **stand down** step down, resign, abdicate, quit, give up, retire, withdraw. **stand for** tolerate, put up with, take, accept, allow, permit. **stand in for** deputize for, cover for, understudy, replace, substitute for. **stand out 1** show, catch the eye, stick out, jut out, project. **stand up for** defend, stick up for, side with, fight for, support, protect, champion, uphold. **stand up to** face, confront, brave, defy, oppose, resist, withstand, endure.

▣ **stand by** let down. **stand down** join. **stand up for** attack. **stand up to** give in to.

standard — *noun* **1** an established or accepted model; a thing with which others are compared so as to be measured or judged. **2** a level of excellence, value, or quality. **3** (*often* **standards**) a principle of behaviour or morality adhered to. **4** a flag or other emblem, especially one carried on a pole. **5** an upright pole or support. **6** something, especially a song, that has remained popular over the years. — *adj.* **1** of the normal or accepted kind, without variations or additions. **2** typical; average; unexceptional. **3** accepted as supremely authoritative: *the standard text on the subject.* **4** *said of language* accepted as correct by educated native speakers. [from Old French *estandart*]

▣ *noun* **1** norm, average, type, model, pattern, example, guideline, benchmark, touchstone, yardstick, rule, measure, rule, criterion, requirement, specification. **2** level, grade, quality. **3** principle, scruple, ethic, ideal. **4** flag, ensign, pennant, pennon, colours, banner. *adj.* **1** normal, regular, accepted, recognized, classic, basic, staple. **2** average, typical, stock, unexceptional, usual, customary. **3** official, orthodox, approved, set, established, definitive. ▣ *adj.* **1** abnormal, irregular. **2** exceptional.

standard-bearer *noun* **1** a person carrying a flag. **2** the leader of a movement or cause.

standard deviation *Maths.* (ABBREV. **SD**) a measure of the spread of a sample of numbers about their arithmetic mean, widely used in statistics. It is equal to the square root of the variance (the mean of the squares of the deviations of each number from the mean of the sample).

Standard English the form of English taught in schools, and used, especially in formal situations, by the majority of educated English speakers.

standard error or **standard error of the mean** *Maths.* (ABBREV. **SE, SEM**) a measure of the extent to which the mean of a sample of a population represents the mean of the population from which the sample is drawn. It is equal to the standard deviation divided by the root of the number of observations, and is widely used in statistics.

standardization or **standardisation** *noun* standardizing or being standardized.

standardize or **standardise** *verb* to make (all examples of something) uniform in kind, size, shape, etc.

▣ normalize, equalize, homogenize, stereotype. ▣ differentiate.

standard lamp a lamp on a pole with a base that sits on the floor.

standard temperature and pressure (ABBREV. **STP**) *Physics* the standard conditions that are used as a basis for experimental measurements and calculations involving quantities that vary with temperature and pressure, by convention a standard temperature of $273.15°$K ($0°$C) and a standard pressure of 101,325 pascals (1 atmosphere); formerly known as normal temperature and pressure.

stand-by *noun* **1** a state of readiness to act, eg in an emergency. **2** a person or thing in this role. **3** *said of air travel* a system of allocating spare seats to passengers without a reservation, once the booked seats have been taken.

stand-in *noun* a deputy or substitute.

standing — *noun* **1** position, status, or reputation. **2** duration. — *adj.* **1** done, taken, etc in or from a standing position: *a standing ovation.* **2** permanent; regularly used: *a standing joke.*

standing order 1 an instruction from an account-holder to a bank to make fixed payments from the account to a third party at regular intervals. **2** an order placed with a shopkeeper for a regular supply of something.

standing wave *Physics* a wave that results from interference between waves of the same wavelength travelling in opposite directions, eg on a guitar string, where a wave passes along the string and is reflected back along itself when it reaches the end of the string. Also called STATIONARY WAVE.

stand-off or **stand-off half** *noun Rugby* a half-back who stands away from the scrum and acts as a link between the scrum-half and the three-quarters.

stand-offish *adj.* unfriendly or aloof.

▣ aloof, remote, distant, unapproachable, unfriendly, unsociable, uncommunicative, reserved, cold. ▣ friendly.

standpipe *noun* a vertical pipe leading from a water supply, especially one providing an emergency supply in the street when household water is cut off.

standpoint *noun* a point of view.

▣ position, stance, viewpoint, angle, point of view, attitude.

standstill *noun* a complete stop, with no progress being made at all.

▣ stop, halt, pause, rest, stoppage, jam, hold-up, impasse, deadlock, stalemate. ▣ advance, progress.

stand-up comedy (*also* **stand-up**) comic monologue that is delivered without any support, usually before an audience.

stank see STINK.

stanza /ˈstanzə/ *noun* a verse in poetry. [from Italian *stanza*]

stapes /ˈsteɪpiːz/ *noun* (PL. **stapes**) *Anat.* a small stirrup-shaped bone in the middle ear. Together with two other bones, the malleus and incus, it transmits sound waves from the eardrum to the inner ear. [from late Latin *stapes*, stirrup]

staphylococcus /ˌstafɪloʊˈkɒkəs/ *noun Biol.* a spherical Gram-positive bacterium of the genus *Staphylococcus*, that occurs on the skin and mucous membranes of humans and other animals. Some species can cause boils and abscesses, food poisoning, pneumonia, and osteomyelitis (inflammation of the bone marrow). [from Greek *staphyle*, bunch of grapes + *kokkos*, a grain]

staple[1] — *noun* **1** a U-shaped wire fastener for paper, forced through the paper from a special instrument into which it is loaded. **2** a U-shaped metal nail. — *verb* to fasten or attach with a staple or staples. [from Anglo-Saxon *stapol*, post, support]

staple[2] — *adj.* **1** principal; main: *staple foods.* **2** of principal importance as a traded article. — *noun* a staple product or ingredient. [from Old Dutch *stapel*, shop, warehouse]

▣ *adj.* **1** principal, essential, necessary, key, main, chief, major, standard, basic, fundamental, primary. ▣ *adj.* **1** minor.

stapler *noun* an instrument for driving staples through paper.

star — *noun* **1** a celestial body, often visible in the night sky, consisting of a sphere of gaseous material held together entirely by its own gravitational field, and generating heat and light energy by means of nuclear fusion reactions deep within its interior. **2** loosely used to refer to these bodies and the planets, comets, and meteors. **3** a representation of such a body in the form of a figure with five or more radiating points, often used as a symbol of rank or excellence. **4** (**the stars**) **a** the planets regarded as an influence on people's fortunes. **b** a horoscope. **5** a celebrity, especially from the entertainment world. **6** a principal performer. **7** an asterisk. — *verb* (**starred, starring**) **1** *trans., intrans.* to feature or appear as a principal performer. **2** to decorate with stars. **3** to asterisk. — **see stars** to see spots of light before one's eyes, eg as a result of a heavy blow to the head. [from Anglo-Saxon *steorra*]

Types of star include: nova, supernova, pulsar, falling star, shooting star, meteor, comet, Halley's comet, red giant, supergiant, white dwarf, red dwarf, brown dwarf, neutron star, Pole Star, Polaris, North Star.

starboard /ˈstɑːbəd, ˈstɑːbɔːd/ — *noun* the right side of a ship or aircraft, as viewed when facing forwards. — *adj., adv.* of, on, or towards the right side. [from Anglo-Saxon *steorbord*, steering board]

starch — *noun* **1** *Biochem.* a carbohydrate that occurs in all green plants, where it serves as an energy store, usually in the form of small white granules in seeds, tubers, etc. **2** a preparation of this substance used to stiffen cloth fabrics and to make paper. Starch extracted from potatoes and cereals is also widely used in the food industry. **3** stiffness of manner; over-formality. — *verb* to stiffen with starch. [from Anglo-Saxon *stercan*, to stiffen]

starchily *adv.* in a starchy way.

starchiness *noun* a starchy quality.

starchy *adj.* (**starchier, starchiest**) **1** like or containing starch. **2** stiff in manner; over-formal.

star cluster *Astron.* a group of stars physically associated in space, and held together by mutual gravitational attraction.

star-crossed *adj. literary* ill-fated; doomed.

stardom *noun* the state of being a celebrity.

stardust *noun* an imaginary dust that blinds the eyes to reality and fills them with romantic illusions.

stare — *verb intrans.* to look with a fixed gaze. — *noun* **1** an act of staring. **2** a fixed gaze. — **be staring someone in the face 1** *said of a solution, etc* to be readily apparent, but unnoticed. **2** *said of a misfortune, etc* to be menacingly imminent. **stare someone out** or **down** to stare more fixedly at someone staring back, causing them to look away. [from Anglo-Saxon *starian*]

. . . .
◨ *verb* gaze, look, watch, gape, *colloq.* gawp, gawk, goggle, glare. *noun* GAZE, GLARE.
. . . .

starfish *noun* the popular name for any of about 16,000 species of marine invertebrate animals belonging to the class Asteroidea, and having a number of arms (usually five) radiating outward from a central disc-like body.

star fruit the smooth-skinned yellow fruit of a SE Asian tree, the carambola, star-shaped in cross-section.

stargazer *noun colloq.* **1** *facetious* an astronomer or astrologer. **2** a daydreamer.

stargazing *noun* **1** studying the stars. **2** daydreaming.

stark — *adj.* **1** severely bare, harsh, or simple. **2** plain; unembellished: *the stark truth.* **3** utter; downright. — *adv.* utterly; completely. [from Anglo-Saxon *stearc*, hard, strong]

. . . .
◨ *adj.* **1** bare, barren, bleak, austere, harsh, severe, grim, dreary. **2** bald, plain, simple, unembellished. **3** utter, unmitigated, total, consummate, absolute, sheer, downright, out-and-out, flagrant, arrant.
. . . .

starkers *adj. colloq.* stark-naked.

stark-naked *adj.* completely naked. [from Middle English *stert-naked*, from Anglo-Saxon *steort*, tail + *nacod*, naked]

starlet *noun* a young actress, especially in films, regarded as a star of the future.

starlight *noun* the light from the stars.

starling *noun* a small common songbird with dark glossy speckled feathers and a short tail. [from Anglo-Saxon *stærling*]

starlit *adj.* lit by the stars.

starry *adj.* (**starrier, starriest**) **1** filled or decorated with stars. **2** shining brightly.

starry-eyed *adj.* **1** navely idealistic or optimistic. **2** radiantly happy or affectionate.

Stars and Stripes (**the Stars and Stripes**) the national flag of the USA.

star-studded *adj. colloq., said of the cast of a film, etc* featuring many well-known performers.

START *abbrev.* Strategic Arms Reduction Talks (or Treaty).

start — *verb* **1** *trans., intrans.* to begin; to bring or come into being. **2** *trans., intrans.* (*also* **start up** or **start something up**) to set or be set in motion, or put or be put into a working state. **3** (*also* **start off** or **out**) to be at first: *started out as an accountant.* **4** (*also* **start off** or **out**) to begin a journey, or an enterprise compared to a journey, eg a career. **5** (*also* **start something up**) to establish it or set it up. **6** (*also* **start something off**) to initiate it or get it going; to cause or set off. **7** *intrans.* to begin a journey: *started for home at midday.* **8** *intrans.* to flinch or shrink back suddenly and sharply, eg in fear or surprise. **9** *intrans., colloq.* to pick a quarrel. **10** to drive (an animal) from a lair or hiding-place. — *noun* **1** the first or early part. **2** a beginning, origin, or cause. **3** the time or place at which something starts. **4** an advantage given or held at the beginning of a race or other contest. **5** a help in or opportunity for beginning, eg in a career. **6** a sudden flinching or shrinking back. — **for a start** as an initial consideration; in the first place. **start on someone** to become suddenly and violently hostile towards them; to turn on them. **to start with 1** in the beginning. **2** in the first place. [from Middle English *sterten*]

. . . .
◨ *verb* **1** begin, commence. **5** establish, set up, found, institute. **6** initiate, originate, create, introduce, pioneer, inaugurate, launch, open, instigate, activate, trigger, set off. **7** set out, set off, leave, depart. **8** jump, jerk, twitch, flinch, recoil. *noun* **1** beginning, opening. **2** beginning, commencement, outset, inception, birth, dawn, break, onset, origin, cause, initiation, introduction, inauguration, launch, foundation. **6** jump, jerk, twitch, spasm.
◧ *verb* **1** stop, finish, end. *noun* **1, 2, 3** finish, end.
. . . .

starter *noun* **1** a person who gives the signal for a race to begin. **2** any of the competitors, horses, greyhounds, etc assembled for the start of a race. **3** (**starter motor**) an electric motor that is used to start the engine of a motor vehicle. **4** *colloq.* the first course of a meal. — **for starters** *colloq.* in the first place; for a start.

starting-block *noun Athletics* a device consisting of a shaped block against which an athlete braces the feet at the start of a race, especially a sprint.

startle *verb* **1** to give a sudden fright to. **2** to surprise. [from Anglo-Saxon *steartlian*, to stumble or struggle]

. . . .
◨ **1** scare, frighten, alarm, upset, disturb. **2** surprise, amaze, astonish, astound, shock.
. . . .

startling *adj.* that startles, surprising.

startup *noun* a business that has just been established.

star turn the principal item or performer in a show.

starvation *noun* a potentially fatal form of malnutrition caused by eating insufficient quantities of food over a long period, or by total lack of food, eg under conditions of famine or extreme poverty.

. . . .
◨ hunger, undernourishment, malnutrition, famine.
◧ plenty, excess.
. . . .

starve *verb* **1** *intrans.* to suffer extreme ill-health, or die, through lack of food. **2** to cause (a person or animal) to suffer or die by depriving them of food. **3** *intrans.*, *colloq.* to be very hungry. **4 (starve something** or **someone of something)** to cause them to suffer a severe lack of it: *starved the project of funds.* **5 (starve someone into something)** to force them into behaviour of a particular kind by withholding or preventing access to food. [from Anglo-Saxon *steorfan*, to die]

· · · · · · · · · · · · · · · · · · · ·
◫ **1** hunger, fast. **4** deprive of, refuse, deny.
◲ **1,2** feed.
· ·

starving *adj.* **1** suffering or dying through lack of food. **2** *colloq.* very hungry.

· · · · · · · · · · · · · · · · · · · ·
◫ **1** underfed, undernourished. **2** ravenous, famished.
· ·

Star Wars *colloq.* the US Strategic Defence Initiative, SDI.

stash *slang* — *verb* to put into a hiding-place. — *noun* a hidden supply or store, or its hiding-place.

Stasi /'stɑːsɪ/ *abbrev.* the former East German secret police, abolished in 1990. [from German, shortened from *Staatssicherheitsdienst*, state security service]

state — *noun* **1** the condition, eg of health, appearance, or emotions, in which a person or thing exists at a particular time. **2** a territory governed by a single political body; a nation. **3** any of a number of locally governed areas making up a nation or federation under the ultimate control of a central government, as in the US. **4** (*often* **State** or **the State**) the political entity of a nation, including the government and all its apparatus, eg the civil service and the armed forces. **5** *colloq.* an emotionally agitated condition. **6** *colloq.* a confused or untidy condition. — *adj.* **1** relating to or controlled or financed by the State, or a federal state. **2** ceremonial: *a state visit by the Queen.* — *verb* **1** to express clearly; to affirm or assert. **2** to specify. — **lie in state** *said of a dead person* to be ceremonially displayed to the public before burial. **the States** the United States of America. [from Latin *status*, from *stare*, to stand]

· · · · · · · · · · · · · · · · · · · ·
◫ *noun* **1** condition, shape, form, situation, position, circumstances, case. **2** nation, country, land, territory, kingdom, republic. **5** panic, *colloq.* flap, *colloq.* tizzy. *adj.* **1** national, governmental, public. **2** official, formal, ceremonial, pompous, stately. *verb* **1** say, declare, announce, express, articulate, voice, affirm, assert. **2** specify, formulate, present.
· ·

State Enrolled Nurse a nurse qualified to perform many nursing tasks. See also STATE REGISTERED NURSE.

stateless *adj.* having no nationality or citizenship.

stateliness *noun* a stately quality.

stately *adj.* (**statelier, stateliest**) noble, dignified and impressive in appearance or manner.

· · · · · · · · · · · · · · · · · · · ·
◫ grand, imposing, impressive, dignified, majestic, regal, royal, imperial, noble, august, lofty, pompous, solemn, ceremonious.
◲ informal.
· ·

stately home a large grand old private house, usually one open to the public.

statement *noun* **1** a thing stated, especially a formal written or spoken declaration. **2** a record of finances, especially one sent by a bank to an account-holder detailing the holder's transactions within a particular period. **3** the act of stating.

· · · · · · · · · · · · · · · · · · · ·
◫ **1** account, report, bulletin, communiqué, announcement, declaration, proclamation, testimony. **3** announcement, declaration, communication, utterance.
· ·

state of affairs a situation or set of circumstances.

state of emergency the suspension of normal law and

order procedures and the introduction of strict control of the population by the military, in order to deal with a crisis, revolution, or other trouble.

state of play the situation at a particular moment.

state of the art the current level of advancement achieved by the most modern, up-to-date technology or thinking in a particular field.

state-of-the-art *adj.* most modern and best.

State Registered Nurse in England and Wales, a nurse with advanced training, qualified to perform all nursing tasks. See also STATE ENROLLED NURSE, REGISTERED GENERAL NURSE.

stateroom *noun* **1** a large room in a palace, etc used for ceremonial occasions. **2** a large private cabin on a ship.

Stateside or **stateside** *colloq.* — *adj.* of or in the USA. — *adv.* to or towards the USA.

statesman *noun* (PL. **statesmen**) an experienced and distinguished politician.

statesmanlike *adj.* **1** diplomatic. **2** suitable for or worthy of a statesman or stateswoman.

statesmanship *noun* the skill of a statesman or stateswoman.

stateswoman *noun* (PL. **stateswomen**) an experienced and distinguished female politician.

static — *adj.* **1** not moving; stationary. **2** fixed; not portable. **3** tending not to move around or change. **4** relating to statics. — *noun* **1** (*in full* **static electricity**) an accumulation of electric charges that remain at rest instead of moving to form a flow of current, eg electricity produced by friction between two materials, such as hair and a plastic comb. **2** a sharp crackling or hissing sound that interferes with radio and television signals, and is caused by static electricity or atmospheric disturbance. [from Greek *statikos*, bringing to a standstill]

· · · · · · · · · · · · · · · · · · · ·
◫ *adj.* **1** stationary, motionless, immobile, unmoving, still, inert. **3** constant, changeless, unvarying, stable, fixed.
◲ *adj.* **1** mobile, moving. **2** mobile, portable. **3** varying. **4** dynamic.
· ·

statics *sing. noun* the branch of mechanics dealing with the action of forces on objects in equilibrium.

station — *noun* **1** a stopping-place for passenger trains or buses, with facilities for refuelling, ticket-purchasing, etc. **2** a local headquarters or depot, eg of a police force. **3** a building equipped for some particular purpose, eg electricity generation. **4** a radio or television channel, or the buildings from which it is broadcast. **5** a position within a class structure. **6** a post or place of duty. — *verb* (**stationed, stationing**) to appoint to a post or place of duty. [from Latin *statio*, from *stare*, to stand]

· · · · · · · · · · · · · · · · · · · ·
◫ *noun* **2** headquarters, depot, base. **5** status, standing, position, rank, level, grade, class. **6** post, place, location, position. *verb* appoint, assign, send, post, garrison, install, establish, locate.
· ·

stationary *adj.* **1** not moving; still. **2** not changing. [related to STATION]

· · · · · · · · · · · · · · · · · · · ·
◫ STATIC, FIXED. **1** motionless, immobile, unmoving, still, inert, standing, resting, parked, moored.
◲ **1** mobile, moving, active.
· ·

stationary wave *Physics.* same as STANDING WAVE.

stationer *noun* a person or shop selling stationery. [from Latin *statio*, shop]

stationery *noun* paper, envelopes, pens, and other writing materials.

stationmaster *noun* the official in charge of a railway station.

station wagon *North Amer.*, *esp. US* an estate car.

statistical *adj.* relating to or determined by statistics.

statistical linguistics the study of language using statistical techniques, especially the study of the frequency and distribution of specific letters, words, and forms in texts and spoken language.

statistically *adv.* according to statistics.

statistician *noun* a person who collects and analyses statistics.

statistics *noun* **1** *sing. Maths.* the branch of mathematics concerned with the collation, classification, and interpretation of numerical data, usually by analysing a representative sample of a population (a group of people, objects or items of data). It also includes the analysis of possible relationships (correlations) between different sets of data, and the prediction of events on the basis of probability. **2** (*usually* **statistics**) an item of numerical information collected and presented in an ordered way. [from German *Statistik*, study of political facts and figures, from Latin *status*, state]

statue *noun* a sculpted, moulded, or cast figure, especially of a person or animal, usually life-size or larger, often erected in a public place. [from Latin *statua*]

- - - - - - - - - - - - - - - - - - - -
▣ figure, head, bust, effigy, idol, statuette, carving, bronze.
- -

statuesque *adj.*, *said of a human figure* like a statue, tall and well-proportioned or dignified and imposing in appearance.

statuette *noun* a small statue.

stature /ˈstatʃə(r)/ *noun* **1** height of body. **2** greatness; eminence. [from Latin *statura*, from *stare*, to stand]

status *noun* **1** rank or position in relation to others, within society, an organization, etc. **2** legal state, eg with regard to adulthood, marriage, or citizenship. **3** importance. [from Latin *status*]

- - - - - - - - - - - - - - - - - - - -
▣ **1** rank, grade, degree, level, class, station, standing, position. **2** state, condition. **3** prestige, eminence, distinction, importance, consequence.
▣ **3** unimportance, insignificance.
- -

status quo /ˈsteɪtəs kwoʊ/ (*usually* **the status quo**) the situation at a given moment, usually before a significant event such as a war. [from Latin, = the state in which]

status symbol a possession or privilege regarded as an indication of a person's high (especially social) status.

statute *noun* **1** a law made by the legislative assembly of a country and recorded in a formal document. **2** a permanent rule drawn up by the leader or leaders of an organization. [from Latin *statutum*, that which is set up]

statute book a formal written record of all the laws passed by a parliament, etc.

statutorily *adv.* according to statute.

statutory *adj.* **1** required or prescribed by law or a rule. **2** usual or regular, as if prescribed by law.

staunch[1] *adj.* loyal; trusty; steadfast. [from Old French *estanche*, watertight]

- - - - - - - - - - - - - - - - - - - -
▣ loyal, faithful, stalwart, strong, stout, firm, sound, true, trusty, reliable, dependable, steadfast.
▣ unfaithful, weak, unreliable.
- -

staunch[2] *verb* to stop the flow of (especially blood from a wound). [from Old French *estanchier*]

stave — *noun* **1** any of the vertical wooden strips joined to form a barrel or tub. **2** any (especially wooden) bar, rod, or shaft, eg a rung on a ladder. **3** *Mus.* same as STAFF *noun* **5 4** a verse of a poem or song. — *verb* **1** (PAST TENSE AND PAST PARTICIPLE **stove, staved**) (*often* **stave something in**) to smash a hole in it. **2** (PAST TENSE AND PAST PARTICIPLE **staved**) (*usually* **stave something off**) to delay the onset of it; to ward it off. [a back-formation from STAVES, plural of STAFF]

staves plural of STAFF, STAVE.

stay[1] — *verb* (PAST TENSE AND PAST PARTICIPLE **stayed**) **1** *intrans.* to remain in the same place or condition, without moving or changing. **2** *intrans.* to reside temporarily, eg as a guest. **3** *intrans.* to remain or linger in order to share or join in something: *will you stay for dinner?* **4** to suspend or postpone (eg legal proceedings). **5** to control or restrain (eg anger). **6** *intrans. Scot.* to reside permanently; to live. — *noun* **1** a period of temporary residence; a visit. **2** a suspension of legal proceedings, or a postponement of a legally enforceable punishment: *grant a stay of execution.* — **stay in** to remain indoors, especially not to go out socially. **stay put** *colloq.* to remain where one or it is. **stay up** to remain out of bed beyond one's usual bedtime. [from Latin *stare*, to stand]

- - - - - - - - - - - - - - - - - - - -
▣ *verb* **1** remain, continue, last, endure, abide, linger, persist. **2** reside, dwell, *formal* sojourn. **3** remain, linger, stop. **4** suspend, halt, postpone, defer. **6** reside, dwell, live, settle. *noun* **1** visit, holiday, stop-over, *formal* sojourn.
▣ *verb* **1** move, change. **2, 3** go, leave, depart.
- -

stay[2] *noun* **1** a prop or support. **2** any of a number of strips of bone or metal sewn into a corset to stiffen it. **3** (**stays**) a corset stiffened in this way. [from Old French *estaye*]

stay[3] *noun* a rope or cable with which a pole, etc is anchored to the ground to keep it upright. [from Anglo-Saxon *stæg*]

stay-at-home *colloq.* — *adj.* tending to prefer the peaceful routine of domestic life to a busy and varied social life. — *noun* a stay-at-home person.

stayer *noun colloq.* a person or animal with great powers of endurance.

staying power stamina; endurance.

STD *abbrev.* **1** sexually transmitted disease. **2** subscriber trunk dialling.

STD code a telephone code for a town or other area, used before a subscriber's individual number when telephoning from outside the area.

stead /sted/ — **in someone's stead** in place of them. **stand someone in good stead** to prove useful to them. [from Anglo-Saxon *stede*, place]

steadfast *adj.* firm; resolute; determinedly unwavering. [from Anglo-Saxon *stede*, place + *fæst*, fixed]

- - - - - - - - - - - - - - - - - - - -
▣ firm, resolute, determined, unwavering, steady, constant.
- -

steadfastly *adv.* in a steadfast way.

steadfastness *noun* being steadfast.

Steadicam *noun trademark* a harness device fitted with shock absorbers, on which a film camera is mounted to produce steady shots while the camera operator moves.

steadily *adv.* in a steady way.

steadiness *noun* being steady.

steady — *adj.* (**steadier, steadiest**) **1** firmly fixed or balanced; not tottering or wobbling. **2** regular; constant; unvarying. **3** stable; not easily disrupted or undermined. **4** having a serious or sober character. — *verb trans., intrans.* (**steadies, steadied**) to make or become steady or steadier. — *adv.* in a steady manner. — *interj.* (**steady on!**) an exhortation to be careful or restrained. — **go steady with someone** *colloq.* to have a steady romantic relationship with them. [see STEAD]

- - - - - - - - - - - - - - - - - - - -
▣ *adj.* **1** stable, balanced, poised, fixed, immovable, firm. **2** regular, even, uniform, consistent, unvarying, unchanging, constant, persistent, unremitting, incessant, uninterrupted, unbroken. **3** stable, settled, still, calm, imperturbable. **4** serious, sober, sensible, steadfast. *verb* balance, poise, stabilize, fix, secure, brace, support.
▣ *adj.* **1** unsteady, wobbly, shaky. **2** variable. **3** unstable.
- -

steady-state theory *Astron.* in cosmology, the generally unaccepted theory that the universe has always existed. In order to account for the observed expansion of the universe, it is postulated that there is continuous spontaneous creation of matter.

steak noun **1** fine quality beef for frying or grilling, or a thick slice of this. **2** beef for stewing or braising in chunks. **3** a thick slice of any meat or fish. [from Norse *steik*, roast]

steakhouse noun a restaurant specialising in beef steaks.

steal — verb (PAST TENSE **stole**; PAST PARTICIPLE **stolen**) **1** to take away (another person's property) without permission or legal right, especially secretly. **2** intrans. to take other people's property, especially habitually. **3** to obtain by cleverness or trickery: *steal a kiss*. **4** to fraudulently present (another person's work, ideas, etc) as one's own. **5** intrans. to go stealthily. — noun colloq. **1** a bargain; a thing easily obtained. **2** North Amer., esp. US an act of stealing. [from Anglo-Saxon *stelan*]

■ verb **1** pilfer, filch, *colloq.* pinch, *slang* nick, take, snatch, swipe, poach, embezzle. **2** thieve, shoplift, poach, embezzle. **4** lift, plagiarize, pirate, poach. **5** creep, tiptoe, slip, slink, sneak.
◨ verb **1** return, give back.

stealth noun **1** softness and quietness of movement, avoiding notice. **2** secretive or deceitful behaviour. [related to STEAL]

stealthily adv. in a stealthy way.

stealthy adj. (**stealthier, stealthiest**) acting or done with stealth; furtive.

■ surreptitious, clandestine, covert, secret, unobtrusive, quiet, furtive, sly, cunning, sneaky, underhand.
◨ open.

steam — noun **1** the gaseous state of water, ie water at a temperature higher than its boiling point. It is colourless, forming a mist of tiny water droplets, and is often used as a source of power or energy, eg in steam engines. **2** colloq. power, energy, or speed: *run out of steam*. **3** attributive powered by steam: *a steam generator*. — verb **1** intrans. to give off steam. **2** to cook or otherwise treat by exposure to steam. **3** intrans. to move under the power of steam. **4** intrans., colloq. to go at speed. — **be steamed up** colloq. to be very angry or excited. **let off steam** to release anger or energy built up inside one. **steam up** *said of a transparent or reflective surface* to make or become clouded by tiny water droplets formed from condensed steam. **under one's own steam** by one's own efforts alone. [from Anglo-Saxon]

■ noun **1** vapour, mist, haze, condensation, moisture, dampness.

steamer noun **1** a ship whose engines are powered by steam. **2** a two-tier pot in which food in the upper tier is cooked by the action of steam from water heated in the lower tier.

steam iron an electric iron in which steam from a built-in water tank is released on to the laundry through holes in the iron's base, to help smooth out creases.

steamroller — noun a large vehicle, originally and still often steam-driven, with wheels consisting of huge solid metal cylinders, driven over newly made roads to flatten the surface. — verb colloq. **1** to use overpowering force or persuasion to secure the speedy movement or progress of. **2** to crush (opposition, etc).

steam turbine Engineering a balanced wheel, with a large number of blades round its rim, which converts the kinetic energy of moving steam into the mechanical energy of rotation. Steam turbines are often used to drive electricity generators in power stations.

steamy adj. (**steamier, steamiest**) **1** full of, or made cloudy by, steam. **2** colloq. involving or featuring sexual passion; erotic.

stearic acid /stɪˈarɪk/ Chem. a saturated long-chain fatty acid, consisting of a colourless waxy solid that is soluble in alcohol and ether but insoluble in water. It is the commonest fatty acid in animal and vegetable fats and oils, and is used as a lubricant, and in pharmaceutical products, cosmetics, candles, and food packaging. Its sodium and potassium salts are used to make soap. Also called OCTADECANOIC ACID. [from Greek *stear, steatos*, suet, tallow]

steed noun literary a horse thought of as something to ride on. [from Anglo-Saxon *steda*, stallion]

steel — noun **1** any of a number of iron alloys containing small amounts of carbon and, in some cases, additional elements, eg chromium, nickel, manganese, silicon, molybdenum. **2** a rough-surfaced rod made of this alloy, on which knives are sharpened by hand. **3** hardness or strength, especially of a person's character. — verb (usually **steel oneself**) to harden oneself or prepare oneself emotionally, especially for something unpleasant or unwelcome. [from Anglo-Saxon *style*]

steel band a band, of a kind originating in the West Indies, with percussion instruments made from steel petrol drums.

steel blue a deep greyish-blue colour.

steel wool thin strands of steel in a woolly mass, used for polishing and scouring.

steelworks sing. or pl. noun a factory where steel is manufactured.

steely adj. (**steelier, steeliest**) **1** hard and unyielding: *a steely gaze*. **2** steel-blue.

steep [1] adj. **1** rising or sloping sharply. **2** colloq., said of a price, rate, etc unreasonably high. [from Anglo-Saxon *steap*]

■ **1** sheer, precipitous, abrupt, sudden, sharp. **2** excessive, extreme, stiff, unreasonable, high, exorbitant, extortionate.
◨ **1** gentle, gradual. **2** moderate, low.

steep [2] verb trans., intrans. to soak thoroughly in liquid. — **be steeped in something** to be closely familiar with something (eg a subject of knowledge) or influenced by it. [from Middle English *stepen*]

steepen verb trans., intrans. (**steepened, steepening**) to make or become steep or steeper.

steeple noun **1** a tower forming part of a church or temple, especially one with a spire. **2** the spire itself. [from Anglo-Saxon *stepel*]

steeplechase — noun **1** a horse race round a course with hurdles, usually in the form of man-made hedges. **2** a track race for humans, with very high hurdles and a water jump. — verb intrans. to take part in a steeplechase.

steeplechaser noun a horse that runs in a steeplechase.

steeplejack noun a person who repairs steeples and tall chimneys.

steeply adv. with a steep incline, decline, or slope; abruptly.

steepness noun being steep.

steer [1] verb **1** trans., intrans. to guide or control the direction of (a vehicle or vessel). **2** to guide the course or movements of, eg with tuition, persuasion, or force. **3** to follow (a particular course). — **steer clear of someone** or **something** to avoid them. [from Anglo-Saxon *styran*]

■ **1** pilot, guide, direct, control. **2** guide, direct.

steer [2] noun a young bull or male ox, especially one castrated and reared for beef. [from Anglo-Saxon *steor*]

steerage noun **1** old use the cheapest accommodation on board a passenger ship, traditionally near the rudder. **2** the act or practice of steering.

steering committee 1 a committee deciding on the nature and order of topics to be discussed by a parliament, etc. **2** a committee in charge of the overall direction pursued by a business or other organization.

steering wheel a wheel turned by hand to control the wheels of a vehicle or the rudder of a vessel.

stegosaurus *noun* a herbivorous dinosaur, up to 7.5m in length, that lived during the Jurassic period. It had a small head, a high domed back bearing two rows of large vertical bony plates, and a long tail. [from Greek *stegos*, roof + *saurus*, lizard]

stein /stiːn/ *noun* a large metal or earthenware beer mug, often with a hinged lid. [from German *stein*]

stele /'stiːlɪ/ or **stela** *noun* (PL. **stelae** /'stiːliː/) an ancient stone pillar or upright slab, usually carved or engraved. [from Greek *stele*]

stellar /'stɛlə(r)/ *adj.* **1** of, like, or relating to a star or stars. **2** *slang* excellent. [from Latin *stella*, star]

stem[1] — *noun* **1** the central part of a plant, growing upward from the root, or the part by which a leaf, flower, or fruit is attached to a branch. **2** the long thin supporting part of a wine glass. **3** any long slender part. **4** *Linguistics* the usually unchanging base of a word, to which inflectional affixes are added. See also ROOT — *verb intrans.* (**stemmed**, **stemming**) (**stem from something** or **someone**) to originate or derive from them. [from Anglo-Saxon *stemn*]

. . . .

▣ *noun* **1** stalk, shoot, stock, branch, trunk.

. . . .

stem[2] *verb* (**stemmed**, **stemming**) to stop (the flow of something). [from Norse *stemma*]

. . . .

▣ stop, halt, arrest, staunch, block, dam, check, curb, contain.

. . . .

stench *noun* a strong and extremely unpleasant smell. [from Anglo-Saxon *stenc*, smell]

. . . .

▣ stink, reek, *colloq.* pong, smell, odour.

. . . .

stencil — *noun* **1** a drawing or printing plate with parts cut out to form lettering or a design that is copied on to a surface by laying the plate on the surface and inking or painting over the cut out parts. **2** the lettering or design produced in this way. — *verb* (**stencilled**, **stencilling**) to print or produce by means of a stencil. [from Old French *estinceller*, to sparkle]

Sten gun a lightweight portable machine-gun, the standard submachine-gun of the British Army from 1942 onwards. [named after *Shepherd* and *Turpin*, its designers, and *Enfield* as in BREN GUN]

stenographer *noun North Amer., esp. US* a shorthand typist.

stenographic *adj.* relating to or recorded in shorthand.

stenography *noun* the skill or practice of writing in shorthand. [from Greek *stenos*, narrow + *graphein*, to write]

stentorian *adj. literary, said of a voice* loud and strong. [from *Stentor*, a Greek herald in the Trojan War who according to Homer had a voice as loud as 50 men (*Iliad* 5.7835)]

Step *noun trademark* a method of exercise based on stepping on and off a small platform of adjustable height, usually in time to music.

step — *noun* **1** a single complete action of lifting then placing down the foot in walking or running. **2** the distance covered in the course of such an action. **3** a movement of the foot (usually one of a pattern of movements) in dancing. **4** (*often* **steps**) a single (often outdoor) stair, or any stair-like support used to climb up or down. **5** the sound of a foot being laid on the ground in walking. **6** a single action or measure taken in proceeding towards an end or goal. **7** a degree or stage in a scale or series. **8** a way of walking; gait. **9** (**steps**) a stepladder. — *verb intrans.* (**stepped**, **stepping**) **1** to move by taking a step or steps, especially slowly, quietly or carefully. **2** (*usually* **step on something**) to lay one's foot on it. **3** (**step into something**) to enter into

it or become involved in it, especially easily or casually. **4** to go or come: *step this way.* — **in step 1** walking or marching in unison, with corresponding feet hitting the ground at the same time. **2** in harmony or unison. **out of step** not in step. **step by step** gradually. **step down** to resign from a position of authority. **step something down** to reduce the rate, intensity, etc of it. **step in 1** to take up a position or role as a substitute or replacement. **2** to intervene in an argument. **step on someone** *colloq.* to treat them harshly or with contempt. **step on it** *colloq.* to hurry up. **step out 1** to walk quickly and confidently with long strides. **2** *colloq.* to go out socially. **step something up** to increase the rate, intensity, etc of it. **watch one's step 1** to walk with careful steps, avoiding danger. **2** to proceed with caution, taking care not to anger or offend others. [from Anglo-Saxon *steppe*]

. . . .

▣ *noun* **1, 2** pace, stride. **4** rung, stair. **5** footstep, tread, footfall. **6** move, act, action, deed, measure, procedure, process, proceeding. **7** stage, phase, degree, rank, level, point. **8** gait, walk. *verb* **1** pace, stride, walk. **2** tread, stamp, trample, walk. **step down** stand down, resign, abdicate, quit, leave, retire, withdraw. **step up** increase, raise, augment, boost, build up, intensify, escalate, accelerate, speed up.

▣ **step up** decrease.

. . . .

step *combining form* indicating a relationship not by blood but through a second or later marriage or partnership. [from Anglo-Saxon *steop*, originally orphan]

stepbrother and **stepsister** *noun* the son or daughter of a stepfather or stepmother.

stepchild *noun* a stepson or stepdaughter.

stepfather and **stepmother** *noun* the second or later husband of a mother or wife of a father.

stephanotis /stɛfə'nəʊtɪs/ *noun* a twining evergreen perennial plant (*Stephanotis floribunda*), native to Madagascar, and having glossy oval leaves and heavily scented white waxy tubular flowers. It is often used in bridal bouquets, and is also a popular house plant. [from Greek *stephanos*, wreath]

stepladder *noun* a short ladder with flat steps, not rungs, made free-standing by means of a supporting frame attached by a hinge at the ladder's top.

step-parent *noun* a stepfather or stepmother.

steppe *noun* an extensive dry grassy and usually treeless plain, especially that in SE Europe and Asia extending E from the Ukraine through to the Manchurian plains of China. Large areas of steppe are important for wheat-growing (eg in Ukraine). [from Russian *step*]

stepping-stone *noun* **1** a large stone in a stream, etc, with a surface above the water level, stepped on to cross the stream. **2** a means of gradual progress.

stepson or **stepdaughter** *noun* the son or daughter of a second or later husband or wife, from an earlier marriage or partnership.

-ster *suffix* denoting a person with regard to some characteristic, activity, membership of a group, etc: *youngster/ trickster/gangster.*

steradian /stə'reɪdɪən/ *noun Geom.* (ABBREV. sr) the SI unit of measurement for solid (three-dimensional) angles. It is equal to the solid angle formed at the centre of a sphere when an area on the surface of the sphere equal to the square of the sphere's radius is joined to the centre. [from Greek *stereos*, solid + RADIAN]

stereo — *noun* **1** stereophonic reproduction of sound: *broadcast in stereo.* **2** (PL. **stereos**) a hi-fi system giving a stereophonic reproduction of sound. — *adj.* stereophonic.

stereo *combining form* forming words meaning 'solid, three-dimensional'. [from Greek *stereos*, solid]

stereochemistry *noun Chem.* the branch of chemistry that is concerned with the study of the three-dimensional arrangement of atoms within molecules, and the way in which such arrangements affect the chemical properties of the molecules. [from Greek *stereos*, solid]

stereophonic *adj. Electron.* denoting the reproduction of sound by means of two or more independent sound channels leading to separate loudspeakers, in order to simulate the depth and physical separation of different sounds that would be experienced at a live performance.

stereophonically *adv.* by means of stereophony.

stereophony *noun Physics* the reproduction of sound by means of two or more independent sound channels leading to separate loudspeakers, in order to simulate the depth and physical separation of different sounds that would be experienced at a live performance. [from Greek *stereos*, solid]

stereoscopic *adj. Optics* denoting an instrument such as a special type of camera or microscope that produces an apparently binocular (three-dimensional) image by presenting a slightly different view of the same object to each eye.

stereoscopically *adv.* by stereoscopic means.

stereoscopic photography *Photog.* the recording and presentation of paired images which give the viewer an impression of solidity and depth. A basic system was developed in 1845 using two cameras 65mm apart (the width between the human eyes), which produced apparently three-dimensional images when viewed in a device that allowed each eye to see only its appropriate right-eye and left-eye record. Twin-lens or stereoscopic cameras produce pairs of colour transparencies which may be mounted, or shown on two projectors each fitted with a polarizing filter orientated at right angles to each other. The viewer wears spectacles with corresponding polarizing filters so that each eye sees only the correct image. Similar principles are applied in cinematography.

stereotype — *noun* **1** an over-generalized idea, impression, or point of view allowing for no individuality or variation. **2** a person or thing conforming to such an idea, etc. **3** a solid metal printing plate cast from a mould taken from a plate on which the text consists of individual letters pieced together. — *verb* to think of or characterize in an over-generalized way.
. . . .
◼ *noun* **1** formula, convention, mould, pattern, model. *verb* categorize, pigeonhole, typecast, standardize, formalize, conventionalize.
◪ *verb* differentiate.
. . . .

stereotyped *adj.* **1** *Printing* produced by means of a stereotype. **2** *said of opinions, etc* fixed, unchangeable; conventionalized, conforming to a stock image or cliché.

sterile *adj.* **1** biologically incapable of producing offspring, fruit, or seeds. **2** made free of germs. **3** producing no results; having no new ideas. [from Latin *sterilis*, barren]
. . . .
◼ **1** infertile, barren, unproductive, arid, bare. **2** germ-free, aseptic, sterilized, decontaminated, disinfected, antiseptic, uncontaminated.
◪ **1** fertile, fruitful. **2** septic, contaminated.
. . . .

sterility *noun* being sterile, inability to reproduce.

sterilization or **sterilisation** *noun* **1** treatment of food, surgical or laboratory equipment, etc, with heat, chemicals or radiation in order to destroy all living micro-organisms. **2** a surgical operation that is performed on a human or animal so that offspring can no longer be produced. It may be achieved by vasectomy in men, cutting and tying of the Fallopian tubes in women, or complete removal of the sex organs in other mammals.

sterilize or **sterilise** *verb* to make sterile.
. . . .
◼ decontaminate, disinfect, fumigate, purify, clean, cleanse.
◪ contaminate, infect.
. . . .

sterling — *noun* British money. — *adj.* **1** of British money. **2** good quality; worthy; reliable. **3** authentic; genuine. **4** *said of silver* of at least 92.5 per cent purity. [from Anglo-

Saxon *steorra*, star, from the markings on early Norman pennies]

stern[1] *adj.* **1** extremely strict; authoritarian. **2** harsh, severe, or rigorous. **3** unpleasantly serious or unfriendly in appearance or nature. [from Anglo-Saxon *styrne*]
. . . .
◼ **1** strict, severe, authoritarian, rigid, inflexible, unyielding. **2** harsh, severe, hard, tough, rigorous, stringent, relentless, unrelenting. **3** grim, forbidding, stark, austere.
◪ **1** lenient. **2** mild. **3** pleasant.
. . . .

stern[2] *noun* the rear of a ship or boat. [from Norse *stjorn*, steering]

sternal *adj.* relating to or in the region of the sternum.

sternly *adv.* with a stern manner.

sternness *noun* being stern.

sternum *noun* (PL. **sternums, sterna**) the breastbone, the broad vertical bone in the chest to which the ribs and collarbone are attached. [from Greek *sternon*, chest]

steroid /ˈstɛrɔɪd, ˈstɪərɔɪd/ *noun* **1** *Biochem.* any of a large group of fat-soluble organic compounds that have a complex molecular structure consisting of four carbon rings, and are widely distributed in living organisms. **2** *Medicine* a drug containing such a compound. **3** an anabolic steroid. [from STEROL + -OID]

sterol /ˈstɪərɒl, ˈstɛrɒl/ *noun Biochem.* any of a group of colourless waxy solid steroid alcohols found in plants, animals, and fungi, eg cholesterol. [a shortening of CHOLESTEROL and similar words]

stertorous /ˈstɜːtərəs/ *adj. formal, said of breathing* noisy; with a snoring sound. [from Latin *stertere*, to snore]

stet *verb* (**stetted, stetting**) *Printing* in proof-reading, an instruction to ignore a correction and let the existing text stand. [from Latin *stet*, let it stand]

stethoscope *noun* an instrument for listening to sounds made inside the body, eg the heartbeat, consisting of a small concave disc, placed on the body, with attached tubes carrying the sound to earpieces. [from Greek *stethos*, chest +*skopeein*, to look at]

stetson *noun* a man's broad-brimmed felt hat with a high crown, concave at the top, worn especially by cowboys. [named after John Stetson (1830–1903), American hatmaker]

stevedore /ˈstiːvədɔː(r)/ *noun* a person employed to load and unload ships; a docker. [from Spanish *estibador*, packer]

stew — *verb* **1** to cook (especially meat) by long simmering. **2** to cause (tea) to become bitter and over-strong by letting it brew for too long. **3** *intrans. colloq.* to be in a state of worry or agitation. — *noun* **1** a dish of food, especially meat, cooked by stewing. **2** *colloq.* a state of worry or agitation. — **stew in one's own juice** *colloq.* to suffer the consequences of one's own (often ill-advised) actions. [from Old French *estuve*, stove]
. . . .
◼ *verb* **1** boil, simmer, braise, casserole.
. . . .

steward — *noun* **1** an attendant on a passenger ship or aircraft. **2** a person supervising crowd movements during a sporting event or public march. **3** a person overseeing catering and associated arrangements in a hotel or club. **4** a person employed to manage another person's property and affairs, eg on a country estate. **5** a senior official monitoring the conduct of jockeys during a horse race. — *verb* to serve as a steward of. [from Anglo-Saxon *stigweard*, hall-keeper]

stewardess *noun* a female attendant on a passenger ship or aircraft.

stewed *adj. colloq.* drunk.

stick[1] *noun* **1** a twig or thin branch taken from or which has fallen from a tree. **2** any long thin piece of wood shaped for a particular purpose, eg striking the ball in hockey, or playing a percussion instrument. **3** a long thin piece of anything, eg celery. **4** (*usually* **sticks**) a piece of furniture, especially one of few. **5** *colloq.* verbal abuse, criticism, or mockery. **6** (**the sticks**) *colloq.* a rural area when considered remote or unsophisticated. **7** *colloq.* a person: *a funny old stick.* — **get hold of the wrong end of the stick** to misunderstand a situation, a statement, etc. [from Anglo-Saxon *sticca*]

....

▣ **1** branch, twig. **2** baton, wand, staff, sceptre, cane, birch, rod, pole, stake.

....

stick ² *verb* (PAST TENSE AND PAST PARTICIPLE **stuck**) **1** to push or thrust (especially something long and thin or pointed). **2** to fasten by piercing with a pin or other sharp object: *stick it up with drawing-pins.* **3** to fix with an adhesive or something similar. **4** *intrans.* to be or stay fixed with or as if with an adhesive. **5** *intrans.* to remain persistently: *an episode that sticks in my mind.* **6** *trans., intrans.* to make or be unable to move; to jam or lock. **7** to confine. **8** (**stick to something**) **a** to remain faithful to something undertaken (eg a promise). **b** not to stray from something (eg a matter under discussion). **9** *intrans., said of criticism, etc* to continue to be considered valid. **10** *colloq.* to place or put: *just stick it on the table* **11** *colloq.* to bear or tolerate: *could not stick it any longer.* — **stick around** *colloq.* to remain or linger. **stick at something 1** to continue doggedly with it. **2** to hesitate or refuse to do it for reasons of principle: *will stick at nothing in order to succeed.* **stick by someone** to remain loyal or supportive to them. **stick in one's throat** *colloq.* to be extremely difficult to say or accept, usually for reasons of principle. **stick out 1** to project or protrude. **2** to be obvious or noticeable; to stand out. **stick something out 1** to cause it to project or protrude. **2** *colloq.* to endure it. **stick out for something** to continue to insist on it; to refuse to yield. **stick together** to remain loyal and supportive to each other. **stick up** *colloq.* to project upwards; to stand up. **stick up for someone** to speak or act in their defence. [from Anglo-Saxon *stician*]

....

▣ **1** push, thrust, poke, stab, jab, pierce, puncture. **2** fasten, secure, fix, pin, attach, affix. **3** glue, gum, paste, cement, bond, fuse, weld, solder. **4** adhere, cling, hold, bond, fuse. **5** remain, linger, persist. **10** put, place, lay. **11** bear, stand, tolerate, put up with. **stick at 1** persevere with, *colloq.* plug away at, continue with, carry on with. **stick out 1** protrude, jut out, project, extend. **stick up for** stand up for, speak up for, defend, champion, support, uphold.

▣ **stick at 1** give up. **stick up for** attack.
....

sticker *noun* an adhesive label, especially one displaying a message or advertisement in the window of a shop, a car, etc.

stickiness *noun* a sticky quality.

sticking-plaster *noun* adhesive plaster used to dress wounds.

stick insect a tropical insect with a long twig-like body and legs.

stick-in-the-mud *noun colloq.* a person boringly opposed to anything new or adventurous.

stickleback *noun* a small spiny-backed fish of northern rivers. [from Anglo-Saxon *sticel*, prick + BACK]

stickler *noun* (**a stickler for something**) a person who fastidiously insists on it. [from Anglo-Saxon *stihtan*, to set in order]

sticky *adj.* (**stickier, stickiest**) **1** able or likely to stick to other surfaces. **2** *said of the weather* warm and humid; muggy. **3** *colloq., said of a situation, etc* difficult; awkward; unpleasant. — **a sticky end** *colloq.* an unpleasant end or death.

....

▣ **1** adhesive, gummed, tacky, gluey, gummy, viscous, glutinous, *colloq.* gooey. **2** humid, clammy, muggy, close, oppressive, sultry. **3** difficult, tricky, thorny, unpleasant, awkward, embarrassing, delicate.

▣ **1** dry. **2** fresh, cool. **3** easy.
....

sticky-fingered *adj. colloq.* prone to pilfering.

sticky tape a strong tape for binding, fastening or joining, with an adhesive substance on one side.

sticky wicket *noun colloq.* a difficult or awkward situation.

stiff — *adj.* **1** not easily bent or folded; rigid. **2** *said of limbs, joints, etc* lacking suppleness; not moving or bending easily. **3** *said of a punishment, etc* harsh; severe. **4** *said of a task, etc* difficult; arduous. **5** *said of a wind* blowing strongly. **6** *said of a manner* not natural and relaxed; overformal. **7** thick in consistency; viscous. **8** *colloq., said of an alcoholic drink* not diluted or only lightly diluted; strong. — *adv. colloq.* to an extreme degree: *bored me stiff.* — *noun slang* a corpse. — **have** or **keep a stiff upper lip** to show or maintain self-control and resignation in the face of disappointment or unpleasantness. [from Anglo-Saxon *stif*]

....

▣ *adj.* **1** rigid, inflexible, unbending, unyielding, hard, solid, hardened, solidified. **2** tight, taut, tense. **3** harsh, severe, strict, rigorous. **4** difficult, hard, tough, arduous, laborious, awkward, exacting. **6** formal, ceremonious, pompous, prim, cold. **7** thick, viscous, firm, congealed, set.

▣ *adj.* **1** flexible, yielding. **2** supple. **4** easy. **6** informal.
....

stiffen *verb trans., intrans.* (**stiffened, stiffening**) to make or become stiff or stiffer.

....

▣ harden, solidify, tighten, tense, brace, reinforce, starch, thicken, congeal, coagulate, set.

....

stiffly *adv.* in a stiff way.

stiff-necked *adj.* arrogantly obstinate.

stiffness *noun* a stiff quality.

stiffware *noun* software that is difficult or impossible to modify because of having being customized or having incomplete documentation, etc.

stifle *verb* **1** *intrans.* to experience difficulty in breathing, especially because of heat and lack of air. **2** to kill by stopping the breathing; to smother. **3** to suppress (a feeling or action). [perhaps from Old French *estouffer*, to smother]

....

▣ **2** smother, suffocate, asphyxiate, strangle, choke. **3** suppress, quell, check, curb, restrain, repress, muffle, dampen, deaden, silence.

....

stifling *adj.* unpleasantly hot or airless.

stigma *noun* (PL. **stigmas, stigmata** sense 4) **1** shame or social disgrace. **2** a blemish or scar on the skin. **3** *Bot.* in a flower, the sticky surface at the tip of the style that receives pollen. **4** *Zool.* any of a variety of pigmented markings or spots, eg the wingspot of certain butterflies. **5** (**stigmata**) *Christianity* marks resembling the wounds of Christ's crucifixion, said to have appeared on the bodies of certain holy people. [from Greek *stigma*, tattoo-mark, brand]

....

▣ **1** shame, disgrace, dishonour, stain, blot. **2** mark, spot, blemish, scar, brand.

▣ **1** credit, honour.
....

stigmatization or **stigmatisation** *noun* stigmatizing or being stigmatized.

stigmatize or **stigmatise** *verb* to describe or regard as shameful.

stilboestrol or *North Amer.* **stilbestrol** /stɪlˈbiːstrəl/ *noun* a synthetic oestrogen. [from Greek *stilbein*, to shine]

stile *noun* a step, or set of steps, built into a fence or wall. [from Anglo-Saxon *stigel*]

stiletto *noun* (PL. **stilettos**) **1** (*also* **stiletto heel**) a high thin heel on a woman's shoe. **2** *colloq.* a shoe with such a heel. **3** a dagger with a narrow tapering blade. [from Italian *stiletto*, diminutive of *stilo*, dagger]

still ¹ — *adj.* **1** motionless; inactive. **2** quiet and calm; tranquil. **3** *said of a drink* not fizzy. — *adv.* **1** continuing as before, now or at some future time. **2** up to the present time, or the time in question; yet. **3** even then; nevertheless. **4** quietly and without movement: *sit still.* **5** *with comparatives* to a greater degree; even: *older still.* — *verb* **1** *trans., intrans.* to make or become still. **2** to calm, appease, or put an end to. — *noun* **1** stillness; tranquillity. **2** a photograph, especially of an actor in or a scene from a cinema film, used for publicity purposes. [from Anglo-Saxon *stille*]

⊟ *adj.* **1** stationary, motionless, immobile, stagnant, inert, inactive. **2** smooth, undisturbed, unruffled, calm, tranquil, serene, restful, peaceful, quiet, silent, noiseless. *adv.* **3** nevertheless, nonetheless, notwithstanding, however. *verb* **2** calm, soothe, tranquillize, subdue, quieten, silence, appease, pacify, quell, settle. *noun* **1** stillness, peace, calm, tranquillity.
⊞ *adj.* **1** active. **2** disturbed, agitated. *verb* **2** agitate, stir up.

still² *noun* an apparatus in which an alcoholic spirit is distilled. [see DISTIL]

stillborn *adj.* **1** dead when born. **2** *said of a project, etc* doomed from the start.

still life *noun* (PL. **still lifes**) **1** a painting, drawing, or photograph of an object or objects, eg a bowl of fruit, rather than of a living thing. **2** this kind of art or photography.

stillness *noun* being still; a still quality.

still room 1 a room in which distilling is carried out. **2** a housekeeper's pantry in a large house.

stilt *noun* **1** either of a pair of long poles with supports for the feet part way up, on which a person can walk around supported high above the ground. **2** any of a set of props on which a building, jetty, etc is supported above ground or water level. [from Middle English *stilte*]

stilted *adj.*, *said of language* unnatural-sounding, especially over-formal. [see STILT]

⊟ unnatural, artificial, stiff, wooden, forced, constrained.
⊞ natural, fluent, flowing.

Stilton *noun* a strong white English cheese, often with blue veins. [from *Stilton* in Cambridgeshire, S England]

stimulant *noun, adj.* any substance, especially a drug, that produces an increase in the activity of a particular body system or function, eg caffeine, nicotine, amphetamines.

stimulate *verb* **1** to cause physical activity, or increased activity, in (eg an organ of the body). **2** to initiate or get going. **3** to excite or arouse the senses of; to animate or invigorate. **4** to create interest and enthusiasm in (someone). [from Latin *stimulare*]

⊟ **2** initiate, instigate, trigger off, goad, provoke, incite, induce, urge, impel. **3** rouse, arouse, excite, animate, invigorate, fire, inflame. **4** inspire, motivate, spur, prompt, encourage.
⊞ **4** discourage.

stimulating *adj.* that stimulates; exciting.

stimulation *noun* **1** stimulating. **2** something that stimulates.

stimulus *noun* (PL. **stimuli**) **1** a change in some aspect of the external or internal environment of an organism that causes a response in a cell, tissue, or organ, eg in the nervous system of animals. **2** something that stimulates. [from Latin *stimulus*, goad]

⊟ **2** incentive, encouragement, inducement, spur, goad, provocation, incitement.
⊞ **2** discouragement.

sting — *noun* **1** in certain animals and plants, a defensive puncturing organ that can pierce skin and inject poison or

venom, eg the spine of a stingray, the hairs of a stinging nettle. **2** the injection of poison from an animal or plant. **3** a painful wound resulting from the sting of an animal or plant. **4** any sharp tingling pain. **5** any sharply wounding quality or effect, eg that of a vicious insult. **6** *slang* a trick, swindle, or robbery. — *verb* (PAST TENSE AND PAST PARTICIPLE **stung**) **1** to pierce, poison, or wound with a sting. **2** *intrans.* to produce a sharp tingling pain. **3** (**sting someone into something**) to goad or incite them into action of a particular kind. **4** *slang* to cheat, swindle or rob; to cheat by overcharging. [from Anglo-Saxon *stingan*, to pierce]

⊟ *noun* **3** prick, bite, nip, wound. **4** smart, tingle. *verb* **1** prick, bite, hurt, injure, wound. **2** smart, tingle, prick, burn, hurt.

stingily *adv.* in a stingy way.

stinginess *noun* being stingy.

stinging *adj.* that stings.

stinging nettle same as NETTLE.

stingray *noun* a ray with a long whip-like tail tipped with spikes capable of inflicting severe wounds.

stingy *adj.* (**stingier, stingiest**) ungenerous; mean; miserly. [from *stinge*, a dialect form of STING]

⊟ mean, miserly, niggardly, *colloq.* tight-fisted, parsimonious, penny-pinching.
⊞ generous, liberal.

stink — *noun* **1** a strong and very unpleasant smell. **2** *colloq.* an angry complaint or outraged reaction; a fuss: *kick up a stink.* — *verb* (PAST TENSE **stank, stunk**; PAST PARTICIPLE **stunk**) **1** *intrans.* to give off a stink. **2** (*usually* **stink something out**) to fill a place with a stink. **3** *intrans. colloq.* to be contemptibly bad or unpleasant. **4** *intrans. colloq.* to be morally disgusting. [from Anglo-Saxon *stincan*, to smell]

⊟ *noun* **1** smell, odour, stench, *colloq.* pong, *slang* niff. *verb* **1** smell, reek, *colloq.* pong, *slang* hum.

stink bomb a small bomb-like container releasing a foul-smelling gas when broken as a practical joke.

stinker *noun colloq.* **1** a very difficult task, question, etc. **2** a dishonest, cheating, or otherwise unpleasant person.

stinkhorn *noun* a fungus (*Phallus impudicus*), found in woodland. When immature it resembles a white egg, which then ruptures to release the fast-growing fruiting body, which consists of a white spongy hollow stem and a swollen conical ridged cap which is covered wtih dark olive-green slime containing the spores. Its pungent nauseating smell attracts insects, which eat the slime and disperse the spores.

stinking — *adj.* **1** that stinks. **2** *colloq.* very unpleasant. — *adv. colloq.* extremely; disgustingly: *stinking rich.*

stint — *verb trans., intrans.* (**stint on something**) to be mean or grudging in the giving or supplying of it. — *noun* an allotted amount of work. — **without stint** liberally; unreservedly. [from Anglo-Saxon *styntan*, to dull]

⊟ *noun* spell, stretch, period, time, shift, turn, bit, share, quota.

stipend /'staɪpend/ *noun* a salary or allowance, especially one paid to a member of the clergy. [from Latin *stipendium*, tax]

stipendiary /staɪ'pendɪərɪ, stɪ'pendɪərɪ/ — *adj.* receiving a stipend. — *noun* (PL. **stipendiaries**) a person receiving a stipend.

stipendiary magistrate *Legal* in England and Wales, a salaried and legally qualified magistrate, found in London and other large towns. Most magistrates are lay people receiving only travelling expenses and a small allowance, and having no formal legal training.

stipple — *verb* **1** to paint or draw in dots or dabs, rather than lines or masses of colour. **2** to give a finish of tiny raised bumps to (wet cement, plaster, etc), creating a grainy effect. — *noun* a pattern produced by stippling. [from Dutch *stippelen*, diminutive of *stippen*, to dot]

stipulate *verb* to state as a necessary condition. [from Latin *stipulari*]
. . . .
☐ specify, lay down, require, demand, insist on.
. . . .

stipulation *noun* **1** stipulating. **2** a contract or a condition of agreement.
. . . .
☐ **2** specification, requirement, demand, condition, proviso.
. . . .

stir[1] — *verb* (**stirred**, **stirring**) **1** to mix or agitate (a liquid or semi-liquid substance) by repeated circular strokes with a spoon or other utensil. **2** to arouse the emotions of; to move. **3** *intrans.* to make a slight or single movement. **4** (*also* **stir something up**) to cause or provoke (eg trouble). **5** *intrans.* to get up after sleeping; to become active after resting. **6** *intrans. colloq.* (*also* **stir it**) to make trouble. — *noun* **1** an act of stirring (a liquid, etc). **2** an excited reaction; a commotion: *cause a stir* [from Anglo-Saxon *styrian*]
. . . .
☐ *verb* **1** mix, blend, beat. **2** move, touch, affect, inspire, excite, thrill. **3** move, budge, tremble, quiver, flutter, rustle. **4** disturb, rouse, arouse, awaken, animate, stimulate, spur, prompt, provoke, incite, agitate. *noun* **2** activity, movement, bustle, flurry, commotion, fuss, ado, uproar, tumult, disturbance, disorder, agitation, excitement, ferment.
☒ *verb* **4** calm. *noun* **2** calm.
. . . .

stir[2] *noun slang* prison.

stir-crazy *adj. North Amer., esp. US slang* emotionally disturbed as a result of being confined, especially in prison.

stir-fry — *verb* to cook lightly by brisk frying on a high heat with little oil. — *noun* a dish of stir-fried food.

stirrer *noun colloq.* a person who enjoys stirring up trouble.

stirring *adj.* arousing strong emotions.

stirrup *noun* **1** either of a pair of metal loops hanging on straps from a horse's saddle, serving as the rider's footrests. **2** any strap or loop supporting or passing under a foot. [from Anglo-Saxon *stigrap*, from *stigan*, to mount + *rap*, rope]

stirrup cup an alcoholic drink given to a person, originally a rider, about to leave.

stirrup pump a portable hand-operated pump that draws water from a bucket, etc, used in fighting small fires.

stitch — *noun* **1** a single interlinking loop of thread or yarn in sewing or knitting. **2** a complete movement of the needle or needles creating such a loop. **3** any of various ways in which such loops are interlinked. **4** a single interlinking loop of surgical suture. **5** a sharp ache in the side resulting from physical exertion. **6** *colloq.* the least scrap of clothing: *without a stitch on.* — *verb* (*also* **stitch something up**) to join or close it, or decorate it, with stitches. — **in stitches** *colloq.* helpless with laughter. **stitch someone up** *slang* to trick them, especially to betray or double-cross them. [from Anglo-Saxon *stice*, prick]

stitchwort /ˈstɪtʃwɜːt/ *noun Biol.* a perennial plant, found in woods and hedgerows throughout Europe, that has thin brittle stems, narrow leaves, and small white flowers, so called because it was formerly used to treat a 'stitch' or pains in the side.

stoat *noun* a small flesh-eating mammal, closely related to the weasel, and having a long slender body and reddish-brown fur with white underparts. In northern regions the fur turns white in winter, during which time it is known as ermine and is highly prized by the fur trade. Stoats are found throughout Europe and Asia, and also in N America, where they are known as short-tailed weasels. [from Middle English *stote*]

stock — *noun* **1** (*also* **stocks**) the total amount of goods of a particular kind stored in a shop, warehouse, etc. **2** a supply kept in reserve. **3** equipment or raw material in use: *rolling stock.* **4** liquid in which meat or vegetables have been cooked, used as a base for a soup, sauce, etc. **5** the shaped wooden or plastic part of a rifle or similar gun, held against the firer's shoulder. **6** farm animals; livestock. **7** the money raised by a company through the selling of shares. **8** the total shares issued by a particular company or held by an individual shareholder. **9** a group of shares bought or sold as a unit. **10** ancestry; descent: *of peasant stock.* **11** any of various Mediterranean plants of the wallflower family, cultivated for their bright flowers. **12** (**stocks**) a wooden device into which an offender was formerly fastened to be displayed for public ridicule, held by the head and wrists, or wrists and ankles. **13** reputation; standing. — *adj.* **1** of a standard type, size, etc, constantly in demand and always kept in stock. **2** *said of a phrase, etc* much used, especially so over-used as to be meaningless. — *verb* **1** to keep a stock of (something) for sale. **2** to provide with a supply: *a well-stocked drinks cabinet.* — **in stock** currently held for sale on the premises. **out of stock** not in stock. **stock up on something** to acquire or accumulate a stock of it. **take stock** to make an inventory of all stock held on the premises at a particular time. **take stock of something** to make an overall assessment of something (especially circumstances). [from Anglo-Saxon *stocc*, stick]
. . . .
☐ *noun* **1** goods, merchandise, wares, commodities, inventory, range, variety, assortment. **2** supply, fund, reservoir, store, reserve, stockpile, hoard. **6** livestock, animals, cattle, horses, sheep, herds, flocks. **10** parentage, ancestry, descent, extraction, family, line, lineage, pedigree, race, breed, species, blood. *adj.* **1** standard, basic, regular, ordinary, run-of-the-mill, usual, traditional, conventional. **2** set, stereotyped, clichéd, hackneyed, overused, banal, trite. *verb* **1** keep, carry, sell, trade in, deal in, handle. **2** supply, provide. **stock up on** gather, accumulate, amass, lay in, store, save, hoard, stockpile.
☒ *adj.* **1** unusual. **2** original.
. . . .

stockade /stɒˈkeɪd/ — *noun* a fence or enclosure made from tall heavy posts, built for defence. — *verb* to protect or defend with a stockade. [from Spanish *estacada*]

stockbroker *noun* a person who buys and sells stocks and shares for customers in return for a fee.

stockbroking *noun* the buying and selling of stocks and shares for clients.

stock car a car modified for a kind of track racing in which deliberate colliding is allowed.

stock cube a small cube of compressed meat or vegetable extract, added to water to make stock.

stock exchange a market for the trading of stocks and shares by professional dealers on behalf of customers; also a building housing this.

stockily *adv.* in a stocky way.

stockiness *noun* being stocky.

stockinet or **stockinette** *noun* a stretchy knitted fabric used especially for undergarments. [perhaps a contraction of *stocking-net*]

stocking *noun* **1** either of a pair of close-fitting coverings for women's legs, self-supported or supported by suspenders, made of fine semi-transparent nylon or silk. **2** a sock. [related to STOCK]

stockinged *adj., said of the feet* wearing only socks, stockings, or tights, and not shoes.

stock-in-trade *noun* the basic equipment, techniques, personal qualities, etc needed for a particular trade or activity.

stockist *noun* a person or shop that stocks a particular item.

stock market a stock exchange, or the trading carried on there.

stockpile — *noun* an accumulated reserve supply. — *verb* to accumulate a (usually large) reserve supply of.

stockroom *noun* a storeroom, especially in a shop.

stock-still *adj., adv.* motionless.

stocktaking *noun* **1** the process of making a detailed inventory of all stock held on the premises of a shop, factory, etc at a particular time. **2** the process of making an overall assessment (eg of the present situation).

stocky *adj.* (**stockier, stockiest**) *said of a person or animal* broad and strong-looking, especially when not tall.

· · · · · · · · · · · · · · · · · · · ·

☐ sturdy, solid, thickset, chunky, short, squat, dumpy, stubby.
☒ tall, skinny.

· ·

stockyard *noun* a large yard or enclosure in which cattle are kept temporarily, eg to be sorted for market.

stodge — *noun* food that is heavy, filling, and usually fairly tasteless. — *verb* to stuff with food.

stodginess *noun* a stodgy quality.

stodgy *adj.* (**stodgier, stodgiest**) **1** of the nature of stodge. **2** boringly conventional or serious.

Stoic any of the philosophers belonging to a school of the Hellenistic-Roman age, founded by Zeno of Citium at the end of the 4cBC. The main emphasis of their philosophy was on the development of self-sufficiency in the individual, whose duty was to conform only to the dictates of natural order to which all people belonged equally.

stoic *noun* **1** a stoical person. **2** *Philos.* See STOIC. [from Greek *Stoa Poikile*, Painted Porch, where Zeno taught]

stoical *adj.* **1** accepting suffering or misfortune uncomplainingly. **2** indifferent to both pain and pleasure.

· · · · · · · · · · · · · · · · · · · ·

☐ **1** patient, long-suffering, uncomplaining, resigned, philosophical. **2** indifferent, impassive, unemotional, phlegmatic, dispassionate, cool.

· ·

stoically *adv.* in a stoical way, stoical.

stoichiometry /stɔɪkaɪ'ɒmətrɪ/ *noun Chem.* the branch of chemistry that is concerned with the relative proportions in which atoms or molecules react together to form chemical compounds. [from Greek *stoicheion*, element]

stoicism /'stoʊɪsɪzm/ *noun* **1** acceptance of suffering and misfortune. **2** (**Stoicism**) the philosophy of the Stoics.

stoke *verb* (*often* **stoke up**) **1** to put coal or other fuel in (eg the furnace of a boiler). **2** to arouse or intensify (eg passion or enthusiasm). **3** *intrans. colloq.* to fill oneself with food. [from Dutch *stoken*]

stokehold *noun* the boiler room on a steamship.

stoker *noun* a person who stokes a furnace, especially on a steamship or steam train.

stole[1] see STEAL.

stole[2] *noun* **1** a woman's scarf-like garment, often of fur, worn round the shoulders. **2** a scarf-like garment worn ceremonially by members of the clergy, with ends hanging down in front. [from Greek *stole*]

stolen see STEAL.

stolid *adj.* showing little or no interest or emotion; impassive. [from Latin *stolidus*, dull]

· · · · · · · · · · · · · · · · · · · ·

☐ slow, heavy, dull, bovine, wooden, stoical, impassive, unemotional, phlegmatic.
☒ lively, interested.

· ·

stolidity or **stolidness** *noun* being stolid.

stolidly *adv.* in a stolid way.

stolon /'stoʊlən/ *noun Bot.* a runner. [from Latin *stolo stolonis*, twig, sucker]

stoma /'stoʊmə/ *noun* (PL. **stomata**) **1** a small opening or pore in the surface of a living organism, eg a mouth-like opening in animals, or one of the tiny pores on the stems and undersurfaces of leaves in plants. **2** *Medicine* the opening that is made in the abdominal wall during a surgical operation such as a colostomy. See also STOMATA.

stomach — *noun* **1** the large sac-like organ situated be-

tween the oesophagus and the duodenum, into which food passes after it has been swallowed. It secretes gastric juice containing hydrochloric acid and the enzyme pepsin, which initiates protein digestion. Contractions of the muscular stomach walls reduce the partially digested food to a semiliquid mass. **2** *loosely* the area around the abdomen; the belly. **3** (**the stomach for something**) *colloq.* courage; determination: *do you have the stomach for a fight?/has no stomach for exercise.* — *verb* **1** *colloq.* to bear or put up with: *cannot stomach his arrogance.* **2** to digest (food) easily. [from Greek *stomachos*, from *stoma*, mouth]

· · · · · · · · · · · · · · · · · · · ·

☐ **1** *colloq.* tummy. **2** belly, abdomen, gut, paunch, pot. *verb* **1** bear, stand, abide, tolerate, put up with, endure, suffer, take.

· ·

stomach ache a pain in the abdominal area, especially from indigestion.

stomach pump a device for drawing out stomach contents, usually a syringe with an attached tube passed down the throat.

stomata /'stoʊmətə/ *pl. noun* **1** see STOMA. **2** *Bot.* the specialized pores present in large numbers on the aerial parts of a plant, particularly on the undersurface of the leaf. They allow the exchange of air and carbon dioxide between the plant and the surrounding atmosphere, and the loss of water vapour from the plant during the process of *transpiration*. Each pore is surrounded by two *guard cells*, which control the opening and closing of the stomata in response to the general availability of water to the plant.

stomatal /'stoʊmətəl, 'stɒmətəl/ *adj.* relating to or in the region of a stoma.

stomp — *verb intrans.* to stamp or tread heavily. — *noun* a kind of lively jazz dancing with stamping movements. [see STAMP]

stone — *noun* **1** the hard solid material of which rocks are made. **2** a small fragment of rock, eg a pebble. **3** a shaped piece of stone designed for a particular purpose, eg millstone. **4** a gemstone. **5** the hard seed of any of several fruits, eg peach. **6** a hard and often painful mass formed within the gall bladder, kidney, etc, and usually requiring surgical removal. **7** (PL. **stone**) a UK measure of weight equal to 14 pounds or 6.35 kilograms. **8** a dull light grey colour. — *verb* **1** to pelt with stones. **2** to remove the stone from (fruit). — *adv. in compounds* completely: *stone-deaf/ stone-cold.* — **leave no stone unturned** to try all possibilities or make every possible effort. **a stone's throw** *colloq.* a short distance. [from Anglo-Saxon *stan*]

Stone Age the earliest period in human history, during which primitive tools and weapons were made of stone.

stonechat *noun* a small brownish European bird whose song is like two stones knocking together.

stone circle *Archaeol.* a near-circular or circular ring of prehistoric standing stones (or *henges*) of the late Neolithic and Early Bronze Age found in N Europe (particularly in Britain and Ireland). Their exact function is unknown, although they may have been temples in which celestial events, the passing of the seasons, and the fertility of the land and people could be celebrated.

stonecrop *noun* any of about 300 species of succulents, mostly perennials, of the genus *Sedum*, native to north temperate regions, and having fleshy leaves that may be very narrow or almost circular, and star-like flowers with five petals, which are usually yellow, but sometimes white or red. Some species are popular ornamentals for rock gardens.

stone curlew a large wading bird like a plover, that nests on stony ground.

stoned *adj. slang* **1** under the influence of drugs. **2** very drunk.

stonemason *noun* a person skilled in shaping stone for building work.

stonewall *verb intrans.* to hold up progress intentionally, eg by obstructing discussion or by batting extremely defensively in cricket.

stoneware *noun* hard coarse pottery made of clay with a high silica content or of clay with flint mixed in.

stonewashed *adj.*, *said of a fabric* given a faded appearance through the abrasive action of small pieces of pumice stone.

stonily *adv.* in a stony way.

stony *adj.* (**stonier**, **stoniest**) **1** covered with stones. **2** having a hard unfriendly or unfeeling appearance or quality: *stony-hearted*. **3** *colloq.* stony-broke.

. . . .

☰ **1** pebbly, shingly, rocky. **2** hard, cold, icy, indifferent, unfeeling, blank, expressionless, heartless, callous, hostile, unfriendly.
✑ **2** warm, soft-hearted, friendly.
. . . .

stony-broke *adj.*, *colloq.* having absolutely no money; penniless.

stood see STAND.

stooge *noun* **1** a performer serving to provide a comedian with opportunities for making jokes, often also the butt of the jokes. **2** an assistant, especially one given unpleasant tasks or otherwise exploited.

stool *noun* **1** a seat without a back. **2** a footstool. **3** a single piece of faeces. — **fall between two stools** to lose two opportunities by hesitating between them or trying for both. [from Anglo-Saxon *stol*]

stoolball *noun* an old-fashioned 11-a-side bat-and-ball game resembling cricket and rounders. The batter uses a wooden bat resembling a tennis racket to defend a wicket or stool (a wooden board 1.4m from the ground), which the underarm bowler attempts to hit. Runs are scored in a similar way to cricket.

stool-pigeon *noun* **1** a police informer. **2** a decoy bird, originally a pigeon stuck to a stool, used by a hunter to lure others.

stoop¹ — *verb intrans.* **1** to bend the upper body forward and down. **2** to walk with head and shoulders bent forward. **3** (**stoop to something**) to lower oneself to do it; to deign or condescend to do it. — *noun* a stooped posture. [from Anglo-Saxon *stupian*]

. . . .

☰ **1** hunch, bow, bend, lean, duck, squat, crouch. **3** descend to, sink to, lower oneself to, resort to, go so far as to, condescend to, deign to.
. . . .

stoop² *noun North Amer., esp. US* an open porch; a veranda. [from Dutch *stoep*]

stoop³ see STOUP.

stop — *verb* (**stopped**, **stopping**) **1** *trans., intrans.* to bring or come to rest, a standstill or an end; to cease or cause to cease moving, operating, or progressing. **2** to give up or refrain from: *stop it!* **3** to prevent. **4** to withhold or keep back. **5** (*also* **stop something up**) to block, plug, or close it. **6** to deduct (money) from wages. **7** to instruct a bank not to honour (a cheque). **8** *colloq.* to stay or reside temporarily. **9** *Mus.* to adjust the vibrating length of (a string) by pressing down with a finger. **10** *slang* to receive (a blow). — *noun* **1** an act of stopping. **2** a place stopped at, eg on a bus route. **3** the state of being stopped; a standstill. **4** a device that prevents further movement. **5** a full stop. **6** a set of organ pipes of uniform tone; a keyboard knob that brings them all into use at once. **7** (*also* **f-stop**) any of a graded series of sizes that a camera's aperture can be adjusted to. **8** a speech sound made by suddenly releasing a build-up of air behind the lips, teeth, tongue, etc. — **pull out all the stops** to make one's best effort. **put a stop to something** or **someone** to cause them to end, especially abruptly. **stop at nothing** to be prepared to do anything, no matter how unscrupulous, in order to achieve one's aim. **stop down** to reduce the size of the aperture in a camera. **stop off** or **over** to break one's journey. [from Anglo-Saxon *stoppian*]

. . . .

☰ *verb* **1** halt, cease, end, finish, conclude, terminate, discontinue. **2** quit, give up, *colloq.* pack in, refrain from, desist from. **3** prevent, bar, frustrate, thwart, intercept, hinder, impede, check, restrain. **5** seal, close, plug, block, obstruct, stem, staunch. *noun* **1** rest, break, pause, cessation, discontinuation. **2** station, halt, terminus, destination. **3** halt, standstill, stoppage, end, finish, conclusion, termination.
✑ *verb* **1** start, begin, continue. *noun* **1** start, beginning, continuation.
. . . .

stopcock *noun* a valve controlling the flow of liquid in a pipe, operated by an external lever usually controlled by the level of the liquid in a cistern, etc.

stopgap *noun* a temporary substitute.

stop-off *noun* a brief or temporary stop during a longer journey.

stopover *noun* same as STOP-OFF.

stoppage *noun* **1** an act of stopping or the state of being stopped. **2** an amount deducted from wages. **3** a stopping of work, as in a strike.

. . . .

☰ **1** stop, halt, standstill, blockage, obstruction, check, hindrance. **3** strike, walkout, sit-in, shutdown, closure.
✑ **1** start, continuation.
. . . .

stopper *noun* a cork, plug, or bung.

stop press **1** late news inserted into a newspaper after printing has begun, in a specially reserved space. **2** the space itself.

stopwatch *noun* a watch for accurate recording of elapsed time, used for timing races, etc.

storage *noun* **1** the act of storing or the state of being stored. **2** space used for storing things. **3** the process of storing information in a computer's memory.

storage device *Comput.* any piece of computer equipment, such as a magnetic disk, on which data may be stored.

storage heater an electric heater consisting of a casing enclosing a stack of bricks with a high heat capacity. It accumulates and stores heat, usually overnight during off-peak periods, and then slowly releases it by convection to the surrounding air during the daytime.

store — *noun* **1** a supply kept in reserve. **2** a shop, especially when large and one of a chain. **3** (*also* **stores**) a place where stocks or supplies are kept, eg a warehouse. **4** a computer's memory. — *verb* **1** to put aside for future use. **2** (*also* **store something up**) to build up a reserve supply of it. **3** to put something (eg furniture) into a warehouse for temporary safekeeping. **4** to put into a computer's memory. — **in store** **1** kept in reserve; ready to be supplied. **2** destined to happen; imminent. **set** or **lay store by something** to value something (especially a quality or attribute) highly. [from Latin *instaurare*, to provide or restore]

. . . .

☰ *noun* **1** stock, supply, provision, fund, reserve, mine, reservoir, hoard, cache, stockpile, accumulation. **3** storeroom, storehouse, warehouse, repository, depository. *verb* **1** save, keep, reserve, put aside, set aside, lay by, lay down. **2** accumulate, hoard, stockpile, lay in, lay up.
✑ *verb* **1** use.
. . . .

storehouse *noun* a place where things are stored.

storey *noun* (PL. **storeys**) a level, floor, or tier of a building. [from Latin *historia*, picture, story, from the pictures with which medieval windows were decorated]

. . . .

☰ floor, level, stage, tier, flight, deck.
. . . .

stork *noun* **1** any of various species of large wading bird, related to the heron, with long legs, a long bill and neck, and usually with loose black and white plumage, mostly found near water in warm regions of the world. In folklore the white stork is associated with childbirth. **2** (**the stork**) this bird as the imaginary bringer of babies. [from Anglo-Saxon *storc*]

storm — *noun* **1** an outbreak of violent weather, with severe winds and heavy falls of rain, hail, or snow, often with thunder and lightning. **2** a violent reaction, outburst or show of feeling. **3** a furious burst, eg of gunfire or applause. — *verb* **1** *intrans.* to go or come loudly and angrily. **2** to say or shout angrily. **3** *Mil.* to make a sudden violent attack on. — **a storm in a teacup** *colloq.* much fuss about something unimportant. **take someone** or **something by storm 1** to enthral or captivate them totally and instantly. **2** *Mil.* to capture a place by storming. [from Anglo-Saxon *storm*]

◼ *noun* **1** tempest, squall, thunderstorm, blizzard, gale, hurricane, whirlwind, tornado, cyclone. **2** outburst, uproar, furore, outcry, row, rumpus, commotion, stir, rage. **3** burst, outbreak. *verb* **1** stride, march. **2** roar, thunder. **3** charge, rush, attack, assault, assail.

storm centre 1 the centre of a storm, where air pressure is lowest. **2** any focus of trouble or controversy.

storm door a second outer door, giving extra protection from bad weather.

storming *adj. colloq., said of a performance* very impressive.

storm petrel see PETREL.

stormtrooper *noun* **1** a soldier trained in methods of sudden violent attack. **2** *Hist.* a member of a branch of the Nazi army with a terrorist function.

stormy *adj.* (**stormier, stormiest**) **1** affected by storms or high winds. **2** violent; passionate: *a stormy relationship.*

◼ TEMPESTUOUS, TURBULENT, WILD, RAGING. **1** squally, windy, gusty, blustery, rough, choppy, foul. **2** violent, frenzied, passionate, intense.
◼ **1** calm.

story *noun* (PL. **stories**) **1** a written or spoken description of an event or series of events, real or imaginary. **2** (*also* **short story**) a piece of fiction much shorter than a novel, usually published as one of a collection. **3** the plot of a novel, play, or film. **4** a news article. **5** *colloq.* a lie. — **the story goes that …** it is widely said or believed that … [from Latin *historia*]

◼ **1** tale, fable, myth, legend, romance, fiction, yarn, anecdote, episode, history, chronicle, record, account. **3** plot, storyline, narrative. **4** article, feature, report. **5** lie, falsehood, untruth.

storyline *noun* the plot of a novel, play, or film.

stoup or **stoop** /stuːp/ *noun* a basin for holy water. [from Norse *staup*]

stout — *adj.* **1** rather fat. **2** hard-wearing; robust. **3** courageous; steadfastly reliable. — *noun* dark beer with a strong malt flavour. [from Dutch *stout*]

◼ *adj.* **1** fat, plump, portly, corpulent, overweight, heavy, bulky, brawny, beefy, hulking, burly. **2** strong, tough, durable, hard-wearing, thick, sturdy, robust, hardy, vigorous. **3** brave, courageous, valiant, plucky, fearless, bold, intrepid, dauntless, resolute, stalwart, steadfast, trusty, reliable.
◼ *adj.* **1** thin, lean, slim. **2** weak. **3** cowardly, timid.

stout-hearted *adj.* courageous; steadfastly reliable.

stoutly *adv.* in a stout way.

stoutness *noun* being stout.

stove[1] *noun* **1** a domestic cooker. **2** any cooking or heating apparatus, eg an industrial kiln. [from Anglo-Saxon *stofa*]

stove[2] see STAVE.

stow *verb* (*often* **stow away**) **1** to pack or store, especially out of sight. **2** *intrans.* to hide on a ship, aircraft, or vehicle in the hope of travelling free. [from Anglo-Saxon *stow, place*]

◼ **1** put away, store, load, pack, cram, stuff, *colloq.* stash.
◼ **1** unload.

stowage *noun* **1** a place for stowing things. **2** a charge made for stowing goods.

stowaway — *noun* a person who stows away on a ship, etc. — *adj.* **1** travelling as a stowaway. **2** able to be folded up and carried or stored easily.

STP *abbrev.* standard temperature and pressure.

strabismus *noun Medicine* a squint. [from Greek *strabismos*]

straddle *verb* **1** to stand or sit with one leg or part on either side of. **2** to part (the legs) widely. **3** *colloq.* to adopt a neutral or non-committal attitude towards. [related to STRIDE]

strafe /strɑːf/ *verb* to attack with heavy machine-gun fire from a low-flying aircraft. [from German *strafen*, to punish]

straggle *verb intrans.* **1** to grow or spread untidily. **2** to lag behind or stray from the main group or course.

straggler *noun* a person who trails along behind.

straggly *adj.* (**stragglier, straggliest**) straggling.

straight — *adj.* **1** not curved, bent, curly, or wavy. **2** without deviations or detours; direct. **3** level; not sloping, leaning, or twisted. **4** frank; open; direct. **5** respectable; not dishonest, disreputable, or criminal. **6** neat; tidy; in good order. **7** successive; in a row. **8** *said of a drink, especially alcoholic* undiluted; neat. **9** with all debts and favours paid back. **10** not comic; serious. **11** *colloq.* conventional in tastes and opinions. **12** *slang* heterosexual. — *adv.* **1** in or into a straight line, position, or posture. **2** following an undeviating course; directly. **3** immediately. **4** honestly; frankly. — *noun* **1** a straight line or part, eg of a race track. **2** *slang* a heterosexual person. **3** *Cards* a running sequence of five cards, irrespective of suit. — **go straight** *colloq.* to renounce criminal activities and live an honest life. **the straight and narrow** an honest, respectable, sober way of life. **straight away** immediately. **straight up** *colloq.* honestly; really. [from Anglo-Saxon *streht*, from *streccan*, to stretch]

◼ *adj.* **1** upright, vertical. **2** direct, undeviating, unswerving. **3** level, even, flat, horizontal. **4** frank, candid, open, direct, forthright, straightforward, blunt. **5** respectable, honest, law-abiding, upright, trustworthy, reliable, honourable, fair, just. **6** tidy, neat, orderly, shipshape, organized. **8** undiluted, neat, unadulterated, unmixed. *adv.* **2, 3** directly. **4** honestly, frankly, candidly, directly, point-blank. **straight away** at once, immediately, instantly, right away, directly, now, there and then.
◼ *adj.* **1** bent, crooked, curved, wavy, curly. **3** sloping. **4** evasive. **5** dishonest. **6** untidy. **8** diluted. **straight away** later, eventually.

straighten *verb* (**straightened, straightening**) (*often* **straighten out** or **up**) **1** *trans., intrans.* to make or become straight. **2** to resolve, disentangle, or put into order.

◼ **1** unbend, flatten, level, align. **2** resolve, settle, clear up, sort out, disentangle, tidy, neaten, order, arrange.
◼ **1** bend, twist. **2** confuse, muddle.

straight face an unsmiling face hiding a desire to laugh.

straight fight a contest in which there are only two candidates or sides.

straightforward *adj.* **1** without difficulties or complications; simple. **2** honest and frank.

◼ **1** easy, simple, uncomplicated, clear. **2** honest, truthful, sincere, genuine, frank, candid, direct, forthright, open.
◼ **1** complicated. **2** evasive, devious.

straight man a comedian's stooge.

strain[1] — *verb* **1** to injure or weaken (oneself or a part of one's body) through over-exertion. **2** *intrans.* to make violent efforts. **3** to make extreme use of or demands on. **4** to pass through or pour into a sieve or colander. **5** (**strain something off**) to remove it by the use of a sieve or colander. **6** to stretch or draw tight. **7** (**strain at something**) to tug it forcefully. **8** *intrans.* to feel or show reluctance or disgust; to balk. — *noun* **1** an injury caused by over-exertion, especially a wrenching of the muscles. **2** an extreme or excessive effort made by, or demand made on, the mind or the body. **3** the fatigue resulting from such an effort. **4** an absence of friendliness and openness; tension. **5** *Physics* a measure of the deformation of an object when it is subjected to stress. It is equal to the change in dimension, eg change in length, divided by the original dimension, eg original length. **6** (*also* **strains**) a melody or tune, or a snatch of one. **7** one's tone in speech or writing. [from Old French *estraindre*, from Latin *stringere*, to stretch tight]

    ▣ *verb* **1** pull, wrench, twist, sprain, weaken, tire, tax, overtax. **2** labour, try hard, struggle, exert oneself. **4** sieve, sift, screen, filter, purify. **6** stretch, extend, tighten, tauten. *noun* **1** pull, wrench, sprain, injury. **2** effort, struggle, exertion, pressure, force, stress, burden. **3** tiredness, weariness, fatigue, exhaustion. **4** tension, stress, anxiety.

strain[2] *noun* **1** a group of animals (especially farm livestock), or plants (especially crops), that is artificially maintained by inbreeding, etc, in order to retain certain desirable characteristics. **2** a group of bacteria or viruses of the same species that possess a particular characteristic that distinguishes them from other such groups of the same species. **3** an element of a person's character, especially when inherited. [from Anglo-Saxon *streon*, a begetting]

    ▣ **1** stock, breed, pedigree, blood, variety, type. **3** trait, streak, vein, tendency.

strained *adj.* **1** *said of an action, a person's manner, etc* not natural or easy; forced. **2** *said of an atmosphere* not friendly or relaxed; tense.

    ▣ TENSE, UNCOMFORTABLE. **1** forced, constrained, laboured, false, artificial, unnatural, stiff, self-conscious, uneasy, awkward. **2** unfriendly, cool.
    ▣ RELAXED. **1** natural. **2** friendly.

strainer *noun* a sieve or colander.

strait — *noun* **1** (*often* **straits**) a narrow strip of water that links two larger areas of ocean or sea. **2** (**straits**) difficulty; hardship: *dire straits*. — *adj.*, *old use* narrow; strict. [from Old French *estreit*, from Latin *stringere*, to draw tight]

straitened *adj.* — **in straitened circumstances** having very little money or assets.

straitjacket *noun* **1** a jacket used to restrain the arms of a person with violent tendencies, with long sleeves crossed at the chest and tied behind. **2** a thing that prevents freedom of development or expression.

strait-laced *adj.* strictly correct in moral behaviour and attitudes; prudish or puritanical.

    ▣ prudish, stuffy, starchy, prim, proper, strict, narrow, narrow-minded, puritanical, moralistic.
    ▣ broad-minded.

strand[1] — *verb* **1** to run (a ship) aground. **2** to leave in a helpless position, eg without transport. — *noun literary* a shore or beach. [from Anglo-Saxon *strand*, seashore]

    ▣ *verb* **1** ground, beach, wreck. **2** maroon, abandon, forsake, leave high and dry, leave in the lurch.

strand[2] *noun* **1** a single thread, fibre, length of hair, etc, whether alone or twisted or plaited with others to form a rope, cord, or braid. **2** a single element or component part.

    ▣ **1** fibre, filament, wire, thread, string, piece, length.

strange *adj.* **1** not known or experienced before; unfamiliar or alien. **2** not usual, ordinary, or predictable; difficult to explain or understand; odd. **3** vaguely ill or ill at ease. [from Latin *extraneus*, foreign]

    ▣ **1** new, novel, untried, unknown, unheard-of, unfamiliar, foreign, alien, exotic. **2** odd, peculiar, *colloq.* funny, curious, queer, weird, bizarre, abnormal, irregular, uncommon, unusual, exceptional, extraordinary, mystifying, perplexing, unexplained.
    ▣ **1** well-known, familiar. **2** ordinary, common.

strangely *adv.* in a strange way; as a strange circumstance.

strangeness *noun* a strange quality.

stranger *noun* **1** a person whom one does not know. **2** a person from a different place, home town, family, etc. **3** (**a stranger to something**) a person unfamiliar with or inexperienced in something (usually an experience).

    ▣ **2** newcomer, visitor, guest, non-member, outsider, foreigner, alien.
    ▣ **2** local, native.

strangle *verb* **1** to kill or attempt to kill by squeezing the throat with the hands, a cord, etc. **2** to hold back or suppress (eg a scream or laughter). **3** to hinder or stop the development or expression of. [from Latin *strangulare*]

    ▣ **1** throttle, choke, asphyxiate, suffocate, stifle, smother. **2** suppress, hold back, contain, restrain. **3** suppress, gag, repress, inhibit.

stranglehold *noun* **1** a choking hold in wrestling. **2** a position of total control; a severely repressive influence.

strangler *noun* a person who strangles.

strangulate *verb* **1** *Medicine* to press or squeeze so as to stop the flow of blood or air. **2** to strangle. [see STRANGLE]

strangulation *noun* being strangled.

strap — *noun* **1** a narrow strip of leather or fabric by which a thing is hung, carried, or fastened. **2** (*also* **shoulder strap**) either of a pair of strips of fabric by which a garment hangs from the shoulders. **3** (**the strap**) a leather belt used to give a beating as punishment; such a beating. **4** a hanging loop providing a hand-hold for a standing passenger on a bus or train. — *verb* (**strapped**, **strapping**) **1** (**strap someone** or **something in** or **up**) to fasten or bind them with a strap or straps. **2** to beat with a strap. [a dialect form of STROP]

    ▣ *noun* **1** thong, tie, band, belt, leash. *verb* LASH. **1** fasten, secure, tie, bind. **2** beat, flog, belt, whip.

strapping *adj.* tall and strong-looking.

strata /ˈstrɑːtə/ see STRATUM.

stratagem /ˈstratədʒəm/ *noun* a trick or plan, especially one for deceiving an enemy or gaining an advantage. [from Greek *strategema*, act of generalship]

    ▣ plan, scheme, plot, ruse, ploy, trick, dodge, manoeuvre, device, artifice, wile, subterfuge.

strategic *adj.* **1** relating to strategy or a strategy. **2** *said of weapons* designed for a direct long-range attack on an enemy's homeland, rather than for close-range battlefield use.

▣ **1** tactical, planned, calculated, deliberate, advantageous, key, vital.

strategically *adv.* in a strategic way.

strategic capability *Politics* the capability of states with long-range nuclear missiles and aircraft to make war or carry out reprisals. Various categories include first-strike capability, second-strike capability, and the ability to carry out a pre-emptive strike.

strategic studies the academic study of the military, political, economic, and technological factors which affect the relations between nations. It reviews the continuous process of military relations between nations in war and peace, and has risen to particular prominence in the age of nuclear weapons (compare MILITARY SCIENCE).

strategist *noun* a person skilled in strategy.

strategy *noun* (PL. **strategies**) **1** the process of, or skill in, planning and conducting a military campaign. **2** a long-term plan for future success or development. [from Greek *strategia*, from *stratos*, army + *agein*, to lead]

▣ **1** tactics, planning, policy, approach, procedure. **2** plan, programme, scheme, design.

strath *noun Scot.* a broad flat valley. [from Gaelic *srath*]

strathspey /straθˈspeɪ/ *noun* (PL. **strathspeys**) a Scottish folk dance similar to but slower than the reel, or a piece of music for it. [from *Strathspey* (the valley of the River Spey) in Scotland]

stratification *noun* **1** the formation of strata. **2** a stratified condition.

stratify *verb* (**stratifies, stratified**) **1** *Geol.* to deposit (rock) in layers or strata. **2** to classify or arrange into different grades, levels, or social classes. [from Latin *stratum* (see STRATUM) + *facere*, to make]

stratigraphy /strəˈtɪɡrəfɪ/ *noun Geol.* the branch of geology concerned with the origin, composition, and age of rock strata, especially sedimentary rocks, and the sequence in which they have been laid down. It has important applications in prospecting for minerals, especially petroleum, and the interpretation of archaeological excavations.

stratosphere /ˈstratəsfɪə(r)/ *noun Meteorol.* the layer of the Earth's atmosphere that extends from about 12km to about 50km above the Earth's surface, and contains the ozone layer. It lacks clouds and winds, and its temperature remains relatively constant. [from STRATUM + *sphere* as in ATMOSPHERE]

stratospheric /stratəˈsferɪk/ *adj.* of or in the stratosphere.

stratum /ˈstrɑːtəm/ *noun* (PL. **strata**) **1** a layer of sedimentary rock. **2** a layer of cells in living tissue. **3** a layer of the atmosphere or the ocean. **4** a level, grade, or social class. [from Latin *stratum*, something spread]

stratus /ˈstrɑːtəs, ˈstreɪtəs/ *noun* (PL. **strati**) *Meteorol.* a horizontal sheet of low grey layered cloud. [see STRATUM]

straw *noun* **1** the dried cut stems and leaves of cereal crops that remain after removal of the grains by threshing. Straw may be ploughed back into the soil, burned as stubble, or used as litter or feedstuff for animal livestock. It is also used for thatching, and woven into hats, baskets, etc. **2** a single stalk. **3** a thin hollow tube for sucking up a drink. **4** a pale yellow colour. — **clutch at straws** to resort in desperation to an alternative that is unlikely to succeed. **the last straw** the last in a whole series of disagreeable incidents, breaking one's tolerance or resistance. **the short straw** the worst of all possible outcomes or options. [from Anglo-Saxon *streaw*]

strawberry *noun* (PL. **strawberries**) **1** a trailing perennial plant of the genus *Fragaria*, that produces white flowers and propagates by means of runners or stolons. It is widely cultivated in temperate regions for its edible fruit. **2** the juicy red 'fruit' of this plant, which consists of tiny pips or *achenes* (the true fruits) embedded in the surface of a swol-

len fleshy receptacle. It may be eaten raw, preserved by canning or freezing, or used to make jam. It is also used as a flavouring in confectionery. **3** the flavour or colour of the fruit. [from Anglo-Saxon *strawberige*, perhaps from the straw-like appearance of the plant stem]

strawberry blonde *noun* a woman with reddish-blonde hair.

strawberry mark a reddish birthmark.

straw poll or **straw vote** an unofficial vote, especially taken on the spot, to get some idea of general opinion.

stray /streɪ/ — *verb intrans.* **1** to wander away from the right path or place, usually unintentionally. **2** to move away unintentionally from the main or current topic in thought, speech, or writing. **3** to depart from an accepted or required pattern of moral behaviour. — *noun* a lost or homeless pet or child. — *adj.* **1** *said of a dog, cat, etc* lost or homeless. **2** not the result of a regular or intended process; random; casual. [from Old French *estraier*, to wander]

▣ *verb* **1** wander (off), get lost, ramble, roam, rove, meander, straggle. **2** digress, diverge, drift, wander, ramble. **3** deviate, err. *adj.* **1** lost, abandoned, homeless, wandering, roaming. **2** random, chance, accidental, freak, odd, casual.

streak — *noun* **1** a long irregular stripe or band. **2** a flash of lightning. **3** an element or characteristic: *a cowardly streak.* **4** a short period; a spell: *a lucky streak.* **5** *colloq.* a naked dash through a public place. — *verb* **1** to mark with a streak or streaks. **2** *intrans.* to move at great speed; to dash. **3** *intrans., colloq.* to make a dash naked through a public place. [from Anglo-Saxon *strica*, stroke]

▣ *noun* **1** line, stroke, smear, band, stripe, strip, layer, vein. **3** element, strain, trait, characteristic. *verb* **1** band, stripe, fleck, striate, smear, daub. **2** speed, tear, dash, hurtle, sprint, gallop, fly, dart, flash, whistle, zoom, whizz.

streaked *adj.* having streaks.

streaker *noun colloq.* a person who makes a naked dash in public (see STREAK *verb* 3).

streakiness *noun* a streaky quality.

streaky *adj.* (**streakier, streakiest**) **1** marked with streaks. **2** *said of bacon* with alternate layers of fat and meat.

stream — *noun* **1** a very narrow river; a brook or rivulet. **2** any constant flow of water or other liquid. **3** a continuously moving line or mass, eg of vehicles. **4** an uninterrupted burst or succession, eg of insults. **5** general direction, trend, or tendency. **6** any of several groups into which school pupils are broadly divided according to ability, subdivided into classes. — *verb* **1** *intrans.* to flow or move continuously and in large quantities or numbers. **2** *intrans.* to float or trail in the wind. **3** to divide (pupils) into streams. [from Anglo-Saxon *stream*]

▣ *noun* **1** river, creek, brook, beck, burn, rivulet, tributary. **2** flow, run, gush, flood, deluge, cascade, torrent. **4** string, burst, volley, torrent, flood. **5** drift, flow, course, trend, tendency, current. *verb* **1** run, flow, course, pour, spout, gush, flood, cascade. **2** float, trail, fly, flutter.

streamer *noun* **1** a long paper ribbon used to decorate a room. **2** a roll of coloured paper that uncoils when thrown. **3** a long thin flag.

▣ **1** ribbon, banner. **3** pennant, pennon, flag, ensign, standard.

streaming *noun* the placing of children into higher or lower groups or classes according to their general ability. In the UK, it was general practice before the introduction of comprehensive education, and is being reintroduced in some schools, particularly at secondary level.

streamline *verb* to make streamlined.

streamlined *adj.* **1** *said of a vehicle, aircraft, or vessel* shaped so as to move smoothly and efficiently with minimum resistance to air or water. **2** *said of an organization, process, etc* extremely efficient, with little or no waste of resources, excess staff, unnecessary steps, etc.

  ▣ **1** aerodynamic, smooth, sleek, graceful. **2** efficient, well-run, rationalized, organized, slick.
  ▣ **2** inefficient.

streamlining *noun* **1** a condition of air or fluid flow such that no turbulence occurs. **2** the design of machinery or apparatus so that its shape creates a minimum of turbulence, either when moving (as in motor cars and aircraft), or when static (as in fixed structures that stand in a flow of air or water). **3** the refining of any system to optimize efficiency.

street *noun* **1** a public road, especially one in a town with pavements and buildings at the side or sides. **2** the road and the buildings together. **3** the people in the buildings or on the pavements: *tell the whole street.* — **on the street** or **streets** *colloq.* **1** homeless. **2** practising prostitution, especially soliciting. **streets ahead of someone** or **something** *colloq.* much more advanced than or superior to them. **up someone's street** *colloq.* suited to their tastes or abilities. **walk the streets 1** to walk from street to street. **2** to solicit as a prostitute on the street. [from Anglo-Saxon *stræt*]

streetcar *noun North Amer., esp. US* a tram.

street credibility (*also* **street cred**) *colloq.* popularity with or acceptability from fashionable urban society.

street hockey a form of hockey played on roller skates, first popularized in the USA, and now also played in the UK. It is so called because it was first played by children on street corners, although it is now generally played in enclosed areas, such as playgrounds.

streetwalker *noun colloq.* a prostitute who solicits.

streetwise *adj. colloq.* experienced in, and able to survive, the ruthlessness of urban life.

strength *noun* **1** the quality or degree of being physically or mentally strong. **2** the ability to withstand pressure or force. **3** degree or intensity, eg of emotion or light. **4** potency, eg of a drug or alcoholic drink. **5** forcefulness of an argument. **6** a highly valued quality or asset. **7** the number of people, etc needed or normally expected in a group, especially in comparison to those actually present or available: *with the workforce only at half strength.* — **go from strength to strength** to achieve a series of successes each surpassing the last. **on the strength of something** on the basis of it; judging by it. [from Anglo-Saxon *strengthu*]

  ▣ **1** power, might, force, vigour, energy, brawn, muscle, sinew, stamina, health, fitness, courage, fortitude, spirit, resolution. **2** toughness, resilience, robustness, sturdiness. **3** intensity, vividness, vehemence, violence. **4** potency, effectiveness, concentration. **5** forcefulness, effectiveness, power, force. **6** forte, asset, advantage.
  ▣ **1** weakness, feebleness, impotence. **2, 3, 4, 5, 6** weakness.

strengthen *verb* (**strengthened, strengthening**) **1** to make stronger. **2** *intrans.* to become stronger.

  ▣ TOUGHEN, HARDEN, INCREASE, INTENSIFY. **1** reinforce, brace, steel, fortify, buttress, bolster, consolidate, substantiate, corroborate, confirm, support, refresh, restore, invigorate.
  ▣ WEAKEN.

strenuosity or **strenuousness** *noun* being strenuous.
strenuous *adj.* requiring, or performed with, great effort or energy. [from Latin *strenuus*]

  ▣ hard, tough, demanding, gruelling, taxing, laborious, uphill,

arduous, tiring, exhausting, active, energetic, vigorous.
  ▣ easy, effortless.

strenuously *adv.* in a strenuous way.

streptococcus /strɛptəˈkɒkəs/ *noun* (PL. **streptococci**) **1** (**Streptococcus**) *Biol.* a genus of non-motile spherical bacteria that occur in pairs or chains. **2** any bacterium of this genus, which includes many harmless species, as well as serious pathogens of humans and animals that cause conditions such as scarlet fever and pneumonia. [from Greek *streptos*, twisted + *kokkos*, berry]

streptomycin /strɛptoʊˈmaɪsɪn/ *noun* an antibiotic used to treat various bacterial infections. [from Greek *streptos*, twisted + *mykes*, fungus]

stress — *noun* **1** physical or mental overexertion. **2** *Physics* the force exerted per unit area on a body that tends to cause that body to deform. **3** a physical or emotional reaction, or both, to a mentally or emotionally demanding event or situation (eg bereavement or overwork) that has a harmful effect on the general health and functioning of the body. Some physical disorders are worsened, if not caused by, mental stress, eg stomach ulcer, eczema, migraine, certain allergies. **4** importance, emphasis, or weight laid on or attached to something. **5** emphasis on a particular syllable or word. — *verb* **1** to emphasize or attach importance to. **2** to pronounce with emphasis. **3** to subject to mental or physical stress. [a shortening of DISTRESS]

  ▣ *noun* **1** pressure, strain, tension, worry, anxiety, weight, burden, trauma. **4** force, weight, emphasis, importance, significance. **5** emphasis, accent, accentuation, beat. *verb* **1** emphasize, accentuate, highlight, underline, underscore. **2** emphasize, accentuate, accent.
  ▣ *noun* **1** relaxation. *verb* **1** understate, downplay.

stressed-out *adj. colloq.* exhausted by psychological stress.

stressful *adj.* affected by or causing stress.

stress-mark *noun* a mark used to indicate stress.

stretch — *verb* **1** *trans., intrans.* to make or become temporarily or permanently longer or wider by pulling or drawing out. **2** *intrans.* to extend in space or time. **3** (*also* **stretch out** or **stretch something out**) to straighten and extend the body or part of the body, eg when waking or reaching out. **4** *trans., intrans.* to make or become tight or taut. **5** (*also* **stretch something out**) to lay it out at full length. **6** *intrans.* to be extendable without breaking. **7** *trans., intrans.* to last or cause to last longer through economical use. **8** (*also* **stretch something out**) to prolong it. **9** to make extreme demands on or severely test (eg resources or physical abilities). **10** to exaggerate (the truth). — *noun* **1** an act of stretching, especially (a part of) the body. **2** a period of time; a spell. **3** an expanse, eg of land or water. **4** capacity to extend or expand. **5** a straight part on a racetrack or course. **6** *colloq.* a difficult task or test: *will be a bit of a stretch.* **7** *slang* a term of imprisonment. — **at a stretch 1** continuously; without interruption. **2** with difficulty. **stretch a point** to agree to something not strictly in keeping with the rules; to bend the rules. **stretch one's legs** to take a short walk to invigorate oneself after inactivity. [from Anglo-Saxon *streccan*]

  ▣ *verb* **1** extend, lengthen, broaden, widen, expand, spread. **2** extend, spread, reach. **3** straighten, extend, hold out, reach out. **4** pull, tighten, tauten, strain. **5** unfold, unroll. **8** prolong, extend, lengthen, protract, draw out. *noun* **2** period, time, term, spell, stint, run. **3** expanse, spread, sweep, space, area, tract. **4** reach, extent.
  ▣ *verb* **1** compress.

stretcher *noun* a length of canvas or other sheeting with poles attached, for carrying a sick or wounded person in a lying position.

stretcher-bearer *noun* a person who carries a stretcher.

stretchiness *noun* a stretchy quality.

stretchy *adj.* (**stretchier, stretchiest**) *said of materials* able or tending to stretch.

strew *verb* (PAST TENSE **strewed**; PAST PARTICIPLE **strewed, strewn**) **1** to scatter untidily: *papers were strewn across the floor.* **2** to cover with an untidy scattering: *the floor was strewn with papers.* [from Anglo-Saxon *streowian*]

strewth *interj.* , *old colloq. use* an expression of surprise or annoyance. [from *God's truth*]

stria /ˈstraɪə/ *noun* (PL. **striae**) *Geol.* , *Biol.* any of a series of parallel grooves in rock, or furrows or streaks of colour in plants and animals. [from Latin *stria*, furrow]

striated /ˈstraɪeɪtɪd/ *adj.* marked with striae, striped.

striated muscle *Anat.* a voluntary muscle.

striation /straɪˈeɪʃən/ *noun* marking with striae.

stricken *adj.* deeply affected, especially by grief or disease. [an old past participle of STRIKE]

strict *adj.* **1** demanding obedience or close observance of rules; severe. **2** *said of instructions, etc* that must be closely obeyed. **3** observing rules or practices very closely: *strict Catholics.* **4** exact; precise: *the strict sense of the word.* **5** complete: *in the strictest confidence.* [from Latin *stringere*, to tighten]

. . . .

◼ **1** severe, stern, authoritarian, no-nonsense, firm. **2** rigid, inflexible, stringent, rigorous. **3** orthodox, religious, conscientious, meticulous, scrupulous, particular. **4** exact, precise, accurate, literal, faithful, true. **5** absolute, utter, total, complete.

◪ **1** easy-going. **2** flexible. **4** loose, rough.

. . . .

strictly *adv.* **1** with a strict manner. **2** (*also* **strictly speaking**) as a strict interpretation: *they have, strictly, broken the law.*

strictness *noun* being strict.

stricture *noun* **1** a severe criticism. **2** *Medicine* abnormal narrowing of a passage. [see STRICT]

stride — *noun* **1** a single long step in walking. **2** the length of such a step. **3** a way of walking in long steps. **4** (*usually* **strides**) a measure of progress or development: *make great strides.* **5** a rhythm, eg in working, aimed for or settled into: *put me off my stride.* **6** (**strides**) *slang* trousers. — *verb* (PAST TENSE **strode**; PAST PARTICIPLE **stridden**) **1** *intrans.* to walk with long steps. **2** *intrans.* to take a long step. **3** to step or extend over. — **take something in one's stride** to achieve it or cope with it effortlessly, as if part of a regular routine. [from Anglo-Saxon *stridan*]

stridency *noun* a strident quality.

strident *adj.* **1** *said of a sound, especially a voice* loud and harsh. **2** forcefully assertive; compelling. [from Latin *stridere*, to creak]

. . . .

◼ **1** loud, clamorous, vociferous, harsh, raucous, grating, rasping, shrill, screeching, discordant, jarring.

◪ **1** quiet, soft.

. . . .

stridently *adv.* in a strident way.

strife *noun* **1** bitter conflict or fighting. **2** *colloq.* trouble of any sort; hassle. [from Old French *estrif*]

. . . .

◼ **1** conflict, discord, dissension, controversy, animosity, friction, rivalry, contention, struggle, fighting, combat, battle, warfare.

◪ **1** peace.

. . . .

strigil /ˈstrɪdʒɪl/ *noun* **1** in ancient Greece and Rome, a scraper used to clean the skin after bathing. **2** in bees, a mechanism for cleaning the antennae. [from Latin *strigilis*]

strike — *verb* (PAST TENSE AND PAST PARTICIPLE **struck**) **1** to hit; to give a blow to; to come or bring into heavy con-

tact with. **2** to make a particular impression on (someone): *they struck me as a strange couple.* **3** to come into the mind of; to occur to. **4** to cause (a match) to ignite through friction. **5** (*usually* **strike at someone** or **something**) to attempt to hit them. **6** *trans., intrans., said of a clock* to indicate the hours, half-hours, and quarter-hours with chimes. **7** *intrans.* to happen suddenly: *disaster struck.* **8** *intrans.* to make a sudden attack. **9** to afflict suddenly; to cause to become by affliction: *struck dumb.* **10** to introduce or inject suddenly: *the thought struck terror into them.* **11** to arrive at or settle (eg a bargain or a balance). **12** to find a source of (eg oil). **13** (**strike on something**) to come upon or arrive at something (especially an idea) by chance. **14** *intrans.* to stop working as part of a collective protest against an employer. **15** to dismantle (a camp). **16** to make (a coin) by stamping metal. **17** to adopt (a posture or attitude). **18** to lower (a flag). **19** *trans., intrans.* to draw (a line) in order to cross something out. — *noun* **1** an act of hitting or dealing a blow. **2** a usually collective on-going refusal to work, as a protest against an employer. **3** a prolonged refusal to engage in a regular or expected activity, eg eating, as a protest. **4** a military attack, especially by aircraft. **5** a discovery of a mineral source, eg gold. **6** the knocking down of all pins with a single ball in tenpin bowling. **7** *Cricket* the position of being the batsman bowled at: *take strike.* **8** *Baseball* a ball swung at but missed by the batter. — **on strike** taking part in an industrial or other strike. **strike it lucky** or **rich** to enjoy luck or become rich suddenly and unexpectedly. **strike something** or **someone off** to remove their name from a professional register, eg of doctors, because of misconduct. **strike out 1** to aim blows wildly. **2** to set out determinedly on a journey or effort. **3** *Baseball* to be dismissed by means of three strikes (see STRIKE *noun* 8). **strike someone out** *Baseball* to dismiss a batter by means of three strikes (see STRIKE *noun* 8). **strike something out** to cross it out or efface it. **strike up** *said of a band, etc* to begin to play. **strike something up** to start something (especially a conversation or friendship). [from Anglo-Saxon *strican*]

. . . .

◼ *verb* **1** hit, knock, collide with, slap, smack, thump, *colloq.* wallop, beat, pound, hammer, buffet. **2** impress, affect, touch. **12** find, discover, unearth, uncover, reach. **14** stop work, down tools, work to rule, walk out, protest, revolt. *noun* **1** hit, blow, stroke. **2** industrial action, work-to-rule, go-slow, stoppage, sit-in, walkout. **4** raid, attack, bombardment. **strike something out** cross out, delete, efface, cancel, remove.

◪ **strike something out** add.

. . . .

strike-breaker *noun* a person who continues to work while others strike, or who is brought in to do the job of a striking worker.

strike pay an allowance paid by a trade union to a member on strike.

striker *noun* **1** a worker taking part in a strike. **2** *Football* a player with an attacking role.

striking *adj.* **1** impressive or arresting. **2** noticeable; marked. **3** on strike.

. . . .

◼ **1** impressive, arresting, dazzling, stunning, astonishing, extraordinary, remarkable, outstanding, memorable. **2** noticeable, marked, conspicuous, salient.

◪ **1** unimpressive. **2** inconspicuous.

. . . .

string — *noun* **1** thin cord, or a piece of this. **2** any of a set of pieces of stretched wire, catgut, or other material vibrated to produce sound in various musical instruments. **3** (**strings**) the orchestral instruments in which sound is produced in this way, usually the violins, violas, cellos, and double basses collectively; also used of the players. **4** a set of things, eg pearls threaded together. **5** a series or succession. **6** (**strings**) undesirable conditions or limitations: *no strings attached.* **7** any cord-like thing, eg a nerve or tendon. — *verb* (PAST TENSE AND PAST PARTICIPLE **strung**) **1** to fit or provide with a string or strings. **2** to tie with string. **3** to thread (eg beads) on a string. **4** to remove the stringy parts from (eg a bean pod). **5** (*also* **string out**) to extend in a string. — **pull strings** *colloq.* to use one's influence, or relationships with influential people, to get something done. **pull the strings** *colloq.* to be the ultimate, although not usually apparent, controller of a situation or person. **string someone along** to keep them in a state of deception or false hope. **string along with someone** to go along with them for company. **string something out** to extend or stretch it in a long line. **string someone up** *colloq.* to kill them by hanging. **string something up** to hang, stretch, or tie it with string, or as if with string. [from Anglo-Saxon *streng*]

▣ *noun* **1** twine, cord, rope, cable, line, strand, fibre. **5** series, succession, sequence, chain, line, row, file, queue, procession, train. *verb* **2** tie, lash, bind, strap. **3** thread, link, connect.

stringency *noun* being stringent.
stringent *adj.* **1** *said of rules, terms, etc* severe; rigorous; strictly enforced. **2** marked by a lack of money. [from Latin *stringere*, to draw together]

▣ **1** strict, severe, rigorous, tough, rigid, inflexible, binding, tight.
▣ **1** lax, flexible.

stringently *adv.* in a stringent way.
stringer *noun* **1** a horizontal beam in a framework. **2** a journalist employed part-time to cover a particular town or area.
stringiness *noun* a stringy quality.
stringy *adj.* (**stringier, stringiest**) **1** like string, especially thin and thread-like. **2** *said of meat or other food* full of chewy fibres.
strip — *noun* **1** a long narrow piece. **2** a lightweight uniform worn by members of a sports team. **3** a striptease performance. — *verb* (**stripped, stripping**) **1** (*also* **strip something off**) to remove it by peeling or pulling off; to remove the surface or contents of something in this way. **2** (**strip someone of something**) to divest or dispossess them of something (eg property or dignity). **3** to remove the clothes of. **4** *intrans.* (*also* **strip off**) to take one's clothes off. **5** (*also* **strip something down**) to take it completely to pieces; to dismantle it. [from Anglo-Saxon *strypan*]

▣ *noun* **1** ribbon, strap, belt, band, stripe, lath, slat, piece, bit, slip, shred. *verb* **1** peel, skin, flay, denude, clear, empty, gut, ransack, pillage, plunder, loot. **2** divest of, deprive of. **3** undress, disrobe, unclothe, uncover, expose, lay bare. **4** undress, disrobe.
▣ *verb* **1** cover, fill. **3** dress, clothe. **4** dress, get dressed.

strip cartoon a sequence of drawings, eg in a newspaper, telling a comic or adventure story.
strip club a club in which striptease artistes perform.
stripe — *noun* **1** a band of colour. **2** a chevron or coloured band on a uniform, indicating rank. — *verb* to mark with stripes. [from Old Dutch *stripe*]

▣ *noun* **1** band, line, bar, strip, streak, fleck. **2** chevron, flash.

striped *adj.* having or marked with stripes.
strip light or **strip lighting** a light or lighting using tube-shaped fluorescent lamps.
stripling /'strɪplɪŋ/ *noun*, *literary* a boy or youth. [a diminutive of STRIP]
stripper *noun* **1** a striptease artiste. **2** a substance or appliance for removing paint, varnish, etc.
strip search a thorough search of the body of a person who has been made to take off his or her clothes, to check for concealed drugs or smuggled items.

strip-search *verb* to search (a person's naked body).
striptease *noun* an entertainment in which a person undresses to music in a slow and sexually exciting way.
stripy *adj.* (**stripier, stripiest**) marked with stripes; striped.
strive *verb intrans.* (PAST TENSE **strove**; PAST PARTICIPLE **striven**) **1** to try extremely hard; to struggle. **2** to contend; to be in conflict. [from Old French *estriver*]

▣ **1** try, attempt, endeavour, struggle, strain, toil, labour. **2** fight, contend, compete.

strobe /strəʊb/ *noun* **1** same as STROBE LIGHTING. **2** a stroboscope. [from Greek *strobos*, whirling]
strobe lighting equipment for producing a powerful rapidly flashing light which, directed on a moving body, creates an effect of jerky movement, widely used in discotheques, etc.
strobilus /strəʊ'baɪləs/ *noun Bot.* a conical reproductive structure composed of spore-bearing leaves, known as *sporophylls*, occurring in cone-bearing plants (eg pine and other conifers) and horsetails. Also called CONE. [from Greek *strobile*, a conical plug of lint, *strobilos*, a spinning top, whirl, pine cone]
strobo-flash *noun* photographic recording of a moving object by a series of brief exposures at regular intervals using sequential electronic flash lighting during the period when the camera shutter is open. In cinematography, strobe-lighting with electronic flash sychronized to the camera frame rate produces sharp images of fast moving subjects.
stroboscope *noun* an instrument that uses a flashing light (strobe light) to measure or set the speed of rotating shafts, propellers, etc. When the speed of the strobe light is equal to that of the rotating object, the latter appears to be stationary. Stroboscopes are used to set the ignition timing of car engines. [from Greek *strobos*, whirling + -SCOPE]
strode see STRIDE.
stroke — *noun* **1** an act of striking; the way a thing is struck, especially the technique used in striking a ball in sport. **2** a single movement with a pen, paintbrush, etc, or the line or daub produced. **3** a single complete movement in a repeated series, as in swimming or rowing. **4** the total linear distance travelled by a piston in the cylinder of an engine. **5** a particular named style of swimming. **6** the striking of a clock, or its sound. **7** a gentle caress or other touching movement. **8** (**stroke of**) an act or occurrence that reveals the presence of something, eg genius or luck. **9** a sloping line used to separate alternatives in writing or print; a solidus. **10** a sudden interruption to the supply of blood to the brain, caused by thrombosis (formation of a blood clot in an artery), embolism (a detached clot circulating in the bloodstream), or haemorrhage (the rupture of a blood vessel in or leading to the brain). It causes a sudden loss of consciousness, often resulting in paralysis of one side of the body, which may be temporary or permanent, and is often accompanied by loss of speech. Stroke is one of the major causes of death worldwide. **11** *colloq.* the least amount of work: *not done a stroke all day.* — *verb* **1** to caress in kindness or affection, often repeatedly. **2** to strike (a ball) smoothly and with seeming effortlessness. — **at a stroke** with a single action. **on the stroke of …** precisely at (a particular time). [from Anglo-Saxon *strac*]

▣ *noun* **1** blow, hit, knock, swipe. **2** line, streak, daub, flourish. **3** movement, action, move, sweep. **7** caress, touch, pat, rub. *verb* **1** caress, fondle, pet, touch, pat, rub, massage.

stroll — *verb intrans.* to walk in a slow leisurely way. — *noun* a leisurely walk. [perhaps from German *strolchen*, from *Strolch*, tramp]

▣ *verb* saunter, amble, dawdle, ramble, wander. *noun* saunter, amble, walk, constitutional, turn, ramble.

strong *adj.* **1** exerting or capable of great force or power. **2** able to withstand rough treatment; robust. **3** *said of views, etc* firmly held or boldly expressed. **4** *said of taste, light, etc* sharply felt or experienced; intense; powerful. **5** *said of coffee, alcoholic drink, etc* relatively undiluted with water or other liquid; concentrated. **6** *said of an argument* having much force; convincing. **7** (**strong on something**) excelling in it; well-skilled or versed in it. **8** *said of language* bold or straightforward; rude or offensive. **9** *said of prices, values, etc* steady or rising. **10** *said of a syllable* stressed. **11** *said of a group, etc* numbering so many: *a gang fifty strong.* — **come on strong** *colloq.* to be strongly, often disconcertingly, persuasive or assertive. **going strong** *colloq.* flourishing; thriving. [from Anglo-Saxon *strang*]

⊟ **1** powerful, mighty, potent, lusty, strapping, stout, burly, well-built, beefy, brawny, muscular, sinewy, athletic, fit, healthy. **2** tough, resilient, durable, hard-wearing, heavy-duty, robust, hardy, sturdy, solid, firm, sound. **4** intense, deep, vivid, fierce, violent, powerful, sharp, keen, pungent, piquant, hot, spicy. **5** undiluted, concentrated, potent. **6** convincing, persuasive, cogent, effective, telling, forceful, weighty, compelling, urgent.
⊞ **1** weak, feeble. **4** mild, bland. **6** unconvincing.

strongarm — *adj. colloq.* **1** aggressively forceful. **2** making use of physical violence or threats. — *verb* to compel with aggressive forcefulness or threats of violence.

strongbox *noun* a safe, or other sturdy lockable box for storing money or valuables.

stronghold *noun* **1** a fortified place of defence, eg a castle. **2** a place where there is strong support (eg for a political party).

⊟ BASTION **1** citadel, fort, fortress, castle, keep, refuge.

strongly *adv.* **1** in a strong way. **2** to a strong degree: *strongly flavoured.*

strong point a feature or attribute in which a person excels.

strongroom *noun* a room in which valuables or prisoners are held for safekeeping, designed to be difficult to penetrate.

strong verb in English, German, etc, an irregular verb with different vowels in different tenses, as *sing, sang, sung* and *write, wrote, written.*

strontium *noun Chem.* (SYMBOL **Sr**, ATOMIC NUMBER **38**) a soft silvery-white highly reactive metal that is a good conductor of electricity. It is used in certain alloys, and as a 'getter' for removing traces of gas from vacuum tubes. Its compounds burn with a bright red flame and are used in flares and fireworks. The radioactive isotope strontium-90 occurs in radioactive fallout, and is a recognized health hazard because it becomes incorporated into bone. [from the name *Strontian* in Scotland, where it was discovered]

strop — *noun* a strip of coarse leather or other abrasive material on which razors are sharpened. — *verb* (**stropped**, **stropping**) to sharpen (a razor) on a strop. [from Latin *struppus*, thong]

stroppy *adj.* (**stroppier**, **stroppiest**) *colloq.* quarrelsome, bad-tempered, and awkward to deal with. [probably from OBSTREPEROUS]

strove see STRIVE.

struck past tense and past participle of STRIKE. — **struck on someone** or **something** *colloq.* infatuated with them; enthusiastic about them.

structural *adj.* of or relating to structure, or a framework.

structural formula *Chem.* a formula that is used to represent the exact arrangement of the atoms within a molecule of a chemical compound, as well as its composition.

structuralism *noun* an approach to various areas of study, eg literary criticism and linguistics, which seeks to identify underlying patterns or structures, especially as they might reflect patterns of behaviour or thought in society as a whole.

structuralist — *noun* a person who believes in structuralism. — *adj.* relating to or characterized by structuralism.

structurally *adv.* in a structural way; as regards structure.

structure — *noun* **1** the way in which the parts of a thing are arranged or organized. **2** a thing built or constructed from many smaller parts. — *verb* to put into an organized form or arrangement. [from Latin *structura*, from *struere*, to build]

⊟ *noun* CONSTRUCTION. **1** framework, fabric, form, shape, design, configuration, conformation, make-up, formation, arrangement, organization, set-up. **2** building, edifice, erection. *verb* construct, assemble, build, erect, form, shape, design, arrange, organize.

strudel /ˈstruːdəl/ *noun* a baked roll of thin pastry with a filling of fruit, especially apple. [from German *strudel*, whirlpool, from the rolling]

struggle — *verb intrans.* **1** to move the body around violently in an attempt to get free. **2** to strive vigorously or make a strenuous effort under difficult conditions. **3** to make one's way with great difficulty. **4** to fight or contend. — *noun* **1** an act of struggling. **2** a task requiring strenuous effort. **3** a fight or contest. [from Middle English *strogelen*]

⊟ *verb* **2** strive, work, toil, labour, strain, agonize. **4** fight, battle, wrestle, grapple, contend, compete, vie. *noun* **1** effort, exertion, pains, work, labour, toil. **2** difficulty, problem. **3** fight, contest, battle, skirmish, encounter, clash, conflict, strife.
⊞ *verb* **2** give up. *noun* **1** submission, co-operation.

strum — *verb trans., intrans.* (**strummed**, **strumming**) to play (a stringed musical instrument, or a tune on it) with sweeps of the fingers or thumb rather than with precise plucking. — *noun* an act or bout of strumming.

strumpet *noun, old use* a prostitute, or a woman who engages in casual sex.

strung see STRING.

strut[1] — *verb intrans.* (**strutted**, **strutting**) to walk in a proud or self-important way. — *noun* a strutting way of walking. [from Anglo-Saxon *strutian*]

strut[2] *noun* a bar or rod used to support weight or take pressure; a prop.

strychnine /ˈstrɪkniːn/ *noun* a deadly poison obtained from the seeds of a tropical Indian tree, used medicinally in small quantities as a nerve stimulant. [from Greek *strychnos*, nightshade]

stub — *noun* **1** a short piece, eg of a cigarette or a pencil, left after the rest has been used up. **2** the part of a cheque or ticket kept by the issuer as a record. — *verb* (**stubbed**, **stubbing**) **1** to accidentally bump the end of (one's toe) against a hard surface. **2** (*also* **stub something out**) to extinguish a cigarette or cigar by pressing the end against a surface. [from Anglo-Saxon *stubb*]

⊟ *noun* **1** end, stump, remnant, *colloq.* fag end, *slang* dog-end, butt. **2** counterfoil.

stubbiness *noun* being stubby.

stubble *noun* **1** the mass of short stalks left in the ground after a crop has been harvested. **2** a short early growth of beard. [from Old French *estuble*]

stubbly *adj.* **1** characterized by or having stubble. **2** of the nature of stubble.

stubborn *adj.* **1** resolutely or unreasonably unwilling to change one's plans or opinions; obstinate. **2** determined; unyielding. **3** difficult to treat, remove, or deal with: *stubborn stains.*

⊟ UNYIELDING. **1** obstinate, stiff-necked, mulish, pig-headed, obdurate, intransigent, rigid, inflexible, unbending. **2** determined, resolute, dogged, persistent, tenacious, headstrong, self-willed, wilful. **3** difficult, unmanageable.

▣ **1** flexible. **2** yielding.

· ·

stubbornly *adv.* in a stubborn way.

stubbornness *noun* being stubborn.

stubby *adj.* (**stubbier, stubbiest**) short and broad or thickset.

STUC *abbrev.* Scottish Trades Union Congress.

stucco /ˈstʌkoʊ/ — *noun* (PL. **stuccos, stuccoes**) any kind of plaster or cement used for coating, or moulding decorative shapes on to, outside walls. — *verb* (**stuccos** or **stuccoes, stuccoed** or **stucco'd**) to coat with or mould out of stucco. [from Italian *stucco*, from Old German *stucchi*, coating]

stuck past tense and past participle of STICK². — *adj.* **1** unable to move, leave, etc. **2** unable to make further progress with a task, problem, puzzle, etc. — **be stuck for something** *colloq.* to be in need of it or at a loss for it. **be stuck with someone** or **something** to be unable to get rid of an unwelcome person or thing. **get stuck in** *slang* to set about an activity with energy or aggression. **stuck on someone** *colloq.* fond of or infatuated with them.

· ·

▣ *adj.* **1** fast, jammed, trapped, stranded. **2** beaten, defeated, *colloq.* stumped, baffled.

▣ *adj.* **1** loose, free.

· ·

stuck-up *adj. colloq.* snobbish; conceited.

· ·

▣ snobbish, *colloq.* toffee-nosed, *colloq.* snooty, supercilious, haughty, high and mighty, condescending, conceited, *colloq.* big-headed, proud, arrogant.

▣ humble, modest.

· ·

stud¹ — *noun* **1** a rivet-like metal knob fitted on to a surface, eg of a garment, for decoration. **2** any of several knob-like projections on the sole of a sports boot, giving added grip. **3** a fastener, eg fixing a collar to a shirt, consisting of two small discs on either end of a short bar or shank. **4** a press stud. — *verb* (**studded, studding**) **1** to fasten or decorate with a stud or studs. **2** (**be studded with something**) to be covered with a dense scattering of it. [from Anglo-Saxon *studu*, post]

stud² *noun* **1** a male animal, especially a horse, kept for breeding. **2** (*also* **stud farm**) a place where animals, especially horses, are bred. **3** a collection of animals kept for breeding. **4** *colloq.* stud poker. **5** *slang* a man who has or claims great sexual energy and prowess. — **at stud** or **out to stud** kept for breeding purposes. [from Anglo-Saxon *stod*]

student *noun* **1** a person following a formal course of study, especially in further education. **2** (**a student of something**) a person with an informed interest in a subject. [from Latin *studere*, to be zealous]

· ·

▣ **1** undergraduate, postgraduate, scholar, schoolboy, schoolgirl, pupil, disciple, learner, trainee, apprentice.

· ·

studied *adj.*, *said of an attitude, expression, etc* carefully practised and adopted or produced for effect; unspontaneous and affected.

· ·

▣ deliberate, conscious, premeditated, planned, calculated, contrived, forced, unnatural, affected.

▣ unplanned, spontaneous, impulsive, natural.

· ·

studio *noun* (PL. **studios**) **1** the workroom of an artist or photographer. **2** a room in which music recordings, cinema films, or television or radio programmes are made. **3** (**studios**) the premises of a company making any of these. [from Italian; see STUDY]

· ·

▣ **1** workroom, workshop.

· ·

studio couch a couch, often backless, that converts into a bed.

studio flat a small flat with one main room acting as living, eating, sleeping, and often cooking area.

studious *adj.* **1** having a serious, hard-working approach to study. **2** painstaking or painstakingly carried out. [see STUDY]

· ·

▣ **1** scholarly, academic, intellectual, bookish, serious, thoughtful, reflective, diligent, hard-working, industrious. **2** careful, attentive, thorough, painstaking, meticulous, assiduous.

▣ **1** lazy, idle. **2** negligent.

· ·

studiously *adv.* in a studious way.

studiousness *noun* being studious.

stud poker a form of poker in which bets are placed on hands in which some of the cards are laid face up.

study — *verb* (**studies, studied**) **1** *trans., intrans.* to devote oneself to the gaining of knowledge of (a subject); to take an educational course in (a subject). **2** to look at or examine closely, or think about carefully. — *noun* (PL. **studies**) **1** the act or process of studying. **2** (**studies**) work done in the process of acquiring knowledge. **3** a careful and detailed examination or consideration: *undertook a careful study of the problem*. **4** a work of art produced for the sake of practice, or in preparation for a more complex or detailed work. **5** a piece of music intended to exercise and develop the player's technique. **6** a private room where quiet work or study is carried out. [from Latin *studere*, to be zealous, from *studium*, zeal]

· ·

▣ *verb* **1** read, learn, revise, *colloq.* swot, research. **2** examine, scrutinize, analyse, peruse, pore over, scan, survey, contemplate, ponder, consider. *noun* **1** reading, homework, preparation, learning, revision, *colloq.* swotting, research. **3** examination, scrutiny, inspection, analysis, contemplation, consideration, investigation, inquiry, survey, review, critique, report, paper. **6** office, *colloq.* den.

· ·

study skills the ability to study effectively and to use and develop skills, such as effective reading (how to skim, scan, slow down at important stages, make notes, use an index, etc), information gathering and the proper use of library and resource centre facilities, revision techniques, and an understanding of one's own learning strategies.

stuff — *noun* **1** any material or substance. **2** luggage or equipment; belongings. **3** *literary* matter; essence: *the very stuff of life*. **4** *old use* cloth, especially woollen. — *verb* **1** to fill the hollow or hollowed-out part of (eg a chicken or pepper) with a seasoned mixture of other foods. **2** to fill to capacity or over. **3** to cram or thrust into something. **4** to fill out the disembodied skin of (an animal) to recreate its living shape. **5** to feed (oneself) gluttonously. **6** (*also* **stuff something up**) to block something (eg a hole, or the nose with mucus). **7** *slang* to defeat overwhelmingly. **8** *slang* to dispose of (something angrily rejected) however one wishes: *you can stuff your job!* **9** *offensive slang* to have sexual intercourse with (a woman). — **do one's stuff** *colloq.* **1** to display one's talent or skill. **2** to perform the task required of one. **get stuffed!** *coarse slang* an expression of anger or contemptuous dismissal. **know one's stuff** *colloq.* to have a thorough knowledge of the subject with which one is concerned. [from Old French *estoffe*]

· ·

▣ *noun* **1** material, substance. **2** belongings, possessions, things, goods, luggage, baggage, paraphernalia, *colloq.* gear, kit, tackle, equipment, materials. **3** matter, essence. **4** cloth, fabric, material. *verb* **2** fill, pack, stow, load, cram, crowd. **3** cram, force, push, shove, ram, wedge, jam, squeeze. **5** gorge, guzzle, gobble, sate, satiate.

▣ *verb* **2** empty, unload. **5** nibble.

· ·

stuffed shirt *derog. colloq.* a conservative or pompous person.

stuffily *adv.* in a stuffy way.

stuffiness *noun* being stuffy.

stuffing *noun* 1 padding used to stuff children's toys, cushions, animal skins, etc. 2 a seasoned mixture of foods with which another item of food is stuffed. — **knock the stuffing out of someone** *said of an arduous task, etc* to deprive them rapidly of strength or force; to exhaust them.

......

▣ 1 padding, wadding, quilting. 2 filling, forcemeat.

......

stuffy *adj.* (**stuffier, stuffiest**) 1 lacking fresh, cool air; badly ventilated. 2 *colloq.* pompous. 3 *colloq.* boringly formal, conventional, or unadventurous; staid.

......

▣ 1 musty, stale, airless, unventilated, suffocating, stifling, oppressive, heavy, close, muggy. 3 staid, strait-laced, prim, formal, conventional, old-fashioned, unadventurous, dull, dreary, uninteresting.

▣ 1 airy, well-ventilated. 3 informal, lively.

......

stultify *verb* (**stultifies, stultified**) 1 to make (eg efforts) appear useless or foolish. 2 to dull the mind of, eg with tedious tasks. [from Latin *stultus*, foolish + *facere*, to make]

stultifying *adj.* that stultifies.

stumble — *verb intrans.* 1 to lose one's balance and pitch forwards after accidentally catching or misplacing one's foot. 2 to walk unsteadily. 3 to speak with frequent hesitations and mistakes. 4 to make a mistake in speech or action. — *noun* an act of stumbling. — **stumble across** or **on something** to find or encounter it by chance. [from Middle English *stomble*]

......

▣ *verb* 1 trip, slip, fall, lurch, reel, stagger, flounder. 3 stammer, stutter, hesitate, falter. **stumble across** or **on** find, discover, encounter, come across, chance upon, happen upon.

......

stumbling block 1 an obstacle or difficulty. 2 a cause of failure or faltering.

......

▣ 1 obstacle, hurdle, barrier, bar, obstruction, hindrance, impediment, difficulty, snag.

......

stump — *noun* 1 the part of a felled or fallen tree left in the ground. 2 the short part of anything, eg a limb, left after the larger part has been removed. 3 *Cricket* any of the three thin vertical wooden posts forming the wicket; (**stumps**) the whole wicket, including the bails. — *verb* 1 to baffle or perplex. 2 *intrans.* to walk stiffly and unsteadily, or heavily and noisily. 3 *Cricket* to dismiss (a batsman stepping wholly beyond the crease) by disturbing the wicket with the ball. — **stump up** *colloq.* to pay up. [from Middle English *stumpe*]

......

▣ *noun* 2 end, remnant, stub. *verb* 1 perplex, puzzle, baffle, mystify, confuse, bewilder, *colloq.* flummox, defeat, outwit, confound. **stump up** pay, hand over, *colloq.* fork out, *colloq.* shell out, donate, contribute, *slang* cough up.

▣ **stump up** receive.

......

stumpiness *noun* being stumpy.

stumpy *adj.* (**stumpier, stumpiest**) short and thick.

stun *verb* (**stunned, stunning**) 1 to make unconscious, eg by a blow to the head. 2 to make unable to speak or think clearly, eg through shock. 3 *colloq.* to impress greatly; to astound. [from Old French *estoner*, to astonish]

......

▣ 1 knock out. 2 daze, stupefy, dumbfound, *colloq.* flabbergast, shock, overcome, confound, confuse, bewilder. 3 amaze, astonish, astound, stagger, impress, dazzle.

......

stung see STING.

stunk see STINK.

stunner *noun colloq.* a person or thing of overwhelming beauty or attractiveness.

stunning *adj. colloq.* 1 outstandingly beautiful. 2 extremely impressive.

......

▣ 1 beautiful, lovely, gorgeous, ravishing. 2 striking, impressive, dazzling, brilliant, spectacular, remarkable, wonderful, marvellous.

▣ 1 ugly. 2 awful.

......

stunningly *adv.* in a stunning way.

stunt[1] *verb* to prevent (growth or development) to the full, or prevent the full growth or development of. [from Anglo-Saxon *stunt*, dull, stupid]

......

▣ stop, arrest, check, restrict, slow, retard, hinder, impede, dwarf.

▣ promote, encourage.

......

stunt[2] *noun* 1 a daring act or spectacular event intended to show off talent or attract publicity. 2 a dangerous or acrobatic feat performed as part of the action of a film or television programme.

......

▣ 1 feat, exploit, act, trick, turn, performance.

......

stunted *adj.* dwarfed, under-developed.

stuntman or **stuntwoman** *noun* a person hired to take the place of an actor when stunts are being filmed.

stupa /ˈstuːpə/ *noun* an Indian cairn or mound originally constructed over the ashes of an emperor or some other great person, such as the Buddha. Later they were used to house the ashes of Buddhist monks and holy relics. [from Sanskrit *stūpa*]

stupefaction *noun* stupefying or being stupefied.

stupefy *verb* (**stupefies, stupefied**) 1 to make senseless, eg with drugs or alcohol. 2 to amaze or astound. 3 to confuse or bewilder. [from Latin *stupere*, to be struck senseless + *facere*, to make]

......

▣ 1 daze, stun, knock out, numb. 2 amaze, astound, stagger, shock, dumbfound.

......

stupefying *adj.* that stupefies.

stupendous *adj.* 1 astounding. 2 *colloq.* astoundingly huge or excellent. [from Latin *stupere*, to be stunned]

......

▣ STUNNING. 1 amazing, astounding, staggering. 2 huge, enormous, gigantic, colossal, vast, prodigious, phenomenal, tremendous, fabulous, fantastic, superb, wonderful, marvellous.

▣ 2 ordinary, unimpressive.

......

stupendously *adv.* in a stupendous way.

stupid *adj.* 1 having or showing a lack of common sense, or a slowness to understand. 2 made senseless or stupefied, eg with drugs. 3 *colloq.* trivial; unimportant. [from Latin *stupidus*, senseless]

......

▣ 1 silly, foolish, irresponsible, ill-advised, foolhardy, rash, senseless, mad, idiotic, half-witted, feeble-minded, simple-minded, slow, *colloq.* dim, dull, *colloq.* dense, *colloq.* thick, *colloq.* dumb, inane, puerile, meaningless, nonsensical, absurd. 2 dazed, groggy, dopey, stupefied, stunned, unconscious, senseless.

▣ 1 sensible, wise, clever, intelligent. 2 alert.

......

stupidity *noun* a stupid state or condition; extreme foolishness.

stupidly *adv.* in a stupid way.

stupor / 'stjuːpə(r)/ *noun* a state of near-unconsciousness in which there is little or no response to external stimuli. It is usually caused by drugs, alcohol, etc. [from Latin *stupor*, insensibility]

⊟ daze, stupefaction, torpor, lethargy, inertia, trance, coma, numbness, insensibility, unconsciousness, semi-consciousness.
⊟ alertness, consciousness.

sturdily *adv.* in a sturdy way.
sturdiness *noun* being sturdy.
sturdy *adj.* (**sturdier, sturdiest**) **1** *said of limbs, etc* thick and strong-looking. **2** strongly built; robust. **3** healthy; vigorous; hardy. [from Old French *estourdi*, stunned]

⊟ **1** powerful, muscular, athletic, well-built. **2** strong, robust, durable, well-made, stout, substantial, solid. **3** fit, healthy, vigorous, hardy, flourishing, hearty.
⊟ **1, 3** puny. **2** weak, flimsy.

sturgeon *noun* a large long-snouted fish of northern seas, from which caviar is obtained. [from Old French *sturgeon*]
stutter — *noun* **1** an inability to utter, without hesitation, certain speech sounds especially at the beginnings of words, resulting in repetition of the sounds; a stammer. **2** the resulting repetition. — *verb trans., intrans.* (**stuttered, stuttering**) to speak or say with a stutter. [from obsolete *stut*]

⊟ STAMMER, FALTER, MUMBLE.

STV *abbrev.* **1** Scottish Television. **2** single transferable vote (a method of voting for proportional representation).
sty[1] *noun* (PL. **sties**) a pen in which pigs are kept. [from Anglo-Saxon *stig*, pen, hall]
sty[2] or **stye** *noun* (PL. **sties, styes**) a tiny swelling on the eyelid, at the base of the lash. [from Anglo-Saxon *stigan*, to rise]
style — *noun* **1** a manner or way of doing something, eg writing, speaking, painting, or designing buildings. **2** a distinctive manner that characterizes a particular author, painter, film-maker, etc. **3** the characteristic appearance of something designed or made by a particular person or in a particular era: *a twenties-style dress.* **4** kind; type; make. **5** a striking quality, often elegance or lavishness, considered desirable or admirable: *she dresses with style.* **6** the state of being fashionable: *gone out of style.* **7** a pointed tool used for engraving. **8** *Bot.* in a flower, the often elongated part of the carpel that connects the stigma to the ovary. — *verb* **1** to design, shape, or groom in a particular way. **2** to name or designate: *a self-styled expert.* [from Latin *stilus*, writing tool, literary style]

⊟ *noun* **1** technique, approach, method, manner, mode, fashion, way. **2** wording, phrasing, expression, tone, touch. **3** appearance, design, pattern, shape, form, cut. **4** sort, type, kind, genre, variety, make, brand. **5** elegance, smartness, chic, flair, panache, stylishness, taste, polish, refinement, sophistication, urbanity, affluence, luxury, grandeur. **6** fashion, vogue, trend, mode. *verb* **1** design, cut, tailor, fashion, shape, groom, adapt. **2** designate, term, name, call, address, title, dub, label.
⊟ *noun* **5** inelegance, tastelessness.

stylish *adj.* elegant; fashionable.

⊟ smart, elegant, chic, fashionable, modish, in vogue, *colloq.* trendy, *colloq.* natty, *colloq.* snazzy, *colloq.* classy, polished, refined, sophisticated, urbane.
⊟ old-fashioned, shabby.

stylishly *adv.* in a stylish way.
stylist *noun* **1** a trained hairdresser. **2** a writer, artist, etc who pays a lot of attention to style.
stylistic *adj.* relating to artistic or literary style.
stylistically *adv.* in a stylistic way; as regards style.
stylistics *sing. noun Linguistics* the systematic study of style, ranging from features of language which can be identified with an individual (eg Shakespeare's style, Joyce's style), to those which identify major occupation groups (eg legal style, journalistic style), and those characteristic of speakers and writers in particular situations (eg parliamentary style).
stylize or **stylise** *verb* to give a distinctive or elaborate style to, especially creating an impression of unnaturalness.
stylized or **stylised** *adj.* conventionalized, not naturalistic.
stylobate / 'staɪləbeɪt/ *noun Archit.* a continuous platform of masonry supporting a row of columns. Greek Doric columns had no pedestal and were built on a stepped stylobate. [from Greek *stylobates*, from *stylos* a column + *bates*, from *bainein*, to walk, tread]
stylometry / staɪ'lɒmətrɪ/ or **stylometrics** *sing. noun* a method of studying literary style by means of a statistical analysis of a text. Such studies have an important function in plotting historical changes in style, and in investigating questions of disputed authorship. [from Greek *stylos*, style + *metron*, a measure]
stylus *noun* (PL. **styluses, styli**) **1** the needle-like part on the end of the arm of a record-player, that picks up the sound from the record's grooves. **2** the cutting tool used to produce the grooves in a record. [related to STYLE]
stymie / 'staɪmɪ/ — *verb* (**stymies, stymied, stymieing** or **stymying**) to prevent, thwart, or frustrate. — *noun* (PL. **stymies**) **1** *Golf* a situation in which an opponent's ball blocks the path between one's own ball and the hole, possible before the introduction of markers. **2** any tricky situation.
styptic / 'stɪptɪk/ *Medicine* — *noun* any substance that is used to stop or prevent bleeding, either by causing the blood vessels to contract, or by accelerating the clotting of the blood. It is used to treat minor cuts, as well as bleeding disorders such as haemophilia. — *adj.*, *said of a substance* having an astringent action. [from Greek *styptikos*, contracting]
SU *abbrev.* Scripture Union.
suave / swaːv/ *adj.* **1** polite and charming, especially insincerely so. **2** *loosely* smart and fashionable. [from Latin *suavis*, sweet]

⊟ **1** polite, courteous, charming, agreeable, affable, smooth, unctuous, sophisticated, urbane, worldly.
⊟ **1** rude, unsophisticated.

suavely *adv.* with a suave manner.
suavity / 'swaːvɪtɪ/ *noun* being suave; suave behaviour.
sub *colloq.* — *noun* **1** a submarine. **2** a substitute player. **3** (*also* **subs**) a subscription fee. **4** a small loan or an advance payment of wages, to help one subsist. **5** a subeditor. — *verb* (**subbed, subbing**) **1** *intrans.* to act as a substitute. **2** *trans., intrans.* to subedit or work as a subeditor.
sub- *prefix* forming words meaning: **1** under or below: *submarine.* **2** secondary; lower in rank or importance: *sublieutenant.* **3** imperfectly; less than: *subhuman.* **4** a part or division of: *subcommittee.* [from Latin *sub*, under, near]
subaltern / 'sʌbəltən/ *noun* any army officer below the rank of captain. [from Latin *subalternus*, from *sub*, under + *alter*, another]
subaqua *adj.* of, for, or for use in underwater activities. [from SUB- + Latin *aqua*, water]
subatomic *adj.* **1** smaller than an atom. **2** existing or occurring within an atom.
subatomic particle *Physics* a general term for any particle that is smaller than an atom, eg electron, neutron, proton, neutrino, quark, meson. All subatomic particles are

either bosons (force particles) or fermions (matter particles).

subconscious — *noun* **1** the mental processes of which a person is not consciously aware. **2** *Psychol.* in psychoanalysis, the part of the mind that contains all the memories, associations, and feelings that can readily be brought back to conscious awareness after having been repressed. — *adj.* denoting mental processes of which a person is not consciously aware.

∙∙∙∙∙∙∙∙∙∙∙∙∙∙∙∙∙∙∙∙∙∙∙∙∙

🔳 *adj.* subliminal, unconscious, intuitive, inner, innermost, hidden, latent, repressed, suppressed.

🔳 *adj.* conscious.

∙∙

subconsciously *adv.* in a subconscious way; in the subconscious.

subcontinent *noun* a large part of a continent that is distinctive in some way, eg by its shape or culture.

subcontract — *noun* a secondary contract, by which the hired person or company hires another to carry out the work. — *verb* to employ (a worker), or pass on (work), under the terms of a subcontract.

subcontractor *noun* a person or company employed under the terms of a subcontract.

subculture *noun* the customs, tastes, and activities of a particular group within society.

subcutaneous /sʌbkjʊˈteɪnɪəs/ *adj. Medicine* under the skin. [from Latin *sub*, under + *cutis*, skin]

subdirectory *noun Comput.* a directory of files that is contained within another, parent directory.

subdivide *verb* to divide (a part) into even smaller parts.

subdivision *noun* **1** a second or further division. **2** a section produced by subdividing.

subdue *verb* to overpower and bring under control; to suppress or conquer (feelings or an enemy). [from Latin *subducere*, to remove]

∙∙∙∙∙∙∙∙∙∙∙∙∙∙∙∙∙∙∙∙∙∙∙∙∙

🔳 overcome, quell, suppress, repress, overpower, crush, defeat, conquer, vanquish, subject, subjugate, humble, break, tame, master, discipline, control, check, moderate, reduce.

🔳 arouse, awaken.

∙∙

subdued *adj.* **1** *said of lighting, etc* soft, or made softer; toned down. **2** *said of a person* uncharacteristically quiet or in low spirits.

∙∙∙∙∙∙∙∙∙∙∙∙∙∙∙∙∙∙∙∙∙∙∙∙∙

🔳 **1** soft, dim, shaded, muted, hushed, sober, restrained, unobtrusive, low-key, subtle. **2** quiet, serious, grave, solemn, sad, downcast, dejected, crestfallen.

🔳 **1** bright, loud. **2** lively, excited.

∙∙

subedit *verb trans., intrans.* (**subedited**, **subediting**) to act as a subeditor of (a text, newspaper, etc).

subeditor *noun* **1** a person who selects and prepares material to be printed, eg in a newspaper or magazine, for the ultimate approval of an editor. **2** a person who assists with various editing tasks.

subfusc /ˈsʌbfʌsk/ — *adj.* dusky; sombre. — *noun* dark formal clothes worn at some universities. [from Latin *subfuscus*, dark brown]

subito /ˈsuːbɪtoʊ/ *adv. Mus.* suddenly, immediately, as in *piano subito*, suddenly soft. [from Italian *subito*]

subject — *noun* (with stress on *sub-*) **1** a matter or topic under discussion or consideration. **2** an area of learning that forms a course of study. **3** a person or thing represented by an artist or writer. **4** a person on whom an experiment or operation is performed. **5** a person under the ultimate rule of a monarch or government; a citizen. **6** *Grammar* a word or phrase referring to the person or thing that performs the action of an active verb or receives the action of a passive verb. *The doctor* is the subject in *the doctor saw us,* and *we* is the subject in *we were seen by the doctor.* — *adj.* (with stress on *sub-*) (*often* **subject to**

something or someone) **1** showing a tendency; prone. **2** exposed; open. **3** governed; dependent. **4** ruled by a monarch or government. — *adv.* (**subject to something**) conditionally upon it: *you may go, subject to your parent's permission.* — *verb* (with stress on *-ject*) (*often* **subject someone to something** or **someone**) **1** to cause them to undergo or experience something unwelcome. **2** to make one person subordinate to or under the control of another. [from Latin *subjectus*, thrown under]

∙∙∙∙∙∙∙∙∙∙∙∙∙∙∙∙∙∙∙∙∙∙∙∙∙

🔳 *noun* **1** topic, theme, matter, issue, question, point, case, affair, business. **2** discipline, field. **4** participant, client, patient, victim. **5** citizen, national. *adj.* **1** liable, likely, disposed, inclined, prone. **2** open, exposed, vulnerable, susceptible. **3** dependent, contingent, conditional, governed, bound. **4** ruled, subjugated, subordinate, inferior, answerable, obedient. *verb* **1** submit, expose, lay open. **2** subjugate, subdue.

🔳 *noun* **5** monarch, ruler, master. *adj.* **2** invulnerable. **3** unconditional.

∙∙

subjection *noun* subjecting or being subjected.

∙∙∙∙∙∙∙∙∙∙∙∙∙∙∙∙∙∙∙∙∙∙∙∙∙

🔳 subjugation, defeat, captivity, bondage, slavery, enslavement, oppression, domination, mastery.

∙∙

subjective *adj.* **1** based on personal thoughts and feelings; not impartial or objective. See also OBJECTIVE. **2** *Grammar* indicating or referring to the subject of a verb; nominative.

∙∙∙∙∙∙∙∙∙∙∙∙∙∙∙∙∙∙∙∙∙∙∙∙∙

🔳 **1** personal, individual, idiosyncratic, emotional, intuitive, instinctive, partial, biased, prejudiced.

🔳 **1** objective, impartial, unbiased.

∙∙

subjectively *adv.* in a subjective way.

sub judice /sʌb ˈdʒuːdɪsɪ/ under consideration by a court, and therefore not to be publicly discussed or remarked on. [Latin, = under a judge]

subjugate *verb* to bring under one's control; to make obedient or submissive. [from Latin *sub*, under + *jugum*, yoke]

subjugation *noun* subjugating or being subjugated.

subjunctive *Grammar* — *noun* **1** a set of verb forms, or mood, used to express condition, wish or uncertainty, eg 'If I *were* you' and 'I suggest he *leave* now'. **2** a verb form of this kind. — *adj.* in or of the subjunctive. [from Latin *subjungere*, to join to]

sublet *verb* (**subletting**; PAST AND PAST PARTICIPLE **sublet**) to rent out to another person (property one is renting from someone else).

sublimate — *noun Chem.* the solid product formed during the process of sublimation. — *verb* **1** *Chem.* to carry out the process of sublimation. **2** *Psychol.* to channel an undesirable impulse towards the attainment of a more morally or socially acceptable goal. [from Latin *sublimare*, to elevate or exalt]

sublimation *noun* **1** *Chem.* the conversion of a solid, eg iodine or dry ice (solid carbon dioxide), directly into a gas or vapour without the intermediate formation of a liquid; the reverse process, in which the vapour condenses to form a solid or *sublimate*. **2** *Psychol.* the channelling of an undesirable impulse towards the attainment of a more morally or socially acceptable goal.

sublime — *adj.* **1** of the highest or noblest nature, usually morally or spiritually. **2** overwhelmingly great; supreme. — *verb trans., intrans., Chem.* to change from a solid to a vapour without passing through the liquid state. — **from the sublime to the ridiculous** passing in consideration from something serious or elevated to something silly or trivial. [from Latin *sublimis*, in a high position]

∙∙∙∙∙∙∙∙∙∙∙∙∙∙∙∙∙∙∙∙∙∙∙∙∙

🔳 *adj.* GREAT. **1** exalted, elevated, high, lofty, noble. **2** grand, imposing, magnificent, glorious, supreme, transcendent.

🔳 *adj.* **1** base. **2** lowly.

∙∙

sublimely *adv.* to a sublime degree.

subliminal *adj.* existing or occurring below the threshold of ordinary awareness. [from Latin *sub*, under + *limen*, threshold]

subliminal advertising advertising in the form of pictures shown during a film or television programme for a split second only, so that the viewer's subconscious mind registers them without the viewer knowing.

subliminally *adv.* in a subliminal way.

sublimity *noun* **1** being sublime. **2** something that is sublime.

sub-machine gun a lightweight portable machine-gun fired from the shoulder or hip.

submarine — *noun* a vessel, especially military, able to travel beneath the surface of the sea. — *adj.* under the surface of the sea.

submariner *noun* a person who goes to sea in a submarine.

submerge *verb* **1** to immerse in water or other liquid. **2** *intrans.* to sink under the surface of water or other liquid. **3** to overwhelm or inundate, eg with work. [from Latin *sub*, under + *mergere*, to plunge]

⊟ **1** submerse, immerse, plunge, duck, dip, drown. **2** sink, go down, plunge, dive, duck. **3** overwhelm, swamp, flood, inundate, deluge.
⊟ **2** surface.

submerged *adj.* under the surface of water, especially in the sea or in a lake or river: *a submerged rock.*

⊟ underwater, sunk, sunken, hidden, concealed, unseen.

submersible — *adj.*, *said of a vessel* able to operate under water. — *noun* a submersible vessel; a submarine.

submersion *noun* submersing or being submersed.

submission *noun* **1** an act of submitting. **2** a thing submitted, eg for consideration or approval. **3** submissiveness.

⊟ **1** surrender, capitulation, resignation, acquiescence, assent, compliance, obedience, deference. **2** presentation, offering, contribution, entry, suggestion, proposal. **3** submissiveness, meekness, docility, passivity, deference, subservience.
⊟ **3** intransigence, intractability.

submissive *adj.* willing or tending to submit; meek; obedient.

⊟ yielding, unresisting, resigned, patient, uncomplaining, accommodating, biddable, obedient, deferential, ingratiating, subservient, humble, meek, docile, subdued, passive.
⊟ intransigent, intractable.

submissively *adv.* in a submissive way.

submissiveness *noun* being submissive.

submit *verb* (**submitted, submitting**) **1** *intrans.* (*also* **submit to someone**) to give in, especially to the wishes or control of another person; to stop resisting them. **2** *trans., intrans.* to offer (oneself) as a subject of experiment or other treatment. **3** to offer or present (eg a proposal) for formal consideration by others. [from Latin *sub*, beneath + *mittere*, to send]

⊟ **1** yield, give in, surrender, capitulate, knuckle under, bow, bend, succumb, agree, comply. **3** present, tender, offer, put forward, suggest, propose, table, state, claim, argue.
⊟ **1** resist. **3** withdraw.

subnormal *adj.* less than normal, especially with regard to intelligence.

subordinate /sə'bɔːdɪnət, sə'bɔːdɪneɪt/ — *adj.* (pronounced -nat) (*often* **subordinate to someone**) lower in rank or importance than them; secondary. — *noun* (pronounced -nat) a subordinate person or thing. — *verb* (pronounced -nate) (*often* **subordinate one person** or **thing to another**) to regard or treat as them as subordinate. [from Latin *sub*, below + *ordo*, rank]

⊟ *adj.* secondary, auxiliary, ancillary, subsidiary, dependent, inferior, lower, junior, minor, lesser. *noun* inferior, junior, assistant, attendant, second, aide, dependant, *colloq.* underling.
⊟ *adj.* superior, senior. *noun* superior, boss.

subordinate clause *Grammar* a clause that acts like a noun, adjective, or adverb and is not able to function as an independent sentence, as in 'the book *that you gave me for Christmas* was fascinating'.

subordination *noun* subordinating or being subordinated.

suborn /sə'bɔːn/ *verb* to persuade (someone) to commit a crime or other wrong, eg with a bribe. [from Latin *sub*, secretly + *ornare*, to equip]

subplot *noun* a subsidiary plot coinciding with the main action in a play or story.

subpoena /sə'piːnə, səb'piːnə/ — *noun* a written order legally obliging a person to appear in a court of law at a specified time; a summons. — *verb* (**subpoenaed** or **subpoena'd**) to serve with a subpoena. [from Latin *subpoena*, under penalty]

subroutine /'sʌbruːtiːn/ *noun Comput.* a self-contained part of a computer program which performs a specific task and which can be called up at any time during the running of the main program.

subscribe *verb* **1** *trans., intrans.* to contribute or undertake to contribute (a sum of money), especially on a regular basis. **2** (*usually* **subscribe to something**) to undertake to receive regular issues of a magazine, etc in return for payment. **3** (**subscribe to something**) to agree with or believe in a theory, idea, etc. **4** to write one's name at the bottom of (a document, picture, etc). [from Latin *sub*, at the bottom + *scribere*, to write]

⊟ **1** contribute, give. **3** agree with, support, endorse, back, advocate, believe in.

subscriber *noun* **1** a person who subscribes. **2** the user of a telephone line.

subscriber trunk dialling a telephone system in which customers make long-distance calls direct, without the help of an operator.

subscript *adj. Printing, said of a character* set below the level of the line, as the number 2 in H_2O. — *noun* a subscript character. [related to SUBSCRIBE]

subscription *noun* **1** a payment made in subscribing. **2** an advance order, especially of a book before its official publication. **3** the act of subscribing. [related to SUBSCRIBE]

⊟ **1** membership fee, dues, payment, donation, contribution, offering.

subsequent *adj.* (*also* **subsequent to something**) happening after or following it. [from Latin *sub*, after + *sequi*, to follow]

⊟ following, later, future, next, succeeding, consequent, resulting, ensuing.
⊟ previous, earlier.

subsequently *adv.* later; thereafter.

subservience *noun* a subservient state.

subservient *adj.* **1** ready or eager to submit to the wishes of others, often excessively so. **2** subordinate. [from Latin *sub*, under + *servire*, to serve]

· · · · · · · · · · · · · · · · · · · ·

■ **1** servile, deferential, fawning, ingratiating. **2** subordinate, secondary, ancillary.

· · · · · · · · · · · · · · · · · · · ·

subset *noun* **1** *Maths.* a set that forms part of a larger set. A set X is said to be a subset of a set Y if all members of set X are included in set Y. **2** *Biol.* a term used in immunology for a functionally or structurally different population of cells within a single cell type.

subside *verb intrans.* **1** *said of land, buildings, etc* to sink to a lower level; to settle. **2** *said of noise, feelings, etc* to become less loud or intense; to die down. [from Latin *sub*, down + *sidere*, to settle]

· · · · · · · · · · · · · · · · · · · ·

■ **1** sink, collapse, settle, descend, fall, drop. **2** decrease, lessen, diminish, wane, moderate, abate, die down, quieten, ease.

✦ **2** rise, increase.

· · · · · · · · · · · · · · · · · · · ·

subsidence /səbˈsaɪdəns/ *noun* subsiding, settling, sinking.

subsidiarity *noun* the concept of a central governing body permitting its member states, branches, etc to take decisions on issues thought to be best dealt with at a local level.

subsidiary — *adj.* **1** of secondary importance; subordinate. **2** serving as an addition or supplement; auxiliary. — *noun* (PL. **subsidiaries**) **1** a subsidiary person or thing. **2** a company controlled by another, usually larger, company or organization. [related to SUBSIDE]

· · · · · · · · · · · · · · · · · · · ·

■ *adj.* **1** secondary, subordinate, lesser, minor. **2** auxiliary, supplementary, additional, ancillary, assistant, supporting, contributory. *noun* **2** branch, offshoot, division, section, part.

✦ *adj.* **1** primary, chief, major.

· · · · · · · · · · · · · · · · · · · ·

subsidize or **subsidise** *verb* **1** to provide or support with a subsidy. **2** to pay a proportion of the cost of (a thing supplied) in order to reduce the price paid by the customer. **3** *loosely* to pay the expenses of. [related to SUBSIDE]

· · · · · · · · · · · · · · · · · · · ·

■ **1** support, back, underwrite, sponsor, finance, fund, aid.

· · · · · · · · · · · · · · · · · · · ·

subsidy *noun* (PL. **subsidies**) **1** a sum of money given, eg by a government to an industry, to help with running costs or to keep product prices low. **2** financial aid of this kind. [related to SUBSIDE]

· · · · · · · · · · · · · · · · · · · ·

■ **1** grant, allowance, contribution. **2** assistance, help, aid, sponsorship, finance, support, backing.

· · · · · · · · · · · · · · · · · · · ·

subsist *verb intrans.* **1** (**subsist on something**) to live or manage to stay alive by means of it. **2** *formal* (**subsist in something**) to be based on it; to consist of it: *the team's success subsists in their fitness.* [from Latin *subsistere*, to stand still or firm]

subsistence *noun* **1** the means of existence; livelihood. **2** *attributive said of wages, etc* just enough to provide basic necessities.

· · · · · · · · · · · · · · · · · · · ·

■ **1** living, survival, existence, livelihood, maintenance, support, keep, sustenance, nourishment, food, provisions, rations.

· · · · · · · · · · · · · · · · · · · ·

subsistence farming farming in which almost all the produce is used to feed and support the farmer's family, with no surplus left to sell.

subsoil *noun Geol.* the layer of soil that lies beneath the topsoil (the layer that is normally used for cultivation). It contains chemical compounds that have leached from the topsoil, but very little organic matter.

subsonic *adj.* relating to, being, or travelling at speeds below the speed of sound.

subspecies *noun Biol.* a taxonomic subdivision of a species, with some morphological differences from the other subspecies and often with a different geographical distribution or ecology.

substance *noun* **1** the matter or material that a thing is made of. **2** a particular kind of matter with a definable quality: *a sticky substance.* **3** the essence or basic meaning of something spoken or written. **4** touchable reality; tangibility: *ghosts have no substance.* **5** solid quality or worth: *food with no substance.* **6** foundation; truth: *no substance in the rumours.* **7** wealth and influence: *woman of substance.* [from Latin *substantia*]

· · · · · · · · · · · · · · · · · · · ·

■ **1** matter, material, stuff, fabric. **3** essence, pith, gist, meaning, significance, force. **4** tangibility, concreteness, reality, actuality. **5** body, solidity. **6** foundation, ground, basis, truth.

· · · · · · · · · · · · · · · · · · · ·

substandard *adj.* below the required or acceptable standard; inferior.

· · · · · · · · · · · · · · · · · · · ·

■ inferior, second-rate, imperfect, damaged, shoddy, unacceptable, inadequate, poor.

✦ superior, first-rate, perfect.

· · · · · · · · · · · · · · · · · · · ·

substantial *adj.* **1** considerable in amount, extent or importance. **2** of real value or worth. **3** *said of food* nourishing. **4** solidly built. **5** existing as a touchable thing; material; corporeal. **6** relating to a thing's basic nature or essence; essential. **7** wealthy and influential; well-to-do. [see SUBSTANCE]

· · · · · · · · · · · · · · · · · · · ·

■ **1** large, big, sizeable, ample, generous, great, considerable, significant, important. **2** worthwhile, valuable. **4** well-built, stout, sturdy, strong, tough, durable, sound. **5** tangible, material, corporeal, real, actual.

✦ **1** small. **2** insignificant. **4** flimsy.

· · · · · · · · · · · · · · · · · · · ·

substantially *adv.* in a substantial way; to a substantial degree.

substantiate *verb* to prove or support; to confirm the truth or validity of. [see SUBSTANCE]

· · · · · · · · · · · · · · · · · · · ·

■ prove, verify, confirm, support, corroborate, authenticate, validate.

✦ disprove, refute.

· · · · · · · · · · · · · · · · · · · ·

substantiation *noun* **1** proof, validation. **2** being proved or validated.

substantive /səbˈstæntɪv/ — *adj.* **1** of significant importance or value. **2** relating to the essential nature of something. — *noun Grammar* a noun. [from Latin *substantivus*]

substantively *adv.* in a substantive way.

substitute — *noun* a person or thing that takes the place of, or is used instead of, another. — *verb* **1** (**substitute something** or **substitute one thing for another**) to use or bring into use as a substitute. **2** (**substitute for someone** or **something**) to act as a substitute. — *adj.* acting as a substitute. [from Latin *sub*, under + *statuere*, to set]

· · · · · · · · · · · · · · · · · · · ·

■ *noun* reserve, stand-by, *colloq.* temp, supply, locum, understudy, stand-in, replacement, relief, surrogate, proxy, agent, deputy, makeshift, stopgap. *verb* **1** change, exchange, swap, switch, interchange. **2** stand in for, *colloq.* fill in for, deputize for, understudy, relieve, replace. *adj.* reserve, temporary, acting, surrogate, proxy, replacement, alternative.

· · · · · · · · · · · · · · · · · · · ·

substitution *noun* **1** the process of substituting or being substituted. **2** something that is substituted.

substrate *noun* **1** *Biol.* the material or medium on which a living organism (eg a plant or bacterium) grows, or to which it is attached. It may provide nutrients (eg agar, used for growing bacterial cultures), or it may merely provide support (eg soil). **2** *Electron.* a piece of ceramic, semiconductor material, plastic, glass, etc, on which an integrated circuit is fabricated, and which provides mechanical support or insulation. **3** *Biochem.* the substance on which an enzyme acts during a biochemical reaction. **4** any surface to which a substance such as a paint, dye, or laminate adheres. [from Latin *substernere, -strātum*, to spread beneath]

substratum /ˈsʌbˈstrɑːtəm/ *noun* (PL. **substrata**) *technical* **1** an underlying layer. **2** a foundation or foundation material.

subsume *verb* **1** to take into, or regard as part of, a larger, more general group or category. **2** *loosely* to take over. [from Latin *sub*, under + *sumere*, to take]

subsumption *noun* subsuming or being subsumed.

subtend *verb, said of a line or a side of a geometric figure* to be opposite to (an arc or an angle). [from Latin *sub*, under + *tendere*, to stretch]

subterfuge *noun* a trick or deception that evades, conceals, or obscures; also, trickery in general: *a clever subterfuge/resorted to subterfuge.* [from Latin *subter*, secretly + *fugere*, to flee]

- trick, stratagem, scheme, ploy, ruse, dodge, manoeuvre, deception, pretence, artifice, trickery, deviousness, evasion.
- openness, honesty.

subterranean *adj.* existing or operating underground, or in secret. [from Latin *sub*, under + *terra*, earth]

subtext *noun* **1** an unstated message conveyed through the form of a play, film, book, or picture. The subject may be implied by the use of pauses or silence, or by the shape of the plot or the patterns of imagery used. **2** more loosely, anything implied but not stated in ordinary speech or writing, especially in extended conversation.

subtitle *noun* **1** (*usually* **subtitles**) a printed translation of the dialogue of a foreign film, appearing bit by bit at the bottom of the screen. **2** a second title, usually expanding on or explaining the main title.

subtle /ˈsʌtl/ *adj.* **1** not straightforwardly or obviously stated or displayed. **2** *said of distinctions, etc* difficult to appreciate or perceive. **3** *said of flavours, etc* extremely faint or delicate. **4** carefully or craftily discreet or indirect. [from Latin *sub*, under + *tela*, web]

- **1** understated, implied, indirect. **2** fine, nice, refined, sophisticated, deep, profound. **3** faint, delicate, mild. **4** discreet, tactful, shrewd, astute, artful, cunning, crafty, sly, devious.
- **1** blatant, obvious. **4** indiscreet, tactless, direct, open.

subtlety /ˈsʌtltɪ/ *noun* (PL. **subtleties**) **1** being subtle; subtle behaviour. **2** a subtle point or argument.

subtly /ˈsʌtlɪ/ *adv.* in a subtle way.

subtract *verb* to take (one number or quantity) from another; to deduct. [from Latin *sub*, away + *trahere*, to draw]

- deduct, take away, remove, withdraw, debit.
- add.

subtraction *noun* the process of subtracting.

subtropical *adj.* relating to or typical of the areas of the world that lie between the tropics and the temperate zone, and that have a near-tropical climate or experience tropical conditions for part of the year.

suburb *noun* (*often* **suburbs**) a district, especially residential, on the edge of a town or city. [from Latin *sub*, near + *urbs*, city]

- suburbia, commuter belt, residential area, outskirts.
- centre, heart.

suburban *adj.* **1** of or in a suburb. **2** narrow in outlook; narrowly genteel or middle-class.

suburbia *noun often derog.* suburbs and their inhabitants and way of life regarded collectively.

subvention *noun* a grant or subsidy. [from Latin *subvenire*, to come to help]

subversion *noun* the act or practice of subverting (usually a government).

subversive — *adj.* likely or tending to subvert or undermine government or authority. — *noun* a subversive person.

- *adj.* seditious, treasonous, treacherous, traitorous, inflammatory, incendiary, disruptive, rabble-rousing. *noun* seditionist, terrorist, freedom fighter, dissident, traitor, quisling, fifth columnist, agitator, rabble-rouser.
- *adj.* loyal.

subvert *verb* **1** to undermine or overthrow (a government or other legally established body). **2** to corrupt (a person); to undermine (a principle, etc). [from Latin *subvertere*, to overturn]

subway *noun* **1** a passage for pedestrians under a road or railway. **2** an underground passage for pipes and cables. **3** *North Amer., esp. US* an underground railway.

succeed *verb, usually intrans.* **1** to achieve an aim or purpose. **2** to develop or turn out as planned. **3** to do well in a particular area or field. **4** *trans.* to come next after; to follow. **5** (*also* **succeed to something**) to take up a position, etc, following on from someone else. [from Latin *succedere*, to go next after]

- **1**, triumph, win. **3** thrive, flourish, prosper, make good, get on, make it. **4** follow, replace.
- **1, 3** fail. **4** precede.

succeeding *adj.* that follows or comes next.

- following, next, subsequent, ensuing, coming, to come, later, successive.
- previous, earlier.

success *noun* **1** the quality of succeeding or the state of having succeeded; a favourable development or outcome. **2** the attainment of fame, power, or wealth. **3** a person who has attained any such quality, or who is judged favourably by others. **4** a thing that turns out as planned, or that is judged favourably by others.

- **1** triumph, victory. **2** luck, fortune, prosperity, fame, power. **3** celebrity, star, somebody, winner. **4** hit, sensation, bestseller.
- FAILURE.

successful *adj.* **1** resulting in success. **2** achieving the required outcome. **3** prosperous, flourishing.

- **1** victorious, winning, lucky, fortunate, money-making, lucrative, profitable, rewarding. **2** fruitful, productive. **3** prosperous, wealthy, thriving, flourishing, booming, famous, well-known, popular, leading, top, bestselling.
- **2** unsuccessful, fruitless. **3** unknown.

successfully *adv.* in a successful way; with success.

succession *noun* **1** a series of people or things coming one after the other. **2** the right or order by which one person or thing succeeds another. **3** the sequential development of plant communities on a site, especially a lake in which silting occurs. — **in succession** one after the other.

- **1** sequence, series, order, progression, run, string, chain, cycle, flow, line, train, procession.

successive *adj.* immediately following another or each other.
. . . .
▣ consecutive, sequential, following, succeeding.
. . . .

successively *adv.* in a successive way; with one following another.

successor *noun* a person who follows another, especially who takes over the job or position of another.

succinct /sək'sɪŋkt/ *adj.*, *said of something written or said* brief and precise; concise. [from Latin *succinctus*]
. . . .
▣ short, brief, terse, pithy, concise, compact, condensed, summary.
▣ long, lengthy, wordy, verbose.
. . . .

succinctly *adv.* in a succinct way.

succinctness *noun* a succinct quality.

Succoth same as SUKKOTH.

succour /'sʌkə(r)/ *formal* — *noun* help or relief in time of distress or need. — *verb* to give succour to. [from Latin *succurrere*, to run to help]

succubus /'sʌkjʊbəs/ *noun* (PL. **succubi**) a female evil spirit which is supposed to have sexual intercourse with sleeping men. See also INCUBUS. [from Latin *succuba*, prostitute]

succulence *noun* a succulent quality.

succulent — *noun* a plant which has fleshy stems and leaves adapted for storing water. Succulents are common in arid regions and also in places where water is present but not readily available because the soil contains high levels of salts, eg saltmarshes. Such plants often have thick waxy cuticles, or reduced or inrolled leaves, eg cacti, *Sedum* species (stonecrops). — *adj.* **1** relating to such a plant. **2** *said of food* tender and juicy. [from Latin *sucus*, juice]
. . . .
▣ *adj.* **2** tender, fleshy, juicy, moist, luscious, mouthwatering, delicious, lush, rich.
▣ *adj.* **2** tough, dry.
. . . .

succumb /sə'kʌm/ *verb intrans.* (**often succumb to someone** or **something**) **1** to give in to pressure, temptation, or desire. **2** to die of something (especially a disease). [from Latin *sub*, under + *cumbere*, to lie down]
. . . .
▣ **1** give way, yield, give in, submit, knuckle under, surrender, capitulate.
▣ **1** overcome, master.
. . . .

such — *adj.* **1** of that kind, or the same or a similar kind: *you cannot reason with such a person.* **2** so great: *not such a fool as to believe that.* — *adv.* extremely: *such a lovely present.* — *pron.* a person or thing, or people or things, like that or those just mentioned: *chimps, gorillas, and such.* — **as such 1** in or by itself alone. **2** as it is described. **such as ...** for example ... [from Anglo-Saxon *swilc*]

such-and-such — *adj.* of a particular but unspecified kind. — *pron.* a person or thing of this kind.

suchlike — *adj.* of the same kind. — *pron.* things of the same kind.

suck — *verb* **1** *trans.*, *intrans.* (*also* **suck something in** or **up**) to draw (liquid) into the mouth. **2** to draw liquid from (eg a juicy fruit) with the mouth. **3** (*also* **suck something in** or **up**) to draw it in by suction. **4** to rub (eg one's thumb or a pencil) with the tongue and inside of the mouth, with an action similar to sucking in liquids. **5** to draw the flavour from (eg a sweet) with squeezing and rolling movements inside the mouth. **6** to draw milk from (a breast or udder) with the mouth. **7** *intrans.*, *North Amer. slang* to be contemptible or contemptibly bad. — *noun* an act or bout of sucking. — **suck up to someone** *colloq.* to flatter them or be obsequious to them, in order to gain favour. [from Anglo-Saxon *sucan*]

. . . .
▣ *verb* **3** draw in, imbibe, absorb, soak up.

sucker *noun* **1** in certain animals, an organ that is adapted to adhere to surfaces by suction, in order to assist feeding, locomotion, etc. **2** a similar man-made device designed to adhere to a surface by creating a vacuum. **3** a shoot arising from an underground stem or root that grows underground and then emerges to form a new plant capable of independent existence. **4** *colloq.* a person easily deceived or taken advantage of. **5** *colloq.* a person who is gullible or vulnerable in some way: *a sucker for lending money.*

suckle *verb* **1** to feed (a baby) with milk from one's breast or udder. **2** *trans.*, *intrans.* to suck milk from (a breast or udder). [related to SUCK]

suckling *noun* a young baby or animal still suckling its mother's breast.

sucrose /'suːkrəʊs/ *noun*, *Chem.* (FORMULA $C_{12}H_{22}O_{11}$) a white soluble crystalline sugar consisting of a molecule of glucose linked to a molecule of fructose. It occurs in most plants, and is extracted from sugar cane and sugar beet for use as a sweetener in food and drinks. Also called CANE SUGAR. [from French *sucre*, sugar]

suction *noun* **1** the act or power of sucking. **2** a drawing or adhering force created by a difference or reduction in air pressure. [from Latin *sugere*, to suck]

sudden *adj.* happening quickly or unexpectedly. — **all of a sudden** suddenly. [from Old French *soudain*]
. . . .
▣ unexpected, unforeseen, surprising, startling, abrupt, sharp, quick, swift, prompt, hasty, impetuous, impulsive, *colloq.* snap.
▣ expected, predictable, gradual, slow.
. . . .

sudden death *Sport* a method of deciding a tied contest by declaring the winner to be the player or team that scores first in an extra period.

sudden infant death syndrome (ABBREV. SIDS) *Medicine* the sudden unexpected death of an apparently healthy baby, often at night, for which no adequate cause can be found on clinical or post-mortem examination. See also COT DEATH.

suddenly *adv.* unexpectedly and without warning.

suddenness *noun* being sudden.

sudorific /sjuːdə'rɪfɪk/ *Medicine* — *adj.*, *said of a drug* causing sweating. — *noun* a sudorific drug. [from Latin *sudor*, sweat + *facere*, to make]

suds *pl. noun* a mass of bubbles produced on water when soap or other detergent is dissolved. [perhaps from Old Dutch *sudse*, marsh]

sue /suː, sjuː/ *verb trans.*, *intrans.* to take legal proceedings against (a person or company). [from Old French *suir*, from Latin *sequi*, to follow]

suede /sweɪd/ *noun* soft leather given a velvet-like finish. [from French *gants de Suède*, gloves from Sweden]

suet /'suːɪt, 'sjuːɪt/ *noun* hard fat from around the kidneys of sheep or cattle, used to make pastry and puddings. [from Latin *sebum*, fat]

Suff. *abbrev.* Suffolk.

suffer *verb* (**suffered**, **suffering**) **1** *intrans.* to undergo or endure physical or mental pain or other unpleasantness. **2** to undergo (pain, etc). **3** (**suffer from something**) to be afflicted with an illness. **4** *intrans.* to deteriorate (as a result of something). **5** to tolerate: *not suffer fools gladly.* *old use* to allow: *suffer little children to come unto me.* [from Latin *sub*, under + *ferre*, to bear]
. . . .
▣ **1** hurt, ache, agonize, grieve, sorrow. **2** undergo, go through, experience, feel, endure, sustain. **5** tolerate, endure, bear, support.
. . . .

sufferance *noun* — **on sufferance** tolerated, but not welcomed or encouraged.

sufferer *noun* a person who suffers.
suffering *noun* pain or distress.

....

▣ pain, discomfort, agony, anguish, affliction, distress, misery, hardship, ordeal, torment, torture.
▣ ease, comfort.

....

suffice /səˈfaɪs/ *verb* **1** *intrans.* to be enough, or be good enough for a particular purpose. **2** *trans.* to satisfy (a person). — **suffice it to say ...** it is enough to say ... [from Latin *sufficere*]
sufficiency *noun* (PL. **sufficiencies**) a sufficient amount.
sufficient *adj.* enough; adequate. [from Latin *sufficere*, to suffice]

....

▣ enough, adequate,
▣ insufficient, inadequate.

....

sufficiently *adv.* in a sufficient way; to a sufficient degree.
suffix — *noun* a word element added to the end of a word or word stem to mark a grammatical inflection or form a derivative, eg the *s* in *monkeys* and the *tude* in *certitude*. — *verb* to add as a suffix. [from Latin *suffixus*, fixed underneath]
suffocate *verb* **1** to cause to die from lack of air, eg with an obstruction over the mouth and nose. **2** *intrans.* to die from lack of air. **3** *intrans.* to experience difficulty in breathing because of heat and lack of air; to stifle. **4** to subject to an oppressive amount of something. [from Latin *suffocare*, from *sub*, under + *fauces*, throat]

....

▣ STIFLE, CHOKE. **1** asphyxiate, smother, strangle, throttle. **2** asphyxiate. **4** smother.

....

suffocating *adj.* that suffocates.
suffocation *noun* suffocating or being suffocated.
suffragan /ˈsʌfrəɡən/ *noun* **1** a bishop appointed as assistant to another bishop. **2** any bishop considered as an archbishop's subordinate. [from Latin *suffraganeus*, assistant]
suffrage *noun* the right to vote in political elections. [from Latin *suffragium*, a vote]
suffragette *noun* any of a group of women who campaigned strenuously for women's suffrage in Britain in the early 20c.
suffuse *verb*, *said of colour, light, etc* to cover or spread throughout. [from Latin *suffundere*, to pour beneath]
suffusion *noun* suffusing or being suffused.
Sufi /ˈsuːfɪ/ *noun* an adherent of Sufism; a Muslim mystic.
Sufism /ˈsuːfɪzm/ *Relig.* an Islamic mystical movement which represents a move away from the legalistic approach in Islam to a more personal relationship with God, and whose adherents aspire to lose themselves in the ultimate reality of the Divinity by constant repetition of the *dhikr* or 'mentioning of God'. [from Arabic *çuf*, probably 'man of wool', from *çuf*, wool (as worn by ascetics)]
sugar — *noun* **1** any of a group of white crystalline carbohydrates that are soluble in water and typically have a sweet taste. Sugars are widely used as sweeteners in confectionery, desserts, soft drinks, etc. **2** common name for sucrose (table sugar), which is obtained from the pith of sugar cane, or from sugar beet. **3** *colloq.* a term of endearment. — *verb* (**sugared, sugaring**) **1** to sweeten with sugar. **2** to sprinkle or coat with sugar. — **sugar the pill** to make something unpleasant easier to deal with or accept. [from Arabic *sukkar*]
sugar beet a variety of beet (*Beta vulgaris*), widely cultivated in Europe and the USA for its large white conical root, which contains up to 20 per cent sucrose (sugar). It is the most important source of sugar in temperate regions.
sugar cane a tall tropical grass (*Saccharum officinarum*) that resembles bamboo but has soft jointed stalks up to 6m

in height. It is native to Asia, but is cultivated in tropical and subtropical regions worldwide as one of the two main sources of sugar (the other is sugar beet). The stalks are cut once a year, crushed, and soaked in water to extract the juice which contains sugar (sucrose or cane sugar). The sugary solution is then concentrated by evaporation, and sucrose gradually crystallizes out, leaving a residue of molasses. The raw sugar is brown, and can be purified further to give white sugar. Cuba and India are the two largest producers of cane sugar.
sugar daddy *colloq.* an elderly man with a young girlfriend on whom he lavishes money and gifts.
sugared *adj.* **1** sugar-coated, candied. **2** containing sugar.
sugariness *noun* a sugary quality.
sugar maple a N American maple tree from whose sap sugar is obtained.
sugar soap a substance for cleaning or stripping paint.
sugary *adj.* **1** like sugar in taste or appearance. **2** containing much or too much sugar. **3** *colloq.* exaggeratedly or insincerely pleasant or affectionate; cloying.
suggest *verb* **1** to put forward as a possibility or recommendation. **2** to make one think of; to create an impression of. **3** to cause one to think or conclude. [from Latin *suggerere*, to put under]

....

▣ **1** propose, put forward, advocate, recommend, advise, counsel. **2** evoke, indicate. **3** imply, insinuate, hint, intimate.

....

suggestible *adj.* easily influenced by suggestions made by others.
suggestion *noun* **1** a thing suggested; a proposal or recommendation. **2** a hint or trace. **3** the creation of a belief or impulse in the mind of a hypnotised person. **4** the act of suggesting.

....

▣ **1** proposal, proposition, motion, recommendation, idea, plan. **2** hint, suspicion, trace, indication. **4** intimation, implication, insinuation, innuendo.

....

suggestive *adj.* **1** (**suggestive of something**) causing one to think of it; creating an impression of it. **2** provoking thoughts or feelings of a sexual nature.

....

▣ **1** evocative, reminiscent, expressive, meaning, indicative. **2** indecent, immodest, improper, indelicate, off-colour, risqué, smutty, provocative.
▣ **1** inexpressive. **2** decent, clean.

....

suggestively *adv.* in a suggestive way.
suicidal *adj.* **1** involving or indicating suicide. **2** that will result in suicide or ruin. **3** *said of a person* inclined or likely to commit suicide.
suicide *noun* **1** the act, or an instance, of killing oneself deliberately. **2** a person who deliberately kills himself or herself. **3** the bringing about of one's own downfall, often unintentionally: *the minister's speech was political suicide*. [from Latin *sui*, of oneself + *caedere*, to kill]
suit — *noun* **1** a set of clothes, usually a jacket with trousers or a skirt, made from the same material and designed to be worn together. **2** an outfit worn on specific occasions or for a specific activity. **3** *facetious* a bureaucratic or administrative official. **4** any of the four groups into which a pack of playing-cards is divided. **5** a legal action taken against someone; a lawsuit. — *verb* **1** *trans., intrans.* to be acceptable to or what is required by. **2** to be appropriate to, in harmony with, or attractive to. — **follow suit 1** to play a card of the same suit as the card first played. **2** to do the same as someone else has done. **suit oneself** to do what one wants to do, especially without considering others. [from Old French *sieute*, from *sivre*, to follow]

....

▣ *noun* **2** outfit, costume, dress, clothing. *verb* **1** satisfy, answer, please, gratify. **2** match, tally with, agree with, harmonize with, fit, befit, become.

∎ *verb* **1** displease. **2** clash.

....

suitability *noun* being suitable.
suitable *adj.* that suits; appropriate or agreeable.

....

∎ appropriate, fitting, convenient, opportune, apt, apposite, relevant, applicable, fit, adequate, satisfactory, acceptable, becoming, seemly, proper, right.
∎ unsuitable, inappropriate.

....

suitably *adv.* in a suitable way.
suitcase *noun* a portable travelling case for clothes, with flat stiffened sides and a handle.
suite /swiːt/ *noun* **1** a set of rooms forming a self-contained unit within a larger building. **2** a matching set of furniture. **3** *Mus.* a set of instrumental movements in related keys. **4** a group of followers or attendants. [from French *suite*]
suitor /ˈsuːtə(r)/ *noun* **1** *old use* a man courting a woman for love or marriage. **2** a person who sues; a plaintiff. [see SUIT]
Sukkoth or **Succoth** /ˈsʊkoʊt, ˈsʊkoʊθ/ a Jewish harvest festival commemorating the period when the Israelites lived in tents in the desert during the Exodus from Egypt. Also called FEAST OF TABERNACLES. [from Hebrew *sukkoth*, huts]
sulk — *verb intrans.* to be silent or unsociable out of petty resentment or bad temper. — *noun* (*also* **the sulks**) a bout of sulking. [perhaps from Anglo-Saxon *aseolcan*, to slack or be slow]

....

∎ *verb* mope, brood, pout.

....

sulkily *adv.* with a sulky manner.
sulkiness *noun* being sulky.
sulky *adj.* (**sulkier, sulkiest**) sulking; inclined to sulk.

....

∎ brooding, moody, morose, resentful, grudging, disgruntled, put out, sullen.
∎ cheerful, happy.

....

sullen *adj.* **1** silently and stubbornly angry or unsociable. **2** *said of skies, etc* dismal. [from Latin *solus*, alone]

....

∎ **1** silent, unsociable, aloof, surly, cross, bad-tempered, sour, sulky, moody, morose, obstinate, stubborn. **2** dark, gloomy, sombre, dismal, cheerless, dull, leaden, heavy.
∎ **1** sociable, good-tempered, cheerful. **2** fine, clear.

....

sullenly *adv.* with a sullen manner.
sullenness *noun* being sullen.
sully *verb* (**sullies, sullied**) **1** to tarnish or mar (a reputation, etc). **2** *literary* to make dirty. [from Anglo-Saxon *sylian*, to defile]

....

∎ **1** stain, tarnish, spoil, mar, spot, blemish, besmirch, disgrace, dishonour. **2** dirty, soil, defile, pollute, contaminate, taint.
∎ **2** cleanse.

....

sulphate *noun* a salt of sulphuric acid.
sulphide *noun* a compound containing sulphur and another element.
sulphonamide /sʌlˈfɒnəmaɪd/ *noun Chem.* **1** an amide of a sulphonic acid. **2** *Medicine* any of a group of drugs containing such a compound that prevent the growth of bacteria, formerly widely used to treat bacterial infections in humans, and to prevent infections of wounds and burns during World War II, but now largely superseded by antibiotics such as penicillin.
sulphur /ˈsʌlfə(r)/ *noun* (SYMBOL **S**, ATOMIC NUMBER **16**) a yellow solid non-metallic element that forms several allotropes, including two stable crystalline forms. Also called BRIMSTONE. [from Latin *sulfur*]

sulphur dioxide *Chem.* (FORMULA SO_2) a colourless gas with a strong pungent odour that is soluble in water and alcohol. It is a reducing agent, and is used as a bleach for paper and straw, and as a food preservative, fumigant, and solvent. It is also used in metal refining, paper pulping, and the manufacture of sulphuric acid. It is produced by the burning of fossil fuels and other sulphur-containing compounds, and is a major cause of acid rain and other forms of atmospheric pollution.
sulphuric acid *Chem.* (FORMULA H_2SO_4) a colourless odourless oily liquid that is highly corrosive, and strongly acidic when diluted with water. It is widely used in the manufacture of organic chemicals, fertilizers, explosives, detergents, paints, and dyes, and as a laboratory reagent. Dilute sulphuric acid is used as an electrolyte in car batteries, and for electroplating.
sulphurous *adj.* of, like, or containing sulphur.
sulphurous acid *Chem.* (FORMULA H_2SO_3) a colourless weakly acidic solution of sulphur dioxide in water, that is a reducing agent and is used as a bleach, antiseptic, and preservative, and in brewing and wine-making, paper and textile manufacture, and the refining of petroleum products.
sultan *noun* the ruler of any of various Muslim countries, especially the former ruler of the Ottoman empire. [from Arabic *sultan*]
sultana *noun* **1** the wife or concubine of a sultan. **2** the mother, sister, or daughter of a sultan. **3** a pale seedless raisin.
sultrily *adv.* in a sultry way.
sultriness *noun* being sultry.
sultry *adj.* (**sultrier, sultriest**) **1** *said of the weather* hot and humid; close. **2** *said of a person* having an appearance or manner suggestive of sexual passion; sensual. [from obsolete *sulter*, to swelter]

....

∎ **1** hot, sweltering, stifling, stuffy, oppressive, close, humid, muggy, sticky.
∎ **1** cool, cold.

....

sum — *noun* **1** the amount produced when numbers or quantities are added together. **2** an amount of money. **3** an arithmetical calculation, especially of a basic kind. — *verb* (**summed, summing**) (*usually* **sum up** or **sum something up**) **1** to summarize. **2** to express or embody the complete character or nature of. **3** to make a quick assessment of. **4** *said of a judge* to review the main points of a case before the jury retires. — **in sum** briefly; to sum up. [from Latin *summa*, top]

....

∎ *noun* **1** total, sum total, aggregate, whole, entirety, number, quantity, amount. **3** tally, reckoning, score. *verb* **4** review, recapitulate.

....

sumac /ˈsjuːmak/ *noun Bot.* **1** any tree or shrub of the genus *Rhus.* **2** its dried leaves and shoots, used in dyeing. [from Arabic *summaq*]
Sumatran rhinoceros /sʊˈmɑːtrən/ a species of rhinoceros found in Asia, and having two horns. It is unusual in that the young are covered with thick brown hair, which is gradually lost as the animal matures.
summarily *adv.* in a summary way.
summarize or **summarise** *verb* to make or present a summary of.

....

∎ outline, précis, condense, abridge, abbreviate, shorten, sum up, encapsulate, review, recapitulate.
∎ expand (on).

....

summary — *noun* (PL. **summaries**) a short account outlining the main points. — *adj.* done or performed quickly and without the usual attention to details or formalities. [from Latin *summarium*]

....

∎ *noun* synopsis, résumé, outline, abstract, précis,

condensation, abridgement, summing-up, review, recapitulation. *adj.* brief, cursory, hasty, prompt, direct, unceremonious, arbitrary.

E3 *adj.* lengthy, careful.

· ·

summary offence *Legal* an offence subject to trial in a magistrates' or (in Scotland) sheriff court (courts of *summary jurisdiction*). Basically, most summary offences are the less serious criminal cases, although the magistrates' and sheriff courts may also try certain indictable offences such as theft.

summation *noun* **1** the process of finding the sum; addition. **2** a summary or summing-up. [from Latin *summare*, to sum up]

summer — *noun* **1** the warmest season of the year, between spring and autumn, extending from about May to Sep in the N hemisphere. **2** *literary* a time of greatest energy, happiness, etc; a heyday. — *adj.* of, occurring in, or for use in the summer. [from Anglo-Saxon *sumer*]

summerhouse *noun* any small building or shelter designed to provide shade in a park or garden.

summer school a course of study held during the summer, eg at a university.

summertime *noun* the season of summer.

summer time time one hour ahead of Greenwich Mean Time, adopted in Britain during the summer months for daylight-saving purposes.

summery *adj.* typical of or suitable for summer.

summing-up *noun* a review of the main points, especially of a legal case by the judge before the jury retires.

summit *noun* **1** the highest point of a mountain or hill. **2** the highest attainable level of achievement or development, eg in a career. **3** (*also* **summit meeting** or **conference**) a conference between heads of government or other senior officials. [from Latin *summum*, highest]

· ·

E3 1 top, peak, pinnacle, apex, crown. **2** top, peak, pinnacle, zenith, acme, culmination, height.

E3 1 bottom, foot. **2** nadir.

· ·

summon *verb* (**summoned, summoning**) **1** to order (a person) to come or appear, eg in a court of law. **2** to order or call upon (someone) to do something. **3** (**summon something up**) to gather or muster (eg one's strength or energy). [from Latin *summonere*, to warn secretly]

· ·

E3 1 call, send for, invite, beckon. **2** ask, bid, order, command. **3** gather, assemble, muster, mobilize, rouse, arouse.

· ·

summons — *noun* (PL. **summonses**) **1** a written order legally obliging a person to attend a court of law at a specified time. **2** any authoritative order to come or to do something. — *verb* to serve with a summons.

sumo /'suːmoʊ/ *noun* traditional Japanese wrestling between contestants of great bulk, won by forcing the opponent to the ground or out of the circular unroped ring. [from Japanese *sumo*]

sump *noun* **1** a small tank inside a vehicle engine from which oil is carried around the moving parts. **2** any pit into which liquid drains or is poured. [from Dutch *somp*]

sumptuary *adj.* **1** relating to or regulating expense. **2** controlling extravagance. [from Latin *sumptuarius*, from *sumptus*, cost]

sumptuous *adj.* superbly rich and luxurious. [from Latin *sumptuosus*, from *sumptus*, cost]

· ·

E3 luxurious, plush, lavish, extravagant, opulent, rich, costly, expensive, splendid, magnificent, gorgeous, superb, grand.

E3 plain, poor.

· ·

sum total the complete or final total.

Sun or **Sun.** *abbrev.* Sunday.

sun — *noun* **1** (*usually* **the Sun**) the central object of the solar system, around which the planets revolve, held in their orbits by its gravitational pull. It is the nearest star to Earth, and its heat and light energy enable living organisms to survive on Earth. **2** the heat and light of this star. **3** any star with a system of planets revolving around it. — *verb* (**sunned, sunning**) to expose (oneself) to the sun's rays. — **under the sun** anywhere; on earth. [from Anglo-Saxon *sunne*]

sunbathe *verb intrans.* to expose one's body to the sun, in order to get a suntan.

· ·

E3 sun oneself, bask, tan, brown, bake.

· ·

sunbathing *noun* exposing oneself to the sun.

sunbeam *noun* a ray of sunlight.

sunbed *noun* a bed-like device with sun-lamps fitted above (and often beneath a transparent screen one lies on), for artificially tanning the whole body.

sunburn *noun* soreness and reddening of the skin caused by over-exposure to the sun.

sunburnt *adj.* sore and red from over-exposure to the sun.

· ·

E3 burnt, red, blistered, peeling.

· ·

sundae /'sʌndeɪ/ *noun* a portion of ice-cream topped with fruit, nuts, syrup, etc.

Sunday *noun* **1** the first day of the week and for most Christians the day of worship and rest. **2** *colloq.* a newspaper appearing on this day. — **a month of Sundays** a very long time. [from Anglo-Saxon *sunnan dæg*, day of the sun]

Sunday best one's best clothes, (especially formerly) considered the most suitable for wearing to church.

Sunday school a class for the religious instruction of children, held on Sundays, usually in church buildings.

sundew *noun Bot.* an insectivorous plant of the genus *Drosera*, found in bogs and on sandy heaths where nitrogen is scarce. The leaves are covered with long sticky hairs that trap insects which are then digested by the plant, providing it with an important source of extra nitrogen.

sundial *noun* an instrument that uses sunlight to tell the time, by the changing position of the shadow that a vertical arm casts on a horizontal plate with graded markings.

sundown *noun* sunset.

sundry — *adj.* various; assorted; miscellaneous. — *noun* (*in pl.* **sundries**) various small unspecified items; oddments. — **all and sundry** everybody. [from Anglo-Saxon *syndrig*]

· ·

E3 *adj.* various, diverse, miscellaneous, assorted, varied, different, several, some, a few.

· ·

sunfish *noun* a large and distinctive fish that is widespread in open waters of tropical and temperate seas, and has a compressed almost circular body, 1m to 2m in length, a small mouth, and teeth fused into a sharp beak.

sunflower *noun* a tall annual plant (*Helianthus annuus*) that produces large yellow flowerheads up to 30cm in diameter on tall stems up to 3m in height. It is widely cultivated for its seeds, which are rich in edible oil, and as a garden plant. Sunflower-seed oil is used as a cooking oil, and in the manufacture of margarine, soap, paints, and varnishes.

sung see SING.

sunglasses *pl. noun* glasses with tinted lenses, worn to protect the eyes from sunlight, not to correct eyesight.

sunk see SINK.

sunken past participle of SINK. — *adj.* **1** situated or fitted at a lower level than the surrounding area. **2** *said of the cheeks, etc* made hollow through ill health.

· ·

E3 *adj.* **1** recessed, lower, depressed, concave. **2** hollow, haggard, drawn.

. . . .

sunlamp *noun* a lamp emitting light similar in nature to sunlight, used therapeutically and for artificially tanning the skin.

sunlight *noun* light from the sun.

sunlit *adj.* lit by the sun.

sun lounge a room with large windows for letting in maximum sunlight.

Sunni /'sʊnɪ, 'sʌnɪ/ *noun* one of the two main branches of the Islamic religion, regarding the teachings of Mohammed himself as supremely authoritative. See also SHIA. [from Arabic *sunnah*, rule]

Sunnite — *noun* an adherent of the Sunni. — *adj.* relating to the Sunni.

sunny *adj.* (**sunnier, sunniest**) **1** filled with sunshine or sunlight. **2** cheerful; good-humoured.

. . . .

⊟ **1** fine, cloudless, clear, summery, sunlit, bright, brilliant. **2** cheerful, happy, joyful, smiling, beaming, radiant, good-humoured, light-hearted, buoyant, optimistic.
⊟ **1** sunless, dull. **2** gloomy.

. . . .

sunrise *noun* the sun's appearance above the horizon in the morning; also, the time of day represented by this.

. . . .

⊟ dawn, sun-up, daybreak, daylight.

. . . .

sunroof *noun* a transparent panel in a car roof, for letting in sunlight, often opening for ventilation.

sunset *noun* the sun's disappearance below the horizon in the evening; also, the time of day represented by this.

. . . .

⊟ sundown, dusk, twilight, gloaming, evening, nightfall.

. . . .

sunshade *noun* **1** a sort of umbrella for protecting one from the sun. **2** an awning.

sunshine *noun* **1** fair weather, with the sun shining brightly. **2** the light or heat of the sun. **3** a place where one can be in the light or heat of the sun. **4** an informal term of address, often used in a condescending or scolding tone.

sunspot *noun* **1** *Astron.* a relatively dark patch on the Sun's surface (the photosphere), representing a region that is cooler than the rest of the photosphere, and caused by an intense magnetic field erupting from within the Sun. **2** *colloq.* a holiday resort renowned for sunny weather.

sunstroke *noun* a severe condition of collapse and fever brought on by over-exposure to the sun.

suntan *noun* a browning of the skin through exposure to the sun or a sun-lamp.

sun-tanned *adj.* having a suntan, brown-skinned.

suntrap *noun* a sheltered place which receives a large amount of sunshine.

sun-up *noun* sunrise.

sup[1] — *verb* (**supped, supping**) **1** to drink in small mouthfuls. **2** *colloq.* to drink (alcohol). — *noun* a small mouthful; a sip. [from Anglo-Saxon *supan*]

super[1] — *adj., interj., colloq.* extremely good; excellent. — *noun* something of superior quality or grade, eg petrol. [from Latin *super*, above]

super[2] *noun colloq.* **1** a superintendent. **2** a supernumerary, especially a supernumerary actor.

super- *combining form* forming words meaning: **1** great or extreme in size or degree: *supertanker*. **2** above or beyond: *supernatural* **3** outstanding: *superhero*. [from Latin *super*, above]

superannuated *adj.* **1** made to retire and given a pension; pensioned off. **2** old and no longer fit for use. [from Latin *super*, above + *annus*, year]

superannuation *noun* **1** an amount regularly deducted from wages as a contribution to a company pension. **2** the pension received. **3** retirement.

superb *adj.* **1** *colloq.* outstandingly excellent. **2** magnificent; majestic. [from Latin *superbus*, proud]

. . . .

⊟ **1** excellent, first-rate, first-class, superior, choice, fine, exquisite, wonderful, marvellous. **2** magnificent, splendid, grand, majestic, imposing, impressive, breathtaking.
⊟ **1** bad, poor, inferior.

. . . .

superbly *adv.* in a superb way.

superbug *noun* a strain of bacteria that is resistant to antibiotics.

supercharge *verb* **1** to increase the power and performance of (a vehicle engine). **2** to charge or fill (eg an atmosphere) with an intense amount of an emotion, etc.

supercharger *noun Engineering* a mechanical pump or compressor that is used to increase the amount of air taken into the cylinder of an internal combustion engine, in order to burn the fuel more rapidly and so increase the power output.

supercilious *adj.* **1** self-important. **2** arrogantly disdainful. [from Latin *super*, above + *cilium*, eyelid]

. . . .

⊟ **1** self-important, condescending, haughty, arrogant, lordly, pretentious, snobbish, *colloq.* snooty. **2** disdainful, scornful, sneering.

. . . .

superciliously *adv.* with a supercilious manner.

superciliousness *noun* a supercilious quality.

superconductivity *noun Physics* the complete loss of electrical resistance exhibited by many metals and alloys at temperatures close to absolute zero (−273°C). Various materials, eg certain ceramics, have recently been discovered that show superconductivity at much higher temperatures, close to that of liquid nitrogen. Superconducting coils are used in some large electromagnets and particle accelerators, where they produce very strong magnetic fields.

superconductor *noun Physics* a material which exhibits superconductivity.

supercooling *noun Physics* the cooling of a liquid to a temperature below that considered to be its freezing point.

superego *noun Psychol.* in psychoanalysis, the part of the mind that is concerned with moral conscience or judgement, and so sets standards for the ego, causing it discomfort when it accepts unworthy impulses from the id.

supererogation *noun* the doing of more than is required. [from Latin *super*, above + *erogare*, to pay out]

superficial *adj.* **1** of, on, or near the surface. **2** not thorough or in-depth; cursory. **3** only apparent; not real or genuine. **4** lacking the capacity for sincere emotion or serious thought; shallow. [from Latin *super*, above + *facies*, face]

. . . .

⊟ **1** surface, external, exterior. **2** cursory, sketchy, hasty, hurried, passing, casual. **3** apparent, seeming, cosmetic, outward, skin-deep. **4** shallow, frivolous, lightweight.
⊟ **1** internal. **2** thorough. **3** real, genuine. **4** deep.

. . . .

superficiality *noun* a superficial quality.

superficially *adv.* in a superficial way.

superfluidity *noun Physics* the property of zero resistance to flow (ie zero viscosity) exhibited by liquid helium at temperatures below −271°C. At these temperatures, helium exhibits unusual properties, including the ability to creep out of a container in apparent defiance of gravity.

superfluity *noun* (PL. **superfluities**) **1** being superfluous. **2** a thing that is superfluous. **3** a superabundance.

superfluous *adj.* more than is needed or wanted; surplus. [from Latin *superfluus*, overflowing]

. . . .

⊟ extra, spare, excess, surplus, redundant, supernumerary, unnecessary, unwanted, uncalled-for, excessive.

◫ necessary.

supergiant *noun* a bright star of enormous size and low density, such as Betelgeuse and Antares.

supergrass *noun slang* a police informer whose information has led to large numbers of arrests.

superheterodyne receiver *Radio* a radio receiver in which the frequency of the incoming signal is reduced by mixing it with another signal generated inside the receiver. The resulting intermediate frequency is easier to amplify and manipulate than the initial frequency.

super high frequency *Radio* (ABBREV. **SHF**) a radio frequency in the range 3,000 to 30,000MHz.

superhighway *noun* 1 *North Amer.* a fast dual carriageway. 2 (*in full* **information superhighway**) the use of computer networks as a means of rapid worldwide communication and access to information.

superhuman *adj.* beyond ordinary human ability or knowledge.

superimpose *verb* to lay or set (one thing) on top of another.

superimposition *noun* 1 superimposing or being superimposed. 2 something that is superimposed.

superintend *verb* to be in overall charge of; to supervise. [from Latin *superintendere*]

⊟ supervise, oversee, overlook, inspect, run, manage, administer, direct, control, handle.

superintendence *noun* superintending.

superintendent *noun* 1 a police officer above the rank of chief inspector. 2 a person who superintends.

superior — *adj.* (*often* **superior to someone** or **something**) 1 higher in rank or position. 2 better in a particular way. 3 of high quality. 4 arrogant; self-important. 5 *Printing*, *said of a character* set above the level of the line; superscript. — *noun* 1 a person of higher rank or position. 2 the head of a religious community. [from Latin *superus*, set above]

⊟ *adj.* 1 higher, greater, senior. 2 better, greater, preferred. 3 excellent, first-class, first-rate, *colloq.* top-notch, *colloq.* top-flight, exclusive, choice, select, fine, de luxe. 4 arrogant, lordly, self-important, pretentious, snobbish, *colloq.* snooty, haughty, supercilious, disdainful, condescending, patronizing. *noun* 1 senior, elder, better, boss, chief, principal, director, manager, supervisor.
◫ *adj.* INFERIOR. 1 lower. 2 worse. 3 average. 4 humble. *noun* 1 inferior, junior, assistant.

superiority *noun* 1 a superior state. 2 pre-eminence. 3 advantage.

⊟ 1 supremacy, ascendancy. 2 pre-eminence, predominance. 3 advantage, lead, edge.
◫ 1 inferiority.

superior planet *Astron.* a planet whose orbit around the Sun lies outside that of the Earth, ie Mars, Jupiter, Saturn, Uranus, Neptune, and Pluto.

superlative — *adj.* 1 superior to all others; supreme. 2 *Grammar*, *said of an adjective or adverb* expressing the highest degree of a particular quality, eg *nicest*, *most beautiful*. — *noun Grammar* the superlative form, or an adjective or adverb in this form. [from Latin *superlativus*]

⊟ *adj.* 1 best, greatest, highest, supreme, transcendent, unbeatable, unrivalled, unparalleled, matchless, peerless, unsurpassed, unbeaten, consummate, excellent, outstanding.
◫ *adj.* 1 poor, average.

superman *noun* (PL. **supermen**) 1 a man with extraordinary strength or ability. 2 a fictional man with superhuman powers.

supermarket *noun* a large self-service store selling food and other goods.

supernatant / suːpəˈneɪtənt/ *noun Chem.* the clear layer of liquid above a precipitate or a sediment that has settled. [from SUPER- + Latin *natare*, to swim, float]

supernatural — *adj.* of, relating to, or being phenomena that cannot be explained by the laws of nature or physics. — *noun* (**the supernatural**) supernatural phenomena.

⊟ *adj.* paranormal, unnatural, abnormal, metaphysical, spiritual, psychic, mystic, occult, mysterious, miraculous, magical, ghostly.
◫ *adj.* natural, normal.

supernova *noun* (PL. **supernovae**, **supernovas**) a star that suddenly becomes millions of times brighter as a result of a catastrophic explosion, so that it may dominate an entire galaxy of stars. A supernova explosion occurs when a massive star has exhausted all the nuclear fuel in its central core, which then collapses. Supernovas occur relatively rarely, and take several weeks or months to fade.

supernumerary — *adj.* additional to the normal or required number; extra. — *noun* (PL. **supernumeraries**) 1 a supernumerary person or thing. 2 an actor without a speaking part. [from Latin *super*, above + *numerus*, number]

superoxide *noun Chem.* 1 any of various chemical compounds that are very powerful oxidizing agents and contain the O_2^- ion, which is highly toxic to living tissues. 2 any oxide that reacts with an acid to form hydrogen peroxide and oxygen.

superphosphate *noun Chem.* the most important type of phosphate fertilizer, made by treating calcium phosphate in the form of the mineral apatite, bone ash, or slag with sulphuric acid (which yields a fertilizer containing 16 to 20 per cent phosphorus) or phosphoric acid (which yields a fertilizer containing 45 to 50 per cent phosphorus).

superpower *noun* a nation with outstanding political, economic, or military influence, especially the USA or the former USSR.

superscript *Printing* — *adj.*, *said of a character* set above the level of the line, as the number 2 in 10^2. — *noun* a superscript character. [from Latin *super*, above + *scribere*, to write]

supersede *verb* 1 to take the place of (often something outdated or no longer valid). 2 to set aside in favour of another. [from Latin *supersedere*, to sit above]

⊟ REPLACE. 1 succeed, supplant, usurp, oust, displace.

supersession *noun* superseding or being superseded.

supersonic *adj.* 1 faster than the speed of sound. 2 *said of aircraft* capable of supersonic speeds. [from Latin *super*, above + *sonus*, sound]

supersonically *adv.* in a supersonic way.

superstar *noun* an internationally famous celebrity, especially from the world of film, popular music, or sport.

superstition *noun* 1 belief in an influence that certain (especially commonplace) objects, actions, or occurrences have on events, people's lives, etc. 2 a particular opinion or practice based on such belief. 3 any widely held but unfounded belief. [from Latin *superstitio*, fear of the supernatural]

⊟ 3 myth, old wives' tale, fallacy.

superstitious *adj.* 1 relating to or involving superstition. 2 believing, following, or practising superstition.

⊟ 1 mythical, false, fallacious, illogical, irrational, groundless.

⊞ **1** logical, rational.

superstring *noun Physics* a theory that has been proposed to explain the properties of elementary particles and the forces between them, and that takes account of both quantum theory and relativity.

superstructure *noun* any part built above another (especially main) part, eg those parts of a ship above the main deck.

supertax *noun colloq.* a surtax.

supertitle same as SURTITLE.

supervene *verb intrans.* to occur as an (especially unexpected) interruption to some process. [from Latin *supervenire*, to come upon]

supervention *noun* supervening.

supervise *verb* to be in overall charge of; to oversee. [from Latin *supervidere*, to see over]

⊞ oversee, overlook, watch over, look after, superintend, run, manage, administer, direct, preside over, control, handle.

supervision *noun* supervising; inspection; control.

⊞ surveillance, care, charge, superintendence, running, management, administration, direction, control, guidance, instruction.

supervisor *noun* a person who supervises.

⊞ overseer, inspector, superintendent, boss, chief, director, administrator, manager, foreman, forewoman.

supervisory *adj.* relating to or involving supervision.

supine /'suːpaɪn, 'sjuːpaɪn/ *adj.* **1** lying on one's back. **2** passive or lazy. [from Latin *supinus*]

supper *noun* **1** a light evening meal. **2** a late-night snack taken in addition to and later than the main evening meal. [from Old French *soper*]

supplant /sə'plɑːnt/ *verb* to take the place of, often by force or unfair means. [from Latin *supplantare*, to trip up]

⊞ replace, supersede, usurp, oust, displace, overthrow, topple, unseat.

supple *adj.* **1** *said of joints, etc* bending easily; flexible. **2** *said of a person* having flexible joints. [from Latin *supplex*, bending the knees]

⊞ **1** flexible, bending, pliant, pliable, plastic, elastic. **2** lithe, graceful, loose-limbed, double-jointed.
⊠ **1** stiff, rigid, inflexible.

supplely or **supply** *adv.* in a supple way.

supplement — *noun* **1** a thing added to make something complete or to make up a deficiency. **2** an extra section added to a book or document to give additional information or to correct previous errors. **3** a separate part added to a newspaper or magazine on certain occasions, eg on Sundays. — *verb* to add to, or make up a lack of. [from Latin *supplementum*, a filling up]

⊞ *noun* **1** addition, extra. **2** appendix, codicil, postscript, addendum. **3** insert, pull-out. *verb* add to, augment, boost, reinforce, fill up, top up, complement, extend, eke out.
⊠ *verb* deplete, use up.

supplementary *adj.* additional; added to supply what is needed.

⊞ additional, extra, auxiliary, secondary, complementary, accompanying.

supplementary benefit a former name for INCOME SUPPORT.

supplementation *noun* **1** supplementing. **2** something that is added.

suppleness *noun* a supple quality.

supplicant — *noun* a person who supplicates or entreats. — *adj.* supplicating; entreating.

supplicate *verb trans., intrans.* (**supplicate someone** or **to someone**) to make a humble and earnest request or entreaty to them. [from Latin *supplicare*, to beg on one's knees]

supplication *noun* **1** supplicating. **2** an earnest or humble petition. **3** an earnest prayer or entreaty for a special blessing.

supplier *noun* a person or organization that supplies a particular commodity.

⊞ dealer, seller, vendor, wholesaler, retailer.

supply — *verb* (**supplies, supplied**) **1** (*often* **supply someone with something** or **something to someone**) to provide or furnish them with it. **2** to satisfy (eg a need); to make up (a deficiency). — *noun* (PL. **supplies**) **1** an amount supplied, especially regularly. **2** an amount that can be drawn from and used; a stock. **3** (**supplies**) necessary food or equipment gathered or taken on a journey, etc. **4** a source of some public utility, eg water or gas. **5** *Econ.* the total supply of a commodity being produced for sale. **6** degree of availability: *in short supply.* **7** a person, especially a teacher, acting as a temporary substitute. **8** the act of supplying. [from Latin *supplere*, to fill up]

⊞ *verb* **1** provide, furnish, equip, outfit, stock, fill, give, donate, endow, contribute, yield, produce, sell. *noun* **1** amount, quantity. **2** stock, fund, reservoir, source, store, reserve, stockpile, hoard. **3** stores, provisions, food, equipment, materials, necessities.
⊠ *verb* **1** take, receive.

supply-side *noun* an economic approach based on the theory that supply creates demand, and proposing that the most effective method of increasing national output and the level of employment is through the removal of tax disincentives. Thus, if personal taxes are reduced, people work harder and there will be a significant rise in output; also, if taxes on profit are reduced it will encourage investment which will again improve output.

support — *verb* **1** to keep upright or in place; to keep from falling; to bear the weight of. **2** to give active approval and encouragement to. **3** to provide with the means necessary for living or existing. **4** to maintain a loyal interest in the fortunes of (a sporting team), especially by regular attendance at matches. **5** to reinforce the disputed accuracy or validity of (eg a theory or claim). **6** to speak in favour of (a proposal, etc). **7** to play a part subordinate to (a leading actor). **8** to perform as an introduction to (the main item in a musical concert, etc). **9** to bear or tolerate. — *noun* **1** the act of supporting or the state of being supported. **2** a thing that supports. **3** a person or group that supports; a supporting act in a concert, etc. [from Latin *supportare*, to hold up]

⊞ *verb* **1** hold up, bear, carry, sustain, brace, reinforce, strengthen, prop, buttress, bolster. **2** back, promote, foster, encourage, help, aid, assist. **3** maintain, keep, provide for, feed, nourish, finance, fund, subsidize, underwrite. **5** confirm, verify, authenticate, corroborate, substantiate, document. **6** back, endorse, second, defend, champion, advocate. **9** bear, stand, tolerate, put up with, endure, abide. *noun* **1** backing, approval, encouragement, allegiance, loyalty, defence, protection, patronage, sponsorship, comfort, relief, help, aid, assistance. **2** prop, stay, post, pillar, brace, crutch, foundation, underpinning.

◨ *verb* **2** oppose. **3** live off. **5** contradict, refute. *noun* **1** opposition, hostility.

....

supporter *noun* a person who supports a cause or proposal, or who supports an institution such as a sports team or political party.

....

▣ advocate, champion, defender, seconder, patron, sponsor, helper, ally, friend, fan, follower, adherent.

◨ opponent.

....

supporting *adj.* giving support.

supportive *adj.* providing support, especially active approval and encouragement.

....

▣ encouraging, helpful, caring, attentive, sympathetic, understanding, comforting, reassuring.

◨ discouraging.

....

suppose *verb* **1** to consider likely or probable; to regard as certain or probable. **2** to treat (a possibility) as a fact for the purposes of forming an argument or plan: *let us suppose he does not come.* **3** *said of a theory* to require (a factor or assumption) to be true in order to be itself valid. [from Latin *supponere*, to substitute]

....

▣ **1** guess, conjecture, surmise, believe, think, consider, judge, assume, presume, expect, infer, conclude. **2** imagine, fancy, pretend, postulate, hypothesize.

....

supposed *adj.* generally believed to be so or such (but considered doubtful by the speaker). — **supposed to ... 1** expected or required to be or do something: *are we supposed to reply?* **2** *often ironical, as a reproof* reputed to have or be something: *you are supposed to be an adult.*

....

▣ alleged, reported, rumoured, assumed, presumed, reputed, putative, imagined, hypothetical. **supposed to 1** meant to, intended to, expected to, required to, obliged to.

◨ known, certain.

....

supposedly /sə'pəʊzɪdlɪ/ *adv.* as is supposed.

supposition *noun* **1** the act of supposing. **2** that which is supposed; a mere possibility or assumption, not a fact.

....

▣ ASSUMPTION, CONJECTURE, SPECULATION. **1** presumption. **2** guess, theory, hypothesis, idea, notion.

....

suppositional *adj.* hypothetical, conjectural, supposed.

supposititious *adj.* based on supposition; hypothetical.

suppository *noun* (PL. **suppositories**) *Medicine* a soluble container of medicine that is solid at room temperature and can be inserted into the rectum or vagina. [from Latin *suppositorium*, from *supponere*, to place underneath]

suppress *verb* **1** to hold in or restrain (feelings, etc). **2** to put a stop to or crush (eg a rebellion). **3** to prevent from broadcasting or circulating; to prevent from being broadcast, circulated, or otherwise made known. **4** to moderate or eliminate (interference) in an electrical device. [from Latin *supprimere*, to press down]

....

▣ **1** restrain, check, stifle, smother, repress, inhibit, hold back, contain. **2** crush, stamp out, quash, quell, subdue. **3** silence, gag, stifle, smother, censor, conceal, withhold, hold back.

◨ **2** incite.

....

suppression *noun* **1** suppressing or being suppressed. **2** stopping. **3** concealing.

suppressor *noun* **1** a person who suppresses. **2** a device for suppressing electrical interference.

suppurate /'sʌpjʊreɪt/ *verb intrans.*, *said of a wound, etc* to gather and release pus. [from Latin *suppurare*]

suppuration *noun* **1** the process of suppurating. **2** the formation or secretion of pus. **3** the coming to a head of a boil or similar eruption.

supra /'suːprə/ *adv.* above; further up the page or earlier in the book. [from Latin *supra*]

supra- *combining form* forming words meaning 'above, beyond': *supranational.* [from Latin *supra*, above]

supranational *adj.* **1** in or belonging to more than one nation. **2** overriding national sovereignty.

supremacy *noun* **1** supreme power or authority. **2** the state of being supreme.

supreme *adj.* **1** of highest rank, power or importance; greatest. **2** most excellent; best. **3** greatest in degree; utmost. [from Latin *supremus*, highest]

....

▣ GREATEST, TOP. **1** highest, first, leading, foremost, chief, principal, head, sovereign, pre-eminent, predominant, prevailing. **2** best, unsurpassed, second-to-none, incomparable, matchless, consummate, transcendent, superlative, prime. **3** utmost, extreme, ultimate, final, culminating, crowning.

◨ **1** lowest, minor. **2** worst, poor. **3** least.

....

supremely *adv.* to a supreme degree.

supremo *noun* (PL. **supremos**) *colloq.* **1** a supreme head or leader. **2** a boss. [from Spanish; see SUPREME]

sur-[1] *prefix* forming words meaning 'over, above, beyond'. [from French *sur*]

sur-[2] *prefix* a form of *sub-* used before some words beginning with *r*: *surrogate.*

sura or **surah** /'sʊərə/ *noun* a chapter of the Koran. [from Arabic *sura*, step]

surcharge — *noun* **1** an extra charge. **2** an alteration printed on or over something, especially a new valuation on a stamp. **3** an amount over a permitted load. — *verb* **1** to impose a surcharge on. **2** to print a surcharge on or over. **3** to overload.

surd /sɜːd/ *noun* **1** *Maths.* an irrational number that is a root of a rational number, so can never be determined exactly, eg 3. **2** an arithmetic expression involving the sum or difference of such numbers, eg 3 or 6. [from Latin *surdus*, deaf]

sure — *adj.* **1** confident beyond doubt in one's belief or knowledge; convinced. **2** guaranteed or certain (to happen, etc). **3** (**sure of something**) unquestionably destined for it or assured of it. **4** undoubtedly true or accurate: *a sure sign.* **5** reliably stable or secure. — *adv. colloq.* certainly; of course. — **be sure to ...** not to fail to do something. **for sure** definitely; undoubtedly. **make sure** to take the necessary action to remove all doubt or risk; to be certain. **sure enough** *colloq.* in fact; as was expected. **to be sure** certainly; admittedly. [from Old French *sur*, from Latin *securus*, with care]

....

▣ *adj.* CERTAIN. **1** convinced, assured, confident, decided, positive. **2** guaranteed, bound. **4** definite, unmistakable, accurate, precise, unerring, unfailing, infallible, unquestionable, indisputable, undoubted, undeniable. **5** safe, secure, solid, firm, steady, stable, reliable, dependable, steadfast, unwavering.

◨ *adj.* UNCERTAIN. **1** unsure, doubtful. **5** unsafe, insecure.

....

sure-fire *adj. colloq.* sure to succeed; infallible.

sure-footed *adj.* **1** not stumbling or likely to stumble. **2** not making, or not likely to make, mistakes.

surely *adv.* **1** without doubt; certainly. **2** *used in questions and exclamations* it must be that ...; it is hoped or expected that: *surely you are not leaving already!*

sureness *noun* being sure.

surety /'ʃʊərətɪ/ *noun* (PL. **sureties**) **1** security against loss or damage, or a guarantee that a promise will be fulfilled; also, a thing given as security. **2** a person who agrees to become legally responsible for another person's behaviour. [see SURE]

surf — *noun* the foam produced by breaking waves. — *verb* **1** *intrans.* to go surfing. **2** to move through (the Internet or television channels).

surface — *noun* **1** the upper or outer side of anything, often with regard to texture or appearance. **2** the upper level of a body or container of liquid. **3** external appearance, rather than underlying reality. **4** a geometric figure that is flat or two-dimensional, not solid. **5** *attributive* **a** at, on, or relating to a surface. **b** superficial: *surface politeness.* — *verb* **1** to give the desired finish or texture to the surface of. **2** *intrans.* to rise to the surface of a liquid. **3** *intrans.* to become apparent; to come to light. **4** *intrans. colloq.* to get out of bed. [from French *surface*]

. . . .

🔳 *noun* **1** outside, exterior, covering, skin, side, face, plane. **2** top. **3** appearance, façade, veneer. **5** external, exterior, outer, superficial, outward, shallow. *verb* **1** finish, cover, veneer, overlay. **2** rise, come up. **3** emerge, appear, materialize, come to light.
🔳 *noun* **1** inside, interior. **2** bottom. **5** internal, inner. *verb* **2** sink. **3** disappear, vanish.

. . . .

surface mail mail sent overland or by ship, as opposed to *airmail.*

surface tension *Physics* the force that causes a liquid to behave as if it has an elastic surface skin. It is caused by the attraction between molecules of a liquid at its surface, which causes the liquid to change shape in order to mimimize its surface. For this reason a water drop on a flat surface tends to dome upwards, but if detergent is added to it, reducing surface tension, the water will spread out and wet the surface. Surface tension is responsible for capillary action. See also CAPILLARITY.

surfactant *noun Chem.* **1** any soluble substance that reduces the surface tension of a liquid, or reduces the surface tension between two liquids or between a solid and a liquid. Surfactants are used as detergents, wetting agents, emulsifiers, and foaming agents. **2** *Zool.* a substance secreted by the cells lining the alveoli of the lungs that prevents the walls of the alveoli from sticking together. [a contraction of *surface-active agent*]

surfboard *noun* a long narrow shaped fibreglass board that a surfer stands or lies on.

surfcasting *noun* fishing from the shore by casting into surf.

surfeit /'sɜːfɪt/ — *noun* **1** an excess. **2** the stuffed or sickened feeling resulting from any excess, especially overeating or over-drinking. — *verb* to feed or otherwise indulge until stuffed or disgusted. [from Old French *surfait,* excess]

. . . .

🔳 *noun* **1** excess, surplus, superfluity, glut.

. . . .

surfer *noun* a person who goes surfing.

surfing *noun* the sport of riding a surfboard along on the crests of large breaking waves.

surge — *noun* **1** a sudden powerful mass movement, especially forwards. **2** a sudden sharp increase. **3** a violent rush of emotion. **4** a rising and falling of a large area of sea, without individual waves; a swell. — *verb intrans.* to well up, move, increase, or swell suddenly and with force. [from Latin *surgere,* to rise]

. . . .

🔳 *noun* **1** rush, gush, pouring, flow. **2** upsurge, rise, escalation. **4** rise, swell, billowing. *verb* gush, rush, rise, swell.

. . . .

surgeon *noun* **1** a doctor specializing in surgery. **2** a military doctor. [from Old French *surgien,* from Greek *kheirurgia*; see SURGERY]

surgery *noun* (PL. **surgeries**) **1** the treatment of disease or injury by cutting into the patient's body to operate directly on, or remove, the affected part. **2** the place where, or period of the day during which, a community doctor or dentist carries out treatment. **3** a set period during which

a local MP or councillor is available to be consulted by the public. [from Greek *kheirurgia,* from *kheir,* hand + *ergon,* work]

surgical *adj.* relating to, for use in, or by means of surgery.

surgically *adv.* by means of surgery.

surgical spirit methylated spirit, with small amounts of castor oil, oil of wintergreen and other substances, used for cleaning wounds and sterilising medical equipment.

surliness *noun* being surly.

surly *adj.* (**surlier, surliest**) abrupt and impolite in manner or speech. [from obsolete *sirly,* haughty]

. . . .

🔳 gruff, brusque, abrupt, rude, churlish, bad-tempered, cross, crabbed, grouchy, crusty, sullen, sulky, morose.
🔳 friendly, polite.

. . . .

surmise /sə'maɪz/ — *verb* to conclude from information available; to infer. — *noun* **1** a conclusion drawn from such information. **2** the act of drawing such a conclusion; conjecture. [from Old French *surmettre,* to accuse]

surmount /sə'maʊnt/ *verb* **1** to overcome (problems, obstacles, etc). **2** to be set on top of; to crown. [from Old French *surmunter*]

surmountable *adj.* capable of being surmounted.

surname *noun* a family name or last name, as opposed to a forename or Christian name. [from French *surnom*]

surpass /sə'pɑːs/ *verb* **1** to go or be beyond in degree or extent; to exceed. **2** to be better than. [from French *surpasser*]

. . . .

🔳 BETTER. **1** beat, outdo, exceed, outstrip. **2** excel, outshine, eclipse, transcend.

. . . .

surpassed *adj.* bettered.

surplice *noun* a loose wide-sleeved white linen garment worn ceremonially over the robe of members of the clergy and choir singers. [from Latin *superpellicium,* overgarment]

surplus — *noun* **1** an amount exceeding the amount required or used. **2** *Commerce* the amount by which income is greater than expenditure. — *adj.* left over after needs have been met; extra. [from French *surplus*]

. . . .

🔳 *noun* **1** excess, residue, remainder, balance, superfluity, glut, surfeit. *adj.* extra, spare, remaining, unused, excess, superfluous, redundant.
🔳 *noun* **1** lack, shortage.

. . . .

surprise — *noun* **1** a feeling of mental disorientation caused by an encounter with something sudden or unexpected; also, the thing encountered. **2** the act of catching someone unawares; the state of being caught unawares. — *verb* **1** to cause to experience surprise by presenting with or subjecting to something unexpected. **2** to come upon unexpectedly or catch unawares. **3** to capture or attack with a sudden unexpected manoeuvre. — **take someone by surprise** to surprise them abruptly; to catch them unawares. [from Old French *surprendre,* to take over]

. . . .

🔳 *noun* **1** amazement, astonishment, incredulity, wonder, bewilderment, dismay, shock, start. *verb* **1** startle, amaze, astonish, astound, stagger, *colloq.* flabbergast, bewilder, confuse, disconcert, dismay.
🔳 *noun* **1** composure.

. . . .

surprised *adj.* **1** taken unawares. **2** shocked, startled, amazed.

. . . .

🔳 **2** startled, amazed, astonished, astounded, staggered, *colloq.* flabbergasted, thunderstruck, dumbfounded, speechless, shocked, nonplussed.
🔳 **2** unsurprised, composed.

. . . .

surprising *adj.* causing surprise.
. . . .
⊟ amazing, astonishing, astounding, staggering, stunning, incredible, extraordinary, remarkable, startling, unexpected, unforeseen.
⊞ unsurprising, expected.
. . . .

surreal *adj.* dreamlike, in the style of Surrealism.

Surrealism a movement in modern art and literature, the basic idea of which was to free the artist from the demands of logic, and to penetrate beyond everyday consciousness to the 'super-reality' that lies behind.

Surrealist — *noun* an adherent of Surrealism. — *adj.* relating to or characteristic of Surrealism.

surrealistic *adj.* suggestive or characteristic of Surrealism.

surrender — *verb* (**surrendered, surrendering**) **1** *intrans.* to admit defeat by giving oneself up to an enemy; to yield. **2** (**surrender to something**) to allow oneself to be influenced or overcome by a desire or emotion; to give in. **3** to give or hand over, voluntarily or under duress. — *noun* the act of surrendering. [from Old French *surrendre*]
. . . .
⊟ *verb* **1** capitulate, submit, resign, concede, yield, give in, give up. **2** yield to, give way to, give in to, cede to. **3** give up, hand over, cede, relinquish, abandon, renounce, forego, waive. *noun* capitulation, resignation, submission, yielding, relinquishment, renunciation.
. . . .

surreptitious *adj.* done secretly or sneakily. [from Latin *sub*, secretly + *rapere*, to snatch]
. . . .
⊟ furtive, stealthy, sly, covert, veiled, secret, clandestine, underhand, unauthorized.
⊞ open, obvious.
. . . .

surreptitiously *adv.* in a surreptitious way.

surreptitiousness *noun* being surreptitious.

surrogacy *noun* (PL. **surrogacies**) **1** the state of being surrogate or a surrogate. **2** the use of a surrogate, especially a surrogate mother.

surrogate /ˈsʌrəgət, ˈsʌrəgeɪt/ — *adj.* standing in for another. — *noun* a surrogate person or thing. [from Latin *sub*, in the place of + *rogare*, to ask]

surrogate mother a woman who carries and gives birth to a baby on behalf of another couple, especially through artificial insemination with the man's sperm.

surround — *verb* **1** to extend all around; to encircle. **2** to exist as a background situation to; to make up the particular context or environment of. **3** (**surround oneself with people** or **things**) to maintain around oneself a large following of people or collection of things. — *noun* a border or edge, or an ornamental structure fitted round this. [from Old French *suronder*]
. . . .
⊟ *verb* **1** encircle, ring, girdle, encompass, envelop, encase, enclose, hem in, besiege.
. . . .

surrounding *adj.* that surrounds; encompassing, neighbouring.
. . . .
⊟ encircling, encompassing, bordering, adjacent, adjoining, neighbouring, nearby.
. . . .

surroundings *pl. noun* environment; the places and things round about.
. . . .
⊟ environment, neighbourhood, vicinity, locality, setting, background, milieu, ambience.
. . . .

surtax *noun* an additional tax, especially on incomes above a certain level.

surtitle or **supertitle** *noun* each of a sequence of captions projected on to a screen visible to the audience above the stage during the performance of a foreign-language opera or play, giving a running translation of the libretto or dialogue as it is performed. The term was first used in Canada in the 1980s; *supertitle* is more common in the USA.

surveillance /səˈveɪləns/ *noun* the act of keeping a close watch over a person, eg a suspected criminal. [from French; see SURVEY]

surveillance TV closed circuit television with security applications, such as supervision of customer areas in banks, building societies, supermarkets, and shopping complexes, and the monitoring of unattended locations. Small monochrome cameras sensitive to low light levels are fitted with wide-angled lens to give maximum coverage from a fixed or remotely-controlled viewpoint; pictures may be recorded or viewed from a central location.

survey — *verb* (with stress on -*vey*) (**surveys, surveyed**) **1** to look at or examine at length or in detail, in order to get a general view. **2** to examine (a building) in order to assess its condition or value. **3** to measure land heights and distances in (an area) for the purposes of drawing a detailed map. — *noun* (with stress on *sur*-) (PL. **surveys**) **1** a detailed examination or investigation, eg to find out public opinion or customer preference. **2** an inspection of a building to assess condition or value. **3** a collecting of land measurements for map-making purposes. [from Old French *surveoir*, from Latin *super*, over + *videre*, to see]
. . . .
⊟ *verb* **1** view, contemplate, observe, scan, scrutinize, examine, inspect, study, research, review, consider. **2** examine, inspect, value, assess, evaluate, estimate. **3** measure, plot, plan, map, chart, reconnoitre. *noun* **1** review, overview, scrutiny, examination, investigation, study, poll. **2** inspection, valuation, assessment, appraisal.
. . . .

surveyor *noun* a person who surveys land or buildings.

survival *noun* **1** surviving, living on. **2** anything that continues to exist after others of its kind have disappeared, or beyond the time to which it naturally belongs.

survive *verb* **1** *intrans.* to remain alive or relatively unharmed in spite of a dangerous experience. **2** to come through (a dangerous experience) alive or relatively unharmed. **3** to live on after the death of. **4** *intrans.* to remain alive or in existence. [from Latin *super*, beyond + *vivere*, to live]
. . . .
⊟ **1** live, hold out. **2** withstand, weather. **3** outlive, outlast. **4** last, endure, stay, remain, live, exist.
⊞ **1** succumb, die.
. . . .

surviving *adj.* that survives, living on.

survivor *noun* a person who survives.

sus same as SUSS.

susceptibility *noun* (PL. **susceptibilities**) **1** the state or degree of being susceptible. **2** (**susceptibilities**) feelings; sensibilities.

susceptible *adj.* **1** (**susceptible to something**) suffering readily from something (eg a disease or something unwelcome); prone to it. **2** in whom strong feelings, especially of love, are easily aroused. **3** (*often* **susceptible to something**) capable of being influenced by something (eg persuasion). **4** (**susceptible of something**) open to it; admitting of it: *a ruling susceptible of several interpretations*. [from Latin *suscipere*, to take up]
. . . .
⊟ **1** prone to, inclined to, disposed to, given to, subject to. **2** sensitive, tender. **3** receptive, responsive, impressionable, suggestible, weak, vulnerable.
⊞ **1** resistant to, immune to.
. . . .

sushi /ˈsuːʃɪ/ *noun* a Japanese dish of small cakes of cold rice topped with raw fish or vegetables. [from Japanese *sushi*]

suspect — *verb* (with stress on *-spect*) **1** to consider likely. **2** to think (a person) possibly or probably guilty of a crime or other wrongdoing. **3** to doubt the truth or genuineness of. — *noun* (with stress on *sus-*) a person suspected of committing a crime, etc. — *adj.* (with stress on *sus-*) thought to be possibly false, untrue or dangerous; dubious. [from Latin *suspicere*]

◫ *verb* **1** believe, fancy, feel, guess, suppose, consider. **2** distrust, mistrust. **3** doubt, call into question. *adj.* suspicious, doubtful, dubious, questionable, debatable, unreliable, *colloq.* iffy, *colloq.* dodgy, *colloq.* fishy.

◱ *adj.* acceptable, reliable.

suspend *verb* **1** to hang or hang up. **2** to bring a halt to, especially temporarily. **3** to delay or postpone. **4** to remove from a job, a team, etc temporarily, as punishment or during an investigation of a possible misdemeanour. **5** to keep small insoluble solid particles more or less evenly dispersed throughout a fluid (a liquid or a gas). [from Latin *suspendere*]

◫ **1** hang, dangle, swing. **2** adjourn, interrupt, discontinue, halt, cease. **3** delay, defer, postpone, put off, shelve. **4** dismiss, expel, exclude, debar.

◱ **2** continue. **4** reinstate.

suspended animation a state in which a body's main functions are temporarily slowed down to an absolute minimum, eg in hibernation.

suspended sentence a sentence of imprisonment not actually served unless the offender commits another crime within a specified period.

suspender belt a woman's belt-like undergarment with attached suspenders.

suspenders *pl. noun* **1** elastic straps for holding up women's stockings. **2** elastic straps for holding up men's socks. **3** *North Amer.* braces for trousers.

suspense *noun* a state of nervous or excited uncertainty. [related to SUSPEND]

◫ uncertainty, insecurity, anxiety, tension, apprehension, anticipation, expectation, expectancy, excitement.

◱ certainty, knowledge.

suspenseful *adj.* full of suspense.

suspension *noun* **1** the act of suspending or the state of being suspended. **2** a system of springs and shock absorbers that connect the axles of a car to the chassis, and absorb some of the unwanted vibrations transmitted from the road surface. **3** a system in which small insoluble solid particles are more or less evenly dispersed throughout a fluid (a liquid or a gas).

◫ **1** adjournment, interruption, break, intermission, respite, remission, stay, moratorium, delay, deferral, postponement, abeyance.

◱ **1** continuation.

suspension bridge a bridge in which the road or rail surface hangs on vertical cables themselves attached to thicker cables stretched between towers.

suspicion *noun* **1** the feeling of suspecting. **2** an act of suspecting; a belief or opinion based on intuition or slender evidence. **3** a slight quantity; a trace. **above suspicion** too highly respected to be suspected of a crime or wrongdoing. **under suspicion** suspected of a crime or wrongdoing. [related to SUSPECT]

◫ **1** doubt, scepticism, distrust, mistrust, wariness, caution, misgiving, apprehension. **2** idea, notion, hunch, belief, opinion. **3** trace, hint, suggestion,

soupçon, touch, tinge, shade, glimmer, shadow.

◱ **1** trust.

suspicious *adj.* **1** (*often* **suspicious of** or **about something**) suspecting or tending to suspect guilt, wrongdoing, or danger. **2** arousing suspicion; dubious.

◫ **1** doubtful, sceptical, unbelieving, suspecting, distrustful, mistrustful, wary, chary, apprehensive, uneasy. **2** dubious, questionable, suspect, irregular, shifty, *colloq.* shady, *colloq.* dodgy, *colloq.* fishy.

◱ **1** trustful, confident. **2** trustworthy, innocent.

suspiciously *adv.* in a suspicious way.

suss or **sus** *slang verb* (*also* **suss someone** or **something out**) **1** to discover them, or discover their character, especially by intuition. **2** to assess or establish by taking a look. — *noun* **1** a suspect. **2** suspicion, or suspicious behaviour. [a shortening of SUSPECT or SUSPICION]

sussed *adj. colloq.* well-informed; in the know.

sustain *verb* **1** to maintain the energy or spirits of; to keep going. **2** to suffer or undergo (eg an injury). **3** to judge (especially a barrister's objection to an opposing barrister's question or comment in court) to be valid. **4** to bear the weight of; to support. **5** to keep in existence, especially over a long period; to maintain. [from Latin *sustinere*]

◫ **1** maintain, keep going, nourish, provide for, help, aid, assist, comfort, relieve. **2** suffer, receive, undergo, experience. **3** uphold, accept. **4** support, bear, carry, hold. **5** maintain, keep up, continue, prolong.

sustained *adj.* maintained, usually for a long time without a break.

◫ prolonged, protracted, long-drawn-out, steady, continuous, constant, perpetual, unremitting.

◱ broken, interrupted, intermittent, spasmodic.

sustained-yield cropping *Environ.* the removal of a natural resource, eg trees, fish, at at a rate that does not irreparably deplete or damage the population.

sustenance *noun* that which keeps up energy or spirits, especially food and drink. [related to SUSTAIN]

◫ nourishment, food, drink, refreshments, provisions, fare, maintenance, subsistence, livelihood.

suttee /ˈsʌtiː/ *noun* **1** a former Hindu custom in which a widow sacrifices herself by being burned alive on her dead husband's funeral fire. **2** a Hindu woman who sacrifices herself in this way. [from Sanskrit *sati*, true wife]

suture /ˈsuːtʃə(r)/ — *noun* **1** the thread used in sewing up wounds. **2** a stitch or seam made with such thread. — *verb* to sew up (a wound). [from Latin *sutura*, seam]

suzerain /ˈsuːzəreɪn/ *noun* **1** a nation or state that has control over another. **2** a feudal lord. [from French *suzerain*]

suzerainty /ˈsuːzərəntɪ/ *noun* the position or power of a suzerain.

svelte /svɛlt/ *adj.* of attractively slim build. [from French *svelte*]

SW *abbrev.* **1** short wave. **2** south-west or south-western.

swab /swɒb/ — *noun* **1** a piece of cotton wool or gauze used to clean wounds, apply antiseptics, etc. **2** a sample of some bodily fluid taken for examination. **3** a mop used for cleaning floors, ships' decks, etc. **4** *slang* a worthless person. — *verb* (**swabbed**, **swabbing**) to clean or clean out with, or as if with, a swab. [from Old Dutch *swabbe*]

swaddle /ˈswɒdl/ *verb* **1** to bandage. **2** to wrap (a baby) in swaddling clothes. [from Anglo-Saxon *swæthel*, bandage]

swaddling clothes strips of cloth formerly wrapped round a newborn baby to restrict movement.

swag — *noun* **1** *slang* stolen goods. **2** *Austral.* a traveller's pack or rolled bundle of possessions. **3** a garland hung between two points, or a carved representation of one. — *verb intrans.* (**swagged, swagging**) to sway or sag. [from Norse *sveggja*, to cause to sway]

swagger — *verb intrans.* (**swaggered, swaggering**) **1** to walk with an air of self-importance. **2** to behave arrogantly. — *noun* **1** a swaggering way of walking or behaving. **2** *colloq.* the quality of being showily fashionable or smart. — *adj., colloq.* showily fashionable or smart. [see SWAG]

....

◧ *verb* **1** parade, strut. **2** bluster, boast, crow, brag, *colloq.* swank. *noun* **1** bluster, boasting, self-importance, arrogance. **2** show, ostentation.

....

swagger-stick *noun* a short cane carried by a military officer.

swagman *noun Austral.* a traveller on foot, especially an itinerant workman, who carries a swag.

Swahili /swɑˈhiːlɪ/ *noun* **1** a group of Bantu-speaking peoples of the coast and islands of E Africa. **2** the language spoken by these people, today spoken as a lingua franca throughout E Africa.

swain *noun, old use, poetic* **1** a country youth. **2** a young male lover or suitor. [from Anglo-Saxon *swan*]

swallow[1] — *verb* **1** to transfer (food or drink) from the mouth to the oesophagus (gullet) by a muscular movement of the tongue. **2** *intrans.* to move the muscles of the throat as if performing such an action; to gulp. **3** (*also* **swallow something up**) to make it an indistinguishable and inseparable part of a larger mass; to engulf or absorb it. **4** to stifle or repress (one's pride, tears, etc). **5** to accept (an insult, etc) meekly and without retaliation. **6** *colloq.* to believe unquestioningly. — *noun* **1** an act of swallowing. **2** an amount swallowed at one time. [from Anglo-Saxon *swelgan*]

....

◧ *verb* **1** eat, drink, consume, devour, gobble up, guzzle, gulp, quaff, *colloq.* knock back, *colloq.* down. **3** engulf, enfold, envelop, absorb, assimilate. **4** stifle, smother, repress, hold back, contain, suppress. **5** accept, take. **6** believe, *colloq.* buy.

....

swallow[2] *noun* a small fast-flying insect-eating bird with long pointed wings and a long forked tail. [from Anglo-Saxon *swalwe*]

swallow dive a dive during which the arms are held out at chest level until just before the entry into water.

swallowtail butterfly a large colourful butterfly with hindwings extended into slender tails. The adults and larvae are usually distasteful to predators.

swam see SWIM.

swami /ˈswɑːmɪ/ *noun* a Hindu religious teacher. [from Hindi *svami*, lord, master]

swamp — *noun* an area of land that is permanently waterlogged but has a dense covering of vegetation, especially trees and shrubs, eg mangroves in certain tropical regions, reeds or willows in some temperate regions. — *verb* **1** to overwhelm or inundate. **2** to cause (a boat) to fill with water. **3** to flood. [from Old Dutch *somp*]

....

◧ *noun* bog, marsh, fen, slough, quagmire, quicksand, mire, mud. *verb* **1** overwhelm, overload, inundate, besiege, beset. **2** engulf, submerge, sink. **3** flood, inundate, deluge, drench, saturate, waterlog.

....

swampy *adj.* (**swampier, swampiest**) having many swamps; of the nature of or like a swamp.

swan — *noun* any of six species of a large graceful aquatic bird with a long slender neck, powerful wings, and webbed feet, belonging to the same family (Anatidae) as ducks and geese. — *verb intrans.* (**swanned, swanning**) *colloq.*

(**swan off, around,** *etc*) to spend time or wander irresponsibly or idly. [from Anglo-Saxon]

swank *colloq.* — *verb intrans.* to boast or show off. — *noun* boastfulness.

swanky *adj.* (**swankier, swankiest**) *colloq.* **1** boastful. **2** showily smart or fashionable.

swan song the last performance or piece of work by a musician, artist, etc before death or retirement.

swap or **swop** — *verb* (**swapped, swapping**) **1** (**swap things** or **one thing for another**) to exchange them. **2** *intrans.* (*often* **swap with someone**) to exchange something one has for something they have. — *noun* **1** an exchange. **2** a thing exchanged or offered in exchange. [from Middle English *swappen*]

....

◧ *verb* EXCHANGE, TRADE. **1** switch, transpose, interchange, barter, traffic.

....

SWAPO *abbrev.* South-West Africa People's Organization.

swarm[1] — *noun* **1** a large group of bees flying off in search of a new home. **2** any large group of insects or other small creatures on the move. **3** a crowd of people on the move. — *verb intrans.* **1** to gather, move, or go in a swarm. **2** (**be swarming with people** or **things**) *said of a place* to be crowded or overrun with them. [from Anglo-Saxon *swearm*]

....

◧ *noun* **3** crowd, throng, mob, mass, multitude, host, army, horde, herd, flock, drove. *verb* **1** flock, congregate, mass, crowd, throng, flood, stream. **2** be crowded with, be teeming with, be crawling with, be bristling with, abound in.

....

swarm[2] *verb trans., intrans.* (*often* **swarm up**) to climb (especially a rope or tree) by clasping with the hands and knees or feet.

swarthiness *noun* having a dark complexion.

swarthy *adj.* (**swarthier, swarthiest**) of dark complexion. [from Anglo-Saxon *sweart*]

....

◧ dark, dark-skinned, dark-complexioned, dusky, black, brown, tanned.

◨ fair, pale.

....

swashbuckling *adj., said of a story, film, etc* full of adventure and excitement. [from obsolete *swash*, to make noisy violent movements + BUCKLER]

swastika *noun* a plain cross with the ends bent at right angles, usually clockwise, an ancient religious symbol and the adopted badge of the Nazi party. [from Sanskrit *svastika*, from *svasti*, wellbeing]

swat — *verb* (**swatted, swatting**) to crush (especially a fly) with a heavy slapping blow. — *noun* such a blow. [from Old French *esquatir*, to crush]

swatch /swɒtʃ/ *noun* **1** a sample, especially of fabric. **2** a collection of fabric samples.

swath /swɔːθ, swɒθ/ or **swathe** /sweɪð/ *noun* **1** a strip of grass or corn, etc cut by a scythe, mower, or harvester; also, the width of this. **2** a broad strip, especially of land. [from Anglo-Saxon *swæth*, track]

swathe[1] /sweɪð/ — *verb* to wrap or bind in fabric, eg clothes or bandages. — *noun* a bandage; a wrapping, especially of cloth. [from Anglo-Saxon *swathian*]

swathe[2] see SWATH.

sway — *verb* **1** *trans., intrans.* to swing or cause to swing from side to side, especially slowly and smoothly. **2** *intrans.* to waver between two opinions or decisions. **3** to persuade to take a particular view or decision. — *noun* **1** a swaying motion. **2** control or influence. — **hold sway** to have authority or influence. [perhaps from Norse *sveigja*, to bend]

....

◧ *verb* **1** rock, roll, swing, wave, bend, incline, lean. **2** waver, oscillate, fluctuate. **3** influence, affect, persuade, induce, convince, convert.

. . . .

swear *verb* (PAST TENSE **swore**; PAST PARTICIPLE **sworn**) **1** *intrans.* to use indecent or blasphemous language. **2** to promise or assert solemnly or earnestly, as if by taking an oath. **3** (**swear to something**) to solemnly state it to be unquestionably true. **4** (**swear someone to something**) to bind them to a solemn promise: *I swore him to secrecy.* — **swear by someone** or **something 1** to appeal to a deity as a witness of one's solemn promise or statement. **2** *colloq.* to put complete trust in something (eg a certain product or remedy). **swear someone in** to introduce them formally into a post, or into the witness box, by requesting them to take an oath. **swear off something** *colloq.* to promise to renounce it or give it up. [from Anglo-Saxon *swerian*]

. . . .

■ **1** curse, blaspheme. **2** vow, promise, pledge, avow, attest, asseverate, testify, affirm, assert, declare, insist.

. . . .

swear word a word regarded as obscene or blasphemous.

. . . .

■ expletive, four-letter word, curse, oath, imprecation, obscenity, profanity, blasphemy.

. . . .

sweat — *noun* **1** the salty moisture that the body gives off through the skin's pores during physical exertion, exposure to heat, nervousness or fear. **2** the state, or a fit, of giving off such moisture. **3** *colloq.* any activity that causes the body to give off such moisture. — *verb* (PAST TENSE AND PAST PARTICIPLE **sweated, sweat**) **1** *intrans.* to give off sweat through one's pores. **2** *intrans.* to release a sweat-like moisture, as cheese does when warm. **3** *intrans. colloq.* to be nervous, anxious or afraid. **4** to exercise (eg a racehorse) strenuously, to the point of producing sweat. **5** to cook (eg onions) slowly so as to release and retain the juices. — **in a sweat** *colloq.* in a worried or anxious state. **no sweat!** *slang* **1** that presents no problems. **2** okay! **sweat blood** *colloq.* **1** to work extremely hard. **2** to be in a state of extreme anxiety. **sweat it out** *colloq.* to endure a difficult or unpleasant situation to the end, especially to wait at length in nervous anticipation. [from Anglo-Saxon *swætan*]

. . . .

■ *noun* **1** perspiration, moisture, stickiness. **3** toil, labour, drudgery, chore. *verb* **1** perspire, swelter.

. . . .

sweatband *noun* a strip of elasticated fabric worn around the wrist or head to absorb sweat when playing sports.

sweated labour hard work for long hours with poor pay and conditions; also, people carrying out this work.

sweater *noun* a knitted jersey or pullover, of a kind worn before and after hard exercise.

sweatshirt *noun* a long-sleeved jersey of a thick soft cotton fabric with a fleecy lining, originally worn for sports.

sweatshop *noun* a workshop or factory in which sweated labour is demanded.

sweatsuit *noun* a loose-fitting suit of sweatshirt and trousers, usually tight-fitting at the wrists and ankles, worn especially by athletes.

sweaty *adj.* (**sweatier, sweatiest**) **1** causing sweat. **2** covered with sweat, wet or stained with sweat. **3** smelling of sweat.

. . . .

■ **2** sweating, perspiring, damp, moist, clammy, sticky.
▣ **2** dry.

. . . .

Swede /swiːd/ *noun* a native or citizen of Sweden.

swede /swiːd/ *noun* a large turnip with yellow flesh, originally introduced from Sweden.

Swedish — *noun* **1** the language of Sweden. **2** (**the Swedish**) the people of Sweden; Swedes. — *adj.* relating to Sweden or its people or language.

sweep — *verb* (PAST TENSE AND PAST PARTICIPLE **swept**) **1** (*also* **sweep up** or **sweep something up**) to clean (a room, a floor, etc), or remove (dirt, dust, etc), with a brush or broom. **2** to take, carry, or push suddenly and with irresistible force. **3** to force or inspire into taking an unwanted or unintended direction or course of action. **4** to lift, gather, or clear with a forceful scooping or brushing movement. **5** *intrans.* to move, pass, or spread smoothly and swiftly, or uncontrollably. **6** *intrans.* to walk (especially with garments flowing) impressively or arrogantly. **7** to pass quickly over, making light contact. **8** *intrans.* to extend curvingly and impressively into the distance. **9** *said of emotions, etc* to affect suddenly and overpoweringly. **10** to cast or direct (eg one's gaze) with a scanning movement. — *noun* **1** an act of sweeping. **2** a sweeping movement. **3** a sweeping line, eg of a road or landscape. **4** *colloq.* a sweepstake. **5** *colloq.* a chimney-sweep. — **sweep something under the carpet** to hide or ignore something (especially unwelcome facts, difficulties, etc). [from Anglo-Saxon *swapan*, to sweep]

. . . .

■ *verb* **1** brush, dust, clean, clear, remove. **5** pass, sail, fly, glide, skim, glance, whisk, tear, hurtle. *noun* **2** swing, stroke, movement, gesture. **3** arc, curve, bend, range, span, stretch, vista.

. . . .

sweeper *noun* **1** a person who sweeps. **2** a device or machine used for sweeping. **3** *Sport* a player covering the whole area behind a line of defenders.

sweeping — *adj.* **1** *said of a search, change, etc* wide-ranging and thorough. **2** *said of a statement* too generalized; indiscriminate. **3** *said of a victory, etc* impressive; decisive. — *noun* (*usually* **sweepings**) a thing swept up.

. . . .

■ *adj.* **1** wide-ranging, broad, extensive, far-reaching, thorough, comprehensive, general, global, across-the-board, radical, wholesale. **2** generalized, oversimplified, simplistic, indiscriminate, general, global, all-inclusive, all-embracing, blanket.
▣ *adj.* **1** narrow. **2** specific.

. . . .

sweepingly *adv.* **1** with a sweeping gesture or movement. **2** indiscriminately, comprehensively.

sweepstake *noun* **1** a system of gambling in which the prize money is the sum of the stakes of all those betting. **2** a horse race in which the winning owner receives sums of money put up by all the other owners.

sweet — *adj.* **1** tasting like sugar; not sour, salty or bitter. **2** pleasing to any of the senses, especially smell and hearing. **3** *said of air or water* fresh and untainted. **4** *said of wine* having some taste of sugar or fruit; not dry. **5** likeable; charming. **6** *colloq.* (**sweet on someone**) fond of them; infatuated with them. — *noun* **1** any small sugar-based confection for sucking or chewing. **2** a dessert. **3** a person one loves or is fond of. [from Anglo-Saxon *swete*]

. . . .

■ *adj.* **1** sugary, syrupy, sweetened. **2** pleasant, delightful, lovely, attractive, beautiful, perfumed, fragrant, aromatic, melodious, harmonious, euphonious, dulcet, soft, mellow, luscious, delicious. **3** fresh, clean, unpolluted, pure, clear. **5** charmig, agreeable, likeable, lovable, appealing, winsome, cute, pretty. **6** kind, nice, considerate, thoughtful, generous, affectionate, tender. *noun* **2** dessert, pudding, *colloq.* afters.
▣ *adj.* **1** savoury, salty, sour, bitter. **2** unpleasant, ugly, malodorous, discordant. **3** foul. **6** nasty, mean.

. . . .

Sweets include: barley sugar, bull's eye, butterscotch, caramel, chewing gum, chocolate, fondant, fruit pastille, fudge, gobstopper, gumdrop, humbug, jelly, jelly bean, liquorice, liquorice allsort, lollipop, *trademark* Mars, marshmallow, marzipan, nougat, peppermint, praline, rock, Edinburgh rock, toffee, toffee apple, truffle, Turkish delight.

sweet-and-sour — *adj.* cooked in a sauce that combines sugar with vinegar or fruit juice. — *noun* a sweet-and-sour dish.

sweetbread *noun* the pancreas of a young animal, especially a calf, used as food.

sweetcorn *noun* kernels of a variety of maize, eaten young while still sweet.

sweeten *verb* (**sweetened, sweetening**) **1** to make (food) sweet or sweeter. **2** (*also* **sweeten someone up**) *colloq.* to make them more agreeable or amenable, eg by flattery. **3** *colloq.* to make (eg an offer) more acceptable or inviting, by making changes or additions.

◫ **1** sugar, honey. **2** mellow, soften, soothe, appease.
  3 temper, cushion.
▣ **1** sour. **2** embitter.

sweetener *noun* **1** an agent for sweetening food, especially one other than sugar. **2** *colloq.* an additional and usually illicit inducement made to an offer to make it more attractive, especially a bribe.

sweetheart *noun* **1** a term of endearment. **2** *old use* a lover.

sweetie *noun colloq.* **1** a sweet confection for sucking or chewing. **2** a term of endearment. **3** a lovable person.

sweetly *adv.* in a sweet way.

sweetmeat *noun* any small sugar-based confection or cake.

sweetness *noun* a sweet quality.

sweet nothings the endearments that lovers say to each other.

sweet pea a European climbing plant with delicate fragrant brightly-coloured flowers.

sweet pepper 1 a fruit native to the New World, consisting of a hollow fleshy pod, usually red, green, or yellow in colour. **2** the plant which produces such fruit.

sweet potato the potato-like root of a tropical American climbing plant, with pinkish violet or grey skin and yellow or pink, slightly sweet flesh.

sweet talk *colloq.* flattery intended to persuade.

sweet-talk *verb colloq.* to persuade with flattery.

sweet tooth a fondness for sweet foods.

sweet-toothed *adj.* fond of sweet things.

sweet william a perennial plant (*Dianthus barbatus*), native to S Europe, having elliptical leaves sheathing its stem, and dense compact heads of dark red or pink flowers; garden varieties also include white and spotted forms.

swell — *verb* (PAST TENSE **swelled**; PAST PARTICIPLE **swollen**, **swelled**) **1** *intrans.* (*also* **swell up** or **out**) to become bigger or fatter through injury or infection, or by filling with liquid or air. **2** (*also* **swell something up** or **out**) to make it bigger or fatter. **3** *trans., intrans.* to increase or cause to increase in number, size, or intensity. **4** *intrans.* to become visibly filled with emotion, especially pride. **5** *intrans., said of the sea* to rise and fall in smooth masses, without forming individual waves. **6** *intrans., said of a sound* to become louder, then die away. — *noun* **1** a heaving of the sea without waves. **2** an increase in number, size or intensity. **3** an increase in volume of sound or music, followed by a dying away. **4** *old colloq. use* a person who dresses smartly and fashionably. **5** *old colloq. use* a prominent member of society. — *adj. chiefly North Amer. colloq.* excellent. [from Anglo-Saxon *swellan*]

◫ *verb* **1** expand, dilate, puff up, bulge, balloon, billow. **2** expand, dilate, inflate, blow up, puff up, bloat, distend, fatten. **3** increase, enlarge, extend, grow, augment, heighten, intensify. *noun* **2** increase, rise, surge, enlargement.
▣ *verb* **1** shrink, contract. **3** decrease, dwindle.

swelling *noun* an area on the body swollen through injury or infection.

◫ lump, tumour, bump, bruise, blister, boil, inflammation, bulge, protuberance, puffiness, distension, enlargement.

swelter — *verb intrans.* (**sweltered, sweltering**) to sweat heavily or feel oppressively hot. — *noun* a sweltering feeling or state. [from Anglo-Saxon *sweltan*, to die]

sweltering *adj., said of the weather* oppressively hot.

◫ hot, tropical, baking, scorching, stifling, suffocating, airless, oppressive, sultry, steamy, sticky, humid.
▣ cold, cool, fresh, breezy, airy.

swept see SWEEP.

swerve — *verb intrans.* **1** to turn or move aside suddenly and sharply, eg to avoid a collision. **2** to deviate from a course of action. — *noun* an act of swerving; a swerving movement. [from Middle English *swerve*]

◫ *verb* **1** turn, bend, veer, swing, shift, sheer. **2** deviate, stray, wander, diverge, deflect.

swift — *adj.* **1** fast-moving; able to move fast. **2** done, given, etc quickly or promptly. — *noun* a small fast-flying insect-eating bird similar to the swallow but with longer wings and a shorter tail. [from Anglo-Saxon *swift*]

◫ *adj.* FAST, QUICK, RAPID, SPEEDY, EXPRESS. **1** agile, nimble, *colloq.* nippy. **2** hurried, hasty, flying, short, brief, sudden, prompt, ready.
▣ *adj.* SLOW. **1** sluggish. **2** unhurried.

swiftly *adv.* quickly.

swiftness *noun* being swift.

swig *colloq.* — *verb trans., intrans.* (**swigged, swigging**) to drink in gulps, especially from a bottle. — *noun* a large draught, or gulp.

swill — *verb* **1** to rinse by splashing water round or over. **2** *colloq.* to drink (especially alcohol) greedily. — *noun* **1** any mushy mixture of scraps fed to pigs. **2** disgusting food or drink. **3** *colloq.* a gulp of beer or other alcohol. [from Anglo-Saxon *swilian*, to wash]

swim — *verb* (**swimming**; PAST TENSE **swam**; PAST PARTICIPLE **swum**) *usually intrans.* **1** to propel oneself through water by moving the arms and legs or (in fish) the tail and fins. **2** *trans.* to cover (a distance) or cross (a stretch of water) in this way. **3** to float. **4** (**be swimming in** or **with something**) to be flooded or awash with it. **5** to be affected by dizziness. **6** to move or appear to move about in waves or whirls. — *noun* **1** a spell of swimming. **2** the general flow of events. — **in the swim** *colloq.* up to date with, and often involved in, what is going on around one. [from Anglo-Saxon *swimman*]

swim bladder *Zool.* in bony fishes, an internal structure that can be filled with air and so used to control buoyancy of the fish in the water.

swimmer *noun* a person who swims.

swimming *noun* the act of propelling oneself through water without any mechanical aids.

swimming baths (*also* **swimming bath**) a swimming pool, usually indoors.

swimming costume a swimsuit.

swimmingly *adv. colloq.* smoothly and successfully.

swimming pool an artificial pool for swimming in.

swimsuit *noun* a garment worn for swimming.

◫ swimming costume, bathing costume, bathing suit, bikini, trunks.

swindle — *verb* to cheat or trick; to obtain by cheating or trickery. — *noun* **1** an act of swindling. **2** anything that is not what it is presented as being. [from German *schwindeln*, to be giddy]

. . . .

■ *verb* cheat, defraud, diddle, *colloq.* do, overcharge, fleece, *colloq.* rip off, trick, deceive, dupe, *colloq.* con, *slang* sting. *noun* FRAUD, DECEPTION. **1** fiddle, racket, sharp practice, *colloq.* rip-off, double-dealing, trickery. **2** sham, *colloq.* con.

. . . .

swindler *noun* a person who swindles.

. . . .

■ cheat, fraud, impostor, *colloq.* con man, trickster, shark, rogue, rascal.

. . . .

swine *noun* (PL. **swine, swines** in sense 2) **1** a pig. **2** a despicable person. [from Anglo-Saxon *swin*, pig]

swing — *verb* (PAST TENSE AND PAST PARTICIPLE **swung**) **1** *trans., intrans.* to open, close, or move to and fro in a curving motion, pivoting from a fixed point. **2** *trans., intrans.* to move or cause to move or turn with a sweeping or swaying movement or movements. **3** *intrans.* to undergo a sudden sharp change or changes, eg of opinion, mood or direction. **4** *colloq.* to arrange or fix; to achieve the successful outcome of. **5** *colloq.* to determine or settle the outcome of (eg an election in which voters were initially undecided). **6** *intrans., colloq.* to throw a punch at someone. **7** *intrans., colloq., said of a social function* to be lively and exciting. **8** *intrans., colloq.* to enjoy oneself with vigour and enthusiasm. **9** *intrans., colloq.* to be promiscuous. **10** *intrans.* to be hanged. **11** *Mus.* to perform as swing. — *noun* **1** an act, manner, or spell of swinging. **2** a swinging movement. **3** a seat suspended from a frame or branch, for a child to swing on. **4** a sudden sharp change, eg in mood or pattern of voting. **5** a swinging stroke with a golf club, cricket bat, etc; the technique of a golfer. **6** *Mus.* jazz or jazz-like dance music with a simple regular rhythm, popularized by bands in the 1930s. **7** usual routine or pace: *get back into the swing of things.* — **in full swing** at the height of liveliness. **swing the lead** *slang* to make up excuses to avoid work. **swings and roundabouts** *colloq.* a situation in which advantages and disadvantages are equal. [from Anglo-Saxon *swingan*]

. . . .

■ *verb* **1** hang, dangle, wave, spin, rotate, pivot. **2** sway, rock. **3** veer, swerve, turn, oscillate, fluctuate, vary. *noun* **1** oscillation, fluctuation, variation. **2** sway, rock, rhythm, movement, motion. **4** change, shift.

. . . .

swingboat *noun* a fairground ride in the form of a boat-shaped swinging carriage.

swing bridge a bridge that swings open to let boats through.

swing door a door hinged so as to open in both directions.

swingeing *adj.* hard to bear; severe. [from Anglo-Saxon *swengan*, to shake]

. . . .

■ harsh, severe, stringent, drastic, punishing, devastating, excessive, extortionate, oppressive, heavy.

🔄 mild.

. . . .

swinger *noun, old slang use* **1** a person who has a very active social life, especially with much dancing and drinking. **2** a promiscuous person.

swinging *adj.* **1** moving or turning with a swing. **2** *colloq.* lively and exciting.

swinish *adj.* **1** like a swine. **2** filthy. **3** voracious.

swipe — *verb* **1** to hit with a heavy sweeping blow. **2** (**swipe at someone or something**) to try to hit them. **3** *colloq.* to steal. **4** to pass (a credit or debit card, etc) through an electronic reading terminal. — *noun* a heavy sweeping blow. [from Anglo-Saxon *swipian*, to beat]

. . . .

■ *verb* **1** hit, strike, slap, *colloq.* whack, *colloq.* wallop, *slang*

sock. **2** lunge at, lash out at. **3** steal, pilfer, filch, *colloq.* pinch, *slang* nick. *noun* stroke, blow, slap, smack, clout, *colloq.* whack, *colloq.* wallop.

. . . .

swirl — *verb trans., intrans.* to flow or cause to flow or move with a whirling or circling motion. — *noun* such a motion.

. . . .

■ *verb* spin, twirl, whirl, twist, churn.

. . . .

swish [1] — *verb trans., intrans.* to move or cause to move with a brushing or rustling sound. — *noun* a brushing or rustling sound or movement. [imitative]

swish [2] *adj., colloq.* smart and stylish.

Swiss — *adj.* of or relating to Switzerland, its people, or the dialects of German and French spoken by them. — *noun* (PL. **Swiss**) **1** a native or citizen of Switzerland. **2** either of the dialects of German and French spoken in Switzerland.

Swiss cheese plant monstera.

Swiss roll a cylindrical cake made by rolling up a thin slab of sponge spread with jam or cream.

Switch *noun trademark* a method of paying for goods in the UK, using a plastic card which automatically debits the relevant amount from the user's bank account.

switch — *noun* **1** a manually operated or automatic device that is used to open or close an electric circuit, eg a lever or button that makes or breaks a pair of contacts, or a solid-state switch with no moving parts, eg a transistor. **2** a change; an exchange or change-over. **3** a long flexible twig or cane. **4** *North Amer., esp. US* a set of railway points. — *verb* **1** (**switch something on** or **off**) to turn an appliance on or off by means of a switch. **2** *trans., intrans.* to exchange (one thing or person for another), especially quickly and without notice. **3** *trans., intrans.* to transfer or change over (eg to a different system). **4** to beat with a switch. — **switch off** *colloq.* to stop paying attention. **switch someone on** *colloq.* to make them aware of something. **switch something on** *colloq.* to bring on eg charm or tears at will, to create the required effect.

. . . .

■ *noun* **2** change, alteration, shift, exchange, swap, interchange, change-over, substitution, replacement. *verb* **2** change, exchange, swap, trade, interchange, substitute. **3** transfer, change over, shift, turn.

. . . .

switchback *noun* **1** a road with many twists and turns and upward and downward slopes. **2** a roller-coaster.

switchboard *noun* **1** a board on which incoming telephone calls are connected manually or electronically. **2** a board from which various pieces of electrical equipment are controlled.

switched-on *adj., colloq.* **1** well informed or aware. **2** under the influence of drugs.

swivel — *noun* a joint between two parts enabling one part to turn or pivot independently of the other. — *verb trans., intrans.* (**swivelled, swivelling**) to turn or pivot on a swivel, or as if on a swivel. [from Anglo-Saxon *swifan*, to turn round]

. . . .

■ *verb* turn, pivot, spin, rotate, revolve, twirl.

. . . .

swivel chair a chair in which the seat pivots on the base, and can be spun right round.

swizz *noun colloq.* a thing that, in reality, is disappointingly inferior to what was cheatingly promised.

swizzle — *noun* **1** a frothy cocktail with a rum or gin base. **2** *colloq.* a swizz. — *verb colloq.* to cheat with a swizz.

swizzle-stick *noun* a thin stick used to stir cocktails and other drinks.

swollen past participle of SWELL. — *adj.* bigger or fatter than normal.

☐ *adj.* bloated, distended, puffed up, puffy, inflamed, enlarged, bulbous, bulging,

☐ *adj.* shrunken, shrivelled.

....

swoon — *verb intrans.* **1** to faint. **2** (**swoon over someone** or **something**) to go into raptures or fits of adoration for them. — *noun* an act of swooning. [from Middle English *iswowen*]

swoop — *verb intrans.* **1** to fly down with a fast sweeping movement. **2** to make a sudden forceful attack; to descend or pounce. — *noun* **1** an act of swooping. **2** a swooping movement. [from Anglo-Saxon *swapan*, to sweep]

....

☐ *verb* **1** dive, plunge, drop, fall. **2** descend, pounce, lunge, rush. *noun* **1** dive, plunge, drop, descent, lunge, rush, attack, onslaught.

....

swop see SWAP.

sword *noun* **1** a weapon like a large heavy knife, with a long blade sharpened on one or both edges. **2** (**the sword**) violence or destruction, especially in war. — **cross swords with someone** to encounter them as an opponent. [from Anglo-Saxon *sweord*]

....

☐ **1** blade, foil, rapier, sabre, scimitar.

....

sword dance **1** in Scotland, a dance, often by a solo dancer, with steps over an arrangement of swords laid on the ground. **2** in northern England, a dance for a group of dancers carrying long flexible swords with which they perform a number of movements and create various patterns.

swordfish *noun* a large sea-fish with a very long and pointed upper jaw used as a weapon.

sword of Damocles /ˈdaməkliːz/ literary any imminent danger or disaster.

swordplay *noun* **1** the activity or art of fencing. **2** lively argument.

swordsman *noun* a man skilled in fighting with a sword.

swordsmanship *noun* skill in using a sword.

swordstick *noun* a hollow walking-stick containing a short sword or dagger.

swordtail *noun* a small colourful freshwater fish native to streams and swamps of Central America, up to 12cm in length, and green in colour with an orange side stripe. In the male the lower edge of the tail is prolonged to form the 'sword'. It is a popular aquarium fish, with many varieties produced by selective breeding.

swore see SWEAR.

sworn past participle of SWEAR. — *adj.* bound or confirmed by, or as if by, having taken an oath: *sworn enemies.*

swot *colloq.* — *verb* (**swotted, swotting**) **1** *intrans.* to study hard and seriously. **2** (*also* **swot something up**) to study it intensively, especially at the last minute. — *noun* a person who studies hard, especially single-mindedly or in order to impress a teacher. [a variant of SWEAT]

....

☐ *verb* STUDY, REVISE, CRAM. **1** work. **2** learn, memorize, *colloq.* mug up (on), *colloq.* bone up on.

....

swum see SWIM.

swung see SWING.

sybarite /ˈsɪbəraɪt/ *noun* a person devoted to a life of luxury and pleasure. [originally an inhabitant of *Sybaris*, an ancient Greek city in S Italy, noted for its luxury]

sybaritic /sɪbəˈrɪtɪk/ *adj.* luxurious.

sycamore *noun* **1** a deciduous tree of Europe and Asia, with large five-pointed leaves and seed-cases that spin when they fall. **2** *North Amer.* any American plane tree. **3** the wood of any of these trees. [from Greek *sykomoros*, from *sykon*, fig]

sycophancy /ˈsɪkəfənsɪ/ *noun* the behaviour of a sycophant, flattery.

sycophant /ˈsɪkəfənt/ *noun* a person who flatters in a servile way; a crawler. [from Greek *sykophantes*, informer, swindler]

sycophantic /sɪkəˈfantɪk/ *adj.* characteristic of a sycophant or sycophancy.

SYHA *abbrev.* Scottish Youth Hostels Association.

syllabary /ˈsɪləbərɪ/ *noun* a writing system in which the basic units, or *graphemes*, correspond to spoken syllables. Examples of syllabic writing systems include the ancient Cypriot syllabary of the 6c–3cBC; and present-day Amharic, Cherokee, and Japanese *kana*.

syllabi /ˈsɪləbaɪ/ see SYLLABUS.

syllabic /sɪˈlabɪk/ *adj.* relating to syllables, or the division of words into syllables.

syllabification *noun* division into syllables.

syllabify *verb* (**syllabifies, syllabified**) to divide (a word) into syllables.

syllable *noun* **1** each of the distinct parts that a spoken word can be divided into. Each part consists of one or more sounds and usually includes a vowel. The word *telephone* has three syllables, *tiger* has two, and *book, dance,* and *shape* have one each. **2** the slightest sound: *they hardly uttered a syllable all evening.* — **in words of one syllable** in simple language; frankly. [from Greek *syllabe*]

syllabub or **sillabub** *noun* a frothy dessert made by whipping a sweetened mixture of cream or milk and wine.

syllabus *noun* (PL. **syllabuses, syllabi**) a series of topics prescribed for a course of study; also, a booklet or sheet listing these. [from a misreading of Latin *sittybas*, from Greek *sittyba*, book-label]

....

☐ curriculum, course, programme, schedule, plan.

....

syllogism /ˈsɪlədʒɪzm/ *noun* an argument in which a conclusion, valid or invalid, is drawn from two independent statements using logic, as in *All dogs are animals, foxhounds are dogs, therefore foxhounds are animals.* [from Greek *syllogismos*, a reasoning together]

syllogistic *adj.* relating to or involving syllogism.

sylph *noun* **1** in folklore, a spirit of the air. **2** a slender, graceful woman or girl. [word created by Paracelsus, a medieval alchemist]

sylph-like *adj.* like a sylph, slim.

sylvan *adj. literary* of woods or woodland; wooded. [from Latin *silva*, a wood]

symbiosis /sɪmbɪˈoʊsɪs/ *noun* (PL. **symbioses**) **1** a close association between two organisms of different species, usually to the benefit of both partners. In many cases such a relationship is essential for mutual survival, eg a lichen represents a symbiotic relationship between a fungus and an alga. **2** *Psychol.* a mutually beneficial relationship between two people who are dependent on each other. [from Greek *syn*, together + *bios*, livelihood]

symbiotic *adj.* relating to or involving symbiosis.

symbol *noun* **1** a thing that represents or stands for another, usually something concrete or material representing an idea or emotion, eg the colour red representing danger. **2** a letter or sign used to represent a quantity, idea, object, operation, etc, such as the × used in mathematics to represent the multiplication process or £ used for pound sterling. [from Greek *symbolon*, token]

....

☐ SIGN. **1** representation, figure, image, mark, token, emblem, badge, logo. **2** character, ideogram.

....

Symbols include: badge, brand, cipher, coat ofarms, crest, emblem, hieroglyph, icon, ideogram, insignia, logo, logogram, monogram, motif, pictograph, swastika, token, totem, trademark; ampersand, asterisk, caret, dagger, double-dagger, obelus.

symbolic *adj.* **1** (*often* **symbolic of something**) being a symbol of it; standing for it. **2** relating to symbols or symbolism.

. . . .

▣ **1** representative, emblematic, token. **2** figurative, metaphorical, allegorical.

. . . .

symbolically *adv.* in a symbolic way.

symbolic interactionism a sociological theory which attempts to explain patterns of behaviour in terms of the meanings and symbols that people share in everyday interaction.

symbolism *noun* **1** the use of symbols, especially to express ideas or emotions in literature, cinema, etc. **2** (*often* **Symbolism**) a 19c movement in art and literature making extensive use of symbols.

symbolist *noun* an artist or writer who uses symbolism (see also SYMBOLISM).

symbolize or **symbolise** *verb* to be a symbol of; to stand for.

. . . .

▣ represent, stand for, denote, mean, signify, typify, exemplify, epitomize, personify.

. . . .

symmetrical *adj.* having symmetry.

. . . .

▣ balanced, even, regular, parallel, corresponding, proportional. ▨ asymmetric, irregular.

. . . .

symmetrically *adv.* in a symmetric way.

symmetry *noun* (PL. **symmetries**) **1** exact similarity between two parts or halves, as if one were a mirror image of the other. **2** the arrangement of parts in pleasing proportion to each other; also, the aesthetic satisfaction derived from this. [from Greek *syn*, together + *metron*, measure]

. . . .

▣ **1** parallelism, correspondence. **2** balance, evenness, regularity, proportion, harmony, agreement.
▨ **1** asymmetry. **2** irregularity.

. . . .

sympathetic *adj.* **1** (*also* **sympathetic to someone** or **something**) feeling or expressing sympathy for them. **2** amiable, especially because of being kind-hearted. **3** acting or done out of sympathy. **4** in keeping with one's mood or feelings; agreeable. **5** *Biol.* or or relating to the sympathetic nervous system.

. . . .

▣ **1** understanding, supportive, comforting, consoling, commiserating, pitying, well-disposed, interested, concerned, solicitous, caring, compassionate. **2** amiable, friendly, kind-hearted, warm-hearted. **4** agreeable, congenial, like-minded, compatible.
▨ **1** unsympathetic, indifferent. **2** callous. **4** antipathetic.

. . . .

sympathetically *adv.* in a sympathetic way.

sympathetic nervous system *Zool.* in vertebrates, a subdivision of the autonomic nervous system. The activity of the sympathetic nervous system tends to increase the heart rate, constrict blood vessels, and generally prepare the body for action. It has the opposite effects to the parasympathetic nervous system.

sympathize or **sympathise** *verb intrans.* (**sympathize with someone**) to feel or express sympathy for them.

. . . .

▣ understand, commiserate with, pity, feel for, empathize with, identify with, respond to.
▨ ignore, disregard.

. . . .

sympathizer or **sympathiser** *noun* a person who sympathizes.

sympathy *noun* (PL. **sympathies**) **1** a deep and genuine understanding of the sadness or suffering of others, often shown in expressions of sorrow or pity. **2** (*often* **sympathy for** or **with someone**) loyal or approving support for them or agreement with them. **3** affection between people resulting from their understanding of each other's personalities. [from Greek *syn*, with + *pathos*, suffering]

. . . .

▣ **1** understanding, comfort, consolation, condolences, commiseration, pity, compassion, tenderness, kindness, warmth. **2** support, approval, agreement, accord, harmony. **3** empathy, fellow-feeling, affinity, rapport.
▨ **1** indifference, insensitivity, callousness. **2** disapproval, disagreement.

. . . .

symphonic *adj.*, *said of music* suitable for performance by a symphony orchestra.

symphony *noun* (PL. **symphonies**) **1** a long musical work in several parts, or movements, played by a full orchestra. **2** an instrumental passage in a musical work which consists mostly of singing. **3** *literary* a pleasing combination of parts, eg shapes or colours. [from Greek *syn*, together + *phone*, sound]

symphony orchestra a large orchestra capable of playing large-scale orchestral music.

symposium *noun* (PL. **symposia**, **symposiums**) **1** a conference held to discuss a particular (especially academic) subject. **2** a collection of essays by different writers on a single topic. [from Greek *symposion*, a drinking-party with intellectual discussion]

symptom *noun* **1** *Medicine* an indication of the presence of a disease or disorder, especially something perceived by the patient and not outwardly visible, eg pain, nausea, dizziness. **2** an indication of the existence of a (usually unwelcome) state or condition: *increasing crime as a symptom of moral decline*. [from Greek *symptoma*, happening, attribute]

. . . .

▣ **2** sign, indication, evidence, manifestation, expression, feature, characteristic, mark, token, warning.

. . . .

symptomatic *adj.* serving as a symptom.

. . . .

▣ indicative, typical, characteristic, associated, suggestive.

. . . .

synagogue /ˈsɪnəgɒg/ *noun* **1** a Jewish place of worship and religious instruction. **2** a Jewish religious assembly or congregation. [from Greek *synagoge*, assembly]

synapse /ˈsaɪnaps/ *noun Anat.* in the nervous system, a region where one neurone (nerve cell) communicates with the next. There is a minute gap between the two cells, across which nerve impulses are transmitted by means of a chemical substance known as a *neurotransmitter*. [from Greek *synapsis*, contact, junction]

synapsis /sɪˈnapsɪs/ *noun* **1** *Biol.* the pairing of chromosomes of paternal and maternal origin during meiosis. **2** *Medicine* a synapse. [from Greek *synapsis*, contact, junction]

synch or **sync** /sɪŋk/ *colloq.* — *noun* synchronization, especially of sound and picture in film and television. — *verb* to synchronize.

synchromesh *noun* a gear system which matches the speeds of the gear wheels before they are engaged, avoiding shock and noise in gear-changing. [a shortening of *synchronized mesh*]

synchronic or **synchronical** *adj. Linguistics* concerned with the study of a language as it exists at a particular point in time, without reference to its past history or development: the opposite of *diachronic*.

Synchronism a US movement in abstract art (c.1913–18). As in Orphism, faceted Cubist-inspired shapes combined with rich colours were characteristic of the style.

synchronization or **synchronisation** *noun* the process of synchronizing or being synchronized.

synchronize or **synchronise** *verb* **1** *trans., intrans.* to happen or cause to happen, move, or operate in exact time with (something else or each other). **2** to project (a film) or broadcast (a television programme) so that the action, actors' lip movements, etc precisely match the sounds or words heard. [from Greek *syn*, together + *chronos*, time]

synchronized swimming a sport in which a swimmer or group of swimmers performs a sequence of gymnastic and balletic movements in time to music. Individual and group competitions have recently become official events in the Olympic Games.

synchronous *adj.* in time with something; synchronized.

synchrotron /'sɪŋkroʊtrɒn/ *noun Physics* a particle accelerator that is used to accelerate electrons and protons which travel around a hollow ring at increasing speed. Synchrotrons are an important experimental tool in particle physics. [from Greek *syn*, together + *chronos*, time + ELECTRON]

syncline /'sɪŋklaɪn/ *noun Geol.* a large generally U-shaped fold in the stratified rocks of the Earth's crust. [from Greek *syn*, together + *klinein*, to cause to lean]

syncopate *verb* to alter (the rhythm of music) by putting the stress on beats not usually stressed. [see SYNCOPE]

syncopation *noun* **1** syncopating. **2** the beat or rhythm produced by syncopating.

syncope /'sɪŋkəpɪ/ *noun* **1** *Medicine* a fit of fainting. **2** the dropping of a letter or syllable in the middle of a word, eg in *o'er*, the poetic version of *over*. [from Greek *synkope*, a cutting short]

sync pulse 1 *Broadcasting* in a television signal, a pulse transmitted at the beginning of each line and field to ensure correct scanning rate on reception. **2** *Cinema* in motion pictures, a series of signals linked to the camera frame rate recorded on the separate sound magnetic tape for subsequent matching to the picture (see also SYNCHRONIZATION).

syndic /'sɪndɪk/ *noun* the person representing a university, company, or other body in business or legal matters. [from Greek *syndikos*, advocate, representative]

syndicalism *noun* a form of trade-unionism favouring the transfer of the ownership of factories, etc to the workers themselves. [from French *syndicalisme*, from Greek *syndikos*, representative]

syndicate — *noun* (pronounced -kɪt) **1** any association of people or groups working together on a single project. **2** a group of business organizations jointly managing or financing a single venture. **3** an association of criminals organizing widespread illegal activities. **4** an association of journalists selling material to a variety of newspapers. — *verb* (pronounced -keɪt) **1** to form into a syndicate. **2** to organize or sell by means of a syndicate. [from Old French *syndicat*, from Greek *syndikos*, representative]

syndication *noun* syndicating or being syndicated.

syndrome *noun* **1** a set of symptoms that represent a specific (physical or mental) illness. **2** a pattern or series of events, observed qualities, etc characteristic of a particular problem or condition. [from Greek *syndrome*, a running together]

synecdoche /sɪ'nekdəkɪ/ *noun* a figure of speech in which a part of something is used to refer to or denote the whole thing, or the whole to refer to or denote a part, as *wiser heads* meaning *wiser people*. [from Greek *synekdoche*, a receiving together]

synergy /'sɪnədʒɪ/ or **synergism** /'sɪnədʒɪzm/ *noun Biol.* the phenomenon in which the combined action of two or more compounds, especially drugs or hormones, is greater than the sum of the individual effects of each compound. [from Greek *synergia*, co-operation]

synod /'sɪnɒd/ *noun* a local or national council of members of the clergy; also, a meeting of this. [from Greek *synodos*, meeting]

synonym *noun* a word having the same, or very nearly the same, meaning as another. [from Greek *syn*, with + *onoma*, name]

synonymous *adj.* (*often* synonymous with something) **1** having the same meaning. **2** very closely associated in the mind: *for many, football is synonymous with hooliganism.*

⬛ **1** interchangeable, substitutable, the same, identical. **2** tantamount, equivalent, corresponding, similar, comparable.
🔁 **1** antonymous, opposite.

synopsis /sɪ'nɒpsɪs/ *noun* (PL. **synopses**) a brief outline, eg of the plot of a book; a summary. [from Greek *syn*, together + *opsis*, view]

⬛ outline, abstract, summary, résumé, précis, digest, condensation, abridgement, review, recapitulation.

synoptic *adj.* of the nature of a synopsis; giving or taking an overall view.

Synoptic Gospels the Gospels of Matthew, Mark, and Luke, which describe the events of Christ's life from a similar point of view.

synovia /sɪ'noʊvɪə, saɪ'noʊvɪə/ *noun* an oily liquid produced by the body to lubricate the joints. [a term invented by Paracelsus]

synovial *adj.* relating to or in the region of the synovia.

syntactic or **syntactical** *adj.* relating or belonging to syntax.

syntax *noun* the positioning of words in a sentence and their relationship to each other; also, the grammatical rules governing this. [from Greek *syn*, together + *tassein*, to put in order]

synthesis /'sɪnθəsɪs/ *noun* (PL. **syntheses**) **1** the process of putting together separate parts to form a complex whole. **2** the result of such a process. **3** *Chem.* any process whereby a complex chemical compound is formed from simpler compounds or elements, especially via a series of chemical reactions. [from Greek *syn*, together + *thesis*, a placing]

synthesize or **synthesise** *verb* **1** to combine (simple parts) to form (a complex whole). **2** to create by chemical synthesis.

⬛ **1** combine, amalgamate, integrate, unify, merge, blend. **2** compound, alloy.
🔁 **1** separate. **2** analyse, resolve.

synthesizer or **synthesiser** /'sɪnθəsaɪzə(r)/ *noun* an integrated set of electronic devices for generating and modifying musical sounds. It usually includes one or more keyboards, loudspeakers, oscillators, filters, and devices for frequency and amplitude modulation. One of the earliest and best known was developed by Robert A Moog (1934–), synthesizers could produce only one note at a time, but more recently polyphonic types have been developed, including digital systems based on microprocessors. There are a wide variety of types and sizes used in the production of both live and pre-recorded music.

synthetic *adj.* **1** created artificially by combining chemical substances; not natural; man-made. **2** not sincere; sham. [from Greek *synthetikos*, skilled at putting together]

⬛ SIMULATED, ARTIFICIAL, FALSE, FAKE, MOCK. **1** manufactured, man-made, ersatz, imitation. **2** insincere, sham, bogus, affected.
🔁 GENUINE, REAL. **1** natural. **2** sincere.

synthetically *adv.* in a synthetic way.

syphilis /'sɪfɪlɪs/ *noun Medicine* a sexually transmitted disease caused by infection with the bacterium *Treponema pallidum*, characterized by painless ulcers which appear on the genitals, and heal spontaneously after several weeks, to be followed by fever, headache, fatigue, and a faint red rash. If untreated with antibiotics, the disease may over a period of years result in heart damage, blindness, paralysis, and death. [from *Syphilus*, the infected hero of a 16c Latin poem]

syphilitic *adj.* relating to or affected with syphilis.

syphon see SIPHON.

Syriac /'sɪrɪak/ — *noun* **1** the ancient Aramaic dialect of Syria. **2** a modern form of this dialect, spoken by c.1m people in the Middle East and the USA. — *adj.* relating to or spoken or written in either of these dialects.

syringa /sɪ'rɪŋgə/ *noun* **1** the mock orange shrub. **2** the lilac shrub. [see SYRINGE]

syringe — *noun* **1** a medical instrument for injecting or drawing off liquid, consisting of a hollow cylinder with a plunger inside and a thin hollow needle attached. **2** a similar device used in gardening, cooking, etc. — *verb* to clean, spray or inject using a syringe. [from Greek *syrinx*, tube]

syrinx /'sɪrɪŋks/ *noun* (PL. **syringes, syrinxes**) **1** a panpipe or set of panpipes. **2** *Zool.* the sound-producing organ of a bird, consisting of several vibrating membranes. [from Greek *syrinx*, a reed, panpipes]

syrup *noun* **1** a sweet sticky almost saturated solution of sugar in water, obtained from various plants, eg sugar-cane, maple, corn, or manufactured commercially, eg golden syrup. It is widely used in cooking, baking, etc. **2** a solution of sugar in water used to preserve canned fruit. **3** any sugar-flavoured liquid medicine. **4** *colloq.* exaggerated sentimentality or pleasantness of manner. [from Arabic *sharab*]

syrupy *adj.* of the consistency of or like syrup.

system *noun* **1** a set of interconnected or interrelated parts forming a complex whole: *the transport system/the human digestive system.* **2** an arrangement of mechanical, electrical or electronic parts functioning as a unit. **3** a way of working; a method. **4** efficiency of organization; methodicalness. **5** one's mind or body regarded as a set of interconnected parts: *get the illness out of your system.* **6** (**the system**) society, or the network of institutions that control it, usually regarded as an oppressive force. [from Greek *systema*]

⊟ **1** structure, set-up, arrangement. **3** method, mode, technique, procedure, process, routine, practice, usage, rule. **4** organization, co-ordination, orderliness, systematization, methodology, logic, order, plan, scheme.

systematic *adj.* **1** making use of, or carried out according to, a clearly worked-out plan or method. **2** methodical.

⊟ **1** ordered, well-ordered, planned, well-planned, organized, well-organized, structured, systematized, standardized. **2** methodical, logical, orderly, businesslike, efficient.

⊟ **1** unsystematic, arbitrary. **2** disorderly, inefficient.

systematically *adv.* in a systematic way.

systematics *sing. noun Biol.* the scientific study of the classification of living organisms into a hierarchical series of groups which emphasizes their natural interrelationships. The main categories of modern classifications are (in order of increasing generality) species, genus, family, order, class, phylum (in animals) or division (in plants), and kingdom.

systematization or **systematisation** *noun* systematizing or being systematized.

systematize or **systematise** *verb* to organize or arrange in a methodical way.

system building *Archit.* methods designed to increase the speed of construction by manufacturing component parts of a building ready for later assembly on site. Many modern buildings are constructed from prefabricated components, such as steel and timber frames, preformed roofing and exterior wall cladding, and windows.

system date *Comput.* the current date as specified by an operating system, used to record a user's operations or to begin pre-set programs, etc.

systemic /sɪ'sti:mɪk, sɪ'stemɪk/ *adj. Medicine, Biol.* relating to or affecting the whole body or the whole plant.

systemically *adv.* in a systemic way.

systems analysis 1 the detailed analysis of all phases of activity of a commercial, industrial, or scientific organization, usually with a computer, in order to plan more efficient methods and better use of resources, or to determine whether computerization of certain processes would be appropriate. **2** *Comput.* the detailed investigation and analysis of some human task, usually in business, commerce, management, industry, or scientific research, in order to determine whether and how it can be computerized, followed in appropriate cases by the design, implementation, and evaluation of a computer system that can perform the task.

systems analyst a person who carries out systems analysis.

systole /'sɪstəlɪ/ *noun Medicine* contraction of the heart muscle, during which blood is pumped from the ventricle into the arteries. Together with *diastole* (relaxation of the muscle) it represents a single heartbeat. [from Greek *systole*]

systolic *adj. Medicine* relating to systole, when the heart pumps out blood.

T

T^1 or **t** *noun* (PL. **Ts, T's, t's**) **1** the twentieth letter of the English alphabet. **2** something shaped like a T, eg a pipe which is used to join three separate pipes together. — **to a T** exactly; perfectly well.

T^2 *abbrev. Mus.* tenor.

T^3 *symbol Chem.* tritium.

t or **t.** *abbrev.* **1** ton. **2** tonne. **3** troy (weight).

TA *abbrev.* Territorial Army.

Ta *symbol Chem.* tantalum.

ta *interj. Brit. colloq.* thank you. [imitative of a young child's pronunciation]

tab^1 — *noun* **1** a small flap, tag, strip of material, etc attached to an article, for hanging it up, opening it, holding it, etc for identification. **2** a small strip of material attached to a garment for hanging it up. **3** *North Amer.* a bill, eg in a restaurant. — *verb* (**tabbed, tabbing**) to fix a tab to. — **keep tabs on someone** or **something** *colloq.* to keep a close watch or check on them. **pick up the tab** *North Amer.* to pay the bill. [probably originally a dialect word]

. . . .

⊟ *noun* **1** flap, tag, marker, label, sticker, ticket.

. . . .

tab^2 *noun* a key on a typewriter or word processor which sets and then automatically finds the position of the margins and columns needed to arrange information in a table. [an abbreviation of TABULATOR]

tabard /'tabəd/ *noun* a short, loose, sleeveless jacket or tunic, worn especially by a knight over his armour, or, with the arms of the king or queen on the front, by a herald. [from Old French *tabart*]

Tabasco /tə'baskou/ *noun trademark* a hot sauce made from a pungent type of red pepper. [named after *Tabasco* in Mexico]

tabbouleh /'tabuleɪ/ *noun* a Mediterranean salad made with cracked wheat which has been soaked especially in lemon juice and mixed with chopped vegetables, especially tomatoes, cucumber, and garlic. [from Arabic *tabbula*]

tabby — *noun* (PL. **tabbies**) **1** (*also* **tabby cat**) **a** a usually grey or brown cat with darker stripes. **b** any female domestic cat. **2** a kind of silk with irregular wavy shiny markings. — *adj.* having darker stripes or wavy markings. [from *Al-Attabiyah* in Baghdad where the silk was first made]

tabernacle /'tabənakl/ *noun* **1** (*also* **Tabernacle**) *Hist.* the tent carried by the Israelites across the desert during the Exodus, used as a sanctuary for the Ark of the Covenant. **2** *RC Church* a receptacle in which the consecrated bread and wine are kept. **3** a place of worship of certain nonconformist Christian denominations. — **Feast of Tabernacles** see SUKKOTH. [from Latin *tabernaculum*, tent]

tabla /'tablə, 'tablɑː/ *noun* a pair of small drums played with the hands in Indian music. [from Hindi, from Arabic]

tablature /'tablətʃə(r)/ *noun* an old system of musical notation (chiefly of the 16c and 17c), tailored to a particular instrument or group of instruments, and indicating the keys, frets, etc, to be used rather than the pitch to be sounded. Nowadays tablature is used only for the guitar and ukulele. [from French, from medieval Latin *tabulatura*, from Latin *tabula*, a board]

table — *noun* **1** a piece of furniture consisting of a flat horizontal surface supported by a leg or legs. **2** the people sitting at a table. **3** the food served at a particular table or in a particular house: *keeps a good table.* **4** a group of words, figures, etc arranged systematically in columns and rows. **5** a multiplication table. **6** any flat level surface. **7** *Hist.* a slab of stone or wood inscribed with laws. **8** a tableland. **9** a broad flat surface cut on a gem. — *verb* **1** *Brit.* to put forward for discussion. **2** *North Amer.* to postpone discussion of a bill, etc indefinitely. **3** to make or enter into a table; to tabulate. — **at table** having a meal. **on the table** under discussion. **turn the tables on someone** to reverse a situation, so that they are at a disadvantage where previously they had an advantage. [from Latin *tabula*, board, tablet]

. . . .

⊟ *noun* **1** counter, worktop, desk, bench, stand, board, slab. **4** diagram, chart, graph, timetable, schedule, programme, list, inventory, catalogue, index, register, record. *verb* **1** propose, suggest, submit, put forward.

. . . .

tableau /'tablou/ *noun* (PL. **tableaux**) **1** a picture or pictorial representation of a group or scene. **2** (*also* **tableau vivant**) a group of people on stage forming a silent motionless scene from history, literature, etc. [from French]

tablecloth *noun* an often decorative cloth for covering a table, especially during meals.

table d'hôte /tɑːbl 'dout/ *noun* (PL. **tables d'hôte**) a meal with a set number of choices and a set number of courses offered for a fixed price, especially to residents in a hotel. [from French *table d'hôte*, host's table]

tableland *noun Geol.* a broad high plain or a plateau, usually with steep sides and rising sharply from the surrounding lowland.

table licence a licence to sell and serve alcohol only with meals.

table linen tablecloths and napkins.

table mat a mat for protecting the top of a table from the heat of dishes from the oven and warmed plates.

tablespoon *noun* **1** a spoon which is larger than a dessert spoon and is used for serving food. **2** the amount a tablespoon will hold.

tablespoonful *noun* (PL. **tablespoonfuls**) the amount a tablespoon will hold.

tablet *noun* **1** a small, solid, measured amount of a medicine or drug; a pill. **2** a solid flat piece of something, eg soap. **3** a slab of stone or wood on which inscriptions may be carved. [from Old French *tablete*, from Latin *tabula*, board]

table tennis a game based on tennis which is played indoors on a table with small bats and a light hollow ball.

tableware *noun* dishes, plates, cutlery, etc for use at table.

tabloid *noun* a newspaper with relatively small pages (approximately 12x16in, 30x40cm), especially one written in an informal and often sensationalist style and with many photographs. See also BROADSHEET. [from TABLET]

taboo or **tabu** /tə'buː/ — *noun* **1** anything which is forbidden for religious reasons or by social custom. **2** any system which forbids certain actions as being unclean or holy. — *adj.* forbidden or prohibited as being a taboo. — *verb* to forbid (a custom, the use of a word, etc) as a taboo. [from Tongan (the language of Tonga) *tabu*, unclean, holy]

◼ *noun* **1** ban, interdiction, prohibition, restriction, anathema, curse. *adj.* forbidden, prohibited, banned, proscribed, unacceptable, unmentionable, unthinkable. *verb* forbid, prohibit, ban, proscribe.

◪ *adj.* permitted, acceptable. *verb* permit, allow.

tabor /ˈteɪbə(r)/ *noun* a small, single-headed drum played with one hand while the same player plays a pipe or fife with the other. [from Old French *tabour*]

tabular /ˈtabjʊlə(r)/ *adj.* arranged in systematic columns; in the form of or according to a table. [from Latin *tabularis*, from *tabula*, board]

tabulate /ˈtabjʊleɪt/ *verb* to arrange (information) in tabular form. [from Latin *tabulare*, from *tabula*, board]

tabulation *noun* tabulating.

tabulator *noun* **1** see TAB². **2** a machine which reads data from a computer storage device, especially from punched cards, and prints it out on continuous sheets of paper.

Tachism or **Tachisme** /ˈtaʃɪzm/ *noun Art* a term used, especially in France, to describe a movement in mid-20c abstract painting which coincided with the development of action painting in the US. Paint was laid on in thick patches intended to be interesting in themselves, irrespective of whether a motif was represented. [from French *tache*, blob (of paint)]

tachograph /ˈtakɒgraːf/ *noun* a device which records the speed a vehicle travels at and the distance travelled in a particular period of time, used especially in lorries and coaches. [from Greek *tachos*, speed]

tachometer /taˈkɒmɪtə(r)/ *noun* a device which measures the speed of a machine or vehicle.

tachycardia /takɪˈkaːdɪə/ *noun Medicine* abnormally rapid beating of the heart. [from Greek *tachys*, swift + *kardia*, heart]

tacit /ˈtasɪt/ *adj.* understood but not actually stated; implied; inferred. [from Latin *tacitus*, silent]

◼ unspoken, unexpressed, unvoiced, silent, understood, implicit, implied, inferred.

◪ express, explicit.

tacitly *adv.* without speaking, silently.

◼ implicitly, by implication, by inference, silently, on the quiet.

tacitness *noun* silence.

taciturn /ˈtasɪtɜːn/ *adj.* saying little; quiet and uncommunicative. [from Latin *taciturnus*, from *tacere*, to be silent]

◼ silent, quiet, uncommunicative, unforthcoming, laconic, reticent, reserved, withdrawn, aloof, distant, cold.

◪ talkative, communicative, forthcoming.

taciturnity *noun* a taciturn or uncommunicative quality.

tack — *noun* **1** a short nail with a sharp point and a broad flat head. **2** a long loose temporary stitch used especially to hold material together while it is being sewn properly. **3** the direction of a sailing ship which is sailing into the wind at an angle, stated in terms of the side of the sail that the wind is blowing against: *on the starboard tack*. **4** a sailing ship's zigzag course formed by sailing with first one side of the sail to the wind and then the other. **5** a direction, course of action, or policy. **6** riding harness, saddle, and bridle, etc for a horse. **7** stickiness. — *verb* **1** (*also* **tack something down**) to fasten or attach it with tacks. **2** to sew with long loose temporary stitches. **3** (*also* **tack something on**) to attach or add it as a supplement. **4** *intrans., said of a sailing ship or its crew* to sail into the wind at an angle with first one side of the sail to the wind and then the other so as to sail in a zigzag course and be able to progress forwards. **5** to change the tack of (a ship) to the opposite one. **6** *in-*

trans. to change one's direction, course of action, or policy abruptly. [from Middle English *tak*]

◼ *noun* **1** nail, pin, drawing-pin, staple. **3**, **4**, **5** course, path, direction, line, bearing, heading. **5** approach, method, way, technique, procedure, plan, tactic, attack. *verb* **1**, **3** attach, affix. **1** fasten, fix, nail, pin, staple. **2** stitch, baste. **3** add, append.

tackily *adv.* in a tacky way.

tackiness *noun* **1** a tacky quality. **2** stickiness. **3** vulgarity.

tackle — *noun* **1** *Sport* an act of trying to get the ball away from a player on the opposing team. **2** the equipment needed for a particular sport or occupation. **3** a system of ropes and pulleys for lifting heavy objects. **4** the ropes and rigging on a ship. — *verb* **1** to grasp or seize and struggle with, especially to try and restrain. **2** to try to deal with or solve (a problem). **3** *trans., intrans. Sport* to try to get the ball from (a player on the opposing team). [from Middle English *takel*, gear]

◼ *noun* **1** attack, challenge, interception, intervention, block. **2** equipment, tools, implements, apparatus, rig, outfit, gear, trappings, paraphernalia. *verb* **1**, **2** grapple with. **1** grab, seize, grasp, struggle with, restrain, pinion. **2** begin, embark on, set about, try, attempt, undertake, take on, challenge, confront, encounter, face up to, deal with, attend to, handle. **3** intercept, block, halt, stop.

◪ *verb* **1** avoid, sidestep.

tacky¹ *adj.* (**tackier**, **tackiest**) slightly sticky.

tacky² *adj.* (**tackier**, **tackiest**) *colloq.* **1** shabby. **2** showing a lack of taste or refinement.

◼ **1** shabby, scruffy, tatty, threadbare, shoddy, dingy, tattered, ragged, untidy, messy, sloppy, *colloq.* grotty. **2** tasteless, vulgar, tawdry, flashy, gaudy, kitschy, *slang* naff.

taco /ˈtakəʊ/ *noun* (PL. **tacos**) in Mexican cooking, a thin flat corn disc (tortilla), fried and filled with meat. [from Mexican Spanish]

tact *noun* **1** an awareness of the best or most considerate way to deal with others so as to avoid offence, upset, antagonism, or resentment. **2** skill or judgement in handling difficult situations; diplomacy. [from Latin *tactus*, touch]

◼ **1** tactfulness, delicacy, sensitivity, thoughtfulness, consideration, understanding. **2** diplomacy, discretion, prudence, judgement, perception, discernment, skill, adroitness, finesse.

◪ **1** tactlessness. **2** indiscretion.

tactful *adj.* having or showing tact.

◼ diplomatic, discreet, politic, judicious, prudent, careful, delicate, subtle, sensitive, perceptive, discerning, understanding, thoughtful, considerate, polite, skilful, adroit.

◪ tactless, indiscreet, thoughtless, rude.

tactic *noun* a tactical manoeuvre. [from Greek *taktikos*, fit for arranging]

◼ manoeuvre, plan, stratagem, scheme, way, means, method, procedure, ruse, ploy, subterfuge, trick, device, shift, move, approach, course.

tactical *adj.* **1** relating to or forming tactics. **2** skilful; well-executed and well-planned. **3** *said of a bomb, missile, etc* used to support other military operations.

◼ **1** strategic, planned, calculated. **2** shrewd, skilful, clever, smart, prudent, politic, judicious, artful, cunning.

tactically *adv.* in a tactical way; as regards tactics.

tactical voting the practice of voting for a candidate one does not support but who is the most likely to defeat another candidate that one supports even less.

tactician /tak'tɪʃən/ *noun* a person who is good at tactics or successful planning.

tactics *noun* **1** (*sing.*) the art or science of employing and manoeuvring troops to win or gain an advantage over the enemy. **2** (*sing.*) skill in or the art of using whatever means are available to achieve an end or aim. **3** (*pl.*) the plans, procedure, means, etc followed.

● STRATEGY. **3** campaign, plan, policy, approach, line of attack, moves, manoeuvres.

tactile /'taktaɪl/ *adj.* **1** of or having a sense of touch. **2** perceptible to the sense of touch. [from Latin *tactilis*, from *tangere*, to touch]

tactless *adj.* lacking tact.

● undiplomatic, indiscreet, indelicate, inappropriate, impolitic, imprudent, careless, clumsy, blundering, insensitive, unfeeling, hurtful, unkind, thoughtless, inconsiderate, rude, impolite, discourteous.
● tactful, diplomatic, discreet.

tadpole *noun* the larval stage of many frogs and toads, resembling a fish, which lives in water and initially has a round or oval body, a characteristic fin-covered tail, and gills. [from Middle English *taddepol*, from *tadde*, toad + *pol*, head]

taekwondo /'taɪ'kwɒn'dɒʊ/ *noun* a Korean martial art and combat sport similar to karate. [from Korean *tae*, kick + *kwon*, fist + *do*, method]

taffeta /'tafɪtə/ *noun* a stiff shiny cloth woven from silk or some silk-like material, eg rayon. [from Persian *taftan*, to twist]

taffrail /'tafrɪl/ *noun* a rail round a ship's stern. [from Dutch *tafereel*, panel]

Taffy *noun* (PL. **Taffies**) *slang, often offensive* a Welshman. [from Welsh *Dafydd*, David]

tag[1] — *noun* **1** a piece of material, paper, leather, etc that carries information (eg washing instructions or the price) about the object to which it is attached. **2** an electronic device such as a bracelet or anklet which transmits radio signals and is used to supervise the movements of a prisoner or offender outside of prison. **3** a metal or plastic point on the end of a shoelace or cord. **4** a loose hanging flap or piece of loose hanging cloth. **5** a trite or common quotation used especially for effect. **6** the final speech in a play, or refrain in a song, added to make the moral or point clear. — *verb* (**tagged**, **tagging**) **1** to put a tag or tags on. **2** to attach or fasten (something). **3** (**tag along**, **on**, *etc*) to follow or accompany, especially when uninvited. [from Middle English *tagge*]

● *noun* **1** label, sticker, tab, ticket, mark, identification, note, slip, docket. *verb* **1** label, mark, identify, designate, term, call, name, christen, nickname, style, dub. **2** add, append, annex, adjoin, affix, fasten. **3** follow, shadow, tail, trail, accompany.

tag[2] — *noun* a children's game in which one child chases the others and tries to catch or touch one of them, who then becomes the chaser. — *verb* (**tagged**, **tagging**) to catch or touch in or as if in the game of tag.

Tagalog /tə'gɑːlɒg/ — *noun* an Austronesian language spoken as a first language by c.12 million people on the island of Luzon in the Philippines. A standardized version of the language, known as Pilipino, is taught along with English in schools. — *adj.* relating to or spoken or written in Tagalog.

tagliatelle /taglɪə'tɛlɪ, taljə'tɛlɪ/ *noun* pasta made in the form of long narrow ribbons. [from Italian *tagliatelle*]

tahini /tə'hiːnɪ/ *noun* a thick paste made from ground sesame seeds. [from Arabic *tahine*, from *tahan*, to grind]

Tai /taɪ/ — *adj.* denoting a family of c. 40 languages used in SE Asia, principally in Thailand, Laos, Vietnam, and parts of China. — *noun* the languages forming this family.

t'ai chi /'taɪ 'tʃiː/ or **t'ai chi ch'uan** a Chinese system of exercise and self-defence in which good balance and coordination mean that minimum effort is used, developed especially by doing extremely slow and controlled exercises. [from Chinese, = great art of boxing]

taiga /'taɪgə/ *noun* Geog. in northern parts of the N hemisphere, the large area of predominantly coniferous forest located S of the arctic and subarctic tundra regions. [from Russian *taiga*]

tail[1] — *noun* **1** the often quite long and relatively thin part of an animal's body that projects from the lower or rear end of the back; the feathers that project from the rear of a bird's body; the end part of a snake's body. **2** anything which has a similar form, function, or position as a creature's tail: *the tail of a shirt*/kite. **3** a lower, last, or rear part: *the tail of the storm*. **4** the rear part of an aircraft including the rudder and tailplane. **5** the trail of luminous particles following a comet. **6** (**tails**) the reverse side of a coin, that side which does not bear a portrait or head. **7** (**tails**) a tailcoat. **8** (**tails**) evening dress for men, usually including a tailcoat and white bow tie. **9** *colloq.* a person who follows and keeps a constant watch on someone else. **10** *offensive slang* women thought of as sexual objects. — *verb* **1** to remove the stalks (from fruit or vegetables). **2** (**tail someone** or **tail after someone**) to follow them closely. — **tail away** or **off** to become gradually less, smaller, or weaker. **turn tail** to turn round and run away. **with one's tail between one's legs** completely defeated or humiliated. [from Anglo-Saxon *tægel*]

● *noun* **3** end, extremity, rear, rear end, rump, behind, *facetious* posterior, appendage. *verb* **2** follow, pursue, shadow, dog, stalk, track, trail. **tail away** or **off** decrease, decline, drop, fall away, fade, wane, dwindle, taper off, peter out, die (out).
● **tail away** or **off** increase, grow.

tail[2] *noun* Legal a limiting of who may inherit property to one person and that person's heirs, or to some other particular class of heirs. [from Old French *taillier*, to cut]

tailback *noun* a long queue of traffic stretching back from an accident, roadworks, etc blocking the road.

tailboard *noun* a hinged or removable flap at the rear of a lorry, cart, or wagon.

tailcoat *noun* a man's formal black jacket which is cut away below the waist in the front and has a long divided, tapering tail which is slit to the waist.

tailed *adj.* **1** having a tail. **2** with the tail removed.

tail end the very end or last part.

tailgate *noun* **1** the rear door which opens upwards on a hatchback vehicle. **2** the lower gate of a canal lock. **3** *North Amer.* a tailboard.

tailless *adj.* lacking a tail.

tail-light *noun* North Amer. the usually red light on the back of a car, train, bicycle, etc.

tailor — *noun* a person who makes suits, jackets, trousers, overcoats, etc to measure, especially for men. — *verb* (**tailored**, **tailoring**) **1** *trans., intrans.* to make and style (garments) so that they fit well. **2** to make suitable for particular or special circumstances. [from Old French *taillour*]

● *noun* outfitter, dressmaker. *verb* FIT, ALTER. **1** cut, trim, style. **2** suit, fashion, shape, mould, modify, adapt, adjust, accommodate.

tailor-bird *noun* a small Asian bird that sews leaves together to make a nest.

tailored *adj.* **1** tailor-made. **2** *said of a person* dressed in clothes which fit well.

tailoress *noun rare* a female tailor.

tailor-made — *adj.* **1** *said of clothes* made by a tailor to fit a particular person well. **2** well suited or adapted for a particular purpose. — *noun* a tailor-made piece of clothing.
. . . .

▣ *adj.* **1** made-to-measure. **2** ideal, perfect, right, suited, fitted, suitable, fit, appropriate.

▣ *adj.* **2** unsuitable.
. . . .

tailpiece *noun* **1** a piece at the end or tail. **2** a design or engraving at the end of a chapter. **3** a strip of wood at the bottom of some stringed instruments (eg a violin) from which the strings are stretched across the bridge to the pegs.

tailplane *noun* a small horizontal wing at the rear of an aircraft.

tailspin *noun* an aircraft's spiral dive with the nose facing down.

tail wind a wind blowing in the same direction as that in which a ship, aircraft, etc is travelling.

taint — *verb* **1** to affect with pollution, putrefaction, or contamination. **2** *intrans.* to become polluted, contaminated, or spoiled. **3** to contaminate morally; to infect with evil. **4** to affect slightly with something bad. — *noun* **1** a spot, mark, or trace of decay, contamination, infection, or something bad or evil. **2** a corrupt or decayed condition. [from Middle English *taynt*, struck or Old French *teint*, from Latin *tingere*, to dye]
. . . .

▣ *verb* **1, 2, 3** corrupt. **1, 3** contaminate, pollute. **1** adulterate. **2** spoil, go off, decay, putrefy. **3** deprave, pervert, defile. **4** stain, blemish, blot, smear, tarnish, sully, harm, damage, shame, disgrace, dishonour, blight, spoil, ruin. *noun* CONTAMINATION, INFECTION, POLLUTION, SHAME, DISGRACE, DISHONOUR. **1** stain, blemish, fault, flaw, defect, spot, blot, smear, stigma. **2** corruption.
. . . .

tainted *adj.* contaminated, polluted.

taipan /ˈtaɪpan/ *noun* a venomous snake native to NE Australia and New Guinea, one of the world's most deadly snakes, and the largest Australian snake. It is brown with a paler head. [an Aboriginal name]

take — *verb* (PAST TENSE **took**; PAST PARTICIPLE **taken**) **1** (*often* **take something down**, **off**, **out**, *etc*) to reach out for and grasp, lift, pull, etc (something chosen or known); to grasp, enter, etc for use: *take a book from the shelf / take my car if you like.* **2** to carry, conduct, or lead to another place: *take him some grapes / talents which will take her far.* **3** to do or perform: *take a walk / take one's revenge.* **4** to get, receive, occupy, obtain, rent, or buy: *take a holiday / take two eggs.* **5** to agree to have or accept: *take advice / take office / will you take a cheque?* **6** to accept as true or valid: *take her word for it.* **7** to adopt or commit oneself to: *take a decision / take her side in the argument.* **8** to endure or put up with: *cannot take his arrogance.* **9** to need or require: *it will take all day to finish / a verb which takes a direct object.* **10** to use as a means of transport: *take the bus.* **11** to make (a written note of something): *take the minutes of the meeting / take notes.* **12** to make (a photographic record); to make a photographic record of (someone or something): *decided to take a few colour slides / shall I take you by the bridge?* **13** to study or teach: *take French at night school.* **14** to remove, use, or borrow without permission: *took her coat by mistake.* **15** to proceed to occupy: *take a seat.* **16** to come or derive from: *a quotation taken from Proust.* **17** to have room for or strength to support: *the shelf won't take any more books.* **18** to consider as an example. **19** to consider or think of in a particular way; to mistakenly consider (someone) to be someone or something: *took her to be a teacher / do you take me for a fool?* **20** to capture or win. **21** (**take to someone** or **be taken with someone**) to be charmed and delighted by them. **22** to eat or drink: *take medicine / take sugar in coffee.* **23** to conduct or lead: *this road will take you to the station.* **24** to be in charge or control of; to run: *take the meeting.* **25** to react to or receive in a specified way: *take the news well.* **26** to feel: *take pride in one's work.* **27** to turn to for help, refuge, etc. **28** (*also* **take something away** or **off**) to subtract it. **29** to go down or into: *took the first road on the left.* **30** to deal with or consider: *take the first two questions together.* **31** *intrans.* to have or produce the expected or desired effect: *the vaccination didn't take.* **32** *intrans.*, *said of seeds, etc* to begin to send out roots and grow. **33** to measure: *take a temperature.* **34** (**be taken ill**, etc) to become suddenly ill, etc. **35** to understand. **36** to have sexual intercourse with. — *noun* **1** a scene filmed or piece of music recorded during an uninterrupted period of filming or recording. **2** the amount or number taken (eg of fish caught) at one time. **3** the amount of money taken in a shop, business, etc over a particular period of time: *the day's take.* **4** a view or interpretation: *a good take of that song.* — **take someone aback** to surprise or shock them. **take after someone** to be like a parent or relation in appearance or character. **take against someone** to dislike them immediately. **take someone apart** to criticize or defeat them severely. **take something apart** to separate it into pieces or components. **take someone back** to make them remember the past. **2** to receive back a former partner, lover, etc, after an estrangement. **take something back 1** to withdraw or retract a statement or promise. **2** to regain possession of something. **3** to return something to an original or former position. **4** to return something bought from a shop for an exchange or refund. **take a degree** to study for and obtain a university or college degree. **take something down 1** to make a written note or record of it. **2** to demolish or dismantle it. **3** to lower it. **take someone down 1** to escort them to dinner. **2** to make less powerful or self-important; to humble: *take him down a peg or two.* **take someone in 1** to include them. **2** to give them accommodation or shelter. **3** to deceive or cheat them. **take something in 1** to include it. **2** to understand and remember it. **3** to make a piece of clothing smaller. **4** to do paid work in one's home: *take in washing.* **5** to include a visit to it: *we can take in a restaurant on the way home.* **take it 1** to be able to bear suffering, trouble, difficulty, etc: *tell me the worst, I can take it.* **2** to assume: *I take it that you'll be able to come.* **take it from me** you can believe me. **take it out of someone** *colloq.* to exhaust their strength or energy. **take it out on someone** *colloq.* to vent one's anger or frustration on an innocent person. **take it upon oneself** to take responsibility. **take off 1** *said of an aircraft or its passengers* to leave the ground. **2** to depart or set out, especially by aeroplane: *took off for Madrid.* **3** *colloq.*, *said of a scheme, product, etc* to become popular and successful and expand quickly. **take someone off 1** to imitate or mimic them. **take something off 1** to remove something, especially clothing. **2** to deduct something. **3** to spend a period of time away from work on holiday, resting, etc. **take on** *colloq.* to be greatly upset or distraught. **take someone on 1** to give them employment. **2** to challenge or compete with them: *decided to take them on at snooker.* **take something on 1** to agree to do it; to undertake it. **2** to acquire a new meaning, quality, appearance, etc. **3** *said of an aircraft, ship, etc* to admit new passengers, fuel, cargo, etc on board. **take something out 1** to remove or extract it. **2** to obtain on application: *take out insurance / take out a warrant.* **take someone out 1** to go out with them or escort them in public. **2** *slang* to kill, defeat, or destroy them. **take over** or **take something over** to assume control, management, or ownership of it. **take to someone** or **something 1** to develop a liking for them. **2** to begin to do something regularly. **3** to turn to something as a remedy or for refuge. **take someone up 1** to become their patron or supporter. **2** *said of an activity, interest, etc* to absorb them. **take something up 1** to lift or raise it. **2** to use or occupy space or time. **3** to become interested in it and begin to do it: *take up the violin.* **4** to shorten a piece of clothing. **5** to resume a story, account, etc after a pause. **6** to assume or adopt: *take up residence in July.* **7** to accept an offer. **take someone up on something 1** to accept their offer, proposal, challenge, etc. **2** to discuss a point or issue first raised by them. **take something up with someone** to discuss a matter with them: *take it up with your MP.* **take**

up with someone to become friendly with them; to begin to associate with them. [from Anglo-Saxon *tacan*]

. . . .

■ *verb* 1 seize, grab, snatch, grasp, hold, catch. 2 convey, carry, bring, transport, ferry, accompany, escort, lead, guide, conduct, usher. 4, 5, 6 accept. 4 get, obtain, acquire, receive, derive, adopt, assume, secure, gain, pick, choose, select. 8 bear, tolerate, stand, stomach, abide, endure, suffer, undergo, withstand. 9 need, necessitate, require, demand, call for. 14 remove, take away, steal, filch, purloin, *colloq.* pinch, *slang* nick, appropriate, abduct, carry off. 20 capture, occupy, win, carry, conquer. **take aback** surprise, astonish, astound, shock, stagger, stun, startle, disconcert, bewilder, dismay, upset. **take after** resemble, look like, be like, favour. **take something apart** take to pieces, dismantle, disassemble, analyse. **take something back** 1 withdraw, retract, recant, repudiate, deny. 2 reclaim, repossess, regain, get back. 3 return, replace, restore. **take something down** 1 note, record, write down, put down, set down, transcribe. 2 dismantle, disassemble, demolish, raze, level. 3 lower, drop. **take in** *someone* 2 receive, shelter, accommodate. 3 deceive, fool, dupe, *colloq.* con, mislead, trick, hoodwink, *colloq.* bamboozle, cheat, swindle. *something* 1 contain, include, comprise, incorporate, embrace, encompass, cover. 2 absorb, assimilate, digest, realize, appreciate, understand, comprehend, grasp, admit. 5 visit, see, call in at, call in on. **take off** 2 leave, depart, go, decamp, disappear. *someone* imitate, mimic, parody, caricature, satirize, mock, *Brit. colloq.* send up. *something* 1 remove, divest, shed, discard, drop, *old use, literary* doff. 2 subtract, deduct, take away, discount. **take on** *someone* 1 employ, hire, enlist, recruit, engage, retain. 2 challenge, compete with, face, fight, oppose. *something* 1, 2 acquire, assume, get. 1 accept, undertake, tackle, face, contend with. **take something up** 1 raise, lift. 2 occupy, fill, engage, engross, absorb, monopolize, use up. 3 start, begin, embark on, pursue, carry on, continue. 5, 6 accept. 5 adopt, assume.
E3 1 leave, refuse.

. . . .

takeaway — *noun* 1 a cooked meal prepared and bought in a restaurant but taken away and eaten somewhere else, eg at home. 2 a restaurant which provides such meals. — *adj.* 1 *said of cooked food* prepared in a shop or restaurant for the customer to take away. 2 *said of a shop or restaurant* providing such meals.

take-home pay the salary that one actually receives after tax, national insurance, and pension contributions have been deducted.

take-off *noun* 1 an instance of an aircraft leaving the ground. 2 an act of imitating or mimicking. 3 a place from which one takes off, jumps, etc; a starting-point. See also TAKE OFF.

. . . .

■ 2 imitation, mimicry, impersonation, parody, caricature, spoof, *Brit. colloq.* send-up, travesty.

. . . .

takeover *noun* the act of taking control of something, especially a company by buying the majority of its shares.

. . . .

■ merger, amalgamation, combination, incorporation.

. . . .

taker *noun* a person who takes or accepts something, especially a bet.

take-up *noun* the act or extent of claiming or accepting something, eg state benefit.

take-up rate the number of people who claim a benefit to which they are entitled or who accept an offer.

taking — *adj.* attractive; charming. — *noun* (**takings**) the amount of money taken at a concert, in a shop, etc; receipts.

. . . .

■ *noun* receipts, gate, proceeds, returns, profits, gains, revenue, yield, income, earnings, pickings.

. . . .

talc or **talcum** *noun* 1 *Geol.* a soft greasy white, green, or grey mineral form of magnesium silicate, which when purified consists of a white powder. It is used in talcum powder and other cosmetics, French chalk, lubricants, and paper coatings, and as a filler in paints, plastics, and rubber. 2 talcum powder. [from Persian *talk*]

talcum powder a fine, often perfumed, powder made from purified talc, used on the body.

tale *noun* 1 a story or narrative. 2 a false or malicious story or piece of gossip; a lie. — **tell tales** to disclose secret or private information, especially about another person's wrongdoing to someone in authority. [from Anglo-Saxon *talu*]

. . . .

■ 1 story, yarn, anecdote, *colloq.* spiel, narrative, account, report, rumour, tall story, old wives' tale, superstition, fable, myth, legend, saga. 2 lie, fib, falsehood, untruth, fabrication.

. . . .

tale-bearer *noun* a person who repeats malicious or false gossip.

talent *noun* 1 a special or innate skill, aptitude, or ability, especially for art, music, etc. 2 high general or mental ability. 3 a person or people with such skill or ability. 4 *colloq.* attractive members of the opposite sex as a group. 5 *Hist.* a measure of weight and unit of currency used eg by the ancient Greeks and Romans. [from Anglo-Saxon *talente*, from Latin *talentum*]

. . . .

■ *noun* 1, 2 genius, flair, aptitude, skill, ability, capacity. 1 gift, endowment, feel, knack, bent, faculty, strength, forte.
E3 1 weakness. 2 inability.

. . . .

talented *adj.* having talent or aptitude.

. . . .

■ gifted, brilliant, well-endowed, versatile, accomplished, able, capable, proficient, adept, adroit, deft, clever, skilful.
E3 inept.

. . . .

talent scout or **talent spotter** a person whose job is to find and recruit talented amateurs, especially singers and dancers, for professional engagements.

talisman / 'talɪzmən, 'talɪsmən/ *noun* (PL. **talismans**) a small object such as a stone which is supposed to have magic powers to protect its owner from evil, bring good luck, or work magic; a charm or amulet. [from Greek *telesma*, rite, consecrated object]

. . . .

■ token, totem, symbol, charm, amulet, fetish, idol.

. . . .

talismanic / talɪz'manɪk, talɪs'manɪk/ *adj.* of the nature of a talisman.

talk — *verb* 1 *intrans.* (*often* **talk to** or **with someone**) to express one's ideas, feelings, and thoughts by means of spoken words; to have a conversation or discussion. 2 to discuss: *talk business.* 3 *intrans.* to use or be able to use speech: *is the baby beginning to talk yet?* 4 to express in speech; to utter: *talk nonsense.* 5 *intrans.* to gossip. 6 (*intrans.*) to give away secret information. 7 to use (a language) or speak in it: *talk Dutch.* 8 to get (oneself) into a certain state by talking: *talked themselves hoarse.* 9 *intrans.* to have influence: *money talks.* 10 *intrans.* to give a talk or lecture: *our guest speaker will talk on potholing.* — *noun* 1 a conversation or discussion. 2 (*often* **talks**) a formal discussion or series of negotiations. 3 an informal lecture. 4 gossip or rumour, or the subject of it: *the talk of the town.* 5 fruitless or impractical discussion or boasting: *his ideas are just talk.* 6 a particular way of speaking or communicating: *baby talk.* — **now you're talking** *colloq.* now you are saying something welcome. **talk back** to answer rudely, impudently, or boldly. **talk big** *colloq.* to talk boastfully. **talk someone down 1** to silence them by speaking more loudly or aggressively. **2** to help a pilot or aircraft to land by sending instructions over the radio. **talk down to someone** to talk patronizingly or condescendingly to them. **talk someone into something** to persuade them to do something. **talk someone out of something** to dissuade them from doing something. **talk something out 1** to resolve a problem or difference of opinion by discussion. **2** *Brit.* to defeat a bill or motion in parliament by prolonging discussion of it until there is not enough time left to vote on it. **talk something over** to discuss it thoroughly. **talk round something** to discuss all aspects of a subject, problem, etc without reaching a decision or coming to a conclusion. **talk someone round** to bring them to one's own way of thinking by talking persuasively. **you can't talk** *colloq.* you are in no position to criticize or disagree. [from Middle English *talken*]

⬛ *verb* **1**, **4** speak, utter, articulate. **1** communicate, converse, confer, chat. **2** discuss, negotiate. **5** gossip, chat, natter, chatter. **6** tell, confess, *slang* grass, *colloq.* spill the beans, *colloq.* let the cat out of the bag. *noun* **1**, **2** dialogue, conference. **1** conversation, chat, chatter, *colloq.* natter, gossip. **2** discussion, meeting, consultation, negotiation. **3** lecture, seminar, symposium, speech, address, discourse, sermon, *colloq.* spiel. **4** gossip, hearsay, rumour, tittle-tattle. **6** language, dialect, slang, jargon, speech, utterance, words. **talk into** persuade, convince, bring round, encourage, coax, sway, win over. **talk out of** dissuade, discourage, deter, put off. **talk over** discuss, debate, consider, argue about, *colloq.* chew over.

🅴 **talk into** dissuade. **talk out of** persuade, convince.

talkative *adj.* talking a lot.

⬛ garrulous, voluble, vocal, communicative, forthcoming, unreserved, expansive, chatty, gossipy, verbose, wordy.

🅴 taciturn, quiet, reserved.

talker *noun* a person who talks, especially at length or in some specified way.

talkie *noun colloq.* a cinema film with sound, especially one of the first such films.

talking-point *noun* a subject for discussion.

talking-shop *noun* a place for discussion and argument and not action.

talking-to *noun colloq.* a ticking-off; a scolding or reproof.

⬛ lecture, *colloq.* dressing-down, telling-off, *colloq.* ticking-off, scolding, reprimand, rebuke, reproof, reproach, criticism.

🅴 praise, commendation.

tall *adj.* **1** of above average height. **2** having a stated height: *six feet tall.* **3** difficult to believe; extravagant: *a tall story.* **4** difficult or demanding: *a tall order.* [from Middle English *tal*, from Anglo-Saxon *getæl*, swift, ready]

⬛ **1**, **2** high. **1** lofty, elevated, soaring, towering, great, giant, gigantic.

🅴 **1** short, low, small.

tallboy *noun* a tall chest of drawers, sometimes on short legs and with an upper and slightly smaller section standing on a larger lower one.

tallow *noun* hard fat from sheep and cattle melted down and used to make candles, soap, etc. [from Middle English *talg*]

tally — *noun* (PL. **tallies**) **1** an account or reckoning, eg of work done, debts, or the score in a game. **2** *Hist.* a stick which could have notches cut in it to show debts and accounts, and which could then be split in half lengthways so that each party had a record of the deal. **3** a distinguishing or identifying mark or label. **4** a counterpart; a corre-

sponding part. — *verb* (**tallies**, **tallied**) **1** *intrans.* to agree, correspond, or match. **2** to record or mark (a number, score, etc) on, or as if on, a tally. [from Latin *talea*, stick]

⬛ *noun* **1** record, count, total, score, reckoning, account. *verb* **1** agree, concur, tie in, square, accord, harmonize, coincide, correspond, match, conform, suit, fit. **2** add up, total, count, reckon, figure.

🅴 *verb* **1** disagree, differ.

tally clerk a person who checks a ship's cargo against an official list.

tally-ho *interj.* a cry to the hounds at a hunt when a fox has been sighted.

tallyman *noun* **1** a person who keeps a tally. **2** a person who sells goods on credit, especially from door to door.

Talmud /ˈtalmʊd, ˈtalmʌd/ *noun* the body of Jewish civil and canon law. [Hebrew, = instruction]

Talmudic /talˈmʊdɪk, ˈtalmʌdɪk/ *adj.* relating to or contained in the Talmud.

Talmudist *noun* a scholar of the Talmud.

talon /ˈtalən/ *noun* a hooked claw, especially of a bird of prey. [from Latin *talus*, heel]

talus /ˈteɪləs/ *noun* (PL. **tali**) *Anat.* the ankle bone. [from Latin *talus*, ankle]

tamable or **tameable** *adj.* capable of being tamed.

tamari /taˈmɑːrɪ/ *noun* a concentrated sauce made of soya beans and salt, used especially in Japanese cookery. [from Japanese]

tamarind /ˈtamərɪnd/ *noun* **1** a tropical evergreen tree which bears yellow flowers and brown seed-pods. **2** the pod of this tree, filled with a reddish-black slightly acid pulp used as food and to make cooling drinks. [from Arabic *tamr-hindi*, Indian date]

tamarisk /ˈtamərɪsk/ *noun* a tropical or Mediterranean shrub or tree with slender branches and small pink or white flowers, usually found on seashores. [from Latin *tamarix*]

tambour /ˈtambʊə(r)/ *noun* **1** a drum. **2** a frame for embroidery consisting of two hoops which hold the fabric taut while stitches are sewn. **3** an embroidery done on such a frame. [from Old French]

tambourine /tambəˈriːn/ *noun* a small round drum with skin stretched tight on one side only, with small discs of metal in the rim that jingle when the drum is struck with the hand. [from Old Dutch *tamborijn*, small drum]

tame — *adj.* **1** *said of animals* used to living or working with people; not wild or dangerous. **2** *said of land, etc* changed by people from a natural wild state; cultivated. **3** docile, meek, and submissive. **4** dull and unexciting; insipid: *a tame ending to an otherwise exciting story.* — *verb* **1** to make (an animal) used to living or working with people. **2** to make meek and humble; to deprive the spirit of; to subdue. [from Anglo-Saxon *tam*]

⬛ *adj.* **1** domesticated, broken in, trained, disciplined. **3** docile, meek, submissive, manageable, tractable, amenable, gentle, unresisting, obedient, biddable. **4** dull, boring, tedious, uninteresting, humdrum, flat, bland, insipid, weak, feeble, uninspired, unadventurous, unenterprising, lifeless, spiritless. *verb* **1** domesticate, housetrain, break in, train, discipline. **2** repress, suppress, quell, subdue, temper, soften, mellow, calm, pacify, humble, master, subjugate, conquer, bridle, curb.

🅴 *adj.* **1** wild. **3** unmanageable, rebellious. **4** exciting.

tamely *adv.* in a tame way.

tameness *noun* a tame quality.

tamer *noun* a person who tames animals.

Tamil /ˈtamɪl/ — *noun* **1** a member of a people living in S India and Sri Lanka. **2** the language spoken by this people. — *adj.* of or relating to this people or their language.

tam-o'-shanter /tamə'ʃantə(r)/ *noun* a Scottish flat round cloth or woollen cap which fits tightly round the brows and has a full crown, often with a bobble in the middle. [after the hero of Robert Burns's poem]

tamoxifen /tə'mɒksɪfɛn/ *noun Medicine* a drug that inhibits the effects of oestrogens, and is used in the treatment of advanced breast cancer. It has been suggested that it may have useful preventive effects in certain women at relatively high risk of developing breast cancer. It is also used to stimulate ovulation in the treatment of infertility.

tamp *verb* **1** to fill up (a hole containing explosive) with earth, cement, etc before setting off the explosion. **2** to drive or force down (eg ballast on a railway) by repeated blows.

tamper *verb intrans.* (**tampered, tampering**) **1** to interfere or meddle, especially in a harmful way. **2** to attempt to corrupt or influence, especially by bribery. [a form of TEMPER]

· · · · · · · · · · · · · · · · · · · ·

⊟ **1** interfere, meddle, *colloq.* mess, tinker, fiddle. **2** fix, rig, manipulate, juggle, alter.

· ·

tamper-evident *adj.*, *said of packaging* designed in such a way that it is obvious when it has been tampered with.

tampion or **tompion** *noun* a plug, especially a protective plug placed in the muzzle of a gun when not in use. [from French *tampon*, from *tapon*, a plug of cloth]

tampon — *noun* a plug of cottonwool or other soft absorbent material inserted into a cavity or wound to absorb blood and other secretions, especially one for use in the vagina during menstruation. — *verb* (**tamponed, tamponing**) to insert a tampon in. [from Old French, from *tape*, plug]

tam-tam *noun* a percussion instrument similar to a gong, but made of thinner metal and having no central boss. While a gong produces a definite pitch, the tam-tam's sound is made up of a dissonant mixture of frequencies varying with the size of the instrument. [from Hindi]

tan¹ — *noun* **1** the brown colour of the skin after exposure to the sun's ultraviolet rays. **2** a tawny brown colour. **3** oak bark or other material, used especially for tanning hides. — *adj.* tawny brown in colour. — *verb* (**tanned, tanning**) **1** *trans., intrans.* to make or become brown in the sun. **2** to convert (hide) into leather by soaking it in a solution containing tannin, mineral salts, or manmade chemicals. **3** *colloq.* to beat. [from Latin *tannum*, oak bark]

tan² *abbrev. Maths.* tangent (see TANGENT 2).

tandem — *noun* **1** a type of long three-wheeled bicycle for two people, with two seats and two sets of pedals placed one behind the other. **2** a team of two horses harnessed one behind the other, or a carriage drawn by it. **3** any two people or things which follow one behind the other. — *adv.* one behind the other, especially on a bicycle, or with two horses harnessed one behind the other: *ride tandem / drive tandem.* — **in tandem 1** with one behind the other. **2** together or in partnership. [a pun on Latin *tandem*, at length, at last]

tandoori /tan'dʊərɪ, tʌn'dʊərɪ/ *noun* food cooked on a spit over charcoal in a clay oven. [from Hindi *tandoor*, clay oven]

tang *noun* **1** a strong or sharp taste, flavour, or smell. **2** a trace or hint. **3** the pointed end of a knife, sword, chisel, etc that fits into and is held firmly by the handle. [from Norse *tange*, point]

· · · · · · · · · · · · · · · · · · · ·

⊟ **1, 2** taste, flavour, savour, smack, whiff. **1** sharpness, bite, piquancy, pungency, smell, aroma, scent. **2** tinge, touch, trace, hint, suggestion, *literary* soupçon, overtone.

· ·

tangent — *noun* **1** *Geom.* a straight line that touches a curve at one point, and has the same gradient (slope) as the curve at the point of contact. At a maximum or minimum, the tangent to a curve has a gradient of zero. **2** (ABBREV. **tan**) *Maths.* in trigonometry, a function of an angle in a right-angled triangle, defined as the length of the side opposite the angle divided by the length of the side adjacent to it. — *adj.* being or forming a tangent. — **at a tangent** in a completely different direction or course. [from Latin *tangere*, to touch]

tangential /tan'dʒɛnʃəl/ *adj.* **1** of or along a tangent. **2** not of central importance to; incidental; peripheral.

tangentially *adv.* in the direction of a tangent; at a tangent.

tangerine — *noun* **1** a tree producing a variety of mandarin orange with a loose reddish-orange skin and flesh. **2** an orange produced by this tree. **3** the reddish-orange colour of this fruit. — *adj.* reddish-orange. [named after *Tangier*, a port on the Moroccan coast]

tangibility *noun* the quality of being tangible.

tangible /'tandʒɪbl/ *adj.* **1** able to be felt by touch. **2** real or definite; material: *tangible evidence.* [from Latin *tangibilis*]

· · · · · · · · · · · · · · · · · · · ·

⊟ PALPABLE, SOLID, CONCRETE, MATERIAL, SUBSTANTIAL, PHYSICAL, REAL, PERCEPTIBLE, DISCERNIBLE.
1 touchable, tactile. **2** actual, evident, manifest, definite, positive.

⊟ INTANGIBLE. **2** abstract, unreal.

· ·

tangibly *adv.* in a tangible way.

tangle — *noun* **1** an untidy and confused or knotted state or mass, eg of hair or fibres. **2** a confused or complicated state or situation. — *verb* **1** *trans., intrans., said especially of hair, fibres, etc* to become or make them untidy, knotted, and confused. **2** (**tangle with someone**) *colloq.* to become involved with them, especially in conflict, a struggle, or an argument. **3** *colloq.* to trap or hamper the movement of. [from Middle English *tanglen*]

· · · · · · · · · · · · · · · · · · · ·

⊟ *noun* MESS, MUDDLE, JUMBLE, MAZE, LABYRINTH. **1** knot, snarl-up, twist, coil, convolution, mesh, web. **2** mix-up, confusion, entanglement, embroilment, complication.
verb **1** knot, snarl, ravel, twist, coil, interweave, interlace, intertwine. **2** get involved with, argue with, take on, fight. **3** entangle, catch, ensnare, entrap, enmesh, embroil, implicate, involve, muddle, confuse.

⊟ *verb* **1, 3** disentangle.

· ·

tangled *adj.* full of tangles.

· · · · · · · · · · · · · · · · · · · ·

⊟ knotty, snarled, matted, tousled, dishevelled, messy, muddled, jumbled, confused, twisted, convoluted, tortuous, involved, complicated, complex, intricate.

· ·

tango — *noun* (PL. **tangos**) a dance of Argentinian origin with dramatic stylized body positions and long pauses, or a piece of music for this. — *verb intrans.* (**tangoes, tangoed**) to perform this dance. [from American Spanish *tango*]

tangy *adj.* (**tangier, tangiest**) having a fresh sharp smell or flavour.

· · · · · · · · · · · · · · · · · · · ·

⊟ sharp, biting, acid, tart, spicy, piquant, pungent, strong, fresh.

⊟ tasteless, insipid.

· ·

tank — *noun* **1** a large container for holding, storing, or transporting liquids or gas. **2** the amount a tank will hold. **3** a heavy steel-covered vehicle armed with guns and moving on Caterpillar tracks. — *verb* (*often* **tank up** or **tank something up**) **1** to fill the tank of (a vehicle) with fuel. **2** *trans., intrans. slang* to drink or cause to drink heavily and become very drunk. **3** to store in a tank. **4** *intrans.* to move like a tank, especially quickly and heavily. [from Gujurati (Indian language) *tankh*, reservoir, and Portuguese *tanque*, pond]

▣ *noun* **1** container, reservoir, cistern, aquarium, vat, basin.

tankard /'taŋkəd/ *noun* a large silver, pewter, or pottery drinking-mug, often with a hinged lid, used especially for drinking beer. [from Middle English]

tanker *noun* **1** a ship or large lorry which transports liquid in bulk. **2** an aircraft which transports fuel and is usually able to refuel other aircraft in flight.

tankful *noun* (PL. **tankfuls**) the amount a tank will hold.

tanned *adj.* **1** having a suntan. **2** *said of hide* cured, treated.

▣ **1** brown, bronzed, sunburnt.

tanner[1] *noun* a person who tans leather, especially as a profession.

tanner[2] *noun Brit. old colloq. use* a sixpence.

tannery *noun* (PL. **tanneries**) a place where hides are tanned.

tannic acid or **tannin** any of several substances obtained from certain tree barks and other plants, used in tanning leather, dyeing, ink-making, and in medicine, also occurring in, and giving a distinctive flavour to, red wine and tea.

tanning *noun* **1** browning of the skin due to exposure to ultraviolet light. **2** converting hides into leather.

Tannoy /'tanɔɪ/ *noun trademark* a communication system with loudspeakers, used for making announcements in public buildings, eg railway stations.

tansy /'tanzɪ/ *noun* (PL. **tansies**) a wild plant with small heads of yellow flowers and pungent leaves used in cooking and formerly in medicine. [from Greek *athanasia*, immortality]

tantalization or **tantalisation** *noun* the process of tantalizing or being tantalized.

tantalize or **tantalise** *verb* to tease or torment (someone) by keeping something wanted just out of reach. [named after *Tantalus*, in Greek mythology]

▣ tease, taunt, torment, torture, provoke, lead on, titillate, tempt, entice, bait, balk, frustrate, thwart.

▣ gratify, satisfy, fulfil.

tantalizing or **tantalising** *adj.* teasing; tormenting.

tantalizingly or **tantalisingly** *adv.* in a tantalizing way.

tantalum /'tantələm/ *noun Chem.* (SYMBOL **Ta**, ATOMIC NUMBER 73) a hard bluish-grey metal that is resistant to corrosion and has a high melting point. It is used to make certain alloys, especially for nuclear reactors, as well as electronic components, chemical equipment, and dental and surgical instruments. [named after Tantalus because of certain supposedly tantalizing characteristics of its chemistry]

tantalus /'tantələs/ *noun* a case in which decanters holding whisky, sherry, etc are visible but locked up.

tantamount *adj.* — **tantamount to something** having the same effect or result as something; as good as it; equivalent to it. [from Old French *tant amunter* or Italian *tanto montare*, to amount to as much]

▣ **tantamount to** as good as, equivalent to, commensurate with, equal to, synonymous with, the same as.

Tantra or **tantra** /'tantrə, 'tʌntrə/ *noun* any of a number of Hindu or Buddhist texts giving religious teaching and ritual instructions which may include descriptions of spells, magical formulas, mantras, meditative practices, and rituals to be performed. The practice of Tantra requires instruction by a guru. [from Sanskrit *tantra*, thread, fundamental doctrine]

tantrum *noun* a fit of childish or petulant bad temper.

▣ temper, rage, fury, storm, outburst, fit, scene, *colloq.* paddy.

Taoism /'taʊɪzm, 'daʊɪzm/ *noun* **1** a Chinese philosophical system based on the teachings of Lao-tzu (c.6CBC) and others, advocating a life of simplicity and non-interference with the natural course of events. **2** a religion supposedly based on this system of philosophy, but also including magic, alchemy, and the worship of many gods. [from Chinese *tao*, way]

Taoist /'taʊɪst, 'daʊɪst/ — *noun* a follower of Taoism. — *adj.* characteristic of or relating to Taoism.

tap[1] — *noun* **1** a quick or light touch, knock, or blow, or the sound made by this. **2** tap-dancing. **3** a piece of metal attached to the sole and heel of a shoe for tap-dancing. — *verb* (**tapped**, **tapping**) **1** to strike or knock lightly. **2** to strike or knock lightly with (something). **3** (*also* **tap something out**) to produce it by tapping: *tap out a message.* **4** (**tap at** or **on something**) to strike it with a light but audible blow. [from Middle English *tappen*]

▣ *noun* **1** knock, rap, beat, pat, touch. *verb* **1**, **2** strike, knock, rap, beat, drum. **2** hit, pat, touch.

tap[2] — *noun* **1** a device consisting of a valve, with a handle for opening and shutting it, attached to a pipe for controlling the flow of liquid or gas. **2** a peg or stopper, especially in a barrel. **3** a receiver for listening to and recording private conversations, attached secretly to a telephone wire. **4** an act of attaching such a receiver to a telephone wire. **5** *Medicine* the withdrawal of fluid from a place, especially from a cavity in the body. **6** a screw for cutting an internal thread. — *verb* (**tapped**, **tapping**) **1** to get liquid from (a barrel, cavity in the body, etc) by piercing it or opening it with, or as if with, a tap. **2** to let out (liquid) from a vessel by opening, or as if by opening, a tap. **3** to get sap from (a tree) by cutting into it. **4** to attach a receiver secretly to (a telephone wire) so as to be able to hear private conversations. **5** to start using (a source, supply, etc). **6** *colloq.* (**tap someone for something**) to obtain money from them. — **on tap** **1** *said of beer* stored in casks from which it is served. **2** ready and available for immediate use. [from Anglo-Saxon *tæppa*]

▣ *noun* **1** stopcock, valve, faucet, spigot, spout. **2** stopper, plug, bung. *verb* **1**, **2** bleed, milk, drain. **2** siphon (off). **5** use, utilize, exploit, mine, quarry.

tapas /'tapas/ *pl. noun* light savoury snacks or appetizers, especially those based on Spanish foods and cooking techniques, and served with drinks. [from Spanish *tapas*]

tap dance — *noun* a dance performed wearing shoes with metal on the soles and toes so that the dancer's rhythmical steps can be heard clearly. — *verb intrans.* to perform a tap-dance.

tap dancer a person who tap-dances.

tap dancing dancing wearing shoes fitted with taps.

tape — *noun* **1** a narrow strip of woven cloth used for tying, fastening, etc. **2** (*in full* **magnetic tape**) a strip of thin plastic or metal wound on spools, used for recording sounds or images. **3** anything which has been recorded on magnetic tape; a tape or video-recording. **4** (*in full* **adhesive tape**) a strip of thin paper or plastic with a sticky surface, used for fastening, sticking, etc. **5** a string or paper ribbon stretched above the finishing line on a race track. **6** a tape-measure. — *verb* **1** to fasten, tie, or seal with tape. **2** (*trans., intrans.*) to record (sounds or images) on magnetic tape. — **have something** or **someone taped** *colloq.* to understand them or be able to deal with them. [from Anglo-Saxon *tæppe*]

▣ *noun* **1** band, strip, binding, ribbon. **2**, **3** cassette, video. *verb* **1** bind, secure, stick, seal. **2** record, video.

tape deck a tape recorder and player used to record sound or video signals on to magnetic tape, or to play back such a recording. It usually forms part of an integrated sound system that may also include a compact-disc player, record turntable, radio tuner, etc.

tape measure a length of plastic, cloth, or thin flexible metal tape, marked with inches, feet, and yards or centimetres and metres for measuring.

taper — *noun* **1** a long thin candle. **2** a long waxed wick or spill for lighting candles or fires. **3** a gradual lessening of diameter or width towards one end. — *verb trans., intrans.* (**tapered, tapering**) (*also* **taper off**) **1** to make or become gradually narrower towards one end. **2** to make or become gradually less. [from Anglo-Saxon *tapor*]

⊞ *noun* **1** candle. **2** spill, wick. *verb* **1** narrow, thin, slim, attenuate. **2** decrease, reduce, lessen.

⊞ *verb* **1** widen, flare, swell. **2** increase.

tape-record *verb* to record (sounds) on magnetic tape.

tape recorder a machine that is used to record sound or video signals on magnetic tape, and play them back.

tape-recording *noun* **1** recording sound on tape. **2** a sound recording made on tape.

tapered or **tapering** *adj.* having a taper.

tapestried *adj.* covered or decorated with tapestry.

tapestry /'tapǝstrɪ/ *noun* (PL. **tapestries**) **1** a thick woven textile with an ornamental design (often a picture) on it, used for curtains, wall-hangings, chair coverings, etc. **2** embroidery or an embroidery usually done with wool on canvas, which imitates the designs and pictures and the heavy texture of tapestry. [from Old French *tapisserie*, carpeting]

tapeworm *noun Zool.* any of a group of segmented flatworms that live as parasites in the intestines of humans and other vertebrates.

tapioca /tapɪ'ouka/ *noun* hard white grains of starch from the cassava plant, often made into a pudding with sugar and milk. [from Tupí (S American Indian language) *tipioca*, juice squeezed out]

tapir /'teɪpǝ(r), 'teɪpɪǝ(r)/ *noun* (PL. **tapir, tapirs**) any of three species of brown or black-and-white nocturnal mammal, related to the horse and rhinoceros, and similar in size to a donkey, but with shorter legs and a long flexible snout. Tapirs are found near water in tropical forests of Central and S America and SE Asia, where they browse on water plants and low-growing vegetation on land. [from Tupíf (S American Indian language) *tapíra*]

tappet *noun* a lever or projection that transmits motion from one part of a machine to another, especially in an internal-combustion engine from the camshaft to the valves. [from TAP¹]

taproom *noun* a bar serving alcoholic drinks, especially beer direct from casks.

taproot *noun Bot.* a long straight main root of a plant, from which smaller lateral roots develop. In certain plants, eg carrot, it functions as a food store.

taps *pl. noun* **1** a bugle call for lights out, also used at military funerals. **2** in the Guide movement, a song sung at the end of a meeting or round a campfire in the evening.

tar¹ — *noun* **1** a dark sticky pungent liquid obtained by distillation of coal or wood, or by petroleum refining. It consists of a mixture of hydrocarbons, phenols, and free carbon, and is used in road construction, and as a wood preservative and antiseptic. **2** a similar substance, especially the residue formed from smoke from burning tobacco. — *verb* (**tarred, tarring**) to cover with tar. — **tar and feather someone** to cover them with tar and then feathers as a punishment. **tarred with the same brush** having the same faults. [from Anglo-Saxon *teoru*]

tar² *noun old colloq. use* a sailor. [perhaps an abbreviation of TARPAULIN]

taramasalata /tarǝmǝsǝ'lɑːtǝ/ *noun* a creamy pink pâté made from the smoked roe of fish, especially cod, and ol-

ive oil and garlic. [from modern Greek, from *taramus*, preserved roe, and *salata*, salad]

tarantella /tarǝn'telǝ/ *noun* a lively country dance from S Italy, or a piece of music for it. [named after *Taranto* in S Italy]

tarantula /tǝ'rantjʊlǝ/ *noun* **1** a European wolf spider, named after the town of Taranto in Italy, where according to legend its bite was fatal unless the bitten person danced until exhausted. **2** any of a family of large tropical spiders with a fist-sized body and long hairy legs, which live in short burrows in the ground, and run down their prey instead of trapping it in webs. They hunt nocturnally, and although capable of catching small birds, they feed mainly on small insects which they kill instantly by injecting a poison. [from Italian *tarantola*]

tarboosh /tɑː'buːʃ/ *noun* a hat like a fez, sometimes worn with a turban. [from Arabic *tarbush*]

tardily *adv.* slowly, late.

tardiness *noun* being late or delayed.

tardy *adj.* (**tardier, tardiest**) **1** slow to move, progress, or grow; sluggish. **2** slower to arrive or happen than expected; late. [from Latin *tardus*, slow]

⊞ SLOW. **1** slow-moving, sluggish, lethargic, unresponsive. **2** late, delayed, unpunctual, behindhand.

tare¹ *noun* **1** any of several vetches, especially those grown for food or fodder. **2** (*usually* **tares**) *Biblical* a weed which grows in cornfields. [from Middle English]

tare² *noun* **1** the weight of the wrapping paper or container in which goods are packed. **2** an allowance made for this. **3** the weight of a vehicle without its fuel, cargo, or passengers. [from Arabic *tarhah*, that which is thrown away]

target — *noun* **1** an object aimed at in shooting practice or competitions, especially a flat round board marked with concentric circles and with a bull's-eye in the centre. **2** any object or area fired or aimed at. **3** a person or thing which is the focus of ridicule or criticism. **4** a result aimed at; a goal. **5** *old use* a small buckler or round shield. — *verb* (**targeted, targeting**) **1** to direct or aim (something). **2** to make (a person, place, or thing) a target or the object of an attack. [from Old French *targe*, shield]

⊞ *noun* **3** butt, mark, victim, prey, quarry. **4** goal, aim, object, end, purpose, intention, ambition, destination, objective.

Targum or **targum** /tɑː'guːm, 'tɑːgǝm/ *noun Relig.* an Aramaic version or paraphrase of the Hebrew Scriptures, probably originally composed orally (c.1cBC) when the Torah was read aloud in the synagogues, since most Jews of the time understood Aramaic rather than Hebrew, and later written in the rabbinic period. [from Chaldaean *targūm*, interpretation]

tariff *noun* **1** a list of prices or charges: *a hotel tariff.* **2** the tax or duty to be paid on a particular class of goods imported or exported. **3** a list of such taxes and duties. [from Arabic *tarif*, explanation]

⊞ **1** price list, schedule, charges, rate. **2** tax, duty, levy, toll, customs, excise.

tarlatan /'tɑːlǝtǝn/ *noun* an open, transparent muslin, used for stiffening garments. [from French *tarlatane*]

tarmac *noun* **1** tarmacadam. **2** a surface covered with tarmac, especially an airport runway.

tarmacadam *noun* a mixture of small stones bound together with tar, used to make road surfaces, etc.

tarn *noun Geol.* a small, often circular, mountain lake, especially one formed in a cirque. [from Norse *tjörn*]

tarnish — *verb* **1** to make (metal) dull and discoloured, especially through the action of air or dirt. **2** *intrans., said of metal* to become dull and discoloured. **3** to spoil or damage (eg someone's reputation). — *noun* **1** a loss of shine or lustre. **2** a discoloured or dull film on the surface of metal. [from Old French *ternir*, to make dull]

◼ *verb* **1, 2** discolour, corrode, rust, dull, dim, darken, blacken. **3** sully, taint, stain, blemish, spot, blot, mar, spoil.
◼ *verb* **1** polish, brighten.

tarnishable *adj.* capable of tarnishing.

taro /ˈtɑːroʊ/ *noun Bot.* a plant of the genus *Colocasia* of the arum family, widely cultivated in the Pacific islands for its edible rootstock. [from Polynesian]

tarot /ˈtaroʊ/ *noun* **1** a pack of 78 playing cards consisting of four suits of 14 cards and a fifth suit of 22 trump cards. It is used for playing several different games or in fortune-telling. **2** any of the 22 trump cards in this pack, which are decorated with allegorical pictures. [from Italian *tarocchi*]

tarpaulin /tɑːˈpɔːlɪn/ *noun* heavy canvas which has been made waterproof, especially with tar; also, a sheet of this. [from TAR¹ + PALL¹]

tarragon *noun* a European herb with narrow, pungent leaves used in cooking, eg for flavouring vinegar. [from Greek *drakon*, dragon]

tarriness *noun* a tarry quality.

tarry¹ *verb intrans.* (**tarries, tarried**) **1** to linger or stay in a place. **2** to be slow or late in coming, doing something, etc. [from Middle English *taryen*, to delay]

tarry² *adj.* (**tarrier, tarriest**) like tar or covered with tar.

tarsal /ˈtɑːsl/ *adj. Anat.* relating to the bones of the tarsus (the foot and ankle). — *noun* in terrestrial vertebrates, any of the bones that form the tarsus. [from Greek *tarsos*, the flat of the foot]

tarsus /ˈtɑːsəs/ *noun* **1** *Anat.* the bones forming the upper part of the foot and ankle. **2** *Biol.* the extremity of a limb in insects, usually a five-jointed foot. **3** *Anat.* the firm connective tissue that supports and stiffens the eyelid. [from Greek *tarsos*, the flat of the foot]

tart¹ *adj.* **1** sharp or sour in taste. **2** *said of a remark, etc* brief and sarcastic; cutting. [from Anglo-Saxon *teart*, rough]

◼ SHARP, ACID. **1** sour, bitter, vinegary, tangy, piquant, pungent. **2** biting, cutting, trenchant, incisive, caustic, astringent, acerbic, scathing, sardonic.
◼ SWEET, BLAND.

tart² — *noun* **1** a pastry case, especially one without a top, with a sweet filling such as fruit or jam. **2** *derog. slang* a female prostitute or a promiscuous woman. — *verb* (*usually* **tart someone** or **something up**) *slang* to decorate or embellish them, especially in a showy or tasteless way. [from Old French *tarte*]

◼ *noun* **1** pie, flan, pastry, tartlet, patty. **2** prostitute, call girl, *colloq.* hooker, whore, harlot, scarlet woman, slut, trollop, *slang* scrubber, *slang* tramp.

tartan *noun* **1** a distinctive checked pattern which can be produced with checks of different widths and different colours, especially one of the very many designs which are each associated with a different Scottish clan. **2** a woollen cloth or garment woven with such a design. [from Old French *tiretaine*]

Tartar /ˈtɑːtə(r)/ — *noun* **1** (*also* **Tatar**) a member of a group of peoples, including Mongols and Turks, which overran Asia and parts of Europe in the Middle Ages. **2** (*also* **Tatar**) a member of a people related to the Turks living especially in Soviet central Asia. **3** (*also* **Tatar**) the language spoken by this people. **4** (**tartar**) a violent or fierce person. — *adj.* relating to the Tartars or their language. [from Latin *Tartarus*, from Persian *Tatar*, perhaps influenced by Greek *Tartaros*, hell]

tartar /ˈtɑːtə(r)/ *noun* **1** a hard deposit, consisting mostly of calcium salts, that forms on the teeth. **2** a deposit that forms a hard brownish-red crust on the insides of wine casks during fermentation. [from Greek *tartaron*]

tartaric acid an organic acid consisting of a white or colourless crystalline solid, that occurs naturally in grapes and other fruit, and can also be manufactured synthetically. It is used in baking powder, food additives, dyeing, tanning, textile processing, printing, mirror silvering, photographic chemicals, and ceramics.

tartar sauce or **tartare sauce** /ˈtɑːtə(r) sɔːs, tɑːˈtɑː(r) sɔːs/ mayonnaise flavoured with chopped pickles, capers, olives, and parsley, often served as a dressing for fish. [from French *sauce tartare*]

tartly *adv.* with a tart manner.

tartness *noun* being tart, sharpness.

tartrazine /ˈtɑːtrəziːn/ *noun Food Science* a yellow powder, soluble in water, that is used as an artificial colouring in foods, drugs, and cosmetics. It can produce allergic reactions in some people, and has been associated with hyperactivity in children. [from TARTAR]

tarty *adj.* (**tartier, tartiest**) *derog. slang* **1** *said of a woman or women's clothing* blatantly sexual or promiscuous. **2** cheap, showy, and vulgar.

task *noun* a piece of work to be done or required, especially one which is unpleasant or difficult; a chore. — **take someone to task** to scold or criticize them. [from Old French *tasque*]

◼ job, chore, duty, charge, imposition, assignment, exercise, mission, errand, undertaking, enterprise, business, occupation, activity, employment, work, labour, toil, burden.

task force 1 *Mil.* a temporary grouping of different units, eg land, sea, and air forces, under a single commander to undertake a specific mission. **2** any similar grouping of individuals for a specific purpose.

taskmaster or **taskmistress** *noun* a man or woman who sets and supervises the work of others, especially strictly or severely.

Tasmanian devil a small ferocious bear-like marsupial now found only in Tasmania.

Tass *noun* the official news agency of the former Soviet Union. [an acronym of Russian *Telegrafnoe Agentsvo Sovietskovo Soyuza*, Telegraph Agency of the Soviet Union]

tassel — *noun* **1** a decoration (eg on a curtain, cushion, or lampshade) consisting of a hanging bunch of threads tied firmly at one end and loose at the other. **2** a tassel-like flower-head on some plants, especially maize. — *verb* (**tasselled, tasselling**) **1** to adorn with tassels. **2** *intrans., said of maize* to grow tassels. [from Old French *tassel*]

tastable *adj.* capable of being tasted.

taste — *verb* **1** *trans., intrans.* to perceive the flavour of (food, drink, or some other substance) by means of the sensation produced on the surface of the tongue. **2** to try or test a food or drink by eating or drinking a small amount of it. **3** *trans., intrans.* to be aware of or recognize the flavour of: *I can taste nutmeg in this cake.* **4** (**taste of something**) to have a particular flavour. **5** to eat or drink, especially in small quantities or with enjoyment: *had not tasted food for days.* **6** to experience: *taste defeat.* — *noun* **1** the particular sensation produced when food, drink, or other substances are placed on the tongue. **2** the quality or flavour of a food, drink, or other substance that is perceived by this sense: *dislike the taste of onions.* **3** an act of tasting or a small quantity of food or drink tasted. **4** a first, usually brief experience of something. **5** a liking or preference: *a taste for exotic holidays / the film was not to her taste.* **6** the ability to judge and appreciate, what is suitable as well as being fine, elegant, or beautiful: *show good taste in clothes / a joke in poor taste.* — **to taste** as needed to give a pleasing flavour: *add water to taste.* [from Old French *taster*]

◼ *verb* **2** sample, nibble, sip, try, test, savour, relish. **3** discern, perceive, distinguish, differentiate. **6** experience, undergo,

feel, encounter, meet, know. *noun* **2** flavour, savour, relish, smack, tang. **3** bit, piece, morsel, titbit, bite, nibble, mouthful, sip, drop, dash, soupçon, sample. **4** experience, encounter. **5** liking, fondness, partiality, preference, inclination, leaning, desire, appetite. **6** discrimination, discernment, judgement, perception, appreciation, sensitivity, refinement, polish, culture, cultivation, breeding, decorum, finesse, style, elegance, tastefulness.
🔲 *noun* **2** blandness. **5** distaste. **6** tastelessness.

taste bud any of the cells on the surface of the tongue which are sensitive to flavour.

tasteful *adj.* showing good judgement or taste.

🔲 in good taste, refined, polished, cultured, cultivated, elegant, smart, stylish, aesthetic, artistic, harmonious, beautiful, exquisite, delicate, graceful, restrained, well-judged, judicious, correct, fastidious, discriminating.
🔲 tasteless, garish, tawdry.

tastefully *adv.* in a tasteful way.
tastefulness *noun* a tasteful quality.
tasteless *adj.* **1** lacking flavour. **2** showing a lack of good taste or judgement.

🔲 **1** flavourless, insipid, bland, mild, weak, watery, flat, stale, dull, boring, uninteresting, vapid. **2** in bad taste, inelegant, graceless, unseemly, improper, indiscreet, crass, rude, crude, vulgar, kitschy, *slang* naff, cheap, tawdry, flashy, gaudy, garish, loud.
🔲 **1** tasty. **2** tasteful, elegant.

tastelessly *adv.* in a tasteless way.
tastelessness *noun* being tasteless.
taster *noun* a person whose job is to taste and judge the quality of food or drink.
tastily *adv.* in a tasty way.
tastiness *noun* a tasty quality.
tasting *noun* a social event at which wine or some other food or drink is sampled.
tasty *adj.* (**tastier, tastiest**) **1** having a good, especially savoury, flavour. **2** *colloq.* interesting or attractive.

🔲 LUSCIOUS, *colloq.* SCRUMPTIOUS. **1** palatable, appetizing, mouthwatering, delicious, flavoursome, succulent, *colloq.* yummy, tangy, piquant, savoury, sweet.
🔲 **1** tasteless, insipid.

tat¹ *noun Brit. colloq.* rubbish or junk. [a shortening of TATTY]
tat² *verb trans., intrans.* (**tatted, tatting**) to make (lace for trimming) by hand with a small shuttle from sewing-thread.
ta-ta /tə'tɑː/ *interj. Brit. colloq.* good-bye.
Tatar /'tɑːtə(r)/ see TARTAR.
tatter *noun* (*usually* **tatters**) a torn ragged shred of cloth, especially of clothing. — **in tatters 1** *said of clothes* in a torn and ragged condition. **2** *said of an argument, theory, etc* completely destroyed. [from Middle English, from Norse *torturr*, rag]

🔲 rags, shreds, ribbons, pieces.

tattered *adj.* ragged or torn.

🔲 ragged, frayed, threadbare, ripped, torn, tatty, shabby, scruffy.
🔲 smart, neat.

tattily *adv.* in a tatty way.

tattiness *noun* being tatty.
tatting *noun* **1** delicate knotted lace trimming made by hand with a small shuttle from sewing-thread. **2** the process of making such lace.
tattle — *noun* idle chatter or gossip. — *verb* **1** *intrans.* to chat or gossip idly. **2** *trans.* to give away (secrets) by chatting idly or gossiping. [from Old Dutch *tatelen*]
tattler *noun* a chatterer, a gossip.
tattoo¹ /tə'tuː/ — *verb* (**tattoos, tattooed**) to mark (coloured designs or pictures) on (a person or part of the body) by pricking the skin and putting in indelible dyes. — *noun* (PL. **tattoos**) a design tattooed on the skin. [from Tahitian *tatau*]
tattoo² /tə'tuː/ *noun* (PL. **tattoos**) **1** a signal by drum or bugle calling soldiers to quarters, especially in the evening. **2** an outdoor military entertainment with marching troops, military bands, etc, usually given in the evening. **3** a rhythmic beating, tapping, or drumming. [from earlier *taptoo*, from Dutch *taptoe*, the tap of a barrel (is to be) shut]
tattooer or **tattooist** *noun* a person who tattoos skin.
tatty *adj.* (**tattier, tattiest**) *colloq.* shabby and untidy. [from TATTER]
taught /tɔːt/ see TEACH.
taunt — *verb* to tease, say unpleasant things to, or jeer at in a cruel and hurtful way. — *noun* a cruel, unpleasant, and often hurtful or provoking remark.

🔲 *verb* tease, torment, provoke, bait, goad, jeer, mock, ridicule, gibe, *colloq.* rib, deride, sneer, insult, revile, reproach. *noun* jeer, catcall, gibe, dig, sneer, insult, reproach, taunting, teasing, provocation, ridicule, sarcasm, derision, censure.

taunting — *noun* teasing, goading. — *adj.* that taunts.
tauntingly *adv.* with taunts.
taupe /toʊp/ — *noun* a brownish-grey colour. — *adj.* of this colour. [from French *taupe*, mole]
Taurean /tɔː'rɪən/ — *noun* a person born under the sign Taurus. — *adj.* relating to this sign.
Taurus /'tɔːrəs/ *noun* **1** *Astron.* the Bull, a conspicuous northern constellation of the zodiac, which includes the Crab Nebula, the Pleiades (Seven Sisters) and Hyades star clusters. Its brightest star is the red giant Aldebaran. **2** the second sign of the zodiac, the Bull. **3** a person born between 21 Apr and 20 May, under this sign. [from Latin *taurus*, bull]
taut *adj.* **1** pulled or stretched tight. **2** showing nervous strain or anxiety. **3** *said of a ship* in good condition. [from Middle English *toht*, tight]

🔲 **1, 2** strained, tense. **1** tight, stretched, contracted, unrelaxed, stiff, rigid.
🔲 **1, 2** relaxed. **1** slack, loose.

tauten *verb trans., intrans.* (**tautened, tautening**) to make or become taut.
tautological or **tautologous** *adj.* relating to or involving tautology.

🔲 repetitive, superfluous, redundant, pleonastic, verbose, wordy.
🔲 succinct, economical.

tautology /tɔː'tɒlədʒɪ/ *noun* (PL. **tautologies**) **1** the use of words which repeat the meaning found in other words already used, as in *I myself personally*. **2** *Logic* a statement which is necessarily always true. [from Greek *tautologos*, from *tauto*, same + *legein*, to say]

🔲 **1** repetition, duplication, superfluity, redundancy, pleonasm.

tavern *noun* an inn or public house. [from Latin *taberna*, shed]

taverna /tə'vɜːnə/ *noun* in Greece, a type of guesthouse with a bar, popular as holiday accommodation; also, a Greek restaurant. [from modern Greek, from Latin *taberna*, shed]

tawdrily *adv.* in a tawdry way.

tawdriness *noun* being tawdry.

tawdry *adj.* (**tawdrier, tawdriest**) cheap and showy and of poor quality. [from *St Audrey lace*, lace sold at fairs held on the feast day of St Audrey, 17 Oct]

◨ cheap, vulgar, tasteless, fancy, showy, flashy, gaudy, garish, tinselly, *colloq.* tacky, *slang* naff.

◪ fine, tasteful.

tawny — *noun* a yellowish-brown colour. — *adj.* (**tawnier, tawniest**) of this colour. [from Old French *taune*]

tawny owl a tawny-coloured European owl.

taws or **tawse** /tɔːz/ *noun Scot.* a leather strap divided into strips at one end, formerly used for corporal punishment in schools. [pl. of obsolete *taw*, whip]

tax — *noun* **1** a contribution towards a country's expenses raised by the government from people's salaries, property, and from the sale of goods and services. **2** a strain, burden, or heavy demand. — *verb* **1** to impose a tax on (a person, goods, etc) or take tax from (a salary). **2** to put a strain on or make a heavy demand on. **3** (**tax someone with something**) to accuse them of it. **4** *Legal* to assess (costs). [from Latin *taxare*, to appraise]

◨ *noun* **1** levy, charge, rate, duty, tariff, customs, contribution. **2** burden, load, strain, imposition. *verb* **1** levy, charge, demand, exact, assess, impose. **2** burden, load, strain, stretch, try, tire, weary, exhaust, drain, sap, weaken.

Taxes include: airport tax, capital gains tax, capital transfer tax, community charge, corporation tax, council tax, customs, death duty, estate duty, excise, income tax, inheritance tax, PAYE, poll tax, property tax, rates, surtax, tithe, toll, value added tax (VAT).

taxable *adj.* capable of being taxed.

taxation /tak'seɪʃən/ *noun* the act or system of imposing taxes.

tax-deductible *adj.*, *said of expenses, etc* eligible for deduction from taxable income.

tax-free *adj.*, *adv.* without payment of tax.

tax haven a country or state with a low rate of taxation compared to one's own.

taxi — *noun* (PL. **taxis**) a car which may be hired together with its driver to carry passengers on usually short journeys, and which is usually fitted with a taximeter for calculating the fare. — *verb* (**taxis, taxied, taxiing** or **taxying**) **1** *intrans.*, *said of an aircraft or its pilot* to move along the ground slowly before or after take-off or landing under its own power. **2** to cause (an aircraft) to move in this way. **3** *intrans.*, *trans.* to travel or cause to be conveyed in a taxi. [a shortening of *taximeter cab*]

taxicab *noun* same as TAXI *noun*.

taxidermist *noun* a person who practises taxidermy.

taxidermy /'taksɪdɜːmɪ/ *noun* the art of preparing, stuffing, and mounting animal skins and birds so that they present a lifelike appearance. [from Greek *taxis*, arrangement + *derma*, skin]

taximeter *noun* a meter fitted to a taxi which monitors the time taken and the distance travelled, and displays the fare due. [from French *taximètre*, from *taxe*, tax + *mètre*, meter]

taxing *adj.* requiring a lot of mental or physical effort; demanding.

◨ difficult, tough, hard, severe, demanding, arduous,
strenuous, gruelling, tiring, exhausting, stressful.

taxi rank a place where taxis stand until hired.

taxis *noun Biol.* the movement of a single cell (eg a gamete, bacterium, or protozoan) in response to an external stimulus from a specific direction (eg light). Such behaviour is only shown by cells that possess some means of locomotion. [from Greek *taxis*, from *tassein* to arrange]

taxonomic *adj.* relating to or involving classification.

taxonomist *noun* a scientist who classifies plants and animals.

taxonomy /tak'sɒnəmɪ/ *noun Biol.* the theory and techniques of describing, naming, and classifying living and extinct organisms on the basis of their anatomical and morphological features (*classical taxonomy*), similarities in the structure of their proteins and nucleic acids (*biochemical taxonomy*), the number, size, and shape of their chromosomes (*cytotaxonomy*), or quantitative assessments of their similarities and differences (*numerical taxonomy*). [from Greek *taxis*, arrangement + *nomos*, law]

taxpayer *noun* a person who pays or is liable for tax or taxes.

TB *abbrev.* tuberculosis.

Tb *symbol Chem.* terbium.

tbsp *abbrev.* tablespoon or tablespoonful.

Tc *symbol Chem.* technetium.

t-cell *noun* a kind of lymphocyte involved in cellular immunity that matures in the thymus gland in mammals. [from the initial letter of THYMUS + CELL]

TCM *abbrev.* traditional Chinese medicine.

TCP *abbrev. trademark* an antiseptic and disinfectant. [from the full name *trichlorophenylmethyliodosalicyl*]

Te *symbol Chem.* tellurium.

te see TI.

tea *noun* **1** a small evergreen tree or shrub, especially *Camellia sinensis* (of the camellia family), which has pointed leathery leaves and white fragrant flowers, and grows to a height of about 4m in the wild, although in cultivation it is pruned to the height of a small shrub to encourage the production of new shoots. Tea is native to Burma and Assam, but is now cultivated in China, Japan, India, Sri Lanka, and elsewhere for its leaves. The shoot tips with the first two leaves are picked, allowed to wither, and then rolled, fermented, and dried. When infused with boiling water they make a popular beverage. **2** the dried leaves of this plant prepared for sale. **3** a beverage prepared by infusing the dried leaves of this plant with boiling water. It contains tannins, which give the drink its characteristic flavour, and caffeine, which is a stimulant, and it may be served either hot or iced. **4** a similar drink made from the leaves or flowers of other plants: *peppermint tea*. **5** a light afternoon meal at which tea, sandwiches, and cakes are served. **6** *Brit.* a light cooked meal, usually less substantial than the midday meal, served early in the evening. [from S Chinese *te*]

tea bag a small bag or sachet of thin paper containing tea, infused in boiling water in a pot or cup.

tea break a pause for tea or other refreshments in working hours.

tea caddy a small container for tea leaves.

teacake *noun* a glazed currant bun, usually eaten toasted.

teach *verb* (PAST TENSE AND PAST PARTICIPLE **taught**) **1** to give knowledge to; to instruct in a skill or help to learn. **2** to give lessons in (a subject). **3** *intrans.* to give lessons in a subject, especially professionally. **4** *said of circumstances, experience, etc* to cause to learn or understand, especially by example, experience, or punishment: *experience had taught her to be cautious.* **5** to encourage (someone) to do what is required or acceptable (often with irony, as in the first example): *I'll teach you to be so rude / that'll teach you to be more polite.* — **teach school** *North Amer.* to be a teacher in a school. [from Anglo-Saxon *tæcan*]

◨ **1, 2** coach, tutor, lecture (in). **1** instruct, train, school, educate, drill, ground, verse, discipline, enlighten, edify,

inform, advise, counsel, guide, direct. **2** impart, inculcate.
🔳 **1, 2** learn.

. . . .

teachable *adj.* **1** able, willing, or quick to learn. **2** capable of being taught.

teacher *noun* a person who teaches, especially professionally in a school.

. . . .

🔳 schoolteacher, master, mistress, schoolmaster, schoolmistress, educator, pedagogue, tutor, lecturer, professor, don, instructor, trainer, coach, adviser, counsellor, mentor, guide, guru.
🔳 pupil.

. . . .

tea chest a tall light wooden box in which tea is packed for export, or for storing things in.

teach-in *noun* an informal lecture, demonstration and discussion, or a series of these given one after the other and usually on the same day, by experts in a particular subject.

teaching *noun* **1** the work or profession of a teacher. **2** that which is taught, especially guidance or doctrine.

. . . .

🔳 **1** education, instruction, tuition, training, grounding, schooling, pedagogy, indoctrination. **2** dogma, doctrine, tenet, precept, principle.

. . . .

teaching hospital a large hospital where medical students are taught.

tea cloth 1 a small cloth for decorating and protecting the surface of a table or trolley. **2** a tea towel.

tea-cosy *noun* a cover to keep a teapot warm.

teacup *noun* **1** a medium-sized cup used especially for drinking tea. **2** the amount a teacup will hold.

teacupful *noun* (PL. **teacupfuls**) the amount a teacup will hold.

teahouse *noun* a restaurant in China or Japan where tea and light refreshments are served.

teak *noun* **1** a large tree which grows in India, Malaysia, etc. **2** its hard yellowish-brown wood used for making furniture. [from Malayalam (S Indian language) *tekka*]

teal *noun* any of several kinds of small freshwater duck of Europe and America. [from Middle English *tele*]

tea leaf 1 a leaf of the tea plant, or a part of the leaf. **2** (**tea leaves**) the leaves remaining in the pot or cup after the tea made from them has been drunk. **3** *slang* a thief.

team — *noun* **1** a group of people forming one side in a game. **2** a group of people working together. **3** two or more animals working together, especially in harness together. — *verb* **1** (**team someone with someone** *also* **team someone up with someone**) to form them into a team for some common action. **2** *intrans.* (**team up with someone**) to form a team, an association, or a friendship with someone. **3** to harness (horses, oxen, etc) together. **4** to match (clothes). [from Anglo-Saxon *team*, childbearing, offspring]

. . . .

🔳 *noun* **1, 2** squad. **1** side, line-up, eleven, fifteen. **2** shift, crew, gang, band, group, company, stable. *verb* **1, 2** join. **1** pair (off), couple, put together. **2** pair up with, pair off with, co-operate with, collaborate with, work together with, unite with, combine with, band together with, make friends with.

. . . .

team spirit willingness to work together as part of a team and suppress individual needs and desires.

teamster *noun* **1** a driver of a team of animals. **2** *North Amer., esp. US* a lorry-driver.

team-work *noun* co-operation between those who are working together on a task.

teapot *noun* a pot with a spout and handle used for making and pouring tea.

tear[1] /tɪə(r)/ *noun* **1** a drop of clear saline liquid, secreted by the lachrymal gland, that moistens and cleans the front of the eyeball, or overflows from it in response to irritation of the eye, or as a result of emotion, especially sorrow. **2** any pear or tear-shaped drop or blob. — **in tears** crying; weeping. [from Anglo-Saxon *tear*]

. . . .

🔳 **in tears** crying, weeping, sobbing, wailing, whimpering, blubbering, sorrowful, distressed.

. . . .

tear[2] /teə(r)/ — *verb* (PAST TENSE **tore**; PAST PARTICIPLE **torn**) **1** to pull or rip apart by force. **2** (**tear at something**) to pull it violently or with tearing movements. **3** to make (a hole, etc) by, or as if by, tearing or ripping. **4** *intrans.* to come apart; to be pulled or ripped apart: *material that tears easily.* **5** (*also* **tear someone away**) to remove or take them by force; to force or persuade them to leave. **6** *intrans.* (**tear along, away, off**, etc) to rush; to move with speed or violence. — *noun* **1** a hole or other damage caused by tearing. **2** an act of tearing. **3** damage: *wear and tear.* — **be torn** to be unable to decide between two or more options. **tear a strip off someone** *colloq.* to rebuke or reprimand them severely. **tear someone apart** to cause them severe suffering or distress. **tear something down** to pull it down or demolish it using force. **tear one's hair out** to be in despair with impatience and frustration. **tear into someone** to attack them physically or verbally. **tear something up 1** to tear it into pieces, especially to destroy it. **2** to remove from a fixed position by violence: *the wind tore up several trees.* [from Anglo-Saxon *teran*]

. . . .

🔳 *verb* **1, 3** rip, rend, rupture, gash. **1** divide, sever, shred, scratch, lacerate, mutilate, mangle. **2, 4** pull, snatch, grab, claw. **4** wrest. **6** dash, rush, hurry, speed, race, run, sprint, fly, shoot, dart, bolt, *colloq.* belt, career, charge. *noun* **1** rip, rent, slit, hole, split, rupture, scratch, gash, laceration. **tear down** demolish, destroy, raze, knock down, pull down, bulldoze, flatten. **tear into** attack, assail, let fly at, *colloq.* lay into, *colloq.* go for, lambaste. **tear up 1** rip up, shred, rend, destroy.

. . . .

tearaway /ˈteərəweɪ/ *noun Brit. colloq.* an undisciplined and reckless young person.

teardrop *noun* a single tear.

tear duct a short tube opening in the inner corner of the eye, for carrying tears to the eye or draining them into the nose.

tearful *adj.* **1** inclined to cry or weep. **2** with much crying or weeping; covered with tears. **3** causing tears to be shed; sad.

. . . .

🔳 **1, 3** *literary* lachrymose. **1** emotional, *colloq.* weepy. **2, 3** sad. **2** crying, weeping, sobbing, whimpering, blubbering, sorrowful, upset, distressed. **3** upsetting, distressing, mournful, doleful.
🔳 **1, 2** happy. **2** smiling, laughing.

. . . .

tearfully *adv.* in a tearful way.

tearfulness *noun* being tearful.

tear gas a gas which causes stinging, blinding tears, and temporary loss of sight, used eg to control riots.

tearing *adj.* furious; overwhelming: *a tearing hurry.*

tear-jerker *noun colloq.* a sentimental play, film, book, etc intended to make people feel sad and cry.

tear-jerking *adj.* sentimental.

tearless *adj.* without tears or sorrow.

tearoom *noun* a restaurant where tea, coffee, cakes, etc are served.

tea rose a hybrid rose which is supposed to smell of tea.

tear-stained *adj., said of the face or cheeks* marked with the traces of tears.

tease — *verb* **1** *trans., intrans.* to annoy or irritate deliberately or unkindly. **2** *trans., intrans.* to laugh at or make fun of playfully or annoyingly. **3** to persuade (someone) to agree to something, especially by continual coaxing. **4** *trans., intrans.* to arouse (someone) sexually without satisfying that desire. **5** to comb wool, flax, hair, etc to remove tangles and open out the fibres. **6** to raise a nap on (cloth) by scratching or brushing, especially with teasels. **7** to backcomb (the hair). — *noun* **1** a person or thing that teases. **2** an act of teasing. — **tease something out 1** to separate it from something in which it is entangled. **2** to clarify an obscure point by discussion, etc. [from Anglo-Saxon *tæsan*, to card]

◫ *verb* **1** annoy, provoke, irritate, pester, torment, *colloq.* wind up. **2** mock, gibe, banter, chaff, *colloq.* rib.

teasel or **teazel** or **teazle** /'ti:zl/ *noun* **1** a plant whose prickly flower heads were formerly used to raise a nap on woollen or woven cloth. **2** an artificial substitute for the teasel. [from Anglo-Saxon *tæsel*]

teaser *noun* **1** a puzzle or tricky problem. **2** a person who enjoys teasing others.

teashop *noun* a (usually small) restaurant where tea and light refreshments are served; also, a shop where tea is sold.

teasing — *noun* the act or practice of teasing. — *adj.* that teases; taunting, tantalizing.

teasingly *adv.* in a teasing way.

teaspoon *noun* **1** a small spoon for use with a teacup. **2** the amount a teaspoon will hold.

teaspoonful *noun* (PL. **teaspoonfuls**) the amount a teaspoon will hold.

teat *noun* **1** the nipple of a breast or udder. **2** a piece of shaped rubber attached to a bottle through which a baby can suck milk. [from Old French *tete*]

tea towel a cloth for drying dishes after they have been washed.

tea tray a tray on which tea, usually with sandwiches and cakes, is served.

tea trolley a small trolley from which tea, sandwiches, and cakes are served.

tec *noun colloq.* a detective.

tech /tɛk/ *noun colloq.* a technical college.

tech. *abbrev.* **1** technical. **2** technology.

techie /'tɛkɪ/ *noun slang* a devotee of or expert in (some aspect of) technology. [shortened from TECHNICAL (expert) or TECHNICIAN]

technetium /tɛk'niːʃɪəm/ *noun Chem.* (SYMBOL Tc, ATOMIC NUMBER 43) a radioactive metallic element that is produced artificially by bombarding molybdenum with neutrons. It has 16 radioactive isotopes, and there are no known natural sources of the element. [from Greek *technetos*, artificial]

technical /'tɛknɪkl/ *adj.* **1** having knowledge of, specializing in, or relating to a practical skill or applied science, especially those sciences which are useful to industry. **2** *said especially of language* relating to a particular subject or requiring knowledge of a particular subject to be understood. **3** according to a strict interpretation of the law or rules. **4** of or showing a quality of technique: *playing of technical brilliance.* [from Greek *technikos*, from *techne*, art]

◫ **1** mechanical, scientific, technological, electronic, computerized, specialized, expert, professional.

technical college a college of further education that teaches practical skills and applied sciences necessary to industry and business.

technical drawing 1 the drawing of plans, machinery, electrical circuits, etc with compasses, rulers, etc for business and industry. **2** a drawing done for business or industry.

technical hitch a mechanical fault.

technicality /tɛknɪ'kalətɪ/ *noun* (PL. **technicalities**) **1** a technical detail or term. **2** a usually trivial or petty detail caused by a strict interpretation of the law or rules. **3** the state of being technical.

technical knockout a decision by a referee that a boxer has been defeated even though he or she has not been knocked out.

technically *adv.* in a technical way; strictly speaking: *technically, they are criminals.*

technician /tɛk'nɪʃən/ *noun* **1** a person specialized or skilled in a practical art or science: *a dental technician.* **2** a person employed to do practical work in a laboratory. [from Greek *techne*, art]

Technicolor /'tɛknɪkʌlə(r)/ *noun trademark* a process of producing colour cinema film by placing several copies of a scene, each one produced using different colour filters, on top of each other.

technique /tɛk'niːk/ *noun* **1** proficiency or skill in the practical or formal aspects of an art, especially painting, music, sport, etc: *a singer with a beautiful voice but poor technique.* **2** mechanical or practical skill or method: *study the techniques of film-making.* **3** a way of achieving one's purpose skilfully; a knack. [from French, from Greek *technikos*, from *techne*, art]

◫ **1, 2** art, craft, skill. **1** execution, delivery, artistry, craftsmanship, facility, proficiency, expertise, *colloq.* know-how, manner, style. **2** method, system, procedure. **3** knack, touch, approach, way.

techno /'tɛknoʊ/ *noun* a style of pop music that makes use of electronic effects, especially to produce unmelodic sounds. [from TECHNOLOGY]

techno- *combining form* forming words denoting technology: *technophobia.*

technobabble *noun colloq.* language that overuses technical jargon, eg specialized words, acronyms, and abbreviations used in computing, etc.

technocracy /tɛk'nɒkrəsɪ/ *noun* (PL. **technocracies**) the government of a country or management of an industry by technical experts. [from Greek *techne*, art + -CRACY]

technocrat /'tɛknəkrat/ *noun* a member of or believer in technocracy.

technocratic *adj.* relating to or typical of technocracy.

technological *adj.* relating to or involving technology.

technologist *noun* a person skilled in technology and its applications.

technology /tɛk'nɒlədʒɪ/ *noun* (PL. **technologies**) **1** the practical use of scientific knowledge in industry and everyday life. **2** practical sciences as a group. **3** the technical skills and achievements of a particular time in history, civilization, or group of people. [from Greek *technologia*, systematic treatment]

tectonics /tɛk'tɒnɪks/ *sing. noun* **1** *Geol.* the study of structures which form the earth's crust and the forces which change it. See also PLATE TECTONICS. **2** the art or science of building and construction. [from Greek *tekton*, builder]

Ted *noun Brit. colloq.* a Teddy boy.

teddy¹ *noun* (PL. **teddies**) (*also* **teddy bear**) a child's stuffed toy bear. [named after 'Teddy', the pet name of Theodore Roosevelt, who was well known as a bear hunter]

teddy² *noun* (PL. **teddies**) a woman's one-piece undergarment consisting of a chemise and panties.

Teddy boy *Brit. colloq.* an unruly or rowdy adolescent, especially one in the 1950s who dressed in Edwardian-style clothes. [from *Teddy*, a familiar form of *Edward*]

Te Deum /tiː 'diːəm/ (PL. **Te Deums**) a Latin hymn of praise and thanksgiving, or a musical setting of it. [from its first words *Te Deum laudamus*, You God we praise]

tedious /'tiːdɪəs/ *adj.* tiresomely long-winded or dull; monotonous. [from Latin *taedere*, to weary]

◫ boring, monotonous, uninteresting, unexciting, dull,

laborious, long-winded, long-drawn-out, dreary, drab, banal, humdrum, tiresome, wearisome, tiring.

■ lively, interesting, exciting.

tediously *adv.* in a tedious way.

tediousness *noun* being tedious.

tedium /'tiːdɪəm/ *noun* tediousness; boredom. [from Latin *taedere*, to weary]

■ boredom, monotony, dullness, dreariness, uneventfulness, uniformity, routineness, banality, wearisomeness.

tee[1] *noun* a phonetic spelling for the letter *T*. See also T[1].

tee[2] *noun* **1** *Golf* **a** a small peg with a concave top, or a small pile of sand, used to support a ball when the first shot is taken at the beginning of a hole. **b** the small area of level ground where the first shot is taken at the beginning of a hole. **2** a mark aimed at in quoits or curling. — **tee off** to play one's first ball at the beginning of a golf hole. **tee up** to place a golf ball on a tee ready for a stroke.

teem[1] *verb intrans.* **1** (**teem with people** or **things**) to be full of them or abound in them: *a resort teeming with tourists.* **2** to be present in large numbers; to be plentiful: *fish teem in this river.* [from Anglo-Saxon *teman*, to give birth]

■ **1** swarm with, crawl with, abound in, bristle with, be alive with, be full of, be thick with, be packed with, be bursting with, be brimming with, overflow with, be seething with.

teem[2] *verb intrans.* (*usually* **teem down**) *said of water, especially rain* to pour in torrents. [from Norse *toema*, to empty]

teen *noun* **1** (**teens**) the years of a person's life between the ages of 13 and 19. **2** (**teens**) the numbers from 13 to 19. **3** *colloq.* (*usually* **teens**) a teenager. [from Anglo-Saxon *tien*, 10]

teenage /'tiːneɪdʒ/ *adj.* **1** (*also* **teenaged**) in one's teens. **2** relating to or suitable for people in their teens.

■ **1** adolescent, young, youthful, juvenile, immature.

teenager /'tiːneɪdʒə(r)/ *noun* a person aged between 13 and 19.

■ adolescent, youth, boy, girl, minor, juvenile.

teeny or **teensy** *adj.* (**teenier, teeniest**) *colloq.* tiny. [from TINY + WEE[1]]

teenybopper *noun colloq.* a young teenager, usually a girl, who enthusiastically follows the latest trends in clothes and pop music.

teeny-weeny or **teensy-weensy** *adj. colloq.* very tiny.

teepee /'tiːpiː/ *see* TEPEE.

tee shirt *see* T-SHIRT.

teeter *verb intrans.* (**teetered, teetering**) **1** (**teeter about, along,** *etc*) to stand or move unsteadily; to wobble. **2** to hesitate or waver. [from Middle English *titeren*]

■ WAVER. **1** totter, wobble, sway, rock, tremble. **2** hesitate, dither, falter, *colloq.* dilly-dally, shilly-shally.

teeth /tiːθ/ *see* TOOTH.

teethe /tiːð/ *verb intrans.* (**teethed, teething**) *said of a baby* to develop or cut milk teeth. [from Middle English *tethen*]

teething /'tiːðɪŋ/ *noun* cutting teeth.

teething ring a small hard ring for a baby to chew while teething.

teething troubles problems or difficulties at the beginning of a project, or with a new piece of machinery, etc.

teetotal /tiː'toʊtl/ *adj.* never taking alcoholic drink. [probably connected with 'total abstinence (from alcohol)'; used by a campaigner for total abstinence in a speech in 1833]

■ TT, temperate, abstinent, abstemious, sober, *colloq.* on the wagon.

teetotaller /tiː'toʊtələ(r)/ *noun* a person who abstains from alcoholic drink.

tefillen or **tephillin** /tə'fɪlɪn/ *pl. noun Judaism* phylacteries consisting of two black leather cubes with leather straps, bound over the head and arm, and worn during Jewish morning prayers, except on sabbaths and festivals. Also, the scriptural texts contained in the cubes. [from Hebrew *tephillāh*, prayer]

TEFL *abbrev.* teaching English as a foreign language.

Teflon /'teflɒn/ *noun trademark* PTFE (polytetrafluoroethene), a polymer with a high melting point, which is resistant to chemical attack. It is widely used to coat the inside of cooking pans to give them a non-stick surface.

tel. *abbrev.* telephone.

tele- *combining form* forming words meaning: **1** at, over, or to a distance: *telegram.* **2** television: *teletext.* **3** telephone: *telesales.* [from Greek *tele*, far]

tele-ad /'telɪad/ *noun* an advertisement placed in a newspaper by telephone.

telebanking *noun* a system which enables banking transactions to be carried out by means of a telecommunications network. This is most commonly achieved through a view data system or an interactive computer link, or sometimes over an interactive cable television network, with provision for the user to send signals to the bank.

telecast /'telɪkɑːst/ — *verb* (PAST TENSE AND PAST PARTICIPLE **telecast, telecasted**) to broadcast by television. — *noun* a television broadcast.

telecaster *noun* a television broadcaster.

telecommunication or **telecommunications** *noun* any process or group of processes that allows the transmission of audible or visible information, or data, over long distances by means of electrical or electronic signals, eg telephone, radio, television, telegraph, fax, radar, data transmission.

telecommuter *noun* a person working at home and communicating with an office by telephone, computer link, etc.

telecommuting *noun* same as TELEWORKING.

teleconferencing *noun* the facility for conducting conferences or meetings between people in two or more remote locations by video, audio, and/or computer links which allow communication in real time between the participants.

telecottage *noun* a building situated in a rural area and equipped with computers and electronic communication links, used by a number of people for teleworking.

telegram *noun* a message sent by telegraph and delivered in printed form, now used (in the UK) only for messages sent abroad and replaced by *Telemessage* for inland messages.

telegraph /'telɪɡrɑːf/ — *noun* a system of or instrument for sending messages or information to a distance, especially by sending electrical impulses along a wire. — *verb* **1** *trans., intrans.* to send (a message) to (someone) by telegraph. **2** to give a warning of (something which is to happen) without being aware of doing so. **3** *intrans.* to signal. [from French *télégraphe*]

telegrapher /tə'leɡrəfə(r)/ or **telegraphist** *noun* a person who operates a telegraph.

telegraphese /tɒlɪɡrɑː'fiːz/ *noun* the jargon or abbreviated language used for telegrams.

telegraphic /telɪ'ɡrafɪk/ *adj.* **1** of or by telegraph or telegram. **2** concisely worded.

telegraphically *adv.* by means of the telegraph.

telegraphy /tə'leɡrəfɪ/ *noun* the science or practice of sending messages by telegraph.

telekinesis /ˌtelɪkɪˈniːsɪs, ˌtelɪkaɪˈniːsɪs/ *noun* the moving of objects at a distance without using physical force, eg by willpower. [from TELE- + Greek *kinesis*, movement]

telekinetic /ˌtelɪkɪˈnetɪk, ˌtelɪkaɪˈnetɪk/ *adj.* relating to or involving telekinesis.

telemarketing *noun* a marketing system that uses the telephone to recruit and provide a service for prospective clients.

Telemessage *noun Brit. trademark* a message sent by telex or telephone and delivered in printed form, replacing the telegram within the UK.

telemeter /təˈlemɪtə(r)/ *noun Engineering* an instrument that is used to take measurements and send the readings obtained, usually by means of electrical or radio signals, to a location remote from the site of measurement. Telemeters are used to relay information from spacecraft, to transmit meteorological data, and to determine the conditions inside nuclear reactors.

telemetric /ˌtelɪˈmetrɪk/ *adj.* involving or by means of a telemeter.

telemetry /təˈlemɪtrɪ/ *noun* scientific measurement of distances.

teleological *adj.* relating to or involving teleology.

teleologist *noun* a believer in or supporter of teleology.

teleology /ˌtelɪˈɒlədʒɪ/ *noun* the doctrine that the universe, all phenomena, and natural processes are directed towards a goal or are designed according to some purpose. [from Greek *telos*, end + -LOGY]

telepathic *adj.* relating to or involving telepathy.

telepathically *adv.* in a telepathic way; by means of telepathy.

telepathist *noun* a person who studies or practises telepathy.

telepathy /təˈlepəθɪ/ *noun* the communication of thoughts directly from one person's mind to another's without using any of the five known senses. [from TELE- + Greek *pathos*, feeling]

▉ mind-reading, thought transference, sixth sense, ESP, extra-sensory perception, clairvoyance.

telephone — *noun* 1 an instrument with a mouthpiece and an earpiece mounted on a handset, for transmitting human speech in the form of electrical signals or radio waves, enabling people to communicate with each other over a distance. Most modern telephones have a push-button dialling mechanism. 2 the system of communication that uses such an instrument. — *verb* 1 to seek or establish contact and speak to (someone) by telephone. 2 to send (a message, etc) by telephone. 3 *intrans.* to make a telephone call. — **on the telephone** 1 connected to the telephone system. 2 talking to someone by means of the telephone.

▉ *noun* 1 phone, handset, receiver, *colloq.* blower. *verb* PHONE. 1, 3 ring (up), call (up). 1 dial, *colloq.* buzz, contact, get in touch with.

telephone box or **telephone booth** a small enclosed or partly-enclosed compartment containing a telephone for public use.

telephone directory or **telephone book** a book listing the names, addresses, and telephone numbers of telephone subscribers in a particular area.

telephone exchange see EXCHANGE.

telephonic /ˌtelɪˈfɒnɪk/ *adj.* relating to or involving the telephone.

telephonist /təˈlefənɪst/ *noun* a telephone switchboard operator.

telephony /təˈlefənɪ/ *noun* the use or system of communication by means of the telephone.

telephoto /ˌtelɪˈfoʊtoʊ/ *adj.* relating to telephotography.

telephotographic /ˌtelɪfoʊtəˈɡræfɪk/ *adj.* relating to or involving telephotography.

telephotography /ˌtelɪfəˈtɒɡrəfɪ/ *noun* the photographing of distant objects with lenses which produce large images.

telephoto lens a camera lens which produces large images of distant or small objects.

teleprinter /ˈtelɪprɪntə(r)/ *noun* an apparatus with a keyboard which types messages as they are received by telegraph and transmits them as they are typed.

Teleprompter *noun trademark* a device placed next to a television or film camera and out of sight of the audience, which displays the script to the speaker.

telesales *pl. noun* (*also* **teleselling**) the selling of goods or services by telephone.

telescope /ˈtelɪskoʊp/ — *noun* 1 an optical instrument containing a powerful magnifying lens or mirror that makes distant objects appear larger. 2 a radio telescope. — *verb* 1 *intrans.* to be in the form of several cylinders which slide into each other for opening and closing, like the sections of a folding telescope. 2 to collapse part within part like a folding telescope. 3 *trans., intrans.* to crush or compress, or become crushed or compressed, under impact. [from TELE- + Greek *skopeein*, to see]

▉ *verb* 3 contract, shrink, compress, condense, abridge, squash, crush, reduce.

telescopic /ˌtelɪˈskɒpɪk/ *adj.* 1 of or like a telescope; performed with a telescope. 2 able to be seen only through a telescope. 3 *said of a lens* able to discern and magnify distant objects. 4 made in sections which slide into each other.

telescopically *adv.* in a telescopic way.

telescopic sight a small telescope used as a sight on a rifle.

teleshopping *noun* the purchase or ordering of goods from home, using an electronic communications network. A list of food and goods available to the shopper are displayed on a television screen, and these can be ordered directly over the communications link.

teletext /ˈtelɪtekst/ *noun* a news and information service that is produced and regularly updated by a television company, eg Ceefax, operated by the BBC. It is transmitted using the spare lines in the video signal, and can be viewed on television sets fitted with a suitable receiver and decoder.

telethon /ˈtelɪθɒn/ *noun* a usually day-long television programme broadcast to raise money for charity. [from TELEVISION + MARATHON]

Teletype /ˈtelɪtaɪp/ *noun trademark* a type of teleprinter.

televangelist *noun North Amer., esp. US* an evangelical preacher who preaches and conducts religious services regularly on television. [from TELEVISION + EVANGELIST]

televise *verb* to broadcast by television.

television *noun* 1 an electronic system that is used to convert moving images and sound into electrical signals, which are then transmitted by radio waves or by cable to a distant receiver that converts the signals back to images and sound. It is widely used for entertainment and educational purposes. 2 (*also* **television set**) a device with a picture tube and loudspeakers that is used to receive picture and sound signals transmitted in this way. 3 television broadcasting in general. See also COLOUR TELEVISION.

▉ TV, *colloq.* TELLY. 2 receiver, set, *colloq.* the box, *colloq.* goggle-box, *colloq.* idiot box. 3 the small screen.

televisual /ˌtelɪˈvɪʒʊəl/ *adj.* of or suitable for being broadcast by television.

televisually *adv.* in a televisual way; by means of television.

teleworking *noun* working from home by means of an electronic communication link with an office.

telex /ˈteleks/ (*also* **Telex**) — *noun* 1 *Telecomm.* an international telecommunications network that uses teleprinters (devices that transmit and receive telegraph messages in the form of coded electrical signals) and radio and satellite links to enable subscribers to the network to send and receive messages to each other. Unlike fax, telex can transmit one message to several receivers simultaneously. **2** a teleprinter used in such a network. **3** a message received or sent by such a network. — *verb trans., intrans.* to send a message to someone via such a network. [from TELE-PRINTER + EXCHANGE]

tell[1] *verb* (PAST TENSE AND PAST PARTICIPLE **told**) **1** (**tell someone something** or **tell something to someone**) to inform or give information to someone in speech or writing. **2** *trans., intrans.* (**tell of something** or **tell someone of something**) to relate or give an account of something. **3** to command or instruct. **4** to express in words: *tell lies.* **5** to discover or distinguish: *you can tell it by its smell / it is sometimes difficult to tell Brie from Camembert.* **6** (**tell on someone**) to give away secrets about them. **7** to make known or give away. **8** (**tell on someone**) *said of an ordeal, etc* to have a noticeable effect on them. **9** *intrans., trans.* to know or recognize (something) definitely: *can never tell when he's lying.* **10** to assure. **11** (**tell against someone**) *said of evidence, circumstances, etc* to be unfavourable to their case, cause, etc. — **all told** in all; with all taken into account: *there were thirty all told.* **take a telling** to do as one is told without having to be asked again. **tell people** or **things apart** to distinguish between them. **tell someone off 1** to scold or reprimand them. **2** to count them off and detach them on some special duty. **you're telling me!** *colloq.* an exclamation of agreement. [from Anglo-Saxon *tellan*]

....

▪ **1** inform, notify, let know, acquaint, impart, communicate. **2** relate, report, narrate, recount, announce, describe, portray, mention. **3** order, command, direct, instruct, authorize. **4** speak, utter, say, state. **5** differentiate, distinguish, discover, recognize, identify, discern. **6** inform on, *slang* grass on, *slang* shop, betray, denounce. **7** confess, divulge, disclose, reveal. **8** affect, have an effect on, take its toll of, exhaust, drain, change, transform, alter. **9** recognize, see, understand, comprehend. **tell off 1** scold, chide, *colloq.* tick off, upbraid, reprimand, rebuke, reprove, lecture, berate, *colloq.* dress down, reproach, censure.

....

tell[2] or **tel** *noun Archaeol.* especially in the Middle East, an artificial mound or hill formed from the accumulated remains of former settlements. [from Arabic *tall*, hill]

teller *noun* **1** a person who tells especially stories. **2** a bank employee who receives money from and pays it out to members of the public. **3** a person who counts votes.

telling *adj.* having a great or marked effect.

....

▪ effective, forceful, powerful, convincing, cogent, persuasive, impressive.

....

tellingly *adv.* in a telling way.
telling-off *noun* a mild scolding.

....

▪ scolding, *colloq.* ticking-off, reprimand, rebuke, reproof, lecture, *colloq.* dressing-down, reproach.

....

telltale — *noun* **1** a person who spreads gossip and rumours, especially about another person's private affairs or misdeeds. **2** any of various devices for recording or monitoring a process, machine, etc. — *adj.* revealing or indicating something secret or hidden.

....

▪ revealing, revelatory, give-away, noticeable, perceptible, unmistakable.

....

tellurian /tɛˈlʊərɪən, tɛˈljʊərɪən/ — *adj.* of or living on the earth. — *noun* an inhabitant of the earth, especially in science fiction. [from Latin *tellus*, earth]

tellurium /tɛˈlʊərɪəm, tɛˈljʊərɪəm/ *noun Chem.* (SYMBOL **Te**, ATOMIC NUMBER 52) a brittle silvery-white metalloid element obtained from gold, silver, and copper ores. It is added to alloys of lead or steel to increase their hardness, and is also used in semiconductors, glass, and ceramics, and as a catalyst. [from Latin *tellus*, earth]

telly *noun* (PL. **tellies**) *colloq.* television; a television set.

telophase /ˈtɛloʊfeɪz/ *noun Biol.* the final stage of cell division, that occurs once in mitosis and twice in meiosis. The two sets of chromosomes aggregate at opposite poles of the spindle, and a nuclear membrane forms around each set, resulting in the production of two daughter nuclei. [from Greek *telos*, end, purpose]

Telstar *noun* any of a series of communications satellites, industrially funded but launched by NASA. *Telstar 1* was the first satellite to relay live television pictures across the Atlantic Ocean, in Jul 1962.

Telugu /ˈtɛlʊɡuː/ — *noun* a Dravidian language of SE India and parts of Malaysia with c.35–55 million speakers. — *adj.* relating to or spoken or written in Telugu.

temazepam /təˈmazɪpam/ *noun* a drug used to treat insomnia, and as a sedative.

temerity /tɪˈmɛrɪtɪ/ *noun* rashness or boldness; an unreasonable lack of fear. [from Latin *temeritas*]

....

▪ audacity, boldness, impudence, impertinence, cheek, gall, *colloq.* nerve, *colloq.* brass (neck), daring, rashness, recklessness, impulsiveness.

▣ caution, prudence.

....

temp — *noun* an employee, especially a secretary, typist, or other office worker, employed on a temporary basis. — *verb intrans.* to work as a temp.

temp. *abbrev.* **1** temperature. **2** temporary.

temper — *noun* **1** a characteristic state of mind; mood or humour: *have an even temper.* **2** a state of calm; composure; self-control: *lose one's temper.* **3** a state of uncontrolled anger: *in a temper.* **4** a tendency to have fits of uncontrolled anger. **5** the degree of hardness and toughness of metal or glass. — *verb* (**tempered**, **tempering**) **1** to soften or make less severe: *temper firmness with understanding.* **2** *Engineering* to heat a metal, hardened alloy (eg steel), or glass to a certain temperature and then allow it to cool slowly, in order to toughen it by reducing its hardness and making it less brittle. **3** to bring clay, plaster, or mortar to the desired consistency by moistening it with water and kneading it. **4** to tune (the notes on a keyboard instrument) so that the intervals between them are correct. — **out of temper** irritable; peevish; fractious. [from Latin *temperare*, to mix in due proportion]

....

▪ *noun* **1** mood, humour, nature, temperament, character, disposition, constitution. **2** calm, composure, self-control, *colloq.* cool. **3** anger, rage, fury, passion, tantrum, *colloq.* paddy, annoyance, irritability, ill-humour. *verb* **1** moderate, lessen, reduce, calm, soothe, allay, assuage, palliate, mitigate, modify, soften. **2** harden, toughen, strengthen.

▣ *noun* **3** calmness, self-control.

....

tempera /ˈtɛmpərə/ *noun* **1** a method of painting in which powdered pigment is mixed with an emulsion made usually of egg yolks and water. **2** an emulsion, especially one made with egg yolks and water, into which powdered pigments are mixed to produce paint. **3** a painting produced using tempera. [from Italian *temperare*, to mix in due proportion]

temperament *noun* **1** a person's natural character or disposition which governs the way he or she behaves and thinks. **2** a sensitive, creative, and excitable or emotional personality. **3** an adjustment made to the intervals between notes on an instrument's keyboard to allow the instrument to play in any key. [from Latin *temperamentum*, a mixing in due proportion, in this case of the four humours believed in the Middle Ages to govern one's physical and mental characteristics]

▣ **1** nature, character, personality, disposition, tendency, bent, constitution, make-up, soul, spirit, mood, humour, temper, state of mind, attitude, outlook.

temperamental *adj.* **1** given to extreme changes of mood; quick to show emotion, anger, irritability, etc. **2** *said of a machine, etc* not working reliably or consistently. **3** of or caused by temperament.

▣ **1, 2** unpredictable, unreliable. **1** moody, emotional, neurotic, highly-strung, sensitive, touchy, irritable, impatient, passionate, fiery, excitable, explosive, volatile, mercurial, capricious. **3** natural, inborn, innate, inherent, constitutional, ingrained.
▣ **1** calm, level-headed, steady.

temperamentally *adv.* in a temperamental way.

temperance / 'tempərəns/ *noun* **1** moderation, self-restraint, especially in controlling one's appetite or desires. **2** moderation or complete abstinence from alcoholic drink. [from Latin *temperantia*, moderation, sobriety]

▣ SOBRIETY. **1** moderation, restraint, self-restraint, self-control, self-discipline, self-denial, continence. **2** teetotalism, prohibition, abstinence, abstemiousness.
▣ **1** intemperance, excess.

temperate *adj.* **1** moderate and self-restrained, especially in appetite, consumption of alcoholic drink, and behaviour. **2** not excessive; moderate. **3** *said of a climate or region* having temperatures which are mild, and neither tropical nor polar. [from Latin *temperatus*]

▣ **1, 2** moderate, reasonable, sensible, restrained. **1** teetotal, abstinent, abstemious, sober, continent, controlled, even-tempered, calm, composed. **2, 3** mild. **2** equable, balanced, stable. **3** clement, balmy, fair, gentle, pleasant, agreeable.
▣ **2, 3** extreme. **2** intemperate, excessive.

temperately *adv.* in a temperate way.
temperateness *noun* a temperate quality.
temperate zones those parts of the earth having moderate temperatures, lying between the tropic of Cancer and the Arctic Circle, and the tropic of Capricorn and the Antarctic Circle.
temperature / 'tempərətʃə(r)/ *noun* **1** the degree of hotness or coldness of an object or medium (eg air or water), as measured by a thermometer. Heat always flows from a region of higher temperature to one of lower temperature. **2** a body temperature above normal (37°C or 98.6°F), regarded as an indicator of ill health if it is significantly higher than normal. Also called FEVER. [from Latin *temperatura*, proportion]
tempest *noun* **1** a violent storm with very strong winds. **2** a violent uproar. [from Latin *tempestas*, season, storm]

▣ storm, thunderstorm, gale, hurricane, typhoon, wind, gust, squall.

tempestuous / tem'pestjʊəs/ *adj.* **1** of or like a tempest; very stormy. **2** *said of a person, behaviour, etc* violently emotional; passionate.

▣ STORMY, ROUGH, WILD, VIOLENT, FURIOUS, RAGING. **1** windy, gusty, blustery, squally, thundery. **2** turbulent, tumultuous, heated, passionate, intense.
▣ CALM.

tempestuously *adv.* in a tempestuous way.
tempestuousness *noun* a tempestuous quality.
tempi / 'tempi:/ *see* TEMPO.

template / 'templeɪt/ or **templet** *noun* **1** a piece of metal, plastic, or wood cut in a particular shape and used as a pattern when cutting out material, drawing, etc. **2** a small wooden beam or block placed in a wall to help spread and support the weight or load. **3** the coded instructions carried by a molecule for the formation of a new molecule of the same type. [from Latin *templum*, small piece of timber]
temple [1] *noun* **1** a building in which people worship, especially in ancient and non-Christian religions, and in particular Christian sects such as the Mormons. **2** *Hist.* either of the two successive religious buildings built by the Jews in Jerusalem, one before and one after the exile in Babylon. **3** a place devoted to a particular purpose: *a temple to literature*. **4** *North Amer., esp. US* a synagogue, especially in Reform or Conservative Judaism. [from Latin *templum*]

▣ **1, 3** shrine, sanctuary. **1** church, tabernacle, mosque, pagoda.

temple [2] *noun* either of the flat parts of the head at the side of the forehead in front of the ear. [from Latin *tempus*]
temple [3] *noun* a device in a loom which keeps the cloth stretched. [from Latin *templum*, small piece of timber]
templet / 'templət/ *see* TEMPLATE.
tempo / 'tempoʊ/ *noun* (PL. **tempos, tempi**) **1** the speed at which a piece of music should be or is played. **2** rate or speed. [from Italian *tempo*]

▣ SPEED. **1** time, rhythm, metre, beat, pulse. **2** velocity, rate, pace.

temporal [1] / 'tempərəl/ *adj.* **1** of or relating to time, often in being relatively short. **2** of worldly or secular life as opposed to religious or spiritual life. **3** *Grammar* relating to tense or the expression of time. [from Latin *temporalis*, from *tempus*, time]

▣ **2** secular, profane, worldly, earthly, terrestrial, material, carnal, fleshly, mortal.
▣ **2** spiritual.

temporal [2] / 'tempərəl/ *adj.* of or close to the temples on either side of the head. [from Latin *tempus*, temple]
temporally *adv.* in a temporal way.
temporarily *adv.* in a temporary way; not permanently.

▣ provisionally, for the time being, for the present, ad hoc.

temporariness *noun* being temporary.
temporary / 'tempərərɪ/ — *adj.* lasting, acting, used, etc for a limited period of time only. — *noun* (PL. **temporaries**) a worker employed temporarily; a temp. [from Latin *temporarius*, from *tempus*, time]

▣ *adj.* impermanent, provisional, interim, acting, makeshift, stopgap, temporal, transient, transitory, passing, ephemeral, evanescent, fleeting, brief, short-lived, momentary.
▣ *adj.* permanent, everlasting.

temporization or **temporisation** / tempəraɪ'zeɪʃən/ *noun* avoidance of a decision or commitment.
temporize or **temporise** *verb intrans.* **1** to avoid taking a decision or committing oneself to some course of action, to gain time and perhaps win a compromise. **2** to adapt oneself to circumstances or what the occasion requires. [from Latin *tempus*, time]
temporizer or **temporiser** *noun* a person who temporizes.
tempt *verb* **1** to seek to attract and persuade (someone) to do something, especially something wrong or foolish. **2** to attract or allure. **3** to be strongly inclined to do something. **4** to risk provoking, especially by doing some-

thing foolhardy: *tempt fate*. [from Latin *temptare*, to probe, test]

▣ **1** entice, coax, persuade, woo, bait, lure, seduce, provoke, incite. **2** allure, attract, draw, invite, tantalize.
▣ **1** discourage, dissuade. **2** repel.

temptation /tɛmpˈteɪʃən/ *noun* **1** an act of tempting or the state of being tempted. **2** something that tempts.

▣ ENTICEMENT, INDUCEMENT. **1** coaxing, persuasion, seduction. **2** allure, appeal, attraction, draw, bait, lure, pull.

tempter *noun* **1** a person who tempts. **2** (**the Tempter**) *Relig.* the Devil.
tempting *adj.* that entices or attracts.

▣ attractive, inviting, enticing, alluring, seductive, tantalizing, desirable, eye-catching, *colloq.* mouth-watering.

temptingly *adv.* in a tempting way.
temptress *noun* a female tempter.
tempura /ˈtɛmpʊrə/ *noun* a Japanese dish of seafood or vegetables deep-fried in batter. [from Japanese]
Ten. *abbrev.* Tennessee.
ten — *noun* **1** the number or figure 10; any symbol for this number. **2** the age of 10. **3** something, especially a garment or a person, whose size is denoted by 10. **4** a playing card with 10 pips. **5** a set of 10 things, people, etc. **6** 10 o'clock. **7** a score of 10 points. — *adj.* **1** 10 in number. **2** aged 10. [from Anglo-Saxon *ten*]
tenability /tɛnəˈbɪlətɪ, tiːnəˈbɪlətɪ/ *noun* being tenable.
tenable /ˈtɛnəbl, ˈtiːnəbl/ *adj.* **1** able to be believed, upheld, or maintained. **2** *said of a post or office* to be held or occupied for a specified period only or by a specified person. [from Latin *tenere*, to hold]

▣ **1** credible, defensible, justifiable, reasonable, rational, sound, arguable, believable, defendable, plausible, viable, feasible.
▣ **1** untenable, indefensible, unjustifiable.

tenacious /təˈneɪʃəs/ *adj.* **1** holding or sticking firmly. **2** clinging persistently to a particular purpose, principle, policy, etc. **3** *said of memory* retaining information extremely well; retentive. [from Latin *tenere*, to hold]

▣ **1** adhesive, clinging, secure. **2** determined, persistent, dogged, single-minded, resolute, steadfast, obstinate, stubborn, intransigent.

tenaciously *adv.* in a tenacious way.
tenaciousness /təˈneɪʃəsnəs/ or **tenacity** /təˈnasɪtɪ/ *noun* being tenacious.

▣ determination, persistence, doggedness, single-mindedness, resolution, steadfastness, obstinacy, stubbornness, intransigence.

tenancy /ˈtɛnənsɪ/ *noun* (PL. **tenancies**) **1** the temporary renting of property or land by a tenant. **2** the period during which property or land is so rented.
tenant — *noun* **1** a person who pays rent to another for the use of property or land. **2** an occupant. — *verb* to occupy as a tenant. [from Latin *tenere*, to hold]

▣ *noun* **1** renter, lessee, leaseholder, lodger. **2** occupier, occupant, resident, inhabitant.

tenanted *adj.* occupied by a tenant.
tenant farmer a farmer who farms land rented from another person, especially on an estate.

tenantry *noun* all of the tenants, usually of an estate or a landlord.
Tencel /ˈtɛnsɛl/ *noun trademark* a fabric made from a fibre originally created from wood pulp.
tench *noun* (PL. **tench**) a European freshwater fish with a dark green or brownish body, related to the carp. [from Old French *tenche*]
Ten Commandments or **Decalogue** the fundamental laws of the Jews, which, according to the Bible, were given by God to Moses on Mt Sinai and set the terms of God's covenant with the Jewish people.
tend¹ *verb* **1** to take care of; to look after; to wait on. **2** (**tend to something**) to attend to it: *tended to all his needs*. [from ATTEND]

▣ LOOK AFTER. **1** care for, cultivate, keep, maintain, manage, handle, guard, protect, watch over, mind, nurture, nurse. **2** minister to, serve, attend to.
▣ NEGLECT, IGNORE.

tend² *verb intrans.* **1** (**tend to** or **towards something**) to be likely or inclined to it. **2** to move slightly, lean, or slope in a specified direction. [from Latin *tendere*, to stretch]

▣ INCLINE, LEAN. **2** bend, bear, head, aim, lead, go, move, gravitate.

tendency /ˈtɛndənsɪ/ *noun* (PL. **tendencies**) **1** a likelihood of acting or thinking, or an inclination to act or think, in a particular way. **2** a general course, trend, or drift. **3** a faction or group within a political party or movement.

▣ **1** bias, partiality, predisposition, propensity, readiness, liability, susceptibility, proneness, inclination, leaning, bent, disposition. **2** trend, drift, movement, course, direction, bearing, heading.

tendentious /tɛnˈdɛnʃəs/ *adj.* having a particular bias, tendency, or underlying purpose.

▣ biased, weighted, partial, partisan, one-sided.

tender¹ *adj.* **1** soft and delicate; fragile. **2** *said of meat* easily chewed or cut. **3** easily damaged or grieved; sensitive: *a tender heart*. **4** easily hurt when touched, especially because of having been hurt before: *her arm is still bruised and tender*. **5** loving and gentle: *tender words*. **6** easily moved to love, pity, guilt, etc: *a tender conscience*. **7** youthful and vulnerable: *of tender years*. **8** requiring gentle or careful handling. [from Old French *tendre*, from Latin *tener*]

▣ **1** soft, succulent, fleshy, dainty, delicate, fragile, frail, weak, feeble. **3**, **5** sensitive, tender-hearted, soft-hearted. **4** sore, painful, aching, smarting, bruised, inflamed, raw. **5** fond, affectionate, loving, amorous, romantic, sentimental, emotional, warm. **6** kind, gentle, caring, humane, considerate, compassionate, sympathetic. **7** young, youthful, immature, green, raw, new, inexperienced, impressionable, vulnerable.
▣ **1**, **2** tough. **1** hard. **3** hard-hearted, callous. **7** mature.

tender² — *verb* **1** to offer or present (an apology, resignation, etc). **2** (**tender for something**) to make a formal offer to do work or supply goods for a stated amount of money and within a stated period of time. — *noun* a formal offer, usually in writing, to do work or supply goods for a stated amount of money and within a stated period of time. — **put something out to tender** to invite tenders for a job or undertaking. [from Latin *tendere*, to stretch]

▣ *verb* **1** offer, proffer, extend, give, present, submit, propose, suggest, advance, volunteer. **2** bid for, apply for. *noun* offer, bid, estimate, quotation, proposal, proposition, suggestion, submission.

. . . .

tender [3] *noun* **1** (*often in compounds*) a person who looks after something or someone: *bartender*. **2** a small boat which carries stores or passengers to and from a larger boat. **3** a railway wagon attached to a steam-engine to carry fuel and water.

tender [4] see TEND [1].

tenderfoot *noun* (PL. **tenderfeet, tenderfoots**) an inexperienced newcomer or beginner.

tender-hearted *adj.* kind and sympathetic; easily made to feel love or pity.

. . . .

■ kind, gentle, caring, humane, considerate, compassionate, sympathetic, soft-hearted, sensitive.

. . . .

tender-heartedly *adv.* in a tender-hearted way.
tender-heartedness *noun* being tender-hearted.
tenderize or **tenderise** *verb* to make (meat) tender by pounding it or by adding an acidic substance.
tenderizer or **tenderiser** *noun* a pounding instrument or a substance that tenderizes meat.
tenderloin *noun* a cut from the tenderest part of the loin of pork, beef, etc.
tenderly *adv.* in a tender way.
tenderness *noun* being tender.
tendinitis or **tendonitis** /tendə'naɪtɪs/ *noun* inflammation of a tendon.
tendon /'tendən/ *noun* a cord of strong, fibrous tissue that joins a muscle to a bone or some other structure. [from Latin *tendo*]
tendril /'tendrɪl/ *noun* Bot. a long, often spirally twisted, thread-like extension of a stem, leaf, or petiole, by means of which many climbing plants attach themselves to solid objects for support. [from Old French *tendron*, shoot]
tendrilled *adj.* having a tendril or tendrils.
tenement /'tenəmənt/ *noun* **1** North Amer., Scot. a large building divided into several self-contained flats or apartments. **2** a self-contained flat or room within such a building. [from Latin *tenementum*, from *tenere*, to hold]
tenet /'tenɪt, 'tiːnɪt/ *noun* a belief, opinion, or doctrine. [from Latin *tenet*, he, she, or it holds]
tenfold — *adj.* **1** 10 times as much or as many. **2** divided into, or consisting of, 10 parts. — *adv.* by 10 times as much.
ten-gallon hat North Amer., esp. US a hat worn by cowboys, with a broad brim and high crown.
Tenn. *abbrev.* Tennessee.
tenner *noun colloq.* a £10 note.
tennis *noun* **1** (*in full* **lawn tennis**) a game in which two players or two pairs of players use rackets to hit a light ball across a net on a grass-covered or hard rectangular court. **2** real tennis. [from Old French *tenetz*, hold!, take!]
tennis elbow painful inflammation of the elbow caused by over-exercise (typically by playing tennis) or over-work.
tenon /'tenən/ — *noun* a projection at the end of a piece of wood, etc, formed to fit into a socket or mortise in another piece. — *verb* **1** to fix with a tenon. **2** to cut a tenon in. [from Latin *tenere*, to hold]
tenor /'tenə(r)/ *noun* **1** a singing voice of the highest normal range for an adult man; also, a singer having this voice. **2** an instrument, eg a viola, recorder, or saxophone, with a similar range. **3** music written for a voice or instrument with such a range. **4** the general course or meaning of something written or spoken. **5** a settled or general course or direction, eg of a person's life. [from Latin *tenor*, from *tenere*, to hold]
tenpin bowling a game in which 10 skittles are set up at the end of an alley and a ball is rolled at them with the aim of knocking as many down as possible.
tense [1] *noun* Grammar a form of verb that shows the time of its action in relation to the time of speaking and

whether that action is completed or not. [from Latin *tempus*, time]

tense [2] — *adj.* **1** feeling, showing, or marked by emotional, nervous, or mental strain. **2** tightly stretched; taut. **3** causing tension or excitement. — *verb trans., intrans.* to make or become tense. [from Latin *tendere*, to stretch]

. . . .

■ *adj.* **1** nervous, anxious, worried, jittery, uneasy, apprehensive, edgy, fidgety, restless, jumpy, overwrought, keyed up, *colloq.* wired. **2** tight, taut, stretched, strained, stiff, rigid. **3** stressful, exciting, worrying, fraught. *verb* tighten, contract, brace, stretch, strain.

☒ *adj.* **1** calm, relaxed. **2** loose, slack. *verb* loosen, relax.

. . . .

tensely *adv.* in a tense way.
tenseness *noun* being tense.
tensile /'tensaɪl, 'tensɪl/ *adj.* **1** able to be stretched. **2** relating to or involving stretching or tension. [from Latin *tensilis*, from *tendere*, to stretch]
tensile strength Physics a measure of the ability of a material to resist tension, equal to the minimum stress (force per unit cross-sectional area) required to break it. The tensile strength of a material is influenced by the way in which it is manufactured, and by processes such as tempering.
tensility /ten'sɪlɪtɪ/ *noun* a tensile quality or condition.
tension /'tenʃən/ — *noun* **1** an act of stretching, the state of being stretched, or the degree to which something is stretched. **2** mental or emotional strain, excitement, or anxiety, usually accompanied by physical symptoms. **3** strained relations or underlying hostility between people, countries, etc. **4** Physics a force which causes a body to be stretched or elongated. **5** electromotive force. **6** Knitting the tightness or looseness of wool as one knits, measured as the number of stitches to the inch. — *verb* to give the required tightness or tension to. [from Latin *tensio*, from *tendere*, to stretch]

. . . .

■ *noun* **1, 2** strain, stress, pressure. **1** tightness, tautness, stiffness. **2** nervousness, anxiety, worry, uneasiness, apprehension, edginess, restlessness, suspense.

☒ *noun* **1** looseness. **2** calm(ness), relaxation.

. . . .

tent — *noun* **1** a shelter made of canvas or other material supported by poles or a frame and fastened to the ground with ropes and pegs, that can be taken down and carried from place to place. **2** anything like a tent in form or function, especially a clear plastic device placed over the head and shoulders to control the oxygen supply to a sick person. — *verb* **1** (*intrans.*) to camp in a tent. **2** to cover or shelter with a tent. [from Old French *tente*, from Latin *tendere*, to stretch]

. . . .

■ *noun* **1** tepee, wigwam, marquee, big top.

. . . .

tentacle /'tentəkl/ *noun* **1** any of the long thin flexible appendages growing on the head or near the mouth of many invertebrate animals (eg sea anemone, octopus) used as sense organs, or for defence, grasping prey, or attachment to surfaces. **2** in certain insectivorous plants (eg sundew) any of the sticky hairs on the leaves that serve to trap insects. [from Latin *tentare*, to feel]
tentacled *adj.* having tentacles.
tentacular /ten'takjʊlə(r)/ *adj.* belonging to or like a tentacle.
tentative /'tentətɪv/ *adj.* **1** not finalised or completed; provisional. **2** showing uncertainty, hesitancy, or caution. [from Latin *tentare*, to try]

. . . .

■ **1** experimental, exploratory, speculative, provisional, indefinite, unconfirmed. **2** hesitant, faltering, cautious, unsure, uncertain, doubtful, undecided, diffident.

☒ DEFINITE, DECISIVE. **1** conclusive, final.

. . . .

tentatively *adv.* in a tentative way.

tentativeness *noun* being tentative.

tenter *noun* a frame on which cloth is stretched, especially so that it dries without losing its shape.

tenterhook *noun* a sharp hooked nail used for fastening cloth to a tenter. — **on tenterhooks** in a state of impatient suspense or anxiety.

tenth — *noun* **1** one of 10 equal parts. **2** the last of 10; the next after the ninth. **3** *Mus.* an interval of an octave plus a third. **4** *Mus.* a note which is an octave plus a third above or below another. — *adj.* being the last of 10 or in an equivalent position. — *adv.* **1** in tenth position. **2** as the tenth point, etc.

tenthly *adv.* as the tenth point, etc.

tenuous /ˈtɛnjʊəs/ *adj.* **1** slight; with little strength or substance. **2** thin; slim. [from Latin *tenuis*, thin]

⊟ **1** slight, insubstantial, flimsy, fragile, delicate, weak, shaky, doubtful, dubious, questionable. **2** thin, slim, slender, fine.
⊟ **1** strong, substantial.

tenuously *adv.* in a tenuous way.

tenuousness *noun* being tenuous.

tenure /ˈtɛnjə(r)/ *noun* **1** the holding of an office, position, or property. **2** the length of time an office, position, or property is held. **3** the holding of a position, especially a university teaching job, for a guaranteed length of time or permanently. **4** the conditions by which an office, position, or property is held. [from Latin *tenere*, to hold]

tenured *adj.* having tenure of office or property.

tepee or **teepee** /ˈtiːpiː/ *noun* a Native American tent formed of skins stretched over a conical frame of poles. [from Dakota (Native American language) *tipi*]

tepid /ˈtɛpɪd/ *adj.* **1** slightly or only just warm; lukewarm. **2** not enthusiastic. [from Latin *tepidus*]

⊟ LUKEWARM, COOL. **2** half-hearted, unenthusiastic, apathetic.
⊟ COLD, HOT. **2** passionate.

tepidity *noun* a tepid quality.

tepidly *adv.* in a tepid way; to a tepid degree.

tequila /təˈkiːlə/ *noun* a Mexican spirit used as the basis for many alcoholic drinks. [named after *Tequila*, a district in Mexico]

ter- *prefix* forming words meaning 'three, threefold, thrice'. [from Latin *ter*, thrice]

terabyte /ˈtɛrəbaɪt/ *noun Comput.* a unit of storage capacity equal to 2^{40} or $1,099,511,627,776$ bytes. [from Greek *teras*, monster, + BYTE]

teraflop *noun Comput.* a processing speed of a trillion calculations per second.

teratogen /təˈratoʊdʒɪn/ *noun Medicine* an agent or procedure that interferes with the normal development of the fetus, and leads to the development of physical abnormalities. [from Greek *teras*, *-atos*, monster]

terbium /ˈtɜːbɪəm/ *noun Chem.* (SYMBOL Tb, ATOMIC NUMBER 65) a silvery metal that is a member of the lanthanide series, and is used in semiconductor devices and phosphors. [from *Ytterby* in Sweden, where it was discovered]

terce /tɜːs/ *noun* the third of the canonical hours, originally said at the third hour (ie 9am). See also COMPLINE, LAUDS, MATINS, NONE[2], SEXT, VESPERS. [from Latin *tertia pars*, third part]

tercel /ˈtɜːsl/ or **tiercel** *noun* a male hawk. [from Old French *tercel*]

tercentenary /tɜːsɛnˈtiːnərɪ, tɜːsɛnˈtɛnərɪ/ or **tercentennial** /tɜːsɛnˈtɛnɪəl/ — *noun* (PL. **tercentenaries**) a three-hundredth anniversary. — *adj.* of three hundred years. [from Latin *ter*, thrice + CENTENARY]

tercet /ˈtɜːsɪt/ *noun* a set of three lines in a poem which rhyme or which are connected by rhyme to a preceding

or following group of three lines. [from Italian *terzetto*, from *terzo*, third]

teredo /tɛˈriːdoʊ/ *noun* (PL. **teredos**) any of several molluscs which bore into wooden ships. [from Greek *teredon*, boring worm]

tergiversate /ˈtɜːdʒɪvɜːseɪt/ *verb intrans. formal* **1** to turn one's back. **2** to change sides. **3** to speak or act evasively. [from Latin *tergum*, back + *versare*, to turn]

tergiversation /tɜːdʒɪvɜːˈseɪʃən/ *noun formal* **1** turning one's back. **2** evasion.

term *noun* **1** a word or expression, especially one used with a precise meaning in a specialized field: *a scientific term.* **2** (**terms**) language used; a particular way of speaking: *criticized him in no uncertain terms.* **3** a limited or clearly defined period of time. **4** the end of a particular time, especially the end of pregnancy when the baby is about to be born. **5** (**terms**) a relationship between people or countries: *be on good terms.* **6** (**terms**) the rules or conditions of an agreement: *terms of sale.* **7** (**terms**) fixed charges for work or a service. **8** one of the usually three divisions into which the academic and school year is divided. **9** the time during which a court is in session. **10** *Maths.* a quantity which is joined to another by either addition or subtraction. **11** *Maths.* one quantity in a series or sequence. **12** *Logic* a word or expression which may be a subject or a predicate of a proposition. — *verb* to name or call. — **come to terms** to give way or submit; to yield. **come to terms with someone** or **something 1** to come to an agreement or understanding with someone. **2** to find a way of living with or tolerating some personal trouble or difficulty. **in terms of** ... in relation to ...; using the language and value of ... as a basis. [from Latin *terminus*, boundary]

⊟ *noun* **1** word, expression, name, designation, appellation, title, epithet, phrase. **2** words, language, terminology, phraseology. **3** time, period, course, duration, spell, span, stretch, interval, space. **5** relations, relationship, footing, standing, position. **6** conditions, specifications, stipulations, provisions, provisos, qualifications, particulars. **7** rates, charges, fees, prices, tariff. **8** semester, session. *verb* call, name, dub, style, designate, label, tag, title, entitle.

termagant /ˈtɜːməgənt/ *noun* a scolding, brawling, and overbearing woman. [from Old French *Tervagan*, a mythical deity believed in the Middle Ages to be worshipped by Muslims and introduced into morality plays as a scolding, overbearing character]

terminability *noun* being terminable.

terminable *adj.* able to come or be brought to an end. [from Latin *terminus*, boundary]

terminal /ˈtɜːmɪnl/ — *adj.* **1** *said of an illness* causing death; fatal. **2** *said of a patient* having an illness which will cause death. **3** *colloq.* extreme; acute: *terminal laziness.* **4** forming or occurring at an end, boundary, or terminus. **5** of a term or occurring at every term. — *noun* **1** an arrival and departure building at an airport. **2** a large station at the end of a railway line or for long-distance buses and coaches. **3** a point in an electric circuit or electrical device at which the current leaves or enters it, or by which it may be connected to another device. **4** a device consisting usually of a keyboard and visual display unit, which allows a user to communicate with and use a distant computer. **5** an installation at the end of a pipeline or at a port where oil is stored and from where it is distributed. [from Latin *terminalis*, from *terminus*, boundary]

⊟ *adj.* **1** fatal, deadly, lethal, mortal, incurable. **4** last, final, concluding, ultimate, extreme, utmost.
⊟ *adj.* **4** initial.

terminally *adv.* **1** in a terminal way. **2** fatally.

terminal velocity the constant velocity reached by an object falling through a fluid (a gas or liquid) under the influence of gravity, with no net force acting on it.

terminate *verb* **1** *trans., intrans.* to bring or come to an end. **2** *intrans. formal* to end or conclude in a specified way or at a specified time: *the conference terminated in/ with a panel discussion*. **3** to end (a pregnancy) artificially before its term. **4** to form a boundary or limit to. **5** *intrans. formal* to stop; to go no further: *the train terminates at Vienna*. [from Latin *terminare*, to set a limit to]

■ **1** finish, conclude, cease, end, stop, close, discontinue, cut off, abort.

▣ **1** begin, start, initiate.

terminate-and-stay-resident program *Comput.* (ABBREV. **TSR**) a program which remains in memory once activated, even while it is not running, and which can be reactivated quickly using a pre-set key, etc.

termination *noun* **1** an act of ending or the state of being brought to an end. **2** an artificially induced miscarriage or abortion. **3** a final result.

■ **1** finish, end, ending, conclusion, cessation, completion, close, discontinuation, lapse, expiry.

terminological *adj.* relating to or involving terminology.
terminologically *adv.* as regards terminology.
terminologist *noun* an expert in terminology.
terminology /tɜːmɪˈnɒlədʒɪ/ *noun* (PL. **terminologies**) the words and phrases used in a particular subject or field. [from Latin *terminus*, term]

■ language, jargon, phraseology, vocabulary, words, terms, nomenclature.

terminus /ˈtɜːmɪnəs/ *noun* (PL. **termini**, **terminuses**) **1** the end of a railway line or bus route, usually with a station. **2** an extreme or final point. **3** a stone marking a boundary. [from Latin *terminus*, boundary, limit]

■ **1** depot, station, garage, terminal. **2** end, close, termination, extremity, limit, boundary, destination, goal, target.

termite /ˈtɜːmaɪt/ *noun* any of about 200 species of social insect that live in highly organized colonies of up to a million insects, found mainly in the tropics, although a few species occur in the USA. Many termites feed on living plants and are regarded as pests, while wood-boring species cause damage to trees, structural timber of buildings, etc. [from Latin *termes*, white ant]

terms of reference a description or definition of the basis and scope of an undertaking, inquiry, etc.

tern *noun* any of several sea-birds which are smaller than gulls and have long wings and a long forked tail. [from Scandinavian]

ternary /ˈtɜːnərɪ/ *adj.* **1** having three parts. **2** *Maths.* using three as a base. [from Latin *ternarius*]

terpene /ˈtɜːpiːn/ *noun Chem.* any of a group of unsaturated hydrocarbons that are present in plant resins and also form the main constituents of essential oils such as rose and jasmine oil. They are used in the manufacture of camphor and menthol. [from *terpentin*, an old form of TURPENTINE]

terpsichorean /tɜːpsɪkəˈriːən/ *adj.* of or relating to dancing.

terrace /ˈterəs/ — *noun* **1** each one of a series of raised level banks of earth, like large steps on the side of a hill, used for cultivation. **2** a row of identical and connected houses, properly one overlooking a slope, or the street on to which they face. **3** a raised, level, paved area by the side of a house. **4** (*usually* **terraces**) open areas rising in tiers round a sports ground, where spectators stand. — *verb* to form into a terrace or terraces. [from Latin *terracea*]

terrace house or **terraced house** *Brit.* a house which is part of a terrace.

terracotta /terəˈkɒtə/ — *noun* **1** an unglazed brownish-orange earthenware made from a mixture of sand and clay and used for pottery, statuettes, and building. **2** its brownish-orange colour. — *adj.* made of, or the colour of, terracotta. [from Italian *terracotta*, baked earth]

terra firma dry land as opposed to water or air; solid ground. [from Latin *terra firma*, firm land]

terrain /təˈreɪn, ˈtereɪn/ *noun* a stretch of land, especially with regard to its physical features or as a battle area. [from Latin *terrenus*, from *terra*, earth]

■ land, ground, territory, country, countryside, landscape, topography.

terrapin /ˈterəpɪn/ *noun* **1** in the UK, any small freshwater turtle. **2** in the USA, an edible turtle. [from a Native American language]

terrarium /təˈreərɪəm/ *noun* (PL. **terraria**, **terrariums**) **1** an enclosed area or container in which small land animals are kept. **2** a large globe-shaped sealed glass jar in which plants are grown. [from Latin *terra*, earth]

terrestrial /təˈrestrɪəl/ — *adj.* **1** relating to dry land or to the Earth. **2** denoting animals or plants that are found on dry land, rather than in aquatic environments or in the air. **3** of this world; worldly; mundane. **4** *said of broadcast signals* sent by a land transmitter and not by satellite. — *noun* an inhabitant of the earth. [from Latin *terrestris*, from *terra*, earth]

■ *adj.* **3** earthly, worldly, global, mundane.

▣ *adj.* **2** aquatic, aerial. **3** celestial, cosmic, heavenly. **4** satellite.

terrible *adj.* **1** *colloq.* very bad: *a terrible singer*. **2** *colloq.* very great; extreme: *a terrible gossip*. **3** causing great fear or terror. **4** causing suffering or hardship and requiring great strength or fortitude. [from Latin *terribilis*, from *terrere*, to frighten]

■ AWFUL, FRIGHTFUL, DREADFUL, APPALLING. **1** bad, shocking, unpleasant, obnoxious, outrageous, foul, vile, disgusting, revolting, repulsive, offensive, hateful, abhorrent. **3** terrifying, frightening, gruesome, horrific, horrid, horrible, hideous. **4** harrowing, distressing, grave, serious, extreme, desperate.

▣ **1** excellent, wonderful, superb.

terribly *adv.* **1** *colloq.* very: *terribly happy*. **2** in a terrible way; to a great degree: *hurts terribly*.

■ AWFULLY, FRIGHTFULLY, EXTREMELY. **1** very, much, greatly, exceedingly, decidedly. **2** severely.

terrier *noun* any of several breeds of small dog originally to hunt animals in burrows. [from Old French *chien terrier*, dog of the earth]

terrific *adj.* **1** *colloq.* marvellous; excellent. **2** *colloq.* very great or powerful: *a terrific storm*. **3** very frightening; terrifying. [from Latin *terrificus*, frightful]

■ **1, 2** tremendous, great, amazing, stupendous, breathtaking. **1** excellent, wonderful, marvellous, super, smashing, outstanding, brilliant, magnificent, superb, *colloq.* fabulous, *colloq.* fantastic, sensational. **2** huge, enormous, gigantic, intense, extreme, excessive, awesome. **3** terrifying, fearful, fearsome, frightening.

▣ **1** awful, terrible, appalling.

terrifically *adv.* **1** in a terrific way. **2** *colloq.* extremely.
terrified *adj.* extremely frightened.

■ fearful, alarmed, petrified, panic-stricken, terror-stricken, *colloq.* scared stiff, frightened to death.

terrify *verb* (**terrifies, terrified**) to make very frightened; to fill with terror. [from Latin *terrificare*]

⊟ petrify, horrify, appal, shock, terrorize, intimidate, frighten, scare, alarm, dismay.

terrifying *adj.* causing extreme fright.

⊟ petrifying, horrifying, horrific, appalling, hair-raising, bloodcurdling, *colloq.* spine-chilling, dreadful, frightful, awful, frightening, *colloq.* scary, alarming, intimidating.

terrine /tɛˈriːn/ *noun* **1** an oval or round earthenware dish in which food may be cooked and served. **2** food cooked or served in such a dish, especially pâté. [from Old French *terrin*, earthen]

territorial /tɛrɪˈtɔːrɪəl/ — *adj.* **1** of or relating to a territory. **2** limited or restricted to a particular area or district. **3** *said especially of birds and animals* likely to establish their own territory and defend it from others of the same species. — *noun* (**Territorial**) *Brit.* a member of the Territorial Army.

territorial waters the sea surrounding a state which is considered to belong to it.

territory /ˈtɛrɪtərɪ/ *noun* (PL. **territories**) **1** a stretch of land; a region. **2** the land under the control of a ruler, government, or state. **3** an area of knowledge, interest, or activity. **4** an area or district for which a travelling salesman or distributor is responsible. **5** an area which a bird or animal treats as its own and defends against others of the same species. **6** (*often* **Territory**) part of a country (usually a federal state such as the USA) with an organized government but without the full rights of a state. [from Latin *territorium*, the land round a town]

⊟ **1** sector, region, area, district, zone, tract, terrain. **2, 3** province, domain, preserve. **2** country, land, state, dependency.

terror *noun* **1** very great fear or dread. **2** something or someone which causes such fear. **3** *colloq.* a troublesome or mischievous person, especially a child. **4** a time of, or government by, terror. [from Latin *terror*]

⊟ **1** fear, panic, dread, trepidation, horror, shock, fright, alarm, dismay, consternation, terrorism, intimidation.

terrorism *noun* the systematic and organized use of violence and intimidation to force a government, community, etc to act in a certain way or accept certain demands.

terrorist — *noun* a person who practises terrorism. — *adj.* relating to or involving terrorism.

terrorize or **terrorise** *verb* **1** to frighten greatly. **2** to control or coerce (someone) by threatening violence.

⊟ **1** frighten, scare, alarm, terrify, petrify, horrify, shock. **2** threaten, menace, intimidate, oppress, coerce, bully, browbeat.

terror-stricken *adj.* feeling very great uncontrollable fear.

terry — *noun* an absorbent fabric with uncut loops on one side used especially for towels. — *adj.* made of this fabric.

terse *adj.* **1** *said of language* brief and concise; succinct. **2** abrupt and rude; curt. [from Latin *tersus*, rubbed clean]

⊟ SHORT. **1** brief, succinct, concise, compact, condensed, laconic, epigrammatic, pithy, incisive. **2** curt, brusque, abrupt, snappy, rude.
⊟ **1** long-winded, verbose.

tersely *adv.* in a terse way.
terseness *noun* a terse quality.

tertiary /ˈtɜːʃərɪ/ — *adj.* **1** third in order, degree, importance, etc. **2** *said of education* coming after secondary, eg university or college. See also PRIMARY, SECONDARY. **3** *Geol.* (**Tertiary**) relating to the first period of the Cenozoic era, lasting from about 65 million to 2 million years ago, and subdivided into the Palaeocene, Eocene, Oligocene, Miocene, and Pliocene epochs. During this period mammals evolved rapidly, although many large mammals died out at the end of the period when the climate became colder, and flowering plants became widespread. Mountain ranges such as the Alps, Himalayas, Andes, and Rockies were formed towards the beginning of the period. **4** relating to rocks formed during this period. — *noun* (PL. **tertiaries**) **1** (**Tertiary**) the first geological period of the Cenozoic era. **2** a lay person who is affiliated to a monastic order and who follows a slightly modified form of that order's rule. [from Latin *tertius*, third]

Terylene /ˈtɛrɪliːn/ *noun trademark* a light tough synthetic fabric of polyester fibres.

terza rima /ˈtɛətsə ˈriːmə/ *Prosody* an Italian verse-form in triplets, rhyming *aba bcb cdc*. [Italian, = third rhyme]

TESL *abbrev.* teaching English as a second language.

tesla /ˈtɛslə/ *noun Physics* (ABBREV. **T**) the SI unit of magnetic flux density, defined as a magnetic flux of one weber per square metre. [named after the US physicist Nikola Tesla]

TESSA *abbrev.* Tax-Exempt Special Savings Account.

tessellate /ˈtɛsɪleɪt/ *verb* to form into or mark like a mosaic, especially with tesserae or checks. [from Latin *tessella*, small square piece of stone]

tessellated *adj.* chequered.

tessellation /tɛsɪˈleɪʃən/ *noun* a regular pattern of small squares, such as that found on mosaic tiles. [from Latin *tessellare*]

tessera /ˈtɛsərə/ *noun* (PL. **tesserae**) a square piece of stone, glass, etc used in mosaics. [from Latin *tessera*]

tessitura /tɛsɪˈtʊərə/ *noun* the natural range of the pitch or compass of a particular voice or of a vocal or instrumental part in a particular piece. A particular singer or vocal part may be said to have or require a high or low tessitura. [from Italian *tessitura*, texture]

test[1] — *noun* **1** a critical examination or trial of a person's or thing's qualities, abilities, etc. **2** anything used as the basis of such an examination or trial, eg a set of questions or exercises: *long-distance running is a test of endurance.* **3** a short, minor, usually written examination: *a spelling test.* **4** a test match. **5** *Chem.* anything used to distinguish, detect, or identify a substance; a reagent. — *verb* **1** to examine (someone or something, abilities, qualities, etc), especially by trial. **2** *trans., intrans.* to examine (a substance) to discover whether another substance is present or not: *test the water for microbes.* **3** *intrans.* to achieve a stated result in a test: *test positive for the virus.* [from Old French, from Latin *testa* or *testum*, earthenware pot]

⊟ *noun* **1** trial, try-out, experiment, examination, assessment, evaluation, check, investigation, analysis, proof, probation, ordeal. *verb* **1, 2** examine, check, investigate, analyse, screen. **1** try, assess, evaluate, prove, verify.

test[2] *noun Biol.* a hard outer covering or shell of certain invertebrates. [from Latin *testa*, tile]

testa *noun Biol.* the hard outer covering of a seed.

testable *adj.* capable of being tested.

testaceous /tɛˈsteɪʃəs/ *adj.* **1** *Biol.* covered by a protective shell-like material, or consisting of such a material. **2** of a reddish-brown colour.

testament /ˈtɛstəmənt/ *noun* **1 a** a written statement of one's wishes, especially of what one wants to be done with one's property after death. **b** a will: *last will and testament.* **2** proof, evidence, or tribute. **3** a covenant between God and Man. **4** (**Testament**) **a** either of the two main divisions of the Bible, the *Old Testament* and the *New Testament*. **b** a copy of the New Testament. [from Latin *testamentum*, from *testis*, witness]

testamentary *adj.* **1** relating to a test or will. **2** bequeathed or done by will.

testate /'tɛsteɪt/ *adj. Legal* having made and left a valid will. [from Latin *testari*, to make a will]

testator /tɛ'steɪtə(r)/ *noun Legal* a person who leaves a will at death.

testatrix /tɛ'steɪtrɪks/ *noun Legal* a female testator.

test case *Legal* a case whose outcome will serve as a precedent for all similar cases in the future.

test drive a trial drive of a car by a prospective owner to test its performance.

test-drive *verb* to test (a car) by taking a trial drive.

tester *noun* **1** a person who tests. **2** a thing used for testing.

testes /'tɛstiːz/ See TESTIS.

testicle /'tɛstɪkl/ *noun* a testis. [from Latin *testis*, witness (of male virility)]

testicular /tɛ'stɪkjʊlə(r)/ *adj.* relating to or affecting the testicles.

testify *verb* (**testifies, testified**) **1** *intrans.* to give evidence in court. **2** (**testify to something**) to serve as evidence or proof of it. **3** *intrans.* to make a solemn declaration (eg of one's faith). **4** to declare solemnly: *testify one's sorrow*. [from Latin *testificari*, from *testis*, witness]

....

■ **1** give evidence. **2, 4** declare, assert, attest, certify. **2** show, display, manifest, evidence, evince, bear witness to, vouch for, corroborate. **4** state, avow, vouch, affirm, swear.

....

testily *adv.* in a testy way.

testimonial /tɛstɪ'moʊnɪəl/ *noun* **1** a letter or certificate giving details of one's character, conduct, and qualifications. **2** a gift presented (often in public) as a sign of respect or as a tribute to personal qualities or services.

....

■ **1** reference, character, credential, certificate, recommendation, endorsement, commendation. **2** tribute.

....

testimony /'tɛstɪmənɪ/ *noun* (PL. **testimonies**) **1** a statement made under oath, especially in a law court. **2** evidence: *a testimony to her intelligence*. **3** a declaration of truth or fact. [from Latin *testimonium*, from *testis*, witness]

....

■ **1, 2** evidence. **1** statement, affidavit, submission, deposition, declaration, profession, attestation, affirmation. **2** support, proof, verification, confirmation, witness, demonstration, manifestation, indication.

....

testiness *noun* being testy.

testing *noun* the assessment of an individual pupil's level of knowledge, skill, etc by a variety of methods. In schools, it may be a formal examination based on course work, or continuous assessment over a term or a year, or a combination of the two.

testis /'tɛstɪs/ *noun* (PL. **testes**) *Anat.* in male animals, either of the two reproductive glands that produce sperm and, in vertebrates, also secrete male sex hormones, eg testosterone. During development the testes of mammals usually descend from the body cavity into the scrotum, so that the sperm are stored at slightly below body temperature. [from Latin *testis*]

test match in various sports, especially cricket, a match forming one of a series played by the same two international teams.

testosterone /tɛ'stɒstəroʊn/ *noun Physiol.* the main male sex hormone, a steroid that is secreted primarily by the testes. It controls the growth and functioning of the male sex organs, and the appearance of male secondary sexual characteristics such as beard growth and deepening of the voice. [from Latin *testis*, testicle]

test paper 1 a list of questions forming a short, minor examination. **2** paper which has been soaked in some substance so that it changes colour when it comes into contact with certain chemicals.

test pilot a pilot who tests new aircraft by flying them.

test tube a thin glass tube closed at one end, used in chemical tests or experiments.

test-tube baby 1 *Medicine* a baby born as a result of fertilization (under laboratory conditions) of one of the mother's ova by male sperm, followed by implantation of the fertilized ovum in the mother's uterus (womb). **2** formerly, a child born as a result of artificial insemination.

testy *adj.* (**testier, testiest**) showing irritability or touchiness. [from Old French *testif*, headstrong]

....

■ irritable, bad-tempered, short-tempered, tetchy, cross, crusty, grumpy, surly, crotchety, crabby, touchy, prickly, peevish.

....

tetanus /'tɛtənəs/ *noun* **1** *Medicine* an infectious and potentially fatal disease caused by the bacterium *Clostridium tetani*, which usually enters the body through a wound and releases a toxin that affects the nervous system. The main symptoms are fever and painful muscle spasms that result in rigidity, especially of the mouth and facial muscles, and may lead to convulsions and inability to breathe. Also called LOCKJAW. **2** the state of prolonged contraction of a muscle caused by rapidly repeated stimuli. [from Greek *tetanos*, from *teinein*, to stretch]

tetchily *adv.* in a tetchy way.

tetchiness *noun* being tetchy.

tetchy /'tɛtʃɪ/ *adj.* (**tetchier, tetchiest**) irritable; peevish.

tête-à-tête /teɪtɑ'teɪt/ — *noun* (PL. **tête-à-têtes**) a private conversation or meeting between two people. — *adj., adv.* in private; intimate, intimately. [from French *tête-à-tête*, head to head]

tether /'tɛðə(r)/ — *noun* a rope or chain for tying an animal to a post or confining it to a particular spot. — *verb* (**tethered, tethering**) to tie or restrain with a tether. — **at the end of one's tether** having reached the limit of one's patience, strength, resources, etc. [from Norse *tjothr*]

....

■ *noun* chain, rope, cord, line, lead, leash, bond, fetter, shackle, restraint, fastening. *verb* tie, fasten, secure, restrain, chain, rope, leash, bind, lash, fetter, shackle, manacle.

....

tetra /'tɛtrə/ *noun* any of many small colourful freshwater fish from S and Central America, about 3cm to 10cm in length. It is a popular aquarium fish. [a shortening of the former genus name *Tetragonopterus*]

tetra- *combining form* forming words meaning 'four'. [from Greek *tetra-*, from *tettares*, four]

tetrachloromethane /tɛtrəklɔːroʊ'miːθeɪn/ *noun Chem.* (FORMULA CCl_4) a toxic colourless strong-smelling liquid, insoluble in water, formerly used as a solvent for fats, waxes, lacquers, and rubber, as a dry-cleaning reagent, and in certain types of fire-extinguisher. It is now known to be carcinogenic, and has been largely replaced by safer chemicals. Also called CARBON TETRACHLORIDE.

tetracycline /tɛtrə'saɪklɪn/ *noun Medicine* any of a group of antibiotics obtained from *Streptomyces* bacteria and used to treat a wide range of bacterial infections, eg acne, respiratory infections, syphilis.

tetrad /'tɛtrad/ *noun* a group of four. [from Greek *tetras*]

tetragon /'tɛtrəgon/ *noun* a plane figure with four angles and four sides. [from Greek *tetragonon*]

Tetragrammaton /tɛtrə'gramətən/ *noun* the Hebrew name of God written using four letters, in the English alphabet given as either YHWH (Yahweh) or JHVH (Jehovah). [from Greek, *tetra*, four + *gramma*, letter]

tetrahedron /tɛtrə'hiːdrən/ *noun* a solid figure having four plane faces with three angles each; a three-sided pyramid. [from Greek *tetraedron*]

tetrameter /tɛˈtramɪtə(r)/ *noun* a line of verse with four measures. [from Greek *tetrametros*, from *tetra*, four + *metron*, measure]

tetrapod /ˈtɛtrəpɒd/ *noun Zool.* an animal with four limbs, adapted for living on land. Tetrapods include amphibians, reptiles, birds, and mammals. [from Greek *tetrapous*, four-footed]

Teuton /ˈtjuːtən/ *noun* **1** any speaker of a Germanic language. **2** *Hist.* a member of an ancient Germanic tribe from N Europe. [from Latin *Teutoni* or *Teutones*, the Teutons]

Teutonic /tjʊˈtɒnɪk/ — *adj.* **1** relating to the Germanic languages or peoples speaking these languages. **2** German. — *noun* Germanic.

Tex. *abbrev.* Texas.

Tex-Mex /teksˈmeks/ *adj., said of food, music, etc* typically Mexican but with elements either taken from, or adapted through contact with, American culture.

text *noun* **1** the main body of printed words in a book as opposed to the notes, illustrations, etc. **2** the actual words of an author or piece of written work as opposed to commentary on them. **3** a short passage from the Bible taken as the starting-point for a sermon or quoted in authority. **4** a theme or subject. **5** a book, novel, play, etc forming part of a course of study. **6** the words written or displayed on a visual display unit. [from Latin *texere*, to weave]

⊟ **1** words, wording, content, matter, body. **3** reading, passage, paragraph, sentence. **4** subject, topic, theme. **5** book, textbook, source.

textbook *noun* **1** a book containing the standard principles and information of a subject. **2** (*attributive*) conforming or as if conforming to the guidance of a textbook; exemplary.

textile — *noun* **1** any cloth or fabric made by weaving or knitting. **2** fibre, yarn, etc suitable for weaving into cloth. — *adj.* of, relating to, manufacturing, or suitable for being woven into, such cloth. [from Latin *textilis*, from *texere*, to weave]

text linguistics the study of the structure of all forms of linguistic text which have a communicative function, eg essays, notices, road signs, scripts, poems, and conversations. This includes analysis of the ways in which elements of the text cohere in a sequence, and of the ways in which the content is structured from the point of view of grammar, vocabulary, pronunciation, and graphic layout.

text messaging the sending of written messages on mobile phones, using the key pad and display.

textual /ˈtɛkstjʊəl/ *adj.* relating to, found in, or based on a text or texts.

textually *adv.* **1** in or as regards the text. **2** in the words of the text.

textural *adj.* relating to texture.

texture /ˈtɛkstʃə(r)/ — *noun* **1** the way the surface of a material or substance feels when touched. **2** the way that a piece of cloth looks or feels, caused by the way in which it is woven. **3** the structure of a substance as formed by the size and arrangement of the smaller particles which form it, especially as seen, touched, or tasted: *cheese with a crumbly texture*. **4** the structure of a piece of music, writing, work of art, etc as formed by the individual parts which form it. — *verb* to give a particular texture to (eg food or fabric). [from Latin *texere*, to weave]

⊟ *noun* **1** feel, surface, grain. **2** weave, tissue, fabric. **3**, **4** structure, composition, character, quality. **3** consistency, constitution.

textured *adj.* having a texture.

texturize or **texturise** *verb* to give a particular texture to (eg food or fabric).

TGWU *abbrev.* Transport and General Workers' Union.

Th *symbol Chem.* thorium.

Th. *abbrev.* Thursday.

-th or **-eth**[1] *suffix* forming ordinal numbers and fractions from cardinal numbers: *fourth / one fiftieth*. [from Anglo-Saxon *-tha*, *-the*]

-th[2] *suffix* forming nouns denoting an action or process, or a state or condition: *death / filth / width*. [from Anglo-Saxon *-thu*, *-tho*, *-th*]

Thai /taɪ/ — *noun* the official language of Thailand, the largest of the Tai language family of SE Asia. It is spoken by c.30 million people and has a wide range of dialects. — *adj.* relating to or spoken or written in Thai.

thalamus /ˈθaləməs/ *noun* (PL. **thalami**) *Anat.* in the forebrain of vertebrates, either of two egg-shaped masses of grey matter that lie within the cerebral hemispheres. The thalamus relays sensory nerve impulses to the cerebral cortex. [from Greek *thalamos*, inner room, bedroom]

thalassaemia or **thalassemia** /θalə'siːmɪə/ *noun Medicine* a hereditary disorder, most common in the Mediterranean region, characterized by the presence of an abnormal form of haemoglobin in the red blood cells. The main symptom is anaemia, which may be severe if the disorder is inherited from both parents. [from Greek *thalassa*, sea + *haima*, blood]

thalassotherapy /θəlasoʊˈθerəpɪ/ *noun* a form of treatment to detoxify and relax the body, involving the application of mud and seaweed compresses, seawater baths, and massage. [from Greek *thalassa*, sea]

thalidomide /θəˈlɪdəmaɪd/ *noun* a drug formerly used as a sedative but withdrawn in 1961 because it was found to cause malformation of the fetus if taken by the mother in early pregnancy.

thallium /ˈθalɪəm/ *noun Chem.* (SYMBOL **Tl**, ATOMIC NUMBER 81) a soft bluish-white metal that is used in electronic equipment, experimental alloys, and optical glass. Its compounds, which are highly poisonous, are used as pesticides. [from Greek *thallos*, a green shoot, so called because of the bright green line in its spectrum]

thalloid *adj. Bot.* relating to a thallus.

thallus /ˈθaləs/ *noun* (PL. **thalluses**, **thalli**) *Biol.* in fungi, lichens, seaweeds, etc, a flattened and sometimes branched structure that is not differentiated into stems, leaves, and roots. [from Greek *thallos*, young shoot]

than — *conj.* **1** used to introduce the second part of a comparison, or that part which is taken as the basis of a comparison: *she is older than he is*. **2** used to introduce the second, and usually less desirable or rejected, option in a statement of alternatives: *would rather go swimming than play football*. **3** except; other than: *be left with no alternative than to resign*. — *prep.* in comparison with: *someone older than him*. [from Anglo-Saxon *thonne*]

thanatology /θanəˈtɒlədʒɪ/ *noun Medicine* the medical and legal study of death, its causes and phenomena. [from Greek *thanatos*, death + -LOGY]

thane *noun Hist.* **1** in Anglo-Saxon England, a person holding land from the king or some other superior in exchange for military service. **2** a person holding land from a Scottish king (but not in return for military service); a Scottish feudal lord. [from Anglo-Saxon *thegn*]

thank — *verb* **1** to express gratitude to: *thanked him for his help*. **2** to hold responsible for: *have only yourself to thank for your failure*. — *noun* (*usually* **thanks**) **1** gratitude or an expression of gratitude. **2** thank you: *thanks for the present*. — **no thanks to someone** or **something** in spite of them; no gratitude being due to them. **thank God** or **goodness** or **heavens** an expression of relief. **thanks to ...** as a result of ...; because of ... **thank you** a polite expression acknowledging a gift, help, or offer. [from Anglo-Saxon *thancian*]

⊟ *verb* **1** say thank you, be grateful, appreciate, acknowledge, recognize, credit. *noun* **1** gratitude, gratefulness, appreciation, acknowledgement,

recognition, credit, thanksgiving, thank-offering.
thanks to as a result of, because of, owing to, due to, on account of, through.

thankful *adj.* feeling or showing gratitude or relief.

▣ grateful, appreciative, obliged, indebted, relieved, happy, pleased, contented.
▣ ungrateful, unappreciative.

thankfully *adv.* 1 in a thankful manner. 2 in a way that invites one's thanks: *thankfully, it didn't rain.*
thankfulness *noun* being thankful.
thankless *adj.* bringing no thanks, pleasure, or profit.

▣ unrecognized, unappreciated, unrequited, unrewarding, unprofitable, fruitless.
▣ rewarding, worthwhile.

thanklessly *adv.* in a thankless way.
thanklessness *noun* being thankless.
thanksgiving *noun* 1 a formal act of giving thanks, especially to God. 2 (**Thanksgiving** or **Thanksgiving Day**) *North Amer.* a public holiday for giving thanks, occurring on the fourth Thursday in November in the USA and the second Monday in October in Canada.
that — *adj.* (PL. **those**) 1 indicating the thing, person, or idea already mentioned, specified, or understood. 2 indicating someone or something that is farther away or is in contrast: *not this book, but that one.* — *pron.* (PL. **those**) 1 the person, thing, or idea just mentioned, already spoken of, or understood. 2 a relatively distant or more distant person, thing, or idea. — *rel. pron.* used instead of *which, who,* or *whom,* to introduce a relative clause which defines, distinguishes, or restricts the person or thing mentioned in the preceding clause: *all the children that were late.* — *conj.* used to introduce a noun clause, or a clause showing reason, purpose, consequence, a result, or expressing a wish or desire: *spoke so quickly that no one could understand/ oh, that the holiday would never end!* — *adv.* 1 to the degree or extent shown or understood: *won't reach that far.* 2 *colloq., dialect* to such a degree that; so: *they are that unsociable they never leave the house.* — **all that** *colloq.* very: *not all that good.* **that's that** that is the end of the matter. [from Anglo-Saxon *thæt*]
thatch — *noun* 1 a roof covering of straw, reeds, etc. 2 anything resembling such a roof, especially thick hair on the head. — *verb trans., intrans.* to cover (a roof or building) with thatch. [from Anglo-Saxon *theccan*]
thatcher *noun* a person who thatches.
thaw — *verb* 1 *trans., intrans. said of snow or ice* to melt or cause it to melt. 2 *trans., intrans.* (*also* **thaw out** or **thaw something out**) *said of anything frozen, eg food* to become or cause it to become unfrozen; to defrost. 3 *intrans.* to become warm enough to begin to melt snow and ice: *it is beginning to thaw.* 4 *trans., intrans.* (*also* **thaw out** or **thaw something out**) to make or become less stiff and numb with cold. 5 *trans., intrans.* (*also* **thaw out** or **thaw something out**) to make or become more friendly or relaxed. — *noun* an act or process of thawing. 2 a period of weather warm enough to begin to thaw ice and snow. [from Anglo-Saxon *thawian*]

▣ *verb* 1 melt, soften, liquefy, dissolve. 2 defrost, unfreeze, de-ice. 4 warm, heat up.
▣ *verb* 1, 2, 3 freeze.

the — *definite article* 1 used to refer to a particular person or thing, or group of people or things, already mentioned, implied, or known. 2 used to refer to a unique person or thing: *the Pope.* 3 used before a singular noun to refer to all the members of that group or class: *a history of the novel.* 4 used before certain titles and proper names.

5 used before an adjective or noun describing an identified person: *William the Conqueror.* 6 used after a preposition to refer to a unit of quantity, time, etc: *a car which does forty miles to the gallon / paid by the hour.* — *adv.* 1 used before comparative adjectives or adverbs to indicate (by) so much or (by) how much: *the sooner the better.* 2 used before superlative adjectives and adverbs to indicate an amount beyond all others: *like this book the best.* [from Anglo-Saxon *the,* who, which, that, replacing *se,* that]
theatre / 'θɪətə(r)/ *noun* 1 a building or area outside specially designed for the performance of plays, operas, etc. 2 a large room with seats rising in tiers, eg for lectures. 3 (*also* **the theatre**) the writing and production of plays in general. 4 *Brit.* a specially equipped room in a hospital where surgery is performed. 5 a scene of action or place where events take place: *theatre of war.* 6 (**the theatre**) the world and profession of actors and theatre companies. 7 *North Amer.* a cinema. [from Greek *theatron,* from *theaesthai,* to see]
theatre-in-the-round *noun Theatr.* a style of staging plays in a theatre with a central stage surrounded on all sides by the audience. Modern theatre-in-the-round developed in the 1930s, particularly for avant-garde productions in Russia, England, and the USA.
Theatre of the Absurd a term for certain plays of the 1950s, in which the absurdity of man's condition was mirrored in a dramatic form of unreal situations without traditional narrative continuity or meaningful and coherent dialogue. The term is applied to works by Samuel Beckett (notably *Waiting for Godot,* 1953), Eugène Ionesco, Jean Genet, Arthur Adamov, and Harold Pinter. See also ABSURDISM.
theatrical / θɪ'atrɪkl/ — *adj.* 1 of theatres or acting. 2 *said of behaviour, a gesture, etc* done only for effect; artificial and exaggerated. — *noun* (**theatricals**) dramatic performances.

▣ *adj.* 1 dramatic, thespian. 2 melodramatic, histrionic, mannered, affected, camp, artificial, pompous, ostentatious, showy, extravagant, exaggerated, overdone.

theatricality *noun* a theatrical quality.
theatrically *adv.* in a theatrical way.
thee *pron. old use, dialect* the objective form of *thou.* [from Anglo-Saxon]
theft *noun* 1 stealing; an act of stealing. 2 something stolen. [from Anglo-Saxon *thiefth*]

▣ 1 robbery, thieving, stealing, pilfering, larceny, shoplifting, kleptomania, fraud, embezzlement.

their *adj.* 1 of or belonging to them. 2 his or her: *has everyone got their books with them?* [from Norse *thierra*]
theirs *pron.* a person or thing that belongs to them. — **of theirs** belonging to them.
theism / 'θiːɪzm/ *noun* the belief in the existence of God or a god, especially one revealed supernaturally to man. See also DEISM. [from Greek *theos,* god]
theist / 'θiːɪst/ *noun* a person who believes in theism.
theistic / θiː'ɪstɪk/ *adj.* relating to or involving theism.
them — *pron.* 1 people or things already mentioned or spoken about, or understood or implied. 2 *colloq., dialect* those. 3 *old use* themselves. — *adj. colloq., dialect* those. [from Norse *thiem*]
theme / θiːm/ *noun* 1 the subject of a discussion, speech, or piece of writing. 2 *Mus.* a short melody which forms the basis of a piece of music and which is developed and repeated with variations. 3 a repeated or recurring image or idea in literature or art. 4 a brief essay or written exercise. [from Greek *thema*]

▣ 1 subject, topic, matter, thread, keynote, idea, gist, essence, burden, argument, thesis. 2, 3 motif, leitmotif. 4 thesis, dissertation, composition, essay, text.

theme park a large amusement park in which all of the rides and attractions are based on a particular theme, such as outer space.

theme song or **theme tune** a song or melody that is associated with, and usually played at the beginning and end of, a film, television, or radio programme, or which is associated with a particular character.

themselves *pron.* **1** the reflexive form of *they* and *them*: *they helped themselves.* **2** used for emphasis: *they did it themselves.* **3** their normal selves: *they aren't feeling themselves today.* **4** colloq. himself or herself: *nobody needs to blame themselves.*

then — *adv.* **1** at that time. **2** soon or immediately after that: *looked at him, then turned away.* **3** in that case; that being so; as a necessary consequence: *what would we do then? / if you're tired, then you should rest.* **4** also; in addition. **5** used to continue a narrative after a break or digression: *by the time she got to the top, then, it had started to snow.* **6** used especially at the end of questions which ask for an explanation, opinion, etc, or which ask for or assume agreement: *your mind is made up, then? / that was a bit of a shock, then, wasn't it?* — *noun* that time: *until then.* — *adj.* being or acting at that time: *the then Prime Minister.* — **then and there** at that very time and on that very spot. [from Anglo-Saxon *thonne*]

thence /ðens/ *adv. old use, formal* **1** from that place or time. **2** from that cause; therefore. [from Middle English *thennes*]

thenceforth or **thenceforward** *adv. old use, formal* from that time or place forwards.

theo- *combining form* forming words meaning 'of God or a god'. [from Greek *theos*, god]

theocracy /θɪˈɒkrəsɪ/ *noun* (PL. **theocracies**) government by a deity or by priests representing a deity; also, a state ruled in this way. [from Greek *theos*, god + *kratos*, power]

theocrat /ˈθɪəkrat/ *noun* a divine or deified ruler.

theocratic *adj.* relating to or involving theocracy.

theocratically *adv.* in a theocratic way.

theodolite /θɪˈɒdəlaɪt/ *noun* an instrument for measuring horizontal and vertical angles when surveying land. [from Latin *theodolitus*]

theolinguistics *sing. noun* the study of language used in the theory and practice of religious belief, eg by theologians, biblical scholars, ministers, and preachers, etc.

theologian /θɪəˈlɒdʒɪən/ *noun* a person who studies, or is an expert in, theology.

theological *adj.* relating to or involving theology.

theologically *adv.* in a theological way; as regards theology.

theology /θɪˈɒlədʒɪ/ *noun* (PL. **theologies**) **1** the study of God, religion, religious belief, and revelation. **2** a particular system of theology and religion: *Catholic theology.* [from Greek *theos*, god + *logos*, reason]

theorbo /θɪˈɔːbəʊ/ *noun* a type of large lute with six strings above a fretted fingerboard, and seven or eight additional unstopped bass strings with a separate pegbox. It was widely used in the 17c as a continuo instrument. [from Italian *teorba*, variant of *tuorba*, travelling bag]

theorem /ˈθɪərəm/ *noun Maths.* a scientific or mathematical statement which makes certain assumptions in order to explain observed phenomena, and which has been proved to be correct. [from Greek *theorema*, subject for contemplation]

⊞ formula, principle, rule, statement, deduction, proposition, hypothesis.

theoretical or **theoretic** *adj.* **1** concerned with or based on theory rather than practical knowledge or experience. **2** existing in theory only; hypothetical. **3** dealing with theory only; speculative.

⊞ **1** pure, ideal. **2** hypothetical, conjectural. **3** speculative, abstract, academic, doctrinaire.

⊟ **1** practical, applied, concrete.

theoretically *adv.* in a theoretical way; in terms of theory rather than practice.

theoretician /θɪərɪˈtɪʃən/ *noun* someone who specializes in or is concerned with the theoretical aspects of a subject rather than its practical use.

theorist *noun* **1** a person who speculates or invents theories. **2** a theoretician.

theorize or **theorise** *verb intrans.* to devise theories; to speculate.

⊞ speculate, suppose, guess, conjecture, postulate, propound, hypothesize, formulate.

theory /ˈθɪərɪ/ *noun* (PL. **theories**) **1** a series of ideas and general principles which seek to explain some aspect of the world: *theory of relativity.* **2** an idea or explanation which has not yet been proved; a conjecture. **3** the general and usually abstract principles or ideas of a subject: *music theory.* **4** an ideal, hypothetical, or abstract situation. **5** ideal, hypothetical, or abstract reasoning: *a good idea in theory.* [from Greek *theoria*, from *theoreein*, to view]

⊞ **1, 2** idea, notion. **1** philosophy, system. **2** hypothesis, supposition, assumption, presumption, surmise, guess, conjecture, speculation, thesis. **4** abstraction, plan, proposal, scheme.

⊟ **2, 3** practice. **2** certainty.

theosophic /θɪəˈsɒfɪk/ or **theosophical** *adj.* relating to or involving theosophy.

theosophically *adv.* in a theosophical way.

theosophist *noun* a person who believes in theosophy.

theosophy /θɪˈɒsəfɪ/ *noun* (PL. **theosophies**) a religious philosophy which is based on the belief that a knowledge of God can be achieved through intuition, mysticism, and divine inspiration, especially a modern movement which combines this with elements from Hinduism and Buddhism, such as a belief in reincarnation. [from Greek *theos*, god + *sophia*, wisdom]

therapeutic /θerəˈpjuːtɪk/ *adj.* **1** of, concerning, or contributing to the healing and curing of disease. **2** bringing a feeling of general well-being. [from Greek *therapeuein*, to take care of, to heal]

⊞ **1** remedial, curative, healing, restorative, tonic, medicinal, corrective. **2** good, beneficial.

⊟ HARMFUL, DETRIMENTAL.

therapeutically *adv.* in a therapeutic way.

therapeutics *sing. noun Medicine* the branch of medicine concerned with the treatment and cure of diseases.

therapist /ˈθerəpɪst/ *noun Medicine* a person who treats physical or mental diseases and disorders of a particular kind by means other than surgery or drugs, eg speech therapist, physiotherapist.

therapy /ˈθerəpɪ/ *noun* (PL. **therapies**) the treatment of physical or mental diseases and disorders by means other than surgery or drugs. [from Greek *therapeuein*, to take care of, to heal]

⊞ treatment, remedy, cure, healing, tonic.

there — *adv.* **1** at, in, or to a place or position. **2** at that point in speech, a piece of writing, a performance, etc: *don't stop there.* **3** in that respect: *I agree with him there.* **4** used to begin a sentence when the subject of the verb follows the verb instead of coming before it: *there are no mistakes in this.* **5** used at the beginning of a sentence to emphasise or call attention to that sentence: *there goes the last bus.* **6** used after a noun for emphasis: *that book there is the one you need.* **7** *colloq., dialect* used between a noun and *this* or *that*, etc for emphasis: *that there tractor.* — *noun* that place or point. — *interj.* used to express sympathy, satisfaction, approval, encouragement, etc or to comfort. — **have been there before** *slang* to have been in the same, especially unpleasant, situation before. **there and then** at that very time and on that very spot. **there you are 1** *said when giving something to someone* this is what you need or want. **2** expressing satisfaction or triumph. [from Anglo-Saxon *thær*]

thereabouts or **thereabout** *adv.* near that place, number, amount, degree, or time.

thereafter *adv. formal* from that time on.

thereby *adv. formal* **1** by that means. **2** in consequence.

therefore *adv.* for that reason; as a consequence.

. . . .

▤ so, then, thus, consequently, as a result.

. . . .

therein *adv. formal* in or into that or it.

thereof *adv. formal* of or from that or it.

thereon *adv. formal* on or onto that or it.

thereto *adv. formal* to that or it; in addition.

thereunder *adv. formal* under that or it.

thereupon *adv. formal* **1** on that matter or point. **2** immediately after it or that.

therm /θɜːm/ *noun* a unit of heat equal to 100,000 British thermal units, used to measure gas used or sold. [from Greek *therme*, heat]

thermal — *adj.* **1** of, caused by, or producing heat. **2** *said of clothing* designed to prevent the loss of heat from the body. — *noun* a rising current of warm air, used by birds, gliders, and hang-gliders to move upwards. [from Greek *therme*, heat]

Thermalite *noun trademark* a manufactured material used to make building-blocks, light and effective as insulation.

thermally *adv.* in a thermal way; by means of heat.

thermal printer *Comput.* a printer which uses heat-sensitive paper, producing visible characters by the action of heated wires.

thermic lance a torch-like cutting device for resistant steel and alloys which depends on the fact that iron will burn in oxygen. It consists of a main nozzle (for a stream of oxygen) with a subsidiary nozzle for acetylene which preheats the metal to the temperature at which it will begin to burn in the stream of oxygen.

thermion /'θɜːmɪən/ *noun* an electrically charged particle emitted by an extremely hot or incandescent substance. [from Greek *therme*, heat]

thermionic *adj.* relating to thermions.

thermionic emission *Physics* the emission of electrons from a heated material, usually a metal surface.

thermionics *pl. noun Physics* the branch of electronics concerned with the study of the processes involved in thermionic emission. It is mainly concerned with the design of thermionic valves and electron guns, which draw away electrons emitted from a heated metal surface, so producing a beam of electrons that can be used for a range of different purposes.

thermionic valve *Electron.* an electron tube (vacuum tube) that emits electrons from an electrically heated cathode into a vacuum. Formerly widely used in amplifiers, switches, and other electrical devices, thermionic valves have now largely been superseded by transistors.

thermistor /θɜːˈmɪstə(r)/ *noun Physics* a device in which the electrical resistance decreases rapidly as its temperature rises. Thermistors are used in electronic circuits for measuring or controlling temperature, eg electronic switches and thermometers. [a contraction of *thermal resistor*]

thermo- *combining form* forming words denoting heat. [from Greek *therme*, heat]

thermocouple *noun* a device for measuring temperature, consisting of two different metallic conductors welded together at their ends to form a loop. When the

two junctions are kept at different temperatures, a voltage is generated between them, the size of which can be measured and is directly related to the temperature difference between the two junctions.

thermodynamic /θɜːməʊdaɪˈnæmɪk/ *adj.* relating to or involving thermodynamics.

thermodynamically *adv.* in a thermodynamic way; in terms of thermodynamics.

thermodynamics *sing. noun Physics* the branch of physics concerned with the study of the relationship between heat and other forms of energy, especially mechanical energy, and the behaviour of physical systems in which temperature is an important factor.

thermoelectric *adj.* relating to or involving thermoelectricity.

thermoelectricity *noun Electr.* an electric current generated by a difference in temperature in an electric circuit, especially between a pair of junctions where two different metals are in contact, eg a thermocouple. Thermoelectric devices incorporating a radioactive heat source are used to power heart pacemakers.

thermography /θɜːˈmɒɡrəfɪ/ *noun* **1** a technique for the conversion of invisible heat energy into a visible picture, used for military purposes, and for nocturnal studies of wildlife. **2** *Medicine* the analysis of heat emitted from the skin of a patient's body as infrared radiation, which is converted to a visible image representing warmer and cooler regions of the skin, and is used in the diagnosis of certain medical disorders, eg underlying tumours. It is widely used in mammography to detect breast cancer.

thermoluminescence dating *Archaeol.* a method of dating ancient pottery, burnt flint, calcite, and sediments by measuring the energy accumulated in the crystal lattice of its inclusions of quartz, through the breakdown over time of naturally occurring uranium.

thermometer /θəˈmɒmɪtə(r)/ *noun* an instrument for measuring temperature, often consisting of a narrow calibrated sealed glass tube filled with a liquid whose properties vary with temperature, eg mercury, which expands (rises) as the temperature increases, and contracts (falls) as it decreases.

thermonuclear *adj.* **1** using or showing nuclear reactions which can only be produced at extremely high temperatures. **2** relating to or involving thermonuclear weapons.

thermopile /'θɜːməʊpaɪl/ *noun Physics* a device consisting of several thermocouples connected together, that is used to detect and measure the intensity of thermal radiation.

thermoplastic — *noun Chem.* a polymer that can be repeatedly softened and hardened, without any appreciable change in its properties, by heating and cooling it. — *adj.* denoting such a material.

Thermos /'θɜːmɒs/ *noun trademark* (also **Thermos flask**) a kind of vacuum flask. [from Greek *thermos*, hot]

thermosetting *adj.*, *said of plastics* becoming permanently hard after a single melting and moulding.

thermosphere *noun* the layer of the Earth's atmosphere that is situated above the mesosphere, and in which the temperature rises steadily with increasing height, although the actual heat content is very low because the air is so thin. The thermosphere includes the ionosphere.

thermostat /'θɜːməstat/ *noun* a device that is used to maintain the temperature of a system at a constant preset level. [from THERMO- + Greek *states*, causing to stand]

thermostatic *adj.* relating to or operated by a thermostat.

thermostatically *adv.* by means of a thermostat.

thesaurus /θɪˈsɔːrəs/ *noun* (PL. **thesauruses**, **thesauri**) **1** a book which lists words and their synonyms according to sense. **2** any book, eg a dictionary or encyclopedia, which gives information about a particular field, quotations, etc. [from Greek *thesauros*, treasury]

these see THIS.

thesis /'θiːsɪs/ *noun* (PL. **theses**) **1** a long written essay or report, especially one based on original research and presented for an advanced university degree such as the MSc,

MLitt, or PhD. **2** an idea or proposition to be supported or upheld in argument. **3** an unproved statement put forward as a basis for argument or discussion. [from Greek *thesis*, a setting down]

. . . .

■ **1** dissertation, essay, composition, treatise, paper, monograph. **2** subject, topic, theme. **3** idea, opinion, view, theory, hypothesis, proposal, proposition, premise, statement, argument, contention.

. . . .

Thespian / ˈθɛspɪən/ — *adj.* of or relating to tragedy, or to drama and the theatre in general. — *noun facetious* an actor or actress. [from Greek *Thespis* (lived c.534BC), Greek poet and reputed founder of Greek tragedy]

they *pron.* **1** the people, animals, or things already spoken about or being indicated. **2** people in general. **3** people in authority. **4** *colloq.* he or she: *anyone can help if they want.* [from Norse *their*]

they'd *contr.* **1** they had. **2** they would.

they'll *contr.* **1** they will. **2** they shall.

they're *contr.* they are.

they've *contr.* they have.

thiamine / ˈθaɪəmiːn/ *noun Biochem.* a member of the vitamin B complex that is found in yeast, wheatgerm, peas, beans, and green vegetables. It is required for the metabolism of carbohydrates, and deficiency of the vitamin causes the disorder beriberi. Also called VITAMIN B₁. [from Greek *theion*, sulphur + AMINE]

thick — *adj.* **1** having a relatively large distance between opposite sides. **2** having a specified distance between opposite sides: *one inch thick*. **3** having a large diameter: *a thick rope*. **4** *said of a line, handwriting, etc* broad. **5** *said of liquids* containing a lot of solid matter; viscous: *thick soup*. **6** having many single units placed very close together; dense: *thick hair*. **7** difficult to see through: *thick fog*. **8** (**thick with something**) covered with or full of it: *a room thick with smoke*. **9** great in number: *insults were flying thick and fast*. **10** *said of speech* not clear. **11** *said of an accent* marked; pronounced. **12** *colloq.*, *said of a person* stupid; dull. **13** *colloq.* (**thick with someone**) friendly or intimate: *is very thick with the new manager*. **14** *colloq.* unfair: *that's a bit thick!* — *adv.* thickly. — *noun* (**the thick**) **1** the busiest, most active, or most intense part: *in the thick of the fighting*. **2** the thickest part of anything. — **as thick as thieves** very friendly. **through thick and thin** whatever happens; in spite of any difficulties. [from Anglo-Saxon *thicce*]

. . . .

■ *adj.* **1, 2, 4, 11** broad. **1, 2** wide. **4** fat, heavy, solid. **5** viscous, coagulated, clotted, concentrated, condensed. **6, 7** dense, impenetrable. **6** close, compact. **8** full of, packed with, crowded with, chock-a-block with, swarming with, teeming with, bristling with, brimming with, bursting with. **9** numerous, abundant. **12** stupid, foolish, slow, dull, dim-witted, brainless, simple.

◧ *adj.* **1, 3, 4, 5** thin. **1** slim, slender, slight. **6** sparse. **12** clever, *colloq.* brainy.

. . . .

thicken *verb* (**thickened, thickening**) **1** *trans., intrans.* to make or become thick or thicker. **2** *intrans.* to become more complicated: *the plot thickens*.

. . . .

■ **1** condense, stiffen, congeal, coagulate, clot, cake, gel, set.
◧ thin.

. . . .

thickening *noun* **1** something used to thicken liquid. **2** the process of making or becoming thicker. **3** a thickened part.

thicket *noun* a dense mass of bushes and trees. [from THICK]

. . . .

■ wood, copse, coppice, grove, spinney, undergrowth.

. . . .

thickhead *noun colloq.* a stupid person.

thick-headed *adj. colloq.* **1** stupid. **2** unable to think clearly because of a cold, too much alcohol, etc.

thickly *adv.* in a thick way; so as to be thick.

thickness *noun* **1** the state, quality, or degree of being thick. **2** a layer. **3** the thick part of something.

. . . .

■ **1** width, breadth, diameter, density, viscosity, bulk, body. **2** layer, stratum, ply, sheet, coat.
◧ **1** thinness.

. . . .

thickset *adj.* **1** heavily built; having a thick, short body. **2** growing or planted close together.

thick-skinned *adj.* not easily hurt by criticism or insults; insensitive.

. . . .

■ insensitive, unfeeling, callous, tough, hardened, hard-boiled.
◧ thin-skinned, sensitive.

. . . .

thief *noun* (PL. **thieves**) a person who steals, especially secretly and often without violence. [from Anglo-Saxon *theof*]

. . . .

■ robber, bandit, mugger, pickpocket, shoplifter, burglar, housebreaker, plunderer, poacher, stealer, pilferer, filcher, kleptomaniac, swindler, embezzler.

. . . .

thieve *verb trans., intrans.* to steal.

thieving — *noun* stealing. — *adj.* that thieves.

thievish *adj.* given to stealing.

thievishly *adv.* in a thievish way.

thievishness *noun* being thievish.

thigh /θaɪ/ *noun* the fleshy part of the leg between the knee and hip in humans, or the corresponding part in animals. [from Anglo-Saxon *theoh*]

thigh bone the bone of the leg between the hip-joint and the knee.

thimble / ˈθɪmbl/ *noun* **1** a small metal, ceramic, or plastic cap worn on the finger to protect it and push the needle when sewing. **2** a metal ring with a concave groove on the outside, fitted into a loop formed by splicing a rope in order to prevent chafing. [from Anglo-Saxon *thymel*]

thimbleful *noun* (PL. **thimblefuls**) the amount a thimble will hold, especially used for a very small quantity of liquid.

thin — *adj.* (**thinner, thinnest**) **1** having a relatively short distance between opposite sides. **2** having a relatively small diameter: *thin string*. **3** *said of a line, handwriting, etc* narrow or fine. **4** *said of people or animals* not fat; lean (often too lean). **5** *said of liquids* containing very little solid matter. **6** set far apart; not dense or crowded: *thin hair*. **7** rarefied: *thin air*. **8** few in number: *good books are thin on the ground*. **9** weak; lacking in body: *thin blood*. **10** not convincing or believable: *a thin disguise*. **11** *colloq.* difficult; uncomfortable; unpleasant: *have a thin time of it.* — *adv.* thinly. — *verb trans., intrans.* (**thinned, thinning**) (*usually* **thin out** or **thin something out**) to make or become thin, thinner, sparser, or less dense. [from Anglo-Saxon *thynne*]

. . . .

■ *adj.* **1, 2, 4** slim, slender. **1, 3** narrow. **2, 3** fine, attenuated, delicate, light, flimsy, filmy, gossamer, sheer, see-through, transparent, translucent. **4** lean, skinny, bony, skeletal, scraggy, scrawny, lanky, gaunt, spare, slight, underweight, undernourished, emaciated. **5** runny, watery, diluted. **6, 8** sparse, scarce. **6** scattered, scanty, skimpy, scant. **9, 10** poor, inadequate, deficient. **9** meagre, weak, feeble. *verb* narrow, attenuate, diminish, reduce, trim, weed out, weaken, dilute, water down, rarefy, refine.
◧ *adj.* **1, 2, 3, 5, 6, 8** thick. **1, 2, 3** broad. **4** fat. **5, 6** dense. **5** solid. **8** plentiful, abundant. **9** strong.

. . . .

thin air nowhere: *disappear into thin air*.

thin client *Comput.* a computer from which all operations are carried out on a central server, and that has no peripheral devices (such a disk drive) attached.

thine *old use, dialect* — *pron.* something which belongs to thee. — *adj.* (used before a vowel instead of *thy*) of or belonging to thee. — **of thine** of or belonging to thee. [from Anglo-Saxon *thin*]

thing *noun* 1 any object, especially one that is inanimate. 2 any object that cannot, need not, or should not be named. 3 any fact, quality, idea, etc that can be thought about or referred to. 4 an event, affair, or circumstance: *things are getting out of hand*. 5 a quality: *generosity is a great thing*. 6 *colloq.* a person or animal, especially when thought of as an object of pity: *poor thing!* 7 a preoccupation, obsession, or interest: *have a thing about horses*. 8 what is needed or required: *it's just the thing*. 9 an aim: *the thing is to do better next time*. 10 (**things**) personal belongings, especially clothes. — **do one's own thing** *colloq.* to do what one likes doing best, or what it is natural for one to do. **make a thing of something** to make a fuss about it or exaggerate its importance. **one of those things** something that must be accepted or cannot be avoided. [from Anglo-Saxon *thing*]

⊟ 1 article, object, entity, creature, body, substance, device, contrivance, gadget, tool, implement, instrument, apparatus, machine, mechanism. 3 item, detail, particular, feature, factor, element, point, fact, concept, thought. 4 circumstance, eventuality, happening, occurrence, event, incident, phenomenon, affair, proceeding, action, act, deed. 7 obsession, preoccupation, fixation, fetish, phobia, *colloq.* hang-up. 9 aim, task, job, responsibility. 10 belongings, possessions, effects, paraphernalia, stuff, goods, luggage, baggage, equipment, *colloq.* gear, *slang* clobber, odds and ends, bits (and pieces).

thingummy or **thingamy** /ˈθɪŋəmɪ/ or **thingummy-jig** or **thingummybob** *noun* (PL. **thingummies**) *colloq.* someone or something whose name is unknown, forgotten, or deliberately not used.

think — *verb* (PAST TENSE AND PAST PARTICIPLE **thought**) (*often* **think something** or **think about** or **of something**) 1 *intrans., trans.* a to have or form ideas in the mind. b to have as a thought in one's mind. 2 *trans., intrans.* to consider, judge, or believe: *thought the world was flat / think of oneself as a great singer*. 3 *trans., intrans.* to intend or plan; to form an idea of: *think about going to London / couldn't think of being so unkind / think no harm*. 4 *trans., intrans.* to imagine, expect, or suspect: *did not think there would be any trouble*. 5 (**think of someone** or **something**) to keep them in one's mind; to consider them: *think of the children first*. 6 *trans., intrans.* (**think of something** or **to do something**) to remember it: *did not think to tell her / couldn't think of his name*. 7 (**think of something**) to form or have an idea about it: *think of a plan*. 8 to have one's mind full of. 9 to bring into a specified condition by thinking. — *noun colloq.* an act of thinking. — **think better of something** or **someone** 1 to change one's mind about something on further thought. 2 to think that someone would not be so bad as to do something wrong: *I thought better of him than that*. **think highly** or **well** or **badly**, *etc* **of someone** to have a high, good, bad, etc opinion of them. **think little of something** or **not think much of something** to have a very low opinion of it. **think something out** 1 to consider or plan it carefully. 2 to solve a problem by thinking about all the aspects of it. **think something over** to consider all the advantages and disadvantages of an action, decision, etc; to reflect on it. **think something through** to think carefully about all the possible consequences of a plan, idea, etc, especially so as to reach a conclusion as to its wisdom or value. **think twice about something** to hesitate before doing something; to decide in the end not to do it. **think something up** to invent or devise it. [from Anglo-Saxon *thencan*]

⊟ *verb* 1, 3, 4 contemplate. 1 reason, ponder, meditate (on), ruminate, muse (on), cogitate, reflect (on), deliberate. 2 believe, hold, consider, regard, esteem, deem, judge, estimate, reckon, calculate, determine, conclude, reason. 3 intend, plan. 4 conceive, imagine, suppose, presume, surmise, expect, foresee, envisage, anticipate. 5, 6 remember. 5 consider, take account of, take into account. 6 recall, recollect. 7 See THINK UP. **think out** 1 consider, examine, scrutinize, investigate, sift, analyse, plan, formulate, frame. 2 solve, resolve, work out, figure out. **think over** ponder, mull over, chew over, ruminate on, meditate on, contemplate, muse on, reflect on, deliberate, weigh up. **think through** consider, examine, scrutinize, investigate, sift, analyse. **think up** devise, contrive, dream up, imagine, conceive, visualize, invent, design, create, concoct.

thinker *noun* a person who thinks, especially deeply and constructively or in a specified way: *an original thinker / a shallow thinker*.

⊟ philosopher, theorist, ideologist, brain, intellect, mastermind.

thinking — *noun* 1 the act of using one's mind to produce thoughts. 2 opinion or judgement: *what is your thinking on this?* — *adj.*, *said of people* using the mind intelligently and constructively. — **put on one's thinking-cap** *colloq.* to think carefully or reflect, especially to try to solve a problem or come up with an idea.

⊟ *noun* 1 reasoning, ratiocination, meditation, contemplation, cogitation, reflection, deliberation, consideration. 2 theory, idea, opinion, view, outlook, position, judgement, assessment, philosophy, thoughts, conclusions. *adj* reasoning, rational, intellectual, intelligent, cultured, sophisticated, philosophical, analytical, reflective, contemplative, thoughtful.

think tank *colloq.* a group of experts who research into an area to find solutions to problems and think up new ideas.

thinly *adv.* in a thin way; so as to be thin.

thinner *noun* a liquid such as turpentine that is added to paint or varnish to dilute it.

thinness *noun* being thin.

thin-skinned *adj.* sensitive; easily hurt or upset.

⊟ sensitive, touchy, irritable, vulnerable, susceptible, defenceless.
⊡ thick-skinned.

thio- /θaɪoʊ/ *combining form Chem.* forming words denoting the presence of sulphur in a compound. [from Greek *theion*, sulphur]

thiosulphate /θaɪoʊˈsʌlfeɪt/ *noun Chem.* an ester or salt of thiosulphuric acid (an unstable acid that readily decomposes to form sulphur and sulphurous acid), containing the $S_2O_3^{2-}$ ion. Thiosulphates are used in photography as fixing agents.

third — *adj.* 1 coming next after second in time, place, order, or rank; last of three. 2 being one of three equal parts. 3 being the forward gear which is one faster than second in a gearbox, eg in a motor vehicle. — *noun* 1 one of three equal parts. 2 (*also* **third gear**) the gear which is one faster than second in a gearbox, eg in a motor vehicle. 3 the third position in time, place, order, or rank; also, the person or thing occupying this position. 4 *Mus.* an interval of three notes (counting inclusively) along the diatonic scale. 5 *Mus.* a note which is separated by such an interval from another. 6 *Brit.* (*also* **third class**) an honours degree of the third, and usually lowest, class. — *adv.* in the third position: *come third in the race*. [from Anglo-Saxon *thridda*]

third class the class or rank next (especially in quality) after second.

third-class *adj.*, *adv.* of or in the position, class, or rank next after or below the second.

third degree prolonged and intensive interrogation, usually involving physical and mental intimidation.

third-degree adj. Medicine denoting the most serious of the three degrees of burning, with damage to the lower layers of skin tissue.

third dimension the depth or thickness of an object which distinguishes a solid object from a flat one.

thirdly adv. in the third place; as the third reason, etc.

third party a person who is indirectly involved, or involved by chance, in a legal action, contract, etc between usually two principals.

third-party adj., said of insurance covering damage done by or injury done to a person other than the insured.

third person see PERSON.

third-rate adj. of very bad or inferior quality.

. . . .

▣ low-grade, poor, bad, inferior, mediocre, indifferent, shoddy, cheap and nasty.
▣ first-rate.

. . . .

Third Reich the enlarged Germany planned by Hitler. [from German *Reich*, kingdom]

third wave (also **Third Wave**) the age of information technology, regarded as successor to the agrarian and industrial ages.

Third Way politics that are neither traditionally left- nor right-wing, but incorporate elements of both.

Third World (the **Third World**) the developing or underdeveloped countries in Africa, Asia, and Latin America.

thirst — noun 1 the need to drink, or the feeling of dryness in the mouth that this causes. 2 a strong and eager desire or longing. — verb intrans. 1 to have a great desire or long for something. 2 old use to be thirsty. [from Anglo-Saxon *thyrstan*]

. . . .

▣ noun 1 thirstiness, dryness, drought. 2 desire, longing, yearning, hankering, craving, hunger, appetite, lust, passion, eagerness, keenness. verb 1 long, yearn, hanker, crave, hunger.

. . . .

thirstily adv. with a thirsty manner.

thirstiness noun being thirsty.

thirsty adj. (**thirstier, thirstiest**) 1 needing or wanting to drink. 2 eager or longing. 3 causing thirst.

. . . .

▣ 1 dry, parched, colloq. gasping, dehydrated, arid. 2 eager, avid, greedy, longing, yearning, hankering, desirous, craving, hungry, burning, itching, dying.

. . . .

thirteen — noun 1 the number or figure 13; any symbol for this number. 2 the age of 13. 3 something, especially a garment or a person, whose size is denoted by the number 13. 4 a set of 13 people or things. — adj. 1 13 in number. 2 aged 13. [from Anglo-Saxon *threotine*]

thirteenth noun, adj. 1 the position in a series corresponding to 13 in a sequence of numbers. 2 one of 13 equal parts.

thirties pl. noun 1 the period of time between one's thirtieth and fortieth birthdays. 2 the range of temperatures between thirty and forty degrees. 3 the period of time between the thirtieth and fortieth years of a century.

thirtieth noun, adj. 1 the position in a series corresponding to 30 in a sequence of numbers. 2 one of 30 equal parts.

thirty — noun (PL. **thirties**) 1 the number or figure 30; any symbol for this number. 2 the age of 30. 3 a set of 30 people or things. — adj. 1 30 in number. 2 aged 30. [from Anglo-Saxon *thritig*]

thirty-eighth parallel the boundary line proposed for the partition of Korea at the Potsdam Conference (1945), after the defeat of Japan (which had annexed Korea in 1910). Since the Korean War, the 38th parallel again forms the line of division between North and South Korea.

this — pron. (PL. **these**) 1 a person, animal, thing, or idea already mentioned, about to be mentioned, indicated, or otherwise understood from the context. 2 a person, animal, thing, or idea which is nearby, especially which is closer to the speaker than something else. 3 the present time or place. 4 an action, event, circumstance: *what do you think of this?* — adj. 1 being the person, animal, thing, or idea which is nearby, especially closer to the speaker than something else: *this book or that one*. 2 being the person, animal, thing, or idea just mentioned, about to be mentioned, indicated, or otherwise understood. 3 relating to today, or time in the recent past ending today: *this morning / have been working on it these last few days*. 4 colloq. (used instead of *a* or *the* for emphasis) being a person, animal, thing, or idea not yet mentioned: *then I had this bright idea.* — adv. to this (extreme) degree or extent: *I didn't think it would be this easy.* — **this and that** colloq. various minor unspecified actions, objects, etc. [from Anglo-Saxon *thes*]

thistle / ˈθɪsl/ noun any of several plants with prickly purple flowers, the national emblem of Scotland. [from Anglo-Saxon *thistel*]

thistledown noun the fluffy hairs attached to thistle seeds.

thither / ˈðɪðə(r)/ adv. old use, literary, formal to or towards that place. [from Anglo-Saxon *thider*]

thixotropy / θɪkˈsɒtrəpɪ/ noun Physics the property of certain fluids, especially gels, which show a decrease in viscosity when stirred or shaken, eg 'jelly' paints. [from Greek *thixis*, action of touching, + *tropos*, turn]

tho' poetic same as THOUGH.

thole[1] / θəʊl/ or **tholepin** noun either one of a pair of pins in the side of a boat to keep an oar in place. See also ROWLOCK. [from Anglo-Saxon *thol*]

thole[2] / θəʊl/ verb Scot. old use to endure or tolerate. [from Anglo-Saxon *tholian*, to suffer]

tholos or **tholus** / ˈθəʊləs/ noun (PL. **tholoi, tholi**) a term loosely applied to any round building. More specifically, a dome-shaped or 'beehive' tomb common in the Mycenaean period, and the name by which the classical Greek tomb at Epidaurus (c.350BC) is known.

Thomism / ˈtəʊmɪzm/ noun in Christian philosophical theology, the name given to the doctrines of Thomas Aquinas (1225–74), and to later schools claiming descent from him.

thong / θɒŋ/ noun a narrow strip of leather used eg to fasten something, or as the lash of a whip. [from Anglo-Saxon *thwang*]

thoracic / θɔːˈrasɪk/ adj. relating to or in the region of the thorax.

thorax / ˈθɔːraks/ noun (PL. **thoraxes, thoraces**) the part of the body between the head and abdomen, in humans the chest, and in insects the middle section that bears the wings and legs. [from Greek *thorax*, breastplate]

thorium / ˈθɔːrɪəm/ noun Chem. (SYMBOL **Th**, ATOMIC NUMBER 90) a silvery-grey radioactive metal used in X-ray tubes, photoelectric cells, and sunlamps. The isotope thorium-232 is used as a nuclear fuel in breeder reactors, as it decays to form uranium-233 when bombarded with neutrons. [from *Thor*, the Scandinavian god of thunder]

thorn noun 1 a hard, sharp point sticking out from the stem or branch of certain plants. 2 a shrub bearing thorns, especially a hawthorn. 3 a constant irritation or annoyance: *a thorn in one's side*. [from Anglo-Saxon]

. . . .

▣ 1 spike, point, barb, prickle, spine, bristle, needle.

. . . .

thorny adj. (**thornier, thorniest**) 1 full of or covered with thorns. 2 difficult; causing trouble or problems.

. . . .

▣ 1 spiky, pointed, barbed, prickly, spiny, bristly. 2 difficult, troublesome, problematic, knotty, complex, intricate, awkward, delicate, ticklish.

. . . .

thorough /'θʌrə/ *adj.* **1** *said of a person* extremely careful and attending to every detail. **2** *said of a task, etc* carried out with great care and great attention to detail. **3** complete; absolute: *a thorough waste of time.* [from Anglo-Saxon *thurh*]

⊞ **1, 2** painstaking, scrupulous, meticulous. **1** conscientious, efficient. **2** sweeping, all-embracing, comprehensive, all-inclusive, exhaustive, thorough-going, intensive, in-depth. **3** full, complete, total, entire, utter, absolute, perfect, pure, sheer, unqualified, unmitigated, out-and-out, downright.
⊟ **1, 2** superficial, careless.

thoroughbred — *noun* **1** an animal, especially a horse, bred from the best specimens carefully developed by selective breeding over many years. **2 (Thoroughbred)** a breed of racehorse descended from English mares and Arab stallions of the early 18c. **3** a racehorse belonging to this breed. — *adj.* **1** *said of an animal, especially a horse* bred from the best specimens; pure-bred. **2 (Thoroughbred)** of or being a Thoroughbred.

thoroughfare *noun* **1** a public road or street. **2 a** a road or path that is open at both ends. **b** the right of passage through this.

thoroughgoing *adj.* **1** extremely thorough. **2** utter; out-and-out: *a thoroughgoing villain.*

⊞ **1** sweeping, all-embracing, comprehensive, all-inclusive, exhaustive, thorough, intensive, in-depth, painstaking, meticulous. **2** utter, absolute, unqualified, unmitigated, out-and-out, downright.

thoroughly *adv.* in a thorough way; to a thorough degree.
thoroughness *noun* being thorough.
those see THAT.
thou[1] /ðaʊ/ *pron. old use, dialect* you (singular). [from Anglo-Saxon *thu*]
thou[2] /θaʊ/ *noun* (PL. **thou, thous**) **1** *colloq.* a thousand. **2** a unit of length equal to one thousandth of an inch.
though /ðəʊ/ — *conj.* **1** despite the fact that. **2** if or even if: *I wouldn't marry him though he was the richest man in the world.* **3** and yet; but: *we like the new car, though not as much as the old one.* — *adv.* however; nevertheless. — **as though** ... as if ... [from Norse *tho*]

⊞ *conj.* ALTHOUGH. **1** notwithstanding, while, allowing, granted. **2** even if. *adv.* however, nevertheless, nonetheless, yet, still, even so, all the same, for all that.

thought /θɔːt/ — past tense and past participle of THINK. — *noun* **1** an idea, concept, or opinion. **2** the act of thinking. **3** serious and careful consideration: *give some thought to the problem.* **4** the faculty or power of reasoning. **5** the intellectual ideas which are typical of a particular place, time, group, etc: *recent scientific thought.* **6** intention, expectation, or hope. **7 a** consideration or kindness. **b** an action which shows these qualities. [from Anglo-Saxon *thoht*]

⊞ **1** idea, notion, concept, conception, belief, conviction, opinion, view, judgement, assessment, conclusion. **2** thinking, meditation, contemplation, cogitation, reflection, deliberation. **3** consideration, attention, heed, regard, study, scrutiny, introspection. **6** plan, design, intention, purpose, aim, hope, dream, expectation, anticipation. **7** *consideration* thoughtfulness, kindness, care, concern, compassion, sympathy, *action* gesture, touch.

thoughtful *adj.* **1** thinking deeply, or appearing to think deeply; reflective. **2** showing careful or serious thought: *a thoughtful reply.* **3** thinking of other people; considerate.

⊞ **1** reflective, pensive, wistful, dreamy, abstracted,

contemplative, introspective, thinking, absorbed, studious, serious, solemn. **2** considered, well-thought-out, well-judged, prudent, careful, cautious, wary. **3** considerate, kind, unselfish, helpful, caring, attentive, heedful, mindful.
⊟ **2** thoughtless, insensitive, selfish.

thoughtless *adj.* **1** not thinking about other people; inconsiderate. **2** showing a lack of careful or serious thought; rash.

⊞ **1** inconsiderate, unthinking, insensitive, unfeeling, tactless, undiplomatic, unkind, selfish, uncaring. **2** absent-minded, inattentive, heedless, mindless, foolish, stupid, silly, rash, reckless, ill-considered, imprudent, careless, negligent, remiss.
⊟ **1** thoughtful, considerate. **2** careful.

thousand /'θaʊzənd/ — *noun* (PL. **thousands, thousand**) **1** the number or figure 1,000; any symbol for this number, eg M. **2** anything having 1,000 parts, etc. **3** (*usually* **thousands**) *colloq.* a large unspecified number or amount. — *adj.* numbering 1,000. — **one in a thousand** an extremely rare or special person or thing. [from Anglo-Saxon *thusend*]

thousandth *noun, adj.* **1** the position in a series corresponding to 1,000 in a sequence of numbers. **2** one of 1,000 equal parts.

thrall /θrɔːl/ *noun* **1** a person who is in the power of another person or thing; a slave. **2** (*also* **thraldom**) the state of being in the power of another person or thing; slavery: *be held in thrall by her beauty.* [from Anglo-Saxon *thræl*]

thrash — *verb* **1** to beat soundly, especially with blows or a whip. **2** to defeat thoroughly or decisively. **3** (*usually* **thrash about, around,** *etc*) to move around violently or wildly. **4** (*trans., intrans.*) to thresh (corn, etc). — *noun* **1** an act of thrashing. **2** *colloq.* a party. **3** *colloq.* thrash metal music. — **thrash something out** to discuss a problem, etc thoroughly to try to solve it. [from Anglo-Saxon *therscan*]

⊞ *verb* **1, 2** beat, *colloq.* clobber, *colloq.* wallop, *colloq.* hammer. **1** punish, whip, lash, flog, scourge, cane, belt, spank, lay into. **2** defeat, trounce, *colloq.* slaughter, crush, overwhelm, rout. **3, 4** thresh. **3** flail, toss, jerk. **thrash out** discuss, debate, negotiate, work out, settle, resolve.

thrashing *noun* **1** a beating. **2** threshing.
thrash metal a style of music combining heavy metal and punk rock rhythms, often with violent lyrics or subject matter.
thread /θred/ — *noun* **1** a very thin strand of glass, silk, cotton, or wool, especially when several such strands are twisted together for sewing. **2** any naturally formed very thin strand of fibre, such as that forming a spider's web. **3** anything like a thread in length and narrowness. **4** the projecting spiral ridge round a screw, bolt, or in a nut. **5** a continuous connecting element or theme in a story, argument, etc: *lost the thread of what he was saying.* **6** a thin seam or vein of ore or coal. — *verb* **1** to pass a thread through (eg the eye of a needle). **2** to pass (tape, film, etc) into or through something to put it into its correct position. **3** to string (beads) on a thread or length of string. **4** (*trans., intrans.*) to make (one's way) carefully (through eg narrow streets or crowded areas). **5** to streak (hair, the sky, etc) with narrow patches of a different colour. **6** to provide (eg a bolt) with a screw thread. — **hang by a thread** to be in a very precarious or dangerous state or position. [from Anglo-Saxon *thræd*]

⊞ *noun* **1, 2, 3** strand, fibre, filament. **1** cotton, yarn. **3** string, line. **5** course, direction, drift, tenor, theme, motif, plot, storyline.

threadbare adj. **1** said of material or clothes worn thin; shabby. **2** said of a person wearing such clothes. **3** said of a word, excuse, etc commonly used and meaningless; hackneyed; feeble.

....

▤ **1**, **2** ragged, scruffy, shabby. **1** worn, frayed, moth-eaten. **3** hackneyed, overused, old, stale, tired, trite, commonplace, stock, stereotyped.

▣ **1** new. **3** fresh.
....

threadworm noun Zool. a nematode worm of the genus Enterobius, which resembles a small piece of thread and lives as a parasite in the large intestine of humans, mainly affecting children. It rarely causes any symptoms apart from itching around the anus.

threat /θrɛt/ noun **1** a warning that one is going to or might hurt or punish (someone). **2** a sign that something dangerous or unpleasant is or may be about to happen. **3** a source of danger. [from Anglo-Saxon threat, affliction]

....

▤ **1**, **3** menace. **2** warning, omen, portent, presage, foreboding. **3** danger, risk, hazard, peril.
....

threaten verb (**threatened**, **threatening**) **1** to make a threat against. **2** to be a source of danger to. **3** to give warning that (something unpleasant or dangerous is or may be about to happen). **4** (intrans.) said of something unpleasant or dangerous to seem likely to happen: a storm was threatening.

....

▤ **1**, **2** menace. **1** intimidate, browbeat, pressurize, bully, terrorize. **2** endanger, jeopardize, imperil. **3** warn, portend, presage, forebode, foreshadow. **4** impend, be in the offing, approach, loom (up).
....

threatening adj. **1** making or containing threats. **2** imminent.

....

▤ **1** menacing, intimidatory, warning, cautionary, ominous, inauspicious, sinister, grim. **2** looming, impending, imminent, nigh.
....

three — noun **1** the number or figure 3; any symbol for this number, eg III. **2** the age of 3. **3** something, especially a garment or a person, whose size is denoted by the number 3. **4** a playing-card with 3 pips. **5** a set of 3 things or people. **6** 3 o'clock. **7** a score of 3. — adj. **1** 3 in number. **2** aged 3. — pron. 3 things or people. [from Anglo-Saxon thrie]

three-dimensional adj. **1** having or appearing to have three dimensions, ie height, width, and depth. **2** said especially of fictional characters developed or described in detail and therefore lifelike.

threefold — adj. **1** three times as much or as great. **2** divided into, or consisting of, three parts. — adv. by three times as much.

three-legged race a race run between pairs of runners who have their adjacent legs tied together.

three-line whip a written notice to politicians belonging to a particular party that they must attend a vote in parliament and vote in the way in which they are instructed.

three-peat or **threepeat** — verb trans., intrans. to win a sporting event three times, especially in succession. — noun a third, especially successive, win of a sporting event.

threepence noun Brit. Hist. in the UK before the introduction of decimal currency, the sum of three pence (3d).

threepenny /ˈθrʌpnɪ, ˈθrɛpnɪ/ adj. Brit. Hist. **1** worth or costing threepence. **2** of little worth or value.

threepenny bit or **threepenny piece** Brit. Hist. a coin worth threepence.

three-ply — noun anything which has three layers or strands bound together, especially wood or wool. — adj. having three layers or strands.

three-point turn a reversing of the direction of a motor vehicle by moving forward, then backward, then forward again while turning round.

three-quarter — adj. being three-quarters of the full amount or length. — noun Rugby any of the four players positioned between the full back and the scrum half and stand-off half.

three Rs see R¹.

threesome noun a group of three.

three-strikes noun a system of law originating in the US whereby a person found guilty of three criminal offences is automatically jailed. [from the baseball term three strikes and you're out]

threnodial /θrəˈnoʊdɪəl/ or **threnodic** adj. relating to or of the nature of a threnody.

threnodist noun a person who composes or performs a threnody.

threnody /ˈθrɛnədɪ, ˈθriːnədɪ/ noun (PL. **threnodies**) a song or ode of lamentation, especially for a person's death. [from Greek threnos, lament + oide, song]

threonine /ˈθriːənaɪn/ noun Biochem. an amino acid that is found in certain proteins. [a rearrangement of Greek erythro-, red]

thresh verb trans., intrans. **1** to separate the grain or seeds from the stalks of cereal plants by beating, a procedure that is now often performed by a combine harvester at the time of cutting. **2** to beat or strike. **3** (**thresh about** or **around**) to move violently or wildly. [from Anglo-Saxon therscan]

thresher noun **1** a machine or person that threshes corn, etc. **2** a large shark with a long whip-like tail.

threshold /ˈθrɛʃhoʊld, ˈθrɛʃoʊld/ noun **1** a piece of wood or stone forming the bottom of a doorway. **2** any doorway or entrance. **3** a starting-point: on the threshold of a new career. **4** Biol. the minimum intensity of a stimulus, eg pain, that is required to produce a response in a cell or organism, and below which there is no response. **5** Biol. the membrane potential that must be reached before an impulse is initiated in a nerve cell. **6** Physics the minimum value of a quantity or variable that must be reached before it has a specified effect. [from Anglo-Saxon therscold]

....

▤ **1** doorstep, sill. **2** doorway, door, entrance. **3** starting-point, beginning, start, outset, opening, brink, verge, dawn.
....

threw /θruː/ see THROW.

thrice /θraɪs/ adv. old use, literary three times; three times as much. [from Anglo-Saxon thriwa]

thrift noun **1** careful spending, use, or management of resources, especially money. **2** a wild plant with narrow bluish-green leaves and dense round heads of pink flowers, usually found near the coast. [from Norse, = prosperity]

....

▤ **1** economy, husbandry, saving, conservation, frugality, prudence, carefulness.

▣ **1** extravagance, waste.
....

thriftily adv. in a thrifty way.

thriftiness noun being thrifty.

thriftless adj. not thrifty; extravagant.

....

▤ spendthrift, extravagant, profligate, prodigal, wasteful, improvident, ne'er-do-well.

▣ thrifty, economical.
....

thrifty adj. (**thriftier, thriftiest**) showing thrift.

....

▤ economical, saving, frugal, sparing, prudent, careful, provident.

▣ extravagant, profligate, prodigal, wasteful.
....

thrill — *verb* **1** to cause to feel a sudden strong glowing, tingling, or throbbing sensation, especially of excitement, emotion, or pleasure. **2** *intrans.* to feel such a sensation. **3** *trans., intrans.* to vibrate or quiver. **4** *intrans. said of a feeling* to pass quickly with a glowing or tingling sensation: *excitement thrilled through her.* — *noun* **1** a sudden tingling feeling of excitement, happiness, or pleasure. **2** something, eg an event, which causes such a feeling. **3** a shivering or trembling feeling caused especially by fear, terror, or distress. [from Anglo-Saxon *thyrlian*, to pierce]

■ *verb* **1** excite, electrify, galvanize, exhilarate, rouse, arouse, move, stir, stimulate. **2, 3** tremble, quiver, shake. **2** flush, glow, tingle, throb, shudder. **3** vibrate. *noun* **1, 2** excitement, adventure, pleasure. **1** stimulation, charge, *colloq.* kick, *colloq.* buzz, sensation, glow, tingle, throb. **3** shiver, shudder, quiver, tremor.

◨ *verb* **1** bore.

thriller *noun* an exciting novel, play, or film, usually involving crime, espionage, or adventure.

thrilling *adj.* that thrills, exciting.

■ exciting, electrifying, exhilarating, *colloq.* high-octane, stirring, breathtaking, tense, nail-biting, heart-stopping, cliffhanging, *colloq.* white-knuckle, dramatic, sensational.

thrillingly *adv.* in a thrilling way.

thrips *noun* (PL. **thrips, thripses**) a minute slender black insect which lives on flowers. [from Greek *thrips*, woodworm]

thrive *verb* (PAST TENSE **throve, thrived**; PAST PARTICIPLE **thriven, thrived**) *intrans.* **1** to grow strong and healthy. **2** to prosper or be successful, especially financially. [from Norse *thrifa*, to grasp]

■ FLOURISH, GROW, BLOOM, BLOSSOM. **2** prosper, boom, increase, advance, develop, gain, profit, succeed.

◨ LANGUISH, FAIL, DIE. **2** stagnate.

thriving *adj.* that thrives; prosperous.

■ flourishing, blooming, blossoming, prosperous, booming, expanding, growing, profitable, successful, lucrative, fruitful, productive.

thro' or **thro** through.

throat *noun* **1** the top part of the passage which leads from the mouth and nose to the stomach. **2** the front part of the neck. **3** something resembling a throat in form or function, especially a narrow passageway or opening. — **cut one's own throat** to cause one's own ruin or downfall. **cut someone's throat** to kill or injure someone by slitting open their throat. **stick in one's throat** *said of an unwelcome or unpalatable thought* to be impossible to say, believe, or accept. [from Anglo-Saxon *throte*]

throatily *adv.* in a throaty way.

throatiness *noun* being throaty.

throaty *adj.* (**throatier, throatiest**) *said of a voice* deep and hoarse.

throb — *verb intrans.* (**throbbed, throbbing**) **1** to beat, especially with unusual force in response to excitement, emotion, exercise, or pain. **2** to beat or vibrate with a strong, regular rhythm. — *noun* a regular beat; pulse. [from Middle English *throbben*]

■ *verb* BEAT, PULSE, POUND, THUMP. **1** pulsate, palpitate. **2** vibrate. *noun* pulse, pulsation, beat, palpitation, vibration, pounding, thumping.

throe *noun* (*usually* **throes**) a violent pang or spasm, especially during childbirth or before death. — **in the**

throes of something involved in a difficult or painful struggle with it; suffering under it: *in the throes of a severe storm.* [from Middle English *throwe*]

thrombin /ˈθrɒmbɪn/ *noun Biochem.* an enzyme that causes the blood to clot by converting the soluble protein fibrinogen into the insoluble protein fibrin, which then forms a network of fibres.

thrombosis /θrɒmˈbəʊsɪs/ *noun* (PL. **thromboses**) *Pathol.* the formation of a thrombus (blood clot) in a blood vessel, obstructing the flow of blood to the tissue supplied by the vessel. Formation of a thrombus in an artery to the heart (coronary thrombosis) causes heart attack, and the formation of a blood clot in an artery to the brain is one cause of stroke. [from Greek *thrombosis*, curdling]

thrombotic *adj.* relating to or caused by thrombosis.

thrombus /ˈθrɒmbəs/ *noun Pathol.* a blood clot in a blood vessel. [from Greek *thrombus*, clot]

throne — *noun* **1** the ceremonial chair of a monarch or bishop, used on official occasions. **2** the office or power of the sovereign: *come to the throne.* — *verb* to place on a throne. [from Greek *thronos*, seat]

throng — *noun* a crowd of people or things, especially in a small space; a multitude. — *verb* **1** to crowd or fill: *people thronging the streets.* **2** *intrans.* to move in a crowd; to come together in great numbers: *an audience thronging into a theatre.* [from Anglo-Saxon *gethrang*]

■ *noun* crowd, multitude, horde, mass, host, swarm, flock, herd. *verb* CROWD, SWARM, CRAM, PACK. **1** fill. **2** flock, herd.

throstle /ˈθrɒsl/ *noun old use, poetic* a song thrush. [from Anglo-Saxon *throstle*]

throttle /ˈθrɒtl/ — *noun* **1** a valve which regulates the amount of fuel, steam, etc supplied to an engine; also, the pedal or lever that controls this. **2** the throat or windpipe. — *verb* to injure or kill by choking or strangling. **1** to prevent from being said, expressed, etc; to suppress. **2** to control the flow of (fuel, steam, etc to an engine) using a valve. — **throttle back** or **down** to reduce the speed of an engine by closing the throttle to reduce the amount of fuel, steam, etc supplied to it. [from Middle English *throtelen*, to strangle]

■ *verb* **1** strangle, choke, asphyxiate, suffocate, smother, stifle. **2** gag, silence, suppress, inhibit.

through /θruː/ — *prep.* **1** going from one side or end of to the other: *a road through the village.* **2** from place to place within; everywhere within: *searched through the house.* **3** from the beginning to the end of: *read through the magazine / all through the night.* **4** *North Amer.* up to and including: *Tuesday through Thursday.* **5** because of: *lost his job through stupidity.* **6** by way of, means of, or agency of; by: *related through marriage.* — *adv.* **1** into and out of; from one side or end to the other. **2** from the beginning to the end. **3** into a position of having completed, especially successfully: *sat the exam again and got through.* **4** to the core; completely: *soaked through.* **5** *Brit.* in or into communication by telephone: *put the caller through.* — *adj.* **1** *said of a journey, route, train, ticket, etc* going all the way to one's destination without requiring a change of line, train, etc or a new ticket. **2** *said of traffic* passing straight through an area, town, etc without stopping. **3** going from one surface, side or end to another: *a through road.* — **be through** to have no further prospects or intentions in some regard: *is through as a businessman.* **be through with someone** to have no more to do with them. **be through with something** to have finished or completed it. **through and through** completely. [from Anglo-Saxon *thurh*]

■ *prep.* **1** between. **2, 3** throughout. **3** during, in. **5** because of, as a result of, thanks to. **6** by, via, by way of, by means of, using. *adj.* **1** direct, express, non-stop. **be through** be finished, be ended, be completed, be done.

throughout — *prep.* **1** in all parts of. **2** during the whole of. — *adv.* **1** in every part; everywhere: *a house with carpets throughout.* **2** during the whole time: *remain friends throughout.*

throughput *noun* the amount of material put through a process, especially a computer or manufacturing process.

through-ticketing *noun* an arrangement whereby passengers can use a ticket to travel over more than one railway network.

throw — *verb* (PAST TENSE **threw**; PAST PARTICIPLE **thrown**) **1** *trans., intrans.* to propel or hurl through the air with force, especially with a rapid forward movement of the hand and arm. **2** to move or hurl into a specified position, especially suddenly or violently. **3** to put into a specified condition, especially suddenly: *threw them into confusion.* **4** to direct, cast, or emit: *a candle throwing shadows on the wall / throw a glance.* **5** *colloq.* to puzzle or confuse. **6** *said of a horse* to make (its rider) fall off. **7** *Wrestling, Judo* to bring (one's opponent) to the ground. **8** to move (a switch or lever) so as to operate a mechanism. **9** to make (pottery) on a potter's wheel. **10** *colloq.* to lose (a contest) deliberately, especially in return for a bribe. **11** *trans., intrans.* to roll (dice) on to a flat surface. **12** to obtain (a specified number) by throwing dice. **13** to have or suffer: *throw a tantrum.* **14** to give (a party). **15** to deliver (a punch). **16** to cause (one's voice) to appear to come from elsewhere. — *noun* **1** an act of throwing or instance of being thrown. **2** the distance something is thrown. **3** *colloq.* an article, item, turn, etc: *sell them at £2 a throw.* **4** *Geol.* the amount by which a fault in a stratum is displaced vertically. — **throw something about** or **around** to throw it in various directions; to scatter it. **throw something away 1** to discard it or get rid of it. **2** to fail to take advantage of it; to waste or lose it through lack of care. **throw something back** to delay or hinder its progress to a specified extent: *the problem threw us back six months.* **throw someone back on something** to force them to rely on it. **throw back to something** to revert to some earlier, ancestral character or type. **throw something in 1** to include or add it as a gift or as part of a bargain at no extra cost. **2** to contribute a remark to a discussion, especially casually. **throw in one's hand** *colloq.* to give up or abandon what one is doing. **throw in the towel** or **sponge** *colloq.* to give up or abandon a struggle. **throw oneself into something** to begin doing it with great energy or enthusiasm. **throw something off 1** to get rid of it: *throw off a cold.* **2** to write or say it in an offhand or careless way. **3** to remove clothing hurriedly. **throw something on** to put on clothing hurriedly. **throw oneself on something** to rely or depend on someone's goodwill, sympathies, mercy, etc. **throw something open 1** to open it suddenly and widely. **2** to allow anyone to enter or take part in it. **throw someone out 1** to expel them. **2** to confuse or disconcert them. **throw something out 1** to get rid of it; to reject or dismiss it. **2** to say it in a casual or offhand manner. **3** to cause it to extend or project, especially from a main body: *throw out a new wing.* **throw someone over** to leave or abandon someone, especially a lover. **throw people together** *said of circumstances, etc* to bring them into contact by chance. **throw something together** to construct it hurriedly or temporarily. **throw up** *colloq.* to vomit. **throw something up 1** to give it up or abandon it. **2** to build or erect it hurriedly. **3** to cause it to come to light **throw up one's hands** to raise them in the air quickly, usually as a sign of despair, horror, etc. [from Anglo-Saxon *thrawan*, to twist]

. . . .

🔲 *verb* **2** hurl, heave, lob, pitch, *colloq.* chuck, *colloq.* sling, cast, fling, toss, launch, propel, send. **4** shed, cast, emit, radiate, give off, project, direct. **5, 7** *colloq.* floor. **5** perplex, baffle, confound, confuse, disconcert, astonish, dumbfound. **6** unseat, unsaddle, unhorse. **7** bring down, upset, overturn, dislodge. *noun* **1** heave, lob, pitch, sling, fling, toss, cast. **throw away 1** discard, jettison, dump, *slang* ditch, scrap, dispose of, throw out. **2** waste, squander, fritter away, *colloq.* blow. **throw off 1, 3** shed, cast off. **1** drop, abandon, shake off, get rid of, elude. **throw out** *someone* **1** evict, turn out, expel, *Brit. colloq.* turf out, eject, *something*

1 reject, discard, dismiss, turn down, jettison, dump, *slang* ditch, throw away, scrap. **throw together** *something* construct, erect, improvise, put together, *colloq.* knock up, *colloq.* cook up, concoct. **throw up** vomit, spew, regurgitate, disgorge, retch, heave, *something* **1** abandon, give up, renounce, relinquish, resign, quit, leave. **3** bring to light, unearth, reveal, expose, uncover, bring up.

🔳 **1** keep, preserve, salvage, rescue.

. . . .

throwaway *adj.* **1** meant to be thrown away after use. **2** said or done casually or carelessly.

throwback *noun* reversion to earlier or ancestral characteristics, or an instance of this.

throw-in *noun* *Football, Basketball* an act of throwing the ball back into play from a sideline.

thru *North Amer., esp. US* same as THROUGH.

thrum¹ — *verb* (**thrummed, thrumming**) **1** *trans., intrans.* to strum idly (on a stringed instrument). **2** *intrans.* to drum or tap with the fingers. **3** *intrans.* to hum monotonously. — *noun* repetitive strumming, or the sound of this. [imitative]

thrum² *noun* **1** an unwoven end of thread remaining on a loom when the woven fabric has been cut away, or a group of such threads. **2** any loose thread or fringe. [from Anglo-Saxon *thrum*]

thrush¹ *noun* any of several common small or medium-sized songbirds with brown feathers and a spotted chest. [from Anglo-Saxon *thrysce*]

thrush² *noun* **1** a fungal infection, especially of children, which causes white blisters in the mouth, throat, and lips. **2** a similar infection in the vagina. **3** an inflammation affecting the sole of a horse's hoof.

thrust — *verb* (PAST TENSE AND PAST PARTICIPLE **thrust**) **1** to push suddenly and violently. **2** (**thrust something on** or **upon someone**) to force them to accept it; to impose it on them. **3** (**thrust through something**) to pierce or stab it. **4** (**thrust at something**) to make a lunge at it. **5** (**thrust into, through,** etc) to force one's way. — *noun* **1** a sudden or violent movement forward, a push or lunge. **2** *Aeron.* the force produced by a jet or rocket engine that propels an aircraft or rocket forward. The magnitude of thrust depends on the mass and velocity of the gases expelled from the rear of the vehicle. **3** an attack or lunge with a pointed weapon; a stab. **4** an attack, especially by a military force on the enemy's territory, or a verbal attack on a person. **5** the strong continuous pressure that one part of an object exerts against another. **6** the main theme, message, or gist, eg of an argument. **7** determination; drive. [from Norse *thrysta*]

. . . .

🔲 *verb* **1** push, impel, drive, propel, shove, butt, ram, jam, wedge, stick, poke, prod, plunge. **2** impose on, press on, force on. **3** pierce, stab, jab. **4** lunge at. *noun* **1** push, shove, poke, prod, lunge. **2** drive, impetus, momentum. **3** stab.
6 gist, essence, drift, tenor, theme, point, substance.

. . . .

thrust stage *Theatr.* a stage that extends beyond the proscenium arch into the auditorium.

thud — *noun* a dull sound like that of something heavy falling to the ground. — *verb intrans.* (**thudded, thudding**) to move or fall with a thud. [from Anglo-Saxon *thyddan*, to strike]

. . . .

🔲 *noun, verb* thump, clump, knock, clunk, smack, *colloq.* wallop, crash, bang, thunder.

. . . .

thug /θʌg/ *noun* **1** a violent or brutal man or criminal. **2** (**Thug**) *Hist.* a member of a religious organization of robbers and murderers in India. [from Hindi *thag*, thief, cheat]

. . . .

🔲 **1** ruffian, tough, robber, bandit, mugger, killer,

murderer, assassin, gangster, hooligan.

....

thuggery *noun* violent behaviour.

thuggish *adj.* characteristic of a thug; violent, brutal.

thulium /ˈθjuːlɪəm/ *noun Chem.* (SYMBOL **Tm**, ATOMIC NUMBER **69**) a soft silvery-white metal that is a member of the lanthanide series and is used as a source of X-rays and gamma rays. The dust of this metal is a fire hazard. [from Latin *Thule*]

thumb /θʌm/ — *noun* **1** in humans, the two-boned digit on the inner side of the hand, set lower than and at a different angle to the other four digits. **2** the part of a glove or mitten covering this finger. **3** in other animals, the digit corresponding to the human thumb. — *verb* **1** *trans., intrans.* (**thumb through something**) to turn over the pages of a book, magazine, etc to glance at the contents. **2** to smudge or wear with the thumb. **3** to ask for or obtain (a lift) in a motor vehicle by signalling to passing drivers with the thumb. **4** *intrans.* to travel by thumbing lifts; to hitchhike. — **all thumbs** awkward and clumsy. **thumbs down** a sign indicating failure, rejection, or disapproval. **thumbs up** a sign indicating success, best wishes for success, satisfaction, or approval. **under someone's thumb** completely controlled or dominated by someone. [from Anglo-Saxon *thuma*]

thumb index a series of notches, each with a letter or word in them, cut into the outer edges of pages of a book for quick reference.

thumbnail — *noun* the nail on the thumb. — *adj.* brief and concise.

thumbscrew *noun Hist.* an instrument of torture which crushes the thumbs.

thumbtack *noun North Amer.* a drawing-pin.

thump — *noun* a heavy blow, or the dull sound of a blow. — *verb* **1** to beat or strike with dull-sounding heavy blows. **2** *intrans.* to throb or beat violently. **3** (*also* **thump something out**) to play (a tune), especially on a piano, by pounding heavily on the keys. **4** (**thump along, around,** *etc*) to move with heavy pounding steps. [imitative]

....

◨ *noun* knock, blow, punch, clout, box, cuff, smack, *colloq.* whack, *colloq.* wallop, crash, bang, thud, beat, throb. *verb* **1** hit, strike, knock, punch, clout, box, cuff, smack, thrash, *colloq.* whack, *colloq.* wallop, bang, batter. **2** pound, hammer, beat, throb.

....

thumping *colloq.* — *adj.* very big: *a thumping lie.* — *adv.* very: *a pair of thumping great boots.*

thunder — *noun* **1** a deep rumbling or loud cracking sound heard after a flash of lightning, caused by the lightning causing gases in the atmosphere to expand suddenly. **2** a loud deep rumbling noise. — *verb* (**thundered, thundering**) **1** *intrans.* said of thunder: to sound or rumble. **2** *intrans.* to make a noise like thunder while moving: *tanks thundering over a bridge.* **3** to say or utter in a loud, often aggressive, voice. [from Anglo-Saxon *thunor*]

....

◨ *noun* **2** boom, reverberation, crash, bang, crack, clap, peal, rumble, roll, roar, blast, explosion. *verb* **2, 3** roar, bellow. **2** boom, resound, reverberate, crash, bang, crack, clap, peal, rumble, roll, blast. **3** shout, yell, bawl, cry.

....

thunderbolt *noun* **1** a flash of lightning immediately followed by thunder. **2** a sudden and unexpected event. **3** a supposed destructive stone, missile, etc falling to earth in a flash of lightning.

thunderclap *noun* a crash of thunder, something startling or unexpected.

thundercloud *noun* a large cloud charged with electricity which produces thunder and lightning.

thundering *colloq.* — *adj.* very great: *a thundering idiot.* — *adv.* very: *a thundering great error.*

thunderous *adj.* like thunder, especially in being very loud, threatening, or violent.

....

◨ booming, resounding, reverberating, roaring, loud, noisy, deafening, ear-splitting.

....

thunderously *adv.* with a thunderous noise.

thunderstorm *noun* a storm with thunder and lightning and usually heavy rain.

thunderstruck *adj.* overcome by surprise; astonished.

thundery *adj.* warning of, or likely to have or bring, thunder.

Thur or **Thur.** *abbrev.* Thursday.

thurible /ˈθjʊərɪbl/ *noun* a censer. [from Latin *thus*, incense]

Thurs or **Thurs.** *abbrev.* Thursday.

Thursday *noun* the fifth day of the week. [from Anglo-Saxon *thunresdæg*, the day of Thunor, the god of thunder]

thus *adv.* **1** in the way or manner shown or mentioned; in this manner. **2** to this degree, amount, or distance: *thus far.* **3** therefore; accordingly. [from Anglo-Saxon *thus*]

....

◨ SO. **1** like this, in this way, as follows. **3** hence, therefore, consequently, then, accordingly.

....

thwack /θwak/ — *noun* a blow with something flat, such as a bat, or the noise made by it. — *verb* to strike (something) with such a noise. [imitative]

thwart /θwɔːt/ — *verb* to prevent or hinder (a person, plans, etc). — *noun* a seat for a rower lying across a boat. [from Norse *thvert*, across]

....

◨ *verb* frustrate, foil, stymie, defeat, hinder, impede, obstruct, block, check, baffle, stop, prevent, oppose.
◨ *verb* help, assist, aid.

....

thy *adj. old use, dialect* of or belonging to thee. [from Middle English, from THINE]

thyme /taɪm/ *noun* any of several herbs and shrubs, especially those with sweet-smelling leaves which are used to season food. [from Greek *thymon*]

thymine /ˈθaɪmiːn/ *noun Biochem.* one of the bases, derived from pyrimidine, that is found in the nucleic acid DNA. [from Greek *thymos*, thymus gland]

thymus /ˈθaɪməs/ *noun* (PL. **thymi**) (*in full* **thymus gland**) *Anat.* in vertebrates, a gland just above the heart, which in the newborn plays an important role in the development of the immune response to invasion of the body by pathogens or other foreign particles. It enlarges between birth and puberty, and gradually shrinks during adulthood. [from Greek *thymos*]

thyroid /ˈθaɪrɔɪd/ — *noun Physiol.* (*in full* **thyroid gland**) in vertebrates, a shield-shaped gland situated in the neck, in front of the trachea. It secretes several hormones, including thyroxine, which controls growth, development, and metabolic rate. Deficiency of iodine in the diet can lead to enlargement of the thyroid, forming a goitre. — *adj.* **1** relating to the thyroid gland or thyroid cartilage. **2** shield-shaped. [from Greek *thyreoeides*, shield-shaped]

thyroid cartilage the principal cartilage in the larynx which projects in men to form the Adam's apple.

thyroid hormone *Physiol.* any of various hormones, especially thyroxine and triiodothyronine, that are secreted by the thyroid gland and are required for normal mental and physical development, and for the growth and functioning of the body tissues.

thyroxine or **thyroxin** /θaɪəˈrɒksɪn/ *noun* **1** *Physiol.* an iodine-containing compound that is the principal hormone secreted by the thyroid gland. **2** a synthetic form of this compound, administered in order to treat underactivity of the thyroid gland.

thyself *pron. old use, dialect Relig.* **1** the reflexive form of *thou* and *thee.* **2** used for emphasis.

Ti *symbol Chem.* titanium.

ti or **te** /tiː/ *noun Mus.* in tonic sol-fa, the seventh note of the major scale. [earlier *si*, from the initial sounds of *Sancte Iohannes* in a medieval Latin hymn, certain syllables and sounds of which were used in naming the notes of the scale]

tiara /tɪˈɑːrə/ *noun* **1** a women's jewelled ornament for the head, similar to a crown. **2** the pope's three-tiered crown. [from Greek]

Tibetan /tɪˈbɛtən/ — *noun* **1** a native or citizen of Tibet (the Tibet Autonomous Region of China). **2** the main language of Tibet. — *adj.* relating to Tibet or its people or language, etc.

tibia /ˈtɪbɪə/ *noun* (PL. **tibias, tibiae**) **1** the inner and usually larger of the two bones between the knee and ankle in man, or the bone corresponding to this in other animals; the shinbone. **2** the fourth joint of an insect's leg. [from Latin *tibia*, shinbone]

tic *noun* **1** an habitual nervous, involuntary movement or twitch of a muscle, especially of the face. **2** an habitual and usually involuntary response or behaviour. [from French *tic*]

tick[1] — *noun* **1** a usually soft regular tapping or clicking sound, such as that made by a watch or clock. **2** *Brit. colloq.* a moment. **3** a small mark, usually a line with an acute angle at the bottom, used to show that something is correct, to mark off items on a list which have been dealt with, etc. — *verb* **1** *intrans. said of a clock* to make a sound like a tick. **2** (*usually* **tick away**) *said of time* to pass steadily. **3** to mark with a written tick. **4** (*also* **tick something off**) to count something (eg an item on a list) by marking a tick beside it. — **tick someone off** *colloq.* to scold them mildly. **tick over 1** to function or work quietly and smoothly at a relatively gentle or moderate rate. **2** *said of an engine* to idle. **what makes someone tick** *colloq.* their underlying character and motivation. [from Middle English *tek*, little touch]

■ *noun* **1** click, tap, stroke, tick-tock. **2** moment, instant, flash, *colloq.* jiffy, second, minute. **3** mark, *North Amer.* check. *verb* **1** click, tap, beat. **3, 4** mark, indicate, *North Amer.* check (off). **tick off** scold, chide, reprimand, rebuke, reproach, reprove, upbraid, tell off.
🄴 **tick off** praise, compliment.

tick[2] *noun* **1** any of several bloodsucking, spider-like insects living on the skin of some animals, eg dogs and cattle. **2** any of several bloodsucking flies living on the skins of eg sheep and birds. [from Anglo-Saxon *ticia*]

tick[3] *noun* **1** the strong cover of a mattress, pillow, or bolster. **2** (*also* **ticking**) the strong, coarse, usually striped, cotton fabric from which such covers are made. [from Greek *theke*, case]

tick[4] *noun Brit. colloq.* credit: *buy it on tick.* [a shortening of TICKET]

ticker *noun* **1** anything that ticks, eg a watch. **2** *colloq.* the heart.

ticker-tape *noun formerly* continuous paper tape with messages, especially up-to-date share prices, printed by a telegraph instrument.

ticket — *noun* **1** a printed piece of paper or card which shows that the holder has paid a fare (eg for travel on a bus or train) or for admission (eg to a theatre or cinema), or has the right to use certain services (eg a library). **2** an official notice issued to someone who has committed a motor offence, such as speeding or parking illegally. **3** a tag or label, especially one showing the price, size, etc of the item to which it is attached. **4** *North Amer.* a list of candidates put up for election by a particular political party. **5** the principles of a particular political party. **6** *slang* a certificate discharging a soldier from the army. **7** *slang* a licence or permit, especially one allowing the holder to work as a ship's master or pilot. **8** *colloq.* exactly what is required, proper, or best: *just the ticket.* — *verb* (**ticketed, ticketing**) to give or attach a ticket or label to. [from Old French *estiquier*, to attach, stick]

■ *noun* **1** pass, card, certificate, token, voucher, coupon, docket, slip. **3** label, tag, sticker.

ticket of leave a pass issued to convicts in Australia as a reward for good behaviour; it was a form of parole which could be issued for four, six, or eight years, depending on whether the sentence was for seven years, fourteen years, or life. About 30 per cent of convicts received tickets of leave by 1840.

ticking-off *noun colloq.* a mild scolding.

■ scolding, telling-off, reprimand, rebuke, reproof, lecture, *colloq.* dressing-down, reproach.

tickle — *verb* **1** to touch (a person or part of the body) lightly and so as to provoke a tingling or light prickling sensation or laughter. **2** *intrans. said of a part of the body* to feel a tingling or light prickling sensation. **3** *colloq.* to amuse or entertain. **4** to catch (a fish, especially a trout) by rubbing it gently underneath so that it moves backwards into one's hands allowing one to put one's fingers into its gills. — *noun* **1** an act of tickling. **2** a tingling or light prickling sensation. — **tickled pink** or **to death** *colloq.* very pleased or amused. [from Middle English *tikelen*]

■ *verb* **3** excite, thrill, delight, please, gratify, amuse, entertain, divert.

ticklish *adj.* **1** sensitive to tickling. **2** *said of a problem, etc* difficult to manage or deal with; needing careful handling.

■ SENSITIVE. **2** delicate, touchy, thorny, awkward, difficult, tricky, critical, risky, hazardous, *colloq.* dodgy.
🄴 **2** easy, simple.

ticklishness *noun* being ticklish.

tick-tack *noun* a system of communication based on hand signals, used eg by bookmakers at a racecourse to exchange information about the odds they are offering.

tidal /ˈtaɪdl/ *adj.* relating to or affected by tides.

tidally *adv.* **1** in a tidal way. **2** by the tide or tides.

tidal wave 1 a popular (but unscientific) name for a tsunami. **2** a loose term for an unusually large ocean wave.

tidbit *noun North Amer.* a titbit.

tiddler *noun Brit. colloq.* **1** a small fish, especially a stickleback or a minnow. **2** a small person or thing.

tiddly[1] *adj.* (**tiddlier, tiddliest**) *Brit. colloq.* slightly drunk.

tiddly[2] *noun Brit. colloq.* little.

tiddlywinks *sing. noun* a game in which players try to flick small flat plastic discs into a cup using larger discs.

tide *noun* **1** the twice daily rise and fall of the water level in the oceans and seas that is caused by the gravitational pull of the Sun and especially the Moon. Two fixed 'bulges' of water are pulled out on either side of the Earth, which moves through them as it rotates, giving high tides and low tides. *Spring tides* occur at full and new moon, while *neap tides* occur at quarter moon. **2** the level of the water, especially the sea, as affected by this: *high tide.* **3** a sudden or marked trend: *the tide of public opinion.* **4** (*in compounds*) a time or season, especially of some festival: *Whitsuntide.* — *verb* **1** (*intrans.*) to drift with or be carried on the tide. **2** (**tide someone over**) to help them deal with a problem, difficult situation, etc for a time. [from Anglo-Saxon *tid*]

■ *noun* **2** ebb, flow, stream, current, flux, movement. **3** course, direction, drift, trend, tendency. **tide over** help through, see through, keep going, help out.

tidemark *noun* **1** a mark showing the highest level that the tide has reached or usually reaches. **2** *Brit. colloq.* a mark left on a bath which shows how high it was filled. **3** *Brit. colloq.* a dirty mark on the skin which shows the limit of washing.

tideway *noun* a channel in which a tide runs, especially that part of a river which has a tide.

tidily *adv.* in a tidy way; so as to be tidy.

tidiness *noun* being tidy; a tidy state.

tidings *pl. noun* news. [from Anglo-Saxon *tidung*]

tidy — *adj.* (**tidier**, **tidiest**) **1** neat and in good order. **2** methodical. **3** *colloq.* large; considerable. — *verb* (**tidies**, **tidied**) (*also* **tidy something away** or **up**) to make it neat; to put things away or arrange them neatly. [from Middle English, *seasonable*]

▪▪▪▪▪▪▪▪▪▪▪▪▪▪▪▪▪▪▪▪▪

◘ *adj.* **1**, **2** neat, orderly, methodical, systematic, organized. **1** clean, spick-and-span, shipshape, smart, spruce, trim, well-kept, ordered, uncluttered. **3** large, substantial, sizable, considerable, good, generous, ample. *verb* neaten, straighten, order, arrange, clean, smarten, spruce up, groom.

◪ *adj.* **1**, **2** untidy, messy, disorganized. **3** small, insignificant.

▪▪▪▪▪▪▪▪▪▪▪▪▪▪▪▪▪▪▪▪▪

tie — *verb* (**tying**) **1** to fasten with a string, ribbon, rope, etc. **2** to make (string, ribbon, etc) into a bow or knot, or to make a bow or knot in. **3** (*intrans.*) to be fastened with a knot, string, ribbon, etc: *a dress that ties at the back.* **4** (*intrans.*) to have the same score or final position as another competitor or entrant (in a game, contest, etc). **5** (*also* **tie someone down**) to limit or restrict the way they lead their life: *be tied down by family responsibilities.* **6** *Mus.* **a** to mark (notes of the same pitch) with a curved line showing that they are to be played as a continuous sound rather than individually. **b** *Mus.* to play (notes of the same pitch) in this way. — *noun* **1** a narrow strip of material worn, especially by men, round the neck under a shirt collar and tied in a knot or bow at the front. **2** a strip of ribbon, rope, cord, chain, etc for binding and fastening. **3** something that limits or restricts one's freedom. **4** a link or bond: *ties of friendship.* **5** a match, competition, etc in which the result is an equal score for both sides; also, the score or result achieved. **6** *Brit.* a game or match to be played, especially in a knockout competition. **7** a rod or beam holding parts of a structure together. **8** *Mus.* a curved line above two or more notes of the same pitch showing that they are to be played as a continuous sound rather than individually. **9** *North Amer.* a sleeper. — **tie someone down** to bind them to a decision or commitment. **tie in with something** to be in or be brought into connection; to correspond or be made to correspond. **tie up to** to moor or dock. **tie someone up 1** to bind them securely. **2** to keep them busy. **3** to block or restrict their progress, movement, or operation. **tie something up 1** to attach and fasten it securely with string, especially to make into a parcel with string. **2** to invest money, funds, etc so that it cannot be used for other purposes. **3** *colloq.* to finish or finalize it. **tie up with something** to be in or be brought into connection; to correspond or be made to correspond. [from Anglo-Saxon *tiegan*]

▪▪▪▪▪▪▪▪▪▪▪▪▪▪▪▪▪▪▪▪▪

◘ *verb* **1**, **2** knot. **1**, **3** fasten, secure. **1** moor, tether, attach, join, connect, link, unite, rope, lash, strap, bind. **4** draw. **5** restrain, restrict, confine, limit, hamper, hinder. *noun* **2** knot, fastening, band, ribbon, tape. **3**, **4** obligation, commitment, duty. **3** restraint, restriction, limitation, hindrance. **4** connection, link, liaison, relationship, bond, affiliation. **5** draw, dead heat, stalemate, deadlock. **tie up** *someone* **1**, **3** restrain. **1** bind, rope, lash, truss. **2** occupy, engage, engross. **3** restrict, confine, limit, hamper, hinder, *something* **1** wrap up, moor, tether, attach, secure, rope, lash, bind, truss. **3** conclude, terminate, wind up, settle, *colloq.* wrap up.

▪▪▪▪▪▪▪▪▪▪▪▪▪▪▪▪▪▪▪▪▪

tie beam a horizontal beam connecting the lower ends of rafters so that they do not move apart.

tie-break or **tie-breaker** *noun* an extra game, series of games, or question that decides which of the competitors or teams is to win a match which has ended in a draw.

tied cottage *Brit.* a cottage on an employer's land which is rented out to employees.

tied house *Brit.* a public house which may only sell the beer of a particular brewery.

tie-dyed *adj.* treated with tie-dyeing.

tie-dyeing *noun* a technique of dyeing fabrics to produce patterns, in which parts of the fabric are tied tightly to stop them absorbing the dye.

tie-in *noun* **1** a connection or link. **2** something which is presented at the same time as something else, especially a book which is published to coincide with a film or television programme.

tie-pin or **tieclip** *noun* an ornamental clasp fixed to a tie to hold it in place.

tier /tɪə(r)/ — *noun* any series of levels placed one above the other, eg of seats in a theatre. — *verb* to place in tiers. [from Old French *tire*, sequence]

▪▪▪▪▪▪▪▪▪▪▪▪▪▪▪▪▪▪▪▪▪

◘ *noun* floor, storey, level, stage, stratum, layer, belt, zone, band, echelon, rank, row, line.

▪▪▪▪▪▪▪▪▪▪▪▪▪▪▪▪▪▪▪▪▪

tiercel /'tɪəsl/ see TERCEL.

tiff — *noun* a slight, petty quarrel. — *verb intrans.* to have a tiff; to squabble.

▪▪▪▪▪▪▪▪▪▪▪▪▪▪▪▪▪▪▪▪▪

◘ *noun* argument, quarrel, squabble, *colloq.* spat, set-to, difference, disagreement, contretemps. *verb* argue, quarrel, squabble, *colloq.* spat, bicker.

▪▪▪▪▪▪▪▪▪▪▪▪▪▪▪▪▪▪▪▪▪

tiffin /'tɪfɪn/ *noun old use* a light meal taken in the middle of the morning, especially by members of the British raj in India. [from obsolete *tiff*, to sip]

tig same as TAG².

tiger /'taɪgə(r)/ *noun* **1** a carnivorous cat (*Panthera tigris*), and the largest member of the cat family (Felidae), native to Asia, and having a fawn or reddish coat with black or brownish-black transverse stripes, and white underparts. **2** the male of this species. **3** a fierce, cruel person. **4** an economy, especially of a country in eastern Asia, that has the potential to perform extremely well. [from Greek *tigris*]

tigerish *adj.* like a tiger, especially fiery-tempered.

tiger lily a tall lily with black or purple-spotted orange or yellow flowers.

tiger moth any of several moths with long striped and spotted wings.

tight — *adj.* **1** fitting very or too closely. **2** stretched so as not to be loose; tense; taut. **3** fixed or held firmly in place: *a tight knot.* **4** (*usually in compounds*) made so as to not let air, water, etc pass in or out: *watertight.* **5** difficult or posing problems: *in a tight spot.* **6** strictly and carefully controlled: *keep a tight rein on one's emotions.* **7** *said of a contest or match* closely or evenly fought. **8** *said of a schedule, timetable, etc* not allowing much time. **9** *colloq.* mean; miserly. **10** *colloq.* drunk. **11** *said of money or some commodity* in short supply; difficult to obtain. — *adv.* tightly; soundly; completely. [from Norse *thettr*]

▪▪▪▪▪▪▪▪▪▪▪▪▪▪▪▪▪▪▪▪▪

◘ *adj.* **1** close-fitting, close, snug, compact, cramped, constricted. **2** taut, stretched, tense, rigid, stiff. **3** firm, fixed, fast, secure. **4** sealed, hermetic, -proof, impervious, airtight, watertight. **6** strict, severe, stringent, rigorous. **9** mean, stingy, miserly, niggardly, parsimonious, tight-fisted. **10** drunk, intoxicated, *colloq.* sloshed, *colloq.* sozzled, *colloq.* plastered, *coarse slang* pissed, tipsy, *Brit. colloq.* tiddly, *colloq.* merry, maudlin.

◪ *adj.* **1**, **2**, **3** loose. **2** slack. **4** open. **6** lax. **9** generous.

▪▪▪▪▪▪▪▪▪▪▪▪▪▪▪▪▪▪▪▪▪

tighten *verb trans., intrans.* (**tightened**, **tightening**) to make or become tight or tighter.

. . . .
🔲 tauten, tense, stiffen, narrow, close, constrict, squeeze.
🔲 loosen, relax.
. . . .

tight-fisted *adj.* mean and ungenerous with money.
. . . .
🔲 mean, stingy, miserly, *colloq.* mingy, niggardly, penny-pinching, sparing, parsimonious, *colloq.* tight, grasping.
🔲 generous, charitable.
. . . .

tight-knit *adj.* closely organized or united.

tight-lipped *adj.* with the lips firmly closed in determination to say or reveal nothing.

tightly *adv.* in a tight way; so as to be tight.

tightness *noun* being tight.

tightrope *noun* 1 a tightly-stretched rope or wire on which acrobats balance. 2 a difficult situation which requires careful, fair handling if a potential disaster is to be avoided.

tights *pl. noun* a close-fitting usually nylon or woollen garment covering the feet, legs, and body to the waist, worn by women, dancers, acrobats, etc.

tigress / 'taɪgrɪs/ *noun* 1 a female tiger. 2 a fierce or passionate woman.

tike /taɪk/ same as TYKE.

tikka / 'tɪkə/ *noun* in Indian cookery, meat that is marinated in yoghurt and spices and cooked in a clay oven. [from Hindi]

tilde / 'tɪldə, 'tɪldeɪ/ *noun* a mark [~] placed over an n in Spanish to show that it is pronounced *ny* and over *a* and *o* in Portuguese to show they are nasalized. [from Spanish]

tile — *noun* 1 a flat, thin slab of fired clay, or a similar one of cork or linoleum, used to cover roofs, floors, walls, etc. 2 a tube-shaped piece of clay used for building drains. 3 a small, flat, rectangular piece used in some games. — *verb* to cover with tiles. — **on the tiles** having a wild time socially, usually including a lot of drinking and dancing. [from Anglo-Saxon *tigele*, from Latin *tegula*]

tiler *noun* a maker or setter of tiles.

tiling *noun* 1 tiles as a group. 2 a tiled area. 3 the act of covering a surface with tiles.

till¹ — *prep.* up to the time of: *wait till tomorrow.* — *conj.* up to the time when: *go on till you reach the station.* See also UNTIL. [from Anglo-Saxon *til*]

till² *noun* a container or drawer in which money taken from customers is put, now usually part of a cash register. [from Middle English *tylle*, to draw]

till³ *verb* to prepare and cultivate (land) for growing of crops. [from Anglo-Saxon *tilian*, to aim at]
. . . .
🔲 cultivate, work, plough, dig, farm.
. . . .

tillable *adj., said of land* capable of being tilled; arable.

tillage *noun* 1 the preparing and cultivating of land for crops. 2 land which has been tilled.

tiller¹ *noun* the lever used to turn the rudder of a boat. [from Old French *telier*, weaver's beam]

tiller² *noun* 1 a sapling. 2 a shoot growing from the bottom of the original stalk. 3 a sucker. [from Anglo-Saxon *telgor*, twig]

tiller³ *noun* a person who tills the land.

tilt — *verb* 1 *trans., intrans.* to slope or cause to slope; to be or put in a slanting position. 2 *intrans.* (**tilt at someone** or **something**) to charge at or attack them. 3 *intrans.* to fight on horseback with a lance; to joust. 4 to point (a lance) or attack with (a lance) as if in a joust. 5 to forge (steel, etc) using a tilt-hammer. — *noun* 1 a slant; a sloping position or angle. 2 an act of tilting. 3 a joust. 4 a thrust, charge, or attack with a lance during a joust. 5 an attack, disagreement, or contest. — **at full tilt** at full speed or with full force. [from Anglo-Saxon *tealt*, tottering]

. . . .
🔲 *verb* 1 slope, incline, slant, list, tip, lean. *noun* 1 slope, incline, angle, inclination, slant, pitch, list.
. . . .

tilth / tɪlθ/ *noun Agric.* the physical condition of the soil surface after cultivation, eg after ploughing. It may be fine or coarse, depending on the size of the clods of soil. [from Anglo-Saxon]

tilt-hammer *noun* a heavy pivoted hammer lifted by a cam, used in forging.

timber / 'tɪmbə(r) — *noun* 1 wood, especially prepared for building or carpentry. 2 trees suitable for this; forest or woodland. 3 a wooden beam in the framework of especially a ship or house. — *interj.* used to warn that a tree has been cut and is going to fall. — *verb* (**timbered, timbering**) 1 to provide timber or beams for. 2 to cover in timber. [from Anglo-Saxon]
. . . .
🔲 *noun* 1, 2 wood. 2 trees, forest. 3 beam, lath, plank, board.
. . . .

timbered *adj.* 1 built completely or partly of wood. 2 *said of land* covered with trees; wooded.

timber line the line or level of high ground above which trees do not grow.

timbre / 'tmbrə, 'tambə(r), 'tɪmbə(r)/ *noun* the distinctive quality of the tone produced by a musical instrument or voice, as opposed to pitch and loudness. [from Old French, = bell]

timbrel / 'tɪmbrəl/ *noun* a small tambourine. [from Old French *timbre*, bell]

time — *noun* 1 the continuous passing and succession of minutes, days, years, etc. 2 a particular point in time expressed in hours and minutes, or days, months and years, and as can be read from a clock or watch or told by a calendar. 3 any system for reckoning or expressing time: *East European Time.* 4 (*also* **times**) a point or period which is marked by some event or some particular characteristic: *at the time of her marriage* / *Edwardian times.* 5 the period required or available for, suitable for, or spent doing some particular activity. 6 an unspecified interval or period: *stayed there for a time.* 7 one of a number or series of occasions or repeated actions: *been to Spain three times.* 8 (**times**) expressing multiplication: *three times two is six.* 9 a period or occasion, especially a personal one, characterized by some quality or experience: *a good time* / *hard times.* 10 a particular period being considered, especially the present. 11 *colloq.* a prison sentence: *do time.* 12 an apprenticeship. 13 the point at which something ends, eg a section of a game. 14 *Brit.* the time when a public house must close. 15 the moment at which childbirth or death is expected. 16 the hours and days that one spends at work. 17 a rate of pay for work: *double time.* 18 *Mus.* any of several different rhythms and speeds: *waltz time.* 19 *Mus.* the speed at which a piece of music is to be played. — *adj.* that can be set to function at a particular moment or during a particular period: *a time switch on a heating system.* — *verb* 1 to measure the time taken by (an event, journey, etc). 2 to arrange, set, or choose the time for. 3 *trans., intrans.* to keep or beat, or cause to keep or beat, time (with). — **against time** with as much speed as possible because of the need or wish to finish by a certain time. **ahead of time** earlier than expected or necessary. **all in good time** in due course; soon enough. **all the time** continually. **at times** occasionally; sometimes. **behind time** late. **behind the times** out-of-date; old-fashioned. **for the time being** meanwhile; for the moment. **from time to time** occasionally; sometimes. **have no time for someone** or **something** to have no interest in or patience with them; to despise them. **have the time of one's life** to enjoy oneself very much. **in good time** early. **in no time** very quickly. **in one's own time** 1 in one's spare time when not at work. 2 at the speed one prefers. **in time** early enough. **in time with someone** or **something** at the same speed or rhythm as them. **kill time** to pass time aimlessly while waiting on events. **make good time** to travel as quickly as, or more quickly than, one had expected or hoped. **no time at all** *colloq.* a very short time. **on time** at the right time; not late. **pass the time of day** to exchange greetings and have a brief, casual conversation. **take one's time** not to hurry; to work as slowly as one wishes. **time and time again** again and again; repeatedly. **time out of mind** for longer than anyone can remember. [from Anglo-Saxon *tima*]

▱ *noun* **2**, **4** date, day, hour. **4**, **5**, **6** period. **4** moment, point, juncture, instance, occasion, stage, age, era, epoch, heyday, peak. **5** season, session, span, duration, interval. **6** spell, stretch, term, space, while. **10** age, era, epoch, life, lifetime, generation. **18** tempo, beat, rhythm, metre, measure. *verb* **1** measure, clock, meter. **2** regulate, control, set, schedule, timetable.

time-and-motion study a study of the way work is done in a factory, company, etc with a view to increasing efficiency.

time bomb a bomb that has been set to explode at a particular time.

time capsule a box containing objects chosen as typical of the current age, buried or otherwise preserved for discovery in the future.

time clock an apparatus with a clock which stamps on cards the time of arrival and departure of eg factory workers.

time code a series of digitally coded signals appearing sequentially (as hours, minutes, and seconds) on a magnetic tape of a video or audio recording, and sometimes on film, to provide specific identification and location of each frame, etc, in editing and postproduction.

time exposure a photograph taken by exposing the film to the light for a relatively long period of time, usually a few seconds.

time-honoured *adj.* respected and upheld because of being a custom or tradition.

timekeeper *noun* **1** a person who records the time, eg that worked by employees or taken by a competitor in a game. **2** a clock or watch, especially thought of in terms of its accuracy: *a good timekeeper*. **3** an employee thought of in terms of punctuality.

timekeeping *noun* **1** beating, marking, or observing time. **2** punctuality.

time lag the interval or delay between connected events or phenomena.

time-lapse photography a series of photographs taken of a subject at regular intervals and from the same viewpoint, to record some process or development, such as plant growth, cloud formation, metallic corrosion, or traffic flow. When filmed as successive single frames, subsequent projection at normal speed provides a rapid presentation of changes which are slow or gradual in real time.

timeless *adj.* **1** not belonging to or typical of any particular time or date. **2** unaffected by time.

▱ **2** ageless, immortal, everlasting, eternal, endless, permanent, changeless, unchanging.

timelessly *adv.* **1** in a timeless way. **2** with no reference to time.

timelessness *noun* being timeless.

time limit a fixed length of time during which something must be done and finished.

timeliness *noun* being timely; punctual, opportune.

timely *adj.* coming at the right or a suitable moment.

▱ well-timed, seasonable, suitable, appropriate, convenient, opportune, propitious, prompt, punctual.
▰ ill-timed, unsuitable, inappropriate.

time out *North Amer.* a brief pause or period of rest, especially in a game. — **take time out from something** to take a break from some activity, eg work.

▱ break, pause, rest, interval, interlude, intermission.

timepiece *noun* an instrument for keeping time, especially one which is larger than a watch but which does not chime.

timer *noun* **1** a device like a clock which switches an appliance on or off at pre-set times. **2** a person or instrument that records the time taken by someone or something.

time-served *adj.* having completed an apprenticeship; fully trained.

timeserver *noun* a person who changes his or her behaviour or opinions to fit those held by people in general or by someone in authority.

time-sharing *noun* **1** a scheme whereby a person buys the right to use a holiday home for the same specified period within the year for an agreed number of years. **2** a system which allows many users with individual terminals to use a single computer at the same time.

time sheet a record of the time worked by a person on a daily, weekly, or monthly basis, and often used as a basis for calculating pay.

time signal a signal, especially broadcast on the radio, which gives the exact time.

time signature *Mus.* a sign consisting of two numbers one above the other (the lower one indicating the value of the note used as the basic beat and the upper one the number of these to the bar), placed after the key signature at the beginning of a piece of music to show the rhythm it is to be played in, or in the middle of a piece where the rhythm changes.

timetable — *noun* **1** a list of the departure and arrival times of trains, coaches, buses, etc. **2** a plan showing the order of events, especially of classes in a school. — *verb* to arrange or include in a timetable; to schedule or plan.

▱ *noun* SCHEDULE. **2** programme, agenda, calendar, diary, rota, roster, list, listing, curriculum. *verb* schedule, plan, list, roster, programme, organize, arrange.

time warp in science fiction, etc, a hypothetical distortion in the time continuum, allowing one to pass from the present to the past or the future, or to stand still in the present.

timeworn *adj.* worn through long use; old.

time zone any one of the 24 more or less parallel sections into which the world is divided longitudinally, all places within a given zone generally being at the same standard time.

timid *adj.* easily frightened or alarmed; nervous; shy. [from Latin *timidus*]

▱ shy, bashful, modest, shrinking, retiring, nervous, apprehensive, afraid, timorous, fearful, cowardly, faint-hearted, spineless, irresolute.
▰ brave, bold, audacious.

timidity *noun* a timid state; nervousness, shyness.

timidly *adv.* in a timid way.

timing *noun* the regulating and co-ordinating of actions and events to achieve the best possible effect, especially the regulating of the speed of dialogue, action, and interaction between characters in a play, film, etc.

timorous /ˈtɪmərəs/ *adj.* very timid; frightened. [from Latin *timere*, to fear]

timorously *adv.* timidly.

timorousness *noun* a timid quality or state.

timothy grass /ˈtɪməθɪ/ *Bot.* a perennial grass (*Phleum pratense*) used for fodder and pasture. [named after Timothy Hanson, who promoted its cultivation in America in the early 18c]

timpani or **tympani** /'tɪmpənɪ/ *pl. noun* a set of two or three kettledrums. [from Italian]

timpanist or **tympanist** *noun* a person who plays the timpani.

tin — *noun* **1** *Chem.* (SYMBOL **Sn**, ATOMIC NUMBER **50**) a soft silvery-white metal that exists as three different allotropes, and is obtained from ores such as cassiterite (tinstone). It is used as a thin protective coating for steel, eg in 'tin' cans, and as a component of various alloys, eg bronze, pewter, solder. Tin compounds are used in dyeing, and as fungicides and catalysts. **2** an airtight metal container, often composed of steel coated with a thin layer of tin, used for storing food. **3** any of several containers of different shapes and sizes made usually of tin or aluminium and in which food is cooked. **4** the amount a tin will hold. **5** a strip of tin along the bottom of the front wall of a squash court. **6** *Brit. slang* money. — *adj.* made of tin. — *verb* (**tinned, tinning**) **1** to pack (food) in tins; to can. **2** to cover or coat with tin. [from Anglo-Saxon]

tincture /'tɪŋktʃə(r)/ — *noun* **1** a slight flavour, trace, or addition. **2** a slight trace of colour; hue; tinge. **3** a solution of a drug in alcohol for medicinal use. — *verb* to give a trace of a colour, flavour, etc to. [from Latin *tinctura*, dyeing]

tinder /'tɪndə(r)/ *noun* dry material, especially wood, which is easily set alight and can be used as kindling. [from Anglo-Saxon *tynder*]

tinder-box *noun* **1** *Hist.* a box containing tinder, a flint and steel for striking a spark to light a fire. **2** a volatile and potentially dangerous situation.

tine *noun* a slender prong or tooth, eg of a comb, fork, or antler. [from Anglo-Saxon *tind*]

tinea /'tɪnɪə/ *noun Medicine* any of a group of common fungal infections of the skin, and sometimes the nails, eg athlete's foot, which affects the skin between the toes. [from Latin *tinea*, moth, bookworm, etc]

tinfoil *noun* tin, aluminium or other metal in the form of very thin, paper-like sheets, used especially for wrapping food.

tinful *noun* (PL. **tinfuls**) the amount a tin will hold.

ting *noun* a high, metallic tinkling sound such as that made by a small bell. [imitative]

ting-a-ling *noun* a ringing or tinkling.

tinge /tɪndʒ/ — *noun* **1** a trace or slight amount of colour. **2** a trace or hint of (eg a quality or feeling). — *verb* **1** to give a slight colour to. **2** to give a trace or hint of a feeling, quality, etc to. [from Latin *tingere*]

> 🞐 *noun* TOUCH, TRACE, SUGGESTION, HINT. **1** tint, dye, colour, shade. **2** smack, flavour, pinch, drop, dash, bit, sprinkling, smattering. *verb* **1** tint, dye, stain, colour, shade. **2** suffuse, imbue.

tingle — *verb trans., intrans.* to feel or cause to feel a prickling or slightly stinging sensation, as with cold or embarrassment. — *noun* a prickling or slightly stinging sensation. [from Middle English *tinglen*, a variant of *tinklen*, to tinkle]

> 🞐 *verb* sting, prickle, tickle, itch, thrill, quiver, vibrate. *noun* stinging, prickling, pins and needles, tickle, tickling, itch, itching, thrill, throb, quiver, shiver, goose pimples.

tingling or **tingly** *adj.* that tingles.

tin god *noun* **1** a self-important pompous person. **2** a person or thing held in excessively or unjustifiably high esteem.

tin hat *slang* a military steel helmet.

tininess *noun* a tiny size.

tinker — *noun* **1** a travelling mender of pots, pans, and other household utensils. **2** *Scot., Irish* a Gypsy. **3** *colloq.* a mischievous or impish person, especially a child. — *verb intrans.* (**tinkered, tinkering**) **1** (*often* **tinker about** or **around**) to work in an unskilled way, meddle or fiddle

with machinery, etc, especially to try to improve it. **2** to work as a tinker. [from Middle English *tinkere*, worker in tin]

> 🞐 *verb* **1** fiddle, play, toy, trifle, potter, dabble, meddle, tamper.

tinkle — *verb* **1** *trans., intrans.* to make or cause to make a sound of or like the ringing or jingling of small bells. **2** *intrans. colloq.* to urinate. — *noun* **1** a ringing or jingling sound. **2** *colloq.* a telephone call. **3** *colloq.* an act of urinating. [from Middle English *tinken*, to click or tink]

> 🞐 *verb* **1** ring, jingle, jangle, clink, chink, chime. *noun* **1** ring, jingle, jangle, clink, chink, chime.

tinkly *adj.* (**tinklier, tinkliest**) tinkling.

tinned *adj.* **1** coated or plated with tin. **2** preserved in tins, canned.

tinnily *adv.* with a tinny sound.

tinniness *noun* a tinny quality.

tinnitus /tɪ'naɪtəs, 'tɪnɪtəs/ *noun Medicine* any noise (ringing, buzzing, whistling, etc) in the ears that is not caused by external sounds. It is frequently associated with deafness due to ageing or continuous exposure to loud noise, but may also be caused by ear infections or disease, high blood pressure, or drugs such as aspirin or quinine. [from Latin *tinnire* to ring]

tinny *adj.* (**tinnier, tinniest**) **1** of or like tin, especially in appearance or taste. **2** not solid and durable; flimsy; shoddy. **3** *said of sound* thin and high-pitched.

tin-opener *noun* any of several tools for opening tins of food.

tin plate thin sheet iron or steel coated with tin.

tinpot *adj. Brit. colloq.* cheap; of poor quality.

tinsel /'tɪnsl/ — *noun* **1** a long strip of glittering coloured metal or plastic threads used as a decoration especially at Christmas. **2** anything which is cheap and showy. — *adj.* of or like tinsel, especially in being cheap and showy. [from Old French *estincele*, spark]

tinselly *adj.* **1** like or full of tinsel. **2** gaudy.

tinsmith *noun* a worker in tin and tin plate.

tint — *noun* **1** a variety or (usually slightly) different shade of a colour. **2** a variety of a colour, especially one made softer by adding white. **3** a pale or faint colour used as a background for printing. **4** shading produced by engraving parallel lines close together. **5** a hair dye. — *verb* to give a tint to; to colour slightly. [from Latin *tingere*, to colour]

> 🞐 *noun* **1** colour, hue, shade, tincture, tinge, tone, cast, streak. **5** dye, stain, rinse, wash. *verb* dye, colour, tinge, streak, stain, taint, affect.

tintinnabulation /tɪntɪnabju'leɪʃən/ *noun* a ringing of bells. [from Latin *tintinnabulum*, bell]

tiny /'taɪnɪ/ *adj.* (**tinier, tiniest**) very small. [from Middle English *tine*]

> 🞐 minute, microscopic, infinitesimal, *colloq.* teeny, small, little, slight, negligible, insignificant, diminutive, petite, dwarfish, *humorous* pint-size, pocket, miniature, *colloq.* mini.
> 🞐 huge, enormous, immense.

tip¹ — *noun* **1** the usually small pointed end of something. **2** a small piece forming an end or point: *a rubber tip on a walking-stick.* **3** a tea leaf-bud. — *verb* (**tipped, tipping**) **1** to put or form a tip on. **2** (**tip in**) to attach (a loose sheet) into a book. **3** to remove a tip from. — **on the tip of one's tongue** about to be or almost said, but not able to be because not quite remembered. [from Middle English]

> 🞐 *noun* **1** end, extremity, point, nib, apex, peak, pinnacle,

summit, acme, top, cap, crown, head. *verb* **1** cap, crown, top, surmount.

. . . .

tip² — *verb* (**tipped, tipping**) **1** *trans., intrans.* (*also* **tip up** or **tip something up**) to lean or cause to lean or slant. **2** (*also* **tip something out**) to remove or empty (something) from its container, surface, etc by overturning or upsetting that container or causing that surface to slant. **3** *Brit.* to dump (rubbish). — *noun* **1** a place for tipping rubbish, coal, etc. **2** *colloq.* a very untidy place. — **tip over** *trans., intrans.* to knock or fall over; to overturn. [from Middle English *typen*, to overturn]

. . . .

⊟ *verb* **1** lean, incline, slant, list, tilt, overbalance. **2, 3** dump. **2** spill, pour out, empty, unload. *noun* dump. **1** rubbish heap, refuse heap. **2** pigsty, *colloq.* hole. **tip over** overturn, upset, capsize, topple over.

. . . .

tip³ — *noun* **1** a gift of money given to a servant, waiter, taxi driver, etc in return for service done well. **2** a piece of useful information; a helpful hint or warning. **3** a piece of inside information which may lead to financial gain, such as the name of a horse likely to win a race, or a company whose shares are likely to become more valuable. — *verb* (**tipped, tipping**) to give a tip to. — **tip someone off** to give them a piece of useful or secret information. [perhaps from TIP⁴]

. . . .

⊟ *noun* **1** gratuity, gift, perquisite. **2, 3** tip-off, information, inside information. **2** clue, pointer, hint, suggestion, advice, warning, forecast. *verb* reward, remunerate. **tip off** advise, suggest, warn, caution, forewarn, inform, tell.

. . . .

tip⁴ — *noun* a light blow or tap. — *verb* (**tipped, tipping**) to hit or strike lightly. [from Middle English]

tip-off *noun* a piece of useful or secret information, or the disclosing of this.

tipped *adj.* having a tip.

tippet /'tɪpɪt/ *noun* **1** a shoulder-cape of fur or cloth. **2** a long band of cloth or fur worn as part of some official costumes, eg by the clergy over the surplice during morning and evening prayers. [from TIP¹]

Tipp-Ex or **Tippex** /'tɪpeks/ *noun* trademark a correction fluid, usually opaque white, for covering over mistakes in typing or writing.

tipple *colloq.* — *verb trans., intrans.* to drink alcohol regularly in relatively small amounts. — *noun* a person's favourite alcoholic drink.

tippler *noun* a habitual drinker of alcohol.

tipsily *adv.* in a tipsy way.

tipsiness *noun* being tipsy.

tipstaff /'tɪpstɑːf/ *noun* (PL. **tipstaffs, tipstaves**) **1** a metal-tipped staff which is a symbol of office. **2** a sheriff's officer. [from TIP¹ + STAFF]

tipster *noun* a person who gives tips, especially as to which horses to bet on.

tipsy *adj.* (**tipsier, tipsiest**) *colloq.* slightly drunk. [from TIP²]

. . . .

⊟ *colloq.* squiffy, *Brit. colloq.* tiddly, *colloq.* merry, maudlin, drunk, intoxicated, *colloq.* tight, *colloq.* sloshed, *colloq.* sozzled, *colloq.* plastered, *coarse slang* pissed.

. . . .

tiptoe — *verb intrans.* to walk quietly or stealthily on the tips of the toes. — *noun* the tips of the toes. — *adv.* on the tips of the toes.

tiptop *colloq.* — *adj., adv.* excellent; first-class. — *noun* the very best; the height of excellence.

TIR *abbrev. Transports Internationaux Routiers* (French), International Road Transport, a continental haulage organization.

tirade /taɪə'reɪd, tɪ'reɪd/ *noun* a long angry speech or denunciation. [from French]

. . . .

⊟ harangue, philippic, diatribe, denunciation, onslaught, speech.

. . . .

tiramisu /tɪrəmə'zuː/ *noun* a dessert made with pieces of sponge soaked in coffee and marsala, layered with mascarpone and chocolate. [from Italian *tira mi sù*, = pick me up]

tire¹ *verb* **1** to make physically or mentally weary and in need of rest. **2** *intrans.* to become physically or mentally weary. **3** (**tire of something**) to become bored or impatient with it. [from Anglo-Saxon *teorian*]

. . . .

⊟ **1** weary, fatigue, wear out, exhaust, drain, enervate. **2** slow down, droop, flag, falter, fade. **3** weary of, *colloq.* get fed up with, lose patience with, have had enough of, lose interest in.
⊟ᴲ **1** enliven, invigorate, refresh.

. . . .

tire² *North Amer.* same as TYRE.

tired *adj.* **1** wearied; exhausted. **2** (**tired of something** or **someone**) no longer interested in them; bored with them. **3** lacking freshness and showing the effects of time and wear, especially in being limp and grubby or hackneyed.

. . . .

⊟ **1** weary, drowsy, sleepy, flagging, fatigued, worn out, exhausted, *colloq.* dog-tired, drained, jaded, fagged, *colloq.* bushed, whacked, *colloq.* shattered, *colloq.* beat, *colloq.* dead beat, *colloq.* all in, *colloq.* knackered. **2** *colloq.* fed up with, bored with, sick of. **3** old, stale, past its sell-by date, musty, fusty, worn out, hackneyed, trite.
⊟ᴲ **1** lively, energetic, rested, refreshed. **3** new.

. . . .

tiredly *adv.* in a tired way.

tiredness *noun* being tired, weariness.

tireless *adj.* never becoming weary or exhausted.

. . . .

⊟ untiring, unwearied, unflagging, indefatigable, energetic, vigorous, diligent, industrious, resolute, determined.
⊟ᴲ tired, lazy.

. . . .

tirelessly *adv.* in a tireless way.

tirelessness *noun* being tireless.

tiresome *adj.* troublesome and irritating; annoying; tedious.

. . . .

⊟ troublesome, trying, annoying, irritating, exasperating, wearisome, dull, boring, tedious, monotonous, uninteresting, tiring, fatiguing, laborious.
⊟ᴲ interesting, stimulating, easy.

. . . .

tiresomely *adv.* in a tiresome way.

tiresomeness *noun* being tiresome.

tiring *adj.* that tires.

. . . .

⊟ wearying, fatiguing, exhausting, draining, demanding, exacting, taxing, arduous, strenuous, laborious.

. . . .

tiro or **tyro** /'taɪrəʊ/ *noun* (PL. **tiros, tyros**) a beginner or novice. [from Latin, = recruit]

'tis *contr. old use + poetic* it is.

tissue /'tɪʃuː, 'tɪsjuː/ *noun* **1** a group of cells with a similar structure and particular function in an animal or plant: *muscle tissue*. **2** a piece of thin soft disposable paper used as a handkerchief or as toilet paper. **3** (*in full* **tissue paper**) fine thin soft paper, used eg for protecting fragile objects. **4** fine thin delicate woven fabric. **5** an interwoven mass or collection: *a tissue of lies*. [from Old French *tissu*, woven cloth]

. . . .

⊟ **1** substance, matter, material. **4** fabric, stuff, gauze. **5** web, mesh, network, structure, texture.

. . . .

tissue culture *Biol.* the growth of isolated plant or animal cells, tissues, or organs under controlled conditions in a sterile growth medium. Important applications include the large-scale propagation of plants, development of disease-free plants, and the production of drugs from plant tissues. Tissue culture is also used for medical research on the behaviour of cancer cells, and the growth of human skin cultures to provide tissue grafts for patients with burns.

tit¹ *noun* any of several small agile songbirds. [from Middle English *tite*]

tit² — **tit for tat** blow for blow; repayment of injury with injury.

tit³ *noun* **1** *slang* a teat. **2** *coarse slang* a woman's breast. [from Anglo-Saxon *titt*]

Titan /'taɪtn/ *noun* **1** in Greek mythology, any of the 12 children of Uranus and Gaea, members of the older generation of Gods. **2** *Astron.* Saturn's largest natural satellite, the second-largest moon in the solar system.

titan /'taɪtn/ *noun* a person or thing of very great strength, size, intellect, or importance.

titanic /taɪ'tanɪk/ *adj.* having great strength or size; colossal; gigantic.

titanium /tɪ'teɪnɪəm, taɪ'teɪnɪəm/ *noun Chem.* (SYMBOL **Ti**, ATOMIC NUMBER 22) a silvery-white metal that is used to make strong, light, corrosion-resistant alloys for components of aircraft, missiles, etc. Its oxide is used as a dielectric in capacitors, and as a white pigment (titanium white). [from TITAN]

titbit *noun* a choice or small tasty morsel eg of food or gossip. [from TIDE 4 + BIT¹]

. . . .
◰ morsel, scrap, appetizer, snack, delicacy, dainty, treat.
. . . .

titfer /'tɪtfə(r)/ *noun slang* a hat. [shortened from rhyming slang *tit for tat* (see TIT²)]

tithable /'taɪðəbl/ *adj.* subject to the payment of tithes.

tithe /taɪð/ — *noun* **1** (*often* **tithes**) *Hist.* a tenth part of a person's annual income or produce, paid as a tax to support the church or clergy in a parish. **2** a tenth part. — *verb* **1** to demand a tithe or tithes from. **2** *intrans.* to pay a tithe or tithes. [from Anglo-Saxon *teotha*, tithe, tenth]

Titian /'tɪʃən/ — *noun* a bright reddish-gold colour. — *adj.* of this colour. [named after the painter TITIAN]

titillate /'tɪtɪleɪt/ *verb* **1** to excite gently, especially in a sexual way. **2** to tickle. [from Latin *titillare*]

. . . .
◰ TICKLE. **1** stimulate, arouse, *colloq.* turn on, excite, thrill, provoke, tease, tantalize, intrigue, interest.
. . . .

titillating *adj.* that titillates.

titillation /tɪtɪ'leɪʃən/ *noun* **1** titillating or being titillated. **2** something that titillates.

titivate /'tɪtɪveɪt/ *verb trans., intrans. colloq.* to smarten up or put the finishing touches (to). [earlier *tidivate*, from TIDY + *vate* from words such as *elevate* and *cultivate*]

titivation /tɪtɪ'veɪʃən/ *noun* titivating.

title /'taɪtl/ — *noun* **1** the distinguishing name of a book, play, work of art, piece of music, etc. **2** an often descriptive heading, eg of a chapter in a book or a legal document. **3** a word of address used before a person's name to show acquired or inherited rank, an honour, occupation, or attainment. **4** a title page. **5** (*often* **titles**) written material on film giving credits, dialogue, etc. **6** *Legal* a right to the possession or ownership of property. **7** *Sport* a championship. **8** a book or publication. **9** a book or publication as distinct from a copy and as listed in a catalogue. — *verb* to give a title to. [from Latin *titulus*]

. . . .
◰ *noun* **1, 2, 3** name, appellation. **2** heading, headline, caption, legend, inscription. **3** style, designation, label, epithet, nickname, pseudonym, rank, status, office, position. **6** right, claim, entitlement, ownership, deeds,

prerogative, privilege. *verb* entitle, name, call, dub, style, term, designate, label.
. . . .

titled *adj.* having a title, especially one that shows noble rank.

title deed a document proving legal ownership.

title page the page at the beginning of a book which gives the name and address of the publisher, the title, author, and cataloguing information, etc.

title role the role of the character in a play or film from which that play or film takes its name, eg *King Lear*.

titmouse /'tɪtmaʊs/ *noun* (PL. **titmice**) same as TIT¹. [from Middle English *titemose*]

titrate /taɪ'treɪt, 'taɪtreɪt/ *verb Chem.* to determine the concentration of a chemical substance in a solution by the process of titration. [from French *titre*, title, qualification]

titration /taɪ'treɪʃən/ *noun Chem.* a method of *volumetric analysis* (a form of chemical analysis) in which the concentration of a particular solution is determined by adding measured amounts of another solution of known concentration until the end-point is reached, as indicated by a colour change or precipitation.

titre /'taɪtə(r), 'tiːtə(r)/ *noun* **1** *Chem.* the concentration of a solution as determined by titration with a standard solution of known concentration. **2** *Biol.* the concentration of a particular virus present in a suspension. **3** the concentration of an antibody present in a sample of serum.

titter *colloq.* — *verb intrans.* (**tittered**, **tittering**) to giggle or snigger. — *noun* a giggle or snigger.

. . . .
◰ *verb, noun* laugh, chortle, chuckle, giggle, snigger, snicker.
. . . .

tittle *noun* **1** a small written or printed sign, mark, or dot. **2** a very small particle. [from Latin *titulus*, title]

. . . .
◰ **2** bit, jot, iota, trace, speck, grain, hint, mite.
. . . .

tittle-tattle — *noun* idle or petty gossip or chatter. — *verb intrans.* to gossip or chatter idly.

. . . .
◰ *noun* gossip, chitchat, chatter, rumour, scandal, hearsay. *verb* gossip, chatter, tattle, *colloq.* natter, tell tales.
. . . .

titty *noun* (PL. **titties**) a child's word for TIT³.

titular /'tɪtjʊlə(r)/ *adj.* **1** having the title of an office or position but none of the authority or duties. **2** being or having a title. [from Latin *titulus*, title]

. . . .
◰ **1** honorary, formal, official, so-called, nominal, token.
. . . .

titularly *adv.* **1** in respect of name, style, or title. **2** in name only.

tizzy or **tizz** *noun* (PL. **tizzies**) *colloq.* a nervous, highly excited, or confused state.

T-junction *noun* a junction at which one road meets another at a right angle but does not cross it.

Tl *symbol Chem.* thallium.

TLA *abbrev. Comput.* three letter acronym.

TLC *abbrev. facetious* tender loving care.

Tm *symbol Chem.* thulium.

TN *abbrev.* Tennessee.

TNT *abbrev.* trinitrotoluene.

to — *prep.* **1** towards; in the direction of; with the destination of. **2** used to express a resulting condition, aim, or purpose: *turn to stone* / *boil the fruit to a pulp* / *made to order* / *to my surprise*. **3** as far as; until: *a lie from beginning to end* / *five miles from the house to the station* / *bear the scars of the attack to this day*. **4** used to introduce the indirect object of a verb: *he sent it to us*. **5** used to express addition: *add one to ten*. **6** used to express attachment, connection, contact, or possession: *put his ear to the door* / *the key to the* *lock*. **7** before the hour of: *ten minutes to three*. **8** used to express response or reaction to a situation, event, etc: *rise to the occasion / dance to the music*. **9** used to express comparison or proportion: *win by two goals to one / second to none*. **10** used before an infinitive or instead of a complete infinitive: *he asked her to stay but she didn't want to*. — *adv*. **1** in or into a nearly closed position: *pulled the window to*. **2** back into consciousness: *he came to a few minutes later*. **3** near at hand. **4** in the direction required. — **to and fro** backwards and forwards. **toing and froing** movement backwards and forwards in an agitated way. [from Anglo-Saxon]

toad *noun* **1** a tailless amphibian belonging to the family Bufonidae of the order Anura (which also includes frogs), and having a short squat head and body, and dry skin covered with warts that contain poison glands which help to deter predators. **2** an obnoxious or repellent person. [from Anglo-Saxon *tade*]

toadflax *noun* a plant with flax-like leaves and yellow flowers.

toad-in-the-hole *noun Brit*. sausages cooked in Yorkshire pudding batter.

toadstool *noun* any of various fungi, most of which are poisonous or inedible, that produce a fruiting body consisting of an umbrella-shaped cap, on the underside of which are numerous spore-bearing gills, supported by a stem. See also MUSHROOM.

toady — *noun* (PL. **toadies**) a person who flatters someone else, does everything he or she wants, and hangs on his or her every word; a sycophant. — *verb trans., intrans*. (**toady to someone**) to flatter them and behave obsequiously towards them.

. . . .

◼ *noun* flatterer, sycophant, *colloq*. crawler. *verb* flatter, *colloq*. suck up to, fawn on, curry favour with, dance attendance on, pay court to, *colloq*. butter up.

. . . .

toadyish *adj*. characteristic of a toady.

toadyism *noun* the activities and behaviour of a toady.

toast — *verb* **1** to make (especially bread) brown by exposing it to direct heat, eg under a grill. **2** *intrans*. said especially of bread to become brown in this way. **3** *trans., intrans*. to make or become warm by being exposed to heat, eg a fire. **4** to drink ceremonially in honour of or to the health or future success of. — *noun* **1** bread which has been browned by being exposed to direct heat, eg under a grill. **2** an act of drinking to a person's honour, health, or future success. **3** a person whose honour, health, or future success is drunk to. **4** a very admired person or thing: *her singing is the toast of the festival*. **5** the wish conveyed when drinking to someone's honour, etc. [from Latin *tostus*, roasted; sense 4 of the verb and senses 2, 3, 4, and 5 of the noun reflect the idea that a woman's name (ie as the person whose health is being drunk to) would flavour the wine like spiced toast]

. . . .

◼ *verb* **1** grill, brown, roast, heat, warm. **4** drink to, honour, salute, pledge. *noun* **2** drink, pledge, tribute, salute, compliment, health.

. . . .

toasted *adj*. cooked or heated by toasting.

toaster *noun* an electric machine for toasting bread.

toasting-fork *noun* a fork with a long handle, used to toast bread in front of a fire.

toastmaster or **toastmistress** *noun* a man or woman who announces the toasts to be drunk at a ceremonial dinner.

toast rack a small rack for holding slices of toast.

tobacco /tə'bakoʊ/ *noun* (PL. **tobaccos, tobaccoes**) **1** a fast-growing annual or shrubby perennial plant of the genus *Nicotiana*, belonging to the same family (Solanaceae) as the potato. It is thought to be native to tropical America, and has large leaves and tubular greenish, yellow, pink, or red flowers. The leaves of certain species, especially *N.*

tabacum, contain nicotine, a poisonous alkaloid compound that is an addictive stimulant. The plant requires a warm humid climate and a fertile well-drained soil. Much of the tobacco that is used in cigars is grown in the Caribbean. **2** the dried leaves of this plant, which are used to make cigarettes, cigars, pipe tobacco, and snuff. [from Spanish *tabaco*]

tobacconist *noun* a person or shop that sells tobacco, cigarettes, cigars, pipes, etc.

to-be *combining form* forming words meaning 'of the future, soon to become': *mother-to-be*.

toboggan /tə'bɒgən/ — *noun* a long, light sledge which curves up at the front, used for riding over snow and ice. — *verb intrans*. to ride on a toboggan. [from Native American *topagan*]

tobogganing *noun* the activity or sport of riding on a toboggan.

tobogganist or **tobogganer** *noun* a person who rides on a toboggan.

toccata /tɒ'kɑːtə/ *noun* a piece of music for a keyboard instrument intended to show off the performer's skill and touch in a series of runs and chords before breaking into a fugue. [from Italian, *toccare*, to touch]

tocopherol /tɒ'kɒfərɒl/ *noun* vitamin E. [from Greek *tokos*, offspring + *pherein*, to bear; so called from its apparent necessity for reproduction]

tocsin /'tɒksɪn/ *noun* an alarm bell or warning signal. [from French]

tod *noun* — **on one's tod** *Brit. colloq*. alone. [rhyming slang *on one's Tod Sloan*, on one's own]

today — *noun* **1** this day. **2** the present time. — *adv*. **1** on or during this day. **2** nowadays; at the present time. [from Anglo-Saxon *to dæg*]

toddle — *verb intrans*. **1** to walk with unsteady steps, as or like a young child. **2** *colloq*. to take a casual walk; to stroll or saunter. **3** (**toddle off**) *colloq*. to leave; to depart. — *noun* **1** a toddling walk. **2** *colloq*. a casual walk or stroll. [originally a dialect form; origin unknown]

toddler *noun* a very young child who is just beginning or has just learnt to walk.

toddy *noun* (PL. **toddies**) a drink made of spirits, sugar, hot water, lemon juice, and sometimes spices. [from Hindi *tari*, from *tar*, palm]

to-do /tə'duː/ *noun* (PL. **to-dos**) *colloq*. a fuss, commotion, or bustle.

toe — *noun* **1** in humans, any of the five digits at the end of each foot, whose main function is to assist balance and walking. **2** the front part of a shoe, sock, etc covering the toes. **3** in other animals, the digit corresponding to the human toe. **4** the lower, often projecting end of eg a tool or area of land. — *verb* **1** to kick, strike, or touch with the toes. **2** to provide (eg a stocking, sock, or shoe) with a toe. — **on one's toes** alert and ready for action. **toe the line** *colloq*. to act according to the rules. **tread on someone's toes** to offend or upset them. **turn up one's toes** *colloq*. to die. [from Anglo-Saxon *ta*]

toe-cap *noun* a piece of metal or leather covering the toe of a boot or shoe.

toehold *noun* **1** a place to anchor one's toes, eg when climbing. **2** a small initial or beginning position.

toenail *noun* a nail covering a toe.

toerag *noun slang* a despicable or contemptible person.

toff *noun Brit. slang* an upper-class and usually smartly dressed person. [from *tuft*, a titled undergraduate]

toffee /'tɒfɪ/ *noun* a sticky sweet which is usually either chewy or hard, made from boiling sugar and butter, and sometimes nuts, etc.

toffee apple an apple covered with a thin layer of toffee on a stick.

toffee-nosed *adj. Brit. colloq*. conceited; stuck-up.

tofu /'toʊfuː/ *noun* a curd made from soya beans, with a creamy colour and bland flavour, used especially in Japanese cooking. [from Japanese, from Chinese *dou fu*, rotten beans]

tog[1] — *noun* (**togs**) clothes. — *verb trans., intrans.* (**togged, togging**) (**tog up** or **tog oneself up**) to dress in one's best or warmest clothes. [from Middle English, from Latin *toga*, *toga*]

tog[2] *noun* a unit for measuring the warmth of fabrics and clothes. [perhaps from TOG[1]]

toga /ˈtoʊɡə/ *noun Hist.* a loose outer garment worn draped round the body by a citizen of ancient Rome. [from Latin]

togaed /ˈtoʊɡəd/ *adj.* wearing a toga.

together — *adv.* **1** with someone or something else; in company: *travel together.* **2** at the same time: *all arrived together.* **3** so as to be in contact, joined, or united. **4** by action with one or more other people: *managed to persuade him together.* **5** in or into one place: *gather together.* **6** continuously: *chatting on the phone for hours together.* **7** *colloq.* into a proper or suitable order or state of being organized: *get things together.* — *adj. colloq.* well organized; competent. — **together with** ... in company with ...; in addition to ... [from Anglo-Saxon *to gæthere*]

. . . .

⊟ *adv.* **1, 4** collectively, en masse. **1** hand in hand, side by side, shoulder to shoulder, in a row. **2** simultaneously, at the same time, all at once. **4** jointly, in concert, in unison, in collaboration, as one. **6** continuously, consecutively, successively, in succession.
⊞ *adv.* **1, 4** separately, individually, alone.

. . . .

togetherness *noun* a feeling of closeness, mutual sympathy, and understanding, and of belonging together.

toggle — *noun* **1** a fastening, eg for garments, consisting of a small bar of wood, plastic, etc which will pass one way only through a loop of material, rope, etc. **2** a pin, bar, or crosspiece placed through a link in a chain, loop in a rope, etc to prevent the chain, rope, etc from slipping. **3** *Comput.* a keyboard command which turns a particular feature (eg bold type or read-only mode) alternately on or off. — *verb* **1** to provide or fasten with a toggle. **2** *Comput.* **a** (**toggle something on** or **off**) to turn a particular feature, eg bold type or read-only mode alternately on and off using the same keyboard command. **b** *intrans.* to move between different features, modes, files, etc using a keyboard command. [originally a nautical term; origin unknown]

toggle switch 1 *Electr.* a switch consisting of a projecting spring-loaded lever that can be moved to either of two positions, as a result of which an electric circuit is either opened or closed. **2** *Comput.* a key on a computer keyboard that operates in a similar manner, and is used to turn a particular feature, such as bold type, on or off.

toil[1] — *verb intrans.* **1** to work long and hard; to labour. **2** to make progress or move forwards with great difficulty or effort. — *noun* long, hard work. [from Old French *toiler*, to contend]

. . . .

⊟ *verb* labour, work, slave, drudge, *colloq.* sweat (blood), *colloq.* grind, *colloq.* slog, *colloq.* graft, *colloq.* plug away, persevere, strive, struggle. *noun* labour, hard work, donkeywork, drudgery, *colloq.* sweat, *colloq.* graft, industry, application, effort, exertion, *colloq.* elbow-grease.

. . . .

toil[2] *noun* (*usually* **toils**) a trap or snare. [from French *toile*, cloth, from Latin *tela*, web]

toilet /ˈtɔɪlət/ *noun* **1** a bowl-like receptacle for the body's waste matter, with a water supply for washing this into a drain. **2** a room containing such a receptacle. **3** (*also* **toilette**) the act of washing, dressing, and arranging one's hair. [from French *toilette*, cloth]

. . . .

⊟ **1, 2** lavatory, WC, *Brit. colloq.* loo, *Brit. slang* bog, *North Amer. slang* can, *North Amer. slang* john, urinal. **2** bathroom, cloakroom, washroom, rest room, public convenience, ladies, gents, convenience, powder room.

. . . .

toilet paper or **toilet tissue** thin absorbent paper used for cleaning the body after urination and defecation.

toilet roll a roll of toilet paper.

toiletry *noun* (PL. **toiletries**) an article or cosmetic used when washing, arranging the hair, and making up.

toilet water a light perfume containing a lot of alcohol.

toilsome *adj.* involving long, hard work.

toilworn *adj.* wearied by hard work.

Tokay /toʊˈkeɪ/ *noun* a sweet, heavy, aromatic wine made at *Tokay* in Hungary.

token /ˈtoʊkən/ — *noun* **1** a mark, sign, or distinctive feature. **2** anything serving as a reminder or souvenir; a keepsake. **3** a voucher worth a stated amount of money which can be exchanged for goods of the same value. **4** a small coin-like piece of metal or plastic which is used instead of money, eg in slot machines. — *adj.* done or given as a token and therefore of no real value. — **by the same token** also; in addition; for the same reason. [from Anglo-Saxon *tacen*]

. . . .

⊟ *noun* **1** symbol, emblem, representation, mark, sign, indication, manifestation, demonstration, expression, evidence, proof, clue. **2** reminder, warning, memorial, memento, souvenir, keepsake. **3** gift token, voucher, coupon. **4** counter, disc. *adj.* symbolic, emblematic, nominal, minimal, perfunctory, superficial, cosmetic, hollow, insincere.

. . . .

tokenism /ˈtoʊkənɪzm/ *noun* the principle or practice of doing very little of something in pretence that one is committed to it, eg of employing one black person to avoid charges of racism.

Tok Pisin /tɒk ˈpɪzɪn/ an English-based Melanesian pidgin spoken by about 1 million people in Papua New Guinea. Strongly influenced by native languages, it is now spoken by some as a mother tongue, and has thus become a creole.

tolbooth or **tollbooth** /ˈtoʊlbuːð, ˈtoʊlbuːθ, ˈtɒlbuːð, ˈtɒlbuːθ/ *noun* **1** an office where tolls are or were collected. **2** *old use Scot.* a town hall. **3** *Scot.* a prison.

told /toʊld/ SEE TELL.

tolerability *noun* being tolerable.

tolerable /ˈtɒlərəbl/ *adj.* **1** able to be borne or endured. **2** fairly good.

. . . .

⊟ **1** bearable, endurable, sufferable. **2** acceptable, passable, adequate, reasonable, fair, average, all right, *colloq.* OK, not bad, *colloq.* so-so, unexceptional, ordinary, run-of-the-mill.
⊞ **1** intolerable, unbearable, insufferable. **2** excellent.

. . . .

tolerably *adv.* in a tolerable way; to a tolerable degree.

tolerance *noun* **1** the ability to be fair towards and accepting of other people's religious, political, etc beliefs or opinions. **2** the ability to resist or endure pain or hardship. **3** *Medicine* the ability of a person to adapt to the effects of a drug, so that increased doses are required to produce the same effect. **4** *Biol.* lack of reactivity to a particular antigen that would normally cause an immune response. **5** *Biol.* the ability of a plant or animal to survive extreme environmental conditions, eg drought, low temperature. **6** the amount by which a measurement is permitted to vary from a standard or specification.

. . . .

⊟ **1, 2** toleration, patience. **1** open-mindedness, broad-mindedness, magnanimity, sympathy, understanding, forbearance, lenity, indulgence, permissiveness. **2** resistance, resilience, toughness, endurance, stamina. **6** variation, fluctuation, play, allowance, clearance.
⊞ **1** intolerance, prejudice, bigotry, narrowmindedness.

. . . .

tolerant *adj.* **1** tolerating the beliefs and opinions of others. **2** capable of enduring unfavourable conditions, etc. **3** indulgent, permissive. **4** able to take drugs without showing serious side effects.

⊟ **1** open-minded, fair, unprejudiced, broad-minded, liberal, charitable, kind-hearted, sympathetic, understanding, forgiving. **2** patient, forbearing, long-suffering. **3** lenient, indulgent, easy-going, permissive, lax, soft.

⊟ **1, 3** intolerant, unsympathetic. **1** biased, prejudiced, bigoted.

tolerate /'tɒləreɪt/ *verb* **1** to bear or endure (pain or hardship); to put up with. **2** to be able to resist the effects of (a drug). **3** to treat fairly and accept (a person with different religious, political, etc beliefs or opinions). **4** to allow to be done or exist. [from Latin *tolerare*]

⊟ **1** endure, suffer, put up with, bear, stand, abide, stomach, swallow, take. **3** receive, accept. **4** admit, allow, permit, condone, countenance, indulge.

toleration *noun* **1** the act of tolerating. **2** the practice of allowing people to practise religions which are different to the established religion of the country.

⊟ **1** tolerance, open-mindedness, broad-mindedness, magnanimity, sympathy, understanding, forbearance, patience, lenity, indulgence, permissiveness.

toll¹ /təʊl/ — *verb* **1** *trans., intrans.* to ring (a bell) with slow, measured strokes. **2** *said of a bell* to announce, signal, or summon by ringing with slow measured strokes. — *noun* the act or sound of tolling. [from Middle English *tollen*, to entice, lure]

⊟ *verb* RING, PEAL, CHIME, KNELL, SOUND, STRIKE. **2** announce, call.

toll² /təʊl/ *noun* **1** a fee or tax paid for the use of some bridges and roads. **2** the cost in damage, injury, or lives of some disaster. [from Anglo-Saxon *toll*]

⊟ **1** charge, fee, payment, levy, tax, duty, tariff, rate, penalty, demand. **2** loss, cost.

tollgate *noun* a gate or barrier across a road or bridge which is not lifted until travellers have paid the toll.

Toltec *noun* a member of a people (or peoples) dominant in most of central Mexico between c.900 and 1150, the last such culture prior to the Aztecs.

toluene /'tɒljuiːn/ *noun Chem.* (FORMULA **C₆H₅CH₃**) a toxic organic compound, consisting of a colourless flammable liquid, derived from benzene and insoluble in water, used as an industrial solvent and as an intermediate in the manufacture of the explosive trinitrotoluene (TNT), high-octane petrol, and various other organic chemicals.

tom *noun* a male of various animals, especially a male cat. [an abbreviation of the name *Thomas*]

tomahawk /'tɒməhɔːk/ *noun* a small axe used as a weapon by Native Americans. [from Algonkian (Native American language group) *tamahaac*]

tomato /tə'mɑːtoʊ/ *noun* (PL. **tomatoes**) **1** a round or oval fleshy, juicy fruit, usually red or yellow in colour, eaten as a vegetable eg in salads. **2** the plant bearing this fruit. [from Aztec *tomatl*]

tomb /tuːm/ *noun* **1** a chamber or vault for a dead body, either below or above ground, and often serving as a monument; a grave. **2** a hole cut in the earth or rock for a dead body. **3** (**the tomb**) *poetic* death. [from Greek *tymbos*]

⊟ **1** grave, burial-place, vault, crypt, sepulchre, catacomb, mausoleum, cenotaph.

tombola /tɒm'boʊlə/ *noun* a lottery in which winning tickets are drawn from a revolving drum. [from Italian *tombolare*, to tumble]

tomboy /'tɒmbɔɪ/ *noun* a girl who likes rough and adventurous games and activities.

tombstone *noun* an ornamental stone placed over a grave, on which the dead person's name, etc is engraved.

tomcat *noun* a male cat.

Tom, Dick and **Harry** anybody at all; people in general.

tome /toʊm/ *noun* a large, heavy, and usually learned book. [from Greek *tomos*, slice]

tomfool /tɒm'fuːl/ — *noun* an absolute fool. — *adj.* absolutely foolish. [from Middle English *Thome fole*, Tom the fool]

tomfoolery *noun* (PL. **tomfooleries**) stupid or foolish behaviour, or an instance of it; nonsense.

Tommy *noun* (PL. **Tommies**) *colloq.* a private in the British army. [from *Tommy* Atkins, the name used on specimens of official forms]

tommy-gun *noun* a type of submachine gun. [named after J T Thompson (1860–1940), its American inventor]

tommyrot *noun colloq.* absolute nonsense.

tomography /toʊ'mɒgrəfɪ/ *noun Medicine* a diagnostic scanning technique, especially one involving the use of X-rays or ultrasound, in which a clear image of internal structures in a single plane of a body tissue at a specified depth and angle is obtained. [from Greek *tomos*, cut + -GRAPHY]

tomorrow — *noun* **1** the day after today. **2** the future. — *adv.* **1** on the day after today. **2** in the future. [from Anglo-Saxon *tomorgen*]

tomtit *noun* a tit, especially a bluetit.

tom-tom /'tɒmtɒm/ *noun* a usually small-headed drum beaten with the hands. [from Hindi *tam-tam*, imitative]

-tomy /təmɪ/ *combining form* (PL. **-tomies**) *Medicine* forming words denoting removal by surgery: *episiotomy*. [from Greek *tome*, from *temnein*, to cut]

ton /tʌn/ *noun* **1** *Brit.* (*in full* **long ton**) a unit of weight equal to 2240lb (approximately 1016.05kg). **2** *North Amer.* (*in full* **short ton**) a unit of weight equal to 2000lb (approximately 907.2kg). **3** (*in full* **metric ton**; *also* **tonne**) a unit of weight equal to 1000kg (approximately 2204.6lb). **4** (*in full* **displacement ton**) a unit used to measure the amount of water a ship displaces, equal to 2240lb or 35 cubic feet of seawater. **5** (*in full* **register ton**) a unit (originally a *tun* of wine) used to measure a ship's internal capacity, equal to 100 cubic feet. **6** (*in full* **freight ton**) a unit for measuring the space taken up by cargo, equal to 40 cubic feet. **7** (*usually* **tons**) *colloq.* a lot. **8** *colloq.* a speed, score, sum, etc of 100. See also TONNAGE. [a variant of TUN]

tonal /'toʊnl/ *adj.* of or relating to tone or tonality.

tonality /toʊ'nalɪtɪ/ *noun* (PL. **tonalities**) **1** *Mus.* the organization of all of the notes and chords of a piece of music in relation to a single tonic. **2** the colour scheme and tones used in a painting.

tone — *noun* **1** a musical or vocal sound with reference to its quality and pitch. **2** *Mus.* a sound having a definite pitch. **3** a quality or character of the voice expressing a particular feeling, mood, etc. **4** the general character or style of spoken or written expression. **5** *Mus.* the interval between, or equivalent to that between, the first two notes of the major scale. **6** high quality, style, or character: *his coarse jokes lowered the tone of the meeting*. **7** the quality, tint, or shade of a colour. **8** the harmony or general effect of colours. **9** firmness of the body, a bodily organ or muscle. — *verb* **1** (*intrans.*) (**tone in**) to fit in well; to harmonize. **2** to give tone or the correct tone (to). **3** (*intrans.*) to take on a tone or quality. — **tone down** or **tone something down** to become or make it softer or less harsh in tone, colour, force, etc. **tone up** or **tone something up** to become or make it stronger, healthier, more forceful, etc. [from Greek *tonos*, tension]

⊟ *noun* **1, 2, 3** note. **3** timbre, pitch, volume, intonation, modulation, inflection, accent, stress, emphasis, force, strength. **4** mood, spirit, humour, temper, character, quality, feel, style, effect, vein, tenor, drift, air, manner, attitude. **7** tint, tinge, colour, hue, shade, cast, tonality. *verb* **1** match, co-ordinate, blend, harmonize. **tone down** moderate, temper, subdue, restrain, soften, dim, dampen, play down, reduce, alleviate, mitigate.

· ·

tone-deaf *adj.* unable to distinguish accurately between notes of different pitch.

tone-deafness *noun* being tone-deaf.

tone language a language in which differing pitch levels, or tones, are used to alter the meaning of a word, or to signal a grammatical feature such as a change of tense. In Mandarin Chinese, for example, the word *ma* can mean 'mother', 'horse', 'hemp', or 'scold', depending on the tone used.

toneless *adj.* without variation in sound, pitch, expression, etc.

tonelessly *adv.* in a toneless manner.

tone pad *Comput.* an electronic device similar to a remote control for a television, etc, which allows data to be input into a central computer from a distance, usually via a telephone link.

tone poem a piece of music not divided into movements and which is based on a story or literary or descriptive theme.

tong /tɒŋ/ *noun* a Chinese guild or secret society, especially one responsible for organized crime and gang warfare. [from S Chinese dialect *tong*, meeting hall]

tongs *pl. noun* a tool consisting of two arms joined by a hinge or pivot, for holding and lifting objects. [from Anglo-Saxon *tang*]

tongue /tʌŋ/ — *noun* **1** in certain animals, the fleshy muscular organ attached to the floor of the mouth, covered with a mucous membrane, and bearing groups of taste buds on its upper surface. Its functions include tasting, licking, and manipulating food in preparation for chewing and swallowing. In human beings it is the main organ of speech. **2** the tongue of some animals, eg the ox and sheep, used as food. **3** the ability to speak. **4** a particular language. **5** a particular manner of speaking: *a sharp tongue*. **6** anything like a tongue in shape. **7** a narrow strip of land that reaches out into water. **8** the clapper in a bell. **9** a flap in the opening of a shoe or boot. **10** a projecting strip along the side of a board that fits into a groove in another. — *verb* **1** to touch or lick with the tongue. **2** *intrans. Mus.* to play a wind instrument by tonguing. **3** *Mus.* to produce (notes) by tonguing. — **find one's tongue** to be able to speak again after a shock which has left one speechless. **hold one's tongue** to say nothing; to keep quiet. **lose one's tongue** to be left speechless with shock, horror, etc. **speak in tongues** *Biblical* to speak in wholly or partly unknown languages. **with one's tongue in one's cheek** or **tongue in cheek** with ironic, insincere, or humorous intention. [from Anglo-Saxon *tunge*]

· ·

◧ *noun* **3** speech, discourse, utterance, articulation. **4, 5** language. **5** parlance, vernacular, idiom, dialect, patois.

· ·

tongue-tie *noun* a speech impediment which is caused by an abnormally small fold of skin under the tongue not allowing full movement of the tongue.

tongue-tied *adj.* **1** speechless, especially because of shyness or embarrassment. **2** suffering from tongue-tie.

· ·

◧ **1** speechless, dumbstruck, inarticulate, silent, mute, dumb, voiceless.

◨ **1** talkative, garrulous, voluble.

· ·

tongue-twister *noun* a phrase or sentence that is difficult to say quickly, usually because it contains a series of similar consonant sounds, eg *She sells sea shells on the sea shore.*

tonguing *noun Mus.* a way of playing a wind instrument which allows individual notes to be articulated separately by the tongue opening and blocking the passage of air.

tonic /'tɒnɪk/ — *noun* **1** a medicine that increases strength, energy, and the general wellbeing of the body. **2** anything that is refreshing or invigorating. **3** same as TONIC WATER. **4** *Mus.* the first note of a scale, the note on which a key is based. — *adj.* **1** increasing strength, energy, and wellbeing. **2** invigorating. **3** *Mus.* of or being the tonic. **4** producing (especially muscular) tension. [from Greek *tonikos*]

· · · · · · · · · · · · · · · · · · · ·

◧ *noun* **1, 2** pick-me-up, restorative. **1** cordial. **2** stimulant, *colloq.* shot in the arm, boost, fillip, refresher, bracer.

· ·

tonic sol-fa a way of teaching music which represents notes by syllables, with *doh* as the keynote for major keys and *lah* that for minor keys.

tonic water a fizzy soft drink flavoured with quinine.

tonight — *noun* the night of this present day. — *adv.* on or during the night of the present day. [from Anglo-Saxon *to niht*]

tonnage /'tʌnɪdʒ/ *noun* **1** the space available in a ship for carrying cargo, measured in tons. **2** the total carrying capacity of a country's merchant shipping, measured in tons. **3** a duty or tax on ships based on their cargo-carrying capacity. **4** a duty on cargo by the ton. See also TON. [originally a tax or duty levied on each *tun* of wine carried by a ship]

tonne /tʌn/ *noun* a unit of weight equal to 1000kg (2204.6lb) (see also TON 3). [from French]

tonner /'tʌnə(r)/ *noun* (*in compounds with a numeral*) a ship, lorry, etc that can carry the specified number of tons: *a 10-tonner*.

tonsil /'tɒnsɪl/ *noun* either of two almond-shaped lumps of tissue at the back of the mouth. They produce lymphocytes (white blood cells associated with antibody formation) and have an important role in preventing infection. During childhood they often become swollen, resulting in tonsillitis. [from Latin *tonsillae*, pl.]

tonsillectomy /tɒnsɪ'lektəmɪ/ *noun* (PL. **tonsillectomies**) a surgical operation to remove the tonsils.

tonsillitis /tɒnsɪ'laɪtɪs/ *noun* inflammation of the tonsils.

tonsorial /tɒn'sɔːrɪəl/ *adj. often facetious* relating to barbers or hairdressing. [from Latin *tondere*, to clip or shave]

tonsure /'tɒnʃə(r)/ — *noun* **1** a shaved patch on the crown of a monk's or priest's head. **2** the act of shaving the crown of a monk's or priest's head as part of the rite of entering a monastic order or the priesthood. — *verb* to shave the head of, especially as a tonsure. [from Latin *tonsura*, from *tondere*, to clip or shave]

tonsured *adj.* wearing a tonsure.

tontine /'tɒntiːn, tɒn'tiːn/ *noun* an annuity scheme in which several subscribers share a common fund, with their individual benefits increasing as members die until only one member is left alive and receives everything or until a specified date at which the proceeds will be shared amongst the survivors. [named after Lorenzo *Tonti* (c. 1653), the Italian-born Parisian banker who invented it]

ton-up *adj. old slang use, usually said of a motorcyclist* travelling or having travelled at more than 100mph, especially often and recklessly.

too *adv.* **1** to a greater extent or more than is required, desirable, or suitable: *too many things to do.* **2** in addition; as well; also: *enjoy swimming and like cycling too.* **3** what is more; indeed: *they need a good holiday, and they'll get one, too!* [a stressed form of TO]

· · · · · · · · · · · · · · · · · · · ·

◧ **1** excessively, inordinately, unduly, over, overly, unreasonably, ridiculously, extremely, very. **2** also, as well, in addition, besides, moreover, likewise.

· ·

took see TAKE.

tool — *noun* **1** an implement, especially one used by hand, for cutting, digging, etc, such as a spade, hammer, etc.

2 the cutting part of a machine tool. **3** a thing used in or necessary to a particular trade or profession: *books are the tools of a librarian's job.* **4** a person who is used or manipulated by another, especially for selfish or dishonest reasons. **5** *coarse slang* a penis. — *verb* **1** to work or engrave (eg stone or leather) with tools. **2** (*also* **tool up** *or* **tool something up**) to equip a factory, etc or become equipped with the tools needed for production. **3** (**tool along**, **around**) *colloq.* to drive or ride casually. [from Anglo-Saxon *tol*]

▣ *noun* **1** implement, instrument, utensil, gadget, device, contrivance, contraption, apparatus, appliance, machine, means, vehicle, medium, agency, agent, intermediary. **4** puppet, pawn, dupe, stooge, minion, hireling, cat's paw.

Types of tool include: bolster, caulking-iron, crowbar, hod, jackhammer, jointer, mattock, pick, pick-axe, plumbline, sledgehammer; chaser, clamp, dividers, dolly, drill, hacksaw, jack, pincers, pliers, protractor, punch, rule, sander, scriber, snips, socket wrench, soldering iron, spraygun, tommy bar, vice; auger, awl, brace and bit, bradawl, chisel, file, fretsaw, hammer, handsaw, jack plane, jig saw, level, mallet, plane, rasp, saw, screwdriver, set square, spirit level, tenon saw, T-square; billhook, chainsaw, chopper, dibber, fork, grass rake, hay fork, hoe, pitchfork, plough, pruning knife, pruning shears, rake, scythe, secateurs, shears, shovel, sickle, spade, thresher, trowel; needle, scissors, pinking shears, bodkin, crochet hook, forceps, scalpel, tweezers, tongs, cleaver, steel, gimlet, mace, mortar, pestle, paper-cutter, paperknife, stapler, pocket knife, penknife.

toolbag *noun* a bag for carrying and storing tools.

toolbox *noun* a box for carrying and storing tools.

tooled-up *adj. slang* carrying a weapon, especially a gun.

toolkit *noun* a set of tools, especially those required for a particular trade or purpose.

toolmaker *noun* a person who makes or repairs machine tools.

toolmaking *noun* **1** producing tools. **2** the production or repair of machine tools.

toot — *noun* a quick, sharp blast of a trumpet, whistle, horn, etc. — *verb trans., intrans.* to sound or cause (a trumpet, horn, etc) to sound with a quick, sharp blast. [imitative]

tooth — *noun* (PL. **teeth**) **1** in vertebrates, any of the hard structures, usually embedded in the upper and lower jawbones, that are used for biting and chewing food. **2** in invertebrates, any similar structure that is used for rasping or grinding food, or that resembles a vertebrate tooth. **3** one of many equally spaced projections around the edge of a gear wheel. **4** anything like a tooth in shape, arrangement, or function, such as one of a series of cogs on a wheel or points on a comb. **5** an appetite or liking, especially for sweet foods: *a sweet tooth.* **6** (**teeth**) enough power or force to be effective. — *verb* **1** to provide with teeth. **2** *intrans.* said of cogs: to interlock. — **in the teeth of something** against it; in opposition to it. **long in the tooth** *colloq.* old. **set one's teeth on edge** to cause a sharp pain in the teeth such as that caused by eating something very cold; to cause to wince; to irritate severely. **take the teeth out of something** to make it harmless. **tooth and nail** fiercely and with all one's strength. [from Anglo-Saxon *toth*]

toothache *noun* an ache or pain in a tooth, usually as a result of dental caries (tooth decay). It also occurs during teething.

toothbrush *noun* a brush for cleaning the teeth.

toothily *adv.* in a toothy manner.

toothless *adj.* **1** without teeth. **2** powerless or ineffective.

toothpaste *noun* a paste used to clean the teeth.

toothpick *noun* a small sharp piece of wood, plastic, etc for picking out food from between the teeth.

toothpowder *noun* a powder used to clean the teeth.

toothsome *adj.* appetising; delicious; attractive.

toothy *adj.* (**toothier, toothiest**) showing or having a lot of especially large, prominent teeth.

tootle — *verb intrans.* **1** to toot gently or continuously. **2** (**tootle about**, **round**) *colloq.* to go about casually, especially by car. — *noun* **1** a tootling sound. **2** *colloq.* a trip or drive. [from TOOT]

tootsie or **tootsy** *noun* (PL. **tootsies**) *colloq.* **1** a foot. **2** a toe.

top¹ — *noun* **1** the highest part, point, or level of anything. **2** the highest or most important rank or position, or the person holding this: *top of the class.* **3** the upper edge or surface of something: *the table-top.* **4** a lid or piece for covering the top of something. **5** a garment for covering the upper half of especially a woman's body. **6** the highest or loudest degree or pitch: *the top of one's voice.* **7** (**the tops**) *colloq.* the very best person or thing. **8** (*usually* **tops**) the part of a root vegetable that is above the ground. **9** *Brit.* top gear. — *adj.* **1** at or being the highest. **2** being the most important. — *verb* (**topped**, **topping**) **1** to cover or form the top of, especially as a finishing or decorative touch: *top a cake with cream.* **2** to remove the top of. **3** to rise above or be better than; to surpass. **4** to reach the top of. **5** to be the top or leader of. **6** *slang* to kill. **7** *Golf* to hit the upper half of (the ball). — **from top to toe** completely; from head to foot. **on top of something 1** in control of it. **2** in addition to it. **3** very close to it. **on top of the world** in the very best of spirits. **top something off** to put a finishing or decorative touch to it. **top something out** to put the highest stone on a building. **top something up 1** to refill (a glass, container, etc) that has been partly emptied. **2** to provide money to bring (a grant, wage, money supply, etc) to the required or desirable total. **top someone up** to refill their partly emptied glass, container, etc: *let me top you up with more coffee.* [from Anglo-Saxon]

▣ *noun* **1** head, tip, vertex, apex, crest, crown, peak, pinnacle, summit, acme, zenith, culmination, height. **4** lid, cap, cover, cork, stopper. *adj* **1** highest, topmost, upmost, uppermost, upper. **2** superior, head, chief, leading, first, foremost, principal, sovereign, ruling, pre-eminent, dominant, prime, paramount, greatest, maximum, best, finest, supreme, crowning, culminating. *verb* **1** tip, cap, crown, cover, finish (off), decorate, garnish. **3** beat, exceed, outstrip, better, excel, best, surpass, eclipse, outshine, outdo, surmount, transcend. **5** head, lead, rule, command. **top something up 1** refill, replenish, recharge, reload. **2** add to, supplement, augment, increase, boost.

▣ *noun* **1** bottom, base, nadir. *adj.* **1** bottom, lowest. **2** inferior.

top² *noun* a wooden or metal toy which spins on a pointed base. — **sleep like a top** to sleep very soundly. [from Anglo-Saxon]

topaz / ˈtoʊpaz/ *noun* an aluminium silicate mineral, found in gneisses and granites, that sometimes occurs in the form of enormous hard crystals, the pale yellow variety being most highly prized as a semi-precious gemstone. [from Greek *topazos*]

top boot a high boot with a band of different coloured leather round the top.

top brass *colloq.* the highest-ranking (especially military) officers or personnel.

topcoat *noun* an overcoat.

top coat a final coat of paint.

top dog *colloq.* the most important or powerful person in a group.

top dollar *colloq.* the highest amount of money possible to pay.

top drawer the highest level, especially of society.

top-dress *verb* to apply a top-dressing to.

top-dressing *noun Agric.* **1** manure or fertilizer applied to a growing crop. **2** the application of manure or fertilizer to a growing crop.

tope¹ /təʊp/ *verb intrans.* to drink alcohol to excess. [a variant of obsolete *top*, to drink]

tope² /təʊp/ *noun* a small shark found in European waters. [from a Norfolk dialect word]

toper *noun* a drunkard.

top-flight *adj.* of the best or highest quality.

topgallant *noun* the mast or sail above the topmast and topsail.

top gear *Brit.* the combination of gearwheels which allows a vehicle to travel at its fastest speed.

top hat a man's tall, cylindrical hat, often made of silk, worn as part of formal dress.

top-heavy *adj.* **1** having the upper part too heavy for, or disproportionately large in comparison with, the lower. **2** *said of a company, administration, etc* having too many senior staff in proportion to junior staff.

topi or **topee** /ˈtəʊpi/ *noun* (PL. **topis, topees**) a helmet-like lightweight hat worn in hot countries as protection against the sun. [from Hindi, = hat]

topiary /ˈtəʊpɪərɪ/ — *noun* (PL. **topiaries**) **1** the art of cutting trees, bushes, and hedges into ornamental shapes. **2** an example of this. — *adj.* of or relating to topiary work. [from Latin *topia*, landscape gardening]

topic /ˈtɒpɪk/ *noun* a subject or theme. [from Greek *topos*, place]

■ subject, theme, issue, question, matter, point, thesis, text.

topical *adj.* **1** relating to matters of interest at the present time; dealing with current affairs. **2** relating to a particular place; local. **3** of a topic or topics.

■ **1** current, contemporary, up-to-date, up-to-the-minute, recent, newsworthy, relevant, popular, familiar.

topicality *noun* being topical.

topically *adv.* in a topical way; so as to be topical.

topknot *noun* a crest, tuft of hair, piece of added hair, or a knot of ribbons, etc, on the top of the head.

topless *adj.* **1** having no top. **2** *said of a woman's clothing* leaving the breasts exposed. **3** *said of a woman* with her breasts exposed. **4** *said of a place* where women go topless: *topless beaches.*

topmast *noun* the second mast, usually directly above the lower mast.

topmost *adj.* being the very highest of all.

■ highest, top, upmost, uppermost, upper, superior, leading, first, foremost, principal.

top-notch *adj. colloq.* of the very best quality; superb.

topographical /tɒpəˈɡræfɪkl/ *adj.* relating to or involving topography.

topographically *adv.* in a topographical way; in terms of topography.

topography /təˈpɒɡrəfɪ/ *noun* (PL. **topographies**) **1** the natural and man-made features on the surface of land, such as rivers, mountains, valleys, bridges, and railway lines; also, a description or map of these. **2** the describing or mapping of such features. **3** the mapping or describing of the surface of any object or body. [from Greek *topos*, place + *graphein*, to describe]

topological /tɒpəˈlɒdʒɪkl/ *adj.* relating to or involving topology.

topologically *adv.* in a topological way; in terms of topology.

topology /təˈpɒlədʒɪ/ *noun Geom.* the branch of geometry concerned with those properties of a geometrical figure that remain unchanged even when the figure is deformed by bending, stretching, twisting, etc. For example, a ring shape (torus) painted on a rubber sheet can be distorted by stretching, but will always have a hole at its centre. The standard map of the London Underground system is a topological diagram, because it shows the lines joining the various stations, but is not to scale, ie the distances are distorted. [from Greek *topos*, place + -LOGY]

topper *noun colloq.* a top hat.

topping — *noun* something that forms a covering or garnish for food. — *adj. Brit. old colloq. use* excellent.

topple *verb* **1** *intrans.* (*also* **topple over**) to fall; to seem about to fall because top-heavy. **2** to cause to fall. **3** to overthrow. [from TOP¹]

■ **1, 2** overbalance, tumble, overturn, capsize. **1** totter, fall, collapse. **2** knock down, knock over, upset. **3** overthrow, oust, dethrone, depose.

topsail /ˈtɒpsl, ˈtɒpseɪl/ *noun* a square sail set across the topmast.

top-secret *adj.* very secret, especially officially classified so.

topside — *noun* **1** a lean cut of beef from the rump. **2** the side of a ship above the waterline. — *adj., adv.* on deck.

topsoil *noun* the uppermost layer of soil, rich in organic matter, that is disturbed during cultivation, eg ploughing. Most plant roots develop in this layer.

topspin *noun* a spin given to a ball by hitting it sharply on the upper half with a forward and upward stroke to make it travel higher, further, or more quickly.

topsy-turvily *adv.* in a topsy-turvy way.

topsy-turviness *noun* being topsy-turvy.

topsy-turvy /tɒpsɪˈtɜːvɪ/ *adj., adv.* **1** upside down. **2** in confusion. [from TOP¹ + obsolete *terve*, to turn over]

toque /təʊk/ *noun* a woman's small, close-fitting, brimless or nearly brimless hat. [French]

tor *noun* a high rock or a pile of rocks or boulders found on the summit of a hill in an area of hard bedrock, eg on Dartmoor in the UK. [from Anglo-Saxon *torr*]

Torah /ˈtɔːrə/ *noun Judaism* **1** the Pentateuch. **2** the scroll on which this is written, used in a synagogue. **3** the whole body of Jewish literature and law, both written and oral, and including the Old Testament and Talmud. [from Hebrew, instruction]

torc see TORQUE.

torch *noun* **1** *Brit.* a small portable light powered by electric batteries. **2** a piece of wood or bundle of cloth, etc used to give light. **3** any source of heat, light, illumination, enlightenment, etc. — **carry a torch for someone** (especially unrequited) love for them. [from Old French *torche*, from Latin *torquere*, to twist]

torchlight *noun* the light of a torch or torches.

tore See TEAR².

toreador /ˈtɒrɪədɔː(r)/ *noun* a bullfighter, especially one on horseback. [from Spanish]

torero /tɒˈreərəʊ/ *noun* (PL. **toreros**) a bullfighter on foot. [from Spanish]

torii /ˈtɔːriː/ *noun* a Japanese Shinto temple gateway, generally orange-red in colour, but sometimes unpainted, giving the name of the deity. At shrines of the harvest god, or the fox deity (Inari), those wanting good fortune may donate torii with their names. [from Japanese]

torment /ˈtɔːment, tɔːˈment/ — *noun* (with stress on *tor-*) **1** very great pain, suffering, or anxiety. **2** something that causes this. — *verb* (with stress on *-ment*) **1** to cause great pain, suffering, or anxiety to. **2** to pester or harass (eg a child or animal). [from Latin *tormentum*]

■ *noun* **1** anguish, distress, misery, affliction, suffering, pain, agony, ordeal, torture, persecution. **2** bane, scourge, trouble, bother, nuisance, plague. *verb* **1** afflict, distress, harrow, pain, torture, persecute. **2** tease, provoke, annoy, vex, trouble, worry, harass, hound, pester, bother, bedevil, plague.

. . . .

tormentil /'tɔːməntɪl/ *noun* a perennial plant (*Potentilla erecta*) with leaves composed of three (sometimes more) leaflets, silvery below, with margins toothed owards the tip. It bears clusters of bright yellow flowers, and is widely distributed on cultivated land, heaths, and garden lawns. [from Old French *tormentille*, from Latin *tormentum*, torment, because it was used to numb pain]

tormentor *noun* a person who torments.

. . . .

☰ persecutor, torturer, nuisance.

. . . .

torn see TEAR².

tornado /tɔːˈneɪdoʊ/ *noun* (PL. **tornadoes**) *Meteorol.* a violently destructive storm consisting of a funnel-shaped rotating column of air which can be seen extending downward from thunder clouds to the ground surface, tracing a narrow path across the land. Tornadoes can reach speeds of over 350kph, and cause considerable destruction in the Gulf states and central and S plains of the USA, and Australia. [from Spanish *tronada*, thunderstorm]

. . . .

☰ whirlwind, *North Amer.* twister, storm, tempest, gale, cyclone, hurricane.

. . . .

Toronto blessing a form of charismatic religious activity involving weeping, fainting, and other emotional reactions. [named after *Toronto* in Canada, where it originated]

torpedo /tɔːˈpiːdoʊ/ — *noun* (PL. **torpedos, torpedoes**) 1 a long, self-propelling, underwater missile which explodes on impact with its target (usually a ship) and can be fired from submarines, ships, and aircraft. 2 any of several rays found in warm seas with organs on the head which can give an electric shock. 3 *North Amer.* a small container holding an explosive charge, used in warfare as eg a firework or fog-signal. — *verb* (**torpedoes, torpedoed**) 1 to attack with torpedos. 2 to wreck or destroy (eg a plan). [from Latin *torpedo*, numbness, electric ray, from *torpere*, to be numb]

torpedo boat a small fast warship armed with torpedos.

torpedo ray See ELECTRIC RAY.

torpid /'tɔːpɪd/ *adj.* 1 lacking in energy or liveliness. 2 unable to move or feel; numb. 3 *said of a hibernating animal* dormant. [from Latin *torpidus*, from *torpere*, to be numb]

. . . .

☰ 1 sluggish, lethargic, slow, dull, lifeless, inert, inactive, apathetic, drowsy, sleepy. 2 numb, nerveless, dead, deadened, insensible.

. . . .

torpidity *noun* a torpid state; numbness.

torpidly *adv.* with a torpid manner.

torpor /'tɔːpə(r)/ *noun* 1 drowsiness, sluggishness, apathy. 2 numbness. [from Latin *torpere*, to be numb]

torque /tɔːk/ *noun* 1 (*also* **torc**) *Hist.* a necklace made of metal twisted into a band, worn by the ancient Britons and Gauls. 2 *Physics* a measure of the tendency of a force to cause an object to rotate about an axis. It is defined as the magnitude of the force multiplied by the distance between the force and the point about which it causes rotation. [from Latin *torquere*, to twist]

torr /tɔː(r)/ *noun Physics* a unit of pressure equal to 133.3 pascals, that will support a column of mercury 1mm high. It is used to measure very low pressures, eg in high-vacuum technology. [named after the Italian mathematician Evangelista Torricelli]

torrent *noun* 1 a great rushing stream or downpour of water, lava, etc. 2 a violent or strong flow, eg of questions, abuse, etc. [from Latin *torrens*, boiling]

. . . .

☰ STREAM, GUSH, RUSH, FLOOD, SPATE, DELUGE, CASCADE. 1 downpour, cloudburst. 2 volley, outburst.

☲ TRICKLE.

. . . .

torrential /təˈrenʃəl/ *adj.*, *said of rain, etc* falling in torrents; extremely heavy.

torrid *adj.* 1 *said of the weather* so hot and dry as to scorch the land. 2 *said of land* scorched and parched by extremely hot, dry weather. 3 passionate; intensely emotional. [from Latin *torridus*, from *torrere*, to parch]

. . . .

☰ 1 hot, blazing, sweltering, blistering, scorching, tropical. 2 arid, parched, scorched, waterless, desert. 3 passionate, erotic, red-hot, sexy, *colloq.* steamy.

. . . .

torsion *noun* 1 the act or process of twisting something by applying force to one end while the other is held firm or twisted in the opposite direction. 2 the state of being twisted in this way. [from Latin *torsio*, from *torquere*, to twist]

torsional *adj.* relating to or involving torsion.

torso /'tɔːsoʊ/ *noun* (PL. **torsos**) 1 the main part of the human body, without the limbs and head. 2 a nude statue of this. [from Italian, from Latin *thyrsos*, stalk]

tort /tɔːt/ *noun Legal* any wrongful act other than breach of contract for which an action for damages or compensation may be brought. [from Latin *tortum*, wrong]

tortilla /tɔːˈtiːjə, tɔːˈtɪlə/ *noun* a Mexican thin round maize cake cooked on a griddle and usually eaten hot with a filling or topping of meat or cheese. [from Spanish *torta*, cake]

tortoise /'tɔːtəs, 'tɔːtɔɪz/ *noun* any of various slow-moving toothless reptiles having a high domed shell into which the head, short scaly legs, and tail can be withdrawn for safety. Tortoises are found in warm regions, and live on land, unlike turtles, which are aquatic. [from Latin *tortuca*]

tortoiseshell — *noun* 1 the brown and yellow mottled shell of a sea turtle, used in making combs, jewellery, and decorative inlay in furniture. 2 a butterfly with mottled orange or red and brown or black wings. 3 a domestic cat with a mottled orange and brown coat. — *adj.* made of or mottled like tortoiseshell.

tortuous /'tɔːtjʊəs/ *adj.* 1 full of twists and turns. 2 not straightforward, especially in being devious or involved. [from Latin *tortuosus*, from *torquere*, to twist]

. . . .

☰ CIRCUITOUS, ROUNDABOUT, INDIRECT, CONVOLUTED, COMPLICATED, INVOLVED. 1 twisting, winding, meandering, serpentine, zigzag.

☲ 1 straight. 2 straightforward.

. . . .

torture /'tɔːtʃə(r)/ — *noun* 1 the infliction of severe pain or mental suffering, especially as a punishment or as a means of persuading someone to give information. 2 great physical or mental suffering, or a cause of this. — *verb* 1 to subject to torture. 2 to cause to experience great physical or mental suffering. 3 to force out of a natural state or position; to distort. [from Latin *tortura*, torment]

. . . .

☰ *noun* 1 persecution, crucifixion. 2 pain, agony, suffering, affliction, distress, misery, anguish, torment. *verb* 1, 2 crucify, rack, martyr. 2 agonize, excruciate, persecute, torment, afflict, distress.

. . . .

torturous *adj.* 1 causing torture. 2 causing distortion.

torus /'tɔːrəs/ *noun* 1 *Anat.* a rounded swelling or projection on a body part. 2 *Bot.* the receptacle of a flower, ie the tip of the flower stalk, on which the sepals, petals, stamens, and carpels are borne. 3 *Geom.* a curved surface with a hole in it, resembling a doughnut, obtained by rotating a circle about an axis lying in the same plane as the circle. [from Latin *torus*, bulge, swelling]

Tory — *noun* (PL. **Tories**) **1** a member or supporter of the British Conservative Party. **2** *Hist.* a member or supporter of a major English political party from the 17c to mid-19c which favoured royal authority over that of Parliament, supported the established Church, and was against political and social reform, superseded by the Conservative Party. See also WHIG. **3** *North Amer. Hist.* a supporter of the British Crown during the American Revolution. — *adj.* **1** relating to or supporting the Tories. **2** Conservative. [from Irish Gaelic *tórai*, bandit, outlaw]

Toryism /ˈtɔːrɪˌɪzm/ *noun* the principles of the Tories; Conservatism.

toss — *verb* **1** to throw up into the air. **2** (*usually* **toss something away, aside, out,** *etc*) to throw it away or discard it casually or carelessly. **3** (*also* **toss about, around,** *etc*) to move restlessly or from side to side repeatedly: *toss sleeplessly all night.* **4** *trans., intrans.* (*also* **toss about** or **toss something about**) to be thrown or throw it from side to side repeatedly and violently: *a ship tossed by the storm.* **5** to jerk (the head), especially as a sign of impatience or anger. **6** *trans., intrans.* to throw (a spinning coin) into the air and guess which side will land facing up, as a way of making a decision or settling a dispute. **7** to settle a dispute with (someone) by tossing a coin: *toss him for the last cake.* **8** to coat (food, especially salad) by gently mixing it in a dressing. **9** *said of a horse, etc* to throw (its rider). **10** *said of an animal* to throw (a person) into the air with its horns. **11** to discuss or consider in, or as if in, light-hearted or casual debate: *toss various ideas back and forth in one's head.* — *noun* **1** an act or an instance of tossing. **2** a fall from a horse. **3** *coarse slang* the slightest amount: *not give a toss.* — **argue the toss** to dispute a decision. **toss off** *Brit. coarse slang* to masturbate. **toss something off 1** to drink it quickly, especially in a single swallow. **2** to produce it quickly and easily. **toss up** to throw a spinning coin into the air and guess which side will land facing upwards, as a way of making a decision or settling a dispute.

∙∙∙∙∙∙∙∙∙∙∙∙∙∙∙∙∙∙∙∙∙∙

▣ *verb* **1** flip, cast, fling, throw, *colloq.* chuck, *colloq.* sling, hurl, lob. **3** thrash, squirm, wriggle. **4** roll, heave, pitch, jolt, shake, rock. *noun* **1** flip, cast, fling, throw, pitch.

∙∙∙∙∙∙∙∙∙∙∙∙∙∙∙∙∙∙∙∙∙∙∙∙∙∙∙∙∙∙∙∙∙∙∙∙

toss-up *noun* **1** *colloq.* an even chance or risk. **2** an act of tossing a coin.

tot[1] *noun* **1** a small child; a toddler. **2** a small amount of spirits: *a tot of whisky.*

tot[2] *verb* (**totted, totting**) **1** (*also* **tot something up**) to add it together. **2** (*also* **tot up**) *said of money, etc* to increase. [an abbreviation of TOTAL]

total /ˈtoʊtl/ — *adj.* whole; complete. — *noun* the whole or complete amount, eg of various things added together. — *verb* (**totalled, totalling**) **1** *trans., intrans.* (*also* **total to**) to amount to a specified sum. **2** (*also* **total something up**) to add it up to produce a total. **3** *North Amer. slang* to wreck or destroy (especially a vehicle) completely. [from Latin *totalis*, from *totus*, all]

∙∙∙∙∙∙∙∙∙∙∙∙∙∙∙∙∙∙∙∙∙∙

▣ *adj.* full, complete, entire, whole, integral, all-out, *colloq.* full-on, utter, absolute, unconditional, unqualified, outright, undisputed, perfect, consummate, thoroughgoing, sheer, downright, thorough. *noun* sum, whole, entirety, totality, all, lot, mass, aggregate, amount. *verb* **1** amount to, come to, reach. **2** add (up), sum (up), tot (up), count (up), reckon.

▣ *adj.* partial, limited, restricted.

∙∙∙∙∙∙∙∙∙∙∙∙∙∙∙∙∙∙∙∙∙∙∙∙∙∙∙∙∙∙∙∙∙∙∙∙

total internal reflection *Optics* the complete reflection of a ray of light at the boundary of one medium with another, eg glass and air. It forms the basis for the reflection of light inside optical fibres, so that all of the light is reflected back into the fibre and 'trapped'.

totalitarian /toʊtælɪˈtɛərɪən/ — *adj.* of or relating to a system of government by a single party which allows no opposition and which demands complete obedience to the State. — *noun* a person in favour of such a system.

totalitarianism *noun* totalitarian practices and systems.

totality /toʊˈtælɪtɪ/ *noun* **1** completeness. **2** a complete number or amount.

Totalizator *noun,* also called **the Tote,** a method of placing bets at horse race or greyhound meetings. All money invested is returned to winning punters, less expenses and taxes.

totalizer or **totaliser** /ˈtoʊtəlaɪzə(r)/ *noun* same as TOTALIZATOR.

totally /ˈtoʊtəlɪ/ *adv.* **1** completely. **2** absolutely.

total recall *Psychol.* the power of remembering accurately in full detail.

Tote see TOTALIZATOR.

tote *verb* (**tote something about** or **around**) *colloq.* to carry, drag, or wear it.

tote bag a large bag for carrying shopping.

totem /ˈtoʊtəm/ *noun* **1** a natural object, especially an animal, used as the badge or sign of a tribe or an individual person among North American Indians. **2** an image or representation of this. [from Ojibwa (N American Indian language) *nintotem*, my totem, from *ote*, to live in a village]

totemic /toʊˈtɛmɪk/ *adj.* **1** relating to a totem or totems. **2** having or characterized by totems.

totemism /ˈtoʊtəmɪzm/ *noun* the rituals, customs, and taboos associated with the use of totems as the foundation of a social system of obligation and restriction.

totem pole 1 a large wooden pole on which totems are carved and painted. **2** an order of rank; a hierarchy.

totter — *verb intrans.* (**tottered, tottering**) **1** to move unsteadily or weakly. **2** to sway or tremble as if about to fall. **3** *said of a system of government, etc* to be on the verge of collapse. — *noun* a weak and unsteady movement or gait. [from Middle English *toteron*]

∙∙∙∙∙∙∙∙∙∙∙∙∙∙∙∙∙∙∙∙∙∙

▣ *verb* **1, 2** teeter. **1** stagger, reel, lurch, stumble, falter. **2** waver, sway, rock, shake, quiver, tremble.

∙∙∙∙∙∙∙∙∙∙∙∙∙∙∙∙∙∙∙∙∙∙∙∙∙∙∙∙∙∙∙∙∙∙∙∙

tottery *adj.* shaky.

totting-up *noun* **1** adding-up. **2** *Brit.* accumulation of penalties for motoring offences, eventually resulting in disqualification.

totty *noun slang* young women or girls, especially when considered sexually attractive.

toucan /ˈtuːkən/ *noun* a tropical American fruit-eating bird with a huge beak and brightly coloured feathers. [from Tupff (S American Indian language) *tucana,* imitative of its cry]

touch /tʌtʃ/ — *verb* **1** to bring something (eg one's hand) into contact, especially lightly, with (something), especially so as to feel: *he touched her cheek gently.* **2** *said of an object* to come into contact with (something else): *the branch touched the window.* **3** (*intrans.*) to feel, push, or strike something lightly, especially with the hand and foot. **4** (*intrans.*) to be in contact with something else without overlapping. **5** to make (someone) feel pity, sympathy, quiet pleasure, etc: *was touched by his sad story.* **6** to have an effect on. **7** to be of concern to: *a matter which doesn't touch you.* **8** to have dealings with: *wouldn't touch a job like that.* **9** to use, especially to eat or drink: *I never touch chocolate.* **10** to reach: *the temperature touched 100°.* **11** to be as good as; to equal or rival: *no one can touch her at chess.* **12** to mark slightly or delicately; to make a usually slight, sometimes harmful, impression on: *a sky touched with pink.* **13** to draw or paint with light strokes. **14** (**touch on** or **upon something**) to speak of or discuss briefly or in passing. **15** to disturb by handling, meddling, etc: *someone's touched my papers.* **16** (**touch someone for something**) *slang* to ask for and receive money as a loan or gift from them: *tried to touch him for £50.* — *noun* **1** an act of touching or the sensation of being touched. **2** the sense by which the existence, nature, texture, and quality of objects can be perceived through physical contact with the hands, feet, skin, lips, etc. **3** the particular texture and qualities of an object as perceived through contact with the hands, feet, etc: *the silky touch of the fabric against her skin.* **4** a small amount or quantity; a trace or hint. **5** a slight attack (eg of an illness). **6** a slight stroke or mark. **7** a detail which adds to or complements the general pleasing effect or appearance: *put the finishing touches to the portrait / a few vases of flowers are an elegant touch.* **8** a distinctive or characteristic style or manner: *a woman's touch.* **9** a musician's individual manner or technique of touching or striking the keys of a keyboard instrument or strings of a string instrument to produce a good tone. **10** an artist's or writer's individual style or manner of working. **11** the ability to respond or behave with sensitivity and sympathy: *have a wonderful touch with animals.* **12** contact; communication: *out of touch with recent developments / in touch with old school friends.* **13** (**a touch** ...) *colloq.* a bit ...; rather: *a touch too much make-up.* **14** *Rugby etc* the ground outside the touchlines. **15** *slang* an act of asking for and receiving money from someone as a gift or loan. **16** *slang* a person who can be persuaded to give or lend money: *a soft touch.* **17** a test with, or as if with, a touchstone. — **touch and go** of a very uncertain outcome. **touch down** *said of an aircraft or spacecraft* to land. **touch something down** *Rugby* to put the ball on the ground behind the goal-line, either behind one's own as a defensive move or behind the opponent's when scoring a try. **touch something off 1** to cause it to explode, eg by touching it with a flame. **2** to cause it to begin; to trigger it. **touch someone up** *slang* to touch or fondle them so as to excite sexually; to molest them sexually. **touch something up** to improve it by adding small details to or correcting or hiding the minor faults of. [from Old French *tuchier*]

◫ *verb* **1**, **2** brush, graze, stroke, pat, tap, hit, strike, contact. **1** feel, handle, finger, caress, fondle. **4** meet, abut, adjoin, border. **5** move, stir, impress, inspire, influence, upset, disturb. **7** affect, concern, regard. **10** reach, attain. **11** equal, match, rival, better. **14** mention, broach, speak of, remark on, refer to, allude to, cover, deal with. *noun* **1** brush, stroke, caress, pat, tap, contact. **3** feel, texture. **4** trace, hint, spot, dash, pinch, soupçon, suspicion, suggestion, speck, jot, tinge, smack. **10** style, method, manner, technique, approach. **11** skill, art, knack, flair.

touchdown *noun* **1** the point of contact of an aircraft with the ground on landing. **2** *Rugby* the action of touching the ball down to score.

touché /tuːˈʃeɪ/ *interj.* an expression used to acknowledge: **1** a hit in fencing. **2** a point scored in an argument or made in retaliation. [French, = touched]

touched *adj.* **1** feeling pity, sympathy, quiet pleasure, etc. **2** *colloq.* slightly mad.

◫ **1** moved, stirred, affected, impressed, disturbed. **2** mad, crazy, deranged, disturbed, eccentric, *colloq.* dotty, daft, *colloq.* barmy, *slang* loopy.

touchily *adv.* in a touchy manner.
touchiness *noun* being touchy.
touching — *adj.* causing one to feel pity or sympathy; moving. — *prep.* concerning.

◫ *adj.* moving, stirring, affecting, poignant, pitiable, pitiful, pathetic, sad, emotional, tender. *prep.* concerning, regarding, about, as to, with reference to, in respect of.

touchingly *adv.* in a touching way.
touch judge *Rugby* a linesman.
touchline *noun Football, Rugby* either of the two lines marking the side boundaries of the pitch.
touchpaper *noun* paper steeped in saltpetre for firing gunpowder.
touch screen *Comput.* a visual display unit screen that doubles as an input device, and is operated by being touched.

touchstone *noun* **1** a test or standard of judging the quality of something. **2** a hard black flint-like stone used for testing the purity and quality of gold and silver alloys which, when rubbed on this stone, leave a coloured mark which indicates the amount of alloy.

touch-tone *adj.* describing telephones that have push buttons that cause distinct tones to sound.

touch-type *verb intrans.* to type without looking at the typewriter keyboard.

touch-typing *noun* the act or skill of typing without watching the keyboard.

touch-typist *noun* a person who is skilled in touch-typing.

touchwood *noun* wood which can be used as tinder, especially because it is dry or decayed.

touchy *adj.* (**touchier**, **touchiest**) *colloq.* **1** easily annoyed or offended. **2** needing to be handled or dealt with care and tact.

◫ **1** irritable, irascible, quick-tempered, bad-tempered, grumpy, grouchy, crabbed, cross, peevish, captious, edgy, over-sensitive.
◱ **1** calm, imperturbable.

touchy-feely *adj. colloq.* involving emotions and personal contact as distinct from intellectual activity.

tough /tʌf/ — *adj.* **1** strong and durable; not easily cut, broken, torn, or worn out. **2** *said of food* difficult to chew. **3** *said of people and animals* strong and fit and able to endure hardship. **4** difficult to deal with or overcome; testing. **5** severe and determined; resolute. **6** rough and violent; criminal. **7** *colloq.* unlucky; unjust; unpleasant: *tough luck.* — *noun* a rough, violent person, especially a bully or criminal. — **get tough with someone** *colloq.* to begin to deal with them more strictly or severely. [from Anglo-Saxon *toh*]

◫ *adj.* **1**, **3** strong, resilient, hardy, sturdy, solid, robust. **1** durable, resistant, rigid, stiff, inflexible, hard, leathery. **3** fit, muscular. **4** arduous, laborious, exacting, hard, difficult, puzzling, perplexing, baffling, knotty, thorny, troublesome. **5** harsh, severe, strict, stern, firm, resolute, determined, tenacious, unyielding, uncompromising. **6** rough, violent, vicious, callous, hardened, obstinate. *noun* brute, thug, bully, ruffian, hooligan, lout, *slang* yob.
◱ *adj.* **1**, **3** fragile, delicate, weak. **2** tender. **4** easy, simple. **5** gentle, soft.

toughen *verb* (**toughened**, **toughening**) (*also* **toughen up** or **toughen someone up**) to become or make them tough or tougher.

◫ harden, strengthen, fortify.

tough love care for others that involves them taking the initiative to improve themselves, correct faults, etc.

toughly *adv.* in a tough way.
toughness *noun* a tough quality.
toupee /ˈtuːpeɪ/ *noun* a small wig or hair-piece worn usually by men to cover a bald patch. [from French *toupet*, tuft of hair]

tour /tʊə(r)/ — *noun* **1** an extended journey round a place stopping at various places along the route and usually returning to one's starting-point at the end: *a coach tour of Italy.* **2** a visit round a particular place: *a tour of the cathedral.* **3** a journey round a place with frequent stops for business or professional engagements along the route, eg by a theatre company or a sports team visiting from abroad. **4** an official period of duty or military service, especially abroad. — *verb* **1** *trans., intrans.* to make a tour of (a place). **2** *said of a theatre company* to travel from place to place giving performances (of a play). [from Old French, from Greek *tornos*, tool for making circles] noun **1**, **2** circuit, round, visit. **1** expedition, journey, trip, outing, excursion, drive, ride. verb **1** visit, go round, sightsee, explore, travel, journey.

tour de force /tʊə də fɔːs/ (PL. **tours de force**) a feat of strength or skill; an outstanding performance or effort. [French, = turning movement]

Tourette's syndrome /tʊˈrɛts ˈsɪndrəʊm/ Medicine a disorder that usually starts in childhood, and is characterized by severe and multiple nervous tics, and coprolalia (involuntary obscene speech). Its cause is unknown. [named after the French physician Gilles de la Tourette]

tourism noun **1** the practice of travelling to and visiting places for pleasure and relaxation. **2** the industry providing services, eg accommodation and catering, for tourists.

tourist — noun **1** a person who travels for pleasure and relaxation. **2** a member of a sports team visiting from abroad. — adj. of or suitable for tourists, often in being cheap or reasonably priced.

 noun **1** holidaymaker, North Amer. vacationer, visitor, sightseer, tripper, excursionist, traveller, voyager, globetrotter.

tourist class the cheapest class of passenger accommodation on a ship or in an aircraft.

touristy adj. derog. designed for or full of tourists.

tourmaline /ˈtʊəməliːn/ noun Geol. any of a group of aluminium silicate minerals containing boron, and found in many igneous and metamorphic rocks. Tourmaline crystals, which may be transparent or coloured, are used as semi-precious gemstones, especially the pink, blue, and green varieties. [from Sinhalese tormalliya, cornelian]

tournament /ˈtʊənəmənt/ noun **1** a competition, eg in tennis or chess, between many players for a championship, usually played in heats. **2** Hist. in the Middle Ages, a competition in which knights on horseback fought with usually blunted lances and swords. [from Old French torneiement]

 1 championship, series, competition, contest, match, event, meeting.

tournedos /ˈtʊənədəʊ/ noun (PL. **tournedos**) a small round thick fillet of beef. [from French]

tourney /ˈtʊənɪ/ — noun (PL. **tourneys**) a medieval tournament. — verb intrans. (**tourneys**, **tourneyed**) to take part in a medieval tournament. [from Old French torneie]

tourniquet /ˈtʊənɪkeɪ/ noun a bandage or other device for tying very tightly round an arm or leg to stop the flow of blood through an artery. [from French tourner, to turn]

tousle /ˈtaʊzl/ — verb to make (especially hair) untidy; to tangle or dishevel. — noun a tousled mass. [from Middle English touselen]

tout /taʊt/ — verb **1** intrans. to try persistently to persuade people to buy something, give support, etc: tout for trade. **2** to try persistently to persuade (someone) to buy (something). **3** to advertise or praise strongly or aggressively. **4** intrans. to spy on racehorses in training to gain information about their condition and likely future performance. — noun **1** a person who buys up large numbers of tickets for a popular sporting event, concert, etc and sells them at inflated prices to members of the public. **2** a person who spies on racehorses in training and passes information about their condition, etc to people wishing to bet on them. **3** a person who touts for trade, especially persistently or aggressively. [from Middle English tuten, to peep out]

 verb **2** sell, hawk, peddle. **3** advertise, promote, colloq. plug, colloq. hype.

tow[1] /təʊ/ — verb **1** to pull (a ship, barge, car, trailer, etc) by rope, chain, or cable behind the vehicle one is driving. **2** said of a vehicle to pull (a ship, barge, car, etc) along by rope, chain, or cable. — noun **1** an act of towing or the state of being towed. **2** something towed, eg a car. — **in tow 1** (also on or under tow) said of a vehicle being towed. **2** said of a person following or accompanying as a companion or escort: she arrived late with several men in tow. **3** said of a person under one's protection, guidance, or control. [from Anglo-Saxon togian]

 verb PULL, TUG, DRAW, TRAIL, DRAG, LUG, HAUL, TRANSPORT.

tow[2] /təʊ/ noun coarse, short, or broken fibres of flax or hemp prepared for spinning into rope. [from Anglo-Saxon tow-]

towards or **toward** prep. **1** in the direction of: travel towards Boston / turn towards him. **2** in relation or regard to: a strange attitude towards the new manager. **3** as a contribution to: donate £1000 towards the cost of a new hospital. **4** near; just before: towards midnight. [from Anglo-Saxon toweard, future]

 1 to. **2** regarding, with regard to, with respect to, concerning, about, for. **4** approaching, nearing, close to, nearly, almost.

towbar noun a short rigid bar at the back of a car for towing a caravan or trailer.

tow-coloured adj., said of hair very fair.

towel — noun **1** a piece of absorbent cloth or paper for drying oneself, washed dishes, etc. **2** a sanitary towel. — verb (**towelled**, **towelling**) **1** to rub, wipe, or dry with a towel. **2** slang to thrash. [from Old French toaille]

towelling noun **1** an absorbent cotton cloth for making towels. **2** slang a thrashing.

tower — noun **1** a tall, narrow, usually circular or square structure forming part of a larger, lower building such as a church or castle or standing alone, built for defence, as a lookout, for machinery, etc. **2** a fortress, especially one with one or more towers: the Tower of London. — verb intrans. (**towered**, **towering**) (often **tower above something** or **someone**) to reach a great height or rise high above them. — **a tower of strength** someone who is a great help or support. **tower over someone** to be considerably taller than or superior to them. [from Anglo-Saxon torr]

 noun **1** steeple, spire, belfry, turret, fortification, bastion, citadel. **2** fort, fortress, castle, keep. verb rise, rear, ascend, mount, soar, loom. **tower over** overlook, dominate, surpass, transcend, exceed, top.

tower block a very tall residential or office building.

towering adj. **1** reaching a great height; very tall or elevated. **2** said of an achievement, genius, etc extremely impressive. **3** said of rage, fury, etc intense; violent.

 GREAT, COLOSSAL. **1**, **2** monumental, gigantic, imposing, impressive. **1** soaring, tall, high, lofty, elevated. **2** magnificent, sublime, supreme, surpassing, overpowering, extreme, inordinate.

 1 small, tiny. **2** minor, trivial.

tow-head /ˈtəʊhɛd/ noun a person with very fair or tousled hair.

tow-headed adj. **1** fair-haired. **2** having tousled hair.

towline or **towrope** noun a rope, chain, or cable used for towing.

town noun **1** an urban area with relatively defined boundaries and a name, smaller than a city but larger than a village. **2** the central shopping or business area in a neighbourhood. **3** the principal town in an area, or the capital city of a country, regarded as a destination: *went into town on Thursday.* **4** the people living in a town. **5** city or urban life in general as opposed to the countryside and rural life. **6** the permanent residents of a town as opposed to *gown,* the members of its university. **— go out on the town** *colloq.* to enjoy the entertainments offered by a town, especially its restaurants and bars. **go to town** *colloq.* to do something very thoroughly or with great enthusiasm or expense. [from Anglo-Saxon *tun,* enclosure, manor]

. . . .

🖃 **1** market town, county town, new town, city, metropolis, conurbation. **2** city centre, *North Amer.* downtown.

. . . .

town clerk *Brit. Hist.* (until 1974) a secretary and legal advisor to a town council.

town council an elected governing body of a town.

town councillor a member of a town council.

town crier *Hist.* a person whose job is to make public announcements in the streets of a town.

townee or **townie** *noun colloq., often derog.* a person living in a town, especially as opposed to a person living in the countryside or a member of a town's university.

town gas a flammable gas, obtained from coal and consisting of a mixture of methane, hydrogen, and carbon, formerly used as an industrial and domestic fuel, and now largely superseded by natural gas.

town hall the building where the official business of a town is carried out.

town house 1 a terraced house, especially a fashionable one, and often with the living room on an upper floor. **2** a person's house in town as opposed to his or her house in the country.

town planning the planning and designing of the future development of a town.

townscape *noun* the general appearance of or visual impression created by a town.

townsfolk *pl. noun* the people living in a town or city.

township *noun* **1** *South Afr.* an urban area where black and coloured citizens live. **2** *Brit. Hist.* a division of a large parish. **3** *North Amer.* a subdivision of a county with some degree of local government. **4** *North Amer.* an area of land or district 36 miles square. **5** *Austral.* a small town or settlement.

townsman and **townswoman** *noun* a man or woman living in a town or city.

townspeople *pl. noun* the people living in a town or city.

towpath *noun* a path beside a canal or river formerly used by horses towing barges.

toxaemia /tɒkˈsiːmɪə/ *noun* **1** *Medicine* blood poisoning caused by the presence of a bacterial toxin in the bloodstream, released from a local site of bacterial infection such as an abscess. It may also occur as a result of kidney failure. **2** a serious complication that sometimes occurs in late pregnancy, characterized by a sudden increase in blood pressure, oedema (abnormal retention of fluid in the body tissues), and the excretion of protein in the urine. [from Greek *toxikon,* poison for the tips of arrows + *haima,* blood]

toxaemic *adj.* relating to or affected with toxaemia.

toxic *adj.* **1** poisonous. **2** of or caused by a poison or toxin. [from Greek *toxikon pharmakon,* poison for the tips of arrows, from *toxon,* bow]

. . . .

🖃 **1** poisonous, harmful, noxious, unhealthy, dangerous, deadly, lethal.

🖾 **1** harmless, safe.

. . . .

toxicity /tɒkˈsɪsɪtɪ/ *noun* (PL. **toxicities**) **1** the degree to which a substance is poisonous. **2** the state of being poisonous.

toxicologist *noun* an expert in toxicology.

toxicology /tɒksɪˈkɒlədʒɪ/ *noun* the scientific study of poisons.

toxic shock syndrome a potentially fatal condition in women, marked by flu-like symptoms and a drop in blood pressure, caused by blood-poisoning which is itself caused by a toxin developing in a high-absorbency tampon which is kept too long in the body during menstruation.

toxin *noun* any poison produced naturally by plants, animals, bacteria, etc, especially in a body.

toxocara /tɒksəˈkɑːrə/ *noun Zool.* any of various roundworms, especially *Toxocara canis* and *T. cati,* which live as parasites in the intestines of dogs and cats, respectively. When transmitted to humans they cause the disease toxocariasis, which often results in damage to the retina of the eye. [from Greek *toxikon,* poison for the tips of arrows + *kara,* head]

toxoid *noun Biol.* a toxin that has been treated so as to remove its toxic properties without destroying its ability to stimulate the production of antibodies, eg chemically treated preparations of diphtheria and tetanus toxins are used as vaccines.

toy — noun 1 an object made, especially for a child, to play with. **2** *often derog.* anything, especially a gadget, intended to be or thought of as being for amusement or pleasure rather than practical use. **3** something which is very small, especially a dwarf breed of dog. — *adj.* **1** made to be played with, especially in imitation of something real: *a toy oven.* **2** being a dwarf breed. — *verb intrans.* **1** (**toy with someone**) to flirt or amuse oneself amorously with them. **2** (**toy with something**) to play with it in an idle way and without much interest: *toy with one's food.* [from Middle English *toye,* dalliance]

. . . .

🖃 *noun* **1** plaything, game, doll, knick-knack. *verb* PLAY WITH. **1** trifle with, dally with, sport with. **2** tinker with, fiddle with.

. . . .

TQM *abbrev.* total quality management.

toy boy *colloq.* a usually young man who is the lover of a woman much older than himself.

trabeated construction /ˈtrabɪeɪtɪd, ˈtreɪbɪeɪtɪd/ *Archit.* a method of building in which vertical load-bearing posts are used to support horizontal beams, without the use of arches and vaults. Classical Greek architects used this method, especially for large public buildings, with columns supporting the structure externally and internally. [from Latin *trabs,* beam]

trace[1] — *noun* **1** a mark or sign that some person, animal, or thing has been in that place. **2** a track or footprint. **3** a very small amount that can only just be detected. **4** a tracing. **5** a line marked by the moving pen of a recording instrument. **6** a visible line on a cathode ray tube showing the path of a moving spot. **7** a supposed physical change in the brain or cells of the nervous system caused by learning. — *verb* **1** to track and discover by or as if by following clues, a trail, etc. **2** to follow step by step: *trace the development of medicine.* **3** to make a copy of (a drawing, design, etc) by covering it with a sheet of semi-transparent paper and drawing over the visible lines. **4** to outline or sketch (an idea, plan, etc). **5** (*also* **trace back** or **trace something back**) to date or be dated back to a specified time: *can trace the name back to the sixteenth century.* [from Old French, from Latin *trahere,* to draw]

. . . .

🖃 *noun* **1** mark, token, sign, indication, evidence, record, relic, remains, remnant, vestige. **2** trail, track, spoor, footprint, footmark. **3** hint, suggestion, suspicion, soupçon, dash, drop, spot, bit, jot, touch, smack, shadow. **4** copy, drawing, sketch, outline. *verb* **1** find, discover, detect, unearth, track (down), trail, stalk, hunt, seek, follow, pursue, shadow. **2** mark, record, map, chart, depict. **3, 4** sketch, outline, delineate. **3** copy, draw.

. . . .

trace[2] *noun* either of two ropes, chains, or straps attached to an animal's collar, etc for pulling a carriage, cart, etc. — **kick over the traces** to become independent or rebellious. [from Old French *trais*, from Latin *trahere*, to pull]

trace element a chemical element that is required in very small quantities for the growth, development, and general health of a living organism, eg zinc, copper, molybdenum. Trace elements are usually toxic if absorbed in large quantities.

tracer *noun* 1 a person or device that traces. 2 a bullet, etc which leaves a smoke-trail behind it by which its flight path can be seen. 3 a substance, especially a radioactive element, whose course through the body, or effect on it, can be observed.

tracer bullet or **tracer shell** a bullet or shell containing a charge of chemical compound (such as phosphorus) which glows brightly as it travels through the air, indicating in darkness or the fog of war the path of the bullet or shell and its efficacy in reaching its target.

tracery /ˈtreɪsərɪ/ *noun* (PL. **traceries**) 1 ornamental open stonework used to form a decorative pattern, especially in the top part of a Gothic window. 2 a finely patterned decoration or design.

trachea /trəˈkɪə/ *noun* (PL. **tracheae**) the passage which carries air into and out of the lungs from the larynx; the windpipe. [from Greek *tracheia arteria*, rough artery]

tracheotomy /trækɪˈɒtəmɪ/ or **tracheostomy** /trækɪˈɒstəmɪ/ *noun* (PL. **tracheotomies, tracheostomies**) *Medicine* a surgical operation in which an incision is made through the front of the neck into the trachea (windpipe), usually to provide an alternative airway when breathing is obstructed, eg during diphtheria, or when the larynx is blocked by a tumour. [from TRACHEA + Greek *tome*, a cutting]

trachoma /trəˈkoʊmə/ *noun* *Medicine* a contagious eye disease, common in the Third World, caused by the bacterium *Chlamydia trachomatis*, which is transmitted by flies. The main symptoms are inflammation and scarring of the conjunctiva, redness, and pain. If untreated it may spread to the cornea, causing blindness. [from Greek *trachoma*, roughness]

tracing *noun* 1 a copy of a drawing made on semi-transparent paper. 2 an act of tracing.

tracing paper thin, semi-transparent paper used for tracing drawings.

track — *noun* 1 a mark or trail left by the passing of a person, animal, or thing, especially a footprint. 2 a rough path, especially one beaten by feet. 3 a specially prepared course, especially for racing. 4 a railway line, ie the parallel rails, the space in between, and the sleepers and stones below. 5 a length of railing along which something, eg a curtain, moves. 6 the groove cut in a record by the recording instrument. 7 one of several items, eg a song or movement of a symphony, recorded on a disc or tape. 8 one of several paths on magnetic recording tape that receives information from a single input channel. 9 one of a series of parallel paths on magnetic recording tape that contains a single sequence of signals. 10 *Comput.* an area that is created on the surface of a magnetic disc during the process of formatting, and within which data can be stored. 11 the line or course of travel or movement. 12 the line or course of thought, reasoning, etc. 13 the predetermined line of travel of an aircraft. 14 the continuous band of metal plates used instead of wheels on heavy vehicles designed to travel over rough surfaces, eg a tank. 15 the distance between a pair of wheels as measured between those parts of the wheels which actually touch the ground. — *verb* 1 to follow the marks, footprints, etc left by (a person or animal). 2 to follow and usually plot the course of (a spacecraft, satellite, etc) by radar. 3 *intrans.* to move a television or film camera in towards, parallel to, or away from the object being filmed. 4 *said of stylus or laser beam* to extract information from (a recording medium, eg a vinyl record or a compact disc). 5 *intrans. said of a vehicle's rear wheels* to run exactly in the course of the front wheels. — **across the tracks** *colloq.* a socially disadvantaged area of town. **in one's tracks** exactly where one is standing. **keep** or **lose**

track of something to keep or fail to keep oneself informed about its progress or whereabouts. **make tracks** *colloq.* to leave; to set out. **on the track of someone** or **something** following, pursuing, or looking for them. **track someone** or **something down** to search for and find them after a thorough search or by following a track. **the wrong side of the tracks** a poor or disadvantaged urban area. [from Old French *trac*]

⊞ *noun* 1 footstep(s), footprint(s), footmark(s), scent, spoor, trail, wake, mark, trace. 2 path, footpath, bridle path, way, lane, trail. 11, 12 course, direction. 11 path, route, orbit, line. 12 drift, sequence, argument. *verb* 1 stalk, trail, hunt, trace, follow, pursue, chase, dog, tail, shadow. **track down** find, discover, trace, hunt down, run to earth, sniff out, ferret out, dig up, unearth, expose, catch, capture.

trackball or **trackerball** *noun Comput.* a ball mounted in a small box linked to a computer terminal, rotated with the palm to move a cursor correspondingly on a screen.

tracker dog a dog specially trained to search for people, especially criminals.

track event *Athletics* a race. See also FIELD EVENT.

tracking *noun* 1 the balance of the arm on a gramophone so that the needle remains correctly positioned in the groove. 2 *Electr.* a leakage of current between two insulated points caused by moisture, dirt, etc.

tracking station a station equipped with radar to follow and plot the courses of spacecraft, satellites, etc.

track record a record of past performance.

track shoe a shoe with a spiked sole worn by a runner.

tracksuit *noun* a warm suit worn by athletes, etc when exercising, or to keep the body warm before and after performing.

tract[1] *noun* 1 an area of land, usually of indefinite extent. 2 a system in the body with a particular function formed by a series of connected organs and glands: *the digestive tract*. 3 a short essay or book, especially on a religious subject. [from Latin *trahere*, to draw]

⊞ 1 stretch, extent, expanse, plot, lot, territory, area, region, zone, district, quarter. 3 booklet, essay, monograph.

tractability *noun* being tractable.

tractable *adj.* easily managed, controlled, or used. [from Latin *tractabilis*]

⊞ pliant, pliable, flexible, manageable, compliant, amenable, biddable, docile, submissive.

⊟ intractable.

tractably *adv.* in a tractable way.

Tractarianism /trækˈtɛərɪənɪzm/ *noun Relig.* the system of religious opinion which sought the revival of high doctrine and ceremonial in the Church of England, promulgated in the *Tracts for the Times* (1833–41) by Keble, Newman, Pusey, Hurrell, Fronde, and others; also known as the Oxford Movement. It led to Anglo-Catholicism and ritualism, and has remained influential in certain quarters of Anglicanism.

traction *noun* 1 the action of pulling, state of being pulled, or the force used in pulling. 2 *Medicine* a steady pulling on a muscle or limb using a series of pulleys and weights, to correct some condition or problem. 3 the grip of a wheel, tyre, etc on the surface on which it moves. [from Latin *tractio*, from *trahere*, to pull]

tractional or **tractive** *adj.* relating to or involving traction.

traction engine a heavy steam-powered road vehicle formerly used for pulling heavy loads, eg farm machinery, and as a mobile power source.

tractor *noun* 1 a slow-moving motor vehicle with two large rear wheels for pulling especially farm machinery, heavy loads, etc. 2 a traction engine. [from Latin *trahere*, to pull]

trad — *noun Brit. colloq.* traditional jazz, the style of jazz music first played in the 1920s and 1930s and which originated in New Orleans. — *adj.* traditional.

trade — *noun* 1 the buying and selling of goods or services. 2 business and commerce, especially as opposed to a profession or landed property; also, the people involved in this. 3 a personal occupation or job, especially one requiring skill; a craft: *a carpenter by trade.* 4 the people and companies engaged in a particular business or occupation: *the building trade.* 5 customers: *the lunchtime trade.* 6 business at a particular time or for a particular market: *the tourist trade / a seasonal trade in woolly hats.* 7 (**trades**) the trade winds. — *verb* 1 (**trade in something**) to buy and sell a particular type of goods. 2 *intrans.* to engage in trade (with a person or country). 3 to exchange (one commodity) for another. — **trade something in** to give it as part payment for something else. **trade something off** to give it in exchange for something else, usually as a compromise. **trade on something** to take unfair advantage of a factor, especially a person's generosity. [from Middle English, = course, path]

■ *noun* 1, 2, 3 business. 1, 2 commerce. 1 traffic, dealing, buying, selling, shopkeeping, barter, exchange, transactions, custom. 3 occupation, job, profession, calling, craft, skill. *verb* 1, 2 traffic in, do business in, deal in. 1 buy, sell, peddle. 3 exchange, swap, switch, barter, bargain.

trade cycle the pattern of changing levels of activity in an economy over a period of time. High points of activity are *booms*, and low points are *recessions* or *slumps*. Economists have identified that a typical trade cycle lasts seven or eight years, though much longer trends have also been identified.

trade gap the amount by which a country's imports are greater than its exports.

trade-in *noun* a commodity that is traded in exchange for another, especially a used vehicle.

trademark *noun* 1 (*in full* **registered trademark**) a name, word, or symbol, especially one that is officially registered and protected by law, used to represent a company or individual and shown on all of the goods made or sold by that company or individual. 2 a distinguishing characteristic or feature.

■ 1 brand, label, name, sign, symbol, logo, insignia, crest, emblem, badge. 2 hallmark, stamp, speciality, feature, attribute, quality, characteristic, idiosyncrasy, peculiarity, quirk.

tradename *noun* 1 a name given to an article or product, or group of these, by the trade which produces them. 2 a name under which a company or individual does business. 3 a name serving as a trademark.

trade-off *noun* an exchange, especially a compromise.

trader *noun* 1 a person who trades, often one who owns or runs a shop, or who trades in a particular group of goods. 2 a ship used for trade.

■ 1 merchant, tradesman, broker, dealer, buyer, seller, vendor, supplier, wholesaler, retailer, shopkeeper, trafficker, peddler.

tradescantia /tradɪˈskanʃɪə/ *noun* any of several widely cultivated plants with attractive, often variegated, leaves. [named after John Tradescant (c.1567–1637), English gardener, naturalist, and traveller]

tradesman or **tradeswoman** *noun* (PL. **tradesmen**) 1 a person engaged in trade, especially a shopkeeper. 2 a skilled worker.

tradespeople *pl. noun* people engaged in trade.

Trades Union Congress a national organization formed from representatives of the individual trade unions, which meets annually to discuss working conditions and the economy in the country at large.

tradeswoman *noun* (PL. **tradeswomen**) a woman engaged in trade, especially a shopkeeper.

trade union or **trades union** an organization of workers or employees formed to protect their interests and to improve working conditions.

trade unionism the principles and practices of trade unions.

trade unionist a member of a trade union.

trade wind a wind that blows continually towards the equator and is deflected westward by the eastward rotation of the earth.

trading estate *Brit.* an area in a town which is developed for industry and business.

trading post a store in a remote or sparsely populated region.

trading stamp a stamp given to a customer in return for a certain amount of money spent on goods in a store, and which may be collected and exchanged for an item supplied by the company issuing the trading stamp.

tradition /trəˈdɪʃən/ *noun* 1 the handing down of doctrines, beliefs, customs, etc from generation to generation. 2 a doctrine, belief, custom, story, etc that is passed on. 3 a particular body of doctrines, beliefs, customs, etc belonging to a particular group of people, religion, country, family, etc. 4 the continuous development of a body of artistic, literary, or musical principles or conventions. [from Latin *traditio*, from *tradere*, to give up]

■ 1, 2 convention, custom, usage, folklore. 2 ritual, institution, way, habit, routine.

traditional *adj.* 1 belonging to or derived from tradition. 2 of the nature of or being a tradition.

■ CONVENTIONAL, CUSTOMARY, HABITUAL, USUAL, ACCUSTOMED, ESTABLISHED, FIXED, LONG-ESTABLISHED, TIME-HONOURED, OLD, HISTORIC. 1 folk, oral, unwritten.

🔁 1 new, modern, contemporary. 2 unconventional, innovative.

traditionalism *noun* belief in the importance of, respect for, and often excessive following of tradition.

traditionalist — *noun* a person who favours tradition. — *adj.* relating to or involving tradition.

traditional jazz see TRAD.

traditionally *adv.* in a traditional way; in terms of tradition.

traduce /trəˈdjuːs/ *verb* to say or write unpleasant things about; to malign. [from Latin *traducere*, to lead across]

traducement *noun* traducing, slander.

traducer *noun* a person who traduces, a slanderer.

traffic — *noun* 1 the vehicles, ships, aircraft, etc moving along a route. 2 the movement of vehicles along a route. 3 illegal or dishonest trade. 4 trade; commerce. 5 the transporting of goods or people on a railway, air, or sea route, etc. 6 the goods or people transported along a route. 7 dealings or communication between groups or individuals. — *verb* (**trafficked, trafficking**) 1 (**traffic in something**) to deal or trade in it, especially illegally or dishonestly. 2 to deal in (a particular type of goods). [from Old French *traffique*]

■ *noun* 1 vehicles, shipping. 4 trade, commerce, business, dealing, trafficking, barter, exchange. 5 transport, transportation. 6 freight, passengers. 7 communication, dealings, relations. *verb* 2 peddle, buy, sell, trade, do business in, deal in, barter.

traffic calming the control of traffic in built-up areas by the use of various devices designed to reduce speed and volume, such as ramps and sleeping policemen.

traffic island see ISLAND.

trafficker /'træfɪkə(r)/ *noun* a dealer or trader, usually in illegal goods.

traffic lights a system of red, amber, and green lights which controls traffic at road junctions, pedestrian crossings, etc.

traffic warden *Brit.* a person whose job is to control the parking of vehicles in towns and report parking offences.

tragedian /trə'dʒiːdɪən/ *noun* **1** an actor who specialises in tragic roles. **2** a person who writes tragedies.

tragedienne /trədʒiːdɪ'ɛn/ *noun* an actress who specializes in tragic roles.

tragedy /'trædʒədɪ/ *noun* (PL. **tragedies**) **1** a serious drama, film, opera, etc in which the main character or characters are eventually destroyed through a combination of events, circumstances, and personality problems. **2** such plays as a group or genre. **3** any sad play, film, book, etc, especially one ending with an unnecessary or untimely death. **4** a serious disaster. **5** any sad event. [from Greek *tragoidia*, from *tragos*, goat + *oide*, song]

⊟ **4** calamity, disaster, catastrophe. **5** adversity, misfortune, unhappiness, affliction, blow.

tragic /'trædʒɪk/ *adj.* **1** sad, especially because of death or destruction; intensely distressing. **2** relating to or in the style of tragedy. [from Greek *tragikos*]

⊟ **1** sad, sorrowful, miserable, unhappy, unfortunate, unlucky, ill-fated, pitiable, pathetic, heartbreaking, shocking, appalling, dreadful, awful, dire, calamitous, disastrous, catastrophic, deadly, fatal.
⊟ **1** happy, comic, successful.

tragically *adv.* in a tragic way; so as to be tragic.

tragicomedy *noun* (PL. **tragicomedies**) a play or event which includes a mixture of both tragedy and comedy. [from Latin *tragicomoedia*]

tragicomic *adj.* having the nature of a tragicomedy, combining comedy and tragedy.

tragicomically *adv.* in a tragicomic way.

trail — *verb* **1** *trans., intrans.* to drag or be dragged loosely along the ground or other surface, especially behind one. **2** *intrans.* (usually **trail along**, **behind**, *etc*) to walk or move along slowly and wearily. **3** to drag (a limb, etc) especially slowly and wearily: *a bird trailing a broken wing.* **4** *trans., intrans.* to fall or lag behind (eg a competitor) in eg a race or contest, often by a stated number of points. **5** to follow the track or footsteps of. **6** *trans., intrans.* to grow or encourage (a plant) to grow so long that it droops over or along a surface towards the ground. — *noun* **1** a track, series of marks, footprints, etc left by a passing person, animal, or thing, especially one followed in hunting. **2** a rough path or track through a wild or mountainous area. **3** anything which drags or is drawn behind. **4** the part of a gun carriage that rests on the ground when the limber is detached. — **trail away** or **off** *said especially of a sound* to become fainter. [from Middle English *trailen*]

⊟ *verb* **1, 3** drag, pull, dangle. **1** extend, stream. **2** straggle, dawdle, lag, loiter, linger. **5** track, stalk, hunt, follow, pursue, chase, shadow, tail. *noun* **1, 2** track, path.
1 footprints, footmarks, scent, trace. **2** footpath, road, route, way.

trailblazer *noun* a person who blazes a trail; a pioneer (see BLAZE[2]).

⊟ pioneer, pathfinder, innovator, inventor, discoverer, developer.

trailblazing — *noun* breaking new ground, pioneering. — *adj.* pioneering.

trailer *noun* **1** a usually two-wheeled cart for towing behind a car, used eg for transporting small boats. **2** the rear section of an articulated lorry, as opposed to the cab. **3** *North Amer.* a caravan. **4** a series of brief extracts from a film or programme prepared as an advertisement for it.

train — *noun* **1 a** a string of railway carriages or wagons with a locomotive. **b** *loosely* a locomotive. **2** a back part of a long dress or robe that trails behind the wearer. **3** the attendants following or accompanying an important person. **4** a connected series of events, actions, ideas, or thoughts. **5** a number of things in a string or connected line, eg a line of animals or vehicles carrying baggage. **6** a line of gunpowder, etc laid to fire a charge. **7** a set of connected wheels which act on each other to transmit motion. — *verb* **1** to teach or prepare (a person or animal) for something through instruction, practice, or exercises. **2** *intrans.* to be taught, or prepare oneself to be taught, through instruction, practice, or exercises: *trained as a nurse.* **3** (**train for something** or **train someone for something**) to prepare oneself or prepare them for performance (eg in a sport) by instruction, practice, exercise, diet, etc: *training for the marathon.* **4** to point or aim (eg a gun) at or focus (eg a telescope) on a particular object or in a particular direction: *the guns were all trained on the front gates.* **5** to make (a plant, tree, etc) grow in a particular direction: *train the ivy along the wall.* **6** *intrans.* to travel by train. [from Old French *trahiner*, to drag]

⊟ *noun* **3** retinue, entourage, attendants, court, household, staff, followers, following. **4** sequence, succession, series, progression, order, chain, string. **5** line, file, procession, convoy, cortège, caravan. *verb* **1, 2** drill, exercise, work out, practise, rehearse, prepare. **1** teach, instruct, coach, tutor, educate, improve, school, discipline. **4** point, direct, aim, level.

train-bearer *noun* a person who carries the train of a person's dress or robe.

trained *adj.* having received training; prepared; tamed.

trainee *noun* a person who is being trained for a job.

⊟ apprentice, pupil, learner, student, probationer.

trainer *noun* **1** a person who trains racehorses, athletes, sportsmen and women, etc. **2** *Brit.* a soft running shoe with a thick sole. **3** a machine or device used in training, eg an aircraft with two sets of controls for training pilots.

⊟ **1** teacher, instructor, coach, tutor, handler.

training *noun* **1** the act or process of being prepared for something, of being taught or learning a particular skill and practising it until the required standard is reached: *go into training for the marathon.* **2** the state of being physically fit: *out of training.*

⊟ **1** teaching, instruction, coaching, tuition, education, schooling, discipline, preparation, grounding, drill, exercise, working-out, practice, learning, apprenticeship.

trainspotter *noun* **1** a person who notes the numbers of railway locomotives or rolling stock as a hobby. **2** *colloq.* a person who takes an obsessive interest in a trivial subject.

trainspotting *noun* the activity of a trainspotter.

traipse or **trapes** /treɪps/ — *verb intrans.* to walk or trudge along idly or wearily. — *noun* a long, tiring walk.

trait /treɪt, treɪ/ *noun* a distinguishing feature or quality, especially of a person's character. [from French, from Latin *trahere*, to draw]

⊟ feature, attribute, quality, characteristic, idiosyncrasy, peculiarity, quirk.

traitor /'treɪtə(r)/ *noun* 1 a person who commits treason and betrays his or her country to the enemy. 2 a person who betrays a friend's trust. [from Latin *tradere*, to give up]

⊟ BETRAYER. 1 turncoat, renegade, deserter, defector, quisling, collaborator. 2 informer, deceiver, double-crosser.
⊞ 1 loyalist. 2 supporter, defender.

traitorous *adj.* like a traitor; treacherous.

traitorously *adv.* in a traitorous way.

traitress *noun old use* a female traitor.

trajectory /trə'dʒektərɪ/ *noun* (PL. **trajectories**) *Physics* the curved path followed by an object that has been projected into the air (a *projectile*), eg a rocket, guided missile, or bullet. [from Latin *trajectorius*, casting over]

tram *noun* 1 an electrically-powered passenger vehicle which runs on rails laid in the streets. 2 a truck or wagon running on rails in a mine.

tramcar *noun* same as TRAM 1.

tramline *noun* 1 (*often* **tramlines**) either of a pair of rails forming the track on which trams run. 2 (**tramlines**) *colloq.* the lines marking the sides of a tennis or badminton court and the lines parallel to them inside the court.

trammel /'traml/ — *noun* 1 a dragnet for fishing in which a fine inner mesh is carried by fish through the coarse outer mesh, thus trapping the fish in a pocket. 2 (*usually* **trammels**) anything which hinders or prevents free action or movement. — *verb* (**trammelled**, **trammelling**) 1 to catch or entangle, especially in a trammel. 2 to hinder or prevent the free movement of. [from Old French *tramail*, net]

tramp — *verb* 1 *intrans.* (*usually* **tramp about**, **up**) to walk with firm, heavy footsteps. 2 *intrans.* to make a journey on foot, especially heavily or wearily: *tramp over the hills.* 3 to walk heavily and wearily on or through: *tramp the streets.* 4 to walk (a specified distance) heavily and wearily: *tramp six miles across the open moor.* 5 *intrans.* to live as a tramp. 6 to tread or trample. — *noun* 1 a person with no fixed home or job, who travels from place to place on foot and who lives by begging and doing odd jobs. 2 a long and often tiring walk especially in the country. 3 the sound of heavy, rhythmic footsteps. 4 (*in full* **tramp steamer**) a cargo boat with no fixed or regular route. 5 *slang* a promiscuous or immoral woman. 6 an iron plate on the sole of a shoe to protect it, eg when digging. [from Middle English *trampen*]

⊟ *verb* 1, 2, 3, 4 walk, march, plod, trudge. 1 tread, stamp, stomp, stump. 2 trail, trek, hike, traipse, ramble, roam, rove. *noun* 1 vagrant, vagabond, hobo, down-and-out, *slang* dosser. 2 walk, march, trek, hike, ramble. 5 slut, *slang* tart, *slang* scrubber, trollop, whore.

trample — *verb trans.*, *intrans.* 1 (**trample something** or **on something**) to tread on it heavily or roughly: *trampled on the flower-bed.* 2 to press or be pressed down by treading or being trodden on: *cigarette ash trampled into the carpet.* 3 to treat someone dismissively or with contempt: *trampled all over them / trampled over their feelings.* — *noun* an act of trampling or the sound made by trampling. [from Middle English *tramplen*, to stamp]

⊟ *verb* 1, 2 tread (on). 2, 3 stamp (on), crush, squash, flatten.

trampoline /'trampəliːn/ — *noun* a piece of tough canvas attached to a framework by cords or rope and stretched tight, for acrobats, gymnasts, children, etc to jump on. — *verb intrans.* to jump, turn somersaults, etc on a trampoline. [from Italian *trampolino*, springboard]

tramway *noun* 1 a system of tracks for trams. 2 a tram system.

trance /trɑːns/ *noun* 1 a sleep-like or half-conscious state in which one loses the ability to react to stimuli such as pain. 2 a dazed or absorbed state. 3 a usually self-induced state in which one may experience religious or mystical ecstasy. 4 (*also* **trance music**) a type of repetitive electronic dance music. [from Latin *transire*, to go across]

⊟ 1 dream, reverie. 2 daze, stupor, unconsciousness. 3 hypnosis, spell, ecstasy, rapture.

trannie or **tranny** *noun* (PL. **trannies**) 1 *Brit. colloq.* a transistor radio. 2 *slang* a transvestite.

tranquil /'traŋkwɪl/ *adj.* quiet; peaceful; undisturbed. [from Latin *tranquillus*]

⊟ serene, peaceful, restful, still, undisturbed, untroubled, quiet, hushed, silent, calm, composed, cool, imperturbable, unexcited, placid, sedate, relaxed, *colloq.* laid-back.
⊞ agitated, disturbed, troubled, noisy.

tranquillity *noun* a tranquil state or quality; calmness.

⊟ serenity, peace, restfulness, stillness, quietness, hush, silence, calm, composure, imperturbability.

tranquillize or **tranquillise** *verb trans.*, *intrans.* to make or become calm, peaceful, or less tense or restore or be restored to such a state, especially through drugs.

tranquillizer /'traŋkwɪlaɪzə(r)/ or **tranquilliser** *noun* a drug that acts on the central nervous system and has a calming and relaxing effect. Major tranquillizers, eg chlorpromazine, are used to treat severe mental disorders such as schizophrenia. Minor tranquillizers, eg diazepam, are used to relieve anxiety and tension, but may become addictive if taken for prolonged periods.

⊟ sedative, opiate, narcotic, barbiturate.

tranquilly *adv.* in a tranquil way.

trans *abbrev.* 1 transitive. 2 translation; translated.

trans- *prefix* forming words meaning: 1 across; beyond; on the other side of: *transatlantic.* 2 through. 3 into another state or place: *transform.* [from Latin *trans*, across]

transact /tran'zakt/ *verb* to conduct or carry out (business). [from Latin *transigere*, to force through]

transaction *noun* 1 something transacted, especially a business deal. 2 (**transactions**) the published reports of papers read, discussions, decisions taken, etc at a meeting of a learned society. 3 an act of transacting.

⊟ 1, 3 arrangement, negotiation. 1 deal, bargain, agreement, business, affair, matter, enterprise, undertaking, deed, action. 2 proceedings, papers, records. 3 execution, discharge.

transactor *noun formal* a person who transacts, a negotiator.

transalpine *adj.* situated or happening beyond the Alps (originally as viewed from Rome). [from Latin *transalpinus*]

transatlantic *adj.* 1 crossing the Atlantic. 2 situated on the other side of the Atlantic. 3 relating to or originating from the other side of the Atlantic.

transceiver /tran'siːvə(r)/ *noun* a piece of radio equipment which both receives and transmits signals.

transcend /tran'sɛnd/ *verb* 1 to be beyond the limits or range of: *transcend the bounds of human experience.* 2 to be better or greater than; to surpass or excel. 3 to overcome or surmount: *transcend all difficulties.* [from Latin *transcendere*, to climb over]

⊟ 1, 2 surpass, pass, exceed, go beyond. 2 excel, outshine, eclipse, outdo, outstrip, beat.

transcendence or **transcendency** *noun* transcending.

transcendent *adj.* **1** going beyond in excellence; surpassing or excelling. **2** beyond usual human knowledge or experience. **3** *said especially of a deity* existing outside the material or created world and independent of it.

⊟ **1** surpassing, supreme, sublime, superlative, incomparable, matchless, peerless, unparalleled, unsurpassable. **2** ineffable, superhuman, supernatural, spiritual, numinous.

transcendental /transən'dɛntl/ *adj.* **1** going beyond usual human knowledge or experience. **2** going beyond in excellence; surpassing or excelling. **3** supernatural or mystical. **4** vague, abstract, or abstruse.

transcendentalism *noun* any philosophical system concerned with what is constant, innate, and a priori, independent of and a necessary prerequisite to experience.

transcendentally *adv.* in a transcendental way.

transcendental meditation a system of meditation for relieving anxiety, promoting spiritual wellbeing, and achieving physical and mental relaxation through the (usually silent) repetition of a mantra.

transcendental number *Maths.* an irrational number (a number that cannot be expressed as a ratio of two integers) that is not algebraic, eg π.

transcontinental — *adj.*, *said especially of a railway* crossing a continent. — *noun* something that crosses a continent, eg a railway.

transcribe /tran'skraɪb/ *verb* **1** to write out (a text) in full, eg from notes: *take shorthand notes to be transcribed later.* **2** to copy (a text) from one place to another: *transcribed the poem into her album.* **3** to write out (a spoken text); to convert (a text) from one form of notation to another. **4** *Mus.* to arrange (a piece of music) for an instrument or voice that it was not originally composed for. **5** to record any form of information on a suitable storage medium. **6** *Comput.* to transfer data from one computer storage device to another, eg from tape to disk, or from the main memory of a computer to a storage device, or from a storage device to the main memory. [from Latin *transcribere*]

⊟ **1, 2, 3** write out, write up. **2** copy, reproduce, rewrite. **3** take down, note, record, transliterate, translate, render.

transcript /'transkrɪpt/ *noun* a written or printed copy, especially a legal or official copy of court proceedings. [from Latin *transcriptum*]

⊟ transcription, copy, reproduction, duplicate, transliteration, translation, version, note, record, manuscript.

transcription *noun* **1** the act of transcribing. **2** something transcribed; a transcript. [from Latin *transcriptio*]

transducer /trans'djuːsə(r)/ *noun* **1** *Electr.* a device that converts energy from one form to another, eg a loudspeaker, which converts electrical energy into sound waves. **2** *Electr.* a device that converts a physical quantity, such as sound, light, or temperature, into an electrical signal, eg a microphone or photoelectric cell. Because electrical signals can be measured, transducers are used in many types of sensor. [from Latin *transducere*, to lead across]

transept *noun* each of the two arms forming the part of a cross-shaped church that is at right angles to the nave; also, the area formed by these two arms. [from Latin *transeptum*, from *trans*, across + *saeptum*, enclosure]

trans-fatty acid an acid formed when unsaturated fats are converted into saturated fats by hydrogenation.

transfer /trans'fɜː(r) 'transfɜː(r)/ — *verb* (**transferred**, **transferring**) (with stress on *-fer*) **1** *trans.*, *intrans.* to move from one place, person, or group to another. **2** *intrans.* to change from one vehicle, line, or passenger system to another. **3** *Legal* to give the right to or ownership of (property) to someone. **4** to move (a design) from one surface to another. — *noun* (with stress on *trans-*) **1** an act of transferring or the state of being transferred. **2** a design or picture that can be transferred from one surface to another. **3** any person or thing that is transferred. **4** *Legal* the changing of the right to property from one person to another; conveyance. **5** *Legal* any document which records such a change in the right to property. **6** *North Amer.* a ticket allowing a passenger to continue a journey on another route. [from Latin *transferre*, to carry across]

⊟ *verb* **1, 2** change. **1** move, shift, remove, relocate, transplant, transpose. **3** assign, consign, grant, hand over, convey, transmit. *noun* **1** change, change-over, transposition, move, shift, removal, relocation, displacement, transmission, handover, transference.

transferable /trans'fɜːrəbl/ *adj.* capable of being transferred.

transference *noun* **1** the act of transferring from one person, place, or group to another. **2** *Psychol.* an unconscious transferring of one's emotions, fears, anxieties, etc to another person or thing, especially to a psychoanalyst during therapy.

transfer orbit *Astron.* the flight path taken by a spacecraft as it moves from one orbit to another.

transfer pricing *Commerce* the price charged when an article is passed from one part or department of a company to another. When such a transfer is across national boundaries, as with multinational companies, the company may avoid taxes in one country by artificially fixing the price.

transfer RNA *Genetics* (ABBREV. **tRNA**) a small molecule of RNA (ribonucleic acid) whose function is to carry specific amino acids from the cytoplasm to the specialized structures known as ribosomes that are the site of protein manufacture in living cells.

transfiguration *noun* **1** a change in appearance, especially to something more beautiful, glorious, or exalted. **2** (**Transfiguration**) **a** *Christianity* the radiant change in Christ's appearance described in Matthew 17.1–2. **b** a Church festival held on 6 Aug to commemorate this.

transfigure /trans'fɪgə(r)/ *verb* to change the appearance of, especially so as to make more beautiful, glorious, or exalted. [from Latin *transfigurare*]

transfix *verb* **1** to cause (someone) to be unable to move through surprise, fear, horror, etc. **2** to pierce through with, or as if with, a pointed weapon. [from Latin *transfigere*, to pierce through]

⊟ **1** fascinate, spellbind, mesmerize, hypnotize, paralyse. **2** impale, spear, skewer, spike, stick.

transfixion *noun* transfixing or being transfixed.

transform *verb* **1** to change the appearance, nature, or function of completely and often dramatically. **2** *intrans.* to undergo a complete and often dramatic change of appearance, function, or nature. **3** *Maths.* to change the form but not the value of (an equation or algebraic expression). **4** to change the voltage or type of (a current), eg from alternating to direct. [from Latin *transformare*]

⊟ **1, 2** change, alter, adapt. **1** convert, remodel, reconstruct, transfigure, revolutionize.
🗷 **1** preserve, maintain.

transformation *noun* **1** transforming or being transformed. **2** a change of form, constitution, or substance.

⊟ ALTERATION, MUTATION, CONVERSION, METAMORPHOSIS, TRANSFIGURATION. **2** change, revolution.
🗷 **1** preservation, conservation.

transformational grammar *Linguistics* a system of generative grammar in which elements or structures can be derived from others or related to others by using a set of rules to convert the basic structure of a sentence into the forms in which they will occur in the language.

transformer *noun Electr.* an electromagnetic device, usually consisting of two coils of wire (the input or *primary* and the output or *secondary*) wound on the same iron core, and used to transfer electrical energy from one alternating current circuit to another, with an increase or decrease in voltage. Transformers are used to provide a low-voltage domestic supply from high-voltage mains electricity, and to provide even lower voltages for the operation of electrical appliances, eg television sets.

transfuse /trans'fjuːz/ *verb* 1 to transfer (blood or plasma from one person) into the blood vessels of another. 2 to cause to pass, enter, or diffuse through. 3 to cause (fluid) to pass from one vessel to another. [from Latin *transfundere*, to pour out]

transfusion /trans'fjuːʒən/ *noun* 1 (*in full* **blood transfusion**) the introduction of whole blood directly into a person's bloodstream by allowing it to drip under gravity through a needle inserted in a vein. 2 the introduction of a component of whole blood (eg plasma) or saline solution into a person's bloodstream in a similar manner, eg to treat shock.

transgenic /trans'dʒɛnɪk/ *adj. Genetics* containing genetic material introduced, usually in the form of DNA, from another species.

transgress *verb* 1 *trans., intrans.* to go beyond the limits set by, break, or violate (divine law, a rule, etc). 2 to overstep (a limit or boundary). [from Latin *transgredi*, to step across]

> ⊟ 1 offend (against), sin (against), disobey. 2 overstep, infringe.

transgression *noun* 1 the act of breaking rules, divine law, etc. 2 a fault, crime, or sin.

transgressor *noun* a person who transgresses, a sinner.

tranship /tran'ʃɪp/ same as TRANSSHIP.

transhumance /trans'hjuːməns/ *noun* the transfer of livestock, most often cattle or sheep, between summer and winter pastures. It is characteristic of many mountainous regions, where entire families may move with their flocks to high altitude pastures, and of Arctic regions where livestock are moved to more northerly pastures in summer. [from Spanish *trashumar*, from Latin *trans*, across, beyond + *humus* ground]

transience or **transiency** *noun* a transient quality.

transient /'transɪənt/ — *adj.* lasting, staying, or visiting for a short time only; passing quickly. — *noun* 1 a temporary resident or worker. 2 a short, sudden surge of voltage or current. [from Latin *transire*, to cross over]

> ⊟ *adj.* transitory, passing, flying, fleeting, brief, short, momentary, ephemeral, short-lived, temporary, short-term.
> ⊞ *adj.* lasting, permanent.

transiently *adv.* in a transient way.

transistor /tran'zɪstə(r)/ *noun* 1 *Electron.* a semiconductor device with three electrodes, used as a switch or to amplify (strengthen) electric current in electronic circuits. Transistors have superseded valves because they are smaller, more efficient, and cheaper to produce. They are used to amplify signals in radio receivers, television sets, etc, and complex circuits containing thousands of transistors can be constructed on silicon chips. 2 (*in full* **transistor radio**) a small portable radio using transistors. [from TRANSFER + RESISTOR]

transistorize or **transistorise** *verb* to fit with a transistor or transistors.

transistorized or **transistorised** *adj.* equipped or powered with transistors.

transit — *noun* 1 the carrying or movement of goods or passengers from place to place or across or through a place. 2 a route or passage: *transit by sea*. 3 *North Amer.*,

esp. US the transport of passengers or goods on public, usually local, routes. 4 the passage of a heavenly body across a meridian. — *verb* (**transited, transiting**) to pass across or through. — **in transit** *said of goods or passengers* in the process of being taken from or travelling from one place to another. [from Latin *transitus*, from *transire*, to cross over]

> ⊟ *noun* 1 movement, transfer, transportation, conveyance, carriage, haulage, shipment. 2 passage, journey, travel, route. **in transit** on the way, en route, travelling.

transit camp a camp for the temporary accommodation of soldiers, refugees, etc on the way to their permanent destination.

transit instrument an astronomical instrument for observing the passage of a heavenly body across the meridian; generally a telescope mounted on a fixed horizontal axis so as to sweep the meridian in a vertical plane. It may be used for correcting clocks, and as a means of determining longitude.

transition *noun* 1 a change or passage from one place, state, subject, etc to another. 2 *Mus.* a change from one key to another. 3 *Archit.* the gradual change from one style to another, especially from Norman to Early English. [from Latin *transitio*, from *transire*, to cross over]

> ⊟ 1 passage, passing, progress, progression, development, evolution, flux, change, alteration, conversion, transformation, shift.

transitional or **transitionary** *adj.* involving transition; temporary.

> ⊟ provisional, temporary, passing, intermediate, developmental, changing, fluid, unsettled.
> ⊞ initial, final.

transitionally *adv.* in a transitional period, during a transition.

transition element *Chem.* in the periodic table, any of a group of metallic elements that have only partially filled inner electron shells, eg copper, cobalt, iron. As a result, they tend to show variable valency and form highly coloured compounds. Many of them are used as catalysts. Also called transition metal.

transitive /'transɪtɪv/ *adj. Grammar, said of a verb* having a direct object, such as the verb *hit* in the phrase *hit the ball*. [from Latin *transitivus*]

transitively *adv.* in a transitive way.

transit lounge an airport lounge for passengers waiting for a connecting flight.

transitorily *adv.* briefly, for a short time.

transitoriness *noun* being transitory.

transitory /'transɪtərɪ/ *adj.* lasting only for a short time; transient. [from Latin *transitorius*, from *transire*, to cross over]

> ⊟ transient, passing, flying, fleeting, brief, short, momentary, ephemeral, short-lived, temporary, short-term.
> ⊞ lasting, permanent.

transit visa a visa which allows a person to pass through a country but not to stop in it.

translate *verb* 1 to express (a word, speech, written text, etc) in another language, with the same meaning. 2 *intrans.* to do this, especially as a profession. 3 *intrans. said of a written text, etc* to be able to be expressed in another language: *poetry does not always translate well*. 4 to put or express (eg an idea) in plainer or simpler terms. 5 to interpret the significance or meaning of (an action, behaviour, etc). 6 *trans., intrans.* to change or be changed into or show or be shown as: *need to translate their ideas into reality*. 7 to change or move from one state, condition, person, place, etc to another. **8** *Ecclesiastical* to transfer (a bishop) from one see to another. **9** to move (the relics of a saint) from one place to another. **10** *Relig.* to remove to heaven, especially without death. [from Latin *translatum*, from *transferre*, to carry across]

⊟ **1, 5** interpret, render. **4** paraphrase, simplify, decode, decipher. **7** change, alter, convert, transform, move, transfer.

translation *noun* **1** a word, speech, written text, etc that has been put into one language from another. **2** the act of translating. **3** *Genetics* in a living cell, the process by which the coded genetic information within messenger RNA molecules is used to specify the order in which individual amino acids are added to a growing chain of protein that is being manufactured within the cell. Translation takes place on specialized structures called *ribosomes*.

⊟ **1, 2** rendering. **1** version, paraphrase, gloss, crib. **2** interpretation, simplification, transliteration, transcription, rewording, rephrasing, change, alteration, conversion, transformation.

translational *adj.* relating to or involving translation.
translator /trəns'leɪtə(r), tranz'leɪtə(r)/ *noun* a person who translates, especially as a profession.
transliterate /trənz'lɪtəreɪt, trans'lɪtəreɪt/ *verb* to write (a word, name, text, etc) in the letters of another alphabet. [from TRANS- + Latin *litera*, letter]
transliteration *noun* **1** the process of transliterating. **2** a letter or word that is transliterated.
translocation /transloʊ'keɪʃən/ *noun Bot.* in higher plants, the transport of soluble organic compounds (manufactured in the leaves by photosynthesis) to the rest of the plant via the specialized conducting tissue known as phloem.
translucence or **translucency** *noun* a translucent quality.
translucent /trans'ljuːsənt/ *adj.* **1** allowing light to pass and be diffused through; semi-transparent. **2** clear. [from Latin *translucere*, to shine through]
translucently *adv.* in a translucent way.
transmigrate *verb intrans.* **1** *said of a soul in some beliefs* to pass into another body at death. **2** to move from one home or abode to another; to migrate. [from Latin *transmigrare*]
transmigration /transmaɪ'greɪʃən/ *noun* the act or process of transmigrating.
transmissible *adj.* capable of being transmitted.
transmission *noun* **1** an act of transmitting or the state of being transmitted. **2** something transmitted, especially a radio or television broadcast. **3** the system of parts in a motor vehicle which transfers power from the engine to the wheels. [from Latin *transmissio*]

⊟ **1** broadcasting, diffusion, spread, communication, conveyance, carriage, transport, shipment, sending, dispatch, relaying, transfer. **2** broadcast, programme, show, signal.
⊟ **1** reception.

transmit *verb* (**transmitted, transmitting**) **1** to pass or hand on (especially a message or infection). **2** *trans., intrans.* to send out (signals) by radio waves. **3** *trans., intrans.* to broadcast (a radio or television programme). **4** to allow the passage of (eg light or sound); to act as a medium for. [from Latin *transmittere*]

⊟ **1** communicate, impart, convey, disseminate, carry, bear, transport, send, dispatch, forward, relay, transfer, diffuse, spread, network. **2** broadcast, radio.
⊟ RECEIVE.

transmitter *noun* **1** a person or thing that transmits. **2** *Radio* the equipment that converts electrical signals into modulated radio waves for broadcasting. **3** *Telecomm.* the part of a telephone mouthpiece that converts sound waves into electrical signals. **4** *Physiol.* a neurotransmitter.
transmogrification /transmɒgrɪfɪ'keɪʃən/ *noun* a strange transformation.
transmogrify /trans'mɒgrɪfaɪ/ *verb* (**transmogrifies, transmogrified**) *facetious* to transform, especially in shape or appearance and often in a surprising or bizarre way.
transmutable *adj.* capable of being changed into something else.
transmutation *noun* the process of transmuting; change of form.
transmute /trans'mjuːt/ *verb* **1** to change the form, substance, or nature of. **2** to change (one chemical element) into another. **3** *Alchemy* to change (base metal) into gold or silver. [from Latin *transmutare*]

⊟ **1** change, alter, transform, convert, metamorphose, modify, mutate.

transom /'transəm/ *noun* **1** a horizontal bar of wood or stone dividing a window, or placed across the top of a door separating it from a window or fanlight above. **2** a lintel. **3** (*in full* **transom window**) a small window over the lintel of a door or larger window. **4** any of several crossbeams in the stern of a boat. [from Old French *traversin*]
transparency *noun* (PL. **transparencies**) **1** the state of being transparent. **2** a small photograph on glass or rigid plastic mounted in a frame and viewed by being placed in a projector or other device which shines light behind it.

⊟ **1** clarity, translucence, sheerness, plainness, distinctness, clearness, lucidity, explicitness, perspicuity, intelligibility. **2** slide, photograph, picture.

transparent /trans'peərənt/ *adj.* **1** able to be seen through; clear. **2** easily seen through, understood, or recognized; obvious; evident. **3** frank and open; candid. [from Latin *transparere*, to shine through]

⊟ **1** clear, see-through, translucent, sheer. **2** plain, distinct, clear, lucid, explicit, perspicuous, unambiguous, unequivocal, apparent, visible, obvious, evident, manifest, patent, undisguised, open, candid, straightforward.
⊟ **1** opaque. **2** unclear, ambiguous.

transparently *adv.* in a transparent way; openly, visibly.
transpiration /transpɪ'reɪʃən/ *noun* **1** transpiring. **2** exhalation through the skin. **3** emission of water vapour in plants.
transpire *verb* **1** *intrans.* *said especially of something secret* to become known or clear: *it later transpired that he had been in Paris.* **2** *intrans.* *loosely* to happen: *what transpired next?* **3** *trans., intrans. Bot.*, *said of a plant* to lose water vapour to the atmosphere by evaporation, especially through the stomata on the lower surfaces of leaves. **4** to give off in the form of vapour. [from Latin *transpirare*, to breathe through]

⊟ **1** turn out, come to light, come out, become apparent, appear, prove. **2** happen, occur, take place, ensue, come about, come to pass, befall.

transplant /trans'plɑːnt, 'transplɑːnt/ — *verb* (with stress on *-plant*) **1** to transfer (an organ, skin, etc) from one person or part of the body to another. **2** to move (especially a growing plant) from one place to another. — *noun* (with stress on *trans-*) **1** an operation in which an organ, skin, etc is transferred from one person or part of the body to another. **2** anything which has been transplanted, especially an organ, skin, or plant. [from Latin *transplantare*]

. . . .

■ *verb* **2** uproot, repot, move, shift, displace, remove, transfer, relocate, resettle.

. . . .

transplantation *noun* the transfer of an organ or tissue from one person (the donor), who may be alive or recently dead, to another (the recipient), or from one part of the body to another.

transport — *verb* **1** to carry (goods, passengers, etc) from one place to another. **2** *Hist.* to send to a penal colony overseas. **3** (*usually* **be transported**) to be affected with strong feelings: *was transported with grief.* — *noun* **1** the transporting of people, goods, etc from place to place; also, a system or business for this. **2** a means of getting or being transported from place to place: *I have no transport at the moment.* **3** (*often* **transports**) strong emotion, especially of pleasure or delight; ecstasy. **4** a ship, aircraft, lorry, etc used to carry soldiers or military equipment and stores. **5** *Hist.* a criminal or convict who has been sentenced to transportation. [from Latin *transportare*]

. . . .

■ *verb* **1** convey, carry, bear, take, fetch, bring, move, shift, transfer, ship, haul, remove, deport. **3** delight, enrapture, entrance, captivate, *colloq.* carry away. *noun* **1, 2** conveyance, carriage. **1** transfer, transportation, shipment, shipping, haulage, removal. **3** rapture, ecstasy, frenzy, fit.

. . . .

transportable *adj.* capable of being transported.

transportation /transpɔ:ˈteɪʃən/ *noun* **1** the act or transporting or process of being transported. **2** a means of being transported; transport. **3** *Hist.* the punishment of prisoners by sending them to a penal colony overseas.

transport café *Brit.* an inexpensive restaurant on or near a main road, used especially by lorry drivers.

transporter *noun* someone or something that transports, especially a heavy vehicle for carrying large goods.

transposable *adj.* capable of being transposed.

transpose *verb* **1** to cause (two or more things, letters, words, etc) to change places. **2** to change the position of (a thing) in a sequence or series. **3** *Mus.* to perform or rewrite in a different key. **4** *Maths.* to move (a term) to the other side of an equation and reverse the sign accompanying it. [from Middle English *transposen*, to transmute]

. . . .

■ **1** swap, exchange, switch, interchange. **2** transfer, shift, rearrange, reorder, change, alter, move, substitute.

. . . .

transposition /transpəˈzɪʃən/ *noun* **1** transposing or being transposed. **2** something transposed.

transputer /transˈpjuːtə(r)/ *noun Comput.* a chip capable of all the functions of a microprocessor, including memory, and able to process in parallel rather than sequentially. [from TRANSISTOR + COMPUTER]

transsexual *noun* **1** a person belonging anatomically to one sex who adopts the physical characteristics or social behaviour, etc of the opposite sex. **2** a person who has had medical or surgical treatment to alter the external sexual features to resemble those of the opposite sex.

transship /tranzˈʃɪp/ *verb trans., intrans.* (**transshipped, transshipping**) to transfer from one ship or form of transport to another.

transshipment *noun* the process of transshipping; changing from one conveyance to another.

transubstantiate /transəbˈstanʃɪeɪt/ *verb* to change into another substance. [from Latin *transubstantiare*]

transubstantiation /transəbstanʃɪˈeɪʃən/ *noun Christianity* the doctrine, especially in the Roman Catholic and Eastern Orthodox churches, that the bread and wine become the actual body and blood of Christ when consecrated during the Eucharist, but with their appearance remaining unchanged.

transuranic /transjʊˈranɪk/ *adj. Chem.* having an atomic number greater than that of uranium.

transuranic element *Chem.* any chemical element with an atomic number greater than 92 (the atomic number of uranium). Such elements are artificially manufactured and radioactive, most of them having short half-lives.

transverse /ˈtransvɜːs/ *adj.* placed, lying, built, etc crosswise or at right angles. [from Latin *transvertere*, to turn across]

. . . .

■ cross, crosswise, transversal, diagonal, oblique.

. . . .

transversely *adv.* in a transverse direction or position.

transverse stage *Theatr.* an open stage positioned in the middle of an auditorium and stretching from wall to wall, dividing the audience into two groups facing each other across the acting area.

transverse wave *Physics* a wave motion in which the disturbance of the medium occurs at right angles to the direction of propagation of the wave, eg ripples on water.

transvestism *noun* the practices of transvestites.

transvestite /transˈvestaɪt/ *noun* a person, especially a man, who derives sexual pleasure from wearing the clothes of the opposite sex. [from Latin *trans*, across + *vestire*, to dress]

trap — *noun* **1** a device or hole, usually with bait attached, for catching animals. **2** a plan or trick for surprising a person into speech or action, or catching someone unawares: *a speed trap.* **3** a trapdoor. **4** a bend in a pipe, especially a drainpipe, which fills with liquid to stop foul gases passing up the pipe. **5** a light, two-wheeled carriage pulled by a single horse. **6** a device for throwing a ball or clay pigeon into the air. **7** a box-like compartment from which a greyhound is released at the beginning of a race. **8** a bunker or other hazard on a golf course. **9** *slang* the mouth. **10** (**traps**) *Jazz* drums or other percussion instruments. — *verb* (**trapped, trapping**) **1** to catch (an animal) in a trap. **2** to catch (a person) out or unawares, especially with a trick. **3** to set traps in (a place). **4** to stop and hold in or as if in a trap. **5** *intrans.* to act as a trapper. [from Anglo-Saxon *treppe*]

. . . .

■ *noun* **1** snare, net, noose, booby trap, pitfall. **2** trick, wile, ruse, stratagem, device, trickery, artifice, deception, ambush, danger, hazard. *verb* **1, 2** entrap, ensnare, enmesh. **1** snare, net, catch, take. **2** trick, deceive, dupe, ambush, corner.

. . . .

trapdoor *noun* a small door or opening in a floor or ceiling.

trapes /treɪps/ *see* TRAIPSE.

trapeze /trəˈpiːz/ *noun* a swing-like apparatus consisting of a short horizontal bar hung on two ropes, on which gymnasts or acrobats perform tricks. [from French *trapèze*, trapezium]

trapezium /trəˈpiːzɪəm/ *noun* (PL. **trapeziums, trapezia**) **1** *Brit.* a quadrilateral with one pair of opposite sides parallel. **2** *North Amer., esp. US* a quadrilateral with no sides parallel (see also TRAPEZOID 1). **3** any quadrilateral that is not a parallelogram. [from Greek *trapezion*, from *trapeza*, table]

trapezoid /ˈtrapɪzɔɪd, trəˈpiːzɔɪd/ *noun* **1** *Brit.* a quadrilateral with no sides parallel. **2** *North Amer., esp. US* a quadrilateral with one pair of opposite sides parallel (see also TRAPEZIUM 1). [from Greek *trapeza*, table]

trapper *noun* a person who traps animals and sells their fur.

trappings *pl. noun* clothes or ornaments suitable for a particular occasion, ceremony, office, or person. [from Old French *drap*, cloth]

Trappist — *noun* a member of a branch of the Cistercian order of monks with a severe rule which includes a vow of silence. — *adj.* relating to the Trappists. [from *La Trappe*, in France, where the order was founded]

traps *pl. noun* personal luggage. [from Old French *drap*, cloth]

trash *noun* **1** *North Amer., esp. US* rubbish; waste material or objects. **2** nonsense. **3** a worthless person or worthless people. **4** a worthless object or worthless objects. [from Middle English *trasches*]

⊟ **1, 2, 4** rubbish, garbage, junk. **1, 3** scum, dregs. **1** refuse, waste, litter, sweepings, offscourings.

trashcan *noun North Amer., esp. US* a dustbin.

trashily *adv.* in a trashy way.

trashiness *noun* a trashy quality.

trashy *adj.* (**trashier, trashiest**) of no value or worth.

⊟ worthless, valueless, cheap, rubbishy, inferior, tawdry, third-rate.

trattoria /tratəˈrɪə, trəˈtɔːrɪə/ *noun* (PL. **trattorias, trattorie**) an Italian restaurant. [from Italian *trattoria*]

trauma /ˈtrɔːmə, ˈtraʊmə/ *noun* (PL. **traumas, traumata**) **1** a physical injury or wound. **2** a state of shock caused by a physical wound or injury. **3** an emotional shock which may have long-term effects on behaviour or character. [from Greek *trauma*, wound]

⊟ **1** injury, wound, hurt, damage. **2** pain, suffering, anguish, agony, torture. **3** ordeal, shock, disturbance, upheaval, strain, stress.

traumatic /trɔːˈmatɪk, traʊˈmatɪk/ *adj.* **1** relating to, resulting from, or causing physical wounds. **2** of or causing an emotional shock with long-term effects. **3** *colloq.* distressing; frightening; unpleasant.

⊟ **1, 2** painful, hurtful, injurious, wounding. **3** upsetting, distressing, shocking, disturbing, unpleasant, frightening, stressful.

⊟ **1, 2** healing, relaxing.

traumatically *adv.* in a traumatic way.

traumatize or **traumatise** *verb* to cause physical or emotional trauma to.

travail /ˈtraveɪl/ — *noun* **1** painful or extremely hard work or labour. **2** the pain of childbirth; labour. — *verb intrans.* to work hard or with pain, especially in childbirth. [from Old French]

travel — *verb usually intrans.* (**travelled, travelling**) **1** to go from place to place; to journey, especially abroad or far from home. **2** *trans.* to journey through, across, or over (a region, country, etc). **3** *trans.* to journey across (a stated distance). **4** to be capable of withstanding a usually long journey: *these wines don't travel well.* **5** to journey from place to place as a sales representative. **6** to move: *light travels in a straight line.* **7** to move or pass deliberately and steadily from one point to another: *her eyes travelled over the horizon.* **8** *said especially of machinery* to move along a fixed course. **9** *colloq.* to move quickly. — *noun* **1** an act of travelling. **2** (*usually* **travels**) a journey or tour, especially abroad: *get back from one's travels.* **3** the distance or speed travelled by machinery. [from Middle English]

⊟ *verb* **1, 2, 3** journey, voyage, go. **1** proceed, progress, wander, ramble, roam, rove, tour, wend. **2** cross, traverse. *noun* **1** travelling, touring, tourism, globetrotting.

⊟ *verb* **1** stay, remain.

travel agency an office dealing in airline, coach, ship, and train tickets, hotel accommodation, etc for journeys and holidays.

travel agent a person who runs a travel agency.

travelled *adj., combining form* **1** having travelled, especially abroad a lot. **2** travelled along; frequented: *a well-travelled road.*

traveller *noun* **1** a person who travels. **2** *old use* a travelling sales representative. **3** *Brit. colloq.* a gypsy.

⊟ **1** tourist, explorer, voyager, globetrotter, holidaymaker, tripper, excursionist, passenger, commuter, wanderer, rambler, hiker, wayfarer, migrant, nomad, gypsy, itinerant, tinker, vagrant. **2** salesman, saleswoman, representative, rep, agent.

traveller's cheque a cheque issued by a bank, which can be exchanged for the currency of another country when in that country.

travelling *adj.* **1** *said of a person* that travels, usually in the course of business or as a way of life. **2** *said of a machine* that moves along a fixed track.

⊟ **1** touring, wandering, roaming, roving, wayfaring, migrant, migratory, nomadic, itinerant, peripatetic, vagrant, homeless. **2** moving, mobile.

travelogue /ˈtravəlɒg/ *noun* a film, article, talk, etc about travel, especially an individual's trip to a particular place or region.

travel sickness nausea and vomiting experienced as a result of motion during travel by car, boat, aircraft, etc.

traversal /trəˈvɜːsl/ *noun* the action of traversing or crossing.

traverse /ˈtravɜːs, trəˈvɜːs/ — *verb* (with stress either on *trav-* or on *-verse*) **1** to go across or through. **2** to lie or reach across: *a bridge traversing a deep gorge.* **3** *trans., intrans.* to climb, walk, or ski at an angle across (a slope) rather than straight up or down. **4** *intrans.* to move sideways or to one side. **5** to examine or consider (a subject, problem, etc) carefully and thoroughly. **6** to move (especially the barrel of a large gun) to one side while keeping it horizontal. **7** to oppose or thwart. **8** to survey by traverse. — *noun* (with stress on *trav-*) **1** an act of crossing or traversing. **2** a path or passage across eg a rock face or slope. **3** something that lies across. **4** a sideways movement. **5** the movement of the barrel of a large gun to one side while being kept horizontal. **6** a survey by measuring straight lines from point to point and the angles between. **7** an obstruction. — *adj.* (with stress on *trav-*) being or lying across; oblique. [from Latin *traversare*]

⊟ *verb* **1, 2** cross, pass over. **1** negotiate, pass (through). **2** bridge, span.

travesty /ˈtravəstɪ/ — *noun* (PL. **travesties**) a ridiculous or crude distortion: *a travesty of justice.* — *verb* (**travesties, travestied**) to make a travesty of. [from French *travestir*, to disguise]

⊟ *noun* mockery, parody, *colloq.* take-off, send-up, farce, caricature, distortion, sham, apology.

travolator or **travelator** /ˈtravəleɪtə(r)/ *noun* a moving ramp which transports people or goods horizontally, or at a slight incline (see also ESCALATOR).

trawl /trɔːl/ — *noun* **1** (*in full* **trawl-net**) a large bag-shaped net with a wide mouth, used to catch fish at sea. **2** a wide-ranging or extensive search. — *verb trans., intrans.* **1** to search (the sea, an area of sea, etc) for (fish) with a trawl. **2** to search through (a large number of things, people, etc) thoroughly, especially before finding the one required: *had to trawl through hundreds of applications.* [from Old Dutch *tragel*]

trawler *noun* **1** a fishing boat used in trawling. **2** a person who trawls.

tray *noun* **1** a flat piece of wood, metal, plastic, etc usually with a low edge, for carrying dishes, crockery, etc. **2** a very shallow lidless box forming a drawer in eg a wardrobe or trunk, or used for displaying articles in a cabinet. [from Anglo-Saxon *trig*]

treacherous /ˈtretʃərəs/ *adj.* **1** not able to be trusted; ready or likely to betray. **2** having hidden hazards and dangers. [from Old French *trechier*, to cheat]

▪ **1** traitorous, disloyal, unfaithful, faithless, unreliable, untrustworthy, false, untrue, deceitful, double-crossing. **2** dangerous, hazardous, risky, perilous, precarious, icy, slippery.
▪ **1** loyal, faithful, dependable. **2** safe, stable.

treacherously *adv.* in a treacherous way.
treacherousness *noun* **1** being treacherous. **2** treachery.
treachery /ˈtretʃərɪ/ *noun* (PL. **treacheries**) betraying someone or their trust, disloyalty; also, an act of betrayal or disloyalty.

▪ treason, betrayal, disloyalty, infidelity, falseness, duplicity, double-dealing.
▪ loyalty, dependability.

treacle /ˈtriːkl/ *noun* **1** (*also* **black treacle**) the thick dark sticky liquid that remains after the crystallization and removal of sugar from extracts of sugar cane or sugar beet. **2** molasses. [from Greek *theriake*, an antidote to the bites of wild beasts, from *therion*, wild beast. The word gradually came to be applied to the sugary substance in which the antidote was taken rather than to the antidote itself]

tread /tred/ — *verb* (PAST TENSE **trod**; PAST PARTICIPLE **trodden, trod**) **1** (**tread on something**) to put a foot or feet on it; to walk or step on it. **2** *intrans.* to step or walk in a certain way. **3** to crush or press (eg into the ground) with a foot or feet; to trample: *tread grapes / was treading ash into the carpet.* **4** to wear or form (a path, hole, etc) by walking. **5** to perform by walking. **6** (**tread on someone**) to suppress them; to treat them cruelly. **7** *said of a male bird* to copulate with (a female bird). — *noun* **1** a manner, style, or sound of walking: *a heavy tread.* **2** an act of treading. **3** a mark made by treading; a footprint or track. **4** the thick, grooved, and patterned surface of a tyre that grips the road. **5** that part of a wheel that touches the rail. **6** that part of a rail that the wheels touch. **7** that part of the sole of a shoe that touches the ground. **8** the horizontal part of a step or stair on which the foot is placed. — **tread water** to keep oneself afloat and upright in water by making a treading movement with the legs and a circular movement with the hands and arms. [from Anglo-Saxon *tredan*]

▪ *verb* **1, 2** walk (on), step (on). **2** pace, stride, march, tramp, trudge, plod. **3** stamp, trample, press, crush, squash. *noun* **1, 2** step. **1, 3** footstep. **1** walk, footfall, gait. **2** pace, stride. **3** footprint, footmark.

treadle /ˈtredl/ — *noun* a pedal for one or both feet that drives a machine, eg a sewing-machine or loom. — *verb intrans.* to work a treadle. [from Anglo-Saxon *tredel*, step]

treadmill *noun* **1** an apparatus for producing motion consisting of a large wheel turned by people (especially formerly prisoners) or animals treading on steps inside or around it. **2** a monotonous and dreary routine. **3** an exercise machine consisting of a continuous moving belt whose speed can be regulated to make the user walk, jog, or run.

treason /ˈtriːzn/ *noun* **1** (*also* **high treason**) disloyalty to or betrayal of one's country, sovereign, or government. **2** any betrayal of trust or act of disloyalty. [from Old French *traison*]

▪ TREACHERY, DISLOYALTY, PERFIDY. **1** subversion, sedition, mutiny, rebellion. **2** duplicity, deceit.
▪ LOYALTY.

treasonable *adj.* of, being or involving treason.

▪ traitorous, disloyal, false, subversive, seditious, mutinous, perfidious.
▪ loyal.

treasonably *adv.* in a treasonable way.
treasure /ˈtreʒə(r)/ — *noun* **1** wealth and riches, especially in the form of gold, silver, precious stones, and jewels, etc which have been accumulated over a period of time and which can be hoarded. **2** any thing of great value. **3** *colloq.* a much loved and valued helper, friend, etc. — *verb* **1** to value greatly or think of as very precious. **2** (*usually* **treasure something up**) to preserve it or collect it for future use or as something of value: *treasured up all his old school photographs.* [from Old French *tresor*]

▪ *noun* **1** fortune, wealth, riches, money, cash, gold, jewels, hoard, cache. *verb* **1** prize, value, esteem, revere, worship, love, adore, idolize, cherish. **2** preserve, guard.
▪ *verb* **1** disparage, belittle.

treasure hunt **1** a hunt for treasure. **2** a game in which players try to be the first to find a hidden prize by solving a series of clues whose answers lead to its location.

treasurer *noun* **1** the person in a club, society, etc who is in charge of the money and accounts. **2** an official responsible for public money, eg in a local council.

treasure-trove *noun Legal* treasure or money that is found hidden usually in the earth and whose owner is unknown, deemed to be the property of the Crown. [from Old French *trover*, to find]

treasury *noun* (PL. **treasuries**) **1** a place where treasure is stored. **2** (**Treasury**) the government department in charge of a country's finances, especially the collection and distribution of income from tax, etc; also, the building which houses this. **3** the income or funds of a state, government, organization, or society. **4** a store of valued items, eg a book containing popular poems, stories, or quotations.

Treasury bench the front bench in the House of Commons where the Prime Minister, Chancellor of the Exchequer, and other senior members of the Government sit.

treat /triːt/ — *verb* **1** to deal with or behave towards (a person or thing) in a certain manner: *treated him badly / treat it as a joke.* **2** to care for or deal with (a person, illness, injury, etc) medically. **3** to put through a process or apply something to: *treat the wood with creosote.* **4** (**treat someone to something**) to provide them with food, drink, entertainment, or a gift at one's own expense: *she treated herself to a new dress.* **5** to speak or write about; to discuss. **6** (**treat of something**) to deal with or discuss a subject, especially in writing. **7** (**treat with someone**) to negotiate with another nation, person, etc to settle a dispute, end a war, etc. — *noun* **1** an outing, meal, present, etc given as a gift by one person to another. **2** any source of pleasure or enjoyment, especially when unexpected. — **a treat** *colloq.* very good or well: *they looked a treat.* [from Old French *traitier*]

▪ *verb* **1, 5, 6** deal with. **1** manage, handle, use, regard. **2** tend, nurse, minister to, attend to, care for, heal, cure. **4** pay for, buy, stand, give, provide, entertain, regale, feast. **5, 6** consider, discuss, cover. *noun* **1** excursion, outing, party, celebration, feast, banquet, gift, surprise. **2** thrill, pleasure, delight, enjoyment, fun, entertainment, indulgence, gratification.

treatise /'tri:tɪz/ *noun* a formal piece of writing with deals with a subject in depth. [from Old French *tretis*, from *traitier*, to treat]

▣ essay, dissertation, thesis, monograph, paper, pamphlet, tract, study, exposition.

treatment *noun* **1** the medical or surgical care given to a patient, or to cure an illness. **2** an act or the manner of dealing with someone or something, often in a literary, musical, or artistic context: *rough treatment / the painter's characteristic treatment of light and shadow.* — **the full treatment** *colloq.* the appropriate or usual treatment, especially when lavish or generous.

▣ **1** healing, cure, remedy, medication, therapy, surgery, care, nursing. **2** management, handling, use, usage, conduct, discussion, coverage.

treaty /'tri:tɪ/ *noun* (PL. **treaties**) **1** a formal agreement between states or governments. **2** an agreement between two parties or individuals, especially for the purchase of property. [from Old French *trete*]

▣ AGREEMENT. **1** pact, convention, covenant, compact, alliance. **2** contract, bond.

treble /'trebl/ — *noun* **1** anything which is three times as much or as many. **2** *Mus.* a soprano; a person, especially a boy, having a soprano singing voice; a part written for this voice. **3** *Mus.* an instrument with a similar range; in a family of instruments, the member with the highest range. **4** a high-pitched voice or sound. **5** the higher part of the audio frequency range of a radio, record, etc. **6** a cumulative bet on three races in which the original money bet plus winnings on the first race is (if successful) bet on the second, and then the total bet on the third. **7** the narrow inner ring of a dartboard, which scores three times the stated score; also, a hit on this. — *adj.* **1** three times as much or as many; threefold; triple. **2** for, being, or having a treble voice. **3** *said of a voice* high-pitched. — *adv.* with a treble voice: *sing treble.* — *verb trans., intrans.* to make or become three times as much. [from Latin *triplus*, triple]

treble chance a way of betting with football pools in which the chance of winning depends on the number of draws and home and away wins forecast by the competitor.

treble clef a sign at the beginning of a piece of written music which places the note G (a fifth above middle C) on the second line of the staff.

trebly *adv.* three times as much; to a threefold degree.

trecento /treɪ'tʃɛntoʊ/ *noun* the 14c, usually with reference to Italian art. [Italian, = three hundred (shortened from *mille trecento*, thirteen hundred)]

treddle same as TREADLE.

tree — *noun* **1** *Bot.* a tall woody perennial plant which typically has one main stem or trunk, and usually only bears branches on its upper part, so giving rise to a distinct crown of foliage. Apart from the loss of leaves in deciduous species, the aerial parts do not die back at the end of each growing season. **2** anything like a tree, especially in having branches leading from a main trunk, eg a diagram with a branched structure: *a family tree.* **3** (*also in compounds*) a wooden frame or support for holding things: *shoe tree.* **4** *old use* a cross for crucifixion. **5** *old use* a gallows or gibbet. — *verb* to drive or chase up a tree. — **at the top of the tree** at the top of one's profession. **up a tree** *North Amer. colloq.* in difficulties. [from Anglo-Saxon *treow*]

▣ *noun* bush, shrub, evergreen, conifer.

Trees include: acacia, acer, alder, almond, apple, ash, aspen, balsa, bay, beech, birch, blackthorn, bluegum, box, cedar, cherry, chestnut, coconut palm, cottonwood, cypress, date palm, dogwood, Dutch elm, ebony, elder, elm, eucalyptus, fig, fir, gum, hawthorn, hazel, hickory, hornbeam, horse chestnut, Japanese maple, larch, laurel, lime, linden, mahogany, maple, monkey-puzzle, mountain ash, oak, palm, pear, pine, plane, plum, poplar, prunus, pussy willow, redwood, rowan, rubber tree, sandalwood, sapele, sequoia, silver birch, silver maple, spruce, sycamore, teak, walnut, weeping willow, whitebeam, willow, witch hazel, yew, yucca; bonsai, conifer, deciduous, evergreen, fruit, hardwood, ornamental, palm, softwood.

tree creeper a small bird that runs up tree trunks in search of insects on which to feed.

tree fern a fern with a thick woody stem covered in dead leaf bases and bearing a crown of leaves at its apex, found mainly in tropical regions, and so called because it resembles a tree in size and shape.

tree frog a frog adapted to live in trees, that has sucker-like discs on its fingers and toes to facilitate climbing.

tree hugger *derog.* an environmentalist. [from the practice of hugging a tree to prevent its being cut down]

treeless *adj.* having no trees.

tree line same as TIMBER LINE.

tree shrew a small SE Asian mammal with a long tail (which may be bushy or have a tufted tip) and a long thin shrew-like muzzle. It lives in trees and on the ground, feeds on insects and fruit, and resembles ancestral mammals of 220 million years ago.

tree snake any snake which spends much of its life in trees. The term is applied to many unrelated species.

tree surgeon a person who is skilled in tree surgery.

tree surgery *Bot.* the treatment of diseased or damaged trees, especially by cutting off dead branches, filling cavities, and providing supports.

treetop *noun* the top of a tree.

trefoil /'trefɔɪl, 'tri:fɔɪl/ *noun* **1** a leaf which is divided into three sections. **2** any plant having such leaves, eg clover. **3** anything with three lobes or sections. **4** a carved ornament or decoration with three lobes or sections. [from Latin *trifolium*, from *tres*, three + *folium*, leaf]

trefoil arch *Archit.* an arch constructed in a trefoil shape with two rounded arches on either side of and below a third arch whose central point is drawn from the cusp formed by the arcs of the two lower arches.

trek — *verb intrans.* (**trekked, trekking**) **1** to make a long, hard journey. **2** *South Afr.* to make a journey by ox-wagon. — *noun* **1** a long, hard journey. **2** *South Afr.* a journey by ox-wagon. [from Dutch *trekken*, to draw (a vehicle or load)]

▣ *verb* hike, walk, tramp, march, trudge, plod, journey, rove, roam. *noun* **1** hike, walk, tramp, march, journey, expedition, safari.

trellis /'trelɪs/ — *noun* a frame or network of narrow wooden strips used to support climbing plants. — *verb* (**trellised, trellising**) to provide or support with a trellis. [from Old French *trelis*]

trellised *adj.* **1** having or formed like a trellis. **2** trained on a trellis.

tremble — *verb intrans.* **1** to shake, eg with cold, fear, weakness, etc. **2** to quiver or vibrate. **3** to feel fear or anxiety. — *noun* **1** a trembling movement; a shudder or tremor. **2** (**trembles**) a disease of livestock, especially cattle, causing muscular weakness, shaking, and constipation. — **go in fear and trembling of someone** or **something** *often facetious* to be extremely afraid of them. [from Latin *tremere*, to shake]

▣ *verb* **1, 2** shake, quake, shiver, shudder. **2** vibrate, quiver,

wobble, rock. *noun* **1** shake, vibration, quake, shiver, shudder, quiver, tremor, wobble.
⊟ *noun* **1** steadiness.

trembling *adj.* **1** that trembles. **2** afraid.
tremblingly *adv.* with trembling.
trembling poplar the aspen.
trembly *adj.* (**tremblier, trembliest**) trembling or likely to tremble.
tremendous /trə'mendəs/ *adj.* **1** enormous; huge. **2** *colloq.* very good or remarkable. [from Latin *tremendus*, to be trembled at]

⊟ STUPENDOUS, TOWERING. **1** huge, immense, vast, colossal, gigantic, formidable. **2** wonderful, marvellous, sensational, spectacular, extraordinary, amazing, incredible, terrific, impressive.
⊟ **2** ordinary, unimpressive.

tremendously *adv.* in a tremendous way; to a tremendous degree.
tremolo /'treməloʊ/ *noun* (PL. **tremolos**) *Mus.* **1** a trembling effect produced by rapidly repeating a note or notes, produced especially by a stringed or keyboard instrument. **2** a similar effect produced in singing by fluctuating the pitch of the note sung. **3** a device in an organ for producing a trembling effect. [from Italian]
tremor /'tremə(r)/ *noun* **1** a shaking or quivering. **2** a slight vibration or trembling movement, especially a slight earthquake. **3** a thrill. [from Latin *tremor*]

⊟ **1, 2** vibration, shake, quiver. **2** tremble, shiver, quake, quaver, wobble, shock, earthquake. **3** thrill, frisson.
⊟ **1** steadiness.

tremulous /'tremjʊləs/ *adj.* **1** trembling, especially with fear, worry, nervousness, or excitement. **2** *said of a line drawn, words written, etc* written by a shaky hesitant hand and so weak and wavering. [from Latin *tremulus*, from *tremere*, to shake]
tremulousness *noun* a tremulous quality.
trench — *noun* **1** a long narrow ditch dug in the ground, especially one used to protect soliders from enemy gunfire. **2** a long narrow deep depression in the sea floor, usually having steep sides. **3** a long narrow depression in the Earth's surface, produced by erosion or by movements of the Earth's crust. — *verb* **1** to dig a trench or trenches (in). **2** to provide (a place) with a trench as fortification. [from Old French *trenche*, cut]
trenchancy *noun* a trenchant quality.
trenchant /'trentʃənt/ *adj.* **1** cutting; keen. **2** that gets to the heart of the matter. **3** forthright; vigorous. [from Old French *trenchant*, cutting]

⊟ **2** incisive, penetrating, acute, astute, perceptive, perspicacious, effective. **3** forthright, vigorous, blunt, terse, no-nonsense.

trenchantly *adv.* in a trenchant way.
trench coat a waterproof coat with a belt and epaulettes, based on the style of a military raincoat.
trencher *noun* **1** *Hist.* a wooden plate or board for serving food. **2** (*in full* **trencher-cap**) a square flat hat worn by academics; a mortarboard. [from Old French *trenchour*, from *trenchier*, to cut]
trencherman *noun* a person who eats well or heartily.
trench warfare warfare in which each side uses trenches from which to attack the enemy.
trend — *noun* **1** a general direction or tendency. **2** the current general movement in fashion, style, or taste. — *verb intrans.* to turn or have a tendency to turn in a specified direction: *trend north / trend towards socialism*. [from Anglo-Saxon *trendan*]

⊟ *noun* **1** course, flow, drift, tendency, inclination, leaning. **2** fashion, vogue, craze, *colloq.* rage, mode, style, look.

trendily *adv.* in a trendy way.
trendsetter *noun* a person who sets a fashion.
trendsetting *noun* creating a new fashion.
trendy — *adj. Brit. colloq.* (**trendier, trendiest**) following the latest fashions, often without thinking or using one's own discrimination or taste. — *noun* (PL. **trendies**) a trendy person.

⊟ *adj.* fashionable, up-to-date, *colloq.* with it, in, *colloq.* cool.

trepan /trɪ'pan/ — *noun* a small cylindrical saw formerly used for removing part of a bone, especially the skull, during surgery. — *verb* (**trepanned, trepanning**) to remove (a piece of bone) with a trephine. [from Greek *trypaein*, to bore]
trephine /trɪ'fiːn, trɪ'faɪn/ — *noun* a surgical instrument used for removing circular sections of bone, especially from the skull, during surgery, now used instead of the trepan. — *verb* to remove (a piece of bone) with a trephine. [from Latin *tres fines*, three ends]
trepidation /trepɪ'deɪʃən/ *noun* fear or nervousness. [from Latin *trepidare*, to hurry with alarm]
trespass /'trespəs/ — *verb intrans.* (*often* **trespass on** or **upon someone** or **something**) **1** to enter someone else's property without the right or permission to do so. **2** to intrude into a person's time, privacy, rights, etc. **3** *old use* to sin. — *noun* **1** the act of entering someone else's property without the right or permission to do so. **2** an intrusion into someone's time, privacy, etc. **3** *old use* a sin. [from Latin *transpassare*, to step across]

⊟ *verb* **1, 2** invade, intrude (on), encroach (on), infringe, violate. **1** poach. **3** offend, sin. *noun* **2** invasion, intrusion, encroachment, infringement, violation. **3** sin, offence, misdemeanour, contravention.

trespasser *noun* **1** a person who trespasses. **2** *old use* a sinner.

⊟ **1** intruder, poacher, offender, criminal.

tress *noun* **1** a long lock or plait of hair. **2** (**tresses**) a woman's or girl's long hair. [from Old French *tresse*]
trestle /'tresl/ *noun* a support, eg for a table, consisting of a horizontal beam resting at each end on a pair of legs sloping outwards. [from Old French *trestel*, from Latin *transtrum*, transom]
trestle table a table consisting of a board or boards supported by trestles.
trews /truːz/ *pl. noun* trousers, especially of tartan cloth. [from Irish and Scots Gaelic *triubhas*]
tri- *combining form* forming words meaning 'three, three times, threefold'. [from Latin *tres* and Greek *treis*, three]
triad /'traɪad/ *noun* **1** any group of three people or things. **2** a chord consisting of three notes, usually a base note and those notes a third and a fifth above it. **3** any of several Chinese secret societies, especially one involved in organized crime or drug trafficking. **4** in Welsh literature, a group of three sayings, stories, etc about related subjects. [from Greek *treis*, three]
triadic /traɪ'adɪk/ *adj.* relating to or consisting of triads.
trial /'traɪəl/ — *noun* **1** a legal process by which a person accused of a crime or misdemeanour is judged in a court of law. **2** an act of trying or testing; a test. **3** trouble, worry, or vexation, or a cause of this: *her son is a great trial to her*. **4** *Sport* a preliminary test of a player's or athlete's skill and fitness, especially before choosing which players or athletes to include in a team. **5** a test of a vehicle's perfor-

mance held especially over rough ground or a demanding course. **6** a competition, usually over rough ground, to test skills in handling high-performance cars or motorcycles. **7** any competition testing the skills of animals: *sheepdog trials*. **8** an attempt. — *adj*. done, used, etc for the purpose of testing. — *verb* to test (especially a new product). — **on trial 1** the subject of a legal action in court. **2** undergoing tests or examination before being permanently accepted or approved. **trial and error** the trying of various methods, alternatives, etc until the correct or suitable one is found. [from Old French, from *trier*, to try]

. . . .

目 *noun* **1** litigation, lawsuit, hearing, inquiry, tribunal. **2** experiment, test, examination, check, dry run, dummy run, practice, rehearsal, audition, contest. **3** affliction, suffering, grief, misery, distress, ordeal, hardship, ordeal, trouble, nuisance, vexation, tribulation. *adj* experimental, test, pilot, exploratory, provisional, probationary.

目 *noun* **3** relief, happiness.

. . . .

trial run a test of a vehicle, piece of machinery, etc or rehearsal of a play, to assess effectiveness.

triangle /ˈtraɪangl/ *noun* **1** a plane (two-dimensional) figure with three sides and three angles, whose sum is always 180°; a three-sided polygon. **2** anything with a similar shape. **3** a musical percussion instrument consisting of a metal bar shaped into a triangle with one corner left open that is struck with a small hammer. **4** an emotional relationship or love affair involving three people. [from Latin *triangulum*]

triangular /traɪˈangjʊlə(r)/ *adj*. **1** in the shape of a triangle. **2** involving three people or parties.

triangularity *noun* a triangular form.

triangularly *adv*. in a triangular way.

triangulate /traɪˈangjʊleɪt/ *verb* to survey (an area) by dividing it up into a series of triangles, eg when map-making.

triangulation /traɪangjʊˈleɪʃən/ *noun* the process or result of triangulating.

Triassic /traɪˈasɪk/ *adj. Geol*. relating to the earliest period of the Mesozoic era, lasting from about 250 million to 210 million years ago. During this time the first dinosaurs and large sea reptiles appeared, and ammonites were common. The first small mammals also appeared, and conifers became widespread, forming luxuriant forests. [from Latin *trias*, triad]

triathlete /traɪˈaθliːt/ *noun* an athlete who competes in the triathlon.

triathlon /traɪˈaθlɒn/ *noun* an athletic contest consisting of three events, usually swimming, running, and cycling. [from TRI- + DECATHLON]

tribal /ˈtraɪbl/ *adj*. of a tribe or tribes.

tribalism /ˈtraɪbəlɪzm/ *noun* **1** the system of tribes as a way of organizing society. **2** the feeling of belonging to a tribe.

tribally *adv*. in a tribal way; in terms of tribes.

tribe *noun* **1** a group of families, clans, or communities who are linked by social, economic, and political ties, who often have a common ancestor and usually have a common culture, dialect, and leader. **2** a group of people with a common interest, profession, etc. **3** *Hist*. any of the three divisions of the ancient Romans, the Latins, Etruscans, and Sabines. **4** *Hist*. any of the twelve divisions of the Israelites, each of which was believed to be descended from one of the twelve patriarchs. **5** *Biol*. in plant and animal classification, a subdivision of a family, consisting of several similar or closely related genera. [from Latin *tribus*, one of the divisions of the ancient Roman people]

. . . .

目 **1** race, nation, people, clan, sib, family, house, dynasty, blood, stock. **2** group, caste, class, division, branch.

. . . .

tribesman or **tribeswoman** *noun* (PL. **tribesmen**) a man, or woman, who belongs to a tribe.

tribulation /trɪbjʊˈleɪʃən/ *noun* great sorrow or trouble, or a cause of this. [from Latin *tribulatio*, from *tribulare*, to afflict]

. . . .

目 affliction, suffering, grief, misery, distress, adversity, hardship, trouble.

. . . .

tribunal /traɪˈbjuːnəl/ *noun* **1** a court of justice. **2** a group of people appointed to inquire into some matter or dispute and to adjudicate or give judgement. **3** a seat or bench in a court for a judge or judges. [from Latin *tribunus*]

tribune [1] /ˈtrɪbjuːn/ *noun* **1** *Hist*. a high official elected by the ordinary people of ancient Rome to defend their rights and interests. **2** a champion or defender of the rights of the common people. [from Latin *tribunus*]

tribune [2] /ˈtrɪbjuːn/ *noun* **1** a raised area, dais, or stand. **2** a bishop's throne. [from Latin *tribuna*]

tributary /ˈtrɪbjʊtərɪ/ — *noun* (PL. **tributaries**) **1** a stream or river flowing into a larger river or lake. **2** a person or nation paying tribute to another. — *adj*. **1** *said of a stream or river* flowing into a larger river or lake. **2** paid or owed as tribute. **3** paying tribute. [from Latin *tributarius*]

tribute /ˈtrɪbjuːt/ *noun* **1** something given or said as an expression of praise, thanks, admiration, or affection. **2** a sign or evidence of (something valuable, effective, worthy of praise, etc): *her success was a tribute to all her hard work*. **3** *Hist*. a sum of money paid regularly by one nation or ruler to another in return for protection or as an acknowledgement of submission. [from Latin *tributum*]

. . . .

目 **1, 2** acknowledgement, recognition. **1** praise, commendation, compliment, accolade, homage, respect, honour, credit. **3** payment, levy, charge, tax, duty.

. . . .

tricarboxylic acid cycle /traɪkɑːbɒkˈsɪlɪk/ *Biochem*. Kreb's cycle.

trice *noun* — **in a trice** in a very short time; almost immediately. [from Middle Dutch *trisen*, to pull or haul]

triceps /ˈtraɪseps/ *noun* any muscle attached to a bone or bones in three places, especially the large muscle at the back of the arm which straightens the elbow. [from Latin *triceps*, three-headed]

triceratops /traɪˈserətɒps/ *noun* a four-legged herbivorous dinosaur, with a bony frill round its neck, one horn over each eye and one on its nose. [from Greek *trikeratos*, three-horned + *ops*, face]

trichinosis /trɪkɪˈnoʊsɪs/ *noun Medicine* a disorder caused by infestation with a parasitic nematode worm (*Trichinella spiralis*), usually as a result of eating raw or partially cooked pork containing the worm's larvae. The main symptoms are nausea, diarrhoea, fever, and pain and stiffness in the muscles. [from Greek *trichinos*, of hair + -OSIS]

trichloromethane /traɪklɔːroʊˈmiːθeɪn/ *noun Chem*. same as CHLOROFORM.

trichology /trɪˈkɒlədʒɪ/ *noun* the scientific study of the hair and its diseases. [from Greek *trix*, hair + -LOGY]

trick — *noun* **1** something which is done or said to cheat, deceive, fool, or humiliate someone. **2** a deceptive appearance, especially one caused by the light; an illusion. **3** a mischievous act or plan; a prank or joke. **4** a clever or skilful act or feat which astonishes, puzzles, or amuses. **5** a habit or mannerism: *he has a trick of scratching his nose when he's angry*. **6** a special technique or knack: *the trick of the trade*. **7** a feat of skill which can be learned. **8** the cards played in one round of a card game and which are won by one of the players. **9** *slang* a prostitute's client. **10** *Naut*. a period of duty at the helm. — *adj*. **1** intended to deceive or give a certain illusion: *trick photography*. **2** able to or designed for the performing of tricks. — *verb* **1** to cheat, deceive, or defraud. **2** (**trick someone into** or **out of something**) to make them do as one wants, or to gain something from them, by cheating or deception: *tricked him into donating his life savings*. — **do the trick** *colloq*. to do or be what is necessary to achieve something. **trick or**

treat *chiefly North Amer.* the children's practice of dressing up on Hallowe'en to call at people's houses for small gifts, threatening to play a trick if they are not given one. **trick someone** or **something out** or **up** to dress or decorate them fancily. **up to one's tricks** *colloq.* behaving in one's usual deceitful or tiresome way. [from Old French *trique*]

....

■ *noun* **1** fraud, swindle, deception, deceit, artifice, ruse, wile, dodge, subterfuge, trap, device. **2**, **4** illusion. **3** hoax, practical joke, joke, *colloq.* leg-pull, prank, antic, caper, frolic. **4** feat, stunt. **6** knack, technique, secret. *adj.* **1** false, mock, artificial, imitation, ersatz, fake, forged, counterfeit, feigned, sham, bogus. *verb* **1**, **2** dupe, fool, beguile. **1** deceive, delude, mislead, hoodwink, bluff, hoax, *colloq.* pull someone's leg, cheat, swindle, *colloq.* diddle, defraud, *colloq.* con, *slang* sting, trap, outwit.

■ *adj.* **1** real, genuine.
....

trickery *noun* (PL. **trickeries**) an act or the practice of deceiving or cheating.

....

■ deception, illusion, sleight-of-hand, pretence, artifice, guile, deceit, dishonesty, cheating, swindling, fraud, imposture, double-dealing, *colloq.* monkey business, *slang* funny business, chicanery, skulduggery, *colloq.* hocus-pocus.
🖙 straightforwardness, honesty.
....

trickily *adv.* in a tricky way.
trickiness *noun* being tricky.
trickle — *verb* **1** *trans., intrans.* to flow or cause to flow in a thin slow stream or drops. **2** *intrans.* to move, come, or go slowly and gradually. — *noun* a thin slow stream, flow, or movement. [from Middle English *triklen*]

....

■ *verb* **1** dribble, run, leak, ooze, exude, drip, drop, filter, percolate. *noun* dribble, drip, drop, leak, seepage.
🖙 *verb* STREAM, GUSH. *noun* stream, gush.
....

trickster *noun* a person who deceives or cheats, or plays tricks.

tricky *adj.* (**trickier**, **trickiest**) **1** difficult to handle or do; needing skill and care. **2** inclined to trickery; sly; deceitful. **3** clever in tricks; resourceful; adroit.

....

■ **1** difficult, awkward, problematic, complicated, knotty, thorny, delicate, ticklish. **2** crafty, artful, cunning, sly, wily, foxy, subtle, deceitful, devious, slippery, scheming.
🖙 **1** easy, simple. **2** honest.
....

tricolour /ˈtrɪkələ(r)/ *noun* a three-coloured flag, especially one with three equal stripes of different colours, such as the French and Irish flags. [from Latin *tricolor*]
tricoloured /ˈtraɪkʌləd/ *adj.* three-coloured.
tricot /ˈtriːkoʊ/ *noun* **1** a hand-knitted woollen fabric. **2** a soft, slightly ribbed cloth for women's garments. [from French *tricot*, knitting]
tricycle /ˈtraɪsɪkl/ — *noun* **1** a vehicle with three wheels, two at the back and one at the front, driven by pedals. **2** a light, three-wheeled car for the use of a disabled person. — *verb intrans.* to ride a tricycle.
tricyclist /ˈtraɪsɪklɪst/ *noun* a person who rides a tricycle.
trident /ˈtraɪdənt/ *noun* **1** *Hist.* a spear with three prongs, especially as carried by a sea-god, such as Neptune or Britannia, or a Roman gladiator. **2** (**Trident**) a ballistic missile with several warheads which can each be programmed to attack a different target, fired from a submarine. [from Latin *tridens*, having three teeth]
Tridentine /traɪˈdentaɪn/ — *adj.* relating to the Council of Trent (1545–63) or the traditional Catholic beliefs and doctrines reaffirmed there as a reaction to Protestantism and the Reformation. — *noun* a member of the Roman Catholic Church who follows the traditional doctrine af-

firmed at the Council of Trent. [from Latin *Tridentum*, Trent]
Trident missile the US Navy's third-generation submarine-launched ballistic missile system, following on from the earlier Polaris and Poseidon missiles.
tried *adj.* **1** tested and proved to be good, efficient, etc. **2** (*in phrases and compounds*) having had one's patience put to strain: *sorely tried.*
triennial /traɪˈɛnɪəl/ *adj.* **1** happening once every three years. **2** lasting three years. [from Latin *triennis*]
triennially *adv.* every three years.
trier *noun* a person who tries hard.
trifle /ˈtraɪfl/ — *noun* **1** anything of very little value. **2** a very small amount. **3** a dessert made typically of sponge-cake soaked in sherry and spread with jam or jelly and fruit and topped with custard and whipped cream. — *verb* **1** (**trifle with someone** or **something**) to treat a person or a person's feelings frivolously and insensitively. **2** *intrans.* to act, behave, or talk idly. **3** (**trifle something away**) to spend or pass time idly; to waste an opportunity, etc. [from Old French *trufe*, mockery, deceit]

....

■ *noun* **1** toy, plaything, trinket, bauble, knick-knack, triviality, nothing. **2** little, bit, spot, drop, dash, touch, trace. *verb* **1**, **2** toy (with), play (with), dally (with). **1** flirt with. **2** dabble, fiddle, meddle, fool.
....

trifling *adj.* **1** unimportant; trivial. **2** frivolous.

....

■ **1** small, paltry, slight, negligible, inconsiderable, unimportant, insignificant, minor, trivial, petty, worthless. **2** silly, frivolous, idle, empty.
🖙 IMPORTANT, SIGNIFICANT, SERIOUS.
....

trig *noun colloq.* trigonometry.
trigger — *noun* **1** a small lever which releases a catch or spring to set a mechanism going, especially one which is squeezed to fire a gun. **2** anything which starts a train of actions or reactions. — *verb* (**triggered**, **triggering**) (*also* **trigger something off**) to start a train of actions, reactions, events, etc. [from Dutch *trekken*, to pull]

....

■ *noun* **1** lever, catch, switch. **2** spur, stimulus, impetus, cause. *verb* cause, start, initiate, activate, set off, spark off, provoke, prompt, elicit, generate, produce.
....

trigger-happy *adj. colloq.* likely to shoot or react violently without thinking or with very little provocation.
triglyceride /traɪˈɡlɪsəraɪd/ *noun Biochem.* any of a large number of chemical compounds, consisting of a glycerol molecule combined with three fatty acids, that are present in most fats.
triglyph /ˈtraɪɡlɪf/ *noun Archit.* a tablet with three parallel grooves, forming part of a Doric frieze. [from Greek *triglyphos*, from *glyphein*, to carve]
trigonometrical /ˌtrɪɡənəˈmetrɪkl/ or **trigonometric** *adj.* relating to or involving trigonometry.
trigonometrical point a fixed point, often a point on a hilltop, whose position as the vertex of a triangle is calculated astronomically and which is used as an aid to mapmaking.
trigonometric function or **trigonometric ratio** *Maths.* any function of an angle that is defined by the relationship between the angles and sides in a right-angled triangle, eg sine, cosine, tangent, secant, cosecant, cotangent.
trigonometry /ˌtrɪɡəˈnɒmətrɪ/ *noun Maths.* the branch of mathematics that is concerned with the relationships between the sides and angles of triangles, especially by use of the trigonometric functions (sine, cosine, and tangent). It is an important mathematical tool, and also has practical applications in navigation and surveying. [from Greek *trigonon*, triangle + *metron*, measure]

trig point *noun colloq.* same as TRIGONOMETRICAL POINT.

trike *noun colloq.* a tricycle.

trilateral /traɪˈlatərəl/ *adj.* having three sides. [from Latin *tri*, three + *latus*, side]

trilaterally *adv.* **1** on three sides. **2** concerning three countries or parties.

trilby /ˈtrɪlbɪ/ *noun* (PL. **trilbies**) *Brit.* a soft felt hat with an indented crown and narrow brim. [named after *Trilby*, the heroine of the novel of the same name by George du Maurier, in the stage version of which such a hat was worn]

trilingual /traɪˈlɪŋɡwəl/ *adj.* **1** able to speak three languages fluently, as or like a native speaker. **2** written or spoken in three languages. [from TRI- + Latin *lingua*, tongue]

trill — *noun* **1** *Mus.* a sound produced by playing or singing a note and a note higher than it repeatedly and in rapid succession. **2** a shrill warbling sound made by a songbird. **3** a consonant sound, especially an 'r' sound, produced by rapidly vibrating the tongue. — *verb trans., intrans.* to play, sing, or pronounce (something) with a trill. [from Italian *trillo*]

trillion /ˈtrɪlɪən/ *noun* **1** in North America, and increasingly in the UK, a million millions (10^{12}). **2** formerly in Britain, a million million millions (10^{18}). **3** (*also* **trillions**) *colloq.* an enormous number or amount. [from TRI- + MILLION]

trillionth *noun, adj.* a million millionth.

trilobite /ˈtraɪləbaɪt/ *noun* **1** *Zool.* an extinct marine arthropod having a flat oval body divided lengthwise into three lobes. Trilobites were abundant from the Cambrian to the Permian periods. **2** the fossilized remains of this animal. [from Greek *trilobos*, three-lobed]

trilogy /ˈtrɪlədʒɪ/ *noun* (PL. **trilogies**) a group of three plays, novels, poems, operas, etc which are related, often by theme. [from Greek *trilogia*]

trim — *verb* (**trimmed**, **trimming**) **1** to make neat and tidy, especially by clipping. **2** (*also* **trim something away** or **off**) to remove it by, or as if by, cutting: *trim hundreds of pounds off the cost.* **3** to make less by, or as if by, cutting: *trim costs.* **4** to decorate with ribbons, lace, ornaments, etc. **5** to adjust the balance of (a ship, submarine, or aircraft) by moving its cargo, ballast, etc. **6** to arrange (a ship's sails) to suit the weather conditions. **7** *intrans.* to hold a neutral or middle course between two opposing individuals or groups. **8** *intrans.* to adjust one's behaviour to suit current trends or opinions, especially for self-advancement. — *noun* **1** a haircut which neatens but does not change a person's hairstyle. **2** proper order or condition: *in good trim.* **3** material, ornaments, etc used as decoration. **4** the decorative additions to a car, including the upholstery, internal and external colour scheme, and chrome and leather accessories. **5** the set or balance of a ship on the water. **6** *said of a ship* the state of being ready, especially with the sails in proper order, for sailing. **7** the inclination of an aircraft in flight, especially with reference to the horizon. **8** parts removed by trimming. — *adj.* (**trimmer**, **trimmest**) **1** in good order; neat and tidy. **2** clean-cut; slim. [from Anglo-Saxon *trymian*, to strengthen]

🔲 *verb* **1** neaten, tidy, adjust, arrange, order. **2, 3** cut. **2** clip, crop, dock, prune, pare, shave. **4** decorate, ornament, embellish, garnish, dress, array. *noun* **2** condition, state, order, form, shape, fitness, health. *adj.* **1** neat, tidy, orderly, shipshape, spick-and-span, spruce, smart, dapper. **2** slim, slender, streamlined, compact.
🔁 *adj.* **1** untidy, scruffy.

trimaran /ˈtraɪməran/ *noun* a boat with three hulls placed side by side. [from TRI- + CATAMARAN]

trimester /traɪˈmɛstə(r)/ *noun* a period of three months, especially in the US one forming an academic term. [from Latin *trimestris*, of three months]

trimly *adv.* in a trim way.

trimmer *noun* **1** a person or thing that trims. **2** a person who adjusts his or her behaviour to suit current trends and opinions, especially for self-advancement. **3** a short horizontal beam on a floor into which the ends of joists are fitted.

trimming *noun* **1** ribbon, lace, or other decoration added to clothing, etc. **2** (**trimmings**) the traditional or usual sauce, garnish, accompanying vegetables, etc served with a particular dish. **3** (**trimmings**) parts cut or trimmed off.

🔲 **1, 2** extra(s). **1** decorations, ornaments, frills, accessories. **2** garnish, sauce. **3** cuttings, parings, clippings, ends.

trimness *noun* being trim.

Trinitarian /trɪnɪˈtɛərɪən/ — *noun* a person who believes in the doctrine of the Trinity. — *adj.* relating to or believing in the doctrine of the Trinity. See also UNITARIAN.

Trinitarianism *noun* the beliefs of the Trinitarians.

trinitrotoluene /traɪnaɪtrəʊˈtɒljuːiːn/ *noun Chem.* a highly explosive yellow crystalline solid that is used as an explosive, and in certain photographic chemicals and dyes. [from TRI- + NITRO- + *toluene*, a liquid organic chemical]

trinity /ˈtrɪnɪtɪ/ *noun* (PL. **trinities**) **1** the state of being or a group of three. **2** (**Trinity**) in Christian theology, the unity of three persons, the Father, Son, and Holy Spirit, in a single Godhead. **3** (**Trinity** or **Trinity Sunday**) the Sunday after Whit Sunday, kept as a festival in honour of the Trinity. **4** (**Trinity** or **Trinity term**) the university or law term beginning after Easter. [from Latin *trinitas*]

trinket *noun* a small, worthless article, especially a cheap ornament or piece of jewellery.

🔲 bauble, jewel, ornament, knick-knack.

trinketry *noun* a collection of such articles.

trio /ˈtriːəʊ/ *noun* (PL. **trios**) **1** a group of three. **2** *Mus.* a group of three instruments, players, or singers, or a piece of music composed for it. **3** *Mus.* a contrastive central section of a minuet, scherzo, or march. [from Italian]

🔲 **1** threesome, triad, triumvirate, trinity, triplet, trilogy.

trip — *verb* (**tripped**, **tripping**) **1** *intrans.* (*also* **trip over** or **up**) to stumble. **2** (*also* **trip over** or **up**) to cause to stumble. **3** *trans., intrans.* (*also* **trip up**) to make or cause to make a mistake. **4** (*also* **trip up**) to catch (someone) in a fault or mistake. **5** *intrans.* (*usually* **trip along**) to walk, skip, or dance with short light steps. **6** *intrans.* to move or flow smoothly and easily: *words tripping off the tongue.* **7** *intrans.* to take a trip or excursion. **8** *intrans. slang* to experience the hallucinatory effects of a drug, especially LSD. **9** *trans., intrans.* to activate or cause (a device or mechanism) to be activated, especially suddenly. **10** to perform (a dance) with quick, light, agile steps. — *noun* **1** a short journey or excursion, usually to a place and back again. **2** a catching of the foot; a stumble. **3** a short light step or skip. **4** a striking part or catch which activates a mechanism. **5** an error or blunder. **6** *slang* a hallucinatory experience caused by taking a drug, especially LSD. **7** *slang* an intensely emotional experience. [from Old French *triper*]

🔲 *verb* **1** stumble, slip, fall, tumble, stagger, totter. **4** catch out, trap. **5** dance, skip, gambol, caper, tiptoe. *noun* **1** outing, excursion, tour, jaunt, ride, drive, spin, journey, voyage, expedition, foray.

tripartite /traɪˈpɑːtaɪt/ *adj.* **1** divided into three parts. **2** involving or concerning three parts, groups, people, etc. [from Latin *tripartitus*]

tripe *noun* **1** parts of the stomach of a cow or sheep, used as food. **2** *colloq.* nonsense; rubbish. [from Old French]

triple / 'trɪpl/ — *adj.* **1** three times as great, as much, or as many. **2** made up of three parts or things. **3** *Mus.* having three beats to the bar. — *verb trans., intrans.* to make or become three times as great, much, or many. — *noun* **1** three times the (usual) amount. **2** a group or series of three. [from Latin *triplus*]

∎ *adj.* **1, 2** treble, triplicate, threefold. **2** three-part, three-ply, three-way. *verb* treble, triplicate.

triple bond *Chem.* a covalent bond formed between two atoms that share three pairs of electrons between them.

triple glazing three layers of glass separated by air spaces to give improved thermal and acoustic insulation. It provides insulation significantly greater than that from double glazing.

trip hop a type of dance music developed from hip-hop and involving associations with a hallucinatory 'trip'.

triple jump an athletic event in which competitors try to cover the greatest distance with a type of jump consisting of a hop, skip, and a jump.

triple point *Chem.* the temperature and pressure at which the solid, liquid, and gaseous phases of a particular substance are in equilibrium.

triplet *noun* **1** one of three children or animals born to the same mother at the same time. **2** a group or set of three. **3** *Mus.* a group of three notes played in the time usually given to two. **4** a group of three rhyming verses in a poem. [from TRIPLE]

triple time musical time with three beats to the bar. Simple triple time has beats divisible by two, as in 3:2, 3:4, 3:8. Compound triple time has beats divisible by three, as in 9:4, 9:8, 9:16.

triplicate — *adj.* **1** having three parts which are exactly alike. **2** being one of three identical copies. **3** tripled. — *noun* any of three identical copies or three parts which are exactly alike. — *verb* to make three copies of. — **in triplicate** three times; on three separate copies of the same document. [from Latin *triplicatus*]

triplication / trɪplɪ'keɪʃən/ *noun* the process of triplicating.

triply / 'trɪplɪ/ *adv.* three times as much.

tripod / 'traɪpɒd/ *noun* **1** a stand with three legs for supporting a camera. **2** a stool or table with three legs or feet. [from Latin *tripus*]

tripos / 'traɪpɒs/ *noun* an honours examination for the BA degree at Cambridge University. [from Latin *tripus*, tripod]

tripper *noun* **1** *Brit. often derog.* a person who goes on a journey for pleasure; a tourist. **2** *slang* a person who takes a drug, especially LSD, and experiences its hallucinatory effects.

triptych / 'trɪptɪk/ *noun* a picture or carving on three panels which are joined together by hinges to form a single work of art, often used as an altarpiece. See also DIPTYCH. [from Greek *triptychos*, threefold]

tripwire *noun* a hidden wire which sets off a mechanism of some kind, such as an alarm or bomb, when someone trips over it.

trireme / 'traɪriːm/ *noun* an ancient Greek warship with three banks of rowers on each side. [from Latin *triremis*]

trisect / traɪ'sɛkt/ *verb* to divide into three usually equal parts. [from TRI- + Latin *secare*, to cut]

trisection *noun* trisecting, dividing into three equal parts.

trite *adj., said of a remark, phrase, etc* having no meaning or effectiveness because repeated or used so often; hackneyed. [from Latin *tritus*, rubbed]

∎ banal, commonplace, ordinary, run-of-the-mill, stale, tired, worn, threadbare, unoriginal, hackneyed, overused, stock, stereotyped, clichéd, *colloq.* corny.
✷ original, new, fresh.

tritely *adv.* in a trite way.

triteness *noun* a trite quality.

tritium / 'trɪtɪəm/ *noun Chem.* (SYMBOL ³H or T) a radioactive isotope of hydrogen that contains two neutrons and one proton in its nucleus. It undergoes radioactive decay to form beta particles, and is used in scientific research to label compounds with radioactivity so that they can be traced by the radiation they emit. It is also used in hydrogen bombs and luminous paints. [from Greek *tritos*, third]

triumph / 'traɪəmf/ — *noun* **1** a great or notable victory, success, or achievement. **2** the great joy or feeling of elation felt on winning a great victory, etc. **3** *Hist.* the procession accompanying the entry into ancient Rome of a general who had won a great victory over a foreign enemy. — *verb intrans.* **1** to win a victory or be successful. **2** to celebrate a victory or success. **3** to enjoy a feeling of triumph over someone. [from Latin *triumphus*]

∎ *noun* **1** win, victory, conquest, *colloq.* walkover, success, achievement, accomplishment, feat, coup, masterstroke, hit, sensation. **2** exultation, jubilation, rejoicing, celebration, elation, joy, happiness. *verb* **1** win, succeed, prosper, conquer, vanquish, overcome, overwhelm, prevail, dominate. **2** celebrate, rejoice. **3** glory, gloat.
✷ *noun* **1** failure, fiasco. *verb* **1** lose, fail.

triumphal / traɪ'ʌmfl/ *adj.* of or celebrating a triumph.

triumphal arch *Archit.* a free-standing gateway of purely aesthetic or symbolic function, usually monumental in proportion and built of stone. Triumphal arches were first built in Rome in the 2cBC, usually to celebrate a military victory. The most famous example today is the Arc de Triomphe de l'Etoile in Paris, built in 1806–35.

triumphant *adj.* **1** having won a victory or achieved success. **2** feeling or showing great joy or elation at, or celebrating, a victory or success.

∎ **1** winning, victorious, conquering, successful. **2** exultant, jubilant, rejoicing, celebratory, glorious, elated, joyful, proud, boastful, gloating, swaggering.
✷ **1** defeated. **2** humble.

triumphantly *adv.* in a triumphant way.

triumvir / traɪ'ʌmvə(r)/ *noun* (PL. **triumviri, triumvirs**) any one of a group of three people sharing office or supreme power. [from Latin, *trium virorum*, of three men]

triumviral *adj.* relating to or designating a triumvir.

triumvirate / traɪ'ʌmvɪrət/ *noun* a group of three people sharing office or supreme power.

trivalence / traɪ'veɪləns/ or **trivalency** *noun* being trivalent.

trivalent / traɪ'veɪlənt/ *adj. Chem.* having a valency of three. [from TRI- + Latin *valere*, to be strong]

trivet / 'trɪvɪt/ *noun* **1** a three-legged stand or bracket which hooks on to a grate for holding cooking vessels over a fire. **2** a stand for a hot dish, pot, teapot, etc at table. [from Anglo-Saxon *trefet*]

trivia / 'trɪvɪə/ *pl. noun* unimportant or petty matters or details. [from Latin *trivium*, place where three ways meet]

∎ trifles, details, inessentials, incidentals, trivialities, minutiae.

trivial / 'trɪvɪəl/ *adj.* **1** of very little importance. **2** *said of a person* only interested in unimportant things; frivolous. **3** commonplace; ordinary.

∎ **1, 2** frivolous. **1** unimportant, insignificant, inconsequential, incidental, minor, petty, paltry, trifling, small, little, inconsiderable, negligible, worthless, meaningless. **3** banal, trite, commonplace, everyday.
✷ **1** important, significant, profound.

triviality *noun* (PL. **trivialities**) **1** being trivial. **2** something that is trivial.

....

◨ **1** unimportance, insignificance, pettiness, smallness, worthlessness, meaninglessness, frivolity. **2** trifle, detail, technicality.
◨ **1** importance. **2** essential.

....

trivialization /trɪvɪəlaɪˈzeɪʃən/ or **trivialisation** *noun* trivializing or being trivialized.

trivialize or **trivialise** /ˈtrɪvɪəlaɪz/ *verb* to make or treat as if trivial or unimportant.

trivially *adv.* in a trivial way; to a trivial extent.

Trivial Pursuit *trademark* a board quiz game developed in Canada in 1979.

trochee /ˈtrəʊkiː/ *noun Prosody* a foot consisting of one long syllable followed by one short one. [from Greek *trochaios pous*, running foot]

trod, trodden see TREAD.

troglodyte /ˈtrɒglədaɪt/ *noun* a person who lives in a cave. [from Greek *troglodytes*, one who creeps into holes]

troika /ˈtrɔɪkə/ *noun* **1** a Russian vehicle drawn by three horses abreast. **2** a team of three horses harnessed abreast. **3** any group of three people working as a team, especially sharing power. [from Russian]

Trojan /ˈtrəʊdʒən/ — *noun* **1** *Hist.* a citizen or inhabitant of ancient Troy in Asia Minor. **2** a person who works, fights, etc extremely hard or courageously. — *adj.* relating to ancient Troy or its inhabitants or citizens. [from Latin *Trojanus*, from *Troja*, Troy]

troll[1] /trəʊl/ *noun Scandinavian Mythol.* an imaginary, ugly, evil-tempered, human-like creature, usually a dwarf or a giant. [from Norse]

troll[2] /trəʊl/ — *verb* **1** *trans., intrans.* to fish by trailing bait on a line through water. **2** *intrans. old use, facetious* to stroll or saunter. — *noun* the bait used in trolling, or a line holding this. [from Middle English *trollen*, to roll or stroll]

trolley /ˈtrɒlɪ/ *noun* (PL. **trolleys**) **1** *Brit.* a small cart or basket on wheels used for conveying luggage, shopping, etc. **2** *Brit.* a small table, usually with a shelf underneath, mounted on castors or wheels, used for conveying food, crockery, etc in the home or a restaurant. **3** a bed on wheels for transporting patients in hospital. **4** *Brit.* a small wagon or truck running on rails. **5** a trolley wheel. **6** *Brit.* a trolley bus. **7** *North Amer.* a trolley car. — **off one's trolley** *colloq.* daft; crazy. [probably from TROLL[2]]

trolley bus a vehicle providing public transport which receives power from a trolley wheel and overhead electric wires.

trolley car *North Amer.* a vehicle providing public transport which runs on rails like a tram and receives power from a trolley wheel and overhead electric wires.

trolley wheel a small grooved wheel which collects current from an overhead electric wire and transmits it down a pole to power the vehicle underneath.

trollop /ˈtrɒləp/ *noun* a promiscuous or disreputable woman. [perhaps from TROLL[2]]

trombone /trɒmˈbəʊn/ *noun* a brass musical wind instrument, on which the pitch of notes is altered by sliding a tube in and out. [from Italian *tromba*, trumpet]

trombonist /trɒmˈbəʊnɪst/ *noun* a person who plays the trombone.

trompe l'oeil /trɒmp ˈlɜːɪ/ (PL. **trompe l'oeils**) a painting or decoration which gives a convincing illusion of reality. [French, = deceives the eye]

troop — *noun* **1** (*usually* **troops**) armed forces; soldiers. **2** a group or collection, especially of people or animals. **3** a division of a cavalry or armoured squadron. **4** a large group of Scouts, divided into patrols. — *verb intrans.* (**troop along, off,** *etc*) to move as a group. — **troop the colour** to parade the regiment's flag ceremonially. [from Old French *trope*]

....

◨ *noun* **1** army, military, soldiers, servicemen, servicewomen. **2** contingent, division, company, squad, team, crew, gang, band, bunch, group, body, pack, herd, flock, horde, crowd, throng, multitude. **3** squadron, unit. *verb* go, march, parade, stream, flock, swarm, throng.

....

trooper *noun* **1** a private soldier, especially one in a cavalry or armoured unit. **2** a cavalry soldier's horse. **3** *North Amer., esp. US* a policeman mounted on a horse or motorcycle. **4** *Brit.* a troop-ship.

troop-ship *noun* a ship for transporting soldiers.

trope /trəʊp/ *noun* a word or expression used figuratively. [from Greek *tropos*, turn]

trophy /ˈtrəʊfɪ/ *noun* (PL. **trophies**) **1** a cup, medal, plate, etc awarded as a prize for victory or success in some contest, especially in sport. **2** something which is kept in memory of a victory or success, eg in hunting. **3** a memorial of victory, especially in ancient Greece or Rome, originally captured weapons, armour, and other spoils, set up on or near the field of victory. **4** a representation of such a memorial, eg on a medal or monument. — *adj. said of someone's partner* regarded as a status symbol for them: *a trophy wife*. [from Greek *tropaion*]

....

◨ **1** cup, prize, award. **2** souvenir, memento.

....

tropic — *noun* **1** either of two imaginary circles running round the earth at 23° 2´ north (the *Tropic of Cancer*) or 23° 2´ south (the *Tropic of Capricorn*) of the equator. **2** (**tropics**) the part of the earth lying between these two circles, noted for its hot dry weather. — *adj.* same as TROPICAL. [from Greek *tropikos*]

tropical *adj.* **1** relating to, found in, or originating from the tropics. **2** very hot; passionate. **3** luxuriant.

....

◨ **2** hot, torrid, sultry, sweltering, stifling, steamy, humid.
◨ **2** arctic, cold, cool, temperate.

....

tropically *adv.* in a tropical way or situation.

tropical medicine *Medicine* the branch of medicine that specializes in diseases that are prevalent in tropical regions. The most important tropical diseases worldwide are malaria, schistosomiasis, leprosy, and river blindness, all of which are potentially curable, although the facilities for their treatment are often inadequate in the countries where they occur.

Tropic of Cancer see TROPIC.

Tropic of Capricorn see TROPIC.

tropism /ˈtrəʊpɪzm/ *noun Biol.* the growth movement of a plant in response to an external stimulus such as gravity or light, usually by curving towards or away from the source. For example, plant roots grow vertically downward in response to gravity (positive geotropism). [from Greek *tropos*, turning]

troposphere /ˈtrɒpəsfɪə(r)/ *noun Meteorol.* the lowest layer of the Earth's atmosphere, extending from the Earth's surface to a height of about 8km over the Poles, and about 17km over the Equator. Weather conditions, in the form of clouds, convection currents, etc, occur within the troposphere, and the temperature steadily decreases with increasing height. [from Greek *tropos*, turn + SPHERE]

Trot *noun derog. colloq.* **1** a Trotskyist. **2** any supporter of the extreme left.

trot — *verb* (**trotted, trotting**) **1** *intrans. said of a horse* to move at a steady, fairly fast pace, moving each diagonal pair of legs together to give a bouncy gait. **2** to cause (a horse) to move in this way. **3** *intrans.* to move or proceed at a steady, fairly brisk pace. — *noun* **1** the pace at which a horse, rider, etc moves when trotting. **2** an act of trotting. **3** (**the trots**) *slang* diarrhoea. — **on the trot** *colloq.* **1** one after the other. **2** continually moving about; busy. **trot something out** *colloq.* to produce a story, excuse, etc habitually and unthinkingly. [from Old French *troter*]

⊟ *verb* **3** jog, run, scamper, scuttle, scurry.

troth /trəʊθ, trɒθ/ *noun old use* faith or fidelity. — **plight one's troth** to promise to be faithful and true in marriage. [from Anglo-Saxon *treowth*, truth]

Trotskyism /'trɒtski:ɪzm/ *noun* a development of Marxist thought by Leon Trotsky (1879–1940). Essentially a theory of permanent revolution, Trotskyism stressed the internationalism of socialism and encouraged revolutionary movements abroad, which conflicted with Stalin's 'socialism in one country'.

Trotskyist or **Trotskyite** /'trɒtski:aɪt/ — *noun* a supporter of Trotskyism. — *adj.* relating to or involving Trotskyism.

trotter *noun* **1** a horse trained to trot in harness. **2** (*usually* **trotters**) a pig's foot used as food.

troubadour /'tru:bədʊə(r)/ *noun Hist.* any of a number of lyric poets in S France and N Italy in the 11c to 13c who wrote, usually in Provençal, about a highly idealized form of love. [from Provençal *trobar*, to find]

trouble /'trʌbl/ — *noun* **1** distress, worry, or concern, or a cause of this. **2** bother or effort, or a cause of this: *go to a lot of trouble / the dog was no trouble.* **3** a problem or difficulty: *your trouble is that you're too generous.* **4** (*often* **troubles**) public disturbances and unrest. **5** illness or weakness: *heart trouble.* **6** malfunction; failure: *engine trouble.* **7** the state of expecting a child when not married: *get into trouble.* — *verb* **1** to cause to feel distress, worry, concern, anger, or sadness to. **2** to cause physical distress or discomfort to. **3** *used in polite requests* to put to inconvenience: *might I trouble you to open the window a little?* **4** *intrans.* to make any effort or take pains: *he didn't even trouble to tell me what had happened.* **5** to disturb or agitate (eg the surface of water). — **be asking for trouble** *colloq.* to behave in a way likely to bring problems or difficulties on oneself. **in trouble** in difficulties, especially because of doing something wrong or illegal. **take trouble over** or **with something** to perform or treat it carefully and assiduously. [from Old French *trubler*, from Latin *turbare*, to disturb]

⊟ *noun* **1** annoyance, irritation, bother, nuisance, inconvenience, misfortune, adversity, trial, tribulation, pain, suffering, affliction, distress, grief, woe, heartache, concern, uneasiness, worry, anxiety, agitation. **2** effort, exertion, pains, care, attention, thought. **3** problem, difficulty. **4** unrest, strife, tumult, commotion, disturbance, disorder, upheaval. **5** disorder, complaint, ailment, illness, disease, disability, defect. **6** problem(s), malfunction, failure, breakdown. *verb* **1**, **2** bother, torment, afflict. **1**, **5** agitate, disturb, ruffle. **1** annoy, vex, harass, inconvenience, upset, distress, sadden, burden, pain, worry, disconcert, perplex.
⊟ *noun* **1** relief, calm. **4** order. **5** health. *verb* **1** reassure, help.

troubled *adj.* in a state of agitation or distress.

⊟ agitated, disturbed, worried, anxious, ill at ease, uneasy, fretful, ruffled, sad, unhappy.

troublemaker *noun* a person who continually and usually deliberately causes trouble, worry, problems, etc to others.

⊟ agitator, rabble-rouser, incendiary, instigator, ringleader, stirrer, mischief-maker.
⊟ peacemaker.

troubleshooter *noun* **1** a person who is employed to find and solve problems, eg with machinery or in a company. **2** a person employed to mediate in disputes.

troubleshooting *noun* the solving of problems.

troublesome *adj.* **1** causing worry or difficulty. **2** difficult to keep under control.

⊟ **1** annoying, irritating, vexatious, irksome, bothersome, inconvenient, difficult, hard, tricky, thorny, taxing, demanding, laborious, tiresome, wearisome. **2** unruly, rowdy, turbulent, trying, unco-operative, insubordinate, rebellious.
⊟ **1** easy, simple. **2** helpful.

troublesomely *adv.* in a troublesome way.

troublous *adj. old use, literary* full of troubles; disturbed.

trough /trɒf/ *noun* **1** a long narrow open container used for feeding animal livestock. **2** a channel, drain, or gutter. **3** a long narrow hollow between two waves. **4** *Meteorol.* a long narrow area of low atmospheric pressure; the opposite of a ridge. **5** a low point. [from Anglo-Saxon *trog*]

⊟ **2** gutter, conduit, trench, ditch, gully, channel, groove, furrow, hollow. **4**, **5** depression, low. **5** drop, slump, downturn.

trounce /traʊns/ *verb* to beat or defeat completely.

⊟ defeat, rout, beat, thrash, *colloq.* wallop, *colloq.* slaughter, *colloq.* hammer, *slang* wipe the floor with.

trouncing *noun* a beating.

troupe /tru:p/ *noun* a group or company of performers. [from French, from Latin *troppus*, troop]

trouper *noun* **1** a member of a troupe. **2** an experienced, hard-working, and loyal colleague.

trouser *verb colloq.* to gain or take (something, especially money); to pocket.

trouser- *combining form* of trousers: *trouser-buttons.*

trousers /'traʊzəz/ *pl. noun* an outer garment for the lower part of the body, reaching from the waist and covering each leg separately down to the ankle. — **wear the trousers** *colloq.* to be the member of a household who makes the decisions. [from Irish and Scots Gaelic *triubhas*, trews]

⊟ pants, slacks, jeans, denims, Levis *trademark*, flannels, *colloq.* bags, dungarees, breeches, shorts.

trousseau /'tru:səʊ/ *noun* (PL. **trousseaux**, **trousseaus**) a bride's set of new clothes and linen, traditionally bought for her wedding and for married life. [from French, *trousse*, bundle]

trout /traʊt/ *noun* (PL. **trout**, **trouts**) **1** any of several usually freshwater fish of the salmon family. **2** *derog. slang* an unpleasant, interfering old person, usually a woman. [from Anglo-Saxon *truht*]

trove see TREASURE-TROVE.

trowel /'traʊəl/ *noun* **1** a small, hand-held tool with a flat blade, used for applying and spreading mortar, plaster, etc. **2** a similar tool with a slightly curved blade, used for potting plants, etc. [from Latin *trulla*, scoop]

troy *noun* (*in full* **troy weight**) a system of weights used for precious metals and gemstones, with 12 ounces or 5760 grains to the pound. [from *Troyes* in France]

truancy *noun* playing truant.

⊟ absence, absenteeism, shirking, *colloq.* skiving.
⊟ attendance.

truant /'tru:ənt/ — *noun* someone who stays away from school or work without good reason or without permission. — *verb intrans.* to be a truant. — *adj.* that is deliberately absent. — **play truant** to stay away from school without good reason and without permission. [from Old French]

■ *noun* absentee, deserter, runaway, idler, shirker, *colloq.* skiver, dodger. *adj.* absent, missing, runaway.

truce /tru:s/ *noun* 1 an agreement to stop fighting, usually temporarily. 2 a temporary break in fighting, hostilities, feuding, etc. [from Middle English *trewes*, from Anglo-Saxon *treow*, truth]

■ CEASE-FIRE, PEACE, ARMISTICE. 2 cessation, moratorium, suspension, stay, respite, *colloq.* let-up, lull, rest, break, interval, intermission.
◨ WAR, HOSTILITIES.

truck [1] — *noun* 1 *Brit.* an open railway wagon for carrying goods. 2 *North Amer.* a heavy motor vehicle for transporting goods; a lorry. 3 a frame with four or more wheels supporting a railway carriage. 4 any wheeled vehicle, trolley, or cart for moving heavy goods. — *verb* 1 to put on or transport by truck. 2 *intrans. chiefly North Amer.* to work as a truck driver.

■ *noun* 1, 3 wagon. 2 *Brit.* lorry, van, trailer. 4 float, cart, barrow.

truck [2] — *noun* 1 exchange of goods; commercial dealings. 2 payment of wages in goods rather than money. 3 *colloq.* small goods or wares. 4 *colloq.* odds and ends; rubbish. 5 *North Amer., esp. US* market-garden produce, such as vegetables and fruit. — *verb trans., intrans.* to give (goods) in exchange; to barter. — **have no truck with someone** or **something** have no part in or dealings with them. [from Old French *troquer*, to exchange]

trucker *noun North Amer.* a person who drives a lorry, especially over long distances.

trucking *noun* transporting by trucks.

truckle — *noun* (*in full* **truckle-bed**) a low bed that may be wheeled under a larger bed for storage. — *verb intrans.* to submit or give in passively or weakly. [from Latin *trochlea*, pulley]

truculence /'trʌkjʊləns/ or **truculency** *noun* 1 being truculent. 2 truculent behaviour.

truculent /'trʌkjʊlənt/ *adj.* aggressively defiant, quarrelsome, or discourteous. [from Latin *trux*, wild, fierce]

■ aggressive, belligerent, bellicose, defiant, disobedient, quarrelsome, argumentative, obstreperous, rude, discourteous, disrespectful.

truculently *adv.* with a truculent manner.

trudge — *verb* 1 *intrans.* (*usually* **trudge along, over,** *etc*) to walk with slow and weary steps. 2 to cover (a stated distance, ground, etc) slowly and wearily. — *noun* a long and tiring walk.

■ *verb* TRAMP, PLOD, TRAIPSE, TREK, HIKE, WALK, MARCH. 1 clump, stump, lumber, slog, labour. *noun* tramp, traipse, slog, haul, trek, hike, walk, march.

true — *adj.* 1 agreeing with fact or reality; not false or wrong: *a true story.* 2 real; genuine; properly so called: *the spider is not a true insect.* 3 accurate or exact: *a photograph doesn't give a true idea of the size of the building.* 4 faithful; loyal: *be true to one's word.* 5 conforming to a standard, pattern, type, or expectation: *behave true to form.* 6 in the correct position; well-fitting; accurately adjusted. 7 *said of a compass bearing* measured according to the earth's axis and not magnetic north. 8 honest; sincere: *twelve good men and true.* — *adv.* 1 certainly: *true, she isn't very happy here.* 2 truthfully. 3 faithfully. 4 honestly. 5 accurately or precisely. 6 accurately in tune: *sing true.* 7 conforming to ancestral type: *breed true.* — *verb* to bring or restore (eg machinery) into an accurate or required position. — **come true** *said of a dream, hope, etc* to happen in

reality. **out of true** not in the correct position; not straight or properly balanced. [from Anglo-Saxon *treow*]

■ *adj.* 1 truthful, veracious, honest, sincere, correct, right, factual. 2 real, genuine, authentic, actual, veritable, legitimate, valid, rightful, proper. 3 exact, precise, accurate. 4 faithful, loyal, constant, steadfast, staunch, firm, trustworthy, trusty, honourable, dedicated, devoted.
◨ *adj.* 1, 2 false. 1 wrong, incorrect. 3 inaccurate. 4 unfaithful, faithless.

true airspeed *Aeron.* (ABBREV. **TAS**) the actual speed of an aircraft as it moves through the air, calculated by correcting the value obtained from an airspeed indicator (the *indicated airspeed*) for altitude, temperature, density, and pressure.

true-blue — *adj.* 1 extremely loyal. 2 *Brit.* being an extremely orthodox supporter of the Conservative party. — *noun* a true-blue person.

true-love *noun* a beloved person; a sweetheart.

trueness *noun* being true.

true north the direction of the north pole (rather than the direction of magnetic north).

truffle /'trʌfl/ *noun* 1 any of several dark round fungi which grow underground and are considered a delicacy. 2 a usually round sweet made typically with cream, butter, chocolate, and rum, and coated in cocoa. [from Latin *tuber*, lump, swelling]

trug *noun Brit.* a shallow rectangular basket used for carrying garden tools, plants, etc. [perhaps a variant of TROUGH]

truism /'tru:ɪzm/ *noun* a statement which is obviously true; a commonplace.

■ truth, platitude, commonplace, cliché.

truly *adv.* 1 really: *truly believe it to be for the best.* 2 genuinely; honestly. 3 faithfully. 4 accurately; exactly. 5 properly; rightly. 6 very.

■ 1, 2 really, genuinely, sincerely, honestly, truthfully. 1 undeniably, indubitably, indeed, in fact, in reality. 4 exactly, precisely, correctly. 5 rightly, properly, rightfully, legitimately. 6 very, greatly, extremely.
◨ 4 falsely, incorrectly.

trump [1] — *noun* 1 (**trumps**) the suit of cards which has been declared to have a higher value than any other suit. 2 (*also* **trump card**) a a card of this suit, which has a higher value than a card of the other suits. b a secret advantage. 3 *colloq.* a helpful, reliable, or fine person. — *verb* 1 *trans., intrans.* to defeat (an ordinary card or a trick with no trumps) by playing a trump. 2 to win a surprising victory or advantage over (a person, plan, idea, etc). — **come up** or **turn up trumps** *said of a person* to be unexpectedly useful or helpful in difficult circumstances. **trump something up** to invent or make up false evidence, accusations, etc. [a variant of TRIUMPH]

trump [2] *noun old use, poetic* a trumpet. — **the last trump** *Relig.* the trumpet call to wake the dead on the Day of Judgement. [from Old French *trompe*]

trumped-up *adj., said of evidence, accusations, etc* invented or made up; false.

trumpery /'trʌmpəri/ — *noun* (PL. **trumperies**) 1 showy but worthless articles. 2 rubbish. — *adj.* showy but worthless. [from Old French *tromper*, to deceive]

trumpet — *noun* 1 a brass musical instrument with a narrow tube and flared bell and a powerful, high, clear tone. 2 anything like this in shape, such as the corona of a daffodil or a horn, or sound. 3 the loud cry of an elephant. — *verb* (**trumpeted, trumpeting**) 1 *intrans. said of an elephant* to make a loud cry. 2 *intrans.* to blow a trumpet. 3 to make known or proclaim loudly. [from Old French *trompette*]

▣ *noun* **1** bugle, horn, clarion. **3** blare, blast, roar, bellow, cry, call. *verb* **1** blare, blast, roar, bellow. **3** shout, proclaim, announce, broadcast, advertise.

trumpeter *noun* a person who plays the trumpet.

trumpeter swan a black-billed American swan, the largest of the world's swans.

truncate /trʌŋ'keɪt/ — *verb* to cut so as to shorten. — *adj.*, *said eg of a leaf* having the base or tip cut square. [from Latin *truncare*]

▣ *verb* shorten, abbreviate, curtail, cut, lop, dock, prune, pare, clip, trim, crop.
▣ *verb* lengthen, extend.

truncation *noun* the process of truncating or being truncated.

truncheon /'trʌntʃən/ *noun* **1** a short, thick heavy stick, carried by police officers. See also BATON. **2** a staff of authority or office. [from Old French *tronchon*, stump]

trundle /'trʌndl/ *verb trans., intrans.* (*usually* **trundle along, through**) to move or roll heavily and clumsily. [from Anglo-Saxon *trendel*]

trunk *noun* **1** the main stem of a tree without the branches and roots. **2** a person's or animal's body without the head and limbs. **3** the main part of anything. **4** a large rigid box or chest for storing or transporting clothes and personal items. **5** *North Amer.* the boot of a car. **6** the long, muscular nose of an elephant. **7** (**trunks**) men's close-fitting shorts or pants worn especially for swimming. [from Latin *truncus*]

▣ **1** shaft, stock, stem, stalk. **2, 3** torso, body, frame. **4** case, suitcase, chest, coffer, box, crate.

trunk call *Brit.* a long-distance telephone call.

trunk line 1 a main telephone line between large towns or cities. **2** a main railway line.

trunk road a main road between large towns.

truss — *noun* **1** a framework, eg of wooden or metal beams, supporting a roof, bridge, etc. **2** a belt, bandage, or other device worn to support a hernia. **3** a bundle of hay or straw. **4** a cluster of flowers or fruit at the top of a main stalk or stem. **5** *Archit.* a corbel. — *verb* (*often* **truss something** or **someone up**) **1** to tie up or bind (someone) tightly. **2** to tie up the wings and legs of (a fowl) before cooking. **3** to support (a roof, bridge, etc) with a truss. [from Old French *trousse*]

▣ *noun* **1, 2** support, brace. **1** prop, stay, shore, strut, joist. **2** binding, bandage. *verb* **1** tie, strap, bind, pinion, fasten, secure, bundle, pack.
▣ *verb* **1** untie, loosen.

trust — *noun* **1** belief or confidence in, or reliance on, the truth, goodness, character, power, ability, etc of someone or something. **2** charge or care: *the child was placed in my trust*. **3** the state of being responsible for the conscientious performance of some task: *be in a position of trust*. **4** a task assigned to someone in the belief that they will perform it well and conscientiously. **5** credit: *put it on trust*. **6** an arrangement by which money or property is managed by one person for the benefit of someone else. **7** an amount of money or property managed by one person for the benefit of another. **8** a group of business firms working together to control the market in a particular commodity, beat down competition, and maximise profits. **9** same as HOSPITAL TRUST. — *adj.* held in trust. — *verb* **1** (**trust someone** or **trust in someone**) to have confidence or faith in them; to depend or rely on them: *we must trust her to cope*. **2** to allow (someone) to use or do something in the belief that they will behave responsibly, honestly,

etc: *I wouldn't trust him with your new car.* **3** (**trust something** or **someone to someone**) to give them into the care of that person: *trusted the children to their grandfather*. **4** *trans., intrans.* to be confident; to hope or suppose: *I trust you had a good journey*. **5** to give credit to. — **take something** or **someone on trust** to accept or believe them without verification. [from Norse *traust*]

▣ *noun* **1** faith, belief, credence, credit, hope, expectation, reliance, confidence, assurance, conviction, certainty. **2** care, charge, custody, safekeeping, guardianship, protection, responsibility, duty. *verb* **1** rely on, depend on, count on, bank on, swear by. **3** entrust, commit, consign, confide, give, assign, delegate. **4** believe, imagine, assume, presume, suppose, surmise, hope, expect.
▣ *noun* **1** distrust, mistrust, scepticism, doubt. *verb* **1** distrust, mistrust, doubt, disbelieve.

trustafarian *noun Brit., facetious* a young person who adopts the attitudes and style of someone who rejects conventional society, but who in fact has money in a trust fund. [from TRUST FUND + RASTAFARIAN]

trustee *noun* **1** a person who manages money or property for someone else. **2** a member of a group of people managing the affairs and business of a company or institution.

trusteeship *noun* the status or position of a trustee.

trustful or **trusting** *adj.* willing to have confidence or trust in others; confiding.

▣ credulous, gullible, naïve, innocent, unquestioning, unsuspecting, unguarded, unwary.
▣ distrustful, suspicious, cautious.

trustfully or **trustingly** *adv.* in a trustful or trusting way.

trustfulness *noun* being trustful.

trust fund money or property held in trust, eg until the owner comes of age.

trustily *adv.* faithfully, honestly.

trustiness *noun* being trusty.

trustworthily *adv.* in a trustworthy way.

trustworthiness *noun* being trustworthy.

trustworthy *adj.* able to be trusted or depended on.

▣ honest, upright, honourable, principled, dependable, reliable, steadfast, true, responsible, sensible.
▣ untrustworthy, dishonest, unreliable, irresponsible.

trusty — *adj.* (**trustier, trustiest**) able to be trusted or depended on. — *noun* (PL. **trusties**) a trusted person, especially a convict given special privileges for good behaviour.

truth /truːθ/ *noun* **1** the state of being true, genuine, or factual. **2** the state of being truthful; sincerity; honesty. **3** that which is true. **4** that which is established or generally accepted as true: *scientific truths*. **5** strict adherence to an original or standard. — **to tell the truth** or **truth to tell** really; actually. [from Anglo-Saxon *treowth*]

▣ **1** genuineness, authenticity, realism, exactness, precision, accuracy, validity, legitimacy. **2** truthfulness, veracity, candour, frankness, honesty, sincerity, integrity, uprightness, faithfulness, fidelity, loyalty, constancy. **3** facts, reality, actuality, fact, axiom, maxim, principle, truism.
▣ **1** falseness. **2** deceit, dishonesty. **3** lie, falsehood.

truthful *adj.* **1** *said of a person* telling the truth. **2** true; realistic.

▣ **1** veracious, frank, candid, straight, honest, sincere. **2** true, veritable, exact, precise, accurate, correct, realistic, faithful, trustworthy, reliable.

▣ **1** untruthful, deceitful. **2** false, untrue.

. . . .

truthfully *adv.* in a truthful way.

truthfulness *noun* being truthful.

try — *verb* (**tries, tried**) **1** *trans., intrans.* to attempt or make an effort (at); to seek to attain or achieve. **2** (*also* **try something out**) to test it or experiment with it in order to assess its usefulness, value, quality, etc. **3** to judge or conduct the legal trial of (someone). **4** to examine all the evidence in (a case) in a law court. **5** to exert strain or stress on: *try the limits of his patience.* — *noun* (PL. **tries**) **1** an attempt or effort. **2** *Rugby* the score of three points (in Rugby League) or five points (in Rugby Union) gained by a player who succeeds in placing the ball over the opponent's goal line with his or her hand. — **try one's hand at something** to see if one can do it, especially at a first attempt. **try something on** to put on (clothes, shoes, etc) to check the fit and appearance. **try it on** *Brit. colloq.* to attempt to deceive someone, or to test their patience or tolerance. **try something** or **someone out** to test their qualities or capabilities. [from Old French *trier*, to sift]

. . . .

▤ *verb* **1** attempt, endeavour, venture, undertake, seek, strive. **2, 5** test. **2** experiment with, sample, taste, inspect, examine, investigate, evaluate, appraise. **4** hear, judge. **5** tax, strain, stress, stretch. *noun* **1** attempt, go, *colloq.* bash, *colloq.* crack, *colloq.* shot, *colloq.* stab, endeavour, effort, experiment, test, trial, sample, taste.

. . . .

trying *adj.* causing strain or anxiety; stretching one's patience to the limit.

. . . .

▤ annoying, irritating, aggravating, vexatious, exasperating, troublesome, tiresome, wearisome, difficult, hard, tough, arduous, taxing, demanding, testing.

▣ easy.

. . . .

try-on *noun Brit. colloq.* an attempt to deceive, or to test a person's patience.

try-out *noun colloq.* a test or trial.

trypsin /'trɪpsɪn/ *noun Biochem.* a digestive enzyme secreted by the pancreas that catalyses the partial breakdown of protein. [from Greek *tripsis*, rubbing, because it was first obtained by rubbing down the pancreas with glycerine]

tryptophan or **tryptophane** /'trɪptoʊfan/ *noun Biochem.* an essential amino acid that is found in proteins.

trysail /'traɪsl/ *noun* a small strong fore-and-aft sail used in a storm.

tryst /trɪst, traɪst/ *old use Scot. literary* — *noun* **1** an arrangement to meet someone, especially a lover. **2** the meeting itself. **3** (*also* **trysting-place**) the place where such a meeting takes place. — *verb intrans.* to make a tryst. [from Old French *triste*, a hunter's station]

tsar or **czar** or **tzar** /zɑː(r), tsɑː(r)/ *noun* **1** *Hist.* the title given to the former emperor of Russia. **2** a despot or tyrant. [from Latin *Caesar*, family name of the earliest Roman emperors]

tsarevitch or **czarevitch** or **tzarevitch** /'zɑːrəvɪtʃ, 'tsɑːrəvɪtʃ/ *noun Hist.* the title given to the eldest son of a tsar or tsarina.

tsarina or **czarina** or **tzarina** /zɑː'riːnə/ *noun Hist.* **1** the title given to a woman who ruled Russia as empress. **2** the title given to the wife or widow of a tsar.

TSB *abbrev.* Trustee Savings Bank.

tsetse /'tsetsɪ/ *noun* (*in full* **tsetse-fly**) an African fly which feeds on human and animal blood and transmits several dangerous diseases including sleeping sickness. [from Tswana (a southern African language) *tsetse*]

T-shirt or **tee shirt** *noun* a light casual shirt, often made of stretchy material, with no collar and usually short sleeves.

T-square *noun* a T-shaped ruler for drawing right angles.

TSR *abbrev. Comput.* terminate-and-stay-resident.

tsunami /tsʊ'nɑːmɪ/ *noun* (PL. **tsunamis**) a fast-moving highly destructive wave that steadily increases in height as it approaches the shore, associated with movement of the Earth's surface under the sea, such as a volcanic eruption or a landslide. It is sometimes loosely referred to as a tidal wave, but is not associated with the tides. [from Japanese *tsu*, harbour + *nami*, wave]

TT *abbrev.* **1** teetotal. **2** Tourist Trophy.

TTL *abbrev.* Through The Lens.

tuatara /tʊə'tɑːrə/ *noun* a rare lizard-like reptile, native to islands off the coast of New Zealand, green or orange-brown in colour, and up to 650mm in length. In the male there is a crest of tooth-like spines along the back. It is nocturnal, and feeds on invertebrates, small vertebrates, and birds' eggs. [from Maori, = spine on the back]

tub *noun* **1** any of various large, low, round wooden, metal, or plastic containers, usually for holding water. **2** a small, round plastic or cardboard container for holding cream, ice-cream, yoghurt, etc. **3** a bath. **4** the amount a tub will hold. **5** *colloq.* a slow and often clumsy boat. [from Middle English *tubbe*]

. . . .

▤ **1, 3** bath. **1, 4** vat, tun, butt, cask, barrel, keg, basin.

. . . .

tuba /'tjuːbə/ *noun* a musical instrument made from brass tubing curved elliptically, with three to five valves, a mouthpiece set at right angles, and a wide upturned bell. It is the largest and lowest in pitch of the brass instruments and was included as an orchestral instrument from the mid-19c. It is made in various sizes, some of which are known by other names. [from Latin and Italian *tuba*]

tubbiness *noun* being tubby.

tubby *adj.* (**tubbier, tubbiest**) *colloq.* rather fat. [from TUB]

. . . .

▤ plump, podgy, chubby, fat, overweight, rotund, stout, corpulent.

. . . .

tube *noun* **1** a long hollow cylinder used for conveying liquids or as a container. **2** a similar long hollow structure in an animal or plant body: *bronchial tubes*. **3** a cylindrical container made from soft metal or plastic with a cap at one end, used for holding paste which is got out by squeezing. **4** *Brit.* an underground railway, especially in London; also a train running on this. **5** a cathode ray tube. **6** *North Amer.* a thermionic valve. **7** *slang* a television set. — **go down the tubes** *slang* to fail dismally; to be ruined. [from Latin *tubus*, pipe]

. . . .

▤ **1** hose, pipe, cylinder, duct, conduit, spout, channel.

. . . .

tubeless *adj.*, *said of a tyre* having no inner tube.

tuber /'tjuːbə(r)/ *noun* **1** *Bot.* in certain plants, a swollen underground root (eg dahlia tuber) or stem (eg potato tuber) which functions as a food storage organ, enabling the plant to survive between one growing season and the next. It also allows the propagation of new plants from buds on the surface of the stem tubers. **2** *Anat.* a thickened region or swelling. [from Latin *tuber*, swelling]

tubercle /'tjuːbəkl/ *noun* **1** a small round swelling or lump, eg on a bone. **2** a small round swelling in an organ, especially one caused by a bacillus and characteristic of tuberculosis. [from Latin *tuberculum*, small swelling]

tubercular /tjʊ'bɜːkjʊlə(r)/ or **tuberculous** *adj.* **1** affected by or suffering from tuberculosis. **2** of or having tubercles.

tuberculin /tjʊ'bɜːkjʊlɪn/ *noun* a preparation in the form of a sterile liquid prepared from a culture of the bacillus which causes tuberculosis, used to test for and treat the disease.

tuberculin-tested *adj.*, *said of milk* from cows that have been tested for and certified free from tuberculosis.

tuberculosis /tjʊbɜːkjʊ'loʊsɪs/ *noun* (ABBREV. **TB**) any of various infectious diseases of humans and animals, caused by the bacterium *Mycobacterium tuberculosis*. [from Latin *tuberculum*, small swelling]

tuberculous see TUBERCULAR.

tuberous /'tjuːbərəs/ adj. 1 having tubers. 2 of the nature of or like a tuber.

tubful noun (PL. **tubfuls**) the amount a tub will hold.

tubing noun a length of tube or system of tubes, or material for this.

tub-thumper noun a passionate or ranting public speaker or preacher.

tub-thumping noun declamatory or rousing public speaking.

tubular /'tjuːbjʊlə(r)/ adj. 1 made or consisting of tubes or tube-shaped pieces. 2 shaped like a tube.

tubular bells a set of brass tubes tuned to different pitches, suspended in a large frame in the same arrangement as a keyboard, and struck with a short mallet to simulate the sounds of bells. They are used in orchestral and operatic music, and are also known as *chimes*.

tubule /'tjuːbjuːl/ noun a small tube in an animal or plant body.

TUC abbrev. Trades Union Congress.

tuck — verb 1 (**tuck something in, up**, *etc*) to push or fold the outer edges of something together or into a specified position, especially to make it secure or tidy. 2 (*usually* **tuck something up**) to draw or put it into a folded position: *tucked her legs up*. 3 (**tuck someone in** or **up**) to fold the edges of the bedclothes tightly round them. 4 to put in a confined or hidden place: *tuck it away out of sight*. 5 to make a tuck or tucks in (a piece of clothing, etc). — noun 1 a flat pleat or fold sewn in a garment or piece of material. 2 *Brit. colloq.* food, especially sweets, cakes, and pastries eaten by school children. — **tuck something away** *colloq.* to eat large quantities of food heartily. **tuck in** or **tuck into something** *colloq.* to eat heartily or greedily. [from Anglo-Saxon *tucian*, to disturb]

⊟ verb 1 fold, pleat, gather, crease. 4 insert, push, thrust, stuff, cram. noun 1 fold, pleat, gather, pucker, crease.

tucker noun *Hist.* a piece of material, lace, etc drawn over the bodice of a low-cut dress. — **best bib and tucker** *colloq.* best clothes. [from TUCK]

tuck shop *Brit.* a small shop selling sweets, cakes, pastries, etc in or near a school.

Tudor /'tjuːdə(r)/ — adj. 1 relating to the royal family which ruled England from 1485 to 1603 or this period in English history. 2 in or of the style of architecture characteristic of this period, which involved using a lot of wood both internally and externally. — noun a member of the House of Tudor.

Tue or **Tue.** abbrev. Tuesday.

Tues or **Tues.** abbrev. Tuesday.

Tuesday noun the third day of the week. [from Anglo-Saxon *Tiwesdaeg*, Tiw's day (Tiw being the Anglo-Saxon god of war)]

tufa /'tjuːfə/ noun *Geol.* a deposit of calcium carbonate, usually consisting of white spongy porous masses in the form of an incrustation around a spring or along a stream, especially in an area of limestone rock. [from Italian, from Latin *tofus*, soft stone]

tufaceous /tjʊ'feɪʃəs/ adj. 1 consisting of tufa. 2 of the nature or texture of tufa.

tuff noun a rock composed of fine volcanic fragments and dust. [from French *tuf*, from Latin *tofus*, soft stone]

tuffaceous /tʌ'feɪʃəs/ adj. 1 consisting of volcanic tuff. 2 having the properties of tuff.

tuffet noun 1 a low seat. 2 a small mound. [a variant of TUFT]

tuft noun a small bunch or clump of grass, hair, feathers, wool, etc attached or growing together at the base. [from Middle English]

⊟ knot, clump, cluster, bunch, crest, beard, tassel.

tufted adj. 1 having or forming a tuft or tufts. 2 growing in tufts.

tufty adj. (**tuftier, tuftiest**) 1 covered with or full of tufts. 2 forming a tuft or tufts; consisting of or growing in tufts.

tug — verb trans., intrans. (**tugged, tugging**) 1 to pull sharply and strongly (at). 2 to tow (a ship) with a tugboat. — noun 1 a strong sharp pull. 2 a hard struggle. 3 a small boat with a very powerful engine, for towing larger ships and barges. [from Middle English *toggen*, from Anglo-Saxon *teon*]

⊟ verb 1 pull, tow, haul, drag, heave, wrench, jerk, pluck. noun 1 pull, haul, heave, wrench, jerk, pluck.

tugboat noun same as TUG noun 3.

tug-of-love noun a dispute over the guardianship of a child, eg between divorced parents.

tug-of-war noun 1 a contest in which two people or teams pull at opposite ends of a rope, trying to pull their opponents over a centre line. 2 any hard struggle between two opposing sides.

tuition /tjʊ'ɪʃən/ noun 1 teaching or instruction, especially when paid for, or in a college or university. 2 the fee paid for teaching or instruction. [from Latin *tuitio*, protection]

⊟ 1 teaching, instruction, coaching, training, lessons, schooling, education.

tulip /'tjuːlɪp/ noun 1 any spring-flowering perennial plant of the genus *Tulipa*, which has an underground bulb and produces a single cup-shaped flower in a variety of bright colours on a long leafy stem. Tulips are native to the Mediterranean region, but several thousand ornamental garden varieties are cultivated on a commercial scale in the Netherlands for export. 2 the flower of this plant. [from Turkish *tulbend*, turban]

tulip tree a tall N American tree of the magnolia family, with tulip-like flowers.

tulle /tjuːl/ noun a delicate thin netted cloth made of silk or rayon. [from *Tulle* in France, where it was first made]

tum noun a child's word for 'stomach'.

tumble — verb 1 intrans. (*usually* **tumble down, over**, *etc*) to fall headlong, especially suddenly or clumsily. 2 to cause to fall over. 3 intrans. to fall or collapse suddenly, especially in value or amount. 4 (**tumble about, around**, *etc*) to roll over and over or toss around helplessly. 5 intrans. to perform as an acrobat, especially turning somersaults. 6 intrans. to move or rush in a confused, hasty way: *tumble out of the car*. 7 to rumple or disorder: *tumble the bedclothes*. 8 (**tumble to something**) *colloq.* to understand, realize, or become aware of it suddenly: *tumbled to their intentions*. 9 to dry (wet clothes or washing) in a tumble-drier. — noun 1 an act of tumbling. 2 a fall. 3 a somersault. 4 a confused or untidy state or heap. [from Anglo-Saxon *tumbian*]

⊟ verb 1, 2 trip, topple. 1 fall, stumble, drop, flop. 2 knock down, unseat, overthrow. 3 collapse, plummet. 4 pitch, roll, toss. noun 1, 2 fall. 1 stumble, trip. 2 drop, plunge, roll, toss.

tumbledown adj., *said of a building* falling to pieces; in a dilapidated condition.

⊟ ramshackle, rickety, dilapidated, unstable, shaky, unsteady, unsafe, ruinous, neglected.

tumble-drier or **tumble-dryer** noun a machine for drying wet clothes and washing them in a current of warm air.

tumble-dry verb trans., intrans. (**tumble-dries, tumble-dried**) to dry (laundry) in a tumble-drier.

tumbler noun 1 a large drinking glass without a stem or handle. 2 the amount a tumbler will hold. 3 an acrobat.

especially one who performs somersaults. **4** a tumble-drier. **5** the part of a lock which holds the bolt in place until it is moved by a key. **6** the part of a firearm which is released by the trigger and forces the hammer forward. **7** (*also* **tumbler-box**) a machine with a revolving drum in which gemstones are polished.

tumblerful *noun* (PL. **tumblerfuls**) the amount a tumbler will hold.

tumbleweed *noun* a plant that snaps off above the root, curls into a ball and rolls around in the wind.

tumbling-barrel *noun* same as TUMBLER 7.

tumbrel or **tumbril** /'tʌmbrəl/ *noun* **1** a two-wheeled cart which tips over backwards to empty its load, used eg on farms. **2** *Hist.* a similar cart used to take those sentenced to death to the guillotine during the French Revolution. [from Old French *tomberel*, from *tomber*, to fall]

tumescence /tjʊ'mɛsəns/ *noun* **1** becoming tumid. **2** a swelling.

tumescent *adj.* swollen or becoming swollen, especially with blood as a response to sexual stimulation. [from Latin *tumescere*, to swell up]

tumid /'tju:mɪd/ *adj.* **1** swollen or enlarged. **2** *said of writing, speech, etc* bombastic; inflated. [from Latin *tumidus*, from *tumere*, to swell]

tumidity *noun* being tumid.

tumidly *adv.* in a tumid manner.

tummy *noun* (PL. **tummies**) a child's word for 'stomach'. [a childish pronunciation of STOMACH]

tummy-button *noun colloq.* the navel.

tumorous /'tju:mərəs/ *adj.* relating to or of the nature of a tumour.

tumour /'tju:mə(r)/ *noun* **1** *Pathol.* an abnormal growth of tissue that may be malignant (cancerous) or benign, and develops within or on the surface of normal body tissue. **2** any swelling that is not caused by inflammation. [from Latin *tumor*, from *tumere*, to swell]

tumular or **tumuli** see TUMULUS.

tumult /'tju:mʌlt/ *noun* **1** a great or confused noise, especially made by a crowd; an uproar. **2** a violent or angry commotion or disturbance. **3** the state of feeling confused and usually violent emotions: *a mind in tumult.* [from Latin *tumultus*, from *tumere*, to swell]

. . . .

▣ COMMOTION, TURMOIL. **1, 2** rumpus, uproar. **1** pandemonium, noise, clamour, din, racket, hubbub, hullabaloo, row. **2** disturbance, upheaval, stir, agitation, unrest, disorder, chaos, riot, fracas, brawl, affray, strife.
▣ PEACE, CALM. **3** composure.
. . . .

tumultuous /tjʊ'mʌltjʊəs/ *adj.* **1** with great noise or confusion: *a tumultuous welcome.* **2** disorderly; unruly. **3** agitated.

. . . .

▣ **1, 2** riotous, rowdy, noisy. **1** hectic, boisterous. **2, 3** violent, wild. **2** disorderly, unruly. **3** turbulent, stormy, raging, fierce, restless, agitated, troubled, disturbed, excited.
▣ CALM, PEACEFUL, QUIET.
. . . .

tumultuously *adv.* in a tumultuous way, uproariously.

tumulus /'tju:mjʊləs/ *noun* (PL. **tumuli**) *Archaeol.* an ancient burial mound or barrow. [from Latin, *tumere*, to swell]

tun *noun* **1** a large cask, especially for ale or wine. **2** *Hist.* the amount such a cask holds, being 252 gallons of wine or 216 gallons of ale, used as a unit of measure for liquids. [from Middle English *tunne*]

tuna /'tju:nə/ *noun* (PL. **tuna, tunas**) **1** any of several large marine fish with a streamlined body, pointed head, and coarse oily flesh, related to the mackerel, and found in warm temperate and tropical seas, eg bluefin tuna, yellowfin tuna, albacore (an important food fish). Tuna are the only fish that have a body temperature higher than that of the surrounding water. **2** the flesh of this fish used as food. [from Greek *thynnos*]

tunable or **tuneable** /'tju:nəbl/ *adj.* capable of being tuned.

tundra /'tʌndrə/ *noun Geog.* the vast relatively flat treeless zone, with permanently frozen subsoil, found mainly in the arctic regions of Alaska, N Canada, and Siberia. Its vegetation consists of dwarf trees and shrubs, grasses, sedges, mosses, and lichens. [from Lappish]

tune — *noun* **1** a pleasing succession of musical notes; a melody. **2** the correct, or a standard, musical pitch. **3** harmony; agreement: *in tune with current fashions.* — *verb* **1** *trans., intrans.* (*also* **tune up**) to adjust (a musical instrument or instruments, their keys or strings, etc) to the correct or a standard pitch. **2** *trans., intrans.* (*also* **tune in**) to adjust (a radio receiver) to pick up signals from a required frequency or station, or for a particular programme: *tune in to the local radio station.* **3** to adjust (an engine, machine, etc) so that it runs properly and efficiently. — **call the tune** *colloq.* to be in charge. **change one's tune** to change one's attitude, opinions, approach, or way of talking. **in tune 1** *said of a voice or musical instrument* having or producing the correct or a required pitch: *sing in tune.* **2** having the same pitch as other instruments or voices: *the two guitars are not in tune.* **out of tune** not in tune. **to the tune of** . . . *colloq.* amounting to the sum or total of . . . [a Middle English variant of TONE]

. . . .

▣ *noun* **1** melody, theme, motif, song, air, strain. *verb* **1, 3** set, regulate, adjust. **1** pitch, harmonize.
. . . .

tuneful *adj.* **1** having a good, clear, pleasant, etc tune; melodious. **2** full of music.

. . . .

▣ MELODIOUS. **1** melodic, catchy, musical, euphonious, harmonious, pleasant, mellow, sonorous.
▣ **1** tuneless, discordant.
. . . .

tunefully *adv.* in a tuneful way.

tunefulness *noun* being tuneful.

tuneless *adj.* without a good, pleasant, etc tune; not melodious.

tunelessly *adv.* in a tuneless way.

tunelessness *noun* being tuneless.

tuner *noun* **1** a person whose profession is tuning instruments, especially pianos. **2** *Electron.* an electronic circuit that acts as a filter for radio or television broadcast signals, by selecting one specific frequency, eg the channel selector on a television set. **3** a knob, dial, etc, that is used to adjust a radio to different wavelengths corresponding to different stations. **4** a radio that is part of a stereo sound system.

tungsten /'tʌŋstən/ *noun Chem.* (SYMBOL **W**, ATOMIC NUMBER **74**) a very hard silvery-white metal that is resistant to corrosion and has the highest melting point of any metal. It is used in steel alloys for turbine blades and cutting tools, and in filaments for electric light bulbs, X-ray tubes, and television sets. Tungsten carbides are used as abrasives. Also called WOLFRAM. [from Swedish, = heavy stone]

tunic /'tju:nɪk/ *noun* **1** a loose, sleeveless garment reaching usually to the hip or knee and usually with a belted or gathered waist, as worn in ancient Greece and Rome, or as a type of simple modern dress. **2** a close-fitting usually belted jacket with a high collar worn as part of a soldier's or policeman's uniform. **3** *Biol.* a covering membrane or layer. [from Latin *tunica*]

tuning-fork *noun* a two-pronged metal instrument invented in 1711 by the English trumpeter John Shore (c.1662–1752). When the tuning fork is struck and made to vibrate, it produces a single note virtually free from overtones, to which voices and instruments can adjust their pitch.

tunnel — *noun* **1** a man-made underground passage for pedestrians, vehicles, trains, etc through or under some obstruction such as a hill or river. **2** an underground passage dug by an animal such as a mole. **3** a period of difficulty, problems, stress, or exceptionally hard work: *light at the end of the tunnel.* — *verb* (**tunnelled, tunnelling**) **1** *intrans.* (*often* **tunnel through, under,** *etc*) to make a tunnel (through, under, etc). **2** *intrans.* to pass through, or as if through, a tunnel. **3** (**tunnel one's way**) to make one's way by digging a tunnel. [from Old French *tonel,* cask]

▣ *noun* **1, 2** passage, gallery. **1** passageway, subway, underpass, mine, shaft, chimney. **2** burrow, hole. *verb* **1** burrow, dig, excavate, mine, sap.

tunnel vision 1 a medical condition in which one is unable to see objects other than those straight ahead. **2** the inability or unwillingness to consider other viewpoints on or the wider implications of a situation.

tunny *noun* (PL. **tunnies**) (*also* **tunny-fish**) tuna. [from Greek *thynnos*]

tup *Brit.* — *noun* a ram. — *verb* (**tupped, tupping**) *said of a ram* to copulate with (a ewe). [from Middle English *tupe*]

tuppence, tuppenny SEE TWOPENCE, TWOPENNY.

turban *noun* **1** a man's headdress consisting of a long cloth sash wound round the head or a cap, worn especially by Muslims and Sikhs. **2** a woman's headdress or hat similar to this. [from Persian *dulband*]

turbaned *adj.* wearing a turban.

turbid /ˈtɜːbɪd/ *adj.* **1** *said of liquid, etc* cloudy; not clear. **2** thick or dense. **3** in turmoil or confusion. [from Latin *turbidus,* from *turba,* disturbance]

▣ **1** cloudy, muddied, opaque. **3** confused, disordered, turbulent, tumultuous, unsettled, agitated.

turbidity *noun* a turbid quality.

turbidly *adv.* in a turbid way.

turbine /ˈtɜːbaɪn/ *noun* a balanced wheel, with a large number of blades around its rim, that converts the kinetic energy of a moving fluid (such as water, steam, or gas) that passes over the blades into the mechanical energy of rotation. Steam turbines and water turbines are used to drive electricity generators in power stations, and gas turbines are used to power jet-propelled aircraft. [from Latin *turbo,* whirlwind]

turbo- *combining form* forming words meaning 'having or driven by a turbine'. [from Latin *turbo,* whirlwind]

turbocharger *noun* a supercharger operated by the exhaust gases of an engine, thereby boosting its power.

turbofan *noun* a jet engine driven by a gas turbine in which part of the power developed is used to drive a fan which blows air out of the exhaust and so increases thrust.

turbojet *noun* a jet engine consisting of a compressor and a turbine in which the gas energy produced is directed through a nozzle to produce thrust; also, an aircraft powered by this.

turboprop *noun* a jet engine in which the turbine drives a propeller; also, an aircraft powered by this.

turbot *noun* (PL. **turbot, turbots**) a large flatfish highly valued as food. [from Old French]

turbulence /ˈtɜːbjʊləns/ *noun* **1** a disturbed, wild, or unruly state. **2** *Meteorol.* the irregular movement of the atmosphere, causing gusts of wind. **3** *Physics* the movement of particles of a fluid (a liquid or a gas) in an irregular manner so that there are continual changes in the magnitude and direction of motion, eg during the flow of air across an aircraft wing, or the movement of a liquid through a pipe. [from Latin *turbulentia,* from *turba,* turmoil]

turbulent /ˈtɜːbjʊlənt/ *adj.* **1** violently disturbed; wild; unruly. **2** *Meteorol.* in a state of turbulence; stormy. **3** causing disturbance or unrest.

▣ **1** rough, choppy, stormy, blustery, tempestuous, raging, furious, violent, wild, tumultuous, unbridled, boisterous, rowdy, disorderly, unruly, undisciplined, obstreperous, rebellious, mutinous, riotous, agitated, unsettled, unstable, confused, disordered.

Ｆ3 **1** calm, composed.

turd *noun* **1** *coarse slang* a lump of excrement. **2** *coarse slang* a worthless or despicable person. [from Anglo-Saxon *tord*]

tureen /tjʊˈriːn/ *noun* a large deep dish with a cover from which soup, especially soup, is served at table. [from Old French *terrin,* earthen]

turf — *noun* (PL. **turfs, turves**) **1** the surface of the soil consisting of grass and matted roots. **2** a square piece cut from this. **3** a slab of peat. **4** (**the turf**) horse-racing, the race-course, or the racing world. **5** *slang* area of operation or influence; territory. — *verb* to cover with turf. — **turf something** or **someone over, out,** *etc Brit. colloq.* to throw or expel them: *turfed him out of the house / turf the book over here.* [from Anglo-Saxon]

turf accountant *Brit.* a bookmaker.

turf war *colloq.* a dispute over territory or an area of influence by rival groups.

turfy *adj.* (**turfier, turfiest**) **1** covered with or consisting of turf. **2** like turf. **3** associated with turf.

turgescence /tɜːˈdʒesəns/ *noun* **1** swelling up. **2** swollenness.

turgescent /tɜːˈdʒesənt/ *adj.* swelling; growing big. [from Latin *turgere,* to swell]

turgid /ˈtɜːdʒɪd/ *adj.* **1** swollen; inflated or distended. **2** *said of language* sounding important but meaning very little; pompous. [from Latin *turgere,* to swell]

▣ **2** bombastic, pompous, high-sounding, grandiloquent, overblown, pretentious.

turgidity *noun* a turgid quality.

turgidly *adv.* in a turgid way.

Turk — *noun* **1** a person from the modern state of Turkey or the former Ottoman Empire. **2** any speaker of a Turkic language. **3** *derog.* a wild or unmanageable person. — *adj.* Turkish. [from Persian and Arabic]

turkey /ˈtɜːkɪ/ *noun* (PL. **turkeys**) **1** a large game bird related to the grouse and pheasant, indigenous to woodland in N and Central America; domesticated varieties are now intensively farmed in most parts of the world. It has dark plumage with a green sheen, and a bare blue or red head with red wattles (loose flaps of skin). The male has a fanlike tail and a large protuberance on its neck. **2** the flesh of this bird used as food, eaten particularly at Christmas and (in the USA) at Thanksgiving. **3** *North Amer. slang* a stupid or inept person. **4** *North Amer. slang* a play, film, etc that is a complete failure. — **talk turkey** *North Amer. slang* to talk bluntly or frankly; to talk business. [originally used of a guinea fowl imported from Turkey, and later wrongly applied to the American bird]

Turkic — *noun* the family of Asian languages to which Turkish, Tatar, Uzbek, etc belong. — *adj.* of this family of languages or the people who speak them.

Turkish — *adj.* of Turkey, its people, language, etc. — *noun* the official language of Turkey.

Turkish bath a bath in which the bather first sweats in a hot room filled with steam, is then washed and massaged, and finally takes a cold shower.

Turkish coffee strong, usually very sweet black coffee.

Turkish delight a sticky, jelly-like sweet usually flavoured with rose water or lemon and dusted with icing sugar.

turmeric /ˈtɜːmərɪk/ *noun* **1** an E Indian plant of the ginger family. **2** the dried powdered underground stem of this plant, used as a spice (eg in curry powder) and as a yellow dye. [from Latin *terra merita,* merited earth]

turmoil /ˈtɜːmɔɪl/ *noun* wild confusion, agitation, or disorder; upheaval: *a mind in turmoil.*

▣ confusion, disorder, tumult, commotion, disturbance,

trouble, disquiet, agitation, turbulence, stir, ferment, flurry, bustle, chaos, pandemonium, bedlam, noise, din, hubbub, row, uproar.

F3 calm, peace, quiet.

. . . .

turn — verb **1** trans., intrans. to move or go round in a circle or with a circular movement. **2** trans., intrans. to change or cause to change position so that a different side or part comes to the top or front: turn the pages slowly / turn to face the sun / turn it inside out. **3** intrans. to change direction or take a new direction: turn left at the corner. **4** trans., intrans. to direct, aim, or point or be directed, aimed, or pointed: turn one's thoughts to supper. **5** to go round: turn the corner. **6** trans., intrans. to become or cause to become or change to something specified: turn the book into a film / love which turned to hate / turn nasty. **7** trans., intrans. to change or cause to change colour: the shock turned his hair white / the leaves begin to turn in September. **8** trans., intrans. said of milk to make or become sour. **9** to make into a circular or rounded shape, especially on a lathe or potter's wheel. **10** to perform with a rotating movement: turn somersaults. **11** intrans. to move or swing around a point or pivot: a gate turning on its hinge / turn on one's heels. **12** to pass the age or time of: turn forty. **13** (**turn to someone** or **something**) to appeal to or have recourse to them for help or support. **14** (**turn to something**) to come to consider or pay attention to it: the conversation turned to discussing holiday plans. **15** (also **turn something out**) to put it into a specified position by, or as if by, inverting it; to tip it out: turned the dough out on to the table. **16** trans., intrans. said of the stomach to feel or cause it to feel nausea or queasiness. **17** trans., intrans. said of the head to become or cause it to become giddy. **18** to translate. **19** (**turn against someone** or **turn one person against another**) to become or make them hostile or unfriendly. **20** to remake (part of a piece of clothing, sheet, etc) by putting the worn outer part on the inside: turn a collar. **21** to give an elegant form to. **22** intrans. said of the tide to begin to flow in the opposite direction. **23** to make (a profit, etc). — noun **1** an act of turning; a complete or partial rotation: a turn of the wheel. **2** a change of direction, course, or position: a turn to the right. **3** a point or place where a change of direction occurs. **4** a direction, tendency, or trend: the twists and turns of the saga. **5** a change in nature, character, condition, course, etc: a turn for the worse / an unfortunate turn of events. **6** an opportunity or duty that comes to each of several people in rotation or succession: her turn to bat. **7** inclination or tendency: be of a pessimistic turn of mind. **8** a distinctive style or manner: a blunt turn of phrase. **9** an act of a stated kind, usually good or malicious. **10** colloq. a sudden feeling of illness, nervousness, shock, faintness, etc: gave her quite a turn. **11** a short walk or ride. **12** each of a series of short acts or performances, eg in a circus or variety theatre; also, each performer. **13** a single coil or twist of eg rope or wire. **14** (**the turn of the month, year, century,** etc) the end of one month, year, century, etc and the beginning of the next. **15** Mus. an ornament in which the principal note is preceded by the note next above it and followed by that next below it. — **at every turn** everywhere, at every stage; continually. **by turns** one after another in order; in succession. **in turn** one after another in order; in succession. **on the turn 1** said of the tide starting to change direction. **2** said of milk on the point of going sour. **out of turn 1** out of the correct order. **2** at a moment that is inappropriate or discourteous: he apologized for speaking out of turn. **serve a turn** to be enough or adequate for present purposes or needs. **take turns** or **take it in turn** said of two or more people to share a task by acting or working one after the other in rotation. **to a turn** cooked to exactly the right degree. **turn and turn about** one after the other; each taking a turn. **turn aside** to move or direct one's attention away from the original direction. **turn something aside** to deflect it; to turn (one's eyes, gaze, face, concentration, etc) to another direction. **turn away** to look away; to move or turn to face the opposite direction. **turn someone away** to send them away or reject them; to refuse them admittance. **turn back** or **turn someone back** to return or cause them to return in the opposite direction. **turn one's back**

on someone or **something** to leave them for good; to have no more to do with them. **turn something down** to reduce the level of light, noise, etc produced by something by, or as if by, turning a control. **turn someone** or **something down** to refuse or reject them. **turn one's hand to something** to undertake a task, etc, or have the ability for it. **turn in 1** to bend inwards. **2** colloq. to go to bed. **turn someone** or **something in** to hand them over to someone in authority. **turn something in** to give, achieve, or register a good performance, score, etc. **turn someone** or **something loose** to set a person or animal free. **turn off 1** to leave a straight course or a main road: followed the car until it turned off down a side street. **2** said of a road to lead from a main road. **turn someone off** colloq. to cause them to feel dislike or disgust, or to lose (especially sexual) interest. **turn something off 1** to cause water, electricity, etc, or a machine to stop flowing or operating by, or as if by, turning a knob or pushing a button or switch. **2** to operate a knob, button, tap, switch, etc so that something stops. **turn on** or **upon someone** to attack them physically or verbally, usually suddenly or violently. **turn someone on** colloq. **1** to cause them to feel excitement, pleasure, or (especially sexual) interest. **2** to cause them to feel a heightened sense of awareness, especially with hallucinogenic drugs. **turn on** or **upon something** to depend on it: the whole argument turns on a single point. **turn something on 1** to cause electricity, etc, or a machine to flow or operate by or as if by turning a knob. **2** to operate a knob, button, tap, switch, etc so that something begins to work. **turn out 1** to bend outwards. **2** to happen or prove to be: she turned out to be right. **3** to leave home for a public meeting or event: hundreds of people turned out to vote. **4** colloq. to get out of bed. **turn someone out 1** to send them away; to make them leave; to expel them. **2** to call soldiers, a guard, etc for duty. **turn something out 1** to put a light, etc out or off by or as if by turning a knob. **2** to make or produce something. **3** to empty or clear a room, etc, especially for cleaning or to check the contents. **turn someone** or **something out** to dress, equip, or groom them: was well turned out. **turn over** to roll oneself over when in a lying position. **2** said of an engine to start and run at low speed. **turn over something** to handle or do business to the amount specified: turned over five million in the first year. **turn something over 1** to turn it so that the hidden or reverse side becomes visible or faces upwards. **2** to roll it over. **3** to start an engine so that it runs at low speed. **4** to consider it carefully. **turn someone** or **something over 1** to surrender them to an authority. **2** slang to rob them. **turn round 1** to turn to face in the opposite direction. **2** said of a loaded vehicle to arrive, be unloaded, and depart again. **turn something round** to receive and deal with a matter, the arrival of loaded vehicles, etc in the appropriate manner: able to turn an order round in an hour. **turn to something** to begin a task, undertaking, etc. **turn up 1** to appear or arrive. **2** to be found, especially by accident or unexpectedly. **turn something up 1** to increase the flow, intensity, or strength of sound, light, etc produced by a machine by, or as if by, turning a knob. **2** to discover facts, evidence, etc. **3** to shorten a piece of clothing or its hem by folding part up and stitching it in place. **4** to turn it so as to make the hidden or reverse side visible. [from Anglo-Saxon turnain and Old French torner]

. . . .

E3 verb **1** revolve, circle, spin, twirl, whirl, twist, gyrate, rotate, roll. **2** move, shift, invert, reverse. **3** bend, veer, swerve. **6** change, alter, modify, convert, transform. **7** discolour, fade, blanch. **8** sour, curdle, spoil. **9** mould, shape, form, fashion, remodel. **11** pivot, hinge, swivel. **13** resort to, have recourse to, apply to, appeal to. noun **1** revolution, cycle, round, circle, rotation, spin, twirl, twist, gyration. **2, 3** bend, curve, loop, reversal. **3** corner, turning. **5** change, alteration, shift, deviation. **6** go, chance, opportunity, occasion, stint, period, spell. **12** act, performance, performer. **turn aside** deviate, depart, diverge, something deflect, ward off, fend off, parry, avert. **turn someone away** reject, dismiss, rebuff, exclude. **turn something down** lower, lessen, quieten, soften, mute, muffle. **turn**

someone or something down reject, decline, refuse, spurn, rebuff, repudiate. **turn in 2** go to bed, retire. **turn someone** or **something in** hand over, give up, surrender, deliver, hand in, tender, submit, return, give back. **turn off 1, 2** branch off, deviate, divert. **1** leave, quit, depart from. **turn someone off** repel, sicken, nauseate, disgust, offend, displease, disenchant, alienate, bore, discourage, put off. **turn something off** SWITCH OFF. **1** turn out, stop, shut down, unplug, disconnect. **turn on** or **upon someone** attack, round on, fall on. **turn someone on** AROUSE, STIMULATE, EXCITE, THRILL, PLEASE, ATTRACT. **turn on** or **upon something** hinge on, depend on, rest on. **turn something on** switch on. **1** start (up), activate, connect. **turn out 2** happen, come about, transpire, ensue, result, end up, become, develop, emerge. **turn someone out 1** evict, throw out, expel, deport, banish, dismiss, discharge, drum out, kick out, colloq. sack. **turn something out 1** switch off, turn off, unplug, disconnect. **2** produce, make, manufacture, fabricate, assemble. **3** empty, clear, clean out. **turn someone** or **something out** present, dress, clothe. **turn something over 1** overturn, upset, upend, invert, capsize, keel over. **4** think over, think about, mull over, ponder, deliberate, reflect on, contemplate, consider, examine. **turn someone** or **something over 1** hand over, surrender, deliver, transfer. **turn up 1** attend, come, arrive, appear, colloq. show up. **turn something up 1** amplify, intensify, raise, increase. **2** discover, find, unearth, dig up, expose, disclose, reveal, show.

🔁 **turn someone away** accept, receive. **turn something down** turn up. **turn someone** or **something down** accept. **turn in 2** get up. **turn someone** or **something in** keep. **turn off 1, 2** join. **turn someone off** turn on. **turn something off 1** turn on. **turn someone on** TURN OFF. **turn something on 1** turn off. **turn someone out** admit. **turn something out 1** turn on. **3** fill. **turn up 1** stay away. **turn something up 1** turn down.

turnabout or **turnaround** noun **1** an act of turning to face the opposite way. **2** a complete change or reversal of direction or opinion.

turncoat noun a person who turns against or leaves his or her party, principles, etc and joins the opposing side.

turner noun a person or thing that turns, especially a person who works with a lathe.

turning noun **1** a place where one road branches off from another. **2** a road which branches off from another. **3** the art of using a lathe to form curves in wood, metal, etc. **4** (**turnings**) the shavings from an object turned on a lathe.

🔁 **1, 2** turnoff, fork. **1** junction, crossroads, turn.

turning circle noun the smallest possible circle in which a vehicle can turn round.

turning point noun a time or place at which a turn or significant change is made.

🔁 crossroads, watershed, crux, crisis.

turnip noun **1** a plant of the cabbage family with a large round white or yellowish root. **2** the root of this vegetable used as food or animal fodder. [from TURN, with reference to its rounded shape + Latin napus, turnip]

turnkey noun (PL. **turnkeys**) Hist. a person who keeps the keys in a prison; a gaoler.

turnoff noun **1** a road which branches off from a main road. **2** colloq. a person or thing that causes reluctance, dislike, or disgust.

turn of phrase one's way of expressing oneself, especially if distinctive; an instance of this: has an amusing turn of phrase.

turn-on noun slang a person or thing that causes especially sexual excitement.

turn-out noun **1** the number of people attending a meeting, celebration, event, etc. **2** an outfit or set of clothes or equipment. **3** the quantity of goods produced or on display.

🔁 **1** attendance, audience, gate, crowd, assembly, congregation. **2** appearance, outfit, dress, clothes.

turnover noun **1** the total value of sales in a business during a certain time. **2** the rate at which stock is sold and replenished. **3** the rate at which money or workers pass through a business. **4** Biol. within a living organism, eg in bone tissue, the rate at which molecules that are undergoing breakdown are being replaced by new molecules. **5** Biol. in an ecosystem, the rate at which members of a population of plants or animals that are lost as a result of death or emigration are being replaced by reproduction or by the immigration of new members. **6** a small pastry with a fruit or jam filling.

turnpike noun **1** Hist. a gate or barrier across a road or bridge which is not lifted until travellers have paid the toll. **2** North Amer., esp. US a motorway on which a toll is paid.

turnstile noun a revolving gate with metal arms which allows only one person to pass through at a time, usually after payment of a fee.

turntable noun **1** the revolving platform on which a record turns on a record-player. **2** a revolving platform for turning railway engines and other vehicles.

turn-up noun **1** Brit. a piece of material folded up at the bottom of a trouser-leg. **2** (**a turn-up for the book**) an unexpected and usually pleasant surprise; a surprising piece of good luck.

turpentine /'tɜːpəntaɪn/ noun **1** a thick oily resin obtained from certain trees, eg pines. **2** (in full **oil of turpentine**) a clear essential oil distilled from this resin used in many commercial products, especially solvent and paint thinners. [from Greek terebinthos, a tree yielding turpentine]

turpitude /'tɜːpɪtjuːd/ noun baseness; vileness; depravity. [from Latin turpitudo]

turquoise /'tɜːkwɔɪz, 'tɜːkwɑːz/ noun **1** Geol. a hard opaque mineral, light blue or green in colour, consisting of copper aluminium phosphate, and formed by the alteration of aluminium-rich rock by surface waters. It is a valuable gemstone and ornamental material. **2** the colour of this stone. [from Old French turkeis, Turkish, as first brought from Persia through Turkey or Turkestan]

turret /'tʌrɪt/ noun **1** a small tower on a castle or other building. **2** (in full **gun-turret**) a small revolving tower-like structure on warships, tanks, etc on which guns are mounted. **3** that part of a lathe which holds the cutting tool. [from Latin turris, tower]

turreted adj. **1** having turrets. **2** formed like a tower or a long spiral.

turtle /'tɜːtl/ noun **1** any of several large marine reptiles of the order Chelonia, with a short broad body protected by a bony shell which tends to be flatter than that of its land-dwelling relatives (the tortoises), and limbs that have evolved as flippers. All turtles return to land to lay their eggs, and several species have become endangered as a result of their exploitation for food (including their eggs) and tortoiseshell. **2** North Amer. a tortoise or terrapin. — **turn turtle** said of a boat, etc to turn upside down; to capsize. [from Latin tortuca]

turtledove noun any of several wild doves noted for their soft cooing and apparent affection for mates and young. [from Latin turtur]

turtleneck noun a high round close-fitting neck; also, a piece of clothing having this, especially a jersey.

turtle soup soup made from the flesh and fat of a female turtle.

turves see TURF.

Tuscan /'tʌskən/ — adj. **1** denoting an order of classical architecture, introduced by the Romans. It is a simplified version of Doric with an unfluted shaft on the column and minimal decoration on capital and entablature. **2** relating to Tuscany in Italy. — *noun* a native of Tuscany.

tusk *noun* one of a pair of long, curved, pointed teeth which project from the mouth of certain animals including the elephant, walrus, and wild boar. [from Anglo-Saxon *tusc*]

tusked *adj.* having tusks.

tusker *noun* an elephant, walrus, wild boar, etc with well-developed tusks.

tussle — *noun* a sharp or vigorous struggle or fight. — *verb intrans.* to struggle or fight vigorously. [from Middle English *tusen*]

. . . .

▣ *noun* fracas, *colloq.* punch-up. *verb* fight, brawl, *colloq.* scrap, scuffle, skirmish.

. . . .

tussock /'tʌsək/ *noun* a clump of grass or other vegetation.

tussocky *adj.* **1** full of tussocks. **2** forming tussocks.

tut or **tut-tut** — *interj.* an expression of mild disapproval, annoyance, or rebuke. — *verb intrans.* (**tutted, tutting**) to express mild disapproval, annoyance, or rebuke by saying 'tut' or 'tut-tut'. — *noun* an act of saying 'tut' or 'tut-tut'. [originally a conventional spelling representation of the sound, also represented by *tch* or *tsk*, made with the tongue against the inner gums to express mild disapproval, etc]

tutelage /'tjuːtɪlɪdʒ/ *noun* **1** the state or office of being a guardian. **2** the state of being under the care of a guardian. **3** tuition or instruction. [from Latin *tutela*, guard]

tutelary /'tjuːtɪlərɪ/ *adj.* **1** having the power or role of a guardian over someone. **2** of a guardian. **3** giving protection. [from Latin *tutelaris*, from *tutela*, guardian]

tutor /'tjuːtə(r)/ — *noun* **1** a university or college teacher who teaches students individually or in small groups, or who is responsible for the general welfare and progress of a certain number of students. **2** a private teacher. **3** *Brit.* an instruction book. — *verb trans., intrans.* (**tutored, tutoring**) to act as a tutor to (a pupil). [from Latin *tutor*, guardian]

. . . .

▣ *noun* **1** teacher, instructor, coach, educator, lecturer, supervisor, guide, mentor, guru, guardian. *verb* teach, instruct, train, drill, coach, educate, school, lecture, supervise, direct, guide.

. . . .

tutorial /tjuː'tɔːrɪəl/ — *noun* a lesson given by a university or college tutor to an individual student or small group of students. — *adj.* of a tutor or tuition by a tutor.

tutorially *adv.* **1** in a tutorial way. **2** by a tutor, in a tutorial.

tutorship *noun* the office or position of tutor.

tutti /'tʊtɪ/ *Mus.* — *adv.* with all the instruments and singers together. — *noun* a piece of music to be played or sung by all the instruments and singers together. [from Italian]

tutti-frutti /tuːtɪ'fruːtɪ/ *noun* an ice cream or other sweet containing or flavoured with mixed fruits. [from Italian, = all fruits]

tut-tut see TUT.

tutu /'tuːtuː/ *noun* a female ballet dancer's very short, stiff, spreading skirt. [from French]

tu-whit tu-whoo /tʊ'wɪt tʊ'wuː/ a conventional spelling representation of an owl's hoot.

tux *noun North Amer. colloq.* a tuxedo.

tuxedo /tʌk'siːdoʊ/ *noun* (PL. **tuxedos**) a dinner jacket, or an evening suit which includes such a jacket. [named after a fashionable club at *Tuxedo* Park, New York]

TV *abbrev.* television.

TVEI *abbrev.* Technical and Vocational Education Initiative, a scheme intended to give school students more job-oriented and technological courses.

TVP *abbrev.* textured vegetable protein, a form of protein from vegetable sources which has a meat-like texture, used in food as a substitute for meat.

TWA *abbrev.* Trans-World Airlines.

twaddle /'twɒdl/ — *noun colloq.* nonsense; senseless or silly writing or talk. — *verb intrans.* to speak or write nonsense.

twain *noun old use* two: *in twain.* [from Anglo-Saxon *twegen*]

twang — *noun* **1** a sharp ringing sound like that produced by plucking a tightly-stretched string. **2** a nasal quality or tone of voice. **3** *colloq.* a local or regional intonation. — *verb trans., intrans.* to make or cause to make a twang. [imitative]

twangy *adj.* (**twangier, twangiest**) making a twanging sound.

twat /twat, twɒt/ *noun coarse slang* **1** a worthless, unpleasant, or despicable person. **2** the female genitals.

tweak — *verb* **1** to pull or twist with a sudden jerk. **2** to adjust (something) slightly in order to improve it.— *noun* **1** a sudden sharp pull or twist. **2** a slight adjustment made to improve something. [related to TWITCH]

. . . .

▣ *verb, noun* twist, pinch, squeeze, nip, pull, tug, jerk, twitch.

. . . .

twee *adj. Brit. colloq.* too pretty, sweet, quaint, or sentimental. [from *tweet*, a childish pronunciation of SWEET]

. . . .

▣ sweet, cute, pretty, dainty, quaint, sentimental, affected, precious.

. . . .

tweed *noun* **1** a thick, rough woollen cloth usually with coloured flecks in it, made originally in Scotland and used for suits, jackets, etc. **2** (**tweeds**) clothes, especially a suit, made of this material. [from Scots *tweeding*, twilling or *tweeled*, twilled]

tweedy *adj.* (**tweedier, tweediest**) **1** of or like tweed. **2** typical of people who enjoy a hearty, outdoor life and pastimes such as fishing and shooting, for which it is traditional to wear tweed clothing.

tweely *adv.* in a twee way.

'tween *contr. old use* between.

tweeness *noun* a twee quality.

tweet — *noun* a melodious chirping sound made by a small bird. — *verb intrans.* to chirp melodiously. [imitative]

tweeter *noun* a loudspeaker used to reproduce high-frequency sounds. See also WOOFER.

tweezers *pl. noun* a small pair of pincers for pulling out individual hairs, holding small objects, etc. [from obsolete *tweeze*, a surgeon's case of instruments]

twelfth *noun* **1** one of 12 equal parts. **2** the last of 12; the next after the eleventh. *adj.* coming after the eleventh. *adv.* **1** in twelfth position. **2** as the twelfth point, etc. [from Anglo-Saxon *twelfta*]

Twelfth Day the twelfth day after Christmas, 6 Jan.

twelfthly *adv.* as the twelfth point, etc.

twelfth man *Cricket* a reserve member of a team.

Twelfth Night the evening before the twelfth day after Christmas (5 Jan) or the evening of the day itself (6 Jan).

twelve — *noun* **1** the number or figure 12; any symbol for this number. **2** the age of 12 years. **3** something, especially a garment or a person, whose size is denoted by 12. **4** a set of 12 things, people, etc. **5** a score of 12 points. **6** 12 o'clock. **7** *Brit.* a film classified as being suitable for people of twelve years and over. — *adj.* **1** 12 in number. **2** aged 12. [from Anglo-Saxon *twelf*]

twelvefold — *adj.* **1** 12 times as much or as many. **2** divided into or consisting of 12 parts. — *adv.* by 12 times as much.

twelvemonth *noun old use* a year.

twelve-tone *adj. Mus.* of or relating to music based on a pattern formed from the 12 notes of the chromatic scale.

twenties *pl. noun* **1** the period of time between one's 20th and 30th birthdays. **2** the range of temperatures between

20 and 30 degrees. **3** the period of time between the 20th and 30th years of a century.

twentieth *noun, adj.* **1** the position in a series corresponding to 20 in a sequence of numbers. **2** one of 20 equal parts.

twenty — *noun* (PL. **twenties**) **1** the number or figure 20; any symbol for this number. **2** the age of 20. **3** a set of 20 people, things, etc. **4** a bank note worth 20 pounds. **5** a score of 20 points. — *adj.* **1** 20 in number. **2** aged 20. [from Anglo-Saxon *twentig*]

twenty-four seven *slang* all the time (twenty-four hours, seven days a week).

twerp or **twirp** *noun colloq.* a silly or contemptible person.

twice *adv.* **1** two times; on two occasions. **2** double in amount: *twice as much*. [from Middle English *twiges*, from Anglo-Saxon *twige*]

twiddle — *verb* **1** to twist (something) round and round: *twiddle the knob on the radio.* **2** (**twiddle with something**) to play with it or twist it round and round idly. — *noun* **1** an act of twiddling. **2** a curly mark or ornament. — **twiddle one's thumbs 1** to move one's thumbs in a circular movement round and round each other, usually as a sign of boredom. **2** to have nothing to do. [perhaps from TWIRL, TWIST, TWITCH, FIDDLE]

⊟ *verb* **1** turn, twirl, swivel, twist, wiggle, adjust. **2** fiddle with, finger.

twiddler *noun* a person who twiddles.

twiddly *adj.* (**twiddlier, twiddliest**) full of twiddles, ornamented.

twig[1] *noun* a small shoot branch of a tree, bush, etc. [from Anglo-Saxon]

twig[2] *verb trans., intrans.* (**twigged, twigging**) *colloq.* to understand (a joke, situation, etc), especially suddenly. [from Irish Gaelic *tuigim*, I understand]

twiggy *adj.* **1** like a twig. **2** full of twigs.

twilight /ˈtwaɪlaɪt/ — *noun* **1** the faint light in the sky when the sun is just below the horizon immediately before sunrise or especially immediately after sunset. **2** the time of day when this occurs. **3** dim light or partial darkness. **4** a period of decline in strength, health, or importance, especially after a period of vigorous activity: *the twilight of his life.* — *adj.* of or at twilight; shadowy; dim. [from Anglo-Saxon *twi*, two + LIGHT]

⊟ *noun* **2, 3** dusk, gloaming. **2** sunset, evening. **3** half-light, gloom, dimness.

twilight zone 1 a decaying area of a city or town situated typically between the main business and commercial area and the suburbs. **2** any indefinite or intermediate state or position.

twilit *adj.* lit by or as if by twilight.

twill — *noun* a strong woven cloth worked to give an appearance of parallel diagonal lines. — *verb* to weave (fabric) with a twill. [from Anglo-Saxon *twilic*, woven of double thread]

twilled *adj.* woven with a twill.

twilling *noun* weaving cloth with a twill.

twin — *noun* **1** either of two people or animals born to the same mother at the same time. **2** either of two people or things that are very like or closely associated with each other. **3** (**the Twins**) Gemini. **4** (*also* **twin crystal**) a compound crystal consisting of two crystals or parts of crystals which have grown together so that each one or part is a mirror image of the other. — *adj.* **1** being one of or consisting of a pair born of the same mother at the same time. **2** being one of or consisting of very similar or closely connected parts. — *verb* (**twinned, twinning**) **1** *trans., intrans.* to bring or come together closely or intimately. **2** to link (a town) with a counterpart in another country to encourage cultural, social, and economic exchanges

and co-operation. **3** *intrans.* to give birth to twins. **4** *trans., intrans.* to form into or grow as a twin crystal. [from Anglo-Saxon *twinn*]

⊟ *noun* **2** double, lookalike, likeness, duplicate, clone, match, counterpart, corollary, fellow, mate. *adj.* **2** identical, matching, corresponding, symmetrical, parallel, matched, paired, double, dual, duplicate, twofold. *verb* **1** match, pair, couple up, link, join.

twin bed a single bed which is one of a matching pair.

twine — *noun* **1** strong string or cord made of twisting two or more threads of cotton, hemp, etc together. **2** a coil or twist. **3** an act of twisting or clasping. — *verb* **1** to twist together; to interweave. **2** to form by twisting or interweaving. **3** *trans., intrans.* to twist or coil round: *ivy twining round the old tree trunk.* [from Anglo-Saxon *twin*, double or twisted thread]

⊟ *noun* **1** string, cord, thread, yarn. *verb* TWIST, WREATHE, ENTWINE. **2** plait, braid, knit, weave. **3** wind, coil, spiral, loop, curl, bend, wrap, surround, encircle.

twin-engined *adj.* having a pair of engines.

twinge /twɪndʒ/ — *noun* **1** a sudden sharp stabbing or shooting pain. **2** a sudden sharp pang of emotional pain, bad conscience, etc. — *verb trans., intrans.* to feel or cause to feel a sharp pain or pang. [from Anglo-Saxon *twengan*, to pinch]

⊟ *noun* PANG, SPASM, THROE, PRICK. **1** pain, throb, stab, stitch, pinch.

twinkle — *verb* **1** *intrans. said of a star, etc* to shine with a bright, flickering light. **2** *intrans. said of the eyes* to shine or sparkle with amusement or mischief. **3** to give off (light) with a flicker. — *noun* **1** a gleam or sparkle in the eyes. **2** a flicker or glimmer of light. **3** an act of twinkling. — **in a twinkle** or **in the twinkle of an eye** in a moment or very short time. [from Anglo-Saxon *twinclian*]

⊟ *verb* SPARKLE. **1, 2** glitter. **1** shimmer, glisten, glimmer, flicker, wink, flash, glint, gleam, shine. *noun* **1, 2** sparkle. **2, 3** scintillation, glitter, shimmer, glimmer. **2** flicker, wink, flash, glint, gleam, light.

twinkling — *adj.* shining brightly; scintillating. — *noun* **1** the time occupied by a wink; an instant. **2** scintillation of the stars. — **in a twinkling** or **in the twinkling of an eye** in a moment or very short time.

twinkly *adj.* (**twinklier, twinkliest**) twinkling.

twinset *noun Brit.* a matching sweater and cardigan.

twin town a town which has been linked to a town abroad to encourage cultural, social, and economic exchanges and co-operation.

twirl — *verb trans., intrans.* to turn, spin, or twist round. — *noun* **1** an act of twirling. **2** a curly mark or ornament, especially one made with a pen. [from TWIST + WHIRL]

⊟ *verb* spin, whirl, pirouette, wheel, rotate, revolve, swivel, pivot, turn, twist, gyrate, wind, coil. *noun* **1** spin, whirl, pirouette, rotation, revolution, turn, twist, gyration, convolution, spiral, coil.

twirly *adj.* full of twirls, twirling.

twirp see TWERP.

twist — *verb* **1** *trans., intrans.* to wind or turn round, especially by moving only a single part, or different parts in opposite directions: *twist the knob / he twisted round in his seat.* **2** *intrans.* to follow a winding course: *a road twisting through the mountains.* **3** *trans., intrans.* to wind around or together: *twist the pieces of string together / a piece of wire* was twisted round his leg. **4** to force or wrench out of the correct shape or position with a sharp turning movement: twist an ankle. **5** to distort the form, meaning, implication, or balance of: twisted his face into an ugly sneer / twist her words / a twisted mind. **6** to remove or break off with a sharp turning movement: twist the button off. **7** to form by winding or weaving. **8** intrans. to dance the twist. **9** trans., intrans. to take or give a spiral or coiled form (to). — noun **1** the act of twisting. **2** something formed by twisting or being twisted. **3** a turn or coil; a bend. **4** a sharp turning movement which pulls something out of shape; a wrench. **5** an unexpected event, development, or change, eg of direction. **6** a distortion of form, nature, or meaning. **7** an eccentricity or perversion. **8** a length of thread, cord, silk, etc formed by twisting two or more strands together. **9** a twisted roll of bread or tobacco. **10** a curl of citrus peel used to flavour a drink. **11** a screw of paper, especially one containing a collection of small items such as sweets. **12** (usually **the twist**) a dance, popular in the 1960s, involving twisting movements of the legs and hips. — **round the twist** colloq. mad; crazy. **twist someone's arm** colloq. to apply especially moral pressure to someone to make them act in the way one wants. [from Middle English twisten, to divide]

⊟ verb **1** turn, screw, spin, swivel, wriggle, writhe. **2** wind, zigzag, bend, coil, spiral, curl, wreathe. **3** twine, entwine, intertwine, weave, entangle. **4** wrench, rick, sprain, strain. **5** change, alter, garble, misquote, misrepresent, distort, contort, warp, pervert. noun **1, 3** turn, spin, roll. **3** bend, curve, arc, curl, loop, zigzag, coil, spiral, convolution, squiggle, tangle. **5** change, variation, break, surprise, turnabout. **6, 7** perversion. **6** distortion, contortion. **7** quirk, eccentricity, oddity, peculiarity.

twisted adj. **1** full of twists; out of shape. **2** colloq. mentally sick or perverted.

⊟ WARPED. **1** coiled, curled, spiral, bent, curved, distorted, contorted. **2** perverted, deviant, unnatural.
⊟ **1** straight.

twister noun **1** Brit. colloq. a dishonest or deceiving person; a swindler. **2** North Amer. a tornado.
twisty adj. (**twistier, twistiest**) **1** full of twists or turns. **2** dishonest.
twit[1] noun colloq. a fool or idiot. [perhaps from TWIT[2]]
twit[2] verb (**twitted, twitting**) to tease or criticize, usually pleasantly or affectionately. [from Anglo-Saxon ætwitan, to reproach]
twitch — verb **1** intrans. to move jerkily. **2** (**twitch something** or **twitch at something**) to pull or pluck it sharply or jerkily. — noun **1** a sudden sharp pull or jerking movement. **2** a sudden spasm of a muscle, especially one caused by nervousness; a tic. [related to Anglo-Saxon twiccian, to pluck]

⊟ verb JERK. **1** jump, start, blink, tremble, shake. **2** pull, tug, tweak, snatch, pluck. noun JERK. **2** spasm, convulsion, tic, tremor, jump, start.

twitcher noun **1** a person or thing that twitches. **2** colloq. a bird-watcher whose main interest is to spot as many rare birds as possible.
twitchily adv. in a twitchy way.
twitchy adj. (**twitchier, twitchiest**) colloq. nervous.
twitter — noun **1** a light, repeated chirping sound made by especially small birds. **2** colloq. a nervous or excited state: be all of a twitter. — verb (**twittered, twittering**) **1** intrans. said especially of a bird to make a light, repeated chirping sound or similar high-pitched trembling sounds. **2** to say or utter with such a chirping sound. **3** intrans. to make small nervous or excited movements. [imitative]

⊟ verb **1** chirp, chirrup, tweet, cheep, sing, warble, whistle, chatter.

twittery adj. habitually twittering.
two — noun **1** the number or figure 2; any symbol for this number. **2** the age of 2. **3** something, especially a garment or a person, whose size is denoted by the number 2. **4** something with 2 parts or members. **5** a playing-card with 2 pips. See also DEUCE[1]. **6** 2 o'clock. **7** a score of 2. — adj. **1** 2 in number. **2** aged 2. — pron. two people or things. — **in two** in or into two pieces. **put two and two together** to come to a usually obvious conclusion from the available evidence. **that makes two of us** colloq. the same is true of me too. [from Anglo-Saxon twa]
two-bit adj. North Amer. colloq. cheap; petty; small-time.
twoc /twɒk/ verb trans. colloq. to steal (a car). [from taking without owner s consent, the technical name for this offence]
two-edged adj. double-edged.
two-faced adj. deceitful; hypocritical; insincere.

⊟ hypocritical, insincere, false, lying, deceitful, treacherous, double-dealing, devious, untrustworthy.
⊟ honest, candid, frank.

twofold — adj. **1** twice as much or as many. **2** divided into or consisting of two parts. — adv. by twice as much.
two-handed adj. **1** having, needing, or for two hands or people. **2** able to use both hands equally well.
twopence or **tuppence** /'tʌpəns/ noun Brit. **1** the sum of two pence, especially before the introduction of decimal coinage. **2** a coin of the value of two pence in decimal coinage. — **not care twopence** colloq. to not care at all.
twopenny or **tuppenny** /'tʌpnɪ/ adj. Brit. **1** worth or costing twopence. **2** colloq. cheap; worthless.
two-piece — adj., said of a suit, etc having two matching or complementary pieces or parts. — noun a two-piece suit, etc.
two-ply — adj. having two strands or layers. — noun (PL. **two-plies**) knitting wool or yarn made of two strands of wool twisted together.
two-seater noun a vehicle, aircraft, or seat for two people.
two-sided adj. **1** having two sides which are different. **2** having two aspects; controversial.
twosome noun **1** a game, dance, etc for two people. **2** a pair of people; a couple.
two-step noun a ballroom dance in duple time, or a piece of music for it.
two-stroke adj., said of an internal combustion engine having a cycle consisting of one up and one down stroke of a piston.
two-time verb trans., intrans. colloq. to deceive or be unfaithful to (a husband, wife, lover, etc).
two-timer noun colloq. a person who two-times another.
two-tone adj. having or made up of two colours or two shades of the same colour, or two sounds.
two-way adj. **1** able to move, moving, or allowing movement in two opposite directions: a two-way street. **2** said of a radio, telephone, etc able to both send and receive messages. **3** said of communication between two people or groups in which both participate equally and responsibility and gains are shared. **4** able to be used in two ways.
TX abbrev. Texas.
tycoon /taɪ'kuːn/ noun a rich and powerful businessman or businesswoman. [from Japanese taikun, great prince]

⊟ industrialist, entrepreneur, captain of industry, magnate, mogul, baron, supremo, capitalist, financier.

tying see TIE.

tyke /taɪk/ *noun* **1** a dog, especially a mongrel. **2** *Brit. originally dialect* a rough or coarse man. **3** *colloq.* a small, often cheeky child. [from Norse *tik*, bitch]

tympanic /tɪm'panɪk/ *adj.* **1** relating to or in the region of the eardrum. **2** relating to or representing a drum.

tympanic membrane same as TYMPANUM 1.

tympani, tympanist see TIMPANI.

tympanum /'tɪmpənəm/ *noun* (PL. **tympana, tympanums**) **1** *Anat.* the eardrum. **2** *Archit.* the recessed usually triangular face of a pediment. **3** *Archit.* a space between a lintel and an arch over it. **4** a drum or drumhead. [from Greek *tympanon*, kettledrum]

Tynwald /'tɪnwɒld/ *noun* the parliament of the Isle of Man. [from Norse *thing*, assembly + *völlr*, field]

type /taɪp/ — *noun* **1** a class or group of people, animals, or things which share similar characteristics; a kind or variety. **2** the general character, nature, or form of a particular class or group. **3** *colloq.* a person, especially of a specified kind: *a quiet type of person.* **4** a person, animal, or thing that is a characteristic example of its group or class. **5** a small metal block with a raised letter or character on one surface, used for printing. **6** a set of such blocks. **7** a set of such blocks of a particular kind: *italic type.* **8** printed letters, characters, words, etc. **9** *Biol.* the actual specimen on which the description of a new species or genus is based. — *verb* **1** *trans., intrans.* to write (words, text, etc) using a typewriter or word processor. **2** to be a characteristic example or type of; to typify. **3** *Medicine, Biol.* to decide the type of (eg a blood sample); to classify. [from Greek *typos*, blow, mark]

⊟ *noun* **1, 3** sort. **1** kind, form, genre, variety, strain, species, breed, group, class, category, subdivision, classification. **2** description, designation, stamp, mark, order, standard. **4** archetype, embodiment, prototype, original, model, pattern, specimen, example. **8** print, printing, characters, letters, lettering, face, fount, font.

typecast — *verb* (PAST TENSE AND PAST PARTICIPLE **type-cast**) to cast (an actor or actress) regularly in the same kind of part. — *adj., said of an actor or actress* regularly cast in the same kind of part.

typeface *noun* a set of letters, characters, etc of a particular design or style.

typescript *noun* any typewritten document, manuscript, or copy.

typeset *verb* (**typesetting**; PAST TENSE AND PAST PARTICIPLE **typeset**) *Printing* to arrange (type) or set (a page, etc) in type ready for printing.

typesetter *noun* a person or machine that sets type ready for printing.

typewrite *verb trans., intrans.* (PAST TENSE **typewrote**; PAST PARTICIPLE **typewritten**) to produce (text) with a typewriter.

typewriter *noun* a machine with a keyboard for writing in characters resembling print.

typewriting *noun* **1** the act or process of using a typewriter. **2** text produced by a typewriter.

typhoid /'taɪfɔɪd/ — *noun* (also **typhoid fever**) *Medicine* a serious and sometimes fatal infection of the digestive system caused by the bacterium *Salmonella typhi*, transmitted by contaminated food and drinking water, and characterized by fever, a rash of red spots on the front of the body, abdominal pain, and sometimes delirium. — *adj.* relating to or resembling typhus. [from Greek *typhos*, fever + *eidos*, likeness]

typhoon /taɪ'fuːn/ *noun Geol.* a tropical storm, characterized by revolving winds, that occurs over the NW Pacific Ocean and the South China Sea. [from Chinese *da feng*, great wind or Greek *typhon*, whirlwind]

⊟ whirlwind, cyclone, tornado, *North Amer.* twister, hurricane, tempest, storm, squall.

typhus /'taɪfəs/ *noun Medicine* any of a group of infectious diseases caused by rickettsiae (small spherical or rodlike parasitic micro-organisms) and transmitted to humans by lice, fleas, ticks, or mites carried by rodents. The main symptoms are fever, severe headache, a red skin rash, and delirium. [from Greek *typhos*, fever]

typical /'tɪpɪkl/ *adj.* (*often* **typical of someone** or **something**) **1** having or showing the usual characteristics; being a characteristic or representative example. **2** showing the usual, expected, undesirable characteristics of behaviour, attitude, etc: *a hostile reaction is typical of him.* **3** of, relating to, or being a representative or characteristic specimen or type. **4** foreshadowing; symbolic. [from Latin *typicalis*, from Greek *typos*, blow, mark]

⊟ **1, 3** characteristic, representative. **1** standard, normal, usual, average, conventional, orthodox, stock, model. **3** distinctive, illustrative, indicative.
⊞ **1** atypical, unusual.

typically *adv.* in a typical way; as is typical.

typify /'tɪpɪfaɪ/ *verb* (**typifies, typified**) **1** to be an excellent or characteristic example of. **2** to represent by a type or symbol; to symbolize. [from Greek *typos*, blow, mark + Latin *facere*, to make]

⊟ **1** embody, epitomize, encapsulate, personify, characterize, exemplify, illustrate. **2** symbolize, represent.

typing /'taɪpɪŋ/ *noun* typewriting.

typist /'taɪpɪst/ *noun* a person who types, especially as an occupation.

typo /'taɪpəʊ/ *noun* (PL. **typos**) an error made in the typesetting of a text, such as the use of one letter in mistake for another. [an abbreviation of *typographical error*]

typographer *noun* a person skilled in typography.

typographic or **typographical** *adj.* **1** relating to or involving printing or typography. **2** printed.

typographically *adv.* in a typographic way; in terms of typography.

typography /taɪ'pɒgrəfɪ/ *noun* **1** the art or occupation of composing type and arranging texts for printing. **2** the style and general appearance of printed matter which has been typeset. [from Latin *typographia*]

tyrannical /tɪ'ranɪkl/ or **tyrannous** /'tɪrənəs/ *adj.* of or like a tyrant; oppressive; despotic.

⊟ dictatorial, despotic, autocratic, absolute, arbitrary, authoritarian, domineering, overbearing, high-handed, imperious, magisterial, ruthless, harsh, severe, oppressive, overpowering, unjust, unreasonable.
⊞ liberal, tolerant.

tyrannically or **tyrannously** *adv.* in a tyrannical way.

tyrannize or **tyrannise** /'tɪrənaɪz/ *verb trans., intrans.* to rule or treat (a person or people) in a cruel, unjust, and oppressive way.

⊟ oppress, subjugate, persecute, terrorize, trample on, grind down.

tyrannosaur /tɪ'ranəsɔː(r)/ or **tyrannosaurus** *noun* the largest flesh-eating dinosaur, which lived during the Cretaceous period, and grew to a height of 6m, walking on its hind legs, the front legs being much reduced. It is thought to have used the powerful claws on its hind legs to kill its prey, which consisted mainly of herbivorous dinosaurs. [from Greek *tyrannos*, tyrant, after DINOSAUR]

tyranny /'tɪrənɪ/ *noun* (PL. **tyrannies**) **1** cruel, unjust, and oppressive use of authority or power. **2** absolute, cruel, and oppressive government by a single tyrant or group of tyrannical people. **3** a state under such government. **4** a cruel, unjust, or oppressive act. [from Latin *tyrannia*, from Greek *tyrannos*, tyrant]

⋯⋯⋯⋯⋯⋯⋯⋯⋯⋯⋯⋯⋯⋯⋯

▣ **1, 2** dictatorship, despotism, autocracy, absolutism, totalitarianism. **1** authoritarianism, imperiousness, ruthlessness, harshness, severity, oppression, injustice.
▣ **1** democracy, freedom.
⋯⋯⋯⋯⋯⋯⋯⋯⋯⋯⋯⋯⋯⋯⋯⋯⋯

tyrant /ˈtaɪərənt/ *noun* **1** a cruel, unjust, and oppressive ruler with absolute power. **2** a person who uses authority or power cruelly and unjustly. [from Greek *tyrannos*]

⋯⋯⋯⋯⋯⋯⋯⋯⋯⋯⋯⋯⋯⋯⋯

▣ DICTATOR, DESPOT, AUTOCRAT, ABSOLUTIST. **2** authoritarian, bully, oppressor, slave-driver, taskmaster.
⋯⋯⋯⋯⋯⋯⋯⋯⋯⋯⋯⋯⋯⋯⋯⋯⋯⋯⋯⋯⋯

tyre /taɪə(r)/ *noun* a thick rubber usually air-filled or hollow ring placed over a wheel, and forming the contact with the ground. Tyres usually no longer have inner tubes, and grip is improved by a carefully designed tread and a system of grooves and slits (sipes) which aid in water dispersal. [a variant of *tire*, headdress]

tyro See TIRO.

tyrosine /ˈtaɪərəʊsiːn/ *noun Biochem.* an amino acid that is found in proteins. [from Greek *tyros*, cheese]

tzar, tzarevitch, tzarina See TSAR.

tzatziki /tsatˈsɪkɪ/ *noun* a Greek dish made of yoghurt and finely chopped cucumber, flavoured with mint and garlic, and eaten as a dip. [from modern Greek]

tzigane /tsɪˈɡɑːn/ *noun* a Hungarian gypsy. [from Hungarian *cigány*, gypsy]

u

U[1] or **u** *noun* (PL. **Us, U's, u's**) **1** the twenty-first letter of the English alphabet. **2** anything shaped like the letter.

U[2] *adj. Brit. colloq., said especially of language* typical of or acceptable to the upper classes (see NON-U).

U[3] *abbrev.* **1** unionist. **2** united. **3** *Brit.* universal, denoting a film designated as suitable for people of all ages.

U[4] *symbol Chem.* uranium.

UB40 *noun* in the UK, a registration card issued by the Department of Employment to an unemployed person.

über- /'u:bə/ *combining form* meaning the supreme form of something: *über-nerd.*

ubiquitous /juˈbɪkwɪtəs/ *adj.* found or seeming to be found everywhere; ever-present. [from Latin *ubique*, everywhere]

. . . .

⊟ omnipresent, ever-present, everywhere, universal, global, pervasive, common, frequent.

⊟ rare, scarce.

. . . .

ubiquity /juˈbɪkwɪtɪ/ *noun* existence everywhere.

U-boat *noun* a German submarine (especially of World Wars I and II). [from German *Unterseeboot*, undersea-boat]

UCCA *abbrev.* Universities Central Council on Admissions.

udder *noun* in certain mammals, such as cows and goats, the bag-like structure which hangs beneath the body and contains the mammary glands that secrete milk. Each gland has its own teat or nipple from which the milk is sucked. [from Anglo-Saxon *uder*]

UDI *abbrev.* Unilateral Declaration of Independence.

UEFA *abbrev.* Union of European Football Associations.

UFC *abbrev.* Universities Funding Council.

UFO *noun* (PL. **UFOs, UFO's**) *colloq.* an unidentified flying object, any unrecognizable flying vehicle presumed to be from another planet or outer space.

ufology /juˈfɒlədʒɪ/ *noun* the study of unidentified flying objects.

UGC *abbrev.* University Grants Committee (replaced, 1979, by UFC).

ugh /ʌx, ɜːg/ *interj.* an exclamation of dislike or disgust, also used to represent a cough or grunt.

Ugli *noun trademark* (PL. **Uglis, Uglies**) a fruit that is a cross between a grapefruit, a tangerine, and a seville orange, with wrinkly green and yellow skin. [from UGLY, from its appearance]

ugly *adj.* (**uglier, ugliest**) **1** unpleasant to look at. **2** morally repulsive or offensive. **3** threatening or involving danger or violence. **4** bad-tempered.

. . . .

⊟ **1** unattractive, unsightly, plain, unprepossessing, ill-favoured, hideous, monstrous, misshapen, deformed. **2** repulsive, offensive, disgusting, revolting, vile, frightful, terrible, unpleasant, disagreeable, nasty, horrid, objectionable. **3** dangerous, threatening, alarming, grave, nasty.

⊟ **1** attractive, beautiful, handsome, pretty.

. . . .

ugly duckling a person or thing initially thought ugly or worthless but growing to be outstandingly beautiful or highly valued.

UHF *abbrev.* ultra-high frequency.

UHT *abbrev.* **1** ultra-heat-treated. **2** ultra-high-temperature.

UK *abbrev.* United Kingdom.

UKAEA *abbrev.* United Kingdom Atomic Energy Authority.

ukase /juˈkeɪz/ *noun* a command issued by a supreme ruler, especially the Tsar in Imperial Russia. [from Russian *ukaz*]

ukulele or **ukelele** /juːkəˈleɪlɪ/ *noun* a small guitar, usually with four strings. [from Hawaiian *ukulele*, jumping flea]

ulcer *noun* **1** *Pathol.* an open sore, often accompanied by inflammation, on the surface of the skin or of a mucous membrane lining a body cavity, eg peptic ulcer. **2** a continuing source of harm or evil. [from Latin *ulceris*]

ulcerate *verb trans., intrans.* to form an ulcer on or in a part of the body.

ulceration *noun* the process or result of ulcerating.

ulcerous *adj.* **1** like an ulcer. **2** affected with ulcers.

ulna *noun* (PL. **ulnae, ulnas**) *Anat.* the inner and longer of the two bones of the human forearm, or the corresponding bone in the forelimb or wing of other vertebrates. [from Latin *ulna*, elbow, arm]

ulnar *adj.* of or in the region of the ulna.

ulster *noun* a man's loose heavy double-breasted overcoat. [from Ulster, Northern Ireland, where it was first made]

ult. *abbrev.* **1** ultimate or ultimately. **2** ultimo.

ulterior *adj., said of motives, etc* other than what is apparent or admitted. [from Latin, from *uls*, beyond]

. . . .

⊟ secondary, hidden, concealed, undisclosed, unexpressed, covert, secret, private, personal, selfish.

⊟ overt.

. . . .

ultimate — *adj.* **1** last or final. **2** most important; greatest possible. **3** fundamental; basic. **4** *colloq.* best; most advanced. — *noun* (**the ultimate**) *colloq.* the best or most advanced one of its kind. [from Latin *ultimus*, last]

. . . .

⊟ *adj.* **1** final, last, closing, concluding, eventual, terminal, furthest, remotest. **2** greatest, highest, supreme, extreme, utmost. **3** fundamental, primary, basic. **4** best, greatest, highest, supreme, superlative, perfect.

. . . .

ultimately *adv.* in the end; finally.

. . . .

⊟ finally, eventually, at last, in the end, after all.

. . . .

ultimatum /ʌltɪˈmeɪtəm/ *noun* (PL. **ultimatums, ultimata**) a final statement declaring an intention to take hostile action unless a specified condition is fulfilled. [see ULTIMATE]

ultimo *adj., in business letters* of last month: *your letter of the tenth ultimo.* [from Latin *ultimus*, last]

ultra- *combining form* forming words meaning: **1** beyond in place, range, or limit: *ultra-microscopic.* **2** extreme or extremely: *ultra-Conservative.* [from Latin *ultra*, beyond]

ultra-high frequency (ABBREV. **UHF**) a radio frequency between 300 and 3,000MHz.

ultramarine *noun* a deep blue pigment used in paints, originally made by grinding lapis lazuli, a blue stone from Asia. [from Latin *ultra marinus*, overseas, from where the stone was imported]

ultramontane — *adj.* **1** beyond the mountains, especially the Alps. **2** *RC Church* denoting a faction in favour of supreme papal authority on doctrinal matters. — *noun* **1** a person living on the other side of the Alps. **2** *RC Church* a member of the ultramontane faction. [from Latin *ultra*, beyond + *mons*, mountain]

ultrasonic *adj.* relating to or producing ultrasound.

ultrasonically *adv.* in an ultrasonic way; by ultrasonic means.

ultrasonics *sing. noun* the study of ultrasound, a branch of physics.

ultrasound *noun* sound consisting of waves with frequencies higher than 20,000 Hz, and which are therefore above the upper limit of normal human hearing. It is widely used in medical diagnosis, sonar systems, and for cleaning and degreasing industrial tools, and detecting flaws and impurities in metals.

ultrasound scan a medical examination of an internal part, especially a fetus, by directing ultrasound waves through it to produce an image on a screen.

ultraviolet (ABBREV. **UV**) *adj.* denoting electromagnetic radiation with wavelengths in the range 4 to 400nm, ie in the region between violet light and X-rays. [from ULTRA- + VIOLET, because it is beyond the violet end of the visible spectrum]

ululate /'juːljʊleɪt, 'ʌljʊleɪt/ *verb intrans.* to howl, wail, or screech. [from Latin *ululare*]

ululation *noun* a howling or wailing.

umbel *noun Bot.* an inflorescence (flower-head) in which a cluster of flowers with stalks of equal length arise from the same point on the main stem. This umbrella-shaped arrangement is found in plants belonging to the family Umbelliferae, eg cow parsley, hogweed. [from Latin *umbella*, sunshade]

umbellate *adj.* **1** constituting an umbel. **2** having an umbel or umbels.

umbelliferous *adj. Bot.* denoting a plant with flowers growing in umbels.

umber *noun* a dark yellowish-brown mineral in soil, used as a pigment in paints. [from Italian *terra di umbra*, shadow earth or Umbrian earth]

umbilical *adj.* relating to the umbilicus or the umbilical cord.

umbilical cord a long flexible tube-like organ by which a fetus is attached to the placenta, and through which it receives nourishment.

umbilicus *noun Medicine* the navel. [from Latin *umbilicus*]

umbra *noun* (PL. **umbrae**, **umbras**) **1** the darkest part of a shadow, at the centre. **2** any shadow, especially that cast by the moon on the earth during an eclipse of the sun. [from Latin *umbra*, shade, shadow]

umbrage *noun* offence, especially in the phrases *give umbrage / take umbrage*. [from Old French *ombrage*, from Latin *umbra*, shadow]

umbrella *noun* **1** a device carried to give shelter against rain, etc, consisting of a rounded fabric canopy on a lightweight folding framework fitted around a central handle. **2** a thing, eg an organization, providing protection or overall cover for a number of others. [from Italian *ombrella*, from *ombra*, shade]

umbrella bird any of three species of bird with black plumage, native to tropical forests of S America. It has a crest of raised feathers on the crown of its head which, when opened during courtship, resembles an umbrella.

UMIST *abbrev.* University of Manchester Institute of Science and Technology.

umlaut /'ʊmlaʊt/ *noun* in Germanic languages: **1** a change in the pronunciation of a vowel under the influence of a front vowel in a following syllable (especially in a suffix). **2** a mark consisting of two dots placed above a vowel that undergoes or has undergone this change. [from German *um*, around + *Laut*, sound]

umpire — *noun* a person supervising play in various sports, eg cricket and tennis, enforcing the rules and deciding disputes. — *verb trans., intrans.* to act as umpire in a match. [from Old French *nomper*, not a peer or equal]

     ▣ *noun* referee, judge, adjudicator, arbiter, arbitrator, mediator, moderator. *verb* referee, judge, adjudicate, arbitrate, mediate, moderate, control.

umpteen *adj. colloq.* very many; innumerable. [from obsolete *umpty*, a great deal + *-teen*, from *thirteen*, etc]

     ▣ a good many, innumerable, numerous, plenty, *colloq.* millions, countless.
     ▣ few.

umpteenth *noun, adj.* the latest or last of very many.

UN *abbrev.* United Nations.

un- *prefix* forming words denoting the opposite or reversal of the root word: *unacceptable / unplug / unperson*. [from Anglo-Saxon *un*]

'un *contr. colloq.* one: *that's a nice 'un.*

unable *adj.* not having sufficient strength, skill, or authority; not able to do something.

     ▣ incapable, powerless, impotent, unequipped, unqualified, unfit, incompetent, inadequate.
     ▣ able, capable.

unaccountable *adj.* **1** impossible to explain. **2** not answerable or accountable.

     ▣ **1** inexplicable, unexplainable, unfathomable, impenetrable, incomprehensible, baffling, puzzling, mysterious, astonishing, extraordinary, strange, odd, peculiar, singular, unusual, uncommon, unheard-of.
     ▣ **1** explicable, explainable.

unaccountably *adv.* in an unaccountable way; so as to be unaccountable.

unaccustomed *adj.* **1** (**unaccustomed to something**) not used or accustomed to it. **2** not usual or customary.

     ▣ **1** unused to, unacquainted with, unfamiliar with, unpractised at, inexperienced in. **2** strange, unusual, uncommon, different, new, unexpected, surprising, uncharacteristic, unprecedented.
     ▣ **1** accustomed to, familiar with. **2** customary, usual, normal.

unadopted *adj., said of a road* for which the local authority has no responsibility regarding maintenance, etc.

unadulterated *adj.* **1** pure or neat; not mixed with anything else. **2** sheer; absolute.

unadvised *adj.* **1** not advised; without advice. **2** unwise; ill-advised.

unadvisedly /ʌnəd'vaɪzɪdlɪ/ *adv.* in an unadvised way; against advice.

unaffected *adj.* **1** sincere or genuine, not pretended or affected; free from pretentiousness. **2** not affected.

     ▣ **1** sincere, honest, genuine, straightforward, unpretentious, unassuming, unsophisticated, plain, simple, unspoilt, artless, naïve, ingenuous. **2** untouched, unchanged, unaltered, unmoved, unconcerned, indifferent, impervious.

1 affected, pretentious, insincere. **2** moved, influenced, touched, swayed.

unalienable same as INALIENABLE.

unalloyed *adj.*, *said of joy, pleasure, etc* pure; sheer; not mixed with feelings of sadness or anxiety.

unanimity *noun* unanimous agreement.

consensus, unity, agreement, concurrence, accord, like-mindedness, concord, harmony, unison, concert.

disagreement, disunity.

unanimous *adj.* **1** all in complete agreement. **2** *said of an opinion, decision, etc* shared or arrived at by all, with none disagreeing. [from Latin *unus*, one + *animus*, mind]

1 united, as one, in agreement, in accord. **2** concerted, joint, common, harmonious.

DIVIDED. **1** disunited.

unanswerable *adj.* that can not be denied or disproved.

unapproachable *adj.* whose manner discourages in-formality; unfriendly; stand-offish.

unfriendly, stand-offish, aloof, withdrawn, reserved, distant, unsociable, inaccessible, remote, forbidding.

approachable, friendly.

unarmed *adj.* without weapons.

defenceless, unprotected, exposed, open, vulnerable, weak, helpless.

armed, protected.

unasked *adj.* **1** not asked. **2** not asked for; uninvited.

2 uninvited, unbidden, unrequested, unsought, unsolicited, unwanted, voluntary, spontaneous.

2 invited, wanted.

unassailable *adj.* not able to be challenged or destroyed.

unassuming *adj.* modest or unpretentious.

modest, unpretentious, simple, restrained, unassertive, unobtrusive, retiring, humble, meek, self-effacing.

presumptuous, assertive, pretentious.

unattached *adj.* **1** not in a steady romantic or sexual rela-tionship with another person. **2** not attached, associated, or connected.

1 free, available, single, unmarried, footloose, fancy-free. **2** independent, unaffiliated.

COMMITTED. **1** engaged, married.

unattended *adj.* **1** not accompanied or watched over. **2** not listened to or paid attention.

1 unaccompanied, unescorted, alone, unsupervised, unguarded, unwatched. **2** ignored, disregarded.

1 attended, escorted.

unavailing *adj.*, *said of efforts, etc* futile; of no avail.

unaware *adj.* having no knowledge of something; not aware.

oblivious, unconscious, ignorant, uninformed, unknowing, unsuspecting, unmindful, heedless, blind, deaf.

aware, conscious.

unawares *adv.* **1** unexpectedly; by surprise. **2** without knowing or realizing.

unbalanced *adj.* **1** not in a state of physical balance. **2** lacking mental balance; deranged. **3** lacking impartiality; biased.

1 unsteady, unstable, unequal, uneven, asymmetrical, lopsided. **2** deranged, disturbed, demented, irrational, unsound, insane, mad, crazy, lunatic. **3** biased, prejudiced, one-sided, partisan, unfair, unjust.

2 sane. **3** unbiased.

unbearable *adj.* too unpleasant to bear; intolerable.

intolerable, unacceptable, insupportable, insufferable, unendurable, excruciating.

bearable, acceptable.

unbearably *adv.* in an unbearable way; to an unbearable degree.

unbecoming *adj.* **1** not suited to the wearer. **2** not proper or fitting.

1 unattractive, unsightly. **2** unseemly, improper, unsuitable, inappropriate.

1 attractive. **2** proper, fitting, suitable.

unbeknown or **unbeknownst** *adv.* (**unbeknown to someone**) *colloq.* unknown to them; without their knowl-edge.

unbelief *noun* lack of (especially religious) belief.

atheism, agnosticism, scepticism, doubt, incredulity, disbelief.

belief, faith.

unbelievable *adj.* **1** too unusual or unexpected to be be-lieved. **2** *colloq.* remarkable; astonishing.

1 incredible, inconceivable, unthinkable, unimaginable, astonishing, staggering, extraordinary, impossible, improbable, unlikely, implausible, unconvincing, far-fetched, preposterous. **2** remarkable, incredible, astonishing, staggering, extraordinary.

1 believable, credible.

unbelievably *adv.* in an unbelievable way; so as to be un-believable.

unbeliever *noun* a person who does not believe (espe-cially in a particular religion).

unbelieving *adj.* not believing, without belief.

unbend *verb* (PAST TENSE AND PAST PARTICIPLE **unbent**) **1** *intrans.* to become less formal in manner or behaviour. **2** *trans.* to straighten or release from a bent position.

unbending *adj.* strict or severe; inflexible.

unbidden *adj.*, *adv. literary* not requested, solicited, or summoned up; spontaneous or spontaneously.

unblushing *adj.* shameless; brazen.

unborn *adj.* **1** *said of a baby* not yet born. **2** of or in the fu-ture.

1 embryonic. **2** coming, future, expected, awaited.

unbosom *verb* (**unbosomed**, **unbosoming**) (*often un-bosom oneself*) to speak openly about what is on one's mind; to free oneself of worries or troubles by talking about them.

unbounded *adj.* limitless; infinite.

limitless, unlimited, infinite, boundless, endless, immeasurable, unrestricted, unrestrained, unchecked, unbridled, vast.

limited, restrained.

unbowed *adj.* **1** not bowed or bent. **2** not conquered or forced to yield.

unbridled *adj.* fully and freely felt or expressed; unrestrained.

⬛ unrestrained, unchecked, uncontrolled, immoderate, excessive.

unburden *verb* (**unburdened, unburdening**) **1** to remove a load or burden from. **2** (*often* **unburden oneself**) to relieve oneself of troubles or worries by confessing them to another person.

uncalled-for *adj.*, *said of a remark, etc* not warranted or deserved, especially unjustifiably rude or aggressive.

⬛ gratuitous, unprovoked, unjustified, unwarranted, undeserved, unnecessary, needless.
🔁 timely.

uncannily *adv.* in an uncanny way.

uncanniness *noun* being uncanny.

uncanny *adj.* **1** strange or mysterious. **2** beyond ordinary human ability.

⬛ **1** weird, strange, queer, bizarre, mysterious, unaccountable, incredible, remarkable, extraordinary, fantastic, eerie, *colloq.* creepy, *colloq.* spooky. **2** unnatural, unearthly, supernatural.

uncared-for *adj.* not well looked-after; neglected.

unceremonious *adj.* **1** without ceremony; informal. **2** with no regard for politeness or dignity; direct and abrupt.

uncertain *adj.* **1** not sure, certain or confident. **2** not definitely known or decided. **3** not to be depended upon. **4** likely to change. **5** lacking confidence; hesitant.

⬛ **1** unsure, unconvinced, doubtful, dubious, undecided, ambivalent, hesitant, wavering, vacillating. **2** undecided, unknown, undetermined, unsettled, unresolved, unconfirmed, indefinite, vague. **3** unreliable, unpredictable, unforeseeable, risky, *colloq.* iffy, dubious, shaky, unsteady. **4** changeable, variable, erratic, inconstant, irregular. **5** hesitant, insecure, wavering, vacillating.
🔁 **1** certain, sure. **3, 4** steady, predictable.

uncertainty *noun* (PL. **uncertainties**) **1** an uncertain state. **2** something that is uncertain.

⬛ **1** doubt, scepticism, irresolution, dilemma, hesitation, misgiving, confusion, bewilderment, perplexity, puzzlement, unreliability, unpredictability, insecurity.
🔁 CERTAINTY.

uncertainty principle *Physics* the notion that it is impossible to determine the exact position and momentum of a moving particle simultaneously. Also called **Heisenberg uncertainty principle**.

uncharted *adj.* **1** *said of territory, etc* which has never been fully explored or mapped in detail. **2** not yet examined or investigated.

⬛ UNEXPLORED, VIRGIN. **1** undiscovered. **2** unplumbed, foreign, alien, strange, unfamiliar, new.
🔁 FAMILIAR.

unchristian *adj.* against the principles or spirit of Christianity; uncharitable.

uncial /ˈʌnʃəl/ — *adj.*, *said of a form of writing* in large rounded letters with flowing strokes, of a kind used in ancient manuscripts. — *noun* **1** an uncial letter or form of writing. **2** a manuscript written in uncials. [from Latin *uncia*, inch]

uncircumcised *adj.* **1** not circumcised. **2** not Jewish; gentile.

uncivil *adj.* lacking courtesy; rude.

unclasp *verb* **1** to unfasten the clasp on. **2** to relax one's clasp on. **3** to cause (one's hand) to relax and open up.

uncle *noun* **1** the brother or brother-in-law of a father or mother; the husband of an aunt. **2** *colloq.* a form of address used by a child to a male friend of his or her parents. **3** *slang* a pawnbroker. [from Latin *avunculus*]

unclean *adj.* **1** morally or spiritually impure. **2** *said of an animal* regarded for religious reasons as unfit to be used as food.

⬛ **1** impure, corrupt, defiled, sullied, tainted.

unclear *adj.* not clear; uncertain; vague.

⬛ indistinct, hazy, dim, obscure, uncertain, unsure, doubtful, dubious, vague, indefinite, ambiguous, equivocal.
🔁 clear, evident.

Uncle Sam a nickname for the US government, or a personification of the USA. [supposedly from the initials 'US' stamped on boxes of meat supplied to the government in the War of 1812 by Samuel Wilson (1766–1854) of Troy, New York, who was locally known as Uncle Sam]

Uncle Tom *offensive* a black person who behaves subserviently to whites.

unclothe *verb* **1** to take the clothes off. **2** to uncover or reveal.

uncomfortable *adj.* **1** not comfortable. **2** feeling, involving, or causing discomfort or unease.

⬛ **1** cramped, hard, cold, ill-fitting, irritating, painful, disagreeable. **2** awkward, embarrassed, self-conscious, uneasy, troubled, worried, disturbed, distressed, disquieted, conscience-stricken.
🔁 **1** comfortable. **2** relaxed.

uncomfortably *adv.* in an uncomfortable way; so as to be uncomfortable.

uncommon *adj.* **1** rare or unusual. **2** remarkably great; extreme.

⬛ **1** rare, scarce, infrequent, unusual, abnormal, atypical, unfamiliar, strange, odd, curious, bizarre, extraordinary, distinctive. **2** remarkable, great, outstanding, extreme, exceptional, special, notable.
🔁 **1** common, usual, normal.

uncommonly *adv.* in an uncommon way; to an uncommon degree.

uncompromising *adj.* **1** refusing to compromise or submit. **2** sheer; out-and-out.

⬛ **1** unyielding, unbending, inflexible, unaccommodating, rigid, firm, strict, tough, hard-line, inexorable, intransigent, stubborn, obstinate, diehard.
🔁 **1** flexible.

unconcern *noun* lack of interest or concern; indifference.

unconcerned *adj.* **1** indifferent. **2** not anxious.

⬛ **1** indifferent, apathetic, uninterested, unmoved, uncaring, unsympathetic, callous, aloof, remote, distant, detached, dispassionate, uninvolved, nonchalant. **2** relaxed, cool, composed, complacent, untroubled, unworried, unruffled, carefree, oblivious.
🔁 CONCERNED. **1** interested. **2** worried.

unconcernedly *adv.* with an unconcerned manner.

unconditional adj. straightforward, with no conditions imposed; absolute.

■ unqualified, unreserved, unrestricted, absolute, unlimited, utter, full, total, complete, entire, wholehearted, thoroughgoing, downright, outright, positive, categorical, unequivocal.

✷ conditional, qualified, limited.

unconditionally adv. in an unconditional way; without conditions.

unconscionable adj. 1 without conscience or scruples. 2 outrageous; unthinkable; unreasonable; excessive.

unconscious — adj. 1 said of a person or animal in a state of insensibility, characterized by loss of awareness of the external environment, and inability to respond to sensory stimuli. 2 denoting any mental activity of which a person is unaware: unconscious actions. 3 (unconscious of something) not actively thinking about it. — noun Psychol. (the unconscious) in psychoanalysis, the part of the mind that contains memories, thoughts, and feelings of which one is not consciously aware, but which may be manifested as dreams, psychosomatic symptoms, or certain patterns of behaviour.

■ adj. 1 stunned, knocked out, out, colloq. out cold, colloq. out for the count, concussed, comatose, senseless, insensible. 2 involuntary, automatic, reflex, instinctive, impulsive, innate, subconscious, subliminal, repressed, suppressed, latent, unwitting, inadvertent, accidental, unintentional. 3 unaware of, oblivious of, blind to, deaf to, heedless of, unmindful of, ignorant of.

✷ adj. 1 conscious. 2 intentional. 3 aware of.

unconsciously adv. not consciously, unintentionally.

unconstitutional adj. not allowed by or consistent with a nation's constitution.

uncork verb 1 to remove the cork from (a bottle). 2 colloq. to release (eg emotion) from a pent-up state.

uncouple verb to undo the coupling of or between; to disconnect.

uncouth adj. coarse in behaviour, manners or language. [from Anglo-Saxon uncuth, unfamiliar (ie with social graces)]

■ coarse, crude, vulgar, rude, ill-mannered, unseemly, improper, clumsy, awkward, gauche, graceless, unrefined, uncultivated, uncultured, uncivilized, rough.

✷ polite, refined, urbane.

uncover verb (uncovered, uncovering) 1 to remove the cover from. 2 to reveal or expose. 3 intrans. to take off one's hat as a mark of respect.

■ 1 unveil, unmask, unwrap, strip, bare, open. 2 expose, reveal, show, disclose, divulge, leak, unearth, exhume, discover, detect.

✷ 1 cover. 2 conceal, suppress.

uncrowned adj. 1 said of a monarch not yet crowned. 2 having the status but not a formal title; denoting an acknowledged master of expert in something: the uncrowned king of swindlers.

UNCTAD abbrev. United Nations Conference on Trade and Development.

unction noun 1 Christianity the act of ceremonially anointing a person with oil. 2 the oil used. 3 ointment of any kind. 4 soothing words or thoughts. 5 the kind of sincerity in language or tone of voice that provokes, or is the result of, deep emotion. 6 affected charm, sincerity, or religious feeling. [from Latin ungere, to anoint]

unctuous adj. 1 insincerely and excessively charming. 2 oily; greasy. [from Latin unctuosus]

uncured adj., said of food, especially meat and fish not dried, salted, or smoked.

uncut adj. 1 not cut. 2 said of a book whose pages have not been cut open. 3 said of a book, film, etc with no parts cut out. 4 said of a gemstone not cut into a regular shape.

undated adj. not dated; lacking a date.

undeceive verb to free from a mistaken belief; to reveal the truth to.

undecided adj. 1 not having decided; not able to decide. 2 about which no decision has been made.

■ 1 uncertain, unsure, in two minds, ambivalent, doubtful, hesitant, wavering, irresolute, uncommitted. 2 unsettled, open, indefinite, vague, debatable, moot.

✷ DECIDED, CERTAIN, DEFINITE.

undeniable adj. 1 not able to be denied; obviously true. 2 clearly and indisputably excellent.

■ 1 irrefutable, unquestionable, incontrovertible, sure, certain, undoubted, proven, clear, obvious, patent, evident, manifest, unmistakable.

✷ QUESTIONABLE.

undeniably adv. so as to be undeniable.

under — prep. 1 below or beneath; on the downward-facing surface of. 2 at the foot of. 3 less than; short of. 4 lower in rank than. 5 during the reign or administration of. 6 subjected to, receiving, or sustaining: under consideration / under pressure. 7 in the category or classification of. 8 according to: under the terms of the agreement. 9 in view of; because of: under the circumstances. 10 propelled by: under sail. 11 said of a field planted with (a particular crop). — adv. 1 in or to a lower place, position, or rank. 2 into a state of unconsciousness. — adj. 1 lower. 2 subordinate. — under way in motion; in progress. [from Anglo-Saxon under]

■ prep. 1, 2 below, beneath, underneath. 3 less than, lower than, short of, below. 4 lower than, subordinate to, inferior to. adv. 1 below, beneath, underneath. under way moving, in motion, in progress, going, in operation, started, begun, afoot.

✷ prep. 1, 2 over, above. 3 more than, over, above. 4 over, above, superior to. adv. 1 over, above.

under- combining form forming words meaning: 1 beneath or below: underfoot. 2 too little in quantity or degree; insufficient or insufficiently: underexpose / underpay. 3 lower in rank or importance: under-secretary. 4 less than: underbid. 5 less or lower than expectations or potential: underdeveloped.

underachieve verb intrans. to be less successful than expected, especially academically; to fail to fulfil one's potential.

underachiever noun a person who is less successful than expected.

under-age adj. 1 said of a person below an age required by law. 2 said of an activity, etc carried on by an under-age person.

underarm adj. adv., said of a style of bowling in sports with the arm kept below the level of the shoulder.

underbelly noun (PL. underbellies) 1 the part of an animal's belly facing the ground. 2 any underside that resembles a belly. 3 (also soft underbelly) any unprotected part vulnerable to attack.

undercarriage noun 1 the landing-gear of an aircraft, including wheels, shock absorbers, etc. 2 the chassis of a road vehicle.

undercharge verb 1 to charge (a person) too little money. 2 to put an insufficient charge in (eg an electrical circuit or explosive device).

underclothes pl. noun or **underclothing** noun underwear.

undercoat — *noun* **1** a layer of paint applied as preparation for the top or finishing coat. **2** the kind of paint used. **3** a layer of fur or hair beneath the top layer. — *verb* to apply an undercoat to.

undercover *adj.* working, or carried out, in secret.

■ secret, *colloq.* hush-hush, private, confidential, underground, clandestine, surreptitious, furtive, covert, spy, intelligence, hidden, concealed.

🖪 open, unconcealed, overt.

undercurrent *noun* **1** an unseen current under the (often still) surface of a body of water. **2** an underlying trend or body of opinion, especially different from the one perceived.

■ **1** undertow. **2** aura, atmosphere, feeling, sense, movement, tendency, trend, drift, undertone, overtone, hint, suggestion, tinge, flavour.

undercut — *verb* (**undercutting**; PAST TENSE AND PAST PARTICIPLE **undercut**) **1** to offer goods or services at a lower price than (a competitor). **2** to cut away the underside of. **3** to apply backspin to (a ball). — *noun* the underside of a sirloin, ie the fillet.

underdog *noun* **1** the less highly regarded competitor, not expected to win. **2** the losing competitor. **3** a person dominated by another.

underdone *adj.* not cooked to the proper or required degree.

underemployed *adj.* **1** given less work than could realistically be done. **2** given work that fails to make good use of the skills possessed.

underemployment *noun* **1** insufficient use of something. **2** a state of having too large a part of a labour force unemployed.

underestimate — *verb* to make too low an estimate of the value, capacity, or extent of. — *noun* too low an estimate.

■ *verb* underrate, undervalue, misjudge, miscalculate, minimize, belittle, disparage, dismiss.

🖪 *verb* overestimate, exaggerate.

underfelt *noun* an old type of underlay, made of felt.

underfoot *adv.* under the feet of a walking or running person or people.

undergarment *noun* an item of underwear.

undergo *verb* (**undergoes**; PAST TENSE **underwent**; PAST PARTICIPLE **undergone**) to endure, experience, or be subjected to. [from Anglo-Saxon *undergan*]

■ endure, experience, suffer, sustain, submit to, bear, stand, weather, withstand.

undergraduate *noun* a person studying for a first degree in a higher education establishment.

underground — *noun* (*usually* **the underground**) **1** a place or area below ground level. **2** a system of electric trains running in tunnels below ground. **3** a secret paramilitary organization fighting a government or occupying force. **4** any artistic movement seeking to challenge or overturn established (usually social as well as artistic) views and practices. — *adj.* **1** existing or operating below the surface of the ground. **2** of or belonging to any political or artistic underground. — *adv.* **1** to a position below ground level. **2** into hiding.

■ *noun* **2** metro, tube, *North Amer., esp. US* subway. **3** resistance. *adj.* **1** subterranean, buried, sunken. **2** undercover, revolutionary, subversive, secret, covert, radical, experimental, avant-garde, alternative, unorthodox, unofficial.

undergrowth *noun* a thick growth of shrubs and bushes among trees.

■ brush, scrub, vegetation, ground cover, bracken, bushes, brambles, briars.

underhand or **underhanded** — *adj.* **1** secretively deceitful or dishonest; sly. **2** underarm. — *adv.* in an underhand way.

■ *adj.* **1** sly, crafty, sneaky, stealthy, surreptitious, furtive, clandestine, devious, dishonest, deceitful, deceptive, fraudulent, *colloq.* crooked, *colloq.* shady, unscrupulous, unethical, immoral, improper.

🖪 *adj.* **1** honest, open, above board.

underlay — *verb* (PAST TENSE AND PAST PARTICIPLE **underlaid**) to lay underneath, or support or provide with something laid underneath. — *noun* a thing laid underneath another, especially felt or rubber matting laid under a carpet for protection.

underlie *verb* (**underlying**; PAST TENSE **underlay**; PAST PARTICIPLE **underlain**) **1** to lie underneath. **2** to be the hidden cause or meaning of (an attitude, event, etc), beneath what is apparent, visible, or superficial.

underline *verb* **1** to draw a line under (eg a word or piece of text). **2** to emphasize.

■ UNDERSCORE. **2** stress, emphasize, accentuate, italicize, highlight, point up.

🖪 **2** play down, *colloq.* soft-pedal.

underling *noun derog.* a subordinate.

underlying *adj.* **1** lying under or beneath. **2** fundamental, basic: *the underlying causes.*

■ **2** basic, fundamental, essential, primary, elementary, root, intrinsic, latent.

undermentioned *adj.* mentioned or named below or later in the text.

undermine *verb* **1** to dig or wear away the base or foundation of. **2** to weaken or destroy, especially gradually and imperceptibly.

■ **1** excavate, mine, tunnel. **2** weaken, destroy, erode, wear away, sap, sabotage, subvert, vitiate, mar, impair.

🖪 **2** strengthen, fortify.

underneath — *prep., adv.* beneath or below; under. — *noun* a lower or downward-facing part or surface. [from Anglo-Saxon *underneothan*]

underpants *pl. noun* a man's undergarment covering the body from the waist or hips to (especially the tops of) the thighs.

underpass *noun* **1** a tunnel for pedestrians under a road or railway; a subway. **2** a road or railway passing under another.

underpin *verb* (**underpinned**, **underpinning**) **1** to support from beneath, usually temporarily, with brickwork or a prop. **2** *fig.* to give strength or support to.

underplay *verb* to understate or reduce the emphasis on.

underprivileged *adj.* deprived of the basic living standards and rights enjoyed by most people in society.

■ disadvantaged, deprived, poor, needy, impoverished, destitute, oppressed.

🖪 privileged, fortunate, affluent.

underproduce *verb trans., intrans.* to produce less than the required or potential amount of something.

underproduction *noun* producing less than expected or possible.

underrate *verb* to underestimate.

■ underestimate, undervalue, belittle, disparage, depreciate, dismiss.

🔁 overrate, exaggerate.

underrated *adj.* 1 underestimated. 2 rated at less than real worth.

underseal — *noun* an anti-rusting substance painted on to the underside of a motor vehicle. — *verb* to apply such a substance to.

under-secretary *noun* (PL. **under-secretaries**) a subordinate to a secretary of state, especially a junior minister or senior civil servant.

undersell *verb* (PAST TENSE AND PAST PARTICIPLE **undersold**) to sell goods or services at a lower price than (a competitor).

undersexed *adj.* experiencing sexual desire less frequently or less intensely than the average person.

undershoot *verb* (PAST TENSE AND PAST PARTICIPLE **undershot**) 1 *said of an aircraft* to land short of (a runway). 2 to fall short of (a target, etc).

underside *noun* the downward-facing side or surface.

undersigned *adj.* whose names are signed below: *we, the undersigned, ...*

undersized *adj.* of less than the usual size.

■ small, tiny, minute, miniature, pygmy, dwarf, stunted, underdeveloped, underweight, puny.

🔁 oversized, big, overweight.

underskirt *noun* a thin skirt-like undergarment worn under a dress or skirt.

understaffed *adj.* having insufficient staff.

understand *verb* (PAST TENSE AND PAST PARTICIPLE **understood**) 1 to grasp with the mind the meaning, nature, explanation, or implication of. 2 to know, believe, or infer, from information received. 3 to have a sympathetic awareness of the character or nature of. 4 *intrans.* to grasp what is said. 5 *intrans.* to be sympathetic. [from Anglo-Saxon *understandan*]

■ 1 grasp, comprehend, take in, follow, *colloq.* get, *colloq.* cotton on to, fathom, penetrate, make out, discern, perceive, see, realize, recognize, appreciate, accept. 2 know, believe, infer, think, hear, learn, gather, assume, presume, suppose, conclude. 3 sympathize with, empathize with, commiserate with. 4 see, follow, *colloq.* cotton on, realize. 5 sympathize.

🔁 1, 3, 4 misunderstand.

understandable *adj.* capable of being understood; reasonable.

understandably *adv.* 1 in an understandable way. 2 so as to be understood.

understanding — *noun* 1 the act of understanding, or the ability to understand. 2 a person's perception or interpretation of information received. 3 an informal agreement. 4 a sympathetic harmony of viewpoints. 5 a condition agreed upon: *on the understanding that you stay for six months.* — *adj.* sympathetic to, or keenly aware of, the feelings and opinions of others.

■ *noun* 1 comprehension, intelligence, intellect, discernment, appreciation, awareness, perception, interpretation, insight, wisdom, sense. 2 perception, interpretation, impression, belief, idea, notion, opinion, grasp, judgement, appreciation, awareness, knowledge. 3 agreement, arrangement, pact. 4 accord, harmony, sympathy, empathy. *adj.* sympathetic, compassionate, kind, considerate, sensitive, patient, tolerant, forbearing, forgiving, tender, loving.

🔁 *adj.* unsympathetic, insensitive, impatient, intolerant.

understate *verb* to describe as being less or more moderate than is really the case, or to express in very restrained or moderate terms, often for ironic or dramatic effect.

■ underplay, play down, *colloq.* soft-pedal, minimize, make light of, belittle, dismiss.

🔁 exaggerate.

understatement *noun* something that is understated.

understood past tense and past participle of UNDERSTAND. — *adj.* 1 implied but not expressed or stated. 2 realized without being, or needing to be, openly stated.

■ 1 implied, implicit, tacit, unstated, unspoken, unwritten. 2 assumed, presumed, inferred, accepted, tacit.

understudy — *verb trans., intrans.* (**understudies, understudied**) to study (a role), or study the role of (an actor), so as to be able to take over if the need arises. — *noun* (PL. **understudies**) a person who understudies.

■ *noun* stand-in, substitute, replacement, reserve, deputy, double.

undertake *verb* (PAST TENSE **undertook**; PAST PARTICIPLE **undertaken**) 1 to accept (a duty, responsibility, or task). 2 to promise or agree. 3 to overtake on the inside lane of a motorway. [from Middle English *undertaken*, to entrap]

■ 1 take on, accept, assume, tackle, try, attempt, endeavour, embark on, begin, commence. 2 promise, agree, pledge, guarantee, contract, covenant.

undertaker *noun* a person whose job is organizing funerals and preparing dead bodies for burial or cremation.

undertaking *noun* 1 a duty, responsibility, or task undertaken. 2 a promise or guarantee. 3 the work of an undertaker.

■ 1 duty, responsibility, task, project, enterprise, venture, business, affair, operation, attempt, endeavour, effort. 2 promise, pledge, guarantee, commitment, vow, word, assurance.

undertone *noun* 1 a quiet tone of voice. 2 an underlying quality, emotion, or atmosphere. 3 a subdued sound or shade of a colour.

■ 1 murmur, whisper. 2 undercurrent, hint, suggestion, trace, tinge, touch, flavour, feeling, atmosphere.

undertook see UNDERTAKE.

undertow *noun* 1 the strong current that flows away from the shore underneath a breaking wave. 2 any undercurrent that flows in the opposite direction to the surface current.

undervalue *verb* to place too low a value on.

■ underrate, underestimate, misjudge, minimize, depreciate, disparage, dismiss.

🔁 overrate, exaggerate.

underwater *adj., adv.* below the surface of water.

■ *adj.* subaquatic, undersea, submarine, submerged, sunken.

underwear *noun* clothes worn under shirts, trousers, dresses, and skirts.

▣ underclothes, undergarments, lingerie, *colloq.* undies, *colloq.* smalls.

underwent see UNDERGO.

underworld *noun* **1** the world of organized crime. **2** *Mythol.* a world beneath the earth's surface, the home of the souls of the dead.

underwrite *verb* (PAST TENSE **underwrote**; PAST PARTICIPLE **underwritten**) **1** to agree to finance (a commercial venture), and accept the loss in the event of failure. **2** to agree to buy, or find a buyer for, leftover shares from (a sale of shares to the public). **3** to issue (an insurance policy), accepting the risk involved.

▣ **1** sponsor, fund, finance, subsidize, back, guarantee. **3** insure.

underwriter *noun* a person who underwrites insurance.

undesirable — *adj.* unpleasant or objectionable in some way. — *noun* a person or thing considered undesirable.

▣ *adj.* unpleasant, objectionable, unwanted, unwelcome, unacceptable, unsuitable, disagreeable, distasteful, repugnant, offensive, obnoxious.
▣ *adj.* desirable, pleasant.

undesirably *adv.* in an undesirable way; to an undesirable extent.

undid see UNDO.

undies *pl. noun colloq.* items of (especially women's) underwear.

undo *verb* (**undoes**; PAST TENSE **undid**; PAST PARTICIPLE **undone**) **1** *trans., intrans.* to open, unfasten, or untie. **2** to cancel or reverse the effect or result of. **3** *facetious, literary* to bring about the downfall of: *I am undone!*

▣ **1** open, unfasten, untie, unbuckle, unbutton, unzip, unlock, unwrap, unwind, loose, loosen, separate. **2** cancel, annul, nullify, invalidate, offset, neutralize, reverse, overturn, upset, quash, defeat, undermine, subvert, mar, spoil, ruin, wreck, shatter, destroy.
▣ **1** fasten, do up.

undoing *noun* downfall or ruin, or the cause of it.

▣ downfall, ruin, ruination, collapse, destruction, defeat, overthrow, reversal, shame, disgrace. *cause* weakness.

undone *adj.* **1** unfinished. **2** unfastened. **3** ruined.

▣ **1** unfinished, uncompleted, incomplete, unaccomplished, unfulfilled, outstanding, left, omitted, neglected, forgotten. **2** unfastened, untied, unlaced, unbuttoned, unlocked, open, loose.
▣ **1** done, accomplished, complete. **2** fastened.

undoubted *adj.* beyond doubt or question; clear; evident.

▣ clear, evident, obvious, patent, sure, certain, definite, unchallenged, undisputed, acknowledged, unquestionable, indisputable, incontrovertible, undeniable, indubitable.

undoubtedly *adv.* without doubt, certainly.

undreamed-of or **undreamt-of** *adj.* not imagined, especially thought never to be likely or possible.

undress — *verb* **1** to take the clothes off. **2** *intrans.* to take one's clothes off. — *noun* **1** nakedness, or near-nakedness. **2** casual or informal dress. **3** ordinary uniform as opposed to full military dress.

▣ *verb* STRIP, DISROBE. **2** *colloq.* peel off.

undue *adj.* inappropriately or unjustifiably great; excessive.

▣ excessive, extreme, immoderate, inordinate, undeserved, unreasonable, disproportionate, uncalled-for, unwarranted, unnecessary, needless, extravagant, improper.
▣ reasonable, moderate, proper.

undue influence a strong influence over another person, considered to have prevented that person from exercising free will.

undulant fever a remittent fever with swelling of the joints and enlarged spleen; it is caused by the bacterium which produces brucellosis in animals and is transmitted to man by goat's or cow's milk.

undulate *verb intrans.* **1** to move in or like waves. **2** to be wavy. [from Latin *unda*, wave]

undulation *noun* **1** undulating. **2** a wave-like motion or form. **3** waviness. **4** a wave.

unduly *adv.* excessively; unreasonably.

▣ too, over, excessively, unreasonably, immoderately, inordinately, disproportionately, unjustifiably, unnecessarily.
▣ reasonably, moderately.

undying *adj.* everlasting; eternal.

unearned *adj.* **1** *said of income* gained through investments, interest on savings, etc, rather than as wages or fees. **2** not deserved.

unearned income income, such as dividends and interest earned on savings, that is not remuneration for work done.

unearth *verb* **1** to dig up out of the ground. **2** to discover by searching or rummaging.

▣ **1** dig up, exhume, disinter, excavate, uncover, expose. **2** discover, find, detect, *colloq.* dig up, uncover, expose, reveal.
▣ **1** bury.

unearthliness *noun* an unearthly state or quality.

unearthly *adj.* **1** weird; ghostly. **2** *colloq.* outrageous, especially outrageously early: *at this unearthly hour.* **3** not of this earth; heavenly or hellish.

▣ **1** weird, ghostly, supernatural, eerie, uncanny, strange, *colloq.* spine-chilling. **2** unreasonable, outrageous, ungodly.
▣ **2** reasonable.

unease or **uneasiness** *noun* an uneasy state or quality.

uneasily *adv.* in an uneasy way.

uneasy *adj.* (**uneasier, uneasiest**) **1** nervous, anxious, or unsettled; ill at ease. **2** unlikely to prove lasting; unstable. **3** causing anxiety; unsettling.

▣ **1** uncomfortable, unsettled, nervous, anxious, worried, apprehensive, tense, strained, agitated, shaky, jittery, edgy, upset, troubled, disturbed, unsettled, restless, impatient, unsure, insecure. **3** unsettling, unnerving, disconcerting.
▣ **1** calm, composed.

uneaten *adj.* not eaten.

uneconomic *adj.* not conforming to the principles of sound economics, especially unprofitable.

uneconomical *adj.* not economical; wasteful.

unemployed — *adj.* **1** not having a paid job. **2** not in use. — *noun* (**the unemployed**) unemployed people.

▣ *adj.* **1** jobless, out of work, laid off, redundant, unwaged,

colloq. on the dole, idle, unoccupied. **2** unused, redundant.
🔄 *adj.* EMPLOYED, OCCUPIED.
....

unemployment *noun* **1** the state of being unemployed. **2** the number of unemployed people.

unemployment benefit *Brit.* formerly, a regular payment made to an unemployed worker through the national insurance scheme. Now replaced by JOBSEEEKER'S ALLOWANCE.

unequal *adj.* **1** not equal in quantity, value, or rank. **2** not evenly matched or balanced. **3 (unequal to something)** unable to carry it out, deal with it, etc. **4** not uniform; varying.
....
🔄 **1** different, varying, dissimilar, unlike, unfair, unjust, biased, discriminatory. **2** unmatched, uneven, unbalanced, disproportionate, asymmetrical, irregular. **4** varying, irregular, different, dissimilar, unlike.
🔄 EQUAL.
....

unequalled *adj.* not matched by any other; without equal; supreme.

unequivocal *adj.* clearly stated or expressed; unambiguous.
....
🔄 unambiguous, explicit, clear, plain, evident, distinct, unmistakable, express, direct, straight, definite, positive, categorical, incontrovertible, absolute, unqualified, unreserved.
🔄 ambiguous, vague, qualified.
....

unerring /ʌnˈɜːrɪŋ/ *adj.* consistently true or accurate; never making an error or missing the mark.

UNESCO *abbrev.* United Nations Educational, Scientific, and Cultural Organization.

uneven *adj.* **1** not smooth or flat; bumpy. **2** *said of a contest* with sides poorly matched; unequal. **3** not uniform or consistent; varying.
....
🔄 **1** rough, bumpy. **2** unequal, inequitable, unfair, unbalanced, one-sided. **3** irregular, varying, variable, intermittent, spasmodic, fitful, jerky, unsteady, changeable, fluctuating, erratic, inconsistent, patchy.
🔄 **1** flat, level. **2** even, equal. **3** regular, uniform, consistent.
....

uneventful *adj.* during which nothing interesting or out of the ordinary happens; uninteresting, routine.
....
🔄 uninteresting, unexciting, quiet, unvaried, boring, monotonous, tedious, dull, routine, humdrum, ordinary, commonplace, unremarkable, unexceptional, unmemorable.
🔄 eventful, memorable.
....

uneventfully *adv.* routinely; without much happening.

unexampled *adj.* **1** unprecedented. **2** unequalled.

unexceptionable *adj.* so inoffensive, excellent, or suitable as to make criticism or objection impossible.

unexceptional *adj.* ordinary; run-of-the-mill.
....
🔄 ordinary, run-of-the-mill, average, normal, usual, typical, unremarkable, unmemorable, indifferent, mediocre, unimpressive.
🔄 exceptional, impressive.
....

unfailing *adj.* remaining constant; never weakening or failing.

unfailingly *adv.* without fail.

unfair *adj.* **1** not fair or just. **2** involving deceit or dishonesty.
....
🔄 **1** unjust, inequitable, partial, biased, prejudiced, bigoted, discriminatory, unbalance, one-sided, partisan, arbitrary,

undeserved, unmerited, unwarranted, uncalled-for. **2** deceitful, dishonest, unethical, unscrupulous, unprincipled, wrongful.
🔄 **1** fair, just, unbiased, deserved.
....

unfairness *noun* being unfair; an instance of this.

unfaithful *adj.* **1** breaking faith with a sexual partner by having a sexual relationship with someone else. **2** not loyal. **3** not true to a promise. **4** not accurate as a copy or reproduction.
....
🔄 **1** adulterous, two-timing. **2** disloyal, treacherous, unreliable, fickle, inconstant, false, untrue, deceitful, dishonest, untrustworthy, duplicitous, double-dealing, faithless. **3** false, untrue, unreliable, untrustworthy, duplicitous, double-dealing.
🔄 **1** faithful, true. **2** loyal, faithful, reliable. **3** true, reliable. **4** faithful.
....

unfathomable *adj.* **1** that cannot be understood or fathomed. **2** too deep to measure or fathom.

unfavourable *adj.* **1** not encouraging or helping; adverse. **2** not liking, agreeing, or approving.
....
🔄 **1** discouraging, adverse, inauspicious, unpromising, ominous, threatening, hostile, inopportune, untimely, unseasonable, disadvantageous, ill-suited, unfortunate, unlucky, bad, poor. **2** hostile, unfriendly, uncomplimentary, negative, contrary.
🔄 FAVOURABLE. **1** auspicious, promising.
....

unfavourably *adv.* in an unfavourable way; so as to be unfavourable.

unfeeling *adj.* unsympathetic; hard-hearted.
....
🔄 unsympathetic, hard-hearted, heartless, pitiless, uncaring, insensitive, cold, hard, stony, callous, cruel, inhuman.
🔄 sensitive, sympathetic.
....

unfettered *adj.* not controlled or restrained.

unfit *adj.* **1** not meeting required standards; not good enough. **2** not fit, especially physically.
....
🔄 **1** unsuitable, inappropriate, unsuited, ill-equipped, unqualified, ineligible, untrained, unprepared, unequal, incapable, incompetent, inadequate, ineffective, useless. **2** out of condition, unhealthy, flabby, feeble, decrepit.
🔄 **1** fit, suitable, competent. **2** fit, healthy.
....

unfitted *adj.* **1** not provided with fittings. **2** not adapted or suited.

unflappability *noun* being unflappable.

unflappable *adj. colloq.* never becoming agitated or alarmed; always remaining calm.

unfledged *adj.* **1** *said of a bird* not yet having developed adult flight feathers. **2** young and inexperienced.

unflinching *adj.* showing a fearless determination in the face of danger or difficulty.

unfold *verb* **1** to open out the folds of; to spread out. **2** *intrans.* to be opened out or spread out. **3** *intrans.* to develop, or be revealed, gradually.
....
🔄 **1** open, spread, flatten, straighten, stretch out, undo, uncurl, unfurl, unroll, uncoil, unwrap, uncover. **2** open, spread out, undo, unfurl, uncurl, unroll, uncoil. **3** develop, evolve.
🔄 **1** fold, wrap.
....

unforgiven *adj.* not forgiven.

unforgiving *adj.* not ready or disposed to forgive; intolerant.

unfortunate — *adj.* 1 having bad luck. 2 resulting from or constituting bad luck: *an unfortunate injury.* 3 regrettable. — *noun* an unfortunate person.

◨ *adj.* 1 unlucky, luckless, hapless, unsuccessful, doomed, ill-fated. 2 unlucky, unhappy, ill-fated, hopeless, calamitous, disastrous, ruinous. 3 regrettable, lamentable, deplorable, adverse, unfavourable, unsuitable, inappropriate, inopportune, untimely, ill-timed, poor, wretched, unhappy.
◨ *adj.* FORTUNATE. 2 favourable, appropriate, happy.

unfortunately *adv.* as is unfortunate; regrettably.

unfounded *adj.* not based on fact; without foundation; groundless.

◨ baseless, groundless, unsupported, unsubstantiated, unproven, unjustified, idle, false, spurious, trumped-up, fabricated.
◨ substantiated, justified.

unfreeze *verb* (PAST TENSE **unfroze**; PAST PARTICIPLE **unfrozen**) 1 *trans., intrans.* to thaw or cause to thaw. 2 to free (eg prices or funds) from a restriction or control imposed, eg by a government.

unfrock same as DEFROCK.

unfunny *adj.* not funny; not amusing.

unfurl *verb trans., intrans.* to open out from a rolled-up or tied-up state.

ungainliness *noun* an ungainly manner.

ungainly *adj.* (**ungainlier**, **ungainliest**) awkward and ungraceful in movement. [from obsolete *gainly*, graceful]

◨ clumsy, awkward, gauche, inelegant, *colloq.* gawky, uncoordinated, lumbering, unwieldy.
◨ graceful, elegant.

ungodliness *noun* being ungodly.

ungodly *adj.* 1 wicked or sinful. 2 *colloq.* outrageous, especially outrageously early.

◨ 1 sinful, wicked, impious, irreligious, godless, blasphemous, profane, immoral, corrupt, depraved. 2 unreasonable, outrageous, intolerable, unearthly, unsocial.

ungovernable *adj., said of a temper, etc* uncontrollable.

unguarded *adj.* 1 without guard; unprotected. 2 showing a lack of caution or alertness.

◨ 1 undefended, unprotected, exposed, vulnerable, defenceless. 2 unwary, careless, incautious, imprudent, impolitic, indiscreet, undiplomatic, thoughtless, unthinking, heedless, foolish, foolhardy, rash, ill-considered.
◨ 1 defended, protected. 2 guarded, cautious.

unguent /ˈʌŋgwənt/ *noun* ointment. [from Latin *unguere*, to anoint]

ungulate *Biol.* — *adj.* hoofed. — *noun* a hoofed mammal. [from Latin *ungula*, hoof, claw]

unhand *verb old use, literary* to let go of; to take one's hands off.

unhappily *adv.* in an unhappy way, sadly.

unhappiness *noun* being unhappy, sadness.

unhappy *adj.* (**unhappier**, **unhappiest**) 1 sad; in low spirits. 2 being the result of, or bringing, misfortune; unfortunate.

◨ 1 sad, sorrowful, miserable, melancholy, depressed, dispirited, despondent, dejected, downcast, crestfallen, long-faced, gloomy. 2 unfortunate, unlucky, ill-fated, unsuitable, inappropriate, inapt, ill-chosen, tactless, awkward, clumsy.

◨ 1 happy. 2 fortunate, suitable.

unhealthily *adv.* in an unhealthy way.

unhealthiness *noun* an unhealthy state.

unhealthy *adj.* (**unhealthier**, **unhealthiest**) 1 suffering from, or showing evidence of, ill health. 2 damaging to health. 3 causing or likely to cause anxiety or worry; psychologically damaging. 4 flouting or corrupting moral standards.

◨ 1 unwell, sick, ill, poorly, ailing, sickly, infirm, invalid, weak, feeble, frail, unsound. 2 unwholesome, insanitary, unhygienic, harmful, detrimental. 3 morbid, unnatural, harmful, detrimental.
◨ 1 healthy, fit. 2 wholesome, hygienic.

unheard *adj.* 1 not heard. 2 not heeded; ignored.

unheard-of *adj.* 1 not known to have ever happened or been done before; unprecedented. 2 not at all famous; unknown.

◨ 1 unprecedented, unimaginable, undreamed-of, unthinkable, inconceivable. 2 unknown, unfamiliar, new, unusual, obscure.
◨ 1 normal. 2 famous.

unhinge *verb* to cause (a person, or a person's mind) to become unbalanced.

unhinged *adj.* 1 *said of a door, etc* off the hinges. 2 *said of a person* deranged, crazy.

unholy *adj.* (**unholier**, **unholiest**) 1 wicked; sinful; irreligious. 2 *colloq.* outrageous; frightful.

◨ 1 wicked, evil, sinful, impious, irreligious, iniquitous, immoral, corrupt, depraved. 2 outrageous, frightful, ungodly, unearthly, shocking.
◨ 1 holy, pious, godly.

unholy alliance an alliance that seems unnatural, especially because it is between adversaries, often formed for malicious purposes against a third party.

unhorse *verb* to throw or force (a rider) off a horse.

uni *noun colloq.* a university.

uni- *combining form* forming words meaning 'one, a single': *unidirectional.* [from Latin *unus*, one]

unicameral *adj.* having only one law-making body or chamber.

UNICEF *abbrev.* United Nations Children's Fund.

unicellular *adj.* denoting an organism or structure that consists of a single cell, eg bacteria, protozoa, and many spores.

unicorn *noun* a mythical animal in the form of a (usually white) horse with a long straight horn on its forehead. [from Latin *cornu*, horn]

unicycle *noun* an acrobat's cycle consisting of a single wheel with a seat and pedals attached.

unicyclist *noun* a person who rides a unicycle.

unidentified *adj.* 1 not identified. 2 too strange to identify.

◨ 1 unknown, unrecognized, unmarked, unnamed, nameless, anonymous, incognito. 2 unfamiliar, strange, mysterious.
◨ 1 identified, known, named.

unidentified flying object see UFO.

unification *noun* the act of unifying, or the state of being unified. [from UNI- + Latin *facere*, to make]

uniform — *noun* a distinctive set of clothing worn by members of a particular organization or profession. — *adj.* not changing or varying in form or nature. [from UNI- + Latin *forma*, form]

◨ *noun* outfit, costume, livery, insignia, regalia, robes, dress,

suit. *adj.* unvarying, unchanging, constant, unbroken, homogeneous, consistent, regular, equal, smooth, even, flat, monotonous, same, identical, like, alike, similar.
🔁 *adj.* varied, changing, different.

uniformed *adj.* wearing a uniform.

uniformitarianism *noun Geol.* the principle which states that the results of past geological events resemble the results of geological processes and phenomena occurring in the present, and can be used to explain them.

uniformity *noun* a uniform state or quality.

uniformly *adv.* in a uniform way.

unify *verb* (**unifies, unified**) to bring together to form a single unit or whole. [from UNI- + Latin *facere*, to make]

🔁 unite, join, bind, combine, integrate, merge, amalgamate, consolidate, coalesce, fuse, weld.
🔁 separate, divide, split.

unilateral *adj.* affecting, involving, or done by only one person or group among several. [from UNI- + Latin *latus*, side]

unilateralism *noun* a policy or practice of unilateral action, especially unilateral nuclear disarmament.

unilateralist — *noun* a person who supports unilateralism. — *adj.* relating to or involving unilateralism.

unilaterally *adv.* in a unilateral way; by or on one side alone.

unimpeachable *adj.* indisputably reliable or honest.

uninspired *adj.*, *said of a performance, etc* lacking feeling or imagination; dull.

uninspiring *adj.* that fails to inspire interest, enthusiasm, or emotion.

uninterested *adj.* not taking an interest; not interested. See also DISINTERESTED.

🔁 indifferent, unconcerned, uninvolved, bored, listless, apathetic, unenthusiastic, blasé, impassive, unresponsive.
🔁 interested, concerned, enthusiastic, responsive.

union *noun* **1** the act of uniting or the state of being united. **2** an association of people or groups united in a common (especially political) purpose. **3** a trade union. **4** an organization concerned with the welfare of the students in a college, university, etc; also, the building housing this, often also the site of canteen and recreational facilities. **5** agreement or harmony. **6** *formal* marriage; wedlock. **7** *Maths.* a set comprising the members of two smaller sets. **8** *formal* sexual intercourse. [from Latin *unio*, from *unus*, one]

🔁 **1** fusion, unification, unity, alliance, coalition, association, confederation, amalgamation, merger, combination, mixture, synthesis, blend. **2** association, alliance, coalition, league, federation, confederation, confederacy. **5** agreement, harmony, accord, unity, unanimity.
🔁 **1** separation, alienation, estrangement.

union flag the Union Jack.

unionism *noun* **1** the principle or policy of combining. **2** the principles and practices of trade unions.

unionist *noun* **1** a person supporting or believing in trade unions. **2** a person in favour of creating or maintaining a political union between states or countries, especially (**Unionist**) between Northern Ireland and Britain.

unionization or **unionisation** *noun* the process or policy of unionizing.

unionize or **unionise** *verb* **1** to recruit into a trade union. **2** to organize (a workforce), or the workforce of (a company), into a trade union.

Union Jack the national flag of the United Kingdom, combining the crosses of St George, St Andrew, and St Patrick.

unique *adj.* **1** being the only one of its kind; having no equal. **2** (**unique to something** or **someone**) belonging solely to or associated solely with them. **3** *colloq.* extremely unusual or excellent. [from Latin *unicus*, from *unus*, one]

🔁 **1** *being the only one* single, one-off, sole, only, lone, solitary. *having no equal* unmatched, matchless, peerless, unequalled, unparalleled, unrivalled, incomparable, inimitable.
🔁 COMMON.

uniquely *adv.* in a unique way; to a unique degree.

unisex *adj.* suited to, for use by, or wearable by, both men and women.

unison *noun* **1** *Mus.* sameness of pitch in voices or instruments; the state of singing or playing all in the same pitch. **2** the state of acting all in the same way at the same time. **3** complete agreement. [from UNI- + Latin *sonus*, sound]

🔁 **2** concert, co-operation. **3** unanimity, unity.

unit — *noun* **1** a single item or element regarded as the smallest subdivision of a whole; a single person or thing. **2** a set of mechanical or electrical parts, or a group of workers, performing a specific function within a larger construction or organization. **3** a standard measure of a physical quantity, such as time or distance, specified multiples of which are used to express its size, eg SI units. **4** *Physics* a kilowatt-hour. **5** an item of furniture combining with others to form a set; a set of such items. **6** any whole number less than 10. **7** any subdivision of a military force. — *adj.* relating to the quantity of one: *unit mass*. [see UNITY]

🔁 *noun* **1** item, part, element, constituent, piece, entity, one. **2** section, module, component. **5** module.

Unitarian — *noun* a member of a religious group originally comprising Christians who believed God to be a single entity rather than a Trinity of Father, Son, and Holy Spirit, now including members holding a broad spectrum of beliefs. — *adj.* relating to this group. See also TRINITARIAN.

Unitarianism *noun* the beliefs of Unitarians.

unitary *adj.* **1** of a unit or units. **2** characterized by unity or uniformity.

unite *verb* **1** *trans., intrans.* to make or become a single unit or whole. **2** *trans., intrans.* to come together in a common purpose or belief. **3** to have (eg features or characteristics) in combination. [from Latin *unire*]

🔁 **1, 2** join, link, couple, marry, ally, co-operate, band, associate, federate, confederate, combine, pool, amalgamate, merge, blend, unify, consolidate, coalesce, fuse. **3** combine, marry, blend, ally.
🔁 **1, 2** separate, sever.

united *adj.* **1** joined together, combined. **2** in combination, resulting from union.

🔁 **1** allied, affiliated, corporate, unified. **2** combined, pooled, collective, concerted, one, unanimous, agreed, in agreement, in accord, like-minded.
🔁 DISUNITED.

unit price the price per item of goods supplied.

unit trust 1 an investment scheme in which clients' money is invested in various companies, with the combined shares purchased divided into units which are allocated in multiples to each client according to the individual amount invested. **2** a financial organization operating such a scheme.

unity *noun* (PL. **unities**) **1** the state of being a single unified whole; oneness. **2** a single unified whole. **3** agreement or harmony between different members or elements. **4** *Maths.* the number 1. [from Latin *unitas*, from *unus*, one]

. . . .

☐ **1** integrity, oneness, wholeness, union, unification. **3** agreement, harmony, accord, concord, peace, consensus, unanimity, solidarity.

☒ **1** disunity. **3** disunity, disagreement, discord, strife.

. . . .

Univ. *abbrev.* University.
univalency *noun Chem.* a univalent state.
univalent *adj. Chem.* monovalent, ie describing an atom of an element that has a valency of one.
universal *adj.* **1** of the universe. **2** of, relating to, or affecting the whole world or all people. **3** of, relating to, or affecting all the people or things in a particular group. **4** *colloq.* widespread; general; all-round.

. . . .

☐ **2** worldwide, global. **3** all-embracing, all-inclusive, across the board, total, whole, entire. **4** widespread, general, common, all-round.

. . . .

universal indicator *Chem.* a mixture of several chemical indicators, used to measure the pH (relative acidity or alkalinity) of a solution, that shows a whole range of different colours corresponding to different pH values.
universality *noun* being universal.
universal joint or **universal coupling** a joint allowing movement in all directions.
universally *adv.* in a universal way; everywhere.
universe *noun* **1** the cosmos, ie the whole of space and all the galaxies, stars, planets, moons, asteroids, and other bodies contained within it. **2** the world; all people. [from Latin *universus*, whole]
university *noun* (PL. **universities**) **1** a higher education institution with the authority to award degrees, traditionally in non-vocational subjects. **2** its buildings, staff, or students. [from Latin *universitas*, group of scholars]
univocalic — *adj.* using only one vowel. — *noun* writing, especially verse, that uses only one vowel throughout, as in *no fool so gross to bolt Scotch collops hot*, from a poem by C C Bombaugh written in 1890.
UNIX or **Unix** *noun trademark Comput.* a type of operating system designed to handle large file transfers and allow multi-user access of data. [from UNI-, influenced by *Multics*, an operating system developed in the 1960s]
unkempt *adj.* **1** *said of hair* uncombed. **2** *said of general appearance* untidy; dishevelled. [from Anglo-Saxon *uncembed*, uncombed]

. . . .

☐ **1** uncombed, tousled, untidy. **2** untidy, dishevelled, rumpled, ungroomed, messy, scruffy, shabby, slovenly.
☒ TIDY. **2** well-groomed.

. . . .

unkind *adj.* unsympathetic, cruel, or harsh.

. . . .

☐ unsympathetic, cruel, harsh, inhuman, inhumane, callous, hard-hearted, unfeeling, insensitive, thoughtless, inconsiderate, uncharitable, nasty, malicious, spiteful, mean, malevolent, unfriendly, uncaring.
☒ kind, considerate.

. . . .

unknown — *adj.* **1** not known; unfamiliar. **2** not at all famous. — *adv.* (**unknown to someone**) without their knowledge. — *noun* an unknown person or thing.

. . . .

☐ *adj.* **1** unfamiliar, unheard-of, strange, alien, foreign, mysterious, dark, obscure, hidden, concealed, undisclosed, secret, untold, new, uncharted, unexplored, undiscovered, unidentified, unnamed, nameless, anonymous, incognito.
☒ *adj.* WELL-KNOWN. **1** known, familiar.

. . . .

unknown quantity a person or thing whose precise identity, nature, or influence is not known or cannot be predicted.
unladen *adj.* not carrying a load.
unleaded *adj.*, *said of petrol* not containing lead additives, eg antiknocking agents.
unlearn *verb* (PAST TENSE AND PAST PARTICIPLE **unlearnt**, **unlearned**) **1** to try actively to forget; to rid one's memory of. **2** to free oneself from (eg an acquired habit).
unlearned [1] /ʌnˈlɜːnɪd/ *adj.* having no learning; uneducated.
unlearned [2] or **unlearnt** *adj.* **1** *said of a lesson, etc* not learnt. **2** *said of a skill, etc* not acquired by learning; instinctive; innate.
unleash *verb* **1** to release (eg a dog) from a leash. **2** to release or give free expression to (eg anger).
unleavened *adj.*, *said of bread* made without yeast, and therefore rather flat and hard.
unless *conj.* if not; except if. [from Middle English *unlesse*]
unlettered *adj.* **1** uneducated. **2** illiterate.
unlike — *prep.* **1** different from. **2** not typical or characteristic of. — *adj.* different; dissimilar.
unlikelihood or **unlikeliness** *noun* an unlikely state.
unlikely *adj.* **1** probably untrue. **2** not expected or likely. **3** not obviously suitable; improbable.

. . . .

☐ **1** implausible, far-fetched, unconvincing, unbelievable, incredible, unimaginable, improbable, dubious, suspect, suspicious, questionable. **2** unexpected, doubtful, questionable, improbable.
☒ LIKELY. **1** plausible.

. . . .

unlimited *adj.* **1** not limited or restricted. **2** *loosely* very great or numerous.

. . . .

☐ **1** limitless, unrestricted, unbounded, boundless, infinite, endless, absolute, unconditional, unqualified, all-encompassing, total, complete, full, unconstrained, unhampered. **2** countless, incalculable, immeasurable, vast, great, immense, extensive, indefinite.
☒ LIMITED.

. . . .

unlined *adj.* **1** not having a lining: *an unlined jacket*. **2** free from lines: *she had a youthful unlined face*.
unlisted *adj.* not entered on a list, especially on a list of telephone numbers or companies quoted on the Stock Exchange.
unlit *adj.* not having lights or lighting.
unload *verb* **1** *trans., intrans.* to remove (cargo) from (a vehicle). **2** *trans., intrans.* to remove the ammunition from (a gun). **3** to dispose of. **4** to relieve (oneself or one's mind) of troubles or anxieties by telling them to another; to get rid of (troubles) in this way.

. . . .

☐ **1** unpack, empty, offload, discharge, dump. **4** unburden, relieve, offload.
☒ **1, 2** load.

. . . .

unlock *verb* **1** to undo the lock of. **2** to free from being locked up. **3** to release or let loose.

. . . .

☐ **1** unbolt, unlatch, unfasten, undo, open. **2, 3** free, release.
☒ **1** lock, fasten.

. . . .

unlooked-for *adj.* **1** unexpected. **2** not deliberately encouraged or invited.
unloose or **unloosen** *verb* (**unloosened**, **unloosening**) **1** to make less tight; to loosen. **2** to set free.
unloved *adj.* not loved.

. . . .

☐ unpopular, disliked, hated, detested, unwanted, rejected, spurned, loveless, uncared-for, neglected.
☒ loved.

. . . .

unluckily *adv.* 1 in an unlucky way; as a result of bad luck. 2 I am sorry to say; unfortunately.

unlucky *adj.* (**unluckier, unluckiest**) 1 bringing, resulting from, or constituting bad luck. 2 having, or tending to have, bad luck.

. . . .

▣ ILL-FATED, ILL-STARRED, JINXED, DOOMED, CURSED. 1 unfavourable, inauspicious, ominous. 2 unfortunate, luckless, unsuccessful.
▣ LUCKY.

. . . .

unmade *adj.* 1 not yet made. 2 *said of a bed* with bedclothes not rearranged neatly after being slept in. 3 *said of a road* with no proper surface (eg of tarmac).

unmake *verb* to cancel or destroy the (especially beneficial) effect of.

unman *verb* (**unmanned, unmanning**) *old use, literary* to cause to lose self-control, especially to overcome with emotion.

unmanned *adj.* 1 *said especially of a vehicle or spacecraft* not manned, especially controlled remotely or automatically. 2 *old use, literary* deprived of self-control.

unmannerliness *noun* being unmannerly.

unmannerly *adj.* bad-mannered; impolite.

unmarried *adj.* not married, usually when never having been married.

. . . .

▣ single, on one's own, unwed, unattached, available, celibate.
▣ married.

. . . .

unmask *verb* 1 to remove a mask or disguise from. 2 to reveal the true identity or nature of.

. . . .

▣ UNVEIL, UNCLOAK, UNCOVER. 1 bare. 2 disclose, expose, reveal, show, discover, detect.
▣ MASK, DISGUISE. 2 conceal.

. . . .

unmentionable — *adj.* not fit to be mentioned or talked about, especially because considered indecent. — *noun* (**unmentionables**) *humorous* underwear.

. . . .

▣ *adj.* unspeakable, unutterable, taboo, indecent, shocking, scandalous, shameful, disgraceful, abominable.

. . . .

unmerciful *adj.* 1 merciless. 2 unpleasantly great or extreme.

unmistakable or **unmistakeable** *adj.* too easily recognizable to be mistaken for anything or anyone else.

. . . .

▣ clear, plain, distinct, patent, glaring, explicit, unambiguous, unequivocal, positive, definite, sure, certain, unquestionable, indisputable, undeniable, pronounced, obvious, evident, manifest.
▣ unclear, ambiguous.

. . . .

unmistakably or **unmistakeably** *adv.* in an unmistakable way; as is unmistakable.

unmitigated *adj.* 1 not lessened or made less severe. 2 unqualified; absolute; out-and-out: *an unmitigated rogue.*

unmoved *adj.* 1 still in the same place. 2 not persuaded. 3 not affected by emotion.

. . . .

▣ 2 resolute, resolved, determined, unimpressed, firm, adamant, inflexible, unbending, undeviating, unwavering, steady, unchanged. 3 unaffected, indifferent, impassive, dispassionate, unresponsive, untouched, unshaken, dry-eyed, unfeeling, cold.
▣ MOVED. 3 affected, shaken.

. . . .

unnamed *adj.* 1 not named or specified; anonymous. 2 not baptized.

unnatural *adj.* 1 contrary to the way things usually happen in nature. 2 contrary to ordinary human nature, especially intensely evil, cruel, or disgusting. 3 insincere; affected.

. . . .

▣ 1 abnormal, anomalous, freakish, irregular, unusual, strange, odd, peculiar, queer, bizarre, extraordinary, uncanny, supernatural. 2 inhuman, perverted. 3 affected, insincere, artificial, false, feigned, unspontaneous, contrived, laboured, stilted, forced, strained, self-conscious, stiff.
▣ 1 natural, normal. 3 natural, sincere.

. . . .

unnaturally *adv.* in an unnatural way; to an unnatural degree.

unnerve *verb* 1 to weaken the courage or confidence of. 2 to cause to feel ill at ease.

. . . .

▣ 1 discourage, demoralize, intimidate, daunt, frighten, scare. 2 disconcert, upset, worry, shake, *colloq.* rattle, confound, fluster.
▣ 1 nerve, brace, steel.

. . . .

unnerving *adj.* that unnerves, unsettling.

unnilpentium *noun Chem.* (SYMBOL **Unp**, ATOMIC NUMBER **105**) an artificially manufactured metallic element that has six isotopes, all with half-lives of a fraction of a second; sometimes referred to as nielsbohrium.

unnilquadium *noun Chem.* (SYMBOL **Unq**, ATOMIC NUMBER **104**) a radioactive metallic element, formed by bombarding californium with carbon nuclei, that has 10 isotopes with half-lives of up to 70 seconds.

unnilseptium *noun Chem.* (SYMBOL **Uns**, ATOMIC NUMBER **107**) an artificially manufactured radioactive chemical element.

unnumbered *adj.* 1 not given a number. 2 too numerous to be counted; innumerable.

UNO *abbrev.* United Nations Organization.

unobtrusive *adj.* not noticeable or prominent.

. . . .

▣ inconspicuous, unnoticeable, unostentatious, unpretentious, restrained, low-key, subdued, quiet, retiring, unassertive, self-effacing, humble, modest.
▣ obtrusive, ostentatious.

. . . .

unpack *verb* 1 to take out of a packed state. 2 to empty (eg a suitcase) of packed contents.

unpaid *adj.* not paid: *unpaid bills / an unpaid job.*

. . . .

▣ outstanding, overdue, unsettled, owing, due, payable. *work* voluntary, honorary, unsalaried, unwaged, unremunerative, free.
▣ paid.

. . . .

unparalleled *adj.* so remarkable as to have no equal or parallel.

. . . .

▣ unequalled, unmatched, matchless, peerless, incomparable, unrivalled, unsurpassed, supreme, superlative, rare, exceptional, unprecedented.

. . . .

unparliamentary *adj.* contrary to the established procedures by which, or to the spirit in which, a parliament is conducted.

unperson *noun* a person whose existence is officially denied or ignored, often by removing his or her name from official records.

unpick *verb* to undo (stitches); to take (a sewn article) to pieces by undoing the stitching.

unpleasant *adj.* not pleasant; disagreeable.

. . . .

▣ disagreeable, nasty, objectionable, offensive, distasteful, unpalatable, unattractive, repulsive, bad, troublesome, ill-natured.

🔁 pleasant, agreeable, nice.

unpleasantly *adv.* in an unpleasant way; to an unpleasant extent.

unpleasantness *noun* 1 the quality of being unpleasant. 2 *euphemistic* an unpleasant incident, especially a disagreement involving open hostility.

unplug *verb* to remove the plug from.

unpopular *adj.* generally disliked.

▣ disliked, hated, detested, unloved, unsought-after, unfashionable, undesirable, unwelcome, unwanted, rejected, shunned, avoided, neglected.
🔁 popular, fashionable.

unpopularity *noun* an unpopular state or quality.

unpractical *adj.* having no practical skills; not good at practical tasks. See also IMPRACTICAL.

unpractised *adj.* 1 having had little or no practice or experience. 2 not or not yet put into practice.

unprecedented *adj.* not known to have ever happened before; without precedent.

▣ new, original, revolutionary, unknown, unheard-of, exceptional, remarkable, extraordinary, abnormal, unusual, freakish, unparalleled, unrivalled.
🔁 usual.

unprepossessing *adj.* 1 unappealing; unattractive. 2 not creating or likely to create a good impression.

unprincipled *adj.* having or showing a lack of moral principles.

unprintable *adj.* not fit to be printed, especially because of being obscene or libellous.

unprofessional *adj.* violating the rules governing, or the standards of conduct expected of, members of a particular profession.

▣ amateurish, inexpert, unskilled, sloppy, incompetent, inefficient, casual, negligent, lax, unethical, unprincipled, improper, unseemly, unacceptable, inadmissible.
🔁 professional, skilful.

unprotected sex sexual intercourse without the use of a condom or other contraception.

unputdownable *adj. colloq.*, *said of a book* so absorbing as to compel one to read to the end without a break.

unqualified *adj.* 1 not having any formal qualifications; lacking the formal qualifications required for a particular job, etc. 2 not limited or moderated in any way. 3 absolute; out-and-out: *an unqualified success.* 4 not competent.

▣ 1 untrained, inexperienced, unskilled, amateur. 2 unmitigated, unreserved, wholehearted, outright, unconditional, unrestricted. 3 absolute, out-and-out, categorical, utter, total, complete, thorough, consummate, downright. 4 incompetent, incapable, ill-equipped, ineligible, unfit.
🔁 1 qualified, professional. 2 conditional, tentative.

unquestionable *adj.* beyond doubt or question.

unquestionably *adv.* as cannot be questioned; undoubtedly.

unquestioning *adj.* not arguing or protesting; done, etc without argument or protest.

unquestioningly *adv.* without questioning or protesting.

unquiet *literary* — *adj.* anxious; ill at ease; restless. — *noun* disquiet.

unquote *interj.* used in speech to indicate the end of a quotation. See also QUOTE.

unravel *verb trans., intrans.* (**unravelled, unravelling**) 1 to take or come out of a knitted or woven state back into a strand or strands. 2 to take or come out of a tangled state. 3 to make or become clear after being confusing or obscure.

▣ 1 unwind, undo. 2 untangle, disentangle, unwind, undo, free, extricate, separate. 3 resolve, sort out, solve, work out, figure out, puzzle out, penetrate, interpret, explain.
🔁 2 tangle. 3 complicate.

unread *adj.* 1 *said of a book, etc* that has not been read. 2 *said of a person* having read few books.

unreadable *adj.* 1 illegible. 2 too difficult to read. 3 not worth reading.

unready *adj.* 1 not ready. 2 not acting quickly; hesitant.

unreal *adj.* 1 not real; illusory or imaginary. 2 *colloq.* exceptionally strange, ridiculous, or excellent.

▣ 1 false, artificial, synthetic, mock, fake, sham, imaginary, visionary, fanciful, make-believe, *colloq.* pretend, fictitious, made-up, fairy-tale, legendary, mythical, illusory, immaterial, insubstantial, hypothetical. 2 fantastic.
🔁 1 real, genuine.

unreality *noun* lack of reality.

unrelenting *adj.* 1 refusing to change viewpoint or chosen course of action. 2 not softened by feelings of mercy or pity. 3 constant; relentless; never stopping.

▣ 1 uncompromising, inexorable. 2 remorseless, unmerciful, merciless, pitiless, unsparing. 3 relentless, constant, continual, perpetual, continuous, steady, unabated, incessant, unceasing, ceaseless, endless, unremitting, unbroken, remorseless.
🔁 3 spasmodic, intermittent.

unremitting *adj.* not easing off or abating; constant; never stopping.

unrequited *adj.*, *said of love* not felt in return by the loved person.

unreserved *adj.* 1 not booked or reserved. 2 open and sociable in manner; showing no shyness or reserve. 3 not moderated or limited; unqualified.

unreservedly *adv.* without reservation.

unrest *noun* 1 a state of (especially public) discontent bordering on riotousness. 2 anxiety; unease.

▣ 1 discontent, dissension, disaffection, protest, rebellion. 2 anxiety, unease, worry, turmoil, agitation, restlessness, dissatisfaction.
🔁 PEACE, CALM.

unrivalled *adj.* far better than any other; unequalled.

▣ unequalled, unparalleled, unmatched, matchless, peerless, incomparable, inimitable, unsurpassed, supreme, superlative.

unroll *verb trans., intrans.* 1 to open out from a rolled state. 2 *intrans.* to become unrolled.

unruffled *adj.* 1 *said of a surface* smooth. 2 *said of a person* not agitated or flustered.

▣ 1 undisturbed, smooth, level, even. 2 collected, composed, cool, calm, tranquil, serene, peaceful, untroubled, imperturbable.
🔁 2 anxious, troubled.

unruliness *noun* 1 being unruly. 2 unruly behaviour.

unruly *adj.* (**unrulier, unruliest**) noisily disobedient or disorderly, especially habitually.

▣ uncontrollable, unmanageable, ungovernable, intractable, disorderly, insubordinate, disobedient, wayward, wild, rowdy, wilful, headstrong, obstreperous, riotous, rebellious, mutinous, lawless.

▣ manageable, orderly.

unsaddle *verb* **1** to take the saddle off (a horse). **2** to throw (a rider) from a horse; to unhorse.

unsafe *adj.* **1** not safe or secure; dangerous. **2** *said of a conclusion or decision* based on insufficient or suspect evidence.

▣ **1** dangerous, perilous, risky, hazardous, treacherous, unstable, precarious, insecure, vulnerable, exposed. **2** unsound, unreliable, uncertain.
▣ SAFE. **1** secure.

unsaid *adj.* not said, especially when it might have been or should have been said. See also UNSAY.

unsaturated *adj. Chem.* **1** *said of an organic chemical compound* containing at least one double or triple bond between its carbon atoms, eg unsaturated fats. **2** *said of a solution* not containing the maximum amount of a solid or gas (*solute*) that can be dissolved in it.

unsavoury *adj.* unpleasant or distasteful.

unsay *verb* (PAST TENSE AND PAST PARTICIPLE **unsaid**) to take back or withdraw (something said). See also UNSAID.

unscathed *adj.* not harmed or injured.

▣ unhurt, uninjured, unharmed, undamaged, untouched, whole, intact, safe, sound.
▣ hurt, injured.

unscramble *verb* **1** to interpret (a coded or scrambled message). **2** to take out of a jumbled state and put in order.

unscrew *verb* **1** to remove or loosen by taking out screws, or with a twisting or screwing action. **2** to loosen (a screw).

unscrupulous *adj.* without scruples or moral principles.

▣ unprincipled, ruthless, shameless, dishonourable, dishonest, *colloq.* crooked, corrupt, immoral, unethical, improper.
▣ scrupulous, ethical, proper.

unseasonable *adj.* **1** not appropriate to the time of year. **2** coming at a bad time; inopportune.

unseat *verb* **1** to remove from an official post or position, especially a parliamentary seat. **2** to throw or knock off a seat, or off a horse.

unseemliness *noun* being unseemly.

unseemly *adj.* not fitting, especially because of being indecent.

▣ improper, indelicate, indecorous, unbecoming, undignified, unrefined, disreputable, discreditable, undue, inappropriate, unsuitable.
▣ seemly, decorous.

unseen *adj.* **1** not seen or noticed. **2** *of a text for translation* not seen in advance by the examinee.

▣ **1** unnoticed, unobserved, undetected, invisible, hidden, concealed, veiled, obscure.
▣ **1** visible.

unselfish *adj.* having or showing concern for others; generous-spirited.

▣ selfless, altruistic, generous-spirited, self-denying, self-sacrificing, disinterested, noble, magnanimous, generous, liberal, charitable, philanthropic, public-spirited, humanitarian, kind.
▣ selfish.

unsettle *verb* **1** to disturb from a fixed or stable position or state. **2** to cause to become ill at ease.

▣ **1** disturb, upset, unbalance, shake. **2** trouble, bother, discompose, ruffle, fluster, agitate, *colloq.* rattle, disconcert, confuse, *colloq.* throw.

unsettled *adj.* **1** lacking stability; changing or likely to change. **2** not relaxed or at ease. **3** *said of a debt* unpaid.

▣ **1** changeable, variable, unpredictable, inconstant, unstable, insecure, unsteady, shaky, undecided, uncertain, unresolved, undetermined, open, doubtful. **2** anxious, uneasy, disturbed, upset, troubled, agitated, tense, edgy, flustered, shaken, unnerved, disoriented, confused. **3** unpaid, outstanding, owing, payable, overdue.
▣ **1** certain, settled. **2** composed. **3** paid.

unshakable or **unshakeable** *adj.*, *said of beliefs, or the person holding them* firm; steadfast.

▣ firm, well-founded, fixed, stable, immovable, unassailable, unwavering, constant, steadfast, staunch, sure, resolute, determined.
▣ insecure.

unsightliness *noun* being unsightly.

unsightly *adj.* (**unsightlier**, **unsightliest**) not pleasant to look at; ugly.

▣ ugly, unattractive, unprepossessing, hideous, repulsive, repugnant, *colloq.* off-putting, unpleasant, disagreeable.
▣ attractive.

unskilled *adj.* not having or requiring any special skill or training.

▣ untrained, unqualified, inexperienced, unpractised, inexpert, unprofessional, amateurish, incompetent.
▣ skilled.

unsociable *adj.* disliking or avoiding the company of other people.

▣ unfriendly, aloof, distant, standoffish, withdrawn, introverted, reclusive, retiring, reserved, taciturn, unforthcoming, uncommunicative, cold, chilly, uncongenial, unneighbourly, inhospitable, hostile.
▣ sociable, friendly.

unsocial *adj.* **1** annoying, or likely to annoy, other people; antisocial. **2** *said of working hours* falling outside the normal working day.

unsold *adj.* not sold.

unsophisticated *adj.* **1** not sophisticated. **2** free from insincerity or artificiality.

▣ **1** unrefined, plain, simple, straightforward, uncomplicated, uninvolved. **2** artless, guileless, innocent, ingenuous, naïve, inexperienced, unworldly, childlike, natural, unaffected, unpretentious.
▣ **1** sophisticated, worldly.

unsound *adj.* **1** not reliable; not based on sound reasoning. **2** not firm or solid. — **of unsound mind** *Legal* mentally ill; insane.

▣ **1** faulty, flawed, defective, ill-founded, fallacious, false, erroneous, invalid, illogical. **2** unstable, unsteady, wobbly, shaky, insecure, unsafe, weak, frail. **of unsound**

mind insane, unbalanced, deranged.
🔊 SOUND.

. . . .

unsparing *adj.* **1** giving generously or liberally. **2** showing no mercy.

unspeakable *adj.* **1** not able to be expressed in words. **2** too bad, wicked, or obscene to be spoken about.

. . . .

🔲 **1** unutterable, inexpressible, indescribable. **2** awful, dreadful, frightful, terrible, horrible, shocking, appalling, monstrous, inconceivable, unbelievable.

. . . .

unspent *adj.* not spent.

unstinting *adj.* giving (eg praise) generously or liberally.

unstop *verb* **1** to free from being stopped or blocked. **2** to draw out the stop or stopper from.

unstoppable *adj. colloq.* whose progress can not be stopped.

unstrung *adj.* **1** with strings removed. **2** unnerved.

unstuck *adj.* loosened or released from a stuck state. — **come unstuck** *said of a plan, etc* to go wrong.

unstudied *adj.* not affected; natural and spontaneous.

unsung *adj.*, *said of people or their achievements* not praised or recognized.

🔲 unpraised, unacknowledged, unrecognized, unhonoured, overlooked, disregarded, neglected, forgotten, unknown, obscure.
🔊 honoured, famous, renowned.

. . . .

unsure *adj.* **1** uncertain, doubtful: *he was unsure if the painting was genuine.* **2** precarious: *an unsure foothold.* **3** insecure; not assured: *he was unsure of himself in large gatherings of people.* **4** untrustworthy: *an unsure character.*

. . . .

🔲 **1** uncertain, doubtful, dubious, suspicious, sceptical, unconvinced, unpersuaded, undecided, hesitant, tentative.
🔊 **1** certain, sure. **3** sure, confident, assured.

. . . .

unswerving *adj.* not deviating from a belief or aim; steadfast.

untamed *adj.* not tame; wild.

untangle *verb* to disentangle.

. . . .

🔲 disentangle, extricate, unravel, undo, resolve, solve.
🔊 tangle, complicate.

. . . .

untaxed *adj.* **1** not taxed. **2** not charged with any fault.

unthinkable *adj.* **1** too unusual to be likely; inconceivable. **2** too unpleasant to think about.

. . . .

🔲 **1** inconceivable, unimaginable, unheard-of, unbelievable, incredible, impossible, improbable, unlikely, implausible, unreasonable, illogical, absurd, preposterous. **2** outrageous, shocking.

. . . .

unthinking *adj.* **1** inconsiderate. **2** careless.

. . . .

🔲 **1** thoughtless, inconsiderate, insensitive, tactless, indiscreet, rude, impulsive, instinctive, unconscious, automatic, mechanical. **2** careless, heedless, negligent, rash.
🔊 CONSIDERATE.

. . . .

unthrone *verb* to dethrone.

untidily *adv.* in an untidy or disorderly way.

untidy — *adj.* (**untidier, untidiest**) not tidy; messy, disordered. — *verb* (**untidies, untidied**) to make untidy (something that was previously tidy).

. . . .

🔲 *adj.* messy, cluttered, disordered, disorderly, muddled, jumbled, unsystematic, chaotic, topsy-turvy,

scruffy, dishevelled, unkempt, slovenly, sloppy, slipshod.
🔊 *adj.* tidy, neat.

. . . .

untie *verb* **1** to undo from a tied state. **2** to remove the constraints on; to set free.

. . . .

🔲 **1** undo, unfasten, unknot, unbind. **2** free, release, loose, loosen.
🔊 TIE. **1** fasten.

. . . .

until — *prep.* **1** up to the time of. **2** up to the time of reaching (a place); as far as: *slept until Paris.* **3** (*with a negative*) before: *not until Wednesday.* — *conj.* **1** up to the time that. **2** (*with a negative*) before: *not until I say so.* [see TILL[1]]

untimeliness *noun* being untimely.

untimely *adj.* **1** happening before the proper or expected time. **2** coming at an inappropriate or inconvenient time.

. . . .

🔲 **1** early, premature, unseasonable. **2** ill-timed, inopportune, inconvenient, awkward, unsuitable, inappropriate, unfortunate, inauspicious.
🔊 TIMELY. **2** opportune.

. . . .

unto *prep. old use* to.

untold *adj.* **1** not told. **2** too severe to be described. **3** too many to be counted.

. . . .

🔲 **2** indescribable, unimaginable. **3** uncounted, unnumbered, unreckoned, incalculable, innumerable, uncountable, countless, infinite, measureless, boundless, inexhaustible, undreamed-of, unimaginable.

. . . .

untouchable — *adj.* **1** not to be touched or handled. **2** discouraging physical contact. **3** above the law. — *noun* **1** an untouchable person or thing. **2** *formerly* in India, a member of the lowest social class, or caste, whose touch was regarded by members of higher castes as a contamination.

untoward *adj.* **1** inconvenient; unfortunate. **2** adverse; unfavourable.

untried *adj.* **1** not attempted or tested. **2** not yet submitted to a legal trial.

. . . .

🔲 **1** untested, unproved, experimental, exploratory, new, novel, innovative, innovatory.
🔊 TRIED. **1** tested, proven.

. . . .

untrue *adj.* **1** not true. **2** not accurate. **3** unfaithful.

. . . .

🔲 **1, 2** false, fallacious, deceptive, misleading, wrong, incorrect, inaccurate, mistaken, erroneous. **3** unfaithful, disloyal, untrustworthy, dishonest, deceitful, untruthful.
🔊 **1, 2** true, correct. **3** faithful, honest.

. . . .

untruth *noun* **1** the fact of being untrue. **2** a lie.

. . . .

🔲 **1** fiction, invention, fabrication, falsehood, untruthfulness. **2** lie, *colloq.* fib, *colloq.* whopper, story, tale, fiction, invention, fabrication, falsehood, deceit.
🔊 TRUTH.

. . . .

untruthful *adj.* not truthful; lying.

. . . .

🔲 lying, deceitful, dishonest, *colloq.* crooked, hypocritical, two-faced, insincere, false, untrue.
🔊 truthful, honest.

. . . .

unused *adj.* **1** brand new; never used. **2** (**unused to something**) not used or accustomed to it.

. . . .

🔲 **1** new, fresh, blank, clean, untouched, left-over,

remaining, surplus, extra, spare, available, unexploited, unemployed, idle.

☒ **1** used.

unusual *adj.* not usual; uncommon; rare.

▤ uncommon, rare, unfamiliar, strange, odd, curious, queer, bizarre, *colloq.* left-field, unconventional, irregular, abnormal, extraordinary, remarkable, exceptional, different, surprising, unexpected.
☒ usual, normal, ordinary.

unusually *adv.* in an unusual way; to an unusual degree.

unutterable *adj.* so extreme or intense as to be impossible to express in words.

unvarnished *adj.*, *said of an account or report* not exaggerated or embellished.

unveil *verb* **1** to remove a veil from (a person's face). **2** *intrans.* to remove one's veil. **3** to remove a curtain or other covering from (a plaque, etc) as part of a formal opening ceremony. **4** to reveal or make known for the first time.

▤ **1, 3** uncover, expose, bare, reveal. **4** reveal, disclose, divulge, discover.
☒ **1, 3** cover. **4** conceal, hide.

unveiling *noun* **1** removal of a veil. **2** the ceremony of opening or presenting something new.

unvoiced *adj.* **1** unspoken. **2** *Phonetics* pronounced without vibrating the vocal cords; voiceless.

unwaged *adj.* not in paid employment.

unwell *adj.* ill.

▤ ill, sick, poorly, indisposed, *Brit.* off-colour, ailing, sickly, unhealthy.
☒ well, healthy.

unwieldiness *noun* being unwieldy.

unwieldy *adj.* large and awkward to carry or manage; cumbersome. [from WIELD]

▤ unmanageable, cumbersome, awkward, clumsy, bulky, massive, hefty, weighty, ponderous, inconvenient, ungainly.
☒ handy, dainty.

unwilling *adj.* having or showing a lack of willingness; reluctant.

▤ reluctant, disinclined, loath, slow, unenthusiastic, grudging, indisposed, resistant, opposed, averse.
☒ willing, enthusiastic.

unwind *verb* (PAST TENSE AND PAST PARTICIPLE **unwound**) **1** *trans.*, *intrans.* to take or come out of a coiled or wound position. **2** *intrans. colloq.* to relax.

▤ **1** unroll, uncoil, untwist, unravel, unreel, unwrap, undo, disentangle. **2** relax, wind down, calm down.
☒ **1** wind, coil, roll.

unwise *adj.* not prudent; ill-advised; foolish.

unwisely *adv.* in an unwise way.

unwitting *adj.* **1** not realizing or being aware. **2** done without being realized or intended. [from WIT]

▤ **1** unaware, unknowing, unsuspecting. **2** unconscious, involuntary, accidental, chance, inadvertent, unintentional, unintended, unplanned, unthinking.
☒ KNOWING, CONSCIOUS. **2** deliberate.

unwittingly *adv.* without knowing.

unwonted *adj.* not usual or habitual. [from WONT]

unwound see UNWIND.

unwritten *adj.* **1** not recorded in writing or print. **2** *said of a rule or law* not formally enforceable, but traditionally accepted and followed.

▤ **1** verbal, oral, word of mouth, unrecorded. **2** tacit, implicit, understood, accepted, recognized, traditional, customary, conventional.
☒ **1** written, recorded.

unzip *verb* (**unzipped**, **unzipping**) to unfasten or open by undoing a zip.

up — *prep.* at or to a higher position on, or a position further along: *climbed up the stairs / walking up the road.* — *adv.* **1** at or to a higher position or level: *lift it up / turn up the volume / prices went up.* **2** at or to a place higher up, or a more northerly place. **3** in or to a more erect position: *stood up.* **4** fully or completely: *use up / eat up.* **5** into the state of being gathered together: *saved up for it / parcel up the presents.* **6** in or to a place of storage or lodging: *put them up for the night.* **7** out of bed: *got up.* **8** to or towards: *went up to the town / travelling up to London / walked up to him.* — *adj.* **1** placed in, or moving or directed to, a higher position. **2** out of bed: *he's not up yet.* **3** having an advantage; ahead: *two goals up / £5 up after the first bet.* **4** *said of a road* under repair. **5** appearing in court: *up before the judge.* **6** *said of the sun* above the horizon. **7** relating to or providing (especially rail) transport to, rather than away from, a major place: *the up train.* — *verb* (**upped**, **upping**) **1** to raise or increase. **2** *intrans. colloq.* to proceed boldly or unexpectedly to act or speak; to get up (and do something): *he upped and left her.* — *noun* **1** a success or advantage. **2** a spell of good luck or prosperity. — **be well up on** or **in something** to have a thorough knowledge of it. **it's all up with someone** *colloq.* there is no hope for them. **not up to much** *colloq.* not good at all; no good. **on the up-and-up** *colloq.* **1** steadily becoming more successful. **2** honest; on the level. **something is up** something is wrong or amiss. **up against someone** or **something 1** situated or pressed close against them. **2** faced with difficulties, etc. **up and about** or **up and doing** out of bed and active. **up for something 1** presented or offered for (eg discussion or sale). **2** under consideration for a job or post. **up front** *colloq.* **1** openly or candidly. **2** *said of money paid* in advance. **up to ...** **1** immersed or embedded as far as ... **2** dependent on: *it's up to you.* **3** capable of ...; equal to: *are you up to meeting them?* **4** thinking about doing or engaged in doing: *was up to his usual tricks.* **5** as good as: *not up to his standard.* **up to the minute** completely up to date. **up with ...** **1** abreast of ... **2** even with ... **3** an expression of enthusiastic approval or support: *up with Christmas!* **what's up?** what's the matter? what's wrong? [from Anglo-Saxon *up* or *upp*]

up-and-coming *adj.* beginning to become successful or well known.

upbeat — *adj. colloq.* cheerful; optimistic. — *noun Mus.* the unstressed beat, at which a conductor raises the baton.

upbraid *verb* to scold or reproach. [from Anglo-Saxon *upbregdan*]

▤ reproach, scold, reprimand, admonish, rebuke, reprove, chide, castigate, berate, criticize, censure.
☒ praise, commend.

upbringing *noun* the all-round instruction and education of a child, intended to form his or her character and values.

▤ bringing-up, raising, rearing, breeding, parenting, care, nurture, cultivation, education, training, instruction, teaching.

up-country — *adj.*, *adv.* to or in the regions away from the coast; inland. — *noun* the inland regions.

update — *verb* (with stress on -*date*) to make or bring up to date. — *noun* (with stress on *up*-) an act of updating.

· ·

▤ *verb* modernize, revise, amend, correct, renew, renovate, revamp.

· ·

up-end *verb* **1** to turn upside down. **2** to put into disorder or disarray.

upfront *adj. colloq.* **1** candid; open. **2** *said of money* paid in advance.

upgrade *verb* **1** to promote (a person). **2** to increase the grade or status of (a job or post). **3** to improve the quality of. **4** to improve (a computer or other piece of equipment) by replacing an out-of-date component with a new one.

· ·

▤ 1 promote, elevate. **2** elevate, promote, advance, raise. **3** improve, enhance.
▣ DOWNGRADE. **1** demote.

· ·

upheaval *noun* a change or disturbance that greatly disrupts.

· · · · · · · · · · · · · · · · · · · ·

▤ disruption, disturbance, upset, chaos, confusion, disorder, turmoil, *colloq.* shake-up, revolution, overthrow.

· ·

upheld see UPHOLD.

Up-Helly-Aa /ˌʌpˈhɛlɪɑː/ *noun* a midwinter festival, derived from an older Celtic fire festival, held on the last Tuesday of January in Lerwick, Shetland. It now includes guisers and the ceremonial burning of a replica Viking long boat. [from *up*, at an end, finished + Scots *haliday*, holiday; ie the end of the Yule holiday]

uphill — *adj.* **1** sloping upwards; ascending. **2** *said of a task, etc* requiring great effort; arduous. — *adv.* up a slope.

· · · · · · · · · · · · · · · · · · · ·

▤ *adj.* **2** hard, difficult, arduous, tough, taxing, strenuous, laborious, tiring, wearisome, exhausting, gruelling, punishing.
▣ *adj.* **2** easy.

· ·

uphold *verb* (PAST TENSE AND PAST PARTICIPLE **upheld**) **1** to support (an action), defend (a right) or maintain (the law). **2** to declare (eg a court judgement) to be correct or just; to confirm.

· · · · · · · · · · · · · · · · · · · ·

▤ 1 support, maintain, stand by, defend, champion, advocate, promote, back, sustain, fortify, strengthen, justify, vindicate. **2** confirm, endorse, hold to.
▣ REJECT. **1** abandon.

· ·

upholster *verb* (**upholstered**, **upholstering**) to fit with upholstery. [from UPHOLD, in the obsolete meaning 'to keep in good condition']

upholstered *adj.* fitted with upholstery.

upholsterer *noun* a person who upholsters furniture.

upholstery *noun* **1** the springs, stuffing, and covers of a chair or sofa. **2** the work of an upholsterer.

UPI *abbrev.* United Press International.

upkeep *noun* the task of keeping something in good order or condition, or the cost of this.

· · · · · · · · · · · · · · · · · · · ·

▤ maintenance, preservation, conservation, care, running, repair, support, sustenance, subsistence, keep.

· ·

upland *noun* (*often* **uplands**) a high or hilly region.

uplift — *verb* (with stress on *-lift*) **1** to fill with an invigorating happiness, optimism, or awareness of the spiritual nature of things. **2** *formal* to lift up; to collect. — *noun* (with stress on *up-*) an uplifting influence or effect.

uplifting *adj.* cheering, inspiring with hope.

upload *verb intrans., trans. Comput.* to send (data) from one computer to another, eg by means of a telephone line and modem.

up-market *adj.* high in price, quality, or prestige.

upmost *adj., adv.* uppermost.

upon *prep.* on or on to. — **upon my word**! *old use* an exclamation of surprise.

upper — *adj.* **1** higher; situated above. **2** high or higher in rank or status. — *noun* **1** the part of a shoe above the sole. **2** *slang* a drug that induces euphoria. — **on one's uppers** *colloq.* extremely short of money; destitute.

· · · · · · · · · · · · · · · · · · · ·

▤ *adj.* HIGHER. **1** loftier. **2** superior, senior, top, topmost, uppermost, high, elevated, exalted, eminent, important.
▣ *adj.* LOWER. **2** inferior, junior.

· ·

upper-case *adj.* consisting of capital letters.

upper class the highest social class; the aristocracy.

upper-class *adj.* belonging or relating to the upper class.

upper crust *noun. colloq.* the upper class.

upper-crust *adj. colloq.* same as UPPER-CLASS.

uppercut *noun* a forceful upward blow with the fist, usually under the chin.

upper hand (**the upper hand**) a position of advantage or dominance.

upper house or **upper chamber** the second and normally smaller part of a two-chamber (bicameral) parliament, such as the House of Lords in the UK.

uppermost *adj., adv.* at, in or into the highest or most prominent position.

· · · · · · · · · · · · · · · · · · · ·

▤ *adj.* highest, loftiest, top, topmost, greatest, supreme, first, primary, foremost, leading, principal, main, chief, dominant, predominant, paramount, pre-eminent.
▣ *adj.* lowest.

· ·

uppish or **uppity** *adj. colloq.* arrogant or snobbish. [from UP]

upright — *adj.* **1** standing straight up; erect or vertical. **2** having integrity or moral correctness. — *adv.* into an upright position. — *noun* **1** a vertical (usually supporting) post or pole. **2** an upright piano.

· · · · · · · · · · · · · · · · · · · ·

▤ *adj.* **1** erect, vertical, perpendicular, straight. **2** righteous, good, virtuous, upstanding, noble, honourable, ethical, principled, incorruptible, honest, trustworthy.
▣ *adj.* **1** horizontal, flat. **2** dishonest.

· ·

upright piano a piano with strings arranged vertically in a case above the keyboard.

uprising *noun* a rebellion or revolt.

· · · · · · · · · · · · · · · · · · · ·

▤ rebellion, revolt, mutiny, rising, insurgence, insurrection, revolution.

· ·

uproar *noun* an outbreak of noisy and boisterous behaviour, especially angry protest. [from Dutch *oproer*, from *oproeren*, to stir up]

· · · · · · · · · · · · · · · · · · · ·

▤ noise, din, racket, hubbub, *colloq.* hullabaloo, pandemonium, tumult, turmoil, turbulence, commotion, confusion, disorder, clamour, outcry, furore, riot, rumpus.

· ·

uproarious *adj.* **1** *said of laughter* loud and unrestrained. **2** provoking such laughter.

uproariously *adv.* in an uproarious way, with uproar.

uproot *verb* **1** to pull (a plant) out of the ground completely, with the root attached. **2** to take completely away from surroundings settled into.

· · · · · · · · · · · · · · · · · · · ·

▤ 1 pull up, rip up, root out, weed out. **2** move, remove, displace, eradicate, destroy, wipe out.

· ·

ups-a-daisy or **upsy-daisy** *interj.* an expression of encouragement to a child one is lifting up, or helping up from a fall.

ups and downs spells of success and failure; changes of fortune.

upscale *adj. colloq.* of or designed to appeal to the wealthier in society; up-market.

upset — *verb* (with stress on *-set*) (**upsetting**; PAST TENSE AND PAST PARTICIPLE **upset**) **1** to cause to be emotionally distressed. **2** to ruin or spoil (eg plans). **3** to disturb the proper balance or function of (a person's stomach). **4** to knock over. — *noun* (with stress on *up-*) **1** a disturbance, eg of plans or digestion. **2** an unexpected result or outcome. — *adj.* emotionally distressed.

....

☰ *verb* **1** distress, grieve, dismay, trouble, worry, agitate, disturb, bother, fluster, ruffle, discompose, shake, unnerve, disconcert, confuse, disorganize. **4** tip, spill, overturn, capsize, topple, overthrow, destabilize, unsteady. *noun* **1** disturbance, disruption, upheaval, *colloq.* shake-up, reverse, surprise, shock, trouble, bother, worry, agitation. *stomach upset* disorder, complaint, *colloq.* bug, illness, sickness. *adj.* distressed, grieved, hurt, annoyed, dismayed, troubled, worried, agitated, disturbed, bothered, shaken, disconcerted, confused.

....

upset price the lowest price a seller will accept, and the price at which bidding starts at an auction.

upsetting *adj.* causing upset.

upshot *noun* (**the upshot**) the final outcome or ultimate effect.

....

☰ result, consequence, outcome, issue, end, conclusion, finish, culmination.

....

upside *noun* **1** the upper part or side of anything. **2** *colloq.* a positive or favourable aspect.

upside down *adj., adv.* (*also, as adj.,* **upside-down**) **1** with the top part at the bottom; upturned or inverted. **2** in or into complete confusion or disorder.

....

☰ **1** inverted, upturned, wrong way up, upset, overturned. **2** disordered, muddled, jumbled, confused, topsy-turvy, chaotic.

....

upsides *adj.* (**upsides with someone**) *Brit. colloq.* even with them, especially through revenge or retaliation.

upstage — *adj., adv.* **1** at or towards the back of a theatre stage. **2** *slang* arrogant or arrogantly. — *verb* **1** to move upstage and force (an actor) to turn his or her back to the audience when speaking to one. **2** to direct attention away from (a person) on to oneself.

upstairs — *adj., adv.* **1** on or to an upper floor. **2** *colloq.* in or to a senior or more senior position. — *noun* an upper floor, especially the part of a house above the ground floor.

upstanding *adj.* **1** honest; respectable; trustworthy. **2** having a healthily erect posture. — **be upstanding** *formal* to stand up.

upstart *noun derog.* an arrogant young person with rapidly acquired power or wealth.

upstream *adv.* towards the source of a river or stream and against the current.

upsurge *noun* a sudden sharp rise or increase; a surging up.

upsy-daisy see UPS-A-DAISY.

uptake — **quick** or **slow on the uptake** *colloq.* quick or slow to understand or realize.

upthrust *noun Physics* the upward force that tends to make an object immersed in a liquid float.

uptight *adj. colloq.* **1** nervous; anxious; tense. **2** angry; irritated. **3** *North Amer., esp. US* strait-laced; conventional.

up to date or **up-to-date 1** containing all the latest facts or information. **2** knowing or reflecting the latest trends.

....

☰ CURRENT, LATEST. **2** modern, contemporary, fashionable, *colloq.* trendy, recent, new.
🔁 OUT OF DATE, OLD-FASHIONED.

....

upturn — *noun* an increase in (especially economic) activity; an upward trend. — *verb* to turn over, up, or upsidedown.

....

☰ *noun* revival, recovery, upsurge, upswing, rise, increase, boost, improvement.
🔁 *noun* downturn, drop.

....

UPVC *abbrev.* unplasticized polyvinyl chloride.

upward — *adv.* (**upwards**) to or towards a higher place, a more important or senior position, or an earlier era. — *adj.* moving or directed upwards. — **upwards of** ... more than: *upwards of a thousand people.*

upwardly *adv.* in an upward direction. — **upwardly mobile** *colloq.* moving, or in a position to move, into a higher social class or income bracket.

upwind — *adv.* **1** against the direction of the wind; into the wind. **2** in front in terms of wind direction; with the wind carrying one's scent towards (eg an animal one is stalking). — *adj.* going against or exposed to the wind.

uracil /'juərəsɪl / *noun Biochem.* one of the bases, derived from pyrimidine, that is present in the nucleic acid RNA. [from UREA + ACETIC]

uraemia or **uremia** *noun Medicine* the presence of excessive amounts of urea and other nitrogenous waste products in the blood, one of the first symptoms of kidney failure. [from Greek *ouron*, urine + *haima*, blood]

Uralic — *adj.* denoting a family of languages descended from an ancestor spoken in the N Ural Mountains over 7,000 years ago. The major languages include Finnish, Estonian, and Lapp, with an isolated member, Magyar, spoken in Hungary. — *noun* the languages forming this family.

uraninite *noun Geol.* a hard slightly greasy black, brown, grey, or greenish mineral form of uranium oxide that is often associated with thorium, lead, radium, or the rare earth elements, and is highly radioactive. It is the principal ore of uranium.

uranium *noun Chem.* (SYMBOL **U**, ATOMIC NUMBER **92**) a dense silvery-white radioactive metal, originally discovered in pitchblende in 1789, but now mainly obtained from the ore uraninite. [after the planet *Uranus*, discovered shortly before the metal]

urban *adj.* of, relating to, or situated in a town or city; not rural. [from Latin *urbs*, city]

....

☰ town, city, inner-city, metropolitan, municipal, civic, built-up.
🔁 country, rural.

....

urbane *adj.* **1** having refined manners; courteous. **2** sophisticated; civilized; elegant. [from Latin *urbanus*, of the town]

urban guerrilla a person carrying out terrorist activities in urban areas.

urbanity *noun* an urbane quality.

urbanization or **urbanisation** *noun* the process of urbanizing.

urbanize or **urbanise** *verb* to make (a district) less rural and more town-like.

urban legend or **myth** a story or anecdote of modern life, often untrue or apocryphal.

urban renewal project the demolition of old or run-down areas in a city to allow construction of new buildings, or the installation of modern amenities and the repair of structurally sound buildings in such areas.

urchin *noun* **1** a mischievous child. **2** a dirty, raggedly dressed child. **3** a sea-urchin. [from Old French *heriüon*, from Latin *ericus*, hedgehog]

Urdu /ˈɜːduː, ˈʊədu:/ — *noun* the official literary language of Pakistan, related to Hindi but with many words from Arabic and Persian. — *adj.* in or relating to Urdu.

urea *noun Biochem.* a compound, white and crystalline when purified, formed during amino acid breakdown in the liver of mammals, and excreted in the urine. It is also manufactured synthetically for use as a component of plastics, pharmaceuticals, fertilizers, and animal-feed additives. [from Greek *ouron*, urine]

ureter / jʊˈriːtə(r)/ *noun Anat.* one of the two tubes through which urine is carried from the kidneys to the bladder. [from Greek *oureter*, from *ouron*, urine]

urethra / jʊˈriːθrə/ *noun* (PL. **urethras, urethrae**) the tube through which urine passes from the bladder out of the body. [from Greek *ourethra*, from *ouron*, urine]

urethritis *noun* inflammation of the urethra.

urge — *verb* **1** to persuade forcefully or incite. **2** to beg or entreat. **3** to advise or recommend earnestly. **4** (*also* **urge someone** or **something on**) to drive (eg horses) onwards. — *noun* a strong impulse, desire, or motivation. [from Latin *urgere*]

⊟ *verb* **1** persuade, encourage, press, push, incite, drive, impel, goad, spur, constrain, compel, force, hasten, induce, instigate. **2** beg, entreat, implore, beseech, plead. **3** advise, counsel, recommend, advocate, encourage, exhort. *noun* impulse, desire, wish, inclination, compulsion, impetus, drive, eagerness, fancy, longing, yearning, *colloq.* itch.
⊞ *verb* **1, 3** discourage, dissuade, deter. *noun* disinclination.

urgency *noun* an urgent state or condition.

⊟ hurry, haste, importance, seriousness, gravity, imperativeness, need, necessity, pressure, stress.

urgent *adj.* **1** needing immediate attention or action. **2** *said of a request, etc* forcefully and earnestly made. [from Latin *urgere*, to urge]

⊟ **1** immediate, instant, top-priority, important, critical, crucial, imperative, exigent, pressing. **2** compelling, persuasive, earnest, eager, insistent, persistent.
⊞ **1** unimportant.

urgently *adv.* with urgency.

uric *adj.* relating to or present in urine.

uric acid *Biochem.* an organic acid that is the main form in which nitrogenous waste products are excreted by birds and reptiles.

urinal *noun* **1** any receptacle designed for men to urinate into. **2** a room containing such receptacles. [from Old French, from Latin *urinalis*, of urine]

urinary *adj.* of or relating to urine or the passing of urine.

urinate *verb intrans.* to discharge urine.

urination *noun* the act of urinating.

urine /ˈjʊərɪn/ *noun Zool.* a liquid, consisting mainly of water containing urea, uric acid, and other nitrogenous waste products, that is produced by the kidneys and stored in the bladder. [from Latin *urina*, from Greek *ouron*]

URL *abbrev. Comput.* Uniform Resource Locator, an address of a location on the World Wide Web.

urn *noun* **1** a vase with a rounded body, a small narrow neck, and a (usually square) base. **2** such a vase used to contain a dead person's ashes. **3** a large metal cylinder with a tap and an internal element for heating water or making large quantities of tea or coffee. [from Latin *urna*]

urology *noun Medicine* the branch of medicine concerned with the treatment of diseases and disorders of the male and female urinary tracts, and the male genital tract. [from Greek *ouron*, urine + -LOGY]

ursine *adj.* **1** of or relating to bears. **2** bear-like. [from Latin *ursus*, bear]

US *abbrev.* United States (of America).

us *pron.* **1** the speaker or writer together with another person or other people; the object form of *we*. **2** all or any people; one. **3** *colloq.* me: *give us a hand.* — **be us** *colloq.* to be suited to us: *breakdancing is just not us.* [from Anglo-Saxon *us*]

USA *abbrev.* United States of America.

usable *adj.* capable of being used.

⊟ working, operational, serviceable, functional, practical, exploitable, available, current, valid.
⊞ unusable, useless.

USAF *abbrev.* United States Air Force.

usage *noun* **1** the act or way of using. **2** custom or practice. **3** the way language is used in practice; a word or expression commonly used. [from Old French *usage*]

⊟ **1** treatment, handling, management, control, running, operation, employment, application, use. **2** tradition, custom, practice, habit, convention, etiquette, rule, regulation, form, routine, procedure, method.

use¹ — *verb* **1** to put to a particular purpose. **2** to consume; to take as a fuel. **3** to treat (a person) as a means to benefit oneself; to exploit. **4** *slang* to take (especially drugs or alcohol) habitually. **5** *old use* to behave (well or badly) towards. — **used to something** or **someone** accustomed to them: *she's not used to exercising / they're not used to us yet.* — *verb aux.* was or were formerly: *they used to be friends / she didn't used to be / used not to be so grumpy.* **be used up** *colloq.* be tired or exhausted. **use something up 1** to exhaust supplies, etc. **2** to finish off an amount left over. [from Latin *uti*, to use]

⊟ **1** utilize, employ, exercise, practise, operate, work, apply, wield, handle, treat, manipulate, exploit, enjoy. **2** consume, exhaust, expend, spend. **3** exploit, manipulate. **use up 1** finish, exhaust, drain, sap, deplete, consume, devour, absorb.

use² *noun* **1** the act of using. **2** the state of being (able to be) used: *go out of use / not in use.* **3** a practical purpose a thing can be put to. **4** the quality of serving a practical purpose: *it's no use complaining / is this spanner any use?* **5** the ability or power to use (eg a limb). **6** the length of time for which a thing is, will be, or has remained serviceable: *should give you plenty of use.* **7** the habit of using; custom. — **have no use for something** or **someone 1** to have no need of them. **2** *colloq.* to dislike or despise them. **make use of someone** to exploit a person. **make use of something** to put it to a practical purpose. [from Latin *usus*, from *uti*, to use]

⊟ **1** usage, application, employment, operation, exercise. **2** application, usage, operation. **4** usefulness, value, worth, profit, service, advantage, benefit, good, avail, help, point, object, end, purpose.

used *adj.* not new; second-hand.

⊟ second-hand, cast-off, *colloq.* hand-me-down, nearly new, worn, dog-eared, soiled.
⊞ unused, new, fresh.

useful *adj.* **1** serving a helpful purpose, or various purposes. **2** (*often* **useful at something**) *colloq.* skilled or proficient in it. — **come in useful** to prove to be useful.

⊟ **1** handy, convenient, all-purpose, practical, effective, productive, fruitful, profitable, valuable, worthwhile, advantageous, beneficial, helpful. **2** proficient, skilled, practised, experienced, expert, able, skilful, handy.
⊞ USELESS, INEFFECTIVE. **1** worthless.

useless *adj.* **1** serving no practical purpose. **2** (*often useless at something*) *colloq.* not at all proficient at it.

⊟ **1** futile, fruitless, unproductive, vain, idle, unavailing, hopeless, pointless, worthless, unusable, broken-down, *colloq.* clapped out, unworkable, impractical. **2** incompetent, ineffective, inefficient, weak.
⊟ USEFUL. **1** helpful. **2** proficient, effective, skilled.

uselessly *adv.* in a useless way; so as to be useless.

user *noun* a person who uses something.

user-friendly *adj.* designed to be easy or pleasant to use, or easy to follow or understand.

user name *Comput.* the name used by an individual to gain access to a computer network.

usher — *noun* **1** a person who shows people to their seats, eg in a church or theatre. **2** a court official who guards the door and maintains order. **3** an official who escorts, or introduces people to, dignitaries on ceremonial occasions. — *verb* **1** (**usher someone in** or **out**) to conduct or escort them into or out of a building, room, etc. **2** (**usher something in**) *literary* to be a portent of it; to herald it. [from Old French *ussier*, from Latin *ostiarius*, doorkeeper]

⊟ *noun* **1** usherette, steward. **2** doorkeeper, attendant. **3** escort, guide, attendant. *verb* **1** escort, accompany, conduct, lead, direct, guide, show, pilot, steer.

usherette *noun* a woman who shows people to their seats in a theatre or cinema.

USM *abbrev.* Unlisted Securities Market.

USN *abbrev.* United States Navy.

USS *abbrev.* United States Ship or Steamer.

USSR *abbrev.* Union of Soviet Socialist Republics.

usual — *adj.* done, happening, etc most often; customary. — *noun* (**the usual**) *colloq.* the thing regularly requested, done, etc. — **as usual** as regularly happens. [from Latin *usualis*]

⊟ *adj.* normal, customary, conventional, regular, routine, habitual, typical, accustomed, familiar, common, everyday, general, ordinary, unexceptional, expected, predictable, stock, standard, accepted, recognized.
⊟ *adj.* unusual, strange, rare.

usually *adv.* ordinarily, normally.

⊟ ordinarily, normally, generally, as a rule, typically, traditionally, regularly, commonly, by and large, on the whole, mainly, chiefly, mostly.
⊟ exceptionally.

usurer /ˈjuːʒərə(r)/ *noun* a moneylender.

usurious /jʊˈzjʊərɪəs/ *adj.* **1** relating to or involving usury. **2** *said of interest* excessive.

usurp /jʊˈzɜːp/ *verb* to take (eg power) or assume (eg authority) by force, without right, or unjustly. [from Latin *usurpare*, to take possession of by use]

⊟ take over, assume, seize, take, commandeer, steal, annex, appropriate, arrogate.

usurpation *noun* the act of usurping.

usurper *noun* a person who usurps.

usury /ˈjuːʒərɪ/ *noun* **1** the practice of lending money at an unfairly or illegally high rate of interest. **2** such a rate of interest. [from Latin *usura*, from *uti*, to use]

UT or **Ut.** *abbrev.* Utah.

utensil *noun* an implement or container, especially for everyday use. [from Latin *utensilis*, fit for use]

⊟ tool, implement, instrument, device, contrivance, gadget, apparatus, appliance.

uterine *adj.* **1** relating to or in the region of the uterus. **2** *said of siblings* having the same mother but different fathers.

uterus *noun* (PL. **uteri**) *Anat.* in the lower abdomen of female mammals, the pear-shaped hollow muscular organ (extending upward from the vagina, and linked to the oviducts or Fallopian tubes) in which the embryo or fetus develops and is nourished until birth. Also called WOMB. [from Latin *uterus*]

utilitarian — *adj.* **1** intended to be useful rather than beautiful. **2** caring (too much) about usefulness and not (enough) about beauty. **3** of or relating to utilitarianism. — *noun* a supporter of utilitarianism. [see UTILITY]

utilitarianism *noun* a set of values based on the belief that an action is morally right if it benefits the majority of people.

utility — *noun* (PL. **utilities**) **1** usefulness. **2** a useful thing. See also PUBLIC UTILITY. — *adj.* designed for usefulness, rather than beauty. [from Latin *utilis*, useful, from *uti*, to use]

⊟ *noun* **1** usefulness, use, value, profit, advantage, benefit, avail, service, convenience, practicality, efficacy, efficiency, fitness, serviceableness.

utilization or **utilisation** *noun* utilizing or being utilized.

utilize or **utilise** *verb* to make practical use of; to use. [see UTILITY]

utmost — *adj.* **1** greatest possible. **2** furthest; outermost. — *noun* the greatest possible degree or extent: *tried his utmost to win.* [from Anglo-Saxon *utemest*]

⊟ *adj.* **1** greatest, maximum, highest, supreme, paramount, extreme. **2** furthest, farthest, furthermost, remotest, outermost, ultimate, final, last. *noun* best, hardest, most, maximum.

utopia *noun* any imaginary place or situation of ideal perfection.

utopian *adj.* unrealistically ideal.

utricle /ˈjuːtrɪkl/ *noun* **1** *Medicine* the larger of the cavities of the inner ear. **2** *Biol.* any pouch-like part in plants and animals. [from Latin *utriculus*, small bag]

utter[1] *verb* (**uttered, uttering**) **1** to express or give out as speech or a sound; to speak. **2** *Legal* to put (counterfeit money) into circulation. [from Middle English *uttren*, from Anglo-Saxon *ut*, out]

⊟ **1** speak, say, express, articulate, voice, vocalize, verbalize, enunciate, sound, pronounce, deliver, state, declare, announce, proclaim, tell, reveal, divulge.

utter[2] *adj.* complete; total; absolute. [from Anglo-Saxon *utor*, outer]

⊟ absolute, complete, total, entire, thoroughgoing, out-and-out, downright, sheer, stark, arrant, unmitigated, unqualified, perfect, consummate.

utterance *noun* **1** the act of uttering; the ability to utter. **2** a thing uttered.

⊟ **1** expression, articulation, delivery, declaration, announcement, proclamation, pronouncement. **2** statement, remark, comment, expression, articulation, delivery, speech, declaration, announcement, proclamation, pronouncement.

....

utterly *adv.* completely, absolutely.

....

⊟ absolutely, completely, totally, fully, entirely, wholly, thoroughly, downright, perfectly.

....

uttermost *adj.* utmost.

U-turn *noun* **1** a manoeuvre in which a vehicle is turned to face the other way in a single continuous movement. **2** a complete reversal of direction, eg of government policy.

....

⊟ **2** about-turn, volte-face, reversal, backtrack.

....

UV or **uv** *abbrev.* ultraviolet.

UVF *abbrev.* Ulster Volunteer Force.

uvula / ˈjuːvjʊlə/ *noun* (PL. **uvulas, uvulae**) the fleshy part of the soft palate that hangs over the back of the tongue at the entrance to the throat. [from Latin *uvula*, small grape]

uvular / ˈjuːvjʊlə/ *adj.* relating to or produced by the uvula.

uxorious *adj.* greatly or submissively fond of one's wife. [from Latin *uxor*, wife]

Uzi / ˈuːzɪ/ *noun* an Israeli sub-machine gun.

V

V¹ or **v** *noun* (PL. **Vs, V's, v's**) **1** the twenty-second letter of the English alphabet. **2** a thing shaped like the letter V.

V² *abbrev.* volt.

V³ *symbol* **1** *Chem.* vanadium. **2** the Roman numeral for 5.

v or **v.** *abbrev.* **1** verb. **2** versus. **3** very. **4** *vide* (Latin): see, refer to.

VA or **Va.** *abbrev.* Virginia.

vac *noun colloq.* a vacation, especially between terms at a university or college.

vacancy *noun* (PL. **vacancies**) **1** the state of being vacant. **2** an unoccupied job or post. **3** an unoccupied room in a hotel or guesthouse.

. . . .

◼ **2** job, post, opening, position, situation, place, opportunity.

. . . .

vacant *adj.* **1** empty or unoccupied. **2** having, showing, or suggesting an absence of thought, concentration, or intelligence. [from Latin *vacare*, to be empty]

. . . .

◼ **1** empty, unoccupied, unfilled, free, available, not in use, unused, uninhabited, void. **2** blank, expressionless, vacuous, inane, inattentive, absent, absent-minded, unthinking, dreamy.

◲ **1** occupied, engaged.

. . . .

vacantly *adv.* absently, without concentration: *stared vacantly into the distance.*

vacate *verb* to leave or cease to occupy (a house or an official position). [from Latin *vacare*, to be empty]

. . . .

◼ leave, depart, evacuate, abandon, withdraw from, quit.

. . . .

vacation — *noun* **1** *North Amer., esp. US* a holiday. **2** a holiday between terms at a university, college, or court of law. — *verb intrans. North Amer., esp. US* to take a holiday. [from Latin *vacatio*, freedom, exemption]

vaccinate /'vaksɪneɪt/ *verb* to administer a vaccine to, giving immunity from a disease.

vaccination /vaksɪ'neɪʃən/ *noun* the act or process of inoculating with a vaccine.

vaccine /'vaksiːn, 'vaksɪn/ *noun Medicine* a liquid preparation containing dead or weakened micro-organisms (such as bacteria or viruses), or products derived from them, which have lost their virulence but still behave as antigens. Vaccines are used in vaccination to confer temporary or permanent immunity to a bacterial or viral disease by stimulating the body to produce antibodies to a specific bacterium or virus. They are usually either injected into the bloodstream or given by mouth. [from Latin *vaccinus*, from *vacca*, cow]

vacillate /'vasɪleɪt/ *verb intrans.* to change opinions or decisions frequently; to waver. [from Latin *vacillare*]

vacillation /vasɪ'leɪʃən/ *noun* constant wavering or hesitation; indecision.

vacuity /va'kjuːɪtɪ/ *noun* (PL. **vacuities**) **1** the state or quality of being vacuous. **2** a foolish thought or idea. **3** *formal* an empty space.

vacuole /'vakjʊoʊl/ *noun Biol.* a space within the cytoplasm of a living cell that is filled with air or liquid (eg water or cell sap), and is surrounded by a membrane known as a *tonoplast* that controls the movement of substances in to and out of the vacuole. [from French *vacuole*, little vacuum]

vacuous *adj.* **1** unintelligent; stupid; inane. **2** *said of a look or expression* blank; conveying no feeling or meaning. **3** empty. **4** having no meaning or purpose. [from Latin *vacuus*, empty]

vacuously *adv., said of an expression* without feeling or meaning; blankly: *then he stared vacuously back at me.*

vacuum /'vakjʊəm/ — *noun* (PL. **vacuums**, or in technical use **vacua**) **1** a space from which all matter has been removed. **2** a space from which all or almost all air or other gas has been removed. **3** a feeling or state of emptiness. **4** a condition of isolation from outside influences. **5** *colloq.* a vacuum cleaner. — *verb trans., intrans.* (**vacuumed, vacuuming**) *colloq.* to clean with a vacuum cleaner. [from Latin *vacuus*, empty]

. . . .

◼ *noun* **3** emptiness, void, nothingness, vacuity, space.

. . . .

vacuum cleaner an electrically powered cleaning device that lifts dust and dirt by suction.

vacuum flask a container for preserving the temperature of liquids, especially drinks. It consists of a double-skinned glass bottle with a vacuum sealed between the layers, fitted inside a protective metal or plastic container.

vacuum-packed *adj.* sealed in a container from which most of the air has been removed.

vacuum tube 1 *Electr.* an electron tube containing an electrically heated electrode (the cathode) that emits electrons which flow through a vacuum to a second electrode (the anode). Also called VALVE. **2** a thermionic valve.

vade-mecum /veɪdɪ'miːkəm/ *noun* a handbook of practical information carried for frequent reference. [from Latin *vade mecum*, literally 'go with me']

vagabond — *noun* a person who lives an unsettled wandering life, especially one regarded as lazy or worthless. — *adj.* wandering; roving. [from Latin *vagari*, to wander]

vagary /'veɪgərɪ/ *noun* (PL. **vagaries**) an unpredictable and erratic act or turn of events. [from Latin *vagari*, to wander]

vagina /və'dʒaɪnə/ *noun* in the reproductive system of most female mammals, the muscular canal that leads from the cervix of the uterus to the exterior. It receives the penis during sexual intercourse, and is the passage down which the fetus passes at the time of birth. [from Latin *vagina*, sheath]

vaginal *adj.* relating to or associated with the vagina.

vaginismus /vadʒɪ'nɪzməs/ *noun Medicine* spasmodic contraction of the muscles surrounding the vagina, which may be associated with fear of or aversion to sexual intercourse, or have physical causes.

vagrancy *noun* the unsettled state of a vagrant.

vagrant — *noun* a person who has no permanent home or place of work. — *adj.* **1** wandering; roving. **2** uncertain; unsettled. [from Old French *wakerant*, roaming]

vague *adj.* **1** of an indistinct or imprecise nature. **2** thinking, expressing, or remembering without clarity or precision. [from Latin *vagus*, wandering]

....

⊟ **1** indistinct, imprecise, ill-defined, blurred, hazy, dim, shadowy, misty, fuzzy, nebulous, obscure, indefinite, unclear, undefined, undetermined, unspecific, generalized, inexact. **2** uncertain, imprecise, loose, woolly, ambiguous, evasive.
⊡ CLEAR. **1** definite.

....

vaguely *adv.* in a vague or uncertain manner; roughly or imprecisely: *was vaguely thinking of going out.*

vagueness *noun* a vague state; unclear or indistinct thought.

vagus /'veɪgəs/ *Anat.* in vertebrates, the tenth cranial nerve, branches of which carry motor nerve fibres to many internal organs, such as the heart, lungs, stomach, kidneys, and liver. [from Latin *vagus*, wandering]

vain *adj.* **1** having too much pride in one's appearance, achievements, or possessions; conceited. **2** having no useful effect or result; futile. — **in vain** without success; fruitlessly. **take someone's name in vain** to refer to them in a disrespectful way, especially in anger or surprise. [from Latin *vanus*, empty]

....

⊟ **1** conceited, proud, self-satisfied, arrogant, self-important, egotistical, *colloq.* big-headed, swollen-headed, *colloq.* stuck-up, affected, pretentious, ostentatious, swaggering. **2** useless, worthless, futile, abortive, fruitless, pointless, unproductive, unprofitable, unavailing, hollow, groundless, empty, trivial, unimportant.
⊡ **1** modest, self-effacing. **2** fruitful, successful.

....

vainglorious *adj. literary* boasting; extremely proud.

vainglory *noun literary* extreme boastfulness; excessive pride in oneself. [from Old French *vaine gloire*]

vainly *adv.* **1** in a vain manner. **2** unsuccessfully.

valance *noun* a decorative strip of fabric hung over a curtain rail or round the frame of a bed. [possibly from Old French *valer*, to descend]

vale *noun literary* a valley. [from Latin *vallis*]

valediction *noun* a farewell. [from Latin *vale*, farewell + *dicere*, to say]

valedictory *adj.* signifying or accompanying a farewell: *gave a valedictory wave.*

valence *noun Chem.* same as VALENCY.

valence electron *Chem.* an electron in one of the outer shells of an atom that participates in the formation of chemical bonds with other atoms, resulting in the production of molecules.

valency or **valence** *noun* (PL. **valencies**, **valences**) *Chem.* a positive number that denotes the combining power of an atom of a particular element. It is equal to the number of hydrogen atoms or their equivalent with which it could combine to form a compound, eg in water (H_2O), hydrogen has a valency of one and oxygen has a valency of two. [from Latin *valentia*, strength, capacity]

valentine *noun* **1** a card or other message given, often anonymously, as a token of love or affection on St Valentine's Day (14 Feb). **2** the person it is given to.

valerian /və'lɪərɪən/ *noun* **1** any of a family of small flowering plants of Europe and Asia. Its roots have medicinal properties. **2** a sedative drug prepared from its root. [from medieval Latin *valeriana herba*, from the name *Valerius*]

valet — *noun* a man's personal servant. — *verb* (**valeted**, **valeting**) **1** *intrans.* to work as a valet. **2** to clean out (a car) as a service. [from French *valet*, related to VARLET]

valeta see VELETA.

valetudinarian *formal* — *adj.* **1** relating to or suffering from a long-term or chronic illness. **2** anxious about one's health; hypochondriac. — *noun* a valetudinarian person. [from Latin *valetudo*, state of health]

Valhalla in Norse mythology, a great hall built by Odin to house warriors who die bravely in battle. [from Norse *Valhöll*, from *valr*, the slain + *höll*, hall]

valiant *adj.* outstandingly brave and heroic. [from Latin *valere*, to be strong]

....

⊟ brave, heroic, courageous, gallant, fearless, intrepid, bold, dauntless, plucky, indomitable, staunch.
⊡ cowardly, fearful.

....

valiantly *adv.* bravely; heroically: *the doctors worked valiantly to save many lives.*

valid *adj.* **1** based on truth or sound reasoning. **2** *said of a ticket or official document* legally acceptable for use. **3** *said of a contract* drawn up according to proper legal procedure. [from Latin *validus*, strong]

....

⊟ **1** logical, well-founded, well-grounded, sound, good, cogent, convincing, telling, conclusive, reliable, substantial, weighty, powerful, just. **2, 3** official, legal, lawful, legitimate, authentic, bona fide, genuine, binding, proper.
⊡ INVALID. **1** false, weak. **2, 3** unofficial.

....

validate *verb* to make valid; to confirm the validity of.

validation *noun* making valid; validating.

validity *noun* **1** the state of being valid or acceptable for use. **2** soundness of an argument or proposition.

valine /'veɪliːn, 'valiːn/ *noun Biochem.* an essential amino acid that is found in proteins. [from *valeric acid*]

valise /və'liːz/ *noun North Amer., esp. US* a small overnight case or bag. [from French *valise*, suitcase]

Valium /'valɪəm/ *noun trademark* a type of tranquillizing drug.

Valkyrie /val'kaɪərɪ/ *Scandinavian Mythol.* a handmaiden of Odin, one of twelve who accompanied the souls of slain heroes to Valhalla. [from Norse *Valkyrja*, from *valr*, the slain + *kjosa*, to choose]

valley *noun* (PL. **valleys**) **1** a long flat area of land, usually containing a river or stream, flanked on both sides by higher land, eg hills or mountains. **2** any trough or hollow between ridges, eg on an M-shaped roof. [from Latin *vallis*]

....

⊟ **2** hollow, depression.

....

valorous *adj. literary* showing valour; courageous.

valour *North Amer.* **valor** *noun* courage or bravery, especially in battle. [from Latin *valere*, to be strong]

valuable — *adj.* of considerable value or usefulness. — *noun* (usually **valuables**) personal possessions of high financial or other value.

....

⊟ *adj.* precious, prized, valued, costly, expensive, high-priced, dear, treasured, cherished, estimable, helpful, worthwhile, useful, beneficial, invaluable, constructive, fruitful, profitable, important, serviceable, worthy, handy.
⊡ *adj.* worthless, useless.

....

valuably *adv.* to a valuable degree or extent.

valuation *noun* **1** an assessment of the monetary value of something, especially from an expert or authority. **2** the value arrived at.

value — *noun* **1** worth in monetary terms. **2** the quality of being useful or desirable; the degree of usefulness or desirability. **3** the quality of being a fair exchange: *value for money.* **4** (**values**) moral principles or standards. **5** *Maths.* a quantity represented by a symbol or set of symbols. **6** *Mus.* the duration of a note or rest. — *verb* **1** to consider to be of a certain value, especially a high value; to esteem. **2** to assess the value of. [from Latin *valere*]

....

⊟ *noun* **1** cost, price, rate, worth. **2** worth, use, usefulness, utility, merit, importance, desirability, benefit, advantage, significance, good, profit. *verb* **1** prize, esteem, appreciate, treasure, hold dear, respect, cherish. **2** evaluate, assess,

estimate, price, appraise, survey, rate.
☷ *verb* **1** disregard, neglect. **2** undervalue.

value-added tax a tax on goods and services sold. It is calculated on the difference between the cost of raw materials and production, and the market value of the final product.

valued *adj.* considered valuable or precious; highly prized: *a valued friend.*

value judgement an assessment of worth or merit based on personal opinion rather than objective fact.

valueless *adj.* having little or no value.

valuer *noun* a person who makes a valuation, especially professionally.

valve *noun* **1** any device that regulates the flow of a fluid (a liquid or gas) through a pipe by opening or closing an aperture, or that allows flow in one direction only. **2** *Anat.* in certain tubular organs, a flap of membranous tissue that allows flow of a body fluid, such as blood, in one direction only, eg the valves in the heart and veins. **3** *Electron.* a thermionic valve. **4** any of a set of finger-operated devices that control the flow of air through some brass musical instruments, producing different notes. **5** *Bot.* any of the sections that are formed when a capsule or other dry fruit opens to shed its seeds at dehiscence. **6** *Zool.* either half of the hinged shell of a bivalve mollusc such as a cockle or clam. [from Latin *valva*, folding door]

valvular *adj.* **1** having valves. **2** functioning as a valve.

vamoose /vəˈmuːs/ *verb intrans. North Amer., esp. US slang* (usually as a command) to depart hurriedly; to clear off. [from Spanish *vamos*, let us go]

vamp¹ *colloq.* — *noun* a woman who flaunts her sexual charm, especially in order to exploit men. — *verb* **1** to seduce (a man) with intent to exploit. **2** *intrans.* to behave like a vamp. [a shortening of VAMPIRE]

vamp² — *noun* the part of a shoe or boot that covers the toes. — *verb* **1** (**vamp something up**) **a** to refurbish it or do it up; to prepare something old or out of date for re-use by making alterations. **b** to make up from bits and pieces. **2** to improvise (a simple musical accompaniment). [from Old French *avanpi*, forefoot]

vampire *noun* **1** a dead person who supposedly rises from the grave at night to suck the blood of the living. **2** a person who ruthlessly exploits others. [from German *Vampir*]

vampire bat a bat of Central and S America that pierces the skin of animals and humans and sucks their blood.

van¹ *noun* **1** a commercial road vehicle with storage space at the rear, lighter than a lorry or truck. **2** *Brit.* a railway carriage in which luggage and parcels are carried, often also where the guard travels. [a shortening of CARAVAN]

van² *noun* **1** a vanguard. **2** the forefront: *in the van of progress.* [a shortening of VANGUARD]

vanadium /vəˈneɪdɪəm/ *noun Chem.* (SYMBOL **V**, ATOMIC NUMBER 23) a soft silvery-grey metal that is used to increase the toughness and shock resistance of steel alloys, eg for components of cars. Its compounds are used in ceramics and glass, and as industrial catalysts. [after *Vanadis*, a name of the Norse goddess Freyja]

Van Allen belt *Astron.* either of two rings of intense radiation that encircle the Earth at distances of about 1,000km to 5,000km and 15,000km to 25,000km. They consist of electrically charged particles trapped by the Earth's magnetic field, the outer zone consisting mainly of electrons, and the inner one of protons. [named after the US physicist James Van Allen (1914–), who identified them]

Vandal — *noun* a member of a Germanic people, originally perhaps from the Baltic area, who settled in the Danube valley in the 4c AD, invaded Gaul, conquered Roman Africa, and sacked Rome. — *adj.* relating to the Vandals.

vandal *noun* a person who wantonly damages or destroys works of art or other property.

vandalism *noun* wanton damage to works of art or other property.

vandalize or **vandalise** *verb* to inflict wilful and senseless damage on (property).

van der Waals' force /ˈvan də wɑːlz/ *Physics* any of the weak attractive forces that exist between atoms or molecules. [named after the Dutch physicist Johannes Diderik van der Waals (1837–1923), who discovered the equation]

vane *noun* **1** a weathervane. **2** each of the blades of a windmill, propeller, or revolving fan. [from obsolete *fane*, flag, weathercock]

vanguard *noun* **1** the part of a military force that advances first. **2 a** a person or group that leads the way, especially by setting standards or forming opinion. **b** a leading position: *in the vanguard of discovery.* [from French *avant-garde*, advance guard]

vanilla — *noun* **1 a** a Mexican climbing orchid. **b** its pod. **2** a flavouring substance obtained from the pod, used in ice cream, chocolate, and other foods. — *adj* ordinary or bland. [from Spanish *vainilla*, small pod]

vanish *verb intrans.* **1** to disappear suddenly. **2** to cease to exist; to die out. [from Latin *evanescere*, from *vanus*, empty]

☷ **1** disappear, fade, dissolve, evaporate, disperse, melt, depart, exit. **2** die out, fizzle out, peter out.
☷ **1** appear, materialize.

vanishing cream moisturizing cream that leaves no trace on the skin.

vanishing point 1 the point at which parallel lines extending into the distance appear to meet. **2** the point at which something disappears completely.

vanitas /ˈvanɪtas/ *noun Art* a type of still-life picture, produced mainly by 17c Dutch artists, in which symbolic motifs such as skulls, hourglasses, and old books feature as reminders of the vanity of earthly pleasures and the transience of human life and aspirations. [from a phrase in the Vulgate (Eccles. 1.2): *vanitas vanitatum, omnia vanitas*, vanity of vanities, all is vanity]

vanity *noun* (PL. **vanities**) **1** the quality of being vain or conceited. **2** a thing one is conceited about. **3** futility or worthlessness. [from Latin *vanitas*]

☷ **1** conceit, conceitedness, pride, arrogance, self-conceit, self-love, self-satisfaction, narcissism, egotism, pretension, ostentation, affectation, airs, *colloq.* big-headedness, swollen-headedness. **3** worthlessness, uselessness, emptiness, futility, pointlessness, unreality, hollowness, fruitlessness, triviality.
☷ **1** modesty.

vanity bag or **vanity case** a woman's small case for cosmetics and make-up.

vanity publishing publication by the author, at his or her own expense.

vanity unit a piece of furniture combining a dressing-table and washbasin.

vanquish *verb literary* to defeat or overcome. [from Latin *vincere*]

vantage *noun* an advantage, especially in tennis. [from Old French *avantage*, related to ADVANTAGE]

vantage point a position affording a clear overall view or prospect.

vapid /ˈveɪpɪd, ˈvapɪd/ *adj.* **1** dull; uninteresting. **2** having little taste, colour, or smell. [from Latin *vapidus*, flat-tasting]

vapidity *noun* a vapid state or condition.

vaporization or **vaporisation** *noun* the act or process of vaporizing.

vaporize or **vaporise** *verb* **1** to convert into vapour. **2** *intrans.* to become vapour; to evaporate. **3** to destroy by reducing to vapour.

vapour *noun* **1** a gas that can be condensed to a liquid by pressure alone, without being cooled. It consists of atoms or molecules, dispersed in the air, that have evaporated from the surface of a substance that normally exists in the form of a liquid or solid: *water vapour*. **2 (the vapours)** *old use* a feeling of depression, or of faintness, formerly thought to be caused by gases in the stomach. [from Latin *vapor*]

◗ **1** steam, mist, fog, smoke, breath, fumes, haze, damp, dampness, exhalation.

vapour pressure *Chem.* the pressure exerted by the atoms or molecules of a vapour. If the vapour is in equilibrium with the liquid with which it is in contact, the pressure is referred to as the saturated vapour pressure.

vapour trail a white trail of condensed water vapour from the engine exhausts of a high-flying aircraft.

variability *noun* the state or condition of being variable.

variable — *adj.* **1** varying or tending to vary; not steady or regular; changeable. **2** that can be varied or altered. — *noun* **1** a thing that can vary unpredictably in nature or degree. **2** a factor which may change or be changed by another. **3** *Maths.* in an algebraic expression or equation, a symbol, usually a letter, for which one or more quantities or values may be substituted, eg in the expression $3x$, x is a variable. **4** *Astron.* denoting a star whose brightness changes over a period of time.

◗ *adj.* **1** changeable, inconstant, varying, shifting, mutable, unpredictable, fluctuating, fitful, unstable, unsteady, wavering, vacillating, temperamental, fickle. **2** changeable, alterable, flexible.
◗ *adj.* FIXED. **1** stable. **2** invariable.

variably *adv.* in a way that varies or is changeable.

variance *noun* **1** the state of being different or inconsistent: *there was some variance between them*. **2** *Statistics* a quantity equal to the square of the standard deviation. — **at variance** in disagreement or conflict. [from Latin *varientia* difference, related to VARY]

◗ **1** variation, difference, discrepancy, divergence, inconsistency, disagreement, disagreement, disharmony, conflict, discord, division, dissent, dissension, quarrelling, strife.
◗ **1** agreement, harmony.

variant — *noun* **1** a form of a thing that varies from another form, eg the ending of a story, or one of several permissible spellings of a word. **2** an example that differs from a standard. — *adj.* **1** different. **2** differing from a standard.

variation *noun* **1** the act or process of varying or changing. **2** a thing that varies from a standard. **3** the extent to which a thing varies from a standard. **4** a passage of music in which the main melody is repeated with some (slight) changes. **5** *Biol.* differences in characteristics, eg size, colouring, between individual members of the same plant or animal species, due to environmental differences, differences in genetic make-up, or (more often) both. **6** differences in characteristics between parents and their offspring, due to mutations, or (more often) to the rearrangement of genetic material that occurs during sexual reproduction.

◗ **1** diversity, variety, deviation, discrepancy, diversification, alteration, change, difference, departure, modification, modulation, inflection, novelty, innovation. **2** deviation, discrepancy, difference, departure, modification, novelty, innovation. **3** alteration, change, deviation, discrepancy, difference.
◗ **1** monotony, uniformity.

varicoloured *adj.* having parts in different colours. [from Latin *varius*, various + COLOUR]

varicose *adj.* **1** *Medicine* denoting a superficial vein that is abnormally swollen and twisted, so that it produces a raised and often painful knot on the skin surface, usually of the legs. **2** denoting an ulcer that forms as a result of the development of such a vein. [from Latin *varix*, varicose vein]

varied *adj.* having variety; diverse.

◗ assorted, diverse, miscellaneous, mixed, various, sundry, heterogeneous, different, wide-ranging.
◗ standardized, uniform.

variegated /ˈveərɪɡeɪtɪd, ˈveərɪəɡeɪtɪd/ *adj. Bot.* denoting leaves or flowers with patches of two or more colours. [from Latin *variegatus*, from *varius*, changing]

◗ multicoloured, particoloured, varicoloured, speckled, mottled, dappled, pied, streaked, motley, many-coloured, kaleidoscopic.
◗ monochrome, plain.

variegation *noun Bot.* in certain plants, the occurrence of patches of two or more colours on the leaves or flowers.

variety *noun* (PL. **varieties**) **1** any of various types of the same thing; a kind or sort. **2** the quality of departing from a fixed pattern or routine; diversity. **3** a plant or animal differing from another in certain characteristics, but not enough to be classed as a separate species; a race, breed, or strain. **4** a form of theatrical entertainment consisting of a succession of acts of different kinds. [from Latin *varietas*]

◗ **1** sort, kind, class, category, species, type, breed, brand, make, strain. **2** difference, diversity, dissimilarity, discrepancy, variation, multiplicity, assortment, miscellany, mixture, collection, medley, potpourri, range.
◗ **2** uniformity, similitude.

varifocal — *adj.* having variable focal lengths. — *pl. noun* spectacles with varifocal lenses, for a wide range of vision.

various *adj.* **1** several different: *worked for various companies*. **2** different; disparate; diverse: *their interests are many and various*. [from Latin *varius*, changing]

◗ **1** several, many, different, assorted, miscellaneous. **2** different, disparate, differing, diverse, varied, varying, assorted, miscellaneous, heterogeneous, distinct, diversified, mixed.

variously *adv.* in different ways or at different times.

varlet *noun old use* **1** a menial servant. **2** a rascal or rogue. [from Old French *vaslet*]

varmint *noun North Amer., esp. US slang* a troublesome animal or person. [a variant form of VERMIN]

varnish — *noun* **1** an oil-based liquid containing resin, painted on a surface such as wood to give a hard transparent and often glossy finish. **2** any liquid providing a similar finish, eg on fingernails. **3** a superficial attractiveness or impressiveness, especially masking underlying shoddiness or inadequacy; a gloss. — *verb* **1** to apply varnish to. **2** to make superficially appealing or impressive. [from French *vernis*]

◗ *noun* **1, 2** lacquer, glaze, resin, polish, gloss, coating.

varsity *noun colloq.* (PL. **varsities**) **1** *Brit.* a university, especially with reference to sport. **2** *North Amer.* the principal team representing a college in a sport.

vary *verb* (**varies, varied**) **1** *intrans.* to change, or be of different kinds, especially according to different circumstances. **2** *trans., intrans.* to make or become less regular or uniform and more diverse. [from Latin *variare*, from *varius*, various]

⊟ CHANGE, ALTER, MODULATE, DIVERSIFY, REORDER, TRANSFORM, ALTERNATE, INFLECT, PERMUTATE, DIVERGE, DIFFER, DISAGREE, DEPART, FLUCTUATE.

varying *adj.* changing, especially according to circumstances.

varyingly *adv.* in a changing way; with change.

vas /vas/ *noun* (PL. **vasa**) *Biol.* a vessel, tube, or duct carrying liquid. [from Latin *vas*, vessel]

vascular *adj. Biol.* relating to the blood vessels of animals or the sap-conducting tissues (*xylem* and *phloem*) of plants. [from Latin *vasculum*, from *vas*, vessel]

vascular bundle *Bot.* in higher plants (eg flowering plants, conifers, ferns), any of numerous thin strands of vascular tissue (conducting tissue), running upwards through the roots and stem and extending into the leaves, composed of xylem (which transports water and mineral salts absorbed by the roots) and phloem (which conducts sugars manufactured during photosynthesis in the leaves).

vascular tissue *Biol.* describing tissue within which water, nutrients, and other materials are transported from one part of a living organism to another, ie the blood vessels of animals, and the xylem and phloem of plants.

vas deferens /'vas 'defərenz/ (PL. **vasa deferentia**) *Biol.* the duct from each testicle that carries sperm to the penis. [from Latin *deferre*, to carry away]

vase /vɑːz, veɪz/ *noun* an ornamental glass or pottery container, especially one for holding cut flowers. [from Latin *vas*, vessel]

vasectomy *noun* (PL. **vasectomies**) *Medicine* a surgical operation involving the tying and cutting of the vas deferens in order to produce male sterility without loss of sexual desire or potency. [from Latin *vas*, vessel + -ECTOMY]

Vaseline /'vasəliːn/ *noun trademark* an ointment consisting mainly of petroleum jelly.

vasoconstrictor *noun Physiol.* any agent (eg a hormone, drug, or nerve) that stimulates blood vessels to contract, so that they become narrower. [from Latin *vas*, vessel]

vasodilator *noun Physiol.* any agent (eg a hormone, drug, or nerve) that stimulates blood vessels to dilate, so that they become wider. [from Latin *vas*, vessel]

vasopressin /veɪzoʊ'prɛsɪn/ *noun Physiol.* a hormone, released by the pituitary gland, that increases blood pressure and the absorption of water by the kidneys, so that less water is excreted from the body. [from Latin *vas*, vessel]

vassal *noun* **1** *Hist.* a person acting as a servant to, and fighting on behalf of, a medieval lord in return for land or protection. **2** a person or nation dependent on or subservient to another. [from Latin *vassus*, servant]

vassalage *noun Hist.* the condition of vassals; a system of using vassals.

vast *adj.* extremely great in size, extent, or amount. [from Latin *vastus*, desolate, huge]

⊟ huge, immense, massive, gigantic, enormous, great, colossal, *colloq.* seismic, extensive, tremendous, sweeping, unlimited, fathomless, immeasurable, never-ending, monumental, monstrous.

vastly *adv.* to a considerable extent: *was vastly different.*

vastness *noun* a vast state or space; immensity.

VAT *abbrev.* value-added tax.

vat *noun* a large barrel or tank for storing or holding liquids, especially alcoholic drinks. [Anglo-Saxon *fæt*]

Vatican *noun* (*usually* **the Vatican**) **1** the palace and official residence of the pope in Rome. **2** the authority of the pope. [from Latin *Mons Vaticanus*, Vatican Hill]

vatman *noun* (PL. **vatmen**) *Brit.* a customs and excise officer responsible for collecting VAT.

vaudeville /'voʊdvɪl/ *noun North Amer., esp. US* variety entertainment; music hall. [from French *vaudeville*, originally of 15c songs composed in *Vau de Vire* in Normandy]

vault[1] — *noun* **1** an arched roof or ceiling, especially in a church. **2** an underground chamber used for storage, or as a burial tomb. **3** a wine cellar. **4** a fortified room for storing valuables, eg in a bank. **5** *poetic* the sky or heaven. — *verb* **1** to build in the shape of an arch. **2** to provide with an arched roof or ceiling. [from Old French *voute*, from Latin *volvere*, to roll]

⊟ *noun* **1** arch, roof, span, concave. **2** cellar, crypt, tomb, mausoleum, cavern. **4** strongroom, depository, repository.

vault[2] — *verb trans., intrans.* to spring or leap over, especially assisted by the hands or a pole. — *noun* an act of vaulting. [from Latin *volvere*, to roll]

⊟ *verb* leap, spring, bound, clear, jump, hurdle, leap-frog.

vaulting *adj.* excessive or immoderate, especially of ambition or pride.

vaulting-horse *noun* a padded wooden block on legs, vaulted over by gymnasts.

vaunt — *verb trans., intrans.* to boast or behave boastfully about. — *noun* a boast. [from Latin *vanitare*, from *vanus*, vain]

⊟ *verb* boast, brag, exult in, flaunt, show off, parade, trumpet, crow.

⊟ *verb* belittle, minimize.

vauntingly *adv.* in a boastful manner.

VC *abbrev.* **1** Vice Chancellor. **2** Victoria Cross.

V-chip *noun* a computer chip installed in a television receiver to control its use, especially by young viewers. [short for *viewer* or *violence*]

vCJD *abbrev.* variant Creutzfeldt-Jakob disease.

VCR *abbrev.* video cassette recorder.

VD *abbrev.* venereal disease.

VDQS *abbrev. vins délimités de qualité supérieure* (French) wines of superior quality from approved vineyards.

VDU *abbrev.* visual display unit.

've *contr.* (usually after pronouns) have: *we've/they've.*

veal *noun* the flesh of a calf, used as food. [from Old French *veel*, from Latin *vitulus*, calf]

vector *noun* **1** *Maths.* a quantity which has both magnitude and direction, eg force, velocity, acceleration. It is often represented by an arrow pointing in an appropriate direction, whose length is proportional to its magnitude. See also SCALAR. **2** *Aeron.* the course of an aircraft or missile. **3** *Medicine* any agent, such as an insect, that is capable of transferring a pathogen (a disease-causing microorganism) from one organism to another, eg from an animal to man, usually without itself contracting the disease, eg the vector of the malaria parasite is the *Anopheles* mosquito. **4** *Biol.* in genetic engineering, a vehicle used to transfer DNA from one organism to another to make *recombinant DNA* (DNA containing sequences from different sources). [from Latin *vector*, carrier]

Veda /'veɪdə/ the 'sacred knowledge' of the Hindus (c.1500 BC), contained in the four collections: the *Vedas*, the *Brahmanas* appended to them, and the *Aranyakas* and *Upanishads*, which serve as an epilogue or conclusion. [from Sanskrit *veda*, knowledge]

Vedic /'veɪdɪk/ — *adj.* relating to the Hindu Vedas. — *noun* the old Sanskrit language of the Vedas.

veduta /vɛ'duːtə/ *noun* (PL. **vedute**) *Art* a painting depicting a panoramic view of a place, usually a city, in a topographically accurate and decorative manner. [from Italian *veduta*, view]

veejay or **VJ** *colloq.* — *noun* a person who presents a programme of popular music videos on television. — *verb in-*

trans. to act as a veejay. [from video jockey, by analogy with DISC JOCKEY]

veer — *verb intrans.* **1** to move abruptly in a different direction. **2** *said of the wind* to change direction clockwise. — *noun* a change of direction. [from French *virer*]

◼ *verb* **1** swerve, swing, change, shift, diverge, deviate, turn, sheer.

veg / vɛdʒ/ *colloq.* — *noun* a vegetable or vegetables. — *verb intrans.* (**veg out**) *colloq.* to be inactive or engage in mindless activity, especially after a period of over-exertion.

vegan /'vi:gən/ — *noun* a person who does not eat meat, dairy products, or any foods containing animal fats or extracts, often also avoiding wool, leather, and other animal-based substances. — *adj.* **1** of or for vegans. **2** *said of a meal or diet* excluding such foods. [a contraction of VEGETARIAN]

veganism *noun* the principles and practices adopted by vegans.

vegeburger /'vɛdʒɪbɜ:gə(r)/ *noun* a flat cake resembling and served like a hamburger, made with vegetables, soy beans, etc instead of meat. [from VEGETARIAN + HAMBURGER]

vegetable — *noun* **1** a plant or any of its parts, other than fruits and seeds, that is used for food, eg roots, tubers, stems, or leaves. **2** loosely used to refer to some fruits that are used for food, eg tomato, marrow. **3** the edible part of such a plant. **4** *offensive colloq.* a person almost totally incapable of any physical or mental activity because of severe brain damage. — *adj.* relating to plants. [from Latin *vegetabilis*, from *vegetus*, lively]

Vegetables include: artichoke, aubergine, bean, beetroot, broad bean, broccoli, Brussels sprout, butterbean, cabbage, calabrese, capsicum, carrot, cauliflower, celeriac, celery, chicory, courgette, cress, cucumber, *North Amer.* eggplant, endive, fennel, French bean, garlic, kale, leek, lentil, lettuce, mangetout, marrow, mushroom, okra, onion, parsnip, pea, pepper, petit pois, potato, *colloq.* spud, pumpkin, radish, runner bean, shallot, soya bean, spinach, spring onion, swede, sweetcorn, sweet potato, turnip, watercress, yam, *North Amer.* zucchini.

vegetable marrow a marrow.

vegetable oil any of various oils obtained from plants, used especially in cooking and cosmetics.

vegetal *adj.* consisting of or relating to vegetables or to plant life in general. [from Latin *vegetalis*]

vegetarian — *noun* a person who does not eat meat or fish. — *adj.* **1** of or for vegetarians. **2** denoting food or a diet that contains no meat or fish. [from VEGETABLE + suffix -*arian*]

vegetarianism *noun* the principles and practices adopted by vegetarians.

vegetate *verb intrans.* **1** to live a dull inactive life. **2** to live or grow as a vegetable. [from Latin *vegetare*, to animate]

◼ **1** stagnate, degenerate, deteriorate, rusticate, *colloq.* go to seed, idle, languish.

vegetation *noun* **1** *Bot.* a collective term for plants. **2** *Bot.* the plants of a particular area, which may be very diverse or belong to just one or a few species, depending on climatic conditions, the nature of the soil, and human activity.

vegetative *adj.* **1** of plants or vegetation. **2** *Biol.* denoting asexual reproduction in plants or animals, as in bulbs, corms, yeasts, etc. **3** *Bot.* denoting a phase of plant growth as opposed to reproduction.

vegetative propagation *Bot.* any form of asexual reproduction in plants (ie reproduction without the formation of seeds), which gives rise to new plants known as clones which are genetically identical to the parent plant. Natural methods of vegetative propagation include the production of bulbs, tubers, corms, rhizomes, stolons, etc, and artificial methods include grafting and the taking of cuttings.

veggie /'vɛdʒɪ/ *noun colloq.* **1** a vegetarian. **2** a vegetable.

vehemence /'vɪəməns, 'vi:həməns/ *noun* strong and forceful feeling.

vehement /'vɪəmənt, 'vi:həmənt/ *adj.* expressed with strong feeling or firm conviction; forceful; emphatic. [from Latin *vehemens*, eager]

◼ forceful, emphatic, impassioned, passionate, ardent, fervent, intense, heated, strong, powerful, urgent, enthusiastic, animated, eager, earnest, forcible, fierce, violent, zealous.
◪ apathetic, indifferent.

vehemently /'vɪəməntlɪ, 'vi:həməntlɪ/ *adv.* with strong feeling; forcefully.

vehicle *noun* **1** a conveyance for transporting people or things, especially a self-powered one. **2** a person or thing used as a means of communicating ideas or opinions: *newspapers as vehicles for political propaganda.* **3** a neutral substance in which a drug is mixed in order to be administered, eg a syrup. **4** a substance in which a pigment is transferred to a surface as paint, eg oil or water. [from Latin *vehere*, to carry]

◼ **1** conveyance, transport. **2** means, agency, channel, medium, mechanism, organ.

Vehicles include: plane, boat, ship, car, taxi, hackney carriage, bicycle, *colloq.* bike, cycle, tandem, tricycle, *colloq.* boneshaker, penny-farthing, motorcycle, motorbike, scooter, bus, omnibus, minibus, *colloq.* double-decker, coach, charabanc, caravan, caravanette, camper, train, Pullman, sleeper, wagon-lit, tube, tram, monorail, maglev, trolleybus; van, *trademark* Transit, lorry, truck, juggernaut, pantechnicon, trailer, tractor, fork-lift truck, steamroller, tank, wagon; bobsleigh, sled, sledge, sleigh, toboggan, troika; barouche, brougham, dog-cart, dray, four-in-hand, gig, hansom, landau, phaeton, post-chaise, stagecoach, sulky, surrey, trap; rickshaw, sedan chair, litter. *See also* **aircraft**; **boats and ships**; **car**.

vehicular *adj.* relating to or for the use of vehicles: *no vehicular access.*

veil — *noun* **1** a fabric covering for a woman's head or face, forming part of traditional dress in some societies. **2** a covering of fine netting for a woman's head, which may be attached to a hat or headdress, worn for decoration or ceremonially, eg by a bride. **3** the hoodlike part of a nun's habit. **4** (**the veil**) *literary* the vocation of a nun. **5** anything that covers or obscures: *a veil of secrecy.* — *verb* **1** to cover, or cover the face of, with a veil. **2** to conceal or partly conceal; to disguise or obscure: *veiled threats.* — **draw a veil over something** to conceal it discreetly; to avoid mentioning it. **take the veil** to become a nun. [from Latin *velum*, curtain]

◼ *noun* **5** cover, cloak, curtain, mask, screen, disguise, film, blind, shade, shroud. *verb* **2** screen, cloak, cover, mask, shadow, shield, obscure, conceal, hide, disguise, shade.
◪ *verb* EXPOSE, UNCOVER.

vein *noun* **1** any blood vessel, apart from the pulmonary vein, that carries deoxygenated blood back towards the heart. Veins have thin walls, and contain valves which ensure that blood can only flow in one direction. **2** *loosely* any blood vessel. **3** a thin sheetlike deposit of one or more minerals, eg quartz, deposited in a fracture or joint in the surrounding rock. **4** a streak of different colour, eg in cheese. **5** in a leaf, any of a large number of thin branching tubes containing the vascular (conducting) tissues, ie the xylem and phloem. **6** in an insect, any of the tubes of chitin that stiffen and support the membranous structure of the wings. **7** a mood or tone: *written in a sarcastic vein*. **8** a distinct characteristic present throughout; a streak. [from Latin *vena*]

⊟ **3** stratum, seam, lode, streak. **4** streak, stripe. **7, 8** mood, tone, tenor, frame of mind, mode, style, tendency, bent, strain, temper.

veined *adj.* having veins or different-coloured streaks.

veiny *adj.* streaked with veins; having prominent veins.

Velcro *noun trademark* a fastening material consisting of two nylon surfaces, one of tiny hooks, the other of thin fibres, which bond tightly when pressed together but are easily pulled apart.

veld or **veldt** /felt, velt/ *noun* a wide grassy plane with few or no trees, especially in southern Africa. [from Dutch *veld*, field]

veleta or **valeta** /vəˈliːtə/ *noun* a ballroom dance or dance tune with a fast waltz-like rhythm. [from Spanish *veleta*, weathercock]

vellum /ˈveləm/ *noun* **1** a fine kind of parchment, originally made from calfskin. **2** a manuscript written on such parchment. **3** thick cream-coloured writing-paper. [from Old French *velin*, from *veel*, calf]

velocity *noun* (PL. **velocities**) **1** *technical* rate of motion in a particular direction. **2** *loosely* speed. [from Latin *velox*, swift]

velour or **velours** /vəˈlʊə(r)/ *noun* any fabric with a velvet-like pile, used especially for upholstery. [from French *velours*, related to VELVET]

velvet — *noun* **1** a fabric, usually nylon or silk, with a very short soft closely woven pile on one side. **2** the soft skin that covers the growing antlers of deer, and is rubbed off as they mature. — *adj.* **1** made of velvet. **2** soft or smooth like velvet. — **on velvet** *colloq.* in a comfortable position of safety or wealth. [from late Latin *velvettum*, from Latin *villus*, tuft]

velveteen *noun* cotton fabric with a velvet-like pile.

velvet glove apparent gentleness or lenience concealing strength or firmness, especially with allusion to the phrase *an iron hand in a velvet glove*.

velvet revolution the peaceful transition from communism to democracy in Czechoslovakia in 1989.

velvety *adj.* having the quality of velvet; smooth.

Ven. *abbrev.* Venerable.

vena cava /ˈviːnə ˈkeɪvə/ (PL. **venae cavae**) *Anat.* either of the two large veins (the superior vena cava and the inferior vena cava) that carry deoxygenated blood to the right atrium (auricle) of the heart. [from Latin *vena cava*, hollow vein]

venal *adj.* **1** willing to be persuaded by corrupt means, especially bribery. **2** *said of behaviour* dishonest; corrupt. [from Latin *venum*, goods for sale]

venality *noun* a venal state or conduct; susceptibility to corruption.

venally *adv.* dishonestly; corruptly.

venation *noun Biol.* **1** the arrangement of veins in the wing of an insect. **2** the arrangement of veins in the leaf of a plant. [from Latin *vena*, vein]

vend *verb* to sell or offer for sale (especially small wares). [from Latin *vendere*, to sell]

vendee /venˈdiː/ *noun Legal* a buyer, especially of property.

vendetta *noun* **1** a bitter feud in which the family of a murdered person takes revenge by killing the murderer or a relative. **2** any long-standing bitter feud or quarrel. [from Italian, from Latin *vindicta*, revenge]

⊟ FEUD, BLOOD-FEUD, ENMITY, RIVALRY, QUARREL,

BAD BLOOD, BITTERNESS.

vending machine a coin-operated machine dispensing small wares such as sweets, drinks, and cigarettes.

vendor *noun* **1** *Legal* a seller, especially of property. **2** a seller of goods, especially at a market: *fruit vendor*.

veneer — *noun* **1** a thin layer of a fine material (especially wood) fixed to the surface of an inferior material to give an attractive finish. **2** a false or misleading external appearance, especially of a favourable quality: *a veneer of respectability*. — *verb* to put a veneer on. [from Old French *fornir*, to furnish]

⊟ *noun* **2** front, façade, appearance, gloss, pretence, guise, show, mask.

venerable *adj.* **1** deserving to be greatly respected or revered, especially on account of age or religious association. **2** (**Venerable**) **a** *Church of E.* a title given to an archdeacon. **b** *RC Church* a title given to a person due to be declared a saint. [from Latin *venerabilis*]

⊟ **1** respected, revered, esteemed, honoured, venerated, dignified, grave, wise, august, aged, worshipped.

venerate *verb* to regard with deep respect or awe; to revere. [from Latin *venerari*]

⊟ revere, respect, honour, esteem, worship, hallow, adore.
⊟ despise, anathematize.

veneration *noun* the paying of deep respect; devotion.

venereal *adj.* **1** *said of a disease or infection* transmitted by sexual intercourse. **2** relating to, resulting from, or for the treatment of such diseases. [from Latin *venereus*, from *Venus*, Roman goddess of love]

venereal disease *Medicine* former name for a sexually transmitted disease.

Venetian — *adj.* relating to Venice in NE Italy. — *noun* a native or citizen of Venice. [from Latin *Venetia*, Venice]

Venetian blind a window blind consisting of horizontal slats strung together, one beneath the other, and tilted to let in or shut out light.

vengeance *noun* punishment inflicted as a revenge; retribution. — **with a vengeance 1** forcefully or violently. **2** to a great degree: *foolishness with a vengeance*. [from Old French, from Latin *vindicare*, to avenge]

⊟ retribution, revenge, retaliation, reprisal, requital, tit for tat.
⊟ forgiveness.

vengeful *adj.* **1** eager for revenge. **2** carried out in revenge. [from obsolete *venge*, to avenge]

venial *adj.*, *said of a sin or weakness* forgivable; excusable. [from Latin *venia*, pardon]

veniality *noun* a venial state, with reference to sin or weakness.

venial sin *RC Church* a minor sin, not involving loss of divine grace. See also MORTAL SIN.

venison *noun* the flesh of a deer, used as food. [from Old French, from Latin *venari*, to hunt]

Venn diagram *Maths.* a diagram that is used to illustrate the relationships between mathematical sets, consisting of a rectangle that represents the universal set, within which individual sets are denoted by circles. [named after the English logician John Venn (1834–1923)]

venom *noun* **1** a poisonous liquid that some creatures, including scorpions and certain snakes, inject in a bite or sting. **2** spitefulness, especially in language or tone of voice. [Latin *venenum*, poison]

⊟ **1** poison, toxin. **2** rancour, ill-will, malice, malevolence, spite, bitterness, acrimony, hate, virulence.

venomous *adj.* **1** inflicting venom; poisonous. **2** spiteful.

▣ **1** poisonous, toxic, virulent, harmful, noxious. **2** spiteful, malicious, vicious, vindictive, baleful, hostile, malignant, rancorous, baneful.
▣ HARMLESS.

venous *adj.* relating to or contained in veins. [from Latin *vena*, vein]

vent¹ *noun* a slit in a garment, especially upwards from the hem at the back of a jacket or coat, for style or ease of movement. [from French *fente*, slit]

vent² — *noun* **1** an opening allowing air, gas, or liquid into or out of a confined space. **2** the passage inside a volcano, through which lava and gases escape. **3** *Biol.* the anus of a bird or other small animal. — *verb* **1** to make a vent in. **2** to let in or out through a vent. **3** to release (especially emotion) freely. — **give vent to something** to express one's feelings or emotions openly. [from French *éventer*, to expose to air]

▣ *noun* **1** opening, hole, aperture, outlet, passage, orifice, duct. *verb* **2** release, discharge, emit. **3** express, voice, utter, air.

ventilate *verb* **1** to allow fresh air to circulate throughout. **2** to cause (blood) to take up oxygen. **3** to supply air to (the lungs). **4** to expose to public examination or discussion. [from Latin *ventilare*, from *ventus*, wind]

▣ **1** air, aerate, freshen. **4** air, broadcast, debate, discuss.

ventilation *noun* the act or process of ventilating; circulation of fresh air.

ventilator *noun* **1** a device that circulates or draws in fresh air. **2** a machine that ventilates the lungs of a person whose respiratory system is damaged.

ventral *adj.* **1** *Anat.* denoting the lower surface of an animal that walks on four legs, of any invertebrate, or of a structure such as a leaf or wing. **2** denoting the front surface of the body of an animal that walks upright, eg a human being. **3** denoting a structure that is situated on or just beneath such a surface. [from Latin *venter*, abdomen]

ventrally *adv.* in relation to the abdomen or belly.

ventricle *noun* **1** *Anat.* in mammals, either of the two lower chambers of the heart, which have thick muscular walls. **2** *Anat.* in vertebrates, any of several fluid-filled cavities within the brain. [from Latin *ventriculus*]

ventricular *adj.* relating to or situated in a ventricle.

ventriloquism *noun* the art of speaking in a way that makes the sound appear to come from elsewhere, especially a dummy's mouth; throwing the voice. [from Latin *venter*, belly + *loqui*, to speak]

ventriloquist *noun* a person who performs ventriloquism, especially as entertainment.

ventriloquize or **ventriloquise** *verb intrans.* to perform ventriloquism.

venture — *noun* **1** an exercise or operation involving danger or uncertainty. **2** a business project, especially one involving risk or speculation. **3** an enterprise attempted. — *verb* **1** *trans., intrans.* to be so bold as to; to dare: *ventured to criticize the chairman.* **2** (**venture out** or **forth**) to dare to go out, especially outdoors: *reluctant to venture out in bad weather.* **3** to put forward or present in the face of possible opposition: *ventured a different opinion.* **4** to expose to danger or chance; to risk. — **venture on something** to attempt something dangerous. [shortening of ADVENTURE]

▣ *noun* **1** risk, chance, hazard, speculation, gamble, adventure, fling. **2, 3** undertaking, project, endeavour, enterprise, operation. *verb* **1** dare, make bold, presume.

3 put forward, present, advance, suggest, volunteer. **4** risk, hazard, endanger, imperil, jeopardize, speculate, wager, stake.

venture capital money supplied by individual investors or business organizations for a new, especially speculative, business enterprise.

venturer *noun* **1** a person who takes part in a venture or enterprise. **2** *Hist.* a participant in a trading scheme.

Venture Scout a member of the senior branch of the Scout movement.

venturesome *adj.* **1** prepared to take risks; enterprising. **2** involving danger; risky.

venue *noun* **1** the chosen location for a sports event or entertainment. **2** *Legal* the place where a court case is to be tried, or the district from which the jurors are chosen. **3** a meeting-place. [from Latin *venire*, to come]

venule *noun* *Biol.* **1** a branch of a vein in an insect's wing. **2** any of the small-calibre blood vessels into which the capillaries empty, and which join up to form veins. [from Latin *venula*, diminutive of *vena*, vein]

Venus *Astron.* the second planet from the Sun. It resembles a bright star, and can be seen some time before and after the true stars become visible. For this reason it is sometimes called the 'evening star' or 'morning star'.

Venus flytrap an insectivorous plant (*Dionaea muscipula*), native to the bogs of North and South Carolina, with leaves consisting of two parts hinged together which snap shut when an insect touches the inner surface of the leaf.

veracious *adj. formal* truthful. [from Latin *verus*, true]

veracity *noun formal* truthfulness.

veranda or **verandah** *noun* a sheltered terrace attached to a house or other building. [from Portuguese *varanda*, balcony]

verb *noun* a word that belongs to a grammatical class denoting an action, experience, occurrence, or state, eg *do, feel, happen, remain.* [from Latin *verbum*, word]

verbal *adj.* **1** relating to or consisting of words: *verbal abuse.* **2** spoken, not written: *verbal communication.* **3** *Grammar* relating to verbs.

▣ **1** spoken, oral, written, linguistic. **2** spoken, oral, unwritten, word-of-mouth.

verbalism *noun* excessive attention paid to words used, rather than to ideas expressed, especially in literary criticism.

verbalize or **verbalise** *verb* **1** to express in words. **2** *intrans.* to use too many words; to be verbose.

verbally *adv.* in speech, not in writing: *communicated with them verbally.*

verbal noun a form of a verb that functions as a noun, eg '*to err* is human' and '*swimming* keeps you fit'.

verbatim /vɜːˈbeɪtɪm/ *adj., adv.* using exactly the same words; word-for-word. [from Latin *verbatim*]

▣ word-for-word, exactly, literally, to the letter, precisely.

verbena *noun* any of a group of plants of mild and tropical climates, with clusters of fragrant flowers, used in herbal medicine and cosmetics. [from Latin *verbena*, sacred bough]

verbiage *noun* **1** the use of language that is wordy or needlessly complicated, and often meaningless. **2** such language. [from Old French *verbeier*, to chatter]

verbose *adj.* using or containing too many words; boringly or irritatingly long-winded. [from Latin *verbosus*]

▣ long-winded, wordy, prolix, loquacious, diffuse, circumlocutory.
▣ succinct, brief.

verbosity *noun* using or containing too many words; long-windedness.

verdancy *noun* a lush quality; freshness.

verdant *adj.* 1 covered with lush green grass or vegetation. 2 of a rich green colour. 3 naive or unsophisticated; green. [from Old French *verdeant* from Latin *viridis* green]

verdict *noun* 1 a decision arrived at by a jury in a court of law. 2 any decision, opinion, or judgement. [from Latin *veredictum*, truly said]

■ DECISION, JUDGEMENT, CONCLUSION, FINDING, ADJUDICATION, ASSESSMENT, OPINION.

verdigris /'vɜːdɪgriːs/ *noun Chem.* a bluish-green coating of basic copper salts, especially copper carbonate, that forms as a result of corrosion when copper, brass, or bronze surfaces are exposed to air and moisture for long periods. [from Old French *verd de Grèce*, green of Greece]

verdure /'vɜːdʒə(r)/ *noun literary* lush green vegetation, or its rich colour. [from Latin *viridis*, green]

verge¹ — *noun* 1 a limit, boundary, or border. 2 a strip of grass bordering a road. 3 a point or stage immediately beyond or after which something exists or occurs: *on the verge of tears.* — *verb* 1 to serve as the border or boundary of. 2 (**verge on something**) to be close to being or becoming something specified: *enthusiasm verging on obsession.* [from Latin *virga*, rod]

■ *noun* 1 border, boundary, edge, edging, margin, limit, rim, brim, extreme. 3 threshold, brink. *verb* 2 come close to, approach, border on, near.

verge² *verb intrans.* 1 to slope or incline in a specified direction. 2 (**verge to** or **towards something**) to move or tend to or towards it. [from Latin *vergere*, to bend]

verger *noun* 1 a church official who assists the minister and acts as caretaker. 2 an official who carries the ceremonial staff of a bishop or other dignitary. [from Latin *virga*, rod]

verifiable *adj.* capable of being verified or established as true.

verification *noun* establishing as true or valid; verifying.

verify *verb* (**verifies**, **verified**) to check or confirm the truth or accuracy of. [from Latin *verus*, true + *facere*, to make]

■ check, confirm, corroborate, substantiate, authenticate, bear out, prove, support, validate, testify, attest.
🔁 invalidate, discredit.

verily *adv. old use* truly; really. [related to VERY]

verisimilitude /vɛrɪsɪ'mɪlɪtjuːd/ *noun formal* 1 the quality of appearing to be real or true. 2 a statement or proposition that sounds true but may not be. [from Latin *verus*, true + *similis*, like]

veritable *adj. formal* accurately described as such; real: *a veritable genius!* [from Latin *verus*, true]

veritably *adv. formal* truly, really.

verity *noun* (PL. **verities**) 1 a true statement, especially one of fundamental wisdom or importance; a maxim. 2 truthfulness. [from Latin *verus*, true]

vermicelli /vɜːmɪ'tʃɛlɪ/ *noun* 1 pasta in very thin strands, thinner than spaghetti. 2 tiny splinters of chocolate used for desserts and cake decoration. [from Italian *vermicelli*, little worms]

vermiform *adj.* like a worm; worm-shaped. [from Latin *vermis*, worm]

vermiform appendix *Medicine* the appendix.

vermilion *noun* 1 a bright scarlet colour. 2 a pigment of this colour, consisting of sulphide of mercury. [from Latin *vermiculus*]

vermin *noun* (usually as pl.) 1 a collective name for wild animals that spread disease or generally cause a nuisance, especially rats and other rodents. 2 detestable people. [from Latin *vermis*, worm]

verminous *adj.* like vermin; parasitic; vile.

vermouth /'vɜːməθ/ *noun* an alcoholic drink consisting of wine flavoured with aromatic herbs, originally wormwood. [from German *Wermut*, wormwood]

vernacular /və'nakjʊlə(r)/ — *noun* (usually **the vernacular**) 1 the native language of a country or people, as opposed to a foreign language that is also in use. 2 the form of a language as commonly spoken, as opposed to the formal or literary language. 3 the language or jargon of a particular group. 4 *humorous* slang or indecent language. — *adj.* 1 of or in the vernacular. 2 local; native. [from Latin *vernaculus*, native]

■ *noun* 1, 2 language, speech, tongue, dialect, idiom. 3 language, jargon, idiom, parlance. *adj.* 1 popular, vulgar, informal, colloquial, common, indigenous, local, native. 2 indigenous, local, native.

vernal *adj.* relating or appropriate to spring. [from Latin *ver*, spring]

vernal equinox *Astron.* the equinox that occurs annually around 21 Mar, when the Sun's path crosses the celestial equator S–N, so that day and night are of equal length.

vernalization or **vernalisation** *noun Bot.* the process whereby germinating seeds or seedlings are exposed to low temperatures in order to ensure that they flower subsequently.

vernally *adv.* as regards spring; in spring.

vernier *noun* a small sliding device on some measuring instruments, eg barometers and theodolites, used to measure fractions of units. [named after the French scientific instrument-maker Pierre Vernier (1584–1638)]

veronica *noun* a plant of the foxglove family, of mild and cold climates, with small blue, pink, or white flowers.

verruca /və'ruːkə/ *noun* (PL. **verrucas**, **verrucae**) *Medicine* a wart, especially one on the sole of the foot. [from Latin *verruca*, wart]

versatile *adj.* 1 adapting easily to different tasks. 2 having numerous uses or abilities. [from Latin *versatilis*, from *vertere*, to turn]

■ 1 adaptable, flexible, resourceful, handy. 2 multipurpose, multifaceted, all-round, many-sided, general-purpose, functional, adjustable, variable.
🔁 INFLEXIBLE.

versatility *noun* the ability to be adaptable.

verse *noun* 1 a division of a poem; a stanza. 2 poetry, as opposed to prose. 3 a poem. 4 a division of a song. 5 any of the numbered subdivisions of the chapters of the Bible. [from Latin *versus*, line, row]

■ 2 poetry, rhyme, metre, doggerel.

versed *adj.* (**versed in something**) familiar with it or skilled in it.

■ familiar with, skilled at, proficient at or in, practised in, experienced at or in, acquainted with, knowledgeable about, conversant with, qualified in, competent at or in, accomplished at.

versification *noun* composing verses or turning into verses.

versifier *noun* a person who writes verses.

versify *verb* (**versifies**, **versified**) 1 *intrans.* to write poetry. 2 to express as, or turn into, a poem. [from Latin *versificare*, to put into verse]

version *noun* any of several types or forms in which a thing exists or is available, eg a particular edition or translation of a book, or one person's account of an incident. [from Latin *versio*, from *vertere*, to turn]

. . . .

■ type, kind, variant, form, model, style, design, rendering, reading, interpretation, account, translation, adaptation, portrayal.

. . . .

verso *noun* (PL. **versos**) **1** the back of a loose sheet of printed paper. **2** the left-hand page of two open pages. See also RECTO. [Latin *verso folio*, turned leaf]

versus *prep.* **1** (in a contest or lawsuit) against. **2** *colloq.* in comparison to. [from Latin *versus*]

vertebra *noun* (PL. **vertebrae**) *Anat.* in vertebrates, any of the small bones or cartilaginous segments that form the backbone. Each vertebra contains a central canal through which the spinal cord passes. [from Latin *vertebra*, from *vertere*, to turn]

vertebral *adj.* relating to the vertebra.

vertebrate — *noun Zool.* any animal that has a backbone consisting of bony or cartilaginous vertebrae enclosing a spinal cord. Vertebrates include fish, amphibians, reptiles, birds, and mammals. — *adj.* relating to an animal that has a backbone.

vertex *noun* (PL. **vertexes**, **vertices**) **1** the highest point; the peak or summit. **2** *Maths.* the point opposite the base of a geometric figure, eg the pointed tip of a cone. **3** *Maths.* the point where the two sides of an angle meet in a polygon, or where three or more surfaces meet in a polyhedron. [from Latin *vertex*, summit, whirlpool]

vertical — *adj.* **1** perpendicular to the horizon; upright. **2** running from top to bottom, not side to side. **3** of or at a vertex. **4** relating to, involving, or running through all levels within a hierarchy, all stages of a process, etc, rather than just one. — *noun* a vertical line or direction.

. . . .

■ *adj.* **1** upright, perpendicular, upstanding, erect, on end.
E3 *adj.* **1, 2** horizontal.

. . . .

vertical integration *Commerce* a business situation in which a company expands by buying up its suppliers and/or its customers, thus controlling all the processes of production, from raw materials through to sale of the final product.

vertically *adv.* in a vertical or upright position.

vertical take-off a take-off by an aircraft directly upwards from a stationary position.

vertiginous *adj.* **1** so high or whirling as to bring on vertigo; dizzying. **2** relating to vertigo.

vertigo *noun* a whirling sensation felt when the sense of balance is disturbed; dizziness; giddiness. [from Latin *vertigo*, from *vertere*, to turn]

. . . .

■ dizziness, giddiness, light-headedness.

. . . .

vervain *noun* a wild verbena. [from Old French *vervaine*]

verve *noun* great liveliness or enthusiasm. [from French *verve*]

. . . .

■ vitality, vivacity, enthusiasm, animation, liveliness, energy, dash, élan, sparkle, vigour, gusto, life, relish, spirit, force.
E3 apathy, lethargy.

. . . .

very — *adv.* **1** to a high degree or great extent: *very kind.* **2** (used with *own*, *same*, and with superlative adjectives) absolutely; truly: *the very same day / my very best effort.* — *adj.* **1** absolute: *the very top.* **2** precise; actual: *this very minute.* **3** mere: *shocked by the very thought.* — **not very** not at all; the opposite of. **very good** or **very well** expressions of consent and approval. [from Old French *verai*, from Latin *verus*, true]

. . . .

■ *adv.* **1** extremely, greatly, highly, deeply, truly, *colloq.* terribly, remarkably, excessively, exceeding(ly), acutely, particularly, really, absolutely, noticeably, unusually. *adj.* **1** true, genuine,

real, actual. **2** precise, actual, exact, same, selfsame, identical. **3** mere, sheer, pure, utter, simple, perfect, plain, bare.
E3 *adv.* **1** slightly, scarcely.

. . . .

very high frequency (ABBREV. **VHF**) a band of radio frequencies between 30 and 300 MHz.

Very light a coloured flare fired from a pistol, as a signal or to illuminate an area. [invented by E W Very (1852–1910), US naval ordnance officer]

very low frequency (ABBREV. **VLF**) *Radio* a radio frequency in the range 3 to 30kHz.

Vesak or **Wesak** /'wesak/ *noun* the most widely celebrated of Buddhist festivals, held in May to commemorate the birth, enlightenment, and death of Buddha.

vesicle *noun* **1** *Biol.* any small sac or cavity, especially one filled with fluid, within the cytoplasm of a living cell. **2** *Medicine* a small blister in the skin, containing serum (a clear fluid), usually associated with herpes, eczema, or other skin disorders. **3** *Geol.* a cavity formed by trapped gas bubbles during the solidification of molten lava. [from Latin *vesica*, bladder]

vespers *sing. noun* an evening service in some Christian churches; evensong. [from Latin *vesper*, evening]

vessel *noun* **1** a container, especially for liquid. **2** a ship or large boat. **3** a tube or duct carrying liquid, eg blood or sap, in animals and plants. [from Latin *vasis*]

vest — *noun* **1** an undergarment for the top half of the body. **2** *North Amer., esp. US* a waistcoat. — *verb* **1** (**vest something in someone** or **someone with something**) to give or bestow legally or officially: *by the power vested in me / the chairman is vested with absolute authority.* **2** *intrans.* to put on ecclesiastical robes. [from Latin *vestis*, clothing]

vestal — *adj.* virginal; chaste. — *noun* **1** a chaste woman, especially a nun. **2** a vestal virgin. [from Latin *vestalis*, of *Vesta*, the Roman goddess of the hearth and home]

Vestal Virgin in ancient Rome, one of the aristocratic virgin priestesses of Vesta, the goddess of the hearth.

vested interest 1 an interest a person has in the fortunes of a particular system or institution because that person is directly affected or closely associated. **2** a person or company with such an interest.

vestibule *noun* an entrance hall. [from Latin *vestibulum*]

vestige *noun* **1** a slight amount; a hint or shred. **2** a surviving trace of what has almost disappeared. **3** *Biol.* a small, fairly functionless part in an animal or plant, once a fully developed organ in ancestors. [from Latin *vestigium*, footprint]

. . . .

■ **1** hint, shred, trace, suspicion, indication, sign, evidence, whiff, inkling, glimmer, token, scrap. **2** trace, remains, remainder, remnant, residue, sign, evidence.

. . . .

vestigial *adj. Biol.*, *said of an organ* having no function: *a vestigial wing.*

vestment *noun* **1** any of various garments worn ceremonially by members of the clergy and church choir. **2** any ceremonial robe. [from Latin *vestis*, clothing]

vestry *noun* (PL. **vestries**) a room in a church where the vestments are kept, often also used for meetings, Sunday school classes, etc. [from Latin *vestis*, clothing]

vet[1] — *noun* a veterinary surgeon. — *verb* (**vetted**, **vetting**) to examine or investigate (especially a person) thoroughly, to check for suitability or reliability.

. . . .

■ *verb* investigate, examine, check, scrutinize, scan, inspect, survey, review, appraise, audit.

. . . .

vet[2] *noun colloq. North Amer., esp. US* a veteran.

vetch *noun* any of various climbing plants of the pea family with blue or purple flowers, and pods used as fodder. [from Latin *vicia*]

veteran *noun* **1** a person with many years of experience in a particular activity. **2** an old and experienced member of the armed forces. **3** *North Amer., esp. US* an ex-serviceman or woman. [from Latin *veteranus*, old]

. . . .

▣ **1** old hand, old stager, old-timer, master, pastmaster, *colloq.* pro, warhorse.
▨ **1** novice, recruit.

. . . .

veteran car a very old motor car, specifically one made before 1905.

Veterans' Day 11 Nov, a public holiday in the USA, in honour of veterans of all wars. It was originally instituted as *Armistice Day* after World War I, and was known by that name until 1954.

veterinary — *adj.* concerned with diseases of animals. — *noun* (PL. **veterinaries**) *colloq.* a veterinary surgeon. [from Latin *veterinae*, cattle]

veterinary surgeon or **veterinarian** a person qualified to treat diseases of animals.

veto — *noun* (PL. **vetoes**) **1** the right to formally reject a proposal or forbid an action, eg in a law-making assembly; the act of using such a right. **2** *colloq.* any prohibition or refusal of permission. — *verb* (**vetoes, vetoed**) **1** to formally and authoritatively reject or forbid. **2** *loosely* to forbid. [from Latin *veto*, I forbid]

. . . .

▣ *noun* **2** prohibition, refusal, rejection, ban, embargo, *colloq.* thumbs-down. *verb* REJECT, TURN DOWN, FORBID, DISALLOW, BAN, PROHIBIT, RULE OUT, BLOCK.
▨ *noun* **2** approval, assent. *verb* APPROVE, SANCTION.

. . . .

vex *verb* **1** to annoy or irritate. **2** to worry. [from Latin *vexare*, to shake, to annoy]

. . . .

▣ **1** irritate, annoy, provoke, *colloq.* aggravate, exasperate, put out, pester, harass, *colloq.* hassle, *colloq.* needle, torment. **2** trouble, upset, worry, bother, disturb, distress, agitate, fret.
▨ **1** calm, soothe.

. . . .

vexation *noun* **1** the state or feeling of being vexed. **2** a thing that vexes.

vexatious *adj.* vexing; annoying.

vexed *adj.*, *said of an issue, etc* much discussed or debated.

. . . .

▣ controversial, contested, disputed, difficult.

. . . .

vexing *adj.* irritating; annoying.

VGA *abbrev. Comput.* video graphics array, a computer monitor screen display system able to display several colours at a resolution of 640 x 480 pixels.

VHF *abbrev. Radio* very high frequency.

VHS *abbrev.* Video Home Service.

via *prep.* by way of or by means of; through. [from Latin *via*, way]

viability *noun* feasibility; capable of being maintained.

viable *adj.* **1** *said of a plan, etc* having a chance of success; feasible; practicable. **2** *said of a plant, etc* able to exist or grow in particular conditions. **3** *said of a foetus or baby* able to survive independently outside the womb. [from French *viable*, from Latin *vita* life]

. . . .

▣ **1** feasible, practicable, possible, workable, usable, operable, achievable, sustainable.
▨ **1** impossible, unworkable.

. . . .

viaduct *noun* a bridge-like structure of stone arches supporting a road or railway across a valley, etc. [from Latin *via*, way + *ducere*, to lead]

Viagra /vaɪˈagrə, viːˈagrə/ *noun trademark* a drug used to treat male impotence.

vial *noun* a small medicine bottle. [related to PHIAL]

viands /vaɪəndz/ *pl. noun formal* items of food; provisions. [from Old French *viande*, food, from Latin *vivenda*]

viaticum /vaɪˈatɪkəm/ *noun* (PL. **viaticums, viatica**) **1** the Eucharist given to a dying person. **2** *formal* provisions for a journey. [from Latin *viaticum*, from *via*, way]

vibes *pl. noun colloq.* feelings, sensations, or an atmosphere experienced or communicated. [shortening of *vibration*]

vibrancy *noun* **1** vibrating; quivering. **2** excitement.

vibrant *adj.* **1** extremely lively or exciting; made strikingly animated or energetic. **2** *said of a colour* strong and bright. **3** vibrating. [from Latin *vibrare*, related to VIBRATE]

. . . .

▣ **1** animated, vivacious, lively, sparkling, spirited, thrilling, dynamic, electrifying, electric. **2** vivid, strong, bright, brilliant, colourful.

. . . .

vibrantly *adv.* in a vibrant or exciting way.

vibraphone *noun* a musical instrument in which horizontal metal bars of different lengths are made to resound electrically when struck with hammers. [from VIBRATE + -PHONE]

vibraphonist *noun* a person who plays the vibraphone.

vibrate *verb* **1** *trans., intrans.* to move a short distance back and forth very rapidly. **2** *intrans.* to ring or resound when struck. **3** *intrans.* to shake or tremble. **4** *intrans.* to swing back and forth; to oscillate. [from Latin *vibrare*, tremble]

. . . .

▣ **1** pulsate, throb. **2** resonate, reverberate. **3** shake, tremble, quiver, shudder, shiver. **4** oscillate, sway, swing.

. . . .

vibration *noun* **1** a vibrating motion. **2** a single movement back and forth in vibrating. **3** (**vibrations**) *colloq.* feelings, sensations, or an atmosphere experienced or communicated.

vibrato /vɪˈbrɑːtoʊ/ *noun* (PL. **vibratos**) a faint trembling effect in singing or the playing of string and wind instruments, achieved by vibrating the throat muscles or the fingers. [from Italian *vibrato*]

vibrator *noun* **1** any device that produces a vibrating motion, eg for massage. **2** a battery-powered vibrating dildo.

vibratory *adj.* causing vibration.

vicar *noun* **1** *Church of E.* the minister of a parish. **2** *RC Church* a bishop's deputy. [from Latin *vicarius*, deputy, substitute]

vicarage *noun* a vicar's residence or benefice.

vicar-apostolic *noun RC Church* a member of the clergy appointed, with the rank of bishop, to a country with no established church structure.

vicar-general *noun RC Church* an official assisting a bishop in administrative matters.

vicarial *adj.* of or serving as a vicar.

vicarious /vɪˈkɛərɪəs/ *adj.* **1** experienced not directly but through witnessing the experience of another person: *vicarious pleasure in seeing his children learn.* **2** undergone on behalf of someone else. **3** standing in for another. **4** *said of authority, etc* delegated to someone else. [from Latin *vicarius*, substituted]

Vicar of Christ the pope, regarded as representative of Christ on earth.

vice¹ *noun* a tool with heavy movable metal jaws, usually fixed to a bench, for gripping an object being worked on. [from French *vis*, screw]

vice² *noun* **1** a habit or activity considered immoral, evil, or depraved, especially involving prostitution or drugs. **2** such activities collectively. **3** a bad habit; a fault in one's character. [from Latin *vitium*, blemish]

. . . .

▣ **1** sin. **2** evil, evildoing, depravity, immorality, wickedness, sin, corruption, iniquity, profligacy, degeneracy. **3** fault, failing, defect, shortcoming, weakness, imperfection, blemish, bad habit.

▣ VIRTUE. **2** morality.
....

vice³ *prep.* **1** in place of. **2** following on from or succeeding. [from the Latin root *vic-*, turn, alteration]

vice- *combining form* forming words meaning 'next in rank to, and acting as deputy for': *vice-admiral* / *vice-president*. [related to VICE³]

vice-chancellor *noun* the deputy chancellor of a university, responsible for most administrative duties.

vicegerency *noun* the office of vicegerent.

vicegerent /vaɪsˈdʒɛrənt/ *noun* a person appointed to act in place of a superior. — *adj.* acting in this capacity. [from VICE³ + Latin *gerere*, to manage]

viceregal /vaɪsˈriːɡəl/ *adj.* relating to a viceroy.

viceroy /ˈvaɪsrɔɪ/ *noun* a governor of a province or colony ruling in the name of, and with the authority of, a monarch or national government. [from French *viceroy*]

viceroyalty or **viceroyship** *noun* the office or position of viceroy.

vice squad a branch of the police force investigating crimes relating to vice, especially prostitution.

vice versa *adv.* with the order or correspondence reversed; the other way round: *from me to you and vice versa*. [from Latin *vice versa*, the position being reversed, related to VICE³]

vicinity *noun* (PL. **vicinities**) **1** a neighbourhood. **2** the area immediately surrounding. **3** the condition of being close; nearness. [from Latin *vicinus*, neighbour]
....

▣ **1** neighbourhood, area, locality, district. **2** precincts, environs. **3** nearness, closeness, proximity.
....

vicious *adj.* **1** violent or ferocious. **2** spiteful or malicious. **3** extremely severe or harsh. **4** *said of reasoning, etc* incorrect or faulty; unsound. [from Latin *vitiosus*, faulty]
....

▣ **1** violent, ferocious, savage, wild. **2** malicious, spiteful, vindictive, virulent, cruel, mean, nasty, slanderous, venomous, defamatory. **3** severe, harsh, barbarous, brutal, cruel, punishing, merciless, relentless, bitter.
▣ **2** kind.
....

vicious circle 1 a situation in which any attempt to resolve a problem creates others which in turn recreate the first one. **2** an incorrect form of reasoning in which one proposition is supposedly proved on the basis of another which itself depends for its proof on the truth of the first.

viciously *adv.* in a vicious or spiteful way.

viciousness *noun* a vicious or spiteful state or manner.

vicissitude /vɪˈsɪsɪtjuːd/ *noun* an unpredictable change of fortune or circumstance. [from Latin *vicissim* by turns]

victim *noun* **1** a person or animal subjected to death, suffering, ill-treatment, or trickery. **2** a person or animal killed in a sacrifice or ritual. [from Latin *victima*, beast for sacrifice]
....

▣ **1** sufferer, casualty, prey, scapegoat, martyr, fatality. **2** sacrifice.
▣ **1** offender, attacker.
....

victimization or **victimisation** *noun* unfair or vindictive treatment.

victimize or **victimise** *verb* **1** to single out for hostile or unfair treatment. **2** to cause to be a victim.
....

▣ **1** oppress, persecute, discriminate against, pick on, prey on, bully, exploit.
....

victor *noun* the winner or winning side in a war or contest. [from Latin *victor*, from *vincere*, to conquer]

victoria *noun* a large red sweet variety of plum, named after Queen Victoria.

Victorian — *adj.* **1** relating to or characteristic of Queen Victoria or the period of her reign (1837–1901). **2** *said of attitudes or values* typical of the strictness or conventionality of this period. — *noun* a person who lived during this period.

Victoriana *pl. noun* objects from, or in a style typical of, the Victorian period in Britain.

victorious *adj.* **1** winning a war or contest. **2** marking or representing a victory.
....

▣ TRIUMPHANT, CONQUERING, CHAMPION. **1** winning, unbeaten, successful, prize-winning, top, first.
▣ **1** defeated, unsuccessful.
....

victory *noun* (PL. **victories**) **1** success against an opponent in a war or contest. **2** an occurrence of this. [from Latin *victoria*]
....

▣ TRIUMPH, SUCCESS. **1** superiority, mastery, vanquishment, subjugation, overcoming. **2** conquest, win.
▣ DEFEAT, LOSS.
....

victual /ˈvɪtl/ — *noun* (*usually* **victuals**) food; provisions. — *verb* (**victualled**, **victualling**) **1** to supply with victuals. **2** (*intrans.*) to obtain supplies. [from Latin *victualis*, relating to living]

victualler /ˈvɪtlə(r)/ *noun formal* **1** a shopkeeper selling food and drink. **2** (*in full* **licensed victualler**) *Brit.* a publican licensed to sell food and alcoholic liquor for consumption on the premises.

vicuna /vɪˈkjuːnjə/ *noun* **1** a S American mammal related to the llama. **2** a cloth or yarn made from its wool. [from Spanish *vicuna*]

vide *verb* (as an instruction in a text) refer to; see. [Latin]

videlicet /vɪˈdɛlɪsɪt/ *adv. formal* (especially in writing) namely; that is. [Latin *videre licet* it is allowed to see]

video — *noun* (PL. **videos**) **1** the recording, reproducing, or broadcasting of visual (especially televised) images on magnetic tape. **2** a videocassette or videocassette recorder. **3** a film or programme pre-recorded on videocassette: *now available as a video*. — *adj.* relating to the process of or equipment for recording by video. — *verb* (**videos**, **videoed**) to make a videocassette recording of. [Latin *videre*, to see]

video camera *Photog.* a portable camera that records moving visual images directly on to videotape, which can then be played back on a videocassette recorder and viewed on the screen of a television receiver.

videocassette *noun* a cassette containing videotape, for use in a videocassette recorder.

videocassette recorder (ABBREV. **VCR**) a machine for recording on magnetic tape the sound and video signals of a television broadcast, so that they can be played back on a standard television receiver at a later date. It is also used to play back pre-recorded tapes of motion pictures.

video disc *Telecomm.* a rotating flat circular plate for the reproduction of pre-recorded video programmes on a television receiver.

video game an electronically operated game involving the manipulation of images produced by a computer program on a visual display unit.

video nasty *colloq.* an explicitly shocking violent or pornographic film available as a videocassette.

video RAM or **VRAM** *Comput.* video random access memory, a part of a computer's memory in which data controlling the visual display is stored, sometimes physically separate from the main memory.

video recorder a videocassette recorder.

videotape *noun* magnetic tape on which visual images and sound can be recorded.

videotext *noun* any system in which computerized information is displayed on a television screen, eg teletext.

vie /vaɪ/ *verb intrans.* (**vying**) (**vie with someone for something**) to compete or struggle with them for some gain or advantage. [from Old French *envier*, to challenge or invite]

🔁 struggle, compete, contend, contest, fight, strive, rival.

Vietnamese — *noun* **1** (PL. **Vietnamese**) a native or citizen of Vietnam. **2** an Austro-Asiatic language spoken by c.50 million people in Vietnam, Laos, and Cambodia. — *adj.* relating to Vietnam or its people or language.

view — *noun* **1** an act or opportunity of seeing without obstruction: *a good view of the stage.* **2** something, especially a landscape, seen from a particular point: *a magnificent view from the summit.* **3** range or field of vision: *out of view.* **4** a scene recorded in photograph or picture form. **5** a description or impression: *the book gives a view of life in Roman times.* **6** an opinion; a point of view: *can we have your view on unemployment?* **7** a way of considering or understanding something: *a short-term view of the situation.* — *verb* **1** to see or look at. **2** to inspect or examine. **3** to consider or regard. **4** *trans., intrans.* to watch (a programme) on television; to watch television. — **have something in view** to have it as a plan or aim. **in view of something** taking account of it; because of it. **on view** displayed for all to see or inspect. **with a view to something** with the hope or intention of achieving it: *bought the house with a view to retiring there.* [from French *vue*]

🔁 *noun* **1** look, glimpse, survey, inspection, examination, observation, scrutiny, scan. **2** sight, scene, vision, vista, outlook, prospect, perspective, panorama, landscape. **3** sight. **4** scene, vista, picture, composition. **5** description, account, impression, picture, portrait, portrayal, sketch, glimpse, perception. **6** opinion, attitude, belief, judgement, estimation, feeling, sentiment, impression, notion. **7** perception, consideration, understanding, outlook, attitude. *verb* **1** see, look at, watch, observe, scan, survey, witness, perceive. **2** examine, inspect, look at, observe. **3** consider, regard, contemplate, judge, think about, speculate. **4** watch, see.

viewdata *noun* a system by which computerized information can be displayed on a television screen by means of a telephone link with a computer source.

viewer *noun* **1** any device used for viewing something, especially a photographic slide. **2** a person watching television.

🔁 **2** watcher, spectator, observer.

viewfinder *noun* a device on a camera showing the field of vision covered by the lens.

viewing *noun* an act or opportunity of seeing or inspecting something, eg an exhibition or a house for sale.

viewpoint *noun* an interpretation of facts received; an opinion or point of view.

🔁 opinion, point of view, attitude, position, perspective, slant, standpoint, stance, angle, feeling.

vigil *noun* **1** a period of staying awake, usually to guard or watch over a person or thing. **2** the day before a major religious festival, traditionally spent in prayer. **3** a night-time religious service or session of prayer. [from Latin *vigil*, awake, watchful]

vigilance *noun* the state of being watchful or observant. [from Latin *vigilare*, to keep awake]

vigilant *adj.* ready for possible trouble or danger; alert; watchful.

🔁 watchful, alert, attentive, observant, on one's guard, on

the lookout, cautious, wide awake, sleepless, unsleeping.

🔁 careless.

vigilante /vɪdʒɪˈlantɪ/ *noun* a self-appointed enforcer of law and order.

vignette /viːnˈjet/ *noun* **1** a decorative design on a book's title page, traditionally of vine leaves. **2** a photographic portrait with the background deliberately faded. **3** a short literary essay, especially describing a person's character. [from French *vignette*, little vine]

vigorous *adj.* **1** strong and active. **2** forceful; energetic: *had a vigorous approach to life.*

🔁 ENERGETIC, ROBUST. **1** healthy, strong, active. **2** forceful, lively, dynamic, spirited, full-blooded, strenuous, sound, brisk, forcible, powerful, stout, effective, efficient, enterprising, flourishing, intense.

🔁 WEAK, FEEBLE.

vigorously *adv.* forcefully; energetically.

vigour *noun* **1** great strength and energy of body or mind. **2** liveliness or forcefulness of action. **3** healthy growth (in plants, etc). [from Latin *vigor*]

🔁 **1** strength, energy, health, robustness, stamina, liveliness, vitality, spirit, verve, resilience, soundness. **2** liveliness, animation, forcefulness, dynamism, vitality, gusto, spirit, verve, activity, power, potency, force, might, dash. **3** vitality, robustness.

🔁 WEAKNESS.

viking *noun* (*often* **Viking**) any of the Scandinavian seafaring peoples who raided and settled in much of NW Europe between the 8c and 11c. [perhaps from Anglo-Saxon *wicing*, pirate]

vile *adj.* **1** evil or wicked. **2** physically repulsive; disgusting. **3** *colloq.* extremely bad or unpleasant. [from Latin *vilis*, worthless, base]

🔁 **1** evil, bad, wicked, sinful, base, contemptible, debased, depraved, degenerate, wretched, worthless, miserable, mean, impure, corrupt, despicable, disgraceful, degrading, vicious, appalling. **2, 3** disgusting, foul, nauseating, sickening, repulsive, repugnant, revolting, noxious, offensive, nasty, loathsome, horrid.

🔁 **1** pure, worthy. **2, 3** pleasant, lovely.

vilification *noun* speaking evil; defamation.

vilify *verb* (**vilifies, vilified**) to say insulting or abusive things about; to malign or defame. [from Latin *vilificare*, to make worthless or base]

villa *noun* **1** a large country house or mansion. **2** a good-sized (especially detached) suburban house. **3** a seaside house let to holidaymakers. [from Latin *villa*, country house]

village *noun* **1** a group of houses, shops, and other buildings smaller than a town and larger than a hamlet, especially in or near the countryside. **2** the people living in it, regarded as a community: *the village has started to gossip.* **3** a residential complex for participants in a major (usually international) sporting event. [from Old French *village*, from Latin *villaticus*]

villager *noun* an inhabitant of a village.

villain *noun* **1** the principal wicked character in a story. **2** any violent, wicked, or unscrupulous person. **3** *colloq.* a criminal. [originally 'a rustic', from Old French *vilein*, serf, from Latin *villanus*, worker on a country estate]

🔁 **2, 3** evildoer, *literary* miscreant, scoundrel, rogue, *old use* malefactor, criminal, reprobate, rascal.

villain of the piece 1 the villain in a story. 2 the person responsible for some trouble or mischief.

villainous *adj.* 1 like or worthy of a villain. 2 *colloq.* extremely bad: *a villainous storm.*

. . . .

◼ BAD, CRIMINAL, EVIL, VICIOUS, CRUEL, VILE, DISGRACEFUL, TERRIBLE. 1 sinful, wicked, notorious, depraved.
🔁 GOOD.

. . . .

villainy *noun* (PL. **villainies**) wicked or vile behaviour, or an act of this kind.

villein /ˈvɪlən/ *noun Hist.* a feudal peasant worker owing allegiance directly to a lord. [a Middle English variant of VILLAIN]

villeinage /ˈvɪlənɪdʒ/ *noun Hist.* the position or status of villeins.

villus /ˈvɪləs/ *noun* (PL. **villi**) *Anat.* any of many tiny finger-like projections that line the inside of the small intestine. The villi absorb the products of digestion, and their presence greatly increases the surface area over which absorption can take place. [from Latin *villus*, wool]

vim *noun colloq.* energy; liveliness. [from Latin *vis*, force]

vinaigrette /vɪnəˈɡrɛt/ *noun* a salad dressing made by mixing oil, vinegar, and seasonings, especially mustard. [from French, from *vinaigre*, vinegar]

vindicate *verb* 1 to prove to be blameless or beyond criticism. 2 to show to have been worthwhile or justified: *the year's results vindicated their cautious planning.* [Latin *vindicare*, to lay claim to, to avenge]

. . . .

◼ 1 clear, acquit, excuse, exonerate, absolve, rehabilitate. 2 justify, uphold, support, maintain, defend, establish, advocate, assert, verify.

. . . .

vindication *noun* proof of blamelessness or worth: *this was a vindication of all they had done.*

vindicatory *adj.* serving to vindicate or prove worthwhile.

vindictive *adj.* 1 feeling or showing spite or hatred. 2 seeking revenge. 3 serving as revenge or retribution. [from Latin *vindicta* vengeance, related to VINDICATE]

. . . .

◼ 1 spiteful, malevolent, malicious, venomous. 2 vengeful, revengeful, unforgiving, implacable, resentful. 3 punitive.
🔁 FORGIVING.

. . . .

vindictively *adv.* spitefully; with malicious revenge.

vindictiveness *noun* a maliciously spiteful state or character.

vine *noun* 1 any of various climbing plants that produce grapes. 2 any climbing or trailing plant, including ivy. [from Latin *vinum*, wine]

vinegar *noun* 1 a sour liquid consisting of a dilute solution of acetic acid, produced by the bacterial fermentation of alcoholic beverages such as cider or wine. It is used as a food flavouring, and as a preservative for pickles. 2 the quality of being bad-tempered or peevish. [from French *vinaigre*, from *vin*, wine + *aigre*, sour]

vinegary *adj.* sour like vinegar.

vineyard *noun* a plantation of grape-bearing vines, especially for wine-making.

vingt-et-un /vantɛˈan/ *noun* the card game pontoon. [from French *vingt-et-un*, twenty-one]

viniculture *noun* the cultivation of grapes for making wine. [from Latin *vinum*, wine or CULTURE]

viniculturist *noun* a cultivator of grapes for making wine.

vino /ˈviːnoʊ/ *noun slang* wine, especially of poor quality. [from Spanish and Italian *vino*]

vinous *adj.* 1 of or like wine. 2 resulting from excess of wine: *a vinous complexion.* [from Latin *vinum*, wine]

vintage — *noun* 1 the grape-harvest of a particular year. 2 the wine produced from a year's harvest. 3 the time of year when grapes are harvested. 4 a particular period, espe-

cially when regarded as productive: *literature of a postwar vintage.* — *adj.* 1 *said of wine* of good quality and from a specified year. 2 typical of someone's best work or most characteristic behaviour: *the remark was vintage Churchill.* [from Old French *vintage*, from Latin *vinum*, wine]

. . . .

◼ *noun* 1 year, harvest, crop. 2 year. 4 period, era, epoch, generation, origin. *adj.* CHOICE, BEST, FINE, PRIME, SELECT, SUPERIOR, RARE, MATURE, CLASSIC, VENERABLE, VETERAN.

. . . .

vintage car *Brit.* an old motor car, specifically one built between 1919 and 1930.

vintner *noun formal* a wine-merchant. [from Old French *vinetier*, from Latin *vinum* wine]

vinyl *noun* 1 any of a group of tough plastics manufactured in various forms, eg paint additives and carpet fibres. 2 *colloq.* plastic long-playing records regarded collectively, as distinct from cassettes and compact discs.

viol /vaɪəl/ *noun* any of a family of Renaissance stringed musical instruments played with a bow. [from Old Provençal *viola*]

viola[1] *noun* a musical instrument of the violin family, larger than the violin and lower in pitch. [Italian]

viola[2] *noun* any of a group of flowering plants including the violet and pansy. [from Latin *viola*]

violate *verb* 1 to disregard or break (a law or agreement, or an oath). 2 to treat (something sacred or private) with disrespect; to profane. 3 to disturb or disrupt (eg a person's peace or privacy). 4 to rape or sexually abuse. [from Latin *violare*, to treat violently]

. . . .

◼ 1 contravene, disobey, disregard, transgress, break, flout, infringe. 2 profane, dishonour, desecrate, defile. 3 disturb, disrupt, invade, wreck. 4 rape, ravish, abuse, debauch.
🔁 1 observe.

. . . .

violation *noun* an act or the process of violating.

violator *noun* a person who violates an agreement or oath.

violence *noun* 1 the state or quality of being violent. 2 violent behaviour. — **do violence to someone** or **something** 1 to harm them physically. 2 to spoil or ruin them. 3 to distort their meaning or significance. [from Latin *violentus*, from *vis*, force]

. . . .

◼ 1 ferocity, fierceness, severity, vehemence, might, intensity, tumult, turbulence, wildness, force, strength, power. 2 brutality, destructiveness, cruelty, bloodshed, murderousness, savagery, passion, fighting, frenzy, fury, hostilities.

. . . .

violent *adj.* 1 marked by or using extreme physical force. 2 using, or involving the use of, such force to cause physical harm. 3 impulsively aggressive and unrestrained in nature or behaviour. 4 intense, extreme, vehement: *they took a violent dislike to me.*

. . . .

◼ 1 rough, forceful, forcible, aggressive, destructive, devastating, injurious. 3 brutal, aggressive, bloodthirsty, impetuous, hotheaded, headstrong, murderous, savage, wild, cruel, vicious, unrestrained, uncontrollable, ungovernable, passionate, furious, intemperate, maddened, outrageous, riotous, fiery. 4 intense, extreme, strong, severe, vehement, sharp, acute, powerful, painful, agonizing, harsh.
🔁 1 calm. 3 peaceful, gentle. 4 moderate.

. . . .

violently *adv.* 1 in a violent or aggressive way. 2 extremely; severely; ardently: *she was violently opposed to our involvement.*

violet *noun* 1 any of a group of flowering plants of mild climates with large purple or blue petals; or of various similar but unrelated plants, eg the African violet. 2 a bluish-purple colour. [from Latin *viola*]

violin *noun* **1** a musical instrument with a shaped body and a neck along which four strings are stretched. It is held with one end under the chin and played with a bow. **2** any of the violinists in an orchestra or group: *was first violin*. [from Italian *violino*, little viola]

violinist *noun* a violin-player.

violist *noun* a viola- or viol-player.

violoncellist *noun formal* a cellist.

violoncello *noun* (PL. **violoncellos**) *formal* a cello. [from Italian *violoncello*, a diminutive form]

VIP *abbrev.* very important person.

viper *noun* **1** any of a large family of poisonous snakes found in Europe, Asia, and Africa, characterized by long tubular fangs through which venom is injected into the prey. **2** the common European viper, which is the only poisonous snake in the UK. Also called ADDER. **3** a treacherous or spiteful person. [from Latin *vipera*]

virago /vɪ'reɪgoʊ/ *noun* (PL. **viragoes, viragos**) *literary* a loudly fierce or overbearing woman. [from Latin *virago*, manlike woman]

viral *adj.* relating to or caused by a virus.

virgin — *noun* **1** a person, especially a woman, who has never had sexual intercourse. **2** a member of a religious order of women sworn to chastity. **3** *colloq.* someone who is inexperienced in a specified area: *a computing virgin*. **4** (**the Virgin**) *RC Church* a name for Mary, the mother of Jesus Christ. **5** (**Virgin**) a portrait or statue of Mary. **6** (**the Virgin**) the sign or constellation Virgo. — *adj.* **1** never having had sexual intercourse; chaste. **2** in its original state; never having been used. [from Latin *virgo*]

⊟ *noun* **1** maiden, celibate, vestal. **2** vestal. *adj.* **1** virginal, chaste, intact, immaculate, maidenly, pure, modest, undefiled. **2** new, fresh, spotless, stainless, undefiled, untouched, unsullied.

virginal¹ *adj.* **1** of or appropriate to a virgin. **2** in a state of virginity.

virginal² *noun* a 16c–17c keyboard instrument like a small harpsichord but with strings set at right angles to the keys (as in the clavichord). [perhaps so called because it was mostly played by young women]

Virgin Birth *Relig.* the birth of Christ of the Virgin Mary, regarded as an act of God.

virginity *noun* the state of being a virgin.

Virgo *noun* (PL. **Virgos**) **1** *Astron.* the Maiden, a large northern constellation of the zodiac, lying between Leo and Libra. It is the second-largest constellation in the sky, and its brightest star is Spica. **2** the sixth sign of the zodiac, the Virgin. **3** a person born under this sign, between 23 Aug and 22 Sep. [from Latin *virgo*, virgin]

virile *adj.* **1** *said of a man* having a high level of sexual desire. **2** displaying or requiring qualities regarded as typically masculine, especially physical strength. **3** *said of a man* able to produce children. **4** relating to or possessing the features of a mature adult male. [from Latin *virilis*, manly]

⊟ **2** manly, macho, robust, vigorous, lusty, forceful, strong, rugged, red-blooded. **3** potent. **4** man-like, masculine, male.
⊟ **2** effeminate. **3** impotent.

virility *noun* the state of being virile; showing masculine physical strength.

virological *adj.* relating to the study of viruses.

virology *noun Medicine* the branch of microbiology concerned with the study of viruses and viral diseases.

virtual *adj.* **1** being so in effect or in practice, but not in name: *a virtual state of war*. **2** nearly so: *the virtual collapse of the steel industry*. **3** computer simulated. **4** taking place via the Internet. [from Latin *virtualis*, related to VIRTUE]

⊟ **1** effective, essential, practical, implied, implicit.

virtually *adv.* **1** in practice, though not strictly speaking: *was virtually in charge of us*. **2** almost; nearly: *the war is virtually over*.

⊟ PRACTICALLY, ALMOST, NEARLY, AS GOOD AS, IN ESSENCE, IN EFFECT.

virtual reality a computer simulation of a real or artificial environment that gives the user the impression of actually being within the environment and interacting with it. A special visor is worn, containing two tiny television screens (one for each eye), and the user may wear special gloves fitted with sensors.

virtue *noun* **1** a quality regarded as morally good: *he has many virtues, including honesty*. **2** moral goodness; righteousness. **3** an admirable quality or desirable feature: *the virtue of this one is its long life*. **4** virginity, especially in women. — **by** or **in virtue of something** because of it; on account of it. [from Latin *virtus*, moral excellence, bravery]

⊟ **2** goodness, morality, righteousness, rectitude, uprightness, worthiness, probity, integrity, honour, incorruptibility, justice, high-mindedness, excellence. **3** advantage, asset, merit, credit, strength, quality, worth.
⊟ **1, 2** vice.

virtuosity *noun* brilliance of technique.

virtuoso *noun* (PL. **virtuosos**) **1** a person with remarkable artistic skill, especially a brilliant musical performer. **2** (*attributive*) highly skilful; brilliant: *a virtuoso performance*. [from Italian *virtuoso*, learned, skilful]

⊟ **1** expert, master, maestro, prodigy, genius.

virtuous *adj.* possessing or showing virtue; morally sound.

⊟ good, moral, righteous, upright, worthy, honourable, irreproachable, incorruptible, exemplary, unimpeachable, high-principled, blameless, clean-living, excellent, innocent.
⊟ immoral.

virtuously *adv.* in a virtuous way; with moral rightness.

virulence *noun* **1** causing extreme harm; poisonousness. **2** bitter hostility.

virulent *adj.* **1** *said of a disease* having a rapidly harmful effect. **2** *said of a disease or the organism causing it* extremely infectious. **3** *said of a substance* highly poisonous. **4** bitterly hostile; acrimonious. [from Latin *virulentus*, venomous]

⊟ **1** malignant, pernicious. **3** poisonous, toxic, venomous, deadly, pernicious, lethal. **4** hostile, acrimonious, resentful, spiteful, bitter, vicious, venomous, vindictive, malevolent, malicious.
⊟ **3, 4** harmless.

virus *noun* **1** a non-cellular micro-organism, only visible under an electron microscope, that infects the cells of animals, plants, and bacteria, and can only survive and reproduce within such cells. **2** the organism that causes and transmits an infectious disease. **3** *loosely* a disease caused by such an organism. **4** anything that damages or corrupts. **5** (*in full* **computer virus**) a computer program, written anonymously, that can make copies of itself and spread from one computer to another within a network. Many viruses instruct a computer to change or delete data (eg by erasing hard disks), and they can be spread via floppy disks. [from Latin *virus*, venom]

visa /'viːzə/ *noun* a permit stamped into a passport to allow the holder to enter or leave the country issuing it. [from Latin *visa*, from *videre*, to see]

visage /'vɪzɪdʒ/ *noun literary* **1** the face. **2** the usual expression of a face; a countenance. [from French *visage*, face]

vis-à-vis — *prep.* in relation to; with regard to. — *adv.* face-to-face. — *noun* (PL. **vis-à-vis**) a counterpart or opposite number. [from French *vis-à-vis*, face to face]

viscacha /vɪ'skɑːtʃə/ *noun* a cavy-like rodent, native to S America, that resembles a large chinchilla, and lives among rocks or in burrows. [from Spanish, from Quechua *huiscacha*]

viscera /'vɪsərə/ — *pl. noun Anat.* the internal organs of the body, especially those found in the abdominal cavity. — *adj.* relating to these organs. [from Latin *viscera*, plural of *viscus*; see VISCUS]

visceral /'vɪsərəl/ *adj.* **1** relating to the viscera. **2** relating to the feelings, especially the basic human instincts as distinct from the intellect.

viscid /'vɪsɪd/ *adj.* glutinous; viscous. [from Latin *viscum*, bird-lime]

viscose *noun* **1** cellulose in a viscous state, able to be made into thread. **2** rayon, a fabric made from such thread.

viscosity *noun* (SYMBOL **h**) a measure of the resistance of a fluid (a liquid or gas) to flow, caused by internal friction which results in different rates of flow in different parts of the liquid, eg treacle has a higher viscosity than water. The viscosity of liquids decreases with increasing temperature, while that of gases increases.

viscount /'vaɪkaʊnt/ *noun* a member of the British nobility below an earl and above a baron in rank. [from Old French *visconte*]

viscountcy /'vaɪkaʊntsɪ/ or **viscountship** /'vaɪkaʊntʃɪp/ *noun* the rank of viscount.

viscountess /'vaɪkaʊntɪs/ *noun* **1** the wife or widow of a viscount. **2** a woman of the rank of viscount in her own right.

viscous *adj.* **1** of a thick semi-liquid consistency, not flowing easily. **2** *said of liquid* sticky. [from Latin *viscosus*, sticky, from *viscum*, bird-lime]

viscus *noun Medicine* any of the body's large internal organs. See also VISCERA. [from Latin *viscera*]

Vishnu the second Hindu deity in the Hindu triad (Trimurti), the preserver of the universe and the embodiment of goodness and mercy.

visibility *noun* **1** the state or fact of being visible. **2** the range in which one can see clearly in given conditions of light and weather: *poor visibility / visibility down to 50 yards*.

visible *adj.* **1** able to be seen. **2** able to be realised or perceived; apparent. [from Latin *visibilis*, from *videre*, to see]

☰ NOTICEABLE, PERCEPTIBLE, DISCERNIBLE, DETECTABLE, OBSERVABLE, DISTINGUISHABLE, CONSPICUOUS, CLEAR, OBVIOUS, MANIFEST, OPEN, PLAIN, PATENT. **2** apparent, discoverable, evident, unconcealed, undisguised, unmistakable, palpable.

◳ INDISCERNIBLE, HIDDEN. **1** invisible.

visible spectrum *Physics* the range of wavelengths of electromagnetic radiation that can be seen by the human eye, ie visible light, ranging from about 390nm to 780nm. The visible spectrum can be produced by dispersing white light through a prism.

visibly *adv.* so as to be visible or discernible: *they were visibly annoyed*.

Visigoth a member of a Germanic people who fled from the Huns in AD 376 into the Roman empire and founded several Visigothic kingdoms which, by the 6c, extended through Portugal, most of Spain, and S Gaul.

vision *noun* **1** the ability to see objects outside the body. Nerve impulses from specialized receptor cells (rods and cones) in the retina are relayed via the optic nerve to the brain, where they are interpreted as a three-dimensional image of the object being viewed. **2** an image conjured up vividly in the imagination. **3** the ability to perceive what is

likely, and plan wisely for it; foresight. **4** an image communicated supernaturally, eg by God. **5** the picture on a television screen, or its quality. **6** a person or thing of overwhelming beauty. [from Latin *visio*, sight]

☰ **1** sight, seeing, eyesight. **2** idea, ideal, conception, insight, view, picture, image, fantasy, dream, daydream, hallucination, illusion, delusion. **3** foresight, perception, discernment, far-sightedness, penetration. **4** dream, apparition, mirage, phantom, ghost, chimera, spectre, wraith.

visionary — *adj.* **1** showing or marked by great foresight or imagination. **2** possible only in the imagination; impracticable; fanciful. **3** capable of seeing supernatural images; seeing such images often. — *noun* (PL. **visionaries**) **1** a person of great foresight. **2** *Relig.* a person to whom supernatural visions are attributed. **3** a person who dreams up idealistic schemes.

☰ *adj.* **1** imaginative, forward-looking, advanced, progressive, prophetic. **2** idealistic, impractical, impracticable, fanciful, unrealistic, unworkable, romantic, speculative, utopian, dreamy, unreal, illusory, imaginary. **3** psychic. *noun* **1** prophet, mystic, seer. **3** idealist, romantic, dreamer, daydreamer, fantasist, utopian, rainbow-chaser.

◳ *noun* **3** pragmatist.

vision mixer *Telecomm.* **1** equipment used in video and film production for the combination of visual material from several sources (eg multiple cameras, videotape, etc), and with facilities for transition effects between scenes and image combination at the time of shooting, to create the visual effects required by the director. **2** the operator of this equipment.

visit — *verb* (**visited, visiting**) **1** *trans., intrans.* to go or come to see (a person or place) socially or professionally. **2** *trans., intrans.* to go or come to stay (with) temporarily. **3** (**visit something on someone**) to inflict harm or punishment on them. **4** to enter the mind of temporarily. **5** (**visit someone with something**) *old use* to afflict or trouble them: *were visited with dire consequences*. — *noun* **1** an act of visiting; a social or professional call. **2** a temporary stay. **3** a sightseeing excursion. [from Latin *visitare*, from *visere*, to go to see]

☰ *verb* **1** call on, call in, look in, drop in on, *colloq.* stop by, *colloq.* pop in, see, look up. **2** stay (with), *colloq.* stop (with), stop over. *noun* stay, stop, *formal* sojourn.

visitant *noun* **1** *Relig.* a person appearing in a supernatural vision; an apparition. **2** a migratory bird, staying temporarily.

visitation *noun* **1** an official visit or inspection. **2** an event regarded as a divine punishment or reward. **3** an instance of seeing a supernatural vision. **4** (**the Visitation**) the visit made by the Virgin Mary to her cousin Elizabeth (Luke 1.39–56); the Christian festival commemorating this, held on 2 Jul.

visiting card a card with one's name and address printed on it, left instead of a formal visit.

visitor *noun* **1** someone who visits a person or place. **2** a migratory bird present in a place for a time: *winter visitors*.

☰ **1** caller, guest, company, tourist, holidaymaker.

visor *noun* **1** the movable part of a helmet, covering the face. **2** (*in full* **sun visor**) a translucent device shaped like the peak of a cap, worn to shade the eyes. **3** a small movable panel above the windscreen on the inside of a motor vehicle, folded down to shade the eyes from sunlight. [from Old French *viser*, from *vis*, face]

vista *noun* **1** a view into the distance, especially when bounded narrowly on both sides, eg by rows of trees. **2** a mental vision extending far into the future or past. [from Italian *vista*, view]

. . . .

▣ **1** view, prospect, panorama, perspective, scene. **2** *future* vision, prospect, outlook.

. . . .

visual *adj.* **1** relating to or received through sight or vision: *a visual image.* **2** creating vivid mental images: *visual poetry.* **3** creating a strong impression through what is seen, rather than what is said or heard: *a very visual play.* [from Latin *visus*, sight]

visual aid a picture, film, or other visual material used as an aid to teaching or presenting information.

visual arts (*usually* **the visual arts**) art-forms involving appreciation with the eyes, eg painting, sculpture, film, etc, as distinct from literature, music, etc.

visual display unit (ABBREV. **VDU**) a screen on which information from a computer is displayed.

visualization or **visualisation** *noun* **1** the act or process of visualizing. **2** *Psychol.* a technique for improving performance, in which a person learns to create a mental picture of the successful performance of the tasks that are to be achieved. Visualization is also used to increase self-confidence, relieve stress, etc.

visualize or **visualise** *verb* to form a clear mental image of.

. . . .

▣ picture, envisage, imagine, conceive.

. . . .

visually *adv.* as regards sight or vision: *the performance is visually stunning.*

visual purple see RHODOPSIN.

vital — *adj.* **1** relating to or essential for life: *the vital organs.* **2** determining life or death, or success or failure: *a vital error.* **3** essential; of the greatest importance. **4** full of life; energetic. — *noun* (**vitals**) the vital organs, including the brain, heart, and lungs. [from Latin *vita*, life]

. . . .

▣ *adj.* **2** life-or-death, decisive, critical, crucial. **3** essential, critical, crucial, important, imperative, key, significant, basic, fundamental, necessary, requisite, indispensable, urgent, forceful. **4** lively, energetic, spirited, vivacious, vibrant, vigorous, dynamic, animated, living, alive.

🄴 *adj.* **3** inessential, peripheral. **4** dead.

. . . .

vitality *noun* **1** liveliness and energy. **2** the state of being alive; the ability to stay alive.

. . . .

▣ LIFE. **1** liveliness, animation, vigour, energy, vivacity, spirit, sparkle, exuberance, *colloq.* go, strength, stamina.

. . . .

vitalization or **vitalisation** *noun* the act or process of vitalizing.

vitalize or **vitalise** *verb* to fill with life or energy.

vitally *adv.* essentially, urgently: *it is vitally important to go.*

vital statistics 1 statistics concerning births, marriages, deaths and other matters relating to population. **2** *colloq.* a woman's bust, waist, and hip measurements.

vitamin *noun Biochem.* any of various organic compounds that occur in small amounts in many foods, and are also manufactured synthetically. Trace amounts of vitamins are essential for the normal growth and functioning of the body. [from Latin *vita*, life + AMINE]

vitamin A a fat-soluble organic compound found in liver, fish oils, dairy products, and egg yolk. It is required for normal growth and especially the functioning of the light-sensitive rods and cones of the retina of the eye. Deficiency causes night blindness and retarded growth. Also called *retinol.*

vitamin B₁ thiamine.

vitamin B₂ riboflavin.

vitamin B₆ any of three interconvertible organic com-

pounds found in milk, eggs, liver, cereal grains, yeast, and fresh vegetables. Vitamin B_6 is required for the metabolism of amino acids, and deficiency of the vitamin can cause dermatitis and nervous disorders. Also called PYRIDOXINE.

vitamin B₇ nicotinic acid.

vitamin B₁₂ a member of the vitamin B complex that is found in raw liver, and is required for the oxidation (breakdown) of fatty acids, the manufacture of DNA, and the formation of red blood cells. Deficiency of the vitamin causes pernicious anaemia. Also called CYANOCOBALAMIN.

vitamin B complex any of a group of water-soluble vitamins found in yeast, liver, and wheat germ, and referred to either by individual B numbers, eg vitamin B_1, vitamin B_2, or by specific names, eg thiamine, riboflavin.

vitamin C a water-soluble crystalline organic compound found in fresh fruits, especially citrus fruits and blackcurrants, and green vegetables. It is required for the maintenance of healthy bones, cartilage, and teeth, and deficiency of the vitamin causes scurvy. Also called ASCORBIC ACID.

vitamin D either of two fat-soluble steroid compounds, vitamin D_2 (calciferol) and vitamin D_3 (cholecalciferol), found in fish liver oils, egg yolk, and milk, and also formed from cholesterol derivatives in the skin on exposure to sunlight. Vitamin D is required for the deposition of adequate amounts of calcium and phosphates in the bones and teeth, and deficiency in children causes rickets.

vitamin E any of various closely related fat-soluble organic compounds found in wholemeal flour, wheat-germ, and green vegetables. Vitamin E has strong antioxidant properties and may be required for maintenance of the structure of cell membranes. Deficiency causes infertility in some animals, and has been associated with muscular dystrophy in humans. Also called TOCOPHEROL.

vitamin K any of various closely related fat-soluble organic compounds found in green leafy vegetables, and also manufactured by bacteria in the intestines, as a result of which deficiency is rare. It is required for the production of several proteins involved in blood clotting.

vitiate /'vɪʃɪeɪt/ *verb* **1** to impair the quality or effectiveness of (eg an argument); to make faulty or defective. **2** to make (eg a legal contract) ineffectual or invalid. [from Latin *vitiare*, from *vitium*, blemish]

vitiation *noun* the act or process of vitiating.

viticulture *noun* the cultivation of grapes for making wine; viniculture. [from Latin *vitis*, vine + CULTURE]

vitreous *adj.* **1** relating to or consisting of glass. **2** like glass in hardness, sheen, or transparency: *vitreous china.* [from Latin *vitrum*, glass]

vitreous humour a jelly-like substance inside the eye, between the lens and the retina.

vitrification *noun Engineering, Geol.* the formation of glass or a glassy material under conditions of intense heat.

vitrified *adj.* made into glass or something like glass.

vitrify *verb trans., intrans.* (**vitrifies, vitrified**) to make into or become glass or something like glass, especially by heating. [from Latin *vitrum*, glass + *facere*, to make]

vitriol *noun* **1** concentrated sulphuric acid. **2** a sulphate of a metal, originally one of a glassy appearance. **3** extremely bitter or hateful speech or criticism. [from Latin *vitreus*, of glass]

vitriolic *adj.* extremely bitter or hateful, especially with reference to speech or criticism.

. . . .

▣ bitter, hateful, abusive, virulent, vicious, venomous, malicious, caustic, biting, sardonic, scathing, destructive.

. . . .

vituperate *verb* **1** to attack with abusive criticism or disapproval. **2** *intrans.* to use abusive language. [from Latin *vituperare*, to blame]

vituperation *noun* abusive criticism or language.

vituperative *adj.* abusive.

viva[1] /'viːvə/ *interj.* long live (someone or something named). [from Spanish and Italian *viva*]

viva[2] /'vaɪvə/ — *noun* (*in full* **viva voce**) (PL. **vivas, viva voces**) an oral examination, usually for an academic qualification. — *verb* (**vivas, vivaed**) to examine orally. [from Latin *viva voce*, by the living voice]

vivace /vɪ'vɑːtʃɪ/ *adj., adv. Mus.* in a lively manner. [from Italian]

vivacious *adj.* attractively lively and animated, especially with reference to a person. [from Latin *vivax*, lively]

⊟ lively, animated, spirited, high-spirited, effervescent, ebullient, cheerful, sparkling, bubbly.

vivaciously *adv.* in an attractive, lively way.

vivacity *noun* liveliness, animation, especially with reference to a person.

vivarium /vaɪ'veərɪəm/ *noun* (PL. **vivariums, vivaria**) any place or enclosure in which live animals are kept, especially in conditions resembling their natural habitat. [from Latin *vivarium*, from *vivere*, to live]

viva voce /'vaɪvə 'voʊtʃɪ/ in speech; orally.

vivid *adj.* 1 *said of a colour* strong and bright. 2 creating or providing a clear and immediate mental picture: *gave a vivid account of the incident* / *has a vivid imagination*. 3 full of life; vivacious. [from Latin *vividus*, lively]

⊟ 1 bright, strong, colourful, intense, rich, vibrant, brilliant, glowing, dazzling. 2 clear, distinct, graphic, striking, sharp, memorable, powerful, expressive, dramatic, lifelike, realistic. 3 vivacious, animated, lively, spirited, vigorous, flamboyant.
⊞ 1 colourless, dull. 2 vague.

vividly *adv.* brightly, clearly, intensely.

vividness *noun* brightness, clarity, intensity.

viviparity /vɪvɪ'parɪtɪ/ *noun* the condition of giving birth to a live offspring.

viviparous /vɪ'vɪpərəs/ *adj.* 1 *Zool.*, *said of an animal* giving birth to live young that have developed within the mother's body, as in humans and most other mammals, instead of laying eggs that develop outside the body. See also OVIPAROUS. 2 *Bot.* denoting a form of asexual reproduction in which new young plants start to develop on the parent plant while still attached to it, as in the spider plant and certain grasses. [from Latin *vivus*, alive + *parere*, to produce]

vivisect *verb* to perform vivisection on.

vivisection *noun* 1 strictly, the practice of dissecting living animals for experimental purposes. 2 loosely used to refer to any form of animal experimentation. [from Latin *vivus*, living + *secare*, to cut]. See also ANIMAL EXPERIMENTATION.

vivisectionist *noun* a person who practises or advocates vivisection.

vixen *noun* 1 a female fox. 2 a fierce or spiteful woman. [from Anglo-Saxon *fyxen*]

viz or **viz.** *adv.* namely; that is. [an abbreviation of Latin *videlicet*, from *videre*, to see + *licet*, it is allowed]

vizier /vɪ'zɪə(r)/ *noun* a high-ranking government official in certain Muslim countries. [from Arabic *wazir*, porter, bearer of a burden]

VLF *abbrev. Radio* very low frequency.

VMH *abbrev.* Victoria Medal of Honour.

V-neck *noun* 1 the open neck of a garment cut or formed to a point at the front. 2 a garment, especially a pullover, with such a neck.

V-necked *adj., said of clothing* having a V-neck.

VOA *abbrev.* Voice of America.

voc. *abbrev.* vocative.

vocab *noun colloq.* vocabulary.

vocable /'voʊkəbl/ *noun Linguistics* 1 a spoken word or single sound in a word. 2 a spoken or written word regarded as a series of sounds or letters, rather than as a unit of meaning. [from Latin *vocabulum*, from *vox*, voice]

vocabulary *noun* (PL. **vocabularies**) 1 the words used in speaking or writing a particular language. 2 the words, or range of words, known to or used by a particular person or group. 3 a list of words with translations in another language alongside. 4 a range of artistic or stylistic forms and techniques.

⊟ 1 language, words. 2 language, words, vernacular, idiom, jargon. 3 glossary, lexicon, dictionary, word-book.

vocal — *adj.* 1 relating to or produced by the voice. 2 expressing opinions or criticism freely and forcefully. — *noun* (**vocals**) the parts of a musical composition that are sung, as distinct from the instrumental accompaniment. [from Latin *vocalis*, from *vox*, voice]

⊟ *adj.* 1 spoken, said, oral, uttered, voiced. 2 articulate, eloquent, expressive, noisy, clamorous, shrill, strident, outspoken, frank, forthright, plain-spoken.
⊞ *adj.* 1 unspoken. 2 inarticulate, silent.

vocal cords *Anat.* in mammals, the two folds of tissue within the larynx that vibrate and produce sound when air is expelled from the lungs. Changes in the tension of the vocal cords, and in the speed of the air flow over them, affect the pitch and volume of the sound produced.

vocalist *noun* a singer, especially in a pop group.

vocalization or **vocalisation** *noun* the act or process of forming sounds.

vocalize or **vocalise** *verb* 1 to utter or produce with the voice. 2 to express in words; to articulate.

vocally *adv.* with the voice; loudly.

vocation *noun* 1 a particular occupation or profession, especially regarded as needing dedication and skill. 2 a feeling of being especially suited for a particular type of work. 3 *Relig.* a divine calling to adopt a religious life or perform good works. [from Latin *vocare*, to call]

⊟ 1 calling, pursuit, career, métier, mission, profession, trade, employment, work, role, post, job, business, office. 2 mission.

vocational *adj.* concerned with, or in preparation for, a particular trade or profession: *vocational training*.

vocational education education aimed at preparing students for their present or future employment. It may take place in colleges of further education, universities, or in the workplace itself. It is also increasingly being offered to secondary school pupils in a wide variety of subjects, and in the form of work experience.

vocationally *adv.* as regards vocation or profession.

vocative /'vɒkətɪv/ *Grammar* — *noun* 1 in some languages, the particular form of a word used when a person or thing is addressed directly. 2 a word in this form. — *adj.* in the vocative. [from Latin *vocare*, to call]

vociferate /və'sɪfəreɪt/ *verb trans., intrans. formal* 1 to exclaim loudly and forcefully. 2 to shout or cry in a loud voice; to bawl. [from Latin *vox*, voice + *ferre*, to carry]

vociferous *adj.* 1 loud and forceful, especially in expressing opinions. 2 expressed loudly and forcefully.

⊟ NOISY, VOCAL, CLAMOROUS, LOUD, OBSTREPEROUS, STRIDENT, VEHEMENT, THUNDERING.
⊞ QUIET.

vociferously *adv.* loudly and forcefully.

vociferousness *noun* loudness, forcefulness.

Vodafone *noun trademark* 1 a UK cellular phone system. 2 a cellular phone.

vodka *noun* a clear alcoholic spirit of Russian origin, traditionally made from rye, sometimes from potatoes. [from Russian *vodka*, from *voda*, water]

vogue / voʊɡ/ *noun* **1** (*usually* **the vogue**) the current fashion or trend in any sphere. **2** a period of being fashionable or popular: *enjoyed a long vogue.* — **in vogue** in fashion. [French *vogue*]

▣ **1** fashion, trend, craze, mode, style, custom, fad, *colloq.* the rage, *colloq.* the thing, *colloq.* the latest. **2** popularity, prevalence.

vogue word a word that is currently fashionable.

voice — *noun* **1** the ability to speak; the power of speech: *lost his voice.* **2** a way of speaking or singing peculiar to each individual: *couldn't recognize the voice.* **3** a tone of speech reflecting a particular emotion: *in a nervous voice.* **4** the sound of a person speaking: *heard a voice.* **5** the ability to sing, especially to sing well: *has no voice / has a lovely voice.* **6** expression in the form of spoken words: *gave voice to their feelings.* **7** a means or medium of expression or communication: *newspapers as the voice of the people.* **8** *Grammar* the status or function of a verb in being either active or passive. — *verb* **1** to express in speech. **2** *Phonetics* to pronounce with a vibration of the vocal cords. — **in good voice** singing well. **with one voice** unanimously. [from Latin *vox*]

▣ *noun* **1** speech, language, utterance, articulation. **3** tone, intonation, inflection. **6** expression, utterance, articulation, words, say, vote, opinion, view, decision, option, will. **7** mouthpiece, medium, instrument, organ. *verb* **1** express, say, utter, air, articulate, speak of, verbalize, assert, convey, disclose, divulge, declare, enunciate.

voice-box *noun colloq.* the larynx.

voiced *adj.* **1** expressed in speech. **2** *Phonetics* pronounced with a vibration of the vocal cords, as is *z*, but not *s*.

voiceless *adj. Phonetics* not voiced.

voice mail a system by which telephone messages can be stored in a central location and picked up later.

voice-over *noun* the voice of an unseen narrator in a film or television advertisement or programme.

void — *adj.* **1** not valid or legally binding: *declared the contract null and void.* **2** containing nothing; empty or unoccupied. **3** (**void of something**) free from it. — *noun* **1** an empty space. **2** a space left blank or unfilled. **3** a feeling of absence or emptiness strongly felt. — *verb* **1** to make empty or clear. **2** to invalidate or nullify. **3** to empty (the bladder or bowels). [from Old French *voide*, empty]

▣ *adj.* **1** invalid, cancelled, ineffective, annulled, inoperative. **2** empty, emptied, unfilled, unoccupied, vacant, free, clear, bare, blank, drained. *noun* **1** emptiness, space, vacuity, vacuum, chasm, cavity, gap, hollow, opening. **2** blank, space, gap. **3** emptiness, blankness, vacuity, worthlessness, futility, lack, want, need, deficiency.
▣ *adj.* **1** valid. **2** full.

voile / vɔɪl, vwɑːl/ *noun* any very thin semi-transparent fabric. [from French *voile*, veil]

vol or **vol.** *abbrev.* volume.

volatile *adj.* **1** changing quickly from a solid or liquid into a vapour. **2** explosive. **3** easily becoming angry or violent. **4** *said of a situation, etc* liable to change quickly, especially verging on violence. [from Latin *volare*, to fly]

▣ *adj.* UNSTABLE. **3** temperamental, mercurial, unpredictable, fickle, capricious, restless. **4** changeable, unpredictable, inconstant, variable, erratic, unsteady, unsettled.
▣ STABLE. **4** constant, steady.

volatility *noun* a volatile state.

volatilization or **volatilisation** *noun* the process of evaporating or causing to evaporate.

volatilize or **volatilise** *verb trans., intrans.* to change, or cause to change, from a solid or liquid into a vapour.

vol-au-vent / 'vɒloʊvɒn/ *noun* a small round puff-pastry case with a savoury filling. [from French *vol-au-vent*, literally 'flight in the wind']

volcanic *adj.* **1** relating to or produced by a volcano or volcanoes. **2** easily erupting into anger or violence: *a volcanic temper.*

volcano *noun* (PL. **volcanoes**) **1** any of various cracks or vents in the Earth's crust through which lava (molten rock), gas, steam, ash, or solid rock material may be forced out on to the Earth's surface, often forming a more or less conical hill or mountain with a central crater. **2** a situation, or a person, likely to erupt into anger or violence. [from Latin *Vulcanus*, Roman god of fire]

vole *noun* a small rodent related to the lemming, with a smaller tail, blunter snout, and smaller eyes and ears than a mouse, found in Europe, Asia, N Africa, and N America. [originally *vole-mouse*, from Norwegian *voll*, field + *mus*, mouse]

volition *noun* the act of willing or choosing; the exercising of one's will: *did it of her own volition.* [from Latin *velle*, to will]

volitional *adj.* relating to volition or the exercise of will.

volley — *noun* (PL. **volleys**) **1** a firing of several guns or other weapons simultaneously. **2** an aggressive outburst, especially of criticism or insults. **3** *Sport* a striking of the ball before it bounces. — *verb* (**volleys**, **volleyed**) **1** to fire (weapons) in a volley. **2** *Sport* to strike (a ball) before it bounces. [from French *volée*, flight]

▣ *noun* **1**, **2** barrage, bombardment, hail, shower, burst, blast, discharge, explosion.

volleyball *noun* a game for two teams of six players each, in which a large ball is volleyed back and forth over a high net with the hands.

volt *noun* (SYMBOL **V**) the SI unit of voltage, potential difference, or electromotive force. It is equal to the potential difference between two points if one joule of energy is required to move one coulomb of electric charge from one point to the other. One volt will send a current of one ampere across a resistance of one ohm. [named after the Italian physicist Alessandro Volta (1745–1827)]

voltage *noun Electr.* potential difference expressed as a number of volts.

volte-face / 'vɒltfɑːs/ *noun* a sudden and complete reversal, of opinion or policy. [from French *volte-face*, literally 'turning face']

voltmeter *noun Electr.* an instrument that measures voltage.

volubility *noun* the act or process of speaking insistently or volubly.

voluble *adj.* **1** speaking or spoken insistently, uninterruptedly, or with ease. **2** tending to talk at great length. [from Latin *volubilis*, from *volvere*, to roll]

▣ **1** fluent, articulate, *derog.* glib. **2** talkative, forthcoming, garrulous, *formal* loquacious.

volubly *adv., said of talking* at great length; fluently.

volume *noun* **1** the amount of three-dimensional space occupied by an object, gas, or liquid. **2** loudness of sound; the control that adjusts it on a radio, hi-fi system, etc. **3** a book, whether complete in itself or one of several forming a larger work. **4** an amount or quantity, especially when large: *the volume of traffic.* — **speak volumes** to be very significant; to say a lot: *their refusal to answer spoke volumes.* [from Latin *volumen*, roll, scroll]

▣ **1** size, bulk, mass. **2** amplitude, loudness, sound. **3** book, tome, publication. **4** amount, quantity, capacity, size, bulk, mass, body, dimensions, aggregate.

volumetric analysis *Chem.* a method of chemical analysis in which the unknown concentration of a solution of known volume is determined by adding known volumes of standard solutions of known concentration until the chemical reaction between the reagents is complete.

voluminous *adj.* 1 *said of clothing* flowing or billowing out; ample. 2 *said of a writer* producing great quantities of writing. 3 *said of writing* enough to fill many volumes.

. . . .

⊞ 1 roomy, billowing, ample, huge, large, capacious, spacious, vast.

. . . .

voluntarily *adv.* willingly; of one's free will.

voluntary — *adj.* 1 done or acting by free choice, not by compulsion. 2 working with no expectation of being paid or otherwise rewarded. 3 *said of work* unpaid. 4 *said of an organization* staffed by unpaid workers; supported by donations of money freely given. 5 *said of a movement, muscle, or limb* produced or controlled by the will. — *noun* (PL. **voluntaries**) a piece of music, usually for organ, played before, during, or after a church service. [from Latin *voluntarius*, from *velle*, to will]

. . . .

⊞ *adj.* 1 willing, unforced, spontaneous, free, optional. 2 unpaid. 3 unpaid, honorary, gratuitous. 5 conscious, deliberate, purposeful, intended, intentional, wilful.

⊟ *adj.* 1 compulsory. 5 involuntary.

. . . .

voluntary muscle *Anat.* muscle that is under conscious control, and produces voluntary movements by pulling against the bones of the skeleton, to which it is attached by means of tendons. Also called STRIATED MUSCLE.

volunteer — *verb* 1 *trans., intrans.* (**volunteer for something**) to offer one's help or services freely, without being persuaded or forced. 2 *intrans.* to go into military service by choice, without being conscripted. 3 to give (information, etc) unasked. 4 *colloq.* to constrain (someone) to perform a task or give help: *I'm volunteering you for playground duty.* — *noun* 1 a person who volunteers. 2 a person carrying out voluntary work. 3 a member of a non-professional army of voluntary soldiers set up during wartime.

. . . .

⊞ *verb* 1 step forward. 3 offer, propose, put forward, present, suggest, advance.

. . . .

voluptuary — *noun* (PL. **voluptuaries**) a person addicted to luxury and sensual pleasures. — *adj.* promoting or characterized by luxury and sensual pleasures. [from Latin *voluptas*, pleasure]

voluptuous *adj.* 1 relating to or suggestive of sensual pleasure. 2 *said of a woman* strikingly attractive sexually. [from Latin *voluptas*, pleasure]

. . . .

⊞ 1 sensual, erotic, licentious, luxurious. 2 shapely, *colloq.* sexy, seductive, provocative, enticing.

. . . .

voluptuously *adv.* in a voluptuous way; sensually.

voluptuousness *noun* sensuousness; strong sensual gratification.

volute *noun* 1 a spiral. 2 a scroll carved in stone, especially at the top of a column. 3 one single twist in a spiral shell. [from Latin *volvere*, to roll]

vomit — *verb* (**vomited, vomiting**) 1 *trans., intrans.* to eject the contents of the stomach forcefully through the mouth as a reflex action; to be sick. 2 to emit or throw out with force or violence. — *noun* the contents of the stomach ejected during this process. [from Latin *vomere*]

. . . .

⊞ *verb* 1 be sick, bring up, heave, retch, *colloq.* throw up, *colloq.* puke.

. . . .

voodoo — *noun* 1 witchcraft of a type originally practised by the Black peoples of the West Indies and southern US. 2 the beliefs and practices of the religious cult that developed it, including serpent-worship and human sacrifice. — *verb* to bewitch using, or as if using, voodoo methods. [from *vodu*, (in various W African languages) spirit, demon]

Voortrekker /fɔː'trɛkə(r)/ *noun* one of the Afrikaner (Boer) farmers from Cape Colony who took part in the Great Trek into the Transvaal in 1836 and following years. They established independent republics in the interior (the Orange Free State and the South African Republic).

voracious *adj.* 1 eating or craving food in large quantities. 2 extremely eager in some respect: *a voracious reader.* [from Latin *vorare*, to devour]

voraciously *adv.* in a voracious or eager way; greedily.

voracity *noun* extreme greed or eagerness.

vortex *noun* (PL. **vortexes, vortices**) 1 a whirlpool or whirlwind; any whirling mass or motion. 2 a situation or activity into which all surrounding people or things are helplessly and dangerously drawn. [from Latin *vortex*, from *vortere*, to turn]

vortical *adj.* resembling or characteristic of a vortex.

Vorticism a modern art movement started in England in 1913, partly inspired by the Futurists.

votary *noun* (PL. **votaries**) 1 a person bound by solemn vows to a religious life. 2 a person dedicated to a particular cause or activity. [from Latin *vovere*, to vow]

vote — *noun* 1 a formal indication of choice or opinion, eg in an election or debate. 2 the right to express a choice or opinion, especially in a national election. 3 a choice or opinion expressed in this way: *a vote in favour of the motion.* 4 the support given by a certain sector of the population, or to a particular candidate or group, in this way: *will attract the middle-class vote.* — *verb* 1 *intrans.* to cast a vote (for or against). 2 to decide, state, grant, or bring about by casting votes. 3 to declare support for by casting a vote. 4 *colloq.* to declare or pronounce by general consent: *the show was voted a success.* 5 *colloq.* to propose or suggest. — **vote someone** or **something down** to reject or defeat them by voting. **vote someone in** to appoint them by voting; to elect them. [from Latin *votum*, wish]

. . . .

⊞ *noun* 1 ballot, poll, election, referendum. 2 franchise, suffrage. *verb* 1 ballot. 2 elect, choose, opt for, plump for, return, declare. 3 choose, opt for, plump for.

. . . .

vote of confidence or **vote of no confidence** a vote taken to show whether the majority support or disapprove of a person or group in authority or leadership.

voter *noun* a person who votes, or is eligible to vote, in an election.

votive *adj. Relig.* done or given in thanks to a deity, or to fulfil a vow or promise. [from Latin *vovere*, to vow]

vouch *verb intrans.* (**vouch for someone** or **something**) to give a firm assurance or guarantee of their authenticity, trustworthiness, etc. [from Old French *voucher*, to call upon to defend]

. . . .

⊞ guarantee, support, back, endorse, confirm, certify, affirm, assert, attest to, speak for, swear to, uphold.

. . . .

voucher *noun* 1 a ticket or paper serving as proof, eg of the purchase or receipt of goods. 2 a ticket exchangeable for goods or services of a specified value; a token: *gift voucher.*

voucher scheme *Education* a scheme giving parents a voucher equivalent in value to the average cost of a child's education, which they are then entitled to spend at the school of their choice.

vouchsafe *verb trans., intrans. literary* to agree or condescend (to do, give, grant, or allow): *vouchsafed me no reply / did not vouchsafe to reply.* [from VOUCH in the sense 'voucher' + SAFE]

voussoir /vuːˈswɑː(r)/ — *noun Archit.* one of the wedge-shaped stones that form part of the centre line of an arch. Also known as an *arch stone*. — *verb* to form (an arch) with voussoirs. [from French, from Latin *volutus*, from *volvere*, to roll]

vow — *noun* a solemn and binding promise, especially one made to or in the name of a deity. — *verb* to promise or declare solemnly, or threaten emphatically; to swear. [from Latin *vovere*]
. . . .
◼ *noun* promise, oath, pledge. *verb* promise, pledge, swear, dedicate, devote, profess, affirm.
. . . .

vowel *noun* 1 any speech-sound made with an open mouth and no contact between mouth, lips, teeth, or tongue. 2 a letter, used alone or in combination, representing such a sound in English the letters *a e i o u* and in some words *y*. [from Latin *vocalis*, from *vox*, voice]

vox pop *Broadcasting* popular opinion derived from comments given informally by members of the public.

vox populi /vɒks ˈpɒpjʊlaɪ/ public opinion; popular belief. [from Latin *vox populi*, voice of the people]

voyage — *noun* a long journey to a distant place, especially by air or sea or in space. — *verb intrans.* to go on a voyage; to travel. [from Old French *voiage*, from Latin *viaticum*]
. . . .
◼ *noun* journey, trip, passage, expedition, crossing.
. . . .

voyager *noun* a person who goes on a voyage.

voyeur /vwaɪˈɜː(r)/ *noun* 1 a person who derives gratification from furtively watching the sexual attributes or activity of others. 2 a person who observes, especially with fascination or intrusively, the feelings of others. [from French *voyeur*, one who sees]

voyeurism /vwaɪˈɜːrɪzm/ *noun* the practice of spying on others as a means of sexual gratification.

voyeuristic /vwaɪəˈrɪstɪk/ *adj.* characteristic of a voyeur; spying intrusively.

VR *abbrev.* virtual reality.

VRAM same as VIDEO RAM.

vs or **vs.** *abbrev.* versus.

V-sign *noun Brit.* a sign made by raising the first two fingers, an expression of victory with the palm turned outwards or an offensive gesture of contempt with the palm inwards.

VSO *abbrev.* Voluntary Service Overseas.

VSOP *abbrev.* very special old pale: a port, sherry, or brandy between 20 and 25 years old.

VT or **Vt.** *abbrev.* Vermont.

VTOL *abbrev.* vertical take-off and landing.

VTR *abbrev.* videotape recorder.

vulcanite *noun* hard black vulcanized rubber.

vulcanization or **vulcanisation** *noun Chem.* the process whereby natural or artificial rubber is hardened and its elasticity increased by treating it with sulphur or sulphur compounds at high temperatures.

vulcanize or **vulcanise** *verb* to subject natural or artificial rubber to the process of vulcanization. [see VOLCANO]

vulg. *abbrev.* vulgar.

vulgar *adj.* 1 marked by a lack of politeness or social or cultural refinement; coarse. 2 of or relating to the form of a language commonly spoken, rather than to formal or literary language; vernacular.
. . . .
◼ 1 unrefined, uncouth, coarse, common, crude, ill-bred, impolite, rude, indecent, suggestive, risqué, indelicate, indecorous, tasteless, flashy, gaudy, tawdry. 2 common, vernacular, informal, popular, ordinary, general.
◪ 1 tasteful, correct, decent.
. . . .

vulgar fraction a fraction expressed as one number above another, rather than in decimal form.

vulgarism *noun* 1 a vulgar expression in speech. 2 an example of vulgar behaviour.

vulgarity *noun* (PL. **vulgarities**) coarseness in speech or behaviour, or an instance of it.

vulgarization or **vulgarisation** *noun* the act or an instance of vulgarizing.

vulgarize or **vulgarise** *verb* 1 to make vulgar. 2 to make, or spoil by making, common or popular.

vulgarly *adv.* 1 in a vulgar or coarse way. 2 *old use* among people generally.

Vulgate a Latin translation of the Christian Bible from Hebrew by Jerome (c.405 AD), recognized in 1546 as the official Latin text of the Roman Catholic Church. [from Latin *vulgata editio*, popular edition]

vulnerability *noun* a state of being vulnerable or easily harmed.

vulnerable *adj.* 1 easily hurt or harmed physically or emotionally. 2 easily tempted or persuaded. 3 (**vulnerable to something** or **someone**) unprotected against physical or verbal attack from them. [from Latin *vulnerare*, to wound]
. . . .
◼ SUSCEPTIBLE. 1 sensitive, wide open. 2 weak.
3 unprotected against, exposed to, defenceless against, wide open to.
◪ 1, 2 strong. 3 protected against.
. . . .

vulpine *adj.* 1 relating to or resembling a fox or foxes. 2 *formal* cunning like a fox. [from Latin *vulpes*, fox]

vulture *noun* 1 any of various large birds of prey with brown or black plumage, long broad wings, a bare head, and a strongly curved beak, found in both temperate and tropical regions. They feed on carrion and, unlike other birds of prey, they rarely hunt live food. 2 an American vulture or condor, sometimes referred to as a buzzard. 3 a person who exploits, or prepares to exploit, the downfall or death of another. [from Latin *vultur*]

vulva *noun Medicine* the parts surrounding the opening to the vagina; the female genitals. [from Latin *vulva*, wrapping, womb]

vv or **vv.** *abbrev.* 1 versus. 2 vice versa.

VW *abbrev.* Volkswagen.

vying present participle of VIE.

W

W¹ or **w** *noun* (PL. **Ws, W's, w's**) the twenty-third letter of the English alphabet.

W² *symbol Chem.* tungsten. [from German *Wolfram*]

W³ *abbrev.* **1** watt. **2** West. **3** *Physics* work.

w *abbrev.* **1** *Cricket* wicket. **2** wide. **3** wife. **4** with.

WA *abbrev.* Washington.

WAAC *abbrev.* Women's Army Auxiliary Corps (now WRAC).

WAAF *abbrev.* Women's Auxiliary Air Force (later WRAF).

wacky *adj.* (**wackier, wackiest**) *colloq. orig. North Amer., esp. US* eccentric; crazy. [perhaps from WHACK]

wad /wɒd/ *noun* **1** a compressed mass of soft material used for packing, padding, stuffing, etc. **2** a thick sheaf or bundle of banknotes, etc. [from Latin *wadda*, from Arabic]

. . . .

■ **1** chunk, plug, ball, *colloq.* wodge, lump, hunk, mass. **2** bundle, roll, *colloq.* wodge.

. . . .

wadding /'wɒdɪŋ/ *noun* material used as padding or stuffing.

waddle /'wɒdl/ *verb intrans., said of a duck, or of a person derog.* to sway from side to side in walking. [perhaps related to WADE]

. . . .

■ totter, wobble, sway, rock, toddle, shuffle.

. . . .

wade *verb trans., intrans.* to walk through deep water; to cross (a river, etc) by wading. — **wade in** to involve oneself unhesitatingly and enthusiastically in a task, etc. **wade into someone** to attack or criticize them fiercely. **wade through something** to make one's way laboriously through it: *wading through legal documents.* [from Anglo-Saxon *wadan*, to go]

wader *noun* **1** a general term for any long-legged bird that wades in marshes, or along the shores of rivers, lakes, or seas, eg curlew, plover, heron, stork, sandpiper, flamingo. Their beaks are usually specially adapted for extracting food from water, sand, or mud. **2** (**waders**) thigh-high waterproof boots used by anglers, etc.

wadi /'wɒdɪ/ *noun* a rocky river bed in N Africa and Arabia, dry except during the rains. [from Arabic *wadi*]

wafer *noun* **1** a thin, light, finely layered kind of biscuit, served eg with ice cream. **2** a thin disc of unleavened bread or rice paper served to communicants at Holy Communion. **3** *Hist.* a thin disc of sticky paste or other adhesive material for sealing letters. **4** *Hist.* a small flat edible capsule of medicine. [from Middle English *wafre*, from Old Dutch *wafer*, variant of *wafel*, waffle]

waffle¹ /'wɒfl/ *noun* a light-textured cake made of batter, with a distinctive grid-like surface pattern. [from Old Dutch *wafel*]

waffle² /'wɒfl/ — *verb intrans.* to talk or write at length but to little purpose. — *noun* talk or writing of this kind.

. . . .

■ *verb colloq.* rabbit on, *colloq.* witter on, jabber, prattle, blether. *noun* wordiness, padding, blether, prattle, nonsense, *colloq.* gobbledygook, *colloq.* hot air.

. . . .

waffle iron a flat double-sided hinged mould for cooking waffles.

waffler *noun* a person who waffles.

waft /wɒft, wɑːft/ — *verb trans., intrans.* to float or cause to float or drift gently, especially through the air. — *noun* a whiff, eg of perfume. [from Middle English *waughter* or *wafter*, escort vessel]

. . . .

■ *verb* drift, float, blow, transport, transmit. *noun* whiff, scent, breath, puff, draught, current, breeze.

. . . .

wag — *verb* (**wagged, wagging**) **1** *trans., intrans.* to wave to and fro vigorously; *said of a dog or its tail* to wave (its tail) as a sign of pleasure. **2** to shake (one's finger) up and down at someone, while giving advice, a warning, or rebuke. **3** *intrans., said of the tongue, chin, or beard* to move busily in chatter. — *noun* **1** a wagging movement. **2** a habitual joker; someone with a roguish sense of humour; a wit. [from Anglo-Saxon *wagian*]

. . . .

■ *verb* **1, 2** waggle. **1** shake, wave, wiggle, sway, swing, bob, nod, oscillate, flutter, vibrate, quiver, rock.

. . . .

wage — *verb* to fight (a war or battle). — *noun* **1** (*sing., pl.*) a regular, especially daily or weekly rather than monthly, payment from an employer to an especially unskilled or semi-skilled employee. See also SALARY. **2** (**wages**) *literary* reward, recompense, or repayment: *the wages of sin is death.* [from Old French *wagier*, to pledge]

. . . .

■ *verb* carry on, conduct, engage in, undertake, practise, pursue. *noun* **1** pay, fee, earnings, salary, wage-packet, payment, stipend, remuneration, *formal* emolument, allowance, hire, reward, compensation, recompense.

. . . .

wager *old use* — *noun* a bet on the outcome or result of something. — *verb* (**wagered, wagering**) to bet; to stake in a bet. [from Old French *wagier*, to pledge]

waggish *adj.* **1** amusing. **2** mischievous.

waggle *verb trans., intrans.* to move or cause to move to and fro. [from WAG]

wagon or **waggon** *noun* **1** a four-wheeled vehicle for carrying loads, especially horse-drawn; a cart. **2** an open truck or closed van for carrying railway freight. **3** a tea trolley. — **on the wagon** *colloq.* temporarily abstaining from alcohol. **off the wagon** *colloq.* no longer abstaining from alcohol. [from Dutch *wagen*]

wagoner or **waggoner** *noun* the driver of a wagon.

waif *noun* **1** an orphaned, abandoned, or homeless child. **2** any pathetically undernourished-looking child. **3** something unclaimed and apparently ownerless. [from Old French *waif, guaif*, stray beast]

. . . .

■ **1** orphan, stray, foundling.

. . . .

waif-like *adj.* like a waif; thin and underfed.

waifs and strays **1** homeless people, especially children. **2** unclaimed articles; odds and ends.

wail — *noun* a long-drawn-out mournful or complaining cry. — *verb intrans., trans.* **1** to make, or utter with, such a cry. **2** *said eg of a siren* to make a similar noise. [perhaps related to Norse *wæla*, to wail]

· · · · · · · · · · · · · · · · · · · ·

▣ *noun* moan, cry, howl, lament, complaint, weeping. *verb* **1** moan, cry, howl, lament, weep, complain, yowl.

· ·

wainscot /ˈweɪnskət/ *noun Hist.* wooden panelling or boarding covering the lower part of the walls of a room. [perhaps from Dutch *wagen-schot*, wagon partition]

wainscoting or **wainscotting** /ˈweɪnskətɪŋ/ *noun* a wainscot, or material for this.

waist *noun* **1** the narrow part of the human body between the ribs and hips. **2** the part of a garment covering this. **3** a narrow middle part of something such as a violin or a wasp. **4** the middle part of a ship. [from Anglo-Saxon *wæstm*, form, figure]

waistband *noun* the reinforced strip of cloth on a skirt, trousers, etc, that goes round the waist.

waistcoat *noun* a close-fitting, sleeveless, usually waist-length garment worn especially by men under a jacket.

wait *verb* **1** (**wait for something**) to delay action, or re-main in a certain place, in expectation of, or readiness for, something: *wait for the bus / wait till you're older.* **2** *in-trans., said of a task, etc* to remain temporarily undealt with: *that can wait.* **3** to postpone action for (a period of time). **4** to await (one's turn, etc). **5** *colloq.* to delay eating (a meal) till someone arrives: *won't wait dinner.* **6** *intrans.* to park one's vehicle briefly at the kerb, etc: *no waiting.* **7** *intrans.* to serve as a waiter or waitress. — **wait on some-one 1** to serve them with food as a waiter or waitress. **2** to act as a servant or attendant to someone. **3** *dialect* to wait for someone. **4** *old use* to pay a respectful visit to someone. **wait up for someone** to delay going to bed at night waiting for someone's arrival or return, or some other event. **you wait!** an expression used to warn or threaten. [from Old French *waitier*, *guaitier*, from Old German *wahten*, to watch]

· · · · · · · · · · · · · · · · · · · ·

▣ **1, 3** delay, linger, hold back, hesitate, pause, *colloq.* hang around, hang fire, remain, rest, stay.

▣ **1, 3** proceed, go ahead.

· ·

Waitangi Day /waɪˈtaŋi/ 6 Feb, the national day of New Zealand, commemorating the Treaty of Waitangi made between Britain and the Maori chiefs in 1840.

waiter or **waitress** *noun* a man, or woman, who serves people with food at a restaurant, etc.

waiting list a list of people waiting for something cur-rently unavailable.

waiting-room *noun* a room for people to wait in, eg at a railway station, doctor's surgery, etc.

waive *verb* **1** to refrain from insisting upon; to give up (a claim, right, etc). **2** to refrain from enforcing (a rule, pen-alty, etc). [from Old French *weyver*, *guaiver*, to abandon]

· · · · · · · · · · · · · · · · · · · ·

▣ **1** renounce, relinquish, give up, forego, resign, surrender, yield.

· ·

waiver *noun* the relinquishment of a right, etc, or a written statement confirming this.

wake¹ — *verb* (PAST TENSE **woke**; PAST PARTICIPLE **wo-ken**) **1** *trans., intrans.* (*also* **wake up** or **wake someone up**) to rouse or be roused from sleep. **2** *trans., intrans.* (*also* **wake up** or **wake someone up**) to stir or be stirred out of a state of inactivity, lethargy, etc. **3** (**wake up** or **wake someone up to something**) to become or make them aware of a fact, circumstance, situation, etc. — *noun* **1** a watch or vigil kept beside a corpse. **2** *dialect* an annual holiday. [from Middle English *waken*, from Anglo-Saxon *wacan*, to become awake, and *wacian*, to stay awake]

· · · · · · · · · · · · · · · · · · · ·

▣ *verb* **1** rouse, bring round, come to, get up, rise, arise. **2**

stimulate, stir, activate, arouse, animate, excite, fire, galvanize. **3** alert, notify, warn. *noun* **1** vigil, watch, death-watch, funeral.

▣ *verb* **1** sleep.

· ·

wake² *noun* a trail of disturbed water left by a ship, or of disturbed air left by an aircraft. — **in one's wake** wherever one has been. **in the wake of someone** or **something** coming after them; resulting from them. [from Norse *vök*, hole or channel in the ice]

· · · · · · · · · · · · · · · · · · · ·

▣ wash, trail, track, path, train, aftermath, backwash, rear, waves.

· ·

wakeful *adj.* **1** not asleep; unable to sleep. **2** *said of a night* sleepless. **3** vigilant; alert; watchful.

wakefully *adv.* in a wakeful way.

waken *verb* (**wakened, wakening**) **1** *trans., intrans.* to rouse or be roused from sleep, or from inactivity or lethargy. **2** *intrans.* (**waken to something**) to become aware of a fact, situation, etc. [from Anglo-Saxon *wæcnan*]

waking hours the part of the day that one spends awake.

Waldenses /wɒlˈdensiːz/ or **Waldensians** a small Chris-tian community that began as a reform movement initiated in the 12c by Peter Waldo in Lyons, France.

Waldsterben /ˈvɒːldstɜːbən/ *noun Environ.* the dying back of first the shoots and then the larger branches of trees, especially pine trees, as a result of air pollution. [German, = forest death]

wale *noun* **1** a raised mark on the skin; a weal. **2** a ridge on cloth, eg the rib on corduroy. **3** *Naut.* a course of planking running along the top edge of a ship's side. [from Anglo-Saxon *walu*, ridge]

walk — *verb* **1** *intrans.* to go in some direction on foot, moving one's feet alternately and always having one or other foot on the ground. **2** *intrans.* to go or travel on foot; to do this for exercise. **3** to travel (a distance) by walking: *walked three miles.* **4** to go about (the streets, countryside, etc) on foot. **5** to accompany, support, or propel (someone who is on foot). **6** to take (a dog) out for exercise. **7** *intrans., old use* to live one's life or behave in a certain manner: *walk in fear / walk tall.* **8** *intrans. facetious* to disappear; to be stolen: *my pen has walked.* — *noun* **1** the motion, or pace, of walking: *she slowed to a walk.* **2** an outing or journey on foot, especially for exercise. **3** a distance walked or for walking: *a three-minute walk.* **4** one's distinctive manner of walking: *they recognized your walk.* **5** a path, especially a broad formal one. **6** a route for walking: *some nice walks in these parts.* — **walk all over someone** *colloq.* to treat them inconsiderately or arrogantly. **walk away from someone** *colloq.* to outdistance them. **walk away from something 1** to ignore or abandon a commitment, respon-sibility, etc. **2** to escape unhurt from an accident, etc. **walk away with something** to win a prize or reward effortlessly. **walk into something** to involve oneself in trouble or diffi-culty through one's own unwariness. **walk off** to depart. **walk off with something 1** to win a prize or reward effort-lessly. **2** *colloq.* to steal it. **walk out 1** *said of factory workers, etc* to leave the workplace in a body, in declaration of a strike. **2** to depart abruptly from a meeting, etc in protest. **walk out on someone** to abandon or desert them. **walk out with someone** *old use* to court someone of the oppo-site sex. [from Anglo-Saxon *wealcan*]

· · · · · · · · · · · · · · · · · · · ·

▣ *verb* **1, 2** step, stride, pace, proceed, advance, march, plod, tramp, traipse, trek, trudge, saunter, amble, stroll, tread, hike, promenade, move, *slang* hoof it. **3, 4** tramp, march, plod, traipse, roam, trek, hike, trudge, pace. **5** accompany, escort, march. *noun* **1** stroll, saunter, amble, march. **2, 3** stroll, ramble, hike, saunter, amble, march, tramp, trek, traipse. **4** carriage, gait, step, pace, stride. **5** footpath, path, walkway, avenue, pathway, promenade, alley, esplanade, lane, pavement, sidewalk. **6** route, trail, footpath, path.

· ·

walkabout *noun* **1** a casual stroll through a crowd of ordinary people by a celebrity, especially a member of the royal family. **2** *Austral.* (*usually in* **go walkabout**) a walk alone in the bush by an Australian Aboriginal.

walker *noun* a person who walks, especially for pleasure.

· ·

⊟ pedestrian, rambler, hiker.

· ·

walkie-talkie *noun colloq.* a portable two-way radio carried by police, etc.

walking *adj.* **1** in human form: *a walking encyclopedia.* **2** for the use of walkers: *walking shoes.*

walking stick *noun* a stick used for support or balance in walking.

Walkman *noun trademark* a small portable audio cassette recorder, or radio, with headphones.

walk of life one's occupation or profession.

· ·

⊟ occupation, profession, trade, field, area, sphere, line, activity, arena, course, pursuit, career, vocation, calling, métier.

· ·

walk-on *adj., said of a part in a play, opera, etc* not involving any speaking or singing.

walkout *noun* a sudden departure, especially of a workforce in declaration of a strike. strike, stoppage, industrial action, protest,

walkover *noun colloq.* an easy victory.

· ·

⊟ *colloq.* pushover, *colloq.* doddle, child's play, *colloq.* piece of cake, *colloq.* cinch.

· ·

walkway *noun* a paved path or passage for pedestrians.

wall — *noun* **1** a solid vertical brick or stone construction of narrow width, substantial height, and variable height, serving eg as a barrier, territorial division, or protection. **2** the side of a building or room. **3** anything in some way suggestive of a wall: *a wall of fire / a wall of secrecy.* **4** *Biol.* an outer covering, eg of a cell; the side of a hollow organ or cavity. **5** a sheer rock face. — *verb* **1** to surround with a wall: *a walled garden.* **2** (*usually* **wall something off** or **in**) to separate or enclose it with a wall. **3** (**wall something** or **someone up**) to block an opening with, or seal something behind, brickwork, etc; to imprison someone in this way. — **go to the wall** *said of a business* to fail. **have one's back to the wall** to be making one's last desperate stand. **up the wall** *colloq.* crazy. **walls have ears** an exhortation to speak discreetly. [from Anglo-Saxon *weall*, from Latin *vallum*, rampart]

· ·

⊟ *noun* **1, 2** partition, screen, panel, divider, bulkhead. **3** obstacle, obstruction, barrier, block, impediment, fortification, barricade, rampart, parapet, stockade, embankment, bulwark, palisade. **4** enclosure, membrane, side.

· ·

wallaby *noun* (PL. **wallabies**) any of more than 20 species of a plant-eating marsupial, belonging to the same family (Macropodidae) as, but smaller than, the kangaroo, and native to Australia and Tasmania. Some wallabies are no larger than rabbits, and several species are endangered. [from Aboriginal *walaba*]

wallah /ˈwɒlə/ *noun Anglo-Indian* (*in compounds*) a person performing a specified task: *the tea wallah.* [from Hindi -*wala*]

wallbars *pl. noun* a series of horizontal wooden bars supported by uprights lining the walls of a gymnasium, for climbing, hanging from, etc.

wallet *noun* **1** a flat folding case made eg of leather, for holding banknotes, etc, carried in the pocket or handbag. **2** any of various kinds of especially plastic folders or envelopes for holding papers, etc. [from Middle English *wallet*]

walleye /ˈwɔːlaɪ/ *noun* **1** an eye in which the iris has a chalky appearance. **2** an eye that squints away from the

nose, so that an abnormal amount of the white shows. [from Norse *wagleygr*]

walleyed *adj.* having a walleye.

wallflower *noun* **1** a sweet-smelling plant with yellow, orange or red flowers. **2** *colloq.* a person who sits all evening at the edge of the dance floor, waiting in vain to be asked to dance.

Walloon /wɒˈluːn/ — *noun* **1** a member of the French-speaking population of S Belgium. **2** their language, a dialect of French. — *adj.* relating to, or belonging to, the Walloons. [from French *Wallon*, from Germanic; literally foreigner]

wallop /ˈwɒləp/ *colloq.* — *verb* (**walloped, walloping**) to hit or spank vigorously. — *noun* a hit or a thrashing. [from Old French *waloper, galoper*, to gallop]

walloping — *noun* a thrashing. — *adj.* great; whopping: *a walloping great hole.*

wallow *verb intrans.* (*often* **wallow in something**) **1** to lie or roll about in water, mud, etc. **2** to revel or luxuriate in admiration, etc. **3** to indulge excessively in self-pity, etc. **4** *said of a ship* to roll from side to side making poor headway. **5** *said of an enterprise, project, etc* to fail to progress with speed and efficiency. [from Anglo-Saxon *wealwian*]

· ·

⊟ **1** loll, lie, roll, wade, welter, lurch, flounder, splash. **2** revel, indulge, luxuriate, relish, bask, enjoy, glory, delight.

· ·

wallpaper — *noun* **1** paper used to decorate the interior walls and ceilings of houses, etc. **2** something of a bland or background nature. **3** *Comput.* a background on a computer screen.— *verb* to cover (walls) or the walls of (a room) with wallpaper.

wall-to-wall *adj.* **1** *said of carpeting* covering the entire floor of a room. **2** *facetious* ever-present; inescapable: *wall-to-wall Muzak.*

wally *noun* (PL. **wallies**) *colloq.* an ineffectual or foolish person. [from the name *Walter*]

walnut *noun* **1** any of various deciduous trees of the genus *Juglans*, found in N temperate regions, with large compound leaves, cultivated for its timber and for its edible nut, which is rich in protein and fat. **2** the round nut produced by this tree, consisting of a wrinkled two-lobed seed surrounded by a hard shell. **3** the hard durable dark-brown or black wood of this tree, which has an attractive grain and is highly prized for furniture-making, cabinet-work, and panelling. [from Anglo-Saxon *wealhhnutu*, foreign nut]

Walpurgis Night /valˈpɜːɡɪs, valˈpʊəɡɪs/ the eve of 1 May, when according to German popular superstition witches rode on broomsticks and he-goats to revel with the Devil on high places.

walrus *noun* (PL. **walruses, walrus**) a large marine mammal (*Odobenus rosmarus*) belonging to the family Odobenidae, related to the seal, and found in the northern waters of the Atlantic and Pacific oceans. Walruses are usually over 3m in length, and have grey, wrinkled, almost hairless skin, flippers, a broad bristly snout, and two long tusks. [from Dutch *walrus*, literally whale-horse]

walrus moustache a thick drooping moustache.

waltz /wɔːlts/ — *noun* **1** a slow or fast ballroom dance in triple time. **2** a piece of music for this dance. — *verb intrans.* **1** to dance a waltz. **2** *colloq.* to go or move with easy confidence. [from German *Walzer*, from *walzen*, to roll, dance]

wampum /ˈwɒmpəm/ *noun Hist.* shells strung together for use as money among the Native Americans. [from Algonkin (Native American language group) *wampumpeag*, white string of beads]

WAN *abbrev. Comput.* wide area network, a network of computers spread over a wide area, linked by means of telephone lines, etc.

wan /wɒn/ *adj.* (**wanner, wannest**) pale and pinched-looking from illness, exhaustion, or grief. [from Anglo-Saxon *wann*, dusky, lurid]

wand *noun* **1** a slender rod used eg by magicians or fairies for performing magic. **2** a conductor's baton. **3** a rod carried as a symbol of authority. **4** a slender young shoot; a flexible cane or switch. [from Norse *vöndr*, shoot]

⊟ **3** rod, staff, mace, sceptre. **4** cane, switch, stick, sprig, twig.

wander — *verb* (**wandered, wandering**) **1** to walk or travel about, with no particular destination; to ramble. **2** *said of a stream, etc* to follow a meandering course. **3** to stray, eg from the right path, or from the point of an argument, etc. **4** *said of people, their wits, etc* to become confused, incoherent, or irrational, eg in delirium or advanced age. **5** *said of one's thoughts, etc* to flit randomly. — *noun* a ramble or stroll. [from Anglo-Saxon *wandrian*]

⊟ *verb* **1** roam, ramble, rove, meander, saunter, stroll, prowl, drift, range, straggle. **2** meander. **3** stray, digress, diverge, deviate, depart, go astray, swerve, veer, err. **4** ramble, rave, babble, gibber. *noun* ramble, stroll, saunter, meander, prowl, excursion.

wanderer *noun* a person or animal that wanders.

⊟ itinerant, traveller, voyager, drifter, rover, rambler, stroller, stray, straggler, ranger, nomad, Gypsy, vagrant, vagabond, rolling stone .

wanderlust /ˈwɒndəlʌst/ *noun* an urge to rove; a liking for keeping on the move. [from German *Wanderlust*, from *wandern*, to travel + *Lust*, desire]

wane — *verb intrans.* **1** *said of the moon* to grow narrower as the sun illuminates less of its surface. **2** to decline in glory or influence. — *noun* the process of waning or declining. — **on the wane** decreasing or declining. [from Anglo-Saxon *wanian*, to lessen]

⊟ *verb* **1** decline, diminish, decrease, weaken, subside, fade, dwindle, ebb, lessen, abate, sink, drop, taper off, dim, droop, contract, shrink, fail, wither.
⊟ *verb* WAX. **2** increase.

wangle — *verb* to contrive or obtain by persuasiveness or subtle manipulation. — *noun* an act of wangling.

⊟ *verb* contrive, manipulate, arrange, engineer, fix, scheme, manoeuvre, work, pull off, manage, fiddle.

wank *verb intrans. coarse slang* to masturbate.

wanker *noun coarse slang* **1** a person who masturbates. **2** used as a general term of abuse.

wanly *adv.* with a pale or weak appearance.

wannabe /ˈwɒnəbi/ *noun* someone who aspires, usually ineffectually, to a particular lifestyle or image. [representing a colloquial pronunciation of *want to be*]

wanness /ˈwɒnnɪs/ *noun* being wan; pallor.

want — *verb* **1** to feel a need or desire for. **2** (**want to do something** or **want someone to do something**) to wish or require that they do it: *do you want to say something?* / *she doesn't want you to leave.* **3** (**want in, out**, etc) *colloq.* to desire to get in, out, etc. **4** *colloq.* ought; need: *you want to take more care* / *we want to turn left at the school.* **5** *colloq.* to need (a certain treatment, etc): *he wants his head examined.* **6** (**want something** or **want for something**) to feel the lack of it: *want for nothing.* **7** to require the presence of: *you are wanted next door.* **8** to desire (someone) sexually. **9** *old use* to fall short by a certain amount: *it wants two minutes to midnight.* — *noun* **1** a need or requirement. **2** *old use* lack: *a want of discretion.* **3** a state of need; destitution: *those in want.* — **for want of something** in the absence of it: *for want of a better word.* **in want of something** needing it. [from Norse *vanta*, to be lacking]

⊟ *verb* **1** desire, wish, crave, covet, fancy, long for, pine for, yearn for, hunger for, thirst for. **2** desire, wish, require, call for, demand. **4** ought, need, should, must. **6** lack, miss. **7** need, require, call for. **8** desire, *colloq.* fancy. *noun* **1** need, requirement, wish, desire, longing, demand, appetite. **2** lack, dearth, insufficiency, deficiency, shortage, inadequacy. **3** poverty, privation, destitution.

wanted *adj.* being sought by the police on suspicion of having committed a crime, etc.

wanting *adj.* **1** missing; lacking. **2** (**wanting in something**) not having enough of it: *wanting in tact.* **3** not up to requirements: *has been found wanting.*

⊟ **1** absent, missing, lacking, short, insufficient. **2** lacking in. **3** inadequate, imperfect, faulty, defective, substandard, poor, deficient, unsatisfactory.
⊟ **1, 2** sufficient. **3** adequate.

wanton — *adj.* **1** motivelessly cruel. **2** motiveless: *wanton destruction.* **3** *old use, said of a woman* sexually immoral. **4** *old use* playfully fanciful; whimsical. — *noun old use* a wanton woman. — *verb intrans.* (**wantoned, wantoning**) *old use* to play about, flirt, or trifle wantonly. [from Middle English *wantowen*, from Anglo-Saxon *wan-*, not + *togen*, disciplined]

⊟ *adj.* **1** malicious, malevolent. **2** arbitrary, unprovoked, unjustifiable, unrestrained, rash, reckless, wild. **3** immoral, promiscuous, shameless.

wantonly *adv.* in a wanton manner.

wantonness *noun* being wanton.

WAP Wireless Application Protocol, a system allowing access to the Internet through a mobile telephone.

wapiti /ˈwɒpɪtɪ/ *noun* a large deer of N America. [from Algonkian (Native American language group) *wapiti*]

war — *noun* **1** an openly acknowledged state of armed conflict, especially between nations: *declared war on the French.* **2** a particular armed struggle: *the Iran-Iraq war.* **3** fighting as a science: *the arts of war.* **4** open hostility between people. **5** any long-continued struggle or campaign: *the war against drug-dealing.* **6** fierce rivalry or competition in business: *a trade war.* — *verb intrans.* (**warred, warring**) **1** to fight wars. **2** to conflict with one another: *warring emotions.* — **go to war** to begin an armed conflict. **have been in the wars** *colloq.* to have, or show signs of having, sustained injuries. [from Old French *werre*]

⊟ *noun* **1** warfare, hostilities, fighting, conflict, combat. **2** conflict. **3** warfare, fighting, battle. **4** strife, struggle, contest, contention, enmity. **5** battle, struggle, campaign. *verb* **1** wage war, fight, take up arms, clash, battle, skirmish. **2** struggle, contest, contend.
⊟ *noun* **1, 3, 4** peace.

war baby a baby born during a war, especially a serviceman's illegitimate child.

warble[1] *verb intrans., trans.* **1** *said of a bird* to sing melodiously. **2** *said of a person* to sing in a high, tremulous voice; to trill. [from Old French *werbler*]

warble[2] *noun* a swelling under the hide of horses or cattle, especially one containing a maggot.

warbler *noun* any of several small songbirds.

war crime a crime, eg ill-treatment of prisoners, massacre of civilians or racial minorities, etc, committed during, and in connection with, a war.

war criminal a person who commits a war crime.

war cry 1 a cry used to rally or hearten troops, or as a signal for charging. **2** a slogan or watchword.

ward — *noun* **1** any of the rooms in a hospital with beds for patients. **2** any of the areas into which a town, etc is divided for administration or elections. **3** *Legal* a person, especially a minor, under the protection of a guardian or court. **4** a projection inside a lock that fits into a notch in its key, ensuring that the lock cannot be turned by the wrong key. **5** *old use* a watch or guard kept over something. — *verb* (*usually* **ward something off**) **1** to fend off, turn aside, or parry a blow. **2** to keep trouble, hunger, disease, etc away. [from Anglo-Saxon *weard*, protector]

. . . .

▣ *noun* **1** room, apartment, unit. **2** division, area, district, quarter, precinct, zone. **3** charge, dependant, protégé(e), minor. *verb* FEND OFF, STAVE OFF, BEAT OFF, DEFLECT, REPEL, TURN ASIDE, TURN AWAY. **1** parry, block. **2** avert, forestall, thwart, avoid, evade.

. . . .

-ward see -WARDS.

war dance a dance performed by primitive tribes before going into battle, or after victory.

warden *noun* **1** a person in charge of a hostel, student residence, old people's home, etc. **2** (*in compounds*) a public official responsible in any of various ways for maintaining order: *traffic warden* / *game warden*. **3** *North Amer.* the officer in charge of a prison. [from Old French *wardein*]

. . . .

▣ **1** superintendent, administrator, custodian, curator, steward, guardian, watchman, caretaker, janitor. **2** ranger, steward, keeper, superintendent. **3** governor, warder, superintendent, administrator.

. . . .

warder *noun* a prison officer. [from Middle English *wardere*, from Old French *warder*, *garder*, to guard]

. . . .

▣ prison officer, jailer, keeper, guard, wardress, custodian.

. . . .

wardress *noun* a female warder.

wardrobe *noun* **1** a cupboard in which to hang clothes. **2** a personal stock of garments. **3** the stock of costumes belonging to a theatrical company. [from Old French *garderobe*]

. . . .

▣ **1** cupboard, closet. **2** clothes, garments, outfits, attire.

. . . .

wardrobe mistress or **wardrobe master** the woman or man in charge of a theatrical company's costumes.

wardroom *noun* the officers' quarters on board a warship.

-wards or **-ward** *combining form* forming words denoting direction: *westwards* / *backwards* / *homeward*. [from Anglo-Saxon -*weardes*, genitive of -*weard*, towards]

ware *noun* **1** (*in compounds*) manufactured goods of a specified material or for a specified range of use: *glassware* / *kitchenware*. **2** (*often in compounds*) a particular type of pottery: *Delftware*. **3** (**wares**) goods that one has for sale. [from Anglo-Saxon *waru*]

. . . .

▣ **3** goods, merchandise, commodities, stock, products, produce, stuff.

. . . .

warehouse *noun* **1** a building in which goods are stored. **2** a large, especially wholesale, shop.

. . . .

▣ **1** store, storehouse, depot, depository, repository, stockroom, entrepôt.

. . . .

warfare *noun* **1** the activity of waging war. **2** violent conflict.

. . . .

▣ **1** war, fighting, hostilities, conflict, combat, battle, arms. **2** strife, struggle, contest, conflict, contention, discord, blows. ⏍ PEACE.

. . . .

warfarin /ˈwɔːfərɪn/ *noun Medicine* a crystalline substance that is used as an anticoagulant to prevent the clotting of blood, or to break up existing clots in blood vessels, eg in coronary thrombosis. It is also used as a rat poison. [from *Wisconsin Alumni Research Foundation* (the patent owners) and coum*arin*, an anticoagulant]

war game **1** a mock battle or military exercise providing training in tactics, etc. **2** an elaborate game in which players use model soldiers, knights, etc to enact imaginary battles, etc.

warhead *noun* the front part of a missile, etc containing the explosives.

warhorse *noun* **1** *Hist.* a powerful horse on which a knight rode into battle. **2** an old soldier or politician still full of fight. **3** a standard, reliable, frequently used, over-familiar musical composition, etc.

warily *adv.* cautiously, watchfully.

wariness *noun* being wary.

warlike *adj.* **1** fond of fighting; aggressive; belligerent. **2** relating to war; military.

. . . .

▣ **1** belligerent, aggressive, bellicose, pugnacious, combative, militaristic, bloodthirsty, warmongering, hostile, antagonistic, unfriendly. **2** military, martial. ⏍ FRIENDLY, PEACEABLE.

. . . .

warlock *noun* a wizard, male magician, or sorcerer. [from Anglo-Saxon *warloga*]

warlord *noun* a powerful military leader.

warm — *adj.* **1** moderately, comfortably, or pleasantly hot. **2** *said of clothes* providing and preserving heat. **3** *said of work* making one hot. **4** kind-hearted and affectionate. **5** *said of an environment, etc* welcoming and congenial. **6** enthusiastic; whole-hearted: *warm support*. **7** *old use* vehement; indignant: *was warm in her denial of the charge*. **8** *said of colours* suggestive of comfortable heat, typically deep and containing red or yellow. **9** *said of a trail or scent* still fresh enough to follow. **10** *in a children's game, etc* close to guessing correctly or finding the thing sought. **11** *old use, said of one's situation* awkward or dangerous. — *verb* **1** *trans., intrans.* to make or become warm or warmer. **2** (*usually* **warm to something**) to gain in enthusiasm for a task as one performs it. **3** (**warm to someone**) to gain in affection or approval for them. — **warm up** or **warm something up** **1** to become or make it warm or warmer. **2** to re-heat food. **3** *said of a party, etc* to become or make it livelier. **4** *said of an engine* to reach, or bring it up to, an efficient working temperature. **5** to exercise the body gently in preparation for a strenuous work-out, race, athletic contest, etc. [from Anglo-Saxon *wearm*]

. . . .

▣ *adj.* **1** heated, tepid, lukewarm, cosy. **3** hot. **4** kind-hearted, affectionate, kindly, genial, friendly, amiable, cordial, affable, hearty, sympathetic, tender. **5** welcoming, congenial, friendly, hospitable, genial. **6** enthusiastic, wholehearted, earnest, ardent, fervent, vehement, passionate, zealous. **8** rich, intense, mellow, cheerful. **warm up 1** heat up. **2** heat up, reheat. **3** hot up.

⏍ *adj.* **1, 2** cool. **4** indifferent, cool, cold. **5** unwelcoming, unfriendly, cold. **6** cool, indifferent. **8** cool, cold. **9, 10** cold.

. . . .

warm-blooded *adj.* **1** *said of an animal* maintaining its internal body temperature at a relatively constant level, usually above that of the surrounding environment, eg mammals, birds. Also called HOMOIOTHERMIC. **2** *said of a person* passionate, impulsive, or ardent.

warm boot *Comput.* a reboot activated by pressing a computer's reset key or a combination of keys, rather than by switching off and on again at the power source.

warm-down *noun* gentle exercise for relaxation after more strenuous physical exercise.

war memorial a monument commemorating members of the armed forces who died in war.

warm front *Meteorol.* the edge of a mass of warm air pushing against a mass of cold air.

warm-hearted *adj.* kind, affectionate, and generous.

warming-pan *noun Hist.* a long-handled copper or brass lidded container for hot coals, slid into a bed to warm it up.

warmly *adv.* 1 so as to be warm. 2 enthusiastically; affectionately.

warmonger *noun* a person who tries to precipitate war, or whips up enthusiasm for it.

warmth *noun* 1 the condition of being warm; moderate, pleasant, or comfortable heat. 2 affection or kind-heartedness. 3 passion; vehemence: *the warmth of her denial.* 4 strength or intensity: *the warmth of her love for him.*

....

■ 1 warmness, heat. 2 affection, kind-heartedness, friendliness, cordiality, tenderness. 3 passion, vehemence, ardour, enthusiasm, eagerness, fervour, zeal.
Ⓔ 1 coldness. 2 unfriendliness. 3 indifference.

....

warm-up *noun* the act of exercising the body in preparation for an athletic contest, etc.

warn *verb* 1 (*usually* **warn someone of** or **about something**) to make aware of possible or approaching danger or difficulty. 2 to advise strongly: *warned them to book early.* 3 to rebuke or admonish, with the threat of punishment for a repetition of the offence; to caution. 4 to inform in advance: *warned him she might be late.* 5 (**warn someone off**) to order them to go away. [from Anglo-Saxon *wearnian*]

....

■ 1 alert, forewarn, put on one's guard. 2 advise, counsel, urge. 3 rebuke, admonish, caution, reprimand, reprove. 4 inform, notify, advise, tip off.

....

warning — *noun* something that happens, or is said or done, that serves to warn. — *adj.* intended, or serving, to warn.

....

■ *noun* caution, alert, admonition, advice, notification, notice, advance notice, counsel, hint, lesson, alarm, threat, tip-off, omen, augury, premonition, presage, sign, signal, portent.

....

warning coloration *Zool.* brightly coloured patterns occurring on some animals, especially poisonous, unpalatable, or stinging insects. These deter unpleasant predators which learn to associate the coloration with unpalatable prey and avoid it, eg the black-and-yellow stripes on the abdomen of the wasp.

warningly *adv.* so as to warn.

warnography *noun* the presentation of images of war for pleasure. [from WAR + PORNOGRAPHY]

warp — *verb trans., intrans.* 1 *said of wood and other hard materials* to become or cause to become twisted out of shape through the shrinking and expanding effects of damp and heat. 2 to become or cause to become distorted, corrupted, or perverted. 3 *Naut., said of a vessel* to move it, or be manoeuvred, by hauling on a rope fixed to a position on a wharf. — *noun* 1 an unevenness or twist in wood, etc. 2 a distortion or abnormal twist in personality, etc. 3 a shift or displacement in a continuous dimension, especially time: *caught in a time warp.* 4 *Naut.* a rope used for warping a vessel. 5 *Weaving* the set of threads stretched lengthways in a loom, under and over which the widthways set of threads (the *weft* or *woof*) are passed. [from Anglo-Saxon *weorpan*, to throw]

....

■ *verb* 1 twist, bend, contort, deform, distort, kink, misshape. 2 distort, corrupt, pervert, twist, deviate. *noun* 1 twist, bend, contortion, deformation, distortion. 2 distortion, twist, bias, kink, irregularity, turn, bent, defect, deviation, quirk, perversion.

Ⓔ *verb* 1 straighten.

....

warpaint *noun* paint put on the face by primitive peoples when going to war.

warpath *noun* the march to war, especially *Hist.* among Native Americans. — **on the warpath** 1 setting off to fight. 2 *colloq.* in a fighting mood; in angry pursuit.

warrant — *noun* 1 a written legal authorization for doing something, eg arresting someone, or searching property. 2 a certificate such as a licence, voucher, or receipt, that authorizes, guarantees, or confirms something. 3 a justification: *has no warrant for making such an accusation.* 4 a certificate appointing a warrant officer in the armed services. — *verb* 1 to justify: *the circumstances are suspicious enough to warrant a full investigation.* 2 *old use* to assert with confidence; to be willing to bet: *I'll warrant he knows nothing of this.* 3 to guarantee (goods, etc) as being of the specified quality or quantity; to confirm as genuine, worthy, etc. [from Old French *warant, guarant*]

....

■ *noun* 1, 2 authorization, authority, sanction, permit, permission, licence, guarantee, warranty, security, commission, voucher. *verb* 1 justify, excuse, necessitate, require, approve, call for, commission. 3 guarantee, pledge, certify, assure, declare, affirm, vouch for, answer for, underwrite, uphold, endorse, license.

....

warrantable *adj.* 1 that may be permitted. 2 justifiable.

warrant officer in the armed services, an officer intermediate between a commissioned and non-commissioned officer.

warrantor *noun* a person who gives a warrant or warranty.

warranty *noun* (PL. **warranties**) 1 an assurance of the quality of goods being sold, usually with an acceptance of responsibility for repairs during an initial period of use; a guarantee. 2 an undertaking or assurance expressed or implied in certain contracts.

warren *noun* 1 an underground labyrinth of interconnecting tunnels linking numerous rabbit burrows. 2 an overcrowded dwelling or district. 3 any maze of passages. [from Old French *warenne*]

warrior *noun* 1 a skilled fighting man, especially of earlier times. 2 any distinguished soldier. 3 a person notable for stoutness of spirit or indomitability. [from Old French *werreieor*]

warship *noun* a ship equipped with guns, etc for naval battles.

wart *noun* 1 a small and usually hard benign growth with a horny surface, found on the skin, especially of the fingers, hands, and face, and transmitted by a virus. 2 a small protuberance on a plant surface or the skin of an animal. — **warts and all** *colloq.* with any blemishes or defects remaining. [from Anglo-Saxon *wearte*]

warthog /ˈwɔːthɒg/ *noun* a hairy wild pig of Africa, which has wart-like lumps on its face, and two tusks.

wartime *noun* a period during which a war is going on.

Warwicks. *abbrev.* Warwickshire.

wary *adj.* (**warier, wariest**) 1 alert; vigilant; cautious; on one's guard. 2 distrustful or apprehensive. 3 (*often* **wary of something** or **someone**) cautious; suspicious: *should be wary of such invitations.* [from Anglo-Saxon *wær*, to beware]

....

■ 1, 3 alert, vigilant, cautious, on one's guard, heedful, attentive, watchful, wide-awake, suspicious, guarded, careful, chary, on the lookout, prudent. 2 distrustful, apprehensive, suspicious, chary.
Ⓔ UNWARY, CARELESS, HEEDLESS.

....

was *see* BE.

Wash. *abbrev.* Washington.

wash — *verb* 1 to cleanse with water and usually soap or detergent. 2 *intrans.* to cleanse oneself, or one's hands

and face, with water, etc. **3** *intrans., said of a fabric or dye* to withstand washing without change or damage. **4** *trans., intrans.* (*usually* **wash** or **wash something off, out,** etc) *said of dirt or a stain* to be removed, or remove it, through washing. **5** *said of an animal* to lick itself, its young, etc clean. **6** to moisten or flush (eg an injured part) with liquid. **7** (*usually* **wash against** or **over something**) *said of a river, the sea, waves, etc* to flow against or over a place, land-feature, etc. **8 a** (*usually* **wash something down** or **away**) *said of flowing water* to sweep objects along with it. **b** (*usually* **wash down** or **away**) *said of substances, etc* to be swept along by water. **9** *said of flowing water* to gouge out (a channel, etc) in the landscape. **10** to apply watercolour thinly to (a surface, eg a wall). **11** *intrans. colloq.* to stand the test; to bear investigation: *that excuse won't wash.* **12** *Mining* to separate (ore) from earth with a flow of water. **13** *literary* to spread over: *washed with the pale light of morning.* — *noun* **1** the process of washing or being washed. **2** this process undertaken by a laundry. **3** a quantity of clothes, etc for washing, or just washed. **4** the breaking of waves against something; the sound of this. **5** the rough water or disturbed air left by a ship or aircraft. **6** a lotion or other preparation for cleansing or washing. **7** kitchen slops or brewery waste, etc for giving to pigs; pigswill. **8** a thin application of water colour. — **be washed out 1** *colloq.,* *said of a person* to be worn out and faded-looking. **2** *said of fabric* to be faded through washing. **3** *said of an outdoor occasion, eg a sports match* to be cancelled because of rain or other bad weather. **be washed up** *colloq.* **1** *said of a person* to be exhausted and incapable of further productivity. **2** *said of plans, etc* to have come to nothing. **come out in the wash** to turn out satisfactorily in the end. **wash something down 1** to wash walls, etc from top to bottom. **2** to ease a pill down one's throat, or accompany food, with a drink. **wash one's hands of something** or **someone** to abandon responsibility for them. **wash up** or **wash something up** to wash dishes. [from Anglo-Saxon *wæscan*]
....
■ *verb* **1** clean, cleanse, launder, scrub, swab down, rinse, swill, shampoo. **2** bathe, bath, shower, douche. *noun* **1** cleaning, cleansing, bath, bathe, scrub, shower, shampoo, washing, rinse. **2** laundry, laundering, cleaning. **3** laundry. **5** wake, backwash, trail.
....

washable *adj.* able to be washed without damage.

washbasin or **washhand basin** *noun* a shallow sink in which to wash one's face and hands.

washcloth *noun North Amer.* a facecloth or flannel.

washed-out *adj.* **1** *colloq., said of a person* worn out and faded-looking. **2** *said of fabric* faded through washing.

washed-up *adj. colloq., said of a person* exhausted and incapable of further productivity.

washer *noun* **1** *combining form* a machine for washing: *a dishwasher.* **2** a flat ring of rubber or metal for keeping a joint tight, or one of linen for reinforcing the punched holes in ring-binder paper.

washerwoman *noun Hist.* a woman paid to wash clothes.

washhouse *noun Hist.* **1** an outhouse or basement room for washing clothes. **2** a public building for washing clothes in.

washing *noun* clothes to be, or which have just been, washed.

washing-machine *noun* a machine for washing clothes.

washing-powder *noun* powdered detergent for washing clothes.

washing soda sodium carbonate crystals, used for washing and cleaning.

washing-up *noun* **1** washing dishes after a meal, etc. **2** dishes for washing.

wash leather a chamois leather.

washout *noun* **1** *colloq.* a failure or flop. **2** a rained-off event, eg a match.

....
■ **1** failure, *colloq.* flop, disaster, disappointment, fiasco, debacle.
■ **1** success, triumph.
....

washroom *noun North Amer.* a lavatory.

washstand *noun Hist.* a small table in a bedroom for holding a jug and basin for washing oneself.

washy *adj.* (**washier, washiest**) *colloq.* **1** *said of a drink* watery; weak. **2** feeble; lacking liveliness or vigour. **3** *said of colours* faded-looking or pallid.

wasn't *contr.* was not.

WASP *abbrev. North Amer. often derog.* White Anglo-Saxon Protestant.

wasp *noun* any of numerous stinging insects having slender bodies and narrow waists, belonging to the same order (Hymenoptera) as bees and ants, and found worldwide. They include both social and solitary species. [from Anglo-Saxon *wæsp*]

waspish *adj.* sharp-tongued; caustic.

wasp waist a slender waist.

wasp-waisted *adj.* having a slender waist.

wassail /ˈwɒseɪl, ˈwɒsl/ *noun old use* **1** a festive bout of drinking. **2** a toast made at such an occasion. [from Norse *ves heill*, be in good health]

wast /wɒst/ a form of the past tense of the verb *be* used with the pronoun *thou.*

wastage *noun* **1** the process of wasting; loss through wasting. **2** the amount so lost. **3** loss or reduction through use, natural decay, etc. **4** (*also* **natural wastage**) reduction of staff through retirement or resignation, as distinct from dismissal or redundancy.

waste — *verb* **1** to use or spend purposelessly, extravagantly, or to too little useful effect; to squander. **2** to fail to use or make the best of (an opportunity, etc). **3** to throw away unused. **4** to offer (advice, sympathy, etc) where it is unheeded or unappreciated: *shall not waste any more sympathy on them.* **5** *trans., intrans.* (*also* **waste away**) to lose or cause to lose flesh or strength. **6** *old use* to devastate (territory); to lay waste. — *adj.* **1** rejected as useless or excess to requirements. **2** *said of ground* lying unused, uninhabited, or uncultivated. **3** *Physiol.* denoting material excreted from the body in the urine or faeces. — *noun* **1** the act, or an instance, of wasting; the condition of being wasted. **2** failure to take advantage of something: *a waste of talent.* **3** material that is no longer needed and must be disposed of, eg household waste, nuclear waste. **4** refuse; rubbish. **5** *Physiol.* matter excreted from the body. **6** a devastated or barren region: *reduced to a muddy waste.* **7** (*often* **wastes**) a vast tract of uncultivated land, expanse of ocean, etc: *the Arctic wastes.* — **go** or **run to waste** to be wasted. **lay something waste** to devastate an area, etc. [from Old French *wast, guast*]
....
■ *verb* **1** squander, misspend, misuse, fritter away, dissipate, lavish, throw away, *colloq.* blow. **2** squander, throw away, *colloq.* blow. **4** squander. **5** wither, shrivel, shrink, become emaciated, consume, erode, exhaust, drain, destroy. *adj.* **1** useless, worthless, unwanted, excess, unused, left-over, superfluous, supernumerary, extra. **2** disused, uninhabited, uncultivated, barren, desolate, empty, bare, devastated, unprofitable, wild, dismal, dreary. *noun* **1** squandering, dissipation, prodigality, wastefulness, extravagance, loss, misapplication, misuse, abuse, neglect. **2** squandering, neglect, loss. **3, 4** rubbish, refuse, *North Amer.* trash, *North Amer.* garbage, leftovers, debris, dregs, effluent, litter, scrap, slops, dross.
■ *verb* **1** economize. **3** preserve.
....

waste disposal the depositing of waste from domestic, industrial, or agricultural sources, the environmental consequences of which are a source of major concern.

wasteful *adj.* causing waste; extravagant.

- ▣ extravagant, spendthrift, prodigal, profligate, uneconomical, thriftless, unthrifty, ruinous, lavish, improvident.
- ▣ economical, thrifty.

wasteland *noun* a desolate and barren region.

- ▣ wilderness, desert, waste, wild(s), void.

waste paper paper discarded as rubbish.

waste-paper basket or **waste-paper bin** a basket or other container for waste paper and other office or household waste.

waste pipe a pipe carrying waste material or waste water from a sink, etc.

waste product 1 a useless by-product of a manufacturing process, etc. **2** a substance excreted from the body during the metabolic and physiological processes.

waster *noun* an idler, good-for-nothing, or wastrel.

wastrel / 'weɪstrəl/ *noun* an idle spendthrift; a good-for-nothing.

watch — *verb* **1** *trans., intrans.* to look at or focus one's attention on (someone or something moving, doing something, etc). **2** *trans., intrans.* to pass time looking at (television, a programme, entertainment, sports event, etc). **3** to guard, look after, or keep an eye on. **4** to keep track of, follow, or monitor: *watch developments in the Middle East.* **5** to keep (eg a building or person) under observation or surveillance. **6** (**watch something** or **watch for something**) to await one's chance, opportunity, etc. **7** to keep checking on, in case controlling measures or adjustments are necessary. **8** (**watch oneself**) *colloq.* to take care in one's behaviour or actions. **9** to pay proper attention to: *watch where you're going!* **10** to take care: *watch you don't slip.* — *noun* **1** a small instrument for telling the time, usually worn strapped to the wrist or in the waistcoat pocket. **2** the activity or duty of watching or guarding: *keep watch / stayed on watch.* **3** *Naut.* any of the four-hour shifts during which particular crew members are on duty; those on duty in any shift. **4** *old use* a body of sentries on look-out duty; a watchman or body of watchmen. — **keep a watch on something** or **someone** to keep them under observation. **on the watch for something** seeking or looking out for it. **watch it!** be careful! **watch out** to be careful. **watch out for something** or **someone** to be on one's guard against them; to look out for them. **watch over someone** or **something** to guard, look after, or tend to them. [from Anglo-Saxon *wæccan* or *wacian*, to watch]

- ▣ *verb* **1** look at, observe, see, regard, stare at, peer at, gaze at, view, note, notice, mark. **2** see, view, spectate. **3** guard, look after, keep an eye on, mind, protect, superintend, take care of, keep. **4** keep track of, follow, monitor, observe, survey, track. **7** monitor, observe, keep an eye on, keep under observation. **8, 10** take care, be careful. **9** pay attention, be careful, take care, take heed, look out. *noun* **1** timepiece, wristwatch, chronometer. **2** vigilance, watchfulness, vigil, observation, surveillance, notice, lookout, attention, heed, alertness, inspection, supervision. **watch out for** notice, be vigilant, look out for, keep one's eyes open for. **watch over** guard, look after, stand guard over, keep an eye on, protect, tend to, mind, shield, defend, shelter, preserve.

watchdog *noun* **1** a dog kept to guard premises, etc. **2** a person or group of people guarding against unacceptable standards, behaviour, etc.

- ▣ **1** guard dog, house-dog. **2** inspector, ombudsman, scrutineer, monitor, guardian, custodian, protector, vigilante.

watchful *adj.* alert, vigilant, and wary.

- ▣ alert, vigilant, wary, attentive, wide awake, heedful, observant, guarded, on one's guard, chary, cautious, suspicious.
- ▣ unobservant, inattentive.

watchfully *adv.* in a watchful way.

watchfulness *noun* being watchful.

watching brief an instruction to a barrister to follow a case on behalf of a client not directly involved.

watchmaker *noun* a person who makes and repairs watches and clocks.

watchman *noun* a man employed to guard premises at night.

- ▣ guard, security guard, caretaker, custodian.

watchnight service a church service lasting through midnight on Christmas Eve or New Year's Eve.

watchtower *noun* a tower from which a sentry keeps watch.

watchword *noun* **1** a catchphrase encapsulating the principles, or used to inspire the members, of a party, group, profession, etc. **2** *old use* a password.

water — *noun* **1** (FORMULA. H_2O) a colourless odourless tasteless liquid that freezes to form ice at $0°C$ and boils to form steam at $100°C$, at normal atmospheric pressure. **2** (*also* **waters**) an expanse of this; a sea, lake, river, etc. **3** (**waters**) the sea round a country's coasts, considered part of its territory. **4** the level or state of the tide: *at high/ low water.* **5** a solution of a substance in water: *rose water.* **6** (**waters**) water at a spa, etc, containing minerals and formerly considered good for one's health. **7** *Physiol.* any of several fluids secreted by the body, especially urine. **8** (**waters**) the amniotic fluid surrounding the fetus in the womb. **9** the degree of brilliance and transparency of a diamond. — *verb* **1** to wet, soak, or sprinkle with water. **2** to irrigate (land). **3** to dilute (wine, etc). **4** *intrans., said of the mouth* to produce saliva in response to a stimulus activated by the expectation of food. **5** *intrans., said of the eyes* to fill with tears in response to irritation. **6** *trans., intrans.* to let (animals) drink, or (of animals) to drink: *fed and watered.* **7** to give a wavy appearance to the surface of, by wetting and pressing: *watered silk.* — **by water** by ship. **hold water** to prove sound; to be valid. **in deep water** in trouble, danger, or difficulty. **like water** *colloq.* in large quantities; freely; lavishly: *spending money like water.* **make one's mouth water** to make one's saliva flow; to stimulate one's appetite for something. **of the first water** of the highest class; first-class; prize. **pass water** to urinate. **test the water** or **waters** to test for a response to an intended course of action. **throw cold water on something** *colloq.* to be discouraging or unenthusiastic about an idea, etc. **tread water** to keep oneself afloat and upright in deep water, gently moving one's legs and arms to maintain the position. **under water** under the surface of the water. **water something down 1** to dilute or thin it with water. **2** to reduce the impact of something; to make it less controversial or offensive. **water under the bridge** experiences that are past and done with. [from Anglo-Saxon *wæter*]

- ▣ *noun* **2** sea, ocean, lake, river, stream. *verb* **1** wet, soak, spray, sprinkle, moisten, dampen, drench, flood, hose. **3** dilute, thin, water, weaken, adulterate, mix. **4** salivate. **water down 1** dilute, thin, water, weaken, adulterate, mix. **2** tone down, soften, qualify, weaken.
- ▣ *verb* **1** dry out, parch. **2** drain.

water bed a waterproof mattress filled with water, or a bed equipped with this.

water biscuit a plain crisp biscuit made from water and flour, eaten with cheese, etc.

water boatman a predatory aquatic bug, distributed worldwide, that swims upside-down in water, using its paddle-like hindlegs. Its forelegs are used to grasp prey.

waterborne *adj.* carried by water.

water buffalo an important domestic animal belonging to the cattle family, native to India, Sri Lanka, and SE Asia. It may be black, grey, pink, or white in colour, and has huge ridged horns that curve outwards and upwards. It is noted for its docility, and it provides meat and milk, the skin being used for leather. Wild water buffalo have black coats, are much more aggressive, and live in small herds in swampy areas or by rivers.

water bus a passenger boat sailing regularly across a lake, along a river, etc.

water cannon a device that sends out a powerful jet of water, used for dispersing crowds.

water chestnut 1 an aquatic annual plant (*Trapa natans*), native to Asia, Africa, and warm parts of Europe. It produces white flowers and triangular woody fruits, which are rich in starch and fat, and are an important food source in many parts of Asia. **2** a sedge (*Eleocharis tuberosa*), grown in China, that produces edible tubers. **3** the tuber of this plant, eaten as a vegetable, especially in Chinese and Japanese cuisine.

water closet *formal, technical* a lavatory whose pan is mechanically flushed with water.

watercolour *noun* **1** a paint thinned with water, not oil. **2** a painting done in such paint.

water-colourist *noun* an artist who works in water colours.

water-cooled *adj., said of an engine, etc* cooled by circulating water.

water cooler a tank dispensing cool water, usually in a workplace.

watercourse *noun* the bed or channel of a stream, river, or canal.

watercress *noun* a cress that grows in water, whose sharp-tasting leaves are used in salads, etc.

water cycle *Chem.* the continuous movement of water between the oceans, the atmosphere, and the land, mainly involving such processes as evaporation and precipitation (eg in the form of rain or snow), and also including interactions with living organisms.

water-diviner *noun* a person who detects underground sources of water, usually with a divining-rod; a dowser.

waterfall *noun* a sudden interruption in the course of a river or stream where water falls more or less vertically for a considerable distance, eg over the edge of a plateau, or where overhanging softer rock has been eroded away.
. . . .
▣ fall, cascade, force, chute, cataract, torrent.
. . . .

waterfowl *noun* **1** a bird living on or near water, especially a swimming bird such as a duck. **2** (*pl.*) swimming game birds in general.

waterfront *noun* the buildings or part of a town along the edge of a river, lake, or the sea.

Watergate *noun* a US political scandal (1972–4) that led to the first resignation of a president in US history (Richard Nixon, in office 1968–74). It was named from the hotel and office complex in Washington, DC, the home of the Democratic Party headquarters, where, during the 1972 presidential campaign, burglars were caught whose connections were traced to the White House and to the Committee to Re-elect the President.

waterglass *noun* a solution of potassium or sodium silicate in water, used as protective coating, an adhesive, and, especially formerly, for preserving eggs.

waterhole *noun* a pool or spring in a desert area, where animals can drink.

water ice sweetened fruit purée frozen and served as a dessert; a sorbet.

watering can a water-container with a handle and spout, for watering plants.

watering hole 1 a waterhole. **2** *facetious* a public house.

watering place *noun Hist.* a spa or other place where people go to drink mineral water or bathe.

water jump in a steeplechase, etc, a jump over a water-filled ditch.

water level 1 the height reached by the surface of a body of water. **2** the level below which the ground is waterlogged; a water table. **3** a waterline.

water lily any of various aquatic perennial plants of the genera *Nymphaea* or *Nuphar*, found in both tropical and temperate regions, with large flat circular leaves and conspicuous white, pink, red, or yellow bowl-shaped flowers that float on the surface of still or very slow-moving water.

waterline *noun* the level reached by the water on the hull of a floating vessel.

waterlogged *adj.* **1** saturated with water. **2** *said of a boat* so filled or saturated with water as to be unmanageable.

Waterloo *noun* the challenge that finally defeats one: *meet one's Waterloo.* [after the battle of Waterloo (1815) where Napoleon I was finally defeated]

water main a large underground pipe carrying a public water supply.

watermark — *noun* **1** the limit reached by the sea at high or low tide. **2** a manufacturer's distinctive mark in paper, visible when the paper is held up to the light. — *verb* to impress (paper) with a watermark.

water meadow a meadow kept fertile by periodic flooding from a stream.

water melon a melon native to Africa, with dark green coarse skin and red flesh.

watermill *noun* a mill whose machinery is driven by a water wheel.

water of crystallization *Chem.* water that is chemically incorporated in definite proportions in crystalline compounds, and can be removed by heating. Such compounds are called *hydrates.* For example, copper(II) sulphate, $CuSO_4.5H_2O$, has five molecules of water of crystallization associated with each molecule of copper(II) sulphate.

water pistol a toy pistol that fires squirts of water.

water pollution *Environ.* the contamination of seas, lakes, rivers, and other bodies of water with artificial fertilizers, pesticides, sewage, industrial waste, and other materials that are considered to be detrimental to living organisms.

water polo a seven-a-side ball game for swimmers; a similar game for canoeists.

water power the power generated by moving water (including tides and waves) that is used to drive machinery, eg turbines for generating hydroelectricity.

waterproof — *adj.* impenetrable by water; treated or coated so as to resist water. — *verb* to treat so as to make waterproof. — *noun* a raincoat.

water rat or **water vole** a swimming rodent inhabiting stream banks.

water rate a charge made for the use of the public water supply.

watershed *noun* **1** the high land separating two river basins. **2** a crucial point after which events take a different turn.

waterside *noun* the edge of a river, lake, or sea.

water ski a ski on which to glide over water, towed by a powered boat.

water-ski *verb intrans.* (**water-skis, water-skied** or **water-ski'd**) to travel on water skis.

water-skiing *noun* the sport or activity of travelling on water skis.

water softener a substance or device used in water to remove minerals, especially calcium, that cause hardness and prevent lathering.

waterspout *noun Meteorol.* a tornado that occurs over open water, mainly in the tropics, and consists of a rotating column of water and spray. Waterspouts are potentially hazardous to shipping.

water table *Geol.* the level below which porous rocks are saturated with groundwater.

watertight *adj.* **1** so well sealed as to be impenetrable by water. **2** *said of an argument, etc* without any apparent flaw or weakness; completely sound.

· · · · · · · · · · · · · · · · · · · ·

⊟ **1** waterproof, sound, hermetic. **2** impregnable, unassailable, airtight, flawless, foolproof, firm, incontrovertible.
⊟ **1** leaky.

· ·

water tower a tower supporting an elevated water tank, from which water can be distributed at uniform pressure.

water vapour water in the form of droplets suspended in the atmosphere, especially where evaporation has occurred at a temperature below boiling point.

water vole SEE WATER RAT.

waterway *noun* a channel, eg a canal or river, used by ships or smaller boats.

waterwheel *noun* a wheel that is turned by the force of flowing or falling water on blades or buckets around its rim, formerly used as a source of energy to drive machinery, etc, but now largely superseded by the turbine.

water wings an inflatable device that supports the chest and terminates in wing-like projections, used by children learning to swim.

waterworks *noun* **1** (*sing., pl.*) an installation where water is purified and stored for distribution to an area. **2** (*pl.*) *euphemistic* one's bladder and urinary system. **3** (*pl.*) *facetious* tears; weeping.

watery *adj.* **1** of, or consisting of, water: *the watery depths.* **2** containing too much water; over-diluted; weak or thin: *watery tea.* **3** *said of the sun or sunlight* weak and pale, as when alternating with showers. **4** *said of eyes* inclined to water. **5** *said of a smile, etc* half-hearted; feeble.

· · · · · · · · · · · · · · · · · · · ·

⊟ **1** liquid, fluid, moist, wet, damp. **2** weak, thin, watered-down, diluted, runny, soggy, insipid, tasteless, flavourless, *colloq.* wishy-washy. **3** weak, pale, thin. **4** moist. **5** half-hearted, feeble, weak.
⊟ **1** dry.

· ·

watt *noun* (SYMBOL **W**) *Physics* the SI unit of power, defined as the power that gives rise to the production of energy at the rate of one joule per second. Electrical power is equal to the current (in amperes) multiplied by the voltage (in volts). [named after the UK engineer James Watt]

wattage *noun* electrical power expressed in watts.

watt hour a unit of electrical energy, the amount of work done by one watt in one hour.

wattle *noun* **1** rods, branches, etc forming a framework for a wall, especially when interwoven. **2** a loose fold of skin hanging from the throat of certain birds, fish, and lizards. **3** any of various Australian acacia trees.

wattle and daub wattle plastered with mud, as a building material.

wattmeter *noun Physics* an instrument for measuring the power consumption (usually in watt-hours or units) in an electric circuit. [named after James Watt]

wave — *verb* **1** *intrans., trans.* to move (one's hand) to and fro in greeting, farewell, or as a signal; to hold up and move (some other object) in this way for this purpose: *waved her hand to her father / waved their handkerchiefs.* **2** to say (especially goodbye) in this way: *waved them farewell.* **3** (**wave someone off**) to see them off on a journey. **4** *trans., intrans.* to move or cause to move or sway to and fro. **5** to direct with a gesture of the hand: *waved the waiter away.* **6** to put a gentle curl into (hair) by artificial means. — *noun* **1** any of a series of moving ridges on the surface of the sea or some other body of water; such a ridge as it arches and breaks on the shore, etc. **2** *Physics* a regularly repeated disturbance or displacement in a medium (eg water or air). Both electromagnetic radiation (eg light and radio waves) and sound travel as waves. **3** any of the circles of disturbance moving outwards from the site of a shock such as an earthquake. **4** a loose soft curl, or series of such curls, in the hair. **5** a surge or sudden feeling: *a wave of nausea.* **6** a sudden increase in something: *a wave of car thefts / a heat wave.* **7** an advancing body of people: *waves of invaders.* **8** any of a series of curves in an upward-and-downward-curving line or outline. **9** an act of waving the hand, etc. — **wave someone** or **something aside** to dismiss them as unimportant or intrusive. [from Anglo-Saxon *wafian*, to wave]

· · · · · · · · · · · · · · · · · · · ·

⊟ *verb* **1, 5** gesture, gesticulate, beckon, sign, signal, indicate, direct. **4** brandish, flourish, flap, flutter, shake, sway, swing, waft, quiver, ripple. **6** curl, perm, set. *noun* **1** breaker, roller, billow, ripple, tidal wave, wavelet, undulation, white horse. **5** surge, swell, upsurge, ground swell, rush. **6** outbreak, stream, flood, rash.

· ·

waveband *noun Radio* a range of frequencies in the electromagnetic spectrum occupied by radio or television broadcasting transmission of a particular type. Broadcasting systems that require a large waveband, eg FM radio, use higher frequencies, which have a larger frequency range.

wavelength *noun Physics* **1** the distance between two successive peaks or two successive troughs of a wave. It is equal to the velocity of the wave divided by its frequency, ie for waves of a given velocity, the higher the frequency the shorter the wavelength. The wavelengths of electromagnetic waves range from several kilometres for some radio waves to less than 10^{-10}m (for red light) to 4×10^{-7}m (for violet light). **2** the length of the radio wave used by a particular broadcasting station. — **on the same wavelength** *said of two or more people* speaking or thinking in a way that is mutually compatible.

wave power or **wave energy** energy or power derived from the movement of the ocean waves, especially when used for the generation of electricity.

waver *verb intrans.* (**wavered, wavering**) **1** to falter, lessen, weaken, etc. **2** to hesitate through indecision. **3** *said of the voice* to become unsteady through emotion, etc. **4** to shimmer or flicker. **5** to vary or fluctuate between extremes: *wavering between elation and despair.* [from Norse *vafra*, to flicker]

· · · · · · · · · · · · · · · · · · · ·

⊟ *verb* **1** falter, lessen, weaken, flag, fail, totter, rock. **2** hesitate, dither, vacillate. **3** shake, wobble, tremble. **5** fluctuate, vary, seesaw, oscillate.

· ·

wavy *adj.* (**wavier, waviest**) **1** *said of hair* falling in waves. **2** *said of a line or outline* curving alternately upward and downward.

· · · · · · · · · · · · · · · · · · · ·

⊟ **1** curly. **2** winding, zigzag, undulating, curvy, rippled, ridged, sinuous.

· ·

wax ¹ — *noun* **1** *Chem.* any of a wide variety of solid or semi-solid organic compounds that are typically shiny, easily moulded when warm, and insoluble in water. Mineral waxes, eg paraffin wax, consist of mixtures of hydrocarbons, and are used in candles, polishes, and protective coatings. Natural waxes produced by plants or animals, eg beeswax, and the waxy coatings of certain leaves and fruits, are esters of fatty acids. **2** beeswax. **3** sealing-wax. **4** the sticky, yellowish matter that forms in the ears. — *verb* to use or apply a natural or mineral wax, eg prior to polishing. [from Anglo-Saxon *weax*]

wax ² *verb intrans.* **1** *said of the moon* to appear larger as more of its surface is illuminated by the sun. **2** to increase in size, strength, or power. **3** *facetious* to become (eg eloquent, lyrical) in one's description of something. [from Anglo-Saxon *weaxan*, to grow]

· · · · · · · · · · · · · · · · · · · ·

⊟ **2** grow, increase, rise, swell, develop, enlarge, expand, magnify, mount, fill out, become.

◨ **1** wane. **2** decrease, wane.

....

waxen adj. made of, or similar to, wax.

waxwing noun Zool. a songbird of the N hemisphere, which has greyish-brown plumage with a black tail, and a crest on the head. In some individuals there are red wax-like tips to some of the wing feathers. It inhabits woodland and gardens, and feeds on berries and insects.

waxwork noun **1** a lifelike model, especially of someone celebrated, made of wax. **2** (**waxworks**) an exhibition of these.

waxy adj. (**waxier, waxiest**) like wax in appearance or feel.

way — noun **1** a route, entrance, exit, etc providing passage or access somewhere; also, the passage or access provided: *the way into the house / is this the way?* **2** the route, road, or direction taken for a particular journey: *on the way to school / are you going my way?* **3** (*often in compounds*) a track or road: *motorway / London Way*. **4** a direction: *a one-way street / a two-way radio*. **5** position: *the wrong way up*. **6** a distance in space or time: *a little way ahead / Christmas is a long way off*. **7** one's district: *if you're round our way*. **8** the route or path ahead; room to move or progress: *block someone's way / moved out of the way / clear the way for reform*. **9** a means. **10** a distinctive manner or style: *a funny way of walking*. **11** a method: *an easy way to cook fish / do it your own way*. **12** (**ways**) customs: *their ways are not ours*. **13** a characteristic piece of behaviour: *can't stand the way he ignores women*. **14** a habit or routine: *get into the way of taking regular exercise*. **15** a typical pattern or course: *it's always the way*. **16** (**his, her**, etc, **way** or **own way**) what one wants oneself, as opposed to what others want: *always wanting their own way*. **17** a mental approach: *different ways of looking at it*. **18** a respect: *correct in some ways*. **19** an alternative course, possibility, choice, etc: *can't have it both ways / that way we'll save money*. **20** a state or condition: *is in a bad way*. **21** scale: *is in business in a big way*. **22** (**the, this**, or **that way**) the manner or tendency of a person's feelings, wishes, etc: *if that's the way you want it / I didn't know you felt that way*. **23** used with many verbs to indicate progress: *ate their way through the food*. **24** Naut. headway: *made little way that day*. **25** used in indicating the number of portions something is divided into: *divided it three ways*. — adv. colloq. far; a long way: *way back in the 60s*. — **be on** or **get on one's way** to make a start on a journey. **by the way** incidentally; let me mention while I remember. **by way of** ... as a form or means of: *he grinned by way of apology*. **by way of a place** by the route that passes through it: *went by way of Lincoln*. **come someone's way** *said of an opportunity, etc* to become available to them, especially unexpectedly. **give way 1** to collapse or subside. **2** to fail or break down under pressure, etc. **3** to yield to persuasion or pressure. **go out of one's way** to make special efforts. **have a way with someone** to be good at dealing with them: *has a way with customers*. **have a way with one** colloq. to have an attractive manner. **have something one's own way** to get what one wants with something. **in its**, etc **own way** as far as it, etc goes; within limits: *is all right in its way*. **in no way** not at all. **in the way of** ... in the nature of: *haven't got much in the way of cash*. **lead** or **show the way** to act as a guide or inspiration to others. **learn one's way around** to accustom oneself to one's new environment, duties, etc. **look the other way** to pretend not to notice something. **lose one's way** to leave one's intended route by mistake. **make one's way 1** to go purposefully. **2** to progress or prosper: *making her way in life*. **make way for someone** or **something 1** to stand aside, or make room, for them. **2** to be replaced by them. **no two ways about it** that's certain; no doubt about it. **no way** *slang* absolutely no possibility. **on the way out** becoming unfashionable. **on the way to** ... progressing towards: *well on the way to becoming a millionaire*. **pay one's way** to pay one's own debts and living expenses. **put someone out of the way** *euphemistic* colloq. to kill. **see one's way to** or **clear to doing something** to be agreeable to it. **that's the way!** a formula of encouragement or approval. **under way** in motion; progressing. [from Anglo-Saxon *weg*]

....

◨ noun **1** route, direction, course, path, road, channel, passage, access. **2** route, direction, course, path, road. **3** track, road, lane, street, avenue, highway. **7** district, area, neighbourhood. **8** path, route, road, thoroughfare, passage. **9, 11** method, approach, manner, technique, procedure, means, mode, system, fashion. **10, 13** characteristic, idiosyncrasy, trait, style, nature. **14** habit, routine, custom, practice, usage. **by the way** incidentally, in passing.

....

waybill noun a list giving details of goods or passengers being carried. [from WAY]

wayfarer noun old use a traveller, especially on foot. [from WAY + FARE]

wayfaring noun, adj. travelling, journeying by road.

waylay verb (PAST TENSE AND PAST PARTICIPLE **waylaid**) **1** to lie in wait for and ambush. **2** to wait for and delay with conversation. [from WAY + LAY²]

wayleave noun permission given to pass over another's ground, usually on payment of a fee. [from WAY + LEAVE²]

way of life a style of living; the living of one's life according to certain principles.

way-out adj. slang excitingly unusual, exotic, or new.

-ways combining form forming words denoting direction or manner: *lengthways / edgeways*. [from WAY¹]

ways and means methods, especially of obtaining funds; resources.

wayside — noun the edge of a road, or the area to the side of it. — adj. growing or lying near the edge of roads. — **fall by the wayside** to fail or give up in one's attempt to do something; to drop out.

wayward adj. undisciplined, self-willed, headstrong, wilful, or rebellious. [from AWAY + -WARD]

....

◨ undisciplined, self-willed, headstrong, wilful, rebellious, unmanageable, obstinate, disobedient, insubordinate, intractable, unruly, stubborn, incorrigible, capricious, perverse, contrary, changeable, fickle, unpredictable.
◨ tractable, good-natured.

....

wazir / wɑːˈzɪə(r)/ noun a vizier, a high-ranking official in Muslim countries. [from Arabic *wazir*]

WBA abbrev. World Boxing Association.

WBC abbrev. World Boxing Council.

WC abbrev. (PL. **WCs, WC's**) water closet.

W/ Cdr abbrev. Wing Commander.

we pron. used as the subject of a verb: **1** to refer to oneself in company with another or others. **2** to refer to people in general: *the times we live in*. **3** by a royal person and by writers and editors in formal use, to refer to themselves or the authority they represent. **4** affected to mean 'you': *how are we feeling today?* [from Anglo-Saxon *we*]

WEA abbrev. Workers' Educational Association.

weak adj. **1** lacking physical strength. **2** not functioning effectively: *a weak heart*. **3** liable to give way: *a weak link*. **4** lacking power: *militarily weak*. **5** Commerce dropping in value: *a weak dollar*. **6** too easily influenced by others. **7** yielding too easily to temptation. **8** lacking full flavour: *weak tea*. **9** said of an argument unsound or unconvincing. **10** faint: *a weak signal*. **11** half-hearted: *a weak smile*. **12** (**weak on** or **in something**) defective in some respect; having insufficient of something. [from Norse *veikr*]

....

◨ **1** feeble, frail, exhausted, sickly, delicate, debilitated. **2** infirm, unhealthy, sickly, debilitated. **3** flimsy, fragile. **4** powerless, impotent, vulnerable, unprotected, unguarded, defenceless, exposed. **6, 7** spineless, cowardly, indecisive, ineffectual, irresolute. **8** insipid, tasteless, watery, thin, diluted, runny. **9** unsound, unconvincing, inconclusive, lame, inadequate, defective, deficient, untenable, poor, lacking.

10 faint, slight, low, soft, muffled, dull, imperceptible.
▣ STRONG. **4** powerful.

....

weaken verb (**weakened, weakening**) **1** trans., intrans. to make or become weaker. **2** intrans. to yield to pressure or persuasion.

....

▣ **1** enfeeble, exhaust, debilitate, sap, undermine, dilute, diminish, lower, lessen, reduce, moderate, mitigate, temper, soften (up), thin, water down, tire, flag, fail, give way, droop, fade, abate, ease up, dwindle. **2** yield, give way, submit, capitulate, succumb, give in, admit defeat, colloq. cave in, acquiesce, accede.
▣ **1** strengthen.

....

weak-kneed adj. cowardly; feeble.

weakling noun **1** a physically weak person or animal. **2** someone weak in a certain respect: a moral weakling.

weak-minded adj. **1** of feeble intelligence. **2** lacking will or determination.

weak moment a lapse of self-discipline.

weakness noun **1** the condition of being weak. **2** a fault or failing. **3** (**a weakness for something**) a liking for it.

....

▣ **1** feebleness, debility, infirmity, impotence, frailty, powerlessness, vulnerability. **2** fault, failing, flaw, shortcoming, blemish, defect, deficiency, foible. **3** liking, inclination, fondness, penchant, passion, soft spot.
▣ **1, 2** strength. **3** dislike.

....

weak verb Grammar a verb inflected by the addition of a regular suffix, eg walked, and not by a change of the main vowel, as with sang and sung.

weal[1] noun a long, raised, reddened mark on the skin caused eg by a slash with a whip or sword. [a variant of WALE]

weal[2] noun old use welfare: the common weal. [from Anglo-Saxon wela]

wealth noun **1** riches and property, or the possession of them. **2** abundance of resources: the country's mineral wealth. **3** a large quantity: a wealth of examples. [from Middle English welthe, from Anglo-Saxon wela WEAL[2]]

....

▣ **1** money, cash, riches, assets, affluence, prosperity, funds, mammon, fortune, capital, opulence, means, substance, resources, goods, possessions, property, estate. **2** riches, assets, resources. **3** abundance, plenty, bounty, fullness, profusion, store.
▣ **1** poverty.

....

wealthy adj. (**wealthier, wealthiest**) **1** possessing riches and property; rich. **2** (**wealthy in something**) well supplied with it; rich in it: wealthy in timber.

....

▣ **1** rich, prosperous, affluent, well off, moneyed, opulent, comfortable, colloq. well-heeled, well-to-do, colloq. flush, colloq. loaded, colloq. rolling in it.
▣ **1** poor, impoverished.

....

wean[1] verb **1** to accustom (a baby) to taking food other than its mother's milk: weaned on to solid foods. **2** to break (someone) gradually of a bad habit, etc: how to wean him from drugs. [from Anglo-Saxon wenian, to accustom]

wean[2] noun Scot. a child. [from WEE + ane, one]

weapon noun **1** an instrument or device used to kill or injure people in a war or fight. **2** something one can use to get the better of others: patience is our best weapon. [from Anglo-Saxon wæpen]

Weapons include: gun, airgun, pistol, revolver, automatic, trademark Colt, trademark Luger, magnum, Mauser, six-gun, six-shooter, rifle, air rifle, trademark Winchester rifle, carbine, shotgun, blunderbuss, musket, elephant gun, machine gun, kalashnikov, sub-machine gun, Uzi, tommy gun, stengun, Bren gun, cannon, field gun, gatling gun, howitzer, mortar, turret gun; knife, bowie knife, flick-knife, stiletto, dagger, dirk, poniard, sword, épée, foil, rapier, sabre, scimitar, bayonet, broadsword, claymore, lance, spear, pike, machete; bomb, atom bomb, H-bomb, cluster bomb, depth charge, incendiary bomb, Mills bomb, mine, landmine, napalm bomb, time bomb; bow and arrow, longbow, crossbow, blowpipe, catapult, boomerang, sling, harpoon, bolas, rocket, bazooka, ballistic missile, Cruise missile, trademark Exocet, colloq. Scud, torpedo, hand grenade, flame-thrower; battleaxe, pole-axe, halberd, tomahawk, cosh, cudgel, knuckleduster, shillelagh, truncheon; gas, CS gas, mustard gas, tear gas.

weaponry noun weapons, armament.

wear — verb (PAST TENSE **wore**; PAST PARTICIPLE **worn**) **1** to be dressed in, or have on one's body. **2** to have (one's hair, beard, etc) cut a certain length or in a certain style. **3** to have (a certain expression). **4** intrans., said of a carpet or garment to become thin or threadbare through use. **5** to make (a hole, bare patch, etc) in something through heavy use. **6** intrans. to bear intensive use; to last in use: doesn't wear well. **7** colloq. to accept (an excuse, story, etc) or tolerate (a situation, etc). **8** to tire: worn to a frazzle. **9** (**wear on someone**) to irritate them: all that noise is very wearing on us. — noun **1** (often in compounds) clothes suitable for a certain purpose, person, occasion, etc: menswear. **2** the amount or type of use that eg clothing, carpeting, etc gets: subjected to heavy wear. **3** damage caused through use: machinery showing signs of wear. — **wear away** or **wear something away** to become or make it thin or disappear completely through rubbing, weathering, etc. **wear down** or **wear something down** to become or make it shallower or shorter through rubbing, friction, etc. **wear someone down** to tire them, especially with persistent objections or demands. **wearing thin** said of an excuse, etc becoming unconvincing or ineffective through over-use. **wear off** said of a feeling, pain, etc to become less intense; to disappear gradually. **wear on** said of time to pass: as the year wore on. **wear out** or **wear something out** to become or make it unusable through use. **wear someone out** to tire them utterly; to exhaust them. **wear through** said of clothing, etc to develop a hole through heavy wear. [from Anglo-Saxon werian]

....

▣ verb **1** dress in, have on, put on, don, sport, carry, bear, display, show. **2** have, sport. **3** have, bear. **4** deteriorate, rub, fray, abrade. **5** rub, grind. noun **1** clothes, clothing, dress, garments, outfit, costume, attire. **3** damage, wear and tear, deterioration, abrasion, friction, erosion, corrosion. **wear off** disappear, decrease, abate, dwindle, diminish, subside, wane, weaken, fade, lessen, ebb, peter out. **wear out** something deteriorate, wear through, erode, impair, consume, fray. someone tire (out), exhaust, fatigue, enervate, sap.
▣ **wear off** increase.

....

wearable adj. capable of being worn.

wear and tear damage sustained in the course of continual or normal use.

wearer noun a person who is wearing something.

wearily adv. with a weary manner.

weariness noun being weary.

wearing adj. exhausting.

....

▣ exhausting, tiring, fatiguing, wearisome, tiresome, trying, taxing, oppressive, irksome, exasperating.
▣ refreshing.

....

wearisome adj. tiring, tedious, or frustrating.

weary — adj. (**wearier, weariest**) **1** tired out; exhausted. **2** (**weary of something**) tired by it; fed up with it. **3** tiring, dreary, or irksome. — verb **1** trans., intrans. to make or become weary. **2** intrans. (**weary of something**) to get tired of it. [from Anglo-Saxon *werig*]

. . . .

▣ adj. **1** tired, exhausted, fatigued, sleepy, worn out, drained, drowsy, jaded, colloq. all in, colloq. done (in), fagged out, colloq. knackered, colloq. dead beat, colloq. dog-tired, whacked. **2** tired of, sick of, fed up of. **3** tiring, dreary, irksome, fatiguing, exhausting, wearisome, wearing, taxing, trying.

▣ adj. **1** refreshed. **3** refreshing.

. . . .

weasel noun a small nocturnal carnivorous mammal, closely related to the stoat and found in most N temperate regions, with a slender body, short legs, and reddish-brown fur with white underparts. It feeds on rodents and small birds, and will sometimes kill animals several times its own size, eg rabbits. [from Anglo-Saxon *wesle*]

weather — noun the atmospheric conditions in any area at any time, with regard to sun, cloud, temperature, wind, rain, etc. — adj. Naut. on the side exposed to the wind. — verb (**weathered, weathering**) **1** trans., intrans. to expose or be exposed to the effects of wind, sun, rain, etc; to alter or be altered in colour, texture, shape, etc through such exposure. **2** to come safely through (a storm or stormy situation). **3** Naut. to get to the windward side of (a headland, etc). — **keep a weather eye open** to keep alert for developments. **make heavy weather of something** to make unnecessarily slow and difficult progress with a task. **under the weather** colloq. not in good health. [from Anglo-Saxon *weder*]

. . . .

▣ noun climate, conditions, temperature. verb **1** expose, toughen, season, harden. **2** come through, survive, live through, ride out, rise above, stick out, endure, withstand, surmount, stand, brave, overcome, resist, pull through, suffer.

▣ verb **2** succumb.

. . . .

Types of weather include: breeze, wind, squall, gale, hurricane, tornado, typhoon, monsoon, cyclone, whirlwind, chinook, mistral, cloud, mist, dew, fog, smog, rain, drizzle, shower, deluge, downpour, rainbow, sunshine, heatwave, haze, drought, storm, tempest, thunder, lightning, frost, hoar frost, hail, sleet, snow, snowstorm, ice, black ice, thaw, slush.

weatherbeaten adj. **1** said of the skin or face tanned or lined by exposure to sun and wind. **2** worn or damaged by exposure to the weather.

weatherboard noun **1** a sloping board fitted to the bottom of a door, to exclude rain. **2** any of a series of overlapping horizontal boards covering an exterior wall.

weathercock noun **1** a weathervane in the form of a farmyard cock. **2** derog. a fickle, unreliable person who frequently changes loyalties.

weathering noun Geol. the physical disintegration and chemical decomposition of rocks on or just beneath the Earth's surface, involving little or no transport of the altered rock material, which occurs as a result of exposure to wind, rain, humidity, extremes of temperature (eg frost), atmospheric oxygen, etc.

weatherman noun colloq. a person who presents the weather forecast on radio or television.

weatherproof adj. designed or treated so as to keep out wind and rain.

weathervane noun a revolving arrow that turns to point in the direction of the wind, having a fixed base with arms for each of the four compass points, mounted eg on a church spire.

weave¹ — verb (PAST TENSE **wove**; PAST PARTICIPLE **woven**) **1** trans., intrans. to make (cloth or tapestry) in a loom, passing threads under and over the threads of a fixed warp; to interlace (threads) in this way. **2** to construct any-

thing (eg a basket, fence, etc) by passing flexible strips in and out between fixed canes, etc; to make by interlacing or intertwining. **3** to devise (a story, plot, etc); to work (details, facts, etc) into a story, etc. — noun the pattern or compactness of the weaving in a fabric: *an open weave*.

. . . .

▣ verb **1** knit, interlace, lace, plait, braid, intertwine, entwine, intercross, wind, twist, zigzag, criss-cross. **3** devise a story, etc create, compose, construct, contrive, put together, fabricate. work details, etc in intertwine, interlace, knit, entwine.

. . . .

weave² verb intrans. (PAST TENSE AND PAST PARTICIPLE **weaved**) to move to and fro or wind in and out. — **get weaving** colloq. to get busy; to hurry. [from Middle English *weve*]

weaver noun a person who weaves. [from Anglo-Saxon *wefian*]

weaverbird noun Zool. a small sparrow-like bird with a conical bill, found in Africa and Asia, that has bright plumage during the breeding season. The male builds an elaborate flask-shaped nest from strands of grass or palm fronds.

web noun **1** a network of slender threads constructed by a spider to trap insects. **2** old use a piece of weaving or tapestry on a loom. **3** a membrane connecting the toes of a swimming bird or animal. **4** Printing a continuous roll of paper fed through rollers in an offset lithographic printing process. **5** any intricate network: *a web of lies, intrigue, etc*. **6** (**the Web**) short for WORLD WIDE WEB. [from Anglo-Saxon *webb*]

. . . .

▣ **1** cobweb, gossamer. **5** network, net, netting, lattice, mesh, webbing, interlacing, weft, snare, tangle, trap.

. . . .

webbed adj. **1** having a web. **2** said of fingers or toes partially joined together by a membrane of skin.

webbing noun strong jute or nylon fabric woven into strips for use as belts, straps, and supporting bands in upholstery.

weber /ˈveɪbə(r), ˈwiːbə(r)/ noun Physics (SYMBOL **Wb**) the SI unit of magnetic flux (the total size of a magnetic field). [named after the German scientist Wilhelm Weber (1804–91)]

web-footed or **web-toed** adj. having webbed feet.

web page one of a number of sections of information on an Internet website.

website noun a location connected to the Internet, often providing information on the World Wide Web for an organization.

Wed or **Wed**. abbrev. Wednesday.

wed verb (**wedding**; PAST TENSE AND PAST PARTICIPLE **wedded, wed**) **1** trans., intrans. old use to marry. **2** old use to join in marriage. **3** (**wed one thing to** or **with another**) to unite or combine: *wed firmness with compassion*. [from Anglo-Saxon *weddian*, to promise, marry]

we'd contr. we would; we should.

wedded adj. **1** (**wedded to something**) devoted or committed to a principle, activity, etc. **2** married; in marriage: *wedded bliss*.

wedding noun **1** a marriage ceremony, or the ceremony together with the associated celebrations. **2** any of the notable anniversaries of a marriage, especially the *silver wedding* (25 years), *ruby wedding* (40 years), *golden wedding* (50 years), or *diamond wedding* (60 years). [see WED]

. . . .

▣ **1** marriage, matrimony, nuptials, wedlock.

▣ divorce.

. . . .

wedding breakfast the celebratory meal served after a wedding ceremony.

wedding cake a rich iced fruit cake usually in several tiers, served to wedding guests.

wedding ring a ring, especially in the form of a plain gold band, given by a bridegroom to his bride, or by a bride and bridegroom to each other, for wearing as an indication of married status.

wedge — *noun* **1** a piece of solid wood, metal, or other material, tapering to a thin edge, driven into eg wood to split it, or pushed into a narrow gap between moving parts to immobilize them. **2** a wedge-shaped section usually cut from something circular. **3** a shoe heel in the form of a wedge, tapering towards the sole. **4** *Golf* a club with a steeply angled wedge-shaped head for lofting. — *verb* **1** to fix or immobilize in position with, or as if with, a wedge. **2** to thrust or insert: *wedged herself into the corner.* — **drive a wedge between people** to cause ill-feeling or division between people formerly friendly or united. **the thin end of the wedge** something that looks like the small beginning of a significant, usually unwanted, development. [from Anglo-Saxon *wecg*]

⊟ *noun* **1** chock. **2** lump, chunk, wodge, block. *verb* JAM. **1** chock, block, lodge. **2** thrust, cram, pack, ram, squeeze, stuff, push, crowd, force.

Wedgwood /ˈwedʒwʊd/ *noun trademark* a type of pottery decorated with white classical figures applied over a distinctive blue background. [named after the English potter Josiah Wedgwood (1730–95)]

wedlock *noun old use* the condition of being married. — **born out of wedlock** born to parents not married to each other; illegitimate. [from Anglo-Saxon *wedlac*]

Wednesday *noun* the fourth day of the week. [from Anglo-Saxon *Wodnes dæg*, the day of Woden (the chief god of the Germanic peoples)]

Weds or Weds. *abbrev.* Wednesday.

wee[1] *adj.* (**weer, weest**) *colloq. esp. Scot.* small; tiny. [from Middle English *we*, bit, from Anglo-Saxon *wæg*, weight]

wee[2] or **wee-wee** *colloq.* — *verb intrans.* (**wees, weed**) to urinate. — *noun* **1** an act of urinating. **2** urine.

weed — *noun* **1** any plant that grows wild and has no specific use or aesthetic value. **2** any plant growing where it is not wanted, especially one that is thought to hinder the growth of cultivated plants such as crops or garden plants. **3** a plant growing in fresh or salt water, eg pondweed, seaweed. **4** *colloq.* marijuana. **5** (**the weed**) *old colloq. use* tobacco. **6** *derog.* an unmanly man, especially of gangling build. — *verb* **1** *trans., intrans.* to uproot weeds from (a garden, flowerbed, etc). **2** (*also* **weed out**) to identify and eliminate eg those who are unwanted or ineffective from an organization or other group. [from Anglo-Saxon *weod*]

weedkiller *noun* a substance used to kill unwanted plants.

weeds *pl. noun old use* the black mourning clothes worn by a widow. [from Anglo-Saxon *wæd*, garment]

weedy *adj.* (**weedier, weediest**) **1** overrun with weeds. **2** *said of a plant* straggly in growth. **3** *derog., said of a person* of gangling or otherwise weak build. **4** feeble; ineffectual.

⊟ **1** overgrown. **2** straggly, drawn, leggy. **3** gangling, puny, scrawny, skinny, undersized, thin, weak, frail. **4** feeble, *colloq.* wet, *colloq.* wimpish, weak-kneed.

week — *noun* **1** a sequence of seven consecutive days, usually beginning on Sunday. **2** any period of seven consecutive days. **3** the working days of the week, as distinct from the weekend. **4** the period worked per week: *works a 45-hour week.* — *adv.* by a period of seven days before or after a specified day: *Friday week* (= the Friday after the next one) / *a week last Friday* (= the Friday before the last one) / *a week on Friday/next Friday* (= the Friday after the next one). — **week in, week out** endlessly; relentlessly. [from Anglo-Saxon *wice*]

weekday *noun* any day except Sunday, or except Saturday and Sunday.

weekend *noun* the period from Friday evening to Sunday night.

weekly — *adj.* occurring, produced, or issued every week, or once a week. — *adv.* every week, or once a week. — *noun* (PL. **weeklies**) a magazine or newspaper published once a week.

weeny *adj.* (**weenier, weeniest**) *colloq.* tiny. [from WEE + TINY or TEENY]

weep — *verb* (PAST TENSE AND PAST PARTICIPLE **wept**) **1** *intrans.* to shed tears as an expression of grief or other emotion. **2** (**weep for something** or **weep something**) *poetic* to lament or bewail it: *wept for her lost youth* / *no poet wept his passing.* **3** *intrans., trans., said of a wound, seal, etc* to exude matter; to ooze. — *noun* a bout of weeping. [from Anglo-Saxon *wepan*]

⊟ *verb* **1** cry, sob, moan, wail, bawl, blubber, snivel, whimper, *colloq.* blub. **2** lament, bewail, mourn, grieve.

⊞ *verb* **2** rejoice.

weeping *adj., said of a tree variety* having low-drooping branches.

weepy — *adj.* (**weepier, weepiest**) **1** tearful. **2** *said of a story, etc* making one weep; poignant; sentimental. — *noun* (PL. **weepies**) *colloq.* a film, novel, etc of this kind.

weevil *noun* any of several beetles with an elongated proboscis, that as both adults and larvae can damage fruit, grain, nuts, and trees; any insect that damages stored grain. [from Anglo-Saxon *wifel*]

wee-wee see WEE[2].

weft *noun Weaving* the threads that are passed over and under the fixed threads of the warp in a loom. [from Anglo-Saxon *weft*]

weigh *verb* **1** to measure the weight of. **2** *trans., intrans.* to have (a certain weight): *weighs 8kg* / *books weigh heavy.* **3** (*also* **weigh something out**) to measure out a specific weight of it: *weighed out a pound of flour.* **4** (*also* **weigh something up**) to consider or assess (facts, possibilities, etc). **5** to balance (something) in one's hand so as to feel its weight. **6** (**weigh on** or **upon someone**) to oppress them: *her worries weighed heavily on her.* **7** (**weigh with someone**) to impress them favourably: *your previous experience should weigh with the appointments board.* **8** to raise (the anchor) of a ship before sailing: *weighed anchor at dawn.* — **weigh someone down** to burden, overload, or oppress them. **weigh in** *said of a wrestler or boxer before a fight, or of a jockey after a race* to be weighed officially. **weigh in with something** *colloq.* to contribute a comment, etc to a discussion. [from Anglo-Saxon *wegan*]

⊟ **4** consider, assess, examine, contemplate, evaluate, size up, meditate on, mull over, ponder, think over, *colloq.* chew over, reflect on, deliberate, discuss. **6** oppress, burden, *colloq.* get down, weigh down, depress, afflict, trouble, worry. **weigh down** burden, oppress, overload, load, bear down, weigh upon, press down, *colloq.* get down, depress, afflict, trouble, worry.

⊞ **weigh down** lighten, hearten.

weighbridge *noun* an apparatus for weighing vehicles with their loads, consisting of a metal plate set into a road surface and connected to a weighing device.

weigh-in *noun* the official weighing in of a wrestler, boxer, or jockey.

weight — *noun* **1** the heaviness of something; the amount anything weighs. **2** *Physics* (SYMBOL **W**) the gravitational force acting on a body at the surface of the Earth or another planet, star, or moon. Units of measurement are the newton, dyne, or pound-force. Weight = mass × acceleration due to gravity; therefore an object of constant mass weighs more on the Earth than on the Moon. **3** any system of units for measuring and expressing weight: *imperial weight* / *troy weight.* **4** a piece of metal of a standard weight, against which to measure the weight of other objects. **5** (*often in compounds*) a heavy object used to compress, hold down, or counterbalance: *paperweight* / *counterweight.* **6** a heavy load. **7** *Athletics* a heavy object for lifting, throwing, or tossing. **8** a mental burden: *took a weight off my mind.* **9** strength or significance in terms of amount: *the weight of the evidence.* **10** the main thrust or force: *the weight of the argument.* **11** influence, authority, or credibility: *opinions that carry little weight.* **12** *Statistics* a number denoting the frequency of some element within a frequency distribution. — *verb* **1** to add weight to, eg to restrict movement. **2** to burden or oppress. **3** to arrange so as to have an unevenness or bias: *a tax system weighted in favour of the wealthy.* — **pull one's weight** to do one's full share of work, etc. **throw one's weight about** *colloq.* to behave domineeringly. **throw one's weight behind something** to give one's full support to it. **worth one's** or **it's weight in gold** exceptionally useful or helpful. [from Anglo-Saxon *wiht*]

■ *noun* **1** heaviness, gravity, burden, load, pressure, mass, force, ballast, tonnage, poundage. **9** significance, importance, preponderance. **10** thrust, force, substance, consequence, impact, moment. **11** influence, authority, credibility, value, *colloq.* clout, power. *verb* **1** load, weigh down. **2** burden, oppress, handicap. **3** bias, unbalance, slant, prejudice.
❌ *noun* **1** lightness.

weighted mean *Maths.* see MEAN³ 2b.
weighting *noun* a supplement to a salary, usually to compensate for high living costs: *London weighting.*
weightless *adj.* **1** weighing nothing or almost nothing. **2** *said of an astronaut in space* not subject to earth's gravity, so able to float free.
weightlessness *noun* being weightless.
weightlifter *noun* a person who specializes in weightlifting.
weightlifting *noun* the sport or exercise of lifting barbells.
weight-training *noun* muscle-strengthening exercises performed with the aid of weights and pulleys.
weighty (**weightier**, **weightiest**) *adj.* **1** heavy. **2** important, significant, or grave.

■ **1** heavy, substantial, bulky, burdensome. **2** important, significant, grave, consequential, crucial, critical, momentous, serious, solemn.
❌ **1** light. **2** unimportant.

weir /wɪər/ *noun* **1** a shallow dam constructed across a river to control its flow. **2** a fish-trap built across a river in the form of a fence. [from Anglo-Saxon *wer*, enclosure]
weird *adj.* **1** eerie; uncanny; supernatural. **2** queer; strange; bizarre. [from Anglo-Saxon *wyrd*, fate]

■ **1** eerie, uncanny, supernatural, unnatural, ghostly, *colloq.* creepy, *colloq.* spooky, freakish, grotesque. **2** queer, strange, bizarre, mysterious, *slang* far-out, *slang* way-out.
❌ **2** normal, usual.

weirdly *adv.* in a weird way.
weirdness *noun* being weird.
weirdo /ˈwɪərdəʊ/ *noun* (PL. **weirdos**) *colloq.* someone who behaves or dresses bizarrely.
welch same as WELSH.
welcome — *verb* **1** to receive (a guest, visitor, etc) with a warm greeting or kindly hospitality. **2** to encourage visits from: *the museum welcomes children.* **3** to invite (suggestions, contributions, etc). **4** to approve of (an action, etc): *welcomed her intervention.* **5** to respond with pleasure to: *welcomed the long summer evenings.* — *interj.* an expression of pleasure on receiving someone: *welcome home!* — *noun* the act of welcoming; a reception. — *adj.* **1** warmly received: *was made welcome.* **2** gladly permitted or encouraged (to do or keep something): *you're welcome to borrow it / she's welcome to my old bicycle.* **3** much appreciated: *a welcome cup of tea.* — **welcome with open arms**

to receive warmly, gladly, gratefully, or thankfully. **you're welcome**! *used in response to thanks* not at all; it's a pleasure. [from Anglo-Saxon *wilcuma*, a welcome guest]

■ *verb* **1** greet, hail, receive, salute, meet. **2** accept. **5** embrace. *noun* reception, greeting, salutation, hospitality, acceptance. *adj.* **3** pleasing, pleasant, agreeable, gratifying, appreciated, delightful, refreshing, desirable.
❌ *verb* **1** snub, reject. **3, 4** reject. *adj.* **1** unwelcome.

weld — *verb* **1** *Engineering* to join two pieces of metal by heating them to melting point and fusing them together, or by applying pressure alone. Welding produces a stronger joint than soldering. **2** to unite or blend together. — *noun* a joint between two metals formed by welding. [a past participle of obsolete *well*, to melt, weld]

■ *verb* JOIN, FUSE, BOND. **2** unite, blend, bind, connect, seal, link, cement.
❌ *verb* **2** separate.

welder *noun* a person who welds.
welfare *noun* **1** the health, comfort, happiness, and general wellbeing of a person, group, etc. **2** social work concerned with helping those in need. **3** financial support given to those in need. [from WELL¹ + FARE]

■ **1** wellbeing, health, prosperity, happiness, benefit, good, advantage, interest, success. **3** benefit.

welfare economics *Econ.* an economic theory devoted to studying how best to distribute the gross national product and a nation's wealth among competing claimants, and the extent to which government interferes with market forces.
welfare state a system in which the government uses tax revenue to look after citizens' welfare, with the provision of free health care, old-age pensions, and financial support for the disabled or unemployed.
well¹ — *adv.* (**better**, **best**) **1** competently; skilfully. **2** satisfactorily: *all went well.* **3** kindly: *was well treated.* **4** thoroughly; properly; carefully; fully: *wash it well / wasn't attending very well.* **5** intimately: *don't know her well.* **6** successfully; prosperously: *do well / live well.* **7** approvingly: *thinks well of you.* **8** by a long way: *well past midnight / well ahead.* **9** justifiably: *can't very well ignore him.* **10** conceivably; quite possibly: *may well be right.* **11** understandably: *if she objects, as well she may.* **12** very much: *well worth doing.* **13** used in combination for emphasis: *I'm jolly well going to.* — *adj.* **1** healthy. **2** in a satisfactory state. **3** sensible; advisable: *would be well to check.* — *interj.* **1** used enquiringly in expectation of a response, explanation, etc. **2** used variously in conversation, eg to resume a narrative, preface a reply, express surprise, indignation, doubt, etc. — **all very well** *colloq.*, *said in response to a consoling remark* satisfactory or acceptable only up to a point. **as well 1** too; in addition. **2** (*also* **just as well**) for all the difference it makes: *I may as well tell you.* **3** (*also* **just as well**) advisable; sensible: *would be as well to buy it now.* **4** (*also* **just as well**) a good thing; lucky: *it was just as well you came when you did.* **as well as**... in addition to... **do well out of something** to profit from it. **leave** or **let well alone** not to interfere in things that are satisfactory as they are. **mean well** to have helpful or kindly intentions. **very well** an expression of acceptance in complying with an order, accepting a point, etc. **well and good** used to show acceptance of facts or a situation. **well and truly** thoroughly; completely. **well away 1** making rapid progress; having got into one's stride. **2** *colloq.* drunk, asleep, etc. **well done!** an expression used to congratulate someone on an achievement, etc. **well enough** satisfactory within limits. **well off 1** wealthy; financially comfortable. **2** fortunate; successful. **well out of something** fortunate to be free of it. **well up in something** having a thorough knowledge of it. [from Anglo-Saxon *wel*]

□ adv. **1** competently, skilfully, properly, ably, expertly, rightly, correctly, successfully. **2** satisfactorily, adequately, suitably, sufficiently. **3** kindly, generously, agreeably, pleasantly. **4** thoroughly, properly, carefully, fully, completely, greatly, considerably. **6** successfully, prosperously, comfortably, splendidly. **7** approvingly, favourably. **8** substantially, considerably, far. **10** conceivably, quite possibly, easily. adj. **1** healthy, in good health, fit, able-bodied, sound, robust, strong, thriving, flourishing. **2** satisfactory, right, all right, good, pleasing, proper, agreeable, fine, lucky, fortunate. **well off 1** rich, wealthy, affluent, prosperous, well-to-do, moneyed, thriving, successful, comfortable.
□ adv. **1** badly, inadequately, incompetently, wrongly. **2, 3** badly. adj. **1** ill, unwell. **2** bad. **well off 1** poor.

well² — noun **1** a lined shaft that is sunk from ground level to a considerable depth below ground in order to obtain a supply of water, oil, gas, etc. **2** a natural spring of water, or a pool fed by it. **3** a shaft, or shaft-shaped cavity, eg that made through the floors of a building to take the staircase: *stairwell*. **4** *Naut*. an enclosure in a ship's hold round the pumps. **5** (*in compounds*) a reservoir or receptacle: *inkwell*. **6** *Legal* the open space in the centre of a law court. **7** a plentiful source of something: *she's a well of information*. — verb intrans. (**well up**) *said of a liquid* to spring, flow, or flood to the surface. [from Anglo-Saxon *wella*]

□ noun **2** spring, wellspring, fountain, fount, source, reservoir, wellhead, waterhole. verb flow, spring, surge, gush, stream, brim over, jet, spout, spurt, swell, pour, flood, run, rise.

we'll contr. we will; we shall.
well-advised adj. sensible: *you'd be well-advised to comply*.
well-appointed adj., *said of a house, etc* well furnished or equipped.
well-balanced adj. **1** satisfactorily proportioned. **2** sane, sensible, and stable.

□ **1** symmetrical, even, harmonious. **2** sane, rational, sensible, stable, reasonable, level-headed, well-adjusted, sound, sober, colloq. together.
□ **1** asymmetrical. **2** unbalanced.

well-behaved adj. behaving with good manners or due propriety.
wellbeing noun welfare.

□ welfare, happiness, comfort, good.

well-born adj. descended from an aristocratic family.
well-bred adj. having good manners; showing good breeding.

□ well-mannered, polite, well-brought-up, mannerly, courteous, civil, refined, cultivated, cultured, genteel.
□ ill-bred.

well-built adj. **1** strongly built. **2** of muscular or well-proportioned bodily build.
well-connected adj. having influential or aristocratic friends and relations.
well-disposed adj. inclined to be friendly.
well-earned adj. thoroughly deserved.
well-founded adj., *said of suspicions, etc* justified; based on good grounds.
well-groomed adj., *said of a person* of smart, neat appearance.
well-grounded adj. **1** *said of an argument, etc* soundly based. **2** having had a good basic training.

wellhead noun **1** the source of a stream; a spring. **2** an origin or source. **3** the rim or structure round the top of a well.
well-heeled adj. colloq. prosperous; wealthy.
well-informed adj. **1** having sound, reliable information on something particular. **2** full of varied knowledge.
wellington noun a waterproof rubber or plastic boot loosely covering the foot and calf. [named after the first Duke of Wellington]
well-intentioned adj. having good intentions, if an unfortunate effect.
well-judged adj. neatly calculated; judicious.
well-knit adj. **1** *said of a person* sturdily and compactly built. **2** compactly or soundly constructed.
well-known adj. familiar or famous.

□ familiar, famous, renowned, celebrated, famed, eminent, notable, noted, illustrious.
□ unknown.

well-mannered adj. polite.
well-meaning adj. well-intentioned.
well-meant adj. intended well.
well-nigh adv. almost; nearly.
well-oiled adj. **1** colloq. drunk. **2** fig. smoothly operating from thorough practice.
well-preserved adj. **1** in good condition; not decayed. **2** youthful in appearance; showing few signs of age.
well-read adj. having read and learnt much.
well-rounded adj. **1** pleasantly plump. **2** having had a broadly based, balanced upbringing and education. **3** well constructed and complete.
well-spoken adj. having a courteous, fluent, and usually refined way of speaking.
wellspring noun **1** a spring or fountain. **2** a rich or bountiful source.
well-thought-of adj. approved of; respected.

□ respected, highly regarded, esteemed, admired, honoured, revered.
□ despised.

well-timed adj. timely; opportune.
well-to-do adj. wealthy; financially comfortable.
well-tried adj. found reliable from frequent testing.
well-turned adj. **1** *old use* attractively formed: *a well-turned ankle*. **2** neatly expressed: *a well-turned phrase*.
well-versed adj. thoroughly trained.
well-wisher noun someone concerned for one's welfare.
well-woman clinic *Medicine* a clinic that specializes in the diagnosis and treatment of minor gynaecological and sexual disorders, and also offers advice on related health matters.
well-worn adj. **1** much worn or used; showing signs of wear. **2** *said of an expression, etc* over-familiar from frequent use; trite.

□ OVERUSED. **1** worn out, threadbare, shabby. **2** trite, stale, hackneyed, tired, timeworn, unoriginal, commonplace, stereotyped, colloq. corny.
□ **2** original.

welly noun (PL. **wellies**) colloq. a wellington.
Welsh — noun **1** the Celtic language of Wales. **2** (**the Welsh**) the people of Wales. — adj. **1** of or belonging to Wales. **2** of or in the language of Wales. [from Anglo-Saxon *welisc*, from *wealh*, Briton, foreigner]
welsh or **welch** verb intrans. **1** (**welsh on something**) to fail to pay one's debts or fulfil one's obligations. **2** (**welsh on someone**) to fail to keep one's promise to them.
Welshman or **Welshwoman** noun a person from Wales.

Welsh rabbit or **Welsh rarebit** a dish of melted cheese served on toast.

welt — noun 1 a reinforcing band or border, eg the ribbing at the waist of a knitted garment. 2 *Shoemaking* a strip of leather fitted round the upper, as a means of attaching it to the sole. 3 a weal raised by a lash or blow. — verb 1 to fit a welt. 2 to beat or thrash.

welter — noun a confused mass. — verb intrans. (**weltered, weltering**) (**welter in something**) to lie, roll, or wallow in it. [from Dutch *welteren*]

welterweight noun 1 a class for boxers and wrestlers of not more than a specified weight (66.7kg in professional boxing, similar but different weights in amateur boxing and wrestling). 2 a boxer or wrestler of this weight.

welwitschia /wɛl'wɪtʃɪə/ noun a peculiar gymnosperm (cone-bearing plant), *Welwitschia mirabilis*, found only in the deserts of SW Africa, where it obtains moisture from sea fogs. It usually lasts for over a century and has a turnip-like stem which produces two strap-shaped leaves several metres long, which grow throughout the life of the plant. [named after an Austrian traveller F Welwitsch]

wen noun a cyst on the skin, usually of the scalp. [from Anglo-Saxon *wenn*]

wench old colloq. use — noun 1 a girl; a woman. 2 a servant girl. 3 a prostitute. — verb intrans. 1 to associate with prostitutes. 2 to go courting girls. [from Anglo-Saxon *wencel*, a child]

wend verb — **wend one's way** to go steadily and purpose-fully on a route or journey. [from Anglo-Saxon *wendan*, to go]

Wendy house a small playhouse for children, constructed of wood or cloth.

went see GO.

wept see WEEP.

were see BE.

we're contr. we are.

weren't contr. were not.

werewolf /'weəwʊlf, 'wɪəwʊlf/ noun (PL. **werewolves**) *Folklore* a person who changes periodically into a wolf. [from Anglo-Saxon *werwulf*, man-wolf]

wert old use a form of the past tense of the verb *be* used with the pronoun *thou*.

Wesleyan — adj. relating to John Wesley, or to Methodism, the Protestant movement founded by him. — noun a follower of Wesley or Methodism.

west — noun 1 (also **the west** or **the West**) the direction in which the sun sets, or any part of the earth, a country, town, etc lying in that direction. 2 (**the West**) a the countries of Europe and N America, in contrast to those of Asia; also formerly, the non-communist bloc as distinct from the communist or former communist countries of the East. b *Hist.* the part of the US to the west of the Mississippi. — adj. 1 in the west; on the side that is on or nearer the west. 2 *said of a wind* blowing from the west. — adv. toward the west. — **go west** colloq. to be lost or destroyed. [from Anglo-Saxon *west*]

westbound adj. going or leading towards the west.

West Country the SW counties of England – Somerset, Devon, and Cornwall.

westering adj., *said of the sun* sinking towards the west.

westerlies or **Westerlies** *Meteorol.* winds that blow W–E, most often over the middle latitudes of both hemispheres. In the N hemisphere the westerlies blow from the SW, and in the S hemisphere they blow from the NW.

westerly — adj. 1 *said of a wind* coming from the west. 2 looking, lying, etc towards the west. — adv. to or towards the west. — noun (PL. **westerlies**) a westerly wind. See also WESTERLIES.

western — adj. 1 of or in the west. 2 facing or directed towards the west. — noun (**Western**) a film or story about 19c cowboys in the west of the USA.

westerner noun a person who lives in or comes from the west, especially the western part of the USA.

westernmost adj. situated furthest west.

West Highland white terrier a small muscular terrier developed in Scotland, which has a thick coat of white straight hair, a rounded head, and short pointed erect ears.

West Indian — noun a native or inhabitant of the West Indies. — adj. relating to the West Indies.

westward or **westwards** adv., adj. towards the west.

wet — adj. (**wetter, wettest**) 1 covered or soaked in water, rain, perspiration, or other liquid. 2 *said of the weather* rainy. 3 *said of paint, cement, etc* not yet dried. 4 covered with tears: *wet cheeks*. 5 *said of a baby* having a urine-soaked nappy. 6 derog. colloq., *said of a person* feeble; ineffectual. 7 *North Amer. Hist.* allowing the sale of alcoholic drink. 8 *Chem.*, *said of processes, etc* using liquid. — noun 1 moisture. 2 rainy weather; rain. 3 derog. a feeble, ineffectual person. 4 colloq. a moderate Conservative. — verb (**wetting**; PAST TENSE AND PAST PARTICIPLE **wet, wetted**) 1 to make wet; to splash or soak. 2 to urinate involuntarily on: *wet the bed*. — **wet behind the ears** colloq. immature or inexperienced. **wet through** completely wet. [from Anglo-Saxon *wæt*]

⊟ adj. 1 damp, moist, soaked, soaking, sodden, saturated, soggy, sopping, watery, waterlogged, drenched, dripping, spongy, dank, clammy. 2 raining, rainy, showery, teeming, pouring, drizzling, humid. 6 ineffectual, feeble, weak, weedy, colloq. wimpish, spineless, soft, namby-pamby, irresolute, timorous. noun 1 moisture, wetness, damp, dampness, liquid, water, clamminess, condensation, humidity. 2 rain, drizzle. verb 1 splash, soak, spray, sprinkle, saturate, drench, steep, moisten, damp, dampen, water, irrigate, imbue, dip.

⊟ adj. 1, 2 dry. 6 strong. noun 1, 2 dryness. verb 1 dry.

wet blanket a dreary, pessimistic person who dampens the enthusiasm and enjoyment of others; a killjoy.

wet dream an erotic dream that causes emission of semen.

wether noun a castrated ram. [from Anglo-Saxon *wether*]

wet nurse *Hist.* a woman employed to breastfeed another's baby.

wet suit a tight-fitting rubber suit permeable by water, but conserving body heat, worn by divers, canoeists, yachtsmen, etc.

we've contr. we have.

WFTU abbrev. World Federation of Trade Unions.

whack colloq. — verb to hit sharply and resoundingly. — noun 1 a sharp, resounding blow, or the sound of this. 2 one's share of the profits, work, etc. — **have a whack at something** to try it. [imitative]

⊟ verb hit, strike, smack, thrash, slap, beat, colloq. bash, bang, cuff, thump, box, buffet, rap, colloq. wallop, colloq. belt, colloq. clobber, colloq. clout, slang sock. noun 1 smack, slap, blow, hit, rap, stroke, thump, cuff, box, bang, colloq. clout, colloq. bash, colloq. wallop. 2 share, stint.

whacked adj. exhausted.

whacking — noun a beating. — adj. colloq. enormous; huge.

whale — noun any of various large marine mammals belonging to the order Cetacea, distributed worldwide, and having a torpedo-shaped body, two flippers, flat horizontal tail blades, and a blow-hole on the top of the head for breathing. — verb intrans. to hunt whales. — **a whale of a …** colloq. a hugely enjoyable (time, evening, etc). [from Anglo-Saxon *hwæl*]

whalebone noun the light flexible horny substance of which the plankton-filtering plates in the mouths of toothless whales are composed, used especially formerly for stiffening corsets, etc.

whale oil oil obtained from whale blubber.

whaler *noun* a person or ship engaged in whaling.

whale shark the largest of all fishes, widely distributed in surface waters of tropical seas, up to 18m in length, and weighing up to 20 tonnes. It feeds mainly on small planktonic organisms.

whaling *noun* the activity of hunting and killing whales.

whammy *noun colloq.* (PL. **whammies**) (*usually* **double whammy**) a stunning blow.

wharf *noun* (PL. **wharfs**, **wharves**) a landing-stage built along a waterfront for loading and unloading vessels. [from Anglo-Saxon *hwearf*]

- - - - - - - - - - - - - - - - - - - -
🔳 dock, quay, quayside, jetty, landing-stage, dockyard, marina, pier.
- -

wharfage *noun* **1** dues paid for the use of a wharf. **2** accommodation for vessels at a wharf.

wharfinger *noun* the owner or supervisor of a wharf.

what — *adj.*, *pron.* **1** used in seeking to identify or classify a thing or person: *what street are we in? / what woman do you mean? / tell me what flowers these are / what is that bird?* **2** used in exclamations: *what lies they tell! / what a fool! / what awful clothes! / what she puts up with!* **3** used as a relative, meaning 'the, all, or any (things or people) that': *it is just what I thought / what you need is a holiday / they gave what money they could / what little they have is used sparingly.* — *adv.* to what extent: *what does that matter?* — **give someone what for** *colloq.* to scold or punish them. **know what's what** *colloq.* to know what really goes on, counts, etc; to know the truth of the matter. **so what?** or **what of it?** *colloq.* why is that important? **what ... for?** what is the reason ...?: *what did you do that for?* **what have you** *colloq.* other such things. **what's more** ... and, more importantly: *they came, and what's more, they stayed all evening.* **what with** ... because of ...; taking account of: *we were exhausted, what with all the delays.* [from Anglo-Saxon *hwæt*]

what-d'you-call-it *noun colloq.* a thing whose name one can't remember.

whatever — *adj.*, *pron.* **1** used as an emphatic form of what: *whatever shall I do? / take whatever you want / take whatever money you need.* **2** no matter what: *I must finish, whatever happens.* **3** ... at all: *has nothing whatever to do with you.* **4** *colloq.* some or other: *has disappeared, for whatever reason.* **5** used to express uncertainty: *a didgeridoo, whatever that is.* — **... or whatever** *colloq.* ... or some such thing.

whatnot *noun* **1** a stand with shelves for ornaments, etc. **2** *colloq.* a whatsit. **3** *colloq.* and other similar things: *grammar and whatnot.*

what's-his-name or **what's-her-name**, *etc colloq.* a substitute for an unknown or forgotten name.

whatsit *noun colloq.* some unspecified thing, or one whose name one can't remember. [from *what is it?*]

whatsoever *pron.*, *adj.* **1** *poetic* whatever: *whatsoever things are lovely.* **2** used after the noun or pronoun in negative sentences: at all: *had no encouragement whatsoever / none whatsoever.*

wheat *noun* a cereal of the genus *Triticum*, belonging to the grass family (Gramineae), and the most important cereal crop in terms of harvested area, native to the Middle East but now cultivated in temperate regions worldwide. It bears a dense cylindrical head of flowers and is the only cereal suitable for making bread, because it contains the elastic protein gluten. There are numerous species and cultivars with different growth properties and yielding different qualities of flour, such as bread wheat (*Triticum aestivum*), and durum wheat (*Triticum durum*), which is used to make pasta. Wheat is also used in breakfast cereals, and soft wheat flour is used in cakes, biscuits, and pastry. [from Anglo-Saxon *hwæte*]

wheat beer beer brewed from malted wheat.

wheatear *noun* a migratory songbird with a white belly and rump. [probably changed from *white arse*]

wheaten *adj.* **1** made of wheat flour or grain. **2** wholemeal.

wheat germ the vitamin-rich embryo of wheat, present in the grain.

wheatmeal *noun* brown flour containing more than 85 per cent of the powdered whole grain (bran and germ), but not as much as wholemeal flour. Its nutritional value is almost as high as that of wholemeal flour, and it is more digestible and yields a more attractive loaf.

wheatsheaf *noun* a sheaf of wheat.

Wheatstone's or **Wheatstone bridge** *Physics* an electric circuit, consisting of four resistors connected in a loop, for measuring the resistance of one resistor of unknown value by comparing it with three other resistors of known values. [named after the English physicist Sir Charles Wheatstone (1802–75)]

wheedle *verb intrans.*, *trans.* to coax or cajole.

- - - - - - - - - - - - - - - - - - - -
🔳 cajole, coax, persuade, inveigle, charm, flatter, entice, court, draw.
🔳 force.
- -

wheedler *noun* a person who wheedles.

wheel — *noun* **1** a circular object of varying design rotating on an axle, on which a vehicle moves along the ground. **2** such an object serving as part of a machine or mechanism. **3** a steering-wheel, spinning-wheel, or water wheel. **4** (**wheels**) *chiefly North Amer. colloq.* a motor vehicle for personal use. **5** (**wheels**) the workings of an organization, etc: *the wheels of justice.* **6** *Hist.* a circular instrument of torture on which the victim was stretched. **7** *Betting* a disc or drum on the results of whose random spin bets are made: *a roulette wheel.* **8** a circling or pivoting movement, eg of troops. **9** any progression that appears to go round in a circle: *the wheel of fortune.* — *verb* **1** to fit with wheels: *wheeled vehicles.* **2** to push (a wheeled vehicle or conveyance) or (someone or something) in or on it. **3** *intrans.*, *said of troops, birds, etc* to sweep round in a curve. **4** (*also* **wheel round**) to turn round suddenly; to pivot on one's heel. — **at** or **behind the wheel 1** in the driver's seat. **2** in charge. **wheel and deal** to engage in tough business dealing or bargaining. **wheel something out** to suggest ideas, etc that have often been considered before. [from Anglo-Saxon *hweol*]

- - - - - - - - - - - - - - - - - - - -
🔳 *noun* **8** turn, pivot, circle, revolution, rotation, gyration, roll, spin, twirl, whirl. *verb* **3** turn, circle, orbit, spin, twirl, whirl, swing, roll, revolve, swivel, rotate, gyrate.
- -

wheelbarrow *noun* a hand-pushed cart with a wheel in front and two legs at the rear.

wheelbase *noun* the distance between the front and rear axles of a vehicle.

wheelchair *noun* a chair with wheels in which invalids can be conveyed or convey themselves.

wheel clamp a locking device fitted to a wheel of an illegally parked vehicle in order to immobilize it.

wheeler-dealer *noun* a person who uses wheeler-dealing to achieve success.

wheeler-dealing or **wheeling and dealing** tough dealing and bargaining in pursuit of one's political or business interests.

wheelhouse *noun* the shelter on a ship's bridge in which the steering-gear is housed.

wheelie bin *Brit. colloq.* a large dustbin in a wheeled frame.

wheel window same as ROSE WINDOW.

wheelwright *noun* a craftsman who makes and repairs wheels and wheeled carriages.

wheeze — *verb intrans.* to breathe in a laboured way with a gasping or rasping noise, when suffering from a lung infection, etc. — *noun* **1** a wheezing breath or sound. **2** *colloq.* a bright idea; a clever scheme. [from Norse *hvæza*]

- - - - - - - - - - - - - - - - - - - -
🔳 *verb* pant, gasp, cough, hiss, rasp, whistle.
- -

wheezily *adv.* with wheezing.

wheezy *adj.* (**wheezier, wheeziest**) wheezing.

whelk *noun* an edible shellfish with a thick spiral shell. [from Anglo-Saxon *weoloc*]

whelp — *noun* **1** the young of a dog or wolf; a puppy. **2** *old use* an impudent boy or youth. — *verb intrans.* to give birth to puppies or cubs. [from Anglo-Saxon *hwelp*]

when — *adv.* at what time?; during what period?; how soon?: *when does the plane arrive?* / *I cannot remember when I last saw them.* — *conj.* **1** at the time, or during the period, that: *locks the door when she goes to bed* / *it happened when I was abroad.* **2** as soon as: *I'll come when I've finished.* **3** at any time that; whenever: *come when you can.* **4** but just then: *was about to leave when the telephone rang.* **5** at which time; for at that time: *ring tomorrow, when I'll have more information.* **6** in spite of the fact that; considering that: *why stand when you can sit?* — *pron.* what or which time: *they stayed talking, until when I can't say* / *since when she hasn't spoken to me* / *an era when life was harder.* [from Anglo-Saxon *hwænne*]

whence or **from whence** — *adv.* **1** from what place?: *enquired whence they had come.* **2** from what cause or circumstance?: *can't explain whence the mistake arose.* — *conj.* **1** to the place from which; from where: *returned to the village whence they had come.* **2** from which cause or circumstance: *has red hair, whence his nickname 'Ginger'.* [from Middle English *hwannes*]

whenever — *conj.* **1** at any or every time that: *gets furious whenever he fails to get his way.* **2** if ever; no matter when: *I'll be here whenever you need me.* — *adv.* **1** an emphatic form of *when*: *whenever could I have said that?* **2** used to indicate that one does not know when: *at Pentecost, whenever that is.* — **... or whenever** *colloq.* ... or some such time.

whensoever *adv.* if ever; no matter when.

where — *adv.* **1** in, at, or to which place?; in what direction?: *where is she going?* / *I don't know where this road takes us.* **2** in what respect?: *showed me where I'd gone wrong.* — *pron.* what place?: *where have you come from?* — *conj., pron.* **1** in, at, or to the, or any, place that; in, at, or to which: *went where he pleased* / *the village where I was born.* **2** in any case in which: *keep families together where possible.* **3** the aspect or respect in which: *that's where you are wrong.* **4** and there: *stopped at Bradford, where we picked up Jane.* [from Anglo-Saxon *hwær*]

whereabouts — *adv.* (with stress on *-bouts*) where or roughly where? — *sing. or pl. noun* (with stress on *where-*) the position or rough position of a person or thing.

. . . .

◧ *noun* position, location, place, situation, site, vicinity.

. . . .

whereas *conj.* **1** when in fact: *she thought she'd failed, whereas she'd done well.* **2** but, by contrast: *I'm a pessimist, whereas my husband is an optimist.*

whereby *rel. pron.* by means of which.

wherefore — *conj., adv. old use Legal* for what reason? — *noun* a reason, as in *the whys and wherefores.*

wherein *old use Legal* — *adv., conj.* in what place?; in what respect?: *wherein is the justification?* — *rel. pron.* in which place or thing.

whereof *rel. pron. old use* of which: *the circumstances whereof I told you.*

whereon *rel. pron. old use* on which.

wheresoever *adv. old use* no matter where.

whereupon *conj.* at which point.

wherever — *rel. pron.* in, at, or to any or every place that: *takes it wherever she goes.* — *conj.* in, at, or to whatever place: *they were welcomed wherever they went.* — *adv.* **1** no matter where: *I won't lose touch, wherever I go.* **2** an emphatic form of *where: wherever can they be?* **3** used to indicate that one does not know where: *the Round House, wherever that is.* — **... or wherever** *colloq.* ... or some such place.

wherewithal — *rel. pron. old use* with which. — *noun* (**the wherewithal**) the means or necessary resources, especially money.

wherry *noun* (PL. **wherries**) **1** a long light rowing-boat, especially for transporting passengers. **2** a light barge.

whet *verb* (**whetted, whetting**) **1** to sharpen (a bladed tool) by rubbing it against stone, etc. **2** to intensify (someone's appetite or desire). [from Anglo-Saxon *hwettan*]

. . . .

◧ **1** sharpen, hone, file, grind. **2** stimulate, intensify, stir, rouse, arouse, provoke, kindle, quicken, incite, awaken, increase.

◲ **1** blunt. **2** dampen.

. . . .

whether *conj.* **1** used to introduce an indirect question: *asked whether it was raining.* **2** used to introduce an indirect question involving alternative possibilities: *was uncertain whether or not he liked her.* **3** used to state the certainty of something, whichever of two circumstances applies: *promised to marry her, whether or not his parents agreed* / *the rules, whether fair or unfair, are not our concern.* [from Anglo-Saxon *hwæther*]

whetstone *noun* a stone for sharpening bladed tools.

whew /hju:/ *interj. colloq.* an expression of relief or amazement.

whey *noun* the watery content of milk, separated from the curd in making cheese, junket, etc. [from Anglo-Saxon *hwæg*]

which *adj., pron.* **1** used like *what* in seeking to identify or specify a thing or person, usually from a known set or group: *which twin did you mean?* / *can't decide which book is better* / *which did you choose?* **2** used like *that* to introduce a defining or identifying clause: *animals which hibernate* / *the evidence on which it is based* / *look for the house which lies back from the road.* **3** used to introduce a commenting clause: in this use *that* is not available: *the house, which lies back from the road, is painted red.* **4** used as a relative, meaning 'any that': *take which books you want* / *tell me which you fancy.* [Anglo-Saxon *hwilc*]

whichever *rel. pron., rel. adj.* **1** the one or ones that; any that: *take whichever are suitable* / *take whichever coat fits better.* **2** according to which: *at 10.00 or 10.30, whichever is more convenient.* — *adj., pron.* no matter which: *we'll be late, whichever way we go* / *I'll be satisfied, whichever you choose.*

whiff *noun* **1** a slight smell. **2** a puff or slight rush: *a whiff of smoke.* **3** a hint: *at the first whiff of scandal.* [imitative]

. . . .

◧ **1** odour, smell, aroma, sniff, scent. **2** puff, breath, draught. **3** hint, trace.

. . . .

Whig *Brit. Hist.* — *noun* a member of the Whigs, a British political party that emerged in 1679–80 as a group agitating for the exclusion of James, Duke of York (later James VII and II) on the grounds of his Catholicism. See also TORY. — *adj.* relating to the Whigs. [probably from *whiggamore*, a 17c Scottish Presbyterian rebel]

Whiggery *noun* Whig principles.

Whiggish *adj.* relating to or resembling Whigs.

while — *conj.* **1** at the same time as. **2** for as long as; for the whole time that: *guards us while we sleep.* **3** during the time that: *happened while we were abroad.* **4** whereas: *he likes camping, while she prefers sailing.* **5** although: *while I see your point, I still cannot agree.* — *adv.* at or during which: *all the months while I was ill.* — *noun* a space or lapse of time: *after a while.* — *verb* (usually **while away time,** *etc*) to pass time in a leisurely or undemanding way. — **in between whiles** during the intervals. **make it worth someone's while** *colloq.* to reward them well for their trouble. **worth one's while** worth one's time and trouble. [from Anglo-Saxon *hwil*]

whilst *conj.* while.

whim *noun* a sudden fanciful idea; a caprice.

. . . .

◧ fancy, caprice, notion, quirk, freak, humour, conceit, fad, vagary, urge.

. . . .

whimper — *verb* (**whimpered**, **whimpering**) 1 *intrans.* to cry feebly or plaintively. 2 *trans.* to say plaintively. — *noun* a feebly plaintive cry. [imitative]

▣ *verb* 1 cry, sob, weep, snivel, whine, grizzle, mewl. 2 moan, *colloq.* whinge. *noun* sob, snivel, whine, moan.

whimsical *adj.* 1 delicately fanciful or playful. 2 odd, weird, or fantastic. 3 given to having whims.

▣ 2 odd, weird, queer, unusual, peculiar, fantastic, quaint, eccentric, curious. 3 impulsive, capricious, *colloq.* dotty, eccentric.

whimsicality *noun* a whimsical quality.
whimsically *adv.* in a whimsical way.
whimsy *noun* (PL. **whimsies**) 1 quaint, fanciful humour. 2 a whim. [see WHIM]
whin *noun* gorse. [probably from Norse *whin*]
whine — *verb usually intrans.* 1 to whimper. 2 to cry fretfully. 3 to complain peevishly. 4 to speak in a thin, ingratiating, or servile voice. 5 *trans.* to say peevishly. — *noun* 1 a whimper. 2 a continuous high-pitched noise. 3 a thin, ingratiating nasal tone of voice. [from Anglo-Saxon *hwinan*]

▣ *verb* 1, 2 cry, sob, whimper, grizzle, moan, wail. 3, 5 complain, carp, grumble, *colloq.* whinge, *colloq.* gripe, *colloq.* grouch, *North Amer. slang* kvetch. *noun* 1 whimper, cry, sob, moan, wail.

whinge — *verb intrans. colloq.* to complain irritably. — *noun* a peevish complaint. [from Anglo-Saxon *hwinsian*, to whine]
whinny — *verb intrans.* (**whinnies**, **whinnied**) *said of a horse* to neigh softly. — *noun* (PL. **whinnies**) a gentle neigh. [imitative]
whip — *noun* 1 a lash with a handle, for driving animals or thrashing people. 2 a member of a parliamentary party responsible for members' discipline, and for their attendance to vote on important issues. 3 a notice sent to members by a party whip requiring their attendance for a vote, urgency being indicated by the number of underlinings: *a three-line whip*. 4 a dessert of any of various flavours made with beaten egg-whites or cream. 5 a whipper-in. — *verb* (**whipped**, **whipping**) 1 to strike or thrash with a whip. 2 to lash with the action or force of a whip: *a sharp wind whipped their faces*. 3 *trans., intrans.* to move or cause to move with a whip-like motion: *the branch whipped back*. 4 (*usually* **whip something off, out**, *etc*) to take or snatch it: *whipped out a revolver*. 5 *intrans., trans.* to move smartly: *whipped out of sight*. 6 to rouse, goad, drive, or force into a certain state: *whipped the crowd into a fury*. 7 *colloq.* to steal. 8 to beat (egg-whites, cream, etc) until stiff. 9 to wind cord round (a rope, etc) to prevent fraying. 10 to oversew. 11 *colloq.* to outdo, outwit, or defeat. — **have the whip hand over someone** *colloq.* to have an advantage over them. **whip something up** 1 to arouse support, enthusiasm, or other feelings. 2 to prepare a meal, etc at short notice. [from Middle English *whippe*]

▣ *noun* 1 lash, scourge, switch, birch, cane, horsewhip, riding-crop, cat-o'-nine-tails. *verb* 1 beat, flog, lash, flagellate, scourge, birch, cane, strap, thrash, punish, chastise, discipline, *formal* castigate. 2 lash, thrash. 3 pull, jerk, snatch, whisk. 4 whisk, pull, jerk, snatch, tear. 5 dash, dart, rush, tear, fly, flit, flash. 6 rouse, goad, drive, spur, push, urge, stir, agitate, incite, provoke, instigate.

whipcord *noun* 1 strong, fine, tightly twisted cord. 2 cotton or worsted cloth with a diagonal rib.
whiplash *noun* 1 the lash of a whip, or the motion it represents. 2 (*also* **whiplash injury**) a popular term for a neck injury caused by the sudden jerking back of the head and neck, especially as a result of a motor-vehicle collision.
whipper-in *noun* an assistant to a huntsman, who controls the hounds.
whipper-snapper *noun* old *colloq. use* a cheeky young lad; any lowly person who behaves impudently.
whippet *noun* a slender dog like a small greyhound, used for racing.
whipping-boy *noun* 1 *Hist.* a boy who is educated with a prince and given whatever beatings the prince has deserved. 2 anyone on whom the blame for others' faults falls.
whipping cream cream that will thicken when whipped.
whipping-top *noun* a top kept spinning by the lash of a whip.
whippoorwill /'wɪppʊəwɪl, 'wɪppəwɪl/ *noun* a species of nightjar native to N America. [imitative of call]
whippy *adj.* (**whippier**, **whippiest**) *said of a stick or cane* springy; flexible.
whip-round *noun* a collection of money hastily made among a group of people.
whipstock *noun* the handle of a whip.
whirl — *verb* 1 *intrans.* to spin or revolve rapidly. 2 *trans., intrans.* to move with a rapid circling or spiralling motion. 3 *intrans., said of the head* to feel dizzy from excitement, etc. — *noun* 1 a circling or spiralling movement or pattern: *a whirl of smoke / whirls of colour*. 2 a round of intense activity: *a whirl of parties*. 3 a dizzy state. [from Norse *hvirfla*, to turn]

▣ *verb* 1, 2 swirl, spin, twirl, pivot, pirouette, turn, twist, rotate, revolve, gyrate, swivel, wheel, circle, reel, roll. 3 spin, reel. *noun* 1 spin, swirl, twirl, spiral, twist, gyration, revolution, pirouette, turn, wheel, rotation, circle, reel, roll. 2 bustle, flurry, hubbub, hurly-burly, confusion, tumult, uproar, commotion, agitation. 3 daze, giddiness.

whirligig *noun* 1 a spinning toy, especially a top. 2 a merry-go-round. 3 a dizzying round of activity, progression of events, etc. [from Middle English *whirligigge*, spinning toy]
whirlpool *noun* a violent almost circular eddy of water that occurs in rivers or seas at a point where several strong currents of water travelling in different directions converge, eg at the foot of a waterfall. Floating objects may be drawn into a depression at the whirlpool's centre.
whirlwind — *noun* a violently spiralling column of air. — *adj.* rapid: *a whirlwind courtship*.

▣ *noun* tornado, cyclone, vortex. *adj.* swift, rapid, lightning, quick, speedy, hasty, impulsive, headlong, impetuous, rash.
▣ *adj.* deliberate, slow, cautious.

whirlybird *noun colloq.* a helicopter.
whirr or **whir** — *verb intrans.* (**whirred**, **whirring**) to turn or spin with a humming noise. — *noun* a whirring sound. [probably from Scandinavian *whirr*]
whisk — *verb* 1 (**whisk something off** or **away**) to brush or sweep it lightly: *whisked the crumbs off the table*. 2 to transport rapidly: *was whisked into hospital*. 3 to move with a brisk waving motion: *whisked its tail from side to side*. 4 to beat (egg-whites, cream, etc) till stiff. — *noun* 1 a whisking movement or action. 2 a hand-held implement for whisking egg-whites, etc. 3 a flexible implement for swatting flies. [related to Norse *visk*, wisp]

▣ *verb* 1 brush, sweep, flick, wipe, twitch. 2 rush, hurry, speed, hasten, race. 4 whip, beat.

whisker *noun* 1 any of the long coarse hairs growing round the mouth of a cat, mouse, etc. 2 (**whiskers**) a man's beard, especially the parts growing on his cheeks. 3 the tiniest possible margin; a hair's breadth: *within a whisker of death / escaped by a whisker*. [related to Norse *visk*, wisp]

whiskery *adj.* having whiskers.

whiskey *noun* (PL. **whiskeys**) *Irish, North Amer., esp. US* whisky.

whisky *noun* (PL. **whiskies**) an alcoholic spirit distilled from a fermented mash of cereal grains, eg barley, wheat, or rye. [from Gaelic *uisge beatha*, literally 'water of life']

whisper — *verb* (**whispered, whispering**) **1** *intrans., trans.* to speak or say quietly, breathing rather than voicing the words. **2** *intrans., trans.* to speak or say in secrecy or confidence. **3** *intrans., trans.* to spread a rumour; to rumour: *it's whispered that she's leaving him.* **4** *intrans., said of a breeze, etc* to make a rustling sound in leaves, etc. — *noun* **1** a whispered level of speech: *spoke in a whisper.* **2** (*often* **whispers**) a rumour or hint; whispered gossip: *have been whispers about their divorce.* **3** a soft rustling sound: *the whisper of the breeze.* [from Anglo-Saxon *hwisprian*]

■ *verb* **1** murmur, breathe, mutter, mumble, hiss. **3** gossip, intimate, insinuate, divulge, hint. **4** rustle, sigh. *noun* **1** undertone, murmur, hiss. **2** rumour, hint, suggestion, suspicion, breath, whiff, report, innuendo, insinuation, trace, tinge, soupçon. **3** rustle, sigh.

🞄 *verb* **1** shout.

whist *noun* a card game for usually two pairs of players, in which the object is to take a majority of 13 tricks, each trick over six scoring one point. [originally *whisk*]

whist drive a gathering for whist-playing, with a change of partner after every four games.

whistle — *noun* **1** a shrill sound produced through pursed lips or through the teeth, used to signal, to express surprise, etc. **2** any of several similar sounds, eg the call of a bird, or the shrill sigh of the wind. **3** any of many devices producing a similar sound, etc, eg one operated by steam on a railway locomotive or kettle, or one blown by a referee to regulate play on the pitch. **4** a simple wind instrument consisting of a wooden or metal pipe with finger holes. — *verb* **1** *intrans., trans.* to produce a whistle through pursed lips or teeth; to perform (a tune), signal, communicate, or summon with this sound. **2** *intrans., trans.* to blow a whistle, or play on a whistle. **3** *intrans., said of a kettle or locomotive* to emit a whistling sound. **4** *intrans., said of the wind* to make a shrill sound. **5** *intrans., trans., said of a bird* to sing. **6** *intrans., said of a bullet, etc* to whizz through the air. — **blow the whistle on someone** or **something** *colloq.* **1** to expose illegal or dishonest practices to the authorities. **2** to declare something to be illegal. **wet one's whistle** *colloq.* to have a drink; to quench one's thirst. **whistle for something** *colloq.* to expect it in vain. [from Anglo-Saxon *hwistlian*, to whistle]

whistle-stop *adj.* **1** *said of a politician's tour* with a number of short stops, originally at railway stations, for delivering electioneering addresses to local communities. **2** *said of any tour* very rapid, with a number of brief stops.

Whit — *noun* Whitsuntide. — *adj.* of or belonging to Whitsuntide.

whit *noun* (*with a negative*) the least bit: *not a whit worse.* [variant of *wight*, creature]

white — *adj.* **1** of the colour of snow, the colour that reflects all light. **2** (*often* White) *said of people* belonging to one of the pale-skinned races; relating to such people. **3** abnormally pale, from shock or illness. **4** *said eg of a rabbit or mouse* albino. **5** *said of hair* lacking pigment, as in old age. **6** *said of a variety of anything* pale-coloured, as distinct from darker types: *white grapes.* **7** *said of wine* made from white grapes or from skinned black grapes. **8 a** *said of flour* having had the bran and wheat germ removed. **b** *said of bread* made with white flour. **9** *said of coffee or tea* with milk or cream added. **10** *poetic, said of the soul, etc* pure; innocent. — *noun* **1** white colour or colouring matter, eg paint; white clothes: *dressed all in white.* **2** (*often* White) a white person. **3** (*also* **egg-white**) the clear fluid surrounding the yolk of an egg; albumen. **4** the white part of the eyeball, surrounding the iris. **5** *Games* something white, eg a playing-piece in chess or draughts, a ball in snooker, or ring on an archery target; the player of the white pieces in

a board game. **6** (**whites**) household linen, or white clothes, worn eg for cricket or tennis. — **bleed someone white** to drain or deprive them gradually of resources, wealth, etc. [from Anglo-Saxon *hwit*]

■ *adj.* **1** light, snowy, milky, creamy, ivory, hoary. **3** pale, pallid, wan, ashen, colourless, anaemic, pasty. **5** silver, grey. **10** pure, innocent, immaculate, spotless, stainless, undefiled.

🞄 *adj.* **1, 9** black. **3** ruddy. **6** red, black. **7** red. **8** brown, wholemeal, wholewheat. **10** defiled.

white ant a termite.

whitebait *noun* the young of various fish, eg herrings, fried and eaten whole.

white blood cell or **white corpuscle** a colourless blood cell, containing a nucleus, whose main functions are to engulf invading micro-organisms and foreign particles, to produce antibodies, or to remove cell debris from sites of injury and infection. There are three main types (monocytes, granulocytes, and lymphocytes), all of which are formed in the bone marrow. Also called LEUCOCYTE.

White Canon another name for PREMONSTRATENSIAN.

white-collar *adj.* denoting non-manual workers, in clerical or other professions. See also BLUE-COLLAR.

white dwarf a small faint hot star that has reached the last stage of its life, having exhausted the nuclear fuel in its central core and started to collapse under its own gravity. The mass of a white dwarf is similar to that of the Sun, but its diameter is about the same as that of the Earth.

white elephant a possession or piece of property that is useless or unwanted, especially if inconvenient or expensive to keep.

White Ensign see ENSIGN.

white feather a symbol of cowardice. — **show the white feather** to behave in a cowardly fashion.

white fish a general name for white-fleshed sea fish, including whiting, cod, sole, haddock, and halibut.

white flag the signal used for offering surrender or requesting a truce.

whitefly *noun* a small sap-sucking bug, whose body and wings are covered with a white waxy powder. The immature stages are immobile, and are typically found on the underside of leaves. It commonly produces honeydew, and is attended by ants.

white gold a pale lustrous alloy of gold, containing eg platinum or palladium.

white goods large, traditionally white, kitchen appliances such as washing machines, dishwashers, and cookers.

white-headed boy *ironic* a favourite or protégé.

white heat 1 a temperature of metals, etc greater than red heat, at which white light is emitted. **2** *colloq.* the intensest possible keenness, activity, or excitement: *the white heat of technology.*

white hope someone of whom great achievements are expected.

white horse a white wave crest on a choppy sea.

white-hot *adj.* **1** so hot that white light is given off. **2** intense; passionate.

white knight a person who rescues a company financially, especially from an unwanted takeover bid.

white-knuckle *adj. colloq.* causing extreme anxiety, alarm, or terror: *a white-knuckle ride.*

white lead a mixture of lead carbonate and lead hydroxide in the form of a white powder, used as colouring matter, etc.

white lie a forgivable lie, especially one told to avoid hurting someone's feelings.

white light light, such as that of the sun, containing all the wavelengths in the visible range of the spectrum.

white magic magic used for beneficial purposes, eg to oppose evil, cure disease, etc.

white matter pale fibrous nerve tissue in the brain and spinal cord.

white meat a pale-coloured meat, eg veal, chicken, and turkey. **b** in poultry, the paler meat of the breast as opposed to the darker meat of the leg, etc.

whiten *verb trans., intrans.* (**whitened, whitening**) to make or become white or whiter; to bleach.

. . . .

▣ bleach, blanch, whitewash, pale, fade.
▣ blacken, darken.

. . . .

whitener *noun* **1** a person or thing that whitens. **2** an artificial substitute for milk in coffee, etc.

whiteness *noun* a white state or quality.

white noise noise in which there are a large number of frequencies of roughly equal intensity.

white-out *noun* **1** conditions of poor visibility in snowy weather, when the overcast sky blends imperceptibly with the white landscape. **2** a dense blizzard.

white paper (*also* **White Paper**) a government policy statement printed on white paper, issued for the information of parliament.

white pepper light-coloured pepper made from peppercorns from which the dark outer husk has been removed.

white pudding a spicy sausage made from minced pork, oatmeal, and suet.

White Russian a member of the counter-revolutionary forces led by ex-tsarist officers, who fought unsuccessfully against the Bolshevik Red Army during the Russian Civil War (1918–22).

white sauce thick sauce made from flour, fat, and milk.

white slave a girl or woman held against her will, and forced into prostitution.

white spirit a colourless liquid distilled from petroleum and containing a mixture of hydrocarbons, used as a solvent and thinner for paints and varnishes.

white sugar refined sugar.

white tie 1 a white bow tie, part of men's formal evening dress. **2** *as an instruction on an invitation* formal evening dress for men.

white trash *North Amer. derog.* poor white people, especially those living in the southern states of the US.

white van man *Brit. colloq.* a man who drives a white van as part of his job, regarded as being an average person with typical attitudes that are sometimes aggressive or ill-informed. [coined by David Garfinkel in a column in *The Sun* newspaper]

whitewash — *noun* **1** a mixture of lime and water, for giving a white coating to especially outside walls. **2** measures taken to cover up eg a disreputable affair, clear a stained reputation, etc. — *verb* to coat, clean up, or conceal with whitewash.

white whale a white toothed whale of arctic waters, related to the dolphin.

whitewood *noun* **1** the light-coloured timber of any of various trees. **2** unstained wood; wood prepared for staining.

whither *old use* — *adv.* **1** to what place?: *whither did they go?* **2** in what direction? towards what state?: *whither education?* — *conj., rel. pron.* **1** to the, or any, place that; towards which: *went whither he was instructed / the mountain pass whither they were headed.* **2** towards which place: *some miles away lay London, whither they turned their steps next day.* [from Anglo-Saxon *hwider*]

whiting[1] *noun* a small edible fish related to the cod. [from Middle English *hwitling* or Old Dutch *witinc*]

whiting[2] *noun* ground and washed white chalk, used in putty, whitewash, and silver cleaner. [see WHITE]

whitish *adj.* somewhat white; nearly white.

whitlow *noun* an inflammation of the finger or toe, especially near the nail. [from Middle English *whitflawe*, white flaw]

Whitsun or **Whitsuntide** *noun* the week beginning with Whit Sunday.

Whit Sunday or **Whitsunday** in the Christian Church, the seventh Sunday after Easter, commemorating the day

of Pentecost, on which by tradition those newly baptized wore white robes. [from Anglo-Saxon *hwita sunnandæg*, white Sunday]

whittle *verb* **1** to cut, carve, or pare (a stick, piece of wood, etc). **2** to shape or fashion by this means. **3** (**whittle something away**) to consume it bit by bit; to eat away at it or erode it. **4** (**whittle something down**) to reduce it gradually or persistently: *whittled down the guest list from 200 to 150.* [from Anglo-Saxon *thwitan*, to cut]

. . . .

▣ **1** carve, cut, scrape, shave, trim, pare. **2** shape, hew. **3** consume, erode, eat away, wear away. **4** diminish, reduce, undermine.

. . . .

whizz or **whiz** *colloq.* — *verb intrans.* (**whizzed, whizzing**) **1** to fly through the air, especially with a whistling noise. **2** to move fast. — *noun* an expert.

whizz kid *colloq.* someone who achieves success early, through ability, inventiveness, dynamism, or ambition.

WHO *abbrev.* World Health Organization.

who *pron.* **1** used in seeking to identify a person or people, as the subject of a verb and also commonly as the object of a verb or preposition in place of the more formal *whom*: *who is at the door? / who did you give it to? / asked who else he had seen.* **2** used like *that* to introduce a defining clause: *the boy who was on the train / anyone who wants this can have it.* **3** used to add a commenting clause; in this use, *that* is not available: *Julius Caesar, who was murdered in 44 BC.* — **know who's who** know the important people and what they do. [from Anglo-Saxon *hwa*]

whoa /woʊ/ *interj.* a command to stop, especially to a horse.

who'd *contr.* **1** who would. **2** who had.

whodunit or **whodunnit** *noun colloq.* a detective novel, play, etc; a mystery. [from *who done it?*, facetiously illiterate for *who did it?*]

whoever *pron.* **1** used as an emphatic form of *who* or *whom*: *whoever is that at the door? / ask whoever you like.* **2** no matter who: *I don't know them, whoever they are / whoever is appointed faces a huge task.* **3** used to indicate that one does not know who: *St Fiacre, whoever he was.* — **... or whoever** *colloq.* ... or some other such person or people.

whole — *noun* **1** all of; not less than. **2** something complete in itself, especially if consisting of integrated parts: *elements that together form a whole.* — *adj.* **1** all of; no less than. **2** in one piece: *swallowed it whole.* **3** unbroken: *only two cups left whole.* **4** *said of food* processed as little as possible. **5** *old use* healthy; well: *the miracle that made him whole.* **6** *colloq.* huge; vast: *a whole pile of work to do.* — *adv. colloq.* completely; altogether; wholly: *a whole new approach.* — **a whole lot** *colloq.* a great deal. **as a whole** in general; taken as a complete group, etc rather than as individuals. **on the whole** considering everything. [from Anglo-Saxon *hal*, healthy]

. . . .

▣ *noun* **1** total, aggregate, sum total, entirety, totality, all, fullness. **2** unit, entity, ensemble, lot, piece. *adj.* **1** complete, entire, integral, full, total, unabridged, uncut, undivided, unedited. **3** intact, unharmed, undamaged, unbroken, inviolate, perfect, mint, unhurt. **5** well, healthy, fit, sound, strong. **on the whole** all things considered, all in all, by and large, in general, generally, generally speaking, as a rule, mostly, for the most part.
▣ *noun* PART. *adj.* **1** partial. **3** damaged. **5** ill.

. . . .

wholehearted *adj.* sincere and enthusiastic.

. . . .

▣ sincere, enthusiastic, unreserved, unstinting, unqualified, passionate, earnest, committed, dedicated, devoted, heartfelt, emphatic, warm, unfeigned, genuine, complete, true, real, zealous.
▣ half-hearted.

. . . .

wholeheartedly adv. in a wholehearted way.

wholemeal adj. 1 said of flour made from the entire wheat grain. 2 said of bread made from wholemeal flour.

wholeness noun a whole or complete state.

wholesale — noun the sale of goods in large quantities to a retailer. — adj., adv. 1 of, or by, this type of sale. 2 on a huge scale and without discrimination: wholesale destruction. See also RETAIL.

....

⊟ adj. 2 mass, indiscriminate, extensive, sweeping, wide-ranging, broad, outright, total, massive, comprehensive, far-reaching.

⊟ adj. 2 partial.

....

wholesaler noun a wholesale supplier.

wholesome adj. 1 attractively healthy: a wholesome appearance. 2 promoting health. 3 old use morally beneficial. 4 sensible; prudent: a wholesome respect for mountains.

....

⊟ healthy, salubrious, salutary, beneficial, nourishing, nourishing, invigorating, bracing, hygienic, sanitary. 3 improving, edifying, uplifting, pure, virtuous, righteous, honourable, respectable, moral, decent, clean, proper.

⊟ UNWHOLESOME. 1, 2 unhealthy.

....

wholesomely adv. in a wholesome way.

wholesomeness noun being wholesome.

whole-tone scale Mus. either of two scales produced by beginning on one of any two notes a chromatic semitone apart and ascending or descending in whole tones for an octave. There may be no tonic (or other) relationship between the individual notes in the series.

wholly adv. completely; altogether.

....

⊟ completely, altogether, entirely, totally, fully, purely, absolutely, utterly, comprehensively, perfectly, thoroughly, all, exclusively, only.

⊟ partly.

....

whom pron. used as the object of a verb or preposition, as the objective case of who; it is now often replaced by who, especially in less formal usage: 1 in seeking to identify a person: whom do you want? / to whom are you referring? 2 used like that as a relative in a defining clause: I am looking for the woman whom I met at the reception. 3 used to introduce a commenting clause: in this use that is not available: the woman, whom I met at the reception, has disappeared. [from Anglo-Saxon hwam]

whomever pron. formal used as the object of a verb or preposition to mean 'any person or people that': I will write to whomever they appoint.

whomsoever pron. whomever.

whoop — noun 1 a loud cry of delight, triumph, etc. 2 a noisy indrawn breath typical in whooping cough. — verb intrans., trans. to utter, or say with, a whoop. — **whoop it up** colloq. to celebrate noisily.

whoopee interj. expressing exuberant delight. — **make whoopee** to celebrate exuberantly.

whooper swan a swan that is easily distinguished by its straight neck and yellow-and-black bill, so called because it makes loud whooping calls when in flight. It breeds in Iceland, N Europe, and Asia, and migrates S in winter.

whooping cough Medicine pertussis, a highly contagious disease mainly affecting children, caused by infection of the respiratory tract with the bacterium Bordetella pertussis. It is characterized by bouts of violent coughing followed by a sharp drawing in of the breath which produces a characteristic 'whooping' sound.

whoops interj. an exclamation of surprise or concern made when one has a slight accident, makes an error, etc or sees someone else do so.

whop verb (**whopped, whopping**) colloq. 1 to hit; to thrash. 2 to defeat soundly.

whopper old colloq. use noun 1 anything very large: a whopper of a fish. 2 a lie.

whopping adj. colloq. huge; enormous.

whore /hɔ:(r)/ — noun old offensive use 1 a prostitute. 2 a sexually immoral or promiscuous woman. — verb intrans. 1 said of a man to have sexual relations with prostitutes. 2 said of a woman to be a prostitute. [from Anglo-Saxon hore]

who're contr. who are.

whorehouse noun old colloq. use a brothel.

whorl /wɔːl, wɜːl/ noun 1 Bot. a circular arrangement of several petals, leaves, or other identical structures around the same point on a plant. 2 Zool. one of the coils in the spiral shell of a mollusc. 3 a type of fingerprint in which there is a spiral arrangement of the ridges on the skin. [from Anglo-Saxon hwyrfel]

who's contr. 1 who is. 2 who has.

whose pron., adj. 1 belonging to which person or people: whose is this jacket? / we do not know whose these are. 2 used to introduce a defining clause: of whom or which: children whose parents are divorced / buildings whose foundations are sinking. 3 used to add a commenting clause: my parents, without whose help I could not have succeeded. 4 whoever's or whichever's: take whose advice you will.

whosoever pron. whoever.

why — adv. for what reason: why do you ask? / did not say why she was leaving. — rel. pron. for, or because of, which: no reason why I should get involved. — interj. 1 expressing surprise, indignation, impatience, recognition, etc: why, you little monster! 2 used to challenge an implied criticism: why, have you any objection? — noun a reason: the whys and wherefores. — **why not** used to make or agree to a suggestion: why don't you ask her? / 'Like a drink?' 'Why not.'. [from Anglo-Saxon hwi]

WI abbrev. 1 West Indies. 2 Wisconsin. 3 in the UK, Women's Institute.

wick noun the string running up through a candle and projecting at the top, that burns when lit and draws up the wax into the flame. — **get on someone's wick** slang to be a source of irritation to them. [from Anglo-Saxon weoce]

wicked adj. 1 evil; sinful; immoral. 2 mischievous; playful; roguish. 3 colloq. bad: wicked weather. 4 slang excellent. [from Anglo-Saxon wicca, wizard]

....

⊟ 1 evil, sinful, immoral, depraved, corrupt, vicious, unprincipled, iniquitous, heinous, debased, abominable, ungodly, unrighteous, shameful. 2 mischievous, playful, naughty, roguish. 3 bad, unpleasant, dreadful, awful, nasty, foul, vile, terrible, atrocious, harmful, offensive, distressing, worthless, difficult, severe, intense, injurious, troublesome, fierce.

⊟ GOOD. 1 upright.

....

wickedly adv. in a wicked way.

wickedness noun a wicked state; wicked activity or behaviour.

wicker adj., said of a fence, basket, etc made of interwoven twigs, canes, rushes, etc. [from Scandinavian wicker]

wickerwork noun articles made of such material.

wicket noun 1 Cricket a row of three small wooden posts stuck upright in the ground behind either crease; the playing area between these; a batsman's stand at the wicket, or his or her dismissal by the bowler: 45 runs for two wickets. 2 a small door or gate, especially one that can open separately within a large door or gate. [from Old French wiket]

wicket-keeper noun Cricket the fielder who stands immediately behind the wicket.

wide — adj. 1 large in extent from side to side. 2 measuring a certain amount from side to side. 3 said of the eyes open to the fullest extent. 4 said of a range, selection, etc covering a great variety. 5 extensive; widespread: wide support. 6 said of a gap large: a wide difference. 7 general, as opposed to particular: consider the wider implications. 8 (**wide of something**) off the mark: his aim was wide of the target. — adv. **1** over an extensive area: *travelling far and wide.* **2** to the fullest extent: *with legs wide apart.* **3** (**wide of something**) off the mark: *shot wide of the target.* — *noun Cricket* a ball bowled out of the batsman's reach. — **wide awake** fully awake or alert. **wide open 1** open to the fullest extent. **2** *colloq.* vulnerable; exposed to attack. [from Anglo-Saxon *wid*]

⊟ *adj.* **1** broad, roomy, spacious, vast, immense, loose, baggy. **2** broad. **3** dilated, expanded, full. **4** extensive, wide-ranging, comprehensive. **5** extensive, widespread, wide-ranging, far-reaching, general. **6** vast, immense. **7** general, broad. **8** off the mark, off-target. *adv.* **2** fully, completely, all the way. **3** astray, off course, off target, off the mark.
⊞ *adj.* **1, 4, 7** narrow. **5** limited, restricted. **8** near. *adv.* **3** on target.

-wide *combining form* forming words meaning 'throughout the extent of': *nationwide.*
wide-angle lens a camera lens with an extra-wide range of view.
wide boy *colloq.* a shrewd but dishonest operator in business undertakings.
widely *adv.* **1** over a wide area or range. **2** to a great extent.
widen *verb trans., intrans.* (**widened, widening**) to make, or become, wide or wider.

⊟ distend, dilate, expand, extend, spread, stretch, enlarge, broaden.
⊞ narrow.

wideness *noun* a wide state or quality.
wide-ranging *adj.*, *said of interests, discussions, etc* covering a large variety of subjects or topics.
widespread *adj.* **1** extending over a wide area. **2** affecting or involving large numbers of people: *widespread agreement.*

⊟ EXTENSIVE, PREVALENT, SWEEPING, UNIVERSAL, COMMON, FAR-REACHING, PERVASIVE. **2** general, wholesale, unlimited.
⊞ LIMITED.

widgeon see WIGEON.
widget /ˈwɪdʒɪt/ *noun* a gadget; any small manufactured item or component. [perhaps an alteration of GADGET]
widow — *noun* **1** a woman whose husband is dead and who has not remarried. **2** *colloq.* a woman whose husband spends much time away from her on some especially sporting pursuit: *golf widows.* — *verb* to leave (someone) a widow or widower. [from Anglo-Saxon *widewe*]
widower *noun* a man whose wife is dead, and who has not remarried.
width *noun* **1** extent from side to side. **2** wideness. **3** the distance from side to side across a swimming-pool. [see WIDE]

⊟ **1, 2** breadth, diameter, wideness, compass, thickness, span, range, measure, girth, beam, amplitude, extent.

widthways *adv., adj.* across the width: *folded widthways.*
wield *verb* **1** to brandish or use (a tool, weapon, etc). **2** to have or exert (power, authority, influence, etc). [from Anglo-Saxon *wieldan*, to control]

⊟ **1** brandish, flourish, swing, wave, handle, ply, manage, manipulate. **2** have, exert, hold, possess, employ, exercise, use, utilize, maintain, command.

wife *noun* (PL. **wives**) **1** the woman to whom a man is married; a married woman. **2** *old use, dialect* (*often in compounds*) a woman: *housewife / fishwife.* [from Anglo-Saxon *wif*]

⊟ **1** spouse, partner, mate, better half, other half, bride.

wifely *adj.* of, or considered suitable to, a wife.
wig *noun* an artificial covering of hair for the head. [see PERIWIG]
wigeon or **widgeon** *noun* a wild duck of marshy regions.
wigged *adj.* wearing a wig.
wigging *noun colloq.* a scolding.
wiggle *verb trans., intrans. colloq.* to move, especially jerkily, from side to side or up and down. [related to Anglo-Saxon *wegan*, to move, and Dutch *wiggelen*, to totter]
wiggly *adj.* (**wigglier, wiggliest**) wriggly, wavy.
wight *noun old use* a human creature. [from Anglo-Saxon *wiht*]
wigwam *noun* **1** a domed tent-like Native American dwelling made of arched poles covered with skins, bark, or mats. **2** often applied to the cone-shaped dwelling more correctly known as a tepee. [from Abenaki (Native American language) *wikewam*, house]
wild — *adj.* **1** *said of animals* untamed; undomesticated; not dependent on man. **2** *said of plants* growing in a natural, uncultivated state. **3** *said of country* desolate, rugged, inhospitable, or uninhabitable. **4** *said of peoples* savage; uncivilized. **5** unrestrained; uncontrolled: *wild fury.* **6** frantically excited: *the spectators went wild.* **7** distraught: *wild with grief.* **8** dishevelled; disordered: *wild attire.* **9** *said of the eyes* staring; scared-looking. **10** *said of weather* stormy: *a wild night.* **11** *said of plans, hopes, etc* crazy; impracticable; unrealistic: *succeeded beyond their wildest dreams.* **12** *said of a guess* very approximate, or quite random. **13** (**wild about someone** or **something**) intensely fond of them or keen on them. **14** *colloq.* furious. **15** *slang* enjoyable; terrific. — *noun* **1** (**the wild**) a wild animal's or plant's natural environment or life in it: *returned the cub to the wild.* **2** (**the wild**) lonely, sparsely inhabited regions away from the city. — **run wild 1** *said of a garden or plants* to revert to a wild, overgrown, uncultivated state. **2** *said eg of children* to live a life of freedom, with little discipline or control. [from Anglo-Saxon *wilde*]

⊟ *adj.* **1** untamed, undomesticated, natural. **3** desolate, rugged, inhospitable, uninhabitable, uncultivated, waste. **4** savage, uncivilized, barbarous, primitive. **5** unrestrained, uncontrolled, unruly, unmanageable, violent, turbulent, rowdy, lawless, disorderly, riotous, boisterous. **6** *colloq.* mad, *colloq.* crazy. **7** distraught, frenzied, demented. **8** dishevelled, disordered, untidy, unkempt, messy, tousled. **10** stormy, tempestuous, rough, blustery, choppy. **11** *colloq.* crazy, impracticable, unrealistic, irrational, outrageous, preposterous, wayward, extravagant, reckless, rash, imprudent, foolhardy, foolish.
⊞ *adj.* **1** tame, domesticated. **2** cultivated. **4** civilized. **5** restrained. **6** calm. **8** tidy. **11** sensible.

wild boar a wild ancestor of the domestic pig, native to Europe, NW Africa, and S Asia, and having thick dark hair. The male has tusks.
wild card 1 a competitor lacking the usual or statutory qualifications. **2** *Comput.* a symbol, eg an asterisk, that can be used to represent any character or set of characters in a certain position, in order to identify text strings with variable contents. For example, the specification 'c*.doc' can be used to denote all file-names that start with 'c' and end with '.doc'.
wildcat — *noun* **1** (*often* **wild cat**) an undomesticated cat of Europe and Asia, which has a longer stouter body and longer legs than those of a domestic cat, and a thick bushy tail which is shorter and ringed, with a black tip. It feeds mainly on hares, grouse, rabbits, and small rodents, but will also attack poultry and lambs. **2** (*often* **wild cat**) any of several small or medium-sized cats, eg lynx, ocelot, as opposed to the lion, tiger, leopard, cheetah, and other

large cats. — *adj.* **1** *said of an industrial strike* not called or approved by a trade union. **2** *said of a business scheme* financially unsound or risky; speculative. **3** *said of an oil well* exploratory; experimental.

wildebeest /ˈwɪldəbiːst/ *noun* (PL. **wildebeest**, **wilde-beests**) either of two species of large antelope that live in herds on the grasslands of Africa, and resemble cattle in appearance, having a large head, a short thick neck, tufts of hair growing from the throat, and an upright mane. Both sexes have large curved horns. Wildebeest is the main prey of the lion. Also called GNU. [from Afrikaans, from Dutch *wilde*, wild + *beest*, ox]

wilderness *noun* **1** an uncultivated or uninhabited region. **2** a desolate, pathless area. **3** an overgrown tangle of weeds, etc. **4** *Hist.* a part of a garden or estate deliberately left wild for romantic effect. **5** any daunting maze. **6** *Politics* the state of being without office or influence after playing a leading role. — **a voice crying in the wilderness** someone with an important message or warning who goes unheeded (in allusion to Matthew 3.3). [from Anglo-Saxon *wilddeor*, wild beast]

· · · · · · · · · · · · · · · · ·

■ **1** desert, wasteland, waste, wilds, jungle.

· ·

wildfire *noun Hist.* a highly flammable liquid used in warfare. — **spread like wildfire** *said eg of disease, rumour, etc* to spread rapidly and extensively.

wildfowl *sing. or pl. noun* a game bird or game birds, especially waterfowl.

wildfowler *noun* a person who hunts and kills wildfowl.

wildfowling *noun* the activity or sport of hunting and killing wildfowl.

wild goose chase a search that is bound to be unsuccessful.

wildlife *noun* wild animals, birds, and plants in general.

wildly *adv.* in a wild way; to a wild extent.

wildness *noun* a wild state or quality.

wild pansy SEE HEARTSEASE.

wild type the form of a species typically occurring under natural breeding conditions, as distinct from mutant types.

Wild West (**the Wild West**) *Hist.* the part of the USA west of the Mississippi, settled during the 19c and legendary for the adventures of its cattlemen and the struggle to gain territory from the Native American population.

wile — *noun* **1** (**wiles**) charming personal ways. **2** a piece of cunning; a ruse, trick, manoeuvre, or stratagem. — *verb* **1** *old use* (**wile someone away**) to lure or entice them. **2** (**wile away time**) to pass time pleasantly; to while away time. [from Anglo-Saxon *wil*; related to GUILE]

· ·

■ *noun* **2** ruse, trick, manoeuvre, stratagem, ploy, device, contrivance, guile, subterfuge, cunning, dodge, deceit, cheating, trickery, fraud, craftiness, chicanery.

▣ *noun* **2** guilelessness.

· ·

wilful *adj.* **1** deliberate; intentional. **2** headstrong, obstinate, or self-willed. [see WILL²]

· ·

■ **1** deliberate, conscious, intentional, voluntary, premeditated. **2** self-willed, obstinate, stubborn, pigheaded, obdurate, intransigent, inflexible, perverse, wayward, contrary.

▣ **1** unintentional. **2** good-natured.

· ·

wilfully *adv.* in a wilful way.

wilfulness *noun* being wilful.

wili /ˈviːliː/ (PL. **wilis**) in Slavic folklore, the spirit of a betrothed maiden who has died before her wedding day. They haunt highways at night, compelling any passing youth to dance with them until he drops dead. The legend was recorded by Heinrich Heine and used in the ballet *Giselle* by Théophile Gautier.

wiliness *noun* being wily.

will¹ *verb aux.* used: **1** especially in the second and third persons, to form a future tense. **2** in the first person, to express intention or determination: *we will not give in.* **3** to make requests: *please will you shut the door?* **4** to express commands: *you will apologize to your mother immediately!* **5** to indicate ability: *the table will seat ten.* **6** to indicate readiness or willingness: *any of our branches will exchange the goods / the car simply will not start.* **7** to make an invitation: *will you have a coffee?* **8** to indicate what is bound to be the case: *accidents will happen / the experienced teacher will know when a child is unhappy.* **9** to state what applies in certain circumstances: *an unemployed young person living at home will not receive housing benefit.* **10** to express an assumption or probability: *that will be Ted at the door.* **11** to suggest obstinate resistance to advice: *she will leave her clothes on the floor.* **12** to mean 'will be so good' or 'wish': *consider, if you will... /make what you will of that.* See also SHALL, WON'T. [from Anglo-Saxon *wyllan*]

will² — *noun* **1** the power of conscious decision and deliberate choice of action: *free will / exercise one's will.* **2** one's own preferences, or one's determination in effecting them: *a clash of wills / I did it against my will.* **3** desire or determination: *the will to live.* **4** a wish or desire: *what is your will?* **5** instructions for the disposal of a person's property, etc after death, or the document containing these. **6** one's feeling towards someone else: *felt no ill-will towards her.* — *verb* **1** to try to compel by, or as if by, exerting one's will: *willed herself to keep going.* **2** *formal* to desire or require that something be done, etc: *Her Majesty wills it.* **3** to bequeath in one's will. — **at will** as and when one wishes. **with a will** eagerly; enthusiastically. **with the best will in the world** (*with a negative*) no matter how willing one is or how hard one tries. [from Anglo-Saxon *willa*]

· · · · · · · · · · · · · · · · · · · ·

■ *noun* **1** volition, choice, discretion, decision, option. **2** choice, preference, decision. **3** desire, determination, purpose, resolve, resolution, willpower. **4** wish, desire, inclination, feeling, fancy, disposition, mind, aim, intention, command. *verb* **1** compel, force, push. **2** desire, want, order, command, decree, ordain. **3** bequeath, leave, hand down, pass on, transfer, confer, dispose of.

· ·

willies *pl. noun* (**the willies**) *colloq.* a feeling of anxiety or unease.

willing *adj.* **1** ready, glad, or not disinclined (to do something). **2** eager and co-operative. **3** voluntarily given. [see WILL²]

· ·

■ **1** disposed, inclined, agreeable, compliant, ready, prepared, consenting, content, amenable, biddable, pleased, well-disposed, favourable, happy. **2** eager, enthusiastic, co-operative.

▣ **1, 2** unwilling, disinclined, reluctant.

willingly *adv.* with a willing manner; readily.

willingness *noun* being willing.

will-o'-the-wisp *noun* **1** a light sometimes seen over marshes, caused by the combustion of marsh gas (methane). Also called IGNIS FATUUS. **2** something elusive, such as an unattainable goal. [literally 'Will of the torch']

willow *noun* **1** a deciduous tree or shrub of the genus *Salix* found mainly in the N hemisphere, generally growing near water, and having slender flexible branches, narrow leaves, and spikes or catkins of male and female flowers. It is widely cultivated as an ornamental plant, eg weeping willow. **2** the durable yellowish-brown wood of this tree, which is used to make cricket bats, wicker baskets, high-quality drawing charcoal, and furniture. [from Anglo-Saxon *welig*]

willow herb a plant with willow-like leaves and purple flowers.

willow pattern a design used on pottery, usually in blue on a white background, showing a Chinese landscape with a willow tree, bridge, and figures.

willowy *adj., said of a person, especially a woman* slender and graceful.

willpower *noun* the determination, persistence, and self-discipline needed to accomplish something.

willy or **willie** *noun* (PL. **willies**) *colloq. especially childish* a penis.

willy-nilly *adv.* whether one wishes or not; regardless. [originally *will I, nill I* (or *will ye, he,* etc), will I, will I not]

wilt — *verb intrans.* **1** *Bot., said of a plant organ or tissue* to droop or become limp because there is insufficient water to maintain the individual cells in a turgid state. **2** to droop from fatigue or heat. **3** to lose courage or confidence. — *noun Bot.* one of a number of plant diseases, often caused by fungal infection, in which wilting is the main symptom. [a variant of *wilk,* to wither]

· ·

■ *verb* DROOP, SAG. **1** wither, shrivel, fade. **2** flop, flag, sink, weaken, languish. **3** flag, weaken, wane, languish, fail, ebb.

🔁 *verb* **3** perk up.

· ·

Wilts. *abbrev.* Wiltshire.

wily *adj.* (**wilier, wiliest**) cunning. [from WILE]

· ·

■ cunning, shrewd, scheming, artful, crafty, foxy, intriguing, tricky, underhand, shifty, deceitful, deceptive, astute, sly, guileful, designing, *colloq.* crooked, *colloq.* fly.

🔁 guileless.

· ·

wimp[1] *colloq.* — *noun* a feeble person. — *verb intrans.* (**wimp out**) to back out of doing something through feebleness.

wimp[2] *noun Comput.* a user interface incorporating windows, icons, pull-down menus, and a pointing device such as a mouse or trackball.

win — *verb* (**winning;** PAST TENSE AND PAST PARTICIPLE **won**) **1** *trans., intrans.* to be victorious, come first, or beat one's opponent or rivals in (a contest, race, conflict, war, bet, election, etc). **2** to compete or fight for, and obtain (a victory, prize, etc). **3** to obtain by struggle or effort: *win someone's heart / win a contract.* **4** to earn and get: *win respect.* **5** *old use* to gain the hand of in marriage: *wooed and won her.* **6** to secure for: *her dazzling smile won her the part.* **7** (*also* **win through** or **out**) to be successful, or succeed in getting somewhere, after a struggle. — *noun* a victory or success. — **win someone over** or **round** to persuade them to come over to one's side or opinion. **you can't win** there's no way to succeed, please someone, etc. [from Anglo-Saxon *winnan*]

· ·

■ *verb* **1** be victorious, come first, finish first, triumph, succeed, prevail, overcome, conquer, carry off. **2, 3, 4** gain, acquire, achieve, attain, accomplish, receive, procure, secure, obtain, get, earn, catch. **6** get, net, secure. *noun* victory, success, triumph, conquest, mastery. **win over** or **round** persuade, prevail upon, convince, talk round, convert, sway, influence, charm, allure.

🔁 *verb* LOSE. **1** fail. *noun* defeat.

· ·

wince — *verb intrans.* to shrink back, start, or grimace, eg in pain or anticipation of it; to flinch. — *noun* a start or grimace in reaction to pain, etc. [from Old French *wencier, guenchier*]

winceyette *noun* a soft cotton cloth with a raised brushed surface on both sides. [from Scot. *wincey,* linen or cotton cloth with a mixture of wool]

winch — *noun* **1** a drum-shaped roller round which a rope or chain is wound for hoisting or hauling heavy loads; a windlass. **2** a crank or handle for setting a wheel, axle, or machinery in motion. — *verb* (*usually* **winch something up** or **in**) to hoist or haul it with a winch. [from Anglo-Saxon *wince*]

wind[1] — *noun* **1** the movement of air, especially horizontally, across the Earth's surface as a result of differences in atmospheric pressure between one location and another. **2** a current of air produced artificially, by a fan, etc. **3** an influence that seems to pervade events: *a wind of change.* **4** one's breath or breath supply: *short of wind.* **5** the scent of game, or, for animals, the scent of a hunter or predator, carried by the wind. **6** gas built up in the intestines; flatulence. **7** empty, pompous, or trivial talk. **8** the wind instruments of an orchestra; their players. — *verb* to deprive of breath temporarily: *was winded by her fall.* — **before the wind** *said of a ship* sailing with the wind coming from behind it. **break wind** to discharge intestinal gas through the anus. **down wind from something** receiving, or liable to receive, air laden with the smell, pollutants, etc, from it. **get wind of something** to have one's suspicions aroused or hear a rumour, especially of something unfavourable or unwelcome. **get the wind up** *colloq.* to become anxious or alarmed. **get one's second wind** to recover breath after initial exertion sufficiently to carry on with ease. **in the wind** about to happen. **like the wind** swiftly. **put the wind up someone** *colloq.* to make them anxious or alarmed. **sail close to the wind** to be in danger of going beyond an approved limit. **see which way the wind blows** to assess current opinions, likely developments, etc. **take the wind out of someone's sails** to thwart someone's confident progress; to deflate or humble someone. [from Anglo-Saxon]

· ·

■ *noun* **1** air, breeze, gale, hurricane, tornado, cyclone, bluster, gust, current, air-current. **2** draught, breeze, puff, breath, blast, gust, current, air-current.

· ·

wind[2] *verb* (PAST TENSE AND PAST PARTICIPLE **wound**) **1** (*often* **wind** or **wind something round** or **up**) to wrap or coil, or be wrapped or coiled. **2** *intrans., trans.* to progress on a path with many twists and turns: *winding lanes / the procession wound its way through the streets.* **3** (*also* **wind something up**) to tighten the spring of a clock, watch, or other clockwork device by turning a knob or key. — **wind down 1** *said of a clock or clockwork device* to slow down and stop working. **2** *said of a person* to begin to relax, especially after a spell of tension or stress. **wind something down 1** to lower it by turning a handle. **2** to reduce the resources and activities of a business or enterprise. **wind up** *colloq.* to end up: *wind up in jail.* **wind someone up 1** to make them tense, nervous, or excited. **2** *colloq.* to taunt or tease them. **wind something up 1** to raise it by turning a handle. **2** to tighten the spring of a clock or clockwork device. **3** to conclude or close down a business or enterprise. [from Anglo-Saxon *windan*]

· ·

■ **1** wrap, coil, twist, turn, curl, twine, encircle, furl, wreath, roll, reel. **2** curve, bend, loop, spiral, zigzag, twine, deviate, meander, ramble. **wind down 2** relax, unwind, quieten down, ease up, calm down. **wind up** end up, finish up, find oneself, settle. **wind someone up 1** annoy, irritate, disconcert. **2** taunt, tease, *colloq.* kid, trick, fool. **wind something up 3** close down, end, conclude, terminate, finalize, finish, liquidate.

· ·

windbag *noun colloq.* a person full of pompous, tedious, or trivial talk.

wind band a musical ensemble made up of wind instruments.

windbreak *noun* a barrier, eg in the form of a fence or line of trees, giving protection from the wind.

windcheater *noun* a windproof jacket usually of close-woven fabric.

windchill *noun* the extra chill given to air temperature by the wind.

wind cone a windsock.

winder *noun* a person or thing that winds.

windfall *noun* **1** a fruit, especially an apple, blown down from its tree. **2** an unexpected financial gain, or other piece of good fortune. **3** a payment made to customers of a financial institution when it is demutualized.

⊟ **2** bonanza, godsend, jackpot, treasure-trove, stroke of luck, find.

winding-sheet *noun* a sheet for wrapping a corpse in; a shroud.

wind instrument a musical instrument such as a clarinet, flute, or trumpet, played by blowing air through it.

windjammer *noun Hist.* a large fast merchant sailing-ship.

windlass /'wɪndləs/ *noun* a drum-shaped axle round which a rope or chain is wound for hauling or hoisting weights. [from Norse *windass*, from *vinda*, to wind + *ass*, beam]

windmill *noun* **1** a mechanical device operated by wind-driven sails or vanes that revolve about a fixed shaft, formerly used in W Europe to mill flour. Lightweight metal windmills are used in many developing countries to pump water (eg for land drainage) and to generate electricity. **2** a toy with a set of plastic or paper sails mounted on a stick, that revolve in the wind. — **tilt at windmills** to attack imaginary opponents (with reference to Cervantes' hero *Don Quixote*, who in a crazed state gave battle to windmills, thinking them to be knights).

window *noun* **1** an opening in a wall to look through, or let in light and air; a wooden or metal frame fitted with panes of glass for placing in such an opening; a pane. **2** the area behind a shop's window, in which to display goods on sale: *the skirt in the window.* **3** a glass-covered opening eg at a railway, theatre, etc, at which to purchase one's ticket. **4** a gap in a schedule, etc available for some purpose. **5** *Comput.* an enclosed rectangular area on the visual display unit of a computer, which can be used as an independent screen. Many operating systems allow several windows to be displayed simultaneously, so that a different file can be worked on or a different program run in each window. [from Norse *windauga*, literally 'wind eye']

⊟ **1** pane, light, opening, skylight, rose window, casement, oriel, dormer.

window box a box fitted along an exterior window ledge, for growing plants.

window-dressing *noun* **1** the art of arranging goods in a shop window. **2** the art or practice of giving something superficial appeal by skilful presentation.

Windows *pl. noun trademark* an operating system for personal computers.

window-shopping *noun* the activity of eyeing goods in shop windows as the next-best thing to buying them.

windowsill or **window ledge** *noun* the interior or exterior ledge running along the bottom of a window.

windpipe *noun* the passage running from the back of the throat to the lungs, through which air is drawn into, and expelled from, the body; the trachea.

wind power a renewable energy source generated from winds in the Earth's atmosphere, used to drive machinery, generate electricity, etc.

windscreen *noun* the front window of a motor vehicle.

windscreen-wiper *noun* a device fitted to the windscreen of a motor vehicle, consisting of a rubber blade on an arm moving in an arc, to keep the windscreen clear of rain.

windshield *noun North Amer.* a windscreen.

windsock *noun* an open-ended cone of fabric flying from a mast, eg at an airport, showing the direction and speed of the wind.

windsurfing *noun* the sport of riding the waves on a sailboard; sailboarding.

windswept *adj.* **1** exposed to strong winds. **2** dishevelled from, or otherwise showing the effects of, exposure to the wind.

wind tunnel *Aeron.* an experimental chamber in which fans blow a controlled stream of air past stationary models of aircraft, cars, trains, etc (or their components), in order to test their aerodynamic properties by simulating the effects of movement through air.

windward — *noun* the side of a boat, etc facing the wind. — *adj.* on this side.

windy *adj.* (**windier**, **windiest**) **1** exposed to, or characterized by, strong wind: *a windy place / a windy day.* **2** *colloq.*, *said of speech or writing* long-winded or pompous. **3** *colloq.* nervous; uneasy.

⊟ **1** breezy, blowy, blustery, squally, windswept, stormy, tempestuous, gusty.
⊟ **1** calm.

wine *noun* **1** an alcoholic drink made from the fermented juice of grapes, or one made from other fruits, plants, etc. **2** the dark red colour of red wine. [from Anglo-Saxon *win*, from Latin *vinum*]

winebibber *noun old use* someone who drinks wine to excess.

wine cellar 1 a cellar in which to store wines. **2** the stock of wine stored there.

wine glass a drinking-glass typically consisting of a bowl on a stem, with a wide base flaring out from the stem.

winery *noun* (PL. **wineries**) a place where wine is prepared and stored.

wineskin *Hist.* the skin of a goat or sheep sewn up and used for holding wine.

wing — *noun* **1** one of the two modified forelimbs of a bird or bat that are adapted for flight. **2** one of two or more membranous outgrowths that project from either side of the body of an insect and enable it to fly. **3** one of the flattened structures that project from either side of an aircraft body. **4** any of the corner sections of a vehicle body, forming covers for the wheels. **5** a part of a building projecting from the central or main section. **6** the left or right flank of an army or fleet in battle formation. **7** *Football* either edge of the pitch, or the player at either extreme of the forward line. **8** (**wings**) the area at each side of a stage, where performers wait to enter, out of sight of the audience. **9** a group with its own distinct views and character, within a political party or other body. **10** in the Royal Air Force, a unit consisting of several squadrons. **11** (**wings**) *literary* a miraculous surge of speed: *fear lent him wings.* — *verb* **1** to wound in the wing, arm, or shoulder; to wound superficially. **2** (**wing one's way**) to make one's way by flying, or with speed. **3** *poetic* to fly over, or skim lightly. **4** to send (eg an arrow) swiftly on its way. — **in the wings** waiting for one's turn to perform. **on the wing** flying; in flight. **spread one's wings 1** to use one's potential fully. **2** to escape from a confining environment in order to do this. **take wing** to fly off. **under someone's wing** under their protection or guidance. [from Norse *vængre*]

⊟ *noun* **5** annexe, extension. **9** branch, arm, section, faction, group, grouping, flank, circle, coterie, set.

wing chair an armchair that has a high back with forward-projecting lugs.

wing commander in the Royal Air Force, an officer of the rank below group captain.

winger *noun Football* a player in wing position.

wingless *adj.* not having wings.

wing nut a metal nut with flattened projections for easy turning on a bolt with the finger and thumb.

wingspan *noun* the distance from tip to tip of the wings of an aircraft, or a bird's wings when outstretched.

wink — *verb intrans., trans.* **1** to shut an eye briefly as a form of informal communication with someone, especially as a conspiratorial signal. **2** (**wink at something**) to ignore an offence or improper procedure deliberately; to pretend not to notice it. **3** *said of lights, stars, etc* to flicker or twinkle. — *noun* an act of winking. — **tip someone the wink** *colloq.* to give them a useful hint, valuable information, etc, especially in confidence. [from Anglo-Saxon *wincian*]

. . . .

⊟ *verb* **3** blink, flutter, glimmer, glint, twinkle, gleam, sparkle, flicker, flash. *noun* blink, flutter, sparkle, twinkle, glimmering, gleam, glint.

. . . .

winker *noun old colloq. use* a flashing direction-indicator on a motor vehicle.

winkle — *noun* a small edible snail-shaped shellfish; a periwinkle. — *verb* (**winkle something out**) to force or prise it out. [see PERIWINKLE[2]]

winkle-picker *noun colloq.* a shoe with a long narrow pointed toe.

winner *noun* a person, animal, or vehicle, etc that wins a contest, etc.

. . . .

⊟ champion, victor, prizewinner, medallist, title-holder, world-beater, conqueror.

⊟ loser.

. . . .

winning — *adj.* **1** attractive or charming: *a winning smile.* **2** securing victory: *the winning shot.* — *noun* (**winnings**) money won, especially in gambling.

. . . .

⊟ *adj.* **1** charming, attractive, winsome, captivating, engaging, fetching, enchanting, endearing, delightful, amiable, alluring, lovely, pleasing, sweet. **2** victorious, successful, conquering, triumphant, unbeaten, undefeated.

⊟ *adj.* **1** unappealing. **2** losing.

. . . .

winningly *adv.* in a winning way; attractively, persuasively.

winning post *Racing* the post marking the point where a race finishes.

winnow *verb* **1** to separate chaff from (grain) by blowing a current of air through it or fanning it. **2** (**winnow something out**) to blow (chaff) from grain, to identify and reject what is unwanted from a group or mass. **3** to sift (evidence, etc). [from Anglo-Saxon *windwian*, from *wind*, wind]

. . . .

⊟ **2** separate out, select. **3** sift, screen.

. . . .

wino *noun* (PL. **winos**) *slang* someone, especially a down-and-out, addicted to cheap wine.

winsome *adj. old use* charming; captivating. [from Anglo-Saxon *wynsum*, joyous]

winsomely *adv.* in a winsome way.

winsomeness *noun* a winsome state or quality.

winter — *noun* the coldest season of the year, coming between autumn and spring. — *adj.* of or belonging to winter. — *verb intrans.* (**wintered**, **wintering**) to spend the winter in a specified place, usually other than one's normal home. [from Anglo-Saxon *winter*]

wintergreen *noun* **1** an evergreen plant from which an aromatic oil, used medicinally and as a flavouring, is obtained. **2** this oil.

winter sports sports held on snow or ice, eg skiing and tobogganing.

wintertime *noun* the season of winter.

wintriness *noun* a wintry condition.

wintry *adj.* (**wintrier**, **wintriest**) **1** *said of weather, etc* like or characteristic of winter. **2** unfriendly, cold, or hostile: *a wintry expression.*

. . . .

⊟ COLD, FROSTY, ICY, HARSH. **1** chilly, freezing, frozen, snowy. **2** unfriendly, hostile, bleak, cheerless, desolate, dismal.

. . . .

winy *adj.* (**winier**, **winiest**) having a wine-like flavour.

wipe *verb* **1** to clean or dry with a cloth, on a mat, etc. **2** to dry (dishes). **3** (**wipe something away** or **off**) to remove it by wiping. **4** *Comput.* to erase material from a tape or disk. **5** to remove or get rid of: *wiped the incident from his memory.* **6** to pass (a cloth, etc) over, or rub (a liquid, etc) on to, a surface. — **wipe something out 1** to clean out the inside of it. **2** to remove or get rid of it: *wipe out the memory.* **3** to destroy or obliterate it. [from Anglo-Saxon *wipian*]

. . . .

⊟ **1** clean, dry, dust, brush, mop, swab, sponge, clear. **3** remove, erase, take away, take off. **4** erase, delete. **5** remove, erase, get rid of. **wipe out 2** remove, get rid of, erase, expunge, blot out, efface. **3** obliterate, destroy, eradicate, massacre, exterminate, annihilate, raze, abolish.

. . . .

wiper *noun* same as WINDSCREEN-WIPER.

wire — *noun* **1** metal drawn out into a narrow flexible strand. **2** a length of this, usually wrapped in insulating material, used for carrying an electric current. **3** a cable connecting point with point in a telecommunications system. **4** a telegram or telegraph. **5** a fence, barrier, etc made of wire; wire netting. — *verb* **1** to send a telegram to; to send (a message) by telegram. **2** (*also* **wire something up**) to fit up or connect up an electrical apparatus, system, etc with wires. **3** (*also* **wire something up**) to fasten or secure it with wire. — **get one's wires crossed** to misunderstand or be confused about something. [from Anglo-Saxon *wir*]

wired *adj. colloq.* **1** in a tense, nervous state. **2** connected to the Internet.

wire-haired *adj.*, *said of a dog breed* having a coarse, usually wavy coat.

wireless *noun old use* **1** a radio. **2** wireless telegraphy.

wireless telegraphy the transmission of signals by means of electromagnetic waves.

wire netting wires twisted into network for use as fencing, etc.

wiretap *verb* (**wiretapped**, **wiretapping**) to tap (a telephone) or the telephone of (someone).

wire wool a mass of fine wire used for scouring.

wireworm *noun* the hard-bodied worm-like larva of certain beetles, destructive to plant roots.

wiring *noun* **1** the arrangement of wires that connects the individual components of electric circuits into an operating system, eg the mains wiring of a house. **2** the act of securing with, connecting with, or communicating by wire.

wiry *adj.* (**wirier**, **wiriest**) **1** of slight build, but strong and agile. **2** resembling wire. **3** *said of hair* coarse and wavy.

. . . .

⊟ **1** muscular, sinewy, lean, tough, strong.

⊟ **1** puny.

. . . .

Wis. *abbrev.* Wisconsin.

wisdom *noun* **1** the ability to make sensible judgements and decisions, especially on the basis of one's knowledge and experience; prudence and common sense. **2** learning; knowledge. **3** the weight of informed opinion: *the current wisdom on whether or not to smack children.* **4** *old use* wise sayings. [from Anglo-Saxon *wisdom*]

. . . .

⊟ **1** judgement, judiciousness, prudence, reason, sense, sagacity, astuteness, discernment, penetration, foresight, comprehension, enlightenment. **2** understanding, knowledge, learning, intelligence, erudition.

⊟ **1** folly, stupidity.

. . . .

wisdom literature in the Hebrew Bible, a group of writings, usually including Proverbs, Ecclesiastes, the Song of Songs, and Job. The literature is usually traced to a special class of sages in Israel who sought to draw lessons for life from general human experience rather than from revealed religious truths. The influence of wisdom may also be found in other Biblical stories (eg Esther) and in some of the Psalms; in the Apocrypha it also includes Ecclesiasticus and the Wisdom of Solomon.

wisdom tooth any of the last four molar teeth to come through, at the back of each side of the upper and lower jaw.

wise[1] *adj.* **1** having or showing wisdom; prudent; sensible. **2** learned. **3** astute; shrewd; sagacious. **4** (*in compounds*) knowing the ways of: *streetwise / worldly-wise*. — **be wise to something** *colloq.* to be aware of or informed about it. **none the wiser** knowing no more than before. **put someone wise** *colloq.* to give them necessary information. **wise up** to find out the facts about something. [from Anglo-Saxon *wis*]

⊞ **1, 3** judicious, prudent, sensible, reasonable, well-advised, rational, sound, astute, shrewd, clever, sagacious, experienced, discerning, perceptive, understanding, aware, long-sighted. **2** informed, well-informed, erudite, enlightened, knowing, intelligent, clever.
Ⓕ **1, 3** foolish, stupid, ill-advised.

wise[2] *noun old use* way: *in no wise to blame.* [from Anglo-Saxon *wise*, manner]

-wise *combining form* forming words denoting: **1** direction or manner: *lengthwise / clockwise / likewise / otherwise.* **2** respect or relevance: *money-wise / business-wise.* [from WISE[1]]

wiseacre /ˈwaɪzeɪkə(r)/ *noun derog.* someone who assumes an air of superior wisdom. [from Old Dutch *wijsegger*, soothsayer]

wisecrack *noun* a smart, clever, knowing remark.

wise guy *colloq.* someone full of smart comments; a know-all.

wisely *adv.* in a wise way; with wisdom.

wise man *old use* **1** a wizard. **2** one of the Magi.

wish — *verb* **1** to want; used especially in expressing one's desire. **2** to desire, especially vainly or helplessly (that something were the case): *I wish you'd sit still/I wish I'd known.* **3** (**wish for something**) **a** to long, especially vainly, for it: *often wished for a quieter life.* **b** to make a wish for it: *wished for a new bicycle.* **4** to express a desire for (luck, success, happiness, etc) to come to someone: *wish you all the best.* **5** to say (good afternoon, etc) to: *wished them good day.* **6** (**wish something on someone**) (*with a negative*) to desire it to be inflicted on them: *wouldn't wish it on my worst enemy.* **7** *colloq.* to impose or inflict: *expect she'll wish herself on us for Christmas.* — *noun* **1** a desire. **2** (*usually* **wishes**) what one wants to be done, etc: *we want to respect your wishes.* **3** (**wishes**) a hope expressed for someone's welfare: *best wishes to your parents.* **4** in fairy tales, traditional ritual, etc, the stating of a desire in expectation or hope of its being magically fulfilled: *make a wish.* — **wish someone joy of something** *ironic* to wish them well of some liability, commitment, etc that one is glad to be rid of. [from Anglo-Saxon *wyscan*]

⊞ *verb* **1** desire, want, prefer, need, ask, bid, require, order, instruct, direct, command. **3** *long for* yearn for, hanker after, covet, crave, aspire to, hope for, hunger for, thirst after. *noun* **1** desire, want, hankering, aspiration, inclination, hunger, thirst, liking, preference, yearning, urge, whim, hope. **2** bidding, will, order, command, request.

wishbone *noun* a V-shaped bone in the breast of poultry.

wishful thinking an over-optimistic expectation that something will happen, arising from one's desire that it should.

wishy-washy *adj.* **1** *said eg of colours* pale and insipid. **2** lacking character; insipid. **3** watery; weak.

wisp *noun* **1** a strand; a thin fine tuft or shred. **2** something slight or insubstantial: *a wisp of a child.*

⊞ **1** shred, strand, thread, twist, piece, lock.

wispy *adj.* (**wispier, wispiest**) wisp-like; light and fine in texture, flimsy, insubstantial.

⊞ light, fine, thin, straggly, flimsy, insubstantial, frail, attenuated, fragile, delicate, ethereal, gossamer, faint.
Ⓕ substantial.

wisteria or **wistaria** /wɪˈstɪərɪə/ *noun* a deciduous climbing shrub of the genus *Wisteria*, native to E Asia and N America, and having leaves divided into leaflets, and lilac, violet, or white flowers borne in long pendulous clusters. It is often grown for ornament, and can reach a considerable age, developing thick gnarled stems. [named after the American anatomist C Wistar (or Wister)]

wistful *adj.* sadly or vainly yearning. [from old word *wist*, intent]

⊞ melancholy, sad, forlorn, disconsolate, longing, mournful, thoughtful, pensive, musing, reflective, wishful, contemplative, dreamy, dreaming, meditative.

wistfully *adv.* in a wistful way.

wistfulness *noun* a wistful quality.

wit[1] *noun* **1** humour; the ability to express oneself amusingly. **2** a person with this ability. **3** humorous speech or writing. **4** (*also* **wits**) common sense; intelligence; resourcefulness. — **at one's wits' end** *colloq.* reduced to despair; utterly at a loss. **have or keep one's wits about one** to be, or stay, alert. **live by one's wits** to live by cunning. **scared,** *etc* **out of one's wits** extremely scared, etc. [from Anglo-Saxon *wit*, mind, thought]

⊞ **1, 3** humour, repartee, jocularity, drollery, facetiousness, banter, levity. **2** humorist, comedian, comic, satirist, joker, wag. **4** intelligence, cleverness, brains, sense, reason, common sense, wisdom, understanding, judgement, insight, intellect.
Ⓕ **1** seriousness. **4** stupidity.

wit[2] — **to wit** *old use Legal* that is to say; namely. [from Anglo-Saxon *witan*, to know]

witch *noun* **1** a person, especially a woman, supposed to have magical powers used usually, but not always, malevolently. **2** a frighteningly ugly or wicked old woman. **3** a dangerously or irresistibly fascinating woman. [from Anglo-Saxon *wicca*]

⊞ **1** sorceress, enchantress, occultist, magician. **2** hag. **3** enchantress, siren.

witchcraft *noun* magic or sorcery of the kind practised by witches.

⊞ sorcery, magic, wizardry, occultism, the occult, the black art, black magic, white magic, enchantment, necromancy, voodoo, spell, incantation, divination.

witch doctor a member of a tribal society who is believed to have magic powers, and to be able to cure or harm people by means of them.

witchery *noun* **1** the activities of witches. **2** a bewitching or spellbinding influence; fascination.

witch hazel **1** a N American shrub with narrow-petalled yellow flowers, from whose bark an astringent lotion is produced, used to treat bruises, etc. **2** another name for wych-elm. [from Anglo-Saxon *wice*]

witch hunt the hunting down and persecution of an individual or number of individuals, for alleged political or other types of heresy, behaviour considered dangerous to society, etc.

with *prep.* **1** in the company of: *went with her.* **2** used after verbs of partnering, co-operating, associating, etc: *danced with him / plays with Arsenal.* **3** used after verbs of mixing: *mingled with the crowd.* **4** by means of; using: *raised it with a crowbar.* **5** used after verbs of covering, filling, etc: *plastered with mud / filled with rubbish.* **6** used after verbs of providing: *equipped with firearms.* **7** as a result of: *shaking with fear.* **8** bearing; announcing: *rang with bad news.* **9** in the same direction as: *drift with the current.* **10** at the same time or rate as: *discretion comes with age.* **11** used after verbs of conflict: *quarrelled with her brother / clashes with the curtains.* **12** used after verbs of agreeing, disagreeing, and comparing: *compared with last year / agrees/ disagrees with the evidence.* **13** used in describing: *a man with a limp.* **14** used in stating manner: *won with ease / answered with a nod.* **15** because of having: *with your talents, you'll surely get the job.* **16** in spite of having: *with all his money he's still unhappy.* **17** in (the specified circumstances): *I can't go abroad with my mother so ill.* **18** featuring; starring: *'Treasure Island' with Robert Newton.* **19** in the care of: *left it with the porter.* **20** used after verbs of parting: *parted with her sadly / dispensed with his crutches.* **21** regarding: *what shall we do with this? / I can't do a thing with my hair / what's wrong with you?* **22** used after adverbs and adverbial phrases in exclamations expressing a wish or order: *down with tyranny! / into bed with you!* **23** *colloq.* understanding: *are you with me?* **24** loyal to; supporting: *we're with you all the way.* **— with it** *colloq.* fashionable; trendy. **with that** ... at that point ...; thereupon ... [from Anglo-Saxon *with*]

withal *old use* **— adv. 1** as well; into the bargain. **2** for all that; nevertheless. **— prep.** with: *flesh to bait fish withal.* [from WITH + ALL]

withdraw *verb* (PAST TENSE **withdrew**; PAST PARTICIPLE **withdrawn**) **1** *intrans.* to move somewhere else, especially more private: *withdrew into her bedroom.* **2** *trans., intrans., said of troops* to move back; to retreat or order to retreat. **3** to pull in or back: *withdrew his head into the carriage/ withdrew her hand from his.* **4** to take (money) from a bank account for use. **5** *intrans., trans.* to back out or pull out of an activity: *withdrew from the contest.* **6** to take back, or say that one doesn't mean (what one has said): *I withdraw that remark.* **7** *intrans.* (**withdraw from something**) to stop oneself taking a drug to which one is addicted. **8** *intrans.* to become uncommunicative or unresponsive. **9** to discontinue or cancel: *withdraw a service / withdraw an offer.* [from WITH (= away from) + DRAW]

....

■ **1** retire, leave, depart, go (away), absent oneself. **2** move back, fall back, retreat. **3** draw back, pull back, take away, remove, draw out, pull out, extract, shrink back, recoil. **5** back out, drop out, secede. **6** take back, recant, retract, disclaim, abjure. **9** discontinue, cancel, rescind, revoke, recall.

....

withdrawal *noun* **1** the act or process of withdrawing. **2** a removal of funds from a bank account. **3** *Medicine* the breaking of a drug addiction, with associated physical and psychological symptoms (known as *withdrawal symptoms*), eg trembling, sweating, vomiting, and depression. **4** a retreat into silence and self-absorption. **5** (*also* **withdrawal method**) an unreliable method of contraception in which the penis is removed from the vagina before ejaculation has occurred.

....

■ **1** departure, exit, exodus, retirement, retreat, extraction, removal, repudiation, recantation, disavowal, abjuration, revocation, recall, secession.

....

withdrawal symptom any of a number of symptoms such as pain, nausea, or sweating, experienced by someone who is deprived of a drug to which they have become addicted.

withdrawn *adj.* unresponsive, shy, or reserved.

....

■ unresponsive, shy, reserved, unsociable, introvert, quiet, retiring, aloof, detached, shrinking, uncommunicative, unforthcoming, taciturn, silent.

■ extrovert, outgoing.

....

withe *noun* a pliable branch or twig, especially from the willow tree. [from Anglo-Saxon *withthe*]

wither *verb intrans., trans.* (**withered, withering**) **1** *said of plants* to fade or cause to fade, dry up, and die. **2** to fade or cause to fade and disappear: *love that never withers.* **3** to shrivel or cause to shrivel and decay: *withered old bodies.* [possibly a variant of WEATHER]

....

■ **1** fade, dry up, shrivel, die, wilt, droop. **2** fade, languish, decline, wane, disappear, perish. **3** decay, disintegrate, waste, shrink.

■ FLOURISH, THRIVE.

....

withered *adj.*, *said of a limb* thin and stunted, from illness, etc.

withering *adj.*, *said of a glance, remark, etc* such as makes one shrivel up; bitterly contemptuous.

....

■ scornful, contemptuous, scathing, snubbing, humiliating, mortifying, wounding, devastating.

■ encouraging, supportive.

....

withers *pl. noun* the ridge between the shoulder blades of a horse. [from older *wither*, against]

withhold *verb* (PAST TENSE AND PAST PARTICIPLE **withheld**) to refuse to give or grant; to hold back: *withhold evidence / withhold payment.* [from WITH (= away from) + HOLD]

....

■ keep back, retain, hold back, suppress, restrain, repress, control, check, reserve, deduct, refuse, hide, conceal.

■ give, accord.

....

within **— prep. 1** inside; enclosed by: *within these four walls / circles within circles.* **2** not outside the limits of; not beyond: *live within one's means / within sight.* **3** in less than (a certain time or distance): *finished within a week / within a hair's breadth of death.* **— adv.** *old use* inside: *apply within / a voice from within.* [from Anglo-Saxon *withinnan*]

without **— prep. 1** not having the company of: *went home without him.* **2** deprived of: *can't live without her.* **3** not having: *a blue sky without a cloud.* **4** lacking: *books without covers.* **5** not (behaving as expected or in a particular way): *answered without smiling / did it without being told.* **6** not giving, showing, etc: *complied without a murmur.* **7** not encountering (some expected circumstance): *managed without difficulty / completed the rescue without anyone getting hurt.* **8** not having (something required); in neglect of (a usual procedure): *entered without permission / imprisoned without trial.* **9** not using; not having the help of: *opened it without a key.* **10** if it had not been for: *would have died without their help.* **11** *old use* outside: *without the walls.* **— adv.** *old use* outside. [from Anglo-Saxon *withutan*]

withstand *verb* to resist or brave: *withstand storms / withstand insults.* [from Anglo-Saxon *withstandan*]

....

■ resist, brave, oppose, stand fast, stand one's ground, stand, stand up to, confront, face, cope with, take on, thwart, defy, hold one's ground, hold out, last out, hold off, endure, bear, tolerate, put up with, survive, weather.

■ give in, yield.

....

withy *noun* (PL. **withies**) a withe.

witless *adj.* **1** stupid; brainless. **2** crazy. [see WIT[1]]

witness **— noun 1** someone who sees, and can therefore give a direct account of, an event, occurrence, etc. **2** a person who gives evidence in a court of law. **3** a person who adds his or her own signature to confirm the genuineness of a signature just put on a document, etc. **4** proof or evidence of anything. **— verb 1** to be present as an observer at (an event, etc). **2** to add one's own signature to confirm the genuineness of (a signature on a document, etc). **3** *said of a* *period or place, or of a person* to be the setting for, or to live through certain events: *a century that witnessed great medical advances.* **4** *trans., intrans.* (**witness something** or **witness to something**) to confirm it: *I can witness to his generosity.* — *prep.* as shown by: *politicians do not get everything right, witness the poll tax.* — **bear witness to something** to be evidence of it; to give confirmation of it: *a chaotic mess that bore witness to the struggle / was at home all evening, as my husband will bear witness.* **be witness to something** to be in a position to observe it: *have never before been witness to such cruelty.* [from Anglo-Saxon *witnes*, from *witan*, to know]

- *noun* **1** onlooker, eyewitness, looker-on, observer, spectator, viewer, watcher, bystander. **2** testifier, attestant. *verb* **1** see, observe, notice, note, view, watch, look on, mark, perceive. **2** endorse, sign, countersign. **3** see. **4** confirm, bear out, corroborate, testify to, attest to, bear witness to.

witness box or **witness stand** the enclosed stand from which a witness gives evidence in a court of law.

witticism *noun* a witty remark.

wittily *adv.* in a witty way.

wittiness *noun* a witty quality.

wittingly *adv.* knowingly; consciously. [from Anglo-Saxon *witan*, to know]

witty *adj.* (**wittier, wittiest**) able to express oneself cleverly and amusingly. [see WIT¹]

- humorous, amusing, comic, sharp-witted, droll, funny, facetious, fanciful, jocular, whimsical, original, brilliant, clever, ingenious, lively, sparkling.
- dull, unamusing.

wives see WIFE.

wizard — *noun* **1** a man supposed to have magic powers; a magician or sorcerer. **2** *colloq.* (**wizard at** or **with something**) a person extraordinarily skilled in some way. — *adj. old colloq. use* marvellous. [from Middle English *wisard*, from *wis*, wise]

- *noun* **1** sorcerer, magician, warlock, enchanter, necromancer, occultist, witch, conjurer. **2** expert at, adept at, *colloq.* whizz at, ace at, master of, virtuoso, maestro, prodigy, genius, *colloq.* star.

wizened *adj.* shrivelled or wrinkled, especially with age. [from Anglo-Saxon *wisnian*, to dry up]

- shrivelled, wrinkled, shrunken, dried up, withered, gnarled, thin, worn, lined.

WNO *abbrev.* Welsh National Opera.

WNP *abbrev.* Welsh National Party.

WO *abbrev.* Warrant Officer.

woad /wəʊd/ *noun* **1** a plant from whose leaves a blue dye is obtained. **2** this dye used by ancient Britons to paint their bodies. [from Anglo-Saxon *wad*]

wobble — *verb* **1** *intrans., trans.* to rock or cause to rock, sway, or shake unsteadily. **2** *intrans., said of the voice* to be unsteady. **3** *intrans.* to be undecided; to waver. — *noun* a wobbling, rocking, or swaying motion. [from German *wabbeln*]

- *verb* **1** rock, shake, sway, teeter, totter, tremble, quake, seesaw, vibrate, oscillate. **2** shake, tremble, quiver. **3** waver, dither, hesitate, shilly-shally, vacillate, dodder, fluctuate.

wobbliness *noun* being wobbly.

wobbly *adj.* (**wobblier, wobbliest**) unsteady; shaky.

- unstable, shaky, rickety, unsteady, *colloq.* wonky, teetering, tottering, doddering, doddery, uneven, unbalanced, unsafe.
- stable, steady.

wodge *noun colloq.* a lump, wad, or chunk. [a variant of WEDGE]

woe — *noun* **1** grief; misery. **2** affliction; calamity. — *interj. old use* an exclamation of grief. — **woe betide** ... *old use, facetious* may evil befall, or evil will befall, whoever offends in some specified way. **woe is me** *old use* alas! [from Anglo-Saxon *wa*]

woebegone /'wəʊbɪɡɒn/ *adj.* dismally sorrowful. [from *begone*, surrounded]

woeful *adj.* **1** mournful; sorrowful. **2** causing woe. **3** disgraceful; pitiful.

woefully *adv.* **1** sorrowfully. **2** disgracefully.

woefulness *noun* a woeful quality.

wog *noun Brit. offensive slang* any non-white person. [perhaps from GOLLIWOG]

wok *noun* an almost hemispherical pan used in Chinese cookery. [from S Chinese *wok*]

woke, woken see WAKE.

wold *noun* a tract of open rolling upland. [from Anglo-Saxon *wald, weald*, forest]

wolf — *noun* (PL. **wolves**) **1** either of two species of carnivorous mammal belonging to the dog family (Canidae), and having erect ears, a long muzzle, and a long bushy tail. **2** *colloq.* a man with an insatiable appetite for sexual conquests. — *verb* (*usually* **wolf something down**) *colloq.* to gobble it greedily. — **cry wolf** to give a false alarm. **keep the wolf from the door** to ward off hunger. **wolf in sheep's clothing** a dangerous or powerful person who appears to be harmless. [from Anglo-Saxon]

wolfcub *noun* **1** a young wolf. **2** (**Wolfcub**) formerly, a Cub Scout.

wolfish *adj.* **1** like a wolf. **2** rapacious. **3** ravenous.

wolfishly *adv.* in a wolfish way.

wolfram /'wʊlfrəm/ *Chem. noun* the old name for tungsten. [from German]

wolfsbane /'wʊlfsbeɪn/ *noun* a poisonous yellow-flowered plant; the aconite.

wolf whistle a whistle usually directed at a woman by a man, as a coarse expression of admiration for her appearance.

woman — *noun* (PL. **women**) **1** an adult human female. **2** women generally. **3** one's wife or girlfriend. **4** *old use, affected* a female servant or domestic daily help. **5** feminine instincts: *the woman in her longed for a child.* — *adj.* female: *a woman doctor.* [from Anglo-Saxon *wifman*, from *wif*, wife + *man*, man, human]

- *noun* **1** female, lady, girl.

-woman *combining form* forming words denoting: **1** a woman associated with a specified activity: *policewoman.* **2** a woman who is a native of a specified country or place: *Irishwoman.*

womanhood *noun* **1** the state of being a woman; female adulthood. **2** womankind.

womanish *adj. derog.* **1** associated with women. **2** *said of a man, or his behaviour or appearance* effeminate; unmanly.

womanize or **womanise** *verb intrans. derog. colloq.*, *said of a man* to frequent the company of, or have casual affairs with, women.

womanizer *noun* a person who womanizes.

womankind *noun* women generally.

womanliness *noun* a womanly quality.

womanly *adj.* **1** feminine. **2** considered natural or suitable to a woman.

- FEMININE. **1** female. **2** ladylike, womanish.

woman of the world a woman who is mature and widely experienced.

womb /wu:m/ *noun* **1** the uterus, the organ in female mammals in which the young develop till birth. **2** a place of origin: *the womb of civilization.* **3** *literary* a deep dark centre: *in the womb of the earth.* [from Anglo-Saxon *wamb*]

wombat *noun* a nocturnal marsupial of Australia and Tasmania, well adapted for burrowing, with a compact body, short legs, a large flat head, and no tail. It is the only marsupial with continuously growing incisor teeth. It feeds on grasses, tree roots, and the bark of shrubs. [from Aboriginal *wambat*]

women see WOMAN.

womenfolk *pl. noun* **1** women generally. **2** the female members of a family or society. **3** a man's female relations.

women's liberation a movement, started by women, aimed at freeing them from the disadvantages they suffer in a male-dominated society.

women's studies the study of the history, literature, and contemporary role of women.

won see WIN.

wonder — *noun* **1** the state of mind produced by something extraordinary, new, or unexpected; amazement; awe. **2** something that is a cause of awe, amazement or bafflement; a marvel. — *adj.* notable for accomplishing marvels: *a wonder drug.* — *verb* (**wondered, wondering**) **1** *trans., intrans.* to be curious: *often wondered about her background.* **2** (*also* **wonder at something**) to be surprised by it: *shouldn't wonder if she won / hardly to be wondered at.* **3** to be uncertain or undecided: *I wonder whether to go.* **4** used politely to introduce requests: *I wonder if you could help me?* — **do** or **work wonders** to achieve marvellous results. **no, little,** or **small wonder** it is hardly surprising. [from Anglo-Saxon *wundor*]

▣ *noun* **1** awe, amazement, astonishment, admiration, wonderment, fascination, surprise, bewilderment. **2** marvel, phenomenon, miracle, prodigy, sight, spectacle, rarity, curiosity. *verb* **1** ask oneself, ponder, speculate, question, conjecture, puzzle, inquire, query, think, meditate. **2** be surprised, be amazed, marvel. **3** doubt, ponder, ask oneself, question, query, conjecture.

wonderful *adj.* **1** arousing wonder; extraordinary. **2** excellent; splendid.

▣ **1** amazing, extraordinary, astonishing, astounding, startling, surprising, incredible, remarkable, staggering, strange. **2** excellent, splendid, marvellous, magnificent, oustanding, superb, admirable, delightful, phenomenal, sensational, stupendous, tremendous, *colloq.* super, *colloq.* terrific, *colloq.* brilliant, *colloq.* great, *colloq.* fabulous, *colloq.* fantastic, *slang* stellar.
▣ **1** ordinary. **2** appalling, dreadful.

wonderfully *adv.* in a wonderful way; to a wonderful extent.

wonderland *noun* **1** an imaginary place full of marvels. **2** a scene of strange unearthly beauty.

wonderment *noun* **1** surprise. **2** curiosity. **3** something that stimulates wonder.

wondrous *adj.* wonderful, strange, or awesome.

wondrously *adv.* in a wondrous way; to a wondrous extent.

wonk *noun colloq.* **1** a serious or studious person. **2** a person who is excessively interested in details of political policy.

wonky *adj.* (**wonkier, wonkiest**) *colloq.* unsound, unsteady, wobbly, crooked or ill-made.

wont *old use* — *adj.* habitually inclined, or accustomed. — *noun* a habit that one has: *it was her wont to rise early.* [from Anglo-Saxon *gewunod*, accustomed]

won't *contr.* will not.

wonted *adj.* customary: *with none of his wonted cheerfulness.*

woo *verb* (**woos, wooed**) **1** *old use, said of a man* to try to win the love of (a woman) especially in the hope of marrying her. **2** to try to win the support of: *woo the voters.* **3** to pursue or seek (fame, success, fortune, etc). [from Anglo-Saxon *wogian*]

▣ **1** court, chase, pursue. **2** cultivate, attract, encourage. **3** pursue, seek, look for.

wood — *noun* **1** *Bot.* the hard tissue (secondary xylem) that forms the bulk of woody trees and shrubs. The central *heartwood* provides structural support, enabling many trees to grow to a great height, and is surrounded by the *sapwood*, which is involved in the transport of water from the roots to all other parts of the plant. **2** this material obtained from trees and used as building timber, firewood, and fencing, and for furniture-making, etc. **3** (*also* **woods**) an expanse of growing trees. **4** *Golf* a club with a head made of wood. **5** *Bowls* a bowl. **6** casks or barrels made of wood, for wine or beer: *matured in wood.* — *adj.* made of, or using, wood. — **not see the wood for the trees** to fail to grasp the broad issue because of over-attention to details. **out of the woods** free at last of trouble or danger. **touch wood** (*usually as an exclamation*) to touch something wooden as a superstitious guard against bad luck: *no problems so far, touch wood!* [from Anglo-Saxon *wudu*]

▣ *noun* **2** timber, lumber, planks. **3** forest, woods, woodland, trees, plantation, thicket, grove, coppice, copse, spinney.

wood alcohol methanol.

woodbine *noun* honeysuckle. [from Anglo-Saxon *wudubinde*]

woodchuck *noun* a N American marmot. [from Cree (N American Indian language) *otchek*, marten]

woodcock *noun* a long-billed game bird related to the snipe, but with a bulkier body and shorter, stronger legs.

woodcut *noun* a design cut into a wooden block, or a print taken from it.

woodcutter *noun* a person who fells trees and chops wood.

wooded *adj.*, *said of land* covered with trees.

▣ forested, timbered, woody, tree-covered, *literary* sylvan.

wooden *adj.* **1** made of wood. **2** *said of an actor, performance, etc* stiff, unnatural, and inhibited; lacking expression and liveliness.

▣ **1** timber, woody. **2** stiff, unnatural, inhibited, stilted, lifeless, spiritless, emotionless, unemotional, expressionless, rigid, leaden, awkward, clumsy, deadpan, blank, empty, slow.
▣ **2** lively.

wooden-headed *adj.* dull-witted; unintelligent.

woodenly *adv.* in a wooden manner.

woodenness *noun* being wooden.

wooden spoon a booby prize.

woodland *noun* (*also* **woodlands**) an area of land planted with relatively short trees that are more widely spaced than those in a forest.

woodlouse *noun* (PL. **woodlice**) an insect-like creature with a grey, oval, plated body, found in damp places, under stones, bark, etc.

woodpecker *noun* any of about 200 species of tree-dwelling bird found in woodland throughout the world except for Australasia and Madagascar. They are usually brightly patterned with black, white, green, or red, and have a straight pointed chisel-like bill that is used to bore into tree bark in search of insects, and to drill nesting holes.

wood pigeon a common pigeon of the woods, with a white marking round its neck; the ring dove.

wood pulp crushed wood fibres used in paper-making.

woodruff *noun* a white-flowered, sweet-smelling plant. [from Anglo-Saxon *wuduroffe*]

woodwind *noun* orchestral wind instruments made, or formerly made, of wood, including the flute, oboe, clarinet, and bassoon; the section of the orchestra composed of these.

woodwork *noun* **1** the art of making things out of wood; carpentry. **2** the wooden parts of any structure.

woodworm *noun* (PL. **woodworm**, **woodworms**) the larva of any of several beetles, that bores into wood.

woody *adj.* (**woodier, woodiest**) **1** *said of countryside* wooded. **2** resembling, developing into, or composed of wood: *plants with woody stems*.

woody nightshade a purple-flowered climbing plant with poisonous red berries.

wooer *noun* a person who woos.

woof[1] — *noun* the sound of a dog's bark. — *verb intrans.* to give a bark. [imitative]

woof[2] *noun* Weaving the weft. [from Middle English *oof*, with *w* added by association with WEFT and WARP]

woofer /'wʊfə(r)/ *noun* Electron. a large loudspeaker for reproducing low-frequency sounds. See also TWEETER.

wool — *noun* **1** the soft wavy hair of sheep and certain other animals. **2** this spun into yarn for knitting or weaving. **3** fluffy, curly, or tangled material resembling this: *steel wool*. — *adj.* made of wool; relating to wool or its production. — **pull the wool over someone's eyes** *colloq.* to deceive them. [from Anglo-Saxon *wull*]
....
⊟ *noun* **1** fleece, down.
....

wool-gathering *noun* absent-mindedness; day-dreaming.

woollen — *adj.* **1** made of wool. **2** producing, or dealing in, goods made of wool: *woollen manufacturers*. — *noun* **1** (*often* **woollens**) a woollen, especially knitted, garment. **2** a woollen fabric.

woolliness *noun* a woolly quality.

woolly — *adj.* (**woollier, woolliest**) **1** made of wool, like wool, or covered with wool or wool-like fibres, etc; fluffy and soft. **2** vague and muddled: *woolly thinking / woolly-minded*. — *noun colloq.* a woollen, usually knitted garment.
....
⊟ *adj.* **1** woollen, fleecy, woolly-haired, downy, shaggy, fuzzy, frizzy. **2** vague, muddled, unclear, confused, ill-defined, hazy, blurred, indefinite, nebulous. *noun* jumper, sweater, jersey, pullover, cardigan.
⊟ *adj.* **2** clear, distinct.
....

woolly monkey a New World monkey with a large round head, a long grasping tail, and a short dense dark woolly coat. It feeds on fruit and some insects, and if food is plentiful will eat until its abdomen is markedly swollen.

woolly rhinoceros an extinct rhinoceros, once native to Europe and N Asia, about 3.5m in length, and having a thick coat of long hair, and a snout with two horns. It was hunted by humans in Europe 30,000 years ago.

woolsack *noun* the seat of the Lord Chancellor in the House of Lords, a large square wool-stuffed sack.

woozily *adv.* in a woozy manner.

woozy *adj.* (**woozier, wooziest**) *colloq.* feeling dazed, dizzy, or confused, with senses blurred and hazy.

wop *noun offensive slang* a member of a Latin or Mediterranean race, eg an Italian, especially as an immigrant or visitor. [perhaps from Italian dialect *guappo*, swaggerer]

Worcester sauce /'wʊstə(r)/ a strong-tasting sauce used as a seasoning, made with soy sauce, vinegar, and spices. [from *Worcester*, in England, where it was originally made]

word — *noun* **1** the smallest unit of spoken or written language that can be used independently, usually separated off by spaces in writing and printing. **2** a brief conversation on a particular matter: *I'd like a word with you.* **3** any brief statement, message, or communication: *a word of caution / a word to all pet-owners.* **4** news or notice: *any word of Kate? / I sent word she'd arrive tomorrow.* **5** a rumour: *the word is they are bankrupt.* **6** one's solemn promise: *give one's word / word of honour.* **7** an order: *expects her word to be obeyed / just say the word.* **8** a word given as a signal for action: *wait till I give the word.* **9** what someone says: *remembered her mother's words.* **10** (**words**) language as a means of communication: *impossible to convey in words.* **11** (**words**) discussion in contrast to action. **12** (**words**) the lyrics of a song, etc; the speeches an actor must learn for a particular part. **13** (**the Word**) *Relig.* the teachings contained in the Bible. **14** a watchword: *mum's the word.* **15** *Comput.* **a** a group of bits or bytes that can be processed as a single unit by a computer. The size of a word varies according to the size of the computer. **b** in word processing, any group of characters separated from other such groups by spaces or punctuation, whether or not it is a real word. — *verb* to express in carefully chosen words: *worded her refusal tactfully.* — **as good as one's word** careful to keep one's promise. **have words with someone** *colloq.* to quarrel with them. **in a word** briefly. **in other words** saying the same thing in a different way. **in so many words** explicitly; bluntly. **my word** or **upon my word** an exclamation of surprise. **of many** or **few words** inclined to be talkative (or reserved). **say the word** to give one's consent or approval for some action to proceed. **take someone at his** or **her word** to take an offer, undertaking, etc literally. **take someone's word for it** to accept what someone says as true, without verification. **word for word** repeated in exactly the same words, or translated into exactly corresponding words. [from Anglo-Saxon]
....
⊟ *noun* **1** term, name, vocable, expression, utterance, designation. **2** conversation, chat, talk, discussion, consultation. **3** message, note, remark, warning. **4** information, news, notice, report, communication, message, bulletin, communiqué, statement, dispatch, declaration, account. **6** promise, pledge, oath, assurance, vow, guarantee. **7** order, command, decree, commandment. **8** *colloq.* go-ahead, *colloq.* green light. **9** advice, message, comment, assertion. **11** talk, discussion, chat. **12** lyrics, libretto, lines, text, book. *verb* express, put, phrase, couch, say, explain, write. **have words** have an argument, dispute, quarrel, bicker, row, squabble, disagree, have an altercation.
....

word-blindness *noun* dyslexia.

wordclass *noun* a set of words that share the same grammatical properties, such as inflectional forms or position in a sentence structure: otherwise known as *part of speech*. The grouping of words into classes was first carried out by the Greeks, and there are eight classes recognized in most grammars: noun, verb, adjective, adverb, pronoun, preposition, conjunction, and interjection.

word game any game or puzzle in which words are constructed, deciphered, etc.

wordily *adv.* in a wordy manner.

wordiness *noun* being wordy.

wording *noun* one's choice and arrangement of words in expressing something.

word of honour one's solemn promise.

word of mouth spoken, in contrast to written, communication.

word-perfect *adj.* able to repeat something accurately from memory.

word-processing *noun* the production of text using a word-processor.

word processor *Comput.* a computer system or program that allows the input, processing, storage, and retrieval of text, and so can perform electronically the tasks of typing and editing letters, documents, and books.

wordy *adj.* (**wordier, wordiest**) using too many words to say something; long-winded, especially pompously so.

. . . .

◫ verbose, rambling, long-winded, *formal* loquacious, garrulous, prolix, diffuse, discursive.

▣ concise.

. . . .

wore see WEAR.

work — *noun* **1** physical or mental effort made in order to achieve or make something; labour, study, research, etc. **2** employment: *out of work.* **3** one's place of employment: *leaves work at 4.30.* **4** a task or tasks to be done: *often brings work home with her* / housework. **5** the product of mental or physical labour: *his work has improved* / a splendid piece of work. **6** a literary, artistic, musical, or dramatic composition or creation: *the complete works of Milton.* **7** anything done, managed, made, achieved, etc; activity for some purpose: *good work!* / *works of charity.* **8** (*in compounds*) things made in the material or with the tools specified; the production of such things: *basketwork* / *needlework.* **9** (*in compounds*) the parts of a building, etc using a specified material: *stonework* / *paintwork.* **10** (**works**) building or repair operations: *roadworks* / *the clerk of works.* **11** (**works**) (*often in compounds*) a rampart or defence: *earthworks.* **12** (**works**) *colloq.* the operating parts of eg a watch or machine; the mechanism. **13** (**works**) (*often in compounds*) the place of manufacture of a specified product: *gasworks.* **14** *colloq.* (the **works**) everything possible, available, or going; the lot: *has a headache, fever, cold – the works!* **15** *Physics* the transfer of energy that occurs when force is exerted on a body to move it. — *adj.* relating to, suitable for, etc work: *work clothes.* — *verb* **1** *intrans.* to do work; to exert oneself mentally or physically; to toil, labour, or study. **2** *intrans., trans.* to be employed; to have a job; to perform the tasks and duties involved in a job; to impose tasks on; to cause to labour: *works her staff hard.* **3** to impose tasks on; to cause to labour: *works her staff hard.* **4** *trans., intrans.* to operate, especially satisfactorily: *learn to work a drill* / *does this radio work?* **5** *intrans., said of a plan, idea, etc* to be successful or effective. **6** *intrans.* to function in a particular way: *most relationships don't work like that.* **7** *intrans., said of a craftsman* to specialize in the use of a specified material: *works in brass.* **8** to shape or fashion (metals or other materials); to make by doing this: *earrings worked in silver.* **9** to cultivate (land). **10** to extract materials from (a mine). **11** to knead (eg dough). **12** to cover (an area) as a salesman, etc. **13** *old use* to sew, embroider, etc (eg a handkerchief). **14** to achieve (miracles, wonders, etc). **15** *colloq.* to manipulate (a system, rules, etc) to one's advantage. **16** (*also* **work someone up**) to rouse or stir up: *work oneself into a rage* / *too worked-up to think.* **17** *trans., intrans.* to make (one's way), or shift or cause to shift gradually: *work one's way forward* / *worked the nail out of his sole.* **18** *intrans., said eg of a screw* to become gradually (loose, free, etc). **19** *intrans., said of the face or features* to move uncontrollably with emotion; to contort. **20** to exercise (a part of the body). **21** to earn (one's sea passage) by unpaid work on board. — **give someone the works** *colloq.* to use every measure available in dealing with someone, by way of eg punishment, coercion, or welcome. **have one's work cut out** *colloq.* to be faced with a challenging task. **make short work of something** or **someone** to deal with them rapidly and effectively. **a ... piece** or **bit of work** *colloq.* a person, especially with regard to an unfavourable aspect of character or disposition: *a nasty piece of work.* **work in** *said of workers protesting against closure, redundancy, etc* to occupy work premises and take over the running of the business. **work something in 1** to add and mix an ingredient into a mixture. **2** to find a place for something; to fit it in. **work something off** to get rid of energy or the effects of a heavy meal by energetic activity. **work on something 1** to try to perfect or improve it. **2** to use it as a basis for one's decisions and actions: *working on that assumption.* **work on someone** *colloq.* to use one's powers of persuasion on them. **work out 1** to be successfully achieved: *if things work out.* **2** to perform a set of energetic physical exercises. **work something out** to solve it; to sort

or reason it out. **work someone over** *slang* to beat them up. **work to rule** to reduce efficiency by working strictly to official working rules, especially as a form of industrial action. **work someone up** to excite or agitate them. **work something up** to summon up an appetite, enthusiasm, energy, etc. **work up to something** to approach a difficult task or objective by gradual stages. [from Anglo-Saxon *weorc*]

. . . .

◫ *noun* **1** toil, labour, drudgery, effort, exertion, industry, *colloq.* slog, *colloq.* graft, *colloq.* elbow-grease. **2** occupation, job, employment, profession, trade, business, career, calling, vocation, line, métier, livelihood, craft, skill. **4** task, assignment, undertaking, job, chore, responsibility, duty, commission. **6** creation, production, achievement, composition, opus. **12** machinery, mechanism, workings, action, movement, parts, installations. **13** factory, plant, workshop, mill, foundry, shop. *verb* **1** labour, toil, drudge, slave. **2** be employed, have a job, earn one's living. **4** function, go, operate, perform, run, handle, manage, use, control. **8** manipulate, knead, mould, shape, form, fashion, make, process. **9** cultivate, farm, dig, till. **14** bring about, accomplish, achieve, create, cause, *colloq.* pull off. **work out 1** develop, evolve, go well, succeed, prosper, turn out, *colloq.* pan out. **work something out 1** solve, resolve, calculate, figure out, puzzle out, sort out, understand, clear up. **work someone up** excite, agitate, incite, stir up, move. **work something up** rouse, arouse, animate, stimulate, inflame, spur, instigate, generate.

▣ *noun* **2** play, rest, hobby. *verb* **1** play, rest. **2** be unemployed. **4** fail.

. . . .

workability *noun* being workable.

workable *adj.* **1** *said of a scheme, etc* able to be carried out; practicable. **2** *said eg of a material, mineral source, etc* able to be worked.

workaday *adj.* **1** ordinary; commonplace. **2** suitable for a work day; practical or everyday; not fine.

workaholic *noun colloq.* a person addicted to work. [formed after ALCOHOLIC]

workbasket or **workbox** *noun* a basket or box for holding sewing materials and implements.

workbench *noun* a usually purpose-built table for a mechanic or craftsman.

workday *noun North Amer.* a working day.

worker *noun* **1** a person who works. **2** a person employed in manual work. **3** an employee as opposed to an employer. **4** a male social insect, eg honeybee, ant, that is sterile and whose sole function is to maintain the colony and forage for food. See also DRONE.

. . . .

◫ **1** employee, working man, working woman, wage-earner, breadwinner, proletarian. **2** labourer, tradesman, tradeswoman, artisan, craftsman, craftswoman, hand, operative.

. . . .

workforce *noun* the number of workers engaged in a particular industry, factory, etc; the total number of workers potentially available.

. . . .

◫ workers, employees, personnel, labour force, staff, labour, work-people, shop floor.

. . . .

workhouse *noun Hist.* an institution where the poor can be housed and given work to do.

work-in *noun* the occupation of work premises by employees, especially in protest at closure.

working — *noun* **1** (*also* **workings**) the operation or mode of operation of something. **2** the steps, usually noted down, by which the answer to a mathematical problem is reached. **3** (**workings**) excavations at a mine or quarry. — *adj.* **1** *said of a period of time* devoted to work, or denoting that part that is devoted to work. **2** adequate for one's purposes: *a working knowledge of French.* **— in working order** functioning properly.

▣ *noun* **1** operation, functioning, running, routine, manner, method, action. *adj.* **1** employed, active.

▣ *adj.* **1** idle, inactive, rest.

working capital money used to keep a business, etc going.

working class the wage-earning section of the population, employed especially in manual labour.

working-class *adj.* relating to the working class.

working day 1 a day on which people go to work as usual. **2** the part of the day during which work is done: *an eight-hour working day.*

working majority *Politics* a majority sufficient to enable a party in office to carry through its legislative programme without the risk of parliamentary defeat.

working party a group of people appointed to investigate and report on something.

workload *noun* the amount of work expected of a person or machine.

workman *noun* **1** a man employed to do manual work. **2** anyone performing a craft.

workmanlike *adj.* suitable to, or characteristic of, a good workman.

workmanship *noun* the skill of a craftsman, especially where evident in the appearance of a finished product.

▣ skill, craft, craftsmanship, expertise, finish, art, handicraft, handiwork, technique, execution, manufacture, work.

workmate *noun colloq.* someone who works alongside one in one's place of work; a fellow-worker or colleague.

work of art 1 a painting or sculpture of high quality. **2** anything constructed or composed with obvious skill.

workout *noun* a session of physical exercise or training.

workpiece *noun* an object that is being worked on with a machine or tool.

workplace *noun* an office, factory, or other premises where a person is employed.

works council or **works committee** *Industry* a body on which representatives of both employer and employee meet to deal with labour relations within a business.

workshop *noun* **1** a room or building where construction and repairs are carried out. **2** a course of study or work, especially of an experimental kind, for a group of people on a particular project.

▣ **1** works, workroom, atelier, studio, factory, plant, mill, shop. **2** study group, seminar, symposium, discussion group, class.

workshy *adj. colloq.* lazy; inclined to avoid work.

work station a person's seat at a computer terminal.

work study an investigation of the most efficient way of doing a job, especially with regard to time and effort.

work surface or **worktop** a flat surface constructed along the top of kitchen installations such as fridge and cupboards, on which to prepare food, etc.

work-to-rule *noun* a period of working to rule by employees.

world *— noun* **1** the earth; the planet we inhabit. **2** any other planet or potentially habitable heavenly body. **3** the people inhabiting the earth; mankind: *tell the world.* **4** human affairs: *the present state of the world.* **5** (*also* **World**) a group of countries characterized in a certain way: *the Third World / the New World.* **6** (*also* **World**) the people of a particular period, and their culture: *the Ancient World.* **7** a state of existence: *in this world or the next.* **8** (**the world**) human existence, especially regarded as oppressive and

materialistic, or as distinct from spiritual or intellectual life: *escape from the world.* **9** one's individual way of life or range of experience: *one's own narrow world.* **10** an atmosphere or environment: *enter a world of make-believe.* **11** a particular area of activity: *the world of politics.* **12** a class of living things: *the insect world.* **13** *colloq.* a great deal; a lot: *did her a world of good / are worlds apart. — adj.* relating to, affecting, or important throughout the whole world: *world championships / a world power.* **— be** or **mean all the world to someone** to be important or precious to them. **the best of both worlds** the benefits of both alternatives with the drawbacks of neither. **bring someone into the world** to give birth to or deliver a baby. **come into the world** to be born. **come** or **go up** or **down in the world** to rise (or fall) in social status. **for all the world as if** ... exactly as if ... **in the world** used for emphasis: *how in the world...? / without a care in the world.* **not for the world** not for anything: *wouldn't hurt her for the world.* **on top of the world** *colloq.* supremely happy. **out of this world** *colloq.* extraordinarily fine; marvellous. **think the world of someone** to love or admire them immensely. [from Anglo-Saxon *weorold*]

▣ *noun* **1** earth, globe. **2** planet, star, heavenly body. **3** everybody, everyone, mankind, human race, humankind, humanity, people, universe. **6** times, epoch, era, period, age, days. **7** life. **8** reality. **9** sphere, realm, domain. **10** realm. **11** field, area, province. **12** kingdom, realm, system, society.

world-beater *noun* a person, product, etc that is supreme in its class.

world-class *adj. Sport* of the highest standard in the world.

world-famous *adj.* well known throughout the world.

worldliness *noun* a worldly quality.

worldly *adj.* (**worldlier, worldliest**) **1** relating to this world; material, not spiritual or eternal: *worldly possessions.* **2** over-concerned with possessions, money, luxuries, etc; materialistic. **3** shrewd about the ways of the world; knowing and sophisticated in one's outlook.

▣ **1** temporal, earthly, material, mundane, terrestrial, physical, secular, unspiritual, profane. **2** materialistic, selfish, ambitious, grasping, greedy, covetous, avaricious. **3** worldly-wise, sophisticated, urbane, cosmopolitan, experienced, knowing, *colloq.* streetwise.

▣ **1** spiritual, eternal. **3** unsophisticated.

worldly-wise *adj.* knowledgeable about life; not easily impressed.

world music popular folk music originating in non-western, especially African, cultures.

world-shaking *adj. colloq.* important; significant; momentous.

world war a war in which most of the major world powers take part, especially those of 1914–18 (*World War I*) and 1939–45 (*World War II*).

worldweary *adj.* tired of the world; bored of life.

worldwide *adj., adv.* extending or known throughout the world.

World Wide Web *Comput.* same as INTERNET.

worm *— noun* **1** *Zool.* any member of several unrelated groups of small soft-bodied limbless invertebrates (animals with no backbone) that are characteristically long, slender, and cylindrical in shape, eg annelids (segmented worms such as the earthworm) and flatworms (such as tapeworms). **2** any superficially similar but unrelated animal, eg the larva of certain insects. **3** a mean, contemptible, weak, or worthless person. **4** *Mech.* the spiral thread of a screw. **5** (**worms**) any disease characterized by the presence of parasitic worms in the intestines of humans or animals. **6** *Comput.* an unauthorized computer program designed to sabotage a computer system, especially by reproducing itself throughout a computer network. A worm differs from a virus in that it is an independent program rather than a piece of coding. — *verb* **1** (**worm one's way**) to wriggle or manoeuvre oneself gradually: *wormed their way to the front.* **2** (**worm one's way into something**) to insinuate oneself into someone's favour, affections, etc. **3** (*also* **worm something out**) to extract information, etc little by little: *wormed the secret out of them.* **4** to treat an animal that has worms, especially to rid it of these. [from Anglo-Saxon *wyrm*]

wormcast *noun* a coiled heap of sand or earth excreted by a burrowing worm.

worm-eaten *adj.*, *said eg of furniture* riddled with wormholes.

worm gear 1 a gear consisting of a shaft with a spiral thread that engages with and drives a toothed wheel. **2** (*also* **worm wheel**) the toothed wheel driven in this way.

wormhole *noun* a hole left by a burrowing grub, in eg furniture, books, or fruit.

wormwood *noun* **1** a bitter-tasting herb from which the flavouring for absinthe is obtained. **2** *old use* acute bitterness or chagrin, or a cause of this. [from Anglo-Saxon *wermod*]

wormy *adj.* (**wormier**, **wormiest**) like or full of worms.

worn past participle of WEAR. — *adj.* **1** haggard with weariness. **2** showing signs of deterioration through long use or wear. — **worn out 1** exhausted. **2** too badly worn to be any further use; threadbare.

- **1** exhausted, tired, weary, spent, fatigued, careworn, drawn, haggard, jaded. **2** shabby, threadbare, worn out, tatty, tattered, frayed, ragged. **worn out 1** exhausted, tired out, weary, *colloq.* done in, *colloq.* all in, *colloq.* dog-tired, *colloq.* knackered. **2** shabby, threadbare, useless, used, tatty, tattered, on its last legs, ragged, *colloq.* moth-eaten, frayed, decrepit.
- **worn out 1** fresh. **2** new, unused.

worried *adj.* anxious, concerned, fretting.

- anxious, concerned, troubled, fretting, uneasy, ill at ease, apprehensive, bothered, upset, fearful, afraid, frightened, on edge, overwrought, tense, strained, nervous, disturbed, distraught, distracted, fretful, distressed, agonized.
- calm, unworried, unconcerned.

worrier *noun* a person who worries, especially habitually.

worrisome *adj. old use* causing worry; perturbing; vexing.

worry — *verb* (**worries**, **worried**) **1** *intrans.* to be anxious. **2** to cause anxiety to. **3** to bother or harass. **4** *said of a dog* to tear and pull about with the teeth; to chase and bite (sheep, etc). **5** (**worry at something**) to try to solve a problem, etc. — *noun* (PL. **worries**) **1** a state of anxiety. **2** a cause of anxiety. — **not to worry** *colloq.* an expression of reassurance. [from Anglo-Saxon *wyrgan*, to strangle]

- *verb* **1** be anxious, be troubled, be distressed, agonize, fret. **2** upset, unsettle, disturb, perturb. **3** bother, harass, irritate, annoy, vex, *colloq.* hassle, tease, nag, harry, plague, pester, torment. **4** attack, go for, savage. *noun* **1** anxiety, apprehension, unease, misgiving, fear, disturbance, agitation, torment, misery, perplexity. **2** concern, problem, trouble, responsibility, burden, care, trial, annoyance, irritation, vexation.
- *verb* **1** be unconcerned. **2** comfort. *noun* **2** comfort, reassurance.

worry beads a string of beads for fiddling with, to calm the nerves.

worse — *adj.* comparative of BAD. **1** more bad: *to be blind or deaf — which is worse?* **2** more ill. **3** more grave, serious, or acute. **4** inferior in standard. — *noun* something worse: *worse was to follow.* — *adv.* less well; more badly. — **go**

from bad to worse to get worse; to deteriorate. **might do worse than** ... should consider (doing something). **none the worse for** ... unharmed by (an accident, bad experience, etc). **the worse for something** showing the bad effects of it. **the worse for wear 1** worn or shabby from use. **2** in poor condition. **worse off** in a worse situation, especially financially. [from Anglo-Saxon *wyrsa*]

worsen *verb intrans.*, *intrans.* (**worsened**, **worsening**) to make or become worse.

- exacerbate, aggravate, intensify, heighten, get worse, weaken, deteriorate, degenerate, decline, sink, go downhill.
- improve.

worship — *verb* (**worshipped**, **worshipping**) **1** *trans.*, *intrans.* to honour (God or a god) with praise, prayer, hymns, etc. **2** to love or admire, especially blindly; to idolize. **3** to glorify or exalt (material things, eg money). — *noun* **1** the activity of worshipping. **2** (**His** or **Your Worship**) the title used to address or refer to a mayor or magistrate. [from Anglo-Saxon *weorthscipe*, 'worthship']

- *verb* REVERE, REVERENCE, ADORE, EXALT, GLORIFY, VENERATE. **1** honour, praise, pray to. **2** love, admire, idolize, adulate, deify. *noun* **1** veneration, reverence, adoration, devotion(s), homage, honour, glory, glorification, exaltation, praise, prayer(s), love, adulation, deification, idolatry.
- *verb* **2**, **3** despise, hate.

worshipful *adj.* **1** full of reverence or adoration. **2** (*usually* **Worshipful**) used as a term of respect in the titles of certain dignitaries. **3** worshipping; adoring.

worshipper *noun* a person who worships.

worst — *adj.* **1** most bad, awful, unpleasant, etc. **2** most grave, severe, acute, or dire. **3** most inferior; lowest in standard. — *noun* the worst thing, part, or possibility: *hope the worst is over.* — *adv.* most severely; most badly: *the worst I've ever played.* — *verb* to defeat; to get the better of. — **at its**, etc **worst** in the worst state or severest degree. **at the worst** taking the most unfavourable or pessimistic view. **do your worst** a formula rejecting or defying a threat, etc. **get the worst of something** to lose a fight, argument, etc. **if the worst comes to the worst** if the worst happens. [from Anglo-Saxon *wyrst*]

worsted /ˈwʊəstɪd, ˈwɜːstɪd/ *noun* **1** a fine strong woollen yarn. **2** fabric woven from this. [from *Worstead*, in Norfolk]

wort /wɜːt/ *noun* **1** *combining form* a plant: *liverwort.* **2** *Brewing* a dilute solution or infusion of malt, fermented to make beer and whisky. [from Anglo-Saxon *wyrt*, plant, root]

worth — *noun* **1** value; importance; usefulness. **2** financial value. **3** the quantity of anything that can be bought for a certain sum, accomplished in a certain time, etc: *lost a thousand pounds' worth of equipment / three days' worth of work.* — *adj.* **1** having a value of: *a stamp worth £15.* **2** *colloq.* having money and property to the value of: *she's worth two million.* **3** justifying, deserving, meriting, repaying, or warranting: *worth consideration.* — **for all one is worth** with all one's might. **for all it's**, etc **worth** to the utmost. **for what it's**, etc **worth** worthless though it, etc may be. **worth it** worthwhile. [from Anglo-Saxon *weorth*]

- *noun* **1** worthiness, merit, value, benefit, advantage, importance, significance, use, usefulness, help, assistance, avail, utility, quality, good, virtue, excellence, credit, desert(s). **2** value, cost, rate, price.
- *noun* **1**, **2** worthlessness.

worthily *adv.* in a worthy way; so as to be worthy.

worthiness *noun* a worthy quality.

worthless *adj.* of no value or merit.

- valueless, useless, pointless, meaningless, futile, unavailing, unimportant, insignificant, trivial, unusable, cheap, poor, rubbishy, trashy, trifling, paltry, contemptible, despicable, good-for-nothing, vile. 🔁 valuable, worthy.

worthlessly *adv.* in a worthless way.

worthlessness *noun* being worthless.

worthwhile *adj.* worth the time, money, or energy expended; useful, beneficial, or rewarding.

🔳 profitable, useful, beneficial, helpful, constructive, rewarding, valuable, worthy, good, gainful, justifiable, productive. 🔁 worthless.

worthy — *adj.* (**worthier, worthiest**) 1 *often condescending* admirable; excellent; deserving: *support worthy causes.* 2 (**worthy of something**) deserving it. 3 (**worthy of someone**) suitable to them. — *noun, often condescending* an esteemed person; a dignitary: *the village worthies.*

🔳 *adj.* 1 admirable, excellent, deserving, praiseworthy, laudable, creditable, commendable, valuable, worthwhile, respectable, reputable, good, honest, honourable, decent, upright, righteous. 3 fit, appropriate. 🔁 *adj.* UNWORTHY. 1 disreputable.

would *verb aux.* past tense of WILL used: 1 in reported speech: *said she would leave at 10.* 2 to indicate willingness, readiness, or ability: *was asked to help, but would not / the radio would not work.* 3 in expressing probability: *they would surely have heard.* 4 in indicating habitual action: *would always telephone at 6.* 5 in implying that some happening is predictable or unsurprising: *'She refused.' 'She would.'.* 6 to suggest obstinate resistance to advice: *he would have his own way.* 7 in expressing frustration at some happening: *it would rain, just as we're setting out.* 8 in expressing condition: *in your place, I would have told her.* 9 in making polite invitations, offers, or requests: *would you like to go? / would you rather have a red one? / would you ring her back?* 10 in formulating a desire: *wish she would stop talking.* 11 in politely expressing and seeking opinions: *I would suggest / would you not agree?* — **would that** ... *old use* if only: *would that I were twenty again.* [from Anglo-Saxon *wolde,* past tense of *wyllan*]

would-be *adj.* hoping or aspiring to be: *a would-be actor.*

wouldn't *contr.* would not.

wound[1] see WIND[2].

wound[2] — *noun* 1 any external injury to living tissue of a human, animal, or plant, caused by physical means such as cutting, piercing, crushing, or tearing. Wounds include bruises, grazes, cuts, and burns. 2 an incision made by a surgeon. 3 an injury caused to pride, feelings, reputation, etc. — *verb trans., intrans.* 1 to inflict a wound on (a person, creature, limb, etc). 2 to injure (feelings, etc). [from Anglo-Saxon *wund*]

🔳 *noun* 1 injury, trauma, hurt, cut, gash, lesion, laceration, scar. 3 hurt, distress, trauma, torment, heartbreak, harm, damage, anguish, grief, shock. *verb* 1 damage, harm, hurt, injure, hit, cut, gash, lacerate, slash, pierce. 2 injure, distress, offend, insult, pain, mortify, upset, slight, grieve.

wove, woven see WEAVE.

wow[1] *colloq.* — *interj.* an exclamation of astonishment or admiration. — *noun* a huge success. — *verb* to impress hugely. [perhaps originally Scot.]

wow[2] *noun Electron.* a repeated waver in the pitch of reproduced sound, usually caused by an irregularity in the operating speed of the recording or reproducing apparatus. [imitative]

WPC *abbrev.* woman police constable.

wpm *abbrev.* words per minute.

WRAC *abbrev.* Women's Royal Army Corps.

wrack *noun* 1 seaweed, especially one of the large brown

varieties, floating, cast-up, or growing on the beach. 2 destruction. 3 a wreck or wreckage. [from Old Dutch or Old German *wrak,* related to Anglo-Saxon *wræc,* misery, and *wrecan,* to wreak; in sense 2, a variant of RACK[2]]

WRAF *abbrev.* Women's Royal Air Force.

wraith *noun* 1 a ghost; a spectre. 2 a person of spectral thinness and pallor. [originally Scot.]

wrangle — *verb intrans.* to quarrel or argue noisily or bitterly. — *noun* a bitter dispute. [from German *wrangeln,* related to WRING]

🔳 *verb* argue, quarrel, disagree, dispute, bicker, altercate, contend, fall out, row, squabble, *colloq.* scrap, fight, spar. *noun* argument, quarrel, dispute, controversy, squabble, tiff, row, bickering, disagreement, clash, altercation, contest, *colloq.* slanging match, set-to. 🔁 *verb* agree. *noun* agreement.

wrap — *verb* (**wrapped, wrapping**) 1 to fold or wind round something. 2 (*also* **wrap something up**) to cover or enfold it. — *noun* 1 a shawl or stole for the shoulders. 2 a protective covering. — **keep something under wraps** *colloq.* to keep it secret. **take the wraps off something** *colloq.* to reveal it to the public for the first time. **wrapped up in something** absorbed in it; engrossed by it. **wrap round** 1 *said eg of a piece of clothing* to pass right round with an overlap. 2 *Comput., said of text on a screen* to start a new line automatically as soon as the last character space on the previous line is filled. **wrap up** 1 to dress warmly. 2 *slang* to be quiet. **wrap something up** *colloq.* to finish it off or settle it finally.

🔳 *verb* FOLD, WIND, BIND. 2 cover, envelop, enfold, enclose, shroud, surround, muffle, cocoon, cloak, roll up, bundle up, pack, pack up, package, parcel, immerse. **wrap something up** finish off, settle, conclude, end, bring to a close, terminate, wind up, complete, round off. 🔁 *verb* UNWRAP.

wraparound or **wrapround** *adj., said especially of clothing* designed to wrap round.

wrapper *noun* 1 a paper or cellophane cover round a packet, sweet, etc. 2 the dust jacket of a book.

🔳 1 wrapping, packaging, envelope, cover. 2 jacket, dust jacket, sleeve, paper.

wrapping *noun* (*usually* **wrappings**) any of various types of cover, wrapper, or packing material.

wrasse /ras/ *noun* a brightly coloured bony sea fish. [from Cornish *wrach*]

wrath /rɒθ/ *noun literary* anger; fury. [from Anglo-Saxon *wræththo*]

wrathful *adj. literary* angry.

wrathfully *adv. literary* angrily.

wreak *verb* 1 to cause (havoc, damage, etc) on a disastrous scale. 2 to take (vengeance or revenge) ruthlessly on someone. 3 to give unrestrained expression to (one's anger or hatred). [from Anglo-Saxon *wrecan*]

🔳 1 cause, create, bring about, unleash, perpetrate, bestow, inflict. 2 carry out, exercise, execute, inflict, bestow. 3 vent, express, unleash.

wreath /riːθ/ *noun* 1 a ring-shaped garland of flowers and foliage placed on a grave as a tribute, or hung up as a decoration. 2 a victor's crown of especially laurel leaves. 3 (*usually* **wreaths**) a ring, curl, or spiral of smoke, mist, etc. [from Anglo-Saxon *writha,* something coiled, related to WRITHE]

🔳 2 coronet, chaplet, crown, festoon. 3 band, ring.

wreathe /riːð/ verb **1** to coil, twine, or intertwine. **2** to hang or encircle with flowers, etc. **3** to cover or surround (in smoke, mist, etc). **4** intrans. said of smoke, etc to curl, coil, or spiral. — **wreathed in smiles** smiling broadly or joyously.

wreck — noun **1** the destruction, especially accidental, of a ship at sea. **2** a hopelessly damaged sunken or grounded ship. **3** a crashed aircraft; a ruined vehicle. **4** colloq. someone in a pitiful state of fitness or mental health. **5** something in so advanced a state of deterioration that it cannot be salvaged. **6** colloq. a mess or shambles. **7** the remains of something destroyed: a wreck of his former self. — verb **1** to break; to destroy. **2** to spoil (eg plans, hopes, a holiday, relationship, etc). **3** to cause the wreck of (a ship, etc). [from Middle English wrec, from Old Danish wræce]

. . . .

◨ noun **1** ruin, destruction, devastation, ruination, loss. **3** write-off. **4** mess, disaster. **5** ruin. **6** mess, colloq. shambles, disaster. verb **1** break, destroy, demolish, devastate, shatter, smash, ruin, ravage. **2** spoil, play havoc with, shatter, destroy, smash, ruin.

◳ verb **1** conserve, repair.

. . . .

wreckage noun the remains of things that have been wrecked.

. . . .

◨ remains, debris, rubble, ruin, fragments, flotsam, pieces.

. . . .

wrecker noun **1** someone who criminally ruins anything. **2** Hist. someone who deliberately causes a wreck in order to plunder the wreckage. **3** North Amer. a person whose job is to demolish buildings, vehicles, etc. **4** North Amer. a breakdown vehicle.

Wren noun a member of the Women's Royal Naval Service. [from the initials WRNS]

wren noun a very small songbird with short wings and an erect tail. [from Anglo-Saxon wrenna]

wrench — verb **1** (often **wrench something off** or **out**) to pull or twist it violently. **2** (**wrench someone away**) to force them to leave. **3** to sprain (an ankle, etc). — noun **1** a violent pull or twist. **2** a spanner-like tool for gripping and turning nuts and bolts, etc. **3** a painful parting or separation: leaving home was always a wrench. [from Anglo-Saxon wrencan]

. . . .

◨ verb **1** yank, wrest, jerk, pull, tug, wring, distort. **3** sprain, strain, rick, tear, twist, rip.

. . . .

wrest verb **1** to pull or wrench away, especially from someone else's grasp or possession. **2** to extract with force or difficulty: wrested an admission from her. **3** to grab (victory) from the expected victor. **4** to distort or twist (words) from their true meaning. [from Anglo-Saxon wræstan]

wrestle — verb **1** trans., intrans. to fight by trying to grip, throw, and pinion one's opponent; to do this as a sport; to force to some position in this way: wrestled him to the floor. **2** intrans. to struggle intensely. — noun **1** a spell of wrestling. **2** a struggle. [from Anglo-Saxon wrestlian]

. . . .

◨ verb GRAPPLE, FIGHT, SCUFFLE, TUSSLE. **2** struggle, strive, contend, contest, vie, battle.

. . . .

wrestler noun a person who wrestles.

wrestling noun the activity or sport of wrestlers.

wretch noun **1** a miserable, unfortunate, pitiful creature. **2** humorous a shamelessly wicked person. [from Anglo-Saxon wrecca]

. . . .

◨ RASCAL, SCOUNDREL, ROGUE. **1** villain, good-for-nothing, ruffian, vagabond, miscreant, outcast.

. . . .

wretched adj. **1** pitiable. **2** miserable; unhappy; distressed; distraught. **3** inferior; poor; lowly: a wretched hovel. **4** infuriating: a wretched bore.

. . . .

◨ **1** pitiable, pitiful, pathetic, unfortunate, sorry, hopeless, poor. **2** miserable, unhappy, sad, distressed, distraught, melancholy, depressed, dejected, disconsolate, downcast, forlorn, gloomy, doleful, broken-hearted, crestfallen. **3** inferior, poor, low, lowly, contemptible, despicable, vile, worthless, shameful, mean, paltry. **4** dreadful, awful, deplorable, appalling.

◳ **1** enviable. **2** happy. **3** excellent.

. . . .

wretchedly adv. in a wretched condition or way.

wretchedness noun a wretched state or quality.

wrick same as RICK².

wriggle — verb **1** intrans., trans. to twist to and fro. **2** intrans., trans. to make (one's way) by this means. **3** intrans. (**wriggle out of something**) to manage cleverly to evade an awkward situation, disagreeable obligation, etc. — noun a wriggling action. [from Old German wriggeln]

. . . .

◨ verb **1** squirm, writhe, wiggle, worm, twist, snake, squiggle, zigzag, waggle. **2** squirm, writhe, worm, twist, snake. **3** dodge, extricate oneself from. noun wiggle, twist, squirm, jiggle, jerk, turn, twitch.

. . . .

wriggly adj. (**wrigglier**, **wriggliest**) inclined to wriggle.

wright noun (usually in compounds) a maker or repairer: playwright / shipwright. [from Anglo-Saxon wryhta]

wring verb (PAST TENSE AND PAST PARTICIPLE **wrung**) **1** (also **wring something out**) to force liquid from it by twisting or squeezing. **2** to force (information, a consent, etc) from someone. **3** to break (the neck) of a bird, etc by twisting. **4** to keep clasping and twisting (one's hands) in distress. **5** to crush (someone's hand) in one's own, by way of greeting. **6** to tear at (the heart as the supposed seat of the emotions). — **wringing wet** soaking wet; saturated. [from Anglo-Saxon wringan]

. . . .

◨ **1** squeeze, twist, wrench, wrest, extract, mangle, screw. **2** exact, extort, coerce, force. **5** shake, squeeze. **6** distress, pain, hurt, rack, rend, pierce, torture, wound, stab, tear.

. . . .

wringer noun Hist. a machine with two rollers for squeezing water out of wet clothes.

wrinkle¹ — noun **1** a crease or line in the skin, especially of the face, appearing with advancing age. **2** a slight crease or ridge in any surface. — verb trans., intrans. to develop or cause to develop wrinkles. [from Anglo-Saxon wrinclian, to wind round]

. . . .

◨ noun **1** line. **2** crease, ridge, furrow, corrugation, fold, gather, pucker, crumple. verb crease, corrugate, furrow, fold, crinkle, crumple, shrivel, gather, pucker.

. . . .

wrinkle² noun colloq. a useful tip; a handy hint. [perhaps from Anglo-Saxon wrenc, trick]

wrinkly adj. (**wrinklier**, **wrinkliest**) having wrinkles.

wrist noun **1** the joint between the hand and the forearm. **2** the region surrounding the wrist joint. **3** the part of a sleeve covering this. [from Anglo-Saxon]

wristlet noun a decorative or supporting band for the wrist.

wristwatch noun a watch worn strapped to the wrist.

writ noun a legal document by which one is summoned, or required to do or refrain from doing something. [from Anglo-Saxon writ]

write verb (PAST TENSE **wrote**; PAST PARTICIPLE **written**) **1** trans., intrans. to produce (letters, symbols, numbers, words, sentences, etc) on a surface, especially paper, usually using a pen or pencil. **2** to compose or create (a book, music, etc) in manuscript, typescript, on computer, etc; to be the author or composer of. **3** *intrans.* to compose novels, contribute articles to newspapers, etc, especially as a living. **4** to put down; to inscribe. **5** to make or fill in (a document, form, etc): *write a prescription.* **6** *trans., intrans.* to compose (a letter, etc). **7** to say in a letter, article, book, etc. **8** to put up-to-date information in (one's diary, etc). **9** to include (a condition, etc) in a contract, etc: *wrote a new stipulation into his will.* **10** to fill (pages, sheets, etc) with writing. **11** to display all too clearly: *guilt written all over his face.* **12** *Comput.* to transfer (data) to a memory or storage device. **— write something down 1** to put it down or record it in writing. **2** to reduce its accounting value. **write down to someone** to write in a simplified style for their benefit. **write in** to write a letter formally to an organization, television programme, etc. **write off** to write and send a letter of request. **write something off 1** to damage a vehicle beyond repair. **2** to cancel a debt. **3** to discontinue a project, etc because it is likely to fail. **4** to dismiss something as being of no importance. **write something out 1** to write it in full; to copy or transcribe it. **2** to remove a character or scene from a film, serial, etc. **write something up 1** to write or rewrite it in a final form. **2** to bring a diary, accounts, etc up to date. **3** to write about it or review it, especially approvingly. [from Anglo-Saxon *writan*]

....

▣ **1, 4** pen, record, jot down, set down, inscribe, transcribe, scribble, scrawl. **2** compose, create, pen. **5** scribble, scrawl, compose, pen, fill in, complete. **6** compose, pen, draft, draw up, scribble, scrawl, correspond, communicate. **7** say, state, claim. **write something off 1** wreck, destroy, crash, smash up. **2** cancel, disregard, cross out, delete.

....

write-off *noun* something that is written off, especially a motor vehicle involved in an accident.
writer *noun* **1** a person who writes, especially as a living; an author. **2** someone who has written a particular thing.

....

▣ AUTHOR. **1** wordsmith, novelist, dramatist, essayist, playwright, columnist, diarist, hack, penpusher, scribbler, secretary, copyist, clerk, scribe.

....

writer's cramp painful cramp of the hand brought on by intensive writing.
write-up *noun* a written or published account, especially a review.
writhe *verb intrans.* **1** to twist violently to and fro, especially in pain or discomfort; to squirm. **2** *colloq.* to feel painfully embarrassed or humiliated. [from Anglo-Saxon *writhan*, to twist]

....

▣ SQUIRM. **1** wriggle, thresh, thrash, twist, wiggle, toss, coil, contort, struggle.

....

writing *noun* **1** written or printed words. **2** handwriting. **3** a literary composition, or the art or activity of literary composition. **4** (*usually* **writings**) a literary work: *Bacon's writings.* **5** a form of script: *Chinese writing.* **— in writing** *said of a promise or other commitment* in written form, especially as being firm proof of intention, etc.

....

▣ **1** script, print, scrawl, scribble, hand, handwriting. **2** handwriting, calligraphy, penmanship, scrawl, scribble, hand. **3** document, letter, book, composition, letters, literature. **4** work, publication.

....

writing paper paper for writing letters on.
written past participle of WRITE. — *adj.* expressed in writing, and so undeniable: *a written undertaking.*
written word (**the written word**) written language, as distinct from spoken language.
WRNS *abbrev.* Women's Royal Naval Service.

wrong — *adj.* **1** not correct. **2** mistaken: *quite wrong about her motives.* **3** not appropriate or suitable: *always saying the wrong thing / wrong way up.* **4** not good; not sensible; unjustifiable: *wrong to waste the good weather.* **5** morally bad: *wrong to tell lies.* **6** defective or faulty: *something wrong with the radio.* **7** amiss; causing trouble, pain, etc: *wouldn't cry unless something was wrong with her.* **8** *said of one side of a fabric, garment, etc* intended as the inner, unseen, side. **9** not socially acceptable: *get in with the wrong class of people.* — *adv.* **1** incorrectly: *spelt wrong.* **2** improperly; badly: *timed it wrong.* — *noun* **1** whatever is not right or just: *know right from wrong / do wrong.* **2** any injury done to someone else: *did her wrong.* — *verb* **1** to treat unjustly. **2** to judge unfairly. **— get on the wrong side of someone** *colloq.* to antagonize them. **get something wrong 1** to give the incorrect answer to it, or do it incorrectly. **2** to misunderstand it. **go wrong 1** *said of plans, etc* to fail to go as intended. **2** to make an error. **3** to stray morally; to fall into bad ways. **4** *said of a mechanical device* to stop functioning properly. **in the wrong** guilty of an error or injustice. [from Anglo-Saxon *wrang*]

....

▣ *adj.* **1** incorrect, inaccurate, mistaken, erroneous, false, fallacious, imprecise. **2** mistaken, in error, erroneous. **3** inappropriate, unsuitable, unseemly, improper, indecorous, unconventional, unfitting, incongruous, inapt. **4** bad, unjustifiable, stupid, *colloq.* wicked. **5** unjust, unethical, unfair, unlawful, immoral, illegal, illicit, dishonest, criminal, *colloq.* crooked, reprehensible, blameworthy, guilty, to blame, bad, wicked, sinful, iniquitous, evil. **6** defective, faulty, out of order. **7** amiss, awry. *adv.* **1** inaccurately, incorrectly, wrongly, mistakenly, erroneously, faultily. *noun* **1** sin, misdeed, offence, crime, immorality, sinfulness, transgression, wickedness, wrongdoing, *old use* trespass, unfairness, injustice, iniquity, inequity, infringement, abuse, error. **2** injury, grievance, injustice. *verb* **1** ill-treat, mistreat, maltreat, injure, ill-use, abuse, oppress, cheat, hurt, harm, discredit, dishonour, malign. **2** misrepresent.

◪ *adj.* **1, 2** correct, right. **3** suitable, appropriate, right. **5** good, moral. **8** right. *adv.* right. *noun* **1** right.

....

wrongdoer *noun* a person guilty of an immoral or illegal act.

....

▣ offender, law-breaker, transgressor, criminal, delinquent, felon, miscreant, evildoer, sinner, trespasser, culprit.

....

wrongdoing *noun* evil or wicked action or behaviour.
wrongfoot *verb* **1** *Tennis,* to catch (one's opponent) off balance by making an unpredictable shot, etc to a point away from the direction in which they are moving or preparing to move. **2** to contrive to place (an opponent in a dispute, etc) at a tactical or moral disadvantage; to disconcert.
wrongful *adj.* unlawful; unjust.

....

▣ unlawful, illegal, illegitimate, illicit, dishonest, criminal, unjust, immoral, improper, unfair, unethical, blameworthy, dishonourable, wrong, reprehensible, wicked, evil.

◪ rightful.

....

wrongfully *adv.* wrongly, unjustly, unlawfully.
wrongly *adv.* in the wrong direction or way.
wrote see WRITE.
wroth *adj. old use* angry; full of wrath. [from Anglo-Saxon *wrath*]
wrought *adj.* **1** *old use* made, formed, shaped, or fashioned. **2** *old use* decorated or ornamented. **3** *said of metal* beaten into shape as distinct from being cast. [an old past participle of WORK]
wrought iron a malleable form of iron with a very low carbon content, but containing small amounts of slag as evenly distributed threads or fibres that render it tough

and ductile. It is resistant to corrosion, easily welded, and used to make ornamental ironwork, chains, bolts, pipes, rivets, anchors, etc.

wrought-iron *adj.* made of wrought iron.

wrought-up *adj.* over-excited; agitated.

wrung see WRING.

WRVS *abbrev.* Women's Royal Voluntary Service.

wry *adj.* **1** slightly mocking or bitter; ironic. **2** *said of a facial expression* with the features twisted into a grimace, in reaction to a bitter taste, etc. **3** twisted to one side; awry. [from Anglo-Saxon *wrigian*, to turn, twist]

▣ **1** ironic, sardonic, dry, sarcastic, mocking, droll. **3** twisted, distorted, deformed, contorted, warped, uneven, crooked.
▣ **3** straight.

WS *abbrev.* Writer to the Signet.

wt *abbrev.* weight.

wurst / vʊəst, wɜːst/ *noun* any of various types of large German sausage. [from German literally 'something rolled', related to Latin *vertere*, to turn]

wuss / wʊs/ *noun slang* an ineffectual or cowardly person.

wuther *verb intrans.* (**wuthered**, **wuthering**) *dialect*, *said of the wind* to roar or bluster. [related to Norse *hvitha*, squall]

WV or **W. Va.** *abbrev.* West Virginia.

WVS *abbrev.* Women's Voluntary Service (now WRVS).

WWF *abbrev.* World Wide Fund for Nature (earlier World Wildlife Fund).

WWW *abbrev.* World Wide Web.

WY or **Wy.** *abbrev.* Wyoming.

wych-elm *noun* a tree of the elm family native to N Europe and Asia, with drooping branches and smooth bark. [from Anglo-Saxon *wice*]

wych hazel same as WITCH HAZEL.

Wyo. *abbrev.* Wyoming.

WYSIWYG — *abbrev. Comput.* what you see is what you get, ie the type and characters appearing on screen are as they will appear on the print-out. — *noun* a word-processing facility giving text on screen that closely approximates to printed text, with italic and bold type, etc as required.

X

X¹ or **x** *noun* (PL. **Xs**, **X's**, **x's**) **1** the twenty-fourth letter of the English alphabet. **2** anything in the shape of an X. **3** an unknown or unnamed person.

X² *symbol* **1** *Maths.* (**x**) an unknown quantity. **2** the Roman numeral for 10. **3** a film classified as suitable for people over the age of 17 (in the USA) or 18 (in the UK; now replaced by '18'). **4** a mark used to symbolize a kiss, to indicate an error, the signature of an illiterate person, etc.

x *Maths.* see X².

xanthoma /zanˈθəʊmə/ *noun* (PL. **xanthomata**) *Medicine* a small yellowish lump or swelling in the skin, often on the eyelid. It is formed by deposits of fat, and is usually a symptom of high blood cholesterol. [from Greek *xanthos*, yellow]

X-chromosome *noun Biol.* the sex chromosome that when present as one half of an identical pair determines the female sex in most animals, including humans. There is only one X-chromosome present in the male sex in most animals. See also Y-CHROMOSOME.

Xe *symbol Chem.* xenon.

Xenical /ˈzɛnɪkəl/ *noun trademark* a drug that aids weight control by preventing the absorption of dietary fat.

xenoglossia /zɛnəʊˈɡlɒsɪə/ *noun* the spontaneous use of a language which the speaker has never heard or learned. No scientifically attested case of xenoglossia has ever come to light. See also GLOSSOLALIA. [from Greek *xenos*, strange, foreign + *glossa*, tongue]

xenolith /ˈzɛnəlɪθ/ *noun Geol.* a piece of foreign material that occurs within a body of igneous rock. [from Greek *xenos*, stranger + *lithos*, stone]

xenon /ˈzɛnɒn/ *noun Chem.* (SYMBOL **Xe**, ATOMIC NUMBER **54**) a colourless odourless inert gas (one of the rare or noble gases) that is present in minute traces in the atmosphere. It is used in fluorescent lamps, photographic flash tubes, and lasers. [from Greek *xenos*, stranger]

xenophobe /ˈzɛnəfəʊb/ *noun* a person who practises xenophobia.

xenophobia /zɛnəˈfəʊbɪə/ *noun* intense fear or dislike of foreigners or strangers. [from Greek *xenos*, stranger + PHOBIA]

xenophobic /zɛnəˈfəʊbɪk/ *adj.* relating to or practising xenophobia.

xerographic /zɪərəˈɡrafɪk/ *adj.* relating to or involving xerography.

xerography /zɪˈrɒɡrəfɪ/ *noun* an electrostatic printing process used to make photocopies of printed documents or illustrations. An image of the object to be copied is transferred to a charged drum, and the charge is erased by light reflecting off the white areas of the article. Resinous ink powder (*toner*) adheres to the areas of the drum that remain charged, and is then transferred to paper and fixed to it by heat. [from Greek *xeros*, dry + -GRAPHY]

xerophyte /ˈzɪərəʊfaɪt/ *noun Bot.* a plant that is adapted to grow under conditions where water is very scarce, such as the desert cactus, and showing any of a number of structural modifications, eg swollen stems that serve as a water store. [from Greek *xeros*, dry + *phyton*, plant]

Xerox /ˈzɪərɒks/ — *noun trademark* **1** a type of photographic process used for copying documents. **2** a copying-machine using this process. **3** a photocopy made by such a process. — *verb* (**xerox**) to photocopy (something) using this process. [see XEROGRAPHY]

Xmas /ˈkrɪsməs, ˈɛksməs/ *noun colloq.* Christmas. [formed by substituting *X* for Christ, this being identical to Greek chi = ch]

X-rated *adj.* graphically violent or sexually explicit.

X-ray — *noun* **1** an electromagnetic ray which can pass through many substances that light cannot pass through, producing on photographic film an image of the object passed through. **2** a photograph taken using X-rays. **3** a medical examination using X-rays. — *verb* to take a photograph of (something) using X-rays. [called X because at the time of discovery in 1895, the nature of the rays was unknown]

X-ray astronomy *Astron.* the study of X-ray emissions from celestial objects, using instruments on rockets or satellites (because X-rays from space cannot penetrate the Earth's atmosphere).

X-ray crystallography *Chem.* the study of the arrangement of atoms within a crystal by analysis of the diffraction pattern obtained when a beam of X-rays is passed through the crystal. A pattern of spots, corresponding to the arrangement of atoms, is produced on a photographic plate.

X-ray diffraction *Chem.* the characteristic interference pattern produced when X-rays are passed through a crystal, due to the fact that the wavelengths of X-rays are of a similar size to the distance between atoms in crystals. X-ray diffraction forms the basis of X-ray crystallography.

xylem /ˈzaɪləm/ *noun Bot.* the plant tissue that transports water and mineral nutrients from the roots to all other parts of the plant. It consists of vertical chains of two types of conducting cell (vessels and tracheids), and woody fibres. See also PHLOEM. [from Greek *xylon*, wood]

xylene /ˈzaɪliːn/ or **xylol** /ˈzaɪlɒl/ *noun* a hydrocarbon existing in three isomeric forms, a colourless liquid obtained from coal tar, etc and used eg as a solvent and in the preparation of specimens for microscopy. [from Greek *xylon*, wood]

xylophone /ˈzaɪləfəʊn/ *noun* a musical instrument consisting of a series of wooden, or sometimes metal, bars of different lengths, played by being struck by wooden hammers. [from Greek *xylon*, wood + *phone*, sound]

xylophonist /zaɪˈlɒfənɪst/ *noun* a person who plays the xylophone.

Y

Y[1] or **y** *noun* (PL. **Ys, Y's, y's**) **1** the twenty-fifth letter of the English alphabet. **2** a thing shaped like the letter Y.

Y[2] *abbrev.* yen.

Y[3] *symbol* **1** *Chem.* yttrium. **2** *Maths.* (**y**) the second of two unknown quantities. See also X, Z.

y *symbol Maths.* See Y[3].

-y[1] *suffix* forming adjectives with the sense of 'full of', 'characterized by', 'having the quality of', 'keen on', etc: *spotty* / *icy* / *shiny* / *horsey*. [from Anglo-Saxon *-ig*]

-y[2] an element forming words that are. **1** diminutives or nouns used as terms of affection: *doggy* / *daddy*. **2** nouns denoting people or things with a particular characteristic: *fatty*. [originally Scots, used in names]

-y[3] an element forming nouns denoting. **1** a quality or state: *jealousy* / *modesty*. **2** an action: *entreaty* / *expiry*. [from Old French *-ie*]

Y2K *noun* the year 2000, especially with reference to the millennium bug. [from *Year* + *2K*, abbreviated form of 2000]

yacht /jɒt/ *noun* a boat or small ship, usually with sails and often with an engine, built for racing or cruising.

yacht club a club for yacht-owners.

yachting *noun* sailing in yachts, especially as a sport.

yachtsman or **yachtswoman** *noun* a person who sails a yacht.

yack *derog. slang* — *verb* (**yacked, yacking**) *intrans.* to talk at length and often foolishly or annoyingly. — *noun* persistent foolish or annoying chatter. [imitative]

yah *interj.* **1** an exclamation of scorn or contempt. **2** *colloq.* yes.

yahoo *noun* a lout or ruffian. [named after the Yahoos, a race of dirty, drunken beasts, in Swift's *Gulliver's Travels*]

yak[1] *noun* (PL. **yaks, yak**) a type of long-haired ox found in Tibet. [from Tibetan *gyag*]

yak[2] see YACK.

yakitori *noun* a Japanese dish of boneless pieces of chicken grilled on skewers and basted with a thick sweet sauce of sake, mirin, and soy sauce. [from Japanese, from *yaki*, grill + *tori*, bird]

Yale lock *trademark* a type of lock operated by a flat key with a notched upper edge. [from Linus Yale (1821–68), US locksmith]

yam *noun* **1** any of various perennial climbing plants of the genus *Dioscorea*, cultivated in tropical and subtropical regions for its thick edible tuber. **2** the thick starchy tuber of this plant. **3** *North Amer.* a sweet potato. [from Portuguese *inhame*]

yammer — *verb* (**yammered, yammering**) **1** *intrans.* to complain whiningly; to grumble. **2** *intrans.* to talk loudly and at length. **3** *trans.* to say, especially to make (a complaint), loudly and longly. — *noun* the act or sound of yammering. [from Anglo-Saxon *geomrian*]

yang see YIN.

Yank *noun colloq.* a person from the United States. [a shortening of YANKEE]

yank *colloq.* — *noun* a sudden sharp pull. — *verb trans.*, *intrans.* to pull suddenly and sharply.

⊟ *noun, verb* jerk, tug, pull, wrench, snatch, haul, heave.

Yankee *noun* **1** *Brit. colloq.* a person from the United States. **2** *North Amer., esp. US* a person from New England or from any of the northern states of America. [perhaps from Dutch *Jan Kees*, John Cheese, the nickname given by the New York Dutch to the British settlers in Connecticut]

yap — *verb intrans.* (**yapped, yapping**) **1** *said of a puppy or small dog* to give a high-pitched bark. **2** *derog. colloq.*, *said of a person* to talk continually in a shrill voice, often about trivial matters. — *noun* a short high-pitched bark. [imitative]

⊟ *verb* **1** bark, yelp. **2** chatter, jabber, babble, prattle, yatter, *colloq.* jaw.

yappy *adj.* (**yappier, yappiest**) *said of a dog* inclined to yap or bark.

Yard *noun* (**the Yard**) *colloq.* New Scotland Yard, the headquarters of the London Metropolitan Police.

yard[1] *noun* **1** a unit of length equal to 3 feet (0.9144m). **2** *Naut.* a long beam hung on a mast, from which to hang a sail. [from Anglo-Saxon *gierd, rod*]

yard[2] *noun* **1** (*often in compounds*) an area of (enclosed) ground near a building. **2** (*often in compounds*) an area of enclosed ground used for a special (business) purpose: *a shipyard*. **3** *North Amer.* a garden. [from Anglo-Saxon *geard*, fence, enclosure]

yardage *noun* the length (or, rarely, the area or volume) of something, measured in yards.

yard-arm *noun Naut.* either of the tapering end-sections of a yard.

Yardie *noun* a member of a criminal organization, originally from and based in Kingston, Jamaica, involved in drug-dealing and related crime. [from Jamaican English *yard*, home, dwelling, or (by Jamaicans abroad) Jamaica]

yardstick *noun* **1** a standard for comparison. **2** a stick exactly one yard long, used for measuring.

⊟ MEASURE. **1** criterion, gauge, standard, benchmark, touchstone, comparison.

yarmulka or **yarmulke** /ˈjɑːməlkə/ *noun* a skullcap worn by Jewish men. [from Yiddish]

yarn *noun* **1** thread spun from wool, cotton, etc. **2** a story or tale, often lengthy and incredible. **3** *colloq.* a lie. — **spin a yarn** *colloq.* to tell a long or untruthful story. [from Anglo-Saxon *gearn*]

⊟ **1** thread, fibre, strand. **2** story, tale, anecdote, fable, fabrication, tall story, *colloq.* cock-and-bull story.

yarrow *noun* a strong-scented composite plant with heads of small white flowers. [from Anglo-Saxon *gearwe*]

yashmak *noun* a veil worn by Muslim women, covering the face below the eyes. [from Arabic *yashmaq*]

yaw — *verb intrans.* **1** *said of a ship* to move temporarily from, or fail to keep to, the direct line of its course. **2** *said of an aircraft* to deviate horizontally from the direct line of its course. **3** to move unsteadily; to zigzag. — *noun* an act of yawing.

yawl *noun* **1** a type of small fishing or sailing-boat, especially one with two masts. **2** a ship's small boat, usually with four or six oars. [from Dutch *jol*]

yawn — *verb intrans.* **1** to open the mouth wide and take a deep involuntary breath when tired or bored. **2** *said of a hole, gap, etc* to be or become wide open. — *noun* **1** an act of yawning. **2** *colloq.* a boring or tiresome event, person, etc. [from Anglo-Saxon *ganian*, to yawn, and *geonian*, to gape widely]

yawning *adj.*, *said of a hole, etc* wide; large.
. . . .
◨ wide, gaping, large, huge, vast, cavernous.
. . . .

yaws *sing. noun* an infectious skin disease of tropical countries, causing red swellings.

Yb *symbol Chem.* ytterbium.

Y-chromosome *noun Biol.* the smaller of the two sex chromosomes, whose presence determines the male sex in most animals. In male humans there is one Y-chromosome and one X-chromosome. There is no Y-chromosome in human females. See also X-CHROMOSOME.

yd *abbrev.* yard.

ye[1] *pron. old use, dialect* you (plural). [from Anglo-Saxon *ge*]

ye[2] *definite article old or affected use* the: *Ye Olde Englishe Tea Shoppe.* [from the use of *y* by medieval printers as a substitute for the old letter representing the *th*-sound]

yea / jeɪ/ *interj. old use* yes. [from Anglo-Saxon *gea*]

yeah *interj. colloq.* yes.

year *noun* **1** the period of time the earth takes to go once round the sun, about 365¼ days; the equivalent time for any other planet. **2** (*also* **calendar year**) the period from 1 Jan to 31 Dec, being 365 days, except in a leap year, when it is 366 days. **3** any period of twelve months. **4** a period of less than 12 months during which some activity is carried on: *At this college, the academic year runs from September to June.* **5** a period of study at school, college, etc over an academic year: *she's in third year now.* **6** students at a particular stage in their studies, considered as a group: *had a meeting with the third year this morning.* See also YEARS. — **year in, year out** happening, done, etc every year, with tedious regularity. [from Anglo-Saxon *gear*]

yearbook *noun* a book of information updated and published every year, especially one recording the events, etc of the previous year.

yearling — *noun* an animal which is a year old. — *adj.*, *said of an animal* one year old.

yearly — *adj.* **1** happening, etc every year. **2** valid for one year. — *adv.* every year.
. . . .
◨ *adj.* ANNUAL. **1** per year, per annum, perennial. *adv.* annually, every year, once a year, perennially.
. . . .

yearn / jɜːn/ *verb intrans.* **1** (**yearn for** or **after something** or **to do something**) to feel a great desire or longing; to long for it. **2** (**yearn to** or **towards someone**) to feel compassion for them. [from Anglo-Saxon *giernan*, to desire]
. . . .
◨ **1** long for, desire, want, wish for, pine for, crave, covet, hunger for, hanker for, ache for, languish for, *colloq.* itch for.
. . . .

yearning *noun* a strong desire or longing.

year out a year taken out of studying and spent travelling or gaining work experience. Also called GAP YEAR.

years *pl. noun* **1** age: *he is wise for his years.* **2** *colloq.* a very long time. **3** some period of time in the past or future: *in years gone by.*

yeast *noun* any of various single-celled fungi belonging to the genus *Saccharomyces* of the subdivision Ascomycetes, which are round or oval in shape. [from Anglo-Saxon *gist*]

yeasty *adj.* **1** (tasting or smelling) of yeast. **2** frothy. **3** trivial.

yell — *noun* a loud shout or cry. — *verb intrans., trans.* to shout or cry out. [from Anglo-Saxon *gellan*]
. . . .
◨ *noun* shout, cry, scream, roar, bellow, shriek, howl, screech, squall, whoop. *verb* shout, cry out, scream, bellow, roar, bawl, shriek, squeal, howl, *colloq.* holler, screech, squall, yelp, yowl, whoop.
◨ *noun* whisper. *verb* whisper.
. . . .

yellow — *adj.* **1** of the colour of gold, butter, egg-yolk, a lemon, etc. **2** *derog. colloq.* cowardly: *a yellow streak.* (= a tendency to cowardice). **3** *often offensive* (when used as a term of racial description) having a yellow or yellowish skin. **4** (any shade of) the colour of gold, butter, egg-yolk, etc. **5** something (eg material or paint) yellow in colour. — *verb trans., intrans.* to make or become yellow. [from Anglo-Saxon *geolu*]

yellow-bellied *adj. slang* cowardly.

yellow card *noun Football* a yellow-coloured card shown by the referee as a warning to a player being cautioned for a serious violation of the rules. See also RED CARD.

yellow fever *noun* an acute viral disease of tropical America and West Africa transmitted by the bite of a mosquito, causing high fever, jaundice and haemorrhaging.

yellowhammer *noun* a small brownish bunting, the male of which has a yellow head, neck, and breast.

yellowish *adj.* somewhat yellow; close to yellow.

yellowness *noun* a yellow state or quality.

Yellow Pages *trademark* a telephone directory, or a section of one, printed on yellow paper, in which entries are classified and arranged together according to the nature of the trade or profession of the individuals or companies listed and the services they offer.

yellow spot see FOVEA.

yelp *verb intrans. noun, said of a dog, etc* (to give) a sharp, sudden cry. [from Anglo-Saxon *gielpan*, to boast]
. . . .
◨ *verb, noun* yap, bark, squeal, cry, yell, yowl.
. . . .

yen[1] *colloq.* — *noun* a desire. — *verb* (**yenned, yenning**) (**yen for something**) to feel a longing for it. [from South Chinese dialect *yeen*]

yen[2] *noun* (PL. **yen**) the standard unit of Japanese currency. [from Japanese]

yeoman /ˈjəʊmən/ *noun* (PL. **yeomen**) **1** *Hist.* a farmer who owns and works his own land, often serving as a foot-soldier when required. **2** *Mil.* a member of the yeomanry (sense 2). [from Middle English *yoman*; perhaps from earlier *yongman*, young man]

yeomanry /ˈjəʊmənrɪ/ *noun* (PL. **yeomanries**) **1** *Hist.* the class of land-owning farmers. **2** a volunteer cavalry force formed in the 18c, now mechanized and forming part of the Territorial Army.

yep *interj. colloq.* yes.

yes — *interj.* used to express agreement or consent. — *noun* (PL. **yesses**) an expression of agreement or consent.

yes-man *noun derog.* a person who always agrees with the opinions and follows the suggestions of a superior, employer, etc, especially to curry favour with them.

yesterday — *noun* **1** the day before today. **2** the recent past. — *adv.* **1** on the day before today. **2** in the recent past. [from Anglo-Saxon *giestran dæg*]

yesteryear *noun literary* **1** the past in general. **2** last year.

yet — *adv.* **1** (*also* **as yet**) up till now or then; by now or by that time: *he had not yet arrived.* **2** at this time; now: *you can't leave yet.* **3** at some time in the future; before the matter is finished; still: *she may yet make a success of it.* **4** (used for emphasis with another, more, or a comparative) even; still: *yet bigger problems / yet another mistake.* — *conj.* but; however; nevertheless. — **nor yet ...** and not ... either. **yet again** once more. [from Anglo-Saxon *giet*]

yeti *noun* the abominable snowman, an ape-like creature supposed to live in the Himalayas. [from Tibetan]

yew *noun* 1 (*also* **yew tree**) a type of evergreen tree with dark needle-like leaves and red berries. 2 its wood. [from Anglo-Saxon *iw*]

Y-fronts *pl. noun* men's or boys' underpants with a Y-shaped front seam.

YHA *abbrev.* Youth Hostels Association.

Yid *noun offensive* a Jew. [from YIDDISH]

Yiddish *noun, adj.* (of or in) a language spoken by many Jews, based on medieval German, with elements from Hebrew and several other, especially Slavic, languages. [from German *jüdisch*, Jewish]

yield — *verb* 1 to produce an animal product such as meat or milk, or a crop. 2 to give or produce: *shares yield dividends.* 3 *trans., intrans.* to give up or give in; to surrender. 4 *intrans.* to break or give way under force or pressure. — *noun* 1 the amount produced. 2 the total amount of a product produced by an animal or plant, or harvested from a certain area of cultivated land. [from Anglo-Saxon *gieldan*, to pay]

. . . .

▣ *verb* 1 produce, supply, provide, generate, return, bear, bring forth. 2 give, produce, generate, bring in, supply, provide, furnish, return, earn, pay. 3 give up, relinquish, abandon, abdicate, cede, part with, relinquish, surrender, give in, capitulate, concede, submit, succumb, admit defeat, bow, *colloq.* cave in, knuckle under, resign oneself, go along with, permit, allow, acquiesce, accede, agree, comply, consent. 4 give way, break, cave in, collapse. *noun* 1 product, produce, output, return, earnings, profit, revenue, takings, proceeds, income. 2 harvest, crop, produce, output.

▣ *verb* 3 resist, withstand. 4 hold.

. . . .

yielding *adj.* 1 submissive. 2 flexible. 3 able to or tending to give way.

yin *noun Chinese Philos.* one of the two opposing and complementary principles of traditional Chinese philosophy, religion, medicine, etc, being the negative, feminine, dark, cold, passive element or force as opposed to the positive, masculine, light, warm, active **yang**. [from Chinese *yin*, dark, *yang*, bright]

yippee *interj. colloq.* used to show excitement, delight, etc.

ylang-ylang /ˈiːlaŋˈiːlaŋ/ an evergreen tree (*Cananga odorata*) that grows to a height of 25m, native to Malaysia and the Philippines, and cultivated elsewhere. It has large elliptical leaves, and dull yellow fragrant flowers. Ylang-ylang or macassar oil from the flowers is used in perfumes and aromatherapy. [from Tagalog]

YMCA *abbrev.* in the UK, the Young Men's Christian Association, a charity which promotes the spiritual, social, and physical welfare of boys and young men.

YMHA *abbrev.* Young Men's Hebrew Association.

yob *noun slang* a bad-mannered, aggressive young person (usually male); a lout or hooligan. [a slang reversed form of *boy*]

yobbo *noun* (PL. **yobbos**) *slang.* same as YOB.

yodel — *verb trans., intrans.* (**yodelled, yodelling**) to sing (a melody, etc), changing frequently from a normal to a falsetto voice and back again. — *noun* an act of yodelling. [from German dialect *jodeln*]

yodeller *noun* a person who yodels or is yodelling.

yoga *noun* 1 a system of Hindu philosophy showing how to free the soul from reincarnation and reunite it with God. 2 any of several systems of physical and mental discipline based on this, especially (in western countries) a particular system of physical exercises. [from Sanskrit, = union]

yoghurt or **yogurt** or **yoghourt** *noun* a type of semi-liquid food made from fermented milk, often flavoured with fruit. [from Turkish *yoghurt*]

yogi *noun* a person who practises the yoga philosophy and the physical and mental disciplines associated with it.

yoke — *noun* 1 a wooden frame placed over the necks of oxen to hold them together when they are pulling a plough, cart, etc. 2 a frame placed across a person's shoulders, for carrying buckets. 3 something oppressive; a great burden: *the yoke of slavery.* 4 *technical* the part of a garment that fits over the shoulders and round the neck. — *verb trans.* (**yoke one thing to another** or **two things together**) 1 to join them under or with a yoke (sense 1). 2 to join or unite them. [from Anglo-Saxon *geoc*]

. . . .

▣ *noun* 1 harness. 3 burden, bondage, enslavement, slavery, oppression, subjugation, servility. *verb* 1 harness, hitch. 2 join, unite, couple, link, connect, tie, bracket.

. . . .

yokel *noun derog.* an unsophisticated (usually male) person from the country.

yolk *noun* the yellow part of a bird's or reptile's egg. [from Anglo-Saxon *geolca*, from *geolu*, yellow]

Yom Kippur /jɒm kɪˈpʊə(r)/ the Day of Atonement, an annual Jewish religious festival devoted to repentance for past sins and celebrated with fasting and prayer. [from Hebrew]

yon *adj. literary, dialect* that or those. [from Anglo-Saxon *geon*]

yonder *adj., adv.* (situated) in or at that place over there. [from Middle English]

yonks *noun colloq.* a long time.

yoo-hoo *interj. colloq.* used to attract someone's attention.

yore — **days of yore** *literary* times past or long ago. [from Anglo-Saxon *geara*, formerly]

yorker *noun Cricket* a ball pitched to a point directly under the bat. [probably from the name *Yorkshire*]

Yorkist *Hist.* — *noun* a supporter of the House of York in the Wars of the Roses. See also LANCASTRIAN. — *adj.* relating to the House of York.

Yorks. *abbrev.* Yorkshire.

Yorkshire fog *Bot.* a grass (*Holcus lanatus*) with greyish-green leaves covered with soft hair, which has long white, green, pink, or purple spikelets borne in dense hairy flower-heads.

Yorkshire pudding a baked cake-like pudding of unsweetened batter, served especially with roast beef. [from the name *Yorkshire* in England]

Yorkshire terrier a small long-haired breed of dog.

you *pron.* 1 the person or persons, etc spoken or written to. 2 any or every person: *you don't often see that nowadays.* — **something is you** or **really you,** etc *colloq.* it suits you: *that hat is just you.* [from Anglo-Saxon *eow*, originally accusative and dative of *ge*, ye]

you'd *contr.* 1 you would. 2 you had.

you'll *contr.* 1 you will. 2 you shall.

young — *adj.* 1 in the first part of life, growth, development, etc; not old. 2 in the early stages: *The evening is still young.* — *pl. noun* 1 young animals or birds: *Some birds feed their young on insects.* 2 (**the young**) young people in general. [from Anglo-Saxon *geong*]

. . . .

▣ *adj.* 1 youthful, juvenile, baby, infant, junior, adolescent. 2 immature, early, new, recent, green, growing, fledgling, unfledged, inexperienced. *noun* 1 offspring, babies, issue, litter, progeny, brood, children, family. 2 youth, teenagers, adolescents, children.

▣ *adj.* OLD. 1 adult. 2 mature.

. . . .

young offender institution a place where young criminals between the ages of 14 and 20 are detained and given education and training. Young offender institutions replaced *youth custody centres.*

youngster *noun colloq.* a young person.

. . . .

▣ child, boy, girl, toddler, youth, teenager, *colloq.* kid.

. . . .

your *adj.* belonging to you. [from Anglo-Saxon *eower*, genitive of *ge*, ye]

you're *contr.* you are.

yours *pron.* **1** something belonging to you. **2** (**yours faithfully** or **sincerely** or **truly**) expressions written before a signature at the end of a letter (see FAITHFULLY, SINCERELY, TRULY). — **... of yours** ... of or belonging to you: *a book of yours.*

yourself *pron.* (PL. **yourselves**) **1** the reflexive form of **you**. **2** used for emphasis. **3** your normal self: *don't seem yourself this morning.* **4** (**by yourself**) alone; without help.

yours truly *colloq.* used to refer to oneself, especially with irony or affected condescension: *then yours truly had to go and fetch it.*

youth *noun* **1** (the state of being in) the early part of life, between childhood and adulthood. **2** the enthusiasm, rashness, etc associated with people in this period of life. **3** a boy or young man. **4** (*pl.*) young people in general.

· · · · · · · · · · · · · · · · · · · ·

▣ **1** adolescence, immaturity. **3** boy, young man, adolescent, youngster, juvenile, teenager, *colloq.* kid. **4** young people, the young, younger generation.
◪ **1** adulthood.

· ·

youth club a place or organization providing leisure activities for young people.

youth custody centre see YOUNG OFFENDER INSTITUTION.

youthful *adj.* **1** young, especially in manner or appearance. **2** *said of someone who is not young* young-looking, or having the energy, enthusiasm, etc of a young person. **3** of or associated with youth: *youthful pleasures.*

· · · · · · · · · · · · · · · · · · · ·

▣ **1** young, boyish, girlish, childish, immature, juvenile, inexperienced, fresh. **2** young-looking, active, lively, well-preserved. **3** childish.

· ·

youthfully *adv.* with a youthful manner.

youthfulness *noun* being youthful; a youthful quality.

youth hostel a hostel providing simple overnight accommodation, especially one that belongs to the Youth Hostels Association.

youth hosteller a person who stays at youth hostels, especially regularly.

Youth Training Scheme see YTS.

you've *contr.* you have.

yowl *verb intrans. noun, said especially of an animal*

(to make) a sad cry or howl. [from Middle English *youlen*]

yo-yo — *noun* (PL. **yo-yos**) **1** a toy consisting of a pair of wooden, metal, or plastic discs joined at their centre with a deep groove between them, and with a piece of string attached to and wound round the joining axis within the groove, the toy being repeatedly made to unwind from the string by the force of its weight and rewind by its momentum. **2** anything which resembles such an object in upward and downward movement or variation. — *verb intrans.* (**yo-yoes**, **yo-yoed**) to rise and fall repeatedly; to fluctuate repeatedly in any way. [originally a trademark]

yr *abbrev.* **1** year. **2** your.

YTS *abbrev.* Youth Training Scheme, a British government-sponsored scheme to give training and work-experience to unemployed school-leavers.

ytterbium /ɪ'tɜːbɪəm/ *noun Chem.* (SYMBOL **Yb**, ATOMIC NUMBER **70**) a silvery-white metallic element, one of the rare earth metals. [from the name *Ytterby*, a quarry in Sweden]

yttrium /'ɪtrɪəm/ *noun Chem.* (SYMBOL **Y**, ATOMIC NUMBER **39**) a silvery-grey metal that is used in alloys to make superconductors and strong permanent magnets. Its compounds are used in lasers, microwave filters, and red phosphors for colour television sets. [see YTTERBIUM]

Yuan drama /jʊ'ɑːn/ music theatre written and produced in China during the Yuan dynasty (1280–1369).

yucca *noun* any of a number of household and garden plants, originally from southern USA and Central America, grown for their attractive sword-like leaves and clusters of white flowers.

yucky *adj.* (**yuckier**, **yuckiest**) *colloq.* disgusting; unpleasant; messy. [from *Yuck* or *yuk*, an expression of disgust]

Yule *noun old use, literary, dialect* **1** Christmas. **2** (**Yuletide**) the Christmas period. [from Anglo-Saxon *geol*]

yummy *adj.* (**yummier**, **yummiest**) *colloq.* delicious. [from YUM-YUM]

yum-yum *interj.* an expression of delight at or appreciative anticipation of something, especially delicious food. [imitative]

yuppie or **yuppy** *noun* (PL. **yuppies**) *derog. colloq.* an ambitious young professional person working in a city job. [from *young urban professional*, or *young upwardly-mobile professional*]

yuppie flu *colloq. Medicine* myalgic encephalomyelitis.

YWCA *abbrev.* (in the UK) the Young Women's Christian Association.

YWHA *abbrev.* Young Women's Hebrew Association.

Z

Z¹ or **z** *noun* (PL. **Zs, Z's, z's**) **1** the last letter of the English alphabet. **2** anything in the shape of this letter.

Z² *symbol Maths.* (**z**) a third unknown quantity.

zabaglione /zabaˈljoʊnɪ/ *noun* a dessert made from egg-yolks, sugar, and wine whipped together. [from Italian *zabaglione*]

zakat *noun* the obligatory alms tax of 2½ per cent payable by all Muslims as an annual levy on income and capital. It is the third of the five 'pillars' of Islam. [from Persian, from Arabic *zakāh*]

ZANU *abbrev.* Zimbabwe African National Union.

zany *adj.* (**zanier, zaniest**) amusingly crazy. [from *Zanni*, a N Italian dialect form of *Gianni* or *Giovanni*, John, name of a character in medieval comedies]

⁝⁝⁝⁝⁝⁝⁝⁝⁝⁝⁝⁝⁝⁝⁝⁝⁝⁝

  ▤ *colloq.* crazy, *slang* loony, *colloq.* wacky, clownish, comical, funny, amusing, eccentric, droll.
  ▣ serious.

⁝⁝⁝⁝⁝⁝⁝⁝⁝⁝⁝⁝⁝⁝⁝⁝⁝⁝⁝⁝⁝⁝⁝⁝⁝⁝⁝⁝⁝⁝⁝

zap *verb* (**zapped, zapping**) *colloq.* **1** to hit, destroy, shoot, etc, especially suddenly. **2** *Comput.* to delete all the data in (a file) or from (the main memory of a computer). **3** *intrans.* to change television channels frequently using a remote-control device. **4** *trans., intrans.* to move quickly or suddenly. [imitative]

zapper *noun colloq.* a remote-control device for a television or video recorder.

ZAPU *abbrev.* Zimbabwe African People's Union.

zarzuela /θɑːθʊˈeɪlɑ/ *noun* a type of popular Spanish opera with spoken dialogue. The modern form of zarzuela may be serious or comic in character. [probably from *La Zarzuela*, a royal palace near Madrid, where productions were first staged in the 17c]

zeal *noun* great, and sometimes excessive, enthusiasm or keenness. [from Greek *zelos*]

⁝⁝⁝⁝⁝⁝⁝⁝⁝⁝⁝⁝⁝⁝⁝⁝⁝⁝⁝⁝

  ▤ ardour, fervour, passion, fire, fanaticism, enthusiasm, keenness, eagerness, spirit, zest, gusto, verve, warmth, devotion, earnestness, dedication.
  ▣ apathy, indifference.

⁝⁝⁝⁝⁝⁝⁝⁝⁝⁝⁝⁝⁝⁝⁝⁝⁝⁝⁝⁝⁝⁝⁝⁝⁝⁝⁝⁝⁝⁝⁝

zealot /ˈzɛlət/ *noun* **1** (**Zealot**) *Hist.* a member of the Zealots, a militant Jewish sect which came into prominence in Palestine in the 1c AD. **2** *often derog.* a single-minded and determined supporter of a political cause, religion, etc.

⁝⁝⁝⁝⁝⁝⁝⁝⁝⁝⁝⁝⁝⁝⁝⁝⁝⁝

  ▤ **2** fanatic, extremist, militant, partisan, bigot.

⁝⁝⁝⁝⁝⁝⁝⁝⁝⁝⁝⁝⁝⁝⁝⁝⁝⁝⁝⁝⁝⁝⁝⁝⁝⁝⁝⁝⁝⁝⁝

zealous /ˈzɛləs/ *adj.* enthusiastic; keen.

⁝⁝⁝⁝⁝⁝⁝⁝⁝⁝⁝⁝⁝⁝⁝⁝⁝⁝

  ▤ ardent, fervent, impassioned, passionate, enthusiastic, keen, eager, burning, intense, spirited, fanatical, militant, devoted, earnest.
  ▣ apathetic, indifferent.

⁝⁝⁝⁝⁝⁝⁝⁝⁝⁝⁝⁝⁝⁝⁝⁝⁝⁝⁝⁝⁝⁝⁝⁝⁝⁝⁝⁝⁝⁝⁝

zealously *adv.* enthusiastically.

zebra /ˈzɛbrə, ˈziːbrə/ *noun* (PL. **zebras, zebra**) any of three species of a stocky black-and-white striped mammal with a stubby mane, belonging to the same family (Equidae) as the horse and ass, and found in Africa, south of the Sahara. [from an African language]

zebra crossing *Brit.* a pedestrian crossing marked by black and white stripes.

zebu /ˈziːbjuː/ *noun* a domesticated ox found in parts of Africa and Asia. [from French *zébu*]

zed *Brit. noun* the name of the letter Z. [from French *zède*, from Greek *zeta*]

zee *North Amer. noun* the name of the letter Z.

Zend-Avesta *noun* the Zoroastrian sacred writings, comprising the scriptures (the *Avesta*) and a commentary on them (the *Zend*). [from Old Persian *zand*, commentary, *avastak*, text]

zenith *noun* **1** *Astron.* the point on the celestial sphere that is directly above the observer. It is diametrically opposite the nadir. See also NADIR. **2** the highest point. [from Arabic *samt-ar-ras*, direction of the head]

⁝⁝⁝⁝⁝⁝⁝⁝⁝⁝⁝⁝⁝⁝⁝⁝⁝⁝

  ▤ **2** high point, top, summit, peak, height, pinnacle, apex, optimum, climax, culmination, acme, meridian, vertex.
  ▣ NADIR.

⁝⁝⁝⁝⁝⁝⁝⁝⁝⁝⁝⁝⁝⁝⁝⁝⁝⁝⁝⁝⁝⁝⁝⁝⁝⁝⁝⁝⁝⁝⁝

zeolite *noun Geol.* any of a group of hydrated aluminosilicate minerals, usually containing sodium, potassium, or calcium. They are widely used as 'molecular sieves' for separating substances, and as water softeners. [from Greek *zeein* to boil (in allusion to the fact that many swell up when heated with a blowpipe) + *lithos*, stone]

zephyr /ˈzɛfə(r)/ *noun literary* a light, gentle breeze. [from Greek *Zephyros*, the west wind]

zero — *noun* (PL. **zeros**) **1** the number or figure 0. **2** the point on a scale (eg on a thermometer) which is taken as the base from which measurements may be made: *5 degrees below zero.* **3** zero hour. See also ABSOLUTE ZERO. — *adj.* **1** of no measurable size. **2** *colloq.* not any; no. — *verb* (**zeroes, zeroed**) to set to zero on a scale. — **zero in on something 1** to aim for it; to move towards it. **2** to focus one's attention on it. **3** to aim a weapon at it. [from French *zéro*, from Arabic *sifr*]

⁝⁝⁝⁝⁝⁝⁝⁝⁝⁝⁝⁝⁝⁝⁝⁝⁝⁝⁝⁝

  ▤ *noun* **1** nothing, nought, nil, *slang* zilch, duck, love.

⁝⁝⁝⁝⁝⁝⁝⁝⁝⁝⁝⁝⁝⁝⁝⁝⁝⁝⁝⁝⁝⁝⁝⁝⁝⁝⁝⁝⁝⁝⁝

zero grazing a feeding system, often used on extensively stocked farms, where freshly cut grass is fed to livestock which are confined in a building, yard, or paddock. It makes use of grass from, eg, outlying or unfenced pastures, and reduces wastage from the fouling and selective grazing that often occurs when animals are allowed to graze freely.

zero hour 1 the exact time fixed for something to happen. **2** the time at which a military operation, etc is fixed to begin.

zero-rated *adj., said of goods* on which the buyer pays no VAT, and on which the seller can claim back any VAT he or she has paid.

zero tolerance total non-tolerance of something, especially crime or a social wrong.

zest *noun* **1** keen enjoyment; enthusiasm. **2** something that adds to one's enjoyment of something. **3** *Cookery* the peel of an orange or lemon, used for flavouring.

▣ **1** enjoyment, enthusiasm, gusto, appetite, keenness, zeal, exuberance, interest. **2** spice, tang, relish, savour, piquancy.

▣ **1** apathy.

zestful *adj.* keen; full of enjoyment.

zestfully *adv.* with zest.

zeugma /'zjuːgmə/ *noun* a figure of speech in which an adjective or verb is applied to two nouns although strictly it is appropriate to only one of them, as in *weeping eyes and hearts*. [from Greek *zeugma*, yoking together]

ziggurat /'zɪgʊrat/ *noun* a pyramid-like temple in ancient Mesopotamia. [from Assyrian *ziqquratu*, mountaintop]

zigzag — *noun* **1** (*usually* zigzags) one of two or more sharp bends to right and left in a path, etc. **2** a path, road, etc with a number of such bends. — *adj.*, *said of a path, road, etc* having sharp bends to right and left. — *verb* (**zigzagged, zigzagging**) to move in a zigzag path or manner. [from French *zigzag*, from German *Zickzack*]

▣ *adj.* meandering, crooked, serpentine, sinuous, twisting, winding. *verb* meander, snake, wind, twist, curve.

▣ *adj.* straight.

zilch *noun* slang nothing.

zillion *noun colloq.* a very large but unspecified number. [by analogy with *million*, *billion*, etc]

Zimmer *noun trademark* a three-sided tubular metal frame, used as a support for walking by the disabled or infirm. [the name of the original manufacturer]

zinc *noun Chem.* (SYMBOL **Zn**, ATOMIC NUMBER **30**) a brittle bluish-white metal that occurs in the ores zinc blende (sphalerite) and smithsonite. It is used in dry batteries, various alloys, eg brass and bronze, and as a corrosion-resistant coating to galvanize steel. Its compounds are used in medicines and pigments. [from German *Zink*]

zincite *noun Geol.* a yellow, orange, or dark red mineral form of zinc oxide, often also containing small amounts of manganese, that is an important ore of zinc.

zinc ointment a soothing antiseptic ointment containing zinc oxide.

zine /ziːn/ *noun slang* a magazine, especially one aimed at a special-interest group. [a shortening of MAGAZINE]

zing — *noun* **1** a short high-pitched humming sound, as made by a bullet or vibrating string. **2** *colloq.* zest or vitality. — *verb intrans.* to move very quickly, especially making a high-pitched hum. [imitative]

zinnia *noun* an originally tropical American plant cultivated for its showy flowers. [named after J G Zinn (1727–59), German botanist]

Zionism /'zaɪənɪzm/ *noun* the movement which worked for the establishment of a national homeland in Palestine for Jews and now supports the state of Israel.

Zionist /'zaɪənɪst/ *noun* a supporter of Zionism. — *adj.* characteristic of or supporting Zionism.

zip — *noun* **1** (*also* zip fastener) a device for fastening clothes, bags, etc, in which two rows of metal or nylon teeth are made to fit into each other when a sliding tab is pulled along them. **2** a whizzing sound. **3** *colloq.* energy; vitality. **4** *Comput.* a type of file which has been compressed into a standard format. — *verb* (**zipped, zipping**) **1** *trans., intrans.* (*also* zip up) to fasten, or be fastened, with a zip fastener. **2** (*intrans.*) to make, or move with, a whizzing sound. [imitative]

zip code in the US, a postal code, having the form of a five-figure number. [from zone improvement plan]

zipper *North Amer.* a zip fastener.

zippy *adj.* (**zippier, zippiest**) *colloq.* lively; quick.

zircon *noun Geol.* a hard mineral form of zirconium silicate, which is the main ore of zirconium, and an important source of hafnium and thorium. It occurs in various coloured forms, and colourless varieties are used as semi-precious gemstones. [from German *Zirkon*; originally from Persian *zargun*, golden]

zirconium *noun Chem.* (SYMBOL **Zr**, ATOMIC NUMBER **40**) a silvery-grey metal that is resistant to corrosion and absorbs neutrons, used in certain alloys, and as a coating for fuel rods in nuclear reactors. [from ZIRCON]

zither *noun* a musical instrument consisting of a flat wooden sound-box, one section of which has frets on it, over which strings (usually metal) are stretched, the instrument being played resting on a table or on the player's knees. [from German *Zither*]

Zn *symbol Chem.* zinc.

zodiac *noun* **1** (the zodiac) *Astron.* the band of sky that extends 8° on either side of the Sun's ecliptic (apparent path). It is divided into 12 equal parts, each containing one of the zodiacal constellations, ie Aries, Taurus, Gemini, Cancer, Leo, Virgo, Libra, Scorpius, Sagittarius, Capricornus, Aquarius, and Pisces. **2** *Astrol.* a chart or diagram, usually circular, representing this belt. [from Old French *zodiaque*, from Greek *zoidiakos*, from *zoidion*, a figure of a small animal]

The signs of the zodiac (with their symbols) are: Aries (Ram), Taurus (Bull), Gemini (Twins), Cancer (Crab), Leo (Lion), Virgo (Virgin), Libra (Balance), Scorpio (Scorpion), Sagittarius (Archer), Capricorn (Goat), Aquarius (Water-bearer), Pisces (Fishes).

zombie or **zombi** *noun* **1** a corpse brought to life again by magic. **2** *derog. colloq.* a slow-moving, stupid, unresponsive, or apathetic person. [from Kongo (W African language) *zumbi*, fetish]

zonal *adj.* **1** relating to a zone or zones. **2** arranged in zones.

zone — *noun* **1** an area or region of a country, town, etc, especially one marked out for a special purpose or by a particular feature. **2** any of the five horizontal bands into which the Earth's surface is divided by the Arctic Circle, the Tropic of Cancer, the Tropic of Capricorn and the Antarctic Circle. — *verb* **1** (zone something off) to divide it into zones; to mark it as a zone. **2** to assign to a particular zone. [from Latin *zona*, girdle]

▣ *noun* REGION, AREA, SECTION, SECTOR, BELT. **1** district, territory.

zonked *adj.* **1** *colloq.* exhausted. **2** *slang* under the influence of drugs or alcohol. [imitative]

zoo *noun* a place where wild animals are kept for the public to see, and for study, breeding, etc. [a shortening of ZOOLOGICAL GARDEN]

zoological /zuːə'lɒdʒɪkəl, zoʊə'lɒdʒɪkəl/ *adj.* relating to or involving zoology.

zoological garden *formal* a zoo.

zoologically *adv.* in a zoological way; in terms of zoology.

zoologist /zʊ'ɒlədʒɪst, zoʊ'ɒlədʒɪst/ *noun* a person who studies zoology.

zoology /zʊ'ɒlədʒɪ, zoʊ'ɒlədʒɪ/ *noun* the scientific study of animals, including their structure, function, behaviour, ecology, evolution, and classification. [from Greek *zoion*, animal + -LOGY]

zoom — *verb* **1** *intrans., trans.* (*often* zoom over, past, etc) to move or cause to move very quickly, making a loud, low-pitched, buzzing noise. **2** (zoom away, off, etc) to move very quickly. **3** *intrans.* to increase quickly: *prices have zoomed in the past year.* — *noun* the act or sound of zooming. — **zoom in on someone** or **something** to direct a camera towards them, using a zoom lens to make them appear closer. [imitative]

▣ *verb* **1, 2** race, rush, tear, dash, speed, fly, hurtle, streak, flash, shoot, whirl, dive, buzz, zip. **3** soar, *colloq.* skyrocket, spiral.

zoom lens a type of camera lens which can be used to make a distant object appear gradually closer or further away without the camera being moved and without loss of focus.

zoophyte /'zoʊəfaɪt/ *noun Biol.* any of various invertebrate animals which resemble plants, such as sponges, corals and sea anemones. [from Greek *zoion*, animal + *phyton*, plant]

zooplankton /zoʊə'plaŋktən/ *noun Zool.* the part of the plankton that is composed of passively drifting or floating microscopic animals.

Zoroastrian /zɒroʊ'astrɪən/ — *noun* a follower of Zoroastrianism. — *adj.* relating to or characteristic of Zoroastrianism.

Zoroastrianism /zɒroʊ'astrɪənɪzm/ *noun* an ancient religion of Persian origin founded or reformed by the Iranian religious leader and prophet Zoroaster (c.630–c.553 BC), which teaches the existence of two continuously opposed divine beings, one good and the other evil.

zoster *noun* **1** an ancient Greek waist-belt for men. **2** *Medicine* herpes zoster or shingles. [from Greek *zoster*, girdle]

zouk /zuːk/ *noun* a style of dance music originating in the French Antilles combining Latin American, African, and Western disco rhythms. [from French]

Zr *symbol Chem.* zirconium.

zucchini /zʊ'kiːnɪ/ *noun* (PL. **zucchini**, **zucchinis**) *North Amer., Austral.* a courgette. [from Italian *zucchini*]

zygote /'zaɪgoʊt/ *noun Biol.* the cell that is formed as a result of the fertilization of a female gamete (ovum or egg cell) by a male gamete (sperm or pollen grain). [from Greek *zygon*, yoke]

zymase /'zaɪmeɪs/ *noun* any enzyme that catalyzes the fermentation of carbohydrates to ethanol (ethyl alcohol). [from Greek *zyme*, leaven]

zymotic /zaɪ'mɒtɪk/ *adj.* **1** relating to or causing fermentation. **2** relating to, causing, or like an infectious disease. [from Greek *zymosis*, fermentation]